The World Travel Guide is distributed in the United States of America exclusively by:

SF Communications, Inc
207 Park Avenue
Suite 107
Falls Church
VA 22046
Tel: (1 800) 322 3834
Fax: (703) 534 3844

David Frank	**President**
Diane Lee	**Marketing**
Leesa Rangnath	**Customer Service**
Donna Romano	**Sales**

British Library Catologuing in Publication Data

The World Travel Guide: Incorporating the ABTA/ANTOR Factfinder - 12th Edition
1. World Visitors' Guides
910'. 2 '02

ISBN: 0 946393 23 0
ISSN: 0267 8748

Typesetting and Colour Reproduction by Alphabet Set, London SW3;
Target Litho, London EC2; and Alphachannel, London EC2.
Printed by Passmore International, Basildon.

Editor
Sally McFall
Art Editor
Karen Harkness
Production Manager
Gavin Crosswell
Production & World Cup Design
Annmarie Kiddle
Assistant Editor
Nonke Beyer
Researchers
Michael Curtis, Lucie Tobin, Helen Thomas, Patrick Fitzgerald, Reid Savage, Suzy Dittmar, Graham Lowing, Karin Schulz, Tim Robinson, Mike Swindell, Dr Glyn Williams, Amanda Betley, Mike Wickenden
Cover Design
Terry Pottle of Design8
Advertisement Manager
Kerian Sydes
Copy Controller
Huw Jones
Cartographer
David Burles
Additional Cartography
Euromap
Technical Manager
Tim Smith

Customer Services Manager
Steve Mitchell
Booksales Manager
Steve Collins
Circulation Manager
Martin Newman
Circulation Controller
Louise Barclay
USA Co-ordinator
David Frank
Sales Administration
Alison Hierlehey, Sioban Hierlehey, Barbara Mitchell
Financial Director
Bruce Law
Financial Controller
Kay White
Sales Director
David Itzkin
Sales Consultant
George Armstrong
Marketing Director
Philip Barklem
Production Director
Brian Quinn
Publisher
Tony Oakland

The Publishers would like to thank all the tourist offices, embassies, high commissions, consulates, airlines and other organisations and individuals who assisted in the preparation of this edition. Special thanks to Patrick Brown and all at Alphabet Set.

Most of the photographs used in this publication were supplied by the respective tourist office, embassy, high commission or airline. The Publishers would also like to thank other organisations and individuals whose photographs appear.

IMPORTANT NOTICE

The information in the *World Travel Guide* is compiled from many sources: embassies, national tourist offices, health organisations and governmental bodies. Whilst every effort is made by the Publishers to ensure the accuracy of the information contained in this edition of the *World Travel Guide,* the Publishers accept no responsibility for any loss occasioned to any person acting or refraining from acting as a result of the material contained in this publication or liability for any financial or other agreements which may be entered into with any advertisers, organisations or individuals listed in the text.

By its very nature much of the information contained in this publication is susceptible to change or alteration, for instance, in response to changing political, health and environmental situations. These changes or alterations are beyond the control of the Publishers. To assist users in obtaining up-to-date information, the Publishers have provided as many contact telephone, fax and telex numbers as possible. In particular, the Code-Link™ information is available in respect of many countries. In any case of doubt, or in response to any change in a domestic or international situation, users are urged to verify information upon which they are relying with the relevant authority.

Columbus Press Limited is part of the Columbus Holdings Group.
Directors: Nigel Barklem; Philip Barklem; Bruce Law; Tony Oakland; Brian Quinn; Patrick Stephenson; Nigel Wray.

World Travel Guide

COLUMBUS PRESS

ALLIANCE OF CANADIAN TRAVEL ASSOCIATIONS

The **Alliance of Canadian Travel Associations,** also known as ACTA, is a national non-profit trade association which was established in 1977 to become autonomous from the American Society of Travel Agents (ASTA Canada).
ACTA's mission is to represent the interests of its members, primarily retail and wholesale, to the public, to governments, to suppliers and other bodies to further develop high professional standards among members, and to support and assist them in maximizing their economic objectives.
ACTA's executive board of directors consists of 20 travel industry professionals working to improve the industry and assist ACTA members in reaching their professional objectives.
ACTA's seven provincial associations are a powerful source for its strength as a national association. Each association is represented by a provincial president who is a full voting member on the national body's executive board of directors.
In addition to the services provided by the provincial associations, ACTA also provides the following national level programs and services.

Membership
Membership fees support the efforts and activities of the executive board and working committees of both the national and provincial associations.

Canadian Travel Industry Identification Card
A new worldwide travel industry identification card has recently been released. This card provides photo-identification proof that the bearer is a bona-fide travel industry professional.

Conferences and international travelmarts
Another of ACTA's objectives is to raise industry professional standards by continually developing and implementing educational programs to improve the skills of agency managers and travel consultants.

AMS ACTA Marketing Services
AMS ACTA Marketing Services is another benefit exclusive to ACTA members. Through AMS, ACTA members receive substantial savings on over 2000 products and services from some 15 ACTA-preferred suppliers.

Industry and government relations
ACTA maintains continuous and effective representation and dialogue with industry and government bodies on those issues and matters of concern and of relevance to its members.

International industry representation
ACTA keeps abreast of international developments in the travel industry and represents the views of its members worldwide throughout its alliance with affiliated associations in other countries.

Committees and research
ACTA conducts constant review and research to further streamline and maximize membership benefits.

Alliance of Canadian Travel Associations
Suite 1106, 75 rue Albert Street,
Ottawa, Canada K1P 5E7
Tel: (613) 238 1361. Fax: (613) 238 8949.

'Many of our members from all sectors of the travel trade use the *World Travel Guide* and find it an invaluable source of information.
Tom Reilly, Executive Director

ASSOCIATION OF BRITISH TRAVEL AGENTS

ABTA

The Association of British Travel Agents (ABTA), formed in 1950, is a company limited by guarantee. It is a self-regulatory trade body representing over 2500 travel agents and about 700 tour-operator member companies throughout Britain. With many members having branch offices, there are nearly 8000 ABTA outlets overall, accounting for over 90% of the travel trade in Britain. ABTA provides a conciliation and arbitration service for all consumers purchasing package holidays from ABTA members.

ABTA, as the representative of the travel industry, maintains dialogue with governments and other authoritative bodies, both in the UK and abroad. It endeavours to create a favourable trading environment for its members and seeks to encourage the best possible standards for consumers.

Association of British Travel Agents
55-57 Newman Street
London W1P 4AH
Tel: (071) 637 2444. Fax: (071) 637 0713.

'The *World Travel Guide* is by far one of the most useful tools of the trade, and one which expert travel agents rely upon.'
Mike Grinrod, President

ASSOCIATION OF NATIONAL TOURIST OFFICE REPRESENTATIVES IN GREAT BRITAIN

'Most informative source of destination information.'

Orestis Rossides, Chairman

ANTOR, the Association of National Tourist Offices in the United Kingdom, has a membership of over 80 National Tourist Offices representing countries from all over the world, with vastly different attractions, resources, geographical features and cultural heritages. This voluntary non-political organisation has been established since the early 1950s and serves the dual role of a forum for the exchange of views and experiences of its members and of a driving force for joint promotional activities aimed at both the trade and the consumer.

Drawing on broad knowledge and experience, ANTOR brings a fully international approach to problems affecting all aspects of the travel industry, with which ANTOR works in close partnership. It maintains contact with the media and other organisations in the travel industry, such as ABTA, and is frequently called on for its views on matters relating to the industry as a whole.

ANTOR thus aims, through mutual cooperation, to co-ordinate and improve services that government tourist offices offer to the British travel industry and to the consumer. ANTOR's regular business meetings for its members are also often addressed by leading tourism experts.

Association of National Tourist office Representatives in Great Britain
42d Compayne Gardens
London
NW6 3RY
Tel: (071) 624 5817.

NATIONAL BUSINESS TRAVEL ASSOCIATION

Founded in 1968 as the National Passenger Traffic Assocation, the NBTA has grown to include travel managers from the largest corporations in America and the world, as well as allied suppliers. Today NBTA members account for more than $30 billion in travel expenditures.

NBTA includes three major membership categories. Direct members are business travel managers who are responsible for negotiating and acquiring travel services for a particular corporation. Allied members are suppliers who provide services and equipment to Direct members. Associate members are other travel-related companies and individuals. Additionally, NBTA operates in cooperation with regional affiliates.

The National Business Travel Association is the authoritative voice and action arm of corporate travel managers and suppliers who arre involved in business travel.

The purposes of NBTA are to:

- Enhance the value of travel managers in meeting corporate travel needs and financial goals.
- Provide a forum for members to network and act on matters affecting business travel.
- Serve as a spokesman and cultivate a positive public image of the corporate travel industry.
- Educate members about industry matters, evolving issues and technology.
- Advocate and protect the interests of members and their corporations on legislative and regulatory matters.
- Promote the safety, security, efficiency and quality of travel.
- Enhance the professionalism and recognition of the industry and individual members.
- Provide an authoritative database and information on corporate travel.

Institute of Travel & Toursim
113 Victoria Street
St Albans
Hertfordshire AL1 3TJ.
Tel: (0727) 54395. Fax: (0727) 47415.

INSTITUTE OF TRAVEL & TOURISM

The Institute of Travel & Tourism was inaugurated in 1956 to set, maintain and improve standards within the Travel and Tourism industry and to establish a body which would recognise those attaining high standards. It aims to help managers and potential managers develop and maintain their professional knowledge by awarding a recognised professional qualification, which entitles members to use designatory letters after their names.

The Institute runs a series of one-day seminars. In 1992, some of the subjects covered include old Print and Brochure Production, Travel Legislation and Law, Choosing and Using Technology, BS5750, Financial Management and Business Strategies in the 1990s.

The Institute holds an Annual Conference each autumn. The 1992 Conference was held in September in The Kruger National Park in South Africa, and was the most exciting Conference to date. The theme for the Conference was 'Getting the Lion's share', looking at how companies maintain their competitive edge.

'The World Travel Guide would be the choice for professional travel agents to give their customers the very best service.'

Linda Gibson, Chief Executive

Institute of Travel & Tourism
113 Victoria Street
St Albans
Hertfordshire AL1 3TJ
Tel: (0727) 54395. Fax: (0727) 47415.

WORLD ASSOCIATION OF TRAVEL AGENTS

WATA, the **World Association of Travel Agencies**, is a non-profit making organisation created by independent travel agents for the benefit of all travel agencies around the world. It helps locally respected agencies combine their personal touch with the influence gained by global recognition. Since its foundation in 1949, WATA has become a truly well-respected name in the travel industry worldwide. With over 200 members from 189 cities in 84 countries, WATA today has established an international network of travel agents who enjoy some unique privileges and benefits.

WATA's basic idea is to bring local (preferably privately owned) travel agencies into an international network, so that every member is offered all the facilities and advantages of being associated with an international body – in addition to enjoying local prominence. As a consequence, a substantial volume of business to the agency's turnover can be expected.

WATA maintains a permanent secretariat at its headquarters in Geneva to cover the Association's administrative needs. WATA headquarters also provides information, assistance and a number of services to individual members. These include the offices of an Ombudsman between members and other sections of the travel trade plus assistance in the recovery of outstanding payments anywhere in the world.

1) The General Assembly: for unparalleled opportunities
Held every second year, the WATA General Assembly provides a forum for discussion of the Association's business and an unparalleled opportunity to 'talk travel' with fellow members from the four corners of the globe.

2) Regional Assemblies: for local discussions
Held in those years without a General Assembly, these shorter meetings provide the chance to discuss regional travel problems and technical difficulties.

3) Senior Employees Assembly: another perspective
This new Assembly aims to familiarise employees who are actually involved in the day-to-day running of WATA agencies to become acquainted with the advantages and possibilities WATA offers.

Membership in WATA is open to any travel agency, preferably privately owned, which can prove a sound financial structure, adheres to the highest professional standards expected in the industry and enjoys a prominent standing in the local community.
All WATA members have the same rights, privileges and obligations within the association.

- Members must adhere strictly to the WATA ethics.
- Members must favour the WATA organisation.
- The collaboration between member agencies must be genuine.
- Members must assist at the general and regional assemblies.

Please apply for an Application form and a copy of the Articles of Association.
The Secretary General
WATA
PO Box 2317
1211 Geneva 1
Switzerland
Tel: (022) 731 4760. Fax: (022) 732 8161.

'The best informed travel agents use the *World Travel Guide.*'
Hervé Choisy, Secretary General

AMERICAN SOCIETY OF TRAVEL AGENTS

You are invited to join the family, to take advantage of excellent networking opportunites and develop contacts worldwide.

ASTA International, with over 3000 members in 125 countries, is the forum for not only those providing receptive services for travellers from the United States but also for the growing number of travel organisers for whom the USA is the destination.

Overall, ASTA has 20,000 members, and business opportunities will be found at the annual World Congress ('93 in St Louis), the annual International Convention ('93 in Queensland, Australia and '94 in New York), and four regional domestic conferences.

Membership – from just $235 per year – represents a superb value today, and, besides the networking challenges outlined above, includes the monthly International 'ASTA Notes' and the acclaimed 'ASTA Agency Management' publication, plus access to local Chapter activities in your country – there are nearly 50 Chapters worldwide – and many other benefits.

Interested? You should be!

Membership details from:
American Society of Travel Agents
1101 King Street
Alexandria
Virginia 22314
USA
Tel: (703) 739 2782. Fax: (703) 684 8319. Telex: 440203.

'All segments of travel and tourism are united under the ASTA umbrella. Through unity the industry can better achieve its mutual goals: professionalism, profitablitly and progress.'
Earlene Causey, ASTA President and CEO

CONTENTS

Countries marked in RED appear in colour, the section having been sponsored by the tourist board or tourism authority to help promotion of the destination for business and leisure travel.

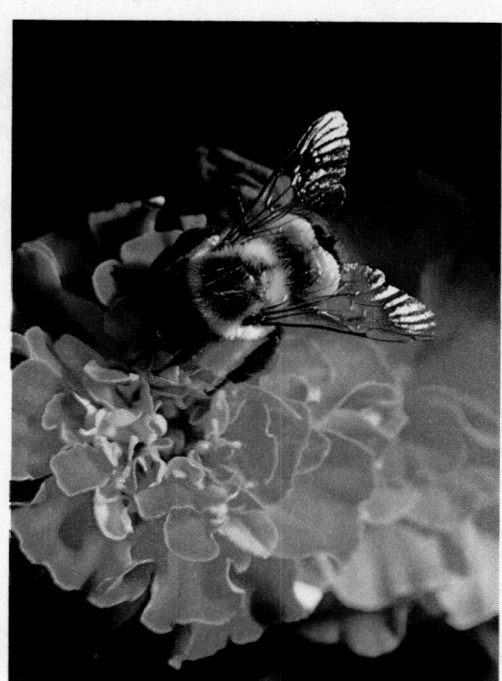

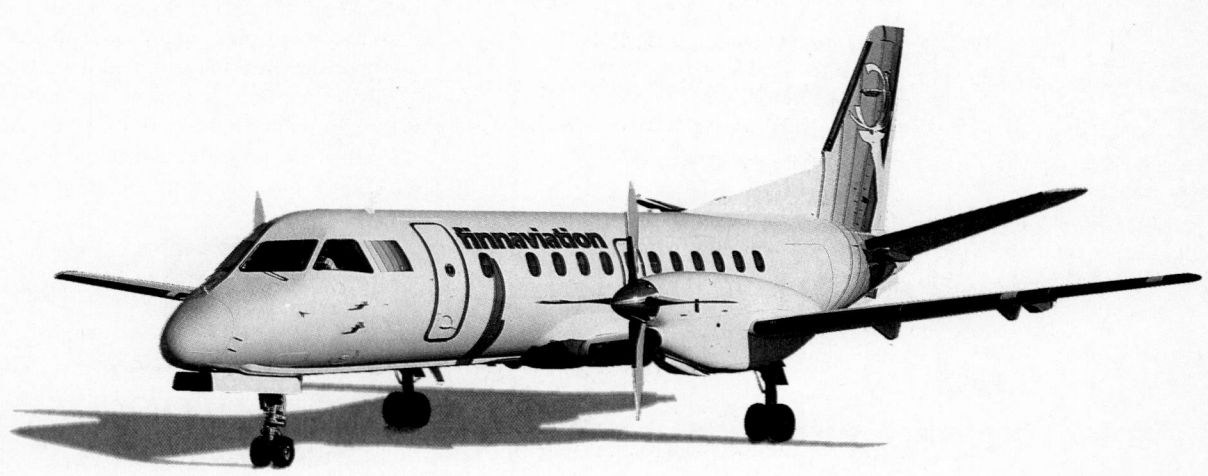

• STOP PRESS •

The new address for the
China International Travel Service (CITS)
is as follows:

Head Office
103 Fuxingmennei Avenue
Beijing 100800, China
Tel: 601 1122
Telex: 22350 CITSH CN
Fax: 601 2013/512 2068
24 -hour Tel: 601 2055

We look forward to hearing from you!

TABA
CAIRO
ALEXANDRIA

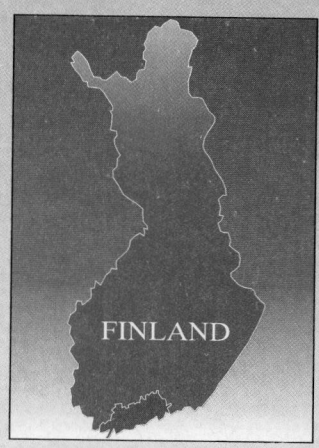

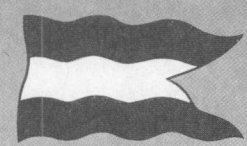

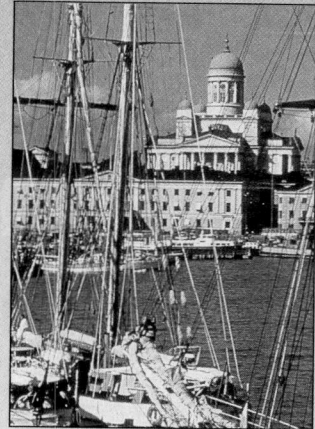

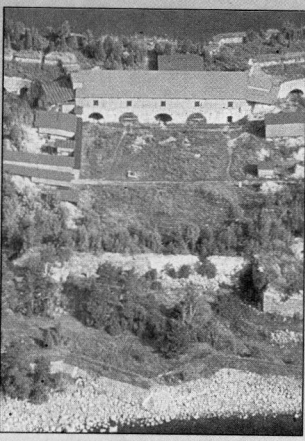

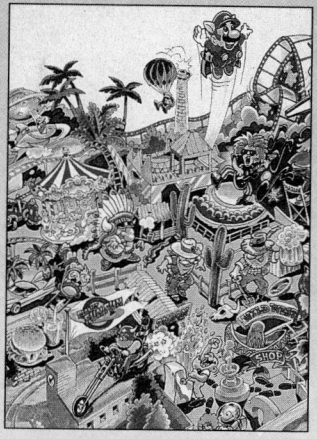

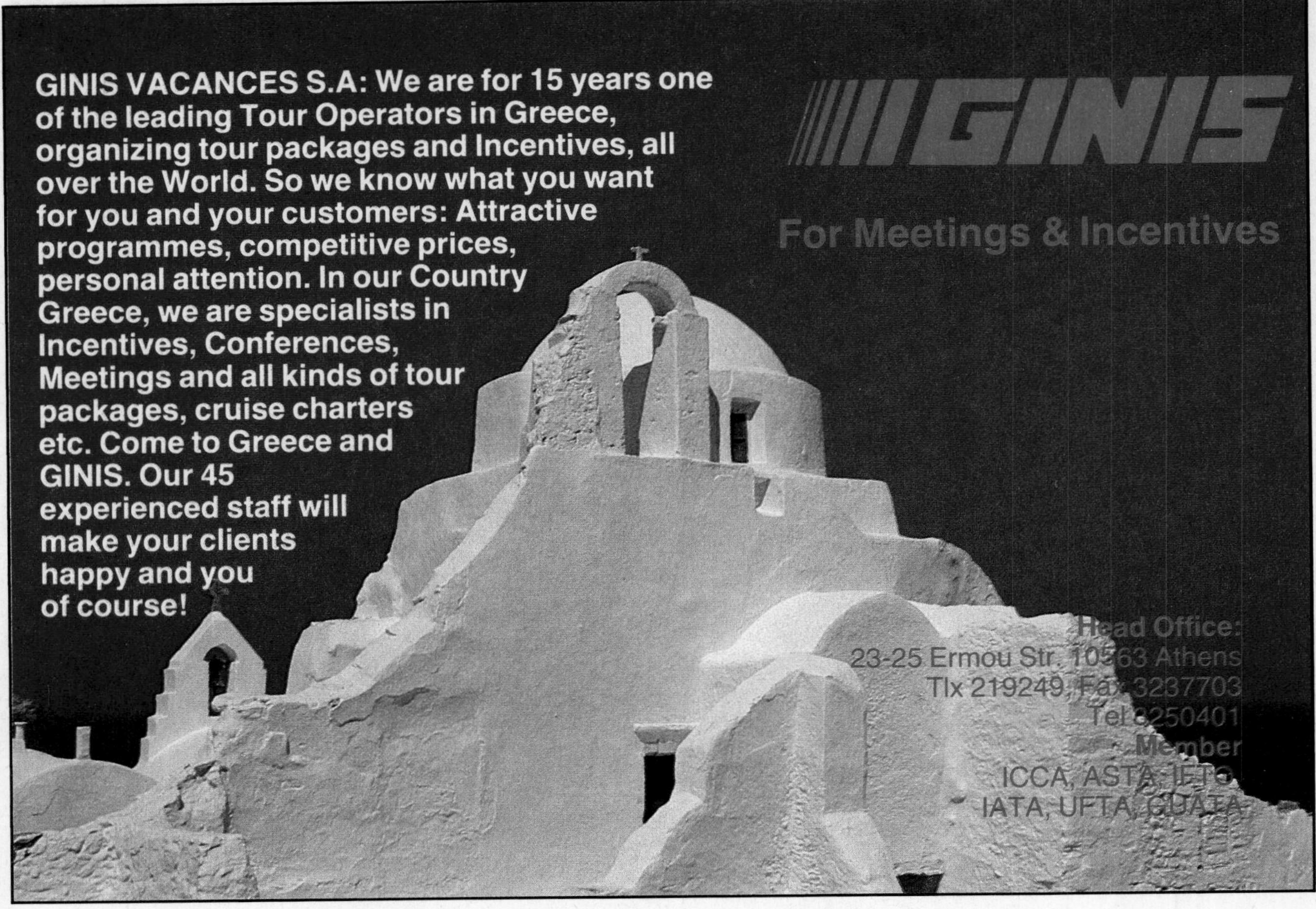
GINIS VACANCES S.A: We are for 15 years one of the leading Tour Operators in Greece, organizing tour packages and Incentives, all over the World. So we know what you want for you and your customers: Attractive programmes, competitive prices, personal attention. In our Country Greece, we are specialists in Incentives, Conferences, Meetings and all kinds of tour packages, cruise charters etc. Come to Greece and GINIS. Our 45 experienced staff will make your clients happy and you of course!
GINIS
For Meetings & Incentives
Head Office:
23-25 Ermou Str. 10563 Athens
Tlx 219249, Fax 3237703
Tel 3250401
Member
ICCA, ASTA, IFTO
IATA, UFTA, GUATA

check-in

YOUR GUIDE TO THE CMP TRAVELGROUP OF PUBLICATIONS

Presenting *Check-in*, the newsletter of the CMP Travel Group, to the readers of The World Travel Guide.

We invite you use *Check-in* as your guide to our media network of travel publications: *Business Travel News, Tour & Travel News, Travel Counselor, Tour & Travel Marketplace* and the *Special Supplements Division*—designed to deliver the highest quality editorial products and read by the most qualified professionals in the industry.

TOUR & TRAVEL NEWS: A NEW LOOK FOR '93

Tour & Travel News, the weekly newspaper for the retail travel industry, is the only trade publication to focus all of its attention on the role of retailers and the many travel products they sell and recommend. To help our over 207,000* readers find the information they need quickly and with regularity, each issue is separated into easy to locate departments and destination sections . In addition, *Tour & Travel News' Travel USA* special pullout sections will continue to be a strong focus in our editorial line-up, publishing six times in 1993.

And now, *Tour & Travel News* has a new look: headlines that are easier to read and provide more detail; better information graphics; improved paperstock; and new features that highlight the news in each issue, including a Late News Report and News Summary.

TOUR&TRAVEL NEWS

All-Inclusives: How Many Are Too Many?

Club Vacations Cuts Charters, Gets Marsans

AmEx Promotes Use Of Agents

Can Egypt Save Its Ancient Ruins?

BUSINESS TRAVEL NEWS COVERS CORPORATE TRAVEL

Business Travel News is a bi-weekly newspaper written for corporate executives responsible for business travel and meetings purchasing, policy-making and negotiating; and for travel agency personnel who specialize in the business travel and meetings field. Established in 1984, *Business Travel News,* the only newspaper in the business travel and meetings market, reaches over 266,000** readers and offers advertisers unmatched timeliness and immediacy.

Business Travel NEWS

THE 25 MOST INFLUENTIAL EXECUTIVES

Riding With The Recovery

OUTLOOK '93

No Celebrating Yet For Airlines

Perspective '92: The Top 10 Stories

1992

The editorial focus of *Business Travel News* is on news, news analysis, and instructional features. Regular departments cover suppliers, business travel technology, travel management, U.S. destinations and international business travel. Special supplements include *Meetings Today* and the *Official Business Travel Handbook.*

Business Travel News
Tour & Travel News

Travel Counselor
Tour & Travel Marketplace
Special Supplements

World Travel Guide Special Edition 1993

Travel Counselor: Value-Added For CTCs & Career Travel Agents

The CMP Travel Group will continue to publish four editions of *Travel Counselor* under the direction of ICTA, the Institute of Certified Travel Agents, in 1993. *Travel Counselor* addresses the needs of those travel agents who have chosen to build their careers in the industry—the key decision makers at the very core of retail and commercial travel.

H. Wayne Berens, CTC, ICTA chairman, says,"We intend to make *Travel Counselor* one of the most valuable tools in professional travel counselors' libraries."

Direct Response With Tour & Travel Marketplace

Tour & Travel Marketplace is the most active direct-response publication in the industry. Delivered bi-monthly with *Tour & Travel News,* TTM offers an exciting vehicle that guarantees prompt delivery and response, with a special editorial platform–Marketplace Spotlights.

Special Supplements: The Creative Approach

In addition to its many features, departments, sections and special reports, *Business Travel News* and *Tour & Travel News* publish dozens of market driven special sections, sales guides, private-label publications, newsletters and in-flight magazines and supplements.

If you are looking for a creative approach that goes beyond the scope of our editorial calendars, please give us a call.

For More Information About The CMP Travel Group, Check-In With:

Jerry R. Landress
Vice President/Group Publisher
(516) 562-5704

- **Business Travel News:**
  Bill Besch, Divisional Director of Marketing Product Development
  (516) 562-5772
- **Tour & Travel News:**
  Bob Sullivan, Publisher
  (516) 562-5708
- **Travel Counselor:**
  Joanne N. Nelson, Director of Advertising
  (516) 562-5701
- **Tour & Travel Marketplace/ Special Supplements Division:**
  Doug Corper, Director
  (516) 562-5961

*November 1991 BPA projected research study of pass-along receivership
**BPA Supplementary Audit Publication Research Study November 1989

FUN ISLAND

Treat yourself to a dream holiday.... in the sublime serenity of Fun Island – Bodufinolhu, the tropical Island Resort set amidst the cluster of tiny islands in the fascinating Maldives.... where, nature's unspoilt natural beauty meets the luxurious style of living!

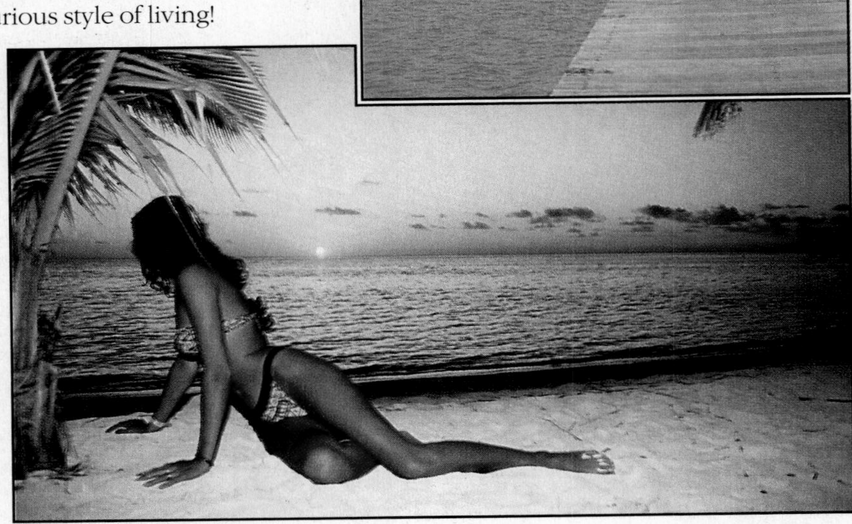

Situated in the eastern reef of South Malé Atoll, 38km from Malé International Airport, Fun Island captivates the imagination with its endless stretches of lovely, white sandy beaches and the warm turquoise lagoon.

Its charm is enhanced by two virgin islets across the channel which can be waded in at low tide...
Total seclusion... it's a perfect hideaway for honeymooners!

The resort offers luxury accommodation, in its 100 elegantly furnished, beach-fronted guest rooms containing en suite bath facilities, air-conditioning, hot and cold fresh water, IDD telephone and mini-bar. Two restaurants, three well-stocked bars and rich, choice buffets... Apart from that, open-air B-B-Qs and exciting "Maldivian Nights" add a few climatic moments to an unforgettable holiday.

You have a wide range of water sports facilities to choose from – snorkelling, water skiing, sailing, day/night fishing, windsurfing or scuba diving. The magnificent underwater world and the giant house reef abounding in many-hued corals and tropical fish is really a diver's dream.

Excellent diving! The resort boasts of a fully equipped diving base with qualified instructors.

When the sun goes down... disco!
Or relax... on the picturesque open-air deck in the quietness of the cool sea breeze... the best entertainment of all – doing nothing. Interesting excursions, picnics and much more..., complemented with our incomparable hospitality, will make your holiday a dream come true.

It's a totally amazing experience!

FUN ISLAND (Bodufinolhu) South Malé Atoll, Maldives.

Villa Building, PO Box 2073, Malé 20-02, Maldives
Tel: 444558/324478 Fax: 443958/327845 Tlx: 77099 FUNISLE MF

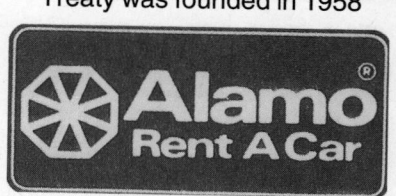

3 PLACES TO BE IN '94

Holidayworld – Ireland's Travel and Tourism Exhibitions open to: Trade Professional and Public.
Well promoted, organised and presented.
Expected attendance in excess of 100,000 over the three exhibitions.
If you want to sell and promote your products in Ireland (population in excess of 5m) then join us at:

BELFAST
KING'S HALL
JAN 5 • 9
1994

DUBLIN
R.D.S.
JAN 19 • 23
1994

CORK
SILVER SPRINGS
JAN 28 • 30
1994

Enquiries to:
Maureen Ledwith/Edmund Hourican
Holiday and Leisure Fair Ltd.
6 Sandyford Office Park,
Dublin 18, Ireland.
Tel: ++ 010 3531 2954911
Fax: ++ 010 3531 2957417

BTL
DESIGN: PAULO MOEDAS
PORTUGAL
BOLSA DE TURISMO
DE LISBOA
LISBOA TRAVEL MARKET
19.23 JAN.94
ASSOCIAÇÃO INDUSTRIAL PORTUGUESA
FEIRA INTERNACIONAL DE LISBOA

Efficient services at
competitive rates offer
excellent value for money.

At the crossroads of the
compass points, we have
an edge in opening
new markets.

Whichever way you look at it, Seychelles
and well equipped to play a key role in
people, cargo and servic

The Authentic Route to Paradise...

Choose the authentic gateway. Sundays, Mondays, and Fridays from Gatwick, to an environment untouched by pollution, with an unrivalled display of shimmering beaches, glistening waves, unspoilt splendour and rare harmony.

Discover marine life at its best. A feast for diving enthusiasts. Where the treasures of bygone pirates still lie hidden, and the climate begs to be savoured.

Flying with us brings the golden, sundrenched and incomparable Seychelles so much closer – now only a short dream away.

Our modern Boeing 767 200 ER will seat you in comfort and style whilst our friendly cabin crew and experienced pilots will ensure that your holiday starts the moment you board the flight.

While you're there, discover the islands at your leisure with our island hopping flights.

Phone Air Seychelles 0293-536313 for further information

DESIGNALINE ADVERTISING (R.S.A.) D/3785/E

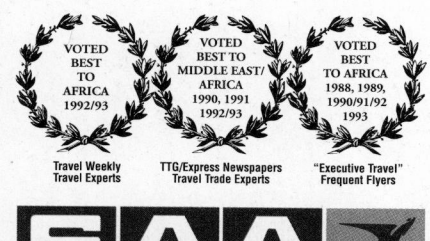

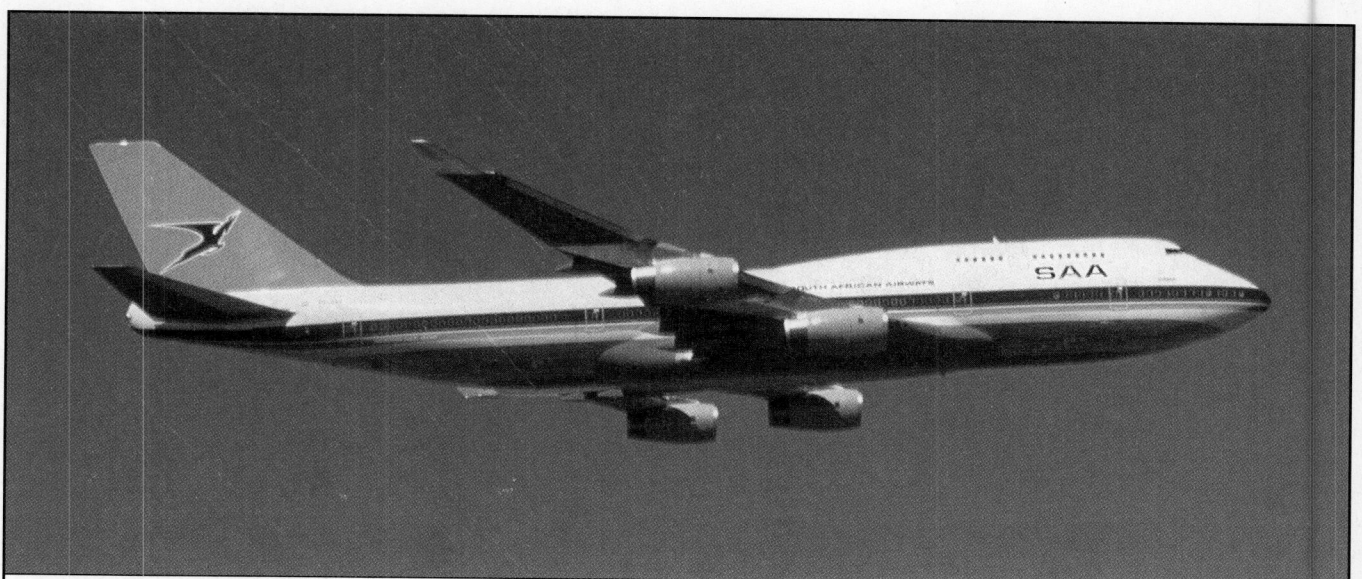

Once Upon a Time...
is NOW in a land not so far away. A land where castles rise from the sand. Where guests are offered the sea and shore in royal fashion.
Where bountiful, complimentary meals, snacks and spirits appear at every turn.
Your castle in the heart of the Caribbean is Jack Tar Village, where activities are numerous, a Robert Trent Jones-designed golf course challenges your skills and an exciting casino and live entertainment add sparkle to your nights.
In this land, relaxation reigns.
There's nothing to spoil the fun--
no hassles, no tips, (no dragons),
no kidding.
Jack Tar Village-
Your Castle
in the Sand
For reservations or information call
(214) 987-4909 • Mex (800) 952-2582 • US (800) 999-9182
JACK TAR VILLAGE®
BEACH RESORT & CASINO PUERTO PLATA, D.R.

monomotor
THE SERVICE GARANTEE

Armação De Pera

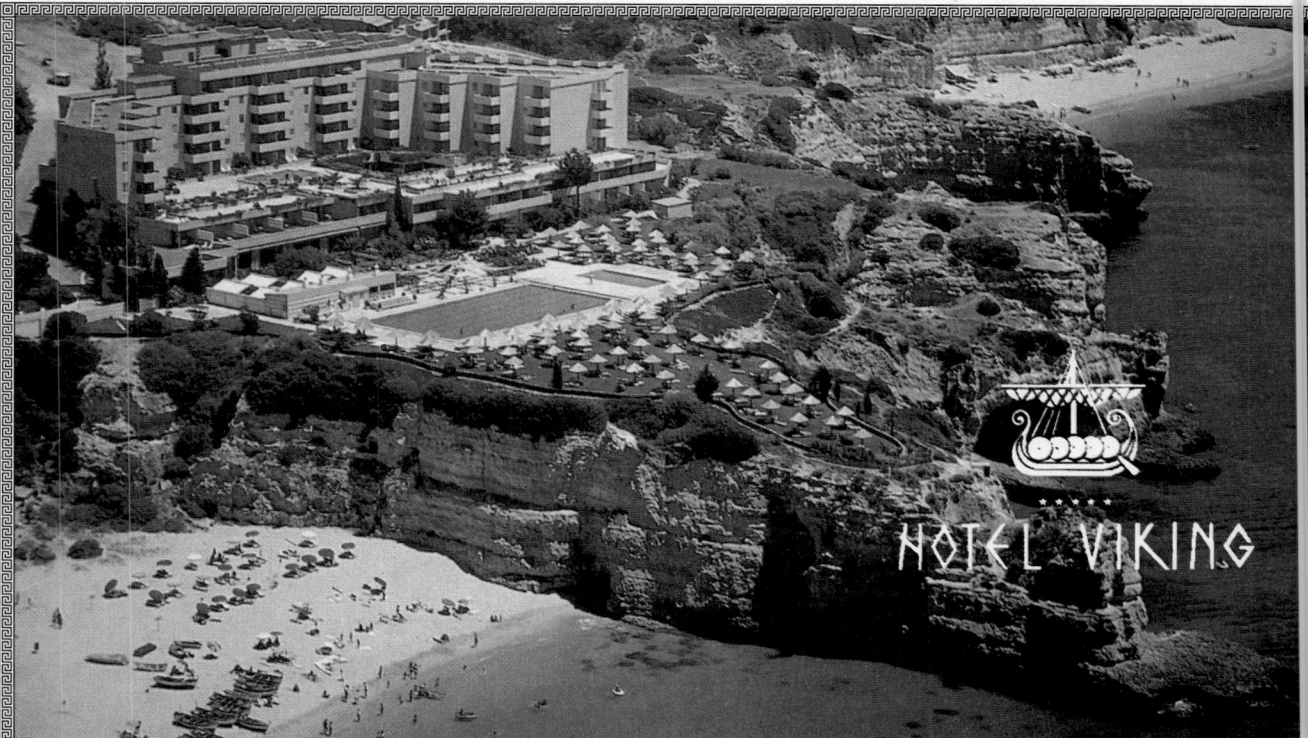

Armação de Pêra is situated in an enviable position in the Algarve between Albufeira and Portmão, where the municipalities of Lago, Silvas and Albufeira meet on the coast.
Perfect for a quiet holiday, the many attractions of the Algarve, from golf courses to stunning beaches, rocks and coves are within easy reach by car.
Armação is linked with the tuna fishing activities and the tradition remains very much alive.
Resorts are set on dramatic cliffs which lead down to the Atlantic Ocean and the beautiful sandy beaches of Armação de Pêra and Praia Senhora da Rocha (the beach of Our Lady of the Rocks). It takes its name from the Romanesque chapel which is perched seemingly precariously – above it Immediately west of this beach, the sea has carved a series of caverns, vaults, grottos in the area of Furnas. These caves (Mesquita, Ruazes, Pontal) are well worth visiting.

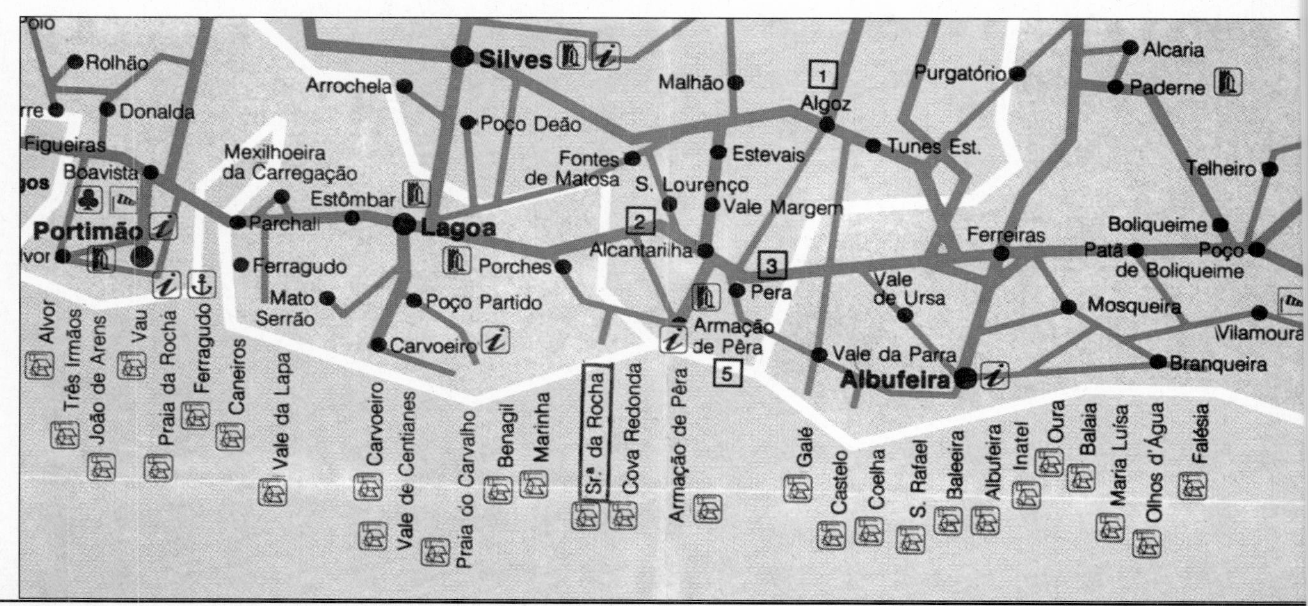

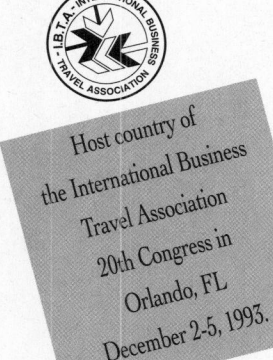

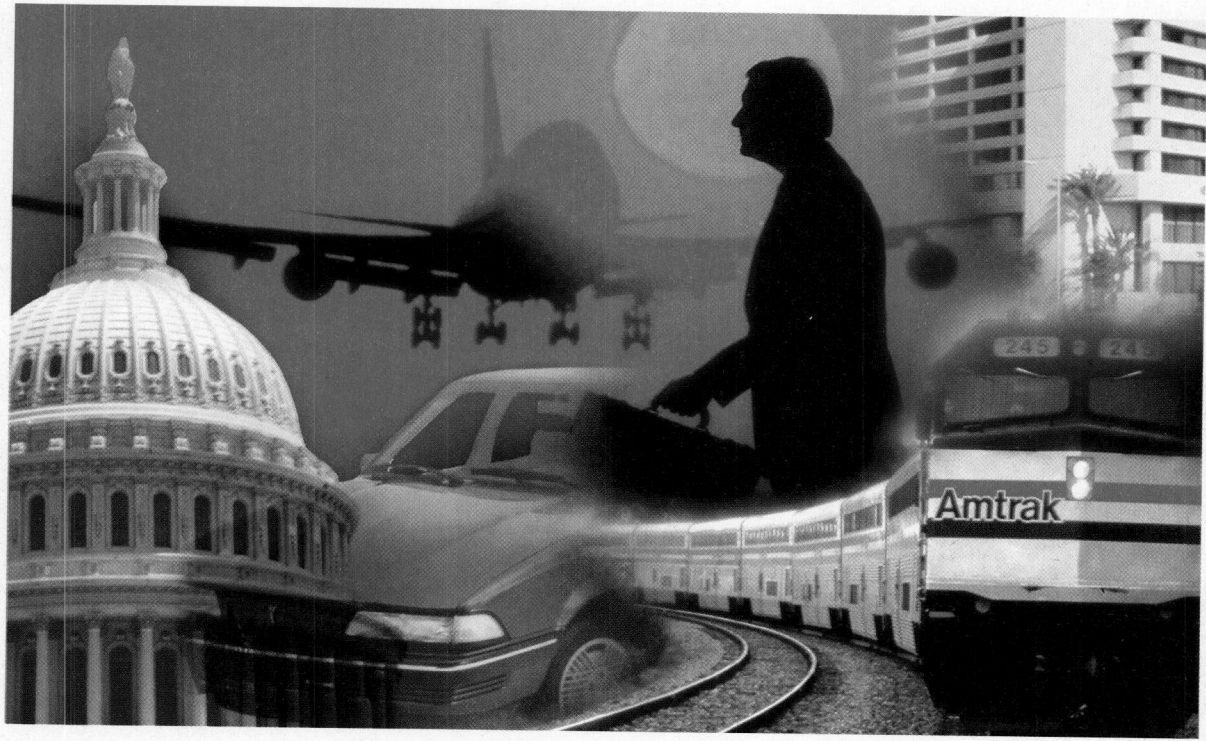

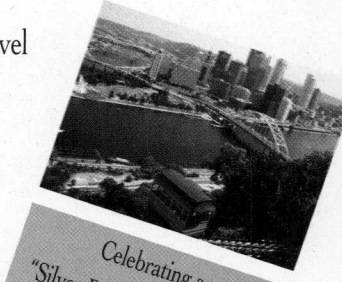

MAP INDEX

At the beginning of each entry in the World Travel Guide is a black-and-white map showing the main towns, rivers and geographical features of the country. In addition, more detailed information is contained in the following regional, city and expanded colour maps. All maps were compiled by David Burles, apart from the World Cup 1994 maps which were compiled by Euromap. All are in black and white unless otherwise specified.

INTRODUCTION
How to Use this Book

Welcome to the 1993 12th edition of the *World Travel Guide*; now at over 1300 pages it is even more comprehensive.
Last year saw some dramatic developments in Eastern Europe, especially the final separation of the former Czechoslovakia into the Czech and Slovak Republics and the continuing civil war in Yugoslavia. The users of this book will notice that each of the independent republics of the former Yugoslavia – Bosnia-Hercegovina, Croatia and Slovenia – now appear in alphabetical order as individual entries, and the remaining republics of Montenegro and Serbia appear together under the Yugoslavia entry. The former Yugoslav republic of Macedonia also has a separate country entry, although it is as yet not recognised by the international community. Also, there are individual entries for the Czech Republic and the Slovak Republic listed in the correct alphabetical order. All information given in these entries is correct at the time of going to press, although travellers should check with the respective Embassy or High Commission as regulations are likely to change. However, information has been retained in sections on the former republics of Yugoslavia and certain other countries currently experiencing civil unrest, such as Somalia, or international detachment, such as Iraq, that may not be useful in the present circumstances, but may prove so again if the situations are resolved in the near future.
Below is a brief description of all the sections contained in the book. In addition to the country-by-country entries, which occupy the vast majority of the text, attention is also drawn to the various sections at the front and the back of the book, all of which are the source of much useful additional information. These will be referred to in the text where necessary.

INTERNATIONAL ORGANISATIONS

This is a list of organisations concerned with world trade, which can be used as a supplement to the Business Profile section in each country entry. Some of these organisations, such as the Commonwealth, though not primarily trade organisations, nevertheless make decisions and form political alliances of economic significance.

Country-by-Country Guide

Every country in the world is included, listed alphabetically and broken down under various headings which are described in greater detail below. It has been almost impossible to update some of the Middle Eastern countries and Yugoslavia accurately, due to ongoing circumstances in those areas. A note has been made at the top of the entry for the countries concerned. For some countries, not all headed sections would be relevant, in which case they have been omitted. In others, the amount of information which it is necessary to convey has resulted in the extending and subdividing of some of the sections. Despite the problems which are caused by attempting to describe both very large and very small countries within a common framework, every effort has been made to standardise the way in which the information is presented. The only significant exception to this is the entry for the United States of America, which is divided into detailed sections on each gateway city.
Certain islands, states and territories do not have their own entry in the *World Travel Guide*, but are instead grouped together; this applies particularly to some island groups in the Pacific and the Caribbean. Examples include Niue, which can be found under *New Zealand*; the Faroe Islands, which can be found under *Denmark*; Svålbard, which can be found under *Norway*; the Galapagos Islands, which can be found under *Ecuador*; and Easter Island, which can be found under *Chile*. In other cases, countries may, correctly or not, be known popularly by more than one name; Sri Lanka/Ceylon, Cambodia/Kampuchea, Myanmar/Burma, Côte d'Ivoire/Ivory Coast, for instance. A further complication is caused by areas which are politically an integral part of a country with its own entry; thus the Canary and Balearic Islands have their own sub-sections at the end of Spain, while information on Madeira and the Azores may be found at the end of the entry on Portugal. If in doubt as to where information may be found, please refer to the *Contents* pages. The entries for countries which appear in colour have been sponsored by the National Tourism Office or Tourism Representative in the UK. They are designed to assist the travel trade in the presentation and marketing of these countries as destinations for both business and holiday travel. The use of colour for a particular country does not imply a different editorial approach.

MAPS

Each country section is headed by a map of the country, showing its location within a more general region. Over the years, we have introduced more maps of major cities of the world and, for certain countries, more detailed regional maps showing areas of particular interest to the tourist or business traveller – these are now listed in the separate *Map Contents*. Comments and suggestions from users of the book concerning cities and areas which could be further covered in this way will be gratefully received.
More detailed maps of the Middle East, Europe, the Caribbean and the South Pacific countries may be found in the regional maps section at the front of the book. Attention is also drawn to the two world maps, one of which shows time zones. All maps in the book are for reference purposes only, and have no political significance.
Time Zones: The World Time Zones map at the front of the book shows the time in each part of the world. All time zones are based on the Greenwich Meridian, zero degrees longitude. Note that in many countries some form of Daylight Saving Time/Summertime is observed, during which clocks will be altered to make maximum use of daylight. This will be specified under each country's entry. It is noteworthy that many parts of the world are moving towards standard regional Daylight Saving Times (a process associated with the formation of regional trade blocs, similar to the EC); some countries in the Tropics have adopted Daylight Saving Time/Summertime only for commercial reasons. (Although the EC has requested that all clock changes should be standardised, the UK only comes into line with the rest of Europe for the start of daylight saving and finishes daylight saving two weeks earlier in the year than most of the other European countries.)

CONTACT ADDRESSES

Addresses are given in the following order: the name and address of the national Tourist Board within the particular country; the diplomatic representation of the particular country in either the UK or mainland Europe; the name and address of the country's Tourist Board in the UK, where applicable; the British Embassy or High Commission in the particular country; the country's diplomatic representation and Tourist Board in the USA; the US Embassy in the country in question; the country's diplomatic representation and Tourist Board in Canada; and the Canadian Embassy or High Commission in the country. Addresses of Consulates or sections specifically handling visa applications can also be found here. In a few cases it has not been possible to follow this format and alternative addresses have been given.

GENERAL DETAILS

GEOGRAPHY: The country's location is followed by a list of the main geographical features. **Population** figures given at the head of this section are taken from the most reliable statistics available.
LANGUAGE: Information is given about the principal official, spoken and understood languages.
RELIGION: The main religious denominations are given.
TIME: Information on national and regional time-zones is given, together with details of Daylight Saving Time/Summertime where appropriate. This supplements the information in the time-zone charts (see above).
ELECTRICITY: Information is included on voltages and, where available, on cycles (in Hertz) and the types of plugs used. These can vary within a country. Various travel plugs enable visitors to use their appliances without changing to the locally used plug.
COMMUNICATIONS: Information is given on the **Telephone, Fax, Telex/telegram** and **Postal** services available. If a country is available through the IDD (International Direct Dialling) system, the country code is given; dialling this code from any other country will connect it with the country in question. The **Press** section lists the main English-language papers published in that country and, where none exist, the most important papers published in the national language(s).
International Radio Services: The chart shows a selection of frequencies for receiving the **BBC World Service** and **Voice of America** in each country (except Canada and the USA) in MHz. Reception quality can vary; as a general rule, lower frequencies give better results early in the morning and late at night, higher ones in the middle of the day. Variations in sunspot activity may also adversely affect reception and from time to time the BBC makes further changes in broadcasting frequencies to counter this. The most up-to-date information is available in the World Service magazine *London Calling*.

PASSPORT/VISA

Information is presented by means of a quick-glance table on the passport and visa requirements for British, Australian, Canadian, American and Japanese nationals, as well as holders of other EC passports. Information, where available, is also given on types and prices of visas and their duration, application requirements, the length of time an application takes to process and the procedures to be followed when renewing visas. There is also some information for visitors seeking temporary residence. Other relevant information is included where necessary.
In many cases, the same regulations for passports and visas (or other identity documents) apply equally to all countries who are members of a particular international organisation (such as the Commonwealth or the EC). Occasionally, in the notes following the charts, the organisation only, rather than the often lengthy list of member states, will be referred to. For this reason, lists giving the membership of the EC, British Dependent Territories, the Commonwealth, the CFA (French Community in Africa), the Arab League, ECOWAS (Economic Community of West African States) and other organisations may be found in the *International Organisations* section.
In the interests of clarity and brevity, various groups of people who are often exempt from passport and visa requirements have generally not been referred to in the charts or notes. These include holders of seamen's books, UN travel passes, service or diplomatic passports and stateless persons. Information may be obtained from the relevant Embassy or High Commission.
Unless otherwise stated in the chart, all travellers should be in possession of a return ticket and/or sufficient funds for the duration of their stay. In many cases they will be required to prove this on arrival in the country, or when they apply for their visa prior to departure.
The Visa sections of Embassies or High Commissions are normally open Monday to Friday with varying opening hours. During peak holiday times visas can often take longer to issue.
Note: *Although every effort has been made to ensure the accuracy of the information included in this section, entry requirements may be subject to change at short notice. If in doubt, check with the Embassy or High Commission concerned, being sure to state the nature of the visit (ie business, touristic, transit) and the intended length of stay, and to confirm exactly what documentation will be required for the application. Remember that Transit visas may be required for stopovers.*
Entry and other restrictions: Nationals of Israel, South Africa and Taiwan especially (though not exclusively) may be subject to restrictions when visiting other countries. These range from limiting the categories of persons who may visit to a total ban on entering a country, even for transit purposes. Travellers whose passports indicate that they have entered these countries may also be subject to restrictions. Some countries enforce stricter regulations for those crossing land borders. Travellers from Commonwealth countries who have passports conferring less than full British citizenship may also be subject to additional requirements (this affects nationals of up to 20% of the countries listed in this guide). In such cases it is advisable to check with the relevant embassy or with the Foreign Office well in advance. Brief details follow.
British passports: Under the terms of the British Nationality Act 1981, which came into force on January 1, 1983, 'citizenship of the United Kingdom and Colonies' has been divided into three categories:
British Citizen, for those closely connected with the UK. The holder has automatic right of abode in the UK.
British Dependent Territories Citizen, for those with certain specific ties with one or more of the dependent territories.

British Overseas Citizen, for those citizens of the UK and Colonies who do not acquire either of the above citizenship.
Since January 1, 1983, no endorsement about immigration status has been necessary on passports issued to British citizens as they will automatically be exempt from UK immigration control and have the right to take up employment or to establish themselves in business in another member state of the EC.
Visitors should check with the relevant Embassy or Consulate if they have any queries regarding what level of citizenship is necessary to qualify for entry to any country destination without possession of a visa.
All applications and enquiries should be made to the Passport Office, Clive House, Petty France, London SW1 (who also handle visa requirements relating to **British Dependent Territories**), or to its regional offices in Belfast, Glasgow, Liverpool, Newport and Peterborough.

MONEY

The entries for each country provide information on currency denominations, currency restrictions, recent exchange rates for Sterling and the US Dollar and banking hours. Where necessary, information is also included on matters relating to currency exchange and the use of travellers cheques and credit cards. The following sections are intended as a general guide; details are given in the individual country entries.
Currency: The denominations of notes and coins given are correct at the time of going to press, but new ones may be introduced or old ones withdrawn, particularly in countries with high rates of inflation. In some countries, certain foreign currencies may be accepted instead of or in addition to the local currency. In most cases, UK Sterling and US Dollar bank notes and travellers cheques can be exchanged at banks and bureaux de change. Sometimes, however, a **Currency exchange** section is included, giving additional information and local regulations. In certain countries of the world, some foreign currencies are more readily accepted than others, and details are included where this is likely to affect a visitor carrying Sterling notes or travellers cheques. The French Franc, for instance, is advisable for countries of the French Monetary Area (for a list of countries in the French Monetary Area, see below under *International Organisations*), and the US Dollar is more readily accepted throughout much of South America and the Caribbean. In general, the Pound Sterling and US Dollar are almost universally negotiable. Banks may recommend one in preference to the other, depending on the exchange rates, and will also be able to offer up-to-date information as to the acceptability of Sterling in a particular country.
It is worth remembering that certain currencies can be reconverted into Sterling only at very disadvantageous rates; others cannot be reconverted at all. In some cases, banknotes of a very low value will not be negotiable in the UK, whilst denominations which are considered too high may attract a less favourable rate of exchange. However, US travellers can expect to get a better rate for US$100 notes than for US$5, but please note that many banks will refuse to exchange US$1 notes. Coins should not be brought back, as UK banks will not be able to exchange them, or may do so only at a very disadvantageous rate. Some countries prohibit reconversion except at airports or borders, and then only up to a certain limit. It is often advisable only to change the amount necessary.
Currency restrictions permitting, it may be advisable to change enough money in the UK to cover immediate expenses such as taxi fares from the airport, in the event of the airport bank not being open (these banks do not always keep normal banking hours, see individual country entries under **Travel – International**). Visitors should also note that each country has specific Bank Holidays (see **Public Holidays**).
Credit cards: Information has been given on the acceptability of credit cards, although space clearly does not permit a list of organisations which will accept any particular card. Most of the major credit card companies produce booklets providing information.
Travellers cheques: These are widely accepted as shown. In some places there are preferences, usually for either Dollar or French Franc travellers cheques.
Exchange rate indicators: A selection of exchange rates, spanning the past four years, have been included in each country entry. These figures are usually middle rates, ie the average of buying and selling prices. Some countries operate a 2- or 3-tiered exchange rate, in which case the rates quoted are the most advantageous, and are the ones which would apply to a foreign visitor. It must be stressed that these figures are only a guide, enabling the visitor to judge the approximate value of each currency over the period. Exchange rates will vary from bank to bank, both in the UK and in the country itself. The figures are based on rates supplied by the *Financial Times*.
Subject to availability, permitted currencies can usually be bought in UK banks before departure. It is not, however, possible to indicate whether it is more profitable to buy foreign currency in the UK or in the country being visited. Exchange rates fluctuate from day to day and a British bank would not know what rates were being offered in a foreign country at any given time, nor what commission rates were likely to be charged. In almost all cases it is best to obtain travellers cheques, either in Sterling or, for countries where Sterling is not easily negotiable, in US Dollars. The advantages of these being both widely accepted and easily refundable more than offset the small profits that may be made by buying foreign currency in the UK.
Currency restrictions: Most countries permit the unlimited import of foreign currency, although it is often subject to declaration on arrival. In such cases the export of foreign currency will usually be limited to the amount imported and declared. Some countries insist on the exchange of a certain quantity of foreign currency for each day of the visit and this may need to be done in advance. In some cases, receipts must be kept in order to reconvert surplus local currency on departure; in others, special forms or permits may be required.
The import and export of local currency is often prohibited, or limited to certain amounts or denominations of coins or banknotes.
Travellers should note that black market transactions are not necessarily favourable, in some cases illegal, and are always unaccountable (which may cause problems when leaving a country) and often result in severe punishment (including, in some places, a possible death sentence).
Further details and up-to-date information may be obtained from UK banks, or from the relevant Embassy, High Commission or Tourist Office. For addresses, see the section at the start of each country entry.

DUTY FREE

All duty-free allowances, including differentials for EC and non-EC travellers, are given where applicable, as well as information on prohibited items and any other relevant details.
The import or export of animals, plants, meat or meat products, commercial samples and certain other goods may involve complicated regulations or restrictions, and details given in the text are not necessarily exhaustive and should only be used as a general guide. Further information may be obtained from the appropriate High Commission, Embassy or Tourist Board, HM Customs and Excise *or* the British Overseas Trade Board.
On January 1, 1993, the Single European Market was introduced which enables travellers between EC member countries to import larger quantities of duty-paid goods. A separate paragraph within the duty-free section for EC member countries gives exact quantities of the goods affected.

PUBLIC HOLIDAYS

This section lists all public, statutory holidays which will affect the traveller during the period March 1993 to March 1994. The holidays given are usually those when businesses and banks will close. Note that the dates for Islamic holidays are approximate, since they must accord with sightings of the moon. The dates given are correct within one or two days. For further information relating to the Islamic way of life, see the *World of Islam* section at the back of the book. (Similar variations of dating occur for Hindu, Buddhist and Chinese holidays.)
In some cases, official dates for public holidays had not been fixed at the time of going to press. Check with the respective Tourist Office, Embassy or High Commission for further details.

HEALTH

Vaccination requirement and/or recommendations are presented in a quick-glance chart. Wherever an immunisation is considered 'advisable', we strongly advise that precautions are taken, even though they may not be strictly necessary. Occasionally this advice may conflict with advice given by the relevant Tourist Board or Embassy, but we feel that the recommendations of the Department of Health and the WHO are worth heeding, on the principle of safeguarding against even a minimal risk. It is important to note that general standards of hygiene and sanitation may be higher in tourist areas and city centres. Where immunisation is required, vaccination should be taken well in advance so that adequate intervals between doses can be maintained: rapid courses do not guarantee the same level of immunisation. Children and pregnant women my require special vaccination procedures. (See the immunisation chart in the *Health* section, to be found at the back of this book.)
The information contained in the *Health* section of the book and in the individual country entries has been compiled from several sources including the Department of Health, the World Health Organisation, the London School of Hygiene and Tropical Medicine and the *British Medical Journal* (official publication of the British Medical Association).
We would particularly like to thank: Dr G R Williams, MRCP, DTMH, Consultant Physician in Infectious Diseases at the Ayrshire General Hospital, for his help in updating the *Health* section and, in particular, the chart of vaccination and prophylaxis requirements and programmes; and Dr Paul Clarke of MASTA and the London School of Hygiene and Tropical Medicine in London.

TRAVEL

This information is divided into sections for **International** and **Internal** travel for the country. As the information on **AIR** and **ROAD** sub-sections tends to be different, depending on whether international or internal travel is being discussed, they are therefore dealt with twice, once as *international* and once as *internal*. Information within the sub-sections for **SEA (or SEA/RIVER/LAKE)** and **RAIL** will be included, where applicable, in the relevant section. The **URBAN** sub-section only occurs in the **Internal** section.

–International

AIR: The name and code of the major *airline* serving the country is given (usually the national airline). In almost all cases the **Approximate flight time** from London and other major cities to the main airport is also given; it must be stressed that these figures *are* approximate, and depend on a number of factors including the airline taken, the number and duration of stopovers and the route. Information is also supplied on the major **International airports**, including the distance from the city centre. Where available, additional details of available modes of transport and a list of airport facilities are also included.
SEA: Where applicable, ferry and cruise ports will be mentioned and details, where available, will be given of international ferry services.
RAIL: Where applicable, the main international rail routes are described. The section also covers special fares and reductions available, for example, the *Inter-Rail* ticket scheme. The respective Tourist Board or national Railway Office can be contacted for details.
ROAD: The main links between countries are described with details of ferry crossings where appropriate. Where crossing borders by road is likely to cause difficulties or inconvenience this is noted.

–Internal

AIR: Where appropriate, further information is given on internal air services and domestic airports.
SEA/RIVER/LAKE: Where applicable, ferry ports will be mentioned and details, where available, will be given of internal ferry services. Main river and lake services will also be mentioned.
RAIL: The main internal rail routes are described. The section also covers special fares and reductions available. Prices have normally not been included, as these are subject to change, often at short notice. Contact the respective Tourist Board or national Railway Office for details.
ROAD: The main road routes are described, as are the quality and extent of the major bus, coach, taxi and car hire services. Driving regulations and documentation required are also referred to.
URBAN: Where appropriate, many countries also have a section giving details of travel facilities in and around the main cities.
For some countries, a **Journey time chart** has also been included, giving the approximate journey times between the capital and major towns/cities/islands in the country. These figures are based on the fastest and most direct services, and are intended only as a guide.
ACCOMMODATION
Details are given in this section on the range of available **Hotel** accommodation including government

classifications, regulations etc, according to the latest information available at the time of going to press. The *World Travel Guide* provides details of the national hotel association where possible, together with specific information on the national **Grading** system. The national grading system should not be confused with local award schemes such as the AA or Michelin star systems. Information is also included on other forms of accommodation, including **SELF-CATERING, GUEST-HOUSES, CAMPING/CARAVANNING** and **YOUTH HOSTELS**.

RESORTS & EXCURSIONS

This section offers a description of the country's main tourist regions, most popular resorts and the facilities provided in and around them. Any recommended places of interest and excursions are also included. Some countries may be extremely difficult to visit at the present time for political reasons. However, some description of those areas which would normally be of interest to travellers is given for future reference in the event of them becoming accessible again. Where information is available, advice is given on the current political and travel situation and whether special permission is needed for travel within the country.

Sub Divisions

The *Resorts & Excursions* sections of many countries have been subdivided using the heading style shown above. **Note:** In some cases, the divisions in the *Resorts & Excursions* section will not correspond exactly with administrative boundaries. These divisions have been made in an attempt to group towns or regions together for touristic purposes, and have no political significance.

SOCIAL PROFILE

This section describes the range of leisure activities and facilities available, especially those with a national or regional flavour.
FOOD & DRINK: Information is included on the national cuisine and recommended dishes, bars, restaurants, national drinks and licensing hours.
NIGHTLIFE: Information on the extent and range of the main forms of evening entertainment within the main centres of the country.
SPORT: Descriptions of sporting facilities and spectator sports are included.
SPECIAL EVENTS: Special events including festivals, ceremonies, celebrations, exhibitions and sporting occasions which might be of interest to a foreign visitor.
SOCIAL CONVENTIONS: Includes information on customs or expected modes of behaviour, the required style of dress and acceptable or unacceptable gifts. **Photography:** Any general restrictions on photography, such as the photographing of military installations etc, are indicated. **Tipping:** Where to tip, roughly how much to tip and where not to tip at all. In a few cases other categories have also been included where necessary.

BUSINESS PROFILE

Information is presented under the following headings:
ECONOMY: There is a brief description of the economy of each country. The section also identifies the country's principal exports and imports and its major trading partners. Important recent economic developments and future prospect are also mentioned. The section is largely descriptive and does not provide detailed trade or other economic statistics.
BUSINESS: This section includes the best times to visit the country, the necessity or otherwise for visiting cards, prior appointments, translation/interpreter services and punctuality, the required style of dress for business meetings as well as business/office hours and other useful tips and advice.
COMMERCIAL INFORMATION: The national chamber of commerce in each country is in a position to be able to offer detailed commercial advice and information to any prospective business traveller. For this reason the address, telephone number and fax number of the chamber of commerce and/or other relevant organisation(s) has been included in this section.
CONFERENCES/CONVENTIONS: A brief description of the conference/convention scene within the country is included here along with the name, address, telephone and fax number of the national conference organisation. Where appropriate, a description of the organisation itself and the facilities it can provide is also included.

HISTORY & GOVERNMENT

This section has been devised in order to help all users of the book understand something of the history and constitution of the country. It is divided into two categories and every effort has been made within each to give a balanced and factual account of the most important features. Inevitably, many of the events referred to can lend themselves to interpretations other than those which may be stated or implied within the text and the publishers consequently wish to stress that no general political or historiographical stance has been adopted. The inclusion of the *History & Government* section has established the *World Travel Guide* as a leading reference work for the travel trade, and forms an informative epilogue to the entry on each country, providing the visitor with important background information, which is as accurate as possible at the time of going to press; this is not always easy. Last year, for instance, the dramatic and fast-moving events in the former Yugoslavia and the moves to create the separate states of the Czech Republic and Slovak Republic at times overwhelmed our best efforts. All of this has once again thrown the world of international travel into turmoil and at the time of writing the results of the conflict are still far from clear. It is nevertheless hoped that the *History & Government* entries will provide a useful summary of events.

CLIMATE

This section includes a brief description of the country's climate, including recommendations on clothing. The information is supplemented by at least one climate graph per country, giving average maximum and minimum monthly temperatures, precipitation and humidity; where available, sunshine hours have also been included.
Attention is also drawn to the *Weather* section at the back of the book.

Appendices

INTERNATIONAL TRAVEL TRADE PRESS

This section gives an overview of major travel trade publications worldwide. Information is included on each publication's contents, markets, country of origin, circulation, frequency of publication, language, methods of distribution and publisher.

GOLF

This section gives an overview of the increasing importance of golf to the traveller. Graham Lowing's survey provides an introduction and insight into destinations and trends.

HEALTH

This section contains essential information for anyone travelling abroad, particularly to tropical countries, and supplements the information contained in the *Health* section of each country's entry. Information is included on special and rare diseases, malaria prophylaxis, accidents and bites, pregnancy, contraception, immunisation, sources of advice and specialist associations. There are maps showing yellow fever endemic areas, areas of malaria risk and where chloroquine-resistance of *plasmodium falciparum* has been reported. It is vital for travellers to obtain up-to-date information on countries they intend to visit as local circumstances are liable to change rapidly.

COUNTRY CURRENCY CODES

This new section lists the country currency codes assigned by the International Standards Organisation.

THE DISABLED TRAVELLER

This section is designed to provide the travel trade with information relevant to the booking of holidays for handicapped people. A selection of sources of further information is also given. Note that certain operators cater exclusively for the special needs of handicapped people, while others draw attention to suitable destinations and accommodation in their brochures.

WEATHER

This section is intended as a general introduction to the way in which weather conditions can affect individuals, and supplements the information contained in the *Climate* section of each country's entry. Information is included on humidity, wind and wind-chill factor, temperature range, precipitation and precautions. There is also an example of a climate chart, giving conversions between Fahrenheit and Centigrade, and millimetres and inches.

THE WORLD OF BUDDHISM

This section is intended to give a brief introduction to the religious and cultural attitudes of Buddhism, and supplements information contained in the *Public Holidays*, *Social Profile*, *Business Profile* and *History & Government* sections of countries where Buddhism is practised. Information is included on basic religious tenets, social customs and conventions.

THE WORLD OF CHRISTIANITY

This section is intended to give a brief introduction to the religious and cultural attitudes of Christians, and supplements information contained in the *Public Holidays*, *Social Profile*, *Business Profile* and *History & Government* sections of countries where Christianity is practised. Information is included on basic religious tenets, social customs and conventions.

THE WORLD OF ISLAM

This section is intended to give an introduction to the religious and cultural attitudes of Muslims, and supplements information contained in the *Public Holidays*, *Social Profile*, *Business Profile* and *History & Government* sections of countries where Islam is practised. Information is included on the basic religious tenets, social customs and conventions, women and Islam and the Islamic calendar.

CRS & CODELINK

This section offers an overview of current developments in the CRS market as well as an insight into Codelink™, the Columbus Press-developed bar-code reference system.

TRAVEL CONTACTS

This section provides a selective list of ground operators in most countries of the world. These companies are approved by *Travel Contacts* whose directory (established 1980) is available free to anyone needing reliable ground handling services. Listed companies are chosen because they have been proved to offer professional, honest and efficient service. Nevertheless, neither *Columbus Press* nor *Travel Contacts Ltd* can accept any liability for any information contained within this section, nor for any business dealings which may be entered into with any company listed in the text. A copy of the directory is available from: Travel Contacts Ltd, 45 Idmiston Road, London SE27 9HL. Tel: (081) 766 7868. Fax: (081) 766 6123.

FINAL NOTE

If there is anything which you would like to see expanded, clarified or included for the first time, or if you come across any information which is no longer accurate, we would be very grateful if you could let us know. Such suggestions will be considered for future editions of the *World Travel Guide*. Address your suggestions to:
The Editor, World Travel Guide, Columbus Press, Charles House, Charles Square, London N1. Tel: (071) 729 4535.
You may have noticed that we have moved (or will have done by the time this book is published) from our old address in Luke Street EC2 to larger premises. This has been made necessary by the rapid expansion of the company to cater for an ever-increasing stable of comprehensive publications for the travel trade worldwide. We would like to thank you for your support over the last twelve editions of the *World Travel Guide*, during which time the title has become *the* destination source book for the trade worldwide. We look forward to supplying you with travel information for many years to come.

Lincoln Sea
ARCTI
Ellesmere I.
Greenland Sea
GREENLAND (Den.)
Beaufort Sea
Baffin Bay
Jan Mayen (Nor.)
Victoria I.
Baffin I.
Norwegian
Arctic Circle
Alaska (US)
Gt. Bear Lake
ICELAND
Faroe Is. (Den.)
NORW
Gt. Slave Lake
Hudson Bay
CANADA
UNITED KINGDOM
North Sea
Gulf of Alaska
DENMARK
NETH.
Aleutian Is.
L. Winnipeg
NORTH
IRELAND
Newfoundland
Vancouver I.
L. Superior
ATLANTIC
BELG.
FRANCE
L. Huron
St Pierre et Miquelon (Fr.)
SWITZ
L. Michigan
L. Ontario
OCEAN
ANDORRA
L. Erie
Corsica
UNITED STATES OF AMERICA
Azores (Port.)
PORTUGAL
SPAIN
Sardinia
Balearic Is.
Gibraltar (UK)
Bermuda (UK)
Madeira (Port.)
MOROCCO
Turks & Caicos Is. (UK)
HAITI
DOMINICAN REPUBLIC
Puerto Rico (US)
Canary Is. (Sp.)
ALGERIA
Gulf of Mexico
BAHAMAS
Virgin Is. (US,UK)
Anguilla (UK)
Tropic of Cancer
Cayman Is. (UK)
CUBA
ST KITTS-NEVIS
W. SAHARA
ANTIGUA & BARBUDA
Montserrat (UK)
Hawaii (US)
MEXICO
Guadeloupe (Fr.)
MAURITANIA
JAMAICA
DOMINICA
Martinique (Fr.)
BELIZE
MALI
PACIFIC
Caribbean Sea
ST LUCIA
CAPE VERDE
SENEGAL
ST VINCENT
GUATEMALA
Aruba (Neths.)
Neths. Antilles
THE GAMBIA
BURKINA FASO
BARBADOS
EL SALVADOR
GRENADA
GUINEA-BISSAU
GUINEA
OCEAN
HONDURAS
TRINIDAD & TOBAGO
NICARAGUA
VENEZUELA
GUYANA
CÔTE D'IVOIRE
BENIN
COSTA RICA
SURINAME
SIERRA LEONE
PANAMA
French Guiana (Fr.)
LIBERIA
GHANA
TOGO
COLOMBIA
Equator
SÃO TOMÉ & PRÍNCIPE
Galapagos Is. (Ec.)
ECUADOR
EQUAT. GUINEA
KIRIBATI
Tokelau (NZ)
Ascension (UK)
Samoa (US)
Cook Is. (NZ)
PERU
BRAZIL
St Helena (UK)
Niue (NZ)
French Polynesia
BOLIVIA
SOUTH
Walvis Bay
Pitcairn Is. (UK)
Tropic of Capricorn
PARAGUAY
ATLANTIC
Easter I. (Chile)
CHILE
URUGUAY
OCEAN
ARGENTINA
Tristan da Cunha (UK)
Gough I. (UK)
Falkland Is. (UK)
Tierra del Fuego
S. Georgia (UK)
S. Sandwich Is. (UK)
Drake Passage
Scotia Sea
Antarctic Circle
Antarctic Peninsula
Weddell Sea

OCEAN
Franz Josef Land
Severnaya Zemlya
Kara Sea
Laptev Sea
Novaya Zemlya
Barents Sea
New Siberian Is.
East Siberian Sea
Wrangel I.
Chukchi Sea
FINLAND
L. Ladoga
RUSSIAN FEDERATION
ESTONIA
LATVIA
LITHUANIA
BELARUS
COMMONWEALTH OF INDEPENDENT STATES
L. Baikal
Sea of Okhotsk
Kamchatka
Bering Sea
UKRAINE
MOLDOVA
ROMANIA
BULG.
MACEDONIA
Black Sea
GEORGIA
ARMENIA
AZER-BAIJAN
Caspian Sea
KAZAKHSTAN
L. Balkhash
Aral Sea
UZBEKISTAN
TURKMENISTAN
KIRGHIZIA
TAJIKISTAN
MONGOLIA
Sakhalin
Kurile Is.
Aleutian Is.
Hokkaido
TURKEY
CYPRUS
Crete
SYRIA
LEB.
ISRAEL
JORDAN
IRAQ
IRAN
AFGHANISTAN
CHINA
DEMOCRATIC PEOPLE'S REP. OF KOREA
REP. OF KOREA
JAPAN
Honshu
Kyushu
Shikoku
East China Sea
Ryukyu Is.
EGYPT
KUWAIT
BAHRAIN
QATAR
The Gulf
SAUDI ARABIA
U.A.E.
OMAN
PAKISTAN
NEPAL
BHUTAN
BANGLADESH
Hong Kong (UK)
Macau (Port.)
TAIWAN
PACIFIC
INDIA
MYANMAR
LAOS
Hainan I.
Arabian Sea
Red Sea
SUDAN
YEMEN
DJIBOUTI
Socotra (Yem.)
Bay of Bengal
THAILAND
VIETNAM
CAMBODIA
South China Sea
Philippine Sea
PHILIPPINES
Northern Mariana Is.
Guam (US)
Marshall Is.
OCEAN
ETHIOPIA
SOMALIA
SRI LANKA
BRUNEI
MALAYSIA
Belau (US)
Federated States of Micronesia
UGANDA
KENYA
MALDIVES
SINGAPORE
Borneo
W. SAMOA
RWANDA
BURUNDI
L. Victoria
Sumatra
Irian Jaya
PAPUA NEW GUINEA
NAURU
KIRIBATI
ZAÏRE
TANZANIA
COMOROS
SEYCHELLES
British Indian Ocean Territory (UK)
INDONESIA
Java
SOLOMON IS.
TUVALU
Tokelau (NZ)
ZAMBIA
MALAWI
Samoa (US)
MADAGASCAR
ZIMBABWE
Coral Sea
VANUATU
FIJI
TONGA
MOZAMBIQUE
MAURITIUS
Réunion (Fr.)
INDIAN OCEAN
AUSTRALIA
New Caledonia (Fr.)
Niue (NZ)
Wallis & Futuna (Fr.)
SWAZILAND
SOUTH AFRICA
LESOTHO
Tasman Sea
North I.
Tasmania
NEW ZEALAND
South I.
Prince Edward Is. (S. Af.)
Crozet Is. (Fr.)
Kerguelen Is. (Fr.)
SOUTHERN OCEAN
ANTARCTICA

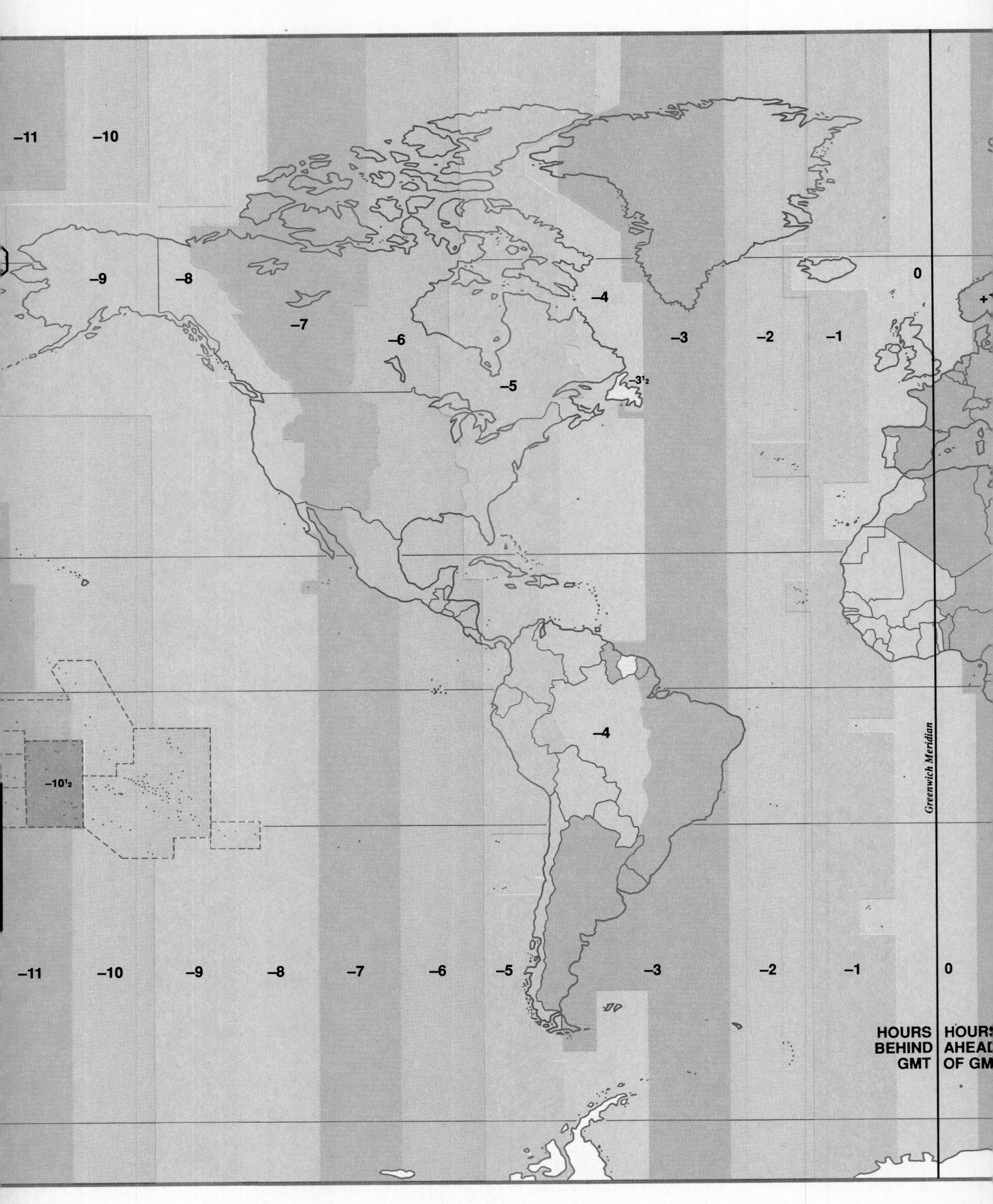

–11
–10
–9
–8
–7
–6
–5
–4
–3½
–3
–2
–1
0
–4
–10½
–11
–10
–9
–8
–7
–6
–5
–3
–2
–1
0
Greenwich Meridian
HOURS BEHIND GMT

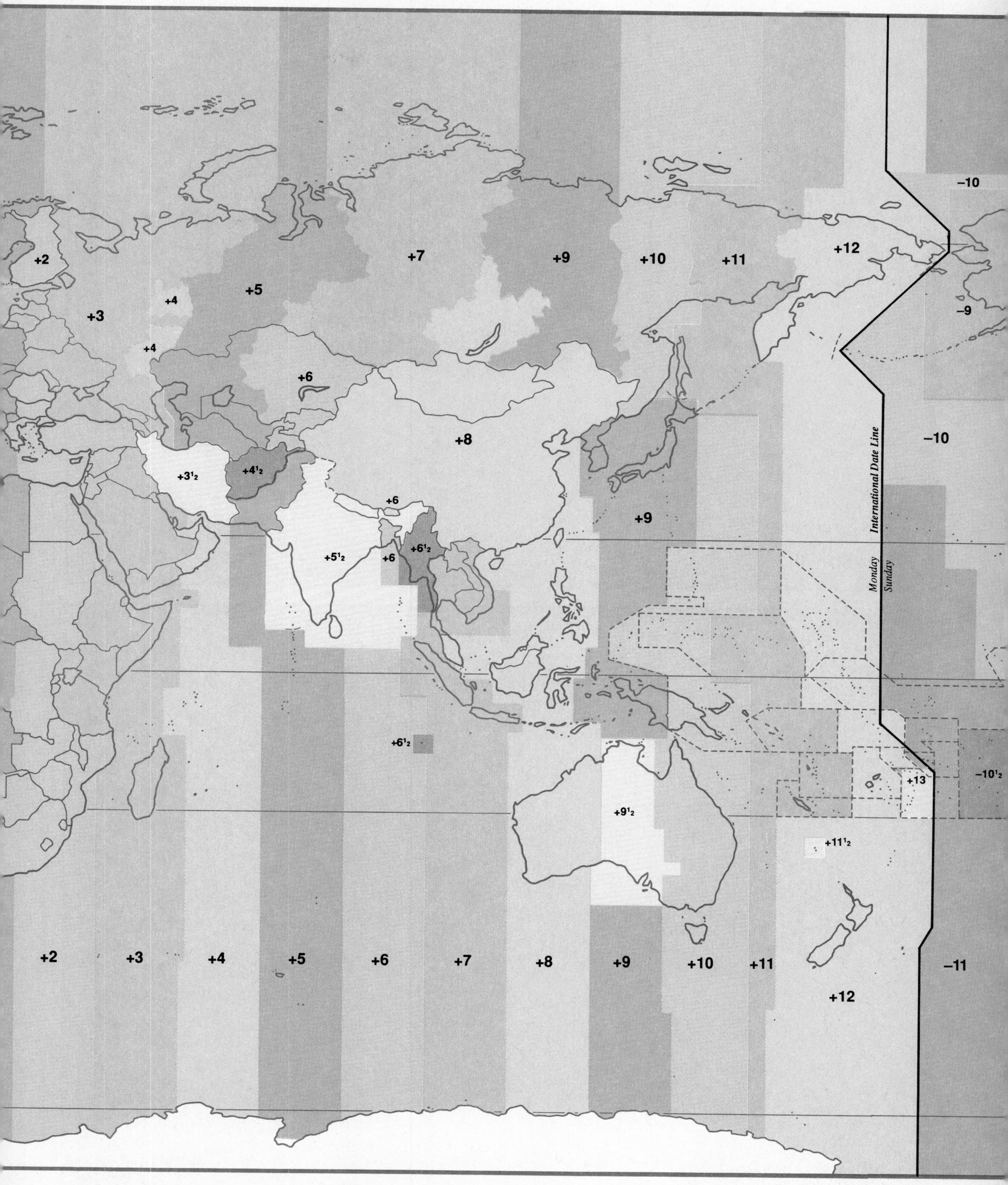

+2
+3
+4
+4
+5
+7
+9
+10
+11
+12
−10
−9
+6
+8
−10
+3½
+4½
+6
+9
International Date Line
+5½
+6
+6½
Monday
Sunday
+6½
+13
−10½
+9½
+11½
+2
+3
+4
+5
+6
+7
+8
+9
+10
+11
−11
+12

Europe

0 Km 600
0 Miles 400

1 Amsterdam
2 Brussels
3 Luxembourg City
4 Ljubljana
5 Zagreb
6 Sarajevo
7 Skopje

Reykjavik
ICELAND
Arctic Circle
Lappland
Faroes (Den.)
ATLANTIC OCEAN
North Sea
NORWAY
Bergen
Oslo
SWEDEN
Stockholm
Göteborg
FINLAND
Helsinki
St Petersburg
Tallinn
ESTONIA
LATVIA
Riga
LITHUANIA
Vilnius
Minsk
BELARUS
RUSSIAN FEDERATION
Nizhny Novgorod
Moscow
COMMONWEALTH OF INDEPENDENT STATES
KAZAKHSTAN
N. IRELAND
SCOTLAND
Edinburgh
IRELAND
Dublin
UNITED KINGDOM
ENGLAND
WALES
Birmingham
London
DENMARK
Copenhagen
Hamburg
NETHS.
FEDERAL REP. OF GERMANY
Berlin
Köln
Bonn
BELGIUM
LUX.
Paris
FRANCE
Warsaw
POLAND
Prague
CZECH REP.
Kiev
UKRAINE
Munich
Bratislava
SLOVAK REP.
Vienna
AUSTRIA
Bern
SWITZ.
Budapest
HUNGARY
MOLDOVA
Kishinev
Odessa
ROMANIA
Bucharest
Lyon
SLOVENIA
CROATIA
Milan
Turin
Marseille
MONACO
BOSNIA-HERZ.
YUGOSLAVIA
Belgrade
Sofia
BULGARIA
Black Sea
Caspian Sea
Tbilisi
GEORGIA
AZERBAIJAN
Baku
ARMENIA
Yerevan
Tabriz
IRAN
PORTUGAL
Lisbon
Madrid
SPAIN
Barcelona
Seville
Gibraltar (Brit.)
Balearic Is.
Corsica
SAN MARINO
Sardinia
Rome
ITALY
Naples
Tirana
ALBANIA
MACEDONIA
Istanbul
Ankara
TURKEY
GREECE
Athens
Ceuta (Sp.)
Melilla (Sp.)
Algiers
Rabat
MOROCCO
ALGERIA
Tunis
TUNISIA
Sicily
MALTA
Mediterranean Sea
Crete
CYPRUS
Nicosia
SYRIA
LEB.
IRAQ
Baghdad
D A Burles

A
FRANCE
ANDORRA
Andorra la Vella
SPAIN
0 Km 20
0 Miles 20

B
SWITZ.
AUSTRIA
LIECHTENSTEIN
Vaduz
0 Km 10
0 Miles 10

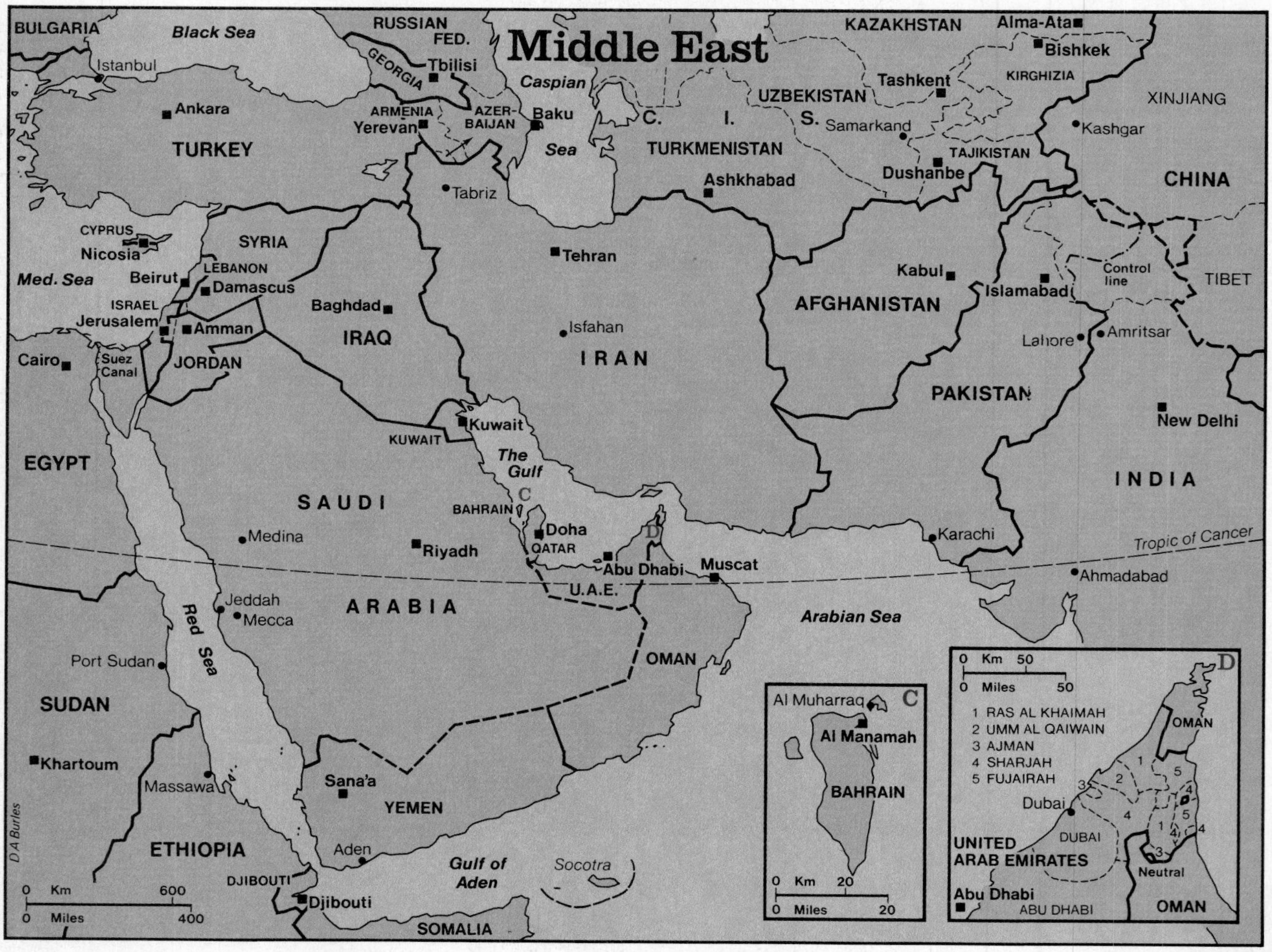

Middle East

BULGARIA
Black Sea
RUSSIAN FED.
Istanbul
GEORGIA
Tbilisi
Caspian Sea
ARMENIA
Yerevan
AZERBAIJAN
Baku
Ankara
TURKEY
Tabriz
KAZAKHSTAN
Alma-Ata
Bishkek
KIRGHIZIA
Tashkent
UZBEKISTAN
C. I. S.
Samarkand
TURKMENISTAN
Ashkhabad
TAJIKISTAN
Dushanbe
XINJIANG
Kashgar
CHINA
CYPRUS
Nicosia
SYRIA
Med. Sea
Beirut
LEBANON
Damascus
ISRAEL
Jerusalem
Amman
JORDAN
Baghdad
IRAQ
Tehran
Isfahan
IRAN
Kabul
AFGHANISTAN
Islamabad
Control line
TIBET
Lahore
Amritsar
PAKISTAN
New Delhi
Cairo
Suez Canal
EGYPT
Kuwait
KUWAIT
The Gulf
SAUDI ARABIA
BAHRAIN
C
Doha
QATAR
D
Abu Dhabi
U.A.E.
Muscat
Medina
Riyadh
Karachi
INDIA
Tropic of Cancer
Ahmadabad
Jeddah
Mecca
Red Sea
Arabian Sea
Port Sudan
OMAN
SUDAN
Khartoum
Massawa
Sana'a
YEMEN
ETHIOPIA
Aden
Gulf of Aden
Socotra
DJIBOUTI
Djibouti
SOMALIA
0 Km 600
0 Miles 400
D A Burles

C
Al Muharraq
Al Manamah
BAHRAIN
0 Km 20
0 Miles 20

D
0 Km 50
0 Miles 50
1 RAS AL KHAIMAH
2 UMM AL QAIWAIN
3 AJMAN
4 SHARJAH
5 FUJAIRAH
OMAN
Dubai
DUBAI
UNITED ARAB EMIRATES
Neutral
Abu Dhabi
ABU DHABI
OMAN

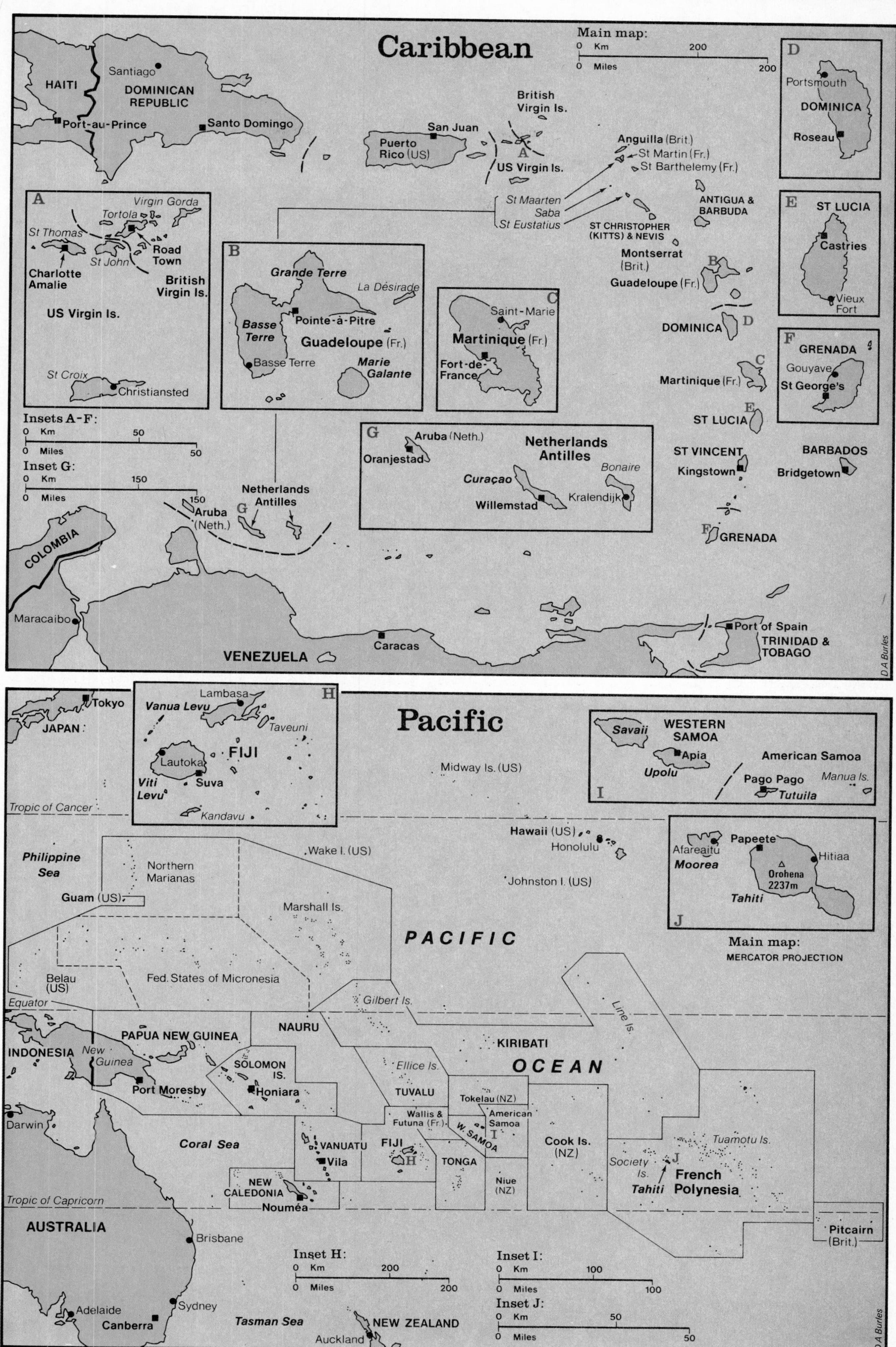
Caribbean
Main map:
0 Km 200
0 Miles 200
HAITI
DOMINICAN REPUBLIC
Santiago
Port-au-Prince
Santo Domingo
San Juan
Puerto Rico (US)
British Virgin Is.
US Virgin Is.
Anguilla (Brit.)
St Martin (Fr.)
St Barthelemy (Fr.)
St Maarten
Saba
St Eustatius
ANTIGUA & BARBUDA
ST CHRISTOPHER (KITTS) & NEVIS
Montserrat (Brit.)
Guadeloupe (Fr.)
DOMINICA
Martinique (Fr.)
ST LUCIA
ST VINCENT
Kingstown
BARBADOS
Bridgetown
GRENADA
Port of Spain
TRINIDAD & TOBAGO
Caracas
VENEZUELA
Maracaibo
COLOMBIA
Aruba (Neth.)
Netherlands Antilles
Insets A-F:
0 Km 50
0 Miles 50
Inset G:
0 Km 150
0 Miles 150
A
Virgin Gorda
Tortola
St Thomas
St John
Road Town
Charlotte Amalie
British Virgin Is.
US Virgin Is.
St Croix
Christiansted
B
Grande Terre
La Désirade
Basse Terre
Pointe-à-Pitre
Guadeloupe (Fr.)
Basse Terre
Marie Galante
C
Saint-Marie
Martinique (Fr.)
Fort-de-France
D
Portsmouth
DOMINICA
Roseau
E
ST LUCIA
Castries
Vieux Fort
F
GRENADA
Gouyave
St George's
G
Aruba (Neth.)
Oranjestad
Netherlands Antilles
Bonaire
Curaçao
Willemstad
Kralendijk
D A Burles
Pacific
Tokyo
JAPAN
H
Lambasa
Vanua Levu
Taveuni
FIJI
Lautoka
Viti Levu
Suva
Kandavu
Midway Is. (US)
I
Savaii
WESTERN SAMOA
Apia
Upolu
American Samoa
Pago Pago
Manua Is.
Tutuila
Tropic of Cancer
Hawaii (US)
Honolulu
J
Papeete
Afareaitu
Moorea
Hitiaa
Orohena 2237m
Tahiti
Philippine Sea
Northern Marianas
Wake I. (US)
Johnston I. (US)
Guam (US)
Marshall Is.
PACIFIC
Main map:
MERCATOR PROJECTION
Belau (US)
Fed. States of Micronesia
Equator
Gilbert Is.
Line Is.
PAPUA NEW GUINEA
NAURU
KIRIBATI
INDONESIA
New Guinea
SOLOMON IS.
Ellice Is.
OCEAN
Port Moresby
Honiara
TUVALU
Tokelau (NZ)
Darwin
Wallis & Futuna (Fr.)
American Samoa
W. SAMOA
Coral Sea
VANUATU
Vila
FIJI
TONGA
Cook Is. (NZ)
Tuamotu Is.
Society Is.
Tahiti
French Polynesia
NEW CALEDONIA
Nouméa
Niue (NZ)
Tropic of Capricorn
AUSTRALIA
Brisbane
Pitcairn (Brit.)
Inset H:
0 Km 200
0 Miles 200
Inset I:
0 Km 100
0 Miles 100
Inset J:
0 Km 50
0 Miles 50
Adelaide
Sydney
Canberra
Tasman Sea
NEW ZEALAND
Auckland
D A Burles

INTERNATIONAL ORGANISATIONS

Listed below are major international organisations concerned with economics and trade.

ASOCIACION LATINOAMERICANA DE INTEGRACION – ALADI

(Latin American Integration Association – LAIA)
Cebollatí 1461, Casilla 577, Montevideo, Uruguay.
Tel: (2) 401 121. Fax: (2) 490 649. Telex: 26944.
Members: Argentina, Bolivia, Brazil, Chile, Colombia, Ecuador, Mexico, Paraguay, Peru, Uruguay, Venezuela.

ASSOCIATION OF SOUTH EAST ASIAN NATIONS – ASEAN

Jalan Sisingamangaraja, PO Box 2072, Jakarta, Indonesia.
Tel: (21) 712 272. Telex: 47214.
Members: Brunei, Indonesia, Malaysia, Philippines, Singapore, Thailand.

CARIBBEAN COMMUNITY & COMMON MARKET – CARICOM

Bank of Guyana Building, PO Box 10827, Georgetown, Guyana.
Tel: (2) 69280. Fax: (2) 56194. Telex: 2263.
Members: Antigua & Barbuda, Bahamas, Barbados, Belize, Dominica, Dominican Republic, Grenada, Guyana, Haiti, Jamaica, Montserrat, St Kitts & Nevis, St Lucia, St Vincent & the Grenadines, Trinidad & Tobago.

CENTRAL AMERICAN COMMON MARKET – CACM

(Mercado Común Centroamericano)
4a Avenida 10-25, Zona 14, Apartado Postal 1237, 01901 Guatemala City, Guatemala.
Tel: (2) 682 151. Fax: (2) 681 071. Telex: 5676.
Members: Costa Rica, Guatemala, El Salvador, Honduras, Nicaragua.

THE COLOMBO PLAN FOR CO-OPERATIVE ECONOMIC AND SOCIAL DEVELOPMENT IN ASIA AND THE PACIFIC

12 Melbourne Avenue, PO Box 596, Colombo 4, Sri Lanka.
Tel: (1) 581 813. Fax: (1) 580 721. Telex: 21537.
Members: Afghanistan, Australia, Bangladesh, Bhutan, Cambodia, Canada, Fiji, India, Indonesia, Iran, Japan, Laos, Malaysia, Maldives, Myanmar, Nepal, New Zealand, Pakistan, Papua New Guinea, Philippines, Singapore, Sri Lanka, South Korea, Thailand, United Kingdom, United States of America.

COMMONWEALTH

Marlborough House, Pall Mall, London SW1Y 5HX, England.
Tel: (071) 839 3411. Fax: (071) 930 0827. Telex: 27678.
Members: Antigua & Barbuda, Australia, Bahamas, Bangladesh, Barbados, Belize, Botswana, Brunei, Canada, Cyprus, Dominica, The Gambia, Ghana, Grenada, Guyana, India, Jamaica, Kenya, Kiribati, Lesotho, Malawi, Malaysia, Maldives, Malta, Mauritius, Namibia, Nauru, New Zealand, Nigeria, Pakistan, Papua New Guinea, St Kitts & Nevis, St Lucia, St Vincent & the Grenadines, Seychelles, Sierra Leone, Singapore, Solomon Islands, Sri Lanka, Swaziland, Tanzania, Tonga, Trinidad & Tobago, Tuvalu, Uganda, United Kingdom, Vanuatu, Western Samoa, Zambia, Zimbabwe.
Dependencies & Associated States: *Australia:* Australian Antarctic Territory, Christmas Island (Pacific), Cocos Islands, Coral Sea Islands Territory, Heard & McDonald Islands, Norfolk Island; *New Zealand:* Cook Islands, Niue, Ross Dependency, Tokelau; *United Kingdom:* Anguilla, Ascension Island, Bermuda, British Antarctic Territory, British Indian Ocean Territory, British Virgin Islands, Cayman Islands, Channel Islands, Falkland Islands, Gibraltar, Hong Kong, Isle of Man, Montserrat, Pitcairn Islands, St Helena, South Georgia, South Sandwich Islands, Tristan da Cunha, Turks & Caicos Islands.

CO-OPERATION COUNCIL FOR THE ARAB STATES OF THE GULF

PO Box 7153, Riyadh 11462, Saudi Arabia.
Tel: (1) 482 7777. Fax: (1) 482 9089. Telex: 403635.
Members: Bahrain, Kuwait, Oman, Qatar, Saudi Arabia, United Arab Emirates.
Council of Arab Economic Unity
PO Box 925100, Amman, Jordan.
Tel: (6) 664 326. Telex: 21900.
Members: Egypt, Iraq, Jordan, Kuwait, Libya, Mauritania, Palestine Liberation Organisation, Somalia, Sudan, Syria, United Arab Emirates, Yemen.

ECONOMIC COMMUNITY OF WEST AFRICAN STATES – ECOWAS

Abuja, Nigeria.
Tel: (9) 523 1858.
Members: Benin, Burkina Faso, Cape Verde, Côte d'Ivoire, The Gambia, Ghana, Guinea, Guinea-Bissau, Liberia, Mali, Mauritania, Niger, Nigeria, Senegal, Sierra Leone, Togo.

THE EUROPEAN COMMUNITY – EC

No final decision has been made on a headquarters for the Community. Meetings of the principal organs take place in *Brussels, Luxembourg* and *Strasbourg*.
Members: Belgium, Denmark, France, Federal Republic of Germany, Greece, Ireland, Italy, Luxembourg, The Netherlands, Portugal, Spain, United Kingdom.

EUROPEAN FREE TRADE ASSOCIATION – EFTA

9-11 rue de Varembé, 1211 Geneva 20, Switzerland.
Tel: (22) 749 1111. Fax: (22) 733 9291. Telex: 22660.
Members: Austria, Finland, Iceland, Liechtenstein, Norway, Sweden, Switzerland.

THE FRANC ZONE

Direction Générale des Services Etrangers (Service des Relations avec la Zone Franc), Banque de France, 39 rue Croix-des-Petits-Champs, BP 140-01, Paris Cedex 01, France.
Tel: (1) 42 92 31 26. Fax: (1) 42 96 47 18. Telex: 220932.
Members: Benin, Burkina Faso, Cameroon, Central African Republic, Chad, Comoro Islands, Congo, Côte d'Ivoire, Equatorial Guinea, French Republic*, Gabon, Mali, Niger, Senegal, Togo.
* Metropolitan France, Mayotte, St Pierre and Miquelon, and the Overseas Departments and Territories.

GENERAL AGREEMENT ON TARIFFS AND TRADE – GATT

Centre William Rappard, 154 rue de Lausanne, 1211 Geneva 21, Switzerland.
Tel: (22) 739 5111. Fax: (22) 731 4206. Telex: 412324.

LEAGUE OF ARAB STATES

Arab League Building, Tahrir Square, Cairo, Egypt.
Tel: (2) 752 966 or 750 511. Fax: (2) 775 626. Telex: 92111.
Members: Algeria, Bahrain, Djibouti, Egypt, Iraq, Jordan, Kuwait, Lebanon, Libya, Mauritania, Morocco, Oman, Palestine, Qatar, Saudi Arabia, Somalia, Sudan, Syria, Tunisia, United Arab Emirates, Yemen Republic.

NORDIC COUNCIL

Tyrgatan 7, Box 19506, 10432 Stockholm, Sweden.
Tel: (8) 143 420. Fax: (8) 117 536. Telex: 12 867.
Members: Denmark (with the autonomous territories of the Faroe Islands and Greenland), Finland (with the autonomous territory of the Aland Islands), Iceland, Norway, Sweden.

ORGANISATION FOR ECONOMIC CO-OPERATION AND DEVELOPMENT – OECD

2 rue André-Pascal, 75775 Paris Cedex 16, France.
Tel: (1) 45 24 82 00. Fax: (1) 45 24 85 00. Telex: 620160.
Members: Australia, Austria, Belgium, Canada, Denmark, Finland, France, Federal Republic of Germany, Greece, Iceland, Ireland, Italy, Japan, Luxembourg, The Netherlands, New Zealand, Norway, Portugal, Spain, Sweden, Switzerland, Turkey, United Kingdom, United States of America.

ORGANISATION OF AFRICAN UNITY – OAU

PO Box 3243, Addis Ababa, Ethiopia.
Tel: (1) 517 700. Fax: (1) 512 622. Telex: 21046.
Members: Algeria, Angola, Benin, Botswana, Burkina Faso, Burundi, Cameroon, Cape Verde, Central African Republic, Chad, Comoro Islands, Congo, Côte d'Ivoire, Djibouti, Egypt, Equatorial Guinea, Ethiopia, Gabon, The Gambia, Ghana, Guinea, Guinea-Bissau, Kenya, Lesotho, Liberia, Libya, Madagascar, Malawi, Mali, Mauritania, Mauritius, Mozambique, Namibia, Niger, Nigeria, Rwanda, São Tomé & Príncipe, Senegal, Seychelles, Sierra Leone, Somalia, Sudan, Swaziland, Tanzania, Togo, Tunisia, Uganda, Zaïre, Zambia, Zimbabwe.

ORGANISATION OF AMERICAN STATES – OAS

1889 F Street, NW, Washington, DC 20006, USA.
Tel: (202) 458 3000. Telex: 440118.
Members: Antigua & Barbuda, Argentina, Bahamas, Barbados, Bolivia, Brazil, Canada, Chile, Colombia, Costa Rica, Cuba*, Dominica, Dominican Republic, Ecuador, El Salvador, Grenada, Guatemala, Guyana, Haiti, Honduras, Jamaica, Mexico, Nicaragua, Panama, Paraguay, Peru, St Kitts & Nevis, St Lucia, St Vincent & the Grenadines, Suriname, Trinidad & Tobago, United States of America, Uruguay, Venezuela.
* The Cuban government was suspended fom OAS activities in 1962.

ORGANISATION OF THE PETROLEUM EXPORTING COUNTRIES – OPEC

Obere Donaustrasse 93, 1020 Vienna, Austria.
Tel: (1) 211 120. Fax: (1) 264 320. Telex: 134474.
Members: Algeria, Ecuador, Gabon, Indonesia, Iran, Iraq, Kuwait, Libya, Nigeria, Qatar, Saudi Arabia, United Arab Emirates, Venezuela.

SOUTH PACIFIC FORUM

(c/o South Pacific Bureau for Economic Co-operation – SPEC).
GPO Box 856, Suva, Fiji.
Tel: 312 600. Telex: 2229.
Members: Australia, Cook Islands, Fiji, Kiribati, Marshall Islands, Federated States of Micronesia, Nauru, New Zealand, Niue, Papua New Guinea, Solomon Islands, Tonga, Tuvalu, Vanuatu, Western Samoa.

SOUTHERN AFRICAN DEVELOPMENT CO-ORDINATION CONFERENCE – SADCC

Private Bag 0095, Gaborone, Botswana.
Tel: 51863. Telex: 2555.
Members: Angola, Botswana, Lesotho, Malawi, Mozambique, Namibia, Swaziland, Tanzania, Zambia, Zimbabwe.

UNION OF THE ARAB MAGHREB

Quartier Administratif, Rabat, Morocco.
The location of the Union's Secretariat rotates with the chairmanship.
Members: Algeria, Libya, Mauritania, Morocco, Tunisia.

UNITED NATIONS

United Nations Plaza, New York, NY 10017, USA.
Tel: (212) 963 1234.
Members: All sovereign countries except: Andorra, China (Taiwan), Kiribati, Democratic People's Republic of Korea, Republic of Korea, Monaco, Nauru, Switzerland, Tonga, Tuvalu, Vatican City.

UNITED NATIONS CONFERENCE ON TRADE AND DEVELOPMENT – UNCTAD

Palais des Nations, 1211 Geneva 10, Switzerland.
Tel: (22) 734 6011. Fax: (22) 733 6542. Telex: 289696.

UN INTERNATIONAL BANK FOR RECONSTRUCTION AND DEVELOPMENT – IBRD (WORLD BANK)

1818 H Street, NW, Washington, DC 20433, USA.
Tel: (202) 477 1234. Fax: (202) 477 6391. Telex: 248423.

UN INTERNATIONAL MONETARY FUND (IMF)

700 19th Street, NW, Washington, DC 20431, USA.
Tel: (202) 623 7430. Fax: (202) 623 4661. Telex: 440040.

IMPLICATIONS OF THE EC DIRECTIVE ON PACKAGE TRAVEL

By December 31, 1992, all Member States of the European Community should have implemented the *Council Directive of June 1990* which introduces new standards for the relationship between package organisers and consumers.

Needless to say, the degree of implementation throughout Europe is not uniform. In the United Kingdom, specific legislation, the *Package Travel Regulations 1992*, has given the *Directive* statutory effect. Other member states, whilst having adopted the *Directive*, have not brought in specific legislation. In some states, the existing regulatory framework of the travel industry on consumer protection is very much along the lines of the *Directive*. Other states are still considering what to do.

So, the effect at the moment is that whilst there is in theory a common set of legal obligations throughout the Community, in practice there are wide discrepancies between Member States in how these are put into operation. Thus, it is questionable to what extent the European Council's twin aims of increased consumer protection and harmonisation to enhance free competition throughout Europe have actually been achieved. Readers based in or operating from Europe who think they may be effected as package organisers are advised to take advice on their position under the laws of the country or countries in which they operate. Non-European operators selling packages in Europe may well be caught by the *Directive*.

The detailed provisions of the *Directive* are complicated and will vary from state to state. The principle objectives and their effect on the operator–supplier relationship are set out below. If there is one underlying theme to the *Directive*, it may be said to be one of increased quality control throughout the industry, effecting both the consumer–organiser relationship and dealings between the organiser and its suppliers, whether they be airlines, hoteliers or local agents. It is also important to bear in mind that business-to-business dealings are covered by the *Directive*, so business travel, incentive travel and conference and meetings organisers are included.

The principle elements of the *Directive* can be summarised as follows:

(1) In *Article 3*, a tightening up of the content of descriptive matter and brochures. Essential information relating to transport accommodation, passport and visa requirements and price must be included in the brochure. *Article 4* requires the organiser to provide, before the contract is concluded, general information on passport, visas and health requirements and, before the package starts, details of the journey such as intermediate stops and transport connections, contact addresses and an insurance policy to cover cancellation, accidents and repatriation. In the United Kingdom, failure to provide this information at the proper time has become a criminal offence. So, those dealing with organisers can expect them to be more demanding than ever to obtain accurate information to pass on to their clients. Suppliers can also now expect organisers to require the suppliers to take some financial responsibility for the accuracy of information provided.

(2) *Article 4* also lays down minimum requirements for the contents of any contract governing the package.

(3) *Article 5* has a great impact in many states. Organisers are now responsible to the consumer for the proper performance of the package contract, irrespective of whether the organiser is actually going to perform that contract or whether it is to be done by other suppliers of services. So, the organiser is now, in effect, primarily responsible for everything that happens on the package. Because of this, the organiser will now be insisting on quality control, ensuring that a supplier can and will perform to the standards the organiser has promised to the consumer. Alert suppliers will recognise these new obligations on organisers and satisfy their requirements. Suppliers can also expect organisers to be contracting on a much more rigorous basis and seeking indemnities from suppliers against any liability they incur to consumers.

(4) *Article 7* now requires any organiser to provide financial security for the refund of consumer's deposits and for their repatriation in the event of the organiser's insolvency. Thus, bonding must now become a universal concept throughout the European travel industry. Bonding can be an expensive business, cutting into organiser's profit margins with an obvious effect on their position in contractual negotiations.

The *Directive* may look intimidating, but if used to prove the quality of services and relationships, it will be no bad thing. It should help to introduce higher standards in the information given to consumers, the contractual relationships between organisers and suppliers and the financial stability of tour organisers.

For further information, contact:
Tim Robinson
Head of the Travel Law Unit
Nicholson Graham & Jones
25-31 Moorgate
London EC2R 6AR
Tel: (071) 628 9151
Fax: (071) 638 3102.

AFGHANISTAN

Location: Southwest Asia; northwest part of Indian sub-continent.

Note: At present, few visitors are entering Afghanistan due to the political situation and the British and US Embassies in Kabul are closed. Information is included below in case of future change. Check with the appropriate government office (Foreign Office for British citizens) for up-to-date information.

Afghan Tourist Organisation (ATO)
Shar-i-Nau
Ansari Wat
Kabul,
Afghanistan
Tel: (93) 30323.

Embassy of the Republic of Afghanistan
31 Prince's Gate
London
SW7 1QQ
Tel: (071) 589 8891. Fax: (071) 581 3452. Telex: 916641. Opening hours (visa applications): 0900-1600 Monday to Friday.

Afghanaid
292 Pentonville Road
London
N1 9NR
Tel: (071) 278 2832. Fax: (071) 837 8155.

British Embassy
Karte Parwan
Kabul,
Afghanistan
Tel: (93) 30511.
The Embassy is presently closed.

Embassy of the Republic of Afghanistan
2341 Wyoming Avenue, NW
Washington, DC
20008
Tel: (202) 234 3770. Fax: (202) 328 3516. Telex: 248206.

Embassy of the United States of America
Wazir Akbar Khan Mena
Kabul,
Afghanistan
Tel: (93) 62230.
The Embassy is presently closed.

AREA: 652,225 sq km (251,773 sq miles).
POPULATION: 18,614,000 (1986 estimate). The United Nations estimate that there are approximately 5.5 million refugees as a result of the fighting, of whom 3.15 million live in camps in Pakistan and about 2.35 million in Iran; their estimate of the population within the country is 14,709,000 (1987).
POPULATION DENSITY: 28.5 per sq km.
CAPITAL: Kabul. **Population:** 1,036,407 (1982).
GEOGRAPHY: Afghanistan is a landlocked country, sharing its borders with the CIS to the north, China to the northeast, Pakistan to the east and south, and Iran to the west. On the eastern tip of the Iranian plateau, central Afghanistan is made up of a tangled mass of mountain chains. The Hindu Kush is the highest range, rising to more than 7500m (24,600ft). The Bamian Valley separates the Hindu Kush from Koh-i-Baba, the central mountain range, and source of the Helmand River. To the north and southwest of these mountains alluvial plains provide fertile agricultural soil. To the northeast is Kabul, the capital. The other major cities are Jalalabad, Kandahar, Mazar-i-Sharif and Herat.
LANGUAGE: The official languages are Pashtu and Dari Persian. The more educated Afghans speak English. Some French, German and Russian is also spoken.
RELIGION: Islamic majority (mostly Sunni), with Hindu, Jewish and Christian minorities.
TIME: GMT + 4.5.
ELECTRICITY: 220 volts AC, 50Hz.
COMMUNICATIONS: Telephone/Fax: No IDD. There is a severe shortage of lines for operator-connected international calls. **Telex/telegram:** May be sent from the Central Post Office, Kabul (closes at 2100). **Post:** Airmail takes about a week to Europe. **Press:** *The Kabul New Times* is the main English-language newspaper.
BBC World Service and Voice of America frequencies: From time to time these change. See the section *How to Use this Book* for more information.

BBC:

MHz	15.31	11.95	9.740	15.57

A service is also available on 1413kHz.

Voice of America:

MHz	11.97	9.670	6.040	5.995

PASSPORT/VISA

Regulations and requirements may be subject to change at short notice, and you are advised to contact the appropriate diplomatic or consular authority before finalising travel arrangements. Details of these may be found at the head of this country's entry. Any numbers in the chart refer to the footnotes below.

	Passport Required?	Visa Required?	Return Ticket Required?
Full British	Yes	Yes	Yes
BVP	Not valid	-	-
Australian	Yes	Yes	Yes
Canadian	Yes	Yes	Yes
USA	Yes	Yes	Yes
Other EC	Yes	Yes	Yes
Japanese	Yes	Yes	Yes

Entry restrictions: Nationals of Israel are refused entry.
PASSPORTS: Valid passports are required by all.
British Visitors Passport: Not accepted.
VISAS: Required by all.
Types of visa: Enquire at Embassy or Grazandoy office (Kabul) for details about visiting Afghanistan. At time of writing, tourist visas are not being issued. When a business visa is required, it is necessary to write first to the Export Promotion Department, Ministry of Commerce, Darulaman Wat, Kabul, describing the purpose of the visit. 2 to 3 weeks should be allowed for authorisation to be granted. Transit visas are required by all transiting passengers except those continuing their journey on the same aircraft and holding confirmed reservations and valid documents for onward travel.
Application to: Consulate (or Consular Section at Embassy). For addresses, see top of entry.
Application requirements: (a) Authorisation. (b) Valid passport. (c) 3 photos. (d) Fee (£20 for UK citizens).
Note: Exit and re-entry permits must be obtained before attempting to leave Afghanistan.

MONEY

Currency: Afghani (Af) = 100 puls. Notes are in denominations of Af1000, 500, 100, 50, 20 and 10. Coins are in denominations of Af5, 2 and 1, and 50 and 25 puls.
Credit cards: Diners Club and Access/Mastercard are accepted but it is advisable to check with your credit card company for details of merchant acceptability and other services which may be available.
Exchange rate indicators: The following figures are included as a guide to the movements of the Afghani against Sterling and the US Dollar:

Date:	Oct '89	Oct '90	Oct '91	Oct '92
£1.00=	99.25	99.25	99.25	99.25
$1.00=	62.85	50.81	57.19	62.54

Currency restrictions: The import of local currency is unrestricted, the export is limited to Af1000. The import of foreign currency is unlimited if declared; the declared sum is the maximum allowed for export.
Banking hours: Generally 0800-1200 and 1300-1630 Saturday to Wednesday, 0800-1300 Thursday. Some banks are closed Wednesday.

DUTY FREE

The following goods can be taken into Afghanistan without incurring customs duty:
Any amount of perfume.
Prohibited items: Alcohol. The export of antiques, carpets and furs is prohibited without licence. All valuable goods (radios, cameras etc) must be registered on arrival.

PUBLIC HOLIDAYS

Public holidays observed in Afghanistan are as follows:
Mar 21 '93 Nauroz (New Year's Day, Iranian calendar). **Mar 25** Start of Eid al-Fitr. **Apr 27** Revolution Day. **May 1** Workers' Day. **Jun 1** Start of Eid al-Adha. **Jun 30** Ashoura. **Aug 18** Independence Day. **Aug 30** Mouloud (Prophet's Birthday). **Jan '94** Leilat al-Meiraj. **Mar** Nauroz *and* Eid al-Fitr.
Note: Muslim festivals are timed according to local sightings of various phases of the Moon and the dates given above are approximations. During the lunar month of Ramadan that precedes Eid al-Fitr, Muslims fast during the day and feast at night and normal business patterns may be interrupted. Some disruption may continue into Eid al-Fitr itself. Eid al-Fitr and Eid al-Adha may last anything from two to ten days, depending on the region. For more information see the section *World of Islam* at the back of the book.

HEALTH

Regulations and requirements may be subject to change at short notice, and you are advised to contact your doctor well in advance of your intended date of departure. Any numbers in the chart refer to the footnotes below.

	Special Precautions?	Certificate Required?
Yellow Fever	Yes	1
Cholera	Yes	2
Typhoid & Polio	Yes	-
Malaria	3	-
Food & Drink	4	

[1]: Certificate required if arriving from endemic or infected areas.
[2]: Following WHO guidelines issued in 1973, a cholera vaccination certificate is no longer a condition of entry to Afghanistan. However, cholera is a serious risk in this country and precautions are essential. Up-to-date advice should be sought before deciding whether these precautions should include vaccination as medical opinion is divided over its effectiveness. See the *Health* section at the back of the book.
[3]: Malarial risk exists from May to November below 2000m.
[4]: All water should be regarded as being potentially contaminated. Milk is unpasteurised and should be boiled. Powdered or tinned milk is available and is advised, but make sure that it is reconstituted with pure water. Avoid dairy products which are likely to have been made from unboiled milk. Only eat well-cooked meat and fish, preferably served hot. Pork, salad and mayonnaise may carry increased risk. Vegetables should be cooked and fruit peeled.
Rabies is present. For those at high risk, vaccination before arrival should be considered. If you are bitten abroad seek medical advice without delay. For more information consult the *Health* section at the back of the book.
Bilharzia (schistosomiasis) is present. Avoid swimming and paddling in fresh water. Swimming pools which are well-chlorinated and maintained are safe.
Health care: Medical insurance is strongly recommended.

TRAVEL - International

AIR: Afghanistan's national airline is *Bakhtar Afghan Airlines (FG)*, which merged with *Ariana Afghan*

Airlines in 1985.
Approximate flight times: From Kabul to *Moscow* is 6 hours and to *Tashkent* is 1 hour 30 minutes.
International airport: *Kabul Airport (KBL)* is 16km (10 miles) from the city. Airport facilities include banking, buffet-bar, car park, post office and restaurant (opening hours: 0700-2400).
Taxis are available to the city centre (travel time – 30 minutes). Airport facilities in Kabul have been expanded recently and new airports have been built near the border.
Departure tax: Af200 for all international departures; transit passengers are exempt.
RAIL: Afghanistan's rail network consists of a short spur from the CIS, crossing the Amu Darya at Hairatan, where it stops. There are plans to extend it to Kabul but these continue to be disrupted by the activities of guerrillas.
ROAD: Overland travel is currently very risky, especially in eastern Afghanistan. Buses operate along the Asia Highway, which links Afghanistan to Iran and Pakistan and there are good road links from Mazar-i-Sharif and Herat to the CIS.

TRAVEL - Internal

AIR: Internal flights connect Kabul with Herat, Kandahar and Mazar-i-Sharif.
ROAD: There are over 18,000km (11,000 miles) of roads, of which 2800km (1700 miles) are paved. An arc of all-weather roads runs from Mazar-i-Sharif through Kabul and Kandahar to Herat. Bus services operate from Kabul to the provinces. **Documentation:** An International Driving Permit is required.
URBAN: Buses, trolleybuses and taxis operate in Kabul. It is essential to check these services with relevant airline offices.

ACCOMMODATION

HOTELS: The only top-class hotel in the country is the Intercontinental in Kabul. There is a 5% government tax, but no service charge. Elsewhere in the city there is limited moderate and low-class accommodation; prices often include service charges. Only basic accommodation is available elsewhere. In some rural areas there are hotels run by the provincial authority, but these are of a low standard. The Afghan Tourist Organisation deals with all bookings. See front of section for address and telephone number.
CAMPS AND LODGES: There are campsites along the Central Route, including Bande Amir and various tourist lodges for visitors to Nuristan.

RESORTS & EXCURSIONS

Kabul: The capital has little remaining from its historic past. The *Garden of Babur* and a well-presented museum are amongst the few conventional attractions for tourists. Travel outside Kabul is not generally permitted to tourists but, if allowed, it is worth trying to visit the *Valley of Paghman*, 90 minutes by road west of the capital, where the rich have second houses; and, to the north, **Karez-i-Amir, Charika** and the *Valley of Chakardara*.
Jalalabad: The capital of Nangarhar Province is an attractive winter resort, with many cypress trees and flowering shrubs.
Hindu Kush: Consisting of two huge mountain ranges, the region is wild and remote, and although one can travel by car the steepness of the routes makes vehicles prone to breakdowns. The Hindu Kush is best left for travellers prepared to rough it. For those who make the journey, the mountain, valley and lake scenery is stupendous. **Bamian** is the main centre.

SOCIAL PROFILE

FOOD & DRINK: Indian-style cuisine. Most modern restaurants in Kabul offer international cuisine as well as Afghan specialities such as *pilaus*, *kebabs*, *bolani* and *ashak*. Traditional foods and tea from *chaikhanas* are found in all areas at cheap prices including service. Afghan dishes can be very good, but very spicy, so visitors with a weak palate should take care when ordering. There are few bars outside luxury hotels and restaurants and alcohol is available only for non-Muslims.
NIGHTLIFE: Traditional music and dance is performed in hotels and restaurants.
SHOPPING: Special purchases include Turkman hats, Kandahar embroidery, Istaff pottery, local glassware from Herat, nomad jewellery, handmade carpets and rugs, Nuristani woodcarving, silkware, brass, copper and silver work. **Note:** Many craft items may only be exported under licence. **Shopping hours:** Generally 0800-1200 and 1300-1800 Saturday to Wednesday, 0800-1300 Thursday. Some shops close all day Wednesday.
SPORT: The national sport is the **Buzkashi,** a fiercely competitive equestrian event dating from the time of Alexander the Great. It resembles a rather lawless version of polo, with the ball being replaced by the headless body of a goat. Played in Kabul at the Ghazi Stadium (late October) and at Kunduz during the Afghan New Year.
SOCIAL CONVENTIONS: Outside Kabul, Afghanistan is still very much a tribal society. Religion and traditional customs have a strong influence within the family, and there are strict male and female roles in society. It is considered insulting to show the soles of the feet. Guests may have to share a room as specific accommodation is rarely set aside. Women are advised to wear trousers or long skirts and avoid revealing dress. Handshaking is acceptable as a form of greeting although nose-rubbing and embracing are traditional. Smoking is a common social habit and cheap by European standards. It is a compliment to accept an offered cigarette from your host. **Photography:** Care should be taken when using cameras and videos. Military installations should not be photographed.

BUSINESS PROFILE

ECONOMY: Agriculture accounts for over 60% of Gross Domestic Product and the majority of the population exist at subsistence level. Their position has been exacerbated by the 11-year war: since 1979 it is estimated that one-third of the country's farms have been abandoned. This has led to recurring food shortages, with the result that the Govern-ment has been obliged to import large quantities of foodstuffs. Afghanistan has significant deposits of natural gas, coal, salt, barite and other ores. Hydroelectricity accounts for 80% of energy production. There is some manufacturing industry, principally textiles, chemical fertilisers, leather and plastics. The CIS was Afghanistan's largest trading partner by a considerable margin, but there are also important trade links with India and Pakistan.
Although the country has appreciable economic potential, the dislocation wrought by years of occupation and civil war will take years to repair.
BUSINESS: Price bargaining is expected and oral agreements are honoured. Formal wear is expected and meetings should be pre-arranged. **Office hours:** Generally 0800-1200 and 1300-1630 Saturday to Wednesday and 0830-1330 Thursdays, but some offices are closed all day Wednesday. **COMMERCIAL INFORMATION:** The following organisations can offer advice: Afghan Chamber of Commerce and Industry, Mohd Jan Khan Wat, Kabul. Tel: (93) 26796. Telex: 245; *or*
Federation of Afghan Chambers of Commerce and Industry, Durulaman Wat, Kabul. Tel: (93) 41041. Telex: 34.

HISTORY & GOVERNMENT

HISTORY: The history of Afghanistan has been closely tied to that of Persia, India and Russia, with all of whom Afghanistan has regularly been in conflict. Contact with Britain came about in the early 1800s. By the end of the First Afghan War (1839-42) British influence had spread throughout the country and, despite local discontent, the country was used as a pawn in the imperialist conflicts between Russia and Britain. It was not until the 1919 Treaty of Rawalpindi that Britain recognised Afghanistan's independence.
During the 1920s King Amanullah brought about the modernisation of industry and trade, education and communications, but during the next 15 years a rapid succession of coups brought one ruler after another to power. Relations with the then USSR were strengthened during the mid-1950s, with economic aid given to Afghanistan. Zahir Shar, the last king of Afghanistan, was overthrown by a military coup in 1973. Afghanistan was declared a republic. In 1978 the People's Democratic Party of Afghanistan (PDPA) came to power under Nur Mohammad Taraki; the PDPA was declared the sole legal party. Taraki was deposed just a year later by Hafizullah Amin, who was

CODE-LINK™

You will notice that throughout the World Travel Guide there are Code-Link symbols. These enable users of Computer Reservation Systems to make instant information up-dates. For more details about how Code-Link can help your agency, refer to the Introduction.

AFGHANISTAN	HEALTH REGULATIONS	VISA REGULATIONS
GALILEO/WORLDSPAN	 TI-DFT/KBL/HE	TI-DFT/KBL/VI
SABRE	 TIDFT/KBL/HE	 TIDFT/KBL/VI

Code-Link

To access this information on your CRS, swipe the barcode with a light pen or type in the text under the barcode. For more information, see the introduction *How to Use This Book*.

himself deposed (and killed) three months later in a coup engineered by the KGB and backed by the USSR. Babrak Karmal was installed as President. During the next decade, the Soviet military commitment in Afghanistan rose to approximately 115,000 troops as an alliance of opposition groups collectively known as the Mujaheddin waged an increasingly savage guerrilla war against the Karmal regime. In 1986 Dr Najibullah Ahmadzai, previously head of KHAD (the security service), replaced Karmal and began to seek a negotiated end to the war. This was finally agreed in April 1988 and, monitored by the UN, the USSR pulled its last troops out in February 1989. Meanwhile, there was growing exasperation abroad with the inability of the guerrilla factions to agree amongst themselves and their intransigence towards brokered solutions.
The situation on the ground seemed to be consigned to a long period of political and military stalemate. In April 1992 this suddenly gave way. Over a matter of days, the Kabul regime had all but collapsed. Najibullah sought the protection of the UN mission in Afghanistan while his erstwhile subordinates negotiated the formal transfer of power to the Mujaheddin. The new regime has pledged itself to the prompt introduction of *Shari'a* (Islamic law).
However, there have been repeated outbreaks of fighting betwen different Mujaheddin factions, particularly those led by Ahmed Shah Massoud and Hekmatyar respectively. Unless a lasting solution is found quickly to the competing claims of Afghanistan's numerous, heavily armed factions, the country risks degeneration Somalia-style.
GOVERNMENT: Afghanistan is formally governed by a coalition comprised of various groups belonging to the Mujaheddin which ousted the Najibullah government in April 1992. A mutually acceptable candidate, the prominent Islamist, Professor Burhanuddin Rabbani, holds the post of President. A nominee of the Hekmatyar faction, Abdul Faird, is Prime Minister. The writ of the central government – such as it exists – barely runs except in the capital. Outside Kabul, the country is divided in a patchwork of chiefdoms effectively governed by the prevailing militia.

CLIMATE

Although occupying the same latitudes as South-Central USA, the mountainous nature of much of Afghanistan produces a far colder climate. Winter may be considered permanent in regions above 2500m (8200ft); regions above 4000m (13,000ft) are uninhabitable. Being landlocked, there are considerable differences in temperature between summer and winter and between day and night in lowland regions and in the valleys. The southern lowlands have intensely hot summers and harsh winters.
Required clothing: Warm clothing for winter, especially in the north. Lightweight for summer and rainwear for spring.

KABUL Afghanistan (1815m)

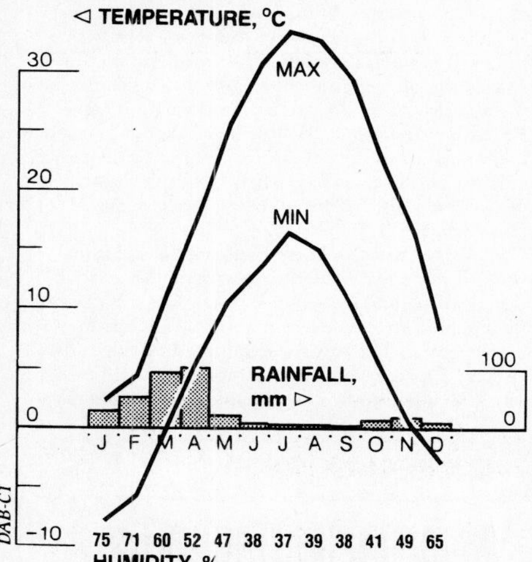

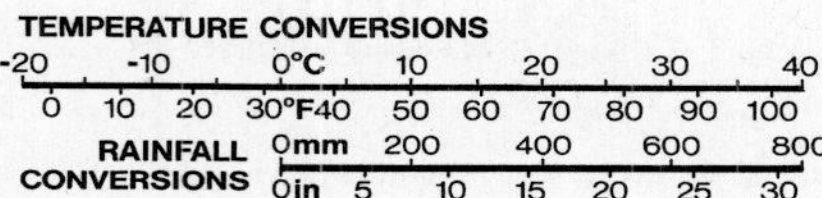

ALBANIA

Location: Eastern Europe, Adriatic and Ionian Coast.

Tirana Travel Agency (formed by the formerly state-owned Albturist)
c/o Hotel Tirana
Skanderbeg Square
Tirana, Albania
Tel: (42) 34572. Fax: (42) 34359. Telex: 2113 *or* 2148.
Embassy of the Republic of Albania
131 rue de la Pompe
75016 Paris, France
Tel: (1) 45 53 51 32. Fax: (1) 45 53 89 38. Telex: 611534.
Albturist (Travel Agency)
c/o Regent Holidays (UK) Limited
15 John Street
Bristol BS1 2HR
Tel: (0272) 211 711. Fax: (0272) 254 866. Telex: 444606. Opening hours: 0900-1730 Monday to Friday.
Embassy of the Republic of Albania
320 East 79th Street
New York, NY 10021
Tel: (212) 249 2059. Fax: (212) 535 2917.
The Embassy also deals with enquiries from Canada.
Embassy of the United States of America
Room 2921
Rruga Labinoti 103
Tirana, Albania
Tel: (42) 32875 *or* 33520. Fax: (42) 32222.

AREA: 28,748 sq km (11,100 sq miles).
POPULATION: 3,250,000 (1990).
POPULATION DENSITY: 113.1 per sq km.
CAPITAL: Tirana. **Population:** 225,700 (1987).
GEOGRAPHY: Albania shares borders with Montenegro and Serbia to the north, with Macedonia to the northeast, and with Greece to the south; to the west are the Adriatic and Ionian Seas. Most of the country is wild and mountainous, with extensive forests. There are fine sandy beaches and, inland, many beautiful lakes.
LANGUAGE: The official language is Albanian. Greek is widely spoken in the south.
RELIGION: The Government closed all churches and mosques in 1967 and declared atheism as part of the constitution in 1976, but they were reopened in 1990 and are now widely in use. An estimated 70% of the population are Muslims, 18% Greek Orthodox and Roman Catholic. There are also Protestant minorities.
TIME: GMT + 1 (GMT + 2 in summer).
ELECTRICITY: 220 volts AC, 50Hz.
COMMUNICATIONS: Telephone: IDD is available to major towns. Country code: 355. Direct dialling to Shkodër is to be installed soon. **Post:** All mail to and from Albania is subject to long delays, sometimes up to 2 months. Letters should be sent recorded delivery to avoid loss. The postal and telecommunication sytems are to undergo extensive modernisation in the near future. Post office hours: 0900-1300 and 1600-1900 Monday to Saturday. **Press:** Publications that diverge from the Party line have only been permitted since 1990. There are 43 national and 34 regional newspapers, although regular editions cannot be guaranteed due to frequent paper shortages. The main newspapers are published twice a week, although the *Rilindja Demokratike*, the organ of the ruling Democratic Party, is published five times a week with a circulation of 70,000. The only daily, the *Zëri i Popullit* (Voice of the People), is the Socialist Party (formerly the Communist Party) newspaper, the daily circulation of which has been reduced from 180,000 in 1990 to 15,000 in 1992. Over 30 magazines are published in Albania.
BBC World Service and Voice of America frequencies: From time to time these change. See the section *How to Use this Book* for more information.

BBC:				
MHz	17.64	15.07	9.410	6.195
Voice of America:				
MHz	1764	15.07	9.410	6.180

PASSPORT/VISA

Regulations and requirements may be subject to change at short notice, and you are advised to contact the appropriate diplomatic or consular authority before finalising travel arrangements. Details of these may be found at the head of this country's entry. Any numbers in the chart refer to the footnotes below.

	Passport Required?	Visa Required?	Return Ticket Required?
Full British	Yes	No	No
BVP	Not valid	-	-
Australian	Yes	Yes	Yes
Canadian	Yes	No	Yes
USA	Yes	No	Yes
Other EC	Yes	No	No
Japanese	Yes	Yes	Yes

PASSPORTS: A valid passport is required by all.
British Visitors Passport: Not acceptable.
VISAS: Required by all except nationals of:
(a) countries referred to in the chart above;
(b) Austria, Bulgaria, Finland, Iceland, Liechtenstein, Norway, Sweden, Switzerland and Turkey.
Note: Nationals of other countries can obtain visas at Tirana airport or at the border point. A fee is payable, although an additional passport photo is not required. In some cases proof of sufficient funds to cover stay is required.
Types of visa: Business and Tourist. Tourist visas cost £14 each for groups and £20 for individuals.
Validity: Duration of visas is individually specified for each visit.
Application to: Embassy (or Consular Section at Embassy) or Tourist Board. For addresses, see top of entry.
Application requirements: (a) Application form(s). (b) 4 photos. (c) Valid passport. (d) Sufficient funds to cover duration of stay. (e) For business, letters from company and from sponsor etc.
Working days required: Minimum of 4 weeks.
Temporary residence: Apply to the Albanian Embassy in Paris (by invitation only).

MONEY

Currency: Lek (Lk) = 100 qindarka. Notes are in denominations of Lk500, 100, 50, 25, 10, 5, 3 and 1. Coins are in denominations 50, 20, 10 and 5 qindarkas.
Currency exchange: All bills are normally settled in cash; cheques are never used. Only actually needed amounts should be changed. Many bureaux de change do not have large amounts of small change, visitors are therefore advised to carry notes in small denominations. Banks offer the best rate of exchange.
Credit cards: American Express and Eurocard are accepted in a few of the large hotels and in foreign currency shops.
Eurocheques are cashed by some banks on presentation of own passport. Some hotels also accept Eurocheques.
Exchange rate indicators: The following figures are included as a guide to the movements of the Lek against Sterling and the US Dollar:

Date:	Oct '89	Oct '90	Oct '91	Oct '92
£1.00=	9.95	9.98	10.01	173.97*
$1.00=	6.30	5.11	5.77	109.62*

Note [*]: Since the middle of 1992 exchange rates are

tied to the US Dollar.
Currency restrictions: The import and export of local currency is prohibited. Foreign currency must be declared on arrival. The export of foreign currency is limited to the amount declared.
Banking hours: *April to September*: 0700-1400 Monday to Saturday. *October to March*: 0730-1430 Monday to Saturday.

DUTY FREE

The following items may be taken into Albania without incurring customs duty:
A reasonable quantity of tobacco products;
Alcoholic beverages;
Perfumes for personal use.
Prohibited items: Firearms, ammunition, narcotics and drugs. Special export permits are required for precious metals, antique coins and scrolls, antiques, national costumes of artistic or folkloristic value, books and works of art which form part of the national heritage and culture.
Note: Passage through Customs can be difficult.

PUBLIC HOLIDAYS

Public holidays observed in Albania are as follows:
May 1 '93 Labour Day. **Nov 28** Independence Day 1912. **Nov 29** Liberation Day. **Jan 1 '94** New Year's Day. **Jan 11** Proclamation of the Republic 1946.

HEALTH

Regulations and requirements may be subject to change at short notice, and you are advised to contact your doctor well in advance of your intended date of departure. Any numbers in the chart refer to the footnotes below.

	Special Precautions?	Certificate Required?
Yellow Fever	No	1
Cholera	Yes	No
Typhoid & Polio	Yes	No
Malaria	No	-
Food & Drink	2	-

[1]: A yellow fever vaccination certificate is required from travellers over one year of age if arriving from infected or endemic areas.
[2]: Mains water is normally chlorinated, and whilst relatively safe may cause mild abdominal upsets. Bottled water is available and is advised. Drinking water outside main cities and towns is likely to be contaminated and sterilisation is considered essential. Milk is pasteurised and dairy products are safe for consumption. Local meat, poultry, seafood, fruit and vegetables are generally considered safe to eat.
Rabies is present. For those at high risk, vaccination before arrival should be considered. If you are bitten abroad seek medical advice without delay. For more information consult the *Health* section at the back of the book.
Health care: Medical insurance is not strictly essential as all tourists in Albania receive free medical treatment, even when no Reciprocal Health Agreement exists.

TRAVEL - International

AIR: The national carrier is *Albanian Airlines*. Established in August 1992 in co-operation with *Tyrolean Airways*, the airline operates services to major European cities. Other airlines offering services to Tirana are *Ada Air*, *Alitalia*, *Hemus Air*, *Malev*, *Olympic Airways*, *Swissair* and *Tarom*.
Approximate flight time: From *London* to Tirana is 4 to 5 hours (including stopover times, the best being Zurich, 45 minutes, and Rome, 1 hour 30 minutes). Other connections are slow. Passengers may travel via Zurich, Athens, Rome, Vienna, Bucharest, Paris or Budapest.
International airport: *Tirana Rinas (TIA)* is 29km (18 miles) from the capital. There is a small duty-free shop. *Albanian Airlines* shuttle to the city centre (travel time – 40 minutes). Taxis are also available from and to the airport.
Departure tax: US$10 levied on all flights.
SEA: The main ports are Durrës, Vlorë and Sarandë. Durrës has ferry connections to Italy (to Bari is 10 hours, to Brindisi and to Trieste is 23 hours) and to Slovenia (to Koper is 22 hours); Vlorë has ferry connections to Bari (travel time – 11 hours); and Sarandë has a connection from Corfu for day trippers. Other ports in southern Albania can also be reached from Bari, Brindisi and Ortona (all Italy) as well as Corfu and Igoumenitsa (Greece).
RAIL: There is an international freight link from Shkodër in Albania to Podgorica (formerly Titograd) in Montenegro.
ROAD: There are road links to all neighbouring countries with border crossings at Hani i Hotit (Podgorica in Montenegro), Morina (Prizren in Kosovo), Qafa e Thaës (Struga and Ohrid in Macedonia), Kapshtica (Florina in Greece) and Kakavia (Igoumenitsa in Greece). There is an international private bus service between Tirana and Sofia. It is now permitted to travel in a private car; however, due to the problems caused by lack of fuel and the need to keep the vehicle under constant supervision or locked away at night, this is not recommended. A fully comprehensive insurance policy is absolutely essential.

TRAVEL - Internal

RAIL: The total rail network runs to approximately 720km and is single-track and unelectrified along the whole of its length. Trains are diesel, dilapidated and mostly overcrowded.
ROAD: There are around 18,000km of roads in Albania, but only 7500km are considered main roads. Maintained by the State they are more or less suitable for motor vehicles, although only 2850km are paved, and of those, three-quarters are in a very poor condition. Motorways are planned for the future. All roads are currently used in equal measure by pedestrians, cyclists, ox- and horse-drawn wagons, agricultural vehicles and herds of cattle and poultry. There are strict speed limits according to type of vehicle and type of road as well as within towns. Normal rules and international road signs apply. However, due to vandalism of the existing signposts and the lack of useable road maps, drivers can discover that finding their way around the country is problematic. Petrol is expensive and scarce, while lead-free fuel is unavailable. Albanian diesel is of a very poor quality. Fuel-vouchers can be obtained at some shops. There is a road toll of Lk125 per day for cars. **Bus:** The major form of transportation within Albania. The main routes from Shkodër, Korcë, Sarandë, Gjirokastër and Durrës to Tirana are operated by private bus companies.
URBAN: A cheap, flat-fare urban **bus** service operates in Tirana, although the buses are hopelessly overcrowded and pickpocketing is rife. **Taxis** can be found in Tirana in front of the main hotels housing foreigners.
JOURNEY TIMES: The following chart gives approximate journey times from Tirana (in hours and minutes) to other major cities/towns in Albania.

	Road
Durrës	1.00
Elbasan	1.00
Shkodër	3.00
Berat	3.30
Vlorë	3.30
Korcë	5.00

ACCOMMODATION

HOTELS: All the formerly state-run hotels are now run as private businesses. Standards range from basic to very basic while prices for foreigners have risen enormously. Bed capacity is still very limited and cannot cater to the increase in foreign visitors. Rooms are often unhygenic and without shower or WC; water- and power-cuts should be expected. New hotels are being planned. On occasions, private accommodation in apartments or rooms is available.

RESORTS & EXCURSIONS

During the Communist reign, foreign visitors were few and far between and were only allowed to travel in groups to a limited number of destinations within Albania. Having recognised the scenic beauty and cultural heritage of Albania, the Government intends to develop the tourism potential of the country with plans for the construction of new hotels, tourist villages and motorway connections.
For the tourist there is much to discover: extensive beaches, mountain scenery such as Mount Dêja with numerous valleys, rivers, lakes such as Lake Préspa, outstanding flora and fauna and sites of great archaeological and historical interest.
In Roman times, **Apollonia** was a large, prosperous city at the mouth of the Vjosë. The amphitheatre, a colonnade of shops and several other parts of the Roman city centre are open to the public. Unfortunately, some of the statues and other portable objects were removed before 1946 and sent to other countries. Those remaining have been placed in the well-organised museum which is to be found on the site of a 13th-century monastery. In the courtyard of the monastery is a Byzantine-style church believed to have been built in the 14th century.
Known as the 'city of a thousand windows', **Berat** has been declared a 'Museum City'. Built on the slopes of a mountain, the old Turkish part of the town is very picturesque, being largely encompassed by the medieval fortress. To house the increasing population, a new town has been built further down the valley beside the largest textile combine in the country. The *Onufri Museum* houses restored icons in an orthodox church.
The town of **Butrint** has been known as a settlement since 1000BC. It belonged to the Greek and Roman Empires during its long history and both have left a rich legacy. Several excavations dating from the 1st and 4th centuries AD can now be visited, among them a theatre, the *Dionysos Altar*, Roman houses and baths. The *Baptistery*, with a floor of colourful mosaics, is not to be missed.
The important port of **Durrës** is the second largest city in Albania with the second largest concentration of industry. The city was colonised by the Greeks in 627BC and was named *Epidamos*, which later became *Dyrrachium* under the Romans. From the *Venetian Tower* at the harbour the *Medieval Town Wall* leads to the *amphitheatre* dating back to the 2nd century BC and containing an early Christian crypt with a rare wall mosaic. Between the 1st and 3rd centuries Durrës was an important port and trading centre on the *Via Egnatia* trading route between Rome and Byzantium (Istanbul). Following a number of earthquakes, much of ancient Durrës sank into the sea or collapsed and was subsequently built over. Today the city is best known for the nearby beach resort of *Durrës Plazh*.
Gjirokastër has also been designated a 'Museum City' as so many of the houses retained their traditional wood- and stone-work. The narrow and winding cobbled streets ensure the virtual exclusion of motor traffic. The town is dominated by the 13th-century *Fortress* which was extended by Ali Pasha in 1811. It now contains an armaments museum; the

ALBANIA	**HEALTH REGULATIONS**	**VISA REGULATIONS** Code-Link
GALILEO/WORLDSPAN	 TI-DFT/TIA/HE	TI-DFT/TIA/VI
SABRE	TIDFT/TIA/HE	 TIDFT/TIA/VI

To access this information on your CRS, swipe the barcode with a light pen or type in the text under the barcode. For more information, see the introduction *How to Use This Book*.

collection ranges from medieval armour to a shot-down US reconnaissance aircraft. The view is not to be missed. The surrounding area is renowned for its many mineral springs.

Visible for miles around, **Krujë** is an attractive medieval town perched on top of a mountain. It was the centre of Albanian resistance to the Ottoman Turks under Skanderberg, the national hero, and the *Skanderberg Museum* is to be found inside the recently restored castle. The street leading up to the castle is built in the style of a Turkish bazaar.

Korcë was the seat of government during the Turkish reign. In the 18th century, the city was able to exploit its location at the crossroads of several caravan routes and become a major trading point. Standing beneath dramatic mountains near the Greek border, Korcë is home to the *Mirahor Mosque*, dating back to 1466, the *Museum for Medieval Art* and a listed though decaying bazaar quarter.

The charming resort of **Pogradec** near the Macedonian border stands beside *Lake Ohrid*, rich in trout, carp and sardines.

Albania's southern coastline remains completely unspoilt. Situated opposite Corfu, **Sarandë** is now much visited by day trippers who come to enjoy this previously inaccessible resort.

Situated on the lake of the same name that divides Albania from Montenegro, **Shkodër** is dominated by the ruins of the *Fortress of Rozafa*, from where a spectacular panorama of the surrounding countryside, Lake Shkodër and the *Lead Mosque* can be enjoyed. A museum is dedicated to one of the greatest Albanian writers, *Migjeni*.

Tirana has only been the capital of Albania since 1920, although the *Ethem-Bey Mosque* and *Clocktower* date back to the early 19th century. The old bazaar quarter was demolished in 1961 to make way for the *Palace of Culture*. The city centre and the government buildings on *Skanderberg Square* date back to the Italian era, creating the impression of a provincial Italian town, while the *Pyramid*, which was built as a museum for Enver Hoxha, is to be turned into an international Cultural Centre. Today, Tirana is not only the most populous city in Albania, but also the political, economic, cultural and spiritual centre of the country with national museums of Archaeology, History and Art. The best view over the city is to be had from the *Heroes' Cemetery* which contains the *Mother Albania Monument*.

Vlorë is not only a major port, but of great historical importance, for it was here in 1912 that the Assembly was convened which first proclaimed Albania as an independent state and set up the first National Government, headed by Ismail Qemal. In recognition of this it was proclaimed a 'Hero City' in 1962. The *Muradite Mosk* (1538-42) was designed by the famous architect Mimar Sinan whose family originates in Albania.

SOCIAL PROFILE

FOOD & DRINK: Private restaurants are appearing overnight in Albania and usually offer better food than the hotels. In the more popular places it is necessary to reserve a table and to be punctual. Food is typically Balkan with Turkish influences evident on any menu – *byrek, kofte, shish kebab*. Albanian specialities include *fërgesë tiranë*, a hot fried dish of meat, liver, eggs and tomatoes, and *tavllë kosi* or *tavllë elbanasi*, a mutton and yoghurt dish. Fish specialities include the *koran*, a trout from Lake Ohrid and the *Shkodër carp*. In summer *tarator*, a cold yoghurt and cucumber soup, is particularly refreshing. Popular Albanian desserts include *oshaf*, a fig and sheep's milk pudding, cakes soaked in honey and candied fruits or *reçel*. Guests of honour are quite often presented with baked sheep's head. A favourite in the south is *kukurez* (stuffed sheep's intestines). Continental breakfasts are usually served in hotels, but in the country the Albanian breakfast of *pilaf* (rice) or *paça* (a wholesome soup made from animals' innards) may not be to everyone's taste. **Drink:** Due to the collapse of Albanian industry, nearly all drinks have to be imported and include Austrian canned beer, Macedonian wine, Cola imitations and ouzo from Greece. Good local wines have become rare, as has *Raki*, a clear local liqueur. Albanian cognac, with its distinctive aroma, is sometimes available in hotel shops. Both Turkish coffee (*kafe Turke*) and Italian expresso (*ekspres*) are equally popular.

NIGHTLIFE: The most popular form of nightlife is the *Nhiro*, the evening stroll along the main thoroughfare in each town and village. Cultural life in the form of theatre, opera and concerts struggles to survive, while the first discos and games arcades are beginning to appear. Some hotels have music and dancing, although these are at the mercy of frequent power cuts in winter.

SHOPPING: Special purchases include carpets, filigree silver and copper, woodcarvings, ceramic and any kind of needlework. Old markets are often worth exploring. Haggling is very much the order of the day as the prices for foreigners are generally much higher than those for locals. **Shopping hours:** Generally 0700-1200 and 1600-1900 Monday to Saturday (although regional variations are possible). Many shops open on Sundays.

SOCIAL CONVENTIONS: One-third of the population live in urban areas, with the rest pursuing a relatively quiet rural existence. Many Albanian characteristics and mannerisms resemble those of the mainland Greeks, most notably in the more rural areas; for instance, a nod of the head means 'no' and shaking one's head means 'yes'. Handshaking is the accepted form of greeting. Albanians should be addressed with *Zoti* (Mr) and *Zonja* (Mrs). The former widespread greeting of *Shoku* (Comrade) has all but disappeared. Small gifts are customary when visiting someone's house, although flowers are not usually given. Any attempt to speak Albanian is greatly appreciated. Visitors should accept offers of raki, coffee or sweets. Dress is generally informal.

Bikinis are acceptable on the beach; elsewhere women are expected to dress modestly although attitudes are becoming increasingly relaxed. Offices and restaurants are often unheated. Visitors should be aware that foreigners tend to be charged a lot more than locals, with this applying to entry fees as well as general merchandise. Smoking is permitted except where the sign *Ndalohet te pi duhan* is displayed. It is also worth noting that the crime rate has risen, especially theft, and visitors should be careful not to overtly display valuables. Passports which allow entry to EC countries without a visa, foreign currency and cameras are mostly at risk, although all possessions should be kept close at hand at all times. Avoid remote areas and streets, especially at night. **Tipping:** Previously frowned upon by the authorities, tips are gratefully received in restaurants or for any service provided.

BUSINESS PROFILE

ECONOMY: Albania is Europe's poorest country and faces a very difficult period trying to adjust to its new status after years of isolation. However, it is blessed with considerable natural resources: it is one of the world's largest producers of chromium, and also has considerable reserves of copper, nickel, pyrites and coal. There are also substantial oil deposits, both on- and offshore. Both the mining and oil industries are handicapped by lack of investment and poor equipment, which the Government is trying to rectify through international joint ventures rather than selling property immediately. Agriculture, which still provides for 30% of GNP and employs half the workforce, is undergoing upheaval following decollectivisation. Albania is gradually taking its place within the international community. Membership of the IMF, the World Bank and the European Bank for Reconstruction and Development was secured in 1991. Having decided on a gradual transition to a market economy Albania faces a difficult interim period; the favoured joint ventures are to bring much-needed technology and expertise. However, it may be some time before the national economic indicators approach the European average. This is particularly true since, after an initial rush following the introduction of democratic government, foreign investors are now shunning Albania in favour of better prospects elsewhere in Eastern Europe. In the longer term this course may prove to be more prudent.

BUSINESS: Punctuality is expected. Business cards are common and European practices are observed. **Office hours:** *April to September:* 0700-1400 Monday to Saturday and 1700-2000 Monday and Tuesday. *October to March:* 0730-1430 Monday to Saturday and 1600-1900 Monday and Tuesday.

COMMERCIAL INFORMATION: The following organisation can offer advice: Dhoma e Tregtisë e Republikës të Shqiperisë (Chamber of Commerce of the Republic of Albania), Rruga Konferenca e Pezës 6, Tirana. Tel: (42) 27997. Telex: 2179.

HISTORY & GOVERNMENT

HISTORY: Despite Albania's geographical inaccessibility, the country has suffered continual invasions over the last 1000 years. From 1467, the country endured the often corrupt and repressive rule of the Turks as part of the Ottoman Empire. Independence came in 1912, after several demands for autonomy had been ruthlessly suppressed, but the country at once became involved in the chaos of the Balkan War and, subsequently, in the 1914-1918 war. During the reign of King Zog (1928-39), relations with Italy deteriorated, and in April 1939 Albania was conquered by Mussolini's forces. Resistance to the occupation was centred on the Communist-led National Liberation Front, which ultimately took power in November 1944. The new regime, under the communist leader Enver Hoxha, was initially close to the Tito government in neighbouring Yugoslavia but broke off contact following the latter's expulsion from the Soviet bloc in 1948. Soviet efforts at rapprochement with Yugoslavia precipitated Albania's own secession from the bloc in 1961 and its alliance with China. The post-Mao liberalisations in China were bitterly denounced by the Albanian government, which embarked forthwith on a policy of almost total isolation from the rest of the world. Only with the death of Enver Hoxha in 1985 and his replacement by the ALP's First Secretary, Ramiz Alia, did Albania start to develop foreign links once again. The closest of these appear to be with Western European nations (mostly neighbouring Greece, but also Italy and France), principally for economic reasons. To the north, relations with Yugoslavia have been particularly sensitive recently due to ethnic unrest in the southern Yugoslavian province of Kosovo, which has a substantial ethnic Albanian population. However, the Government's main concern in recent years has been that the unstable regional situation as a whole should prompt a groundswell of discontent within Albania itself. The Government knows that its future survival depends on opening up Albania's uniquely rigid political and economic system, but it is nonetheless proceeding cautiously, not least because of the powerful conservative grouping within the ALP backed by the still-powerful *Sigurimi* secret police, which is still opposed to reform. In the face of continuing discontent, the Government agreed to hold elections in 1991. The Communist Party won and managed to hold onto office for a month before a general strike brought it down. New elections in March 1992 brought a landslide victory for the Democratic Party. The new government needs to act urgently to arrest the continuing deterioration of the Albanian economy. Having decided that the country could not stand a Polish-style economic 'Big Bang', the Government has embarked on a more moderate reform programme. **GOVERNMENT:** Legislative power rests with the elected 250-seat People's Assembly. Executive power is held by the Council of Ministers drawn from the largest party in the Assembly and headed by the Prime Minister, Sali Berisha. The former Communist leader, Ramiz Alia, is President and Head of State.

CLIMATE

Warm, dry periods from June to September, cool and wet from October to May. May/ June and mid-September to mid-October are best months for visits. **Required clothing:** Leightweight – summer. Winter – warm.

TIRANA Albania (114m)

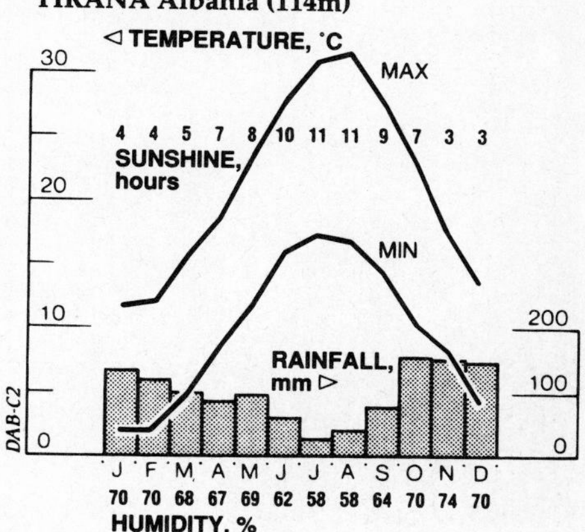

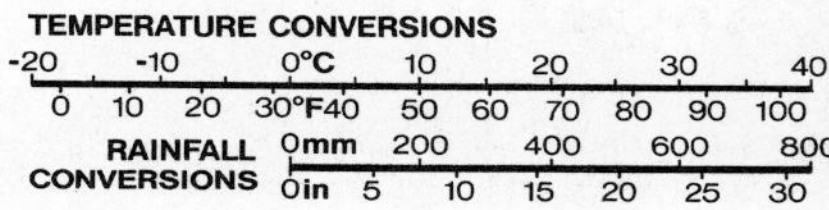

ALGERIA

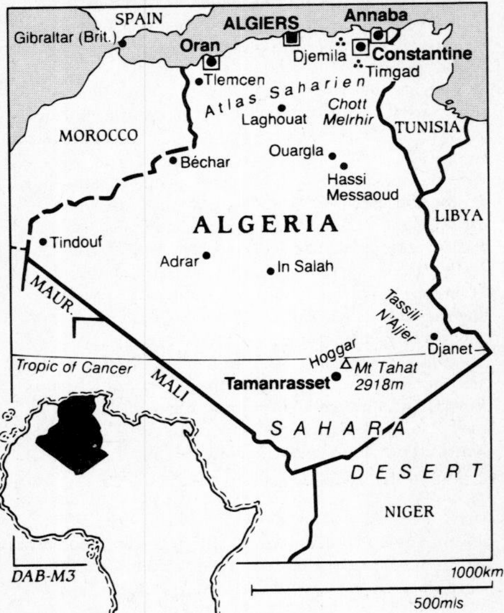

☐ *international airport*

Location: North Africa, Mediterranean Coast.

Office National Algérien de l'Animation de la Promotion et de l'Information Touristique (ONAT)
25-27 rue Khélifa-Boukhalfa
16000 Algiers, Algeria
Tel: (2) 743 376. Fax: (2) 743 214. Telex: 66339.

Embassy of the Democratic and Popular Republic of Algeria
54 Holland Park
London W11 3RS
Tel: (071) 221 7800. Fax: (071) 221 0448. Opening hours: 0930-1700 Monday to Friday.

Algerian Consulate
6 Hyde Park Gate
London SW7 5EW
Tel: (071) 221 7800. Fax: (071) 221 0448. Opening hours (for visa applications): 0930-1130 Monday to Friday.

Air Algérie
10 Baker Street
London W1M 1DA
Tel: (071) 487 5709 *or* (071) 487 5903 (reservations). Fax: (071) 935 1715. Telex: 24606 ALGAIR. Opening hours: 0930-1730 Monday to Friday.

British Embassy
BP 43, Résidence Cassiopée, Bâtiment B

Bou-Saada, the happy one

ALGERIA

A country of contrasts. . . A country of diversity. . . From the clear waters and Golden Beaches of the Mediterranean coast to the fertile plains, the snow-capped mountains and particularly the oases of the south, Algeria is yours to discover.

For all ground arrangements in Algeria including regularly scheduled tours:
Office National Algerien De Tourisme (O. N. A. T.)

Tel: (02) 74 33 76 - (02) 74 33 77.
Fax: (02) 61 97 64 - (02) 74 32 14.
Telex: 66383.

3 FLIGHTS PER WEEK FROM HEATHROW BY BOEING 737

Every Tuesday, Friday and Sunday at 1530 we invite you to be our guest and enjoy the comfort warmth and friendliness of traditional Algerian hospitality aboard our direct flight to Algiers and onwards to Africa, the Middle East or any of 26 other destinations within Algeria. The guest is king. Welcome aboard.

YOUR LINK WITH ALGERIA FOR BUSINESS OR PLEASURE

For further information please contact:
Air Algerie, 10 Baker Street, London WIM 1DA.
Tel: (071) 487 5903. Fax: (071) 935 1715. Telex: 24606 ALGAIR G.

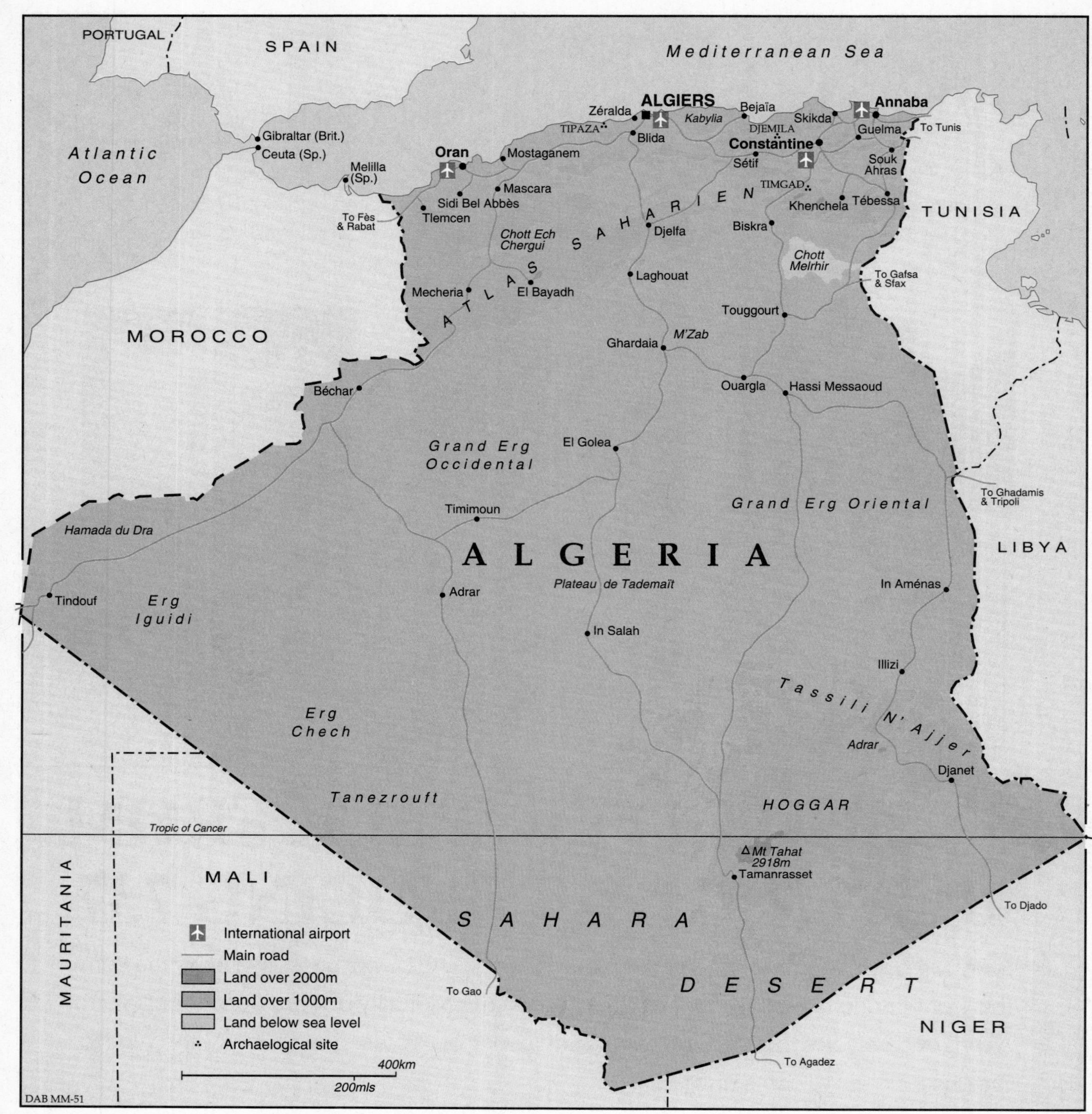

7 chemin des Glycines
DZ 16000 Alger-Gare
Algiers, Algeria
Tel: (2) 605 601. Fax: (2) 604 410. Telex: 66151.

Embassy of the Republic of Algeria
2118 Kalorama Road, NW
Washington, DC 20008
Tel: (202) 265 2800. Fax: (202) 667 2174. Telex: 892443.

Embassy of the United States of America
BP 549
4 Chemin Cheikh Bachir El-Ibrahimi
16000 Alger-Gare
Algiers, Algeria
Tel: (2) 601 186. Fax: (2) 603 979. Telex: 66047.

Algerian Embassy
435 Daly Avenue
Ottawa, Ontario
K1N 6H3
Tel: (613) 232 9453/4. Fax: (613) 232 9099.

Canadian Embassy
PO Box 225
27 bis rue Ali Massoudi
Alger-Gare
16000 Algiers, Algeria
Tel: (2) 606 611. Fax: (2) 605 920. Telex: 66043.

AREA: 2,381,741 sq km (919,595 sq miles).
POPULATION: 24,960,000 (1990).
POPULATION DENSITY: 10.5 per sq km.
CAPITAL: Algiers (El Djazaïr). **Population:** 1,721,607 (1983).
GEOGRAPHY: Algeria is situated along the North African coast, bordered to the east by Tunisia and Libya, to the southeast by Niger, to the southwest by Mali, and to the west by Mauritania and Morocco. It is Africa's second largest country, with 1000km (600 miles) of coastline. Along the coastal strip are the main towns, fertile land, beach resorts and 90% of the population. Further south lies the area of the *Hauts Plateaux*, mountains of to 2000m (6600ft) covered in cedar, pine and cypress forests with broad arable plains dividing the plateaux. The remaining 85% of the country is the Sahara Desert in its various forms, sustaining only 500,000 people, many of whom are nomadic tribes with goat and camel herds. The oil and minerals boom has created new industrial centres like Hassi Messaoud, which have grown up within previously barely inhabited regions of the northern Sahara. The plains of gravel and sand in the deep south are interrupted by two mountain ranges: the dramatic *Hoggar* massif, rising to almost 3000m (9800ft), and the *Tassili N'Ajjer* or 'Plateau of Chasms'. Both have long been important centres of Tuareg culture.
LANGUAGE: The official language is Arabic, but French is still used for most official and business transactions. Berber dialects are still spoken in the south. In general, English is spoken only in major business or tourist centres.
RELIGION: Over 90% of the population adhere to Islam, mostly to the Sunni branch.
TIME: GMT + 1.
ELECTRICITY: 127/220 volts, AC 50Hz. The European 2-pin plug is standard.
COMMUNICATIONS: Telephone: IDD is available. Country code: 213. There are public telephones in all post offices, leading hotels and on many main streets. **Telex/telegram:** Telex facilities are available at the main post office in Algiers (address below) and also at the El-Aurassi hotel. Telegrams can be sent from any post office between 0800 and 1900 hours. The main post office in Algiers has a 24-hour service. **Post:** Mail posted in any of the main cities along the coast takes three to four days to reach Europe; posted elsewhere, it could take very much longer. A letter delivery service operates Saturday to Thursday. Parcels sent by surface mail may take up to two months to reach Algeria. All parcels sent by air or surface mail are subject to long delays in customs. Post office hours: generally 0800-1700 Saturday to Wednesday and 0800-1200 Thursday, but the main post office in Algiers (at 5 blvd Mohamed Khémisti) is open around the clock. **Press:** The main daily newspapers are El Watan, El Moudjahid, *Le*

El Kautara, the desert door.

Matin, *L'Opinion* and *Alger Republicain* printed in French.
BBC World Service and Voice of America frequencies: From time to time these change. See the section *How to Use this Book* for more information.

BBC:

MHz	17.70	15.07	12.09	9.410

Voice of America:

MHz	11.97	9.670	6.040	5.995

PASSPORT/VISA

Regulations and requirements may be subject to change at short notice, and you are advised to contact the appropriate diplomatic or consular authority before finalising travel arrangements. Details of these may be found at the head of this country's entry. Any numbers in the chart refer to the footnotes below.

	Passport Required?	Visa Required?	Return Ticket Required?
Full British	Yes	Yes	Yes
BVP	Not valid	-	-
Australian	Yes	Yes	Yes
Canadian	Yes	Yes	Yes
USA	Yes	Yes	Yes
Other EC	Yes	Yes	Yes
Japanese	Yes	Yes	Yes

Restricted entry: Those with Israeli stamps on their passports will have great difficulty entering Algeria. Nationals of Israel will automatically be refused entry.
PASSPORTS: Valid passport required by all.
British Visitors Passport: Not acceptable.
VISAS: Required by all except nationals of Andorra, Argentina, Benin, Bosnia-Hercegovina, Croatia, Libya, Liechtenstein, Mali, Malta, Mauritania, Monaco, Morocco, San Marino, Senegal, Slovenia, Syria, Tunisia, Yemen and all other former Yugoslav republics.
Types of visa: Transit, Tourist and Business. Cost depends on visa type.
Validity: Tourist: approximately 30 days. Transit: approximately 48 hours. Business: approximately 15 days.
Application to: Consulate (or Consular Section at Embassy). For addresses, see top of entry.
Application requirements: (a) Completed application form. (b) 2 passport-size photos. (c) Applicants for business visas need a letter from their sponsoring company.
Working days required: Generally 2 or 3 days but less in urgent cases. Nationals of The Netherlands and Portugal who are not resident in the UK must expect a delay of 3 or 4 weeks.
Temporary residence: Apply at Consulate.
Note: Exit permits are required for alien residents and those who have stayed in Algeria for more than 3 months.

MONEY

Currency: Dinar (AD) = 100 centimes. Notes are in denominations of AD200, 100, 50, 20 and 10. Coins are in denominations of AD5 and 1, and 50, 20, 10, 5, 2 and 1 centimes.
Currency exchange: In the past, difficulties have arisen when trying to exchange currency in Algeria, with only one national bank *(La Banque d'Extérieure d'Algérie)* able to exchange foreign currency at branches in major business centres. Difficulties are now decreasing and it is possible, for example, to exchange currency at some of the larger hotels. However, the facilities for currency exchange remain limited. Passengers arriving by plane during daylight hours are strongly advised to exchange a good deal of the money they intend to spend during their stay at the bank in the airport.
Credit cards: Limited acceptance of Visa, American Express, Diners Club and Access/Mastercard. Check with your credit card company for details of merchant acceptability and other services which may be available.
Travellers cheques: Only top-class (4-star and above) hotels and government-run craft (souvenir) shops can accept these.
Exchange rate indicators: The following figures are included as a guide to the movements of the Dinar against Sterling and the US Dollar:

Date:	Oct '89	Oct '90	Oct '91	Oct '92
£1.00=	12.80	18.25	36.64	33.95
$1.00=	8.11	9.34	21.11	21.39

Currency restrictions: Unlimited amounts of foreign currency (except for gold coins) may be imported, but it must all be declared. Visitors must fill in the currency declaration form at the same time as they complete their disembarkation card and have the form stamped by customs on arrival (even if the customs officer does not ask to see the form). At Algiers airport this should be done at the special customs desk sit-

ALGERIA	HEALTH REGULATIONS	VISA REGULATIONS (Code-Link)
GALILEO/WORLDSPAN	 TI-DFT/ALG/HE	 TI-DFT/ALG/VI
SABRE	 TIDFT/ALG/HE	TIDFT/ALG/VI

To access this information on your CRS, swipe the barcode with a light pen or type in the text under the barcode. For more information, see the introduction *How to Use This Book.*

uated after Passport control but before baggage claim and customs. Every time they exchange currency they will be given a receipt and the amount exchanged will be entered onto this form. This form and the receipts *must* be surrendered on departure from Algeria. Visitors are required to produce their currency declaration forms when paying hotel bills to ensure that the Dinars being used to pay the bill have been legally changed from foreign currency. Visitors must change the equivalent of at least AD1000 *on entry* (AD500 for minors) and only amounts larger than AD1000 can be reconverted into foreign currency on departure. Visitors wishing to purchase tickets in Algeria for international transportation (air/rail/bus/sea) must exchange foreign currency specifically for this purpose *in excess of the AD1000 minimum obligatory exchange* and produce the exchange receipt and currency declaration form when purchasing their tickets. The import and export of local currency is limited to AD50.
Note: Because of the very strict adherence of the authorities to these regulations, visitors are strongly advised not to be associated with the black market, which tends to concentrate on the French Franc and portable electronics.
Banking hours: 0900-1630 Sunday to Thursday.

DUTY FREE

The following goods may be taken into Algeria by persons over 17 years of age without incurring customs duty:
200 cigarettes or 50 cigars or 250g of tobacco;
1 bottle of spirits (opened).
Prohibited items: Gold, firearms and drugs may not be imported. Gold, firearms and jewellery may not be exported.
Note: Personal jewellery weighing in excess of 100g is subject to a temporary importation permit which will ensure its re-exportation. Alternatively it can be left with customs on arrival. It is compulsory to declare all gold, pearls and precious stones on arrival in the country.

PUBLIC HOLIDAYS

Public holidays observed in Algeria are as follows:
Mar 25 '93 Eid al-Fitr, end of Ramadan. **May 1** Labour Day. **Jun 1** Eid al-Adha, Feast of the Sacrifice. **Jun 19** Anniversary of Ben Bella's Overthrow. **Jun 21** Islamic New Year. **Jun 30** Ashoura. **Jul 5** Independence. **Aug 30** Mouloud (Birth of Mohammed). **Nov 1** Anniversary of the Revolution. **Jan 1 '94** New Year. **Jan** Leilat al-Meiraj (Ascension of Mohammed). **Feb** Beginning of Ramadan. **Mar** Eid al-Fitr.
Note: Muslim festivals are timed according to local sightings of various phases of the Moon and the dates given above are approximations. The Algerian observance of Ramadan (lasting one lunar month and culminating in the feast days of Eid al-Fitr) has recently relaxed, and restaurants in Algiers and other business centres will be open during the day. However, in the towns and oases of the south where religious observance tends to be more orthodox, some difficulty might be had in finding eating places and getting transport during the daylight hours. For a more detailed description of Ramadan and its meaning see *World of Islam* at the back of this book.

HEALTH

Regulations and requirements may be subject to change at short notice, and you are advised to contact your doctor well in advance of your intended date of departure. Any numbers in the chart refer to the footnotes below.

	Special Precautions?	Certificate Required?
Yellow Fever	Yes	1
Cholera	No	No
Typhoid & Polio	Yes	-
Malaria	2	-
Food & Drink	3	-

[1]: A certificate is required by travellers over one year of age arriving from endemic or infected areas.
[2]: Malarial risk cannot be excluded from October to May in the Sahara region.
[3]: Mains water is normally chlorinated, and whilst relatively safe may cause mild abdominal upsets. Bottled water is available and is advised for the first few weeks of the stay. Drinking water outside main cities and towns is likely to be contaminated and sterilisation is considered essential. Milk is unpasteurised and should be boiled. Powdered or tinned milk is available and is advised, but make sure that it is reconstituted with pure water. Local meat, poultry, seafood, fruit and vegetables are generally considered safe to eat.
Bilharzia (schistosomiasis) is present. Avoid swimming and paddling in fresh water. Swimming pools which are well-chlorinated and maintained are safe.
Health care: Medical insurance is strongly recommended. Health care facilities are generally of a high standard in the north but more limited in the south. Emergency cases will be dealt with free of charge.

Oasis

TRAVEL - International

AIR: Algeria's national airline is *Air Algérie (AH)*.
Approximate flight time: From *London* to Algiers is 2 hours 30 minutes.
International airports: *Algiers (ALG)* (Houari Boumediène) is 20km (12 miles) east of Algiers. Coaches depart every 30 minutes to the city. Taxi fare to the city is approximately AD100 (travel time – 30 minutes). Airport facilities include banking and exchange (0600-2400), a state-run duty-free and craft shop (0600-2400), car park, garage, left luggage *(consigne)*, post office, car hire (ONAT), and 24-hour restaurant and bar.
Oran (ORN) (Es Senia) is 10km (6 miles) from the city,

Ghardaia, the seven holy cities . . . pyramid of cubes

linked by taxis and a regular bus service. The taxi fare is approximately AD100. Airport facilities include banking, limited catering and car hire (ONAT).
Annaba (AAE) (El Mellah) is 12km (7.5 miles) from the city. Bus service departs to the city every 30 minutes. Coach service is available on request and taxis are also available; maximum taxi fare to the city is AD100. There are no duty-free shops but there are restaurant, banking and car hire facilities (ONAT).
Constantine (Ain El Bey) is 9km (6 miles) from the city. There are bus and taxi links with the city and limited airport facilities.
SEA: The main ports are Algiers, Annaba, Arzew, Béjaia and Oran. Regular shipping lines serve Algiers from Mediterranean ports. The two major shipping lines are *Compagnie Nationale de Algérie Navigation* and *Compagnie de Navigation Mixte*.
RAIL: There is a daily through train, the *Transmaghreb*, from Casablanca via Oran in Algiers to Tunis.
ROAD: The main road entry points are Maghnia (Morocco), Souk-Ahras, Tebessa and El Kala (Tunisia), Fort Thiriet (Libya), In Guezzam (Niger) and Bordj Mokhtar (Mali). There is a good network of paved roads in the coastal regions and paved roads connect the major towns in the northern Sahara. Further south, the only substantial stretches of paved roads are on the two trans-Saharan 'highways', one of which runs to the west through Reggane and up through Morocco to the coast, while the other runs through Tamanrasset and Djanet on its way to Ghardaia and Algiers. The precise route taken by trans-Saharan travellers often depends on the season. Please note that many desert 'roads' are up to 10km (6-mile) wide ribbons of unimproved desert and are suitable only for well-maintained 4-wheel drive vehicles. **Coach:** Services run by *SNTV (National Travel and Transport Company)* with four international routes, from Libya, Tunisia, Morocco and Niger.

El Oued, town with a thousand domes

TRAVEL - Internal

AIR: *Air Algérie* operates very frequent services from Algiers domestic airport (adjacent to Algiers international) to the major business centres of Annaba, Constantine and Oran. Less frequent services run from Algiers, Oran, Constantine and Annaba to the other less important commercial centres and gateway oases such as Ghardaia (six hours from Algiers) and Ouargla, as well as important oil towns such as In Amenas and Hassi Messaoud. Services are generally reliable, but air travel to the far south may be subject to delay during the dry summer months because of sand storms. Despite this, air is by far the most practical means of transport to the far south for the visitor with limited resources of time; Djanet and Tamanrasset are the oasis gateways to the *Tassili N'Ajjer* and the *Hoggar* respectively.
Note: The London office of *Air Algérie* can provide a timetable of services and prices, make reservations and issue tickets. There is an *Air Algérie* office in every town which is served by *Air Algérie*. Reservations and itineraries can be arranged from these offices, but as some of the more isolated offices are not connected by computer or telex, reservations should be confirmed well in time. Offices are *very* busy in the major towns.
SEA: Government ferries service the main coastal ports: Algiers, Annaba, Arzew, Béjaia, Djidjelli, Ghazaouet, Mostaganem, Oran and Skikda.
RAIL: There are 4000km (2500 miles) of railway in Algeria. Daily but fairly slow services operate between Algiers and Oran, Béjaia, Skikda, Annaba and Constantine.
ROAD: Road surfaces are reasonably good. All vehicles travelling in the desert should be in good mechanical condition, as breakdown facilities are virtually non-existent. Travellers *must* carry full supplies of water and petrol. **Coach:** Relatively inexpensive coaches link major towns. Services are regular but this mode of travel is not recommended for long journeys, such as travel to the south from the coastal strip. Services leave from the coach stations close to the centres of Algiers and Oran. **Car hire:** Can be arranged through the state-run travel agency ONAT at the airport on arrival or in most towns. Many hotels can also arrange car hire. **Documentation:** An International Driving Permit is required. A *carnet de passage* may be required if one's own car is to be used. Cars are allowed entry for three months without duty. Insurance must be purchased at the border. Proof of ownership is essential. Enquire at ONAT for details.
URBAN: Municipal **bus** services operate in Algiers, its suburbs and the coastal area. 10-journey carnets and daily, weekly or longer duration passes are available. There are also two public elevators and a funicular which leads up to the hill overlooking the old *souk* in Algiers. A metro is planned. **Taxis:** All taxis are metered and are plentiful in most cities and major towns, though busy during the early evening in the main cities as many people use them to return home after work. The habit of taxi sharing is extensive. The amount on the meter is the correct fare, but there are surcharges after dark. Travellers should not use unlicensed taxis, which are likely to be uninsured.
JOURNEY TIMES: The following chart gives approximate journey times (in hours and minutes) from Algiers to other major cities/towns in Algeria.

	Air	Road
Constantine	0.45	4.00
Ghardaia	0.55	6.00
Oran	0.50	4.00
Tlemcen	1.00	6.00
Béjaia	0.45	3.00
Biskra	1.15	5.00
El Oued	1.25	6.00
Annaba	0.55	6.00
H. Messaoud	1.05	8.00

ACCOMMODATION

The government department ONAT *(Office National Algérien de l'Animation de la Promotion et de l'Information Touristique)* produces a brochure listing hotels, hotel tariffs, car hire prices, transfer (hotel/air-

port) charges and specially arranged tours. This brochure is available from *Air Algérie* offices.
HOTELS: In general, good hotel accommodation in Algeria is limited. The business centres, and in particular Algiers, tend to have either extremely expensive luxury hotels or cheaper hotels primarily suited to the local population visiting on business or for social purposes. Oran or Algiers are full of cheaper hotels, but they tend to be crowded and difficult to get into, even with a confirmed booking. For assurance on business, reserve rooms only at the best hotels. **Grading:** All hotels are subject to government regulations and are classified by a star rating: deluxe (**5-star**), second class (**4/3-star**) and tourist class (**2/1-star**).
The Coast: The hotels in the resorts along the Mediterranean coast are increasing in number, and many are of a reasonably high standard. Often the good hotels in these resorts run their own nightclubs. The Government travel agency, ONAT, which has offices all over the country, owns the majority of the best hotels, and its network of higher standard accommodation is growing year by year. ONAT offices will make reservations, but only in their own hotels. Winter rates for coastal resorts apply from October 1 to May 31, and summer rates for the remainder of the year.
The Oases: Good hotels in the gateway oases of the mid-south such as Ghardaia and Ouargla are few and far between, and during the season (any time other than high summer, which runs from late June to early September) it is vital to book well in advance. Once again ONAT can help, especially during high season when room availability is limited. It is generally wiser

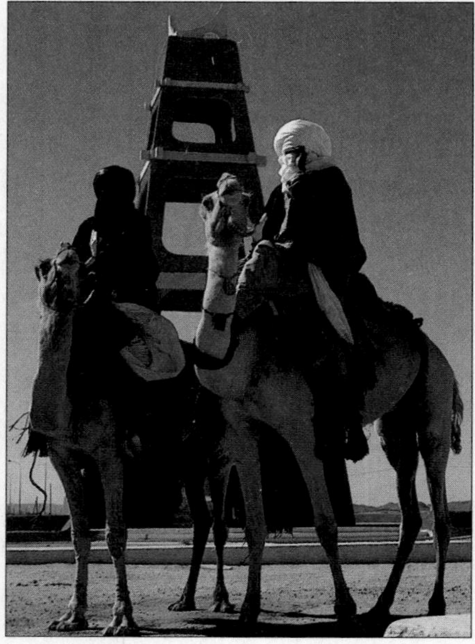
Kings of the desert

in season to book through ONAT for the first night or so, and look around once there if not satisfied.
The Far South: Hotels in the very far south are extremely limited; for instance the only hotel in Djanet, a favourite stopping place for trans-Saharan expeditions and gateway oasis for trips to the *Tassili N'Ajjer*, is the Hotel Zeribas, a *campement* of 20 straw huts. In Tamanrasset, better class hotels have been built since the oasis became a fashionable winter resort. Room availability is, however, still limited.
CAMPING/CARAVANNING: Camping is free on common land or on the beaches but permission from the local authorities is necessary. Campsites with good facilities are found in Larhat, Ain el-Turk and Annaba.
YOUTH HOSTELS: There is a good network of youth hostels throughout the country, costing approximately AD10 per night.

RESORTS & EXCURSIONS

For the purposes of this section the country has been divided into three regions: The Coastal Strip, The Hauts Plateaux and The Sahara.

The Coastal Strip

The capital city, **Algiers**, has been a port since Roman times and many impressive ruins can be seen, such as those at Djemila, Timgad and especially Tipaza (see below), which are all in good condition because of the

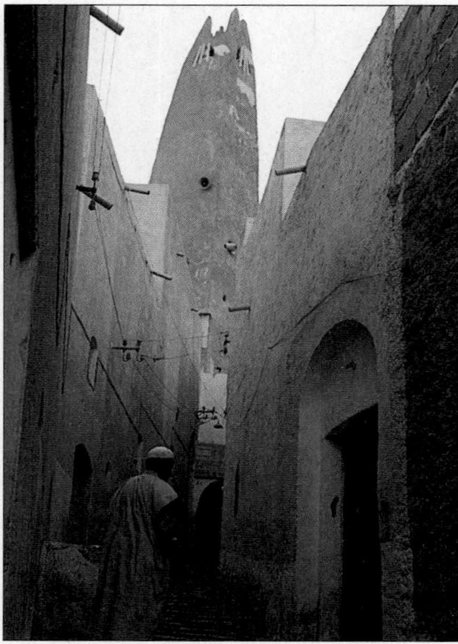
Ghardaia, architectural jewel

dry desert climate. The city was commercialised by the French in the mid-19th century and much of the fabric of the city dates from this time. However, it still has a Maghreb feel to it, with many zig-zag alleyways, mosques, a *casbah*, *medersas* (study houses) and the beautiful Turkish houses and palaces much admired by Le Corbusier. The *Bardo Ethnographic and Local Art Museum* and the *National Museum of Fine Arts* are amongst the finest in North Africa. Despite these attractions, it is not likely that anyone but the business traveller will want to spend much time in the capital; it is an unavoidable stop en route to either the coast or the far south, the place to arrange itineraries and accommodation for onward internal travel.
Within easy reach of Algiers along the coast lie some fine resorts. **Zeralda** is a beach resort with a holiday village and a replica nomad village. **Tipaza** has exceptional Roman, Punic and Christian ruins, and a Numidian mausoleum. The **Chiffa Gorges** and **Kabylia** in the mountains provide more rural scenery. Fig and olive groves in summer become ski resorts in the winter.
To the east of Algiers, the **Turquoise Coast** offers rocky coves and long beaches within easy reach of the city, equipped with sports, cruise and watersports facilities. The **Sidi Fredj** peninsula has a marina, an open-air theatre and complete amenities including sporting facilities.
The western coast around Algeria's second city, **Oran**, has a similar range of beaches, historic remains and mosques. Along the coast from the city, which is primarily a business centre and an oil depot, there are a number of resorts, many with well-equipped hotels.

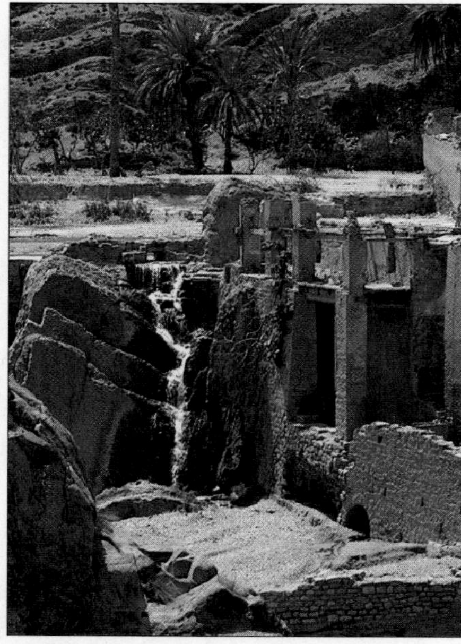
Bou-Saada

Notable beaches include *Ain El Turk*, *Les Andalouses*, *Canastel*, *Kristel*, *Monastagem* and *Sablettes*. Les Andalouses is the most developed and offers all types of watersports facilities and nightclub entertainment as well as first-class accommodation.

The Hauts Plateaux

Tlemcen was an important imperial city from the 12th to 16th centuries, when Morocco ruled the whole of the Maghreb. It stands in the wooded foothills of the Tellein Atlas and is a pleasant retreat from the stifling heat of high summer. Sights include the *Grand Mosque*, the *Mansourah Fortress* and the *Almohad ramparts*.
Constantine, to the east, is a natural citadel lying across the River Rhumnel. Founded by the Carthaginians, who called it Cirta, it is the oldest continuously inhabited city in Algeria. Sights include the *Ahmed Bey Palace* (one of the most picturesque in the Maghreb) and the *Djamma el-Kebir Mosque*.

The Sahara

The Sahara is the most striking and also most forbidding feature of the country. Relatively uninhabited, the area is drawing increasing numbers of winter tourists. Accommodation, though generally good value, is often scarce in oasis regions, and during the season it is advisable to book in advance through ONAT or a hotel representative. *Air Algérie* operates frequent flights from Algiers to Ghardaia, Djanet and Tamanrasset, as well as to several smaller towns, oases and oil settlements, but services can be delayed in high summer due to adverse weather conditions. Roads are much improved, although summer sand storms and winter rains can make all but the major routes hazardous.
The best way to enter the south is to cross the El Kantara Gorges in the south of Constantine. The sudden glimpse of the Sahara through the El Kautara Gorges is breathtaking. These gorges are said to separate the winter areas from the land of everlasting summer and are called *Fouur Es Sahra* (the Sahara's mouth) by the inhabitants. Further down, most Algerian oases generally defy the European cliché of a small patch of palms forever threatened by encroaching dunes: they are often fairly large towns with highly organised, walled-in gardens for the date palms, and mosques, shops and monuments. Favourite starting places for exploring the Sahara are **Laghouat,** a town with a geometric plan, or the **M'Zab Valley,** which has seven typical holy towns and is inhabited by a Muslim fundamentalist sect called the Mozabites. Each town is distinguished by a minaret with four spires, a striking characteristic of all mozabite towns. The most famous among them is **Ghardaïa,** coiled within a group of bare, ochre rocks. The streets, made of clay or paving stones, curl up through the blue and beige buildings towards the white obelisk of the minaret. Not far from Ghardaïa, situated on a hill, is the holy town of **Beni-Isgheu,** the four gates of which are constantly guarded. The special feature of this town is its permanent auction market. In the east of the M'Zab region is **Ouargla**, referred to as 'the golden key to the desert'. This town is well worth visiting for its malekite (another Islamic sect) minaret overlooking an expansive landscape. At the foot of the minaret lies the market square, the porticos of the *souks* and the terraced house roofs of the inhabitants. Further on there is an oasis surrounded by palm trees and beyond that lie the beaches of the Sebkha. Deeper into the south lies the town of **El Goléa**, referred to as 'the pearl of the desert' or 'the enchanted oasis' because of its luxuriant vegetation and abundant water. The town is dominated by an old *ksar* (fort) whose ruins are well-preserved. Moving ever further south one comes to the *Hoggar Mountains*, an impressive, jagged range reaching as far as Libya and surrounded by desert on all sides. It consists of a plateau made of volcanic rock and consists of eroded cliffs and granite needles forming fascinating shapes in pink, blue or black basalt. At the top of the *Assekreu* nestles the famous refuge of Charles de Foucault at 2800m. *Mount Tahat*, which belongs to the **Atakor Massif,** can be seen in the distance, reaching 3000m at its highest point. The picturesque capital, **Tamanrasset,** is situated at the heart of the Hoggar Mountains and is full of life and character and is an important stopping place for commercial traffic travelling to and from West Africa. 'Tam' is the best base for exploring the moonlike Hoggar Mountains and the open desert to the south and west. Being a large town with many hotels and restaurants, tourists often stay in the town and use it as a base for touring the Hoggar Mountains (the Assekreu and Charles de Foucault's hermitage) or hiking in the company of camel drivers who carry their

luggage. It is also a popular winter holiday resort and a centre for oil exploration and exploitation. It is visited regularly by the camel caravans of *Les hommes A* (the Touaregs), who are the ancient nomadic inhabitants of this wide region. They make their way around the inscrutable desert through an ancient knowledge of landmarks passed on from father to son. These nomads have a fair complexion, a blue veil over their faces and are often very tall. The tiny oasis of **Djanet,** another watering hole for commercial traffic and trans-Saharan expeditions, can be found in the *Tassili N'Ajjer*, or 'Plateau of Chasms'. This is a vast volcanic plateau crossed by massive gorges gouged out by rivers which have long since dried out or gone underground. The Tassili conceals a whole group of entirely unique rupestrian paintings (rock paintings) which go back at least as far as the neolithic age. The paintings, depicting daily life, hunting scenes and herds of animals, have a striking beauty and reveal ways of life several thousand years old. They spread out over a 130,000 sq km surface (50,000 sq miles) and form an extraordinary open-air museum which has been miraculously conserved due to the pure quality of the air. Tours are available, lasting from one day to up to two weeks, of the Tassili Plateau and the rupestrian paintings, as well as long-distance car treks in the Ténéré. These visits are organised by private agencies run by the Touaregs and most of them offer a high-quality service. Tourists are collected at the airport (either Djanet or Tamanrasset) and the agency provides them with transportation (usually in 4-wheel drive vehicles), mattresses and food, but travellers must bring their own sleeping bags.

SOCIAL PROFILE

FOOD & DRINK: Algiers and popular coastal towns have a fair selection of good restaurants, serving mainly French and Italian-style food, though the spicy nature of the sauces sets the cuisine apart from its European counterparts. Even classic dishes will have an unmistakeable Algerian quality. Fish dishes are exceptionally good. Menus generally feature a soup or salad to start, roast meat (lamb or beef) or fish as a main course and fresh fruit to finish. In the towns you will find stalls selling *brochettes* (kebabs) in French bread and covered in a spicy sauce (if desired). The range of foodstuffs in the south is limited, and it can be more a question of doing something with whatever is available. Local cooking, which you might be served as a guest of a household, will often consist of roast meat (generally lamb), *cous-cous* with a vegetable sauce (excellent if fresh) and fresh fruit to finish. Food is no longer expensive because of the devaluation of Algerian money and is of very good quality.
Drink: The sale of alcohol is not encouraged and it is available only in the more expensive restaurants and hotels. There are no licensing hours and hotel bars tend to stay open for as long as there is custom. Algeria produces some good wines but very few of them seem to be served in the country itself. If available try Medea, Mansourah and Mascara red wines and Medea, Mascara and Lismara rosés. The major hotels may have a reasonable cellar of European wines. Alcohol in Algeria is generally not cheap. All visitors are advised to respect Muslim attitudes to alcohol.
NIGHTLIFE: The main towns offer reasonable entertainment facilities, including hotel restaurants, nightclubs, discotheques, folk dancing and traditional music. In Oran and Algiers, some cinemas show French and English films.
SHOPPING: Possible souvenirs include leatherware, rugs, copper and brassware, local dresses and jewellery. Berber carpets are beautifully decorated and from the Sahara comes finely-dyed basketwork and primitive-style pottery. Bargaining is customary in street markets and smaller shops. The rue Didouche Mourad is the best shopping street in Algiers. There are two state-run craft centres with fixed prices. One is located at Algiers airport. **Shopping hours:** *Winter:* 0800-1800 Saturday to Wednesday. *Summer:* 0800-1830 Saturday to Wednesday.
SPORT: Horseracing is popular. The northern coastline offers **fishing, swimming** and **sailing,** mainly in Algiers and Annaba. **Football** is also popular.
SOCIAL CONVENTIONS: French-style courtesy should be adopted with new acquaintances. The provision and acceptance of hospitality are as important a part of Algerian culture as elsewhere in the Arab world. In the main cities the urban population lives at a frantic pace much akin to European urban dwellers, but in the south and in rural areas people are much more open and friendly. Algerian women have strict social and dress codes (only one eye is allowed to be revealed in public) and Western women should respect Muslim tradition and cover themselves as much as possible or they may

incite hostility. For more information see the section *World of Islam* at the back of the book. **Photography:** Military installations and personnel should not be photographed and visitors are advised to make sure there is nothing that could be of a governmental or military nature around their prospective object. **Tipping:** 10% is usual.

BUSINESS PROFILE

ECONOMY: Petroleum and natural gas resources have overtaken agriculture in importance. Algeria has the fourth highest GNP per capita in Africa. Most of the country consists of the Sahara desert, and despite investments in the agricultural sector (the main crops being grapes, cereals and citrus fruits), Algeria is far from self-sufficent in foodstuffs. The largest export sector is that of petroleum products, although Algeria is somewhat constrained in its earnings from this source by the requirements of OPEC, to which it belongs. Other exports are fruit and minerals, principally iron ore and phosphates. The country's major trading partners are France, Germany, Italy and Spain. From these it imports most industrial equipment and consumer goods. Since 1972 all international trading has been carried out by a number of state trading organisations, although this is likely to change in the near future with the liberalisation of commerce proposed by the Algerian government. Management decisions and financial control are being devolved to individual enterprises. Previous tight restrictions on foreign investment have been relaxed since the passage of new legislation in March 1990.

BUSINESS: Suits should always be worn in winter months, shirt sleeves during the summer. Prior appointments are necessary for larger business firms. Businessmen generally speak Arabic or French and, as a great deal of bargaining is necessary, it is rarely convenient to carry out transactions through an interpreter. Patience is always important. Visitors are usually entertained in hotels or restaurants, where Algerian businessmen are seldom accompanied by their wives. Only rarely are visitors entertained at home. If visiting during Ramadan (and this should be avoided if possible) care should be taken to observe local custom in public places. (For a more detailed description see *World of Islam* at the back of this book.) The climate is best between October and May. **Office hours:** Generally 0800-1200 and 1400-1730 Saturday to Wednesday.

COMMERCIAL INFORMATION: The following organisations can offer advice:
Arab-British Chamber of Commerce, 6 Belgrave Square, London SW1X 8PH. Tel: (071) 235 4363. Fax: (071) 245 6688. Telex: 22171 ARABRIG; *or*
Chambre Nationale de Commerce (CNC), BP 100, Palais Consulaire, rue Amilcar Cabral, Algiers, Algeria. Tel: (2) 575 555. Telex: 61345.

HISTORY & GOVERNMENT

HISTORY: The present borders of Algeria as well as Tunisia and Libya were determined when the region became part of the Ottoman Empire, with each of the countries being an administrative sub-division. The coming of the Ottoman Empire lead to the Spanish losing the coastal strip which they had held. It subsequently became a pirate base for attacking European fleets. The French launched a military attack in 1830 and having obtained a toe-hold in North Africa held on and expanded it. Algeria achieved independence in 1962, despite opposition from many French quarters. The victorious FLN *(Front de Libération Nationale)* under Ahmed Ben Bella pursued orthodox socialist policies. Ben Bella was subsequently deposed by the Minister of Defence Houari Boumediène, who ruled until his death in 1978. After the 1986 revision of the National Charter, the official political emphasis has been more on 'pragmatic socialism' rather than Marxism, as a result of which private enterprise and market forces assumed a more important role in society and the economy. Further government decrees loosened restrictions on political organisation and press comment, giving A;geria probably the liveliest media in the Arab world. In the international arena, by this time, Algeria enjoyed a considerable reputation as an 'honest broker', mediating in a number of complex international disputes including the Iran-Iraq war. Algeria has also recently joined the Union of the Arab Maghreb, a regional grouping with Tunisia, Morocco, Libya and Mauritania which is designed to promote political and economic co-operation. However, domestic issues have dominated the agenda in Algeria since the turn of the 90s, beginning with multi-party municipal and local elections which were held for the first time in June 1990: the ruling FLN secured a majority of the seats, but Islamic parties made a strong showing. Prominent among these was the *Front Islamique du Salut* (FIS, Islamic Salvation Front) whose growing support have since changed the face of Algerian politics. In May the following year, the Government was forced to resign by a FIS-led general strike. Only decisive action by President Chadli, backed by the security forces, prevented an outright FIS takeover. Nonetheless, the Government persevered with its democratisation programme, holding general elections as scheduled in January 1992, which resulted in a comprehensive victory for the FIS, but was followed by the military's decision to annul the result. The country has since been governed under a state of emergency. Against this background, at the end of June 1992, the state president Mohamed Boudiaf was assassinated.

Algiers

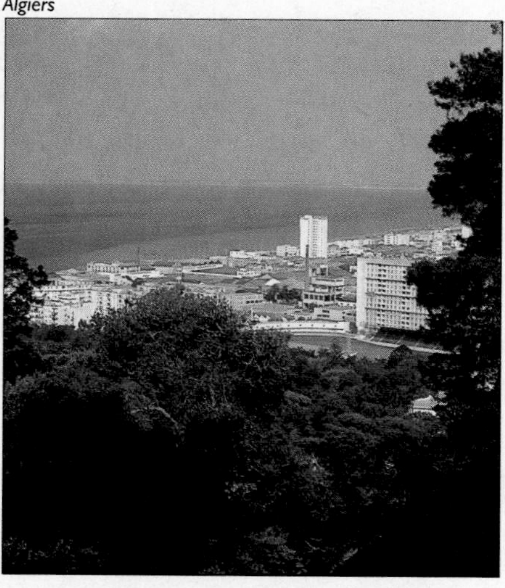

GOVERNMENT: Since 1962 the country has been a single-party state with the *Front de Libération Nationale* as the only party. Power is shared between the Head of State and the unicameral 281-member National People's Assembly, both elected by universal adult suffrage. Moves towards a multi-party system have been suspended for the time being, and the country is now governed by a Higher State Council.

CLIMATE

Summer temperatures are high throughout the country, particularly in the south where it is very dry and very hot. During this time road travel is difficult and air travel prone to delay due to sandstorms. Northern cities have high humidity, while those along the coast are cooled by sea breezes. In the winter the oases of the far south are pleasant, and attract many visitors. The desert temperature drops dramatically at night. Coastal towns are prone to storms from the sea. Rainfall is relatively low throughout the country, and in the far south is virtually unknown.

Required clothing: Cotton and linen lightweights for winter months and evenings in desert areas. Woollens and light rainwear are advised for the winter along the coastal strip and the *Hauts Plateaux*.

ALGIERS Algeria (60m)

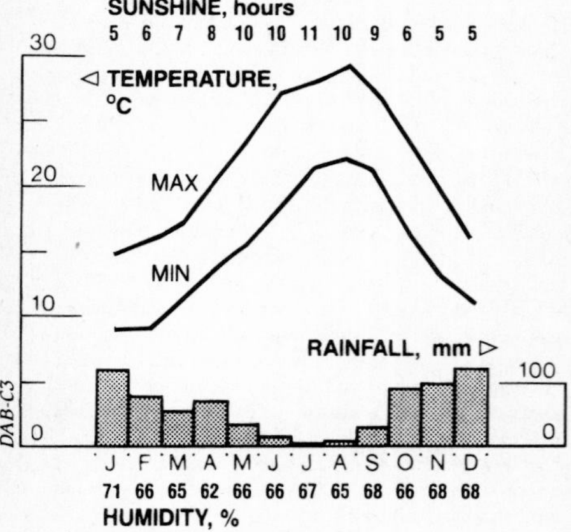

Tassili

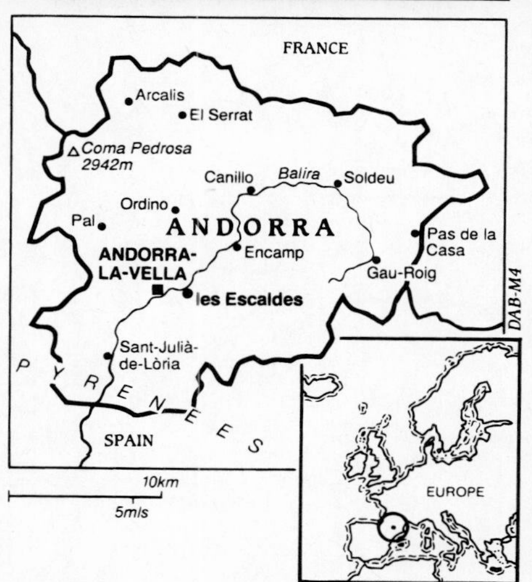

Location: Western Europe; border of France and Spain.

Sindicat d'Initiativa de las Valls d'Andorra
Carrer Dr Vilanova
Andorra la Vella, Andorra
Tel: 20214. Fax: 25823.
Andorran Delegation
63 Westover Road
London SW18 2RF
Tel: (081) 874 4806.
British Consulate (in Barcelona)
Edificio Torre de Barcelona
13th Floor, Avenida Diagonal 477
08036 Barcelona
Spain
Tel: (3) 419 9044. Fax: (3) 405 2411. Telex: 52799 BRBARE.
Andorran Delegation
120 East 55th Street
New York, NY 10022
Tel: (212) 688 8681. Fax: (212) 688 8683.
Embassy of Spain
Suite 802
350 Sparks Street
Ottawa, Ontario
K1R 7S8
Tel: (613) 237 2193. Fax: (613) 236 1502.

AREA: 467.76 sq km (180.6 sq miles).
POPULATION: 50,887 (1989).
POPULATION DENSITY: 108.8 per sq km.
CAPITAL: Andorra la Vella. **Population:** 19,003 (1989).
GEOGRAPHY: Andorra is situated in the Pyrenées, bordered by France to the north and east and Spain to the south and west. The landscape consists of gorges and narrow valleys surrounded by mountains. Much of the landscape is forested, but there are several areas of rich pastureland in the valleys. There are four rivers and several mountain lakes. Ski resorts and the spa town of Les Escaldes are Andorra's main attractions.
LANGUAGE: The official language is Catalan. Spanish and French are also spoken.
RELIGION: Roman Catholic.
TIME: GMT + 1 (GMT + 2 in summer).
ELECTRICITY: Sockets: 240 volts AC, 50Hz. Lighting: 125 volts AC.
COMMUNICATIONS: Telephone: Full IDD is available. Country code: 33 628. **Telex:** Some telex services are available; enquire at hotels. **Post:** Internal mail services are free; international mail takes about a week within Europe. A *Poste Restante* service is available in Andorra la Vella. Post office hours: 0900-1300 and 1500-1700 in Andorra la Vella, otherwise variable. **Press:** Andorra has two weekly publications, *Andorra 7* and *Poble Andorra*.
BBC World Service and Voice of America frequencies: From time to time these change. See the section *How to Use this Book* for more information.

BBC:				
MHz	15.07	12.10	9.410	3.955
Voice of America:				
MHz	11.97	9.670	6.040	5.995

PASSPORT/VISA

Important note: all regulations and requirements may be subject to change at short notice, and you are advised to contact the appropriate diplomatic or consular authority before finalising travel arrangements. Details of these may be found at the head of this country's entry. Any numbers in the chart refer to the footnotes below.

	Passport Required?	Visa Required?	Return Ticket Required?
Full British	1	2	No
BVP	Valid	2	No
Australian	Yes	2	Yes
Canadian	Yes	2	Yes
USA	Yes	2	Yes
Other EC	1	2	No
Japanese	Yes	2	Yes

PASSPORTS: [1] Valid passport required by all except for nationals of France and Spain, providing they hold a valid ID card; and nationals of UK holding a BVP.
British Visitors Passport: Acceptable. A BVP can be used for holidays or unpaid business trips of up to 3 months.
VISAS: [2] There are no visa requirements for entry into Andorra. However, as Andorra is bordered by France and Spain the relevant regulations for these countries should be studied. Visitors wishing to have their passport stamped with the Andorran coat of arms should apply to the Sindicat d'Initiativa in the capital.
Validity: Stays of up to 3 months are allowed without a visa.
Temporary residence: Apply in person at any police station in Andorra.

MONEY

Currency: Although most currencies are accepted, the main currencies in circulation are Spanish Pesetas and, to a lesser extent, French Francs. Please consult the entries for *Spain* and *France* later in this book.
Currency exchange: Andorran banks and bureaux de change will exchange foreign currency.
Credit cards: Diners Club, Visa, American Express and Access/Mastercard are accepted. Check with your credit card company for details of merchant acceptability and other services which may be available.
Currency restrictions: There are no frontier formalities when entering the country, but French and Spanish authorities may carry out formalities on departure.
Banking hours: 0900-1300 and 1500-1700 Monday to Friday; 0900-1200 Saturday.

DUTY FREE

Andorra is a duty-free zone and there is little point buying duty-free items to take in. See also under *Food & Drink* below.
Prohibited/restricted items: Controlled drugs, firearms, pornography, radio transmitters, certain foodstuffs, plants, flowers, animals and birds and items made from endangered species are prohibited. No works of art and certain other items can be exported without permission.

PUBLIC HOLIDAYS

Public holidays observed in Andorra are as follows:
Apr 9 '93 Good Friday. **Apr 12** Easter Monday. **Sep 8** National Holiday. **Dec 25-26** Christmas. **Jan 1 '94** New Year's Day.
In July, August and September, parishes have their own public holidays during which festivals are held (see *Special Events* in the *Social Profile* section).

HEALTH

Important note: all regulations and requirements may be subject to change at short notice, and you are advised to contact your doctor well in advance of your intended date of departure. Any numbers in the chart refer to the footnotes below.

	Special Precautions?	Certificate Required?
Yellow Fever	No	No
Cholera	No	No
Typhoid & Polio	No	-
Malaria	No	-
Food & Drink	No	-

Health care: Most health costs are covered by UK health agreements but additional insurance is advised. Please note that as entry to Andorra is usually through France or Spain, their health regulations should also be complied with.

TRAVEL - International

AIR: Andorra's nearest international airport is *Barcelona (BCN)* in Spain, 225km (141 miles) from Andorra. For more information on the airport and its facilities, please consult the entry for *Spain* later in the book. Shared taxis and buses are available.
Toulouse (TLS), in France, is 180km (113 miles) from Andorra.
The nearest airport is *Seo de Urgel*, which is served by three flights a day from Barcelona. It is 20km (12 miles) from Andorra.
RAIL: Routes from Perpignan, Villefranche, Toulouse and Barcelona go to La Tour de Carol, 20km (12 miles) from Andorra. The nearest station is L'Hospitalet, but buses run from both L'Hospitalet and La Tour de Carol.
ROAD: Mountainous roads over the Envalita pass to Perpignan, Tarbes and Toulouse (France); and southwards to Barcelona and Lérida (Spain). Buses run regularly from Barcelona. Taxis may also be taken and sharing is commonly practised to cut costs.

TRAVEL - Internal

ROAD: A good road runs from the Spanish to the French frontiers through Saint Julia, Andorra la Vella, Les Escaldes, Encamp, Canillo and Soldeu. There is one major east–west route and a minor road to El Serrat, which are closed in winter. The bus journey from La Tour de Carol takes 2 hours 20 minutes and runs once daily at 1330. From L'Hospitalet the service takes 2 hours 40 minutes and runs early enough to permit a day return trip from France. A seasonal service runs from Ax-les-Thermes, and services may be available from Seo de Urgel in Spain. There are also internal buses and minibuses linking the villages on the 186km (115 miles) of road.**Documentation:** A national driving licence is sufficient.

ACCOMMODATION

HOTELS: There are over 200 hotels and inns (9000 beds in total), principally catering for the summer months, although some stay open all year round. Rooms during the summer months (July to August) should be booked well in advance. Hotels (and restaurants) are registered with the Sindicat d'Initiativa and are bound to keep to the registered prices and services.
MOUNTAIN REFUGES: These offer cheap and basic accommodation; normally they will have one room available for visitors, and may or may not have a hearth and bunk beds. Enquire locally concerning locations and prices.
CAMPING: There are 25 campsites in Andorra, most of which are close to the main towns and well-signposted. Several have shops and other facilities. There are also facilities for caravans.

RESORTS & EXCURSIONS

The country is mountainous, traversed by a main road which runs roughly northeast to southwest, along which most of the settlements are to be found. Many of these are villages or hamlets with Romanesque churches and houses built in the local style; others, off the main road, are even more unspoilt, and provide spectacular views across the rugged countryside. For the visitor however, Andorra's two greatest attractions are the fact that it is both a duty-free state and a centre for winter sports, a combination which has led to a great deal of overt commercialism, particularly in the main towns of Andorra La Vella and Les Escaldes.
Andorra La Vella, the country's capital, lies at the junction of two mountain streams. Sights there include a fine

For **CODE-LINK**™ symbols, refer to **France** or **Spain** entries.

12th-century church and the 'Casa de la Val', the ancient seat of government.

Adjoining the capital is the spa town of **Les Escaldes** which also has examples of Romanesque architecture. These towns are also the centre of the colourful Andorran local festival in early September, in honour of La Vierge de Meritxell. 18km (11 miles) from Les Escaldes, off the main road, is the hamlet of **El Serrat**, which commands a breathtaking view across the mountains. The town of **Encamp**, between the capital and the French frontier, is also worth a visit.

Ski resorts: There are several ski resorts in the country, most of which offer good facilities. The main ski resort in Andorra is **Soldeu**, the first major settlement on the road after the French frontier at Port d'Envarlira. Both nursery slopes and skiing for intermediates are available with a good ski school offering tuition at reasonable prices. There are also ski centres at **Pas de la Casa/Grau Roig**, on the French frontier, and at **Arcalis, Arinsal, and Pal,** all north of **Andorra la Vella**.

The Sindicat d'Initiativa can provide details on prices, snow conditions, as well as other information about tourist opportunities in the country; address at top of entry.

SOCIAL PROFILE

FOOD & DRINK: Cuisine is mainly Catalan, and generally expensive. Quality and prices in the 250 or so restaurants are similar to those in small French and Spanish resort towns. Local dishes include *coques* (flavoured flat cakes), *trinxat* (a potato and cabbage dish), local sausages and cheeses, and a variety of dishes of pork and ham. **Drink:** Alcoholic drinks bought in shops and supermarkets are cheap (Andorra being a duty-free zone), but prices in bars can be expensive. They do, however, stay open late.

NIGHTLIFE: There are centres around the bars and hotels. Discotheques can be found during both summer and winter.

SHOPPING: There is duty-free shopping for all goods. Petrol, alcohol, cameras and watches etc can be purchased at low prices. Electrical goods are very good value.

SPORT: There is excellent **skiing**, mainly around Soldeu (see above, under *Resorts & Excursions*, for further information). A bus service picks up skiers from hotels and inns, and takes them to the slopes, returning in the evening. There are many good nursery slopes. Other available activities include **horseriding, tennis, swimming, trout fishing, clay pigeon shooting, hiking** and **rock climbing. Football, rugby** and **basketball** are the most popular spectator sports.

SPECIAL EVENTS: Regional festivals take place annually in the following locations:

Andorra la Vella: From the first Saturday in August for three days.

Canillo: From the third Saturday in June for 3 days.

Encamp: 3-day festival in August.

Escaldes-Engordany: 3-day festival in July.

La Massana: 3-day festival in August.

Ordino: 2-day festival in September.

Santa Julia de Loria: From the last Sunday in July for three days.

SOCIAL CONVENTIONS: Normal social courtesies should be extended when visiting someone's home. Handshaking is the accepted form of greeting. Dress is informal and smoking is very common; customs are similar to those of Spain. **Tipping:** Service charges are usually included in the bill. Porters and waiters expect a further 10%.

BUSINESS PROFILE

ECONOMY: Andorra is principally an agricultural country with some mineral resources. Potatoes and tobacco are the main products, although there is some livestock farming. The principal raw materials are lead, iron and alum. The country's energy requirements are met by the government-owned electricity company which can supply around 60% of Andorran requirements. As a duty-free zone the economy has expanded rapidly in recent years, trading in both European and foreign goods. The main sources of government revenue are taxes on petrol, tourism and consumer goods. There is some concern about the long-term implications of Spanish membership of the EC and the likely resulting fall in tax revenues. Andorra's main trading partners are neighbouring France and Spain.

BUSINESS: Suits are recommended at all times with white shirt and black shoes. Prior appointments are necessary and meetings tend to be formal. Lunch is usually after 1430 and can extend through the afternoon until 2100-2200. Although English is widely spoken a knowledge of Spanish or French is appreciated. **Office hours** vary considerably. It is advisable to arrange business appointments in advance.

HISTORY & GOVERNMENT

HISTORY: Andorra is one of the oldest nations in Europe, originally established by Charlemagne as a buffer state against the Iberian Muslims. As a result of the *Paretages* of 1278 and 1288, control of the country was split between the Spanish Bishop of Urgel and a nominee appointed by the King of France and, subsequently, by the French Emperors and Presidents; a state of affairs which has continued to the present day. The country is therefore a co-principality, unique in having two Heads of State.

With the exception of a brief period during the Napoleonic Wars, the country has retained its independence ever since. Following a Council of Europe investigation in 1988, elections were held in Andorra for the first time. The issues that ruffled the normally staid face of Andorran politics concerned the denial of trade union rights for the vast majority of salaried workers in Andorra who originate in Spain and France, and the smallness of the electorate permitted to vote. The Government's response to these developments has produced an improvement in relations with its neighbours. The Spanish agreed in 1990 to represent Andorran interests abroad, including at diplomatic level.

GOVERNMENT: Andorra has no formal constitution. The arrangements which have evolved historically are now enshrined in the Decree of January 15, 1981, with a Head of Government elected by the Council General. The Co-Princes nominate two Permanent Delegates who in turn nominate the *Veguers*. The *Veguers* live in Andorra and are entrusted with the administration of justice, law and order. The administration is in the hands of a General Council with 28 members, four from each of the seven parishes, elected by universal suffrage (a concept introduced very recently; until 1970, only third-generation Andorran males were entitled to vote). The Council elects a President and a Vice-President. The General Council voted in June 1990 to establish a Special Commission to draft a constitution which is intended to promulgate popular sovereignty and legitimise the Co-Princes; a draft was completed in the spring of 1992.

CLIMATE

Temperate climate with warm summers and cold winters. Rain falls throughout the year.

Required clothing: Lightweights for the summer and warm mediumweights during winter. Waterproofing is advisable throughout the year.

LES ESCALDES Andorra (1080m)

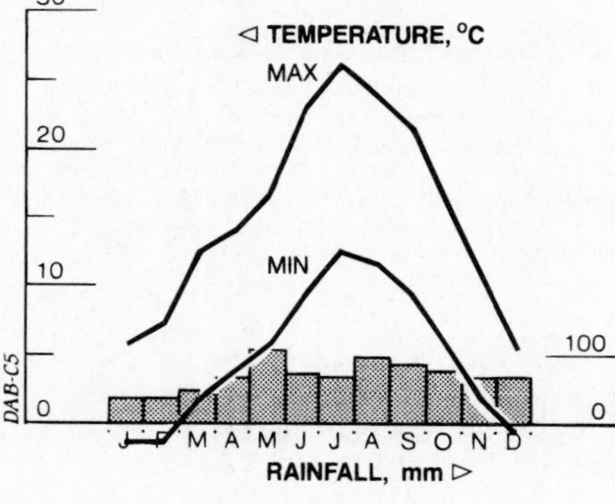

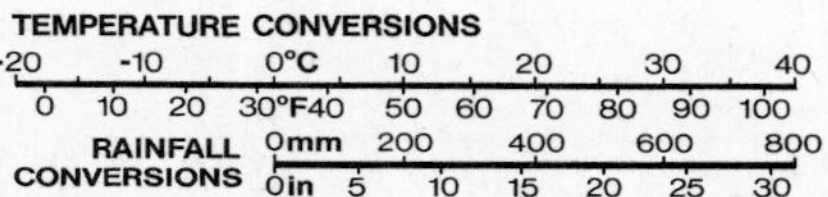

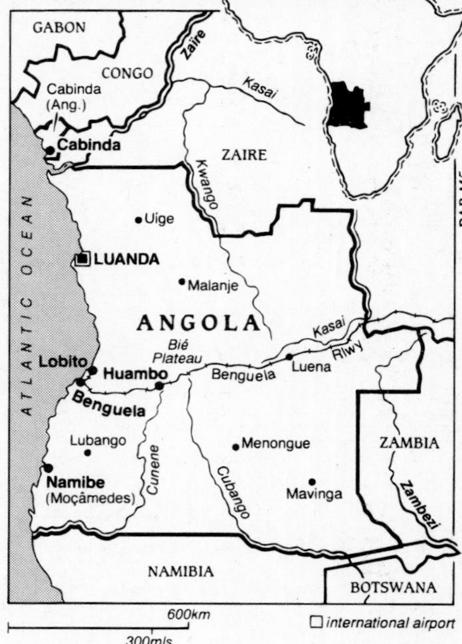

Location: Southwest Africa.

Note: Angola has been riven by civil war for nearly 20 years. Although elections were recently held, there is a probability that fighting may once again resume, particularly in the interior of the country and around the capital. Check with the appropriate government office (Foreign Office for British citizens) for up-to-date information.

National Tourist Agency
CP 1240, Palácio de Vidro
Luanda, Angola
Tel: 372 750.

Embassy of the People's Republic of Angola
98 Park Lane
London W1Y 3TA
Tel: (071) 495 1752. Fax: (071) 495 1635. Telex: 8813258. Opening hours: 0930-1200 and 1330-1500 Monday to Friday (closed on Wednesdays).

Ministry of External Relations
Avenida Comte Gica
Luanda, Angola
Telex: 4127 *or* 4186 MIREX AN.

British Embassy
CP 1244
Rua Diogo Cão 4
Luanda, Angola
Tel: 334 582. Fax: 333 331. Telex: 3130.

AREA: 1,246,700 sq km (481,354 sq miles).
POPULATION: 10,020,000 (1990 estimate).
POPULATION DENSITY: 8 per sq km.
CAPITAL: Luanda. **Population:** 1,200,000 (1982 estimate).

GEOGRAPHY: Angola is bordered by Zaïre to the north, Zambia to the east, Namibia to the south and the Atlantic Ocean to the west. Mountains rise from the coast, levelling to a plateau which makes up most of the country. The country is increasingly arid towards the south; the far south is on the edge of the Namib Desert. The northern plateau is thickly vegetated. Cabinda is a small enclave to the north of Angola proper, surrounded by the territories of Zaïre and Congo. The discovery of large oil deposits off the coast of the enclave has led to it becoming the centre of Angola's foreign business interests. The oil industry, based primarily at Malongo, is run jointly by Gulf Oil and Sonangol, the Angolan state oil producers.

LANGUAGE: The official language is Portuguese. African languages (Ovimbundu, Kimbundu, Bakongo and Chokwe) are spoken by the majority of the population.

RELIGION: 12% Roman Catholic, 4% Protestant; Animist.

TIME: GMT + 1.
ELECTRICITY: 220 volts AC, 60Hz. Plugs are of the Continental-style round 2-pin type.
COMMUNICATIONS: Telephone: Until recently all calls had to be made through the international operator, booking at least six hours in advance; direct calls to Luanda (but not to the rest of the country) are becoming increasingly possible. **Telex/telegram:** Telegram services are fairly reliable, occasionally subject to delay. Telex facilities are available in main hotels. **Post:** Airmail between Europe and Angola takes five to ten days. Surface mail between Europe and Angola takes at least two months. There is a fairly reliable internal service. Most correspondence is by telex. **Press:** The daily newspaper is *O Jornal de Angola*; *Diario da República* is an official government news-sheet. There are no English-language newspapers.
BBC World Service and Voice of America frequencies: From time to time these change. See the section *How to Use this Book* for more information.

BBC:

MHz	21.66	17.88	15.40	6.600

Voice of America:

MHz	21.49	15.60	9.525	6.035

PASSPORT/VISA

Important note: all regulations and requirements may be subject to change at short notice, and you are advised to contact the appropriate diplomatic or consular authority before finalising travel arrangements. Details of these may be found at the head of this country's entry. Any numbers in the chart refer to the footnotes below.

	Passport Required?	Visa Required?	Return Ticket Required?
Full British	Yes	Yes	Yes
BVP	Not valid	-	-
Australian	Yes	Yes	Yes
Canadian	Yes	Yes	Yes
USA	Yes	Yes	Yes
Other EC	Yes	Yes	Yes
Japanese	Yes	Yes	Yes

PASSPORTS: Valid passports required by all including nationals of Angola.
British Visitors Passport: Not accepted.
VISAS: Required by all except those continuing their journey to a third country without leaving the airport. Some business travellers are allowed entry, but only as guests of an accepted business firm; tourist travel is not allowed in Angola at this time.
Types of Visa: Business. Single: £63.
Exit permits: Required by all visitors; must be issued by the same consulate that issued the visa.
Application to: Consulate (or Consular Section at Embassy). For addresses, see top of entry.
Working days required: Applications should be made well in advance.

MONEY

Currency: Kwanza (Kz) = 100 lwei (Lw). Notes are in denominations of Kz5000, 1000, 500, 100, 50 and 20. Coins are in denominations of Kz20, 10, 5, 2 and 1, and Lw50.
Credit cards: Credit cards are generally not accepted. American Express and Diners Club enjoy limited acceptance. Amex is accepted at the Le Méridien Presidente Hotel in Luanda; otherwise check with your credit card company for details of merchant acceptability and other services which may be available.
Exchange rate indicators: The following figures are included as a guide to the movements of the Kwanza against Sterling and the US Dollar:

Date:	Oct '89	Oct '90	Oct '91	Oct '92
£1.00=	48.59	56.27	103.41	950.40
$1.00=	30.77	28.80	59.59	598.87

Currency restrictions: All imported currency should be declared on arrival. The local currency import limit is Kz15,000; there is no limit on the import of foreign currency, subject to declaration on arrival. Export of local currency is prohibited; up to Kz5000 equivalent of foreign currency may be exported by those leaving on a return ticket purchased in Angola.
Banking hours: 0845-1600 Monday to Friday.

DUTY FREE

The following items may be imported into Angola without payment of duty:
A reasonable amounts of tobacco and perfume.
Prohibited items: Firearms, ammunition and alcohol.

PUBLIC HOLIDAYS

Public holidays observed in Angola are as follows:
Mar 27 '93 Victory Day. **Apr 14** Youth Day. **May 1** Workers' Day. **Aug 1** Armed Forces Day. **Sep 17** National Heroes' Day (Birthday of Dr Agostinho Neto). **Nov 11** Independence Day. **Dec 1** Pioneers' Day. **Dec 10** Anniversary of the Foundation of the MPLA. **Dec 25** Family Day. **Jan 1 '94** New Year's Day. **Feb 4** Outbreak of the armed struggle against Portuguese colonialism.

HEALTH

Important note: all regulations and requirements may be subject to change at short notice, and you are advised to contact your doctor well in advance of your intended date of departure. Any numbers in the chart refer to the footnotes below.

	Special Precautions?	Certificate Required?
Yellow Fever	1	-
Cholera	Yes	2
Typhoid & Polio	Yes	-
Malaria	Yes	-
Food & Drink	3	-

[1]: Vaccination essential if travelling from an infected area; pregnant women and infants under nine months should not be vaccinated and therefore should avoid exposure to infection.
[2]: Following WHO guidelines issued in 1973, a cholera vaccination certificate is no longer a condition of entry to Angola. However, cholera is a serious risk in this country and precautions are essential. Up-to-date advice should be sought before deciding whether these precautions should include vaccination as medical opinion is divided over its effectiveness. See the *Health* section at the back of the book.
[3]: All water should be regarded as being potentially contaminated. Water used for drinking, brushing teeth or making ice should have first been boiled or otherwise sterilised. Milk is unpasteurised and should be boiled. Powdered or tinned milk is available and is advised, but make sure that it is reconstituted with pure water. Avoid dairy products which are likely to have been made from unboiled milk. Only eat well-cooked meat and fish, preferably served hot. Pork, salad and mayonnaise may carry increased risk. Vegetables should be cooked and fruit peeled.
Malaria risk (and of other insect-born diseases) exists all year throughout the country, including urban areas. The malignant *falciparum* form is prevalent. Resistance to chloroquine and sulfadoxine/pyrimethane has been reported.
Rabies is present. For those at high risk, vaccination before arrival should be considered. If you are bitten abroad seek medical advice without delay. For more information consult the *Health* section at the back of the book.
Bilharzia (schistosomiasis) is present. Avoid swimming and paddling in fresh water. Swimming pools which are well-chlorinated and maintained are safe.
Health care: Full health insurance is essential. There are three main hospitals in Luanda: the Hospital Americo Boavida, the Hospital Josefina Machel, and the Hospital do Prenda. There are also hospital facilities in the other main towns. Medical treatment is free although often inadequate, and visitors should travel with their own supply of remedies for simple ailments such as stomach upsets; pharmaceutical supplies are usually very difficult to obtain.

TRAVEL - International

AIR: Angola's national airline is *TAAG Angola Airlines (DT)*.
Approximate flight time: From *London* to Luanda is 19 hours 30 minutes (this includes a stopover of 5 hours in Lisbon).
International airport: *Luanda (LAD)* is 4km (2.5 miles) from the city. There are no taxis: visitors must be met by their sponsors. Airport facilities include restaurant and currency exchange.
Note: Most British and American visitors with business interests in the Cabinda enclave bypass Luanda by flying to Gabon by *UTA*, then on by private jet. On arrival, they are taken immediately by helicopter to the Malongo Base. This is only possible by special arrangement with the Gabonese and Angolan Governments as no visas are available at present.
SEA: The main ports are Cabinda, Lobito, Luanda and Namibe.
RAIL/ROAD: All land frontiers are currently closed. Plans to re-open the Benguela railway seem unlikely to achieve fruition until a greater degree of peace is achieved.

TRAVEL - Internal

Note: All travel in the country is very strictly controlled. Tourist travel is not allowed in Angola at this time, but some business travel is permitted. Most of the country is only accessible by air.
AIR: *TAAG Angola Airlines* operate flights within Angola. There are scheduled services between major towns. Also, private jets are operated by some Portuguese, French and Italian business interests (trading most notably in oil and diamonds) in the north of the country, particularly to and from the Cabinda enclave, which is only accessible by air (see above for information on travelling directly to Cabinda from Gabon). Helicopter access to Cabinda is possible as well. Passengers on internal flights must carry official authorisation (*guia de marcha*); contact the Ministry of External Relations in Luanda (address at top of entry) for further information.
Approximate flight times: From Luanda to *Benguela* and *Cabinda* is 50 minutes, to *Huambo* is 1 hour, to *Namibe* is 1 hour 45 minutes and to *Lubango* is 1 hour 10 minutes.
RAIL: Due to the instability of the political situation, rail services are erratic. Trains run on three separate routes inland from Luanda: to Malanje (daily), Lobito to Dilolo (the Benguela Railway, daily), and Mocamedes to Menongue (daily). There are no sleeping cars and no air-conditioned services, though food and drink are available on some journeys.
ROAD: There were once nearly 8000km (5000 miles) of tarred roads but much of the infrastructure was destroyed in the conflict after 1975. Many roads are unsuitable for travel at the present time, and local advice should be sought and followed carefully. Identity papers must be carried.
Documentation: An International Driving Permit is required.
URBAN: Local buses run in Luanda. A flat fare is charged.

ACCOMMODATION

Many hotels in Angola have recently undergone refurbishment, and have air-conditioning, a private bath or shower, a phone, radio and TV. However, there is a general shortage of accommodation, and it is advisable to book well in advance (at least one month prior to departure); accommodation cannot be booked at the airport. Most bookings must be made by the person, company or organisation being visited through the state hotel

ANGOLA | **HEALTH REGULATIONS** | **VISA REGULATIONS** | Code-Link

GALILEO/WORLDSPAN

TI-DFT/LAD/HE

TI-DFT/LAD/VI

SABRE

TIDFT/LAD/HE

TIDFT/LAD/VI

To access this information on your CRS, swipe the barcode with a light pen or type in the text under the barcode. For more information, see the introduction *How to Use This Book*.

organisation, ANGHOTEL. Tel: 392 648. Telex: 3492 ANGOTE AN. There is also accommodation in Kissama National Park (see *Resorts & Excursions* below).

RESORTS & EXCURSIONS

In **Luanda** the main places to visit are the fortress (containing the *Museum of Armed Forces*), the *National Museum of Anthropology* and the *Museum of Slavery*, 25km (16 miles) along the coast from Luanda.

The **Kissama National Park** lies 70km (45 miles) south from Luanda, and is home to a great variety of wild animals. Accommodation is available in bungalows located in the middle of the Park, but visitors must bring their own food. The park is closed during the rainy season.

The **Kalandula Waterfalls**, located in the Malange area, make an impressive spectacle, particularly at the end of the rainy season.

There are plenty of beaches: Luanda itself is built around a bay and there are bathing beaches (*Ilha*) five minutes from the centre of the city. Watersports are possible on the *Mussulo Peninsula*. 45km (28 miles) south of Luanda is *Palmeirinhas*, a long-deserted beach. The scenery is magnificent, but bathing is hazardous. Fishing is possible both here and at *Santiago* beach, 45km (28 miles) north of Luanda.

SOCIAL PROFILE

FOOD & DRINK: Tables should be booked well in advance in the few restaurants and hotels, although only the Le Méridien Presidente Hotel can really offer high-class service. Notice needs to be given for extra guests. **NIGHTLIFE:** There are some nightclubs and cinemas in Luanda. Cinema seats should be booked in advance. **SHOPPING:** Traditional handicrafts are sold in the city; shopping is not easy outside the main cities. **SPORT: Watersports** are available on Mussolo peninsula, **swimming** is available on Ilha beaches and Palmeirinhas. Santiago has **fishing**. **SOCIAL CONVENTIONS:** Normal social courtesies should be observed. **Photography:** It is inadvisable to photograph public places, public buildings or public events. Copies of photography permits should be deposited with the British Embassy; permits should be carried at all times. **Tipping:** Where service charge is not added to the bill, 10% is acceptable, although tipping is not officially encouraged. Tipping can be in kind (eg cigarettes).

BUSINESS PROFILE

ECONOMY: Angola is rich in natural resources, including oil, coffee and diamonds. Agriculture employs over 50% of the population. Gulf Oil and Texaco have developed major oilfields off the shore of Cabinda (an enclave in the north of the country) but the country has only one refinery and so exports most of its oil in the crude form; plans to develop the country's refining capacity have been shelved since the collapse of the oil price in the late 1980s (Angola is not a member of OPEC). The economy was adversely affected by the departure of 700,000 Portuguese after independence and the consequences of civil strife and the South African incursions. Since then the economy has for the most part been centrally planned with a dominant state sector. Import controls and austerity measures forced on the authorities by the civil war have further inhibited economic growth. Capital and technical expertise are being sought from the West to help further development of resources. Angola's largest trading partners are Portugal, Brazil, France and the USA, from whom it imports much of its food and almost all its manufactured equipment.
BUSINESS: Lightweight suits are recommended. Many Angolan business people dress casually, wearing safari suits and open neck shirts. Any dark colours can be worn for social occasions. As Portuguese is the official language, a knowledge of this is an advantage in business transactions; French and Spanish are also useful. There are limited translation services. Avoid June to September as Angolans tend to take their holidays at this time. **Office hours:** 0730-1200 and 1430-1800 Monday to Thursday, 0730-1230 and 1430-1730 Friday.
COMMERCIAL INFORMATION: The following organisation can offer advice: Associação Comercial de Luanda (Chamber of Commerce), CP 1275, Edifício Palácio de Comércio, Luanda. Tel: 322 453.

HISTORY & GOVERNMENT

HISTORY: Angola was made part of the Congo Kingdom in the 14th century by Wene and was flourishing a century later when the first Portuguese explorers reached the country. Relations between the Europeans and the Congo kings were good and missionaries were sent over. The kings' sons were sent to Lisbon for education until the 17th century, when the slave trade soured all trust between the two countries. An estimated one million slaves were shipped to Portuguese Brazil between the 16th and 17th century. The formal abolition of the slave trade in 1836 following the loss of Brazil resulted in the Portuguese intensifying colonisation of Angola. An unsuccessful rebellion in 1962 by supporters of the Popular Movement for the Liberation of Angola (MPLA) and a party later known as the National Front for the Liberation of Angola (FNLA) was followed by severe repression. In 1964 members of FNLA formed the National Union for the Total Independence of Angola (UNITA). Guerrilla warfare tactics threw the Government into confusion, and in 1975 South Africa aided troops fighting against the MPLA. A new radical military government in Lisbon opted for rapid decolonisation, effected in November 1975. The tenuous tripartite agreement collapsed and civil war followed, pitting MPLA (supported by the then USSR and Cuba), against FNLA and UNITA (backed by South Africa, USA and Britain). MPLA achieved formal victory in February 1976 but never fully defeated UNITA who, with South African support, sustained a continuous guerrilla war in the south and centre of the country. During 1988, a provisional agreement was reached on the mutual withdrawal of foreign troops by South Africa, Cuba and Angola with concerted behind-the-scenes pressure on the part of both superpowers. It took another three years before the Government and UNITA finally reached a political settlement at the end of May 1991. The main provision of the accord stipulated the holding of national legislative and presidential elections, scheduled for the autumn of 1992. These were held simultaneously at the end of September under the supervision of the United Nations and contested by 18 parties. The real competition, however, was between the MPLA and UNITA. The MPLA took a comfortable majority in the legislature, while the presidential election favoured – with most returns in – a victory for President Eduardo Dos Santos. Alleging widespread fraud and malpractice, UNITA's Savimbi declared that his troops would resume the war unless the full results were withheld and the election declared null and void. After frantic mediation by the United Nations, who had organised the election, and the South African foreign minister, Pik Botha, UNITA's closest foreign ally, full-scale war was averted, although there was an outbreak of heavy fighting in the capital a fortnight after the poll. The presidential result narrowly deprived Dos Santos of an outright majority, so that a run-off election between the President and Jonas Savimbi will have to be held within a few months. Whatever the final arithmetic, political realities will dictate that the MPLA and UNITA must collaborate in the process of national reconstruction. Angola needs a period of sustained peace in order to rebuild its shattered economy and organise the resettlement of the large numbers of people displaced by the 15-year-long civil war.
GOVERNMENT: Under the constitution of the 'Second Republic of Angola', a unicameral 223-seat legislature and executive president are elected by universal adult suffrage.

CLIMATE

The north of the country is hot and wet during the summer months (November to April); winters are slightly cooler and mainly dry. The south is hot throughout much of the year with a slight decrease in temperature in winter (May to October). **Required clothing:** Lightweight cottons and linens throughout the year in the south. Tropical clothing for summers in the north. Nights can be cold, so warm clothing should be taken. Waterproofing is advisable for the rainy season throughout the country.

LUANDA Angola (45m)

◁ TEMPERATURE, °C
MAX
MIN
30
20
10
0
SUNSHINE, hours
7 7 7 7 8 7 6 5 5 5 7 7
RAINFALL, mm ▷
100
0
J F M A M J J A S O N D
79 78 79 82 82 82 82 83 82 81 81 80
HUMIDITY, %
DAB-C6

ANGUILLA

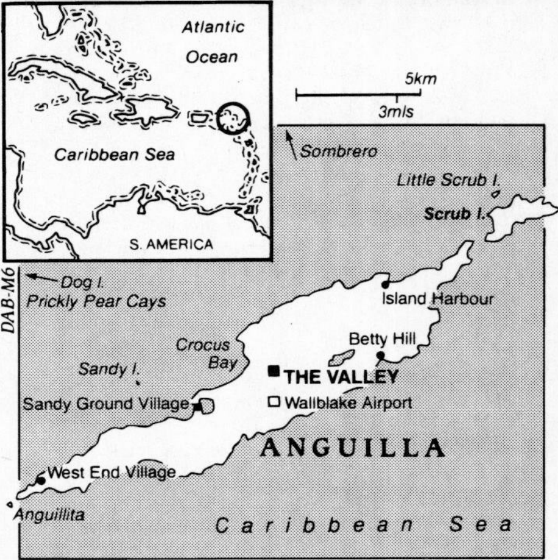

Location: Caribbean; Leeward Islands.

Department of Tourism
The Secretariat
The Valley, Anguilla
Tel: 2759/2451. Fax: 2751. Telex: 9313 ANG GOVT LA.
Anguilla Tourist Office
3 Epirus Road
London SW6 7UJ
Tel: (071) 937 7725. Fax: (071) 938 4793. Opening hours: 0930-1700 Monday to Friday.
Anguilla Tourist Information Office
c/o Medhurst & Associates
271 Main Street
Northport, NY
11768
Tel: (516) 261 1234. Fax: (516) 261 9606. Opening hours: 0930-1700 Monday to Friday.

AREA: Anguilla: 91 sq km (35 sq miles). **Sombrero:** 5 sq km (3 sq miles). **Total:** 96 sq km (38 sq miles).
POPULATION: 6800 (1986 estimate).
POPULATION DENSITY: 70.8 per sq km.
CAPITAL: The Valley. **Population:** 500.
GEOGRAPHY: Anguilla, the northernmost of the Leeward Islands, also comprises the island of Sombrero, lying 48km (30 miles) north of Anguilla, and several small islets or cays. The nearest islands are St Maarten, 8km (5 miles) south of Anguilla, and St Kitts and Nevis, 112km (70 miles) to the southeast. The islands are mainly flat – the highest point, Crocus Hill, is only 60m (214ft) above sea level – with arguably some of the best beaches in the world.
LANGUAGE: English is the official and commercial language.
RELIGION: Roman Catholic, Anglican, Baptist, Methodist and Moravian with Hindu, Jewish and Muslim minorities.
TIME: GMT - 4.
ELECTRICITY: 110/220 volts AC, 60Hz.
COMMUNICATIONS: Telephone: Full IDD is available. Country code: 1 809 497 (including area code). **Fax:** Cable and Wireless operate fax services. **Telex/telegram:** Cable and Wireless (West Indies) Ltd have telex facilities available to the public at their office. Cables may be sent from Cable and Wireless (West Indies) Ltd Public Booth, The Valley, which controls all British-owned cables in the area. **Post:** The General Post Office is in The Valley, open 0800-1530 Monday to Friday and 0800-1200 Saturday. There is a 'travelling service' to other districts on Anguilla. Airmail to Europe takes from four days to two weeks to arrive. **Press:** The government of Anguilla publishes two monthly papers: *The Government Information Service Bulletin* and *The Official Gazette*, both English-language. There is also one weekly – *The Vantage*.
BBC World Service and Voice of America frequencies: From time to time these change. See the section *How to Use this Book* for more information.

BBC:

MHz	17.84	15.22	9.915	6.195

Voice of America:

MHz	15.21	11.70	6.130	0.930

PASSPORT/VISA

Regulations and requirements may be subject to change at short notice, and you are advised to contact the appropriate diplomatic or consular authority before finalising travel arrangements. Details of these may be found at the head of this country's entry. Any numbers in the chart refer to the footnotes below.

	Passport Required?	Visa Required?	Return Ticket Required?
Full British	Yes	No	Yes
BVP	Not valid	-	-
Australian	Yes	No	Yes
Canadian	Yes	No	Yes
USA	Yes	No	Yes
Other EC	Yes	No	Yes
Japanese	Yes	No	Yes

PASSPORTS: Valid passport required by all.
British Visitors Passport: Not accepted.
VISAS: May be required by some nationals; check with the Passport Office, Clive House, Petty France, London SW7.

MONEY

Currency: Eastern Caribbean Dollar (EC$) = 100 cents. Notes are in denominations of EC$100, 20, 10, 5 and 1. Coins are in denominations of 50, 25, 10, 5, 2 and 1 cents.
Currency exchange: Currency may be exchanged in the capital.
Credit cards: American Express is most widely used, although Visa has limited acceptance. Check with your credit card company for details of merchant acceptability and other services which may be available.
Travellers cheques: US currency cheques are the most easily exchanged.
Exchange rate indicators: The following figures are included as a guide to the movements of the EC Dollar against Sterling and the US Dollar:

Date:	Oct '89	Sep '90	Oct '91	Oct '92
£1.00=	4.27	5.27	4.69	4.27
$1.00=	2.70	2.70	2.70	2.70

Note: The EC Dollar is tied to the US Dollar.
Currency restrictions: Free import and export of both local and foreign currency if declared.
Banking hours: 0800-1500 Monday to Thursday, 0800-1700 Friday.

DUTY FREE

The following goods can be taken into Anguilla without incurring customs duty:
200 cigarettes or 50 cigars or 250g of tobacco;
1 quart of wine or spirits.
Prohibited items: Weapons and non-prescribed drugs.

PUBLIC HOLIDAYS

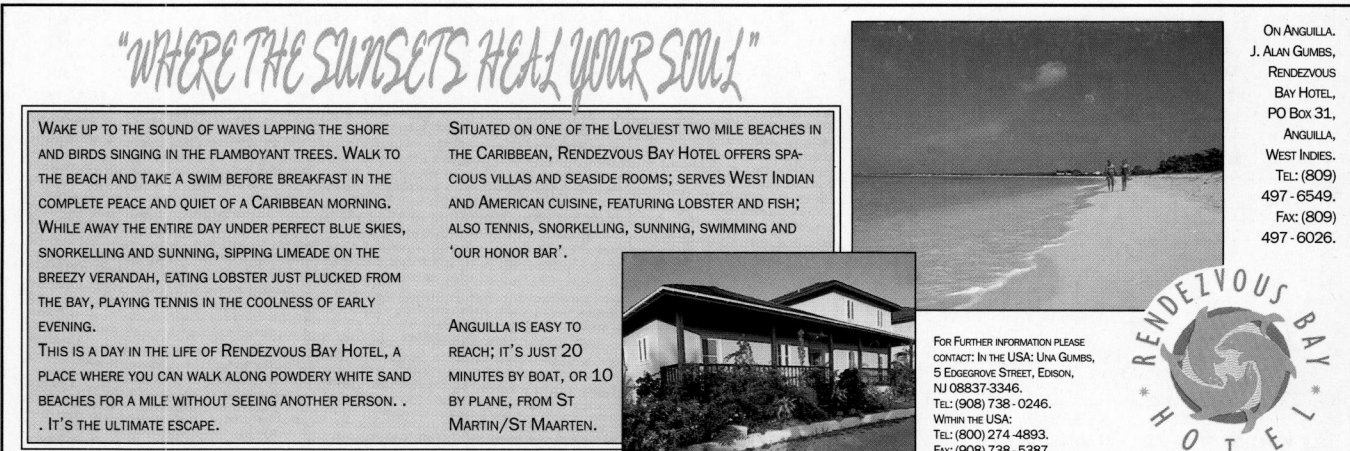

Public holidays observed in Anguilla are as follows:
Apr 9 '93 Good Friday. **Apr 12** Easter Monday. **May 3** Labour Day. **May 31** Whit Monday. **Jun 1** Anguilla Day. **Jun 11** Queen's Official Birthday. **Aug 2** August Monday. **Aug 5** August Thursday. **Aug 6** Constitution Day. **Dec 17** Separation Day. **Dec 25** Christmas. **Dec 27** Boxing Day. **Jan 1 '94** New Year's Day.

HEALTH

Regulations and requirements may be subject to change at short notice, and you are advised to contact your doctor well in advance of your intended date of departure. Any numbers in the chart refer to the footnotes below.

	Special Precautions?	Certificate Required?
Yellow Fever	No	No
Cholera	No	No
Typhoid & Polio	No	-
Malaria	No	-
Food & Drink	1	-

[1]: Water precautions recommended except in major hotels and restaurants.
Health care: There are three government-appointed medical practitioners on Anguilla, two private practitioners and a 24-bed hospital located in The Valley. There are also health centres at The Valley, East End, South Hill and West End. Minor emergency treatment is usually free for UK citizens with proof of UK residence. Health insurance is recommended as costs for other categories of treatment are high.

TRAVEL - International

AIR: Anguilla is served by *LIAT (LI)* (Leeward Islands Air Transport) based on Antigua. The airline's local office is at Gumb's Travel Agency.
Approximate flight times: From Anguilla to *London* is 12 hours (including a stopover time in Antigua of 2 hours 30 minutes), to *Los Angeles* is 10 hours and to *New York* 6 hours.
International airport: *Wallblake Airport (AXA)* is 3km (2 miles) from The Valley. *Air Anguilla, Carib Aviation* and *Tyden Air* offer air taxi services, with several daily flights to and from St Maarten, St Thomas, Tortola and St Kitts.
SEA: The main port is Road Bay where there is a jetty capable of handling ships of up to 1000 tons. Ferries operate between Blowing Point, Anguilla and Marigot on St Maarten at regular intervals between 0800-1700.

TRAVEL - Internal

ROAD: The road network is good but basic and the main road is of asphalt, stretching throughout the 25km (16-mile) length of Anguilla. Unpaved roads lead to beaches. **Taxis** are available at the airport and seaports with fixed prices to the various hotels. Island tours can be arranged on an individual basis. In addition, there are numerous **car rental** agencies available, including *Apex* and *Budget*. Bicycles and mopeds can also be hired.
Documentation: A temporary licence, valid for three months, can be issued at the police headquarters in The Valley on presentation of a national driving licence.

ACCOMMODATION

Accommodation on Anguilla ranges from luxury-class hotels to guest-houses, apartments, villas and cottages. Many establishments are situated right on the beach and offer boat services, snorkelling, fishing and scuba diving equipment. There are new resorts at Cap Juluca, Coccoloba and The Great House. For further details contact the Tourist Office. Twelve hotels are currently members of the Anguilla Hotel Association, PO Box 321, The Valley. Tel: 2944. Fax: 3091. Telex: 9327.
Grading: International standards apply. There are four hotels in the deluxe class, six first class and two second class.

RESORTS & EXCURSIONS

Anguilla is small and secluded; the main resorts are based around the hotels, many of which are situated off the islands' white coral beaches. Most excursions will be a leisurely exploration of other equally idyllic beaches. The visitor should see, however, *Wallblake House*, an impressively restored plantation house whose foundations date back to 1787. Other historical landmarks include *The Fountain*, a huge underground cave with a constant supply of fresh water at *Shoal Bay*. The ruins of the *Dutch Fort*, built in the 1700s, are located at **Sandy Hill,** famous as the scene of fierce fighting during the second French invasion of Anguilla in 1796. The *Tomb of Governor Richardson* (1679-1742) is well preserved, located at Sandy Hill. Also of interest are the *Salt Ponds* at **Sandy Ground** and **West End,** where salt is collected. There are over 30 beaches on Anguilla, some of which stretch for miles, dotted with hidden coves and grotto-like rock areas. Boats are available for charter. Some of the best beaches are *Rendezvous, Shoal Bay, Road Bay, Maundays Bay, Cove Bay, Meads Bay* and *Crocus Bay*. For the visitor who enjoys solitude and privacy, charter a boat to **Sandy Island,** fringed with coconut palms, 15 minutes from Sandy Ground Harbour; or **Sombrero Island,** 48km (30 miles) northwest of Anguilla, which has a picturesque lighthouse. The even smaller sandy cays of **Scub, Dog** and **Prickly Pear Islands** are within reach of Anguilla by power boat.

SOCIAL PROFILE

FOOD & DRINK: Restaurants offer a mixture of Continental, American and Anguillan dishes. Seafoods include lobster, whelk and a variety of fish.
NIGHTLIFE: Anguilla's nightlife is centred on the hotels.
SHOPPING: The Department of Tourism sponsors handicrafts and the island-built racing boats are world-famous. Souvenirs will also include shells and small models of island sloops. There are a few small boutiques with limited stocks of swimwear, and a gift shop offering international name brands in bone china, crystals, and jewellery. **Shopping hours:** 0800-1200 and 1300-1700 Monday to Friday, 0800-1600 Saturday.
SPORT: Boat racing is the national sport, and dominates all holidays and festivals. For the visitor, all watersports, including **snorkelling, scuba diving** and **fishing,** are widely available.
SPECIAL EVENTS: May 1 '93 *Fun Day*. **May 30** *AXA Athletics Day*. **May-Jun** *Shell Cup*. **Jun** *Leeward Islands Cricket Tournament*. **Jul** *Leeward Islands Basketball Tournament*. **Aug** *Carnival* (beginning with Friday preceding August Monday and lasting a week; Calypso competitions, street dancing, house parties and pageants). **Dec** *Barclays Cup*. **Jan '94** *Heineken Cup*.
Boat races are held on almost every holiday; the most impressive are held on Anguilla Day, August Monday,

August Thursday and New Year's Day. Athletics competitions are held on Anguilla Day.
SOCIAL CONVENTIONS: The Government is anxious to set limits to the commercialisation of the island and visitors will find that social life is centred on the tourist areas. The atmosphere is relaxed and English customs prevail. Beachwear should be confined to resorts. **Tipping:** 10% should be left in restaurants.

BUSINESS PROFILE

ECONOMY: Anguilla's economy is based on agriculture and fisheries. Lobster fishing is the most productive activity; livestock and crop growing (solely for internal consumption) are also important. Anguilla produces salt, the bulk of which is sold to Trinidad for use in its petroleum industry. Boat-building is the island's other major employer. The expanding tourist industry has ensured steady economic growth since the 1980s, although the pace has been restrained by the Govern-ment's concern to avoid the excesses of development experienced in resorts elsewhere. Nonetheless, un-employment is high; estimated at 40% of the population. The residents pay no income tax and the Anguillan government receives development aid from Britain.
BUSINESS: Anguilla is a small island with few business opportunities as such; however, lightweight suits or shirt and tie should be adequate for meetings. **Office hours:** 0800-1200 and 1300-1600 Monday to Friday.
COMMERCIAL INFORMATION: The following organisation can offer advice: Anguilla Chamber of Commerce, PO Box 321, The Valley. Tel: 2701. Telex: 9327.

HISTORY & GOVERNMENT

HISTORY: The name 'Anguilla', meaning 'eel', was given to the island by the Spanish because of the island's eel-like shape. It was the British, however, who first settled on Anguilla in the 17th century and the island was administered in conjunction with the Leeward Islands. During the early part of the 19th century Anguilla became incorporated into St Kitts and Nevis, despite opposition from the islanders. By 1967 the islands became a State in association with the UK. Anguilla seceded unilaterally from the government of St Kitts and was formally granted the status of British Dependent Territory in 1980.
GOVERNMENT: Anguilla is a separate dependency under the British Government, and the 1982 constitution provided that executive power should be in the hands of the Governor, who administers external affairs. The Executive Council advises the Governor. The legislature is the House of Assembly, seven members of which are elected by universal adult suffrage. The Governor is appointed by the British Monarch.

CLIMATE

Hot throughout the year tempered by trade winds in local areas. Although rain showers can occur at all times, the main rainy season is between October and December. The hurricane season is July to October.
Required clothing: Lightweight cottons and linens throughout the year. Waterproofing is advisable during the rainy season.

PLYMOUTH Montserrat (40m)

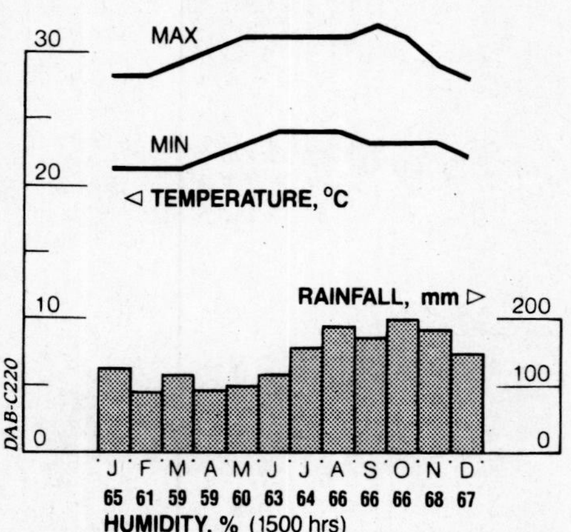

ANTARCTICA

Location: South Pole.

British Antarctic Survey
High Cross
Madingley Road
Cambridge CB3 0ET
Tel: (0223) 61188. Fax: (0223) 62616. Telex: 817725.

Antarctica covers an area of 36 million square kilometres (14 million square miles) around the South Pole and is covered with an ice sheet on average of two kilometres deep. It has no permanent human population other than personnel at a number of research stations run by different nations.
The constitutional position of Antarctica is governed by the terms of the Antarctic Treaty of 1959 (which came into effect in 1961) and signed initially by Argentina, Australia, Chile, France, New Zealand, Norway, the United Kingdom, Belgium, Japan, South Africa, the USSR and the USA. The first seven of these have historic claims to the ice-bound continent (none of which were or are generally recognised) and the Treaty preserves the *status quo*, neither recognising nor repudiating the old claims, but forbidding their expansion in any way. The terms of the Treaty also forbid absolutely the assertion of new claims.
Since 1961, a further 28 states have acceded to the Treaty, (making a total of 40 states). Twenty-six states have full consultative status and seventeen maintain research stations throughout the year
The discovery in 1987 by the British Antarctic Survey of a 'hole' in the ozone layer of the Earth's atmosphere – conclusively proved to have been caused by terrestrial use of the CFC group of gases (chlorofluorocarbons) – did more than perhaps any other single event, bar nuclear accidents, to bring ecology to prominence in the international political agenda.
The Antarctic Treaty made no provision for mineral exploitation and in November 1988, after six years of negotiations, an Antarctic Minerals Convention was finally opened for signing. This was intended to regulate but not prevent the extraction of minerals and caused much protest from environmental lobbyists.
The preservation of Antartica as perhaps the last great wilderness on earth seemed to get a step nearer at the 15th Consultative Conference of parties to the Treaty in October 1989. Some areas of the continent were designated worthy of special protection, with strict regulations covering sea pollution.
At the Antarctic Treaty Consultative Meetings in 1991, provisional agreement was reached on a new Environmental Protocol to the Antarctic Treaty, which guarantees a further ban on mining for 50 years and provides for a fully comprehensive regime of environmental protection.

SOUTH POLE (2800m)

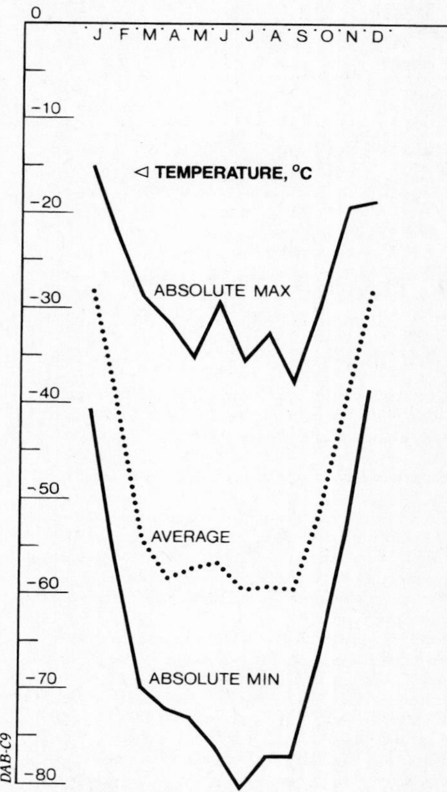

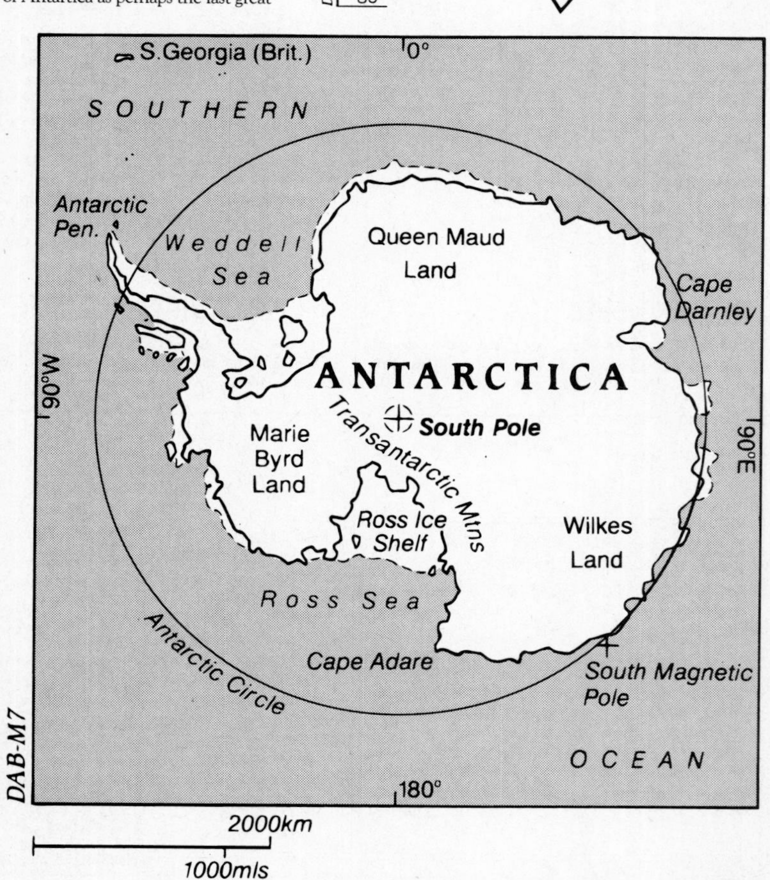

ANTIGUA & BARBUDA

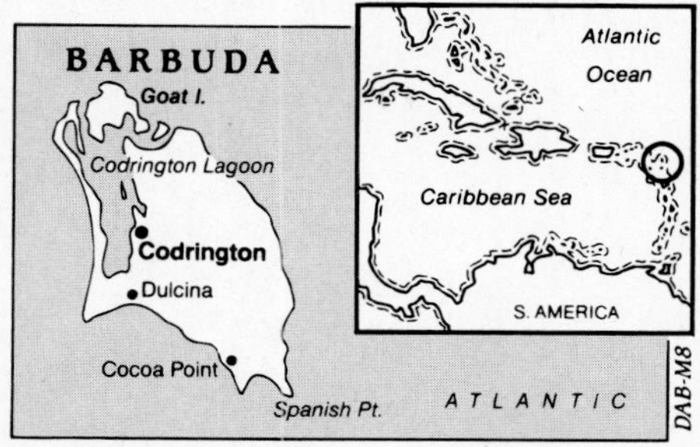

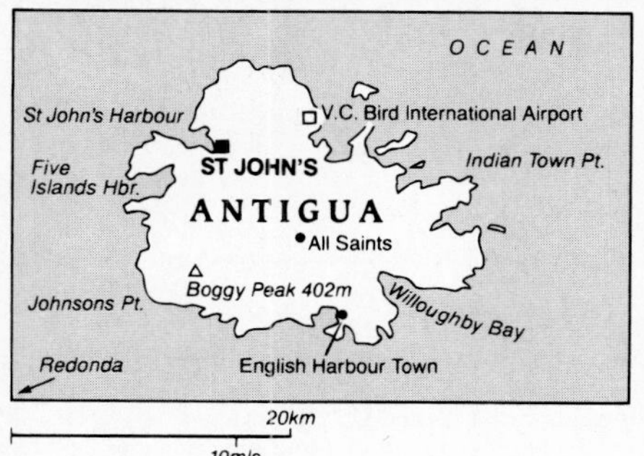

Location: Caribbean, Leeward Islands.

Antigua Department of Tourism
PO Box 363
Long and Thames Streets
St John's, Antigua
Tel: 20029 *or* 20480. Fax: 22483. Telex: 2122.

Antigua & Barbuda High Commission
15 Thayer Street
London W1M 5LD
Tel: (071) 486 7073/4/5. Fax: (071) 486 9970.
Opening hours: 0900-1730 Monday to Friday.

Antigua & Barbuda Tourist Office
Address as above.
Tel: (071) 486 7073/4/5. Fax: (071) 486 9970.
Opening hours: 0900-1730 Monday to Friday.

British High Commission Office
PO Box 483
11 Old Parham Road
St John's, Antigua
Tel: 462 0008. Fax: 462 2806. Telex: 2113 UKREP ANT AK.

Embassy of Antigua & Barbuda
Suite 4M, 3400 International Drive, NW
Washington, DC
20008
Tel: (202) 362 5122. Fax: (202) 362 5225. Telex: 8221130.

Antigua Department of Tourism
Suite 311, 610 Fifth Avenue, New York, NY 10020
Tel: (212) 541 4117. Fax: (212) 757 1607.

United States Embassy
Queen Elizabeth Highway
St John's, Antigua
Tel: 23505/6. Fax: 23516. Telex: 2140 USEMB.

Embassy of Antigua & Barbuda
Suite 205, Place de Ville, Tower B
112 Kent Street
Ottawa, Ontario K1P 5P2
Tel: (613) 234 9143. Fax: (613) 232 0539.

Antigua Department of Tourism & Trade
Suite 304
60 St Clair Avenue East
Toronto, Ontario M4T 1N5
Tel: (416) 961 3085. Fax: (416) 961 7218.

AREA: Antigua: 280 sq km (110 sq miles); Barbuda: 160 sq km (60 sq miles); Redonda: 1.6 sq km (0.6 sq miles). Total: 441.6 sq km (170.5 sq miles).
POPULATION: 78,400 (1989 estimate).
POPULATION DENSITY: 177.5 per sq km (1989).
CAPITAL: St John's. **Population:** 36,000 (1986 estimate).
GEOGRAPHY: Antigua & Barbuda comprise three islands, Antigua, Barbuda and Redonda. Low-lying and volcanic in origin, they are part of the Leeward Islands group in the northeast Caribbean. **Antigua's** coastline curves into a multitude of coves and harbours (they were once volcanic craters) and there are more than 365 beaches of fine white sand, fringed with palms. The island's highest point is Boggy Peak (402m, 1319ft); its capital is St John's. **Barbuda** lies 40km (25 miles) north of Antigua and is an unspoiled natural haven for wild deer and exotic birds. Its 8km (5-mile) long beach is reputed to be amongst the most beautiful in the world. The island's village capital, Codrington, was named after the Gloucestershire family that once leased Barbuda from the British Crown for the price of 'one fat pig per year if asked for'. There are excellent beaches and the ruins of some of the earliest slave plantations in the West Indies. The coastal waters are rich with all types of crustaceans and tropical fish. **Redonda,** smallest in the group, is little more than an uninhabited rocky islet. It lies 40km (25 miles) southwest of Antigua.
LANGUAGE: English is the official language. English *patois* is widely spoken.
RELIGION: Anglican, Methodist, Moravian, Roman Catholic, Pentecostal, Baptist and Seventh Day Adventists.
TIME: GMT - 4.
ELECTRICITY: 220/110 volts AC, 60Hz. European 3-pin plugs.
COMMUNICATIONS: Telephone: IDD is available

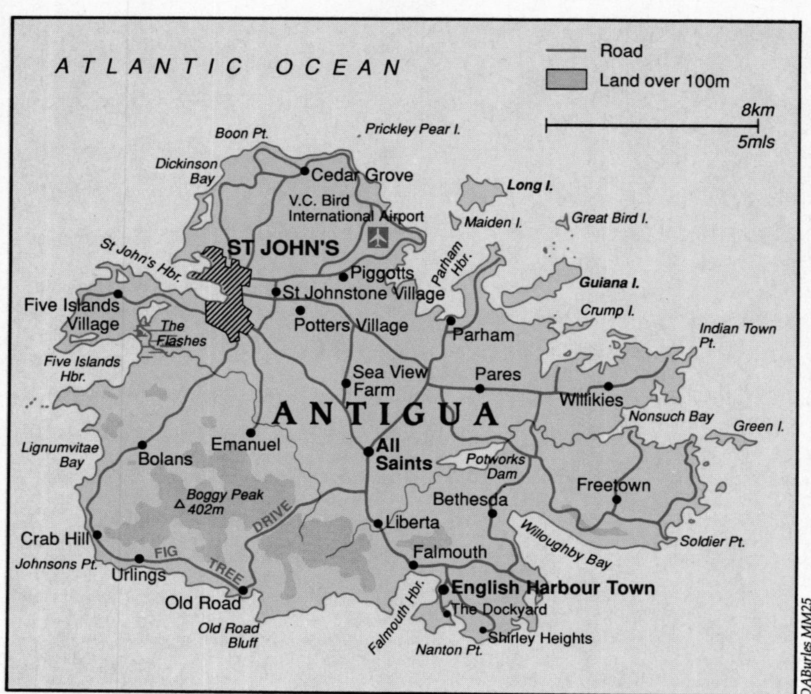

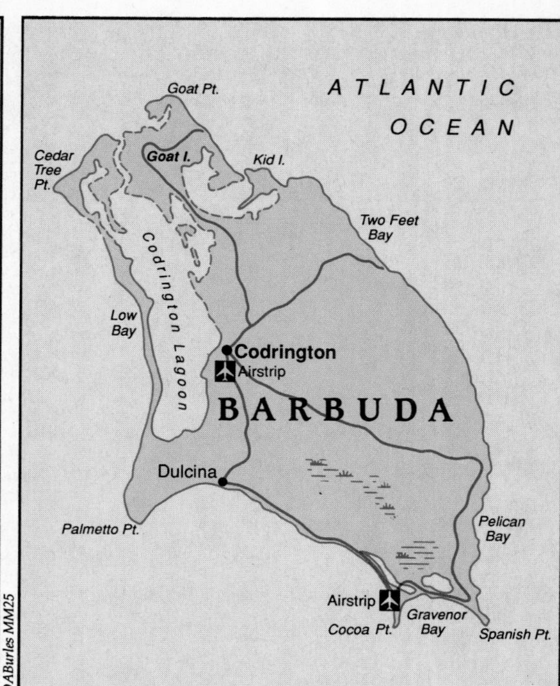

to all numbers. Country code: 1 809 46. No area codes. **Fax:** Services are available from Cable and Wireless. Many hotels have fax facilities. **Telex/telegram:** These facilities are offered by Cable & Wireless (West Indies). **Post:** A *Poste Restante* service is available at the post office in St John's. Post office hours: 0800-1200 and 1300-1600 Mondays to Fridays. **Press:** All newspapers printed on the islands are weekly, many with political or governmental associations. All are in English. The main newspapers are *The Nation*, *The Worker's Voice*, *Rappore* and *The Sentinel*.

BBC World Service frequencies: From time to time these change. See the section *How to Use this Book* for more information.

BBC:				
MHz	17.72	11.78	9.915	5.965

PASSPORT/VISA

Regulations and requirements may be subject to change at short notice, and you are advised to contact the appropriate diplomatic or consular authority before finalising travel arrangements. Details of these may be found at the head of this country's entry. Any numbers in the chart refer to the footnotes below.

	Passport Required?	Visa Required?	Return Ticket Required?
Full British	1/2	No	Yes
BVP	2	–	–
Australian	Yes	No	Yes
Canadian	1	No	Yes
USA	1	No	Yes
Other EC	Yes	No	Yes
Japanese	Yes	No	Yes

PASSPORTS: [1] Nationals of Canada, the USA and the UK (but see note 2 below) do not require a passport, providing that they have other documents with proof of identity, such as a birth certificate, a citizenship card/naturalization certificate, or a voters' registration card. A valid passport is required by all other nationals.

British Visitors Passport: [2] Although the immigration authorities of this country may in certain circumstances accept British Visitors Passports for persons arriving for holidays or unpaid business trips of up to 3 months, travellers are reminded that no formal agreement exists to this effect and the situation may, therefore, change at short notice. In addition, UK nationals using a BVP and returning to the UK from a country with which no such formal agreement exists may be subject to delays and interrogation by UK immigration officials.

VISAS: Required by all except:

(a) nationals of countries referred to on the chart above (but note that nationals of Germany require visas for visits exceeding 30 days);

(b) citizens of Commonwealth countries;

(c) UK nationals;

(d) nationals of Argentina, Austria, Brazil, Finland, Liechtenstein, Malta, Mexico, Monaco, Norway, Peru, San Marino, Suriname, Sweden, Switzerland, Turkey and Venezuela.

These exemptions are valid for up to 6 months. Nationals of all other countries require a visa.

Types of visa: *Single visa*, cost £24. *Multiple visa*, cost £28.

Validity: The single visa is valid for 3 months, the multiple visa for 6 months.

Application to: Consulate (or Consular Section at Embassy or High Commission). For address, see top of entry.

Application requirements: (a) Completed form. (b) 2 identical passport photos. (c) Valid passport. (d) Payment (by postal order or cash only). (e) Onward or return ticket. (f) Evidence of sufficient funds to cover duration of stay.

Working days required: 2-4.

Temporary residence: Applications should be sent to the Prime Minister's Office, Factory Road, St John's Road, Antigua, (tel: 20773), but it is advisable to enquire first at the Embassy or High Commission.

MONEY

Currency: Eastern Caribbean Dollar (EC$) = 100 cents. Notes are in denominations of EC$100, 20, 10, 5 and 1. Coins are in denominations of EC$1 and 50, 25, 10, 5, 2 and 1 cents. US currency is accepted almost everywhere.

Currency exchange: Although the EC Dollar is tied to the US Dollar, exchange rates will vary at different exchange establishments. There are international banks in St John's and US Dollars and Sterling can be exchanged at hotels and in the larger shops.

Credit cards: Diners Club, Visa, and American Express are accepted. Check with your credit card company for details of merchant acceptability and other services which may be available.

Travellers cheques: Can be exchanged at international banks, hotels and the larger stores.

Exchange rate indicators: The following figures are included as a guide to the movements of the EC Dollar against Sterling and the US Dollar:

Date:	**Oct '89**	**Oct '90**	**Oct '91**	**Oct '92**
£1.00=	4.27	5.23	4.69	4.27
$1.00=	2.70	2.70	2.70	2.69

Note: The EC Dollar is tied to the US Dollar.

Currency restrictions: Free import and export of both local and foreign currency if declared.

Banking hours: 0800-1400 Monday to Thursday (*Barclays* 0800-1400 Monday, Tuesday and Wednesday); 0800-1400 and 1500-1700 Friday.

DUTY FREE

The following items may be taken into Antigua & Barbuda without payment of customs duty:

200 cigarettes or 50 cigars or 250g (8oz) of tobacco;
1 litre (1qt) of wine or spirits;
6oz of perfume.

Prohibited items: Weapons and non-prescribed drugs (list available from Tourist Office).

PUBLIC HOLIDAYS

Public holidays observed in Antigua & Barbuda are as follows:

Apr 9 '93 Good Friday. **Apr 12** Easter Monday. **May 3** Labour Day. **May 31** Whit Monday. **Jul 5** Caricom Day. **Aug 2-3** Carnival. **Nov 1** Independence Day. **Dec 25** Christmas Day. **Dec 26** Boxing Day. **Jan 1 '94** New Year's Day.

ANTIGUA & BARBUDA	**HEALTH REGULATIONS**	**VISA REGULATIONS** Code-Link
GALILEO/WORLDSPAN	 TI-DFT/ANU/HE	 TI-DFT/ANU/VI
SABRE	 TIDFT/ANU/HE	TIDFT/ANU/VI

To access this information on your CRS, swipe the barcode with a light pen or type in the text under the barcode. For more information, see the introduction *How to Use This Book*.

Main picture: English Harbour, Antigua Sailing Week. Inset: Bird sanctuary, Barbuda

HEALTH

Regulations and requirements may be subject to change at short notice, and you are advised to contact your doctor well in advance of your intended date of departure. Any numbers in the chart refer to the footnotes below.

	Special Precautions?	Certificate Required?
Yellow Fever	No	1
Cholera	No	No
Typhoid & Polio	No	-
Malaria	No	-
Food & Drink	2	-

[1]: A yellow fever certificate is required of travellers aged one year or over arriving from infected areas.
[2]: Mains water is normally chlorinated, and whilst relatively safe may cause mild abdominal upsets. Bottled water is available and is advised for the first few weeks of the stay. Milk is pasteurised and dairy products are safe for consumption. Local meat, poultry, seafood, fruit and vegetables are generally considered safe to eat.
Health care: Health insurance is recommended as medical treatment is expensive.

TRAVEL - International

AIR: Antigua & Barbuda is served by several international airlines, including *British Airways*. *LIAT (Leeward Islands Air Transport)* provides scheduled passenger flights from Antigua to over 20 islands in the West Indies. Subsidiary companies *(Four Island Air Services Ltd* and *Inter Island Air Services Ltd)* of *LIAT* run flights within the Leeward Islands.
Approximate flight times: From St John's to *London* is 8 hours, to *Los Angeles* is 9 hours and to *New York* is 3.5 hours.
International airport: *VC Bird International (ANU)*, formerly Coolidge International, is 10km (6 miles) northeast of St John's. The airport provides access to major international centres, such as London, New York, Miami, Frankfurt, Toronto and Montreal, with feeder services to all the Eastern Caribbean islands, the US Virgin Islands and Puerto Rico. Taxi service to city and hotels. Facilities include full outgoing duty-free shopping (liquor, perfume, straw items, T-shirts, souvenirs and handicrafts), restaurant (0730-2000), bar (0730-2400), and currency exchange (0900-1500).
Departure tax: US$8.
SEA: St John's has a deep-sea harbour served by cruise liners from the USA, Puerto Rico, the UK, Europe and South America. Fly-cruises from London are available with *Holland America*, *Royal Caribbean*, *Cunard*, *Costa*, *Sunline*, *Sitmar* and *Princess* Cruises. Many smaller ships sail to other Caribbean islands.

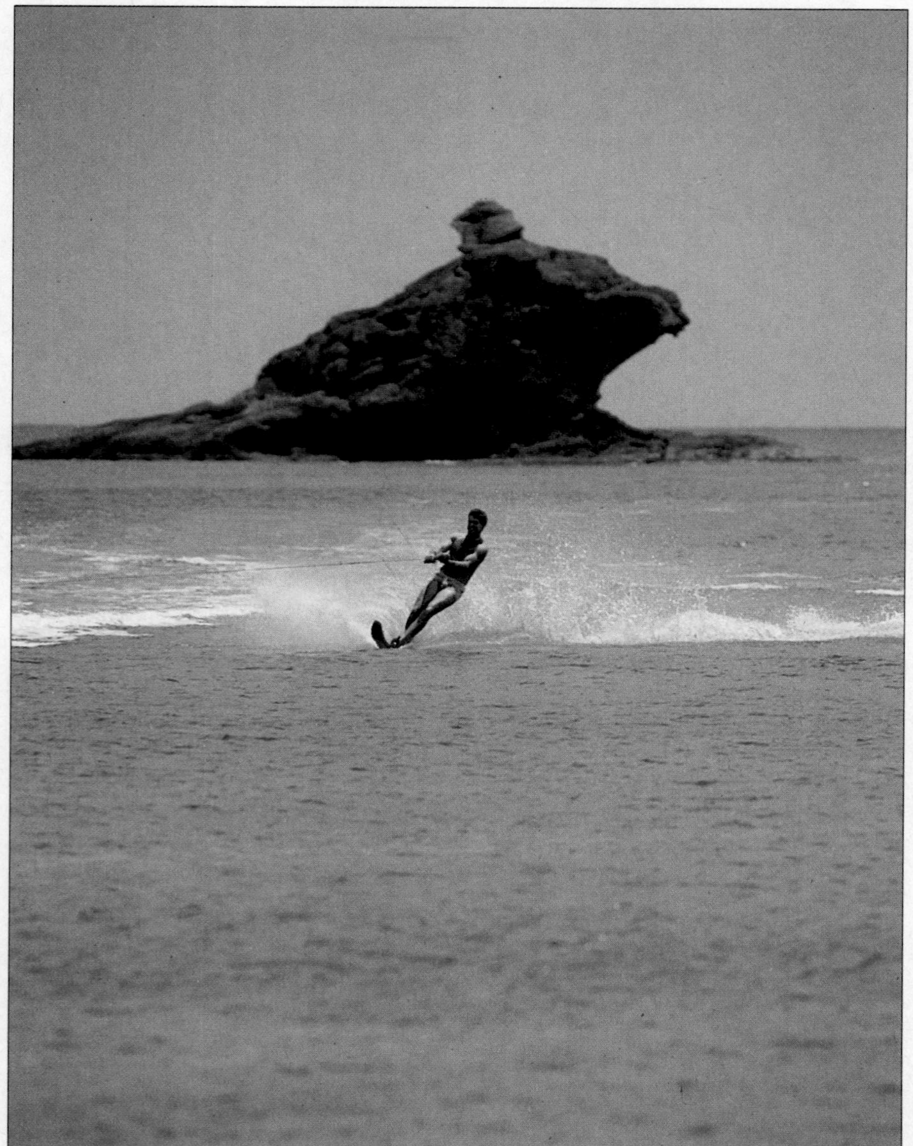

TRAVEL - Internal

AIR: A small airstrip at Codrington on Barbuda is equipped to handle light aircraft.
SEA: Local boats are available for excursions.
ROAD: There are nearly 1000km (600 miles) of roads in the country, about 140km (90 miles) of which are all-weather. Driving is on the left. The speed limit outside towns is 88kmph (55mph). **Buses:** The bus network is small, the buses infrequent. **Taxis:** Available everywhere with standardised rates. US Dollars are more readily accepted by taxi drivers. **Car hire:** This can be organised from your home country but is almost as easy to do on arrival. There are several reputable car hire companies on Antigua (some of which also hire out mopeds and bicycles). Rental rates are for the day and there is no mileage charge. **Documentation:** A national licence is accepted but a local driver's permit must be obtained. This is a simple formality and does not require a test. The permit is issued from a police station on presentation of a valid driver's licence plus a small fee.
JOURNEY TIMES: The following chart gives approximate journey times (in hours and minutes) from St John's to other major towns/resorts/centres in Antigua.

	Road
VC Bird (airport)	0.10
Dickenson Bay	0.10
English Harbour	0.35
St James's	0.35
Royal Antiguan	0.15
Half Moon Bay	0.30
Long Bay	0.35
Jolly Beach	0.20
Shirley Heights	0.35

ACCOMMODATION

Accommodation must be booked well in advance during Tennis Weeks, International Sailing Week and Carnival Week (see *Special Events* in the *Social Profile* section). No special accommodation facilities exist for students and young travellers and there are no official camping sites in Antigua or Barbuda. Sleeping and living on the beaches is not permitted.
HOTELS: Hotel rates are considerably cheaper in the summer months (May to November). A government tax of 7% is added to hotel bills. 90% of hotels belong

to the Antigua Hotels & Tourist Association, PO Box 374, Redcliffe Street, St John's, Antigua. Tel: 20374 *or* 23702. Fax: 23702. Telex: AK 2172. **Grading:** There are three grades of hotel: *Deluxe* (20% of all graded hotels), *Superior* (60% of all graded hotels) and *Standard* (20% of all graded hotels). A full list of hotels and guest-houses, with rates, is available from the tourist office, and at *VC Bird International Airport* in Antigua.
ANTIGUA: Most of the larger hotels have rooms with either full air-conditioning or with fans and provide a choice of meal plans. The more luxurious establishments offer a large variety of watersports, tennis and evening entertainments. Guest-houses, much cheaper than the hotels, provide basic but clean accommodation, sometimes with meals. Self-catering accommodation is available for the budget vacationer.
BARBUDA: Currently there are three hotels, two villas and a couple of guest-houses. The newest resort is the Palmétto Point Beach Resort.

RESORTS & EXCURSIONS

ANTIGUA: Antiguans claim to have a different beach for every day of the year and their island's many beautiful soft, sandy beaches and coves certainly constitute its main attraction. The most popular resorts have hotels located either on beaches or close by, many of them taking their names from the beaches. But for the energetic, there's plenty to see and do away from the beaches. The island is rich in colourful bird and insect life; off-shore, beneath the waters of the Caribbean, are splendid tropical fish and coral; and there are several sites of historic interest.
An excursion to **Bird Island** can be made from Dickenson Bay. Many hotels offer excursions in glass-bottomed boats for a leisurely view of the reef. A restored pirate ship sails around the island and take passengers for day or evening trips; food, unlimited drink and entertainment are included.
Nelson's Dockyard in English Harbour is one of the safest landlocked harbours in the world. It was used by Admirals Nelson, Rodney and Hood as a safe base for the British navy during the Napoleonic wars. *Clarence House*, overlooking Nelson's dockyard, was once the home of the Duke of Clarence, later King William IV. It is now the Governor General's summer residence, and is periodically open to visitors.
Shirley Heights and **Fort James** are two examples of the efforts made by the British to fortify the colony during the 18th century. Shirley Heights was named after General Shirley, later Governor of the Leeward Islands in 1781. One of the main buildings, known as the *Block House*, was erected as a stronghold in the event of a siege by General Mathew in 1787. Close by is the cemetery, containing an obelisk commemorating the soldiers of the 54th Regiment.
St John's Cathedral appears on postcards and in almost all visitors' photographs. The church was originally built in 1683, but was replaced by a stone building in 1745. An earthquake destroyed it almost a century later, and in 1845 the cornerstone of the present Anglican cathedral was laid. The figures of St John the Baptist and St John the Divine erected at the south gate were supposedly taken from one of Napoleon's ships and brought to the island by a British man-of-war.
The Market is situated in the east of St John's, and makes a lively and colourful excursion, especially on the busy Saturday mornings.
Indian Town, one of Antigua's national parks, is at the northeastern point of the island. Breakers roaring in with the full force of the Atlantic behind them have carved *Devil's Bridge* and have created blow-holes with fuming surf.
A newer sight is the lake that now monopolises the countryside in the centre of Antigua. The result of the **Potworks Dam**, it is Antigua's largest man-made lake, with a capacity of one thousand million gallons.
Fig Tree Drive is a scenic route through the lush tropical hills and picturesque fishing villages along the southwest coast. Taxis will take visitors on a round-trip. At **Greencastle Hill** there are megaliths said to have been erected for the worship of the Sun God and Moon Goddess.
Parham, in the east of the island, is notable for its octagonal church, built in the mid-18th century, which still retains some Stucco work.
BARBUDA: Less developed than Antigua, Barbuda has a wilder, more spontaneous beauty. Deserted beaches and a heavily wooded interior abounding in birdlife, wild pigs and fallow deer are the main attractions of this unspoilt island. A visit to **Codrington**, the main village, makes an interesting excursion: the settlement is on the edge of a lagoon and the inhabitants rely largely on the sea for their existence.
REDONDA: This uninhabited rocky islet, lying about 56km (35 miles) northeast of Antigua, was once an important source of phosphates and guano (the remains of some of the mining buildings can still be seen) but for more than a century its chief claim to fame has been its association with a fairly harmless brand of English eccentricity. In 1865, Redonda was 'claimed' by Matthew Shiell as a kingdom for his son, Philippe. King Philippe I's 'successor', the poet John Gawsworth, appointed many leading literary figures of his day as dukes and duchesses of his kingdom; the lucky peers included JB Priestley, Dylan Thomas and Rebecca West. The current king lives in Sussex, but his subjects are not likely to produce any great works of fiction as they are all either goats, lizards or seabirds. The island is also well known amongst birdwatchers for its small population of burrowing owls, a bird now extinct on Antigua.

Blue Waters, Antigua

SOCIAL PROFILE

FOOD & DRINK: Casual wear is accepted in all bars and restaurants. There are no licensing restrictions, but excessive consumption of alcohol is frowned upon and further service will be refused. Antigua's gastronomic speciality is lobster, with red snapper and occasionally other fish running a close second when available. Larger hotels offer a wide selection of imported meats, vegetables, fruits and cheeses. Local specialities include barbecued free-range chicken, roast suckling pig, pilaffs, curries, goat water, fungi and saltfish. **Drink:** Imported wines and spirits are available as well as imported sodas and local fruit drinks. Local drinks include ice-cold fruit juice, coconut milk, Antiguan-produced red and white rums (*Cavalier*), rum punches, and beer from Barbados (*Banks*) and Jamaica (*Red Stripe*). There is a 7% government tax on most restaurant bills.
NIGHTLIFE: There is a wide choice of restaurants and bars around main tourist areas. Steel bands, com-

bos and limbo dancers travel round hotels, performing nightly during the winter season (November to April). There are three casinos on the island and two nightclubs/discotheques. Some hotels have their own discotheques. Two theatre groups perform at the University.

SHOPPING: Uniquely Antiguan purchases include straw goods, pottery, *batik* and silk-screen printed fabrics, and jewellery incorporating semi-precious Antiguan stones. English bone china and crystal, and French perfumes, watches and table linens are all available at very attractive prices. The *Heritage Quay Tourist Complex* is a shopping and entertainment complex with 40 duty-free shops, a theatre, restaurants and a casino and supper club. It forms part of the newest development in downtown St John's. **Shopping hours:** 0800-1200 and 1300-1630 Monday to Saturday, although some shops and chemists do not close for lunch. Early closing on Thursday.

SPORT: Cricket: This, the national game, is played to the highest international standard. In Viv Richards, Antigua has produced one of the finest cricketers the game has ever seen. **Tennis:** Antigua has many lawn tennis courts. Professionals descend for the International Tennis Weeks in January (Men) and April (Women), both for competition and to train for the international tennis circuit. **Horseriding:** This can be organised through hotels. On public holidays, there is horseracing at Cassada Gardens. **Squash:** The Bucket Club allows temporary membership for visitors. **Golf:** There are two first-class golf courses: the spectacular 18-hole golf course at Cedar Valley; and the 9-hole course at Half Moon Bay. Daily, weekly and monthly memberships at Cedar Valley include tennis privileges as well as golf. **Watersports:** Most resort hotels offer some facilities for most watersports. **Windsurfing** is popular and boards are easy to find. **Water-skiing** and sunfish **sailboating** are also available from most of the larger resorts' hotels. Deep-sea fishing (see below) and **scuba diving** are easily arranged and **snorkelling** equipment is cheap and easy to hire from hotels. There are very fine coral reefs in Antiguan and Barbudan coastal waters. **Swimming:** There are more than 365 beaches, all of them open to the public. **Sailing:** Antigua offers spectacular sailing and is famous for its international sailing regatta held once a year during April or May. The less adventurous may wish to hire a dinghy and find their own secluded cove or sheltered beach and anchor for a day of peace and quiet. **Deep-sea fishing:** There is excellent year-round fishing for wahoo, kingfish, mackerel, dorado, tuna and barracuda. Small to very large yachts can be chartered. There is an annual Sportfishing Tournament at the end of April to early May. The tournament record is a 56lb kingfish. **Crab-racing:** A sport for the very, very lazy, crab-racing is staged in certain bars once or twice a week. A punter may win enough to pay for his next round of drinks, but stakes are moderate and the crabs are unlikely to make anyone a millionaire.

SPECIAL EVENTS: The following is a selection of events in Antigua from March 1993 to March 1994: **Apr 25-May 1 '93** *Antigua Sailing Week*. **Jul 26-Aug 3** *Carnival*.

SOCIAL CONVENTIONS: Dress is informal unless formal dress is specifically requested. As a gesture towards the islanders themselves, it is preferable not to wear scanty clothing or beachwear in towns or villages. Relatives and good friends generally embrace. Friends tend to drop by unannounced but an invitation is necessary for acquaintances or business associates. Although gifts will generally be well received, they are normally only given on celebratory occasions. Flowers are appropriate for dinner parties; bring a bottle only when specifically requested. Smoking is accepted in most public places. **Tipping:** 10% is included on hotel bills for staff gratuities, plus a 7% government tax. Taxi drivers expect 10% of the fare and dockside and airport porters expect EC$1 per bag.

BUSINESS PROFILE

ECONOMY: Antigua was one of the first Caribbean islands to actively encourage tourism, beginning in the late 1960s. The late 1980s have seen another phase of major development and tourism is today the main source of revenue. There are more than 30 luxury hotels and over 50 guest-houses and apartments, and further expansions of the facilities are planned. Fears of over-reliance on tourism have, however, led the Government into attempts to diversify the economy towards manufacturing, agriculture and fisheries. Local agriculture has been promoted to reduce dependency on imported food, although the lack of water resources is

proving to be a major handicap. There are a number of light industries producing rum, clothing and household appliances; there is also an electronic assembly plant producing goods for export. Offshore banking and other financial services are the newest addition to the economy. On top of these, Antigua receives rent for two American military bases and significant overseas aid. Even so, the island has a large trade and balance-of-payments deficit. Antigua and Barbuda's main trading partners are the United States, the UK and Canada, and countries within the CARICOM Caribbean trading bloc, of which Antigua/Barbuda is a member. Puerto Rico is an important export market.

BUSINESS: A lightweight or safari suit, a long- or short-sleeved shirt and a tie are suitable for most business visits. Handshaking is the normal greeting for acquaintances and for formal introductions. Calling cards are expected from people who do not live on the islands. **Office hours:** 0800-1200 and 1300-1600 Monday to Friday. **Government office hours:** 0800-1630 Monday to Thursday, 0800-1500 Friday.

COMMERCIAL INFORMATION: The following organisation can offer advice: Antigua and Barbuda Chamber of Commerce, PO Box 774, Cross and Redcliffe Streets, St John's, Antigua. Tel: 462 0743. Telex: 2105.

CONFERENCES/CONVENTIONS: 10% of the membership of the Antigua Hotels & Tourist Association (see *Accommodation* for details) offer meeting facilities. Information is available direct from the Tourist Office or the AHTA.

HISTORY & GOVERNMENT

HISTORY: The most important settlers were the Arawak Indians, who arrived in the 1st century AD. Many prehistoric sites have been identified and excavated. Europeans had no knowledge of the island's existence until the second voyage of Christopher Columbus to the West Indies in 1493. Without landing, Columbus named the island Santa Maria de la Antigua. Barbuda, whose association with Antigua dates back to the time of Codrington, was annexed to the territory in 1860. The small island of Redonda became part of Antigua in 1872. During the 20th century, economic problems contributed to the

growth of an independence movement and internal autonomy was achieved in February 1967 when Antigua, Barbuda and Redonda became an Associated State. In 1981, the country became fully independent as Antigua & Barbuda. Vere C Bird and his Antiguan Labour Party (ALP) have long dominated Antiguan politics. Except for a brief spell in opposition in the 1970s, he has been in power since 1946, first as Chief Minister, later as Premier and currently as Prime Minister. The ALP won 16 out of 17 seats in the House of Representatives in 1984, and repeated the victory at the most recent poll held in March 1989.

GOVERNMENT: Antigua & Barbuda is a constitutional monarchy, with the British Sovereign as Head of State. The Prime Minister advises the appointment of Governor-General, who represents the Sovereign. Parliament has supreme legislative power and comprises the Senate, with 17 appointed members, and the House of Representatives, with 17 members elected by universal adult suffrage from single-member constituencies. The judiciary is fully autonomous, and Antigua & Barbuda shares it with five other Eastern Caribbean states. Barbuda has its own local council with wide-ranging powers.

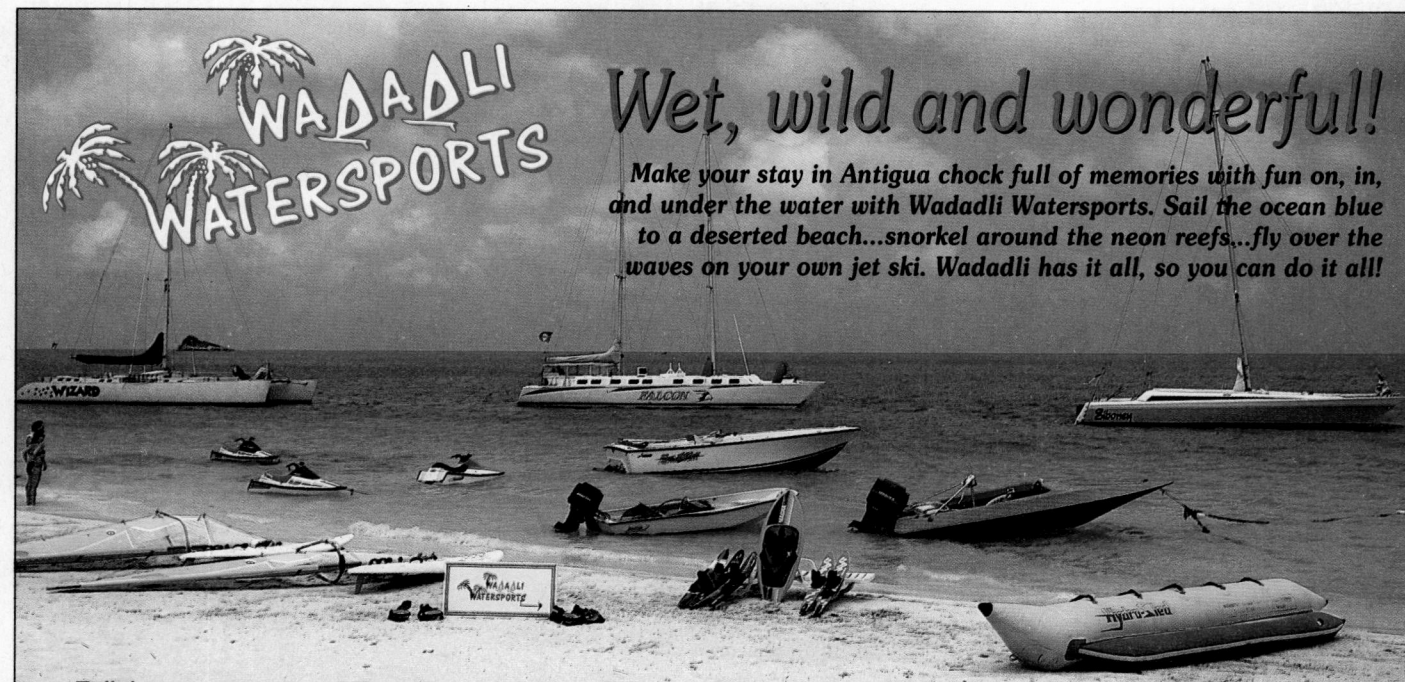

CLIMATE

The islands enjoy a very pleasant tropical climate which remains pleasantly warm and relatively dry throughout the year.

Required clothing: Lightweight cottons or linen, with rainwear needed from September to December.

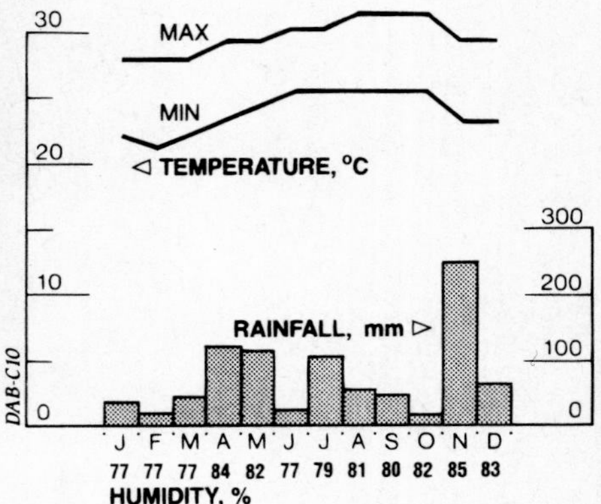

TEMPERATURE CONVERSIONS
-20 -10 0°C 10 20 30 40
0 10 20 30°F40 50 60 70 80 90 100

RAINFALL CONVERSIONS
0mm 200 400 600 800
0in 5 10 15 20 25 30

ARGENTINA

Location: Southeastern South America.

Secretaría de Turismo de la Nación
Calle Suipacha 1111, 21°
1368 Buenos Aires, Argentina
Tel: (1) 312 5621. Fax: (1) 313 6834. Telex: 24882.
Embassy of the Argentine Republic
53 Hans Place
London SW1X 0LA
Tel: (071) 584 6494. Fax: (071) 589 3106. Opening hours: 0900-1700 Monday to Friday.
Consular Section: Tel: (071) 589 3104. Opening hours: 1000-1300 Monday to Friday.
British Embassy
Casilla 2050
Dr Luis Agote 2412/52
1425 Buenos Aires, Argentina
Tel: (1) 803 7070/1. Fax: (1) 803 1731.
Embassy of the Argentine Republic
1600 New Hampshire Avenue, NW
Washington, DC
20009
Tel: (202) 939 6400. Fax: (202) 332 3171.
Consulate General of the Argentine Republic
12 West 56th Street
New York, NY
10019
Tel: (212) 603 0400. Fax: (212) 397 3523.
Argentina Government Tourist Office
12 West 56th Street
New York, NY
10019
Tel: (212) 603 0443. Fax: (212) 397 3523.
Embassy of the United States of America
Unit 4334
Avenida Colombia 4300
1425 Buenos Aires, Argentina
Tel: (1) 774 7611 *or* 8811 *or* 9911. Fax: (1) 775 4205.
Telex: 18156.
Embassy of the Argentine Republic
Suite 620
Royal Bank Center
90 Sparks Street
Ottawa, Ontario
K1P 5B4
Tel: (613) 236 2351/4. Fax: (613) 235 2659.
Canadian Embassy
Casilla 1598
Edificio Brunetta, 25°
Calle Suipacha 1111
1368 Buenos Aires, Argentina
Tel: (1) 312 9081. Telex: 21383.

AREA: 2,766,889 sq km (1,068,302 sq miles).
POPULATION: 32,370,298 (1991).
POPULATION DENSITY: 11.7 per sq km.
CAPITAL: Buenos Aires. **Population:** 11,382,002 (1990 estimate).
GEOGRAPHY: Argentina is situated in South America, east of the Andes, and is bordered by Chile to the west, the Atlantic Ocean to the east and Uruguay, Bolivia, Paraguay and Brazil to the north and northeast. There are four main geographical areas: the Andes, the North and Mesopotamia, the Pampas and Patagonia. The climate and geography of Argentina vary considerably, ranging from the great heat of the Chaco, through the pleasant climate of the central Pampas to the sub-Antarctic cold of the Patagonian Sea. Mount Aconcagua soars almost 7000m (23,000ft) and waterfalls at Iguazú stretch around a massive semi-circle, thundering 70m (230ft) to the bed of the Paraná River. In the southwest is a small Switzerland with a string of beautiful icy lakes framed by mountains.
LANGUAGE: Spanish is the official language. English, German, French and Italian are also spoken.
RELIGION: 90% Roman Catholic, 2% Protestant.
TIME: GMT - 3.
ELECTRICITY: 220 volts AC, 50Hz.
COMMUNICATIONS: Telephone: IDD is available (but not generally in use). Country code: 54. The system is often overburdened. **Telex/telegram:** Telex service from ENTEL (state-owned) in Buenos Aires. A cable service to other Latin American countries exists, run by All America Cables Limited. **Post:** Mail to Europe takes up to five days. **Press:** The *Buenos Aires Herald* is the leading English-language newspaper in Latin America. Argentina's principal dailies include *Clarín*, *Crónica*, *El Cronista Comercial*, *La Nación*, *La Razón* and *Ambito Financiero*.
BBC World Service and Voice of America frequencies: From time to time these change. See the section *How to Use this Book* for more information.

BBC:				
MHz	15.26	15.19	11.75	9.915
Voice of America:				
MHz	15.21	11.74	9.815	6.030

PASSPORT/VISA

Regulations and requirements may be subject to change at short notice, and you are advised to contact the appropriate diplomatic or consular authority before finalising travel arrangements. Details of these may be found at the head of this country's entry. Any numbers in the chart refer to the footnotes below.

	Passport Required?	Visa Required?	Return Ticket Required?
Full British	Yes	No	Yes
BVP	Not valid	-	-
Australian	Yes	Yes	Yes
Canadian	Yes	No	Yes
USA	Yes	No	Yes
Other EC	Yes	No	Yes
Japanese	Yes	No	Yes

PASSPORTS: Valid passport required by all except nationals of Bolivia, Brazil, Chile, Paraguay and Uruguay who, for journeys that do not go beyond Argentina and these 5 countries, may use their ID cards.
British Visitors Passport: Not accepted.
VISAS: Required by all for business purposes. For tourist visits, visas are required by all except:
(a) nationals of the countries shown in the chart above;
(b) nationals of Austria, Barbados, Bolivia, Brazil, Chile, Colombia, Costa Rica, Dominican Republic, Ecuador, El Salvador, Finland, Guatemala, Haiti, Honduras, Liechtenstein, Mexico, Monaco, Norway, Paraguay, Peru, Sweden, Switzerland and Uruguay.
Types of visa: Tourist, Business and Resident.
Application to: Consulate (or Consular Section at Embassy). For addresses, see top of entry.
Application requirements: (a) Passport. (b) Application forms. (c) Fee (£9.50). (d) Letter from employer if on business or from bank and employer if a tourist.
Working days: 1.
Note: Minors travelling to or from Argentina, if unaccompanied by their fathers, must carry the father's or other legal guardian's authorisation to travel, which must be certified by an Argentine Consul if issued abroad.

MONEY

Currency: Peso. Introduced in 1992, it replaces the Austral which is being phased out.
Currency exchange: Banks and *cambios* are available in all the major cities.
Credit cards: Diners Club, American Express and Access/Mastercard are accepted. Check with your credit card company for details of merchant acceptability and other services which may be available.
Travellers cheques: It is often difficult to exchange these in the smaller towns, except at branches of the Bank of London and South America. Citibank will exchange travellers cheques for US Dollars in cash at 1% commission.
Exchange rate indicators: The following figures are included as a guide to the movements of the Peso against Sterling and the US Dollar:

Date:	**Oct '89**	**Oct '90**	**Oct '91**	**Oct '92**
£1.00=	1029.98	10,862.8	17,195.08	1.57
$1.00=	652.29	5560.71	9907.85	0.99

Currency restrictions: The import and export of both local and foreign currency is unlimited.
Banking hours: 1000-1500 Monday to Friday.

DUTY FREE

The following goods may be imported into Argentina without incurring customs duty:
400 cigarettes;
50 cigars;
2 litres of alcohol;
5kg of foodstuffs;
Goods to the value of US$200.
For those arriving from Bolivia, Brazil, Chile, Paraguay or Uruguay:
200 cigarettes;
20 cigars;
1 litre of alcohol;
2kg of foodstuffs;
Goods to the value of US$100.
Prohibited items: Animals and birds from Africa or Asia (except Japan), parrots and fresh foodstuffs such as meat, dairy products and fruit.
Note: All gold must be declared. It is wise to arrange Customs clearance for expensive consumer items (cameras, typewriters etc) in order to forestall any problems.

PUBLIC HOLIDAYS

Public holidays observed in Argentina are as follows:
Apr 8-9 '93 Easter. **May 1** Labour Day. **May 25** Anniversary of the 1810 Revolution. **Jun 10** Assertion Day. **Jun 20** National Flag Day. **Jul 10** Independence Day. **Aug 17** Death of General José de San Martin. **Oct 12** Discovery of America. **Dec 25** Christmas. **Jan 1 '94** New Year's Day.

HEALTH

Regulations and requirements may be subject to change at short notice, and you are advised to contact your doctor well in advance of your intended date of departure. Any numbers in the chart refer to the footnotes below.

	Special Precautions?	Certificate Required?
Yellow Fever	1	No
Cholera	No	No
Typhoid & Polio	2	-
Malaria	3	-
Food & Drink	4	-

[1]: Yellow fever risk in the northeastern forest area only. Vaccination advised only if intending to visit this area. A certificate is not required for entry.
[2]: Protection is advised for both polio and typhoid in the form of vaccinations.
[3]: Malaria risk, primarily in the benign *vivax* form, exists from October through May below 1200m in rural areas of Iruya, Orán, San Martín, Santa Victoria Dep. (Salta Prov.) and Ledesma, San Pedro and Santa Barbara Dep. (Jujuy Prov.). Protection is advised.
[4]: Tap water is considered safe to drink. Drinking water outside main cities and towns may be contaminated and sterilisation is advisable. Milk is pasteurised and dairy products are safe for consumption. Local meat, poultry, seafood, fruit and vegetables are generally considered safe to eat.
Rabies is present. For those at high risk, vaccination before arrival should be considered. If bitten abroad seek medical advice without delay. For more information consult the *Health* section at the back of the book.
Other diseases of which there is a noteworthy level of risk are trypanosomiasis, gastroenteritis, viral hepatitis, intestinal parasitosis and anthrax.
Health care: Medical insurance is recommended. Medical facilities are generally of a high standard.

TRAVEL - International

AIR: Argentina's national airline is *Aerolíneas Argentinas (AR)*.
Approximate flight times: From Buenos Aires to *London* is 18 hours (including a good connection in Madrid), to *Los Angeles* is 16 hours and 5 minutes, to *New York* is 14 hours and 15 minutes, to *Singapore* is 29 hours 30 minutes and to *Sydney* is 16 hours.
International airport: *Buenos Aires (BUE)* (Ezeiza), 50km (31.5 miles) from the city. There is an hourly coach service to the city as well as taxis. The airport has a bank, restaurant, *cambio*, duty-free shop and a car rental facility. There is also a coach connection to *Jorge Newbery* airport (locally called *Aeroparque*) hourly for domestic flight connections. A taxi service is available. There are frequent flights from Buenos Aires to all neighbouring republics.
Departure tax: US$13 for international flights; US$3 for domestic. Passengers in transit and children under two years of age are exempt.
SEA: The main ports are Buenos Aires, La Plata (Ensenada), Rosario and Bahía Blanca. Two Italian ocean lines (*Italmar* and *Costa*) run services from Spanish and Italian ports. There are ferry connections down the Paraná River from Paraguay and ferries and hydrofoils link Buenos Aires with Montevideo in Uruguay.
RAIL: Argentina's rail network connects with all surrounding countries, although there is currently no passenger service into Chile. The timetables and journey times are often disrupted and delays must be expected.
ROAD: There are well-maintained road routes from Uruguay, Brazil, Paraguay, Bolivia and Chile. **Coach:** Direct daily services between Buenos Aires, Puerto Alegre, Sao Paolo and Rio de Janeiro.

TRAVEL - Internal

AIR: Domestic flights from *Jorge Newbery* (Aeroparque) and *Córdoba* (Pajas Blancas) to destinations throughout Argentina run by *Aerolíneas Argentinas*, *Austral* and the army airline *LADE*. Air travel is the most efficient way to get around, but the services are very busy and subject to delay. You are advised to book in advance for all flights. It is possible to buy a 30-day unlimited travel ticket from *Aerolíneas* or *Austral*.
RAIL: The domestic rail network extends over 35,000km (21,000 miles), which makes it one of the largest in the world. The coaches are comfortable and air-conditioned. There are restaurant and sleeping facilities for first-class passengers, and most long-distance trains run several times a week. Low-class rail travel is also good value. One can purchase a permit to travel anywhere in Argentina for a limited period, but rail travellers are warned that once out of Buenos Aires information is very hard to come by.
ROAD: Cross-country highways are well built and equipped, but road conditions off the main routes can be unreliable. Nonetheless, buses are considered to be a more reliable form of long-distance transport than trains. **Car hire:** There are a number of agencies in Buenos Aires. **Documentation:** International Driving permit is required and this must be stamped at the offices of the *Automóvil Club Argentino*.
URBAN: The **metro** *(subte)* service in Buenos Aires operates from early morning to late at night on a fixed fare basis; tokens can be purchased at booking offices. **Bus** services are provided by *colectivo* minibuses operating 24 hours a day on a flat fare; however, these are often crowded. There are extensive bus services in other towns, including trolleybuses in Rosario. **Taxis** are available in most cities and large towns and can either be hailed on the street or found at taxi ranks. They are usually recognisable by their yellow roofs.
JOURNEY TIMES: The following chart gives approximate journey time (in hours and minutes) from Buenos Aires to other major cities/towns in Argentina.

	Air	Road	Rail
Córdoba	1.00	8.00	9.00
Bariloche	1.30	20.00	30.00
Cataratas	1.30	17.00	24.00
Mendoza	1.30	15.00	20.00
Mar del Plata	0.40	4.00	4.00
Salta	2.00	15.00	20.00
Ushuaia	3.00	30.00	-

ACCOMMODATION

HOTELS: Hotels range in standard from the most luxurious in Buenos Aires to the lowest class in the rural areas. In Buenos Aires, the cheaper hotels can mostly be found around Avenida de Mayo. Generally service is excellent. All hotels add 3% tourism tax, 24% service charge for food and drink and 15% room tax. Most are air-conditioned, many have fine restaurants. The national hotel association is the Asociación de Hoteles en la Argentina, Calle Rivadavia 1157, Piso 9, Capital Federal, Buenos Aires. Tel: (1) 371 160/382 039. Fax: (1) 370 669. **Grading:** The *Dirección de Turismo* fixes maximum and minimum rates for 1-, 2- and 3-star hotels, guest-houses and inns; 4- and 5-star hotels are free to charge any rate they choose. All hotels, guest-houses and inns, as well as campsites, are graded according to the number of beds available and the services supplied.
SELF-CATERING: It is possible to rent cheap self-catering apartments and flats, with or without maid service, either by the day or week. Some can provide meals. Most apartments are in Buenos Aires.
CAMPING/CARAVANNING: Most resort cities welcome campers, and there are motels, campsites and caravan sites throughout Argentina. You will find a campsite in virtually every major region you wish to visit. Dormobiles are for hire.

RESORTS & EXCURSIONS

BUENOS AIRES: The capital city, which dominates the commercial life of the country, is also an elegant shoppers' paradise and a cosmopolitan cultural centre, and takes pride in *The National Art Museum*, the *Folk Art Museum* and the *Teatro*. There are now few reminders of the city's past, although the immense cathedral, which contains the remains of San Martín, Argentina's liberator, is one exception. The district of *La Boca*, one of the older areas and the home of the tango, is worth a night-time visit. The city has numerous parks and squares and is well served by public transport.
THE NORTH: To the northwest of the capital lie the most ancient cities in the country. **Córdoba** is interesting for its architecture and scenery, and **Salta** for its colonial cathedral containing a gold altar. **Tucumán,** the 'Garden of Argentina', is set in a landscape of great natural beauty. The squares of the city are planted with palm and orange trees, and it has some of the finest colonial churches in the country. One of the most famous sights in the whole of Argentina is the **Iguazú Falls** in the northeast of the country, on the border with Brazil and Paraguay, around which a vast tourist industry has been built up.
COASTAL RESORTS: One of the most popular resorts on the Atlantic coast, with several kilometres of fine beaches, is **Mar del Plata**. Others include **Villa Gezell**, **Pinamar**, **Miramar** and **Necochea** (which has, reputedly, the largest casino in the world). New resorts are constantly springing up along this developing area of coastline. Most can offer deep-sea fishing and other watersports. **Bahía Blanca**, the largest southern city, is mainly commercial but it is also the gateway to the fascinating lakeland around **Bariloche**.
THE ANDES: This region has many national parks with abundant wildlife, as well as opportunities for shooting and fishing. Skiing is available at **Cerro Chapelco Tronador** and **San Martín de los Andes.** The foothills of the Andes, west of the capital, are noted for their vineyards. The Andes proper contain many spectacular natural features, including **Mount Aconcagua**, one of the highest in the Western hemisphere.

SOCIAL PROFILE

FOOD & DRINK: North American, Continental and Middle Eastern cuisine is generally available, whilst local food is largely a mixture of Basque, Spanish and Italian. Beef is of a particularly high quality, and meat-eaters should not miss out on the chance to dine at a *parillada*, or grill room, where a large variety of barbecue-style dishes can be had. In general, restaurants are good value, and are classified by a fork sign with three forks implying a good evening out. Hotel residents are usually asked to sign a charge slip. **Drink:** Local distilleries produce name brands of most well-known spirits. Whiskies and gins are excellent, as are classic and local wines. Caribbean and South American rum add flavour to cocktails. There are no licensing laws.
NIGHTLIFE: Buenos Aires' nightlife is vibrant. There are many theatres and concert halls featuring foreign artists. Economic instability has meant a contraction of some of the more extravagant nightclubs for which Buenos Aires was famous, though there are still a large number of smaller intimate *boîtes* (clubs) and many stage shows. There are casinos throughout Argentina.
SHOPPING: Special purchases from Argentina include leather goods of all descriptions (gloves, coats, jackets and purses etc), hand-embroidered blouses and vicuña woollen goods. **Shopping hours:** 0900-1900 Monday to Friday.
SPORT: Football, tennis, golf, polo, horse racing and motor racing are all very popular. **Football** is obsessively followed; the national team were world champions in 1978 and 1986, and runners-up in the World Cup of 1990. Palermo Park has a golf course and public **tennis** courts. **Swimming** is enjoyed in rivers, lakes and small resorts along the Atlantic coast; **water-skiing** along the San Antonio River in the Tigre Delta Region; yachting and **boating** along the River Plate; and **fishing** on the Atlantic coast off the piers. There is very fine freshwater fishing along the Paraná River and in Argentina's many artificial lakes with fine trout and salmon. **Skiing:** There is excellent skiing on the eastern slopes of the Andes, with an increasing number of ski resorts and runs. The season is generally May to September. An all-season resort is being built on the slopes of Mount Tronador, an extinct volcano. *Bariloche* is the oldest, most established, and best-equipped ski resort. The runs at *San Antonio*, *San Bernado*, *La Canaleta*, *Puente del Inca* and *Las Cuevas* on the border of Argentina and Chile, offer the most exciting skiing. There are also skiing facilities and resort hotels at *Chapelco*, *Vallecitos* and *Esquel*. One note of caution: there is a chronic shortage of accommodation at these resorts, though the situation is being rectified as quickly as possible. It is vital to book early.
SPECIAL EVENTS: The following is a selection of the special events occurring annually in Argentina:
Jan *Sea Festival*, Mar del Plata; *Jineteada* (breaking in horses) and *Folklore Festival*, Diamante, Prov. Entre Ríos; *Chaya* (a musical instrument) *Festival*, La Rioja; *Doma* (breaking in horses) *and Folklore Festival*, Intendente Alvear, Prov. La Pampa; *Folklore Festival*, Cosquín, Prov. Córdoba.
Feb *Carnival*, Esquina, Prov. Corrientes; *Pachamama* (Mother Earth) *Festival*, Amaicha del Valle, Prov. Tucumán; *Trout Fishing Festival*, Río Grande.
Mar *Grape Harvest Festival*, Mendoza.
Apr *Holy Week*, Salta; *Festival of Our Lady Del Valle*, Catamarca.
Jul *Poncho Week*, Catamarca; *Simoca Fair*, Simoca, Prov. Tucumán; *Santiago Week*, Santiago del Estero; *Dorado Fishing Competition*, Formosa.

ARGENTINA | **HEALTH REGULATIONS** | **VISA REGULATIONS** | Code-Link

GALILEO/WORLDSPAN

TI-DFT/BUE/HE

TI-DFT/BUE/VI

SABRE

TIDFT/BUE/HE

TIDFT/BUE/VI

To access this information on your CRS, swipe the barcode with a light pen or type in the text under the barcode. For more information, see the introduction *How to Use This Book*.

Aug *Snow Festival*, Río Turbio, Prov. Santa Cruz; *Jujuy Week*, Jujuy; *Dorado Festival*, Posadas, Prov. Misiones; *Snow Festival*, Bariloche.
Sep *Chamamé Festival*, Corrientes (music); *Agriculture Festival*, Esperanza, Prov. Santa Fé.
Nov *Sea Salmon Fishing Contest*, Comodoro Rivadavia.
Dec *Gaucho Festival*, Gral. Madaria, Prov. Buenos Aires; *Trout Festival*, San Junín de los Andes, Prov. Neuquén.
SOCIAL CONVENTIONS: Entertaining often takes place in the home and it is customary to send flowers to the hostess the following day. Avoid casual discussion of the Falklands/Malvinas war. Dress is not usually formal, though clothes should be conservative away from the beach. Formal wear for official functions and dinners, particularly in exclusive restaurants. Smoking is prohibited on public transport, in cinemas and theatres. **Tipping:** Tips are theoretically outlawed but hotels or restaurants will add 24% service and tax charge and 10% on top of bill will suffice. The same applies in bars. Taxi drivers tend to expect tips from visitors.

BUSINESS PROFILE

ECONOMY: Argentina is rich in natural resources and also has a large and profitable agricultural sector; the country is one of the world's major exporters of wheat and also produces maize, oilseeds, sorghum, soya beans and sugar. Beef is no longer the dominant trading commodity that it once was. Agriculture accounts for 70% of export earnings, and although it has been affected by Argentina's economic crisis, it has not suffered as badly as the inefficient industrial sector. Steel and petrochemicals are two key industries which have recently been released from state control and are looking for new business. The state telephone company is expected to join the private sector soon. Farming products aside, Argentina exports textiles and some metal and chemical products. Brazil is the largest of the country's South American trading partners. There is comparatively little trade with neighbouring Chile with whom political relations are very bad. Further afield, Argentina has important trading relationships with both superpowers: the United States is the main source of manufactured products while the CIS buys large quantities of grain from the Argentinian surplus. The fastest growing aspects of the country's foreign trade are, however, Japan and the EC, especially Germany and The Netherlands. Trade relations with the UK have improved sharply in the last few years in line with the diplomatic rapprochement. Throughout the 1980s, the Argentinian economy has been stricken by the twin scourges of hyper-inflation and a massive foreign debt. Austerity measures introduced by President Alfonsín – in particular, the 1988 'Primavera' plan – were well received by international financiers but sparked major civil disorder inside Argentina, with serious clashes between demonstators and the army. Within a year, Alfonsín was voted out of office. Carlos Menem's administration retained some of the policies of his predecessor but attempted to accelerate the privatisation programme and liberalise other parts of Argentina's vast public sector. The Government has also embarked on a comprehensive overhaul of the country's financial system, including a planned devaluation and renaming of the currency (from *austral* to *peso*).
BUSINESS: Business cards are usually given and businessmen will expect to deal with someone of equal status. Punctuality is expected by visitors. Literature is in Spanish, although many Argentinian business people speak English or Italian as their second language.
Office hours: 0900-1900 Monday to Friday.
COMMERCIAL INFORMATION: The following organisation can offer advice: Cámara Argentina de Comercio, Avenida Leandro N., Alem 36, 1003 Buenos Aires. Tel: (1) 331 8051. Fax: (1) 331 8055. Telex: 18542.
CONFERENCES/CONVENTIONS: For more information contact: Asociación de Organizadores de Congresos de la Argentina, CP 1022, Avenida Callao 449, Piso 9, Capital Federal, Buenos Aires. Tel: (1) 464 726.

HISTORY & GOVERNMENT

HISTORY: Between the mid-19th century and 1946 Argentina swung from civilian to military rule and from radical to conservative policies. In 1943 a military coup resulted in the rise of Lt General Perón Sosa as President who instigated a policy of extreme nationalism and social improvement. He founded the Peronista movement and when he was overthrown in 1955 he continued to direct the movement from his Spanish exile. The ensuing administrations failed to secure the allegiance of either the people or the trade unions and Perón was re-elected as President in 1973. On his death a year later his wife, Isabelita Perón,

took over but chaos ensued and she was deposed by a military coup in 1976. Argentina suffered rampant inflation and social, political and financial disarray. Elections in October 1983 (which were partly the result of economic problems, opposition to the military's violation of human rights and the unsuccessful Falklands/Malvinas War) produced a victory for the revitalised Radical Party and Dr Raúl Alfonsín Foukes became President. Alfonsín successfully held his position despite repeated stirrings from the military; most notably in December 1988, when the country's largest military base became the focus of a major uprising. The economy proved, however, to be Alfonsín's undoing. By the time of his departure from office in June 1989 Argentina was racked by 4-digit annual inflation and still financially crippled by massive foreign debts. He duly lost the election to the Peronist challenger, Carlos Menem. Menem immediately announced harsh economic austerity measures including hefty price rises for public services, a wage freeze and a programme of privatisation to slim down Argentina's sprawling and inefficient public sector. Following discrete bilateral discussions with the UK late in 1989, Menem announced the formal ending of hostilities over the Falklands/Malvinas; diplomatic relations were resumed in February 1990. This rapprochement was only made possible, however, by the two parties agreeing to exclude the question of Falklands/Malvinas sovereignty from the discussions. In February 1992, Britain and Argentina opened negotiations on oil exploration. There are potentially large reserves in the seabed around the islands but no test drilling has been done since an inconclusive survey in the 1970s. Since 1991, however, the Menem government has been more preoccupied with domestic issues. The Argentinian economy has shown some improvement during 1992. In particular, the country's once notorious annual inflation is now running at 18%.
GOVERNMENT: With civilian rule, executive power is in the hands of an elected President who serves a 6-year term. Congress, made up of an elected 254-member Chamber of Deputies and a nominated 46-member Senate, is vested with legislative power.

CLIMATE

The north is subtropical with rain throughout the year, while Tierra del Fuego in the south has a sub-arctic climate. The main central area is temperate but can be hot and humid during summer (December to February) and cool in winter.
Required clothing: European clothes for the main central area. Lightweight cottons and linens in the north. Warm clothes are necessary in the south and during cool winter months in the central area. Waterproofing is advisable for all areas.

BUENOS AIRES Argentina (25m)

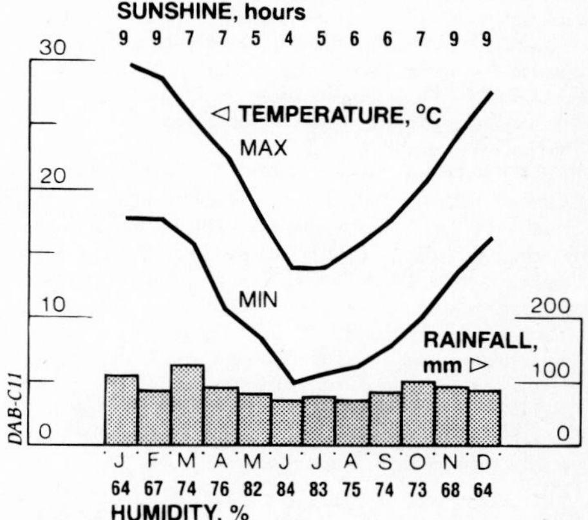

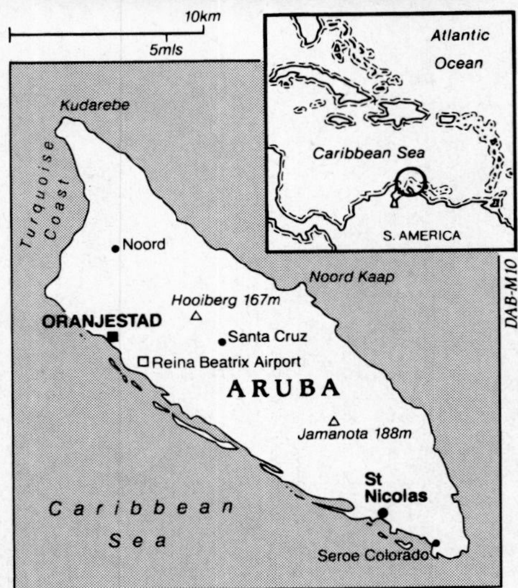

Location: South Caribbean.

Note: On January 1, 1986, the island of Aruba achieved internal independence; it is now administratively separate from the Netherlands Antilles, although it remains an integral part of the Kingdom of the Netherlands.

Aruba Tourism Authority
LG Smith Boulevard 172
Eagle, Aruba
Tel: (8) 23777. Fax: (8) 34702. Telex: 5006 ARTUR.

Aruba Tourism Authority
Amaliastraat 16
2514 JC The Hague
The Netherlands
Tel: (31-70) 356 6220. Fax: (31-70) 360 4877.

Note: The Tourism Authority also acts as diplomatic representative in the UK.

Aruba Tourism Authority
Suite 204
86 Bloor Street West
Toronto, Ontario
M4T 1N5
Tel: (416) 975 1950. Fax: (416) 975 1947.

AREA: 193 sq km (74.5 sq miles).
POPULATION: 62,365 (1989).
POPULATION DENSITY: 323.1 per sq km.
CAPITAL: Oranjestad.
GEOGRAPHY: Aruba is the smallest island in the Leeward group of the Dutch Caribbean islands, which also includes Bonaire and Curaçao. They are popularly known as the ABCs. As the westernmost island of the group, Aruba is the final link in the long Antillean chain, lying 29km (18 miles) off the Venezuelan coast. The island is 30km (20 miles) long and six miles across at its widest and has a flat landscape dominated by Yamanota Mountain (188m). The west and southwest coast, known as the Turquoise Coast, boasts seven miles of palm-fringed powder-white sands, while in complete contrast the east coast has a desolate, windswept shoreline .
LANGUAGE: The official language is Dutch. English and Spanish are also spoken. The islanders also speak a local language called Papiamento, which is a combination of Dutch, Spanish, Portuguese, English and African.
RELIGION: 80% of the population are Roman Catholic. The remainder are either Protestant or Jewish.
TIME: GMT - 4.
ELECTRICITY: 110 volts AC, 60Hz.
COMMUNICATIONS: Telephone: IDD available. Country code: 2978. **Telex/telegram:** Facilities exist at the Telegraph and Radio Office in the Post Office Building in Oranjestad and at Lands Radio Dienst. Most hotels can offer telex, fax and telegram service to residents. Post offices are open from 0730-1200 and 1300-1630. **Press:** The oldest established newspaper (in Dutch) is *Amigoe di Aruba* and the English-language daily is *The News*.
BBC World Service and Voice of America frequencies: From time to time these change. See the section *How to Use this Book* for more information.

BBC:

MHz	17.72	11.78	9.915	5.965

Voice of America:

MHz	15.21	11.70	6.130	0.930

PASSPORT/VISA

Regulations and requirements may be subject to change at short notice, and you are advised to contact the appropriate diplomatic or consular authority before finalising travel arrangements. Details of these may be found at the head of this country's entry. Any numbers in the chart refer to the footnotes below.

	Passport Required?	Visa Required?	Return Ticket Required?
Full British	Yes	No	Yes
BVP	Not valid/2	-	-
Australian	Yes	No	Yes
Canadian	1	No	Yes
USA	1	No	Yes
Other EC	Yes	No	Yes
Japanese	Yes	No	Yes

PASSPORTS: Valid passport required by all except:
[1] nationals of Canada and the USA holding a voter's registration card, birth certificate, affidavit of birth, or a passport which has expired within the last 5 years.
British Visitors Passport: [2] Should be considered as unacceptable. Although the immigration authorities of this country may in certain circumstances accept British Visitors Passports for persons arriving for holidays or unpaid business trips of up to 3 months, travellers are reminded that no formal agreement exists to this effect and the situation may, therefore, change at short notice. In addition, UK nationals using a BVP and returning to the UK from a country with which no such formal agreement exists may be subject to delays and interrogation by UK immigration.
VISAS: All nationals are allowed to stay in Aruba for 90 days without a visa provided they have a return or onward ticket. For stays of over 90 days the traveller will be issued with a Temporary Certificate of Admission by the Immigration authorities on arrival in Aruba. Visits in excess of 90 days require a visa.

MONEY

Currency: Aruba Florin/Guilder (Afl) = 100 cents. Notes are in denominations of Afl100, 50, 25, 10 and 5. Coins are in denominations of Afl1, and 100, 50, 25, 10 and 5 cents.
Currency exchange: The US Dollar is widely accepted in Aruba.
Exchange rate indicators: The following figures are included as a guide to the movements of the Aruba Florin against Sterling and the US Dollar.

Date:	Oct '89	Oct '90	Oct '91	Oct '92
£1.00=	2.83	3.49	3.11	2.83
$1.00=	1.79	1.79	1.79	1.78

Currency restrictions: No limit on import or export of foreign currency. Import and export of local currency is Afl200. Exchange of local currency is difficult outside of Aruba.
Banking hours: 0800-1200 and 1400-1800 Monday to Friday.

DUTY FREE

The following items may be taken into Aruba by those over 18 years of age without payment of duty:
200 cigarettes or 50 cigars or 250g of tobacco;
2 litres of alcoholic beverages;
0.25 litre of perfume (if more is taken the whole is dutiable);
Gifts to a value of AFL100.
Note: A duty-free allowance is only available to persons over 21 years of age.

PUBLIC HOLIDAYS

Public holidays observed in Aruba are as follows:
Apr 9-12 '93 Easter. **Apr 30** Queen's Day. **May 1** Labour Day. **May 28** Ascension Day. **Dec 25-26** Christmas. **Jan 1 '94** New Year's Day. **Feb 22** Carnival Monday. **Mar 18** National Anthem & Flag Day.

HEALTH

Regulations and requirements may be subject to change at short notice, and you are advised to contact your doctor well in advance of your intended date of departure. Any numbers in the chart refer to the footnotes below.

	Special Precautions?	Certificate Required?
Yellow Fever	No	1
Cholera	No	No
Typhoid & Polio	2	-
Malaria	No	-
Food & Drink	3	-

[1]: A yellow fever vaccination certificate is required for travellers over six months of age coming from infected areas. Pregnant women should not normally be vaccinated and should avoid exposure to infection.
[2] Vaccinations are recommended for both typhoid and polio.
[3]: Tap water is considered safe to drink. Milk is pasteurised and dairy products are safe for consumption. Local meat, poultry, seafood, fruit and vegetables are generally considered safe to eat.
Health care: There are excellent medical facilities at the Horacio Oduber Hospital. Many hotels also have doctors on call. Full medical insurance is strongly advised. There is no Reciprocal Health Agreement with the UK.

TRAVEL - International

AIR: Aruba's national airline is *Air Aruba (FQ)*.
Approximate flight times: From Oranjestad to *London* is 11 hours 40 minutes (including a good connection, normally in Amsterdam), to *Los Angeles* is 10 hours and to *New York* is 4 hours.
International airport: *Reina Beatrix (AUA)* is 5km (3 miles) southeast of Oranjestad. Airport facilities include a duty-free shop. Taxi service is available between the airport and the city.
The limited airport bus service must be paid for with prepaid travel coupons issued by travel agents.
Departure tax: Approximately AFL17.50 or US$9.50 per person for all travellers over two years of age.
SEA: Aruba has extensive virtually duty-free shopping facilities and many cruise ships call in on their Caribbean itineraries.

TRAVEL - Internal

AIR: *Air Aruba* offers several daily flights between Aruba, Bonaire and Curaçao.
ROAD: The road system throughout the island is very good. Driving is on the right and international signs are used. **Bus:** Public bus service runs between the towns and hotels on Eagle Beach and Palm Beach about ten times daily, except on Sundays and public holidays. Check with the tourist office or hotels for schedule. **Taxis:** The main taxi office is at the Boulevard Centre in Oranjestad: Tel: 22116 or 21604. Taxis are not metered. Rates are fixed and should be checked before getting into the cab. There is no need to tip drivers except for help with unusually heavy luggage. **Car hire:** There are plenty of cars available for hire and renting a car is one of the most pleasant ways to explore the island. Most major companies have offices in Aruba (*Hertz, National, Budget* and *Avis*); there are also many well-established local car rental firms. It is also possible to rent scooters, motorcycles and cycles. Minimum age for renting a car is 21. Hotels can assist with bookings.
Documentation: A valid foreign licence or International Driving Permit are both acceptable.
JOURNEY TIMES: The following chart gives approximate journey times (in hours and minutes) from Aruba to other major centres.

	Air
Amsterdam	9.00
Bonaire	0.30
Curaçao	0.20
Caracao	0.20
Las Piedras	0.20
Caracas	1.15
Miami	2.00
New York	4.00

ACCOMMODATION

HOTELS: The majority of hotels are concentrated in the Palm Beach resort area on the south coast, offering accommodation of a very high standard. Many of these luxury hotels have beach frontage and their own swimming pools, plus extensive sport, entertainment and shopping facilities for residents. Rates are considerably lower in the summer, which is the island's low season. Some tour operators offer out-of-season accommodation packages. Rooms are subject to 6% government room tax and many hotels also add 10-15% service charge. **Grading:** All hotels are graded into first class and deluxe. About 40% of all hotels are of the deluxe standard (high-rise hotels with good facilities) and about 60% are first-class hotels (low-rise establishments). For more information contact Aruba Tourism Authority (see above for address) *or* the Aruba Hotel and Tourism Association, PO Box 542, Oranjestad, Aruba. Tel: 33188. Fax: 24202.
GUEST-HOUSES: There is limited scope for this kind of accommodation. Many guest-houses are in the Malmok area not far from the main hotel area. Contact the tourist office for details.
SELF-CATERING: Although prices are reasonable there is not much choice. Contact tourist office for details.

RESORTS & EXCURSIONS

Aruba's principal attraction is its beaches; these include *Arashi Beach* (near California Point on the northwest tip, particularly good for snorkelling), *Spaans Lagoen* and *Commandeurs Baai*, *Bachelor's Beach* (good for windsurfing), and the particularly shallow areas of *Baby's Beach* and the 'Grapefield' (all on the south coast). Near Baby Beach, at Seroe Colorado, is *Rodger's Beach*, where the surf is a little stronger. Beaches on the north coast include *Boca Prins*, *Dos Playas* and *Andicouri*. One of the attractions on this shore is the **Natural Bridge**, an arch carved from coral cliffs by the ocean surf. The bridge is the biggest in the Caribbean and Aruba's most famous natural wonder. So too is the surf on this coast, but visitors are warned that it can be very rough. Local advice concerning conditions for surfing on the island at should be followed carefully, but there will usually be one beach to suit all levels of skill and courage.

Not all of the coast is completely deserted; for instance, much of the **Turquoise Coast** (also known as Palm Beach), the seven or so miles of sand and palm trees on the west and southwest shores of the island, has now been developed into a unique hotel resort. Low-rise resort hotels are more common on the stretch of beach between the point to the north of Druif Bay and the capital. Visitors after more isolated relaxation will need to seek out some of the more remote sunbathing and swimming spots (of which there are plenty) or turn their attention to the **Cunucu**, the interior, a land of cactus, windswept divi-divi trees, old villages and hamlets and unsignposted dirt roads stretching across the often mysterious landscape. The distinctive shape of the divi-divi trees (also known as *watapanas)* has become Aruba's unofficial trademark; blown by the southwesterly tradewinds, the trees grow at alarming angles. The island can easily be driven round in a day, and cars can be hired without difficulty; see the *Travel* section above for further information.

Aruba's Dutch heritage is always present, and nowhere more so than in the capital of **Oranjestad**, characterised by pastel-coloured gabled buildings, and a windmill brought piece by piece from Holland, now used as a restaurant. There are three museums here open to the public: the *Historical Museum*, the *Archaeological Museum* and the *Numismatic Museum*. Oranjestad has a daily floating market in the *Paardebaai* (Schooner Harbour) where traders sell fresh fish and fruit and vegetables from the mainland out of their boats. The capital is also famous for its shopping district, centred on Nassaustraat.

One of the roads north from the capital runs inland, passing the **Bubali Bird Sanctuary.** On the northern tip of the island is the **California Lighthouse** set in an area of desolate sand dunes. Off this coast is the wreck of a German freighter from the Second World War which is now the home of exotic fish and a very popular spot for scuba divers.

There are several systems of caves on Aruba. **Fontein** was once used by the Arawak Indians who were the original inhabitants of the island. On the walls of the caves are ancient drawings thought to be part of the Indian sacrificial rite. Nearby, the caves at **Quadiriki** are a haven for wild parrots. **Arikok,** which has been designated a national park, has by far the best preserved Indian drawings on the island. Inland is the old settlement of **Santa Cruz**, named after what is allegedly the place where the first cross was raised on Aruba. **Hooiberg** (Mount Haystack) looms out of the flat landscape of the interior to the northwest of Santa Cruz. A series of several hundred steps leads up to the 165m (540ft) peak, from where it is possible to see across to Venezuela. Northwest of the town is **Noord**, noted for its church of Santa Anna with its beautiful hand-carved oak altar. The road from Noord turns north to the California Lighthouse (see above). North from Santa Cruz, turning back towards the coast, the road to Ayo passes spectacular boulders, the result of some unexplained geological catastrophe. The road continues to the coast at **Bushiribana**, centre of the island's former gold-mining industry. Gold was discovered here in 1824 and mined until the beginning of the First World War. Kettles and ovens used in the smelting process have been preserved; nearby are the ruins of a pirate's castle. Gold was also mined at **Balashi** in the south.

In the southeastern part of the island is Aruba's second largest town, **San Nicolas**, which owed its prosperity to the oil refinery, once one of the largest in the world, which was closed in March 1985. To the east is the area known as **Seroe Colorado,** notable not only for several fine beaches but also for being the home of the local iguana community.

SOCIAL PROFILE

FOOD & DRINK: Not much food is grown locally, which may account for the lack of variety in the local cuisine. Aruban specialities include *stobà* (lamb or goat stew), *cala* (bean fritters), *pastechi* (meat-stuffed turnovers), *ayacas* (leaf-wrapped meat roll) and *sopito* (fish chowder). There is a wide range of international cuisine and several of the more famous fast-food chains have premises on the island.
NIGHTLIFE: There are several cinemas screening current American, European and Latin American films. The highlight of Aruba's nightlife, however, is the casinos, of which there are eight, open from 2100 to the early morning. There are several discotheques in Oranjestad, as well as nightclubs offering revues and live music.
SHOPPING: As a 'free zone', duty on most items in Aruba is so low that shopping here can have obvious advantages. Stores carry goods from all parts of the world and there are some excellent buys, including perfume, linens, jewellery, watches, cameras, crystal, china and other luxury items plus a range of locally made handicrafts. **Shopping hours:** 0800-1200 and 1400-1800 Monday to Saturday. For cashback on duty-free goods contact the Department of Economic Affairs, LG Smith Boulevard, 15 Oranjestad, Aruba.
SPORT: The island's clear warm waters and excellent facilities make it a haven for all kinds of watersports. There is **surfing** on the north coast at Dos Playas and Andicouri beaches, but surfers are warned to pay attention to the strong currents in the area. The clear waters offer visibilities of as much as 30m (90ft), and, with the coral reef, offer good **snorkelling** and **scuba diving.** There are several companies able to hire out equipment for either sport; details from most hotels. There is good **fishing** in the area (sailfish, wahoo, blue and white marlin, tuna and bonito) and there are companies chartering boats and fishing equipment; enquire at hotel or tourist office. The principal hotels have extensive sporting facilities including **waterskiing** and **tennis.** The island also has a **bowling** rink (Camacuri Bowling Centre) and a 9-hole **golf** course claimed to be the most unusual in the Caribbean. **Volleyball, soccer** and **baseball** are played at the Wilhelmina Stadium.
SPECIAL EVENTS: The following list is a selection of some of the events celebrated in Aruba in 1993/94. For further information contact the Aruba Tourism Authority. **Apr 30-May 2 '93** *National Drag Races*. **May 26-Jun 6** *Aruba Hiwinds* (windsurfing competition). **Jun 4-6 & 11-13** *Aruba Jazz & Latin Music Festival*. **Jun 20-25** *Site University*. **Jun 24** *St Johns Day*. **Sep** *ATEX*. **Oct 21-31** *Aruba International Dance Festival*. **Oct-Nov** *International Fishing Tournament*. **Nov** *Eurostyle O'Neil Catamaran Regatta*. **Feb 21 '94** *Carnival Grand Parade*.
SOCIAL CONVENTIONS: Much of the social activity will take place in hotels where the atmosphere will be informal, often American in feel. The islanders do not wear shorts in town though it is acceptable for visitors to do so. Bathing suits are strictly for beach or pool wear only. In the evenings people tend to dress up, especially when visiting the casinos. Jackets are required for men at night in certain nightclubs, restaurants and casinos. **Tipping:** Hotels add a 10-15% service charge to bills which covers most services. Restaurants may add service to the bill, if not, 10-15% is normal. Taxi drivers receive a tip only if they help with luggage. Allow approximately AFL2.5.

BUSINESS PROFILE

ECONOMY: In 1824 gold was discovered in Balashi, bolstering Aruba's economy until 1916 when gold yields became so poor the mines were left to fall into ruin. In 1929 Aruba's industry was rekindled with the opening of the Lago oil refinery in San Nicolaas, Aruba's second city, which for many years was the largest refinery in the world. This closed in 1985, however, and brought an end to the industry, a large increase in unemployment and a dramatic drop in government revenue. Since then tourism has become the island's major industry but Aruba is now looking once again to develop an oil business: exploration for oil and gas has already begun in Aruban waters. For the present, revenue other than tourism derives from Aruba's freeport status, ship bunkering and repair facilities, and transshipment of oil products (mainly between Venezuela and the US). Light industry is limited to the production of some tobacco products, drinks and consumer goods.
BUSINESS: Office hours: 0800-1700 Monday to Friday.
COMMERCIAL INFORMATION: The following organisation can offer advice: Aruba Chamber of Commerce and Industry, PO Box 140, Zoutmanstraat 21, Oranjestad, Aruba. Tel: (8) 21566/23423. Telex: 5174.

HISTORY & GOVERNMENT

HISTORY: Aruba was discovered in 1499 by Alonzo de Ojeda, who claimed the island for Spain. The Spaniards considered the island not worth colonising and left the original Arawak Indian inhabitants to live in virtual peace. The Spaniards' lack of interest resulted in the island's becoming a haven for pirates and buccaneers. Spanish 'occupation' continued unchallenged, however, until 1634, by which time the war with Holland was well into its seventh decade. Dutch war interests then switched to the Caribbean and the Dutch fleet took over the neglected territory with little opposition. In 1643 the Dutch appointed a governor in charge of Aruba and the rest of the Netherlands Antilles. Except for a brief period in the early 19th century when the British took possession, Aruba has remained under peaceful Dutch jurisdiction ever since. On January 1, 1986, Aruba achieved internal autonomy separating it administratively from the the rest of the Netherlands Antilles, although it remains an integral part of the Kingdom of the Netherlands. This is the first step towards full independence, planned to take place within the next ten years, although economic problems resulting in part from the closure of the oil refinery may cause this to be postponed.
GOVERNMENT: Aruba is a separate entity within the Kingdom of the Netherlands, with a Governor (appointed by the queen of the Netherlands), a 21-member elected parliament and a council of ministers.

CLIMATE

With a median temperature of 83°F, this dry and sunny island is made pleasantly cool throughout the year by constant trade winds. Showers of short duration occur during the months of October, November and December.
Required clothing: Lightweights for all seasons.

WILLEMSTAD Curaçao (8m)

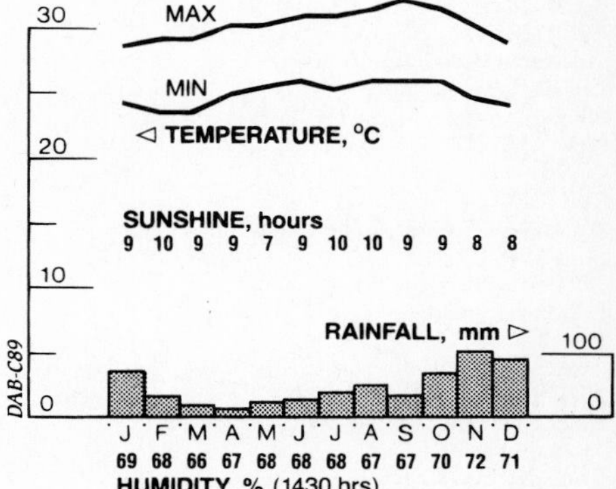

ARUBA | **HEALTH REGULATIONS** | **VISA REGULATIONS** | Code-Link

GALILEO/WORLDSPAN

TI-DFT/AUA/HE

TI-DFT/AUA/VI

SABRE

TIDFT/AUA/HE

TIDFT/AUA/VI

To access this information on your CRS, swipe the barcode with a light pen or type in the text under the barcode. For more information, see the introduction *How to Use This Book*.

AUSTRALIA

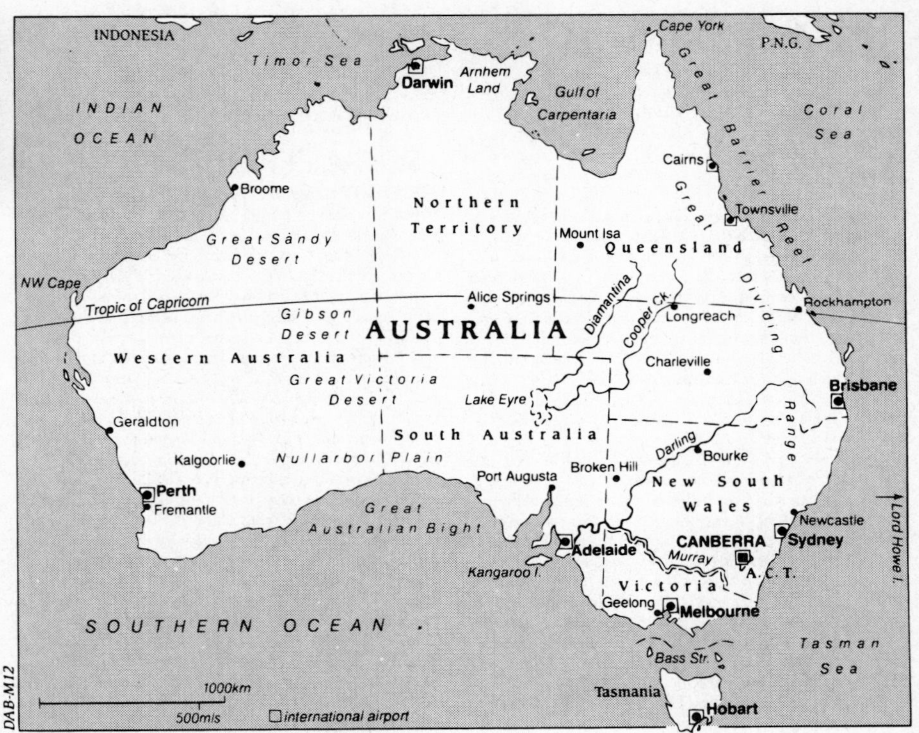

Location: Indian/Pacific Oceans.

Australian Tourist Commission
Level 13
80 William Street
Woolloomooloo
Sydney, NSW 2011
Australia
Tel: (2) 360 1111. Fax: (2) 331 6469.

High Commission of the Commonwealth of Australia
Australia House
The Strand
London WC2B 4LU
Tel: (071) 379 4334 *or* 438 8818 (visa enquiries and immigration). Fax: (071) 240 5333. Telex: 27565.
Opening hours: 0900-1700 Monday to Friday (1000-1600 Monday to Friday for visas).

Australian Consulate
Chatsworth House
Lever Street
Manchester M1 2DL
Tel: (061) 228 1344. Fax: (061) 236 4074.
and
Hobart House
80 Hanover Street
Edinburgh EH2 2DL
Tel: (031) 226 6271. Fax: (031) 225 1078.

Australian Embassy
Fitzwilton House
Wilton Terrace
Dublin 2, Republic of Ireland
Tel: (1) 761 517. Fax: (1) 785 185.

Australian Tourist Commission
First Floor, Gemini House
10-18 Putney Hill
London SW15 6AA
Tel: (081) 780 1424 (recorded message) *or* 780 2227 (general enquiries). Fax: (081) 780 1496. Opening hours: 0900-1730 Monday to Friday.

British High Commission
Commonwealth Avenue
Yarralumla
Canberra, ACT 2600
Australia
Tel: (6) 706 6666. Fax: (6) 273 3236. Telex: 71 62222.
Consulates in: Adelaide, Brisbane, Melbourne, Perth, Sydney and Darwin.

Embassy of the Commonwealth of Australia
1601 Massachusetts Avenue, NW
Washington, DC
20036-2273
Tel: (202) 797 3000. Fax: (202) 797 3168.

Australian Consulate General
International Building
636 5th Avenue
New York, NY
10020
Tel: (212) 245 4000.

Australian Tourist Commission
Suite 1200
2121 Avenue of the Stars
Los Angeles, CA
90067
Tel: (213) 552 1988. Fax: (213) 552 1215. Telex: 4720767 AUSTOUR.

Embassy of the United States of America
Moonah Place
Canberra, ACT 2600
Australia
Tel: (6) 270 5000. Fax: (6) 270 5970. Telex: 62104.
Consulates in Melbourne, Sydney, Perth and Brisbane.

Australian High Commission
Suite 710
50 O'Connor Street
Ottawa, Ontario
K1P 6L2
Tel: (613) 236 0841. Fax: (613) 236 4376.

Australian Consulate
Suite 314, 3rd Floor
175 Bloor Street East
Toronto, Ontario
M4W 3R8
Tel: (416) 323 1155. Fax: (416) 323 3910.

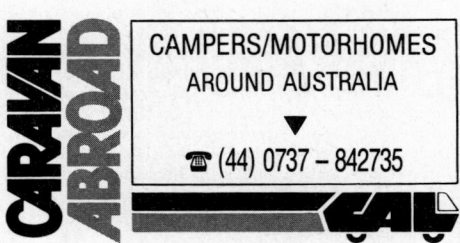

Australian Tourist Commission
Suite 1730
2 Bloor Street West
Toronto, Ontario
M4W 3E2
Tel: (416) 925 9575. Fax: (416) 925 9312.

Note: Addresses of Government and Tourist Representatives for individual states can be found at the head of each state entry.

AREA: 7,682,300 sq km (2,966,151 sq miles).
POPULATION: 17,086,200 (1990 estimate).
POPULATION DENSITY: 2.2 per sq km.
CAPITAL: Canberra. **Population:** 284,990 (1990).
GEOGRAPHY: Australia is bounded by the Arafura Sea and Timor Seas to the north, the Coral and Tasman Seas of the South Pacific to the east, the Southern Ocean to the south, and the Indian Ocean to the west. Its coastline covers 36,738km (22,814 miles). Most of the population has settled along the eastern and south-eastern coastal strip. Australia is the smallest continent (or the largest island) in the world. About 40% of the continent is within the Tropics and Australia is almost the same size as the mainland of the United States of America. The terrain is extremely varied, ranging from tortured red desert to lush green rainforest. Australia's beaches and surfing are world-renowned, while the country is also rich in reminders of its long, if often mysterious, past. These range from prehistoric Aboriginal art to Victorian colonial architecture. The landscape consists mainly of a low plateau mottled with lakes and rivers and skirted with coastal mountain ranges, highest in the east with the Great Dividing Range.
There are jungles in the far northeast (Cape York Peninsula). The southeast is a huge fertile plain. Further to the north lies the enormous Great Barrier Reef, a 2012km (1250-mile) strip of coral that covers a total area of 350,000 sq km. Although Australia is the driest land on Earth it, nevertheless, has enormous snow-fields the size of Switzerland. It is a country with a sense of space. There are vast mineral deposits. More detailed geographical descriptions of each state can be found under the individual state entries below.
LANGUAGE: The official language is English. Many other languages are retained by minorities, including Italian, German, Greek and Chinese dialects and Aboriginal languages.
RELIGION: Mainly Protestant, with a large Roman Catholic minority and smaller minorities of all other major religions.
TIME: Australia spans three time zones:
Northeast/southeast: GMT + 10.
Central: GMT + 9.5.
West: GMT + 8.
Some states operate daylight saving time during the Australian summer. Clocks in these states will be put forward by one hour in October and put back again in March.
ELECTRICITY: 240/250 volts AC, 50Hz. 3-pin plugs are in use, however sockets are different than those found in most countries and an adaptor socket may be needed. Outlets for 110 volts for small appliances are found in most hotels.
COMMUNICATIONS: Telephone: There are full facilities for national and international telecommunications. Full IDD is available. Code: 61. Pay-phones are red, green, gold or blue. Only local calls can be made from red phones. Green, gold and blue phones also have International Direct Dialling (IDD) and Subscriber Trunk Dial (STD). The minimum cost of a local phone call is 30c. Phonecards are available at newsagents, supermarkets and chemists and can be bought in denominations of A$2, 5, 10 and 20 and used for local, STD or international calls. Creditphones, which take most major credit cards, can be found at airports, city centre locations and many hotels. **Fax:** The Overseas Telecommunications Commission accepts documents over the counter for transmission. Free collection by courier is available in Brisbane, Sydney, Melbourne, Perth and Adelaide. Fax number guides are available at post offices, and prices vary. **Telex/telegram:** Services are run by the Overseas Telecommunications Commission and local offices. There are telex facilities at central post offices in Brisbane, Canberra, Sydney, Melbourne, Perth, Adelaide, Newcastle and Hobart. The OTC also operates a 24-hour public telex at Sydney, Brisbane, Canberra and Melbourne. Cables can be sent Urgent (2-4 hours delivery), Ordinary (4-6 hours), or Letter rate (24 hours). Telegrams may be sent through the telephone operator. Hotels usually add a surcharge. **Post:** There are post offices in all the main towns of every state. Opening hours are 0900-1700 Monday to Friday. Stamps are often available at hotel and motel reception areas and selected newsagents. *Poste Restante* facilities are available throughout the country; mail should be addressed to the nearest post office. **Press:** The main daily newspapers are *The Australian* and the *Australian Financial Review*. The weekly newspapers with the largest circulation are *The Bulletin*, the *Sunday Telegraph*, the *Sunday Mail* and the *Sunday Sun*. Newspapers have a generally high circulation throughout the continent.
BBC World Service and Voice of America frequencies: From time to time these change. See the section *How to Use this Book* for more information.

BBC:				
MHz	17.83	15.34	9.740	7.150
Voice of America:				
MHz	18.82	15.18	9.525	1.735

PASSPORT/VISA

Regulations and requirements may be subject to change at short notice, and you are advised to contact the appropriate diplomatic or consular authority before finalising travel arrangements. Details of these may be found at the head of this country's entry. Any numbers in the chart refer to the footnotes below.

	Passport Required?	Visa Required?	Return Ticket Required?
Full British	Yes	Yes	No
BVP	Not valid	-	-
Australian	-	-	-
Canadian	Yes	Yes	Yes
USA	Yes	Yes	Yes
Other EC	Yes	Yes	No
Japanese	Yes	Yes	Yes

PASSPORTS: Valid passport required by all.
British Visitors Passport: Not acceptable.
VISAS: Required by all except New Zealand citizens travelling on New Zealand passports.
Types of visa: *Visitor* (less than 3 months); *Visitor* (3 months and over); *Working Holiday; Business*.
Cost: Working Holiday: £55; Visitor (over 3 months): £15.
Validity: Varies according to type of visa, purpose of trip and validity of passport. Visitor Visa (to be used within 4 years or life of passport, whichever is shorter) is valid for 3 months and over; Visitor Visa (to be used within 1 year) is valid for up to 3 months; Working Holiday Visa is valid for 12 months.
Application to: Consulate (or Consular Section at Embassy or High Commission). For addresses, see top of entry.
Application requirements: (a) Completed application form. (b) Valid passport. (c) Separate passport-size photo. (d) Proof of sufficient funds for duration of stay. (e) A first-class stamped, self-addressed envelope large enough for return of passport if applying by mail. (f) Business visitors should, if possible, provide details of purpose of visit on company notepaper.
Note: Embassy representatives must submit applications to the office closest to the client's house. Delays will otherwise occur.
Working days required: Normally 1-5 days if applying in person; 21 days if applying by post.
Note: The Australian High Commission has asked that ABTA members should not sign visitor application forms on behalf of their clients. Travellers should also take particular note of the declarations relating to health, drugs and criminal convictions, as difficulties will arise if incorrect information is given.
Temporary residence: Applicants for temporary residence in Australia should consult the Embassy or High Commission and complete the relevant forms.

MONEY

Currency: Australian Dollar (A$) = 100 cents. Notes are in denominations of A$100, 50, 20, 10 and 5. Coins are in denominations of A$2 and 1, and 50, 20, 10 and 5 cents.
Currency exchange: Exchange facilities are available for all incoming and outgoing flights at all international airports in Australia. International-class hotels will exchange major currencies for guests. It is recommended that you change your money at the airport or at city banks.
Credit cards: Visa, Diners Club, Access/Mastercard, Carte Blanche and American Express are accepted. Use may be restricted in small towns and Outback areas. Check with your credit card company for details of merchant acceptability and other services which may be available.
Travellers cheques: These are accepted in major currencies at banks or large hotels. However, some banks may charge a small fee for cashing travellers cheques.
Exchange rate indicators: The following figures are included as a guide to the movements of the Australian Dollar against Sterling and the US Dollar.

Date:	Oct '89	Sep '90	Oct '91	Oct '92
£1.00=	2.01	2.46	2.18	2.22
$1.00=	1.27	1.26	1.26	1.39

Currency restrictions: No limit to amount of currency imported. Export restricted to A$5000, unless specially authorised.
Banking hours: 0930-1600 Monday to Thursday; 0930-1700 Friday. These hours vary throughout the country.

DUTY FREE

The following items may be taken into Australia without payment of duty:
250 cigarettes or 250g of tobacco or cigars;
1 litre of any alcoholic liqueur;
Other goods to a value of A$400.
Prohibited items: There are very strict regulations against the import of non-prescribed drugs, weapons, firearms and certain foodstuffs and other potential sources of disease and pestilence. For more information, read the Australian Customs information leaflets and *Australia, A Protected Place*. They are available from the Australian Tourist Commission.
There are severe penalties for drug trafficking.

PUBLIC HOLIDAYS

The following Public Holidays are observed throughout Australia:
Apr 9-12 '93 Easter. **Jun 14** Queen's Official Birthday. **Jan 1 '94** New Year's Day. **Jan 3** New Year additional holiday.

HEALTH

Regulations and requirements may be subject to change at short notice, and you are advised to contact your doctor well in advance of your intended date of departure. Any numbers in the chart refer to the footnotes below.

	Special Precautions?	Certificate Required?
Yellow Fever	No	1
Cholera	No	No
Typhoid & Polio	No	-
Malaria	No	-
Food & Drink	No	-

[1]: A yellow fever certificate is required from travellers over one year of age arriving within six days of a visit to any region in any country that has had an instance of yellow fever in the previous ten years. See *Health* section at the back of this book.
Health care: There are strict Customs and Health controls on entering and leaving the country, and Australian law can inflict severe penalties on health infringements. Australia reserves the right to isolate any person who arrives without the required certificates. Carriers are responsible for expenses of isolation of all travellers arriving by air who are not in possession of the required vaccination certificates. All arriving aircraft are sprayed before disembarkation to prevent the spread of disease-carrying insects. Standards of hygiene are high in Australia, especially in food preparation. Doctors and dentists are highly trained and hospitals are well equipped. There is a Reciprocal Health Agreement with the UK, New Zealand, Italy, Malta and Sweden in emergencies only, which allows residents from these five countries free hospital treatment; prescribed medicines, ambulances and treatment at some doctor's surgeries must be paid for. Personal insurance for illness and accidents is highly recommended for all visitors. Those wishing to benefit from the Agreement should enrol at a *Medicare* office; this can be done *after* treatment.

TRAVEL - International

AIR: The national airline is *Qantas (QF)*.
Approximate flight times: From *London* to Adelaide is 23 hours 55 minutes, to Brisbane is 23 hours 55 minutes, to Cairns is 25 hours 45 minutes, to Darwin is 21 hours 50 minutes, to Melbourne is 24 hours 25 minutes, to Perth is 21 hours 40 minutes, to Sydney is 21 hours 45 minutes and to Townsville is 26 hours 5 minutes.
From *Los Angeles* to Perth is 21 hours and to Sydney is 17 hours 55 minutes.
From *New York* to Perth is 27 hours 35 minutes and to Sydney is 21 hours 5 minutes.
From *Singapore* to Sydney is 9 hours 15 minutes and to Perth is 5 hours.
Approximately 30 international airlines fly to Australia.
International airports: Canberra, Sydney, Adelaide, Melbourne, Perth, Darwin, Brisbane, Hobart, Townsville and Cairns. All airports have a duty-free shop, bank/exchange facilities and car hire; these will almost always be available on arrival and departure of international flights.
Canberra Airport is 10km (6 miles) east of the city. Transport into the city is available by taxi or rental car (travel time – 20 minutes). **Note:** Until recently *Canberra Airport* served domestic flights exclusively. However *Britannia Airways* now fly to Canberra from *Luton Airport*, north of London.
Sydney Airport (Kingsford Smith) is 12km (7 miles) south of the city (travel time – 35 minutes). Coaches meet all incoming international and domestic flights. The international terminal is separate to the domestic terminal. Passengers may be set down at city airline terminals and city hotels, motels and guest-houses on request. There are also buses and taxis. Airport facilities include a duty-free shop, banks, restaurant (open one hour before and after every flight), car hire, car park and a travellers' information desk (open from 0530 to one hour after last flight).
Adelaide Airport is 6km (4 miles) south of the city (travel time – 25 minutes). Coaches meet all international and domestic flights. Buses and taxis are available to the city and hotels. Airport facilities include a duty-free shop, restaurant, bar (open two hours before and one hour after flights) and car hire.
Melbourne Airport is 22km (14 miles) northwest of the city (travel time – 35 minutes). Skybus Coach or taxis are available to the city centre. Airport facilities include a buffet (open 0630), restaurant, bar (open 90 minutes before first departure), public bar (open 1000-2200), banks, post office, car park and duty-free shop.
Perth Airport is 10km (6 miles) northeast of the city (travel time – 35 minutes). There are separate international and domestic terminals. Airporter bus runs 0500-2100 and meets both international and domestic flights. Taxis are also available. Airport facilities include banks, duty-free shop, 24-hour restaurant, buffet, bar (open 0900-0100; from 0100-0900, open one hour before and after arrival of international aircraft), car park, garage and gift shop (access from public area 0500-2400; access from transit/departure lounge 2400-0500).
Brisbane Airport is 13km (8 miles) northeast of the city (travel time – 35 minutes). Coach services are available to the city, Gold Coast, Sunshine Coast and major hotels. Coaches meet all international flights. Taxis are also available. Airport facilities include a car park, duty-free shop and a bar-buffet.
Darwin Airport is 8km (5 miles) from the city (travel time – 15 minutes). Coaches and taxis meet all incoming international daytime flights and all flights operated by *Ansett Australia Airlines*, *Ansett WA* and *Australian Airlines*. Airport facilities include a general goods kiosk (open 0700 to last departure) and bar (open 1100 to last departure).
Hobart Airport is 22km (14 miles) east of the city (travel time – 35 minutes). Coaches meet all incoming flights. Buses and taxis are available to the city. Airport facilities include a restaurant and bar (open 0630-2100).
Cairns Airport (Queensland) is 6km (4 miles) from the city (travel time – 15 minutes). Coaches meet all incoming flights, plus airport bus, limousines, car rental, taxis to city and other areas by arrangement. Airport facilities include a duty-free shop, restaurant (open 0600), bar (open 30 minutes before first flight to 30 minutes after last flight).
Townsville Airport (Queensland) is 5km (3 miles) from the city (travel time – 10 minutes). Coaches meet all incoming flights operated by *Qantas* and *Ansett*. The first coach leaves at 0735 and the last at 1949. Buses and taxis are available to city and hotels.
All other state capital cities are served by connections from the above international airports.
Departure tax: A$20 is levied on international departures. Tax stamps may be purchased at Australian airports or any Australian post office and must be paid in Australian currency in Australia only. Children under 12 years and those in transit for not more than 24 hours are exempt.
SEA: Cruise liners dock at Sydney, Melbourne, Hobart, Perth (Port of Fremantle), Adelaide and Brisbane.

TRAVEL - Internal

AIR: Australians rely on aviation to get from place to place as inhabitants of smaller countries rely on trains and buses. The network of scheduled services extends to more than 150,000km (95,000 miles) and covers the whole continent. Both first-class and second-class service is available, with meals and hostess service on many routes. Recent deregulation of Australia's domestic airlines means that flight services are more competitively priced. Aircraft can be chartered by pilots who pass a written examination on Australian air regulations and have their licences validated for private operations within Australia.
The four major **domestic airlines** are: *Ansett Australia Airlines (AN)*, *Australian Airlines (TN)*, *East-West Airlines (EW)* and *Compass Airlines (YM)*.
Ansett Airlines and *Australian Airlines* serve the major resorts and cities throughout Australia.
East-West Airlines operate throughout New South Wales,

with services to Queensland, Norfolk Island, Victoria, Tasmania, Northern Territory and Western Australia. *Compass Airlines* operate throughout Queensland, New South Wales, Victoria, Southern Australia and Western Australia.

In addition, *Ansett Express (WX)*, *Hazelton Airlines (ZL)* and *Eastern Australia Airlines (UN)* operate throughout New South Wales; *Ansett WA (MV)* operates throughout Western Australia; *Air North (HS)* operates throughout the Northern Territory; *Lloyd Aviation (UD)* operates throughout South Australia; *Kendell Airlines (KD)* operates throughout Victoria and South Australia; *Sunstate Airlines* operates throughout Victoria and Queensland; *Australian Regional Airlines (TN)* operates throughout Queensland; and *Airlines of Tasmania (IP)* operates throughout Tasmania.

Nearly all the domestic airlines operate special deals or air-passes at greatly reduced prices. Contact *Qantas* for telephone numbers.

SEA: There are 36,738km (22,600 miles) of coastline and many lakes, inland waterways and inlets, all of which can be used for touring by boat. From paddle steamers along the Murray River to deep-sea fishing cruisers along the vast Barrier Reef, all are available for charter or passenger booking. Most tour operators also handle shipping cruises. There is a regular car ferry service linking Victoria with Tasmania.

RAIL: Over 40,000km (24,850 miles) of track cover the country, but only one service spans the continent from coast to coast – the thrice-weekly *Indian Pacific*, running 4000km (2480 miles) on standard 1435mm (56.5-inch) gauge from Sydney on the east coast to Perth on the west coast, a journey time of three days, including a 500km (300-mile) stretch of straight track, the longest in the world. For most of the year, a twice-weekly service is provided by the *Trans-Australian* running from Adelaide to Perth (two days). Other express service links (not always daily) from the state capitals are as follows:

The *Melbourne Sydney Express* links Sydney and Melbourne overnight, and the *Intercapital Daylight Express* provides a daytime service. The *Ghan* links Adelaide to Alice Springs (overnight). The *Overland* links Melbourne with Adelaide (overnight). The *Brisbane Limited Express* links Brisbane with Sydney (overnight). The *Canberra Monaro Express* and the fast *XPT* link Canberra with Sydney in four or five hours. The *Sunlander* and the *Queenslander* link Brisbane with Cairns (one and a half days). The *Prospector* links Perth with Kalgoorlie (eight hours). The *Vinelander* links Melbourne with Meldura (overnight); the *Sunraysia* provides a daytime service on the same route. The *Spirit of Capricorn* links Brisbane with Rockhampton (overnight). The *Pacific Coast Motorail* links Sydney with Murwillumbah (overnight).

Both first- and second-class tickets are available, with sleeping accommodation on longhauls. Reservations for seats and sleeping berths are essential on all long-distance trains and are accepted up to six months in advance. Several routes have motorail facilities. Long-distance trains are air-conditioned and have excellent catering facilities and hot water.

Luggage allowance: All interstate rail passengers are allowed 80kg (176lb). Medium-sized suitcases and hand luggage can be placed in the passengers' compartments. Large suitcases must be carried in the guard's van and checked in 30 minutes prior to departure.

Sleeping berths: Single and twin apartments are available for a surcharge on most inter-capital overnight services. 'Twinettes' have two sleeping berths and individual showers. 'Roomette' (single compartment) cars have showers at the end of each car.

Cheap fares: Unlimited travel, valid from 14 to 60 days, is available with an *Austrailpass*, which must be purchased outside Australia, and can only be used by non-Australian passport holders. First- and second-class passes are available. Each state operator offers its own *Austrailpass* scheme. The *Kangaroo Road 'n Rail Pass* is also available, offering unlimited travel on both the rail and Greyhound bus networks throughout the country. It is also possible to obtain discounts on certain rental car schemes. **Note:** An *Austrailpass* or *Kangaroo Road'n Rail Pass* does not include meal or sleeping berth charges. A surcharge must be paid on the *XPT Express* service in New South Wales. The passes must be used within six months of issue.

Representative in the UK: Railways of Australia, c/o *Compass Travel*, PO Box 113, Peterborough PE1 1LE. Tel: (0733) 51780. Fax: (0733) 892 601. Most major tourist attractions can be reached by train; tickets for multiple destinations can be purchased from travel agents outside Australia. **Note:** Booking domestic travel for Australia outside the country can result in discounts of up to 30%. Contact the respective Tourist Boards.

Pensioners: Some fares in Australia quote children and pensioners as half-price, particularly on coaches and trains. Please note that these only apply to *Australian* pensioners.

ROAD: Traffic drives on the left. Road signs are international. The speed limit is 60kmph (35mph) per hour in cities and towns and 100kmph (62mph) per hour on country roads and highways unless signs indicate otherwise. Seatbelts must be worn at all times and driving licences must be in the driver's possession when driving. Driving off major highways in the Outback becomes more difficult between November and February because of summer rain, as many roads are little more than dirt tracks. Road travel is best between April and October. Distances between towns can be considerable, and apart from ensuring that all vehicles are in peak condition it is advisable to carry spare water, petrol and equipment. Travellers are advised to check with local Automobile Associations before departure in order to obtain up-to-date information on road and weather conditions.

Coach: Major cities are linked by an excellent national coach system, run by *Australian Coachlines* (combining *Pioneer Express* and *Greyhound Australia)* and *Bus Australia*. Tasmania also has its own coach service, *Tasmanian Redline Coaches*. There are numerous other companies operating state and interstate services. The main coach express routes are: Sydney to Adelaide, Melbourne (inland) and Canberra; Canberra to Melbourne; Melbourne to Adelaide and Broken Hill; Adelaide to Alice Springs, Perth and Brisbane; Darwin to Alice Springs and Kakadu; Alice Springs to Ayers Rock; Cairns to Brisbane; Brisbane to Sydney (inland and coastal) and Melbourne. Coach passes are available for travel on the express services for between 7 and 90 days, eg the *Aussie Discoverer*, the *Eastern Discoverer*, the *Aussiepass*, the *Bus Australia Pass*, the *Down Under Pass* etc. These normally give unlimited travel throughout the country. The *Kangaroo Road'n Rail Pass* offers unrestricted rail and coach travel throughout mainland Australia on *Railways of Australia* and *Australian Coachlines* coaches. It is advisable to purchase all these passes before departure from country of origin. Coaches are one of the cheapest ways to travel around Australia, as well as one of the most comfortable, with air-conditioning, big adjustable seats and on-board bathrooms; some also have television and the latest videos.

Representation in the UK: *Australian Coachlines (Greyhound International* and *Pioneer Express)*: c/o Greyhound World Travel, Sussex House, London Road, East Grinstead, West Sussex RH19 1LD. Tel: (0342) 317 317. Fax: (0342) 328 519; *or* Destination Marketing Ltd, 2 Cinnamon Row, Plantation Wharf, York Place, London SW11 3TW. Tel: (071) 978 5222. Fax: (071) 924 3171. For *Bus Australia:* c/o Australian Destination Centre, 27 High Street, Windsor, Berkshire SL4 1LH. Tel: (0753) 855 457. Fax: (0753) 830 629.

Car hire: Available at all major airports and major hotels to those over 21 years old. **Documentation:** International, foreign or national Driving Permits, translated into English, are generally valid for three months. These must be carried on the person while driving.

URBAN: Comprehensive public transport systems are provided in all the main towns. The state capitals have suburban rail networks, those in Sydney and Melbourne being particularly extensive, and trams run in Melbourne and Adelaide. Meter-operated taxis can be found in all major cities and towns. There is a minimum 'flagfall charge' and then a charge for the distance travelled. Taxi drivers do not expect to be tipped. A small additional payment may be required for luggage and telephone bookings. Some taxis accept payment by credit card. For further details, see individual state entries.

JOURNEY TIMES: The following chart gives approximate journey times (in hours and minutes) from Sydney to other major cities in Australia.

	Air	Rail	Coach	Sea
Canberra	0.40	5.00	4.00	-
Adelaide	1.55	28.40	23.40	-
Brisbane	1.15	16.00	16.30	-
Darwin	5.00	-	92.50	-
Melbourne	1.15	13.00	14.30	-
Perth	4.35	65.45	60.00	-
Hobart	2.05	-	-	14.00

ACCOMMODATION

HOTEL/MOTEL: Every state has a selection of hotels run by international chains such as the Hilton and Intercontinental. More authentic accommodation for the tourist can be found outside the cities. The smaller hotels are more relaxed, and offer more of the flavour of their location. The highways out of the state cities are lined with good quality motels offering self-contained family units, and often an in-house restaurant service. Most hotels and motels provide rooms with telephones, private shower and/or bath, toilet, small fridge and tea- and coffee-making facilities. Check-out time is 1000 or 1100. Hotel/motels and motor inns have licensed restaurant and a residents' bar; some may provide a public bar (see also paragraph below). Motels in rural areas will normally only be able to offer breakfast. Motor inns in rural areas will probably have a licensed restaurant, and possibly a residents' bar as well. Private hotels are not permitted to provide bars. The principal difference between a hotel and a motel in Australia is that a hotel must, by law, provide a public bar among its facilities. For this reason there are many motels which are hotels in all but name, offering an excellent standard of comfort and service but preferring to reserve their bar exclusively for the use of their guests, rather than for the public at large.

Grading: Hotels and motels in Australia are graded in a star rating system by the Australian Automobile Clubs. In most cases, different rooms will be offered at different rates depending on their size, aspect or facilities; this is particularly true of seafront hotels. In general, hotels in cities cost more than their rural counterparts. The fact that an establishment is unclassified does not imply that it is inferior. It may still be in the process of being classified or is as yet not covered by the grading scheme. The following grading definitions are intended as a guide only and are subject to change:

5-star accommodation: International-style establishments offering a superior standard of appointments, furnishings and decor with an extensive range of first-class guest services. A variety of room styles and/or suites available. Choice of dining facilities, 24-hour room service and additional shopping or recreational facilities available.

4-star accommodation: Exceptionally well-appointed establishments with high-quality furnishings and a high degree of comfort. Fully air-conditioned. High standards of presentation and guest services provided. Restaurant and meals available on premises.

3-star accommodation: Well-appointed establishments offering a comfortable standard of accommodation with above average floor coverings, furnishings, lighting and ample heating/cooling facilities.

2-star accommodation: Well-maintained establishments offering an average standard of accommodation with average furnishings, bedding, floor coverings, lighting and heating/cooling facilities.

1-star accommodation: Establishments offering a basic

AUSTRALIA	HEALTH REGULATIONS	VISA REGULATIONS Code-Link
GALILEO/WORLDSPAN	 TI-DFT/SYD/HE	 TI-DFT/SYD/VI
SABRE	  TIDFT/SYD/HE	 TIDFT/SYD/VI

To access this information on your CRS, swipe the barcode with a light pen or type in the text under the barcode. For more information, see the introduction *How to Use This Book.*

standard of accommodation. Simply furnished, adequate lighting. Motel units all have private facilities. Resident manager.
Note: Some hotels are graded with an additional *open* or *hollow* star. This indicates a slightly higher grade of facilities than the normal facilities for its classification. For more information on accommodation classification contact the RAC Touring and Travel Administration, 550 Princes Highway, Noble Park, VIC 3174.
Information is also available from the Australian Hotels Association, Level 5, 8 Quay Street, Sydney, NSW 2000. Tel: (2) 281 6944/22. Fax: (2) 281 1857 *and* the Motor Inn, Motel and Accommodation Association, Level 12, 309 Pitt Street, Sydney, NSW 2000. Tel: (2) 261 3793.
GUEST-HOUSES, HOMESTAY, SELF-CATERING & FARMSTAY HOLIDAYS: Service apartments and self-contained flats are available at main tourist resorts, especially along the east coast. Many of the less accessible areas have accommodation on farmsteads, from guest-houses on the huge sheep stations to basic staff quarters on smaller arable farms, giving an insight into an alternative aspect of Australian life. There are many homes and farms which open their doors to foreign visitors and offer splendid hospitality. For specific information on farmstay holidays, contact Australian Farmhost & Farm Holidays, PO Box 65, Culcairn, NSW 2660. Tel: (60) 298 621. Fax: (60) 29 8770. For information on home holidays, contact Home Hospitality, 50 Rosemead Road, Hornsby, NSW 2077. Tel: (2) 568 2331. Fax: (2) 564 2601. Bed & breakfast private home accommodation is available throughout Australia. For information on bed & breakfast accommodation, contact Bed & Breakfast Australia, 5 Yarabah Avenue, Gordon, NSW 2072. Tel: (2) 498 5344. Fax: (2) 498 6438. Some hotels have self-catering apartments. For more information contact the Australian Tourist Commission. Guest-houses are not allowed to serve alcohol. **Grading:** Holiday units and apartments are classified according to a 5-star system with criteria comparable to those for hotels and motels above.
COUNTRY PUB ACCOMMODATION: These offer cold beer, meals and simple but comfortable accommodation for travellers from A$30 a night. Pubs tend to be easy to find and advance reservations are not always necessary. However, standards may vary according to the type of pub and its location. For further information, contact Australian Pub Stays, First Floor, Albert Park Hotel, 83 Dundas Place, Albert Park, VIC 3206. Tel: (3) 696 0422. Fax: (3) 696 0329.
YOUTH HOSTELS: Found throughout the country, but there are greater concentrations near cities and densely populated areas. Associations responsible are affiliated to most other international organisations. Further details may be obtained from the Australian Youth Hostel Association, National Office, 10 Mallett Street, Camperdown, NSW 2050. Tel: (2) 565 1699. Fax: (2) 565 1325.
ON-CAMPUS ACCOMMODATION: University colleges and halls of residence offer inexpensive accommodation for both students and non-students during the vacation periods (May, August and late November to late February).
CAMPING/CARAVANNING: Camping tours cover most of the country, especially the wilder areas. Participants generally join a group under an experienced guide team and everyone helps with cooking, washing etc. All equipment and transport is supplied; some also provide portable showers. More rugged tours with Land Rovers are available, offering limited facilities, although company equipment is again provided with a driver/guide and cook. This can be one of the best ways to explore the Australian Outback. Camping site information is available from all major tourist centres. It is inadvisable to camp on undesignated sites.
A number of companies can arrange **motor camper** rentals, with a range of fully-equipped vehicles. Full details can be obtained from the Australian Tourist Commission. **Grading:** Caravan parks are classified according to a 5-star system with criteria similar to those for hotels and motels above.

RESORTS & EXCURSIONS

Australia's main tourist attractions are Sydney, the Great Barrier Reef, the Gold Coast of Queensland, and Ayers Rock, in the rugged Outback of the Northern Territory. Other attractions in the continent range from the wild flowers of Western Australia to the wines of the Barossa Valley, and from Western Australia's ghost towns to the remarkable wildlife on the island of Tasmania. It is possible to visit the relatively undisturbed Aboriginal communities on Bathurst and Melville Islands, about 80km (50 miles) north of Darwin, providing valuable insights into the continent's ancient indigenous culture. The Australian coastline has thousands of miles of beautiful beaches. Information on resorts, excursions and places of interest within Australia is given under each individual state entry below.
The range of adventure and special interest holidays is almost limitless. Many of the safari tours include luxury transport, and comfortable accommodation is available at many of the sheep stations. Further details may be obtained from the many brochures and leaflets published by the Australian Tourist Commission.

SOCIAL PROFILE

FOOD & DRINK: There are numerous speciality dishes and foods including Sydney rock oysters, *barramundi* (freshwater fish), tiger prawns, macadamia nuts and *yabbies* (small freshwater lobsters). Beef is the most popular meat and lamb is also of a high quality. There is a wide variety of excellent fruits and vegetables. Service is European style and varies from waitress and waiter service to self-service. Bistros, cafés, family-style restaurants and 'pub' lunches at the counter offer good food at reasonable prices. Some restaurants will allow guests to bring their own alcohol and are called 'BYO' restaurants. Being a country of immigrants, Australia also offers an enormous variety of cuisines, eg Italian, French, Greek, Spanish, Chinese, Vietnamese, Malaysian, Thai, Japanese, Indian, African, Lebanese and Korean. **Drink:** The major vineyards (wineries) are outside Perth, Sydney, Melbourne, Hobart, Canberra and Adelaide. The largest single wine-making region is in the Barossa Valley, South Australia, two hours drive from Adelaide, where high-quality red and white wines are produced. Most restaurants and all hotels are licensed to serve alcohol; private hotels and guest-houses cannot be by law. Australian wines are good and inexpensive. Beer is served chilled. Licensing hours in public bars 1000-2200 Monday to Saturday, however most pubs are open until 2400; Sunday varies. Restaurants, clubs and hotel lounges have more flexible hours. Drinking age is 18 years or over.
SHOPPING: Special purchases include excellent local wines; wool, clothing and leather and sheepskin products; opal and other precious or semi-precious stones; and modern art sculpture and paintings. Exhibitions of bark paintings, boomerangs and other tribal objects are on view and for sale in Darwin, Alice Springs and the state capitals; many depict stories from the Dreamtime. A brochure titled *Shopping Guide to Australian Crafts* gives crafts outlets in all major cities, their opening hours and the type of goods they offer, and is available free of charge from The Crafts Council of Australia, 35 George Street, The Rocks, Sydney, NSW 2000. Tel: (2) 241 1701. Many cities and towns have small shops devoted to the sale of 'Australiana', where Australian souvenirs, ranging from T-shirts to boomerangs, can be bought. **Shopping hours:** Opening hours for most stores in the cities are 0900-1700 Monday to Thursday, 0900-2100 Friday and 0900-1700 Saturday, except in South Australia and Western Australia where shops are open all day Saturday. Late-night shopping is available on Friday to 2100 in Melbourne, Adelaide, Brisbane, Hobart and Darwin. Late-night shopping is available Thursday at the same time in Sydney, Canberra and Perth. Corner stores, restaurants and snack bars are open in most cities until well into the night.
SPORT: The national sports are **cricket** and **rugby**, both played successfully at international level. Australian-rules football and **European football** are also very popular. **Tennis:** The *Australian Open* is played at the National Tennis Centre in Melbourne early in the year, attracting top tennis players from all over the world. There are also many other tournaments throughout the country and tennis courts are available in most areas for the tennis enthusiast. **Golf:** Some of the world's finest courses can be found in Australia, with spectacular settings and excellent facilities. **Racing:** The main event in the Australian horseracing calendar is the annual *Melbourne Cup*, run on the first Tuesday in November. **Skiing:** Possible during June to August in the mountainous areas of the southeast. One of the best locations is Mount Kosciusko, south of Sydney, at 2126m (7300ft). **Watersports:** Water-skiing, deep-sea fishing, sailing, windsurfing, swimming, surfing and skindiving predominate, especially along the 2500km (1500 miles) of the Great Barrier Reef, where there are numerous tiny islands much used by snorkellers, scuba divers and wildlife enthusiasts. **Special interest holidays:** A huge range of these is available – farming, flying and gliding, ballooning, cycling, rafting, golfing, pony trekking, bushwalking, visiting national parks, gemstone fossicking, etc. For further details, see under the individual state entries below or contact the Australian Tourist Board.
SPECIAL EVENTS: For a selection of festivals and special events occurring in each state and territory throughout Australia during 1993-94 consult the regional sections below.
SOCIAL CONVENTIONS: A largely informal atmosphere prevails; shaking hands is the customary greeting. Casual wear is worn everywhere but the most exclusive restaurants, social gatherings and important business meetings. Some restaurants may have 'no smoking' areas. **Tipping:** Not as common as it is in Europe and America nor is a service charge added to the bill in restaurants. 10% for food and drink waiters is usual in top-quality restaurants, but is optional elsewhere. However, with taxis it is not usual to tip but round up the cost to the next dollar.

BUSINESS PROFILE

ECONOMY: Australia has a highly diverse economy and a standard of living comparable with Western industrialised countries. Manufacturing contributes approximately one-sixth of GDP, principally from iron, steel and engineering. There is a strong agricultural base which contributes 40% of export earnings although the relative importance of this sector has diminished in recent years due to exceptional growth in exploitation of mineral deposits. Australia has vast reserves of coal, oil, natural gas, nickel, zircon, iron ore, bauxite and diamonds (in the Kimberley Mountains). In 1986 Australia overtook the US as the world's leading exporter of coal which now accounts for 15% of export earnings. Uranium is another key export product: Australian ore fuels many of the Western nations' nuclear power plants. Minerals now contribute the largest slice, and petroleum products and agricultural goods contribute roughly equal amounts to the balance of payments. The main agricultural industry, sheep, has suffered a downturn in recent years as textile manufacturers have turned to man-made fibres instead of wool and Arab countries, traditionally major importers of live sheep, have cut their demand for various reasons. Australia's largest trading partner is Japan – both for imports and exports – followed by the United States (a key export market), New Zealand, China and the European Community nations (principally the UK and Germany). Japanese investment in Australia, particularly in property and tourist ventures, accelerated during the late 1980s to the point where large swathes of the eastern seaboard are Japanese-owned. During the 1980s there was a marked shift in Australian trading patterns towards the fast-growing economies of the Pacific Rim, a trend which seems likely to continue. The recession of the late 1980s and early 1990s has hit the Australian economy hard, exemplified by the financial demise of several of Australia's internationally-known entrepreneurs. But the effects go much wider: unemployment is at its highest since the 1930s and several key industries, such as wool, are facing possibly terminal decline. Despite this, Australia's relative proximity to fast-growing Pacific Rim region and its economic compatibility (abundant raw materials in a region where they are, China apart, relatively scarce) should be of great benefit. The large and increasing proportion of Australian trade is now carried out with East Asia and ethnic Asians now account for more than half the recent immmigrants into Australia.
BUSINESS: Suits are necessary in Sydney and Melbourne. Brisbane business people may wear shirts, ties and shorts; visiting business people should wear lightweight suits for initial meeting. Prior appointments necessary. A great deal of business is conducted over drinks. Best months for business travel are March to November. **Office hours:** 0900-1700 Monday to Friday.
COMMERCIAL INFORMATION: The following organisations can offer advice: Australian Chamber of Commerce, PO Box E139, Queen Victoria Terrace, Canberra, ACT 2600. Tel: (6) 285 3523. Fax: (6) 285 3590. Telex: 62507; *or*
International Chamber of Commerce, PO Box E118, Queen Victoria Terrace, Canberra, ACT 2600. Tel: (6) 295 1961. Fax: (6) 295 0170.
Note: Routine commercial enquiries should be directed to the Consulate General. The federal chambers of commerce are able to provide further information. Consult regional entries below.
CONFERENCES/CONVENTIONS: The Australian Tourist Commission (addresses at the beginning of entry) is the first point of contact for information about conferences and conventions in Australia. It publishes a *Meeting Planners' Guide to Australia* which gives extensive information on meeting facilities in all major cities and their surrounding areas, as well as details on the cities themselves and various activities outside the boardroom. There is also a nationwide organisation overseeing conference and convention activity throughout the country: Australian Association of Convention Bureaux, Level 1, 80 William Street, Woolloomooloo, NSW 2011. Tel: (2) 360 3500. Fax: (2) 331 7767. Over 5000 conference and convention establishments belong to this association. More detailed information about specific venues is available from the regional Convention and Visitors' Bureaux in each State and Territory (see regional entries

below). These can also provide details of the many private companies throughout Australia offering conference and convention services.

HISTORY & GOVERNMENT

HISTORY: *Terra Australis*, as the continent was first known to Europeans, is thought to have been inhabited by man for at least 40,000 years. The aboriginal population, whose modern remnants are today known simply as Aborigines, are thought to have migrated from southern India or Sri Lanka but, as theirs is not a written culture, the history of the continent prior to the arrival of Europeans remains a mystery. The first major European settlement was initiated in 1606 by the Dutch East India Company, who charted and claimed for their mother country 320km (200 miles) of the northwest coast which they named New Holland. The explorations of Captain James Cook, 150 years later, opened up the east coast. It was a timely expansion of the British Empire: having just lost her American colonies, Britain was in need of a new prison colony. By 1868, when transportation ended, Britain had sent more than 160,000 convicts to Australia. They were settled around the coast, enabling Britain to claim the whole continent; several of modern Australia's biggest cities grew from penal settlements. The colonisers treated the Aborigines with appalling brutality but as long as European settlement was confined to the coast, the majority of tribes were able to live as before. This ended in 1851 when, following an exodus to the gold fields of California, the administrators sought to stem the tide by offering rewards for the discovery of gold in Australia. The subsequent gold rush prompted the first wave of voluntary migration to the continent in modern times; the population doubled within months of the discovery of gold in Victoria. Around the same time, the interior was charted for the first time while towns sprang up both there and on the littoral. The aboriginals, meanwhile, had been driven into barren areas or, alternatively, into a life of virtual slavery. Most of the colony was granted the right to self-government in the 1850s. The Commonwealth of Australia, a Federation of States, was set up in 1901, establishing Australia as an independent democracy. Close links remained, nonetheless, reflected in the despatch of troops to fight alongside the British during the both World Wars. The politics of the country remained under firm British supervision until years after the Second World War. In the aftermath, Australia assumed some of the trappings of a regional power, taking control of some of Germany's former territories in the area and developing links with Japan, India and South-East Asia. It also joined in a secretive strategic alliance with Britain, the USA, Canada and New Zealand, and this remains the country's principal defence commitment. Between 1949 and 1972, Australian governments were composed of coalitions between the Liberal and Country parties. Sir Robert Menzies was the dominant political figure, serving 16 years as Prime Minister. In 1972, the coalition was finally defeated at the polls and the Labour Party under Gough Whitlam took office with a comparatively radical agenda. There followed one of the most controversial periods of recent Australian history culminating in the Whitlam government being dismissed by the Governor-General, Sir John Kerr, in circumstances still hotly disputed. The immediate beneficiary was the Liberal Party leader, Malcolm Fraser, who won the next elections in December 1975. Fraser remained in office until 1983, when Labour was returned to power under the leadership of the ex-trade union leader Bob Hawke. Under Hawke, Labour won four elections: his principal opposition came from within his own party, particularly from his acerbic Treasury Minister, Paul Keating, who eventually deposed him as leader in 1991. Keating's major priority is to try and guide the country out of recession, and the Liberal-National coalition, headed by Liberal Party leader John Hewson, will confront Labour at the polls early in 1993 as favourite to win. Aboriginal rights have become a major political issue in Australia during the 1980s and recent Labour governments have taken some measures to improve the generally poor circumstances of most Aboriginal lives and to show more sensitivity towards their historic and abused land rights.

GOVERNMENT: Constitutional monarchy with bicameral legislature. Executive power is held by the British Monarch, who appoints the Governor-General. The Federal parliament holds legislative power, led by the Prime Minister, currently the Labour leader Paul Keating. Each state also has its own legislature.

CLIMATE

Australia is in the southern hemisphere and the seasons are opposite to those in Europe and North America. There are two climatic zones: the tropical zone (in the north above the Tropic of Capricorn) and the temperate zone. The tropical zone (consisting of 40% of Australia) has two seasons, summer ('wet') and winter ('dry') and the temperate zone has all four seasons.

November/March: (spring-summer) Warm or hot everywhere, tropical in the north, and warm to hot with mild nights in the south.

April/September: (autumn-winter) Northern and central Australia have clear warm days, cool nights; the south has cool days with occasional rain but still plenty of sun. Snow is totally confined to mountainous regions of the southeast.

Note: For further details, including climate statistics, see under individual state entries.

Required clothing: Lightweights during summer months with warmer clothes during the cooler winter period in most of the southern states. Lightweight cottons and linens all year in the central/northern states with warm clothes only for cooler winter evenings and early mornings. Sunglasses, sunhats and sunblock lotion are recommended year round in the north and during the summer months in the south.

AUSTRALIAN CAPITAL TERRITORY

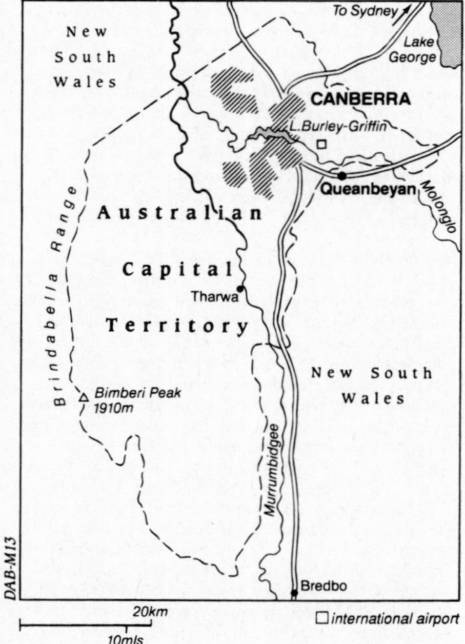

ACT Tourism Commission
Level 8, CBS Towers
Cnr Akuna and Bunda Streets
Canberra, ACT 2600
Australia
Tel: (6) 205 0666. Fax: (6) 205 0629.

British High Commission
Consular Section
Level 10, CBS Tower
Corner Akuma and Bunda Streets
Canberra City, ACT 2601
Australia
Tel: (6) 257 2434 (passports) *or* 257 1982 (entry clearances). Fax: (6) 257 5857. Telex: 7162690.

AREA: 2438 sq km (1511 sq miles).
POPULATION: 284,412 (1990).
POPULATION DENSITY: 115 per sq km.
CAPITAL: Canberra (also national capital).
Population: 281,572 (1990).

GEOGRAPHY: Canberra is located in New South Wales on the western slopes of the Great Dividing Range, and was conceived in the early 1900s in order to create a capital city in a federal state separate from any of the uniting states. Roughly half the population is under 26. Spectacular green countryside is ringed by mountains nearly 600m (2000ft) above sea level. Lake Burley Griffin, a man-made lake, is now the main feature of this constantly expanding modern capital. Hills, trees and greenery remain prominent among the architecture of a city that is attractive, tidy, spacious and efficient as befits the national capital city, although it somewhat lacks the charm of slow historical development.

TIME: GMT + 10 (GMT + 11 from October to March).

PUBLIC HOLIDAYS

The following Public Holidays are observed in the Australian Capital Territory:
Mar 1 '93 Trades & Labour Day. **Mar 15** Canberra Day. **Apr 9-12** Easter. **Apr 26** Anzac Day. **Jun 14** Queen's Birthday. **Aug 2** Bank Holiday. **Oct 4** Labour Day. **Dec 25** Christmas Day. **Dec 27** Boxing Day. **Jan 1 '94** New Year's Day. **Jan 3** New Year additional holiday. **Jan 26** Australia Day. **Mar 7** Trades & Labour Day. **Mar 21** Canberra Day.

TRAVEL

AIR: Until recently there were no direct international flights to Canberra. However, *Britannia Airways* have introduced direct flights to the city from Luton Airport, north of London. These are charter flights, running approximately twice a month (November-March) via Cairns or Adelaide. Travel by air to Canberra is also possible via direct flights from Sydney and Melbourne. The city centre is 8km (5 miles) from Canberra Airport. Canberra is part of a national network of internal flights.

RAIL: Through trains run from Canberra to Sydney and Melbourne, with connections to other states. Economy *Aussiepass* tickets apply on both local and interstate systems.

ROAD: Main road links, which are used by coach services, connect Canberra to Sydney (travel time – 4 hrs, 15 mins) and to Melbourne (travel time – 14 hrs, 30 mins), thereby allowing access to all other parts of the country. *Aussiepass* and *Eaglepass* tickets apply.

URBAN: Bus: An internal bus network operates for the city of Canberra. Pre-purchase day tickets and 10-journey multi-tickets are available. There is a *Canberra Explorer Bus* linking major attractions in the city that visitors can board or depart from at any point. **Taxis:** Radio-controlled, metered taxis are available at all hours.

ACCOMMODATION

Note: More detailed coverage of the range of accommodation available in Australia may be found by consulting the *Accommodation* section in the general entry for Australia above.

HOTELS: Accommodation includes international chain hotels such as those run by Trusthouse Forte and Hilton. There are also small private hotels and it is possible to stay at several of the Territory's sheep stations.

CAMPING/CARAVANNING: A number of companies can arrange **motor camper** rentals, with a range of fully equipped vehicles. Full details can be obtained from the Tourist Board.

RESORTS & EXCURSIONS

Canberra is an elegant city of wide streets, gardens and parkland. The old *Parliament House* is impressive enough, but has been surpassed by its replacement, a grand modern edifice completed in 1988, Australia's bicentennial year. The *War Memorial*, Byzantine in style, constructed from cream-coloured sandstone with a copper dome, is deservedly the city's most popular attraction, and is the scene of the annual Anzac Parade. *Lake Burley Griffin*, a vast man-made waterway named after Canberra's architect, features prominently throughout the city area. Cruises and boating are popular. Near *Tidbinbilla Deep Space Tracking Station*, 70km (40 miles) southeast of the city, is *Tidbinbilla Nature Reserve* where visitors have the opportunity to hand-feed kangaroos. The *Canberra Space Centre* contains model spacecraft and space photographs. *Blundell's Cottage*, which pre-dates the lake, is a stone-slab construction calling to mind the location's earlier incarnation as a sheep station.

The new *Museum of Australia*, north of the lake, will be a further cultural addition to the present *Australian National Gallery*, *National Library* and *National Science and Technology Centre*.

There are several hills in the immediate area of Canberra; from the 195m *Telecom Telecommunications Tower*, topping the 825m-high *Black Mountain*, there is an excellent view of the area for those who don't feel dizzy in revolving restaurants (meal optional).

Helicopter and ballooning trips provide other ways of taking in the view.

The *Snowy Mountains* are to the south of Canberra, in New South Wales, and provide excellent opportunities for winter skiing and summertime pursuits such as bush-walking, horse-riding and watersports. Trips from Canberra can be arranged.

SOCIAL PROFILE

FOOD: Restaurants and hotels serve trout from the streams and lakes of the Snowy Mountains. Beef and lamb come from the farmlands surrounding Canberra. ACT *Barbecue and Picnic Facilities* is a brochure giving details of 60 picnic locations in Canberra.
NIGHTLIFE: Despite the daytime orderliness, nightlife is actively promoted by the large range of pubs, restaurants and nightclubs. There are many film shows.
SHOPPING: A wide range of goods, including Australian arts and crafts, is available from department stores and specialist shops. Galleries and museums are often open outside normal trading hours.
Shopping hours: Opening hours for most stores in the city are 0900-1730 Monday to Thursday, 0900-2100 Friday and 0900-1600 Saturday.
SPORT: The state follows the national passion for **football**, **cricket** and **rugby**, and Lake Burley Griffin gives facilities for all aspects of **watersports. Skiing** is possible during the winter months at high altitudes in the mountains. Tours from Canberra provide the tourist with the opportunity to visit working sheep properties with demonstrations of **sheep-mustering, sheep-shearing** and even **boomerang** throwing.
SPECIAL EVENTS: The following is a selection of events and festivals taking place in Australian Capital Territory:
Mar 6-15 '93 *Canberra Festival*, Canberra; *Canberra Balloon Festival*, Parliament House. **Mar 7** *Black Opal Stakes Horseraces*, Canberra. **Mar 23-28** *Australian Swimming Championships*, ACT. **Sep 18-Oct 17** *Floriade*, Canberra. **Oct** *Australian Theatre Festival*, Canberra Theatre Centre.
For a full list of special events contact the Canberra Tourist Bureau.

BUSINESS PROFILE

COMMERCIAL INFORMATION: The following organisation can offer advice: Canberra Chamber of Commerce Inc, Level 6, 54 Marcus Clarke Street, Canberra, ACT 2600. Tel: (6) 247 3888. Fax: (6) 257 3648.
CONFERENCES/CONVENTIONS: Canberra has recently completed its National Convention Centre with seating facilities for 2500. Other major convention centres include Australian Institute of Sport, Park Hyatt Pavilion and Capital Parkroyal. For more information on conferences and conventions in Australian Capital Territory contact the Australian Tourist Commission *or* the Canberra Visitors & Convention Bureau, Unit 1, JAA House, 19 Napier Close, Deakin, ACT 2601. Tel: (6) 385 3900. Fax: (6) 282 2725.

CLIMATE

Very warm with little rainfall during summer months. Winters can be cold and snow may fall occasionally. Rainfall can be heavy in winter.
Required clothing: Lightweights during summer months with warmer mediumweight clothes necessary in winter. Waterproofing advisable throughout the year, especially in winter.

CANBERRA, ACT (559m)

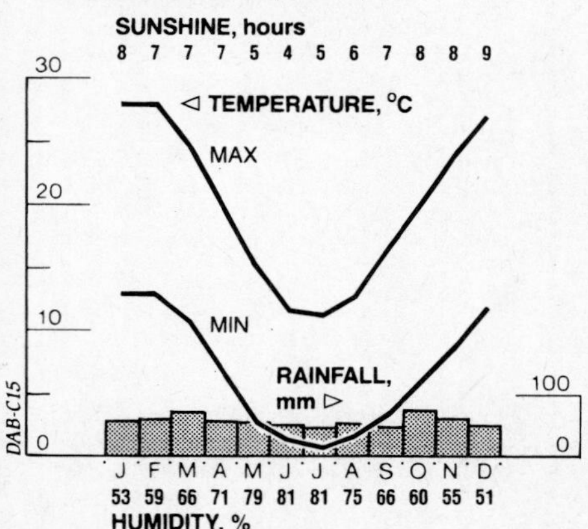

NEW SOUTH WALES

New South Wales Travel Centre
19 Castlereagh Street
Sydney, NSW 2001
Australia
Tel: (2) 231 4444. Fax: (2) 232 6080.
New South Wales Tourism Commission
5th & 6th Floors
140 George Street
Sydney, NSW 2000
Tel: (2) 931 1111. Fax: (2) 931 1424.
New South Wales Tourism Commission
7th Floor, 75 King William Street
London EC4N 7HA
Tel: (071) 522 0306. Fax: (071) 522 0309.
British Consulate-General
Level 16, The Gateway
1 MacQuarie Place
Sydney Cove
Sydney, NSW 2000
Australia
Tel: (2) 247 7521 *or* 247 9731 (consular section). Fax: (2) 233 1826. Telex: 71 20680 BRITN AA.

AREA: 801,600 sq km (309,417 sq miles).
POPULATION: 5,844,900 (1990).
POPULATION DENSITY: 7.3 per sq km.
CAPITAL: Sydney. **Population:** 3,656,900 (1990).
GEOGRAPHY: The landscape ranges from the subtropical north to the Snowy Mountains in the south. There are over 1300km (800 miles) of coastline with golden beaches, and picturesque waterways and rivers include the 1900km (1200-mile) River Murray.
TIME: GMT + 10 (GMT + 11 from October to March) except in the Broken Hill Area which keeps GMT + 9.5.

PUBLIC HOLIDAYS

The following Public Holidays are observed in New South Wales:
Apr 9-12 '93 Easter. **Apr 26** Anzac Day. **Jun 14** Queen's Birthday. **Aug 2** Bank Holiday. **Oct 4** Labour Day. **Dec 25** Christmas Day. **Dec 27** Boxing Day. **Dec 28** Christmas Day Holiday. **Jan 1 '94** New Year's Day. **Jan 3** New Year additional holiday. **Jan 26** Australia Day.

TRAVEL

AIR: Sydney is an international gateway to Australia, and international flights from Europe, New Zealand, Asia, Africa and the Americas all serve the city. Flights to and from Europe take about 24 hours. The main domestic airlines operating in New South Wales are: *Aeropelican (PO)*, *Aquatic Air (Seaplane)*, *Crane Air (FD)*, *Eastern Airlines (UN)*, *Hazelton Air Services (ZL)*, *Kendall Airlines (KD)*, *Macknight Airlines (MT)*, *Norfolk Airlines (UG)*, *Oxley Airlines (VQ)*, *Yanda Air Services (ST)*, *Sunstate Airlines (OF)*, *Western NSW Airlines (FO)*, *Ansett NSW (WX)*, *Ansett Airlines (AN)* and *Australian Airlines (TN)*.
Airports: *Kingsford Smith* is Sydney's international airport; it is 11km (7 miles) from the city centre (travel time – 35 minutes). For more information, see general introduction to Australia above.
SEA: Sydney is a major international port, and cruise lines call from Europe, the Far East and the USA. There are also many day and half-day cruises from Sydney Harbour, offering everything from sightseeing tours to nearby attractions such as wildlife and aboriginal communities, the Blue Mountains and the Hunter Valley wine region, to night-time cabaret showboats.
RAIL: Sydney has through trains to all other state capitals. An internal system of railways runs throughout the state, connecting all the most important towns, tourist resorts and running through to Canberra in the south. Fast *XPT* trains run on some routes.
ROAD: Sydney is the focal point of a network that connects every major city. Road distances from many places, however, are enormous, and a journey by even the fastest coach to Darwin, on the northern coast, takes over 92 hours. The state is well served with an excellent road system, as required by the most heavily populated region of the country. Main highways are the *Barrier Highway*, running west to Adelaide, the *Hume Highway* running south to Canberra and Melbourne, the *New England Highway* running north to Brisbane, the *Pacific Highway* running along the coast to Brisbane and Melbourne, and the *Mitchell Highway* running northeast to Charleville and connecting to the routes to Mount Isa and Darwin in the north. The state is well served by national coach operators and regional bus lines.
URBAN: Sydney's extensive electrified suburban **rail** network includes a city centre underground link and a monorail link. There are also **bus** and **ferry** services. Weekly and other period passes are available, as are multi-journey tickets. The Sydney Explorer Bus stops at over 20 attractions on its route and visitors can join or leave it at any point. A special *Sydney Pass*, valid for three days, offers unlimited travel in Sydney on buses, ferries, harbour cruises, the Sydney Explorer Bus and the Airport Express Bus for A$35.

ACCOMMODATION

HOTELS: Sydney offers excellent hotels run by all the international chains, and many medium to small houses. Further outside the city you can stay on one of the sheep stations to the west of the capital among some of the best sheep country in the world. The state is well travelled by the native Australians, and so offers an excellent network of accommodation outside the larger cities, mostly of motel or similar class.
CAMPING/CARAVANNING: A number of companies can arrange **motor camper** rentals, with a range of fully equipped vehicles. Full details can be obtained from the Tourist Board.
Note: For more detailed coverage of the range of accommodation available in Australia, see the *Accommodation* section in the general entry for Australia above.

SYDNEY

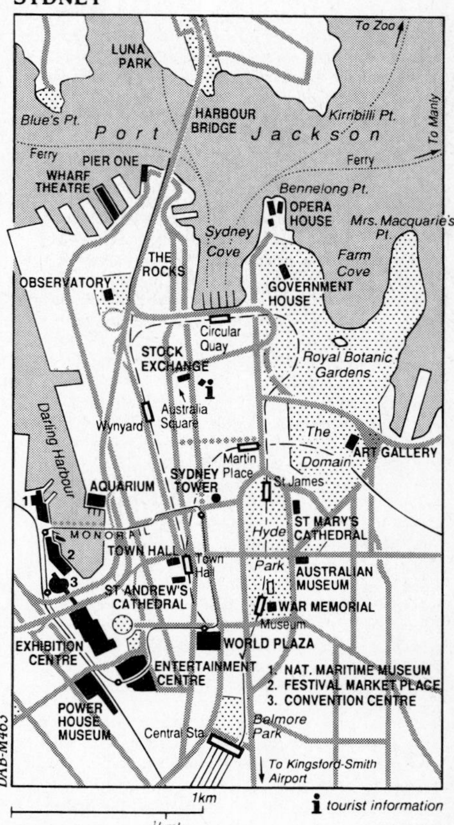

RESORTS & EXCURSIONS

New South Wales is perhaps the most varied of all the states; the landscape ranges from snow-capped mountains with excellent skiing facilities to long, golden sandy beaches, and from the utter emptiness of the Outback to the cosmopolitan vitality of the state capital.
Sydney: The state capital is perhaps best known abroad for the *Opera House*, a building whose distinctive shape is echoed by the sails of the boats in the almost equally famous harbour. Tours of the Opera House are available every day (0900-1600), except Christmas Day and Good Friday. Sydney is also a major commercial and business centre with first-class conference and exhibition facilities. The city centre skyline rivals that of Manhattan, with the added attraction that Sydney is far more likely to be seen under a clear blue sky. There is a spectacular view of the city and its surroundings from the 305m (1000ft) high *Sydney Tower* above the Centrepoint Shopping Complex (opening times: 0930-2130 Monday to Friday, 0900-1130 Saturday). The city itself is also the home of more than enough concert halls, museums, art galleries and theatres to lay the ghost forever of Australia as a cultural wasteland. Among the many other interesting sights Sydney has to offer are the *Taronga Park Zoo*, the *Royal Botanic Gardens*, the *Harbour Bridge*, the *Art Gallery of New South Wales*, the *Australian Museum* and *The Rocks* area (the birthplace of the country) now restored to its original state – cobbled streets, gas lamps, craft shops and tiny restaurants. Apart from exploring the various quarters on foot, such as *Chinatown*, *Paddington*, *Kings Cross*, all bustling with life 24 hours a day, and *Darling Harbour*, Sydney's premier urban development project featuring exhibition halls, museums, gardens, an aquarium, restaurants and a shopping complex, the city can also be enjoyed from the water with numerous harbour cruises departing from Circular Quay. Other ways of seeing the city are from the bright red *Sydney Explorer* bus which stops at 20 popular tourist spots on its 18km (11-mile) loop around the city (cost: A$10) or from the monorail train. Sydney is also justly famous for its many excellent beaches in and around the city, such as *Manly*, to the north (15 minutes by hydrofoil), or *Watson's Bay*, to the south. Most beaches are within reach of public transport. For reasons of safety, swim in the areas marked with flags only.
Nearby *Botany Bay*, the first foothold of British settlers, is still a botanist's delight with mangrove swamps and native wildlife.
Outside Sydney: New South Wales caters for all kinds of holiday, whatever the time of year. The region of *Mount Kosciusko* and the *Snowy Mountains* in the southeast of the state is popular during the skiing season (June to September). In summer bushwalking is a popular activity in this region; cruises are offered to *Grace Lea Island* on *Lake Eucumbene*. Resorts in the Snowy Mountain region include *Charlotte Pass*, *Guthega*, *Perisher Valley*, *Thredbo* and *Smiggin Holes*. For those in search of sun, the beaches in the state are excellent – Sydney's famous surf beaches of *Bondi*, *Avalon* and *Palm Beach* are matched by the resorts to the south and to the north above Port Jackson. Visits to the *Hunter Valley* wine district and the *Kuring-gai Chase National Park* with its Koala Sanctuary are also recommended. To the west of Sydney are the *Blue Mountains* and the *Warrumbungle National Park* with its bizarre rock outcrops. *Lightning Ridge*, to the northwest, is a frontier town where the world's only source of black opal is to be found. *Broken Hill*, close to the state frontier with South Australia, is another mining town, now with golf courses, swimming pools and bowling clubs. 113km (70 miles) from the town, by a good road, are the *Menindee Lakes*, an area of water eight times the size of Sydney Harbour and a major attraction for motor boat and sailing craft owners.
Norfolk Island: Situated 1400km (870 miles) off the east coast of Australia, Norfolk Island is best reached by plane from Sydney. Its history as a penal colony has left the island with some of Australia's finest Georgian colonial architecture. Many of the island's small population are directly related to the mutineers of *HMS Bounty* who settled in the area. A variety of accommodation is available. **Note:** Norfolk Island comes under the control of the Australian government not New South Wales.
Lord Howe Island: Situated 700km (400 miles) northeast of Sydney, Lord Howe Island is made up of 1300 sq hectares of both rich low land and mountains covered with lush vegetation, surrounded by white sandy beaches. It also has the southernmost coral reef in the world and boasts some of the rarest flora, bird and marine life to be found anywhere.

SOCIAL PROFILE

FOOD & DRINK: International cuisine, with local speciality seafood. Fine red and white wines from the Hunter Valley.
NIGHTLIFE: The Kings Cross area of Sydney is an exciting nightlife area. There are also some night-time cruises offering dinner and dancing. Sydney is known as a city that never sleeps.
SHOPPING: Best buys are Australian opals and gemstones, Aboriginal arts and crafts, and woollen and sheepskin goods. In Sydney, shops are open 0830-1730 Monday to Friday and 0830-1600 Saturday, and many shops also stay open until 2100 Thursday and 1000-1600 Sunday.
SPORT: The coastline of New South Wales has some of the best **surfing** conditions in the world, stretching for over 2000km (1250 miles) to the north and south of Sydney, and the port itself has facilities for all kinds of **maritime sports**. Of note is the annual **boat race** from Sydney to Hobart in Tasmania in December, covering over 2000km (1250 miles). South of Sydney are the mountains of the Great Dividing Range, with Australia's highest mountain, Mount Kosciusko, at 2139m (7314ft), offering **skiing** from June to September.
SPECIAL EVENTS: The following is a selection of festivals and special events taking place in New South Wales:
Mar 13 '93 *Toohey's Canterbury Guinness Stakes & Cup Horseracing*. **Apr** *Australian Motorcycle Grand Prix*, Eastern Creek. **Apr 2-13** *Royal Easter Agricultural Show*, Sydney. **Apr 9-12** *Griffith Food & Wine Festival*, Griffith. **May** *Manly Food & Wine Festival*, Manly Beach. **Jun** *Sydney Film Festival*, Sydney. **Jun 9-10** *Darling Harbour Jazz Festival*, Tumbalong Park. **Sep 26** *Grand Final Football/Rugby League*, Sydney. **Nov** *PGA Golf Tournament*, Windsor. **Nov 16-18** *Horticultural Field Day*, Orange. **Mar 25-Apr 5 '94** *Royal Easter Show*, Homebush.
For a full list of special events contact the New South Wales Tourism Commission.

BUSINESS PROFILE

COMMERCIAL INFORMATION: The following organisation can offer advice: State Chamber of Commerce and Industry, PO Box 4280, 93 York Street, GPO Sydney, NSW 2001. Tel: (2) 290 5400. Fax: (2) 290 3278. Telex: 127113.
CONFERENCES/CONVENTIONS: Sydney has launched a major initiative to become an important convention and meeting destination. The Sydney Convention and Exhibition Centre at Darling Harbour has facilities for up to 5000 people. Other major convention centres include Centrepoint Exhibition and Convention Centre, University of NSW, RAS Exhibition Centre, Sydney Opera House, Powerhouse Museum, Sydney Town Hall, University of Sydney, YWCA, Queen Victoria Building, Bankstown Town Hall, Bondi Surf Bathers' Life Saving Club, Curzon Hall, Film Australia, Hills Centre, Taronga Centre and the NSW Harness Racing Club. For more information on conferences and conventions in NSW contact the Australian Tourist Commission *or* the Sydney Convention & Visitors Bureau, Level 13, 80 William Street, Woolloomooloo, NSW 2011. Tel: (2) 331 4045. Fax: (2) 360 1223.

CLIMATE

Warm semi-tropical summers particularly in lower central area. Mountains in the west are cooler, particularly in winter. Rainfall is heaviest from March to June.
Required clothing: Lightweight cottons and linens in summer months. Warmer clothes are needed in winter, although temperatures can be high.

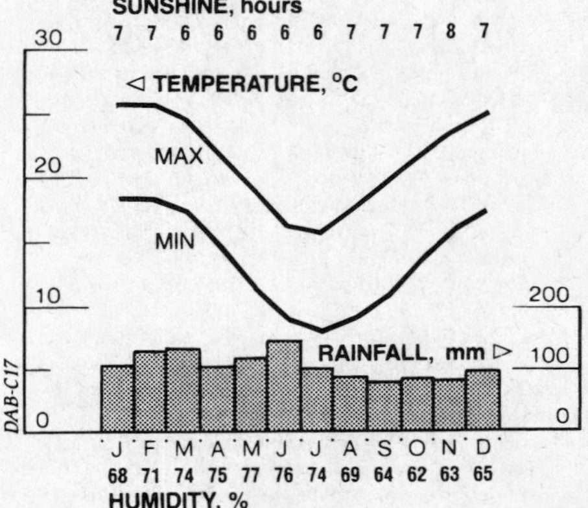

NORTHERN TERRITORY

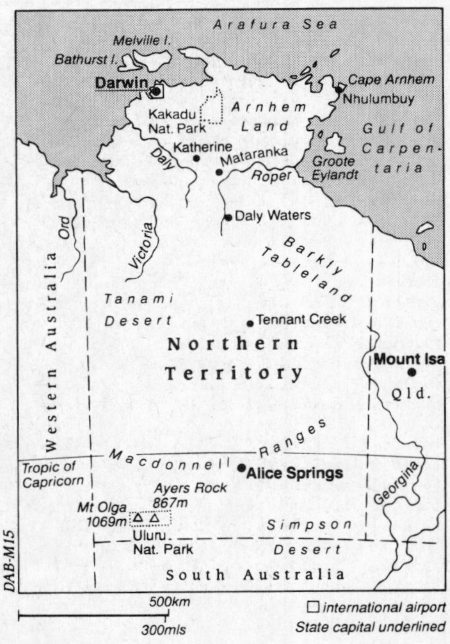

Northern Territory Tourist Commission
PO Box 2532
67 Stuart Highway
Alice Springs, NT 0870
Australia
Tel: (89) 518 555.
Northern Territory Tourist Commission
Suite 1230, 12th Floor
2121 Avenue of the Stars
Los Angeles, CA 90067
Tel: (310) 277 7877. Fax: (213) 277 3061. Telex: 3720296.

AREA: 1,346,200 sq km (836,659 sq miles).
POPULATION: 157,800 (1990).
POPULATION DENSITY: 0.1 per sq km.
CAPITAL: Darwin. **Population:** 73,300 (1990).
GEOGRAPHY: A wilderness roughly 1670km (1038 miles) north–south and 1000km (620 miles) east–west, the Northern Territory comprises nearly one-sixth of Australia. The geography of the Northern Territory is the closest to the popular image of the Great Australian Outback.
The northern area centred on the capital, **Darwin**, is tropical with rich vegetation and a varied coastline. Beyond Darwin, 200km (125 miles) east, is World Heritage-listed *Kakadu National Park*, which is part of the 12,600 sq km (4500 sq-mile) area of Arnhem Land. It is an area of vast flood plains and rocky escarpments steeped in natural and cultural heritage. Aboriginal peoples have lived here for at least 40,000 years. Katherine township is 350km (220 miles) from Darwin and a further 30km (20 miles) northeast is *Katherine Gorge National Park* with 13 gorges towering up to 60m (200ft) high.
The southern part of the Northern Territory is centred on the town of **Alice Springs**, which is almost at the geographical centre of Australia and the starting point of many of the Red Centre's unique and natural wonders, including Ayers Rock and the Uluru National Park. Other notable features of the Red Centre are King's Canyon, Ross River, Trephina, Ormiston and Glen Helen Gorge, the Olgas near Ayers Rock and the Devil's Marbles at Tennant Creek. There are also other parks and reserves with abundant bird and animal life.
TIME: GMT + 9.5 (GMT + 10.5 from October to March).

PUBLIC HOLIDAYS

The following Public Holidays are observed in the Northern Territory:
Apr 9-12 '93 Easter. **Apr 26** Anzac Day. **May 3** May Day. **Jun 14** Queen's Birthday. **Jul 2*** Alice Springs Show Day. **Jul 9*** Tennant Creek Show Day. **Jul 16*** Katherine Show Day. **Jul 23*** Darwin Show Day. **Aug 2** Picnic Day. **Dec 27** Christmas Day. **Dec 28** Boxing Day.

Jan 1 '94 New Year's Day. **Jan 3** New Year additional holiday. **Jan 26** Australia Day.
Note [*]: Regional observance only.

TRAVEL

AIR: The Northern Territory can be reached by international flights to Darwin from the UK, Singapore, Bangkok, Bali, Brunei and Timor. At present there are six international carriers operating to the Northern Territory. Flying time from the United Kingdom is approximately 22 hours, from Singapore approximately 3 hours, from Bangkok approximately 5 hours, from Bali approximately 90 minutes, from Brunei approximately 4 hours and from Timor approximately 2 hours. Connections are available from most Asian ports.
Darwin Airport is 8km (5 miles) from the city centre (travel time –approximately 15 minutes).
Alice Springs Airport is 12km (7.5 miles) from the city centre (travel time – approximately 20 minutes).
There are three domestic airlines (*Australian Airlines, Ansett* and *East-West*) that cover the Territory from all capital cities within Australia with connections from most other towns. Smaller commuter airlines connect some of the remoter areas within the Territory.
SEA: International cruise lines call at Darwin, the Northern Territory's only large port.
RAIL: The main rail service to the Territory is by the *Ghan* from Adelaide which reaches only as far as Alice Springs. There is no internal network.
ROAD: There are three main highways serving the Northern Territory: the *Stuart Highway*, south to Adelaide, Canberra, Melbourne and Sydney; the *Barkly Highway*, east to Mount Isa and Queensland; and the *Victoria Highway*, west to join an unsealed road running across the top of the Western Desert which runs on to Perth. Off these roads there are many uncharted rough tracks often only suitable for 4-wheel drive vehicles, and often ending in impassable desert. The dangers of travelling off main roads in the Northern Territory without a qualified guide cannot be stressed too strongly. **Coach:** The national coach services are run by *Ansett Pioneer, Greyhound* and *Bus Australia*, all of which serve the main townships within the Territory with direct services to all capital cities. Well-equipped coaches take over 92 hours to cover the distance from Darwin to Sydney; from Darwin, coaches depart daily to Kakadu National Park (travel time – 4 hrs, 50 mins) and to Alice Springs (travel time – 19 hours).
URBAN: There are local bus services in Darwin and Alice Springs Monday to Saturday. Darwin Harbour ferries operate Monday to Friday.

ACCOMMODATION

The *Northern Territory Holiday Planner*, published by the Northern Territory Tourist Commission, gives details of tours, holidays and accommodation in the Territory.
HOTELS: International standard hotels are found in Darwin, Alice Springs and Ayers Rock, and a good standard of hotel and motel accommodation can be found in all the major tourist areas and centres of population.
LODGE/MOTEL: Lodges and budget motels are available in some of the remote areas.
CAMPING/CARAVANNING: The Northern Territory contains some of the most inhospitable country in the world. From Alice Springs the nearest major town, in any direction, is 1000km (620 miles) away; clearly, any car or caravan must be in prime mechanical condition. During the wet season from November to April, travel in the Outback is advisable only in suitable cross-country vehicles, as many conventional roads become impassable for ordinary cars. The *Stuart Highway* between Darwin and Alice Springs and through to Adelaide in South Australia is a fully sealed road accessible all year. A number of companies can arrange **motor camper** rentals, with a range of fully equipped vehicles. Full details can be obtained from the Tourist Commission.

RESORTS & EXCURSIONS

The Northern Territory is a huge and diverse region. The north, the 'Top End' of Australia, is subtropical, with such high rainfall in the rainy season that much of it is accessible only by air. The south of the territory is an arid desert, known as the 'Red Centre'.
Aboriginal lands and sacred sites: There are many places and objects in the Territory that are of special significance to the Aboriginal people and laws protecting these sacred sites carry heavy penalties for entering, damaging or defacing them. It is necessary to obtain a permit before entering Aboriginal lands. These permits are not issued lightly, nor are they generally issued for touristic purposes. Some areas that have historic significance to the Aborigines *are* open to the public (for example, Ayers Rock and Corroboree Rock near Alice Springs, and Ubirr Rock in Kakadu National Park – see below). Visitors are welcome at these places but due respect should be shown for the site and its historical significance. For further information, maps and permit applications advice, contact the Tourist Commission at their London office.

The Top End

The territorial capital, **Darwin**, which was savaged by Cyclone Tracy on Christmas Eve 1974, has been rebuilt as a modern provincial city. Darwin and the rest of the Top End has two distinct seasons. In the summer or 'Wet' season, from November to April, monsoon conditions mean late afternoon thunderstorms, high humidity and heavy downpours. This is the green season when the waterfalls flow and the wildlife abounds. From May through to October is the 'Dry' season, with unlimited sunshine and balmy evenings. The wetlands begin to dry out, confining the bird and animal life to ever smaller areas.
The Top End is the area to see lush tropical vegetation, either in Darwin's *Botanical Gardens*, the *Crocodile Farm* just outside Darwin, the Territory's various National Parks, or at **Katherine Gorge** on the road south (see below). Also south of Darwin are the **Howard Springs** and **Berry Springs** Nature Parks, **Territory Wild Life Park** and the **Fogg Dam** bird sanctuary. There are many good opportunities for swimming and fishing near the city, for example at **Mindil Beach**, **Mandorah Beach** or **Fannre Bay**.
KAKADU NATIONAL PARK: This may be found about a 2-hour drive to the east of Darwin down the Arnhem Highway. The park includes the flood plains between the Wildman and the Alligator rivers which empty into Van Diemen Gulf to the north. It is bordered by the **Arnhem Land escarpment**, where the spectacular waterfalls of *Jim Jim* and *Twin Falls* cascade hundreds of feet into crystal clear rock pools below. At **Ubirr** (Obiri Rock) and **Nourlangie Rock** are fascinating galleries of Aboriginal rock painting, many dating back over 20,000 years. These paintings show mythical and spiritual figures and an ancient lifestyle which still holds great significance for the Aboriginal people today.
Within the park there are three resort-style hotels and a number of camping and caravan sites from which to explore this beautiful area. Numerous creeks, rivers and *billabongs* provide excellent fishing, particularly for the much prized *barramundi*, which is found in abundance here. Thousands of birds inhabit the wetlands – over 260 species – and wildlife abounds throughout the year. Aerial tours over the Arnhem Land escarpment depart daily and local fishing trips can be easily arranged. A popular way to explore the waterways is on a boat cruise on the *South Alligator River* or scenic *Yellow Waters*, giving access to nature at its best. It is possible to spot crocodiles basking on the riverbanks, buffaloes wallowing in the mud, and the graceful *jabiru* (Australia's only stork) wading amongst the water lilies. Kakadu National Park is the habitat for all wildlife common to Northern Australia and as such provides a diverse and exciting experience in the tropical Top End. Tours and safaris from 2 to 21 days are available by air, coach or 4-wheel drive from Darwin.
KATHERINE GORGE/NITMILUK NATIONAL PARK: The township of Katherine is in the area known as the 'Never Never' about 350km (220 miles) southeast of Darwin. This is pioneer territory, made famous by Mrs Aeneas Gunn in her book *We of the Never Never*. This is the centre of a thriving beef cattle industry and the *Old Elsey* and *Springvale Homesteads* are monuments to the Outback settlers who founded the original township. Katherine Gorge, some 30km (20 miles) northeast of the town, is one of Australia's great natural wonders and the famous boat cruises through the spectacular gorges, towering up to 60m (200ft) high, are a highlight of any visit to the region. There are in fact 13 gorges and each has its own glowing colours and fascinating outcrops, steep canyon walls above cool, blue waters. Marked walking tracks are well maintained for easy access to features of interest in the park. Canoeing, swimming and boat tours are all available along with scenic helicopter rides over the gorges. There is a good range of accommodation both in the town and Nitmiluk National Park and campers and caravanners are also well catered for.

The Red Centre

Alice Springs is located in what is almost the geographic centre of the continent. A pleasant solid town, set in red desert country, it is a popular tourist resort and a base for exploring the wonders of the Outback. There are many excellent hotels and motels, a casino, a variety of restaurants and varied sporting facilities ranging from golf and tennis to hot-air ballooning and tandem parachuting. The *Royal Flying Doctor Base* is open most days to the public (excluding Sundays and public holidays) and the *School of the Air* is operational during the school term; visiting hours are 1330-1530 Monday to Friday. There are also museums and preserved buildings which help the visitor to appreciate the history of this remote town. Not least among these are the *Dreamtime Gallery* and the *Centre for Aboriginal Artists and Craftsmen*. The *Old Telegraph Station*, 3km (2 miles) north of the town, is an historical reserve featuring original buildings, restored equipment and an illustrated display including early photographs, papers and documents.
The region around Alice Springs is pitted with colourful gorges, canyons, valley pools and awe-inspiring chasms. These include **Stanley Chasm**, 50km (30 miles) west of Alice, **Glen Helen Gorge**, 140km (9 miles) west, **Ormiston Gorge**, 130km (80 miles) west, Kings Canyon, 310km (186 miles) and **N'Dhala Gorge,** 90km (5.5 miles) east, which is also notable for its ancient rock engravings. **Palm Valley** lies around an hour's drive to the southwest and **Rainbow Valley** to the southeast on the edge of the **Simpson Desert**.
Anzac Hill lies just behind Alice Springs and provides a panoramic view of the town and surrounding ranges. **Château Hornsby**, the Northern Territory's only vineyard, is situated approximately 15km (9 miles) from the town centre and is an unusual venue for barbecues, Outback evenings, Aboriginal Corroborees and even camel safaris.
AYERS ROCK: Alice Springs is also the base for tours to **Ayers Rock** (about 450km (280 miles) or five hours drive away) and the East and Western **MacDonnell Ranges.** Ayers Rock is the world's largest monolith and plays an important part in Aboriginal mythology in which it is known as 'Uluru' and is believed to have been created by ancestors of the Aborigines.
Visitors may climb the rock or explore some of the fascinating caves at its base. Sunset and sunrise must be seen as the sun's rays change the rock's colour from blazing orange to red and even deep purple, depending on the atmospheric conditions.
14km (9 miles) from Ayers Rock is the **Ayers Rock Resort** – a village built to cater for the rapidly growing number of visitors to the area. The resort contains two top-class hotels, lodges, self-catering maisonettes, shops, bank, post office, caravan park and campsites and caters for all the needs of the traveller. Tours depart throughout the day for the Rock and the nearby **Olgas**, as well as other points of interest.
Ayers Rock has its own airport with five daily flights to Alice Springs and direct connections to Sydney and other Australian cities. Car hire is available and all major coach companies service Ayers Rock on a daily basis.
Other points of interest in the Red Centre include Aboriginal tours to **Ipolera** and **Pitjantjatjara** country; and the **Ross River Homestead** for horseriding, log cabins and Outback ambience.

SOCIAL PROFILE

FOOD: *Barramundi* is the local speciality.
NIGHTLIFE: There is plenty of exciting nightlife in Darwin, which also offers the *Diamond Beach Casino*, built in an extraordinary modern architectural style. This 30-million-dollar casino complex also encompasses luxury accommodation, restaurants, discos and sporting and convention facilities and is surrounded by lush gardens perched along the shores of Mindil Beach. Alice Springs also has a casino.
SHOPPING: Darwin specialties include Aboriginal artefacts and Outback clothing. Aboriginal items, bush clothing and opals are available in Alice Springs.
SPECIAL EVENTS: The following is a selection of festivals and special events taking place in the Northern Territory:
Mar 27-Apr 3 '93 *National Track Cycling Championships*, Alice Springs. **Apr 9-12** *Gemboree 93*, Alice Springs. **Apr 24-May 1** *Arafura Sports Festival*, Marrara. **May** *Aussie Masters Swim Championships*, Darwin. **Jul** *Darwin to Ambon Yacht Race*, Darwin.
For a full list of special events contact the Northern Territory Tourist Commission.

BUSINESS PROFILE

COMMERCIAL INFORMATION: The following organisation can offer advice: Northern Territory Confederation of Industry and Commerce Inc, PO Box 1825, 5/2 Shepherd Street, Darwin, NT 0800. Tel: (89) 815 755. Fax: (89) 811 405.
CONFERENCES/CONVENTIONS: Major convention centres in Darwin are The Beaufort Hotel, Darwin Performing Arts Centre, Diamond Beach Hotel Casino, Marrara International Indoor Sports Stadium and the Sheraton Darwin. In Alice Springs, the major convention centres are Arulen Arts Centre and Sheraton Alice

Springs. There are also a number of resort convention facilities outside of the cities, such as the Sheraton Ayers Rock and Yulara Resort. For more information on conferences and conventions in the Northern Territory contact the Australian Tourist Commission *or* the Northern Territory Convention Bureau, 1 Smith Street Mall, Darwin, NT 0800. Tel: (87) 815 651.

CLIMATE

Hot most of the year; the coastal areas have heavy monsoonal rain November to March.

Required clothing: Lightweight cottons and linens most of the year. Waterproofing is necessary in the northern areas during the wet season. A warm sweater or jacket is advised for the Centre during winter months, as evenings can be quite cool.

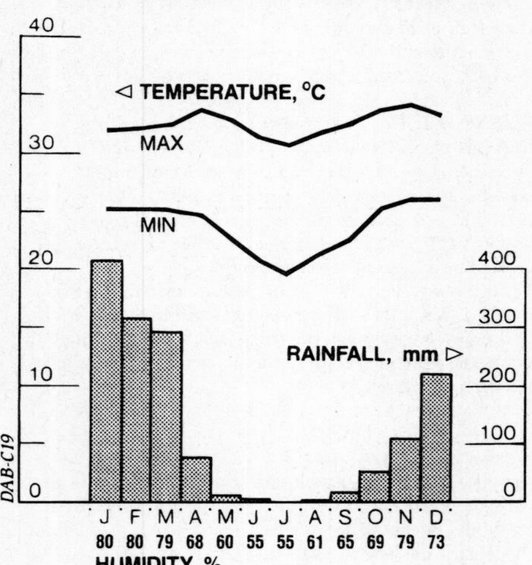

QUEENSLAND

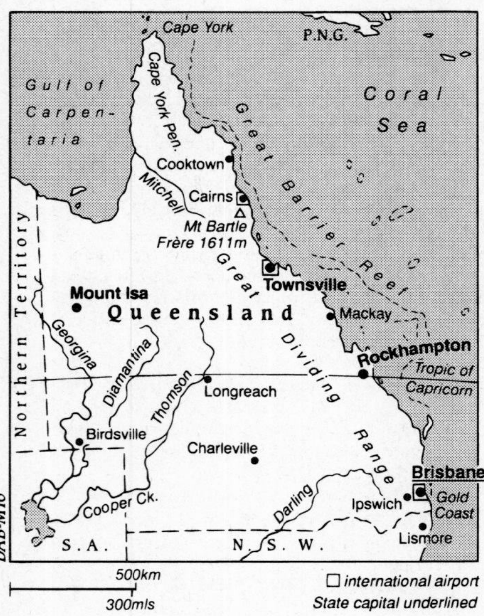

Queensland Tourist and Travel Corporation
36th Floor, Riverside Centre
123 Eagle Street
Brisbane, QLD 4000
Australia
Tel: (7) 833 5400. Fax: (7) 833 5436.

Queensland Tourist and Travel Corporation
Queensland House
392-3 Strand
London WC2R 0LZ
Tel: (071) 836 7242. Fax: (071) 836 5881.

British Consulate-General
BP House
193 North Quay
Brisbane, QLD 4000
Australia
Tel: (7) 236 2575/7 *or* 236 2581. Fax: (7) 236 2576.
Telex: 40556 BRITN AA.

Queensland Tourist and Travel Corporation
Suite 330, Third Floor
Northrop Plaza
1800 Century Park East
Los Angeles, CA
90067
Tel: (213) 788 0997. Fax: (213) 788 0128.

AREA: 1,727,000 sq km (107,334 sq miles).
POPULATION: 2,921,700 (1990).
POPULATION DENSITY: 1.7 per sq km.
CAPITAL: Brisbane. **Population:** 1,301,658 (1990).
GEOGRAPHY: Two and a half times the size of Texas or six times the size of the United Kingdom, more than half of Queensland lies above the Tropic of Capricorn, and it is known as the 'Sunshine State'. Within its borders are the Great Barrier Reef, numerous resort islands, endless kilometres of golden sandy beaches, national park forests, vast plains, lush rainforests, forested mountains and massive wilderness areas for safari touring.
TIME: GMT + 10 (GMT + 11 from October to March).

PUBLIC HOLIDAYS

The following Public Holidays are observed in Queensland:
Apr 9-12 '93 Easter. **Apr 26** Anzac Day. **May 3** Labour Day. **Jun 14** Queen's Birthday. **Dec 25** Christmas Day. **Dec 27** Boxing Day. **Jan 1 '94** New Year's Day. **Jan 3** New Year additional holiday. **Jan 26** Australia Day.

TRAVEL

AIR: The international airport at *Brisbane* is Eagle Farm. Approximate flying time from London is 24 hours. The airport is 13km (8 miles) northeast of the city centre (travel time – approx 35 minutes). Flights from Europe, Asia, the Far East, New Zealand, Canada and the USA all land at Eagle Farm. International travellers can land directly at *Townsville* – 5km (3 miles) from the city – on flights from Europe, Asia, New Zealand and the Far East. Queensland's third international airport is *Cairns*, 6km (4 miles) from the city. It is an excellent gateway both to the Great Barrier Reef and the tropical north, also hosting flights from Europe, Asia, the Far East, New Zealand, Canada and the USA. For more flight details see *Travel* section in the general introduction for Australia above.

The extensive internal airline system means that Queensland is connected with nearly all major Australian gateways. Brisbane is connected directly to Sydney, Melbourne, Adelaide, Alice Springs and Darwin, as well as having interstate connections with Cairns, Mount Isa, Townsville and other smaller airstrips. Cairns and Townsville also offer easy connections to the rest of Australia. The two major domestic airlines are *Australian Airlines* and *Sunstate Airlines*. Airlines such as *Lloyd Air*, *Seair Pacific* and *Sunstate* offer charter flights and feeder services to Queensland's main towns and Barrier Reef island resorts.

RAIL: Queensland has its own railway system, the main route being the *Sunlander* and the *Queenslander* which connects the coast from Brisbane to Cairns. In addition, other services, such as the *Inlander*, *Westlander*, *Midlander* and *Capricornian* open up the Outback to travellers. The 'Sunshine Railpass' allows unlimited travel on Queensland's rail routes. Passes are valid for 14, 21 and 31 days in first- or economy-class, offering excellent travel facilities for those intending extensive travel throughout the state.

ROAD: There is a high standard of highways and road networks offering easy connections between towns and cities. The *Bruce Highway* runs down the whole east coast from Cairns to Brisbane and continues into New South Wales. An extensive coach network offers an easy and cheap way of getting around. The tropical inland areas can be explored with 4-wheel drive vehicles, many of the interior roads being unsealed. Four-wheel drive vehicles and guided self-drive tours are available. The other main highways running into the interior are the *Capricorn Highway* (Rockhampton– Winton), the *Flinders Highway* (Townsville–Mount Isa, connecting with the network in the Northern Territories) and the *Warrego Highway* (Brisbane–Charleville). The *Mitchell* and *Landsborough Highways*, which in places have unsealed road surfaces, run roughly north–south, connecting the main east–west highways and terminating at Sydney. The *Newell Highway* runs inland between Brisbane and Melbourne.

URBAN: Brisbane's recently electrified **rail** system is easy to use for suburban services, particularly cross-river. There are also cross-river **ferries**, and a comprehensive **bus** network with zonal fares and 10-journey pre-purchase fares obtainable through newsagents. Day and other period tickets are also available. The City Sights Bus stops at 20 places of interest around the city for A$9 (adult) and A$5 (children). In Cairns, bus services operate Monday to Saturday and there is a touring bus, Cairns Red Explorer, that departs from the Transit Centre. **Taxis** are also available.

ACCOMMODATION

HOTELS: International standard hotels are available in Brisbane, Cairns and the Gold Coast together with a high standard of hotel/motel accommodation throughout the state. Information about prices and location of accommodation can be obtained through the Queensland Tourist and Travel Corporation office.

MOTELS: These are usually in or on the outskirts of towns and cities and normally offer self-contained rooms at reasonable rates.

SELF-CONTAINED APARTMENTS: These are available throughout the larger resort areas and offer a variety of facilities.

FARMSTAYS/HOMESTAYS: 'Holiday Host' services operate throughout Australia, matching hosts with visitors, in stations, family homes and farm properties.

YOUTH HOSTELS: Budget dormitory-style accommodation is available throughout Queensland.

CAMPING/CARAVANNING: Parks are located in tourist areas around Queensland, and offer facilities of varying standards. Camping is permitted in parks, but permission must be sought from the National Parks Association of Queensland, PO Box 1040, Fortune House, 10/45 Black Street, Milton, QLD 4066. Tel: (7) 267 0878. Fax: (7) 267 0890. A number of companies can arrange **motor camper** rentals, with a range of fully equipped vehicles. Full details can be obtained from the Tourist Board.

Note: More detailed coverage of the range of accommodation available in Australia may be found by consulting the *Accommodation* section in the general entry for Australia above.

RESORTS & EXCURSIONS

Brisbane is the economic hub and state capital of Queensland, with a year-round warm subtropical climate. It is Australia's fastest growing city, a fact which is due almost entirely to the 'discovery' of the region as a holiday paradise, providing easy access to adjacent coastal resorts. In addition to being a gateway to sun, sand, surf and coral, Brisbane itself offers many attractions. Probably the most famous of these is the *Lone Pine Koala Sanctuary*, situated on the slopes above the River Brisbane. The *Botanic Gardens* and *Bunya Park* are also splendid wildlife areas. *Queensland Maritime Museum*, located on Stanley Street in the city's 19th-century dry dock area, offers historic boats and nautical relics. *The City Hall* in King George Square houses an art gallery, museum and library. Other buildings of note include the *State Parliament House* with its glittering copper roof, *St John's Cathedral*, *The Mansions* and the *Old Windmill*, the city's oldest surviving building and once a treadmill worked by convicts. Brisbane is also the cultural centre of the state, attracting major artists and exhibitions to its galleries, museums and entertainment centres. Visits to the *Queensland Museum* in Bowen Bridge Road, and to the art gallery at the *Department of Aboriginal and Islanders Advancement* are recommended for those wishing to learn about the cultural, artistic and scientific history of the state. Brisbane's newest attraction is *World Expo Park*, the site of the 1988 World Expo and now a leisure entertainment centre with high-tech rides and lively night-time entertainment. Outdoor festivals are another major attraction, with themes such as *Ekka* (Royal National Exhibition) and *Warana* (Fun in the Sun). The city now boasts 7-day shopping.

The Gold Coast, probably the best beach area in the country, comprises 42km (26 miles) of white surfing beaches, theme parks (*Sea World* and *Dream World*), a casino, hotels and restaurants. It has year-round sunshine and lively tourist facilities. Surfing and swimming are popular at *Surfers Paradise* beach. Inland are lush green mountains, rainforests, walking trails and scenic villages.

An hour's drive northwards from Brisbane, the

Sunshine Coast offers miles of unspoilt beaches, untouched wilderness, lakes and mountains.
A visit to the **Glasshouse Mountains** is recommended, particularly for the artist or photographer. Nature-lovers will also appreciate the **Lamington National Park** in the McPherson Mountains, and the **Currumbin Bird Sanctuary**, 80km (50 miles) south of Brisbane.
Townsville is North Queensland's largest tropical city, boasting an international airport and a casino. Cruises are available to nearby islands and trips to the Barrier Reef (see below) for diving, walking or white-water rafting.
Charters Towers is 135km (85 miles) west of Townsville, with restored old buildings dating back to the town's gold-mining heyday in the 1870s.
Cairns is the major gateway to the far north. As well as the Barrier Reef (see below), there are rainforests in the **Atherton Tableland** to the west and to the south is **Mission Beach** with 14km (9 miles) of white sandy beaches, looking out to **Dunk Island**. To the north, there is the charming old town of **Port Douglas** which attracts many visitors, as well as **Daintree**, and its daily barge service to **Cape Tribulation National Park**, and **Cooktown**, close to **Endeavour National Park** where excellent examples of Aboriginal rock art can be found, and beyond that is the wilderness of **Cape York Peninsula** to be explored.
Townsville is another gateway to the Great Barrier Reef. This pleasant city, its streets lined with palm trees and tropical flora, has a number of interesting attractions on offer, such as *Great Barrier Reef Wonderland*, the largest coral aquarium in the world, with a transparent walk-in tunnel, and *Magnetic Island*, a resort island with superb beaches, an aquarium, bushwalking trackings and a koala sanctuary only 13km (7 miles) offshore and a 25-minute ferry ride from the city centre.
GREAT BARRIER REEF: This playground and beauty spot is also one of the world's great natural wonders. It stretches for 2000km (1240 miles) along the Queensland coast, its width varying from 25km (15 miles) to 50km (30 miles). There is unique plant and animal life to be found in warm clear waters, with visibility often as deep as 60m (200ft).
Dotted along the coast are 25 island resorts, lying on or between the Barrier Reef and the mainland. For the serious reef enthusiast, Heron or Lady Elliot Islands at **Coral Cays** are renowned as the best diving spots on the reef. **Lizard**, **Bedarra** and **Orpheus Islands** are quiet, secluded and luxurious hideaways. **Hayman Island** is an international resort, with 5-star luxury facilities. **Contiki Whitsunday** and **Great Keppel Islands** cater for lively party-goers and a youthful clientèle. **South Molle**, **Hamilton** and **Lindeman Islands** in the Whitsundays are all-year round resorts with facilities for families. **Quoin Island** in Gladstone Harbour also caters for families. **Tropical Dunk Island** and **Brampton Island** are popular with honeymooners. **Fitzroy**, **Newry** and **Hinchinbrook Islands** offer unspoilt beauty, and Hook, Palm Bay, Wapparaburra Haven and Great Keppel Island have camping facilities. Outside the main reef areas, the islands of Fraser, Moreton, Bribie, North and South Stradbroke offer some of the best unpopulated surfing beaches and national parks in Australia.

SOCIAL PROFILE

FOOD & DRINK: The food of the area relies to a large extent on the sea and the subtropical climate for specialities in cuisine. Local delicacies include mud crabs, king and tiger prawns, mackerel and fresh *barramundi*, as well as avocados, mangoes, pawpaws, pineapples, strawberries, bananas and the highly recommended local speciality, the *macadamia nut*. In Fortitude Valley, just out of Brisbane city centre, there are a number of European, Asian and Chinese restaurants. Brisbane is supplied with local wines from vineyards at Stanhope to the southwest, producing both red and white wines, and from the Hunter Valley near Sydney. All beers on sale are brewed locally.
NIGHTLIFE: Although much of the tourist activity is centred on the beaches and the Barrier Reef, Brisbane offers a wide selection of entertainment. Most of the large hotels have dinner and dancing facilities and there are several nightclubs in the city, especially in World Expo Park where discos and nightclubs abound. The Gold Coast has many nightclubs, as well as Jupiter's Casino. Magnetic Island has the spectacular Sheraton Breakwater Casino on Sir Leslie Thiess Drive, offering a full range of gaming facilities and high-quality entertainment.
SPORT: The geographic proximity to the Barrier Reef and the long stretches of golden beaches in Queensland mean predominant leisure pursuits are associated with the sea. The range is wide, from **surfing** off the beaches to **scuba-diving** on the corals of the Reef; **deep-sea fishing** for black marlin and **sailing** round the islands. There are two **golf** courses in Brisbane, and many others elsewhere in the state. **Squash** and **tennis** are both popular sports, as is **bushwalking**; the Queensland Federation of Bush Walking, PO Box 1537, GPO Brisbane, QLD can supply details.
SPECIAL EVENTS: The following is a selection of festivals and special events taking place in Queensland: **Mar 18-21 '93** *1993 Daikyo Indy Car Grand Prix*, Surfers Paradise. **Apr 3-4** *Kingaroy Peanut Festival*, Kingaroy. **May 3** *World Cup Triathlon Fun Run/Marathon*, Surfers Paradise. **May 15-Jun 18** *International Billfish Tournament*, Sanctuary Cove Marina. **May 27-Jun 6** *Brisbane Biennale International Festival of Music*, Brisbane. **Jul 18** *Jal Gold Coast International Marathon*, Gold Coast. **Sep 24-Oct 3** *Brisbane Warana Festival*, Brisbane. **Feb 25-Mar 6 '94** *Apple & Grape Harvest Festival*, Stanthorpe.
For a full list of special events contact the Queensland Tourist and Travel Corporation.

BUSINESS PROFILE

COMMERCIAL INFORMATION: The following organisation can offer advice: State Chamber of Commerce and Industry, 243 Edward Street, Brisbane, QLD 4000. Tel: (7) 221 1766. Fax: (7) 221 6872. Telex: 145636.
CONFERENCES/CONVENTIONS: Brisbane's major convention centres are Brisbane Entertainment Centre, Brisbane City Hall, Queensland Cultural Centre, RNA Exhibition Grounds, Sheraton Brisbane Hotel, Hilton International Hotel and the Mayfair Crest International Hotel. Cairns' major convention centres are Cairns International, Cairns Civic Centre, Cairns Show Grounds, the Botanical Gardens, Sheraton Mirage Resort and Cairns Hilton. The Gold Coast also has some excellent convention facilities, especially the Hotel Conrad and Jupiter's Casino with seating for 2300 theatre-style. Smaller centres can be found elsewhere along the Gold Coast at Royal Pines Resort and Sheraton Mirage Gold Coast. For more information on conferences and conventions in Queensland contact the Australian Tourist Commission *or* Brisbane Visitor & Convention Bureau, Brisbane City Hall, Brisbane, QLD 4002. Tel: (7) 221 8411. Fax: (7) 229 5126; *or*
Gold Coast Visitor & Convention Bureau, Level 5, Natwest Building, 105 Upton Street, Bundall, QLD 4217. Tel: (75) 740 999. Fax: (75) 740 302; *or*
Far North Queensland Promotion Bureau, PO Box 865, Cairns, QLD 4870. Tel: (70) 513 588. Fax: (70) 510 127.

CLIMATE

Queensland straddles the Tropic of Capricorn and this accounts for the pleasant climate throughout most of the region. Exceptions are the far north and the dry arid western Outback. Brisbane enjoys an average of 7.1 hours of sunshine daily in the winter. July to August is generally humid but sea breezes temper the humidity and make for perfect holiday conditions.
Required clothing: Lightweight cottons and linens throughout most of the year with warmer clothes for cooler winter evenings and early mornings. Waterproofing is advisable throughout the year particularly in coastal areas.

BRISBANE Queensland (42m)

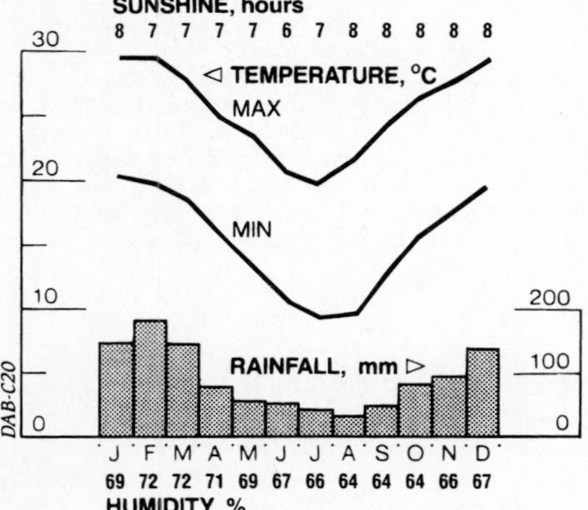

SOUTH AUSTRALIA

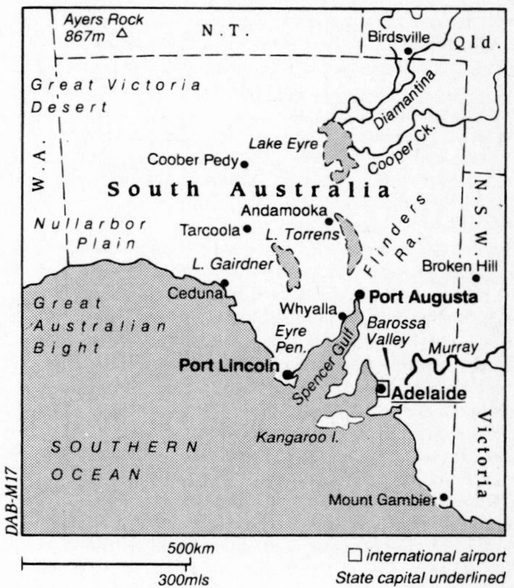

Tourism South Australia
Norwich Centre
55-57 King William Street
Adelaide, SA 5006
Australia
Tel: (8) 239 8800. Fax: (8) 212 4251.
Tourism South Australia
South Australia House
50 Strand
London WC2N 5LW
Tel: (071) 930 7471. Fax: (071) 930 1660.
South Australian Department of Tourism
Suite 1210
2121 Avenue of the Stars
Los Angeles, CA
90067
Tel: (310) 552 2821. Fax: (310) 557 0322.

AREA: 984,377 sq km (380,070 sq miles).
POPULATION: 1,439,200 (1990).
POPULATION DENSITY: 1.5 per sq km.
CAPITAL: Adelaide. **Population:** 1,049,873 (1990 estimate).
GEOGRAPHY: Except for the state capital of **Adelaide,** South Australia is sparsely inhabited – it is four times the area of the UK. It is the country's driest state, a region of rocky plains and desert landscape broken by the fertile wine-growing area of the Barossa Valley. South Australia stretches upwards to the Northern Territory, and eastwards to Queensland, New South Wales and Victoria. The countryside ranges from the beach resorts of the Adelaide suburbs to the vast expanses of isolated, semi-desert Outback, from the craggy mountains of Flinders Ranges to the meandering River Murray. Offshore is the popular resort of Kangaroo Island. Adelaide is an attractive European-style coastal city nestling in the foothills of Mount Lofty Ranges.
TIME: GMT + 9.5 (GMT + 10.5 from October to March).

PUBLIC HOLIDAYS

The following Public Holidays are observed in South Australia:
Apr 9-12 '93 Easter. **Apr 26** Anzac Day. **May 17** Adelaide Cup Day. **Jun 14** Queen's Birthday. **Oct 11** Labour Day. **Dec 27** Christmas Day. **Dec 28** Proclamation Day. **Jan 1 '94** New Year's Day. **Jan 3** New Year additional holiday. **Jan 31** Australia Day.

TRAVEL

AIR: Adelaide receives international flights and direct flights from Europe via Singapore. Approximate flying time from London is 24 hours. The city is already linked to every state capital city. Connecting flights available through Darwin, Alice Springs, Perth, Brisbane, Canberra, Melbourne and Sydney. For more flight details see general introduction above.

There is an excellent system of internal airways, serving all regional towns, and the majority of flights are run by *Ansett Airlines*, *Australian Airlines* and *Compass Airlines*. There are nine government and 20 private airfields in the region.
International Airport: *Adelaide Airport* is 6km (4 miles) from the city centre, a drive of ten minutes.
SEA: Adelaide is an international port, with passenger services from Europe and the Far East.
RAIL: Adelaide, where the popular *Ghan* train departs for Alice Springs, is a major terminal on the national rail network. (See also under general section on internal rail connections above.)
ROAD: The southern territories are fully connected to the national system of coach lines that cross Australia from all the state capitals. Typical coach journey times are: Melbourne to Adelaide – 9.5 hours; Alice Springs to Adelaide – 20 hours; Sydney to Adelaide – 24 hours; Brisbane to Adelaide – 33.5 hours; Perth to Adelaide – 35 hours; Darwin to Adelaide – 46 hours. There are 10,180km (6330 miles) of roads within the State. The main highways north are the *Stuart Highway* to Darwin via Coober Pedy and Alice Springs and the *Birdsville Track* to Queensland. The other main state highways are: the *Eyre Highway* west to Perth, the *Princes Highway* along the coast to Melbourne and the *Sturt Highway* east to Canberra and Sydney.
Car hire services are available at all the main hotels, the railway station and the airport.
URBAN: There is a fully integrated public transport system in Adelaide with **bus**, **tram** and local rail lines plus the *O-Bahn* bus system. Pre-purchase booklets of cash-fare tickets and weekly and other passes are all available. A free bus, known as the Bee-line, number 99B, operates Monday to Saturday in the city. The Adelaide Explorer Bus leaves the South Australian Travel Centre at 18 King William Street and stops at eight major attractions for a charge of A$12 (adult) and A$7 (children). Visitors may alight and rejoin as they please.

ACCOMMODATION

HOTELS: South Australia has 372 hotels and guest-houses, and Adelaide itself contains 126, ranging from budget hostels to 5-star international hotels. There are also 80 bed & breakfast accommodations throughout South Australia, mostly in the Adelaide and Adelaide Hills area.
CAMPING/CARAVANNING: South Australia has almost 200 caravan parks. Typical examples near Adelaide are as follows: *Adelaide Caravan Park*, *West Beach*, *Marineland Village* and *Port Glanville Caravan Park*. They all offer sites with full amenities and power. A number of companies can arrange **motor camper** rentals, with a range of fully equipped vehicles. Full details can be obtained from the South Australian Government Travel Centre. In addition, there are a wide variety of holiday flats and apartments for rent in the state.
Note: More detailed coverage of the range of accommodation available in Australia may be found by consulting the *Accommodation* section in the general entry for Australia above.

RESORTS & EXCURSIONS

Adelaide is the state's capital and by a long way its most populous town. It has to the west a long stretch of attractive coastline with excellent white sandy beaches. The best view of Adelaide and the surrounding countryside can be had from *Mount Lofty*, to the east of the city. The city itself has a European air, primarily because of the large German and southern European minorities. The streets are filled with cafés, European-style churches, art galleries and antique shops. One of the key attractions is the *Festival Theatre* complex in the parkland overlooking the Torrens River. It houses an excellent theatre company, and boasts a concert hall, two theatres, many restaurants and an outdoor amphitheatre. In March every two years an *International Festival* is held, featuring everything from Nureyev to Count Basie, the Royal Shakespeare Company to the Leningrad Ballet. The *South Australian Museum* has the largest collection of Aboriginal artefacts in the world as well as a huge exhibition of Melanesian art and New Guinean wildlife. Adelaide is a spacious city surrounded by parklands, golf courses and the botanical and zoological gardens. The city in recent years has assumed a more youthful appearance, in contrast to its reputation as the 'City of Churches'. It has a wide range of vibrant nightlife and an array of cosmopolitan restaurants. From Adelaide it is easy to travel the 55km (34 miles) to the wine centre of the country, the **Barossa Valley,** originally settled by German refugees in the 1830s and still indelibly marked by their influence on its wineries, restaurants and shops. The main towns are *Tanunda*, *Angaston* and *Nuriootpa*, all notable for Lutheran churches and the vineyards – tours and tastings can be arranged. The other wine regions in South Australia are the Mid North, Riverland, Mclaren Vale and the Coonawarra in the southeast.
Taking a **Murray River** steamer will afford the visitor a view of lush pastureland, limestone cliffs and also the wine country. The Murray–Darling–Murrumbidgee river network is one of the largest in the world – 2600km (1615 miles) from source to sea – and brings irrigation to a wide area. The vegetation and wildlife evoke images of the Deep South and Mississippi in the United States. Opposite Adelaide in the St Vincent Gulf lies Australia's third largest island, **Kangaroo Island** – a natural wildlife sanctuary with a rugged coastline noted for fine fishing and its large sea lion colony at *Seal Bay*. South Australia's best slice of the Outback is to be found in the **Flinders Ranges,** a region of granite peaks and spectacular and colourful gorges, dotted with eucalyptus trees. In the centre of the Flinders area is *Wilpena Pound*, a popular resort area; accommodation is also available at *Arkaroola*, at the northern peak of the Flinders. The opal town of **Coober Pedy** is so hot that 45% of the inhabitants live underground; even the church is underground, and the name of the town in Aboriginal means 'white man lives in a hole.' The area produces 90% of the world's supply of opals and those who wish to dig for the semi-precious stones can obtain a miner's permit.
Andamooka is another mining town and conditions are better here for 'noodlers' (amateur prospectors). Accommodation is limited in the towns.

SOCIAL PROFILE

FOOD & DRINK: The local delicacies are mainly German food in the Barossa region and, on the coast, crabs, whiting, crayfish and other seafood. Kangaroo steak is a speciality of the region and can be ordered in many Australian restaurants. Adelaide has a variety of international cuisine available, including American, Chinese, French, Greek, Italian, Indian, Indonesian, Japanese, Lebanese, Malaysian, Mexican, Mongolian and Vietnamese. There are many excellent seafood restaurants. **Drink:** The local wines and beers are strongly recommended and can be tasted at the Vintage Festival, reminiscent in many ways of German beer festivals in Europe. South Australia contains one of the most important valley regions producing Australian wines, both red and white, and naturally Adelaide and the city environs offer the best selection. There is also a brewery in Adelaide supplying stout and lagers.
NIGHTLIFE: Adelaide has an extraordinary nightlife scene, despite its once conservative image. Another conversion was Adelaide Casino, once a grand Victorian railway station and now a haven for baccarat and roulette players amid its magnificent Corinthian columns (open 1000-0400 Monday to Thursday and continuously from Friday to Sunday). There is also a concentration of nightclubs and discotheques on Hindley Street in the heart of the city, opposite Rundle Mall.
SHOPPING: Excellent quality wines from the Barossa Valley, producing over 60% of the national supply. Adelaide is a city that concentrates on culture, and is full of antique shops and art galleries. Opening hours are the same as for the rest of Australia, except for Saturday when Adelaide's shops are open all day. There are also some street markets in Adelaide which are open on Sunday.
SPORT: The third largest river in the world, the River Murray, winds its way through South Australia providing **cruises, houseboat hire, sailing** and **water-skiing**. One of the sporting specialities is **deep-sea fishing** and **scuba diving** centred on Kangaroo Island. **Ballooning** and **gliding** is popular in the Barossa Valley. Adelaide is the home of the *Australian Formula One Grand Prix*.
SPECIAL EVENTS: South Australia lives up to its name of the *Festival State* with a huge variety of festivals and special events taking place throughout the state all year round. The following is just a selection:
Mar 4-21 '93 *Fiesta 1993 – Adelaide Music Festival*, Adelaide. **Mar 6-7** *Essenfest*, Barossa Valley. **Apr 12-18** *Barossa Valley Vintage Festival*. **May 2-15** *Come Out 1993 Youth Arts Festival*, Adelaide. **May 8** *South Australian Derby*, Adelaide. **May 14-17** *Kernewek Lowender Cornish Festival*, Kadina, Moonta, Wallaroo. **May 15-16** *Gourmet Weekend*, Clare Valley. **May 15-23** *The Great South Australian Bike Ride*, Adelaide. **May 17** *Adelaide Cup*, Morphettville. **Aug 2-8** *Australian International Squash Classic*, Adelaide. **Oct 31** *World Solar Challenge*, Darwin–Adelaide.
For a full list of special events contact Tourism South Australia.

BUSINESS PROFILE

COMMERCIAL INFORMATION: The following organisation can offer advice: Chamber of Commerce and Industry SA Inc, 136 Greenhill Road, Unley, SA 5061. Tel: (8) 373 1422. Fax: (8) 272 9662. Telex: 88370.
CONFERENCES/CONVENTIONS: Adelaide's major convention centres are Adelaide Convention Centre and Exhibition Hall, Adelaide Festival Centre, Hilton International Adelaide, Royal Showground and Exhibition Centre and the new seaside hotel, the Ramada Grand. For more information on conferences and conventions in South Australia contact the Australian Tourist Commission *or* the Adelaide Convention & Tourism Authority, Level 3, 45 Pirie Street, Adelaide, SA 5000. Tel: (8) 212 4794. Fax: (8) 231 9224.

CLIMATE

Warm and temperate with long hot summers and short mild winters, with low rainfall. One of the hottest places in the area in summer is Coober Pedy, 1000km (540 miles) northwest of Adelaide, reaching a temperature of up to 45°C.
Required clothing: Lightweight cottons and linens in summer, warmer mediumweights in winter. Waterproofing is advisable throughout most of the year, particularly in winter.

ADELAIDE S.Australia (43m)

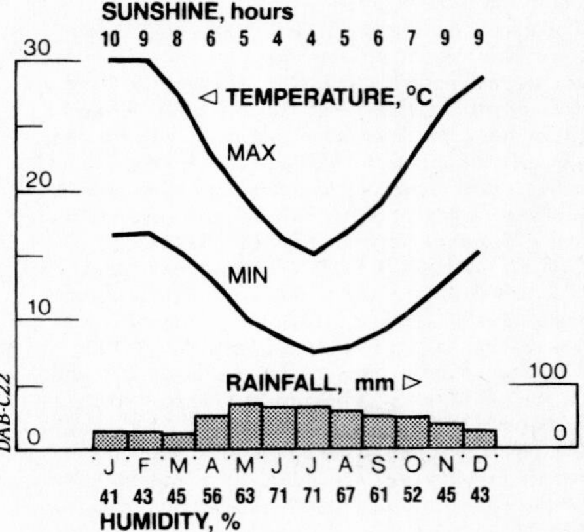

TASMANIA

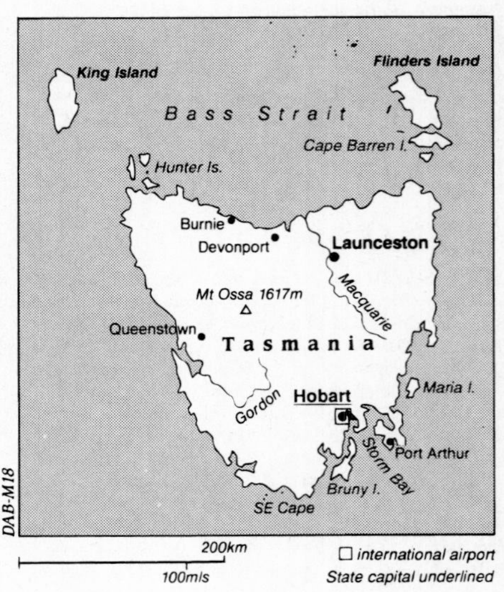

Tourism Tasmania Travel Centre
80 Elisabeth Street
Hobart, TAS 7000
Australia
Tel: (02) 300 286. Fax: (02) 240 289.
Australia's Southern Tourism Promotion
First Floor, Gemini House
10-18 Putney Hill
London SW15 6AA
Tel: (081) 789 7088. Fax: (081) 780 1496.

Australia's Southern Tourism Promotion
12th Floor, Suite 1270
2121 Avenue of the Stars
Los Angeles, CA
90067
Tel: (301) 553 6352. Fax: (301) 277 2883.

AREA: 68,330 sq km (42,467 sq miles).
POPULATION: 457,500 (1990).
POPULATION DENSITY: 6.7 per sq km.
CAPITAL: Hobart. **Population:** 183,550 (1990).
GEOGRAPHY: A separate island located 240km (149 miles) south of Melbourne across Bass Strait. Roughly heart-shaped, Tasmania is 296km (184 miles) long, ranging from 315km (196 miles) wide in the north to 70km (44 miles) in the south. The island has a diverse landscape comprising rugged mountains (snowcapped in winter), dense bushland (including the Horizontal Forest, so-called because the tree trunks are bent over parallel to the ground), tranquil countryside and farmland. Bruny Island, south of Hobart across the D'Entrecasteaux Channel, has superb beaches. The two parts of the island are joined by a narrow isthmus of sand-dunes, the home of fairy penguins from August to April.
TIME: GMT + 10 (GMT + 11 from October to March).

PUBLIC HOLIDAYS

The following Public Holidays are observed in Tasmania: **Mar 1 '93** Labour Day/Eight Hour Day. **Apr 9-12** Easter. **Apr 13** Bank Holiday. **Apr 25** Anzac Day. **Jun 14** Queen's Birthday. **Nov 1** Recreation Day. **Dec 27** Christmas Day. **Dec 28** Boxing Day. **Jan 1 '94** New Year's Day. **Jan 3** New Year additional holiday. **Jan 31** Australia Day. **Feb 1** Australia Day. **Mar 7** Eight Hour Day.

TRAVEL

AIR: Direct international flights to Tasmania run from Christchurch in New Zealand. The airport is 22km (14 miles) from Hobart city centre, a drive of about 35 minutes. *Qantas* operates a direct link with international flights each Thursday. Tasmania is connected to the mainland by internal flights from Sydney and Melbourne, and from there to all the other mainland cities.
SEA: There is a direct ferry, the *Abel Tasman*, which runs thrice-weekly from Melbourne to Devonport on the north coast of the island. A Seacat service operates daily return crossings from George Town in Northern Tasmania to Port Welshpool in Victoria (travel time – 4 hrs, 30 mins one-way).
RAIL: There are no passenger train services.
ROAD: All settlements on the island are linked by a road system running for 22,000km (13,670 miles) over which there are bus services connecting the main towns. The main routes are: the *Lyell Highway* from Hobart to Queenstown, the *Huon Highway* from Hobart to Southport, the *Midland Highway* from Hobart to Launceston, the *Tasman Highway* from Hobart along the east coast and the *Bass Highway* linking the ports of the north coast. **Coach:** Tasmania has its own coach service, *Tasmanian Redline Coaches*, which offers a *Super Tassie Bus Pass* to out-of-state visitors.
URBAN: Local bus networks are operated in Hobart, Launceston and Burnie.

ACCOMMODATION

The Tasmanian Government Tourist Bureau publishes a booklet giving details of 8-16 day rates; available from the Australian Tourist Commission.
HOTELS, MOTELS & GUEST-HOUSES: There are international hotels in Hobart and Launceston and a wide range of tourist hotels, motels and guest-houses in all the major centres. Hotels tend to be slightly more expensive in Hobart and Launceston, and in some of the main tourist areas.
SELF-CATERING: Available in the main centres. For further details, see the main Australia entry.
FARMSTAY/HOMESTAY: See *Accommodation* in the general introduction above.
CAMPING & CARAVANNING: A number of companies can arrange **Motor camper** rentals, with a range of fully equipped vehicles. Full details can be obtained from the Tourist Board. There are a large number of camping and caravan sites in Tasmania. It should be noted that camping is not permitted in any roadside picnic or rest areas.
Note: More detailed coverage of the range of accommodation available in Australia may be found by consulting the *Accommodation* section in the general entry for Australia above.

RESORTS & EXCURSIONS

Hobart, the capital, is Australia's second oldest city after Sydney and is situated on the south side of the island. The city is characterised by strong links with the sea, typified by the wharves, jetties and warehouses – some dating back to the last century – which cluster around the waterfront. Examples of the island's history can be seen in the *Van Diemen's Land Memorial Folk Museum*, the *Tasmanian Maritime Museum* and the *Allport Library and Museum of Fine Arts*. **Mt Wellington**, towering 1270m (4170ft) to the west of the city, provides the backdrop to Hobart. From the lookout at the top (about 20km (12 miles) by road) the clear air offers a spectacular view of Hobart, its suburbs, the Derwent Estuary and Storm Bay. Apart from the view the area offers picnic facilities and walking trails. *The Royal Tasmanian Botanical Gardens* provides a long walk through beautiful scenery, free of charge.
Launceston, the second city, still maintains much of its colonial Georgian flavour. It is the natural gateway for the rural beauty of the island, including the *Cataract Gorge* and the *Launceston Wildlife Sanctuary*. Nearby is the historic town of *Evandale*.
Port Arthur, 100km (82 miles) from Hobart, is the site of an old penal colony built in the early 19th century. Guided tours are available. Not far away is *Eaglehawk Neck*, noted for its bizarre rock formations. There are many National Parks in Tasmania, most of which are within easy reach of Hobart. These include *South West, Ben Lomond, Cradle Mountain-Lake St Clair* and *Frenchman's Cap*, all of which contain examples of the island's unique plant and wildlife.

SOCIAL PROFILE

FOOD & DRINK: Some of the best seafood in the world is available in Tasmania, including Angazie oysters, Atlantic salmon and ocean trout. Freshwater wild brown trout is harvested in the Tasmanian highlands. Goat, quail and venison are the area's speciality meats and other specialities include cheeses, apples, apricots and liqueur honey.
NIGHTLIFE: There are casinos in Hobart and Launceston. Hobart's waterfront area, Salamanca Place, is the home of many night-time haunts in its old stone warehouses, as well as the Wrest Point Hotel casino.
SPORT: The coastline offers all maritime sports and some of the best **sailing** facilities in the world, with crystal clear waters teeming with marine life. Port Arthur offers a base for superb deep sea and trout **fishing**. A wide range of adventure holidays are also available; these include **canoeing**, **hiking** tours, **pony trekking**, **bush-walking**, **gliding** and **rock-climbing**.
SPECIAL EVENTS: The following is a selection of festivals and special events taking place in Tasmania: **Mar 13-27 '93** *1993 Tasmanian Fiva World Rally*. **Mar 20-21** *Floral Garden Week*, Hobart. **Apr 9-12** *Australian National Band Championships*, Launceston. **Apr 28-May 2** *Targa Tasmania*. **Aug** *Australian Masters Squash Association National Titles*. **Oct 30** *Ross Rodeo*, Ross.
For a full list of special events contact Tasbureau or the Australian Tourist Commission.

BUSINESS PROFILE

COMMERCIAL INFORMATION: The following organisations can offer advice:
Hobart Chamber of Commerce, PO Box 969, 65 Murray Street, Hobart, TAS 7000. Tel: (02) 311 007. Fax: (02) 311 639; *or*
Launceston Chamber of Commerce, PO Box 1854, 99 George Street, Launceston, TAS 7250. Tel/Fax: (03) 319 364.
CONFERENCES/CONVENTIONS: The major convention centres in Hobart are Derwent Entertainment Centre; Wrest Point Federal Hotel, Casino and Convention Centre and Sheraton Hobart. Launceston's major convention centres are Launceston Convention Centre/Albert Hall, Federal Launceston Country Club and Casino and Launceston International Hotel. For more information on conferences and conventions in Tasmania contact the Australian Tourist Commission *or* the Tasmanian Convention Bureau, 140 Bathurst Street, Hobart, TAS 7000. Tel: (02) 310 055. Fax: (02) 348 492.

CLIMATE

Similar climate to southern Australia, with warm, dry summers and cold, wet winters. There is often snow above 1000m (3280ft) in July and August.

Required clothing: Cottons and linens in summer, warmer mediumweights in winter. Waterproofing advisable throughout the year particularly in winter.

HOBART Tasmania (54m)

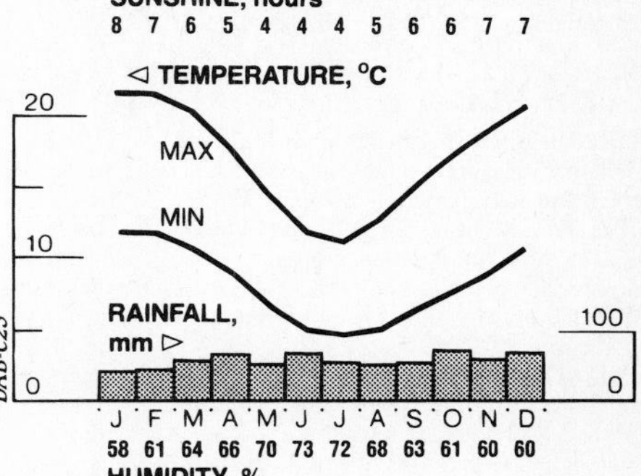

VICTORIA

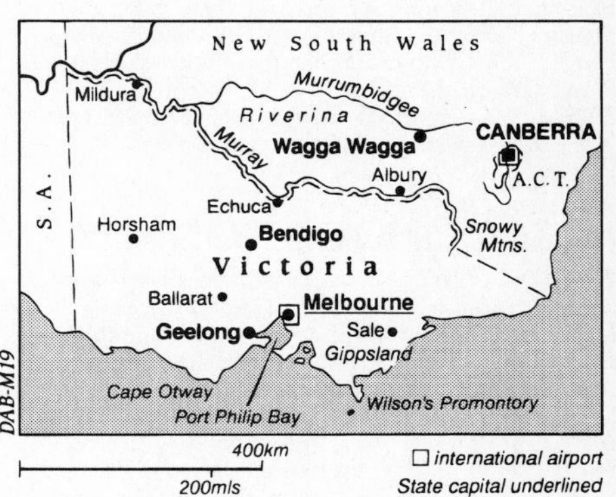

Victorian Tourist Commission
13th Floor
44 Swanston Street
Melbourne, VIC 3001
Australia
Tel: (3) 653 9777. Fax: (3) 653 9744.
Australia's Southern Tourism Promotion
Gemini House
10-18 Putney Hill
London SW15 6AA
Tel: (081) 789 7088. Fax: (081) 780 1496.
British Consulate-General
17th Floor, 90 Collins Street
Melbourne, VIC 3000
Australia
Tel: (3) 650 4155. Fax: (3) 650 2990. Telex: 71 30660.
Australia's Southern Tourism Promotion
Suite 1270
2121 Avenue of the Stars
Los Angeles, CA
90067
Tel: (310) 553 6352. Fax: (310) 277 2883.

AREA: 227,600 sq km (141,454 sq miles).
POPULATION: 4,394,000 (1990).
POPULATION DENSITY: 19.3 per sq km.
CAPITAL: Melbourne. **Population:** 3,080,800 (1990).
GEOGRAPHY: Victoria, Australia's second smallest state, is also the most densely populated and the continent's major agricultural and industrial producer. Located in southeastern Australia, bordered by South Australia and New South Wales, the landscape consists of mountains, rainforests, deserts, snowfields, tobacco plantations, vineyards, potato fields, wheatlands and market gardens. It is possible to drive from a cold, wet Melbourne winter to the dry desert sunshine of Mildura in one day or to be in snow-fields in three hours. The mountain coolness of the alpine region is an easy escape from summer heat.
TIME: GMT + 10 (GMT + 11 from October to March).

PUBLIC HOLIDAYS

The following Public Holidays are observed in Victoria: **Apr 9-13 '93** Easter. **Apr 25** Anzac Day. **Jun 14** Queen's Birthday. **Nov 2** Melbourne Cup Day. **Dec 27** Boxing Day. **Dec 28** Christmas Day. **Jan 1 '94** New Year's Day. **Jan 3** New Year additional holiday. **Jan 31** Australia Day. **Mar 14** Labour Day.

TRAVEL

AIR: The international airport at *Melbourne* (Tullamarine) receives flights from the UK (approximate flying time from London – 24 hours) Europe, Asia and USA. *Tullamarine Airport* is 22km (14 miles) from the city (35 minutes). For more flight details see general introduction above. Internal flights from all state capitals.
SEA: Passenger/vehicle ferry from Tasmania to Melbourne.
RAIL: Daytime and overnight trains link Melbourne and Sydney (13 hours), and an overnight train runs to Adelaide (12 hours). Trains run to other main centres including Canberra (8.5 hours), Brisbane (48 hours), and Perth (72 hours).
ROAD: Connected to all states by coach services. Main coach routes and travelling times are: Melbourne to Canberra – 9.5 hours; Melbourne to Adelaide – 9.5 hours; Melbourne to Sydney – 14.5 hours; Melbourne to Broken Hill – 19 hours; Melbourne to Brisbane – 25 hours. There is a well-developed road system covering 156,700km (97,400 miles) on which local buses operate.
URBAN: Melbourne has an extensive network of electric railways, linked in the city centre by an **underground** loop-line. There is also a **tram** network which has an integrated ticket structure with the **bus** and **rail** systems. Fares are zonal, with travel cards for daily or weekly travel and multi-journey tickets. The Melbourne Explorer Bus goes to major attractions in the city and the visitor may join or leave the bus at any stopping point in its journey.

ACCOMMODATION

HOTELS: A full range of accommodation is available in Victoria, ranging from international standard hotels in Melbourne to farmstay, homestay and self-catering holidays.
CAMPING/CARAVANNING: A number of companies can arrange motor camper rentals, with a range of fully equipped vehicles. Full details can be obtained from the Tourist Board.
Note: More detailed information on the range of accommodation available in Australia may be found by consulting the *Accommodation* section in the general entry for Australia above.

RESORTS & EXCURSIONS

Melbourne is a highly cosmopolitan city of almost three million people with sizeable Italian, Greek and Chinese minorities, each with their own quarter. The architecture is often fascinating, a blend in the suburbs of ornate *stucco* and cast iron and in the city centre a skyline which mixes graceful spires with modern skyscrapers. The *Victorian Arts Centre* consists of the *National Gallery*, which houses Australia's greatest collection of fine art, and the magnificent concert hall and theatre complex, the country's premier venue for the performing arts. Other visits include the various gardens, *Parliament House*, *Captain Cook's Cottage* and other National Trust properties. Also recommended is a trip to the races, a ride in one of Melbourne's trams, a river cruise down the *River Yarra*, or a visit to the *Royal Melbourne Zoo*, one of the finest open-air zoos in the world with no cages, only natural enclosures.
Outside Melbourne: 35km (22 miles) from the state capital are the **Dandenong Ranges,** which provide excellent views of the city over the peaks from the *Summit Lookout*. At Mount Dandenong itself is the sanctuary named after William Ricketts, one of the early champions of Aboriginal rights; his haunting carvings of Aboriginal faces still stare out over the forested landscape. Victoria was also the home of the outlaw Ned Kelly, often regarded as a national hero in Australia, and was the scene of the eventful days of bushranging during the gold rush of the 1850s and 1860s. **Sovereign Hill,** 120km (75 miles) northwest of Melbourne, is an old gold-rush town from this period, now restored to its original condition. Other towns of this era are **Ballarat** and **Bendigo,** respectively 115km (71 miles) and 150km (93 miles) from Melbourne. Nostalgia is also available in the shape of *Puffing Billy*, a train of bright red carriages which runs along the short line from Belgrave to Emerald through the Dandenong Ranges. **Phillip Island Nature Reserve,** 112km from Melbourne, is home to Fairy Penguins and other examples of Antipodean wildlife.
In the east of the state is **Gippsland,** a lush fertile region dotted with lakes and parkland. The west is drier, with huge sheep grazing lands. Towards the centre are the **Grampian Mountains,** famous for wild flowers and birdlife. Another famous wildlife sanctuary is in the **Wilson's Promontory National Park,** southeast of Melbourne and the southernmost tip of the Australian mainland. The **Port Campbell National Park,** southwest of Melbourne, contains some of the most beautiful – and dangerous – coastlines in Victoria. East of Melbourne are the **Gippsland Lakes,** the largest network of inland waterways in Australia.
Victoria, like the rest of Australia, has many fine beaches with opportunities for watersports. These include *Port Phillip Bay*, *Westernport Bay*, *Ninety Mile Beach* (in the Gippsland Lakes area) and those of the *Bellarine Peninsular* near Geelong.

SOCIAL PROFILE

FOOD & DRINK: There is an enormous variety of cuisines available in Melbourne and restaurants offering specific types can be found in sectionalised districts: Lygon Street for Italian, Little Bourke Street for Chinese, Lonsdale Street for Greek, Victoria Street for Vietnamese, Sydney Road for Turkish and Spanish and Acland Street for Middle European. Other cuisines that are well represented in the city's restaurants include French, American, Mexican, Lebanese, African, Malaysian, Afghan, Swiss and Mongolian.
SPORT: Horseracing: The *Melbourne Cup* is the most important event. **Football:** Australian Rules football is a very popular sport, and Melbourne is its focal point during the winter months. **Cricket:** The Melbourne Cricket Ground (MCG) plays host to the highest standard of international and national matches, and is ranked amongst cricket's most sacred turfs.
SPECIAL EVENTS: The following is a selection of festivals and special events taking place in Victoria: **Mar '93** *National Boomerang Throwing Championships*, Leopold. **Mar 1-9** *Moomba International Weightlifting Championships*, Melbourne. **Mar 5-14** *The Ballarat Begonia Festival*, Ballarat; *Moomba Festival*, Melbourne. **Mar 6-7** *Tastes of Rutherglen Wine Festival.* **Mar 13** *Ranges Rodeo*, Tynong. **Mar 14** *Great Melbourne Bike Ride*, Melbourne; *International Dragon Boat Festival*, Melbourne. **Mar 21** *Australian Long Course Fun Run Championship*, Frankston. **Mar 21-27** *Great Ocean Road Ride*, Warrnambool–Queenscliff. **Mar 28** *Walk Against Want*, Albert Park Lake. **Apr 1-24** *Melbourne International Comedy Festival*, Melbourne. **Apr 3-4** *Victorian Wildflower Show*, Melbourne. **Apr 3-12** *Bendigo Easter Fair*. **Apr 4** *The Herald-Sun Banana Run*, Melbourne. **Apr 8-12** *Bell's Beach Easter Surfing Classic*, Torquay. **Apr 20-24** *Australian Open Diving Championships*, Victoria. **Apr 24-May 8** *May Bright Autumn Festival*. **Jun 4-20** *Melbourne International Film Festival*, Melbourne. **Jun 6** *Quantas Melbourne Marathon*, Frankston–Melbourne. **Jul 18-22** *Melbourne Sheep & Woolcraft Show*, Melbourne. **Sep 4-25** *Melbourne Fringe Arts Festival*. **Sep 9-25** *Melbourne International Festival of the Arts*, Melbourne. **Sep 11-Oct 10** *Tesselaar's Tulip Festival*, Silvan. **Oct 9-Nov 13** *Spring Racing Carnival*, Melbourne. **Nov 2** *Melbourne Cup Horserace*, Melbourne. **Jan 18-31 '94** *1994 Ford Australian Open Tennis*.
For a full list of special events contact the Victorian Tourism Commission.

BUSINESS PROFILE

COMMERCIAL INFORMATION: The following organisation can offer advice: State Chamber of Commerce and Industry, Commerce House, World Trade Centre, Melbourne, VIC 3005. Tel: (3) 611 2233. Fax: (3) 611 2266.
CONFERENCES/CONVENTIONS: Ranked 17th in the world for hosting the greatest number of conventions, Melbourne's major convention centres include Dallas Brooks Convention Centre, Melbourne Hilton on the Park, Hyatt on Collins, the Radisson President Hotel and Convention Centre, Regent of Melbourne, Royal Exhibition Building and Convention Centre, Southern Cross Hotel, Victorian Arts Centre, the National Tennis Centre and the World Congress Centre. For more information on conferences and conventions in Victoria contact the Australian Tourist Commission *or* the Melbourne Tourism Authority, Level 5, 114 Flinders Street, Melbourne, VIC 3000. Tel: (3) 654 2288. Fax: (3) 654 8195.

CLIMATE

Hot summers and relatively cold winters. Rainfall is distributed throughout the year. Southern areas can have changeable weather even in summer often with four seasons' weather in one day.
Required clothing: Lightweight cottons and linens in summer, warmer mediumweights in winter. Some warm clothing and waterproofing is advisable throughout the year, particularly in the south.

MELBOURNE Victoria (35m)

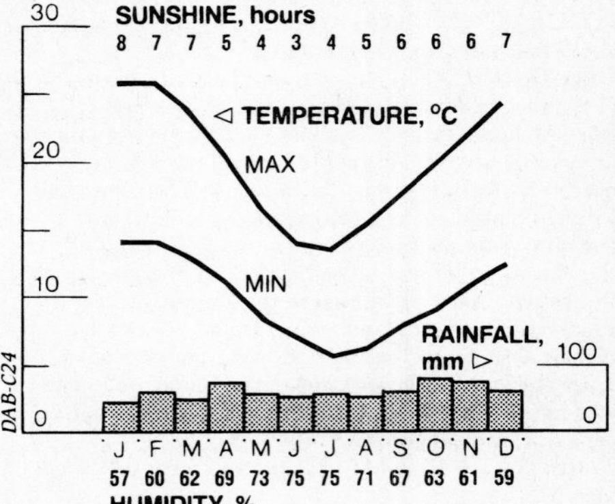

WESTERN AUSTRALIA

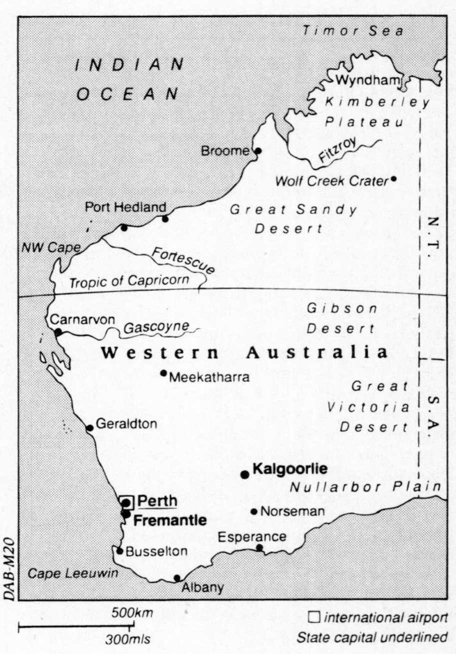

Western Australian Tourist Centre
Forrest Place
Cnr of Wellington Street
Perth, WA 6000
Australia
Tel: (9) 483 1111. Fax: (9) 481 0190.
Western Australia Tourism Commission
6th Floor
16 St George's Terrace
Perth, WA 6000
Tel: (9) 220 1700. Fax: (9) 220 1702.
Western Australia Tourism Commission
115 Strand
London
WC2R 0AJ
Tel: (071) 240 2881. Fax: (071) 379 9826.
British Consulate-General
Prudential Building
95 St George's Terrace
Perth, WA 6000
Australia
Tel: (9) 322 3200. Fax: (9) 481 4755. Telex: 7192493.
Western Australia Tourism Commission
Suite 1210

2121 Avenue of the Stars
Los Angeles, CA 90067
Tel: (213) 557 1987. Fax: (213) 557 0322.

AREA: 2,525,200 sq km (1,569,422 sq miles).
POPULATION: 1,642,700 (1990).
POPULATION DENSITY: 0.6 per sq km.
CAPITAL: Perth. **Population:** 1,193,130 (1990).
GEOGRAPHY: Western Australia covers one-third of Australia; it is larger than Western Europe, but has a population only one-sixth of that of London. It is bordered in the east by South Australia and the Northern Territory and surrounded by the Indian Ocean and in the north by the Timor Sea. On the west coast one is nearer to Bali and Indonesia than to Sydney, making Perth a viable stopover destination enroute to the rest of Australia. To the south, the nearest land mass is Antarctica, 2600km (1600 miles) away. It has mineral wealth in iron, bauxite, nickel, natural gas, oil, diamonds and gold. There are vast wheatlands, forests and deserts, and several national parks. A popular resort is Rottnest Island; there are also many excellent mainland beaches, particularly around Perth. The Kimberleys, in the far north, is one of the oldest geological areas on earth, a region where time and weather have formed deep gorges and impressive mountains, arid red plains and coastal sandstone rich in fossils. In the northwest there are two notable features: Wolf Creek Crater, an immense hole left in the desert by a giant meteorite 50,000 years ago, and the Bungle Bungle, an ancient sandstone massif covering 450 sq km (175 sq miles). Southeast of Perth, near Hyden, there is the 2700-million-year-old Wave Rock.
TIME: GMT + 8 (GMT + 9 from October to March).

PUBLIC HOLIDAYS

The following Public Holidays are observed in Western Australia:
Mar 1 '93 Labour Day/Eight Hour Day. **Apr 9-12** Easter. **Apr 26** Anzac Day. **Jun 7** Foundation Day. **Oct 4** Queen's Birthday. **Dec 27** Christmas Day. **Dec 28** Boxing Day. **Jan 1 '94** New Year's Day. **Jan 3** New Year additional holiday. **Jan 26** Australia Day. **Mar 7** Labour Day.

TRAVEL

AIR: There are international flights to Perth from Europe and Asia. Approximate flying time from London is 22 hours. There are internal flights from all State capitals. *Perth Airport* is 10km (6 miles) from the city (travel time – 35 minutes). *Ansett WA (MV)* is Western Australia's regional airline.
SEA: Port of Fremantle serves Perth. The port is 19km (11 miles) from the city of Perth.
RAIL: The *Indian Pacific* service runs across Australia from Sydney, and the *Trans-Australian* runs from Port Pirie, Adelaide and Melbourne. There is a daily service from Kalgoorlie and Bunbury.
ROAD: The highway network in Western Australia is almost entirely concentrated in the coastal areas. The main exception to this is the *Great Northern Highway* which runs from Perth to Port Headland on the northwest coast. Along the south coast is the *Eyre Highway*, which runs into South Australia. The *Brand/Northwest Coastal Highway* runs from Perth around the west coast to Kimberley. There is only one express coach route from Perth and it goes to Adelaide (travel time – 35 hours).
URBAN: Local **trains** run from Perth to Armadale, Midland and Fremantle. There are **bus** and **ferry** services in Perth itself. A zonal fares structure covers all transport modes; tickets issued on one mode are valid for transfer to either of the others (bus, rail and ferry). A free Clipper Bus service circles the city centre Monday to Friday.

ACCOMMODATION

The Western Australian Tourism Commission provides general information to consumers and travel agents, which can be obtained from their local office (addresses above).
HOTELS: There is a wide range of hotels and motels in Western Australia, including 5-star (luxury), 4-star (deluxe), 3-star (standard) and 2-star (economy).
HOLIDAY FLATS: A wide range of holiday flats are available, both in Perth and the rest of the state.
CAMPING/CARAVANNING: There are many caravan parks and campsites in the state, most of which are located off the main highways. Further information can be obtained from the Western Australian Tourism Commission. A number of companies can arrange **motor camper** rentals, with a range of fully equipped vehicles. Full details can be obtained from the Tourist Commission.
Note: More detailed coverage of the range of accommodation available in Australia may be found by consulting the *Accommodation* section in the general entry for Australia above.

RESORTS & EXCURSIONS

'**Perth** has the climate that California thinks it has' is a popular saying in Western Australia; the city is sunny all year round but made pleasant due to the temperate breezes. It is a boom city and modern skyscrapers overshadow the colonial buildings such as the *Court House*, the *Town Hall* and the *Old Mill*. The *Swan River*, spanned by delicate bridges, winds through the city, and a cruise up river to the vineyards and wine tasting is a top tourist attraction. The *Omni Theatre Planetarium* in West Perth simulates the experience of space flight for the visitor. *Kings Park*, a beautiful parkland in the midst of town, the *West Australian Art Gallery* in James Street and the vast *Entertainment Centre* are also worth seeing.
The west coast beaches are almost always hot and sunny, many within easy reach of Perth.The most popular beach destinations are *Port, Cottesloe, City, Scarborough* and the nude bathing beach at *Swanbourne*. The *Swan River* also provides safe swimming in the suburbs of the city.
Fremantle, just 19km (12 miles) from Perth, is a port city full of charming terraced houses and historic buildings. The *Western Australian Maritime Museum* and *Fishing Boat Harbour*, with its many superb outdoor seafood restaurants, are the main attractions.
Off the coast opposite the natural ocean harbour of Fremantle lies **Rottnest Island,** a wildlife sanctuary named after the nest of the Quokka (a miniature marsupial resembling the wallaby) first found there by the Dutch explorer Van Vlaming in 1696. It is also full of secluded beaches and coves and is ideal for swimming, snorkelling and skindiving.
Outside Perth: Just 17km (11 miles) north of Perth is the new *Underwater World* at **Hillarys Boat Harbour** showing over 4000 sea creatures in their natural environments. *Atlantis Marine Park* in **Yanchep,** an hour's drive north, has performing dolphins. South of Perth is *Cable Ski Park* with thrilling water rides and *Adventure World*, a favourite family entertainment complex on **Bibra Lake** with thrill rides, native animals, parkland and waterways in beautiful surroundings. Set in bushland an hour's drive inland from Perth is **El Caballo Blanco,** where Spanish Andalusian dancing stallions perform. Also nearby is **Pioneer World,** a re-creation of a pioneer town and **Cohunu Wildlife Park,** with abundant wildlife. Further east into the hinterland there is the thriving gold-mining town of **Kalgoorlie** and towns which were once the centre of of Western Australia's gold rush, such as **Coolgardie.** The **Darling Ranges,** behind Perth, are popular among visitors and contain several national parks. The **Avon Valley,** a 90-minute drive from Perth, is an agricultural area of rolling hills and fertile valleys. In this region can be found the town of **York** where the *York Motor Museum* and *The Residency Museum* (showing how life was lived in colonial days) are worth seeing. The southwest region is well known for its coastline and excellent wineries and vineyards. Further north, there are long stretches of undeveloped coastline and rust-coloured landscape. Wildflowers abound in this region during September-October. **Nambung National Park** is well-known for its amazing limestone formations known as The Pinnacles. At **Monkey Mia**, on the coast, there are wild dolphins that come into the shallows to greet visitors. Also in the north of the state lie **The Kimberleys,** a wild region rich in Aboriginal legends, which in recent years has become a thriving diamond-mining centre. It is one of the oldest geological areas on earth. The city of **Broome,** on the north coast, is the pearl capital of the world. At the opposite end of the state is **Albany,** the first European settlement in Western Australia, which has many restored buildings, a whaling museum at *Whaleworld* and some extraordinary natural wonders, such as the *Gap* and the monolithic *Natural Bridge*.

SOCIAL PROFILE

FOOD & DRINK: Excellent seafood from the coast around Perth – king prawns, rock lobster (locals call this crayfish, jewfish barramundi), Westralian *dhufish* and special freshwater lobster called *marron*. There are excellent local wines in Western Australia and important vineyards at Swan Valley, Mount Barker and Margaret River.
NIGHTLIFE: There are many nightclubs in the Northbridge area of Perth and the Burswood Resort and Casino complex is only minutes from Perth city centre.
SHOPPING: Best buys are Argyle diamonds, opals, emu leather products and Aboriginal art. Shops are open all day Saturday and late night Thursday.
SPECIAL EVENTS: The following is a selection of festivals and special events taking place in Western Australia:
Apr 5-10 '93 *Australian Water Polo Championships*, Perth. **Apr 24-May 2** *Fourth Australian Masters Games*, Perth. **Jul 4-14** *National Lacrosse Championships*, Perth. **Sep 17-21** *Commonwealth Bank Rally Australia*, Perth. **Oct 16-24** *Australia & New Zealand Police Games*, Perth. **Dec 1-Jan 1 '94** *Whitbread Round the World Yacht Race*, Fremantle Sailing Club.

BUSINESS PROFILE

COMMERCIAL INFORMATION: The following organisation can offer advice: Western Australian Chamber of Commerce and Industry Inc, 38 Parliament Place, West Perth, WA 6005. Tel: (9) 322 2688. Fax: (9) 481 0980. Telex: 93609.
CONFERENCES/CONVENTIONS: The major convention centres in Perth are the Hilton Hotel, Hyatt Regency Hotel, Observation City Resort Hotel, Perth International Hotel, Sheraton Hotel, the Superdrome and also Burswood Resort and Convention and Exhibition Centre, only 3km (2 miles) from the city centre with seating available for 2000 for conventions or 21,000 for exhibitions. For more information on conferences and conventions in Western Australia contact the Australian Tourist Commission *or* the Perth Convention Bureau, Fourth Floor, 16 St George's Terrace, Perth, WA 6000. Tel: (9) 220 1730. Fax: (9) 220 1702.

CLIMATE

North is tropical with monsoon season. South is subtropical to temperate. Rainfall is distributed throughout the year but varies from area to area. Northern monsoons occur January to March.
Required clothing: Lightweight cottons and linens throughout the year in the north and in summer in the south. Slightly warmer clothes are necessary in cooler winter months; waterproofing is advisable throughout the year.

PERTH W.Australia (60m)

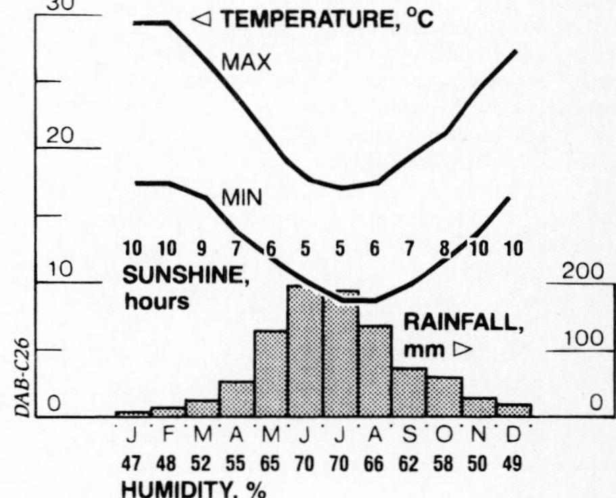

KALGOORLIE W.Australia (380m)

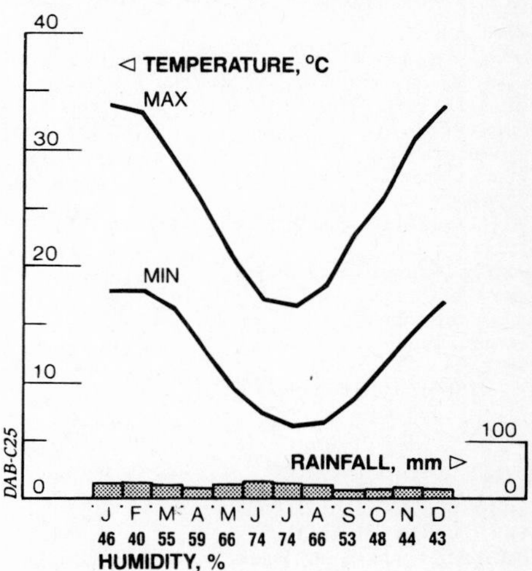

□ international airport

Location: Western Europe.

Österreich Werbung (ANTO)
Margaretenstrasse 1
A-1040 Vienna, Austria
Tel: (1) 588 660 *or* 587 2000. Fax: (1) 588 6620.
Embassy of the Republic of Austria
18 Belgrave Mews West
London SW1X 8HU
Tel: (071) 235 3731. Fax: (071) 235 8025. Telex: 28327.
Opening hours: 0900-1130 Monday to Friday.
Austrian National Tourist Office
30 St George Street
London W1R 0AL
Tel: (071) 629 0461. Fax: (071) 499 6038. Opening hours: 1030-1700 Monday to Friday.
British Embassy
Jaurèsgasse 12
A-1030 Vienna, Austria
Tel: (1) 713 1575. Fax: (222) 712 7316. Telex: 132810.
British Consulates: Innsbruck, Graz, Salzburg and Bregenz.
Embassy of the Republic of Austria
2343 Massachusetts Avenue, NW
Washington, DC 20008-3035
Tel: (202) 483 4474. Fax: (202) 483 2743. Telex: 440010.
Austrian Consulate-General
31 East 69th Street
New York, NY 10021
Tel: (212) 737 6400.
Austrian National Tourist Office
500 Fifth Avenue
New York, NY 10110
Tel: (212) 944 6880.
Embassy of the United States of America
Unit 27937
Boltzmanngasse 16
A-1091 Vienna, Austria
Tel: (1) 315 511; (1) 51451 (consular section). Fax: (1) 310 0682. Telex: 114634.
Canadian Embassy
Dr-Karl-Lueger-Ring 10/IV
A-1010 Vienna, Austria
Tel: (1) 533 3691/5. Fax: (1) 535 4473. Telex: 115320.
Austrian Embassy
445 Wilbrod Street
Ottawa, Ontario
K1N 6M7
Tel: (613) 563 1444. Fax: (613) 563 0038. Telex: 533290.
Austrian National Tourist Board
Suite 3330
2 Bloor Street East
Toronto, Ontario
M4W 1A8
Tel: (416) 967 3381. Fax: (416) 967 4101.

AREA: 83,859 sq km (32,378 sq miles).
POPULATION: 7,812,100 (1991).
POPULATION DENSITY: 93.1 per sq km.
CAPITAL: Vienna (Wien). **Population:** 1,533,176 (1991).

GEOGRAPHY: Austria is a landlocked country, bordered by Switzerland, Liechtenstein, Germany, Czech Republic, Slovakia, Hungary, Slovenia and Italy. It is predominantly Alpine. The imposing Dachstein region of Upper Austria, the massive Tyrolean peaks, the lakes of Carinthia and Salzkammergut, the River Danube and the forests of Styria are amongst the many outstanding features of the country.
LANGUAGE: German is the official language. Regional dialects are pronounced and within the different regions of the country one will encounter marked variations from *Hochdeutsch*, ie 'standard' German.
RELIGION: 89% Roman Catholic, 6% Protestant.
TIME: GMT + 1 (GMT + 2 in summer).
ELECTRICITY: 220 volts AC, 50Hz. Round 2-pin Continental plugs are standard.
COMMUNICATIONS: Telephone: Full IDD facilities available. Country code: 43. Call boxes are painted yellow and found in all areas. International calls can be made from pay-phones with four coin slots. Trunk calls within Austria are approximately 33% cheaper between 1800-2000 hours Monday to Friday and at the weekend (from Friday 1800 to Monday 0800 hrs). **Telex/telegram:** Telex services are available in several main hotels (for residents only) or at the main telecommunications centre in Vienna. Country code: 47. Telegram facilities are available from any post office. **Post:** Letters up to 20g and postcards within Europe are sent airmail. Letters to the UK take two to four days, and to the USA four to six days. Stamps may be purchased in post offices or tobacco shops. Post boxes are painted yellow. A *Poste Restante* service is available at most post offices. Address mail to 'Postlagernd' ('Hauptpostlagernd' if a main post office), followed by the person's name, town, and post code. Post office hours: generally 0800-1200 and 1400-1700/1800 Monday to Friday, but main post offices and those at major railway stations are open for 24 hours seven days a week, including public holidays. **Press:** Newspapers are in German. The *Wiener Zeitung*, established in 1703, is the oldest newspaper in the world. The national daily with the largest circulation is the *Neue Kronen-Zeitung*.
BBC World Service and Voice of America frequencies: From time to time these change. See the section *How to Use this Book* for more information.

BBC:				
MHz	12.09	9.410	6.195	3.955
Voice of America:				
MHz	11.97	9.670	6.040	5.995

PASSPORT/VISA

Regulations and requirements may be subject to change at short notice, and you are advised to contact the appropriate diplomatic or consular authority before finalising travel arrangements. Details of these may be found at the head of this country's entry. Any numbers in the chart refer to the footnotes below.

	Passport Required?	Visa Required?	Return Ticket Required?
Full British	1	No/2	No
BVP	Valid	No	No
Australian	Yes	No	Yes
Canadian	Yes	No	Yes
USA	Yes	No	Yes
Other EC	1	No	No
Japanese	Yes	No/2	No

PASSPORTS: [1] Valid passports required by all except for nationals of EC countries and nationals of Andorra, Finland, Liechtenstein, Malta, Monaco, Norway, San Marino, Sweden, and Switzerland who may enter with a valid national ID card (or BVP for UK nationals).
British Visitors Passport: Acceptable. A BVP can be used for holidays or unpaid business trips to Austria. For further information, see the *Passport/Visa* section of the introduction at the beginning of the book.
VISAS: Required by all except:
(a) nationals of the countries referred to in the chart above for stays of up to 90 days (**[2]** with the exceptions of citizens from the UK and Japan who can stay for a period of up to six months and nationals of Liechtenstein, Luxembourg and Switzerland who can stay for an unlimited period);
(b) nationals of countries referred to above under passport exemptions;
(c) nationals of Argentina, Bahamas, Barbados, Bolivia, Brazil, Chile, Colombia, Costa Rica, Cyprus, Czechoslovakia, Dominican Republic, Ecuador, El Salvador, Guatemala, Hong Kong (British citizens), Iceland, Israel, Jamaica, South Korea, Malaysia, Mexico, New Zealand, Panama, Paraguay, Peru, Poland, Seychelles, Singapore, Trinidad & Tobago, Tunisia, Uruguay and Venezuela for stays of up to 90 days;
(d) nationals of Hungary for stays of up to 30 days.
Note: It is advisable for Romanian nationals to check with the nearest consulate or embassy consular section regarding visa requirements.
Types of visa: Only one type of entry visa is issued, and it is not specified in the visa whether the purpose of the trip is tourism, business or transit; working visas do, however, exist.
Cost: Single entry: £15.15. Multiple entry: £20.20 payable in postal orders or certified bank drafts.
Validity: Up to 3 months. Visas are never extended, but applications for a new visa can be made.
Application to: Consulate (or Consular Section at Embassy). For addresses, see top of entry. Postal applicants should enclose a self-addressed, pre-paid envelope for the return of the passport.
Application requirements: (a) Completed application form. (b) Valid passport. (c) Consular fee. (d) For transit, the visa from the destination country should be obtained first.
Note: Nationals of the following countries must complete the application form *in duplicate* and in addition submit one passport photograph: Albania, Algeria, Bahrain, Cambodia, Cuba, Egypt, Ethiopia, Iran, Iraq, Jordan, North Korea, Kuwait, Lebanon, Libya, Mongolia, Morocco, Oman, Saudi Arabia, Syria, United Arab Emirates, Vietnam, Western Samoa, Yemen, certain South African 'Homeland states' and Palestinians. In certain cases flight tickets, bank statements or other items must also be produced.
Working days required: Visa applications are usually dealt with within 24 hours. If processing takes longer the applicant is informed accordingly. A self-addressed envelope (preferably registered or recorded delivery) is required.
Temporary residence: Apply to Austrian Embassy.

MONEY

Currency: Austrian Schilling (ASch) = 100 Groschen. Bank notes are in denominations of ASch5000, 1000, 500, 100, 50 and 20. Coins are in denominations of ASch1000, 500, 50, 20, 10, 5 and 1, and 50, 10, 5 and 2 Groschen.
Currency exchange: Foreign currencies and travellers cheques are exchanged at all banks, savings banks and exchange counters at airports and railway stations at the official exchange rates. In general, shops, travel agents and hotels also accept foreign currency.
Credit cards: All major credit cards and Eurocheque cards are accepted in large cities and tourist areas, as are travellers cheques.
Exchange rate indicators: The following figures are included as a guide to the movements of the Austrian Schilling against Sterling and the US Dollar:

Date:	**Oct '89**	**Oct '90**	**Oct '91**	**Oct '92**
£1.00=	**20.94**	**20.94**	**20.49**	**17.12**
$1.00=	**13.26**	**11.80**	**11.81**	**10.78**

Currency restrictions: No restrictions except for export of more than ASch100,000 in Austrian currency, for which a permit is required. Gold coins to a limit of 200g per person per trip may be exported, providing the coins do not have legal tender status.
Banking hours: Banks in Vienna are open from 0800-1230 and 1330-1500 Monday, Tuesday, Wednesday and Friday. Thursday hours are from 0800-1230 and 1330-1730 (head offices do not close for the break). Different opening hours may be kept in the various Federal Provinces. The exchange counters at airports and at railway stations are generally open from the first to the last plane or train, which usually means from 0800-2200 including weekends.

DUTY FREE

The following goods can be taken into Austria without incurring any customs duty by visitors over 17 years of age who are either residents of Austria or non-residents arriving from European countries:
200 cigarettes or 50 cigars or 250g of tobacco;
2.25 litres of wine or 2.1 litres of sparkling wine and 1 litre of spirits;
1 bottle of eau de cologne (up to 300g);
50g of perfume
Souvenirs up to a value of ASch400 for non-residents (ASch1000 for Austrian residents).
Note: Arrivals from outside Europe are allowed double the above allowances; to qualify, the visitor must not have stopped for more than 24 hours in another European country en route to Austria.

PUBLIC HOLIDAYS

Public holidays observed in Austria are as follows:
Apr 12 '93 Easter Monday. **May 1** Labour Day. **May 20** Ascension Day. **May 31** Whit Monday. **Jun 10** Corpus Christi. **Aug 15** Assumption. **Oct 16** National Holiday. **Nov 1** All Saints' Day. **Dec 8** Immaculate Conception.

Salzburg Airport

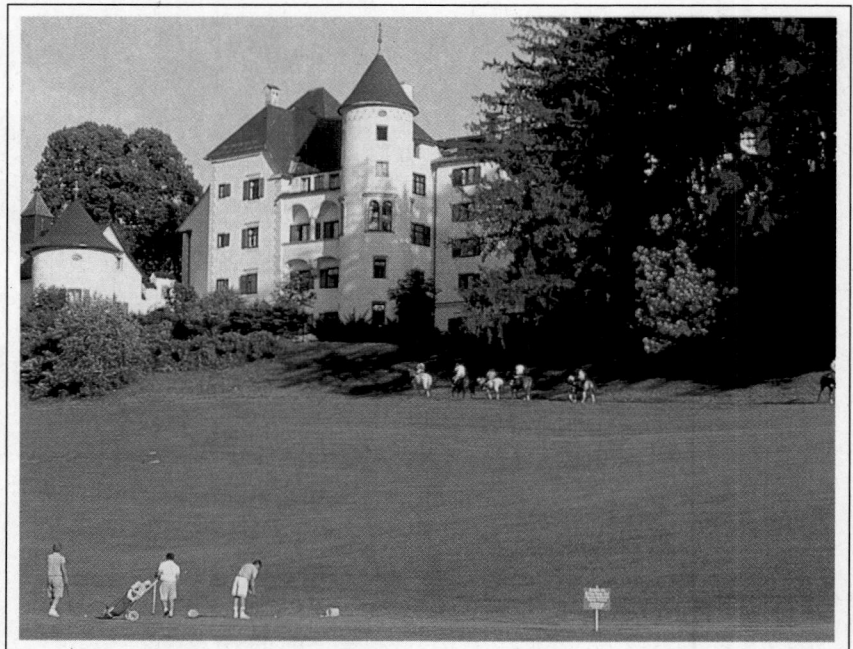

Dec 25 Christmas Day. **Dec 26** St Stephen's Day. **Jan 1 '94** New Year's Day. **Jan 6** Epiphany.

HEALTH

Regulations and requirements may be subject to change at short notice, and you are advised to contact your doctor well in advance of your intended date of departure. Any numbers in the chart refer to the footnotes below.

	Special Precautions?	Certificate Required?
Yellow Fever	No	No
Cholera	No	No
Typhoid & Polio	No	-
Malaria	No	-
Food & Drink	1	-

[1]: Milk is pasteurised and dairy products are safe for consumption. Local meat, poultry, seafood, fruit and vegetables are generally considered safe to eat.

Rabies is present in Austria, although there have been no incidents reported in recent years. For those at high risk vaccination before arrival should be considered. If you are bitten abroad seek medical advice without delay. For more information consult the *Health* section at the back of the book.

Ticks often live in heavily afforested areas during the summer months in some of the more eastern parts of Austria and can create discomfort and, in very rare cases, serious infection to people who are bitten by them. Immunisation is available and travellers likely to find themselves in those woods should take a course of injections. The immunisation consists either of three different shots, which travellers should have injected one year before leaving their country of origin, or of an injection after a tick bite, which is available from every doctor in Austria. For more information contact Immuno Ltd, Arctic House, Rye Lane, Dunton Green, Sevenoaks, Kent, TN14 5HB, UK. Tel: (0732) 458101.

Health care: There is a Reciprocal Health Agreement with the UK but it is of a limited nature, only allowing UK citizens free emergency in-patient treatment at public hospitals. Everything else (including ambulances, prescribed medicines and consultations with general practitioners) must be paid for. Costs are high and medical insurance is, therefore, strongly advised.

TRAVEL - International

AIR: Austria's national airline is *Austrian Airlines (OS)*.

Approximate flight times: From *London* to Innsbruck is 2 hours, to Salzburg is 1 hour 50 minutes and to Vienna is 2 hours 10 minutes.

From *Los Angeles* to Vienna is 15 hours.

From *New York* to Vienna is 9 hours.

From *Singapore* to Vienna is 14 hours.

From *Sydney* to Vienna is 25 hours.

International airports: *Vienna* (Wien–Schwechat), *Graz* (Thalerhof), *Innsbruck* (Kranebitten), *Klagenfurt* (Anna Bichl), *Linz* (Hörsching) and *Salzburg* (Maxglan).

Vienna (VIE) (Wien-Schwechat) is 18km (11 miles) east of the city. There are regular coach, rail and taxi services to the city, including a bus service from the airport to the Vienna Air Terminal, Hilton Hotel. The train services run to Vienna main railway station. Airport facilities include duty-free shop, banks, currency exchange, post office, restaurant, car hire *(Avis, Hertz* and *Inter-rent)*, car park and nursery.

Innsbruck (INN) (Kranebitten) is 5.5km (3.5 miles) from the city. Bus services are available every 15 minutes to the city centre. Taxi services are also available. Airport facilities include duty-free shop, currency exchange, restaurant and car hire *(Avis)*.

Salzburg (SZG) (Maxglan) is 5km (3 miles) west of the city. There are bus services every 15 minutes, taxis and some hotel courtesy coaches. Airport facilities include duty-free shopping, currency exchange, restaurant, bar and car hire *(Avis)*.

Klagenfurt (KLU) (Wörther See) is 3km (2 miles) from the city. Bus and taxi services are available.

Note: Airports have fixed charges for portering.

SEA/RIVER: The quickest and most practical international sea route from London to Vienna is via the Dover–Ostend ferry (3 hours 30 minutes). The distance by road is approximately 1600km (1000 miles). It is a day's drive in summer, but can take longer in winter. Munich is four to five hours from Vienna; Milan and Zurich are a good day's drive.

RAIL: There are daily international services from London to Austrian destinations. The through trains are as follows:

AUSTRIA	HEALTH REGULATIONS	VISA REGULATIONS
GALILEO/WORLDSPAN	TI-DFT/VIE/HE	TI-DFT/VIE/VI
SABRE	TIDFT/VIE/HE	TIDFT/VIE/VI

Code-Link

To access this information on your CRS, swipe the barcode with a light pen or type in the text under the barcode. For more information, see the introduction *How to Use This Book*.

Calais–Basle–Innsbruck *(Arlberg Express)*.
Ostend–Aachen–Cologne–Munich–Salzburg (Note: In winter there is no direct service on this route: change trains at Munich).
Ostend–Brussels–Cologne–Frankfurt–Vienna *(Austria Nachtexpress)*.
Fare reductions are indicated in the international railway fare catalogue (TCV), and Austria is included in the *Eurailpass* and *Eurail Youthpass* scheme.
ROAD: Some tour operators offer package holidays to Austria by coach from the UK. A full list is available from the Tourist Office. See above under *Sea/River* for information on roads into Austria from foreign ports.

TRAVEL - Internal

AIR: Vienna is connected to Graz, Klagenfurt, Linz and Salzburg by both *Austrian Airlines (OS)* and *Austrian Air Services (SO)*. *Tirolean Airlines* run services from Vienna to Innsbruck. **Charter:** A number of companies offer chartering services for single- and twin–engined aircraft and executive jets.
RIVER/LAKE: A number of operators run cruises along the Danube to the Black Sea, and from Bregenz across Lake Constance. On some cruises a passport is needed. They last from one to eight days depending on the itinerary. These services run between spring and autumn. **Ferries:** There are regular passenger boat services from mid-May to mid-September along the Danube and on Austria's lakes. The Danube steamer services are run by the DDSG and other boat trips by private or state-owned companies. International rail tickets are valid on Danube River boats. More information on these services, including connections with Bratislava, Budapest, Belgrade, Istanbul and Yalta can be obtained from: DDSG – Reisedienst, Handelskai 265, A-1021 Vienna. Tel: (1) 217 100.
RAIL: *Austrian Federal Railways (ÖBB)* run an efficient internal service throughout Austria. Tickets can be obtained from any station ticket office or from most Austrian travel agents. Domestic fare reductions include: short-distance return ticket; cross-country pass; provincial pass; senior citizens' pass; school excursions (with up to 70% reductions). For further information consult the Tourist Office. There is a frequent intercity service from Vienna to Salzburg, Innsbruck, Graz and Klagenfurt, and regular car ferry services through the Tauern Tunnel. Information and booking can be obtained from train stations, the Austrian Travel Agency *(Austropa)* and its ticket distribution offices. Railways have fixed charges for portering.
ROAD: Austria has an excellent internal network of roads. Free help is readily given by the Austrian Motoring Association (OAMTC). Information is transmitted in English on radio channels during the summer. Some of the roads are toll roads (a charge is made before entry onto these roads, mainly to help pay for their upkeep). Seat belts must be worn and children under the age of 12 may not sit in the front seat unless a special child's seat has been fitted. Both driver and passenger on a motorbike must wear helmets, and the bike must have lights on at all times. Speed limits are 50kmph (31mph) in built-up areas, 100kmph (62mph) outside built-up areas and 130kmph (81mph) on motorways.
Bus and **coach** services are run by federal and local authorities, as well as private companies. There are over 1800 services in operation. Some 70 international coach services travel to or through Austria and 22 routes with timetables and prices can be found in the Austrian bus guide which can be consulted via the Tourist Office. Coach excursions and sightseeing tours run from most major cities.
Car hire: There are car hire firms with offices in most cities, as well as at airports and major railway stations.
Documentation: British driving licences are generally recognised in Austria and enable the holder to drive in Austria for up to a year. Minimum age is 18. Car registration papers issued in the UK are also valid in Austria, and third-party insurance is law. A Green Card is *strongly recommended.*

URBAN: Vienna has an extensive system of metro, bus, light rail and tramway services. Most routes have a flat fare, and there are pre-purchase multi-journey tickets and passes. Those trams marked *Schaffnerlos* on the outside of the carriage do not have conductors, and there is therefore no way of buying a ticket on board. Tickets are available from newspaper shops or tobacconists called *Trafik*. The classic way to travel round the capital is by horse-drawn carriage *(Fiaker)*; fares should be agreed in advance. There are bus systems in all the other main towns, and also tramways in Linz, Innsbruck and Graz, and trolleybuses in Linz, Innsbruck and Salzburg.
JOURNEY TIMES: The following chart gives approximate journey times (in hours and minutes) from Vienna to other major cities/towns in Austria.

	Air	Road	Rail
Salzburg	0.45	3.00	3.00
Linz	0.45	2.00	2.00
Innsbruck	1.20	5.00	5.30
Bregenz	-	7.00	10.00
Klagenfurt	0.55	4.00	4.20
Graz	0.40	2.40	2.30

ACCOMMODATION

It is advisable to make inquiries and reservations well in advance (especially for July, August, Christmas and Easter). Room reservations are binding for the hotelkeeper and for the guest or travel agency. Compensation may be claimed if reserved rooms are not occupied. Hotels, *pensions* and other forms of tourist accommodation are classified by the Federal Department of Commerce and Industry. See *Grading* section below for details.
HOTELS: 95% of 5-star hotels, 80% of 4-star hotels and 10% of 3-star hotels in Austria belong to the Bundeskammer der Gewerglichen Wirtschaft, Sektion Freundenverkehr (Austrian national hotel association), Wiedner Hauptstrasse 63, A-1045 Vienna, Austria. Tel: (1) 501 050. Fax: (1) 502 06274.
Grading: Classifications are according to the guidelines established by the International Hotel Association and relate to the facilities provided; 5-star for deluxe, 4-star for first class, 3-star for standard, 2-star for economy and 1-star for budget. The facilities offered are as follows:
5-star hotels: Private bathrooms with shower or bath, hand basin and WC with all bedrooms. Telephone, alarm bell, TV on request in all bedrooms. Room service, day and night reception and foreign languages spoken. Restaurant, bars, lifts and garage space (in the cities) in all hotels.
4-star hotels: At least 80% of bedrooms with private bathroom with bath or shower, hand basin and WC. There is a telephone and alarm bell in all rooms, and TV or radio on request in most. Room service and day and night reception, dining rooms, foreign languages spoken, lifts in all hotels.
3-star hotels: All rooms with alarm bell, all with a hand basin and 50% with private bathroom with bath or shower, hand basin and WC. Foreign languages spoken at reception. Lifts and dining room.
2-star hotels: All rooms with hand basin. Toilet facilities may be shared. The dining room may serve as another public room. Some with reception and foreign language capability.
1-star hotels: All rooms have hand basins. Toilet facilities may be shared. The dining room may double as a general public room.
Note: Some hotels may still be under the old grades of A, B, C etc. Full information and hotel list is available from the Austrian National Tourist Office.
SELF-CATERING: Holiday apartments and chalets are available for rent throughout Austria. For full details contact your local travel agent or the following individual agencies:
Vienna: Ruefa Reisen GmbH, Mariahilferstrasse 95, A-1060 Vienna. Tel: (1) 597 016-0. Fax: (1) 597 016-014. Telex: 115475.
Burgenland: Blaguss Reisen GmbH, Untere Hauptstrasse 12, A-7100 Neusiedl am See. Tel: (2167) 8141. Fax: (2167) 8872. Telex: 18160.
Carinthia: Kärntner Landesreisebüro, Neuer Platz 2, A-9020 Klagenfurt. Tel: (463) 56400-0. Fax: (463) 56400-75. Telex: 422118.
Lower Austria: Niederösterreich Reservierungszentrale, Heidenschusse 2, A-1010 Vienna. Tel: (1) 533 3114-34. Telex: 115220.
Salzburg Province: Interhome – Johann Wolfstrasse 7, A-5020 Salzburg. Tel: (662) 845 586. Fax: (662) 845 5895. Telex: 632994.
Ruefa Reisen GmbH – Rainerstrasse 7, A-5020 Salzburg. Tel: (662) 874 561-0. Fax: (662) 874 561-20. Telex: 631186.
Dr Degener GmbH, Linzer Gasse 4, A-5024 Salzburg. Tel: (662) 889 110. Fax: (662) 883 051. Telex: 633596.
Styria: Steiermärkisches Landesreisebüro, Hauptplatz 14, Graz. Tel: (316) 826 456. Fax: (316) 817 261. Telex: 311113.
Tyrol: Tiroler Landesreisebüro, Bozner Platz 7, A-6020 Innsbruck. Tel: (512) 491 626. Fax: (512) 492 854. Telex: 533825.
Upper Austria: Landesfremdenverkehrsamt Zentrale Buchungsstelle, Schillerstrasse 50, A-4020 Linz. Tel: (732) 600 221 *or* 663 024. Fax: (732) 663 0215 *or* 600 220. Telex: 222175.
Oberösterreichisches Landesreisebüro, Hauptplatz 9, A-4010 Linz. Tel: (732) 271 061-0. Fax: (732) 771 061-49. Telex: 21493.
Vorarlberg: Pego, Rental of holiday apartments and chalets all over Austria. Peter Godula, Sägeweg 1, A-6700 Bludenz. Tel: (5552) 65666. Fax: (5552) 63801. Telex: 52169.
FARM HOLIDAYS: Lists of farmhouse accommodation taking paying guests for most provinces in Austria are available at the Austrian National Tourist Office. Listings include farms as well as pensions and inns with an attached farming operation.
CAMPING/CARAVANNING: There are 489 camping sites in Austria, all of which can be entered without any major formalities. One hundred and fifty of these are equipped for winter camping. Reductions in rates for children are available, and for members of FICC, AIT and FIA. It is advisable to take along the camping carnet. Fees are charged on the usual international scale for parking caravans, motorbikes and cars. The parking of caravans without traction vehicle on or beside the public highways (including motorway parking areas) is prohibited. One can park caravans with traction vehicle beside public highways, if the parking regulations are observed. Some mountain roads are closed for caravans. For detailed information contact the automobile clubs or the Austrian National Tourist Office. The address of the Camping Club is as follows: Austrian Camping Club (ÖCC), PO Box 88, 3402 Klosterneuburg. Tel: (2243) 856 100.
Note: When camping in private grounds permission of landowner, police and municipal council is needed.
YOUTH HOSTELS: Youth hostels can be found throughout Austria and are at the disposal of anyone carrying a membership card of the International Youth Hostel Association. It is advisable to book in advance, especially during peak periods. For more details contact the Österreichischer Jugendherbergsverband, Schottenring 28, A–1010 Vienna. Tel: (1) 533 5353 *or* 535 0861.
DISABLED TRAVELLERS: A hotel guide for disabled travellers is available from ANTO or from: Verband der Querschnittgelähmten Österreichs, A-8144 Tobelbad, Styria. For Vienna a special hotel guide for disabled persons has been published. This guide is available from Verband der Querschnittgelahmten Österreichs, Liechtensteinstrasse 57, A-1090 Vienna. Tel: (1) 340 121. There are also hotels with special facilities for disabled persons in towns all over Austria.

RESORTS & EXCURSIONS

Austria is not only famous for the world's premier skiing regions, but also for breathtaking scenery, magnificent mountains and established hiking trails. The western Federal Provinces **Vorarlberg, Tyrol** and **Salzburg Province** are the most popular tourist regions, though the southern **Carinthia** (bordering Italy and Slovenia) is now taking a larger share of the trade due to its mild climate and attractive lakes.

Austria lends itself to walking and climbing as well as skiing, with an extensive network of hiking and mountain routes carefully signposted and cross-referenced to detailed maps. Alpine huts between 915m and 2744m, with resident wardens in the summer, are for rent. Further information can be obtained from the Austrian Alpine Club (*Österreichischer Alpenklub*), Wilhelm-Greil-Strasse 15, A-6020 Innsbruck. Tel: (0512) 595 470.

Skiing facilities can be found in over 600 winter sport resorts between Brand in the west and Semmering in the east. Skiing enthusiasts of all ages and levels have the choice of more than 400 schools and top ski-instructors. **St Anton** is probably the most cosmopolitan with a lively après-ski nightlife. A cable ride to the Vallugagrat offers an ascent with typically stunning Alpine views.

Vienna

The Austrian capital and one of the federal provinces is an important nexus for East-West trade and a frequent host to major congresses either in the *Vienna International Centre* (UNO City) or at the *Austria Center Vienna*. Vienna is situated in the northeast of the country with the Danube running through the northern suburbs of the city. The Ringstrasse is the boundary of the Inner City or Innenstadt, with its fine examples of the city's architecture, shops and hotels. An atmosphere of elegance and style of bygone eras very much prevails in this area, which should be experienced on foot. Art Nouveau buildings line the streets of some suburbs, as Vienna was the birthplace of this then controversial style. The *Austrian National Library* at the Josefsplatz is regarded as an outstanding example of Baroque architecture. The *Schloss Schönbrunn*, home to the Vienna Zoo with its landscaped park, can be compared with the sumptuous palace at Versailles. Many fine art collections like the *Kunsthistorisches Museum*, with the works of Breughel, Dürer and the Akademie der Bildenden Künste (Hieronymus Bosch) are internationally renowned. Opulent balls run from New Year's Eve to *Mardi Gras*, the most famous being the *Opernball*. Spring sees the *Festival of Vienna* with concerts, operas and theatre performances. The *Wiener Oper* itself offers a well-selected programme between September and June. Guided tours of the opera and the stage are held regularly during July and August, and at other times when the performance schedule permits it. Right behind the opera is the *Hotel Sacher*, famous the world over for its chocaholic's dream *Sacher Torte* and other Viennese specialities. There are more than 50 museums open to the public, grand palaces, shops, antique markets, international choirs and orchestras, as well as fine restaurants and cosy coffeehouses, which are very much part of the Austrian culture. The Habsburgs who ruled the country for six centuries resided in the *Hofburg* which has the *Kaiser-Appartements* and the *Crown Jewels*. Essential for any tourist is a visit to the *Spanish Riding School* in the Hofburg, where the famous white Lippizaner stallions perform finely executed dressage manoeuvres to the music of Mozart and the Strauss family (closed during July and August). Vienna was the centre of the cultural Renaissance during the 18th and 19th centuries, and home not only to Mozart and the Strauss' but also to Haydn, Beethoven, Schubert, Bruckner, Brahms and Mahler.

Excursions/sightseeing: Vienna is ideal for art and music enthusiasts. The *Viennese Boys' Choir* and the *Viennese Philharmonic* are internationally renowned. Well worth a visit is the art collection at the *Belvedere*, the *Chapel of the Hofburg*, the *Burgtheater* (known as the Burg), the *Parliament*, the *Old Town Hall*, the University and the Votive church along the Ringstrasse; as well as *St Stephen's Cathedral* and the churches of *St Charles* and *St Rupert*. Not to be missed is the Augustinian Friars and the Capuchin church with the Imperial crypt of the Habsburg family. Vienna's abundance of museums include the *Natural History Museum*, the *Austrian Museum of Applied Arts*, the *Museum of the 20th Century*, the *Museum of Modern Art*, the *Künstlerhaus*, the *Clock and Watch Museum* and the *Technology Museum*. The are also memorial sites for Mozart, Haydn, Beethoven, Schubert, Strauss and Freud.

Burgenland

Austria's youngest Federal Province in the easternmost part of the country is a popular tourist destination. The wooded hills in the south of the region turn into the foothills of the Alps. The northeast largely consists of expanses of the Central European Plain. The mild climate is especially well suited for the cultivation of wine.

Resorts: Eisenstadt, Mogersdorf, Mörbisch, Neusiedl am See, Podersdorf, Raiding Rust, St Margarethen, Bad Tatzmannsdorf and Illmitz.

Excursions/sightseeing: The *Esterhazy Palace*, the *Cathedral* and the *Haydengasse*, as well as the *Bergkirche* and the Franciscan church are well worth a visit in **Eisenstadt**. A thoughtful atmosphere lies over the Jewish Cemetery and the former Jewish Ghetto. The region is dotted with interesting palaces and fortresses. In July and August **Mörbisch** hosts an operetta festival against the backdrop of the Neusiedler Lake. Not to be missed is the *Local History Museum* in **Neusiedl am See. Raiding** is the birthplace of Franz Liszt. Passion plays are staged every five years in **St Margarethen**. The nature reserve of **Illmitz** is ideal for hiking and walks. **Bad Tatzmannsdorf** is a noted spa.

Carinthia

Surrounded by Austria's highest mountain, the Grossglockner (3797m), and the Karawanken in the south, the lifestyle here is friendlier and the summers are warmer. The famous lakes reach water temperatures of 28°C, which earned Carinthia the European Environment Award for their superb water quality. From the **Wörther See** to the *National Park* of **Hohe Tauern**, from the Carinthian summer to the bicycle path on the banks of the Drau, Carinthia offers a variety of excursions even in winter. At this time the lakes become skating rinks and the 10 ski-resorts with 1000km pistes open their doors.

The Provincial capital, **Klagenfurt**, is full of tradition, with more than 50 arcades and the Lindwurm, a medieval dragon, part of the layout. **Villach** combines its flair with a hot spring.

Resorts: Friesach, Heiligenblut, Millstatt, Obervellach, Ossiach, St Veit an der Glan, Villach, Klagenfurt, Veldem and Pörtschach.

Excursions/sightseeing: In **Klagenfurt** the Cathedral, the theatre, the concert hall, the zoo with the reptile house, the birthplace of Robert Musil, the planetarium and several museums are worth visiting. The **Wörther See** has good beaches. The churches and monasteries of **Gurk, Maria Gail, Maria Saal** and **Viktring** are popular, as is the *City Museum* of **Friesach.** Carinthia has a rich legacy of churches, fortresses, palaces and museums – history is always close at hand.

Lower Austria

Lower Austria is the largest Federal Province, encompassing stark mountain scenery, the Alpine foothills, the Danube Valley with its vineyards and the hilly country north of the Danube with its meadows, lakes and ponds.
Resorts: Baden bei Wien, Semmering (spa and ski-resort), Bad Deutsch-Altenburg, Dürnstein, Krems an der Donau, Retz, Rohrau, St Pölten, Wiener Neustadt and Zwettl.
Excursions/sightseeing: The spa of **Baden** has a casino, a summer theatre and a trotting course, whereas **Bad Deutsch-Altenburg** boasts a museum and the Roman archaeological park *Carnuntum*. In **Dürnstein**, the castle ruins, the medieval town centre and church of the same epoch are part of every tour. The sights of **Retz** include subterranean winecellars, well-restored medieval city walls, windmills and a Dominican church. **Rohrau,** Joseph Haydn's birthplace is also worth a visit. **St Pölten** is home to a Cathedral, the bishop's residence, a Franciscan church, a church of the Carmelite Nuns, a museum and several Baroque patrician houses. The *Austrian Military Academy* (an old castle), the Cathedral, a Capuchin church and a former Jesuit church (now the city's museum) can be visited in **Wiener Neustadt**. Well worth a visit is the abbey, the library, the state rooms and the chapter house of **Zwettl**. **Burg Rosenau** hosts a *Museum of Free Masonry*. All over Lower Austria are beautiful and interesting churches, abbeys, castles and palaces.

Salzburg Province

Salzburg is an elegant and spacious town, set against a backdrop of breathtaking mountain scenery. The snow-capped mountains of the Hohen Tauern rise in the south whereas the north offers the hills and lakes of the Salzkammergut. All sights are within walking distance of the old city centre, overlooked by the fortress *Hohensalzburg*. The city is probably best known for Wolfgang Amadeus Mozart who gets commemorated in the yearly *Salzburger Festspiele* which takes place in the *Grossen* and *Kleinen Festspielhaus*, as well as on the Cathedral square or in the University church. Mozart's birthplace in the Getreidegasse and his house at the Marktplatz are museums. Like Vienna, Salzburg is a fine example of Baroque architecture which stands second only to music in the country's cultural history.
Resorts: Badgastein (spa and winter resort), Bad Hofgastein, Grossgmain, Hallein, St Gilgen, Kaprun (glacier skiing in summer), Oberndorf and Zell-am-See.
Excursions/sightseeing: Salzburg: The *Abbey Church of St Peter* with cemetry and catacombs, the Franciscan church, the *Nonnberg Convent*, the *Trinity Church, St Sebastian's Cemetery*, the *Church of Parsch*, the *Palace of the Prince-Archbishops*, the carillon, the *Town Hall*, the *Pferdeschwemme* (a fountain), the festival halls, the *Mirabell Palace* with its landscaped gardens, the *Mönchsbert* and the *Kapuzinerberg*, several museums, the theatre, *Hellbrunn Palace* with the fountains, *Leopoldskron* and *Klessheim Palaces*, *Maria Plain Pilgrimage Church*, the Gaisberg and the Untersberg are ideal for tours and walks.
Salzburg Province: The salt mines and the *Celtic Museum* of **Hallein** are well worth a visit. **Irrsdorf** near Strasswalchen boasts a wonderful carved gate. Further sights include the *Castle Hohenwerfen*, the open-air museum of **Grossgmain**, the *Liechtensteinklamm* as well as the *Krimmler Waterfalls* in the *National Park Hohe Tauern*, the oldest in Austria.

Winter Sports Resorts

Austria is one of the major countries for winter sports in Europe and offers the most up-to-date facilities. The most popular areas for skiing are the provinces of Tyrol, Salzburg and Vorarlberg, with some well-known resorts in Carinthia, Styria and Upper and Lower Austria. Besides skiing, all types of other winter sports can be enjoyed, particularly tobogganing, sleigh rides, skating, curling and bowling. The country has a lively après-ski scene. Contact the ANTO for full details of ski resorts in the country.
Zell-am-See Area: Mid-December to mid-March. Limited though good nightlife. *Kaprun:* Christmas to end of March. Good glacier-skiing. Joint ski-pass **Europa Sportregion**.
Saalbach/Hinterglemm: *Hinterglemm:* Spacious new resort. Intermediates. *Saalbach:* Larger and more expensive, though established. Good entertainment for non-skiiers.
Obertauern: Snow guaranteed. Beginning of December to end of April.
Badgastein Area: *Badgastein:* Numerous downhill and cross-country ski runs. End-December to beginning April. *Bad Hofgastein:* Quiet village, good school. Beginners and intermediates. *Dorfgastein:* Small and friendly. Well-equipped Alpine huts. Beginners and intermediates. *Sportgastein:* This new resort can be reached by car or bus from Badgastein. Joint ski-pass **Gastein Super Ski.**
Pongau: *Flachau:* Beginners and intermediates. A few difficult runs. *St Johann in Pongau:* Runs of all difficulties. Large school. *Wagrain:* Beginners and intermediates. Quiet though good nightlife. *Filzmoos:* Tranquil, friendly atmosphere. Beginners and intermediates. *Altenmarkt:* Several runs. Joint ski-pass **Salzburger Sportwelt Amadé.**

Styria

Styria is a popular and especially attractive holiday destination. In the Dachstein Gebirge overshadowing the Enns Valley skiing is possible all year round. The south of the province is dominated by large vineyards. Styria also has a wealth of green pine forests suitable for rambles and hikes during the summer. In the Provincial capital **Graz**, one should plan a visit to the university and to one of the oldest museums in the world. The *Styrian Armoury*, housing a fine collection of ancient armour, and the *Schloss Eggenberg*, a 17th-century palace, are also not to be missed.
Resorts: Graz, Bruck an der Mur, Eisenerz, Leoben, Murau, Oberzeiring, Piber, Schladming, Stübing/Gratwein, Bad Aussee and Ramsau.
Excursions/sightseeing: The sights of **Graz** include several museums, the Herrengasse, Liberation Square, the *Cathedral*, the *Mausoleum of Emperor Ferdinand II*, the *Leech Church*, the pedestrian zone of the old quarter, numerous patrician houses, a 17th-century castle, *Palais Attems*, *Castle Hill* with the clocktower, the opera, the theatre and the *Maria Trost Pilgrimage Church*. **Eisenerz** boasts a fortified church. Part of any itinerary should be a visit to the museum and the Convent of **Leoben** and to the silver mine in **Oberzeiring**. The studfarm of the famous Lipizzaner breed of horse can be found in **Piber**. Old farm buildings and representative houses of all Austrian provinces are exhibited in the open-air museum of **Stübing/Gratwein**. The whole Province is scattered with churches, convents, palaces and castles.
Resort: *Schladming:* Unpretentious and friendly. Good shopping. Good though restricted nightlife.

Tyrol

Situated in the heart of the Alpine region, it is the most mountainous region of all, with forests, hamlets and alpine pastures, beautiful valleys and mountain lakes. In summer it is a popular destination for hikes; in winter, all winter sports are on offer. Traditional Tyrolean architecture is reflected in the villages, churches and castles.
Innsbruck, the Tyrolean capital and twice home of the Winter Olympics, is the centre of another internationally renowned ski complex comprising six major resorts. An 800-year-old university town, it has numerous fine buildings dating from Austria's cultural Renaissance in the 16th-18th centuries, and a 12th-century castle. For spectacular views over the town and southern Alps, take the funicular to Hungerburg and then the cable car to Hafelekar at 2334m.
Resorts: Innsbruck, Erl, Steinach am Brenner, Hall in Tyrol, Kitzbühel, Kramsach, Landeck, Lienz and Matrei in East Tyrol, Rattenberg, Seefeld in Tyrol and Thiersee.
Excursions/sightseeing: Do not miss the *Golden Roof*, the Herzog-Friedrich-Strasse, *Helbling House*, the *City Tower*, the *Court Church*, the *Hofburg*, the parish *Church of St Jakob*, the Maria-Theresien-Strasse, the *Palace of the Diet*, the *Triumphal Arch*, the *Wilten Basilica, Mount Isel*, the *Ambras Palace*, the *Tyrolean Museum*, the *Landestheater*, a conference centre and the *Seegrube* at **Innsbruck**. Passion plays take place every five years in **Erl**. A sight not to be missed is the Mint Tower at the Hasegg Castle in **Hall in Tyrol**. In **Rattenberg,** a medieval atmosphere prevails. A visit to the *Cathedral Chapter of Stams* and the basilica is recommended.
Resorts: Innsbruck Area: *Igls:* Bobsleigh events. Olympic course nearby. Good après-ski. Mid-December to mid-March. *Innsbruck:* Mid-December to mid-March. Discos, bars.
Axamer Lizum: Snow guaranteed. A few nursery slopes. Evening entertainment in the hotel bars. *Mutters:* Picturesque village with breathtaking views. Good for families, skiers of all levels and non-skiers. *Seefeld:* Comparatively expensive. End December to mid-March. Good après-ski, impressive sports centre.
Ischgl Area: *Ischgl:* Easy-going atmosphere, unsophisticated Tyrolean village. Mid-December to mid-April. *Galtür:* Ideal for families and intermediates. Sports centre.
Kitzbühel Area: *Kitzbühel:* International resort. Good selection of après ski. Mid-December to mid-March. *Kirchberg:* Something for everyone. Mid-December to mid-March. *Fieberbrunn:* Quiet family resort. *Kirchdorf:* Relaxed village atmosphere. Ideal for beginners and intermediates. *St Johann in Tirol:* Beginners and intermediates. Good nightlife.
Zugspitzarea: *Ehrwald:* Easy nursery slopes, ideal for family-skiing. *Lermoos:* Christmas to beginning of April. Good après-ski and leisure activities.
Obergurgl Area: *Hochgurgl:* Small purpose-built resort for all skiiers. *Obergurgl:* Beginning of December to end of April. Friendly and traditional.
Sölden Area: *Sölden:* Beginning of December to end of April. South-facing sunny resort. *Hochsölden:* Secluded. South-facing slopes.
Wilden Kaiser Area: *Söll:* Mid-December to mid-March. Nightlife informal and lively. *Ellmau:* Ideal for intermediates. Downhill and cross-country runs for beginners and intermediates, sledging. *Itter:* Good school. Picturesque surroundings, cosy nightlife. *Westendorf:* Very good après-ski. Mid-December to mid-March.
Stubaital: *Fulpmes:* Good après-ski. *Neustift:* Pretty village, ideal for non-skiers. Mid-December to mid-March.
Zillertal: *Mayrhofen:* Popular. Mid-December to mid-March. *Zell am Ziller:* Small resort. Mid-December to mid-March. Restricted après-ski. *Finkenberg:* 3 nursery slopes, 19 for intermediates. *Fügen and Hochfügen:* Well laid-out, though few slopes. *Gerlos:* Suitable for skiers of all levels. Very good school. Cross-country runs of high standard. *Hinter Tux:* All-year resort. All levels. *Lanersbach:* Intermediate and advanced with nursery slopes.
Serfaus: Quiet après-ski. Reasonable prices. Easy slopes. Mid-December to mid-April.
Nauders: Small with vigorous nightlife. Mid-December to beginning of April.
Arlberg: *St Anton:* Quiet nightlife. Popular with younger people. Beginning of December to mid-April. *St Christoph:* Family resort though no nursery slopes. *Holzgau:* 3 nursery slopes.
Wildschönau: *Niederau:* Mid-December to beginning of April. Very popular, vigorous nightlife. *Auffach:* Perfect for intermediates. School. Friendly and professional. *Oberau:* Ideal for beginners, a favourite for school trips.
Alpbach: Picture postcard village. Christmas to mid-March.

Upper Austria

The south of this Federal Province is dominated by the Salzkammergut lake district. The north offers a relaxed holiday in the many quiet villages and farms – the Mühlviertel. Rolling plains, densely wooded highlands and lush meadows are interspersed with rocks of natural granite. The Pyhrn-Eisenwurzen region is more mountainous, while Innviertel-Hausruckwald (in the west of Upper Austria) is an area of endless farmlands, rivers and forests. The many spas and convalescence centres of this region offer treatment for a wide range of illnesses.
Resorts: Bad Ischl, Hallstadt, St Wolfgang, Mondsee, Gmunden, Braunau, Schärding, Freistadt, Grein, Windischgarsten and Steyr.
Excursions/sightseeing: A tour of the Provice's capital **Linz** is not complete without the *Cathedral*, the old quarter, the *Palace Museum*, *Bruckner House*, *den Pöstlingberg* and a visit to the many churches and monasteries, for example *St Florian*. The summer villa of Emperor Franz Josef can be found in **Bad Ischl**, as well as a salt mine and several museums. **Hallstadt** lend its name to a whole era; the **Mondsee** is one of the warmest lakes in the Salzkammergut. **St Wolfgang** does not only offer a impressive altar, but a rack-railway as well. **Gmunden**, the Nice of Upper Austria, is known for its many cultural festivals. **Braunau's** and **Schärding's** old city centres are not to be missed. **Freistadt** has medieval forts, while **Grein** offers a navigation museum, *Clam Castle* and the old theatre. **Steyr** fascinates with the old inner city, the *Working-World Museum* and the pilgrimage church *Christkindl*.
Resorts: Bad Goisern, Gosau, Obertraun and Grünau in the Salzkammergut and Hinterstoder, Windischgarsten and Spital am Pyhrn (region Pyhrn-Eisenwurzen).

Vorarlberg

Situated at the far western tip of Austria, the scenery of the Vorarlberg is dramatically diverse. The glaciers of the Silvretta mountain ranges drop dramatically to the shores of Lake Constance with its lush vegetation. Bregenz in the summer lends itself to bicycle tours, swimming, sailing or just sightseeing, whereas the winter season populates the numerous slopes and hiking trails of the Vorarlberg.
Excursions/sightseeing: Bregenz is noted for its Upper City with the *Martin's Tower*, the largest floating stage worldwide, the *Congress Centre*, the *Mehrerau Abbey Church*, the *Vorarlberg Country Museum* and the viewing platform on Mount Pfänder, where one can watch the flight of several birds of prey.

Feldkirch: The historical old quarter of which the *Cathedral St Nicholas* is a part, the *Schattenburg* housing the *Local History Museum*, and the *National Conservatoire* can be found here. In **Levis,** near Feldkirch, the *Castle Amberg* and the Hospital should not be missed. **Tosters'** sights include the castle ruin and the *St Corneli Church* with a 1000-year-old yew.
Visitors should pay a visit to the famous Renaissance palace of **Hohenems**. The city is also known for the *Jewish Museum* and the only *Jewish Cemetery* in the Vorarlberg.
Schwarzenberg im Bregenzerwald: A picturesque, completely restored farming village, hometown of the painter Angelika Kaufmann. *The Country Museum* and the church are worth a visit.

Resorts in Other Areas

The following are some additional winter sports resorts:
Brandneuertal: *Bürserberg*: Small village. Beginners and intermediates. *Brand*: Family resort. Selection of leisure activities (paragliding, horseriding, tennis).
Kleinwalsertal: *Hirschegg*: Intermediates. *Riezlern:* Beginners and intermediates.
Montafon: *Schruns:* December to end of April. Large skiing-regions, active nightlife. *Gargellen:* Mid-December to end of April. Relaxed, friendly and reasonable. *Gaschurn:* Mid-December to end of April. Friendly, family atmosphere. *Partenen:* Ideal for intermediates.
Bregenzerwald: *Warth:* Mid-December to end of April. Relatively unknown and secluded near Lech. Intermediates, good après-ski. Lift-pass sharing with *Schröcken, Damüls, Au* and the *Großen Walsertal*.
Arlberg: *Lech:* Beginning of December to end of April. Fashionable and large. *Zürs:* Beginning of December to end of April. Small, expensive town. Lift-pass sharing with *Lech, St Anton im Tyrol, St Christoph im Tyrol, Stuben* and *Dalaas im Klostertal,* with more than 100 lifts.

SOCIAL PROFILE

FOOD & DRINK: Traditional Viennese dishes are *Wiener Schnitzel*, boiled beef *(Tafelspitz)*, calf's liver with herbs in butter *(geröstete Leber)*, *goulash*, and various types of smoked and cured pork. Viennese cuisine is strongly influenced by southeast European cuisine, notably that of Hungary, Serbia, Romania and Dalmatia. Many of the simpler meals are often made with rice, potatoes and dumplings *(Knödel)*, with liquid sauces. The main meal of the day is lunch. *Mehlspeisen* is the national term for cakes and puddings, all of which are wonderfully appetising. There are more than 57 varieties of *Torte*, which are often consumed with coffee at around 3pm. Open all day, the Austrian coffee shop (Kaffeehaus) is little short of a national institution and often provides the social focus of a town or neighbourhood.
Drink: Spirits such as whisky and gin, together with imported beers, tend to be on the expensive side, but local wines (often served in open carafes) are excellent and cheap. Most of the wines are white *(Riesling, Veltliner)* but there are also some good red wines from Baden and Burgenland, as well as imported wines from other European countries. Generally the strict registration laws mean that the quality of the wine will be fully reflected in its price. *Schnaps* is a drink found in most German speaking countries, and is made by distilling various fruits. It is usually very strong, and widely drunk as it is cheap and well flavoured. Most bars or coffee houses have waiter service and bills are settled with the arrival of drinks. All restaurants have waiter service.
Note: There are no national licensing laws in Austria, but each region has local police closing hours. Most coffee houses and bars serve wine as well as soft drinks and beers.
SHOPPING: High quality goods such as handbags, glassware, chinaware and winter sports equipment represent the cream of specialist items found in Austria. A 20% to 32% value-added tax (called MWST) is included in the list price of items sold, and tourists can claim a partial refund on this tax on unused goods which are taken with them when they leave Austria. **Shopping hours:** Shops and stores are generally open Monday to Friday from 0800-1830 with a one or two hour lunch break. Most shops close at noon on Saturday. For information on cashback on purchashed items is Austria Tax-free Shopping, Biberstrasse 10, A-1010 Vienna, Austria.
NIGHTLIFE: The Austrians believe in 'early to bed and early to rise' and consequently nightlife in Vienna is relatively quiet and civilised. One of the best ways to spend an evening is in one of the wine gardens *(Heurigen)* found outside the towns. There are casinos and nightclubs in most of the major cities, which depend largely on the tourist trade, as the native Austrians prefer the theatre and opera.
SPORT: Cycling: Bicycles can be rented in most areas. **Fishing:** Excellent facilities, but permits required. **Gliding:** Facilities available in most areas. **Riding:** Available in most areas. **Hang-gliding:** A growing sport in the mountains. **Swimming, sailing, mountaineering, rambling:** All popular, especially during the summer months. **Skiing**: See *Winter Sports Resorts* section in *Resorts & Excursions* above.
SPECIAL EVENTS: The following is a selection of major events and festivals, many of which occur annually: **Apr 3-12 '93** *Easter Festival*, Salzburg. **May 15-Jun 20** *Vienna Festival*, Konzerthaus. **Jun 15-Sep 20** *Summer Concert Season*. **Jun 16-29** *Schubertiade*, Feldkirch. **Jun 26-Jul 18** *Styriarte*, Graz. **Jun-Sep** *Badener Operetta Days*, Baden. **Jul 20-Aug 22** *Bregenz Festival*, Bregenz. **Jul 26-Aug 31** *Salzburg Festival*, Salzburg. **Jul-Aug** *Morbisch Operetta Festival*, Morbisch; *Carinthia Summer Festival*, Ossiach and Villach. **Aug 15-28** *Festival of Ancient Music*, Innsbruck. **Sep 4-11** *Music Days*, Mondsee. **Sep 10-19** *Haydn Festival*, Eisenstadt. **Sep 12-Oct 3** *International Bruckner Festival*, Linz. **Oct-Nov** *Styrian Autumn*, Graz. **Dec** *Mozart Festival*, Konzerthaus. **Jan 1 '94** *New Year's Day Concert*, Musikverein.
For details of other events celebrated in Austria in 1993-4 consult the Austrian National Tourist Office.
SOCIAL CONVENTIONS: Austrians tend to be quite formal in both their social and business dealings. They do not use first names when being introduced, but after the initial meeting first names are often used. Handshaking is normal when saying hello and goodbye. It is considered impolite to enter a restaurant or shop without saying *Guten Tag* or, more usually, *Grüss Gott;* similarly, to leave without saying *Auf Wiedersehen* can cause offence. Social pleasantries and some exchange of small-talk is appreciated. If invited out to dinner, flowers should be brought for the hostess. The Church enjoys a high and respected position in Austrian society, which should be kept in mind by the visitor. It is customary to dress up for the opera or the theatre. **Tipping** is widespread but large amounts are not expected. On restaurant bills a service charge of 10-15% is included, but it is usual to leave a further 5%. Attendants at theatres, cloakrooms, petrol pumps, etc expect to be tipped ASch2-3. Railway and airports have fixed charges for portering. Taxi drivers expect ASch3-4 for a short trip and 10% for a longer one.

BUSINESS PROFILE

ECONOMY: Austria has enjoyed steady and stable growth with fairly low inflation and unemployment since 1955. It is one of the most prosperous countries in the world. Manufacturing accounts for over 30% of GNP. Since the Second World War, much of the country's industrial capacity has been in state hands and is only gradually being relinquished: given the relative success of those enterprises under the wing of the state holding company, OIAG, this is not surprising. Iron and steel, chemicals, metal working and engineering all fell into this category. Agriculture has proved equally successful with domestic products meeting 90% of the country's food needs. Crops include sugarbeet, potatoes, grain, grapes, tobacco, flax, hemp and wine. Austria has moderate deposits of iron, lignite, magnesium, lead, copper, salt, zinc and silver. Although there are some oil reserves, Austria must import the bulk of its energy requirements; much of it comes from Eastern Europe. Austria is a member of the European Free Trade Association (EFTA) which links European economies outside the EC, although the Government has entered negotiations with the Community to acquire membership. This may be seen as a natural development from Austria's recent export patterns: EC members account for 68% of imports and 63% of exports. Germany is Austria's largest trading partner by a considerable margin, followed by Italy, France and the UK and, outside the EC, Switzerland. The previously substantial trade with both the US and the former USSR has been falling in recent years.
BUSINESS: Austrians are quite formal in their business dealings. A working knowledge of German will be very advantageous. Best times to visit are the spring and autumn months. **Office hours:** 0800-1600 Monday to Friday.
COMMERCIAL INFORMATION: The following organisation can offer advice: Bundeskammer der Gewerblichen Wirtschaft (Federal Economic Chamber), Wiedner Hauptstrasse 63, 1045 Vienna. Tel: (222) 50105. Fax: (222) 50206. Telex: 111871.
CONFERENCES/CONVENTIONS: Austria has 31 conference venues, including over 20 in Vienna and a floating conference centre, the MS *Mozart*, on the river Danube. The provincial capitals of Salzburg, Innsbruck, Graz, Linz, Bregenz, Klagenfurt and Eisenstadt also offer convention venues, as do several health and spa resorts. Furthermore there are 71 hotels in Austria which specialize in the conference/convention field. For more detailed information contact the Österreichischer Kongreßverband (Austrian Convention Association), Judenplatz 3-4, A-1010 Vienna. Tel: (1) 533 5218. Fax: (1) 535 5885.

HISTORY & GOVERNMENT

HISTORY: Austria's history since the 13th century is bound up with that of the Habsburg family. The region was conquered by Charlemagne and remained as a part of the Holy Roman Empire. By the 16th century, the Habsburgs had gained a firm grip on the title of Emperor, although their power owed less to this often empty distinction than to the extensive family lands, many of which were to be found in Austria. Under Charles V, Austria was part of a vast empire, but after Charles' abdication in 1556 the Spanish and Germanic parts of his lands were separated, passing to his son and his brother respectively. The Holy Roman Empire as a political unit became more and more fragmented, leading one 18th-century observer to comment that it was 'neither holy, nor Roman nor an Empire'. It was formally abolished in August 1806, Francis II having already assumed the title of 'Emperor of Austria'; much of the northern and eastern parts of the Empire had by this time been absorbed into Prussia. During the 17th and 18th centuries, Austria and in particular Vienna became one of the major centres of the cultural renaissance associated with the terms 'Baroque' and 'The Enlightenment'; the musical achievements of this period are particularly notable. The Austrian Empire (by this time the Austro-Hungarian Empire) came to an end after the First World War and Austria was declared a republic. In 1938 it was incorporated into the German Reich but was liberated in 1945 and established as a republic once again under the protectorship of the allied powers. Full independence was restored in July 1955, since when Austria has been governed according to an orthodox Western European model. The major parties, who have frequently governed together in coalition, are the ÖVP (Austrian People's Party) and the SPÖ (Socialist Party). The Socialists governed uninterrupted during the 1970s and early 1980s. Their absolute majority was eliminated in 1983 by the emergence of environmentalist parties. The present administration is a coalition between the SPÖ and ÖVP with Socialist leader Franz Vranitsky as Chancellor. The Presidency is a titular post contested by popular election and is currently held by the former Foreign Minister and United Nations Secretary-General, Kurt Waldheim. During his 1986 election campaign new allegations surfaced concerning Waldheim's wartime record which attracted intense international interest. In recent years pursuit of EC membership has emerged as the main foreign policy objective. Austria is one of four countries at the front of the queue to join and hopes to do so by 1995. After national elections in October 1990 the Socialists were once again the largest party in the Nationalrat and Franz Vranitsky was asked by President Waldheim to form a government. Waldheim himself stood down in May 1992, to be replaced by the ÖVP candidate Thomas Klestil, who won 57% of the vote.
GOVERNMENT: Austria is a federal republic with bicameral legislature. The President is elected for a 6-year term, but real executive power is held by the Chancellor.

CLIMATE

Austria enjoys a moderate continental climate: summers are warm and pleasant with cool nights, and winters are sunny, with snow levels high enough for widespread winter sports.
Required clothing: European clothes according to season. Alpine wear for mountain resorts.

VIENNA Austria (203m)

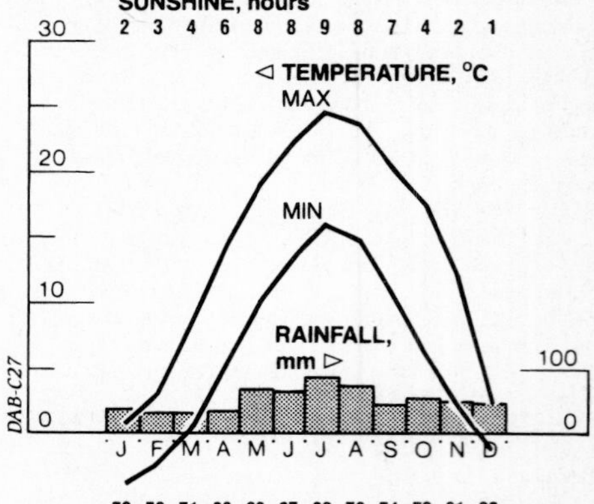

BAHAMAS

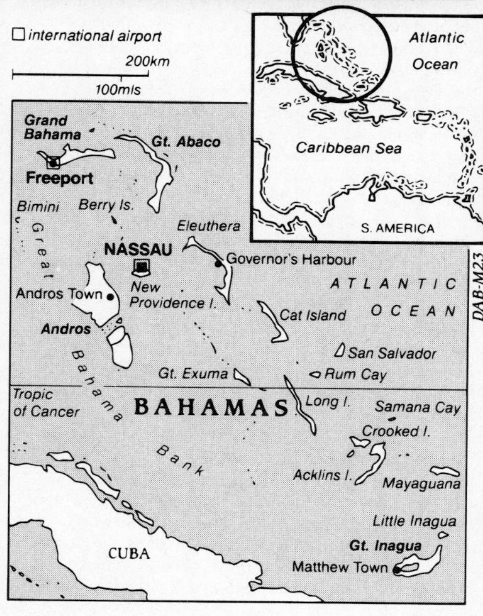

Location: Caribbean; southeast of Florida.

Bahamas Ministry of Tourism
PO Box N-3701
Bay Street
Nassau, The Bahamas
Tel: 322 7500. Fax: 328 0945. Telex: 20164.

High Commission of the Commonwealth of The Bahamas
10 Chesterfield Street
London W1X 8AH
Tel: (071) 408 4488. Fax: (071) 499 9937. Opening hours: 0930-1730 Monday to Friday.

Bahamas Tourist Office
Address as above
Tel: (071) 629 5238. Fax: (071) 491 9311. Opening hours: 0930-1730 Monday to Friday.

British High Commission
PO Box N-7516
3rd Floor, Bitco Building
East Street
Nassau, The Bahamas
Tel: 325 7471/2/3/4. Fax: 323 3871. Telex: 20112 UKREP BS.

Embassy of the Commonwealth of The Bahamas
2220 Massachussetts Avenue, NW
Washington, DC 20008
Tel: (202) 319 2660. Fax: (202) 319 2668. Telex: 4905526.

Bahamas Consulate General
767 Third Avenue
New York, NY 10017
Tel: (212) 421 6420 *or* 421 6925/6.

Bahamas Tourist Office
28th Floor North
150 East 52nd Street
New York, NY 10022
Tel: (212) 758 2777. Fax: (212) 832 0796. Telex: 23 239546.

Embassy of the United States of America
PO Box N-8197
Mosmar Building
Queen Street
Nassau, The Bahamas
Tel: 322 1181 *or* 328 2206. Fax: 328 7838. Telex: 20138 AMEMB.

High Commission for the Commonwealth of The Bahamas
Suite 1020
360 Albert Street
Ottawa, Ontario
K1R 7X7
Tel: (613) 232 1724. Fax: (613) 232 0097.

Bahamas Tourist Office
Suite 1101
121 Bloor Street East
Toronto, Ontario
M4W 3M5
Tel: (416) 968 2999. Fax: (416) 968 6711.

AREA: 13,939 sq km (5382 sq miles).
POPULATION: 254,685 (1990 estimate).
POPULATION DENSITY: 18.3 per sq km.
CAPITAL: Nassau. **Population:** 191,542 (1990 estimate).
GEOGRAPHY: The Bahamas consist of 700 low-lying islands, mostly islets (cays or keys) and rocks. The whole archipelago extends 970km (600 miles) southeastward from the coast of Florida, surrounded by clear, colourful waters. The soil is thin, but on the more developed islands cultivation has produced exotic flowers. On other islands are large areas of pine forest, rocky and barren land, swamp and unspoilt beaches. The Bahamas is divided into two oceanic features, the Little Bahama Bank and the Great Bahama Bank.
LANGUAGE: The official and national language is English.
RELIGION: Baptist, Anglican and Roman Catholic.
TIME: GMT - 5 (GMT - 4 in summer).
ELECTRICITY: 120 volts AC, 60Hz.
COMMUNICATIONS: Telephone: IDD is available. Country code: 1 809. New Providence and all islands have automatic telephone systems. The state telephone company, BaTelCo, offers both manual and automatic-dial mobile radio telephones for use on New Providence Island. **Fax:** This service is available to the public at the Centralised Telephone Office in East Street, Nassau. Machines can also be rented.
Telex/telegram: 24-hour international telex and telegraph facilities are available in Nassau and Freeport; efficient telegram service to all parts of the world.
Post: Postal service to Europe takes up to five days. Post office hours: 0900-1700 Monday to Friday and 0900-1200 Saturday. **Press:** There are three daily newspapers: the *Nassau Daily Tribune*, the *Nassau Guardian* and *Freeport News*.
BBC World Service and Voice of America frequencies: From time to time these change. See the section *How to Use this Book* for more information.

BBC:				
MHz	17.840	15.22	9.915	6.195
Voice of America:				
MHz	15.21	11.70	6.130	0.930

PASSPORT/VISA

Regulations and requirements may be subject to change at short notice, and you are advised to contact the appropriate diplomatic or consular authority before finalising travel arrangements. Details of these may be found at the head of this country's entry. Any numbers in the chart refer to the footnotes below.

	Passport Required?	Visa Required?	Return Ticket Required?
Full British	Yes	2	Yes
BVP	Not valid	-	-
Australian	Yes	No	Yes
Canadian	1	No	Yes
USA	1	No	Yes
Other EC	Yes	2	Yes
Japanese	Yes	No	Yes

PASSPORTS: Valid passport required by all except **[1]** nationals of Canada (for 3 weeks providing they hold a birth certificate, a citizen card or a landed resident card) and the USA (for 8 months providing they hold a birth certificate accompanied by a police clearance record and a driving licence or a voter's registration card).
Note: Expired passports are not considered proper ID, even if they are endorsed with unexpired visas.
British Visitors Passport: Not accepted.
VISAS: Required by all except nationals of:
(a) **[2]** EC countries for visits of less than 8 months (3 months for nationals of Denmark, France, Germany, Ireland and Portugal);
(b) Argentina, Bolivia, Brazil, Chile, Colombia (if travelling via USA), Costa Rica, Ecuador, El Salvador, Guatemala, Honduras, Nicaragua, Panama, Paraguay, Peru, Uruguay and Venezuela, for visits of less than 2 weeks;
(c) Commonwealth countries (with the exception of nationals of the Maldives and Nauru, who *do* require a visa), Fiji, Cayman Islands, Djibouti, South Korea, São Tomé e Principe and Turks & Caicos Islands;
(d) Austria, Finland, Israel, Japan, Mexico and Sweden for visits of less than 3 months;
(e) Iceland, Liechtenstein, Norway, San Marino, Switzerland, Turkey and the USA for visits of less than 8 months.
Types of visa: Tourist – £15 (single entry); £30 (multiple entry).
Validity: Dependent on length of stay and nationality. Applications for extension should be made to the Immigration Department.
Application to: Consulate (or Consular Section at Embassy or High Commission). For addresses, see top of entry.
Application requirements: (a) Application form from Embassy or High Commission. (b) Valid passport. (c) Sufficient funds to cover stay. (d) 2 passport photos. (e) Return or onward ticket.
Working days required: Dependent on nationality of applicant.
Temporary residence: Apply at Immigration Department, PO Box N-831, Nassau, New Providence, the Bahamas.

MONEY

Currency: Bahamian Dollar (Ba$) = 100 cents. Notes are in denominations of Ba$100, 50, 20, 10, 5, 3 and 1, and 50 cents. Coins are in denominations of Ba$5, 2 and 1, and 50, 25, 15, 10, 5 and 1 cents. The Bahamian Dollar has parity with the US Dollar and the latter is also accepted as legal tender.
Credit cards: Diners Club, Access/Mastercard, Visa and American Express are accepted. Check with your credit card company for details of merchant acceptability and other services which may be available.
Exchange rate indicators: The following figures are included as a guide to the movements of the Bahamian Dollar against Sterling and the US Dollar:

Date:	Oct '89	Oct '90	Oct '91	Oct '92
£1.00=	1.58	1.95	1.74	1.59
$1.00=	1.00	1.00	1.00	1.00

Currency restrictions: There is no restriction on the import of foreign currency. Prior permission from the Central Bank of Bahamas is required for the export of local currency in excess of Ba$70 per person. Foreign currency in excess of a value equivalent to US$5000 must be declared on leaving.
Banking hours: 0930-1500 Monday to Thursday, 0930-1700 Friday.

DUTY FREE

The following goods may be taken into The Bahamas without incurring customs duty:
200 cigarettes or 50 cigars or 250g of tobacco;
1 litre of spirits;
50g of perfume.
Note: A duty-free allowance is only available to persons over 17 years of age.
Prohibited items: Firearms, weapons, radio transmitters and drugs.

PUBLIC HOLIDAYS

Public holidays observed in The Bahamas are as follows:
Apr 9 '93 Good Friday. **Apr 12** Easter Monday. **May 31** Whit Monday. **Jun 4** Labour Day. **Jul 10** Independence Day. **Aug 2** Emancipation Day. **Oct 12** Discovery Day. **Dec 25** Christmas Day. **Dec 26** Boxing Day. **Jan 1 '94** New Year's Day.
Note: Holidays which fall on Saturday or Sunday are usually observed on the following Monday.

HEALTH

Regulations and requirements may be subject to change at short notice, and you are advised to contact your doctor well in advance of your intended date of departure. Any numbers in the chart refer to the footnotes below.

	Special Precautions?	Certificate Required?
Yellow Fever	No	1
Cholera	No	No
Typhoid & Polio	Yes	-
Malaria	No	-
Food & Drink	2	-

[1]: A yellow fever vaccination certificate is required from travellers aged over one year arriving within six months of visits to infected areas.
[2]: Water used for drinking, brushing teeth or making ice should usually be boiled or otherwise sterilised. Bottled water is available. Milk is unpasteurised and should be boiled. Powdered or tinned milk is available and is advised, but make sure that it is reconstituted with safe water. Only eat well-cooked meat and fish, preferably served hot. Vegetables should be cooked and fruit peeled.
Health care: There are General Hospitals and two private hospitals on New Providence and Grand Bahama. There are health clinics on the Family Islands. Medical insurance is recommended.

TRAVEL - International

AIR: The Bahamas' national airline is *Bahamasair (UP)*.
Approximate flight times: From *Los Angeles* to Nassau is 7 hours, from *New York* is 3 hours and from *Singapore* is 33 hours.
The number of airlines planning to make direct flights

from Europe is increasing.
International airports: *Nassau International (NAS)* is 16km (10 miles) west of the city. Taxi services are available, but no buses. Airport facilities include banking (0930-1500 Monday to Thursday, 0930-1700 Friday), car parking, car hire (0900-1800), post office, bar/restaurant (0700-2200) and an outgoing duty-free shop (0930-1700).
Freeport International (FPO) is 5km (3 miles) from the city. Only taxis are available. Airport facilities include banking, car hire, car parking, bar/restaurant and a duty-free shop (opening times are as for *Nassau International* above).
There are scheduled turbo-prop services between several airports in Florida and *Treasure Cay (TCB)*, Abaco Island, *Rock Sound (RSD)*, Eleuthera and *Georgetown (GCT)*.
The new international airport at Moss Town, Exuma has been completed.
Departure tax: Ba$13 is levied, except for children under two years and passengers for immediate transit.
SEA: A large number of international passenger ships from New York and Miami call at Nassau. In addition the following cruise ships call there: *Carnavale, Eugenio C, Fairwind, Mermoz, Nordic Prince, Oriana, Queen Elizabeth II, Skyward, Dolphin Sunward II, Southward* and *Sun Viking*. Nassau has direct passenger-cargo connections with the United States, the UK, the West Indies and South America. Facilities for cruisers in Nassau and some harbours of the Family Islands (Eleuthera, Andros and Exuma) are being improved. Contact The Bahamas Tourist Office for an up-to-date list of cruise operators to The Bahamas.

TRAVEL - Internal

AIR: *Bahamasair* links Nassau and Freeport to the Family Islands. Charter services are available from *Trans-Island Airways, Bahamasair Charter, Pinder's Charter Service, Norman Nixon's Charter, Lucaya Beach Air Service* and *Kwin Air*.
Approximate flight times: From Nassau, New Providence Island to *Freeport* is 30 minutes, to *Marsh Harbour* or *Treasure Cay*, Abaco is 35 minutes, to *Governor's Harbour* is 30 minutes, and to *Georgetown* on Exuma is 40 minutes.
SEA: The Family Islands are served by a mail boat which leaves Nassau several times a week carrying mail and provisions to the islands. Passengers share facilities with the crew. Arrangements should be made through boat captains at Potters Cay.
ROAD: Traffic drives on the left. **Bus:** The *jitney* (bus) provides inexpensive touring. Paradise Island is served by a bus service which stops at every hotel. A horse-drawn surrey ride which takes three passengers is available along the streets of Nassau. **Taxis** in New Providence are metered. The rates are government controlled. **Car hire:** *Avis, Budget* and *Hertz* are represented at the airports and in Nassau. Motor scooter hire is also available. **Cycles** can be rented by the day or week. **Documentation:** A British driving licence is valid for up to three months. Motorcycle drivers and passengers are required to wear crash helmets.
JOURNEY TIMES: The following chart gives approximate journey times (in hours and minutes) from Nassau to other major centres.

	Air	Sea
Central Andros, Andros	0.15	3.00
Governors Harbour, Eleuthera	0.30	5.30
Freeport, Grand Bahamas	0.30/0.45	12.00
Marsh Harbour, Abaco	0.45	11.00
George Town, Exuma	0.45	13.00

ACCOMMODATION

The Bahamas offer a wide selection of accommodation, ranging from small, private guest-houses where only lodging is available, to large luxury resorts, complete with swimming pools, private beaches, sailboats, skindiving equipment, full dining facilities and nightclub entertainment. The Bahamas Tourist Office issues a twice-yearly brochure with detailed information on licensed hotels. Information can also be obtained from The Bahamas' Hotel Association, PO Box N-7799, Deans Lane, Nassau, Bahamas. Tel: 322 8398. Fax: 326 5346. Telex: 20392. There is a nationwide toll-free reservation service in the United States. **Classifications:** Many of the larger resorts offer accommodation on either a Modified American Plan (MAP) which consists of room, breakfast and dinner or European Plan (EP) which consists of room only. Accommodation is classified as *Hotels, Colonies, Guest Houses, Apartment Hotels* or *Apartment/Cottage Units*.
HOTELS: Hotels vary in size and facilities. There are luxury hotels offering full porter, bell and room service, planned activities, sports, shops and beauty salon, swimming pool and entertainment; some have a private beach, golf course and tennis courts. Double and single rooms are often the same price. The small hotels are more informal and, while activities are less extensive, they usually offer a dining room and bar. There are new resorts at the Nassau Divi Bahamas Beach Resort and Country Club, situated on New Providence Island, which has sporting facilities and luxury accommodation. The Crystal Palace Casino on Cable Beach has a casino, health spa, luxury accommodation and gourmet restaurants. Some hotels include service charge on the bill.
COTTAGE COLONIES: Separate cottages or villas, with maid service, surrounding a main clubhouse with a bar and dining room – these are 'Cottage Colonies'. They are not equipped with kitchenette and housekeeping facilities for the preparation of meals, although some have facilities for preparing beverages and light snacks. They offer the facilities of a hotel, such as a private beach/swimming pool, and are designed to offer maximum privacy.
GUEST-HOUSES: Often less expensive than hotels and located near downtown Nassau. Many offer European Plan only, but restaurants are plentiful. Rooms may be with or without a bath. In the Family Islands the hotels are small with a casual atmosphere.
APARTMENT HOTELS: These consist of apartment units with complete kitchen and maid service. Other facilities of a hotel (ie swimming pool, sporting activities, restaurant and bar, etc) are normally available on the premises.
APARTMENT/COTTAGE UNITS: These have complete kitchen facilities and some have maid service. Generally, there are no restaurant facilities and tenants are required to prepare their own meals. A few are situated in landscaped estates with their own beach, much like the cottage colonies but without the main clubhouse. Others offer inexpensive accommodation in less spacious but comfortable surroundings. Restaurant and bar facilities are not available.
CAMPING: Not permitted in The Bahamas.

RESORTS & EXCURSIONS

There are over 700 islands in The Bahamas, many of which have escaped the notice of tourists. The islands offer clear warm water and sandy beaches. Several are relatively large – see below for a description of some of these – but others are tiny and uninhabited. All the larger islands offer a high standard of accommodation and leisure facilities.
Nassau, Cable Beach and Paradise Island: The capital of The Bahamas, Nassau stands on **New Providence Island.** In the capital, tourists can shop in the 'straw market', a kind of bazaar, or more sophisticated shops in *Bay Street*. There are two casinos. The islands also have botanical gardens, 18th-century forts and lakes. Sunbathing, diving, fishing and boating are the main daytime amusements. An underwater observatory, *Coral World*, has recently opened.
Grand Bahama Island: The main towns are **Freeport/Lucaya** and **West End,** which both have airports. The island offers wide white sandy beaches, two casinos and good shopping facilities at the *International Bazaar*. The *Rand Memorial Nature Centre* offers an excellent nature walk and the *Garden of the Groves* has exotic flowers, waterfalls and colourful birds. The history of the Lucayan Indians can be learned at the *Grand Bahama Museum*, along with its exhibitions of historic coins and Junkanoo costumes.
Andros: The largest and probably the least well known of the bigger islands. Laced with creeks and densely forested inland, the interior is still largely untouched and natural. Off the eastern shore is the world's largest coral reef outside Australia. Beyond the reef, the ocean floor drops away steeply to a depth of five miles (the Tongue of the Ocean), and deep-water fishing here is a major attraction.
The Abacos: A crescent-shaped chain of islands to the north of New Providence. Many of the towns here have the atmosphere of New England fishing villages. The islands are particularly noted for their tradition of shipbuilding, the original 200-year-old practice of which can still be observed in *Man-O-War Cay*. *Treasure Cay* has an excellent golf course and here, as in the other major islands, there are excellent leisure facilities. Other attractions include *Alton Lowe's Museum* in **New Plymouth,** *Elbow Cay, Green Turtle Cay* and *Marsh Harbour*, the bare-boat charter centre of the northern Bahamas. Scuba divers are drawn to *Pelican Cay National Park*, an underwater preserve where night dives can be arranged.
Eleuthera: A narrow island 177km (110 miles) long but seldom more than 3km wide. Attractions include the *Boiling Hole, Glass Window Bridge, Harbour Island* (with *Dunmore Town*, one of the oldest settlements in The Bahamas), *Spanish Wells*, off the northern tip of the island, *Preacher's Cave* and the underwater caves at *Hatchet Bay*. The scuba diving from Eleuthera is particularly superb.
The Exumas: The waters surrounding this 160km (10-mile) long chain of islands have been described by yachtsmen as being the finest cruising region in the world. There are also spectacular reefs protected by the *National Land and Sea Park*. Inland, several once-great plantation houses now stand ruined and deserted, although the names of their owners still live on in many local family surnames. In April, *Elizabeth Harbour* is the setting for the *Family Island Regatta*.
Cat Island: One of the eastern bulwarks of The Bahamas, Cat Island has 60m (200ft) cliffs (a rare height for The Bahamas), dense natural forest and pre-Columbian Arawak Indian caves. On *Mount Alvernia* is the Hermitage built by Father Jerome. The *Cat Island Regatta* takes place here during the August bank holiday.
Bimini: Lying between Andros and Florida, Bimini is widely regarded as one of the best fishing centres in the world. Hemingway used to live in *Alice Town* in Blue Marlin Cottage, and momentoes of his life can be seen in the local museum.
Berry Island: Popular with fishing enthusiasts and also noted for its serene landscapes and white sand beaches. *Great Harbour Cay* has a championship golf course and a marina. Scuba divers can admire the underwater rock formations and 15ft staghorn coral reefs off *Mamma Rhoda Rock*.
Long Island: This island certainly lives up to its name, being almost 100km (60 miles) long but rarely more than 5km wide. The landscape consists of rugged headlands dropping sharply down to the sea, fertile pastureland, rolling hills and sand beaches washed by surf. At *Conception Island* divers can explore over 30 shipwrecks and tours are arranged from the Stella Maris resort complex at the north end of the island. The *Long Island Regatta* at Salt Pond takes place here in May.
San Salvador: This was Columbus' first landing place in the New World. *Cockburn Town* is the main settlement, which is not far from the spot where Columbus is said to have landed, although other sites also claim this distinction. Game fishing and diving are the most popular pastimes.
The Family Islands: These stretch across a huge area of clear ocean and are fringed with hundreds of kilometres of white sandy beaches. The islands have resort facilities for groups of up to 200 people and are ideal for a relaxing, secluded holiday. Though secluded, the islands are not isolated. They are served by the national flag carrier,

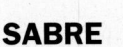

BAHAMAS | **HEALTH REGULATIONS** | **VISA REGULATIONS** | Code-Link

GALILEO/WORLDSPAN

TI-DFT/NAS/HE

TI-DFT/NAS/VI

SABRE

TIDFT/NAS/HE

TIDFT/NAS/VI

To access this information on your CRS, swipe the barcode with a light pen or type in the text under the barcode. For more information, see the introduction *How to Use This Book*.

Bahamasair, from Nassau and Freeport, by *Caribbean Express, Eastern Express, Presidential Airways, Aircoach, Florida Express, Pro Air*, and *Piedmont Airlines* from South Florida.

SOCIAL PROFILE

FOOD & DRINK: There is a wide choice of restaurants and bars. Specialities include conch, grouper cutlets, baked crab and red snapper fillets in anchovy sauce. Fresh fruit is available from the Family Islands, including sweet pineapple, mango, breadfruit and papaya. Table service is usual in restaurants. **Drink:** Local drinks are based on rum. The local rum is *Nassau Royal*, served alone or in coffee. Bars may have counter and/or waiter service.
NIGHTLIFE: Hotels have bars and nightclubs. Beach parties and discotheques are organised regularly. Live entertainment includes calypso, goombay music and limbo dancing. Nightclubs are found in Nassau and Freeport.
SHOPPING: Special purchases include china, cutlery, leather, fabrics, spirits from Britain, Scandinavian glass and silver, Swiss watches, German and Japanese cameras and French perfume. Local products include all types of straw artefacts, sea-shell jewellery and wood carvings.
SPORT: Tennis, squash, baseball, softball, basketball, volleyball, soccer, rugby, golf, American football and **cricket** are all popular. Excellent facilities exist for tennis and squash. **Golf:** Ten 18-hole courses are available and the islands are hosts to major tournaments. **Watersports** are exceptionally well catered for in The Bahamas; **sailing, parasailing, powerboat racing, diving, swimming, snorkelling** and **water-skiing** are all widely available. The temperature of the sea rarely drops below 21°C even in midwinter. Equipment is available from shops, hotels and marinas.
SPECIAL EVENTS: The following is a selection of special events occurring in The Bahamas during 1993-94: **Apr '93** *Family Island Regatta*, Exuma. **Apr 22** *National Trust Earth Week*. **Jun** *Pineapple Festival*, Eleuthera; *Eleuthera Homecoming*, Eleuthera. **Jul-Aug** *Goombay Summer Festival* (parades, dancing and music, beach parties and cook-outs are some of the events on Bay Street in Nassau, and on Cable Beach, Paradise Island and other islands). **Aug** *Cat Island Regatta*, Cat Island; *Bahrefest*, Freeport; *Fox Hill Day* (celebrated on the second Tuesday, this is a local, belated, Emancipation Day celebration). **Sep-Oct** *Discovery Season* (Gospel concerts, art exhibitions, essay competitions, cooking demonstrations, flea markets, concerts, barbecues and special cruises and walking tours to mark the landing of Columbus in the New World on San Salvador, in The Bahamas), Nassau, Freeport, Eleuthera and Andros; *UK Month*. **Oct** *Family Island Regatta*, Eleuthera; *International Festival of Arts*. **Dec 26 and Jan 1 '94** *Junkanoo* (a brilliantly colourful parade, originating in Africa, which takes place in Nassau during the early hours of Boxing Day and New Year's Day, accompanied by a cacaphony of cowbells, horns and whistles, goat-skin drums and other home-made instruments. Throughout the year visitors can have a sampling of Junkanoo at special shows and during other celebrations).
SOCIAL CONVENTIONS: The pace of life is generally leisurely. Informal wear is acceptable in the resorts with some degree of dressing up in the evenings, particularly for dining, dancing and casinos in Nassau or Freeport. Further from the main towns dress is more casual, although there is still a tendency to dress up at night. Small outposts like Green Turtle Cay, for example, will not require more than a shirt and long trousers. It is not acceptable to wear beachwear in towns. **Tipping:** 15% is usual for most services including taxis. Some hotels and restaurants, however, include service charge on the bill.

BUSINESS PROFILE

ECONOMY: One of the wealthiest countries in the Caribbean, tourism is the main industry. Agriculture and fishing, which account for 50% of GNP, have been targetted for development. The Bahamas are also an important offshore banking centre. Most foodstuffs and virtually all other products must be imported, mainly from the US, although oil is purchased firstly from Indonesia and Saudi Arabia. The Government is trying to diversify the economy and offers formal incentives to foreign investors. Tax concessions are available in Freeport on Grand Bahama. Other than the US, the UK and Puerto Rico are The Bahamas' major trading partners.
BUSINESS: Normal courtesies observed, ie appointments and exchanging calling cards. **Office hours:** 0900-1700 Monday to Friday.
COMMERCIAL INFORMATION: The following organisation can offer advice: Bahamas Chamber of Commerce, PO Box N-665, Shirley Street, Nassau, The Bahamas. Tel: 322 2145. Fax: 322 4649.
CONFERENCES/CONVENTIONS: Conference venues can seat up to 2000 people. Information may be obtained from: Bahamas Ministry of Tourism, Groups Department, Suite 415, 255 Alhambra Circle, Coral Gables, FL 33134, USA. Tel: (305) 442 4867. Fax: (305) 448 0532. (The Bahamas Tourist Office also supplies information – see address at top of entry.)

HISTORY & GOVERNMENT

HISTORY: Columbus discovered The Bahamas (and hence America) in 1492. San Salvador was his first landing place in the New World and Cockburn Town, the main settlement, is not far from the spot where Columbus is said to have landed (although other sites also claim this distinction). Subsequently, the Spanish neglected the Lesser Antilles and England colonised The Bahamas during the 17th century, which for the most part remained occupied by Britain until the country achieved independence in 1973. Bahamanian politics have since been dominated by the increasingly controversial figure of Sir Lynden Pindling, who was first elected to the premiership as head of the Progressive Liberal Party in 1967. The PLP and Sir Lynden Pindling were returned to office at each of five subsequent elections despite repeated allegations against Pindling and some of his associates of corruption and involvement in drug trafficking, all of which have been vehemently and repeatedly denied by Pindling. The drugs issue has dominated the political agenda throughout the 1980s, as The Bahamas became used as a transit facility for traffickers between South and North America. Pressure from the United States forced the Government to introduce more stringent measures against trafficking, including changes to the islands' banking secrecy laws, and the two countries have collaborated in joint operations. (The Americans also have military bases on the islands, leased from the British for a 99-year period.) The damage to Pindling's reputation and the islands' deteriorating economic fortunes during the early 1990s – a result of decline in the tourist industry – led to his removal by the electorate at the August 1992 polls. The new premier is the leader of the Free National Movement, Hubert Ingraham, once a minister under Pindling who resigned in 1984 as a gesture of protest when allegations aginst Pindling first surfaced. The Movement holds a commanding 33 of the National Assembly's 45 seats.
GOVERNMENT: The bicameral Parliament, composed of a 16-member Senate and a 49-strong House of Assembly elected by universal suffrage, has legislative powers. The British monarch has formal executive powers, vested in a Governor-General, though in practice the Governor-General almost invariably acts upon the advice of a Cabinet of Ministers appointed from the House of Assembly.

CLIMATE

Apart from Grand Turk in the extreme southeast, The Bahamas are slightly cooler than other Caribbean island groups due to their proximity to the continental North American cold air systems.
Required clothing: Lightweight or tropical, washable cottons all year round. Light raincoats are useful during the wet season.

NASSAU Bahamas (3m)

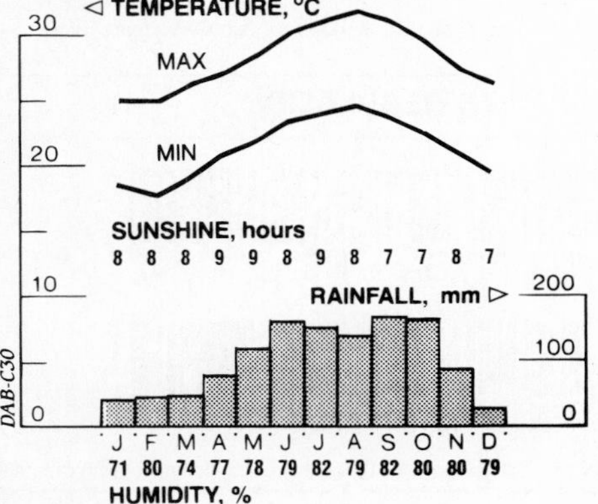

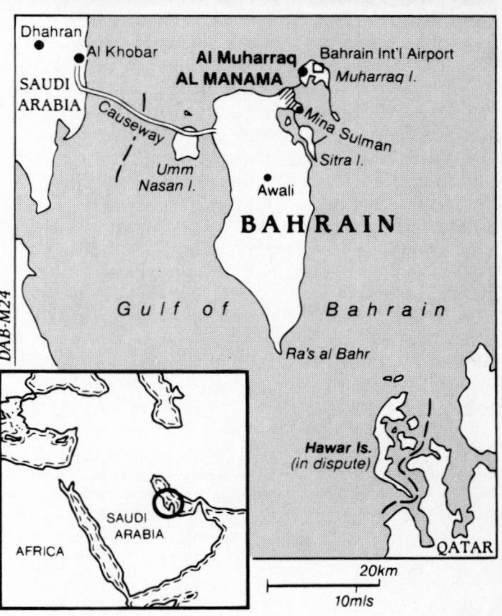

Location: Middle East, Gulf Coast.

Bahrain Tourism Company (BTC)
PO Box 5831
Manama, Bahrain
Tel: 530 530. Telex: 8929.
Embassy of the State of Bahrain
98 Gloucester Road
London SW7 4AU
Tel: (071) 370 5132/3. Fax: (071) 370 7773. Telex: 917829.
Opening hours: 0900-1500 Monday to Friday (0900-1200 for visa enquiries, 1430-1500 for visa collection).
British Embassy
PO Box 114
21 Government Road
Manama, Bahrain
Tel: 534 404. Fax: 531 273. Telex: 8213.
Embassy of the State of Bahrain
3502 International Drive, NW
Washington, DC
20008
Tel: (202) 342 0741/42/43/44.
Also represents Canada.
Embassy of the United States of America
PO Box 26431
House 979, Road 3119
Block 331
Manama, Bahrain
Tel: 273 300. Fax: 272 594. Telex: 9398.
Consulate of the State of Bahrain
1869 René Lévesque Boulevard West
Montréal, Québec
H3H 1R4
Tel: (514) 931 7444.

AREA: 693.15 sq km (267.63 sq miles).
POPULATION: 503,022 (1990 estimate).
POPULATION DENSITY: 725.7 per sq km.
CAPITAL: Manama. **Population:** 138,784 (1990 estimate).
GEOGRAPHY: Bahrain is composed of a group of 33 islands (3 large and 30 small ones), lying halfway down the Arabian Gulf, 25km (15 miles) from the east coast of Saudi Arabia, slightly under 30km (20 miles) off the Qatar peninsula. The islands are low-lying, the highest ground being a hill in the centre of Bahrain. The main island has the valuable asset of an adequate supply of fresh water both on- and off-shore. In the north are extensive date gardens with irrigated fruit and vegetable gardens. A causeway between Bahrain and the east coast of Saudi Arabia recently opened to traffic.
LANGUAGE: The official language is Arabic. English is widely spoken in business and trade circles. Farsi (Persian), Hindi and Urdu are also used.
RELIGION: Muslim, both Shi'ites and Sunnis. Christian, Bahai, Hindu and Parsee minorities.

TIME: GMT + 3.
ELECTRICITY: Manama and other towns: 230 volts, AC single phase and 400 volts, three phase; 50Hz. (Awali, 120 volts AC, 60Hz.)
COMMUNICATIONS: Telephone: Full IDD service is available. Country code: 973. **Fax:** Bahrain International Telecommunications (BATELCO) operate a service from the Sh Mubarak Building on Government Road. **Telex/telegram:** Bahrain possesses one of the most modern international communications networks in the Gulf. A 24-hour service is run by Cable and Wireless, Mercury House, Al-Khalifa Avenue, Manama as well as at the airport. **Post:** Airmail service to Europe takes three to four days. The main post office is at Manama. Efficient 1-day international courier services operate out of Bahrain. **Press:** The main Arabic dailies include *Al-Ayyam* and *Akhbar Al Khaleej*. The English-language daily is the *Gulf Daily News*.
BBC World Service and Voice of America frequencies: From time to time these change. See the section *How to Use this Book* for more information.

BBC:				
MHz	21.47	15.07	11.76	9.410
Voice of America:				
MHz	11.97	9.670	6.040	5.995

PASSPORT/VISA

Regulations and requirements may be subject to change at short notice, and you are advised to contact the appropriate diplomatic or consular authority before finalising travel arrangements. Details of these may be found at the head of this country's entry. Any numbers in the chart refer to the footnotes below.

	Passport Required?	Visa Required?	Return Ticket Required?
Full British	Yes	No	Yes
BVP	Not valid	-	-
Australian	Yes	Yes	Yes
Canadian	Yes	Yes	Yes
USA	Yes	Yes	Yes
Other EC	Yes	Yes	Yes
Japanese	Yes	Yes	Yes

Prohibited entry: Holders of Israeli passports. Holders of passports with visas or endorsements for Israel (valid or expired) are permitted to transit Bahrain provided they do so by the same through aircraft.
PASSPORTS: Valid passport required by all.
British Visitors Passport: Not accepted.
VISAS: Required by all except:
(a) nationals of Kuwait, and the member states of the Gulf Cooperation Council;
(b) citizens of the UK (providing they hold a full passport with at least 6 months' validity).
A long-term 1-2 year visa for working in Bahrain will be supplied if the employing company in Bahrain obtains a 'No Objection Certificate' on behalf of the individual.
Types of visa: Business/Tourist. Cost: £10. Tourist visas can only be issued to those who have contacts within Bahrain. There is also a 72-hour Transit visa.
Application to: Consulate (or Consular Section at Embassy). For addresses, see top of entry.
Application requirements: (a) Letter from company; those not going on business require letter from friends/relatives resident in country and a 'No Objection Certificate' from the Immigration Office, Bahrain. (b) Passport. (c) 1 photo. (d) 1 completed application form. (e) 1 stamped, self-addressed envelope. (f) Fee.
Working days required: 1.

MONEY

Currency: Dinar (BD) = 1000 fils. Notes appear in denominations of BD20, 10, 5, 1 and 0.5 Dinars and 500 fils. Coins are in denominations of 100, 50, 25, 10, 5 and 1 fils.
Credit cards: Diners Club, Access/Mastercard, American Express and Visa are accepted. Check with your credit card company for details of merchant acceptability and other services which may be available.
Exchange rate indicators: The following figures are included as a guide to the movements of the Dinar against Sterling and the US Dollar:

Date:	**Oct '89**	**Oct '90**	**Oct '91**	**Oct '92**
£1.00=	0.59	0.72	0.65	0.61
$1.00=	0.37	0.37	0.38	0.38

Currency restrictions: There are no restrictions on the import or export of either local or foreign currency.
Banking hours: 0800-1200 and usually 1600-1800 Saturday to Wednesday; 0800-1100 Thursday. Many banks are open on both Saturday and Sunday. Government offices, businesses and most offices are closed on Friday, which is a weekly holiday.

DUTY FREE

The following goods may be imported into Bahrain without incurring customs duty:
400 cigarettes or 50 cigars or 225g of tobacco for personal use;
A reasonable amount of perfume for personal use;
2 bottles of wine or spirits (non-Muslim passengers only).
Prohibited items: Firearms, ammunition, drugs, jewellery and all items originating in Israel and South Africa may only be imported under licence. All uncut, bleached or undrilled pearls produced outside the Gulf are under strict import regulations.

PUBLIC HOLIDAYS

Public holidays observed in Bahrain are as follows:
Mar 25 '93 Start of Eid al-Fitr. **Jun 1** Eid al-Adha. **Jun 21** Islamic New Year. **Jun 30** Ashoura. **Aug 30** Mouloud (Prophet's Birthday). **Dec 16** National Day. **Jan 1 '94** New Year's Day. **Jan** Leilat al-Meiraj. **Feb** Beginning of Ramadan. **Mar** Start of Eid al-Fitr.
Note: Muslim festivals are timed according to local sightings of various phases of the Moon and the dates given above are approximations. During the lunar month of Ramadan that precedes Eid al-Fitr, Muslims fast during the day and feast at night and normal business patterns may be interrupted. Many restaurants are closed during the day and there are restrictions on smoking and drinking. Some disruption may continue into Eid al-Fitr itself. Eid al-Fitr and Eid al-Adha may last anything from two to ten days, depending on the region. For more information see the section *World of Islam* at the back of the book.

HEALTH

Regulations and requirements may be subject to change at short notice, and you are advised to contact your doctor well in advance of your intended date of departure. Any numbers in the chart refer to the footnotes below.

	Special Precautions?	Certificate Required?
Yellow Fever	No	1
Cholera	Yes	No
Typhoid & Polio	Yes	-
Malaria	No	-
Food & Drink	2	-

[1]: A yellow fever vaccination certificate is required from travellers over one year old coming from infected areas.
[2]: Water may be contaminated, and that used for drinking, brushing teeth or making ice should have first been boiled or otherwise sterilised. All modern hotels have their own filtration plants. Milk is unpasteurised and should be boiled. Powdered or tinned milk is available and is advised, but make sure that it is reconstituted with pure water. Avoid dairy products which are likely to have been made from unboiled milk. Only eat well-cooked meat and fish, preferably served hot. Pork, salad and mayonnaise may carry increased risk. Vegetables should be cooked and fruit peeled.
Health care: There is a comprehensive medical service, with general and specialised hospitals in the main towns. Medical insurance is essential. Pharmacies are well equipped with supplies.

TRAVEL - International

AIR: Approximate flight times: From Bahrain to *London* is 6 hours, to *Los Angeles* is 21 hours and to *New York* is 14 hours.
International airport: *Bahrain International (BAH)* (Muharraq) is 6.5km (4 miles) northeast of Manama. Taxi services run across the causeway to the main island. Airport facilities include a 24-hour bank, 24-hour duty-free shop, car parking, bar and restaurant.
Departure tax: BD3 for all departing passengers, except for those in direct transit on the same aircraft.
SEA: The main international port is Mina Sulman on the main island. The deep-water oil tanker terminals are on the northeast of the island. There are few regular passenger sailings as it is more usual to travel to Bahrain by air.

TRAVEL - Internal

SEA: Transport between the smaller islands is by motor-boat or dhow. For details contact local travel agents.
ROAD: Manama is served by an excellent road system, largely created during the last few years. The King Fahad Causeway between Bahrain and Saudi Arabia opened in 1986. There are bus and taxi services available to cross from one to the other. However it must be noted that normal Saudi Arabian visa regulations apply. **Bus:** Routes now serve most of the towns and villages, with a standard fare of 50 fils. **Taxi:** Taxis are identifiable by orange and red colouring on their wings. Fares increase by 50% between midnight and 0500 hours. Taxis waiting outside hotels may charge more. Fares should always be agreed beforehand. **Documentation:** An International Driving Permit is necessary and must be endorsed by the Traffic Department before it can be used. All applications must be in person. Holders of licences for the UK, the USA and Australia are not required to take a driving test, but must make application for a licence and take an eyesight test. All others must take a test.

ACCOMMODATION

HOTELS: Bahrain has many first-class hotels catering for the business community, but there is little in the way of cheaper accommodation. Advanced booking is advised. For details contact the nearest Bahrain Embassy.

RESORTS & EXCURSIONS

Bahrain is the largest island in an archipelago off the east coast of Saudi Arabia, accessible by a causeway adjoining the two countries. An adequate freshwater supply, unique in the region, and the benefits of having one of the largest oil refineries in the Gulf, have given the country great prosperity. Watersports, golf, tennis, and horseracing are enjoyed throughout the country.
Manama, Bahrain's capital, is modern, dominated by a Manhattan-style skyline. The souk lies in the centre of the old town, near the archway of *Bab al-Bahrain* and, although much of the surrounding area is modern, the street layout and division of occupations still follows traditional lines: the gold souk, for instance, is to be found to the southeast of the market area and is particularly impressive during the hours of darkness. Much land, including the diplomatic area, has been reclaimed from the sea. The ancient city capital of **Bilas Al Qadir,** which dates from AD900, is just outside the new city.

BAHRAIN	**HEALTH REGULATIONS**	**VISA REGULATIONS** Code-Link
GALILEO/WORLDSPAN	TI-DFT/BAH/HE	TI-DFT/BAH/VI
SABRE	TIDFT/BAH/HE	TIDFT/BAH/VI

To access this information on your CRS, swipe the barcode with a light pen or type in the text under the barcode. For more information, see the introduction *How to Use This Book*.

Excursions: The *Suk-al-Khamis Mosque* built in the 7th century is one of the oldest in the Gulf. Bahrain also has one of the newest: the *Al Fateh Mosque*, completed in 1988 which includes a library and conference hall. Other buildings of note are *Siyadi House*, a typical wood-carved pearl merchant's house from the turn of the century, and the 19th-century house of Shaikh Isa which is a good illustration of the local Islamic architectural style. Visitors can also see the 16th-century Portuguese fort near **Budaiya,** the basket-makers at **Khabadad,** the potteries at **A'ali** and the *Al Areen Wildlife Park*. *Jebel Dukhan* is the highest point in Bahrain, from where the whole south side of the island can be seen. The area around the ruler's country residence at *Shaikhs Beach* has many sandy beaches and apartments. *Zallaq* on the west coast has a sailing club. Near the roundabout on the *King Faisal Highway* Gold Suq dhow builders and fishtrap-makers continue their traditional crafts. Ancient burial mounds can be seen in many places.

SOCIAL PROFILE

FOOD & DRINK: There is a good selection of restaurants serving all kinds of food including Arabic, European, Indian, Chinese, Japanese, Lebanese and American. Arab food is mainly spicy and strongly flavoured. Lamb is the principal meat with chicken, turkey and duck. Salad and dips are common. **Drink:** Water, *arak* (grape spirit flavoured with aniseed) or beer are the most common drinks; the sale of alcohol is not encouraged although it is available to non-Muslims in nightclubs, good restaurants and luxury hotels except during Ramadan. Strong Arabic coffee and tea is also widely available.
NIGHTLIFE: Restaurants, nightclubs and cinemas showing English and Arabic films can be found in main towns.
SHOPPING: There is a wide range of shops with imported goods. Pearls are the main local product. Famous red clay pottery is available from the village of A'ali. There are weavers at Bani Jamra village and basket-makers at Jasra village. **Shopping hours:** 0800-1200 and 1530-1830 Saturday to Thursday. Some shops are open for a few hours on Fridays in the Souk.
SPORT: Football is the national game. There are plans for the construction of an Olympic-sized stadium. The **golf** clubs at Awali also accept temporary membership. Horse and camel **racing** are held on Fridays at Rifaa. **Skindiving, fishing** and **sailing** are popular, particularly at Awali, Zallaq and Nabih Salih. Zallaq has a sailing club and there is a yacht club at Sitra. There are **swimming** pools at the main hotels.
SOCIAL CONVENTIONS: Traditional beliefs and customs are strong influences and people are generally more formal than Westerners. Attitudes to women are more liberal than in most Gulf States. It is acceptable to sit cross-legged on cushions or sofas in people's homes but it is still insulting to display the soles of the feet. It is polite to drink two small cups of coffee or tea when offered. Guests will generally be expected to share a bedroom since guest bedrooms and privacy are almost unknown. Sports clothes may be worn in the street and short dresses are acceptable. Smoking is very common and cheap by European standards. Women should avoid wearing revealing clothing. **Tipping:** 10% is expected, particularly when service is not included, and is normal practice for taxis, porters etc.

BUSINESS PROFILE

ECONOMY: Oil dominates Bahrain's economy, providing almost 85% of export earnings: aluminium accounts for most of the rest. However, the country's oil reserves are dwindling rapidly and the Government is attempting to diversify the economy. As well as aluminium, an iron-ore processing facility and an ammonia-methanol plant have been built. Financial services have experienced rapid growth in recent years as companies trading in the region have set up their regional centres in Bahrain, where the relatively relaxed environment is an important factor in a region where rigorous social mores are often the norm. Japan is Bahrain's main export market, taking around 50% of the total; Britain, the US, Switzerland and France are the other important purchasers. The majority of Bahrainian imports, which cover a wide range of products, come from four countries: Germany, Britain, the US and Japan.
BUSINESS: Businessmen are expected to wear suits and ties. Business must be done on a personal introduction basis. Normal social courtesies should be observed. Bargaining is common practice: Arabs regard their word as their bond and expect others to do the same. The best time to visit is October to April. **Government office hours:** 0700-1300 Saturday to Thursday.
COMMERCIAL INFORMATION: The following organisation can offer advice: Bahrain Chamber of Commerce and Industry, PO Box 248, Manama, Bahrain. Tel: 233 913. Fax: 241 294. Telex: 8691.

HISTORY & GOVERNMENT

HISTORY: During the 15th and 16th centuries the Gulf began to open to European traders and Bahrain came under Portuguese rule between 1521 and 1622. For over 100 years Bahrain was attacked by various tribes and national groups until Mohammad al-Khalifa took control of the island. Bahrain was a British Protectorate between 1861 and 1971; ten years later it took part in formulating the Gulf Co-operation Council (GCC) aimed at economic co-operation between the Gulf states and defence strategy agreements. The discovery of oil in the 1930s instigated a process of social reform, which included education and social services. Tensions still exist between Bahrain and both Iran and Qatar. Both Qatar and Bahrain claim sovereignty over a number of tiny but potentially oil-rich Gulf territories, and several military clashes have occurred in recent years. Since then both countries have submitted their rival claims to the International Court of Justice, from whom a ruling is expected before the end of 1992. Although the Iranians formally dropped a long-standing territorial claim against Bahrain in 1970, since their own revolution they are believed to have given backing to Bahrain's Shi'ite Muslims against the Sunni Muslims to which the ruling dynasty belong. The two traditions are represented roughly equally within the country. The Iranians are alleged to have backed an abortive attempt in 1981 to overthrow the regime. Bahrain's concern about radical Shi'ite activity was overshadowed during 1990 and early 1991 by the Iraqi invasion of Kuwait. Bahrain backed the anti-Iraqi coalition but, given its small size, made a necessarily limited contribution. Perhaps its most valuable service was as a base for British and American aircraft and ships. The country also increased its oil production to compensate for the shortfall on world markets caused by UN sanctions against Iraq. Since the war, Bahrain's foreign policy has concentrated on regional efforts to strengthen the Gulf Co-operation Council as a strategic bloc, and in bilateral matters, on a territorial dispute with Qatar which suddenly flared up again.
GOVERNMENT: Bahrain is a traditional Arab monarchy, ruled since 1782 by the Al-Khalifa dynasty by the Emir through an appointed Cabinet. The current Emir is His Highness Shaikh Isa Bin Sulman Al-Khalifa. There are no popular elections at any level of government, and the National Assembly was abolished in 1975.

CLIMATE

Summer months (June to September) are very hot. The weather is far cooler from December to March, particularly in the evenings. Rainfall is slight and only likely in winter. Spring and autumn are the most pleasant seasons.
Required clothing: Lightweight cottons and linens from spring to autumn, mediumweight clothes from November to March. Warmer clothes are necessary in winter and on cool evenings.

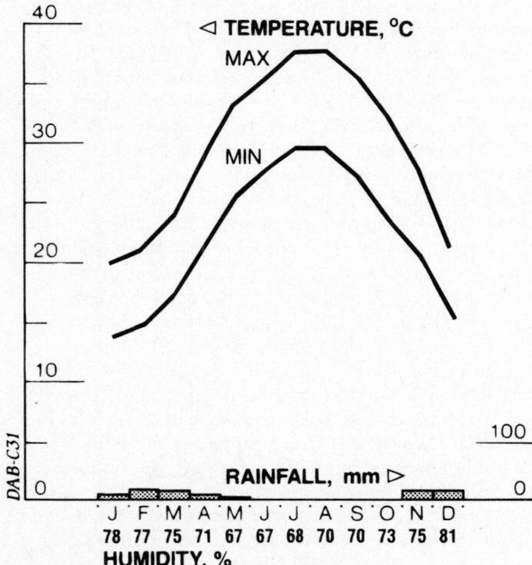

BANGLADESH

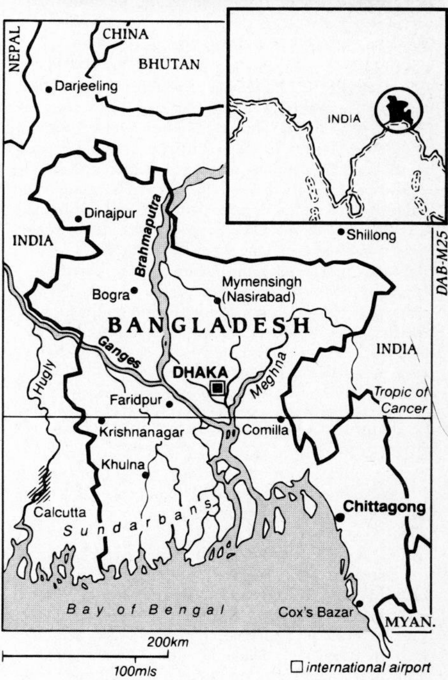

Location: Northeast of Indian sub-continent.

Bangladesh Parjatan Corporation (National Tourist Organisation)
233 Airport Road
Tejgaon
Dhaka 1215, Bangladesh
Tel: (2) 325 155. Telex: 642206.
High Commission for the People's Republic of Bangladesh
28 Queen's Gate
London SW7 5JA
Tel: (071) 584 0081/4. Fax: (071) 225 2130. Telex: 918016 BDTIDN G.
Assistant High Commission
31-33 Guildhall Buildings
12 Navigation Street
Birmingham B2 4BT
Tel: (021) 643 2386. Fax: (021) 643 9004. Opening hours: 0930-1700 Monday to Friday;
and
Bangladesh Consulate
28-32 Princess Street
Manchester M1 4LB
Tel: (061) 236 4853.
British High Commission
PO Box 6079
Abu Bakr House
Plot 7, Road 84, Gulshan Model Town
Dhaka 12, Bangladesh
Tel: (2) 600 133/7 *or* 412 544. Fax: (2) 883 437. Telex: 671066.
Consular & Immigration Section: Tel: (2) 600 224/8.
Embassy of the People's Republic of Bangladesh
2201 Wisconsin Avenue, NW
Washington, DC
20007
Tel: (202) 342 8372. Fax: (202) 333 4971.
Embassy of the United States of America
Diplomatic Enclave
PO Box 323
Madani Avenue
Baridhara Model Town
Dhaka 1212, Bangladesh
Tel: (2) 884 700/22. Fax: (2) 411 648. Telex: 642319.
High Commission for the People's Republic of Bangladesh
Suite 402,
85 Range Road
Ottawa, Ontario
K1N 8J6
Tel: (613) 236 0138. Fax: (613) 567 3213.

Canadian High Commission
PO Box 569
House 16A, Road 48
Gulshan Model Town
Dhaka 12, Bangladesh
Tel: (2) 607 701. Telex: 642328.

AREA: 143,998 sq km (55,598 sq miles).
POPULATION: 108,000,000 (1991).
POPULATION DENSITY: 750 per sq km.
CAPITAL: Dhaka. **Population:** 6,000,000 (1991).
GEOGRAPHY: The People's Republic of Bangladesh, formerly East Pakistan, is bounded to the west and northwest by West Bengal (India), to the north by Assam and Meghalaya (India), to the east by Assam and Tripura (India) and by Myanmar (Burma) to the southeast. The landscape is mainly flat with many bamboo, mango and palm-covered plains. A large part of Bangladesh is made up of alluvial plain, caused by the effects of the two great river systems of the Ganges (Padma) and the Brahmaputra (Jamuna) and their innumerable tributaries. In the northeast and east of the country the landscape rises to form forested hills. To the southeast, along the Burmese and Indian borders, the land is hilly and wooded. About a seventh of the country's area is underwater and flooding occurs regularly.
LANGUAGE: The official language is Bengali (Bangla). English is widely spoken especially in government and commercial circles. Urdu is also spoken.
RELIGION: 86.6% Muslim, 12.1% Hindu, and small Buddhist and Christian minorities. Religion is the main influence on attitudes and behaviour. Since 1988 Islam has been the official state religion.
TIME: GMT + 6.
ELECTRICITY: 220/240 volts AC, 60Hz. Plugs are of the British 5- and 15-amp, 2- or 3-pin (round) type.
COMMUNICATIONS: Telephone: Limited IDD available. Country code: 880. **Fax:** There are facilities at the Sheraton and Sonargaon hotels in Dhaka and services are now widely available throughout the country.
Telex/telegram: There are public telex facilities at the Sheraton and Sonargaon hotels in Dhaka. Telegrams may be sent from main post offices and there are three rates of charge, although service is sometimes unreliable.
Post: Airmail takes three to four days to Europe; surface mail can take several months. Post boxes are blue for air mail and red for surface mail. **Press:** There are nine daily English-language papers, the most popular being the *Bangladesh Observer*, followed by the *Bangladesh Times*, the *Daily Star*, the *Morning Sun* and the *New Nation*. The main English-language weeklies are *Holiday*, *Dialogue*, the *Dhaka Courier* and *Friday*. The main Bengali dailies are *Ittefaq*, *Inquilab*, *Banglar Bani*, *Sangbad*, *Dainik Bangla*, *Meillat* and *Khabar*. All these newspapers are published in Dhaka and circulated throughout the country.
BBC World Service and Voice of America frequencies: From time to time these change. See the section *How to Use this Book* for more information.

BBC:				
MHz	17.79	15.31	11.75	9.740
Voice of America:				
MHz	17.74	15.40	11.71	7.125

PASSPORT/VISA

Regulations and requirements may be subject to change at short notice, and you are advised to contact the appropriate diplomatic or consular authority before finalising travel arrangements. Details of these may be found at the head of this country's entry. Any numbers in the chart refer to the footnotes below.

	Passport Required?	Visa Required?	Return Ticket Required?
Full British	Yes	Yes	Yes
BVP	Not valid	-	-
Australian	Yes	Yes	Yes
Canadian	Yes	No	Yes
USA	Yes	Yes	Yes
Other EC	Yes	Yes	Yes
Japanese	Yes	No	Yes

PASSPORTS: Valid passport required by all.
British Visitors Passport: Not accepted.
VISAS: Required by all except nationals of the Bahamas, Barbados, Bhutan, Botswana, Canada, Cyprus, Fiji, Gabon, Gambia, Ghana, Grenada, Guyana, Jamaica, Japan, Kenya, South Korea, Lesotho, Malawi, Malaysia, Malta, Mauritius, Nauru, New Zealand, Nigeria, Papua New Guinea, the Seychelles, Sierra Leone, Somalia, Sri Lanka, Swaziland, Tanzania, Tonga, Trinidad & Tobago, Tunisia, Vatican City and Zambia if visiting for touristic purposes.
Note: Visas are not required by former Bangladesh nationals holding British passports provided they have Bangladesh passports as well as documentary evidence to prove they are of Bangladeshi origin.
Types of visa: Tourist and Business. As regulations are liable to change at short notice it is advisable to check details with the Embassy, High Commission (or Consular Section at Embassy). Cost: Visas for many nationals are free, but some other nationals (such as Ireland and Malta) must pay a fee. Check with the High Commission or Embassy (or Consular Section at Embassy) to find the cost of particular visas.
Validity: Tourist: 3 months; Business: 3 months.
Application to: Consular Section at Embassy or High Commission. For addresses, see top of entry.
Application requirements: (a) 2 photos. (b) 2 forms. (c) Letter from company for Business visa.
Working days required: 1-5.

MONEY

Currency: Bangladeshi Taka (Tk) = 100 poishas. Notes are in denominations of Tk500, 100, 50, 20, 10, 5, 2 and 1. Coins are in denominations of 100, 50, 25, 10, 5 and 1 poisha.
Currency exchange: All foreign currency exchanged must be entered on currency declaration form. Hotel bills must be paid in a major convertible currency or with travellers cheques. Many shops in the cities will offer better rates of exchange than the banks.
Credit cards: Access/Mastercard (limited), Diners Club and American Express are accepted. Check with your credit card company for details of merchant acceptability and other services which may be available.
Travellers cheques can be exchanged on arrival at Dhaka Airport.
Exchange rate indicators: The following figures are included as a guide to the movements of the Taka against Sterling and the US Dollar:

Date:	**Oct '89**	**Oct '90**	**Oct '91**	**Oct '92**
£1.00=	**49.91**	**68.00**	**63.38**	**63.42**
$1.00=	**31.60**	**34.80**	**36.52**	**39.96**

Currency restrictions: Import and export of local currency is limited to Tk100. Free import of foreign currency is allowed, subject to declaration. Export of foreign currency is limited to the amount declared on import. On departure, up to Tk500 may be reconverted. Banks are allowed to cash travellers cheques up to a value of US$50.
Banking hours: 0900-1300 Saturday to Wednesday, 0900-1100 Thursday.

DUTY FREE

The following goods may be imported into Bangladesh without incurring customs duty:
200 cigarettes or 50 cigars or 250g of tobacco;
2 open bottles of alcohol, total of 0.35 gallon (non-Muslims only);
A reasonable amount of perfume;
Gifts up to value of Tk500.
Note: A Customs Declaration Form will be issued on arrival and should be retained.
Prohibited items: Firearms and animals.

PUBLIC HOLIDAYS

Public holidays observed in Bangladesh are as follows:
Mar 25 '93 Eid al-Fitr, End of Ramadan. **Mar 26** Independence and National Day. **Apr 9** Good Friday. **Apr 12** Easter Monday. **May** Buddha Purinama. **May 1** May Day. **Jun 1** Eid al-Adha, Feast of Sacrifice. **Jun 21** Islamic New Year. **Jul** Jumatul Bida. **Aug 30** Mouloud (Prophet's Birthday). **Sep** Shab-i-Barat and Durga Puja. **Nov 7** National Revolution Day. **Dec 16** Victory Day. **Dec 25** Christmas Day. **Dec 26** Boxing Day. **Jan 1 '94** New Year's Day. **Feb 21** National Mourning Day. **Mar** Eid al-Fitr. **Mar 26** Independence and National Day.
Note: (a) Muslim festivals are timed according to local sightings of various phases of the Moon and the dates given above are approximations. During the lunar month of Ramadan that precedes Eid al-Fitr, Muslims fast during the day and feast at night and normal business patterns may be interrupted. Many restaurants are closed during the day and there may be restrictions on smoking and drinking. Some disruption may continue into Eid al-Fitr itself. Eid al-Fitr and Eid al-Adha may last anything from two to ten days, depending on the region. For more information see the section *World of Islam* at the back of the book. (b) Buddhist festivals are declared according to local astronomical observations and it is only possible to forecast the month of their occurrence.

HEALTH

Regulations and requirements may be subject to change at short notice, and you are advised to contact your doctor well in advance of your intended date of departure. Any numbers in the chart refer to the footnotes below.

	Special Precautions?	Certificate Required?
Yellow Fever	No	1
Cholera	Yes	2
Typhoid & Polio	Yes	-
Malaria	Yes/3	-
Food & Drink	4	-

[1]: A yellow fever certificate is required of all persons (including infants) arriving by air or sea within six days of departure from an infected area, or a country with infection in any part, or a country where the WHO judge yellow fever to be endemic or infected; or has been in such an area in transit; or has come by an aircraft which has come from such an area and has not properly disinfected. Those arriving without a required certificate will be detained in quarantine for six days. For further information, see the *Health* section at the back of the book.
[2]: Following WHO guidelines issued in 1973, a cholera vaccination certificate is no longer a condition of entry to Bangladesh. However, cholera is a serious risk in this country and precautions are essential. Up-to-date advice should be sought before deciding whether these precautions should include vaccination as medical opinion is divided over its effectiveness. See the *Health* section at the back of the book.
[3]: Malaria risks exist throughout the year in the whole country with the exception of Dhaka City. High levels of resistance to chloroquine have been reported in the malignant *falciparum* form.
[4]: All water should be regarded as being potentially contaminated. Water used for drinking, brushing teeth or making ice should have first been boiled or otherwise sterilised. Milk is unpasteurised and should be boiled. Powdered or tinned milk is available and is advised, but make sure that it is reconstituted with pure water. Avoid all dairy products. Only eat well-cooked meat and fish, preferably served hot. Pork, salad and mayonnaise may carry increased risk. Vegetables should be cooked and fruit peeled.
Rabies is present. For those at high risk, vaccination before arrival should be considered. If bitten abroad seek medical advice without delay. For more information consult the *Health* section at the back of the book.
Health care: There are 596 government hospitals and 164 private hospitals in the country. Visitors can be treated at military hospitals. Health insurance is essential.

TRAVEL - International

AIR: Bangladesh's national airline is *Biman Bangladesh Airlines (BG)*.
Approximate flight times: From Dhaka to *London* (direct) is 10 hours 20 minutes, to *Los Angeles* is 22 hours and to *New York* is 23 hours.
International airport: *Dhaka International (DAC)* (Zia International). The airport is 19km (12 miles) north of the city (travel time – 45 minutes). *Biman Bangladesh* coaches run every hour from 0800-2200. To return, pick up the coach from the Tejgaon old airport building, the Golden Gate or Zakaria hotels. Parjatan Coach runs every hour from 0800-2200. Taxi and limousine services are available to the city. Car hire is also possible. Airport facilities include a restaurant, post office, bank, duty-free shop and car parking.
SEA: Ferries from Myanmar and India run to the southern coastal ports. For details contact the Embassy or High Commission of the People's Republic of Bangladesh. The main seaports are Chittagong, Mongla and Chalna.
RAIL: Rail connections (there are no through trains) link Bangladesh with India (West Bengal and Assam). Cycle-rickshaw, bus or porter services provide the cross-border connections.
ROAD: Only two road frontier posts are currently open between Bangladesh and India, at Benopol (for Calcutta) and Chiliharti (for Darjeeling). It is advisable to check when the frontier posts will be open. Conditions are likely to be difficult during monsoon season. All other frontiers posts between the two countries are currently closed; nor is overland travel currently possible between Bangladesh and Myanmar.

TRAVEL - Internal

AIR: Internal services are operated by *Biman Bangladesh Airlines*. Regular flights are run between Dhaka and several other main towns. These are

cheap, and most routes are served at least two or three times a week. Airline buses connect with downtown terminals.
Departure tax: Tk70. Passengers in immediate transit are exempt.
SEA/RIVER: Ferries operate between southern coastal ports and the Ganges River delta, where there are five major river ports: Dhaka, Narayanganj, Chandpur, Barisal and Khulna. Passages should be booked well in advance; for details contact local port authorities. The country has about 8433km (5240 miles) of navigable waterways. River services are operated by the Bangladesh Inland Waterway Transport Corporation, who run 'Rocket' ferries and launches on a number of routes. The 'Rocket' services have three classes of fare; the waterways are the least expensive method of getting around Bangladesh.
RAIL: A rail system of about 2818km (1751 miles) connects major towns, with broad gauge in the west of the country and narrow gauge in the east. The network, which is slow but efficient, is limited by the geography of the country, but river ferries (see above) provide through links. Services are being upgraded. The main line is Dhaka–Chittagong, with several daily trains, some of which have air-conditioned cars. For details contact the Embassy or High Commission of the People's Republic of Bangladesh.
ROAD: There are about 10,407km (6467 miles) of paved roads. It is possible to reach virtually everywhere by road, but given the geography of the country, with frequent ferry crossings a necessity, together with the poor quality of many of the roads, road travel can be very slow. Flooding and storm damage have destroyed many roads and bridges, most recently as a result of the cyclone in April 1991. Bus services serve all major towns; fares are generally low. Traffic drives on the left. **Taxi:** Generally only available at airports and major hotels. Fares should always be agreed upon before travelling. **Car hire:** Self-drive cars may be hired at Dhaka airport, the Bangladesh Tourist Corporation Office or from the major hotels.
Documentation: National driving licence or International Driving Permit accepted. A temporary licence is available on presentation of a valid British or Northern Ireland driving licence.
URBAN: There are **bus** services, which are usually very crowded, in Dhaka provided by the National Road Transport Corporation. The Central Bus Station is on Station Road (Fulbaria); there are also several other terminals which are, in general, for long distance services. Buses and bus stations do not generally have signs in English. There are also an estimated 10,000 independent 'auto-rickshaw' 3-wheeler taxis (avoid night-time use). Conventional **taxis** are also available.
JOURNEY TIMES: The following chart gives approximate journey times (in hours and minutes) from Dhaka to other major cities/towns in Bangladesh.

	Air	Road	Rail
Chittagong	0.35	6.00	6.00
Sylhet	0.30	7.00	7.00
Rajshahi	0.45	12.00	13.00
Khulna	-	10.00	-
Rangpur	-	11.30	11.30
Dinajpur	-	12.00	13.00
Jessore	0.30	9.00	-

ACCOMMODATION

HOTELS: There are a few good hotels, mainly in Dhaka; these include the Sheraton, the Sundarban, the Purbani International and the Sonargaon. All rates are for European Plan. The Bangladesh Parjatan Corporation manages several modern hotels throughout the country. Bills must be paid in hard currency or with travellers cheques.

RESORTS & EXCURSIONS

The country is divided into four administrative areas: Dhaka (north central); Rajshahi (northwest); Khulna (southwest); and Chittagong (southeast). Note that 'Dhaka' is also spelt 'Dacca'. For consistency, the first spelling is used throughout this entry.

Dhaka (North Central)

Dhaka is the historic city and capital of Bangladesh, and lies on the Buriganga River. The river connects the city with all major inland ports in the country, contributing to its trade and commerce, as it has done for centuries.
The old part of the city, to the south of centre and on the banks of the river, is dominated both by the commercial bustle of the waterfront and several old buildings. These include the uncompleted 17th-century *Lalbagh Fort*, the spectacular *Ashan Manzil*, the *Chotta Katra* and a large number of mosques. To the north of this region is the European quarter (also known as British City), which contains the *Banga Bhavan*, the presidential palace, several parks, the *Dhakeswari Temple* and the *National Museum*. To the north and the east are to be found the commercial and diplomatic regions of Dhaka. The *Zoo and Botanical Gardens* are a bus or taxi ride into the suburbs. The waterfront has two main water transport terminals at Saddarghat and Badam Tole, located on the Buckland Road Bund. The famous 'Rocket' ferries dock here and boats can also be hired. There are many buildings of interest along the river and in the old part of the city. The *Khan Mohammed Mirdhai Mosque* and the *Mausoleum of Pari Bibi* are worth a visit, as are the *Baldha Gardens* with their collection of rare plants. There are dozens of mosques and bazaars to visit – the *Kashaitully Mosque* is especially beautiful.
The modern part of the city comprises the diplomatic and commercial regions and is to be found further north in areas such as Motijheel and Gulshan. Buildings of interest include the *Ghana Bhavan* (National Assembly Building) and the *Dhaka Exhibition Fair* building.
City tours are available of Dhaka and its environs: contact the Parjatan Tourist Information Centre for further information.
Outside Dhaka: Sonargaon, about 30km (20 miles) east of Dhaka, was the capital of the region between the 13th and early 17th centuries and retains a number of historical relics of interest although many of these are now in ruins. The **Rajendrapur National Park** about 50km (30 miles) north of the capital is noted for its varied birdlife. Northeast of Dhaka is **Dhamrai** which contains several Hindu temples. Further north still is **Mymensingh,** centre of a region famous for its supply of high-quality jute during the 19th century.

Rajshahi (Northwest)

Rajshahi Division, in the northwest of the country, is often ignored by tourists, but it contains a large number of archaeological sites. The most important of these are at **Paharpur,** where are to be found the vast Buddhist monastery of *Somapuri Vihara* and the *Satyapir Vita* temple; there is also a museum. Other places of interest in the region include the ancient Hindu settlement of **Sherpur**, near Bogra; **Mahastanagar,** also near Bogra, which dates back to the 2nd century BC; **Vasu Vihara,** 14km to the northwest, the site of an ancient but now ruined monastery; **Rajshahi,** on the Ganges, which has a museum displaying many of the archaeological relics of the area; and **Gaur,** very close to the border with the Indian state of West Bengal, which contains a number of old mosques. **Bogra** is a useful base for visiting the archaeological sites of Paharpur, Mahastanagar and Sherpur, although not intrinsically interesting itself.

Khulna (Southwest)

Khulna Division is principally marshland and jungle. The city of the same name is the administrative capital of the division and is mainly a commercial centre, particularly for river traffic. The principal place of interest in this area of the country is the **Sundarbans National Park,** a supreme example of lush coastal vegetation and the variety of wildlife which it can support. The most famous inhabitants of this region are the Royal Bengal Tigers, but spotted deer, monkeys and a great variety of birds are also to be found here. Tours (usually for ten people or more) are organised by Parjatan Tourism during the winter; otherwise boats can be hired from Khulna or Mongla, which is the main port for the Khulna region. Accommodation is available at Heron Point. Other places of interest include the mosque at **Sat Gombad,** and the town of **Bagerhat** (home of Khan Jahan Ali, a well-known Sufi mystic).

Chittagong (Southeast)

Chittagong, the second largest city in the country, is the principal city of the southeastern administrative division of Bangladesh. It is a thriving port set amid lovely natural surroundings studded with green-clad knolls, coconut palms, mosques and minarets, against the background of the blue waters of the Bay of Bengal. The Old City retains many echoes of past European settlement, mainly by the Portuguese, as well as many mosques. These include the 17th-century *Shahi Jama-e-Masjid* – which closely resembles a fort – set astride a hilltop, and the earlier *Qadam Mubarek Mosque*. The *Chilla of Bada Shah* stands to the west of Bakshirhat in the old city. The higher ground to the northwest was, in due course, settled by the British, and this is now where most of the city's commercial activity is conducted. The *Dargah of Sah Amanat* is a holy shrine located in the heart of the town. About five miles from Chittagong is the picturesque *Pahartali Lake* in the railway township of **Pahartali.** The *Tomb of Sultan Bayazid Bostami*, a holy shrine situated on a hillock in **Nasirabad,** is situated four miles to the northwest of the town. At its base is a large tank with several hundred tortoises, supposedly the descendants of evil spirits. In the extreme south of Bangladesh is **Cox's Bazar,** a thriving regional tourist centre with a mixed population of Bengali and Burmese. The town has many thriving cottage industries for weaving silk and making cigars. This is also where the world's longest and broadest beach, *Inani Beach*, can be found; it is 120km (75 miles) long and 55m (180ft) to 90m (300ft) broad (depending on the tide). It has not, however, been developed for tourism. The main tourist beach is *Saikat*, which is also broad and long.

SOCIAL PROFILE

FOOD & DRINK: Limited availability of Western food, although the best hotels and restaurants have continental dishes and Dhaka has many good Chinese restaurants. There are many local specialities, usually served with rice, based on chicken and lamb. Seafood is also recommended, particularly prawns. Kebabs are widely available. Sweets include *keora*, *zorda* and *sundesh*. Table service is usual. **Drink:** Alcoholic drink is expensive and strict Muslim customs severely limit availability and drinking times although leading hotels have bars which will serve drink; soft drinks and tea *(chai)* are freely available. Prices tend to be high.
NIGHTLIFE: Leading hotels have bars, but Western-style nightclubs do not exist. Displays of local dance and music are occasionally to be seen, particularly during religious festivals.
SHOPPING: Hand-loom fabrics, printed saris, coconut masks, bamboo products, mother-of-pearl jewellery, pink pearl, leather crafts, wood and cane handicrafts, folk dolls and horn items are popular purchases. **Shopping hours:** Generally 0900-2000 Saturday to Thursday and 0900-1230 Friday (shops in tourist districts often stay open later).
SPORT: Cricket and **football** are the national sports. Dhaka Metropolitan Soccer League begins its season in April. Games are held in the city stadium and play-

BANGLADESH	HEALTH REGULATIONS	VISA REGULATIONS (Code-Link)
GALILEO/WORLDSPAN	TI-DFT/DAC/HE	TI-DFT/DAC/VI
SABRE	TIDFT/DAC/HE	TIDFT/DAC/VI

To access this information on your CRS, swipe the barcode with a light pen or type in the text under the barcode. For more information, see the introduction *How to Use This Book*.

grounds. **Volleyball, kabadi, badminton, hockey, basketball, tennis** and **rowing** are also popular sports. **Swimming** is available at the Intercontinental Hotel and Dhaka club and on the coast. All other **watersports** are at Kaptai Lake and **sailing** is also popular on the coast.

SOCIAL CONVENTIONS: In someone's home it is acceptable to sit crossed-legged on cushions or the sofa, although it is considered an insult to display the soles of the feet. If a visitor wishes to bring a gift, money must not be given as it may cause offence. Religious customs should be respected by guests. For instance, women should not be photographed unless it is certain that there will be no objection. Women should wear trousers or long skirts; revealing clothes should be avoided, particularly when visiting religious places. Dress is generally informal for men.

Photography: In rural areas people are unused to tourists, who should ask permission before photographs are taken of individuals. Do not photograph military installations.

Tipping: Most services expect a tip in hotels; give 10% for restaurant staff and 5% for taxi drivers.

BUSINESS PROFILE

ECONOMY: Bangladesh is one of the poorest and most overcrowded countries in the world. With few mineral resources, the country depends mainly on an agricultural industry which is frequently hampered by cyclones and flooding. Subsistence crops (wheat, grain and rice) take up the bulk of productive capacity. Tea and jute are the main cash crops – Bangladesh supplies about 90% of the world's raw jute. Production of both has suffered in recent years, again largely due to the weather. Recent attempts to improve the quality of the local tea have been introduced to arrest the drastic decline in export earnings. There are large reserves of natural gas and some deposits of low-grade coal. Most of the manufacturing workforce is based in jute-related industries; the remainder works in textiles, chemicals and sugar. The cotton textile industry did particularly well during the 1980s and has now become a major export earner. Economic policy under the Begum Zia government has involved tentative market reforms, reduction of the bloated state sector, lowering of import barriers and some privatisation. However, Bangladeshi trade patterns have never properly recovered from the split with Pakistan, which used to take much of the country's tea crop: even though direct trade links were re-established in 1976, they have never reached previous levels. Bangladesh relies heavily on foreign aid, which accounts for around 7% of GDP and comes from a variety of sources, notably the World Bank and, increasingly, in the form of bilateral aid from Japan. The USA is substantially the largest export market followed by Italy, Japan, Singapore and the UK. Japan, Canada and Singapore are the country's main suppliers of imports, which are mostly manufactured goods. The hurricane of May 1991 caused irrevocable damage to the economy. The port of Chittagong, through which the bulk of Bangladeshi trade passes, was devastated. The country has now become more reliant than ever on the provision of foreign aid.

BUSINESS: Tropical-weight suits or shirt and tie are recommended. Suits or lounge suits are necessary when calling on Bengali officials. Cards are given and usual courtesies are observed. Visitors should not be misled by the high illiteracy rate and low educational level of most of the population. Given the opportunity, Bangladeshis prove to be good business people and tough negotiators. The best time to visit is October to May. **Office hours:** 0900-1600 Saturday to Thursday.

COMMERCIAL INFORMATION: The following organisation can offer advice: Federation of Bangladesh Chambers of Commerce and Industry (FBCCI), Federation Bhaban, PO Box 2079, 60 Motijheel C/A , 4th Floor, Dhaka 1000. Tel: (2) 250 566. Telex: 642733.

HISTORY & GOVERNMENT

HISTORY: Bangladesh was formerly East Pakistan, a constituent of the original state of Pakistan created by the British in 1947 as part of the partitioning of Britain's former Indian Empire. Tensions arose almost immediately between the two halves of the country, coming to a head in 1970 when Sheikh Mujibur Rahman, leader of the Awami League, won a majority in the elections and demanded greater independence. He was not permitted to become Prime Minister and, after violent protests the country unilaterally seceded from Pakistan in 1971, which precipitated a civil war. A troubled period followed during which floods, famine and economic instability were compounded by a succession of military coups, and the frequent imposition of martial law and states of emergency, but the 1980s were more stable. During this time, Bangladesh improved relations with Pakistan and its principal neighbours, India and Myanmar, and started to make tentative economic progress. General Hussain Mohammed Ershad took power in a military coup in March 1982. Four years later, the country was returned to constitutional government, but Ershad's political vehicle, the Jatiya Dal, managed to retain power for its leader following a dubious election. The Jatiya Dal's main opponent was the Awami League, headed by Sheikh Hasina Wajed; the Bangladesh National Party boycotted the poll. The BNP and Awami were the principal contestants at the next poll in February 1991. Ershad, by now discredited, saw his party limited to just 35 of the 330 national assembly seats. Awami took 84 and the BNP 140. Mrs Khaleda Zia, widow of the founder of modern Bangladesh, was the victor, but soon after the country was devastated by a cyclone. During 1992, the hard-pressed Bangladeshi government, which already presides over one of the world's highest population densities, has been obliged to accommodate thousands of Rohingya Muslims fleeing persecution in neighbouring Myanmar.

GOVERNMENT: After four and a half years of martial law, constitutional government was re-introduced in November 1986. Executive power is wielded by a President, who is elected by universal adult suffrage every five years. The President appoints a Council of Ministers from delegates of the largely elected 330-member Parliament or Jatiya Sangsad, Bangladesh's legislative assembly. Islam was established as the state religion by a majority vote of Jatiya Sangsad in June 1988.

CLIMATE

Very hot, tropical climate with a monsoon season from April to October when temperatures are highest; rainfall averages over 100 inches. The cool season is between November and March.

Required clothing: Lightweight cottons and linens throughout the year. Warmer clothes needed in the evenings during the cool season. Waterproofs are necessary during the monsoon season.

DHAKA Bangladesh (8m)

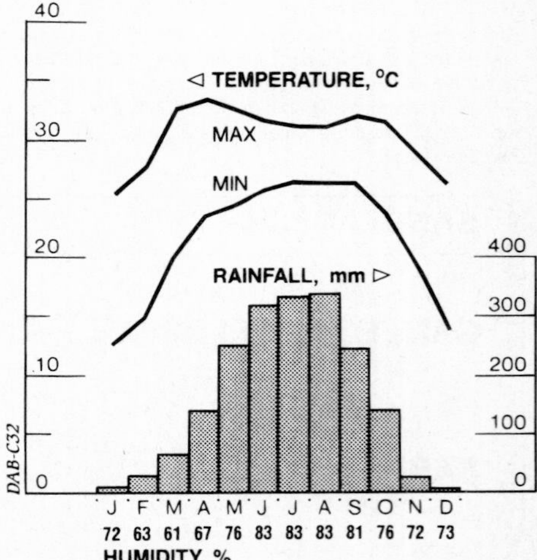

BARBADOS

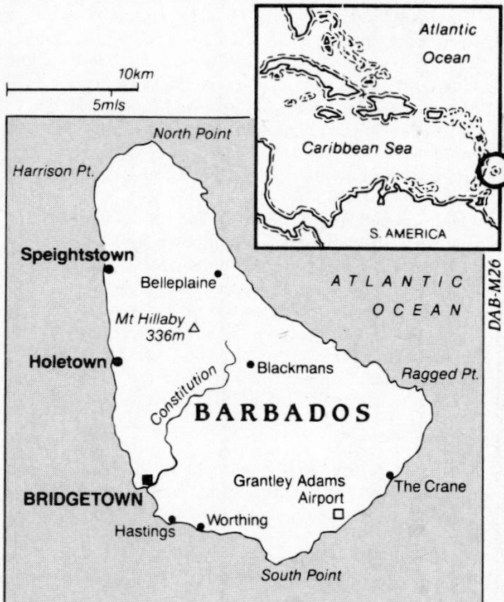

Location: Caribbean, Windward Islands.

Barbados Board of Tourism
PO Box 242
Harbour Road
Bridgetown, Barbados
Tel: 427 2623. Fax: 426 4080. Telex: 2420.
Barbados High Commission
1 Great Russell Street
London WC1B 3NH
Tel: (071) 631 4975. Fax: (071) 323 6872. Telex: 262081. Opening hours: 1000-1530 Monday to Friday (visa section); 0930-1730 Monday to Friday (general enquiries).
Barbados Board of Tourism
263 Tottenham Court Road
London W1P 9AA
Tel: (071) 636 9448. Fax: (071) 637 1496. Opening hours: 0930-1730 Monday to Friday.
British High Commission
PO Box 676
Lower Collymore Rock
St Michael
Barbados
Tel: 436 6694. Fax: 436 5398. Telex: 2219 UKREP BRI.
Embassy of Barbados
2144 Wyoming Avenue, NW
Washington, DC
20008
Tel: (202) 939 9200. Fax: (202) 332 7467. Telex: 64343.
Barbados Board of Tourism
800 Second Avenue
New York NY
10017
Tel: (212) 986 6516 *or* (800) 221 9831. Fax: 573 9850. Telex: 666387.
Embassy of the United States of America
PO Box 302
Canadian Imperial Bank of Commerce Building
Broad Street
Bridgetown, Barbados
Tel: 436 4950. Fax: 429 5246. Telex: 2259.
High Commission for Barbados
Suite 210
151 Slater Street
Ottawa, Ontario
K1P 5H3
Tel: (613) 236 9517. Fax: (613) 230 4362.
Barbados Board of Tourism
Suite 1800
5160 Yonge Street West
North York, Ontario
M2N 6LD
Tel: (416) 512 6569. Fax:(416) 512 6581.
Canadian High Commission
Bishops Court Hill
St Michael, Barbados
Tel: 429 3550. Fax: 429 3780. Telex: 2247.

AREA: 430 sq km (166 sq miles).
POPULATION: 257,082 (1990).
POPULATION DENSITY: 597.9 per sq km.
CAPITAL: Bridgetown. **Population:** 7466 (1980).
GEOGRAPHY: Barbados is the most easterly of the Caribbean chain of islands. It lies well to the east of the West Indies, making it the most windward of the Windward Islands. To the west, coral beaches are made of fine white sand, and the sea endlessly shifts from brilliant blue to emerald green over the natural coral reefs. Along the east coast there is a lively surf as the sea pounds the more rocky shoreline. Trade winds give Barbados a mild subtropical climate. This fertile and well-cultivated land (sugar cane is the main crop) is predominantly flat with only a few gently rolling hills to the north. The coral structure of the island acts as a natural filter, and the water of Barbados is amongst the purest in the world.
LANGUAGE: The official language is English. Local *Bajan Creole* is also spoken.
RELIGION: Mainly Christian, with a Protestant majority. Roman Catholic minority, plus small Jewish, Hindu and Muslim communities.
TIME: GMT - 4 (GMT - 5 in summer).
ELECTRICITY: 110/120 volts AC, 50Hz.
COMMUNICATIONS: Telephone: Inward IDD service is available to some towns. Country code: 1 809. Outgoing IDD calls can be made to all parts of the world. Hotels have telephones available to both residents and non-residents. **Fax:** Available at the largest hotels. Barbados External Telecommunications provides services for members of the public. **Telex/telegram:** Services are provided by Barbados External Telecommunications Ltd. The Bridgetown office has extensive telephone, telex and telegraph facilities. The Cable and Wireless office is at Lower Broad Street, open 0700-1900 Monday to Friday, 0700-1300 Saturday. There is a 24-hour service open at Wildey, St Michael. Telex equipment can be rented. **Post:** Deliveries are made twice a day in Bridgetown and once a day in rural areas. Post boxes, which are red, are plentiful. Post office hours: 0730-1700 Monday to Friday at Bridgetown main office; other branches are open 0730-1200 and 1300-1500 on Mondays, 0800-1200 and 1300-1515 Tuesday to Friday. **Press:** The main dailies are *The Barbados Advocate* and *The Nation*.
BBC World Service and Voice of America frequencies: From time to time these change. See the section *How to Use this Book* for more information.

BBC:				
MHz	17.72	11.78	9.915	5.965
Voice of America:				
MHz	15.21	11.70	6.130	0.930

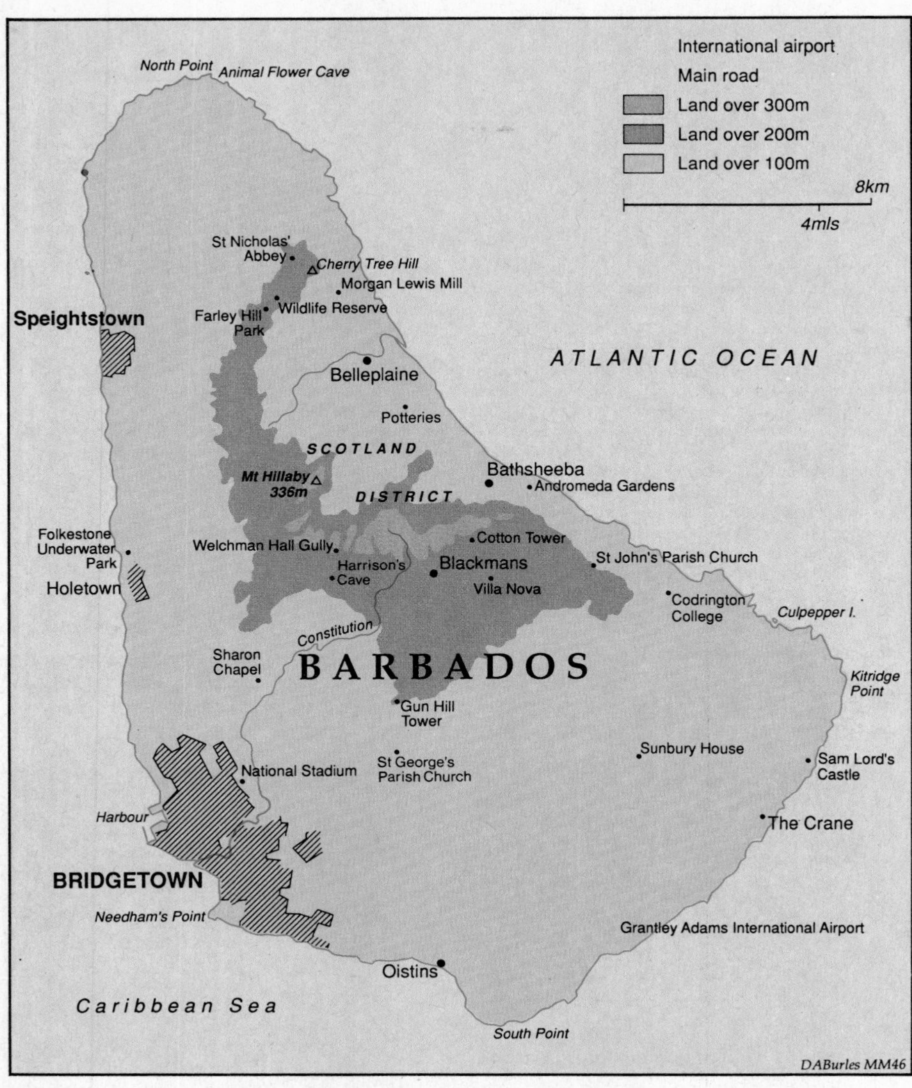

PASSPORT/VISA

Regulations and requirements may be subject to change at short notice, and you are advised to contact the appropriate diplomatic or consular authority before finalising travel arrangements. Details of these may be found at the head of this country's entry. Any numbers in the chart refer to the footnotes below.

	Passport Required?	Visa Required?	Return Ticket Required?
Full British	Yes	No	Yes
BVP	Not valid	-	-
Australian	Yes	No	Yes
Canadian	1	No	Yes
USA	1	No	Yes
Other EC	Yes	2	No
Japanese	Yes	No	Yes

PASSPORTS: Valid passport required by all except:
[1] nationals of the USA and Canada, who hold a valid return ticket, who have embarked in their home country for stays not exceeding 3 months and who have a Naturalisation Certificate or original birth certificate accompanied by one of the following: (a) Driver's Licence with photograph, (b) Senior Citizen's Card with photograph, (c) Univeristy or College acceptance identificaion with photograph, (d) Employment Identification with photograph. Children under 12 years of age accompanied by their parents are exempt.

British Visitors Passport: Not acceptable.

VISAS: Tourist visas are required by all except:
(a) **[2]** nationals of most EC countries for a stay of up to 3 months, nationals of France and Spain for up to 1 month, and nationals of the UK and Portugal for up to 6 months;
(b) nationals of the USA for a stay of up to 6 months;
(c) nationals of Commonwealth countries (but not India and Pakistan) for 6 months;
(d) nationals ofArgentina, Austria, Colombia, Cuba, Fiji, Hong Kong, Iceland, Israel, Japan, Liechtenstein, Malta, Norway, Peru, Sweden, Switzerland, Turkey and Venezuela for a stay of up to 3 months, provided they hold return tickets.
All business visitors require a Business visa. British passport holders should apply for an entry permit for a Business visa on arrival in Barbados at the Immigration Office; this is valid for 6 months. Entry permits held by passport holders of other nationalities are valid for 90 days. If a longer stay is required, apply for renewal at the discretion of the Immigration Office, Barbados.

Types of visa: Tourist and Business; cost £18.

Application to: Consulate (or Consular Section at Embassy or High Commission). For addresses, see top of entry.

Application requirements: (a) 1 form. (b) 1 photo. (c) Valid passport. (d) Company letter where required.

Working days required: 1.

Temporary residence: Enquire at the immigration office in Barbados.

MONEY

Currency: Barbados Dollar (Bds$) = 100 cents. Notes are in denominations of Bds$100, 20, 10, 5, 2 and 1. Coins are in denominations of Bds$1, and 25, 10, 5 and 1 cents.

Currency exchange: The best exchange rates are available at commercial banks. The island is served by the Barbados National Bank and a range of at least six international banks, each with a main office in Bridgetown and further branches in Hastings, Worthing, Holetown and Speightstown.

Credit cards: Diners Club, American Express and Access/Mastercard are accepted in the resorts. Check with your credit card company for details of merchant acceptability and other services which may be available.

Travellers cheques are accepted by all banks and most hotels.

Exchange rate indicators: The following figures are included as a guide to the movements of the Barbados Dollar against Sterling and the US Dollar:

Date:	Oct '89	Oct '90	Oct '91	Oct '92
£1.00=	3.17	3.92	3.49	3.18
$1.00=	2.01	2.01	2.01	2.00

Currency restrictions: Free import of local currency subject to declaration. Export limited to amount declared on import. No restrictions on the import or export of foreign currency.

Banking hours: Generally 0900-1500 Monday to Thursday, 0930-1300 and 1500-1700 Friday.

DUTY FREE

The following items may be taken into Barbados without incurring customs duty:
*200 cigarettes or 500g of other tobacco products**;
*1 bottle of alcoholic beverage**;
150g of perfume;
Gifts up to a value of Bds$100.

Note: For certain items it is now possible, on presentation of airline tickets and travel documents, to obtain duty-free goods any time from the day of arrival in the country. However, tobacco, alcohol and electronic goods must still be bought under the old system immediately prior to embarkation. **[*]** Only for passengers over 18 years of age.

Prohibited items: Restricted import of foreign rum, firearms and ammunition. Permits are needed for plants and animals.

PUBLIC HOLIDAYS

Public holidays observed in Barbados are as follows:
Apr 9 '93 Good Friday. **Apr 12** Easter Monday. **May 1** Whit Monday. **May 3** Labour Day. **Aug 2** Kadooment. **Oct 7** United Nations Day. **Nov 30** Independence Day. **Dec 25-26** Christmas. **Jan 1 '94** New Year's Day. **Jan** Errol Barrow Day.

HEALTH

Regulations and requirements may be subject to change at short notice, and you are advised to contact your doctor well in advance of your intended date of departure. Any numbers in the chart refer to the footnotes below.

	Special Precautions?	Certificate Required?
Yellow Fever	No	1
Cholera	No	No
Typhoid & Polio	Yes	-
Malaria	No	-
Food & Drink	2	-

BARBADOS | **HEALTH REGULATIONS** | **VISA REGULATIONS** | Code-Link

GALILEO/WORLDSPAN

TI-DFT/BGI/HE

TI-DFT/BGI/VI

SABRE

TIDFT/BGI/HE

TIDFT/BGI/VI

To access this information on your CRS, swipe the barcode with a light pen or type in the text under the barcode. For more information, see the introduction *How to Use This Book*.

[1]: A yellow fever vaccination certificate is required from travellers over one year of age coming from countries with infected areas.
[2]: The water on the island of Barbados is considered by some to be the purest in the world; it is filtered naturally by limestone and coral and pumped from underground rivers. Milk is pasteurised and dairy products are safe for consumption. Local meat, poultry, seafood, fruit and vegetables are generally considered safe to eat.
Health care: Excellent medical facilities are available in Barbados, with both private and general wards. There are two large hospitals staffed by highly trained personnel. It is recommended that medical insurance be taken out.

TRAVEL - International

AIR: Barbados is served by *British West Indian Airlines (BW)*.
Approximate flight times: From Barbados to *London* is 7 hours 30 minutes, to *Los Angeles* is 9 hours and to *New York* is 5 hours.
International airport: *Barbados (BGI) (Grantley Adams)* 18km (11 miles) east of Bridgetown, near Christchurch. Facilities include a bank, bar, shops and restaurant. The outgoing duty-free shop carries a range of items including jewellery, perfumes, china, crystal, cameras, shoes and clothing. There is a regular bus service to the city which departs every 10 minutes, and a 24-hour taxi service.
Departure tax: Bds$20 for all departures. Passengers in transit who will be remaining in Barbados for less than 24 hours are exempt.
SEA: Barbados, which has a new deep-sea harbour at Bridgetown, is a port of call for a number of British, European and American cruise lines. Cruises call at Bridgetown and extend to other Caribbean islands. For details contact the Tourist Office. There is a small departure tax.

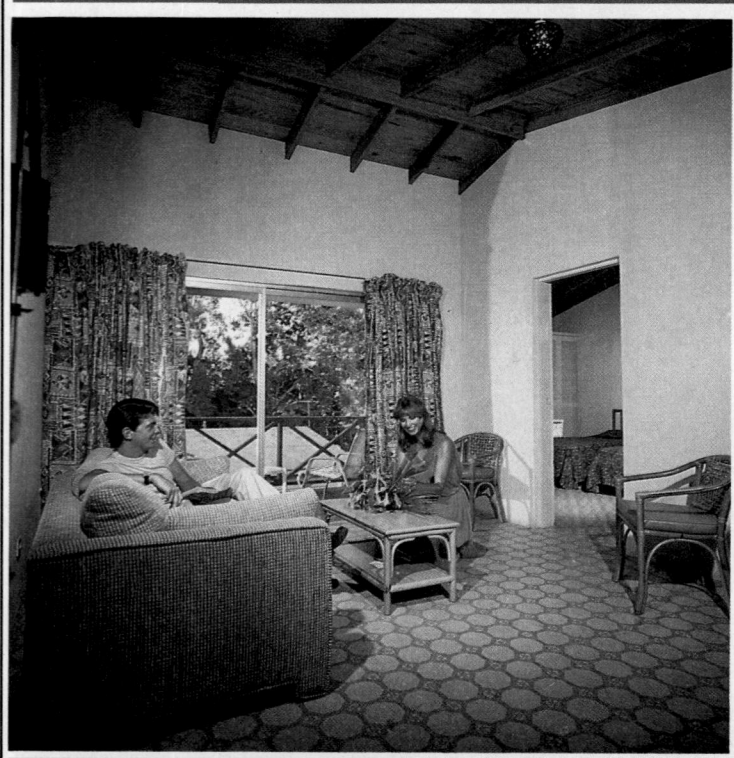

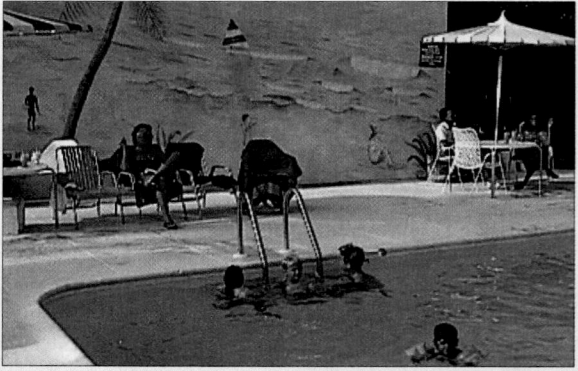

TRAVEL - Internal

AIR: *LIAT* and *BWIA* run inter-Caribbean flights to most of the neighbouring islands. *Tropicair* and *Aero Services* also have chartering facilities.
ROAD: Barbados has a good network of roads which covers the entire island. Driving time to the east coast from Bridgetown has been greatly reduced following the completion of the trans-insular highway. Traffic drives on the left. The road journey from Bridgetown to Speightstown takes about 30 minutes and to Holetown or Oistins about 20 minutes. **Bus:** Frequent, comprehensive coverage of the island, flat rate for all journeys. Although cheap, buses are crowded during the rush hours. All buses terminate at Bridgetown. **Taxi:** Standard rates for all routes throughout the island. Listing available from the Tourist Office. **Car hire:** Anything from a mini-moke to a limousine may be hired at the airport, at offices in Bridgetown and at main hotels. Petrol is comparatively cheap. Cars may be hired by the hour, day or week. **Documentation:** A Barbados driving permit is required. This can be obtained from car hire companies, at the Ministry of Transport (0830-1430 Monday to Friday) or at the airport (0800-2200 every day). There is a registration fee of Bds$10. A valid national licence or an International Driving Permit should also be held.
URBAN: Bridgetown has a local bus network and taxis are available.

ACCOMMODATION

Hotels, apartments, cottages and guest-houses are situated all the way down the coast from Speightstown to Oistins.
HOTELS: Accommodation includes uncompromising luxury and many first-class hotels. Hotel prices range to suit all budgets. Generally the luxury hotels are on the west while the medium-priced can be found along the southwest. The east coast, due to its exposure to the trade

into tourism and light industry. Tourism is now the largest employer on the island and continues to show steady growth. There is also a sizeable trade in high-quality British-manufactured china and glassware, and in souvenirs for tourists. Cotton, flowers and plants are being developed as export industries. Light industries, such as electronic components, have fared less well mainly as a result of falling demand in the United States who are the principal export market for these products. Oil has recently been discovered offshore, but the operations are small scale and the state-owned oil trading concern makes a loss. Barbados receives some overseas aid from British and American sources and is a member of the Caribbean economic community CARICOM. The island is attempting to develop an 'offshore' financial services sector. Barbados has a good transport and communications infrastructure which should do much to assist future economic development.

The main trading partners are the United States – the source of 30% of all imports – the UK and the other CARICOM nations.

BUSINESS: Lightweight tropical suits and shirt and tie are recommended. European courtesies should be observed. **Office hours:** 0800/0830-1600/1630 Monday to Friday.

COMMERCIAL INFORMATION: The following organisation can offer advice: Barbados Chamber of Commerce and Industry, PO Box 189, First Floor, Nemwil House, Lower Collymore Rock, St Michael. Tel: 426 2056. Fax: 429 2907.

CONFERENCES/CONVENTIONS: For the business traveller, conference organiser or incentive group there are a number of hotels with conference and meeting facilities. There are also two conference centres. Contact Barbados Board of Tourism for more information.

HISTORY & GOVERNMENT

HISTORY: The British first occupied Barbados in 1627 and the country remained a colony until 1961, when internal autonomy was achieved. Full independence was granted in 1966. Barbados is part of the British Commonwealth. Politics on the island have since been dominated by the Barbados Labour Party (BLP) and the rival Democratic Labour Party (DLP) which began life after a split in the BLP. The two parties have alternated between government and opposition since independence. The DLP has held office since May 1986, with a substantial majority in the House of Assembly. Erskine Sandiford has been Prime Minister since June 1987, and was returned to power following elections in January 1991. Barbados participates in the Caribbean's principal regional economic and security structures: CARICOM (the Caribbean Common Market) and the US-backed Regional Security System set up following the American invasion of Grenada. The then Government of Barbados backed the invasion, committing some of its own troops to the occupying force. The Government is also one of the main proponents of further regional integration, which it believes to be more important than the trade and political frictions which are presently inhibiting such a development.

GOVERNMENT: The British monarch has executive power, and is represented on Barbados by a Governor-General (currently Sir Hugh Springer). He is advised by the Cabinet and appoints the Prime Minister. The legislature comprises the Governor-General, a Senate and the House of Assembly, members of which are elected by universal adult suffrage.

CLIMATE

The balmy, subtropical climate is cooled by constant sea breezes, but it is sunnier and drier than the other islands. The dry season is from December to June; during the so-called wet season (July to November), some brief rain showers are likely. Average sunshine hours per day: 9-10 from November to March, 7-8 from April to October. **Required clothing:** Lightweight cottons are advised; beachwear is not normally worn in towns.

BRIDGETOWN Barbados (55m)

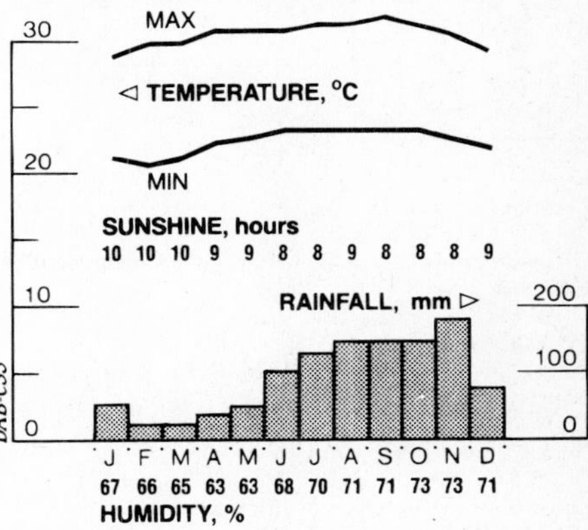

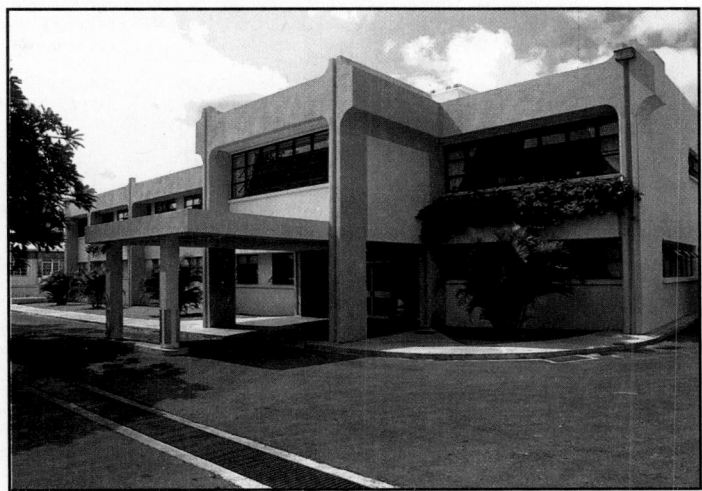

BELGIUM

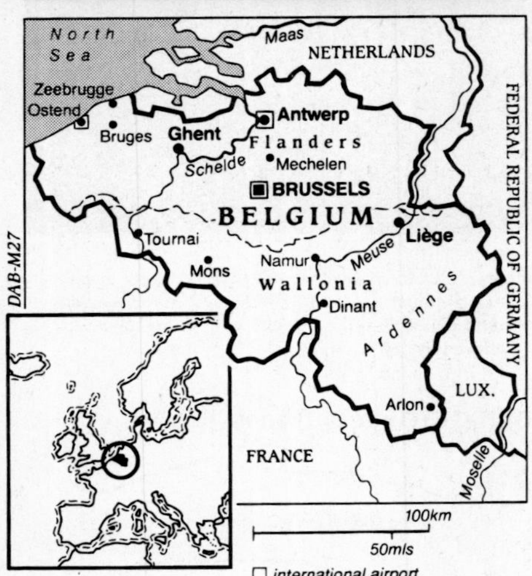

Location: Western Europe.

Office de Promotion du Tourisme de la Communauté Française
61 rue Marché-aux-Herbes
B-1000 Brussels, Belgium
Tel: (2) 504 0390. Fax: (2) 513 6950. Telex: 63245.
Tourist Office for Flanders
Grasmarkt 61
B-1000 Brussels, Belgium
Tel: (2) 513 9090. Fax: (2) 513 8803. Telex: 63245.
Embassy of the Kingdom of Belgium
103 Eaton Square
London SW1W 9AB
Tel: (071) 235 5422 (general enquiries) *or* 235 5144 (visa section). Fax: (071) 259 6213. Telex: 22823 BELAM G. Opening hours: 0830-1230 Monday to Friday (visas); 0900-1300 and 1400-1700 (enquiries).
Belgian Tourist Office
Premier House
2 Gayton Road
Harrow HA1 2XU
Tel: (081) 861 3300. Fax: (081) 427 6760. Opening hours: 0900-1700 Monday to Friday.
British Embassy
85 rue d'Arlon
B-1040 Brussels, Belgium
Tel: (2) 287 6211. Fax: (2) 287 6360.
Consulates in: Antwerp and Liège.
Embassy of the Kingdom of Belgium
3330 Garfield Street, NW
Washington, DC 20008
Tel: (202) 333 6900. Fax: (202) 333 3079. Telex: 440139.
Belgian Consulate General
11th Floor, 50 Rockefeller Plaza
New York, NY 10020
Tel: (212) 586 5110. Fax: (212) 582 9657. Telex: 238824.
Belgian National Tourist Office
745 Fifth Avenue
New York, NY 10151
Tel: (212) 758 8130. Fax: (212) 355 7675. Telex: 237933.
Embassy of the United States of America
27 boulevard du Régent
B-1000 Brussels, Belgium
Tel: (2) 513 3830. Fax: (2) 511 2725.
Embassy of Belgium
Suites 601-604
85 Range Road
Ottawa, Ontario K1N 8J6
Tel: (613) 236 7267. Fax: (613) 236 7882. Telex: 0533568.
Consulates in: Calgary, Edmonton, Halifax, London (Ontario), Montréal, Toronto, Vancouver and Winnipeg.
Belgian Tourist Office
PO Box 760
Succursale NDG
Montréal, Québec
H4A 3S2
Tel: (514) 845 7500. Fax: (514) 489 8965.
Canadian Embassy
2 avenue de Tervueren
B-1040 Brussels, Belgium
Tel: (2) 735 6040. Fax: (2) 735 3383. Telex: 21613.

AREA: 30,519 sq km (11,783 sq miles).
POPULATION: 9,978,681 (1991).
POPULATION DENSITY: 327.2 per sq km.
CAPITAL: Brussels (Bruxelles, Brussel). **Population:** 960,324 (1990).
GEOGRAPHY: Belgium is situated in Europe and bordered by France, Germany, Luxembourg and The Netherlands. The landscape is varied, the rivers and gorges of the Ardennes contrasting sharply with the rolling plains which make up much of the countryside. Notable features are the great forest of Ardennes near the frontier with Germany and Luxembourg and the wide, sandy beaches of the northern coast, which run for over 60km (37 miles). The countryside is rich in historic cities, castles and churches.
LANGUAGE: The official languages are Flemish and French; Flemish is slightly more widely spoken.
RELIGION: Mainly Roman Catholic, with small minorities of Protestants and Jews.
TIME: GMT + 1 (GMT + 2 in summer).
ELECTRICITY: 220 volts AC, 60Hz. Plugs are of the 2-pin round type.
COMMUNICATIONS: Belgium is a major historical European crossroads for communications and possesses a fully integrated service for all aspects of telecommunications. **Telephone:** Full automatic IDD. For operator services dial 1207. Country code: 32. There are call boxes in all major towns and country districts. The cost of local calls is BFr10. Some coinless cardphones are also available. Telecards are available from newsagents, railway stations and post offices. Price: BFr100 and 500. **Telex:** Most major hotels provide this service. **Post:** Airmail takes two to three days to London. A letter sent to Belgium from another country should have a 'B' as a prefix to the Belgian postal district concerned. *Poste Restante* facilities are available in main cities. Post office hours: 0900-1700 Monday to Friday. **Press:** Principal daily newspapers are *Le Soir*, *La Meuse*, *La Lanterne* (French) and *Het Laatste Nieuws*, *De Standaard*, *Het Nieuwsblad*, *De Gentenaar* (Flemish). There is a Dutch-language newspaper, *De Nieuwe Gids*, and one English-language newspaper, *The Bulletin*, printed in Belgium.
BBC World Service and Voice of America frequencies: From time to time these change. See the section *How to Use this Book* for more information.
BBC:

MHz	15.57	12.09	6.195	3.955

A service is also available on 648kHz and 198kHz (0100-0500 GMT).
Voice of America:

MHz	11.97	9.670	6.040	5.995

PASSPORT/VISA

Regulations and requirements may be subject to change at short notice, and you are advised to contact the appropriate diplomatic or consular authority before finalising travel arrangements. Details of these may be found at the head of this country's entry. Any numbers in the chart refer to the footnotes below.

	Passport Required?	Visa Required?	Return Ticket Required?
Full British	1	No	No
BVP	Valid	No	No
Australian	Yes	No	No
Canadian	Yes	No	No
USA	Yes	No	No
Other EC	1	No	No
Japanese	Yes	No	No

PASSPORTS: A valid passport is required by all except [1] nationals of EC countries and nationals of Andorra, Austria, Liechtenstein, Malta, Monaco, San Marino and Switzerland providing they carry a national ID card or, for UK citizens, a BVP.
Note: Where full national passports are required they must be valid for at least 3 months *after* the last day of the intended visit.
British Visitors Passport: A BVP can be used for holidays or unpaid business trips of up to 3 months to Belgium. Please note that children under 16 cannot travel on their brother's or sister's passport.
VISAS: Required by all except:
(a) nationals of countries referred to in the chart above;
(b) nationals of countries referred to under passports;
(c) nationals of Argentina, Brazil, Brunei, Burkino Faso, Chile, Costa Rica, Cyprus, Czechoslovakia, Ecuador, El Salvador, Finland, Guatemala, Honduras, Hungary, Iceland, Israel, Jamaica, South Korea, Malawi, Malaysia, Mexico, New Zealand, Nicaragua, Niger, Norway, Panama, Paraguay, Poland, Singapore, Sweden, Togo, Turkey (if resident in an EC country), Uruguay, Vatican City and Venezuela.
In all cases, this visa-free facility lasts for 3 months within any 6-month period, and is conditional on the length of stay itself being no longer than 3 months.
Types of visa: *Transit:* £8.80. *Visitor's Visa (Tourist and Business):* £19.80 for up to one month, £26.40 for a visa lasting for 3 months and £33 for a visa lasting up to a year.
Validity: *Transit:* 24 hours. *Visitor's Visa:* Up to 3 months. For renewal apply to Embassy.
Application to: Consulate (or Consular Section at Embassy). For addresses, see top of entry.
Application requirements: (a) Application form. (b) Photograph. The required number of each of these varies according to nationality of applicant.
Working days required: 24 hours to 6 weeks, depending on nationality. Postal or personal visits.
Temporary residence: Persons wishing to take up temporary residence should make a special application to the Belgian Embassy.

MONEY

Currency: Belgian Franc (BFr) = 100 centimes. Notes are in denominations of BFr5000, 1000, 500 and 100. Coins are in denominations of BFr50, 20, 5, 1, and 50 centimes.
Credit cards: Access/Mastercard, American Express, Diners Club and Visa are accepted. Check with your credit card company for details of merchant acceptability and other services which may be available.
Travellers cheques: Widely accepted.
Exchange rate indicators: The following figures are included as a guide to the movements of the Belgian Franc against Sterling and the US Dollar:

Date:	Oct '89	Oct '90	Oct '91	Oct '92
£1.00=	62.60	61.25	60.10	50.20

BELGIUM | **HEALTH REGULATIONS** | **VISA REGULATIONS**

Code-Link

GALILEO/WORLDSPAN

TI-DFT/BRU/HE

TI-DFT/BRU/VI

SABRE

TIDFT/BRU/HE

TIDFT/BRU/VI

To access this information on your CRS, swipe the barcode with a light pen or type in the text under the barcode. For more information, see the introduction *How to Use This Book*.

$1.00=	39.64	31.35	34.63	31.63

Currency restrictions: There are no restrictions on the import and export of either local or foreign currency.
Banking hours: 0900-1200 and 1400-1600 Monday to Friday. Some banks open 0900-1200 Saturday.

DUTY FREE

The following goods may be taken into Belgium without incurring customs duty:
(a) Travellers arriving from EC countries:
300 cigarettes or 75 cigars or 400g of tobacco;
5 litres of still wine;
1.5 litres of spirits or 3 litres of sparkling or fortified wine;
8 litres of Luxembourg wines (if imported via the Luxembourg border);
75g of perfume and 0.375 litres of eau de toilette;
Other goods up to BFr25,500.
(b) Travellers arriving from EC countries with duty-paid goods (as of January 1993):
800 cigarettes and 400 cigarillos and 200 cigars and 1kg of tobacco;
90 litres of wine (including up to 60 litres of sparkling wine);
10 litres of spirits;
20 litres of intermediate products (such as fortified wine);
110 litres of beer.
(c) Travellers from non-EC countries:
200 cigarettes or 50 cigars or 250g of tobacco;
2 litres of still wine;
1 litre of spirits or 2 litres of sparkling or fortified wine;
8 litres of Luxembourg wines (if imported via the Luxembourg border);
50g of perfume and 0.25 litres of eau de toilette;
other goods up to BFr2000.
Prohibited items: Unpreserved meat products. Other unpreserved foodstuffs must be declared.

PUBLIC HOLIDAYS

Public holidays observed in Belgium are as follows:
Apr 12 '93 Easter Monday. **May 1** Labour Day. **May 20** Ascension Day. **May 31** Whit Monday. **Jul 21** National Day. **Aug 15** Assumption. **Nov 1** All Saints' Day. **Nov 11** Armistice Day. **Nov 15*** King's Birthday. **Dec 25** Christmas. **Dec 26*** Boxing Day. **Jan 1 '94** New Year's Day.
Note: [*] Administrative/public office only.

HEALTH

Regulations and requirements may be subject to change at short notice, and you are advised to contact your doctor well in advance of your intended date of departure. Any numbers in the chart refer to the footnotes below.

	Special Precautions?	Certificate Required?
Yellow Fever	No	No
Cholera	No	No
Typhoid & Polio	No	-
Malaria	No	-
Food & Drink	No	-

Rabies is present. For those at high risk, vaccination before arrival should be considered. If you are bitten abroad, seek medical advice without delay. For more information consult the *Health* section at the back of the book.
Health care: Medical care is expensive but of a high standard. There is a Reciprocal Health Agreement with the UK. It allows UK citizens a refund of up to 75% of medical costs. To take advantage of the Agreement, UK citizens should obtain form E111 from the post office *before* departure.

TRAVEL - International

AIR: The national airline is *Sabena (SN)*.
Approximate flight times: From *London* to Brussels is 55 minutes and to Antwerp is 50 minutes. From *Los Angeles* to Brussels is 16 hours. From *New York* to Brussels is 10 hours.
International airports: *Brussels Zaventem (BRU)* is 13km (8 miles) northeast of the city (travel time – 35 minutes). Trains to the city (travel time – approx 15 minutes) depart every 20 minutes from 0609-2346. Return from Gare Centrale/Gare du Nord 0539-2314. Buses run to and from the city every 45 minutes 0905-2105. Taxi to the city costs approx BFr1000. Hotel courtesy coaches to Holiday Inn, Novotel and Sofitel. Airport facilities include car parking, car hire (0900-1800), post office, banks (0700-2300), 24-hour restaurant, incoming and outgoing duty-free shops selling a wide range of goods (including mini-computers) and a 24-hour bar.
Antwerp (ANR) (Deurne) is 5.5km (3.4 miles) from the city. There is a regular bus service (no 16) to Central Station (travel time – 20 minutes). Taxis cost approx BFr700. Airport facilities include an outgoing duty-free shop, car hire (0900-1800), bank (0900-1200 and 1400-1600) and bar/restaurant (0800-2300). There is also a regular bus service from Antwerp to *Brussels Airport*, which is free to *Sabena* passengers flying Business class or on a Eurobudget fare.
Ostend (OST), 5km (3.1 miles) from the city, has car parking facilities, car hire, foreign exchange, a restaurant, a bar and a duty-free shop.
Liège (LGG). There are taxis and a regular bus service to the centre 8km (5 miles) away.
Departure tax: BFr115 (Antwerp Deurne); BFr300 (Brussels Zaventem).
SEA: Antwerp is one of Europe's busiest commercial ports, but cross-Channel services generally operate out of Ostend or Zeebrugge. *P&O European Ferries (RTM):* Dover–Ostend (travel time – 4 hours); Felixstowe–Zeebrugge (travel time – 5 hours). *Jetfoil:* Dover–Ostend (1 hour 40 minutes). *North Sea Ferries:* Hull–Zeebrugge.
RAIL: There are good rail links with the rest of Europe. See below under *Travel – Internal* for information on budget travel.
ROAD: Excellent road links of all categories with neighbouring countries. See below under *Travel – Internal* for information on documentation and traffic regulations.

TRAVEL - Internal

AIR: There are no internal domestic flights. *Sabena* does, however, provide non-stop buses from *Brussels Airport* to Antwerp. There is a bus service between Antwerp Town and *Brussels Airport;* this is free to certain passengers.
RAIL: Belgium has a dense railway network with hourly trains on most lines. On the main lines there are more frequent trains. **Fares:** First- and second-class, single and

BRUSSELS

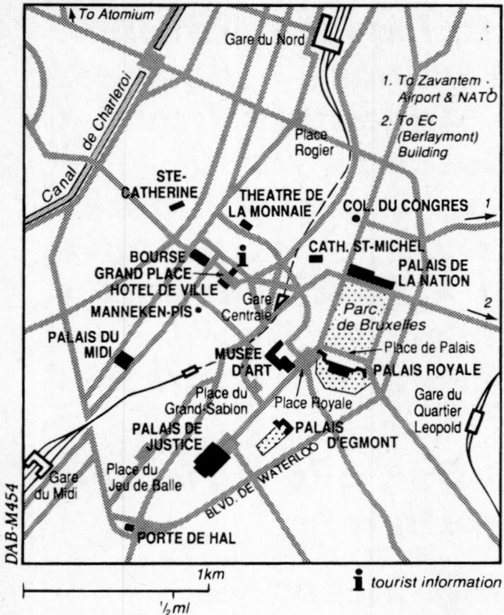

return tickets are available. However, a return ticket is double the single fare and is only valid on the day of issue. Children from 6 - 11 years pay half price.

Tickets at reduced fares: Weekend return fares are available from Friday noon to Sunday noon for the outward journey and from Sunday noon to Monday noon for the return journey (on long holiday weekends these periods are extended). A 50% reduction card, valid for one month, is for sale. It entitles the holder to buy an unlimited number of half-price single tickets.

Runabout tickets: These enable a visitor to travel freely across the whole of the Belgian rail network without any distance limit. They can also be used to and from neighbouring countries, where they are valid as far as, or from, the border. Principal stations in Belgium (and throughout Europe) are able to issue single and return tickets valid from the border to principal foreign stations (in conjunction with a *runabout* ticket). There are four kinds of *runabout* tickets:

(1) *16-day ticket:* valid for 16 consecutive days.

(2) *5-day B-Tourrail ticket:* five days of unlimited travel within a period of 17 days on Belgian Rail.

(3) *5-day TTB (Train, Tram, Bus) ticket:* five days of unlimited travel within a period of 17 days on Belgian Rail, as well as on all buses, trams and underground within Belgium. These tickets are sold in all Belgian Rail stations.

(4) *Benelux 5-day Tourrail ticket:* five days of unlimited travel within a period of 17 days by rail in Belgium, The Nertherlands and Luxembourg. Benelux Tourrail tickets are for sale at Benelux Railway stations.

Rail Europ Senior Card (RES): The RES card is available to men over 65 and women over 60 and entitles the buyer to reductions of up to 30% and 50% on international tickets in 19 European countries. Enquire at Belgian Railways for further information.

ROAD: There are many different brands of petrol available and prices vary. All driving is on the right. Main towns (except in the Ardennes) are connected by toll-free motorways. It is compulsory for seat belts to be worn in the front and back of vehicles. Children under 12 are not permitted to travel in the front seat of a car when there is space in the back. A warning triangle must be displayed at the scene of a breakdown or accident. The speed limit on motorways and dual carriageways is 120kmph (74mph), on single carriageways outside built-up areas is 90kmph (56mph) and in built-up areas is 50kmph (31mph). **Bus:** Extensive regional bus services are operated by the bus companies which publish regional timetables. There are long-distance stopping services between towns, but no express coach services apart from the Sabena airport services (see above under *Air*). **Taxis:** Plentiful in all towns. The tip is included in the final meter price. **Car hire:** Both self-drive and chauffeur-driven cars are available. **Documentation:** A national driving licence is acceptable. EC nationals taking their own cars to Belgium are strongly advised to obtain a Green Card. Without it, insurance cover is limited to the minimum legal cover in Belgium (third party cover is compulsory). The Green Card tops this up to the level of cover provided by the car owner's domestic policy.

URBAN: There is a good public transport system in all the major towns and cities, with metro, tram and bus services in Brussels and Antwerp, bus and tramways in Charleroi and Ostend and bus systems elsewhere. There is a standard flat fare system, with discounts for 5- and 10-journey multi-ride tickets. 1-day tickets and multi-mode tourist travelcards are also available.

JOURNEY TIMES: The following chart gives approximate journey times from Brussels (in hours and minutes) to other major cities/towns in Belgium and neighbouring countries.

	Air	Road	Rail
Paris	0.50	-	2.30
Amsterdam	0.40	-	3.00
Rome	2.00	-	20.00
Cologne	-	-	3.00
London	0.55	-	*8.30
Arlon	-	3.00	2.20
Antwerp	-	0.40	0.41
Bruges	-	1.00	0.53
Ghent	-	0.50	0.28
Liège	-	1.10	1.22
Ostend	-	1.20	1.10
Namur	-	1.00	0.56

Note: [*] Time taken by train and boat; time by rail and jetfoil is 5 hours and 30 minutes.

ACCOMMODATION

HOTELS: Belgium has a large range of hotels from luxury to small family pensions and inns. The best international-class hotels are found in the cities. **Grading:** The Belgian Tourist Board issues a shield to all approved hotels by which they can be recognised. This must be affixed to the front of the hotel in a conspicuous position. Hotels which display this sign conform to the official standards set by Belgian law on hotels which protects the tourist and guarantees certain standards of quality. Some hotels are also graded according to the *Benelux* system in which standard is indicated by a row of 3-pointed stars from the highest (5-star) to the minimum (1-star). However, membership of this scheme is voluntary, and there may be first-class hotels which are not classified in this way. If an establishment providing accommodation facilities is classified under category H or above (1, 2, 3, 4 or 5 stars), it may call itself hotel, hostelry, inn, guest house, motel or other similar names. *Benelux* star ratings comply with the following criteria:

5-star: Luxury hotel, meeting the highest standards of comfort, amenities and service, 24-hour room service, à la carte restaurant, gift shop, parking and baggage service, travel and theatre booking service.

4-star: First-class hotel, with lift, facilities for breakfast in the room, day and night reception, telephone in every room, radio, bar.

3-star: Very good hotel, with lift (if more than 2 floors), day reception, guest wing (food and drink optional).

2-star: Average class hotel, with private bath and WC in at least 25% of rooms, baggage handling facilities, food and drink available.

1-star: Plain hotel, washstand with hot and cold water in every room, breakfast facilities available.

Cat H: Very plain hotel, meets all the fire safety requirements and provides moderate standards of comfort, at least one bathroom for every 10 rooms and accessible to guests at night.

Cat O: Establishments providing accommodation only, with guaranteed safety and hygiene standards only.

For more information on hotels in Belgium contact the Belgian Tourist Board *or* one of the three regional hotel associations, as follows:

Flanders: Horeca Vlaanderen, 111 boulevard Anspach, B-1000 Brussels. Tel: (2) 513 7814. Fax: (2) 513 8954.

Wallonia: Horeca Wallonie, Chausée de Charleroi 83, B-5000 Namur. Tel: (81) 736 367. Fax: (81) 737 689.

Brussels: Horeca Brussels, 111 boulevard Anspach, B-1000 Brussels. Tel: (2) 513 7814. Fax: (2) 513 8954.

FARM HOLIDAYS: In some regions of the country, farm holidays are now available. In the Polders and the Ardennes visitors can (for a small cost) participate in the daily work of the farm. For addresses, the Belgian Tourist Board publishes a brochure called *Budget Holidays*.

SELF-CATERING: There are ample opportunities to rent furnished villas, flats, rooms, or bungalows for a holiday period. There is a particularly wide choice in the Ardennes and on the coast. These holiday houses and flats are comfortable and well equipped. Rentals are determined by the number of bedrooms, the amenities, the location and the season. On the coast, many apartments, studios, villas and bungalows are classified into five categories according to the standard of comfort they offer. Estate agents will supply full details. For the Ardennes region, enquiries should be made to the local tourist office. Addresses of local tourist offices and lists of coastal estate agents can be obtained from the Belgian Tourist Office.

YOUTH HOSTELS: There are two youth hostel associations; the Vlaamse Jeugdherbergcentrale (VJHC) which operates in Flanders, and the Centrale Wallonne (CWAJ) operating in the French-speaking area. The hostels of the former are large, highly organised and much frequented by schools and youth groups; the hostels of the CWAJ are smaller and more informal, similar in some ways to those in France.

A complete list of youth hostels and other holiday homes for young people can be obtained from the Belgian Tourist Office, or by writing direct to 'Info-Jeunes', 27 rue Marché-aux-Herbes, B-1000 Brussels, or to 'Info-Jeugd', Gretry-straat 28, B-1000 Brussels.

CAMPING/CARAVANNING: The majority of campsites are in the Ardennes and on the coast; many of these are excellent. A list of addresses, rates and other information can be obtained from the Belgian Tourist Office. The local 'Verblijftaks' ('Taxe de Sejour') is usually included in the rates charged. On the coast during the summer season a supplement of about 25% is charged on the majority of tariffs. Camping out in places other than the recognised sites is permitted, provided the agreement of the land-owner or tenant has been obtained.

RESORTS & EXCURSIONS

The two main tourist regions in Belgium are the coast and the Ardennes. There are also many historic cities to visit with famous museums, art collections and galleries.

The Coast and West Flanders

The north coast of Belgium stretches for 69km (43 miles) from Knokke near the Dutch border to De Panne on the French border with an unbroken chain of resorts and sandy beaches. Beach cabins and windbreaks have been installed by hotels, agencies and private owners and in some resorts the beach huts are open to the public. Bathing in the sea is free on all beaches and there are facilities for sailing, sand yachting, riding, fishing, rowing, golf and tennis. The promenade is closed to all traffic and the beaches shelve gently and are safe for children.

Resorts: De Panne, Koksijde and Sint Idesbald, Oostduinkerke, Nieuwpoort, Westende and Lombardsijde, Middelkerke, Ostend, Bredene, De Haan, Wenduine, Blankenberge, Zeebrugge and Knokke-Heist.

For nightlife: Ostend, Knokke, Blankenberge and Middelkerke.

For quieter beaches: Zeebrugge, Nieuwpoort, Oostduinkerke, Westende and Lombardsijde and Wenduine.

Places of historical interest: Bruges, Damme, Veurne and Ypres (see also below).

The Ardennes

This area is famous for its cuisine, forests, lakes, streams and grottos. The River Meuse makes its way through many important tourist centres: Dinant, Annevoie with its castle, Yvoir Godinne and Profondeville (well known for watersports), Namur with its cathedral, citadel and many museums, and Houyet offering kayaking and other assorted outdoor activities. The River Semois passes through Arlon and Florenville; nearby are the ruins of Orval Abbey, Bouillon and its castle, Botassart, Rochehaut and Bohan. The Amblève Valley is one of the wildest in the Ardennes and the grottos in the 'Fond de Quarreux' are one of the great attractions of the region. Among these is the Merveilleuse grotto at Dinant and the cavern at Remouchamps. There are prehistoric caverns at Spy, Rochefort, Hotton and Han-sur-Lesse (with an underground lake).

Art treasures from Belgium's history can be seen in the towns of Antwerp, Bruges, Brussels, Ghent, Liège and Tournai (see below). Many castles and abbeys are open to the public. The First World War battlefield and cemeteries of Ypres can also be visited.

Historic Cities

Some of the more popular historic cities in the country are as follows:

Antwerp: A busy city on the banks of the River Scheldt and once one of the most powerful urban centres in Europe. Today Antwerp is characterised by its thriving diamond industry and its successes in the field of petrochemicals. The inhabitants, or *Sinjoors* as they are known, like to perpetuate the city's Baroque image, largely created by the wealth of buildings from the time of Rubens. Well worth a visit is the *Cathedral Of Our Lady* (14th-16th century), both for its architecture – in the Brabant gothic style – and for the Rubens' masterpieces which it houses. Other attractions include the *Grote Markt*, or Main Square, containing the *Town Hall* built by Cornelius de Vriendt in the 1560s and the Brabo fountain commemorating the legend of the city's origin; the *Steen*, a 12th-century fortress now housing the *National Maritime Museum;* the *Royal Museum of Fine*

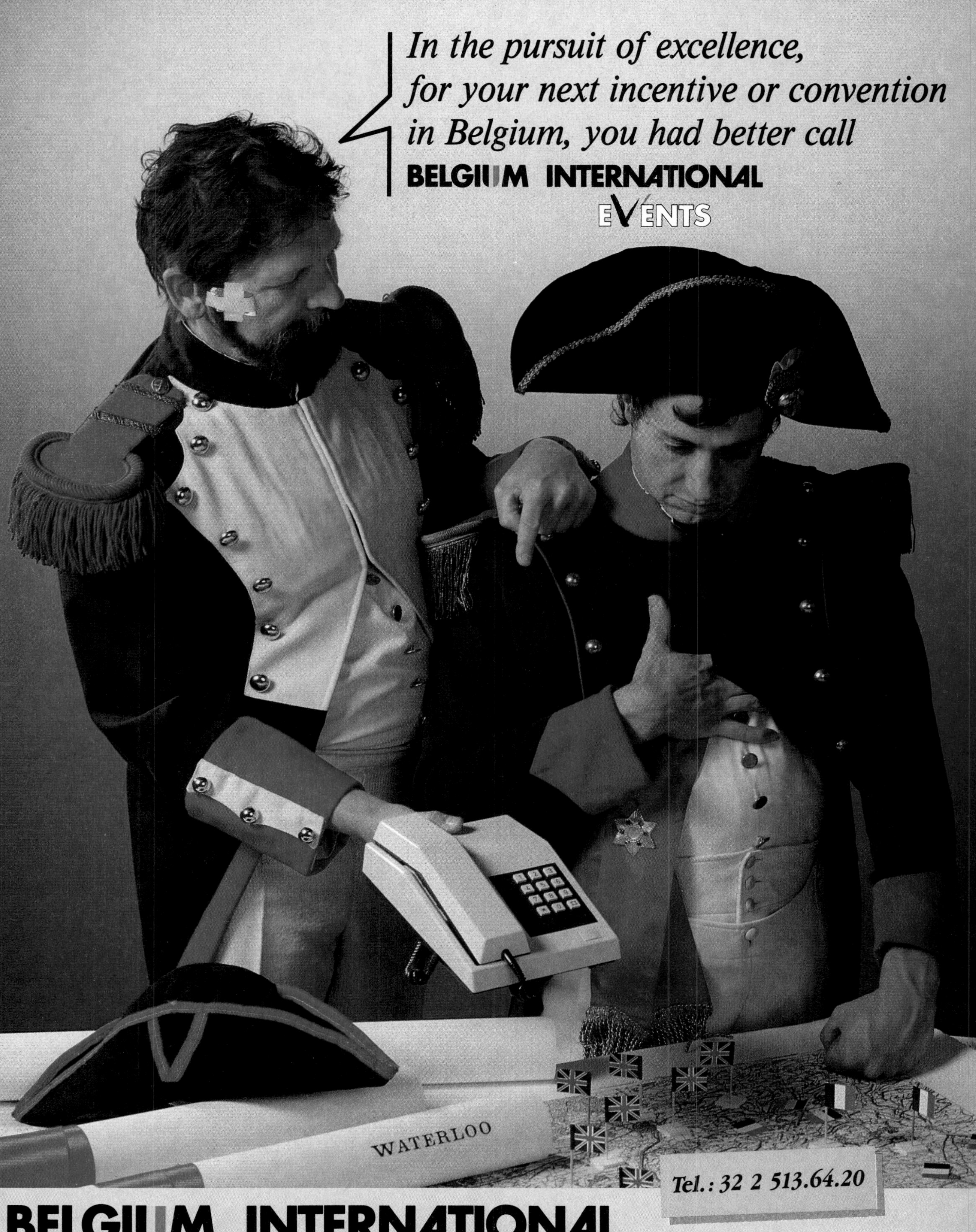

In the pursuit of excellence,
for your next incentive or convention
in Belgium, you had better call
BELGIUM INTERNATIONAL
EVENTS
WATERLOO
Tel.: 32 2 513.64.20

Arts, home to what is arguably the world's finest collection of works by Peter Paul Rubens, as well as 1000 works by other old masters and 1500 more recent works; the *Plantin-Moretus Museum*, where Plantin's printing works were founded in the 16th century, with one of the few remaining copies of the Gutenberg Bible; and many other museums and churches.

Bruges: Like Antwerp, another city whose fortunes in the Middle Ages were built on the cloth trade. The city is close to some excellent beaches and the fertile polder region, dotted with abbeys and parks. Best visited on foot, Bruges offers a variety of attractions including boat trips or walks along the canals and the *Lake of Love*, which in the Middle Ages was the city's internal port; the 14th-century *Town Hall* featuring a façade decorated with bas-reliefs and statues of a Biblical nature; the *Cathedral of the Holy Saviour*, a fine example of 13th-century Gothic architecture and home to many treasures; the *Grote Markt* which was formerly the commercial hub of the city, overlooked by the 83m (272ft) octagonal *Belfry* with its carillon; and several museums.

Brussels: The capital of Belgium, the European Community and NATO. The main sights in Brussels include *St Michael's Cathedral* (13th-16th century) and the famous *Grand-Place* in the heart of the city. It is here that the early 15th-century Gothic-style *Town Hall* and the *Maison du Roi*, containing the *Municipal Museum*, are located. Other attractions include *Mont des Arts*, the park which links the upper and lower parts of the city; the elegant *Place Royale* built between 1774 and 1780 in the style of Louis XVI; the *Manneken Pis* statue which dates from 1619 and symbolises the irreverence of the 'Bruxellois'; and dozens of museums of interest, including the *Museum of Ancient Art* and the *Museum of Modern Art*, opened in 1984. Among other areas worth exploring are the *Ilot Sacré*, the picturesque area of narrow streets to the northeast of the Grand-Place; the fashionable boulevard de Waterloo; the administrative quarter, a completely symmetrical park area commanding a splendid view of the surrounding streets; the *Grand Sablon*, the area containing both the flamboyant Gothic structure of the *Church of Our Lady of Sablon* and the Sunday antique market and lastly the *Petit Sablon*, a square surrounded by Gothic columns, which support 48 small bronze statues commemorating medieval Brussels guilds.

Attractions on the outskirts of the city include the *Royal Castle* at Laeken, the town residence of the Royal Family; the *State Botanical Gardens;* the site of *the Battle of Waterloo*, 18km (11 miles) to the south of Brussels and the *Forest of Soignes*.

Ghent: This former cloth town was once the capital of the Counts of Flanders and was the birthplace of the Emperor Charles V. Although an industrial city, Ghent boasts many historic buildings, including three abbeys. Attractions include *St Bavo's Cathedral*, place of Charles V's baptism and home to *The Adoration of the Mystical Lamb*, the Van Eyck brothers' masterpiece; the *Town Hall*, where the Treaty of Ghent was signed in 1576; the *Castle of the Counts*, a Medieval castle surrounded by the Lieve canal; the medieval town centre; and the *Museum of Fine Arts*.

Liège: An industrial city, situated on the banks of the Meuse, but one with many reminders of a colourful and affluent past. Attractions include the *Church of St James*, an old abbey church of mixed architecture, including an example of the Meuse Romanesque style, with fine Renaissance stained glass; the *Cathedral of St Paul*, founded in the 10th century and boasting a priceless treasury; the 18th-century *Town Hall;* the *Curtius Museum* housing a large collection of coins, Liège furniture and porcelaine; *St Lambert Square*, with the *Perron* fountain of the city's symbol; the *Museum of Modern Art*, displaying the works of Corot, Monet, Picasso, Gauguin and Chagall to name but a few; and the *Romanesque Church of St Bartholemew*, particularly notable for its copper baptismal fonts.

Tournai: One of the oldest cities in the region, the city dates back to the Frankish period in the early Middle Ages. In common with many other Belgian cities, much was destroyed during the two World Wars, although several important buildings have survived while others have been restored. Attractions include the *Cathedral of Notre Dame* (12th century); the *Belfry*, which is the oldest in Belgium; the *Bridge of Holes*, a relic of the old fortified rampart which spanned the Scheldt; the *Museum of Fine Arts*, with works by Rubens and Bruegel; the imposing castle of *Antoing*, parts of which date back to the 5th century; and most recently, *Minibel*, 28km (17 miles) outside the city at the *Château of Beloeil*, a display of scaled-down reproductions of many of Belgium's most interesting treasures and curiosities (including the Brussels Town Hall and Grand Palace, the Bruges Belfry, the Castle of Counts and the Coo Falls).

For more information on these and other cities of historic and cultural interest, consult the *Belgium Historic Cities* booklet available from the Belgian Tourist Office.

SOCIAL PROFILE

FOOD & DRINK: Belgian cuisine is similar to French, based on game and seafood. Each region in Belgium has its own special dish. Butter, cream and wine are generously used in cooking. Most restaurants have waiter service, although self-service cafés are becoming quite numerous. Restaurant bills always include drinks, unless they have been taken at the bar separately. In the latter case this is settled over the counter. **Drink:** Local beers are very good. Two of the most popular are *Lambic*, made from wheat and barley, and *Trappist*. Under a new law, the majority of cafés now have licenses to serve spirits. Beers and wines are freely obtainable everywhere and there are no licensing hours.

NIGHTLIFE: As well as being one of the best cities in the world for eating out (both for its high quality and range), Brussels has a very active and varied nightlife. It has ten theatres producing plays in both Flemish and French. These include the *Théâtre National* and the *Théâtre Royal des Galeries*. The more avant-garde theatres include the *Théâtre Cinq-Quarante* and the *Théâtre de Poche*. Brussels' 35 cinemas, numerous discotheques and many night-time cafés are centred on two main areas: the uptown Porte Louise area and the downtown area between Place Roger and Place de la Bourse. Nightclubs include the famous *Le Crazy*, *Chez Paul*, *Maxim* and *Le Grand Escalier;* jazz clubs include *The Brussels Jazz Club* and *Bloomdido Jazz Café*. Programmes and weekly listings of events can be found in the *BBB Agenda* on sale at tourist offices. This also covers information on the many festivals that take place in Brussels itself. The Belgian Tourist Office should be consulted for folk music or drama festivals elsewhere in Belgium – the most famous of which is the *Festival of Flanders*. The other large cities of Belgium, such as Antwerp, Leuven, Mons, Ghent, Kortrijk and Namur, all have similar (though less extensive) nightlife facilities. Liège is noted for its Walloon opera and for having several theatrical troops; Ghent for its 'illuminations'; while Namur has a large Casino complex.

SHOPPING: Special purchases include ceramics and hand-beaten copperware from Dinant; Belgian chocolates; crystal from Val Saint Lambert; diamonds; jewellery from Antwerp; lace from Bruges, Brussels and Mechelen (Malines), wood carvings from Spa and *bandes dessinées* (comic-strip books) by a number of talented Belgian cartoon artists from Brussels. Main shopping centres are: Brussels, Antwerp, Bruges, Ostend, Namur, Mons, Liège, Ghent and Mechelen. **Shopping hours:** 0900-1800 Monday to Saturday (Friday 0900-2100 in main cities).

SPORT: Golf, tennis, cycling, motor-racing (including the Belgian Grand Prix), **football, basketball, wrestling, horseriding, horse-racing, skiing** and **water-skiing.** The Belgian Alpine Club has a **climbing** school at Freyr. **Bathing, fishing, boating** and **yachting** are also available.

SPECIAL EVENTS: The following is a selection of the major festivals and other special events celebrated in Belgium in 1993:

Jan-Dec '93 *Cultural City of Europe 1993*, Antwerp. **Mar 6** *Dead Rat Ball*, Ostend. **May 9** *Cats Parade*, Ieper. **May 20** *Blood Procession*, Bruges. **Jun** *Procession of the Golden Carriage and the Battle of the Lumeçon*, Mons. **Jun** *Day of the Four Processions*, Tournai. **Jun 20** *Shrimp Festival*, Oostduinkerke. **Jun 29-Jul 1** *Brussels Ommegang*. **Jul 17-27** *Ghent Festival*, Ghent. **Jul** *Bilberry Festival*, Vielsalm. **Aug** *Parade of the Giants*, Ath. **Sep 12** *National Heritage Day*. **Sep** *International Thinking Festival*, St Hubert. **Sep-Dec** *Europalia Mexico*. A full calendar of events is available from the Belgian Tourist Board.

SOCIAL CONVENTIONS: Flemings will often prefer to answer visitors in English rather than French, even if the visitor's French is good. It is customary to bring flowers or a small present for the hostess, especially if invited for a meal. Dress is similar to other Western nations, depending on the formality of the occasion. If black tie/evening dress is to be worn, this is always mentioned on the invitation. Smoking is generally unrestricted. **Tipping:** A 14% service charge is usually included in hotel or restaurant bills. Cloakroom attendants expect BFr5-10, porters approximately BFr30 per piece of luggage. A tip is generally included in taxi fares.

BUSINESS PROFILE

ECONOMY: The traditional industries of steel, motor vehicles and textiles have suffered from the recession of the 1980s, although the governments of Belgium and Luxembourg (who formed a Convention of Economic Union in 1921, as distinct from the Benelux Union or the EC, of which both are members) reached agreement in 1984 on a 10-year joint restructuring plan for their steel industries. Coal mining has also experienced severe difficulties. Belgium relies particularly heavily on export earnings – 70% of GDP is exported, one of the highest proportions in the world – which leaves the country particularly vulnerable to fluctuating patterns of world trade. Equally,

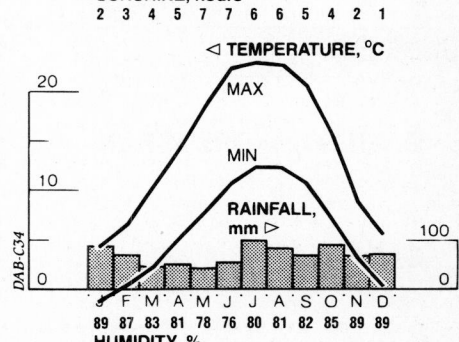

Belgium has few natural resources and must import almost all its fuel and raw materials. Manufactured goods and machinery are the largest export sectors, with the major markets inside the European Community, including France, Germany, The Netherlands and the UK. These are also Belgium's main sources of imported goods.
BUSINESS: Suits should always be worn and business is conducted on a formal basis, with punctuality valued and business cards exchanged. Transactions are usually made in French or English. **Office hours:** 0830-1730 Monday to Friday.
COMMERCIAL INFORMATION: The following organisations can offer advice:
Chambre de Commerce et d'Industrie de Bruxelles, 500 avenue Louise, B-1050 Brussels. Tel: (2) 648 5002. Fax: (2) 640 9328. Telex: 22082; *or*
Kamer van Koophandel en Nijverheid van Antwerpen (Antwerp Chamber of Commerce), Markgravestraat 12, B-2000 Antwerp. Tel: (3) 232 2219. Fax: (3) 233 6442. Telex: 71536.
CONFERENCES/CONVENTIONS: There is an extensive range of meeting venues throughout the country. In 1988 Belgium was the ninth most popular conference destination, whilst Brussels was the fourth most popular city. For more information or assistance in organising a conference or convention in Belgium contact the Belgium Convention and Incentive Bureau *(BECIB)*, Grasmarkt 61, B-1000 Brussels. Tel: (2) 513 2721. Fax: (2) 513 8803/6950.

HISTORY & GOVERNMENT

HISTORY: The area which is now Belgium was part of Charlemagne's empire in the 8th and 9th centuries, but by the 10th century had achieved independence. The Flemish cloth towns enjoyed great financial and political power, but after 1322 the area fell again under French control. A period of instability ended with the accession of Philip of Burgundy (1419), but on the death of his son Charles the Bold (1477), the Low Countries passed to the Hapsburgs. The Protestant northern part rebelled against Philip II of Spain in the 1560s, and soon the division between the southern provinces (under Spanish control) and the northern United Provinces (the basis of the modern-day Netherlands) became established. The Peace of Westphalia (1648) confirmed this position. The region suffered badly as a result of Franco-Spanish conflicts in the subsequent decades, most notably the War of the Spanish Succession (1700-13) which resulted in the Spanish Netherlands passing to the Austrian Hapsburgs until 1794, apart from a short French occupation (1744-48). In 1790, inspired by the events in France, a local rebellion led to the brief establishment of the United States of Belgium, but the country was invaded by France in 1794 and remained annexed until the fall of Napoleon in 1814. The allies subsequently attempted to unite the two Netherlands, but a rebellion in 1830 resulted in the London Conference establishing the Kingdom of Belgium. The late 19th and early 20th century was a period of social and political upheaval, but these problems were overshadowed by the outbreak of the First World War (August 1914), in which Belgium suffered heavily, despite the heroic stand made by King Albert and his army in the first weeks of the war. 1918-39 witnessed the forging of the links between Belgium, The Netherlands and Luxembourg and the emergence of the divisive Walloon/Flemish problem. The country was invaded by the Nazis in 1940 and remained occupied for the rest of the war. King Leopold, hounded by accusations of collaboration, remained in Switzerland after 1945; the present monarch, his nephew Baudouin, succeeded in 1951. Belgium was a founder member of the Benelux Union and the EC, and Brussels is the headquarters of NATO and the EC. Belgium also has a relatively small but important colonial legacy in central Africa (Zaïre, notably) over which it keeps a watching brief. In general, Belgium epitomises a stable, cautiously progressing Western European liberal democracy. The principal problem is the continuing tension between the Flemish-speaking north and the French-speaking south of the country, whose inhabitants are known as Walloons: in early October 1991 this led to the collapse of the 5-party centre-left coalition administration headed by Wilfred Martens, veteran leader of the Flemish Christian Social Party (CVP). The elections left all three leading parties – the Socialists, Christian Social and Liberal parties – with less seats and brought increases for two ecological parties and the exteme right-wing Flemish separatists. Jean-Luc Dehaene emerged at the head of another coalition administration. Belgium has by and large supported the process of European integration enshrined in the 1991 Maastricht treaty.
GOVERNMENT: The country is a hereditary constitutional monarchy (see above) with a bicameral parliament; the Chamber of Deputies is elected by proportional representation, while the Senate is partly elected and partly appointed. The complicated 3-tier system of local government (regional, provincial and communal) is, in view of the cultural and linguistic divisions within the country, likely to remain in a state of flux for some years to come.

CLIMATE

Seasonal and similar to neighbouring countries, with warm weather from May to September and snow likely during winter months.
Required clothing: Waterproofs are advisable at all times of the year.

BRUSSELS Belgium (100m)

SUNSHINE, hours
2 3 4 5 7 7 6 6 5 4 2 1
◁ TEMPERATURE, °C
20
MAX
MIN
10
RAINFALL, mm ▷
100
0
0
DAB-C34
J F M A M J J A S O N D
89 87 83 81 78 76 80 81 82 85 89 89
HUMIDITY, %

BELIZE

Location: Central America, Caribbean coast.

Belize Tourist Board
63 Regent Street
Belize City, Belize CA
Tel: (2) 77213 *or* 77490.

Belize Tourism Industry Association (BTIA)
PO Box 62
99 Albert Street West
Belize City, Belize CA
Tel: (2) 75717 *or* 78709. Fax: (2) 78710.

Belize High Commission
10 Harcourt House
19a Cavendish Square
London W1M 9AD
Tel: (071) 499 9728. Fax: (071) 491 4139. Opening hours: 0900-1700 Monday to Friday.

British High Commission
PO Box 91
Embassy Square
Belmopan, Belize CA
Tel: (8) 22146. Fax: (8) 22761. Telex: 284 UKREP BZE.

Embassy of Belize
2535 Massuchusetts Avenue, NW
Washington DC
20008
Tel: (202) 363 4505. Fax: (202) 362 7468. Telex: 140997 EMBEL.

Embassy of the United States of America
Gabourel Lane and Hutson Street
Belize City, Belize CA
Tel: (2) 77161. Fax: (2) 30802.

High Commission for Belize
Suite 2005, Tower B
112 Kent Street
Place de Ville
Ottawa, Ontario
K1P 5P2
Tel: (613) 232 7389. Fax: (613) 232 5804.

Canadian Consulate
PO Box 610
85 North Street
Belize City, Belize CA
Tel: (2) 31060.

AREA: 22,965 sq km (8867 sq miles).
POPULATION: 190,792 (1991 estimate).
POPULATION DENSITY: 8.3 per sq km.
CAPITAL: Belmopan. **Population:** 3694 (1991 estimate). Belize City has a population of 49,671.
GEOGRAPHY: Belize is situated at the base of the Yucatán Peninsula in Central America, and borders Mexico and Guatemala, with the Gulf of Honduras to the east. The country's area includes numerous small islands (cays) off the coast. The coastal strip is low and swampy, particularly in the north with mangroves, many salt and freshwater lagoons and some sandy beaches crossed by a number of rivers. To the south and west rises the heavily forested Maya mountain range, with the Cockscomb range to the east and the Mountain Pine Ridge in the west. Over 65% of the area of the country is forested. The land to the west along the borders with Guatemala is open and relatively scenic compared to much of the interior. The shallow offshore cays straddle a coral reef second only in size to the Barrier Reef of Australia.
LANGUAGE: English is the official language, but Spanish is spoken by over half the population.
RELIGION: The people of Belize are mainly Roman Catholic (roughly 60% of the population). Other denominations include Anglican, Methodist, Mennonite, Seventh Day Adventist and Pentecostal.
TIME: GMT - 6.
ELECTRICITY: 110/220 volts AC, 60Hz.
COMMUNICATIONS: Telephone: IDD is available. Country code: 501. **Fax:** Limited facilities, but Belize Telecommunications Ltd (BTL) Public Booth in Belize City and some government and company offices have facilities available. **Telex/telegram:** Full services are available from BTL Public Booth and post offices and major hotels in Belize City, Belmopan and San Ignacio. **Post:** Mail to Europe takes up to five days. **Press:** The major weeklies include *Amandala, The Labour Beacon, The Belize Times, The People's Pulse* and *The Reporter*.
BBC World Service and Voice of America frequencies: From time to time these change. See the section *How to Use this Book* for more information.

BBC:

MHz	17.72	11.78	9.590	5.965

Voice of America:

MHz	15.21	11.74	9.815	6.030

PASSPORT/VISA

Regulations and requirements may be subject to change at short notice, and you are advised to contact the appropriate diplomatic or consular authority before finalising travel arrangements. Details of these may be found at the head of this country's entry. Any numbers in the chart refer to the footnotes below.

	Passport Required?	Visa Required?	Return Ticket Required?
Full British	Yes	No	Yes
BVP	Not valid-	-	-
Australian	Yes	No	Yes
Canadian	Yes	No	Yes
USA	Yes	No	Yes
Other EC	Yes	No	Yes
Japanese	Yes	Yes	Yes

PASSPORTS: Valid passport required by all.
British Visitors Passport: Not accepted.
VISAS: Required by all except (for stays of up to 1 month unless otherwise stated):
(a) those exempted in the chart above (USA and UK nationals may stay for up to 6 months without a visa);
(b) nationals of Belgium, Denmark, France, Germany, Greece, Ireland, Italy, Luxembourg, the Netherlands, Portugal and Spain;
(c) nationals of most Commonwealth countries (up to 6 months);
(d) nationals of Finland, Iceland, Liechtenstein, Mexico, Norway, Panama, San Marino, Sweden, Switzerland, Tunisia, Turkey, Uruguay and Venezuela.
Types of visa: Transit, Tourist (single or multiple) and Business (single or multiple).
Cost: Transit, free. Single, £20. Multiple, £30.
Validity: Single visa, up to 6 months maximum. Multiple visa, up to 1 year.
Application to: Consulate (or Consular Section at Embassy or High Commission). For addresses, see top of entry.
Application requirements: (a) Application form. (b) Photo. (c) Sufficient funds to cover stay. (d) Valid passport.
Working days required: 24 hours in person, 2 to 3 days by post.
Temporary residence: Apply to Immigration and Nationality Department, Belmopan, Belize CA. Enquire at the High Commission or Embassy.

MONEY

Currency: Belizean Dollar (Bz$) = 100 cents. Notes are in denominations of Bz$100, 50, 20, 10, 5, 2 and 1. Coins are in denominations of Bz$1 and 50, 25, 10, 5 and 1 cents.
Currency exchange: The Belize currency is tied to the US Dollar at US$1 = Bz$2. Barclays Bank International has a branch in the capital, as well as a few in the country, available for foreign exchange.
Credit cards: American Express, Visa and Access/Mastercard (limited) are accepted. Check with your credit card company for details of merchant acceptability and other services which may be available.
Travellers cheques: These can be changed at the Bellevue Hotel. There is a charge of Bz$1 for cashing travellers cheques.
Exchange rate indicators: The following figures are included as a guide to the movements of the Belize Dollar against the Pound Sterling and the US Dollar:

Date:	Oct '89	Oct '90	Oct '91	Oct '92
£1.00=	3.16	3.90	3.50	3.16
$1.00=	2.00	2.00	2.00	2.00

Currency restrictions: The import and export of local currency is limited to Bz$100. There are no limits on the import of foreign currency; for current export limits, contact the Bank of Belize. It is strongly advised that visitors carry a minimum of Bz$75 for each day they intend to stay in Belize.
Banking hours: 0800-1300 Mon to Thurs; 1500-1800 Fri.

DUTY FREE

The following goods may be taken into Belize without incurring customs duty:
200 cigarettes or 0.25kg tobacco;
20 fl oz of alcoholic beverages;
1 bottle of perfume for personal use.

PUBLIC HOLIDAYS

Public holidays observed in Belize are as follows:
Apr 9-12 '93 Easter. **May 1** Labour Day. **May 24** Commonwealth Day. **Sep 10** St George's Caye Day. **Sep 21** Independence Day. **Oct 12** Pan American Day. **Nov 19** Garifuna Settlement Day. **Dec 25-26** Christmas. **Jan 1 '94** New Year's Day. **Mar 9** Baron Bliss Day.

HEALTH

Regulations and requirements may be subject to change at short notice, and you are advised to contact your doctor well in advance of your intended date of departure. Any numbers in the chart refer to the footnotes below.

	Special Precautions?	Certificate Required?
Yellow Fever	No	1
Cholera	No	No
Typhoid & Polio	Yes	-
Malaria	Yes/2	-
Food & Drink	3	-

BELIZE | **HEALTH REGULATIONS** | **VISA REGULATIONS** | Code-Link

GALILEO/WORLDSPAN
TI-DFT/BZE/HE
TI-DFT/BZE/VI

SABRE

TIDFT/BZE/HE

TIDFT/BZE/VI

To access this information on your CRS, swipe the barcode with a light pen or type in the text under the barcode. For more information, see the introduction *How to Use This Book.*

[1]: A yellow fever vaccination certificate is required from all travellers coming from infected areas. Pregnant woment and children under nine months should not normally be vaccinated.
[2]: Malaria risk exists throughout the year, excluding Belize district and urban areas; predominantly in benign *vivax* form.
[3]: All water should be regarded as being potentially contaminated. Water used for drinking, brushing teeth or making ice should have first been boiled or otherwise sterilised. Milk is unpasteurised and should be boiled. Powdered or tinned milk is available and is advised, but make sure that it is reconstituted with pure water. Avoid all dairy products. Only eat well-cooked meat and fish, preferably served hot. Pork, salad and mayonnaise may carry increased risk. Vegetables should be cooked and fruit peeled.
Rabies is present. For those at high risk, vaccination before arrival should be considered. If you are bitten abroad seek medical advice without delay. For more information consult the *Health* section at the back of the book.

Health care: There is a 174-bed hospital in Belmopan and six other general hospitals. Medical insurance is essential.

TRAVEL - International

AIR: There is no national airline. International services, mainly of a regional nature, are provided by *Tropic Air, Western Caribbean Airways, American Airways, Belize Trans Air, Continental, Taca International* and *Tan/Sahsa.*
Approximate flight times: To Belize from *London* (via Miami) is 11 hours; from *Los Angeles* is 8 hours; from *Miami* is 2 hours; from *Guatemala City* is 2 hours; from *Cancun* is 3 hours; and from *New York* is 5 hours.
International airport: The *Philip S W Goldson International Airport (BZE)* is 16km (10 miles) northwest of Belize City. Facilities include duty-free shop, bank, post office, shops, restaurant, buffet and bar. Taxis are available to the city. A new terminal has recently been completed (1990).
Note: Belmopan, the capital, is 100km (62 miles) from Belize City by road.
Departure tax: Bz$22.50, including a Bz$2.50 Security Tax, is levied on all passengers from the airport, apart from transit passengers and children under 12.
SEA: Over the past ten years Belize has greatly improved its port facilities, but these cater for cargo vessels and no cruise lines call there. There is a motor-yacht link between Punto Gorda and Puerto Barrios in Guatemala.
ROAD: There are road links with Chetumal on the Mexican border, and Melchor de Mencos in Guatemala.

TRAVEL - Internal

AIR: Local services link the main towns. *Maya Airways Ltd* and *Tropic Air* fly three times daily from the municipal airstrip, Belize City, to Ambergris Cay. There are also scheduled flights daily to each of the main towns and charter rates are offered to all local airstrips, of which there are 25. *Island Air* offers scheduled flights between the mainland and San Pedro. Five other companies have charters from Belize City to the outlying districts.
SEA: The sugar industry runs motorboat links along the coast, but there is no scheduled service. Small boats irregularly ply between the small cays off the coast. This

transport used to be the only means of travel to the interior, along the Belize, Hondo and New rivers, but services have dwindled rapidly since the advent of all-weather roads.
Documentation: A national driving licence is acceptable.
ROAD: 1600km (1000 miles) of all-weather roads link the eight towns in the country, though torrential rain seasonally severs these links, particularly at ferry points. Belize has a less developed network of roads than the rest of Central America but it is steadily being improved, especially in the north. There are good daily bus services between the large towns, and to both the Mexican and Guatemalan borders. The Belize stretch of the road to Mexico is currently being improved, while the Belize–Belmopan road is in generally good condition.
JOURNEY TIMES: The following chart gives approximate journey times (in hours and minutes) from Belize City to other major cities/towns in the country:

	Air	Road	Sea
Northern Border	2.20	-	-
Corozal Town	-	2.00	-
Orange Walk Town	1.15	-	-
Belmopan	0.20	1.00	-
Benque Viejo	-	1.45	-
San Ignacio	-	1.30	-
Dangriga	0.30	3.30	-
Punta Gorda	0.45	8.00	-
San Pedro, Ambergris	0.15	-	1.30
Cay Caulker	-	0.45	-
Placentia	0.30	4.00	7.00

ACCOMMODATION

HOTELS: Belize has few first-class hotels, but smaller establishments give good value. There are mountain lodges in the interior and resort hotels on the Caribbean coast. Only limited accommodation is available on some of the larger cays, and resort villages are being built. All approved accommodation is listed by The Belize Tourism Industry Association, (see address and contact numbers above). The BTIA represents 65% of all establishments. **Grading:** Hotels have been divided into three categories according to price and standard. Rates are subject to change without notice. It is advisable to confirm reservations and rates in advance. Classes of hotels are as follows:
Upper: All hotels provide a private bath/shower. There is air-conditioning in all rooms and each hotel has a restaurant and bar.
Middle: All hotels provide a private bath/shower and air-conditioning in all rooms.
Lower: Nearly all provide a private bath/shower.
On the Barrier Reef Cays, there are a number of resort hotels of roughly the same standard as those given above.
APARTMENTS: Long-stay visitors can rent apartments on a monthly basis, while in Chaa-creek, palm-thatched cottages can be rented on a daily basis.
CAMPING/CARAVANNING: Limited campsites are available. There is a caravan site in Corozal Town, and also outside San Ignacio Town. Camping on the beach is forbidden. Camping on private beach yards in Cay Caulker and in Tobacco Caye is available.

RESORTS & EXCURSIONS

For the purposes of this section Belize has been divided into **Mainland Belize, Coastal Belize** and **The Belize Cays**. There is no administrative or political significance in this division which has been made for convenience only.

Mainland Belize

Belmopan is the country's new capital city, carved out of the tropical jungle in the geographic centre of Belize, near the foothills of the beautiful *Maya Mountains*. It has a population of only about 4000, most of whom are civil servants, and is in the first phase of a 20-year development period. The most imposing building is the *National Assembly* on *Independence Hill*, patterned in an ancient Maya motif.
Corozal was settled around 1850 by Mestizo refugees from Mexico; now it is a well-planned community and the centre of Belize's thriving sugar industry.
Mountain Pine Ridge Forest Reserve is located south of the western highway about 115km (70 miles) from Belize City. It is an area of fine views and secluded bustling streams, and contains the *Hidden Valley Falls* which plunge 500m (1600ft) into the valley.
San Ignacio is a quaint, bustling town with a robust, pioneering atmosphere. It is surrounded by hills, and is the administrative centre for the Cayo district. Not far from San Ignacio are several Maya sites including magnificent *Xunantunich* and the 1500-year-old *El Castillo*, the second tallest building in Belize.

Coastal Belize

Belize City is over 300 years old and serves as the main commercial area and seaport. It is the country's biggest city, and has charming colonial architecture, functional wooden buildings and historic cathedrals. Sights to see include the oldest *Anglican cathedral* in Latin America *(St John's)* and *Government House*, the Belize City residence of the British Governor, built in 1814. The archaeological site of *Altun Ha* is on the northern highway between Belize City and Orange Walk.
Cerros is located on the fringe of a beautiful expanse of blue-green water which is ideal for watersports. Across the bay from the town is an interesting archaeological site.
Dangriga (Stann Creek) provides a good jumping-off point for excursions to the offshore islands and nearby forests. These include *Caye Chapel*, a private island paradise with white sand beaches, coral formations, and its own airstrip and marina.
Placentia is a quiet village situated at the tip of the 20km (12-mile) long Placentia peninsula. Its protected lagoon and sandy beaches make it an ideal place for fishing, swimming and sunbathing.

The Belize Cays

Ambergris Cay is the most popular tourist destination in Belize, especially the bustling fishing village of **San Pedro.** 58km (36 miles) north of Belize City, it is accessible by daily scheduled air flights. It has a number of beaches.
Cay Caulker has become increasingly popular in recent years. Its extensive underwater cave system has made it popular with divers, whilst those who wish to explore the reef without getting wet can see photographs of reef fish at the museum (school parties free).
On **Half Moon Cay** at **Lighthouse Reef** is the *Red-Footed Booby Bird Sanctuary*, founded in 1982 to protect the booby and other birds and animals. Scuba divers at Lighthouse Reef have the opportunity to explore walls which have spectacular sheer drops of thousands of feet and the *Blue Hole* (a deep sinkhole), following the webbed feet of Jacques Cousteau in 1984. Boats to both can be hired. There are many other cays with facilities for those interested in fishing, diving and seeing wildlife. Visitors should acquaint themselves with the restrictions on the removal of coral, orchids and turtles, and on spearfishing in certain areas. Wrecks and treasures are also government-protected.

SOCIAL PROFILE

FOOD & DRINK: There is a selection of restaurants which serve American, Chinese, Latin American and Creole food. Service and quality vary but the food is generally cheap. Service is not always very good in some of the more modest places. Bars are plentiful and local drinks include anise and peppermint, known as *A & P*, and the strong *Old Belizero* rum. The local *Belikin* beer is worth sampling.
NIGHTLIFE: There is live dancing late in the evenings at Bellevue Hotel and quiet music at Fort George Bar overlooking the harbour. The native nightspots include the bar on R Front Street and Copa Cabana on New Road complete with flashing lights, tinsel, bamboo, jukebox and live bands at weekends. Other places include the Hard Rock Café and Legends Disco.
SHOPPING: Handicrafts, woodcarvings and straw items are on sale. Jewellery in pink and black coral, and tortoiseshell (not to be imported to the USA) used to be good buys; since 1982 there have been severe restrictions on the export of these and some other goods in the interests of wildlife conservation. 'In-Bond' stores carry watches, perfumes and other duty-free purchases, but Belize is not comparable in size to other free ports in the Caribbean.
Shopping hours: 0800-1200 and 1300-1700 Monday to Saturday; some shops stay open 1900-2100 some evenings.
SPORTS: Attractions include coastal and river **fishing, scuba diving** and **snorkelling** around the reef. **Swimming** is good off the cays and on the southeast coast where many places are developing as **diving** and **watersport** resorts (see *Resorts & Excursions* above). **Soccer, basketball, softball, boxing** and occasional **horseracing** are available. Those not accompanied by a guide holding a government concession require a licence to hunt.
SPECIAL EVENTS: For further details consult the Belize Tourist Board.
Sep 10 '93 *St George's Caye Day Carnival*. **Sep 21** *Independence Day Carnival*. **Nov 19** *Garifuna Settlement Day*.
SOCIAL CONVENTIONS: British influence can still be seen in many social situations. Flowers or confectionery are acceptable gifts to give to hosts if invited to their home for a meal. Dress is casual although beachwear should not be worn in towns. It may be inadvisable to discuss politics particularly if of a partisan nature. Smoking is acceptable everywhere.
Tipping: Few places add service charges, and 10% is normal. Taxi drivers are not tipped.

BUSINESS PROFILE

ECONOMY: Agriculture is the most important economic sector: the main products are citrus fruit, bananas and sugar cane. Timber is also important, especially mahogany and other tropical hardwoods. Fishing and livestock are being developed. The fastest growing area of the Belizean economy is tourism, fuelled by substantial foreign investment, particularly from Canadian sources although it seems likely to remain somewhat limited. There is very little industry and few prospects of future industrial development. Given the low living standards in Belize, markets are limited, although there are some opportunities for the sale of agricultural, construction and consumer goods. The USA is the largest single trading partner, providing half of all imports and taking about 60% of Belizean exports. The UK and the EC are other important trading partners. Belize is a member of

CARICOM, the Caribbean economic community, and provides some transit facilities for trade to and from other countries in the region. Belize is a significant recipient of overseas aid, most recently from the US under the Bush administration programme to eliminate drug trafficking.
BUSINESS: Most businessmen do not wear a jacket or tie, though bush jackets (shirtjacs) are often worn. Appointments should be made and calling cards are acceptable. October to March are the best months for visits. **Office hours:** 0800-1200 and1300-1700 Monday to Thursday; 0830-1200 and1300-1645 Friday.
COMMERCIAL INFORMATION: The following organisation (with which 80% of all businesses are associated) can offer advice: Belize Chamber of Commerce, PO Box 291, 7 Cork Street, Belize City, Belize. Tlx: 121.
CONFERENCES/CONVENTIONS: Facilities are available at a number of venues, and the Chamber of Commerce can supply information.

HISTORY & GOVERNMENT

HISTORY: The region was at the heart of the Mayan empire (circa AD300 to AD800) which subsequently migrated to Yucatán. The country's modern history really begins when Belize, formerly British Honduras, was occupied by the British in 1638-40; with settlements spreading as woodcutting became profitable. By the end of the 18th century, Africans were brought in as slaves to cut the mahogany. Despite attacks from the Spanish, the settlers remained, although it was not until 1862 that the territory was recognised as a British colony. The country achieved internal self-government in 1964. Elections in 1965 brought the leader of the People's United Party (PUP), George Price, to power. A bicameral legislature was then introduced. The PUP won every election held subsequently until 1984, when the United Democratic Party (UDP) took power for the first time. The new government remained committed to the mainstays of Belizean policy: growth through foreign investment, membership of CARICOM (the Caribbean Common Market) and a settlement of the long-running dispute with neighbouring Guatemala. Price was returned to office at the most recent election in September 1989. Tensions have long existed between Belize and Guatemala because, even though the boundary between them was determined in 1859, Guatemala continued to claim sovereignty of Belize. Throughout the 1970s British troops were sent over in response to Guatemalan hostility. As a result of negotiations, Britain agreed to grant Belize independence in 1981. However, the new Guatemalan President, Jorge Serrano, who took office in January 1991, declared his government's urgent desire to reach a settlement. An agreement was duly reached in September 1991 (including the establishment of diplomatic relations) under which Guatemala recognised Belizean sovereignty (although it maintains its territorial claim) in exchange for access to Belizean ports.
GOVERNMENT: Constitutional monarchy: the British Monarch is Head of State, represented in Belize by the Governor-General. The bicameral National Assembly is the legislature, and consists of a Senate and a House of Representatives, members of which are elected by universal adult suffrage. Executive power is in the hands of the Governor-General, advised by the cabinet.

CLIMATE

Subtropical with a brisk prevailing wind from the Caribbean Sea. High annual temperatures and humidity. Dry and hot climate from January to April with monsoon season from June to September.
Required clothing: Lightweight cottons and linens, rainwear.

BELIZE CITY (5m)

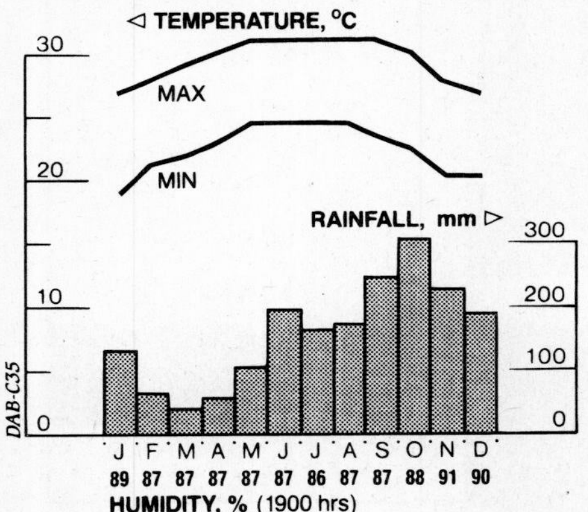

BENIN

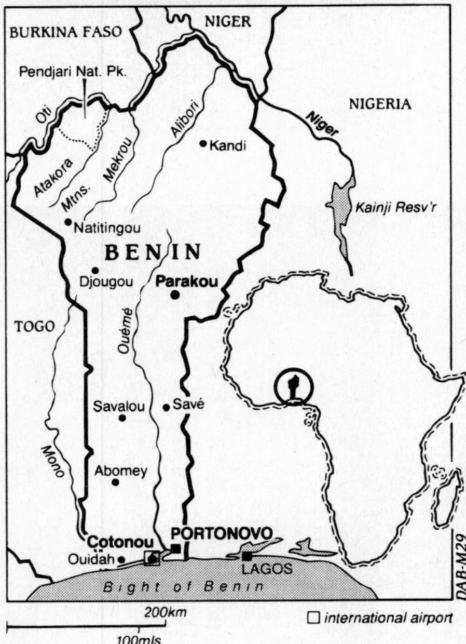

Location: West Africa

Office National du Tourisme et de l'Hôtellerie (ONATHO)
BP 89
Cotonou, Benin
Tel: 312 687. Telex: 5032.
Republic of Benin Consulate
Dolphin House
16 The Broadway
Stanmore
Middlesex HA7 4DW
Tel: (081) 954 8800. Fax: (081) 954 8844. Telex: 24620.
Opening hours: 1000-1230 and 1400-1630 Monday to Friday.
Embassy of the Republic of Benin
87 avenue Victor Hugo
75116 Paris, France
Tel: (1) 45 00 98 82. Telex: 610110.
British Consulate
BP 147
SOBEPAT
Contonou, Benin
Tel: 313 342 *or* 312 058. Telex: 9725047 STIN CTNOU.
Embassy of the Republic of Benin
2737 Cathedral Avenue, NW
Washington, DC
20008
Tel: (202) 232 6656/7/8. Fax: (202) 265 1996. Telex: 64155.
Embassy of the United States of America
BP 2012
rue Caporal Anani Bernard
Cotonou, Benin
Tel: 300 650 *or* 300 513 *or* 301 792. Fax: 301 439 *or* 301 974.
Embassy of the Republic of Benin
58 Glebe Avenue
Ottawa, Ontario
K1S 2C3
Tel: (613) 233 4429 *or* 233 4868 *or* 233 5273. Fax: (613) 233 8952.
Consulates in: Montréal and Calgary.

AREA: 112,622 sq km (43,484 sq miles).
POPULATION: 4,736,000 (1990 estimate).
POPULATION DENSITY: 42.1 per sq km.
CAPITAL: Porto Novo. **Population:** 164,000 (1984 estimate).
GEOGRAPHY: Benin is situated in West Africa, and is bounded to the east by Nigeria, to the north by Niger and Burkina Faso and to the west by Togo. Benin stretches 700km (435 miles) from the Bight of Benin to the Niger River. The coastal strip is sandy with coconut palms. Beyond the lagoons of Porto Novo, Nokoue, Ouidah and Grand Popo is a plateau rising gradually to the heights of the Atakora Mountains. From the highlands run two tributaries of Niger, while southwards the Ouémé flows down to Nokoue lagoon. Mono River flows into the sea at Grand Popo and forms a frontier with Togo.
LANGUAGE: The official language is French. However, many indigenous ethnic groups have their own languages: Bariba and Fulani are spoken in the north, Fon and Yoruba in the south. Some English is also spoken.
RELIGION: 80% Animist/traditional, 13% Muslim, 15% Christian (mainly Roman Catholic). (See *Social Conventions* in the *Social Profile* section below.)
TIME: GMT + 1.
ELECTRICITY: 220 volts AC, 50Hz.
COMMUNICATIONS: Telephone: IDD is available. Country code: 229. There is an additional charge for calls made from a coin box. **Telex:** Public telex facilities are available in Cotonou at post offices and some hotels. **Post:** Airmail takes three to five days to reach Europe. Surface mail letters or parcels take from six to eight weeks. There are good *poste restante* facilities at most main post offices. Post office hours: 0800-1400 Monday to Saturday. **Press:** Exclusively in French. The fortnightly *Journal Officiel de la République* is issued by the government information bureau. *La Nation* replaced the daily *Ehuzu* in 1990 whose publication was suspended in March 1991.
BBC World Service and Voice of America frequencies: From time to time these change. See the section *How to Use this Book* for more information.

BBC:				
MHz	17.79	15.40	15.07	9.410
Voice of America:				
MHz	21.49	15.60	9.525	6.035

PASSPORT/VISA

Regulations and requirements may be subject to change at short notice, and you are advised to contact the appropriate diplomatic or consular authority before finalising travel arrangements. Details of these may be found at the head of this country's entry. Any numbers in the chart refer to the footnotes below.

	Passport Required?	Visa Required?	Return Ticket Required?
Full British	Yes	Yes	Yes
BVP	Not valid	-	-
Australian	Yes	Yes	Yes
Canadian	Yes	Yes	Yes
USA	Yes	Yes	Yes
Other EC	Yes	1	Yes
Japanese	Yes	Yes	Yes

Restricted entry: Holders of passports from South Africa will be denied entry (unless they hold a approval of entry from the Minister of Foreign Affairs of Benin).
PASSPORTS: Valid passport required by all except for nationals of the following countries in possession of a national identity card or expired passport less than 5 years old: Burkina Faso, Cameroon, Central African Republic, Chad, Congo, Côte d'Ivoire, Gabon, Ghana, Madagascar, Mali, Mauritania, Niger, Rwanda, Senegal and Togo.
British Visitors Passport: Not accepted.
VISAS: Required by all except:
(a) nationals listed in *Passports* above;
(b) **[1]** nationals of Denmark, Germany, Italy and France (all other EC nationals *do* require visas);
(c) nationals of Algeria, Bulgaria, Cape Verde, Gambia, Guinea Republic, Guinea Bissau, Liberia, Nigeria, Romania, Sierra Leone and Sweden.
Types of visa: Tourist and Business. Cost: £20.
Validity: Visas are now valid for a period of 15 days only within 3 months of date of issue.
Application to: Consulate (or Consular Section at Embassy). For addresses, see top of entry.
Application requirements: (a) Valid passport. (b) Application form completed in duplicate. (c) 2 passport photos. (d) Valid yellow fever certificate. (e) Prepaid registered envelope large enough to fit passport, if applying by post. (f) Letter from company, if visit is for business purposes.
Working days required: Callers at Consulate are usually able to obtain visa without delay but where authorisation from Benin is required it may take up to 30 days.
Temporary residence: Enquire at Consulate.

MONEY

Currency: CFA Franc = 100 centimes. Notes are in denominations of CFA Fr5000, 1000, 500, 100 and 50. Coins are in denominations of CFA Fr500, 100, 50, 25, 10, 5, 2 and 1. Benin is part of the French Monetary Area. Only currency issued by the 'Banque des Etats de l'Afrique Centrale' is valid; that issued by the 'Banque des Etats de l'Afrique de l'Ouest' is not.
Credit cards: Access/Mastercard, American Express, Diners Club and Visa are accepted on a limited basis. Check with your credit card company for details of merchant acceptability and other services which may be available.
Exchange rate indicators: The following figures are included as a guide to the movements of the CFA Franc against Sterling and the US Dollar:

Date:	Oct '89	Oct '90	Oct '91	Oct '92
£1.00=	505.13	498.37	496.12	413.75
$1.00=	319.90	255.12	285.87	260.71

Currency restrictions: Free import of local and foreign currency, subject to declaration. Export of local currency is limited to CFA Fr75,000 if Benin resident travelling to countries outside the French monetary area, limited to amount declared on arrival if non-resident. EC residents can export an unlimited amount. Export of foreign currency limited is to CFA Fr150,000 for Benin residents; CFA Fr100,000 for non-residents.
Banking hours: 0800-1100 and 1500-1600 Monday to Friday.

DUTY FREE

The following items may be imported into Benin without incurring customs duty:
*200 cigarettes or 100 cigarillos or 25 cigars or 250g of tobacco**;
*1 bottle of wine and 1 bottle of spirits**;
0.5 litres of toilet water and 0.25 litres of perfume.
Note [*]: Only available to persons over 15 years of age.

PUBLIC HOLIDAYS

Public holidays observed in Benin are as follows:
Mar 25 '93 Beginning of Eid al-Fitr. **Apr 1** Youth Day. **Apr 9** Good Friday. **Apr 12** Easter Monday. **May 1** Workers' Day. **May 20** Ascension Day. **May 31** Whit Monday. **Jun 10** Eid al-Adha. **Aug 15** Assumption. **Oct 26** Armed Forces Day. **Nov 1** All Saints' Day. **Nov 30** National Day. **Dec 25** Christmas Day. **Dec 31** Harvest Day. **Jan 1 '94** New Year's Day. **Jan 16** Martyr's Day. **Mar** Beginning of Eid al-Fitr.
Note: Muslim festivals are timed according to local sightings of various phases of the Moon and the dates given above are approximations. During the lunar month of Ramadan that precedes Eid al-Fitr, Muslims fast during the day and feast at night and normal business patterns may be interrupted. Many restaurants are closed during the day and there may be restrictions on smoking and drinking. Some disruption may continue into Eid al-Fitr itself. Eid al-Fitr and Eid al-Adha may last anything from two to ten days, depending on the region. For more information see the section *World of Islam* at the back of the book.

HEALTH

Regulations and requirements may be subject to change at short notice, and you are advised to contact your doctor well in advance of your intended date of departure. Any numbers in the chart refer to the footnotes below.

	Special Precautions?	Certificate Required?
Yellow Fever	Yes	1
Cholera	Yes	2
Typhoid & Polio	Yes	-
Malaria	Yes	-
Food & Drink	3	-

[1]: A yellow fever vaccination certificate is required by all travellers over one year of age.
[2]: Following WHO guidelines issued in 1973, a cholera vaccination certificate is no longer a condition of entry to Benin. However, cholera is a serious risk in this country and precautions are essential. Up-to-date advice should be sought before deciding whether these precautions should include vaccination as medical opinion is divided over its effectiveness. See the *Health* section at the back of the book.
[3]: All water should be regarded as being potentially contaminated. Water used for drinking, brushing teeth or making ice should have first been boiled or otherwise sterilised. Milk is unpasteurised and should be boiled. Powdered or tinned milk is available and is advised, but make sure that it is reconstituted with pure water. Avoid all dairy products. Only eat well-cooked meat and fish, preferably served hot. Pork, salad and mayonnaise may carry increased risk. Vegetables should be cooked and fruit peeled.
Malaria is a risk all year throughout the country. It occurs predominantly in the malignant *falciparum* form. Resistance to choroquine has been reported.
Rabies is present. For those at high risk, vaccination before arrival should be considered. If you are bitten abroad seek medical advice without delay. For more information consult the *Health* section at the back of the book.
Bilharzia (schistosomiasis) is present. Avoid swimming and paddling in fresh water. Swimming pools which are well-chlorinated and maintained are safe.
Trypanosomiasis is present and precautions are recommended.
Meningitis is a risk, depending on the area visited and the time of year.
Health care: Medical insurance is essential.

TRAVEL - International

AIR: Benin's national airline is *Transports Aériens du Bénin TAB (TS)*. Benin also has a shareholding in *Air Afrique*.
Approximate flight times: Not available, but *UTA* operates direct flights to Cotonou from Paris.
International airport: *Cotonou (COO)*, 5km (3 miles) northwest of the city. Taxis are available to the city.
Departure tax: CFA Fr2500 for all passengers leaving Benin.
SEA: Several shipping lines run regular cargo services from Marseille to Cotonou. Local shipping from Lagos arrives in Porto Novo.
RAIL: The railway line from Parakou (via Gaya) to Niamey in Niger, currently under construction, will provide the first rail link into Niger.
ROAD: There are two good main roads, one connecting Cotonou with Niamey in Niger and the other connecting Lagos with Porto Novo, Cotonou, Lomé and Accra; at present, the Nigerian border is closed. Buses and taxis are available. In 1991 work started on a road to link Benin with Togo and Burkina Faso. The first stretch will run from Djougou to Natitingou via Parakou.

TRAVEL - Internal

Note: Foreigners travelling outside Cotonou are subject to restrictions. Visitors are advised to check their position before travelling.
AIR: Government planes run services between Cotonou, Parakou, Natitingou, Djougou and Kandi. It is also possible to charter 2-seater planes.
Departure tax: All internal flights are subject to a CFA Fr250 tax.
RAIL: Benin has about 600km (400 miles) of rail track. Trains run from Cotonou to Porto Novo, to Pobé, to Segboroué and to Parakou. There are no restaurant or sleeper cars but food is available on some services.
Approximate journey times: From Cotonou to *Parakou* is 7-8 hours, to *Segboroué* is 2 hours 30 minutes and to *Pobé* is 4 hours.
ROAD: The roads are in reasonably good condition and many of those which run from Cotonou to Bohicon, and Parakou to Malanville, are bitumen-covered. Tracks are passable during the dry season but often impassable during the rainy season. Traffic drives on the right. Coach services run along major road routes. **Car hire:** A number of local firms are available in Cotonou.
Documentation: International Driving Licence required.
URBAN: Taxis are widely available in the main towns. Settle taxi fares in advance.

ACCOMMODATION

Main hotels in Cotonou are pleasant but elsewhere there is very little accommodation for visitors. Abomey has only a small hotel and motel. Porto Novo has one hotel and Parakou two small hotels. There are two establishments (*campements*) for **game viewing** at Porga near Pendjari National Park.

RESORTS & EXCURSIONS

Abomey, situated about 100km (60 miles) northeast of the capital, was once capital of a Fon kingdom and contains an excellent museum covering the history of the Abomey kingdoms (with a throne made of human skulls) and the *Fetish Temple*. Nearby is the *Centre des Artisanants* where local craft products are sold at reasonable prices.
Cotonou has a market, the *Dan Tokpa*, which is normally open every four days. The museum here is well worth a visit. The lake village of **Ganvie,** 18km (11 miles) northwest of Cotonou, has houses built on stilts and a water-market. About 32km (20 miles) to the east is the town of **Ouidah,** notable for its old Portuguese fort and the *Temple of the Sacred Python*.
Porto Novo, the capital, is the administrative centre of the country, containing many examples of colonial and pre-colonial art and architecture. The *Ethnological Museum* is probably the most notable place of interest for a visitor.
The northwest of the country is the home of the Somba people, whose goods can be bought at the weekly market at **Boukombe**.
Benin has two National Parks. **Pendjari** is normally only open between December and June and has a wide range of wildlife including cheetahs, hippos and crocodiles. Accommodation is available. The **Pendjari National Park** straddles the frontier region between Niger, Benin and Burkina Faso and is less well-developed.

SOCIAL PROFILE

FOOD & DRINK: There is a selection of restaurants and hotels in Cotonou, serving French food with table service, although some also serve local African specialities, particularly seafood. There are no restaurants of any note in Porto Novo.
NIGHTLIFE: Cotonou offers five nightclubs, but elsewhere there is little nightlife except during festivals.
SHOPPING: In Cotonou along the marina there are many stalls selling handicrafts and souvenirs. The Dan Tokpa market borders the Cotonou Lagoon and is stocked with many goods from Nigeria and elsewhere as well as traditional medicines and artifacts. Crafts and local goods can be purchased in many towns and villages elsewhere, particularly in markets. Good buys include ritual masks, tapestries, elongated statues and pottery. **Shopping hours:** 0900-1300 and 1600-1900 Monday to Saturday. Some shops are open 0800-1200 on Sunday.
SPORT: There are limited facilities for **watersports** on the coast, but note that tides and currents render the sea very dangerous and only the strongest swimmers should venture in. In Cotonou, several hotels have **swimming** pools, and there is **tennis** at the Club du Benin and **sailing** at the Yacht Club. A dug-out canoe or motorboat can be hired on Nakoue Lagoon.
SOCIAL CONVENTIONS: Normal courtesies are appreciated; it is customary to shake hands on arrival and departure. However, religious beliefs play a large part in society and these should be respected. Voodoo is perhaps the most striking and best-known religion, and has acquired considerable social and political power. Only priests can communicate with voodoos and spirits of the dead. If travelling, it is advisable to clear itineraries with district or provincial authorities. Casual wear is acceptable in most places. **Tipping:** Normal to tip 10% of bill in hotels and restaurants.

BUSINESS PROFILE

ECONOMY: One of the poorest countries in the world, Benin's economy is principally agricultural. The main commodities are cotton, peanuts, coffee and palm oil. Benin suffered severely from the global recession of the 1980s and the low level of commodity prices. The most promising development of recent years has been the discovery of offshore oil deposits, so that petroleum products are now the country's biggest export earner. There is some light industry, but almost all manufactured and consumer goods have to be imported and the balance of payments shows a large deficit. Membership of the CFA Franc Zone provides a partial cushion but ultimately the country relies heavily on large injections of French aid. As well as the CFA Zone, Benin is a member of the West African economic community ECOWAS. Benin sells its products mainly to France and, in smaller quantities, to The Netherlands, Korea, Japan and India. The country's leading suppliers are Germany and France.
BUSINESS: It is essential to be able to conduct conversations in French. Normal courtesies should be observed and punctuality is especially important. Lightweight tropical suits should be worn. **Office hours:** 0830-1230 and 1500-1830 Monday to Friday.
COMMERCIAL INFORMATION: The following organisation can offer advice: Chambre de

Commerce, d'Agriculture et d'Industrie de la République Populaire du Benin (CCIB), BP 31, avenue du Général de Gaulle, Cotonou, Benin. Tel: 313 299.

HISTORY & GOVERNMENT

HISTORY: Traditionally a sophisticated culture, Benin was used as a trading point during the 18th and 19th centuries. The male population was severely depleted as a result of the slave trade by the 19th century (see Werner Herzog's film, *Cobra Verde*). France first occupied the country in 1872, and in 1904 the territory was incorporated into French West Africa as Dahomey. On December 4, 1958, it became the 'République du Dahomey', self-governing within the French community, and on August 1, 1960, gained full independence from France. Between 1960 and 1972, a succession of military coups brought about many changes of government; the last of these brought Major Mathieu Kérékou to power, who has held on ever since. Having initially pursued strict Marxist-Leninist ideology, Kérékou and the ruling National Council of the Revolution (CNR) have relaxed their previously strict orthodoxy. From 1977 until 1990, Benin was ruled according to the precepts of the *Loi Fondamentale*. This decreed that the sole political party should be the *Parti de la Révolution Populaire du Bénin* (PRPB). The stability of the regime was first threatened during late 1990 with a series of student-led demonstrations whose intensity steadily increased over the following months. These seemed likely to provoke a drastic reaction from the Government. However, with French encouragement, the Kérékou government agreed to hold a presidential election. His principal opponent at the March 1991 poll was Prime Minister Nicéphore Soglo, who beat Kérékou into second place but failed to win an outright majority. In the run-off a fortnight later, Soglo won with two-thirds of the vote. Political violence has since died off and it appears that Benin has successfully effected the transition from dictatorship to a pluralistic political system – an example that many other African governments are trying to emulate. The new government still faces the economic problems that have plagued Benin throughout the 1980s, and these will be more difficult to resolve.
GOVERNMENT: The 64-seat unicameral legislature is elected by universal adult suffrage. This Assembly in turn elects the President who directs the National Executive Council (NEC). Until 1991, candidates for the Assembly were drawn from the PRPB. The March 1991 election saw no less than 24 contesting parties.

CLIMATE

The south has an equatorial climate with four seasons. It is hot and dry from January to April and during August, with rainy seasons May to July and September to December. The north has more extreme temperatures, hot and dry between November and June, cooler and very wet between July and October.
Required clothing: Lightweight cottons and linens. Avoid synthetics. Light raincoat or an umbrella is necessary in rainy seasons and warmer clothes are advised for cool evenings.

COTONOU Benin (10m)

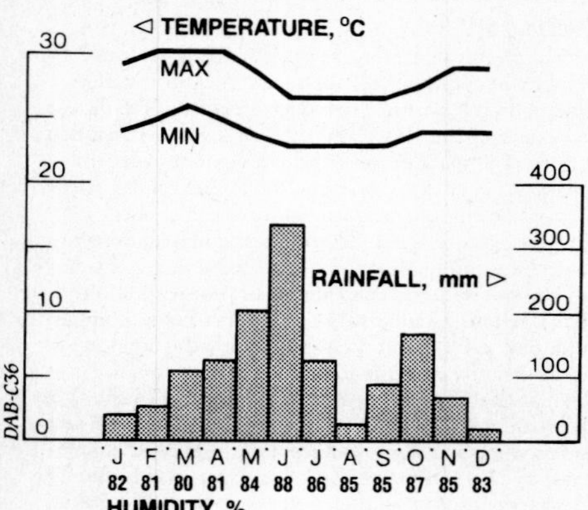

TEMPERATURE CONVERSIONS
-20 -10 0°C 10 20 30 40
0 10 20 30°F40 50 60 70 80 90 100
RAINFALL CONVERSIONS 0mm 200 400 600 800
0in 5 10 15 20 25 30

BERMUDA

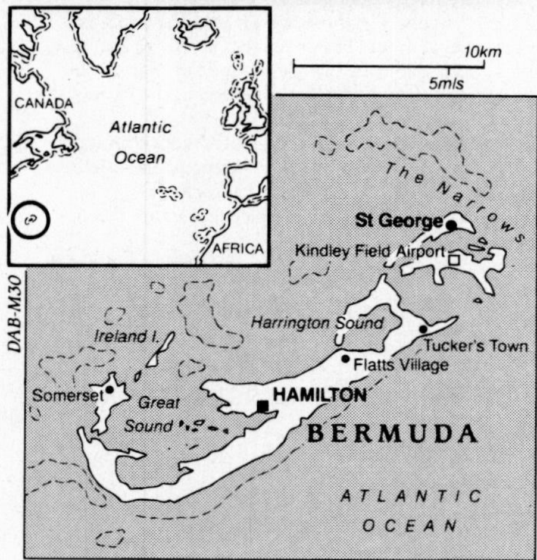

Location: Western Atlantic Ocean.

Bermuda Department of Tourism
Global House
43 Church Street
Hamilton HM 12, Bermuda
Tel: (292) 0023. Fax: (292) 7537.
Bermuda Tourism
BCB Ltd
1 Battersea Church Road
London SW11 3LY
Tel: (071) 734 8813. Fax: (071) 352 6501.
Opening hours: 0900-1700 Monday to Friday.
British Dependent Territories Visas Section
The Passport Office
70-78 Clive House
Petty France
London SW1H 9HD
Tel: (071) 279 3434 (recorded information); (071) 279 4000 (limited enquiries).
Honorary British Trade Correspondent
PO Box HM 655
c/o Visitors' Service Bureau
Front Street
Hamilton HM CX, Bermuda
Tel: (295) 1480.
Bermuda Department of Tourism
Suite 201
310 Madison Avenue
New York, NY 10017
Tel: (212) 818 9800.
US Consulate General
PO Box HM 325
Crown Hill
16 Middle Road
Devonshire, Hamilton
Bermuda
Tel: (295) 1342. Fax: (295) 1592.
Bermuda Department of Tourism
Suite 1004
1200 Bay Street
Toronto, Ontario
M5R 2A5
Tel: (416) 923 9600. Fax: (416) 923 4840.

AREA: 53 sq km (20.59 sq miles).
POPULATION: 59,588 (1990 estimate).
POPULATION DENSITY: 1080 per sq km.
CAPITAL: Hamilton. **Population:** 6000 (1990).
GEOGRAPHY: Bermuda consists of a chain of some 150 coral islands and islets lying 917km (570 miles) off the coast of South Carolina, in the Atlantic Ocean. Ten of the islands are linked by bridges and causeways to form the principal mainland. There are no rivers or streams and the islands are entirely dependent on rainfall for fresh water. Coastlines are characterised by a succession of small bays with beaches of fine pale sand. The surrounding waters are a vivid blue-green. Inland there is an abundance of subtropical plants and flowers.
LANGUAGE: English is the official language. There is a small community of Portuguese speakers.
RELIGION: Anglican, Episcopal, Roman Catholic and other denominations. There are two cathedrals in Bermuda, one Anglican and the other Roman Catholic.
TIME: GMT - 4.
ELECTRICITY: 110 volts AC, 60Hz. American (flat) 2-pin plugs.
COMMUNICATIONS: Telephone: IDD is available. Country code: 1 809 29 or 1 809 23. The internal telephone system is operated by the Bermuda Telephone Company. Bermuda numbers dialled from within Bermuda should be prefixed with the last two digits of the country code (29) but there are no conventional area codes. **Fax:** This service is available from many hotels and offices. **Telex/telegram:** Cable & Wireless Ltd operate Bermuda's international telecommunications system. Cablegrams may be sent from the C & W office in Hamilton. **Post:** Most letters will automatically travel airmail even if surface rates are paid, although paid-for airmail will be given priority. Airmail letters to Europe take five to seven days. *Poste Restante* facilities are available. Post offices are open from 0800-1700 Monday to Friday. In addition, the General Post Office in Hamilton is open on Saturday mornings until 1200. **Press:** The main newspapers are *The Bermuda Sun*, *The Bermuda Times*, *The Mid-Ocean News* (weekly) and *The Royal Gazette* (daily).
BBC World Service and Voice of America frequencies: From time to time these change. See the section *How to Use this Book* for more information.

BBC:				
MHz	17.72	11.78	9.915	5.965
Voice of America:				
MHz	15.21	11.70	6.130	0.930

PASSPORT/VISA

Regulations and requirements may be subject to change at short notice, and you are advised to contact the appropriate diplomatic or consular authority before finalising travel arrangements. Details of these may be found at the head of this country's entry. Any numbers in the chart refer to the footnotes below.

	Passport Required?	Visa Required?	Return Ticket Required?
Full British	1	No	Yes
BVP	Valid	No	Yes
Australian	Yes	No	Yes
Canadian	1	No	Yes
USA	1	No	Yes
Other EC	Yes	No	Yes
Japanese	Yes	No	Yes

Note: Before entering Bermuda, it is *essential* to be in possession of either a return ticket or an onward ticket to country to which one has a legal right of entry. Anyone arriving in Bermuda and intending to return to their own country via another one which requires a visa *must* obtain such a visa before arrival in Bermuda.
PASSPORTS: A valid passport is required by all except: [1] nationals of Canada and the USA provided that they have other documents with proof of identity, such as a birth certificate, a citizenship card/naturalization certificate, or a voters registration card. British citizens may travel on a BVP (see below).
British Visitors Passport: Acceptable. A BVP may be used for holidays or unpaid business trips of up to 3 months providing the user does not travel via the USA.
VISAS: Visas are *not* required for stays of up to 3 weeks *except* for nationals of Albania, Algeria, Bulgaria, Cambodia, China, CIS, Cuba, Czechoslovakia, Georgia, Haiti, Hungary, Iran, Iraq, Jordan, Laos, Lebanon, Libya, Mongolia, Morocco, Nigeria, North Korea, Philippines, Poland, Romania, South Africa, Sri Lanka, Syria, Tunisia, Vietnam and Yugoslavia who *must* obtain a visa.
Types of visa: Tourist and Transit.
Validity: Valid for 3 months from the date of issue.
Application and enquiries to: British Dependent Territories Visas Section. For addresses, see top of entry.
Application requirements: Completed application forms and for business trips, letters from a host. An onward or return ticket is a condition of entry (see note above).
Working days required: 6 to 8 weeks.
Temporary residence: Persons intending to take up residence and/or employment will require prior authorisation from the Department of Immigration, 30 Parliament Street, Hamilton HM 12, Bermuda. Tel: (295) 5151.

MONEY

Currency: Bermuda Dollar (Bda$) = 100 cents. Currency tied to US Dollar. Notes are in denominations of Bda$100, 50, 20, 10, 5 and 2. Coins are in denominations of Bda$1, and 25, 10, 5 and 1 cents.

Currency exchange: US Dollars are generally accepted at par. It is illegal to exchange money other than at authorised banks or bureaux de change.
Credit cards: Access/Mastercard, American Express, Barclaycard and Diners Club are accepted at most large hotels, shops and restaurants. Check with your credit card company for details of merchant acceptability and other services which may be available.
Travellers cheques: US Dollar cheques are widely accepted. There is no bureau de change at the airport, but the bank there is open 1100-1230 and 1300-1600 Monday to Friday.
Exchange rate indicators: The following figures are included as a guide to the movements of the Bermuda Dollar against Sterling and the US Dollar:

Date:	Oct '89	Oct '90	Oct '91	Oct '92
£1.00=	1.57	1.95	1.73	1.59
$1.00=	1.00	1.00	1.00	1.00

Currency restrictions: There is no limit to the import of foreign currency, subject to declaration. The export of foreign currency is limited to the amount declared on import, plus the equivalent of Bda$2000 in foreign currency. There is no limit to the import of local currency. The export of local currency is limited to Bda$250.
Banking hours: 0930-1500 Monday to Thursday, 0930-1600 Friday.

DUTY FREE

The following goods may be taken into Bermuda without incurring customs duty:
200 cigarettes and 50 cigars and 454g of tobacco;
1.136 litres (1 qt) of spirits and wines;
50ml of perfume and 250ml of toilet water.
Prohibited items: Spear guns for fishing, firearms and non-prescribed drugs (including marijuana). All visitors should declare any prescribed drugs on arrival as regulations are strictly observed. Clearance of merchandise and sales materials for use at trade conventions must be arranged in advance with the hotel concerned.

PUBLIC HOLIDAYS

Public holidays observed in Bermuda are as follows:
Apr 9 '93 Good Friday. **May 24** Bermuda Day. **Jun 21** Queen's Birthday. **Jul 29** Cup Match. **Jul 30** Somers Day. **Sep 6** Labour Day. **Nov 11** Remembrance Day. **Dec 25** Christmas Day. **Dec 26** Boxing Day. **Jan 1 '94** New Year's Day.
Note: Holidays falling on a weekend are usually observed the following Monday, when businesses and most restaurants are closed.

HEALTH

Regulations and requirements may be subject to change at short notice, and you are advised to contact your doctor well in advance of your intended date of departure. Any numbers in the chart refer to the footnotes below.

	Special Precautions?	Certificate Required?
Yellow Fever	No	No
Cholera	No	No
Typhoid & Polio	No	-
Malaria	No	-
Food & Drink	No	-

Health care: Health insurance is essential as medical costs are very high. There is no state-run health service. There is a fully-equipped 237-bed hospital near Hamilton.

TRAVEL - International

AIR: Bermuda has no national airline, but *British Airways (BA)* operates regular weekly flights to and from London.
Approximate flight times: to Bermuda from *London* is 7 hours; and from *New York* is 2 hours.
International airport: *Kindley Field (BDA)*, 15km (9.3 miles) from Hamilton. Bermuda Air Services limousines meet all arrivals. Taxis are also available. The journey to Hamilton takes 20-30 minutes. There are no duty-free shops or bureaux de change at the airport. Duty-free goods may, however, be purchased in town shops for collection at the airport on departure. The airport bank is open Monday to Friday 1100-1230 and 1300-1600 and the bar from 1100 until the departure of the last flight.
Departure tax: A tax of Bda$20 is levied except for children under two years and passengers in immediate transit.
SEA: UK cruise ships of the *P&O Line* and *Cunard* occasionally call en route from Australia, New Zealand and Southampton, UK. *Royal Caribbean Cruise Lines, Chandris* and *Kloster Cruise* operate a fly-cruise programme from the UK, via New York, to Bermuda (April to September).

TRAVEL - Internal

SEA: Ferries cross Hamilton Harbour. A reduced service runs on Sundays. Ferry tokens are sold at selected hotels at a discount.
ROAD: The main island has an extensive road network but foreign visitors may not drive cars in Bermuda. Motorcycles may be hired (see below) at more or less standard rates. The speed limit is 32km (20mph) and traffic drives on the left. **Bus:** Buses are modern and punctual. Bermuda's state-run buses (painted pink) are a pleasant and inexpensive way to visit points of interest. The trip from Hamilton to the town of St George's, the northeastern tip of Bermuda, takes about half an hour, with the ride from Hamilton to Somerset, Bermuda's westernmost point, taking around 45 minutes. It is essential to have the correct fare in coins. A route and schedule map is available free, and books of tickets are available at sub-post offices. **Taxi:** All taxis are metered, with a surcharge after midnight; there is a maximum of four passengers per taxi. Taxis displaying small blue flags are driven by qualified guides approved by the Department of Tourism. A 25% surcharge operates between 2400 and 0600. **Carriages:** Horse-drawn carriages are available in Hamilton. **Motorcycle/bicycle hire:** Lightweight motor-assisted bicycles ('livery cycles') may be hired throughout the island. Crash helmets must be worn. Third party insurance must be arranged. Bicycles can also be hired. The Department of Tourism produces a comprehensive sheet giving details of prices and supplies. Minimum age limit is 16 years. **Documentation:** A driving licence is not required for moped or bicycle hire. Again, note that visitors are not allowed to drive cars in Bermuda.
JOURNEY TIMES: The following chart gives approximate journey times from Hamilton (in hours and minutes) to other major towns and the airport on Bermuda.

	Road	Sea
Airport	0.30	-
St George's	0.30	-
Somerset	0.45	0.30
Naval Dockyard	0.45	0.45

ACCOMMODATION

The Bermuda Department of Tourism issues a booklet *Where to stay in Bermuda* listing all accommodation. Another leaflet gives rates and added taxes. Reduced rates are available during the *Rendezvous*, or 'low' season, which runs from November to March, and there are many special package tours for speciality holidays.
HOTELS: Hotels are all of a high standard. The top hotels offer dancing and entertainment. Hotels usually offer a choice between two meal plans. Information is available from the Bermuda Hotel Association, Carmel Buildings, corner of King Street and Reid Street, Hamilton 5-23, Bermuda. Tel: (295) 2127. Fax: (292) 6671. Telex: 3243. **Grading:** There is no formal grading system in Bermuda. MAP and BP. MAP is Modified American Plan; breakfast and dinner included with the price of the room, plus in some places British-style afternoon tea. BP is Bermuda Plan; room and full breakfast only. Large hotels with many facilities make up about 7% of accommodation in Bermuda. Smaller hotels (around 16%) have less than 150 rooms. Normally less expensive than the self-contained resorts, they have limited on-site facilities for shopping and entertainment and are less formal.
GUEST-HOUSES: Guest-houses generally taking less than 12 guests are usually small private homes. Some incorporate several housekeeping units (see below) while others provide shared kitchen facilities. Most of the larger establishments are old Bermudian residences with spacious gardens which have been converted and modernised. A few have their own waterfront and/or pool. Guest-houses make up 50% of accommodation in Bermuda.
Grading: Larger guest-houses may offer the Bermuda Plan or a slightly stripped-down version of the CP (Continental Plan) – room and light breakfast. Smaller places are casual, offering breakfast only. EP (European Plan) consists of room only. All guest-houses offer an informal life-style.
COTTAGE COLONIES: These are typically Bermudian and feature a main club-house with dining room, lounge and bar. The cottage units are spread throughout landscaped grounds and offer privacy and luxury. Though most have kitchenettes for beverages or light snacks they are not self-catering units. All have their own beach and/or pool.
CLUB RESORTS: These are noted for privacy and luxury and are for members or by invitation only. There are two club resorts on the main island.
SELF-CATERING: Housekeeping cottages are large properties situated in landscaped estates with their own beach and pool, much like cottage colonies, but without a main club-house. They are considered to be luxury units. All have kitchen facilities but BP or a reduced CP is available at some establishments. **Apartments:** Apartments can be booked through Happiness Islands, 3 Victoria Avenue, Harrogate HG1 1EQ. Tel: (0423) 526 887. Smaller, less expensive and with fewer amenities than the housekeeping cottages, most holiday apartments are nonetheless comfortable. Some have a pool. All have kitchen and a minimal daily maid service.
CAMPING/CARAVANNING: There are no camping facilities for visitors in Bermuda.

RESORTS & EXCURSIONS

Hamilton is the colony's capital city, situated at the end of Bermuda's *Great Sound* on the inner curve of the 'fish hook'. Here, between Parliament Street and Court Street, is the Cabinet Building where the *Senate* – the Upper House of Bermuda's Parliament – meets. The Lower Chamber of Parliament is housed in the *Sessions House* in Hamilton and is open to the public. Front Street is Hamilton's main street which runs along the water's edge from *Albouy's Point*, site of the Ferrydock and the Royal Bermuda Yacht Club to King Street in the east. Located on Queen Street in Hamilton is *Perot's Post Office*. The Perot stamp, Bermuda's first postage stamp, was printed by Bermuda's Postmaster from 1818 to 1862. Bermuda's stamps make fine gifts for friends who are collectors. In the summer months there are usually up to three cruise ships moored at the city's piers. Ferry trips are available round Hamilton Harbour, and also longer cruises to Great Sound and the rural village of Somerset. The recently restored 19th-century *Fort Hamilton* welcomes visitors to its formidable ramparts, bristling cannon, underground web of limestone tunnels and spectacular view of Hamilton. In **Hamilton**

BERMUDA	HEALTH REGULATIONS	VISA REGULATIONS
GALILEO/WORLDSPAN	TI-DFT/BDA/HE	 TI-DFT/BDA/VI
SABRE	 TIDFT/BDA/HE	TIDFT/BDA/VI

Code-Link

To access this information on your CRS, swipe the barcode with a light pen or type in the text under the barcode. For more information, see the introduction *How to Use This Book*.

parish is the *Blue Grotto Dolphin Show*, with dolphins, sharks, eels and sea horses.
In **Somerset,** on the western end of the island, *Fort Scaur* is a good place to picnic, fish, swim and enjoy the panoramic view of picturesque *Ely's Harbour*.
At the far eastern end of the chain of islands is the 17th-century town of **St George's**, Bermuda's first capital, founded in 1612. It has been the focus of considerable recent restoration; today, the town's narrow winding lanes and historic landmarks appear much as they did more than three centuries ago. At the corner of Duke of Clarence Street and Featherbed Alley is a working model of a 17th-century printing press. Also to be seen are *The Confederate Museum*, a hotel for Confederate officers during America's Civil War; the *Stocks & Pillory*; and the replica of the *Deliverance*, one of Bermuda's first ships. St George's also has many excellent pubs, restaurants and shops. *Gates Fort*, which dates back to 1620, is built on a promontory overlooking the sea and offers a spectacular view of the ocean and harbour. Nearby is *Fort St Catherine*, built in 1622, the largest and one of the most fascinating of the island's fortifications.
At the very tip of Bermuda, on the western side, is **Ireland Island**, with a *Maritime Museum* which displays relics of sunken wrecks and the neo-classical buildings of the Royal Naval dockyard.
Two of the best known caves are *Crystal Cave* and *Leamington Cave*, made up of sprawling underground systems and crystalline tidal pools. They are open daily in season.
The best view of the island is from **Gibb's Hill Lighthouse**, in Southampton parish.
Two notable **churches** on the island include *Old Devonshire Church* and *St Peter's Church*, on Duke of York Street in old St George's.
Everywhere on the island there are circles of stone, called *Moongates*, a design brought to Bermuda in the 1800s by a sea captain who had seen them on a voyage to China. Oriental legend has it that honeymooners should walk through them and make a wish.

SOCIAL PROFILE

FOOD & DRINK: Hotel cooking is usually international with some Bermudian specialities such as Bermuda lobster (in season, September to mid-April), mussel pie, conch stew, fish chowder laced with sherry peppers and rum, and shark. Other seafoods include Rockfish, Red Snapper and Yellowtail. Peculiar to Bermuda is the Bermuda onion; other fine home-grown products include pawpaw and strawberries in January and February, and a variety of local citrus fruit. Traditional Sunday breakfast is codfish and bananas while desserts include sweet potato pudding, bay grape jelly and a syllabub of guava jelly, cream and sherry. There is a vast variety of restaurants, cafés, bars and taverns to suit all pockets. Service will vary although generally table service can be expected. **Drink:** Local drinks and cocktails have Caribbean rum as a base, and have colourful names such as *Dark and Stormy* and the famous *Rum Swizzle*. British, European and American beer is available. It is normal in bars to pay for each drink and to tip the barman. In restaurants, drinks are added to the bill.
NIGHTLIFE: Most hotels offer a variety of entertainment. Dancing, barbecues, nightclubs and discotheques are all available. Local music is a mixture of calypso and Latin American, and steelband music is very popular.
SHOPPING: The best buys are imported merchandise such as French perfumes, English bone china, Swiss watches, Danish silver, American costume jewellery, German cameras, Scottish tweeds, and various spirits and liqueurs. Bermuda-made articles include handicrafts, pottery, cedar ware, fashions, records and paintings by local artists. Antique shops may have the odd good bargain and shops in the countryside offer many souvenirs. Bathing suits, sports clothes and sun straws are other good buys. There is no sales tax or VAT. **Shopping hours:** 0900-1700 Monday to Saturday, with some closing early on Thursdays.
SPORT: Golf: There are eight 18-hole courses, including the *Mid-Ocean Club*, which is world-renowned for its challenge and beauty, and *Port Royal*, situated in beautiful oceanside terrain. There is also one 9-hole layout. For information on Amateur, Professional, and Pro-Am tournaments, write to the Bermuda Golf Association, PO Box 433, Hamilton, Bermuda. **Tennis:** There are almost 100 courts on the island, with a variety of surfaces. Most of the larger Bermuda hotels have their own courts, many of them floodlit for night play. Tournaments are held all year round and several are open to visitors. For information, write to the Bermuda Lawn Tennis Association, PO Box 341, Hamilton, Bermuda. **Swimming:** Bermuda's most famous beaches lie along the island's southern edge. Some of the most beautiful are at Warwick Long Bay, Stonehole, Chaplin and Horseshoe Bay. **Snorkelling and scuba:** Visibility under water is often as much as 200ft in any direction. Experienced scuba divers can go below for a historic 'tour' of old wrecks, cannons and other remnants of past disasters on the reefs. All equipment necessary is easy to hire – please note, however, that spear guns are not allowed. **Fishing:** Bermuda is one of the world's finest fishing centres, especially for light-tackle fishing. Equipment may be rented for shore fishing and there are charter boats for reef and deep-sea fishing. For deep-sea aficionados, wahoo, amberjack, marlin and allison tuna abound. On the reefs, there are amberjack, great barracuda, grey snapper and yellowtail. Shore fisherman can test their skills on bonefish and pompano. The best fishing is during the months from May to November, when trophies are awarded. **Sailing:** The Blue Water Cruising Race, from Marion Massachusetts to Bermuda, takes place in June bi-annually, in odd numbered years. The Newport to Bermuda Ocean Yacht Race is also held bi-annually, in even numbered years. This world-famous June Blue-Water Classic (fondly referred to as the 'Thrash to the Onion Patch') attracts scores of the finest racing craft afloat. The week-long festivities which follow the arrival of the boats are held at the Royal Bermuda Yacht Club. In August the 'Non-Mariners Race' is held. Sailboats and skippers are available for hire from 'Sail Yourself' charter agencies. **Cricket:** The annual Cup Match, an island-wide, 2-day public holiday, is held once a year, when the St George's and Somerset Cricket Clubs vie for the Championship Cup.
SPECIAL EVENTS: Mar '93 *Annual Street Event*, Hamilton. **Apr** *Easter Rugby Classic; Peppercorn Ceremony*, St George; *Agricultural Show*. **May** *Invitational International Race Week; Bermuda Heritage Month*. **Jun 21** *Queen's Birthday Parade*. **Jul 29-30** *Cup Match Cricket Festival*. **Aug/Sep** *Bermuda Hockey Festival*. **Sep/Oct** *Annual Bermuda Triathlon*.
For full details of special events in 1993/94 contact Bermuda Tourism.
SOCIAL CONVENTIONS: Many of these are British influenced, and there is a very English 'feel' to the islands. It is quite customary to politely greet people on the street, even if they are strangers. Casual wear is acceptable in most places during the day, but beachwear should be confined to the beach. Almost all hotels and restaurants require a jacket and tie in the evenings; check dress requirements in advance. Non-smoking areas will be marked. **Tipping:** When not included in the bill, 15% generally for most services. Hotels and guest-houses add a set amount per person in lieu of tips to the bill.

BUSINESS PROFILE

ECONOMY: Bermuda's economy is dominated by two industries: tourism and international financial services, which account for approximately 55% and 40% of GDP respectively. A US Naval Air station accounts for most of the remainder. Offshore banking and related services have been the mainstay of the financial sector, although in recent years insurance has assumed a prominent position. Tax receipts from the 4500 offshore companies registered in Bermuda – which is by no means a tax haven despite the absence of an income tax – and customs duties, go some way to offset the island's large balance of payments deficit: imports at $500 million per annum are approximately five times the size of exports. The small manufacturing base in Bermuda is engaged in boat-building, ship repair, perfume and pharmaceuticals. There is some agriculture, concentrated in the growing of fruit and vegetables, but most of Bermuda's food is imported along with all its oil, machinery and most manufactured goods. Bermuda has recently established an important diamond market. The United States is the largest trading partner followed by Japan, Germany and the UK.
BUSINESS: Lightweight suits or shirt and tie are acceptable, as are Bermuda shorts. Visiting cards and occasionally letters of introduction are used. Codes of practice are similar to those in the UK. **Office hours:** 0900-1700 Monday to Friday.
COMMERCIAL INFORMATION: The following organisation can offer advice: Bermuda Chamber of Commerce, Front Street, PO Box HM 655, Hamilton HM CX. Tel: (295) 4201. Fax: (292) 5779.
CONFERENCES/CONVENTIONS: The Bermuda Department of Tourism (address at top of entry) can give information, including advice on customs arrangements for the speedy handling of materials. The Chamber of Commerce can also offer assistance; *Special Groups and Incentive Services* (published by the Department of Tourism) is a list of members' services available to organisers.

HISTORY & GOVERNMENT

HISTORY: Bermuda was first discovered in 1503 by Juan de Bermudez, the Spanish mariner and was claimed in England's name by Sir George Somers in July 1609. After colonisation, the islands prospered and have continued to do so almost continuously ever since. The tourist industry, catering particularly for the American market, began in Victorian times. Bermuda is the oldest British colony and there are still traces of British culture and customs in almost every aspect of life on the islands. Under the present constitution, which came into force in 1968, the island was granted internal self-government. Bermudan political life revolves around two main political parties: the Progressive Labour Party (PLP), which has close links to the influential trades union movement, and the United Bermuda Party (UBP), dominated by professional and business interests. The UBP has won every election since independence, most recently in 1989 when the UBP took 22 of the national assembly's 40 seats against 15 for the PLP. The current Premier, Sir John Swan, took over the leadership of the UBP in 1982. The Government's principal task at present is to guide the island through an unprecedented recession which saw a drop in GDP of 1% in the last fiscal year. Although independence is seen as inevitable there is little internal pressure for it; indeed, the bulk of the islanders appear to be unenthusastic.
GOVERNMENT: Bermuda is a British Crown Colony. Its bicameral legislature – the Senate with 11 appointed members and the 40-member House of Assembly, elected by universal adult suffrage for a 5-year term – is responsible for most internal affairs, but foreign policy and security matters are decided by the Governor (currently Sir Desmond Langley), who is appointed by and represents the British monarch. He in turn appoints the majority leader in the House of Assembly as Premier; the latter appoints the Cabinet.

CLIMATE

Semi-tropical, with no wet season. The Gulf Stream which flows between Bermuda and the North American continent keeps the climate temperate. A change of seasons comes during mid-November to mid-December, and from late March through April. Either spring or summer weather may occur and visitors should be prepared for both. Showers may be heavy at times but occur mainly at night. Summer temperatures prevail from May to mid-November with the warmest weather in July, August and September – this period is occasionally followed by high winds.
Required clothing: Lightweight cottons and linens. Light waterproofs or umbrella are advisable and warmer clothes for cooler months.

HAMILTON Bermuda (46m)

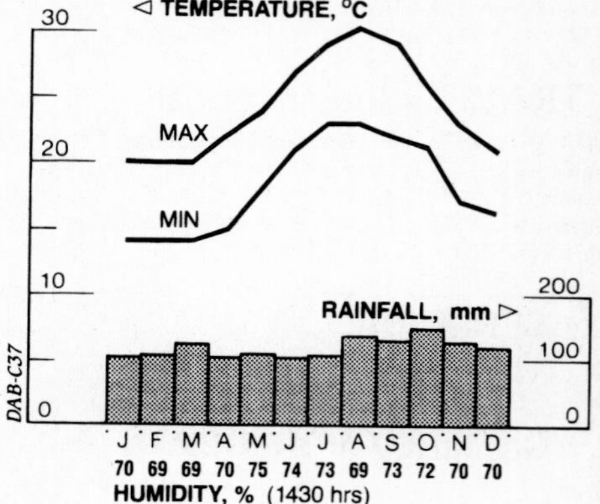

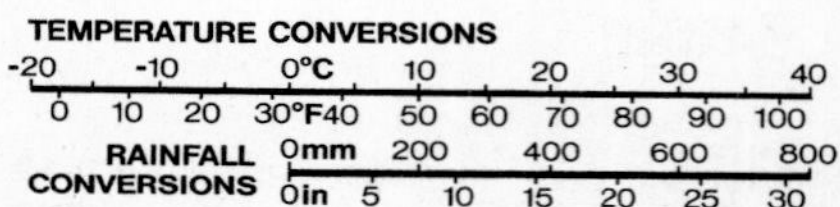

BHUTAN

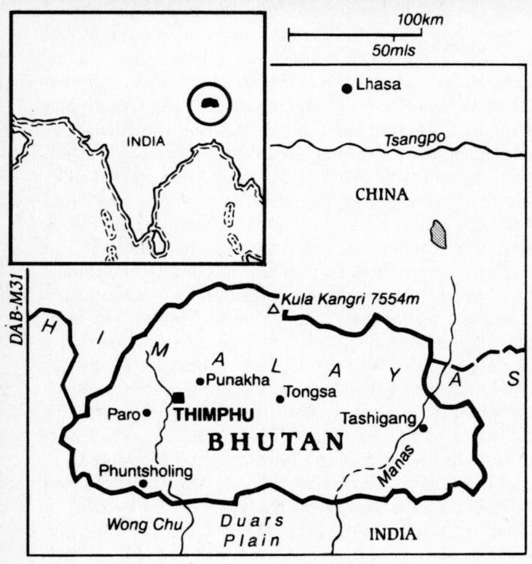

Location: Indian sub-continent; on border between Assam (northeast India) and China.

Bhutan Tourism Corporation Ltd (BTCL)
PO Box 159
Thimphu, Bhutan
Tel: 22647 *or* 23514/6/7. Fax: 24045 *or* 23517. Telex: 890217.
Royal Bhutanese Embassy
Chandragupta Marg
Chanakyapuri
New Delhi 110 021
India
Tel: (11) 609217. Telex: 3162263.
Embassy of India
India House Estate
Lungtenzampa
Thimpu, Bhutan
Tel: 22162. Fax: 23195. Telex: 890211.

AREA: 46,500 sq km (17,954 sq miles).
POPULATION: 1,375,400 (1988 estimate).
POPULATION DENSITY: 29.6 per sq km.
CAPITAL: Thimphu. **Population:** 15,000 (1987 estimate).
GEOGRAPHY: Bhutan is located in the eastern Himalayas, bordered to the north by China and to the south, east and west by India. The altitude varies from 300m (1000ft) in the narrow lowland region to 7000m (22,000ft) in the Himalayan plateau in the north, and there are three distinct climatic regions. The foothills are tropical and home to deer, lion, leopards and the rare golden monkey as well as much tropical vegetation including many species of wild orchids. The Inner Himalaya region is temperate; wildlife includes bear, boar and sambar and the area is rich in deciduous forests. The High Himalaya region is very thinly populated, but the steep mountain slopes are the home of many species of animals including snow leopards and musk deer.
LANGUAGE: Dzongkha is the official language. A large number of dialects are spoken, due to the physical isolation of many villages. Sharchop Kha, from eastern Bhutan, is the most widely spoken. Nepalese is common in the south of the country. English has been the language of educational instruction since 1964 and is widely spoken.
RELIGION: Mahayana Buddhism is the state religion; the majority of Bhutanese people follow the Drukpa school of the Kagyupa sect. Nepalis, who make up about 25% of the population, are Hindu.
TIME: GMT + 6.
ELECTRICITY: 220 volts AC, 50Hz.
COMMUNICATIONS: Telephone: Services are restricted to the main centres. All calls must go through the international operator. **Telex:** Services are available in main centres, but are liable to disruption. **Post:** Airmail letters to Bhutan can take up to two weeks. Mail from Bhutan is liable to disruption, although this is due not to the inefficiency of the service but rather to the highly-prized nature of Bhutanese stamps which often results in their being steamed off the envelopes en route. **Press:** There are very few papers, but *Kuensel*, a government news bulletin, is published weekly in English.
BBC World Service and Voice of America frequencies: From time to time these change. See the section *How to Use this Book* for more information.

BBC:				
MHz	17.79	15.31	11.75	9.740
Voice of America:				
MHz	17.74	15.40	11.71	7.125

PASSPORT/VISA

Regulations and requirements may be subject to change at short notice, and you are advised to contact the appropriate diplomatic or consular authority before finalising travel arrangements. Details of these may be found at the head of this country's entry. Any numbers in the chart refer to the footnotes below.

	Passport Required?	Visa Required?	Return Ticket Required?
Full British	Yes	Yes	Yes
BVP	Not valid	-	-
Australian	Yes	Yes	Yes
Canadian	Yes	Yes	Yes
USA	Yes	Yes	Yes
Other EC	Yes	Yes	Yes
Japanese	Yes	Yes	Yes

Note: All tours are organised by Bhutan Tourism Corporation Ltd (BTCL).
PASSPORTS: Valid passport required by all.
British Visitors Passport: Not accepted.
VISAS: Required by all.
Note: As the only way to enter the country is via India, all travellers must ensure that they have the correct documentation for transiting that country. This will include a double entry visa; a special permit if travelling on the Bagdora–Phuntsoling route; and a special permit if a visit to the Manas Game Sanctuary is planned. Please consult the Passport/Visa section for the entry on India below. Visitors are also advised to contact the Government of India Tourist Office to check exactly what special permits or other documents may be necessary as these regulations are subject to change at short notice. In recent years access to Bhutan has become more difficult, so the Bhutan Tourism Corporation Ltd (BTCL) should also be contacted.
Application to: Visas must be obtained by postal application to the Bhutan Tourism Corporation at least ten weeks in advance. The fee is US$20 (payable in any hard currency); visas will be issued on arrival in Bhutan where the visitor will be met. Application forms may be obtained from the BTCL who should be contacted direct. For addresses, see top of entry.
Working days required: Applications should be made at least ten weeks in advance of the intended date of departure.

MONEY

Currency: Ngultrum (Nu) = 100 chetrums (Ch). The Ngultrum is pegged to the Indian Rupee (which is also acccepted as legal tender). Notes appear in denominations Nu100, 50, 20, 10, 5, 2 and 1. Coins are in denominations of Nu1, and 50, 25, 10 and 5 chetrums.
Credit cards: American Express and Diners Club have very limited acceptability. Check with credit card company for details of merchant acceptability and other services which may be available.
Exchange rate indicators: The following figures are included as a guide to the movements of the Ngultrum/Indian Rupee against Sterling and the US Dollar.

Date:	Oct '89	Oct '90	Oct '91	Oct '92
£1.00	26.74	35.00	44.70	45.00
$1.00	16.93	17.92	25.75	28.35

Currency restrictions: None, but foreign currency must be declared on arrival.

DUTY FREE

The following goods may be taken into Bhutan by travellers aged 17 years or over without incurring customs duty:
200 cigarettes or 50 cigars or 250g of tobacco;
Up to 0.95 litres of spirits;
250ml of toilet water.
Prohibited goods: Narcotics, plants, gold and silver bullion, and obsolete currency. The export of antiques, religious objects, manuscripts, images and anthropological materials is strictly prohibited.

PUBLIC HOLIDAYS

Public holidays observed in Bhutan are as follows:
May '93 Wesak/Buddha Day. **Sep/Oct** Thimphu Tsechu. **Nov 11** Birthday of HM Jigme Singye Wangchuck. **Dec 17** National Day of Bhutan. **May '94** Wesak/Buddha Day.
Note: Buddhist festivals are declared according to local astronomical observations and it is only possible to forecast the month of their occurrence.

HEALTH

Regulations and requirements may be subject to change at short notice, and you are advised to contact your doctor well in advance of your intended date of departure. Any numbers in the chart refer to the footnotes below.

	Special Precautions?	Certificate Required?
Yellow Fever	Yes	1
Cholera	Yes	2
Typhoid & Polio	Yes	-
Malaria	3	-
Food & Drink	4	-

[1]: Vaccination certificate required if coming from an infected area.
[2]: Following WHO guidelines issued in 1973, a cholera vaccination certificate is no longer a condition of entry to Bhutan. However, cholera is a serious risk in this country and precautions are essential. Up-to-date advice should be sought before deciding whether these precautions should include vaccination as medical opinion is divided over its effectiveness. See the *Health* section at the back of this book.
[3]: Malaria risk exists throughout the year in the southern belt of the following five districts: Chirang, Gaylegphug, Samchi, Samdrupjongkhar and Shemgang. Resistance to chloroquine and sulfadoxine/pyrimethane has been reported in the malignant *falciparum* form of the disease.
[4]: All water should be regarded as being potentially contaminated. Water used for drinking, brushing teeth or making ice should have first been boiled or otherwise sterilised. Milk is unpasteurised and should be boiled.

BHUTAN | **HEALTH REGULATIONS** | **VISA REGULATIONS** | Code-Link

GALILEO/WORLDSPAN

TI-DFT/PBH/HE

TI-DFT/PBH/VI

SABRE

TIDFT/PBH/HE

TIDFT/PBH/VI

To access this information on your CRS, swipe the barcode with a light pen or type in the text under the barcode. For more information, see the introduction *How to Use This Book.*

Powdered or tinned milk is available and is advised, but make sure that it is reconstituted with pure water. Avoid all dairy products. Only eat well-cooked meat and fish, preferably served hot. Pork, salad and mayonnnaise may carry increased risk. Vegetables should be cooked and fruit peeled.
Rabies is present. For those at high risk, vaccination should be considered. If you are bitten abroad seek medical advice without delay. For more information consult the *Health* section at the back of the book. *Meningitis* is a sporadic risk and vaccination is advised.
Health care: Full medical insurance is advised. Medical facilities are good but scarce.

TRAVEL - International

AIR: The national airline is *Druk-Air Corporation (Royal Bhutan Airlines)*. There are two ways of travelling to Bhutan: By air to Delhi (see the *Travel* section for India below) and then by *Indian Airlines* to Bagdogra – from here it is a 3-hour drive to the border town of Phuntsholing; *or*
by air to Calcutta (see the *Travel* section for India below) and then by *Druk-Air* to Paro, a small town near Thimphu in western Bhutan.
RAIL: The nearest railhead is Siliguri (India).

TRAVEL - Internal

RAIL: There are no internal services.
ROAD: The country has a fairly good internal road network with 2280km (1417 miles) of surfaced road. The main routes run north from Phuntsholing to the western and central regions of Paro and Thimphu, and east–west across the Pele La Pass linking the valleys of the eastern region. The northern regions of the High Himalayas have no roads. **Buses:** Those services which were formerly government-owned are now privately run, though yaks, ponies and mules are the chief forms of transportation.**Documentation:** International Driving Permit is required.
JOURNEY TIMES: The following chart gives approximate journey times (in hours and minutes) from Thimphu to other major towns:

	Road
Paro	1.30
P'sholing	6.00
W'phodrang	2.15
Punakha	2.30
Bumthang	8.45
Tongsa	6.45

ACCOMMODATION

There are comfortable hotels, cottages and guest-houses (many constructed to accommodate foreign guests during the coronation of the present King in 1974). Hotels have hot and cold running water, electricity and room telephones.

RESORTS & EXCURSIONS

Note: Many areas have now been closed to tourists. Visitors should check with the Bhutan Tourism Corporation.
Thimphu, the capital of Bhutan, lies at a height of over 2400m (8000ft) in the fertile valley transversed by the *Wangchuk River*. In many ways it resembles a large, widely dispersed village rather than a capital. The *Tashichhodzong* is the main administrative and religious centre of the country. It was rebuilt in 1961 after being damaged by fire and earthquake, its hundred-odd spacious rooms house all the government departments and ministries, the *National Assembly Hall*, the *Throne Room of the King* and the country's largest monastery, the summer headquarters of the Je Khempo and 2000 of his monks. The yearly *Thimphu Festival* is held in the courtyard directly in front of the National Assembly Hall. The *Handicraft Emporium* displays a wide assortment of beautifully hand-woven and crafted products which make great souvenirs.
The small town of **Phuntsholing** is a commercial and industrial centre as well as the gateway to Bhutan. A short walk from the hotel is the *Kharbandi Monastery*. Bhutan is well known for its stamps, and the best place to buy them is in Phuntsholing where the *Philatelic Office of Bhutan* has its headquarters. The first and only department store of Bhutan is also in Phuntsholing. **Punakha** is the former capital of the country; situated at a lower altitude it enjoys a comparatively benign climate. The valley contains many sacred temples, including *Machin Lhakhag* where the remains of Ngawang Namgyal, the unifier of Bhutan, are entombed.
Tongsa is the ancestral home of the Royal family. The dzong here commands a superb view of the river valley and contains a magnificent collection of rhino horn sculptures. The **Manas Game Sanctuary** in southeast Bhutan is the home of a wide variety of wildlife, and should not be missed.
Other attractions include: a visit to the *Paro Valley* where the *Taktsang* (Tiger's Nest) *Monastery* clings dizzily to the face of a 900m (2952ft) precipice; the *Drukgyul Dzong* further up the Paro Valley (now in ruins after the earthquake in 1954), which protected Bhutan against numerous Tibetan invasions; the *Paro Watchtower*, which now houses the *National Museum of Bhutan*; the temperate *Punakha Valley* which houses many sacred temples including the *Machin Lhakhag* in the Punakaha Dzong; the 3100m-(10,170ft) high *Dochu La Pass* which commands a breathtaking view of the eastern Himalayan chain; *Bumthang*, starting point for 4- and 7-day cultural tours through the rural villages; and the district of *Wangdiphodrang* known for its slate carving and bamboo weaving.

SOCIAL PROFILE

SHOPPING: Markets are held regularly, generally on a Sunday, and are a rich source of local clothing and jewellery, as well as foodstuffs. The handicraft emporium on the main street in the capital is open daily except Sunday and offers a magnificent assortment of handwoven and handcrafted goods. The Motithang Hotel in Thimphu recently opened a souvenir shop. Silversmiths and goldsmiths in the Thimphu Valley are able to make handicrafted articles to order.**Shopping hours:** 0900-2100 Monday to Sunday.
SPORT: Archery competitions are held frequently, and provide an opportunity for the visitor to appreciate the skills of the Bhutanese in their national sport. **Trekking:** Much of the pleasure of visiting Bhutan is enjoying the breathtaking scenery by trekking around the valleys and the mountain gorges. **Fishing:** The rivers offer superb trout fishing. **Wildlife viewing:** The country boasts over 320 varieties of birds, including the rare black-necked crane. The Manas Game Sanctuary has a wide variety of wildlife (a special permit is necessary). Other sports include **squash**, **golf**, **badminton**, **football**, **basketball** and **volleyball**.
SPECIAL EVENTS: Buddhist festivals, full of dancing and ritual, generally centre on Dzongs (fortified monasteries), the most famous of which is at Paro. More than 40 religious or folk dances are performed by the monks recounting tales of Buddhist history and myth. As the dates for these festivals are based on the Bhutanese lunar calendar, it is difficult to predict them precisely. They are, however, numerous, and visitors should be able to witness and enjoy at least one of these extremely colourful events during their stay.
SOCIAL CONVENTIONS: The lifestyle, manners and customs of the Bhutanese are in many respects unique to the area. The strongest influence on social conventions is the country's state religion, and everywhere one can see the reminders of Buddhism and the original religion of Tibet, Bonism. There are no rigid clan systems, and equal rights exist between men and women. The majority of the Bhutanese live an agrarian lifestyle. The political leaders of the country have historically also been religious leaders (see *Government* section below). For years the country has deliberately isolated itself from visitors, and has only recently opened up to the outside world, a policy which is now to some extent being reversed.
Tipping: Not widely practised.

BUSINESS PROFILE

ECONOMY: Despite being one of the very poorest countries in the world (UN sources list Bhutan as the second poorest country in the world next to Cambodia), there is no unemployment and no starvation. Almost all the working population is involved with agriculture, forestry or fishing. The economy is therefore a mainly subsistence one and dependent on clement conditions. The failure of the 1983 rains, for example, caused a serious decline in production. Since then it has recovered and steadily increased annually, as has the production of cereals and timber – over 70% of the land area is afforested. There is some small scale industry, contributing no more than 5% of gross domestic product, which produces textiles, soap, matches, candles and carpets. The Sixth Plan, covering the years 1987-92, is concentrating on export industries and areas such as power generation which will help these to develop. Tourism and stamps are the main sources of foreign exchange. India accounts for around 90% of both imports and exports.
BUSINESS: Lightweight or tropical suit or a shirt and tie for the south. In the capital, a full business suit and tie are recommended. The best time to visit is October and November.
COMMERCIAL INFORMATION: The following organisation can offer advice: Bhutan Chamber of Commerce and Industry, PO Box 147, Thimphu, Bhutan. Tel: 22742. Telex: 890229.

HISTORY & GOVERNMENT

HISTORY: Existing archives trace Bhutanese history back to AD450 but many of the intervening events remain a mystery. Bhutan has never been conquered or ruled by another foreign power. Britain first came into formal contact with Bhutan in the 18th century, when the East India Company made a treaty with the King in 1774, and again in 1910, when the British government took control of Bhutan's foreign affairs, while agreeing not to interfere with the internal ruling. In 1947 and 1949 agreements were reached with India by which the Indian government advised Bhutan in external relations. Trade agreements with the Indians, essential to sustain the Bhutanese economy, have been the subject of regular rounds of negotiation. The most recent pact, concluded in Thimphu in 1990, was accompanied by diplomatic progress on the still-disputed border between the two countries. Despite its close relations with Delhi, Bhutan has occasionally switched its support to its other great neighbour, China. This has been particularly noticeable in international fora, such as the Non-Aligned Movement and the UN General Assembly. Relations with China have been dominated over the years by the issue of Tibet: thousands of refugees entered Bhutan after the Chinese occupation of Tibet in 1959 and the country has since become a centre for exile politics and consequently of Chinese intelligence activity. Bhutan's small security outfit has occasionally taken measures to prevent – as it sees it – the situation from escalating beyond control. These have included the controversial resettlement of exile communities. In the late 1980s the regime's domestic concerns focussed upon the growing opposition of the Bhutan People's Party, an illegal organisation formed from ethnic Nepalis (who with the indigenous Drupka comprise the country's two main ethnic groups) which has campaigned for greater democracy through demonstrations and occasional acts of violence. The monarch, Jigme Singye Wangchuck, has so far relied on repressive measures to bolster his regime, but may eventually need to follow the political route taken by Nepal itself – where elections were held in 1990 – or risk serious political disturbances. He shows little sign of doing so and although unrest continues, it is as yet far short of seriously threatening the regime. The King would be unwise, however, to interpret this as justifying indefinite inertia on the political front.
CLIMATE: There are four distinct seasons similiar in their divisions to those of western Europe. The Monsoon occurs between June and August when the temperature is normally between 46°-69°F. Temperatures drop dramatically with increases in altitude. Days are usually very pleasant (average about 50°F) with clear skies and sunshine. Nights are cold and require heavy woollen clothing, particularly in winter. Generally October, November and April to mid-June are the best times to visit – rainfall is at a minimum and temperatures are conducive to active days of sightseeing. The foothills are also very pleasant during the winter.
Required clothing: Lightweight cottons in the foothills, also linens and waterproof gear, light sweaters and jackets for the evenings. Upland areas: woollens for evenings, particularly during the winter months.

THIMPHU Bhutan (2987m)

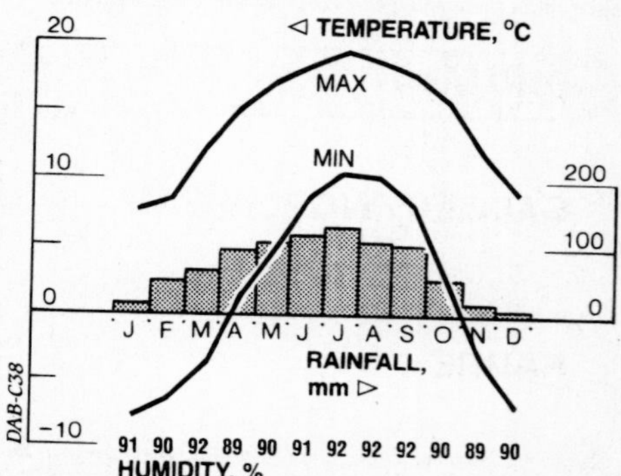

BOLIVIA

Location: South America.

Dirección Nacional de Turismo
Calle Mercado 1328
Casilla 1868
La Paz, Bolivia
Tel: (2) 367 463. Fax: (2) 374 630. Telex: 2534.

Embassy and Consulate of the Republic of Bolivia
106 Eaton Square
London
SW1W 9AD
Tel: (071) 235 2257 *or* (071) 235 4255 (visa enquiries). Fax: (071) 235 1286. Telex: 918885. Embassy opening hours (enquiries): 1000-1300 and 1500-1700 Monday to Friday. Consulate opening hours (visa enquiries): 1000-1300 Monday to Thursday.

British Embassy
Avenida Arce 2732-2754
Casilla 694
La Paz, Bolivia
Tel: (2) 391 063, 329 301 *or* 329 401. Fax: (2) 391 063. Telex: 2341.

Embassy of the Republic of Bolivia
3014 Massachusetts Avenue, NW
Washington, DC
20008
Tel: (202) 483 4410. Fax: (202) 328 3712. Telex: 440049.

Embassy of the United States of America
Casilla 425
Edificio Banco Popular del Perú
Calle Colón 290
La Paz, Bolivia
Tel: (2) 350120. Fax: (2) 359875. Telex: 3268.

Bolivian Embassy
Suite 504
130 Albert Street
Ottawa, Ontario
K1P 5G4
Tel: (613) 236 8237.

Bolivia Instituto Boliviano de Turismo
11231 Jasper Avenue
Edmonton, Alberta T5K OL5
Tel: (403) 488 1525. Fax: (403) 488 0350.

AREA: 1,084,391 sq km (424,164 sq miles).
POPULATION: 7,400,000 (1990 estimate).
POPULATION DENSITY: 6.7 per sq km.
CAPITAL: Administrative: La Paz. **Population:** 1,049,800 (1988). **Legal:** Sucre. **Population:** 95,635 (1988).
GEOGRAPHY: Bolivia is a landlocked country bordered by Peru to the northwest, Brazil to the north and east, Paraguay to the southeast, Argentina to the south, and Peru and Chile to the west. There are three main areas: The first is a high plateau known as the 'Altiplano', a largely barren region lying about 4000m (13,000ft) above sea level. It comprises 10% of the country's area and 70% of the population, nearly one-third of whom are urban dwellers. The second area is a fertile valley situated 1800m to 2700m above sea level. The third area comprises the lowland tropics which stretch down to the frontiers with Brazil, Argentina and Paraguay, taking up some 70% of the land area. Rainfall in this region is high, and the climate is hot.
LANGUAGE: The official language is Spanish. However, the Indians of the Altiplano speak Aymará and, elsewhere, Quechua, the Inca tongue, is spoken. English is also spoken by a small number of officials and businessmen in commercial centres.
RELIGION: Roman Catholic with Protestant minority.
TIME: GMT - 4.
ELECTRICITY: Generally 110/220 volts AC, 50Hz (110/200 volts AC, 50Hz in La Paz). Most houses and hotels have 2-pin sockets for both electrical currents. Variations from this occur in some places.
COMMUNICATIONS: Telephone: IDD is available. Country code: 591. **Fax:** Services available. **Telex/telegram:** Telex facilities are available at La Paz telecommunications centre and some hotels. Telegram facilities are available from the West Coast of America Telegraph Company. Head office at Edificio Electra, Calle Mercado 1150, La Paz. **Post:** Airmail to Europe takes three to four days. A *Poste Restante* service is available. **Press:** Spanish Language only. The main papers published in La Paz are *Presencia*, *Hoy*, *El Diario* and *Ultima Hora*.
BBC World Service and Voice of America frequencies: From time to time these change. See the section *How to Use this Book* for more information.

BBC:				
MHz	17.84	15.22	9.915	9.590
Voice of America:				
MHz	15.21	11.58	9.775	5.995

PASSPORT/VISA

Regulations and requirements may be subject to change at short notice, and you are advised to contact the appropriate diplomatic or consular authority before finalising travel arrangements. Details of these may be found at the head of this country's entry. Any numbers in the chart refer to the footnotes below.

	Passport Required?	Visa Required?	Return Ticket Required?
Full British	Yes	No	Yes
BVP	Not Valid	-	-
Australian	Yes	Yes	Yes
Canadian	Yes	Yes	Yes
USA	Yes	Yes	Yes
Other EC	Yes	1	Yes
Japanese	Yes	Yes	Yes

PASSPORTS: Valid passport required by all.
British Visitors Passport: Not acceptable.
VISAS: Required by all for touristic purposes except:
(a) [1] nationals of EC countries (with the exception of Belgium, France, Greece, Luxembourg, The Netherlands and Portugal who *do* need visas);
(b) nationals of Argentina, Austria, Ecuador, Finland, Iceland, Ireland, Israel, Norway, Sweden, Switzerland, Uruguay, USA and Vatican City.
Types of visa: Tourist, Business (required by all nationals) and Transit (not required by passengers with onward tickets who do not leave the airport or stay overnight). Prices are available on application.
Validity: Tourist visas are valid for 30 days from the date of entry; Business visas for one year, multiple entry.
Application to: Consulate (or Consular Section at Embassy). For addresses, see top of entry.
Application requirements: (a) Photograph (for Business visas a letter from subject's company should accompany application for visa). (b) Completed application form. (c) Passport with remaining validity of at least six months. (d) Fee.
Working days required: Tourist visas are issued immediately; for Business visas allow 7 days.
Temporary residence: Enquire at Bolivian Consulate.

MONEY

Currency: 1 Boliviano (B) = 100 centavos. The Boliviano is tied to the US Dollar. Notes are in denominations of 200, 100, 50, 20, 10, 5 and 2 Bolivianos. Coins are in denominations of 50, 20, 10, 5 and 2 centavos and 1 Boliviano.
Note: The Bolivian peso ceased to be legal tender in 1990.
Currency exchange: Money is usually changed in hotels and cambios. Sterling *cannot* be changed. The decline in inflation over the past few years has been so dramatic that the black market transactions have been virtually wiped out.
Credit cards: Access/Mastercard, Diners Club, Visa and American Express have very limited acceptance. Check with your credit card company for details of merchant acceptability and other services which may be available.
Travellers cheques: United States travellers cheques are probably the best form of currency to take to Bolivia at the present time. Sterling cheques *cannot* be exchanged.
Exchange rate indicators: The following figures are included as a guide to the movements of the Boliviano against Sterling and the US Dollar:

Date:	Nov '89	Oct '90	Oct '91	Oct '92
£1.00=	4.52	6.38	6.35	6.36
$1.00=	2.86	3.26	3.65	4.01

Currency restrictions: There are no restrictions on the import or the export of either local or foreign currency.
Banking hours: 0830-1130 and 1430-1830 Monday to Friday.

DUTY FREE

The following goods may be taken into Bolivia without incurring customs duty:
200 cigarettes and 50 cigars and 0.5kg of tobacco;
1 opened bottle of alcohol.
Note: Cameras must be declared.

PUBLIC HOLIDAYS

Public holidays observed in Bolivia are as follows:
Apr 9 '93 Good Friday. **May 1** Labour Day. **Jun 10** Corpus Christi. **Aug 6** Independence Day. **Nov 1** All Saints' Day. **Dec 25** Christmas Day. **Jan 1 '94** New Year's Day. **Feb/Mar** Two-day Carnival.
Note: There are other additional holidays celebrated in individual provinces and towns. For further details contact the Embassy or Tourist Board.

BOLIVIA | **HEALTH REGULATIONS** | **VISA REGULATIONS** | Code-Link

GALILEO/WORLDSPAN

TI-DFT/LPB/HE

TI-DFT/LPB/VI

SABRE

TIDFT/LPB/HE

TIDFT/LPB/VI

To access this information on your CRS, swipe the barcode with a light pen or type in the text under the barcode. For more information, see the introduction *How to Use This Book*.

HEALTH

Regulations and requirements may be subject to change at short notice, and you are advised to contact your doctor well in advance of your intended date of departure. Any numbers in the chart refer to the footnotes below.

	Special Precautions?	Certificate Required?
Yellow Fever	Yes	1
Cholera	No	No
Typhoid & Polio	Yes	-
Malaria	2	-
Food & Drink	3	-

[1]: A yellow fever vaccination certificate is required from persons travelling to countries with infected local areas and from persons coming from such countries. All travellers going to Beni or Santa Cruz de la Sierra, Bolivia, must be in possession of a valid yellow fever certificate.
[2]: Malaria risk exists throughout the year below 2500m, excluding urban areas, Oruro Department, the provinces of Ingavi, Los Andes, Omasuyos, Pacajes (La Paz Dept), and Southern and Central Potosí Department. Resistance to chloroquine is reported. The disease occurs predominantly in the benign *vivax* form.
[3]: Water used for drinking, brushing teeth or making ice should have first been boiled or otherwise sterilised. Milk is unpasteurised and should be boiled. Powdered or tinned milk is available and is advised, but make sure that it is reconstituted with pure water. Avoid all dairy products which are likely to have been made from local milk. Only eat well-cooked meat and fish, preferably served hot. Pork, salad and mayonnaise may carry increased risk. Vegetables should be cooked and fruit peeled.
Health care: Medical insurance is strongly recommended. All travellers, but especially those with heart conditions, should allow time to acclimatise to the high altitude of La Paz. In case of a medical emergency, La Paz has a good American clinic.

TRAVEL - International

AIR: The national airline is *Lloyd Aéreo Boliviano (LAB)*.
Approximate flight times: From *London* to La Paz is 17 hours and to Santa Cruz is 17 hours.
International airports: *La Paz (LPB)* (El Alto) is 14km (8.5 miles) from La Paz; and *Santa Cruz* (Viru-Viru) is 16km (10 miles) from the centre of Santa Cruz. For passengers arriving at La Paz, *LAB* provide a 24-hour coach service to the city every five minutes. The journey takes 20 minutes. Bus Z also goes to the city from 0600 to 2200, but the journey takes 60 minutes. Taxis are also available to the city. Equivalent services exist for Santa Cruz. Restaurant and duty-free facilities are available at both airports.
Departure tax: US$15 is levied on all international departures. *This cannot be paid in Bolivian currency.*
SEA: Although it recently joined the International Maritime Organisation, Bolivia is wholly landlocked. However, European and US steamship companies serve the Atlantic and Pacific Coasts, navigating the Panama Canal, from which it is possible to reach ports in Peru, Chile, Brazil, Paraguay and Argentina and from there rail connections to La Paz or Santa Cruz. The nearest seaport is Arica in the extreme north of Chile.
LAKE: Steamers cross the lake to the Peruvian port of Puno from Guaqui, the most important port on Lake Titicaca. Situated 90km (56 miles) from La Paz, it is accessible both by road and rail, though generally services are slow.
RAIL: There is a twice-weekly connection from La Paz to Buenos Aires, and a twice-monthly connection to Arica (Chile). There is no service to Brazil via the line to Corumba. There is also a weekly train to Calama (Chile) with bus connections to Antofagasta.
ROAD: The Pan-American Highway which links the Argentine Republic with Peru crosses Bolivian territory from the south to the northwest. Driving in the rainy season may be hazardous. During recent years, much attention has been given to new roads, and the principal highways are now well maintained.**Documentation:** An International Driving Permit is required. This can be issued by *Federación Inter-Americana de Touring y Automovil* on production of a British Licence, but it is wiser to obtain the International Permit before departure.

TRAVEL - Internal

AIR: Airlines operating internal flights are *LAB*, *TAM* (the army airline) and *Aero Xpress (AX)*. Because of the country's topography and tropical regions, air travel is the best method of transport. La Paz (El Alto), which is the highest airport in the world, and Santa Cruz (Viru Viru) are the chief internal airports. Airport taxes for internal flights vary but are usually no more than US$3; please check locally.
RIVER/LAKE: Passenger boats are operated between the various small islands on Lake Titicaca; most of them leave from Copacabana.
RAIL: Bolivia has 3538km (2199 miles) of track which goes to make up separate and unconnected networks in the eastern and western parts of the country. A daily through train or connection links La Paz and Cochabamba, with trains at least twice-weekly on other lines. Some trains have restaurant cars, but there are no sleeping-car services. The railways have recently renewed their rolling stock with Fiat railway carriages from Argentina. There are joint plans with the Brazilians to link Santa Cruz and Cochabamba.
ROAD: The internal road system covers 37,300km (23,178 miles). Work is in progress to improve the condition of major highways. See above for documentation requirements. **Car hire:** *Hertz* and local companies in La Paz. **Bus:** Long bus trips off the main routes can be erratic. **Taxi:** All have fixed rates and sharing taxis is a common practice. Tipping is not necessary.
URBAN: Bus services in La Paz are operated by a confederation of owner-operators. There are also some fixed route taxi 'Trufi' and 'Trufibus' systems which show coloured flags for particular routes. Fares are regulated.
JOURNEY TIMES: The following chart gives approximate journey times from La Paz (in hours and minutes) to other major cities/towns in Bolivia.

	Air	Road	Rail
Cochabamba	0.25	6.00	7.00
Santa Cruz	0.50	24.00	-
Tarija	1.00	18.00	-
Sucre	0.35	11.00	13.00
Potosi	0.40	12.00	12.00
Bemi	0.35	-	-

ACCOMMODATION

It is important to arrive in La Paz as early as possible in the day as accommodation, particularly at the cheaper end of the market, can be hard to find.
HOTELS: Bolivia has several deluxe and first-class hotels. Service charges and taxes amounting to 25-27% are added to bills. Rates are for room only, except where otherwise indicated. There is a wide range of cheap hotel accommodation available, generally of good value. Bolivia's hotel association is the Cámera Hotelera de Santa Cruz, Av. Irala 354. Tel: (3) 33159.
GUEST-HOUSES: Several pensions in La Paz, Cochabamba and Santa Cruz provide the tourist with reasonable comfort at a reasonable price.
CAMPING/CARAVANNING: There are few camping areas anywhere in South America. However, the adventurous traveller may often find adequate lodging for the small fee usually charged at most American or European camping grounds. Despite no formal organisation or marked zones, camping is possible in Bolivia. Mallasa, Valencia and Palca in the river gorge below the suburb of La Florida are recommended, also Chinguihue 10km (6 miles) from the city. Club Andino Boliviano (tel: 794 0160) hires equipment. For details contact the National Institute of Tourism.

RESORTS & EXCURSIONS

La Paz, the seat of national government, is situated 3632m (11,910ft) above sea level and is the world's highest capital city. Mount Illimani stands in the background. The city contains many museums and is well provided with modern and comfortable hotels. Nearby attractions include *Lake Titicaca*, the *Yungas valleys*, the *Chacaltaya* skiing resort and the exceptional rock formations in the Moon Valley.
Cochabamba, known as the garden city, is 2558m (8390ft) above sea level and boasts a long tradition of local culture and folklore.
The state of **Santa Cruz** is rich in natural resources; the city itself, despite considerable modernisation, still retains much of its colonial past. This region is also rich in tradition and folklore. There are abundant opportunities for fishing and hunting, and many natural bathing places. The area's rich cuisine is also to be sampled.
Potosí is known as the imperial city and is situated at the foot of the famous *Rich Mountain*, characteristic for its mineral wealth. In early colonial times, Potosí was the most important and highly populated city on the continent, and is now one of its greatest historical memorials. The 'House of Coins' is just one example of this.
Oruro is a traditional mining centre, and preserver of many relics of a colonial past. Every year one can witness one of the most extraordinary and faithful expressions of folklore in South America during the famous carnival (February/March).
Sucre, in the state of Chuquisaca, played an important part in the struggle for independence, and is rich in museums, libraries and historical archives. Among the most important are the *Cathedral Museum*, the *National Library*, the *Colonial Museum*, the *Anthropological Museum*, the *Natural History Museum* and the *Recoleta Convent*.
Tarija stands 1957m (6480ft) above sea level. The area enjoys an excellent climate, and is festive and hospitable. Graced with beautiful flowers and magnificent wines, Tarija is the ideal place for finding peace and quiet.
The states of **Beni** and **Pando**, situated in the heart of the Bolivian jungle, occupy a region which offers the visitor landscapes of warmth and colour. The 'Golden' Pantiti with many navigable rivers is a popular place for excursions by both land and water. Good hunting and fishing are also possible in the region. The major towns in the area are **Trinidad** and **Cobija.**

SOCIAL PROFILE

FOOD & DRINK: Bolivian food is distinctive and is generally good. National dishes include *empanada saltena* (a mixture of diced meat, chicken, chives, raisins, diced potatoes, hot sauce and pepper baked in dough), *lomo montado* (fried tenderloin steak with two fried eggs on top, rice and fried banana), *picante de pollo* (southern fried chicken, fried potatoes, rice, tossed salad with hot peppers), *chuno* (naturally freeze-dried potato used in soup called *chairo*) and *lechon al horno* (young roast pig served with sweet potato and fried plantains). International and local style restaurants are available in La Paz and other main towns. **Drink:** Bolivian beer, especially *cruzena*, is one of the best on the continent. *Chica* made from fermented cereals and corn is very strong. Mineral water and bottled drinks are available. Local bars are increasing in numbers and are unrestricted with no licensing hours.
NIGHTLIFE: La Paz has many nightclubs, which generally open around midnight. There are also numerous *whiskeria*, local bars. On Fridays and Saturdays there are folk music and dancing shows, which start late evening. Cochabamba and Santa Cruz have several discotheques.
SHOPPING: Special purchases include wood carvings, jewellery, llama and alpaca blankets, Indian handicrafts and gold and silver costume jewellery. **Shopping hours:** 0900-1200 and 1400-1800 Monday to Friday; 0900-1200 some Saturdays.
SPORT: Football is the most popular spectator sport. **Golf**, **mountain climbing** and **safaris** are available. The best months for **skiing** are April, May, September and October. Bolivia has the highest ski run in the world at 5486m (18,000ft) on Mount Chacaltaya. Bolivia also boasts some of the best **lake fishing** in the world, especially for trout.
SPECIAL EVENTS: The following list is a selection of some of the events celebrated in Bolivia in 1993-94. In many places a festival is associated with a local holiday. For further details consult the Embassy or Tourist Board.
Mar '93 *Pujllay Carnival*, Tarabuco. **May** *Fiesta de la Cruz* (Feast of the Cross), Achocalla and Copacabana. **May/Jun** *Gran Poder Festival*, La Paz. **Jun 24** *San Juan Carnival*, La Paz and many other cities and communities. **Jun 28-29** *San Pedro*, Achacachi, Curva, Carabuco, Tiquina and many other villages. **Jul 25** *The Feast of Santiago*. **Sep** *Festival of Madonna of Urkupina*, Cochambamba. **Late Jan '94** *The Alasitas Fair of Miniatures*, La Paz. **Feb 12** *Carnival*, Oruro.
SOCIAL CONVENTIONS: Normal social courtesies in most Bolivian families and respect for traditions should be observed. Remember to refer to rural Bolivians as *campesinos* rather than Indians, which is considered an insult. Western dress and diet are gradually being adopted by the *campesinos* (although further to the north great poverty remains); a suit and tie for men and dress for women should be worn for smart social occasions. Casual wear is otherwise suitable. Smoking is accepted except where indicated. **Tipping:** It is customary to add 10% as a tip to the 13% service charge added to hotel and restaurant bills. Porters also expect tips of B4 for each item of luggage.

BUSINESS PROFILE

ECONOMY: Bolivia has the second lowest per capita income in Latin America, despite having large mineral deposits of natural gas, petroleum, lead, antimony, tungsten, gold and silver. The most important mineral, however, is tin, of which Bolivia is one of the world's leading producers. Falling world prices and inherent economic difficulties throughout the 1980s resulted in a net fall in real incomes for most Bolivians. Agriculture is the other major employer, but suffers from relatively low productivity. During the early 1980s, Bolivia suffered extremely high inflation, vastly fluctuating exchange rates and an ever-worsening overseas debt. Since 1985, however, there has been a marked improvement in national economic performance. Trading prospects have improved as a result but continue to be hampered by poor communications. Oil and gas account for 60% of export earnings; minerals and coffee account for most of the rest. There is a substantial unregistered and illegal trade in coca, the plant source for cocaine, which provides a livelihood for many peasants, although the Government is now co-operating with the

United States in a major continent-wide campaign to eradicate it. Bolivia is a member of the Latin American Integration Association, the River Plate Basin Alliance and, most importantly, of the Andean Pact. Joint ventures through these various organisations, such as the gas pipeline to Brazil, seem to offer the best prospects for Bolivia's economic development. The country's largest trading partners are neighbouring Brazil, Argentina and Chile along with the US, and then Japan and the EC countries. Of the latter, Britain has one of smallest volumes of trade. To reverse this trend, the UK and Bolivia have signed a bilateral investment promotion and protection agreement.

BUSINESS: Suit or a shirt and tie should be worn. Prior appointments are not essential. **Office hours:** 0800-1200 and 1400-1800 Monday to Friday, 0900-1200 some Saturdays.

COMMERCIAL INFORMATION: The following organisation can offer advice: Cámara Nacional de Comercio, Casilla 7, Avenida Mariscal Santa Cruz 1392, La Paz, Bolivia. Tel: (2) 354 255. Fax: (2) 391 004. Telex: 2305.

HISTORY & GOVERNMENT

HISTORY: Bolivia was inhabited by the ancient Aymará civilization, who lived on Lake Titicaca. Later this civilization was conquered by the Incas, who were themselves conquered by the Spanish in 1538. Throughout the country's colonial history it was known as Upper Peru. In 1825 Simon Bolivar led the country to independence. Wars with three neighbouring countries followed (1879-83 War of the Pacific, against Peru and Chile, and the 1928 Chaco Wars against Paraguay), as a result of which Bolivia lost the strip of land leading to the coast. In 1953 Chile declared the port of Arica 'free' and has allowed Bolivia certain privileges in its use. This was not, however, the end of the issue. The continuing dispute brought a break in diplomatic relations in 1978 which was not healed until 1986 and the signing of a bilateral agreement pledging to improve political, social and economic links. Despite pressure from the Organisation of American States to allow Bolivia unimpeded access to the sea, Chile has refused to yield. The recent advent of a civilian government in Chile may offer better prospects for a settlement. Bolivia itself has, meanwhile, entered an unprecedented era of political stability, ending a record of military coups and recurrent internal strife which was little short of ludicrous: there were 192 coups in the 156 years from independence to 1981, an average of one every ten months. Much of the credit is due to President Victor Paz Estenssoro, who was elected in August 1985 at the head of a loose coalition of both left- and right-wing parties. By the time Paz Estenssoro ceded office in August 1989 to Jaime Paz Zamora, rampant hyper-inflation (an estimated 14, 000% in 1985) had been dramatically cut and, after initial unrest over the Government's strict austerity programme, the country had acquired a measure of political stability. The Government has attracted some domestic criticism for its participation in the US-sponsored 'war on drugs' in Latin America, but its dependency on American aid has secured its collaboration. The next round of national elections are due in 1993 and will be, in effect, a referendum on this aspect of government policy.

GOVERNMENT: The bicameral congress is the legislature, made up of the Senate and Chamber of Deputies, who are also elected by universal suffrage.

CLIMATE

Temperate climate but with wide differences between day and night. Wettest period is November to February. The northeast slopes of the Andes are semi-tropical. Visitors often find La Paz uncomfortable because of the thin air due to high altitude. The mountain areas can become very cold at night.

Required clothing: Lightweight linens with a raincoat. A light overcoat is necessary at night, particulaly in the Altiplano and the Puna.

LA PAZ Bolivia (3632m)

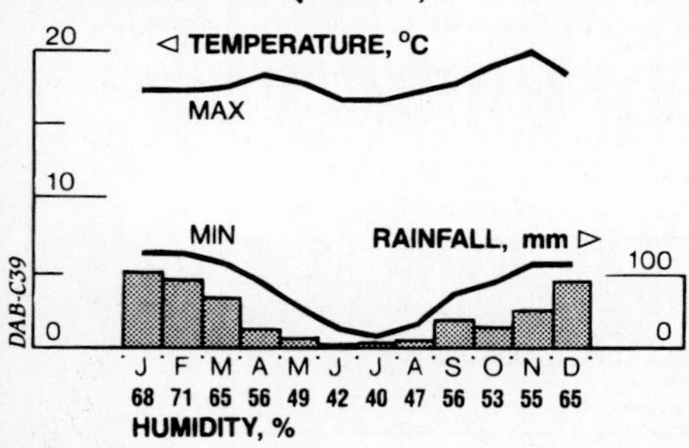

BONAIRE

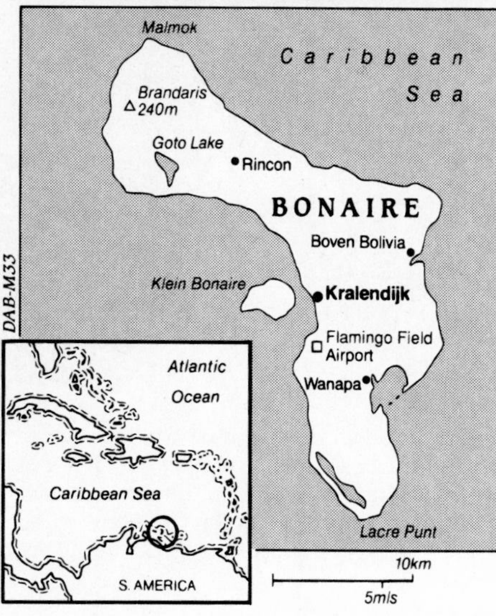

Location: Caribbean, 80km (50 miles) north of Venezuela.

Bonaire Government Tourist Board
Kaya Simon Bolivar 12
Kralendijk
Bonaire, NA
Tel: 8322/8330. Fax: 8408. Telex: 1292.

Office of the Minister Plenipotentiary of the Netherlands Antilles
Badhuisweg 173-175
2597 JP The Hague
The Netherlands
Tel: (070) 351 2811. Fax: (070) 351 2722. Telex: 31161.

Bonaire Government Tourist Board
19th Floor, 275 Seventh Avenue
New York, NY 10001-6788
Tel: (212) 779 0242. Fax: (212) 267 1152.

Bonaire Government Tourist Office
815a Queen Street East
Toronto, Ontario
M4M 1H8
Tel: (416) 465 2958. Fax: (416) 465 5946.

AREA: 288 sq km (111 sq miles).
POPULATION: 11,058 (1990 estimate).
POPULATION DENSITY: 38.4 per sq mile.
CAPITAL: Kralendijk. **Population:** 1700.
GEOGRAPHY: Bonaire is the second largest island of the Antilles in the Dutch Caribbean. The landscape is flat and rocky and, due to low annual rainfall, fairly barren. The island has beautiful palm-fringed beaches and safe waters.
LANGUAGE: Dutch is the official language. Papiamento (a mixture of Portuguese, African, Spanish, Dutch and English) is the commonly used *lingua franca*. English and Spanish are also widely spoken.
RELIGION: Predominantly Roman Catholic with a Protestant minority. There are many evangelical churches of different denominations.
TIME: GMT - 4.
ELECTRICITY: 127 volts AC, 50Hz.
COMMUNICATIONS: Telephone: IDD is available. Country code: 5997. **Telex/telegram:** Facilities are available in the post office in Kralendijk and main hotels. **Post:** Airmail to and from Europe takes four to six days. Surface mail takes up to six weeks. **Press:** The *Beurs- en Nieuwsberichten* is published in Dutch.
BBC World Service and Voice of America frequencies: From time to time these change. See the section *How to Use this Book* for more information.

BBC:				
MHz	17.72	11.78	9.915	5.965
Voice of America:				
MHz	15.21	11.70	6.130	0.930

PASSPORT/VISA

Regulations and requirements may be subject to change at short notice, and you are advised to contact the appropriate diplomatic or consular authority before finalising travel arrangements. Details of these may be found at the head of this country's entry. Any numbers in the chart refer to the footnotes below.

	Passport Required?	Visa Required?	Return Ticket Required?
Full British	Yes	No	Yes
BVP	Valid/1	-	-
Australian	Yes	4	Yes
Canadian	3	4	Yes
USA	2	4	Yes
Other EC	1	4/5	Yes
Japanese	Yes	4	Yes

PASSPORTS: Valid passport required by all except:
(a) **[1]** nationals of Belgium, Luxembourg and The Netherlands holding a tourist card, nationals of Germany holding an identity card and UK nationals holding a British Visitors Passport;
(b) **[2]** nationals of the USA holding voters registration cards or birth certificate, and alien residents of the USA with acceptable documentation;
(c) **[3]** nationals of Canada with birth certificates or proof of citizenship;
(d) nationals of San Marino holding a national ID card.

VISAS: [4] Visas are only required for nationals of the Dominican Republic resident there. All other nationals are allowed to stay in Bonaire for 14 days without a visa (but might need a Certificate of Admission, see below) provided they have a return or onward ticket. All visitors staying more than 90 days require a visa. Transit passengers staying no longer than 24 hours holding confirmed tickets and valid passports do not require visas or Certificates of Admission.
For stays of between 14 and 28 days a **Temporary Certificate of Admission** is required, which in the case of the following countries will be issued by the Immigration authorities on arrival in Bonaire:
(a) **[5]** nationals of Belgium, Germany, Luxembourg, The Netherlands, Spain, and the UK;
(b) nationals of Bolivia, Burkina Faso, Chile, Colombia, Costa Rica, Czechoslovakia, Ecuador, Hungary, Israel, Jamaica, South Korea, Malawi, Mauritius, Niger, The Philippines, Poland, San Marino, Swaziland and Togo.
The following must apply in writing and *before* entering the country even for tourist purposes for a Certificate of Admission: nationals of Albania, Bulgaria, Cambodia, China, Cuba, North Korea, Libya, Romania, USSR, Vietnam and holders of Rhodesian passports issued on or after November 11, 1965.
All other nationals have to apply for the Certificate after 14 days of stay.
Further information about visa requirements may be obtained from the Office of the Minister Plenipotentiary of the Netherlands Antilles; and whilst Royal Netherlands Embassies do not formally represent the Netherlands Antilles in any way, they might also be able to offer limited advice and information. For addresses, see top of this entry and top of *The Netherlands* entry above.
Temporary residence: Enquire at the Office of the Minister Plenipotentiary of the Netherlands Antilles.

MONEY

Currency: Netherlands Antilles Guilder or Florin (NAG) = 100 cents. Notes are in the denominations of NAG250, 100, 50, 25, 10 and 5. Coins are in the denominations of 100, 50, 25, 5, 2.5 and 1 cents. There are in addition a large number of commemorative coins which are legal tender. These range in value from NAG10 to 200. The currency is tied to the the US Dollar.
Credit cards: Access/Mastercard, American Express, Diners and Visa are accepted in large establishments. Check with your credit card company for details of merchant acceptability and other services which may be available.
Travellers cheques: US-currency cheques are the most welcome at points of exchange.
Exchange rate indicators: The following figures are included as a guide to the movement of the

Netherlands Antilles Florin against Sterling and the US Dollar:

Date:	Oct '89	Oct '90	Oct '91	Oct '92
£1.00=	2.84	3.49	3.11	2.83
$1.00=	1.80	1.79	1.80	1.78

Currency restrictions: The import and export of local currency is limited to NAG200; foreign currency is unlimited.
Banking hours: 0830-1200 and 1330-1630 Monday to Friday.

DUTY FREE

The following items may be imported into Bonaire without incurring customs duty:
400 cigarettes or 50 cigars or 250g of tobacco;
2 litres of alcoholic beverages;
250 ml of perfume;
Gifts to a value of NAG100.

PUBLIC HOLIDAYS

Public holidays observed in Bonaire are as follows:
Mar '93 Carnival. **Apr 9** Good Friday. **Apr 12** Easter Monday. **Apr 30** Coronation Day. **May 1** Labour Day. **May 20** Ascension Day. **Sep 6** Bonaire Day. **Dec 25-26** Christmas. **Jan 1 '94** New Year's Day. **Mar** Carnival.
Note: Check with the Tourist Board for full details.

HEALTH

Regulations and requirements may be subject to change at short notice, and you are advised to contact your doctor well in advance of your intended date of departure. Any numbers in the chart refer to the footnotes below.

	Special Precautions?	Certificate Required?
Yellow Fever	No	1
Cholera	No	No
Typhoid & Polio	2	-
Malaria	No	-
Food & Drink	3	-

[1]: A yellow fever certificate is required from travellers over nine months of age coming from infected areas.
[2]: Polio and Typhoid are not endemic in most parts of the Caribbean including Bonaire; however, precautions are advised as a few areas of risk exist within the general region.
[3]: All mains water on the island is distilled from seawater, and is thus safe to drink. Bottled mineral water is widely available. Milk is pasteurised and dairy products are safe for consumption. Local meat, poultry, seafood, fruit and vegetables are generally considered safe to eat.
Mosquitoes may be a nuisance at certain times of year (mainly early to mid summer and early to mid winter) but present no serious hazard. Insect repellant may be useful.
Health care: The St Francis Hospital has 60 beds.

TRAVEL - International

AIR: The national airline of the Netherlands Antilles is *ALM (LM)*. *KLM* also offers daily flights from Amsterdam to Curaçao with connections to Bonaire.
Approximate flight times: From Bonaire to *London* is 11 hours, to *Los Angeles* is 10 hours and to *New York* is 4 hours. These times will vary considerably depending on connections.
International airport: *Flamingo Field (BON)* is 6km (3.5 miles) from Kralendijk.
Departure tax: Approximately NAG20 (US$10) for passengers over two years of age.
SEA: Some good connections to Venezuela and other islands, including the boat to Curaçao and other frequent connections to Aruba.

TRAVEL - Internal

ROAD: A good **taxi** service exists on the island. Taxis are not metered; rates are government-controlled. There are numerous **car hire** firms located at hotels, the airport and the capital city. Bikes and motorbikes can also be hired without any difficulty. Driving is on the right. Roads are reasonably good, although jeeps may be needed for extensive touring of the island.**Documentation:** A national driving licence is acceptable, but drivers must be over 18 years of age.

BONAIRE	HEALTH REGULATIONS	VISA REGULATIONS Code-Link
GALILEO/WORLDSPAN	TI-DFT/BON/HE	TI-DFT/BON/VI
SABRE	TIDFT/BON/HE	TIDFT/BON/VI

To access this information on your CRS, swipe the barcode with a light pen or type in the text under the barcode. For more information, see the introduction *How to Use This Book*.

ACCOMMODATION

HOTELS: There are several large, international standard hotels on the island with good facilities for the holidaymaker, particularly in the provision of watersports equipment etc. Advanced booking (normally through tour company) is essential. For further information contact The Bonaire Hotel and Tourism Association, Kralendijk, Bonaire.
GUEST-HOUSES: The visitor can opt for accommodation in beach villas or private bungalows. Various property companies can be contacted – enquire at Government Tourist Board (address above).
Note: Rates for accommodation will be cheaper in the off-peak season (April 15-December 20).

RESORTS & EXCURSIONS

Bonaire is definitely a place of rest and privacy. The island is ideal for those who want to enjoy a beautiful coastline and the full range of watersports facilities but don't demand too much by way of sophisticated restaurants and nightspots. Bonaire's *Marine Park* is centred on a spectacular coral reef, which is maintained and protected throughout the year by marine experts. There are frequent slide shows on underwater sports and conservation in the hotels and at watersports centres in Kralendijk.
There are several points of interest away from the excellent beaches. The salt flats change colour according to fluctuations in the resident algae population, from a breathtaking fuchsia to subtle pink. Slave huts nearby were inhabited by the salt workers until the abolition of slavery in 1863. The beautiful lagoon of *Goto Meer* is a haven for flocks of flamingoes. Bonaire has its own 13,500-acre game reserve, the *Washington/Slagbaai National Park*, occupying most of the northwestern part of the island and including *Mount Brandaris*, the island's highest point at 784ft. There are two routes through the park, each enabling the visitor to see different aspects of the interesting flora and fauna the island has to offer, in particular the excellent birdlife. In **Kralendijk** itself there are several sites worth visiting, including the lively and architecturally interesting *Fish Market*, or the colourful fruit and vegetable market. There are also some handsome historical buildings along the waterfront, such as *Fort Oranje*.

SOCIAL PROFILE

FOOD & DRINK: The restaurants serve predominantly creole cooking, particularly seafood dishes, including pickled conch shell meat, grilled spicy fish and lobster. Island specialities include Iguana soup and turtle dishes. A wider variety of Chinese, Indonesian, French, Italian and international cooking can also be found. There are many hotels, restaurants, and bars in Kralendijk to choose from. Restaurants and bars are usually closed by midnight.
NIGHTLIFE: This is centred on both the main hotels and restaurants. Having eaten, evening entertainment includes dancing, listening to reggae guitar groups or calypso steel bands, or experiencing the island's casino. The island has two discos.
SHOPPING: The reductions on duty-free imports make the purchase of some perfume, jewellery or alcohol well worthwhile. **Shopping hours:** 0800-1200 and 1400-1800 Monday to Saturday.
SPORT: Watersports predominate, and for almost every visitor will form the central part of any holiday. **Scuba diving, snorkelling, windsurfing** and **water-skiing** are all available with facilities and tuition as necessary. The waters round the island are clear, safe and teeming with fish of every size and hue. **Fishing** and **sailing** charters are popular; half- or full-day cruises can be arranged round the bay or Klein Bonaire, the isle's tiny uninhabited sister island. Every October there is an annual sailing regatta during which there is an enjoyable carnival atmosphere on the island. The focus of the regatta is the new marina, just a few minutes out of Kralendijk: berthing facilities for various types of vessel, a shipyard, and a drydock make Bonaire a pleasure boater's retreat. The main hotels and sporting centres on the island also have **tennis, squash,** and **golf** facilities.
SPECIAL EVENTS: The following list is a selection of some of the events celebrated in Bonaire in 1993-1994. For further details consult the Minister Plenipotentiary of the Netherland Antilles (address above).
Jun 24 '93 *St John's Day Celebrations.* **Jun 28** *St Peter's Day celebrations* (including folk dancing), Rincon. **Sep 6** *Bonaire Day Celebrations.* **Oct** *Sailing regatta.* **Feb 14 '94** *Carnival.*
SOCIAL CONVENTIONS: Dutch customs are still prevalent throughout the islands, although they are increasingly subject to an American influence. Dress is casual and lightweight cottons are advised. Bathing suits should be confined to beach and poolside areas only. It is common to dress up in the evening. **Tipping:** Hotels add a 5-10% government tax and 10% service charge. Tipping is not usually required. There is normally a 10% service charge in restaurants.

BUSINESS PROFILE

ECONOMY: During the 1950s, Bonaire began a gradual climb out of chronic economic depression, aided by investment in tourism and the reactivation of a long-dormant salt industry. The economy gained a further boost in the mid-1970s when the Bonaire Petroleum Corporation (BOPEC) set up an oil transfer depot, a deep-water port with facilities for transferring oil from ocean-going to coastal tankers. Falling oil prices in recent years have badly affected all islands in the Netherlands Antilles, once regarded as among the most affluent in the Caribbean. Oil-related industries have not turned in a profit since 1979 and plans to build a refinery in Bonaire have been indefinitely shelved. The growing practice of transshipping oil whilst still at sea has crippled its land-based transfer industry. All the islands have responded by investing further in tourism, legislating to create tax advantages for overseas investors, and by encouraging agriculture.
BUSINESS: General business practices prevail.
Office hours: 0800-1200 and 1400-1830 Monday to Friday.
COMMERCIAL INFORMATION: The following organisation can offer advice: Bonaire Chamber of Commerce and Industry, PO Box 52, Kaya Princesa Marie 8, Kralendijk, Bonaire. Tel: 5595. Fax: 8995.

HISTORY & GOVERNMENT

HISTORY: Although 'discovered' by the Spanish explorer Amerigo Vespucci in 1499, rock inscriptions in the north of the island indicate a much earlier Amerindian presence. Spanish colonisation, which started in 1527, lasted little more than a century, for by 1634 the Dutch had settled and by 1636 were busy consolidating their position as colonial rulers by conquering and occupying the neighbouring islands. The Dutch West Indies Company introduced economic development schemes, for which they imported hundreds of slave workers. Agriculture and stock management schemes flourished, as did the earlier salt-producing industry. In the early 19th century British and French attacks destabilised the island for a while; at one point it was even leased to a New York merchant. But by 1816 the Dutch had again taken control and introduced further plantation businesses, including the cultivation of brasil wood, aloes and cochenille. Next followed the era of 'Money Order Economy' where economic recession led to the selling of the island's assets and the migration of many Bonairean men to the neighbouring islands of Curaçao and Aruba, from where they sent their earnings home. During the 1950s, however, matters improved and the economy has benefited increasingly from the international tourist trade, the first hotel having opened in 1951.
GOVERNMENT: Bonaire is a constituent island of the Netherlands Antilles; the others being Curaçao, Saba, St Eustatius and St Maarten. The Netherlands Antilles, Aruba and The Netherlands each have equal status within the Kingdom of The Netherlands as regions autonomous in internal affairs. The monarch is represented locally by a Governor, while the Netherlands Antilles are represented in the government of the Kingdom by a Minister Plenipotentiary. Foreign policy and defence matters are decided by a Council of Ministers of the Kingdom, including the Plenipotentiary, and executed under the authority of the Governor. The internal affairs of the Netherlands Antilles are administered by the central government of the Netherlands Antilles, based in Willemstad, Curaçao, which is responsible to the Staten, or legislative assembly. Bonaire may elect by non-compulsory proportional representation adult suffrage three out of 22 members to the Staten. Routine local affairs on each island group (Bonaire, Curaçao and the Windward Islands) are managed by an elected 9-member Island Council, presided over by a Lieutenant-Governor. Internal affairs are managed by an executive council headed by the Lieutenant-Governor. To the central government of the Netherlands Antilles is reserved the right to veto any legislation of the Island Council which conflicts with the Constitution or public interest.

CLIMATE

Hot throughout the year, but tempered by cooling trade winds. The main rainy season is from October to December. The annual mean temperature is 27°C, rainfall 5590mm, windspeed 26kmph and water temperature 26°C.
Required clothing: Lightweights with warmer top layers for the evenings; showerproofs are advisable throughout the year.

BOSNIA-HERCEGOVINA

Location: Ex-Yugoslav republic, southeastern Europe.

Note: Along with the rest of the EC and the US, the UK recognised Bosnia-Hercegovina in April 1992. However, there is no UK, US or Canadian diplomatic presence in Sarajevo. The nearest Embassies are in Belgrade, whose authorities do not recognise the Republic of Bosnia-Hercegovina. The latter's foreign ministry does not have any official diplomatic presence in London, the USA or Canada.

Ministry of International Cooperation
Vojvode Putnika 3
71000 Sarajevo
Bosnia-Hercegovina
Tel: (71) 213 777. Fax: (71) 653 592.
Foreign & Commonwealth Office (Yugoslav Desk)
Tel: (071) 270 3115 *or* 270 3459; (071) 270 3000 (switchboard).
Exports Credit Guarantee Department (Country Policy Desk)
Tel: (071) 512 7000.
Note: All the former Yugoslav republics, including Bosnia-Hercegovina, are off cover for medium- and long-term insurance according to ECGD policy. Short-term cover is now only available from private sector insurers, who will not involve themselves in so risky an area as Bosnia-Hercegovina.

AREA: 51,129 sq km (19,736 sq miles), 20% of the territory of the former Yugoslav federation (its third largest republic).
POPULATION: 4,500,000 (1991), 19% of the total population of the former Yugoslav federation (its third most populous republic).
POPULATION DENSITY: 88 per sq km.
CAPITAL: Sarajevo. **Population:** 448,519 (1991).
GEOGRAPHY: Roughly triangular in shape, and the geopolitical centre of the former Yugoslav federation, Bosnia-Hercegovina shares borders with Serbia and Montenegro in the east and southeast, and Croatia to the north and west, with a short Adriatic coastline of 20km in the southeast, but no ports.
LANGUAGE: Serbo-Croat (Serbs) and Croato-Serb (Croats). The Croats use the Latin alphabet, the Serbs use the Cyrillic. The slavic Muslims use the same language.
RELIGION: 44% Slavic Muslims, 33% Serbian Orthodox and 17% Roman Catholic Croats.
TIME: GMT +1 (GMT + 2 Mar-Sep).
ELECTRICITY: 220 volts AC, 50Hz.
COMMUNICATIONS: Telephone: Formally internationally IDD-connected as part of the former Yugoslav federation. Country code: 38.
Note: All telecommunications services, including facsimile and telex, are now intermittent and uncertain

due to the civil war and the related partition of the republic. This is also true of postal services, internal and international, although Bosnia-Hercegovina is outside the remit of the UN economic sanctions imposed against Serbia and Montenegro in June 1992. **Press/Media:** The main newspaper, *Oslobodjenje*, is still published in Sarajevo. *RTV* is the only TV-radio station operating locally on an intermittent basis. *CNN* is also available via satellite in a number of Sarajevo hotels, notably the Holiday Inn.
BBC World Service and Voice of America frequencies: From time to time these change. See the section *How to use this Book* for more information.

BBC:				
MHz	15.07	12.10	9.410	6.195
Voice of America:				
MHz	9.670	6.040	5.995	1.260

PASSPORT/VISA

The civil war and the related partition of the republic make legal border crossing and airport (Sarajevo) entry for all foreign nationals impossible and should thus not be attempted given the considerable dangers involved.

MONEY

Currency: Yugoslav Dinar (Yu D) = 100 paras; Croatian Dinar (Cr D) = 100 paras. In the Serb-controlled areas, only the Yugoslav Dinar is legal tender, while in Croat-controlled areas only the Croatian Dinar is accepted. The official Sarajevo government does not have the resources to issue its own currency, having previously relied on old Yugoslav Dinars prior to Belgrade's suspension of the issuing of new Yugoslav Dinars in 1991. Due to hyperinflation in all the former Yugoslav republics, the only true repositories of value and means of exchange locally are the German Deutschmark and the US Dollar. Pound Sterling is of relatively little value in the republic and rarely used. Normal banking services in the republic have broken down.
Exchange rate indicators: The following figures are included as a guide to the movements of the Yugoslav Dinar and the Croatian Dinar against Sterling and the US Dollar:

Date:	**Oct '92**
£1.00=	**Yu D325/Cr D681.57**
$1.00=	**Yu D204.79/Cr D429.47**

HEALTH

Regulations and requirements may be subject to change at short notice, and you are advised to contact your doctor well in advance of your intended date of departure. Any numbers in the chart refer to the footnotes below.

	Special Precautions?	Certificate Required?
Yellow Fever	No	No
Cholera	No	No
Typhoid & Polio	No	No
Malaria	No	-
Food & Drink	1	-

[1]: All water should be regarded as being potentially contaminated. Milk is unpasteurised and should be boiled. Avoid dairy products which are likely to have been made from unboiled local milk. Only eat well-cooked meat and fish, preferably served hot. Pork, salad and mayonnaise may carry increased risk. Vegetables should be cooked and fruit peeled.
Rabies is present. For those at high risk, vaccination before arrival should be considered. If you are bitten abroad seek medical advice without delay. For more information consult the *Health* section at the back of the book.
Health care: Due to the ongoing fighting, medical services are extremely stretched and limited. Medical insurance with emergency repatriation is strongly advised.

TRAVEL - International

AIR: There is no national carrier, and no foreign carriers, including *JAT* (the Yugoslav national airline, itself grounded at Belgrade by UN economic sanctions since June 1992) providing services to Sarajevo.
Note: Present Foreign & Commonwealth Office advice is that all UK nationals avoid Bosnia-Hercegovina, and those that remain there leave immediately.

TRAVEL - Internal

RAIL/ROAD: As the entire republic is effectively a partitioned war zone at present, all internal routes are now off-limits to foreign nationals. Sarajevo is the nodal point for all the republic's main communications routes, which go west to Banja Luka, and then to Zagreb, capital of Croatia; north to Doboj, and then to Osijek in Croatia; east to Zvornik, and then to Belgrade; south to Mostar, and then the Adriatic Sea; and southeast to Foca, and then to Podgorica (formerly Titograd), capital of Montenegro.

ACCOMMODATION

With the notable exception of a few city centre hotels used by journalists in Sarajevo (notably the Holiday Inn), no services are presently available to foreign nationals throughout the republic.

SOCIAL PROFILE

FOOD & DRINK: The traditional cuisine of the region includes obvious Turkish influences. Specialities are *bosanski nonac* (bosnian meat and vegetable stew) and *lokum* (Turkish delight) as well as *alva* (crushed nuts in honey).
SPORT: The well-known health spa Jahorina is also renowned for good **skiing**. The Adriatic Coast offers unrestricted fishing, though for fishing in rivers and lakes with nets or traps a special permit is needed. Sometimes visitors can go fishing with regional fishermen. Hotels and regional authorities issue **fishing** permits. The regulations differ in the individual regions; contact the authorities direct. **Football** is a national favourite.
SOCIAL CONVENTIONS: Previously one of the more traditional and stable areas of the former Yugoslav federation, Bosnia-Hercegovina is now its most dangerous place where even foreign nationality or recognised neutral status can not guarantee safety.

BUSINESS PROFILE

ECONOMY: The third poorest and least economically developed of the former Yugoslav republics, Bosnia-Hercegovina accounted for only 12.7% of Yugoslavia's GDP in 1990-91 (approximately US$7 billion), with a GDP per capita of around US$1600 in the same year, on average US$1000 less than across the Federation. Now a predominantly agricultural economy, Bosnia-Hercegovina's traditional industrial base, concentrated on mining and capital goods, largely collapsed in 1991 as a direct result of the demise of the Yugoslav market. Apart from the latter, Bosnia-Hercegovina has always been marginal, accounting for only 10% of Yugoslav foreign trade in 1990-91.
In the same year, as the slavic Muslims and Croats moved to secede from Yugoslavia, the Belgrade government subjected the area to an economic blockade and renounced all responsibility for the republic's share of the former federation's foreign debt at about 15% of the total (US$2.5 billion), which meant that the official government in Sarajevo was internationally bankrupt even before civil war and partition in 1992 completely finished off the area economically.
Consequently, despite being rich in certain natural resources, mainly coal and iron ore, plus immense hydro-electrical potential, the republic is now of no interest to foreign investors, creditors and traders as long as the present chaos continues. UK economic links with Bosnia-Hercegovina are reportedly virtually non-existent.
COMMERCIAL INFORMATION: It is presently unclear as to whether these institutions in Bosnia-Hercegovina are in fact functioning in any normal manner:
Chamber of Economy of Bosnia-Hercegovina, Mis. Irbina 131, 71000 Sarajevo, Bosnia-Hercegovina. Tel: (71) 211 777; *or*
National Bank of Bosnia-Hercegovina, Marsala Tita 25, 71000 Sarajevo, Bosnia-Hercegovina. Tel: (71) 33326.

HISTORY & GOVERNMENT

HISTORY: A province of the Ottoman Empire since 1463, Bosnia-Hercegovina was assigned to the Austro-Hungarian Empire by the Congress of Berlin after the Russo-Turkish War of 1877-78. Formally annexed by Vienna in 1908, the area's turbulent politics and contested status triggered off the First World War in June 1914, when Austrian archduke Franz Ferdinand was assassinated in the Bosnian capital, Sarajevo, by a Serb revolutionary, Gavrilo Princip. The resultant conflagration saw Austria-Hungary, Germany and the Ottoman Turks allied against Serbia, Russia, France, Great Britain and the US. With the approval of the victorious Great Powers, Serbia annexed the area in 1918, as part of the new 'Kingdom of Serbs, Croats and Slovenes', which was renamed 'Yugoslavia' in 1929. After Yugoslavia's dismemberment by the Axis powers during the Second World War, the area was incorporated into a so-called 'Independent State of Croatia', ruled by the fascist Ustasa movement, under the joint sponsorship of both Nazi Germany and its ally Italy, with the Vatican also giving its support. Among other things, this resulted in a Ustasa policy of genocide against the local Serbs (henceforth a numerical minority as a result), often supported and aided by the slavic Muslims who had strongly resented Serb rule before the war. Concomitantly, the area was also the major battleground of the Yugoslav civil war proper between royalist Chetnik forces loyal to the exiled King Peter II and his government in London, and Partisans under the control of the Communist party of Yugoslavia led by Josip Broz Tito. Following the communist takeover in 1945, Bosnia-Hercegovina became a constituent republic of the new Yugoslav federation. Post-communist democratic politics, beginning with the November 1990 elections, brought them out into the open, with extreme nationalists voted into power by each of the republic's three constituencies. Despite the creation of a nominal coalition administration in Sarajevo, complete with a rotating Presidency (beginning with Izetbegovic), Bosnia-Hercegovina effectively fell apart as a functioning and recognisable polity in 1991 on account of local political extremism on all sides and the further disintegration of the Yugoslav federation through civil war; first in Slovenia, then Croatia. As a creation of that federation, Bosnia-Hercegovina did not long survive its demise, being effectively partitioned in 1992 between the various local surrogates of Milosevic's Serbia, taking over 65% of the territory, and those of Tudjman's Croatia, claiming 25%, leaving the slavic Muslims with little more than central Sarajevo. The ongoing civil war that led to this carve-up has displaced 1.5 million people (one-third of the total population) and killed over 10,000. Despite recognising the non-existent 'Republic of Bosnia-Hercegovina' in April 1992, the international community, here particularly the major Western powers, has limited its involvement to punishing Serbia and Montenegro (but not Croatia) by imposing UN-mandated economic sanctions, and providing humanitarian assistance under UN auspices for Sarajevo.
GOVERNMENT: The rump Presidency and military forces loyal to Izetbegovic control only central Sarajevo.

CLIMATE

Dominated by mountainous and hilly terrain, and drained by major rivers to the north (Sava) and east (Drina), Bosnia-Hercegovina has a climate that is as variable as the rest of the former Yugoslav federation, with moderate continental climatic conditions generally the norm (very cold winters and hot summers).
Required clothing: In winter, heavyweight clothing and overcoat. In summer, lightweight clothing and raincoat required, with mediumweight clothing at times in the colder and wetter north, and at higher altitudes elsewhere.

BOTSWANA

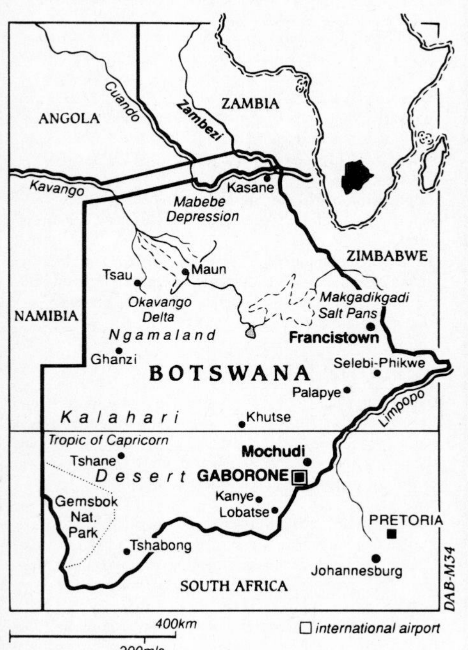

Location: Central Southern Africa.

Tourism Development Unit
Ministry of Commerce and Industry
Private Bag 004
Gaborone, Botswana
Tel: (3) 53024. Fax: (3) 71539. Telex: 2674.

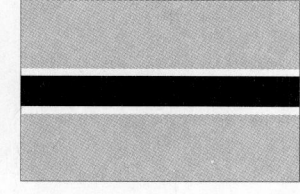

Botswana High Commission
6 Stratford Place
London W1N 9AE
Tel: (071) 499 0031. Fax: (071) 495 8595. Telex: 262897 BOHICO.

Botswana Embassy and Mission to the European Communities
169 avenue de Tervuren
B-1150 Brussels, Belgium
Tel: (2) 735 2070 *or* 753 6110. Fax: (2) 735 6318. Telex: 22849.

British High Commission
Private Bag 0023
Gaborone, Botswana
Tel: (3) 52841/2/3. Fax: (3) 56105. Telex: 2370 UKREP BD.

Embassy of the Republic of Botswana (represents Canada also)
Suite 7m
Intelsat Building
3400 International Drive, NW
Washington, DC 20008
Tel: (202) 244 4990/1. Fax: (202) 244 4164. Telex: 64221.

Embassy of the United States of America
PO Box 90
Gaborone, Botswana
Tel: (3) 53982. Fax: (3) 56947. Telex: 2554.

Consulate of Botswana
14 South Drive
Toronto, Ontario
M4W 1R1
Tel: (416) 324 8239. Fax: (416) 324 8239.

AREA: 582,000 sq km (224,711 sq miles).
POPULATION: 1,300,999 (1990 estimate).
POPULATION DENSITY: 2.2 per sq km.
CAPITAL: Gaborone. **Population:** 129,535 (1990).
GEOGRAPHY: Botswana is bordered by South Africa, Namibia, Zimbabwe and touches Zambia just west of the Victoria Falls. The Kalahari Desert covers most of Botswana. National Parks cover 17% of the country. To the northwest is the Okavango Basin, where the Moremi Wildlife Reserve and the Chobe National Park support abundant wildlife. To the southwest is the Kalahari Gemsbok National Park. The majority of the population lives in the southeast around Gaborone, Serowe and Kanye along the South African border. The vast arid sandveld of the Kalahari occupies much of north, central and western Botswana. The seasonal rains bring a considerable difference to the vegetation, especially in the Makgadikgadi Pans and the Okavango Basin in the north. The latter, after the winter floods, provides one of the wildest and most beautiful nature reserves in Africa.

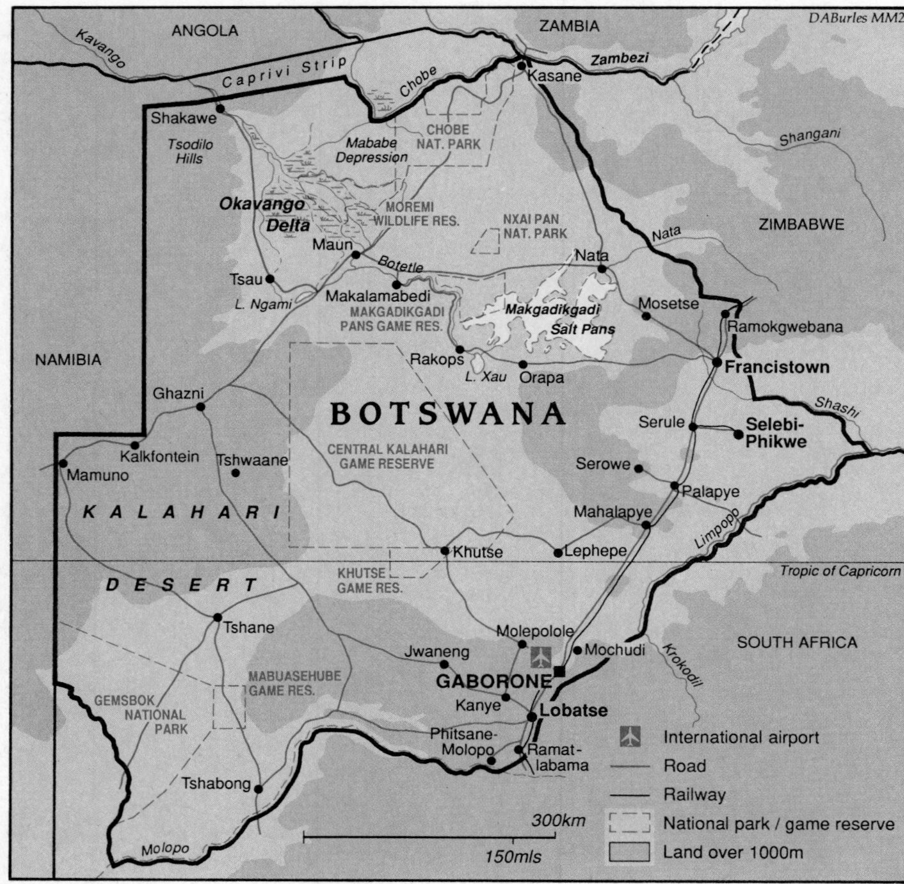

LANGUAGE: English is the official language. Setswana is the national language.
RELIGION: 15% Christian, 85% Traditional.
TIME: GMT + 2 (GMT + 1 in summer).
ELECTRICITY: 220-240 volts AC, 50Hz. 15-amp and 13-amp plug sockets in use.
COMMUNICATIONS: Telephone: IDD is available to over 80 countries. Country code: 267. There are very few public phone boxes. **Fax:** Use of this service is increasing. **Telex/telegram:** There are facilities in Gaborone and other major centres (usually in major hotels and main post offices). **Post:** Airmail service to Europe takes from one to three weeks. There are post offices in all the main towns, although there are no deliveries and post must be collected from boxes. **Press:** The daily newspaper is *The Dikgang Tsa Compieno (Botswana Daily News)*, published in Setswana and English. Periodical newspapers include *The Midweek Sun, Botswana Guardian* and *Business Gazette*.
BBC World Service and Voice of America frequencies: From time to time these change. See the section *How to Use this Book* for more information.

BBC:				
MHz	21.66	11.94	6.190	3.255
Voice of America:				
MHz	21.49	15.60	9.525	6.035

PASSPORT/VISA

Regulations and requirements may be subject to change at short notice, and you are advised to contact the appropriate diplomatic or consular authority before finalising travel arrangements. Details of these may be found at the head of this country's entry. Any numbers in the chart refer to the footnotes below.

	Passport Required?	Visa Required?	Return Ticket Required?
Full British	Yes	No	No
BVP	Not valid	-	-
Australian	Yes	No	No
Canadian	Yes	No	No
USA	Yes	No	No
Other EC	Yes	1	No
Japanese	Yes	No	Yes

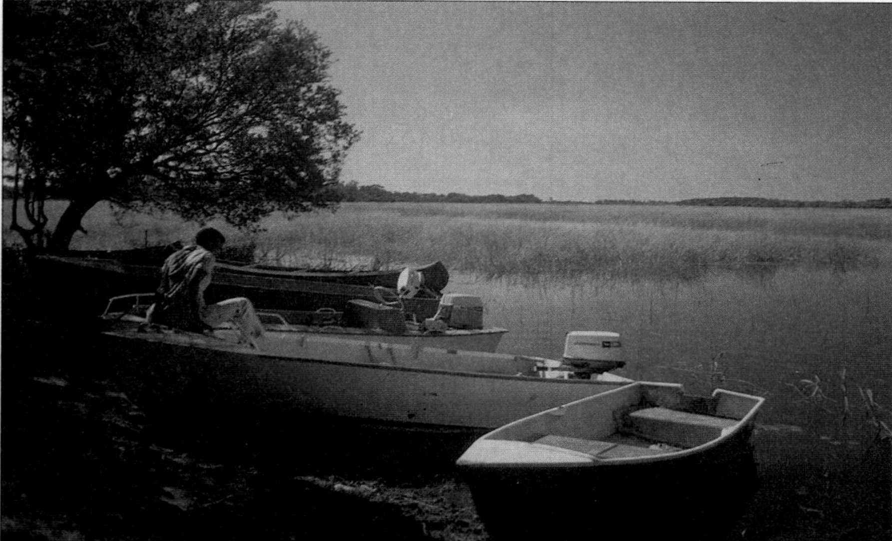

PASSPORTS: Valid passport required by all. All passports must be valid for over 6 months.
British Visitors Passport: Not accepted.
VISAS: Required by all except nationals of the following countries:
(a) Commonwealth countries (*except* Ghana, India, Mauritius, Nigeria, Pakistan and Sri Lanka whose nationals *do* require visas);
(b) Austria, Finland, Iceland, Liechtenstein, Norway, San Marino, South Africa, Sweden, Switzerland, Uruguay, USA, Western Samoa and Yugoslavia;
(c) [1] Belgium, Denmark, France, Germany, Greece, Ireland, Italy, Luxembourg and The Netherlands (nationals of Spain and Portugal *do* require visas).
Types of visa: General entry visa.
Validity: Maximum of 90 days from the date of arrival.
Application requirements: (a) 2 completed application forms. (b) 2 black-and-white photos. (c) £10 fee. (d) Valid passport.
Application to: Consulate (or Consular Section at Embassy or High Commission). For addresses, see top of entry.
Temporary residence: Anyone wishing to stay for more than 90 days should seek permission prior to travelling; contact The Chief Immigration Officer, PO Box 492, Gaborone, Botswana.

MONEY

Currency: Pula (P) = 100 thebes. Notes are in denominations of P50, 20, 10, 5, 2 and 1. Coins are in denominations of P1, and 50, 25, 10, 5, 2 and 1 thebes. Various gold and silver coins were issued to mark the country's tenth anniversary of independence, and are still legal tender.
Credit cards: Access/Mastercard, American Express, Diners Club and Visa are all accepted on a limited basis. Check with your credit card company for details of merchant acceptability and other services which may be available.
Exchange rate indicators: The following figures are included as a guide to the movements of the Pula against Sterling and the US Dollar:

Date:	**Oct '89**	**Oct '90**	**Oct '91**	**Oct '92**
£1.00=	3.19	3.61	3.70	3.43
$1.00=	2.02	1.85	2.13	2.16

Currency restrictions: Visitors may import local currency but export is limited to P500. There is no restriction on the import of foreign currency, but it should be registered with an authorised dealer if it is to be re-exported.
Banking hours: 0900-1430 Monday, Tuesday, Thursday and Friday, 0815-1200 Wednesday and 0815-1045 Saturday.

DUTY FREE

The following goods may be taken into Botswana without incurring any duty:
200 cigarettes and 50 cigars or 350g of tobacco;
2 litres of wine;
1 litre of alcoholic beverages;
50 mls of perfume;
250 mls of toilet water.
Note: Married couples travelling together are only entitled to single allowances. Cameras, films and firearms must be declared.

PUBLIC HOLIDAYS

Public holidays observed in Botswana are as follows:
Apr 9-12 '93 Easter. **May 20** For Ascension Day. **Jul 15-16** President's Day. **Sep 30-Oct 1** Botswana Day. **Dec 25-26** Christmas. **Jan 1-2 '94** New Year.

HEALTH

Regulations and requirements may be subject to change at short notice, and you are advised to contact your doctor well in advance of your intended date of departure. Any numbers in the chart refer to the footnotes below.

	Special Precautions?	Certificate Required?
Yellow Fever	No	-
Cholera	Yes	No
Typhoid & Polio	Yes	-
Malaria	Yes/1	-
Food & Drink	2	-

[1]: *Malaria* risk exists from November to May in the northern part of the country (north of 21 degrees south), predominantly in the malignant *falciparum* form.
[2]: Tap water is considered safe to drink, although drinking water outside main cities and towns may be contaminated and sterilisation is advisable. Milk is pas-

teurised and dairy products are safe for consumption. Local meat, poultry, seafood, fruit and vegetables are generally considered safe to eat.
Rabies is present. For those at high risk, vaccination before arrival should be considered. If you are bitten abroad seek medical advice without delay. For more information consult the *Health* section at the back of the book.
Bilharzia (schistosomiasis) is present. Avoid swimming and paddling in fresh water. Swimming pools which are well-chlorinated and maintained are safe.
Sleeping sickness is transmitted by tsetse flies in the Moremi Wildlife Reserve, Ngamiland and western parts of the Chobe National Park. Protective clothing and fly-spray is recommended.
Tick-bite fever can be a problem when walking in the bush. It is advisable to wear loose-fitting clothes and to search the body for ticks. The disease may be treated with tetracycline, though pregnant women and child-ren who are under eight years of age should not take this medicine.
Health care: The dust and heat may cause a problem for asthmatics and people with allergies to dust. Those with sensitive skin should take precautions. Botswana's altitude, 1000m (3300ft) above sea level, reduces the filtering effect of the atmosphere. Hats and sunscreen are advised.
There are hospitals in Gaborone, Francistown, Kanye, Molepolole, Mochudi, Maun, Serowe, Mahalapye, Lobatse, Selebi-Phikwe, Ramotswa, Jwaneng and Orapa, but only poorly-equipped clinics in the remote villages. There are chemists in all main towns and pharmaceutical supplies are readily available. Health insurance is essential. There is a government medical scheme and medicines supplied by government hospitals are free.

TRAVEL - International

AIR: The national airline is *Air Botswana (BP)* which only operates within Africa. *British Airways* flies direct to Gaborone twice weekly from London.
Approximate flight time: From *London* to Gaborone is 15 hours (including stopovers).
International airport: *Seretse Khama (GBE)*, 15km (9.5 miles) northwest of Gaborone. There are no regular bus or taxi services to and from the airport but the President Hotel, Oasis Motel and Gaborone Sun Hotel run minibuses (combis).
A major new airport at *Kasane* (north Botswana) came into operation during 1991. A connecting flight, via an overnight stay in Gaborone, is available from *British Airways* twice a week.
See below for information on private charters to neighbouring countries.
RAIL: There are good connections between Botswana and South Africa (Mafeking–Ramatlabama–Gaborone) and Botswana and Zimbabwe (Bulawayo–Plumtree–Francistown). A train also runs from Gaborone to Bulawayo. The journey takes 20 hours; passengers are advised to take their own food and drink as the buffet supply has a very limited range (mainly alcoholic). There are four classes, and sleeping compartments are available. Complicated formalities may be necessary for border crossing from Zimbabwe and to or from South Africa, where the South African Customs Union agreement is in operation.
Botswana has assisted in the construction of the Limpopo line from Zimbabwe to Mozambique, an act which will speed up the availability of alternative routes into Botswana. Other plans include extending the network into Namibia.
ROAD: There are reasonable roads running roughly along the same routes as the railway, linking Botswana with South Africa and Zimbabwe.

TRAVEL - Internal

AIR: Major areas of the country are linked by air. There are airports in Francistown, Maun, Selebi-Phikwe, Ghanzi, Pont Drift and Kasane. There are two charter companies in Gaborone: *Kalahari Air Services* (PO Box 10102, Gaborone. Tel: (3) 51804), offering charters to Namibia, South Africa, Lesotho, Swaziland, Zimbabwe and Zambia; and *Okavango Air Services* (PO Box 1966, Gaborone. Tel: (3) 13308).
RAIL: There are rail links between Ramatlabama, Lobatse, Gaborone, Palapye and Francistown. Work on upgrading and extending the rail network continues.
ROAD: Botswana has tarmac roads on the following routes: running from south to north from Lobatse to Francistown up to Ramokgwebana and from Lobatse to Kanye; running from Francistown to Kazungula via Nata; and running from Kanye to Jwaneng. There are approximately 2000km (1200 miles) of bitumised roads in the country. Others are either gravel or sand tracks. There are plans to construct a road network with more major highways. Reserve fuel and at least 20 litres of water should always be carried on journeys into more remote

BOTSWANA	HEALTH REGULATIONS	VISA REGULATIONS Code-Link
GALILEO/WORLDSPAN	 TI-DFT/GBE/HE	 TI-DFT/GBE/VI
SABRE	TIDFT/GBE/HE	 TIDFT/GBE/VI

To access this information on your CRS, swipe the barcode with a light pen or type in the text under the barcode. For more information, see the introduction *How to Use This Book*.

areas, and visitors are advised to make careful enquiries before setting out. **Bus:** There are bus services between Gaborone and Francistown, and from Francistown to Nata and Maun. The bus from Francistown to Maun runs three times a week leaving at about 1100. The journey takes 12-18 hours. There are no published timetables; further details can be obtained locally. Travel within major towns is by taxi. **Car hire:** Hire cars are available in Gaborone, Francistown or Maun. Four-wheel drive vehicles are necessary in many areas. Traffic drives on the left and seat belts must be worn. It is advisable to keep the petrol tank at least half full as distances between towns can be long. There is a speed limit of 110kmph (70mph) outside built-up areas, and about 50kmph (31mph) in built-up areas. Speed limits are strongly enforced with high fines. **Documentation:** International Driving Permit is not legally required, but recommended for stays of up to six months; thereafter, a Botswanan driving licence must be obtained, which will be issued without a test if a valid British licence is produced.

URBAN: There is no public transport within towns except shared taxi or minibus services operating at controlled flat fares. Exclusive use of taxis is sometimes available at a higher charge although fares should always be agreed on before setting off.

JOURNEY TIMES: The following chart gives approximate journey times from Gaborone (in hours and minutes) to other major cities and towns in Botswana:

	Air	Road	Rail
Francistown	0.50	5.00	6.35
Selebi-Phikwe	1.00	4.30	-
Jwangen	-	1.30	-
Orapa	-	5.00	-
Lobatse	0.20	0.45	1.50
Maun	1.30	12.00	-
Kasane	2.50	13.30	-
Tshabong	2.00	15.00	-
Ghanzi	1.25	11.00	-

ACCOMMODATION

Hotels, lodges and camps are not graded in Botswana.

HOTELS: Generally all hotels maintain a reasonable standard, particularly those in main centres in the east of the country. The largest number of hotels and motels are in or near Gaborone (the President and the Sun Hotel being of international standard) and Francistown, some with air-conditioning, swimming pools and facilities for films, bands and discotheques. Most other hotels have fairly basic amenities, although there is a programme for improving facilities. Other towns with hotels and motels are Ghanzi, Kanye, Lobatse, Mahalapye, Maun, Molepolole, Palapye, Selebi-Pikwe, Serowe and Tuli Block.

SAFARI LODGES & CAMPS: Varying standards and facilities are to be found in all the main centres and game reserves. These include Francistown, Kasane, Maun, the Okavango Delta, the western Chobe National Park, the Moremi Wildlife Reserve and Tuli Block. Facilities vary greatly; some are merely campsites with ablution blocks, and can be very reasonably priced, while others consist of luxury groups of chalets or cottages complete with swimming pools, cinemas, conference rooms and shops. Some such as the Tsaro and Xugana Lodges in the Okavango Delta, are hired out as one unit to groups of six. Others, such as Lloyd's Camp in western Chobe and Nxamaseri Camp in the Okavango Delta, provide accommodation in luxury safari tents. Many of these camps are able to hire out equipment and boats, and offer experienced guides.

CAMPING: There are organised campsites at some hotels in the Okavango and Chobe areas. Visitors may camp beside the road. Permission should be sought before camping on private land. Grass fires should not be started, and all litter should be buried or removed. The presence of lions in some of the more remote areas makes it advisable to exercise extreme care.

A booklet entitled *Where To Stay In Botswana*, giving details of prices and facilities, may be obtained from The Tourism Development Unit, at the address at the beginning of the section. The following is an umbrella organisation comprising hotels and lodges, travel agents and tour operators, airlines, and hunters: The Hotel and Tourism Association of Botswana, PO Box 968, Gaborone. Tel: (3) 57144. Fax: (3) 57144.

RESORTS & EXCURSIONS

Gaborone

The capital is situated in the southeast of the country. There is an excellent *National Museum* open from 0900-1800 Monday to Friday and 0900-1700 weekends, with natural history and ethnological exhibitions. As well as permanent displays there are also temporary exhibitions and various symposia and conferences. The visitor will find *Sites of Historic and Natural Interest In and Around Gaborone* a useful pamphlet. Gaborone has several good bookshops and libraries, including the University of Botswana Library which has a 'Botswana Room' devoted solely to publications on the country. There are good craft shops and markets in the town, where pottery, basketwork, leatherwork and handwoven objects may be bought.

Excursions: Nearby is the *Gaborone Dam*, a centre for watersports, and day trips can be made to see local crafts at *Oodi*, *Thamaga* and *Pilane*. A trip to the weaving centre at *Lentswe-La-Udi*, just north of Gaborone, is especially recommended. Local craftwork can be bought here at a fraction of their cost in the big cities. The centre is a non-profit-making organisation, with proceeds going back to the craftspeople. *Mochudi*, also north of Gaborone, is the regional capital of the Kgableng tribe and has an interesting museum (the *Phuthadikabo Museum)* which chronicles the history of the Kgableng people in fascinating detail.

National Parks

Botswana is a vast dry land with over 80% of the country being semi-desert (sand with thorn and scrub bush), so there are many remote areas to visit, with abundant wildlife.

Undoubtedly the most lovely region is the **Okavango Delta** area in the north of the country in the Kgalagadi Desert and easily accessible from **Maun** between June and September. Home to about 36 species of mammals,

200 species of birds, 80 species of fish and a wealth of flora, the Delta was created by shifts of the earth's surface forcing a river system away from its natural path (to the Indian Ocean), to form the greatest inland delta system in the world.

The region is extremely beautiful, covering an area of about 15,000 sq km (6000 sq miles) and composed of vast grass flats, low tree-covered ridges and a widespread network of narrow waterways opening into lagoons. The thick papyrus reeds which thrive in these waters make much of the northern section impenetrable except by dug-out canoe (mokoro). The waters, however, are often a clear blue, and crocodiles, hippos and hundreds of fabulous birds can be seen, as well as elephants, zebra and giraffes. There are three lodges in the swamps; Island Safaris, Crocodile Camp and Okavango River Lodge. At Island Safaris there is a swimming pool, and films are shown. *Chef's Island* may be reached by air or by mokoro and there is a tented camp at *Xaxaba*. The whole area is a designated national park.

Leaving Maun by boat or canoe, with an experienced guide, it is possible to wind one's way through the intricate network of waterways to emerge 640km (400 miles) northwest at *Shakawe* near the Angolan border. These trips can also be made at night, when many of the animals are awake.

The *Gcwihaba Caverns*, about 240km (150 miles) from Tsau, contain beautiful stalactites. The name means 'Hyena's Hole' in the Quing language of the Bushmen.

The **Chobe National Park** with an area of approximately 11,700 sq km (4517 sq miles) is the home of a splendid variety of wildlife, including the white rhinoceros and the elephants who move in their thousands along the well-worn paths of the Chobe River every afternoon to drink. There are also herds of buffalo to be seen at the river's edge, as well as hippo, lechwe, kudu, impala, roan and puku. With the exception of certain sections, which are closed in the rainy season during November to April, the park is open throughout the year. The best time to visit it is between May and September when it is possible to see several thousand animals in a day. An exclusive lodge has recently been completed within the National Park, 12km (8 miles) from *Kasane*, which is situated 69km (42 miles) west of the *Victoria Falls* on a good tarmac road. Although the most developed of Botswana's parks and reserves, many of the roads in the area are passable only by 4-wheel drive vehicles.

One of the most beautiful and perhaps the most spectacular game reserves in southern Africa is the **Moremi Wildlife Reserve,** covering 1812 sq km (700 sq miles) in the northeast corner of the Okavango Delta. The roads are, however, particularly bad in this region. There is a risk from both tsetse fly and malaria.

The **Nxai Pan National Park**, situated only 32km (20 miles) north of the main Francistown to Maun road, is completely flat and covered with grass cropped short by the large quantity of wildlife that visits during the rainy season. The area is famous for the **Makgadikgade Pans,** once a huge prehistoric lake, and now a flat salt sheet which floods in the rainy season and becomes populated by thousands of brilliant pink flamingoes. Enormous herds of zebra and wildebeest also come to drink here. When the Makgadikgade loses its water the animals move on to the *Boteti River* where they remain until the following rainy season, which heralds their movement northwards again to the Nxai Pan. There are basic camping facilities in the area, but essentials such as water, food and petrol should be brought.

The **Tsodilo Hills** are situated north of the Okavango Delta close to the border with the Caprivi Strip (Namibia), and are the site of over 1700 rock paintings, painted between approximately AD1000 and 1800 and mostly portraying animal life. They are thought to be the work of ancestors of the Basarwa and Bantu groups still living in the region (who have labelled the hills Male, Female and Child). There are strong similarities between these paintings and those found on sites in Zimbabwe, Tanzania, South Africa and Lesotho. The hills are reached by air or road but there are no camping facilities or water supply so visitors should allow for water, food and petrol needs.

Khutse Game Reserve is an expanse of dry savannah land which, when filled with water, attracts hundreds of bird species. It is located about 240km (150 miles) northwest of Gaborone. Camping facilities are basic, and water, petrol and food should be brought. There are still a few small bands of Bushmen living in this region, one of the last Stone Age races on earth.

SOCIAL PROFILE

FOOD & DRINK: Restaurants and bars can be found in main towns, often in hotels. Most lodges and safari camps also have restaurants and licensed bars, though food is generally basic outside major hotels and restaurants. **Drink:** There is local beer and in general no restrictions on alcohol.

Sunset in Botswana

SHOPPING: Wood carvings, jewellery, llama and alpaca blankets, Indian handicrafts, gold and silver costume jewellery. **Shopping hours:** 0830-1300 and 1400-1700 Monday to Friday; 0830-1300 Saturday.

SPORT: Safari companies run photographic and sightseeing tours to the magnificent national parks and wildlife reserves in Botswana. For details contact the Tourism Division. Outside protected areas there is limited scope for **hunting**. **Fishing** trips, **water-skiing**, **motorboat** and **canoe** hire are available to varying degrees. Near to Gaborone is an artificial lake with a yacht club offering **sailing,** water-skiing and fishing; use of facilities is available to visitors at the invitation of a club member.

SPECIAL EVENTS: The *Independence Day* and *President's Day* festivities are celebrated with traditional dancing, musical events (including performances by the Defence Force Band) and karate shows.

SOCIAL CONVENTIONS: As most people in Botswana follow their traditional pattern of life, visitors should be sensitive to customs which will inevitably be unfamiliar to them. Outside urban areas, people may well be unused to visitors. Casual clothing is acceptable, and in urban centres normal courtesies should be observed. **Photography:** Airports, official residences and defence establishments should not be photographed. Permission should be obtained to photograph local people. **Tipping:** 10% in urban centres. It is obligatory to tip servants.

BUSINESS PROFILE

ECONOMY: The economy is based on nomadic agriculture, mainly livestock, and cultivation of subsistence crops – maize, sorghum and millet – which have been severely affected by drought in recent years. Cattle produces a large proportion of the country's foreign exchange earnings. The remainder comes from mineral extracts: diamond, nickel, copper and coal are well-established, while soda ash has recently come into production on an industrial scale. Platinum, gold and petroleum deposits have been located in the south and are expected in go into production during the 1990s. Botswana is closely connected to South Africa economically and linked to it, along with Lesotho and Swaziland, in the Southern African Customs Union (SACU), although Botswana has broken its former dependence on the Rand Currency. The bulk of the country's imports come from within SACU, with other African countries and the EC providing most of the rest. Europe is the key export market.

BUSINESS: Lightweight or tropical suits, or safari suits, should be worn. **Office hours:** 0800-1700 April-October; 0730-1630 October-April. **Government office hours:** 0730-1630 all year round.

COMMERCIAL INFORMATION: The Trade and Investment Promotion Agency (TIPA) was created in 1984 to assist potential investors. A brochure *Botswana – a strategic investment opportunity* is available from TIPA (address below). The following organisations can offer advice: Botswana National Chamber of Commerce and Industry, PO Box 20344, Gaborone, Botswana. Tel: (3) 52677.

Trade and Investment Promotion Agency, Ministry of Commerce and Industry, Private Bag 004, Gaborone, Botswana. Tel: (3) 53024. Fax: (3) 71539. Telex: 2674.

HISTORY & GOVERNMENT

HISTORY: Until the early 17th century, Botswana was inhabited by bushmen, who were, to a large extent, overwhelmed by immigrant tribes during the 1600s. Britain came into formal contact with Botswana in the 19th century through the British South Africa Company, who supervised the territory, which became known as Bechuanaland Protectorate. The country achieved independence in 1966 and Seretse Khama became the country's first President, a position he retained until his death in 1980. The party which he led, the Botswana Democratic Party, has dominated the country's politics since independence. It won large majorities in the National Assembly in each of the five elections held since then, most recently in October 1989 when the BDP picked up 65% of the vote. The main opposition party, the Botswana National Front, has made substantial progress against the BDP at local level, but remains a minor force at national level. A newly formed alliance between the BNF and two other opposition parties to create the Botswana People's Progressive Front may boost the opposition enough to mount a serious challenge to the BDP and its leader, Quett Masire, at the 1994 polls. Generally, Botswana proceeds cautiously with respect to its troubled southern neighbour, not least because of its considerable economic dependence. Relations with neighbouring Zimbabwe have also suffered recent strain after political violence drove a large number of refugees across the border into Botswana. Botswana has also been severely affected by the drought that has ravaged the whole of southern Africa.

GOVERNMENT: Executive power is held by the President, who is elected by the legislature, and the National Assembly (34 out of the 38 members of which are elected by universal adult suffrage). The President, currently Dr Masire, appoints a cabinet and receives advice from the House of Chiefs, comprising chiefs from tribes which were once autonomous.

CLIMATE

Mainly temperate climate. Summer is between Oct/April and is very hot combined with the rainy season. Dry and cooler weather between May-Sept. Early mornings and evenings may be cold and frosty in winter. The climate chart below for Francistown represents the wetter north and east of the country. Annual rainfall decreases westwards and southwards.

Required clothing: Lightweights can be worn most of the year during the day, but warmer clothes should be taken for sudden drops in temperature in the winter and during the evenings.

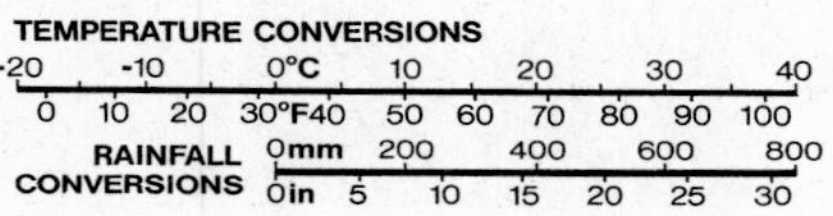

TEMPERATURE CONVERSIONS
-20 -10 0°C 10 20 30 40
0 10 20 30°F40 50 60 70 80 90 100
RAINFALL CONVERSIONS 0mm 200 400 600 800
0in 5 10 15 20 25 30

FRANCISTOWN Botswana (1004m)

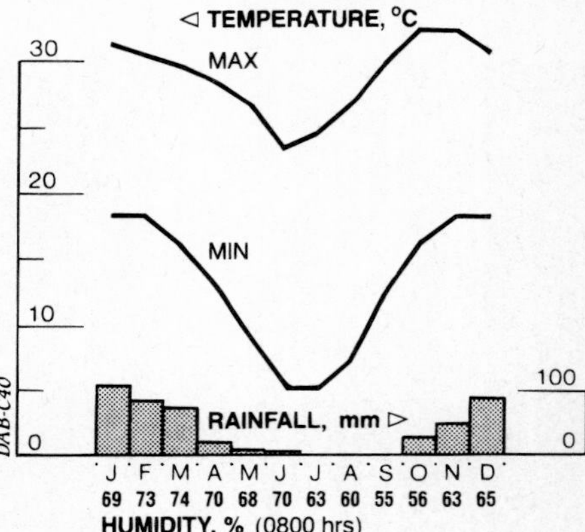

MAUN Botswana (942m)

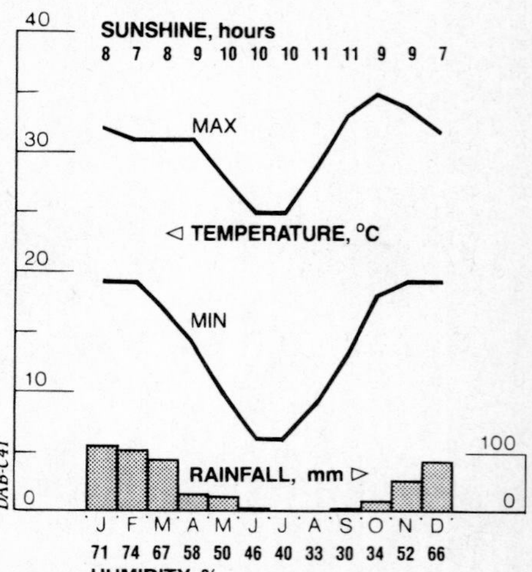

BRAZIL

Location: South America.

Centro Brasileiro de Informação Turística (CEBITUR)
Rua Mariz e Barros 13, 6° andar
Praça de Bandeira
20.270 Rio de Janeiro RJ, Brazil
Tel: (21) 293 1313. Fax: (21) 273 9290. Telex: 21066.

Embassy of the Federative Republic of Brazil *and* **Brazilian Information Office**
32 Green Street
London W1Y 4AT
Tel: (071) 499 0877. Fax: (071) 493 5105. Telex: 261157. Opening hours: 1000-1200 and 1500-1800 Monday to Friday.

Brazilian Consulate General
6 St Albans Street
London SW1Y 4SG
Tel: (071) 930 9055. Fax: (071) 839 8958. Telex: 892849. Opening hours: 1000-1600 Monday to Friday.

British Embassy
Caixa Postal 07-0586
Setor de Embaixadas Sul, Quadra 801
Conjunto K
70.408 Brasília DF, Brazil
Tel: (61) 225 2710. Fax: (61) 225 1777. Telex: 1360.

British Consulate-General
Caixa Postal 669 CEP 20010
Praia do Flamengo
284 2nd Floor
Rio de Janeiro, Brazil
Tel: (21) 552 1422. Fax: (21) 552 5796. Telex: 2121577.
Also in: Belém, Manaus, Recife, Salvador, Belo Horizonte, Fortaleza, São Paulo, Pôrto Alegre, Rio Grande and Santos.

Brazilian Consulate
27th floor, 630 Fifth Avenue
New York, NY 10111
Tel: (212) 757 3080/7.

Embassy of the Federative Republic of Brazil and **Brazilian Tourist Department**
3006 Massachusetts Avenue, NW
Washington, DC 20008
Tel: (202) 745 2700. Fax: (202) 745 2827.

Embassy of the United States of America
Lote 3
Setor de Embaixadas Sul
Avenida das Nações
70.403 Brasília DF
Brazil
Tel: (61) 321 7272. Fax: (61) 225 9136. Telex: 0611091.

Embassy of the Federative Republic of Brazil
450 Wilbrod Street
Ottawa, Ontario
K1N 6M8
Tel: (613) 237 1090. Fax: (613) 237 6144. Telex: 0534222 BRASEMBOTT.

Canadian Embasssy
CP 07-0961 Lote 16
SES Avenida das Nações
70.410 Brasília DF
Brazil
Tel: (61) 223 7515. Fax: (61) 225 5233. Telex: 1296.

AREA: 8,511,996 sq km (3,286,500 sq miles).
POPULATION: 153,322,000 (1991 estimate).
POPULATION DENSITY: 18 per sq km.
CAPITAL: Brasília. **Population:** 1,841,028 (1991 estimate).
GEOGRAPHY: Brazil covers almost half of the South American continent and it is bordered to the north, west and south by all South American countries except Chile and Ecuador; to the east is the Atlantic. Brazil is topographically relatively flat, and at no point do the highlands exceed 3000m (10,000ft). Over 60% of the country is a plateau; the remainder consists of plains. The River Plate Basin (the confluence of the Paraná and Uruguay Rivers, both of which have their sources in Brazil) in the far south is more varied, higher and less heavily forested. North of the Amazon are the Guiana Highlands, partly forested, partly stony desert. The Brazilian Highlands of the interior, between the Amazon and the rivers of the south, form a vast tableland, the Mato Grosso, from which rise mountains in the southwest, that form a steep protective barrier from the coast called the Great Escarpment, breached by deeply cut river beds. The population is concentrated in the southeastern states of Minas Gerais, São Paulo and Paraná. São Paulo has a population of over 10 million, while over 5 million people live in Rio de Janeiro.
LANGUAGE: The official language is Portuguese. French, German and Italian are widely spoken, English to a lesser extent.
RELIGION: Over 90% Roman Catholic.
TIME: Brazil spans several time zones:
Brazilian Standard Time: GMT - 3 (GMT - 2 in summer).
Amazon time zone (except Acre): GMT - 5 (GMT - 4 in summer).
Fernando de Noronha Islands: GMT - 2.
Acre State: GMT - 5.
ELECTRICITY: Bahia (Salvador) 127 volts AC; Brasília 220 volts AC, 60Hz; Rio de Janeiro 110 volts AC, 60Hz; São Paulo 110 volts AC, 60Hz. Plugs are of the 2-pin type.
COMMUNICATIONS: Telephone: The telecommunications systems are state-owned. Full IDD services available for the whole country and abroad. Country code: 55. Public telephones require metal discs called 'fichas', which can be obtained from cash desks or newspaper kiosks. All calls are liable to a 20% tax. **Fax:** Facilities are available in the main post offices of major cities and some 5-star hotels; because this technology is only just being introduced it is advisable to check that this facility is offered at your destination. **Telex/telegram:** International telegram and telex facilities exist in many cities. Offices of *Embratel* in Rio de Janerio (Praca Mauá 7) and São Paulo. Rio's airport provides 24-hour telecommunication services. The domestic telex service now covers the whole of the country. **Post:** Services are reasonably reliable. Sending mail registered or franked will eliminate the risk of having the stamps steamed off. Airmail service to Europe takes four to six days. Surface mail takes at least four weeks. Post offices are open 0900-1300 Monday to Friday and 0900-1300 Saturday. **Press:** The only English newspaper is *The Brazil Herald* in Rio. Also in Rio there is an English-language publication, the *Rio Visitor* which gives tourist information.
BBC World Service and Voice of America frequencies: From time to time these change. See the section *How to Use this Book* for more information.

BBC:				
MHz	15.26	15.19	11.75	6.005
Voice of America:				
MHz	15.21	11.58	9.775	5.995

PASSPORT/VISA

Regulations and requirements may be subject to change at short notice, and you are advised to contact the appropriate diplomatic or consular authority before finalising travel arrangements. Details of these may be found at the head of this country's entry. Any numbers in the chart refer to the footnotes below.

	Passport Required?	Visa Required?	Return Ticket Required?
Full British	Yes	No	2
BVP	Not valid	-	-
Australian	Yes	Yes	2
Canadian	Yes	Yes	2
USA	Yes	Yes	2
Other EC	Yes	1	2
Japanese	Yes	Yes	2

PASSPORTS: Valid passport required by all. Passports must be valid for at least 6 months.
British Visitors Passport: Not acceptable.
VISAS: Required by all except:
(a) **[1]** nationals of EC countries (except nationals of France who *do* require a visa);
(b) nationals of Andorra, Argentina, Austria, Bahamas, Barbados, Chile, Colombia, Finland, Iceland, Liechtenstein, Monaco, Morocco, Norway, Paraguay, Peru, Philippines, Suriname, Sweden, Switzerland, Trinidad & Tobago and Uruguay, Vatican City and Venezuela.
Note: [2] All travellers must be in possession of onward or return tickets.
Types of visa: Tourist, Business, Transit (required by *all* passengers in transit). A fee may be charged if visa is not applied for personally.
Validity: Tourist visas valid for up to 90 days. For an extension of this period apply in Brazil. Tourists are not allowed to work in Brazil.
Application to: Consulate. For addresses, see top of entry.
Application requirements: (a) Valid passport. (b) Application form. (c) Sufficient funds to cover duration of stay. (d) 1 photo. (e) Return or onward tickets.
Note: Visitors on business require a letter from their firm giving full details and confirming financial responsibility for the applicant. Visas will not be granted if the validity of the passport expires within 6 months.
Working days required: 2 clear days.
Temporary residence: Apply to Consulate.

MONEY

Currency: Cruzeiro (Cr) = 100 centavos. Notes are in denominations of Cr50,000, 10,000, 5000, 1000, 500 and 100. Coins are in denominations of Cr20, 10, 5 and 1, and 50, 20, 10 and 1 centavos.
Note: The Cruzeiro replaced the Cruzado in March 1990, and is not to be confused with the pre-1986 Cruzeiro which is not legal tender.
Currency exchange: All banks and cambios exchange recognised travellers cheques and foreign currency.
Credit cards: Access/Mastercard, American Express, Diners Club and Visa are accepted. Check with your

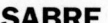

BRAZIL | **HEALTH REGULATIONS** | **VISA REGULATIONS** | Code-Link

GALILEO/WORLDSPAN

TI-DFT/GIG/HE

TI-DFT/GIG/VI

SABRE

TIDFT/GIG/HE

TIDFT/GIG/VI

To access this information on your CRS, swipe the barcode with a light pen or type in the text under the barcode. For more information, see the introduction *How to Use This Book.*

credit card company for details of merchant acceptability and other services which may be available.
Travellers cheques: Tourists cannot exchange US travellers cheques for US banknotes but they can, however, benefit from a 15% discount when paying hotel or restaurant bills in foreign currency or travellers cheques.
Exchange rate indicators: There are frequent currency changes and no stable exchange rate indicators can be given at present. In October 1992 the value of the Cruzeiro against Sterling and the US Dollar was as follows:
£1.00= 12045.60
$1.00= 7590.17
Currency restrictions: Free import and export of local currency. Free import of foreign currency, subject to declaration. Free export of foreign currency up to the amount declared.
Banking hours: 1000-1630 Monday to Friday.

DUTY FREE

The following goods may be taken into Brazil without incurring any duty:
400 cigarettes or 250g of tobacco or 25 cigars;
2 litres of alcohol
Up to US$5000 worth of goods bought duty-free in Brazil.
Prohibited goods: Meat and cheese products from various countries; contact the Consulate for details. Other varieties of animal origin transported from Africa, Asia, Italy, Portugal and Spain. The total value of imported goods may not exceed US$300.

PUBLIC HOLIDAYS

Public holidays observed in Brazil are as follows:
Apr 9 '93 Easter. **May 1** Labour Day. **Sep 7** Independence Day. **Oct 12** Our Lady Aparecida, patroness of Brazil. **Nov 2** All Souls' Day. **Nov 15** Proclamation of the Republic. **Dec 25** Christmas. **Jan 1 '94** New Year's Day. **Feb** Carnival.
Note: It is Government policy in Brazil for certain holidays to be taken on Monday if those holidays fall during the week; however, the church wishes to continue holding festivals on the traditional days. If plans are likely to be affected by such a holiday it is advisable to check the situation with the Information Office before travelling. Please note also that as four of the traditional holidays are fixed by municipalities there may be some variation from region to region.

HEALTH

Regulations and requirements may be subject to change at short notice, and you are advised to contact your doctor well in advance of your intended date of departure. Any numbers in the chart refer to the footnotes below.

	Special Precautions?	Certificate Required?
Yellow Fever	1	1
Cholera	No	No
Typhoid & Polio	Yes	-
Malaria	2	-
Food & Drink	3	-

[1]: A yellow fever vaccination certificate is required from travellers over six months of age arriving from infected regions. Vaccination is strongly recommended for those intending to visit rural areas in Acre, Amazonas, Goiás, Maranhão, Mato Grosso, Matto Gross do Sul, Pará and Rondônia States and the Territories of Amapá and Roraima.
[2]: *Malaria* risk exists throughout the year below 900m in Acre and Rondônia States, in the Territories of Amapá and Roraima, and in some rural areas in Amazonas, Goiás, Maranhão, Mato Grosso and Pará States. The malignant *falciparum* form of the disease is reportedly 'highly resistant' to both chloroquine and sulfadoxine/pyrimethane.
[3]: All water should be regarded as being potentially contaminated. Water used for drinking, brushing teeth or making ice should have first been boiled or otherwise sterilised. Pasteurised milk and cheese is available in towns and is generally considered safe to consume. Milk outside of urban areas is unpasteurised and should be boiled; powdered or tinned milk is available and is advised in rural areas, but make sure that it is reconstituted with pure water. Avoid dairy products which are likely to have been made from local milk. Only eat well-cooked meat and fish, preferably served hot. Pork, salad and mayonnaise may carry increased risk. Vegetables should be cooked and fruit peeled.
Rabies is present. For those at high risk vaccination before arrival should be considered. If you are bitten abroad seek medical advice without delay. For more information consult the *Health* section at the back of the book.
Bilharzia (schistosomiasis) is present. Avoid swimming and paddling in fresh water. Swimming pools which are well-chlorinated and maintained are safe.
Health care: English-speaking medical staff are found mainly in São Paulo and Rio de Janeiro. The main hospital in São Paulo is the Hospital Samaritano. Full insurance is recommended as medical costs are high.

TRAVEL - International

AIR: Brazil's main international airline is *Varig (RG)*.
Approximate flight times: From *London* to Rio de Janeiro is 10 hours 50 minutes and to São Paulo is 11 hours.
From *Los Angeles* to Rio de Janeiro is 13 hours 55 minutes.
From *New York* to Rio de Janeiro is 10 hours 10 minutes.
From *Sydney* to Rio de Janeiro is 19 hours 55 minutes.
International airports: *Rio de Janeiro* (Galeão) *(GIG)*, 20km (12.5 miles) northwest of city. There are regular bus services between the International and Santa Dumont airports, and into the city. Airport facilities include car parking, duty-free shop, banking, restaurant.
São Paulo (Guarulhos) *(GRU)*, 25km (15 miles) northeast of the city. Regular bus and taxi services. Airport facilities include duty-free shops and restaurants.
São Paulo (Viracopos) *(VCP)*, 96km (60 miles) southwest of the city. Airport facilities include banking, a duty-free shop and a restaurant.
São Paulo (Congonhas) *(CGH)*, 14km (8 miles) from the city.
Manàus (Internacional Eduardo Gomes) *(MAO)*, 14km (9 miles) from the city. There are coach services into the city and to other destinations.
Salvador (Dois de Julho) *(SSA)*, 36km (22 miles) from the city. 24-hour taxi facilities are available. Airport facilities include banking, a duty-free shop and a restaurant.
Note: *Brasília* does not have an international airport. All connections are made via Rio de Janeiro. Bus and taxi services are available to all cities.
Departure tax: US$16.50 is levied on international departures.
SEA: Passenger cruises from Europe run by *Lamport* and *Holt* lines. Other cruise lines, some of which also organise cruises down the Amazon are *Lindblad Travel, Delta, Costa* and *Society Expeditions*.
RAIL: Limited rail services link Brazil with Bolivia and Uruguay. For details contact Brazilian Tourist Office.
ROAD: It is possible to drive or take a bus to Brazil from the USA, but it is wise to check any changes in political status or requirements in Central America before travelling. For further information contact the Brazilian Tourist Office. **Documentation:** International Driving Permit required. This must be validated by Automovel Club de Brazil.

TRAVEL - Internal

AIR: There is a shuttle service between São Paulo and Rio de Janeiro, a regular service from São Paulo to Brasília, and a shuttle service from Brasília to Belo Horizonte. There are air services between all Brazilian cities, Brazil having one of the largest internal air networks in the world. At weekends it is advisable to book seats as the services are much used. A monthly magazine *Aeronautico* gives all timetables and fares for internal air travel. Air taxis are available between all major centres.
SEA/RIVER: Ferries serve all coastal ports. River transport is the most efficient method for the Amazon delta.
RAIL: Limited rail connections to most major cities and towns, but there has been a substantial decline in the provision of long-distance services. Because of the great distances and the climate, some of these journeys can be uncomfortable. Daytime and overnight trains with restaurant and sleeping-cars link São Paulo and Rio de Janeiro.
ROAD: Brazil has over 1,600,000km (approximately 1 million miles) of roads. **Bus:** Inter-urban transport is very much road based (accounting for 97% of travellers) compared with air (2.2%) and rail (less than 1%). High quality coaches have been increasingly introduced on the main routes, which are well served. Operators include: Cometa, which operates between São Paulo and Belo Horizonte; Penha (São Paulo–Pôrto Alegre); Reunidas (São Paulo–Aracatuba); Motta (São Paulo–Campo Grande); Garcia (São Paulo–Londrina); Real–Expresso (São Paulo–Rio–Brasília); TransBrasíliana (Rio–Belem); Sulamericana (Curitiba–Foz do Iguazú); and Expresso Brasileiro (São Paulo–Rio). Services connect all inhabited parts of the country. Standards and time-tables vary, and the visitor must be prepared for overnight stops and long waits between connecting stages. **Car hire:** Available in all major centres. Traffic drives on the right. Parking in cities is very difficult and it is best to avoid driving through the often congested city areas if at all possible. **Documentation:** International Driving Licence required. A foreign licence is valid for six months, although a certificate of validity must be obtained from the Brazilian driving authorities.
URBAN: There are extensive bus services in all the main centres, often with express 'executivo' at premium fares run by air-conditioned coaches. Rio and São Paulo both have two-line metros and local rail lines, and there are trolleybuses in São Paulo and a number of other cities. Trolleybuses are increasingly being introduced as an energy-saving measure. Fares are generally regulated with interchange possible between some bus and metro/rail lines, for instance on the feeder bus linking the Rio metro with Copacabana. **Taxi:** In most cities these are identified by red number plates, and are fitted with meters. Willingness immediately to accept a taxi-driver's advice on where to go or where to stay should be tempered by the knowledge that places to which he takes a visitor are more than likely to give him a commission – and the highest commissions will usually come from the most expensive places.
JOURNEY TIMES: The following chart gives approximate journey times (in hours and minutes) from Brasília to other major cities/towns in Brazil.

	Air
Belo Horizonte	1.00
São Paulo	1.20
Rio de Janeiro	1.25
Pôrto Alegre	2.20
Manàus	2.30
Foz do Iguazú	3.25

ACCOMMODATION

HOTELS: Accommodation varies according to region. First-class accommodation is, by and large, restricted to the cities of the south. For further information contact the Associacao Brasileira da Industria de Hoteis, Avenida Nilo Pecanha, 12, 10-1004/5/6, Rio de Janeiro, Brazil. Tel: (21) 2423768. Fax: (21) 33890.
Note: Accommodation for Carnival time should be booked well in advance.
Rio de Janeiro/São Paulo: Many modern hotels, ranging from the very expensive deluxe hotels to moderate priced hotels. It is vital to pre-book well in advance for the Carnival.
Brasília: Small number of good hotels. Most tourists visit Brasília by air from Rio or São Paulo for a day trip, or make a single night stopover. The city is used only for national administration.
Bahia (Salvador): Small number of good hotels, some moderately priced hotels, several demi-pensions.
Amazon Basin: This region is being developed in part as a tourist attraction.
Grading: In 1979 the Federal Tourist Authority began introducing a star range system for hotels. It is now used by most establishments in towns. The classification is not, however, the standard used in Europe and North America. **5-star** is the grade for deluxe hotels. **3-star** hotels are good value for money and offer well-kept accommodation, whilst a **1-star** hotel can only offer basic amenities.
Visitors are reminded that hotel tariffs are subject to alteration at any time, and are liable to fluctuate according to changes in the exchange rate.
Note: The best guide to hotels in Brazil is the *Guia do Brasil Quatro Rodas*, which includes maps.
CAMPING/CARAVANNING: Cars may be hired, and camping arranged on safari tours or group 'exploration' trips in the Amazon region. The road network in Brazil is good and is being expanded, but since many parts of Brazil are wild, or semi-explored, it is wise to drive on main roads, to camp with organised groups under supervision and with official permits, or otherwise to stay in recognised hotels. The country is peaceful, but because it is so large there is a real danger of getting lost, or being injured or killed by natural accident or lack of local knowledge of survival.
Those with an 'international camper's card' pay only half the rate of a non-member (about US$4 per person). The *Camping Clube do Brasil* has 43 sites in 13 states. For those on a low budget, service stations can be used as camping sites. These are equipped with shower facilities and can supply food. For further information contact: Camping Clube do Brazil, Divisao de Campings, Rua Senador Dantas, 75-29 andar, 20000 Rio de Janeiro, Brazil. Tel: (21) 262 7127.
YOUTH HOSTELS: For further information contact: Federacao Brasileira de Albergues da Juventude, Rua General Dionisio, 63 22271, Rio de Janeiro, Brazil. Tel: (21) 286 0303.

RESORTS & EXCURSIONS

For the purposes of this section, the country has been divided into five regions: the northern, the northeastern, the west-central, the southeastern and the southern.

The Northern Region

The states of Amazonas, Pará, Acre and Rondonia cover an area of more than 3,400,000 sq km (1,300,000 sq miles) but have a combined population of little more than 6,000,000. Almost entirely covered with thick rainforest, the north of Brazil is known as the 'exotic Amazon' and is an area where nature prevails over all else (except, perhaps, the slash-and-burn agriculturalists and road-builders).

Manàus is the capital of the state of Amazonas. It contains the Amazonas theatre, with a majestic neo-classical facade, a number of fine restaurants and hotels and a free-trade zone which is excellent for cheap shopping. The Amazon river and its tributaries are ideal for boat excursions, and also offer excellent angling.

Belém has a splendid park and market as well as many fine churches. The *Goeldi Museum* contains the largest collection of tropical plants in the world. **Maray's Island** is the cradle of the Marajoara civilisation; **Santarém, Rio Branco** and **Pôrto Velho** are also all worth a visit.

The Northeastern Region

Known as the 'Golden Coast', this region contains the states of Bahia, Sergipe, Alagoas, Pernambuco, Paraíba, Rio Grande do Norte, Ceará, Piaui and Maranhão. It covers nearly 1,600,000 sq km (600,000 sq miles) and has a population of 35 million. The area is distinctive for its historical and folkloric traditions, as well as for its many beautiful beaches.

Salvador, the capital of Bahia, contains the beautiful arts and crafts market of the *Mercado Modelo*. The number and variety of churches in Salvador is staggering; some of the best include the *Convent of São Francisco de Assis* and the *Church of Nosso Senhor do Bonfim*. Salvador is also renowned for its museums, some of which are converted churches. The area around the city also has many excellent beaches. The towns of **Ilhéus, Pôrto Seguro,** and **Aracaju** all have fine churches and colonial architecture worth visiting. *Recife*, known as the 'Venice of Brazil' on account of the canals and waterways which criss-cross the city, is also well endowed with churches. **Olinda, Caruaru, Natal, Fortaleza, Teresina** and **São Luis** are also notable for their architecture, craftworkers and fine beaches.

The West Central Region

An area of huge marshes traversed by the Araguaia River, it consists of the states of Goiás, Mato Grosso and Mato Grosso do Sul. It covers as area of 1,900,000 million sq km (730,000 sq miles) and has a population of nearly eight million. The region is best known for its pleasant climate, and for its huge cattle ranches and plantations.

Brasília, (which was built miles from anywhere on specially flattened Amazonian rainforest) is known worldwide for its futuristic architecture, which is most notable in the *Praça dos Três Poderes*, *Palácio do Planalto*, and *The National Congress*.

Goiás, 200km (120 miles) to the west, serves as a jumping off point for tourists visiting the *Araguaia River*, *Bananal Island* and the thermal springs of *Caldas Novas*.

Mato Grosso is the gateway to the Pantanal, which is Brazil's largest ecological reserve where farm-hotels house tourists and organise fishing trips and photographic excursions.

The Southeast Region

This comprises the states of São Paulo, Rio de Janeiro, Minas Gerais and Espirito Santo. It covers an area of more than 900,000 sq km (350,000 sq miles) and has a population of nearly 53 million. It is the country's most developed region and offers the best tourist facilities, including a wide variety of scenic and historic resorts.

Rio de Janeiro has one of the most beautiful settings in the world. Renowned for its excellent beaches, such as *Copacabana* and *Ipanema*, the city is chiefly known for its world famous carnival. **São Paulo** is famed throughout the continent for its night-life and its shopping facilities. The gold boom in Minas Gerais during the 18th century produced a number of historic towns, the most famous being **Ouro Preto.** The southeast region has a number of spas, known for their marvellous climate and mineral water; all are well equipped to accommodate the traveller; *Petrópolis*, *Teresópolis* and *Nova Friburgo* are but a few of these.

The Southern Region

This consists of three states, Rio Grande do Sul, Santa Catarina and Paraná, covering an area of over 570,000 sq km (220,000 sq miles). The ideal climate has made this region the most popular among European immigrants. Rio Grande do Sul is one of the richest states in Brazil, and is equipped with good tourist facilities. **Pôrto Alegre,** its capital, offers the visitor fine museums and art centres as well as delightful surrounding countryside. The most popular beaches in this area are the *Tramandai* and *Torres*, respectively 126km (78 miles) and 209km (130 miles) from Porto Alegre. The Gramado and Canela mountains are also popular with tourists. The state of Santa Catarina, with its island capital of *Florianópolis*, also has fine beaches at *Laguna*, *Itapena* and *Camburu*. Paraná is a prime coffee producing state. The train journey between its capital **Curitiba** and **Paranaguá** is a sightseeing must, as is **Vila Velha** (the City of Stone) and – most famous of all – the *Foz do Iguaçu* (Iguazú Falls), the massive waterfalls on the border with Argentina and Paraguay.

SOCIAL PROFILE

FOOD & DRINK: Many regional variations which are very different from North American and European food. One example is Bahian cookery, derived from days when slaves had to cook scraps and anything that could be caught locally, together with coconut milk and palm oil. Specialities include *vatapá* (shrimps, fish oil and coconut milk, bread and rice), *sarapatel* (liver, heart, tomatoes, peppers, onion and gravy), *caruru* (shrimps, okra, onions and peppers). From Rio Grande do Sul comes *churrasco* (barbecued beef, tomato and onion sauce), *galleto al primo canto* (pieces of cockerel cooked on the spit with white wine and oil). From Amazon comes *pato no tucupi* (duck in rich wild green herb sauce), *tacacá* (thick yellow soup with shrimps and garlic). In the northeast dried salted meat and beans are the staple diet. In Rio de Janeiro a favourite dish is *feijoada* (thick stew of black beans, chunks of beef, pork, sausage, chops, pigs' ears and tails on white rice, boiled green vegetables and orange slices). Types of establishments vary. Table service is usual in most restaurants and cafés. If resident in a hotel, drinks and meals can often be charged to account. **Drink:** All kinds of alcoholic drink are manufactured and available and there are no licensing hours or restrictions on drinking. Beer is particularly good and draught beer is called *chopp*. The local liqueur is *cachaça*, a local equivalent of whisky popular with locals, but not so much with visitors. This phenomenally strong spirit is often mixed with sugar, crushed ice and limes to make *caiparinha*, a refreshing if intoxicating cocktail. Southern Brazilian wine is of a high quality. Some bars have waiters and table service.

NIGHTLIFE: The best entertainment occurs in Rio de Janeiro and São Paulo. In Rio the major clubs do not present their main acts until after midnight and the daily

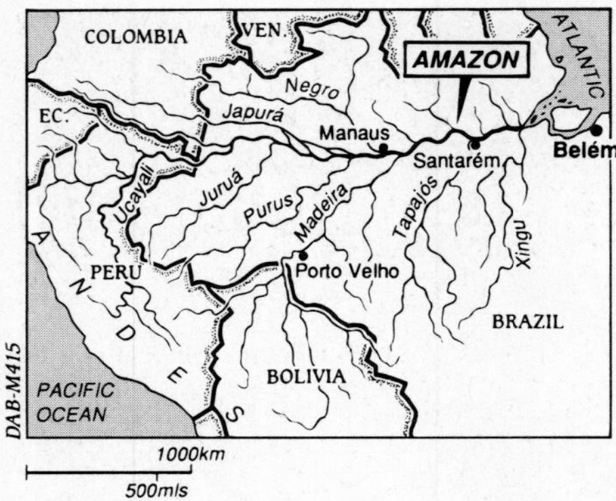

paper gives current information; small clubs *(boites)* provide nightly entertainment throughout the city. São Paulo nightlife is more sophisticated, with greater choice; the shows tend to start earlier.

SHOPPING: In Rio and São Paulo major shops and markets stay open quite late in the evening. Rio and Bahia specialise in antiques and jewellery. Special purchases include: gems (particularly emeralds), jewellery (particularly silver), souvenirs and permissible antiques, leather or snake skin goods. Fashions and antiques, crystal and pottery is a speciality of São Paulo. Belém, the city of the Amazon valley, specialises in jungle items, but be careful that you are not purchasing objects that have been plundered from the jungle, contributing to the general destruction. Check for restrictions on import to your home country of goods made from skins of protected species. **Shopping hours:** 0900-1830 Monday to Friday; 0900-1300 Saturday. Most department stores close at 2200. All the above times are subject to local variations and many shops open until late in the evenings.

SPORT: Association **football** is the national obsession, the national team having won the World Cup on three occasions. **Ball games** and **athletics** are also popular. ***Capoeira,*** a martial art, was developed by black slaves in colonial times disguised as a dance to an African musical rhythm. **Mountain climbing, hang-gliding** and **racing** are popular, and safari trips are available to the Mato Grosso or the Amazon jungle; big game **hunting** is, however, now illegal. **Waterskiing** and underwater **diving** clubs exist all along the coastline. Both deep sea and river **fishing** are available.

SPECIAL EVENTS: There are a number of lavish festivals throughout the year in Brazil, the two most notable being Bahia's carnival just after Christmas (from December to March) and the carnival in Rio de Janeiro (February 12 to 15), widely regarded as the most spectacular and extravagant in the world. For details of exact dates, contact the Tourist Information Office.

Mar-Apr '93 *Carnival*, Pernambuco; *Brazilian Formula One Grand Prix*, São Paulo; *Corpus Christi*, Pernambuco; *Easter Festivities*, Tiradentes. **Apr 18-21** *Independence Festivities*, Minas Gerais. **May-Jun** *Feast of the Holy Ghost*, Maranho. **Jun** *June Festivities*. **Jun 11-26** *Amazon Folklore Festival*, Manaus. **Jul** *Winter Festival*, San Paulo. **Jul 1** *Sea Dragon Regatta*, Ceara. **Jul 2** *Independence of Bahia*, Bahia. **Aug** *Marathon*, Rio de Janeiro; *Competition for Sweets, Liquors and Battidas*, **Pernambuco. Sep 2** *Festival of Our Lady of Aparecida*, San Paulo. **Dec 31** *New Year's Eve Festival.*

SOCIAL CONVENTIONS: Handshaking is customary on meeting and taking one's leave, and normal European courtesies are observed. Frequent offers of coffee and tea are customary. Flowers are acceptable as a gift on arrival or following a visit for a meal. A souvenir from the visitor's home country will be well-received as a gift of appreciation. Casual wear is normal particularly during hot weather. In night clubs casual-smart (eg blazer, no tie) is acceptable. For more formal occasions the mode of dress will be indicated on invitations. Smoking is acceptable unless notified. The Catholic Church is highly respected in the community, something which should be kept in mind by the visitor. **Tipping:** 10% is usual for most services not included on the bill.

BUSINESS PROFILE

ECONOMY: Brazil is the world's fifth largest country, whilst her economy has the tenth highest aggregate national product in the world. Although agriculture remains the largest sector in terms of employment, there are well-developed mineral and manufacturing industries. Brazil is the world's second largest exporter of agricultural products, principally coffee, sugar, soya beans, orange juice, beef poultry and cocoa. Sisal, tobacco, maize and cotton are also produced. Orange juice and coffee are key export earners. Industrial production is concentrated in machinery, electrical goods, construction materials, rubber and chemicals and vehicle production. The large steel industry has experienced bad times due to the fall in world demand and objections by foreign governments to Brazil's protectionist policies (which have been relaxed appreciably since 1988). Vast mineral reserves include iron ore, of which Brazil is the world's largest exporter, bauxite (the ore from which aluminium is produced), gold, titanium, manganese, copper, and tin which is rapidly assuming considerable economic importance. New deposits are discovered almost daily. Oil discoveries have also grown rapidly, although Brazil still imports most of its oil, principally from Iraq and Saudi Arabia. Natural resources are the basis of Brazil's substantial trade surplus of $9 billion (on total exports of $33 billion – 1988 figures): the US, Japan and the EC are the main destinations for Brazilian exports. Despite its healthy trade surplus, the Brazilian economy experienced considerable difficulty during the 1980s through the familiar South American problems of hyper-inflation and enormous overseas debts. On several occasions the Government seemed to have brought inflation under control, albeit at the cost of slowing economic growth, but each time their efforts were frustrated as the pressures which built up within the system burst out into a new spiral of price and wage increases. In 1988, in apparent frustration, the Brazilian government announced a unilateral moratorium on debt and interest repayments to commercial banks: 12 months later, the Government realised the policy had been a costly mistake, and resumed rescheduling negotiations with the banks. By the time President Sarney left office at the end of 1989, a solution to Brazil's economic woes seemed as elusive as ever. His successor, Fernando Collor de Mello, adopted a novel and unique method of economic management. His aim was, quite literally, to remove inflation from the financial system – by removing a large proportion of the money in the economy. Personal bank deposits were frozen. The population was, for the most part, too stunned to object too strenuously. Collor de Mello's strategy – the 'Novo Plan' – also included more orthodox measures such as a reduction in public spending, privatisation of state-owned industries and an overhaul of the tax system. By the autumn of 1990, the economy was showing signs of genuine recovery. By 1992, however, it had become clear that the structural problems persisted as much as before. In the longer term, most Brazilians feel that the best prospects for economic development lie in the exploitation of the interior, and in particular the rainforests. However, unrestrained development is no longer politically possible given the strength of opposition both within the country and internationally. Of interest here is a novel agreement signed between the British and Brazilian governments to create a more ecologically sensitive approach to rainforest development, involving aid and technical assistance. (This may become a pattern for future aid packages to the Third World.) Despite its problems, many observers are optimistic about Brazil's economic prospects, once improved industrial efficiency, careful fiscal management and a sound relationship with overseas creditors have taken root. Brazil's principal trading partners are the United States, Japan, Germany and its fellow members of the newly-formed southern Latin American trading bloc, Mercosur. Brazil also has important trading links with a number of Arab countries, notably Saudi Arabia and, until UN-imposed economic sanctions took effect, Iraq.

BUSINESS: Business suits are worn when meeting senior officials and local heads of business, for semi-formal social functions and in exclusive restaurants and clubs. Exchange of calling cards is usual as is the expectation of dealing with someone of equal business status.

Office hours: 0900-1800 Monday to Friday.

COMMERCIAL INFORMATION: The following organisations can offer advice: Confederacão Nacional do Comércio (CNC) (Chamber of Commerce), SCS, Edif. Presidente Dutra, 4° andar, Quadra 11, 70.327 Brasília DF, Brazil. Tel: (61) 223 0578.

HISTORY & GOVERNMENT

HISTORY: Brazil was first discoverd by the Portuguese Admiral Pedro Alvares Cabral in 1500. The country was colonized later that century. Until the arrival of Jesuit missionaries, plantation owners freely exploited the local inhabitants as slaves. Brazil achieved independence in 1822 with Don Pedro as Constitutional Emperor and Perpetual Defender. The country was declared a republic when Don Pedro was dethroned in 1889, after which it was placed under military rule. Since that date military leaders have played an influential role in the politics of Brazil. From 1964-85 Brazil was under military rule. Pressure for a return to civilian rule gathered momentum during the early 1980s, particularly after the military ceded power in neighbouring Argentina in 1983. The army consented and at the election held in January 1985, Tancredo Neves, a former prime minister and latterly a state governor, became Brazil's first civilian president for 21 years. Neves was the candidate of a liberal alliance formed around the country's main opposition party at the time, the Partido do Movimento Democratico Brasileiro, but which also included dissidents from the then ruling (and now opposition) Partido Democratico Social. Neves died before he was able to take office and was replaced by the deputy president-designate, Jose Sarney. Initial pessimism about the prospects for this little-known and rather colourless figure was shown to be ill-founded as Sarney successfully guided the country through the tricky period of transition between military and civilian rule which many South American countries are now negotiating. A new democratic constitution was drafted and implemented, but the economic problems which dominated his term in office defied solution despite some temporary successes against inflation. The next presidential election, held in late 1989, was a straight fight between two candidates: the Conservative Fernando Collor de Mello and the trades unionist Luis Inacio da Silva (known as Lula), standing for the Workers Party. Collor de Mello eventually won the close-fought poll and immediately set about tackling Brazil's serious economic problems (see *Trading Brief* section above). Once the details of his extraordinary economic experiment became apparent, there was widespread concern that the new government would be unable to weather the political storm which seemed sure to follow. In the event, it never happened – it seemed almost as if the Brazilian people were too astonished to react in opposition. While Collor de Mello's government has achieved some initial success on the economic front, particularly in taming hyper-inflation, there are several problems which have brought unwelcome international attention to Brazil. One is the fate of the country's estimated 8 million 'street children' who are held responible for much urban street crime and now face the threat of murder by hired 'death squads' (it is not clear who is doing the hiring). Another is the destruction of vast tracts of Amazonian rainforest by loggers and ranchers. This attracted widespread international concern; it is now generally recognised that this could have a substantial effect on the environment (see *Trading Brief*). The rate of exploitation has since been substantially reduced. It was appropriate, therefore, that in June 1992 Rio de Janeiro should host the first global summit on environmental issues – the 'Earth Summit'. The outcome of the fortnight-long series of presentations by ministers and others from over 100 countries was broadly disappointing. Two major conventions, on the world climate and on the diversity of species, were finally accepted after extensive dilution. There is a widespread feeling that the industrialised north does not take the issue sufficiently seriously while the developing south resents taking measures which may hinder their economic growth before they have benefitted from that growth. Perhaps the best that can be said of the summit is that, despite some notable absentees such as the EC Environment Commissioner, Carlo Ripa di Meana (who condemned it as an ineffectual talking shop), it took place at all. For its host, the summit was a welcome, albeit brief, respite from mounting domestic problems, in particular, a congressional inquiry which appeared to have uncovered evidence of corruption by the president and members of his family. The crisis, which has yet to be resolved at the time of writing, has all but paralysed the Government and prevented the implementation of measures to tackle Brazil's burgeoning economic crisis.

GOVERNMENT: The 1969 constitution, under which the country was administered as a Federal Republic with a governor and elected legislature for each state, may be reformed shortly in accordance with promises made by Neves.

CLIMATE

Varies from arid scrubland in interior to impassable tropical rainforests of the northerly Amazon jungle and the tropical eastern coastal beaches. The south is more temperate. Rainy seasons occur from January to April in the north, April to July in the northeast and November to March in the Rio/São Paulo area.

Required clothing: Lightweight cottons and linens with waterproofing for rainy season (November-March). Warm clothing needed in south during winter (June-July). Specialist clothing needed for Amazon region. Warm clothing is advised if visiting the southern regions in winter time.

RIO DE JANEIRO Brazil (31m)

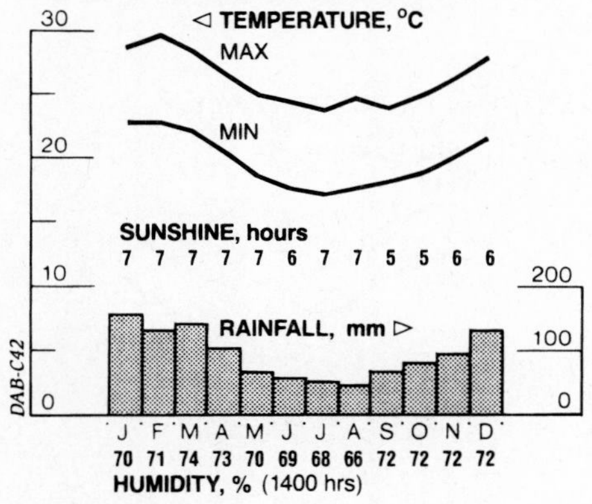

MANAUS Brazil (48m)

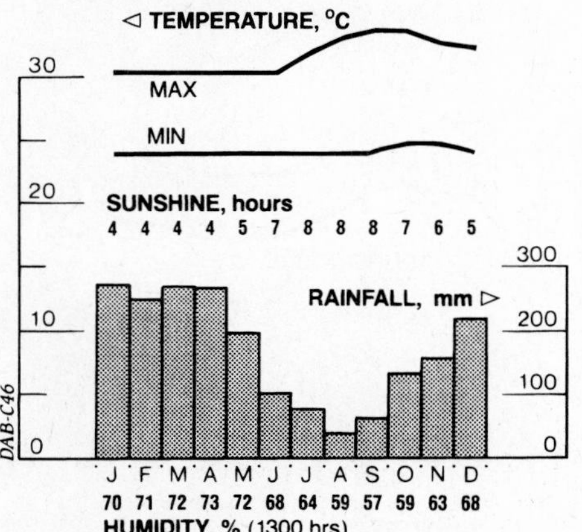

BRITISH DEPENDENT TERRITORIES

Note: The following is a list of the British Dependent Territories; many of these have their own entries in the *World Travel Guide*. For more information on these islands contact the Passport Office in London (for entry requirements), tel: (071) 279 3434; the Royal Commonwealth Society, tel: (071) 930 6733, fax: (071) 930 9705; or the Foreign Office, Atlantic and Indian Ocean Department, tel: (071) 270 3000.

ANGUILLA:
See the section earlier in the *World Travel Guide*.

ASCENSION ISLAND:
Location: South Atlantic, 1131km (703 miles) north-west of St Helena.
Area: 88 sq km (34 sq miles).
Population: 1099 (1991 estimate – excluding British military personnel).
A dependency of St Helena, the main importance of the island is as a communications centre and a military base.

BERMUDA:
See the section earlier in the *World Travel Guide*.

BRITISH INDIAN OCEAN TERRITORY:
Location: Consists of the Chagos Archipelago, 1930km (1199 miles) northeast of Mauritius, and the coral atoll of Diego Garcia.
Area: 60 sq km (23 sq miles) of land and over 54,400 sq km (21,100 sq miles) of sea.
Population: There are no permanent inhabitants. Under the terms of the 1966 agreement the islands are used jointly by the USA and UK governments for military purposes. Following Iraq's invasion of Kuwait in August 1990, Diego Garcia was the base used by the US B-52 bombers taking part in the Allied action in the Gulf.

BRITISH VIRGIN ISLANDS:
See the section later in the *World Travel Guide – Virgin Islands (British)*.

CAYMAN ISLANDS:
See the section later in the *World Travel Guide*.

FALKLAND ISLANDS:
See the section later in the *World Travel Guide*.

GIBRALTAR:
See the section later in the *World Travel Guide*.

HONG KONG:
See the section later in the *World Travel Guide*.

MONTSERRAT:
See the section later in the *World Travel Guide*.

PITCAIRN ISLANDS:
Location: Central South Pacific, equidistant from Panama and New Zealand. The group includes the uninhabited islands of Oeno, Henderson and Ducie.
Area: 35.5 sq km (13.7 sq miles).
Population: 52 on Pitcairn (1990).
Population Density: 12 per sq km (Pitcairn only).
Religion: Seventh Day Adventist.
Health: A yellow fever vaccination certificate is required of all travellers over one year of age coming from infected areas; see *Health* section at back of book. Since 1989 Henderson has been included in the United Nations 'World Heritage List' as a bird sanctuary. For further information, contact the New Zealand High Commission or Embassy.

ST HELENA:
Location: South Atlantic, about 1930km (1200 miles) west of the Angolan coast.
Area: 122 sq km (47 sq miles).
Population: 5644 (1987).
Capital: Jamestown, where about 1413 people live.
Religion: Mostly Anglican.
Money: The St Helena Pound is equivalent to the UK

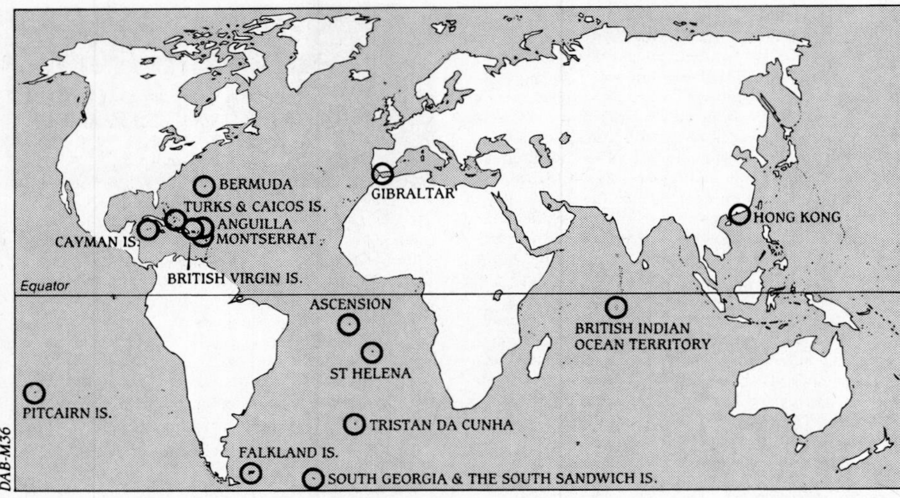

Pound sterling.
Travel: There are no railways or airfields, but *St Helena Shipping Company Limited* operates services to and from the UK six times a year, also stopping at the Canary Islands, Ascension Island and South Africa.
St Helena depends on aid from Britain, although fishing, livestock, handicrafts and timber are important to the economy. There is a chamber of commerce in Jamestown.

SOUTH GEORGIA AND THE SOUTH SANDWICH ISLANDS:
Location: South Atlantic. South Georgia lies about 1300km (800 miles) east-southeast of the Falkland Islands, and the South Sandwich Islands lie about 750km (470 miles) southeast of South Georgia.
Area: South Georgia, 3592 sq km (1387 sq miles), and the South Sandwich Islands, 311 sq km (120 sq miles).
Population: There are no permanent inhabitants.
Dependencies of the Falkland Islands up until 1985, the islands now fall under the jurisdiction of the Commissioner for the territory, the Governor of the Falkland Islands. The islands are used for scientific purposes, and are watched over by a small British garrison.

TRISTAN DA CUNHA:
Location: South Atlantic, 2400km (1500 miles) west of Cape Town, South Africa. The group also includes Inaccessible Island, the three Nightingale Islands and Gough Island.
Area: 98 sq km (38 sq miles).
Population: 309 (1990).
Religion: Anglican with small Roman Catholic minority.
A dependency of St Helena, Tristan da Cunha's economy is based on fishing, handicrafts and stamps.

TURKS AND CAICOS ISLANDS:
See the section later in the *World Travel Guide*.

BRITISH ANTARCTIC TERRITORY:
Location: Within the Antarctic Treaty area.
Area: About 1,710,000 sq km (660,000 sq miles) of land. The territory also includes the South Shetlands and the South Orkneys.
Population: There are no permanent inhabitants, and the territory is used only for scientific purposes.
Since April 1967, these have been administered by the Department of Education and Science and are no longer a British Dependent Territory. See also the *Antarctica* entry earlier in the *World Travel Guide*.

UNITED KINGDOM CROWN DEPENDENCIES: The **Isle of Man** and the **Channel Islands** are not integral parts of the United Kingdom but are dependencies of the Crown and enjoy a high degree of internal self-government. For convenience, information on these islands has been placed at the end of the entry for the *United Kingdom* below.

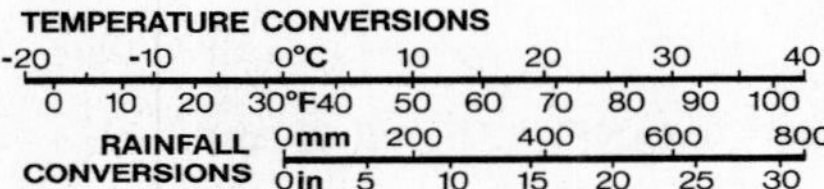

TRISTAN DA CUNHA (23m)

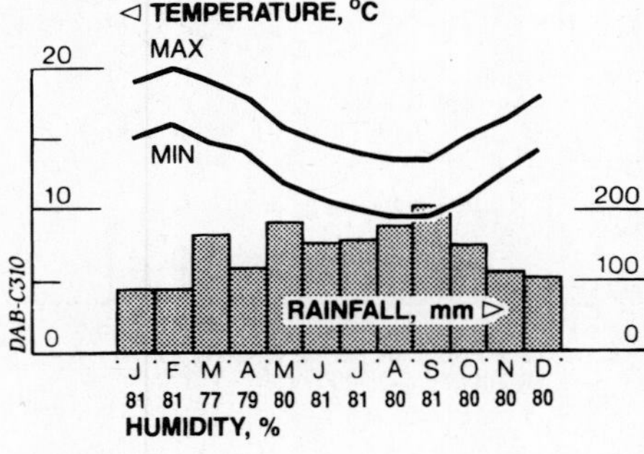

GEORGETOWN Ascension (17m)

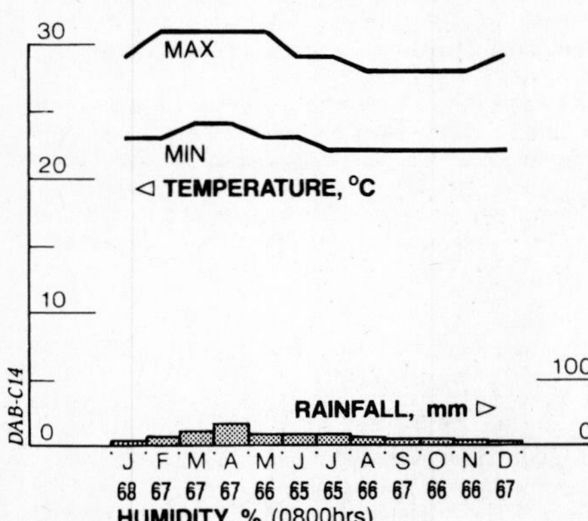

JAMESTOWN St Helena (12m)

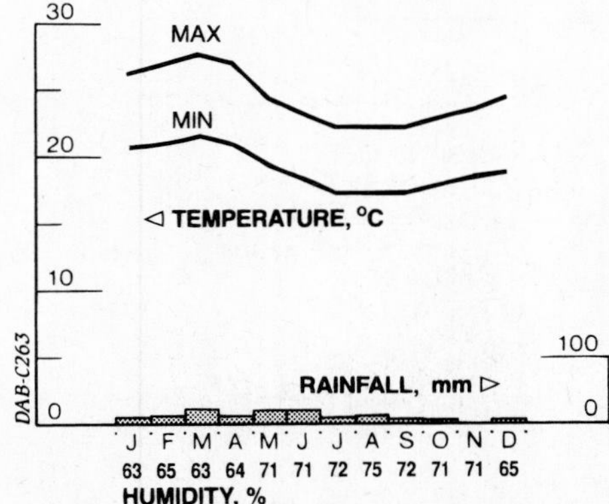

BRUNEI

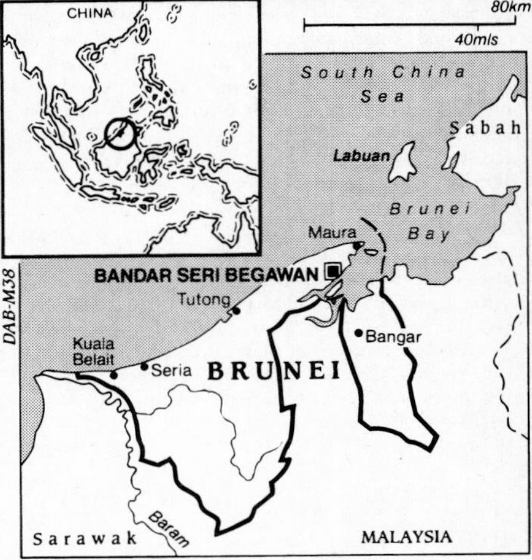

Location: South-East Asia; island of Borneo.

Information Bureau Section
Information Department
Prime Minister's Office
Bandar Seri Begawan 2041, Brunei
Tel: (2) 240 400. Fax: (2) 244 104. Telex: 2614.
High Commission of Negara Brunei Darussalam
19 Belgrave Square
London SW1X 8PG
Tel: (071) 581 0521. Fax: (071) 235 9717. Opening hours: 0930-1300 and 1400-1630 Monday to Friday.
Ministry of Foreign Affairs
Jalan Subok
Bandar Seri Begawan, Brunei
Tel: (2) 241 177. Telex: 2292.
British High Commission
PO Box 2197
3rd Floor, Hong Kong Bank Chambers
Jalan Pemancha
Bandar Seri Begawan, Brunei
Tel: (2) 22231 *or* 23121 *or* 26001. Fax: (2) 26002.
Telex: 2211 UKREP BU.
Embassy of Negara Brunei Darussalam
Suite 300, 3rd Floor
2600 Virginia Avenue, NW
Washington, DC
20037
Tel: (202) 342 0159. Fax: (202) 342 0158. Telex: 904081.
Embassy of the United States of America
3rd Floor, Teck Guan Plaza
Jalan Sultan and Jalan McArthur
Bandar Seri Begawan, Brunei
Tel: (2) 229 670. Fax: (2) 225 293. Telex: 2609 AMEMB.
High Commission of Negara Brunei Darussalam
Suite 248
866 United Nations Plaza
New York, NY
10017
Tel: (212) 838 1600. Fax: (212) 980 6478.
The High Commission also deals with enquiries from Canada.

AREA: 5765 sq km (2226 sq miles).
POPULATION: 249,000 (1989 estimate).
POPULATION DENSITY: 43.2 per sq km.
CAPITAL: Bandar Seri Begawan. **Population:** 50,500 (1986).
GEOGRAPHY: Brunei is a small coastal state in the northwest corner of Borneo, bounded on all landward sides by Sarawak (Malaysia), which splits Brunei into two parts. The landscape is mainly equatorial jungle cut by rivers. Most settlements are situated at estuaries.
LANGUAGE: Malay is the official language. English and Chinese dialects are also spoken.

RELIGION: Most of the Malay population are Sunni Muslims. There are also significant Buddhist, Confucian, Daoist and Christian minorities.
TIME: GMT + 8.
ELECTRICITY: 230 volts AC, 50Hz. Plugs are either round or square 3-pin.
COMMUNICATIONS: Telephone: Full IDD is available. Country code: 673. Public telephones are available in most post office branches and main shopping areas and there is a private internal service. **Telex/telegram:** There are no public telex facilities, but they are available at government, large business offices and major hotels. Telegram facilities are available from the government telecommunications office in Bandar Seri Begawan. **Post:** Airmail letters to Europe take two to five days. **Press:** The only English-language newspaper is the daily *Borneo Bulletin*.
BBC World Service and Voice of America frequencies: From time to time these change. See the section *How to Use this Book* for more information.

BBC:				
MHz	15.36	9.740	6.195	3.915
Voice of America:				
MHz	17.74	11.76	7.275	1.575

PASSPORT/VISA

Regulations and requirements may be subject to change at short notice, and you are advised to contact the appropriate diplomatic or consular authority before finalising travel arrangements. Details of these may be found at the head of this country's entry. Any numbers in the chart refer to the footnotes below.

	Passport Required?	Visa Required?	Return Ticket Required?
Full British	Yes	1	Yes
BVP	Not valid	-	-
Australian	Yes	Yes	Yes
Canadian	Yes	2	Yes
USA	Yes	Yes	Yes
Other EC	Yes	1	Yes
Japanese	Yes	2	Yes

Restricted entry: Nationals of South Africa and Israel are refused entry.
PASSPORTS: A passport valid for travel to Brunei with assured re-entry facilities to country of origin or domicile required by all.
British Visitors Passport: Not accepted.
VISAS: Required by all except:
(a) **[1]** nationals of the United Kingdom for up to 30 days and nationals of Belgium, Denmark, France, Germany, Luxembourg and The Netherlands for up to 14 days (nationals of other EC countries *do* require a visa);
(b) **[2]** nationals of Canada and Japan for up to 14 days;
(c) nationals of Indonesia, South Korea, Maldives, Norway, Philippines, Sweden, Switzerland and Thailand for up to 14 days;
(d) nationals of Malaysia and Singapore for up to 30 days.
Note: Return ticket necessary for visa-free trips.
Types of visa: *Short Visit* and *Transit*. Cost: £5.
Validity: 3 months.
Application and enquiries to: Consulate (or Consular Section at Embassy or High Commission). For addresses, see top of entry.
Application requirements: (a) Passport. (b) Photo. (c) Application form. (d) Fee. (e) Letter of introduction or invitation if on business trip.
Working days required: 1 day if applying in person; 2-3 days by post.

MONEY

Currency: Brunei Dollar (Br$) = 100 sen. Notes are in the denominations Br$1000, 500, 100, 50, 10, 5 and 1. Coins are in the denominations 50, 10, 5 and 1 sen. The Brunei Dollar is officially at a par with the Singapore Dollar.
Currency exchange: Foreign currencies and travellers cheques can be exchanged at any bank.
Credit cards: American Express, Diners Club, Access/Mastercard and Visa are accepted on a limited basis. Check with your credit card company for details of merchant acceptability and other services which may be available.
Exchange rate indicators: The following figures are included as a guide to the movements of the Brunei Dollar against Sterling and the US Dollar:

Date:	**Oct '89**	**Oct '90**	**Oct '91**	**Oct '92**
£1.00=	**3.10**	**3.35**	**2.93**	**2.57**
$1.00=	**1.96**	**1.72**	**1.70**	**1.62**

Currency restrictions: The import and export of local currency is limited to Br$1000 in notes (also Singapore Dollars). Indian and Indonesian banknotes are not exchangeable. Free import and export of other foreign currencies.
Banking hours: 0900-1200 and 1400-1500 Monday to Friday; 0930-1100 Saturday.

DUTY FREE

The following goods may be imported into Brunei without incurring Customs duty:
200 cigarettes or 250g tobacco products;
60ml of perfume and 250ml toilet water.
Note: Import of spirits and wine is not allowed.
Prohibited items: Firearms, non-prescribed drugs and all pornography. The penalty for carrying non-prescribed drugs is death.

PUBLIC HOLIDAYS

Public holidays observed in Brunei are as follows:
Mar 11 '93 Memperingati Nuzul Al-Quran (Anniversary of the Revelation of the Koran). **Mar 25-26** Hari Raya Puasa (End of Ramadan). **Jun 1** Armed Forces Day. **Jun 1** Hari Raya Haji. **Jun 21** Islamic New Year. **Jul 15** Sultan's Birthday. **Aug 30** Hari Mouloud (Prophet's Birthday). **Dec 25** Christmas. **Jan 1 '94** New Year's Day. **Jan** Isra Meraj (Ascension of the Prophet). **Feb** Beginning of Ramadan. **Feb 10** Chinese New Year. **Feb 23** National Day. **Feb/Mar** Hari Raya Puasa (End of Ramadan). **Mar** Memperingati Nuzul Al-Quran (Anniversary of the Revelation of the Koran).
Note: Muslim festivals are timed according to local sightings of various phases of the Moon and the dates given above are approximations. During the lunar month of Ramadan that precedes Hari Raya Puasa, Muslims fast during the day and feast at night and normal business patterns may be interrupted. Restaurants are closed during the day and muslims are prohibited from smoking and drinking. Some disruption may continue into Hari Raya Puasa itself. Hari Raya Puasa and Hari Raya Haji may last anything from two to ten days. For more information see the section *World of Islam* at the back of the book.

HEALTH

Regulations and requirements may be subject to change at short notice, and you are advised to contact your doctor well in advance of your intended date of departure. Any numbers in the chart refer to the footnotes below.

	Special Precautions?	Certificate Required?
Yellow Fever	No	1
Cholera	Yes	2
Typhoid & Polio	Yes	-
Malaria	No	-
Food & Drink	3	-

[1]: A yellow fever vaccination certificate is required from travellers aged one year and over who have visited infected or endemic areas within the previous 6 days.
[2]: Following WHO guidelines issued in 1973, a cholera vaccination certificate is no longer a condition of entry to Brunei.
[3]: All water should be regarded as a possible health risk. Water used for drinking, brushing teeth or making ice should have first been boiled or sterilised. Milk is unpasteurised and should be boiled. Powdered or tinned milk is available and advised, but make sure it is reconstituted with pure water. Avoid all dairy products. Only eat well-cooked meat and fish, preferably served hot. Pork, salad and mayonnaise may carry increased risk. Vegetables should be cooked and fruit boiled.
Health care: Medical insurance is advised. Medical facilities are of a high standard. The health administration of Brunei reserves the right to vaccinate arrivals not in possession of required certificates and to take any other action deemed necessary to ensure arrivals present no health risk.

TRAVEL - International

AIR: Brunei's national airline is *Royal Brunei Airline (RBA) (BI)*. Air carriers to Brunei include *Singapore Airlines, Malaysian Airlines System, Thai International* and *Philippines Airlines*. *RBA* flies to Singapore, Kuching, Kota Kinabalu, Kuala Lumpur, Manila, Bangkok, Taipei, Hong Kong, Perth, Darwin, Dubai, Frankfurt and London.
Approximate flight times: From Brunei to *London* is 17 hours, to *Los Angeles* is 19 hours, to *New York* is 22 hours, to *Singapore* is 2 hours and to *Sydney* is 11 hours.
International airport: *Bandar Seri Begawan (BWN)* is 10km (6 miles) northeast of the city. Taxi services are available to the city with surcharges after 2200. There are two restaurants.
SEA: The port at Muara is the entry point for sea cargo.
ROAD: There are access roads into Brunei from Sarawak at various locations, although some are unpaved.

TRAVEL - Internal

AIR: There are no internal air services.
SEA/RIVER: There are water taxi services to Kampong Ayer, with stations at Jalan Kianggeh and Jalan McArthur. There is a regular service between Brunei and Labuan and Limbang in Sarawak and Bangar in Temburong.
ROAD: There are about 750km (450 miles) of roads in the country. Traffic drives on the left. **Bus:** Services operate to Seria (91km/57 miles from Bandar Seri Begawan), Kuala Belait (16km/10 miles from Seria), Tutong (48km/30 miles from Bandar Seri Begawan), and to Muara (27km/17 miles from Bandar Seri Begawan). There is a bus station in the town centre. **Car hire:** Self-drive cars are available at the airport. It is important to specify whether an air-conditioned car is required. **Documentation:** International Driving Permit legally required. A temporary licence to drive in Brunei is available on presentation of a valid British or Northern Ireland driving licence.
URBAN: Taxis are available in Bandar Seri Begawan. Fares are usually metered. If not they should be agreed before the journey. There is a 50% surcharge after 2300. **Tipping** is not necessary.

ACCOMMODATION

Outside the main towns, accommodation is not available. The main hotels in Bandar Seri Begawan are the Sheraton, Angs Hotel, River Views Inn, National Inn and the Brunei Hotel.

BRUNEI **HEALTH REGULATIONS** **VISA REGULATIONS** Code-Link

GALILEO/WORLDSPAN

TI-DFT/BWN/HE

TI-DFT/BWN/VI

SABRE

TIDFT/BWN/HE

TIDFT/BWN/VI

To access this information on your CRS, swipe the barcode with a light pen or type in the text under the barcode. For more information, see the introduction *How to Use This Book*.

RESORTS & EXCURSIONS

There are beaches with facilities at Kuala Belait, Lumut Beach near Tutong and at Muara. Brunei is a heavily forested state, and most activity is either on the coast or at the river mouths.

The principal tourist sights in **Bandar Seri Begawan**, the capital, are: the minaret crowning the golden-domed *Sultan Omar Ali Saifuddien Mosque*, which stands in the middle of its own artificial lagoon, affording a fine view over the town and stilt village; the *Churchill Memorial*, incorporating the *Churchill Museum* and *Aquarium*; the ancient *Tomb of Sultan Bolkiah*, the fifth sultan and known as the 'singing admiral' for his love of both music and conquest; the *Brunei Museum*; and the new *Malay Technology Museum* showing traditional crafts.

Outside the capital, it is possible to travel up river to visit village settlements, such as **Kampong Parit Resort**, which have largely survived the rapid industrialisation of recent years, following the discovery of oil. **Kampong Ayer**, the water village, is reputed to be the largest collection of stilt habitations in the world. There are splendid traditional longhouses in the Temburong district, at Rampayoh in the Belait district and in more heavily areas of jungle that are accessible only by boat. Waterfalls and lakes can also be seen around **Rampayoh** (beware of leeches); at *Luagan Lalak* there is a picnic area. There is a hill resort at **Tasek Merimbun** where two small lakes flow into a single river.

SOCIAL PROFILE

FOOD & DRINK: European food is served in hotel restaurants, along with Malaysian, Chinese and Indian dishes. Local food resembles Malay cuisine with much use of fresh fish and rice, often quite spicy. **Drink:** Alcohol is prohibited.

SHOPPING: Special purchases include handworked silverware, brassware and bronzeware such as jugs, trays, gongs, boxes, napkin rings, spoons and bracelets; and fine handwoven sarongs, baskets and mats of pandan leaves. Shopping centres at Bandar Seri Begawan, Seria and Kuala Belait offer local products and imported items. The 'Tamu' Night Market in Bandar Seri Begawan is open from early morning to late at night and sells many fruits, spices, poultry and vegetables, as well as antiques. Food is available there at the lowest prices in town. **Shopping hours:** 0800-2130 Monday to Saturday.

SPORT: There are facilities for watching or participating in **tennis, golf, polo, football** and **hockey; swimming, sailing** and **skindiving** are also popular. Hotels will have details.

SOCIAL CONVENTIONS: Shoes should be removed when entering Muslim homes and institutions. There are many honorific titles in Brunei: *Awang* (abbreviated to Awg), for instance, is generally used in the same way as the English 'Mr'; *Dayang* (Dyg) equivalent to 'Ms' or 'Mrs'. Avoid giving or receiving with the left hand. It is widely regarded as discourteous to refuse refreshment when it is offered by a host. Dress is informal except for special occasions. **Tipping:** Most hotels and restaurants add 10% to the bill.

BUSINESS PROFILE

ECONOMY: Brunei's economy depends on its oil and natural gas deposits, which are mostly offshore, and its investments. Although these are not extensive by world standards, Brunei's small population allows a very high standard of living. The Government has made recent efforts to diversify the economy, mainly by providing tax concessions on foreign investment: timber, paper, fertilisers, petro-chemicals and glass are the most promising candidates for development in the growing industrial sector. Some 15% of the land is under cultivation, with rice, cassava and fruit as the main crops. Japan, which takes half of Brunei's oil production, is the country's largest single trading partner, followed by Korea, Singapore, Thailand and Australia.

BUSINESS: Suits are recommended. Business visits are best made outside the monsoon season (between April and November). The services of a translator will not normally be required as English is widely spoken. **Commercial office hours:** 0800-1200 and 1300-1700 Monday to Thursday; 0900-1200 Saturday. **Government office hours:** 0745-1215 and 1330-1630 Monday to Thursday and Saturday.

COMMERCIAL INFORMATION: The following organisation can offer advice: Brunei State Chamber of Commerce, PO Box 2246, Bandar Seri Begawan 1922, Brunei Tel: (2) 236 601. Fax: (2) 228 389. Telex: 2203.

HISTORY & GOVERNMENT

HISTORY: Brunei was, in ancient times, a powerful trading nation controlling most of Borneo and part of the Philippines archipelago. It also had powerful connections throughout South-East Asia and takes its name from a Sanskrit word meaning 'seaform' (it is mentioned in ancient Chinese literature). It is said that the Islamic faith was adopted in the 15th century, a move which angered the Spanish, who eventually attacked Brunei in 1578, occupying it for several years. British influence began in 1846 when the Sultanate of Brunei gave British adventurer James Brooke the area of Sarawak in return for protection against sea-dyak pirates. The following year, a treaty was signed formalising British assistance and in 1888, when Britain declared North Borneo a British Protectorate, Brunei became a British Protected State, under which terms Britain gave advice on all matters except those concerning local customs and religion. Other than a brief period of Japanese occupation during the Second World War, Brunei remained a British Protected State until independence in 1984. Since then, with the benefit of its vast oil wealth, Brunei has undergone steady, if somewhat unequal, development. The country is in many respects comparable to the Gulf sheikhdoms, small, exceedingly wealthy and more or less surrounded by larger, poorer nations. The Government of the country rests in the exclusive hands of His Majesty Paduka Seri Baginda Sultan Haji Hassanal Bolkiah Mu'izzaddin Waddaulah, 29th in the dynasty, 25 years on the throne, and probably the world's richest individual. Political activity in his realm is kept on a very short leash. The Brunei National Democratic Party was formed in 1985 by loyalists, and its membership confined to certain sectors of the population, but was dissolved three years later after calling for the resignation of the Sultan as Head of State. Since then, the Government has invoked the concept of Melayu Islam Beraja (Malay Islamic Monarchy) as a state ideology. There are no plans to introduce elections or party politics.

GOVERNMENT: Brunei is a traditional Islamic monarchy, with supreme political power vested in the Sultan. The North Borneo Liberation Army instigated rebellions in 1962, during which a state of emergency was declared, and as a result the Sultan assumed the power to rule by decree. He is advised by the Privy Council, the Religious Council, the Council of Cabinet Ministers and the Council of Succession.

CLIMATE

Very hot tropical climate most of the year. Heavy rainfall in the monsoon season, October to March. Average temperature is 28°C.

Required clothing: Lightweight cottons and linens most of the year. Waterproofs are needed during the monsoons.

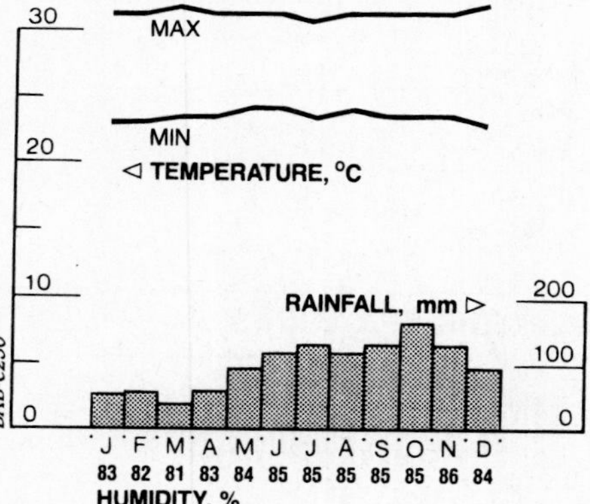

TEMPERATURE CONVERSIONS: -20 -10 0°C 10 20 30 40 / 0 10 20 30°F40 50 60 70 80 90 100

RAINFALL CONVERSIONS: 0mm 200 400 600 800 / 0in 5 10 15 20 25 30

BULGARIA

Location: Eastern Europe.

Balkantourist
Boulevard Vitosha 1
1000 Sofia, Bulgaria
Tel: (2) 43331. Telex: 22568.

Embassy of the Republic of Bulgaria
186-188 Queen's Gate
London SW7 5HL
Tel: (071) 584 9400/9433. Fax: (071) 584 4948. Telex: 25465. Opening hours: 0930-1700 Monday to Friday (0930-1230 visa enquiries).

Bulgarian National Tourist Office
18 Princes Street
London W1R 7RE
Tel: (071) 499 6988. Fax: (071) 499 1905. Telex: 296467. Opening hours: 0900-1700 Monday to Friday.

British Embassy
Boulevard Vasil Levski 65-67
Sofia, Bulgaria
Tel: (2) 879 575. Fax: (2) 656 022. Telex: 22363 PRODROME.

Embassy of the Republic of Bulgaria
1621 22nd Street, NW
Washington, DC 20008
Tel: (202) 387 7969. Fax: (202) 234 7973.

Balkan Holidays (USA) Ltd
Suite 606
41 East 42nd Street
New York, NY 10017
Tel: (212) 573 5530. Fax: (212) 573 5538. Telex: 429767.
Also deals with enquiries from Canada.

Embassy of the United States of America
Unit 25402
Boulevard A Stamboliski 1
Sofia, Bulgaria
Tel: (2) 884 801-05. Fax: (2) 801 977. Telex: 22690 BG.

Embassy of the Republic of Bulgaria
325 Stewart Street
Ottawa, Ontario K1N 6K5
Tel: (613) 232 3215 *or* 232 3453. Fax: (613) 232 9547.

AREA: 110,994 sq km (42,855 sq miles).
POPULATION: 8,989,165 (1990 estimate).
POPULATION DENSITY: 81 per sq km.
CAPITAL: Sofia. **Population:** 1,220,914 (1990).
GEOGRAPHY: Bulgaria is situated in Eastern Europe and bounded to the north by the River Danube and Romania, to the east by the Black Sea, to the south by Turkey and Greece and to the west by Serbia. The Balkan Mountains cross the country reaching to the edge of the Black Sea and its golden

beaches. The land is heavily cultivated, with forests and rivers. Although Bulgaria lies in the southeast corner of Europe the climate is never extreme, even on the red-earthed plains of Southern Thrace, The Black Sea resorts have some of the largest beaches in Europe and offer sunbathing from May until October, while in winter heavy falls of snow are virtually guaranteed in the mountain skiing resorts.
LANGUAGE: Bulgarian is the official language. English is spoken by many in the cities and resorts. Turkish, Russian, German and French are also spoken.
RELIGION: Eastern Orthodox Church; Muslim and Roman Catholic minorities.
TIME: GMT + 2.
ELECTRICITY: 220 volts AC, 50 Hz. Plugs are 2-pin.
COMMUNICATIONS: Telephone: IDD is available to main cities. Country code: 359. Calls from some parts of the country must be placed through the international operator. There are many public telephones in the main towns. **Fax:** Facilities are available at BTA (Bulgarina Telegraph Agency) offfices. **Telex/telegram:** International communications via telex and telegrams are available from Bulgaria. Public telex boothes are available at general post offices and major hotels in Sofia. The General Post Office in Sofia, at 4 Gurko Street, is open 24 hours, with facilites for both telex and telegram. **Post:** Airmail to western Europe takes from four days to two weeks. **Press:** The BTA publishes books, brochures and other literature in 21 languages and the weekly newspaper, *Sofia News*, is available in five languages (including English); the monthly magazine, *Bugaria*, is available in ten languages. Since 1990 the press laws have been liberalised and formerly banned publications are freely availabe. The most important dailies include*Demokratsiya*, *Duma* and *Trud*. **BBC World Service and Voice of America frequencies:** From time to time these change. See the section *How to Use this Book* for more information.

BBC:

MHz	17.64	15.07	9.410	6.180

Voice of America:

MHz	9.670	6.040	5.995	1.197

Radio Varna and BTV broadcast holiday magazine programmes in English.

PASSPORT/VISA

Regulations and requirements may be subject to change at short notice, and you are advised to contact the appropriate diplomatic or consular authority before finalising travel arrangements. Details of these may be found at the head of this country's entry. Any numbers in the chart refer to the footnotes below.

	Passport Required?	Visa Required?	Return Ticket Required?
Full British	Yes	Yes	Yes
BVP	Not valid	-	-
Australian	Yes	Yes	Yes
Canadian	Yes	Yes	Yes
USA	Yes	1	Yes
Other EC	Yes	1	Yes
Japanese	Yes	Yes	Yes

PASSPORTS: A valid passport is required by all.
British Visitors Passport: Not acceptable.
VISAS: Required by all except:
(a) [1] nationals of Denmark (all other EC nationals *do* require visas);
(b) nationals of Austria, Finland, Norway, San Marino, Sweden and residents of the former Eastern bloc countries;
(c) [1] US nationals,with Tourist visas, for up to 4 weeks;
(d) nationals of Cuba, Malta, Tunisia;
(e) those on any holiday pre-arranged through *Balkantourist* or an authorised agent/operator, if in groups of six or more. However, nationals of South Africa and Taiwan must apply for a separate visa even if part of a tour group.
Note: Swiss and EC nationals can obtain visas at the border if travelling by road or air. If travelling by rail, however, a visa is required in advance.
Types of visa: Tourist, Business and Transit; cost: £20 (in cash if applying by person, by postal order if applying by post). Express visas have been introduced for visits of less than 7 working days; these will be issued immediately if applying in person, or by return if applying by post. The cost of an Express visa is £40 (in cash if applying in person, or by postal order if applying by post).
Validity: For tourist and business trips, visas are normally valid for 3 months. Transit visas are for 30 hours. Enquire at Embassy for further details.
Application to: Consulate (or Consular Section at Embassy). For address, see top of entry.
Application requirements: (a) Application form. (b) 1

BULGARIA	**HEALTH REGULATIONS**	**VISA REGULATIONS** Code-Link
GALILEO/WORLDSPAN	 TI-DFT/SOF/HE	TI-DFT/SOF/VI
SABRE	 TIDFT/SOF/HE	TIDFT/SOF/VI

To access this information on your CRS, swipe the barcode with a light pen or type in the text under the barcode. For more information, see the introduction *How to Use This Book.*

photo. (c) Valid passport. (d) If applying for a Business visa, the application must also be accompanied by a letter of invitation from a Bulgarian company and a letter from applicant's company. (e) If applying by post, a registered, stamped, self-addressed envelope large enough for return of passport. (f) For visitors staying with friends or relatives, an official invitation from their hosts, legalised by the respective Bulgarian local authorities, is required.
Working days required: 7.
Temporary residence: Enquire at the Bulgarian Embassy.

MONEY

Currency: Lev (Lv) = 100 stotinki. The plural of Lev is Leva. Notes occur in denominations of Lv200, 100, 50, 20, 10, 5, 2 and 1. Coins are in denominations of Lv5, 2 and 1 and 50, 20, 10, 5, 2 and 1 stotinki.
Currency exchange: A *bordereau* receipt will be given and must be kept until departure.
Credit cards: Diners Club, American Express, Carte Blanche, Eurocard and Visa are accepted. Check with your credit card company for details of merchant availability and other services which may be available.
Exchange rate indicators: The following figures are included as a guide to the movements of the Lev against Sterling and the US Dollar:

Date:	Oct '89	Oct '90	Oct '91	Oct '92
£1.00	1.33	5.37	31.01	43.00
$1.00=	0.84	2.74	17.87	27.10

Currency restrictions: The import and export of local currency is prohibited. There are no restrictions on the amount of foreign currency though amounts over US$5000 have to be declared. The export of foreign currency is limited to the amount declared on import. Local currency can be exchanged at the airport on production of a bordereau.
Banking hours: 0800-1130 and 1400-1800 Monday to Friday; 0830-1130 Saturday.

DUTY FREE

The following goods may be taken into Bulgaria by persons over 18 years of age without paying customs duty:
200 cigarettes or 50 cigars or 250g of tobacco;
1 litre spirits and 2 litres of wine;
100g of perfume;
Objects and foodstuffs intended for personal use during the stay in the holiday;
Gifts to the value of Lv100.
The following goods must be declared:
Objects worth more than Lv60;
Objects intended for other persons;
Antiques, works of art, commercial samples, typewriters, cameras, printed matter and manuscripts, plants, fruits, seeds, firearms and ammunition for hunting purposes;
Currency, securities and precious stones or metals.
Note: (a) The indicated values in local currency are calculated according to the unified state prices for retail sale. (b) Luggage carried by transit passengers may be sealed at customs to avoid another check-up at the exit customs.
Prohibited items: Arms, ammunition, narcotics and pornography.
Export allowance: Articles worth more than Lv50 may be exported duty free if they have been bought with legally exchanged currency, in which case a statement of account must be presented.

Golden Sands

Golden Sands Resort is a harmonious blend of Bulgarian scenery and modern architecture. Restaurants, bars and sports grounds are steeped in verdure and picturesque shaded walks lead to the comfortable hotels. The resort is situated 17km north of Varna – the country's largest Black Sea City, linked by sea and air with Europe's major cities. All in all the resort has 65 3- and 2-star hotels with a total of more than 14,000 beds, 10 deluxe villas (4- and 3- star), 25 2-star bungalows, the Panorama campsite with 100 tent sites, 60 restaurants offering Bulgarian and European cuisine, 12 taverns, 11 cafes and 6 night-clubs.

The Golden Sands Marina has docking facilities for 100 yachts, a 140m long quay and 2 64m-long piers. Windsurfers, water-skis, yachts and row boats can be hired at the yacht club which also offers instruction in sailing, water-skiing, windsurfing and diving.

Available across the resort are 10 tennis courts, a horseriding stable, mini-golf links, bowling and bingo centres, water slides, open-air and indoor swimming pools and play grounds for children.

Fun, Sport & Relaxation

GOLDEN SANDS (Zlanti Piassatisi) – Varna
SALES AND MARKETING DEPARTMENT.
Tel: 052/85 55 25, 95 61 17, 05 53 37.
Fax: 052/85 55 87. Telex: 77508, 77511.

A FAIRY TALE IN WHITE, BLUE AND GREEN

PAMPOROVO TOURIST OFFICE

PAMPOROVO – Location: 1650 metres above sea level, some 80 kilometres away from Plovdiv (Bulgaria's second largest city) and 260 kilometres from the capital Sofia.

CLIMATE: Mountainous with Mediterranean influence, average annual temperature 8.5°c

HOTELS: 7 hotels and 30 chalets with a total of 1500 beds, all rooms with bathrooms and wc.

RESORT AMENITIES: Restaurants, folk-style spots, nightclubs, cates, indoor swimming pools, sauna, fitness centre, physiotherapy, bowling alley, souvenir shops, barber's and hairdresser's, archery, mountain bikes, fishing, guided walking tours and excursions.

SKI FACTS: 25 kilometres downhill ski-runs, 25 kilometres cross-country trails, 1 triple chairlift, 4 single chairlifts, 3 stationary draglifts and a number of baby draglifts providing total capacity 8, 500 skiers per hour; 14 ski-rooms supplying 3, 200 sets of ski-equipment of world famous trademarks; ski-school with 100 English and German speaking instructors, running classes the A-class beginner to the most experienced and sophisticated skiers' E-class; paragliding school; ski kindergarten for children up to 8 years old.

NEW POINTS: Aesthetic dental surgery with the latest modern equipment and high-quality dental services at affordable prices; longevity centre – prophilaxis of ageing and premature senile symptoms and changes. Discover the secret of still active Rhodopean centinarians.

Information and sales: Telephone: +359 3021 438, Marketing department, Fax: +359 3021 263.

PUBLIC HOLIDAYS

Public holidays observed in Bulgaria are as follows:
Mar 3 '93 National Day. **Apr 12** Easter Monday. **May 1** Labour Day. **May 24** Education Day. **Sep 9** National Day. **Dec 25** Christmas. **Jan 1 '94** New Year's Day. **Mar 3** National Day.

HEALTH

Regulations and requirements may be subject to change at short notice, and you are advised to contact your doctor well in advance of your intended date of departure. Any numbers in the chart refer to the footnotes below.

	Special Precautions?	Certificate Required?
Yellow Fever	No	No
Cholera	No	No
Typhoid & Polio	No	-
Malaria	No	-
Food & Drink	1	-

[1]: Mains water is normally chlorinated, and whilst relatively safe may cause mild abdominal upsets. Bottled water is available and is advised for the first few weeks of the stay. Milk is pasteurised and dairy products are safe for consumption. Local meat, poultry, seafood, fruit and vegetables are considered safe to eat.
Health care: There is a Reciprocal Health Agreement with the UK. On the production of a UK passport, hospital and other medical care will be provided free of charge; prescribed medicines must be paid for.

TRAVEL - International

AIR: Bulgaria's national airline is *Balkan-Bulgarian Airlines (LZ).*
Approximate flight times: From Sofia to *London* is 3 hours and to *New York* is 9 hours.
International airports: *Sofia (SOF)*, 10km (6 miles) east of the city (travel time – 20 minutes). Buses run about every ten minutes to the city centre during the day, and about every 20 minutes 2100-0030. Coach by arrangement with *Balkantourist*. Taxis are also available. Airport facilities include banks and currency exchange (24 hours), post office, duty-free shop (stocking spirits, wines, perfume, traditional souvenirs, etc), nursery, restaurant (1100-2230), bar (24 hours), car hire (*Hertz, Avis, Budget* and *Inter-Balkan*) and car park.
Varna (VAR) is 9km (5.5 miles) from the city. Bus service to Varna city centre departs every 20 minutes. Coach service is available by arrangement with *Balkantourist*. Taxi service is also available. Airport facilities include outgoing duty-free shop, banking and currency exchange (24 hours), restaurant (0600-2230), bar (24 hours) and car hire (by prior arrangement with *Balkantourist* in Varna).
Bourgas (BOJ) is 13km (8 miles) from the city. Bus service departs every 20 minutes to the city centre. Coach service is available by prior arrangement with *Balkantourist*. Taxi service is also available. Airport facilities include outgoing duty-free shop, banking and currency exchange (24 hours), restaurant (0600-2230), bar (24-hour) and car hire (by prior arrangement in Bourgas).
SEA: The main international ports are Varna and Bourgas.
RAIL: There are no direct rail services between Bulgaria and western Europe although there are frequent services between Sofia and Belgrade, Bucharest, Thessaloniki and Istanbul. Dining car facilities are available on all routes. First-class travel is recommended.
ROAD: Approach via Koulata on the border of Greece; via Rousse, Kardom and Durankulak on the border of Romania; via Svilengrad and Capitan Andriveevo on the border of Turkey; and via Kalotina, Zlatarevo, Gjueshevo and Vrashkachuka on the border of Yugoslavia.

TRAVEL - Internal

AIR: *Balkan-Bulgarian Airlines* operates eight domestic services connecting Sofia with the coast and main towns. The journeys from Sofia to Varna and Bourgas can be made in under an hour. Air travel is comparatively cheap, and is only slightly more expensive than rail travel.
RIVER: Regular boat and hydrofoil services along the Bulgarian bank of the river link many centres, including Vidin, Lom, Kozloduj; Orjahovo, Nikopol; Svishtov, Tutrakan and Silistra. The official crossing points into Romania are by ferry from Vidin to Calafat and by road bridge from Ruse to Giurgiu.
RAIL: There are over 6500km (4040 miles) of railways in the country. Bulgarian State Railways connect Sofia with main towns. Reservations are essential and first-class travel is advised. For details contact the State Railway Office.
ROAD: There are over 13,000km (8000 miles) of roads linking the major centres and in general the quality is good. Traffic drives on the right. International road signs are used. Speed limits are strictly adhered to: 50kmph (31mph) in built-up areas, 80kmph (50mph) outside built-up areas and 120 kmph (75mph) on motorways. Alcohol is not allowed at all; on-the-spot fines are imposed for offences. Spare parts are easily available. There is a reasonable number of petrol stations (they are marked on a free map supplied by *Balkantourist*). **Taxi:** Available in all towns and also for inter-city journeys. Vehicles are metered, unless they are privately owned. A 5-10% tip is appreciated. **Car hire:** Self-drive cars can be hired through hotel reception desks and through *Hertz-Balkantourist Joint Venture Company* payable in hard currency. There are no fly-drive arrangements through the airlines. Most transactions are in hard currency.
Documentation: An International Driving Licence should be obtained, although foreign driving licences are accepted for short visits. A Green Card is compulsory.
URBAN: Bus, tramway and trolleybus services operate in Sofia; in addition, a metro is under construction. Flat fares are charged and tickets must be pre-purchased. Buses and taxis are provided in all the main towns. There are also trolleybuses in Plovdiv and Varna.
JOURNEY TIMES: The following chart gives approximate journey times from Sofia (in hours and minutes) to other major cities/towns in Bulgaria.

	Air	Road	Rail
Varna	1.00	8.00	7.00
Bourgas	1.00	7.00	6.00
Plovdiv	0.40	2.00	2.00
Rousse	1.00	9.00	8.00
Turnovo	-	3.30	-
Vitosha	-	0.30	-
Borovets	-	1.30	-
Pamporovo	-	3.30	-
Golden Sands	*0.45	*7.00	-
Albena	*0.45	*7.00	-
Sunny Beach	**0.35	**6.30	-

Note: [*] From Varna Airport. [**] From Bourgas Airport.

ACCOMMODATION

HOTELS: Most of the hotels used by Western visitors are owned by *Balkantourist*. Advanced booking is advisable. **Grading:** Hotels are classified as deluxe, first- and second class. Special care has been taken in some hotels

to conform to international standards for these categories.
GUEST-HOUSES: Accommodation is available in small villas with private rooms, particularly near the coast.
CAMPING/CARAVANNING: Camping sites are classified from 'Special' to I and II, and the top two categories have hot and cold water, showers, electricity, grocery stores, restaurants, telephones and sports grounds. The camping areas are located in main tourist areas.
YOUTH HOSTELS: These are situated in 30 main towns. For information contact the Bulgarian Tourist Union, Boulevard Vasil Levski 18, IV/18, Sofia. Tel: (2) 8651 *or* 878 812.

RESORTS & EXCURSIONS

Many tourists will travel in organised groups, but it is possible for tourists to make their own way by train or hired car.

Sofia

Dating back to the 4th century BC, the ancient capital of Sofia has a wealth of different architectural styles including Greek, Roman, Byzantine, Bulgarian and Turkish. The city boasts many theatres and museums (including those of archaeology and ethnography), opera houses and art galleries (including the *National Gallery of Painting and Sculpture* housed in the former Royal Palace of the King) as well as a universities, open-air markets, parks (over 300 of them, including the *Borisova Park*) and sports stadia. Visitors should see the extraordinary *Alexander Nevsky Memorial Church* (which dominates the city with its gold-leaf dome), built to celebrate Bulgaria's liberation from the Turks in the Russo-Turkish war at the end of the last century. The crypt hosts an exhibition of beautiful icons, and the choir is excellent and well worth hearing. Other churches in Sofia include *St Sophia*, which is Byzantine and dates from the 6th century; *St George*, which dates back to the 5th century and contains 14th-century frescoes; and *Sveta Petka Samardshijska*, which is 14th century. There is an archaeological museum housed in the nine cupolas of the *Bouyouk Mosque* (the largest in Sofia). The *Banya Bashi Mosque* is also worth a visit.
An example of modern architecture is the *Battemberg Square*, which contains the *Government Buildings* and nearby some Roman remains (discovered when an underpass was being dug) with a reconstruction of the city as it was in Roman times.
EXCURSIONS & SIGHTSEEING: 121km (75 miles) from Sofia is **Rila Monastery**, perched high up on the side of a mountain in the middle of thick pine forests. Rila has a fascinating collection of murals, wood carvings, old weapons and coins, and manuals and Bibles written on sheepskin. The monastery itself is notable for its delicate and unusual architectural features. Originally founded in the 10th century by the hermit and holy man, Ivan Rilsky, the monastery acted as a repository and sanctuary for Bulgarian culture during the 500-year Turkish occupation from 1396. Fire has destroyed most of the early architecture and the present buildings date from the 19th century, with the exception of the 14th-century *Hrelio's Tower*. There is good accommodation in the monastery and a nearby hotel. Rila is an excellent place from which to start climbs and hikes in the surrounding countryside.
The mountain of **Vitosha** on the outskirts of Sofia is a National Park with chairlifts and cable cars to help with the ascent as it is about 2000m (7000ft) high (see also below). Here, the medieval church of **Boyana** can be seen, with its beautiful and ancient frescoes, painted in about 1200 and thought to be some of the oldest in Bulgaria.

Plovdiv

Founded in 342BC and the country's second largest city, Plovdiv is divided by the Maritsa River and contains both an old quarter and a new commercial section. The old part contains many buildings dating from the 18th and 19th centuries (and earlier) in typical National Revival style. It is possible to wander along the narrow cobbled streets and see Roman ruins (including an amphitheatre), picturesque medieval houses and buildings from the 17th century with their upper sections hanging out into the street and almost touching those opposite. The *Archaeological Museum* has collections of gold Thracian artefacts, including cooking utensils, and the *Ethnographic Museum* is also worth seeing, as are the churches of *St Marina* and *St Nedelya*.
EXCURSIONS & SIGHTSEEING: 8km (5 miles) from Plovdiv is **Batchkovo Monastery**, founded in the 11th century, with some rare frescoes, icons, manuscripts and coins. Batchkovo lies within the area known in ancient times as Thrace (partly occupied by the Rhodope Mountains) and many items of archaeological interest have been discovered, including wonderful gold Thracian objects. The town of **Kazanluk** has a *Museum of Rose Production* and is the centre of Bulgaria's major export: attar of roses. The valley of Kazanluk itself has countless archaeological/historical treasures – Greek, Roman, Thracian and Ottoman. **Turnovo**, ancient capital of Bulgaria in the 13th and 14th centuries, contains extraordinary collections of historic works of art, including church relics. The **Preobrazhenski Monastery** is quite close, as is the open-air folk museum at **Etur**.

The Black Sea Coast

The Bulgarian Black Sea Riviera resorts are ideal for the traditional seaside family holiday. Thickly wooded mountains sweep down into wide bays and long golden beaches stretch four or five miles in length. Some of the resorts along the coast have been called a 'children's playground' as swimming is generally safe, even at 150m (500ft) the water is only is still only shoulder-high. Areas where currents are a problem are clearly marked. The Black Sea is one of the cleanest and clearest seas in the world and has half the salt content of the Mediterranean. Some of the sand is pulled by currents from as far away as the Mediterranean, flowing through the Bosphorus and Dardenelles. Bulgaria offers sunny weather and good, clean air, particularly along the coast; the coast itself has a breeze which blows gently inshore, taking the edge off the heat.
Special children's pools have been installed on many of the beaches; swings, slides, playdomes and donkey rides are also available and a wide range of watersports are available at most resorts.
RESORTS: There are dozens of attractive resorts on the Black Sea Riviera. **Drouzhba** is Bulgaria's oldest Black Sea spa centred on the Grand Hotel Varna, the largest and most luxurious hotel on the Riviera and the pearl of the *Balkantourist* achievements to date. **Albena**, named after a famous local beauty, is situated on the edge of a lovely forest, and is Bulgaria's newest resort (a showcase and vivid monument to contemporary Bulgarian design), with good food and lively nightlife. **Golden Sands**, Bulgaria's second largest resort, is about 15km (9 miles) from Varna with good facilities and probably the best nightlife on the Black Sea Riviera. **Sunny Beach** is a large purpose-built family resort with beautiful and safe

beaches. Close to Sunny Beach can be found the 7th-century fishing village of **Nessebar** with its wooden fishermen's houses and its famous four dozen Byzantine churches. Everywhere in Bulgaria there is a good choice of restaurants and *mehana* (folk taverns), which are full of Bulgarian colour, vigour and friendliness with exceptional cooking and wine. There are discos, cabarets and bars suitable for every pocket and taste. *The Khan's Tent* at **Sunny Beach** is a must as is the *Gorski Tsar* (Forest King) at **Albena.**

Winter Holidays

Bulgaria is a fast-growing destination for Western skiers for adults and children alike. There have been some dramatic improvements in all three major resorts in recent years.
RESORTS: Borovets is a World Cup venue. It is only 70km (45 miles) from Sofia, the capital, at 1300m (4300ft) in the Rila Mountains. There the 2400m (8000ft) Yastrebets (Hawk's Nest) is a steep, twisting red trail for the advanced skier, skied from November until April. Seven comfortable, friendly and well-run hotels provide most of the accommodation and there is a village of timber-framed houses (each sleeping six) nearby. In Bulgarian resorts, hotels usually provide most of the nightlife. There is a disco in the Mousalla and live groups play at the Hotel Bor. There is a wine bar, too, and folk taverns (*mehana*); sleigh rides through the snow are also available.
At **Pamporovo,** 1600m (5315ft) in the Rhodope Mountains near Plovdiv, there is one of the finest ski schools in Europe. The resort has 1440 beds between seven hotels, the main one being the new Perelik (480 beds) which is a mini-resort in itself with shopping arcades, 25m (80ft) swimming pool, solarium, bars and lots more besides. Pamporovo is also the most southerly skiing resort in Europe.
The third resort is **Vitosha,** 1800m (6000ft) high and overlooking Sofia and the home of the National Ski School based on the FIS methods. All the resorts have been purpose-built to blend in with the magnificent natural scenery of mountains and forest. Equipment on hire is all modern and well maintained.
Bulgaria has consistently heavy falls of snow from December until April. Some tour operators actually guarantee snow despite these resorts being so far south under sunny, vivid blue skies. From the restaurant on top of the Pamporovo TV tower you can see as far as Greece and the Aegean. The ski areas may not be quite as extensive as the Alps, but certainly novice and intermediate skiing throughout Bulgaria is considered to be some of the finest in Europe. Off-piste skiing is excellent, and cross-country skiing is becoming more and more popular with trails laid out through towering pines to rival any to be found in the Alps or elsewhere.

Special Interest Tours

These include luxury cruises along the Danube, sailing through seven countries in two brand-new Dutch-built air-conditioned river liners each accommodating 236 passengers. The fascinating tour includes transit to Passau in Germany or Vienna, to begin either a 2- or 3-week cruise to Rousse in Eastern Bulgaria, with excursions at all points of call. Afterwards there is a choice of touring Bulgaria by coach, or staying on the Black Sea Riviera, or at a mountain resort inland. The return trip home is by plane.
Walking holidays have become extremely popular along special routes through the wild mountains and forests. It is possible to travel the country by horse and cart or by narrow gauge railway. There are courses in painting and photography at Plovdiv and the preserved museum town of Koprivshtitsa in the beautiful scenery east of Sofia. There is also the opportunity, once in Bulgaria, of taking special excursions to Moscow or Prague, Istanbul and Warsaw.
As well as the more obvious tourist attractions, Bulgaria is a country of world-famous mineral water spas and increasing interest is being shown in spa holidays. There are over 500 springs. Many medical authorities accept that spa treatments are very effective in dealing with heart conditions, rheumatism, asthma and liver and kidney complaints.
The Bulgarian National Tourist Office will provide more details about *Balkantourist's* full range of amenities on request.

SOCIAL PROFILE

FOOD & DRINK: The main meal is eaten in the middle of the day. Dinner is a social occasion, with dancing in all restaurants. Food is spicy, hearty and good. National dishes include cold yoghurt soup with cucumbers, peppers or aubergines stuffed with meat, *kebapcheta* (small, strongly spiced, minced meat rolls). Fruit is particularly good and cheap throughout the year. *Banitsa* is a pastry stuffed with fruit or cheese. There is a wide variety of national dishes, as well as West European standard dishes, which can be chosen on the spot at any restaurant. All good hotels have restaurants and there are many attractive folk-style restaurants and cafés throughout the country. **Drink:** Coffee, heavily sweetened, is particularly popular. Drinks are also made from infusions of mountain herbs and dried leaves, particularly lime. White wines include *Karlouski Misket*, *Tamianka* and *Evksinograde*. Heavy red wines include *Trakia* and *Mavroud*.
NIGHTLIFE: Some restaurants have folk dancing and music. Opera is performed at the State Opera House in Sofia; other classical concerts include the National Folk Ensemble. There are nightclubs with floor shows and dancing in Sofia, as well as most major towns and all of the resorts.
SHOPPING: The main shopping area of Sofia is the Vitosha Boulevard. Bulgarian products, handicrafts, wines, spirits and confectionery can all be purchased. **Shopping hours:** Shops and stores are generally open Monday to Friday 1000-2000 and Saturday 0800-1400. Many shops open late until 1900.
SPORT: There are facilities for **tennis, mini-golf, horseriding** and **cycling.** *Balkantourist* organises **fishing** tours, and make all the necessary arrangements for permits, guides, equipment and accommodation. **Winter sports:** See *Winter Holidays* in *Resorts & Excursions* section above. **Watersports:** Water-skiing, sailing, surfing and scuba diving are all available on the Black Sea coast.
SPECIAL EVENTS: The following is a selection of the major festivals and other special events celebrated annually in Bulgaria. For a complete list, contact the Bulgarian National Tourist Office.
Last two weeks in Mar *March Musical Days*, Rousse. **Mid-May to mid-Jun** *Sofia Musical Weeks.* **Jun** *Sunny Beach Golden Orpheus Pop Festival.* **First week of Jun** *Kazanluk Rose Festival.* **Aug** *Bourgas International Folklore Festival.* **Sep** *Art, Crafts and Chamber Music*, Plovdiv.

SOCIAL CONVENTIONS: Normal courtesies should be observed and handshaking is the normal form of greeting. Dress should be conservative but casual. If invited to the home, a small souvenir from one's homeland is an acceptable gift. Do not give money. Remember that a nod of the head means 'No' and a shake means 'Yes'. **Tipping:** Until recently not applicable, but 10-12% are appreciated.

BUSINESS PROFILE

ECONOMY: Bulgaria has a strong agricultural sector, in which the main products are wheat, maize, barley, sugar beet, grapes and tobacco, although its relative importance has declined in recent years. Agriculture is mainly organised around large agro-industrial complexes and is relatively efficient; current plans are looking towards further mechanisation of food processing and packaging.
Industry is concentrated in engineering, metals, chemicals and petrochemicals and, recently, electronics and biotechnology. Bulgaria is a major producer of bulk carriers and of fork-lift trucks. Tourism and road transport are both important foreign exchange earners.
The external debt is low by Eastern European standards, although Bulgaria has recently arranged large loans from the West to finance the development of its new industries. Bulgaria's largest trading partner is the CIS (50% of Bulgarian imports; 61% of exports, according to 1987 figures). Elsewhere, Libya and Iraq are important trading partners. The demise of COMECON has eliminated, at a stroke, the major market for Bulgarian goods. At first, this precipitated a major economic collapse for the fledgling Zhelev government, from which it is only now starting to recover. Power cuts and food shortages are now commonplace. The main task facing the Government was to create conditions to attract investment and generate capital internally: without these the economy could not recover. In 1992, with its political position reasonably secure, the Government embarked on a rapid privatisation programme. The legal framework is now in place and the first sell-off of industrial concerns is due to begin in 1992. Foreign investors, who initially steered clear of Bulgaria, are showing an increasing interest in the country. Tourism and agro-industry are thought especially attractive. The Government is also devoting some effort to improving the country's antiquated infrastructure. Trade with the UK is low, although political reforms are likely to encourage improved opportunities in the future.
The country has few energy reserves of its own and has, until now, relied heavily on subsidised Soviet oil and gas, for which they will now have to pay market prices – in scarce hard currency. Oil from Iraq, moreover, is no longer available following UN-imposed sanctions and the destruction of the Iraqi oil industry during the Gulf War.
BUSINESS: Suits and prior appointments necessary. Interpreters can be organised through tourist agencies. If arranged in advance through foreign trading organisations, services are free. It is common for the visiting business person to offer hospitality to the contact in Bulgaria. **Office hours:** 0800-1800 Monday to Satur-day. Shops in Sofia are often open longer hours.
COMMERCIAL INFORMATION: The following organisation can offer advice: Bulgarian Chamber of Commerce and Industry, Boulevard A Stamboliiski 11a, 1040 Sofia, Bulgaria. Tel: (2) 872 631. Fax: (2) 873 209. Telex: 22374.

HISTORY & GOVERNMENT

HISTORY: Despite a turbulent history, Bulgaria is the oldest surviving state in Europe to have kept its original name (AD681), and most of the population are descendents of the Bulgar invasion to the south of the Danube at that time. On two occasions during the medieval period the Bulgarians managed to establish empires which existed in a state of armed conflict with Byzantium. The First Empire is reckoned from the time of Kurt (584-642) and lasted until John Vladislav's defeat by the Byzantines in 1018; the second was the result of an opportunist revolt in 1185 led by John and Peter Asen, who managed to take advantage of an internal weakness at Constantinople; this collapsed in 1258. The history of the Balkans is exceedingly complex, due not least to successive waves of invasions, partitions, sporadic anarchy and internal turmoil. By the 20th century, Bulgaria was ruled by a monarchy which chose to side with the Axis powers in 1939. In 1944, shortly after the death of King Boris, the Soviet-backed Fatherland Front seized power. The monarchy was abolished and a republic declared. The Front, dominated by the Bulgarian Communist Party, took 70% of the vote in a national plebiscite. By the end of 1947, the Communist Party had completed its takeover of the country, instituting a Soviet-style constitution and abolishing all opposition parties. Subsequently, Bulgaria's dominant political figure was Todor Zhivkov, and under his leadership Bulgaria became the staunchest of Moscow's allies. In 1989, under intense domestic and international pressure, Zhivkov resigned. The first multi-party elections for 44 years were held in June 1990: the ruling Communists had restyled themselves the Bulgarian Socialist Party (BSP), and won an absolute majority in the 400-seat National Assembly although not sufficient to effect changes to the constitution. Widespread resentment grew at the desperate economic situation into which the country had plunged. In December 1990, the BSP government resigned after a general strike. Zhelyu Zhelev, the leader of the opposition Union of Democratic Forces (UDF), assumed the presidency. The UDF narrowly won the national assembly elections in October 1991 and formed a government under Dmitur Popov with the support of independent candidates. President Zhelev was re-elected in January 1992. The Popov government fell in October 1992 and has, at the time of writing, yet to be replaced.
GOVERNMENT: Legislative power is held by the 240-seat national assembly, whose members are elected for 4-year terms. The assembly elects a Council of Ministers headed by the Prime Minister. The President of the republic, as Head of State, is also directly elected for a 5-year term.

CLIMATE

Varies according to altitude. Summers are warmest with some rainfall. Cold winters with snow. Frequent rain during spring and autumn.
Required clothing: Mediumweights most of the year, warmer outdoor wear necessary in winter.

SOFIA Bulgaria (550m)

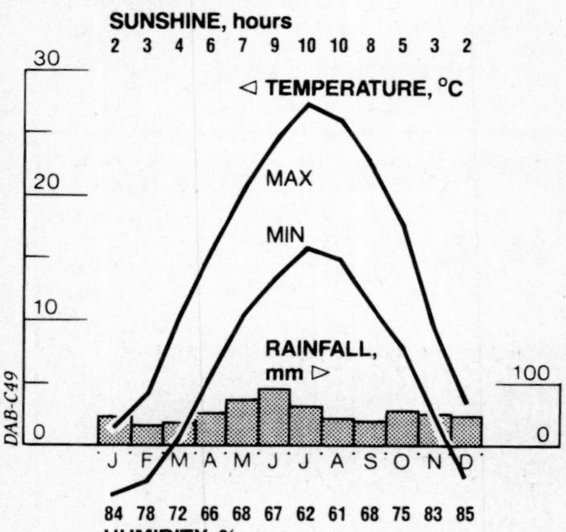

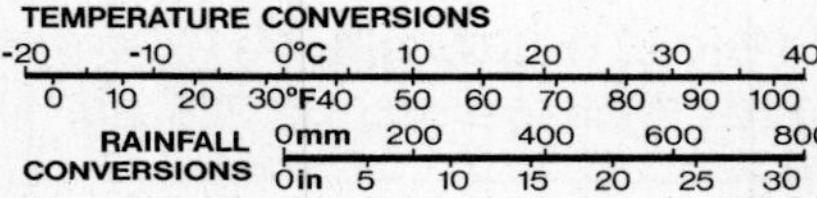

BURKINA FASO

□ international airport

Location: West Africa.

Direction Général du Tourisme et de l'Hôtellerie
BP 624
Ouagadougou, Burkina Faso
Tel: 30 63 96. Telex: 5555 BF SEGEGOUV.
Honorary Consulate of Burkina Faso
5 Cinnamon Row
Plantation Wharf
London SW11 3TW
Tel: (071) 738 1800. Fax: (071) 738 2820. Telex: 296420 AFRO G. Opening hours: 1000-1230 and 1430-1630 Monday to Friday.
The **British Embassy** in **Côte d'Ivoire** deals with enquiries relating to Burkina Faso:
British Embassy
Third Floor, BP 2581
Immeuble Les Harmonies
angle boulevard Carde et avenue Dr Jamot
Plâteau 01
Abidjan 01, Côte d'Ivoire
Tel: 22 68 50/1/2 *or* 32 82 09. Fax: 22 32 21. Telex: 23706.
Embassy of Burkina Faso
2340 Massachusetts Avenue, NW
Washingon, DC
20008
Tel: (202) 332 5577. Telex: 440399.
Embassy of the United States of America
01 BP 35
Rue Raoul Folereau
Ouagadougou 01, Burkina Faso
Tel: 30 67 23. Telex: 5290.
Embassy of Burkina Faso
48 Range Road
Ottawa, Ontario
K1N 8J4
Tel: (613) 238 4796. Telex: 0534413.
Canadian Embassy
BP 548
Ouagadougou, Burkina Faso
Tel: 30 00 30.

AREA: 274,200 sq km (105,870 sq miles).
POPULATION: 9,001,000 (1990 estimate).
POPULATION DENSITY: 32.8 per sq km (1990).
CAPITAL: Ouagadougou. **Population:** 500,000.
GEOGRAPHY: Burkina Faso is situated in West Africa and bordered on the north and west by Mali, on the east by Niger, on the southeast by Benin and on the south by Togo, Ghana and Côte d'Ivoire. The southern part of the country, less arid than the north, is wooded savannah, gradually drying out into sand and desert in the north. The Sahara desert is relentlessly moving south, however, stripping the savannah lands of trees and slowly turning the thin layer of cultivatable soil into sun-blackened rock-hard *lakenite*. Three great rivers, the Black, the Red and the White Volta, water the great plains. The population does not live in the valleys along the river banks due to the diseases prevalent there.
LANGUAGE: The official language is French. Several indigenous languages such as Mossi, More, Dioula and Goumantche are also spoken.
RELIGION: Mainly Animist. 30% Muslim and fewer than 10% Christians (mostly Roman Catholics).
TIME: GMT.
ELECTRICITY: 220/380 volts AC, 50Hz. 2-pin plugs are standard.
COMMUNICATIONS: Telephone: IDD is available. Country code: 226. **Telex/telegram:** There are limited facilities outside Ouagadougou. Main hotels have facilities. **Post:** There are few post offices, but stamps can often be bought at hotels. *Poste Restante* facilities are available but a charge is made for letters collected. There is no local delivery, and all other mail must be addressed to a box number. Airmail to Europe takes up to two weeks. Post office hours are 0700-1230 and 1500-1730 Monday to Friday. The main post office in the capital is open 0830-1200 and 1500-1830 Monday to Saturday. **Press:** French-language only.
BBC World Service and Voice of America frequencies: From time to time these change. See the section *How to Use this Book* for more information.

BBC:				
MHz	21.71	15.07	11.86	6.005
Voice of America:				
MHz	21.49	15.60	9.525	6.035

PASSPORT/VISA

Regulations and requirements may be subject to change at short notice, and you are advised to contact the appropriate diplomatic or consular authority before finalising travel arrangements. Details of these may be found at the head of this country's entry. Any numbers in the chart refer to the footnotes below.

	Passport Required?	Visa Required?	Return Ticket Required?
Full British	Yes	Yes	Yes
BVP	Not valid	-	-
Australian	Yes	Yes	Yes
Canadian	Yes	Yes	Yes
USA	Yes	Yes	Yes
Other EC	Yes	Yes	Yes
Japanese	Yes	Yes	Yes

Restricted entry: Admission is refused to nationals of the South African Republic and Israel (*except* under exceptional circumstances).
PASSPORTS: Valid passport required by all except: nationals of Benin, Central African Republic, Côte d'Ivoire, Guinea Republic, Mali, Mauritania, Niger, Senegal and Togo, providing they hold a valid national ID card.
British Visitors Passport: Not accepted.
VISAS: Required by all, except nationals of Benin, Central African Republic, Côte d'Ivoire, Guinea Republic, Mali, Mauritania, Niger, Senegal, Togo and holders of a re-entry permit.
Types of visa: Tourist, Business and Transit. All cost £17.50.
Validity: Multiple entry: 3 months, with applications for extension to be made to Immigration in Burkina Faso.
Application to: Consulate. For address, see top of entry.
Application requirements: (a) Valid passport. (b) 2 application forms. (c) 2 photos. (d) Sufficient funds to cover duration of stay. (e) Registered, stamped, self-addressed envelope for postal applications. (f) Company letter if on business.
Working days required: Visas can be granted immediately if papers are in order; it takes a few days if the application is made by post.
Temporary residence: Application to be made to Central Government of Burkina Faso. Enquire at Consulate.

MONEY

Currency: CFA Franc (CFA Fr). Notes are in denominations of CFA Fr10000, 5000, 1000, 500, 100 and 50. Coins are in denominations of CFA Fr500, 100, 50, 25, 10, 5, 2 and 1. These notes and coins are legal tender in all the Republics which formerly comprised French West Africa (Benin, Côte d'Ivoire, Mali, Niger, Senegal, Togo and Burkina Faso).
Credit cards: Access/Mastercard (limited) and Diners Club are accepted. Check with your credit card company for details of merchant acceptability and other services which may be available.
Exchange rate indicators: The following figures are included as a guide to the movements of the CFA Franc against Sterling and the US Dollar:

Date:	Oct '89	Oct '90	Oct '91	Oct '92
£1.00=	505.13	498.37	496.13	413.75
$1.00=	319.90	255.12	285.87	260.71

Currency restrictions: No restrictions on import/export of local currency or foreign currency.
Banking hours: 0800-1200 Monday to Friday.

DUTY FREE

The following items may be imported into Burkina Faso by persons over 18 years of age without incurring customs duty:
200 cigarettes or 25 cigars or 100 cigarillos or 250g of tobacco;
1 litre of spirits and 1 litre of wine;
0.5 litre of toilet water and 0.25 litre of perfume.
Note: Sporting guns may only be imported under licence.

PUBLIC HOLIDAYS

Public holidays observed in Burkina Faso are as follows:
Mar 25 '93 Eid al Fitr (End of Ramadan). **Apr 12** Easter Monday. **May 1** Labour Day. **May 20** Ascension Day. **May 31** Whit Monday. **Jun 1** Eid al-Adha (Feast of the Sacrifice). **Aug 4** National Day. **Aug 15** Assumption. **Aug 30** Mouloud (Prophet's Birthday). **Nov 1** All Saints Day (Toussaint). **Dec 25** Christmas. **Jan 1 '94** New Year's Day. **Jan 3** Anniversary of the 1966 *coup d'état*
Note: (a) **May 17** and **Oct 20** are also usually declared holidays by the Government. (b) Muslim festivals are timed according to local sightings of various phases of the Moon and the dates given above are approximations. During the lunar month of Ramadan that precedes Eid al-Fitr, Muslims fast during the day and feast at night and normal business patterns may be interrupted. Many restaurants are closed during the day and there may be restrictions on smoking and drinking. Some disruption may continue into Eid al-Fitr itself. Eid al-Fitr and Eid al-Adha may last anything from two to ten days, depending on the region. For more information, refer to the section *World of Islam* at the back of the book.

HEALTH

Regulations and requirements may be subject to change at short notice, and you are advised to contact your doctor well in advance of your intended date of departure. Any numbers in the chart refer to the footnotes below.

	Special Precautions?	Certificate Required?
Yellow Fever	Yes	1
Cholera	Yes	2
Typhoid & Polio	Yes	-
Malaria	Yes	-
Food & Drink	3	-

[1]: A yellow fever vaccination certificate is required from travellers over one year of age coming from all countries.
[2]: Following WHO guidelines issued in 1973, a cholera vaccination certificate is no longer a condition of entry to Burkina Faso. However, cholera is a serious risk in this country and precautions are essential. Up-to-date advice should be sought before deciding whether these precautions should include vaccination as medical opinion is divided over its effectiveness. See the *Health* section at the back of the book.
[3] All water should be regarded as being potentially contaminated. Drinking water outside main cities and towns is likely to be contaminated and sterilisation is considered essential. Milk is unpasteurised and should be boiled. Powdered or tinned milk is available and is advised, but make sure that it is reconstituted with pure water. Avoid all dairy products. Only eat well-cooked meat and fish, preferably served hot. Pork, salad and mayonnaise may carry increased risk. Vegetables should be cooked and fruit peeled.
Malaria risk exists all year throughout the country, predominantly in the malignant *falciparum* form. Resistance to chloroquine has been reported.
Rabies is present. For those at high risk, vaccination before arrival should be considered. If you are bitten abroad seek medical advice without delay. For more information consult the *Health* section at the back of the book.
Bilharzia (schistosomiasis) is present. Avoid swimming and paddling in fresh water. Swimming pools which are well-chlorinated and maintained are safe.
Health care: Health insurance is strongly recommended.

TRAVEL - International

AIR: Burkina Faso's national airline is *Air Burkina (VH)*. Burkina Faso has a minority shareholding in *Air Afrique*. Other airlines include *Aeroflot, Air Afrique, Air Algérie, Air Ivoire, Ethiopian* and *UTA*.
International airports: *Ouagadougou (OUA)*, 8km (5 miles) from the city, with restaurant and car hire facilities. Taxi service to city. *Borgo* is 16km (10 miles) from Bobo Dioulasso (see below). There are regular and cheap flights between Paris and Ouagadougou.
RAIL: The only route is the international line from Côte d'Ivoire running through to Ouagadougou. Four trains a day run from Ouagadougou to Bobo Dioulasso, of which two are through services to Abidjan in Côte d'Ivoire. Other trains from Bobo cross the border to serve Côte d'Ivoire destinations. Abidjan trains have sleeping and dining cars. Work is under way to extend the line from Ouagadougou to Tambao on the Mali border, but this project may have to be cancelled to meet foreign debt requirements. The existing line is also under threat of closure.
ROAD: Routes are from Ghana, Mali, Côte d'Ivoire, Togo, Benin and Niger, although these are often barely adequate. Regular bus services run during the dry season, from Bobo to Bamako in Mali, and from Ouagadougou to Niamey in Niger. The road from Ghana is being improved.

TRAVEL - Internal

AIR: *Bobo Dioulasso* airport, 16km (10 miles) from Borgo, is the principal airport. Flights run to Bouake, Bamako and Tambao on *Air Volta (VH)*. Air taxis are available.
RAIL: A daily service runs from Ouagadougou to Bobo Dioulasso. There are two classes, with some restaurant cars, sleeping facilities and air-conditioning. This service can become overcrowded.
ROAD: Roads are in general not passable in the rainy season (July-September). Police checkpoints are a common cause of delays. **Bus:** Regular bus services are operated in the dry season and it is necessary to book well in advance. **Taxi:** Shared taxis are available in major centres; fares are negotiable. **Car hire:** Rented from *Burkina Faso Auto Location*, Hotel Independence, Ouagadougou; chauffeur-driven cars are also available. **Documentation:** A temporary licence to drive is available from local authorities on presentation of a valid national driving licence, but an International Permit is recommended.

ACCOMMODATION

HOTELS: There are hotels in Ouagadougou and Bobo Dioulasso and some have air-conditioned rooms and additional facilities. Elsewhere there are small lodges. There is also a group of tourist-class bungalows at Arly National Park. Information can be obtained from the Direction Général du Tourisme et de L'Hôtellerie (address and contact numbers above). **Grading:** Hotels are rated by the Government in stars.

RESORTS & EXCURSIONS

The capital, **Ouagadougou**, has an interesting *Ethnography Museum* containing a substantial collection of Mossi artefacts, the town being the centre of one of the many ancient Mossi kingdoms. There is also a tourist office in the town. Excursions from Ouagadougou include a wildlife-viewing trip to a small artificial lake 18km (11 miles) to the north. **Pabre,** an ancient **Mossi** village, is a short distance from another large reservoir north of the city. At Sabou, crocodiles can be seen at close quarters. However, as far as looking at wildlife is concerned, the three national parks – at *Po*, at '*W*' near the Benin and Niger border, and at *Arly* – are the most important.

SOCIAL PROFILE

FOOD & DRINK: Outside hotels there are a few restaurants in Ouagadougou and in Bobo. Staple foods include sorghum, millet, rice, maize, nuts, potatoes and yams. Local vegetables and strawberries are available in season. Specialities include *brochettes* (meat cooked on a skewer) and chicken dishes. Beer is very reasonably priced.
NIGHTLIFE: There are several nightclubs in Ouagadougou with music and dancing, open-air cinemas and one covered air-conditioned one.
SHOPPING: Bargaining in the traditional market place is recommended. Purchases include wooden statuettes, bronze models, masks, worked skins from the tannery in Ouagadougou, jewellery, fabrics, hand-woven blankets and leather goods and crafts ranging from chess sets to ash trays. **Shopping hours:** 0800-1200 and 1500-1800 Monday to Saturday. Some shops may be open on Sunday and there are daily markets in the main towns.
SPORT: Swimming: There are a couple of hotels with swimming pools in Ouagadougou open to non-residents for a small fee. Due to endemic bilharzia it is not safe to swim in most rivers, lakes or standing water. **Tennis:** Tennis courts are in Ouagadougou and visitors can play at the Burkina Faso Club on invitation of a member. **Fishing:** There are no fishing restrictions on any of the water courses except for the use of poison, explosives, nets with mesh smaller than 3cm (1.2 inches) and electrical equipment. **Horseriding:** Horses are available for hire at the Club Hippique in Ouagadougou.
SPECIAL EVENTS: At 0600 on Fridays *Nabayius Gou* ('the Emperor goes to war') is a traditional 'drama' performed at the Moro Naba Palace in Ouagadougou depicting the magnificently bedecked emperor being restrained by his wife and subjects as he sets off to make war with his brother. The end of *Ramadan* is accompanied by festivals of singing and dancing. Traditional music and dancing can also be seen on festivals and holidays especially in the southwest region which is rich in folklore.
SOCIAL CONVENTIONS: Within the urban areas many French customs prevail. Dress should be casual and appropriate for hot weather. Lounge suits for men and formal wear for women are required for evening entertainment. Outside the cities little has changed for centuries and visitors should respect local customs and traditions. **Tipping:** Service is generally included in the bill (about 10-15%) although it is customary to tip taxi drivers, porters and hotel staff.

BUSINESS PROFILE

ECONOMY: According to World Bank assessments, Burkina is the sixth poorest country in the world. Its economy is predominantly agricultural, employing 80% of the population and contributing 45% of GNP (1986 figures). The sector has recovered from the devastating droughts of the mid-1980s and maintains subsistence agriculture (sorghum, millet, maize and rice) plus cash crops of cotton, groundnuts, sesame and shea-nuts which are a valuable export earner. There is considerable mineral wealth, including gold and manganese, but doubts prevail as to whether exploitation is economically viable. Burkina has a small manufacturing sector producing textiles, sugar and flour. The country depends heavily on overseas aid, particularly from France and the European Community, which is likely to remain the mainstay of the economy for the foreseeable future. Burkina belongs to the CFA Franc Zone. Imports outweigh exports in value by a factor of five. Over one-third of exports are bought by France, which provides a similar quantity of Burkina's imports. Outside the European Community, neighbouring Côte d'Ivoire is Burkina's main trading partner.
BUSINESS: Suits should be worn for Government and official business, otherwise a shirt and tie should suffice. Most officials prefer to wear national dress. French is the main language spoken in business circles and if the visitor does not have command of French, interpreter services should be sought from the British Embassy. **Office hours:**

BURKINA FASO	HEALTH REGULATIONS	VISA REGULATIONS
GALILEO/WORLDSPAN	TI-DFT/OUA/HE	TI-DFT/OUA/VI
SABRE	TIDFT/OUA/HE	TIDFT/OUA/VI

Code-Link

To access this information on your CRS, swipe the barcode with a light pen or type in the text under the barcode. For more information, see the introduction *How to Use This Book*.

0800-1230 and 1500-1730 Monday to Friday.
COMMERCIAL INFORMATION: The following organisation can offer advice: Chambre de Commerce, d'Industrie et d'Artisanat du Burkina, BP 502, Ouagadougou, Burkina Faso. Tel: 30 61 14. Fax: 30 61 16. Telex: 5268.

HISTORY & GOVERNMENT

HISTORY: Burkina Faso was once a part of the Great Mossi Empire, one of the strongest of ancient African kingdoms. The region itself is in the path of several historic migrations of population – in particular those brought about as the edge of the Sahara shifted. Semi-nomadic cattle-herders also crossed the region and their descendants account for a significant proportion of the population. The whole region was annexed by the French in 1896 and in 1919 Upper Volta became a full French colony, its boundaries set by carving a section of land from the colonies of Niger and Senegal. This entity was transferred to Côte d'Ivoire in 1932, only to be reconstituted 30 years later. Upper Volta achieved full independence from France in 1960, and changed its name to Burkina Faso (Land of Dignity) in 1984. The internal history of the country since independence has been characterised by a series of military coups. The most important of these occurred in 1983, when Captain Thomas Sankara, formerly a government minister in previous military regimes during the 1970s, seized power and laid down a new political direction for the country, which had previously pursued an orthodox pro-capitalist scheme of economic development. After renaming the country, Sankara set about reorganising the political and economic system. He openly modelled himself on Flight Lieutenant Jerry Rawlings in neighbouring Ghana and took a radically nationalist stance. Particular emphasis was put on the development of the rural economy, although an unfortunate consequence of this was that the trade unions, whose membership was concentrated in the urban economy, became alienated from the regime. Tensions too were growing within the ruling National Revolutionary Council, which came to a head in October 1987, when Sankara was killed in a revolt led by his second-in-command, Captain Blaise Compaoré. Captain Compaoré disbanded Sankara's National Revolutionary Party (NRP), replacing it with a new group, the Popular Front (FP), of which he is Chairman. This new party is largely supported by former NRP members. Soon after consolidating his position, Campaoré came under pressure from France, in common with the governments of other former French colonies, to introduce democratic reforms. After a boycotted presidential election, the reform programme is now in abeyance while the Government and the main opposition grouping, the Co-ordination des Forces Démocratiques (CFD), negotiate the next stage.
GOVERNMENT: The June 1991 constitution allows for an elected President, who holds executive power, elected for a 7-year term by universal suffrage. Representatives to the legislative assembly, the Assemblée des Députés Populaires, are elected every four years.

CLIMATE

Tropical. The best months are December to March. *Harmattan* wind blows from the east (November to February) with dry and cool weather. Short rains (March and April) followed by dry season (February to May) and main rains (June to October). Rainfall is highest in the southwest and lowest in the northeast.
Required clothing: Lightweights and rainwear for the rainy season. Plenty of scarves and handkerchiefs during the months when *Harmattan* blows.

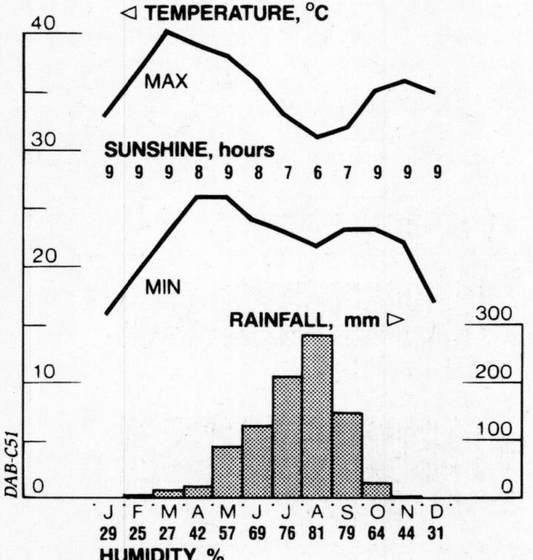

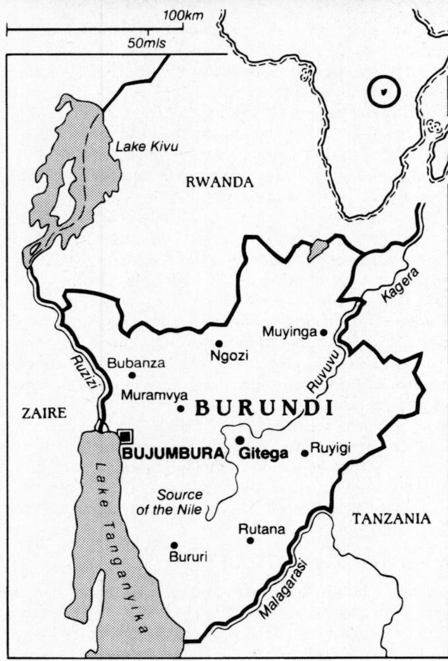

Location: Central Africa.

Office National du Tourisme
BP 902
Bujumbura, Burundi
Tel: (2) 22202. Telex: 5010.
Embassy of the Republic of Burundi
46 square Marie-Louise
1040 Brussels, Belgium
Tel: (2) 230 4535. Fax: (2) 230 7883. Telex: 23572.
British Consulate
BP 1344
43 avenue Bubanza
Bujumbura, Burundi
Tel: (2) 23711. Telex: 5126 INTAC BDI.
Embassy of the Republic of Burundi
Suite 212
2233 Wisconsin Avenue, NW
Washington, DC
20007
Tel: (202) 342 2574.
Embassy of the United States of America
BP 1720
avenue des Etats-Unis
Bujumbura, Burundi
Tel: (2) 23454. Fax: (2) 22926.
Embassy of the Republic of Burundi
Suite 800
151 Slater Street
Ottawa, Ontario
K1P 5H3
Tel: (613) 236 8483. Fax: (613) 563 1827. Telex: 0533393.

AREA: 27,834 sq km (10,747 sq miles).
POPULATION: 5,458,000 (1990 estimate).
POPULATION DENSITY: 196.1 per sq km.
CAPITAL: Bujumbura. **Population:** 215,243 (1987).
GEOGRAPHY: Burundi is situated in the heart of Africa and lies across the main Nile-Congo dividing range, bounded to the west by the narrow plain of the Ruzizi River and Lake Tanganyika. The interior is a broken plateau sloping east to Tanzania and the valley of the Malagarasi River. The southern tributary of the Nile system rises in the south of the country. The landscape is characterised by hills and valleys which are covered with eucalyptus trees, banana groves, cultivated fields and pasture. In the east, the fertile area gives way to savannah grassland, and tea and coffee are now grown on mountainsides.

LANGUAGE: The languages are French and Kirundi, a Bantu language. Kiswahili is also widely spoken.
RELIGION: Mainly Roman Catholic; there are Anglican and Pentecostalist minorities. Local animist beliefs are held by a significant minority.
TIME: GMT + 2.
ELECTRICITY: 220 volts AC, 50Hz.
COMMUNICATIONS: Telephone: IDD is available. Country code: 257. **Telex/telegram:** Facilities are available from *Direction des Télécommunications* in Bujumbura. **Post:** The main post office in Bujumbura is open 0800-1200 and 1400-1600 Monday to Friday and 0800-1100 Saturday. **Press:** No English-language newspapers are published. Most publications are in French (such as *Le Renouveau du Burundi*) or local languages (such as *Ubumwe* in Kirundi). The two main newspapers are government-controlled.
BBC World Service and Voice of America frequencies: From time to time these change. See the section *How to Use this Book* for more information.

BBC:				
MHz	21.47	17.88	15.42	9.630
Voice of America:				
MHz	21.49	15.60	9.525	6.035

PASSPORT/VISA

Regulations and requirements may be subject to change at short notice, and you are advised to contact the appropriate diplomatic or consular authority before finalising travel arrangements. Details of these may be found at the head of this country's entry. Any numbers in the chart refer to the footnotes below.

	Passport Required?	Visa Required?	Return Ticket Required?
Full British	Yes	Yes	Yes
BVP	Not valid	-	-
Australian	Yes	Yes	Yes
Canadian	Yes	Yes	Yes
USA	Yes	Yes	Yes
Other EC	Yes	Yes	Yes
Japanese	Yes	Yes	Yes

PASSPORTS: Valid passport required by all.
British Visitors Passport: Not accepted.
VISAS: Required by all. Passengers arriving at Bujumbura airport without a visa may be deported on the next international flight leaving Bujumbura regardless of its destination.
Types of visa: *Tourist:* US$20. *Business:* price available on application. A Transit visa is not required for passengers continuing their journey to a third country and not leaving the airport. A Re-entry Permit is required for all alien residents.
Application to: Consulate (or Consular Section at Embassy). For addresses, see top of entry.
Application requirements: Details available on application.
Working days required: Applications should be made as far as possible in advance of the intended date of departure.

MONEY

Currency: Burundi Franc (Bufr) = 100 centimes. Notes are in denominations of Bufr5000, 1000, 500, 100, 50, 20 and 10. Coins are in denominations of Bufr10, 5 and 1.
Currency exchange: All exchange transactions must be conducted through one of the main banks in Bujumbura.
Credit cards: Diners Club and Access/Mastercard both have limited acceptance. Check with credit card company for details of merchant acceptability and other services which may be available.
Exchange rate indicators: The following figures are included as a guide to the movements of the Burundi Franc against Sterling and the US Dollar:

Date:	**Oct '89**	**Oct '90**	**Oct '91**	**Oct '92**
£1.00=	**253.50**	**312.62**	**347.50**	**362.52**
$1.00=	**156.67**	**165.45**	**200.23**	**228.43**

Currency restrictions: Unlimited import of foreign currency, subject to declaration; export limited to amount declared on import. Import and export of local currency is limited to Bufr2000.
Banking hours: 0800-1130 Monday to Friday. There are banks in Bujumbura and Gitega.

DUTY FREE

The following goods may be taken into Burundi without incurring customs duty:
1000 cigarettes or 1kg of tobacco;

1 litre of alcohol;
A reasonable amount of perfume.
Note: All baggage must be declared and duty may be required for cameras, radios, typewriters, etc.

PUBLIC HOLIDAYS

Public holidays observed in Burundi are as follows:
Apr 12 '93 Easter Monday. **May 1** Labour Day. **May 20** Ascension Day. **Jul 1** Independence Day. **Aug 15** Assumption. **Sep 3** Anniversary of the Third Republic. **Sep 18** Victory of UPRONA Party. **Nov 1** All Saints' Day. **Dec 25** Christmas Day. **Jan 1 '94** New Year's Day. **Feb 5** Unity Day.

HEALTH

Regulations and requirements may be subject to change at short notice, and you are advised to contact your doctor well in advance of your intended date of departure. Any numbers in the chart refer to the footnotes below.

	Special Precautions?	Certificate Required?
Yellow Fever	Yes	1
Cholera	Yes	2
Typhoid & Polio	Yes	-
Malaria	Yes	-
Food & Drink	3	-

[1]: Yellow fever vaccination certificate is required from travellers over 1 year of age arriving from infected areas.
[2]: Following WHO guidelines issued in 1973, a cholera vaccination certificate is no longer a condition of entry to Burundi. However, cholera is a serious risk in this country and precautions are essential. Up-to-date advice should be sought before deciding whether these precautions should include vaccination as medical opinion is divided over its effectiveness. See the *Health* section at the back of the book.
[3]: All water should be regarded as being potentially contaminated. Water used for drinking, brushing teeth or making ice should have first been boiled or otherwise sterilised. Milk is unpasteurised and should be boiled. Powdered or tinned milk is available and is advised, but make sure that it is reconstituted with pure water. Avoid dairy products which are likely to have been made from local milk. Only eat well-cooked meat and fish, preferably served hot. Pork, salad and mayonnaise may carry increased risk. Vegetables should be cooked and fruit peeled.
Malaria is a risk throughout the year, predominantly in the malignant *falciparum* form. Resistance to choloroquine has been reported.
Rabies is present. For those at high risk vaccination before arrival should be considered. If you are bitten abroad seek medical advice without delay. For more information consult the *Health* section at the back of the book.
Bilharzia (schistosomiasis) is present. Avoid swimming and paddling in fresh water. Swimming pools which are well-chlorinated and maintained are safe.
Health care: Medical insurance is strongly recommended.

TRAVEL - International

AIR: Burundi's national airline is *Air Burundi (PB).*
International airport: *Bujumbura (BJM)* is 11km (7 miles) north of the city. Taxis are available to and from the city.
Departure tax: Bufr2420; US$15 or equivalent for alien residents; transit passengers are exempt.
LAKE: Cargo/passenger steamers ply Lake Tanganyika between Kigoma (Tanzania) and Bujumbura, and less frequently between Kalemi (Zaïre) and Bujumbura. There is also a service to Mpulungu (Zambia). There are three classes. Steamers can often be held up depending on the cargo being loaded or unloaded.
ROAD: It is possible to drive into Burundi from Zaïre, either from the north or south. Road travel from Rwanda is reasonable but, from Tanzania, poor.

TRAVEL - Internal

AIR: There are no regular internal flights.
ROAD: Most roads are sealed. There are main roads east from Bujumbura to Muramvya (once the royal city of Burundi) and south to Gitega. Both journeys can be completed without too much strain during the dry season, but any road travel is very difficult in the rainy season. **Bus:** There are services around Bujumbura and main towns only. Japanese-style minibuses operate within towns and are normally cheaper and less crowded than shared taxis; departures (when the vehicle is full) are normally from bus stands. **Taxi:** *Tanus-tanus* (truck taxis) are usually available but they are often crowded. **Car hire:** *Avis* is represented in Bujumbura, and it may also be possible to arrange some form of car hire via a local garage. **Documentation:** International Driving Permit required.
JOURNEY TIMES: The following chart gives approximate journey times from Bujumbura (in hours and minutes) to other major cities/towns in Burundi.

	Air	Road	Sea
Gitega	-	1.30	-
Resha Gumonge	- 0.45	13.00	
Nyanza Lake	-	-	5.00
Kirundo	0.25	4.00	-
Muyinga	-	5.00	-
Ngozi	-	3.00	-

ACCOMMODATION

HOTELS: Almost all the hotels in the country are situated in the capital, Bujumbura, although there are a few in Gitega, Ngozi and Kirundo. Elsewhere in the country there is virtually no accommodation for visitors.
CAMPING: Generally frowned upon, particularly near towns. Permission should always be obtained from the local authority.

RESORTS & EXCURSIONS

The capital port-city of **Bujumbura**, situated on the shore of Lake Tanganyika, is a bustling town with a population of some 215,000 inhabitants. The area was colonised by the Germans at the end of the 19th century, and there is still architecture dating from that period of Burundi's history, including the *Postmaster's House*. Other attractions include three *museums* and the *Islamic Cultural Centre*. On the lake there are many opportunities for watersports, including sailing, wind-surfing, water-skiing and fishing. There is an excellent market.
Other points of interest in the country include the former royal cities of **Muramvya** and **Gitega** (with its *National Museum*), and the monument near **Rutana** which marks the source of the White Nile.

SOCIAL PROFILE

FOOD & DRINK: The choice is limited. Meals in Bujumbura's hotels are reasonable, but expensive and fairly basic. The French and Greek restaurants in the town are good. There are few restaurants outside the capital and Gitega.
NIGHTLIFE: Several nightclubs, restaurants and bars in Bujumbura.
SPORTS: Bujumbura, on the shores of Lake Tanganyika, offers **watersports** including **sailing, water-skiing** and **fishing.** The public beach lies 5km (3 miles) west of the city. The Entente Sportive Club offers tourist membership for **swimming, tennis, volleyball, basketball** and **golf.** For information on water sports contact the Cercle Nautique. The absence of motor vehicles and the lushness of the sub-tropical flora makes Burundi a superb place for **walking** and **hiking.**
SHOPPING: Local crafts, particularly basketwork. **Shopping hours:** 0800-1200 and 1400-1800 Monday to Friday, 0800-1230 Saturday.
SOCIAL CONVENTIONS: Normal social courtesies apply. However, outside the cities people may not be used to visitors and care and tact must be used in respect of local customs. Inhabitants in major towns generally have a more modern and established way of life. Dress should be reasonably conservative. **Tipping:** As a rule no service charge is levied automatically; 10% is the recommended tip.

BUSINESS PROFILE

ECONOMY: Burundi is one of the world's poorest countries with an economy almost entirely based on agriculture. Cassava and sweet potatoes are the main subsistence crops while the important cash crops are coffee – the country's leading export – tea and cotton. A high dependence on coffee has left Burundi very vulnerable to fluctuations in the world market price; this has been very low throughout most of the 1980s and Burundi's earnings have suffered accordingly. The country's small mining industry produces gold, cassiterite, tungsten and tantalum. Important deposits of vanadium, nickel and uranium have been located and are currently being surveyed. An indigenous textiles industry has recently been developed. For the forseeable future Burundi will remain a major recipient of foreign aid, principally from France, Belgium, Germany – who are also, along with Japan, the main source of Burundi's imports – and from the EC Development Fund and the World Bank. Burundi's major export markets are the countries of the CFA Franc Zone, taking approximately one-third of the total, followed by Belgium-Luxembourg, the United States, the UK, France and The Netherlands.
BUSINESS: Lightweight suits are necessary. April to October and December to January are the best times to visit.
COMMERCIAL INFORMATION: The following organisation can offer advice: Chambre de Commerce et de L'Industrie du Burundi, BP 313, Bujumbura, Burundi. Tel: (2) 22280.

HISTORY & GOVERNMENT

HISTORY: The agricultural Hutu and pastoralist Tutsi have occupied the area for many centuries with the Tutsi occupying the dominant social positions

You will have noticed that throughout the *World Travel Guide* there are Code-Link symbols. These enable users of Computer Reservation Systems to make instant information up-dates. For more details about how Code-Link can help your agency, refer to the Introduction.

Codelink

BURUNDI | **HEALTH REGULATIONS** | **VISA REGULATIONS** | Code-Link

GALILEO/WORLDSPAN

TI-DFT/BJM/HE

TI-DFT/BJM/VI

SABRE

TIDFT/BJM/HE

TIDFT/BJM/VI

To access this information on your CRS, swipe the barcode with a light pen or type in the text under the barcode. For more information, see the introduction *How to Use This Book.*

(though the original relationship was more symbiotic in nature); the society was never highly centralised and proved unable to withstand the advances of the Germans during the scramble for Africa in the 19th century. The country subsequently became part of German East Africa. After 1919, Burundi and neighbouring Rwanda were administered by the Belgians. Both countries gained independence in 1962. In 1966 the reigning King Mwami was deposed by a military coup. His son took the throne, only to be deposed by Captain Micombero, who became Prime Minister and declared Burundi a republic. Micombero was deposed by a military coup in 1976 and Lieutenant Colonel Jean-Baptist Bagaza became President of a military regime, appointed by the supreme revolutionary council. In 1984 Bagaza was re-elected as President of a one-party state, the Union of National Progress (UPRONA). He was deposed in 1987 after a coup led by Major Pierre Buyoya, who suspended the constitution, all state organs, and those of UPRONA. In addition to political instability, Burundi has had to endure the bloody effects of tribal rivalry between the Tutsi – 'the tall ones' – who dominate the army, the Government and the economy, and the pastoral Hutu, who suffer discrimination to an extent possibly unequalled outside South Africa. The antagonism has occasionally flared up into massive violence. In 1972 up to 100,000 Hutu were massacred by the Tutsi, and in 1988, the army was despatched to the north of the country to 'restore order' after several hundred Tutsi were slaughtered by Hutus: in one week, an estimated 20,000 Hutus were massacred in reprisals; a further 60,000 fled to neighbouring Rwanda, Tanzania and Zaïre. Tension between the two communities continued at a high level throughout 1989. That year, in an attempt to defuse the situation, President Buyoya announced plans to combat the extensive discrimination against the Hutu, although the package was strongly resisted by the Tutsi-dominated officer corps. The civil war in neighbouring Rwanda which broke out in the autumn of 1990 has the same two main tribal groups – Tutsi and Hutu – struggling for political control, with the difference that the Hutu have been in control since the 1960s, delivering a timely reminder to Burundi's rulers of the consequences of institutionalised discrimination. There are now signs that Burundi is set to follow the regional trend towards liberalism and political plurality: following approval of a new constitution by referendum in 1992, multi-party elections for a national assembly are scheduled for 1993.
GOVERNMENT: Since the suspension of the 1981 constitution in 1987, Burundi has been ruled by a 31-member Military Committee for National Salvation. There is an appointed civilian Council of Ministers. A new constitution allowing for national assembly elections has been approved.

CLIMATE

A hot equatorial climate is found near Lake Tanganyika and in the Ruzizi River plain. It is often windy on the lake. The rest of the country is mild and pleasant. The rainy season is between October and May and there is a long dry season from June to September.
Required clothing: Lightweight cottons and linens. Waterproofs for rainy season. Warm clothes for the evenings.

BUJUMBURA Burundi (805m)

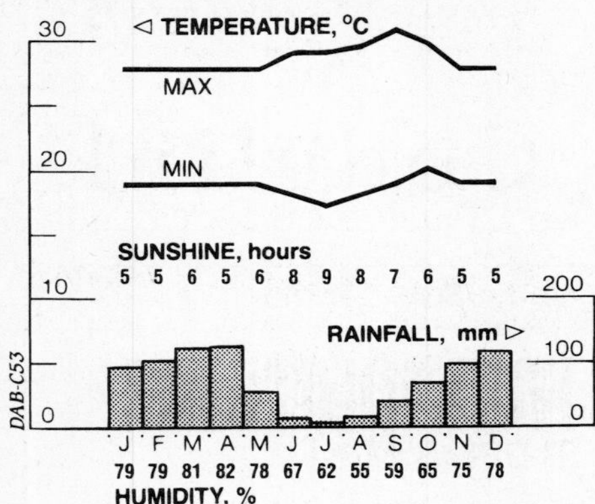

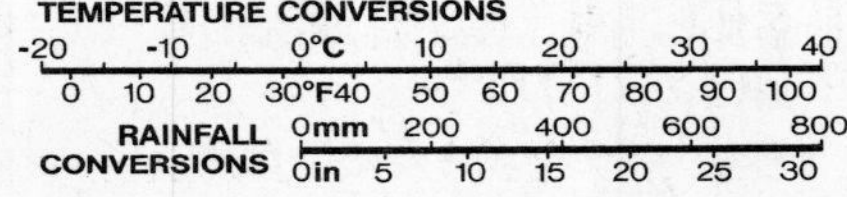

CAMBODIA

Location: South-East Asia.

Note: After the Khmer Rouge takeover in 1975, Cambodia was re-styled Democratic Kampuchea. Following the ousting of the Khmer Rouge by the Vietnamese in 1979, it was renamed the People's Republic of Kampuchea. It reverted to its old name, Cambodia, in April 1989. On October 23, 1991, a peace settlement was officially signed in Paris by all the warring factions. The former monarch, Norodom Sihanouk, returned to Phnom Penh on November 14, 1991, to chair the Supreme National Council which contains representatives from all factions and embodies Cambodian sovereignty as recognised by the United Nations. Diplomatic missions, however, have not yet been set up in Western capitals, although they exist in Hanoi, Ho Chi Minh City, Vientiane (Laos), Beijing, Moscow and Delhi.

Ministry of Information & Culture
corner of 180 Street and Croix Rouge Street
Phnom Penh, Cambodia
Tel: (2) 4769.
Phnom Penh Tourism
313 Quai Karl Marx
corner of of 2 Lenin Boulevard
Phnom Penh, Cambodia
Tel: (2) 3949 *or* 5349 *or* 4059.
Orbitours Pty Ltd
GPO Box 3309
7th Floor, Dymocks Building
428 George Street
Sydney, NSW 2000, Australia
Tel: (2) 221 7322 *or* 800 89 2006 (UK toll free) *or* 800 235 5895 (US toll free). Fax: (2) 221 7425. Telex: AA127081.

AREA: 181,035 sq km (69,898 sq miles).
POPULATION: 8,246,000 (1990 estimate).
POPULATION DENSITY: 45.5 per sq km (1990 estimate).
CAPITAL: Phnom Penh. **Population:** 650,000 (1990).
GEOGRAPHY: Cambodia shares borders in the north with Laos and Thailand, in the east with Vietnam and in the southwest with the Gulf of Thailand. The landscape comprises tropical rainforest and fertile cultivated land traversed by many rivers. In the northeast area rise highlands. The capital is located at the junction of the Mekong and Tonlé Sap rivers. The latter flows from a large inland lake, also called Tonlé Sap, situated in the centre of the country. There are numerous offshore islands along the southwest coast.
LANGUAGE: Khmer. Chinese and Vietnamese are also spoken. French was widely spoken until the arrival of the Pol Pot regime and is spoken by those of the older generation. English is now a more popular language to learn among the younger generation.
RELIGION: 95% Buddhist, the remainder are Muslim and Christian. Buddhism was reinstated as the national religion in the late 1980s, after a ban on religious activity in 1975.
TIME: GMT + 7.
ELECTRICITY: 220 volts AC, 50Hz. Power cuts are frequent. Outside Phnom Penh, electric power is available only in the evenings from around 1830-2130.
COMMUNICATIONS: Telephone: IDD communications have now been restored. Country code: 855. Phnom Penh code: 23. Fax: Not yet available. **Telex/telegram:** International Telex Code is 807. Telegrams are the most popular form of telecommunication. **Post:** Postal services are extremely limited and letters mailed from Cambodia to most destinations (except letters to Eastern Asia and Australia which go through Saigon) must go through Moscow. Airmail to Cambodia can take up to 2-3 months to arrive. The Post & Telephone Office (PTT) in Phnom Penh is located across from the Hotel Monorom at the corner of Achar Mean Boulevard and 126 Street and is open from 0700-1200 and 1300-2300. The main post office in Phnom Penh is located on the western side of 13 Street between 98 Street and 102 Street, open from 0630-2100. General post office hours: 0730-1200 and 1430-1700 Monday to Friday in Phnom Penh. **Press:** The *Phnom Penh Post* is printed in English.
BBC World Service and Voice of America frequencies: From time to time these change. See the section *How to Use this Book* for more information.

BBC:				
MHz	17.79	11.95	9.740	6.195
Voice of America:				
MHz	21.49	15.60	9.525	6.035

PASSPORT/VISA

Regulations and requirements may be subject to change at short notice, and you are advised to contact the appropriate diplomatic or consular authority before finalising travel arrangements. Details of these may be found at the head of this country's entry. Any numbers in the chart refer to the footnotes below.

	Passport Required?	Visa Required?	Return Ticket Required?
Full British	Yes	Yes	Yes
BVP	Not valid	-	-
Australian	Yes	Yes	Yes
Canadian	Yes	Yes	Yes
USA	Yes	Yes	Yes
Other EC	Yes	Yes	Yes
Japanese	Yes	Yes	Yes

PASSPORTS: Valid passport required by all.
British Visitors Passport: Not accepted.
VISAS: Required by all except nationals of Cambodia in possession of valid passports and holders of re-entry permits.
Types of visa: Tourist (usually only obtained through certain tour operators) and Business. Although rare, ordinary Tourist visas can be obtained. However, most tourists, except overseas Cambodians visiting relatives, must book an inclusive tour package.
Validity and cost: Generally around US$100, although the charge is usually included in cost of tourist package. Visa extensions may be granted by the Foreign Ministry in Phnom Penh.
Application to: Consulates (or Consulate section of Embassy) in Hanoi, Saigon, Vientiane (Laos) and Moscow. Business visas are obtainable through the Ministry of Foreign Affairs in Phnom Penh or an official invitation.
Application requirements: (a) Application completed in triplicate. (b) 3 passport-size photos. (c) Photocopy of passport. (d) Curriculum Vitae. (e) Tour itinerary. (f) Business card, if applying for Business visa.
Working days required: Usually 10-14 days. However, visas have been known to take everything from 3 days to 1 month. Once approved it may be collected either at a Cambodian Mission or issued on arrival at Pochentong (Phnom Penh) airport.

MONEY

Currency: Riel (CRl) = 100 sen. Notes are in denominations of (CRl)100, 50, 20, 10, 5 and 1 and 50, 20 and 10 sen. Coin: 5 sen.
Currency exchange: US dollars are widely accepted and exchanged, but other currencies are little recognised.
Credit cards: Not accepted.
Travellers cheques: There is no guarantee of being able to exchange these.
Exchange rate indicators: The following figures are included as a guide to the movements of the Riel against Sterling and the US Dollar:

Date:	**Oct '89**	**Oct '90**	**Oct '91**	**Oct '92**
£1.00=	236.95	898.61	1390.0	3163.0
$1.00=	100.0	460.00	800.92	1993.1

Currency restrictions: Import and export of local currency is prohibited. Foreign currency may be exported up to the limit declared at customs on arrival.
Business hours: 0730-1200 and 1430-1700.

DUTY FREE

The following goods may be taken into Cambodia without incurring customs duty:
200 cigarettes or an equivalent quantity of cigars or tobacco;
1 bottle (opened) of spirits;
A reasonable amount of perfume.

PUBLIC HOLIDAYS

Public holidays observed in Cambodia are as follows:
Apr '93 New Year. **Sep 22** Feast of the Ancestors. **Nov** Full Moon Water Festival. **Jan 7 '94** National Day.
Note: Many of the political holidays are in a state of uncertainty.

HEALTH

Regulations and requirements may be subject to change at short notice, and you are advised to contact your doctor well in advance of your intended date of departure. Any numbers in the chart refer to the footnotes below.

	Special Precautions?	Certificate Required?
Yellow Fever	No	1
Cholera	Yes	2
Typhoid & Polio	Yes	-
Malaria	3	-
Food & Drink	4	-

[1]: A yellow fever vaccination certificate is required by travellers arriving from infected areas.
[2]: Following WHO guidelines issued in 1973, a cholera vaccination certificate is no longer a condition of entry to Cambodia. However, cholera is a serious risk in this country and precautions are essential. Up-to-date advice should be sought before deciding whether these precautions should include vaccination as medical opinion is divided over its effectiveness. See the *Health* section at the back of the book.
[3]: Malaria risk exists all year throughout the country. The malignant *falciparum* strain predominates and is reported to be highly resistant to chloroquine and resistant to sulfadoxine/pyrimethane.
[4]: All water should be regarded as being potentially contaminated. Water used for drinking, brushing teeth or making ice should have first been boiled or otherwise sterilised. Milk is unpasteurised and should be boiled. Powdered or tinned milk is available and is advised, but make sure that it is reconstituted with pure water. Avoid dairy products which are likely to have been made from local milk. Only eat well-cooked meat and fish, preferably served hot. Pork, salad and mayonnaise may carry increased risk. Vegetables should be cooked and fruit peeled.
Plague is present and vaccination is advised. For more information, consult the *Health* section at the back of the book.
Rabies is present. For those at high risk, vaccination before arrival should be considered. If you are bitten abroad seek medical advice without delay. For more information consult the *Health* section at the back of the book.
Bilharzia (schistosomiasis) is present. Avoid swimming and paddling in fresh water. Swimming pools which are well-chlorinated and maintained are safe.
Health care: Health insurance is essential. In 1984 there were 22 hospitals, about 1300 commune infirmaries and about 100 medical posts in the country.

TRAVEL - International

AIR: Cambodia's new international carrier, *Cambodia International Airlines*, started operating to Bangkok in 1992. *Thai International* and *Bangkok Airways* fly to Phnom Penh from Bangkok. *Malaysia Airlines* fly from Kuala Lumpur, *Hang Khong Vietnam (VN)* fly from Hanoi, *Aeroflot (SU)* from Moscow, *Lao International Aviation* from Vientiane and *Kampuchean Airlines (MP)* from Hanoi and Ho Chi Minh City.
International airport: *Pochentong (PNH)* is 10km (6 miles) from Phnom Penh. (*Siem Reap Airport* near Angkor Wat has been closed to international traffic since 1971.)
Departure tax: US$5 levied on all international departures.
SEA: The port of Phnom Penh can be reached via the Mekong delta through Vietnam. A new ocean port has been built at Kompong Som (formerly Sihanoukville).
RAIL/ROAD: The Thai border is closed for all overland access. The main highway links the capital with the Vietnam border.

TRAVEL - Internal

Note: Individual tourism is not often allowed. Orbitours in Sydney, Australia (address at top of entry) organise tours to Cambodia, which may be joined in Bangkok. Regent Holidays in Bristol, UK, also organise tours. Bookings for both need to be made well in advance.
AIR: Internal flights operate between Phnom Penh and Siem Reap (travel time – 45 minutes), Battambang, Koh Kong, Kompong Som and Stung Treng. The price is around US$5000.
SEA: Government-run ferries depart from the Psar Cha Ministry of Transport Ferry Landing on Quai Karl Marx between 102 and 104 streets and go to Kompong Cham, Kratie, Stung Trent, Kompong Chhnang and Phnom Krom
RAIL: Some rail services operate, but foreigners are not allowed to use them. There are plans to restore the international service to Bangkok, but much repair work is needed.
ROAD: Travel permits are required to cross provincial boundaries and most roads are in poor condition, although the highway to Vietnam is open. Care should be taken while driving as Cambodian drivers are prone to recklessness and accidents are relatively frequent. **Bus:** Buses to Phnom Penh suburbs are available from 182 Street next to O Russei Market and the bus station is open from 0530-1730. **Car hire:** Official visitors can arrange to hire a government car and driver. Cars, with or without air-conditioning, are available from The General Directorate of Tourism for about US$20-30.
Taxi: Cruising taxis are non-existent in Cambodia. However, service taxis can be hired at Psar Chbam Pao Shared-Taxi Station between 367 Street and 369 Street. *Samlors*, however, are a slow but inexpensive way to see the city and many drivers, especially those found outside main hotels, speak a little French or English. **Documentation:** An International Driving Permit is required.

ACCOMMODATION

A modern first-class hotel, the *Cambodiana*, is now open in Phnom Penh. Otherwise, small and simple hotels are available in Phnom Penh and most provincial capitals. Camping is not permitted.

RESORTS & EXCURSIONS

Since the ousting of the Pol Pot regime, many aspects of Khmer cultural life have revived. The famed *National Ballet* has been reconstituted by the surviving dancers and performs classical dances for visiting groups. *Buddhist temples* have re-opened and are the sites of various celebrations, especially at Khmer New Year. The interrogation centre of the Pol Pot regime in **Phnom Penh** is now the gruesome *Toul Sleng Museum of Genocide*. Other attractions in the capital are the *Royal Palace*, with its famous *Silver Pavilion*, and the *National Musuem of Khmer Art*. The famous temples at **Angkor,** in the country's northwest, are not accessible by road, but may be reached by special charter flights organised for tourist visitors. The unique echo under the main tower of *Angkor Wat* is worth experiencing. **Oudong,** 30km from Phnom Penh, is located on a hill overlooking vast plains and is famous for the burial chedis of the Khmer kings. **Tonle Bati,** south of Phnom Penh, has interesting ruins and makes an excellent picnic spot.

SOCIAL PROFILE

FOOD & DRINK: Restaurants and other businesses abound in Phnom Penh, although the city remains poor. Food stalls are also common in Phnom Penh and can usually be found in and around the Central Market, O Ressei Market and Tuol Tom Market.
NIGHTLIFE: The *Municipal Theatre* in Phnom Penh stages performances and classical Cambodia music and dance, performed by students, can be seen at the *Fine Arts School* in Phnom Penh.
SHOPPING: Antiques, woodcarvings, *papier maché* masks, brass figurines, kramas (checked scarves), material for *sarongs* and *hols* and items and jewellery made of gold, silver and precious stones are Cambodia's best buys. The Central Market, Tuol Tom Pong Market, Old Market and The Bijouterie d'Etat (State Jewellery Shop) are the best places for buying jewellery and the Fine Arts School sells many of the above goods in its shop. Clothing and materials are available at the Central Market.
SPECIAL EVENTS: Mid-Apr '93 *Chaul Chhnam*, 3-day celebration of the Cambodian New Year. **Late Apr** *Visak Bauchea*, Anniversary of Buddha's Birthday. **May** *Chrat Prea Angkal*, ceremonial beginning of the sowing season. **Late Sep** *Prachum Ben*, offerings made to dead ancestors. **Late Oct/early Nov** *Festival of the Reversing Current*, The Water Festival (Pirogue canoe races are held in Phnom Penh). **Late Jan/early Feb** *Tet*, Vietnamese and Chinese New Year.
SOCIAL CONVENTIONS: Avoid all political topics and all politically related subjects in conversation.
Photography: Permitted, with certain (obvious) restrictions. It is polite to ask permission before photographing Cambodian people, especially monks. Do not allow any type of film to pass through the old-fashioned x-ray machines at the airport. **Tipping:** Modest tips are appreciated in hotels and restaurants.

BUSINESS PROFILE

ECONOMY: The Cambodian economy has been all but destroyed by the war in South-East Asia and the rule of the Khmer Rouge. The country has now recovered from the severe food shortages which followed the ousting of the Khmer Rouge by the Vietnamese, but is still dependent on large quantities of food aid. The transportation infrastructure has suffered greatly from the fighting and restoration of agriculture has been slow. Rice is the staple product in this essentially agricultural economy. The largest export is rubber, most of which goes to the CIS. There are limited mineral resources, mostly of phosphates, iron ore, bauxite, silicon and manganese but these, like the forests which are a valuable potential source of timber, have not been exploited because of the political situation and an inadequate infrastructure. The state agency KAMPEXIM handles all of Cambodia's imports and exports as well as deliveries of foreign aid. The former USSR was until recently the country's largest trading partner. Japan and Australia are the only other trading partners of any consequence. The removal of US sanctions against Cambodia in January 1992, though relatively insignificant in itself, has made foreign companies less reluctant to consider business in the country. And while US sanctions still apply against neighbouring Vietnam, Cambodia has much to benefit from cross-border traffic.
BUSINESS: Shirt and tie should be worn. Some knowledge of French would be useful.
COMMERCIAL INFORMATION: The following organisation can offer advice: Chambre de Commerce et d'Agriculture, Vither Preah Baksei Cham Krong, Phnom Penh.

HISTORY & GOVERNMENT

HISTORY: The Kingdom of Cambodia became a French protectorate in the 19th century and was incorporated into French Indo-China. A democratic monarchy with bicameral parliament, it became an Associated State of the French Union in 1949 and fully independent in 1953. In 1955, King Norodom Sihanouk abdicated in favour of his father,

CAMBODIA | **HEALTH REGULATIONS** | **VISA REGULATIONS** | Code-Link

GALILEO/WORLDSPAN

TI-DFT/PNH/HE

TI-DFT/PNH/VI

SABRE

TIDFT/PNH/HE

TIDFT/PNH/VI

To access this information on your CRS, swipe the barcode with a light pen or type in the text under the barcode. For more information, see the introduction *How to Use This Book.*

Norodom Suramarit, to allow himself to enter politics. Using the title Prince Sihanouk, he founded a mass movement, the Popular Socialist Community, which won every elected seat in Parliament between 1955 and 1966. On the death of his father in 1960, Prince Sihanouk was elected as Head of State. In 1968, the war between the USA and North Vietnam spilled over into Cambodia, and bombing raids forced peasant farmers to abandon their land. In March 1970, Prince Sihanouk was overthrown by a right-wing coup. The Khmer Republic was proclaimed. This was followed by five years of civil war, won in 1975 by the communist Khmer Rouge. Prince Sihanouk returned as Head of State, only to resign after elections the following year. Khieu Samphan became President under the terms of the constitution of the newly-proclaimed Democratic Kampuchea; Pol Pot, a little-known Khmer Rouge leader, became Prime Minister. The new regime attempted a return to 'Year Zero', abolishing currency, destroying temples and churches, slaughtering intellectuals and brainwashing labourers. The hoped-for Utopia did not, however, materialise. In 1978 the Vietnamese invaded Kampuchea and, in January the following year, captured the capital and toppled the regime. The People's Republic of Kampuchea was proclaimed, with Heng Samrin as Head of State. A new constitution was declared in 1981 and, by 1982, Phnom Penh, a ghost city under the Khmer Rouge, was re-occupied by the return of up to 600,000 inhabitants from the countryside. The Vietnamese-controlled government experienced continuing armed opposition from an unlikely coalition of supporters of Prince Sihanouk, the KPNLF (Khmer Peoples' National Liberation Front) and the Khmer Rouge, of which the latter were backed by China and by far the most powerful. The coalition as a whole was supported by the West and collectively recognised as the legitimate government of Cambodia by the United Nations. In May 1988, Vietnam agreed to a phased withdrawal of its troops. Negotiations then began between the Vietnamese-backed government and the tripartite guerrilla alliance began in Paris in July 1989. After more than two years of tortuous negotiations a deal – the Paris Accord – was reached on October 23, 1991. Under its terms, the UN was to provide a peace-keeping force and extensive administrative support (under the rubric of the UN Transitional Authority in Cambodia, UNTAC) while the political factions formed a joint body, entitled the Supreme National Council, to administer the country until elections can be held. Elections are now scheduled for May 1993. In the meantime, the country is under the effective control of the 16,000-strong UN military force and hundreds of UN administrative staff. Cambodia is on the threshold of a sustained period of peace; whether this transpires depends largely on the attitude of the Khmer Rouge who, despite Chinese pressure upon them to support the settlement, still possess the capability to reduce the country, once again, to a state of ruinous civil war.

GOVERNMENT: The country is under the temporary administration of the Supreme National Council, headed by Prince Sihanouk with 12 members (six on the government side and two representatives from each of the three opposition guerrilla factions, including the Khmer Rouge). Legislative and presidential elections are scheduled for May 1993.

CLIMATE

Tropical monsoon climate. Monsoon season from May to October. In the north, winters can be colder.

Required clothing: Tropical and washable cottons all year. Heavy rainwear is needed during the monsoon. Warmer clothes in mountainous regions are advised during winter.

PHNOM PENH Cambodia (12m)

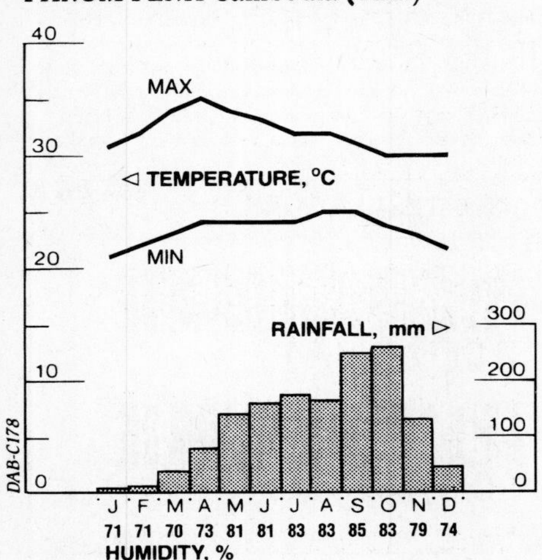

CAMEROON

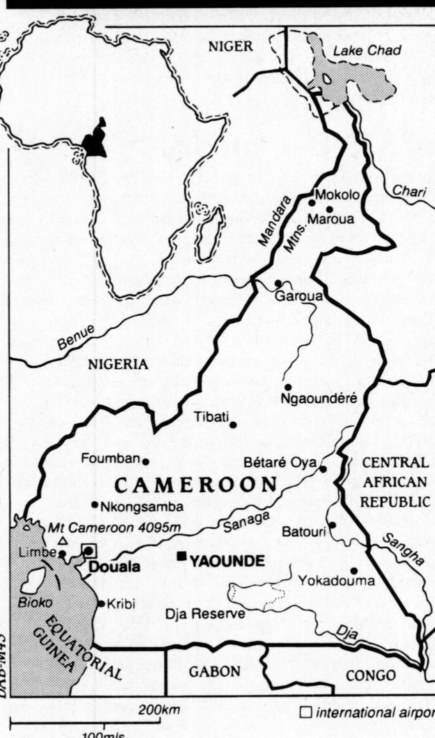

Location: Central Africa.

Société Camerounaise de Tourisme (SOCATOUR)
BP 7138
Yaoundé, Cameroon
Tel: 23 32 19. Telex: 8766.

Embassy of the Republic of Cameroon
84 Holland Park
London W11 3SB
Tel: (071) 727 0771. Fax: (071) 792 9353. Telex: 25176.
Embassy opening hours: 0900-1600. Visa section: 0930-1230 for application *and* 1430-1630 for collection, Monday to Friday.

British Embassy
BP 547
avenue Winston Churchill
Yaoundé, Cameroon
Tel: 22 05 45 *or* 22 07 96. Fax: 22 33 47 *or* 220148. Telex 8200.

British Consulate
BP 1016
rue de l'Hotel de Ville
Douala, Cameroon
Tel: 42 21 77 *or* 42 81 45. Fax: 42 88 96. Telex: 5353 BRITAIN KN.

Embassy of the Republic of Cameroon
2349 Massachusetts Avenue, NW
Washington, DC
20008
Tel: (202) 265 8790/1/2/3/4.

Embassy of the United States of America
BP 817
rue Nachtigal
Yaoundé, Cameroon
Tel: 23 40 14. Telex: 8223.

Embassy of the Republic of Cameroon
170 Clemow Avenue
Ottawa, Ontario
K1S 2B4
Tel: (613) 236 1522. Fax: (613) 238 2967. Telex: 053 3736.

Canadian Embassy
BP 572
Immeuble Stamatiades
Yaoundé, Cameroon
Tel: 23 02 03. Telex: 8209.

AREA: 475,442 sq km (183,569 sq miles).
POPULATION: 11,540,000 (1989 estimate).
POPULATION DENSITY: 24.3 per sq km.
CAPITAL: Yaoundé (constitutional). **Population:** 653,670 (1986).
Douala (economic). **Population:** 1,029,731 (1986).

GEOGRAPHY: Situated on the west coast of Africa, Cameroon is bounded to the west by the Gulf of Guinea, to the northwest by Nigeria, to the northeast by Chad (with Lake Chad at its northern tip), to the east by the Central African Republic and to the south by Congo, Gabon and Equatorial Guinea. The far north of the country is a semi-desert broadening into the vast Maroua Plain, with game reserves and mineral deposits. This is bordered to the west by the lush Mandara Mountains. The Benue River rises here and flows westwards into the Niger. The country to the northwest is very beautiful; volcanic peaks covered by bamboo forest rise to over 2000m (6500ft), with waterfalls and villages scattered over the lower slopes. Further to the south and west are savannah uplands, while dense forest covers the east and south. The coastal strip is tropical and cultivated.
Cameroon derives its name from the 15th-century Portuguese sailor Fernando Po's description of the River Wouri in Douala: *Rio dos Cameroes* ('river of shrimps').

LANGUAGE: The official languages are French and English. They are given equal importance in the Constitution but French is the more commonly spoken. There are many local African languages.

RELIGION: 40% traditional animist beliefs, 40% Christian, 20% Muslim.

TIME: GMT + 1.

ELECTRICITY: 110/220 volts AC, 50Hz. Plugs are round 2-pin; bayonet light-fittings.

COMMUNICATIONS: Telephone: IDD is available to and from Cameroon. Country code: 237. There are no city or area codes. Telephones can usually be found in post offices and restaurants. The main towns in Cameroon are linked by automatic dialling, but this service is often unreliable. **Fax:** Available at Intelcom offices. **Telex/telegram:** Facilities are available at Yaoundé and Douala post offices and at larger hotels but service is slow. Excellent international telex facilities are available at Intelcom. **Post:** Stamps can only be obtained from post offices. Mail takes about a week to reach addresses in Europe. Post office hours: 0730-1800 Monday to Friday. **Press:** The main (official) newspaper is the *Cameroon Tribune*, published daily in French and twice-weekly in English. Other English-language newspapers include the thrice-weekly *Cameroon Outlook*, the fortnightly *Cameroon Information*, the thrice-weekly *Cameroon Times* and the weekly *Gazette*.

BBC World Service and Voice of America frequencies: From time to time these change. See the section *How to Use this Book* for more information.

BBC:				
MHz	25.75	17.88	15.40	7.105
Voice of America:				
MHz	21.49	15.60	9.525	6.035

PASSPORT/VISA

Regulations and requirements may be subject to change at short notice, and you are advised to contact the appropriate diplomatic or consular authority before finalising travel arrangements. Details of these may be found at the head of this country's entry. Any numbers in the chart refer to the footnotes below.

	Passport Required?	Visa Required?	Return Ticket Required?
Full British	Yes	Yes	Yes
BVP	Not valid	-	-
Australian	Yes	Yes	Yes
Canadian	Yes	Yes	Yes
USA	Yes	Yes	Yes
Other EC	Yes	1	Yes
Japanese	Yes	Yes	Yes

PASSPORTS: Valid passport required by all.

British Visitors Passport: Not acceptable.

VISAS: Required by all except:
(a) nationals of Central African Republic, Congo, Gabon, Mali and Nigeria.
(b) [1] nationals of Germany.

Types of visa: 2 types of both Tourist and Business visas: Transit and Short-Stay, approximately £26; Long-stay, £107.

Validity: Short-Stay visas are valid for up to 3 months, Long-Stay visas for up to 1 year. Both types of visa should be used within 3 months of issue. Applications or extensions should be made to the Embassy.

Application to: Consulate (or Consular Section at

Embassy). For addresses, see top of entry.
Application requirements: (a) Valid passport. (b) 2 completed application forms. (c) 2 passport photos. (d) Sufficient funds to cover duration of stay.
Working days required: 48 hours if application is delivered by hand, a few days more if by mail.
Temporary residence: Applicants must have Residence and Work Permits. Immigration authorities in Cameroon must be contacted.

MONEY

Currency:CFA Franc = 100 centimes. Notes are in denominations of CFA Fr10,000, 5000, 1000, 500 and 100. Coins are in denominations of CFA Fr500, 100, 50, 25, 10, 5, 2 and 1. Only notes issued by the 'Banque des Etats de l'Afrique Centrale' are valid; those issued by the 'Banque des Etats de l'Afrique de l'Ouest' are not.
Currency exchange: It is advisable to bring French Francs or US Dollars into the country rather than Sterling.
Credit cards: Access/Mastercard, American Express, Diners Club and Visa are accepted on a limited basis (most major hotels and some restaurants will take them). Check with your credit card company for details of merchant acceptability and other services which may be available.
Travellers cheques: It is easier to convert French Franc cheques; however, it is possible to exchange Sterling travellers cheques.
Exchange rate indicators: The following figures are included as a guide to the movements of the CFA Franc against Sterling and the US Dollar:

Date:	Oct '89	Oct '90	Oct '91	Oct '92
£1.00=	505.13	498.38	496.12	413.75
$1.00=	319.90	255.12	285.87	260.71

Currency restrictions: Import of both local and foreign currency is unlimited, subject to declaration. Export of local currency is limited to CFAFr20,000. There is no limit on export of foreign currency.
Banking hours: 0730-1130 and 1430-1630 Monday to Friday.

DUTY FREE

The following goods may be taken into Cameroon without incurring any customs duty:
400 cigarettes or 125 cigars or 500g of tobacco;
1 litre of spirits and 3 litres of wine;
A reasonable quantity of perfume.
Note: Items such as radios, cameras, typewriters and alcoholic beverages must be declared on arrival, and are usually admitted free of duty if there is only one of each item.

PUBLIC HOLIDAYS

Public holidays observed in Cameroon are as follows:
Mar 25 '93 *Djoulde Soumae* (Eid al-Fitr). **Apr** Reunification Day. **Apr 9** Good Friday. **Apr 12** Easter Monday. **May 1** Labour Day. **May 20** Ascension Day and National Day. **Jun 1** Festival of Sheep. **Jan 1 '94** New Year. **Feb 11** Youth Day. **Mar** Eid a-Fitr.
Note: Muslim festivals are timed according to local sightings of various phases of the moon and the dates given above are approximations. During the lunar month of Ramadan that precedes Eid al-Fitr, Muslims fast during the day and feast at night and normal business patterns may be interrupted. Many restaurants are closed during the day and there may be restrictions on smoking and drinking. Some disruption may continue into Eid al-Fitr itself. Eid al-Fitr and Eid al-Adha may last anything from two to ten days, depending on the region. For more information on muslim festivals, see the section *World of Islam* at the back of the book.

HEALTH

Regulations and requirements may be subject to change at short notice, and you are advised to contact your doctor well in advance of your intended date of departure. Any numbers in the chart refer to the footnotes below.

	Special Precautions?	Certificate Required?
Yellow Fever	Yes	1
Cholera	Yes	2
Typhoid & Polio	Yes	-
Malaria	Yes	-
Food & Drink	3	-

[1]: A yellow fever vaccination certificate is required of all travellers over one year of age.
[2]: Following WHO guidelines issued in 1973, a cholera vaccination certificate is no longer a condition of entry to Cameroon. However, cholera is a serious risk in this country and precautions are essential. Up-to-date advice should be sought before deciding whether these precautions should include vaccination as medical opinion is divided over its effectiveness. See the *Health* section at the back of the book.
[3]: Water precautions recommended outside of main hotels, but all water should be regarded as being potentially contaminated. Water used for drinking, brushing teeth or making ice should have first been boiled or otherwise sterilised. Bottled water is readily available. Milk is unpasteurised and should be boiled. Powdered or tinned milk is available and is advised, but make sure that it is reconstituted with pure water. Avoid dairy products which are likely to have been made from local milk. Only eat well-cooked meat and fish, preferably served hot. Pork, salad and mayonnaise may carry increased risk. Vegetables should always be cooked and fruit peeled.
Malaria risk exists all year throughout the country, predominantly in the malignant *falciparum* form. Resistance to chloroquine has been reported.
Rabies is present. For those at high risk, vaccination before arrival should be considered. If you are bitten abroad seek medical advice without delay. For more information consult the *Health* section at the back of the book.
Bilharzia (schistosomiasis) is present. Avoid swimming and paddling in fresh water. Swimming pools which are well-chlorinated and maintained are safe.
Meningitis risk exists, depending on area visited and time of year.
Health care: Health insurance is strongly advised. There are hospitals in most main towns, with 251 hospitals and health centres throughout the country. There are two hospitals in Yaoundé: the General Hospital and Jamot Hospital. Douala has one large hospital, the Laquintinie Hospital. In addition, there are several medical centres, clinics and private nursing homes located throughout the country. Medical care is competent but expensive, as are medicines. A campaign aiming at 'Health for all by the year 2000' is underway, with the emphasis on the development of preventative medicine.

TRAVEL - International

AIR: Cameroon's national airline is *Cameroon Airlines (UY)*. There are regular flights from Cameroon to Fernando Poo, Nigeria, Côte d'Ivoire, Benin and Togo.
Approximate flight time: From *Paris* to Douala is 6 hours.
International airport: *Douala (DLA)* is 10km (6 miles) southeast of the city. Facilities include a duty-free shop, bar, post office, bank, shops and buffet/restaurant. A bus goes to the city every 15 minutes 0600-2100. Taxis are also available; a surcharge is payable after 2200. International airports are being constructed at Yaoundé and Bafoussam.
SEA: Irregular sailings from European ports to Douala take up to three weeks, with stops in the Canary Islands and West African ports. There are also berths on some cargo boats for six to 12 passengers.
RAIL: There are plans to extend the rail network from Mbalmayo to Bangui in the Central African Republic.
ROAD: There are road connections to Chad, Equatorial Guinea, the Central African Republic, Nigeria and Gabon. Travel on these routes is rough, and should not be attempted in the rainy season. Four-wheel drive vehicles are recommended. The Trans-Africa Highway from Kenya to Nigeria is under construction.

TRAVEL - Internal

AIR: This is the most efficient means of national transport. There are daily flights between Douala and Yaoundé; less regular flights to other interior towns.
RAIL: Rail travel within Cameroon is slow but cheap. Daily trains run from Douala to Yaoundé, with onward connections to N'gaoundéré, and from Douala to N'kongsamba. Couchettes are available on some trains, and a few have air-conditioning and restaurant cars. The final section of the Transcameroon railway was completed in 1987. It runs from Yaoundé to N'gaoundéré covering a distance of 930km (580 miles).
ROAD: There are paved roads from Douala to Yaoundé, Limbé, Buéa, Bafoussam and Bamenda and between main centres. Other roads are generally poorly maintained and become almost impassable during the rainy season. **Bus:** Modern coach services are available between Yaoundé and N'gaoundéré. Bus services also exist between other main centres and more rural areas, but tend to be unreliable and are often suspended during the rainy season. **Car hire:** This is limited and expensive and is available in Douala, Yaoundé and Limbé, with or without a driver. **Documentation:** An International Driving Permit is required.
URBAN: Bus services operate in Douala and Yaoundé at flat fares. Taxis are available at reasonable fixed rates (none are metered). A 10% tip is optional.
JOURNEY TIMES: The following chart gives approximate journey times (in hours and minutes) from Yaoundé:

	Air	Road	Rail
Bafoussam	0.50	4.00	-
Bali	1.10	-	-
Douala	0.30	3.00	4.00
Dschang	.50	-	-
Garoua	2.30	18.00	-
Koutaba	1.25	-	-
Kribi	0.45	-	-
Mamfe	1.00	-	-
Maroua	3.45	24.00	-
N'gaoundéré	2.40	12.00	10.00

ACCOMMODATION

HOTELS: Good accommodation of international standard is available in Douala, Yaoundé, Bamenda, Garoua and Marcua. The good hotels (government-rated 2-star and above) have air-conditioning, sports facilities and swimming pools; most rooms have showers. Most large hotels will accept major credit cards. Rates are for the room only. Cheaper accommodation is also available. The Hotel de Waza, just outside Waza National Park, north of Maroua in the far north of the country, is essentially a *campement* with two pavilions and individual rooms comprised of straw huts. Hotel facilities are in heavy demand: it is advisable to book in advance, and to obtain confirmation of your booking in writing.
CAMPING: Permitted in Boubandjida National Park, on the banks of Mayo Lidi River.

CAMEROON **HEALTH REGULATIONS** **VISA REGULATIONS** Code-Link

GALILEO/WORLDSPAN

TI-DFT/DLA/HE

TI-DFT/DLA/VI

SABRE

TIDFT/DLA/HE

TIDFT/DLA/VI

To access this information on your CRS, swipe the barcode with a light pen or type in the text under the barcode. For more information, see the introduction *How to Use This Book*.

RESORTS & EXCURSIONS

The Centre & East

Like Rome, **Yaoundé,** the capital city, stands on seven hills. There are 13 modern hotels and many markets, museums, shops and cinemas. To the northwest, jungle-clad mountains rise to an altitude of 1000m (3280ft). *Mont Fébé*, which overlooks the city, has been developed as a resort, with a luxury hotel, nightclub, casino, gardens and golf course. Its high altitude ensures a pleasant climate.

Luna Park, a permanent fun-fair and weekend holiday resort 40km (25 miles) north of the capital, can be found on the road to Obala. Further on, one can view the **Nachtigal Falls** on the River Sanga.

East Cameroon is sparsely populated. Its thick forests are home to a small population of lowland gorillas.

The West

Douala, Cameroon's economic capital, is 24km (15 miles) from the sea, on the left bank of the Wouri and dominated by Mount Cameroon. Worth visiting are the cathedral, the shopping avenues , the *Artisanat National* (a craft/souvenir market), *Deido market*, the harbour, the museum, *Wouri Bridge* and the electric coffee-grading plant.

Buéa is a charming town situated on the slopes of Mount Cameroon. For those interested in climbing the mountain (the highest in West Africa but a relatively easy climb), it is necessary to obtain a permit from the local tourist office (these are not issued during the rainy season from March to November).

Limbé (formerly Victoria) is a pleasant port with a botanical garden and 'jungle village'. There are beautiful white sandy beaches a short drive out of town. The tourist season runs between November and February.

Dschang is a mountain resort at an altitude of 1400m (4600ft), where the temperature is pleasantly cool. The road southwards to N'kongsamba and Douala passes through some splendid scenery – spectacular valleys and waterfalls.

Bamenda, in the highlands north of Dschang, has a museum and a craft market.

Foumban, northeast of Dschang, has many traditional buildings dating from its period of German colonization, including *Fon's Palace*. There is also a museum and a market. The town serves as an excellent base for experiencing the Bamileke region's colourful Bamoun festivals and feast days.

Kribi, a small picturesque port and beach resort south of Douala, has perhaps the finest beach in Cameroon, *Londji Beach*. It is also a convenient starting point for tours to pygmy villages and the **Campo Game Reserve** region. Buffaloes, lions and elephants roam the virgin forests inland.

The North

North Cameroon presents unexpected natural landscapes, with an average altitude of 1500m (4900ft) and large plains, reaching an altitude of 300m (1000ft), covered by savannah.

Maroua is located in the foothills of the Mandara Mountains, along the Mayo River. Places worth visiting include the market, the *Diamare Museum* (mainly an ethnographic museum where local craftwares are on sale: jewellery, tooled leather articles, etc), the various African quarters and the banks of the Mayo Kaliao. There is a National Park nearby (see below).

Mokolo is a picturesque village surrounded by a rugged rocky landscape. 55km (34 miles) away is the village of **Rhumsiki,** which features a maze of paths linking the small farms known as the Kapsiki; here live the Kirdi, whose customs and folklore have changed little for centuries.

Going further north, there is a very typical village called **Koza** located at an altitude of 1100m (3600ft). From here the road continues to the village of **Mabas** which gives a panoramic view on the large Bornou plain of Nigeria and where one can still see primitive blast furnaces.

National Parks

The **Kalamaloue Reserve** is small but offers opportunities for viewing several species of antelopes, monkeys and warthogs; some elephants cross the reserve but do not stay long.

Waza National Park covers 170,000 hectares. There is a forest area (open from November to March) and a vast expanse of grassy and wet plains, called 'Yaeres' (open from February to June). Elephants, giraffes, antelopes, hartebeest, cobs, lions, cheetahs and warthogs are numerous. There is also a rich variety of birds: eagles, crested cranes, maribous, pelicans, ducks, geese and numerous guinea-fowl. Accommodation and other facilities are available. There are no vehicles for hire at the park, but buses run from Maroua.

The **Boubandjidah National Park** is on the banks of Mayo Lidi River in the very far north of the country. There are several other parks and reserves which are not open to the public.

SOCIAL PROFILE

FOOD & DRINK: Cooking is often French or Lebanese, while local food can also be very tasty. Luxury items can be extremely expensive. The country abounds in avocado pears, citrus fruits, pineapples and mangoes. Prawns are in plentiful supply in the south. There are many restaurants in big towns and cities, with good service. **Drink:** Most international hotels have bars. There are no licensing hours, and hotel bars stay open as long as there is custom.

NIGHTLIFE: In Douala and Yaoundé particularly, nightclubs and casinos can be found independently or within most good hotels. There are also some cinemas.

SHOPPING: Local handicrafts include highly decorated pots, drinking horns, jugs, bottles and cups, great earthenware bowls and delicate pottery, dishes and trays, mats and rugs woven from grass, raffia, jewellery and camel hair or cotton and beadwork garments.

SPORT: Fishing is good in many rivers and coastal areas. **Swimming** in the sea and swimming pools of luxury hotels, which generally also have **tennis** courts, are both available. A **golf** course is available to hotel residents in Yaoundé. **Football** is a popular spectator sport: the national team reached the quarter-finals of the 1990 World Cup.

SPECIAL EVENTS: Local entertainment troupes may be seen in most regional towns, particularly during festivals.

SOCIAL CONVENTIONS: Handshaking is the customary form of greeting. In the north, where the population is largely Muslim, Islamic traditions should be respected. Visitors should never step inside a Muslim prayer circle of rocks. In other rural areas, where traditional beliefs predominate, it is essential to use tact. **Photography:** Cameras should be used with discretion, particularly in rural areas. Always ask permission before taking a photograph. Do not photograph airports, military establishments, official buildings, or military personnel in uniform. **Tipping:** The average tip for porters and hotel staff should be about 10%, otherwise service charges are usually inclusive.

BUSINESS PROFILE

ECONOMY: Cameroon enjoys one of the most successful economies in Africa by virtue of consistent agricultural performance and the rapid growth of its oil industry. The main agricultural products are cocoa (of which Cameroon is one of the world's largest producers), coffee, bananas, cotton, palm oil, wood and rubber. The country is self-sufficient in oil and has enough surplus to export both crude and refined oil. Natural gas deposits have been located but the currently low world market price inhibits the degree of exploitation. In addition, feasibility studies have been conducted in various parts of the country into the possible extraction of deposits of iron ore, bauxite, copper, chromium, uranium and other metals. Light industries such as food processing, building materials and batteries have helped to diversify the economy further. The Government's economic strategy aims to create a market economy with a substantial level of government participation although a liberal investment code seeks to attract foreign investment. This, coupled with the country's political stability and the continued flow of aid and other foreign capital, makes for generally bright economic prospects. The country has all but recovered from a bad patch during the late 1980s, which was largely the result of a sharp decline in oil revenues. France and The Netherlands are the major export markets followed by Germany, the United States and fellow members of the Central African customs and economic union (known by its French acronym of UDEAC).

COMMERCIAL INFORMATION: The following organisation can offer advice: Chambre de Commerce, d'Industrie et des Mines du Cameroun, BP 4011, Place du Gouvernement, Douala. Tel: 42 28 88. Telex: 5616.

HISTORY & GOVERNMENT

HISTORY: In the 1st century, the Sao people settled around Lake Chad, and it is from them that much of the country's remarkable sculpture originates. Contact with Europe was first made in the 15th century when the Portuguese arrived. Present-day Cameroon was at the heartland of Duala influence (which extended into present-day Nigeria). The area became a German protectorate in 1884. In 1919, after Germany's defeat in the First World War, Cameroon was divided between Britain and France under a League of Nations (and later a United Nations) mandate. French Cameroon achieved independence in 1957. In 1961, a plebiscite was held to decide the future of British Cameroon; the northern provinces voted to become part of Nigeria, while the south opted for union with French Cameroon. Since then the country has enjoyed a largely peaceful period of political development, with the exception of a coup attempt in 1984, since when Amnesty International has noted a marked increase in political repression. The ruling party, the Union Nationale Camerounaise, which has held power ever since independence, was renamed the Rassemblement Démocratique du Peuple Camerounaise in 1985.

There are approximately 200 ethnic groups, the largest of which is the Bamileke, a Bantu-related tribe occupying the west and centre of the country. Equatorial Bantu live in the area between the Congo basin and the plateaux of the interior. Small hunting bands of pygmies (the original inhabitants of central Africa) dwell in the remote Southern forests. Paul Biya succeeded Cameroun's first President, Ahmadou Ahidjo, when the latter retired in 1982, and has since instituted a programme of reform under the banner 'Rigour and Moralisation'. Foreign policy is generally independent, although close links are maintained with Britain and France. In 1990 President Biya announced that Cameroon would follow the political trend in the rest of Africa by introducing political pluralism, but his evident reluctance was matched by ever stronger opposition to his regime and increasingly heavy-handed responses from the security forces. Opposition is being led by Muslims concentrated in the north of the country and by the anglophone communities of western Cameroon who have long complained of discrimination by the predominately francophone regime. Biya was victorious at presidential elections held in October 1992, but his main opponents, John Fru Ndi and Bello Bouba Maigari, backed by outside observers, have alleged widespread fraud and demanded that the Supreme Court annul the poll. At the time of writing, the situation has not been resolved.

GOVERNMENT: The President, as Head of State, and the 180-seat National Assembly, hold executive and legislative power respectively and are both elected for 5-year terms.

CLIMATE:

The south is hot and dry between November and February. There is some rain between March and June but the main rainy season is from July to October. Temperatures in the north vary between very hot and cool. On the Adamaoua Plateau temperatures drop sharply at night; the rainy season there is from May to October. Grassland areas inland are much cooler than the coast with regular rainfall.

Required clothing: Lightweight cotton clothes, canvas or light leather shoes or sandals. Raincoats are necessary for coastal areas.

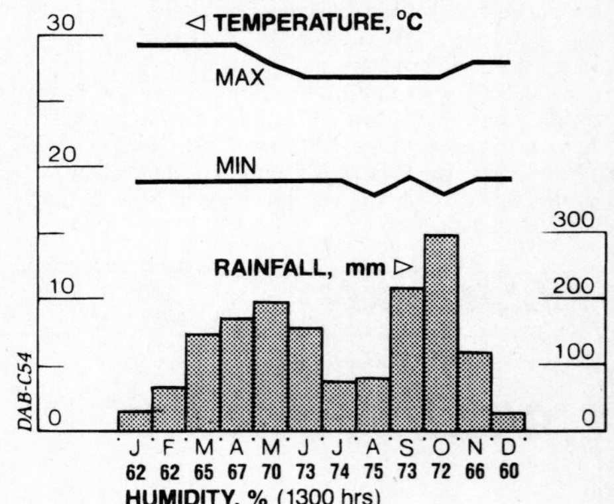

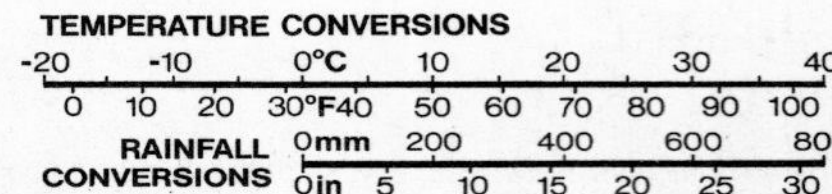

CANADA

Location: North America.

Tourism Canada
(Industry, Science & Technology Canada)
235 Queen Street
Ottawa, Ontario K1A 0H5
Tel: (613) 954 3982. Fax: (613) 954 1894. Telex: 0534123.

Canadian High Commission
Macdonald House
1 Grosvenor Square
London W1X 0AB
Tel: (071) 258 6600. Fax: (071) 258 6333. Telex: 261592. Opening hours: 0900-1700 Monday to Friday.

Immigration Department (Visa Section)
38 Grosvenor Street
London W1X 0AA
Tel: (071) 258 6600. Fax: (071) 258 6506. Opening hours: 0845-1400 Monday to Friday.

Canadian Tourist Office
Canada House
1 Cockspur Street
Trafalgar Square
London SW1Y 5BJ
Tel: (071) 258 6346. Fax: (071) 258 6322. Telex: 261592. Opening hours: 0930-1700 Monday to Friday.

British High Commission
80 Elgin Street
Ottawa, Ontario K1P 5K7
Tel: (613) 237 1530. Fax: (613) 237 7980. Telex: 053 3318 UKREP OTT.
Consulates in: Halifax, St John's, Montréal, Toronto, Vancouver and Winnipeg.

Canadian Embassy
501 Pennsylvania Avenue, NW
Washington, DC 20001
Tel: (202) 682 1740. Fax: (202) 682 7726. Telex: 89664.

Canadian Consulate General
16th Floor, Exxon Building
1251 Avenue of the Americas
New York, NY 10020-1175
Tel: (212) 768 2400. Fax: (212) 486 1295. Telex: 00126242 DOMCAN NYK.
Consulates in: Atlanta, Boston, Buffalo, Chicago, Cleveland, Dallas, Denver, Detroit, Los Angeles, Minneapolis, Princeton, San Francisco and Seattle.

Embassy of the United States of America
PO Box 866, Station 'B'
100 Wellington Street
Ottawa, Ontario K1P 5T1
Tel: (613) 238 5335. Fax: (613) 233 8511. Telex: 053 3582.
Consulates in: Calgary, Halifax, Montréal, Québec and Toronto.

Note: For major regional Tourist Information Offices, please see under Provincial/Territorial entries below.

AREA: 9,970,610 sq km (3,849,674 sq miles).
POPULATION: 26,584,000 (1990 estimate).
POPULATION DENSITY: 2.7 per sq km.
CAPITAL: Ottawa. **Population:** 308,319 (1990).
GEOGRAPHY: Canada is bounded to the west by the Pacific Ocean and Alaska, to the east by the Atlantic Ocean, to the northeast by Greenland, and to the south by the 'Lower 48' of the USA. The polar ice-cap lies to the north. The landscape is diverse, ranging from the Arctic tundra of the north to the great wheatlands of the central area. Westward are the Rocky Mountains, and in the southeast are the Great Lakes, the St Lawrence River and Niagara Falls. The country is divided into ten provinces and two territories. A more detailed description of each province can be found under the separate provincial entries below.
LANGUAGE: Bilingual: French and English. The use of the two languages reflects the mixed colonial history – Canada has been under both British and French rule.
RELIGION: 46.2% Roman Catholic, 17.5% United Church of Canada, 11.8% Anglican, 24.5% other Christian denominations and other religions.
TIME: Canada spans six time zones. Information on which applies where may be found in the regional entries following this general introduction. The time zones are:
Pacific Standard Time: GMT - 8.
Mountain Standard Time: GMT - 7.
Central Standard Time: GMT - 6.
Eastern Standard Time: GMT - 5.
Atlantic Standard Time: GMT - 4.
Newfoundland Standard Time: GMT - 3.5.
Note: From the first Sunday in April to the last Sunday in October, one hour is added for Daylight Saving Time (except in Saskatchewan).
ELECTRICITY: 110 volts AC, 60Hz. American-style (flat) 2-pin plugs are standard.
COMMUNICATIONS: Telephone: Most public telephones operate on 25-cent coins. There is a reduced rate 1800-0800 Monday to Friday, and 1200 Saturday to 0800 Monday. Full IDD is available. Country code: 1. **Fax:** Services are available in commercial bureaux and some hotels and stores all day at locally agreed rates. **Telex/telegram:** Telegrams are handled by Canadian National Telecommunications or Canadian Pacific, and any telegrams must be telephoned or handed in to the nearest Canadian Pacific or Canadian National office (address in local phone book). Services available include *Telepost*, providing first-class door-to-door delivery, and *Intelpost*, which offers satellite communications for documents/photographs to London, Washington DC, New York, Berne and Amsterdam. In Newfoundland & Labrador telegrams are sent through *Terra Nova Tel.* **Post:** All mail from Canada to outside North America is by air. Stamps are available in hotels, chemists and railway stations, or in vending machines outside post offices and shopping centres. *Poste Restante* facilities are available. *Intelpost* is offered at main postal offices for satellite transmission of documents and photographs. Post office hours: generally 0930-1700 Monday to Friday and 0900-1200 Saturday, but times vary according to province and location; city offices will have longer hours. **Press:** There is no national daily newspaper as such, but the Toronto *Globe & Mail* has national distribution. Daily newspapers published in the larger population centres have a wide local and regional circulation. French-language dailies are published in seven cities, including Montréal, Québec and Ottawa.
BBC World Service frequencies: From time to time these change. See the section *How to Use this Book* for more information.

Central, Mountain and Pacific Canada:

MHz	15.22	9.740	9.515	5.975

Atlantic and Eastern Canada:

MHz	15.26	11.78	9.590	5.965

PASSPORT/VISA

Regulations and requirements may be subject to change at short notice, and you are advised to contact the appropriate diplomatic or consular authority before finalising travel arrangements. Details of these may be found at the head of this country's entry. Any numbers in the chart refer to the footnotes below.

	Passport Required?	Visa Required?	Return Ticket Required?
Full British	Yes	No	Yes
BVP	Not valid	-	-
Australian	Yes	No	Yes
Canadian	No	No	No
USA	No	No	No
Other EC	Yes	1	Yes
Japanese	Yes	No	Yes

CANADA | **HEALTH REGULATIONS** | **VISA REGULATIONS** | Code-Link

GALILEO/WORLDSPAN

TI-DFT/YOW/HE

TI-DFT/YOW/VI

SABRE

TIDFT/YOW/HE

TIDFT/YOW/VI

To access this information on your CRS, swipe the barcode with a light pen or type in the text under the barcode. For more information, see the introduction *How to Use This Book*.

PASSPORTS: Valid passport required by all except:
(a) nationals of the USA;
(b) those seeking entry from St Pierre and Miquelon (a French Overseas Territory) who have been lawfully admitted to the USA for permanent residence, provided holding proof of identity;
(c) citizens of Greenland entering from Greenland.
British Visitors Passport: Not acceptable.
VISAS: Required by all except:
(a) nationals of countries shown in the chart above;
(b) [1] nationals of EC countries (with the exception of nationals of Portugal who *do* require visas);
(c) citizens of Andorra, Antigua & Barbuda, Austria, Bahamas, Barbados, Botswana, Brunei, Costa Rica, Cyprus, Dominica, Finland, Grenada, Iceland, Israel, Kiribati, Liechtenstein, Malaysia, Malta, Mexico, Monaco, Namibia, Nauru, New Zealand, Norway, Papua New Guinea, St Kitts & Nevis, St Lucia, St Vincent & the Grenadines, San Marino, Saudi Arabia, Singapore, Solomon Islands, Swaziland, Sweden, Switzerland, Tuvalu, Vanuatu, Venezuela, Western Samoa and Zimbabwe;
(d) citizens of British Dependent Territories: Anguilla, Bermuda, British Virgin Islands, Cayman Islands, Falkland Islands, Gibraltar, Hong Kong, Montserrat, Pitcairn, St Helena, Turks & Caicos Islands.
Note: There are other nationals who do not require visas, but these are subject to change; check with the Consulate prior to travel.
Types of visa: Tourists will be issued a Visitor's visa. Transit visas are necessary for all nationals above who are listed as requiring a Visitor's visa. Although Transit visas are not required by British citizens, they may be required by foreign nationals with British passports; check with the Embassy or High Commission for details (addresses above).
Validity: Up to 6 months depending on circumstances of individual applicant.
Application to: Consulate (or Consular Section at Embassy or High Commission). For addresses, see top of entry.
Application requirements: Visitors to Canada must satisfy an examining officer at the Port of Entry that they are genuine visitors and have sufficient funds to maintain themselves during their stay in Canada and to return to their country of origin, as well as evidence of confirmed onward reservations out of Canada. Persons under 18 years of age who are unaccompanied by an adult should bring with them a letter from a parent or guardian giving them permission to travel to Canada.
Temporary residence: A work permit is required for temporary residence in Canada. Persons who wish to proceed to Canada for the purposes of study or temporary employment should contact the nearest Canadian High Commission, Embassy or Consulate, as authorisation is normally required prior to arrival. Those who will be taking up temporary employment will require an Employment Authorization, for which a fee is charged. Persons going for study purposes must obtain a Student Authorization; a charge is made for this.

MONEY

Currency: Canadian Dollar (Can$) = 100 cents. Notes are in denominations of Can$1000, 100, 50, 20, 10, 5 and 1. Coins are in denominations of Can$1, and 50, 25, 10, 5 and 1 cents.
Credit cards: Most international credit cards are accepted.
Travellers cheques are best bought in Canadian Dollars; these are widely negotiable.
Exchange rate indicators: The following figures are included as a guide to the movements of the Canadian Dollar against Sterling and the US Dollar:

Date:	Oct '89	Oct '90	Oct '91	Oct '92
£1.00=	1.85	2.25	1.96	1.99
$1.00=	1.17	1.15	1.13	1.25

Currency restrictions: There are no restrictions on the import or export of either local or foreign currency if declared.
Banking hours: 1000-1500 Monday to Friday. Business accounts can only be set up on presentation of a letter of credit from a home bank.

DUTY FREE

The following goods may be taken into Canada without incurring customs duty:
200 cigarettes and 50 cigars and 1kg of tobacco per person over 16 years of age;
1 bottle (1.14 litres) of spirits or wine or 24 cans or bottles of beer (equivalent up to 8.5 litres) per person over 18 years of age entering Alberta, Manitoba and Québec, and over 19 years of age entering British Columbia, Northwest Territories, Yukon, New Brunswick, Newfoundland, Ontario, Saskatchewan, Nova Scotia and Prince Edward Island;
A small amount of perfume for personal use;
Gifts not exceeding Can$40 per item.
Prohibited items: The importation of firearms, explosives, endangered species of animals and plants, animal products, meat, food and plant material is subject to certain restrictions and formalities. Dogs and domestic cats may be imported from certain rabies-free countries (including the United Kingdom and the Republic of Ireland) subject to certain restrictions and formalities (but note that rabies is present in Canada and pets will generally face quarantine on returning home). Enquire at the Canadian High Commission or Embassy for further details.
Note: There is a General Sales Tax (GST) in Canada of 7% on all goods and services. Visitors may reclaim this tax on accommodation and any goods purchased and taken out of the country. However, GST is not reclaimable on food, drink, tobacco or any form of transport. To claim a rebate, a GST form must be completed, with all receipts attached, and mailed to the address on the form. GST must be claimed before applying for provincial tax, with the exception of Québec and Manitoba, where the provincial sales tax can be reclaimed at the same time as GST on the GST form. GST forms should be sent to Revenue Canada, Customs and Excise, Visitors Rebate Programme, Ottawa, Ontario K1A 1J5.

PUBLIC HOLIDAYS

Public holidays observed throughout Canada are as follows:
Apr 9 '93 Good Friday. **Apr 12** Easter Monday. **May 24** Victoria Day. **Jul 1** Canada Day. **Sep 6** Labour Day. **Oct 11** Thanksgiving Day. **Nov 11** Remembrance Day. **Dec 25** Christmas. **Dec 26** Boxing Day. **Jan 1 '94** New Year's Day.
Note: In addition, every Province and Territory has its own local holidays; please consult the regional entries below.

HEALTH

Regulations and requirements may be subject to change at short notice, and you are advised to contact your doctor well in advance of your intended date of departure. Any numbers in the chart refer to the footnotes below.

	Special Precautions?	Certificate Required?
Yellow Fever	No	No
Cholera	No	No
Typhoid & Polio	No	-
Malaria	No	-
Food & Drink	1	-

[1]: Tap water is considered safe to drink. Milk is pasteurised and dairy products are safe for consumption. Local meat, poultry, seafood, fruit and vegetables are generally considered safe to eat.
Rabies is present. For those at high risk, vaccination before arrival should be considered. If you are bitten abroad, seek medical advice without delay. For more information consult the *Health* section at the back of the book.
Health care: There are excellent health facilities (similar to the USA). Personal first-aid kits should be carried by travellers to more remote northern areas. Private health insurance up to US$50,000 is absolutely essential as hospital charges are very expensive (from US$650 a day often with 30% surcharge for non-residents imposed in some provinces). Dial '0' for emergencies.
There is no Reciprocal Health Agreement with the UK, but doctors will continue medication for prescriptions issued in Europe.
Note: Visitors intending to stay in Canada for more than six months, either as tourists, students or employees, may be required to take a medical examination. Visitors working in an occupation in which protection of public health is essential may be required to undergo a medical examination even if employment is only temporary. Please check with the Canadian Consulate or High Commission for further information.

TRAVEL - International

AIR: Canada's principal national airline is *Air Canada (AC)*. The other national airline is *Canadian Airlines International (CP)*.
Approximate flight times: From *London* to Calgary is 9 hours, to Halifax is 6 hours 30 minutes, to Montréal is 7 hours, to Toronto is 7 hours 30 minutes and to Vancouver is 10 hours.
From *Los Angeles* to Montréal is 7 hours 5 minutes, to Toronto is 5 hours 25 minutes and to Vancouver is 3 hours 10 minutes.
From *New York* to Montréal is 1 hour 15 minutes, to Toronto is 1 hour 20 minutes and to Vancouver is 8 hours.
From *Singapore* to Montréal is 25 hours, to Toronto is 24 hours and to Vancouver is 16 hours 30 minutes.
From *Sydney* to Montréal is 22 hours 20 minutes, to Toronto is 22 hours 35 minutes and to Vancouver is 18 hours 45 minutes.
International airports: Canada has 13 international airports. All have full banking and catering facilities, duty-free shops and car hire. Airport-to-city bus and taxi services and, in some cases, rail links, are available.
Calgary (YYC) is 19km (11 miles) from the city (travel time – 30 minutes).
Edmonton (YEG) is 28km (19 miles) from the city (travel time – 45 minutes).
Gander (YQX) is 3.2km (2 miles) from the city (travel time – 10 minutes).
Halifax (YHZ) is 41.8km (26 miles) from the city (travel time – 30 minutes).
Hamilton (YHM) is 10km (6 miles) from the city (travel time – 20 minutes).
Montréal (YUL) (Dorval) is 21km (14 miles) from the city (travel time – 25 minutes).
Montréal (YMX) (Mirabel) is 55km (34 miles) from the city (travel time – 60 minutes).
Ottawa (YOW) (Uplands) is 17.5km (11 miles) from the city (travel time – 25 minutes).
St John's (YYT) is 8km (5 miles) from the city (travel time – 10-15 minutes).
Saskatoon (YXE) is 7km (4.5 miles) from the city (travel time – 10 minutes).
Toronto (YYZ) (Lester B Pearson) is 28km (18 miles) from the city (travel time – 20 minutes).
Vancouver (YVR) is 15km (11 miles) from the city (travel time – 20 minutes).
Winnipeg (YWG) is 6.5km (4 miles) from the city (travel time – 20 minutes).
Departure tax: Can$20 (£10) in all Canadian airports for international departures.
SEA: The principal ports of Canada are Montréal, Québec and Toronto on the east coast and Vancouver on the west coast. All are served by international shipping lines, but Montréal is the only port for passenger liners from Europe.
RAIL: The Canadian rail system connects to the USA at several points. Major routes are: New York–Montréal and New York–Toronto. Chicago, Detroit and Buffalo are all connected via terminals in Toronto.
ROAD: The only road access to Canada is through the southern border with the USA or from the west through Alaska. Apart from private motoring, the most popular way of travelling by road is by bus. The biggest coach company in the world is the *Greyhound Bus Company* (see below under *Bus*) and this is one of the most common routes to Canada from the United States. There are many crossing points from the United States to Canada, but some of the most common are:
New York to Montréal/Ottawa; Detroit to Toronto/Hamilton; Minneapolis to Winnipeg; Seattle to Vancouver/Edmonton/Calgary.

TRAVEL - Internal

AIR: There are a number of regional airlines, the principal ones being:
Atlantic Coast: *Air Nova; Air Atlantic*.
Western Canada: *Time Air; Air BC*.
Central Canada: *Nordair Ltd; Québecair (QB)*.
There are also about 75 airlines operating local services. There are reductions for those aged 13-21; and substantial reductions for those under 12. An internal air pass is available on *Air BC* for periods of 14-30 days. This pass, covering Manitoba, Saskatchewan, Alberta and British Columbia, is available in the UK through *Western Canada Airpass* (tel: (0737) 226 881) and may only be purchased outside of Canada.
SEA/RIVER/LAKE/CANAL: Canada has many thousands of miles of navigable rivers and canals, a vast number of lakes and an extensive coastline. The whole country is well served by all manners of boats and ships, particularly the east and west coasts, where the ferries are fast, frequent and good value. The St Lawrence Seaway provides passage from the Atlantic Ocean to the Great Lakes. For further details, see below under regional entries or contact Tourism Canada.
RAIL: *Via Rail Canada* (tel: (514) 871 1331) still operates extensive services across Canada, though in the past year some services have disappeared. The transcontinental Québec–Toronto–Vancouver route no longer runs and has been replaced by a Toronto–Vancouver route operating three times weekly, which goes via Saskatoon, Edmonton and Jasper, the route via Regina having been discontinued. The regional railways are *Ontario Northland, Algoma Central, British Columbia Railway, White Pass* and *Yukon Route*. Rapid inter-city services are

available between Québec, Montréal, Halifax, Toronto, Windsor and Ottawa. Long-distance trains are extremely comfortable, with full restaurant services, air-conditioning etc. Children under two years of age may travel free (one per adult) and children 2-11 years of age pay half fare. Persons over 60 years of age and students carrying student proof will receive a 10% discount. The *Canrailpass* must be purchased outside Canada and a valid passport presented at time of purchase; it allows unlimited travel on the Canadian railway system for a period of 30 days and is only valid on *Via Rail* trains. There is also a *Youth Canrailpass* available to persons up to 24 years of age. Prices on both passes are lower during off seasons. For more details contact the Canadian Tourist Office. In the UK, *Via Rail* representatives can be reached through *Long Haul Leisurail* (tel: (0733) 51780) or *Thistle Air* (tel: (0563) 31121). The *Rocky Mountaineer* service offers the opportunity to travel between Calgary, Banff, Jasper and Vancouver during daylight hours, enabling passengers to view the passing scenery. Customers can purchase either a one-way or round-trip fare. A one-way trip takes two days and covers approximately 443km (275 miles) each day. Included in the price is a one-night stopover in Kamloops, bus transfer from train to Kamloops hotel, two continental breakfasts, two light lunches and complimentary beverages (coffee, tea, fruit juices). Alcoholic beverages, films and souvenirs are available on board at an additional cost. Persons aged over 60 are eligible for various reductions on fares in some parts of the country. For further information on other rail journeys in Canada, contact the Canadian Tourist Office.

ROAD: The road network covers vast distances as the country is over 7600km (4800 miles) from west to east and 4800km (3000 miles) from north to south. The longest road is the Trans-Canada Highway, running west to east for 8000km (5000 miles). Petrol and oil are sold by the litre, and costs per litre should be obtained at time of travel. The *Canadian Automobile Association* is affiliated to most European organisations, giving full use of facilities to members. Road signs are international. Driving is on the right.

Coach: As in the USA, one of the cheapest and most convenient ways of travelling the country apart from private motoring is by coach. Each region is well served by a large network of coach lines, the most extensive being *Greyhound Bus Company*, which extends over 193,000km (120,000 miles) of North America. The *Canadapass* ticket must be purchased outside of North America and entitles the holder to unlimited travel over periods of 7, 15 and 30 days. A supplement may be charged for certain areas of Canada. Daily extensions are available. Further information may be obtained in the UK from *Greyhound World Travel Ltd.* Tel: (0342) 317 317 (reservations). *Grayline Coaches* is another bus company that offers excursions to major Canadian resorts.

Canada also has regional bus services, the most important of which are as follows:

Atlantic Canada: Acadian Lines, Terra Nova Transport, SMT Eastern and CN Roadcruiser.

Central Canada: Canada Coach Lines, Gray Coach Lines, Voyageur and Voyageur Colonial, Grey Goose Bus Lines Limited, Saskatchewan Transportation and Orleans Express.

West Canada: Brewster Transport, Greyhound Lines of Canada and Vancouver Island Coach Lines.

Besides long-distance travel, all these companies operate a range of services, such as regional tours and escorted sightseeing for groups. Children are not charged if under five years old; half the adult fare is charged for children aged between five and 11 years old. Unlimited travel is available on most *Greyhound* bus routes with an *Canadian Excursion Fare* ticket, which can be purchased for a restricted time period covering the whole national network. These tickets must be purchased outside Canada. Persons aged over 65 are eligible for reductions on fares in some provinces.

Bus: Metropolitan buses operate on a flat-fare system (standard fares, irrespective of distance travelled). Fares must be paid exactly, which means that drivers do not carry change or issue tickets. Transfers should be requested when boarding a bus.

Car hire: Available in all cities and from airports to full licence holders over 21 years old. Major companies from which cars can be booked in the UK for use in Canada are *Avis*, *Budget*, *Dollar*, *Hertz*, *Thrifty*, *Tilden* and *Bricar*.

Traffic regulations: Road speeds are in kilometres per hour and are: 100kmph (60mph) on motorways, 80kmph (50mph) on rural highways and 50kmph (30mph) in cities. Seat belts are compulsory in Alberta, British Columbia, Ontario, Québec, Manitoba, New Brunswick, Newfoundland, Nova Scotia and Saskatchewan. Radar detection devices are illegal in Alberta, Manitoba, Newfoundland, Northwest Territories, Ontario and Yukon. Studded tyres are illegal in Ontario, are permitted without seasonal limitations in Northwest Territories, Saskatchewan and Yukon, and are allowed only in winter in other provinces. **Note:** The official date on which winter begins, for this and other purposes, will vary from province to province.

Documentation: An International Driving Licence is recommended though it is not legally required. Visitors may drive on their national driving licences for up to three months in all provinces (six months for holders of UK licences).

JOURNEY TIMES: The following chart gives approximate journey times from Ottawa (in hours and minutes) to other major cities/towns in Canada.

	Air	Road	Rail
Toronto	1.00	5.30	5.30
Montréal	0.30	2.00	2.00
Edmonton	4.30	50.00	50.00
Québec	1.00	6.00	6.00
Halifax	2.00	24.00	24.00
Winnipeg	2.30	32.00	32.00
Calgary	4.00	50.00	
Vancouver	5.00	62.00	110.00
Regina	5.00	40.00	

ACCOMMODATION

There is a wide range of accommodation from hotels to hostels. Standards are high, with full facilities.

HOTELS: International hotel chains are represented in major cities, but advance booking is essential. Guesthouses, farm vacations, bed & breakfast establishments and self-catering lodges are available throughout the country. Hunting and fishing trips to the wilderness areas of the north are often best arranged through *Outfitters*. These are guides (often licensed by the local tourist office) who can arrange supplies, tackle, transport and

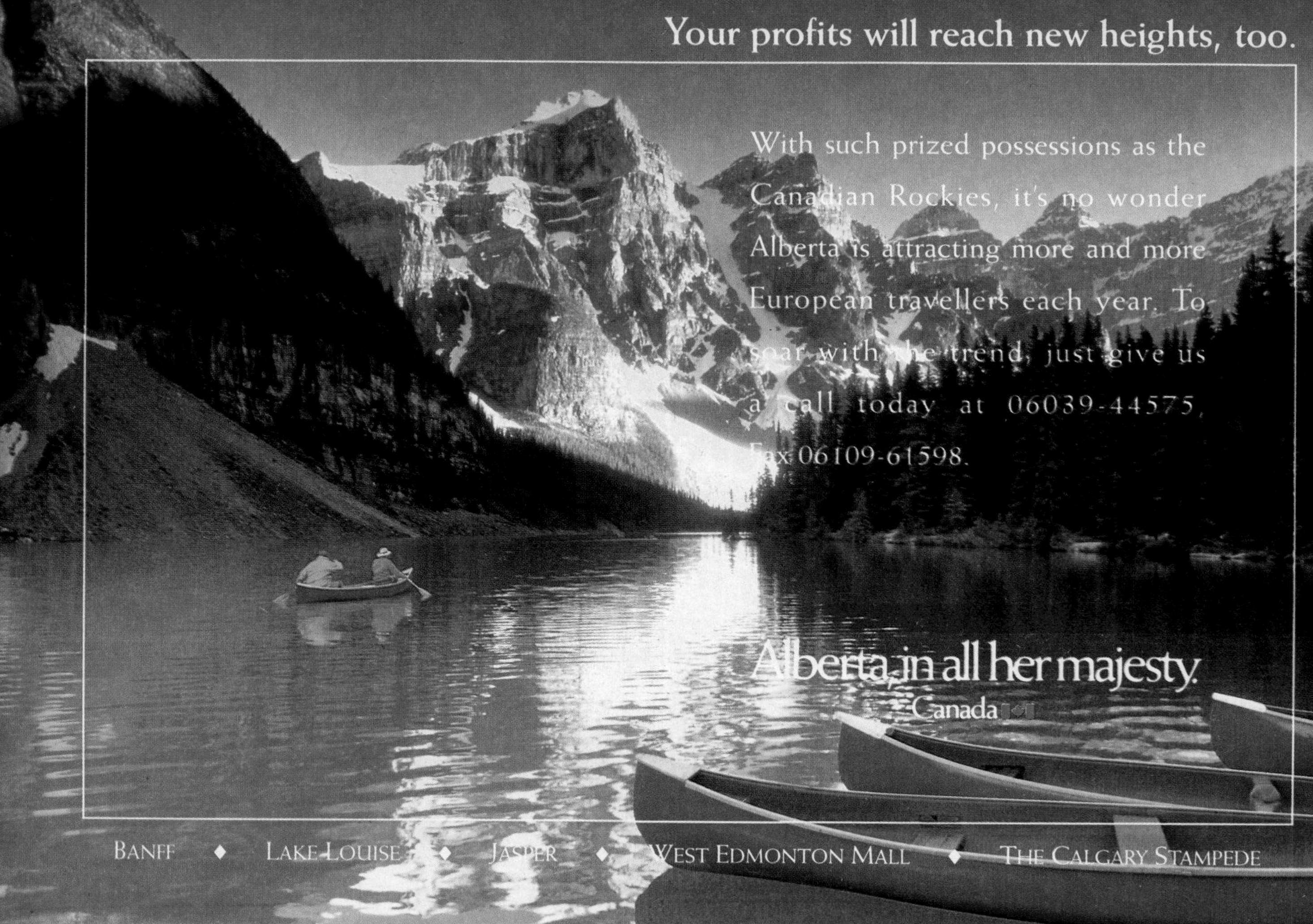

Your profits will reach new heights, too.
With such prized possessions as the Canadian Rockies, it's no wonder Alberta is attracting more and more European travellers each year. To soar with the trend, just give us a call today at 06039-44575, Fax 06109-61598.
Alberta, in all her majesty.
Canada
BANFF ♦ LAKE LOUISE ♦ JASPER ♦ WEST EDMONTON MALL ♦ THE CALGARY STAMPEDE

accommodation. For further information, contact the Canadian Tourist Office or the Hotel Association of Canada, Suite 1505, 155 Carlton Street, Winnipeg, Manitoba R3C 3H8. Tel: (204) 942 0671. **Grading:** There is no national system of accommodation grading. Some provinces operate their own voluntary grading programmes; see regional entries below for details.

CAMPING/CARAVANNING: Mobile trailers and caravans are extremely popular ways of traversing the enormous expanse of the Canadian landscape. There are two different types of vehicle available: a 'motorhome' is a vehicle with connected driving cab and living space, equipped for up to five adults; whilst a 'camper' is a vehicle with a separate driving cab, more like a truck with a caravan on the back, equipped for up to three adults. There are various different models according to the size of the accommodation and facilities required, but most have a fridge, cooker, sink, heater, fitted WC and showers. All vehicles are fitted with power steering and automatic transmission. Petrol consumption is about 24km (15 miles) per imperial gallon (but petrol costs half as much as it does in Europe). Hiring is available to those who hold full licences and are over 25. The cost of hire can vary according to the season. High season runs from June to the end of August, and low season is the rest of the year. During the high season there is a minimum hire of two weeks, but many agents allow a free distance of 75km (47 miles) per day before mileage is charged. Full details can be obtained from the Canadian Tourist Office.
Camping facilities in the National Parks are generally open only from mid-May until the beginning of September.
Further details on accommodation can be found in the regional entries below.

RESORTS & EXCURSIONS

Canada offers a huge range of attractions, from large cosmopolitan cities such as Montréal and Toronto in the south to isolated Inuit (Eskimo) settlements dotted around the frozen shores of Hudson Bay. The contrasting Pacific and Atlantic seaboards and the thousands of lakes and rivers of the interior provide suberb watersports and fishing. The Rocky Mountains and other ranges offer breathtaking scenery on a grand scale. Some of the best resorts are in the series of great National Parks which preserve the wildlife and forests of Canada in their virgin state. Those in the North provide basic amenities for tours of the beautiful northern wilderness. A taste of the pioneering west can be had in the rich farming and grain regions of central Canada. Further west is the New Frontier of Yukon and the Northwest Territories.
A more detailed description of the historic sites and natural attractions of each province can be found in the *Resorts & Excursions* sections in the regional entries below.

SOCIAL PROFILE

FOOD & DRINK: Canadian cuisine is as varied as the country. The hundreds of miles of coastline offer varied seafood, and the central plains provide first-class beef and agricultural produce. The colonial influence is still strong, with European menus available in all major cities. The French influence in Québec is easily discernible in the many restaurants which specialise in French cuisine. Waiter service in restaurants is more common. Dress requirements and billing procedures vary.
Drink: Spirits may only be purchased from specially licensed liquor stores or restaurants displaying the sign 'Licensed Premises' if alcohol is served on the premises. Many allow customers to bring their own beer or wine. A wide variety of alcohol is sold in most hotels, restaurants and bars. A selection of European/American wines and spirits are also imported, although the Canadians prefer their own, such as rye whisky. Bars may have table or counter service and payment is generally made after each drink. Opening hours vary from province to province. Legal age for drinking in bars is 18 or 19 depending on local regulations.
See the *Social Profile* sections in the regional entries below.
NIGHTLIFE: Every major provincial capital in the more populated areas has nightclubs, casinos and hotel dinner/dancing. Ottawa, Toronto, Montréal, Winnipeg and Vancouver are centres for ballet, opera and classical music, with visits from leading orchestras and internationally renowned performers. Entertainment in the more remote towns is scarce.
SHOPPING: Fine examples of Canadian craftware are available, such as artwood carvings, pottery, cottons and native artefacts. Some countries have restrictions against the import of endangered animal species products, such as polar bear, seal, walrus, etc, so check entry regulations in home country before departure. Most provinces, except Alberta, the Northwest Territories andYukon, levy a sales tax which varies from 4% to 11% in shops, restaurants and some hotels. Tax can be refunded when leaving Canada (see the special note above under *Duty Free*). In addition to the provincial tax a general sales tax of 7% was introduced in January 1991. **Shopping hours:** 0900-1800 Monday to Friday, with late-night shopping in some stores up to 2100 Thursday and Friday. Most shops and stores are also open on Saturday and some local stores on Sunday.
SPORT: Facilities for **golf** and **tennis** are excellent throughout the country. Most large hotels have some sports facilities. A number of tour operators offer all-in golfing packages. **Canadian football**, which is similar to American football, is played everywhere, but European football (**soccer**) is becoming increasingly popular. **Hunting, fishing** and **shooting** can be enjoyed in the many wilderness areas; all require licences, which can be obtained locally (Tourism Canada can supply detailed information on this). **Wintersports: Ice hockey** is played at the highest level and top-class competition can be enjoyed as a spectator sport in all the cities throughout Canada. **Skiing** can be enjoyed in innumerable resorts throughout Canada. The Canadian Tourist Office can supply details. **Watersports: Sailing** and other facilities are available throughout the country. For more information, see the regional entries below.
SPECIAL EVENTS: A list of some of the major festivals and special events may be found in the regional entries below.
SOCIAL CONVENTIONS: Handshaking predominates as the normal mode of greeting. Close friends often exchange kisses on the cheeks, particularly in French areas. Codes of practice for visiting homes are the same as in other Western countries: flowers, chocolates or a bottle of wine are common gifts for hosts and dress is generally informal and practical according to climate. It is common for black tie and other required dress to be indicated on invitations. Exclusive clubs and restaurants often require more formal dress. Smoking has been banned in most public areas. Most restaurants, theatres and cinemas, if they permit smoking, have large 'no smoking' areas. **Tipping:** Normal practice, usually 15% of the bill, more if service is exceptional. Waiters, taxi drivers, barbers/hairdressers, bellhops, doormen and porters at hotels should all be tipped this amount. Porters at airports and railway stations generally expect Can$1 per item of luggage.

BUSINESS PROFILE

ECONOMY: Canada is one of the world's major trading nations and the seventh largest exporter and importer, thus qualifying for membership of the so-called G7 group of major industrial economies. The country has immense natural resources and a high standard of living. Agriculture and fisheries are particularly important: Canada exports over half of its agricultural produce – principally grains and oil seeds – and is the world's leading exporter of fish. Timber is another important sector, given that over 40% of the land area is forest. As a mineral producer, Canada exports crude oil and natural gas, copper, nickel, zinc, iron ore, asbestos, cement, coal and potash. Energy requirements are met by a mixture of hydroelectric, nuclear and oil-fired generating stations. The largest economic sector is manufacturing, covering the whole range of activities from heavy engineering and chemicals through vehicle production and agro-business to office automation and commercial printing. Canada has a declining, though nonetheless substantial, trade surplus of Can$5 billion per annum on a net export income of US$121 billion (1987 figures). Slightly over 75% of the country's trade is with the United States, making this the world's largest single bilateral trade route. A free-trade agreement signed with the United States in 1989 has, on provisional figures, already boosted trade still further. The agreement also provided the basis for the North American Free Trade Agreement (NAFTA) which was signed on August 12, 1992 by the Presidents of Canada, the USA and Mexico. After the US, Canada's trade partners are, in order of descending volume: Japan, the UK, Germany, Taiwan and France. UK exporters are well-established in Canada and continue to be well-placed to exploit new market opportunities.
BUSINESS: Usual courtesies observed including exchange of business cards, making appointments etc.
Office hours: 0900-1700 Monday to Friday.
COMMERCIAL INFORMATION: The following organisations can offer advice:
Canadian Chamber of Commerce, Suite 1160, 55 Metcalfe Street, Ottawa, Ontario K1P 6N4. Tel: (613) 238 4000. Fax: (613) 238 7643. Telex: 053-3360; *or*
Canadian Chamber of Commerce, 1080 Beaver Hall Hill, Montréal, Québec H2Z 1T2. Tel: (514) 866 4334. In addition each province has its own regional chamber of commerce. Consult regional entries below for more information.
CONFERENCES/CONVENTIONS: All the major business centres, ie Toronto, Calgary, Edmonton, Montréal, Ottawa and Vancouver, offer extensive convention and conference facilities. For general information on conferences and conventions in Canada, contact Tourism Canada, Industry Science & Technology Canada, Dominion Public Building, Fourth Floor, 1 Front Street West, Toronto, Ontario M5J 1A4. Tel: (416) 973 5082. Fax: (416) 973 8714. Consult regional entries below for more information.

HISTORY & GOVERNMENT

HISTORY: After the American War of Independence, eastern Canada was settled by loyalists from the United States holding allegiance to the defeated British Crown. In 1791 the country was divided between regions occupied by the English speaking and the longer-established Francophone community, but the arrangement did not work and was replaced by a united system 50 years later. Canada suffered a 6-year war during which the Americans made an unsuccessful invasion attempt. Canada became a Dominion of the British Empire in the mid-19th century, with an autonomous government but with the monarch as Head of State. Despite the reservations of the French-speaking population, principally in Québec where a secessionist movement was active as recently as the 1970s, the Canadian government has displayed a strong loyalty to the 'mother country', notably during both World Wars. From 1968 to 1984, politics were dominated by the charismatic figure of Pierre Trudeau, leader of the Liberal Party and 4-times Prime Minister. After his retirement from politics in 1984, his party was eventually ousted by the opposition Progressive Conservatives under Brian Mulroney. The burning domestic issue during his stewardship has been constitutional reform, principally the status of Québec. In April 1987, Mulroney and the provincial premiers reached an agreement at Meech Lake in Québec which was intended to settle the issue. This formally recognised Québec as a 'distinct society' within the federation and set out guarantees protecting its language and cultural identity. Also, the provincial governments were granted important new constitutional powers of their own. The Accord was scuppered in June 1990 by the failure of the legislature in two of the provinces, Newfoundland and Manitoba, to accept the measure. Another attempt was made two years later, in the form of the so-called Charlottetown Accord, which also specified a unique status for Québec. It was put to a national referendum in October 1992 and rejected. The government of Québec, meanwhile, has displayed throughout the same blend of cultural insecurity and economic self-confidence which led it to its demand for independence. In foreign policy, Mulroney immmediately sought to re-establish the 'special relationship' which the USA had held in abeyance during the Trudeau era. In particular, Mulroney considered that Canada's economic health depended on an open trading relationship with the United States. This issue came to a head in 1988, when Mulroney called a general election: this was, in effect, a national referendum on the Free Trade Bill, which proposed the removal of all tariff barriers and restrictions on the movement of goods, labour and capital between Canada and the US (see *Business Profile*). Although the Conservative majority in parliament was reduced, Mulroney was returned to office.
GOVERNMENT: Executive power is vested in the British monarch, the Head of State, who is responsible for electing the Governor-General, presently Ramon John Hnatyshyn. The Prime Minister (presently Brian Mulroney), elected cabinet ministers, a 104-member Senate and a House of Commons make up the Federal Parliament. Members are elected by universal adult suffrage. The ten provinces of Canada each have a Lieutenant Governor and a local legislature, in power for up to five years. There are also two territories (Yukon and the Northwest), constituted by Acts of Parliament. Several recent attempts to amend the Constitution have been rejected by popular referendum.

CLIMATE

Climate graphs for the various provinces and territories may be found in the relevant entries below.
Required clothing: *March:* Moderate temperatures. Winter clothing with some mediumweight clothing.
April: Milder days but the evenings are cool. Mediumweight clothing including a topcoat is recommended.
May: Warm days but cool at night, mediumweight and summer clothing.
June: Warm, summer clothing with some mediumweight clothing for cool evenings. The weather in June is ideal for travel and all outdoor activities.
July/August: These are the warmest months of the year. Lightweight summer clothing is recommended.
September: Warm days and cool evenings. Light to mediumweight clothing.
October: Cool, with the first frost in the air.
November: Cool to frosty. Medium to heavyweight clothing is recommended. First signs of snow. Motorists should have cars prepared for winter and snow tyres are recommended.
December/January/February: Winter temperatures. Winter clothing is necessary (eg overcoat, hat, boots and gloves). Heavy snowfall in most provinces.

ALBERTA

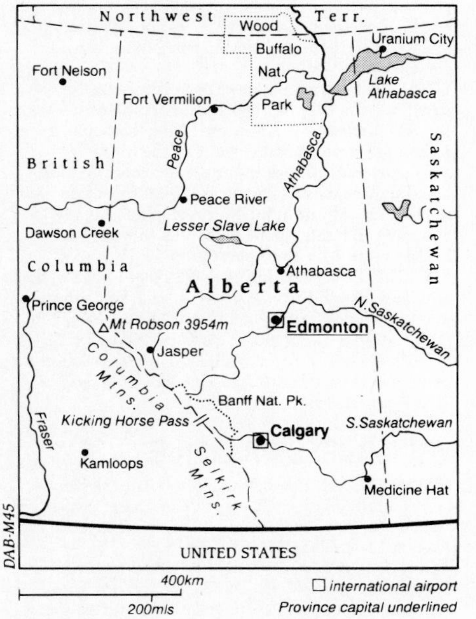

Location: Western Canada.

Tourism Alberta, Parks & Recreation
10155-102 Street
City Centre
Edmonton, Alberta
T5J 4L6
Tel: (403) 427 4321. Fax: (403) 427 0867 *or* 427 5123.
Tourism Alberta, Parks & Recreation
Alberta House
1 Mount Street
London W1Y 5AA
Tel: (071) 491 3430. Fax: (071) 629 2296. Telex: 23461 AGALTA G. Opening hours: 0900-1700 Monday to Friday.
Consulate General of the United States of America
Suite 1050
615 Macleod Trail, SE
Calgary, Alberta
T2G 4T8
Tel: (403) 266 8962. Fax: (403) 264 6630.

AREA: 661,185 sq km (248,799 sq miles).
POPULATION: 2,469,800 (1990).
POPULATION DENSITY: 3.8 per sq km.
CAPITAL: Edmonton. **Population:** 605,538 (1990).
GEOGRAPHY: Alberta is the most westerly of the 'prairie and plains' provinces, bordered to the west by British Columbia and the Rockies; to the southeast by the badlands and desert, while in the north, along the border with the Northwest Territories, there is a wilderness of forests, lakes and rivers. The western, Rocky Mountain border rises to 3650m (11,975ft), has permanent icefields covering 340 sq km (122 sq miles) and releases meltwaters which supply the Mackenzie River flowing to the Arctic, the Saskatchewan River flowing into Hudson Bay and the Columbia River flowing through the Rockies into Idaho and out into the Pacific.
LANGUAGE: Although Canada is officially bilingual (English and French), English is more commonly spoken in Alberta.
TIME: GMT - 7 (GMT - 6 in summer).
Note: Summer officially lasts from the first Sunday in April to the last Sunday in October.

PUBLIC HOLIDAYS

Public holidays as for the rest of Canada (see general section) with the following dates also observed:
Aug 2 '93 Heritage Day. **Feb 15 '94** Family Day.

TRAVEL

AIR: The province is served by *Air Canada (AC)* and *Canadian Airlines International (CP)*. For fares and schedules, contact airlines.
International airports: *Edmonton (YEG)* is 30km (19 miles) from the city (travel time – 40 minutes).
Calgary (YYC) is 17.6km (11 miles) from the city (travel time – 30 minutes).
Both Edmonton and Calgary also receive domestic services; and both have duty-free shops, banks, restaurants and car parking.
LAKES/RIVERS: All the major lakes and rivers are served by government ferries and private cruise lines.
RAIL: *Via Rail* operates two services connecting Edmonton with nationwide points. The *Canadian*, the trans-continental train, crosses the province thrice-weekly originating from Toronto, Ontario in the east through Edmonton and Jasper, to Vancouver in the west and vice versa. This train connects with the *SKEENA* service at Jasper with a thrice-weekly service to Prince Rupert, British Columbia. The *Rocky Mountaineer* is the only other rail service operating into the province. This is an all-daylight tour from either Calgary/Banff or Jasper to Vancouver in the summer months.
ROAD: Coach: *Greyhound Lines* run coach services into Alberta, thereby connecting Edmonton with all other major capitals. The main *Greyhound* terminals are at Edmonton, Banff and Calgary. Coaches are also operated in Alberta by *Brewster Transport* (Banff), and *Gray Lines of Canada* (Calgary), which also organise coach tours in the area. A coach is operated between the two city train stations of Calgary and Edmonton by *Red Arrow* (on behalf of *Via Rail*) four times a day. **Car hire:** Available in all large towns and at Edmonton and Calgary airports.
URBAN: Buses and the light rail system in Calgary are operated on a flat-fare system. Exact fares are required if tickets are purchased on boarding; pre-purchased single- and multi-journey tickets are available. Edmonton, where there is a similar fares system, has buses, trolley-buses and a light rail route. Local buses operate in all other major towns.
JOURNEY TIMES: The following chart give approxi-

mate journey times from Edmonton (in hours and minutes) to other major cities/towns in Alberta.

	Air	Road	Rail
Calgary	1.00	3.00	-
Banff	-	4.30	-
Jasper	-	4.00	4.30

ACCOMMODATION

Accommodation ranges from top-quality hotels to motorway motels, lodge estates and hostels. Banff National Park is famous for its two baronial-quality hotels, offering approximately 2000 rooms. Many lodges offer various levels of self-catering, often in conjunction with fishing and hiking trips. Several agencies offer bed & breakfast and ranch vacations throughout Alberta. For information on bed & breakfast accommodation, contact Alberta's Gem B & B Agency, 11216-48th Avenue, Edmonton, Alberta T6H OC7. Tel: (403) 434 6098. Alberta Tourism, Parks & Recreation publishes a comprehensive guide to the province's accommodation.

Grading: A grading system is being introduced. However, much of Alberta's accommodation is at present already supervised by the provincial government under a voluntary scheme to ensure high standards of cleanliness, comfort, construction and maintenance of furnishings and facilities. Look for the 'Approved Accommodation' sign which means that the establishment conforms to these standards. For more information on accommodation in Alberta contact Alberta Tourism, Parks & Recreation or the Alberta Hotel Association, Suite 401, Centre 104, 5241 Calgary Trail South, Edmonton, Alberta T6H 5G8. Tel: (403) 436 6112. Fax: (403) 436 5404.

CAMPING/CARAVANNING: The northern area of Alberta contains hundreds of lakes and forests, with abundant game such as deer, moose, bears and the rare trumpeter swan. There are numerous campsites in the National Parks. The permanent facilities tend to be more basic in the north. A number of companies can arrange **motor camper** rentals, with a range of fully equipped vehicles. Full details can be obtained from Travel Alberta; see also the *Camping/Caravanning* section in the general introduction above.

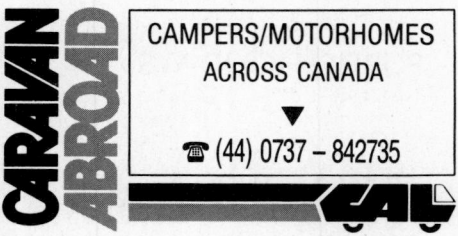

RESORTS & EXCURSIONS

EDMONTON: The provincial capital is the product of two events: the Klondike Gold Rush of 1898 and the oil boom of the late 1960s. This spacious well-planned city is famed for its huge parks on the banks of the North Saskatchewan River. Edmonton's love affair with its past is reflected in the Fort Edmonton Park, a complex of replicas of the city's frontier days; and reaches its apogee in the annual 'Klondike Days' extravaganza, held each July, when Edmontonians relive the days of the Gold Rush. West Edmonton Mall is reputedly the largest shopping mall in the world, with theatres, restaurants, nightclubs, amusement areas (including a miniature golf course, ice rink and swimming pool), aviaries, aquariums and museums. Edmonton also boasts *Fantasyland*, the world's largest indoor amusement park, and Canada's largest planetarium, the *Space Sciences Centre*. There are several theatres and art galleries. On a clear day, an estimated 6500 sq km (2500 sq miles) of Alberta can be seen from *Vista 33* at the Alberta Telephone Tower. *Alberta Wildlife Park* and *Elk Island National Park* are just outside the city.

CALGARY: The province's second city is situated at the western end of the Great Plains in the foothills of the Rocky Mountains. It is probably the fastest growing city in Canada, and hosted the 1988 Winter Olympics. The heart of the city is a pedestrian mall with excellent shopping and restaurants; the *Glenbow Museum*, art galleries and theatres are nearby. The *Calgary Zoo and Prehistoric Park* is one of the best in North America. *Heritage Park* offers a chance to explore an authentic Alberta frontier town as it was 80 years ago. There are panoramic views of the Rocky Mountains from the *Calgary Tower*.

ELSEWHERE: Calgary is the major stopping-off point en route to **Banff National Park,** 130km (80 miles) to the west in the heart of the Canadian Rockies. Banff, the first of the country's national parks, is a spectacular wilderness area with mountain, river and lake scenery – notably *Lake Louise*. Along with **Jasper National Park** to the north it offers a huge range of activities, including boating, canoeing, raft tours, fishing and hiking. The major ski resort in the Rockies, it hosts the annual *Banff Festival of the Arts*. The *Icefields Parkway* (Highway 93), runs the length of the two parks affording magnificent views of the lakes, forests and the glaciers of the *Columbia Icefield*. This route provides the best access to the wilderness trails in the area. On Alberta's southwestern border with the US is **Waterton Lakes National Park,** once joined to Glacier National Park in Montana and the world's first international Peace Park. Scenic views of the stunning lakeland scenery can be experienced on a cruise boat tour around the lake.

In central Alberta, the remains of dinosaurs, first discovered in 1874 in the banks of the Red Deer River, can be seen on the 48km (30-mile) *Dinosaur Trail* near **Drumheller**. Five minutes from the downtown area is the *Royal Tyrell Museum of Palaeontology*, with hands-on exhibitions, ongoing site work and one of the world's largest collections of dinosaur remains. Southwest of Drumheller, the *Dinosaur Provincial Park* continues this theme with reconstructed skeletons of duck-billed dinosaurs. To the south of Calgary, 50km (36 miles) south of Lethbridge, **Head-Smashed-In Buffalo Jump,** designated a UNESCO World Heritage Site in 1981, is among the largest and best-preserved jump sites in the world; it was used by the native people for more than 5600 years to drive thousands of buffalo to their deaths, thus providing them with food, shelter and clothing. The top of the cliff provides an unparalleled view of the surrounding prairie.

SOCIAL PROFILE

FOOD & DRINK: Alberta's prairie is ideal for cattle rearing and its western beef is world-famous. Beef is barbecued, braised, grilled, minced and skewered with different complements such as onions, mushrooms, green peppers, rice, sauces and beans. Unusual beef dishes are *stew* (combination of diced steak, garden vegetables and biscuits cooked in rich gravy), *beef mincemeat* (combines chopped suet, fruits and spices) used in pies and tarts and as a traditional Christmas dish served with ice-cream, cream or rum sauce. Wild berries and nuts are used in desserts. Honey is made from alfalfa and clover nectar and is a widely used sweetener and breakfast food. Apart from traditional foods, Alberta's towns and cities offer an excellent range of international cuisine. **Drink:** Alcohol is sold by 'liquor stores', although beer may be obtained in the majority of hotels. Liquor stores are closed on Sundays, major holidays and election days. There are no standard opening hours; some are open until 2330, many only until 1800. The minimum legal drinking age is 18.

NIGHTLIFE: Edmonton is famous for its night-time entertainment. Nightclubs, cabarets, taverns, lounges and that infamous Alberta watering hole, the beer parlour, combine to provide constant local and international entertainment. Both Calgary and Edmonton enjoy full-scale orchestras.

SHOPPING: Alberta is the only province (apart from the sparsely populated Northwest Territories and the Yukon) that does not apply an extra sales tax on all purchases over and above the general sales tax of 7%. Popular purchases are Hudson's Bay blankets, furs and fur products. The Inuit (Eskimos) produce clothing and tools of a high standard. Artwork includes pottery, ceramics, sculptures and paintings. For shopping hours, see the general entry above.

SPORT: Edmonton is home to four professional sports franchises: **football, baseball, soccer** and **hockey.** Two of the largest **rodeos** in Canada are held in the summer. Many of the rivers running out from the Rocky Mountains provide superb white-water **canoeing**. The large numbers of lakes provide excellent **fishing** and **sailing** facilities. **Skiing** in the Rocky Mountains is fast becoming an international attraction. In winter, **ice hockey** is played at the highest level.

SPECIAL EVENTS: Jun-Aug '93 *Banff Festival of the Arts*. **Jun 25-Jul 4** *Jazz City International*, Edmonton. **Jul** *International Folk Festival* and *Westerner Exhibition*, Red Deer. **Jul 9-18** *Calgary Stampede & Exhibition*. **Jul 22-31** *Klondike Days*, Edmonton. **Aug** *Red Deer International Air Show*, Red Deer. **Sep 1-6** *Spruce Meadows Masters Tournament*, Calgary.

BUSINESS PROFILE

COMMERCIAL INFORMATION: The following organisation can offer advice: Alberta Chamber of Commerce, Suite 1850, 10130-103 Street, Edmonton, Alberta T5J 3N9. Tel: (403) 425 4180.

CONFERENCES/CONVENTIONS: Both Calgary, Banff and Edmonton offer conference and convention venues. Contact the relevant organisation for assistance or advice:

Calgary Conventions & Visitors Bureau, 237-8th Avenue SE, Calgary, Alberta, T2G 0K8. Tel: (403) 263 8510. Fax: (403) 262 3809; *or*

Banff/Lake Louise Tourism Bureau, PO Box 1298, Banff, Alberta T0L 0C0. Tel: (403) 762 3777. Fax: (403) 762 8545; *or*

Edmonton Convention & Tourism Authority, Suite 104, 9797 Jasper Avenue, Edmonton, Alberta T5J 1N9. Tel: (403) 426 4715. Fax: (403) 425 5283.

CLIMATE

Summer, between May and September, is warm, while winters are cold, with particularly heavy snowfalls in the Rockies.

Required clothing: Light to mediumweights during warmer months. Heavyweights are worn in winter, with alpine wear in mountains. Waterproof wear is advisable throughout the year.

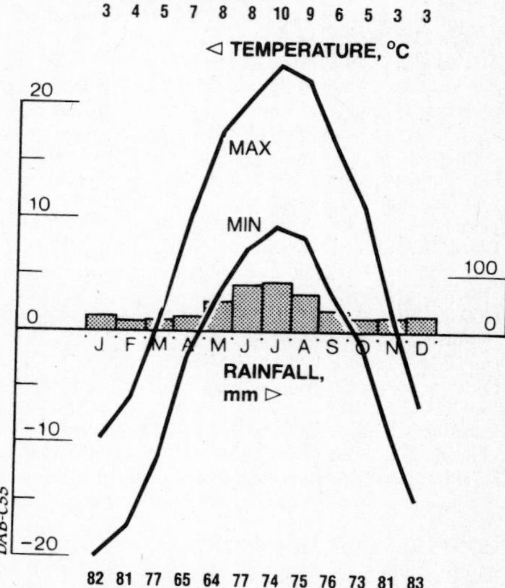

BRITISH COLUMBIA

Location: Western Canada.

Tourism British Columbia
Ministry of Tourism
Parliament Buildings
Victoria, British Columbia

V8V 1X4
Tel: (604) 356 9932. Fax: (604) 660 3383.
Tourism British Columbia
Suite 802
865 Hornby Street
Vancouver, British Columbia
V6Z 2G3
Tel: (604) 660 2861. Fax: (604) 660 3383. Telex: 0453480.
Tourism British Columbia
British Columbia House
1 Regent Street
London SW1Y 4NS
Tel: (071) 930 6857. Fax: (071) 930 2012.
British Consulate General
Suite 800, 1111 Melville Street
Vancouver, British Columbia
V6E 3V6
Tel: (604) 683 4421. Fax: (604) 681 0693. Telex: 0451287 BRITAIN VCR.

AREA: 929,730 sq km (358,969 sq miles).
POPULATION: 3,053,000 (1989 census).
POPULATION DENSITY: 3.3 per sq km.
CAPITAL: Victoria. **Population:** 272,500 (1989).
GEOGRAPHY: British Columbia is Canada's most westerly province, bordered to the south by the USA (Washington and Montana states), to the east by Alberta, to the north by the Northwest and Yukon Territories, and to the west by the Pacific Ocean and the 'Alaskan Panhandle'. It is mainly covered by virgin forests, and encompasses the towering Rocky Mountains, vast expanses of semi-arid sagebrush, lush pastures on Vancouver Island's east coast, farmland in the Fraser River delta, and fruitland in Okanagan Valley. The highest mountain is Fairweather at 4663m (15,298ft). Between the eastern and coastal mountains is a lower central range. The coastal range sinks into the Pacific, with larger peaks emerging at Vancouver and the Queen Charlotte Islands.
LANGUAGE: Although Canada is officially bilingual (English and French), English is more commonly spoken in British Columbia.
TIME: GMT - 8 (GMT - 7 in summer).
Note: Summer officially lasts from the first Sunday in April to the last Sunday in October.

PUBLIC HOLIDAYS

Public holidays as for the rest of Canada (see general section above) with the following date also observed:
Aug 2 '93 British Columbia Day.

TRAVEL

AIR: The following airlines operate in British Columbia: *Air Canada, Air BC, Chilcotin Cariboo Aviation, Canadian Airlines International, North Coast Air Services, Northern Thunderbird Air, Trans-Provincial Airlines* and *Wilderness Airlines*.
International airport: *Vancouver (YVR)*, 15km (11 miles) southwest of the city. It is served by airlines from the USA, Europe and the Far East. The journey to the city centre takes about 20 minutes. Airport facilities include a 24-hour restaurant, car parking, garage, car rental, nursery and duty-free shop.
The other major airports are *Victoria, Prince Rupert* and *Quesnel*.
SEA: Vancouver is an international passenger port, with regular sailings to the Far East and ports on the USA's northeastern coast.
Ferry services to and from all coastal ports and inland waters in British Columbia are available from the following shipping lines: *British Columbia Ferry Corporation, Ministry of Transportation* and *Highways Ferries*. Two ferry services link Vancouver Island with the mainland. The most spectacular route is the 15-hour one-way daylight voyage from Port Hardy on the northern tip of Vancouver Island along the Inside Passage to Prince Rupert
RAIL: *Via Rail* train routes to and within British Columbia are: Edmonton to Prince Rupert via Jasper (Alberta); Victoria to Courtney; Vancouver to Edmonton via Jasper, and on to Toronto three times a week (*Western Transcontinental*). *British Columbia Railways* operate trains from North Vancouver to Lilloet (daily) and on to Prince George (thrice-weekly).
ROAD: The Trans-Canada Highway reaches British Columbia via Calgary (Alberta) and continues through the south of the province to Vancouver. The other main highways are numbers 3, 5, 6, 16, 95 and 97. Apart from Highway 97, which runs northwards to the Yukon Territory, the province's road network is concentrated in the south. Road signs are international. There are good roads south to Seattle in the USA. **Bus:** There are a number of regional services.
URBAN: Bus, LRT and ferry services are provided in Vancouver and by a provincial government corporation (which also serves Victoria). *Metro Transit* operates 'seabuses' on cross-inlet ferry services.
JOURNEY TIMES: The following chart gives approximate journey times from Vancouver (in hours and minutes) to other major cities/towns in British Columbia.

	Air	Road	Rail
Victoria	0.35	2.30	-
Kamloops	0.55	4.00	9.00
Whistler	0.30	2.00	2.30
Prince George	1.20	8.00	12.00

ACCOMMODATION

HOTELS: Accommodation on offer ranges from top-class hotels in Victoria and Vancouver through motels beside the main southern highways to simple cabins high up in the Rockies. Cottages and cabins are widely available on Vancouver Island. 'Ranch Holidays' are popular in the Cariboo Chilcotin region of central British Columbia. Bed & breakfast accommodation can be found by contacting the British Columbia B & B Association, Box 593, 810 West Broadway, Vancouver, British Columbia V5Z 4E2; *or* All Seasons B & B Agency, Box 5511, Station B, Victoria, British Columbia V8R 6S4. Tel: (604) 595 2337. Fax: (604) 655 1422. Tourism British Columbia has an annual guide listing all the agencies providing accommodation in the province.
Grading: Standards are overseen by the Ministry of Tourism and approved hotels display a bright blue 'Approved Accommodation' sign to indicate that the Ministry's standards of courtesy, comfort and cleanliness have been met. For more information contact Tourism British Columbia *or* British Columbia & Yukon Hotels Association, First Floor, Hotel Vancouver, 900 West Georgia Street, Vancouver, British Columbia V6C 2W6. Tel: (604) 681 7164. Fax: (604) 681 7649.
CAMPING/CARAVANNING: There are nearly 10,000 campsites situated in over 150 parks and recreation areas. Most campsites do not have power supply link-ups for caravans. Several of the parks are designated as 'Nature Conservancy Areas', where all motor vehicles are banned and transport must be on foot. The type of parkland available varies from sandy beaches with vehicle access, to lakes and glaciers reached only by aircraft or boat. All campsites have a time limit of 14 days and reservations are not accepted. A number of companies can arrange **motor camper** rentals, with a range of fully equipped vehicles. Full details can be obtained from Tourism British Columbia *or* British Columbia Motels, Campgrounds, Resorts Association, PO Box 12105, Suite 980, Harbour Centre, 555 Hastings Street, Vancouver, British Columbia V6B 4N6. Tel: (604) 682 8883. See also the *Camping/Caravanning* section in the general introduction above.

RESORTS & EXCURSIONS

VANCOUVER: Canada's third largest city is situated in the southwest of the province, overlooking the Burrard Inlet on the Pacific and backed by the Coastal Range of mountains. It is a major port. Downtown Vancouver has the second largest Chinese quarter in North America and a large German and Ukrainian population. Both traditions are reflected in the proliferation of ethnic shops and restaurants. Of the several museums and galleries, most notable are the *Centennial Museum, H R MacMillan Planetarium, University of British Columbia's Museum of Anthropology* (housing excellent examples of Northwest Indian art and artefacts), *Vancouver Art Gallery, Science World* (including four galleries of hands-on exhibits) and the *Maritime Museum*. Main points of interest in the suburbs are *Stanley Park, Vancouver Aquarium* and the *Grouse Mountain Skyride*. The latter offers views of the city and the fjords of the Pacific coast from 1211m (3974ft). During the summer it is a delight for naturalists but in winter, **Whistler,** just north of Vancouver, is the most popular ski resort on the west coast and offers an award-winning design with first-class hotels and restaurants. In addition to 180 varied ski runs covering two enormous mountains, it has facilities for golf, windsurfing, tennis, mountain biking, river rafting, horseriding, hiking, gondola and chairlift rides, shopping and cultural entertainment. Ferries to Vancouver Island pass through the spectacular **Gulf Islands.** A variety of tours and charter boats are available for island-hopping excursions.
VICTORIA: The provincial capital lies at the southern tip of the heavily forested and mountainous Vancouver Island. This most English of Canadian towns is distinguished by Victorian and neo-classical architecture and well-appointed residential areas. In the harbour area are the impressive *Parliament Buildings* and the *Provincial Museum*, which gives an overview of the region's history. Also worth visiting is the *Maltwood Art Gallery, Thunderbird Park* (where visitors may see modern-day Indian carvers at work) and *Craigdarroch Castle* (an impressive 19th-century landmark mansion home). City life is enhanced by more than 60 recreational parks. The *Undersea Gardens* offer a fish's-eye view of harbour life.
Some 20km (12 miles) to the north, the **Butchart Gardens** have delightful English, Japanese and Italian gardens set in a former limestone quarry. **Nanaimo,** the island's major commercial port, is on the coastal route to the north; where there are opportunities for sailing and fishing.
ELSEWHERE: Pacific Rim National Park, 306km (192 miles) north of Vancouver on the west coast, is a popular resort, with sandy beaches offering good surfing and swimming, and wilderness trails through deep, hilly forests. To the east of the province, high in the Rocky Mountains, the huge wilderness areas of **Yoho, Kootenay** and **Glacier National Parks** offer hiking, angling and rafting trips as well as excellent winter sports facilities. Nearby are the hot-spring resorts of **Radium** and **Fairmount** and the **Fort Steel Heritage Park,** which celebrates pioneer days. North of the rich angling and ranching country of the *Cariboo Chilcotin* lie vast tracts of untamed lakeland, forest and wilderness stretching to the border with the Yukon and Northwest Territories. Some sporting resorts in this area are accessible only by air. Many outfitters offer guided hunting and fishing expeditions to this area.
Queen Charlotte Islands, reached by ferry from **Prince Rupert** in the far northwest, is an adventurous side-trip with good hunting opportunities. Another good wilderness route is the **Alaska Highway,** running through **Prince George, Dawson Creek** and **Fort St John** in the northeast. This former fur-trading trail gives good access to the provincial parks of **Stone Mountain** and **Muncho Lake,** which provide basic amenities for striking out into this rugged terrain. Both the scenery and the sporting opportunities en route are excellent.

SOCIAL PROFILE

FOOD & DRINK: The cuisine of the province is enhanced by English traditions. The Pacific Ocean yields a great variety of seafood, including King Crab, oysters, shrimp and other shellfish, as well as cod, haddock and salmon (coho, spring, chum, sockeye and pink) which are smoked, pan-fried, breaded, baked, caned and barbecued, and complemented by local vegetables. Fruits grown in the province include apples, peaches, pears, plums, apricots, strawberries, blackberries, the famous Bing cherries, and loganberries. *Victoria creams*, a famous chocolate delicacy derived from a recipe dating back to 1885, are exported worldwide from British Columbia.
Drink: Sparkling wines are produced in Okanagan Valley and all the usual alcoholic beverages are widely available. Spirits, beer and wine can be served in licensed restaurants, dining rooms, pubs and bars. Taverns (pubs) are open until 0100, bars and cabarets until 0200. The minimum drinking age is 19.
NIGHTLIFE: Major cities and towns have top-class restaurants, nightclubs and bars, sometimes in pub style. Vancouver has an active theatre life. Better nightspots are often to be found in hotels.
SPORT: The hundreds of watersheds among the Rocky Mountains have provided British Columbia with countless rivers and lakes in every park area. **Watersports** ranging from **sailing, canoeing** and even specialist white-water river **rafting** are all available. Campbell River on Vancouver Island is world-famous for salmon **fishing.** The Rocky Mountains are the national centre for snow **skiing,** and attract visitors from the USA and Europe.
SPECIAL EVENTS: May 22-23 '93 *Swiftsure Sailing Race*, Victoria. **Jul** *Vancouver Sea Festival*. **Jul 1-4** *Williams Lake Stampede*, Williams Lake. **Jul 16-18** *Folk Festival*, Vancouver. **Jul 16-25** *July Peach Festival*, Penticton. **Jul 25** *International Bathtub Race*, Nanaimo. **Jul-Aug** *Pacific National Exhibition*, Vancouver. **Aug 6-8** *International Air Show*, Abbotsford. **Sep-Oct** *Wine Festival*, Okanagan.

BUSINESS PROFILE

COMMERCIAL INFORMATION: The following organisation can offer advice: Vancouver Chamber of Commerce, Suite 400, 999 Canada Place, Vancouver, British Columbia V6C 3C1. Tel: (604) 681 2111.
CONFERENCES/CONVENTIONS: There are conference/convention centres in Penticton, Vancouver, Victoria and Whistler as well as over 200 hotels throughout the province which can offer meeting facilities. For more information on conferences and conventions in British Columbia contact: Tourism British Columbia *or* Tourism Vancouver, 562 Burrard Street, Vancouver, British Columbia V6C 2J6. Tel: (604) 682 2222. Fax: (604) 682 1716.

CLIMATE

One of the mildest regions with very warm summers and relatively mild winters. Heavy snowfalls in the Rockies.
Required clothing: Lightweights for most of the summer with warmer clothes sometimes necessary in the evenings. Mediumweights are worn during winter, with Alpine wear in the mountains. Waterproof clothing is advisable throughout the year.

VANCOUVER British Columbia (2m)

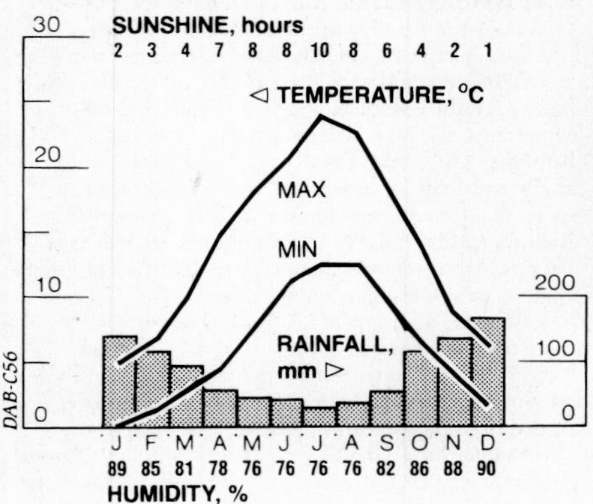

MANITOBA

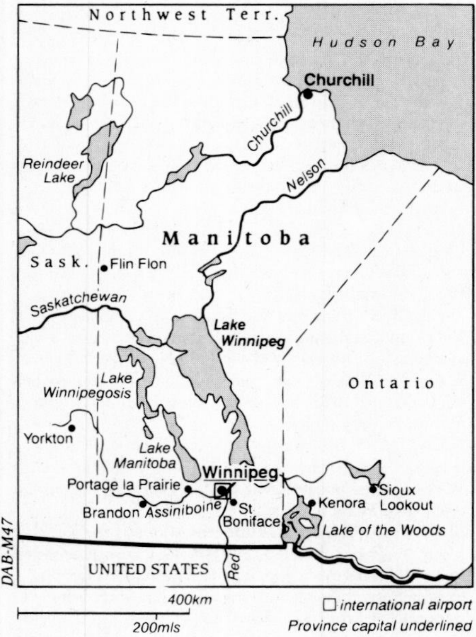

Location: Eastern Central Canada.

Travel Manitoba
Department 147
7th Floor, 155 Carlton Street
Winnipeg, Manitoba
R3C 3H8
Tel: (204) 945 3796. Fax: (204) 945 2302.

AREA: 548,360 sq km (211,722 sq miles).
POPULATION: 1,084,800 (1989 census).
POPULATION DENSITY: 2 per sq km.
CAPITAL: Winnipeg. **Population:** 640,400 (1989).
GEOGRAPHY: Manitoba is bordered by the US state of North Dakota to the south, Saskatchewan to the west, Ontario to the east, and the Northwest Territories to the north. The landscape is diverse, ranging from rolling farmland to sandy beaches on the shores of Lake Winnipeg, and from the desert landscape of the south to northern parkland covered by lakes and forests.
LANGUAGE: Although Canada is officially bilingual (English and French), English is commonly spoken in Manitoba.
TIME: GMT - 6 (GMT - 5 in summer).
Note: Summer officially lasts from the first Sunday in April to the last Sunday in October.

PUBLIC HOLIDAYS

Public holidays are as for the rest of Canada (see general section above) with the following date also observed:
Aug 2 '93 Civic Holiday.

TRAVEL

AIR: The following airlines run inter-provincial flights: *Air Canada (AC)*, *Canadian Airlines International (CP)*, *Frontier Airlines* and *Nordair*. For timetables and fares, contact the airline offices.
International airport: *Winnipeg International Airport (YWG)* is 6.4km (4 miles) northwest of the city (travel time – 15 minutes). Airport facilities include a duty-free shop, a post office, 24-hour restaurant, banks, car rental and car parking.
SEA: The only major coastal port is Churchill on Hudson Bay, which is frozen for much of the year. In summer, there are services to the Northwest Territories and Ontario.
RAIL: *Via Rail* links Saskatchewan and Ontario with Winnipeg and southern Manitoba. A thrice-weekly train runs north from Winnipeg to Hudson Bay, The Pas, Lynn Lake, Thompson and Churchill. For timetables and fares contact a local *Via* office.
ROAD: Excellent road services connect Manitoba with Ontario (through Kenora), Saskatchewan (Regina) and the United States (Fargo,Minnesota and Bismarck,North Dakota). The road system within Manitoba is also excellent and covers over 19,794km (12,300 miles). **Bus:** Services are run by local authorities and interstate services are run by *Greyhound Bus Lines* and *Grey Goose Bus Lines*. For timetables and fares contact local offices. **Taxi:** Available in all larger towns. Taxi drivers expect a 15% tip. **Documentation:** National driving licences are accepted in Manitoba.
URBAN: There are comprehensive bus services in Winnipeg. A flat fare is charged. There are good bus services in other towns.

ACCOMMODATION

Manitoba has a wide selection of accommodation, ranging from first-class hotels in Winnipeg to guest-houses and farm holiday camps among the parklands of the north. Farm vacations are controlled by their own association, ensuring high standards. Bed & breakfast is available at a reasonable price. For information on bed & breakfast accommodation, contact B & B Association of Manitoba, 93 Healy Crescent, Winnipeg, Manitoba R2N 2S2. Tel: (204) 256 6151. For all accommodation details, contact Travel Manitoba *or* the Manitoba Hotel Association, Suite 1505, 155 Carlton Street, Winnipeg, Manitoba R3C 3H8. Tel: (204) 942 0671.
CAMPING/CARAVANNING: The parklands and the enormous spread of lakes and forests in northern Manitoba are major attractions. Camping facilities are widespread. A number of companies can arrange **motor camper** rentals, with a range of fully equipped vehicles. Full details can be obtained from Travel Manitoba.

RESORTS & EXCURSIONS

WINNIPEG: Almost equidistant from the Pacific and Atlantic Oceans, the provincial capital stands in the heart of the vast prairie which covers much of the southern part of the province. This 'Gateway to the North' at the confluence of the Red and Assiniboine Rivers is one of the most culturally and racially varied of Canada's cities. Winnipeg is the fourth largest Canadian city with theatres, galleries, a ballet and an opera. Places of note include the *Legislative Building* with Manitoba's symbol, the *Golden Boy*, balancing triumphantly on its dome; the *Centennial Centre* which features the *Museum of Man and Nature*, re-creating past and present life on the prairies; and the *Commodity Exchange*, the world's largest grain market. *St Boniface*, formerly a separate city, is the French Quarter of Winnipeg. In the suburbs, the *Royal Canadian Mint*, with its high-tech building, and *Lower Fort Garry*, an old fur-trading post, are both worth visiting.
ELSEWHERE: Paddle-steamers offer excursions through the rich farmland of the **Red** and **Assiniboine Rivers**. The *Prairie Dog Central* steam train runs from the city to **Grosse Isle.**
East of the capital along the Trans-Canada Highway is the German-speaking Mennonite town of **Steinbach;** and **Whiteshell Provincial Park,** with over 2500 sq km (1000 sq miles) of wilderness offering fishing, hunting and canoeing. The more developed resorts of **Falcon Lake** and **West**

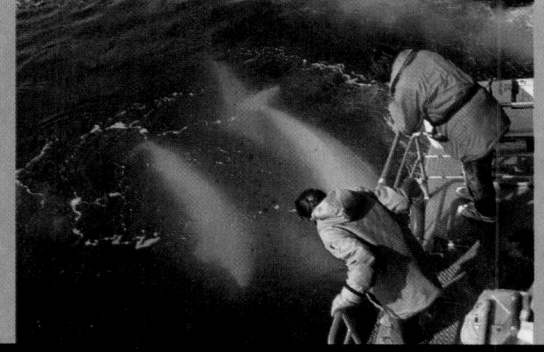

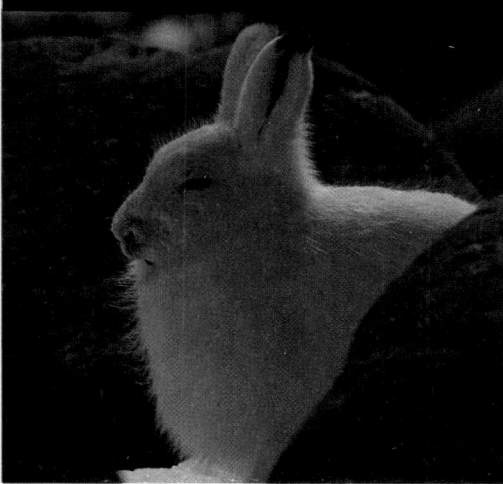

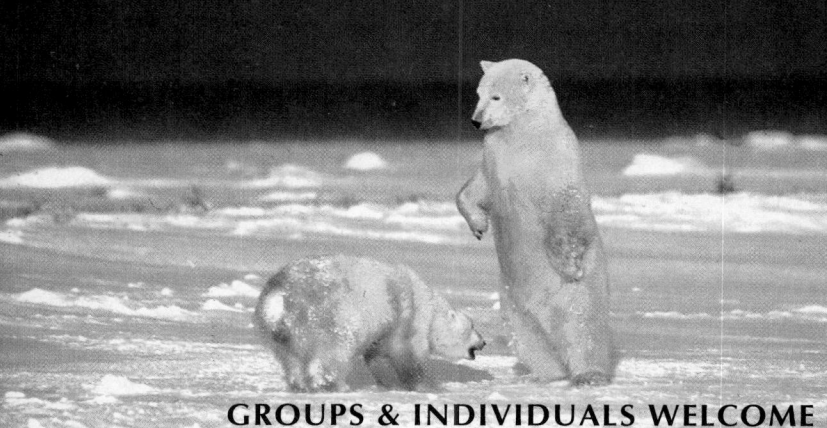

Hawk Lake have good facilities for swimming and sailing. West of Winnipeg the highway cuts through the wheat belt. *Fort la Reine Museum* and the *Pioneer Village* at **Portage la Prairie** reconstruct the town's days as an 18th-century trading post. The **International Peace Garden** on the border with North Dakota has a huge complex of formal gardens and waterways.

Lake Winnipeg has good sandy beaches and boats for hire. The western shore of the lake was once New Iceland, a self-governing area settled by thousands of Icelanders fleeing volcanic eruptions in their homeland. **Gimli**, the major town, still has a large Icelandic population, which stages an annual Icelandic festival. **Hecla Provincial Park,** a group of wooded islands on the lake, offers a resort and conference centre as well as good hiking and camping facilities.

En route to the great northern wilderness, **Riding Mountain National Park** is a vast recreational area providing cross-country skiing, riding and 300km (190 miles) of hiking trails. Ukrainian immigrants colonised the farming area around **Dauphin** in the 1890s and their influence is still felt in the cuisine and costume of the area notably during the annual *Ukrainian Festival.* **The Pas** is the jumping-off point for trips to the lakes and rivers of the northern interior. Near the border with Saskatchewan is the mining and lumbering town of **Flin Flon** (a noted trout-fishing centre) and **Grass River Park**, a huge granite wilderness. **Churchill**, a sub-arctic seaport in the far north-east, is best reached by air across the vast flatlands running into **Hudson Bay.** The area has an abundance of game and wildlife, as well as the world's heaviest concentration of Northern Lights.

SOCIAL PROFILE

FOOD & DRINK: Winnipeg offers opportunities to experience cuisine of the many and diverse cultures that typify the city. Rural Manitoba also offers a wide choice of restaurants from the very expensive to the moderately priced with good home cooking. The best restaurants are usually found in hotels and motels outside the city. It is customary to tip waiters 15% of the bill. **Drink:** The minimum age for drinking is 18, but those under 18 can drink with a meal if it is purchased by a parent or guardian. Off-licence alcohol is available only from government outlets. Opening hours are generally 1100-1400.

NIGHTLIFE: Winnipeg's nightlife is vibrant. The National Film Board of Canada screens top films once a month in the Planetarium Auditorium; admittance is free. Many other cinemas, theatres, clubs, restaurants and bars also provide entertainment. The city also offers romantic dining and moonlit dancing cruises aboard riverboats on its scenic Red and Assiniboine Rivers. The elegant Crystal Casino, Canada's first full-time casino, is located here in the Fort Garry Hotel, offering blackjack, roulette and baccarat.

SHOPPING: There are several nationally known department stores in Winnipeg, with branches throughout Manitoba. City and provincial centres have a variety of unusual shops and boutiques. North of The Pas is an Indian handicraft shop where visitors can watch Indian women making moccasins, mukluks, jackets and jewellery. At the Rock Shop in Fouris, costume jewellery can be bought made from rock from a local quarry and the visitor may obtain a permit to collect his own rock. **Shopping hours:** 1000-1800 Monday to Wednesday and Saturday; 1000-2130 Thursday and Friday (closed Sundays).

SPORT: There are 111 **golf** courses in Manitoba, six of these in Winnipeg. The lakes and parklands of Manitoba mean that **watersports** predominate. **Fishing** for trout, pike, Arctic grayling and walleye is especially popular. Several of the northern lakes are only accessible by air, and charter flights with guides are available from Winnipeg. **Swimming, diving, windsurfing** and **sailing** are also popular. The great outdoors offers excellent opportunities for **canoeing, hiking** and **horseriding**. **Skiing** is available throughout the winter months at the provincial and national parks such as *Mount Agassiz* in *Riding Mountain National Park.*

SPECIAL EVENTS: Mar 29-Apr 3 '93 *Royal Manitoba Winter Fair*, Brandon. **Jul 9-11** *Winnipeg Folk Festival*. **Jul 29-Aug 1** *Canada's National Ukrainian Festival*, Dauphin. **Aug 1-14** *Folklorama*, Winnipeg.

BUSINESS PROFILE

COMMERCIAL INFORMATION: The following organisation can offer advice: Manitoba Chamber of Commerce, Suite 750, 167 Lombard Avenue East, Winnipeg, Manitoba R3B 0V6. Tel: (204) 944 8484.

CONFERENCES/CONVENTIONS: For information on conferences and conventions in Winnipeg contact The Director of Convention Development, Tourism Winnipeg, Suite 232, 375 York Avenue, Winnipeg, Manitoba R3C 3J3. Tel: (204) 943 1970. Fax: (204) 942 4043.

CLIMATE

Summers are warm and sunny. Winters are cold particularly in the north. Rainfall is highest between May and July.

Required clothing: Light to mediumweights in warm months. Heavyweights in winter. Waterproofing is advisable all year.

WINNIPEG Manitoba (254m)

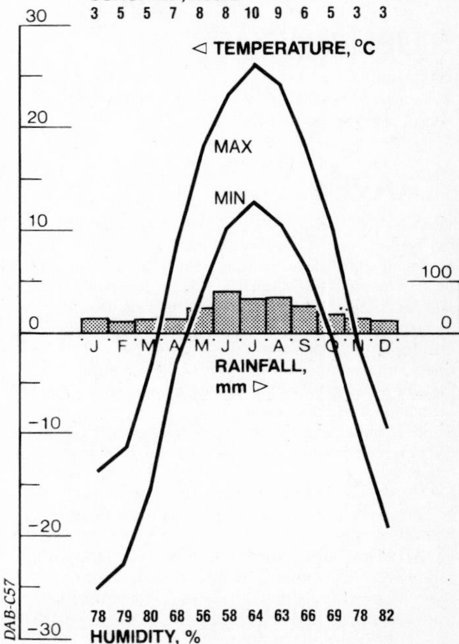

NEW BRUNSWICK

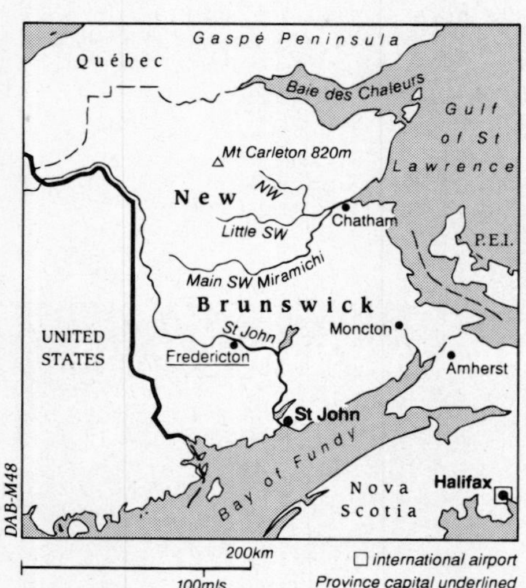

Location: East coast of Canada.

Economic Development and Tourism
PO Box 6000
670 King Street
Fredericton, New Brunswick
E3B 5H1
Tel: (506) 453 3984. Fax: (506) 453 7127.
Tourism New Brunswick
PO Box 12345
Fredericton, New Brunswick
E3B 5C3
Tel: (506) 453 8745. Fax: (506) 453 5370.

AREA: 74,437 sq km (28,354 sq miles).
POPULATION: 726,800 (1992).
POPULATION DENSITY: 9.8 per sq km.
CAPITAL: Fredericton. **Population:** 46,500 (1992).
GEOGRAPHY: New Brunswick, which is below the Gaspé Peninsula, shares its western border with Maine and has 2250km (1400 miles) of coast on the Gulf of St Lawrence and the Bay of Fundy. Its landscape comprises forested hills with rivers cutting through them. The main feature is Saint John River Valley in the south. Northern and eastern coastal regions give way to the extensive drainage basin of the Miramichi River in the central area.
LANGUAGE: New Brunswick is officially bilingual (English and French) with approximately 35% of the population French-speaking.
TIME: GMT - 4 (GMT - 3 in summer).
Note: Daylight savings time officially lasts from the first Sunday in April to the last Sunday in October.

PUBLIC HOLIDAYS

Public holidays are as for the rest of Canada (see general section above), with the following date also observed:
Aug 2 '93 New Brunswick Day.

TRAVEL

AIR: New Brunswick is without an international airport but Fredericton, St John and Moncton are connected to Montréal and Québec by inter-provincial flights operated by *Air Canada (AC)*, *Canadian Airlines International (CP)* and *Air Atlantic*. There are airports offering local services at *Saint John, Fredericton, St Leonard, Edmundston, Campbelton* and *Moncton*.
SEA: Ferries run from Nova Scotia, Maine, Prince Edward Island and Québec to New Brunswick via Saint John and Cape Tormentine.
There is a full coastal ferry service between all ports in the province. For timetables, contact the local tourist office.
RAIL: *Via Rail* runs six times a week from Montréal to Halifax, three times via Mont Joli and three times via Saint John.
ROAD: The Trans-Canada Highway follows the Saint John River Valley from Edmundston in the north to Saint John in the south, with the majority of the highways branching off it. There are over 16,000km (10,000 miles) of roads in the province.

ACCOMMODATION

HOTELS: There are 73 hotels/motels, 64 bed & breakfast inns and 7 resorts. The main centres of population are on the coast, and these offer the best choice of hotel or motel accommodation. There are also numerous guesthouses, bed & breakfast establishments and youth hostels. For information on bed & breakfast accommodation, contact New Brunswick B & B Association, 238 Charlotte Street West, Saint John, New Brunswick E2M 1Y3. Tel: (506) 635 1888. For information on farmhouse accommodation, contact New Brunswick Farm Vacations, Department of Tourism, PO Box 12345, Fredericton, New Brunswick E3B 5C3. Tel: (506) 453 2453. Fax: (506) 453 2416.
Grading: Accommodation is graded by the New Brunswick Grading Authority on a voluntary basis according to the *Atlantic Canada Accommodations Grading Program* as follows:
1-star: Basic, clean, comfortable accommodation.
2-star: Basic, clean, comfortable accommodation with extra amenities.
3-star: Better quality accommodation with a greater range of services.
4-star: High-quality accommodation with extended range of facilities, amenities and guest services.
5-star: Deluxe accommodation with the greatest range of facilities, amenities and guest services.
CAMPING/CARAVANNING: The province's four major parks have extensive campsites and youth hostels. More than a hundred privately owned campsites operate in the area. A number of companies can arrange **motor camper** rentals, with a range of fully equipped vehicles. Details can be obtained from Tourism New Brunswick.

RESORTS & EXCURSIONS

SAINT JOHN: New Brunswick's largest city has been a shipbuilding centre since the last century. Replicas of sailing ships can be seen in the *New Brunswick Museum*. Other historic sites include the *Loyalist Houses* and the *Country Courthouse*. The city was also a bastion for the British Loyalists, who flocked there in May 1783 to escape from the victorious American rebels after the War of Independence, and their historic landing is re-enacted every year in a 5-day celebration.
The **Saint John River Valley** provides a scenic route to the capital, with the uncluttered resort of **Grand Lake** on the way.
FREDERICTON: 110km (70 miles) upriver from Saint John and the Bay of Fundy, Fredericton was once the capital of Acadia. It is the legislative and academic centre of New Brunswick and possesses some fine neo-classical and Victorian architecture such as the *Legislative Building, Christchurch Cathedral* and *Government House*. The *Beaverbrook Art Gallery* is one of the finest in Canada with an extensive collection of Canadian, British and Renaissance paintings and a good group of Salvador Dali's work. Paddle-boats offer cruises and entertainment on the *Saint John River*.
North of the city the highly developed resort of **Mactaquac Park** offers a huge range of outdoor activities. Nearby **King's Landing,** a reconstructed loyalist village, is also worth visiting.
ELSEWHERE: New Brunswick is a maritime province with two coastlines – on the **Gulf of St Lawrence** and the **Bay of Fundy.** Routes along these two coasts provide the best introduction to the area. The eastern shoreline, once a French stronghold, has a temperate climate and some excellent beaches, particularly near **Kouchibouguac Provincial Park.** In the south, **Shediac** hosts an annual lobster festival; at **Parlee**, nearby, is the largest and best beach in the province. Trout-fishing and canoeing on the **Miramichi River**, running into picturesque Miramichi Bay at **Chatham**, are recommended. North of this the area around **Tracadie** is still a French-speaking enclave; deep-sea fishing charters are available here. Nearby, a 500-acre *Acadian Village* re-creates the lifestyle of the 18th-century Breton settlers whose descendants still dominate the northeast corner of the province.
Most of the shipbuilding and fishing towns of the south were founded by British Loyalists fleeing the American War of Independence. The coastline is battered by the tempestuous 15m (50ft) tides of the Bay of Fundy, resulting in dramatic scenery such as the **Hopewell Cape's** sandstone 'flowerpots'. **St Andrews** has some well-preserved 18th-century houses and *The Blockhouse*, built in 1812 to defend the town from American incursions.
St George has a ferry to the little-known and unspoilt **Fundy Islands,** of which *Grand Manan*, the largest, boasts beautiful rare flora and fauna. Whales and dolphins can often be spotted from the shoreline. It is also a centre for collecting *dulse*, an edible seaweed, which is a speciality of the province. **Deer Island** and **Campobello Island** are reached by ferry from **Letete**.
To the east of St John is **Fundy National Park,** the area's most popular resort. Much of it is set on a plateau 300m (985ft) above sea level with 800km (500 miles) of hiking trails. The huge range of organised activities there include an *Arts and Crafts School*. Rowboats and canoes can be rented to navigate the tidal flats where tides can rise by 16m (50ft) a day.
The Fundy tides cause an impressive tidal bore at **Moncton**, the province's second largest city.

SOCIAL PROFILE

FOOD & DRINK: The province is famous for seafood, particularly Atlantic salmon with its delicate flavour, served with butter, new potatoes and *fiddleheads* (young fronds of ostrich fern served with butter and seasoned, or used cold in salads). Apples, blueberries and cranberries are common dessert ingredients. Home-made baked beans and steamed brown bread are served as traditional Saturday-night supper. *Rapée pie*, made with chicken, is an Acadian speciality for Sundays or festivals. Shediac is reputed to be the lobster capital of the world. Fredericton, Saint John and Moncton offer international cuisine as well as local specialities, like New Brunswick *dulse*, an edible seaweed. **Drink:** The minimum drinking age is 19.
NIGHTLIFE: In Saint John some hotels offer live entertainment and bars have music. Moncton also has clubs, lounges and hotels with night-time entertainment. St Andrews has two bars with nightly entertainment as well as many smaller pubs, bars and lounges.
SHOPPING: Special purchases include local and provincial handicrafts which are especially worthwhile in New Brunswick. The best markets in Saint John are between Charlotte and Germain Streets, forming the *Old City Market*. This is open all week, with farmers taking over on Friday and Saturday. Moncton has three large shopping areas: Champlain Place, Moncton Mall and Highfield Square. **Shopping hours:** 0900-1730 Monday to Saturday; 1000-2200 in malls.
SPORT: One of the best centres for **golf** is the picturesque resort town of St Andrews. **Harness racing** is held at Saint John during late August to early September. Harness racing meetings are also held twice a week at Fredericton Raceway. **Skiing** and **skating** are popular winter activities in New Brunswick. New Brunswick is also a maritime sporting province. **Sailing** and **skindiving** are popular, and the annual *Renforth* and *Cocagne Regattas* attract **sculling** crews from all over the world. The best beach in the province for **swimming** is found at Parlee Beach Provincial Park. Deep-sea **fishing** boats are open for charter from all the coastal ports. Grand Manan Island is a **birdwatching** paradise and was the favourite haunt of the famous ornithologist, James Audobon.
SPECIAL EVENTS: Jun 25-Jul 4 '93 *Festival Moncton* (jazz and blues festival with sporting events, fireworks and barbecue). **Jun 27-Jul 6** *Salmon Festival* (salmon supper, as well as a golf tournament, canoe and car rallies, a circus, fireworks, children's events and a parade), Campbellton. **Jun 29-Jul 4** *International Francophone Festival*, Tracadie. **Jun 30-Jul 5** *Festival de Rameurs* (Dory Boat Festival), Petit-Rocher. **Jul 2-11** *Festival Marin* (environmental celebration with seafood dinners, dancing and entertainment on the beach), Bas-Caraquet. **Jul 6-11** *Lobster Festival*, Shediac. **Jul 9-13** *International Festival of Baroque Music*, Ile de Lamèque. **Jul 15-18** *Irish Festival*, Chatham. **Jul 16-24** *Woodstock Old Home Week*, Woodstock. **Jul 18-24** *Loyalist Days Festival*, Saint John. **Jul 23-Aug 1** *Bon Ami Get-Together Festival*, Dalhousie. **Jul 28-Aug 2** *Foire Brayonne* (six days and nights of Brayonne foods, crafts and western and rock music entertainment), Edmundston. **Jul 30-Aug 2** *Buskers on the Boardwalk*, Saint John. **Aug 1-6** *36th Miramichi Folksong Festival*, Newcastle. **Aug 2-6** *Chocolate Fest*, St Stephen. **Aug 6-12** *Acadian Festival*, Caraquet. **Aug 6-15** *Festival By The Sea*, Saint John. **Aug 13-15** *Atlantic Waterfowl Celebration*, Sackville. **Sep 10-12** *Atlantic Balloon Fiesta*, Sussex. **Sep 16-19** *Harvest Jazz & Blues Festival*, Fredericton.

BUSINESS PROFILE

COMMERCIAL INFORMATION: The following organisation can offer advice: Atlantic Provinces Chamber of Commerce, Suite 110, 236 St George Street, Moncton, New Brunswick E1C 1W1. Tel: (506) 857 2883. Fax: (506) 859 6131.
CONFERENCES/CONVENTIONS: For information on conferences and conventions in New Brunswick contact:
Fredericton Visitors & Convention Bureau, PO Box 130, City Hall, Queen Street, Fredericton, New Brunswick E3B 4Y7. Tel: (506) 452 9500. Fax: (506) 452 9509; *or*

Saint John Visitors and Convention Bureau, PO Box 1971, City Hall, Saint John, New Brunswick E2L 4L1. Tel: (506) 658 2990. Fax: (506) 658 2879.

CLIMATE

Summer months (June to August) are warm with cooler evenings. Autumn remains relatively mild. Winters are cold with heavy snows.
Required clothing: Light to mediumweights during summer months, heavyweights in winter. Waterproofing is advisable all year.

ST JOHN New Brunswick (326m)

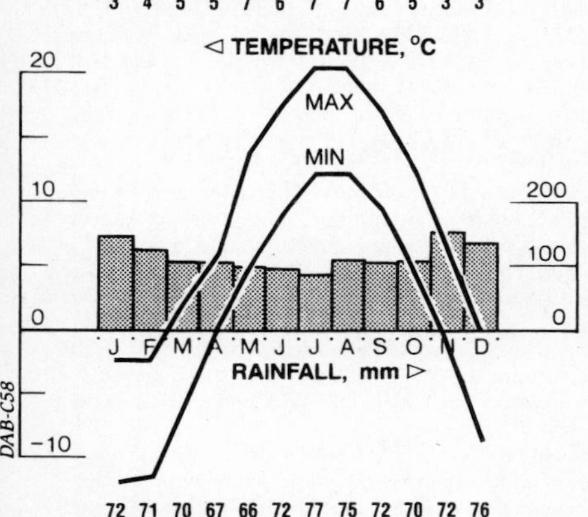

NEWFOUNDLAND & LABRADOR

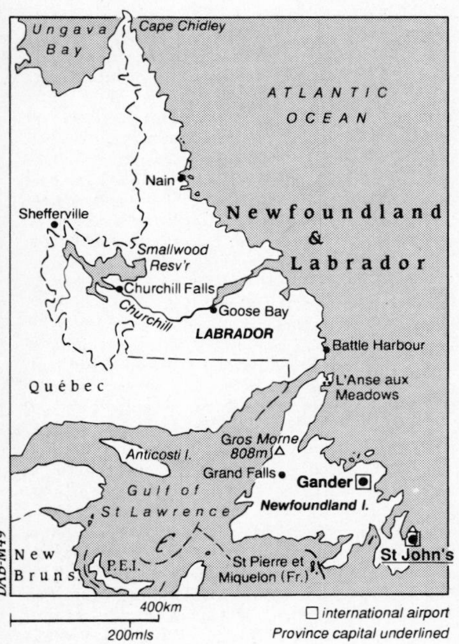

Location: Eastern Canada.

Department of Tourism and Culture
PO Box 8700
4th Floor, West Block
Confederation Building
St John's, Newfoundland
A1B 4J6
Tel: (709) 729 2830. Fax: (709) 729 0057.

AREA: 405,720 sq km (156,185 sq miles).
POPULATION: 575,000 (1992 estimate).
POPULATION DENSITY: 1.4 per sq km.
CAPITAL: St John's. **Population:** 103,000 (1991).
GEOGRAPHY: Newfoundland & Labrador is the most easterly province. It consists of the mainland territory of the Island of Newfoundland at the mouth of the St Lawrence River and the eastern half of the Ungava Peninsula, known as Labrador, which borders on the Canadian Province of Québec. The province stretches about 1700km north to south, and has about 17,000km of coastline, much of it rugged and heavily indented with bays and fjords. The interior of Newfoundland is a combination of forest, heath, lakes and rivers spread over a terrain that ranges from mountainous in the west to rolling hills in the centre and east. Labrador is also mountainous in the west, although its rivers are larger and wilder.
LANGUAGE: Although Canada is officially bilingual (English and French), 95% of this province speaks English as a first language.
TIME: Newfoundland: GMT - 3.5 (GMT - 2.5 in summer).
Labrador: GMT - 4 (GMT - 3 in summer).
Note: Daylight Saving Time officially lasts from the first Sunday in April to the last Sunday in October.
COMMUNICATIONS: Post: Post offices are open 0830-1700 Monday to Friday, 0900-1245 Saturday.

PUBLIC HOLIDAYS

Public holidays as for the rest of Canada (see general section above), with the following dates also observed:
Mar 15 '93 St Patrick's Day. **Apr 24** St George's Day. **May 24** Queen's Birthday. **Jun 21** Discovery Day. **Jul 1** Canada Day. **Sep 6** Labour Day.

TRAVEL

AIR: *Air Canada* (AC) and *Canadian Airlines International* provide services within Canada and to destinations outside the country. *Air Atlantic* and *Air Nova* operate services within the province and to the Maritime Provinces.
International airports: *Gander (YQX)* is 3km (2 miles) from the city centre. Airport facilities include car parking, restaurant, duty-free shop and banks.
St John's (YYT) is 15km (9 miles) from the city. The journey time is about 15 minutes. At present, this airport handles only a few international flights, but it is likely that it will become a full international airport in the near future. Other major airports are at Stephenville, Deer Lake, Happy Valley-Goose Bay, Wabush and Churchill Falls.
SEA: Year-round, daily passenger and automobile service between North Sydney, Nova Scotia and Port aux Basques on Newfoundland's southwest coast. Crossing time: 6 hours. Summer services twice a week between North Sydney and Argentia on Newfoundland Avalon Peninsula, mid-June to mid-September. Crossing time: 12 hours. There is also a summer ferry to the French islands of St Pierre and Miquelon from Fortune on Newfoundland's Burin Peninsula. Crossing time: 90 minutes. Intraprovincial ferries connect island communities with larger towns. Seasonal summer ferry connects southern Labrador and St Barbe on Newfoundland Great Northern Peninsula. Summer coastal boat service is provided by *Marine Atlantic* between Lewisporte on Newfoundland's northeast coast and Happy Valley-Goose Bay in Hamilton Sound, Labrador. Remote communities on the Labrador coast and Newfoundland's south coast are also served by coastal boats.
RAIL: The Québec North Shore and Labrador Railway operates a passenger service between Seven Islands in Québec and Labrador City in western Labrador.
ROAD: A modern paved highway (Route 1, the Trans-Canada Highway) crosses Newfoundland from Port aux Basques in the southwest to the capital of St John's in the east. Distance is 905km (563 miles). Paved secondary roads connect most communities to the main highway. *TerraTransport* operates a cross-island bus service along Route 1. Visitors can reach western Labrador along a partially paved highway from Baie Comeau, Québec. A seasonal gravel highway, dubbed the 'Freedom Road' by residents, connects Labrador City and Wabush with the interior town of Churchill Falls and Happy Valley-Goose Bay in east-central Labrador. There are no services along this latter stretch of road. **Coach:** Long-distance buses connect Port aux Basques, Corner Brook, Gander, St John's and Argentia.

ACCOMMODATION

HOTELS: There are almost 300 establishments in the province with a total of more than 5400 rooms. Most towns offer hotel or bed & breakfast accommodation, although the pre-eminence of the fishing industry means that many of the facilities are seasonal. Most of the settlements in the province are on the coast rather than the wild interior (where some cabins and lodges are, however, available). The *Hospitality Homes Scheme* offers accommodation with families in small coastal communities off the beaten track. As St John's is now an 'oil boom town', accommodation there can be hard to come by, and advance reservations are recommended. For information on hotels, contact Hospitality Newfoundland & Labrador, PO Box 13516, St John's, Newfoundland A1B 4B8. Tel: (709) 722 2000. Fax: (709) 722 8104. For information on bed & breakfast accommodation, contact the Tourism Division of the Department of Development, PO Box 8730, St John's, Newfoundland A1B 4K2. Tel: (709) 729 2830. Tel: (709) 729 5936. **Grading:** Accommodation is graded on a voluntary basis according to the *Atlantic Canada Accommodations Grading Program* as follows:
1-star: Basic, clean, comfortable accommodation.
2-star: Basic, clean, comfortable accommodation with extra amenities.
3-star: Better quality accommodation with a greater range of services.
4-star: High-quality accommodation with extended range of facilities, amenities and guest services.
5-star: Deluxe accommodation with the greatest range of facilities, amenities and guest services.
Note: A new Canadian Select Grading Program is due to start operating during 1993.
CAMPING: The wildness of the province offers superb camping facilities, both for motorhomes and tents. Both national parks (Gros Morne in western Newfoundland and Terra Nova in eastern) as well as more than 50 provincial and 25 private campgrounds provide camping services. Facilities on campsites are basic rather than luxurious, the emphasis being on seclusion and privacy. Full details can be obtained from the Department of Tourism and Culture (see address above).

RESORTS & EXCURSIONS

NEWFOUNDLAND ISLAND: Most of the island's activity and population is based on the Avalon Peninsula to the east. The peninsula is full of old settlements such as *Placentia* where the French once challenged the English for supremacy and *Trinity* which dates from the 16th century. St John's, the provincial capital, is a busy fishing port with a good natural harbour bounded by hills. *Signal Hill,* site of Marconi's first transatlantic radio transmission and Canada's second largest National Historic Park, offers a good overview of the town and harbour to the west. The *Newfoundland Museum* and *Quidi Vidi Battery* are both worth visiting. South of St John's the *Witless Bay Bird Sanctuary* can be toured by boat and the trout fishing is excellent. There are over 60 major seabird colonies along the coast of southern Newfoundland to mid-coast in Labrador. Over 300 species of birds have been identified. The main route off the peninsula leads north and then east through **Terra Nova National Park,** an area of scenic rugged coastline adjoining Bonavista Bay. Fishing trips to the remote and barely accessible interior can be arranged at **Gander** and **Grand Falls**. The **Burin Peninsula** in the south has some beautiful coastal villages. At **Fortune** a ferry runs to the French island of St Pierre. The **Long Range Mountains** dominate the western seaboard, along which runs a 715km (444-mile) coastal road affording good views of the fjords, mountains and beaches. **Corner Brook**, the island's second city, set in a deep inlet halfway up the coast, is an outfitting centre for expeditions to the many lakes and rivers of the interior, many of which are accessible only by air.
The **Great Northern Peninsula** is a wilderness area of outstanding scenic beauty. It is best seen from **Gros Morne National Park,** a blend of rugged mountains, deep fjords and bays on the Gulf of St Lawrence. Local fishing boats can be chartered here. At the northernmost tip of the peninsula at **L'Anse aux Meadows** (which, like Gros Morne, is a UNESCO World Heritage Site) lie the restored remains of the earliest European settlement in the New World, a group of six sod houses built by Norsemen around the year 1000AD.
LABRADOR is a wilderness of only 30,000 inhabitants may be reached by air or by ferry from **St Barbe** on Newfoundland Island; day trips along its coastline are also available from here. Longer trips to the mainland interior should be arranged through the many tour operators and outfitters. Labrador is desolate and, except in the few isolated towns, uninhabited. It can be bitterly cold in winter. Both downhill and cross-country skiing is possible near **Labrador City,** a mining town near the Québec border. **Goose Bay,** a US airbase settlement dating from the Second World War, is the main jumping-off point for hunting and fishing trips to the interior; it can only be reached by air or sea. The main sports fish are salmon, Arctic char, trout and northern pike. The oldest industrial complex in the New World is the 16th century Basque whaling station at **Red Bay** on the southern coast.

SOCIAL PROFILE

FOOD & DRINK: A hearty cuisine making full use of fat pork, molasses, salt fish, salt meat, boiled vegetables and soups. Fish is a staple food, predominantly cod made into stews, fish cakes, fried, salted, dried and fresh.

Salmon, trout, halibut and hake are also available. *Brewis* is a hard water biscuit that needs soaking in water to soften, then gently cooked; often salt or fresh cod is served with *scrunchions*, which are bits of fat pork, fried and crunchy. Another speciality is *damper dog* (a type of fried bread dough), *cod sound pie* (made from tough meat near the cod's backbone), *crubeens* (Irish pickled pigs' feet) and *fat back and molasses dip* (rich mixture of pork fat and molasses for dipping bread). Pies, jams, jellies and puddings are made from wild berries. **Drink:** The minimum drinking age is 19.
NIGHTLIFE: A St John's pub crawl is a real cultural experience, with a particularly strong Irish influence. *Water Street* and *Duckworth Street* offer fine restaurants and nightclubs. Newfoundland also has its own music, mostly Scottish and Irish, which can be found everywhere in local festivals, nightclubs, bars, taverns and concerts. *George Street* in St John's has become a club and restaurant zone and holds a variety of seasonal festivals. However, on the whole, night entertainment in many regions is scarce.
SHOPPING: *Water Street* in downtown St John's is a must for any shopper – it is the oldest shopping street in North America and European merchants, sailors and privateers have bartered here since 1500. Handicrafts, Grenfell parkas and Labradorite jewellery are the most well-known products of the Newfoundland and Labrador area. **Shopping hours:** 1000-1700 Monday to Wednesday, 1000-2200 Thursday to Friday and 1000-1800 Saturday. (Malls generally open 1000-2200 Monday to Saturday.)
SPORT: Skiing is popular at Newfoundland Island's Marble Mountain, 8km (5 miles) east of Corner Brook, the second city of the province. There are also resorts at Smokey Mountain near Labrador City on the mainland and White Hills at Clarenville and **cross-country skiing** at the Menihek Nordic Club in Labrador. **Canoeing, hiking** and **mountain climbing** are popular in the interior, and **sailing, windsurfing** and **scuba diving** are available on the coast. Salmon **fishing** takes place between May 24 and September 15. Fishing in licensed rivers in Newfoundland and in all waters in Labrador needs a qualified guide.
SPECIAL EVENTS: Feb 19-28 '93 *Corner Brook Winter Festival*. **Jul-Aug** *Stephenville Festival of the Arts*. **Jul 15-19** *Exploits Valley Salmon Festival*, Grand Falls. **Jul 22-25** *13th Annual Fish, Fun & Folk Festival*, Twillingate, New World Island. **Jul 23-Aug 1** *Humber Valley Strawberry Festival*, Deer Lake. **Jul 29-Aug 2** *Festival of Flight*, Gander. **Aug 4** *St John's Regatta*. **Aug 6-8** *17th Annual Newfoundland and Labrador Folk Festival*, St John's.

BUSINESS PROFILE

COMMERCIAL INFORMATION: The following organisations can offer advice:
Atlantic Provinces Chamber of Commerce, Suite 110, 236 St George Street, Moncton, New Brunswick E1C 1W1. Tel: (506) 857 2883. Fax: (506) 859 6131; *or*
Enterprise Newfoundland and Labrador Corporation, 136 Crosbie Road, St John's, Newfoundland A1B 3K3. Tel: (709) 729 7000. Fax: (709) 729 7135.
CONFERENCES/CONVENTIONS: For information on conferences and conventions in Newfoundland contact: Meetings and Conventions Co-ordinator, St John's Department of Tourism and Culture, PO Box 8700, St John's, Newfoundland A1B 4J6. Tel: (709) 729 2830. Fax: (709) 729 0057.

CLIMATE

Very cold winters and mild summers.
Required clothing: Light to mediumweights in warmer months, heavyweights in winter. Waterproofing advisable throughout the year.

ST JOHN'S Newfoundland (43m)

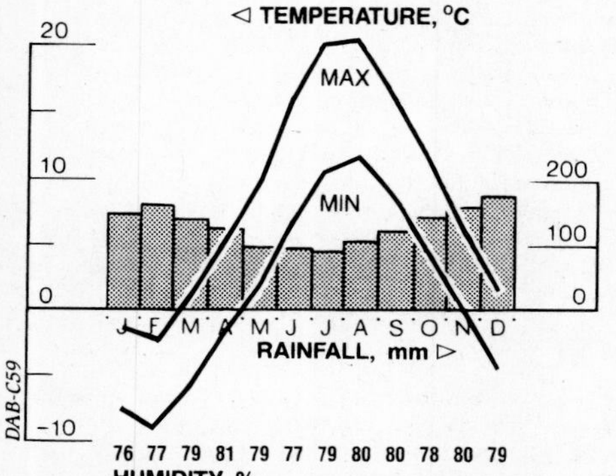

NORTHWEST TERRITORIES

Territory capital underlined

Location: Northern Canada.

TravelArctic
Department of Economic Development and Tourism
PO Box 1320
Yellowknife, Northwest Territories
X1A 2L9
Tel: (403) 873 7200. Fax: (403) 873 0294.

AREA: 3,293,020 sq km (1,271,436 sq miles).
POPULATION: 53,963 (1991 estimate).
POPULATION DENSITY: 0.02 per sq km.
CAPITAL: Yellowknife. **Population:** 13,568 (1990).
GEOGRAPHY: The Northwest Territories covers one-third of Canada, stretching from Ellesmere Island off Greenland's north coast to the Mackenzie Mountain Range at the Yukon border. It is a huge expanse of untouched wilderness, the landscape ranging from lush forests and great rivers to stark northern tundra and Arctic island glaciers. The land rises to over 2000m (7000ft) in the west, where Canada's longest river, the Mackenzie (1800km/1100 miles), is fed by two of the country's largest lakes, the Great Bear and the Great Slave. In the east, towards the northeastern shores of Baffin Bay, there is fjord country.
LANGUAGE: Although Canada is officially bilingual (English and French), English is more commonly spoken in the Northwest Territories.
TIME: East of W 68°: GMT - 4 (GMT - 3 in summer).
W 68° to W 85°: GMT - 5 (GMT - 4 in summer).
W 85° to W 102°: GMT - 6 (GMT - 5 in summer).
West of W 102°: GMT - 7 (GMT - 6 in summer).
Note: Daylight Saving Time officially lasts from the first Sunday in April to the last Sunday in October.

PUBLIC HOLIDAYS

Public holidays are as for the rest of Canada (see general section above) with the following date also observed:
Aug 2 '93 Civic Holiday.

TRAVEL

AIR: The best way to reach the more remote areas within the Territory is by air. Float planes are commonly used to reach the northern lakes. The largest operators into the region are *Canadian Airlines International* and *First Air*. Other operators providing flights into the Northwest Territories include *Air Inuit, Alkan Air Ltd, Calm Air International Ltd,* Delta *Air Charter Ltd* and *NWT Air*.
Scheduled services to connections within the Northwest Territories are run by *Air Providence Ltd, Air Sahtu Ltd, Aklak Air, Buffalo Airways (1986) Ltd, Kenn Borek Air, Northwestern Air Lease Ltd, North-Wright Air Ltd, Ptarmigan Airways Ltd* and *Simpson Air (1981) Ltd.*
International airports: *Yellowknife Airport (YZF)* is less than a kilometre from the town centre (travel time – 10 minutes).
SEA/LAKES: The Mackenzie River is crossed at Fort Providence and at Arctic Red River. The Liard River is crossed at Fort Simpson. Cruises are available from Fort Simpson to the Virginia Falls, as well as cruises on the Great Slave during the summer, with an approximate cost of Can$1000 per person per week. Other local ferries are operated by the provincial government.
ROAD: The major routes are along the Dempster Highway from the Yukon to the Mackenzie Delta, and the Mackenzie Highway from Alberta to the Great Slave Lake region. There are four bus companies that serve the region: *Dempster Highway Bus Service* (tel: (403) 979 4100), *Frontier Coachlines* (tel: (403) 873 4892), *Greyhound Lines of Canada Ltd* (tel: (403) 421 4211) and *North of 60 Bus Lines – Division of Bizzee Bee Enterprises Ltd* (tel: (403) 874 6411 *or* 394 5421).

ACCOMMODATION

HOTELS: Although most of the towns have hotels and bed & breakfast establishments open all year, accommodation can be scarce and often quite basic. Bear in mind the vast area of the region and the long distances between settlements of any size, especially in the Arctic zone. 'Lodges' designed for outdoor activity holidays can be found in many settlements. For details contact the local authorities. TravelArctic publishes an annual travel trade manual detailing accommodation in the region.
CAMPING/CARAVANNING: Camping is only advised in summer as the winter temperatures drop below safety levels. Campsites are run by both government and private organisations. Also 'outposts' (semi-permanent camps) offer tented shelters with beds and meals, often combined with organised trips. A number of companies can arrange **motor camper** rentals, with a range of fully equipped vehicles. Full details can be obtained from TravelArctic.

RESORTS & EXCURSIONS

Most of the province's population and commercial activity is based in Yellowknife and around the Great Slave Lake. In the northern expanse, there are only small settlements of Inuit (Eskimos), living by age-old methods of fishing, hunting and trapping. Inuit peoples and Indians comprise 66% of the Territories' population.
Yellowknife is a busy town perched on the pre-cambrian shield which adjoins the Great Slave Lake. The town's main industries are government/service industries and, to a certain extent, mining. Two major gold finds were made here in the 1930s. Boats and canoes can be hired for trips on the **Mackenzie River** and the **Great Slave** and **Great Bear Lakes.** These tours often follow old trapping and fur-trading routes. An experienced guide is often essential.
Near the capital are the lakeside Dene and Dogrib (Indian) tribal settlements of **Detah, Rae Edzo** and **Snare Lakes,** where a largely traditional way of life is still maintained. **Wood Buffalo National Park,** south of the Great Slave Lake, is home to the world's largest free-roaming bison herd and a noted centre for naturalists and birdwatchers. Two highways serve the Big River Country to the west and visitors may view this area from the road or fly deep into the interior. In the far southwestern corner of this territory lies **Nahanni National Park,** a UNESCO World Heritage Site in the Mackenzie Mountains. Access to the park itself is by air from **Fort Simpson, Fort Liard** or **Watson Lake** as there are no roads in the wilderness area. **South Nahanni River** offers excellent white-water canoeing. Several operators offer boat and raft tours on the river taking in the magnificent 100m (312ft) high **Virginia Falls** (twice the height of Niagara).
The Arctic coastline and islands of the territory have a spectacular landscape of tundra, glaciated mountains and deep fjords. **Baffin Island** has some of the best of the area's rugged beauty; it is most accessible in **Auyuittuq National Park,** a haven for experienced hikers, skiers and climbers with its frozen peaks and glaciers. Much of this rough and forbidding terrain is best visited as part of a package tour or in the company of an outfitter.
From **Frobisher,** trips across the tundra with the native Inuit and overnight accommodation in an igloo can be arranged. **Inuvik,** in the far northwest, sits on the majestic **Mackenzie River Delta** and is accessible by road from Dawson in the Yukon. Cruises on the Delta and Inuit settlements such as **Aklavik** are the main attractions.

SOCIAL PROFILE

FOOD & DRINK: Arctic grayling, char and caribou are specialities. Local *bannick* (a mixture of flour and water mixed with dough when required) dates from the old prospecting rations which kept for weeks in an easily transportable form. Other unusual specialities include *mutuk* (whale fat dipped in whale oil). **Drink:** Most alcohol is imported and supplies vary from town to town. Hotels and restaurants in main towns normally have a good selection, including Canadian whiskies.
SHOPPING: There are over 40 co-operatives in the Territories specialising in handicrafts, furs, fisheries, print shops and retailing. Indian handicrafts and footwear are made locally for sale. The often higher cost of goods (an increase of up to 20% on the rest of Canada) is due to the supply and distribution charges caused by the large distances involved.
SPORT: Fishing on the thousands of clear, unpolluted lakes is the most popular sport. Chief catches are trout, great northern pike and grayling. Numerous outfitters offer inclusive packages often combining boat and air travel to remote regions. **Hunting** for caribou, musk ox and polar bear is available. The many lakes and rivers offer excellent **canoeing** and **rafting.**
SPECIAL EVENTS: Mar 26-28 '93 *Caribou Carnival*, Yellowknife. **Apr 18-24** *Toonik Time*, Iqaluit. **Jun 5-6** *Mixed Slo Pitch Tournament*, Fort Simpson. **Jun 14-19** *NWT Mining Week*, Yellowknife. **Jun 18** *Raven Mad Daze* (summer solstice celebration), Yellowknife. **Jun 18-20** *Kingalik Jamboree* (traditional Inuit games, talent show and live entertainment), Holman. **Jun 18-19** *Midnight Sun Golf Tournament*, Yellowknife. **Jun 19** *Midnight Madness* (summer solstice festival), Inuvik. **Jun 19-21** *Annual Mixed Slo Pitch Tournament*, Hay River. **Jun 21-Jul 1** *Yellowknife Cultural Fair*. **Jun 29-Jul 1** *Kingland Golf Tournament*, Hay River. **Jul 9-12** *8th Annual Midway Lake Music Festival*, Fort MacPherson. **Jul 16-25** *Fifth Annual Great Northern Arts Festival*, Inuvik. **Jul 17-18** *Folk on the Rocks Music Festival*, Yellowknife. **Jul 24-25** *Music Festival*, Inuvik. **Jul 30-Aug 2** *Kelly King 250 Boat Races*, Hay River. **Jul 31-Aug 2** *NWT Merchants Open Golf Tournament*, Fort Smith. **Aug 6-8** *Billy Joss Open Golf Tournament*, Holman. **Aug 23** *Yellowknife Fall Fair*. **Sep 5** *Slave River Journal Triathlon*, Forth Smith. **Oct 8-11** *Delta Days*, Inuvik.

CLIMATE

The region experiences a diverse climate. The north has Arctic and sub-Arctic winters whereas the south is more temperate with mild summers and cold winters.

YELLOWKNIFE NW Territories (215m)

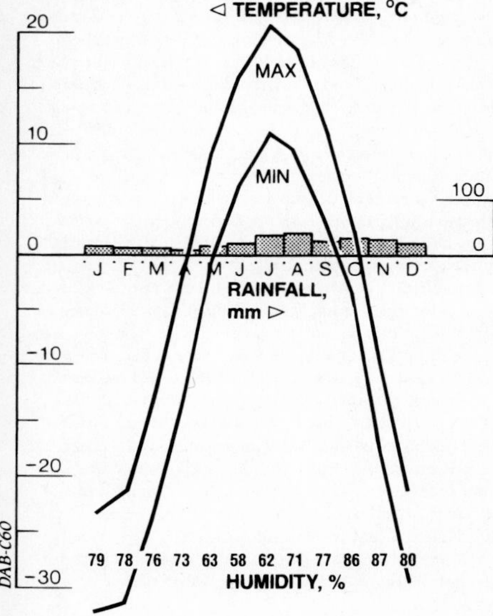

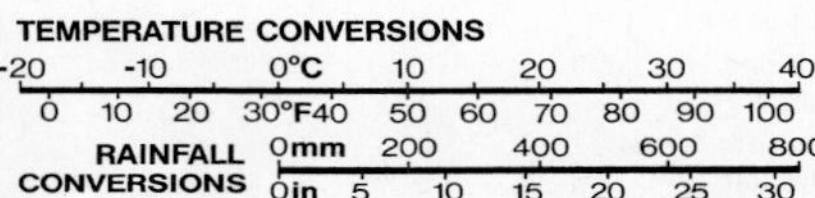

NOVA SCOTIA

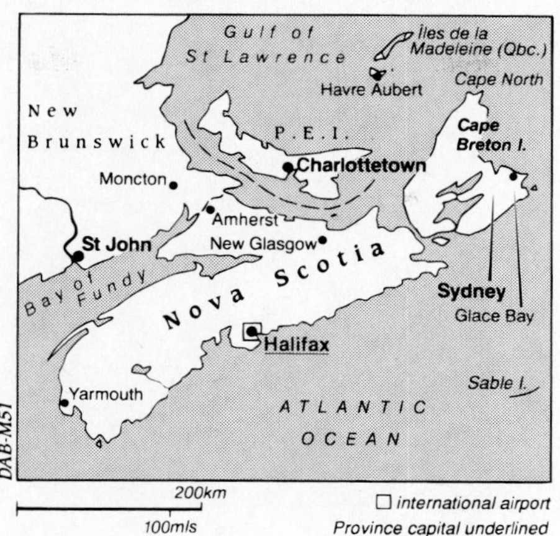

Location: East coast of Canada.

Nova Scotia Tourism and Culture
PO Box 456
Halifax, Nova Scotia
B3J 2R5
Tel: (902) 424 5000. Fax: (902) 424 2668.
The Province of Nova Scotia Trade & Investment Office
Crusader House
14 Pall Mall
London SW1Y 5LU
Tel: (071) 930 6864. Fax: (071) 925 2692. Opening hours: 0900-1700 Monday to Friday.
Consulate General of the United States of America
Suite 910
Cogswell Tower
Scotia Square
Halifax, Nova Scotia
B3J 3K1
Tel: (902) 429 2480. Fax: (902) 423 6861.

AREA: 52,840 sq km (20,402 sq miles).
POPULATION: 885,600 (1989).
POPULATION DENSITY: 16.8 per sq km.
CAPITAL: Halifax. **Population:** 306,300 (1989).
GEOGRAPHY: Nova Scotia comprises the peninsula of Nova Scotia, connected to the mainland by a narrow isthmus, and Cape Breton Island in the northern part of the province, linked by a mile-long causeway. The Atlantic batters the eastern shore. The Bay of Fundy separates the southern part of the peninsula from the mainland, with the Gulf of St Lawrence to the north. The northeast is rural and rocky, while the south and southwest are lush and fertile. Much of the province is covered by rivers. The land rises to 540m (1770ft) on the northeast islands.
LANGUAGE: Although Canada is officially bilingual (English and French), English is more commonly spoken in Nova Scotia.
TIME: GMT - 4 (GMT - 3 in summer).
Note: Daylight Saving Time officially lasts from the first Sunday in April to the last Sunday in October.

PUBLIC HOLIDAYS

Public holidays as for the rest of Canada; see general introduction above.

TRAVEL

AIR: *Air Canada (AC)*, *Canadian Airlines International (CP)* and *Air Atlantic* fly to Halifax from Ottawa, Montréal and Toronto. *Air Atlantic* also offer local flights between Halifax and Sydney.
International airport: *Halifax (YHZ)*, 41.6km (26 miles) from the city. Airport facilities include a duty-free shop, car hire, banks and a restaurant.
SEA: There are regular sailings to Nova Scotia from Portland, Maine (USA), New Brunswick, Prince Edward Island and Newfoundland. Several ferries and shipping lines offer local services in and around the province. Enquire locally for further details.
RAIL: *Via Rail* trains run from Montréal to Halifax *(Ocean)* and from Halifax to Montréal *(Atlantic)* via Saint John three times a week with bus connections to Sydney and Yarmouth.
ROAD: The Trans-Canada Highway enters the province from New Brunswick and ends at North Sydney on the northeast coast. Smaller provincial highways branch off it and circumnavigate the coastline. Ferry services or causeways connect most islands with the mainland. **Car hire:** There are agencies at Halifax and Sydney airports and throughout the province.
URBAN: Comprehensive bus services are provided in the Halifax-Dartmouth area by *Metro Transit,* which operates a zonal fare system. There are connections with the harbour ferry on both sides.

ACCOMMODATION

HOTELS: Nova Scotia offers a wide range of hotels, motels, tourist homes (guest-houses), lodges and campsites. Advance reservations are recommended, especially during the summer. Many establishments are inspected or licensed by the Department of Tourism. Farmhouse holidays are possible and many Nova Scotians provide 'bed and breakfast' for visitors in the tourist season. There are two organisations which can help with bed & breakfast accommodation in Nova Scotia: Halifax Metro Bed & Breakfast, PO Box 1613, Station M, Halifax, Nova Scotia B3J 2Y3. Tel: (902) 374 3546; *or* Cape Breton Bed & Breakfast, PO Box 1750, Sydney, Nova Scotia B1P 6T7. Tel: (902) 562 6300.
Grading: Accommodation is graded on a voluntary basis according to the *Atlantic Canada Accommodations Grading Program* as follows:
1-star: Basic, clean, comfortable accommodation.
2-star: Basic, clean, comfortable accommodation with extra amenities.
3-star: Better quality accommodation with a greater range of services.
4-star: High-quality accommodation with extended range of facilities, amenities and guest services.
5-star: Deluxe accommodation with the greatest range of facilities, amenities and guest services.
For more information about accommodation in the province contact the Tourism Industry Association of Nova Scotia, World Trade and Convention Centre, Suite 5131800 Argyle Street, Halifax, Nova Scotia B3J 3N8.
CAMPING/CARAVANNING: Much of Nova Scotia is luxurious parkland, and one of the best ways to see the province is by hiring a motorhome or camper; a number of companies can arrange rentals, with a range of fully equipped vehicles. Full details can be obtained from the Nova Scotia Tourism and Culture which also publishes a comprehensive guide to accommodation in Nova Scotia.

RESORTS & EXCURSIONS

HALIFAX: The provincial capital is also the commercial, administrative and maritime centre for the whole of Atlantic Canada. Situated at the mouth of the *Bedford Basin*, it is one of the finest natural harbours in the world and has a long and distinguished history as a naval and military base. Harbour tours, deep-sea fishing charters and voyages aboard the schooner *Bluenose II* are available. Despite the town's boom over the past 15 years, the historic 'Waterfront Area', comprising important 18th- and 19th-century buildings, has been kept intact. Excellent shopping, nightlife and restaurants are to be found in both the old and new sections of the town. Worth seeing are: the *Province House*, a Georgian building praised by Dickens in 1842; *St Pauls*, the oldest Protestant church in Canada; the *Nova Scotia Museum;* the *Maritime Museum of the Atlantic*; and *York Redoubt*, a 200-year-old fort overlooking the harbour. Halifax itself is dominated by the *Citadel*, a star-shaped granite fort, which has defended the city since 1749. A good view of the city and bay can be had from its ramparts.
ELSEWHERE: Dartmouth, across the mouth of the harbour from Halifax, is a modern industrial town. West of Halifax, a coastal road skirts around the fishing villages set in the deep bays and inlets of the southern shore. En route to the ferry port of **Yarmouth** are: **Peggy's Cove**, known for its rugged and beautiful coastal scenery and Canada's most photographed lighthouse; **Mahone Bay**; and **Lunenberg**, a German settlement with a maritime museum housed in two ships. North of **Liverpool** on this route is **Kejumjukic National Park** which offers wilderness trails, canoeing and winter sports. After Yarmouth the coastal road runs northeast by French-speaking Acadian villages such as **Metaghan** and **Church Point,** which are dotted along the Bay of Fundy. Nearby, **Port Royal** and **Fort Anne** are the sites of some of the earliest French settlements in Canada. **Grand Pré National Park** commemorates the expulsion of 2000 Acadians from Nova Scotia in 1755.

From **Amherst**, the gateway town to the province, a coastal road on the north shore leads to Cape Breton Island (see below) across a mile-long causeway. The north shore displays strong Scottish influences. Street signs in **Pugwash** are in English and Gaelic and highland games are held annually in **Antigonish**.
Cape Breton Island attracts many fishermen and bird-watchers. Some of the island's most spectacular scenery can be found at the **Cape Breton Highlands National Park.** There is superb inland sailing at **Lake Bras D'Or. Sydney**, a centre of shipping and industry, is the island's main town. Southeast of this is the **Fortress of Louisburgh,** a restored fort and chateau; once the headquarters of the French Fleet in North America, it was demolished by General Wolfe in 1760.

SOCIAL PROFILE

FOOD & DRINK: Seafood features strongly on most menus; popular local dishes include scallops, fried, baked or grilled and usually served with tartar sauce. Fish and clam chowders and *soloman grundy* (a herring dish) are also popular. *Lunenberg sausage* exemplifies the German influence, as do *hugger in buff, fish and scrunchions, Dutch mess* and *house bunkin*, all names for tasty combinations of fish and potatoes covered in cream sauce with onions and salt pork. Desserts make use of plentiful fruit and berries and include a stewed fruit and dumplings dish called *slump* or *fungy*, and baked apple dumplings wrapped in pastry and served with cream, sugar or lemon sauce. **Drink:** Beer and alcoholic beverages are sold by the glass in licensed restaurants (food must also be ordered) and in licensed lounges (opening hours generally 1100-1400). Beer by the bottle and draught beer are sold by the glass in taverns and beverage rooms (opening hours generally 1000-2400), which often offer surprisingly good snacks and light meals. The minimum drinking age is 19.
NIGHTLIFE: Nightclubs are mostly centred on Halifax. Scottish bagpipe music and Gaelic songs can be heard all over the territory in concerts, bars, hotels and restaurants. Professional and amateur theatre is very popular; details of forthcoming attractions are available from Departments of Tourism and Culture.
SPORT: Summer recreations include **golf, harness racing, tennis, horseriding** and **walking** tours of the acres of parkland covering the province. **Skiing** is available in winter near Halifax. Nova Scotia's boundaries enclose more than 2500 sq km (1000 sq miles) of salt and fresh water, and **watersports** predominate. **Sailing, swimming** and deep-sea **fishing** are all popular.
SPECIAL EVENTS: End May-Early Jun '93 *Apple Blossom Festival*, Kentville. **Jun-Aug** *Nova Scotia International Tattoo*, Halifax. **Mid-Jul** *Craft Festival*, Lunenburg. **Early Aug** *Halifax International Buckersfest*, Halifax. **Aug** *Rock-Hound Round-Up*, Parrshoro.

BUSINESS PROFILE

COMMERCIAL INFORMATION: The following organisation can offer advice: Atlantic Provinces Chamber of Commerce, 236 St George Street, Moncton, New Brunswick E1C 1W1. Tel: (506) 857 2883. Fax: (506) 859 6131.
CONFERENCES/CONVENTIONS: Nova Scotia has a wide range of conference and convention venues. The **Halifax Metro Centre** arena in downtown Halifax has facilities for 10,000 people. Connected to this is the **World Trade and Convention Centre,** a striking landmark building made of brick and glass with a sumptuous interior. It has three convention floors, all with excellent catering and audio-visual facilities, and enough room for 2600 people at a stand-up reception or 1700 for a banquet. Certain hotels, such as **Chateau Halifax** and the **Halifax Hilton** in Halifax and the **Holiday Inn** in Dartmouth, also offer good meeting facilities. Also in Dartmouth is another excellent large group facility, the **Dartmouth Sportsplex** arena. The city of Sydney offers **Centre 200,** an arena and convention complex built in celebration of Sydney's bicentennial in 1985, with various flexible meeting rooms for trade shows, receptions and banquets for up to 800. There are also some meeting facilities in more rural settings: **The Pines** resort, overlooking the Annapolis Basin and the Bay of Fundy; **Tales and Trails** lodge, placed along the scenic Fleur-de-Lis Trail; **Keltic Lodge,** overlooking Cape Smoky and the Atlantic Ocean; **Liscombe Lodge,** tucked into the evergreens where the Liscomb River meets the sea; and **Lansdowne Lodge,** east of Truro along the Glooscap Trail and near the beautiful Upper Stewiacke Valley. For more information contact the Nova Scotia Department of Tourism and Culture.

CLIMATE

Very cold winters and mild summers.
Required clothing: Light to mediumweights in summer months. Heavyweights in winter. Waterproofing is advisable all year.

HALIFAX Nova Scotia (8m)

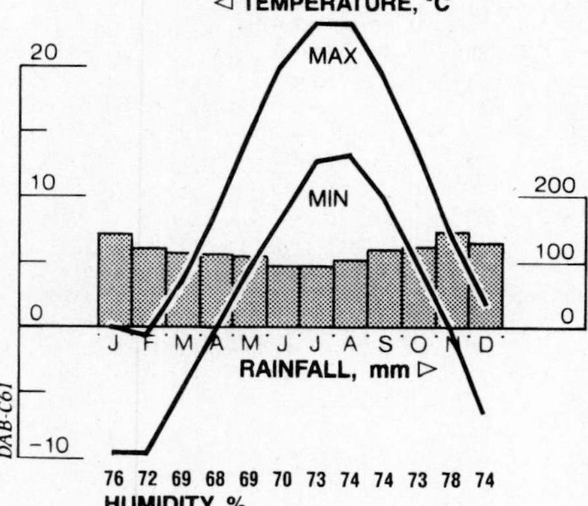

ONTARIO

Location: Eastern central Canada.

Ontario Ministry of Tourism and Recreation
77 Bloor Street W
Queen's Park
Toronto, Ontario M7A 2E5
Tel: (416) 314 0944 (English) *or* 314 0956 (French). Fax: (416) 314 7574.
Ontario Government Office *and* **Ontario Tourism**
21 Knightsbridge
London SW1X 7LY
Tel: (071) 245 1222. Fax: (071) 259 6661. Opening hours: 0900-1700 Monday to Friday.
British Consulate General
Suite 1910, College Park
777 Bay Street
Toronto, Ontario M5G 2G2
Tel: (416) 593 1290. Fax: (416) 593 1229. Telex: 06524486 BRITAIN TOR.
Consulate General of the United States of America
PO Box 135
360 University Avenue
Toronto, Ontario M5G 1S4
Tel: (416) 595 1700. Fax: (416) 595 0051.

AREA: 1,068,582 sq km (412,582 sq miles)
POPULATION: 10,097,774 (1991).
POPULATION DENSITY: 9.4 per sq km.
CAPITAL: Toronto (provincial). **Population:** 3,893,046 (1991).
Ottawa (federal). **Population:** 920,857.
GEOGRAPHY: Ontario is an eastern-central province bordered by Manitoba and Québec, with a northern coastline on the James Bay and Hudson Bay; it also shares the shores of the Great Lakes with the USA. The two main populated areas, around Toronto and Ottawa, are in the southern spur, and the north remains a landscape of forests and lakes. The province contains the Niagara Falls, one of the most spectacular sights in the world.
LANGUAGE: Although Canada is officially bilingual (English and French), English is more commonly spoken in Ontario.
TIME: East of W 90°: GMT - 5 (GMT - 4 in summer). **West of W 90°:** GMT - 6 (GMT - 5 in summer).
Note: Summer officially lasts from the first Sunday in April to the last Sunday in October.

PUBLIC HOLIDAYS

Public Holidays as for the rest of Canada (see general section above), with the following date also observed: **Aug 2 '93** Civic Holiday.

TRAVEL

AIR: Local air services are operated by a number of operators, including *Norontair, Bearskin Lake Air Services, Air Ontario* and *Canadian Partner*, as well as by *Air Canada* and *Canadian Airlines International*. These connect all the large towns. For rates and routes contact local offices.
International airports: *Ottawa (YOW)* (Uplands) is 13km (8 miles) southwest of the city (travel time – 25 minutes).
Toronto (YYZ) (Lester B Pearson) is 35km (22 miles) northwest of the city (travel time – 40 minutes).
SEA: The only port on the James Bay with rail links to the south is Moosonee, which is also the base for a limited local air service. The principal ports receiving sailings from the USA are Windsor (to Detroit/Lake St Clair); Sarnia (to Port Huron/St Clair River); Leamington (to Sandusky/Lake Eire); Kingston, Brockville, Cornwall and Ogdensburg (to USA across the St Lawrence Seaway); and Wolfe Island to New York.
The principal ferry operators in the province are *Toronto Islands Ferries, Pelee Island Transportation Services, Owen Sound Transportation Company* and *Ontario Ministry of Transportation* and local river authorities. For timetables and rates contact local offices.
RAIL: Links to the USA are with *Via Rail* and *Amtrak*. Services run from Toronto to New York via Niagara Falls, and to Chicago via Windsor and Sarnia. *Via Rail* also serves all the major cities of the province, concentrating in the southern region, which holds most of the population. *Ontario Northland Rail* run services from Toronto via North Bay to Moosonee on the James Bay. For details contact local offices.
ROAD: There are several bridges connecting Canadian and USA territories, notably at Cornwall, Fort Erie, Sarnia, Windsor, Sault Ste Marie, Fort Frances, Rainy River and Niagara Falls. A tunnel also connects Windsor to Detroit. The domestic highway network is excellent around the Great Lakes, but does not extend to the north of the province. Good trunk roads run throughout. See also under *Camping/Caravanning*. **Bus:** Services linking most towns are operated by *Greyhound Lines, Gray Coach Lines, Canada Coach Lines, Voyageur Colonial, Canada Coach, Ontario Northland, Chatham Coach* and *Go-Transit*. **Car hire:** Facilities are available from all hotels, at *Ottawa* and *Toronto Airports*, and at main railway stations. Drivers must be over 21 years old and the wearing of seatbelts is strictly enforced.
URBAN: Bus, trolleybus, metro and tramway services are provided by the *Toronto Transit Commission*. Flat fares are charged and there are free transfers. Pre-purchase tokens and multi-tickets may be obtained. Services are integrated with those of the regional *Go-Transit* bus and rail system. Bus services in Ottawa, Carleton and surrounding areas are provided by *OC Transpo*. A flat fare operates with a premium on express routes. There are free transfers, and pre-purchase multi-journey tickets and passes are sold. A 1-day pass (cost: C$5) is available for use on all forms of transport within the Toronto Metropolitan area.
JOURNEY TIMES: The following chart gives approximate journey times from Toronto (in hours and minutes) to other major cities/towns and tourist destinations in the surrounding area.

	Air	Road	Rail
Niagara Falls	-	1.45	2.00
Ottawa	1.00	5.00	4.00
Windsor	1.10	5.00	4.30
London	0.40	2.30	2.15
Sudbury	1.05	6.00	8.00
Sault Ste Marie	1.25	10.00	-
Thunder Bay	1.45	20.00	-

ACCOMMODATION

Most of the accommodation is in the southern spur of the province where the majority of the population is located. **HOTELS:** Hotel costs vary according to class. Both Ottawa and Toronto have international standard hotels. For further information, contact Ontario Hotel & Motel Association, Suite 102, 6725 Airport Road, Mississauga, Ontario L4V 1V2. Tel: (416) 672 9141. Fax: (416) 672 9225.

Grading: Accommodation is graded on an entirely voluntary basis by Ontario Tourism, a private non-profit-making federation of food service, accommodation, recreation and travel associations and businesses. There are over 1000 participating members. For further information, contact Ontario Tourism, Suite 420, 49 The Donway West, Don Mills, Ontario M3C 3M9. Tel: (416) 391 3558. Fax: (416) 391 0773. (There are also several other associations of a less general nature.)

Ontario Tourism grades hotels in Ontario according to a five star system as follows:

1-star: Provides basic furnishings and very limited or no facilities, amenities and guest services.

2-star: Provides more furnishings and some facilities, amenities and guest services.

3-star: Provides better quality furnishings and a more extensive range of facilities, amenities and guest services.

4-star: Provides superior quality furnishings and a complete range of facilities, amenities and guest services.

5-star: Provides deluxe accommodation. Marked superiority in extent and quality of facilities, amenities and guest services.

Just over 75% of participating hotels are in the 3- or 4-star category.

BED & BREAKFAST: There are a number of organisations which can help with bed & breakfast accommodation, including the Federation of Ontario Bed & Breakfast Association, 72 Lowther Avenue, Toronto, Ontario M5R 1C8. Tel: (416) 964 2566; *or* Niagara Region Bed & Breakfast Service, 2631 Dorchester Road, Niagara Falls, Ontario L2J 2Y9. Tel: (416) 358 8988.

SELF-CATERING: Furnished cottages are available throughout the region.

CAMPING/CARAVANNING: The best way to explore the wilderness of the north with its lakes and forestry is to hire a **motorhome** or **camper**. A number of companies can arrange rentals of fully equipped vehicles. Full details can be obtained from Ontario Tourism.

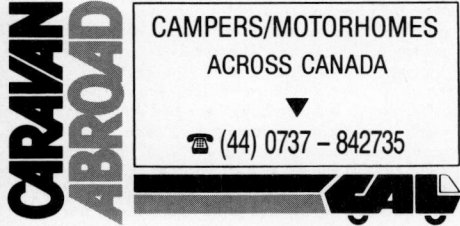

RESORTS & EXCURSIONS

OTTAWA: The federal capital is situated on the south bank of the Ottawa River facing the French-speaking city of Hull in Québec. The imposing Gothic-style *Parliament Buildings* overlook the confluence of the Ottawa, Rideau and Gatineau Rivers and are surmounted by the 92m (302ft) *Peace Tower*, affording a panoramic view of the city and its surroundings. Guided tours are available. The colourful *Changing of the Guard* ceremony takes place here daily in July and August. *Confederation Square*, site of the *National War Memorial*, is the focal point of downtown Ottawa. The *National Arts Centre*, a hexagonal complex on the banks of the Rideau Canal, houses an opera company, theatres, studios and restaurants. The *Rideau Canal* and the *Rideau-Trent-Severn Waterway* are part of a complex of recreational lakes and canals linking Ottawa to Lake Ontario and Georgian Bay. Outstanding among the city's many museums are: the *National Art Gallery*, the *National Museum of Science and Technology* and the *Museum of Civilisation*.

Gatineau Park, an 88,000-acre wilderness area, is only a 15-minute drive north of Parliament Hill. Southeast of the city, **Upper Canada Village** is a reconstructed 19th-century town consisting of historic buildings salvaged from threatened sites on the St Lawrence Seaway.

TORONTO: The provincial capital is Canada's largest city. Its accelerated growth in recent years, with a huge influx of immigrants, has resulted in one of the most vibrant and cosmopolitan cities on the continent. The city is laid out on a rectangular grid broken only by the **Rivers Don** and **Humber,** the banks of which provide a host of recreational amenities. The *CN Tower*, the world's tallest free-standing structure, has glass-fronted elevators rising 553m (1815ft) to indoor and outdoor observation decks which afford a 120km (75-mile) panorama on a clear day. The twin gold towers of the *Royal Plaza* make it the most eye-catching of the many avant-garde commercial buildings in the city. Toronto's latest attraction, *SkyDome*, at the foot of the CN Tower, is a multi-purpose entertainment complex and sports' stadium – the world's first to have a retractable roof. It is home to Toronto Blue Jays baseball team and the Argonauts football team, as well as hosting a multitude of events including rock concerts, opera, exhibitions, cricket, wrestling and motorshows. Together with modern developments the city has seen the renovation of old neighbourhoods, particularly the tree-lined streets of Victorian houses characteristic of the city. In the eastern suburbs the spectacular *Ontario Science Centre* and the *Metro Toronto Zoo* are both worth seeing. The *Art Gallery of Ontario*, the *Royal Ontario Museum* and *Casa Loma*, a fairytale castle to the north of the city, are also noteworthy. Ferries to the *Toronto Islands* depart from *Harbourfront*, one of a group of recreational, shopping and arts complexes, including the artificial island of *Ontario Place*. *Canada's Wonderland* is a huge theme park to the northwest of the city.

Nearby **Niagara Falls** provide a spectacular day's outing from Toronto. **Yonge Street,** reputedly the world's longest street, links Toronto with the vast wilderness of the north and west of the province.

ELSEWHERE: The north shore of Lake Erie is dotted with resorts and good beaches; **St Thomas** and **Port Stanley** are particularly popular. North of this, between Lakes Erie, Ontario and Huron, are **London** and **Stratford,** home of Canada's annual Shakespeare festival. **Windsor,** a beautifully appointed city at the conjunction of Lakes Erie and St Clair, is at the heart of Canada's English culture.

Further north, **Midland** commands a spectacular view of the **Georgian Bay Lake District.**

At the eastern end of Lake Superior, **Sault Ste Marie** straddles the US border and is an important commercial centre. It is also a good jumping-off point for trips to the northern and western wildernesses. A railway (Algoma) and the Trans-Canada Highway head westwards around the north shore of Lake Superior. The principal attraction here is the **Lake Superior Provincial Park,** a region with many beautiful ravines, lakes and waterfalls but chiefly famed for the *Agawa Rock Pictographs*. Nearby is the hunting and fishing resort of **White River.**

The Highway continues to **Thunder Bay,** the western terminus of the St Lawrence Seaway and a noted ski resort, boasting the world's largest ski jump. Fantastic canyons and rock formations can be seen between Thunder Bay and **Lake Nipigon**; the lake itself and the town of the same name are popular resorts in the heart of historic Indian country.

The far north and west of the province is a largely uninhabited wilderness of lakes, swamps and forests. The main trans-Canadian railway crosses Ontario at about N 50°; north of that, there are very few roads and only one railway line, which follows the Moose River to Moose Factory, one of several small settlements on the shores of James and Hudson Bays.

SOCIAL PROFILE

FOOD & DRINK: Chinese, English, French, Greek, Indian, Italian, Israeli, Scandinavian, Spanish and Latin American restaurants and US-style steak houses can all be found in Toronto and Ottawa at varying prices. Toronto is rated as one of the best cities for dining out on the continent. **Drink:** Bars and restaurants offer an international selection of alcohol. Ontario has extensive vineyards providing much of Canada's wine. Each autumn, the *Niagara Grape and Wine Festival* is held. The minimum drinking age is 19. Alcohol is sold in Provincial Liquor Control Board outlets. Domestic beer is available at Brewer's Retail. Domestic wines are sold through company stores. Licensing hours are from 1200-0100. On Sunday drink is served only with meals.

NIGHTLIFE: Both main cities have establishments offering all forms of entertainment, from quiet clubs featuring a lone pianist, through Latin American combos to dance and rock bands and big-name international entertainers. Toronto is also a good jazz and blues town. Theatres with classical entertainment are found in both Ottawa and Toronto and cabaret/dinner theatres are especially popular in Toronto.

SHOPPING: Toronto offers everything from antiques to mink-lined lingerie, if the visitor has the money and time to spend. There are large suburban shopping centres and the *Eaton Centre*, a glass-domed galleria in the heart of the city, is linked to three miles of interconnecting underground shopping with 1000 retail outlets. Toronto's villages are full of colourful streets of renovated Victoriana, with garment shops, art galleries, antique stores and open-air cafés in summer. Yorkville has bath boutiques, expensive toy shops and secondhand and new women's clothes shops. The run-down Queen Street Strip has been taken over by collector's comic book shops, punk day-glo leather emporiums, sci-fi bookstores, junk and antique shops. Ottawa also has a wide choice of shops and handicraft centres.

SPORT: Ottawa and Toronto both have **baseball** and **football** league games for the spectator. Both Toronto and Ottawa have professional NHL **ice hockey** teams. Toronto offers **horseracing** at Greenwood and Woodbine racetracks, **golf** courses, **tennis** courts, **swimming** in pools and in Lake Ontario, **boating,** and cross-country **skiing, riding, cycling** routes and **fishing**. Ottawa offers **boating, cycling,** winter downhill and cross-country **skiing, golf** courses, **tennis** courts and two racetracks.

SPECIAL EVENTS: Mar-Apr '93 *Festival of the Maples*, Lanark County. **Apr-Nov** *Shaw Festival*, Niagara-on-the-Lake. **Apr 3** *Elmira Maple Syrup Festival*. **May to early Sep** *Ontario Place*, Toronto (an entertainment complex on the water featuring music, dance and comedy performances and children's playground and rides). **May to mid-Nov** *Stratford Festival*. **May to early Oct** *Canada's Wonderland Theme Park*, Maple. **May 7-8** *Niagara Blossom Festival Parade*, Niagra Falls. **May 20-24** *Canadian Tulip Festival*, Ottawa. **Jun 5-6** *Molson Canadian London International Air Show*, London. **Jun to mid-Sep** *Blyth Festival* (professional performances of Canadian plays and musicals), Blyth. **Jun 18-26** *Metro International Caravan* (a travel adventure through 40 pavilions of food, drinks and entertainment representing Toronto's many cultures, Toronto). **Jun 18-27** *du Maurier Ltd Downtown Jazz*, Toronto. **Jun 19-20** *Hamilton International Air Show*, Hamilton. **Jun to end Aug** *Changing the Guard*, Ottawa. **Jun 22-27** *Franco-Ontarien Festival*, Ottawa. **Jun 24-Jul 4** *International Freedom Festival*, Windsor. **End Jun to early Jul** *Benson and Hedges Symphony of Fire* (a spectacular fireworks display), Toronto. **Jun 30-Jul 4** *Molson Canadian Hot Air Balloon Festival*, Barrie. **Jul-Aug** *Sunset Ceremony*, Fort Henry, Kingston. **Early Jul** *134th Running of The Queen's Plate*, Toronto. **Jul 1** *Canada Day Celebrations*, Ottawa and throughout province. **Jul 16-18** *Molson Indy Auto Race*, Toronto. **Jul 16-25** *Ottawa Jazz Festival*, Ottawa. **Jul 16-Aug 8** *Festival of the Sound*, Parry Sound. **Jul 19-Aug 2** *Caribana* (Caribbean Festival), Toronto. **Jul 29-Aug 1** *29th Rockhound Gemboree*, Bancroft. **Aug 4-8** *Royal Canadian Henley Regatta*, St Catharines. **Aug 6-8** *Festival of Friends*, Hamilton. **Aug 13-15** *Fergus Championship Supreme Highland Games*, Fergus. **Aug 6, 7, 13, 14, 20, 21** *Six Nations Native Pageant*, Brantford. **Aug 14-22** *Player's Ltd International*, Toronto. **Aug 18-Sep 6** *Canadian National Exhibition*, Toronto. **Aug 19-29** *Central Canada Exhibition*, Ottawa. **Sep 9-12** *Canadian Open Golf Championship*, Oakville. **Sep 9-18** *Festival of Festivals* (a film festival), Toronto. **Sep 11-20** *Western Fair*, London. **Sep 17-27** *Niagara Grape and Wine Festival*, St Catharines. **Oct 8-16** *Oktoberfest*, Kitchener/Waterloo. **Nov 9-20** *Royal Agricultural Winter Fair*, Toronto. **Nov-Jan '94** *Winter Festival of Lights*, Niagara Falls. **Nov 26-Jan 7** *Celebration of Lights*, Sarnia. **Dec-Jan** *Christmas Lights Across Canada*, Ottawa. **Feb 3-6** *Sudbury Snowflake Festival*, Sudbury. **Feb 4-13** *Winterlude*, Ottawa.

BUSINESS PROFILE

COMMERCIAL INFORMATION: The following organisation can offer advice: Ontario Chamber of Commerce, 5th Floor, 2323 Yonge Street, Toronto, Ontario M4P 2C9. Tel: (416) 482 5222.

CONFERENCES/CONVENTIONS: Ontario offers a wide range of conference venues. Ottawa usually hosts between 35-40 major international conferences per year. Some of the organisations which have met in Ottawa recently include Interpol, International Standards Organisation, Human Life International, Lions Club International and the World Tourism Conference. The following organisations can provide assistance and information:

For conferences throughout Ontario: Ontario Association of Convention & Visitors Bureaux, 20 Birch Street, Garson, Ontario P0M 1V0. Tel: (705) 693 2797. (This is an association of Ontario Convention and Visitors Association/Bureaux with common interests such as co-operative marketing and communication between members.)

For conferences in Toronto: Metropolitan Toronto Convention & Visitors Association, PO Box 126, Suite 590, 207 Queen's Quay West, Toronto, Ontario M5J 1A7. Tel: (416) 368 9990. Fax: (416) 867 3995.

For conferences in Niagara Falls: Canada Visitor & Convention Bureau, 5433 Victoria Avenue, Niagara Falls, Ontario L2G 3L1. Tel: (416) 356 6061. Fax: (416) 356 5567.

For conferences in Hamilton: Greater Hamilton Tourism & Convention Services, PO Box 910, Hamilton, Ontario

L8N 3V9. Tel: (416) 546 4222. Fax: (416) 546 4107. *For conferences in Ottawa:* Ottawa Tourism and Convention Authority, 2nd Floor, 111 Lisgar Street, Ottawa, Ontario K2P 2L7. Tel: (613) 237 5150. Fax: (613) 237 7339.

CLIMATE

Summers can be very warm, while spring and autumn are cooler. Winters are cold with snowfall.
Required clothing: Light to mediumweights during warmer months. Heavyweights in winter. Waterproofing is advisable throughout the year.

TORONTO Ontario (35m)

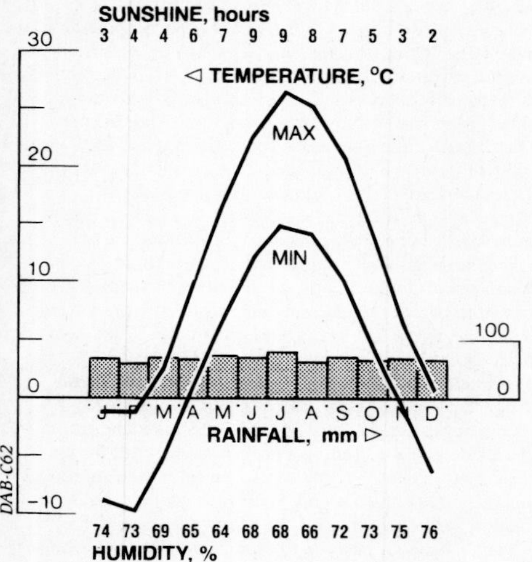

PRINCE EDWARD ISLAND

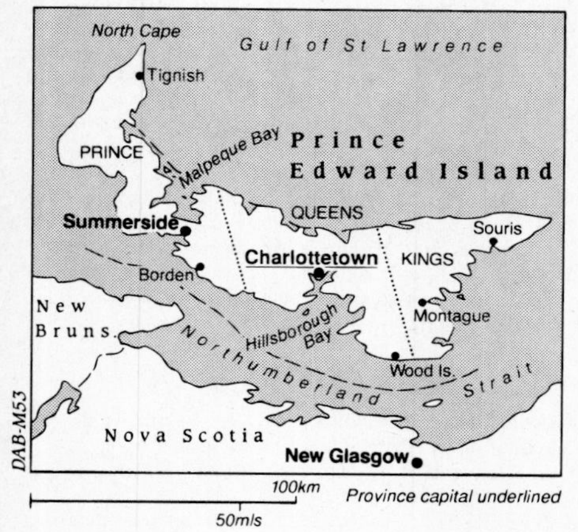

Location: East coast of Canada.

Visitor Information Centre
PO Box 940
Charlottetown, Prince Edward Island
C1A 7M5
Tel: (902) 368 4444. Fax: (902) 368 4438.

AREA: 5660 sq km (2185 sq miles).
POPULATION: 131,000 (1989).
POPULATION DENSITY: 23 per sq km.
CAPITAL: Charlottetown. **Population:** 15,776 (1989).
GEOGRAPHY: Prince Edward Island is a crescent-shaped island in the Gulf of the St Lawrence comprising red farm fields, northern evergreen forests, and white sand beaches. It is 224km (139 miles) long and between 6km (4 miles) and 65km (40 miles) wide.
TIME: GMT - 4 (GMT - 3 in summer).
Note: Daylight Saving Time officially lasts from the first Sunday in April to the last Sunday in October.
LANGUAGE: English and some French are spoken in the province.

PUBLIC HOLIDAYS

Public holidays as for the rest of Canada; see general introduction above.

TRAVEL

AIR: *Charlottetown (YYG)* airport is 3km (2 miles) from the city. *Air Atlantic* and *Air Nova* fly in here. There are no local flights within Prince Edward Island.
Departure tax: There is an airport tax of Can$20.00 (£10).
SEA: *Northumberland Ferries* sail from Wood Islands on the southeast coast to Caribou in Nova Scotia from late April to mid-December (travel time – 75 minutes). Advance reservations are not accepted (tel: (800) 565 0201 for further information). *Marine Atlantic* sails from Borden on the south coast to Cape Tormentine in New Brunswick all year round (travel time – 45 minutes). Advance reservations are not accepted (tel: (902) 855 2030, for further information). *CTMA Ferry* sails to Souris on the east coast from the Magdalen Islands in Québec from early April to the end of January (travel time – 5 hours). Advance reservations are recommended during the summer schedule from mid-June to early September (tel: (418) 986 3278).
RAIL: There are no passenger services on the island.
ROAD: There are three scenic drives following the coast of the island: Lady Slipper Drive (west), Blue Heron Drive (central), and King's Byway (east). Seatbelts for adults and children are mandatory on Prince Edward Island.

ACCOMMODATION

HOTELS: Prince Edward Island offers a wide range of quality accommodation, from conventional hotels to tourist homes, lodges and family farms. Most of the towns have excellent hotels and one is never far from the sea.
BED & BREAKFAST: The *Bed and Breakfast and Country Inns Association* oversees standards of 'Farm Vacations'. For further information, contact Bed & Breakfast, Visitor Services, PO Box 940, Charlottetown, Prince Edward Island C1A 7M5. Tel: (902) 368 5555. Fax: (902) 368 5737. Cottages and apartments can also be rented.
Grading: In 1993, owners of accommodations in Prince Edward Island were invited to participate in the Canada Select Rating Program. This programme is considered to be more stringent than last year's Atlantic Canada Grading Program, so some ratings may have changed. Even some operators who improved their amenities over last year may have received a lower grade under the new national system. Participation in the grading system is voluntary. For further information, contact Canada Select Rating Program, Tourism Industry Association of Prince Edward Island, PO Box 2050, 62 Great George Street, Charlottetown, Prince Edward Island C1A 7N7. Tel: (902) 422 3470. The new star ratings are based on the extent of facilities, quality of facilities, extent of services and amenities.
1 star – Basic, clean, comfortable accommodation.
2 stars – Basic, clean and comfortable with some amenities.
3 stars – Better quality accommodation; greater range of facilities and services.
4 stars – High-quality accommodation; extended range of facilities, amenities and guest services.
CAMPING/CARAVANNING: There are over 65 travel parks for camping near sandy beaches or in the interior. Camping fees vary, depending on the facilities offered. Most private sites accept reservations but the National Park does not. For rates, reservations and other information on provincial parks, contact: Provincial Parks, PO Box 2000, Charlottetown, Prince Edward Island C1A 7N8. For rates and information on the National Park, contact Environment Canada, Canadian Parks Service, Box 487, Charlottetown, Prince Edward Island C1A 7L1. A number of companies can arrange **motor camper** rentals, with a range of fully equipped vehicles. Full details can be obtained from the Visitor Information Centre.

RESORTS & EXCURSIONS

Charlottetown, the provincial capital, is a well-planned colonial seaport with tree-lined streets and rows of wood-frame houses. Main places of interest are *Province House*, a fine Georgian building of Nova Scotia sandstone, the site of the 1864 discussions which led to the Canadian Confederation; and the *Confederation Centre of the Arts*, which houses art galleries, theatres, a restaurant and a museum.
A tourist route known as the *Blue Heron Drive* heads westwards from Charlottetown to **Fort Amherst,** the original French settlement on the island, and on to **Prince Edward Island National Park,** 45km (25 miles) of fine white-sand beaches and red sandstone capes on the north coast. *Green Gables House*, the farmhouse immortalised in the book *Anne of Green Gables* by Lucy Maud Montgomery, is now a museum in **Cavendish,** located within the park. Further along the route, through **Stanley Bridge** where there is a large marine aquarium, is **New London,** where the author was born and wrote and there is now a museum in the house where she lived. **Dunstaffnage,** halfway between Charlottetown and Prince Edward Island National Park has a car museum worth visiting.
A second tourist route, the *Lady Slipper Drive*, circles Prince County, home to most of the province's French-speaking residents. The route passes through **Miscouche,** which has an *Acadian Museum*, and **Mont Carmel,** which has an *Acadian Pioneer Village*. **West Point,** on the western tip of Prince Edward Island, has *Cedar Dunes Provincial Park*, with a century-old wooden lighthouse and a connecting complex housing a museum, restaurant, handicraft shop and guest-rooms.
A third route, the *King's Byway*, traverses the hilly tobacco-growing region of the eastern interior. It passes through **Souris,** where ferries depart regularly for the Québecois **Isles de la Madeleine**; and **North Lake,** where boats can be chartered for what is claimed to be some of the best tuna-fishing in the world. Seal-watching tours have become very popular in the King's Byway region. **Point Prim,** located on a long promontory in the southeast of the Island, has the oldest lighthouse on the island, built in 1846 and still in use. In the interior of the island, accessible by this route, is **Milltown Cross,** offering the *Buffaloland Provincial Park*, home of bison and white-tailed deer, and the *Harvey Moore Migratory Bird Sanctuary*, home to many varieties of duck and geese.

SOCIAL PROFILE

FOOD & DRINK: Shellfish, lobster in particular, is a mainstay of the dinner table. Lobsters are steamed or boiled and included in casseroles and salads. Lobster suppers are a tradition on Prince Edward Island and they are often held in church basements or community halls where fresh lobster is served, along with home-made chowder, rolls, cakes and pies. Seconds are available of everything except lobster. Oysters are also popular; they may be served with tangy sauce, deep-fried, in pies, scalloped, in soufflés, soups and stews. Prince Edward Island is famous for its new potatoes – small, round early potatoes – and a favourite with locals is the new potatoes boiled with their skins, then mashed and served with lots of butter, salt and pepper. The island offers plenty of plain, wholesome, home-cooked food in restaurants. Service is informal and friendly. There are also many seafood outlets where fresh fish and shellfish can be bought in season and taken away for cooking on barbecues or campfires. Waiters expect a 10-15% tip. **Drink:** Most dining rooms are licensed to sell alcohol. Licensed premises are open until 0200 from May to October. Off-licences (liquor stores) are open six days a week from 1000-2200. Only persons over 19 years may buy alcohol.
NIGHTLIFE: Lounges on the island usually have some live entertainment during part or all of the week. Theatres, located mainly in Charlottetown, Victoria, Georgetown, Mont Carmel and Summerside, offer cultural, musical or light entertainment.
SHOPPING: The island's crafts include highly original pottery, weaving, leatherwork, woodwork, quilting, hand-painted silk and jewellery. Various guilds preserve the standards of production. There are also several antique dealers, secondhand stores, auctions, yard sales and flea markets. Main shopping centres can be found in Charlottetown, Summerside, Montague and Cavendish. **Shopping hours:** 0900-1700 Monday to Thursday and Saturday; 0900-2100 Friday.
SPORT: Deep-sea **fishing** is the principal sport. A record catch of bluefin tuna caught by rod and reel was landed in 1978 weighing 572kg (1021 lbs). **Harness racing** is popular, and there are also opportunities for **hiking, horseriding, canoeing, diving, sailing, windsurfing** and **water-skiing**. There are excellent facilities for both **skiing** and **golfing** in some of the area's Provincial Parks, such as *Mill River* in Woodstock and *Brudenell River* in Georgetown. *Brookvale Provincial Ski Park* has the most outstanding facilities for cross-country skiing and was host to the 1991 Canada Winter Games. **Swimming** is also featured in most Provincial Parks, where many of the Island's finest beaches can be found.
SPECIAL EVENTS: Apr 10 '93 *Royal Winnipeg Ballet*. **Apr 24** *Pinch Penny Fair*. **Jun-Sep** *1993 Charlottetown Festival* (theatre performances). **Jun 24-27** *Summerside Highland Gathering*. **Jun 24-Aug 26** *Highland Summer Concert Series* (Thursdays only), Summerside. **Jul-Sep** *Prince Edward Island House Parties*. **Jul 7-Sep 22** *Ceilidh* (evenings of traditional music), Orwell Corner Historic Village. **Jul 17-24** *Summerside Lobster Carnival* (country

music, harness racing, livestock exhibition). **Jul 28-Aug 1** *P.E.I. Potato Blossom Festival*, O'Leary. **Jul 29-Aug 1** *Northumberland Provincial Fisheries Festival*, Murray River. **Aug 3-8** *St Peters Blueberry Festival*, St Peters Park. **Aug 5-8** *Hydroplane Regatta*, Summerside. **Aug 6-7** *Annual Highland Games*, Eldon. **Aug 15** *16th Annual Green Park Blueberry Social*, Port Hill. **Aug 19-22** *1st Annual Lucy Maud Montgomery Festival*, Cavendish. **Aug 19-25** *26th Annual Community Harvest Festival*, Kensington. **Aug 20-21** *National Milton Acorn Festival*, Charlottetown. **Aug 21-22** *Eastern Kings Expedition & Cross Country Relay*. **Aug 22-25** *National Milton Acorn Festival*. **Sep 3-5** *L'Exposition Agricole et Festival Acadien de la Region Evang*, Abram Village.

BUSINESS PROFILE

COMMERCIAL INFORMATION: The following organisation can offer advice: Atlantic Provinces Chamber of Commerce, Suite 110, 236 St George Street, Moncton, New Brunswick E1C 1W1. Tel: (506) 857 2883. Fax: (506) 859 6131.
CONFERENCES/CONVENTIONS: For information on conferences and conventions on Prince Edward Island contact: Prince Edward Island Convention Bureau, 11 Queen Street, Charlottetown, Prince Edward Island C1A 4A2. Tel: (902) 368 3688.

CLIMATE

Temperate climate with cold winters and mild summers.
Required clothing: Light to mediumweights in warmer months, heavyweights in winter. Waterproof wear is advisable all year.

QUEBEC

Location: Eastern Canada.

Tourisme Québec
PO Box 20,000
Québec City, Québec
G1K 7X2
Tel: (514) 873 2015 *or* (418) 643 5959. Fax: (418) 646 8723.
Ministère du Tourisme
Bureau 400
2 place Québec
Québec City, Québec
G1R 2B5
Tel: (418) 643 2230. Fax: (418) 643 3126.
Québec Tourism
59 Pall Mall
London SW1Y 5JH
Tel: (071) 930 8314. Fax: (071) 930 7938. Opening hours: 0900-1700 Monday to Friday (1330-1700 for the library).
British Consulate General
Suite 901
1155 University
Montréal, Québec
H3B 3A7
Tel: (514) 866 5863. Fax: (514) 866 0202. Telex: 05561224 BRITAIN MTL.
Québec Tourism
17 West 50th Street
Rockerfeller Center
New York, NY
10020-2201
Tel: (212) 397 0200. Fax: (212) 757 4753. Telex: 12-6405.
Consulate General of the United States of America
PO Box 939
2 place Terrasse Dufferin
Québec City, Québec
G1R 4T9
Tel: (418) 692 2095. Fax: (418) 692 4640.
Consulate in Montréal.

AREA: 1,667,926 sq km (643,990 sq miles).
POPULATION: 6,688,700 (1989).
POPULATION DENSITY: 4 per sq km.
CAPITAL: Québec City. **Population:** 608,100 (1989).
GEOGRAPHY: The Province of Québec is in the east of Canada, with coasts on the North Atlantic and Hudson and James Bays; the St Lawrence Seaway, the major shipping channel of the Canadian east coast, cuts through the populous south; the cities of Québec and Montréal (Canada's second largest) stand beside it. In the north, the Laurentians resort area has snow-covered mountains and scenic lakes. The far north is a spread of forest and lakes forming one of the largest areas of wilderness in Canada.
LANGUAGE: French is the official language and 95% of the population speak it as a first language; 25% can speak English.
TIME: East of W 63°: GMT - 4 (GMT - 3 in summer).
West of W 63°: GMT - 5 (GMT - 4 in summer).
Note: Daylight Saving Time lasts officially from the first Sunday in April to the last Sunday in October.

PUBLIC HOLIDAYS

Public holidays are as for the rest of Canada (see general section above), with the following date also observed:
Jun 24 '93 Saint Jean Baptiste.

TRAVEL

AIR: Local air services are operated between the cities in the south and float planes serve the lakes and parkland of the north. The main airlines are *Air Alliance*, *Air Alma*, *Air Atlantique*, *Air Canada*, *Air Creebec*, *Air Inuit*, *Air Nova*, *Air Ontario*, *American Airlines*, *Business Express*, *Canadian International*, *Delta Airlines*, *First Air*, *Inter-Canada Airlines*, *Northwest Airlines*, *Ontario Express*, *Skycraft* and *US Air*.
International airports: *Québec (YQB)* and *Mirabel (YMX)*, 55km (34 miles) northwest of Montréal (travel time – 45/60 minutes). A regular bus service and taxis are available to the city.
Dorval (YUL), 22km (15 miles) west of Montréal (travel time – 20/30 minutes). Buses leave from Dorval Airport every 20 minutes to two central locations, costing Can$7 one-way and Can$12 return. Taxi services are also available at a flat fee or metered rate (approx. Can$15-20) or limousine service is available for Can$43 or more.
SEA: Québec City and Montréal are the most important Canadian ports on the St Lawrence Seaway, which links the Atlantic Ocean with the Great Lakes and the industrial heartland of Canada and the USA. Several international passenger carriers sail to both ports; European carriers dock only at Montréal. Most of the province's lakes and rivers are served by local ferries, some of which are able to take heavy lorries. For schedules and fares contact the local shipper.
RAIL: *Via Rail* connects all major provincial towns, and *Amtrak* operates two daily trains to the USA. *Via Rail* services also connect the major cities in the south of the province, with thrice-daily mainline services from Montréal to Québec.
ROAD: The best way of travelling into and around Québec by road is by long-distance coach, especially *Orleans Express*. The services in the southern region are especially frequent. **Motorhomes** and **campers** are best for seeing the northern parklands, and the area is connected to the south by several good highways, although the most extensive network is around the populous areas in the south.
URBAN: Bus and metro services are provided in Montréal at flat fares with free transfers between metro and bus obtainable from machines. Passes and multi-ticket books are sold and metro fares are the lowest in North America. Québec's bus services operate on a flat-fare system. No change is carried on board. Pre-purchase passes are available. There are good bus services in other towns.

ACCOMMODATION

HOTELS: The majority of the population live in the south of the province, where all the large cities offer a large choice of hotel accommodation. Some of the best hotels in the country are in Montréal and Québec City. Outside the cities, accommodation takes on a more rural flavour; lakeside lodges and cabins are very popular. Accommodation is often possible in private homes. For further information on hotels in Québec, contact the Association des Hoteliers de la Province de Québec, Suite 014, 425 rue Sherbrooke est, Montréal, Québec H2L 1J9. Tel: (514) 282 5135. Fax: (514) 849 1157.
BED & BREAKFAST: There are a number of organisations in Québec that provide information regarding bed & breakfast accommodation, including Québec Bed & Breakfast, 3729 avenue Le Corbusier, Ste-Foy, Québec City, Québec G1W 4PE. Tel: (418) 651 1860; *or* Montréal Bed & Breakfast, 4912 Victoria, Montréal, Québec H3W 2N1. Tel: (514) 738 9410.
CAMPING/CARAVANNING: Northern Québec is a vast area of forest and lakes and one of the best areas for wilderness camping in Canada. A number of

companies can arrange **motor camper** rentals, with a range of fully equipped vehicles. Full details can be obtained from Québec Tourism.

RESORTS & EXCURSIONS

Outside the major centres of population in the southeast, Canada's largest province consists of hilly agricultural land along the banks of the **St Lawrence** and vast tracks of barren mountains in the north. The 30-minute drive along the St Lawrence from Québec to the outskirts of **Charlevoix** is along a breathtaking route of towering rock faces, looming canyons and craggy fjords. More than 100,000 lakes provide excellent fishing (chiefly for trout and salmon) whilst in the northern tundra of *Nouveau Québec*, caribou and other game are hunted. La Fédération des pourvoyeurs du Québec Inc (tel: (418) 527 5191) can arrange itineraries, equipment, transport and accommodation in this region.

MONTREAL: Canada's second largest city, on a 27-mile-long island, is a sophisticated cosmopolitan metropolis with an 80% francophone population. Careful central planning for Expo '67 and the 1976 Olympic Games have produced a spacious and beautiful modern city. A series of underground shopping and recreation complexes, linked by walkways and metro, is centred on *Dominion Square*. The *Place des Arts* is the home of the Montréal Symphony and several theatres offering year-round drama, music, ballet and opera. Both the *Montréal Museum of Fine Arts* and the *Museum of Contemporary Arts* have good collections. *Vieux Montréal*, the historic waterfront section, has been carefully restored. Main places of note here are: *Place Jacques Cartier*, the former French governor's residence; *Chateau Ramzay;* and the city's oldest church, *Notre Dame de Bonsecour*. *Mont Royal Park* is the city's highest point, offering an excellent vista from the centre of Montréal. Behind-the-scenes tours of the *Olympic Park*, site of the '76 games, are available.

QUÉBEC CITY: With its old city walls and fortified Citadel, the provincial capital is one of the most European cities in North America; indeed, in 1985, UNESCO declared it a *World Heritage Treasure*. It is the cradle of French culture in Canada with a 95% French-speaking population. The city is split into two levels, connected by stone stairways and a municipal escalator. The 'Upper Town' has some fine 18th- and 19th-century architecture, notably the *Place D'Armes* and the *Chateau Frontenac*. In the 'Lower Town', the network of 17th-century streets centred on *Place Royale* has recently been restored.

ELSEWHERE: Ste Agathe des Monts, 100km (60 miles) north of Montréal, is the hub of a resort area providing some of the best skiing in North America. Further north, the **Mont Tremblant Park** provides boating, hunting and camping as well as winter sports. Northwest of this is **La Verendrye National Park**, a protected lakeland wilderness; and further on, the mining territory centred on **Rouyn-Noranda.**

L'Ile D'Orleans, east of Québec City, is a region of picturesque Québecois villages. Further east are the **Montmorency Falls** and **Ste Anne de Beaupre.** The latter is the main resort in the famous **Laurentians** (or Laurentides) skiing region, which is also a provincial park. Heading northeast from Québec along the southern bank of the St Lawrence, the main route leads first through the farming region of **Bas Saint Laurent** and thence to the **Gaspé Peninsula.** The major attraction here is the **Gaspé National Park.**

Across the mouth of the river is the **Duplessis Peninsula,** site of some of the earliest landfalls in the New World. Remains left by these Viking sailors can be seen in the museum at **Sept-Iles,** the largest city in the area and site of the oldest trading post in Québec. The bizarre geological formations of the nearby **Mingan Archipelago** are best explored by boat.

The **Iles de la Madeleine,** 290km (180 miles) east of Gaspé in the Gulf of St Lawrence, offer miles of white sandy beaches and a host of unspoilt fishing villages.

SOCIAL PROFILE

FOOD & DRINK: Québec proudly reflects a tradition of French culture, never more so than in the restaurants and cuisine of the province. French food here is as excellent as anywhere in Europe. Immigrants from many countries, however, provide a vast selection. Italian, Greek, Japanese, Spanish and English cuisine are all available in Montréal and Québec. International menus are found at all the larger hotels, but the best food is found by wandering around the small backstreets of the cities and sampling the small but excellent restaurants scattered throughout both cities. Specialist dishes include *ragout de boulettes* (pork meatballs with seasoning) and *cretons du Québec* (chilled minced pork). The Ile d'Orleans is an island northeast of Québec City that provides abundant fruits and vegetables for the city. **Drink:** Québec follows French tradition in having excellent standards of wine and spirits to complement the high standard of cuisine. Much is home-produced, although some spirits and the rarer wines are imported from Europe. Taverns and brasseries serve alcoholic beverages from 0800-2400 Monday to Saturday. Cocktail lounges and cabarets stay open until 0200 and 0300 respectively in Montréal. The minimum drinking age is 18.

NIGHTLIFE: Québec City and Montréal offer some of the best nightclubs and cabarets to be found anywhere in Canada. In Montréal the action seldom begins before 2200 and usually continues until 0300 the next morning. Nightlife is concentrated in the western part of the downtown area along Crescent and Bishop Streets and around Ste-Catherine Street, where there are many bars, restaurants and clubs of all kinds. For a particularly French flavour, try the many clubs, bars, restaurants, cafés and bistros further east around St Denis and St Laurent.

SHOPPING: Québec City and Montréal have excellent shopping facilities, both in large department stores and small backstreet markets. Specialities include furs, Indian crafts, *haute couture* and antiques.

SPORT: Sport in Québec is of an international standard, as illustrated by Montréal's hosting of the Olympic Games in 1976. Québec City and Montréal are both on the banks of the St Lawrence River and **watersports** facilities are extensive, especially **sailing, swimming** and **water-skiing.** International downhill **skiing** competitions are held to the north of Montréal at Mont Tremblant and at Mont Sainte-Anne, east of Québec City. Winter sports in general culminate with the Québec Winter Carnival in February of each year, drawing entries from all over North America. **Ice hockey** is played to international standards.

SPECIAL EVENTS: The following is a selection of the special events celebrated annually in Québec:

Mar 17-21 '93 *Maple Festival*, Saint-Georges. **End Mar to early Apr** *Spring Festival* (helicopter rides, raft races, trout fishing), Stoneham. **Apr 29-May 2** *35th Plessisville Maple Tree Festival*, Plessisville. **Jun 6** *Le Tour de l'Ile de Montréal*, Montréal. **Jun 11-13** *Molson Canada Grand Prix*, Montréal. **Jul** *Jazz Festival Montréal*. **Jul 8-18** *International Summer Festival*, Québec City. **Jul-Aug** *Benson & Hedges International Fireworks Competition*, Montréal. **Jul-Aug** *Just for Laughs Festival*, Montréal.

BUSINESS PROFILE

COMMERCIAL INFORMATION: The following organisation can offer advice: Québec Chamber of Commerce, Suite 3030, 500 place d'Armes, Montréal, Québec H2Y 2W2. Tel: (514) 288 9090.

CONFERENCES/CONVENTIONS: Montréal is a major meeting and convention centre and an extensive information booklet is available from the Greater Montréal Convention and Tourism Bureau, Suite 600, 1555 Peel, Montréal, Québec H3A 1X6. Tel: (514) 844 5400. Fax: (514) 844 5757.

For information about conferences and conventions in Québec City contact the Greater Québec Tourism and Convention Bureau, Suite 211, 399 St Joseph Street East, Québec City, Québec G1K 8E2. Tel: (418) 522 3511.

CLIMATE

Summer months (June to August) are warm with cooler evenings. Autumn and Spring are cooler and winters are very cold and snowy.

Required clothing: Lightweights during warmer months. Heavyweights in winter. Waterproofing is advisable all year.

MONTREAL Quebec (17m)

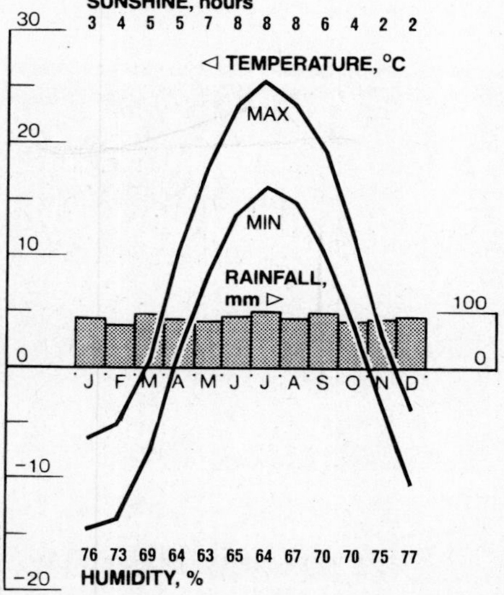

SASKATCHEWAN

Location: Central Canada.

Tourism Saskatchewan
Main Floor
Saskatchewan Trade and Convention Centre
1919 Saskatchewan Drive
Regina, Saskatchewan
S4P 3V7
Tel: (306) 787 2300. Fax: (306) 787 5744.

AREA: 651,900 sq km (251,700 sq miles)
POPULATION: 1,016,944 (1992).
POPULATION DENSITY: 1.8 per sq km.
CAPITAL: Regina. **Population:** 190,000.

GEOGRAPHY: Saskatchewan is bordered by the US states of North Dakota and Montana to the south, Manitoba to the east, the Northwest Territories to the north and Alberta in the west. Its landscape is mainly prairie, forests and lakes. Prince Albert National Park is the entrance to Saskatchewan's wilderness. The highest land is the Cypress Hills in the southwest, 1392m (4566ft) above sea level.

LANGUAGE: Although Canada is officially bilingual (English and French), English is more commonly spoken in Saskatchewan.

TIME: East of W 106°: GMT - 6.

Note: Most of Saskatchewan does not observe Daylight Saving Time in summer.

PUBLIC HOLIDAYS

Public holidays are as for the rest of Canada (see general section above), with the following date also observed:
Aug 2 '93 Civic Holiday.

TRAVEL

AIR: Inter-province flights are offered by *Air Canada*, *Time Air* and *Canadian Airlines* from all provincial capitals to Saskatoon and Regina. The principal local services are operated by *Time Air,Athabasca Airways* and *Prairie Flying Service*; these include charter flights to the lakes and parklands of the north.

International airports: *Saskatoon (YXE)* is 8km (4.5 miles) from the city (travel time – 15 minutes). Airport facilities include left luggage, car hire, car parking and restaurant (0700-2300).

Regina is 5km (3 miles) from the city.

RIVER: Saskatchewan has no coastline. Ferry services on the Saskatchewan River connect the province to Manitoba and Alberta; ferries also link it with Manitoba on the Churchill River. Houseboats may be chartered.

RAIL: The principal routes run by *Via Rail* are from Manitoba (Churchill and Winnipeg) and Alberta (Edmonton). Saskatoon and Regina are connected by bus five times a day.

ROAD: Both the Trans-Canada Highway and the Alaska Highway run across the province. Saskatchewan has over 250,000km (150,000 miles) of road. **Bus:**

Greyhound Bus Lines link Saskatchewan with all other provinces and, within the province, *Greyhound*, *Saskatchewan Transportation Company* and *Moose Mountain Bus Lines* operate between the large cities in the south and to the parklands of the north. **Car hire:** Available in Regina and a number of other cities. Saskatchewan law stipulates that seatbelts must be worn at all times.

ACCOMMODATION

The majority of accommodation suitable for travellers is found in the south of the province, especially in Regina, Saskatoon, Moose Jaw and Weyburn. The parklands in the northern part of the province have mainly camping-style accommodation. 'Houseboat charters' on the lakes are a special feature of Saskatchewan. For further information on hotels in Saskatchewan, contact the Hotel Association of Saskatchewan, Main Floor, Avord Tower, 2202 Victoria Avenue, Regina, Saskatchewan S4P 0R7. Tel: (306) 522 1664. Fax: (306) 525 1657. The *Saskatchewan Accommodation Guide* is available through Tourim Saskatchewan.
Grading: Tourism Saskatchewan's annual guide gives details of hotels, motels, farm vacations and bed & breakfast establishments, using the following definitions:
Mod: Modern room. Includes private bathroom facilities with wash basin, bathtub and/or shower and flush toilet.
Smod: Semi-modern room. Includes wash basin only and a pressurized hot and cold water supply.
Nmod: Non-modern room. Has no plumbing facilities.
Lhk: Light housekeeping unit. Includes kitchen facilities as well as living and sleeping quarters.
CAMPING/CARAVANNING: The parklands offer some of the best camping landscapes in Canada. There are 17 parks, all offering different rates of service and accommodation for those without mobile homes or tents. For details contact the local park authorities. A number of companies can arrange **motor camper** rentals, with a range of fully equipped vehicles. Full details can be obtained from Tourism Saskatchewan.

RESORTS & EXCURSIONS

Half of this vast province comprises designated provincial forest. There are 80 million acres of it north of the 54th parallel, offering unequalled opportunities for 'outdoors' enthusiasts. The south and centre enjoy a more mellow landscape, much of it given over to grain cultivation.
REGINA: The provincial capital was once called 'Pile of Bones' but was renamed in honour of Queen Victoria. Its centrepiece is the *Wascana Centre*, a huge water-park with an the *Mckenzie Art Gallery* and *Centre of Arts*. The park also provides an impressive setting for the *Legislative Buildings* and the *Museum of Natural History*. Regina has long been the base of the Royal Canadian Mounted Police ('The Mounties') and the *RCMP Centennial Museum* offers a quirky insight into the development of Canada's Wild West.
SASKATOON: Built on both banks of the South Saskatchewan River, Saskatoon is one of Canada's fastest growing urban centres. The *Western Development Museum*, *Wanuskewh Heritage Park*, *Forestry Farm Park* and the *Ukrainian Arts and Crafts Museum* are its main attractions.
ELSEWHERE: The Trans-Canada Highway provides the best means of touring the far south, connecting the cities of *Swift Current*, *Moose* and *Regina*. It follows the cavernous **Qu'Appelle Valley,** a sunken garden studded with lakes that runs two-thirds of the way across the province. East of Regina, **Fort Qu'Appelle** and the lakeside recreation parks of **Katepwa Point, Buffalo Pound** and **Echo Valley** are worth visiting. To the west is **Swift Current,** which hosts an annual *Frontier Festival*; and, further west across low-scrub prairie, the afforested oasis of **Cypress Hills Park.** The Yellowhead Highway, running eastwards from Saskatoon to **Yorkton,** near the border with Manitoba, is a good way to tour Saskatchewan's grain belt. This region was once settled by Ukrainians, as testified by the many silver-domed Orthodox churches, such as that at Verigin. Other attractions en route include the **Duck Mountain** and **Good Spirit Provincial Parks.** There is a pioneer village at **Fort Battleford National Historic Park,** northwest of Saskatoon. Manitou Beach has the **Manitou Beach Mineral Spa,** where visitors may relax and float effortlessly in the very salty, warm, mineral-rich waters which are pumped from Little Manitou Lake into pools in the spa and are supposed to provide relief from a variety of ailments.
But Saskatchewan's main attractions are the endless forests and thousands of lakes of the north, accessible by the Northern Woods and Water Route. There are few permanent settlements and many regions are accessible only by air. **Prince Albert** is the main gateway. The closest park is **Prince Albert National Park,** a hilly, forested area with hundreds of lakes, ponds and rivers. Its most developed area is at **Waskesiu Lake,** which has good facilities for camping, organised sports and recreation. Further off to the northwest is **Meadow Lake Park,** which has good accommodation and facilities for hunting and winter sports.
The small airport at **Lac la Ronge,** about 300km (200 miles) north of Prince Albert, is the main base for flights to the very remote northern lakes, such as **Wollaston** and **Athabasca.** Excellent fishing and white-water canoeing are available on the lake and on the **Churchill River,** which passes nearby.

SOCIAL PROFILE

FOOD & DRINK: Whitefish and pickerel are marketed by Indian co-operatives. Wild rice harvested by Indians is an excellent accompaniment to the abundant wild fowl which includes partridge, prairie chicken, wild duck and goose. 'Saskatoons', berries similar to blueberries, are used for jams, jellies and 'Saskatoon pie', eaten with fresh country cream. Other wild berries include pinchberries and cranberries which make a tart and tangy jelly, ideal with wild fowl meals. A good selection of restaurants can be found in all the province's cities and major towns catering to all tastes and pockets.
Drink: The minimum drinking age is 19 (sometimes older). Alcohol is sold only in licensed stores, licensed restaurants, cocktail lounges, dining and beverage rooms. Retail outlets operate throughout the province.
NIGHTLIFE: There are some nightclubs; bars and restaurants in most main towns have live entertainment as well as music and dancing. The best times for nightlife are during the 'period' historical festivals held regularly in all the major towns. The days of the settlers and cowboys are re-created with everyone dressing in costumes and eating traditional foods. The emphasis changes in each town and according to the time of the year, but the largest is at the capital, Regina, a festival lasting several days – the *Buffalo Days*.
SHOPPING: Saskatchewan has many small craft stores that offer original pottery, silkscreens, rock jewellery, potash clocks, embroidered leather, denim, purses, gloves and hats.
SPORT: When the snow melts, parklands are used for **horseriding, camping, canoeing, cycling, white-water rafting** and **cross-country walking.** The majority of the parks provide ancillary services from May to September. Saskatchewan's parks contain over 100,000 lakes and the province is named after the Indian name for the river systems (Kis-is-ska-tche-wan). **Sailing, water-skiing, golf, tennis, swimming** and **fishing** are especially popular in summer months. The **fishing** season is from May to April; fishing licences are required by everyone. **Shooting,** mainly for duck and grouse, is particularly good in the grain region of the southwest. **Wintersports** are the most popular in the region, including **skiing, skating** and **ice fishing.** There are 16 downhill and 39 cross-country ski areas.
SPECIAL EVENTS: May '93 *Vesna Festival*, Saskatoon. **Jun** *Mosaic* (a celebratin of many etnic groups), **Regina and Bazaart** (craft show and sale), Regina.**Jul-Aug '93** *Shakespeare on the Saskatchewan*, Saskatoon. **Jul-Aug** *RCMP Sunset Ceremonies*, Regina. **Jul 8-11** *Big Valley Jamboree* (country music festival), Craven. **Jul 10-11** *Saskatchewan Air Show*, Moose Jaw. **Aug** *Buffalo Days Exhibition* and *Royal Red Arabian Horse Show*, Regina; *Folkfest*, Saskatoon. **Nov 27-Dec 3** *Canadian Western Agribition*, Regina.
There are also about 50 amateur and professional rodeos held annually in various locations.

BUSINESS PROFILE

COMMERCIAL INFORMATION: The following organisation can offer advice: Saskatchewan Chamber of Commerce, 1630 Chateau Towers, 1920 Broad Street, Regina, Saskatchewan S4P 3V2. Tel: (306) 352 2671.
CONFERENCES/CONVENTIONS: For information or assistance contact the Saskatchewan Economic Development and Tourism, 1919 Saskatchewan Drive, Regina, Saskatchewan S4P 3V7. Tel: (306) 787 9575. Fax: (306) 787 0715; *or*
Regina Visitors & Convention Bureau, Tourism Regina, PO Box 3355, Regina, Saskatchewan S4P 3H1. Tel: (306) 789 5099. Fax: (306) 789 3171; *or*
Tourism Saskatoon, PO Box 369, 102-310 Idylwyld Drive, Saskatoon, Saskatchewan S7K 3L3. Tel: (306) 242 1206. Fax: (306) 242 1955.

CLIMATE

Temperate in the south with cold winters in the north. The highest rainfall occurs between April and June. Summers are hot and dry with long hours of sunshine, but winter temperatures are often below freezing.

REGINA Saskatchewan (175m)

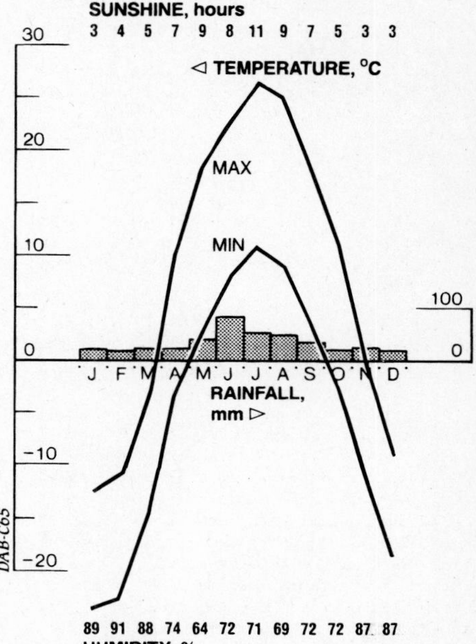

YUKON

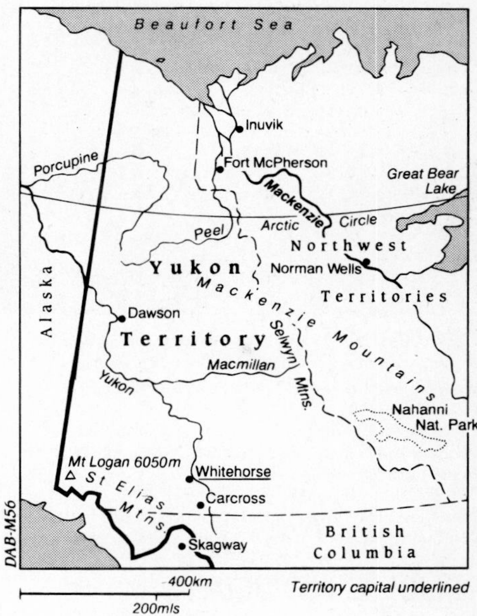

Location: Northwest Canada.

Tourism Yukon
PO Box 2703
Whitehorse, Yukon Territory
Y1A 2C6
Tel: (403) 667 5340. Fax: (403) 667 2634. Telex: 0368260.

AREA: 478,970 sq km (186,299 sq miles).
POPULATION: 29,961 (1991).
POPULATION DENSITY: 0.06 per sq km.
CAPITAL: Whitehorse. **Population:** 21,322 (1991).
GEOGRAPHY: Yukon Territory, Canada's 'last frontier', is largely a mountainous and forested wilderness. It is bisected by the valley of the Yukon River, which passes to the west of the Mackenzie Mountains. Mount Logan in the St Elias Range on the border with Alaska is the

Kluane National Park

second highest peak in North America at 5959m (19,550ft).
LANGUAGE: Although Canada is officially bilingual (English and French), English is more commonly spoken in the territory.
TIME: GMT - 8 (GMT - 7 in summer).
Note: Daylight Saving Time time officially lasts from the first Sunday in April to the last Sunday in October.

PUBLIC HOLIDAYS

Public holidays are as for the rest of Canada (see general section above), with the following dates also observed:
Aug 16 '93 Discovery Day. **Feb 26 '94** Heritage Day.

TRAVEL

AIR: The main international services are run by *Canadian Airlines*. *Canadian Airlines* operates a daily service between Whitehorse, Edmonton and Vancouver. The main local carrier is *Alkan Air*, providing services across the Yukon to Inuvik in the Northwest Territories.
SEA: Cruise ships and ferries operate from Bellingham in Washington (USA) and Prince Rupert in British Columbia, arriving at Skagway in Alaska and connecting to Whitehorse by bus.
ROAD: The major road in the region is the Alaska Highway, running from Alaska to British Columbia through Whitehorse. The Dempster Highway connects Whitehorse with Inuvik in the north. **Coach:** *Gold City Tours* offer a scheduled service from Dawson City to Inuvik in the Northwest Territory. *North West Stage Lines* offer scheduled services to Haines Junction, Destruction Bay, Faro, Ross River and Beaver Creek.
Bus: There is a bus service between Whitehorse and Dawson; daily in summer, three times a week in winter. *Norline* operates to Dawson City; *Greyhound Lines of Canada* operate a 6-times-a-week service in summer from Edmonton to Whitehorse.

ACCOMMODATION

HOTELS: There are 81 hotel/motels with a total of 2483 rooms in the Yukon Territory. There are plans to construct a new 150-room hotel complex with convention facilities and a new 40-room hotel in Whitehorse. Because of the heavy tourist flow through the region in summer, bookings must be made well in advance. Apart from the main settlements with hotels, lodges and motels, accommodation is scarce in wilder areas. Many hotels are closed for the winter. Yukon Territory accommodations are not graded at the present time. For further information, contact British Columbia & Yukon Hotel Association, Yukon Branch, 102 Wood Street, Whitehorse, Yukon Territory Y1A 2E3. Tel: (403) 667 7801. Fax: (403) 668 6075.
BED & BREAKFAST: There are 30 bed & breakfast properties in the Yukon Territory. A free brochure is available listing over 60 bed & breakfast members throughout the Yukon, Alaska, Northwest Territories and British Columbia. Contact Northern Network Bed & Breakfasts, 39 Donjek Road, Whitehorse, Yukon Territory Y1A 3R1. Tel: (403) 667 4315.
CAMPING/CARAVANNING: Camping is only advised in summer and on government or private campsites. A number of companies can arrange **motor camper** rentals, with a range of fully equipped vehicles. Full details can be obtained from Tourism Yukon.

RESORTS & EXCURSIONS

WHITEHORSE: Yukon's capital (since 1953) lies on the west bank of the Yukon River, the water route taken by thousands of eager prospectors during the Klondike Gold Rush of 1898. More than half of the territory's population is concentrated here. The *McBride Museum* houses many of the artefacts of the gold rush era, including *Sam McGee's Cabin*. On the river itself, the *SS Klondike*, a restored sternwheeler vessel, is open for viewing. The *MV Schwatka* offers a 2-hour cruise of the *Miles Canyon* and the *Whitehorse Rapids*.
ELSEWHERE: Carcross, an hour's drive south of Whitehorse, lies between the **Nares** and **Bennett Lakes** at the foot of **Nares Mountain;** the *Caribou*, Yukon's oldest hotel, can be found here. Carcross connects to Skagway in Alaska via the Klondike Highway. **Kluane National Park,** in the southwest corner of the territory, has the tallest mountains in Canada and the largest non-polar icefields in the world. Special flightseeing tours of this park can be arranged from Whitehorse and a variety of other Yukon Territory communities.
Nearby Skagway (Alaska) is **Dyea,** the starting point of the famous *Chilkoot Trail*, where hikers can retrace the footsteps of the gold rush stampeders. **Dawson City,** at the heart of the Klondike, can be reached by road or by the Yukon River. In its brief heyday Dawson was hailed as the 'Paris of the North', having then some 30,000 inhabitants; at the last census there were only 1747. The city is now a designated national historic site, with buildings such as the *Commissioner's Residence* and the *Palace Grand Theatre* bearing witness to its former glories. The latter was built in 1899 from two dismantled steamboats and each summer produces an authentic 1898 vaudeville show – the 'Gaslight Follies'. Tours on the Yukon River on the miniature stern-wheeler *Yukon Lou* visit the *Sternwheelers Graveyard* and *Pleasure Island*. Visitors can pan gold at *Guggieville* or *Claim 33* on Bonanza Creek, the site of the original claim which sparked off the 1898 goldrush.
Expeditions to the wild back-country of the Yukon Territory are best conducted in the company of a licensed outfitter or guide.

SOCIAL PROFILE

FOOD & DRINK: Some of the Yukon's food is very distinctive but difficult to produce commercially. Moose meat is cooked in several ways from steaming to smoked or pot roast, and accompanied by *sourdough* and vegetables. Dall sheep, mountain goat, caribou and porcupine are also eaten. Wild fowl and fish feature in most menus. There are restaurants throughout the area, but the best selection is in Whitehorse, Dawson City and Watson Lake. **Drink:** Most alcohol is imported from other areas of Canada and the USA. A local speciality is *hooch* (a blend of imported and Canadian rum); it is only available in the Yukon Territory.
NIGHTLIFE: Nightlife is best during the historical festivals and carnivals reflecting the pioneer spirit that explored the region (see *Special Events* below). However, Dawson City has legalised gambling, live vaudeville theatre and a floor show at Gertie's featuring cancan girls and honky tonk piano.
SHOPPING: Special items include Indian boots, gold nuggets and the original *parka* coat with a wool lining and waterproof outer cover, dating from prospecting days. Native Indian bone-carving and jewellery are popular souvenirs. Cashback on items purchased can be

claimed back in Revenue Canada, Customs and Excise and Government of Canada offices.
SPORT: The most important sport in the Yukon Territory is **skiing. Canoeing, hiking, mountain climbing, horseriding, dog sledding** and **fishing** are also available in many wilderness areas.
SPECIAL EVENTS: Mid-Mar '93 *Percy De Wolfe Memorial Race and Mail Run*, Dawson City. **Jul 1** *Yukon Gold Panning Championships*, Dawson City. **Jul 23-25** *15th Annual Dawson City Music Festival*. **Jul 24** *International Midnight Dome Race*, Dawson City. **Aug 13-16** *Discovery Days*, Dawson City. **Aug 13-16** *2nd Annual Yukon River Gold Rush Bathtub Race*, Whitehorse. **Sep 5** *The Great Klondike Outhouse Race*, Dawson City. **Sep 10-11** *Klondike Trail of '98 Road Relay*, Whitehorse. **Jan-Dec '94** *Town of Faro's 25th Anniversary*. **Feb 18-27** *Yukon Sourdough Rendezvous*, Whitehorse. **Mid-Mar** *Percy De Wolfe Memorial Race and Mail Run*, Dawson City.

BUSINESS PROFILE

CONFERENCES/CONVENTIONS: For information on conferences and conventions in the Yukon Territory contact Meetings and Convention Bureau, 203-208 Main Street, Whitehorse, Yukon Territory Y1A 2A9. Tel: (403) 668 3331. Fax: (403) 667 7379.

CLIMATE

Summers are warm with almost continuous daylight during June. Winters are bitterly cold.
Required clothing: *Summer* – days can be hot, but sweaters and light jackets are advised for the evenings. *Spring and Autumn* – coats and gloves are required for outdoor activities. *Winter* – thermal underwear, wool sweaters, parkas, wool gloves or mittens and mukluks or felt-lined boots are advised for the winter.

WHITEHORSE Yukon Territory (2128m)

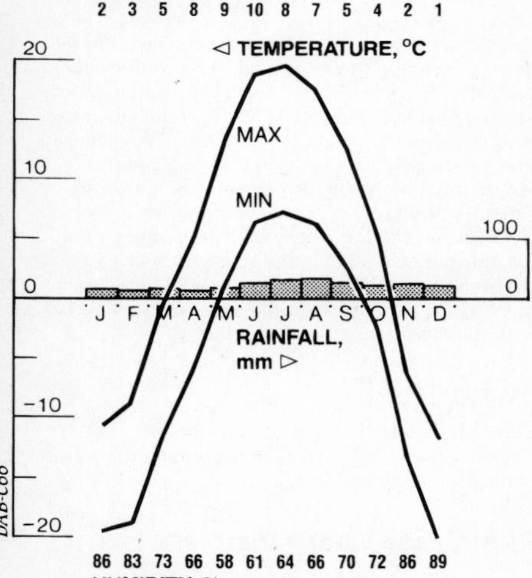

TEMPERATURE CONVERSIONS
-20 -10 0°C 10 20 30 40
0 10 20 30°F 40 50 60 70 80 90 100

RAINFALL CONVERSIONS
0mm 200 400 600 800
0in 5 10 15 20 25 30

CAPE VERDE

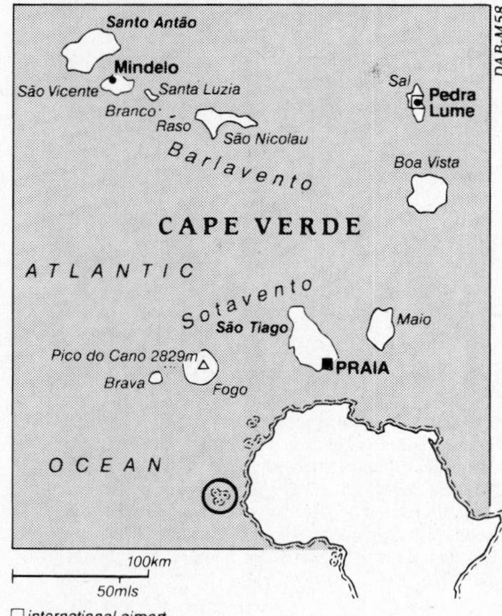

Location: Atlantic Ocean, off coast of West Africa.

Secretaria de Estado de Comércio e Turismo
CP 105
Praia
São Tiago, Cape Verde
Tel: 614 124. Telex: 4232.
Embassy of the Republic of Cape Verde
Koninginnegracht 44
2514 AD The Hague
The Netherlands
Tel: (70) 346 9623. Fax: (70) 346 7702. Telex: 34321 ARCV NL.
Embassy of the Republic of Cape Verde
3415 Massachusetts Avenue, NW
Washington, DC
20007
Tel: (202) 965 6820. Fax: (202) 965 1207.
The Embassy also deals with enquiries from Canada.
Embassy of the United States of America
CP 201
Rua Hoji Ya Yenna 81
Praia
São Tiago, Cape Verde
Tel: 615 616. Fax: 611 355. Telex: 6068 AMEMB.

AREA: 4033 sq km (1557 sq miles).
POPULATION: 347,000 (1987 estimate).
POPULATION DENSITY: 86 per sq km.
CAPITAL: Cidade de Praia. **Population:** 57,748 (1980).
GEOGRAPHY: Cape Verde is situated in the Atlantic Ocean 600km (450 miles) west-northwest of Senegal, and comprises ten volcanic islands and five islets, in two groups: Balavento (Windwards) and Sotavento (Leewards). In the former group are the islands of São Vicente, Santo Antão, São Nicolau, Santa Luzia, Sal and Boa Vista, along with the smaller islands of Branco and Raso; the Sotavento group comprises the islands of São Tiago, Maio, Fogo and Brava, along with the smaller islands of Rei and Rombo. Most have mountain peaks; the highest, Pico do Cano, an active volcano, is on Fogo. The islands are generally rocky and eroded, and have never been able to support more than subsistence agriculture (maize, bananas, sugar cane and coffee are the main crops); low rainfall over the last ten years has crippled food production and forced the islands to depend on international aid.
LANGUAGE: The official language is Portuguese. *Crioulo* is spoken by most of the inhabitants. Some English and French is spoken.
RELIGION: Almost entirely Roman Catholic with a Protestant minority.
TIME: GMT - 1.
ELECTRICITY: 220 volts AC, 50Hz.
COMMUNICATIONS: Telephone: IDD is possible to main cities. Country code: 238. Improvements to rural areas are in progress and the islands have over 12,000 telephones. Some calls to and from Cape Verde must still go through the international operator. **Telex:** This is available in some hotels. **Post:** Postal facilities are not very efficient, deliveries to Europe take over a week. **Press:** Newspapers are in Portuguese. There are two weekly papers with a total circulation of 3000, two quarterly cultural magazines and one monthly newspaper.
BBC World Service and Voice of America frequencies: From time to time these change. See the section *How to Use this Book* for more information.

BBC:				
MHz	21.71	15.07	11.86	6.005
Voice of America:				
MHz	21.49	15.60	9.525	6.035

PASSPORT/VISA

Regulations and requirements may be subject to change at short notice, and you are advised to contact the appropriate diplomatic or consular authority before finalising travel arrangements. Details of these may be found at the head of this country's entry. Any numbers in the chart refer to the footnotes below.

	Passport Required?	Visa Required?	Return Ticket Required?
Full British	Yes	Yes	Yes
BVP	Not valid	-	-
Australian	Yes	Yes	Yes
Canadian	Yes	Yes	Yes
USA	Yes	Yes	Yes
Other EC	Yes	Yes	Yes
Japanese	Yes	Yes	Yes

PASSPORTS: A valid passport is required by all.
British Visitors Passport: Not accepted.
VISAS: Required by all except nationals of Benin, Burkina Faso, Côte d'Ivoire, Cuba, Gambia, Ghana, Guinea-Bissau, Guinea Republic, Liberia, Mali, Mauritania, Niger, Nigeria, Senegal, Sierra Leone and Togo.
Types of visa: Transit, re-entry permit, exit permit.
Application to: Consulate (or Consular Section at Embassy). For addresses, see top of entry. Visitors from countries where there is no Cape Verdian Embassy or Consulate can obtain visas at Cape Verdian Border Services offices at the airports on Sal and Praia.
Application requirements: (a) 2 photographs. (b) 2 application forms.
Working days required: Where there are no complications, visas may be issued immediately, however, it is advisable to anticipate some delay.

MONEY

Currency: Cape Verde Escudo (CVEsc) = 100 centavos. Notes are in denominations of CVEsc2500, 1000, 500, 200 and 100. Coins are in denominations of CVEsc50,

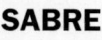

CAPE VERDE	HEALTH REGULATIONS	VISA REGULATIONS
GALILEO/WORLDSPAN	TI-DFT/SID/HE	TI-DFT/SID/VI
SABRE	TIDFT/SID/HE	TIDFT/SID/VI

Code-Link

To access this information on your CRS, swipe the barcode with a light pen or type in the text under the barcode. For more information, see the introduction *How to Use This Book*.

20, 10, 2.5 and 1, and 50 and 20 centavos.
Credit cards: These are not normally accepted but check with the relevant credit card company in case there is now some merchant acceptability.
Exchange rate indicators: The following figures are included as a guide to the movements of the Cape Verde Escudo against Sterling and the US Dollar:

Date:	Oct '89	Oct '90	Oct '91	Oct '92
£1.00=	129.97	130.03	129.43	99.05
$1.00=	82.31	66.56	74.58	62.41

Currency restrictions: The import and export of local currency is prohibited. Import of foreign currency is unlimited; currency declaration is mandatory at entry and departure. The maximum allowable export of foreign currencies is the equivalent of CVEsc20,000 or the amount declared on arrival, whichever is the larger.
Banking hours: 0800-1230 and 1430-1800 Monday to Friday.

DUTY FREE

The following goods may be taken into Cape Verde free of duty:
A reasonable amount of perfume.
Note: Duty-free alcohol and tobacco can be obtained at the international airport on Sal when leaving.

PUBLIC HOLIDAYS

Public holidays observed in Cape Verde are as follows: **Mar 8 '93** Women's Day. **May 1** Labour Day. **Jun 1** Children's Day. **Jul 5** Independence Day. **Sep 12** Day of the Nation. **Dec 25** Christmas Day. **Jan 1 '94** New Year's Day. **Jan 20** National Heroes' Day. **Mar 8** Women's Day.

HEALTH

Regulations and requirements may be subject to change at short notice, and you are advised to contact your doctor well in advance of your intended date of departure. Any numbers in the chart refer to the footnotes below.

	Special Precautions?	Certificate Required?
Yellow Fever	Yes	1
Cholera	No	2
Typhoid & Polio	Yes	-
Malaria	Yes	-
Food & Drink	3	-

[1]: A yellow fever vaccination certificate is required from travellers over one year of age if arriving from infected or endemic areas.
[2]: Following WHO guidelines issued in 1973, a cholera vaccination certificate is not a condition of entry to Cape Verde. However, cholera is a serious risk in this country and precautions are essential. Up-to-date advice should be sought before deciding whether these precautions should include vaccination as medical opinion is divided over its effectiveness. See the *Health* section at the back of the book.
[3]: All water should be regarded as being potentially contaminated. Water used for drinking, brushing teeth or making ice should have first been boiled or otherwise sterilised. Milk is unpasteurised and should be boiled. Powdered or tinned milk is available and is advised, but make sure that it is reconstituted with pure water. Avoid all dairy products. Only eat well-cooked meat and fish, preferably served hot. Pork, salad and mayonnaise may carry increased risk. Vegetables should be cooked and fruit peeled.
Health Care: Health insurance is strongly advised, although in-patient treatment is free in general wards on presentation of a passport. Treatment is private and expensive on small islands.

TRAVEL - International

AIR: The national airline is *Transportes Aéreos de Cabo Verde (TACV)*.
Approximate flight time: From *London* to Lisbon (Portugal) is 3 hours and from Lisbon to Sal is 4 hours. Please note that the stop-over in Lisbon will usually be overnight if flying by *TAP Air Portugal*.
International airports: *Amílcar Cabral (SID)* on Sal is the only airport with a runway long enough to take jets; there are eight others throughout the islands. Since 1987 work has been in progress to expand facilities at *Amílcar Cabral* airport.
SEA: Mindelo is the principal port. São Vincente is served by passenger and cargo ships. There is also a port at Praia.

TRAVEL - Internal

AIR: There are internal flights to all inhabited islands except Brava.
SEA: There are regular boat and ferry services between all the islands.
ROAD: There are over 3050km (1895 miles) of roads on the islands, of which a third are paved. Taxi fares should be agreed in advance. Buses are satisfactory. There is a road improvement programme. **Documentation:** International Driving Permit is recommended, although not legally required.
JOURNEY TIMES: The following chart gives the approximate journey times (in hours and minutes) from Cidade de Praia to other major cities/towns in Cape Verde.

	Air	Sea
San Vincente	0.45	-
Sal	0.45	-
Maio	0.15	-
Boa Vista	0.30	-
Fogo	0.40	-
Brava	-	12.00
St Nicolau	0.50	-

ACCOMMODATION

HOTELS: Hotel accommodation is currently scarce. There are international hotels on Sal Island and a tourist complex at Praia. Otherwise there are small hotels at Mindelo and on Ilha Do Sal (Sal), Fogo and Praia. In total, there are two 4-star, two 3-star and two 2-star hotels on Cape Verde. For further information, contact the Secretaria de Estado de Comércio e Turismo (see above).

RESORTS & EXCURSIONS

Tourism is not currently an important part of Cape Verde's economy, although there are several promotional schemes aimed at changing this. There are many superb diving sites around the islands, several of which have wrecks of ships dating back to the 16th century. Many of the islands have spectacular mountain scenery and beautiful deserted beaches, such as Tarrafal on São Tiago. San Filipe has a spectacular volcano as well as fine beaches. There are good markets on some of the islands, and a number of colourful festivals. Mindelo on São Vincente, with its Portuguese-style buildings, is worth a visit.

SOCIAL PROFILE

FOOD & DRINK: Restaurants are mainly in hotels. The main local culinary speciality is *cachupa*, a mess of maize and beans. Fruits include mangoes, bananas, papayes, goiabas (guavas), zimbrão, tambarinas, marmelos, azedinhas, tamaras and cocos. **Drink:** Beer, wine and local spirits are commonly available; punch is also popular. Soft drinks are expensive.
NIGHTLIFE: There are discos in hotels and several nightclubs.
SHOPPING: Some hotels have boutiques. There are daily markets. The Santa Catarina market is held on Wednesdays and Saturdays. Coconut shells are carved by local craftsmen; there is also pottery, lacework and basketry.
SPORT: Watersports include **sailing, swimming, surfing, diving** and **fishing. Tennis, archery, bodybuilding, snooker** and **ping-pong** are also available. Many facilities are provided by hotels as part of the expanding tourist trade.
SPECIAL EVENTS: There are several annual festivals, the precise dates of which change from year to year. *Todo o Mundo Canta* (a song festival) and *Todo o Mundo Danca* (a dance festival) are held annually in the 5 de Julho amusement park. There is also the *Baia das Gatas* music festival (around August) and *Carnaval* in Mindelo City (around February).
SOCIAL CONVENTIONS: The usual European social courtesies should be observed. **Tipping:** It is normal to give 10%.

BUSINESS PROFILE

ECONOMY: Although most of the population have traditionally been engaged in subsistence agriculture – producing maize and fruit – many years of drought have seen this dwindle to the point where Cape Verde needs large amounts of food aid. Remittances from emigré communities – some 300,000 Cape Verdeans live abroad, mainly in the US – enable the islands to balance their external payments, even though exports, principally fish and fish products, cover less than 5% of imports. Apart from a few fish processing and canning factories, there has been virtually no industry on the islands, and diversification into other industries has continued as part of a 4-year development plan; salt and pozzolana are mined and various manufacturing industries have been introduced; also there are hopes that the tourist trade can be developed without disrupting local lifestyles by directing visitors to less populated islands. Portugal and The Netherlands supply half of Cape Verde's import requirements.
BUSINESS: All correspondence should be in English or French. Most of Cape Verde's business links are with Portugal.
COMMERCIAL INFORMATION: The following organisation can offer advice: Associação Comercial Barlavento (Chamber of Commerce), CP 62, Mindelo, São Vicente. Tel: 313 281.
CONFERENCES/CONVENTIONS: Cape Verde has earned a high reputation internationally as a venue for sensitive inter-government conferences. As facilities improve business communities of the world may follow.

HISTORY & GOVERNMENT

HISTORY: The Portuguese discovered the islands in the 15th century, probably on two separate expeditions; they were uninhabited and there was no evidence of previous settlement. By the late 15th century settlement began on São Tiago, which later became used as a supply point for slaves traded to Brazil and the West Indies. The inhospitable landscape could not support the growing population and extreme poverty has dominated the life of the colony. Cape Verde achieved independence in 1975, shortly after the granting of independence to Guinea-Bissau, with whom Cape Verde had close political associations. The Partido Africano da Independência do Guiné e Cabo Verde (PAICV) took control of the political activities of both countries and full unification was discussed. This proposal was shelved after the 1980 coup in Guinea-Bissau, after which the Cape Verdian branch of PAICV was renamed the Partido Africano da Independência de Cabo Verde (PAIGV) and the two countries pursued their own separate paths of development. At the turn of the 1990s, the Government followed the continental trend and held elections in February 1991. The PAIGV faced the challenge of the Movimento para Democracia (MPD) which duly won both the legislature and the race for the Presidency in which their candidate, ex-supreme court judge Mascarenhas Monteiro, defeated the incumbent Aristides Pereira.
GOVERNMENT: For a decade after January 1981, the only political party in the Republic of Cape Verde has been the PAICV. Following multi-party elections in 1991, the ruling party in the national assembly has been the Movimento para Democracia.

CLIMATE

Generally temperate, but rainfall is very low.
Required clothing: Lightweight throughout the year, tropical for midsummer.

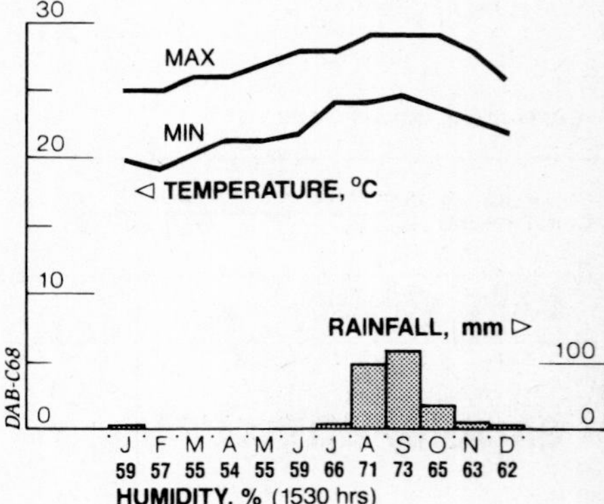

CAYMAN ISLANDS

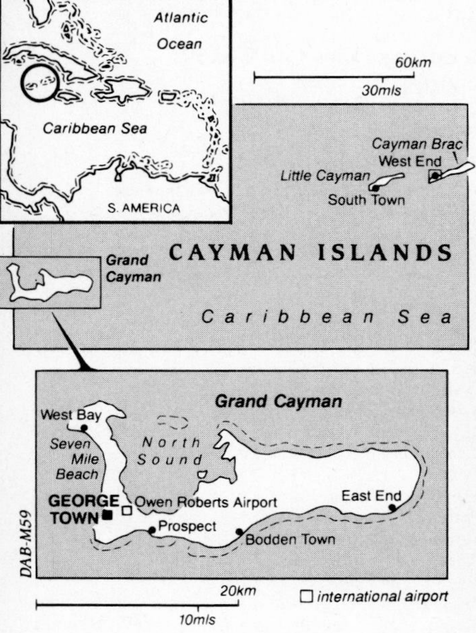

Location: Caribbean; south of Cuba; 720km (480 miles) southwest of Miami.

Cayman Islands Department of Tourism
PO Box 67
Tower Building
George Town
Grand Cayman, British West Indies
Tel: 97999. Fax: 94053. Telex: 4260.
Cayman Islands Government Office *and* **Department of Tourism** *and* **Reservation Service**
Trevor House
100 Brompton Road, Knightsbridge
London SW3 1EX
Tel: (071) 581 9418 (Government office) *or* 581 9960 (Department of Tourism). Fax: (071) 584 4463. Opening hours: 0900-1700 Monday to Friday.
UK Passport Office
Clive House
Petty France
London SW1H 9HD
Tel: (071) 279 3434.
Cayman Islands Department of Tourism Representative: Benelux
Associated Travel Consultants
Leidsestraat 32
1017 BP Amsterdam
The Netherlands
Tel: (20) 626 1197 *or* 627 2190. Fax: (20) 627 4869.
Cayman Islands Department of Tourism Representative: Germany/Switzerland/Austria
Marketing Services International
6000 Frankfurt/Main 1
Liebigstrasse 8
Germany
Tel: (069) 726 342. Fax: (069) 727 714.
Cayman Islands Department of Tourism Representative: Italy
Gandin Associati Martinengo
Via Fratelli
Ruffini 9
20123 Milan
Tel: (02) 480 12068. Fax: (02) 463 532.
Also in: Atlanta, Baltimore, Boston, Chicago, Dallas, Houston, Los Angeles, Miami, San Francisco and Tampa.

AREA: 259 sq km (100 sq miles).
POPULATION: 23,355 (1989).
POPULATION DENSITY: 97.9 per sq km.
CAPITAL: George Town. **Population:** 13,000.
GEOGRAPHY: The Cayman Islands are situated in the Caribbean, 290km (180 miles) northwest of Jamaica, and comprise Grand Cayman, Little Cayman and Cayman Brac. The islands are peaks of a subterranean mountain range extending from Cuba towards the Gulf of Honduras. The beaches are said to be the best in the Caribbean, the most notable being Seven Mile Beach on Grand Cayman. Tall pines line many of the beaches; those located on the east and west coasts are equally well protected offshore by the Barrier Reef.
LANGUAGE: English is the official language, with minority local dialects also spoken.
RELIGION: Mainly Presbyterian with Anglican, Roman Catholic, Seventh Day Adventists, Pilgrims, Pilgrim Holiness Church of God, Jehovah's Witnesses and Bahai minorities on Grand Cayman. Baptists on Cayman Brac.
TIME: GMT - 5.
ELECTRICITY: 110 volts, 60Hz.
COMMUNICATIONS: Telephone: A modern telephone system links the Cayman Islands to the world by

Hand-feeding friendly stingrays at Stingray City, Grand Cayman

submarine cable and satellite; IDD is now possible to North America and Europe. Country code: 1 809 94. **Fax:** This is available at most hotels and banks. Some businesses also have public facilities. **Telex/telegram:** Telecommunications are provided by Cable and Wireless (West Indies) Limited under government franchise. Telex is available from a public booth at the Cable and Wireless office. Many hotels and apartments have their own telex facilities. Public telegraph operates daily 0730-1800, accepting cables from any country. **Post:** Mail is not delivered to private addresses in the Cayman Islands, but collected from numbered PO boxes. *Poste Restante* mail should be addressed 'General Delivery' at the post office. Post office hours: 0830-1530 Monday to Friday, 0830-1200 Saturday. **Press:** *The Daily Caymanian Compass* is published five times a week.

BBC World Service and Voice of America frequencies: From time to time these change. See the section *How to Use this Book* for more information.

BBC:				
MHz	17.72	11.78	9.915	5.965
Voice of America:				
MHz	15.21	11.70	6.130	0.930

PASSPORT/VISA

Regulations and requirements may be subject to change at short notice, and you are advised to contact the appropriate diplomatic or consular authority before finalising travel arrangements. Details of these may be found at the head of this country's entry. Any numbers in the chart refer to the footnotes below.

	Passport Required?	Visa Required?	Return Ticket Required?
Full British	1	No	Yes
BVP	Valid	No	Yes
Australian	Yes	No	Yes
Canadian	1	No	Yes
USA	1	No	Yes
Other EC	Yes	No	Yes
Japanese	Yes	No	Yes

PASSPORTS: [1] Valid passports required by all except nationals of Canada, UK and USA, if proof of nationality is provided and return or onward ticket shows that within 6 months the visitor will leave the Cayman Islands.

British Visitors Passport: Valid.

VISAS: A US visa is required for visitors travelling via the USA, with the exception of participants in the Visa Waiver Scheme (application forms and details available from international carriers). A Cayman Islands visa is required by all except:

(a) nationals of countries referred to in the chart above;

(b) nationals of Andorra, Antigua & Barbuda, Argentina, Austria, Bahamas, Bahrain, Bangladesh, Barbados, Belize, Botswana, Brazil, Chile, Costa Rica, Cyprus, Dominica, Dominican Republic, Ecuador, El Salvador, Finland, Gambia, Ghana, Grenada, Guatemala, Guyana, Haiti, Iceland, India, Israel, Jamaica, Kenya, Kiribati, Kuwait, Lesotho, Liechtenstein, Malawi, Malaysia, Malta, Mauritius, Mexico, Monaco, Nauru, New Zealand, Nigeria, Norway, Oman, Panama, Papua New Guinea, Peru, St Lucia, St Vincent & the Grenadines, San Marino, Saudi Arabia, Seychelles, Sierra Leone, Singapore, Solomon Islands, South Africa, Sri Lanka, Swaziland, Sweden, Switzerland, Tanzania, Tonga, Trinidad & Tobago, Tuvalu, Uganda, Vanuatu, Venezuela, Western Samoa, Zambia and Zimbabwe.

Pirates Week, Grand Cayman

Visitors who wish to conduct business should see the section *Business visits* below.

Types of visa: Tourist, Transit and Business. Visa costs: fee £12; telex charge £8; referral fee £3.

Validity: 1 to 6 months.

Application to: The UK Passport Office. Enquiries may be directed to any Cayman Islands Government or Department of Tourism office (addresses at top of entry).

Application requirements: (a) 2 application forms. (b) Valid passport. (c) 2 passport-size photos. (d) Funds sufficient to cover duration of stay.

Working days required: Dependent upon nature of application. Allow 21 days.

Business visits: For visitors intending to conduct business in the Cayman Islands a Temporary Work Permit must be obtained before arrival, which is issued by the Cayman Islands Department of Immigration (address at top of entry). Visas must be obtained in advance from the Visa Section of the Foreign & Commonwealth Office (tel: (071) 270 3000) who will telex George Town for approval and stamp the visitor's passport.

MONEY

Currency: Cayman Islands Dollar (CI$) = 100 cents. Notes are in denominations of CI$100, 50, 25, 10, 5 and 1. Coins are in denominations of 25, 10, 5 and 1 cents.

Currency exchange: US currency circulates freely. Canadian and British currencies are also acceptable. Credit cards and travellers cheques are preferable to personal cheques.

Credit cards: All accepted. Check with your credit card company for details of merchant acceptability and other services which may be available.

Travellers cheques: In some places these are preferred to credit cards.

Exchange rate indicators: The following figures are included as a guide to the movement of the Cayman Islands Dollar against Sterling and the US Dollar:

Date:	Oct '89	Oct '90	Oct '91	Oct '92
£1.00=	1.34	1.62	1.44	1.30
$1.00=	0.83	0.83	0.83	0.83

Currency restrictions: No restriction on import or export of foreign or local currency.

Banking hours: 0930-1430 Monday to Thursday, 0930-1630 Friday.

DUTY FREE

The following goods may be taken into the Cayman Islands without incurring any customs duty:

200 cigarettes or 50 cigars or 250g of tobacco;
1 quart of strong alcoholic beverages (including wines).

Note: Pets require a permit from Cayman Islands Department of Agriculture.

CAYMAN ISLANDS	**HEALTH REGULATIONS**	**VISA REGULATIONS** Code-Link
GALILEO/WORLDSPAN	TI-DFT/GCM/HE	TI-DFT/GCM/VI
SABRE	TIDFT/GCM/HE	TIDFT/GCM/VI

To access this information on your CRS, swipe the barcode with a light pen or type in the text under the barcode. For more information, see the introduction *How to Use This Book.*

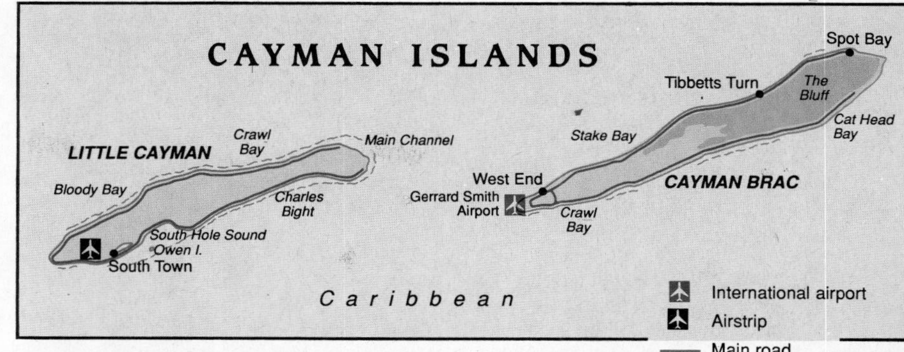

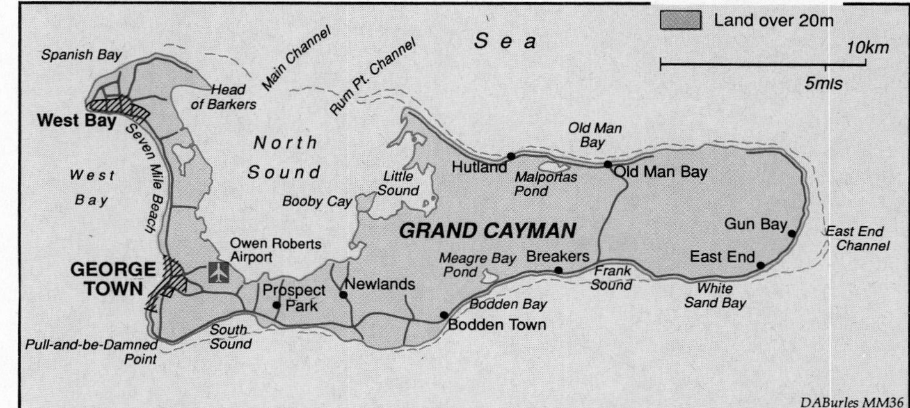

PUBLIC HOLIDAYS

Public holidays observed in the Cayman Islands are as follows: **Apr 9** Good Friday. **Apr 12** Easter Monday. **May 17** Discovery Day. **Jun 14** Queen's Birthday. **Jul 5** Constitution Day. **Nov 8** Remembrance Day. **Dec 25** Christmas Day. **Dec 27** Official Holiday for Christmas Day. **Dec 28** Boxing Day. **Jan 1 '94** New Year's Day. **Feb 16** Ash Wednesday.

HEALTH

Regulations and requirements may be subject to change at short notice, and you are advised to contact your doctor well in advance of your intended date of departure. Any numbers in the chart refer to the footnotes below.

	Special Precautions?	Certificate Required?
Yellow Fever	No	No
Cholera	No	No
Typhoid & Polio	1	No
Malaria	No	No
Food & Drink	No	-

[1]: Vaccinations are recommended.

Health care: Insect repellent is useful to counter mosquitoes and sandflies in some places though there is unlikely to be any serious health risk from these. There is a well-equipped 52-bed hospital in Grand Cayman, as well as private doctors, dentists and opticians. There is a small hospital in Cayman Brac. Health costs are similar to the UK. Private insurance is recommended.

TRAVEL - International

AIR: The Cayman Islands national airline is *Cayman Airways (KX)*.

Approximate flight times: From Miami to Grand Cayman is 1 hour 5 minutes; connection times vary. *Cayman Airways* fly to the Cayman Islands from Miami, New York, Baltimore, Tampa, Atlanta, Houston and Jamaica. The most convenient gateways from UK/Europe are Miami and the British West Indies with same-day onward connections. *Cayman Airways, American Airlines, Northwest* and *United Airlines* have flights from Miami to Grand Cayman. *Northwest* also fly from Raleigh Durham, North Carolina to Grand Cayman.

From *New York* to Grand Cayman is 3 hours 30 minutes.

International airports: *Grand Cayman (GCM)* (Owen Roberts Airport) is 3.5km (2 miles) northeast of the city, and *Cayman Brac (CYB)* (Gerard Smith Airport) is 8km (5 miles) from the town. Taxis meet all flights (10 minutes journey into town). Airport facilities in Grand Cayman include an outgoing duty-free shop for all international departures, car hire, and a bar/restaurant (open for all arrivals and departures) in Grand Cayman.

Departure tax: CI$6 or US$7.50 is payable by all travellers over 12 years old.

SEA: The main port of George Town on Grand Cayman is an important port of call for leading international cruise lines. Passenger lines operate from North America, Mexico and Europe.

TRAVEL - Internal

AIR: The main island of Grand Cayman is connected to Little Cayman and Cayman Brac by internal flights by *Cayman Airways*. There is also a service between Cayman Brac and Little Cayman (see below under *Journey Times*).

ROAD: A good road network connects the coastal towns of all three main islands. **Bus:** A cheap but infrequent bus service runs between George Town and the West Bay residential area, connecting most of the hotels along Seven Mile Beach and also to Bodden Town and East End from George Town. **Taxi:** There are large fleets of taxi cabs. Bicycles are also available. **Car hire:** This is by far the best way to get around. All the major car hire companies are represented in George Town. Driving is on the left and drivers must be over 21. Speed limits are strictly enforced. Full insurance is required and must be arranged with the rental company. There are also two moped and motorbike hire companies. **Documentation:** An International Driving Permit or Tourist Driving Licence (Visitor's Driving Permit) is required, which will be issued on presentation of a valid licence from the traveller's country of origin.

JOURNEY TIMES: The following chart gives approximate journey times (in hours and minutes) from George Town, Grand Cayman, to other major centres in the islands.

	Air	Road	Sea
Cayman Brac	0.30	-	-
Little Cayman	0.35	-	-
Rum Point	-	0.45	1.15
Cayman Kai	-	0.45	-

Cayman Brac to Little Cayman is 10 minutes by air.

ACCOMMODATION

There is a wide variety of accommodation, ranging from luxury hotels and self-catering condominiums to more economical hotels and dive lodges. Most of Grand Cayman's condominiums are superbly situated on beaches and coastal areas and guests can walk out of the apartments onto superb beaches with crystal clear water. Many condominiums have been built in the last few years and are equipped with the latest fittings and furnishings, as well as central facilities such as swimming pools and tennis courts.

HOTELS: The leading hotels are located on the coast. Some of the best known overlook Grand Cayman's renowned *Seven Mile Beach*, a dazzling stretch of fine powdery sand said to be one of the world's most beautiful beaches. There is also a fine selection of diving resort hotels. Hotels providing accommodation with 100 rooms are considered large in the Cayman Islands, and hotels of this size are only found on Grand Cayman. Prices are seasonal, being more expensive in the winter than in the summer (when some hotels offer free accommodation for children under 12). A 6% room tax is payable to the hotel on departure. Most also add a service charge. For more information contact Cayman Islands Reservations in London on (071) 581 9960.

Grading: Hotels vary in standard from *luxury* (very comfortable, with some outstanding features) to *tourist class* (budget hotel).

SELF-CATERING: There is a wide variety of apartments and villas available, from the most luxurious to

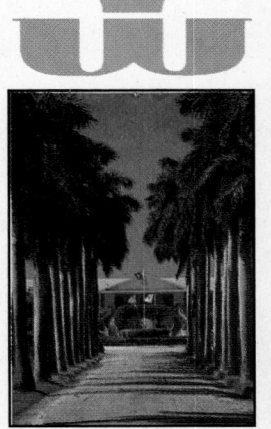

the relatively austere. The Department of Tourism can give full details of these, and also of beach cottages for families, and dive lodges. The following organisation can also be of assistance: Cayman Islands Hotel & Condominium Association (CIHCA), West Bay Road, PO Box 1367, George Town. Tel: 98111.

RESORTS & EXCURSIONS

There are three islands in this British Dependent Territory, which has long been associated with buccaneers and pirates:

Grand Cayman: Most of the population lives on this island, surrounded by water rich in colourful marine life and spectacular coral reefs. There is a 6km (4-mile) stone wall at Bodden Town, known as the Grand Cayman's Wall of China, built to protect residents from pirate attacks. **Seven Mile Beach** is the main tourist centre but, unlike many elsewhere, though highly developed, it retains its charm and the new developments do not overwhelm the visitor. The post office at **Hell** nearby has a lively trade postmarking cards and letters. Close by Seven Mile Beach is the unique **Cayman Turtle Farm** though, owing to conservation pressures, the meat is usually only consumed locally (for more information see *Shopping* in the *Social Profile* section below). The capital of Grand Cayman is **George Town**. Along the harbour front are traditional Caymanian gingerbread-style buildings and, close by, modern banks and finance houses. **Cayman Brac**, where fewer than 2500 people live, gets its name 'Brac' (Gaelic for 'bluff') from the huge bluff which rises 42m (140ft) from the sea. The Brac, which is 143km (89 miles) northeast of Grand Cayman, is about 19km (12 miles) long, and not much more than a mile wide. The rocky cliffs are excellent for exploring and hiking. The area is riddled with caves and some are barely explored. There are dozens of wrecks for divers to explore. It also has a rare bird sanctuary. The island provided the basis for Robert Louis Stevenson's *Treasure Island*.

Little Cayman, the home of 41 people, and many more wild birds and iguanas, is 11km (7 miles) southeast of Cayman Brac. This tiny island is just 16km (10 miles) long, and at no point more than 3km (2 miles) wide. Expert anglers consider that its flats provide the best bone fishing in the world.

SOCIAL PROFILE

FOOD & DRINK: Restaurants are excellent, with several outstanding gourmet establishments, such as The Grand Old House, Hemmingways, The Wharf and the Living Reef. Specialities are turtle steaks, turtle soup, conch chowder and conch salad, red snapper, sea bass and lobster. There are various standards of restaurants with good service, most of which accept credit cards. **Drink:** Bars and restaurants are well stocked with all beverages normally consumed in America and Europe. Draught beer is available in a few bars.

NIGHTLIFE: Grand Cayman has nightclubs featuring international live entertainment and dancing, and weekend dances are held at hotels on Cayman Brac. The islands also have two indoor theatres, two outdoor theatres, while some hotels provide film and slide screenings for guests.

SHOPPING: As a shopping centre, George Town, with fascinating boutiques and duty-free shops, is now one of the leading centres in the Caribbean region. Half a dozen modern and sophisticated shopping centres have recently been established offering prestigious North American and European lines in fashion, furnishings and household goods. Special purchases include china, crystal, silver, woollens and linen, French perfume and local crafts of black coral, sculptures, tortoise and turtle shell jewellery (turtles are bred at Cayman Turtle Farm, which also undertakes conservation measures). *US citizens, and travellers via the US, should note that turtle products cannot be imported into that country, even by persons in transit.* Many luxury goods and essential foodstuffs are duty free but duty of up to 20% is charged on other items. **Shopping hours:** 0900-1700 Monday to Friday, 0830-1230 Saturday.

SPORT: Tennis, cricket, football, rugby, squash and **golf** are popular. The Britannia Golf Course, designed by Jack Nicklaus, may be played either as a 9-hole championship course or as an 18-hole course. **Watersports:** The Cayman Islands have a vast range of watersports, including **swimming, sailing, parasailing** and **windsurfing**, and, especially, **scuba diving** and **fishing**. Divers think of the Cayman Islands as the 'Divers' Islands'. There are over 20 dive operations in the Cayman Islands. On few other islands

TOUR OPERATORS SERVING THE CAYMAN ISLANDS

Cayman Islands UK Tour Operators for 1993

Operator	Telephone
Airtours	0706 240 033
Airwaves	081 875 1188
American Connections	0494 473 273
British Airways Holidays	0293 611 444
Caribbean Connections	0244 329 556
Divers World	081 458 5115
Elegant Resorts	0244 329 671
Frontiers	081 994 6958
Gold Medal TVL	0253 791 222
Harlequin Worldwide	0708 852 780
Hayes & Jarvis	081 748 0088
Interline Holidays	0707 372 886
Jetsave	0342 328 231
Key to America	0784 248 777
Kuoni Travel	0306 740 888
Peregor Travel	08956 30871
Thomas Cook Holidays	0733 332 255
Twicker's World	081 892 7606
Virgin Holidays	0293 562 944

Cayman Islands European Operators for 1993

BENELUX:

Operator	Telephone
Holland Overseas Travel	070 355 9551
Interline Travel	031 2135 17777
Koudijs	01820 14477
Odysseus Travel	03 499 3825
Passe Partout	031 10258 1212

GERMANY:

Operator	Telephone
Airtours International	069 79280
Caribbean Holidays	089 553 434
IPD Tours	8344 051
Mosaic Reisen	0421 328 309
Nova Reisen	089 237 080
Transatlantik Reisen	06221 27181

AUSTRIA:

Operator	Telephone
Airtour Austria	01 534 110
Faraway Farnik	717 970

FINLAND:

Operator	Telephone
Finlandia	90 659 100
Travelpoint	90 131 161

FRANCE:

Operator	Telephone
Airtour Touropa	42 3300 99
Zenith	42 9614 09

SWITZERLAND:

Operator	Telephone
Caribtours	01 463 8863
Kuoni Travel	01 277 4444

NORWAY:

Operator	Telephone
Nordic America	047 259 1160
Paddan Nordmanns Reiser	02 416 582
Passage Tours	02 414 800

SWEDEN:

Operator	Telephone
Paddan Resor AB	031 17 45 40
Stopover World Travel	031 11 67 70
Swansons Travel	0479 14470

ITALY:

Operator	Telephone
Aquadiving Di Blue 'N Green	0721 400 562
Agamare	02 7601 3691
Atitur	02 551 1819
Award – Toledo Executive Travel	02 7601 3621
Chiari Sommariva	02 85041
Columbus	010 5711
Di Lauro Viaggi	02 7609 5231
Donzelli Viaggi	0521 231 203
Fantasia Viaggi	051 251 046
Francorosso Intl. Spa	051 251 084/247 728
Gastaldi Tours	010 28591
Mediolanum	02 7601 3676
Meridiano Viaggi E Turismo	06 436 951
Palatino Viaggi	06 574 3545
Pofinatours	06 4828 280
Press Tours	02 7611 1069
Publitour	02 668 8282
Veronelli	02 937 2915
Viaggidea	02 895 291
VV Tours	02 2900 5444
Zebra Viaggi	0584 45590

can divers enjoy such accessible diving sites; on Seven Mile Beach excellent diving begins 200 yards from the shore. Diving shops and boats are to be found at most hotels. Some diving resorts feature underwater photographic sales, service and training, including camera rentals and repairs, along with overnight processing of slides. The Islands' main hospital in George Town, capital of Grand Cayman, even has its own decompression chamber – the Cayman 'Unbender'. The variety of diving sites ranges from shallow dives near offshore reefs to the famous virgin sites off Cayman Brac, and the famous North Wall dive off Grand Cayman – a sheer drop to the bed of the ocean recognised as the 'Mount Everest' of diving sites and Stingray City, known as the 'best 12ft dive in the world'. The abundance of fish, marine and coral life which can be found in the turquoise waters off the islands is protected by some of the most advanced conservation measures in the region. Scuba divers must be certified by an internationally recognised course. Those who don't make the grade can enjoy the reefs in the air-conditioned comfort of the *Atlantis Submarine*, which offers hour-long dives for up to 46 passengers – highly recommended. **Fishing:** The Cayman Islands established themselves as a leading international game fishing resort in spectacular fashion by holding the first annual *Million Dollar Month Fishing Festival*, in June 1984. Prizes total over one million dollars. Grand Cayman occupies a unique location in the migratory path of the big fish – marlin, tuna, dolphin, swordfish and wahoo – which swim through the deep troughs surrounding the island. Due to the abundance of fish and dependable weather, the Cayman Islands are probably the only place in the Caribbean where the visitor can fish all year round. In 1980, some 200 blue marlin were boated in the Cayman Islands; an average catch of marlin for any Caribbean destination is 25 per year. In one 10-month period, one of the Cayman Islands' leading professional fishermen boated 78, including one of 420lb caught after a five and a half hour battle. The best fishing is between Grand Cayman's west coast and the banks, 7.5km (12 miles) offshore; the Trench, 6-13km (4-8 miles) off the west coast, is particularly good. There is also outstanding fishing for tarpon and bonefish in the inshore lakes of Little Cayman, the smallest of the three islands which make up the Cayman Islands.

SPECIAL EVENTS: The following is a selection of the major festivals and other special events celebrated annually in the Cayman Islands during 1993-94. For a complete list contact the Cayman Islands Department of Tourism.

Apr 2-3 *Batabano*. **Apr 10-11** *Easter Regatta*. **Jun 1-30** *10th Annual Million Dollar Month Fishing Tournament*. **Jun 10-14** *7th Annual Cayman Islands International Aviation Week*. **Jun 14** *Queen's Birthday Celebration*. **Oct 22-31** *Pirates Week*. **Oct 31** *Halloween*.

SOCIAL CONVENTIONS: The mode of life on the Cayman Islands is a blend of local traditions and of American and British patterns of behaviour. Handshaking is the usual greeting. Because of the large number of people with a similar surname, (such as Ebanks and Bodden), a person may be introduced by his Christian name (such as Mr Tom or Mr Jim). Flowers are acceptable as a gift on arrival or following a visit for a meal. Dinner jackets are seldom worn. Short or long dresses are appropriate for women in the evenings. It is normal to prescribe mode of dress on invitation cards. Casual wear is acceptable in most places, but beachwear is best confined to the beach to avoid offence. **Tipping:** 10-15% is normal for most services. Hotels and apartments state specific amount. Restaurant bills usually include 10-15% in lieu of tipping.

BUSINESS PROFILE

ECONOMY: The Cayman Islands have no direct taxation, and have become important as an offshore financial centre and a tax haven. Tourism is the other main source of revenue for the Caymans. There is little agriculture, and most of the foodstuffs for the islands are imported. The standard of living on the islands is generally high, and the per capita income is the highest in the region. The healthy state of the economy has attracted immigrants from Jamaica, Europe and North America who now make up 30% of the working population.

BUSINESS: Business suits when calling on senior officials and local heads of business and also for semi-formal or formal functions. Exchange of calling cards is usual and letters of introduction sometimes used. It is generally easy to gain access to offices of senior government officials, politicians and business executives. Civil servants are precluded from accepting gifts except for diaries or calendars at Christmas. Monetary gifts or expensive presents are not encouraged in the private sector. **Office hours:** 0830-1700 Monday to Friday.

COMMERCIAL INFORMATION: The following organisation can offer advice: Cayman Islands Chamber of Commerce, PO Box 1000, Butterfield House, George Town, Grand Cayman. Tel: 94746. Fax: 90209.

CONFERENCES/CONVENTIONS: Many hotels have conference facilities. Contact the Cayman Islands Department of Tourism for details.

Seven Mile Beach, Grand Cayman

Bodden Town, Grand Cayman

Beach at Cayman Brac

HISTORY & GOVERNMENT

HISTORY: The two smaller Cayman Islands were discovered by Columbus in 1503. Sir Francis Drake explored the area in 1586, but it was 1670 before the islands came under full British rule and the present population is considered to date from that time. Grand Cayman was settled from Jamaica by 1672; Little Cayman and Cayman Brac were settled some time later and maintained a separate administration until 1877. The Governor of Jamaica held administrative responsibility for the islands until 1962, when Jamaica itself became independent. Since then the islands have had their own Governor who is a nominee of the British crown (see *Government*). Despite efforts to develop an orthodox political system during the 1960s, Cayman politics have operated to this day without political parties as such, mainly because of the influence of the Governor over the nomination of executive Committee members. During elections, 'teams' are formed, the main protagonists being the *National* team and the *Unity* team. Demands for independence from Britain have been virtually non-existent in recent years, having dissipated along with political parties in the 1960s. There is, however, pressure for constitutional reform which is currently under consideration both on the islands and in London. As with the rest of the Caribbean, the United States exercises considerable economic and political influence. Both the American and British governments have been concerned about the exploitation of the islands for drug trafficking.
GOVERNMENT: As a British Dependent Territory, the Governor (currently Michael Gore CBE) is appointed by the British monarch. The Governor is responsible for external affairs, security and defence. He is also Chairman of the Executive Council comprising three official and four Elected Members, the latter elected from among the 15 elected representatives in the Legislative Assembly. The three Official Members are the Chief Secretary, the Financial Secretary and the Attorney General. Each member of Executive Council is allocated a portfolio of responsibilities by the Governor. The 15 elected members of the Legislative Assembly represent six districts and a General Election is held every four years (unless the Assembly is dissolved sooner). In 1990 the Assembly passed a motion calling for the creation of an office of Speaker and an appointee was sworn in in February 1991. A Constitutional Review took place in 1991 and the findings are currently being considered.

CLIMATE

Very warm, tropical climate throughout the year. High temperatures are moderated by trade winds. Rainy season from May to October but showers are generally brief.
Required clothing: Lightweight cottons and linens and a light raincoat or umbrella for the rainy season. Warmer clothes may be needed on cooler evenings

CAYMAN ISLANDS

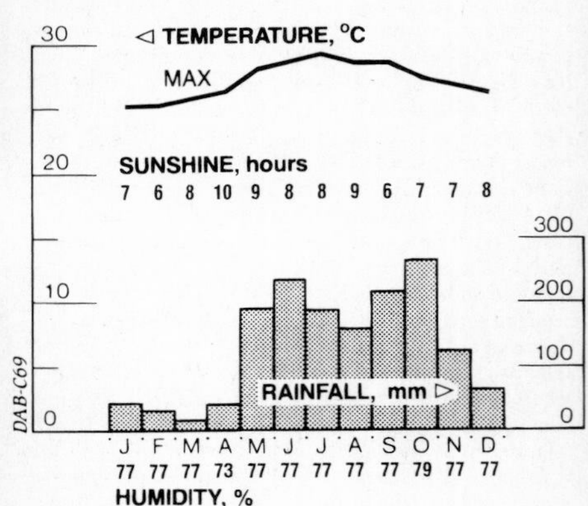

TEMPERATURE CONVERSIONS
-20 -10 0°C 10 20 30 40
0 10 20 30°F40 50 60 70 80 90 100
RAINFALL CONVERSIONS 0mm 200 400 600 800
0in 5 10 15 20 25 30

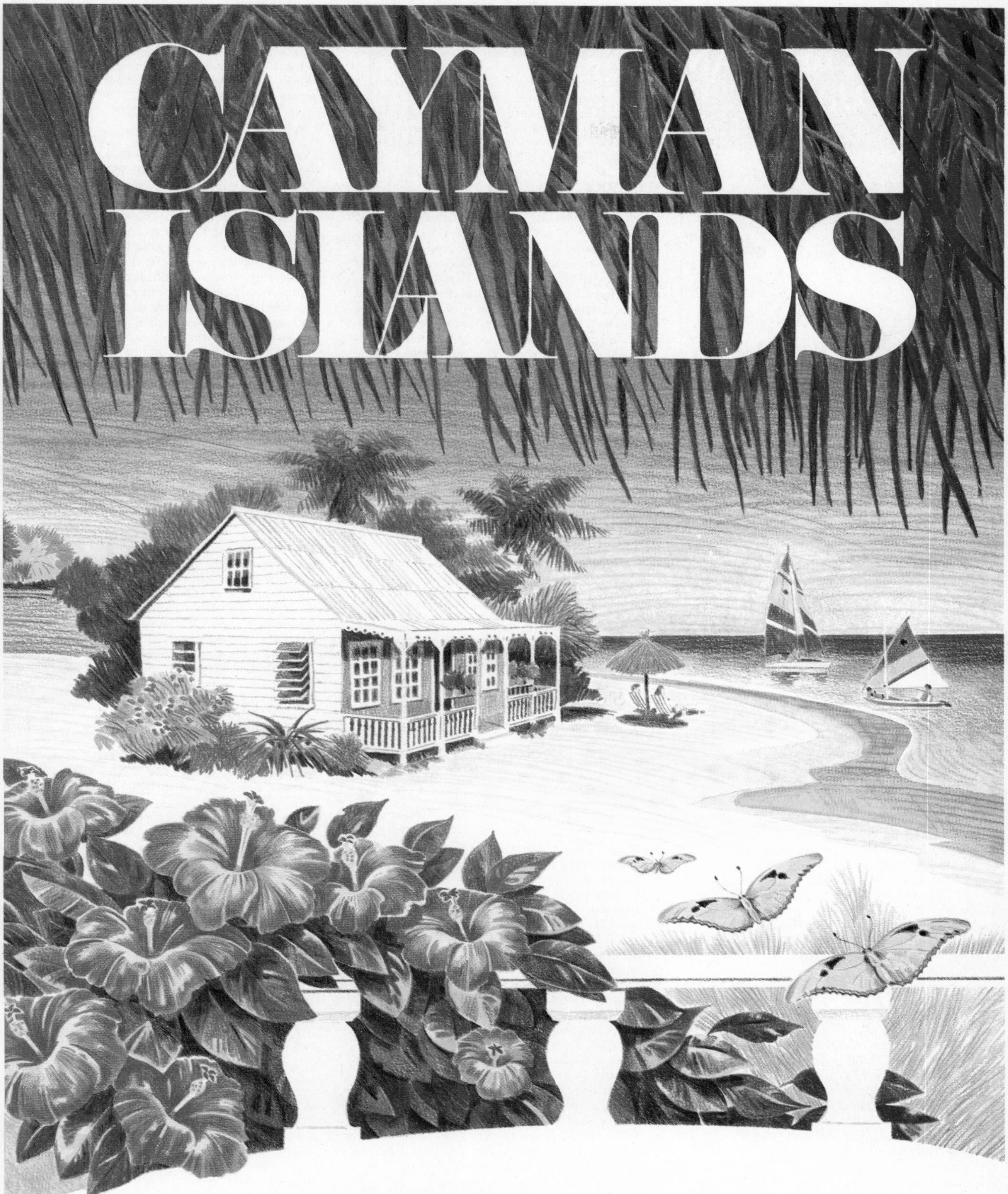

CENTRAL AFRICAN REPUBLIC

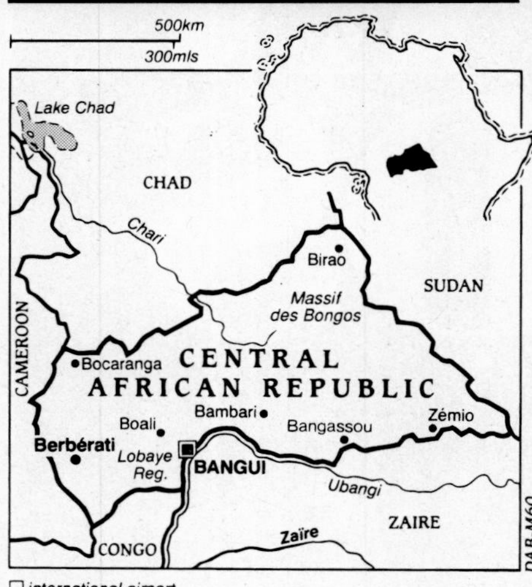

☐ international airport

Location: Central Africa.

Office National Centrafricain du Tourisme (OCATOUR)
BP 655
Bangui, Central African Republic
Tel: 614 566.
Embassy of the Central African Republic
29 boulevard de Montmorency
75116 Paris, France
Tel: (1) 42 24 42 56. Telex: 611908.
British Consulate
c/o SOCACIA
BP 728
Bangui, Central African Republic
Tel: 610 300 *or* 611 045. Fax: 615 130. Telex: 5258 RG.
Embassy of the Central African Republic
1618 22nd Street, NW
Washington, DC 20008
Tel: (202) 483 7800.
Embassy of the United States of America
BP 924, Avenue David Dacko
Bangui, Central African Republic
Tel: 610 200 *or* 612 578 *or* 614 333. Fax: 614 494. Telex: 5287 RC.
Honorary Consulate General of the Central African Republic
3rd Floor, 225 St Jacques Street West
Montréal, Québec H2Y 1M6
Tel: (514) 849 8381.

AREA: 622,984 sq km (240,535 sq miles).
POPULATION: 2,773,000 (1988).
POPULATION DENSITY: 4.5 per sq km.
CAPITAL: Bangui. **Population:** 473,817 (1984).
GEOGRAPHY: The Central African Republic is bordered to the north by Chad, to the east by Sudan, to the south by Zaïre and the Congo and to the west by Cameroon. It is a large, landlocked territory of mostly uninhabited forest, bush and game reserves. The Chari River cuts through the centre from east to west; towards the Cameroon border the landscape rises to 2000m (6560ft) west of Bocaranga in the northwest corner, while the southwest has dense tropical rainforest. Most of the country is rolling or flat plateau covered with dry deciduous forest, except where it has been reduced to grass savannah or destroyed by bush fire. The northeast becomes desert scrubland and mountainous in parts.
LANGUAGE: French is the official administrative language and is essential for business. The native language is Sango.
RELIGION: Animist. One-third of the population is Christian. There is a small Islamic minority.
TIME: GMT + 1.
ELECTRICITY: 220/380 volts AC, 50Hz.
COMMUNICATIONS: Telephone: IDD is available. Country code: 236, although many calls are still directed through the operator. **Telex/telegram:** Telex facilities are available at post offices in Bangui and good hotels. Telegrams may be sent from 1430-1830 on Saturday and from 0800-1830 on Sunday. **Post:** There is a post office in each prefecture. Local postal services are unreliable. Both postal and telecommunications services are in the course of development. Airmail services to Europe take about one week, although it is often much longer; surface mail can take up to three months. *Poste Restante* facilities are available in Bangui. Post office hours: 0730-1130 and 1430-1630 Monday to Friday; open for stamps and telegrams only 1430-1830 Saturday and 0800-1100 Sunday. **Press:** There is one daily newspaper, *E Le Songo*. The weekly publications have limited distribution and are in French.
BBC World Service and Voice of America frequencies: From time to time these change. See the section *How to Use this Book* for more information.

BBC:				
MHz	21.66	17.88	15.42	21.47
Voice of America:				
MHz	21.49	15.60	9.525	6.035

PASSPORT/VISA

Regulations and requirements may be subject to change at short notice, and you are advised to contact the appropriate diplomatic or consular authority before finalising travel arrangements. Details of these may be found at the head of this country's entry. Any numbers in the chart refer to the footnotes below.

	Passport Required?	Visa Required?	Return Ticket Required?
Full British	Yes	Yes	Yes
BVP	Not valid	-	-
Australian	Yes	Yes	Yes
Canadian	Yes	Yes	Yes
USA	Yes	Yes	Yes
Other EC	1	2	Yes
Japanese	Yes	Yes	Yes

PASSPORTS: Valid passport required by all except the following holding a national ID card or passport expired for no more than 5 years:
(a) **[1]** nationals of France;
(b) nationals of Benin, Burkina Faso, Cameroon, Chad, Congo, Côte d'Ivoire, Gabon, Monaco, Niger, Senegal, Togo and Zaïre.
British Visitors Passport: Not accepted.
VISAS: Required by all except:
(a) **[2]** nationals of France; also nationals of Greece provided carrying written proof of travelling on business (all other EC nationals *do* require a visa);
(b) nationals of Benin, Burkina Faso, Cameroon, Chad, Congo, Côte d'Ivoire, Gabon, Israel, Liechtenstein, Madagascar, Monaco, Niger, Romania, Senegal, Sudan, Switzerland, Togo and Zaïre;
(c) nationals of Lebanon provided carrying written proof of purpose of visit.
Types of visa: *Transit:* Visa not required by passengers proceeding by the same aircraft to a third country. *Entry and Exit permits:* It is necessary to obtain entry and exit permits from Bangui Immigration office. Cost: £2-4.
Validity: Check with Embassy for details.
Applications to: Consulate (or Consular Section at Embassy). For addresses, see top of entry.
Application requirements: (a) 4 application forms. (b) 2 photos. (c) Full travel ticket/proof of sufficient funds. (d) Fee. (e) Yellow fever and cholera certificates.
Working days required: Applications are normally processed within 2 working days.

MONEY

Currency: CFA Franc (CFA Fr) = 100 centimes. Notes are in denominations of CFA Fr10,000, 5000, 1000, 500 and 100. Coins are in denominations of CFA Fr100, 50, 25, 10, 5, 2 and 1. These notes are legal tender in the republics which formerly comprised French Equatorial Africa (Chad, Cameroon, Central African Republic, Congo and Gabon). The CFA Fr100 note is not negotiable in the UK. The Central African Republic is part of the French monetary area.
Credit cards: Some major credit cards are accepted. Check with your credit card company for details of merchant acceptability and other services which may be available.
Exchange rate indicators: The following figures are included as a guide to the movements of the CFA Franc against Sterling and the US Dollar:

Date:	**Oct '89**	**Oct '90**	**Oct '91**	**Oct '92**
£1.00=	**505.13**	**498.36**	**496.12**	**413.75**
$1.00=	**319.90**	**255.12**	**285.87**	**260.71**

Currency restrictions: Unlimited import of foreign currency is allowed with export up to the amount imported. Free import of local currency is allowed; export of local currency is unlimited to residents of countries in the French Monetary Zone, but for all others it is CFA Fr75,000.
Banking hours: 0730-1130 Monday to Friday.

DUTY FREE

The following goods may be imported by visitors over 18 years of age into the Central African Republic without incurring customs duty:
1000 cigarettes or cigarillos or 250 cigars or 2kg of tobacco (females may only import cigarettes);
A reasonable quantity of alcoholic beverage and perfume.
Prohibited items: Firearms.
Note: When leaving the Central African Republic any animal skins and diamonds must be declared.

PUBLIC HOLIDAYS

Public holidays observed in the Central African Republic are as follows:
Mar 29 '93 Anniversary of Death of Barthélemy Boganda. **Apr 12** Easter Monday. **May 1** May Day. **May 20** Ascension Day. **May 31** Whit Monday. **Jun 30** National Day of Prayer. **Aug 13** Independence Day. **Aug 15** Assumption. **Nov 1** All Saints' Day. **Dec 1** National Day. **Dec 25** Christmas. **Jan 1 '94** New Year's Day. **Mar 29** Anniversary of Death of Barthélemy Boganda.

HEALTH

Regulations and requirements may be subject to change at short notice, and you are advised to contact your doctor well in advance of your intended date of departure. Any numbers in the chart refer to the footnotes below.

	Special Precautions?	Certificate Required?
Yellow Fever	Yes	1
Cholera	Yes	2
Typhoid & Polio	Yes	-
Malaria	3	-
Food & Drink	4	-

[1]: A yellow fever vaccination certificate is required from travellers over one year of age.
[2]: A cholera vaccination certificate is required of all travellers. Cholera is a serious risk in this country and precautions are essential. See the *Health* section at the back of the book.
[3]: Risk of *malaria* (and of other insect-borne diseases)

CENTRAL AFRICAN REP. | **HEALTH REGULATIONS** | **VISA REGULATIONS** | Code-Link

GALILEO/WORLDSPAN

TI-DFT/BGF/HE

TI-DFT/BGF/VI

SABRE

TIDFT/BGF/HE

TIDFT/BGF/VI

To access this information on your CRS, swipe the barcode with a light pen or type in the text under the barcode. For more information, see the introduction *How to Use This Book.*

exists all year throughout the country. The malignant *falciparum* form is prevalent. Resistance to chloroquine has been reported.
[4]: All water should be regarded as being potentially contaminated. Water used for drinking, brushing teeth or making ice should have first been boiled or otherwise sterilised. Milk is unpasteurised and should be boiled. Powdered or tinned milk is available and is advised, but make sure that it is reconstituted with pure water. Avoid dairy products which are likely to have been made from unboiled milk. Only eat well-cooked meat and fish, preferably served hot. Pork, salad and mayonnaise may carry increased risk. Vegetables should be cooked and fruit peeled.
Rabies is present. For those at high risk, vaccination before arrival should be considered. If you are bitten abroad seek medical advice without delay. For more information consult the *Health* section at the back of the book.
Bilharzia (schistosomiasis) is present. Avoid swimming and paddling in fresh water. Swimming pools which are well-chlorinated and maintained are safe.
Health care: Full health insurance is essential, and should include air evacuation to Europe in case of serious accident or illness. Medical facilities are severely limited outside the major centres and visitors should travel with their own supply of remedies for simple ailments such as stomach upsets; pharmaceutical supplies are usually very difficult to obtain.

TRAVEL - International

AIR: The main airline to serve the Central African Republic is *UTA (UT)*. The Central African Republic is a shareholder in *Air Afrique*.
Approximate flight time: From *London* to Bangui is 9 hours 40 minutes (including approximately 1 hour stopover in Paris). There are also connections between Bangui and Douala (Cameroon), Kinshasa (Zaïre), Lagos (Nigeria) and West Africa.
International airport: *Bangui M'Poko (BGF)*, 4km (2.5 miles) northwest of the city (travel time – 30 minutes). Taxis are available to Bangui and cost CFA Fr10,000-15,000 by day, CFA Fr2000-2500 by night. A bus service to the city meets all flights. Airport facilities include restaurant, post office, shops and car hire.
Departure tax: CFA Fr2000 is levied on all passengers.
RIVER: The Central African Republic has no coastline. The water route by ferry along the Ubangi to Bangui from the Congo or Zaïre is run by the Zaïre government-owned *ONATRA* company. There is a car/passenger ferry between Bangui and Zongo and between Bangassou and Ndu across the Ubangi. Fares are very cheap, although the service breaks down frequently. It is still possible to hire a boat. The price for this may be high. Do not cross the river to Zaïre on Saturday or Sunday, as the customs posts in that country do not work at the weekend.
ROAD: Access from Zaïre, Chad or Cameroon. Good all-weather roads from Yaoundé and N'djamena. From Zaïre it is necessary to get a ferry across Ubangi River from Zongo to Bangui or from Ndu to Bangassou (see above).

TRAVEL - Internal

AIR: *Inter-RCA* operates regular flights to Central African cities from Bangui, including Libreville and N'djamena.
FERRY: River ferries sail from Bangui to several towns further up the Ubangi. Some of them are quite luxurious and the journey can be a marvellous way to travel between the Congo and Central African Republic, although the service may be intermittent and the going slow. Little information on tariffs is available, but the service *officially* operates every two weeks. Information may possibly be obtained from the Embassy in France, but arrangements are best made in Brazzaville, The Congo.
ROAD: Good roads connect the few main towns, but the majority are often impassable during the rainy season and one should expect delays. Outside the urban areas, motor vehicles are rare and spare parts virtually impossible to find. Travellers must carry as large a petrol supply as possible as deliveries to stations outside the towns are infrequent. **Bus:** Local services run between towns; they are a cheap but sometimes a gruelling way to travel. It is also possible to pay for a lift on the numerous goods trucks which drive between the main towns. **Documentation:** International Driving Permit required.
URBAN: Limited bus services run in Bangui on a 2-zone tariff. Taxis are only available in the urban areas; they do not have meters and fares must be negotiated. **Car hire:** Self-drive or chauffeur-driven cars are available from the local *Hertz* agent and other local companies.

ACCOMMODATION

HOTELS: There are good hotels in Bangui, some of which are very exclusive and expensive. The better hotels have air-conditioning and swimming pools. Pre-booking is essential, ideally several weeks in advance. Outside Bangui, accommodation of any standard is very difficult to find, although guest-houses exist in smaller towns.
CAMPING/CARAVANNING: Camping is available at the Centre d'Accueil des Tourists at 'Kilometre Cinq'. Since most of the country is unpopulated or covered by nomadic herdsmen, travelling by vehicle and camping on the landscape is the normal way of life rather than a speciality. There are few organised facilities, so all provisions and requirements should be carried with the vehicles.

RESORTS & EXCURSIONS

In 1900, **Bangui** was a modest village beside the **River Ubangi**; it now extends over nearly 15 sq km (5 sq miles). Built on a rock, it is shaded by tropical greenery and features many modern buildings and avenues lined with mango trees. Places of interest include the colourful *Central Market* (renowned for its malachite necklaces), the *Boganda Museum*, the *Arts and Crafts School*, the cathedral and the *Saint Paul Mission*, whose small brick church overlooks the river, and the Hausa quarter. The *Grande Corniche* leads to the banks of the Ubangi and provides a picturesque view of the fishermen's round huts and canoes.
Outside Bangui: The *Lobaye Region*, 100km (60 miles) from the capital, is the home of pygmies who live in unspoiled forest in encampments of huts made of lianas and roofed with leaves. There are coffee plantations on the fringe of the forest. There are also pygmy villages in the *M'Baiki Region*, 100km (60 miles) southwest of Bangui. The *Boali Waterfalls* are 90km (55 miles) northwest of Bangui, near the charming and picturesque village of Boali. The Waterfalls are 250m (820ft) wide and 50m (165ft) high; the view from the restaurant at the top is stunning. The *Kembe Waterfalls*, west of Bangassou, are also worth a visit.
At **Bouar,** in the east of the country, there is an area of burial mounds with many upright megaliths *(tanjunu)* thought to be thousands of years old. In **Bangassou,** near the Oubangui River on the border with Zaïre, are the extraordinary *Kembe Falls* on the Kotto River.
WILDLIFE SAFARIS: There are a number of National Parks in the Central African Republic, most of which are accessible by 4-wheel drive cars from **Birao,** in the far north of the country between the Chad and Sudanese borders, during the dry season only. The game population of these National Parks is impressive, although the activities of poachers have led to a considerable decrease in the animal population in recent years – elephants and rhinos being the species worst affected. There is no accommodation available: all supplies, including bedding, must be taken. All arrangements are best made on arrival in the country, although time should be allowed for finalising plans.

SOCIAL PROFILE

FOOD & DRINK: The only Western food is in the capital of Bangui. Most of the top-class hotels have good restaurants. The standard of these restaurants is high, but they do tend to be expensive. Otherwise travellers must call at local villages and barter for provisions. Local food is basic. **Drink:** Bars are numerous in Bangui with both table and counter service. Drinking and smoking are not encouraged in Muslim society; in Muslim areas drinking is best done in private.
NIGHTLIFE: The few hotels in Bangui have expensive clubs catering for tourists and businessmen; local nightlife is centred on the district known as 'Kilometre Cinq'.
SHOPPING: Bangui has reasonable shopping facilities, notably for ebony, gold jewellery, butterfly collections and objets d'arts made from butterfly wings. However, one of the best methods of finding bargain souvenirs is by bartering with villagers outside the urban areas for their handmade goods. **Shopping hours:** 0800-1200 and 1600-1900 Monday to Saturday. Some shops close on Monday. The market in Bangui is open from 0730 until dusk.
SOCIAL CONVENTIONS: Dress is informal. Care should be taken to dress modestly in Muslim areas, and Muslim customs should be respected and observed; do not, for instance, show the soles of the feet when sitting. It is customary to shake hands. Women are strictly segregated, especially in towns. In Muslim areas do not smoke or drink in public during Ramadan. **Photography:** Film is expensive and should be sent to Europe for developing. Show caution and discretion when photographing local people, ask for prior permission. Do not photograph military installations or government buildings. **Tipping:** 10% for most services.

BUSINESS PROFILE

ECONOMY: Agriculture, on which most of the population depends, is concentrated on subsistence crops, and coffee, cotton and wood as cash crops for export. Diamonds are the main export commodity, accounting for over 50% of foreign earnings. Other mineral deposits, including uranium and iron, have yet to be exploited. Manufacturing industry is insignificant. The Central African Republic is a member of the CFA Franc Zone and of the Central African customs and economic union, UDEAC. France, which supplies extensive development aid, is the main trading partner for both imports and exports, while Belgium and Luxembourg are the largest single export markets.
BUSINESS: A knowledge of French is essential. Interpreter and translation services may be available at large hotels. Business cards should be in French and English. Formal wear is expected (suits and ties for men). The best months for business visits are between November and May. **Office hours:** 0630-1330 Monday to Friday; 0700-1200 Saturdays.
COMMERCIAL INFORMATION: The following organisation can offer advice: Chambre de Commerce, d'Industrie, des Mines et de l'Artinsinat (CCIMA), BP 813, Bangui. Tel: 614 255. Telex: 5261.

HISTORY & GOVERNMENT

HISTORY: Prior to French colonisation many tribes fled to the area in order to escape the slave trade. In 1910 the area (known as Ubangi-Chari) became incorporated into French Equatorial Africa. Self-government was achieved in 1958 and full independence in 1960, although the country is still effectively controlled by France. The country is very slowly recovering from the effects of the disastrous rule of the self-styled 'Emperor' Bokassa, whose coronation in 1977 is estimated to have used up over a quarter of the country's annual income. He was deposed in 1979, and the country once again became a republic. Since then, it has been governed by two different Heads of State, the first of which was David Dacko, and then André Kolingba, neither of whom has really been able to pull the country out of its economic doldrums – it is underdeveloped, poverty-stricken and corrupt. France continues to maintain a strong presence, notably military garrisons at Bangui and Bouar. Bokassa returned unexpectedly in October 1986 and was immediately imprisoned, a death sentence against him having already been passed *in absentia*. The court case lasted until June 1987, when he was found guilty of murder, conspiracy to murder, illegal detention of prisoners and embezzlement, and the death sentence was confirmed. However, his case went to appeal in February 1988 and the sentence was commuted to life imprisonment; it has since been reduced to 20 years. This was one of the first acts by Kolingba after his resignation from the leadership of the ruling Rassemblement Démocratique Centrafricaine (RDC, the sole legal political party) in order to remain 'above politics' as national president. His position is thus secure from the future whims of the electorate now that the regime has conceded, after repeated refusals amid violent protests and heavy French pressure, the introduction of a multi-party system. A national conference attended by government and recognised opposition parties is to be convened to chart the country's future constitutional course.
GOVERNMENT: After the September 1981 coup, all political and legislative power rested with André Kolingba and the Comité Militaire pour le Redressment Nationale (CMRN). In 1986, the CMRN produced a new constitution allowing for the creation of a sole political party, the Rassemblement Démocratique Centrafricaine. All other political parties were banned. In July 1991, the 52-seat National Assembly, which is elected for a 5-year term (the President is elected for six years), approved legislation to revise the constitution to allow for a multi-party system.

CLIMATE

Hot all year with a defined dry season. Especially hot in the northeast. Monsoon in south (May to October).
Required clothing: Tropical with waterproofing.

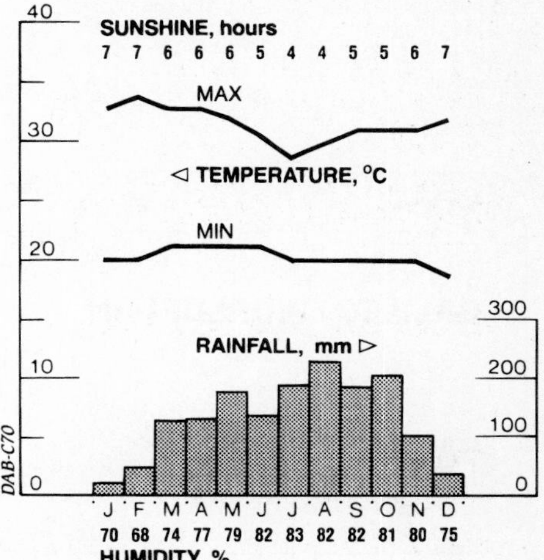

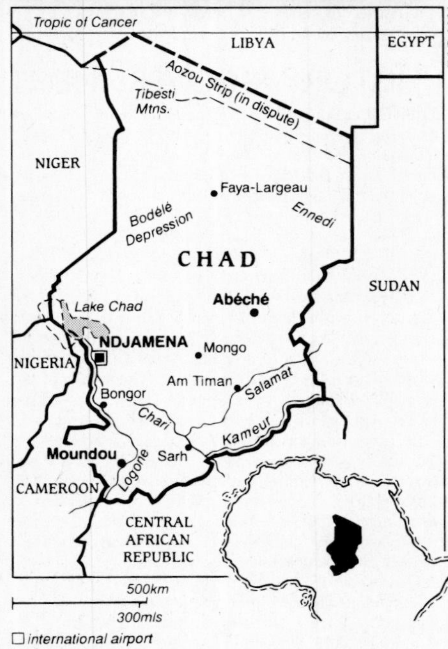

Location: North/Central Africa.

Direction du Tourisme, des Parcs Nationaux et Réserves de Faune
BP 86
N'djaména, Chad
Tel: 51 45 26.

Délégation Régionale au Tourisme
BP 88
Sarh, Chad
Tel: 274.

Embassy of the Republic of Chad
65 rue des Belles Feuilles
75016 Paris, France
Tel: (1) 45 53 36 75. Telex: 610629.

British Consulate
BP 877
avenue Charles de Gaulle (opposite Air Tchad office)
N'djaména, Chad
Tel: 51 30 64. Telex: ACT 5235 KD.

UK Representation:
Worldwide Visas Limited
9 Adelaide Street
London WC2
Tel: (071) 379 0419 *or* 379 0376 *or* 497 2099. Fax: (071) 497 2590.

Embassy of the Republic of Chad (also represents Canada)
2002 R Street, NW
Washington, DC 20009
Tel: (202) 462 4009. Fax: (202) 265 1937.

Embassy of the United States of America
BP 413
avenue Félix Eboué
N'djaména, Chad
Tel: 51 40 09 *or* 51 62 18 *or* 51 62 11. Fax: 51 33 72. Telex: 5203.

AREA: 1,284,000 sq km (495,800 sq miles).
POPULATION: 5,428,000 (1988 estimate).
POPULATION DENSITY: 4.2 per sq km.
CAPITAL: N'djaména. **Population:** 594,000 (1988 estimate).
GEOGRAPHY: Chad is situated in Africa, bounded by Libya to the north, Niger, Nigeria and Cameroon to the west, the Central African Republic to the south, and Sudan to the east. The topography ranges from equatorial forests to the driest of deserts. Lake Chad extends to an area of 25,000 sq km (9652 sq miles) reducing seasonally to 10,000 sq km (3861 sq miles); it is choked with papyrus and covered with islands of floating vegetation. The Chari, Logone, Salamat and Aouk rivers and tributaries run south but are often just dry beds. The Chad basin is bounded by mountains and the Central African Plateau. In the east, the crystalline Ovaddai Range rises 1500m (5000ft). In the northeast lie the pink sandstone heights of Ennedi, and to the north the volcanic Tibesti range, largely sheer cliffs, ravines and canyons set in out of Saharan sand dunes.
LANGUAGE: French is the official language. Other widely spoken languages include Chadian Arabic (North) and Sara (South). The territory's boundaries enclose a small but highly diverse population; not surprisingly, there are over 50 local languages. The principal northern (and mainly Muslim) tribal groups are the Nare Arabs, Toubou, Fulani, Hausa, Kanembou, Boulala and Wadai. The principal southern (and mainly Christian) groups are the Baguirmi, Kotoko, Sara, Massa and Moundang.
RELIGION: 50% Muslim, 45% Animist, 5% Christian (see *Language* above for more information).
TIME: GMT + 1.
ELECTRICITY: 220/380 volts AC, 50Hz.
COMMUNICATIONS: Telephone: Country code: 235. It may be necessary to go through the operator. **Telex/telegram:** Available in major post offices in N'djaména, Sarh, Moundou and Abeche. **Post:** Airmail takes about one week. Post office hours: 0730-1200 Monday to Friday; 1430-1830 Saturday; 0800-1100 Sunday (for the purchase of stamps). **Press:** Newspapers are printed in French and generally have low circulations.
BBC World Service and Voice of America frequencies: From time to time these change. See the section *How to Use this Book* for more information.

BBC:				
MHz	25.75	17.88	15.40	7.105
Voice of America:				
MHz	21.49	15.60	9.525	6.035

PASSPORT/VISA

Regulations and requirements may be subject to change at short notice, and you are advised to contact the appropriate diplomatic or consular authority before finalising travel arrangements. Details of these may be found at the head of this country's entry. Any numbers in the chart refer to the footnotes below.

	Passport Required?	Visa Required?	Return Ticket Required?
Full British	Yes	Yes	Yes
BVP	Not valid	-	-
Australian	Yes	Yes	Yes
Canadian	Yes	Yes	Yes
USA	Yes	Yes	Yes
Other EC	Yes	Yes	Yes
Japanese	Yes	Yes	Yes

PASSPORTS: Valid passport required by all except nationals of Benin, Burkina Faso, Cameroon, Central African Republic, Congo, Côte d'Ivoire, Equatorial Guinea, Mauritania, Niger, Senegal and Togo.
British Visitors Passport: Not accepted.
VISAS: Required by all except nationals of Nigeria and those listed under *Passports* above.
Types of visa: Visitors' visas cost the equivalent of £6. Visitors continuing their journey within 48 hours to a third country by the same or first connecting aircraft do not require Transit visas provided they hold tickets with reserved seats and valid documents for their destination.
Note: Travel outside the capital requires a special authorisation from the Minister of the Interior which must be obtained on arrival. There may be difficulty obtaining it.
Application and enquiries to: Consulate (or Consular Section at Embassy). For address, see top of entry.
Application requirements: (a) Valid passport. (b) 2 photos. (c) 2 forms. (d) Letters of recommendation. (e) Full travel ticket/proof of sufficient funds. (f) Fee approximately FFr200-600.

MONEY

Currency: CFA Franc (CFA Fr) = 100 centimes. Notes are in denominations of CFA Fr10,000, 5000, 1000 and 500. Coins are in denominations of CFA Fr500, 100, 50, 25, 10, 5 and 1. These notes are legal tender in the republics which formerly comprised French Equatorial Africa (Chad, Cameroon, Central African Republic, Congo and Gabon). Chad is part of the French Monetary Area.
Currency exchange: It is advisable to bring Dollars rather than Sterling into the country. CFA Francs can be difficult to exchange outside the French Monetary Area.
Credit cards: Diners Club and Access/Mastercard (limited use) are accepted. Check with your credit card company for details of merchant acceptability and other services which may be available.
Exchange rate indicators: The following figures are included as a guide to the movements of the CFA Franc against Sterling and the US Dollar:

Date:	Oct '89	Oct '90	Oct '91	Oct '92
£1.00=	505.13	498.38	496.12	413.75
$1.00=	319.90	255.12	285.87	260.71

Currency restrictions: Unlimited import of foreign currency is allowed, subject to declaration; export is allowed up to the amount declared on import. There is free import of local currency, subject to declaration. Export of local currency is limited to the amount declared on entry.
Banking hours: 0700-1100 Monday to Saturday, 0700-1030 Friday.

DUTY FREE

The following goods may be imported into Chad without incurring customs duty for passengers over 18 years of age:
400 cigarettes or 125 cigars or 500g of tobacco (women – cigarettes only);
3 bottles of wine;
1 bottle of spirits.

PUBLIC HOLIDAYS

Public holidays observed in Chad are as follows:
Mar 25 '93 Start of Eid al-Fitr. **Apr 12** Easter Monday. **May 1** May Day. **May 25** OAU Foundation Day. **May 31** Whit Monday. **Jun 1** Start of Eid al-Adha. **Aug 11** Independence Day. **Aug 15** Assumption. **Aug 30** Mouloud (Prophet's Birthday). **Nov 1** All Saints' Day. **Nov 28** Proclamation of the Republic. **Dec 1** Victory Day. **Dec 25** Christmas Day. **Jan 1 '94** New Year's Day. **Mar** Start of Eid al-Fitr.
Note: Muslim festivals are timed according to local sightings of various phases of the Moon and the dates given above are approximations. During the lunar month of Ramadan that precedes Eid al-Fitr, Muslims fast during the day and feast at night and normal business patterns may be interrupted. Many restaurants are closed during the day and there may be restrictions on smoking and drinking. Some disruption may continue into Eid al-Fitr itself. Eid al-Fitr and Eid al-Adha may last anything from two to ten days, depending on the region. For more information see the section *World of Islam* at the back of the book.

CHAD	HEALTH REGULATIONS	VISA REGULATIONS
		Code-Link
GALILEO/WORLDSPAN	TI-DFT/NDJ/HE	TI-DFT/NDJ/VI
SABRE	TIDFT/NDJ/HE	TIDFT/NDJ/VI

To access this information on your CRS, swipe the barcode with a light pen or type in the text under the barcode. For more information, see the introduction *How to Use This Book*.

HEALTH

Regulations and requirements may be subject to change at short notice, and you are advised to contact your doctor well in advance of your intended date of departure. Any numbers in the chart refer to the footnotes below.

	Special Precautions?	Certificate Required?
Yellow Fever	Yes	1
Cholera	Yes	2
Typhoid & Polio	Yes	-
Malaria	Yes	-
Food & Drink	3	-

[1]: A yellow fever certificate is required from travellers over one year of age. Risk of infection is highest south of N15°.
[2]: Following WHO guidelines issued in 1973, a cholera vaccination certificate is no longer a condition of entry to Chad. However, cholera is a serious risk in this country and precautions are essential. Up-to-date advice should be sought before deciding whether these precautions should include vaccination as medical opinion is divided over its effectiveness. See the *Health* section at the back of the book.
[3]: All water should be regarded as being potentially contaminated. Water used for drinking, brushing teeth or making ice should have first been boiled or otherwise sterilised. Milk is unpasteurised and should be boiled. Powdered or tinned milk is available and is advised, but make sure that it is reconstituted with pure water. Avoid all dairy products. Only eat well-cooked meat and fish, preferably served hot. Pork, salad and mayonnaise may carry increased risk. Vegetables should be cooked and fruit peeled.
Malaria risk, predominantly in the malignant *falciparum* form, exists all year throughout the country. For more information consult the *Health* section at the back of the book.
Bilharzia (schistosomiasis) is present. Avoid swimming and paddling in fresh water. Swimming pools which are well-chlorinated and maintained are safe.
Meningitis risk is present depending on area visited and time of year.
Health care: Medical facilities are poor, particularly in the north, and health insurance (to include emergency repatriation cover) is essential.

TRAVEL - International

AIR: Within Africa the national airline is *Air Tchad (HT)*. Chad is a shareholder in *Air Afrique*.
There are no direct flights or good connections for those travelling from London. Over-night transit costs may be covered by some airlines.
International airport: *N'djaména (NDJ)* is 4km (2.5 miles) northwest of the city. Taxis are available. There is no duty-free shop.
Departure tax: CFA Fr3000 for international destinations (except CFA Fr1200 if travelling to Benin, Burkina Faso, Central African Republic, Congo, Côte d'Ivoire, Mauritania, Niger, Senegal and Togo). There is also a tourist tax of CFA Fr2500.
RAIL: There is no railway network in Chad. There have been long-standing plans for a rail link with Cameroon but nothing has yet come of these.
ROAD: There are routes from the Central African Republic, Cameroon and Nigeria. Presently the best route from N'djaména to Bangui (car) goes via Bongor, Lai, Doba, Gore (border) and Bossangoa rather than through Sarh. It is possible to enter Chad either by this route or from Maiduguri in Nigeria via a sliver of northern Cameroon. The border between Cameroon and Chad is the River Logone, which flows into Lake Chad. Boats ply across the river (there is no bridge). Roads can be inaccessible during the rainy season.

TRAVEL - Internal

AIR: Air services are run by *Air Tchad (HT)* (when not occupied in military activities). A cotton company, *Coton-Tchad*, runs its own limited flights, and may be able to offer a seat or two, but reports are that there is a considerable demand for this.
ROAD: Travel by road outside N'djaména is only possible in a vehicle with 4-wheel drive and permits are usually needed to do this: certain security conditions and a lack of housing, food, gasoline, and vehicle repair facilities have resulted in the government prohibiting travel, especially in the central and northern areas of the country. This applies even to convoys of vehicles and covers the routes from Libya via Zouar and Faya-Largeau to N'djaména and the road from N'djaména via Ati and Abeche to the Sudanese border. Petrol is expensive. There is an unpaved road running from Maiduguri in Nigeria through Cameroon to N'djaména; this is a major trucking route into Chad. However, its condition varies according to the maintenance it receives and the weather. The rains often render it impassable, the worst season being from the last week of July to the first week of September (when even a Land-Rover won't get through). The Cameroon road from N'Gaoundéré through Garoua, Maroua and the Wazza Game Reserve to N'djaména has paved, all-weather sections but the unimproved sections make this road difficult in the rainy season. Many other roads urgently need repair and international aid is being given for this; it is, however, a huge task.
Documentation: The motorist needs a *carnet de passage* issued by the Tourist Association in the country of origin, an International Driving Permit and either a Green Card for insurance or all risks insurance obtained in Chad.
URBAN: The city of N'djaména has an adequate road system and there are limited self-drive and chauffeured car hire facilities. Minibuses and taxis operate in N'djaména, with a flat fare charged. A 10% tip is expected by taxi drivers.

ACCOMMODATION

HOTELS: There are three good hotels in N'djaména, but accommodation elsewhere is very limited. There are two small hotels at Sarh, a modern hotel complex in Zakouma National Park, and various small hunting hotels in the southwest. It is advisable to book in advance and prospective travellers should contact the Chad Embassy in Paris for latest information. For more information contact: Société Hôtelière et Touristique, BP 478, N'djaména.

RESORTS & EXCURSIONS

Note: Political problems have prevented Chad from developing its considerable tourist potential. Travel outside N'djaména remains dangerous, especially in the north of the country which has yet to recover from the recent war with Libya. Permits are required to travel outside the capital (see *Passport/Visa* and *Travel* above).
N'djaména: The historic quarter and the colourful daily market are both worth a visit, as well as the museum which has collections of the Sar culture dating back to the 9th century.
Zakouma National Park: Located on an immense plain across which the *Bahr Salamat* and its tributaries flow from north to south, here visitors may view rhinos, herds of elephants and a wide range of other species.
Lake Chad: This was once the centre of Africa's lucrative salt trade, but is now shrinking (literally) and sparsely populated.
Tibesti Mountains: An astonishing region of chasms and crags which has seldom been seen by non-Muslims. It remained closed to outsiders during the great era of exploration in the last century and is closed once more as it lies within territory claimed by Libya. The range is said to be home to the best racing camels in the world. The inhabitants, distantly related to the Tuareg of the Western Sahara, were made famous by Herodotus as the *Troglodytes*, stocky but immensely agile cave-dwellers who squeaked like bats and climbed like monkeys.

SOCIAL PROFILE

FOOD & DRINK: There are very few restaurants and those remaining in operation are generally found in hotels in the capital; it is not wise to eat anywhere else. Standard European-style of service is normal. There is an acute shortage of some foodstuffs. There is a limited number of bars due to Muslim beliefs. Drinking and smoking are not encouraged and alcohol is generally only available in the main hotels in N'djaména.
NIGHTLIFE: This is limited and centred in the main towns.
SHOPPING: Chad has an excellent crafts industry. Items include camel-hair carpets, all kinds of leatherware, embroidered cotton cloths, decorated calabashes, knives, weapons, pottery and brass animals. **Shopping hours:** 0900-1230 and 1600-1930 Tuesday to Saturday, being mainly closed Mondays. Food shops open Sunday mornings. The market in the capital is open from 0730 until dusk.
SOCIAL CONVENTIONS: Respect for traditional beliefs and customs is expected. Dress is informal but conservative in respect of Muslim laws. There is strict segregation of women, especially in the towns. It is customary to shake hands. The left hand should never be used for offering or accepting food, nor should the sole of the foot be exposed in the presence of a Muslim. **Tipping:** 10% is normal for most services. US Dollars are a good currency to use.

BUSINESS PROFILE

ECONOMY: Civil war, poor infrastructure, few natural resources and recent droughts have hampered any real development of the economy. Subsistence level farming occupies 80% of the population. The south is the most populous region, particularly around Sarh, where the agricultural Sara people are dominant. Kotoko fishermen and the Massa people live in the southwest. The Boudama and Kouri peoples, who earn their livelihood from fishing and cattle rearing, live on islands in Lake Chad. The central *Sahel* region is the home of traditional pastoral nomads, including the Maba, Dadjo, Barma and many Arab clans. The north is mainly populated by nomadic and highly ethnocentric Toubou, Tuaregs and Arab clans. Food shortage is a problem and many areas of the country rely on international food aid. France is by far the largest trading partner, followed by Nigeria, The Netherlands, Italy, the USA, the UK, Cameroon and Germany.
BUSINESS: A knowledge of French is essential as there are no professional translators available. Best months for business visits are between November and May. **Office hours:** 0730-1400 Monday to Saturday, 0700-1200 Friday.
COMMERCIAL INFORMATION: The following organisation can offer advice: Chambre de Commerce, BP 458, N'djaména, Chad. Tel: 51 52 64.

HISTORY & GOVERNMENT

HISTORY: As well as being an important source of salt, the shores of Lake Chad were for centuries an important marshalling yard for several major trans-Saharan caravan routes. It was a region in which several kingdoms achieved dominance at different times. From the 11th to the 15th century the state of Kanem was one of these, occupying much of the area which makes up present-day Chad. It was largely superseded by the state of Borno which had its centre on the other side of Lake Chad (in present-day Nigeria). Subsequently the area was on the fringes of Arab influence. Chad itself, which lies to the east of the lake, was first defined as an entity in 1910 as one of the four territories of French Equatorial Africa. Chad achieved independence in 1960 with François Tombalbaye, leader of the Parti Progressiste Tchadien (PPT), as Prime Minister. Its history since then has been characterised by political instability and tensions, largely due to the north/south religious and cultural divisions. Since 1979, Chad has been in a state of near-perpetual civil war. The main protagonists were the former Defence Minister, Hissene Habré, and his Libyan-backed erstwhile boss, Goukouni Oueddei. By mid-1983, however, other powers, including France, had become involved. In 1984 heavy fighting resulted in thousands of refugees fleeing Chad to surrounding countries. During 1987 the war intensified, with Libya and particularly Chad, making spectacular raids into each other's territory. However, with the recognition by Libya of the Habré government in N'djaména in November 1988, Chad seemed set to recover some measure of economic, social and political stability for the first time in 20 years. Habré though, quickly fell out with his former army commander Idriss Deby, and then his principal foreign backers, France and the US. Deby's forces routed Habré's and entered the capital, N'djaména, in December 1990. Habré fled to Cameroon.
GOVERNMENT: Two years after independence, Chad was declared a single-party state. Executive and legislative power is wielded by a Council of State, whose members are appointed and led by the Head of State, presently Idriss Deby.

CLIMATE

Hot, tropical climate, though temperatures vary in different areas. Southern rainy season (May to October); central rains (June to September). The north has little rain. The dry season is often windy and cooler during evenings.
Required clothing: Lightweight cottons and linens; warmer clothes for cool evenings. Waterproofing is necessary in the rainy seasons.

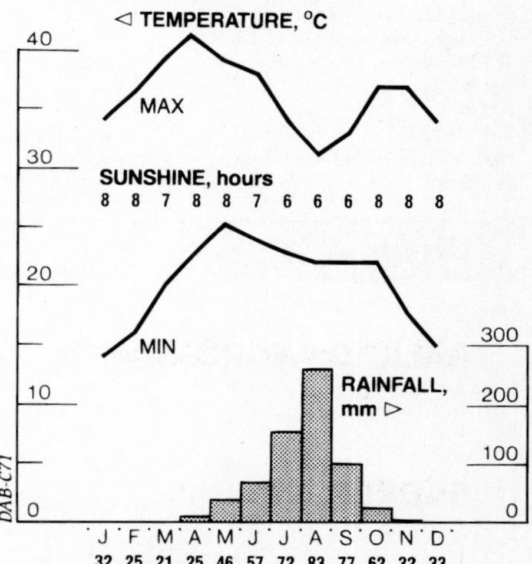

CHILE

Location: West coast of South America.

Servicio Nacional de Turismo (SERNATUR)
(Tourist Office)
Casilla 14082
Avenida Providencia 1550
Santiago, Chile
Tel: (2) 236 0531 *or* 236 1416 *or* 236 1418. Fax: (2) 236 1417. Telex: 240137.

Embassy of the Republic of Chile
12 Devonshire Street
London W1N 2DS
Tel: (071) 580 6392 *or* 580 1023 (visa enquiries). Fax: (071) 436 5204. Telex: 25970.

Chilean Consul General
Address as Embassy
Tel: (071) 580 1023. Opening hours: 0930-1200 Monday, Wednesday and Friday.

British Embassy
Casilla 72-D
Avenida del Bosque
Norte 125
Santiago, Chile
Tel: (2) 231 3737. Fax: (2) 231 9771. Telex: 340483 BRITEMB CK.
Consulates in: Arica, Concepción, Punta Arenas (Magallanes) and Valparaíso.

Embassy of the Republic of Chile
1732 Massachusetts Avenue, NW
Washington, DC
20036
Tel: (202) 785 1746. Fax: (202) 887 5579 *or* 887 5475.

Chilean Consulate General
4th Floor
809 United Nations Plaza
New York, NY
10017
Tel: (212) 980 3366.

Embassy of the United States of America
Agustinas 1343, 5°
Santiago, Chile
Tel: (2) 710 133. Telex: 240062.

Embassy of the Republic of Chile
Suite 605
151 Slater Street
Ottawa, Ontario
K1P 5H3
Tel: (613) 235 4402 *or* 235 9940. Fax: (613) 235 1176.

Chilean Consulate General
Suite 710
1010 Sherbrooke Street West
Montréal, Québec
H3A 2R7
Tel: (514) 499 0405.

Canadian Embassy
10° Casilla 427
Ahumada 11
Santiago, Chile
Tel: (2) 696 2256.

AREA: 756,626 sq km (292,135 sq miles).
POPULATION: 13,385,817 (1991 estimate).
POPULATION DENSITY: 17.7 per sq km.
CAPITAL: Santiago (de Chile). **Population:** 4,385,481 (1990).
GEOGRAPHY: Chile is situated in South America, bounded to the north by Peru, to the east by Bolivia and Argentina, to the west by the Pacific and to the south by the Antarctic. The country exercises sovereignty over a number of islands off the coast, including the Juan Fernández Islands, where Alexander Selkirk (the inspiration for Robinson Crusoe) was shipwrecked, and Easter Island. Chile is one of the most remarkably shaped countries in the world; a ribbon of land, 4200km (2610 miles) long and nowhere more than 180km (115 miles) wide. The Andes and a coastal highland range take up one-third or half of the width in parts, and run parallel with each other from north to south. The coastal range forms high, sloped cliffs into the sea from the northern to the central area. Between the ranges runs a fertile valley, except in the north where transverse ranges join the two major ones, and in the far south where the sea has broken through the coastal range to form an assortment of archipelagos and channels. The country contains wide variations of soil and vast differences of climate. This is reflected in the distribution of the population, and in the wide range of occupations from area to area. The northern part of the country consists mainly of the Atacama Desert, the driest in the world. It is also the main mining area. The central zone is predominantly agricultural. The south is forested, and contains some agriculture; further south, the forests on the Atlantic side give way to rolling grassland on which sheep and cattle are raised.
LANGUAGE: The official language is Spanish, but English is widely spoken.
RELIGION: 89% Roman Catholic, 11% Protestant.
TIME: Mainland and Juan Fernández Islands: GMT - 4 (GMT - 3 from October to March).
Easter Island: GMT - 6 (GMT - 5 from October to March).
ELECTRICITY: 220 volts AC, 50Hz. Two-pin plugs and screw-type bulbs are used.
COMMUNICATIONS: Telephone: Full IDD available. Country code: 56. Compañía de Teléfonos de Chile provides most services though there are a few independent companies. **Fax:** Telex Chile, Transradio Chilena and ITT Communicaciones provide services in main towns. **Telex/telegram:** Telex Chile, Transradio Chilena and ITT Communicaciones Mundiales provide services in main towns. **Post:** Daily airmail services to Europe take approximately three to four days. Post office hours: 0900-1800 Mondays to Fridays, 0900-1300 Saturdays.
Press: Spanish dailies include *El Mercurio*, *La Nación*, *Las Ultimas Noticias*, *La Epoca* and *La Tercera*. Foreign newspapers are available.
BBC World Service and Voice of America frequencies: From time to time these change. See the section *How to Use this Book* for more information.

BBC:				
MHz	15.26	15.19	11.75	9.915
Voice of America:				
MHz	15.21	11.58	9.775	5.995

PASSPORT/VISA

Regulations and requirements may be subject to change at short notice, and you are advised to contact the appropriate diplomatic or consular authority before finalising travel arrangements. Details of these may be found at the head of this country's entry. Any numbers in the chart refer to the footnotes below.

	Passport Required?	Visa Required?	Return Ticket Required?
Full British	Yes	No	Yes
BVP	Not valid	-	-
Australian	Yes	No	Yes
Canadian	Yes	No	Yes
USA	Yes	No	Yes
Other EC	Yes	1	Yes
Japanese	Yes	No	Yes

PASSPORTS: Valid passport required by all except nationals of Argentina, Brazil, Paraguay and Uruguay, who can enter with a special identity card (Cedula de Identitad) for short-term visits (except foreign residents of these countries who *do* need a passport); and nationals of Taiwan, Mexico and Peru who have an official travel document issued by the Organisation of American States.
British Visitors Passport: Not accepted.
VISAS: As the regulations are always subject to change at short notice it is advisable to check with the Chilean Consulate for the latest information. At present, a visa is not required by:
(a) **[1]** nationals of Belgium, Denmark, Germany, Greece, Republic of Ireland, Italy, Luxembourg, The Netherlands, Portugal, Spain and the UK (nationals of France *do* require a visa);
(b) nationals of Argentina, Australia, Austria, Barbados, Bolivia, Brazil, Canada, Colombia, Costa Rica, Cyprus, Ecuador, Finland, Honduras, Iceland, Indonesia, Israel, Jamaica, Japan, Liechtenstein, Malaysia, Malta, Mexico, Morocco, Panama, Paraguay, Peru, San Marino, Singapore, Suriname, Sweden, Switzerland, Tunisia, Turkey, Tuvalu, Uruguay, Venezuela, USA and Yugoslavia.
Types of visa: Residence visa required if intending to carry out paid employment or study in Chile. Visitor's visa required for nationals of countries with no diplomatic relations with Chile. Transit visa required by all, except nationals noted above and those continuing journey on the same day provided they do not leave the airport transit lounge.
Validity: Up to 3 months depending on nationality and purpose of visit.
Application to: Consulate (or Consular Section at Embassy). For address, see top of entry.
Application requirements: Valid passport and return ticket needed.
Working days: Visas are issued within 24 hours.
Temporary residence: Not easy to obtain. Enquire at Embassy.

MONEY

Currency: Peso (Ch$) = 100 centavos. Notes are in denominations of Ch$10,000, 5000, 1000 and 500. Coins are in denominations of Ch$100, 50, 10, 5 and 1.
Currency exchange: Foreign exchange transactions can be conducted through commercial banks, cambios, or authorised shops, restaurants, hotels and clubs. Visitors should not be tempted by the premiums of 10-15% over

CHILE	**HEALTH REGULATIONS**	**VISA REGULATIONS** Code-Link
GALILEO/WORLDSPAN	 TI-DFT/SCL/HE	 TI-DFT/SCL/VI
 **SABRE**	 TIDFT/SCL/HE	TIDFT/SCL/VI

To access this information on your CRS, swipe the barcode with a light pen or type in the text under the barcode. For more information, see the introduction *How to Use This Book*.

the official rate offered by black marketeers.
Credit cards: Diners Club, Visa, American Express and Access/Mastercard are accepted. Check with your credit card company for details of merchant acceptability and other services which may be available.
Travellers cheques: Must be changed before 1200 except in cambios (which in any case tend to offer better rates than banks). There may be some difficulty exchanging travellers cheques outside of major towns.
Exchange rate indicators: The following figures are included as a guide to the movements of the Chilean Peso against Sterling and the US Dollar:

Date:	Oct '89	Oct '90	Oct '91	Oct '92
£1.00=	424.80	607.61	622.65	593.58
$1.00=	269.03	311.04	358.77	374.03

Currency restrictions: There are no restrictions on the import and export of either local or foreign currency.
Banking hours: 0900-1400 Monday to Friday.

DUTY FREE

The following goods may be imported into Chile without incurring customs duty:
400 cigarettes and 500g of tobacco and 50 cigars or 50 cigarillos;
2.5 litres of alcohol (only for visitors over 18 years of age);
A reasonable quantity of perfume.
Prohibited items: Flowers, fruit and vegetables unless permission is sought prior to travelling.

PUBLIC HOLIDAYS

Public holidays observed in Chile are as follows:
Apr 9 '93 Good Friday. **Apr 10** Easter Saturday. **May 1** Labour Day. **May 21** Navy Day. **Jun 10** Corpus Christi. **Jun 29** St Peter's and St Paul's Day. **Aug 15** Assumption. **Sep 18** Independence Day. **Oct 12** Day of Race (Anniversary of the discovery of America). **Nov 1** All Saints' Day. **Dec 8** Immaculate Conception. **Dec 25** Christmas Day. **Jan 1 '94** New Year's Day.

HEALTH

Regulations and requirements may be subject to change at short notice, and you are advised to contact your doctor well in advance of your intended date of departure. Any numbers in the chart refer to the footnotes below.

	Special Precautions?	Certificate Required?
Yellow Fever	No	No
Cholera	No	No
Typhoid & Polio	1	-
Malaria	No	-
Food & Drink	2	-

[1]: Immunisation is recommended.
[2]: All water should be regarded as being potentially contaminated. Water used for drinking, brushing teeth or making ice should have first been boiled or otherwise sterilised. Milk is pasteurised and is safe to drink without boiling, except in very remote areas of the countryside. Only eat well-cooked meat and fish, preferably served hot. Pork, salad and mayonnaise may carry increased risk. Vegetables should be cooked and fruit peeled.
Health care: Health insurance is essential.

TRAVEL - International

AIR: Chile has two national airlines, both privately owned: *LAN-Chile (LA)* and *LADECO (UC)*.
Approximate flight times: From Santiago to *London* is 18 hours 45 minutes, to *Los Angeles* is 15 hours 35 minutes, to *New York* is 14 hours 10 minutes, to *Singapore* is 33 hours 45 minutes and to *Sydney* is 19 hours 5 minutes.
International airports: *Santiago (SCL)* (Comodoro Arturo Merino Benitez). The airport is 16km (10 miles) from Santiago (travel time – 30 minutes). Bus services to the city are available as follows: coach to the city departs every 30 minutes from 0600-2400. Return from Hotel Carrera, Augustinas and Teatinos Streets from 0600-1900. Bus 54 departs to the city every 30 minutes from 0600-2300. Return is from General MacKenna and Morande Street from 0645-2315. Taxis to the city are also available. Airport facilities include bar, bureau de change, car rental, post office and tourist office.
Chacalluta Airport (ARI), 14km (8 miles) northeast of the northern city of Arica, is linked by direct scheduled flights with Miami and several South American capitals.
Departure tax: US$12.50 or the Ch$ equivalent.
SEA: The principal port is Valparaíso. Important shipping lines are *Compañía Argentina de Navegacion Dodero* (CADND) from Buenos Aires; *Cía Sud Americana de Vapores* (CSADV) from New York and European ports; *Delta Line Cruises* from the United States via the Panama Canal and *Royal Netherlands Company* from Rotterdam and Le Havre.
RAIL: The main service is from Santiago to Puerto Montt. From La Paz, Bolivia, there are railways to Arica (on northern border with Peru) and Antofagasta, but with very infrequent trains. There is now no rail connection with Argentina.
ROAD: The Pan American Highway enters Chile through Arica. *TEPSA* buses come to Chile from as far north as Ecuador. There are also services from Brazil to Santiago.

TRAVEL - Internal

AIR: There are frequent services to main towns. The southern part of the country relies heavily on air links. Reservations are essential. Internal passenger air services are operated by the main Chilean airlines *LAN*, *LADECO* and *Aeronorte*, as well as by a number of air taxi companies. Services connecting the main towns are frequent during weekdays, and are fairly regular. There are four 21-day 'Visit Chile' tickets priced from $250 to $500 which cover internal travel. They must be obtained abroad with reservations made well in advance. Once bought, tickets cannot be changed, though reservations can. A coupon ticket on the Santiago–Antofagasta–Arica–Santiago route may suit some travellers better. There are regular flights by *LAN* from Santiago to **Easter Island**, which stop by the island en route to Tahiti. The flights are twice-weekly from November to February, once-weekly at other times; it is essential to book in advance throughout the year. The flight takes five hours. An air taxi runs a daily service during the summer months to the **Juan Fernández Islands** from Valparaíso and Santiago.
Departure tax: US$5 (or Chilean equivalent) per passenger is levied on all flights leaving from Santiago.
SEA: Coastal passenger shipping lines are unreliable and infrequent. Boat services run from Valparaíso to **Easter Island** and **Robinson Crusoe Island** (part of the Juan Fernández Islands) once a month. Contact local travel agents on arrival for details.
RAIL: The State railway runs for 8000km (4971 miles) throughout Chile, beginning in Santiago and ending in Puerto Montt in the south. Services are limited by the geography of the country, but the backbone route (from Santiago to Puerto Montt) has several daily trains with sleeping and restaurant cars, and some air-conditioned accommodation. Principal trains also carry motor cars. For details contact the Chilean Tourist Board.
ROAD: Chile has about 78,000km (48,468 miles) of good roads. The Pan American Highway crosses the country from north to south (a total of 3600km or 2236 miles) from the Peruvian border to Puerto Montt. It is advisable in remoter areas to carry spare petrol and an additional spare tyre. Tyres should be hard-wearing. **Bus:** Intercity buses are cheap and reliable. There is a luxury north–south service running most of the length of the country. Most long-distance coaches have toilets and serve food and drink. Sometimes a lower fare can be negotiated. For details contact the Chilean Tourist Office. **Taxi:** Most have meters, but for long journeys fares should be agreed beforehand. Surcharge of 50% applies on Sundays after 2100 hours. Taxis in Santiago are black and yellow. Tipping is not expected. **Car hire:** Self-drive cars are available at the airport and in major city centres. They are rented on a daily basis plus a mileage charge and 20% tax. A large guarantee deposit is often required. The Automóvil Club de Chile, Avenida Vitacura 8620, Santiago, can supply road maps. **Documentation:** An International Driving Licence is necessary.
URBAN: Santiago has two metro lines, bus, minibus and shared 'Taxibus' services. Taxis are plentiful, the number approaching one per 100 inhabitants, an extremely high figure. The metro, buses and minibuses have flat fares. There is a higher rate for shared taxis. The Santiago underground system is to be expanded. There are bus and taxi services in most other towns.
JOURNEY TIMES: The following chart gives approximate journey times from Santiago (in hours and minutes) to other major cities/towns in Chile.

	Air	Road	Rail
Arica	2.40	28.00	84.00
Concepción	1.30	9.00	7.00
Portillo	2.30	-	-
Puerto Montt	1.45	11.00	17.00
Punta Arenas	3.25	120.00	-
Viña del Mar	-	2.00	-
Easter Island	5.00	-	-

ACCOMMODATION

HOTELS: Chile offers excellent accommodation. Several new luxury hotels have recently opened in Santiago and throughout the country. In all regions of Chile, whatever hotels lack in facilities is made up for by a comfortable homey atmosphere; Chile's famous hospitality is very apparent in provinces where it is common to see the owner or manager sit down to dinner with guests. Advance bookings are essential in resort areas during the high season.
The cost of accommodation in Santiago is rather higher than in the provinces. Rates in Valparaíso, Viña del Mar and other holiday resorts may be increased during the summer holiday from January to March. Members of foreign motoring organisations can obtain discounts at hotels by joining the Automóvil Club de Chile, Avenida Vitacura 8620, Santiago. The address of the Chilean national hotel association is HOTELGA, Elías Fernández Albano 171, Santiago, Chile. Tel: (2) 698 8765. Fax: (2) 598 8850.
Grading: Hotels in Chile are graded from 5 to 2 stars. There are 11 5-star hotels, 58 4-star hotels, 94 3-star hotels and 32 2-star hotels in the country. A description of the facilities included in the Chilean hotel system is as follows:
5-star: Luxurious rooms with air-conditioning, private bathroom and 24-hour room service; garden; restaurant; bar; swimming pool; laundry services; shops; conference rooms; recreational and medical facilities.
4-star: Rooms with air-conditioning and private bathroom; restaurant; bar; laundry services; tourist information; conference rooms; medical and recreational facilities.
3-star: Rooms with private bathrooms; laundry services; first aid and continental breakfast.
2-star: 30% of rooms with private bathroom.
Government tax: VAT of 18% is levied on all hotel bills, except those paid in foreign currencies by foreign visitors for which an export bill is required.
CAMPING/CARAVANNING: Camping facilities exist throughout Chile. A list of campsites may be obtained from Chilean Embassies. Official sites are expensive.
YOUTH HOSTELS: Membership of the Asociación Chilena de Albergues Turísticos Juveniles is required; a card costs US$3.50. For US$7.50 a card including Argentina, Uruguay and Brazil is obtainable. Many hostels are extremely crowded.

RESORTS & EXCURSIONS

In Santiago there are four tourist information centres, including one at the airport. This caters particularly for foreigners just arriving in the country. There are also regional tourist offices throughout the country. Visitors to Chile are faced with a wide variety of excursions from which to choose; for the purposes of this guide, the country has been divided into three geographical areas, ranging from north to south. The *Turistel* series of guide books, sponsored by the telephone company, is published annually. A combined volume of all three parts is also available.

Northern Region

Arica, near the northern border with Peru, is an excellent tourist centre. It has good beaches and the famous *San Marcos Cathedral*. Conditions in the area are ideal for deep-sea fishing. Travelling south through the Atacama Desert, excursions can be made to the hot springs of Mamina and to the oasis of the Pica Valley. The port of **Antofagasta** is the stopping point for air services, for most shipping lines and for rail connections. From here, a visit can be made to *Chuquicamata*, the world's largest open cast copper mine. Visits can also be made from the port at Antofagasta to the archaeological oasis town of **San Pedro de Atacama** and to the geysers at *El Tatio*.
Further south is **Coquimbo,** situated in one of the best harbours on the coast. Nearby is the beautiful bathing resort of **Los Vilos.** Nine miles north of Coquimbo is **La Serena,** the provincial capital. This charming and well laid-out town is graced with fine buildings and streets, as well as by good reproductions of the attractive Spanish colonial style of architecture. The town is at the mouth of the Elqui River and excursions can be made from here to the rich fruit-growing region of the *Elqui Valley*, which is also full of reminiscences of the Chilean Nobel Prize Winner Gabriela Mistral. Tours can also be arranged to the *Tololo Observatory*, the largest in the southern hemisphere.

Central Region and the Islands

This is the most temperate and pastoral region of the country, where the snowcapped peaks of the Andes provide a backdrop for rolling green fields, vineyards and orange groves. **Valparaíso,** the principal port, has many attractions. Only 8km (5 miles) to the north is **Viña del Mar,** Chile's principal and most fashionable seaside resort with casinos, clubs and modern hotels. The *Valparaíso Sporting Club* offers a race course, polo grounds and playing fields.
From Valparaíso there are excellent road and rail services to **Santiago,** where a visitor will find all the conveniences of a modern capital city, including good hotels to suit all tastes. In the northeast of the city is the *San Cristobal Hill* where a zoo, gardens, restaurants

and fine views of the city can be found; the *Club Hippico* and the *Prince of Wales Country Club* provide sporting facilities. From Santiago it is also possible to visit ski resorts such as **Portillo, Farellones** and the newest and most fashionable, **Valle Nevado.** Immediately south of Santiago in the heartland of Chile, one can visit many vineyards where the reputable Chilean wine is produced. Travelling south through the heartland of Chile one reaches **Talca** with its fine parks and museums.
650km (403 miles) west of Valparaíso are the **Juan Fernández Islands,** which can be reached either by plane or boat from the Chilean mainland. Alexander Selkirk was shipwrecked here in the early eighteenth century, and Defoe based his 'Robinson Crusoe' on Selkirk's adventures.
Easter Island is another Pacific Chilean possession, situated 3800km (2361 miles) west of the mainland. It is most famous for the *Moai*, gigantic stone figures up to 9m (30ft) tall which are found all over the island. Other sites include the crater of the volcano *Rano Kao,* the rock carvings at **Oronco** and the museum in the main town of **Hanga Roa.** The best method of travel to the island is by air. Tour guides and guest-house keepers tend to meet every plane, so although it is possible to book good hotel accommodation from Santiago or Valparaíso, it is not essential. Many of the hotels specialise in catering for groups and will arrange tours if asked. Tours can also be arranged with a tour guide. Jeeps, trucks, motorbikes and horses can all be hired.

Southern Region

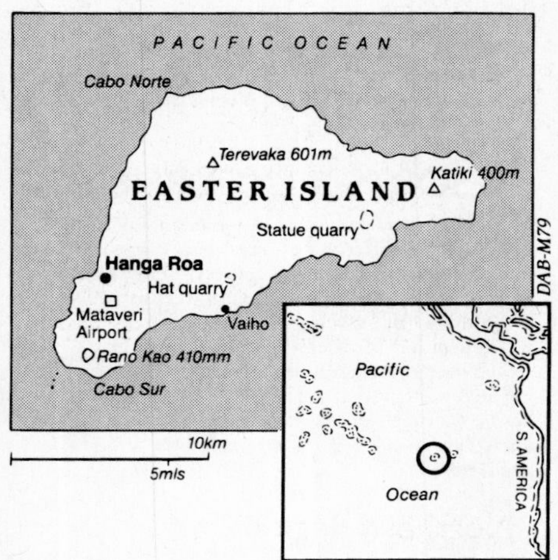

A visit to the impressive waterfalls at **Laguna de Laja** is recommended. **Termuco** marks the beginning of the Lake District, where Lake Villarica and the Trancura and Cincira rivers combine to create beautiful scenery, and an angler's paradise. **Lake Todos** is also well worth a visit. At the southernmost end of the railway line and the Pan American Highway, there is the picturesque town of **Puerto Montt** and, nearby, the colourful small fishing port of **Angelmo.** Inveterate travellers will wish to go on to visit **Chiloe Island** and possibly also the southernmost part of the country, the fjords, spectacular glaciers and harsh landscape of Chilean Patagonia. The whole area of *Magellanes* and *Tierra del Fuego* is worth exploring during the summer season.

SOCIAL PROFILE

FOOD & DRINK: Santiago has many international restaurants; waiter service is normal. The evening will often include floorshows and dancing. Examples of typical national dishes are *empanada* (combination of meat, chicken or fish, with onions, eggs, raisins and olives inside a flour pastry), *humitas* (seasoned corn paste, wrapped in corn husks and boiled), *cazuela de ave* (soup with rice, vegetables, chicken and herbs), *bife a lo pobre* (steak with fried potatoes, onions and eggs) and *parrillada* (selection of meat grilled over hot coals). Seafood is good. Best known are the huge lobsters from Juan Fernández Islands. Abalone, sea urchins, clams, prawns and giant *choros* (mussels) are also common. **Drink:** Chile is famous for its wine. *Pisco* is a powerful liqueur distilled from grapes after wine pressing. Grapes are also used to make the sweet brown *chicha* as well as *aguardiente*, similar to brandy. Beer is drunk throughout the country.
NIGHTLIFE: While many restaurants and hotels offer entertainment there are also a number of independent discotheques and nightclubs. **Casinos:** The Municipal Casino in Viña del Mar offers large gambling salons, full cabaret and *boite* with Chile's best dance bands. A casino operates in Gran Hotel in Puerto Varas between September and March. Arica also has a casino operating throughout the year with baccarat, roulette, Black Jack, a restaurant and late-night cabaret.
SHOPPING: Special purchases include textiles such as colourful handwoven ponchos, vicuna rugs and copper work. Chilean stones such as lapis lazuli, jade, amethyst, agate and onyx are all good buys. **Shopping hours:** 1000-2000 Monday to Friday and 0900-1400 Saturday. The large shopping centres in Santiago are also open 1000-2100 on Sunday.
SPORT: Baseball, tennis, volleyball, hockey, polo, rugby and **football**. The national **golf** championship and the International Horsemanship Championship are held in Viña del Mar in January. The two main **horseraces** of the year are the Derby (Viña del Mar, January) and *El Ensayo* (Santiago, October). The Rod and Gun Club (*Club de Pesca y Caza)* in any city can arrange for licences to **fish** and to **hunt** small game. **Watersports: Skindiving, water-skiing,** and **boating** are available. In the central valley brown trout are found and there is rainbow trout **fishing** in the south. **Winter sports:** The **skiing** season runs from June to September with the best resort at Portillo. Ski-championships are held in Portillo, Farellones and in Valle Nevado in July.
SPECIAL EVENTS: Mar '93 *Los Andes International Fair*. **Mar 25-Apr 4** *Talca International Fair*. **Apr 1-4** *17th National Tourist Industry Congress*, location to be announced.
SOCIAL CONVENTIONS: Handshaking is the customary form of greeting. Most Chileans use a double surname and only the paternal name should be used in addressing them. Normal courtesies should be observed when visiting local people. It is very common to entertain at home and it is acceptable for invitees to give small presents as a token of thanks. Informal, conservative clothes are acceptable in most places but women should not wear shorts outside resort areas. **Tipping:** Restaurants and bars add 10% to bill. However waiters will expect 10% cash tip in addition.

BUSINESS PROFILE

ECONOMY: With a well-developed industrial and service sector, Chile has one of Latin America's strongest economies. However, it still depends on export of primary commodities – metals and ores, fruit, fish and wood – for a large proportion of its export earnings. Chile has a large surplus of fruit and vegetables available for export to North America and Europe but is not entirely self-sufficient in agricultural produce. The industrial base has grown considerably over the last 30 years and now includes steel manufacturing, oil production, shipbuilding, cement and consumer goods. The mainstay of the export economy for the time being is metals and ores: Chile is the world's leading exporter of copper and also produces zinc, iron ore, molybdenum, manganese, iodine and lithium. The United States is the largest trading partner, followed by Japan, Brazil and Germany. Chile has made vigorous efforts in the last few years to open negotiations for a free trade agreement with the United States but has so far been met with indifference in Washington.
BUSINESS: Business people should wear formal clothes in dark colours for official functions, dinners, smart restaurants and hotels. Dress is usually stipulated on invitations. There is a tendency to formality with many old-world courtesies. Best months for business visits are April to December.
COMMERCIAL INFORMATION: The following organisation can offer advice: Cámara de Comercio de Santiago de Chile, Casilla 1297, Santa Lucía 302, 3°, Santiago. Tel: (2) 330 962. Telex: 240868.
CONFERENCES/CONVENTIONS: Information on conferences and conventions can be obtained from the Organización de Profesionales de Congresos y Eventos (OPCE), Toledo 1991, Providencia, Santiago. Tel: (2) 225 6888. Fax: (2) 274 2789.

HISTORY & GOVERNMENT

HISTORY: The Araucanian Indians were the original inhabitants of Chile. The Spanish conquered the country in the 16th century and ruled until the country's independence in 1818 following a war led by Bernard O'Higgins and Jose de San Martín. As a result of the War of the Pacific (1879-1883), Chile gained Tarapacá, Tacna and Arica from Bolivia, and took control of the Atacama. Border disputes between Chile and Bolivia have been a recurrent element in Chile's history ever since. In 1891 civil war broke out and a parliamentary principle of government was established. Elections in 1970 brought Unidad Popular, led by the Marxist Dr Salvador Allende, to power. Violent opposition led to a military coup during which Allende was killed. General Augusto Pinochet Ugarte was declared Supreme Chief of State and President, and remained in power despite considerable opposition from many sectors of society. The ruling military junta assumed wide-ranging powers, its main aim being to eliminate the Communist Party and other leftist opposition. During the 'state of siege', imprisonment of the opposition – many of whom 'disappeared' – censorship and the banning of all political activity were authorised. These powers were gradually relaxed during the 1980s until the Government felt that the Marxist menace was no longer a threat to the country and arranged a gradual return to representative government. The centrist opposition leader, Patricio Aylwin, stood against the General and won in the presidential elections of December 1989. Pinochet, whose days as an absolute ruler ended in March 1990, retains control of the army (and the status of interested spectator) and there remain areas where the civilian administration is constrained in its actions. Defence policy is one of these; the well-documented brutality of Chile's secret police is another. In 1992, the Aylwin government started to tackle this and other of Pinochet's residual and somewhat out-moded powers. Abroad, relations between Chile and its neighbours, including Argentina, have been improving, notably through the creation of the southern cone trading bloc, Mercosur, but also because of growing mutual frustration with the US on a range of issues (environmental protection, trade, drug trafficking).
GOVERNMENT: The new constitution promulgated in 1981, which took effect in 1989, establishes a President as head of the government and a National Assembly with an upper chamber of 26 and a lower chamber with 120 deputies elected by universal suffrage.

CLIMATE

Ranges from hot and arid in the north to very cold in the far south. The central areas have a mild Mediterranean climate with a wet season (May to August). Beyond Puerto Montt in the south is one of the wettest and stormiest areas in the world.
Required clothing: Lightweight cottons and linens in northern and central areas. Rainwear is advised during rainy seasons. Mediumweights and waterproofing are needed in the south.

SANTIAGO Chile (520m)

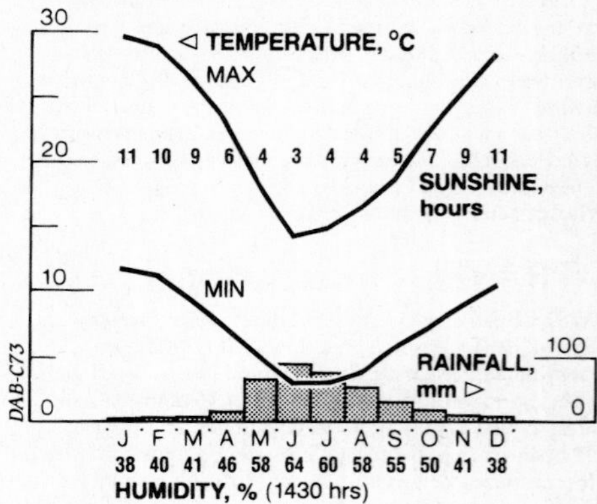

VALDIVIA Chile (9m)

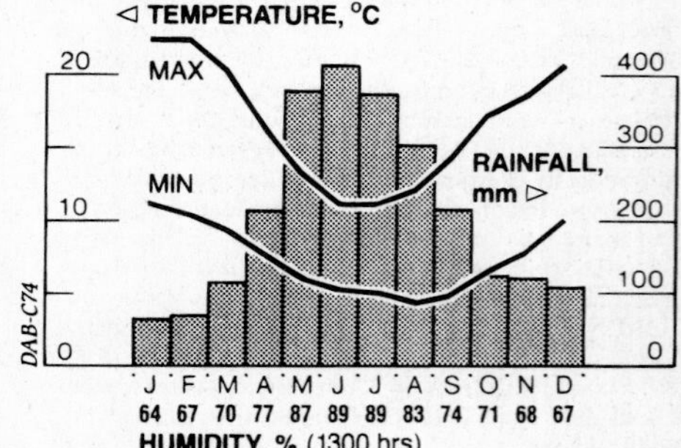

CHINA (PEOPLE'S REPUBLIC OF)

Location: Far East.

China International Travel Service (CITS)
6 Dongchangan Dajie
Beijing
People's Republic of China
Tel: (1) 512 1122. Fax: (1) 512 2068. Telex: 22350.

Embassy of the People's Republic of China
49-51 Portland Place
London W1N 3AH
Tel: (071) 636 9375. Opening hours: 0900-1230 and 1430-1800 Monday to Friday.

Consular Section, Embassy of the People's Republic of China
31 Portland Place
London W1N 3AG
Tel: (071) 636 1835. Fax: (071) 636 9756. Telex: 23851 CHINA G.

Consulate General of the People's Republic of China
Denison House
Denison Road
Victoria Park
Manchester M14 5RX
Tel: (061) 224 7480. Fax: (061) 257 2672. Telex: 667678.

China Tourist Office
4 Glentworth Street
London NW1 5PG
Tel: (071) 935 9427. Fax: (071) 487 5842. Telex: 291221.

British Embassy
11 Guang Hua Lu
Jian Guo Men Wai
Beijing, People's Republic of China
Tel: (1) 532 1961/5. Fax: (1) 532 1939. Ansaphone: (1) 532 2011. Telex: 22191.

British Consulate General
244 Yong Fu Lu
Shanghai 20031
People's Republic of China
Tel: (21) 433 0508 (4 lines) *or* 437 4569 (1 line). Fax: (21) 433 3115. Telex: 33476 BRIT CN; *or*
11 Guang Hua Lu
Jian Guo Men Wai
Beijing, People's Republic of China
Tel: (1) 532 1961/5. Telex: 22191 PRDRM CN.

Embassy of the People's Republic of China
2300 Connecticut Avenue, NW
Washington, DC
20008
Tel: (202) 328 2500. Fax: (202) 232 7855.

Consulate General of the People's Republic of China
520 12th Avenue
New York, NY
10036
Tel: (212) 330 7404.

China National Tourist Office
60 East 42nd Street
New York, NY
10165
Tel: (212) 867 0271. Telex: 662142.

Embassy of the United States of America
3 Xiu Shui Bei Jie
Beijing 100600
People's Republic of China
Tel: (1) 532 3831. Fax: (1) 532 3178. Telex: 22701.

Embassy of the People's Republic of China
511-515 St Patrick Street
Ottawa, Ontario
K1N 5H3
Tel: (613) 234 2706. Fax: (613) 230 9794.

Canadian Embassy
10 San Li Tun Lu
Chao Yang Qu
Beijing, People's Republic of China
Tel: (1) 532 3536. Fax: (1) 532 4072. Telex: 22717.

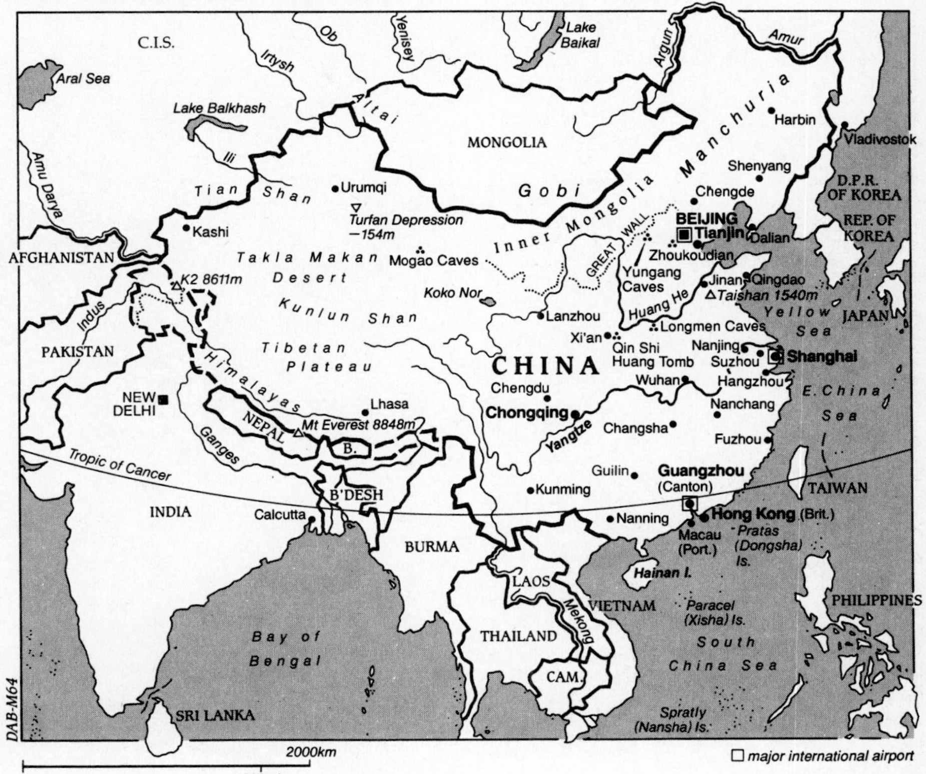

AREA: 9,571,300 sq km (3,695,500 sq miles).
POPULATION: 1,133,682,501 (1990). Roughly a quarter of the world's population live in China.
POPULATION DENSITY: 118.4 per sq km.

Jiayu Pass on the Silk Road, at the western end of the Great Wall

CAPITAL: Beijing (Peking). **Population:** 6,920,000 (1989). The largest city in the country, Shanghai, has a population of over seven million and 39 other cities have a population of over one million.

GEOGRAPHY: China is bounded to the north by the CIS and Mongolia, to the east by North Korea, the Yellow Sea and the South China Sea, to the south by Vietnam, Laos, Myanmar, India, Bhutan and Nepal, and to the west by India, Pakistan, Afghanistan and the CIS. Hong Kong and Macau form enclaves on the southeast coast. China comprises 23 Provinces, 5 Autonomous Regions and 3 Municipalities directly under Central Government. It has a varied terrain ranging from high plateaux in the west to flatlands in the east; mountains take up almost one-third of the land. The most notable high mountain ranges are the Himalayas, the Altai Mountains, the Tianshan Mountains and the Kunlun Mountains. On the China/Nepal border is 8848m (29,198ft) Mount Jolmo Lungma (Mount Everest). In the west is the Qinghai/Tibet Plateau, with an average elevation of 4000m (13,200ft), known as 'The Roof of the World'. At the base of the Tianshan Mountains is the Turfan Depression or Basin, China's lowest area, 154m (508ft) below sea level at the lowest point. China has many great river systems, notably the Yellow (Huang He) and Yangtse Kiang (Chang Jiang). Only 10% of all China is suitable for agriculture.

LANGUAGE: The official language is Mandarin Chinese. Among the enormous number of local dialects, in the south, large groups speak Cantonese, Fukienese, Xiamenhua and Hakka. Mongolia, Tibet and Xinjiang, which are autonomous regions, have their own languages. Translation and interpreter services are good. English is spoken by many guides.

RELIGION: The principal religions and philosophies are Buddhism, Daoism and Confucianism. There are 100 million Buddhists. Also about 20 million Muslims, five million Protestants (including large numbers of Evangelists) and four million Roman Catholics, largely independent of Vatican control.

TIME: GMT + 8 (GMT + 9 in summer). Despite the vast size of the country, Beijing time is standard throughout China.

ELECTRICITY: 220 volts AC, 50Hz.

COMMUNICATIONS: Telephone: IDD is available. Country code: 86. Antiquated internal service with public telephones in hotels and shops displaying telephone unit sign. It is often easier to make international phone calls from China than it is to make calls internally. **Telex/telegram:** Beijing now has an automatic telex service to the UK. Country code: 85. Facilities are available at main and branch post offices in larger towns and cities. A growing number of hotels offer telex and fax facilities but often only incoming. Rates are generally expensive. **Post:** Service to Europe takes about a week. All postal communications to China should be addressed 'People's Republic of China'. **Press:** The main English-language daily is the *China Daily*. There is also the *Beijing Review*, with weekly editions in English, French, Spanish, Japanese and German. National newspapers include *The People's Daily* and *The Guangming Daily*, with many provinces having their own local dailies as well.

BBC World Service and Voice of America frequencies: From time to time these change. See the section *How to Use this Book* for more information.

BBC:				
MHz	21.72	15.36	11.96	7.180
Voice of America:				
MHz	17.74	11.76	7.275	1.575

CHINA	HEALTH REGULATIONS	VISA REGULATIONS
GALILEO/WORLDSPAN	TI-DFT/PEK/HE	 TI-DFT/PEK/VI
SABRE	 TIDFT/PEK/HE	 TIDFT/PEK/VI

Code-Link

To access this information on your CRS, swipe the barcode with a light pen or type in the text under the barcode. For more information, see the introduction *How to Use This Book*.

PASSPORT/VISA

Regulations and requirements may be subject to change at short notice, and you are advised to contact the appropriate diplomatic or consular authority before finalising travel arrangements. Details of these may be found at the head of this country's entry. Any numbers in the chart refer to the footnotes below.

	Passport Required?	Visa Required?	Return Ticket Required?
Full British	Yes	Yes	Yes
BVP	Not valid	-	-
Australian	Yes	Yes	Yes
Canadian	Yes	Yes	Yes
USA	Yes	Yes	Yes
Other EC	Yes	Yes	Yes
Japanese	Yes	Yes	Yes

PASSPORTS: Valid passport required by all.
British Visitors Passport: Not acceptable.
VISAS: Required by all.
Types of visa: *Tourist/UK* (Cost: £25 single entry, £50 double entry, £75 multiple entry. Cash or postal order payable to the Chinese Embassy is preferable, as cheques are not accepted); *Tourist/Other nationals* (Cost: will vary according to nationality; contact the Embassy for further information); *Group; Business* (see below for further information); *Transit* (generally required for people in transit through China for a period of no more than 10 days; these cannot be extended when in China; contact the Embassy for further information). For prices of the last three kinds of visas, apply to the Embassy. It should be noted that it is considerably cheaper to buy visas in Hong Kong, where they cost less than half the price.
Validity: *Tourist* and *Group* visas are normally issued to individuals or groups on package tours, although they are also issued to individuals as well. Visa validity is therefore dependent upon duration of package tour or individual stay. Validity of *Business* visas varies. *Transit* visas are valid for up to 10 days.
Application to: Consulate (or Consular Section at Embassy). For addresses, see top of entry. Applications by post require an additional £5 for postage and handling charges, and a self-addressed envelope must be included. Recorded delivery or registered post is recommended.
Application requirements: For a *Group Visa*, applications should be made to the China National Tourist Office, London, with a confirmation letter or telex from the Chinese travel company concerned, or from the Consulate General of the People's Republic of China in Manchester (see above). For *Tourist* and *Business Visas:* (a) Completed application form. (b) 1 photo. (c) Valid passport with at least 6 months' validity and two blank visa pages left. (d) Sufficient funds for duration of stay. Business visitors can obtain a visa from the Embassy or Consulate only if they have received an invitation from either a Ministry, Corporation, Foreign Trade Corporation or an official Chinese organisation.
Visas can also be issued in Hong Kong on application to the China International Travel Service. Tel: 721 5317. Telex: 38449 CITS HX. This normally takes 3 working days and costs HK$80. Visas can be issued the same day on payment of HK$200.
Working days required: As all visas are granted by the Authorities of China, some time will elapse depending upon the merits of application. Apply as far in advance as possible.
Temporary residence: Enquiries should be made to the Chinese Embassy.
Note: (a) The majority, but not all, visits to China tend to be organised through the official state travel agency *Luxingshe* (China International Travel Service). This liaison with *Luxingshe* is generally handled by the tour operator organising the inclusive holiday chosen by the visitor, though it is possible for individuals to organise affairs in their own right. Once the tour itinerary details have been confirmed to the visitor or visiting group, finances to cover accommodation and the cost of the tour must be deposited with *Luxingshe* through a home bank. Evidence of the payment of funds for the tour must be presented to *Luxingshe* officials on arrival in China. Once again, for package trips all the necessary formalities for a visit to China can be handled by the tour operator concerned.
(b) Under new immigration procedures, it may now be possible for nationals of certain countries (including the UK) to obtain visas on arrival at Beijing Airport. Contact the Embassy or Tourist Office for further details.

MONEY

Currency: 1 Yuan (Renminbi RMB) (¥) = 10 chiao/jiao or 100 fen. Notes are in the denominations of ¥100, 50, 10, 5, 2 and 1, and 5, 2 and 1 chiao/jiao. Coins are in denominations of 5, 2 and 1 fen. In banks and hotels, tourists will only be able to obtain *Foreign Exchange Certificates (FEC)*, which come in the same denominations as RMB but have a slightly higher value.
Currency exchange: RMB (People's money) is not traded outside China and is only available in the form of FEC in exchange for travellers cheques in Hong Kong or within China. There is only one national bank, the People's Bank, which has over 30,000 branches. In hotels and *Friendship Stores* for tourists, imported luxury items such as spirits can only be purchased with *Foreign Exchange Certificates* (FEC), which may be bought with Western currency. FEC must also be used for train tickets, in hotels, in high-class restaurants and admission to certain better-known monuments such as the Forbidden City. In local markets and more remote places, it is often better to use RMB, because people may not have seen FEC before and refuse to take it. It is therefore safer to have both RMB and FEC.
Credit cards: Access/Mastercard, Visa, Diners Club, Federal Card, East-American Visa, Million Card, JCB Card and American Express are valid in major provincial cities in designated establishments.
FEC travellers cheques: Available in Macau or Hong Kong. All major travellers cheques may be exchanged for FEC at banks, but they cannot be used for payment.
Exchange rate indicators: The following figures are

West Lake in Huangzhou

included as a guide to the movements of the Yuan against Sterling and the US Dollar:

Date:	Oct '89	Oct '90	Oct '91	Oct '92
£1.00=	6.01	9.32	9.33	9.02
$1.00=	3.81	4.77	5.37	5.68

Currency restrictions: Import and export of local currency is prohibited. Unlimited foreign currency may be imported but must be declared (also unlimited FEC travellers cheques). The unused amount of foreign currency may be exported.
Banking hours: 0930-1200 and 1400-1700 Monday to Friday, 0900-1700 Saturday.

DUTY FREE

The following items may be imported into China by passengers staying less than six months without incurring customs duty:
400 cigarettes (600 cigarettes for stays of over six months);
2 litres of alcoholic beverage;
A reasonable amount of perfume for personal use.
Prohibited items: Arms, ammunition, radio transmitters/receivers, exposed but undeveloped film.
Note: Baggage declaration forms must be completed upon arrival noting all valuables (cameras, watches, jewellery etc), a copy of which must be presented to customs upon leaving the country for checking.

PUBLIC HOLIDAYS

Public holidays observed in the People's Republic of China are as follows:
Mar 8 '93 International Women's Day. **May 1** Labour Day. **May 4** Chinese Youth Day. **Jun 1** International Children's Day. **Jul 1** Founding of the Communist Party of China. **Aug 1** Army Day. **Oct 1-2** National Days. **Jan 1 '94** Solar New Year. **Feb 10** Chinese New Year. **Mar** International Women's Day.

HEALTH

Regulations and requirements may be subject to change at short notice, and you are advised to contact your doctor well in advance of your intended date of departure. Any numbers in the chart refer to the footnotes below.

	Special Precautions?	Certificate Required?
Yellow Fever	Yes	1
Cholera	2	2
Typhoid & Polio	Yes	-
Malaria	3	-
Food & Drink	4	-

[1]: A yellow fever vaccination certificate is required from travellers if arriving from infected areas.
[2]: Cholera epidemics are very rare, but occasional outbreaks are reported in Southern China. Following WHO guidelines issued in 1973, a cholera vaccination certificate is no longer a condition of entry to China. Up-to-date advice should be sought before deciding whether precautions should include vaccination as medical opinion is divided over its effectiveness. See the *Health* section at the back of the book.
[3]: Malaria risk exists throughout the country below 1500m except in Heilongjiang, Jilin, Inner Mongolia, Gansu, Beijing, Shanxi, Ningxia, Qinghai, Xinjiang (except in the Yili Valley) and Tibet (Xizang, except in the Zangbo Valley in the extreme southeast). North of 33°N, the risk lasts from July to November, between 33°N and 25°N from May to December, and south of 25°N throughout the year. The disease occurs primarily in the benign *vivax* form but the malignant *falciparum* form is also present and has been reported to be 'highly resistant' to chloroquine.
[4]: Outside main centres all water used for drinking, brushing teeth or making ice should have first been boiled or otherwise sterilised. Only eat well-cooked meat and fish, preferably served hot. Pork, salad and mayonnaise may carry increased risk. Vegetables should be cooked and fruit peeled.
Rabies is present, although the Government policy which bans dogs and cats from main cities makes this less of a risk in these areas. For those at high risk, vaccination before arrival should be considered. If you are bitten abroad seek medical advice without delay. For more information consult the *Health* section at the back of the book.
Bilharzia (schistosomiasis) is present in southeastern and eastern China. Avoid swimming and paddling in fresh water. Swimming pools which are well-chlorinated and maintained are safe.
Health care: Medical costs are low. Many medicines common to Western countries are unavailable in China. The hospital system is excellent. There are many traditional forms of medicine still used in China, the most notable being acupuncture. Medical insurance is advised.

TRAVEL - International

AIR: The national airline is CAAC *(CA) (Air China)*.
Approximate flight time: From *London* to Beijing is between 14 and 18 hours depending on the route taken.
From *New York* to Beijing is 22 hours.
From *Los Angeles* to Beijing is 12 hours.
International airports: *Beijing/Peking (BJS/PEK)* airport (Capital International Central) is 30km (18.5 miles) northeast of the city (travel time – 45 minutes by bus, 30 minutes by taxi).
Guangzhou/Canton airport (Baiyun) is 7km (4 miles) from the city (travel time – 20 minutes).
Shanghai (SHA) airport (Hongqiao) is 12km (7.5 miles) southwest of the city (travel time – 20 minutes).
Facilities at the above airports include taxis, duty-free shops, banks/cambios, bars and restaurants.
There are also airports at other major cities throughout the country.
Departure tax: Beijing/Peking: Domestic ¥15, International ¥60. Shanghai: International ¥20. Guangzhou/Canton: Domestic ¥25, International ¥70.
SEA: Principal seaports are Qingdao (Tsingtao), Shanghai, Fuzhou (Foochow), Guangzhou (Canton) and Hong Kong/Kowloon. *Pearl Cruises* operate over 20 cruises a year to China. Other cruise lines are *Lindblad Travel, Royal Viking, Sitmar* and *CTC*. There is a regular (once or twice weekly) ferry service linking Tianjin with Kobe in Japan and the west coast of South Korea.
RAIL: International services run twice a week from Beijing to Moscow (CIS) and Pyongyang (Democratic People's Republic of Korea). A regular train service runs from Hong Kong to Guangzhou (Canton), which is of a higher standard than internal trains in China. There are several trains daily.
ROAD: The principal road routes into China follow the historical trade routes through Myanmar, India, the CIS and Mongolia.

TRAVEL - Internal

Note: All travel destinations and routes are normally organised through *Luxingshe (CITS)*, who ensure that the arrangements for individual itineraries are practical and who provide guides for each party. Independent travel, however, is becoming increasingly possible, and full details of this are available from the China National Tourist Office at the address above. The *Luxingshe (CITS)* guides are generally very helpful and amenable.
AIR: Most long-distance internal travel is by air. The *Civil Aviation Administration of China (CAAC)* operates along routes linking Beijing to over 80 other cities. Tickets will normally be purchased by guides and price will be included in any tour costs. Independent travellers can also book through the local Chinese International Travel Service, which charges a small commission, or they can buy tickets in booking offices. It is advisable to purchase internal air tickets well in advance if the time of travel is to be during May, September or October. Tourist price for a ticket is 70% on a train ticket and 100% on an air ticket. There are many connections to Hong Kong from Beijing/Guangzhou (Peking/Canton) and other cities as well.
SEA/RIVER: All major rivers are served by river ferries. Coastal ferries operate between Dalian, Tianjin (Tientsin), Qingdao (Tsingtao) and Shanghai.
RAIL: Railways provide the principal means of transport for goods and people throughout China. The major routes are from Beijing to Guangzhou, Shanghai, Harbin, Chengdu and Urumqi. There are four types of fare: hard seat, soft seat (only on short-distance trains such as the Hong Kong to Guangzhou (Canton) line), hard sleeper and soft sleeper. Children under 1m tall travel free and those under 1.3m pay a quarter of the fare.
ROAD: 80% of settlements can be reached by road. Roads are not always of the highest quality. Distances should not be underestimated and vehicles should be in

prime mechanical condition as China is still very much an agricultural nation without the mechanical expertise or services found in the West. From Beijing to Shanghai is 1461km (908 miles), and from Beijing to Nanjing (Nanking) is 1139km (718 miles). **Bus:** Reasonable bus services are operated between the main cities. Buses are normally crowded. **Car hire:** Available.

URBAN: There are limited metro services in Beijing and Tianjin, and tramways and trolleybuses in a number of other cities. New lines are under construction in Beijing. Most cities have very extensive bus services. Guides who accompany every visitor or group will ensure that internal travel within the cities is as trouble-free as possible. **Taxi:** Taxis are available in large cities but can be hard to find. It is best to check if the taxi is metered. If not, then it is important to agree a fare beforehand, especially at railway stations where it is best to bargain before gettig into the taxi. Visitors should write down their destination before starting any journey. Taxis can be hired by the day. Most people travel by bicycle or public transport. In most cities, bicycle or other types of rickshaws are also available for short rides.

JOURNEY TIMES: The following chart gives approximate journey times (in hours and minutes) from Beijing to other major cities/towns in China.

	Air	Rail
Tianjin	0.50	1.40
Wuhan	1.45	16.00
Xian	1.55	22.00
Nanjing	1.40	15.30
Shanghai	1.50	20.00
Chengdu	2.25	60.00
Kunming	3.20	80.00
Guangzhou	3.00	37.00
Urumqi	4.00	95.00

ACCOMMODATION

The booking and payment of accommodation is usually arranged beforehand by the organisers of any visit or tour and this restricts choice to a certain degree.

HOTELS: Accommodation is easy to find and cheap by European standards. Most hotels are reasonably clean. Each town has hotels designated for foreigners with special, regular and economy categories, all with private bathroom facilities as well as shops, post office and exchange facilities. Few are centrally heated. Some hotel restaurants offer Western food although Chinese cuisine is excellent.

DORMITORIES: These are found in most tourist centres and provide cheaper accommodation for budget travellers. Standards range from poor to adequate.

RESORTS & EXCURSIONS

China is a vast country, requiring visitors to travel for much of their time in order to see at least a selection of the cultural, historical and natural wonders of the land. Altogether there are 26 provinces, each with their own dialect and regional characteristics. The western provinces of Xinjiang, Tibet, Qinghai, Sichuan and Yunnan occupy an enormous area of land, and Sichuan alone is about the size of France. The state travel agency *Luxingshe (CITS)* tends to organise a good deal of the tours in China, although more and more specialist operators are running packages so visitors are now presented with a considerable choice of excursions.

Beijing and the Northeast

The entire area of **Beijing** within the city limits is in many ways one great historical museum. The city is symmetrical and built as three rectangles, one within the other. The innermost rectangle is the *Forbidden City*, now a museum and public park, but formerly the residence of the Ming and Qing emperors. The second rectangle forms the boundaries of the *Imperial City* where there are several parks and the homes of high government officials. The outer rectangle forms the outer city with its markets and old residential districts. The *Imperial Palace*, lying inside the Forbidden City and surrounded by a high wall and broad moat, is well worth a visit. Dating from the 15th century, the Palace was home to a total of 24 emperors, and today its fabulous halls, palaces and gardens house a huge collection of priceless relics from various dynasties. Other points of interest are the *Coal Hill* (Mei Shan), a beautiful elevated park with breathtaking views; *Beihai Park*, the loveliest in Beijing; *Tiananmen Square*, the largest public square in the world, surrounded by museums, parks, the Zoo and Beijing University; the *Temple of Heaven*, an excellent example of 15th-century Chinese architecture; the *Summer Palace*, the former court resort for the emperors of the Qing Dynasty, looking out over the *Kunming Lake;* the *Great Wall* (see below), the section at Badaling being easily accessible from Beijing; and the *Ming Tombs*, where 13 Ming emperors chose to be buried. Two magnificent tombs here have been excavated, one of which is open to the public.

The **Great Wall**, said to be the only man-made structure visible from the moon, is a spectacular sight which should not be missed. Stretching for a distance of 5400km, it starts at the Shanhaiguan Pass in the east and ends at the Jiayuguan Pass in the west. The section at Badaling, which most tourists visit, is roughly 8m high and 6m wide. Constructed of large granite blocks and bricks some 2600 years ago, the wall is one of the universally acknowledged wonders of the world.

Beidaihe, a small sea-coast resort with beaches, temples and parks, is a popular vacation area 277km (172 miles)

Typical Quilin scenery

The Temple of Heaven, Beijing

from Beijing. Attractions include the *Yansai Lake* and *Shan Hai Guan*, a massive gateway at the very start of the Great Wall.

Chengde is a mountain escape from the summer heat of Beijing and a former retreat of the Qing emperors. There are many temples and parks, including the remains of the *Qing Summer Palace* with its impressive Imperial Garden. The *Eight Outer Temples*, lying at the foot of the hills to the northeast of the Palace, incorporate, amongst others, the architectural styles of the Han, Mongolian and Tibetan peoples. At over 22m (72ft) tall, the colossal wooden image of Buddha in the *Temple of General Peace* is recognised as the largest in the world.

Dalian is China's third port. Formerly occupied by the Soviets, it is an interesting bi-cultural city. There are guided tours of the port, residential areas, parks and the excellent beaches to the south. *Xinghai Park* combines a park with beach and restaurant facilities, while the *Tiger Beach Park* boasts of tiger-shaped rock formations. Shell mosaics and glassware are famous products of Dalian.

Harbin, the capital of Heilongjiang Province, is a Russian-style city and is the industrial centre of the northeast. Attractions include the *Provincial Museum* with its large collection of artefacts, including what are arguably the best-preserved mammoth skeletons in China; *Tai Yang Dao*, or Sun Island; the *Songhau River*, offering boat trips through the very centre of the city; and the *Arts and Crafts Factory*, known for its good selection of jadework. Harbin is host to the annual Harbin Summer Music Festival.

Hohhot (meaning 'green city' in Mongolian) is the capital of the Inner Mongolia Autonomous Region, and probably the most colourful city in China. Traditional Mongolian rodeos are performed for tourists under oriental domes and there are also tours of the grasslands, further displays of horsemanship, and visits to local communes and villages, where it is possible to stay overnight in a Mongolian *yurt*. Hohhot is famous for its woollen products.

A visit to nearby **Kweihua** is also recommended: the monastery's *Five-Pagoda Temple* dates from around 1000BC.

Shenyang is now a large industrial centre, but was once an imperial capital. Remains from this period include the *Imperial Palace* – not unlike the Imperial Palace in Beijing – and two interesting tombs. The *North Imperial Tomb*, about 20km (13 miles) from the city, is the burial place of the founding father of the Qing Dynasty.

The Eastern Provinces

Fuzhou, in Fujian Province on the southeast coast, is a lovely city on the banks of the *Min River*. Dating back some 2000 years (to the Tang Dynasty), the city has numerous parks and temples, as well as bustling shipbuilding and repair centres. Fuzhou also has hot springs dotted throughout the city. Local products include lacquerware, Shoushan stone carvings, paper umbrellas, cork carvings and Fukien black tea.

Hangzhou, about 190km (120 miles) south of Shanghai, is one of China's seven ancient capital cities. Known as 'Paradise on Earth', Hangzhou was also described by Marco Polo as "the most beautiful and magnificent city in the world". Although today's city is a prosperous industrial and agricultural centre, it is nevertheless a beauty spot still visited by Chinese and foreign tourists in great numbers. Attractions include the silk factories and the recently completed zoo. By far the most attractive excursion, however, is to the *West Lake* area, dotted with weeping willows and peach trees, stone bridges, rockeries and painted pavilions. Here can be found the *Pagoda of Six Harmonies*, various tombs and sacred hills, monasteries and temples, not least the *Linyin Temple*.

Nanjing, meaning 'southern capital', has a beautiful setting on the Chang Jiang (Yangste) River at the foot of Zijinshan (Purple Mountain). Another former capital of China, Nanjing is now capital of Jiangsu Province. It abounds with temples, tombs, parks and lakes, museums, hot springs and other places of interest, foremost amongst them being the *Tomb of the Ming Emperor*, where lies the body of Zhu Yuanzhang, founding father of the Ming Dynasty and the only Ming emperor to be buried outside Beijing. The mausoleum of China's first president, Dr Sun Yat-sen, is also here. Other places of interest are the *Yangtse River Bridge* with its observation deck, the *Purple Mountain Observatory* and the *Tombs of the Southern Tang Dynasty*, known as the 'Underground Palace'.

Shanghai is one of the world's largest cities, and is in some ways more like New York than Beijing. Lying at the estuary of the Chang Jiang (Yangtse) River, it is the centre of China's trade and industry. Squares and historical avenues, the old town and magnificent gardens, splendid parks and museums, busy harbours, palaces, pagodas and temples all co-exist in this bustling metropolis. *Yu Yuan Garden* dates back over 400 years: although relatively small, it is impressive thanks to its intricate design, with pavilions, rockeries and ponds recalling an architectural style. The garden is reached via the *Town God Temple Bazaar*, where a variety of small odds and ends can be bought. One of the most well-known Bhuddist temples

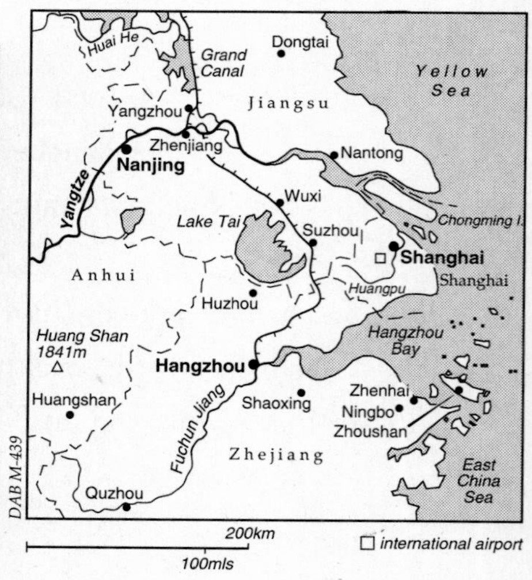

in Shanghai is the *Temple of the Jade Bhudda*, a replica of a palace of the Song Dynasty, and home to the famous 2m (6ft) tall statue of Sakyamuni, carved out of a single piece of white jade. Worth a visit are the *Art and History Museum* (artefacts from all dynasties); the *Carpet Factory*, where a range of carpets can be bought and shipment arranged; the *Jade Carving Factory*, with works of all sizes on show; and the *Children's Palace* – once belonging to a rich businessman, this large house is now at the disposal of the city's children.

Suzhou is one of China's oldest cities, dating back some 2500 years, and is certainly one of her most beautiful. An old proverb says that 'in Heaven there is Paradise; on

The Forbidden City in the heart of Beijing

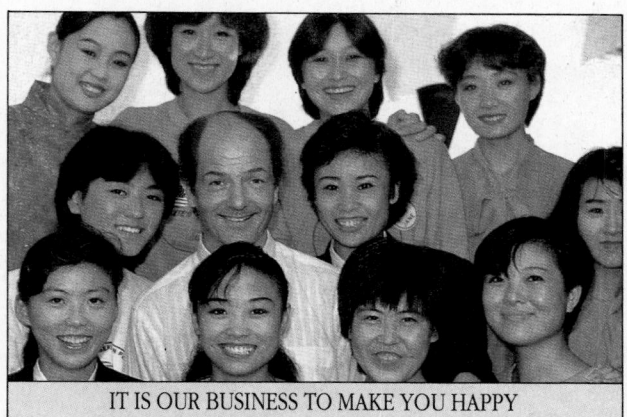

earth, Suzhou': there are indeed many beautiful gardens in this city, and its moderate climate and fertile land make it rich in agricultural produce. There are over 400 historical sites and relics under the protection of the Government, such as the *Gentle Waves Pavilion* and the *Humble Administator's Garden* and the *Lingering Garden* (both fine classical gardens). The *Grand Canal* and *Tiger Hill* are also worth a visit. There are numerous silk mills producing exquisite fabrics, and the local embroidery is an unparalleled art form.

Wuxi is an industrial and resort city on the north bank of Lake Tai, some 125km (75 miles) west of Shanghai. The gardens, parks and sanatoriums around the lake are the main attractions, as is the *Hui Shan Clay Figure Factory*. Wuxi is virtually encircled by the Chang Jiang (Yangtse) River, and so there are plenty of boat trips to be had.

Jinan, the capital of Shandong Province, is known as the 'City of Springs'; these provide the main tourist attraction. The city also has Buddhist relics, parks and lakes. Of particular interest is the *Square Four Gate Pagoda*, the oldest stone pagoda in China.

Qingdao is one of China's most popular coastal resorts and home of the famous brewery making Tsingdao beer. The *Qingdao Aquarium* has hundreds of rare and protected fish on show.

Taiwan is the main island of a group of 78 islands located off the southeast coast of China. For more information on places of interest in Taiwan, please refer to the section entitled *Taiwan, China* further on in the *World Travel Guide*.

Shanghai

The Southern Provinces

Changsha, as well as being the capital of Hunan Province, is a cultural and educational centre. It is close to the birthplace of Mao Zedong at **Shaoshan**. Most attractions revolve around Mao's early life and there are museums and schools dedicated to him. One notable exception is the Han Tomb whose contents – including the 2000-year-old remains of a woman – are now in the *Hunan Provincial Museum*.

Guangzhou (Canton), sometimes known as the 'City of Flowers', is a subtropical metropolis on the south coast and the most important foreign trade centre in China, being only 182km (113 miles) from Hong Kong. Parks, museums, temples, hot springs and trips to nearby mountains (for splendid views) are the main attractions, as are the *Chenhai Tower*, a 15th-century observation tower overlooking the Pearl River, and the *Ancestral Temple* in Hunin, an ancient Taoist temple some 16km (10 miles) southwest of Guangzhou. Cantonese cuisine (the one most familiar to the majority of Westerners) is regarded as being particularly excellent, although it is often too exotic for Western tastes.

Guilin is famous for its spectacular landscape, echoed so evocatively in the paintings and wall hangings well-known in the West. Steep monolithic mountains rise dramatically from a flat landscape of meandering rivers and paddy fields. Visitors can climb the hills, take river trips and visit the parks, lakes and caves.

Kunming is a newer, showcase city with some temples and very pretty lakeside parks. It is known as the 'City of Eternal Spring' because of the pleasant climate throughout the year. Outside of Kunming are the major attractions of *Xi Shan*, the holy mountain, and the petrified limestone forest called *Shilin*, 120km (75 miles) southeast of Kunming.

Hainan Island is a tropical island off the south coast of Guangdong Province with unspoilt beaches, palm groves, fresh seafood and coconuts. In 1989 Hainan Island became a separate province in its own right, and is now one of several Special Economic Zones, a part of China's 'open door' policy (see *History & Government* below).

The Potala Palace in Tibet

The Central Provinces

Chengdu is the capital of Sichuan Province and a great agricultural centre. The attractions include the Tang dynasty shrines, ancient parks and bamboo forests, Buddhist temples and an ancient Buddhist monastery. Chengdu is a base for visiting *Emei Shan*, a famous mountain to which Buddhist pilgrims flock every year, and the holy mountains of *Gongga* and *Siguniang*. There is also the spectacular giant *Stone Buddha*, in **Leshan,** which is an enormous sculpture, carved out of a cliff, on which 100 people can fit on its instep. In Sichuan Province, there is a vast nature reserve where giant pandas can be seen in their natural habitat.

Wuhan spans the Chang Jiang (Yangtse) River. As the capital of Hubei Province, it is an industrial centre. There are, however, Buddhist temples, lakes and parks, as well as the *Yellow Crane Tower* and the *Provincial Museum*, home to the famous Chime Bells manufactured over 2400 years ago.

Xi'an, the capital of Shaanxi Province, was once amongst the largest cities in the world and was also, from the 11th century BC onwards, the capital of 11 dynasties. It was the starting point of the Silk Road and is now, with the exception of Beijing, the most popular tourist attraction in China. The city is most famous for the *Tomb of Emperor Qin Shi Huangdi* and its terracotta figures, over 6000 lifesize warriors and horses buried along with the Qin Dynasty emperor responsible for the unification of China in 200BC. The *Bronze Chariot and Horse Figures* should not be missed: weighing over 1000 tons and made up of over 3000 parts, the figures are the earliest and largest of their kind ever unearthed. Although much of the city was destroyed during the Cultural Revolution, the city still has a great number of tombs, pavilions, museums and pagodas, such as the *Big Wild Goose Pagoda* with its spiral staircase and the *Small Wild Goose Pagoda*.

Close to the industrial city and communications centre of **Zhengzhou** are the cities of **Luoyang** and **Kaifeng**; both were once capitals of dynasties, and both are consequently of historical interest. Near Luoyang are the *Longmen (Dragon Gate) Caves*, over 1300 in all, and they contain over 2100 grottoes and niches, several pagodas, countless inscriptions and about 100,000 images and statues of the Buddha and a marvellous Buddhist shrine dating from the 5th century.

The Northwest Provinces

Lanzhou is an oasis on the ancient trade route known as the Silk Road. The capital of Gansu Province, the town is relatively unspoilt. There is a park and museum, and river trips can be made along the upper reaches of the *Yellow River* to the site of early Buddhist caves.

Dunhuang is a 2000-year-old town on the edge of the desert, once an important Silk Road caravan stop, famous for the *Magao Caves*, the oldest Buddhist shrines in China. These ancient hand-carved shrines are a national treasure and represent a thousand years of devotion to Buddha between the 2nd and 12th centuries. Some 500 exist today, and large areas of frescoes can still be seen. Also worth a visit when in Dunhuang are the *Yang Guan Pass* and the *Mingsha Hill*.

Turfan and **Urumqi** are situated in the far northwest, cities on the edge of the vast deserts of Xinjiang Province. These Muslim cities, lying on the Silk Road, are well known for the distinctive appearance, dress and lifestyle of the inhabitants. Urumqi is the capital of the Xinjiang Uygur Autonomous Region. The city is inhabited by 13 different nationalities, including Mongolian, Kazak, Russian, Tartar and Uzbek. The main inhabitants are the Muslim Uygurs who speak a Turkic language completely unrelated to Chinese. Northwest of Urumqi, a few hours bus ride away, is the beautiful *Lake of Heaven*, a clear turquoise-coloured lake set in the midst of the Tianshan range of mountains. It is possible to go horseriding with the local kazaks in this spectacular scenery. Turfan is the hottest place in China, being the second lowest point on earth next only to the Dead Sea. Nearby are the *Flaming Mountains*, which have the appearance of fire. Museums in both cities trace their fascinating histories.

Tibet (Xizang)

Tibet, known as 'The Roof of the World', has only been open to tourists since 1980. The area was closed to independent travellers in 1988, and it is now only open to tour groups on organised itineraries. About 1000 visas are allocated yearly to visit this remote area. The scenery is spectacular, and the Tibetan culture is one which has a unique fascination.

Lhasa is at an altitude of 3700m (12,000ft). The name means the 'City of Sun', due to the wonderful light and clear skies, which are special to such high mountainous terrain. Despite this, for six months of the year it is impossibly cold. The attraction of Tibet is its isolation from the rest of the world and the preservation of its own way of life and religious traditions, despite efforts, particularly during the Cultural Revolution, to bring Tibet into the fold of the rest of China. The main highlights for tourists lie in the *Potala*, or *Red Palace*, home to successive Dalai Lamas, which dominates Lhasa and the valley. This 17th-century edifice, built on a far more ancient site, is now a museum, the likes of which a visitor will be unlikely to see anywhere else: labyrinths of dungeons and torture chambers beneath the Palace, gigantic bejewelled Buddhas and hoards of treasure, 10,000 chapels with human skull and thigh-bone wall decorations and wonderful Buddhist frescoes, with influences from India and Nepal. Other buildings of interest include the *Drepung Monastery* and the *Jokhang Temple*, with its golden Buddhas.

Some travellers may experience health problems as a result of the altitude, so it is wise to consult your doctor prior to departure.

SOCIAL PROFILE

FOOD & DRINK: Cantonese (the style the majority of Westerners are most familiar with) is only one regional style of Chinese cooking. For a brief appreciation of the cuisine, it is possible to break it down into four major

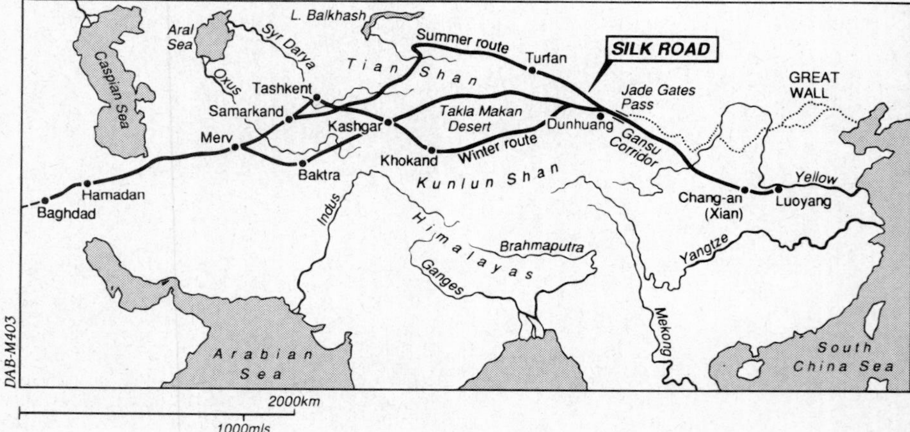

regional categories:
Northern Cuisine: Beijing, which has developed from the Shandong school, is famous for *Beijing Duck*, which is roasted in a special way, and eaten in a thin pancake with cucumber and a sweet plum sauce. Another speciality of the North of China is *Mongolian Hotpot*, which is a Chinese version of fondu. It is eaten in a communal style and consists of a central simmering soup in a special large round pot in which is dipped a variety of uncooked meats and vegetables, which are cooked on the spot. A cheap and delicious local dish is *shuijiao*, which is pasta-like dough wrapped round pork meat, chives and onions, similar in idea to Italian ravioli. These can be bought by the jin (pound) in street markets and small eating houses, and are a good filler if you are out all day and do not feel like a large restaurant dinner. However, it should be noted that in the interests of hygiene, it is best to take one's own chopsticks.
Southern Cuisine: Guangdong (Cantonese) food is famous for being the most exotic in China. The food markets in Guangzhou are a testimony to this, and the Western visitor is often shocked by the enormous variety of rare and exotic animals which are used in the cuisine, including snake, turtle and wildcat.
Eastern Cuisine: Shanghai and Zhejiang cooking is rich and sweet, often pickled. Noted for seafood, hot and sour soup, noodles and vegetables.
Western Cuisine: Sichuan and Hunan food is spicy, often sour and peppery, with specialities such as diced chicken stirred with soy sauce and peanuts, and spicey *doufu* (beancurd).
One of the best-known national drinks is *maotai*, a fiery spirit which is distilled rice wine. Local beers are of good quality, notably *Qingdao*, which is similar to German lager. There are now some decent wines, which are produced mainly for tourists and export.
NIGHTLIFE: Virtually all visitors follow itineraries drawn up in advance when sampling the nightlife of the larger cities, though this is in no way a drawback. Guides will be helpful and discreet, and generally their assistance will be more than welcome. Most tours include a selection of pre-arranged restaurant meals and visits to Chinese opera, ballet and theatre.
SHOPPING: All consumer prices are set by the Government, and there is no price bargaining in shops and department stores, although it is possible to bargain fiercely in small outdoor markets, of which there are many, for items such as jade, antique ceramics and also silk garments. All antiques over 100 years old are marked with a red wax seal by the authorities, and require an export customs certificate. Access to normal shops is available, offering inexpensive souvenirs, work clothes, posters and books; this will prove much easier if accompanied by an interpreter, although it is possible to point or get the help of a nearby English-speaker. Items are sometimes in short supply, but prices will not vary much from place to place. In large cities such as Beijing and Shanghai, there are big department stores with four or five floors, selling a wide range of products. The best shopping is in local factories, shops and hotels specialising in the sale of handicrafts. Arts and crafts department stores offer local handicrafts. Special purchases include jade jewellery, embroidery, calligraphy, paintings and carvings in wood, stone and bamboo. **Shopping hours:** 0900-1900 Monday to Sunday.
SPECIAL EVENTS: The following is a selection of the major festivals and other special events celebrated annually in China. For a complete list of events in all areas, contact the National Tourist Office.
Apr '93 *Weifang International Kite Festival; Third Lunar Month Fair*, Dali; *Qing Ming Festival*. **Jun** *Dragon Boat Festival*. **Sep/Oct** *Mid Autumn Festival*. **Jan 5-Feb 4 '94** *Harbin Ice and Snow Festival*, with magnificent displays of ice sculpture of bizarre subjects such as giant toothbrushes.

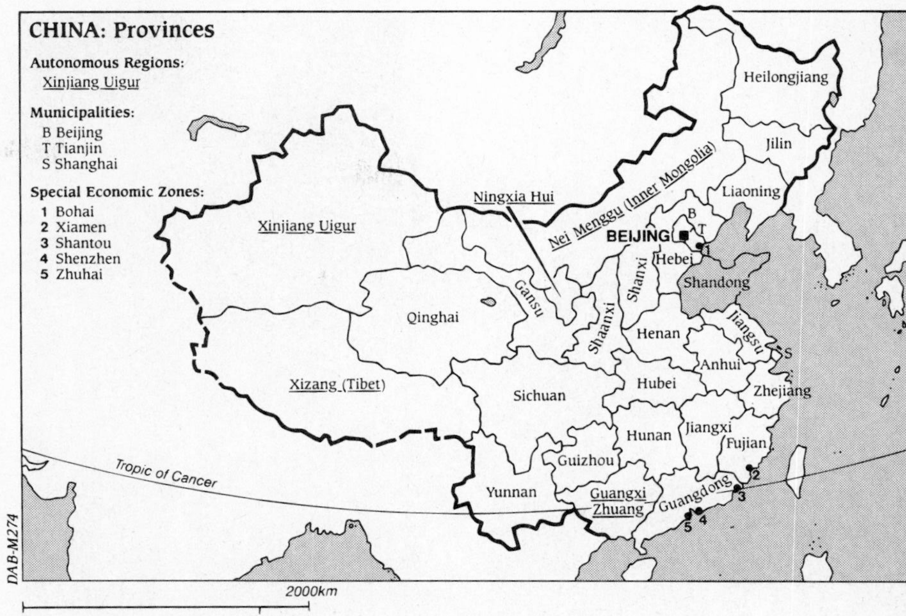

Lunan Stone Forest

Shanghai

Jan/Feb *Spring/New Year Festival*, from the 1st to the 3rd day of of the first month in the lunar calendar (the most important festival in the year for the Chinese, when families get together and share a sumptuous meal); *Lantern Festival*, on the 15th day of the first month in the lunar calendar.

SOCIAL CONVENTIONS: Many cultural differences may create misunderstandings between local people and visitors. Chinese do not usually volunteer information and the visitor is advised to ask questions. Hotels, train dining cars and restaurants often ask for criticisms and suggestions which are considered seriously. Do not be offended by being followed by crowds, this is merely an open interest in visitors who are rare in the remoter provinces. Chinese are generally reserved in manner, courtesy rather than familiarity being preferred. The full title of the country is 'The People's Republic of China', and this should be used in all formal communications. 'China' can be used informally, but there should never be any implication that another China exists. Although handshaking may be sufficient, a visitor will frequently be greeted by applause as a sign of welcome. The usual response is to applaud back. In China the family name is always mentioned first. It is customary to arrive a little early if invited out socially. Toasting at a meal is very common, as is the custom of taking a treat when visiting someone's home, such as fruit, confectionery or a souvenir from a home country. If it is the home of friends or relatives, money might be left for the children. If visiting a school or a factory, a gift from the visitor's home country, particularly something which would be unavailable in China (a text book if visiting a school for example), would be much appreciated. Stamps are also very popular as gifts, as stamp-collecting is a popular hobby in China. A good gift for an official guide is a Western reference book on China. Conservative casual wear is generally acceptable everywhere, but revealing clothes should be avoided since they may cause offence. **Photography:** Not allowed in airports. Places of historic and scenic interest may be photographed, but permission should be sought before photographing military installations, government buildings or other possibly sensitive subjects. **Tipping:** Officially not allowed and sometimes considered insulting.

BUSINESS PROFILE

ECONOMY: The vast Chinese economy has developed in fits and starts since the founding of the People's Republic in 1949. The 1980s proved to be one of the most successful, with an average growth of 9% – the world's highest. Despite some advanced manufacturing and technological enterprises – including a space programme – China's economy is essentially that of a developing country, with the majority of the population employed on the land. China is the world's largest producer of rice and a major producer of cereals and grain. Large mineral deposits, particularly coal and iron ore, provide the raw material for an extensive steel industry. Other important minerals include tungsten, molybdenum, tin, lead, bauxite (aluminium), phosphates and manganese. The 1980s saw a shift in emphasis from heavy to light industry, which now contribute roughly the same proportion to the GNP. Chemicals and high technology industries are receiving much attention at present. China is self-sufficient in oil and developing a petrochemical industry. Trade has been hampered somewhat in recent years by a shortage of foreign exchange, but China has benefited from the availability of soft loans from Western banks. The country's major imports are energy-related products, telecommunications, electronics and transport. Minerals and manufactured goods are the principal imports. The major trading partners are Japan, Hong Kong, the United States and Germany. In economic terms, China has benefited considerably from its 'open door' policy – introduced in the mid-1980s – which abandoned the tight restrictions on foreign trade and encouraged foreign companies both to sell products in China and to establish joint ventures with Chinese commercial organisations. A number of Special Economic Zones (SEZ), operating effectively market economies, have been established in China's southern provinces. Advanced technology enterprises were directed to these new Zones. The China Trade Unit, based in Hong Kong, is responsible for providing British exporters with advice on trade with Southern Chinese provinces, including the SEZs.

BUSINESS: Weights and measures are mainly metric, but several old Chinese weights and measures are still used. Liquids and eggs are often sold by weight. The Chinese foot is 1.0936 of an English foot (0.33m). Suits should be worn for business visits. Appointments should be made in advance and punctuality is expected. Visiting cards should be printed with a Chinese translation on the reverse. Business visitors are usually entertained in restaurants where it is customary to arrive a little early and the host will toast the visitor. It is customary to invite the host or hostess to a return dinner. Business travellers in particular should bear in mind that the United Kingdom government recognises the Government of the People's Republic of China as being the only Government of China; so do most other countries in the world and the United Nations. Best months for business visits are April to June and September to October. **Office hours:** 0800-1200 and 1400-1800 Monday to Saturday.

COMMERCIAL INFORMATION: The following organisations can offer advice:

All-China Federation of Industry and Commerce, 93 Beiheyan Dajie, Beijing 100006. Tel: (1) 554 231. Fax: (1) 512 2631. Telex: 22044; *or*

China Council for the Promotion of International Trade (CCPIT), PO Box 4509, 1 Fu Xing Men Wai Jie, Beijing 100860. Tel: (1) 801 3344. Fax: (1) 801 1370. Telex: 22315.

HISTORY & GOVERNMENT

HISTORY: China can claim to have the world's oldest continuous civilizations. Shang Dynasty 'oracle bone' inscriptions dating back to the 12th century BC are easily recognisable as early forms of the ideograms, some of which are still used today in Chinese calligraphy. During much of China's history, the collapse of a dynasty or the accession of a weak ruler would often result in the country's fragmentation into smaller kingdoms until re-united once again under a new powerful dynasty. In the period of disunion following the Han Dynasty, Buddhism reached China along the silk route from Central Asia. During the Tang Dynasty (AD618-907), the Chinese civilization spread to Korea, Japan and South-East Asia. In the 13th century, the Mongols under Genghis Khan overran Asia and in 1271 Genghis's grandson Kublai Khan founded the Yuan Dynasty. It was during this period that Marco Polo visited China. In 1368 Chinese rule was re-established by the Ming Dynasty, which built the Great Wall to prevent further incursions from the North. Despite this, the Manchus invaded China and founded their own Qing (Ch'ing) Dynasty in 1644.

Modern Chinese history begins in 1840 with the Opium Wars when Britain and other European powers imposed their will upon the ailing Qing Dynasty, forcing the Chinese to recognise the superior military technology of the West. Following the fall of the Qing Dynasty in 1911, Sun Yat-sen founded the Republic of China, but the country was plagued by civil war and warlordism. When the Japanese imperial army invaded China in 1937, during its campaign to establish a Japanese empire throughout eastern Asia, the Chinese armed forces were still too poorly organised to put up much resistance. Eight years of brutal occupation followed, which has continued to sour relations between the two countries to this day. Following the defeat of the Japanese in 1945, civil war ensued between the Nationalists under Chiang Kai-

Yangshuo scenery

shek and the Communists under Mao Zedong. In 1949, the defeated Nationalists fled to Taiwan and the People's Republic of China was founded on the mainland. In the early days of the People's Republic, China forged a close alliance with the Soviet Union, but policy disagreements and personal antipathy between Chinese and Soviet leaders led to a rupture in relations in 1960. Internally, the 1960s were dominated by the convulsions of the Cultural Revolution, an attempt by the party leadership to reinvigorate the party by launching campaigns to reassert their principles on the life of the country. In 1976, the two towering figures of post-revolutionary China, Premier Zhou Enlai and Communist Party Chairman Mao Zedong, both died within months of each other. Hua Guofeng first replaced Zhou as Premier, then went on to replace Mao as Party Chairman, and Zhao Ziyang became Premier. Hua left the Politburo after a series of further changes in the leadership in September 1982. The two prominent figures in the Government were now Zhao and the Chairman of the Communist Party Central Military Commission, Deng Xiaoping. The economic reforms introduced since the late 1970s, in which some market principles have been adopted, have proved broadly successful. However, China's reform programme differed from those which had been adopted by other socialist economies, particularly in Eastern Europe, in allowing a lesser degree of political 'liberalisation' in tandem with the economic measures. The tension between the political opposition, led by student activists demanding political reform, and the party came to a head in 1989 when a group of students and workers occupied Tiananmen Square in central Peking during the visit to the capital of the Soviet leader Mikhail Gorbachev. The square was cleared after Gorbachev's departure with great loss of life, after which the Government took decisive measures to reassert political control and defeat residual threats to socialism. Zhao Ziyang had been replaced as Premier earlier in the year by Li Peng who worked with Deng Xiaoping on the Government's resolution of the internal disorder. Li Peng is one of a new generation of leaders who are gradually assuming control from the octogenarians, who have long dominated Chinese politics. Gorbachev's visit to Peking was part of a gradual improvement in relations between China and the Soviet Union which had taken place since 1985. Contacts between China and some Western countries suffered some damage after the Tiananmen Square incident but have since recovered. Elsewhere, Sino-Vietnamese relations, poor since the military clashes between the two in 1979 and disagreements over Cambodia policy, improved sharply when the two countries were centrally involved in the political settlement reached between the Cambodian government and the main opposing factions in October 1991. The Chinese leadership has monitored, with increasing concern, the escalating ethnic and intercommunal tensions across the border in the CIS. Relations with Britain are dominated by Hong Kong, which China is due to recover in 1997, and have taken a sharp turn for the worse since the appointment of Hong Kong's last British Governor, ex-Cabinet Minister Chris Patten, in 1992.

GOVERNMENT: The National People's Congress (NPC) is the most powerful organ, and elects the President and Vice-President of the People's Republic. It also selects the Premier and Vice-Premier of the State Council (after nomination by the President of the Republic), also Council members and the heads of individual ministries. The State Council reports to the NPC or, when the Congress is not sitting, to its Standing Committee.

The Terracotta Army

CLIMATE

China's enormous size means that it has a great diversity of climates. The northeast experiences hot and dry summers and bitterly cold winters. The north and central region has almost continual rainfall, hot summers and cold winters. The southeast region has substantial rainfall, with semi-tropical summers and cool winters.
Required clothing: *North* – heavyweight clothing with boots and fur hats for the harsh northern winters. Lightweight clothing for summer. *South* – mediumweight clothing for winter and lightweight for summer, with rainwear all year round.

LHASA China (3685m)

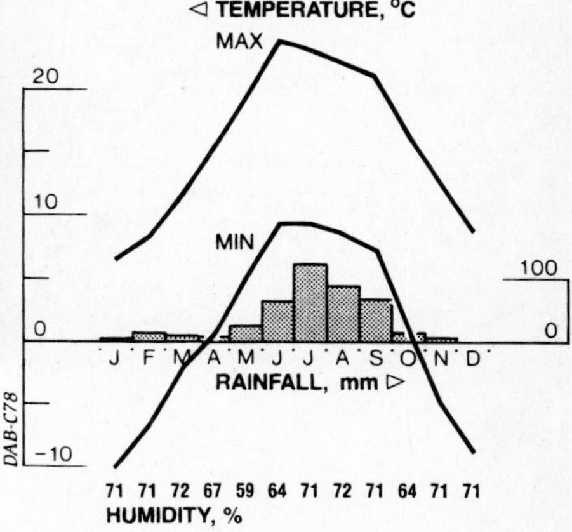

SHANGHAI China (5m)

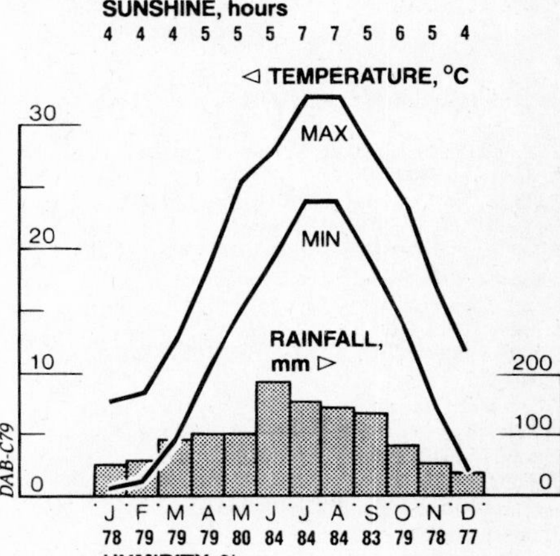

BEIJING China (52m)

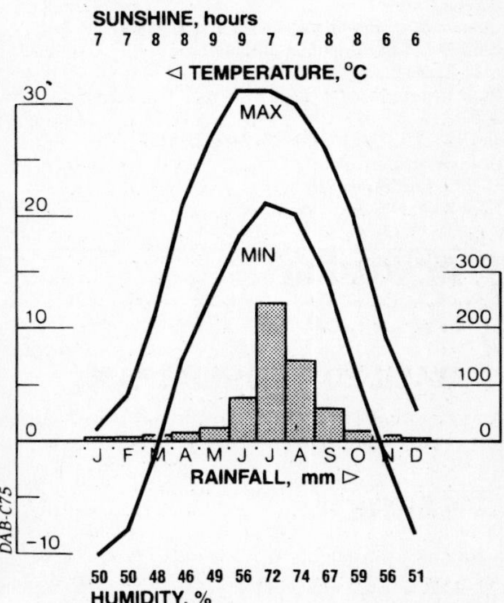

COLOMBIA

Location: Northwest South America.

Corporación Nacional de Turismo
Apdo Aèreo 8400
Calle 28, No 13A-15, Piso 16-18
Santa Fe de Bogotá DC, Colombia
Tel: (1) 283 9466. Fax: (1) 284 3818. Telex: 41350.
Embassy of the Republic of Colombia
3 Hans Crescent
London SW1X 0LR
Tel: (071) 589 9177. Fax: (071) 581 1829. Telex: 916468.
Colombian Consulate
140 Park Lane
London W1Y 3DF
Tel: (071) 495 4233. Fax: (071) 495 4441. Opening hours: 1000-1400 Monday to Friday.
British Embassy
Apdo Aéreo 4508
Torre Propaganda Sancho
Calle 98, No 9-03, Piso 4
Santa Fe de Bogotá DC, Colombia
Tel: (1) 218 5111. Fax: (1) 218 2460. Telex: 44503 BRIT CO.
Consulates in: Barranquilla, Cali and Medellín.
Embassy of the Republic of Colombia
2118 Leroy Place, NW
Washington, DC
20008
Tel: (202) 387 8338. Fax: (202) 232 8643.
Colombian Consulate
10 East 46th Street
New York, NY
10017
Tel: (212) 949 9898.
Colombian Government Tourist Office
140 East 57th Street
New York, NY
10022
Tel: (212) 688 0151. Fax: (212) 752 8932. Telex: 62513.
Embassy of the United States of America
PO Box 3831
Calle 38, No 8-61
Santa Fe de Bogotá, Colombia
Tel: (1) 285 1300/1688. Fax: (1) 288 5687. Telex: 44843.
Embassy of the Republic of Columbia
Suite 1130
360 Albert Street
Ottawa, Ontario
K1R 7X7
Tel: (613) 230 3760/1. Fax: (1) 230 4416. Telex: 053-3780.
Canadian Embassy
Apdo Aéreo 53531
Calle 76, No 11-52
Santa Fe de Bogotá DC, Colombia
Tel: (1) 217 5555. Telex: 44568.

AREA: 1,141,748 sq km (440,831 sq miles).
POPULATION: 32,978,170 (1990 estimate).
POPULATION DENSITY: 28.9 per sq km.
CAPITAL: Santa Fe de Bogotá. **Population:** 4,500,000 (1989).
GEOGRAPHY: Colombia is situated in South America, bounded to the north by the Caribbean, to the northwest by Panama, to the west by the Pacific Ocean, to the southwest by Ecuador and Peru, to the northeast by Venezuela and to the southeast by Brazil. The Andes Mountains extend into the country in three ranges running north to south, dipping finally into the lowlands of the Caribbean coast. Along the southern part of the Pacific coast run wide, marshy lowlands rising to a relatively low but rugged mountain chain. East of this range, the southwestern coastal lowlands extend in a low trough running from the port of Buenaventura on the Pacific coast to the Caribbean. East of this rise the slopes of the Western Cordillera which, with the Central Cordillera range, runs north to the Caribbean lowlands from Ecuador, separated by a valley, filled in the south by volcanic ash to a height of 2500m (8202ft). Further north lies the fertile Cauca Valley, which extends to Cartago where it becomes a deep gorge running between the Cordilleras to the Caribbean lowlands. The Eastern Cordillera, the longest range, rises north of the Ecuadorean border and runs north then northeast towards Venezuela. Flat grassy prairies in the east along with the jungles and towering rainforests of the Amazon make up over half the country's area. There are also two small islands, San Andrés and Providencia, located 480km (298 miles) north of the Colombian coast, that have belonged to Colombia since 1822.
LANGUAGE: Spanish is the official language. Local Indian dialects and some English are also spoken.
RELIGION: 95% Roman Catholic; small Protestant and Jewish minorities.
TIME: GMT - 5.
ELECTRICITY: Mostly 110/120 volts (some 150-volt supplies still exist) AC, 60Hz. American 2-pin plugs are common.
COMMUNICATIONS: Telephone: IDD service to most areas; calls to smaller centres must be made through international operator. Country code: 57. **Fax:** Only the largest hotels have fax services. **Telex/telegram:** Facilities are available at the Tequendama and Hilton hotels in Bogotá or through national ENDT telecommunications offices. Telex facilities also exist at most of the major hotels. **Post:** Post offices are marked *Correos*. Opening hours are 0900-1700 Monday to Friday and 0800-1200 Saturday. There are two types of service: urban post (green letter boxes) and inter-urban and international (yellow boxes). Letters and packets sent by airmail normally take between five and seven days to reach their destination. **Press:** Newspapers are in Spanish. Dailies include *El Espacio*, *El Espectador*, *El Siglo* and *El Tiempo*.
BBC World Service and Voice of America frequencies: From time to time these change. See the section *How to Use this Book* for more information.

BBC:				
MHz	17.84	15.22	9.590	9.915
Voice of America:				
MHz	15.21	11.58	9.775	5.995

PASSPORT/VISA

Regulations and requirements may be subject to change at short notice, and you are advised to contact the appropriate diplomatic or consular authority before finalising travel arrangements. Details of these may be found at the head of this country's entry. Any numbers in the chart refer to the footnotes below.

	Passport Required?	Visa Required?	Return Ticket Required?
Full British	Yes	No	Yes
BVP	Not valid	-	-
Australian	Yes	Yes	Yes
Canadian	Yes	No/2	Yes
USA	Yes	No/2	Yes
Other EC	Yes	1	Yes
Japanese	Yes	No/2	Yes

Security of documents: For about US$20 it is possible to have passports and other important documents photocopied and witnessed by the security police; they can then be kept secure as the photocopy will generally be accepted.
PASSPORTS: Valid passport required by all.
British Visitors Passport: Not accepted.
VISAS: Required by all except:
(a) **[1]** nationals of EC countries (national of Greece, Ireland and Portugal *do* need visas) for stays of up to 90 days;
(b) **[2]** nationals of Canada, Japan and USA for stays of up to 90 days, if travelling as tourists;
(c) nationals of Argentina, Austria, Barbados, Bolivia, Brazil, Chile, Costa Rica, Ecuador, El Salvador, Finland, Guatemala, Israel, South Korea, Liechtenstein, Mexico, Norway, Peru, St Vincent & the Grenadines, Sweden, Switzerland, Trinidad & Tobago, Uruguay and Venezuela for stays of up to 90 days, if travelling as tourists;
(d) nationals of the following countries who hold either a tourist card (valid for 60 days), or a transit card (valid for 15 days, with a possible extension): Antigua & Barbuda, Bahamas, Dominica, Grenada, Guyana, Haiti, Honduras, Jamaica, Panama, Paraguay, St Kitts & Nevis and Suriname.
Visas are required by nationals of all countries for stays of more than 90 days.
Types of visa: Tourist, Business, Working and Student.
Exit visas: All travellers must obtain an exit stamp from the DAS (Security Police) before leaving. This is best obtained at the airport or in main cities.
Application to: Consulate (or Consular Section at Embassy). For addresses, see top of entry.
Application requirements: (a) Recent photo. (b) Completed application form (c) Proof of onward journey. (d) Valid passport.
Working days required: 2 days to 3 months, depending on visa.

MONEY

Currency: Peso (Col$) = 100 centavos. Notes are in denominations of 5000, 2000, 1000, 500, 200, 100, 50, 20, 10, 5, 2 and 1 Col$. Coins are in denominations of 50, 25, 20 and 10 centavos.
Currency exchange: The exchange rate tends to be lower on the Caribbean coast than in Bogotá, Medellín

COLOMBIA | **HEALTH REGULATIONS** | **VISA REGULATIONS** | Code-Link

GALILEO/WORLDSPAN

TI-DFT/BOG/HE

TI-DFT/BOG/VI

SABRE

TIDFT/BOG/HE

TIDFT/BOG/VI

To access this information on your CRS, swipe the barcode with a light pen or type in the text under the barcode. For more information, see the introduction *How to Use This Book*.

and Cali. The US Dollar is the easiest currency to exchange at hotels, banks, shops and travel agencies; but establishments all charge an exchange fee.
Credit cards: All major cards are accepted, but check with your credit card company for details of merchant acceptability and other services which may be available.
Travellers cheques: These are not always easy to change in the smaller towns, except at branches of the Banco de la República. See *Security of documents* in the *Passport/Visa* section above; a photocopied travellers cheque is not of course negotiable but the photocopy will help if they are lost or stolen.
Exchange rate indicators: The following figures are included as a guide to the movements of the Colombian Peso against Sterling and the US Dollar:

Date:	Oct '89	Oct '90	Oct '91	Oct '92
£1.00=	645.10	1053.18	1081.09	936.19
$1.00=	408.54	539.12	622.93	589.91

Currency restrictions: The import of local currency is unlimited; the export is restricted to Col$500 (depends on exchange rate). Free import and export of foreign currency. When leaving Colombia, Col$60 may be reconverted.
Banking hours: 0900-1500 Monday to Friday.

DUTY FREE

The following goods may be taken into Colombia without incurring customs duty:
200 cigarettes and 50 cigars and 500g of tobacco;
6 bottles of wine or spirits;
A reasonable quantity of perfume.
Note: Emeralds and articles in gold or platinum need a receipt from the place of purchase which must be presented to customs on departure.

PUBLIC HOLIDAYS

Public holidays observed in Colombia are as follows:
Mar 19 '93 St Joseph's Day. **Apr 8** Maundy Thursday. **Apr 9** Good Friday. **May 1** Labour Day. **May 20** Ascension Day. **Jun 9** Thanksgiving. **Jun 10** Corpus Christi. **Jun 29** St Peter and Paul. **Jul 20** Independence. **Aug 7** Battle of Boyacá. **Aug 15** Assumption. **Oct 12** Discovery of America. **Nov 1** All Saints' Day. **Nov 11** Independence of Cartagena. **Dec 8** Feast of the Immaculate Conception. **Dec 25** Christmas Day. **Jan 1 '94** New Year's Day. **Jan 6** Epiphany. **Mar 19** St Joseph's Day.

HEALTH

Regulations and requirements may be subject to change at short notice, and you are advised to contact your doctor well in advance of your intended date of departure. Any numbers in the chart refer to the footnotes below.

	Special Precautions?	Certificate Required?
Yellow Fever	1	No
Cholera	Yes	2
Typhoid & Polio	Yes	-
Malaria	3	-
Food & Drink	4	-

[1]: It is recommended that travellers arriving from an affected area or who may visit the following areas considered to be endemic for yellow fever should be vaccinated: middle valley of the Magdalena River, eastern foothills of the frontier with Ecuador to that with Venezuela, Uraba, the southeastern part of the Sierra Nevada de Santa Marta, the forest along the river Guaviare and anywhere on the Pacific coast or in the Llanos Orientales or Amazones regions.
[2]: Following WHO guidelines issued in 1973, a cholera vaccination certificate is not a condition of entry to Colombia. However, cholera is a serious risk in this country and precautions are essential. Up-to-date advice should be sought before deciding whether these precautions should include vaccination as medical opinion is divided over its effectiveness. See the *Health* section at the back of the book.
[3]: Malaria risk exists throughout the year in rural areas below 800m of the Pacific coast, Uraba (Antioquia and Chocó Dep.), Bajo Cauca-Nechi (Córdoba and Antioquia Dep.), Magdalena Medio, Caquetá (Caquetá Intendencia), Sarare (Arauca Intendencia), Catatumbo (Norte de Santander Dep.), Putumayo (Putumayo Intendencia), Ariari (Meta Dep.), Alto Vaupés (Vaupés Comisaria), Amazonas and Guianía (Comisarias). The malignant *falciparum* form of the disease is reported to be 'highly resistant' to chloroquine and 'resistant' to sulfadoxine/pyrimethane.
[4]: All water should be regarded as being potentially contaminated. Water used for drinking, brushing teeth or making ice should have first been boiled or otherwise sterilised. Milk is unpasteurised and should be boiled. Powdered or tinned milk is available and is advised, but make sure that it is reconstituted with pure water. Avoid dairy products which are likely to have been made from unboiled milk. Only eat well-cooked meat and fish, preferably served hot. Pork, salad and mayonnaise may carry increased risk. Vegetables should be cooked and fruit peeled.
Rabies is present. For those at high risk, vaccination before arrival should be considered. If you are bitten abroad seek medical advice without delay. For more information consult the *Health* section at the back of the book.
Hepatitis is a risk. For precautions see the section on *Health* at the back of this book.
Health care: Visitors to Bogotá should take a couple of days to acclimatise themselves to the altitude, which may induce drowsiness. Avoid excessive intake of alcohol. Health facilities in the main cities are good. Medical insurance is essential.

TRAVEL - International

AIR: Colombia's national airline is *Avianca (AV)*.
Approximate flight times: From Bogotá to *London* is 13 hours 45 minutes, to *Los Angeles* is 10 hours 30 minutes, to *New York* is 6 hours 30 minutes, to *Singapore* is 35 hours 15 minutes and to *Sydney* is 29 hours.
International airports: *Bogotá* (El Dorado) *(BOG)* is situated 12km (7.5 miles) from the city. Airport facilities include bank (0700-2200), duty-free shop, bar, restaurant (0700-2200), tourist information and car hire (*Avis, Hertz* and *Dollar*). Bus ('Consul') to city (travel time – 30 minutes) departs every 20 minutes from 0600-1900. Taxis are available.
Barranquilla (Ernesto Cortissoz) *(BAQ)* is 10km (6 miles) from the city. Car rental is available.
Cali (Palmaseca) *(CLO)* is 19km (10 miles) from the city.
Cartegena (Crespo) *(CTG)* is 2km (1 mile) from the city.
Departure tax: US$15 (or the equivalent in Pesos) is charged for all international departures (children under 5 years and passengers for immediate transit are exempt). The tax is doubled to US$30 for travellers who have remained in the country for more than two months. There is also an **exit tax** of US$11 from which travellers whose passports have been endorsed on arrival are exempted.
Note: All air tickets purchased in Colombia for destinations outside the country are liable to a total tax of 15% on one-way tickets and 7.5% on return tickets.
SEA: Shipping companies serve Colombian ports with both passenger and combination passenger/freight vessels. The following ports and lines serve the major routes: US Gulf ports – *Delta Line* cruises; from Europe – *French Line, Italian Line, Pacific Steam Navigation, Royal Netherlands SS Co.* and *Linea 'C'*. Cartegena is an important port of call for the following cruise lines: *Sun Line, Princess Cruises, Delta, Norwegian American, Holland America, Westours, Sitmar* and *Costa*.
RAIL: There are no international rail connections.
ROAD: The Pan Americana Highway, when completed, should make it possible to drive into Colombia from Panama. Vehicles can also be freighted from Panama to one of Colombia's Caribbean or Pacific ports. There are also road links with Ecuador and Venezuela. **Coach/bus:** *TEPSA* buses connect with Venezuela. Coaches are comfortable and services good. There are second-class buses from Maracaibo to Santa Marta and Cartagena, but this method of travelling can be uncomfortable.

TRAVEL - Internal

AIR: Services are offered by *Avianca (SAM)* and 15 smaller companies. There is an excellent internal air network connecting major cities, including those in the Caribbean coastal area. There are also local helicopter flights. There are flights between the mainland and the islands of San Andrés and Providencia operating from most major Colombian cities. San Andrés is a regular stop for *Avianca, SAM, Lacsa* and *Sahsa* airlines.
SEA: There is a ferry service between the mainland and the islands of San Andrés and Providencia, leaving from the Mulle de Pegasos. The journey is long (72 hours), but cheap. Information about other sailings to San Andrés can be obtained from the Maritima San Andrés office. Once on the islands, there are boat trips available to Johnny Cay and the Aquarium.
RIVER: The Magdalena River is the main artery of Colombia some cargo boats take passengers, though this is a slow way to travel. It is possible to hire boats for particular trips. Paddle steamers no longer run services up and down the river and hiring can be expensive. From Leticia, on the Peruvian border, a number of operators run sightseeing tours and jungle expeditions up the Amazon. It is necessary to make enquiries *in situ*, and wise to shop around before booking on any one trip (see also *Resorts & Excursions*).
RAIL: Although trains still carry freight, inter-city passenger services are virtually non-existant. The main route is between Bogotá and Santa Marta on the Caribbean coast, east of Barranquilla. Because of the distances, it is easier to take a plane if speed is important.
ROAD: A good highway links Santa Marta in the east with Cartagena, and passes Barranquilla en route. The brand-new Trans-Caribbean Highway has now placed Barranquilla only five hours away from Venezuela. Northeast of Santa Marta, in the Guajira Peninsula, roads are usually passable except during rainy periods. There is highway transportation between the coastal cities and the capital and other cities of the interior, but much of the highway is rutted. **Bus:** The large distances make air travel advisable. However, the best bus lines are said to be the *Flota Magdalena, Expresso Boliviano* and, especially, the *Expresso Palmita*. About 42 companies with modern buses and minibuses provide transportation between coastal towns and cities. **Car hire:** *Avis, Hertz, Budget* and *National* have car rental offices, but driving in cities is *not recommended*. Traffic drives on the right.
Documentation: An International Driving Permit is recommended, although it is not legally required.
URBAN: Bogotá has extensive trolleybus, bus and minibus services, and a funicular railway; flat fares are charged. There are also shared taxis (*buseta)* which are not expensive and stop on demand. Drivers are authorised to add a supplement for out-of-town trips and to airports. At hotels, the green and cream coloured taxis are available for tourists. They are more expensive than the others. Passengers should insist that meters are used. For those without a meter the fare should be agreed before starting a journey.
JOURNEY TIMES: The following chart gives approximate journey times from Bogotá (in hours and minutes) to other major towns/cities in Colombia.

	Air
Cartagena	1.15
Barranquilla	1.15
Medellín	1.15
Manizales	1.00
Cali	1.00
Bucaramanga	0.45
Cúcuta	1.00
Pereira	1.00
Leticia	2.00

ACCOMMODATION

HOTELS: It is advisable to choose hotels recommended by the Colombian National Tourist Corporation (see address above). The corporation has offices in most towns, on Floor 2 of *El Dorado Airport* and at other main airports. Two tariffs are levied: 'European tariff' from May to November, and 'American tariff' from December to April, which is much higher. It is advisable to make reservations well in advance. There are several hotels and *residencias* on the island of San Andrés, and one on Providencia.
Prices rise on average 10% a year; visitors are advised to check current prices when making reservations. **Grading:** There is a star grading system similar to that operating in Europe.
Note: A 5% tax is added to all hotel bills throughout the country.
CAMPING/CARAVANNING: Camping is possible in Colombia, although there are very few official camping areas. Two of the better campsites in the country are Camping del Sol and Camping de Covenas.

RESORTS & EXCURSIONS

The four major cities in Colombia are Bogotá, Medellín, Cali and Barranquilla.
Bogotá: The capital and largest city, which is situated almost in the centre of the country at an altitude of 2600m (8600ft). The city reflects a blend of Colombian tradition and Spanish colonial influences. Many historical landmarks have been preserved, such as the *Capitol Municipal Palace* and the cathedral on the main square, the *Plaza Bolivar*. Bogotá also contains the *Gold Museum*, with its unique collection of over 100,000 pre-Colombian art-works.
Medellín: Colombia's second city, with over 2 million inhabitants, lies 3300m (5500ft) above sea level in a narrow valley of the central mountain range. It is primarily industrial, and is the centre of the coffee and textile trades. The region has recently acquired a reputation for violence due to the war between the Government and the drug barons.
Cali: The centre of the principal sugar-producing region of the country, where modern technology blends with colonial tradition. Deposits of coal and precious metals are found in this area.
Barranquilla: A busy port and Colombia's fourth city, Barranquilla is located towards the mouth of the Magdalena River. It is one of the nation's main commercial centres. There is a colourful market in the so-called *Zona Negra* on a side channel of the Magdalena.

Other places of interest: Colombia has much to offer those interested in archaeology. *San Augustin Archaeological Park* contains a great number of relics and massive stone statues. The traditional city of **Popayan** is the birthplace of many of Colombia's most illustrious statesmen. As well as containing many fine colonial houses and churches, it is also noted for its Holy Week procession.
Santa Marta was one of the first major cities founded by the Spanish in South America, and its modern hotels and sparkling white beaches now make it just as popular among tourists. **Cartegena**, an ancient walled fortress city on the north coast, is also worth a visit.
Easily reached from Cartegena, by plane or boat, are the islands of **San Andrés** and **Providencia**, nearly 500km (300 miles) north of the Colombian coast. San Andrés was once the headquarters of the English pirate Captain Henry Morgan, the scourge of the Caribbean. The islands are duty free, and consequently often crowded, but there are still several less spoilt parts. Popular excursions include visits by boat to *Johnny Cay* and the *Aquarium*.
Tierradentro, in the southwest of the country, has beautiful man-made burial caves painted with pre-Colombian geometric patterns. In the same region, **Silva** is a beautiful Indian town.
The country also contains much unspoilt countryside; the **Guajura Peninsula** is home to over 100,000 nomadic Indians.

SOCIAL PROFILE

FOOD & DRINK: Restaurants offer international cuisine and table service is the norm. Local dishes are varied and tasty, with a touch of Spanish influence. Recommended dishes are *ajiaco* (chicken stew with potatoes, served with cream, corn on the cob and capers); *arepas* (corn pancakes made without salt, eaten in place of bread); *bandeja* (paisa – meat dish accompanied by cassava), rice, fried plantain (variety of bananas) and red beans, served in the area of Medellín. Seafood, known as *mariscos*, is plentiful on the Caribbean coast. Lobsters in particular are renowned for their flavour. **Drink:** It is safest to drink bottled water. Colombians rarely drink alcohol with meals. *Gaseosa* is the name given to non-alcoholic, carbonated drinks. For a small black coffee, you should ask for a *tinto*, but this term is also used to describe red wine or *vino tinto*. Colombian wines are of poor quality. Chilean and Argentinian wines are available in restaurants at reasonable prices. Colombia produces many different types of rum *(ron)*. *Cañalazo*, a rum-based cocktail taken hot or cold, can be recommended. There are no licensing hours.
NIGHTLIFE: Bogotá's *Colon Theatre* presents ballet, opera, drama and music, with international and local groups. There are many nightclubs and discotheques in the major towns of Colombia.
SHOPPING: Special purchases include local handicrafts, cotton, wool and leather goods, woollen blankets, *ruanas*, and travelling bags. Hotel shops carry excellent gold reproductions of ancient Colombian jewellery. Colombia produces first-grade stones and emeralds are amongst the most perfect in the world. **Shopping hours:** 0900-1230 and 1430-1830 Monday to Saturday.
SPORT: Football is Colombia's main sport, with major league games played throughout the year. **Tennis** is popular; most hotels have facilities. **Mountain climbing** begins 48km (30 miles) east of Santa Marta, with peaks of up to nearly 6000m (19,000ft). A major **cycle** race, the Tour of Colombia, takes place every March and April. **Boxing** and **bullfighting** (the latter at Bogotá, Cali, Medellín, Manizales and Cartagena) are popular sports. **Golf** clubs allow visitors to use their facilities. Good **skiing** can be found on the slopes of Nevado del Ruiz (5400m/17,700ft), 48km (30 miles) from Manizales. **Fishing** is excellent all year round; a licence is required. **Watersports: Water-skiing, boating, sailing** and **skindiving:** Check with authorities before diving, as sharks and barracudas have caused fatalities.
SPECIAL EVENTS: The following is a selection of the major festivals and other special events celebrated in Colombia during 1993. For a complete list contact the Colombian Consulate.
Apr '93 *Festival of the Vallenato Legend*. **Jun** *The Cumbia Festival*, El Banco; *International Film Festival*, Cartagena; *The Porro Festival*, San Pelayo. **Aug** *The Sea Festival*, Santa Marta; *Parade of the Flower Vendors*, Medellín; *The Guabina and Tiple Festival*, Vélez. **Sep** *The National Band Contest*, Paipa. **Nov** *The Plains National Folk and Tourist Festival*, San Martín. **Dec** *The Sugar Cane Fair*, Cali. **Jan '94** *The Manizales Fair*, *Festival of Whites and Blacks*, Pasto. **Feb** *The Barranquilla Carnival*. **Mar** *The International Caribbean Music Festival*, Cartagena; *Easter Week Celebrations*, Mompós, Popayán or Pamplona.
In Bogotá, the open-air *Media Torta* presents music, plays and folk dances on Sunday afternoons and holidays. An amateur theatre group gives frequent performances in English.
SOCIAL CONVENTIONS: Normal courtesies should be observed. It is customary to offer guests black Colombian coffee, well sugared, called *tinto*. Spanish style and culture can still be seen in parts of the country, although in Bogotá, North American attitudes and clothes are becoming prevalent. Casual wear can be worn in most places; formal attire will be necessary for exclusive dining rooms and social functions. Smoking is allowed except where indicated. The visitor is advised that many of the main cities in Colombia are notorious for street crime, particularly at night. Drug-related crimes are a serious problem throughout the country and the visitor should be wary of the unsolicited attention of strangers. See *Security of documents* in the *Passport/Visa* section above. **Tipping:** Taxi drivers do not expect tips. Porters at airports and hotels are usually given a few pesos per item. Many restaurants, bars and cafés add 10% service charge to bill or suggest a 10% tip. Maids and clerks in hotels are rarely tipped. Bogotá's shoeshine boys live on their tips and expect about 50 pesos.

BUSINESS PROFILE

ECONOMY: Colombia is one of South America's stronger economies. Agriculture is extensive and varied, and accounts for 75% of export earnings. Coffee has traditionally been the principal crop (Colombia is the world's second largest producer), but as production has declined and the price fallen, other products have replaced it, including sugar, bananas, cut flowers and cotton. The cattle business may be set for significant expansion in the next few years. The country is self-sufficient in consumer goods and exports of manufactured goods – textiles, leather goods, metal products, chemicals, pharmaceuticals and cement – have been steadily increasing. Colombia has sizeable oil reserves which are now starting to come on stream: British Petroleum has a 40% in a huge recently discovered field at Cusiana in the Andean foothills. Coal deposits are the largest in Latin America but, again, development has also been slow due to financial problems of the state coal company. The country has shown healthy GDP growth throughout the 1980s, averaging 3.5% and has matched the trend so far in the 90s. Colombia is a member of the Andean Pact and of the Asociación Latinoamericano de Integración (ALADI) which is seeking to regularise tariffs throughout South America. The organisation is based in Montevideo, Uruguay. The United States are Colombia's largest trading partner. Germany, Japan and Venezuela follow.
BUSINESS: Business people are expected to dress smartly. English is widely understood in many business circles; the Colombian Ministry of Foreign Affairs has an official translation service, and there are a number of commercial interpreter services. A command of Spanish is always appreciated. Business visitors will sometimes be invited out to dinner, which may be preceded by a long cocktail party, with a meal starting around 2300. The best months for business visits are March to November. The business community generally takes holidays from September to February, the driest months. It is advisable to avoid Barranquilla in June and July. **Office hours:** 0800-1200 and 1400-1730 Monday to Friday.
COMMERCIAL INFORMATION: The following organisations can offer advice:
Confederación Columbiana de Cámaras de Comercio (CONFEMECARAS) (National Chamber of Commerce), Apdo Aéreo 29750, Carrera 13, No 27-47, Of. 502, Santa Fe de Bogotá DC. Tel: (1) 288 1200. Fax: (1) 288 4228. Telex: 44416; *or*
Instituto Colombiana de Comercio Exterior (INCOMEX) (Institute of Foreign Trade), Apdo Aéreo 240193, Calle 28, No 13A-15, Sante Fe de Bogotá DC. Tel: (1) 283 3284. Telex: 44860.
CONFERENCES/CONVENTIONS: For advice and assistance with conferences and conventions in Colombia contact the Colombia Convention Center and Exhibit Corporation, Calle 26A, No 13A-10, Santa Fe de Bogotá. Tel: (1) 281 1099. Telex: 45311-45312.

HISTORY & GOVERNMENT

HISTORY: Prior to the arrival of the Spanish in the 16th century, the territory was inhabited by the highly developed and sophisticated Chibca Indians. Independence was achieved in 1819 and Great Colombia was established, comprising New Granada (as Colombia was then known), Panama, Venezuela and Ecuador. In 1831 New Granada was declared a separate state. Tensions between the two main parties, the Conservatives and the Liberals, and compounded by the authoritarian Church, flared into civil war in 1837-42. In 1851 slavery was abolished. The 1855 Revolution led to the forming of the Republic of Colombia. Several civil wars followed between Conservatives and Liberals in the course of the next century. Colombia was governed by a coalition of Liberal and Conservative parties from 1974 until 1986, when the Liberal Party took power in its own right under the leadership of Dr Virgilio Barco Vargas. These former opponents joined forces to prevent a bid for power by ANAPO (Alianza Nacional Popular) led by the former dictator, General Rojas. At a desperately close election in April 1970, which needed four recounts, Rojas was narrowly defeated by Dr Misael Pastrana Borrero, the candidate for the National Front alliance of Liberals and Conservatives. The 1970 election was a turning point in Colombia's recent history. Disaffected members of ANAPO, who suspected electoral fraud, formed a guerrilla movement known as M-19 (Movimento 19 de Abril, after the date of the election) which waged a major campaign against the Government until the mid-1980s. M-19 was joined in its insurrection by the pro-Soviet Fuerzas Armadas Revolucionarias de Colombia (FARC). In the election of May 1992, Dr Belisario Betancur Cuartas, the conservative candidate became presdident. He introduced some radical reforms, including an amnesty for guerrillas, the release of several hundred prisoners and the reconvening of the Peace Commission to form a truce with the guerrillas. Meanwhile, another potent threat to the Government's authority emerged in the form of organised drug traffickers, who converted their rapidly acquired wealth into substantial political influence, backed up with the very real threat of violence. The recent history has been dominated by this three-cornered struggle between the Government, traffickers and guerrillas. In 1986, Betancur was replaced by the Liberal Virgilio Barco Vargas. Under pressure from the United States, which had launched its much-trumpeted 'war on drugs', the Barco government began a protracted struggle against the Medellín Cartel. The country had to wait until Barco's Liberal Party successor, César Gaviria, took office in the summer of 1990 before any significant results would be seen. The Colombian security forces have now all but dismantled the Medellín Cartel, most of whose principal figures (other than the recent escapee Pablo Escobar) are now dead or in custody. M-19 meanwhile, have made their peace with the Government but FARC is still operating, alongside several smaller groups in a guerrilla coalition known as the Coordinadora Guerrillera Simón Bolívar. And the Medellín Cartel's place in the popular demonology of cocaine has been taken by the Cali Cartel, based in Colombia's second city, who are by repute much more sophisticated. In the murderous *pas de deux* between the Government and the cartels, the latter implicitly agreed not to resort to violence in exchange for government concessions on the fate that the cartel bosses most fear: extradition to the United States. This has now been outlawed in a series of constitutional amendments, introduced soon after Gaviria took office, also allowing for improved judicial procedures and reform of the traditional political patronage. Gaviria's government picked up where Barco's left off on the economic front: Colombia continued to show healthy growth and is now, its reputation notwithstanding, one of the more attractive parts of Latin America for foreign investment. Elections are scheduled for 1994. Former M-19 leader Navarro Wolff's popularity as head of the Democratic Alliance (dubbed AD-M-19) has made him a front-runner.
GOVERNMENT: The President is Head of State, elected by universal adult suffrage for a period of four years. The President appoints and is assisted by a Cabinet. The legislature is the bicameral Congress consisting of a Senate and House of Representatives. All members are elected by universal adult suffrage.

CLIMATE

The climate is very warm and tropical on coast and in the north, with a rainy season from May to November. This varies according to altitude. It is cooler in the upland areas and cold in the mountains. Bogotá is always spring-like, with cool days and crisp nights.
Required Clothing: Lightweight cottons and linens with waterproofing during rainy season in coastal and northern areas. Medium to heavyweights in upland and mountainous areas.

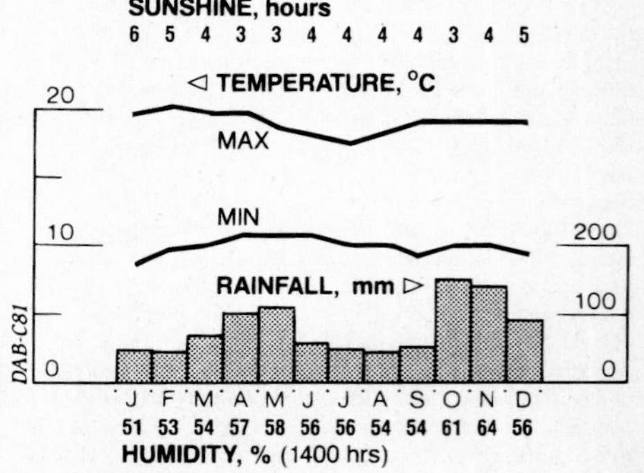

CIS

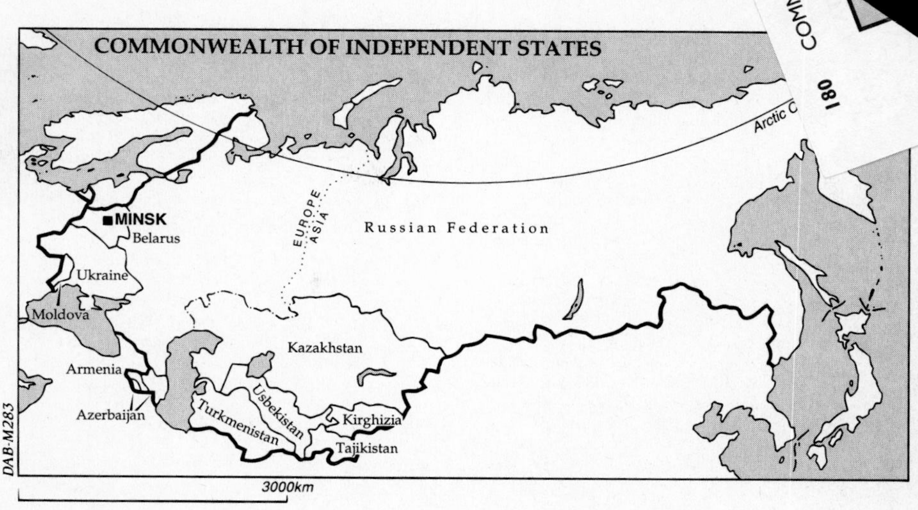

COMMONWEALTH OF INDEPENDENT STATES

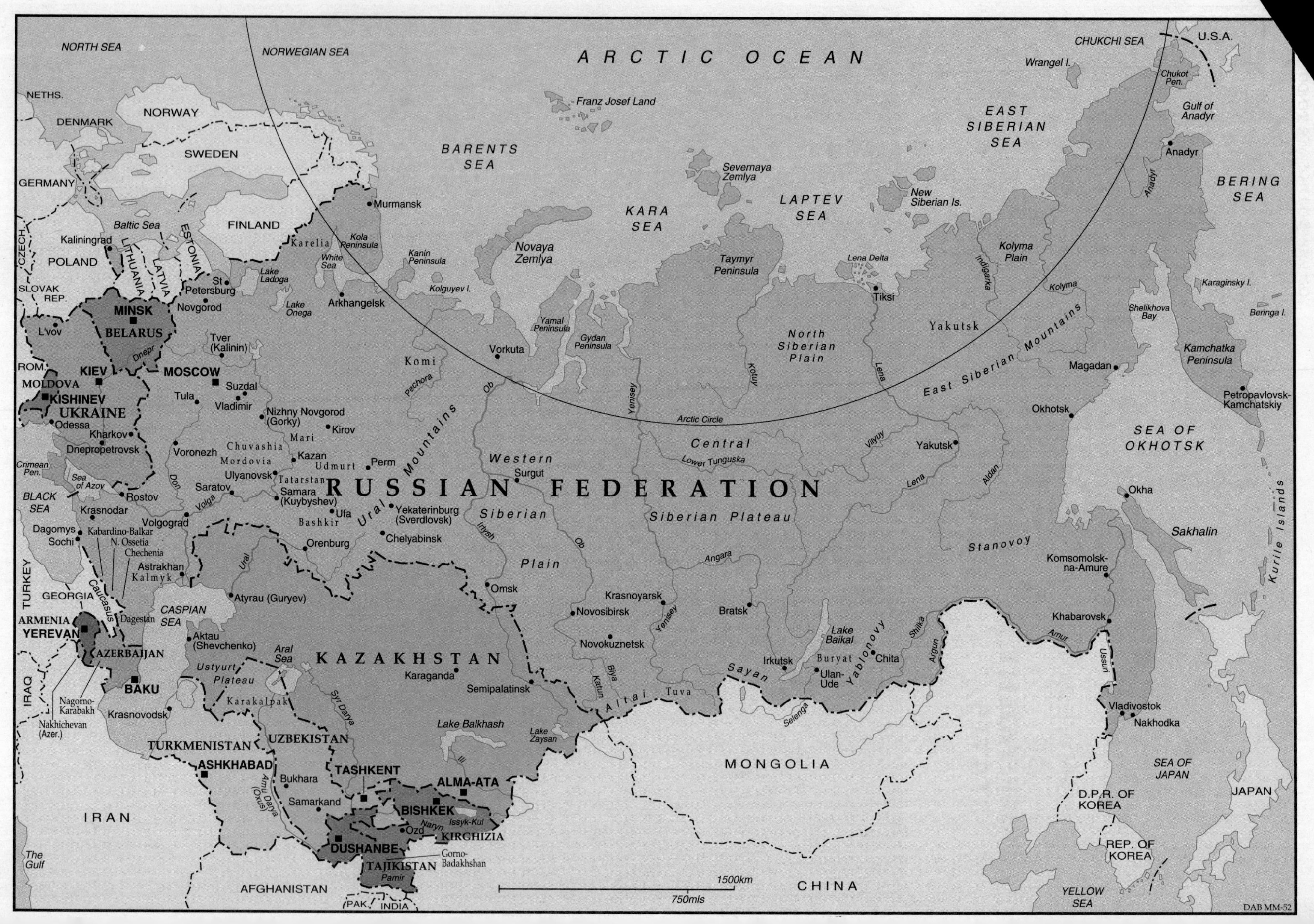

ARCTIC OCEAN
RUSSIAN FEDERATION
KAZAKHSTAN
NORTH SEA
NORWEGIAN SEA
BARENTS SEA
KARA SEA
LAPTEV SEA
EAST SIBERIAN SEA
CHUKCHI SEA
BERING SEA
SEA OF OKHOTSK
SEA OF JAPAN
YELLOW SEA
Baltic Sea
BLACK SEA
Sea of Azov
CASPIAN SEA
Aral Sea
White Sea
The Gulf
Franz Josef Land
Novaya Zemlya
Severnaya Zemlya
New Siberian Is.
Wrangel I.
Kolguyev I.
Karaginsky I.
Beringa I.
Kurile Islands
Sakhalin
Kamchatka Peninsula
Chukot Pen.
Gulf of Anadyr
Shelikhova Bay
Kanin Peninsula
Kola Peninsula
Yamal Peninsula
Gydan Peninsula
Taymyr Peninsula
Crimean Pen.
Lena Delta
North Siberian Plain
Central Siberian Plateau
Western Siberian Plain
Kolyma Plain
Ustyurt Plateau
Ural Mountains
East Siberian Mountains
Yakutsk
Stanovoy
Yablonovy
Sayan
Altai
Caucasus
Pamir
Arctic Circle
Ob
Yenisey
Lena
Kotuy
Lower Tunguska
Angara
Vilyuy
Aldan
Indigarka
Kolyma
Anadyr
Amur
Ussuri
Argun
Shilka
Selenga
Irtysh
Biya
Katun
Ili
Syr Darya
Amu Darya (Oxus)
Ural
Volga
Don
Dnepr
Pechora
Naryn
Lake Ladoga
Lake Onega
Lake Baikal
Lake Balkhash
Lake Zaysan
Issyk-Kul
Murmansk
Arkhangelsk
Vorkuta
Surgut
Omsk
Novosibirsk
Novokuznetsk
Krasnoyarsk
Bratsk
Irkutsk
Ulan-Ude
Chita
Yakutsk
Tiksi
Magadan
Okhotsk
Anadyr
Petropavlovsk-Kamchatskiy
Okha
Komsomolsk-na-Amure
Khabarovsk
Vladivostok
Nakhodka
St Petersburg
Novgorod
Tver (Kalinin)
MOSCOW
Suzdal
Vladimir
Tula
Nizhny Novgorod (Gorky)
Kirov
Perm
Kazan
Samara (Kuybyshev)
Ulyanovsk
Saratov
Voronezh
Volgograd
Rostov
Krasnodar
Sochi
Dagomys
Astrakhan
Ufa
Yekaterinburg (Sverdlovsk)
Chelyabinsk
Orenburg
Kaliningrad
Komi
Karelia
Udmurt
Mari
Chuvashia
Mordovia
Tatarstan
Bashkir
Kalmyk
Buryat
Tuva
Kabardino-Balkar
N. Ossetia
Chechenia
Dagestan
Semipalatinsk
Karaganda
ALMA-ATA
Atyrau (Guryev)
Aktau (Shevchenko)
Karakalpak
BISHKEK
KIRGHIZIA
Ozd
Gorno-Badakhshan
TAJIKISTAN
DUSHANBE
TASHKENT
UZBEKISTAN
Samarkand
Bukhara
TURKMENISTAN
ASHKHABAD
Krasnovodsk
AZERBAIJAN
BAKU
Nagorno-Karabakh
Nakhichevan (Azer.)
ARMENIA
YEREVAN
GEORGIA
UKRAINE
KIEV
Kharkov
Dnepropetrovsk
Odessa
L'vov
MOLDOVA
KISHINEV
BELARUS
MINSK
LITHUANIA
LATVIA
ESTONIA
FINLAND
SWEDEN
NORWAY
DENMARK
NETHS.
GERMANY
POLAND
CZECH.
SLOVAK REP.
ROM.
TURKEY
IRAQ
IRAN
AFGHANISTAN
PAK.
INDIA
CHINA
MONGOLIA
D.P.R. OF KOREA
REP. OF KOREA
JAPAN
U.S.A.
1500km
750mls
DAB MM-52

Location: Eastern Europe; Central and Northern Asia; Far East.

Note: (a) Political and religious unrest in the Trans-Caucasian Republics has made much of the region unsafe for tourists; those intending to visit the region should seek up-to-date advice from the Foreign Office. (b) Georgia is the only republic of the former Soviet Union which has not as yet become a member of the CIS. However, it is included within the CIS section for practical geographical reasons. The Consulate/Embassies of the Russian Federation continue to issue visas valid for Georgia.

Intourist
16 Ul. Mokhovaya
103009 Moscow,
Russian Federation
Tel: (095) 292 2260. Fax: (095) 203 5267. Telex: 411211.

Embassy of the Russian Federation
13 Kensington Palace Gardens
London W8 4QS
Tel: (071) 229 3628. Fax: (071) 727 8625. Telex: 261420 SOCNSLG.

Consulate of the Russian Federation
5 Kensington Palace Gardens
London W8 4QS
Tel: (071) 229 8027. Fax: (071) 229 3215. Opening hours: 1000-1230 Monday to Friday (closed Wednesday).

Intourist Travel Limited
Intourist House
219 Marsh Wall
Meridian Gate II
Isle of Dogs
London E14 9FJ
Tel: (071) 538 8600 (general enquiries) *or* 538 5902 (visas) *or* 538 3202 (reservations) *or* 538 3203 (sales). Fax: (071) 538 5967. Telex: 27232.

BSCC (British-Soviet Chamber of Commerce)
42 Southwark Street
London SE1 1UN
Tel: (071) 403 1706. Fax: (071) 403 1245.

Embassy of the Russian Federation
1125 16th Street, NW
Washington, DC
20036
Tel: (202) 628 7551.

Intourist
Suite 868
630 Fifth Avenue
New York, NY
10111
Tel: (212) 757 3884. Fax: (212) 459 0031.

Embassy of the Russian Federation
285 Charlotte Street
Ottawa, Ontario
K1N 8L5
Tel: (613) 235 4341 *or* 236 1413. Fax: (613) 236 6342.

Consular Section
52 Range Road
Ottawa, Ontario
K1N 8J5
Tel: (613) 236 7220 *or* 236 6215.
Consulate in: Montréal.

Intourist Russian Travel Information Office
Suite 630
1801 McGill College Avenue
Montréal, Québec
H3A 2N4
Tel: (514) 849 6394. Fax: (514) 849 6743. Telex: 055-62018.

The Canadian Embassy
23 Starokonyushenny Pereulok
Moscow 121002,
Russian Federation
Tel: (095) 241 1111 *or* 241 5070. Fax: (095) 241 4400 *or* 241 4232 (nightline). Telex: 413401.

Cathedral of the Dormition, Zagorsk

AREA: 22,227,300 sq km (8,581,969 sq miles).
POPULATION: 290,077,000 (1991 official estimate).
POPULATION DENSITY: 12.9 per sq km.
CAPITAL: Minsk. **Population:** 1,612,000 (1989).
GEOGRAPHY: The Commonwealth of Independent States covers one-sixth of the land in the world. It extends over half of the European landmass and one-third of Asia. From north to south the CIS stretches for almost 5000km (2800 miles). From east to west it extends for almost 10,000km (6214 miles). It shares borders with 15 countries: Norway, Finland, Estonia, Lithuania, Latvia, Poland, Slovakia, Hungary, Romania, Turkey, Iran, Afghanistan, China, Mongolia and North Korea. The topography consists of an immense plain framed by mountains, scattered with plateaux and lakes. The rivers are among the largest in the world and of the great lakes, the Aral Sea, the Caspian Sea and Lake Baikal are the most important. Lake Ladoga and Lake Onega in the northwest are the two largest in Europe. The CIS has more than 60,000km (36,000 miles) of coastline along 13 seas, including the Baltic, Black, East Siberian, Karskaya, Laptef, Barents and Japan. Off the northern coast are the island groups of Novaya Zemlya (New Land), Franz Josef Land, Severnaya Zemlya (North Land) and Novosibirskiye Ostrova. Off the eastern coast lie the islands of Sakhalin and the Kuriles.
LANGUAGE: Russian used to be the only official language, with many local languages and dialects in the individual states and regions. It is still used for inter-state relations though each state has a official internal language. English, French or German are spoken by some people. A knowledge of the Cyrillic alphabet is useful.
RELIGION: The Russian Orthodox church is the largest religious community. Other Christian denominations as well as Jewish and Muslim communities also exist.
TIME: From March 31 to September 28, summertime is observed and clocks are put back one hour. See the *Time Zones* map at the front of the book. For more information, see individual entries below.
ELECTRICITY: 220 volts AC, 50Hz.
COMMUNICATIONS: Telephone: There are limited IDD services to and from Moscow, St Peterburg and Kiev. Some Moscow hotels have telephone booths with IDD. Country Code: 7. When dialling from abroad the 0 of the area code must *not* be omitted. Most other calls are made through the international operator and should be booked well in advance. Local calls can be made free of charge from hotels. **Fax:** Services are being introduced in Moscow and other major centres. **Telex/telegram:** Telex services are available at the offices of the Commercial Department of the British Embassy, Kutuzovsky Prospekt 7/4, 12148 Moscow. Telegrams may be sent from hotels. **Post:** Airmail to western Europe takes over ten days. *Poste Restante* facilities are available at the larger hotels. Inland surface mail is often slow. Post office hours: 0900-2000. **Press:** The most influential newspapers in the Commonwealth are *Pravda* and *Izvestiya*. *TASS*, the main news agency, transmits *Pravda* editorials and distributes news by telegraph and radio throughout the country. Newspapers and magazines are published in some 25 languages, but there are no English-language daily newspapers.
BBC World Service and Voice of America frequencies: From time to time these change. See the section *How to Use this Book* for more information.

CIS	HEALTH REGULATIONS	VISA REGULATIONS (Code-Link)
GALILEO/WORLDSPAN	TI-DFT/SVO/HE	 TI-DFT/SVO/VI
SABRE	 TIDFT/SVO/HE	 TIDFT/SVO/VI

To access this information on your CRS, swipe the barcode with a light pen or type in the text under the barcode. For more information, see the introduction *How to Use This Book*.

Swallow's Nest, Yalta, Ukraine

BBC:				
MHz	17.64	15.07	9.410	6.195
Voice of America:				
MHz	9.670	6.040	5.995	1.197

PASSPORT/VISA

Regulations and requirements may be subject to change at short notice, and you are advised to contact the appropriate diplomatic or consular authority before finalising travel arrangements. Details of these may be found at the head of this country's entry. Any numbers in the chart refer to the footnotes below.

	Passport Required?	Visa Required?	Return Ticket Required?
Full British	Yes	Yes	Yes
BVP	Not valid	-	-
Australian	Yes	Yes	Yes
Canadian	Yes	Yes	Yes
USA	Yes	Yes	Yes
Other EC	Yes	Yes	Yes
Japanese	Yes	Yes	Yes

Note: The following regulations are valid for all members of the CIS, with the exception of the Ukraine and Uzbekistan (see individual entries below). The Consulates/Embassies of the Russian Federation will, until further notice, continue to issue visas for all other member states and Georgia. However, the situation might change at short notice and visitors should check with the consulates/embassies before departure.

PASSPORTS: Valid passport required by all except resident nationals of Bulgaria, Czechoslovakia, Hungary, North Korea, Mongolia, Poland, Romania, Vietnam and former republics of Yugoslavia. British passports must be valid for 10 years and for at least 3 months after returning from the CIS.

British Visitors Passport: Not accepted.

VISAS: Required by all except resident nationals of Bulgaria, Cuba, Czechoslovakia, Hungary, North Korea, Poland, Romania and Vietnam, and nationals of former republics of Yugoslavia if travelling on business (invitation sufficient).

Note: Passengers without valid visas arriving in the Russian Federation from the Ukraine or Belarus are charged a penalty for illegal entry at the rate of US$250 per person.

Types of visa: Entry/exit Tourist; Business (for business or educational visits, trade fairs and exhibitions); and Transit (see below); cost: £5. Tour operators charge £10 plus VAT for obtaining visas for their clients. Generally, all visa types need proof of accommodation. *Transit visas:* Travellers with Transit visas are allowed a maximum of 48 hours to transit provided they are in possession of confirmed onward travel documentation and valid entry requirement for the onward destination. Passengers may leave the airport under certain conditions on a Transit visa, but anyone intending independent excursions must obtain a full visa. It is possible for passengers arriving in the Russian Federation without a Transit visa to obtain it at the Moscow Sheremetjevo Airport, but this is risky and inadvisable, as it is far more costly and passengers may be refused entry and sent back.

Cost: 1 day – US$72; up to 2 days – US$90 and up to 3 days – US$110.

Application to: Consulate (or Consular Section at Embassy). For addresses, see top of entry.

Application requirements: *Tourist visa:* (a) Completed application form. (b) 3 recent identical passport photos. (c) Photocopy of the first 5 pages of a valid passport, trimmed to actual size (if British visitors hold a new EC-format passport, pages 32 and 33 must also be photocopied). (d) A copy of a voucher (exchange order) issued by an authorised travel company with indication of names, dates of entry and exit, itinerary, means of transportation, class of services and amount of money paid by a client. (e) Fee.

Business visa: (a) Completed application form. (b) 3 recent identical passport photos. (c) Photocopy of first 5 pages (plus 32 and 33 if EC-format) of a valid passport. (d) An introductory letter from company or firm indicating the purpose, itinerary, organisation to be visited, period of stay and exact departure dates of flights. (e) An invitation from the organisation, department or institution to be visited in the CIS. (f) Fee.

All postal applications must be accompanied by a large stamped, self-addressed envelope.

Those who are travelling in groups (standard Intourist tours, coach tours, international competition events, package tours, cruises) should submit all documentation to the tour operator making the travel arrangements. Applications should be made directly to the nearest Intourist office.

For visits to relatives/friends in the States, enquire at the Consulate for details of application procedures.

Working days required: Applications for visas may not be made earlier than 3 months before departure, and in no case later than 14 working days before departure, whether by post or personal visit.

MONEY

Currency: Rouble (Rub) = 100 kopeks. Notes are in denominations of Rub10,000, 5000, 1000, 500, 200, 100, 50, 25, 10, 5, 3 and 1. Coins are in denominations of Rub1, and 50, 20, 15, 10, 5, 3, 2 and 1 kopeks, though they are rarely used due to very high inflation. There are also Soviet Olympic coins dated 1977-1980 in denominations of Rub150, 100, 10, 5 and 1. Belarus plans to introduce its own currency in the near future.

Currency exchange: Foreign currency should only be exchanged at official bureaux and all transactions must be recorded on the currency declaration form, which is issued on arrival. It is wise to retain all exchange receipts. Most aspects of a tour, including accommodation, transport and meals, are paid before departure (through Intourist or a recognised tour operator), so large amounts of spending money are not necessary.

Credit cards: Major European and international credit cards, including American Express, Visa and Diners Club, are accepted in the larger hotels and at foreign currency shops and restaurants.

Eurocheques up to Rub300 can be cashed in banks.

Travellers cheques are preferable to cash, but visitors to Moscow would be wise to take some hard currency for purchases.

Exchange rate indicators: The following figures are included as a guide to the movements of the Rouble against Sterling and the US Dollar:

Date:	Oct '89	Oct '90	Oct '91	Oct '92
£1.00=	1.02	1.11	1.02	*0.95
$1.00=	0.64	0.57	0.59	*0.60

Note [*]: Official rate, the market rate differs immensely (£1 = Rub560, $1 = Rub375).

Currency restrictions: The import and export of local currency is prohibited. All remaining local currency must be reconverted at the point of departure. The import of foreign currency is unlimited, subject to declaration. The export of foreign currency is limited to the amount declared on arrival.

Banking hours: 0930-1730 Monday to Friday.

DUTY FREE

The following goods may be imported into the Commonwealth of Independent States without incurring customs duty:

250 cigarettes or 250g of tobacco products;
1 litre of spirits;
2 litres of wine;
A reasonable quantity of perfume for personal use;
Gifts up to a value of Rub1000.

Note: On entering the country, tourists must complete a customs declaration form which must be retained until departure. This allows the import of articles intended for personal use, including currency and valuables which must be registered on the declaration form. Customs inspection can be long and detailed.

Prohibited imports: Military weapons and ammunition, narcotics and drug paraphernalia, pornography, loose pearls and anything owned by a third party that is to be carried in for that third party. If you have any query regarding items that may be imported, an information sheet is available on request from Intourist.

Prohibited exports: As prohibited imports, as well as annulled securities, state loan certificates, lottery tickets, works of art and antiques (unless permission has been

Lake Baikal

granted by the Ministry of Culture), saiga horns, Siberian stag, punctuate and red deer antlers (unless on organised hunting trip), and punctate deer skins.

PUBLIC HOLIDAYS

Until further notice, the public holidays observed in the CIS are as follows:
Mar 8 '93 International Women's Day. **May 1-2** International Labour Day. **May 9** Victory in Europe Day. **Nov 7-8** October Revolution. **Jan 1 '94** New Year's Day. **Jan 7** Russian Orthodox Christmas. **Feb 23** Army & Navy Day. **Mar 8** International Women's Day.

HEALTH

Regulations and requirements may be subject to change at short notice, and you are advised to contact your doctor well in advance of your intended date of departure. Any numbers in the chart refer to the footnotes below.

	Special Precautions?	Certificate Required?
Yellow Fever	No	No
Cholera	No	No
Typhoid & Polio	1	-
Malaria	2	-
Food & Drink	3	-

[1]: There is a risk of typhoid and other tick-borne diseases in east and central Siberia.
[2]: Malaria risk, exclusively in the benign *vivax* form, exists throughout the year in Azerbaijan, Tajikistan and rural areas bordering Iran and Afghanistan.
[3]: All water should be regarded as being a potential health risk. Water used for drinking, brushing teeth or making ice should have first been boiled or otherwise sterilised. Milk is pasteurised and dairy products are safe for consumption. Only eat well-cooked meat and fish, preferably served hot. Pork, salad and mayonnaise may carry increased risk. Vegetables should be cooked and fruit peeled.
Rabies is present. For those at high risk, vaccination before arrival should be considered. If you are bitten abroad, seek medical advice without delay. For more information consult the *Health* section at the back of the book.
Health care: The highly developed health service provides free medical treatment for all citizens. If a traveller becomes ill during a booked tour in the CIS, emergency treatment is free, with small sums to be paid for medicines and hospital treatment. If a longer stay than originally planned becomes necessary because of the illness, the visitor has to pay for all further treatment – a travel insurance is therefore recommended for all travellers. It is advisable to take a supply of those medicines that are likely to be required (but check first that they may be legally imported) as medicines can prove difficult to get hold of.

TRAVEL - International

AIR: The national airline is *Aeroflot Russian International Airlines (SU)*. Certain republics are in the process of establishing new national airlines.
Approximate flight times: From *London* to Moscow or St Petersburg is 3 hours 45 minutes and to Simferopol 4 hours 30 minutes.
From *New York* to Moscow is 9 hours.
From *Singapore* to Moscow is 16 hours.
International airports: *Moscow (SVO)* (Sheremetyevo) is 29km (18 miles) northwest of the city. Coaches depart for the airport from the Central Air Terminal in Moscow, 37 Leningradsky Prospekt (travel time – 35 minutes for domestic flights, 50 minutes for international flights). Taxis are available at the airport to the city centre for approx. US$20 (travel time – 40 minutes). Airport facilities include outgoing duty-free, banks/bureaux de change, restaurants and first aid.
Moscow also has two primarily domestic airports: see *Travel – Internal* below.
St Petersburg (LED) (Pulkovo) is 17km (10.5 miles) south of the city (travel time – 45 minutes). Buses are available to the city centre for Rub10 (travel time – 45 minutes). Taxis are available to the city centre for approx. US$20 (travel time – 40 minutes). Airport facilities include 24-hour banks/bureaux de change, 24-hour tourist information, 24-hour duty-free shops, restaurant (open 0900-2300), bar (open 1000-2000), 24-hour snack bar, 24-hour left luggage and 24-hour first aid.
Intourist offers stopover facilities in Moscow (not exceeding two nights) to transit passengers at special reduced rates including transport, accommodation, full board and guided tour. Four weeks' notice is required.
The following airports also receive international flights: *Minsk*, *Kiev* (from various European countries), *Yerevan* (from the Middle East), *Tashkent* (from South-East Asia), *Irkutsk* (from Mongolia, China and North Korea) and *Khabarovsk* (from Japan).
SEA: Cruise holidays can be arranged by the former Soviet shipping line *CTC Limited*. UK address: 1 Regent Street, London SW1Y 4NN. Tel: (071) 930 5833. Fax: (071) 839 2483. Round-trip cruises include St Petersburg on the Baltic and travel from Tilbury to destinations in Scandinavia (during May and July) or include Odessa (in Georgia) and Yalta (in Ukraine) on the Black Sea and depart from Turkey to destinations in the eastern Mediterranean (during August and September).
RAIL: There are various connections from London. The sleeper coach to Moscow takes about 53 hours. The main routes are:
Harwich–Hook of Holland–Berlin–Warsaw–*Moscow*.
Dover–Ostend–Berlin–Warsaw–*Moscow*.
Services from Harwich are daily, with the train leaving at 0925 from London Liverpool Street Station and the ferry at 1130 from Harwich Docks. Services from Dover are also daily, with the train leaving at 0730 from London Victoria Station and the ferry at 1000 from Dover Docks. There are through trains or coaches from other western and eastern European cities and from Turkey, Iran, Mongolia and China.
ROAD: Foreign tourists may drive their own cars or may hire cars from Intourist (see *Travel – Internal* below). There are road crossing points as follows:
Finland/Russian Federation: Vaalima–Torfianovska; Nuijamaa–Brusnichnoye and Rajajooseppi–Lotta. Poland/Belarus: Terespol–Brest. Poland/Ukraine: Przemsyl–Mostiska. Slovak Republic/Ukraine: Vysné Nemecké–Uzhgorod. Hungary/Ukraine: Zahony–Chop. Romania/Ukraine: Siret–Porubnoye. Romania/Moldova: Albita–Leusheni. Turkey/Georgia: Kemalpasa–Sarpi (presently closed). Those entering by car should have their visas registered at the hotel, motel or campsite where they will stay for the first night; are advised to insure their vehicle with *Ingosstrakh*, which has offices at all crossing points and in most major cities; and should also purchase Intourist service coupons at the border. For information on the documentation required temporarily to import a car, contact Intourist. It should be noted that, once in the CIS, foreigners may only drive on routes agreed beforehand with Intourist (see below).

TRAVEL - Internal

AIR: The internal network radiates from Moscow's three airports. *Aeroflot Russian International Airlines* runs services from Moscow to most major cities. All-inclusive tours are available from Intourist.
Domestic airports: *Vnukovo Airport (VKO)* is 29.5km (18 miles) southwest of Moscow. Coaches go to the airport from the Central Air Terminal (travel time – 75 minutes). Taxis are available to the city. Outgoing duty-free facilities are available at the airport.
Domodedovo (DME) is 40km (25 miles) from Moscow. A coach goes from the Central Air Terminal to the airport (travel time – 80 minutes).
Approximate flight times: From Moscow to *Alma-Ata* is 4 hours 15 minutes, to *Baku* is 3 hours, to *Bratsk* is 6 hours 45 minutes, to *Bukhara* is 3 hours 45 minutes, to *Dzhambul* is 3 hours 45 minutes, to *Donetsk* is 1 hour 30 minutes, to *Yerevan* is 4 hours 30 minutes, to *Irkutsk* is 7 hours, to *Khabarovsk* is 7 hours 30 minutes, to *Kharkov* is 1 hour 15 minutes, to *Kiev* is 1 hour 30 minutes, to *St Petersburg* is 1 hour, to *Lyov* is 2 hours 15 minutes, to *Minsk* is 1 hour 30 minutes, to *Odessa* is 2 hours, to *Samarkand* is 3 hours 45 minutes, to *Tbilisi* is 2 hours 30 minutes, to *Volgograd* is 1 hour 30 minutes and to *Yalta* is 2 hours 15 minutes.
RAIL: The largest and busiest rail network in the world is predominantly for freight traffic. Only a few long-distance routes are open for travel by tourists, and reservations must be made on all journeys. The *Trans-Siberian Express*, probably the most famous train journey in the world, is one of the best ways of seeing the interior of the country; contact Intourist for details.
ROAD: Motoring holidays should be arranged through Intourist and foreigners may only drive on approved routes. It is necessary to pre-plan the itinerary and accommodation requirements. Travellers can take their own car (see *Travel*

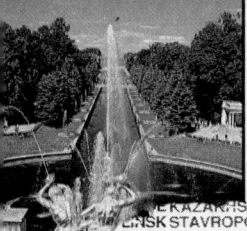

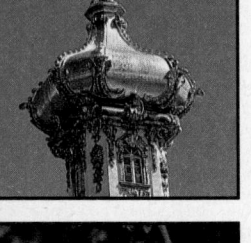

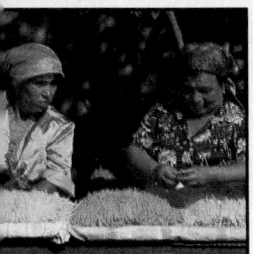

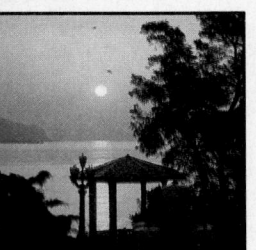

– *International* above) or hire a vehicle through Intourist; tariffs include the cost of insurance. Intourist can arrange to have hire cars waiting at authorised border crossings. Chauffeured cars are available in major cities. Motorists should at all times have the following with them: a valid passport endorsed with a valid visa; a national or international driving licence with a translation; Intourist documentation relating to the route to be taken and the date and place of stopovers (and, where appropriate, recording the hire of the car); a chart of Intourist's routes; tourist papers and Intourist service coupons. Sample distances: Moscow to St Petersburg: 692km (432 miles); Moscow to Minsk: 690km (429 miles); Moscow to Rostov-on-Don: 1198km (744 miles); Moscow to Kiev: 858km (533 miles); Moscow to Odessa: 1347km (837 miles). A motoring guide is available from Intourist. **Bus:** Long-distance coach services operate but they are generally not available for tourist travel.
Traffic regulations: Driving is on the right. Speeds are limited to 60kmph (37mph) in built-up areas and 90kmph (55mph) elsewhere. Hooting the horn is forbidden except when to do so might prevent an accident. Motorists should avoid driving at night if possible. Driving under the influence of drugs or alcohol is forbidden. Every car should be fitted with seat belts, a first-aid kit, a fire extinguisher and an emergency horn or red light. In case of an accident, contact the nearest traffic inspection officer or Intourist office and make sure all participants fill in written statements, to be witnessed by a militia inspector. All repairs will be at the foreign motorist's expense. **Documentation:** An international or national driving licence with an authorised translation is sufficient. Contact Intourist for full details.
URBAN: Public transport in the cities is comprehensive and cheap. Many services are electric traction (metro, tramway, trolleybus). Stations on the Moscow and St Petersburg metros are always elegant and often palatial. Fares are standard for the various modes. Taxis are also available; they can be hailed in the street, hired at a rank or booked by telephone.
JOURNEY TIMES: The following chart gives approximate journey times (in hours and minutes) from Moscow to other major cities/towns in the Commonwealth (for flight times see above).

	Air	Rail	Sea
Khabarovsk	7.30	-	-
Alma-Ata	4.15	-	-
Simferopol	2.30	22.00	-
St Petersburg	1.00	9.00	-
Kiev	1.30	13.00	-
Irkutsk	7.00	88.00	-
Volgograd	1.45	-	-
Yerevan	3.00	-	-
Odessa	2.00	-	-

ACCOMMODATION

The majority of tourists travel with Intourist. Other travel organisations are Sputnik, the International Youth Travel Bureau; the Trade Union Central Council on Tourism & Excursions; and the Centre for International Trade (for business travellers). Camping holidays (in the European part only) can be arranged for June to September only via Intourist.
The hotel capacity is still limited, with differing standards. However, some hotels meet international standards, whereas others are very basic. Several new hotels have been opened in Moscow and St Petersburg, partly as joint-ventures, ie the *Aerostar* (4-star), the *Olympic-Penta* (all rooms with bathroom, air-conditioning, radio, TV, IDD) and the *Novotel* at the Moscow airport. The *Pullman Iris* also offers 4-star comfort. St Petersburg's *Grand Hotel Europe* is one of the first 5-star hotels in the Russian Federation, the *Hotel Helen* is a Russian-Finnish joint-venture, 20km from the St Petersburg airport. Intourist can now arrange bed & breakfast accommodation with English-speaking families in Moscow, St Petersburg, Odessa and other cities.

RESORTS & EXCURSIONS

See individual entries.

SOCIAL PROFILE

FOOD & DRINK: The kind of food visitors will eat from day to day depends on which city they are visiting, as Intourist menus are dependent on local produce and the time of year. Breakfast is often of a Scandinavian type, with cold meats, boiled eggs and bread served with Russian tea. For the midday and evening meal the food is often more traditional, again depending on where in the CIS one is eating. One of the more famous Russian dishes is *borshch*, a beetroot soup served hot with sour cream, and the sister dish of *akroshka*, a kvas soup served cold. Several dishes which are now often seen as international but find their origin in Russia are *beef stroganov* (beef stewed in sour cream with fried potatoes), *bliny* (small pancakes filled with caviar, fish, melted butter or sour cream), *aladyi* (crumpets with the same filling and jam) and especially *ikra* or *krasnaya ikra* (black and red caviar). Local dishes well worth trying include *kotlyety po Pozharsky* (chicken cutlets), *pirozhky* (fried rolls with different fillings, usually meat), *ponchiki* (hot sugared doughnuts), *prostakvasha* (yoghurt), *pelmeni* (meat dumplings), *rossolnik* (hot soup, usually made of pickled vegetables), *shchi* (cabbage soup) and *morozhenoye* (ice cream). Several of the regional specialities are less well-known, such as *chicken tabaka* (Georgian), *shashlik* (Caucasian), *pilaff* (Uzbek), lamb stew with pine nuts (Armenian) and honey cake (Ukrainian).
Intourist meal vouchers are widely acceptable and an increasing number of hotels and restaurants in Moscow accept foreign currency, as do some bars.
Drink: One of the most popular drinks is *chai* (tea served without milk). Coffee is generally available with meals and in cafés, although standards vary. Soft drinks, fruit juices and mineral waters are widely available. Vodka is often flavoured and coloured with herbs and spices such as *zubrovka* (a kind of grass), *ryabinovka* (steeped with ashberries), *starka* (dark, smooth, aged vodka) and *pertsovka* (with hot pepper). Wines produced in areas such as Georgia and the Crimea are excellent. Russian champagne is surprisingly good and reasonably priced. Armenian and Azerbaijani brandies are excellent. *Kvas* is a refreshing and unusual drink and should be tried on a hot day. Drinks are ordered by grams or by the bottle. Former Soviet regulations forbid the serving of more than 100g of vodka per person per meal. Bars and cafés usually close by 2200.
NIGHTLIFE: Theatre, circus, concert and variety performances are the main evening entertainments offered to tourists. The repertoire of theatres provides a change of programme almost nightly. In the course of one month, thirty different productions may be presented by the Bolshoi Opera and Ballet Company. Details of performances can be obtained on arrival. Applications should be made to the service bureau of your hotel. Dancing takes place in many of the Intourist restaurants and night bars, as well as in the main local restaurants.

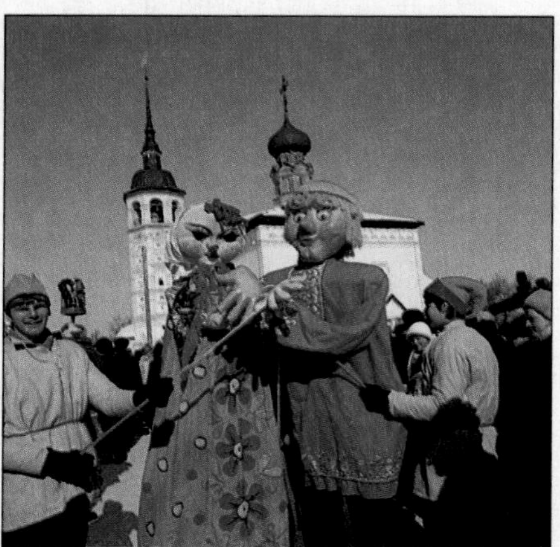

Russian Winter, Carnival Costumes, Suzdal

SHOPPING: Most tourist centres have foreign currency shops, and most consumer goods are now available in Moscow and St Petersburg. A wide range of goods such as watches, cameras, wines and spirits, furs, ceramics and glass, jewellery and toys may be bought for foreign currency only (cash or travellers cheques) at favourable prices. Selected books and records are available at standard prices. In all other shops CIS currencies must be used. A system of queueing is used in local shops for choosing goods, for payment and for collection, so allow some time for souvenir hunting. Most shops are closed on Sundays, but tourist shops are usually open every day. Antiquities, valuables, works of art and manuscripts other than those offered for sale in souvenir shops may not be taken out of the CIS without an export licence. **Shopping hours:** 0900/1000-2000/2100.
SPORT: Hiking trips are available in the Caucasus, at Teberda-Dombay (west); Baksan Elbrus (north). **Skiing:** There is skiing in the same areas. **Fishing:** The Veselovskaye Reservoir in the Rostov-on-Don region is noted for pike, perch, carp, bream, gudgeon, bullhead and roach. **Spectator sports:** Almost every provincial city has a **football** team and larger cities have several clubs organised within factories, unions and government offices. Further information about other sporting events is available from Intourist.
SPECIAL EVENTS: The following is a selection of some of the main events:
May *Moscow Stars' Art Festival*, Moscow. **End of May-early Jun** *'Spring Art' Festival*, Kiev. **Jun** *'White Nights' Art Festival*, St Petersburg. **Nov** *Belarussian Musical Autumn Arts Festival*, Minsk. **Oct** *Melodies of Soviet Trans-Caucasia*, Yerevan, Baku, Tbilisi. **Dec-Jan '94** *Russian Winter Festival*, Moscow. **Mar** *'Mertsishor' Art Festival*, Kishinev.
SOCIAL CONVENTIONS: It is customary to shake hands when greeting someone. All visits to homes and cities are organised on an Intourist itinerary, but visitors will find that, although the people vary from region to region and from city to city, they are welcoming and hospitable. Company or business gifts are well received. Each region has its own characteristic mode of dress, some quite unlike Western styles, and visitors should be aware of this contrast. Conservative wear is suitable for most places and the seasonal weather should always be borne in mind. Smoking is acceptable unless stated otherwise. **Tipping:** Hotels in Moscow and other large cities include a 10-15% service charge. Otherwise 10% is customary.

BUSINESS PROFILE

ECONOMY: The consistent and sometimes rapid growth of the USSR over the last forty years ceased in the 1970s and early 1980s – the 'period of stagnation' – producing serious economic problems. These proved beyond the management capabilities of the last All-Union government of President Gorbachev and has left a daunting legacy for the newly independent republics to cope with. In particular, the Soviet economy has long been hampered by an unwieldy system of economic management under which all production and pricing was centrally administered under the diktats of The Five Year Plan produced by the State Planning Committee (Gosplan). The key advantage enjoyed by the CIS republics is an enormous abundance of natural resources of every description. Energy resources include oil, gas, coal, nuclear fuels and hydroelectric resources. There are deposits of almost every mineral, many of them known to be the world's largest deposits, while countless others have yet to be discovered. There are vast areas of fertile land, forest and fresh water. The fact that the Soviet Union was ultimately unable to feed itself without large imports of grain from the United States, Canada and Argentina is perhaps the most damning indictment of the Soviet economic regime. Much of the blame must be laid at the door of the collective farm system, but an equally important factor is the inadequate infrastructure. Roads and railways are sparse and in poor condition; the telephone system is antique. On top of that, there is a shortage of working transport equipment to exploit what transport systems do exist, leading to poor distribution and consequent shortages and waste. The economy is also paying the price of an obsession with heavy industry, initiated by Stalin and continued by his successors, and consistently high defence spending. The industrial economy is thus extensive, particularly in steel, heavy engineering and chemicals. Light industry, and notably consumer products, are comparatively weak. The consumer sector and agriculture are the areas the republics are most keen to promote. The economic community agreement reached between the republics in the Kazakh capital Alma-Ata in October 1991 allows for co-ordinated policies in energy, transport, the finance and banking systems, customs and tariffs and foreign economic relations and declares that 'private ownership, free enterprise and competition [will] form the basis for economic recovery'. If they are to make the transition successfully, there will also need to be a root and branch reform of the financial system. The Rouble is now desperately weak, and needs substantial international support. A large disparity persists between the nominal official and real (black) market rates. Among the consequences of the financial instability are rocketing inflation – driven up further by the unfreezing of prices at the end of 1991 – capital flight and a shortage of paper money. Foreign trade patterns will have to be re-organised after the dissolution of the Council for Mutual Economic Assistance (COMECON) in April 1991. Yeltsin has instituted a policy of deregulated foreign trade for the Russian Federation, transferring responsibility from designated government ministries to individual producers; the other CIS republics will probably follow this pattern. The barter system which provided the basis of much of the Soviet Union's foreign trade, particularly inside COMECON, has been replaced by hard currency deals. Within the CIS, however, barter remains a common means of conducting transactions.
BUSINESS: For business meetings, people should dress smartly. There are many dialects spoken, but English is a second language for many senior officials. A knowledge of German may also be useful. Appointments should be made at least three days in advance with confirmation. Punctuality is appreciated and visiting cards printed in Russian and English should be carried. Business transactions are likely to take quite a long time. **Office hours:** 0900-1800 Monday to Friday.
COMMERCIAL INFORMATION: See individual entries below.

HISTORY & GOVERNMENT

HISTORY: *PRE-REVOLUTIONARY RUSSIA AND THE SOVIET UNION*

In the course of the 9th century, Viking tribes from Scandinavia moved southward into European Russia, tracing a path along the main waterway connecting the Baltic and Black Seas. The first monarchic dynasty, which ruled until the Mongol invasion of the 13th century, built Kiev as its capital. The Mongol Empire, which stretched across the Asian continent, was divided into a number of 'hordes' or individual kingdoms; Russia was put under the suzerainty of the Khanate of the Golden Horde. The next two centuries saw the rise of Moscow as a provincial capital and centre of the Christian Orthodox Church. In the late 15th century the Grand Prince of Moscow, Ivan III (The Great), annexed the rival principalities of Russia, including the Novgorod republic to the north, thus becoming the first national sovereign and assuming the title of Tsar. The political history of the next 150 years, from 1500 until the mid-17th century, was characterised by struggles between the Tsar and the rich, powerful landed nobility, known as the *boyars*. The Russian empire expanded gradually to acquire land to the south as far as the Caspian Sea and eastwards into Siberia. Russia was also firmly established by now as an important European power. The two most important rulers of Russia in the 17th and 18th centuries were Peter The Great (1682-1725), who cemented the regime and established Russia as a leading European power, and Catherine The Great (1762-96), generally recognised as an astute and energetic ruler, who pursued a policy of enlightened despotism at home while continuing the aggressive foreign policy initiated by Peter. In the first quarter of the 19th century, under Tsar Alexander I, the first steps were taken to dismantle the system of serfdom under which most people continued to live. The process was disrupted, however, by Napoleon's invasion of Russia. The French were driven out in 1812 and Napoleon's army destroyed in the legendary retreat from Moscow. Alexander's successor completed the growth of the empire into the Caucasus (now Georgia) and Armenia and reached agreement with England of the division of Central Asia into spheres of influence. Most of Siberia had been annexed by the 1840s, but the completion of the expansion to the south and east (creating more or less the present frontiers of the CIS) had been completed by 1905. Domestic policies remained conservative in persuasion: pressure for political and economic reform was met only with repression. By February 1917, the populace engulfed Russia in widespread strikes, rioting and army mutinies, which forced the Tsar to abdicate. The liberal Provisional Government which took control was forced out of office by a Bolshevik coup in October. The Bolsheviks (majority faction) were the more radical product of the split in the Social Democratic Party, formed in 1898, upon which much of the organised opposition to the regime was focused. Under the leadership of Vladimir Ilich Ulyanov, better known as Lenin, the Bolsheviks moved quickly to consolidate their position, bringing land, industry and finance under state control. Within two years, having seen off the military challenge of the right-wing White Armies backed by the major European powers, who sought the re-establishment of the Tsarist regime, the Bolsheviks were firmly in control. Lenin died in 1924 and was succeeded by Josef Stalin (Djugashvili) who instituted a crash programme of industrialisation and the forced collectivisation of agriculture. Famine and massive purges were the hallmark of this period. In 1941, the USSR was invaded by Nazi Germany, despite having signed a peace treaty with Hitler in 1939, in the start of what Soviets referred to as the Great Patriotic War. Like Napoleon before him, Hitler's armies were driven out, again with massive loss of life on the Russian side (running into millions of people). A large reconstruction effort had, by the early 1950s, restored much of the war damage. In the meantime, the USSR had become the world's second nuclear power, exploding its first atomic bomb in 1949, and sponsored the formation of a buffer zone of communist-controlled governments in Eastern Europe. The occasional instability of these regimes led the USSR to intervene militarily on two occasions – in Hungary in 1956 and in Czechoslovakia in 1968. Foreign policy has since been dominated by relations with the USA, which fluctuated from outright hostility to the 'Cold Peace' of détente. The two sides came to the brink of nuclear war in the 1962 Cuban missile crisis. The Soviet Union was by now in the hands of Stalin's successor, Nikita Krushchev, who shocked the Communist Party in 1956 by revealing the extent of Stalin's brutality. Also during Krushchev's term, the split with China which fractured the unity of the world communist movement took place: the two countries have been at loggerheads ever since. After Khrushchev's fall from power in 1964, the USSR was led until 1982 by Leonid Brezhnev. In retrospect, the Brezhnev years are seen as a period of stability and relaxation in international tensions (although he took the USSR into Afghanistan) coupled with domestic stagnation and inertia presided over by an ageing and unimaginative party leadership. The very last General Secretary of the Communist Party of the Soviet Union, Mikhail Sergeyevich Gorbachev, took over the leadership in March 1985, after a 3-year interregnum of two General Secretaries, Andropov and Chernenko, who were more often than not indisposed by ill health. Gorbachev instigated a programme of social, political and economic reform, and a wholesale diplomatic offensive abroad, not only on nuclear arms control, but also in regional policies and relations with the Third World. An early success for Gorbachev was the treaty on Intermediate Nuclear Forces, signed in December 1987, which eliminated a whole category of superpower nuclear armaments. Another protracted dispute with the Americans was settled in early 1989, when the last Soviet forces left Afghanistan after a decade of fighting. At home, Gorbachev's programme centred on the slogan-concepts of *perestroika* (restructuring) and *glasnost* (openness). At the heart of the *glasnost* policy was the liberalisation of the media, which has since played an important role in bringing to popular attention policy errors and official mismanagement which was previously hidden from most people. When Gorbachev took office he declared that the 'nationalities problem' – a reference to 100-plus distinct ethnic groups in the Soviet Union – was the most serious facing the nation. He was quickly proved right as the relaxation of the state stranglehold over the country's political and social life allowed simmering aspirations and resentments to come to the surface, particularly in the southern republics of Trans-Caucasia and Central Asia. As the dire state of the economy became apparent, the Soviet Union all but ceased to be a player on the international arena, illustrated by its lack of reaction to the Kuwait crisis of 1990 (where the Soviet Union meekly followed the US line) and the lack of resistance put up to Western terms over the reunification of Germany. Gorbachev made his final stand by setting himself firmly against the dissolution of the USSR, despite growing demand in the republics for independence. The Baltic republics were particularly adamant on this issue and organised plebiscites which proved that independence enjoyed overwhelming popular support. Gorbachev's disastrous decision to send the Red Army into Lithuania in early 1991 to prevent it from seceding marked the beginning of the end. Squeezed by radicals and secessionists on one side and conservative elements in the military and KGB on the other, Gorbachev's position was becoming increasingly untenable. At this point a rival emerged to Gorbachev in the form of the sacked Moscow party boss Boris Yeltsin, who won the election for the presidency of the Russian republic in June 1991. This conferred on Yeltsin a legitimacy which Gorbachev, who had never received any popular mandate, could not match. Meanwhile, the Conservatives in the Party, the army and the KGB looked on with increasing horror and realised that if they were going to arrest the transformation of the country (and with it their own positions), they would need to act quickly. On August 19, while Gorbachev was holidaying in the Crimea, a coup was staged by the 'State Committee for the State of Emergency in the USSR'. Badly planned, it fizzled out after three days, but Gorbachev's position had been completely undermined by the fact that the plotters were his closest associates in the Government. Boris Yeltsin, who co-ordinated and rallied resistance to the coup, came out greatly strengthened. Gorbachev's last attempt to save the USSR was dismissed by the leaders of the republics who spent the remaining months of 1991 consolidating their own positions and convening a series of meetings to sketch out the rough outline of a post-Soviet system. An economic treaty was signed by eight republics at the end of October, and the tripartite agreement between Russia, Ukraine and Belarus, which formed the nucleus of the Commonwealth of Independent States, was settled in the first week of December.

COMMONWEALTH OF INDEPENDENT STATES

The Commonwealth of Independent States (CIS) began as an all-Slav creation, founded on December 8, 1991 by Russia, Ukraine and Belarus in the Belarus capital Minsk. Other republics were then invited to join the fait accompli. This piece of political brinkmanship, although it risked offending the non-Slav states, was all but essential to outmanoeuvre President Gorbachev. This was a principal objective, which was intended to – as indeed it did – leave Gorbachev as President of nothing. The CIS, as conceived, would take on board those multi-lateral issues, such as the future of strategic forces and the space programme, which Gorbachev would otherwise have been left in charge of at the head of a rump Soviet government. Fortunately for the Minsk signatories, all nine other republics signed up within days including, significantly, Kazakhstan, the only republic

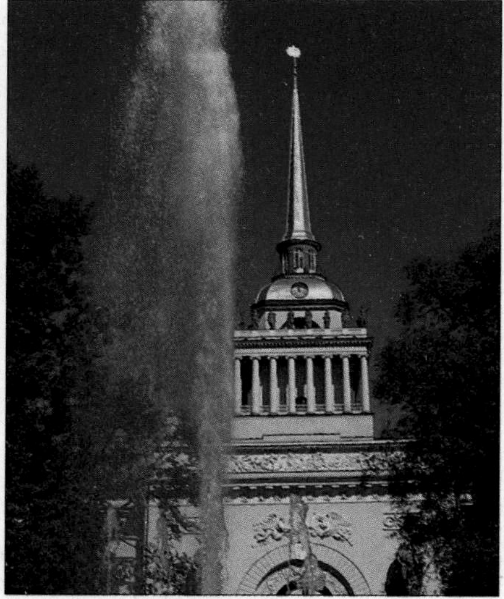

The Admiralty, St Petersburg

outside the original Minsk agreement with strategic systems on its soil. Minsk was chosen as the headquarters of the CIS for much the same reasons that Brussels hosts the European Community: its relative insignificance and lack of stature compared to the grander cities elsewhere. The two principal issues for the CIS are economic co-operation, enshrined in a prior treaty signed in October, and the future of the former Soviet Union's armed forces. Under the current command of Marshal Shaposhnikov, the armed forces will probably be divided up between the republics in rough proportion to their population, although there are numerous difficulties – such as the preponderance of Russians in the officer corps – which have to be settled. Nuclear weapons are under the joint control of those republics – the three Slavs plus Kazakhstan – which host them. Economic affairs will be supervised by the Inter-Republican Economic Committee. The CIS will represent the republics at a number of international fora, including the International Monetary Fund, of which the Soviet Union was a recent associate member. In the case of the United Nations, however, republics have achieved individual membership. It is also intended to have a role in foreign policy co-ordination. The stability of the CIS is less than guaranteed in the long term: its success depends primarily on its success in resolving the military issue and, in the longer term, as a mechanism for resolving disputes and consolidating the economic alliance between the republics. The Popular Front, which forms the new government in Azerbaijan, favours Azeri withdrawal from the CIS.

GOVERNMENT: The Commonwealth of Independent States was established by treaty in December 1991.

CLIMATE

See individual entries.

EUROPEAN STATES

BELARUS

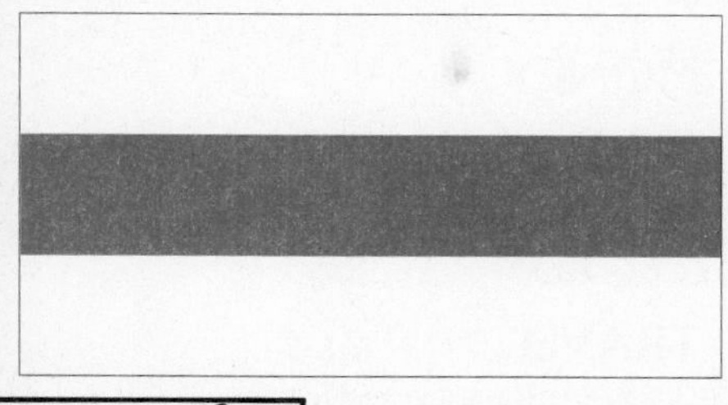

Location: Eastern Europe.

Note: A British Embassy is to open in early 1993. Contact the Foreign Office for further information (tel: (071) 270 3000).

Ministry of Foreign Affairs
pr. Leninsky 8
Minsk, Belarus
Tel: (0172) 272 922.
Embassy of the United States of America
Storovilenskaya 6
Minsk, Belarus
Tel: (0172) 690 802.

AREA: 207,600 sq km (80,154 sq miles).
POPULATION: 10,200,000 (1989).
POPULATION DENSITY: 49 per sq km.
CAPITAL: Minsk. **Population:** 1,612,000 (1989).
GEOGRAPHY: Belarus is bordered by Latvia, Lithuania, Poland, the Ukraine and the Russian Federation. Forests and lakes cover much of its area, the Dnepr and other great rivers flow through it, and it is rich in wildlife. At the same time, there are many ancient Russian cities in this state, and both agriculture and industry are well developed.
LANGUAGE: Predominantly Belarussian and Russian.
TIME: GMT + 2.
COMMUNICATIONS: Belarus has a news agency, *BelTA*, whose headquarters are at vul. Kiraua 26, Minsk, Belarus. Tel: (0172) 271 992. Fax: (0172) 271 346.
TV/Radio: The radio station, *Radio Minsk*, can be contacted at vul. Krasnaya 4, 220807 Minsk, Belarus. Tel: (0172) 338 875. Fax: (0172) 366 643. The television station, *Belarussian Television*, is located in Minsk at vul. A. Makayenka 9, 22087 Minsk. Tel: (0172) 334 501. Fax: (0172) 648 182. Telex: 152267. **Press:** There are four daily newspapers in Belarus: *Belarusskaya Niva, Sovetskaya Belorussiya, Znamya Yunosti* and *Zvyazda*, all printed in Russian.

PASSPORT/VISA

Note: In countries where Belarus has, as yet, no diplomatic representation, the Consulates/Embassies of the Russian Federation will continue to issue visas for Belarus and general Russian visas are valid in Belarus. A Belarussian visa can be obtained at the border points in Brest, Grodno or at Minsk airport. Belarussian visas are not valid for any other member states.

MONEY

There are plans for the introduction of a separate Belarussian currency.

TRAVEL

RAIL: There are 5590km (3494 miles) of track in use.
ROAD: Belarus has a road network of 265,600km (166,000 miles) of which 227,000km (141,875 miles) are paved.
URBAN: The city of Minsk has a metro system which is due to be expanded in 1993.

RESORTS & EXCURSIONS

Minsk: The capital of Belarus, 690km (429 miles) west of Moscow, dates from the 11th century, but little of the old city now survives except a ruined 12th-century Cathedral and a few 17th-century buildings. Modern Minsk is of symmetrical design with wide embankments flanking the Svisloch River. There is a *State Art Museum* and a *World War II Museum*. Tourists are also attracted by *Zhdanovichi*, a lakeland recreation area about 11 miles from the city.

BUSINESS PROFILE

ECONOMY: In comparision to other members of the CIS, Belarus has relatively few natural resources. The national industry and agriculture enjoy similar levels of productivity. The latter mainly produces grain and potatoes; livestock breeding also plays an important part. The manufacturing industry is concentrated in agricultural machines and cars which, together with the chemical industry, forms the major mainstay of the Belarussian economy. The Government has introduced several economic reforms.
COMMERCIAL INFORMATION: The following organisation can offer advice: Chamber of Commerce and Industry of the Republic of Belarus, Ul. Ya. Kolasa 65, 220843 Minsk. Tel: (0172) 660 460.

MOLDOVA

Location: Eastern Europe.

State Department for Tourism
Kishinev, Moldova
Tel: (0422) 233 338.

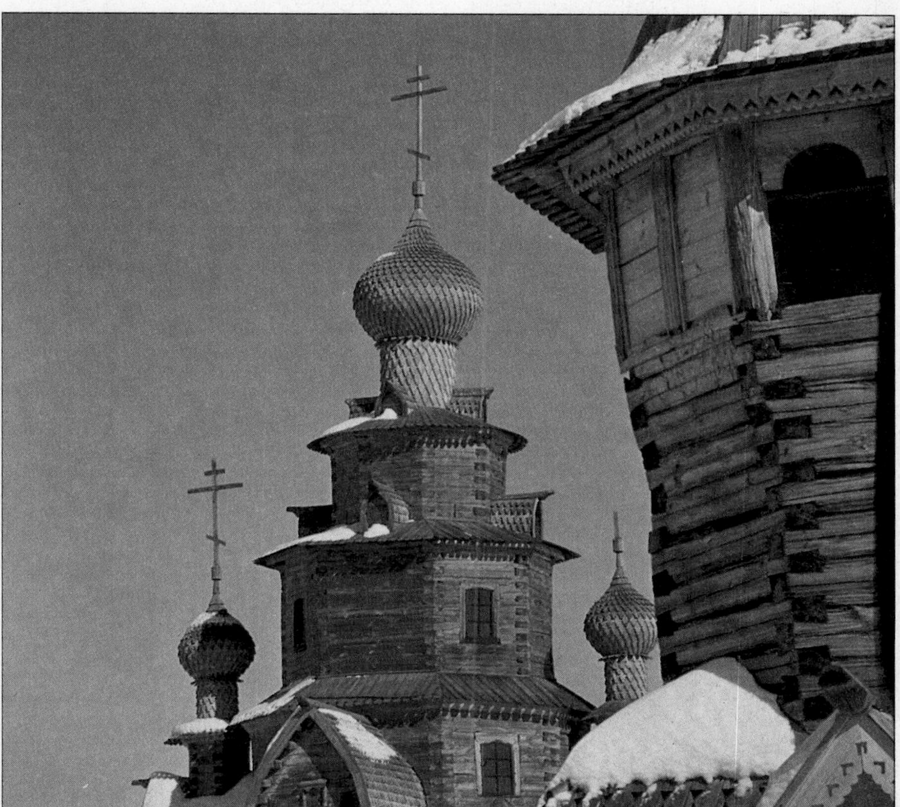

Kizhinev

Embassy of the United States of America
Strada Alexei Mateevich 103
Kishinev, Moldova
Tel: (0422) 233 894 *or* (0873) 151 2442.

AREA: 33,700 sq km (13,011 sq miles).
POPULATION: 4,341,000 (1989).
POPULATION DENSITY: 129 per sq km.
CAPITAL: Kishinev. **Population:** 720,000 (1989).
GEOGRAPHY: Moldova is a small state between the Ukraine and the River Prut, which constitutes the border to Romania.
LANGUAGE: Moldovan.
TIME: GMT + 2.
COMMUNICATIONS: The news agency, *Moldovan Information Agency – Moldovapres*, can be contacted at Str. Puskin 22, 277012 Kishinev, Moldova. Tel: (0422) 233 495. Fax: (0422) 234 371. Telex: 163140.
Radio/TV: *Radio Kishinev* broadcasts in both Romanian and Russian and is located at Str. Prerezhnikov 1, 277028 Kishinev; *Kishinev Television* can be found at the same address.

RESORTS & EXCURSIONS

Kishinev: Northwest of Odessa, Kishinev is the capital of Moldova and about five centuries old. The Republic's famous tradition of folk arts is well supported by its vivacious musical groups, and the vividly coloured costumes and carpets can be seen at their best in the *History and Regional Lore Museum*. A branch of the *Art Museum* is housed in a former 19th-century Cathedral, one of the finest of the city's historical monuments.

BUSINESS PROFILE

ECONOMY: The republic was formerly the largest wine region in the Soviet Union and continues to rely on this revenue. Agriculture plays the predominant part in the national economy, producing fruit and vegetables. Other industry is minimal.
COMMERCIAL INFORMATION: The following organisation can offer advice: Chamber of Commerce and Industry of the Republic of Moldova, Ul. Komsomolskaya 28, 277012 Kishinev. Tel: (0422) 221 552.

UKRAINE

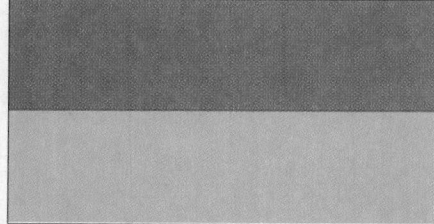

Location: Southeast Europe.

Note: Ukraine is about to open an Embassy in London.

Kievo – Pecherskaya Lavra, Kiev

For further information contact the Foreign Ministry in Kiev (tel: (044) 226 3376) or the Embassy of the Ukraine in Paris (tel: (1) 40 72 86 04).

Association of Foreign Tourism
Ul. Yroslavov Val 36
Kiev, Ukraine
Tel: (044) 212 5570.
British Embassy
Desyatinna 9
252025 Kiev, Ukraine
Tel: (044) 228 0504 *or* 228 0405. Fax: (010871) 144 5257 (satellite link). Telex: 1445256.
Embassy of the United States of America
Yuria Kotsyubinskovo 10
252053 Kiev 53, Ukraine
Tel: (044) 279 0188 *or* 279 1485. Fax: (044) 279 1485. Telex: 131142.

AREA: 603,700 sq km (233,088 sq miles).
POPULATION: 51,704,000 (1989).
POPULATION DENSITY: 86 per sq km.
CAPITAL: Kiev. **Population:** 2,602,000 (1989).
GEOGRAPHY: Ukraine is bordered by Belarus, Poland, Moldova and the Russian Federation. The north of this state is dominated by forests; its other two main features are wooded steppe with beech and oak forests and the treeless steppe. The majestic Dnepr divides Ukraine roughly in half, and flows into the Black Sea to the west of the Crimean peninsula.
LANGUAGE: Predominantly Ukrainian and Russian.
TIME: GMT + 2.
COMMUNICATIONS: The *Ukrainian Press Agency* is independent and can be contacted at vul. Sonyachna 14, 252190 Kiev, Ukraine. Tel/fax: (044) 449 0426. **Radio/TV:** *The State Committee for Television and Radio* at vul. Khreshchatik 26, Kiev, Ukraine (tel: (044) 228 4208) broadcasts in both Ukrainian and Russian, and also broadcasts programmes in Ukrainian to the USA and Europe. **Press:** The main dailies are *Democratychna Ukraina* (in Ukrainian), *Pravda Ukrainy*, *Rabochaya Gazeta* (in Russian and Ukrainian), *Silski Vista* (in Ukrainian) and *Za Vilnu Ukrainu*. *News from Ukraine* is published in English and available in 70 other countries.

PASSPORT/VISA

Note: The Consulates/Embassies of the Russian Federation no longer issue visas for the Ukraine. If transiting between Ukraine and other member states of the CIS, several visas must be held. Travellers who enter the Russian Federation from Ukraine without a Russian Federation visa are charged a penalty of US$250 for illegal entry. Ukrainian visas are *not* valid in the Russian Federation.
For stays up to 30 days, visitors do not have to supply proof of accommodation or an invitation. Visas are issued by Ukrainian consulates and embassies. When travelling direct, visas can be obtained at Kiev airport, Simferopol, and at the ports of Yalta and Odessa; a higher fee, however, is charged in such cases. These regulations do not apply when entering from another CIS member state. As a general rule, visitors should apply for a visa before travelling.
Cost: Individual visitors – US$30. Groups – US$25.

MONEY

Currency: Until recently, the Rouble and the Karbowanez were used simultaneously in Ukraine. An independent currency, the Griwna, is to be introduced at the beginning of 1993.

TRAVEL

SEA/RIVER: The main ports are Yalta and Yevpatoriya (both Crimea) and Odessa. Services are available to the Russian Federation ports of Novorossiysk and Sochi, as well as to Batumi and Sukhumi in Georgia. The republic's most important internal waterway is the River Dnepr.
RAIL: The 22,730km (14,207 miles) of railway track link most towns and cities within the Republic and further links extend from Kiev to all other CIS member states. There are direct lines to Warsaw in Poland, Budapest in Hungary and Bucharest in Romania.
ROAD: Of the 247,300km (154,563 miles) of road network, 201,900km (126,188 miles) are paved.

RESORTS & EXCURSIONS

Kiev: The capital of Ukraine and the third largest city in the CIS, Kiev still retains a charm, even though many of its buildings were destroyed in World War II. Places of interest are the *Cathedral of St Sophia* (built in 1037), the *Monastery of the Caves* (also dating from the 11th century), the medieval *Golden Gate*, the *Cathedral of St Vladimir* and the *Opera House*. The *Museum of Ukrainian Art* has an extensive collection of regional artists' work from the 16th century to the present. The *Historical Museum* contains crafts such as painted blown eggs with their intricate designs. The *Ukrainian Economic Exhibition* charts every aspect of the Ukranian economic achievement. There is a park and a beach on *Trukhaniv Island*.
Odessa: This port contains the magnificent *Potemkin Steps* leading down to its harbour. Also worth visiting are the *Opera House* with its ceiling adorned with scenes from Shakespeare's plays, the *Statue of the Duke of Richelieu*, the *Vorontsov Palace*, the *Assumption Cathedral* and the *Archaeological Museum* with its exhibits from the Black Sea area and Egypt.
Yalta: The Pearl of the Crimea is a charming resort famous for its *Chekhov Museum* in the house where the author lived for the last six years of his life. Here too are the *Wine Tasting Hall* and the *Vorontov Palace* designed by Edward Blore, one of the architects of Buckingham Palace. The famous Yalta Conference of 1945 took place in the *Liwadia Palace*.

BUSINESS PROFILE

ECONOMY: Approximately the size and population of France, Ukraine has only a quarter of its GDP. It is nonetheless the wealthiest republic of the CIS, with rich agricultural and mineral resources and well-established industry. Its only shortage is one of energy. Ukraine has officially endorsed an economic reform programme of privatisation and trade liberalisation, but has shown some reluctance to take the plunge.
COMMERCIAL INFORMATION: The following organisation can offer advice: Chamber of Commerce and Industry, Ul. Bolshaya Zhitomirskaya 33, 252055 Kiev. Tel: (044) 212 2911/3290/2840. Fax: (044) 212 3353. Telex: 131379.

HISTORY & GOVERNMENT

HISTORY: Once it became clear that the future of the Soviet Union as a single entity was in jeopardy, the crucial decision lay in the hands of the reforming ex-Communist President of the Ukraine and leader of the Ukraine National Movement, Leonid Kravchuk.

Kravchuk had secured his own position in the summer by attracting half of the popular vote at the presidential poll, defeating four other candidates, including his principal rival, Vyacheslav Chornovil of the militant nationalist movement Rukh. At the referendum on independence held on December 1, 1991, a majority of over 75% of the electorate voted to leave the Soviet Union. Even those areas in the east of the republic and the Crimea peninsula, which was transferred from Russian to Ukrainian jurisdiction in 1954, delivered a majority in favour. International recognition was forthcoming with little hesitation, assisted by the historical anomaly that Ukraine (and also Belarus) already held their own seats at the UN. The future relationship between Russia and Ukraine was the greatest uncertainty in the dissolution of the USSR, primarily because of the presence of a significant proportion of strategic and tactical nuclear systems in Ukraine, the future distribution of which was – in theory – governed by the US-Soviet START treaty. The new republics agreed to abide by its provisions. More difficult to settle has been the allocation of conventional systems between Russia and the Ukraine, specifically the Black Sea fleet and a number of key tank divisions. Many military and non-military issues were settled by the Minsk treaty of June 1992, including debt and currency questions, but the trickiest problems, the future of the Black Sea fleet and of sovereignty over the Crimean peninsula, have been left to future negotiation. In September, an apparent failure to tackle Ukraine's economic difficulties forced the resignation of independent Ukraine's first Prime Minister, Vladimir Fokin, followed by much of his cabinet. Leonid Kuchma will lead a new-look government. Ukraine's small neighbour, Moldova, tucked up against the Romanian border, is run by an ex-Communist reformer, Mircea Snegur, who won the presidency unopposed in December 1991. Moldova achieved recognition at the United Nations in March 1992. Historically and culturally linked to Romania, Moldova has territorial problems with a region known as Transdniestra which is largely populated by Ukrainians. Fighting broke out in the area in early March, repeating clashes that took place in 1990 and 1991: Igor Smirnov, 'president' of the self-styled republic, declared a state of emergency in the region after an incursion by Moldovan forces. The secessionists managed to secure the backing of ex-Red Army troops. The crisis has done irreparable damage to the economy and forced, on July 1, the resignation of the entire Moldovan government under Prime Minister Valery Muravsky. Andre Sangheli replaced him.

GOVERNMENT: Leonid Kravchuk, a Gorbachev appointee as leader of the Ukrainian Communist Party, has survived the transition to nationalist leader and won control of the presidency by a comfortable majority. The Moldovan Party leader and President Mircea Snegur made a similar transformation to lead his republic's drive for independence. Stanislav Shushkevich leads the Belarus republic.

CLIMATE

Temperate with warm summers, crisp, sunny autumns and cold, snowy winters.

SIMFEROPOL Ukraine (205m)

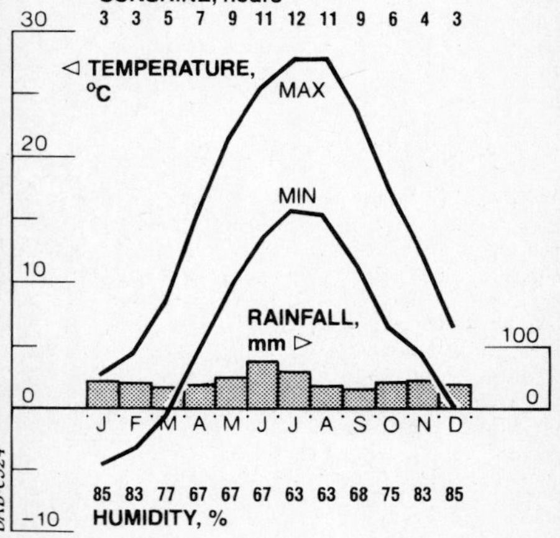

TEMPERATURE CONVERSIONS
-20 -10 0°C 10 20 30 40
0 10 20 30°F40 50 60 70 80 90 100

RAINFALL CONVERSIONS
0mm 200 400 600 800
0in 5 10 15 20 25 30

RUSSIAN FEDERATION

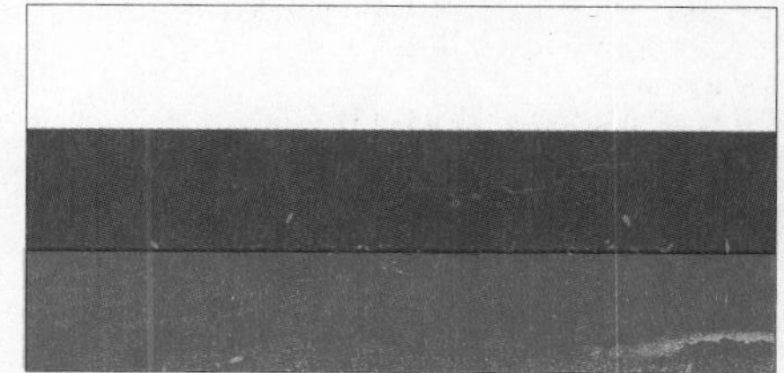

Location: Eastern Europe/Asia.

British Embassy
Sofiyskaya Naberezhnaya 14
Moscow 72, Russian Federation
Tel: (095) 230 6333 (8 lines) *or* 233 3563. Fax: (095) 233 3563. Telex: 413341.
Visa Section: Tel: (095) 233 2766.

British Consulate General
Room 252
Grand Hotel Europe
St Petersburg, Russian Federation
Tel: (0812) 312 0012. Fax: (0871) 144 5137. Telex: 144 5136.

BSCC (British Soviet Chamber of Commerce)
Business Centre
Suite 102, Ground Floor
Bolshoi Strochenovsky per 22/25
Moscow 113054, Russian Federation
Tel: (095) 230 6120. Fax: (095) 230 6124. Telex: 413523 BRISSU.

Embassy of the United States of America
Ulitsa Chaykovskogo 19/21/23
Moscow, Russian Federation
Tel: (095) 252 2450-59. Fax: (095) 255 9965. Telex: 413160 USGSO SU.

US Consulate-General
Ulitsa, Box L
Petra Lavrova Street 15
St Petersburg, Russian Federation
Tel: (0812) 274 8235. Telex: 64-121527.

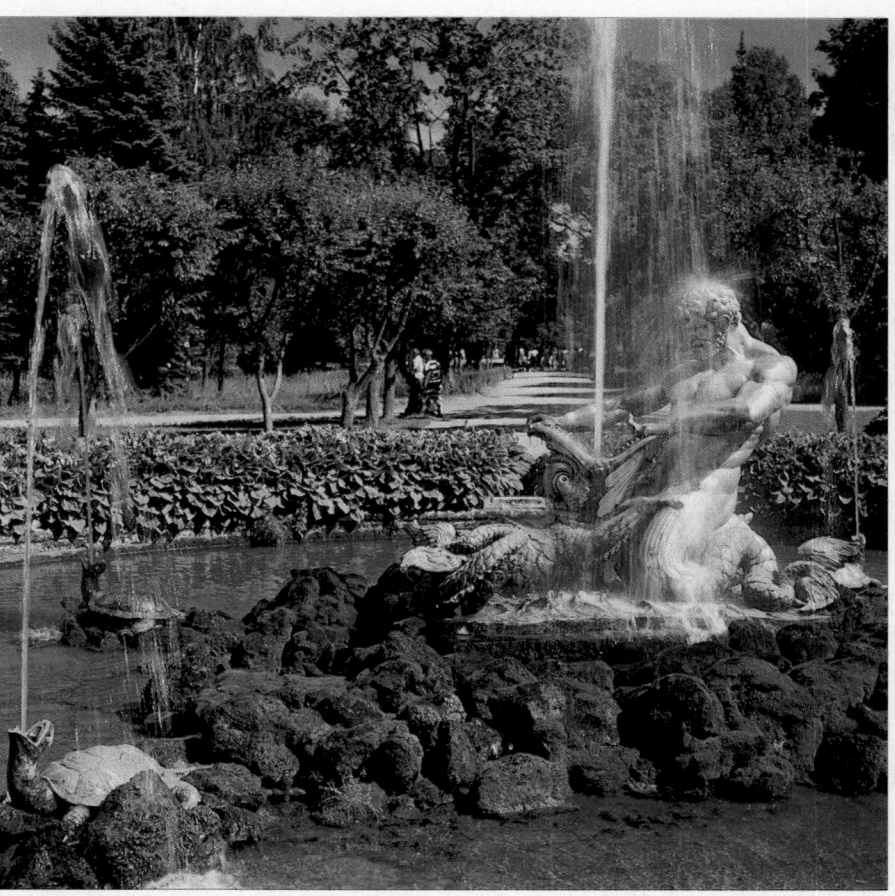

Pan Tours

Although Pan Tours, St. Petersburg, was only set up in 1991, it is now one of the leading international tourism companies in Russia. Since its inception, Pan Tours has shown itself to be an experienced tour operator and ground handler.
Besides St. Petersburg, known as *Venice of the North*, Pan Tours operates in 42 cities of the former USSR, including Moscow, Kiev, Yalta, Irkutsk, Khabarovsk, Novgorod and the towns of the Golden Ring.
The scale of its operations means that Pan Tours is the largest tour operator after Intourist and Sputnik.
One of the principal assets of the company is its experienced staff, many of whom have been working in tourism for as long as 25 years.

We offer the follwing services:

- Meet-and-greet service at the airport or station;
- Transfers by car, coach or minibus;
- Reserved accommodation at the best hotels;
- Arrangement of chauffeur-driven cars;
- Booking of domestic air and rail tickets;
- Provision of qualified multilingual guides;
- Arrangement of sightseeing tours, theatre and ballet tickets;
- Organisation of conferences and symposiums, including hire of halls and facilities;
- Hire of restaurants and banquet halls for special dinners and receptions
- Individual, business and scientific tours.

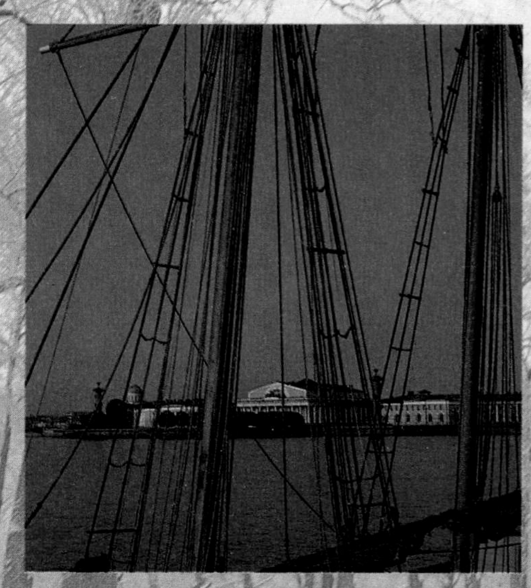

Pan Tours was cheif co-ordinator of the Russian national programme at the World Travel Market in London, November 1992.

On the right are references to our partners in St. Petersburg. In addition, pages 196 and 197 carry advertisements for hotels which are also in partnership with us; the famous *Astoria* hotel and the *Pribaltiyskya* hotel, the largest in St. Petersburg.

Pan Tours is the trade name of J V Panther (St. Petersburg).

St. Petersburg's office phone: (812) 166-2381 166-3558 fax: (812) 166-3558 291-3398 telex: 121634 ITCA SU

PULKOVSKAYA HOTEL

Situated on Victory Square at the south entrance to the great city of St. Petersburg, less than 10 minutes by car from the airport.

It boasts 17 deluxe suites, 80 single and 743 double rooms, a conference hall, restaurants and banquet halls.

ST. PETERSBURG HOTEL

A modern hotel located almost in the centre of the city, its position on the bank of the Neva affords it impressive river views. Its congress hall is one of the best-equipped in St. Petersburg.

There are 4 half-luxe and 6 deluxe suites, and 110 single and 294 double rooms.

KARELIA HOTEL

Especially suitable for sports teams and youth tourism, thanks to its situation in a park-like setting in one of St. Petersburg's new districts. The hotel's interior is decorated with motifs depicting the epic Karelian poem *Kalevala*.

It has 430 double and triple rooms for 1027

OLGINO MOTEL-CAMPING

Situated near the northern border of St. Petersburg, the refreshing atmosphere and majestic calm of the Karelian forest await you.

There are 22 deluxe suites, 15 single and 291 double rooms, as well as 69 wooden summer cottages.

'INTOURIST' BUS COMPANY

The leading tourist transport company in St. Petersburg. Comfortable coaches, minibuses and a range of cars are all at your disposal.

Your can also order taxis for sightseeing tours around St. Petersburg, or even a trip to Helsinki, across the border in Finland.

Moscow's office phone: (095) 208-4743 fax (095) 975-2619 telex: 412045 ABCT SU

Suzdal

AREA: 17,075,400 sq km (6,592,818 sq miles).
POPULATION: 147,386,000 (1989).
POPULATION DENSITY: 8.6 per sq km.
CAPITAL: Moscow. **Population:** 8,967,000.
GEOGRAPHY: The Russian Federation covers almost twice the area of the United States of America, and reaches from Moscow in the west over the Urals and the vast Siberian plains to the Sea of Okhotsk in the east. The border between European Russia and Siberia (Asia) is formed by the Ural Mountains, the Ural River and the Manych Depression. European Russia extends from the North Polar Sea across the Central Russian Uplands to the Black Sea, the Northern Caucasus and the Caspian Sea. Siberia stretches from the West Siberian Plain across the Central Siberian Plateau between Yenisey and Lena, including the Sayan, Yablonovy and Stanovoy ranges in the south to the East Siberian mountains between Lena and the Pacific coast including the Chukotskiy and Kamchatka peninsulas.
LANGUAGE: Russian.
TIME: Moscow, St Petersburg: GMT + 3.
Volgograd: GMT + 4.
Irkutsk: GMT + 8.
Tiksi, Yakutsk: GMT + 9.
Khabarovsk, Okhotsk, Vladivostok: GMT + 10.
Magadan, Sakhalin Island: GMT + 11.
Anadyr, Petropavlosk: GMT + 12.
Eulen: GMT + 13.
COMMUNICATIONS: The state information agency, *Informatsionnoye Telegrafnoye Agentstvo Rossii-Telegrafroye Agentstvo Suverennykh Stran (ITAR-TASS)* can be contacted in Moscow at Tverskoy bul. 10. Tel: (095) 290 3214. Telex: 411186. *Rossiyskoye Informatsionnoye Agentstvo-Novost (RIA – Novosti)* has contacts with foreign press in 110 countries and is located at Zubovsky bul. 4 in Moscow. Tel: (095) 201 2424. Fax: (095) 201 2119. Telex: 411321. *Interfax* and *Postfactum* are independent news agencies, both located in Moscow. **Press:** The main dailies in the Russian Federation are *Pravda* and *Izvestiya*, both published in Moscow.

TRAVEL

SEA: Due to its geographical placement, the Russian Federation has ports on its Pacific and Baltic shores and in the south on the Black Sea. The most important eastern ports are Vladivostok, Magadan, Nakhodka and Petropavlovsk; the most important western ports are St Petersburg and Kaliningrad on the Baltic. The only link to the Atlantic is the port of Murmansk on the Kola peninsula, which never freezes over. Major harbours on the Black Sea are Novorossiysk and Sochi. There are plans to build an extension to the St Petersburg harbour at Ust-Luga. Upgrading of facilities at Kaliningrad and Vyborg is also planned.

RAIL: The 87,090km (54,432 miles) of track are a vital part of the infrastructure due to the poor road system. The *Trans-Siberian Express* runs from Moscow to the Pacific coast of Siberia and on to Japan. There is a daily service, but the steamer from Nakhodka to Yokohama only sails approximately once a week. The through journey from Moscow to Yokohama takes ten days.
ROAD: The European part of the Russian Federation depends heavily on its road network, which totals 854,000km (533,750 miles) throughout the Federation. Of these, 624,100km (390,063 miles) are paved. Generally, the few roads in Siberia and further east are impassable during the winter.

RESORTS & EXCURSIONS

MOSCOW: The capital was founded in 1147, but there is evidence that there has been a settlement here since Neolithic times. The focal point of the city is *Red Square*, on one side of which is the *Kremlin* surrounded by a thick red fortress wall containing 20 towers in all, at intervals. In the Kremlin grounds are *Uspensky Cathedral*, designed by an italian architect (1475-79), containing three of the oldest Russian icons, the 14th-century *Grand Kremlin Palace* and the golden-domed *Belfry of Ivan the Great*. *St Basil's Cathedral* (built 1555-60), at another end of the square, is a well-known and colourful landmark. As the story goes, Ivan the Terrible was so overwhelmed by its beauty that he blinded the architect so that he could never create another building as impressive as this. The *State Historical Museum* is also located in Red Square. Other places of interest are: *Tretyakov Gallery*, containing the work of Russian artists and an extensive collection of icons, among them the 'Trinity' by Andrej Rubljov; the *Pushkin Museum of Fine Arts* with its cosmopolitan collection; the *Moscow Circus*, the old with animal acts and clowns and the new with more technical wonders; and the *Exhibition of Economic Achievements*, where on a large site in the northwest of the city all aspects of Russian life are displayed – agriculture, industry, culture and science. The site also contains a zoo and a circus and there is skating and skiing.
Excursions: The *State Museum of Ceramics*, 10km (6 miles) from the centre of Moscow, has a fascinating collection of Russian china, porcelain and glass. *Arkhangelskoye Estate*, a museum housed in a palace 16km (10 miles) from Moscow, exhibits European paintings and sculptures, but the main attraction is the grounds which are laid out in the French style.
Sergiyev Posad: Situated on two rivers this little town

Kremlin Wall, Moscow

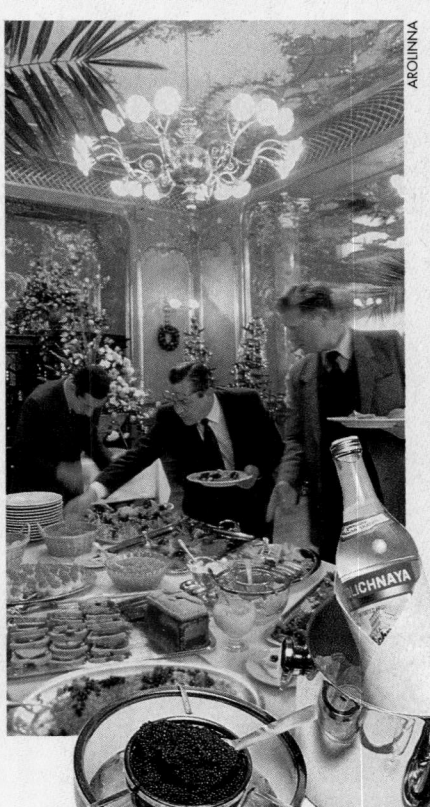

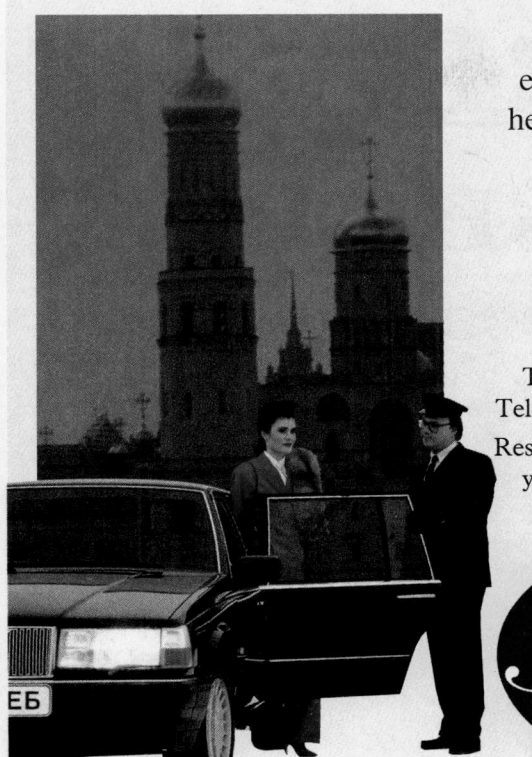

is the centre of the handmade toy industry; the *Toy Museum* has a collection beginning in the Bronze Age. The *Trinity Monastery of St Sergius* dates from the Middle Ages and its Cathedral has wonderful blue domes decorated with gold stars; the museum contains examples of Russian ecclesiastical art and crafts. East of Moscow is **Suzdal,** with over 50 examples of ancient architecture contained within a relatively small area, providing a wonderfully coherent vision of its past. Less than 32km (20 miles) away is **Vladimir,** which played a prominent part in the rise of the Russian state. The city's two magnificent Cathedrals date from the 12th century. Another notable monument is the *Golden Gate*, a unique example of old Russian engineering skills.

ST PETERSBURG: The Federation's second largest city, 715km (444 miles) northwest of Moscow, is known both as a cultural centre at the mouth of the River Neva and for its elegant buildings. In comparison to Moscow, which tended to orientate itself to the east, it always retained a European flair and could be described as a 'Window to the West'. It was built by Peter the Great in 1703 and remained the capital for 200 years of Tsarist Russia. Wide boulevards, slow flowing canals, bridges and some of the best examples of Tsarist architecture made the city known as the Venice of the North. Though badly destroyed in World War II, much of it is now reconstructed. Worth seeing are the *Summer Palace*, the *Winter Palace* and, attached to it, the *Hermitage*, housing the private collection of the Tsars. Exploring the city the visitor will inevitably see the *Alexandrovskaya Column*. *St Isaac's Cathedral* is one of the biggest dome-buildings of the world and, like the *Kazansky Cathedral*, houses a museum. Also worth a visit is the *St Peter and Paul Fort*, a former prison that is now a popular museum. Members of the Romanov dynasty are buried in the Cathedral of the same name. Further sights are the *Cathedral of St Nicholas* (Russian Baroque); the *Alexander Nevsky Monastery*; the *Botanical Gardens*; and the *Museums of Ethnography* and *Russian Art*.

Excursions: *Peteryard* is a former summer palace of Tsar Peter the Great and is known for its beautiful cascades and fountains. *Catherine Palace* is set among spacious gardens in nearby Pushkin.

MURMANSK: Almost due north of St Petersburg, this is the largest city within the Arctic Circle. This important port on the shores of Kola Bay is warmed by the waters of the Gulf Stream and is free of ice throughout the year. The northern lights are seen here in November and December and in March the *Sports Festival of the Peoples of the North* is held.

NOVGOROD: South of St Petersburg, this city was founded over 1100 years ago and was one of the most important towns of ancient Russia. Picturesquely located on the banks of the River Volkhov, the city possesses the oldest stone structure of Russia, *St Sophia's Cathedral* (mid-11th century) with its five naves.

River Volga

The mighty Volga provides an additional road into Russia. Travelling by river from Kazan to Rostov-on-Don makes a pleasant tour.

Kazan: The cultural centre of the Tartars, this city

MOSCOW

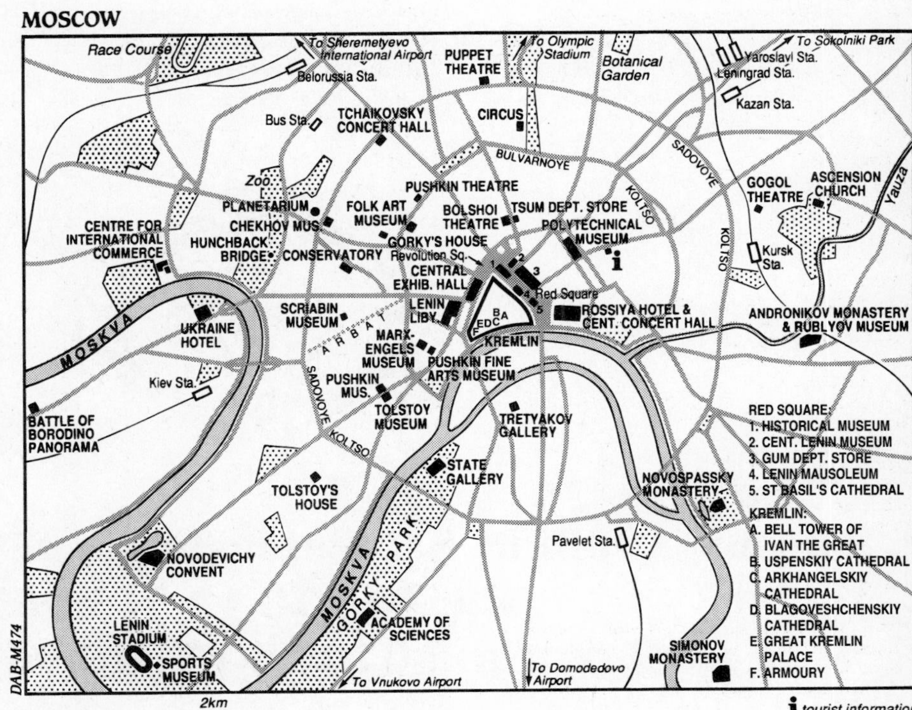

boasts a *Kremlin* dating from the 16th century which, with its towers and churches, is fascinating to visit. The *Tartar State Museum* and the 18th-century *Mosque* are also of interest.
Ulyanovsk: Lenin's birthplace; his parents' house here used to be a popular museum.
Volgograd: Formerly Stalingrad, the *Victory Museum* celebrates the victory over the Nazis, and the whole city is a monument to the year-long battle that took place there.
Rostov-on-Don: Once an Armenian town, its low buildings still show Armenian influences. Especially interesting is the *Cathedral of Resurrection*. There are several parks, four theatres, an orchestra, a racecourse and a beach. Rostov is the gateway to the Caucasus.
Sochi: The most popular resort of the former USSR, and a famous health spa, it is situated on the Black Sea's eastern coast beneath the dramatic Caucasus Mountains. An observation tower on Mt Bolshoi Akhun, 23km (14 miles) from the town, provides a spectacular view of the town, sea and mountains. There is a large *Riviera Park* with many tourist facilities and a *Dendarium* with beautiful and interesting trees and shrubs from all over the world.
Dagomys: A new holiday resort lying to the north of Sochi. Overlooking the Black Sea, it is beautifully located amongst thickly wooded hills and subtropical greenery. The new Intourist complex has a hotel, several restaurants, coffee shops and bars and sports facilities. An esplanade connects the complex with the beach where there are boats and pedaloes for hire. A visit to the Panorama Bar on the top floor of the Dagomys Hotel is recommended. Nearby is the *Dagomys State Tea Farm* where you can sample the fragrant Krasnodar tea accompanied by the delicious local pastries, jams, fruits and nuts whilst enjoying the spectacular mountain scenery.

Siberia

Siberia covers an area of over 12,800,000 sq km (4,000,000 square miles) and contains unimaginably vast stretches of forest and taiga. This 'sleeping land', the literal translation of its name, possesses a million lakes, 53,000 rivers and an enormous wealth of natural resources. Although the temperature in winter falls well below freezing point, the weather in summer can be very warm. Speeding through this country is the famous *Trans-Siberian Railway*, the longest continuous railway in the world, a journey on which is one of the greatest travel adventures. The most scenic part of the journey is between Khabarovsk and Irkutsk.
Khabarovsk on the Amur is the largest industrial centre of eastern Siberia and an important transport junction. The town (founded 1858) was named after the scientist Khabarov. Worth a visit is the regional museum which offers an insight into the different cultures of the Amur people. Among its 100 or so different goods for export are such exotic items as ginseng and Ussuri tigers.
Irkutsk is over 300 years old and owes much of its development to its location at the tradeways to Mongolia and China. At the end of the last century the city began to take on the aspect of a 'boom town' where trade in gold, fur and diamonds had suddenly created new wealth. It was to Irkutsk that many 19th-century revolutionaries, such as the Decembrists, were exiled. The *University of Irkutsk* was the first establishment of higher education in eastern Siberia. In former times as well as today this important Siberian city is one of the world's biggest suppliers of fur.

ST PETERSBURG

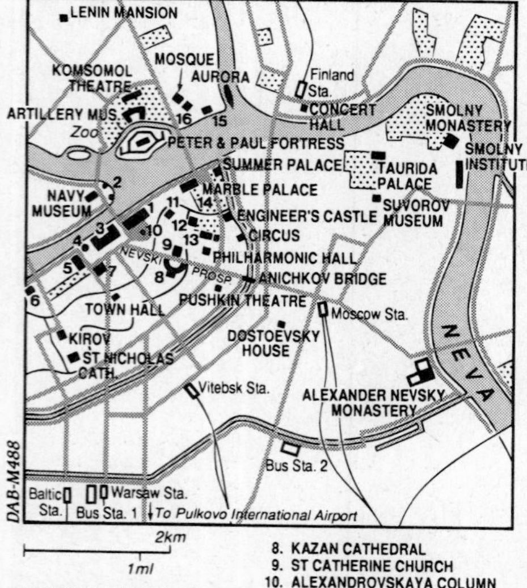

1. WINTER PALACE & HERMITAGE
2. ROSTRAL COLUMNS
3. ADMIRALTY
4. THE BRONZE HORSEMAN (PETER THE GREAT MON.)
5. SENATE
6. HISTORY OF ST PETERSBURG MUSEUM
7. ST ISAAC'S CATHEDRAL
8. KAZAN CATHEDRAL
9. ST CATHERINE CHURCH
10. ALEXANDROVSKAYA COLUMN & Dvortsovaya Square
11. PUSHKIN MUSEUM
12. CHURCH OF THE BLEEDING SAVIOUR
13. RUSSIAN & ETHNOGRAPHIC MUSEUMS
14. *Field of Mars*
15. PETER THE GREAT'S SMALL HSE.
16. MUSEUM OF THE REVOLUTION

BUSINESS PROFILE

ECONOMY: The Russian Federation dominates the CIS economy with 60% of industrial output, 55% of state revenues and 80% of export earnings. The policies which it chooses to adopt, moreover, will set the pace for the other republics. The greatest potential source of friction in the medium- and long-term is likely to be the dominance of the Russian economy within the CIS. Over the next 12 months, this is likely to manifest itself in the form of arguments over the distribution of foreign aid. With an established overseas infrastructure (embassies, banks, trading companies) Russia is in a better position than the other republics (with the possible exception of Ukraine) to exploit aid and trade opportunities. Russia's provisional aid request, satisfaction of which would require no less than a latter-day equivalent of the post-Second World War Marshall Plan (of which the Soviets were not recipients), envisages US$11-billion immediate humanitarian assistance (much of this has already been committed), US$7 billion for debt relief, US$5 billion for currency stabilisation and US$10-12 billion to finance import purchases. The IMF has offered a total of US$24 billion and the G7 summit in Munich in July 1992 agreed to arrange rescheduling of the former Soviet Union's external debt. Donors have made it clear that aid provisions will in future depend on the adoption of suitable economic measures based on the Polish model of 'shock treatment' in sudden removal and price restraint, subsidies, tariff barriers coupled with full-scale privatisation and deregulation. It seems that, despite initial trepidation, the country may be able to withstand the shock, although there are sharp disagreements among Yeltsin's advisers on the speed of implementation.
COMMERCIAL INFORMATION: The following organisation can offer advice: Chamber of Commerce and Industry of the Russian Federation, Ul. Ilynka 6, 103684 Moscow. Tel: (095) 923 4323. Fax: (095) 230 2455. Telex: 411126.

HISTORY & GOVERNMENT

HISTORY: Russia was the heartland of the former Soviet Union, with half its population. The Federation is not a homogenous entity, but hosts nearly 100 distinct nationalities and comprises 16 autonomous republics and 30 autonomous areas. A number of these have been the cause of major secessionist headaches for the Yeltsin government. Throughout 1991 and 1992 there have been outbreaks of fighting in North Ossetia and Chechen-Ingushetia (both of which are now the subject of states of emergency imposed by Moscow) and tension is very high in the autonomous region of Baskiria. The biggest worry is the million-strong region of Tatarstan where an independence referendum in March 1992 drew a 61% vote in favour. Yeltsin's other main problem is the desperate condition of the Russian economy. He has made a series of urgent appeals to the West to provide aid. Bilateral aid has been patchy and the Yeltsin government is increasingly looking to multi-lateral institutions such as the IMF, the World Bank, and the European Bank for Reconstruction and Development for financial support. The Yeltsin team came away from the July 1992 G7 summit in Munich with a provisional agreement on debt rescheduling (Russia's external debt is now estimated at US$37 billion) and an offer of US$24 billion through the IMF, conditional on the execution of the scheduled reform package (see *Economy*). By November 1992, however, only US$1 billion had been released by the IMF; the remainder was stalled because of the deteriorating political situation in Russia. In the hope of unlocking a major potential source of aid, particularly for the eastern part of the country, the Yeltsin government has devoted some attention to improving relations with Japan. The issue which most concerns the Japanese is the future of the Kurile Islands which were occupied by the Red Army in 1945. The Japanese have offered the Russians US$2.5 billion in soft loans and technical assistance with the promise of up to US$15 billion if sovereignty reverts to them. But Yeltsin is constrained, as Gorbachev was, by conservative resistance to territorial concessions. At the other end of Russia's sprawling territory, the Government is hoping to devise a special economic status for Kaliningrad (formerly Königsberg) under which it will become a 'Baltic Hong Kong', specialising in shipping, financial services and entrepôt trade. In the autumn of 1992, such considerations are secondary as the Yeltsin government faces its sternest political test yet. Conservative nationalists and communists have come together under the umbrella of a National Salvation Front, backed by powerful elements in the military, industry and elsewhere, with the aim of replacing Yeltsin with a coalition government. The issue will be settled at the Congress of People's Deputies session which opens in December.

CLIMATE

Northern & Central European Russia: The most varied climate; mildest areas are along the Baltic coast. Summer sunshine may be nine hours a day, but winters can be very cold.
Siberia: Very cold winters, but summers can be pleasant, although they tend to be short and wet. There is considerable seasonal temperature variation.
Southern European Russia: Winter is shorter than in the north. Steppes (in the southeast) have hot, dry summers and very cold winters. The north and northeastern Black Sea has mild winters, but heavy rainfall all the year round.

MOSCOW Russian Federation (156m)

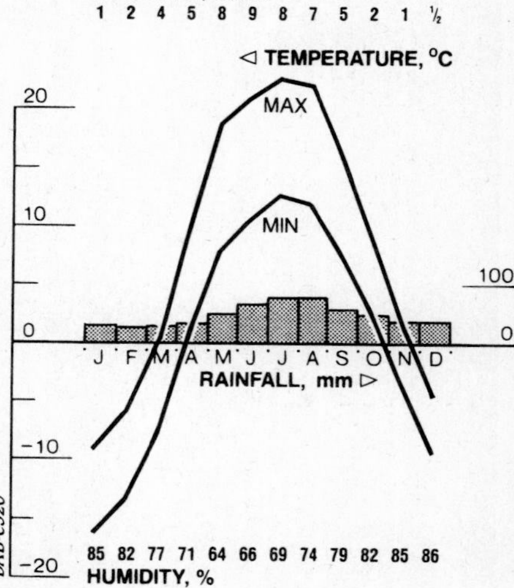

ST PETERSBURG Russian Federation (4m)

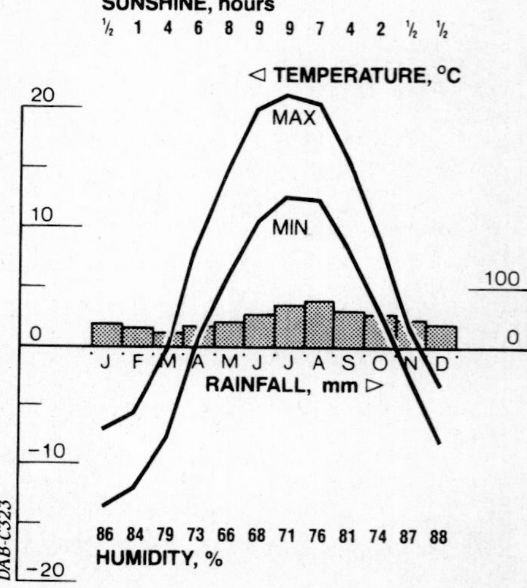

TRANS-CAUCASIA

This region lies between the Black Sea and the Caspian, and consists of the republics of Azerbaijan, Georgia and Armenia (the northern part of which was tragically devastated by the earthquake in 1988). It is bordered to the north by the mighty Caucasian mountain range. Within a relatively small area one can find a great variety of landscapes, from snow-capped mountains – the highest in Europe – to beaches and luxuriant greenery.

ARMENIA

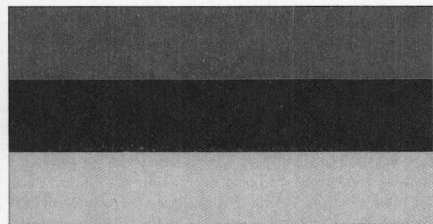

Location: Caucasus, east of Turkey.

Ministry of Foreign Affairs
ul. Antarain 188
375019 Yerevan, Armenia
Tel: (0885) 523 531. Fax: (0885) 565 616. Telex: 243313.
Embassy of the United States of America
c/o Hotel Hrazdan
Yerevan, Armenia
Tel: (0885) 253 5332 *or* 215 1122 *or* 215 1144.

AREA: 29,800 sq km (11,505 sq miles).
POPULATION: 3,283,000 (1989).
POPULATION DENSITY: 110 per sq km.
CAPITAL: Yerevan. **Population:** 1,215,000 (1989).
GEOGRAPHY: Armenia lies on the southern slope of the Armenian Mountains in the Lesser Caucasus and is bordered by Georgia, Turkey and Azerbaijan. Its highest peak is Mt Aragats (4009m), and even its deepest valleys lie 450-700m above sea level. Its biggest lake is Lake Sevan in the east.
LANGUAGE: Armenian, Kurdish and Russian.
TIME: GMT + 3.
COMMUNICATIONS: The state information news agency, *Armen Press*, can be contacted in Yerevan on (0885) 252 7481 *or* 252 6702. **Radio/TV:** *The State Committee for Television and Radio Broadcasting of the Armenian Republic* is located at ul. Mravyana 5, 375025 Yerevan. *Radio Yerevan* broadcasts in Armenian, Kurdish and Russian within Armenia, as well as broadcasting programmes in these three languages plus English, French, Spanish, Turkish, Arabic and Farsi (Persian) outside the country. *Armenian Television* has programmes in Armenian and Russian. **Press:** The main dailies are *Hayastan* and *Hayastani Hanrapetutyun* (published in both Armenian and Russian).

TRAVEL

RAIL: Armenia is linked by railway to Georgia and Azerbaijan and has international links with Turkey and Iran. The network of tracks in service totals 820km (513 miles).
ROAD: The road network comprises 10,200km (6375 miles), of which 9500km (5938 miles) are paved.

RESORTS & EXCURSIONS

Yerevan: The Armenian capital is one of the oldest cities in the world, founded nearly 2800 years ago in the time of ancient Babylon and Rome. On a clear day it is possible to see across the border with Turkey the twin peaks of Mount Ararat, where Noah's ark is said to have settled after the Flood. The *Matenadaran* in the city centre is one of the world's largest repositories of ancient manuscripts.

BUSINESS PROFILE

ECONOMY: The economic blockade of Armenia by its neighbour Azerbaijan threw the Armenian economy into an extreme crisis. The shortages affected fuels, foodstuffs and other important goods and forced the Government to declare a state of emergency in 1992. The reason for this boycott was the ongoing fighting in the Armenian enclave of Nagorno Karabach. Copper mining brings much needed revenue, other deposits include zinc, gold, marble, bauxite and molybdenum. The textile and chemical industry, as well as aluminium production, are also important, whereas the manufacturing industry is mostly concentrated on mechanical engineering. The privatisation of the agricultural sector is reaching completion; commodities include vegetables, tobacco and wine. Being one of the signatory states of the Black Sea treaty, the republic hopes for better regional co-operation. So far the Armenians have taken the most radical steps among the Trans-Caucasians by introducing private land ownership.
COMMERCIAL INFORMATION: The following organisation can offer advice: Chamber of Commerce and Industry of the Republic of Armenia, Ul. Alaverdyana 39, 375033 Yerevan. Tel: (0885) 256 5438. Telex: 243322 AFAZU.

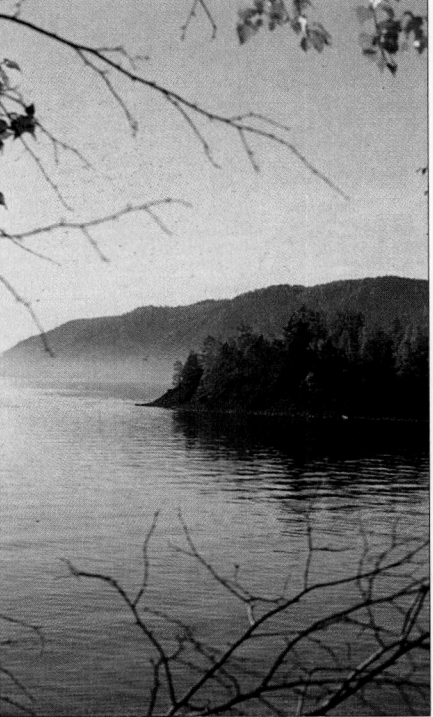

AZERBAIJAN

Location: Caucasus, western Caspian Sea region.

British Trade Office
c/o Starie Hotel, Baku, Azerbaijan
Tel: (0892) 926 307 *or* 925 502.
Embassy of the United States of America
c/o Hotel Intourist
Baku, Azerbaijan. Tel: (0892) 292 6306.

AREA: 86,600 sq km (33,436 sq miles).
POPULATION: 7,029,000 (1989).
POPULATION DENSITY: 81 per sq km.
CAPITAL: Baku. **Population:** 1,757,000 (1989).
GEOGRAPHY: Azerbaijan is bordered by the Russian Federation, Georgia and Iran, and is divided by the state of Armenia into a smaller western part in the Lesser Caucasus and a larger eastern part, stretching from the Greater Caucasus to the Mugan, Mili and Shirvan Steppes and bordered by the Caspian Sea in the east. Its highest peaks are Mt Bazar-Dyuki (4114m) and Sag-Dag (3886m).
LANGUAGE: Azerbaijani.
TIME: GMT + 4.
COMMUNICATIONS: *Azerinform* is the Azerbaijan Information news agency. *The State Committee for Television and Radio* can be contacted at ul. Mekhti Huseina 1, 370011 Baku, Azerbaijan. Tel: (0892) 927 155. *Radio Baku* does broadcasts in Azerbaijani, Russian, Turkish, Arabic and Farsi (Persian), while *Baku Television* broadcasts in Azerbaijani and Russian only.

TRAVEL

SEA: Baku is linked via the Caspian Sea with Krasnovodsk and the ports of Bandar Anzali and Bandar Nowshar in Iran.
RAIL: Azerbaijan is connected with Tbilisi in Georgia and Makhachkala. The rail track to Yerevan in Armenia runs through the autonomous republic of Nakhichevan, connecting with an international line to Tabriz in Iran. A joint-venture between the Iranian and the Azerbaijan governments will see the construction of an additional track to Nakhichevan through Iran, bypassing Armenia.
ROAD: Azerbaijan's road network totals 30,400km (19,000 miles) of which 28,600km (17,875 miles) are paved.

RESORTS & EXCURSIONS

Baku: A city with Islamic roots, Baku is the capital of Azerbaijan and overlooks the Caspian Sea. It has now been developed into one of the most important centres of the oil industry in the CIS. The presence of combustible gases brought fire worshippers from India who built a temple here some 300 years ago. Other monuments include the 15th-century *Palace of the Shirvan Shahs* and the unusually shaped *Maiden's Tower*.

BUSINESS PROFILE

ECONOMY: As none of the Trans-Caucasian states are particularly well placed economically, they will rely heavily on their existing trading links with the former Soviet republics. Azerbaijan has the greatest potential wealth from oil deposits around the capital, Baku. However, production levels have declined drastically in the last year, partly because of equipment failure and a shortage of spare parts. Unemployment has risen sharply and the majority of the population lives below the poverty line. The republic relies mainly on revenue from cotton, grapes and livestock breeding. Industry is dominated by foodprocessing, textiles and steel; other sectors are radio and telecommunications. The petrochemical industry has gone into decline due to decreasing oil production. Azerbaijan is a signatory of the Black Sea conference treaty.

COMMERCIAL INFORMATION: The following organisation can offer advice: Chamber of Commerce and Industry of the Republic of Azerbaijan, Ul. Kommunisticheskaya 31/33, 370601 Baku. Tel: (0892) 398 503.

GEORGIA

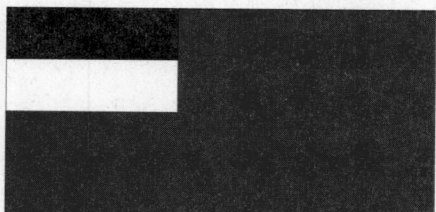

Location: Caucasus, northeast of Turkey.

Note: Although a former Soviet republic, Georgia is not a member of the CIS, even though visas issued by the Consulates/Embassies of the Russian Federation are still valid for Georgia. Touristic travels should be avoided at present as several nationality conflicts, especially in South Ossetia, make the internal situation very unstable. South Ossetia declared independence from Georgia in 1991 and plans to form a union with North Ossetia, part of the Russian Federation.

Embassy of the United States of America
c/o Metechi Palace Hotel
Tbilisi, Georgia
Tel: (08832) 744 623.

AREA: 69,700 sq km (26,911 sq miles).
POPULATION: 5,449,000 (1989).
POPULATION DENSITY: 78 per sq km.
CAPITAL: Tbilisi. **Population:** 1,264,000 (1989).
GEOGRAPHY: Georgia is bordered by the Russian Federation, the Black Sea, Turkey, Armenia and Azerbaijan. The state is crossed by the ranges of the Greater Caucasus (highest peak: Mt Elbrus, nearly 5500m, located in the Russian Federation). High valleys, wide basins, health spas with famous mineral waters, caves and waterfalls combine in this land of varied landscapes and striking beauty.
LANGUAGE: Predominantly Georgian. Russian, Ossetian, Abkhazian and Adzharian are also spoken.
TIME: GMT + 4.
COMMUNICATIONS: *The Georgian News Agency* is located at pr. Rustaveli 42, 380008, Tblisi, Georgia.
Radio/TV: *The Department of Television and Radio Broadcasting* can be contacted at Kostava 68, 380071 Tblisi. Tel: (08832) 362 460. *Radio Tblisi* has programmes in Georgian, Russian, Azerbaijani, Abkhazian, Armenian and Ossetian, while *Tblisi Television* only has programmes in Georgian and Russian.

TRAVEL

SEA: The main ports are Batumi and Sukhumi, providing international connections with the Black Sea and Mediterranean ports.
RAIL: The main tracks, extending to the Russian Federation, run along the Black Sea coast. The line to Armenia continues into eastern Turkey. Further connections exist to Azerbaijan.
ROAD: 35,100km (21,938 miles) of roads, of which nearly all are paved, are presently in use in the republic.

RESORTS & EXCURSIONS

Sukhumi: Of interest are the ruined 11th-century *Castle of the Turkish Bagratid King*, the *Botanical Gardens*, *Shrom Cave* with its amazing stalactites and stalagmites and the monkey-breeding farm.
Batumi: A Black Sea port near the Turkish border, Batumi still has a decidedly Turkish character. Well worth a visit are the mosque, the museum with a superb national costume collection, the circus, park and theatre.
Tbilisi: The capital of Georgia is set in the midst of several mountain ranges in the valley of the River Kura with a Mediterranean climate. It is best seen from the top of Mount Metsminda. In the old part of the town is the *Georgian National Museum*, which houses a good collection of icons, frescoes and porcelain. Also interesting is the open-air *Museum* with its examples of regional farm houses. The distinctive outlines of Georgian churches can be glimpsed among the more modern buildings of this lively, bustling city. Plekhanov Prospekt is the base for the *Georgian State Philharmonic Orchestra* and the internationally known *Georgian National Dance Troupe*.
Mtskheta: This ancient former capital of Georgia contains the *Sveti Tskhoveli Cathedral*, said to have been built on the spot where Christ's crucifixion robe was found in 328AD. The present Cathedral is a good example of 15th-century Georgian architecture.
Gori: The birthplace of Stalin, it also contains the ruins of a 12th-century fortress and a 16th-century church dedicated to St George.
In the southeast of the Caucasian Mountains is the ancient city of **Sheki.**
Shemakha is famous for its carpet factory.

BUSINESS PROFILE

ECONOMY: The economic potential of Georgia lies in the exploration of its natural resources and expanding Black Sea tourism, as there are already a large number of spas and resorts. Known deposits of mangan, coal, oil and peat are to be excavated. The industrial sector is dominated by shipbuilding, foodprocessing and fertilizers. Principal agricultural commodities are tea, wine, fruit (especially citrus fruit), tobacco and vegetables. Georgia signed the treaty of the Black Sea conference in 1992, promoting regional co-operation. All three republics have committed themselves to some degree of market-based economic reform.
COMMERCIAL INFORMATION: The following organisation can offer advice: Chamber of Commerce and Industry of Georgia, Prospekt I. Chavchavadze 11, 380079 Tbilisi. Tel: (08832) 230 045 *or* 220709 *or* 22554. Fax: (08832) 235 760. Telex: 212183.

HISTORY & GOVERNMENT

HISTORY: Historically the most turbulent region of the former Soviet Union, the formation of the CIS has been accompanied by political violence and turmoil in all three constituent states. Elections in Georgia brought to power a veteran dissident, Zviad Gamsakhurdia, as President in a landslide victory with 87% of the poll. However, his erratic and repressive behaviour drew increasing opposition throughout the republic, including the resignation of Prime Minister Tengiz Sigua, until an armed insurrection in December 1991 forced Gamsakhurdia into exile. Tengiz Sigua took over the Government for several months before he was replaced by the former Soviet Foreign Minister, Eduard Schevardnadze. Sigua was reappointed Prime Minister by Schevardnadze in October 1992, after the latter had strengthened his political position with a 96% vote for his sole candidacy in that month's presidential election. Gamsakhurdia has since made three concerted but unsuccessful attempts to storm the capital with loyal troops. Georgia has also suffered secessionist problems with the autonomous province of South Ossetia, which lies inside Georgia, but is heavily populated by ethnic Russians. South Ossetia voted heavily against breaking Georgia's links with Moscow in the referendum on the republic's independence. Since then it has made clear its wish to break away from Georgia and forge closer links with Russia and particularly its sister province of North Ossetia (see *Russian Federation* above). After fighting between South Ossetians and militant Georgian nationalists, Schevardnadze sought out Russia's President Yeltsin and the two leaders signed a co-operation agreement on ethnic disputes at the end of June. The agreement proved impotent, however, to prevent the outbreak of fighting in Abkhazia, another autonomous region in Georgia bordering on the Black Sea, which seeks independence. Georgian troops have waged a bitter struggle with Muslim secessionist guerrillas backed by volunteers from the northern Caucasus. The guerrillas have so far held the upper hand, wresting several tracts of territory from the Georgians through the late summer and autumn of 1992. To the south, the republics of Armenia and Azerbaijan have been locked in an apparently intractable war since 1989. At the heart of the dispute is the enclave of Nagorno-Karabakh. This is an enclosed, mountainous region of Azerbaijan, populated predominantly by Christian Armenians, which holds autonomous status within the largely Muslim Azerbaijani republic. 1991 brought a lull in the fighting, but a new more dangerous phase opened at the end of the year after the dissolution of the Soviet Union. At the end of November, the Azeri parliament voted to annul Nagorno-Karabakh's autonomous status and bring it under full Azeri control. Armenian forces in the enclave, who are heavily armed – to the extent of helicopter gunships – have made clear their intention to keep the Azeris out and hold on to a strip of territory (the Lachin corridor) linking the enclave and Armenia proper. Azerbaijan responded with an economic blockade. The war constantly threatens to draw in other regional powers – Russia on the side of the Armenians; Turkey and possibly Iran supporting the Azeris. While the Nagorno crisis has dominated the political agenda in both Armenia and Azerbaijan, both states have embarked on a course of independence, having secured the backing of their respective populations. In March 1992, the incumbent Communist President of Azerbaijan, Ayaz Mutallibov, was ousted in a coup. After an unsuccessful comeback attempt on Mutallibov's part, national elections were held in the republic in June. These were won by the opposition nationalist, Abulfaz Elchibey. The Popular Front, which Elchibey leads, favours Azeri withdrawal from the CIS. On the issue of Nagorno-Karabakh, Elchibey has declared himself in favour of a UN-sponsored settlement. For the time being, however, with attitudes hardening on both sides, there is no end to the fighting in sight.
GOVERNMENT: President Levon Ter-Petrosyan in Armenia enjoys a power base founded on the strength of the former Communist Party. President Abulfaz Elchibey of Azerbaijan took over from a Communist government in June 1992. In Georgia, Eduard Schevardnadze is the elected President.

CLIMATE

Generally warm, but low temperatures can occur, particularly in the mountains and valleys. Most rainfall in the west.

TBILISI Georgia (490m)

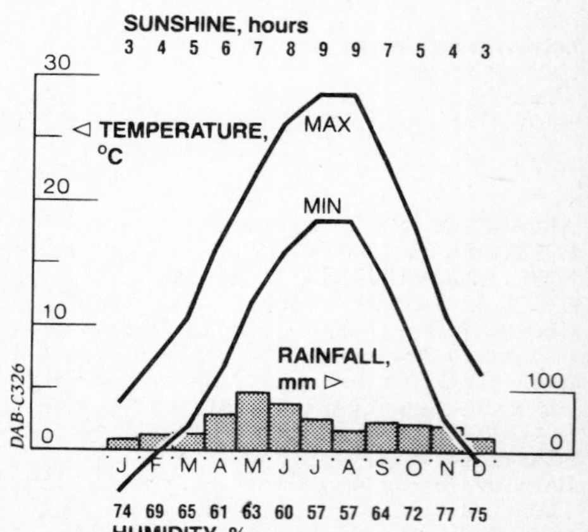

CENTRAL ASIA

This region consists of five states: Kazakhstan, Kirghizia, Tajikistan, Turkmenistan and Uzbekistan. These are lands of mountains and deserts, interspersed with oases of cotton plantations, orchards and vineyards. Until the beginning of the 20th century, they were largely inaccessible to visitors; Central Asia is, however, a richly rewarding area, with many Central Asian cities now open to the public.

Cemetery, Khiva

KAZAKHSTAN

Location: Central Asia, between Caspian Sea and China.

British Embassy
c/o Hotel Kazakhstan
Alma-Ata, Kazakhstan
Tel: (03272) 619 130.
The British Embassy will share premises with the German Embassy as soon as they re-locate. Contact the Foreign Office for further information.
Embassy of the United States of America
c/o Hotel Kazakhstan
Alma-Ata, Kazakhstan
Tel: (03272) 619 056.

AREA: 2,717,300 sq km (1,049,150 sq miles).
POPULATION: 16,538,000 (1989).
POPULATION DENSITY: 6.1 per sq km.
CAPITAL: Alma-Ata. **Population:** 1,132,000 (1989).
GEOGRAPHY: Kazakhstan is the second largest state in the Commonwealth, and is bordered by the Russian Federation, the Caspian Sea, Turkmenistan, Uzbekistan, Kirghizia and China. Its main features are steppe and wheatfields. The Aral Sea and Lake Balkhash are the largest expanses of water.
LANGUAGE: Predominantly Kazakh, also Russian, Uygur and other regional languages and dialects.
TIME: GMT + 6.
COMMUNICATIONS: *KazTAG*, the Kazakh news agency, can be contacted at pr. Kommunistichesky 75, Alma-Ata, Kazakhstan. Tel: (03272) 625 037.
Radio/TV: *The State Committee for Television and Radio* is located at ul. Mira 175, 480013 Alma-Ata. Tel: (03272) 633 716. *Kazakh Radio* has programmes in Kazakh, Russian, Uygur, German and Korean; *Kazakh Television* has programmes in Kazakh, Russian, German and Uygur.
Press: The main dailies are *Freundschaft* (published in German), *Kazakhstanskaya Pravda* (an independent newspaper published in Russian), *Kommuizm Tugi* (published in Uygur), *Lenin Kichi* (published in Korean), *Leninskaya Smena* (published in Russian), and *Leninshilzhas* and *Sosialistik Kazakhstan* (both published in Kazakh).

TRAVEL

RAIL: The total railway track network amounts to 14,460km (8985 miles). Generally, the highest concentration is in the north and connects with the Russian Federation system. The lines from Alma-Ata in the north connect with the Trans-Siberian Railway running west to Chimkent and finally to Orenburg in the Russian Federation. A new link between Druzhba and Alataw Shakou in China, was opened in 1991 and was available to passengers from mid-1992.
ROAD: 164,900km (103,063 miles) of road, of which 61% are paved, are in use.

RESORTS & EXCURSIONS

Alma-Ata, meaning 'Father of Apples' (reference to the local abundance of the fruit), is the capital of Kazakhstan. This relatively young city (founded in 1854) lies at the foot of the majestic Zaili Ala-Tau mountain range. The *State Museum of Kazakhstan* is housed in a former *Cathedral*, which at 56m (183ft) is one of the world's largest wooden structures and which was built without a single iron nail. A magnificent panorama of the city can be viewed from the top of Mount Kok-Tyube (Green Mountain); the summit is reached by funicular.

BUSINESS PROFILE

ECONOMY: Kazakhstan has large natural deposits – iron, nickel, zinc, manganese, coal, chromium, copper, lead, gold and silver are presently being mined. All consumer goods had to be imported from other republics of the then Soviet Union. Therefore, the Government lays priority on the expansion of the manufacturing industry. Agriculture is also important; principal commodities include wheat, meat products and wool. Trade with neighbouring countries has increased rapidly, especially South Korea and China. The irrigation demands on rivers in Kazakhstan and Uzbekistan to feed cotton fields caused the Aral Sea, into which the rivers flow, to shrink by one-third in the space of 20 years – this may qualify as the world's greatest single ecological disaster. Two large oil fields are presently being exploited in an American joint-venture which might give incentive to other such projects. Kazakhstan has also joined the Central Asian economic union ECO.
COMMERCIAL INFORMATION: The following organisation can offer advice: Chamber of Commerce and Industry of Kazakhstan, Prospekt Kommunistichesky 93/95, 480091 Alma-Ata. Tel: (03272) 621 446 *or* 621 620 *or* 620 995. Fax: (03272) 620 594. Telex: 251228 KAZINSU.

KIRGHIZIA

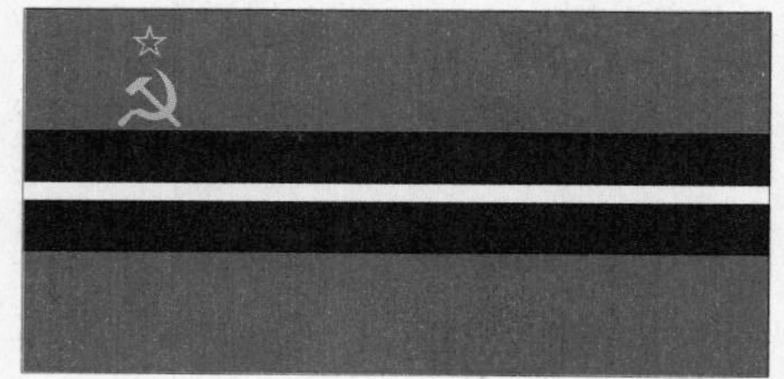

Location: Central Asia, northwest of China.

Ministry of Foreign Affairs
ul. Kirova 205
72003 Bishkek, Kirghizia
Tel: (03312) 225 914.
Embassy of the United States of America
Derzhinsky Prospek 66
Bishkek, Kirghizia
Tel: (03312) 222 270.

AREA: 198,500 sq km (76,640 sq miles).
POPULATION: 4,291,000 (1989).
POPULATION DENSITY: 21.6 per sq km.
CAPITAL: Bishkek (Frunze). **Population:** 626,000 (1989).
GEOGRAPHY: Kirghizia is bordered by Kazakhstan, Uzbekistan, Tajikistan and China. The majestic Tien-Shan Range occupies the greater part of the area. Highest peak: Pik Pobedy (6413m).
LANGUAGE: Predominantly Kirghisian, also Uzbek, Russian, Kazakh and various regional languages and dialects.
TIME: GMT + 6.
COMMUNICATIONS: *KirTAG*, the Kirghisian news agency, is located in Bishkek. **TV/Radio:** *Dom Radio* has programmes in Kirghisian, Russian, Dungan and German and is located at pr. Molodoy, gvardii 63, 720885 Bishkek 10, Kirghizia. The main dailies are published in Bishkek and include *Bishkek Shamy*, *Kyrgyz Tuusu* and *Verherny Bishkek* (Bishkek Evening Newspaper).

RESORTS & EXCURSIONS

Spectacular mountain ranges and valleys are the main attractions of this state, as is Lake Issyk-Kul with its warm, sandy beaches and thermal springs.
Bishkek: The tree-lined roads between the railway station and the centre of the capital house the *Krupskaya Russian Drama Theatre*, the *Kirghiz State Opera & Ballet Theatre*, and the *Chernyshevsky Public Library*. Attractions in the city centre include the *General Frunze Museum*, the *Art Museum* and the *Kirghiz Drama Theatre* on Pervovo Maya Street.

BUSINESS PROFILE

ECONOMY: Agriculture dominates the national economy producing wheat, cotton, tobacco, vegetables and fruit, though the actual cultivable area is small. Of further importance is livestock breeding. Deposits of oil, gas, coal, antimony and mercury are part of Kirghizia's natural resources. The industry concentrates on food-processing, textiles, metal manufacturing and machines. One major problem facing the republic is the inadequate infrastructure. The Government passed a drastic reform programme to encourage economic growth. Kirghizia is a member of ECO.
COMMERCIAL INFORMATION: The following organisation can offer advice: Chamber of Commerce and Industry of the Republic of Kirghizia, Ul. Kirova 205, 720300 Bishkek. Tel: (03312) 264 942. Telex: 251239 SALAM SU.

TAJIKISTAN

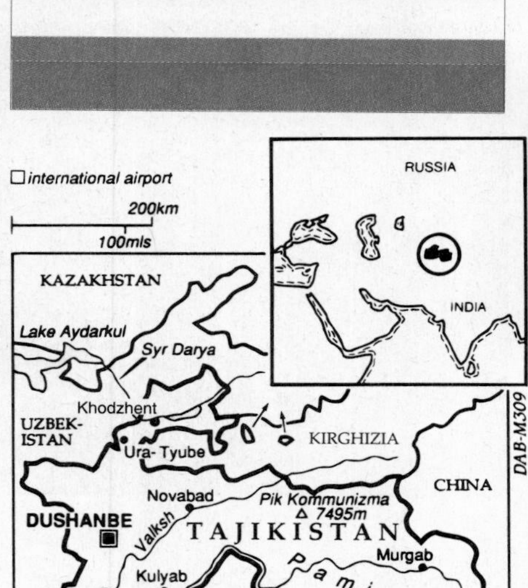

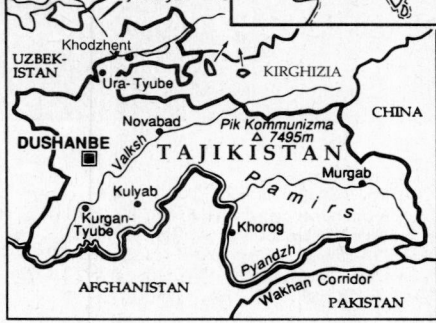

Location: Central Asia, between Afghanistan and China.

Embassy of the United States of America
Interim Chancery
Ainii Street 39
Dushanbe, Tajikistan
Tel: (03772) 248 233.

AREA: 143,100 sq km (55,250 sq miles).
POPULATION: 5,112,000 (1989).
POPULATION DENSITY: 35.7 per sq km.
CAPITAL: Dushanbe. **Population:** 604,000 (1989).
GEOGRAPHY: Tajikistan is bordered by Kirghizia, Uzbekistan, Afghanistan and China. Most of the state is occupied by the Pamir range, with the highest mountains in the CIS. The highest peak reaches 6858m. In the valleys, cotton, maize and fruit are grown.
LANGUAGE: Predominantly Tajik, also Uzbek, Russian and other regional languages and dialects.
TIME: GMT + 5.
COMMUNICATIONS: *Khovar*, the Tajikistan news agency, is located at pr. Lenina 37 in Dushanbe. **Radio/TV:** *The State Television & Radio Corporation* is at ul. Bekhzod 7A, 734013 Dushanbe. *Tajik Radio*, located at Kuchai Chapayev 25, 734025 Dushanbe, has programmes in Tajik, Uzbek, Russian and Farsi (Persian). *Tajik Television*, located at ul. Bekhzod 7A, 734013 Dushanbe, has programmes in Tajik, Uzbek and Russian. **Press:** The main dailies are *Djavononi Todjikiston*, *Omuzgor*, *Sadoi mardum* and *Tochikistoni* (all published in Tajik); *Komsomolets Tajikistana* and *Narodnaya Gazeta* (both published in Russian) and *Sovet Tochikistoni* (published in Uzbek).

RESORTS & EXCURSIONS

Dushanbe: The capital is a modern city with tree-lined roads on the banks of the Dushanbinka River. Near the railway station is the *Historical & Art Museum* opposite the Intourist Office. The colourful municipal market near here (one of two markets) is well worth a visit, not least for its spectacular view of the surrounding mountains. Moscow Square houses the *Ayni Opera & Ballet Theatre*. Further along the main road the *Firdausi Library*, the *Philharmonia* and the *Concert Hall* are to be found.

BUSINESS PROFILE

ECONOMY: Tajikistan's mainstay is its extensive uranium deposits, which will secure a stable income in the future. Agriculture is very limited, and livestock breeding is the most important business.
COMMERCIAL INFORMATION: The following organisation can offer advice: Chamber of Commerce and Industry, Ul. Mazayeva 21, 734012 Dushanbe. Tel: (03772) 279 519.

TURKMENISTAN

Location: Central Asia, northwest of Afghanistan and north of Iran.

Embassy of the United States of America
c/o Yubilenaya Hotel
Ashkhabad, Turkmenistan
Tel: (036320) 244 908.

AREA: 488,100 sq km (188,455 sq miles).
POPULATION: 3,534,000 (1989).
POPULATION DENSITY: 7.2 per sq km.
CAPITAL: Ashkhabad. **Population:** 402,000 (1989).
GEOGRAPHY: Turkmenistan shares borders with Afghanistan, Iran, Uzbekistan and Kazakhstan. To the west is the Caspian Sea. More than 80% of the area of this state is taken up by desert – this includes the Kara-Kum Desert, the largest in the CIS.
LANGUAGE: Predominantly Turkmenian.
TIME: GMT + 5.
COMMUNICATIONS: The news agency is *Turkmen Press* in Ashkhabad. **Radio/TV:** *The State Committee for Television and Radio Broadcasting* is located at Kurortnaya III, 744024 Ashkhabad. *Turkmen Radio* and *Turkmen Television* broadcast in both Turkmenian and Russian. **Press:** *Sovet Turkmenistani* and *Turkmenskaya Iskra* are the main dailies.

TRAVEL

SEA: Services sail via the Caspian Sea to several Iranian ports and Baku (Azerbaijan). One important inland waterway is the Amu-Dar'ya.
RAIL: The main rail connections link Krasnovodsk in the west via Ashkhabad to Chardzhou in the east. Here, a line runs further east to other Central Asian republics and another joins the network of the Russian Federation. There are plans to extend the system to Mashhad in Iran, where direct links to Istanbul in Turkey exist.
ROAD: A new road between Ashkhabad and Tashauz has recently come into service.

RESORTS & EXCURSIONS

Ashkhabad: The capital of Turkmenistan is a green and sprawling city. Many of its sights line Svoboda Prospekt, the main street. The *Fine Arts Museum* is housed in the same attractive building with oriental windows and pillars as the *Museum of Local History & Ethnography*. Two theatres, the glass factories and the hugely popular racecourse are of interest to visitors, as is the *Botanical Garden* behind the *Agricultural College*.

BUSINESS PROFILE

ECONOMY: Turkmenistan became a member of the Central Asian economic union ECO in 1992. As the republic's arable land only makes 2% of the total area, agricultural activities are limited. The major products are cotton, fruit, vegetables and maize.
COMMERCIAL INFORMATION: The following organisation can offer advice: Chamber of Commerce and Industry, Ul. Lakhuti 17, 744000 Ashkhabad. Tel: (036322) 55756.

UZBEKISTAN

Location: Central Asia, northeast of Turkmenistan.

Embassy of the United States of America
Chelanzanskaya 55
Tashkent, Uzbekistan
Tel: (03217) 771 407.

AREA: 447,400 sq km (172,741 sq miles).
POPULATION: 19,906,000 (1989).
POPULATION DENSITY: 45 per sq km.
CAPITAL: Tashkent. **Population:** 2,079,000 (1989).
GEOGRAPHY: Uzbekistan is bordered by Afghanistan, Turkmenistan, Kazakhstan, Kirghizia and Tajikistan and has a colourful and varied countryside. The south and east are dominated by the Tien-Shan and Pamir-Alay mountain ranges, the Kyzyl Kum Desert lies to the northeast. The northwest is bounded by the Aral Sea and the largely uninhabited Ust Urt Plateau with its vast cotton fields.
LANGUAGE: Predominantly Uzbek, also Uygur and Russian.
TIME: GMT + 5.
COMMUNICATIONS: *UzTAG*, the Uzbek news agency, can be contacted at ul. Khamza 2, Tashkent, Uzbekistan. Tel: (03712) 394 982. **Radio/TV:** *The State Committee for Television &Radio* can be contacted at ul. Khorezmskaya 49, Tashkent, Uzbekistan. Tel: (03712) 410 551. *Radio Tashkent* has programmes in Uzbek, Uygur, English, Urdu, Hindi, Farsi (Persian) and Arabic, and can be contacted at at ul. Khorezmskaya 49, 700047 Tashkent, Uzbekistan. Tel: (03712) 330 249. Telex: 116139. *Tashkent Television Studio* is located at ul. Navoi 69, Tashkent. **Press:** The main dailies are *Khaik Suzi*, *Sovet Uzbekistoni* and *Yash Leninchy* (all published in Uzbek); and *Molodets Uzbekistana* and *Pravda Vostoka* (both published in Russian).

PASSPORT/VISA

The Embassies of the Russian Federation no longer issue visas for Uzbekistan. A Russian visa is valid only for transit passengers. All other passengers can obtain visas at the Tashkent airport.
Cost: Up to 7 days – US$30; up to 30 days – US$50; and up to 1 year – US$100.

TRAVEL

The capital, Tashkent, has a metro; the network was expanded in 1991.

RESORTS & EXCURSIONS

Samarkand is a glittering gem from the past, transformed in the 14th century by Tamerlane into one of the world's greatest capitals. Founded over 5000 years ago, the city thrived on its location at one of the major tradeways to China. Muslim architecture is very much part of the general style of the city, the *Mosque of Bibi Khanym* is well worth a visit. Registan Square is hailed as one of the most spacious in Asia. Here tower the colourful medresses *Shir-Dor* and *Tillya-Kari*, as well as the *Ulug-Bek Observatory*. The biggest attraction is the *Town of Graves, Shahi Zinda*. The grave of Tamerlane can be found in the crypt of the *Gur Emir Mausoleum*. Its blue domes rising above the skyline are like a vision from the 'Arabian Nights'.
Tashkent lies in the valley of the River Chirchik and is the fourth-largest city of the CIS. Destroyed by a terrible earthquake in 1966, the city was rebuilt within two to three years by workers from all republics of the former USSR. The capital of Uzbekistan is now an ideal modern city with spacious avenues, parks and ubiquitous fountains to cool the air. Tashkent has been in the past, and continues to be, an important international transport junction.
Bukhara, an ancient holy city which once boasted more than 350 mosques and 100 religious colleges, still retains a wealth of historic monuments, many of which are in the centre of the city, affording a glimpse of how it must have looked in the past. The tallest monument is the *Kalyan Minaret*, or the 'Tower of Death'. Built in 1127, it is 47m high – from here prisoners were once hurled to their death on market days. The narrow, twisting alleyways of the old quarter are fun to explore.

BUSINESS PROFILE

ECONOMY: Cotton dominates the Uzbek economy and the republic is the world's third largest producer. The republic has extensive gas and oil fields. The mining industry concentrates on the large gold deposits, securing Uzbekistan's position as a major world supplier. Of further importance are the manufacturing and chemical industry. However, the level of self-subsistence is relatively low and Uzbekistan has to rely heavily on imports of foodstuffs from other CIS members. To counteract this, plans have been drawn up to expand the cultivation of wheat and fruit. Uzbekistan faces a lot of ecological problems. The indiscriminate use of monocultures (cotton) and highly toxic pesticides resulted in irreparable damages to the environment. The republic is a member of the Central Asian economic zone ECO.
COMMERCIAL INFORMATION: The following organisation can offer advice: Chamber of Commerce and Industry, Prospekt Lenina 16a, 700017 Tashkent. Tel: (03712) 336 282.

HISTORY & GOVERNMENT

HISTORY: The Communist Parties in the five Central Asian republics have fared much better than elsewhere in the former Soviet Union. The essential reason for this is that Communist power, when established in the 1920s, was grafted onto the existing power structure of clan relationships. Nursultan Nazarbayev and Saparmurad Niyazov, leaders of Kazakhstan and Turkmenistan respectively, are the sole survivors from the time when Gorbachev came to power in Moscow in 1985. Niyazov was the first elected Soviet republican leader in 1990, and in 1992 he was re-elected unopposed with 85% of the vote. Turkmenistan has been the republic most reluctant to embrace full independence, largely because of its weak and backward economy. The Niyazov government shows no inclination to introduce economic reform, but hopes to improve collaboration with Pakistan, Iran and Turkey. Kazakhstan is better placed both economically and politically. It has extensive unexploited oil and gas fields and its ex-Soviet nuclear arsenal gives it a political clout unavailable to the other Central Asian states. In Kirghizia, the reformist Askar Akayev was elected unopposed as President in October 1991, while Islam Karimov of Uzbekistan, who came to power in 1989, was elected President of the independent republic in December 1991. Tajikistan has experienced the most upheaval. In September 1991, the former Communist Party boss Rahman Nabiyev returned to power after eight years out of office. The previous years had been led by the Government of Kakhar Makhkamov and a short-lived regime led by Kadreddin Aslonov, who had tried unsuccessfully to ban the Communist Party. Nabiyev then secured the endorsement of the electorate in November 1991 when he won 58% of the vote in defeating seven other candidates. The significant feature of the election was the strong showing of the Islamic Rennaissance Party, whose candidate won 34%. Nabiyev entered into a power-sharing arrangement with the Islamists. Political tension continued, however, culminating in riots in September 1992 in which 1000 people were killed. Nabiyev resigned, and a coalition of Islamic and democratic parties took control under an acting president, Akbarsho Iskanderov. Armed supporters of Nabiyev tried to stage a coup at the end of October but were fought off by the new regime. The turmoil in the republic is probably not over, and has been watched with great concern by Tajikistan's neighbours. All are aware that the strife there could easily erupt in their own provinces as the three main political forces in the region – Islam, communism and liberal democracy – contend for influence. At the moment, the Turkish model of a non-fundamentalist Islamic policy coupled with Western free-market economics finds most favour with the governments of the region. Turkey itself is trying to develop political and economic links with the region, taking advantage of language similarities and with the encouragement of the Americans who view this part of the world as a strategic 'black hole' and wish to counter Iranian influence. Meanwhile, Pakistan is helping the new states with acquiring membership of international organisations and general dealings with the outside world, and the Saudis have chipped in with a gift of one million copies of the Koran. To the east, the Chinese province of Xinjiang is developing closer economic ties with Kazakhstan and Kirghizia, whose peoples have ethnic links with China's 5-million-strong Uygur minority.
GOVERNMENT: In Uzbekistan, the People's Democratic Party of Uzbekistan has 530 out of 550 seats in the Supreme Soviet (national assembly); the Erk (freedom) Party holds the rest. Islam Karimov was elected President of Uzbekistan by an overwhelming majority at the end of December 1991. Tajikistan is currently governed by a coalition of Islamic and democratic parties led by President Akbarsho Iskandarov. Kirghizia's Communist President Askar Akayev was elected unopposed in October 1991. Both Kazakhstan's Nursultan Nazarbayev and Saparmuryad Niyazov in Turkmenistan are long-established Communist-backed rulers.

CLIMATE

Central Asia (plains): Dry, with extremes of temperature. Krasnovodsk and other places on the Caspian Sea have mild winters.
Central Asia (mountains): The mountains have snow all the year round. There is a considerable seasonal temperature variation.

KRASNOVODSK Turkmenistan (–10m)

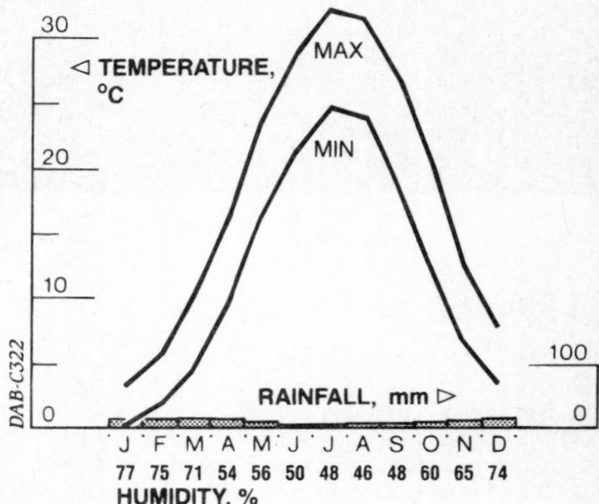

TASHKENT Uzbekistan (479m)

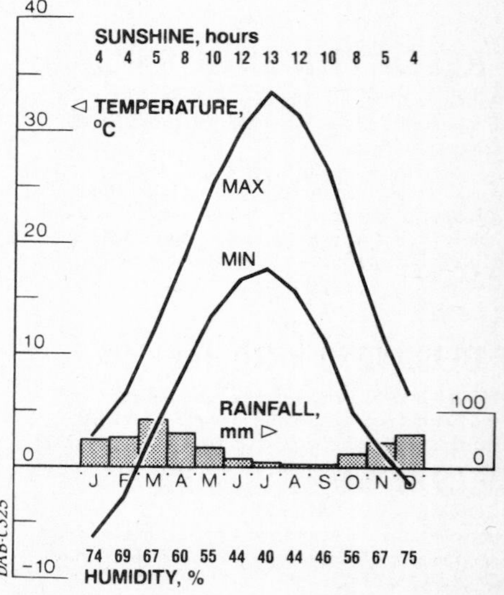

COMORO ISLANDS

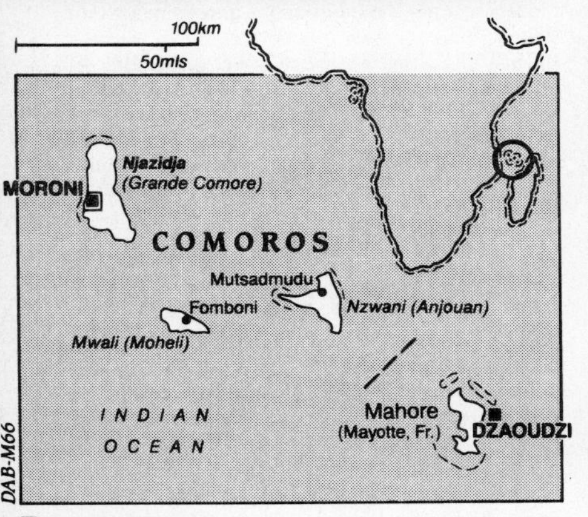

□ international airport

Location: Indian Ocean, between East African coast and Madagascar.

Société Comorienne de Tourisme et d'Hôtellerie (COMOTEL)
Itsandra Hotel
Njazidja
Grand Comoro, Comoros
Tel: 2365.

Embassy of the Federal Islamic Republic of the Comoros
13-15 rue de la Néva
75008 Paris, France
Tel: (1) 47 63 81 78. Telex: 611954.

Note: Britain has no diplomatic representation in the Comoro Islands.

Embassy of the French Republic
BP 465
boulevard de Strasbourg
Moroni, Comoros
Tel: 73 07 53. Telex: 220.

Embassy of the Comoros
2nd Floor
336 East 45th Street
New York, NY 10021
Tel: (212) 972 8010. Fax: (212) 983 4712.

Embassy of the United States of America
PO Box 1318
Moroni, Comoros
Tel: 73 22 03 *or* 73 29 22. Telex: 257.

AREA: 1862 sq km (719 sq miles).
POPULATION: 484,000 (1986 estimate).
POPULATION DENSITY: 259.9 per sq km.
CAPITAL: Moroni. **Population:** 17,267 (1980).
GEOGRAPHY: The Comoro archipelago is situated in the Indian ocean northeast of Madagascar and consists of four main islands of volcanic origin, surrounded by coral reefs: Njazidja (formerly Grande Comore), Nzwani (formerly Anjouan), Mwali (formerly Mohéli) and Mahore (Mayotte). The latter is administered by France but is claimed by the Federal Islamic Republic of the Comoros. The land can only support subsistence agriculture but the surrounding seas are rich in marine life.
LANGUAGE: The official languages are French and Arabic. However, the majority speak Comoran, a blend of Arabic and Swahili.
RELIGION: Muslim with Roman Catholic minority.
TIME: GMT + 3.
ELECTRICITY: 220 volts AC, 50Hz.
COMMUNICATIONS: Telephone: No IDD service. All calls to and from Comoro Islands must be via the international operator. **Post:** Mail to Europe takes at least a week. **Press:** There are no English-language newspapers. The two main weekly papers are *Al Watwany* (state-owned) and *L'Archipel* (independent).
BBC World Service and Voice of America frequencies: From time to time these change. See the section *How to Use this Book* for more information.

BBC:				
MHz	25.75	17.88	11.73	6.005
Voice of America:				
MHz	21.49	15.60	9.525	6.035

PASSPORT/VISA

Regulations and requirements may be subject to change at short notice, and you are advised to contact the appropriate diplomatic or consular authority before finalising travel arrangements. Details of these may be found at the head of this country's entry. Any numbers in the chart refer to the footnotes below.

	Passport Required?	Visa Required?	Return Ticket Required?
Full British	Yes	Yes	Yes
BVP	Not valid	-	-
Australian	Yes	Yes	Yes
Canadian	Yes	Yes	Yes
USA	Yes	Yes	Yes
Other EC	Yes	Yes	Yes
Japanese	Yes	Yes	Yes

PASSPORTS: Valid passport required by all.
British Visitors Passport: Not accepted.
VISAS: Required by all. Issued on arrival by the Immigration Officer to all nationalities.
Types of visa: Transit (valid for 5 days), Tourist, Exit Permit.
Cost: *Transit visas:* free; not required by those continuing their journey by the same or first connecting aircraft from the same or nearest airport. *Tourist visas:* for a stay of up to 45 days, CFr2000; for a stay of up to 90 days, CFr4000. For a stay of 12 months, those without a resident card are charged CFr10,000, and those with a resident card are charged CFr25,000. *Exit permits* cost CFr1500 and are required by all.
Note: All passengers must hold onward or return tickets.
Application to: Consulate (or Consular Section at Embassy). For addresses, see top of entry.

MONEY

Currency: Comoros Franc (CFr) = 100 centimes. Notes are in denominations of CFr5000, 1000, 500, 100 and 50. Coins are in denominations of CFr20, 10, 5, 2 and 1. The Comoran Franc is on a par with the French Franc and French Francs may also be in circulation; enquire at Embassy.
Credit cards: There is limited acceptance of most international credit cards (mainly in hotels), but check with your credit card company for details of merchant acceptability and other services which may be available.
Travellers cheques: French Franc cheques are recommended. The Banque Internationale des Comores (BIC) is the only bank which will change travellers cheques.
Exchange rate indicators: The following figures are included as a guide to the movements of the Comoran Franc against Sterling and the US Dollar:

Date:	Oct '89	Oct '90	Oct '91	Oct '92
£1.00=	505.13	498.38	496.12	413.75
$1.00=	319.91	255.12	285.87	260.71

Currency restrictions: No restrictions on import and export of local and foreign currency.
Banking hours: 0730-1200 Monday to Thursday, 0730-1100 Friday.

DUTY FREE

The following goods may be imported into the Comoros by persons over 18 years of age without incurring any customs duty:
400 cigarettes or 100 cigars or 500g of tobacco;
1 litre of alcoholic beverage;
75cl of perfume.
Prohibited items: Plants or soil.

PUBLIC HOLIDAYS

Public holidays observed in the Comoro Islands are as follows:
Mar 25 '93 Eid al-Fitr (end of Ramadan). **Jun 1** Eid al-Adha (Feast of the Sacrifice). **Jun 21** Muharram, Islamic New Year. **Jun 30** Ashoura. **Jul 6** Independence Day. **Aug 30** Mouloud, Prophet's Birthday. **Nov 27** Anniversary of President Abdallah's Assassination. **Jan '94** Leilat al-Meiraj, ascension of the Prophet. **Feb** Beginning of Ramadan. **Mar** Eid al-Fitr (end of Ramadan).
Note: Muslim festivals are timed according to local sightings of various phases of the Moon and the dates given above are approximations. During the lunar month of Ramadan that precedes Eid al-Fitr, Muslims fast during the day and feast at night and normal business patterns may be interrupted. Many restaurants are closed during the day and there may be restrictions on smoking and drinking. Some disruption may continue into Eid al-Fitr itself. Eid al-Fitr and Eid al-Adha may last anything from two to ten days, depending on the region. For more information see the section *World of Islam* at the back of the book.

HEALTH

Regulations and requirements may be subject to change at short notice, and you are advised to contact your doctor well in advance of your intended date of departure. Any numbers in the chart refer to the footnotes below.

	Special Precautions?	Certificate Required?
Yellow Fever	No	No/1
Cholera	No	No
Typhoid & Polio	Yes	-
Malaria	2	-
Food & Drink	3	-

[1]: Some travellers from areas infected with yellow fever have been asked to provide vaccination certificates.
[2]: Malaria risk exists all year throughout the archipelago, predominantly in the malignant *falciparum* form. Resistance to chloroquine has been reported.
[3]: All water should be regarded as being potentially contaminated. Water used for drinking, brushing teeth or making ice should have first been boiled or otherwise sterilised. Milk is unpasteurised and should be boiled. Powdered or tinned milk is available and is advised, but make sure that it is reconstituted with pure water. Avoid dairy products which are likely to have been made from unboiled milk. Only eat well-cooked meat and fish, preferably served hot. Pork, salad and mayonnaise may carry increased risk. Vegetables should be cooked and fruit peeled.
Health care: Health insurance is strongly advised.

Code-Link

COMORO ISLANDS	HEALTH REGULATIONS	VISA REGULATIONS
GALILEO/WORLDSPAN	TI-DFT/HAH/HE	 TI-DFT/HAH/VI
SABRE	 TIDFT/HAH/HE	 TIDFT/HAH/VI

To access this information on your CRS, swipe the barcode with a light pen or type in the text under the barcode. For more information, see the introduction *How to Use This Book.*

TRAVEL - International

AIR: The national airline is *Air Comores (OR)*.
International airport: *Moroni Hahaya (HAH)*, 20km (12.5 miles) from the city. A bus runs to the town, costing about CFr150. There are also taxis.
Departure tax: CFr500 or FFr100.
Approximate flight time: From *London* to Moroni is 18 hours; this includes a stopover (usually in Paris) of 2 hours 15 minutes.
SEA: There are irregular sailings via Madagascar, Reunion, Mauritius or East Africa (Mombasa, Kenya) to Moroni or Mutsamudu. The *Baraka – Belinga* line sails from the Comoros to France. *Norwegian American* run Arabian Sea cruises from Genoa to Mutsamudu.

TRAVEL - Internal

AIR: Each island has an airfield. *Air Comores* (OR) has four weekly connections between Moroni, Mwali (Mohéli) and Nzwani (Anjouan) and two weekly between Moroni and Dzaoudzi.
SEA: Mahore (Mayotte), Pamanzi and Dzaoudzi islands are linked by a regular ferry service. Travellers can hire motorboats, sailing craft and canoes in port villages and towns, and a boat can be especially useful for Mwali (Mohéli) where the road system is rudimentary.
ROAD: Bush taxis *(taxis-brousse)*, hired vehicles or private cars are the only forms of transport on the islands. Driving is on the right. All the islands have tarred roads. Four-wheel drive vehicles are advisable for the outlying islands and in the interior, especially in the rainy season. Roads are narrow and domestic animals often roam free, so drive slowly. *Tourism Services Comoros* operates minibuses.
Documentation: An International Driving Permit is required.

ACCOMMODATION

Accommodation on the Comoro Islands is being upgraded, but currently there are only a few hotels, located mostly in Moroni, which handle the needs of travelling business people, government officials and other visitors. Room sharing is quite common. There are simple shelters *(gîtes)* on Mahore (Mayotte) and on the slopes of Karthala (an active volcano).

RESORTS & EXCURSIONS

The islands' vegetation is rich and varied: 65% of the world's perfume essence comes from the islands, being processed from the blossoms of ylang-ylang, jasmine and orange. Spices, including nutmeg, cloves, pepper, basil and vanilla, are another mainstay of the economy. Ylang-ylang base has uses in hairdressing, treatment of rheumatism and, mixed with coconut oil, as sun cream. In common with a few other places, such as the wine-growing areas of France, one of the main attractions of the Comoros is also its main non-tourist commercial activity. *Economy* in the *Business Profile* section also has information.
Njazidja (Grand Comore): *Moroni:* The capital is a charming, peaceful town containing a few broad squares and modern government buildings, as well as old, narrow, winding streets and a market place. There are a number of fine mosques including the *Vendredi Mosque*, the top of which provides an attractive view.
Mt Karthala: The more energetic may climb to the top and then descend into the crater of this active volcano. The crater is claimed to be the largest still active anywhere in the world. It is usual to make one overnight stop at the shelter provided.
Itsandra: This fishing village 6km (4 miles) from Moroni has a fine beach and there are opportunities to see dances performed by the local men. The town was once the ancient capital of the island, complete with royal tombs and a fortress.
Excursions: There are hot sulphur springs at *Lac Sale* and a 14th-century village at **Iconi. Mitsamiouli,** a town in the north of the island, is known both for its good diving facilities and for having the best Comoran dancers. There are many bats and spiders on the island, the former often appearing in broad daylight.
Mwali (Mohéli): Dhows are built on the beach at **Fomboni.** There is a fine waterfall at **Miringoni.** Giant turtles may be seen at *Niumashuwa Bay*.
Nzwani (Anjouan): This island is notable for its waterfalls and abundant vegetation. The main town of **Mutsamudou** is built in Swahili-Shirazi style, complete with 17th-century houses with carved doors, twisting alleyways, mosques and a citadel. The ancient capital of **Domoni** is also worth a visit. The best beaches are in the **Bimbini** area. There are perfume distilleries at **Bambao.**
Mahore (Mayotte): This French-administered island is surrounded by a coral reef and has good beaches and excellent skindiving facilities. Tourists may explore the lagoon (claimed to be the largest in the world) by dugout canoe. The town of **Dzaoudzi** contains some old fortifications worthy of a visit. **Pamanzi** is a forested islet 5km (3 miles) offshore, fragrant with a wealth of vegetation. At **Sulu,** a waterfall plunges straight into the sea. There are the remains of an old mosque at **Tsingoni.** Elsewhere, there are 19th-century sugar refineries.

SOCIAL PROFILE

FOOD & DRINK: Restaurants serve good food with spiced sauces, rice-based dishes, cassava, plantain and couscous, barbecued goat meat, plentiful seafood and tropical fruits. There may be restrictions on drink within Muslim circles.
SHOPPING: Comoran products can be purchased at Moroni on Njazidja (Grand Comore). These include gold, pearl and shell jewellery, woven cloth, embroidered skull-caps *(koffia)* and slippers, carved chests, panels and *portes-Cran* (lecterns), pottery and basketry. Most items can be bought in the villages where they are made. **Shopping hours:** 0800-1200 and 1500-1800 Monday to Saturday.
SPORT: There is a sports centre on one of the beaches on Mahore. **Watersports:** There are many excellent **diving** sites in the archipelago. The Trou du Prophète in Misamiouli on Njazidja, Niumashuwa Bay on Mwali and Pamanzi islet off Mahore are particularly fine. There are many excellent beaches on all the islands. *Pirogue* (canoe) **races** are occasionally staged in the lagoon that surrounds Mahore. **Sailing** boats and **canoes** are available for hire in many ports.
SOCIAL CONVENTIONS: Religious customs should be respected, particularly during Ramadan. Dress should be modest although the French residents and tourists tend to be fairly relaxed about what they wear. **Tipping:** This should be 10%.

BUSINESS PROFILE

ECONOMY: The Comoros' economy is severely underdeveloped and depends largely on French aid. The main economic activity is agriculture, which produces vanilla and cloves (the main exports), ylang-ylang (an essence extracted from trees) and copra. There is a small fishing industry, a minimal industrial base devoted mainly to processing vanilla, and a developing tourist industry. Sharp declines in world prices for its principal products have wrought yet further damage to the Comoros' already poor balance of payments. France is the country's major trading partner, providing 42% of Comoros' imports and taking 65% of exports. China, Kenya, Tanzania and Madagascar are the other major importers into the islands.
BUSINESS: Lightweight suit or shirt and tie required. **Office hours:** 0700-1730 Monday to Thursday and 0730-1100 Friday.
COMMERCIAL INFORMATION: The following organisation can offer advice: Chambre de Commerce, d'Industrie et d'Agriculture, BP 763, Moroni, Comoros.

HISTORY & GOVERNMENT

HISTORY: In the early 15th century, the Arabs settled on the islands, each of which was ruled by separate sultans. The islands were ceded to the French in 1841 as protectorates and were proclaimed colonies in 1912. Between 1914 and 1947, the islands received the same supervision as Madagascar. After this date the islands became a French Overseas Territory. Independence was later achieved for all islands except Mayotte (which remained a part of the French Overseas Collectivités Territoriales) as the Federal Islamic Republic of the Comoros. Ahmed Abdallah was elected as the first President; however, he was overthrown by a coup in the same year and was replaced by Ali Soilih. In 1978 Soilih was removed from power and Abdallah regained the Presidency (with the assistance of European mercenaries led by the Frenchman Bob Denard). Abdallah was assassinated in 1989. The Republic continues to claim Mayotte, which is known there as Mahore. Multi-party elections were finally held on February 18, 1990, after initial postponement by the interim President, Saïd Mohamed Djohar, due to civil unrest. However, opposition allegations of fraud led to the result being discounted. On March 4 the election was re-held, with the second round taking place on March 11. Saïd Mohamed Djohar was re-elected. During 1991 political violence flared up on several occasions, but there was apparently no serious threat to the stability of the regime.
GOVERNMENT: Legislative power is in the hands of a National Assembly, each member of which is directly elected. The President, himself elected by universal adult suffrage, appoints a governing Council of Ministers.

CLIMATE

The climate is tropical and very warm. Coastal areas are hot and very humid (December to March), interspaced with rains and seasonal cyclones. The upland areas are cooler, particularly at night, and have higher rainfall.
Required clothing: Lightweight cottons and linens with waterproofing during the rainy season. Warmer garments and rainwear are needed for the mountains.

MORONI Comoros

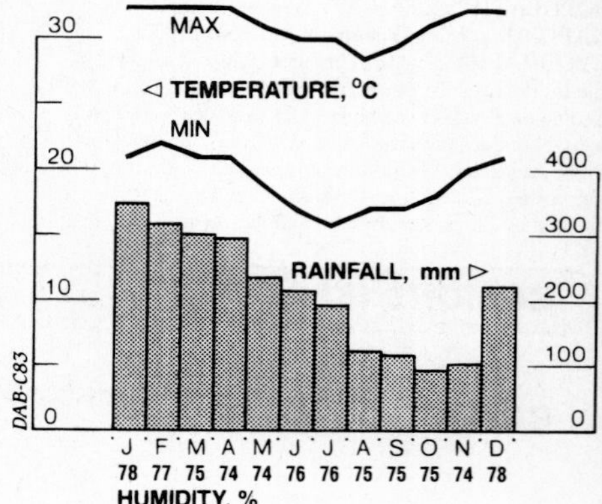

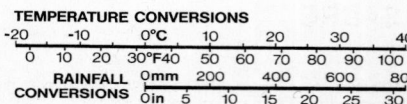

CONGO

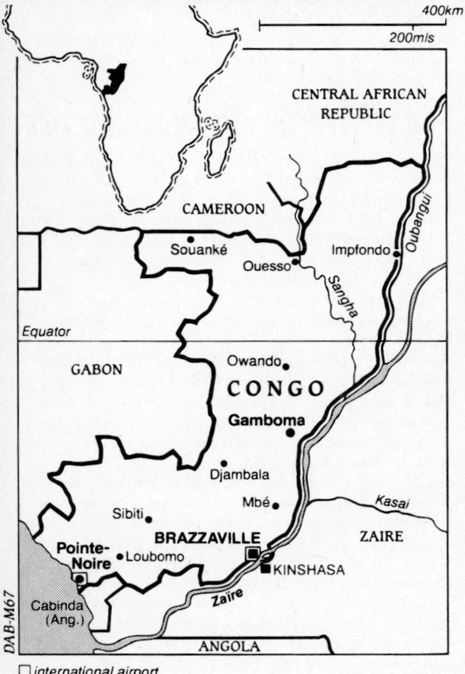

☐ *international airport*

Location: West coast of Central Africa.

Direction Générale du Tourisme et des Loisirs
BP 456
Brazzaville, Congo
Tel: 83 09 53. Telex: 5210.

Consulate of the Republic of the Congo *and* **Tourist Office**
Livingstone House
11 Carteret Street
London SW1H 9DJ
Tel: (071) 222 7575. Fax: (071) 233 2087. Telex: 267526.

Embassy of the Republic of the Congo
37 bis rue Paul Valéry
75016 Paris, France
Tel: (1) 45 00 60 57. Fax: (1) 45 00 96 51. Telex: 611954. Opening hours: 0900-1230 and 1400-1800 Monday to Friday.

British Embassy
BP 1038
avenue du Général de Gaulle
Plateau, Brazzaville
Congo
Tel: 83 49 44. Fax: 83 49 45. Telex: 5385.

Embassy of the Republic of the Congo *(also represents Canada)*
4891 Colorado Avenue, NW
Washington, DC
20011
Tel: (202) 726 5500/1. Telex: 897072

Embassy of the United States of America
BP 1015
avenue Amílcar Cabral
Brazzaville, Congo
Tel: 83 20 70. Telex: 5367.

AREA: 342,000 sq km (132,047 sq miles).
POPULATION: 1,843,421 (1984 estimate).
POPULATION DENSITY: 5.4 per sq km.
CAPITAL: Brazzaville. **Population:** 596,200 (1984).
GEOGRAPHY: The Congo is situated in Africa, bounded to the north by Cameroon and the Central African Republic, to the east by Zaïre, to the southwest by the Atlantic and to the west by Gabon. Vast areas are swamps, grassland or thick forests with rivers virtually the only means of internal travel. The vast River Congo and its major tributaries forms most of the country's border with Zaïre, drawing much of its water from the swamplands in the north of the country. The narrow sandy coastal plain is broken by lagoons behind which rise the Mayombe Mountains. Most of the population lives in the south of the country.
LANGUAGE: The official language is French. Other languages are Likala and Kikongo. English is spoken very little.
RELIGION: The majority are Animist, with 40% Roman Catholic. There are also Protestant and Muslim minorities.
TIME: GMT + 1.
ELECTRICITY: 220/230 volts AC, 50Hz.
COMMUNICATIONS: Telephone: IDD service is available. Country code: 242. Links with Europe are, in general, good. **Telex/telegram:** These services are available in cities at the main post offices and some hotels. **Post:** There is an unreliable internal service. Post office hours: 0730/0800-1200 and 1430-1730 Monday to Friday; and (for stamps and telegrams) 0800-2000 Monday to Saturday and 0800-1200 Sundays and public holidays. **Press:** There are several dailies which are subject to censorship.
BBC World Service and Voice of America frequencies: From time to time these change. See the section *How to Use this Book* for more information.

BBC:				
MHz	21.66	17.88	17.79	15.40
Voice of America:				
MHz	21.49	15.60	9.525	6.035

PASSPORT/VISA

Regulations and requirements may be subject to change at short notice, and you are advised to contact the appropriate diplomatic or consular authority before finalising travel arrangements. Details of these may be found at the head of this country's entry. Any numbers in the chart refer to the footnotes below.

	Passport Required?	Visa Required?	Return Ticket Required?
Full British	Yes	Yes	Yes
BVP	Not valid	-	-
Australian	Yes	Yes	Yes
Canadian	Yes	Yes	Yes
USA	Yes	Yes	Yes
Other EC	Yes	1	Yes
Japanese	Yes	Yes	Yes

PASSPORTS: Valid passport required by all.
British Visitors Passport: Not accepted.
VISAS: Required by all except:
(a) **[1]** nationals of France (for a stay not exceeding 3 months) and Germany (for a stay not exceeding 15 days) for tourist purposes only (other EC nationals *do* require a visa);
(b) nationals of the following countries, providing onward or return tickets and documents for their next destination are held: Benin, Burkina Faso, Cameroon, Central African Republic, Chad, Côte d'Ivoire, Equatorial Guinea, Gabon, Madagascar, Mauritania, Niger, Romania, Senegal, Togo and Zaïre.
Types of visa: Tourist, Business and Transit. *Tourist and Business visas* cost £20 for 15 days single entry; £25 for 15 days, £35 for 30 days, £50 for 90 days multiple entry.
Validity: *Transit visas:* available on arrival for a maximum of 72 hours. *Tourist and Business visas:* enquire at offices listed at top of entry.
Application to: Consulate (or Consular Section at Embassy). For addresses, see top of entry.
Application requirements: (a) 1 completed application form. (b) 1 passport photo. (c) If on business, letter from company on headed paper explaining nature of business.
Working days required: Allow as much time as possible as visa applications are sent to Brazzaville for approval (at least 3 weeks).
Note: Visas are now available from the Consulate in London.

MONEY

Currency: CFA Franc (CFA Fr) = 100 centimes. Notes are in denominations of CFA Fr10,000, 5000, 1000, 500 and 100. Coins are in denominations of CFA Fr100, 50, 25, 10, 5, 2 and 1. The Congo is part of the French Monetary Area. The notes are legal tender in all the republics which formerly comprised French Equatorial Africa (Chad, Congo, Central African Republic, Cameroon and Gabon).
Credit cards: Access/Mastercard and Diners Club are accepted but have limited use. Check with your credit card company for details of merchant acceptability and other services which may be available.
Exchange rate indicators: The following figures are included as a guide to the movements of the CFA Franc against Sterling and the US Dollar:

Date:	**Oct '89**	**Oct '90**	**Oct '91**	**Oct '92**
£1.00=	505.13	498.38	496.12	413.75
$1.00=	319.90	255.12	285.87	260.71

Currency restrictions: There are no import or export restrictions for foreign currency, but declaration must be made. Import of local currency unlimited, export up to CFA Fr25,000.
Banking hours: 0620-1300 Monday to Saturday (counters close at 1130).

DUTY FREE

The following items may be imported into the Congo without incurring customs duty:
200 cigarettes or 1 box of cigars or tobacco (women are permitted to import cigarettes only);
1 bottle of spirits;
2 bottles of wine;
A reasonable quantity of perfume in opened bottles.
Note: A licence is required for sporting guns.

PUBLIC HOLIDAYS

Public holidays observed in the Congo are as follows:
Apr 9 '93 Good Friday. **Apr 12** Easter Monday. **May 1** Labour Day. **Aug 15** Independence Day. **Dec 25** Christmas Day. **Jan 1 '94** New Year's Day.
Note: Due to political change these dates may alter. Check with Tourist Office before travelling.

HEALTH

Regulations and requirements may be subject to change at short notice, and you are advised to contact your doctor well in advance of your intended date of departure. Any numbers in the chart refer to the footnotes below.

	Special Precautions?	Certificate Required?
Yellow Fever	Yes	1
Cholera	Yes	2
Typhoid & Polio	Yes	-
Malaria	Yes	-
Food & Drink	3	-

[1]: A yellow fever vaccination certificate is required for all travellers over one year of age.
[2]: Following WHO guidelines issued in 1973, a cholera vaccination certificate is no longer a condition of entry to

CONGO	**HEALTH REGULATIONS**	**VISA REGULATIONS**
GALILEO/WORLDSPAN	 TI-DFT/BZV/HE	TI-DFT/BZV/VI
SABRE	 TIDFT/BZV/HE	 TIDFT/BZV/VI

Code-Link

To access this information on your CRS, swipe the barcode with a light pen or type in the text under the barcode. For more information, see the introduction *How to Use This Book*.

the Congo. However, cholera is a serious risk in this country and precautions are essential. Up-to-date advice should be sought before deciding whether these precautions should include vaccination as medical opinion is divided over its effectiveness. See the *Health* section at the back of the book.
[3]: All water should be regarded as being potentially contaminated. Water used for drinking, brushing teeth or making ice should have first been boiled or otherwise sterilised. Milk is unpasteurised and should be boiled. Powdered or tinned milk is available and is advised, but make sure that it is reconstituted with pure water. Avoid dairy products which are likely to have been made from unboiled milk. Only eat well-cooked meat and fish, preferably served hot. Pork, salad and mayonnaise may carry increased risk. Vegetables should be cooked and fruit peeled.
Malaria risk exists all year throughout the country, predominantly in the malignant *falciparum* form. Resistance to chloroquine has been reported.
Rabies is present. For those at high risk, vaccination before arrival should be considered. If you are bitten abroad seek medical advice without delay. For more information consult the *Health* section at the back of the book.
Bilharzia (schistosomiasis) is present. Avoid swimming and paddling in fresh water. Swimming pools which are well-chlorinated and maintained are safe.
Health care: Medical and dental facilities are generally very limited outside Brazzaville. Health insurance is essential.

TRAVEL - International

AIR: *UTA* and *Air Afrique* (of which the Congo is a minority shareholder) operate international services to the Congo.
Approximate flight time: From *London* to Brazzaville is 11 hours (including up to 3 hours for stopover in Paris).
International airports: *Brazzaville (BZV)* (Maya Maya) is 4km (2 miles) northwest of the city. Airport facilities include a restaurant and car hire (*Europcar* and *Hertz* are both represented at the airport). Taxis are available to the city.
Pointe Noire (PNR) is 5.5km (3.5 miles) from the city. Taxis are available to the city.
Departure tax: CFA Fr500.
SEA/RIVER: Cargo ships dock at Pointe Noire. An hourly car ferry operates between Kinshasa (Zaïre) and Brazzaville across the Congo River (journey time – 20 minutes). Ferries operate to and from the Central African Republic on the Ubangi.
ROAD: There is a road connection from Lambaréné in Gabon to Loubomo and Brazzaville. The road from Cameroon is usable only during the dry season. Entry can also be made via Zaïre and Angola.

TRAVEL - Internal

AIR: The national airline is *Lina Congo (GC)*. It runs regular services from Brazzaville to Pointe Noire, Boundji, Djambala, Epena, Impfondo, Kindamba, Loubomo, Makoua, Ouesso, Owando, Sibiti, Souanke and Zanaga, as well as to Banjul and Libreville.
Departure tax: CFA Fr500 is levied on all passengers travelling within the Congo.
RIVER: Inland steamers ply from Brazzaville up the Congo and Ubangi. Rivers are vital to internal transport.
RAIL: *Congo-Océan* railway company runs two trains daily (with restaurant car, and with couchettes thrice-weekly) between Brazzaville and Pointe Noire (journey time – 11-15 hours), and railcars daily from Mbinda. Services can be erratic. Advance booking is recommended.
ROAD: Roads are mostly earth tracks, sandy in dry season and impassable in the wet, suitable for Land Rovers only. There are 243km (151 miles) of tarred roads. **Car hire:** There are several car hire firms represented in Brazzaville, lists of which can be obtained from main hotels.
Documentation: An International Driving Permit is required.
URBAN: Brazzaville has a minibus and taxi service and taxis are also available in Pointe Noire and Loubomo. Taxi fares have a flat rate and fares should be agreed beforehand; tipping is not expected.

ACCOMMODATION

There are an adequate number of hotels in Brazzaville, Loubomo and Pointe Noire. Prices and advance bookings can be obtained via *UTA French Airlines*. Outside the towns mentioned above, there is little accommodation for visitors.

RESORTS & EXCURSIONS

The capital city of **Brazzaville** is situated on the west side of *Malebo Pool* on the **River Congo**. Sights to see include the old *Cathedral of St Firmin*, *Poto Poto* suburb, the *Temple Mosque*, the markets at *OIuendze* and *Moungali*, the *National Museum*, the *Municipal Gardens* and the house constructed for De Gaulle when Brazzaville was the capital of Free France.
150km (90 miles) north of the capital is the historic village of **M'Bé**, the capital of King Makoko. Also in this region is *Lake Bleu* and the *Valley of Butterflies*.
To the south of Brazzaville are the *Congo Rapids* (11km/7 miles away by tarred road), the *Foulakari Falls* and the *Trou de Dieu*, above which there is a panoramic view of the surrounding countryside.
The main town on the coast is **Pointe Noire** (with its lively evening market), and there are several good beaches close by in the region known as the **Côte Sauvage.** There are opportunities for fishing all along the coast, as well as inland in the rivers and lakes, such as Lakes *Nango* and *Kayo*. Wildlife and spectacular scenery may both be found at *Mayombé* (150km/90 miles inland) and the *Lagoons of Gounkouati.*

SOCIAL PROFILE

FOOD: Restaurants provide mostly French cuisine and the coast has excellent fish, giant oysters and shrimps. In Brazzaville, the main hotels have good restaurants serving French cuisine, but there are also restaurants specialising in Italian, Lebanese and Vietnamese dishes. Some restaurants, such as those at Nanga Lake and Grand Hotel in Loubomo, specialise in African dishes such as *piri piri chicken* (with pepper), *Mohambe chicken* in palm oil, palm cabbage salad, cassava leaves or *paka paka* in palm oil. Pointe Noire and Loubomo also have restaurants and bars, usually in hotels, with table service. Some bars also have counter service.
NIGHTLIFE: Local groups are popular in the main towns. Brazzaville has several nightclubs, as does Pointe Noire.
SHOPPING: In Brazzaville there are shops, colourful markets and an arts and crafts centre at Poto Poto which displays and sells, amongst other things, local paintings and carved wooden masks and figures. The two main markets are Moungali and Ouendze. Avenue Foch is crowded with street vendors. Basketwork can be bought at the villages of Makana and M'Pila (3km/2 miles from Brazzaville), with pottery and an open-air market. **Shopping hours:** 0800-1200 and 1500-1800 Monday to Saturday. Some shops close on Monday afternoon and a few will open on Sunday morning.
SPORT: Brazzaville has facilities for **sailing, horseriding** and **golf. Angling** along the coast from Pointe Noire is very popular and the Plage Mondaine is a protected beach resort, with **water-skiing** and **yachting.** Lagoons of Gounkouati offer excellent **fishing.**
SPECIAL EVENTS: Details of events for 1993/4 are available from Republic of the Congo Tourist Office.
SOCIAL CONVENTIONS: Normal European courtesies should be observed when visiting people's homes. Gifts are acceptable as a token of thanks especially if invited for a meal. Dress should be casual, and informal wear is acceptable in most places. Artistic carving, traditional dance, and modern and folk songs play an important part in Congolese culture, which is strongly based on tradition. There are large numbers of foreigners resident in the Congo, working as technical assistants, businessmen and traders. **Photography:** Do not photograph public buildings and places. **Tipping:** Normally 10% in hotels and restaurants. Porters do not expect tips.

BUSINESS PROFILE

ECONOMY: There are 14 distinct ethnic groups (the majority of which are Bantu) including Kongos (45%), Tékés and Boubanguis. Nearly half the population live in towns. Subsistence living in forest villages has been increasingly abandoned by each new generation in favour of employment in towns. The Congo relies primarily on its reserves of oil and timber. Roughly 60% of the country is covered by forests, about half of which are exploitable. Forestry is thus an important economic activity and a major employer. This, together with crop farming of both staples (cassava, plantains) and cash crops (sugar, palm oil, cocoa, coffee), means 60% of the labour force work on the land. Even so, the country continues to depend on a large quantity of imported food. A further 20% of workers are employed in various industries, of which the most important is oil. The first oilfield came on stream in 1960 and the industry now accounts for nearly 90% of export earnings, affording the Congo a healthy trade surplus in recent years, even though its contribution to GDP dropped from 40% in 1985 to 15% in 1987 due to the collapse in the world oil price. The strength of the agricultural sector saved the Congo from severe economic difficulty. The bulk of the oil exports are bought by the United States (60%), with Spain and France taking the remainder. France supplies over 60% of the Congo's imports, which largely comprise machinery, transport equipment, iron and steel, as well as foodstuffs. Italy, Spain and Japan provide most of the rest. Congo is a member of the CFA Franc Zone and of the Central African economic and customs union, UDEAC. The country has followed socialist economic policies throughout most of its independence, but at the end of 1989 started to introduce a market economy.
BUSINESS: Jackets and ties are not usually worn by men on business visits but are expected when visiting government officials. A knowledge of French is essential as there are no professional translators available. Normal courtesies should be observed and best months for business visits are January to March and June to September.
Office hours: Usually 0800-1200 and 1500-1800 Monday to Friday, 0700-1200 Saturday.
COMMERCIAL INFORMATION: The following organisation can offer advice: Chambre de Commerce, d'Agriculture et d'Industrie de Brazzaville, BP 92, Brazzaville. Tel: 83 21 15.

HISTORY & GOVERNMENT

HISTORY: Originally part of the kingdom of the Kongo, the area was discovered by the Portuguese in the 15th century and later became a major region for the slave trade. In 1882 the territory was occupied by France, then absorbed into French Equatorial Africa between 1910 and 1958. The Congo was granted full independence as a republic in August 1960. Abbé Fulbert Youlou, a Catholic priest, was elected President and guided the Congo into a single-party state, in accordance with the trend throughout Africa. A series of left-wing military governments followed until elections for the presidency were held in 1979 and brought Colonel Denis Sassou-Nguesso to power, where he has since remained as both head of the ruling Parti Congolais du Travail (PCT) and, since 1984, as head of the Government. Until very recently, Sassou-Nguesso has pursued, in line with his predecessors, a broadly socialist path of development. His position has become gradually less secure since the mid-1980s with civil unrest following the introduction of austerity measures and an attempted coup in July 1987. Within the PCT, however, he remains unassailed, having been elected in 1989 for a third consecutive 5-year term. Since November 1989, the Government has introduced free-market policies, promoting private enterprise and conducting several privatisations. The Government's foreign policy has also been realigned away from the Soviet Union, of which it was a steady ally, towards France. Indications that the PCT was finally preparing to relinquish its firm grip on political power came with the convening of a national conference of all political forces in the country to discuss the political future (this is an increasingly familiar device among Africa's one-party states). The conference, which lasted three months, ended with the public humiliation of President Sassou-Nguesso and his government, and an agreement to introduce a new constitution with legislative and presidential elections scheduled for 1992. At the presidential poll held in August that year, André Milongo, caretaker president of the transition goverment since June 1991, was replaced as president by Pascal Lissouba.
GOVERNMENT: Under the provisions of the constitution adopted in January 1992 after a national referendum, Congo is a multi-party democracy with an elected president, who holds executive power, and a legislature.

CLIMATE

Equatorial climate with short rains from October to December and long rains between mid-January and mid-May. The main dry season is from May to September.
Required clothing: Practical lightweight cottons and linens with a light raincoat or umbrella in the rainy season.

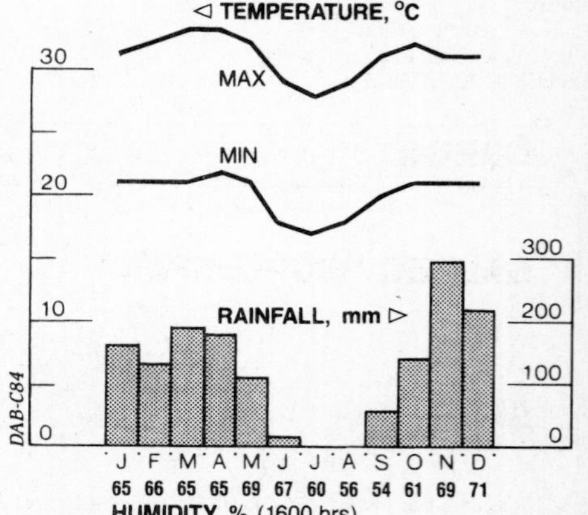

COOK ISLANDS

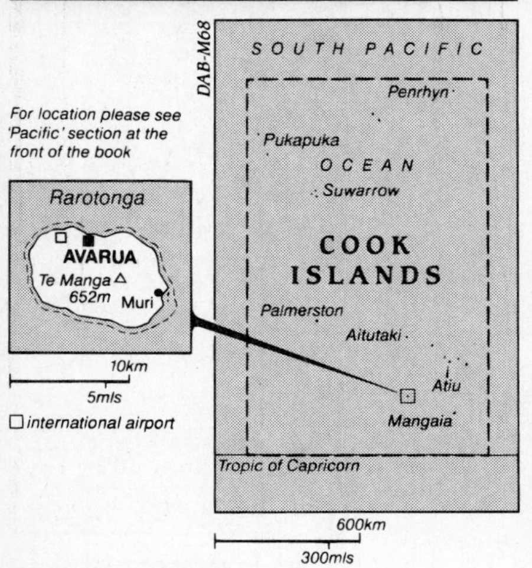

Location: South Pacific, Polynesia.

Cook Islands' Tourist Authority
PO Box 14
Rarotonga, Cook Islands
Tel: 29435. Fax: 21435. Telex: 62054.
Cook Islands Office
PO Box 12-142
Wellington, New Zealand
Fax: (4) 725 121.
Air New Zealand
Elsinore House
77 Fulham Palace Road
London W6 8JA
Tel: (081) 846 9595 (administration) *or* 741 2299 (reservations). Fax: (081) 741 4645. Telex: 265206.
British High Commission
PO Box 1812
9th Floor, Reserve Bank of New Zealand Building
2 The Terrace
Wellington 1, New Zealand
Tel: (4) 726 049. Fax: (4) 711 974. Telex: 3325 UKREP NZ.
Cook Islands Tourist Authority
PO Box 1449
Suite 13, 484 Mobil Avenue
Camarillo, CA 93010
Tel: (805) 388 4673. Fax: (805) 388 8086.
Embassy of the United States of America
PO Box 1190
29 Fitzherbert Terrrace
Thorndon
Wellington, New Zealand
Tel: (4) 472 2068. Fax: (4) 472 3537.
Canadian High Commission
PO Box 12049
61 Molesworth Street
Wellington 1, New Zealand
Tel: (4) 473 9577. Fax: (4) 471 2082. Telex: 3577.

AREA: 237 sq km (91.5 sq miles).
POPULATION: 19,000 (1991 estimate).
POPULATION DENSITY: 80.2 per sq km.
CAPITAL: Avarua (on Rarotonga). **Population:** 9823 (1986, including Rarotonga itself).
GEOGRAPHY: The Cook Islands are situated 3500km (2200 miles) northeast of New Zealand and 1000km (600 miles) southwest of Tahiti in the South Pacific, forming part of Polynesia. The islands fall into two groups: the scattered Northern Group are all coral atolls except Aitutaki, and the islands towards the south, the Southern Group, are of volcanic origin. The islands are self-governing overseas territories of New Zealand. Rarotonga is the largest and highest island with a rugged volcanic interior, its highest peak being Te Manga, at 652m (2140ft). Coral reef surrounds the island and the population lives between reef and hills where rich soil supports both tropical and subtropical vegetation. Most of the island is covered by thick evergreen bush. Most of the larger islands include lagoons surrounded by small areas of fertile land above which rise volcanic hills. The best beaches found on Aitutaki are also part of an 8-island southern group. The northern group comprises seven islands, the largest being Penrhyn, Manihiki and Pukapuka. The Cook Islands have been used as the setting for several films in the last few years, the best known being *Merry Christmas Mr Lawrence*.
LANGUAGE: Maori is the national language. English is widely spoken.
RELIGION: Mainly Cook Islands' Christian Church, also Roman Catholic, Latter Day Saints and Seventh Day Adventists.
TIME: GMT - 10.
ELECTRICITY: 220/230 volts AC, 50Hz.
COMMUNICATIONS: The telecommunications system on the islands is being upgraded in the period 1990-1993.
Telephone: IDD is available. Country code: 682. **Fax:** Many Cook Island organisations have facilities.
Telex/telegram: Services are provided by the Post and Telecommunications Programme in Rarotonga; the most convenient way to use them is via one's hotel. **Post:** Post office hours: 0800-1600 Monday to Friday. **Press:** The daily *Cook Islands News* is published in Maori and English.
BBC World Service and Voice of America frequencies: From time to time these change. See the section *How to Use this Book* for more information.

BBC:				
MHz	17.10	15.36	9.740	7.150
Voice of America:				
MHz	18.82	15.18	9.525	1.735

PASSPORT/VISA

Regulations and requirements may be subject to change at short notice, and you are advised to contact the appropriate diplomatic or consular authority before finalising travel arrangements. Details of these may be found at the head of this country's entry. Any numbers in the chart refer to the footnotes below.

	Passport Required?	Visa Required?	Return Ticket Required?
Full British	Yes	1	Yes
BVP	Not valid	-	-
Australian	Yes	1	Yes
Canadian	Yes	1	Yes
USA	Yes	1	Yes
Other EC	Yes	1	Yes
Japanese	Yes	1	Yes

PASSPORTS: Valid passport required by all, including nationals of New Zealand. Passports should be valid for a further 12 months after intended date of departure.
British Visitors Passport: Not acceptable.
VISAS: [1] Not required by visitors staying a maximum of 31 days who hold confirmed onward/return tickets and documentation required by next country to be visited as well as confirmed accommodation arrangements. Those not satisfying these conditions require an entry permit costing NZ$25 per month (three month maximum) of stay. Visas are required by all business travellers.
Validity: Visitors can extend length of stay on a monthly basis up to an additional 3 months.
Application to: Cook Islands Office (for address, see above).
Temporary residence: Applicants should refer to the Cook Islands Office (for address, see above).

MONEY

Currency: New Zealand Dollar (NZ$) = 100 cents, supplemented by notes and coins minted for local use which are not negotiable outside the Cook Islands. Notes are in denominations of NZ$50, 20, 10 and 3. Coins are in denominations of 50, 10, 5, 2 and 1 cents.
Currency exchange: Exchange facilities are available at the airport and with trade banks.
Credit cards: Visa, Diners Club, Access/Mastercard and American Express are accepted. Check with your credit card company for details of merchant acceptability and other services which may be available.
Travellers cheques: Accepted in hotels and some shops.
Exchange rate indicators: The following figures are included as a guide to the movements of the New Zealand Dollar against Sterling and the US Dollar:

Date:	**Oct '89**	**Oct '90**	**Oct '91**	**Oct '92**
£1.00=	**2.69**	**3.21**	**3.05**	**2.94**
$1.00=	**1.66**	**1.64**	**1.76**	**1.85**

Currency restrictions: There are no currency restrictions.
Banking hours: 0900-1500 Monday to Friday.

DUTY FREE

The following goods may be imported into the Cook Islands by travellers over the age of 18 without incurring customs duty:
200 cigarettes or 50 cigars or 250g of tobacco;
1 litre of spirits or wine or 4.5 litres of beer;
Goods to the value of NZ$250.
Prohibited items: Fruit, meat, livestock, fireworks, firearms, gunpowder and ammunition.

PUBLIC HOLIDAYS

Public holidays observed in the Cook Islands are as follows:
Apr 9 '93 Good Friday. **Apr 12** Easter Monday. **Apr 25** Anzac Day. **Jun 7** Queen's Birthday. **Dec 25** Christmas Day. **Dec 26** Boxing Day. **Jan 1 '94** New Year's Day.

HEALTH

Regulations and requirements may be subject to change at short notice, and you are advised to contact your doctor well in advance of your intended date of departure. Any numbers in the chart refer to the footnotes below.

	Special Precautions?	Certificate Required?
Yellow Fever	No	No
Cholera	No	No
Typhoid & Polio	Yes	-
Malaria	No	-
Food & Drink	1	-

[1]: Water from taps is acceptable to most visitors, and whilst relatively safe may cause mild abdominal upsets. Bottled water is available and is advised for the first few weeks of the stay. Milk is pasteurised and dairy products are safe for consumption. Local meat, poultry, seafood, fruit and vegetables are generally considered safe to eat.
Coral reefs are a hazard. Feet should always be covered. Hands should be kept out of holes and cracks in the reef, as they might contain unpleasant and lethal occupants.
Health care: There is no direct Reciprocal Health Agreement with the UK, but such an agreement exists with New Zealand which may in some circumstances also apply to the Cook Islands; enquire at the Cook Islands Office. There is one government hospital (on Rarotonga) with a total of 151 beds.

TRAVEL - International

AIR: The Cook Islands are served by *Air New Zealand (NZ)*, *Hawaiian Airlines* and *Polynesian Airlines (PH)*. The latter offers a 'Polypass' which allows flights anywhere on the airline's network: Sydney (Australia), Auckland (New Zealand), Western Samoa, American Samoa, Cook Islands, Vanuatu, New Caledonia, Fiji and, on

COOK ISLANDS	HEALTH REGULATIONS	VISA REGULATIONS Code-Link
GALILEO/WORLDSPAN	 TI-DFT/RAR/HE	 TI-DFT/RAR/VI
SABRE	 TIDFT/RAR/HE	 TIDFT/RAR/VI

To access this information on your CRS, swipe the barcode with a light pen or type in the text under the barcode. For more information, see the introduction *How to Use This Book*.

payment of a supplement, Tahiti. The pass is valid for 30 days.
Approximate flight time: From *London* to Rarotonga is 24 hours (including stopover of one hour in Paris).
International airport: *Rarotonga (RAR)* is 3km (2 miles) west of Avarua (travel time – 10 minutes). The airport facilities are open according to flight arrivals and departures and include duty-free shops, bank/bureau de change, bars, shops and car rental (*Avis* and *Budget*). Hotel coaches meet each flight. Taxis and buses are also available.
Departure tax: NZ$20 for passengers over 12 years of age; NZ$10 for 2 to 12 year olds.
SEA: Cargo/passenger lines operating to the Cook Islands are run by the *Cook Islands Shipping Company* and *New Zealand Motor Vessel Company*.
Note: Passengers who embarked in Fiji, Samoa, Tonga and Tahiti are required to have their baggage fumigated on arrival. It is advisable to carry personal articles for immediate need (as fumigation can take up to three hours), and to remove bottles from luggage as they are likely to break during fumigation.

TRAVEL - Internal

AIR: *Cook Island Air* and *Air Rarotonga* run regular inter-island services to Aitutaki, Atiu, Mangaia, Mauke, Mitiaro, Penryhn and Rakahanga.
Inter-island flight times: From Rarotonga to *Aitutaki* is 1 hour, to *Atiu* is 50 minutes, to *Mauke* is 50 minutes and to *Mitiaro* is 1 hour 25 minutes.
ROAD: Driving is on the left. Drivers of all vehicles are required to have a current Cook Islands driver's licence, which costs NZ$2 and is obtainable from the Police Station in Avarua on presentation of an international or Commonwealth licence. **Bus:** There are several companies which operate services around Rarotonga on weekdays as well as Saturdays. Buses are available from 0800-1600 hours from a number of hotels on the Islands. **Taxi:** Available on Rarotonga. **Car hire:** Several companies offer cars for hire from a number of shops and hotels. Motor scooter and bicycle hire is also popular.

ACCOMMODATION

Good class accommodation is still limited, but is increasing yearly. There are now a reasonable number of New Zealand-style motels of international standard. Hotels tend to be quite small and most are situated close to, if not on, a beach. Advance booking is absolutely essential, and it is probably wiser to book via an inclusive tour operator specialising in Pacific destinations.

RESORTS & EXCURSIONS

The developed resorts are situated on **Rarotonga** and **Aitutaki,** and provide various amenities (see *Sport* below). The best swimming beaches are at *Muri Lagoon* and *Titikaveka*. A variety of tours are available, including guided walking trips, sightseeing by air, horse-drawn and motorised drives around the islands and cruises on schooners or yachts to the outer islands. A scenic drive into the *Takuwaine/Avatiu Valleys* offers a panorama of lush tropical scenery. *Papua (Wigmore's) Waterfall*, the only waterfall on the island, is located at **Vaimaanga.** The museum at **Takamoa** has excellent examples of Cook Islands handicrafts. During the year various festivals take place. These are generally celebrated with singing and dancing, often with a strange mixture of traditional ritual grafted on to the somewhat later Christian music and ceremony. The choirs of the Cook Islands are renowned. Places of historical interest include: the *Takamoa Mission House*, built in 1842, and believed to be the second oldest building in the South Pacific; the old *Palace of Makea* at **Taputapuatea;** *Pa's Palace*, built of coral and lime, in **Takitumu;** and *Arai-Te-Tonga (Marae)*, consisting of stone structures which, in the islands' pre-European history, formed a *kouto*, or royal court, where the investiture of chiefs took place. This spot is still regarded as sacred.

SOCIAL PROFILE

FOOD: There are restaurants in hotels, and a variety of independent eating places as well, as a result of the increasing tourist trade. Cantonese cuisine is represented by the *Jade Garden* in Avarua. Other restaurants serve fresh fish or imported beef. Local produce includes citrus and tropical fruits in large varieties, island chestnuts and garden vegetables. Seafood features on many restaurant menus. Local meat and poultry are available.
NIGHTLIFE: Island feast and dance groups feature at various hotels and details are available from local tourist information offices or hotel receptionists.
SHOPPING: Best buys are wood carvings, hand-made *ukuleles*, pearls, shells, woven products, embroidery, Panama hats and baskets. Coins and stamps are considered to be valuable collectors' items. Tiki industries and Island Craft have factories in Avarua and Avatiu where handcarved items can be purchased. There is also a wide range of duty-free items.
Shopping hours: 0800-1600 Monday to Friday and 0800-1200 Saturday. Some stores near tourist areas remain open for longer.
SPORT: Fishing is available at the Deep Sea Fishing Club, and visitors can watch flying fish being netted at night in outrigger canoes equipped with bright lights. The Rarotonga Golf Club has a 9-hole **golf** course. In addition, lawn **bowls** has an enthusiastic following and is a long established sport in Rarotonga. Visitors are also welcome at Rarotonga Sailing Club, where **sailing** races are held on Saturday afternoons from October to May.
Watersports: There is excellent **scuba diving** and **snorkelling** in the clear waters of the islands' many lagoons. It is often possible to hire equipment.
SPECIAL EVENTS: Festivals and special events celebrated in the Cook Islands during 1993/1994 are listed below. For further details contact the Tourist Authority.
Apr (second week) *Dancer of the Year*. **End Jul/beginning Aug (first week)** *Art Exhibition; Constitutional Celebrations*. **Nov** *Food-Festival*. **Nov (third week)** *Tiare* (floral) *Week*. **Feb (third week)** *Cultural Festival Week* (arts, crafts and canoe races).
SOCIAL CONVENTIONS: Casual wear is acceptable. Women are expected to wear dresses for church services and social functions. **Tipping:** Tradition says that all gifts require something in return and tipping is therefore not practised.

BUSINESS PROFILE

ECONOMY: Tourism is the leading industry. The islands depend on extensive aid from New Zealand and are economically underdeveloped through their isolation. The islands produce fresh fruit which is the main export product. The Government is seeking to build up the islands' infrastructure as a precursor to further development.
BUSINESS: Tropical or lightweight suits necessary.
Office hours: 0800-1600 Monday to Friday.
COMMERCIAL INFORMATION: The following organisation can offer advice: Chamber of Commerce, PO Box 242, Rarotonga. Tel: 20295. Fax: 20969. Telex: 62067.

HISTORY & GOVERNMENT

HISTORY: The islands were named in honour of Captain James Cook, who in 1733 became the first European to sight them. However, credit for the first discovery of these islands must go to the Polynesians who discovered them during their great migratory journeys of the 7th and 8th centuries (places of historical interest are listed in *Resorts & Excursions* above). The main island, Rarotonga, was rediscovered by the Bounty Mutineers in 1789. In 1888 they became a British protectorate, and in 1901 became part of New Zealand. In 1965 the islands achieved self-government as a New Zealand dependency.
GOVERNMENT: The Cook Islands are an internally governing state in free association with New Zealand. The Head of State is the British Monarch, who has executive power carried out by the Cabinet, which is responsible to Parliament. Members of Parliament are elected by universal adult suffrage. An advisory body exists called the House of Ariki which is composed of all the paramount chiefs of the Cook Islands. Advice is given on legislation concerning customs and traditions, though the House of Ariki has no powers of legislation itself. New Zealand is responsible for defence and foreign affairs.

CLIMATE

Varies throughout the islands, but generally hot throughout the year, although the trade winds provide some moderating influence. Rainfall is heaviest in Rarotonga, while the northern atolls tend to be drier. The coolest months are May to October. Most rain falls in the warmest period.
Required clothing: Lightweight cottons and linens throughout the year. Warm clothes are advised for cooler evenings. Rainwear advised in the rainy season.

RAROTONGA Cook Is.

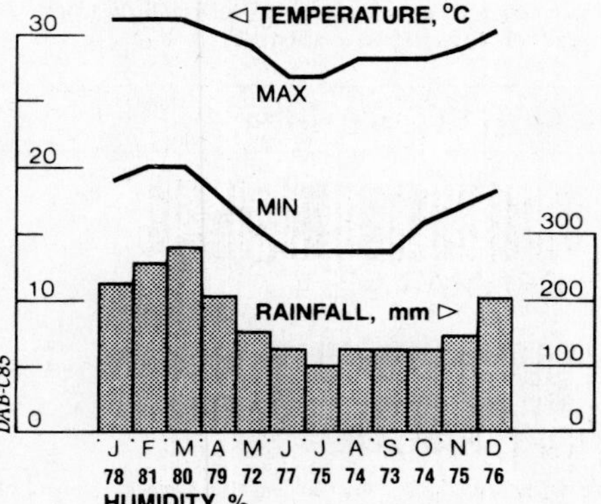

COSTA RICA

Location: Central America.

Instituto Costarricense de Turismo
Apartado 777-1000
Calles 5 y 7
Avenida 4a
1000 San José, Costa Rica
Tel: 23 84 23. Fax: 55 49 97.
Embassy of the Republic of Costa Rica
5 Harcourt House
19A Cavendish Square
London WIM 9AD
Tel: (071) 495 3985. Fax: (071) 495 3992.
Opening hours: 1000-1300 and 1400-1600 Monday to Friday.
Consulate of the Republic of Costa Rica
Flat 2
38 Redcliffe Square
London SW10 9JY
Tel: (071) 373 7973. Fax: (071) 373 7973.
Opening hours: 1000-1300 Monday to Friday.
British Embassy
Apartado 815
Centro Colón 1007
San José, Costa Rica
Tel: 21 55 66. Fax: 33 99 38.
Embassy of the Republic of Costa Rica
Suite 211
1825 Connecticut Avenue, NW
Washington, DC
20009
Tel: (202) 234 2945. Fax: (202) 234 8653.
Costa Rican Tourism Bureau Information Centre
1101 Brickel Avenue
B1V Tower, Suite 801
Miami, FL 33131
Tel: (305) 567 8205. Fax: (305) 358 7951.
Embassy of the United States of America
Apartado 920-1200 Pavas
Pavas Frente Centro Comercial
San José, Costa Rica
Tel: 20 39 39. Fax: 20 23 05.
Embassy of the Republic of Costa Rica
Suite 200
408 Queen Street
Ottawa, Ontario
K1R 5A7
Tel: (613) 234 5762. Fax: (613) 230 2656.
Canadian Embassy
Apartado 10.303,
Edif. Cronos 6°
Avenida Central
Calle 3, San José, Costa Rica
Tel: 23 04 46. Telex: 2179.

AREA: 51,100 sq km (19,730 sq miles).
POPULATION: 2,993,676 (mid-1990 estimate).
POPULATION DENSITY: 58.6 per sq km.

CAPITAL: San José. **Population:** 296,625 (1991).
GEOGRAPHY: Costa Rica, lying between Nicaragua and Panama, is a complete coast-to-coast segment of the Central American isthmus. Its width ranges from 119-282km (74-176 miles). A low, thin line of hills that rises between Lake Nicaragua and the Pacific Ocean in Nicaragua broadens and rises as it enters northern Costa Rica, eventually forming the high, rugged, mountains of volcanic origin in the centre and south. The highest peak is Chirripo Grande which reaches 3820m (12,530ft). More than half the population live on the Meseta Central, a plateau with an equitable climate. It is rimmed to the southwest by the Cordillera range, and provides the setting for the country's capital, San José. There are lowlands on both coastlines, mainly swampy on the Caribbean coast, with grassland savannah on the Pacific side merging into swamps towards the south. Rivers cut through the mountains, flowing down to both the Caribbean and the Pacific.
LANGUAGE: Spanish is the official language. English is also widely spoken.
RELIGION: Roman Catholic.
TIME: GMT - 7 (GMT - 6 from Jan 18-Mar 14)
ELECTRICITY: 110/220 volts, 60Hz. 2-pin plugs are standard.
COMMUNICATIONS: Telephone: IDD is available. Country code: 506. **Fax:** Facilities are available in San José at the Radiografica Costarricense, SA, corner of Calle 1, Avenida 5 (opening hours: 0700-2200).
Telex/telegram: International telex facilities are available in San José at the Radiografica Costarricense, SA, corner of Calle 1, Avenida 5 (opening hours: 0700-2200). Since the abolition of the inland telegram service in the UK, the Costa Rican Government Telegram Company will not accept telegrams destined for the UK. **Post:** Airmail letters to Europe usually take between six and ten days. **Press:** Daily newspapers printed in Spanish include *La Nacíon*, *La Républica* and *La Prensa Libre*. One weekly is printed in English (*The Tico Times*).
BBC World Service and Voice of America frequencies: From time to time these change. See the section *How to Use this Book* for more information.

BBC:				
MHz	17.72	11.78	9.590	5.975
Voice of America:				
MHz	15.21	11.74	9.815	6.030

PASSPORT/VISA

Regulations and requirements may be subject to change at short notice, and you are advised to contact the appropriate diplomatic or consular authority before finalising travel arrangements. Details of these may be found at the head of this country's entry. Any numbers in the chart refer to the footnotes below.

	Passport Required?	Visa Required?	Return Ticket Required?
Full British	Yes	No	Yes
BVP	Not valid	-	-
Australian	Yes	No	Yes
Canadian	Yes	No	Yes
USA	Yes	No	Yes
Other EC	Yes	No/1	Yes
Japanese	Yes	No	Yes

Note: Gypsies, hippies and persons of 'unkempt' appearance will be deported.
PASSPORTS: Valid passport required by all, with a minimum validity of six months at the date of entry.
British Visitors Passport: Not acceptable.
VISAS: Required by all except:
(a) **[1]** nationals of EC countries for a period of 90 days (with the exception of nationals of Greece who *do* need a 30-day visa; French and Irish nationals do not need visas for a period of 30 days);
(b) nationals of Argentina, Austria, Canada, Finland, Hungary, Israel, Japan, Liechtenstein, Norway, Panama, Paraguay, Peurto Rico, Romania, South Korea, Sweden, Switzerland, Uruguay and the USA for a stay of up to 90 days;
(c) nationals of Albania, Antigua, Australia, Bahamas, Barbados, Barbuda, Belize, Bermuda, Bolivia, Brazil, Bulgaria, Cayman Islands, Czechoslovakia, Chile, Colombia, Dominica, Dominican Republic, Ecuador, El Salvador, Grenada, Guatemala, Guyana, Honduras, Iceland, Jamaica, Kenya, Martinique, Mexico, Monaco, New Zealand, Paraguay, Peru, Philippines, Poland, St Lucia, St Vincent, San Marino, Singapore, South Africa, Suriname, Trinidad & Tobago, Vatican City and Venezuela for a period of 1 month.
All other nationals require a visa.
Types of visa: Tourist. Cost: US$20 or equivalent. Transit passengers do not require a visa if they continue their journey within 8 hours.
Validity: Visas are valid for 90 days or 1 month. Contact the Immigration Department in Costa Rica for renewal or extension procedure.
Application to: Consulate (or Consular Section of Embassy). For addresses, see top of entry.
Application requirements: (a) Completed application form. (b) 1 photo. (c) Sufficient funds to cover duration of stay.
Working days required: One day to several weeks, depending on nationality of applicant. (Some visas need the authorisation of the Immigration Department in Costa Rica.)
Temporary residence: A signed contract with the prospective employer is needed. For residence as a retiree, only those with a minimum monthly income of US$600 will be considered.

MONEY

Currency: Costa Rican Colon (CRC) = 100 céntimos. Notes are in denominations of CRC1000, 500, 100, 50, 20, 10 and 5. Coins are in denominations of CRC20, 10, 5, 2 and 1 and 50, 25, 10 and 5 centimos.
Currency exchange: Visitors should consult their banks for the current rate of exchange (there is no direct local quotation for sterling; the cross rate with the US$ is used). *Casas de Cambio* give better rates of exchange than banks and street money charges in San José offer even better rates at times.
Credit cards: Mastercard, American Express, Visa and Diners Club are accepted, but check with your credit card company for details of merchant acceptability and other services which may be available.
Travellers cheques: Should always be in US Dollars.
Exchange rate indicators: The following figures are included as a guide to the movements of the Costa Rican Colón against Sterling and the US Dollar:

Date:	Oct '89	Oct '90	Oct '91	Oct '92
£1.00=	130.51	189.65	227.00	215.67
$1.00=	82.65	97.08	130.80	139.89

Currency restrictions: There are no restrictions on the import and export of either local or foreign currency.
Banking hours: 0900-1600 Monday to Friday.

DUTY FREE

The following goods may be imported into Costa Rica without incurring customs duty:
500g of tobacco produce;
3 litres of alcoholic beverage;
A reasonable quantity of perfume for personal use;
One video camera;
One camera and six rolls of film.

PUBLIC HOLIDAYS

Public holidays observed in Costa Rica are as follows:
Mar 19 '93 Feast of St Joseph. **Apr 8** Maundy Thursday. **Apr 9** Good Friday. **Apr 11** Anniversary of the Battle of Rivas. **May 1** Labour Day. **Jun 10** Corpus Christi. **Jun 29** St Peter and St Paul. **Jul 25** Anniversary of the Annexation of Guanacaste Province. **Aug 2** Our Lady of the Angels. **Aug 15** Assumption. **Sep 15** Independence Day. **Oct 12** Columbus Day. **Dec 8** Immaculate Conception. **Dec 25** Christmas Day. **Jan 1 '94** New Year's Day. **Mar 19** Feast of St Joseph.
Note: Most businesses close for the whole of Holy Week and between Christmas and New Year.

HEALTH

Regulations and requirements may be subject to change at short notice, and you are advised to contact your doctor well in advance of your intended date of departure. Any numbers in the chart refer to the footnotes below.

	Special Precautions?	Certificate Required?
Yellow Fever	No	No
Cholera	No	No
Typhoid & Polio	1	-
Malaria	2	-
Food & Drink	3	

[1]: Vaccination is recommended for both polio and typhoid.
[2]: Malaria risk throughout the year, mostly in the benign *vivax* form, in the rural areas below 500m, of Alajuela, Guanacaste, Limán and Puntarenas.
[3]: Mains water is normally heavily chlorinated, and whilst relatively safe may cause mild abdominal upsets. Drinking water outside main cities and towns may be contaminated and sterilisation is advisable. Bottled water is available and is advised for the first few weeks of the stay. Milk is pasteurised and dairy products are safe for consumption. Local meat, poultry, seafood, fruit and vegetables are generally considered safe to eat.
Bilharzia (schistosomiasis) is present. Avoid swimming and paddling in fresh water. Swimming pools which are well-chlorinated and maintained are safe.
Health care: Health insurance is recommended. Reliable medical services are available in Costa Rica. Standards of health and hygiene are among the best in Latin America.

TRAVEL - International

AIR: The Costa Rican national airline is *Lacsa (LR)*. *Lacsa* fly direct to Costa Rica from Miami, New Orleans, Los Angeles, New York, Mexico, Colombia, Venezuela and Panama. For routes via the USA a change of plane is necessary. Flights with one or two stops which do not go via the USA are available from *Iberia* in Madrid and *KLM* in Amsterdam. They take longer but the need to

COSTA RICA | **HEALTH REGULATIONS** | **VISA REGULATIONS** | Code-Link

GALILEO/WORLDSPAN

TI-DFT/SJO/HE

TI-DFT/SJO/VI

SABRE

TIDFT/SJO/HE

TIDFT/SJO/VI

To access this information on your CRS, swipe the barcode with a light pen or type in the text under the barcode. For more information, see the introduction *How to Use This Book*.

change planes is eliminated.
Approximate flight times: From San José to *London* is 12 hours (including stop-over time), to *Los Angeles* is 11 hours and to *New York* is 7 hours.
International airport: *San José (SJO)* (Juan Santamaria) 18km (11 miles) northwest of the city. Transport to/from city; coach every (20 minutes) 0500-2400. Return pick-ups at various hotels. Bus to city (35 minutes) every 15 minutes 0600-2200. Return from Afajuefa Station service 14th Street, 1/3 Avenue, every 20 minutes. Taxis also available to city.
Departure tax: US$5 (or CRC equivalent) payable if staying more than 48 hours by all passengers leaving Costa Rica. Nationals and alien residents CRC2630.
SEA: *Lauro Lines* run regular services to Puerto Limon from Mediterranean (Genoa, Barcelona). *Costa Lines* run cruises which put in at Puntarenas.
ROAD: The Inter-American Highway runs through Costa Rica from La Cruz on the Nicaraguan border through San José to Progreso on the Panamanian border.

TRAVEL - Internal

AIR: *SANSA*, a national airline, operates cargo and passenger services between San José and provincial towns and villages. A bus is provided from the airline offices in San José to the airport. A number of smaller airlines also provide internal flights. Reservations cannot be made outside Costa Rica.
RAIL: A train service within Costa Rica links San José to Puntarenas on the Pacific coast (two trains daily), and Puerto Limón on the Caribbean coast (once daily).
ROAD: Roads are generally very good. There are 29,586km (18,384 miles) of all-weather highways including 653km (405 miles) of the Inter-American Highway, and highways linking San José with the other principal towns. **Bus:** Regular services to most towns, but buses are often crowded so pre-booking is advisable. Costa Rica offers a wide variety of sightseeing tours. Most tour companies feature bilingual guides and round-trip transportation from hotels. For full details contact the Costa Rica National Tourist Institute. **Taxi:** Numerous and inexpensive in San José. Taxis are coloured red (except those serving the Juan Santamaria International Airport, which are orange). Fares should be negotiated before starting the journey. **Car hire:** *Hertz*, *Rentacar SA* and local firms have offices in San José. Driving is on the right. Distances are measured in kilometres. A speed limit of 88kmph (55 mph) is enforced on most highways.
Documentation: Drivers must have a national driving licence.
URBAN: San José has privately run bus services, charging fares on a 2-zone system.
JOURNEY TIMES: The following chart gives approximate journey times (in hours and minutes) from San José to other major cities/towns.

	Air	Road	Rail
Alajuela	-	0.30	-
Cartago	-	0.30	-
Heredia	-	0.20	-
Puntarenas	-	2.00	4.00
Liberia	0.25	3.00	-
Quepos	0.30	3.30	-
Limón	0.25	2.00	6.00

ACCOMMODATION

HOTELS: There is a good range of reasonably priced hotel accommodation. Most proprietors speak English. San José has many hotels, from the extravagant to smaller, family-run hotels in the less fashionable districts. There are several good hotels out of town near the airport. Larger hotels have swimming pools and other sports facilities. The majority of the hotels have their own restaurants which are generally good and reasonably priced. Hotel tariffs are liable to alteration at any time. A 13% sales tax plus 3% tourism tax is be added to hotel prices. Outside the capital, charges and the standard of comfort are lower. **Grading:** These are graded from A to D according to price range. The A grade category accounts for 20% of all hotels and costs from the equivalent of US$100. About 20% of hotels are in the B range and cost US$50-70. C grade hotels cost US$ 30-50 and D range hotel, about 30%, cost US$10-30. For further information contact: Camara Costarricense de Hoteles y Afines, La Paulina, San José, Costa Rica. Tel: 24 65 72.
CAMPING/CARAVANNING: Facilities at San Antonio de Belen 8km (5 miles) from San José. There is also a small campsite in San Pedro district and south of city on Inter-American highway. There is a camping and caravan site close to Aureola. Most, but not all, national parks (see below) allow camping at designated sites.

RESORTS & EXCURSIONS

One of the Central American states forming the land-bridge between North and South America, Costa Rica has a surprising diversity of terrain (see *Geography* above). In the cities and towns the country's Spanish heritage provides the main features of interest. Elsewhere, Costa Rica's national parks are its greatest glory.

San José

The capital was founded in 1737 and is a pleasant mixture of traditional and modern Spanish architecture. Places of interest include the *Teatro Nacional*, the *Palacio Nacional* (where the legislative assembly meets), and the *Parque Central*, east of which is the Cathedral. There are a number of parks in the city, such as the *Parque Nacional*, the *Parque Bolivar* and the *Parque Morazan*. San José is a good centre for excursions into the beautiful **Meseta Central** region.

Cartago

This town was founded in 1563, but there are no old buildings as earthquakes destroyed the town in 1841 and 1910. However, some of the reconstruction was in the colonial style, the most interesting example being the *Basilica*. Excursions can be made from here to the crater of *Irazu* and to the beautiful valley of *Orosi*.

Carribbean Coast

There are a number of beaches, ports and towns worth visiting. The biggest is **Puerto Limón;** others include *Los Chiles*, *Guapiles*, *Tortuguero*, *Barro Del Colorado*, *Cahuta*, and *Puerto Viejo*.

Pacific Coast

Puntarenas is Costa Rica's principal Pacific port for freight and the beaches around it are rather poor, although **San Lucas Island,** just off the port, has the magnificent beach of *El Coco*. Another island worth a visit is **Isla Del Coco** where a great treasure is supposed to have been buried by pirates. **Puerto Caldera,** a few miles south of Puntarenas, has recently become the country's premier port-of-call for cruise liners. **Puerto Quepos, Nicova, Liberia** and **Samara** are the region's other major towns. There are beautiful beaches in the **Guanacaste** area and near **Quepos** in the south.

National Parks

Well-kept and well-guarded national parks and nature reserves cover 11.23% of the country's territory. The Servicio De Parques Nacionales (SPN) in San José can provide information (and permits where necessary).
Braulio Carrillo National Park is in the central region of the country just 23km (14 miles) north of San José. It has five kinds of forest, some with characteristic rainforest vegetation. Orchids and ferns, jaguars, ocelots and the Baird tapir may be seen here. There are trails through the park and many lookouts.
The **National Park of Poas** contains a smouldering volcano of the same name. It contains the only dwarf cloud-forest in Costa Rica. The crater of the volcano is 1.5km (1 mile) wide and contains a hot-water lake which changes colour from turquoise to green to grey. Access is possible by road.
Tortuguero National Park protects the Atlantic green turtle egg-laying grounds; it is in an area of great ecological diversity. Its network of canals and lagoons serve as waterways for transportation and exploration. There are camping facilities and lodges.
Santa Rosen National Park is in the Dry Pacific climatic zone. There are extensive savannahs and non-deciduous forests. In addition to its abundant wildlife, recreational facilities are provided on some of the beaches.
Corcovado National Park is virgin rainforest containing many endangered species. It has the largest tree in Costa Rica, a ceibo which is 70m (230ft) high. Additionally there is *Cano Island Biological Reserve*, a bird sanctuary.
Cahuita National park protects the only coral reef in the country. Its other attractions include howler and white-faced monkeys and 500 species of fish.
Chirripo National Park contains Costa Rica's highest mountain, 3189m (10,462ft) high. Most notably it contains the quetzal, said to be South America's most beautiful bird.
Other parks are the *Manuel Antonio National Park* , the *Barra de Colorado National Wildlife Refuge* and the *Rafael L Rodriguez National Wildlife Refuge*.
In addition, many of the tiny islands in the **Gulf of Nicoya,** near Puntarenas, are 'biological protection areas'.

SOCIAL PROFILE

FOOD & DRINK: Restaurants in major towns and cities serve a variety of foods including French, Italian, Mexican, North American and Chinese. Food everywhere is good, from the most expensive to the cheapest eating places (which are generally found west of the city centre). Food *sodas* (small restaurants) serve local food. Common dishes include *casado* (rice, beans, stewed beef, fried plantain and cabbage), *olla de came* (soup of beef, plantain, com, yuca, nampi and chayote), *sopa negra* (black beans with a poached egg), and *picadillo* (meat and vegetable stew). Snacks are popular and include *gallos* (filled tortillas), *tortas* (containing meat and vegetables), *arreglados* (bread filled with same), *pan de yuca* (speciality from stalls in San José). There are many types of cold drink made from fresh fruit, milk or cereal flour, for example, *cebada* (barley flour), *pinolillo* (roasted corn), *horchata* (rice flour with cinnamon). Imported alcoholic and soft drinks widely available. Coffee is good value and has an excellent flavour.
NIGHTLIFE: San José especially has many nightclubs and venues with folk music and dance, theatres and cinemas.
SHOPPING: Special purchases include wood and leather rocking chairs (which dismantle for export) as well as a range of local crafts available in major cities and towns. Local markets are also well worth visiting. Prices are slightly higher than many other Latin American countries. Best buys are wooden items, ceramics, jewellery and leather handicrafts. **Shopping hours:** 0850-1200 and 1400-1800 Monday to Saturday.
SPORT: Besides **swimming** in the Carribean Sea and the Pacific, most major towns and resorts have swimming pools open to the public. Horses can be hired for **riding** anywhere. The Barra de Colorado area is world famous for **fishing**. There is good **sea fishing** off Puntarenas, and in the mouth of Rio Chirripo on the Caribbean side near the Nicaraguan border. San José and Puerto Limón have **golf** courses. Association **football** is the national sport, played every Sunday morning between May and October. In San José matches can be seen at the Saprissa Stadium.
SOCIAL CONVENTIONS: Handshaking is common and forms of address are important. Christian names are preceded by Don for a man and Donna for a woman. Normal courtesies should be observed when visiting someone's home and gifts are appreciated as a token of thanks, especially if invited for a meal. For most occasions casual wear is acceptable, but beachwear should be confined to the beach; strapless dresses and shorts are not acceptable for women in San José.
Tipping: It is not necessary to tip taxi drivers. All hotels must add 13% service tax plus 3% tourist tax to the bill by law. Restaurants add a 10% service charge. Tipping is expected by hotel staff, porters and waiters.

BUSINESS PROFILE

ECONOMY: Costa Rica's export earnings are derived partly from agriculture (coffee, bananas, meat, sugar and cocos) and from new non-traditional exports, which amounted to 50% of total exports in 1990. Staple crops are also grown for domestic consumption. Manufacturing industry consists of food processing, textiles, chemicals and plastics and is steadily expanding with government encouragement: new industries include aluminium, following the discovery of a large bauxite deposit. Costa Rica relies heavily on foreign loans and aid, not least because of its considerable overseas debt. Most of this comes through international bodies such as the IMF and from the United States, which is Costa Rica's main trading partner: the USA supplies 43% of imports and takes 44% of the country's exports. Costa Rica has a small net trade surplus with both the USA and the world as a whole.
BUSINESS: Customs tend to be conservative. Advance appointments, courtesy and punctuality are appreciated. It is necessary to have some knowledge of Spanish, although many locals speak English. Best months for business visits are November and December; avoid the last week of September, which is the end of the financial year. **Office hours:** 0800-1130 and 1330-1730 Monday to Friday.
COMMERCIAL INFORMATION: The following organisations can offer advice: Cámara de Comercio de

Costa Rica (Chamber of Commerce), Urbanización Tournón, Apartado 1 114, 1000 San José. Tel: 21 00 05. Telex: 2646 *or* Cámara Nacional de Turismo, Aparto 828 1000, San José, Costa Rica. Tel: 33 88 17. Fax: 55 45 13.

HISTORY & GOVERNMENT

HISTORY: Columbus landed in what is now Costa Rica in 1501. Although it was never heavily colonised, the region came under the captaincy-general of Guatemala. The country declared independence from Spain in 1821, as a member of the United Provinces of Central America, a short-lived confederation whose capital was Guatemala City. This reflected the then dominance of Guatemala in the region, a factor which caused increasing resentment among the other members of the United Provinces and ultimately led to its dissolution into component states in 1840. On the whole, Costa Rica has enjoyed a largely peaceful history, with the notable exception of a civil war in 1948, which followed a disputed presidential election. After the victory of José Figueres Ferrer in the conflict, the army was abolished in a unique political decision which entrusted the defence of the country to a Civil Guard. Costa Rica is the most stable and liberal of the Central American states – it celebrated 100 years of democracy in 1989 – with a high literacy rate and a comfortable standard of living. In February 1986, Oscar Arias Sanchez of the Partido de Liberacíon Nacional was elected president while his party obtained an absolute majority in the Legislative Assembly. In 1987, Arias was awarded the Nobel Peace Prize for his efforts in bringing warring parties elsewhere in central America to the negotiating table. Arias stood down prior to the 1990 national elections to be replaced as PLN candidate by Carlos Manuel Castillo. But faction-fighting within the PLN damaged the party sufficiently to give victory to Rafael Angel Calderon, candidate of the rival Partido Unidad Social Cristiana. Angel was soon confronted with a major national emergency as an earthquake hit the country in April 1991 causing widespread loss of life and damage. Since then the Government has faced some civil unrest following cuts in social programmes to meet IMF budget requirements.
GOVERNMENT: Under the constitution of 1949, executive power is vested in the President, supported by two Vice-Presidents and an appointed Cabinet of Ministers. The President is elected for a 4-year term by universal adult suffrage (voting is obligatory) conditional on one candidate receiving more than 40% of the vote. Legislation is the responsibility of the 57-member National Assembly, which is also elected for a 4-year term of office.

CLIMATE

In the Central Valley where the main centres of population are located the average temperature is 23°C. In the coastal areas the temperature is much hotter. The rainy season starts in May and finishes in November and rain, which usually occurs during the afternoon, can be very heavy. The 'warm' dry season is December to May, though temperature differences between summer and winter are slight.
Required clothing: Lightweight cottons and linens most of the year. Warmer clothes for cooler evenings. Waterproofing during rainy season.

SAN JOSE Costa Rica (1120m)

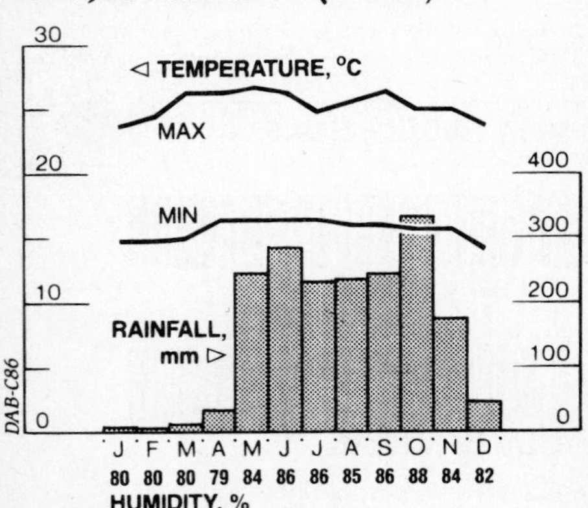

COTE D'IVOIRE

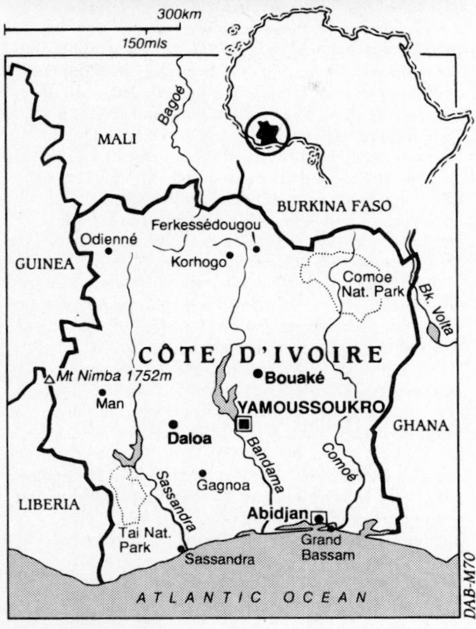

□ international airport

Location: West African coast.

Note: Although the country has not officially changed its name, a speech made by the President in October 1985 requested that the country's name should not be translated from the French, and the Foreign and Commonwealth Office was officially notified of this on December 12 1986.

Direction de la Promotion Touristique
BP V184
Abidjan, Côte d'Ivoire
Tel: 320 011. Telex: 23438.
Embassy of the Republic of Côte d'Ivoire
2 Upper Belgrave Street
London SW1X 8BJ
Tel: (071) 235 6991. Fax: (071) 259 5439. Telex: 23906 IVORY G. Opening hours: 0900-1200 and 1300-1600 Monday to Friday.
British Embassy
01 BP 2581
Third Floor, Immeuble 'Les Harmonies'
angle boulevard Carde et avenue Dr Jamot
Plateau
Abidjan 01, Côte d'Ivoire
Tel: 226 850/1/2 *or* 328 209. Fax: 223 221. Telex: 23706 PRDRME CI.
Embassy of the Republic of Côte d'Ivoire
2424 Massachusetts Avenue, NW
Washington, DC
20008
Tel: (202) 797 0300.
Embassy of the United States of America
01 BP 1712
5 rue Jesse Owens
Abidjan, Côte d'Ivoire
Tel: 210 979 *or* 214 672. Fax: 223 259. Telex: 23660.
Embassy of the Republic Côte d'Ivoire
9 Malborough Avenue
Ottawa, Ontario
K1N 8E6
Tel: (613) 236 9919. Fax: (613) 563 8287.
Canadian Embassy
01 BP 4101
Immeuble Trade Centre
Abidjan 01, Côte d'Ivoire
Tel: 212 009. Telex: 23593.

AREA: 322,462 sq km (124,503 sq miles).
POPULATION: 12,600,000 (1990).
POPULATION DENSITY: 39.1 per sq km.
CAPITAL: Yamoussoukro (administrative & political). **Population:** 200,000 (1986). Abidjan (commercial). **Population:** 1,900,000 (1986).
GEOGRAPHY: Côte d'Ivoire shares borders with Liberia, Guinea, Mali, Burkina Faso and Ghana. There are 600km (370 miles) of coast on the Gulf of Guinea (Atlantic Ocean). The southern and western parts of the country are forested, undulating countryside rising to meet the savannah plains of the north and the mountainous western border. Three rivers, the Sassandra, the Bandama and the Comoé, run directly north–south and on their approach to the coast flow into a series of lagoons. Birdlife is plentiful throughout the country, but particularly so near the coast.
LANGUAGE: The official language is French. Local dialects include Dioula and Baoulé, which tribes use as trading languages.
RELIGION: 60% traditional beliefs, 25% Muslim, 15% Christian.
TIME: GMT.
ELECTRICITY: 220/230 volts AC, 50Hz. Round 2-pin plugs are standard.
COMMUNICATIONS: International telecommunications are only available in major towns/centres.
Telephone: IDD is available. Country code: 225. **Telex:** There are telex facilities at most hotels and the Central Post Office. **Post:** Airmail to Europe takes up to two weeks. Post office opening hours: 0730-1200 and 1430-1800 Monday to Friday. **Press:** All newspapers are in French. *Abidjan 7 Jours*, published weekly, gives local information, including events of interest.
BBC World Service and Voice of America frequencies: From time to time these change. See the section *How to Use this Book* for more information.

BBC:

MHz	21.71	15.07	11.86	6.005

Voice of America:

MHz	21.49	15.60	9.525	6.035

PASSPORT/VISA

Regulations and requirements may be subject to change at short notice, and you are advised to contact the appropriate diplomatic or consular authority before finalising travel arrangements. Details of these may be found at the head of this country's entry. Any numbers in the chart refer to the footnotes below.

	Passport Required?	Visa Required?	Return Ticket Required?
Full British	Yes	No	Yes
BVP	Not valid	-	-
Australian	Yes	Yes	Yes
Canadian	Yes	Yes	Yes
USA	Yes	1	Yes
Other EC	Yes	2	Yes
Japanese	Yes	Yes	Yes

PASSPORTS: Valid passport required by all except nationals of Benin, Burkina Faso, Mali, Mauritania, Niger, Senegal and Togo, if holding ID cards or a passport not expired for longer than 5 years.
British Visitors Passport: Not acceptable.
VISAS: Required by all except nationals of:
(a) **[1]** USA (for a period not exceeding 3 months);
(b) **[2]** Denmark, France, Germany, Italy, Ireland and the UK (all other EC countries *do* need visas);
(c) Andorra, Benin, Burkina Faso, Cameroon, Cape Verde, Central African Republic, Chad, Congo, Finland, Gabon, Gambia, Ghana, Guinea, Guinea-Bissau, Liberia, Madagascar, Mali, Mauritania, Monaco, Niger, Nigeria, Norway, Senegal, Seychelles, Sierra Leone, Sweden, Togo and Tunisia (for a period not exceeding 3 months).
Types of visa: Tourist, Business and Transit. Single entry: £15. Multiple entry: £20. Transit visas are not required by air travellers who do not intend to leave the airport and who have confirmed bookings on the first plane departing for their destination or on one that leaves on the same day they arrived.
Validity: Generally up to 3 months.
Application to: Consulate (or Consular Section at Embassy). For addresses, see top of entry.
Application requirements: (a) Valid passport. (b) 2 application forms. (c) 2 passport-size photos. (d) Business letters if appropriate.
Working days required: 2.

MONEY

Currency: CFA Franc (CFA Fr) = 100 centimes. Notes are in denominations of CFA Fr10,000, 5000, 1000, 500, 100 and 50. Coins are in denominations of CFA Fr100, 50, 25, 10, 5 and 1. Côte d'Ivoire is part of the French Monetary Area and the CFA Franc is tied to the French Franc at CFA Fr50 = FFr1.
Currency exchange: Currency can be exchanged at the

airport, and at banks and hotels.
Credit cards: American Express and Access/Mastercard are widely accepted; Visa and Diners Club have more limited use. Check with your credit card company for details of merchant acceptability and other facilities which may be available.
Travellers cheques: These are accepted in hotels, restaurants and some shops.
Exchange rate indicators: The following figures are included as a guide to the movements of the CFA Franc against Sterling and the US Dollar:

Date:	Oct '89	Oct '90	Oct '91	Oct '92
£1.00=	505.13	498.38	496.12	413.75
$1.00=	319.91	255.12	285.87	260.71

Currency restrictions: The import of both foreign and local currencies is unlimited but all currencies other than the French Franc and the CFA Franc must be declared on arrival. The export of foreign currency according to amount declared and of local currency to CFAfr10,000. There is no restriction on the re-export of unused travellers cheques and letters of credit. Residents and business travellers should enquire at the Consulate.
Banking hours: 0800-1130 and 1430-1630 Monday to Friday.

DUTY FREE

The following goods may be imported into Côte d'Ivoire by passengers over 15 years of age without incurring customs duty:
200 cigarettes or 25 cigars or 250g of tobacco;
1 bottle of wine;
1 bottle of spirits;
A reasonable amount of perfume for personal use.
Prohibited items: Sporting guns may only be imported under licence. Limits are placed on certain personal effects; contact the Consulate prior to departure.

PUBLIC HOLIDAYS

Public holidays observed in Côte d'Ivoire are as follows:
Mar 25 '93 Start of Eid al-Fitr. **Apr 9** Good Friday. **Apr 12** Easter Monday. **May 1** Labour Day. **May 20** Ascension Day. **May 31** Whit Monday. **Jun 1** Start of Eid al-Adha. **Aug 15** Assumption. **Nov 1** All Saints Day. **Nov 15** Peace Day. **Dec 7** Independence Day. **Dec 25** Christmas Day. **Jan 1 '94** New Year's Day. **Mar** Start of Eid al-Fitr.
Note: (a) Holidays that fall on a Sunday are often observed on the following day. (b) Muslim festivals are timed according to local sightings of various phases of the Moon and the dates given above are approximations. During the lunar month of Ramadan that precedes Eid al-Fitr, Muslims fast during the day and feast at night and normal business patterns may be interrupted. Some disruption may continue into Eid al-Fitr itself. Eid al-Fitr and Eid al-Adha may last anything from two to ten days, depending on the region. For more information see the section *World of Islam* at the back of the book.

HEALTH

Regulations and requirements may be subject to change at short notice, and you are advised to contact your doctor well in advance of your intended date of departure. Any numbers in the chart refer to the footnotes below.

	Special Precautions?	Certificate Required?
Yellow Fever	Yes	1
Cholera	Yes	2
Typhoid & Polio	Yes	-
Malaria	Yes	-
Food & Drink	3	-

[1]: A yellow fever vaccination certificate is required from travellers over one year of age coming from all countries.
[2]: Following WHO guidelines issued in 1973, a cholera vaccination certificate is no longer a condition of entry to Côte d'Ivoire. However, cholera is a serious risk in this country and precautions are essential. Up-to-date advice should be sought before deciding whether these precautions should include vaccination as medical opinion is divided over its effectiveness. See the *Health* section at the back of the book.
[3]: All water should be regarded as being potentially contaminated. Water used for drinking, brushing teeth or making ice should have first been boiled or otherwise sterilised. Milk is unpasteurised and should be boiled. Powdered or tinned milk is available and is advised, but make sure that it is reconstituted with pure water. Avoid dairy products which are likely to have been made from unboiled milk. Only eat well-cooked meat and fish, preferably served hot. Pork, salad and mayonnaise may carry increased risk. Vegetables should be cooked and fruit peeled.
Malaria risk (and of other insect-borne diseases) exists all year throughout the country, including urban areas. The malignant *falciparum* form is prevalent. Resistance to chloroquine has been reported.
Rabies is present. For those at high risk, vaccination before arrival should be considered. If you are bitten abroad seek medical advice without delay. For more information consult the *Health* section at the back of the book.
Bilharzia (schistosomiasis) is present. Avoid swimming and paddling in fresh water. Swimming pools which are well-chlorinated and maintained are safe.
Meningitis risk is present depending on area visited and time of year.
Health care: Health facilities are limited; medical insurance is vital.

TRAVEL - International

AIR: The main airline to serve Côte d'Ivoire is *Air Afrique (RK)*, in which Côte d'Ivoire has a shareholding.
Approximate flight time: From *London* to Abidjan is 6 hours.
International airports: *Abidjan (ABJ)* (Port Bouet Airport) is 16km (10 miles) southeast of Abidjan (travel time – 25 minutes). Airport facilities include duty-free shop (24 hours), restaurant, shops and car hire. A bus runs every 10 minutes to the city 0510-2300. Taxi service is available.
Yamoussoukro (San Pedro Airport) has recently been upgraded to international standard.
Departure tax: CFA Fr1200 for international departures, transit passengers are exempt.
SEA: There are no regular passenger sailings but cargo liners provide limited accommodation for passengers travelling from Europe. The *Royal Viking* line operates a cruise to Abidjan.
RAIL: There are two through trains with sleeping and restaurant cars from Abidjan to Ouagadougou (Burkina Faso) daily. Those intending to travel the length of the line should be aware that the Burkina Faso rail network is under constant threat of closure because of financial difficulties; check with appropriate authorities before finalising arrangements.
ROAD: There are road links of varying quality from Kumasi (Ghana) and from Burkina Faso, Guinea and Liberia.

TRAVEL - Internal

AIR: *Air Ivoire (VU)* operates regular internal flights from Abidjan to all major towns.
Approximate flight times: From Abidjan to *Abengourou* is 35 minutes; to *Bondoukou* is 1 hour 20 minutes; to *Bouaké* is 1 hour 20 minutes; to *Bouna* is 1 hour 20 minutes; to *Boundiali* is 2 hours 35 minutes; to *Daloa* is 1 hour; to *Gagnoa* is 50 minutes; to *Guiglo* is 2 hours 15 minutes; to *Korhogo* is 1 hour 30 minutes; to *Man* is 50 minutes; to *Odienne* is 2 hours 20 minutes; to *San Pedro* is 1 hour; to *Sassandra* is 45 minutes; to *Seguela* is 1 hour 20 minutes; to *Tabou* is 1 hour 25 minutes; to *Touba* is 1 hour and to *Yamoussoukro* is 30 minutes.
Departure tax: CFA Fr300 for domestic departures.
RAIL: The Abidjan–Niger railway is one of the most advanced in Africa and runs fast trains several times daily from Abidjan to Bouaké and Ferkessédougou.
ROAD: Côte d'Ivoire has a good road system by West African standards, with over 2000km (1200 miles) of asphalted roads. Petrol stations are frequent except in the north. **Bus:** Small private buses operate throughout the country; they are comfortable and efficient. There are also luxury-class coaches for the longer journeys. **Taxi:** These are available in main cities. **Car hire:** Cars may be hired in Abidjan, main towns and at the airport. **Documentation:** Insurance is compulsory for the driver, as is an International Driving Permit. The motorist must have a customs pass-sheet issued by the Automobile Club of the country of the vehicle's registration.
URBAN: Extensive bus and boat services are operated in Abidjan by *SOTRA* on a 2-tiered fare structure. Taxis are usually red and metered; rates from 2400-0600 are doubled.
JOURNEY TIMES: The following chart gives approximate journey times (in hours and minutes) from Abidjan to other major towns in the Côte d'Ivoire.

	Air	Rail
Agboville	-	2.00
Dimbokro	-	4.00
Bouaké	1.20	6.00
Touba	1.00	-
Tabou	1.20	-
Man	0.50	-
Daloa	1.00	-

ACCOMMODATION

Hotels and restaurants are expensive in the larger towns. There are several hotels of international standard in Abidjan. In general, there is a choice between luxury, medium-range and cheaper accommodation in the larger towns. In all cases it is advisable to book in advance. Further information from the Société Ivoirienne d'Expansion Touristique et Hôtelière (SIETHO), 04 BP 375, avenue Lamblin, Plateau, Abidjan 04. Tel: 322 807 *or* 332 382. **Grading:** Hotels are graded from 1 to 5-star.

RESORTS & EXCURSIONS

Abidjan, the commercial capital and largest city, is dominated by the *Plateau*, the central commercial district. The older, more traditional heart of the city is *Treichville*, home of many bars, restaurants and nightclubs as well as the colourful central market. The city is one of the most expensive in the world. There is a very good museum, the *Ifon Museum*. Suburbs have grown up along the banks of the lagoon; these include Cocody (with the large Hotel Ivoire complex), Marcory and Adjamé.
About 100km (60 miles) east of the capital is the beach resort of **Assouinde**; other places being developed as tourist attractions include **Tiagba**, a stilt-town; **Grand-Bassam,** whose sandy beaches make the place a favourite weekend retreat for the inhabitants of Abidjan; and **Bondoukouo,** one of the oldest settlements in the country.
In the west of the country is the attractive town of **Man**, situated in a region of thickly forested mountains

CÔTE D'IVOIRE | **HEALTH REGULATIONS** | **VISA REGULATIONS** | Code-Link

GALILEO/WORLDSPAN

TI-DFT/ABJ/HE

TI-DFT/ABJ/VI

SABRE

TIDFT/ABJ/HE

TIDFT/ABJ/VI

To access this information on your CRS, swipe the barcode with a light pen or type in the text under the barcode. For more information, see the introduction *How to Use This Book*.

and plateaux. The nearby waterfalls are a popular attraction, as are climbs to the peak of *Mount Tonkoui* and visits to the villages of **Biankouma** and **Gouessesso,** 55km (34 miles) away.

The new administrative and political capital is **Yamoussoukro,** about 230km (143 miles) north of Abidjan. The town has a lively market, an international-standard golf course and several buildings of architectural interest, including the *Palace and Plantations of the President* and the *Mosque*. Also of architectural interest but, above all, of statistical interest, is the recently completed cathedral *Notre Dame de la Paix*. Fractionally smaller than St Peter's in Rome, it incorporates a greater area of stained glass than the total area of stained glass in France. Roman Catholicism is a minority religion in Côte d'Ivoire (some say that the Cathedral could accommodate every Roman Catholic in the country several times over). Yamoussoukro is the birthplace of Félix Houphouët-Boigny, who has been Côte d'Ivoire's president since independence in 1960. The Cathedral was paid for almost entirely out of his own pocket.

Other towns of interest include **Korhogo**, the main city of the north and centre of a good fishing and hunting district; the former capital of **Bingerville**; and the town of **Bouaké** in the centre of the country.

There is a choice of locally organised package tours to provide the traveller with a lightning tour of the country; enquire locally for details. Many of these will include visits to one of the country's national parks, which include the **Comoé** in the northeast and the **Banco National Park,** 3000 hectares of equatorial forest, home to a wide range of wildlife.

SOCIAL PROFILE

FOOD & DRINK: Table service is usual in restaurants; in bars table and/or counter service is available. Abidjan and other centres have restaurants serving French, Italian, Caribbean, Lebanese and Vietnamese food. There is a growing number of African restaurants catering for foreigners. Traditional dishes are *kedjenou* (chicken cooked with different vegetables and sealed in banana leaves), *n'voufou* (mashed bananas or yam mixed with palm oil and served with aubergine sauce) and *attieké* (cassava dish). The best area for spicy African food is the Treichville district of Abidjan. The blue pages of the Abidjan telephone book have a special restaurant section. There are no restrictions on drinking.

NIGHTLIFE: There are nightclubs in most major centres. Abidjan is the most lively area with its hotels and lagoon-side tourist resorts. There are also theatres, casinos, bars and traditional entertainment is offered in some hotels.

SHOPPING: In the markets, hard bargaining is often necessary to get prices down to reasonable levels. Special purchases include wax prints, Ghanaian *kente* cloth, indigo fabric and woven cloth, wooden statuettes and masks, bead necklaces, pottery and basketware. **Shopping hours:** 0800-1200 and 1600-1900 Monday to Saturday.

SPORT: There are many **swimming** pools in main centres and hotels, particularly in Abidjan and the surrounding coastal resorts. All along this stretch of coast there is a dangerous deep current and all but the strongest swimmers should stay near the shore. There is good coastal and river **fishing.** Red carp, barracuda, mullet and sole can all be caught from the shores of the lagoons. Sea trips can be organised through travel agencies to catch sharks, swordfish, bonito and marlin. Most major centres have a **golf** course. In Abidjan there is a course at the Hotel Ivoire on the Riviera. Many hotels have **tennis** courts. Boats and instructors are available in Abidjan at the Marina, Hotel Ivoire, where **water-skiing** facilities are also available.

SPECIAL EVENTS: For a full list of festivals and other special events to be held in Côte d'Ivoire in 1993/1994, and for the exact dates of the selection listed below, contact the Embassy, Consulate or the Direction de la Promotion Touristique (see addresses at head of entry). Those festivals that are also public holidays are listed in the appropriate section above.

Mar '93 *Carnival*, Bouaké. **Easter** *Masks Festival, Popo Carnival* and *Dripi Festival*. **Jun** *Tabaski, Sheep Festival*. **Jul** *Karité*. **Sep/Oct** *Yam Festival*, Agni, Abron and Koulango districts. **Nov** *Carnival de Bassam*, Abissa. **Dec** *Fête des Ignames*, Agni. **Jan '94 (second week)** *Katana Festival*. **Feb** *Seke Festival* and *Houphouët-Boigny Golf Trophy*, Yamoussoukro. **Mar** *Carnival*, Bouaké.

SOCIAL CONVENTIONS: One of the most striking features of Côte d'Ivoire, distinguishing it from many other African countries, is the extreme ethnic and linguistic variety. The size of each of the 60 groups – which include the Akar, Kron, Nzima, Hone, Voltaic and Malinke peoples – varies widely and the area they occupy may cover a whole region. With very few exceptions every Ivorian has a mother tongue which is that of the village, along with traditions, family and social relations within their ethnic group. French has become the official language of schools, cities and government and therefore has an influence on lifestyle even at a modest level. Handshaking is normal. Tropical lightweight clothes are essential, a light raincoat in the rainy season and a hat for the sun. Casual wear is widely acceptable but beachwear should be confined to the beach or poolside. Ties need only be worn for formal occasions.

Small tokens of appreciation, a souvenir from home or a business gift with the company logo are always welcome. Normal courtesies should be observed and it is considered polite to arrive punctually for social occasions. There are no restrictions on smoking. Snakes are regarded as sacred by some ethnic groups.

Tipping: Most hotels and restarants include a service charge in the bill; if not, tip 15%.

BUSINESS PROFILE

ECONOMY: Côte d'Ivoire is the world's largest producer of cocoa and the second largest of coffee and cotton. Timber and fruit are the other main commodities while the Government has successfully encouraged diversification into rice, rubber, sugar and others. Agriculture and forestry thus employ the majority of the population as well as providing the country's major export earners. Côte d'Ivoire has also developed a light industrial sector producing textiles, chemicals and sugar refining and geared towards export markets. There are also assembly plants for cars and other manufactured goods. Significant offshore oil deposits were discovered in the late 1970s but have been developed slowly due to financial and technical problems. France is Côte d'Ivoire's main trading partner and The Netherlands are a key export market. Côte d'Ivoire has comprehensive trading links throughout the European Community and with Nigeria, the CIS and elsewhere.

BUSINESS: French is predominantly used in business circles, although executives in larger businesses may speak English. Translators are generally available. Punctuality is expected, although the host may be late. Visiting cards are essential and given to each person met. It is usual for business visitors to be entertained by local hosts in a hotel or restaurant. Businessmen need only wear cotton safari suits. **Office hours:** 0730-1200 and 1430-1730 Monday to Friday, 0800-1200 Saturday.

COMMERCIAL INFORMATION: The following organisation can offer advice: Chambre de Commerce de la Côte d'Ivoire, 01 BP 1399, avenue Joseph Anoma, Abidjan 01. Tel: 21 46 79. Telex: 23224.

CONFERENCES/CONVENTIONS: In Abidjan, the Palais de Congrès which is part of the Inter-Continental Hotel can host conferences for more than 3000 persons. The political capital Yamoussoukro has a capacity for over 5000. The following organisation can offer advice: Centre de Commerce International d'Abidjan (CCIA), BP 468, Abidjan. Tel: 224 070/72/73. Fax: 227 112. Telex: 23460.

HISTORY & GOVERNMENT

HISTORY: European merchants began to trade in the region during the 15th century, but for many years before that the region had been the centre of several trade routes, dominated by the Dioula. The French had established themselves by the early years of the 19th century, although the whole area of what now forms Côte d'Ivoire was not conquered until the 1890s. It then formed part of French West Africa, until the country was granted independence in August 1960. The current constitution dates from October 1960, and President Félix Houphouët-Boigny has been in power ever since, making him Africa's longest serving ruler. His party, the Parti Démocratique de la Côte d'Ivoire (PDCI), is the only organised political group, although in recent years other candidates have been allowed to contest legislative elections and there have been moves towards a greater degree of local autonomy. Houphouët-Boigny retains close links with the West in general and France in particular. In general, he has pursued an anti-Communist foreign policy and a programme of financial and political austerity at home. The decision in the mid-1980s to build a replica of the Basilica of St Peter, Rome near the capital, Yamassoukrou (Houphouët-Boigny's birthplace), was both bizarre and uncharacteristic, particularly as declining revenue (caused by a steep fall in the world cocoa price) have produced a substantial foreign debt. The estimated cost of US$100 million was considerable for a small and none-too-wealthy African state, and almost incomprehensible given the small proportion of professed Roman Catholics within the country. The completion of Houphouët-Boigny's folly and its blessing by the Pope in 1990 seemed likely to be the swansong for this quirkily effective politician who has dominated Côte d'Ivoire's politics since independence. For in April 1990, 'Le Sage' – as Houphouët-Boigny is reverentially known in some quarters – announced his proposed retirement later in the year and the identity of his chosen successor: the Speaker of the National Assembly, Henri Konan Bédié. He could not resist, however, one more crack at the polls and at the end of October 1990 won a large majority – over 80% of the votes cast – in presidential elections, despite accusations from the opposition of widespread fraud. At the polls for the legislative assembly the following month, political parties other than the ruling PDCI were allowed to stand for the first time, although they managed to win just a dozen of the 170-odd seats. Again, allegations of intimidation and ballot-rigging were rife. In foreign policy, Houphouët-Boigny has often courted controversy: he was almost alone among black African leaders in supporting 'constructive dialogue' with the government of South Africa; he was also one of the first African countries to re-establish diplomatic relations with Israel (which has provided the country with some military and security training). And despite frequent denials, there is compelling evidence that Côte d'Ivoire played a discrete role in supporting the rebel movement in Liberia led by Charles Taylor, which overthrew the government of Samuel Doe in 1990.

GOVERNMENT: The President is elected for a 5-year term, and he appoints the Council of Ministers. The legislature is unicameral. There are 26 Departments, each with an elected local council.

CLIMATE

Four seasons: Dry from December to April, long rains from May to July, a short dry season from August to September, short rains in October and November. In the north the climate is more extreme – rains (May to October) and dry (November to April).

Required clothing: Tropical lightweights; warmer clothing for evenings.

ABIDJAN Côte d'Ivoire (7m)

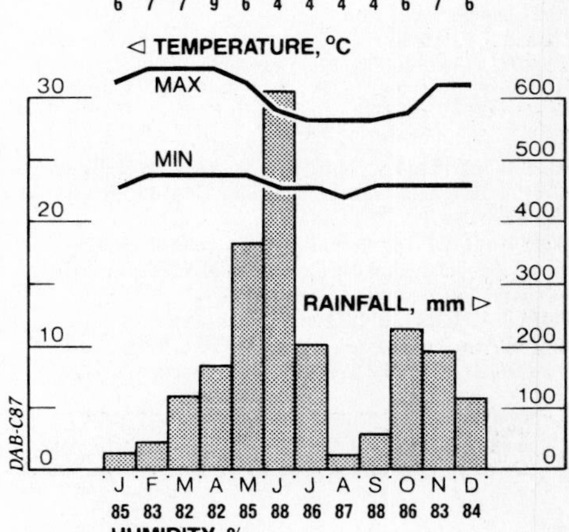

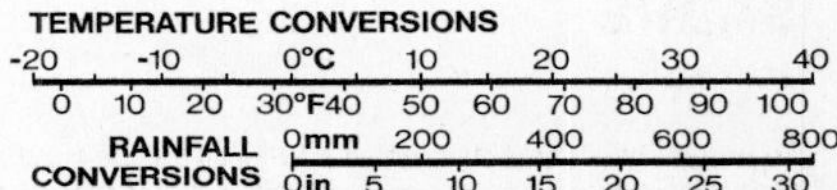

CROATIA

Location: Former Yugoslav republic, southeast Europe.

Note: Due to extreme political instability at the time of writing, travel is not advised. Prospective travellers are advised to contact the Foreign Office (or exterior affairs department of their country) before considering travel. Along with the rest of the EC, the UK recognised Croatia in January 1992. However, there is no UK diplomatic presence in Zagreb, although an Ambassador Designate had been appointed as of July 1992. The nearest UK Embassy is in Belgrade, whose authorities do not recognise the Republic of Croatia.

Ministry of Tourism
Trg Drage Iblera 9
41000 Zagreb, Croatia
Tel: (41) 412 055. Fax: (41) 446 722.
ECGD (Country Policy Desk)
Tel: (071) 512 7000.
Foreign Office Travel Advice Unit
Tel: (071) 270 4129.
Embassy of the Republic of Croatia
18-21 Jermyn Street
London SW1Y 6HP
Tel: (071) 434 2946. Fax: (071) 434 2953.

AREA: 56,538 sq km (21,829 sq miles) or 22% of the territory of the former Yugoslav federation (it was its second largest republic).
POPULATION: 4.688 million (1991 census), or 20% of the total population of the former Yugoslav federation (it was its second most populous republic).
POPULATION DENSITY: 82.7 per sq km
CAPITAL: Zagreb. **Population:** 768,700 (1991). The third largest city in the former Yugoslav federation, whose second largest city, Osijek (867,646), was also in Croatia.
GEOGRAPHY: A long coastal Adriatic region (narrowing as it goes north–south; the major ports being Rijeka, Pula, Zadar, Sibenik, Split and Dubrovnik) and a larger inland area (running west–east from Zagreb to the Danubain border with Serbia), Croatia has borders with Slovenia and Hungary (north), Serbia and Montenegro (east), and Bosnia-Hercegovina (southeast from Zagreb; northeast from the Adriatic coastline).
LANGUAGE: Croato-Serb, with the Latinate alphabet, which is identical in all essential matters to Serbo-Croat (Cyrillic alphabet), used by the local ethnic Serb minority population.
RELIGION: Roman Catholic Croats (75% of the total population) and Eastern Orthodox Serbs (officially 11%; in actuality up to 20%, given that most of the 9% of the population who declared themselves to be 'Yugoslav' in the 1991 census were thought to be Serbs).
TIME: GMT +1 (GMT +2 from March to September).
COMMUNICATIONS: Telephone/fax/telex: Still internationally connected (IDD) as part of the former Yugoslav federation. Country code: 38. All such services, including facsimile and telex, are generally available for communications to and from Western Europe. Apart from a limited telex service, all telephone communications between Zagreb and Belgrade have been indefinitely cut. Internal communications are generally satisfactory, but non-existent in relation to the republic's war zones in northern Dalmatia and eastern Slavonia. **Press:** The main local newspapers, in decreasing order of circulation, are *Vecernji List* (Zagreb), *Slobodna Dalmacija* (Split) and *Novi List* (Rijeka). The state news agency, HINA (Croatian Information and News Agency, Zagreb), produces material in English for international distribution on a daily basis. The state TV-radio station, HTV, also produces a daily (1700-2300) unscrambled programme, including news in English, for a worldwide audience via Eutelsat 1 F5 (21.5DE).
BBC World Service and Voice of America frequencies: From time to time these change. See the section *How to use this Book* for more information.

BBC:

MHz	15.07	12.10	9.410	6.195

Voice of America:

MHz	9.670	6.040	5.995	1.260

Note: CNN is also available via satellite (Astra) in a number of Zagreb, Rijeka, Split and other Adriatic coast hotels.

PASSPORT/VISA

For business visits, UK citizens with a valid passport do not require a visa to enter Croatia and no special permits are requested for stays up to 3 months. UK nationals entering as tourists can also do so with a British Visitors Passport.

MONEY

Currency: Croatian Dinar (Cr D) = 100 paras. Notes are in denominations of Cr D1000, 500, 100, 25, 10, 5 and 1. Coins have not been minted. Although it has never had the foreign exchange reserves to maintain a stable exchange rate, Croatia opted for at least nominal monetary sovereignty in December 23, 1991, when the Croatian Dinar replaced the Yugoslav Dinar (Yu D). The Cr D has been repeatedly devalued.
Currency exchange: As elsewhere in the ex-Yugoslav republics, the only true repositories of value and real mediums of exchange locally are the German DM and the US$ (the UK£ is rarely used in the republic). More foreign exchange is reportedly in circulation in private hands in the republic than ever enters the banking system, which people are extremely wary of, following earlier government seizures of domestic foreign currency accounts for the financing of the war effort. Currency should only be exchanged in banks and authorised dealers.
Exchange rate indicator: The following is included as a guide to the Croatian Dinar against Sterling and the US Dollar.

Date:	Oct '92
£1.00=	681.57
$1.00=	429.47

Note: The unofficial, or black market rate runs up to 400% of the official exchange rate. Uncontrolled and war-related Cr D issuance by the central bank is fuelling local hyper-inflation (+500% in 1991).
Currency restrictions: The Cr D is not convertible anywhere. The import and export of local currency is limited to Cr D5000. The import and export of foreign currency is unrestricted.
Banking hours: 0700-1500 Monday to Friday, 0800-1400 Saturday.

DUTY FREE

No details available at present.

HEALTH

There are no vaccination requirements for any international traveller. Rabies risk exists.

TRAVEL - International

AIR: Croatia's national airline is *Croatian Airlines*. It offers services from several European cities and domestic services. Only a few foreign carriers now have regular services to Zagreb (ZAG).
Approximate flight times: From *London* to Zagreb is 2 hours 5 minutes. From *New York* to Zagreb is 10 hours 35 minutes.
International airports: *Pleso International Airport* (ZAG) (Zagreb) is 17km (10 miles) southwest of the city. An airport bus runs to the city centre (travel time – 25 minutes) and taxis are also available (travel time – 20 minutes). Airport facilities include 24-hour left luggage, banks/bureaux de change, restaurants, snack bars, bars, duty-free shops, post office (0700-1900), tourist information, 24-hour first aid and car rental *(Avis* and *Hertz)*.
Dubrovnik (DBV) is 22km (13 miles) southeast of the city (travel time – 30 minutes). An airport bus runs to the city. Airport facilities include banks/bureaux de change (0600-2400 in summer, 0700-2200 winter), bar, restaurant, duty-free shop (0600-2400 in summer, 0700-220 in winter), shops and car rental (*Avis, Hertz* and *InterRent*).
Departure tax: DM12 (Zagreb) and US$8 (Dubrovnik).
Note: Due to the war, Croatia does not as yet fully control all its airspace.
SEA: There are regular passenger and car-ferry services between Italian, Greek and Croatian ports.

TRAVEL - Internal

AIR: Services are functioning regularly as regards Zagreb–Rijeka, Zagreb–Split, and Zagreb–Ljubljana (Slovenia), but at present there are no services to Dubrovnik and Osijek, and also to Belgrade, Sarajevo (Bosnia-Hercegovina) and Podgorica (Montenegro) due to the war.
Departure tax: DM7 (Zagreb) and US$4 (Dubrovnik).
ROAD/RAIL: The main road–rail route to and from Western Europe now effectively stops at Zagreb (coming from Ljubljana) on account of the war in eastern Slavonia, with extensive detours via Hungary for international traffic going south to and from Serbia, Macedonia and Greece. Otherwise, the routes Zagreb–Rijeka and Zagreb–Varazdin are open, but the Zagreb–Split route involves lengthy diversions from Knin, the centre of Serbian rebellion to Croatian rule from Zagreb, and a major war zone. **Regulations:** Speed limits are 60km/h (38mph) in built-up areas, 120km/h (75mph) on motorways, 80 km/h (50mph) on other roads and 80km/h (50mph) outside built-up areas.
Documentation: International or national Driving Permit. A Green Card should be carried when taking your own car into Croatia. Without it, insurance cover is limited to the minimum legal cover; the Green Card augments this to the level of cover provided by the car owner's domestic policy.

CROATIA	**HEALTH REGULATIONS**	**VISA REGULATIONS** Code-Link
GALILEO/WORLDSPAN	 TI-DFT/ZAG/HE	TI-DFT/ZAG/VI
SABRE	 TIDFT/ZAG/HE	TIDFT/ZAG/VI

To access this information on your CRS, swipe the barcode with a light pen or type in the text under the barcode. For more information, see the introduction *How to Use This Book*.

Note: Present FCO advice is that Croatia can be visited, but that its major Slavonian and Dalmatian war zones, including all points south of Pula on the Adriatic coast, should be avoided at all costs. The local situation, however, is very changeable and the advice of the FCO's travel advice unit should be sought prior to any visit.

ACCOMMODATION

Formerly a major European tourism destination, Croatia has the best of its hotels on its Adriatic coast, although the war has effectively closed all but those on the Istrian peninsula (Rijeka–Pula). Elsewhere, deluxe A-class hotels are only to be found in Zagreb, plus the Plitvice Lakes tourist area on the border with Bosnia-Hercegovina near Bihac (also closed by the war).

RESORTS & EXCURSIONS

Note: The following information reflects the situation before the present conflict and is included in the hope that it will be useful again in the future.
The landscape ranges from small villages in the interior to the dramatic Dalmatian coastline with its numerous resorts, starting from Istria in the north, famous for **Porec, Pula, Opatija** and **Rovinj**. Moving further south, the Split and Makarska regions are well-known tourist centres, as is the old medieval city of Dubrovnik.
Split was founded in the 4th century AD by the Roman Emperor Diocletian. The enormous palace he built and the walled town now form part of the old quarter. The palace is so massive that entire houses have been made out of one room, and streets from the corridors. Concerts, opera and dance all take place within the palace. The southern islands are one of the main tourist attractions in the territory of former Yugoslavia. They have a warm and sunny climate, good beaches, luxurious vegetation and ancient buildings. **Dubrovnik,** an outstandingly beautiful city, was once a free republic and is decked with medieval walls and palaces. Particularly eye-catching are the *Doge's Palace, Onofu's Fountain* and the *Church of St Vlaho*. The summer festival from mid-July to late August attracts world-class performers in music, dance and theatre. **Zagreb,** the capital of Croatia, contains many 13th-century buildings. It is a cultural centre with concerts, opera companies, the World Festival of Animated Cartoons (held every other year), and the International Folklore Festival every year in July. There are museums and art galleries, the *Croatian National Theatre* and interesting churches, the cathedrals of St Mark and St Stephen in particular.
Pula dates from the 5th century BC, and its Roman amphitheatre is still in use. **Opatija** was popular with the Austro-Hungarian nobility and some of its former elegance remains. **Rijeka** is the largest Croatian port, there are museums, art galleries, theatres and a medieval Croatian fortress. In addition there are quieter offshore islands, the most popular being **Brac, Hvar** and **Korcula**. In *Kvarner Bay* are numerous islands: **Krk, Rab** and **Pag** are the best known. From Zadar, the southernmost point of *Kvarner Bay*, visitors can take a water taxi to visit the uninhabited **Kornati Islands.**

SOCIAL PROFILE

FOOD & DRINK: The Adriatic coast is renowned for the variety of seafood dishes, including scampi, *prstaci* (shellfish) and *brodet* (mixed fish stewed with rice) all cooked in olive oil and served with vegetables. In the interior visitors should sample *manistra od bobica* (beans and fesh maize soup). **Drink:** The regional wines are good. Italian expresso is also popular and cheap.
SHOPPING: Traditional handicrafts like embroidery, woodcarvings and ceramics make a good souvenir. **Shopping hours:** 0800-2000 Monday to Friday; and 0800-1500 Saturday.
SPORT: Skiing and **spa resorts** exist at Delnice and Platak. **Fishing** permits are available from hotels or local authorities. Local information is necessary. Fishing on the Adriatic coast is unrestricted, but freshwater angling and fishing with equipment needs a permit. 'Fish-linking' with a local small craft owner is popular. **Sailing** is popular along the coast. Berths and boats can be hired at all ports. Permits are needed for boats brought into the country. **Spectator sports:** Football is one of the more popular.
SPECIAL EVENTS: The following is a selection of the festivals and other special events celebrated annually in Croatia: **May/Jun '93** *The International Flower Fair*. **Jun** *EUORKAZ* (International Festival of Contemporary Theatre). **Jul** *Arts Festival*, Split. *International Festival of Traditional Folklore*, Zagreb. *Film Festival*, Pula. *Arts Festival*, Split. *Moreska* (a richly-costumed tournament commemorating an 11th-century victory over the Moors), Korcula. *Arts Festival*, Opatjia. **Jul-Aug** *Summer Festival*, Dubrovnik. **Aug** *PIF* (The International Puppet Festival). **Sep** *International Autumn Fair*, Zagreb. **Oct** *Jazz Festival*, Zagreb.
SOCIAL CONVENTIONS: People normally shake hands upon meeting and leaving. Smoking is generally acceptable but there are restrictions in public buildings and places and on public transport. **Photography**: Certain restrictions exist and caution is advised. **Tipping:** 10% is expected in hotels, restaurants and taxis.

BUSINESS PROFILE

ECONOMY: The second richest and most economically developed of the former Yugoslav republics, Croatia accounted for 25% of Yugoslavia's GDP (around US$15 billion), 22% of its agricultural and industrial output, and 20% of its exports in 1990-91, with a GDP per capita of around US$3000 in the same year (just above the all-Yugoslav average, but only 60% of that then prevailing in Slovenia). Croatia is presently regressing to south Balkan living standards, with an estimated 30% fall in GDP in 1991. This was variously caused by the collapse of the old all-Yugoslav market, trade with which formerly accounted for 25% of local GDP, and the war, whose costs to date (July 1992) have been estimated at over US$20 billion (75% destroyed property and infrastucture; 25% loss output). Particularly serious losses were those arising out of the collapse of the vitally important Adriatic tourism sector, whose total revenues were around US$6 billion in 1989-90, the last year of relative economic normality in the republic. Chronic political uncertainty has also blocked the repatriation of an estimated US$15-20 billion reportedly held by émigré Croats in foreign banks (particularly in Germany, where there are over 600,000 Croat employees). Without these resources, and particularly tourism earnings, Croatia is not economically viable, and certainly incapable of servicing its agreed share of the former federation's foreign debt (US$2.6 billion, plus around 30% of unallocated federal debt, or around 25% of the total Yugoslav foreign debt). In this regard, Croatia has already asked for a formal debt rescheduling, but this is unlikely to be granted before IMF membership is obtained. The present chaos rules out substantial foreign credits and investments, even from friendly governments (notably Germany) and multi-lateral sources. Local export performance, particularly to EC markets, remains poor, and genuine socio-economic reform (notably privatisation) is as yet largely non-existent, with the needs of a war economy and the statist dogmas of the present government responsible for both problems. UK economic and other links with Croatia are reportedly marginal.
BUSINESS: In many ways one of the more conservative areas of the former Yugoslav federation, Croatia tends towards formal business protocol, but this image of Western-style efficiency is often belied by the fact that things go very slowly on account of the cumbersome bureaucracy. Communication, however, is no problem, as English and German are widely used as second languages. Business cards including professional or academic titles should be exchanged just after formal introductions. There are also a large number of local agents, advisers, consultants and, to a lesser extent, lawyers, willing to act for foreign companies, but none should be engaged before being thoroughly checked in advance.
Office hours: 0800-1600 Monday to Friday.
COMMERCIAL INFORMATION: The following organisations can offer advice:
Chamber of Economy of Croatia, Ruzveltov Trg. 1-2, 41000 Zagreb. Tel: (41) 453 422 *or* 466 455. Fax: (41) 448 618; *or*
ASTRA International Trade Organisation, Ul. Rade Koncara 5, 41000 Zagreb. Tel: (41) 334 911 *or* 334 466. Fax: (41) 339 004; *or*
National Bank of Croatia, Trg. Rackogo 5, 41000 Zagreb. Tel: (41) 445 437 *or* 451 899. Fax: (41) 450 598.

HISTORY & GOVERNMENT

HISTORY: Converted to Roman Catholicism in the 7th century, the Croats established an independent kingdom during the 10th century, when the Serbs also opted for the Eastern Orthodoxy of the Byzantine Empire culminating in the Great Schism of 1054. In 1089, so-called Inner Croatia (principally its central area around Zagreb and Slavonia) became a vassal of Hungary and then the Habsburg Empire, and so remained for eight centuries, while the larger part of Dalmatia was variously controlled by the Byzantines, Venice and Austria. In 1529, following the defeat of the Hungarians by the Ottoman Turks, the Habsburg and Ottoman Empires divided Hungary's territories, thereby creating a militarised border in Croatia between the Islamic and Christian worlds running roughly along the present border between Croatia and Bosnia-Hercegovina. Serbs settled in areas of Croatia known as Krajinas (border lands) which was later the source of much Croat-Serb conflict thereafter. By 1699, when the Ottoman Empire began its long decline, most of modern Croatia was under Habsburg control, except for the Venetian territories of Dalmatia, Istria and Dubrovnik, which finally came to Vienna in 1815 after a brief period of French control under Napoleon. In 1868, Croatia came under strong Hungarian influence (Magyarisation), which ultimately transformed traditional Croat-Serb rivalry into South Slav (Yugoslav) solidarity. Following the destruction of Austro-Hungary during the First World War, a new 'Kingdom of Serbs, Croats and Slovenes' was created in 1918, later renamed 'Yugoslavia' in 1929. During the inter-war period, however, a highly unitary Serb-dominated state produced worsening Croat-Serb conflict which was exploited by the Nazis after the Axis dismemberment of Yugoslavia in 1941. A so-called 'Independent State of Croatia' was established in Zagreb which included the whole of nearby Bosnia-Hercegovina, and was ruled by the indigenous clerico-fascist Ustasa movement. This state adopted a three-pronged policy of genocide, forced conversion (to Catholicism) and deportation against the Serbs under its control, thereby forever compromising Croatian nationalism. Following the communist takeover of 1945, Croatia became a constituent republic of the new Yugoslav federation, whose new ruler, Josip Broz Tito, was a Croat, but opposed to any expression of Croatian nationalism. Thus, in 1971, a mass movement (Maspok) which favoured just such a nationalist revival in Croatia – and was supported by the League of Communists in Croatia – was crushed by Tito with the aid of the federal Yugoslav People's Army (YPA). This added further to the simmering nationalist resentment in the republic, which finally boiled over in the spring of 1990 following multi-party elections in Slovenia and Croatia. In Croatia, the ultra-nationalist Croatian Democratic Union (HDZ), led by Franjo Tudjman, won almost two-thirds of the Croatian assembly seats and immediately declared its intention to seek full independence. In October 1990, the Serb minority in Krajina, under the name of the Serb National Council, declared autonomy within Croatia; disturbances followed when Croatian security forces tried to disarm Serb paramilitary groups. The federal army entered Croatia in force in January 1991 in support of the Serbs. The fighting in Croatia between the YPA and Serb militia on one side and hastily assembled Croat defence forces reached a peak in the late summer. A series of other Serb-dominated Croatian enclaves (Slavonia, Baranja, Srem) announced their union with Krajina. By the time the UN-brokered cease-fire took effect in January 1992, 30% of Croatian territory had been lost to Serb control. The previous month, Croatia had received its much-coveted international recognition from the EC, and the United Nations formally admitted Croatia in May 1992. An uneasy peace under the supervision of the 14,000 strong UN Protection Forces for Yugoslavia (UNPROFOR), has since held in Croatia while the fighting has moved south to Bosnia-Hercegovina. Here, Tudjman and Serbian leader Slobodan Milosevic have shown a brutally pragmatic co-operation in carving up Bosnia-Hercegovina between them. In August 1992, the HDZ further consolidated its position after a comfortable victory in legislative elections in Croatia. Tudjman was re-elected President of Croatia.
GOVERNMENT: The elected national assembly, the Sabor, with 351 seats holds legislative authority. The assembly elects the President of the Republic, in whom executive responsibility is vested, as head of state.

CLIMATE

Croatia has a varied climate, with continental climate conditions in the north and Mediterranean ones on the Adriatic coast.
Required clothing: Mediumweight clothing and heavy overcoats are needed in winter; lightweight clothing and raincoats for summer.

SPLIT Croatia (128m)

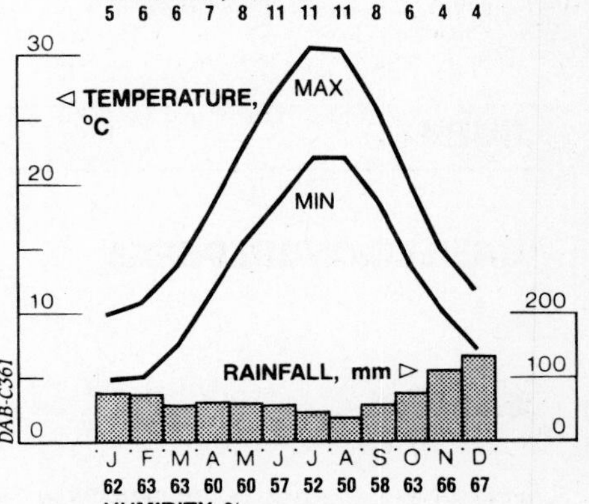

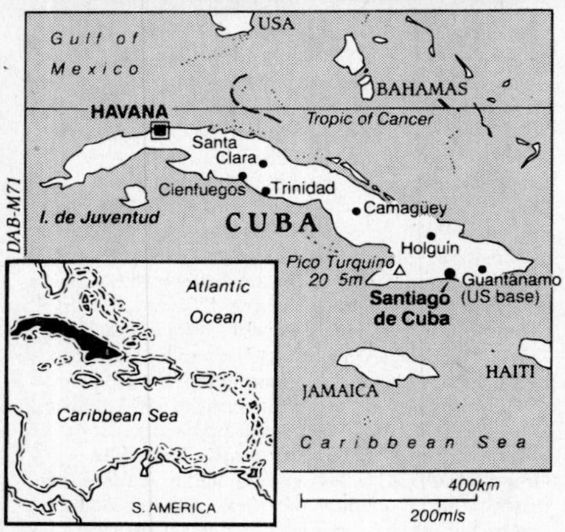

□ *international airport*

Location: Northwest Caribbean.

Empresa de Turismo Internacional (Cubatur)
Apartado 6560
Calle 23, No 156
entre N y O
Vedado
Havana, Cuba
Tel: (7) 324 521. Fax: (7) 333 104. Telex: 511212.
Embassy of the Republic of Cuba
167 High Holborn
London WC1V 6PA
Tel: (071) 240 2488. Fax: (071) 836 2602. Telex: 261094. Opening hours: 0930-1730 Monday to Friday.
Cuban Consulate
15 Grape Street
London WC2 8DR
Tel: (071) 240 2488. Fax: (071) 836 2602. Opening hours: 0930-1200 Monday to Friday.
Cubatur
167 High Holborn
London WC1V 6PA
Tel: (071) 379 1706.
British Embassy
Apartado 1069
Edificio Bolívar
Carcel 101-103
e Morro y Prado
Havana, Cuba
Tel: (7) 623 071/2/3/4/5. Telex: 511656.
Cuban Interests Section
c/o Swiss Embassy
2900 Cathedral Avenue, NW
Washington, DC
20009
Tel: (202) 745 7900. Fax: (202) 387 2564.
US Interests Section
c/o Swiss Embassy
Calzada entre L y M
Vedado
Havana, Cuba
Tel: (7) 333 550-9 *or* 333 543-5 *or* 333 700.
Embassy of the Republic of Cuba
388 Main Street
Ottawa, Ontario
K1S 1E3
Tel: (613) 563 0141. Fax: (613) 562 0068. Telex: 0533135.
Cuba Tourist Board
Suite 705
55 Queen Street East
Toronto, Ontario
M5C 1R5
Tel: (416) 362 0700/01/02. Fax: (416) 362 6799. Telex: 0623258.
Canadian Embassy
Calle 30, No 518
esq. a 7a
Miramar
Havana, Cuba
Tel: (7) 332 516. Fax: (7) 332 044. Telex: 511586.

AREA: 110,860 sq km (42,803 sq miles).
POPULATION: 10,609,000 (1990 estimate).
POPULATION DENSITY: 95.7 per sq km.
CAPITAL: Havana. **Population:** 2,096,054 (1989).
GEOGRAPHY: Cuba is the largest Caribbean island and the most westerly of the Greater Antilles group, lying 145km (90 miles) south of Florida. A quarter of the country is fairly mountainous. West of Havana is the narrow Sierra de los Organos, rising to 750m (2461ft) and containing in the west the Guaniguanicos hills. South of Sierras is a narrow strip of 2320 sq km (860 sq miles) where the finest Cuban tobacco is grown. The Trinidad Mountains in the centre rise to 1100m (3609ft) in the east. Encircling the port of Santiago are the rugged mountains of the Sierra Maestra. A quarter of the island is covered with mountain forests of pine and mahogany.
LANGUAGE: The official language is Spanish. Some English and French are spoken.
RELIGION: Roman Catholic majority.
TIME: GMT - 4 (GMT - 5 Oct-Mar).
ELECTRICITY: 110/120 volts AC, 60Hz. American-style flat 2-pin plugs are generally used, except in certain large hotels where the European round 2-pin plug is standard.
COMMUNICATIONS: Telephone: IDD to Havana only. Country code: 53. All other calls must be made through the international operator, and may be subject to long delays. **Telegram:** From all post offices in Havana and RCA offices in major hotels in large towns. **Post:** Letters to Europe can take several weeks. It is advisable to use the airmail service. **Press:** Papers are in Spanish, although the Communist Party daily newspaper, *Gramma*, publishes weekly editions in English and French. All media is government-controlled.
BBC World Service and Voice of America frequencies: From time to time these change. See the section *How to Use this Book* for more information.

BBC:

MHz	17.840	15.220	9.740	5.975

Voice of America:

MHz	15.21	11.70	6.130	0.930

PASSPORT/VISA

Regulations and requirements may be subject to change at short notice, and you are advised to contact the appropriate diplomatic or consular authority before finalising travel arrangements. Details of these may be found at the head of this country's entry. Any numbers in the chart refer to the footnotes below.

	Passport Required?	Visa Required?	Return Ticket Required?
Full British'	Yes	Yes	Yes
BVP	Not valid	-	-
Australian	Yes	Yes	Yes
Canadian	Yes	Yes	Yes
USA	Yes	Yes	Yes
Other EC	Yes	1	Yes
Japanese	Yes	Yes	Yes

PASSPORTS: Valid passport required by all.
British Visitors Passport: Not acceptable.
VISAS: Required by all except:
(a) [1] nationals of Italy (providing they are travelling as tourists);
(b) nationals of Afghanistan, Albania, Algeria, Benin, Bulgaria, Burkina Faso, Cambodia, Cape Verde, China, Congo, Cyprus, Czech Republic & Slovakia, Finland, Ghana, Guinea, Guinea-Bissau, Guyana, Hungary, Lao, Liechtenstein, North Korea, Mali, Mongolia, Nicaragua, Norway, Poland, Romania, Seychelles, Sweden, Switzerland, Turkey, the former USSR, Vietnam, Yemen and the former Yugoslavia;
(c) holders of a Tourist Card (see below);
(d) nationals of certain countries travelling on certain kinds of official business – enquire at Consulate.
Tourist Cards: Some specialist tour operators can issue a Tourist Card valid for one single trip. Stipulations are that the traveller pre-books and pre-pays hotel accommodation for a minimum of five nights in Cuba through a tour operator officially recognised by Cuba. All passengers must hold tickets and other documentation required for onward or return journey unless issued with special annotation issued by a Cuban consulate. Tourist Cards are valid for 30 days from time of issue and allow a stay in Cuba determined by the duration of the pre-paid arrangements, but not to exceed 30 days. The cost is Cub$7 (or the equivalent in foreign currency).
Types of visa: Tourist (£10); Business (£25); Transit. *Transit visas* are not required by those exempt from visas (above) or passengers continuing their journey within 72 hours and holding reserved onward tickets and enough funds for duration of stay (at least US$50 per day or the equivalent in other currency).
Validity: Tourist visas for up to 6 months. Business visas for 3 months but depends on requirements. Enquire at Consulate.
Application to: Consulate (or Consular Section at Embassy). For addresses, see top of entry.
Application requirements: (a) Valid passport. (b) 2 completed application forms. (c) 2 photos. (d) Details of business contact in Cuba if purpose of travel is business.
Working days required: Tourist visa, 2-3 days. Business visa, 2-3 weeks.
Temporary residence: Enquire at Embassy.

MONEY

Currency: Cuban Peso (Cub$) = 100 centavos. Bank notes are in denominations of Cub$50, 20, 10, 5, 3 and 1. Coins are in denominations of Cub$1 and 40, 20, 5, 2 and 1 centavos.
Currency exchange: Money should be exchanged at official foreign exchange bureaux, banks or international air and sea ports, who issue receipts for transactions. At official tourist shops purchases are made only in US Dollars and in Tourism tokens (see below). Black marketeers may offer as much as 35 times the official rate for US Dollars, but tourists are advised to have nothing to do with them as severe penalties for black marketeering are imposed.
Credit cards: Visa, Access/Mastercard and Diners Club are accepted, but check with your credit card company for details of merchant acceptability and other services which may be available.
Travellers cheques: US Dollar, Sterling and other major currencies are accepted, but US Dollar cheques drawn on a US bank are not acceptable. Do not enter the place and date details on any travellers cheque or it will be refused. The white exchange paper received when a cheque is cashed must be kept with money and shown when money is spent. In general, control of foreign currency is strict.
Tourism tokens: Issued by the National Bank, these are in denominations equivalent to the US Dollar. They are intended to ease the tourist's exchange transactions.
Exchange rate indicators: The following figures are included as a guide to the movements of the Cuban Peso against Sterling and the US Dollar:

CUBA **HEALTH REGULATIONS** **VISA REGULATIONS** Code-Link

GALILEO/WORLDSPAN

To access this information on your CRS, swipe the barcode with a light pen or type in the text under the barcode. For more information, see the introduction *How to Use This Book*.

Date:	Oct '89	Oct '90	Oct '91	Oct '92
£1.00=	1.20	1.55	2.32	1.19
$1.00=	0.76	0.80	1.34	0.75

Currency restrictions: The import and export of local currency is prohibited. There is no limit on the import of foreign currency but it must all be declared on arrival. Generally, a maximum of Cub$10 may be reconverted to foreign currency for re-export at the end of the stay but it may only be reconverted on presentation of a correctly filled out official exchange record.
Banking hours: 0830-1200 and 1330-1500 Monday to Friday, 0830-1030 Saturday.

DUTY FREE

The following goods may be taken into Cuba without incurring customs duty:
200 cigarettes or 25 cigars or 220g of tobacco;
2 bottles of alcoholic beverages;
A reasonable amount of perfume;
Goods from duty-free shop at airport or elsewhere.
Prohibited items: Natural fruits or vegetables, meat and dairy products, weapons and ammunition, all pornographic material and drugs. Certain animal and plant products, including shoes and items made from straw, may be disinfected on entry to Cuba.

PUBLIC HOLIDAYS

Since 1959 there have been no religious or ethnic festivals in Cuba. State holidays observed in Cuba are as follows:
May 1 '93 Labour Day. **Jul 25-27** Revolution Day. **Oct 10** Wars of Independence Day. **Jan 1 '94** Liberation Day.

HEALTH

Regulations and requirements may be subject to change at short notice, and you are advised to contact your doctor well in advance of your intended date of departure. Any numbers in the chart refer to the footnotes below.

	Special Precautions?	Certificate Required?
Yellow Fever	No	No
Cholera	No	No
Typhoid & Polio	1	-
Malaria	No	-
Food & Drink	2	-

[1]: There may be an occasional risk of polio; level of typhoid risk unknown but assumed to be low.
[2]: Mains water is chlorinated and whilst relatively safe, may cause mild abdominal upsets. Bottled water is available and is advised for the first few weeks of stay. Milk is pasteurised and dairy products are safe for consumption. Local meat, poultry, seafoods and fruit are generally considered safe to eat.
Health care: Cuba's medical services are very good and first aid is available free to visitors. However, health insurance is advisable in case emergency repatriation is necessary.

TRAVEL - International

AIR: Cuba's national airline is *Cubana Empresa Consolidada de Aviación (CU)*.
Approximate flight times: From *London* to Havana is 18 hours 50 minutes (including a 4-hour stopover in Madrid), from *Los Angeles* is 9 hours and from *New York* is 5 hours.
International airport: *Havana (HAV)* (International José Martí) is 18km (11 miles) south of the city. Bus and taxi services to the city are available. Airport facilities include duty-free shops, bank, tourist information/hotel reservation and car rental. All incoming visitors will be met by a *Cubatur* (the government tourist company) hostess who will arrange accommodation unless this has been prearranged.
Generally hotels will not accept bookings unless reserved through *Cubatur*. Most large hotels have a *Cubatur* bureau. There are also international airports at Santiago de Cuba, Camagüey, Holguin and Varadero. Facilities at Havana and Santiago de Cuba have recently been upgraded.

TRAVEL - Internal

AIR: *Cubana* operate scheduled services between most main towns, but advance booking is essential as flights are limited.
RAIL: The principal rail route is from Havana to Santiago de Cuba, with two daily trains. Some trains on this route have air-conditioning and refreshments. There are also through trains from Havana to other big towns.
ROAD: Most sightseeing is pre-arranged and even when it is not all internal travel arrangements are made through *Cubatur*. **Bus:** Most tours will include travel by air-conditioned buses. The Cubans themselves use the long-distance buses that link most towns; fares are cheap, services are reliable, but the buses can be very crowded, especially during the rush hour. **Taxi:** Taxis and chauffeur-driven cars are cheap but can be scarce. It is usual to order them through the hotel. Most new taxis have meters but fares should be pre-arranged in those that do not. There are both state-run and private taxi services. **Car hire:** *Havanautos* is the main national car rental agency. **Bicycles** can be hired.
Documentation: National driving licence or International Driving Permit.
URBAN: Buses, minibuses and plentiful shared taxis operate in Havana at low, flat fares. Buses are frequent but often very crowded.
JOURNEY TIMES: The following chart gives approximate jurney times (in hours and minutes) from Havana to other major towns in Cuba.

	Air	Road
Varadero	-	2.00
Trinidad	-	4.00
Santiago de Cuba	1.15	-
Playas del Este	-	0.20
Pinar del Rio	-	1.30

ACCOMMODATION

HOTELS: The range of accommodation available is expanding. The best hotels are in Havana or at Varadero Beach. There are some new hotels in the Guanabo region to serve the beaches there. Since many visitors to Cuba go as part of a package holiday the hotel will have been selected in advance. The hotels are clean, functional and adequate. They do not offer dry-cleaning facilities. Generally speaking, hotels only accept bookings via *Cubatur*.

RESORTS & EXCURSIONS

Since the 1950s, **Havana** has transformed itself from the notorious gambling centre of the Caribbean to the respectable capital of the Republic of Cuba. Apart from seeing the city on organised tours, the visitor can take a bus ride from one end of the town to the other, beginning in the former brothel quarter and ending in the beautiful suburbs of *Vedado* and *Marianao*. *Revolution Square* is an awe-inspiring sight with large tableaux of revolutionary heroes surrounding it. By way of contrast, the *Cathedral Square* in Old Havana has many ancient houses and cobbled streets.
Santa Clara, 288km (179 miles) east of Havana, is a busy city at the centre of the agricultural region.
Trinidad, 444km (276 miles) east of Havana, is an ancient city with the atmosphere of an old colonial town.
Camagüey, 563km (350 miles) east of Havana, is in the centre of a fertile plain and has long been the centre of Cuba's sugar industry. In 1666, it joined the long list of Caribbean ports sacked by Captain Henry Morgan, the notorious English pirate.
Santiago de Cuba, 933km (580 miles) east of Havana, is situated around a large natural harbour and was until 1549 the capital of Cuba. Santiago witnessed the start of the Cuban revolution when, in July 1953, Fidel Castro's troops stormed the Moncada Barracks.
Guama, 179km (111 miles) southeast of Havana in Matanzas Province, is a reconstructed Indian village. Set beside a broad lagoon, the vanished culture of Cuba's first inhabitants, who were wiped out by the early colonisers, is commemorated with sculptures showing Indians taking part in everyday activities. A holiday resort for Cubans has also been constructed here; palm-wood cabins are linked by bridges that cross the lagoon.
Cienfuegos, 325km (202 miles) southeast of Havana, is a prosperous modern city around a fine harbour.
Varadero, 130km (80 miles) northeast of Havana, situated along a sheltered peninsula, is one of the most famous resorts in Cuba. Villas, parks and hotels line a beach ideal for year-round swimming.

SOCIAL PROFILE

FOOD & DRINK: Restaurants (both table- and self-service) are generally expensive and the choice of food can be restricted due to shortages. Cuisine is continental or Cuban with a strong emphasis on seafood (lobster and shrimp are only available in restaurants). Favourite dishes are omelettes, often stuffed with meat and/or cheese; a thick soup made of chicken or black beans; roast suckling pig; chicken and rice; *plantains* (green bananas) baked or fried; and local Cuban ice cream. Tour food served in hotels is not always exciting but it is adequate and will include chicken, fish, ham and cheese, fresh papaya, melon, pineapple, mangoes, bananas, fresh vegetables and green salads. Desserts are sweet and include pastries, flans, caramel custard, guava paste and cheese. **Drink:** Bars generally have waiter and counter service. There are no licensing laws. Cuban coffee is very strong but weaker British coffee is available. Cuban beer is tasty but weak. Spirits are very expensive but rum is good and plentiful and used in excellent cocktails such as *daiquiris* and *mejitos* (pronounced 'mo-hee-to').
NIGHTLIFE: Nightlife is concentrated in Havana, Varadero Beach and the Guanabo, east of Havana. Much entertainment may be planned by the visitor's guide or tour operator, and it is common to attend in organised groups. There is a choice of floor-show entertainments, nightclubs and theatres. The *Tropicana* nightclub stages spectacular open-air shows. Theatre, opera and ballet are staged all year round in Havana and seats are very cheap. Cinemas show films in Spanish, but some have subtitles.
SHOPPING: Special purchases include cigars, rum, and local handicrafts. The main hotels have a few luxury shops (only for tourists) stocked with East European items, especially radios and crystal. There are duty-free shops at the airport and in the centre of Havana.
SPORT: All sporting events are free in Cuba. Cuba participates in many sports in the Olympic Games. **Baseball** is the national sport; **soccer** and a variety of **ball games** are also played. There are many stadia and both playing and watching sport is one of the national pastimes. **Watersports:** Beaches in Cuba tend to be very crowded in summer, while the more remote beaches, which offer good **diving** and **fishing**, are difficult to get to without one's own transport.
SPECIAL EVENTS: July '93 *Carnival*, Havana and Santiago de Cuba. **Jan-Feb '94** *Carnival*, Varadero. For further details of festivals and special events in 1993/1994, contact the Cuban Tourist Board.
SOCIAL CONVENTIONS: Handshaking is the normal form of greeting. Cubans generally address each other as *compañero* but visitors should use *señor* or *señora*. Some Cubans have two surnames after their Christian name and the first surname is the correct one to use. Normal courtesies should be observed when visiting someone's home and a small gift may be given if invited for a meal. Dress is much less formal since the revolution. Cuban men wear *guayabera* (a light pleated shirt worn outside the trousers). Formal wear is not often needed and hats are rarely worn. Men should not wear shorts except on or near the beach. Women wear light cotton dresses or trousers during the day and cocktail dresses for formal evenings. **Tipping:** Following some relaxation in the regulations, tipping is now permitted. Moderate tipping is expected.

BUSINESS PROFILE

ECONOMY: The economy, which is entirely state-controlled, is primarily agricultural. The main crop is sugar, of which Cuba is the world's largest exporter. With the prevailing low world price throughout the 1980s, and the continuing US embargo, the Government has attempted to diversify into other crops. Tobacco and citrus fruits are of increasing importance. Cuban industry is largely devoted to food processing but also produces cement, fertilisers, textiles, prefabricated buildings, agricultural machinery and domestic consumer goods. Tourism is a projected growth industry and Cuba has invested heavily in developing infrastructure for that purpose. Cuba's largest trading partner was the former Soviet Union by a considerable margin: the CIS bought much of the sugar produced on the island and supplied Cuba's oil requirements in exchange. The CIS' decisions to reduce the built-in subsidy which covers this barter trade and demand hard currency payment will cause serious difficulties for the Cubans. The American embargo, through which Cuba was previously able to survive, is now biting much harder. Since the collapse of the Soviet economic bloc, COMECON, Cuba's main trading partners are now Argentina, China and Spain. These latter will now assume increasing importance in Cuba's trading relations, but the withdrawal of CIS support, particularly the provision of cheap oil, threatens to force Cuba back to the pre-industrial era. Hard times are undoubtedly ahead.
BUSINESS: Courtesy is expected and hospitality should not be lavish, being offered to groups rather than individuals. Best months for business visits are November to April.
Office hours: 0830-1230 and 1330-1730 Monday to Friday; some offices also open on alternate Saturdays from 0800-1700.
COMMERCIAL INFORMATION: The following organisation can offer advice: Cámara de Comercio de la República de Cuba, Calle 21, No. 661/701 Calle A, Apartado 4237, Vedado, Havana. Tel: (7) 303 356. Telex: 511752.

HISTORY & GOVERNMENT

HISTORY: Cuba was discovered by Columbus in 1492. In 1502 slavery was introduced and the indigenous population was quickly decimated by disease, fighting and maltreatment. Sugar plantations were developed and slaves were brought in from West Africa to work them. Cuba was also used as a base for Spanish treasure ships and it was from here that the Spanish organised trips to the Americas. In 1885 insurrection broke out as a result of Spain's inhumane treatment of the local inhabitants, and the Spanish-American war of 1898 resulted in Cuba's independence. In the early part of this century, Cuba was governed largely by dictators such as Fulgencio Batista and

Carlos Prío Socarrás. In 1959 Fidel Castro overturned the Batista government and established a socialist state. All US businesses were expropriated in 1960 and diplomatic relations between the two countries were broken by the USA. In 1961, the USA assisted anti-government troops to invade Cuba (unsuccessfully) in what is now known as the Bay of Pigs incident; later that year Castro declared Cuba a Marxist-Leninist state. In 1962, missiles were installed on Cuba that were capable of destroying nuclear weapons in the USA and President Kennedy ordered a naval blockade to prevent shipments of weaponry from the USSR. The confrontation escalated to the threshold of nuclear war, before Kennedy and Krushchev reached a settlement under which Soviet missiles were withdrawn from Cuba in exchange for the dismantling of US missile silos in Turkey. Since the crisis, Cuba for the most part proved a loyal Soviet ally and was the largest recipient of Soviet foreign aid. The other main plank of Cuba's foreign policy is military assistance to weaker Third World nations, principally in the form of combat troops and training personnel. The major foreign engagement, recently ended, has been in Angola. Cuba has also supported guerrillas in Latin America for the export of revolution. At home Cuba has an impressive reputation for the quality of its health care and social services, though not for its overall quality of life or tolerance of opposition. The country is now entering a particularly difficult phase of its history, the outcome of which may decide the forseeable future of the country. A diplomatic offensive which has been under way for several years has scored some successes. There have been notable improvements in relations with its Caribbean neighbours and with Venezuela, Colombia, Peru and Argentina. Cuba has recently been elected to the United Nations Security Council for the first time. Relations with the USA have never been better than cold, and the long-term economic blockade imposed by Washington is now starting to become a real headache for the Government, particularly since the Soviet decision in 1991 to withdraw a large part of its economic and military support – US$5 billion annually and around 14,000 troops – for its erstwhile ally, which has become a real headache for the Government. The Cubans are now preparing to 'go it alone': emergency rationing has been introduced; with oil now very scarce, thousands of bicycles have been imported from China (Cuba's last remaining benefactor) to provide human transport while animals are being reintroduced as beasts of burden on Cuban farms. President Castro has refused to adopt any of the policies of political and economic liberalisation introduced throughout the rest of the former Soviet bloc. The election of President Clinton in the USA will probably make little difference to US policy towards Cuba.

GOVERNMENT: Under the terms of the 1976 constitution, all legislative power in the Republic of Cuba is vested in a 499-member National Assembly of People's Power, which is elected every five years by municipal deputies. A 31-member Council of State is elected by the Assembly from the Assembly. The Council's President is both Head of State and Head of Government. Executive and administrative power is vested in a Council of Ministers, appointed by the Assembly on the Head of State's recommendation. The constitution also guarantees that the Communist Party (PCC) should remain not only the sole legal party in Cuba but 'the leading force of society and state'.

CLIMATE

Hot, subtropical climate all year. Most rain falls between May and October and hurricanes can occur in autumn (August to November). Cooler months are November to April when least rain falls.

Required clothing: Lightweight cottons and linens most of the year; the high humidity makes it unwise to wear synthetics close to the skin. Light waterproofs are advisable all year round.

HAVANA Cuba (24m)

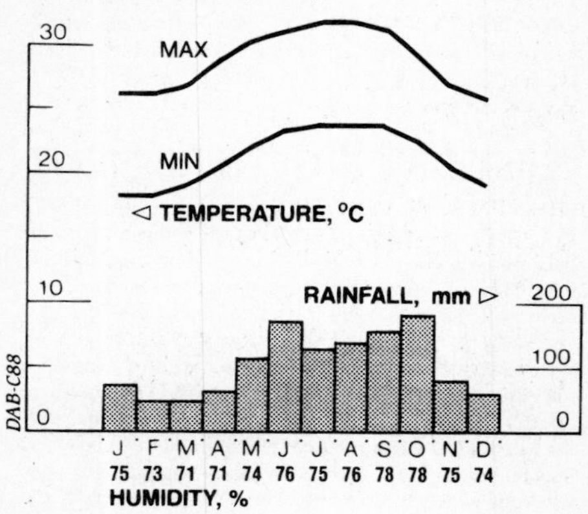

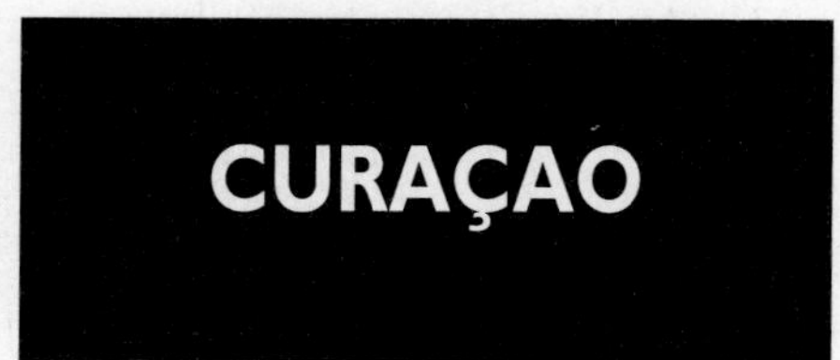

Location: Caribbean, 35 miles north of Venezuela.

Curaçao Tourism Development Foundation (Tourism Development Bureau)
Pietermaai 19
Willemstad
Curaçao NA
Tel: (9) 616 000. Fax: (9) 612 305. Telex: 1450.

Office of the Minister Plenipotentiary for the Netherland Antilles
PO Box 90706
2509 LS The Hague
The Netherlands
Tel: (70) 351 2811. Fax: (70) 351 2722.

British Consulate
PO Box 3803
Bombadiersweg Z/N
Willemstad
Curaçao NA
Tel: (9) 369 533. Fax: (9) 369 533. Telex: 3372 EQIP-NA.

Curaçao Tourist Board
Suite 311
400 Madison Avenue
New York, NY
10017
Tel: (212) 751 8266. Fax: (212) 486 3024. Telex: 237306.
Also deals with enquiries from Canada.

Consulate General of the United States of America
PO Box 158
St Anna Boulevard
Willemstad, Curaçao NA
Tel: (9) 613 066. Fax: (9) 616 489. Telex: 1062.

Consulate of Canada
PO Box 305
Maduro and Curiels Bank N.V.
Plaza Jojo Correa 2-4
Willemstad, Curaçao NA
Tel: (9) 613 515. Fax: (9) 616 019. Telex: 1127.

AREA: 444 sq km (171 sq miles).
POPULATION: 144,952 (1990).
POPULATION DENSITY: 326.5 per sq km.
CAPITAL: Willemstad. **Population:** 70,000 (1990).
GEOGRAPHY: Curaçao, the largest island in the Netherlands Antilles, is geographically part of the Dutch Leeward Islands, also known as the Dutch Antilles. It is flat, rocky and fairly barren due to its low rainfall. There are a large number of excellent beaches.
LANGUAGE: Dutch is the official language. Papiamento (a mixture of Portuguese, African, Spanish, Dutch and English) is the commonly used *lingua franca*; English and Spanish are also widely spoken.
RELIGION: The majority of the population is Roman Catholic, with Protestant minorities, both evangelical and other low-church denominations. There is also a Baha'i temple and a Synagogue.
TIME: GMT - 4.
ELECTRICITY: 110/220 volts AC, 50Hz.
COMMUNICATIONS: Telephone: Good IDD service to Europe. Country code: 599. Radio-telephone and operator services are available. **Telex/telegram:** Facilities available in most large hotels and in the post office in Willemstad. **Post:** Airmail to Europe takes 4-6 days. **Press:** The English-language daily is called *The Guardian*.
BBC World Service and Voice of America frequencies: From time to time these change. See the section *How to Use this Book* for more information.

BBC:				
MHz	17.840	11.78	9.915	5.975
Voice of America:				
MHz	15.21	11.70	6.130	0.930

PASSPORT/VISA

Regulations and requirements may be subject to change at short notice, and you are advised to contact the appropriate diplomatic or consular authority before finalising travel arrangements. Details of these may be found at the head of this country's entry. Any numbers in the chart refer to the footnotes below.

	Passport Required?	Visa Required?	Return Ticket Required?
Full British	Yes	No	Yes
BVP	Valid/1	-	-
Australian	Yes	4	Yes
Canadian	3	4	Yes
USA	2	4	Yes
Other EC	1	4/5	Yes
Japanese	Yes	4	Yes

PASSPORTS: Valid passport required by all except:
(a) **[1]** nationals of Belgium, Luxembourg and The Netherlands holding a tourist card, nationals of Germany holding an identity card and UK nationals holding a British Visitors Passport;
(b) **[2]** nationals of the USA holding voters registration cards or birth certificate, and alien residents of the USA with acceptable documentation;
(c) **[3]** nationals of Canada with birth certificates or proof of citizenship;
(d) nationals of San Marino holding a national ID card.
British Visitors Passports: Acceptable.
VISAS: [4] Visas are only required for nationals of the Dominican Republic resident there. All other nationals are allowed to stay in Curaçao for 14 days without a visa (but might need a Certificate of Admission, see below) provided they have a return or onward ticket. All visitors staying more than 90 days require a visa. Transit passengers staying no longer than 24 hours holding confirmed tickets and valid passports do not require visas or Certificates of Admission.
For stays of between 14 and 28 days a **Temporary Certificate of Admission** is required, which in the case of the following countries will be issued by the Immigration authorities on arrival in Curaçao:
(a) **[5]** Belgium, Germany, Luxembourg, The Netherlands, Spain and the UK;
(b) Bolivia, Burkina Faso, Chile, Colombia, Costa Rica, Czechoslovakia, Ecuador, Hungary, Israel, Jamaica, South Korea, Malawi, Mauritius, Niger, The Philippines, Poland, San Marino, Swaziland and Togo.
The following must apply in writing and *before* entering the country even for tourist purposes for a Certificate of Admission: nationals of Albania, Bulgaria, Cambodia, China, Cuba, North Korea, Libya, Romania, USSR, Vietnam and holders of Rhodesian passports issued on or after November 11, 1965.
All other nationals have to apply for the Certificate after 14 days of stay.
Further information about visa requirements may be obtained from the Office of the Minister Plenipotentiary of the Netherlands Antilles; and whilst Royal Netherlands Embassies do not formally represent the Netherlands Antilles in any way, they might also be able to offer limited advice and information. For addresses, see top of this entry and top of the *Netherlands* entry below.
Temporary residence: Enquire at the Office of the Minister Plenipotentiary of the Netherlands Antilles.

MONEY

Currency: Netherlands Antilles Guilder or Florin (NAG) = 100 cents. Notes are in the denominations of NAG500, 250, 100, 50, 25, 10 and 5. Coins are in the denominations of NAG2.5 and 1, and 50, 25, 10, 5 and 1 cents. There are, in addition, a large number of commemorative coins which are legal tender. These range in value from NAG10 to 200. The currency is tied to the the US Dollar.
Credit cards: Access/Mastercard, Diners Club, American Express and Visa are accepted in large establishments. Check with your credit card company for details of merchant acceptability and other services which may be available.

Travellers cheques: US currency cheques are the most welcome at points of exchange.
Exchange rate indicators: The following figures are included as a guide to the movement of the Netherlands Antilles Guilder against Sterling and the US Dollar:

Date:	Oct '89	Oct '90	Oct '91	Oct '92
£1.00=	2.84	3.49	3.11	2.83
$1.00=	1.80	1.79	1.79	1.78

Currency restrictions: The import and export of local currency is limited to NAG200. Foreign currency is unrestricted.
Banking hours: 0830-1200 and 1330-1630 Monday to Friday.

DUTY FREE

The following items may be taken into Curaçao by those over 15 years of age without payment of duty:
400 cigarettes or 50 cigars or 250g of tabacco;
2 litres of alcoholic beverages;
250ml of perfume;
Gifts up to the value of NAG200.

PUBLIC HOLIDAYS

Public holidays observed in Curaçao are as follows:
Apr 9-12 '93 Easter. **Apr 30** Queen's Day. **May 1** Labour Day. **May 20** Ascension Day. **May 31** Whit Monday. **Jul 2** Curaçao Flag Day. **Dec 25-26** Christmas. **Jan 1 '94** New Year's Day. **Feb*** Carnival.
Note [*]: Check with the tourist board for exact dates before travelling.

HEALTH

Regulations and requirements may be subject to change at short notice, and you are advised to contact your doctor well in advance of your intended date of departure. Any numbers in the chart refer to the footnotes below.

	Special Precautions?	Certificate Required?
Yellow Fever	No	1
Cholera	No	No
Typhoid & Polio	Yes	-
Malaria	No	-
Food & Drink	2	-

[1]: A Yellow Fever certificate is required from travellers over six months of age coming from infected areas.
[2]: All mains water on the island is distilled from seawater, and is thus safe to drink. Bottled mineral water is widely available. Milk is pasteurised and dairy products are safe for consumption. Local meat, poultry, seafood, fruit and vegetables are generally considered safe to eat.
Health care: There is a large and well-equipped modern hospital in Willemstad. Health insurance is recommended.

TRAVEL - International

AIR: The national airline of the Netherlands Antilles is *ALM (LM)*.
Approximate flight times: From *London* to Curaçao is 11 hours (depending on connection time), to *Los Angeles* is 12 hours and to *New York* is 6 hours.
International airport: *Curaçao (CUR)* (Hato) is 12km (7 miles) from Willemstad. Airport facilities include duty-free shop, bar, restaurant, buffet, bank, post office, hotel reservation facilities, car hire and taxis to Willemstad.
Departure tax: US$10 per person; children under two years of age and passengers transiting within 24 hours are exempt.
SEA: Over 200 cruises arrive in Curaçao from America and Europe. A ferry sails regularly between Venezuela and Curaçao.

TRAVEL - Internal

AIR: *Windward Islands Air International (SXM)* operates to Saba (SAB) and St Eustatius (EUX).
ROAD: A good public **bus** service runs throughout the island and many of the main hotels provide their own **minibus** services to Willemstad. **Taxis** are plentiful as are **car rental** firms (both international and local), which are located at the airport and in the main hotels, as well as in the capital. **Documentation:** An International Driving Licence is required.

ACCOMMODATION

HOTELS: There are a dozen or so luxury hotels on Curaçao, all offering air-conditioning, restaurants, swimming pools and/or beach access, and a choice between European Plan (room only) and Modified American Plan (half board). Most also offer some sort of in-house entertainment, a baby-sitting service and cable TV. Some have their own casinos. Out-of-town hotels provide their guests with free transport to and from Willemstad. A 5-10% government tax and 10% service charge are levied on all hotel bills. For more information, contact the Curaçao Hotel & Tourism Association, PO Box 6115, Willemstad, Curaçao NA. Tel: (9) 636 260. Fax: (9) 636 445.
GUEST-HOUSES: For details of more modest accommodation – guest-houses, commercial hotels and self-catering – contact any of the organisations listed at the top of this entry.

RESORTS & EXCURSIONS

Willemstad, the capital, is noted for its very brightly coloured, Dutch-style houses and range of other interesting and complementary architectural styles, including *Cunucu* houses (based on African-style mud and wattle huts), thatched cottages and country houses. It is one of the finest shopping centres in the Caribbean. Monuments of interest in the city include the *Statue of Manuel Piar*, a famous freedom fighter, and two statues associated with the second World War: one given by the Dutch royal family to the people of Curaçao (in recognition of their support), and one in commemoration of those who lost their lives. The mustard-coloured *Fort Amsterdam*, now the seat of government of the Netherlands Antilles, stands at the centre of historic Willemstad, which from 1648-1861 was a fortified town of some strategic importance. The fort's church, still standing, doubled as a storehouse for provisions put by in case of siege; specially designed storerooms for food, sails and other essentials may still be seen. A cannonball is still embedded in the church's southwest wall. Nearby is the present Governor's Residence, dating back to the Dutch colonial days. Also worth seeing are the *Queen Emma Pontoon* bridge and the *Queen Juliana Bridge*. The latter spans the harbour at a height of 490m (1600ft). The harbour itself has a floating market where colourful barges full of agricultural produce can be seen. Near this is the new market building, the design of which is very striking. The market comes to life after 0600 on a Saturday morning. The architecture of the **Scharloo** area, reached by crossing the Wilhelmina draw-bridge, is fascinating, dating from as early as 1700. The *Mikvé Israel Synagogue* is the oldest in the Americas and, like the Jewish *Beth Heim Cemetery*, is worth a visit. Its courtyard museum has a fine collection of historical artefacts.
Excursions: Besides the excellent beaches and hotel resorts, the island itself has a number of other points of interest, which the visitor with only a couple of days on the island can easily see. Just outside Willemstad is the modern site of the Netherlands Antilles University, and further along the western road is the *Landhuis Papaya* (a country house), the *Ceru Grandis* (a 3-storey plantation house) and the driftwood beach of **Boca San Pedro**. Also of note is *Boca Tabla*, the thundering underwater cave of the north coast and the picturesque fishing village of **Westpoint**. **St Christoffel National Park,** occupying the most northwestern part of the island, is a nature reserve dominated by the *St Christoffel Mountain*. There are several caves decorated with Arawak Indian paintings, some unusual rock formations and many fine views across the countryside – the ruins of the *Zorguliet Plantation* and the privately owned *Savonet Plantation* and the *Savonet Museum* may be seen at the base of the mountain; the latter dates back to the 18th century and is still in use today. The indigenous flora includes orchids and some very interesting evergreens. As well as the interesting birdlife, the visitor to St Christoffel Park might see iguanas and the shy Curaçao deer. Well worth a visit are the interesting **Caves of Hato**. Magnificent stalactite formations, wall paintings and underground streams with cascading waterfalls can be seen within the 4900m labyrinth.

SOCIAL PROFILE

FOOD & DRINK: Traditional Dutch food (particularly using fresh seafood and cheeses) is popular, as well as the exciting flavours of Creole food, *criollo*, which also makes good use of the great variety of fresh fish. French, Italian and other international cuisines are also on offer. Restaurant styles vary from informal bistro to the very expensive. **Drink:** A wide variety of alcohol is available.
NIGHTLIFE: There are several discos run by hotels on the island and some hotels have a casino. Performances of drama and music can be found at the *Centro Pro Arte*.
SHOPPING: Curaçao (and other Netherlands Antilles islands) is a thriving centre for duty-free shopping. An enormous range of imported goods is on sale at considerably reduced prices. Locally made curios are available for the tourist, a particularly popular souvenir being 'Curaçao' liqueur, which is made from sun-dried peel of a bitter orange and a mixture of spices. **Shopping hours:** 0800-1200 and 1400-1800 Monday to Saturday.
SPORT: Like the other islands of the Caribbean, **watersports** are widely promoted and facilities on Curaçao itself are well developed. There are excellent beaches for **swimming** (some charge an entrance fee). **Windsurfing, sailing** and **water-skiing** are popular on the island and the hotels and watersports centres are well equipped. **Snorkelling, scuba diving** and **deep-sea fishing** are also popular with the visitor and there are plenty of opportunities to participate in these sports, as well as the chance of lessons for the amateur. Other sports provided on the island include **tennis, squash** and **golf** – at the Shell 9-hole golf course. **Horseriding** is also possible.
SPECIAL EVENTS: Carnivals are staged throughout the island every year during the week preceding Lent. **Apr** *Curaçao Sailing Regatta.* **May 30** *Whit Sunday Parade.* **Apr/May** *International Food Festival.* **May** *Drag Races.* **Nov** *'Sint Nicolaas' arrives at St Anna Bay; Caribbean Jazz Festival.*
SOCIAL CONVENTIONS: The social influences are predominantly Dutch, combined with Indian and African traditions. Dress for men should include tropical lightweight suits for business appointments and, for the customary evening, formal wear. Similarly, women should take some evening wear, but dress for daytime is casual. Swimwear should be confined to the beach and poolside only. **Tipping:** Hotels add a 5-10% government tax and a 10% service charge. Barmen, waiters and doormen expect a 10% tip.

BUSINESS PROFILE

ECONOMY: Curaçao is the most prosperous of the Netherlands Antilles island group. It depends less on oil refining and transshipment – a business which has experienced a marked decline in recent years – than, say, Aruba. The capital Willemstad is the centre of a network of 'offshore' banking facilities and other financial ser-

CURAÇAO	HEALTH REGULATIONS	VISA REGULATIONS Code-Link
GALILEO/WORLDSPAN	 TI-DFT/CUR/HE	 TI-DFT/CUR/VI
SABRE	 TIDFT/CUR/HE	 TIDFT/CUR/VI

To access this information on your CRS, swipe the barcode with a light pen or type in the text under the barcode. For more information, see the introduction *How to Use This Book.*

vices. Curaçao also houses one of the largest dry docks in the Western Caribbean although, far from being lucrative, the Curaçao Dry Dock Company turned in regular losses during the 1980s – a situation since rectified. Import substitution has been successfully pursued, so that a wide range of consumer goods from beer via paint to toilet paper are now produced locally. Venezuela, which supplies the crude oil for refinement, and the USA, which buys most of the finished product, are the largest trading partners.
BUSINESS: Suits should be worn and punctuality is essential. **Office hours:** 0800-1200 and 1330-1630 Monday to Friday.
COMMERCIAL INFORMATION: The following organisation can offer advice: Curaçao Chamber of Commerce and Industry, PO Box 10, Kaya Junior Salas 1, Willemstad, Curaçao NA. Tel: (9) 611 451. Fax: (9) 615 652.

HISTORY & GOVERNMENT

HISTORY: Discovered in 1499 by Alonso de Ojeda, a lieutenant of Columbus, the island was settled by the Spanish in the early 1500s. The Dutch West Indies Company seized control in 1634 and imported thousands of slaves to encourage agriculture and stock management schemes. In the early 19th century, British and French attacks destabilised the island for a while; at one point it was even leased to a New York merchant. But by 1816 the Dutch had taken control again and introduced further plantation businesses: brazil wood, aloes and cochineal. The abolition of slavery in 1863 set off a long period of economic decline, relieved in 1916 by the opening of an oil refinery. This and other oil-related industries became the mainstay of a booming economy, transforming Curaçao into one of the most prosperous islands in the Caribbean. The fall in oil prices, however, again initiated decline. Though this has since been rectified as the island is now quite an interesting offshore finance market.
GOVERNMENT: Curaçao is a constituent island of the Netherlands Antilles; the others being Bonaire, Saba, St Eustatius and St Maarten. The Netherlands Antilles, Aruba and The Netherlands each have equal status within the Kingdom of The Netherlands as regions autonomous in internal affairs. The Dutch monarch is represented locally by a Governor, while the Netherlands Antilles are represented in the government of the Kingdom by a Minister Plenipotentiary. Foreign policy and defence matters are decided by a Council of Ministers of the Kingdom, including the Plenipotentiary, and executed under the authority of the Governor. The internal affairs of the islands are administered by the central government of the Netherlands Antilles, based in Willemstad, Curaçao, responsible to the *Staten*, or legislative assembly. Curaçao may elect by non-compulsory adult suffrage 14 out of 22 members to the Staten. Routine local affairs on each island group (Bonaire, Curaçao and the Windward Islands) are managed by an elected Island Council, presided over by a Lieutenant-Governor.

CLIMATE

Hot throughout the year, but tempered by cooling trade winds. The main rainy season is from October to December. The annual mean temperature is 26°C, rainfall 5148mm, humidity 75.9%. The island lies outside the Caribbean 'hurricane belt'.
Required clothing: Cotton and linen clothing with warmer top layers for the evenings; showerproofs are advisable.

WILLEMSTAD Curaçao (8m)

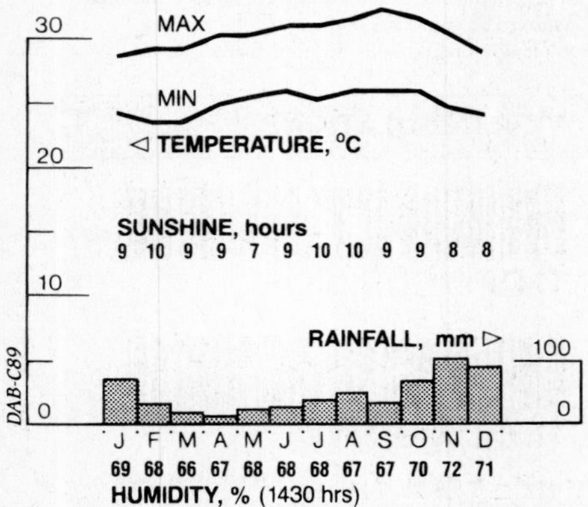

Location: Europe, Eastern Mediterranean.

Note: Since the summer of 1974, the part of the island north of a line drawn roughly between Morphou Bay and Famagusta has been occupied by Turkish troops. All the information given in this section refers to the southern part of the island, the Republic of Cyprus.

Cyprus Tourism Organisation
PO Box 4535, 19 Limassol Avenue
Melkonian Building
Nicosia, Cyprus
Tel: (2) 315 715. Fax: (2) 313 022. Telex: 2165.
High Commission of the Republic of Cyprus
93 Park Street
London W1Y 4ET
Tel: (071) 499 8272. Fax: (071) 491 0691. Telex: 263343.
Consular Section: Tel: (071) 629 5350.
Honorary High Commissions
Glasgow: Tel: (041) 332 6556.
Manchester: Tel: (061) 273 4321.
Cyprus Tourism Organisation
213 Regent Street
London W1R 8DA
Tel: (071) 734 9822/2593. Fax: (071) 287 6534. Telex: 263068. Opening hours: 1000-1800 Monday to Friday.
British High Commission
PO Box 1978, Alexander Pallis Street
Nicosia, Cyprus
Tel: (2) 473 131/7. Fax: (2) 367 198. Telex: 2208 UKREPNIC CY.
Embassy of the Republic of Cyprus
2211 R Street, NW
Washington, DC
20008
Tel: (202) 462 5772. Fax: (202) 483 6710. Telex: 440596.
Consulate General of the Republic of Cyprus
13 East 40th Street
New York, NY
10018
Tel: (212) 686 6016/7/8.
Cyprus Tourism Organisation
13 East Fortieth Street
New York, NY
10016
Tel: (212) 683 5280. Fax: (212) 683 5282.
Also deals with enquiries from Canada.
Embassy of the United States of America
Dositheos Street and Therissos Street
Lykavitos
Nicosia, Cyprus
Tel: (2) 465 151. Fax: (2) 459 571. Telex: 4160.
Honorary Consulate of the Republic of Cyprus
Suite PH2
2930 Edouard Montpetit Street
Montréal, Quebec H3T 1J7
Tel: (514) 735 7233.
Consulate of Canada
PO Box 2125, Margarita House
15 Themistocles Dervis Street
Nicosia, Cyprus
Tel: (2) 451 630. Fax: (2) 459 096. Telex: 2110

AREA: 9251 sq km (3572 sq miles).
POPULATION: 695,000 (1989 estimate, including population of Turkish-occupied region).
POPULATION DENSITY: 75.1 per sq km.
CAPITAL: Nicosia. **Population:** 162,500 (1986).
GEOGRAPHY: Cyprus is an island in the Eastern Mediterranean. The landscape varies between rugged coastlines, sandy beaches, rocky hills and forest-covered mountains. The Troodos Mountains in the centre of the island rise to almost 1950m (6400ft) and provide excellent skiing during the winter. Between these and the range of hills which runs eastward along the north coast and the 'panhandle' is the fertile Messaoria Plain. The Morphou Basin runs around the coast of Morphou Bay in the west.
LANGUAGE: The majority speak Greek and about 25% speak Turkish. The Greek Cypriot dialect is different from mainland Greek. Turkish is spoken by Turkish Cypriots. English, German and French are spoken in tourist centres.
RELIGION: Greek Orthodox, with Muslim minority.
TIME: GMT + 2 (GMT + 3 from the last weekend in March to the last weekend in September).
ELECTRICITY: 240 volts AC, 50Hz. There are two types of plug in use, 5-amp round 3-pin and 13-amp square 3-pin (UK-type).
COMMUNICATIONS: Telephone: Full IDD is available. Country code: 357. **Fax:** This is available at district post offices in Nicosia, Larnaca, Limassol and Paphos. **Telex/telegram:** There are no public telex facilities at present but most hotels will allow guests use of their facilities. A 24-hour service is available via Nicosia. There are telegraph links to the international network through major hotels and the Central Telegraph Office, Egypt Avenue, Nicosia. A 24-hour service is provided with three charge rates. **Post:** There are daily airmail services to all developed countries. Service to Europe takes three days. *Poste Restante* facilities are available in main cities and resorts. Post office opening hours: 0730-1330 Monday to Friday, and 1500-1800 Thursday. **Press:** The only daily newspaper published in English is the *Cyprus Mail*. All others are in Greek and Turkish.
BBC World Service and Voice of America frequencies: From time to time these change. See the section *How to Use this Book* for more information.

BBC:

MHz	17.640	15.070	9.410	6.180

In addition, the CTO sponsors programmes for tourists Monday to Saturday on 603kHz (498m) and FM94.8. The times are as follows: German 0800; English 0830; French 0900; Swedish 0930; Arabic 1000.

Voice of America:

MHz	9.670	6.040	5.995	1.260

PASSPORT/VISA

Regulations and requirements may be subject to change at short notice, and you are advised to contact the appropriate diplomatic or consular authority before finalising travel arrangements. Details of these may be found at the head of this country's entry. Any numbers in the chart refer to the footnotes below.

	Passport Required?	Visa Required?	Return Ticket Required?
Full British	Yes	No	Yes
BVP	Not valid	-	-
Australian	Yes	No	Yes
Canadian	Yes	No	Yes
USA	Yes	No	Yes
Other EC	Yes	1	Yes
Japanese	Yes	No	Yes

PASSPORTS: Valid passport required by all.
British Visitors Passport: Not accepted.
VISAS: Required by all except the following, who can stay for up to 3 months without a visa:
(a) [1] nationals of countries referred to in the chart above (with the exception of nationals of Portugal who *do* require a visa);
(b) nationals of Commonwealth countries except Bangladesh;
(c) nationals of Austria, Bahrain, Fiji, Finland, Iceland, Kuwait, Liechtenstein, Norway, Oman, Qatar, San Marino, Saudi Arabia, Sweden, Switzerland, United Arab Emirates and Yugoslavia.
Types of visa: Ordinary – £1.30; Transit – free. Cash or postal order only. Nationals of Bulgaria, the Baltic States, Czechoslovakia, Egypt, Israel, the USSR and Syria are exempted from visa payment provided they have onward or return tickets and sufficient funds to

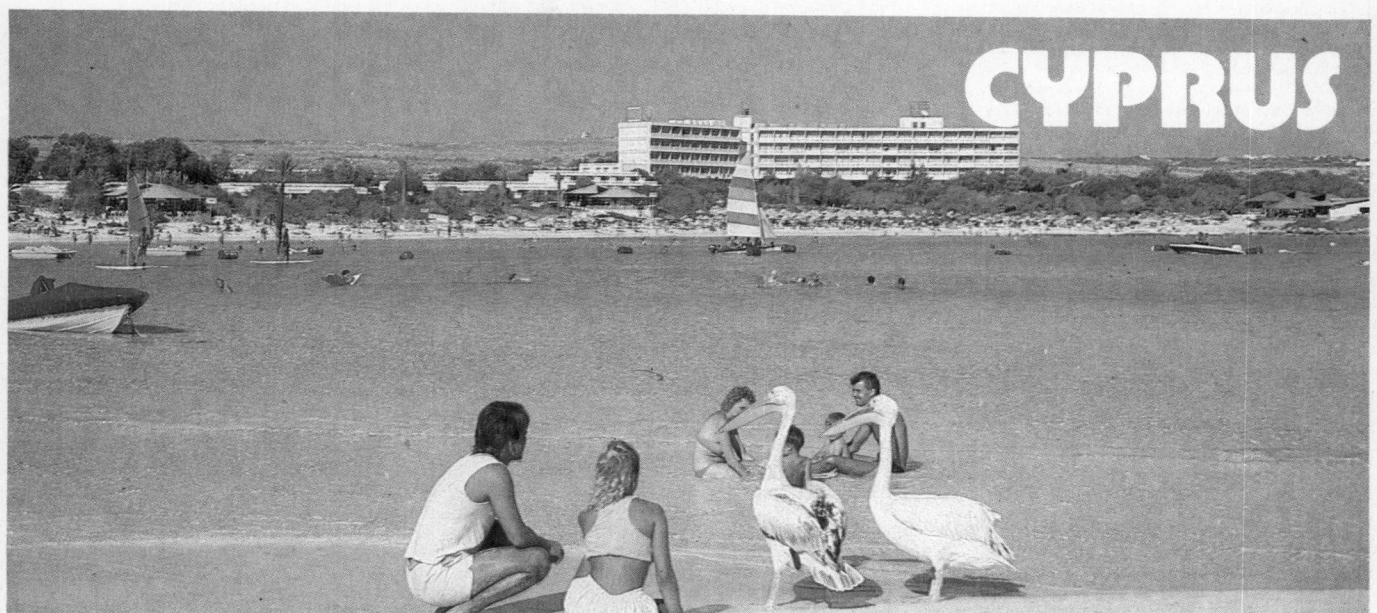

cover the duration of their stay.
Validity: Maximum of 3 months from date of issue.
Transit: Transit visas are valid for travel through Cyprus, providing the traveller does not stay on the island for a period exceeding 5 days, and is in possession of visas and through tickets for the destination country.
Application to: Consulate (or Consular Section at Embassy or High Commission). For addresses, see top of entry.
Application requirements: (a) Passport valid for 3 months if the applicant's country of origin maintains consular representation in Cyprus and for at least 6 months if it does not. (b) 2 completed application forms. (c) 3 photos. (d) Proof of sufficient funds to cover duration of stay. (e) Onward or return ticket. (f) For business trips, an introductory letter from the applicant's company giving details and nature of business to be conducted.
Working days required: Same day, or up to 6 weeks if application needs to be referred to Cyprus.
Temporary residence: Enquire at Embassy or High Commission, addresses above.

MONEY

Currency: Cyprus Pound (C£) = 100 cents. Notes are in denominations of C£10, 5 and 1, and 50 cents. Coins are in denominations of C£50 and 50, 20, 10, 5, 2 and 1 cents. Cents are informally known as 'shillings'.
Currency exchange: Visitors wishing to obtain non-Cypriot currency at Cypriot banks for business purposes are advised that this is only possible by prior arrangement.
Credit cards: Access/Mastercard, American Express, Visa and Diners Club are accepted. Check with your credit card company for details of merchant acceptability and other services which may be available.
Travellers cheques: May be cashed in all banks.
Exchange rate indicators: The following figures are included as a guide to the movements of the Cyprus Pound against Sterling and the US Dollar:

Date:	Oct '89	Oct '90	Oct '91	Oct '92
£1.00=	0.79	0.84	0.80	0.73
$1.00=	0.50	0.43	0.46	0.46

Currency restrictions: Foreign currency of more than the equivalent of US$1000 must be declared. The import and export of local currency is limited to a maximum of C£50.
Banking hours: Generally 0815-1230 Monday to Friday, but certain banks may also open on weekday afternoons except Tuesdays in tourist areas from 1530-1730 (winter) and 1630-1830 (summer).

DUTY FREE

The following goods may be imported into Cyprus without incurring customs duty:
200 cigarettes or 50 cigars or 250g of tobacco;
1 litre of spirits;
0.75 litres of wine;
0.30 litres [1] *of perfume and toilet water;*
Goods (excluding jewellery) up to C£50.
Note: [1] To include no more than 0.15 litre of perfume in one bottle.

PUBLIC HOLIDAYS

Public holidays observed in Cyprus are as follows:
Mar 1 '93 Green Monday. **Mar 25** Greek National Day. **Apr 1** Greek Cypriot Independence. **Apr 16** Good Friday. **Apr 19** Easter Monday. **May 1** May Day. **Jun 7** Kataklysmos. **Aug 15** Dormition (Assumption) of the Virgin Mary. **Oct 1** Cyprus Independence Day. **Oct 28** Greek Independence Day. **Dec 25-26** Christmas. **Jan 1 '94** New Year's Day. **Jan 6** Epiphany. **Mar 14** Green Monday. **Mar 25** Greek National Day.

HEALTH

Regulations and requirements may be subject to change at short notice, and you are advised to contact your doctor well in advance of your intended date of departure. Any numbers in the chart refer to the footnotes below.

	Special Precautions?	Certificate Required?
Yellow Fever	No	No
Cholera	No	No
Typhoid & Polio	1	No
Malaria	No	No
Food & Drink	2	-

CYPRUS — **HEALTH REGULATIONS** — **VISA REGULATIONS** — Code-Link

GALILEO/WORLDSPAN

TI-DFT/LCA/HE

TI-DFT/LCA/VI

SABRE

TIDFT/LCA/HE

TIDFT/LCA/VI

To access this information on your CRS, swipe the barcode with a light pen or type in the text under the barcode. For more information, see the introduction *How to Use This Book*.

[1]: There is a risk of typhoid. No cases of polio have been reported in recent years.
[2]: Milk is pasteurised and tap water is generally safe to drink. Powdered and tinned milk is available. Only eat well-cooked meat and fish, preferably served hot. Pork, salad and mayonnaise may carry increased risk. Vegetables should be cooked and fruit peeled.
Health care: No health agreement exists with the UK but benefits are available if arranged with the Department of Health before departure (see *Health* section at the back of the book).

TRAVEL - International

Note: Since October 1974 the Cyprus Government has declared the ports of Famagusta and Kyrenia and the airport of Ercan as illegal 'ports of entry' to Cyprus. Tourists entering through these illegal ports of entry will be refused entry to the government-controlled areas. Further details can be obtained from the Cyprus Tourism Organisation.
AIR: Cyprus's national airline is *Cyprus Airways (CY)*.
Approximate flight time: From *London* to both Paphos and Larnaca is 4 hours 20 minutes.
From *Paris* to Cyprus is 3 hours 30 minutes.
From *Zurich* to Cyprus is 3 hours.
From *Frankfurt* to Cyprus is 3 hours 30 minutes.
From *Athens* to Cyprus is 1 hour 40 minutes.
From *Stockholm* to Cyprus is 5 hours.
International airports (in the government-controlled part of the island): *Larnaca (LCA)* is 8km (3 miles) south of the city (travel time – 20 minutes). Airport facilities include outgoing duty-free shop, tourist information, car hire, bank/exchange (available 24 hours), bar, restaurant and a Cyprus Hotel Information and Reservation Office.
Paphos (PFO) is 11km (7 miles) east of the city (travel time – 25 minutes). Airport facilities include outgoing duty-free shop, car hire, bank/exchange, bar and restaurant.
SEA: Shipping lines connect the island with Greece, Syria, Israel, Egypt and Italy. For details contact the Cyprus Tourism Organisation.

TRAVEL - Internal

ROAD: Bus: Buses connect all towns and villages on the island. Service is efficient and cheap. Although the local buses are slow, they are a good way of seeing the more remote villages. **Taxi:** Services connect all the main towns on the island. Fares are regulated by the Government and all taxis have meters. *Service Taxis* offer an excellent, cheap service using 7-seat taxis running fixed routes between main points. Taxis run to a timetable and delivery is door to door. Fares under this system are often one-tenth of the usual rate. **Car hire:** Cars are one of the best ways to explore the island. They may be hired at airports and commercial centres, but should be reserved well in advance during the summer season. Reduced tariffs are offered if cars are hired for more than a week. Road signs are in both Greek and English. Traffic drives on the left. **Documentation:** An International Driving Permit or national driving licence is accepted for one year.
URBAN: Nicosia has its own privately run bus company operating efficient services at flat fares. Taxis are widely available; a 15% surcharge is in operation from 2300-0600. Tips are expected.
JOURNEY TIMES: The following chart gives approximate journey times (in hours and minutes) from Nicosia to other main towns and tourist centres in Cyprus.

	Road
Limassol	1.00
Paphos	2.15
Larnaca	0.30
Ayia Napa	1.10
Platres	1.30
Protaras	2.00
Polis	2.30

ACCOMMODATION

Types of accommodation include hotel apartments, tourist apartments, furnished apartments and tourist houses, tourist villas, hotels without a star, guest-houses, camping and youth hostels.
HOTELS: There are over 500 hotels and hotel apartments scattered throughout the island. There are also simple hotels that are ungraded. A service charge of 10% and a 3% tax are added to bills. Most hotels and hotel apartments offer discounts during the low season, which for seaside resorts is from November 1 to March 31 (excluding the period December 20 to January 6) and for hill resorts from October 1 to June 30. There are discounts for children occupying the same room as their parents: *under 1 year* by private arrangement; *1-6 years* 50% discount; *6-10 years* 25% discount. **Grading:** Hotels range from deluxe 5- to 1-star. Hotel apartments are classified A, B or C. The range of accommodation in Cyprus is classified by the Cyprus Tourism Organisation as consisting of hotels with a star classification system; this indicates facilities offered, physical criteria, room size and the cost, according to the class chosen.
For further information contact: The Cyprus Tourism Organisation controls and regulates hotels; *or:* The Cyprus Hotel Association, PO Box 4772, Nicosia, Cyprus. Tel: (2) 445 251. Fax: (2) 365 460. Telex: 4747.
GUEST-HOUSES: Located mainly in Nicosia and Limassol.
CAMPING/CARAVANNING: There are four organised camping sites: Polis (open March-October, tel: (6) 321 526), Troodos (open May-October, tel: (5) 421 624), Forest Beach (east of Larnaca, tel: (4) 622 414) and Ayia Napa (open March-October, tel: (3) 721 946).
YOUTH HOSTELS: These are only open to members of the International Youth Hostels Association: apply either to the Nicosia or Limassol Youth Hostels for membership. There are hostels at 5 Hadjidaki Stree, **Nicosia** (off Themistoklis Dervis Street, tel: (2) 444 808 *or* 442 027); at 37 Eleftherios Venizelos Avenue, **Paphos** (tel: (6) 232 588); **Troodos Mountains** (open April-October, tel: (5) 421 649); and at 27 Nicolaou Rossou Street, **Larnaca** (near St Lazarus Church, tel: (4) 442 027).

RESORTS & EXCURSIONS

NICOSIA: Nicosia, the capital of Cyprus since the 12th century, is situated at the heart of the *Messaoria plain*. It is currently divided by the UN buffer zone that separates the Turkish-occupied north of the island and the government-controlled south. The old city, which has many quaint and ancient shops, is defined by walls built by the Venetians. Other attractions in Nicosia include the *Cyprus Museum*, the *Folk Art Museum*, the old and new *Arch-episcopal palaces*, *St John's Cathedral*, the *Makarios Foundation Art Gallery* and the Byzantine churches. Outside Nicosia, near **Deftera**, there is a new riding school and sports centre. At the end of May the annual *International State Fair* and the *Nicosia Art Festival* are held in Nicosia.
Excursions: Nicosia District extends westwards into the vine-covered **Troodos Mountains**, where there are magnificent forests and valleys, and hill resorts such as **Kakopetria**, and the Byzantine churches in **Galata**. The area offers some interesting excursions including: the *Royal Tombs and Ayios Heraklidios Monastery* at **Tamassos**; the 5-dome church and the mosque in **Peristerona** village; the 12th-century church of *Assinou*, one of the finest examples of Byzantine art in the Middle East, in **Nikitari**; the church of *Stavros tou Ayiasmati* in **Platanistassa**; *St John Lampadistis Monastery* in **Kalopanayotis;** the *Panayia tou Araka Monastery* in **Lagoudera**; and the *Macheras Monastery*, about an hour's drive into the hills southwest of Nicosia. The area has countless other old churches and monasteries, including *Kykkos* (see *Hill Resorts* below) and *Araka*, containing impressive and well-preserved Byzantine frescoes and shrines, and also a few pagan shrines where the ancients worshipped their gods. **Pitsilia District** produces most of the grapes for the Commandaria wine. There are many attractive villages, such as **Zoopygi**, where almond and walnut trees grow, **Kalokhorio** and, further up, **Agros,** a village with a small hotel and a few holiday homes.
LIMASSOL: Limassol is the second largest town in Cyprus and the island's main port. Its modern harbour is constantly being expanded to meet the demands of trade and passenger traffic. Limassol is also the centre of the wine industry in Cyprus; most of the vines used grow on the slopes of the **Troodos Mountains**. In September the town has a wine festival, during which wine and food are served free. At Carnival, held at the start of Lent, the town bursts into celebration with bands, gaily decorated floats and dancing. Limassol is rapidly becoming Cyprus' main tourist centre, with facilities such as the public tourist beach at **Dhassoudi**, backed by cafés and changing rooms. There is also a museum and public gardens with a small zoo and the castle.
Excursions: There are many places of historic and archaeological interest in and around Limassol.
Amathus, 11km (7 miles) east of Limassol, was once the capital of a city-kingdom, but is now in ruins, partly covered by the sea. The *Acropolis*, *Necropolis* and the remains of an early Christian basilica can still be seen, as well as the new excavations in the lower part of the town. Further east lies the *Ayios Georgios Nunnery*, and to the west is *Kolossi Castle*, headquarters of the Knights of St John of Jerusalem. **Curium** has a superb Greco-Roman theatre where concerts and Shakespeare's plays are performed in summer. The town has many sites of interest including the house of Eustolios, in which there are some beautiful mosaics; the *Sanctuary of Apollo Hylates;* the *Stadium;* the *Acropolis* with the ruins of the *Forum;* the *Christian Basilica* and many public buildings. To the south is the *Lady's Mile Beach* and *Akrotiri Salt Lake*, winter home of thousands of flamingoes. Limassol is also a good starting point for an excursion into the Troodos Mountains (see *Excursions* in *Nicosia* above).
PAPHOS: Built on a rocky escarpment, **Upper Paphos** commands a superb view of the coastline and the harbour of **Lower Paphos,** which is ringed by tavernas famous for their fish dishes. It is a place of historic and archaeological interest, including the remains of the *House of Dionysus*, a Roman villa with some fine mosaics, and the nearby *Villa of Theseus*. Other attractions include the *District Museum*, the castle overlooking the harbour, the *Tombs of the Kings*, the remains of the Byzantine castle of *Saranda Kolones* and the *Chrysopolitissa Basilica*, the biggest early Christian Basilica on the island.
Excursions: Paphos is an excellent centre for exploration; eastwards the land rises through the vineyards, the forests and the Cedar Valley; northwards, the road leads over the foothills, passing close to the monastery of *Ayios Neophytos* (founded in AD1220), and down to the little town of **Polis** on the north coast. Polis is an unexploited and virtually undeveloped beach area with one tourist hotel, a campsite and a few self-catering establishments; accommodation is also possible in private homes. Nearby is the fishing harbour of **Latchi**, which offers a variety of fish dishes including grilled swordfish steak. Westwards from Latchi is an unspoilt beach; beyond is the little grotto known as *Fontana Amorosa*. North of **Paphos** is *Coral Bay* which has a bathing beach and several good restaurants. Further on is the fishing village of **Ayios Yeorgios tis Peyias** which has an early Christian basilica; and nearby is *Lara Beach* where a turtle hatchery has been established. In the opposite direction, towards Limassol, is the village of **Yeroskipos**, home of 'Turkish Delight', with a small but interesting folk museum.
LARNACA: Southeast Cyprus provides a complete contrast to the rest of the country. The one-time sleepy little town of Larnaca has now been brought to life by the nearby new international airport. There is also a new harbour with a number of deep-water berths, and a marina which accommodates up to 200 yachts. New hotels and apartment blocks have been built to keep pace with the town's growing popularity as a winter resort. The seafront is fringed by palm trees and cafés and tavernas. Other places of interest include *Ayia Phaneromeni Church*, dating from the 8th century BC and built over a rock cave; *Larnaca Fort*, the *District Museum* and the *Museum of the Pierides Family*, and the ruins of the ancient city of **Kition**. The feast of Kataklysmos (the Greek Orthodox Whitsun) is celebrated throughout Cyprus, but with special enthusiasm in Larnaca. Crowds from all over the district and from Nicosia arrive at the shore for watersports, singing, dancing, eating and drinking.
Excursions: Near the airport is the *Tekke* of **Hala Sultan**, standing in beautiful gardens on the edge of the *Salt Lake*, the winter home of migratory flamingoes. Nearby is the *Church of Panayia Angeloktisti* (meaning 'built by the angels'), containing a fine piece of Byzantine art – a 6th-century life-size mosaic of the Virgin Mary and child.
Westwards is the village of **Lefkara**, famous for its lace, and the *Nunnery of Ayios Minas*; off the Limassol–Nicosia road stands *Stavrovouni Monastery*, the *Royal Chapel in Pyrga* and **Kornos** village, famous for its pottery. Further west is **Khirokitia**, which has the remains of one of the earliest settlements in Cyprus dating from 5800BC (neolithic period). To the east, *Larnaca Bay* has a public bathing beach with facilities comparable to those of Limassol, and several newly built hotels.
FAMAGUSTA DISTRICT: The town of Famagusta is in the zone occupied by the Turks, but much of what was once Famagusta District lies across the divide. There are excellent and comfortable hotels and hotel apartments of all categories. The whole of this area is very fertile, with many of the vegetable crops grown for export. To the southeast of Famagusta is an area famous for silvery beaches ideal for children. The village of **Ayia Napa** has a 16th-century Venetian Monastery, looking down on the fishing harbour. The village caters for the visitor with cafés, restaurants, *bouzouki* and Cypriot dancing shows, but still retains its local atmosphere. Around **Cape Greco** the coastline becomes indented with rocky coves and small sandy beaches, ideal for snorkelling, explorations by boat and picnics. *Fig Tree Bay*, *Flamingo Bay*, *Protaras* and *Pernera* beaches are among the most popular, each with cafés and beach bars. Inland, the little town of **Paralimni** also provides entertainment for the tourist with restaurants, discotheques and cafés.
HILL RESORTS: Platres, 1100m (3700ft) above sea level on the southern approaches to *Mount Olympus*, has many hotels to choose from. It is the ideal base for picnics and excursions through the forests and villages; many mountain villages offer accommodation of different categories with around 1958 beds between them. The

ROYAL ARTEMIS MEDICAL CENTRE AND HEALTH CLUB

PAPHOS, CYPRUS
TEL: 236300. FAX: 243670.

GOOD PRICES ARRANGED FOR ELDERLY PEOPLE STAYING AT THE ARTEMIS HEALTH CLUB ON A MEDIUM TO LONG-TERM BASIS

A private medical, surgical, accident and emergency centre on 24 hour call. We provide specialist health care, first class private rooms, using the most up-to-date equipment and techniques. The clinic offers a team of well-established specialists, all experienced in the latest medical, surgical and health care techniques. Experienced emergency teams with our equipped private ambulance are on call 24 hours a day to visit patients in their hotel room, house or apartment.

The Royal Artemis Medical Centre and Health Club offers a friendly, pleasant environment with luxury single and double rooms which are tastefully decorated, fully air-conditioned with large glass doors leading to the balcony. All rooms include mini refrigerator, bathroom with whirlpool/spa, electrical supply for electric razors, emergency nurse call and maid service button, telephone, satellite and local television, radio and all the required modern medical equipment.

The Medical centre includes fully equipped intensive care vascular monitoring, ultrasound, radiology, biochemistry and other facilities necessary for the most up-to-date treatment of urgent conditions. Dental unit available for any problems you may have with your teeth. Consulting rooms, operating theatres, recovery and x-ray units. Full medical check up unit including cardiography, radiology, biochemical investigation, ultrasound and smear tests for women. Physiotherapy unit including indoor therapeutic salt-water heated swimming pool, spa bath. An experienced acupuncturist is available to help in special conditions.

The Health Club offers accommodation with 24-hour room service and the above mentioned facilities available for your use, as well as the pool bar and cafeteria, restaurant, sunbathing and garden area, pool table and table games.

You will automatically become a member of the Royal Artemis Health Club with the use of the swimming pool and spa free of charge.

The Medical Consultant will advise and hold talks on health related matters free of charge.

The Royal Artemis Medical Centre and Health Club is undoubtedly the international centre that can be trusted with your health and well-being. With experienced, friendly, and welcoming multi-lingual staff who are always available to give you any information you may require, you will feel with the Cypriot hospitality and the beautiful healthy weather that it is a home away from home.

Directors: Ch. Charalambous and Dr. Th. Theophilou.

scenery in this region is truly spectacular. Places of interest include *Phedoulas*, famous for its cherries (and their blossoms in spring) and other fruits; **Kalopanayiotis**, known for its variety of fruit; **Moutoullas**, the source of mineral water which is bottled and exported to the Middle East; **Stavros tis Psokas** where there is a controlled enclosure for the preservation of the *moufflon*, the wild sheep of Cyprus; **Prodromos**, the highest village in the island, 1400m (4600ft) above sea level, and claimed to grow the best apples; *Kykkos Monastery*, which houses a golden icon of the Virgin Mary; *Throni tis Panayias*, the tomb of the late Archbishop Makarios III in a setting so superb that it is worth a visit for this reason alone; the villages of **Moniatis**, **Saittas** and **Phini**, centres of a local pottery industry; *Mesapotamos Monastery* and the *Caledonian Falls*; **Omodhos** village and *Monastery of the Holy Cross* with its small folk art museum; and the *Trooditssa Monastery*.

Kakopetria, 670m (2200ft) above sea level on the north-eastern slopes of Mount Olympus and less than an hour's drive from Nicosia, is popular among those not suited to the higher altitudes. It is a village with a delightful central square shaded by plane trees where apples, pears and peaches grow. Like Platres, it is a centre for excursions into the surrounding landscape of forested mountains, deep gorges and fertile valleys.

WINTER SPORTS: Cyprus is becoming established as a winter destination with some hoteliers and tour operators offering off-peak incentives. Both **Platres** and **Kakopetria** are conveniently placed for the skiing season on Mount Olympus, which usually lasts from January to mid-March, but **Troodos** is actually the nearest resort to the skiing area; it has hotels and cafés. Although Cyprus is not well-known for its skiing, the *Troodos Mountains* offer excellent winter sports facilities and there are three ski-lifts on Mount Olympus. The Ski-Club, which is based in Troodos, has its own shelter and accepts tourists as temporary members. Ski equipment can be hired there.

SOCIAL PROFILE

FOOD & DRINK: Major resorts have bars and restaurants of every category. At larger hotels, the indigenous cuisine tends to have an 'international flavour' although authentic local dishes may also be available. All over the island there are restaurants offering genuine Cypriot food. Charcoal-grilled meat is very popular, as is fresh seafood. Dishes include *kebabs* (pieces of lamb or other meat skewered and roasted over a charcoal fire), *dolmas* (vine leaves stuffed with minced meat and rice), and *tava* (a tasty stew of meat, herbs and onions). One of the best ways of enjoying Cypriot food is by ordering *mezze* (snacks), a large selection of a number of different local dishes. Fresh fruit is plentiful and cheap and very sweet desserts such as *baklava* are widely available. **Drink:** Waiter service is normal and in bars counter service is common. There are no licensing hours. Cyprus produces excellent wines, spirits and beer which can only be bought in the south. Coffee is Greek-style (short, strong and unfiltered), though cappuccino is available in most restaurants and bars. Traditional English tea can be bought everywhere. The highlight of the wine year is the annual wine festival, usually held in September, when free wine flows and local food is on offer. The festival is just one of many celebrated throughout the year in Limassol.

SHOPPING: Uniquely Cypriot purchases include hand-made lace, woven curtains and table cloths, silks, basket work, pottery, silverware and leather goods. Jewellery is an art which has been practised on the island since the Mycenean period; craftsmen working in contemporary and traditional styles produce some very fine pieces. Silver spoons and forks are a traditional symbol of Cypriot hospitality. *Lefkaritika lace* is famous throughout the world as one of the products most closely associated with Cypriot workmanship (the name originates from the village Lefkara, situated on a hill on the the Nicosia–Limassol road). Other products include the simple baskets which have been made on the island for years, leather goods and pottery. The local wines and brandy also make good purchases. Imported goods sell at competitive prices, including cameras, perfume, porcelain, crystal, and of course the finest English fabrics. Shirts made to measure or ready to wear can be found at very low prices. **Shopping hours:** Shops are closed on Wednesday and Saturday afternoons and all day Sunday, but otherwise opening hours are 0800-1300 and 1430-1900 in summer and 0800-1300 and 1430-1730 in winter.

SPORT: Horseriding, tennis, climbing, windsurfing, paragliding, swimming, fishing, sailing, diving, water-skiing, skindiving and, increasingly, **skiing** (see *Resorts & Excursions* above).

SPECIAL EVENTS: For a detailed list of festivals and other special events in Cyprus, please contact the Cyprus Tourism Organisation. The following is a selection of the better-known events:

Apr '93 *Easter Festivities*. **May** *Flower Festival* in all major towns. **May/Jun** *Kataklysmos Festival* (Festival of the Flood) in all seaside towns. **Jun** *Medieval Festival* in Limassol. **Jul** *Regional Festival* in Larnaca. **Aug** *Summer Festival* in Paralimni and *Folk Festival* in Paphos. **Sep** *Wine Festival* in Limassol and *Regional Festivals* in Nicosia and Paphos.

SOCIAL CONVENTIONS: Respect should be shown for religious beliefs. Those visitors who leave the confines of their hotel and beach to explore Cyprus will find a warm reception waiting for them in the many villages. It is customary to shake hands and other normal courtesies should be observed. It is viewed as impolite to refuse an offer of Greek coffee or a cold drink. It is acceptable to bring a small gift of wine or confectionery, particularly when invited for a meal. For most occasions casual attire is acceptable. Beach wear should be confined to the beach or poolside. More formal wear is required for business and in more exclusive dining rooms, social functions etc. **Tipping:** A service charge is added to all bills, but tipping is still acceptable and remains up to the individual.

BUSINESS PROFILE

ECONOMY: Cyprus has recovered well from the trauma of 1974, when almost the entire economy was destroyed or severely disrupted by the Turkish invasion and the ensuing fighting. Despite the lack of a political settlement, the economy in both sectors of the island has recovered well. The southern, Greek Cypriot sector is predominantly agricultural, producing fruit and vegetables – potatoes, barley, citrus fruit and grapes – for export. Tourism is the fastest growing sector, having now recovered to well beyond pre-invasion levels and light manufacturing and principally clothing and footwear is showing steady improvement after major reorganisation during the 1980s. Clothing in particular makes an important contribution to exports. In the Turkish-controlled north of the island, citrus fruit is the main produce. Mining, once an important industry, has declined to minimal levels. Compared to the south, the north remains relatively poor. The UK is the largest single trading partner, while the EC as a whole has now superseded Arab countries (Lebanon, Egypt, The Gulf States and Libya) in trading importance. Britain's sovereign military bases on the southern coast and near the partition boundary are a major source of revenue for the Government.

Under a customs union agreement with the EC, all trade barriers will be abolished by the end of a 15-year transition period ending in 2003. The southern government made a formal application to join the Community in 1990. This was rejected by Brussels, and Cyprus is likely to face continued exclusion until a political settlement is achieved.

BUSINESS: Cypriot businessmen have a tradition of hospitality and courtesy and similar behaviour is expected from visitors. Avoid business visits in July and August. **Office hours:** All offices are closed half-day Wednesday,

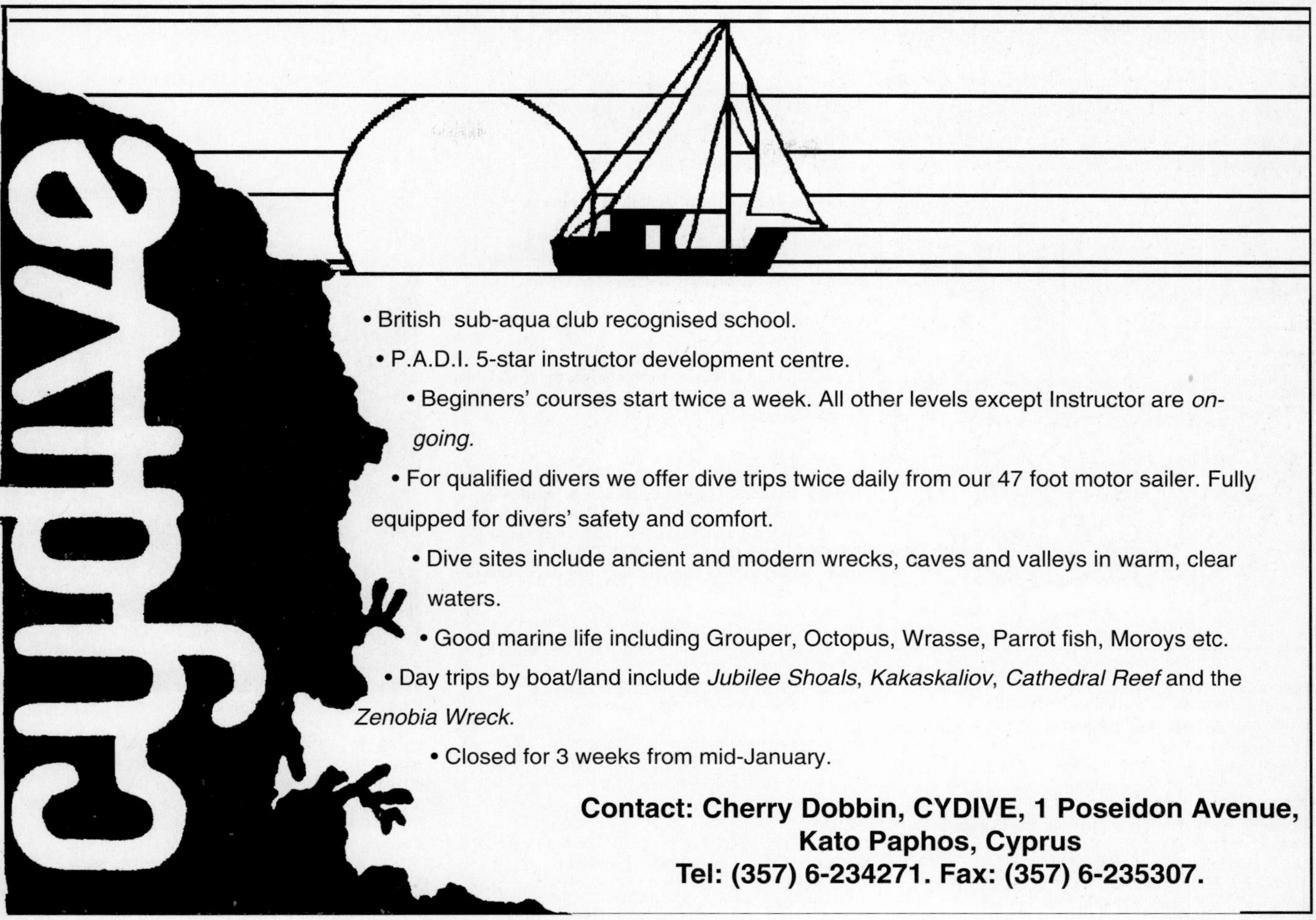

otherwise 0800-1300 and 1600-1900 (summer); 0800-1300 and 1500-1800 (winter) Monday to Friday.
COMMERCIAL INFORMATION: The following organisation can offer advice: Cyprus Chamber of Commerce and Industry, PO Box 1455, 38 Grivas Dhigenis Avenue, Nicosia. Tel: (2) 449 500 *or* 462 312. Fax: (2) 449 048. Telex: 2077 CHAMBER CY.
CONFERENCES/CONVENTIONS: Many hotels have facilities; seating for up to 1200 people is possible. Nicosia is a popular destination for budget-priced conferences and has a number of modern facilities. Advice can be obtained from: Cyprus Tourism Organisation Conference Department, PO Box 4535, Nicosia. Tel: (2) 315 715. Fax: (2) 313 022. Telex: 2165 CYTOUR; *or* Cyprus International Conference Centre, PO Box 5670, Nicosia. Tel: (2) 313 444. Fax: (2) 312 333. Telex: 6393 CICC CY.

HISTORY & GOVERNMENT

HISTORY: Civilisation on the island can be traced back over 8000 years. The island's history, both real and mythical, is turbulent. Like many Mediterranean islands, Cyprus has long been seen as an important strategic base and has suffered a variety of occupations. The Athenians, the Persians, the Egyptians, Alexander the Great and the Romans were the most important invaders during the ancient period, but after the partition of the Roman Empire in the 4th century the island became part of the Eastern Byzantine Empire. The island was a temporary casualty of the Arab invasions between 648 and 746. During the Third Crusade, Richard I of England conquered Cyprus and installed Guy of Lusignan (previously King of Jerusalem), whose house ruled until the island passed to the control of Venice in 1489. From 1571, the Ottomans ruled Cyprus for over three centuries, finally ceding it to Britain in 1878. Independence was achieved in August 1960 after a 4-year military struggle between the British and the guerrillas of EOKA (National Organisation of Cypriot Fighters). The political leader of the liberation movement, Archbishop Makarios (head of the island's Greek Orthodox church) returned from exile and was elected President in December 1959. The island's new constitution was an elaborate compromise between the British and the rival Greek and Turkish communities, between whom there remained considerable distrust. The crisis came to a head in 1974 when Makarios was deposed by a military coup on 15 July (allegedly backed by the military regime then in power in Greece). Five days later, Turkish troops arrived on the northern coast of Cyprus, having been 'invited' by the Turkish Cypriot leader, Rauf Denktash, to intervene to protect the Turkish community on the island. The Greeks failed to respond, largely because of the simultaneous collapse of the military junta in Athens: the Greek Cypriot-controlled National Guard was insufficiently equipped to combat them effectively. After the Turkish army had taken control of the northern third of the island, a ceasefire was arranged under UN auspices. The island has since remained partitioned and United Nations forces maintain a truce between the two sides. In November 1983 the Turkish part of the island proclaimed itself the 'Turkish Republic of Northern Cyprus', but recognition to the self-styled country has been granted only by Turkey and, in November 1991, the autonomous region of Nachichevan in the former Soviet republic of Azerbaijan. For the rest of the international community, the legitimate government of Cyprus is the Greek Cypriot administration in Nicosia. This is currently led by President George Vassiliou, who was elected to office in 1988. Numerous UN-sponsored attempts to reach a political settlement have ended in failure, but the negotiators persevere and another round of talks is currently under way in New York. The main sticking points are: the balance and concentration of power within any unified government; Turkish troop concentrations in the north; and the return of property relinquished by Greek refugees and since occupied by Turkish settlers. This bitter and complex dispute will probably take many years to solve. The Turkish Cypriot leader, Rauf Denktash, who will attend the talks along with President Vassiliou, who was re-elected in April 1990 with 66% of the vote. The legislative assembly in the north is dominated by the Ulusal Birlik Partisi, which won 34 of the the total of 50 seats at the May 1990 poll. The latest elections for the Greek-Cypriot House of Representatives were held in May 1991. AKEL (Communist Party) increased its representation to 18 seats, just behind the 20 seats won by the conservative-liberal alliance of DISY and Komma Phileleftheron.
GOVERNMENT: The 1960 constitution, which allowed for a population-determined sharing of power between the Turkish and Greek communities, officially remains in force but in practice the state organs it established are duplicated in the two zones. Thus executive power in the Republic of Cyprus is vested in a President, elected every five years by universal adult suffrage. He is assisted by a Council of Ministers. A 56-seat Parliament is also elected by universal adult suffrage every five years. The President is currently George Vassiliou, an independent with support from the Communist Party, AKEL. A similar system, with a president and legislative assembly elected for 5- year terms, operates in the self-styled 'Turkish Republic of Northern Cyprus'.

CLIMATE

Warm Mediterranean climate. Hot, dry summers with mild winters during which rainfall is most likely.
Required clothing: Lightweight cottons and linens during summer months; warmer, mediumweights and rainwear during the winter.

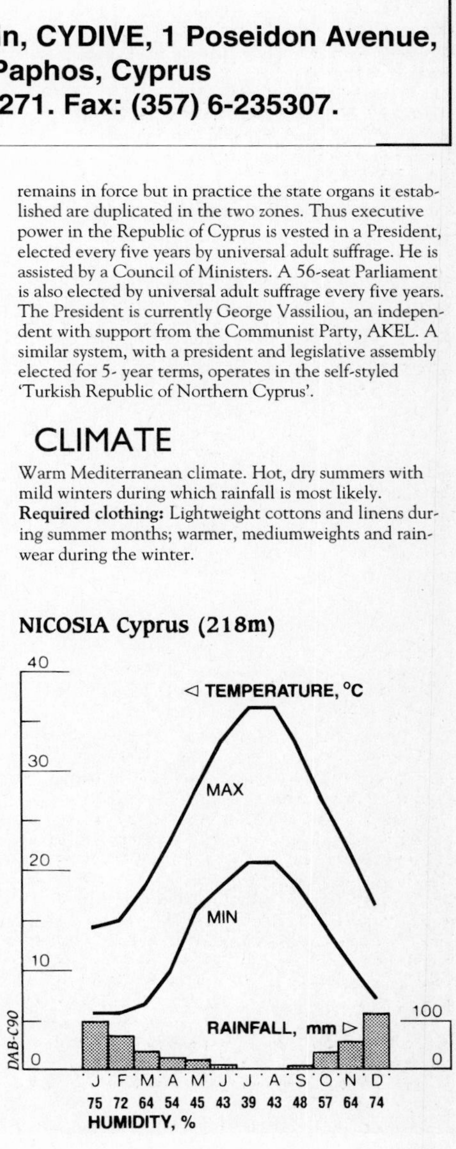

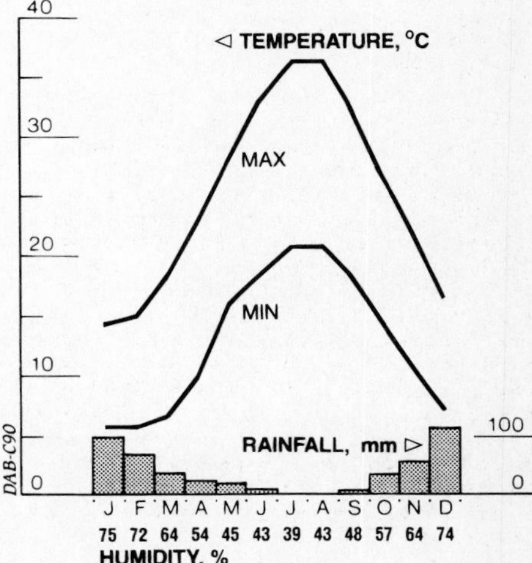

CZECH REPUBLIC

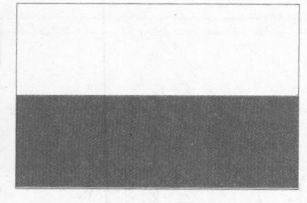

Location: Central Europe.

Ministry of Economy and Tourism of the Czech Republic
Staromestske namesti 6
11000 Prague 1
Czech Republic
Tel: (2) 2897.

Cedok (Travel Bureau Czech Republic and Slovakia)
Na Príkope 18
111 35 Prague 1, Czech Republic
Tel: (2) 212 7111. Fax: (2) 232 1656. Telex: 121109.

Embassy of the Czech Republic and Slovakia
25 Kensington Palace Gardens
London W8 4QY
Tel: (071) 229 1255. Fax: (071) 727 5824. Telex: 28276 OBZALD G. Opening hours: 0900-1700 Monday to Friday.

Consulate of the Czech Republic and Slovakia
30 Kensington Palace Gardens
London W8 4QY
Tel: (071) 727 9431. Fax: (071) 727 5824. Opening hours: 1000-1230 Monday to Friday (except national public holidays – see below).

Czechoslovak Airlines
72-3 Margaret Street
London W1N 7LF
Tel: (071) 255 1366/1898 (reservations). Fax: (071) 323 1633.

Cedok (London) Ltd
(Travel Bureau)
49 Southwark Street
London SE1 1RU
Tel: (071) 378 6009 (general enquiries & independent travellers – 24-hour answering service) *or* 378 1341 (group bookings). Fax: (071) 403 2321. Telex: 21164 CEDOKL G. Opening hours: 0900-1700 Monday to Friday (winter); 0900-1800 Monday to Friday (summer).

British Embassy
Thunovská 14
125 50 Prague 1, Czech Republic
Tel: (2) 533 340 *or* 533 347/8/9 *or* 533 370. Fax: (2) 539 927. Telex: 121011.

Embassy of the Czech Republic and Slovakia
3900 Linnean Avenue, NW
Washington, DC 20008
Tel: (202) 363 6315-8. Fax: (202) 966 8540.

Cedok
Suite 1902, 10 East 40th Street
New York, NY
10016
Tel: (212) 689 9720. Fax: (212) 481 0597. Telex: 62467.

Embassy of the United States of America
Trziste 15
125 98 Prague 1, Czech Republic
Tel: (2) 536 641. Fax: (2) 532 457. Telex: 212196.

Embassy of the Czech Republic and Slovakia
50 Rideau Terrace
Ottawa, Ontario K1M 2A1
Tel: (613) 749 4442 *or* 749 4450. Fax: (613) 749 4989.

Golden Lane, Hradcany Castle, Prague

Cedok Travel Bureau (Cedok Canada)
Suite 201
1212 Pine Street West
Montréal, Québec H3G 1A9
Tel: (514) 849 8983. Fax:(514) 849 4117.

Canadian Embassy
Mickiewiczova 6
125 33 Prague 6, Czech Republic
Tel: (2) 312 0251. Fax: (2) 311 2791. Telex: 121061.

AREA: 78,864 sq km (sq miles).
POPULATION: 10,364,599 (1990 estimate).

Karlstejn

POPULATION DENSITY: 131 per sq km.
CAPITAL: Prague. **Population:** 1,215,076 (1990 estimate).
GEOGRAPHY: The Czech Republic is situated in central Europe, sharing frontiers with Germany, Poland, the Slovak Republic and Austria. Only about one-quarter of the size of the British Isles, the republic is hilly and picturesque, with historic castles, romantic valleys and lakes, as well as excellent facilities to 'take the waters' at one of the famous spas or to ski and hike in the mountains. Among the most beautiful areas are the river valleys of the Vltava and Labe and the Alpine-style mountains. There are two main regions. One is Bohemia, to the west. Besides Prague, the Czech capital, tourists are drawn to the spa towns of Karlovy Vary and Marianske Lazne, and to the beautiful region of gentle hills and woodland known as the Bohemian Forest. The Elbe flows through eastern Bohemia from the Giant Mountains, one of the most popular skiing regions. The second region of Moravia stretches north to south through the central region, offering a variety of wooded highlands, vineyards, folk art and castles. Brno is Moravia's administrative and cultural centre.
LANGUAGE: The official language is Czech (spoken in both Bohemia and Moravia). Slovak, Russian, German and English are also spoken.
RELIGION: Approximately 46% Roman Catholic and 15% Protestant, including Churches such as the Reformed, Lutheran, Methodist, Moravian, Unity of Czech Brethren and Baptist. There is a community of approximately 15,000 Jews, mainly in Prague.
TIME: GMT + 1 (GMT + 2 in summer).
ELECTRICITY: Generally 220 volts AC, 50Hz. Some areas of Prague still use 110 volts. Most major hotels have standard international 2-pin razor plugs. Lamp fittings are normally of the screw type.
COMMUNICATIONS: Telephone: IDD available. Country code: 42. There are public telephone booths, including special kiosks for international calls. Surcharges can be quite high on long-distance calls from hotels. Local calls cost Kcs1. **Telex/telegram:** Facilities are available at all main towns and hotels. **Post:** There is a 24-hour service at the main post office in Prague at Jindrisska Street, Prague 1. *Poste Restante* services are available throughout the country. Post office hours: 0800-1800 Monday to Friday. **Press:** There are English-language newspapers.
BBC World Service and Voice of America frequencies: From time to time these change. See the section *How to Use this Book* for more information.

BBC:				
MHz	15.57	12.09	6.195	3.955
Voice of America:				
MHz	9.670	6.040	5.995	1.197

PASSPORT/VISA

Regulations and requirements may be subject to change at short notice, and you are advised to contact the appropriate diplomatic or consular authority before finalising travel arrangements. Details of these may be found at the head of this country's entry. Any numbers in the chart refer to the footnotes below.

	Passport Required?	Visa Required?	Return Ticket Required?
Full British	Yes	No	No
BVP	Not valid	-	-
Australian	Yes	Yes	No
Canadian	Yes	Yes	Yes
USA	Yes	No	No
Other EC	Yes	No	No
Japanese	Yes	Yes	No

PASSPORTS: Valid passport required by all. Passports must be valid for at least 6 months at the time of application.
British Visitors Passport: Not accepted.
VISAS: Required by all except:
(a) nationals of EC countries;
(b) nationals of other European non-EC countries (with the exception of Albania, Cyprus and Turkey who *do* need visas);
(c) nationals of Cuba;
(d) nationals of the USA.
Types of visa: Tourist, Transit, Double Transit. Costs depend on nationality and cover the range £2-£60. Children aged 15 or under do not have to pay for a visa.
Validity: *Transit:* 48 hours. *Tourist:* 6 months from date of issue for 30-day visit.
Application to: Consulate (or Consular Section at Embassy). For addresses, see top of entry.
Application requirements: (a) 1 application form (2 for double transit). (b) 2 passport-size photos. (c) Passport valid for at least 6 months, with one blank page. (d) Visa fee in the form of cash or postal order.
Working days required: Same day in most cases.
Temporary residence: Special application form required. Enquire at Embassy.

MONEY

Currency: Koruna (Kcs) or Crown = 100 haléru (single: heller). Notes are in denominations of Kcs1000, 500, 100, 50, 20 and 10. Coins are in denominations of Kcs10, 5, 2 and 1, and 50, 20, 10 and 5 haléru.
Currency exchange: Foreign currency (including travellers cheques) can be exchanged at all branches of the State Bank of Czechoslovakia and at exchange offices, Cedok offices, main hotels and road border crossings.
Credit cards: Major cards such as American Express, Diners Club, Visa and Access/Mastercard may be used to exchange currency and are also accepted in better hotels, restaurants and shops. Check with your credit card company for details of merchant acceptability and other services which may be available.
Travellers cheques: These are widely accepted (see listing in *Currency exchange* above).
Exchange rate indicators: The following figures are included as a guide to the movements of the Koruna against Sterling and the US Dollar:

Date:	Oct '89	Oct '90	Oct '91	Oct '92
£1.00=	15.75	58.67	51.81	43.32
$1.00=	9.97	30.03	29.85	27.30

Currency restrictions: The import and export of local currency is not permitted. There is no restriction on foreign currency.
Banking hours: Generally 0800-1700 Monday to Friday.

DUTY FREE

The following goods may be imported into the Czech Republic without incurring customs duty:
250 cigarettes (or corresponding quantity of tobacco products);
1 litre of spirits;
2 litres of wine;
Gifts up to Kcs1000;
Prohibited items: All forms of pornographic literature.

All items of value must be declared at Customs on entry to enable export clearance on departure.

PUBLIC HOLIDAYS

Public holidays observed in the Czech Republic are as follows:

Apr 12 '93 Easter Monday. **May 1** Labour Day. **May 8** National Day, Anniversary of Liberation. **Jul 5** National Day, Day of the Apostles St Cyril and St Methodius. **Jul 6** Day of John Hus Burning. **Oct 28** National Day, Anniversary of Independence. **Dec 24-26** Christmas. **Jan 1 '94** New Year's Day.

HEALTH

Regulations and requirements may be subject to change at short notice, and you are advised to contact your doctor well in advance of your intended date of departure. Any numbers in the chart refer to the footnotes below.

	Special Precautions?	Certificate Required?
Yellow Fever	No	No
Cholera	No	No
Typhoid & Polio	No	-
Malaria	No	-
Food & Drink	1	-

CZECH REPUBLIC	HEALTH REGULATIONS	VISA REGULATIONS
GALILEO/WORLDSPAN	 TI-DFT/PRG/HE	TI-DFT/PRG/VI
SABRE	 TIDFT/PRG/HE	 TIDFT/PRG/VI

Code-Link

To access this information on your CRS, swipe the barcode with a light pen or type in the text under the barcode. For more information, see the introduction *How to Use This Book*.

[1]: Mains water is normally chlorinated, and whilst relatively safe may cause mild abdominal upsets. Bottled water is available and is advised for the first few weeks of the stay. Milk is pasteurised and dairy products are safe for consumption. Local meat, poultry, seafood, fruit and vegetables are generally considered safe to eat.
Health care: No vaccinations are required. There is a Reciprocal Health Agreement with the UK. On the production of a UK passport, hospital and other medical care will be provided free of charge should you fall ill or have an accident while on holiday. Prescribed medicine will be charged for.

TRAVEL - International

AIR: The national airline is *Czechoslovak Airlines (OK)*. There are also some private airlines.
Approximate flight time: From *London* to Prague is 1 hour 45 minutes.
International airports: *Prague (PRG)* (Ruzyne) is 18km (11 miles) from the city (travel time – 30 minutes). Transport to/from city: CSA *Coach* every 40 minutes after flight arrivals 0500-2000 (travel time – 30 minutes); 119 bus approximately every 10 minutes (travel time – 35 minutes); taxis (24-hour service, surcharge at night). Cedok operates frequent shuttle bus services during the summer months to the major hotels in the city. Airport facilities include incoming and outgoing duty-free shops selling food, tobacco products, glass, china, small industrial goods and souvenirs; post office, banking and exchange facilities (24-hour service), a restaurant (1000-2000), a bar (24-hour), car parking and car hire *(Pragocar)*. The Cedok office at the airport is open 0700-1800 Monday to Friday, and 0800-1630 Saturday and Sunday.
RAIL: The most convenient routes to the Czech Republic from Western Europe are via Nuremberg or Vienna. The best train is the Paris–Prague through service, known as the *Zapadni Express* in the Czech Republic. This leaves the French capital at about 2300 and travels overnight via Mainz, Frankfurt and Nuremberg, reaching Prague at 1826. It carries first- and second-class day carriages all the way, couchettes from Paris to Prague, and a dining car from Frankfurt. A daily train via Nuremberg starts from Munich at 1330 and, travelling via Regensburg and Nuremberg, reaches Prague at about 2135. The *Vindobona Express* is a once-daily through train that travels from Vienna to Prague (main station) and on to Berlin. It leaves Vienna at 0930 and reaches Prague at approximately 1515; a dining car is available all the way. There are several other through trains from Prague to Berlin, and also to Moscow, Budapest, Bucharest and other East European destinations.
ROAD: The Czech Republic can be entered via Germany, Poland, the Slovak Republic or Austria. Petrol coupons no longer have be purchased before entering the country and are available at border crossings.

TRAVEL - Internal

AIR: *Czechoslovak Airlines* operates an extensive domestic network that includes flights from Prague to most major cities including Ostrava, Karlovy Vary, Holesov and Brno.
RIVER: Navigable waterways can be found in in the country and the main river ports are located at Prague,

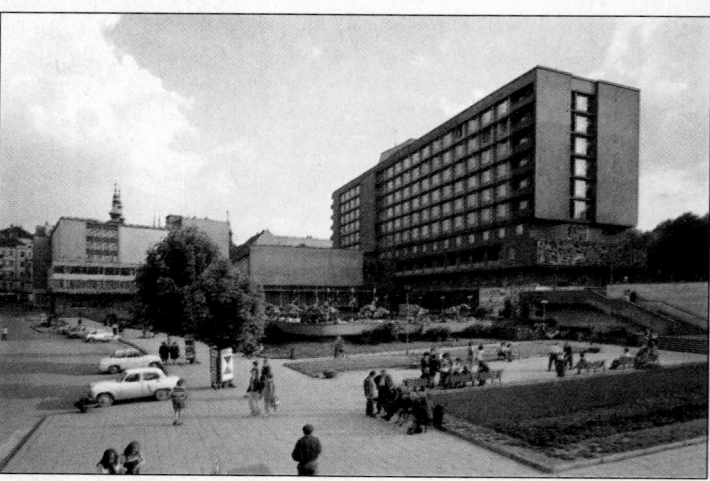

Usti nab Labem and Decin.

RAIL: The rail network is operated by *Czech State Railways*. There are several daily express trains between Prague and main cities and resorts. Reservations should be made in advance on major routes. Fares are low, but supplements are payable for travel by express trains. Details can be obtained from Cedok and other tourist offices.

ROAD: There is a motorway from Prague via Brno to Bratislava. **Bus:** The extensive bus network covers areas not accessible by rail and are efficient and comfortable. **Car hire:** Self-drive cars may be hired through *Pragocar*, *Hertz*, *Avis* etc. Seat belts are compulsory and drinking is absolutely prohibited. Filling stations are quite often closed in the evenings. Another useful address is the Central Automoto Club, Opletalova 29, 11395 Prague 1. Tel: (2) 223 544. **Documentation:** A valid national driving licence is sufficient for car hire.

URBAN: Public transport is excellent. There is a metro service that runs from 0500-2400 and three flat fares are charged. There are also tramway and bus services in Prague (for which tickets must be purchased in advance from tobacconist shops or any shop displaying the sign *Predprodej Jizdenek)*. Buses, trolleybuses and tramways also exist in Brno, Ostrava, Plzen and several other towns. Most services run from 0430-2400. All the cities operate flat-fare systems and pre-purchased passes are available. Tickets should be punched in the appropriate machine on entering the tram or bus. Except on the Prague metro, a separate ticket is required when changing routes. There is a fine for fare evasion. Blue badges on tram and bus stops indicate an all-night service. Taxis are available in all the main towns, and are metered and cheap; higher fares are charged at night.

JOURNEY TIMES: The following chart gives approximate journey times (in hours and minutes) from Prague to other major towns/cities in the Czech Republic.

	Air	Road	Rail
Brno	0.50	2.15	4.45
Karlovy Vary	0.35	3.00	4.45
Ostrava	1.00	6.45	6.00

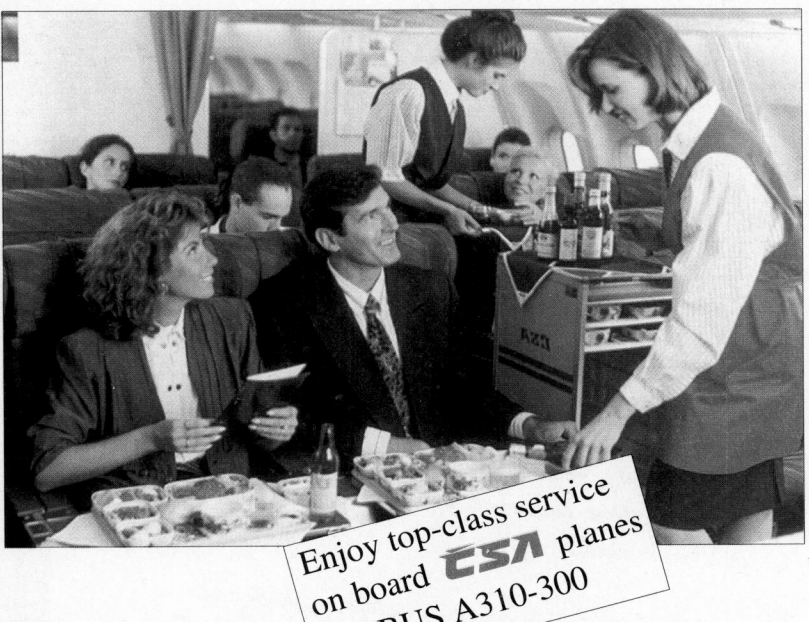

ACCOMMODATION

HOTELS: Prices sometimes compare very favourably with Western hotels, though services and facilities are often more limited. There is an acute shortage of accommodation in the Czech Republic in the peak seasons (May to October, but especially during July and August), and it is wise to pre-book. Accommodation in Prague is difficult to find during the annual *Prague Spring Music Festival* from mid-May to the first week in June. **Grading:** The international 5-star system has recently been introduced for hotel classification, but the old **ABC** system may still be encountered in remote areas. The present system is: **5-star** (formerly **A+** or **Deluxe**), **4-star** (formerly **A**), **3-star** (formerly **B+**), **2-star** (formerly **B**), and **1-star** (formerly **C**). You can expect rooms with private bath or shower in hotels classified 3-star (or B+) and upwards.

MOTELS: Motels are split into two categories. **Grading:** In **B motels** every room is provided with a wash-basin with hot and cold water, and central heating; on every floor there is a separate bathroom and WC for men and women. **A motels** are provided with the following extras: a lift, a bathroom or shower with every room, a radio receiver and in some cases a TV set.

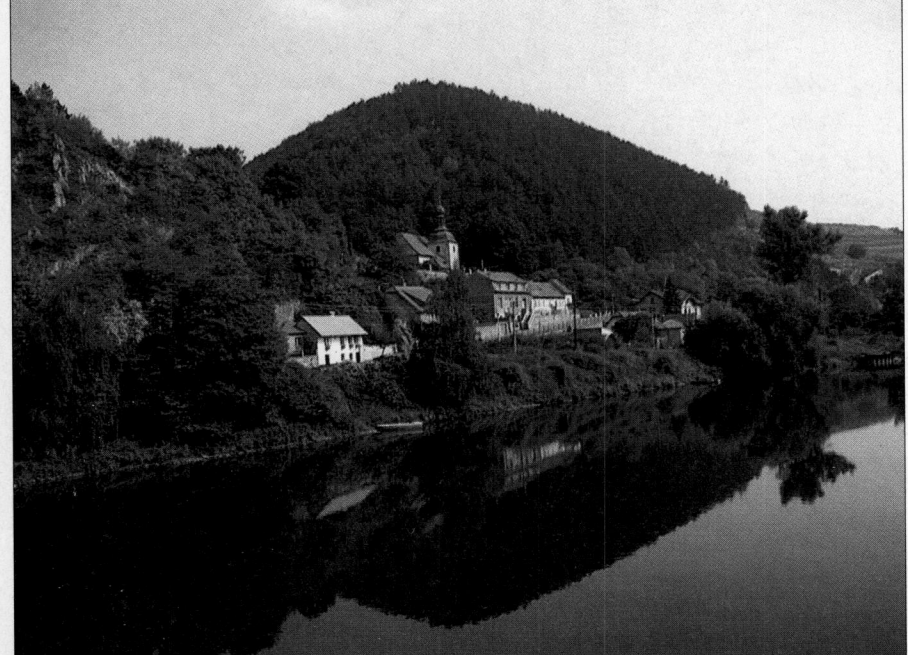

HOTEL PALACE PRAHA
Panská 12, 110 00 Praha 1
Tel: 42 2 219 7111, 236 0008.
Fax: 42 2 235 9373.

November 1992

Dear Judy and Tom,

Frank and I have been having the best time here in Prague, Czechoslovakia! We're staying at the HOTEL PALACE – a 5-star, amazingly luxurious hotel, set in the heart of the business and entertainment district. From the moment we drove up in the Hotel's limousine, we understood why it was chosen as a Preferred Hotel and Resorts Worldwide Hotel! We couldn't ask for better service (around the clock), and it seems like everyone working here is especially dedicated to making our visit a memorable one!

We're staying in the 'Art Nouveau Suite' which is quite spacious and beautifully decorated with original Czech art and the most gorgeous furniture. Oh, I almost forgot – you should see our bathroom – it's ALL MARBLE!

While Frank has been attending meetings in the Palace's state-of-the-art convention facility and entertaining his clients in the Hotel's elegant Club Restaurant, I've been doing a lot of shopping and touristing – which is so convenient from the Hotel – only minutes by foot! Prague is an exciting city – so much to see and do! The concierge department helped us to "get organised", and made all necessary restaurant and theatre reservations upon our arrival – so we never have to worry about being bored!

I'm afraid the PALACE HOTEL has rather spoiled us, and I'm dreading having to go back home, where I have to do everything myself! Oh well, Frank has already promised that we'll come back again for our anniversary in March! I think I'll reserve the Presidential Suite today! Judy maybe you could persuade Tom to bring you here as well?

Love you, miss you and see you soon!

Helen

Car parking facilities are available in both types.
PRIVATE HOUSES: Cedok (London) Ltd can arrange stays in private houses in Prague throughout the year.
SELF-CATERING: Chalet Communities in many parts of the country are available in two categories. **Grading: B chalets** offer drinking water, a WC, the possibility of obtaining meals, and heating in winter. **A chalets** have the following extras: electric lighting in the chalets, a flushing WC, a washroom with running water, washing and ironing facilities, and a sports ground. For further information, contact Cedok (London) Ltd.
CAMPING/CARAVANNING: Campsites have all the regular facilities such as showers, cooking amenities, shops and, in some cases, caravans for hire. A map, marking and listing sites throughout the country, is obtainable through Cedok. **Car camps:** In the **B** category these have a car park, fenced-in campsite, day and night service, a washroom, WC, drinking water and a roofed structure with cookers and washing-up equipment. Car camps in the **A** category are provided with the following extras: sale of refreshments, showers with hot and cold water, flushing WC, washing and ironing facilities, a reception office, a social room, sale of toilet requisites and souvenirs.
YOUTH HOSTELS: Booking through CKM, Jindrisska 28, Prague 2. Tel: (2) 268 507.

RESORTS & EXCURSIONS

Travellers should always make advance hotel bookings when intending to visit the Czech Republic, either through their travel agent or through Cedok (London) Ltd. Visitors may travel alone. Usually they take a package holiday; Cedok offers a large selection.
Prague: Picturesquely sited on the banks of the *Moldau River*, Prague has played an important part in the history of Europe. It is noted for some magnificent Baroque and Romanesque architecture and a cultural scene of elegance. There is the annual *Spring Music Festival*, the excellent Czech Philharmonic Orchestra and the *National Theatre*. The centre is the *Hradcany* complex of the *Castle*, the *St Vitus Cathedral* and all the Palace rooms including the *Vladislav Hall*, once used by Bohemian Kings for jousting. The views over the Moldau (or Vltava), spanned by the medieval *Charles Bridge*, contribute to making Prague one of the loveliest cities in Europe – perhaps less stately than Vienna but with the same grace and enhanced by a sense of intimacy. Worth visiting are the *St Nicholas Cupola*, the Town Hall of the Old City, where you can also see the *Gothic Tyn Church*, and the beautiful 15th-century clock in the *Old Town Square*. The *Little Town* is a quarter of winding narrow streets of small artisan houses and palaces from the 17th and 18th centuries.
Quite near Prague is a grim reminder of the horrors of the Second World War – the site of the concentration camp at **Terezin**, where there is a museum. Also in the area are the castles of *Karlstejn*, *Krivoklat* and *Konopiste*, the historic town of **Kutna Hora** and the dominating cathedral of *St Barbara*.
Brno dates from the 13th century and has a fine museum and the Gothic *Spilberk* castle. There is also an international music festival from September to October.

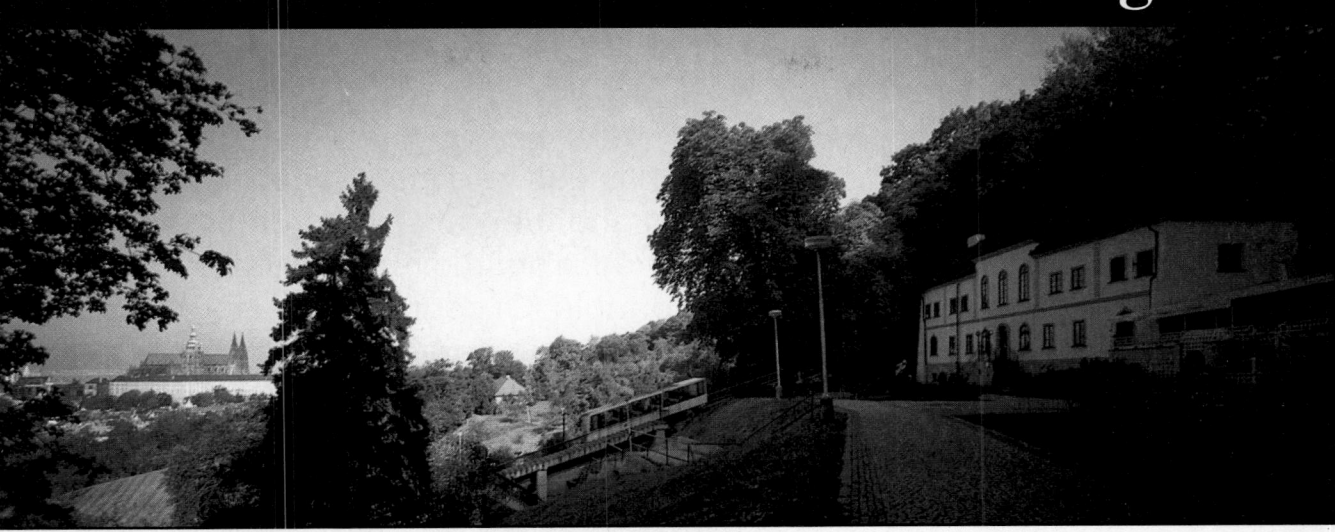

Bohemia: Southern Bohemia, with its lakes and woods, has for a long time been a favourite holiday place for families, since it has many recreation facilities and points of historic interest, such as the medieval town of **Cesky Krumlov** and *Hluboka Castle*, one of the many atmospheric Gothic castles in Bohemia, perched on wooded hillsides and adorned with the round towers and pointed caps so loved by producers of Hammer horror films. With imagination, the visitor can easily picture the lives led by the nobles who once lived here and hunted in the woods. Less well-known but equally characteristic are Bohemia's churches, whose steeples are often capped by onion-shaped cupolas, lending them an Oriental appearance. The country is also famed for its caves: the rock formation of the mountain ranges form underground rivers and chambers decorated above and below with stalactites and stalagmites.
The health resorts or spas of Bohemia remain one of the primary attractions, as they have been for centuries. Beethoven, Edward VII and Goethe all admired the resort of **Marianske Lazne**, formerly **Marienbad**, whilst the town of **Karlovy Vary (Karlsbad)** has attracted the crowned heads of Europe for many years to bathe in the sulphurous waters; there is a bi-annual International Film Festival at Karlovy Vary.
Winter sports: The mountains, forests and lakes are enchanting and ideal for outdoor holidaying as well as winter sports. There are popular winter sports centres in 30 mountain regions, of which the *Giant Mountains* are the best. There are also numerous lakes and rivers amidst the glacial landscape, offering excellent fishing, canoeing, boating and freshwater swimming. The primary watersports areas are in Bohemia.
National Parks: The *Giant Mountains* of northeast Bohemia and the *Eagle Mountains* towards the Polish border are protected as National Parks and thus have an untouched quality rare in Europe.

SOCIAL PROFILE

FOOD & DRINK: Food is often based on Austro-Hungarian dishes; *wiener schnitzel* and sauerkraut, dumplings and pork are very popular. Specialities include *bramborak*, a delicacy of a potato pancake filled with garlic and herbs; and Prague ham. Meat dishes are usually

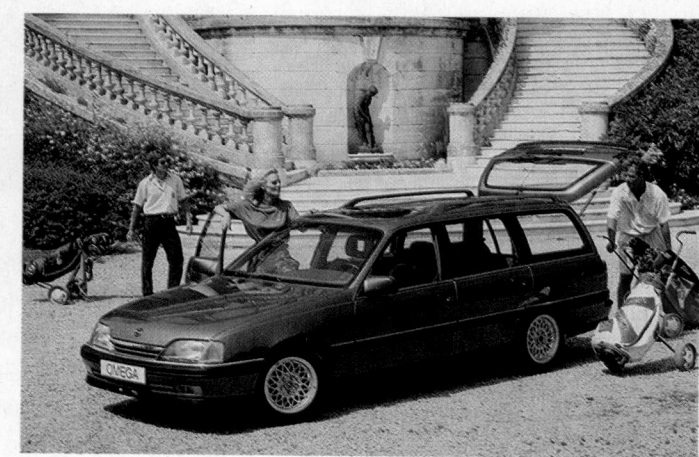

served with large dough called *knedliky*, a type of dumpling, and *zeli* (spiced cabbage). Western-style fresh vegetables are sometimes missing. There is a wide selection of restaurants, beer taverns and wine cellars with counter service, but table service is often available.
Drink: Popular beverages include fresh fruit juices, liqueurs and beers. A particular speciality is *slivovice* (a plum brandy) and *merunkovice* (an apricot brandy). Pilsner beers, *borovicka* (strong gin), *becherovka* (herb brandy) and sparkling wine from the Moravia region are also famous. There are no rigid licensing hours.
NIGHTLIFE: Theatre and opera are of a high standard all over Eastern Europe. Much of the nightlife takes place in hotels, although nightclubs are to be found in major cities.
SHOPPING: Souvenirs include Bohemian glass and crystal, pottery, porcelain, wooden folk carvings, hand-embroidered clothing, and food items. There are a number of excellent shops specialising in glass and crystal, while various associations of regional artists and craftsmen run their own retail outlets (pay in local currency). Other special purchases include pottery (particularly from Kolovce and Straznice); china ornaments and geyserstone carvings from Karlovy Vary; delicate lace and needle embroidery from many Moravian towns; and blood-red garnets and semi-precious stones from Bohemia. **Shopping hours:** 0900-1200 and 1400-1800 Monday to Friday, 0900-1200 Saturday (many shops close all day). In the centre of Prague some shops will stay open through lunch and until late in the evening.
SPORT: Football, volleyball, tennis and **ice hockey** are popular. There is a very good network of marked trails in all mountain areas, and it is possible to plan a **walking** tour in advance.
Winter sports tours can be arranged by Cedok; check for details. The many and varied rivers and lakes provide excellent opportunities for **watersports – canoeing, sailing, water-skiing, fishing,** etc (see *Resorts & Excursions* above).
SPECIAL EVENTS: Most towns have their own folk festivals, with dancing, local costumes and food. These tend to be in the summer months leading up to the harvest festivals in September. The most important festival in 1993/1994 is the *Prague Spring Music Festival* in May. There are also folk festivals at Straznice, Vlcnov, Hluk, Roznov and Domazlice. For further details of special events, contact Cedok, who can also arrange music festival tours.
SOCIAL CONVENTIONS: Dress should be casual, but conservative, except at formal dinners and at quality hotels or restaurants. **Photography:** Areas where there are military installations should not be photographed. **Tipping:** A 5-10% tip will be discreetly accepted; some alteration in customs is to be expected in the wake of political and social changes.

BUSINESS PROFILE

ECONOMY: Of all the Soviet bloc economies, the then Czechoslovakia experienced the highest degree of state control, without even the small-scale private enterprise that existed to some extent in all Eastern European economies. Under central planning, and particularly in the aftermath of the 'Prague Spring', economic development concentrated on heavy industry at the expense of traditional strengths in light and craft-based industries, such as textiles, clothing, glass and ceramics (though these remain significant). These inefficient and, in some cases, redundant industrial monoliths are now a considerable millstone around the economy, particularly in the Slovak Republic. The other problem is a dearth of natural resources – the country has hitherto relied heavily on the Soviet Union for most of their raw materials, particularly oil, supplies of which have been cut to one-third and payment required in hard currency. The oil shortage reached crisis proportions at the end of 1990 and was resolved satisfactorily only after urgent personal discussions between Presidents Havel and Gorbachev. The following year, the Czech government embarked on an ambitious programme of privatisation as the cornerstone of its declared policy of introducing a market economy. This has happened at breakneck speed despite the misgivings of observers from across the political spectrum who have raised questions about the lack of financial infrastructure, possible consequences of extensive foreign ownership, and the use of an untried 'voucher' scheme which gives equity stakes in industrial enterprises to any individuals who apply. The autumn of 1991 saw 1700 enterprises denationalised in the space of just two weeks. This was the first part of a two-phase plan which saw most of Czechoslovak industry and agriculture in private hands by the middle of 1992. However, since the division of the country agreed in June 1992, this is now likely to go ahead only in the Czech Republic. The voucher scheme was not initially popular, but steadily gained credence: 8.5 million people took part in the 1992 privatisation. There has also been extensive fiscal and budgetary reform, with the aim of creating a fully-fledged capitalist financial system with strong safeguards against inflation. Limited currency convertibility has also been introduced as a necessary step towards promoting foreign investment. This is being keenly sought, with joint ventures the favoured method of entering the market. Priority areas are the aircraft and automobile industries, electronics, nuclear energy, textiles, leather and glass, gasification of coal and transport and communications. Agriculture is particularly important as an export sector (beer and timber are much in demand). For the time being, the majority of trade is focused at present is on developing links with Western Europe. The then Czech and Slovak Republic negotiated

WELCOME TO PRAGUE

Pražská
informační
služba
TOURIST SERVICE:
■ INFORMATION
■ GUIDES
■ CITY TOURS
■ TICKETS
■ SPECIAL PROGRAMMES
■ ACCOMMODATION
■ MONEY EXCHANGE
OFFICES
Staroměstské nám. 22
tel.: 22 44 52-3
Na příkopě 20
tel.: 26 40 18-20
Panská 4
tel.: 22 43 11
Main station
PRAGUE INFORMATION SERVICE-
UST OPPOSITE THE OLD TOWN HORLOGE

PRAGUE EXHIBITION GROUNDS

CONTACT WITH COMMERCE – COMMERCÉ WITH CONTACTS

PRAGUE EXHIBITION GROUNDS,
Commercial department,
170 05 Prague 7, Bohemia
Phone: /0042/ (02) 87 29 111;
com. dept.: (02) 37 13 53,
(02) 37 10 43;
management secretariat:
(02) 37 70 98, fax: (02) 37 87 43

EXHIBITION AND FAIRS IN THE MIDDLE OF EUROPE

N.	14. 1. - 17. 1.	**HOBBY 93**
	29.1 - 3.2.	**WOORDWORKING MACHINES** Exhibition of instruments and machines for widespread use in industry and household
B.	5.2 - 6.2.	**HOTEL AND FUN** International specialized fair for equipment for hotels, restaurants and discos
	11.2. - 14.2.	**HOLIDAY WORLD** Fair of travel tourism
	21.2. - 24.2.	**MAN AND NOURISHMENT** International fair of wholesome foodstuffs
AR.	4.3. - 8.3.	**THE WORLD OF CHILDREN** Fair of children's goods and entertainments
	17.3. - 23.3.	**INTERCAMERA** International specialized fair for audiovisual equipment
	14.3. - 25.3.	**PUBLICITY, ADVERTISING** Exhibition of advertisement and propaganda means, massmedia and advertisement
PR.	3.4. - 7.4.	**GARDENING** Contractual and sale exhibition for gardening technology
	4.4 - 9.4.	**RENOVA** Exhibition of construction technologies and restoration of historical sites
	20.4. - 23.4.	**PRAGOMEDICA** International exhibition of medical equipment for diagnoses and therapy
	20.4. - 23.4.	**PRAGOREGULA** International exhibition of measuring, regulation and control equipment
	20.4. - 23.4.	**PRAGOFARMA** International exhibition of farmaceutical products
AY	2.5. - 6.5.	**PRAGOALARM** Exhibition of safety systems and equipment
	2.5. - 6.5.	**FASHION AND COSMETICS** Contractual exhibition
	5.5. - 8.5.	**COM NET** Exhibition of communication and information equipment
MAY	16.5. - 21.5.	**FURNITURES** Exhibition of furnishings for household, restaurants and enterprises
	25.5 - 29.5.	**GRAPHIC SIGNS** Exhibition of sketch designs
	25.5. - 9.6.	**KUK** Exhibition of furnishings and technologies for kitchens and winecellars
JUN.	3.6. - 7.6.	**JAPANEX** Exhibition of Japanese industrial firms
	17.6. - 27.6.	**MOTOR SHOW** International Exhibition of cars and accessories
JUL.	5.7. - 13.7.	**INTERNATIONAL ARTS FAIR**
SEP.	6.9. - 11.9.	**IFABO** International exhibition of office and communication equipment
	7.9. - 12.9.	**RECYCLING** Machines and installations for secondary usage of waste
	20.9. - 25.9.	**THE WORLD OF BEVERAGES** Contractual exhibition for drinks
OCT.	5.10. - 11.10.	**CONSUMER GOODS** International fair of consumer goods
	25.10. - 30.10.	**CHEMICAL INDUSTRY** Exhibition of chemical products and technologies
NOV.	9.11. - 12.11.	**PRAGOSEC** Exhibition of rescue and relieve equipment
	10.11. - 15.11.	**TRANSPAK** Exhibition of packing machines and technologies
	23.11. - 30.11.	**MOTAS** Exhibition of connecting materials
	27.11. - 31.11.	**GASTROPRAG** International exhibition of gastronomy
	29.11. - 4.12.	**BOHEMIA GLASS** Contractual exhibition for glass products
DEC.	9.12. - 24.12	**CHRISTMAS MARKETS** Sale of consumer goods, toys, sport accessories

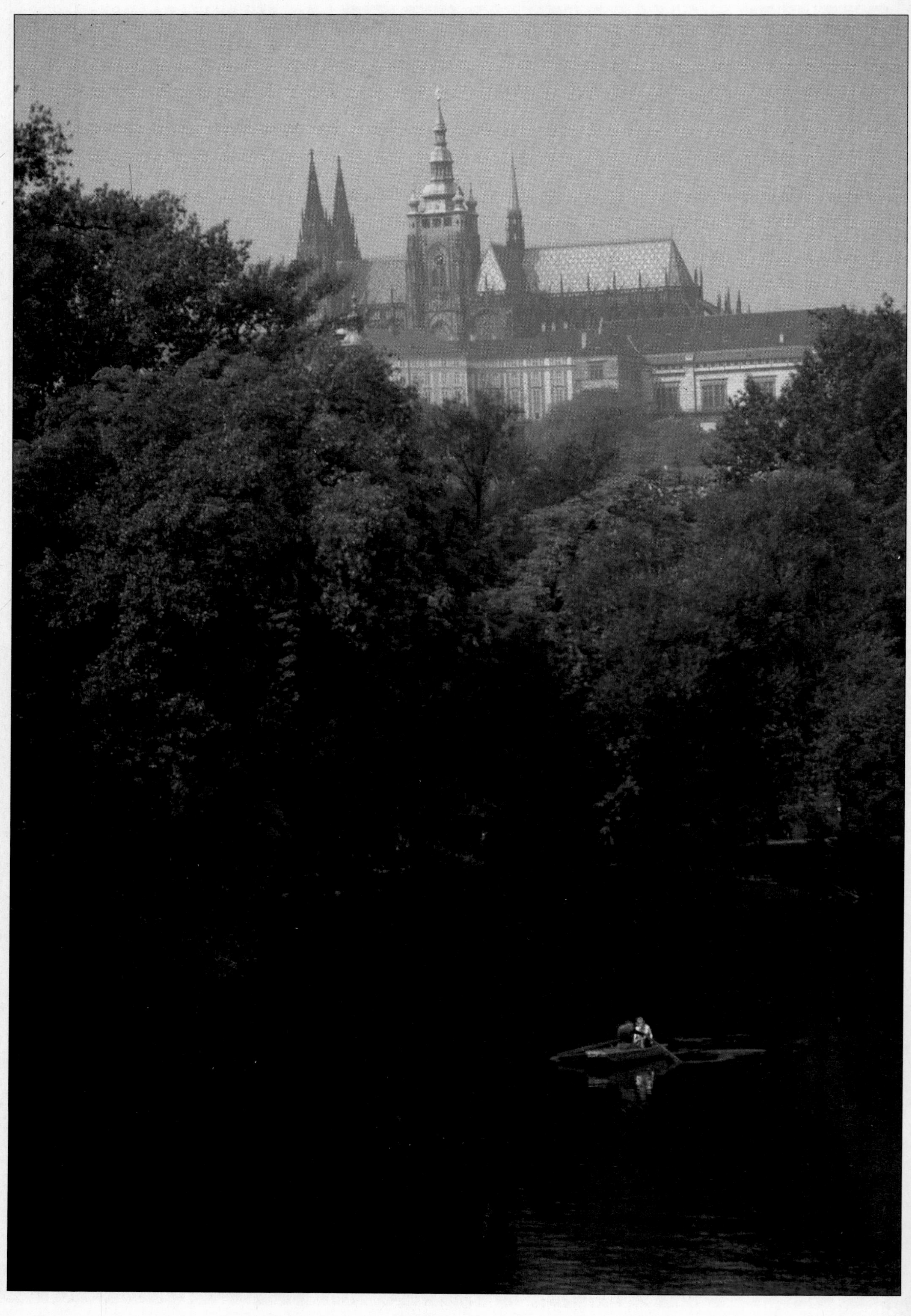

associate membership with the European Community. However, this has been rendered void by the Czech-Slovak split. Future trade patterns are likely to see the Czech Republic improve its links with Austria and Germany.

BUSINESS: Businessmen wear suits. A knowledge of German is useful as English is not widely spoken among the older generations. Long business lunches are usual. Avoid visits during July and August as many businesses close for holidays. **Office hours:** 0800-1600 Monday to Friday.

COMMERCIAL INFORMATION: The following organisation can offer advice: Obchodní a prumyslová komora (Chamber of Commerce and Industry), Argentinská 38, 170 05 Prague 7, Czech Republic. Tel: (2) 872 4111. Fax: (2) 879 134. Telex: 8736.

CONFERENCES/CONVENTIONS: The Prague International Congress Centre can seat up to 2839 persons. There are also facilities in many hotels throughout the country. Trade fairs are held in Brno in May (consumer products) and September (engineering industries). Information can be obtained from BVV, Vystaviste 1, PO Box 491, Brno. Tel: 314 1111. Fax: 333 998.

HISTORY & GOVERNMENT

HISTORY: Czechoslovakia's independence was established in 1918. Before that, Moravia and Bohemia were under Austrian rule and Slovakia came under the aegis of Hungary. During the Second World War the whole country, except for Slovakia, became a German protectorate. After the war, a reconstituted Czechoslovakia was established and Communist successes both in elections and in political life led, in 1948, to the country becoming a People's Republic and adopting a Soviet-style system. This resulted in closer ties being forged with the Soviet Union. Apart from a brief period known as the 'Prague Spring' in 1968, during which a reform-minded government under Alexander Dubcek attempted to introduce a more pluralistic political and economic structure, links between the two countries remained strong. Reactions to the new spirit of *glasnost* were cautious at first, as evinced by a wave of arrests of dissidents in 1988 and 1989. The then Czechoslovakia initially aligned itself with the German Democratic Republic in opposition to political and economic reform. However, during November 1989 large demonstrations took place in all of the country's major cities, culminating in the resignation of the Communist Party leader, Milos Jakes, along with many members of the ruling Politburo. Prime Minister Ladislav Adamec led discussions in the same month with representatives from the main opposition group, Civic Forum, including the playwright Václav Havel. Here, Adamec conceded that the 'leading role' of the Communist Party should end and with it the Party's domination of the Government. These proposals were subsequently endorsed by the National Parliament. Civic Forum's influence over new appointments led to the appointment of Václav Havel as President while the country set about introducing a pluralistic political system and market economy. The country was also set free to pursue its own foreign and defence policies. Multi-party elections for a new national assembly in June 1990 were won by Civic Forum (and its Slovakian ally, Public Against Violence) under the leadership of Marián Calfa. Divisions within the victorious party quickly emerged. The decisive split occurred in January 1991 when the right-wing federal Finance Minister Václav Klaus, the architect and chief engineer of the privatisation programme, left the Forum with his supporters to create the Civic Democratic Party (ODS). With Marián Calfa largely discredited by his previous associations with the Communists, Klaus emerged as the most powerful figure within the federal government. Meanwhile, there was a growing clamour in Slovakia, the eastern part of the country, for greater autonomy and, among a vocal and growing constituency, full independence. Despite the firm opposition of President Havel, who considered that the country can ill afford such diversions at this critical stage in its development, negotiations opened between representatives of the two republican governments in November 1991. The talks broke down within weeks and both sides retired to await the June 1992 national election which promised to be, in effect, a referendum on the future structure of the country. Following the vote, which saw strong support for Slovak separatists, a complete split into two independent countries was quickly accepted as the only viable solution. The date of the formal division was fixed as January 1, 1993.

GOVERNMENT: The country was a federal state of two republics. These will be two distinct nations, provisionally as of January 1, 1993. New constitutions are being drafted for both countries.

CLIMATE

Cold winters, mild summers.

Required clothing: Mediumweights, heavy topcoat and overshoes for winter; lightweights for summer. In all seasons a raincoat may be needed.

PRAGUE Czechoslovakia (197m)

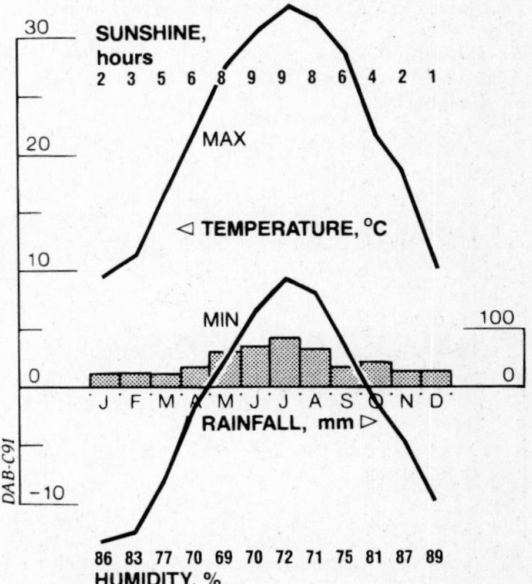

DENMARK

☐international airport

Location: Western Europe.

Danmarks Turistråd (Tourist Office)
Vesterbrogade 6D
DK-1620 Copenhagen V
Denmark
Tel: 33 11 14 15. Fax: 33 93 14 16.

Tourist Office Information Department
Bernstorffsgade 1
DK-1577 Copenhagen V
Denmark
Tel: 33 11 13 25. Fax: 33 93 49 69.

Royal Danish Embassy
55 Sloane Street
London SW1X 9SR
Tel: (071) 333 0200 *or* 333 0265 (visa enquiries, 0900-1000 and 1500-1600 only). Fax: (071) 333 0270 *or* 333 0243 (trade only). Telex: 28103 AMBDKG. Opening hours: 1000-1300 Monday to Friday (telephone enquiries until 1600).

Danish Tourist Board
Sceptre House
169-173 Regent Street
London W1R 8PY
Tel: (071) 734 2637 *or* 287 9585 (trade only). Fax: (071) 494 2170. Opening hours: 1100-1600 Monday to Friday.

British Embassy
Kastelsvej 36-40
DK-2100 Copenhagen Ø
Denmark
Tel: 31 26 46 00. Fax: 31 38 10 12. Telex: 27106.
Consulates in: Aabenraa, Ålborg, Århus, Esbjerg, Fredericia, Odense, Rønne (Bornholm) and Tórshavn (Faroe Islands).

Royal Danish Embassy
3200 Whitehaven Street, NW
Washington, DC
20008-3683
Tel: (202) 234 4300. Fax: (202) 328 1470. Telex: 440081.

Royal Danish Consulate General
825 Third Avenue
New York, NY
10022-7519
Tel: (212) 223 4545.

Danish Tourist Board
18th Floor, 655 Third Avenue
New York, NY
10017
Tel: (212) 949 2333. Fax: (212) 983 5260. Telex: 620681.

Embassy of the United States of America
Dag Hammarskjølds Allé 24
DK-2100 Copenhagen Ø
Denmark
Tel: 31 42 31 44. Fax: 35 43 02 23. Telex: 22216.

Danish Tourist Board
PO Box 115
Postal Station N
Toronto, Ontario
M8V 3S4
Tel: (416) 823 9620. Fax: (416) 823 8860.

Royal Danish Embassy
Suite 702
85 Range Road
Ottawa, Ontario
K1N 8J6
Tel: (613) 234 0704 *or* 234 0116 *or* 234 0204 *or* 234 4619. Fax: (613) 234 7368. Telex: 0533114.
Consulates in: Calgary, Edmonton, Halifax, Montréal, Regina, Saint John, St John's, Toronto, Vancouver and Winnipeg.

Canadian Embassy
Kr. Bernikowsgade 1
DK-1105 Copenhagen K
Denmark
Tel: 33 12 22 99. Fax: 33 14 05 85. Telex: 27036.

AREA: 43,093 sq km (16,638 sq miles).
POPULATION: 5,146,469 (1991 estimate).
POPULATION DENSITY: 119.4 per sq km.
CAPITAL: Copenhagen. **Population:** 464,773 (1991).
GEOGRAPHY: Denmark is the smallest Scandinavian country, consisting of the Jutland peninsula, north of Germany, and over 500 islands of various sizes, some inhabited and linked to the mainland by ferry or bridge. The landscape consists mainly of low-lying, fertile countryside broken by beech woods, small lakes and fjords. Greenland and the Faroe Islands are also under the sovereignty of the Kingdom of Denmark, although both have home rule. The Faroe Islands are a group of 18 islands in the north Atlantic inhabited by a population of 47,449 whose history dates back to the Viking period. Fishing and sheep farming are the two most important occupations. Tórshavn (population 16,189), the capital of the Faroes, is served by direct flights from Copenhagen.
Further information on Greenland may be found by consulting its individual entry later in the *World Travel Guide*.
LANGUAGE: The official language is Danish. Many Danes also speak English, German and French.
RELIGION: Predominantly Evangelical Lutheran with a small Roman Catholic minority.
TIME: GMT + 1 (GMT + 2 in summer).
ELECTRICITY: 220 volts AC, 50Hz. Continental 2-pin plugs are standard. On many campsites, 110-volt power plugs are also available.
COMMUNICATIONS: Telephone: Full IDD is available. Country code: 45. **Fax:** This service is available from many main post offices and from major hotels. **Telex/telegram:** Public telex booth open 24 hours a day at Copenhagen Central Telegraph Office. Telegrams can also be sent by phone; dial 122. **Post:** All telephone and postal rates are printed at the post offices. All post offices offer *Poste Restante* facilities. Post offices are open from 0900-1730 Monday to Friday, and several are open on Saturday from 0900-1200. **Press:** Newspapers are largely regional, the main papers in the capital including *Berlingske Tidende*, *Ekstrabladet*, *Politiken* and *Aktuelt*. There are English-language newspapers available.
BBC World Service and Voice of America frequencies: From time to time these change. See the section *How to Use this Book* for more information.

BBC:

MHz	15.57	12.09	9.410	6.195

A service is also available on 648kHz/463m and 198kHz/1515m (0100-0500 GMT).

Voice of America:

MHz	11.97	9.670	6.040	5.995

PASSPORT/VISA

Regulations and requirements may be subject to change at short notice, and you are advised to contact the appropriate diplomatic or consular authority before finalising travel arrangements. Details of these may be found at the head of this country's entry. Any numbers in the chart refer to the footnotes below.

	Passport Required?	Visa Required?	Return Ticket Required?
Full British	1	2	No
BVP	Valid	No	No
Australian	Yes	No	Yes
Canadian	Yes	No	Yes
USA	Yes	No	Yes
Other EC	1	No	No
Japanese	Yes	No	Yes

PASSPORTS: Valid passport required by all except:
(a) **[1]** nationals of Belgium, France, Germany, Italy, Luxembourg and The Netherlands in possession of a National Identity card, and nationals of the United Kingdom in possession of a BVP (other EC nationals *do* require a passport);
(b) nationals of Austria, Liechtenstein and Switzerland in possession of a National Identity card;
(c) nationals of Finland, Iceland, Norway and Sweden in possession of identification papers if travelling entirely within Scandinavia.
British Visitors Passport: Valid for nationals of the UK who are citizens of the UK or colonies. BVPs can be used for holidays or unpaid business trips to Denmark for up to 3 months. Visits to Denmark, Finland, Iceland, Norway and Sweden as a group must add up to less than 3 months in any 6-month period.
VISAS: Required by all except:
(a) **[2]** nationals of the UK with the exception of holders of passports described as 'British Protected Person' or with endorsement 'holder is subject to control under the Immigration Act 1971' or 'the Commonwealth Immigration Act' (holders of these types of British passport *will* need visas). Note that nationals whose country of origin is Bangladesh, Ghana, India, Nigeria, Pakistan, or Sri Lanka will need an 'exempt' stamp from UK immigration authorities, in addition to an 'indefinite stay' stamp.
(b) nationals of other countries referred to in the chart above;
(c) nationals of Andorra, Argentina, Australia, Austria, Bahamas, Barbados, Belize, Benin, Bolivia, Bosnia-Hercegovina, Botswana, Brazil, Brunei, Chile, Colombia, Costa Rica, Côte d'Ivoire, Croatia, Cyprus, Czechoslovakia, Dominica, Dominican Republic, Ecuador, El Salvador, Fiji, Finland, Gambia, Grenada, Guatemala, Guyana, Haiti, Honduras, Hungary, Iceland, Israel, Jamaica, Kenya, Kiribati, South Korea, Lesotho, Liechtenstein, Lithuania, Malawi, Malaysia, Malta, Mauritius, Mexico, Monaco, Namibia, New Zealand, Nicaragua, Niger, Norway, Panama, Paraguay, Peru, Poland, St Lucia, St Vincent & the Grenadines, San Marino, Seychelles, Sierra Leone, Singapore, Slovenia, Solomon Islands, Suriname, Swaziland, Sweden, Switzerland, Tanzania, Thailand, Togo, Trinidad & Tobago, Tuvalu, Uganda, Uruguay, Vatican City,

DENMARK | **HEALTH REGULATIONS** | **VISA REGULATIONS** | Code-Link

GALILEO/WORLDSPAN

TI-DFT/CPH/HE

TI-DFT/CPH/VI

SABRE

TIDFT/CPH/HE

TIDFT/CPH/VI

To access this information on your CRS, swipe the barcode with a light pen or type in the text under the barcode. For more information, see the introduction *How to Use This Book*.

Venezuela, Zambia and Zimbabwe.
Types of visa: Tourist, Business and Transit. Cost: £14 for Tourist; £9 for Transit, but some free reciprocal arrangements exist. Transit visas are not required by those continuing their journey to a third country on the same day without leaving the airport.
Validity: Variable. Tourist and Business visas normally valid for up to 3 months from date of arrival.
Application to: Consulate (or Consular Section at Embassy). For addresses, see top of entry.
Application requirements: (a) Valid passport. (b) 2 application forms. (c) 2 photographs.
Personal applications should be made to the visa office 0930-1300 Monday to Friday. Postal applicants should enclose a stamped, self-addressed and registered envelope and payment by crossed postal order. Telephone enquiries should be made before 1600. There are special facilities for business travellers, who should phone for details.
Working days required: 6-8 weeks.
Temporary residence: Persons wishing to stay in Denmark for more than 3 months should make their application *in their home country* well in advance of their intended date of departure.

MONEY

Currency: Danish Krone (DKr) = 100 øre. Notes are in denominations of DKr1000, 500, 100 and 50. Coins are in denominations of DKr20, 10, 5 and 1, and 50 and 25 øre.
Currency exchange: Eurocheques are cashed by banks and hotels; they may also be used at most restaurants and shops. Personal cheques cannot be used by foreigners in Denmark. Some banks may refuse to exchange large foreign bank notes.
Credit cards: Access/Mastercard, American Express, Diners Club and Visa are accepted. Check with your credit card company for details of merchant acceptability and other services which may be available.
Travellers cheques: Can be cashed by banks and hotels, and can be used at most restaurants and shops.
Exchange rate indicators: The following figures are included as a guide to the movements of the Danish Krone against Sterling and the US Dollar:

Date:	Oct '89	Oct '90	Oct '91	Oct '92
£1.00=	11.61	11.36	11.24	9.36
$1.00=	7.35	5.81	6.47	5.89

Currency restrictions: No limitations on the import of either local or foreign currencies, although declarations should be made for large amounts. The export of local currency is limited to the amount declared on import, plus any amount acquired by the conversion of foreign currency. There is no limit on the export of foreign currency.
Banking hours: 0930-1600 Monday, Tuesday, Wednesday and Friday; and 0930-1800 Thursday. Several exchange bureaux are open until midnight.

DUTY FREE

The following goods may be imported into Denmark without incurring customs duty by:
(a) Non-Danish residents arriving from an EC country:
1.5 litres of spirits or 3 litres of sparkling wine (under 22%);
5 litres of table wine;
12 litres of beer (if declared also up to DKr4700 for other articles);
300 cigarettes or 150 cigarillos or 75 cigars or 400g of tobacco;
1kg of coffee or 400g of coffee-extracts;
200g of tea or 80g tea-extracts;
75g of perfume;
375ml of toilet water;
Other articles: DKr4700 (single articles up to DKr2725).
(b) Residents of non-EC countries entering from outside the EC (excluding Greenland):
1 litre of spirits or 2 litres of sparkling wine (maximum 22%);
2 litres of table wine;
10 litres of beer;
200 cigarettes or 100 cigarillos or 50 cigars or 250g of tobacco;
500g of coffee or 200g of coffee-extracts;
100g of tea or 40g of tea-extracts;
50g of perfume;
250ml of toilet water;
Other articles: DKr350.
(c) Passengers entering from an EC country with duty-paid goods (as of January 1993):
800 cigarettes and 400 cigarillos and 200 cigars and 1kg of tobacco;
90 litres of wine;
10 litres of spirits;
20 litres of intermediate products (such as fortified wine);
110 litres of beer.
Note: Alcohol and tobacco allowances are for those aged 17 or over only. It is forbidden to import meat or meat products into Denmark.

PUBLIC HOLIDAYS

Public holidays observed in Denmark are as follows:
Apr 8 '93 Maundy Thursday. **Apr 9** Good Friday. **Apr 12** Easter Monday. **May 7** General Prayer Day. **May 20** Ascension Day. **May 31** Whit Monday. **Jun 5** Constitution Day (half-day). **Dec 25** Christmas Day. **Dec 26** Boxing Day. **Jan 1 '94** New Years Day. **Mar 31** Maundy Thursday.

HEALTH

Regulations and requirements may be subject to change at short notice, and you are advised to contact your doctor well in advance of your intended date of departure. Any numbers in the chart refer to the footnotes below.

	Special Precautions?	Certificate Required?
Yellow Fever	No	No
Cholera	No	No
Typhoid & Polio	No	-
Malaria	No	-
Food & Drink	No	-

Diabetic diets are catered for at many restaurants. See *Food & Drink* in the *Social Profile* section.
Health care: Medical facilities in Denmark are excellent. The telephone number for emergencies is 112. Doctors on call in Copenhagen can be reached by dialling 32 84 00 41, 24 hours a day. Doctors' fees for a night call are always paid in cash. Local tourist offices will tell you where to contact a dentist, and Copenhagen has an emergency dental service outside office hours; again, fees are paid in cash.
Medicine can only be bought at a chemist ('Apotek'), open 24 hours in large towns. Only medicine prescribed by Danish or other Scandinavian doctors can be dispensed. Many medicines that can be bought over the counter in the UK can only be obtained with prescriptions in Denmark.
There is a Reciprocal Health Agreement with the UK. In addition to the free emergency treatment at hospitals and casualty departments, this allows UK citizens on presentation of a UK passport (form E111 is not strictly necessary) free hospital treatment if referred by a doctor, and free medical treatment given by a doctor registered with the Danish Public Health Service. It may occasionally be necessary to pay at the time of treatment; if this is so, receipts should be kept to facilitate refunds (see below). The Agreement does not cover the full costs of dental treatment or prescribed medicines, but a partial refund may be allowed, so again – keep receipts. Discounts are sometimes allowed on prescribed medicines at the time of purchase on presentation of a UK passport. The Agreement does not apply in the Faroe Islands. To obtain refunds, UK citizens should apply (with receipts) to the Kommunens Social-og Sundhedsforvaltning before leaving Denmark.

TRAVEL - International

AIR: The national airlines are *SAS (SK)* and *Maersk Air (DM)*. The major carriers are *SAS* and *British Airways*.
Approximate flight times: From *London* to Copenhagen is 1 hour 50 minutes and to Århus is 1 hour 40 minutes. From *Los Angeles* to Copenhagen is 11 hours 15 minutes. From *New York* to Copenhagen is 8 hours 50 minutes. From *Singapore* to Copenhagen is 15 hours 5 minutes. From *Sydney* to Copenhagen is 22 hours 50 minutes.
International airports: *Copenhagen (CPH)* (Kastrup) is 10km (6 miles) southeast of the city (travel time – 30 minutes). Coach departs every 10 minutes and bus every 15 minutes from 0600-2230. Airport facilities include an outgoing duty-free shop (0600-2300), a wide range of car hire firms (0730-2200 weekdays, 0700-1800 Saturday, 1400-2200 Sunday), bank/exchange facilities (0630-2200), and several restaurants and bars (at least one of which will be open between 0600 and 2400).
Århus (AAR) (Tirstrup) is 44km (27 miles) from the city. Buses connect with flight arrivals; taxis are also available. Airport facilities include a duty-free shop (open when flights depart), a wide range of car hire firms (0830-1500 weekdays, except Thursday until 1800), bank/exchange facilities (0800-1500) and a restaurant (open for arrival and departures of flights).
There are direct scheduled services between *Billund (BLL)* and Gatwick (UK); between *Esbjerg (EBJ)* and both Humberside (UK) and Stavanger (Norway); and between *Stauning (STA)* and Aberdeen (UK).
SEA: Denmark's major ports are Copenhagen, Esbjerg, Frederikshavn, Hirtshals and Hanstholm. There are regular ferries to and from the UK, Norway, Sweden, Poland, Iceland, the Faroe Islands and Germany. *Scandinavian Seaways* sail from Newcastle to Esbjerg from May to September, and from Harwich to Esbjerg three to seven times weekly all year round. The major ferry operators from Norway, Sweden and Germany are *Scandinavian Ferry Lines, Flyvebådene, Color Line, Da-No Line, DSB* and *Stena Line*. North Jutland is connected to Iceland, the Faroes, Scotland and Norway during the summer by ferries sailing once a week.
Cruise lines calling at Copenhagen are as follows: *Scandinavian Seaways, Royal Viking, TVI Lines, Lindblad Travel, Lauro, CTC, Norwegian Cruises/Union Lloyd* and *Norwegian American*.
RAIL: Copenhagen is connected by rail to all the other capital cities of Europe, and typical express journey times from Copenhagen are: to London 26 hours; to Hamburg 5 hours; to Berlin 9 hours. All international trains connect with ferries where applicable.
ROAD: All the major road networks of Europe connect with ferry services to Copenhagen; it is advisable to book ferries in advance. For many years the possibility of constructing a bridge or tunnel between Denmark and Sweden has been discussed; nothing has come of this so far.
See below under *Travel – Internal* for information on **documentation** and **traffic regulations**.

TRAVEL - Internal

AIR: The network of scheduled services radiates from *Copenhagen* (Kastrup). Other airports well-served by domestic airlines include Rønne, Odense, Billund, Esbjerg, Karup, Skrydstrup, Sønderborg, Thisted, Ålborg and Århus. Domestic airports are generally situated between two or more cities which are within easy reach of each other. Limousines are often available. Discounts are available on certain tickets bought inside Denmark. Family, children and young person's discounts are also available.
SEA: There are frequent ferry sailings from Zealand to Fyn, Kalundborg to Århus, Ebeltoft to Sjaellands Odde and Rønne to Copenhagen. The larger ferries may have TV, video and cinema lounges, shops, play areas for children and sleeping rooms. Local car ferries link most islands to the road network.
RAIL: The main cities on all islands are connected to the rail network: Copenhagen, Odense, Esbjerg, Horsens, Randers, Herning and Ålborg. There is also a new type of intercity service called the ICB offering faster and more direct transport. The *Danish State Railways (DSB)* operates a number of express trains called *Lyntogs* which

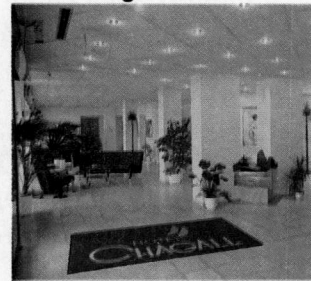

provide long-distance, non-stop travel; it is often possible to purchase newspapers, magazine and snacks on board these trains. Payphones are also available. There is also a new type of intercity train called the IC3 which is even faster and more direct. Seat reservations are compulsory. Children under four years old travel free, and between four and twelve at half price. There are also price reductions for persons over 65 and groups of three people or more. The *Englaenderen* boat-train runs between Esbjerg and Copenhagen and connects with ships from the UK. DSB passenger fares are based on a zonal system. The cost depends on the distance travelled; the cost per kilometre is reduced the longer the journey. Cheap day tickets are available for travel on Tuesday, Wednesday and Thursday. There are fare reductions for adults travelling in groups of three or more. The *Nord-Tourist Pass* allows unlimited travel within Denmark, Sweden, Norway and Finland. As elsewhere in Europe, *Interail* (for travellers under 26) and *Interail Senior* passes are valid in Denmark. Bus and ferry (and, of course, rail) tickets may be purchased at all railway stations.

ROAD: The road system in the Danish archipelago of necessity makes frequent use of ferries. The crossing time from Sjaelland Island (Copenhagen) to Fyn Island (Odense) is about one hour. A combined bridge and tunnel link from Zealand to Fyn has been under construction since 1987; completion of the bridge is expected in 1995 and completion of the tunnel is expected in 1997. This project will result in road connections being available between all the main centres in Denmark. Country buses operate where there are no railways, but there are few private long-distance coaches. Motorways are not subject to toll duty. Emergency telephones are available on motorways and there is a national breakdown network similar to the AA in Britain called *Falck*, which can be called out 24 hours a day (see yellow pages). There are no petrol stations on motorways. Many petrol stations are automatic. A maximum of ten litres of petrol is allowed to be kept as a reserve in suitably safe containers. The Danish Motoring Organisation is Forenede Danske Motorejere (FDM), Firskovvej 32, PO Box 500, DK-2800 Lyngby. Tel: 45 93 08 00.
Cycling: There are cycle lanes along many roads and, in the countryside, many miles of scenic cycle track. Bikes can easily be taken on ferries, trains, buses and domestic air services.
Car hire: Available to drivers over the age of 20, and can be reserved through travel agents or airlines.
Regulations: The wearing of seat belts is compulsory. Motorcyclists must wear helmets and drive with dipped headlights at all times. Headlamps on all vehicles should be adjusted for right-hand driving. Speed laws are strictly enforced, and heavy fines are levied on the spot; the car is impounded if payment is not made. Speed limits are 110kmph (60mph) on motorways, 50kmph (30mph) in built-up areas (signified by white plates with town silhouettes) and 80kmph (50mph) on other roads. All driving signs are international.
Documentation: A national driving licence is acceptable. EC nationals taking their own cars to Denmark are strongly advised to obtain a Green Card. Without it, insurance cover is limited to the minimum legal cover in Denmark; the Green Card tops this up to the level of cover provided by the car owner's domestic policy.

URBAN: Car repair is often available at petrol stations; costs include 22% VAT on labour and materials, which is not refunded when you leave the country.
Parking discs: Parking in cities is largely governed by parking discs, available from petrol stations, post offices, tourist offices, banks and some police stations. These allow up to three hours parking in car parks. Kerbside parking is allowed for one hour 0900-1700 Monday to Friday and 0900-1300 Saturday unless stated otherwise. The hand of the disc should point to the quarter hour following time of arrival. The disc is to be placed on the side of the screen nearest the kerb. **Parking meters:** Where discs do not apply, parking meters regulate parking. Parking on a metered space is limited to three hours 0900-1800 Monday to Friday and 0900-1300 Saturdays. Meter charges differ according to the area of the city.

JOURNEY TIMES: The following chart gives approximate journey times from Copenhagen (in hours and minutes) to other major cities/towns in Denmark.

	Air	Road	Rail
Ålborg	0.45	6.00	6.45
Århus	0.30	4.30	5.00
Billund	0.50	5.00	5.00
Esbjerg	1.00	5.00	5.00
Odense	0.35	3.00	3.00
Sønderborg	0.30	5.30	5.10

ACCOMMODATION

Contact the Danish Tourist Board for information on booking hotels and for details of the savings from the use of a *Scandinavian Bonus Pass* (which must be applied for in advance) or *Inn Cheques*. The Scandinavian Railpass *Nordtourist* is also valid as a *Scandinavian Bonus Pass*.

HOTELS: Travellers without reservations can book at the Tourist Information Department in Copenhagen (see above for address), or at one of the provincial tourist offices. Denmark's fine beaches attract many visitors, and there are hotels and pensions in all major seaside resorts. For more information contact the national hotel association CHR, Vodroffsvej 46, DK-1900 Frederiksberg C. Tel: 31 35 60 88. Fax: 31 35 93 76. **Grading:** There is no hotel grading system in Denmark, the standard is set by price and facilities offered. The Danish Tourist Board publishes an annual list of about 1000 establishments, describing facilities and tariffs; quoted prices are inclusive of MOMS (VAT).

INNS: Excellent inns are to be found all over the country. Some are small and only cater for local custom, but others are tailored for the tourist and have established high culinary reputations for both international dishes and local specialities. For further details contact the Danish Tourist Board or Danish Inn Holidays. Tel: 75 62 35 44.

BED & BREAKFAST: There are private rooms to let, usually for one night, all over Denmark. Prices are in the range DKr150-DKr250 (single/double room) with breakfast extra, but there may be variations from this. A further charge will be made if more beds are required. Signs along the highway with *Zimmer frei* or *Varelse* on them indicate availability of accommodation; those who knock and enquire will find that arrangements are easily made. In Copenhagen rooms can be booked in person through the Tourist Information Depart-ment for a fee of DKr13. Local tourist offices may be contacted, either by writing or in person, to make arrangements; the reservation fee is DKr10.

SELF-CATERING: Chalets are available in various parts of the country.

CAMPING/CARAVANNING: Campers must purchase a camping pass, available at campsites. Over 500 campsites are officially recognised and graded for facilities and shelter. Prices vary greatly; half price for children under four. **Grading:** *3-star sites:* Fulfil the highest requirements. *2-star sites:* Showers, razor points, shops, laundry facilities. *1-star sites:* Fulfil minimum requirements for sanitary installations, drinking water etc.

YOUTH AND FAMILY HOSTELS: There are 100 Youth and Family Hostels scattered around the country, all of which take members of affiliated organisations. A membership card from the National Youth Hostel Association is required.

FARMHOUSE HOLIDAYS: Rooms are often available for rent in farmhouses. Visitors stay as paying guests of the family and, although it is not expected, are welcome to help with the daily chores of the farm. Alternatively, in some cases separate apartments are available close to the main farmhouse. Many farms have their own fishing streams. All holiday homes and farmhouses are inspected and approved by the local Tourist Office. Prices are approximately DKr150 for bed & breakfast and DKr220 for half-board.

HOME EXCHANGE: The organisations listed below can arrange introductions between families interested in home exchange for short periods. The major expense for participants is travel plus a fee of DKr500. The best period (because of school holidays) is from late June to early August. The following organisations can provide further information:

Dansk Bolig Bytte, Hesselvang 20, DK-2900 Hellerup. Tel: 31 61 04 05; *or*
INTERVAC Denmark, c/o J. C. H. Lauritzen, Postboks 34, DK-3000 Helsinger. Tel: 42 19 00 71. Fax: 42 19 32 08; *or*
Haney's Bolig Bytte, v/Ingrid and Erik Haney, Byværnsvej 3, DK-2730 Herlev. Tel: 30 43 17 79. Fax: 42 84 77 79.

RESORTS & EXCURSIONS

Denmark has an abundance of picturesque villages and towns, historical castles and monuments, and a coastline which varies delightfully from broad sandy beaches to small coves and gentle fjords. Throughout the country rolling hills and gentle valleys provide a constant succession of attractive views; there are cool and shady forests of beech trees, extensive areas of heathland, a beautiful lake district, sand dunes and white cliffs resembling those of Dover; nor should one forget the Danish islands, each of which has its own unique attractions. Though there are few holiday resorts of the kind found in, say, France or Spain (the nearest equivalent being the *'Holiday Centre'* (HC), a purpose-built coastal resort), the Danes, who are taking strong measures to keep their coastline clean and tidy, are keen for visitors to sample the many unspoilt beaches.

Incentives offered by the Tourist Board to encourage families to visit the country include discounted passes for children to a large number of parks, museums, zoos etc. There are now nine *Sommerlands* in various locations in Denmark; these are activity parks where a flat entrance fee covers the visitor for use of all the many and varied facilities inside. At *Faarup Sommerland* in Saltum, for example, a fee of about £5.50 covers a visitor for all activities including use of the vast *Aquapark* which was recently completed. The Tourist Board has produced a 15-minute VHS video, *Family Holidays in Denmark*, which is available free on request.

Jutland

This area comprises the greater part of Denmark, extending 400km (250 miles) from the German border to its northernmost tip. Jutland's west coast has superb sandy beaches but bathing there is, however, often unsafe, due to the changing winds and tides. Care should be exercised, and any advice or notices issued by local authorities should be heeded. Also in Jutland is the major port of **Esbjerg**, which receives daily ferries from Britain.
Main towns & resorts: Ålborg, Holstebro, Århus, Vejle, Esbjerg, Frederikshavn, Randers, Viborg, Kolding, Silkeborg, Søndervig (HC), Aggertange (HC), Tranum Klitgård (HC).
Excursions & sightseeing: **Ålborg** contains the largest Viking burial ground, as well as a cathedral, monastery and castle. The largest Renaissance buildings in Denmark are in Ålborg. **Århus** has a collection of over 60 17th- and 18th-century buildings – houses, shops, workshops and so on from all over the country re-erected on a spacious landscaped site; as well as *Marselisborg Castle* and a museum of prehistory. **Esbjerg** and **Fanø** are also historically interesting and have a number of fine beaches. *Rosenholm, Clausholm* and *Voergard* castles are all worth a visit, while *Tivoliland* (Ålborg) and *Legoland* (Billund), which are open from April to September, provide good entertainment for children. *Søhøjlandet* is a new recreational park open to visitors which has chalet accommodation as well.

Fyn

Known as the 'Garden of Denmark', Fyn has some of Denmark's most picturesque and historic castles and manor houses, set in age-old parks and gardens. Odense is famous as the birthplace of the great fairytale writer Hans Christian Andersen. Fyn is connected to Jutland by bridges.
Main towns & resorts: Odense, Nyborg, Svendborg, Middelfart, Bogense, Klinten (HC).
Excursions & sightseeing: Castles and churches are the main attraction in **Fyn**. *Egeskov Castle* is a superb moated Renaissance castle which is fairytale in every detail. Other castles in the area include *Nyborg* (seat of the former National Assembly) and *Valdemar*, which houses a naval museum. There are also a number of beautiful beaches, particularly on the southern islands of **Langeland, Tåsinge** and **Aer. Odense**, the home of Hans Christian Andersen, has a festival every July and August celebrating his life and works. Visitors can see the *Hans Christian Andersen Museum* and his childhood

home. Other museums include a major railway museum and *Fyn Village*, a major cultural centre. Also in Odense is the recently completed *Brandts Klaedefabrik*, a major cultural centre.

Lolland, Falster, Møn & Bornholm

Lolland is generally flat, **Falster** less so, while **Møn** is a haven of small hills and valleys, with the *Møn Klint* chalk cliffs a breathtaking sight. **Bornholm** is set apart from the rest, 150km (90 miles) east of the Danish mainland, and is made up of fertile farmland, white beaches and rocky coastlines.
Main towns & resorts: Nysted, Nykobing, Nakskov, Stege, Sakskøbing, Rønne, Svaneke.
Sightseeing & excursions: *Knuthenborg Park* on **Lolland** is Denmark's largest, with 500 species of trees, flowers and plants; it also contains a safari park. *Ålholm Castle* contains the *Automobile Museum*, with Europe's biggest veteran and vintage car collection. *Corselitse* and the *Pederstrup Museum* are also worth a visit. **Bornholm** contains *Hammershus*, Denmark's largest castle ruin (built in 1260), as well as many fine churches. The small town of **Svaneke** was awarded the European Gold Medal in Architectural Heritage Year (1975).

Zealand

Denmark's capital, **Copenhagen**, is on Zealand and thus there is much commercial activity on the island. But there are also fine beaches, lakes, forests and royal palaces.
Main towns & resorts: Copenhagen (see below), Helsingør, Slagelse, Nastved, Roskilde, Hillerød, Frederikssund, Vedbaek (HC), Karlslunde (HC).
Sightseeing & excursions: At **Helsingør** can be found the old fortress of *Kronborg*, famed not only as the most imposing edifice in Scandinavia, but also as the setting for Shakespeare's *Hamlet*. *Frederiksborg Castle*, equally as impressive, is to be seen at **Hillerød**, which houses the *National History Museum*. The 12th-century cathedral at **Roskilde** and the *Viking Museum* are both worth a visit, while at **Skjoldenasholm** there is a fine *Tram Museum*. Excellent beaches can be found in Zealand, particularly in the north of the island.

Copenhagen

The largest urban centre in Scandinavia, Copenhagen is a city of copper roofs and spires, founded in 1167. It has many old buildings, fountains, statues and squares, as well as the singular attraction of the *Little Mermaid* at the harbour entrance. The *Copenhagen Card* gives unlimited travel on buses and trains and free entry to a large number of museums and places of interest.
Excursions & sightseeing: A number of organised tours are available, taking in most of the famous sights. These include the Vikingland tour to the *Viking Ship Museum;* a Royal tour to the *Christianborg Palace* (the seat of parliament), *Rosenborg Castle* and *Amalienborg Palace;* a coach tour to old-world *Bondebyen* and its open-air museum; and even a brewery tour, which takes in the famous *Carlsberg* and *Tuborg* breweries. *Tivoli*, Copenhagen's world-famous amusement park, is open from late April to mid-September. *Bakken* (in the deer park north of Copenhagen) and the *Charlottenlund Aquarium* are both worth a visit. In 1989 the biggest planetarium in Northern Europe opened its doors.

SOCIAL PROFILE

FOOD & DRINK: Most Danes have *smørrebrød* for their lunch. This is a slice of dark bread with butter and topped with slices of meat, fish or cheese and generously garnished. It bears no resemblance to traditional sandwiches and needs to be eaten sitting down with a knife and fork. Buffet-style lunch (the *koldt bord*) is also popular with a variety of fish, meats, hot dishes, cheese and sweets, usually on a self-service basis. Danes do not mix the various dishes on their plates but have them in strict order. A normal Danish breakfast or *morgencomplet* consists of coffee or tea and an assortment of breads, rolls, jam and cheese, often also sliced meats, boiled eggs and warm Danish pastries. Given its geographical position it is not surprising that shellfish also form an important part of Danish cuisine. Apart from traditional dishes, French or international cuisine is the order of the day. In Copenhagen, superb gourmet restaurants can be found, whilst Ålborg is noted for its impressive number of restaurants. Most towns have 'fast food' outlets for hamburgers and pizzas, and the sausage stalls on most street corners, selling hot sausages, hamburgers, soft drinks and beer, are popular.
Drink: Danish coffee is delicious and if you like it very strong, ask for *mokka*. Denmark also has many varieties of beer, famous breweries being Carlsberg and Tuborg. Most popular is *pilsner* (a lager), but there is also *lager* (a darker beer). The other national drink is *akvavit*, popularly known as *snaps*, which is neither an aperitif, cocktail nor liqueur and is meant to be drunk with food, preferably with a beer chaser. It is served ice cold and only accompanies cold food. There are no licensing hours.

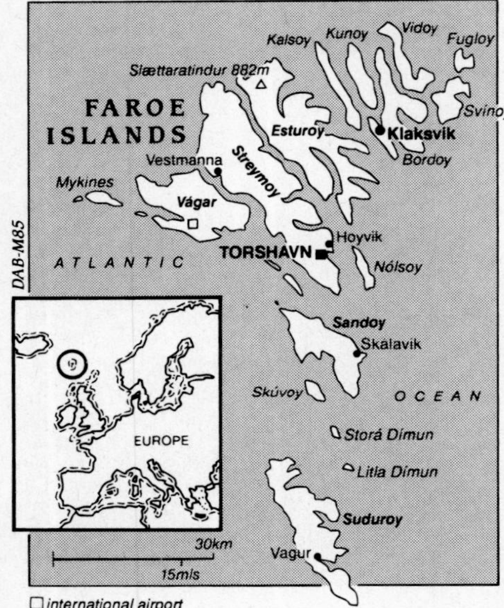

□ international airport

Note: The Danish Hotel and Restaurant Association is introducing a new sign to indicate restaurants where the needs of **diabetics** are given special attention. It consists of the words *'Diabetes mad – sund mad for alle'* ('Food for Diabetics – healthy food for everyone') encircling a chef's head.
NIGHTLIFE: There is a wide selection of nightlife, particularly in Copenhagen, where the first morning restaurants open to coincide with closing time at 0500. Jazz and dance clubs in the capital city are top quality and world-famous performers appear regularly. Beer gardens are numerous.
SHOPPING: Copenhagen has excellent shopping facilities. Special purchases include Bing & Grøndal and Royal Copenhagen porcelain, Holmegaard glass, Georg Jensen silver, furs from AC Bang and Birger Christensen, Bornholm ceramics, handmade woollens from Faroe Islands and Lego toys. Visitors from outside the EC can often claim back on some of the MOMS (VAT) on goods purchased that are sent straight to their home country from the shop in Denmark. **Shopping hours:** 0900-1730 Monday to Thursday, 0900-1900 Friday and 0900-1300 Saturday. Opening hours vary from town to town since shops can regulate their own hours. At some holiday resorts, shops are open on Sunday and public holidays.
SPORT: Swimming, sailing, windsurfing and **skin-diving** may be found at coastal resorts such as Bornholm and on the Jutland Coast; there are 600 harbours and many marinas where boats can be hired. There are also possibilities for freshwater **fishing** on Denmark's numerous lakes and rivers; coastal areas offer sea fishing. **Football** and **badminton** are played at international level. There are about 60 **golf** courses in Denmark of which about half are 18-hole courses. **Riding** schools can be found throughout the country. Enquire at local tourist office for sports facilities.
SPECIAL EVENTS: The following is only a selection of the major festivals and other special events celebrated annually in Denmark. For a complete list (published in several languages) contact the Danish Tourist Board.
1993 *Tønder 750th Town Anniversary*, Tønder (all year); *Ringkøbing 550th Town Anniversary*, Ringkøbing (all year). **Mar 5-7** *Fredericia International Boat Show '93*, Fredericia. **Mar 6-7** *Veteran Car Show*, Herning. **Apr-Sep** *Tivoliland*, amusement park, Ålborg. **Apr 1-4** *Garden '93 Spring Fair*, Ålborg. **Apr 22-Sep 19** *Tivoli in Copenhagen (150th Anniversary)*, Copenhagen. **May 4** *Light Festival*, Haderslev, South Jutland. **May 14-16** *National Horse Show*, Rødding. **May 21-31** *Ålborg Festival*, Ålborg. **May 23** *Wonderful Copenhagen Marathon*, Copenhagen. **May 28-30** *West Jutland Song Festival*, Tarm, West Jutland. **May 29-30** *Carnival*, Copenhagen. **May 1-Sep 19** *Legoland Park*, Billund. **Jun-Jul** *Viking Festival*, Frederikssund. **Jun 17-19** *Summer Jazz in Odense*, Odense. **Jun 24-27** *Skagen Festival*, Skagen. **Jul 2-11** *Copenhagen Jazz Festival*, Copenhagen. **Jul 14-Aug 8** *Hans Christian Andersen Festival*, Odense. **Jul 24-25** *Viking Meet*, Århus. **Jul 26-Aug 1** *World Cup – Single-Hander Europe*, Kaløvig Harbour, Skødstrup. **Jul 30-Aug 5** *Odense Film Festival*, Odense. **Aug 5-7** *Silkeborg Fire Festival Regatta*, Silkeborg. **Aug 6-9** *Cutty Sark Tall Ships Race*, Esbjerg. **Aug 21-Sep 11** *Århus Summer Opera*, Århus. **Sep 4-12** *Århus Festival 1993*, Århus. **Sep 12-13** *Kite Flying*, Århus. **Nov 20-21** *Christmas Fair*, Århus.
SOCIAL CONVENTIONS: Normal courtesies should be observed. Guests should refrain from drinking until the host toasts his or her health. Casual dress is suitable for most places but formal wear is required at more exclusive dining rooms and social functions. Smoking is restricted on public transport and in some public buildings. **Tipping:** Hotels and restaurants quote fully inclusive prices and tipping is not necessary. Taxi fares include tip. Railway porters and washroom attendants receive tips.

BUSINESS PROFILE

ECONOMY: The standard of living is generally high. Since the war industry has rapidly expanded in importance, although by the standards of most industrialised countries, Denmark retains an important agricultural industry. Two-thirds of Danish produce is exported, principally cheese, beef and bacon. Danish manufacturing industry, the largest economic sector, depends on imports of raw materials and components. Iron, steel and other metal industries are the most important, followed by electronics (which is growing especially quickly), chemicals and bio-technology, paper and printing, textiles, furniture and cement. Food processing and drinks also make a significant contribution. The weakest aspect of the Danish economy is its lack of raw materials, particularly oil and other fuels. However, the discovery of offshore deposits has improved the balance of payments in this area, leaving Denmark with a small net trade surplus towards the end of the 1980s. Most of Denmark's trade is conducted within the European Community, of which it is a member. Germany is the largest single trading partner, providing 23% of Denmark's imports and taking 17% of exports. The comparable figures for the UK are 7.5% and 11% respectively. Sweden and the United States are the most important markets outside the Community. According to the Department of Trade and Industry, there are especially good opportunities for British exporters in the following sectors: electrical components, food and drinks, clothing, computer hardware and software, textiles and car components.
BUSINESS: English is widely used for all aspects of business. Local business people expect visitors to be punctual and the approach to business is often direct and straightforward. Avoid business visits from mid-June to mid-August which are prime holiday periods. **Office hours:** 0900-1700 Monday to Friday.
COMMERCIAL INFORMATION: The following organisations can offer advice: Det Danske Handelskammer (Danish Chamber of Commerce), Børsen, DK-1217 Copenhagen K. Tel: 33 91 23 23. Fax: 33 32 52 16; *or*
International Chamber of Commerce Denmark, Børsen, DK-1217 Copenhagen K. Tel: 33 91 23 25. Fax: 33 15 22 66.
CONFERENCES/CONVENTIONS: The Danish Convention Bureau, a non-profitmaking organisation, was established in 1988 by the Danish Tourist Board, the Danish Council of Tourist Trade, Scandinavian Airlines, Danish State Railways, the Danish Hotel and Restaurant Association, Danish Incoming Travel Bureaus and the Danish Association of Multipurpose Halls. The Bureau's aim is to assist decision-makers and planners of meetings, congresses and incentive travel. There are over 100 affiliated companies. For further general information, brochures or to initiate plans for a conference/convention, contact the Danish Convention Bureau, Skindergade 27, DK-1159 Copenhagen K. Tel: 33 32 86 01. Fax: 33 32 88 03.

HISTORY & GOVERNMENT

HISTORY: Canute (Knud), famous for his confrontation with the sea, was an 11th-century king of Denmark who ruled over the first 'northern empire', stretching from England (his dynasty ruled 1016-1042) through Scandinavia to the Baltic provinces which used to form part of the then Soviet Union. Although its power waned during the Middle Ages, amid conflicts between church and state, in favour of Sweden and the German states, Denmark did maintain long-term control over Iceland, Greenland, small Atlantic island groups such as the Faroes, and even, until the early 19th century, over Norway, where Danish was the official language and Danes held all the senior government posts. During the Napoleonic era the Danes sided with the French and, as a result of their defeat, lost their dominance in Scandinavia. Subsequently, after a disastrous war against the Austrians and Prussians, Denmark was forced to relinquish the provinces of Schleswig and Holstein (now part of Germany). Denmark then began the transition from autocratic to parliamentary government, which became fully established after the First World War and was suspended only during the Nazi occupation of the Second World War. A conservative-led coalition government took office in 1982. It was re-elected with a reduced majority at the next scheduled general election in September 1987. In June the following year, Prime Minister Schluter decided to call a snap election on the issue of Denmark's continuing membership of NATO. A three-party coalition of Conservatives, Liberals and Radical Liberals, again led by Schluter, took office in June 1988. Economic issues dominated the political agenda over the next few years, displacing environmental and nuclear concerns. Disagreements over economic and fiscal reform (demanded by the terms of the Single European Market which came into force in 1992) split the coalition and forced a further election in December 1990. Although the Social Democrats emerged as the largest single party, Schluter was yet again able to put together a coalition to form a minority government. His new administration is presently immersed in crisis over Denmark's membership of the European Community, brought about by the rejection of the Maastricht Treaty (which sets out the next stage of development for the EC) in a popular referendum in June 1992. The options facing the Government are partial detachment from the EC or – more likely – the holding of another referendum, suitably reworded, to secure the necessary popular majority. Danish officials are also taking soundings on the feasibility of securing 'opt-outs' on the European single currency and proposed future defence co-operation.
GOVERNMENT: Denmark is a constitutional monarchy. The constitutional charter of 1953 gives the hereditary monarch and the unicameral Parliament *(Folketing)* legislative power. The monarch has no personal political power. Members are elected to the Parliament by proportional representation.

CLIMATE

Summer extends from June to August. Winter is from December to March, wet with long periods of frost. February is the coldest month. Spring and Autumn are generally mild.
The *Faroe Islands* are under the influence of the warm current of the Gulf Stream, and they enjoy a very mild climate for the latitude. Winters are warm, but the islands are cloudy, windy and wet throughout the year. Summers are cool, but with little sunshine.
Required clothing: Lightweight for summer and heavyweight for winter snows.

HOYVIK Faroe Is. (20m)

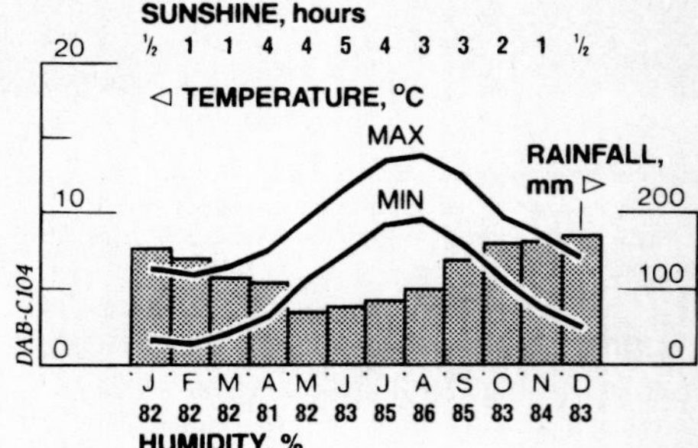

COPENHAGEN Denmark (9m)

SUNSHINE, hours
1 2 4 5 8 8 8 7 5 3 1 ½
TEMPERATURE, °C
MAX
MIN
RAINFALL, mm
20
10
0
100
0
J F M A M J J A S O N D
87 85 82 74 65 65 68 70 80 81 86 88
HUMIDITY, %
DAB-C92

DJIBOUTI

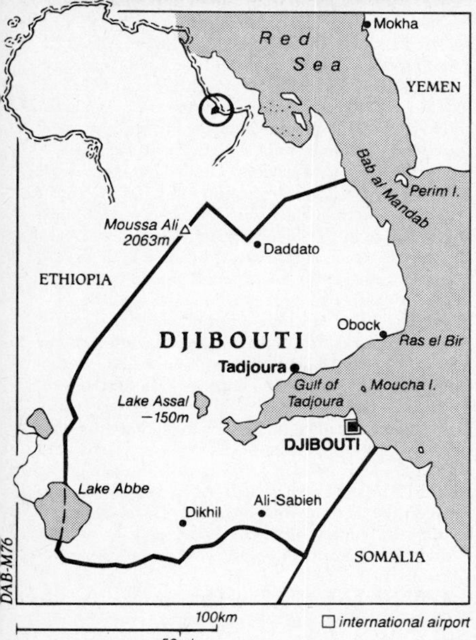

Location: Northeast Africa; Gulf of Aden.

Office National du Tourisme et de l'Artisanat
BP 1938
place du 27 juin
Djibouti
Tel: 352 800. Fax: 356 322. Telex: 5938.
Embassy of the Republic of Djibouti
26 rue Emile Ménier
75116 Paris, France
Tel: (1) 47 27 49 22. Telex: 614970.
British Consulate
BP 81
Gellatly Hankey et Cie
Djibouti
Tel: 355 718. Fax: 353 294. Telex: GELLATLY 5843 DJ.
Embassy of the Republic of Djibouti
Suite 515
1156 15th Street, NW
Washington, DC
20005
Tel (202) 331 0270. Fax: (202) 331 0302. Telex: 4490085.
Also deals with enquiries from Canada.
Embassy of the United States of America
BP 185
Plateau du Serpent
Villa boulevard Maréchal Joffré
Djibouti
Tel: 353 995. Fax: 353 940.

AREA: 23,200 sq km (8958 sq miles).
POPULATION: 510,000 (1989).
POPULATION DENSITY: 22 per sq km.
CAPITAL: Djibouti. **Population:** 220,000 (1981).
GEOGRAPHY: Djibouti is part of the African continent bounded to the northeast and east by the Red Sea, the southeast by Somalia and the south, west and north by Ethiopia. The country is a barren strip of land around the Gulf of Tadjoura, varying in width from 20km (12 miles) to 90km (56 miles), with a coastline of 800km (497 miles), much of it white sandy beaches. Inland is semi-desert and desert, with thorn bushes, steppes and volcanic mountain ranges.
LANGUAGE: The official languages are Arabic and French. Afar and Somali are spoken locally. English is spoken by hoteliers, taxi drivers and traders.
RELIGION: Muslim with Roman Catholic, Protestant and Greek Orthodox minorities.
TIME: GMT + 3.
ELECTRICITY: 220 volts AC, 50Hz.
COMMUNICATIONS: Telephone: IDD available. Country code: 253. **Fax:** There are no facilities for the public. **Telex/telegram:** Telexes and telegrams can be sent from the main post office from 0700-2000. Telegram services are also available at the Telegraph office. **Post:** Letters and parcels to Europe can take about a week by airmail or up to three weeks by surface mail. **Press:** Djibouti has no daily papers. A weekly newspaper, *La Nation de Djibouti*, is published in French.
BBC World Service and Voice of America frequencies: From time to time these change. See the section *How to Use this Book* for more information.

BBC:				
MHz	25.75	17.74	11.73	6.005
Voice of America:				
MHz	21.49	15.60	9.525	6.035

PASSPORT/VISA

Regulations and requirements may be subject to change at short notice, and you are advised to contact the appropriate diplomatic or consular authority before finalising travel arrangements. Details of these may be found at the head of this country's entry. Any numbers in the chart refer to the footnotes below.

	Passport Required?	Visa Required?	Return Ticket Required?
Full British	Yes	Yes	Yes
BVP	Not valid	-	-
Australian	Yes	Yes	Yes
Canadian	Yes	Yes	Yes
USA	Yes	Yes	Yes
Other EC	Yes	1	Yes
Japanese	Yes	Yes	Yes

Prohibited entry and transit: The Government of the Republic of Djibouti refuses admission and transit to nationals of Israel and South Africa.
PASSPORTS: Valid passport required by all.
British Visitors Passport: Not accepted.
VISAS: Required by all ([1] except nationals of France for a maximum stay of 3 months, provided a return ticket is held).
Types of visa: A 3-day (cost: Dfr2500) or 10-day (cost: Dfr5000) Transit visa (Visa d'Escale) can be converted into a permit. Entry visas are valid for a period of 30 days. The issue of these depends on nationality and on the passenger having the appropriate onward or return tickets.
Validity: As stated above and generally non-extendable.
Application to: The Embassy in Paris is at present not issuing visas. However, applications can be made. For address, see top of entry. The visas can be collected at the airport in Djibouti. Nationals of the UK needing visas may apply to the French Consulate (Visa Section) in London.
Application requirements: (a) Valid passport. (b) 2 completed application forms in French. (c) 2 photos. (d) Travel documents, including a photocopy of the return ticket. (e) The equivalent of FFr70 plus FFr25 to cover postage within France or FFr35 to cover postage from abroad; the amount should be sent in the form of a postal or money order, not a cheque. (f) Copy of vaccination certificate for yellow fever.
Working days required: Application normally takes 48 hours to process.
Note: It is obligatory for foreign nationals resident in Djibouti to hold an exit visa.

MONEY

Currency: Djibouti Franc (Dfr) = 100 centimes. Notes are in denominations of Dfr10,000, 5000, 1000 and 500. Coins are in denominations of Dfr500, 100, 50, 20, 10, 5, 2 and 1.
Credit cards: These are only accepted by airlines and some of the larger hotels.
Travellers cheques: French Franc and Sterling cheques are not accepted unless marked as 'External Account' or 'Pour Compte Etranger'. The majority of banks are in the place du 27 juin area.
Exchange rate indicators: The following figures are included as a guide to the movements of the Djibouti Franc against Sterling and the US Dollar:

Date:	Oct '89	Oct '90	Oct '91	Oct '92
£1.00=	275.0	338.0	307.15	285.0
$1.00=	174.2	173.0	176.98	179.58

Currency restrictions: No restrictions on import or export of either foreign or local currency.
Banking hours: 0715-1145 Sunday to Thursday.

DUTY FREE

As for France; see *France* entry below. Firearms must be declared on entry and exit.

PUBLIC HOLIDAYS

Public holidays observed in Djibouti are as follows:
May 1 '93 Workers' Day. **Jun 1** Eid al-Adha. **Jun 21** Muharram (Islamic New Year). **Jun 27** Independence Day. **Aug 30** Mouloud (Prophet's Birthday). **Dec 25** Christmas. **Jan 1 '94** New Years Day. **Mar** Eid al-Fitr.
Note: Muslim festivals are timed according to local sightings of various phases of the Moon and the dates given above are approximations. During the lunar month of Ramadan that precedes Eid al-Fitr, Muslims fast during the day and feast at night and normal business patterns may be interrupted. Many restaurants are closed during the day and there may be restrictions on smoking and drinking. Some disruption may continue into Eid al-Fitr itself. Eid al-Fitr and Eid al-Adha may last anything from two to ten days, depending on the region. For more information see the section *World of Islam* at the back of the book.

HEALTH

Regulations and requirements may be subject to change at short notice, and you are advised to contact your doctor well in advance of your intended date of departure. Any numbers in the chart refer to the footnotes below.

	Special Precautions?	Certificate Required?
Yellow Fever	Yes	1
Cholera	Yes	2
Typhoid & Polio	Yes	-
Malaria	Yes	-
Food & Drink	3	-

[1]: A yellow fever vaccination certificate is required from travellers over one year of age coming from infected areas.

DJIBOUTI	HEALTH REGULATIONS	VISA REGULATIONS
		Code-Link
GALILEO/WORLDSPAN	 TI-DFT/JIB/HE	 TI-DFT/JIB/VI
SABRE	TIDFT/JIB/HE	TIDFT/JIB/VI

To access this information on your CRS, swipe the barcode with a light pen or type in the text under the barcode. For more information, see the introduction *How to Use This Book.*

[2]: Following WHO guidelines issued in 1973, a cholera vaccination certificate is no longer a condition of entry to Djibouti. However, cholera is a serious risk in this country and precautions are essential. Up-to-date advice should be sought before deciding whether these precautions should include vaccination as medical opinion is divided over its effectiveness. See the *Health* section at the back of the book.
[3]: Mains water is normally heavily chlorinated, and whilst relatively safe may cause mild abdominal upsets. Bottled water is available and is advised for the first few weeks of the stay. Drinking water outside main cities and towns is likely to be contaminated and sterilisation is considered essential. Milk is unpasteurised and should be boiled. Powdered or tinned milk is available and is advised, but make sure that it is reconstituted with pure water. Avoid dairy products which are likely to have been made from unboiled milk. Only eat well-cooked meat and fish, preferably served hot. Pork, salad and mayonnaise may carry increased risk. Vegetables should be cooked and fruit peeled.
Malaria, predominantly in the malignant *falciparum* form, is a risk everywhere throughout the year.
Health care: Health insurance is advisable.

TRAVEL - International

AIR: Djibouti does not have a national airline. Services are offered by *Aeroflot (SU)*, *Air France (AF)*, *Air Madagascar (MD)* and *Air Tanzania*.
Approximate flight time: From *London* to Djibouti is 11 hours (including stopovers).
International airport: *Djibouti (JIB)* is 5km (3 miles) south of the city. Taxis are available. There are four or five flights a week from Paris.
Departure tax: Dfr2000, except for *Air France* tickets (tax included in ticket price).
RAIL: The Djibouti–Ethiopian Railway operates regular trains from Addis Ababa and Dire Dawa daily; tourists and business people are prohibited from using the service.
ROAD: There are good roads from Djibouti to Assab (Ethiopia) and going west into Ethiopia via Dikhil. Most other roads are rough but passable throughout the year and there is now a road link with Addis Ababa. Check transit regulations as political conditions in Ethiopia are changeable. There is a bus up to the Somalian border at Loyoda (see below for information on documentation).

TRAVEL - Internal

AIR: Private charters might also be available.
SEA: Ferry services sail to Tadjoura and Obock from Djibouti (three hours).
RAIL: The only service is that provided by the daily train to the border (see above) which tourists and business people are banned from using.
ROAD: Four-wheel drive vehicles for the interior. There is a new highway from Djibouti to Tadjoura. **Car hire:** Available in Djibouti and at the airport. Contact *Red Sea Cars* (tel: 354 646). Four-wheel drive for overland trips are available from *Stophi* (tel: 352 494). It is advisable to carry plenty of water and petrol on any expedition off main routes. **Documentation:** An International Driving Permit is recommended, although it is not legally required. A temporary licence to drive is available from local authorities on presentation of a valid British or Northern Ireland driving licence. Insurance is not required.
URBAN: A minibus service operates in Djibouti, stopping on demand. A flat fare system is used. **Taxi:** These are available in Djibouti and from airport to town; also in Ali-Sabieh, Dikhil, Dorale and Arta. Fares increase by 50% after dark.

ACCOMMODATION

HOTELS: Hotels in Djibouti tend to be expensive and the few cheap hotels are somewhat seedy. The major hotels are the Sheraton, Le Plein Ciel, the Menelik, the Siesta, the Relais and the Ali-Sabieh. Outside Djibouti, accommodation is limited, although attention is being given to upgrading and adding to the accommodation available in the hinterland. The rest shelter at Ali-Sabieh, a provincial town in the hills, has already been enlarged from two rooms to nine, and a large shaded terrace and simple cooking facilities have also been added. Countrywide, however, much remains to be done. The Government would like to establish a network of resthouses similar to the one at Ali-Sabieh throughout the country. In addition, it hopes to build several beach shelters.
Note: *Air France* can book accommodation in advance in the Sheraton and Le Plein Ciel (first-class) hotels through their London office at the same time as issuing the air ticket.

RESORTS & EXCURSIONS

Djibouti is a late 19th-century city with an excellent market near the Mosque, and several good restaurants. Nearby are beaches at **Dorale**, 11km (7 miles) and **Kor Ambad**, 14km (9 miles). Djibouti lies within a geological feature known as the *Afar Triangle*, one of the hottest and most desolate places on Earth. Part of the Great Rift Valley system, it is a wedge of flat desert pushing into the Ethiopian Massif. Much of it is below sea level, indeed **Lake Assal,** 100km (60 miles) to the southwest of Djibouti city, is one of the lowest surface areas anywhere on the planet; like so many places in the country, it is reachable only by 4-wheel drive vehicle. Straddling the Ethiopian frontier is another lake, **Lake Abbe,** the home of thousands of flamingoes and pelicans. A large market can be found at **Ali-Sabieh**, a major stop for the main-line train between Djibouti and Addis Ababa. On the opposite side of the **Gulf of Tadjoura,** an excellent place for skindiving, fishing and underwater photography, are the towns of **Obock** and **Tadjoura,** a town with seven mosques. In the hinterland is the **Goda Mountains National Park**.

SOCIAL PROFILE

FOOD & DRINK: There are restaurants to suit all tastes, serving French, Vietnamese, Chinese, Arab and local specialities. Drink will only be limited in Muslim areas (particularly during Ramadan).
SHOPPING: Lively and colourful local markets are well worth visiting and local crafts and artefacts can be bought. **Shopping hours:** 0800-1200 and 1630-1930 Saturday to Thursday (closed Wednesday).
SPORT: There are beaches at Dorale and Kor Ambade several kilometres from Djibouti with safe **swimming**. The Gulf of Tadjoura (especially Obock) offers many species of fish and coral and is ideal for **diving, spearfishing** and **underwater photography**. The best time for these activities is from September to May when the waters of the Red Sea are clear.
Note: Hunting is forbidden throughout the country.
SOCIAL CONVENTIONS: Casual wear is widely acceptable but visitors are reminded that Djibouti is a Muslim country and certain codes of behaviour should be observed. Beachwear should not be worn in towns. **Tipping:** Not usual for taxi drivers. A tariff is normally set but visitors will be charged at a higher rate. A 10% service charge is usually added to bills.

BUSINESS PROFILE

ECONOMY: Due to the harsh terrain there is little arable farming, and most of the land is desert used by nomads for livestock. There is a small industrial sector. The deep-water port on the Bab-El-Mandeb Straits is vitally important to the country, as it is on the major oil route between the Gulf of Aden and the Red Sea. Djibouti's economic potential lies in the development of its service sector. Transport facilities and banking are the most productive sectors, although Djibouti's economy has suffered throughout the last decade from the political upheaval in the Horn of Africa. The Government hopes to develop Djibouti as a trading centre between Africa and the Middle East and an important telecommunications hub for the region. At present the country is dependent on foreign aid, which it obtains from France and the Middle East. The currency is fixed to the US Dollar. Exports – mostly of food and live animals – barely reach 10% of imports at present: most of the latter originate from France, with Ethiopia, the Benelux countries, Italy and the UK supplying the rest.
BUSINESS: Light, tropical suits should be worn. French and Arabic are the main languages used in business. As there are few, if any, interpreter services of note, a knowledge of either of these languages is essential. Business entertainment will often take place in hotels or restaurants. **Office hours:** 0620-1300 Saturday to Thursday.
COMMERCIAL INFORMATION: The following organisation can offer advice: Chambre Internationale de Commerce et d'Industrie, BP 84, place Lagarde, Djibouti. Tel: 350 826 *or* 350 673. Fax: 350 096.

HISTORY & GOVERNMENT

HISTORY: Djibouti was originally inhabited by nomadic tribes, the main ones being the Afars and the Issas, who are strongly linked to Ethiopia and Somalia respectively. In 1862 the French signed a treaty with the Afar leaders giving them land on the north coast; Djibouti gradually became more firmly associated with France during the course of that century. In 1915 a railway was completed from Djibouti to Addis Ababa. In 1945 French Somaliland (as the area was called) was declared an 'overseas territory'; in 1967 it became the French territory of the Afars and the Issas. Tensions between the Afars, the Issas and the French led to sporadic outbreaks of violence during the late 60s and early 70s; in 1977 the French agreed to withdraw and the country achieved independence with Hassan Gouled Aptidon as President. Gouled has remained in office ever since, featuring as the sole candidate in successive presidential elections. A sizeable French military presence in the country guarantees the survival of the regime, which is threatened by organised opposition – both inside the country and abroad – and by the instability of its two large neighbours, Somalia and Ethiopia, neither of whom enjoy good relations with Djibouti. Since 1991, Gouled has been confronted by a major insurgency launched by well-armed Afar clansmen under the rubric of La Front pour la Restauration de l'Unité et la Democratie (FRUD). Djibouti is also facing possible famine and a growing refugee population from the conflicts across its borders. To that end, Djibouti quickly opened contacts with the new government in Somalia and has been involved in mediation between the factions competing for control in that country. In January 1992, Gouled set up a committee to draft a new constitution allowing for multi-party elections.
GOVERNMENT: The Rassemblement Populaire pour le Progrés (RPP) is the sole legal party. The President is Head of State and is elected by universal adult suffrage. Executive power is vested in the Council of Ministers which, with its leader, the Prime Minister, is responsible to the President.

CLIMATE

Extremely hot and particularly arid between June and August when the dusty Khamsin blows from the desert. Between October and April it is slightly cooler with occasional light rain.
Required clothing: Lightweight cottons and linens. Avoid synthetics. Light raincoat or umbrella may be useful in cooler periods.

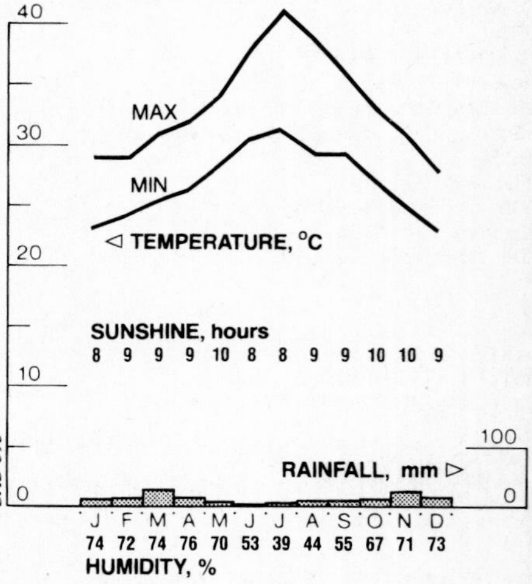

DOMINICA (COMMONWEALTH OF)

Location: Caribbean, Windward Islands.

National Development Corporation (NDC) – Division of Tourism
PO Box 73
Valley Road
Roseau
Tel: 448 2351. Fax: 448 5840.

Dominica High Commission
1 Collingham Gardens
Earls Court
London SW5 0HW
Tel: (071) 370 5194/5. Fax: (071) 373 8743.
Tourist Office: Tel: (071) 835 1937. Fax: (071) 373 8743.
Opening hours: 0930-1730 Monday to Friday.

British High Commission
PO Box 676
Lower Collymore Rock
Bridgetown, Barbados
Tel: 436 6694. Fax: 426 7916 *or* 436 5398. Telex: 2219 UKREP BRI WB.

Caribbean Tourism Organization
20 East 46th Street
New York, NY
10017
Tel: (212) 682 0435. Fax: (212) 697 4258.
Also deals with enquiries from Canada.

High Commission for the Countries of the Organisation of Eastern Caribbean States
Suite 1610
Tower B
112 Kent Street
Place de Ville
Ottawa, Ontario
K1P 5P2
Tel: (613) 236 8952. Fax: (613) 236 3042. Telex: 053-4476.

AREA: 749.8 sq km (289.5 sq miles).
POPULATION: 81,600 (1989).
POPULATION DENSITY: 108.8 per sq km.
CAPITAL: Roseau. **Population:** 11,000 (1987).
GEOGRAPHY: Dominica is the largest and most mountainous of the Windward Islands with volcanic peaks, mountain streams and rivers, dense forests, quiet lakes, waterfalls, geysers and boiling volcanic pools. There are beaches of both black (volcanic) and golden sands while orchids and untamed subtropical vegetation grow in the valleys. Guadeloupe is to the north and Martinique to the south.
LANGUAGE: The official language is English, but a Creole French, the national language, is spoken by most of the population. A dictionary of this language is in preparation. Cocoy, a variant of English, is spoken in the region of Marigot and Wesley.
RELIGION: Roman Catholic majority.
TIME: GMT - 4.
ELECTRICITY: 220/240 volts AC, 50Hz.
COMMUNICATIONS: Telephone: IDD available. Country code: 1 809. **Fax:** Services are available through the Cable & Wireless Company. Opening hours: 0700-2000 Monday to Saturday. **Telex:** Services are also available through the Cable & Wireless Company. Opening hours: 0700-2000 Monday to Saturday. **Post:** There are no *Poste Restante* facilities. Post offices are open 0830-1300 and 1430-1700 Monday and 0830-1300 and 1430-1600 Tuesday to Friday. **Press:** Newspapers are in English. These include *The New Chronicle*, *The Voice of the Island* and the *Official Gazette* published either weekly or every three months.
BBC World Service and Voice of America frequencies: From time to time these change. See the section *How to Use this Book* for more information.

BBC:				
MHz	17.72	11.78	9.915	5.965
Voice of America:				
MHz	15.21	11.70	6.130	0.930

PASSPORT/VISA

Regulations and requirements may be subject to change at short notice, and you are advised to contact the appropriate diplomatic or consular authority before finalising travel arrangements. Details of these may be found at the head of this country's entry. Any numbers in the chart refer to the footnotes below.

	Passport Required?	Visa Required?	Return Ticket Required?
Full British	Yes	No	Yes
BVP	Not valid/2	-	-
Australian	Yes	No	Yes
Canadian	1	No	Yes
USA	1	No	Yes
Other EC	Yes	No	Yes
Japanese	Yes	No	Yes

PASSPORTS: [1] Valid passport required by all except nationals of Canada and the USA who must have suitable ID and return or onward tickets.
British Visitors Passport: [2] Not accepted. Although the immigration authorities of this country may in certain circumstances accept British Visitors Passports for persons arriving for holidays or unpaid business trips of up to 3 months, travellers are reminded that no formal agreement exists to this effect and the situation may, therefore, change at short notice. In addition, UK nationals using a BVP and returning to the UK from a country with which no such formal agreement exists may be subject to delays and interrogation by UK immigration.
VISAS: Not required except for nationals of former Eastern European or communist countries (including Cuba) and South Africa.
Applications to: Dominica High Commission. For addresses, see top of entry.
Temporary residence: Those applying for temporary residence must obtain a work permit.
Note: Business visitors may be required to pay a licence fee of EC$400 per annum (US$154 per year or US$77 for six months).

MONEY

Currency: East Caribbean Dollar (EC$) = 100 cents. Notes are in denominations of EC$100, 20, 5 and 1. Coins are in denominations of 50, 25, 10, 5, 2 and 1 cents. US Dollars are also legal tender.
Credit cards: Visa and Access/Mastercard (limited) are accepted. Check with your credit card company for details of merchant acceptability and other services which may be available.
Travellers cheques are accepted by most hotels.
Exchange rate indicators: The following figures are included as a guide to the movements of the EC Dollar against Sterling and the US Dollar:

Date:	Oct '89	Oct '90	Oct '91	Oct '92
£1.00=	4.26	5.27	4.69	4.27
$1.00=	*2.70	*2.70	*2.70	*2.70

Note [*]: The Eastern Caribbean Dollar is tied to the US Dollar.
Currency restrictions: Unlimited import of local and foreign currency, subject to declaration on arrival. Export of both limited to the amount declared on import.
Banking hours: 0800-1500 Monday to Thursday, 0800-1700 Friday.

DUTY FREE

The following goods may be imported into Dominica without incurring customs duty:
200 cigarettes or 2 packets of tobacco or 24 cigars;
2 bottles of alcoholic beverage.

PUBLIC HOLIDAYS

Public holidays observed on Dominica are as follows:
Apr 9 '93 Good Friday. **Apr 12** Easter Monday. **May 1** May Day. **May 31** Whit Monday. **Aug 2** August Monday. **Nov 3** National Day. **Nov 4** Community Service Day. **Dec 25** Christmas. **Dec 26** Boxing Day. **Jan 1 '94** New Year's Day. **Feb 14-15** Masquerade Carnival.

HEALTH

Regulations and requirements may be subject to change at short notice, and you are advised to contact your doctor well in advance of your intended date of departure. Any numbers in the chart refer to the footnotes below.

	Special Precautions?	Certificate Required?
Yellow Fever	No	1
Cholera	No	No
Typhoid & Polio	2	-
Malaria	No	-
Food & Drink	3	-

[1]: A yellow fever vaccination certificate is required from travellers over one year of age coming from infected areas.
[2]: Polio immunisation is recommended; the risk of typhoid fever is uncertain, but vaccination is recommended.
[3]: Mains water is normally chlorinated, and whilst relatively safe may cause mild abdominal upsets. Bottled water is available and is advised for the first few weeks of the stay. Drinking water outside main cities and towns may be contaminated and sterilisation is advisable. Milk is pasteurised and dairy products are safe for consumption. Local meat, poultry, seafood, fruit and vegetables are generally considered safe to eat.
Health care: Health insurance is recommended.

TRAVEL - International

AIR: The main airline to serve Dominica is *LIAT (LI)*. Others include *Air Angilla*, *Air Martinique* and *Air Guadeloupe*.
Approximate flight times: From Roseau to *London* is 10

DOMINICA | **HEALTH REGULATIONS** | **VISA REGULATIONS** | Code-Link

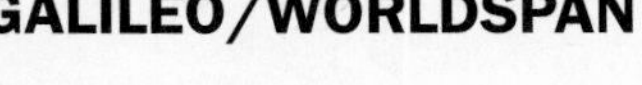
GALILEO/WORLDSPAN

TI-DFT/DOM/HE

TI-DFT/DOM/VI

SABRE

TIDFT/DOM/HE

TIDFT/DOM/VI

To access this information on your CRS, swipe the barcode with a light pen or type in the text under the barcode. For more information, see the introduction *How to Use This Book*.

hours 45 minutes (including a stopover – eg in Antigua, 1 hour 25 minutes), to *Los Angeles* is 10 hours and to *New York* is 7 hours.
International airports (turbo-prop only): *Melville Hall (DOM)* is approximately 56km (35 miles) northeast of Roseau.
Canefield (DCF) is approximately 5km (3 miles) north of Roseau.
Departure tax: EC$20. There is also a Security Check Tax of EC$5.
SEA: *Geest* and several other island-hopping freight lines stop in Dominica. Generally, passenger accommodation is comfortable but numbers are limited, so book well in advance. The *Caribbean Express*, a scheduled ferry service, offers boat connections on a 200-seat catamaran; connections can be made from Guadeloupe, Martinique and Les Saintes. Other cruise liners stop at Woodbridge Bay, 5km (3 miles) outside Roseau. A new cruise ship jetty has been developed and opened at Prince Rupert Bay, Portsmouth.

TRAVEL - Internal

ROAD: There are more than 700km (450 miles) of well-maintained roads on the island and there is little traffic outside Roseau. Driving is on the left. **Bus:** Service exists but is unpredictable. **Taxis** and **minibuses** are the most efficient means of road transport. **Car hire:** Available, but roads can be difficult. Jeep tours operated by local firms offer the best means of sightseeing; all vehicles chartered for this purpose must be hired for at least three hours. **Documentation:** International Driving Permit recommended. A valid foreign licence can be used to get Temporary Visitor's Permit.
JOURNEY TIMES: The following chart gives approximate journey times (in hours and minutes) from Roseau to other places on Dominica.

	Road
Canefield Airport	0.15
Melville H. A'port	1.00
Portsmouth	0.50

ACCOMMODATION

HOTELS: The number of hotels has expanded in recent years; most of the hotels are small to medium sized, and well-equipped; the largest of them has 98 rooms. There are three hotels at the fringe of an area designated as a National Park. Information can be obtained from the Dominica Hotel Association, PO Box 384, Roseau, Dominca. Tel: 448 6565. Fax: 448 2285. **Grading:** Many of the hotels offer accommodation according to one of a number of 'Plans' widely used in the Caribbean; these include Modified American Plan (MAP) which consists of room, breakfast and dinner and European Plan (EP) which consists of room only.
APARTMENTS/COTTAGES: These offer self-catering, full service and maid service facilities and are scattered around the island.
GUEST-HOUSES: There is a variety of guest-houses and inns around the island which offer a comfortable and very friendly atmosphere. There is a 10% Government tax and 10% service charge on rooms.
CAMPING/CARAVANNING: Not encouraged at the present time, though sites may be designated in future. Overnight safari tours are run by local operators.

RESORTS & EXCURSIONS

Roseau, on the southwest coast, is the main centre for visitors. From hotels around here it is possible to arrange jeep safari tours for seeing the hinterland of the country. Canoe trips up the rivers can also be arranged. The beaches are mainly of black volcanic sand, but there are a few white-sand beaches on the northeast of this island. Sports facilities include scuba diving, sailing and sport fishing.
Morne Trois Pitons National Park, covering 7000 hectares (17,000 acres) in the south-central part of Dominica, was established in July 1975. Places of interest in the park include the *Boiling Lake*, the second largest in the world which was discovered in 1922, and the *Emerald Pool, Middleham Falls, Sari Sari Falls, Trafalgar Triple Waterfalls, Freshwater Lake, Boeri Lake* and the *Valley of Desolation*.
Cabrits Historical Park was designated a park in 1987. Attractions include the **Cabrits Peninsular** which contains the historical ruins of *Fort Shirley* and *Fort George*, 18th- and early 19th-century forts, and a museum at Fort Shirley. The usual touring spots in addition to the above include the **Carib Indian Territory**, the *Sulphur Springs*, the *Central Forest Reserve, Botanical Gardens, Titou Gorge, L'Escalier Tête Chien*, several areas of rainforest and a variety of fauna and flora.

SOCIAL PROFILE

FOOD & DRINK: In general it is wise to order the speciality of the house or of the day to ensure freshness. Island cooking includes Creole, Continental and American. Creole dishes include *tee-tee-ree* (tiny freshly spawned fish), *lambi* (conch), *agouti* (a rodent), *manicou*, pig and wild pigeon (smoked meats), and *crabbacks* (backs of red and black crabs stuffed with seasoned crab meat). *Bello Hot Pepper Sauce* is made locally and served everywhere with almost everything. Food prices on Dominica are usually reasonable. Restaurants close at about 2400 weekdays and are open later at weekends. Root vegetables, such as yams and turnips, are often referred to as 'provisions' on a menu. **Drink:** Island fruit juices are excellent as are rum punches, particularly *Anchorage Hotel's* coconut rum punch (made from fresh coconut milk, sugar, rum, bitters, vanilla and grenadine). *Sea moss* is a non-alcoholic beverage made from sea moss or seaweed, with a slightly minty taste. Spirits, local rum especially, are inexpensive. Wines (mainly French and Californian), are expensive. There is a wide choice of beers available. There are no licensing hours.
NIGHTLIFE: Some hotel lounges stay open until 2300 and there is music at weekends at several hotels. A favourite haunt in Roseau, *La Robe Creole*, has stereo music nightly with live bands at weekends. Popular local discotheques include *The Warehouse, Green Grotto, Aquacade* and *Night Box*. There are often folklore evenings with authentic costumes and music. Hotel staff will generally be able to advise visitors as to the best places.
SHOPPING: There is no duty-free shopping, but there are some excellent buys to be found among native handicrafts including hats, bags and rugs made from vetiver grass joined with wild banana strands. The *Carib Reserve Crafts Centre* produces bags made from two layers of reeds that are buried in the ground to achieve a 3-colour effect and covered with a layer of broad banana-type leaf to make them waterproof. There are also two clothing companies and the denim jeans bought here are cheaper than on the other islands to which they are exported. **Shopping hours:** 0800-1300 and 1400-1600 Monday to Friday, 0800-1300 Saturday.
SPORTS: Scuba and **snorkelling** equipment may be hired through hotels and local tour operators. There are facilities for **parasailing, windsurfing** and **water-skiing** at many seaside hotels. Fifteen-minute parasailing flights are available for parties of four or more. Windsurf boards may be hired. Speedboats can be hired for water-skiing. **Motor boats** and **sailing boats** can be chartered at the Anchorage Hotel or through tour operators. **Angling** charters can be arranged for parties of fishermen through the Anchorage Hotel, which also operates a sports tour that includes **horseriding** on a mountain farm. There are a variety of other tours on offer for flora, fauna and **hiking** enthusiasts. Better hotels have swimming pools and of course the sea is warm and clear for **swimming. Tennis** and **squash** facilities are available at some hotels.
SPECIAL EVENTS: The *Quincentennial Commemoration* celebrations continue until November 1993. *Carnival* takes place just before Lent and is preceded by two weeks of celebrations, culminating on February 14-15 1994 in an explosion of parades, with the streets filled with costumed bands, dancing and music. Other events include *DOMFESTA* (the Dominican Festival of Arts, when everyone dresses in national costume) and *Creole Day*, both of which take place in July and August. *Creole Week*, during the last week in October, focuses on a different village or hamlet each year. A week of *Independence Celebrations* accompanies the *National Day* in early November, their climax being on November 3-4. Contact the Tourist Board for exact dates.
SOCIAL CONVENTIONS: Casual dress is normal, but swimwear and shorts are not worn on the streets in town. Evening clothes are informal but conservative. The Catholic Church is one of the most dominant social influences. **Photography:** Visitors should ask 'OK – Alright?' (the accepted opening gambit in a conversation) as a courteous gesture before taking photographs of local people. **Tipping:** A 10% service charge is added by most hotels and some restaurants. Other less touristic places do not add service to the bill and therefore tipping is discretionary, 10%-15% of the bill are acceptable. Taxi rates are set by law and therefore taxi drivers do not expect tips.

BUSINESS PROFILE

ECONOMY: Roughly 60% of the island is under cultivation, with bananas, coconuts, citrus fruits and cocoa being the main produce. The Dominican economy has a little light industry, producing vegetable oil, canned juices, cigarettes and soap, but relies mainly on its agriculture. During the late 1980s, the dominant enterprises went into deficit which prompted urgent efforts to diversify the island's economic base. Industrial development has been hampered, however, by the lack of an adequate infrastructure. Tourism, meanwhile, is not as developed in Dominica as elsewhere in the Caribbean, and Dominica was comparatively tardy in joining the Caribbean economic community CARICOM, largely due to fears about the consequences of opening its inefficient industry up to competition from the rest of the Community. Equipped with guarantees about their protection, however, Dominica finally joined. A series of grants and soft loans have been provided by the UK and the European Community to assist Dominica through this difficult stage in its development. The island's largest trading partners are the UK, the USA, Canada and Japan; Barbados and Guadeloupe are the largest within the Caribbean region.
BUSINESS: Government office hours: 0800-1300 and 1400-1700 Monday, 0800-1300 and 1400-1600 Tuesday to Friday.
COMMERCIAL INFORMATION: The following organisations can offer advice:
Dominica Association of Industry and Commerce (DAIC), PO Box 85, 15 King George V Street, Roseau, Dominica. Tel: 448 2874; *or*
Dominica Export-Import Agency (Dexia), PO Box 173, Roseau, Dominica. Tel: 448 2780. Fax: 448 6308. Telex: 8626; *or*
Dominica National Development Corporation, PO Box 293, Bath Estate, Roseau, Dominica. Tel: 448 2045. Fax: 448 5840.

HISTORY & GOVERNMENT

HISTORY: Columbus discovered the island, which was occupied by Carib Indians (some of whose descendants remain), in 1493 and it was colonised by the French in the 1600s. In 1805 the island became a British possession, and remained under Britain until 1967 when internal self-government was granted, followed by full independence in 1978. Post-independence politics have been somewhat stormy, with two coup attempts during the early 1980s by leftist members of the island's Defence Force. As a result, the Force was abolished and Eugenia Charles was re-elected Dominica's Prime Minister – the first woman in the region to hold the office. She has retained power to date as head of the Dominica Freedom Party, winning three elections in a row, the most recent in May 1990. A former Prime Minister, Patrick John, was implicated in the second coup and imprisoned, but has since been released. John was leader of the Dominica Labour Party, formerly the main opposition, but since merged with other left-wing groupings to form the Labour Party of Dominica, which was led by the now deceased ex-Finance Minister Michael Douglas. In foreign policy, Charles has steered close to the West. French troops were involved in putting down both coups, and Charles was a key figure in the invasion of Grenada, having 'invited' the US to intervene in the island in her capacity as head of the Organisation of Eastern Caribbean States, of which Dominica is a member. Charles has also taken a lead in promoting political and economic unity among its fellow Windward Islands, although proponents of integration face continued resistance borne of political and traditional island rivalries.
GOVERNMENT: The President is Head of State and, in conjunction with a Cabinet, has executive power. The legislature is the unicameral House of Assembly, to which nine members are nominated and 21 elected by universal adult suffrage. The Prime Minister is leader of the majority in the House, currently Dame Mary Eugenia Charles, leader of the Dominican Freedom Party.

CLIMATE

Hot, subtropical climate throughout the year. The main rainy season is between June and October, when it is hottest.
Required clothing: Lightweight cottons and linens. Waterproofing is advisable throughout most of the year.

ROSEAU Dominica (18m)

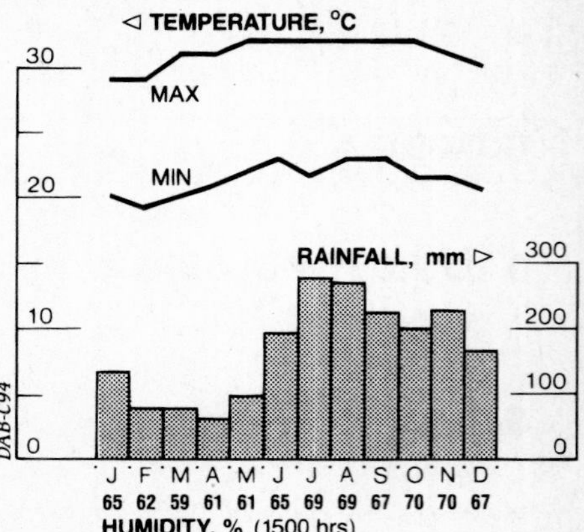

DOMINICAN REPUBLIC

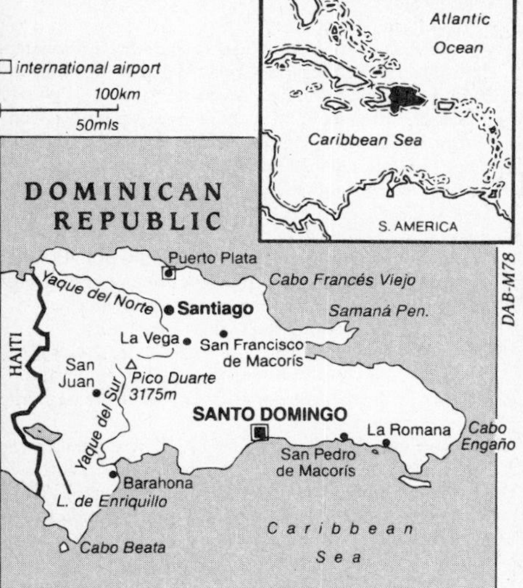

Location: Caribbean, island of Hispaniola; east of Cuba.

Secretaría de Estado de Turismo
Avenida George Washington
Santo Domingo, DN
Tel: 682 8181. Telex: 3460303.

The Caribbean Tourism Organisation
Suite 315
Vigilant House
120 Wilton Road
London SW1V 1JZ
Tel: (071) 233 8382. Fax: (071) 873 8551.

British Consulate
Saint George School
Abraham Lincoln 552
Santo Domingo, DR
Tel: 562 5015/10. Fax: 562 5015. Telex: 3460781.

Embassy of the Dominican Republic
1715 22nd Street, NW
Washington, DC
20008
Tel: (202) 332 6280. Fax: (202) 265 8057.

Dominican Tourist Office Information Centre
485 Madison Avenue
New York, NY
10022
Tel: (212) 867 0833. Telex: 427051 DTIC UI.

Embassy of the United States of America
Unit 5500
Calle César Nicolás Pensón
esq. Calle Leopoldo Navarro
Santo Domingo, DN
Tel: 541 2171. Fax: 686 7437. Telex: 3460013.

General Consulate of the Dominican Republic
Esso Tower
1650 de Maisonneuve West
Montréal, Québec
H3H 2P3
Tel: (514) 933 9008. Fax: (514) 933 8450.

Consulates in: Edmonton, Saint John, St John's and Vancouver.

Dominican Republic Tourist Board
Suite 302
1650 de Maisonneuve West
Montréal, Québec
H3H 2P3
Tel: (514) 933 9008.

Canadian Embassy
PO Box 2054
Malimo Gomez 30
Santo Domingo 1, DN
Tel: 689 0002. Fax: 689 2691. Telex: 346 0270.

AREA: 48,422 sq km (18,696 sq miles).
POPULATION: 7,170,000 (1990).
POPULATION DENSITY: 148.1 per sq km.
CAPITAL: Santo Domingo. **Population:** 1,410,000 (1983).
GEOGRAPHY: The Dominican Republic is in the Caribbean, sharing the island of Hispaniola with Haiti and constituting the eastern two-thirds of land. The landscape is forested and mountainous, with valleys, plains and plateaux. The soil is fertile with excellent beaches on the north, southeast and east coasts, rising up to the mountains.
LANGUAGE: Spanish is the official language. Some English is also spoken.
RELIGION: Roman Catholic; small Protestant and Jewish minorities.
TIME: GMT - 4.

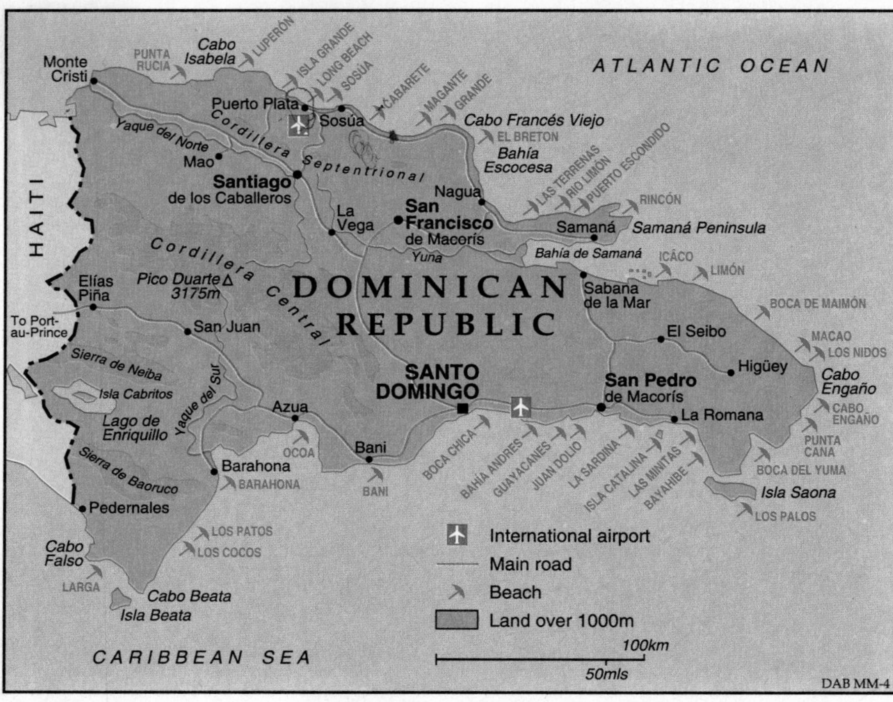

ELECTRICITY: 110 volts AC, 60Hz. There are frequent power cuts and visitors should bring a torch with them.
COMMUNICATIONS: Telephone: Full IDD available. Country code: 1 809. **Fax:** There are facilities at several locations in Santo Domingo; some large hotels also offer this service. **Telex/telegram:** Telexes and telegrams may be sent from RCA Global Communications Inc., Santo Domingo, or from ITT-America Cables and Radio Inc., Santo Domingo. Large hotels have facilities. **Post:** Airmail takes about seven days to reach Europe. It is advisable to post all mail at the Central Post Office in Santo Domingo to ensure rapid handling. **Press:** All daily papers are in Spanish. The English-language *Santo Domingo News* is published weekly on Wednesdays and may be obtained in hotels.
BBC World Service and Voice of America frequencies: From time to time these change. See the section *How to Use this Book* for more information.

BBC:				
MHz	17.840	15.220	9.915	5.975
Voice of America:				
MHz	15.21	11.70	6.130	0.930

PASSPORT/VISA

Regulations and requirements may be subject to change at short notice, and you are advised to contact the appropriate diplomatic or consular authority before finalising travel arrangements. Details of these may be found at the head of this country's entry. Any numbers in the chart refer to the footnotes below.

	Passport Required?	Visa Required?	Return Ticket Required?
Full British	Yes	1	Yes
BVP	Not valid	-	-
Australian	Yes	4	Yes
Canadian	Yes	4	Yes
USA	Yes	4	Yes
Other EC	Yes	1/2	Yes
Japanese	Yes	3	Yes

PASSPORTS: Valid passport required by all.
British Visitors Passport: Not acceptable.
VISAS: Required by all except:
(a) **[1]** nationals of Denmark, Greece, Italy, Spain and the UK for a period of 90 days and for tourist purposes;
(b) **[2]** nationals of Belgium, France and its overseas departments and territories, Germany, Ireland, Luxembourg, The Netherlands, Portugal and foreign nationals who are legal residents of Denmark, France, the UK, Germany, Greece, Ireland, Italy, The Netherlands, Portugal and Spain in possession of a valid passport and a Tourist Card – cost £10 and valid for 60 days from date of entry;

(c) **[3]** nationals of Japan for a maximum of 90 days and for tourist purposes only;
(d) nationals of Argentina, Austria, Costa Rica, Ecuador, Finland, Iceland, Israel, South Korea, Liechtenstein, Norway, Peru, Sweden, Switzerland and Uruguay, for a maximum of 90 days and for tourist purposes only;
(e) **[4]** nationals of Australia, any legal resident of Canada and any legal resident of the USA (including Puerto Rico and the Virgin Islands) in possession of a valid passport and a Tourist Card – cost: £10, valid for 60 days from date of entry;
(f) nationals of Andorra, Antigua & Barbuda, Bahamas, Barbados, Brazil, Bulgaria, Czechoslovakia, Dominica, Hungary, Jamaica, Mexico, Monaco, Paraguay, Poland, Romania, St Lucia, St Vincent & the Grenadines, San Marino, Suriname, Trinidad & Tobago, Turks and Caicos Islands, any legal resident of Venezuela and the former Yugoslavia in possession of a valid passport and a Tourist Card – cost: £10, valid for 60 days from date of entry.
Note: Persons who were born in Cuba are not allowed to enter the Dominican Republic without a visa or a re-entry permit, even if holding a passport of another nationality but keeping the Cuban nationality.
Due to the current upheaval in Yugoslavia, the situation regarding visas is presently unclear. Contact the Embassy for further information. For addresses, see top of entry.
Types of visa: Tourist visa costs £12. There are also Business and Student visas. All visas have to be authorised by the authorities in the Dominican Republic and take anything up to 8 weeks to obtain unless requested by cable (the cost of which must be paid by the applicant).
Validity: Tourist visa is valid for 90 days and one entry. Business and Student visas are valid for up to a year.
Application to: Consulate (or Consular Section of Embassy). For addresses, see top of entry.
Application requirements: (a) Application form. (b) Photo. (c) Proof of sufficient funds to cover stay.
Working days required: 6-8 weeks.
Temporary residence: Consult the Embassy to enquire about Residence visas.
Note: The month in the birth date should be spelled out so as to avoid confusion when entered in the visa.

MONEY

Currency: Dominican Peso (RD$) = 100 centavos. Notes are in denominations of RD$1000, 500, 100, 50, 20, 10, 5 and 1. Coins are in denominations of RD$1, and 50, 25, 10, 5 and 1 centavos.
Currency exchange: The Peso is not available outside of the Dominican Republic. Currency of United States, Canada, Germany, Italy, Mexico, Switzerland and Venezuela may be converted into local currency. At departure all unspent local currency should be reconverted into US Dollars at any bank. Since August 1990 the rate of exchange has been fixed at RD$10.20 for each US Dollar when changing into local currency and US$1 for RD$10.50 when changing back. Controversial legislation in 1990 decreed that all visitors are required to exchange US$100 or equivalent on entry; this may be repealed or modified. All exchange must be done through official dealers; these consist of banks and hotels approved by the Central Bank.
Credit cards: Access/Mastercard, American Express, Diners Club and Visa are accepted. Check with your credit card company for details of merchant acceptability and other services which may be available.
Travellers cheques are accepted by some banks.
Exchange rate indicators: The following figures are included as a guide to the movements of the Dominican Peso against Sterling and the US Dollar:

Date:	Oct '89	Oct '90	Oct '91	Oct '92
£1.00=	10.13	21.25	22.14	20.19
$1.00=	6.41	10.88	12.75	12.73

Note: See *Currency exchange* above for fixed exchange rates.

DOMINICAN REPUBLIC	HEALTH REGULATIONS	VISA REGULATIONS Code-Link
GALILEO/WORLDSPAN	 TI-DFT/SDQ/HE	TI-DFT/SDQ/VI
SABRE	TIDFT/SDQ/HE	 TIDFT/SDQ/VI

To access this information on your CRS, swipe the barcode with a light pen or type in the text under the barcode. For more information, see the introduction *How to Use This Book*.

Currency restrictions: Import and export of local currency is prohibited. Free import of foreign currency allowed but subject to declaration; export is limited to the amount declared.
Banking hours: 0800-1600 Monday to Friday.

DUTY FREE

The following goods may be imported into the Dominican Republic without incurring customs duty:
200 cigarettes or tobacco products to the value of US$5;
1 bottle of alcohol (opened) to the value of US$5;
A reasonable amount of perfume (opened);
Gifts up to a value of US$100.
Prohibited items: Agricultural and horticultural products.

PUBLIC HOLIDAYS

Public holidays observed in the Dominican Republic are as follows:
Apr 9 '93 Good Friday. **Apr 14** Pan-American Day. **May 1** Labour Day. **Jul 16** Foundation of Sociedad la Trinitaria. **Aug 16** Restoration Day. **Sep 24** Las Mercedes. **Oct 12** Columbus Day. **Oct 24** United Nations Day. **Nov 1** All Saints' Day. **Dec 25-26** Christmas. **Jan 1 '94** New Year's Day. **Jan 6** Epiphany. **Jan 21** La Altagracia. **Jan 26** Duarte's Birthday. **Feb 27** Independence Day.

HEALTH

Regulations and requirements may be subject to change at short notice, and you are advised to contact your doctor well in advance of your intended date of departure. Any numbers in the chart refer to the footnotes below.

	Special Precautions?	Certificate Required?
Yellow Fever	No	No
Cholera	No	No
Typhoid & Polio	1	-
Malaria	2	-
Food & Drink	3	-

[1]: Polio is endemic. The risk of contracting typhoid is uncertain, vaccination strongly advised.
[2]: Malaria risk, exclusively in the malignant *falciparum* form, exists throughout the year in urban areas of Dajabón Municipio (Dajabón Prov.), Jimaní Municipio (Independencia Prov.) and Pedernales Municipio (Pedernales Prov.); and rural areas of Bánica, Comendador and El Llano Municipios (Elias Piña Prov.), Guayubín and Pepillo Salcedo Municipios (Montecristi Prov.), Restauración Municipio (Dajabón Prov.) and Pedernales Provincio.
[3]: All water should be regarded as being potentially contaminated and sterilisation should be considered essential. Water used for drinking, brushing teeth or making ice should have first been boiled or otherwise sterilised. Avoid all fresh dairy products; milk is unpasteurised and should be boiled. Powdered or tinned milk is available and is advised, but make sure that it is reconstituted with pure water. Only eat well-cooked meat and fish, preferably served hot. Pork, salad and mayonnaise may carry increased risk. Vegetables should be cooked and fruit peeled.
Rabies is present. For those at high risk, vaccination before arrival should be considered. If you are bitten abroad seek medical advice without delay. For more information consult the *Health* section at the back of the book.
Bilharzia (schistosomiasis) is present. Avoid swimming and paddling in fresh water. Swimming pools which are well-chlorinated and maintained are safe.
Hepatitis is present, precautions strongly advised.
Health care: Health insurance (to include emergency repatriation) is strongly recommended.

TRAVEL - International

AIR: The Dominican Republic's national airline is *Compañía Dominicana de Aviación C por A (DO).*
Approximate flight time: From *London* to Santo Domingo is 11 hours (including a stopover).
International airports: *Santo Domingo (SDQ)* (Internacional de las Americas), 30km (18 miles) east of the city (travel time – 45 minutes). Bus to the city departs from 0700-1730. Return is from Expreso Dominicano bus station. Taxi services are available to Santo Domingo. Airport facilities include outgoing duty-

free shop with perfumes, designer fashions, cigarettes, cameras and spirits; post office; banking and exchange facilities (0800-1730); restaurant (0800-2100); bar (0800-2100) and car hire (*Avis, National, Nelly* and *Quality*).

Puerto Plata International Airport (POP) (La Union). Airport facilities include outgoing duty-free shop with perfumes, spirits, cameras and cigarettes; banking and exchange facilities (0800-1730); restaurant (0800-1900); bar (0800-1900) and car hire (*Avis*).

Departure tax: RD$15 on all international flights; for foreigners living abroad – US$10. Passengers for direct transit and children under 2 years are exempt.

Note: There is a heavy tax payable on tickets purchased in the Dominican Republic.

SEA: *Commodore Cruise Line, Carnival Cruise Lines, Flagship Line, Norwegian American* and *Holland America* stop at the north coast. A cruise port was opened recently in Santo Domingo.

TRAVEL - Internal

AIR: *Compañía Dominicana de Aviación C por A* operates regular flights between Santo Domingo, Santiago, Puerto Plata and Barahona. Planes may also be chartered. For more information contact the airline direct.

ROAD: There is a reasonable network of roads, including the *Sanchez Highway* running westwards from Santo Domingo to Elias Pina on the Haitian frontier; the *Mella Highway* extending eastwards from Santo Domingo to Higuey in the southeast; and the *Duarte Highway* running north and west from Santo Domingo to Santiago and to Monte Cristi on the northwest coast. Not all roads in the Dominican Republic are all-weather and 4-wheel drive vehicles are recommended for wet weather. Checkpoints near military installations are ubiquitous, though no serious difficulties have been reported (those near the Haitian border are most likely to be sensitive). **Bus:** Cheap and efficient air-conditioned bus and coach services run from the capital to other major towns. **Car hire:** There are several car hire companies in Santo Domingo (including *Hertz* and *Avis*). Minimum age for car hiring is 25. A national or international licence can be used, but are only valid for 90 days. Credit cards are recommended for car hire transactions. **Documentation:** Foreign driving licence accepted.

URBAN: Santo Domingo has flat-fare bus and minibus services, and an estimated 7000 shared taxis called *Carro de Conchos*. These operate a 24-hour service, stop on demand and charge higher fares. In old Santo Domingo the streets are narrow with blind corners so care should be taken, particularly as Dominican drivers have a tendency to use their horns rather than their brakes. Horse-drawn carriages are available for rent in most cities for tours around parks and plazas.

JOURNEY TIMES: The following chart gives approximate journey times (in hours and minutes) from Santo Domingo to other major cities and towns in the Dominican Republic.

	Air	Road
Santiago	0.30	4.30
Puerto Plata	0.45	3.15
Samana	0.35	4.30
La Romana	0.25	1.30
Punta Cana	0.30	4.15

ACCOMMODATION

HOTELS: There are many hotels in the Dominican Republic and extensive development is under way. The southeast coast is noted for its modern hotels and beautiful beaches. In the capital the choice runs from clean, neat and cheap to plush, with rates remaining the same

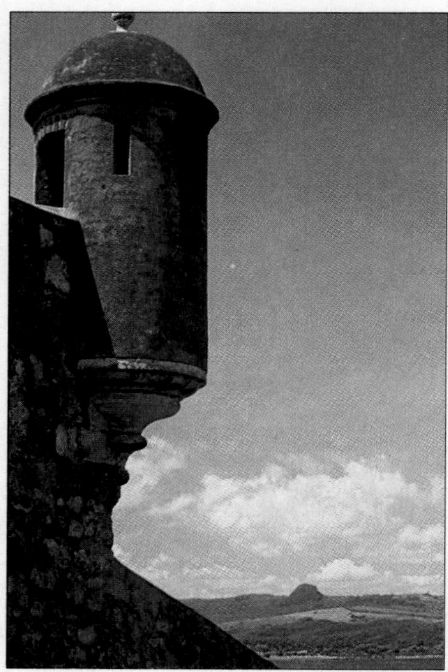

and surrounded by countless stalactites, stalagmites and lush tropical vegetation.

One hour east of Santo Domingo is the city of **La Romana**, home to the understated elegance and graceful charm of the 7000-acre *Casa de Campo* resort, designed by Oscar de la Renta. Nestled within the resort is *Altos de Chavon*, a reconstructed 15th-century Mediterranean-style village for culture and art which is perched high on a cliff overlooking the tropical *Chavon River* and Caribbean Sea. To stage major events, Altos de Chavon hosts a 5000-seat Greek amphitheatre, built in the traditional design of Epidauros.

The Northern, or **Amber Coast**, is so named because some of the most beautiful amber in the world is mined here. The *Amber Museum* houses a good display of unusual amber pieces found in this area.

Puerto Plata (The Silver Port) has some of the finest beaches of the Caribbean Islands. The Atlantic coast of the country is renowned for its miles of unspoilt beaches that surround Puerto Plata. Just two miles from the town is the *Playa Dorada* resort complex, within which is the *Jack Tar Village* resort. Just outside the Playa Dorada complex, in Puerto Plata, is the *Costamber Beach Resort*, with 5km (3 miles) of beach. *Mt Isabel de Torres* features a cable car which climbs over 760m (2500ft) above sea level. The breathtaking view of the Atlantic and the port of Puerto Plata is well worth the 7-minute climb up to the top of the mountain. 10 sq km (4 sq miles) of botanical gardens can be explored here.

The **Samana Peninsula** is located on the northern portion of the island, approximately two hours from Puerto Plata's international airport. Samana, with its transparent blue waters, miles of unspoilt beaches, and dozens of caves waiting to be explored, is a romantic paradise.

Other resorts: The Bahia Beach Resort, Cayo Levantado, El Portillo and Bavaro Beach.

boulevard in Santo Domingo, is known as the world's longest discotheque. Concerts and other cultural events are often held at the *Casa de Francia* and *Plaza de la Cultura* in Santo Domingo.

SHOPPING: Best buys are products made on the island including amber jewellery and decorative pieces which are a national speciality, some pieces encasing insects, leaves or dew drops within ancient petrified pine resin. Larimar or Dominican turquoise is another popular stone. Milky blue and polished pink pieces of conch shell are also made into jewellery. Rocking chairs, wood carvings, macramé, baskets, limestone carvings and tortoiseshell also make good buys. **Shopping hours:** 0800-1200 and 1400-1800 Monday to Saturday.

SPORT: Swimming: Although some shores are rough and rocky, magnificent stretches of beach can be found and many of the hotels have pools. **Scuba diving** and **snorkelling:** Only one place is fully equipped for scuba diving in Santo Domingo: *Mundo Submarino*, where experienced divers only can arrange half-day and all-day trips. Snorkelling gear can be borrowed or rented from resort hotels. **Sailing:** Small sailing craft are available through hotels in Santo Domingo and some north coast hotels. **Fishing:** Charter boats are available through hotels for offshore fishing for marlin, sailfish, dorado, benittos and other game fish. River fishing in flat-bottomed boats with guides can be hired at La Romana, Boca de Yuma and on the north coast. **Tennis:** There are many tennis courts and La Romana boasts a 10-court hillside village. **Golf:** There are championship golf courses at La Romana with other courses near Puerto Plata and the Santo Domingo Country Club.

Horseriding: Dominicans love horseriding and their country offers possibly the best riding in the Caribbean. Regular polo games are held at Sierra Prieta in Santo Domingo and at Casa de Campo near La Romana where guests can join in the twice-weekly competitions.

Baseball: Baseball is another Dominican passion. The professional winter season runs from October to January, and the summer season from April to September. Ask locals or look in the local paper for schedules and the nearest game.

all year because of steady business traffic. At resort hotels winter prices are higher and in summer prices drop by up to 40%. Hotels outside Santo Domingo and La Romana are considerably less expensive whatever the season. Service charge and a 5% Government tax will be added to all bills. **Grading:** There is a 5-star grading system, but visitors should note that even the highest grade is somewhat lower in standard than is general in the Caribbean.

GUEST-HOUSES: Guest-houses are very economical, and best found after arrival in the country.

SELF-CATERING: Self-catering establishments are available in Puerto Plata at very reasonable rates.

CAMPING: There are no official sites, and camping is only possible in rural areas after obtaining permission from the landowner.

RESORTS & EXCURSIONS

Santo Domingo: The colonial section has been carefully restored to retain its original charm, and is home to the first university, cathedral and hospital built in the New World. The modern city of Santo Domingo, by contrast, is a thriving port city, equipped with discotheques, gambling casinos, shops and the *Cultural Plaza* which houses the *Gallery of Modern Art* and the *National Theatre*. Just a few miles east of the city is a remarkable cave complex, *Los Tres Ojos de Agua (The Three Eyes of Water)*, so-called because it contains three turquoise lagoons on three different levels, each fed by an underground river

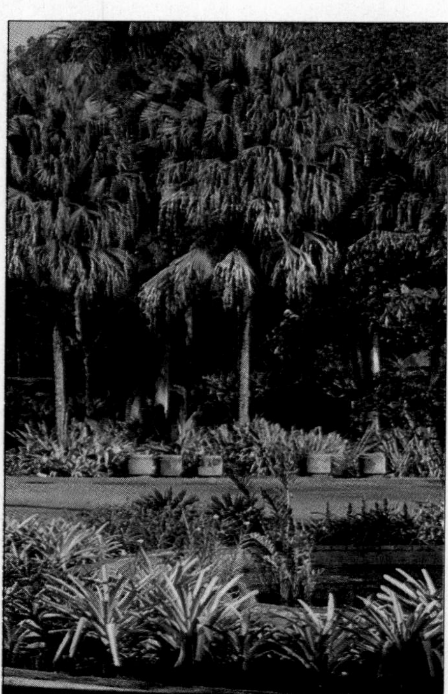

SOCIAL PROFILE

FOOD & DRINK: Native Dominican cooking is appealing. Beef is expensive (Dominicans raise fine cattle, but most is exported) and local favourites are pork and goat meat. There is plenty of fresh fish and seafood, island-grown tomatoes, lettuce, papaya, mangoes and passion fruit and all citrus fruits are delicious. Local dishes include *la bandera* (meaning 'the flag', comprising white rice, red beans, stewed meat, salad and fried green plaintain), *chicharrones* (crisp pork rind), *chicharrones de pollo* (small pieces of fried chicken), *casava* (fried yuca), *moro de habicuelas* (rice and beans), *sopa criolla dominicana* (native soup of meat and vegetables), *pastelon* (baked vegetable cake), *sancocho* (stew with anything up to 18 ingredients). **Drink:** *El Presidente* (Dominican beer) is very good, as are rum drinks such as the local *Brugal* or *Bermudez*. *Rum añejo* (old, dark rum) with ice makes a good after-dinner drink. Native coffee is excellent and very strong. Locally produced beer and rums are cheaper than imported alcohol which tends to be expensive.

NIGHTLIFE: Choice varies from a Las Vegas-style review, discotheques and casinos to a quiet café by the sea in Santo Domingo. Hotels offer more traditional shows including folk music and dancing. Popular dances are the *salsa* and the *merengue* accompanied by a 3-man group called *perico ripiao*. The *Malécon*, along a seaside

SPECIAL EVENTS: The following is a selection of the major festivals and other special events celebrated annually in the Dominican Republic. For a complete list contact the Consulate or Tourist Office Information Centre.

Apr *Las Cachuas de Cabral* (Cabral). **Jun** *Espiritu Santu* (Villa Mella, Santa Maria, San Cristóbal, El Batey and San Juan de la Maguana). **Aug 16** *Restoration Day* (Santo Domingo, La Vega, San Pedro de Macorís and Santiago). **Feb** *Carnival* (Santo Domingo, Samaná, La Vega San Pedro de Macorís, La Romana).

Throughout the year, in addition to the above, various Saint's Days are celebrated in different places.

SOCIAL CONVENTIONS: The Dominican lifestyle is more American than Latin, with no siestas or long, late lunches. The non-Latin ambience is indicated by the fact that, though the culture is rich in Roman Catholic and Spanish influences, 72-hour divorces may be obtained. Daytime dress is generally casual but beachwear and shorts are only acceptable in resorts and pools. Evenings tend to be dressier with jackets (although not necessarily ties) recommended for men at better restaurants, hotels and for social functions.

Tipping: Hotel and restaurant bills automatically include a 10% service charge but an additional tip may be given as an appreciation of good service. Taxi drivers on the fixed routes do not expect tips.

BUSINESS PROFILE

ECONOMY: Sugar is the Dominican Republic's main export earner, and the low world price has done much to depress the economy during the 1980s, while production of other traditional cash crops, principally tobacco, coffee and cocoa, has been in steady decline. Metals and ores, including ferro-nickel, gold and silver, are the other important exports. Oil exploration concessions have been granted, but no deposits have been found to date. Coal deposits have been found but are yet to be exploited. Manufacturing industry is confined to building materials, consumer goods and light engineering. Most of it is state-owned. Tourism is being developed but has yet to make a significant impact on the economy. The United States buy most of the Republic's sugar exports and provides about 30% of imports. Japan is another major source of imports. Trade with the European Community and the UK is steady at a low level.
BUSINESS: It is usual for business people to dress smartly and to deal formally with each other at first, although the general atmosphere is informal. Spanish is the main business language and a knowledge of it will be of assistance. Enquire at hotel for interpreter services.
Office hours: 0830-1200 and 1400-1800 Monday to Friday. **Government office hours:** 0730-1430 Monday to Friday.
COMMERCIAL INFORMATION: The following organisation can offer advice: Cámara de Comercio y Producción del Distrito Nacional, Arz. Nouel 206, Apdo Postal 815, Santo Domingo, DN. Tel: 682 7206. Telex: 346-0877.
There are also official Chambers of Commerce in the larger towns.

HISTORY & GOVERNMENT

HISTORY: Columbus discovered the island of Hispaniola (which he called *La Española*) in 1492 and established it as his main base for the further exploration of the region; in 1697 the western part of the island came under the French, the east remained under Spanish control. In 1795 the city of Santo Domingo (the oldest city in the Americas, founded in 1496 by Columbus' brother) was ceded to the French. The battle of Palo Hincado, in 1808, in which the Dominican General Ramirez inflicted an important defeat on the French, heralded the collapse of French rule. The colony reverted to Spanish sovereignty in 1809, and in 1821 the colonial treasurer, José Nuñez de Caceres, proclaimed Santo Domingo's independence. This independence was short lived and in 1822 the Haitians invaded the colony and occupied it for 22 years, until on February 27, 1844, the independence of the Dominican Republic was proclaimed. After many years of civil war, dictatorship and US occupation, the Republic was ruled by the dictatorship of General Rafael Trujillo (1930-61), whose assassination led to a period of civil unrest. Under the control of President Joaquín Balaguer, who served three terms from 1966, the country has been reasonably stable. The main opposition party won the elections in 1978, despite attempts to disrupt the electoral process by President Balaguer's traditional supporters in the armed forces. After a further defeat in 1982, Dr Balaguer was again elected to the Presidency in 1986. At elections in May 1990, he was returned to office for a further 4-year term. Minor civil unrest accompanied a series of general strikes called in 1991 by the main trade union federation against government austerity measures. These were introduced following a stand-by agreement with the International Monetary Fund.
GOVERNMENT: The bicameral National Congress is the legislature, and members of both houses (Senate and Chamber of Deputies) are elected by universal adult suffrage, as is the President, who has executive power.

CLIMATE

Hot with tropical temperatures all year. Rainy season is from June to October. Hurricanes may sometimes occur during this time.
Required clothing: Lightweight cottons and linens throughout the year. Rainwear is advisable, particularly during the rainy season.

SANTO DOMINGO Dominican Rep. (19m)

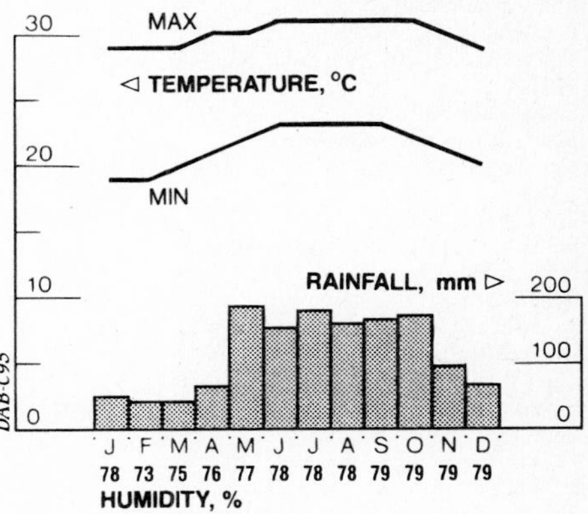

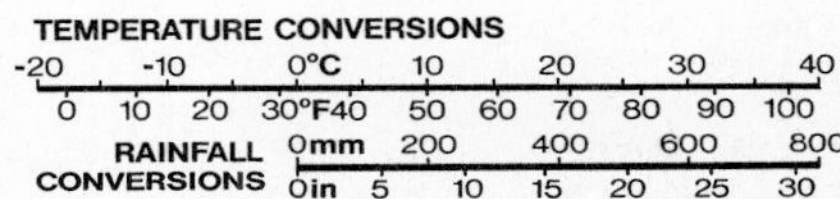

ECUADOR

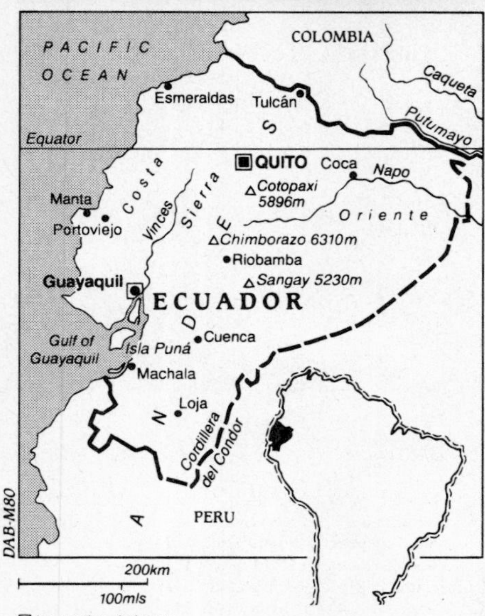

Location: South America.

Asociación Ecuatoriana de Agencias de Viajes y Turismo (ASECUT)
Casilla 1210
Edificio Banco del Pacifico, 5° Piso
Avenida Amazonas 720 y Veintimilla
Quito, Ecuador
Tel: (2) 503 669. Fax: (2) 503 669. Telex: 2749.
Corporación Ecuatoriana de Turismo
Reina Victoria 514 y Roca
Quito, Ecuador
Tel: (2) 527 002. Telex: 21158.
Embassy of the Republic of Ecuador
Flat 3B
3 Hans Crescent
Knightsbridge
London SW1X 0LS
Tel: (071) 584 1367. Fax: (071) 823 9701. Opening hours: 0930-1300 Monday to Friday.
British Embassy
Casilla 314
Calle González Suárez 111
Quito, Ecuador
Tel: (2) 560 670. Fax: (2) 560 730. Telex: 2138 PRODQT ED.
Consulates in: Guayaquil, Cuenca and Galápagos.
Embassy of the Republic of Ecuador
2535 15th Street, NW
Washington, DC 20009
Tel: (202) 234 7200. Fax: (202) 667 3482. Telex: 440129.
Ecuatoriana Airlines
1290 Avenue of the Americas
New York, NY
10014
Tel: (212) 354 1850.
Embassy of the United States of America
PO Box 538
Unit 5309
Avenida 12 Octubre y Patria 120
Quito, Ecuador
Tel: (2) 562 890. Fax: (2) 502 052.
Embassy of the Republic of Ecuador
Suite 1311, 50 O'Connor Street
Ottawa, Ontario
K1N 8L2
Tel: (613) 563 8206. Fax: (613) 235 5776.
Consulate of Ecuador
Suite 625
1010 rue Ste Catherine West
Montréal, Québec
H3B 3R3
Tel: (514) 874 4071. Fax: (514) 931 0252.
Canadian Embassy
Edifico Belmonte 6°
Avenida Corea 126 y Amazonas
Quito, Ecuador
Tel: (2) 458 102.

AREA: 270,670 sq km (104,506 sq miles).
POPULATION: 9,622,608 (1990).
POPULATION DENSITY: 39.8 per sq km (1990).
CAPITAL: Quito. **Population:** 1,281,849 (1990 estimate).
GEOGRAPHY: Ecuador is bounded to the north by Colombia, to the east and south by Peru, and to the west by the Pacific Ocean. There are three distinct zones: the *Sierra* or uplands of the Andes, running from the Colombian border in the north to Peru in the south, of which there are two main ranges, the Eastern and Western Cordilleras (divided by a long valley); the *Costa*, a coastal plain between the Andes and the Pacific with plantations of bananas, cacao, coffee and sugar; and the *Oriente*, the upper Amazon basin to the east, consisting of tropical jungles threaded by rivers. The latter, although comprising 36% of Ecuador's land area, contains only 3% of the population. Colonisation is, however, increasing in the wake of the oil boom.
LANGUAGE: Spanish with Quechua or Indian dialects. Some English is spoken.
RELIGION: 90% are nominally Roman Catholic.
TIME: GMT - 5 (Galapagos Islands GMT - 6).
ELECTRICITY: 110 volts AC, 50Hz.
COMMUNICATIONS: Telephone: IDD is available. Country code: 593. Callers should note that even if the person called is not there a charge may still be made. **Telex/telegrams:** Main hotels in Guayaquil, Quito and Cuenca have telex booths. There is also a service at the offices of IETEL *(Instituto Ecuatoriano de Telecommunicaciones)*. Telegrams may be sent from the chief telegraph office in main towns. There is a 24-hour service in Quito, and a service until 2000 at some hotels. **Post:** Airmail to Europe and the USA takes up to a week, but incoming deliveries are less certain. **Press:** Dailies are in Spanish and include *El Comercio* and *Hoy*, published in Quito; and *El Telégrafo* and *El Universo*, published in Guayaquil.
BBC World Service and Voice of America frequencies: From time to time these change. See the section *How to Use this Book* for more information.

BBC:				
MHz	17.84	15.22	9.915	9.590
Voice of America:				
MHz	18.82	15.18	9.525	1.735

PASSPORT/VISA

Regulations and requirements may be subject to change at short notice, and you are advised to contact the appropriate diplomatic or consular authority before finalising travel arrangements. Details of these may be found at the head of this country's entry. Any numbers in the chart refer to the footnotes below.

	Passport Required?	Visa Required?	Return Ticket Required?
Full British	Yes	No	Yes
BVP	Not valid	-	-
Australian	Yes	No	Yes
Canadian	Yes	No	Yes
USA	Yes	No	Yes
Other EC	Yes	No	Yes
Japanese	Yes	No	Yes

PASSPORTS: Valid passport required by all except nationals of Colombia with an identity card.
Note: Passports must be carried at all times.
British Visitors Passport: Not acceptable.
VISAS: Not required for stays of up to 90 days, *except* for nationals of China, Cuba, North Korea, South Korea and Vietnam.
With the exception of the UK, persons wishing to remain in Ecuador for between 3 and 6 months, for business reasons, require a visa. The cost of the visa will be approximately US$50.
Types of visa: Tourist, Business, Transit or Student (it is illegal to study on a Tourist visa).
Application to: Consulate (or Consular Section at Embassy). For addresses, see top of entry.
Application requirements: (a) 4 passport-size photos. (b) Valid passport. (c) US$50 for student and business visas. (d) Letter from Universities sending and receiving student needed for student visa. (e) Letter from Company sending and receiving businessperson required for business visa.
Working days required: Applications in person – 5.
Temporary residence: Persons wishing to stay longer than 6 months should apply to the Consulate for details of the procedures to be followed.

MONEY

Currency: Sucre (Su) = 100 centavos. Notes are in denominations of Su5000, 1000, 500, 100, 50, 20, 10 and 5. Coins are in denominations of Su50, 20, 10, 5, and 50 centavos.
Currency exchange: It is strongly advised to take US Dollar travellers cheques and currency, as these are the most easily negotiated in Ecuador (though some difficulty may be experienced outside of main towns). The rate of commission varies between 1% and 4%, so it is worth shopping around. *Roderigo Paz* bureaux de change are recommended as being reliable.
Credit cards: Access/Mastercard, American Express, Visa and Diners Club are accepted. Check with your credit card company for details of merchant acceptability and other services which may be available. The American Express office in Avenida Amazonas, Quito is very helpful to foreign travellers.
Travellers cheques: US Dollar travellers cheques are easily changed into US Dollar banknotes at the cambios. US Dollar travellers cheques are generally more easily negotiable than Sterling. See also *Currency exchange* above.
Exchange rate indicators: The following figures are included as a guide to the movements of the Sucre against Sterling and the US Dollar (free market rates):

Date:	**Oct '89**	**Oct '90**	**Oct '91**	**Oct '92**
£1.00=	924.5	1700.8	1930.36	2977.17
$1.00=	585.5	870.65	1112.28	1875.97

Currency restrictions: There are no restrictions on the import and export of either local or foreign currency.
Banking hours: 0900-1330 Monday to Friday; some banks are also open 0900-1330 Saturdays.

DUTY FREE

The following goods may be imported into Ecuador without incurring customs duty:
300 cigarettes or 50 cigars or 200g of tobacco;
1 litre of alcohol;
A reasonable amount of perfume for personal use;
Gifts up to the value of US$200.
Note: Prior permission is required for the import of firearms, ammunition, narcotics, fresh or dry meat and meat products, plants and vegetables.

PUBLIC HOLIDAYS

Public holidays observed in Ecuador are as follows:
Apr 9 '93 Good Friday. **Apr 10** Easter Saturday. **May 1** Labour Day. **May 24** Battle of Pichincha. **Jul 24** Birthday of Simón Bolívar. **Aug 10** Independence of Quito. **Oct 9** Anniversary of the Independence of Guayaquil. **Oct 12** Discovery of America. **Nov 1** All Saints' Day. **Nov 2** All Souls' Day. **Nov 3** Independence of Cuenca. **Dec 6** Foundation of Quito. **Dec 25** Christmas. **Jan 1 '94** New Year's Day. **Jan 6** Epiphany. **Mar 28-29** Carnival.
Note: Check with Tourist Board or Embassy for exact details.

HEALTH

Regulations and requirements may be subject to change at short notice, and you are advised to contact your doctor well in advance of your intended date of departure. Any numbers in the chart refer to the footnotes below.

	Special Precautions?	Certificate Required?
Yellow Fever	Yes	1
Cholera	Yes	No
Typhoid & Polio	Yes	-
Malaria	2	-
Food & Drink	3	-

[1]: Certificate recommended for all travellers over one year arriving from infected areas.
[2]: Malaria risk, predominantly in the benign *vivax* form, exists throughout the year below 1500m in the provinces of Esmereldas, Guayas, Manabí, El Oro, Los Rios, Morona Santiago, Napo, Pastaza, Zamora Chinchipe and Pichincha. Chloroquine-resistant *falciparum* has been reported.
[3]: All water should be regarded as being potentially contaminated. Water used for drinking, brushing teeth or making ice should have first been boiled or otherwise sterilised. Bottled water is available. Milk is unpasteurised and should be boiled. Powdered or tinned milk is available and is advised, but make sure that it is reconstituted with pure water. Avoid dairy products which are likely to have been made from unboiled local milk. Only eat well-cooked meat and fish, preferably served hot. Pork, salad and mayonnaise may carry increased risk. Vegetables should be cooked and fruit peeled.

Rabies is present. For those at high risk, vaccination before arrival should be considered. If you are bitten abroad seek medical advice without delay. For more information consult the *Health* section at the back of the book.
Hepatitis is widespread and inoculation with gamma globulin is highly recommended.
Health care: Medical facilities outside the major towns are extremely limited. Health insurance (to include emergency repatriation) is recommended.

TRAVEL - International

AIR: Ecuador's national airlines are *Ecuatoriana (EU)*, *SAN (MM)* and *TAME (EQ)*.
Approximate flight times: From Quito to *London* is 17 hours, to *Los Angeles* is 9 hours and to *New York* is 9 hours 30 minutes.
International airports: *Quito (UIO)* (Mariscal Sucre) is 8km (5 miles) from the city. There is a bus to the city every 20 minutes from 0600 to 2300. Return is from Ave 10 de Agosto. Taxis are available.
Guayaquil (GYE) (Simon Bolivar) is 5km (3 miles) from the city. There are bus and taxi services into the city.
Departure tax: 10% of ticket price for international departures, plus US$25 payable in US Dollars.
SEA: There are regular passenger/cargo services from Europe, including *Hamburg-South American, Royal Netherlands, Knutsen* and *Johnson Lines*, which take 20-22 days from Rotterdam and Le Havre. Others sail from Antwerp, Genoa and Liverpool, and the US West Coast *(Delta Line Cruises)*. Guayaquil is the main port for both passengers and freight.
ROAD: The Pan-American Highway bisects the country from the Colombian border at Rumichaca south to Quito and on to Riobamba, Cuenca, Loja, and ending at Macara near the border with Peru. See also *Road* in the *Travel – Internal* section below. **Bus:** *TEPSA* buses connect with several countries.

TRAVEL - Internal

AIR: The national airlines *Ecuatoriana (EU)*, *SAN-Saeta (MM)* and *TAME (EQ)* fly frequently between Guayaquil and Quito. A number of small airlines serve the coast and eastern part of the country. Flying is the usual mode of transport for intercity travel. Other airports include *Cuenca, Manta, Esmeraldas, Lago Agrio* and *Coca*.
Departure tax: 12% of ticket price for domestic departures.
Galapagos Islands: There are daily flights at 1300 to the Galapagos Islands on national airlines from both Quito and Guayaquil; note that non-Ecuadoreans have to pay more for their tickets on this route (US$40 is charged for visiting any national park).
SEA/RIVER: Ecuador's rocky coastline makes coast-hopping an inefficient and perhaps dangerous means of transport for the visitor. Several navigable rivers flow westwards into the Amazon basin but this region is often closed to visitors due to a territorial dispute with Peru. Dugout canoes, which carry up to about 25 people, are widely used as a means of transport in roadless areas, particularly in the Oriente jungles and in the northwest coastal regions. There are few passenger services between the mainland and the **Galapagos Islands**; once there, however, tourist boats, local mail steamers and hired yachts may be used to travel between islands.
RAIL: Since the floods of 1983 there have been no through-train services from Guayaquil to Quito. Sections from Riobamba to Quito (223km/139 miles) and from Alausí to Guayaquil (142km/88 miles) are in operation and there are continuing improvements. Although much of the line is in poor condition, the journey offers spectacular views, as the train climbs to 3238m (10,623ft) in 80km (50 miles), reaching its highest point at Urbina (3609m/11,841ft). For railway engineering enthusiasts the construction will be of interest, travelling through the Alausí loop and the Devil's Nose double zigzag.
ROAD: An extensive network of roads spreads out from the main north–south axis of the Pan-American Highway. The Government and *PetroEcuador* are developing highways into the Oriente. In general, road improvements are being put into effect rapidly but, due to the effect of earthquakes and flooding (in the south) during the last ten years, conditions remain variable; potholes and cracks in the road are sometimes sizeable. The roads between Quito and Guayaquil and between Quito, Latacunga, Ambato and Riobamba are completely paved. A road connects Quito, Otavalo, Ibarra and Tulcan. Tulcan is the frontier with Colombia. **Bus:** *TEPSA* buses connect with several countries. Bus travel has improved greatly and is generally more convenient than in the other Andean countries, as distances are shorter and there are more paved roads. The bus service between Quito and Guayaquil and from Quito to the main cities of the highlands needs reservations. **Car hire:** *Avis, Budget, National* and *Hertz* car rentals all operate in Ecuador. **Documentation:** International Driving Permit is required.
URBAN: Quito and Guayaquil have bus and minibus services operating at flat fares.
JOURNEY TIMES: The following chart gives approximate journey times from Quito (in hours and minutes) to other major cities/towns in Ecuador.

	Air	Road	Rail
Guayaquil	0.50	7.00	7.00
Cuenca	1.30	9.30	-
Ambato	-	2.30	-
Riobamba	-	3.30	3.00
Esmereldas	1.00	7.00	-
Puerto Ayora	2.30	-	-

ACCOMMODATION

HOTELS: Rooms should be booked at least a week in advance. Outside the main towns a more or less standard price is charged per person for one night in a *provision residencia*, or a hotel. There is, however, a minimum charge per person. A 10% service charge and 5% tax are added to upper and middle range hotel bills. Cheaper hotels usually charge 5% at the most. Hotel accommodation is very limited on the Galapagos Islands. Further information is available through the national hotel association, Asociacion Hotelera del Ecuador, Avenida America 5378, Quito, Ecuador. Tel: (2) 453 942.
Grading: Hotels in Ecuador have been graded into three main categories according to standard and price bracket. All categories provide at least basic facilities.
CAMPING/CARAVANNING: Camping facilities in Ecuador are run by American or European agencies, but these are very limited. There are two camping sites on the Galapagos Islands.

RESORTS & EXCURSIONS

For the purposes of this section, the country has been divided up into six principal areas: **Quito**, the cities of the **Andean highlands, Guayaquil, The Littoral, The Oriente** and the **Galapagos Islands**.
Quito: The capital city has a setting of great natural beauty, overshadowed by the volcano *Pichinca* with its twin peaks of *Ruca* and *Guagua*. The city has preserved much of its Spanish colonial character, the cathedral in the *Plaza Independencia* and the many old churches and monasteries being among the most notable instances of this. Also in the Plaza is the *Municipal Palace*, the *Archbishop's Palace* and the *Government Palace*. Many of the city's famous churches and monasteries contain priceless examples of Spanish art and sculpture, particularly the convent of *San Francisco* and the Jesuit church of *La Compania*. Other places in Quito worth visiting include the *Alameda Park*, the *Astronomical Observatory*, the *School of Fine Arts* and the modern *Legislative Palace*. As the cultural and political capital, Quito has a number of museums of colonial and modern art.
The Cities of the Andean Highlands: The Pan-American Highway traverses the country from north to south, a spectacular route which passes through all the

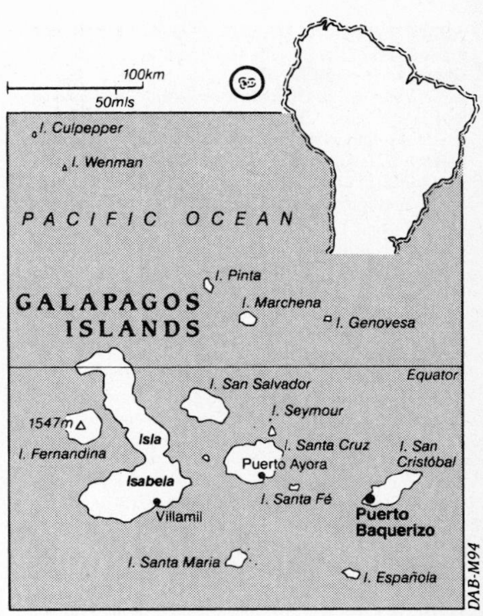

principal cities of the Andean Highlands. **Tulcan**, centre of a rich farming area, is the northernmost of these. Further south is **Chota,** still inhabited by the descendants of former slaves who retain some of their tribal customs. The peak of *Mount Imbabura* signals the approach to the valley of **Otavalo,** the town of the same name being famed for its craftwork and Indian market. Approaching **Quito**, one passes a granite monument which marks the Equator. South of Quito, the region of **Latacunga** and **Ambato** has much fine scenery, marked by an avenue of volcanos. The next city, **Cuenca**, was founded in 1577, and still contains many examples of Spanish colonial architecture. Contrasting with this, a vast cathedral has recently been built. Interesting provincial towns surrounding Cuenca include **Ingapirca,** an ancient Inca settlement. In the highlands of southern Ecuador, **Loja** is the last city of importance on the Pan-American Highway, being originally a trading station on the Spanish 'gold road'.
Guayaquil: Ecuador's biggest city, it is also the chief port and commercial centre. A good starting point for sightseeing is the *Rotonda*, the city's most historic landmark, which faces the beautiful garden promenade of *Paseo de las Colonias*. Across the *Malecon Boulevard* are the *Government Palace* and city hall, while at the northern end one can find the ancient fortress of *La Planchada*. Other places of interest include the church of *Santo Domingo*, the old residential section of *Las Penas* and the *Municipal Museum*.
The Littoral: This is a narrow coastal belt, 560km (350 miles) in length. The chief ports provide visitors with some of the best resorts for deep-sea fishing on the west coast. Particularly attractive are the towns of **Playas Posoria** and **Salinas,** while **Esmeraldas**, one of the country's most important ports, is also known for its beautiful beaches. The region of **Santo Domingo de los Colorados,** situated some 90km (55 miles) west of Quito, is the domain of the Colorados Indians who still practise many of their ancient customs.
The Oriente: The Oriente is a primeval world of virgin forests and exotic flora and fauna, still mainly inhabited by the Indians. The principal towns of the area are **El Puyo, Tena, Macas, Lago Agrio, Sucúa** and **Zamora.** Tourist excursions are available along the rivers, which provide the principal method of transport. **Baños** is worth visiting, taking its name from the numerous springs and pools of hot and cold mineral waters. It is also the gateway to the **Amazon region,**

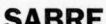

ECUADOR	**HEALTH REGULATIONS**	**VISA REGULATIONS** Code-Link
GALILEO/WORLDSPAN	TI-DFT/UIO/HE	 TI-DFT/UIO/VI
SABRE	 TIDFT/UIO/HE	 TIDFT/UIO/VI

To access this information on your CRS, swipe the barcode with a light pen or type in the text under the barcode. For more information, see the introduction *How to Use This Book*.

passing through the spectacular gorge of the *River Pastaza*. From Baños, one may climb up *Cotopaxi* which, at 5896m (19,344ft), is the highest active volcano in the world. Other volcanoes include *Chimborazo* and *Tungurahua*. All have refuges at the snow-line where intrepid walkers can make overnight stays.
Galapagos Islands: Situated about 800km (500 miles) west of the Ecuadorian mainland, the islands are bleak, barren and rocky. Made famous by Charles Darwin's scientific voyage in the 'Beagle' during the last century, the islands' unique wildlife – which includes giant tortoises, lizards and iguanas – remains the most interesting feature for the modern-day visitor. The islands have been turned into a national park in an attempt to preserve their natural state, and in 1978 UNESCO declared the Galapagos to be 'the universal natural heritage of humanity'. Accommodation and travel can generally be arranged either inclusively from your home country or through local tour operators once in Ecuador. (Shop around and take advice before booking; quality of service and reliability vary greatly.) Accommodation is extremely limited and food is not cheap. There are a few small restaurants. Boat trips around the islands can be arranged locally.

SOCIAL PROFILE

FOOD & DRINK: Avoid unpeeled fruits and raw vegetables. Best of the jungle fruits include *chirimoya*, with a delicious custard-like inside; *mamey*, which has a red, sweet, squash-like meat; *pepinos*, a sweet white and purple striped cucumber-like fruit. Specialities include *llapingachos* (pancakes with mashed potato and cheese); shrimp or lobster *ceviche; locro* (stew of potatoes and cheese); *humitas* (flavoured sweetcorn tamale); and the national delicacy of baked guinea pig. Restaurants have waiter service and there are café-style bars. **Drink:** Ecuador has some of the best beer in South America. International drinks and whiskies are available but expensive. An Ecuadorian speciality is a unique fruit juice called *naranjilla* – a taste somewhere between citrus and peach. Good Chilean wine is available, but is expensive. The best local drink is *paico*, made from fresh lemon. There are no licensing hours.
NIGHTLIFE: There is little nightlife except in Quito and Guayaquil, where there are excellent restaurants and other attractions. In smaller towns, social life takes place in the home and in private clubs. The cinema is the most popular entertainment.
SHOPPING: Bargaining is acceptable in small shops and in markets, but prices are usually fixed in 'tourist stores'. A few stores around the major hotels have fixed prices. In the Province of Azuay, the cities of Cuenca and Gualaceo offer a wide variety of handicrafts at *ferias* or special market days. The top attractions are the ferias of Otavalo, Ambato, Latacunga, Saquisili and Riobamba, held once a week. They offer the visitor excellent bargains for Indian crafts and silver. Principal silver stores are in Quito. Special purchases include native woodcarvings, varnished and painted ornaments made of bread dough, Indian tiles, woollen and orlon rugs, blankets, baskets, leather goods, *shigras* (shoulder bags) and handloomed textiles, aboriginal art and native weapons. **Shopping hours:** 0900-1300 and 1500-1900 Monday to Friday, 0830-1230 Saturday.
SPORT: Soccer: Football is one of the main national sports. Pelota de Guante: **Gloveball** is played with a heavy ball and leather glove. **Golf and tennis:** Popular around Quito and on the coast. **Horseriding and hiking:** Especially in the Sierra country. Jungle tours offered. **Watersports: Swimming, fishing** (the game fishing off the west coast is particularly good), **sailing** and **diving** are all available.
SPECIAL EVENTS: The following is a selection of the major festivals and other special events celebrated annually in Ecuador:
Mar 28-Apr 1 *Holy Week*. **May 24** *Battle of Pichincha*. **Jun** *Corpus Christi* (harvest festivals in mountain villages). **Jun 24** *Feast of John the Baptist*, especially in Otavalo. **Jul 24** *Simón Bolivar's Birthday*. **Aug 10** *Independence Day*. **Sep (first two weeks)** *Yamor's Festival*, Otalavo (native masks, costumes and dances). **Sep 20-26** *Bananas Fair*, Machala. **Sep 24-28** *Lakes Festival*, Ibarra. **Oct 9** *International Fair*, Guayaquil (celebration of town's independence). **Nov 2** *All Souls' Day* (visits to cemeteries). **Dec 24** *Christmas Eve* (costume pageants). **Dec 31** *New Year's Eve* (effigies of old year's events burnt in streets). **Feb** *Carnival* (3-day national celebration).
SOCIAL CONVENTIONS: Casual wear is widely acceptable, but business people are expected to dress smartly. Smart clothes are often required when visiting hotel dining rooms and better restaurants. Beachwear should only be worn on the beach and revealing clothes should not be worn in towns. Smoking is widely accepted. **Photography:** A tip may be requested if you wish to take someone's photograph. **Tipping:** 10% service charge is usually added to the bill in hotels and restaurants. Taxi drivers do not expect tips.

BUSINESS PROFILE

ECONOMY: Ecuador's economy rests on the twin pillars of oil and agriculture, both of which have undergone widely fluctuating fortunes in recent years. Ecuador is the world's largest exporter of bananas, and also grows coffee, cocoa, palm oil and sugar in significant quantities. Fishing is another important sector. Agricultural growth has been stunted by the continuing use of relatively primitive methods: industry has received the bulk of available investment capital in recent years. Crude oil production grew rapidly during the 1970s, until, by the end of the decade, it was the largest single export earner and Ecuador had joined OPEC. It left the organisation in 1985 in an effort to boost exports still further: the Government felt that the allocated OPEC quota was too low. When the world oil price declined sharply shortly afterwards, Ecuador lost substantially. A major earthquake then disrupted production yet further. In the last three years, Ecuador has altered its previous, somewhat isolationist foreign and trade policy and now actively encourages foreign investment to broaden its industrial base, which is concentrated in light manufacturing and consumer products. Indeed, the Government threatened to leave the Andean Pact, the economic bloc comprising Bolivia, Colombia, Peru and Venezuela, unless it adopted a more liberal attitude to inward investment. Ecuador is also a member of ALADI (Asociacíon Latinoamericana de Integracion). The United States is the largest single trading partner, accounting for 50% of Ecuadorean exports and supplying around one-third of imports. Other significant importers are Japan, Germany, Brazil, the UK and Italy.
BUSINESS: Business is conducted in Spanish. Appointments should be made in advance and may be subject to last minute changes, particularly in the case of ministers and government officials. Sales approaches should be low key. The best months are October to mid-December and mid-January to June. **Office hours:** 0900-1300 and 1500-1900 Monday to Friday, 0830-1230 Saturday.
COMMERCIAL INFORMATION: The following organisation can offer advice: Cámara de Comercio de Quito (Quito Chamber of Commerce), Casilla 202, Edificio Las Cameras 6 Piso, Avenida República y Amazonas, Quito. Tel: (2) 435 810. Telex: 2638.
CONFERENCES/CONVENTIONS: The following organisation can provide information: Turisa Williams Congresos, Foch 1206 y Av Amazonas, Edificio Turisa, 2do Piso, Quito, Ecuador. Tel: (2) 552 065. Fax: (2) 500 078. Telex: 2671 TURISA ED.

HISTORY & GOVERNMENT

HISTORY: The ancient kingdom of Quito was established by the Shiris, a tribe that was later conquered by the Incas in the 15th century. In 1533 Sebastián de Balacázar, governor of San Miguel de Piura (the first Spanish town built in Ecuador), undertook the conquest of the Inca kingdom. A year later San Francisco de Quito was founded. The early years under the Spanish were marked by civil strife between rival families contesting for power. In 1739 the viceroyality of New Grenada was created and Quito fell under its jurisdiction until independence. The following century, as the Department of the South, it joined New Grenada and Venezuela to form the Federation of Gran Colombia. In 1828, the country declared war on Peru, whose armies had invaded Gran Colombia. A year later a peace treaty was signed and Ecuador's boundaries were permanently established. Since independence in 1830, Ecuador has been governed by a mixture of civilian and military regimes although civilian administrations have predominated recently and Ecuador is now one of the continent's more stable democracies. Presidential elections in January 1988 brought Rodrigo Borja Cevallos of the Izquierda Democratica (Democratic Left) party to power at the head of a coalition government. He promised to address the country's growing economic problems and modify its isolationist foreign policy. In the latter instance, Ecuador has joined the Contadora group, a political bloc linking countries in northern South America. The Borja government also declared its willingness to settle the long-running border dispute with Peru over ownership of part of the Amazon basin. On the economic front, Ecuador is suffering from having squandered the windfall of the 1970s oil boom. Borja introduced tentative austerity measures – mild by the current standards of the continent – but came up against fierce opposition from the well-organised labour movement. At the next presidential elections in May 1992, Borja did not stand; his party's candidate, Raul Baca, attracted just 8% of the vote. Leading the poll were two right-wingers, Sixto Duran of the newly-formed Republican Unity party and Jaime Nebot Saadi of the Social Christian Party, although neither had sufficent support for a first-round victory. At the run-off in July, Sixto Duran came out on top. Simultaneous local and congressional elections also showed strong preferences for the right.
GOVERNMENT: The constitution was approved by national referendum in 1978, taking effect in 1979. The President, elected for a term of four years, holds executive power. He is assisted by the Vice President and a Cabinet, which includes 12 Ministers and a Secretary General. Legislative power is unicameral and resides in the House of Representatives with 69 members; there are 12 national representatives and the remainder represent the provinces.

CLIMATE

Warm and subtropical. Weather varies within the country due to the Andes mountain range and coastal changes. Andean regions are cooler and it is especially cold at nights in the mountains. Rainfall is high in coastal and jungle areas.
Required clothing: Lightweight cottons and linens, and rainwear in subtropical areas. Warmer clothes are needed in upland areas.

SEYMOUR I. Galapagos Is. (11m)

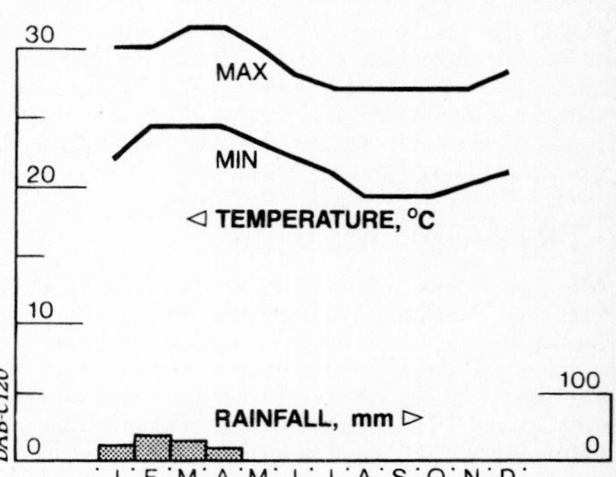

GUAYAQUIL Ecuador (6m)

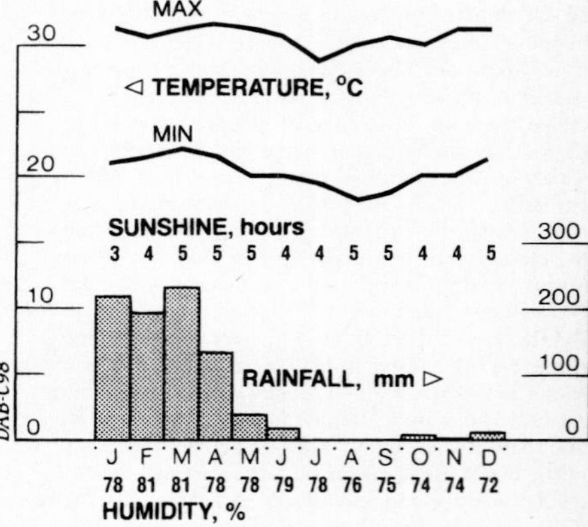

QUITO Ecuador (2818m)

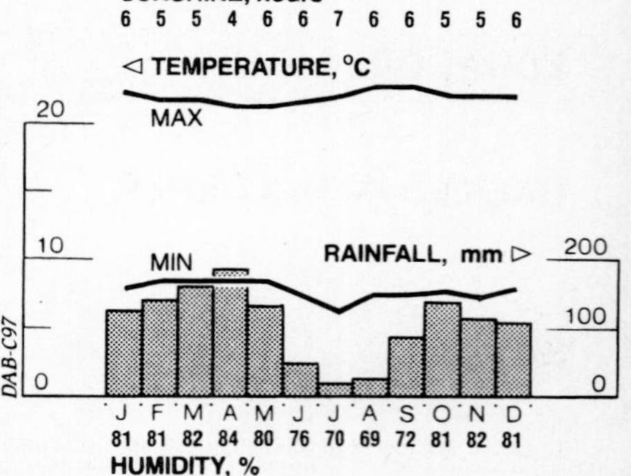

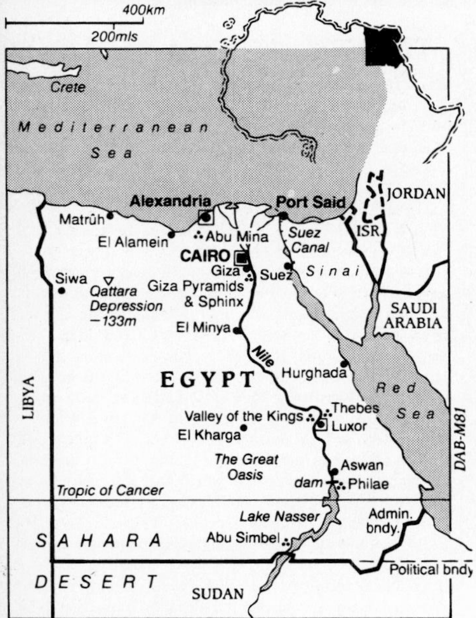

☐ *international airport*

Location: Middle East, North Africa.

Egyptian General Authority for the Promotion of Tourism
Misr Travel Tower
Abasseia Square
Cairo, Egypt
Tel: (2) 823 570. Fax: (2) 282 9771. Telex: 20799.
Embassy of the Arab Republic of Egypt
26 South Street
London W1Y 8EL
Tel: (071) 499 2401. Fax: (071) 355 3568. Telex: 23650 BOSTAN G. Opening hours: 0930-1730 Monday to Friday.
Egyptian Consulate
2 Lowndes Street
London SW1X 9ET
Tel: (071) 235 9777. Fax: (071) 235 5684. Opening hours: 1000-1200 Monday to Friday for personal applications; afternoons only for the collection of visas.
Egyptian State Tourist Office
168 Piccadilly
London W1V 9DE
Tel: (071) 493 5282. Fax: (071) 408 0295. Telex: 23106 EGYSTOG. Opening hours: 0930-1630 Monday to Friday.
British Embassy
Sharia Ahmad Raghab
Garden City
Cairo, Egypt
Tel: (2) 354 0852. Fax: (2) 354 0859. Telex: 94188.
Consulates in: Alexandria, Suez, Port Said and Luxor (honorary).
British Consulate-General
3 Mina Street
Kafr Abdu
Roushdi
Alexandria, Egypt
Tel: (3) 546 7001/2. Fax: (3) 546 7177. Telex: 54578 BRITN UN.
Embassy of the Arab Republic of Egypt
2310 Decatur Place, NW
Washington, DC
20008
Tel: (202) 232 5400. Fax: (202) 332 7894.
Consular Section: Tel: (202) 234 3903.
Egyptian State Tourist Office
630 Fifth Avenue
New York, NY
10111
Tel: (212) 246 6960. Fax: (212) 956 6439.
Embassy of the United States of America
North Gate 8
Kamal El-Din Salah Street
Cairo, Egypt
Tel: (2) 355 7371. Fax: (2) 355 7375. Telex: 93773.
Consulate in Alexandria.
Embassy of the Arab Republic of Egypt
454 Laurier Avenue East
Ottawa, Ontario
K1N 6R3
Tel: (613) 234 4931. Fax: (613) 234 9347.
Consulate in Montréal.
Egyptian Tourist Authority
PO Box 304
Place Bonaventure
40 Frontenac
Montréal, Québec
H5A 1B4
Tel: (514) 861 4420. Fax: (514) 861 8071.
Canadian Embassy
6 Sharia Mohammad Fahmy es-Sayed
Cairo, Egypt
Tel: (2) 354 3110. Fax: (2) 356 3548. Telex: 92677.

AREA: 997,739 sq km (385,229 sq miles).
POPULATION: 53,153,000 (1990 estimate).
POPULATION DENSITY: 53.3 per sq km.
CAPITAL: Cairo (El Qahira). **Population:** 6,052,800 (1986).
GEOGRAPHY: Egypt is bounded to the north by the Mediterranean, to the south by the Sudan, to the west by Libya, and to the east by the Red Sea and Israel. The River Nile divides the country unevenly in two, while the Suez Canal provides a third division with the Sinai Peninsula. Beyond the highly cultivated Nile Valley and Delta, a lush green tadpole of land that holds more than 90% of the population, the landscape is mainly flat desert, devoid of vegetation apart from the few oases that have persisted in the once fertile depressions of the Western Desert. Narrow strips are inhabited on the Mediterranean coast and on the African Red Sea coast, but coastal Sinai is as barren as its interior. The coast south of Suez has fine beaches and the coral reefs just offshore attract many divers. The High Dam at Aswan now controls the annual floods that once put much of the Nile Valley under water; it also provides electricity.
LANGUAGE: Arabic is the official language. English and French are widely spoken.
RELIGION: Islam is the predominant religion. All types of Christianity are also represented, especially the Coptic Church.
TIME: GMT + 2 (GMT + 3 in summer).
ELECTRICITY: Most areas 220 volts AC, 50Hz. Certain rural parts still 110-380 volts AC.
COMMUNICATIONS: Telephone: Full IDD is available. Country code: 20. International telephone calls should be ordered in advance, as the service is subject to delays. **Fax:** Several of the major hotels in Cairo have introduced fax facilities, check with the hotel concerned before travelling. **Telex/telegram:** 24-hour telex facilities are available at: 19 El Alfi Street, Cairo; 26 July Street, Zamalek; 85 Abdel Khalek Sarwat Street, Attaba; El Tayaran Street, Nasser City; and at major hotels. International telex and telegram services are available from the Central Post Offices in Cairo, Alexandria, Luxor and Aswan and main hotels. **Post:** The postal system is efficient for international mail. Airmail to Europe takes about five days. There are *Poste Restante* facilities at the Central Post Office; a small fee is charged when mail is collected. All post offices are open daily 0900-1400 except Fridays, and the Central Post Office in Cairo is open 24 hours. **Press:** The most influential Egyptian daily is *Al-Ahram*, others include *Al-Akhbar* and several weekly and periodical publications. The English-language daily newspaper is the *Egyptian Gazette*, and *The Middle East Observer* is the main weekly English-language business paper.
BBC World Service and Voice of America frequencies: From time to time these change. See the section *How to Use this Book* for more information.

BBC:				
MHz	21.47	17.64	15.07	1.323

A service is also available on 639kHz and 1323kHz.

Voice of America:				
MHz	11.97	9.670	6.040	5.995

PASSPORT/VISA

Regulations and requirements may be subject to change at short notice, and you are advised to contact the appropriate diplomatic or consular authority before finalising travel arrangements. Details of these may be found at the head of this country's entry. Any numbers in the chart refer to the footnotes below.

	Passport Required?	Visa Required?	Return Ticket Required?
Full British	Yes	Yes	Yes
BVP	Not valid	-	-
Australian	Yes	Yes	Yes
Canadian	Yes	Yes	Yes
USA	Yes	Yes	Yes
Other EC	Yes	Yes	Yes
Japanese	Yes	Yes	Yes

Restricted entry and transit: The Government of the Arab Republic of Egypt may refuse admission and transit to nationals of South Africa, Algeria, Morocco, Tunisia, Iraq, Lebanon and Palestinians. Some applications for visas by nationals of these countries may be accepted, but they will have to wait at least two months for the visa to be processed.
PASSPORTS: Valid passport required by all. Passports should be valid for at least 6 months beyond the period of intended stay in Egypt.
British Visitors Passport: Not accepted.
VISAS: Required by all except nationals of Bahrain, Djibouti, Ghana, Guinea, Libya, Malta, Mauritania, Oman, Qatar, Saudi Arabia, Somalia, Sudan, Turkey and United Arab Emirates.
Note: Due to the recent situation in the Middle East region, requirements for visas and other regulations have changed significantly and may change again at short notice; check with the appropriate authority before travelling.
Types of visa: Tourist and Business (both have Single- and Multiple-entry types). Fees vary considerably according to nationality.
Cost: *Tourist* (UK nationals): Single-entry £15, Multiple-entry £18. *Business* (UK nationals): Single-entry £43 and Multiple-entry £67, provided a business letter is forwarded. Payment of fees by cash or postal orders only. Cheques will not be accepted. Visa fees are per passport, not per person.
Validity: Varies, but visas are usually easy to renew within the country.
Note: The situation in the Gulf has resulted in changes to all the regulations in this section. Visitors should consult the Embassy before travelling.
Application to: Consulate (or Consular Section at Embassy). For addresses, see top of entry.

EGYPT | **HEALTH REGULATIONS** | **VISA REGULATIONS** | Code-Link

GALILEO/WORLDSPAN

TI-DFT/CAI/HE

TI-DFT/CAI/VI

SABRE

TIDFT/CAI/HE

TIDFT/CAI/VI

To access this information on your CRS, swipe the barcode with a light pen or type in the text under the barcode. For more information, see the introduction *How to Use This Book*.

Application requirements: (a) 1 photograph. (b) Valid passport. (c) Application form. (d) Business letter for Business visa.
Working days required: 1 month.
Note: All visitors must register with the police within a week of arrival in the country. This registration is generally done by the hotel.

MONEY

Currency: Egyptian Pound (£E) = 100 piastres. Notes are in denominations of £E100, 20, 10, 5 and 1, and 50, 25, 10 and 5 piastres. Coins are in denominations of 10, 5, 2 and 1 piastres.
Currency exchange: It is no longer mandatory to change a minimum of US$150 on arrival. There are five national banks and 78 branches of foreign banks.
Credit cards: Access/Mastercard, American Express, Diners Club and Visa are accepted. Check with your credit card company for details of merchant acceptability and other services which may be available.
Exchange rate indicators: The following figures are included as a guide to the movements of the Egyptian Pound against Sterling and the US Dollar:

Date:	Oct '89	Oct '90	Oct '91	Oct '92
£1.00=	4.16	5.15	5.77	5.24
$1.00=	2.57	2.72	3.32	3.30

Currency restrictions: There are no restrictions on the import of foreign currency provided it is declared on an official customs form. The export of foreign currency is limited to the amount declared. The import and export of local currency is limited to £E100.
Banking hours: 0800-1400 Sunday to Thursday.

DUTY FREE

The following goods may be imported into Egypt without incurring customs duty:
200 cigarettes or 25 cigars or 200g of tobacco;
1 litre of spirits;
A reasonable amount of perfume or eau de cologne;
Gifts up to the value of £E500.
Note: All cash, travellers cheques, credit cards and gold over £E500 must be declared on arrival.
Prohibited items: Drugs, firearms and cotton; for a full list, contact the Egyptian State Tourist Office.

PUBLIC HOLIDAYS

Public holidays observed in Egypt are as follows:
Mar 25 '93 Eid al-Fitr (End of Ramadan). **Apr 19** Sham an-Nessim (Coptic Easter Monday). **Jun 1** Eid al-Adha (Feast of the Sacrifice). **Jun 18** Evacuation Day. **Jun 21** Islamic New Year. **Jul 23** Revolution Day. **Aug 30** Mouloud (Birth of Mohammed). **Oct 6** Armed Forces Day. **Oct 24** Popular Resistance Day. **Dec 23** Victory Day. **Jan 7 '94** Coptic Christmas. **Mar** Eid al-Fitr (End of Ramadan).
Note: Muslim festivals are timed according to local sightings of various phases of the Moon and the dates given above are approximations. During the lunar month of Ramadan that precedes Eid al-Fitr, Muslims fast during the day and feast at night and normal business patterns may be interrupted. Many restaurants are closed during the day and there may be restrictions on smoking and drinking. Some disruption may continue into Eid al-Fitr itself. Eid al-Fitr and Eid al-Adha may last anything from two to ten days, depending on the region. For more information see the section *World of Islam* at the back of the book.

HEALTH

Regulations and requirements may be subject to change at short notice, and you are advised to contact your doctor well in advance of your intended date of departure. Any numbers in the chart refer to the footnotes below.

	Special Precautions?	Certificate Required?
Yellow Fever	No	1
Cholera	Yes	2
Typhoid & Polio	Yes	-
Malaria	3	-
Food & Drink	4	-

[1]: A yellow fever vaccination certificate is required from travellers over one year of age coming from infected areas (see below). Those arriving in transit from such areas without a certificate will be detained at the airport until their onward flight departs. The following countries and areas are regarded by the Egyptian health authorities as being wholly infected with yellow fever: all countries in mainland Africa south of the Sahara with the exception of Lesotho, Mozambique, Namibia, South Africa, Swaziland and Zimbabwe (and including Mali, Mauritania, Niger and Chad); Sudan south of 15°N (location certificate issued by a Sudanese official is required to be exempt from vaccination certificate); São Tomé e Principe; Belize, Bolivia, Brazil, Colombia, Costa Rica, Ecuador, French Guiana, Guatemala, Guyana, Honduras, Nicaragua, Panama, Peru, Suriname, Trinidad & Tobago and Venezuela.
[2]: Following WHO guidelines issued in 1973, a cholera vaccination certificate is no longer a condition of entry to Egypt. However, cholera is a risk in this country and precautions are advised. Up-to-date advice should be sought before deciding whether these precautions should include vaccination as medical opinion is divided over its effectiveness. See the *Health* section at the back of the book.
[3]: Malaria risk, almost exclusively in the benign *vivax* form, exists from June to October in rural areas of the Nile Delta, El Faiyoum area (malignant *falciparum* form), the oases and part of Upper Egypt. There is no risk in Cairo or Alexandria at any time.
[4]: Mains water is normally chlorinated, and whilst relatively safe may cause mild abdominal upsets. Bottled water is available and is advised for the first few weeks of the stay. Milk is unpasteurised and should be boiled. Powdered or tinned milk is available and is advised, but make sure that it is reconstituted with pure water. Avoid dairy products which are likely to have been made from unboiled milk. Only eat well-cooked meat and fish, preferably served hot. Pork, salad and mayonnaise may carry increased risk. Vegetables should be cooked and fruit peeled. Drinking water outside main cities and towns carries a greater risk and should always be sterilised.
Rabies is present. For those at high risk, vaccination before arrival should be considered. If you are bitten abroad seek medical advice without delay. For more information consult the *Health* section at the back of the book.
Bilharzia (schistosomiasis) is present. Avoid swimming and paddling in fresh water. Swimming pools which are well-chlorinated and maintained are safe.
Health care: Public hospitals and chemists are open to tourists. Health insurance is strongly advised.

TRAVEL - International

AIR: The national airline is *Egyptair (MS)*. Charter services fly direct from Gatwick to Egypt.
Approximate flight times: From *London* to Cairo is 4 hours 45 minutes and to Luxor is 5 hours 35 minutes.
From *Los Angeles* to Cairo is 16 hours 40 minutes.
From *New York* to Cairo is 14 hours 35 minutes.
From *Singapore* to Cairo is 11 hours 45 minutes.
From *Sydney* to Cairo is 21 hours 30 minutes.
International airports: *Cairo International (CAI)*, 22.5km (14 miles) northeast of the city at Heliopolis (minimum travel time – 30 minutes, much longer during the rush hour). There are coach services every five to six minutes, and taxis are available to the city centre and the main hotels. Special limousines are offered by local and international operators, also hotel cars. Airport facilities include an incoming and outgoing 24-hour duty-free shop selling a wide range of goods, several 24-hour car hire firms, post office, 24-hour bank and exchange services, restaurants (0900-2100 in the departure lounge and 24 hours outside the airport), 24-hour bar, hotel reservation service, souvenir shops, book shop, and travel insurance services.
El Nouzha (ALY), 7km (4 miles) southeast of Maydan al-Tahir (Alexandria). Regular bus services to downtown Alexandria and to Cairo. Special limousine and local taxis, plus hotel cars are available. Airport facilities include a 24-hour incoming and outgoing duty-free shop, 24-hour car hire, 24-hour bank and exchange services, and a 24-hour bar and restaurant.
Luxor Airport (LXR) is 5.5km (3.5 miles) from Luxor. There is a regular bus service to the city centre. Special limousine and local taxi services are available. Airport facilities include car hire, bank and exchange services, and a bar and restaurant.
Departure tax: £E19.
SEA: The main coastal ports are Alexandria, Port Said and Suez. Ferries operated by *Adriatica (Sealink)* sail from Venice, Italy to Alexandria via Piraeus once a week June 21 to Sept 27, and roughly once a week for the remainder of the year. *Stability Line* also operates from Venice and Brindisi to Alexandria three times a week. A car ferry service also goes from Genoa, Italy to Alexandria. The *Saudi Sea Transport Company* runs a regular car ferry service between Suez and Jeddah. A steamer service travels three days a week up the Nile between Wadi Halfa (Sudan) and Aswan. The *Black Sea Shipping Company* sails from Odessa. Other main passenger lines are: *Grimaldi/Siosa, Rashid* and *Prudential;* and *Soviet Lines* (cruise ships).
RAIL: There are no international rail links to any of Egypt's northern neighbours. The railheads at Aswan and Wadi Halfa (Sudan) are connected by a ferry across Lake Nasser.
ROAD: The road border between Libya and Egypt has now been re-opened. There is a route to Cairo from Israel via El Arish and Port Said, Suez or Ismailia. Group taxis are available from the Israeli border. Also daily coaches leave early in the morning from Tel Aviv and Ashkelon in Israel via El Arish to Cairo and *vice versa*. Fares are US$25 one way and US$45 return. See below for information on **documentation.**

TRAVEL - Internal

AIR: *Egypt Air* operates daily flights between Cairo, Alexandria, Luxor, Aswan, Abu Simbel, New Valley and Hurghada. For schedules contact local offices. *Air Sinai* operates services on the following routes: Cairo to *Tel Aviv;* Cairo to *El Arish;* Cairo to *St Catherine* and *Eilat* (1 hour 15 minutes); and Cairo to *Ras El Nakab, Luxor* and *Sharm El Sheikh*.
SEA/RIVER: There is a hydrofoil service linking Hurghada with Sharm el-Sheikh in Sinai. There are also two new ferries operating a daily ferry service; journey time is 5-6 hours. For more information, contact Red Sea Cruises Company in Hurghada, or the Egyptian Land Company in Cairo at Champolian Street. Tel: (2) 741 467 *or* 751 563. The traditional Nile sailing boats, *feluccas*, can be hired by the hour for relaxing sailing on the Nile. The Sudanese railway system operates a steamer service from Aswan to Wadi Halfa. Regular Nile cruises operate between Luxor and Aswan and sometimes between Cairo and Aswan usually for the following periods: four nights, five days (standard tour); six nights, seven days (extended tour), and 14 nights, 15 days (full Nile cruise). There are over 160 individually-owned boats of all categories operating on the Nile.
RAIL: A comprehensive rail network offering a high standard of service is operated along an east–west axis from Sallom on the Libyan border to Alexandria and Cairo, and along the Nile to Luxor, Aswan and Abu Simbel. There are also links to Port Said and Suez. There are frequent trains from Cairo to Alexandria, and also several luxury air-conditioned day and night trains with sleeping and restaurant cars from Cairo to Luxor and Aswan for the Nile Valley tourist trade. Inclusive tickets with reduced hotel charges are available for Aswan and Luxor. Tourist and student groups, children and holders of Youth Hostel cards can get reductions. A 50% reduction is available for members of the YHA. Vouchers may be obtained on presentation of a membership card from the *Egyptian Youth Hostels Travel Bureau*, 7 Sharia Dr Abdel Hamid Said, Maarouf, Cairo. Tel: (2) 355 0329. For details of other possible reductions, contact the Tourist Office.
ROAD: Besides the Nile Valley and Delta, which hold an extensive road network, there are paved roads along the Mediterranean and African Red Sea coasts. The road looping through the Western Desert oases from Asyut to Giza is now fully paved. The speed limit is usually 90kmph on motorways and 100kmph on the desert motorway from Cairo to Alexandria (there are substantial fines for speeding). Private motoring in the desert regions is not recommended without suitable vehicles and a guide. For more details contact the *Egyptian Automobile Club* in Cairo. **Bus:** The national bus system serves the Nile Valley and the coastal road. Main routes are from Cairo to St Catherine, Sharm el-Sheikh, Dahab, Ras Sudr, El-Tour, Taba and Rafah; from Suez to El-Tour and Sharm el-Sheikh; and from Sharm el-Sheikh to Taba, Newiba, El Tor, Dahab and St Catherine. **Taxi:** Taxis are available in all the larger cities and are metered (see also *Urban* below). Long-distance group taxis for all destinations are cheap. Fares should be agreed in advance. **Car hire:** Car hire is available through *Avis, Hertz, Budget Rental* and local companies. **Documentation:** Own insurance and an International Driving Permit or British driving licence are required to drive any motor vehicle. *Carnet de Passage* or a suitable deposit is necessary for the temporary import of own vehicle. All vehicles (including motor cycles) are required by law to carry a fire extinguisher and a red hazard triangle.
URBAN: The government-owned *Cairo Transport Authority* runs buses and tram services in Cairo and also operates cross-Nile ferries. There is a central area flat fare. In addition, there are other buses and fixed-route shared taxi and minibus services run by private operators. Vehicles normally wait at city terminals to obtain a full load, but there are frequent departures. Fares are three to four times higher than on the buses. Cairo's suburban railways have been upgraded to provide a rapid transit network, including Africa's first underground railway. Alexandria also has buses and tramways, with first- and second-class accommodation and distance-regulated fares.

JOURNEY TIMES: The following chart gives approximate journey times (in hours and minutes) from Cairo to other major cities/towns in Egypt.

	Air	Road	Rail	River
Alexandria	0.30	3.00	2.30	-
Luxor	1.00	12.00	17.00	b
Aswan	2.00	16.00	19.00a	b
Port Said	0.45	3.00	3.00	-
St Catherine	0.30	4.00	-	-
Hurghada	1.00	8.00	-	-
Sharm el-Sh'k	1.30	7.00	-	-
Marsa Matr'h	1.30	5.00	9.00	-
Areish	1.00	5.00	9.00	-
Ismailia	-	2.00	2.30	-
Suez	-	4.00	4.00	-
New Valley	2.00	12.00	-	-

Note: [a] Overnight journey. [b] For further information, see *Sea/River* above.

ACCOMMODATION

Tourism is one of Egypt's main industries, and accommodation is available around all the major attractions and the larger cities. Egypt has all types of accommodation on offer, from deluxe hotels to youth hostels, at prices to suit all pockets.

HOTELS: The main cities have quality hotels moderately priced, which *must* be booked well in advance, especially during the winter months. Smaller hotels are very good value. In 1991 hotel capacity in Egypt had reached 413 hotels and 158 floating hotels with 46,620 rooms and 6504 cabins. Of these hotels over 300 belong to the Egyptian Hotel Association, 8 El Saad El Ali Street, Dokki, Cairo. Tel: (2) 71 2134/348 8468. Fax: (2) 360 8956. Telex: 92355 ANIS UN. **Grading:** The Egyptian Hotel Association grades member hotels on a scale from 5-star to 1-star.

Note: Hotel bills are subject to a tax and service charge of 12%.

CAMPING/CARAVANNING: Travel through the desert wilderness is available through local tour operators. It should be borne in mind that desert travel is extremely hazardous without an experienced guide, ample supplies of water, and a vehicle in good mechanical condition. There are only a few official campsites in the country. Tourists are advised to contact the local Tourist Offices on arrival for further details. The tourist office in Cairo is at 5 Adly Street, Cairo. Tel: (2) 391 5590 *or* 391 8554 *or* 390 3613. There is also an office at Cairo International Airport.

RESORTS & EXCURSIONS

The major attractions in Egypt are Cairo, Alexandria and the northern coast, Nile cruises, Luxor, Abu Simbel, Aswan and the Pharaonic treasures, the Sinai peninsula, and the fabulous Red Sea coastline. Egypt's combination of beach resorts and ancient heritage make it one of the most exciting holiday centres within easy reach of Europe.

Cairo

The capital is a city of astonishing diversity and vitality, uniting elements of Africa, the Orient and Western Europe. Sprawling around the Nile and up towards the Delta, Cairo has a population of 14 million and needs several days to visit properly.

The *Egyptian Museum* contains the largest, and one of the most impressive, collections of Pharaonic and Byzantine art and sculpture from the surrounding area. The witty statues of Akhenaten alone justify a visit, and of course the museum houses the celebrated treasures of Tutankhamun, a minor Pharaoh who ruled for a few years a millenium before Christ. Nearby is *Tehrir (Revolution) Square*, the focal point of downtown Cairo. This area, characterised by tall French neo-classical city blocks, was built in the middle of the 19th century by Pasha Ismail, whose ambitious plans to modernise his country reduced it to a state of bankruptcy (which lasted until Nasser came to power in 1952). The *Cairo Tower*, near the Gezira Sports Club on an island in the Nile, affords a wonderful view of the city; it stands amidst the elegant town-houses of a wealthy neighbourhood that bears a striking resemblance to London's St John's Wood. By contrast there is the hustle and bustle of the *Khan-el-Khalili Bazaar*, where one can bargain for traditional leather work, brassware and excellent inexpensive tailor-made clothing. It is set in an area of narrow winding streets where the local inhabitants will always approach the traveller in the hope of doing a little business. A trip around Old Cairo is an enchanting return to a former age, and there are many fine examples of Islamic art and architecture. The *Citadel* and nearby *Al Rif'ai* and *Sultan Hassan* mosques should not be missed but numerous less well-known attractions may be found around almost every corner (Cairo has over 1000 mosques). There is also a *Coptic and Islamic Museum*.

In Pharaonic times, the east bank of the Nile was for the living and the west was for the dead. Today's west bank is the most modern part of the city – site of the university, the wealthy suburb of Zamalek and the apartment blocks of Dokki – but where the city stops, the Egypt of the *fellahin* (peasants) abruptly starts – date palms, canals, mud villages and lush green fields. To the south, the transition is even more startling. An area of casinos and luxury hotels suddenly gives way to rolling sand dunes and, towering above them, the magnificent pyramids of *Giza*. There are three, the largest being over 137m (450ft) high and containing some three million huge blocks of stone. One can explore deep inside the pyramids by means of labyrinthine tunnels and staircases. Adjacent is the massive *Sphinx*, much admired by Alexander, Caesar, Cleopatra and Napoleon. Camels and horses may be hired and there is a golf course nearby, the night skyline is illuminated by a light show (an unusual but effective way to see the pyramids and Sphinx).

Helwan, a famous winter resort and health spa, is 30km (18 miles) from Cairo. At nearby **Sakkara**, the step pyramids of *Zoser* are even older than those at Giza and there are fine wall reliefs, particularly in the *Necropolis*. Donkey rides can be taken to Sakkara from Giza. 50km (30 miles) further south is **Al Faiyoum,** a salt-water lake visited by Herodotus in 450BC (malaria is a serious risk here).

Nile Cruises

A number of tour operators offer Nile cruises, the majority operate from **Luxor** to **Aswan** or vice versa. Some trips include an extension to **Abydos** and **Denderha**. The Luxor/Aswan cruise lasts four nights/five days; the cruise which includes Abydos and Denderha six nights/seven days, while one or two companies operate long tours on special departure dates only to **Minia** (a charming town with Roman, Greek and Pharaonic ruins) and/or through to **Cairo**.

There are numerous cruise steamers on the Nile, and the majority operate to a very high standard of service. According to the particular vessel used they carry from

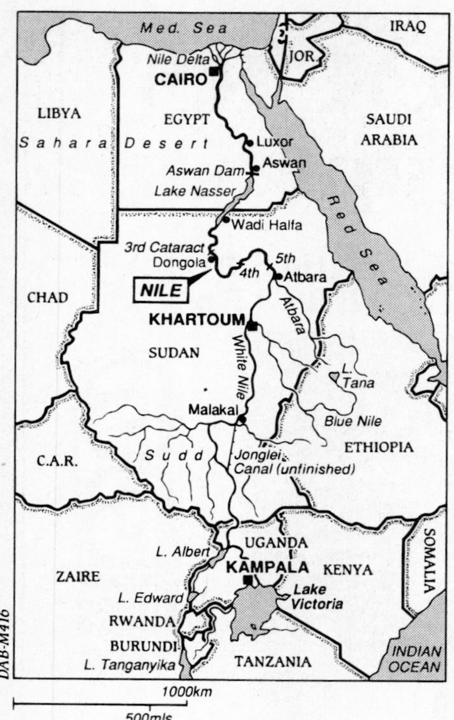

between 50 to 100 passengers, with the facilities varying according to size of the individual vessel. Contacting a specialist operator is recommended for choosing a Nile cruise. Normally you can only book the complete package through the tour operators. Traditional *felluccas* may also be chartered.

The Northern Coast

Alexandria is more modern than Cairo but is graced by numerous Hellenistic and Roman relics from the age when it was the cultural capital of Europe. It remains a popular holiday resort for Egyptians.

The northern beaches stretch from the Libyan border to the Nile delta and along the north of **Sinai**. West of Alexandria, the coast road takes one to the **Mersa Matruh** resort, which has a very fine beach; from there it is possible to head inland to visit the **Siwa Oasis** (site of Amun's oracle, visited by Herodotus and Alexander the Great) on the Libyan border. There are other fine beaches at **Alamein** (where World War II relics are on view), **Baltim, Gamasa, Sidi Kreir** and **Ras El Bar**, where the temperatures are warm enough for bathing until November.

Luxor

Luxor – Homer's 'Hundred-gated Thebes' – is about 500km (300 miles) south of Cairo and contains a vast conglomeration of ancient monuments: the *Temples of Amon* at **Karnak;** colossal statues, obelisks and halls (there is, as at Giza, a *son et lumière* show); the *Valley of the Queens* and the *Valley of the Kings*, where 64 of the Pharaohs are depicted in an enormous relief hewn from the rock. The other temples, tombs and monuments are equally awe-inspiring. Since 1988 visitors have had the opportunity to view these monuments from a hot-air balloon. Many specialist guidebooks are available; the Egyptian State Tourist Office will also be able to supply more detailed information.

Aswan

As well as being a beautiful winter resort with many hotels, Aswan has a huge array of temples, monasteries, the *Elephantine Island's* ancient *Nilometre*, and the *Aswan High Dam*, one of the three largest dams in the world. 2km (1.2 miles) south of Aswan is *Philae*, a classical temple considered to be sufficiently important to be saved from the flooding caused by the opening of the Dam. Further to the south is **Abu Simbel** – surviving largely thanks to a UNESCO-backed project in the 1960s – with the two magnificent temples of Rameses II. 120km (75 miles) north of Aswan is the temple of **Edfu**, one of the best preserved in Egypt. There are three weekly sailings from Aswan down the Nile into the Sudan.

Sinai & The Red Sea

Sinai's diving resorts include **Ras Mohammed, Sharm el Sheikh, Dahah, Neweiba** and **Arish**, most with diving centres offering lessons at all levels. The views across the Gulf of Aqaba to the Saudi Mountains are breathtaking and temperatures are warm until very late in the year. Other watersports are on offer and the whole Sinai east coast has beach resorts with hotels and beach huts where the desert merges into beach fringed by palm trees. **Ras Mohammed,** the southernmost point of the peninsula, is the site of the world's most northerly mangrove forest. In the interior there are the rugged and scenic Sinai Mountains, amongst which is the **Mount Sinai** of the Bible. Nearby is the famous **St Catherine's Monastery.** This was first settled by hermits in the 4th century and attracted an increasing number of pilgrims, particularly after the construction of a sanctuary in 337. Almost every subsequent century saw additions to the architecture of the settlement, as well as intermittent periods of decline and abandonment. Many of the bequests made to the monastery over the years are also on display in the museum. Other attractions in Sinai include Saladin's massive **Qalaat al-Gundi** fortress, one of the region's many reminders of the Crusaders' presence in the Middle East during the 12th and 13th centuries; and **Al-Tur,** on the Red Sea, capital of South Sinai.

The newest tourist attraction in Egypt is perhaps the western coast of the Red Sea. **Hurghada,** some 400km (250 miles) south of Suez, is a well-equipped diving resort with marvellous coral reefs. There is a modern tourist village at **El Gufton** nearby.

SOCIAL PROFILE

FOOD & DRINK: Egyptian cuisine is excellent, combining many of the best traditions of Middle Eastern cooking, and there are both large hotel restaurants and smaller specialist ones throughout the main towns. Some of the larger hotels in Cairo and its environs have excellent kitchens serving the best cosmopolitan dishes. In the centre of Cairo, American-style snack bars are also spreading. Local specialities include bean dishes *(foul)*, kebabs and *humus* (chickpeas). Restaurants have waiter service, with table service for bars. **Drink:** Although Egypt is a Muslim country, alcohol is available in café-style bars and good restaurants.
NIGHTLIFE: Sophisticated nightclubs, discotheques, and good restaurants can be found in Cairo and Alexandria. There is nightlife in Luxor and Aswan, including barbecues along the Nile.
SHOPPING: The most interesting shopping area for tourists in Cairo is the old bazaar, *Khan-el Khalili*, specialising in reproductions of antiquities. Jewellery, spices, copper utensils and Coptic cloth are some of the special items. There are also modern shopping centres available, particularly near Tehrir Square. **Shopping hours:** *Winter:* 0900-2100 every day except Fridays (Islamic Sabbath). During Ramadan, hours vary, with shops often closing on Sunday as well. *Summer:* 0900-1400 and 1700-2100 Saturday to Thursday.
SPORT: Tennis, golf, croquet and **horseriding** clubs are found in both Alexandria and Cairo. For details ask at your hotel. There is a public golf club at the foot of the Giza pyramids. **Watersports:** There are very fine coral reefs in Egyptian waters and **diving** facilities are being expanded year by year. The longest established resorts are on the Gulf of Aqaba, Sharm el-Sheikh, Dahab and Nueweba but specialist diving clubs have opened up on the Red Sea coast at Hurghada and Ras Mohamed. Equipment may be hired and training is available at all levels of ability. See also in *Resorts & Excursions* above, or contact the Egyptian State Tourist Office (address above). **Note:** The Red Sea coral reefs are all protected and persons removing 'souvenirs' will incur heavy fines.
SPECIAL EVENTS: The following is a selection of the major festivals and other special events celebrated in Egypt during 1993/94. For a complete list, contact the Egyptian State Tourist Office.
Feb-Mar '93 *Tennis Tournament, Shooting Festival.* **Mar** *Cairo International Fair; International Windsurfing Festival.*
SOCIAL CONVENTIONS: Islam is the dominant influence and many traditional customs and beliefs are tied up with religion. The people are generally courteous and hospitable and expect similar respect from visitors. Handshaking will suffice as a greeting. Because Egypt is a Muslim country, dress should be conservative and women should not wear revealing clothes particularly when in religious buildings and in towns (although the Western style of dress is accepted in the modern nightclubs, restaurants, hotels and bars of Cairo, Alexandria and other tourist destinations). Official or social functions and smart restaurants usually require more formal wear. Smoking is very common. **Photography:** Tourists will have to pay a fee of £E25 per day to take photographs inside pyramids, tombs and museums. **Tipping:** 10-12% is added to hotel and restaurant bills but an extra tip of 5% is normal. Taxi drivers generally expect 10%.

BUSINESS PROFILE

ECONOMY: On taking power in the 1950s, Nasser quickly instituted a Soviet-style command economy which was closed to Western investment. After his death, his chosen model was gradually dismantled, particularly under Sadat, who followed a policy of *infitah* (openness) towards investment. The Egyptian economy underwent high growth during the 1970s with the rapid expansion of the oil industry, tourism, and Suez canal use (with consequent increase in tariff revenues). However, with the fall in the oil price, Egypt suffered a massive drop in revenues and a severe shortage of foreign currency. The unwieldy and inefficient public sector, which appears all but unreformable, soaks up much of this. Egypt's major industries are textiles, fertilisers, rubber products and cement. There is one major steelworks and several vehicle assembly plants. Agriculture, which generates around 20% of Gross National Product, is largely dependent on cotton, which puts considerable strain on the Nile waters in addition to that imposed by the rapidly growing population, over 90% of whom live within a few miles of the river. The country's major trading partners are the United States and the larger of the European Community economies (Germany, France, Italy and the UK). In 1987 Romania was the second largest export market. The Government is gradually attempting to cut subsidies on foodstuffs, electricity and oil, although many of the poorer Egyptians depend on these and previous attempts to reduce them have met with riots. The country is second only to Israel in the amount of aid it receives from the USA. Since the Gulf War, Egypt has benefitted economically from its improved standing in the international community: in particular, the Cairo government's long-running and difficult negotiations with the International Monetary Fund have entered a more relaxed and productive phase. Egypt's main economic challenge now is the ability of its trade sector to respond to changed conditions in the CIS and Eastern Europe, formerly its largest export market.
BUSINESS: Suits are expected for business persons. Muslim customs should be respected by visiting business persons. English and French are widely spoken in business circles, but business cards in Arabic are appreciated. **Government office hours:** 0900-1400 Saturday to Thursday.
COMMERCIAL INFORMATION: The following organisations can offer advice:
Alexandria Chamber of Commerce, Sharia el-Ghorfa Altogariya, Alexandria. Tel: (3) 808 993; *or*
Cairo Chamber of Commerce, 4 Sharia Midan el-Falaki, Cairo. Tel: (2) 355 8261. Fax: (2) 356 3603. Telex: 92453; *or*
Egyptian-British Chamber of Commerce, PO Box 4EG, Kent House, Market Place, London W1A 4EG. Tel: (071) 323 2856. Fax: (071) 323 5739.
CONFERENCES/CONVENTIONS: Cairo has many hotels and three large meeting halls (seating up to 2000 people) which are equipped for use as conference centres; these include the new Cairo International Conference Centre, 12km (7 miles) east of Cairo International Airport, which has seating for 2500 people, with an exhibition hall, banquet hall and comprehensive facilities.

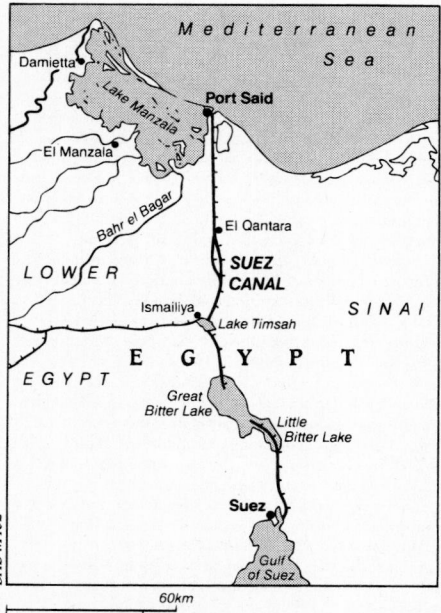

There is also a new convention centre at Alexandria University, which has a main hall with seating for 2400. In 1992 the American Society of Travel Agents (ASTA) held its congress in Cairo. Over 8000 delegates attended. For more information on conference facilities in Egypt contact the tourist office, or Cairo International Conference Centre, El-Nasr Road, Autostrade, Nasr City, Egypt. Tel: (2) 263 4632 *or* 263 4640. Fax: (2) 263 4640. Telex: 20607. For more information on conference facilities in Egypt contact Egyptian General Company for Tourism and Hotels, 4 Latin America St, Cairo. Tel: (2) 32158. Telex: 92363; or the Tourist Office.

HISTORY & GOVERNMENT

HISTORY: The history of Egypt is one of the richest, oldest and most varied of any country in the world, and the country's place in the history of the Middle East is as central now as it was in the fourth millenium BC. The unification of the Lower and the Upper Kingdoms in about 3180BC marks a convenient starting point for Egyptian history. This dynamic, culturally sophisticated and powerful kingdom on the banks of the Nile grew into one of the greatest civilisations of the ancient world. The pre-Hellenic period is reckoned in Kingdoms (Old, Middle and New) and subdivided into Dynasties; the IVth saw the construction of such architectural masterpieces as the Great Pyramid, and the XIth and XIIth saw the zenith of Egyptian power at the start of the second millenium. Tutankhamun, whose magnificent tomb was discovered in 1922, ruled briefly during the XVIIIth dynasty. From the XXth Dynasty onwards the power of Egypt was on the wane, and the country was overrun on several occasions by foreign armies, including those of the Nubians, Ethiopians and Persians. The latest and most permanent of these invasions, which brought the Pharaonic period to an end, was that of Alexander the Great in 332BC. During the Hellenic and Augustan Roman period (which began in AD30 as a result of the defeat of Anthony at the Battle of Actium), the emergence of law and literature in Alexandria allowed seven centuries of comparative peace and economic stability. From the middle of the 4th century, Egypt became part of the Eastern Empire. Then, in 642, an invading Arab army – one manifestation of the rapid Islamic conquests which followed the death of Mohammed – was welcomed by the Coptic Christians in preference to their previous Greek rulers. The Fatamids gained control of the country in the late 10th century but their power declined after a century or so. The subsequent revival of Muslim fortunes, and the reawakening of the spirit of *Jihad* (holy war), was largely associated with the career of Saladin, whose control of Egypt enabled him to reunite much of the Muslim world. The Mamelukes, who ruled Egypt from 1250 to 1517, prevented Mongol and Christian conquests, but were unable to prevent the eventual usurpation of their own power by the Ottoman Turks. Under Ottoman rule, Egypt became a somewhat neglected corner of a large and increasingly moribund empire. The Mamelukes briefly regained power, but the arrival of Napoleon in 1798 brought Egypt once more into violent contact with a European power. By 1805, however, the struggle for independence had been won, Muhammed Ali being recognised as Sultan. A generally pro-Western policy was followed by Muhammed and his successors. The Suez Canal was opened in 1869, but subsequent financial problems and internal struggles led to a British occupation, which was maintained from 1882 to 1936. For the next ten years, Egypt was formally independent though severely constrained by the British. Discontent against the Government culminated in the 1952 revolution by young army officers, led by Colonel Gamal Abdel Nasser. After consolidating his position as President of the new government, Nasser took the Suez Canal into public ownership with all revenues directed to the Egyptian treasury. This led to the Suez Crisis of 1956 in which a combined Anglo-French-Israeli military operation attempted to seize and depose Nasser. The failure of the operation greatly enhanced Nasser's standing and inspired supporters throughout the Middle East who shared his vision of a united Arab world free from foreign interference. Disputes between Arab countries scuppered these plans. The defeat of Arab forces by Israel in the 1967 Six Day War deprived Egypt of the Sinai peninsula and the Gaza strip, land which was recovered only after another defeat by the Israelis in the Yom Kippur war of 1973 and the subsequent Egyptian-Israeli peace initiative which culminated in the 1979 Camp David accord. The treaty was signed on the Egyptian side by Nasser's successor, Anwar El-Sadat, and this, along with the rise of Islamic fundamentalism in Egypt after the Iranian revolution, accounted for his assassination in 1981. Sadat was succeeded by his deputy, Hosni Mubarak, who pursued sinilar policies to his former boss. However, the rapprochement with the Arab world (especially Saudi Arabia), at the Amman Summit in 1987, instigated a new phase of diplomatic relations within the Middle East. The Egyptians have also been closely involved in recent attempts to bring a political solution to the Israeli-Palestinian conflict. Egypt is looking to the new Labour government of Yitzhak Rabin in Israel as the best prospect in recent years for a settlement of the Palestinian issue. Domestically, the Egyptian government continues to worry about the Islamists' persistent political strength and appeal and that the travails of their fundamentalist allies in Algeria and Tunisia will inspire additional support at home. Draconian 'anti-terrorist' legislation has recently been introduced, clearly aimed at the Islamists, who are alleged to have been responsible for a number of terrorist incidents.

GOVERNMENT: The People's Assembly is the legislature. At the General Election of May 1984 the number of members of the Assembly was increased from 392 to 458: 10 nominated by the President and 448 directly elected from 48 constituencies. The Assembly nominates the President, who is elected by popular referendum. The President has executive power and appoints one or more Vice-Presidents, a Prime Minister and a Council of Ministers. There is also a 210-member advisory assembly, the Shura Council.

CLIMATE

Hot, dry summers with mild, dry winters and cold nights. Rainfall is negligible except on the coast. In April the hot, dusty *Khamsin* wind blows from the Sahara.

Required clothing: Lightweight cottons and linens during summer with warmer clothes for winter and cooler evenings.

CAIRO Egypt (95m)

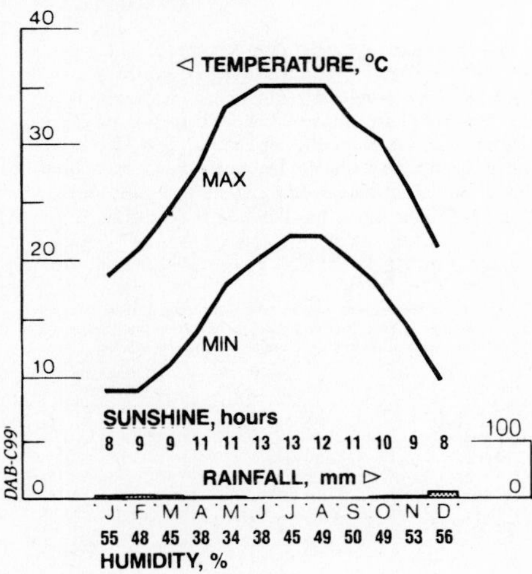

LUXOR Egypt (95m)

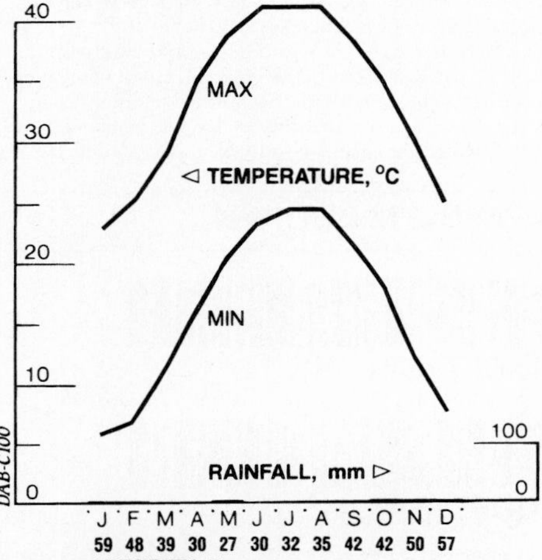

EL SALVADOR

Location: Central America.

Note: The recent history of El Salvador is one of extreme political unrest and instability. Travel to anywhere other than major commercial centres is not recommended; to visit some areas 'safe conduct passes' issued by the military are required. For advice contact the Embassy, at the address below, or the Foreign Office before departure.

Instituto Salvadoreño de Turismo (ISTU)
Calle Rubén Dario 619
San Salvador, El Salvador
Tel: 228 000. Fax: 221 208. Telex: 20775.

Embassy of the Republic of El Salvador
5 Great James Street
London WC1N 3DA
Tel: (071) 430 2141. Fax: (071) 430 0484. Opening hours: 1000-1700 (general enquiries) and 1000-1400 (visa enquiries) Monday to Friday.

British Embassy
PO Box 1591
Paeso General Escalón 4828
San Salvador, El Salvador
Tel: 240 473. Fax: 235 817. Telex: 20033 PRODROME.

Consulate General *and* Embassy of the Republic of El Salvador
2308 California Street, NW
Washington, DC
20008
Tel: (202) 265 9671.

Embassy of the United States of America
Unit 3116
25 Avenida Norte 1230
San Salvador, El Salvador
Tel: 267 100. Fax: 265 839.

Embassy of the Republic of El Salvador
Suite 504
177 Nepean Street
Ottawa, Ontario K2P 0B4
Tel: (613) 238 2939. Fax: (613) 238 6948.

Consulate of Canada
Apartado Postal 3078
111Avenida Las Palmas
Colonia San Benito
San Salvador, El Salvador
Tel: 744 993.

AREA: 21,393 sq km (8260 sq miles).
POPULATION: 5,251,678 (1990 estimate).
POPULATION DENSITY: 245.5 per sq km.
CAPITAL: San Salvador. **Population:** 471,436 (1986).
GEOGRAPHY: El Salvador is located in Central America and is bordered north and west by Guatemala, north and east by Honduras and south and west by the Pacific Ocean. Most of the country is volcanic uplands, along which run two almost parallel rows of volcanoes. The highest are Santa Ana at 2365m (7759ft), San Vicente at 2182m (7159ft) and San Salvador at 1943m (6375ft). Volcanic activity has resulted in a thick layer of

ash and lava on the highlands, ideal for coffee planting. Lowlands lie to the north and south of the high backbone.
LANGUAGE: The official language is Spanish. English is widely spoken.
RELIGION: 99% Roman Catholic and some other Christian denominations.
TIME: GMT - 6.
ELECTRICITY: 110 volts AC, 60Hz.
COMMUNICATIONS: Telephone: IDD available. Country code: 503. IDD is available to Europe, the USA and certain international ports. **Telex:** May be sent from ANTEL. **Post:** Airmail takes up to seven days to reach Britain. Post office hours: 0900-1600 Monday to Friday. **Press:** Four daily newspapers are published in San Salvador, including *Diario de Hoy* and *La Prensa Gráfica*. There are several provincial papers. The *El Salvador News Gazette* is printed in English.
BBC World Service and Voice of America frequencies: From time to time these change. See the section *How to Use this Book* for more information.

BBC:				
MHz	17.72	11.78	9.590	5.975
Voice of America:				
MHz	15.21	11.70	6.130	0.930

PASSPORT/VISA

Regulations and requirements may be subject to change at short notice, and you are advised to contact the appropriate diplomatic or consular authority before finalising travel arrangements. Details of these may be found at the head of this country's entry. Any numbers in the chart refer to the footnotes below.

	Passport Required?	Visa Required?	Return Ticket Required?
Full British	Yes	No	No
BVP	Not valid	-	-
Australian	Yes	Yes	Yes
Canadian	Yes	Yes	Yes
USA	Yes	Yes	Yes
Other EC	Yes	1	Yes
Japanese	Yes	No	Yes

Restricted entry: It is advisable to contact the El Salvador Consulate directly for the latest requirements.
PASSPORTS: Valid passport required by all.
British Visitors Passport: Not acceptable.
VISAS: Required by all except:
(a) **[1]** nationals of Belgium, Denmark, France, Germany, Ireland, Italy, Luxembourg, The Netherlands, Spain and the UK (all other EC nationals *do* require a visa);
(b) nationals of Argentina, Austria, Colombia, Costa Rica, Finland, Guatemala, Honduras, Liechtenstein, Norway, Panama, Sweden and Switzerland;
(c) nationals of Japan.
Note: Nationals of Mexico are required to submit their passport for an approval stamp.
Types of visa: Tourist and Business. Cost: £10 each.
Validity: Business and Tourist: up to 90 days. Visas can be renewed at the Immigration Office in El Salvador.
Application to: Consulate (or Consular Section at Embassy). For addresses, see top of entry.
Application requirements: (a) Application form. (b) Photo. (c) Valid passport.
Working days required: Business visas – 48 hours. Tourist visas – 10 working days.
Temporary residence: Apply to Ministry of Interior in San Salvador.

MONEY

Currency: Colón, ES¢ (colloquially 'Peso') = 100 centavos. Notes are in denominations of ES¢100, 50, 25, 10, 5, 2 and 1. Coins are in denominations of ES¢1, and 50, 25, 10, 5, 3, 2 and 1 centavos. Prices are sometimes shown in US Dollars.
Currency exchange: The legal rate of exchange is 8 Colónes to the US Dollar. Banks generally charge 1 Colón for changing money and cheques. A black market operates for US Dollars (cash only) at the borders and in the capital outside the new post offices, but this is strictly prohibited.
Credit cards: American Express, Visa and Access/Mastercard are widely accepted, whilst Diners Club has more limited use. Check with your credit card company for details of merchant acceptability and other services which may be available.
Travellers cheques: These may be cashed at any bank or hotel on production of a passport.
Note: Visitors should reconvert all unspent Colónes before entering Guatemala or Honduras, as they are neither exchanged or accepted in these countries.
Exchange rate indicators: The following figures have been included as a guide to the movements of the Colón against Sterling and the US Dollar:

Date:	Oct '89	Oct '90	Oct '91	Oct '92
£1.00=	7.89	12.40	13.91	13.83
$1.00=	*5.00	6.35	8.01	8.71

Note [*]: The Colón is tied to the US Dollar.
Currency restrictions: Import of foreign currency is free, subject to declaration. Export of foreign currency is limited to the amount declared on import. On leaving the country Salvadorean Colónes can be exchanged.
Banking hours: 0900-1300 and 1345-1600 Monday to Friday.
Note: All banks are closed for balancing on June 29-30 and December 30-31.

DUTY FREE

The following goods may be imported into El Salvador without incurring customs duty:
1kg of tobacco or 600 cigarettes or 100 cigars;
2 bottles of alcoholic beverage;
A reasonable amount of perfume;
Gifts to the value of US$100.
Note: The following items may also be brought in:
1 photographic or film camera with accessories, and a maximum of 6 films;
1 each of radios, tape recorders and record players for personal use.

PUBLIC HOLIDAYS

Public holidays observed in El Salvador are as follows:
Apr 9-12 '93 Easter. **May 1** Labour Day. **Jun 10** Corpus Christi. **Aug 4-6** San Salvador Festival. **Sep 15** Independence Day. **Oct 12** Discovery of America. **Nov 2** All Soul's Day. **Nov 5** First Call for Independence. **Dec 24-25** Christmas. **Jan 1 '94** New Year's Day.

HEALTH

Regulations and requirements may be subject to change at short notice, and you are advised to contact your doctor well in advance of your intended date of departure. Any numbers in the chart refer to the footnotes below.

	Special Precautions?	Certificate Required?
Yellow Fever	No	1
Cholera	No	No
Typhoid & Polio	Yes	-
Malaria	2	-
Food & Drink	3	-

[1]: A yellow fever vaccination certificate is required from travellers over six months of age coming from infected areas.
[2]: Malaria risk, predominantly in the benign *vivax* form, exists all year throughout the country, but is greater below 600m in the rainy season (May to October).
[3]: All water should be regarded as being potentially contaminated. Water used for drinking, brushing teeth or making ice should have first been boiled or otherwise sterilised. Milk is unpasteurised and should be boiled. Powdered or tinned milk is available and is advised, but make sure that it is reconstituted with pure water. Avoid dairy products which are likely to have been made from unboiled milk. Only eat well-cooked meat and fish, preferably served hot. Pork, salad and mayonnaise may carry increased risk. Vegetables should be cooked and fruit peeled.
Rabies is a serious risk in El Salvador. It is primarily transmitted by dogs and bats, but persons bitten by any animal should seek medical attention promptly. For persons at high risk of exposure on a continuing basis, it may be advisable to have a course of rabies vaccine. Persons taking animals to El Salvador should be certain that the animals are immunised against rabies. See the *Health* section at the back of the book.
Health care: There about 50 state-run hospitals with a total of more than 7000 beds. Health insurance is strongly advised.

TRAVEL - International

AIR: El Salvador's national airline is *TACA International Airlines (TA)*.
Approximate flight time: From *London* to El Salvador *excluding* stopover time in USA (usually overnight) is 10 hours 20 minutes.
International airport: *San Salvador (SAL)* (El Salvador International) is 44km (27 miles) from the city. Airport facilities include a restaurant, duty-free shops and car hire. Coach travel to the city is available 0600-1900. Taxis to the city are also available.
Departure tax: ES¢92 or US$12 is payable when leaving the country via the airport at any time of day or night. It is advisable to carry small denomination notes to pay for this.
SEA: The principal ports are *La Union*, *La Libertad* and *Acajutla* on the Pacific coast.
RAIL: There are rail links to Guatemala. Contact the Embassy for passage details.
ROAD: There are frequent buses from San Salvador to Guatemala City. Scheduled services to Honduras have been suspended, but local buses travel as far as the border. If arriving at the border during off-duty hours (from 1200-1400 and 1800-0800, and from 1200 Saturdays to 2000 Mondays) a duty must be paid in exact cash notes.

TRAVEL - Internal

AIR: Services are available from San Salvador to San Miguel, La Unión and Usulután.
RAIL: There are over 600km (372 miles) of railways, linking San Salvador with Acajutla, Cutuco, San Jeronimo and Angiuatu.
ROAD: There are more than 12,000km (7440 miles) of roads around the country; a third of this network is either paved or improved to allow all-weather use. **Bus:** A good service exists between major towns. **Car hire:** Car rental is available from San Salvador. **Documentation:** A National or International Driving Permit is required. A vehicle may remain in the country for 30 days, and for a further 60 days on application to the Customs and Transport authorities.
URBAN: Bus: City buses offer a good service, but are often crowded. **Taxi:** Plentiful but not metered, so it is advisable to agree fare beforehand. Large hotels have their own taxi services.
JOURNEY TIMES: The following chart gives approximate journey times from San Salvador to other major cities/towns in El Salvador.

	Road
Costa del Sol	0.50
Santa Ana	1.15
San Miguel	3.00

ACCOMMODATION

HOTELS: The main hotels are in the capital, and accommodation should be booked in advance. The situation for foreign visitors remains unstable, and advice

EL SALVADOR | **HEALTH REGULATIONS** | **VISA REGULATIONS** | Code-Link

GALILEO/WORLDSPAN
TI-DFT/SAL/HE
TI-DFT/SAL/VI

SABRE

TIDFT/SAL/HE

TIDFT/SAL/VI

To access this information on your CRS, swipe the barcode with a light pen or type in the text under the barcode. For more information, see the introduction *How to Use This Book*.

should be sought from the Embassy. *Lake Coatepeque* is a popular resort which has good hotels, restaurants and lodging houses. **Grading:** Hotels in El Salvador can be classified into three groups: deluxe, first-class and smaller hotels/guest-houses.

RESORTS & EXCURSIONS

San Salvador: Situated 680m (2240ft) above sea level, San Salvador, which is the second largest city in Central America, is the capital. It has an estimated population of over 800,000. Founded by the Spaniard Gonzalo De Alvarado in 1545, the city is a blend of modern buildings and colonial architecture, broad plazas and monuments, amusement parks and shopping centres. Downtown are the most important public buildings. Standing within a short distance of each other are the *Cathedral*, the *National Palace*, the *National Treasury* and the *National Theatre*. Among the churches to be seen are *St Ignatius Loyola*, once the *Shrine of the Virgin of Guadaloupe*, with its traditional Spanish Colonial facade. The amusement park on San Jacinto Mountain can be reached by cable car and gives a panoramic view of the city. *Balboa Park* and the 1200m (3900ft) rock formation, the *Devil's Doorway*, also give a birds' eye view.
Elsewhere: Excursions can be made by road to **Panchimalco**, around which live the Pancho Indians (pure-blooded descendants of the original Pipil tribes, who retain many of their old traditions and dress); to *Lake Ilopango*, worth a visit for its extraordinary scenery; and to the volcanoes of San Salvador and Izalco (1910m/6270ft).
The town of **Ilobasco** is renowned for its beauty and its craftwork. The *Tazumal Ruins*, situated in the city of **Chalchuapa,** 78km (46 miles) from San Salvador, are worth a visit, as are the *San Andres Ruins*.
El Salvador has a 320km (200-mile) Pacific Coast with resort hotels, unspoiled beaches, fishing villages and pine views. The best resorts tend to be found along the *Costa del Sol*, easily accessible via a modern highway.
For an inland resort, the region of *Lake Coatepeque* at the foot of the *Santa Ana Volcano* is recommended. It has good hotels, restaurants and lodging houses.

SOCIAL PROFILE

FOOD & DRINK: There are numerous Chinese, Mexican, Italian and French and local restaurants, plus several fast food chains. The food market (one of the biggest and cleanest in Latin America) has many stalls selling cheap food.
NIGHTLIFE: San Salvador has a few nightclubs and cocktail lounges with dinner and dancing, some of which require membership. There are many cinemas, some showing English-language films with subtitles; there are also some 'juke box' dance-halls and theatres.
SHOPPING: Various goods can be bought at the *Mercado Cuartel* crafts market, including towels in Maya designs. **Shopping hours:** 0900-1200 and 1400-1800 Monday to Friday, 0800-1200 Saturday.
SPORT: Visitors can watch or take part in **bowling, mini-golf, football** (played regularly at San Salvador's stadium), **horse-racing** and **motor-racing. Basketball, tennis, swimming, fishing, target shooting, wrestling, boxing,** boat and sailing **boat races** are available in private clubs only.
SPECIAL EVENTS: For full details of special events and festivals in El Salvador contact the National Tourism Institute or Embassy.
SOCIAL CONVENTIONS: Conservative casual wear is acceptable. **Photography:** Sensitive (eg military) areas should not be photographed. **Tipping:** 10% in hotels and restaurants. 15% is appropriate for smaller bills. Taxi drivers do not expect tips, except when the taxi has been hired for the day.

BUSINESS PROFILE

ECONOMY: The civil war, together with drought and flooding, has caused economic decline in El Salvador's mainly agricultural economy. The principal commercial crop is coffee, which is the country's major export earner. Other important crops are cotton, sugar, maize, beans and rice. There is a sizeable manufacturing sector – the largest in Central America – which is engaged in producing footwear, textiles, leather goods and pharmaceuticals. El Salvador has a substantial foreign debt and relies heavily on United States aid and loans from the International Monetary Fund. El Salvador is a member of the Central American Common Market. The recent political settlement in El Salvador has been accompanied by the provision of a stand-by facility from the IMF to support an economic programme aimed at reducing inflation to single figures, strengthening the balance of payments and achieveing 3-4% economic growth. The US is the country's largest trading partner, followed by Guatemala, Germany and Japan.
BUSINESS: Business people are expected to wear suits. Although some local business people speak English, a good knowledge of Spanish is important. Visiting cards are essential. The best months for business visits are September to March, avoiding the Christmas period.
Office hours: 0800-1230 and 1430-1730 Monday to Friday.
COMMERCIAL INFORMATION: The following organisation can offer advice: Cámara de Comercio e Industria de El Salvador, 9a Avenida Norte y 5a Calle Poniente, Apartado 1640, San Salvador. Tel: 712 055. Fax: 714 461. Telex: 20753.

HISTORY & GOVERNMENT

HISTORY: A Spanish colony until 1821, the history of El Salvador has been one of frequent military coups and outbursts of political violence. The present constitution for the election of a President and a representative Assembly was adopted in 1983, but since there has been a military coup every five years, the military exerts a strong influence over the political life of the country. As in most of Central America, US influences pervade cultural life and guide political development. A disputed election in 1972, won by a Conservative military candidate, triggered the most recent spell of political violence. It was the assassination in 1980 of Archbishop Romero, a leading critic of civil rights abuses, reputedly by right-wing elements, that accelerated the country's plunge into civil war. Over the next decade, the Government received huge amounts of US military and civil aid and often fought a fairly effective counter-insurgency campaign against leftist guerrillas of the Faribundo Marti Liberation Front (FMLN), who were largely based in the countryside. Peace talks began in earnest in 1989, after a major offensive by the guerrillas persuaded the Government that there would be no outright military victor. Cajoled by President Alfredo Cristiani of the right-wing ARENA party, the military – particularly the hard-line faction associated with Major Roberto d'Aubuisson – reluctantly accepted the need for a settlement. The support given to Democratic Convergence, a political movement loosely allied with the guerrillas, showed they enjoyed significant political support. A formal ceasefire, under UN auspices, came into force at the beginning of February 1992. The process is under the day-to-day supervision of a joint forum of the two sides, entitled the National Commission for the Consolidation of Peace (COPAZ). By mid-summer, normalisation was proceeding according to plan, but was falling behind schedule. The military still exert occasional pressure on the Government to reject the plan.
GOVERNMENT: Executive power in the Republic of El Salvador is vested in a President, elected by universal adult suffrage every five years. He is assisted by a Vice-President and a Council of Ministers. Legislation is formulated by the 60-member National Assembly, elected by universal adult suffrage every three years.

CLIMATE

Hot, subtropical climate affected by altitude. Coastal areas are particularly hot, with a rainy season between May and October. Upland areas have a cooler, temperate climate.
Required clothing: Lightweight cottons and rainwear during the wet season in coastal areas. Waterproof clothing is advisable all year round.

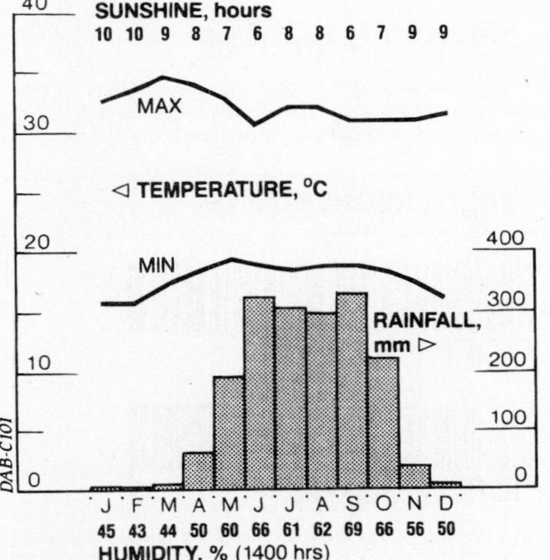

EQUATORIAL GUINEA

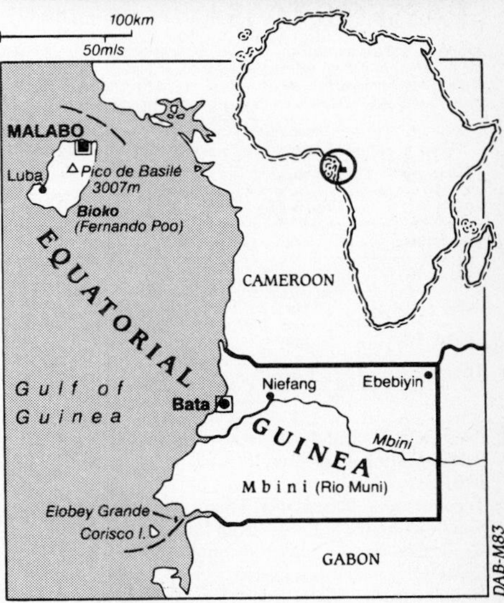

Location: West Africa, Gulf of Guinea.

Embassy of the Republic of Equatorial Guinea
6 rue Alfred de Vigny
75008 Paris, France
Tel: (1) 47 66 44 33 *or* 47 66 95 70.
British Consulate
World Bank Compound
Apartado 801
Malabo
Equatorial Guinea
Tel: 2400. Telex: 5403.
Embassy of the United States
Calle de los Ministros
Apartado 597
Malabo
Equatorial Guinea
Tel: 2406 *or* 2507 *or* 2185. Fax: 2164.
The Canadian Embassy to Equatorial Guinea
c/o The Canadian Embassy
PO Box 4037
Libreville, Gabon
Tel: 743 464 *or* 743 465.

AREA: 28,051 sq km (10,830 sq miles).
POPULATION: 348,000 (1990 estimate).
POPULATION DENSITY: 12.4 per sq km.
CAPITAL: Malabo. **Population:** 15,253 (1983).
GEOGRAPHY: Equatorial Guinea is bordered to the south and east by Gabon, to the north by Cameroon and to the west by the Gulf of Guinea. The country also comprises the island of Bioko, formerly Fernando Poo, 34km (21 miles) off the coast of Cameroon, and the small offshore islands of Corisco, Great Elobey, Small Elobey and Pagalu. The mainland province, Mbini, is mainly forest, with plantations on the coastal plain and some mountains. Bioko rises steeply to two main peaks in the north and the south. The southern area is rugged and inaccessible. Cultivation and settlements exist on the other slopes; above the farming land, the forest is thick. The beaches around the islands are extremely beautiful.
LANGUAGE: Spanish is the official language. African dialects including Fang and Bubi are spoken.
RELIGION: No official religion, but people are mainly Roman Catholic, with an Animist minority.
TIME: GMT + 1.
ELECTRICITY: 220/240 volts.
COMMUNICATIONS: Telephone: IDD is available. Country code: 240. **Post:** Service to Europe takes up to two weeks. **Press:** Equatorial Guinea has two dailies, *Ebano* in Spanish and *Portopoto* in Fang.

BBC World Service and Voice of America frequencies: From time to time these change. See the section *How to Use this Book* for more information.

BBC:				
MHz	25.75	17.88	15.40	7.105
Voice of America:				
MHz	21.49	15.60	9.525	6.035

PASSPORT/VISA

Regulations and requirements may be subject to change at short notice, and you are advised to contact the appropriate diplomatic or consular authority before finalising travel arrangements. Details of these may be found at the head of this country's entry. Any numbers in the chart refer to the footnotes below.

	Passport Required?	Visa Required?	Return Ticket Required?
Full British	Yes	Yes	Yes
BVP	Not valid	-	-
Australian	Yes	Yes	Yes
Canadian	Yes	Yes	Yes
USA	Yes	Yes	Yes
Other EC	Yes	Yes	Yes
Japanese	Yes	Yes	Yes

PASSPORTS: Valid passport required by all.
British Visitors Passport: Not accepted.
VISAS: Required by all.
Types of visas: Business and Tourist. Cost: Ffr350.
Validity: Enquire at Consulate or Embassy.
Application to: Consulate (or Consular Section at Embassy). For addresses, see top of entry. Application should be made well in advance (at least 2 months), unless application is made directly from Paris where it takes 2 days.
Exit permit: Necessary only if visa has run out. This can normally be arranged at the airport.

MONEY

Currency: CFA Franc (CFA Fr) = 100 centimes. Notes are in denominations of CFA Fr10,000, 5000, 1000, 500 and 100. Coins are in denominations of CFA Fr500, 100, 50, 25, 10, 5, 2 and 1. Until December 31, 1984, the currency was the Ekuele (Ek), pegged to the Spanish Peseta. The country is now part of the French monetary area and Ekuele banknotes should not be accepted as they are worthless.
Credit cards: Diners Club accepted on a limited basis. Check with your credit card company for details of merchant acceptability and other services which may be available.
Exchange rate indicators: The following figures are included as a guide to the movements of the CFA Franc against Sterling and the US Dollar:

Date:	**Oct '89**	**Oct '90**	**Oct '91**	**Oct '92**
£1.00=	505.13	498.38	496.13	413.75
$1.00=	319.90	255.12	285.87	260.71

Currency restrictions: The import of local currency is unrestricted. Export of local currency is limited to CFA Fr3000. It is worth remembering that CFA Franc notes cannot easily be exchanged outside the CFA Franc area. There are no restrictions on the import and export of foreign currency.
Banking hours: 0800-1200 Monday to Saturday.

DUTY FREE

The following goods may be imported into Equatorial Guinea without incurring customs duty:
200 cigarettes or 50 cigars or 250g of tobacco;
1 litre of wine;
1 litre of alcoholic beverage;
A reasonable amount of perfume.
Prohibited items: Spanish newspapers.

PUBLIC HOLIDAYS

Public holidays observed in Equatorial Guinea are as follows:
Mar 5 '93 Independence Day. **Apr 9** Good Friday. **Apr 12** Easter Monday. **May 1** Labour Day. **May 25** OAU Day. **Dec 10** Human Rights Day. **Dec 25** Christmas. **Jan 1 '94** New Year's Day. **Mar 5** Independence Day.

HEALTH

Regulations and requirements may be subject to change at short notice, and you are advised to contact your doctor well in advance of your intended date of departure. Any numbers in the chart refer to the footnotes below.

	Special Precautions?	Certificate Required?
Yellow Fever	Yes	1
Cholera	Yes	2
Typhoid & Polio	Yes	-
Malaria	3	-
Food & Drink	4	-

[1]: A yellow fever vaccination certificate is required from travellers coming from infected areas.
[2]: Following WHO guidelines issued in 1973, a cholera vaccination certificate is no longer a condition of entry to Equatorial Guinea. However, cholera is a serious risk in this country and precautions are essential. Up-to-date advice should be sought before deciding whether these precautions should include vaccination as medical opinion is divided over its effectiveness. See the *Health* section at the back of the book.
[3]: Malaria risk, predominantly in the malignant *falciparum* form, all year throughout the country. Resistance to chloroquine has been reported.
[4]: All water should be regarded as being potentially contaminated. Water used for drinking, brushing teeth or making ice should have first been boiled or otherwise sterilised. Milk is unpasteurised and should be boiled. Powdered or tinned milk is available and is advised, but make sure that it is reconstituted with pure water. Avoid dairy products which are likely to have been made from unboiled milk. Only eat well-cooked meat and fish, preferably served hot. Pork, salad and mayonnaise may carry increased risk. Vegetables should be cooked and fruit peeled.
Bilharzia (schistosomiasis) is present. Avoid swimming and paddling in fresh water. Swimming pools which are well-chlorinated and maintained are safe.
Health care: Medical insurance (to include emergency repatriation) is strongly advised.

TRAVEL - International

AIR: Equatorial Guinea's national airline is *Aerolíneas Guinea Ecuatorial*, which operates regular services to some neighbouring countries. There are direct flights from Spain to Malabo.
International airports: There are international airports at *Malabo (SSG)*, 7km (4 miles) from the city centre, and *Bata*, 6km (3.7miles) from the city centre.
Departure tax: In general CFA Fr2250, but note that this will vary according to flight, route and class of travel.
SEA: The main ports are Malabo and Bata, with sailings to Spain and the Canary Islands.
ROAD: Roads link Equatorial Guinea with Cameroon and Gabon (bush taxis are available); road surfaces are not always good. Most travellers enter from Douala in Cameroon.

TRAVEL - Internal

AIR: There are flights between Malabo and Bata every day except Sunday, and it is advisable to book in advance. Light aircraft can be chartered in Malabo with international pilot's qualifications.
Departure tax: CFA Fr1000.
SEA: There is a ferry between Malabo, Bata and Douala. The trip takes about 12 hours. There are four classes of fare.
ROAD: There are few tarred roads in the country. On Bioko, the north is generally better served with tarred roads. Bush taxis connect Malabo with Luba and Riaba and can be hired hourly or daily. There are no car rental facilities.

ACCOMMODATION

Only in Malabo and Bata are the hotels of an acceptable standard for the majority of European travellers. For more information, contact the Embassy in Paris.

RESORTS & EXCURSIONS

Equatorial Guinea is still recovering from the effects of the Macias Nguema dictatorship. The capital, **Malabo,** is a shabby but attractive town, with old Spanish colonial architecture. The *Spanish Cultural Centre* is worth a visit. *Mount Malabo* overlooks the city. **Luba** (an hour's drive from Malabo) has some lovely and deserted beaches.

SOCIAL PROFILE

FOOD & DRINK: There are very few restaurants in Equatorial Guinea and those that exist are mainly restricted to Malabo and Bata, and do not necessarily open every day.
SHOPPING: Shopping hours: 0800-1830 Monday to Friday and 0900-1400 Saturday.
SOCIAL CONVENTIONS: Foreign visitors (especially Europeans) are a comparative rarity in Equatorial Guinea and are liable to be met with much curiosity and, possibly, suspicion. Foreign cigarettes are appreciated as gifts. A knowledge of Spanish is useful. **Photography:** A permit is required. Care should be taken when choosing subjects. **Tipping:** Unless service charges are added to bills, 10-15%.

BUSINESS PROFILE

ECONOMY: Equatorial Guinea produces timber, coffee and bananas for export, and is just self-sufficient in other basic food products. Cocoa production is being re-established on Bioko Island after serious disruption which followed a long period of political instability. Industry is virtually non-existent. There are thought to be mineral deposits inland, including gold and uranium, but prospecting is hampered by the lack of transport systems in the country. Offshore drilling has located deposits of natural gas and preliminary surveys carried out with French and Spanish co-operation in 1984 suggest the presence of oil. Spain remains Equatorial Guinea's principal trading partner, followed by France, Germany and Italy. The country has now joined the Central African Customs and Economic Union, UDEAC, and the CFA Franc Zone. Equatorial Guinea receives large injections of foreign aid from a variety of bilateral and multilateral sources.
BUSINESS: Jackets and ties are only necessary for governmental business. The best time to visit is December to January. Since joining the CFA Franc Zone, external trade has increased. However, it is essential to speak some Spanish as there is no interpreter service and French and pidgin English are only occasionally used. Accommodation arrangements are best made through contacts in Equatorial Guinea.
Office hours: 0800-1700 Monday to Friday.
COMMERCIAL INFORMATION: The following

EQUATORIAL GUINEA — **HEALTH REGULATIONS** — **VISA REGULATIONS** — Code-Link

GALILEO/WORLDSPAN

TI-DFT/SSG/HE

TI-DFT/SSG/VI

SABRE

TIDFT/SSG/HE

TIDFT/SSG/VI

To access this information on your CRS, swipe the barcode with a light pen or type in the text under the barcode. For more information, see the introduction *How to Use This Book.*

organisation can offer advice: Cámara de Comercio, Agrícola y Forestal de Malabo, Apartado 51, Malabo. Tel: 151.

HISTORY & GOVERNMENT

HISTORY: The area now occupied by Equatorial Guinea and the island of Bioko was first colonised by the Portuguese in the late 15th century and developed as a major slave market. The territory was handed over to the Spanish in 1788, who ran it as a protectorate of Spanish Guinea until 1959, when the colony was granted internal self-government. Full independence followed in 1968. The country is still recovering from the effects of the brutal dictatorship of President Macias Nguema. In 1979 he was overthrown in a military coup led by his nephew Lieutenant Colonel Teodoro Obiang Nguema Mbasogo. The general situation has improved slightly since Macias' leadership. The country has been helped by the resumption of international aid (particularly from France and Spain) and by the admission of the country to full membership of the Central African Customs and Economic Union (UDEAC) in December 1983, and by its becoming part of the French monetary area two years later. In 1989, Obiang won an election at which he was the only candidate. Relations with Spain, the former colonial power, remained touchy once the level of aid from Spain was made dependent on progress to democratise the political system. In the main, outside the country, only the Spanish press comments upon (and criticises) Equatorial Guinea's internal affairs. For this reason Spanish newspapers are prohibited. In late 1991, the Government conceded with the introduction of a new draft constitution allowing for the formation of opposition political parties and the separation of the posts of Prime Minister and President. In February 1992, an interim Government was appointed pending the holding of free multi-party elections, although these have yet to be held and reports have continued to emerge of repressive measures against the Government's opponents. It is now widely believed that reforms were announced solely for the purpose of unlocking Spanish and French foreign aid which the country badly needs (70% of GDP derives from overseas aid).
GOVERNMENT: In 1983 a new constitution was adopted by referendum which, although creating democratic institutions, allowed for power to be kept firmly in President Obiang's hands.

CLIMATE

Tropical climate all year round. Rainfall is heavy for most of the year, decreasing slightly in most areas between December and February.
Required clothing: Lightweight cottons and linens.

MALABO Equatorial Guinea (12m)

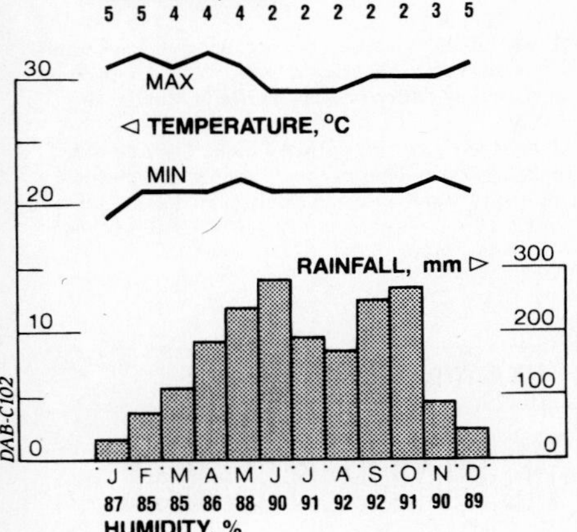

TEMPERATURE CONVERSIONS
-20 -10 0°C 10 20 30 40
0 10 20 30°F40 50 60 70 80 90 100
RAINFALL CONVERSIONS 0mm 200 400 600 800
0in 5 10 15 20 25 30

ESTONIA

☐ international airport

Location: Northern Europe.

National Tourist Board
Suur-Karja 23
EE-0001 Tallinn, Estonia
Tel: (42) 441 239. Fax: (42) 440 963.
Embassy of the Republic of Estonia
18 Chepstow Villas
London W11 2RB
Tel: (071) 229 6700. Fax: (071) 792 0218. Opening hours: 0900-1200 and 1500-1700 Monday to Friday.
British Embassy
Kentmanni 20
EE-0001 Tallinn, Estonia
Tel: (42) 455 328/9 *or* 455 353/4. Fax: (010358) 298 107 (cellular line). Telex: 173974.
Embassy of the Republic of Estonia
Suite 142
9 Rockefeller Plaza
New York, NY
10020
Tel: (212) 247 1450. Fax: (212) 262 0893.
Embassy of the United States of America
Kentmanni 20
EE-0001 Tallinn, Estonia
Tel: (010358) 303 182 (cellular line). Fax: (010358) 306 817 (cellular line).
Consulate General of the Republic of Estonia
Suite 202
958 Broadview Avenue
Toronto, Ontario
M4K 2R6
Tel: (416) 461 0764. Fax: (416) 461 0448.

AREA: 45,215 sq km (17,458 sq miles).
POPULATION: 1,582,000 (1991 estimate).
POPULATION DENSITY: 35 per sq km.
CAPITAL: Tallinn. **Population:** 484,400 (1990 estimate).
GEOGRAPHY: Estonia is the most northerly of the three Baltic Republics and is bordered to the north and west by the Baltic Sea, to the East by the Russian Federation and to the south by Latvia. The country is one of great scenic beauty with many forests, 1500 lakes and 800 islands.
LANGUAGE: Estonian. The Government has pledged to provide all non-ethnic Estonians with one year's free tuition in the Estonian language. Since independence the indiscriminate use of Russian could on occasion cause offence. English should be used if unsure.
RELIGION: Predominantly Protestant (Lutheran).
TIME: GMT + 2 (Summer, GMT + 3).
ELECTRICITY: 220 volts AC, 50Hz. European-style 2-pin plugs are in use.
COMMUNICATIONS: Telephone: IDD service is available. Country code: 701. **Post:** Post to Western Europe takes up to six days. **Press:** Newspapers are published in Estonian. The English-language newspaper *The Estonian Independent* is published weekly.
BBC World Service and Voice of America frequencies: From time to time these change. See the section *How to Use this Book* for more information.

BBC:				
MHz	12.09	9.750	6.195	3.955
Voice of America:				
MHz	11.97	9.670	6.040	5.995

PASSPORT/VISA

Regulations and requirements may be subject to change at short notice, and you are advised to contact the appropriate diplomatic or consular authority before finalising travel arrangements. Details of these may be found at the head of this country's entry. Any numbers in the chart refer to the footnotes below.

	Passport Required?	Visa Required?	Return Ticket Required?
Full British	Yes	No	Yes
BVP	Valid	No	Yes
Australian	Yes	Yes	Yes
Canadian	Yes	Yes	Yes
USA	Yes	Yes/2	Yes
Other EC	Yes	1	Yes
Japanese	Yes	Yes	Yes

PASSPORT: Required by all.
British Visitors Passport: Accepted.
VISA: Required by all except [1] nationals of the Republic of Ireland and the UK. For the latest information contact the relevant authorities *at least 3 weeks* before travelling.
Types of visa: Tourist and Transit. Cost: *Transit:* £5 – *Single entry* – £10; *Multiple entry* – £30. [2] Visas for nationals of the USA are issued free of charge.
Validity: Single entry – 1 month; Transit – 3 days, and Multiple entry – 12 months. Visas for Estonia are also valid for Latvia and Lithuania.
Applications to: Consulate (or Consular Section of Embassy). For addresses, see above.
Application requirements: (a) Completed application form. (b) Valid passport. (c) 1 photo. (d) Company letter for business travellers.
Working days required: Personal – 10-15 min; postal – 2 days.

MONEY

Currency: 1 Kroon = 100 sents. Roubles and kopeks are no longer accepted. Notes are in denominations of 500, 100, 50, 25 *or* 20, 2 and 1 kroon. Coins are in denominations of 1 kroon, and 20, 5, 2 and 1 sents. Definite information was unavailable at time of going to press.
Currency exchange: The value of the kroon has initially been pegged to the Deutschmark at a rate of 8 kroon = DM1 with a 3% band allowed for fluctuation.
Credit cards: Credit cards are accepted on a very limited basis. Check with your credit card company for details of merchant acceptability and other services which may be available.
Exchange rate indicators: The following figures are included as a guide to the value of the Estonian Kroon against Sterling and the US Dollar:

Date:	**Oct '92**
£1.00=	**19.54**
$1.00=	**12.31**

Currency restrictions: The import and export of local and foreign currency is unrestricted.
Banking hours: 0930-1730 Monday to Friday.

DUTY FREE

The following goods may be imported into Estonia without incurring customs duty:
200 cigarettes or 20 cigars or 250g tobacco;
1 litre of spirits and 1 litre of wine;
10 litres of beer.

PUBLIC HOLIDAYS

Public holidays observed in Estonia are as follows:
Apr 9 '93 Good Friday. **Apr 12** Easter Monday. **May 1** Labour Day. **Jun 23** Victory Day (Anniversary of the

Battle of Võnnu). **Jun 26** Midsummer Day. **Dec 25-26** Christmas. **Jan 1 '94** New Year's Day. **Feb 24** Independence Day.

HEALTH

Regulations and requirements may be subject to change at short notice, and you are advised to contact your doctor well in advance of your intended date of departure. Any numbers in the chart refer to the footnotes below.

	Special Precautions?	Certificate Required?
Yellow Fever	No	No
Cholera	No	No
Typhoid & Polio	No	-
Malaria	No	-
Food & Drink	No	-

Rabies is present. For those at high risk, vaccination before arrival should be considered. If you are bitten abroad seek medical advice without delay. For more information consult the *Health* section at the back of the book.
Health care: Medical insurance is recommended.

TRAVEL - International

AIR: Estonia's national airline is *Estonian Airlines*. There are direct weekly flights on Saturdays from Frankfurt/M in Germany to Tallinn and indirect flights to Tallinn via Moscow, Helsinki or Stockholm from all major European cities. Connections to the US are via Helsinki and New York or Los Angeles.
International flight times: From *Frankfurt* to Tallinn takes about 2 hours 30 minutes. From *Los Angeles* to Tallinn takes approximately 22 hours (via Helsinki). From *London* to Tallinn takes approximately 5 hours (via Helsinki). From *New York* to Tallinn takes approximately 13 hours 30 minutes (via Helsinki).
International airport: *Tallinn* (TLL) is located 4km (2.5 miles) southeast of the city. Flight information is in operation 24 hours (tel: (42) 211 092). Bus no 22 runs between the city and the airport (travel time – 20 mins); taxis are also available. The airport facilities include bank (0900-1700), duty-free shops (0900-1800), shops (0900-1800) and car rental (tel: (42) 212 735).
SEA: The *Finnjet* runs daily from Travemünde in Germany to Helsinki, where it connects with the *Tallink* to Tallinn. The *Nord Estonia* runs from Stockholm in Sweden to Tallinn three to four times a week. The crossing takes 14 hours.
RAIL: Estonia has an underdeveloped rail system although there are links to the Russian Federation and Latvia. There are daily trains from Berlin (Germany) to Riga with connections to Tallinn.
ROAD: There are direct routes along the Baltic coast into Latvia and Lithuania and also east into the Russian Federation. Routes are via Poland and Belarus or Poland and Lithuania; border points: Terespol (Poland)–Brest (Belarus) and Ogrodniki (Poland)–Lazdijai (Lithuania).

TRAVEL - Internal

AIR: There are domestic flights from Tallinn to Tartu in the south of the country.
RAIL: The rail system is underdeveloped but rail services to Tartu take about 3 hours 30 minutes from Tallinn.
ROAD: Estonia has a high density of roads although there are few major highways. Lead free and 4-star petrol are only available at two petrol stations in Tallinn and Pärnu. Payment is in local currency only, although credit cards may be accepted on occasions. Breakdown services are not yet available. **Car hire:** Can be arranged through *Hertz* at Tartu mnt. 13, Tallinn. Tel: (42) 421 003.
Documentation: European nationals should be in possession of the new European driving licence.
URBAN: Taxis in Tallinn are inexpensive. All parts of the city can also be reached by bus.

ACCOMMODATION

HOTELS: Since independence there has been a scramble from Western firms to turn the old state-run hotels into modern Western-standard enterprises. There have already been successful Estonian/Finnish joint ventures such as the *Palace Hotel* in Tallinn, which offers every comfort to be expected from a modern Western hotel catering to both tourists and business travellers, such as satellite television, cocktail lounge and conference facilities. Many more such joint ventures with firms from all over western Europe and the United States will ensure that the standard of accommodation in Estonia rapidly reaches western European levels. Outside Tallinn, which for the time being is the main location of the current expansion, Estonia enjoys an adequate range of acceptable accommodation, left over from the pre-independence days, including large hotels and smaller pension-type establishments. For more details contact the Embassy (address at beginning of entry).
YOUTH HOSTELS: The majority of Youth Hostels have saunas and seminar facilities. For further information contact Estonian Youth Hostels, Kentmanni 20, EE-0001 Tallinn. Tel: (42) 442 898. Fax: (42) 446 971.
CAMPING: There are four campsites in Estonia. These are as follows: Camping & Motel Peoleo, 12km (7.5 miles) south of Tallinn; Camping Kernu, 40km (25 miles) south of Tallinn; Motel Valgerrand in Pärnu and Camping Malvaste on the island of Malvaste.

RESORTS & EXCURSIONS

Tallinn, an ancient Hanseatic city and the capital of Estonia, has a wealth of historical and architectural monuments, particularly in the old town centre which is dominated by the soaring steeple of the medieval *Town Hall* (14th-15th centuries), the oldest in northern Europe. At least two-thirds of the original *City Wall* still stands and a superb view of the narrow streets, the gabled roofs and the towers and spires of old Tallinn is afforded from *Toompea Castle*, situated on a cliff-top. A favourite recreation spot is *Kadriorg Park*, which contains the palace built for Peter the Great.
About two hours drive from Tallinn is **Pärnu**, a small town situated on the banks of the Pärnu River where it emerges into the Riga Bay. Established in the 13th century, the town is known as a seaport and a health resort. Among its attractions are its theatre and its 2-mile-long sandy beach which is very popular with Estonians.
Tartu is Estonia's second largest city and lies about 110 miles from Tallinn on the *Emajõgi River*. The city has a very old university and other sights include the *Vyshgorod Cathedral* (13th-15th centuries), the *Town Hall* (18th century) and the university's *Botanical Garden*.

SOCIAL PROFILE

FOOD & DRINK: Hors d'oeuvres are very good and often the best part of the meal. Local specialities include *sult* (jellied veal), *taidetud basikarind* (roast stuffed shoulder of veal) and *rossolye* (vinaigrette with herring and beets). Braised goose stuffed with apples and plums is also a Baltic speciality.
NIGHTLIFE: Tallinn is used to entertaining trippers from over the water in Finland and has a wide range of restaurants, cafés and bars. There is also an opera and ballet theatre.
SHOPPING: Amber and local folk-art are good buys.
SPORT: **Basketball** is very popular. Also cross-country **skiing.** The national **football** team is due to play against Scotland in the qualifying round for the 1994 World Cup.

SPECIAL EVENTS: The following is a selection of major events and festivals. For further information contact the Estonian Embassy or the tourist office.
Apr '93 *Festival Dance '93*, Tallinn. **May** *Cultural Days '93*, Tartu. **Jun** *13th International Hanseatic Days*, Tallinn. **Jul** *Music Festival Pärnu '93*, Pärnu. **Sep** *Flower Fair '93*, Tallinn. **Oct** *16th Rockfestival 'Tartu Autumn'*, Tartu. **Nov** *International Music Festival NYYD '93*, Tallinn. **Dec** Christmas Fair in the Old Centre of Tallinn.
The weekly publication *Tallinn this Week* also lists events.
SOCIAL CONVENTIONS: Handshaking is customary. Normal courtesies should be observed. The Estonians are proud of their culture and their national heritage and visitors should take care to respect this sense of national identity. **Tipping:** Taxi fares and restaurant bills include a tip.

BUSINESS PROFILE

ECONOMY: Economic autonomy was a key demand from Estonia during the negotiations which have led to its independence. The establishment of an Estonian currency, the kroon, and the introduction of export quotas on wood, leather and fur, three of the republic's major products, were important moves en route to full sovereignty. The Baltic states are generally more prosperous than the CIS as a whole, benefiting from a tradition of trading activity in the Baltic and serving as a transit point for goods flowing to and from the the rest of the CIS. In the short term, the Baltic states will be looking to improve their economic links with Scandinavia and the EC. Other than oil-shale, which is present in significant quantities and provides the basis of the country's power generation, Estonia has few raw materials of its own and relies mostly on imported commodities to produce finished goods. Light machinery, electrical and electronic equipment and consumer goods are the main products. Fishing, forestry and dairy farming dominate the agricultural sector. Estonia's infrastructure, particularly the road network, is well-developed by regional standards. In June 1992, Estonia became the first former Soviet republic to introduce its own currency, the kroon, which is now the only legal tender and is fixed in value to the Deutschmark. Some temporary problems with Estonian trade in the rouble zone may occur, but the Estonian move is being watched with great interest by other republics.
BUSINESS: Prior appointments are necessary. Business is conducted formally. Business cards are exchanged after introduction. **Office hours:** 0830-1830 Monday to Friday.
COMMERCIAL INFORMATION: The following organisation can offer advice: Chamber of Commerce and Industry of the Republic of Estonia, Ul. Toomkooli 17, EE-0106 Tallinn. Tel: (42) 444 929. Fax: (42) 443 656. Telex: 173254.

ESTONIA	HEALTH REGULATIONS	VISA REGULATIONS Code-Link
GALILEO/WORLDSPAN	 TI-DFT/TAY/HE	TI-DFT/TAY/VI
SABRE	TIDFT/TAY/HE	TIDFT/TAY/VI

To access this information on your CRS, swipe the barcode with a light pen or type in the text under the barcode. For more information, see the introduction *How to Use This Book*.

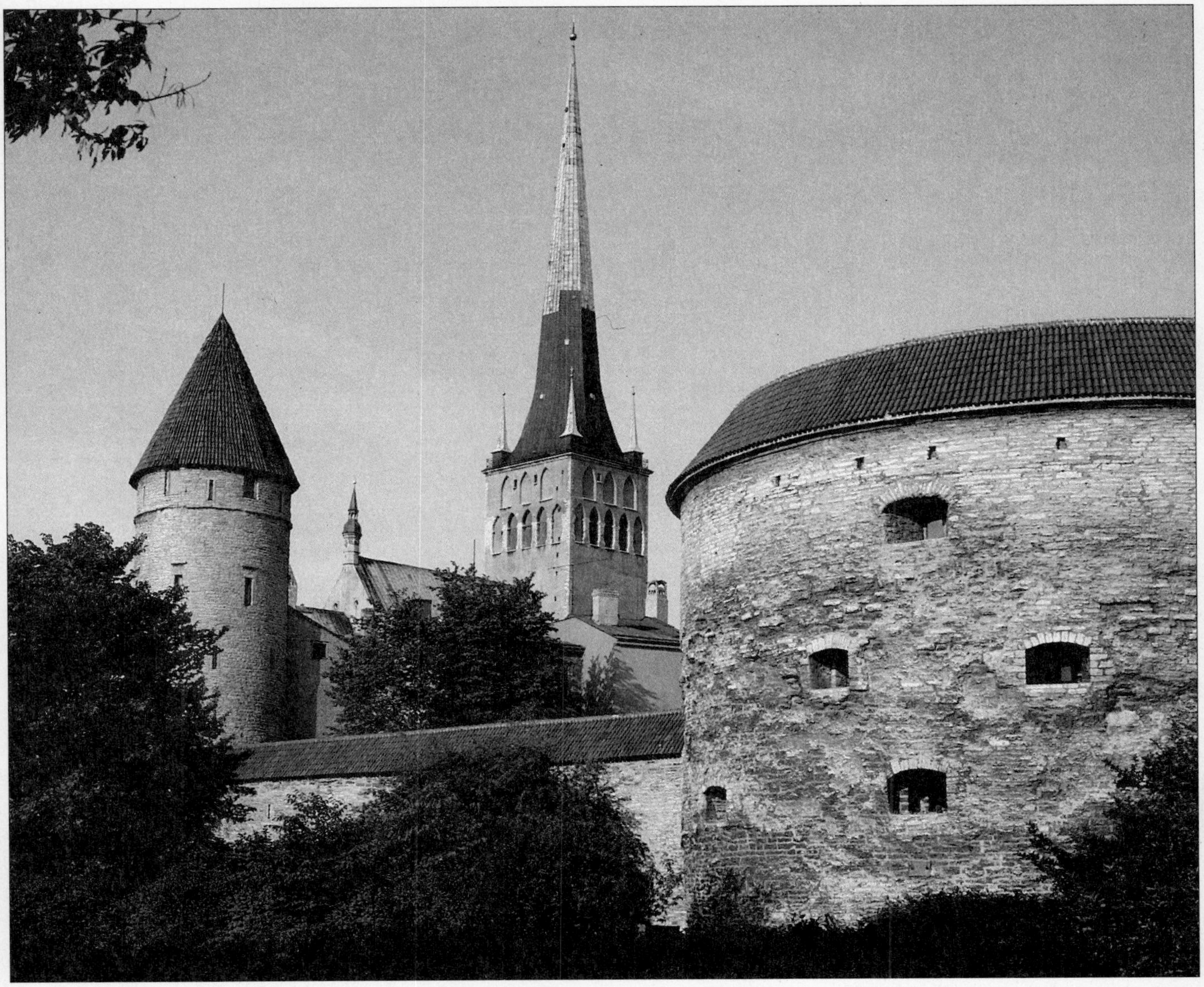

Fat Margaret's Tower, Tallinn

HISTORY & GOVERNMENT

HISTORY: The history of Estonia, and indeed of the other Baltic states, has been one of constant struggle to maintain its independence and national integrity against the predatory instincts of larger neighbours. During the Middle Ages, Danish influence was at a peak in the Baltic region. Estonia was occupied by the Danish King Waldemar II in 1202. After the Livonian War of the 1550s, involving Denmark, Sweden, Poland and Russia in a disputed succession and rival territorial claims, Estonia was taken by the Swedish King Gustavus. The 16th and 17th centuries marked the high point of Swedish imperial power. The Russians were determined, however, to secure a 'window onto the Baltic' for economic as well as strategic reasons: Estonia was duly acquired by the Russians from Sweden at the Treaty of Nystadt (1721). Russia remained in control of Estonia until shortly after the Bolshevik revolution of 1917. At the treaty of Brest-Litovsk the following year, which brought an end to Russian involvement in the First World War, Estonia was ceded. The new Soviet government refused to recognise Estonian independence at first but gave way in February 1920. The new state, along with its Baltic neighbours Lithuania and Latvia, enjoyed just two decades of independent statehood before the Soviet Union took control under the 1939 Nazi-Soviet Pact. Soviet ownership lasted barely 12 months before Estonia was conquered in the German invasion of the Soviet Union. It was retaken by the Red Army in 1944 after which Estonia was constituted as one of the 15 Soviet Socialist Republics. Four decades passed before the advent of Mikhail Gorbachev as Communist Party General Secretary offered the prospect of change for the Baltic states. A key part of the *perestroika* programme was the devolution of power to the republics. Estonia led the way among the Baltic states assisted by the collaboration between nationalist groups and the Communist Party, who joined together in a People's Front (analogous bodies emerged in Latvia and Lithuania) to orchestrate change. Having asserted the right to make their own legislation, measures to establish an Estonian currency, preparatory to full economic autonomy, and restore Estonian as the offical language quickly followed. In March 1990 the Estonian Communist Party voted in favour of full independence from the Soviet Union but allowed for a 6-month transitional period before making the decision final. The same month, elections were held for the Supreme Council (see below), at which the 105 seats were divided between three groups: the Popular Front of Estonia (43 seats); the Association for a Free Estonia and allies (35); and the International Movement of Working People of the Estonian SSR (ex-communists, 27 seats). Arnold Rüütel was elected Chairman of the Supreme Council, and Edgar Savisaar as Prime Minister. Despite vehement opposition, President Gorbachev was powerless to prevent the Estonian drive for independence. Rapid international recognition of Estonia and the others as sovereign states and their admission to the United Nations has completed the transition to full nationhood. Prime Minister Savisaar was replaced in January 1992 by the former Transport Minister Tiit Vähi. The Government asked for, and received, special emergency powers to deal with Estonia's food shortage and general economic crisis. In June 1992, Estonia scored two more firsts with the introduction of its own currency, the kroon, and of a new post-Soviet constitution, accepted in a referendum by 93% of the electorate. Legislative elections held in September 1992 produced an inconclusive result. An unstable coalition government of the Fatherland Alliance, the Moderate Alliance and the National Independence Party is currently in power. Former Foreign Minister Lennart Meri was elected President.

GOVERNMENT: A new constitution was accepted in a referendum in June 1992 under which a 100-seat National Assembly is elected by popular vote. Members elect a President and Council of Ministers.

CLIMATE

Temperate climate, but with considerable temperature variations. Summer is warm with relatively mild weather in spring and autumn. Winter, which lasts from November to mid-March, can be very cold. Rainfall is distributed throughout the year with the heaviest rainfall in August. Heavy snowfalls are common in the winter months

TALLINN Estonia (44m)

SUNSHINE, hours
1 2 5 6 8 10 9 8 5 2 1 ½
20
10
0
−10
MAX
MIN
◁ TEMPERATURE, °C
100
0
J F M A M J J A S O N D
RAINFALL, mm ▷
85 83 80 78 74 77 79 80 83 84 87 87
HUMIDITY, %
DAB-C371

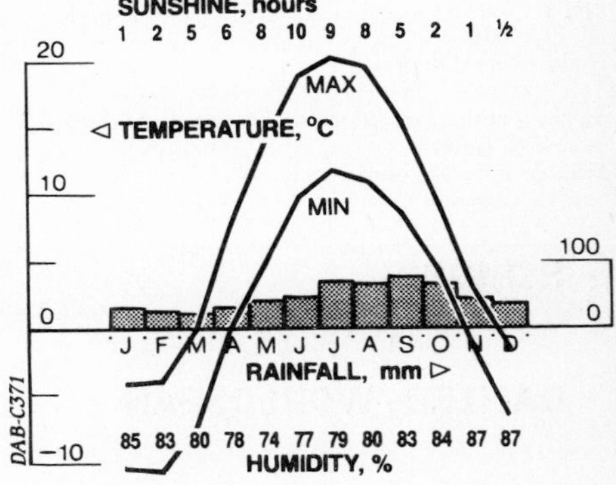

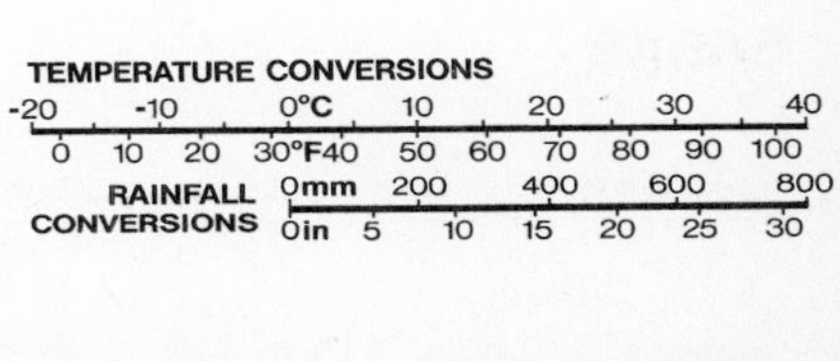

TEMPERATURE CONVERSIONS
-20 -10 0°C 10 20 30 40
0 10 20 30°F 40 50 60 70 80 90 100
RAINFALL CONVERSIONS
0mm 200 400 600 800
0in 5 10 15 20 25 30

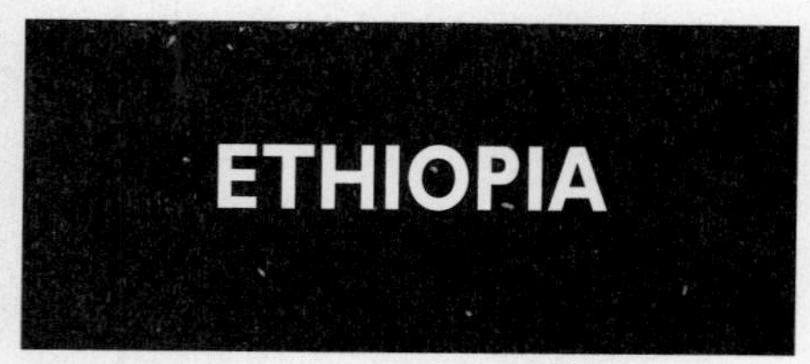

ETHIOPIA

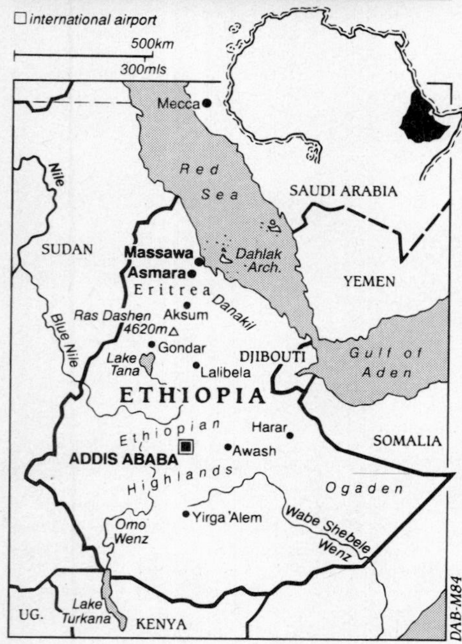

Location: Northeast Africa.

Note: The current situation of widespread famine, and the war between the Marxist regime and the Eritrean and Tigrean secessionists, makes it inadvisable to travel to Ethiopia as a tourist. The information contained here reflects the situation prior to the present instability and is presented in the hope that, when the conflict is resolved, it will again prove useful.

Ethiopian Commission for Hotels and Tourism
PO Box 2183
Addis Ababa, Ethiopia
Tel:(1) 517 470. Telex: 21067.

Embassy of the Ethiopian Transitional Government
17 Prince's Gate
London SW7 1PZ
Tel: (071) 589 7212/5. Telex: 23681. Opening hours: 0900-1300 and 1400-1600 Monday to Friday.

British Embassy
PO Box 858
Fikre Mariam Abatechan Street
Addis Ababa, Ethiopia
Tel: (1) 612 354. Fax: (1) 610 588. Telex: 21299 PROAD ET.

Embassy of the Transitional Government of Ethiopia
2134 Kalorama Road, NW
Washington, DC 20008
Tel: (202) 234 2281/2.

Embassy of the United States of America
Entoto Street
PO Box 1014
Addis Ababa, Ethiopia
Tel: (1) 550 666. Fax: (1) 551 166. Telex: 21282.

Embassy of the Transitional Government of Ethiopia
Suite 208, Tower B
Place de Ville, 112 Kent Street
Ottawa, Ontario
K1P 5P2
Tel: (613) 235 6637 *or* 235 6790. Fax: (613) 235 4638.

Canadian Embassy
PO Box 1130
6th Floor, African Solidarity Insurance Building
Addis Ababa, Ethiopia
Tel: (1) 511 343. Fax: (1) 512 818. Telex: 21053.

AREA: 1,251,282 sq km (483,123 sq miles).
POPULATION: 49,513,000 (1989 estimate).
POPULATION DENSITY: 39.6 per sq km.
CAPITAL: Addis Ababa. **Population:** 1,412,577 (1984).
GEOGRAPHY: Ethiopia is situated in Africa, bordered by the Red Sea, Sudan, Kenya, Somalia and Djibouti. The central area is a vast highland region of volcanic rock forming a watered, temperate zone surrounded by hot, arid, inhospitable desert. The Great Rift Valley, which starts in Palestine, runs down the Red Sea and diagonally southwest through Ethiopia, Kenya and Malawi. The escarpments on either side of the country are steepest in the north where the terrain is very rugged. To the south, the landscape is generally flatter and more suited to agriculture.
LANGUAGE: Amharic is the official language, although about 80 other native tongues are spoken, including Galla in the south. English is the second official language. Italian and French are still widely spoken.
RELIGION: Christianity (Ethiopian Orthodox Church and the Coptic Church), mainly in the north; Islam, mainly in the east and south.
TIME: GMT + 3.
ELECTRICITY: 220 volts AC, 50Hz.
COMMUNICATIONS: Telephone: IDD is available. Country code: 251. Calls out of Ethiopia must be made through the international operator. **Telex/telegram:** International services from local offices and hotels in Addis Ababa and telex offices in Asmara. Telexes may also be sent from the Head Office of the Addis Ababa region of the Telecommunications Services at Churchill Road, opposite Ras Hotel. **Post:** Service to and from Europe takes up to two weeks. **Press:** Newspapers published in the capital include *Addis Zemen*. The English-language daily in Ethiopia is *The Ethiopian Herald*. Other periodicals are also available.
BBC World Service and Voice of America frequencies: From time to time these change. See the section *How to Use this Book* for more information.

BBC:

MHz	21.47	17.64	15.42	9.630

A service is also available on 1413kHz (0100-0500 GMT).

Voice of America:

MHz	21.49	15.60	9.525	6.035

PASSPORT/VISA

Regulations and requirements may be subject to change at short notice, and you are advised to contact the appropriate diplomatic or consular authority before finalising travel arrangements. Details of these may be found at the head of this country's entry. Any numbers in the chart refer to the footnotes below.

	Passport Required?	Visa Required?	Return Ticket Required?
Full British	Yes	Yes	Yes
BVP	Not valid	-	-
Australian	Yes	Yes	Yes
Canadian	Yes	Yes	Yes
USA	Yes	Yes	Yes
Other EC	Yes	Yes	Yes
Japanese	Yes	Yes	Yes

Prohibited entry and transit: (a) Admission or transit facilities will be refused to white nationals of the Republic of South Africa. (b) Entry into Ethiopia can normally only be made by air transport via Addis Ababa international airport, and special permission is necessary for any other entry.
PASSPORTS: Required by all.
British Visitors Passport: Not accepted.
VISAS: Required by all except nationals of Kenya, Djibouti and Sudan.
Types of visa: Business, Transit or Tourist (cost: £7). Transit visas are not required by those continuing their journey to a third country and not leaving the airport.
Validity: 2 months.
Application to: Consulate (or Consular Section at Embassy). For address, see top of entry.
Application requirements: (a) Completed application form. (b) Valid passport. (c) 2 photos. (d) Covering letter if purpose of visit is business. (e) Fee.
Working days required: Immediate (personal); 2 days (postal).
Exit permit: Required by all nationals of Ethiopia and visitors staying more than 15 days in the country.

MONEY

Currency: Ethiopian Birr (Br) = 100 cents. Notes are in denominations of Br100, 50, 10, 5 and 1. Coins are in denominations of 50, 25, 10, 5 and 1 cents.
Credit cards: Access/Mastercard and Diners Club are accepted on a very limited basis (only the Hilton Hotel is certain to accept them).
Exchange rate indicators: The following figures have been included as a guide to the movements of the Birr against Sterling and the US Dollar:

Date:	Aug '89	Oct '90	Oct '91	Oct '92
£1.00=	3.29	4.00	3.56	7.82
$1.00=	2.04	2.04	2.05	4.93

Currency restrictions: The import and export of local currency is limited to Br10.
Banking hours: 0800-1130 and 1300-1600 Monday to Friday; 0800-1200 Saturday. Cash may be withdrawn up to 1100 and 1500 mornings and afternoons respectively.

DUTY FREE

The following goods may be imported into Ethiopia without incurring customs duty:
100 cigarettes or 50 cigars or 250g of tobacco;
1 litre of spirits;
2 bottles or half a litre of perfume;
Gifts up to the value of 10 Br.

PUBLIC HOLIDAYS

Public holidays observed in Ethiopia are as follows:
Mar 2 '93 Battle of Adowa Day. **Mar 25** Eid al-Fitr. **Apr 6** Victory Day. **Apr 12*** Palm Monday. **Apr 16*** Good Friday. **Apr 19*** Easter Monday. **May 1** May Day. **Jun 1** Eid al-Adha. **Aug 30** Mouloud (Birth of the Prophet). **Sep 11** New Year's Day. **Sep 27*** Feast of the True Cross. **Jan 7 '94** * Christmas. **Jan 19*** Epiphany. **Mar 2** Battle of Adowa Day. **Mar** Eid al-Fitr.
Note: [*] indicates Coptic holidays. (a) Ethiopia still uses the Julian calendar, which is divided into 12 months of 30 days each, and a 13th month of five or six days at the end of the year; hence the date for Christmas. The Ethiopian calendar is seven years and eight months behind our own. (b) Muslim festivals are timed according to local sightings of various phases of the Moon and the dates given above are approximations.

HEALTH

Regulations and requirements may be subject to change at short notice, and you are advised to contact your doctor well in advance of your intended date of departure. Any numbers in the chart refer to the footnotes below.

	Special Precautions?	Certificate Required?
Yellow Fever	Yes	1
Cholera	Yes	2
Typhoid & Polio	Yes	-
Malaria	3	-
Food & Drink	4	-

ETHIOPIA | **HEALTH REGULATIONS** | **VISA REGULATIONS** | Code-Link

GALILEO/WORLDSPAN

TI-DFT/ADD/HE

TI-DFT/ADD/VI

SABRE

TIDFT/ADD/HE

TIDFT/ADD/VI

To access this information on your CRS, swipe the barcode with a light pen or type in the text under the barcode. For more information, see the introduction *How to Use This Book*.

[1]: A yellow fever vaccination certificate is required from travellers over one year of age coming from infected areas.
[2]: Following WHO guidelines issued in 1973, a cholera vaccination certificate is no longer a condition of entry to Ethiopia. However, cholera is a serious risk in this country and precautions are essential. Up-to-date advice should be sought before deciding whether these precautions should include vaccination as medical opinion is divided over its effectiveness. See the *Health* section at the back of the book.
[3]: Malaria risk exists throughout the year in all areas below 2000m. Highly chloroquine-resistant *falciparum* reported.
[4]: All water should be regarded as being potentially contaminated. Water used for drinking, brushing teeth or making ice should have first been boiled or otherwise sterilised. Milk is unpasteurised and should be boiled. Powdered or tinned milk is available and is advised, but make sure that it is reconstituted with pure water. Avoid dairy products which are likely to have been made from unboiled milk. Only eat well-cooked meat and fish, preferably served hot. Pork, salad and mayonnaise may carry increased risk. Vegetables should be cooked and fruit peeled.
Rabies is present. For those at high risk, vaccination before arrival should be considered. If you are bitten abroad seek medical advice without delay. For more information consult the *Health* section at the back of the book.
Bilharzia (schistosomiasis) is present. Avoid swimming and paddling in fresh water. Swimming pools which are well-chlorinated and maintained are safe.
Meningitis risk is present, depending on area visited and time of year.
Health care: The high altitude and low oxygen level of much of Ethiopia needs time to be acclimatised to. Those who suffer from heart ailments or high blood pressure should consult a doctor before travelling. See also the section on *Health* at the back of this book.
Health insurance is strongly advised.

TRAVEL - International

AIR: Ethiopia's national airline is *Ethiopian Airlines (ET)*.
Approximate flight time: From *London* to Addis Ababa is 10 hours 35 minutes.
International airports: *Addis Ababa (ADD)* (Bole International) is 8km (5 miles) southeast of the city (travel time – 20 minutes). Coach service departs every 15 minutes to the city. There are full duty-free facilities at the airport and also car rental, banks and bureaux de change, post office, hotel reservation points and a restaurant and bar.
Asmara (Yohannes IV), about 9km (6 miles) from the city centre.
Departure tax: 20 Birr.
SEA: Regular sailings between European ports and Massawa or Assab on Ethiopian Shipping Lines.
RAIL: A 784km (487-mile) rail service between Djibouti and Addis Ababa is run jointly by the two governments; the service is currently closed to visitors.
ROAD: The main route is via Kenya. There is an all-weather road from Moyale on the border via Yabelo, Dila and Yirga to Addis Ababa. See below for information on *documentation*.

TRAVEL - Internal

Note: Travel passes are required for those wishing to travel outside of Addis Ababa. Only guided tourism is permitted; travelling alone is discouraged. In the smaller towns the locals may react with hostility to being photographed. There is a curfew in Addis Ababa from midnight.
AIR: *Ethiopian Airlines* runs internal flights to over 40 towns, although services are erratic and the planes antiquated.
Departure tax: 5 Birr.
RAIL: The only operative line runs between Addis Ababa and Djibouti, via Dire Dawa. The service is closed to visitors.
ROAD: A good network of all-weather roads exists to most business and tourist centres. Otherwise, 4-wheel drive vehicles are recommended. Travel to Eritrea is severely restricted.
Bus: Bus services are run by the Government and private companies and they operate throughout the country. The bus terminus can provide schedules and tickets, although it is unusual for tourists to attempt to use this service. **Taxis:** Available in Addis Ababa, painted blue and white, offer service on a shared basis. Fares should be negotiated before travelling. **Car hire:** Available from Addis Ababa from *National Tour Operations*. Tel: (1) 444 838. Telex: 21370. Traffic drives on the right. **Documentation:** A British driving licence is valid for up to one month, otherwise the visitor needs to obtain a temporary Ethiopian driving licence on arrival.

ACCOMMODATION

HOTELS: Good hotels can be found in Addis Ababa and other main centres and some offer facilities for small exhibitions and conferences. Visitors should remember, however, that travel outside the capital requires a special permit which can take some time to get. There are hotels in the other larger towns; prices are, in general, slightly lower than those in the main centres. There is a 10% service charge and a 2% Government tax on all accommodation. For more information contact the Ethiopian Commission for Hotels and Tourism (address at top of entry).

RESORTS & EXCURSIONS

Addis Ababa, the capital, is at an altitude of 2440m (8000ft) in the central highlands. Places of interest include the university, *St George's Cathedral*, the *Ethnology Museum*, the *Menelik Mausoleum*, the *Trinity Church*, the *Old Ghibbi Palace*, and the market, one of the largest in Africa.
Axum lies in the north and was the ancient royal capital of the earliest Ethiopian Kingdom. It is renowned for multi-storeyed ancient carved granite obelisks.
Gondar was the capital of Ethiopia from 1732 to 1855 and is the site of many ruined castles.
Lalibela is famous for its 12th-century, rock-hewn churches.
Harar, near Agaden, and **Asmara** are best kept away from because of military activity.
National Parks: There are four National Parks in Ethiopia: the *Simyen National Park* (in the Mountain Massif), the *Awash National Park* (east of the capital), the *Omo National Park* (southwest of the capital) and the *Rift Valley National Park* (south of the capital).

SOCIAL PROFILE

FOOD & DRINK: Menus in the best hotels offer international food and Addis Ababa also has a number of good Chinese, Italian and Indian restaurants. Ethiopian food is based on dishes called *we't* (meat, chicken or vegetables, cooked in a hot pepper sauce) served with or on *injera* (a flat spongy bread). Dishes include *shivro* and *misir* (chick peas and lentils, Ethiopian style) and *tibs* (crispy fried steak). There is a wide choice of fish including sole, red sea snapper, lake fish, trout and prawn. Traditional restaurants in larger cities serve food in a grand manner around a brightly coloured basket-weave table called a *masob*. Before beginning the meal guests will be given soap, water and a clean towel, as the right hand is used to break off pieces of *injera* with which the *we't* is gathered up. Cutlery is not used. **Drink:** Ethiopian coffee from the province of Kaffa, with a little rye added for extra aroma, is called 'health of Adam'. Local red and dry white wines are worth trying. *Talla* (Ethiopian beer) has a unique taste. *Kaitaka* (a pure grain alcohol) and *tej* (an alcoholic drink based on fermented honey) are unique.
SHOPPING: Special purchases include local jewellery (sold by the actual weight of gold or silver), woodcarvings, illuminated manuscripts and prayer scrolls, leather shields, spears, drums and carpets. In market places a certain amount of bargaining is expected but prices at shops in towns are fixed. **Shopping hours:** 0800-1230 and 1530-1930 Monday to Friday (with local variations).
SPORTS: Wildlife **safaris** to the National Parks are organised by a number of tour operators. For details contact the Embassy or Tourism Commission. There is excellent **swimming** in the lakes of the Rift Valley, especially Lake Langano (but beware of bilharzia – enquire locally).
SOCIAL CONVENTIONS: Casual wear is suitable for most places, but Ethiopians tend to be fairly formal and conservative in their dress. Private informal entertaining is very common. **Tipping:** In most hotels and restaurants a 10% service charge is added to the bill. Tipping is a fairly frequent custom, but amounts are small.

BUSINESS PROFILE

ECONOMY: The economy is largely dependent on subsistence agriculture. Coffee is the largest single export earner, the bulk of which is bought by the US, and Ethiopia also produces some oil derivatives for overseas sale. Germany is Ethiopia's other main export market, while the CIS, with which the Government is allied, supplies most of the country's manufactured and industrial goods, as well as weapons. Ethiopia is one of the world's least developed countries, with a hostile climate, poor infrastructure and a dearth of skilled labour, exacerbated by long-running civil wars in the northern provinces of Tigre and Eritrea. Much of the economy came under state control during the Mengistu era. It is not clear as yet what approach the new government will take in dealing with Ethiopia's considerable economic difficulties.
BUSINESS: Business persons should wear suits and ties for business visits. English is widely used for trade purposes but Italian and French are also useful. Nonetheless, knowledge of a few words of Amharic will be appreciated. Some of the more useful are *Tena Yistillign* - 'Hello'; *Ishi* - 'Yes'; *Yellem* - 'No'; and *Sint new* - 'How much is this?' Normal courtesies should be observed and business cards can be used. Best months for business visits are October to May. **Office hours:** 0800-1200 and 1300-1600 Monday to Friday, 0800-1200 Saturday.
COMMERCIAL INFORMATION: The following organisation can offer advice: Ethiopian Chamber of Commerce, PO Box 517, Mexico Square, Addis Ababa, Ethiopia. Tel: (1) 518 240. Telex: 21213.

HISTORY & GOVERNMENT

HISTORY: During the Middle Ages, Ethiopia was famous for being the home of Prester John, the mythical Christian King. Although Ethiopia was indeed a Christian kingdom (Ethiopian Coptic) and had been for many centuries, it never fulfilled the expectations of western Christendom of being a staunch ally of Rome in the struggle against the infidel. Later, the Portuguese were equally unsuccessful in their efforts to convert the country to orthodox Catholicism. During the so-called 'colonial period' Ethiopia was the only country in Africa never to be colonised; the most notable casualties were the Italians who suffered a series of devastating defeats at the hands of the Ethiopians in the late 19th century, most notably at the battle of Dogali. The 20th-century history of Ethiopia is dominated by the figure of Haile Selassie who became emperor in 1930 and ruled until the military coup of 1974. The country was occupied by the Italians between 1936 and 1941. The former Italian colony of Eritrea was annexed by Ethiopia in 1962, providing a coastline, but secessionist movements here and in Tigre have removed these areas from the effective control of the Government. In 1977, a further coup brought Lt-Col Mengistu to power. Agricultural backwardness is regarded as the country's major problem, despite frequent attempts at land reform by the military régime since 1974. The Government was pre-occupied with fighting secessionist movements in the provinces of Tigre and Eritrea, and with occasional border clashes with Somalia (one of which escalated into full-scale war during 1977). Three years of severe drought, economic mismanagement and the mutual mistrust between the Government and Western aid agencies were the principal causes of the widely publicised famine in Ethiopia in 1983. The civil war continued unabated until May 1991, when President Mengistu fled the country for Zimbabwe. At this point resistance from the remaining government forces crumbled and the Tigrean-led Ethiopian People's Revolutionary Democratic Front (EPRDF) took control of the capital. The EPRDF leader, Meles Zenawi, took over as head of an interim administration, promising future elections. The EPRDF does not, however, retain undisputed control of the whole country. The northern province of Eritrea is now run from its capital, Asmara, by the Eritrean Peoples Liberation Front and has seceded from Ethiopia. The Oromo Liberation Front is also pushing for the independence of its own province in the west of the country. The OLF was one of six groups which boycotted the election, at which most of the 33 million electorate voted, but which were marred by occasional abuses. The EPRDF dominates the new assembly.
GOVERNMENT: Most of Ethiopia, with the exception of Eritrea, is currently governed by a provisional administration comprising several of the guerrilla factions victorious in the civil war over the Mengistu regime. The leader of the Tigre-based Ethiopian People's Revolutionary Democratic Front, Meles Zenawi, is the head of the new government. Eritrea is under the total effective control of the Eritrean People's Liberation Front which has moved to independence.

CLIMATE

Hot and humid in the lowlands, warm in the hill country and cool in the uplands. Most rainfall is from June to September.
Required clothing: The lightest possible clothing in lowland areas; medium or lightweight in hill country. Warm clothing is needed at night to cope with the dramatic temperature change.

ADDIS ABABA Ethiopia (2450m)

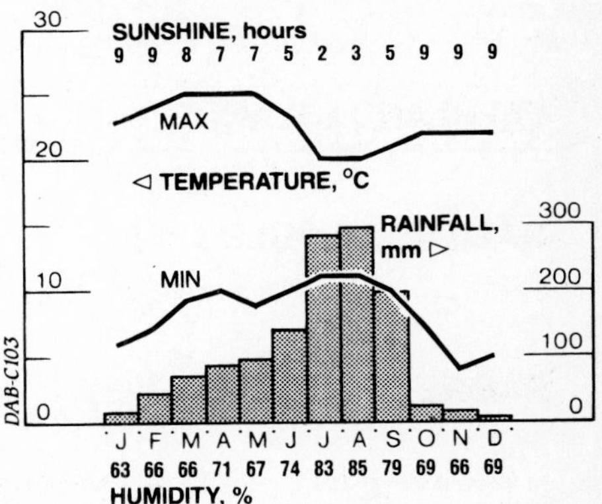

FALKLAND ISLANDS

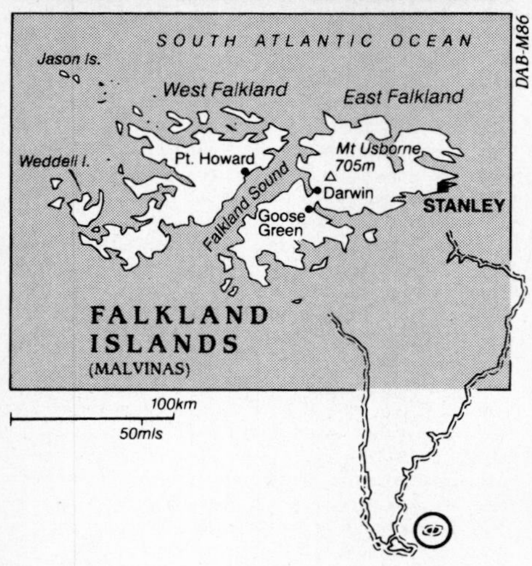

Location: South Atlantic.

Falklands Islands Tourist Board
56 John Street
Port Stanley
Falkland Islands
Tel: 22215. Fax: 22619. Telex: 2433.
Falkland Islands Government Office
Falkland House
14 Broadway
London
SW1H 0BH
Tel: (071) 222 2542. Fax: (071) 222 2375.
This is not a Diplomatic Mission, as the Falkland Islands are a Crown Colony. The office helps to promote trade and investment in the Islands; in dissemination of information to the media and general public on Falkland matters and policy; in processing and assistance of immigrants; and in promoting the Falkland's interest in all respects.
Falkland Islands Tourist Board
Falkland House
14 Broadway
London
SW1H 0BH
Tel: (071) 222 2542. Fax: (071) 222 2375.

AREA: Approx 12,173 sq km (4700 sq miles).
POPULATION: 2121 (1990).
POPULATION DENSITY: 0.2 per sq km.
CAPITAL: Port Stanley. **Population:** 1643 (1990).
GEOGRAPHY: The Falkland Islands are located 560km (350 miles) off the east coast of South America and consist of two main islands and hundreds of small outlying islands, amounting to about two and a half million acres. Generally the main islands are mountainous in the northern areas and low lying and undulating in the south. The highest mountain is Mount Usborne at 712m (2312ft).
LANGUAGE: English.
RELIGION: Christianity.
TIME: GMT - 4 (GMT - 3 from Sep to Apr).
ELECTRICITY: 240 volts AC, 50Hz.
COMMUNICATIONS: Telephone/telex: IDD available. Country code: 500. External communication links are provided by Cable and Wireless plc. Telephone and telex links to the Islands, which are by satellite, provide clear and rapid links to the outside world. The Cable and Wireless office is open daily 0800-2000 for acceptance of traffic and sale of phone cards for use in the international telephone service booths situated in the office. **Fax:** A newly installed system spanning the islands provides international direct dialling facilities, together with telex, facsimile and high-speed data services. **Radio:** Remote areas keep in contact by radio. **Post:** Airmail to Europe takes four to seven days to arrive. **Press:** There are no daily papers on the Falkland Islands, but *Penguin News* (fortnightly) is published in Port Stanley. *The Falklands Island Gazette* is a Government publication.
BBC World Service and Voice of America frequencies: From time to time these change. See the section *How to Use this Book* for more information.

BBC:				
MHz	15.26	15.19	11.75	9.915
Voice of America:				
MHz	15.21	11.58	9.775	5.995

PASSPORT/VISA

Regulations and requirements may be subject to change at short notice, and you are advised to contact the appropriate diplomatic or consular authority before finalising travel arrangements. Details of these may be found at the head of this country's entry. Any numbers in the chart refer to the footnotes below.

	Passport Required?	Visa Required?	Return Ticket Required?
Full British	Yes	No	Yes
BVP	Not valid	-	-
Australian	Yes	No	Yes
Canadian	Yes	No	Yes
USA	Yes	No	Yes
Other EC	Yes	No	Yes
Japanese	Yes	Yes	Yes

PASSPORTS: Valid passports required by all.
British Visitors Passport: Not accepted.
VISAS: Required by all except nationals of the EC and Commonwealth countries, Chile, Finland, Iceland, Liechtenstein, Norway, San Marino, Sweden, Switzerland and Uruguay.
Note: From November 1, 1991, all nationals will need a Visitor's Permit.
Application to: Falkland Islands Government Office. For address, see top of entry.

MONEY

Currency: Falkland Islands Pound (FI£) = 100 pence. Notes are in denominations of FI£50, 20, 10 and 5. Coins are in denominations of FI£1, and 50, 10, 5, 2 and 1 pence. This currency is equivalent to Sterling and Sterling notes and coins are also in use on the Islands.
Currency exchange: Exchange facilities are available in Port Stanley and the Standard Chartered Bank. British Pound Sterling cheques up to £50 from Barclays, Lloyds, Midland and National Westminster can be cashed on production of a valid cheque card. Falklands currency cannot be exchanged anywhere outside the Islands.
Credit cards: Not accepted.
Travellers cheques: May be changed at the Standard Chartered Bank and at some commercial outlets.
Exchange rates: For a guide to the movement of the US Dollar against the Falklands Islands Pound, see the *United Kingdom* section below (FI£1 = UK£1).
Currency restrictions: As for the United Kingdom.
Banking hours: 0800-1700 Monday to Friday.

DUTY FREE

Allowances are as for the United Kingdom.
Prohibited items: Uncooked meat, unboned cured meat and plants can only be imported under licence. It is forbidden to carry livestock at any time on incoming aircraft. There are no restrictions on fruit and vegetables from the United Kingdom for human consumption, or on any dairy produce and dried and tinned vegetables for human consumption.

PUBLIC HOLIDAYS

Public holidays observed in the Falkland Islands are as follows:
Apr 9 '93 Good Friday. **Apr 21** The Queen's Birthday. **Jun 14** Liberation Day. **Oct 5** Bank Holiday. **Dec 8** Battle Day. **Dec 25-29** Christmas. **Jan 1 '94** New Year's Day.

HEALTH

Regulations and requirements may be subject to change at short notice, and you are advised to contact your doctor well in advance of your intended date of departure. Any numbers in the chart refer to the footnotes below.

	Special Precautions?	Certificate Required?
Yellow Fever	No	No
Cholera	No	No
Typhoid & Polio	No	-
Malaria	No	-
Food & Drink	No	-

Health care: Hospital, dental and other medical treatments are usually free, as are prescribed medicines and ambulance travel.

TRAVEL - International

AIR: Travel to and from the Islands is by courtesy of the UK Ministry of Defence. Departures are by Tristar from *Brize Norton*, Oxfordshire, in the UK, with civilian bookings made through the Falkland Islands Government Office. Flights from the UK are via Ascension Island. Return to the UK is arranged through the Secretariat in Port Stanley. *Aerovías DAP* fly weekly from Punta Arenas in southern Chile to Port Stanley.
Approximate flight time: From *Brize Norton* to Mount Pleasant is 18 hours. From *Punta Arenas* to Mount Pleasant is 3.5 to 4.5 hours.
International airport: *Mount Pleasant Airport* is about 56km (35 miles) from Port Stanley. There are duty-free facilitities at the airport. Regular buses from the airport go to the capital.

TRAVEL - Internal

AIR: Most of the settlements and offshore islands in the Falklands can be reached by light aircraft. This service is run by the *Falkland Islands Government Air Service (FIGAS)* (tel: 22215; fax: 22619) which operates five Islander aircraft from the airport. There are no fixed schedules but daily flights operate to all parts of the Islands, subject to demand.
SEA: Boats may be chartered for day trips from Port Stanley and elsewhere in the Islands. Some settlements may be able to offer the use of landing vessels or other crafts to reach the outlying islands.
ROAD: Outside the capital, overland travel is very diffi-

FALKLAND ISLANDS	HEALTH REGULATIONS	VISA REGULATIONS Code-Link
GALILEO/WORLDSPAN	 TI-DFT/MPN/HE	 TI-DFT/MPN/VI
SABRE	 TIDFT/MPN/HE	 TIDFT/MPN/VI

To access this information on your CRS, swipe the barcode with a light pen or type in the text under the barcode. For more information, see the introduction *How to Use This Book*.

cult as the roads are bad and vehicles frequently get bogged down. There is one road linking Port Stanley and the Mount Pleasant airport complex. Land-Rovers are the best form of transport in this terrain. **Bus:** There are routes to and from the airport, also in and around Port Stanley. **Taxi:** A taxi service using Land-Rovers and a specially converted Sherpa van is available. **Car hire:** Land-Rovers and other vehicles can be rented.
JOURNEY TIMES: The following chart gives approximate journey times from Port Stanley to other islands in the surrounding area.

	Air	Road
Mount Pleasant	0.15	0.50
Pebble Island	0.40	-
Port Howard	0.40	-
Sea Lion Island	0.30	-

ACCOMMODATION

Accommodation is limited and must be booked in advance. There are hotels, lodges and boarding houses in the Falkland Islands. There are two hotels in Port Stanley and lodges at Darwin, Pebble Island, Port Howard, San Carlos and Sea Lion Island. Self-catering accommodation is also available throughout the Islands. All ground arrangements can be made through Port Stanley Services Limited, Port Stanley. Tel: 22624. Fax: 22623. Telex: 2438. **Grading:** Although there is no formal grading system the hotels and lodges fall roughly within the British 2/3 crown categories, as used by the English Tourist Board. Contact the Tourism Information Service for full details.

RESORTS & EXCURSIONS

For the purpose of this guide the Falkland Islands and the surrounding islands have been divided into 4 sections: Port Stanley, coastal areas, inland areas and British battle sites.
Port Stanley has pubs, snack bars and restaurants, and there is a golf and race course. The colourful houses on the seafront overlook Stanley Harbour where many different sea birds can be seen and enjoyed. The *Government House* and the *Cathedral* are also worth a visit.
Coastal areas: These offer a chance (in good weather) to explore ships and wrecks abandoned in the last centuries. 19th-century sailing and iron vessels (some of which remain in use for storage) can be seen at Port Stanley and Darwin; Port Stanley used to be a safe anchorage for whalers and merchant vessels travelling around the Horn, though not all of them made it – if conditions are good it may be possible to arrange a dive to see the underwater wrecks. There is a host of unique marine life which can be seen in the clear waters by scuba diving (again weather conditions must be favourable). The marine birdlife is varied, including the famous penguins; the views in winter are made more spectacular by the winter waves, 'grey beards', that can reach a height of 4.5m (15ft).
Inland areas: Here there is a chance to view the varied wildlife, and activities such as fishing, horseriding and walking can be enjoyed often in complete solitude. The Falklands are developing as a tourist area, giving people the opportunity to experience the natural beauty of the islands.
British battle sights: It is a sad fact that many visitors come to the islands to see places made so widely known by the events of the Falkland Islands conflict. As well as the battlefields at Goose Green, San Carlos, Fitzroy, Pebble Island, Mount Tumbledown and Port Stanley itself, there are also military cemeteries, memorials and museums.

SOCIAL PROFILE

FOOD & DRINK: Almost everything is home cooked and many traditional recipes have been handed down through several generations. Food, generally British in character, includes large 'camp breakfasts' and *smoko* (tea and coffee with homemade cakes) with lunch and dinner.
NIGHTLIFE: There is a variety of clubs and societies which welcome visitors. There are several pubs in Port Stanley, as well as restaurants and cafes.
SHOPPING: Costs tend to be high as so much has to be imported, though smaller luxury goods may be cheaper. There is a good range of shops in Port Stanley selling the same type of goods found in a small town in Britain and a variety of souvenirs. Fresh vegetables are available all year round but many Islanders are virtually self-sufficient. Photographers should purchase their film before arrival on the island. **Shopping hours:** 0800-1700 Monday to Friday.
SOCIAL CONVENTIONS: The lifestyle in the Falkland Islands resembles that of a small English or Scottish village/town and communities on the Falkland Islands are highly self-contained. The influx of the British Forces has obviously had an effect on the island. More people now visit the islands (for a variety of reasons – see *Resorts & Excursions*) and the Islanders themselves have benefited from the additional amenities offered by the forces. The British government runs a radio station for the Islanders (FIBS), in conjunction with the British Forces Broadcasting Service; this broadcasts all day on FM and medium wave. The forces also run a limited closed-circuit television network in Port Stanley, another example of the close links that have built up between the Islands and the British Forces/government. The population is very keen to remain under British sovereignty. **Tipping:** If no service charge has been added to the bill, 10% is appropriate. Taxi drivers expect a tip.

BUSINESS PROFILE

ECONOMY: The economy is dominated by fishing and sheep-farming, which is the major employer; wool is the principal export earner, and most of it is sold in Britain. The poor quality of the land precludes crop-growing on any scale larger than allotment. Productivity in sheep-farming has improved sharply since the mid-1980s with the division of the land into smaller working units, coupled with incentives for new farmers to work them. The Falkland Islands Company, a subsidiary of the British conglomerate Coalite, controls a large slice of the economy. There have been several investigations into the possibilities of broadening the base of the economy. Fishing seems to be the most promising sector, and the British government has expanded the exclusion zone around the islands, partly with this in mind. The islands also seem destined to become an important staging post en route to Antarctica, as and when full-scale development begins there in earnest. Trade is almost entirely with the United Kingdom. Commercial links with Argentina were severed after the South Atlantic War in 1982. Since their resumption, trade with Argentina has surpassed previous levels and continues to grow, albeit slowly. The pace has quickened during the last few years and, despite the adamant British refusal to discuss sovereignty, Anglo-Argentinian relations have improved appreciably and especially at the economic and trade level. Fisheries control and aircraft landing rights have already been agreed.
BUSINESS: The Falkland Islands Development Corporation (FIDC), Port Stanley, Falkland Islands, can supply information on business opportunities. Punctuality for meetings is expected.
COMMERCIAL INFORMATION: The following organisation can offer advice: Falkland Islands Development Corporation (FIDC), Port Stanley. Tel: 27211. Fax: 27210. Telex: 2433.

HISTORY & GOVERNMENT

HISTORY: Until the war of 1982 the rainy, windswept Falkland Islands were a lowly, almost forgotten backwater of the British Empire. First occupied by the French in 1764, the Islands were quickly ceded to Spain which then ruled the adjacent territory in Latin America. The British occupation of East Falkland, which had already occurred in 1765, was recognised by the Spanish, who were only established in West Falkland. By 1816, both powers had removed their respective garrisons and the islands had no permanent inhabitants. A vessel from newly independent Argentina was sent in 1820 to establish a permanent settlement but was driven out by a British expedition in 1832. The British declared full sovereignty over the islands the following year. Argentina refused to recognise the British occupation and has maintained a consistent claim to sovereignty ever since. This claim was pursued through diplomatic channels until 1982 when an Argentine force overran the British garrison and established a military base on the 'Islas Malvinas', a name derived from the original French settlers, who named the islands after their home port of St Malo. After various attempts at negotiation and mediation had failed, a British task force, which had been despatched at the start of the crisis, was ordered to continue its journey and engage the Argentines. Argentina formally surrendered on June 14, ten weeks after the invasion. In the contacts between the two governments which have been made since the war, it has become apparent that the issue of sovereignty is a stumbling block and that the Falklands issue will remain a key aspect of Argentine foreign policy in the foreseeable future. Nonetheless, discreet negotiations were opened between the two sides under UN auspices during 1988. The British refused adamantly to discuss sovereignty, but some progress was made on issues such as airline landing rights, fisheries control and other trade matters. The election of the Menem government in Argentina in 1989 was followed by some unexpectedly conciliatory opening gestures, declaring an official end to all hostilities. This led to the resumption of diplomatic relations, first at consular, then in early 1990 at full ambassadorial level. The two countries have since held talks on oil exploration in the region.
GOVERNMENT: The Falkland Islands are a British Crown Colony. The British monarch is represented locally by an appointed Civil Commissioner who is responsible for administration, aided by an Executive Council of six. The Legislative Council has two ex-officio members and six elected by universal suffrage.

CLIMATE

The climate is temperate and largely conditioned by the surrounding sea being cooled by the Antarctic Current.
Required clothing: Much as for the UK; woollens and warm clothing should always be on hand.

STANLEY Falkland Is. (2m)

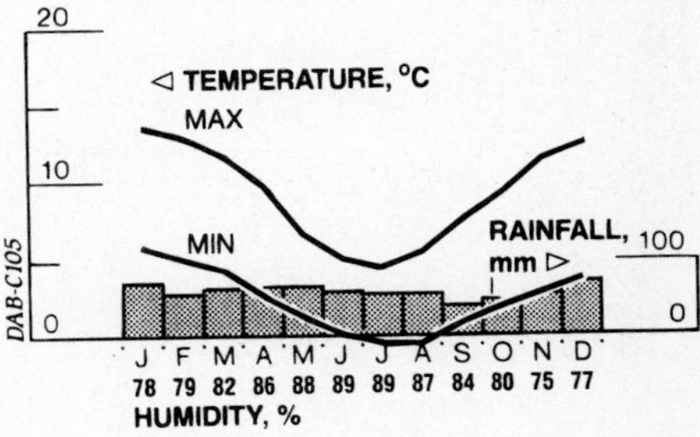

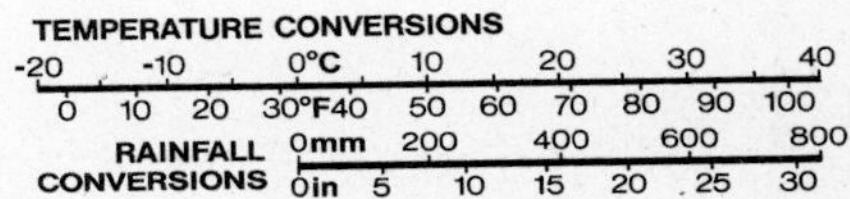

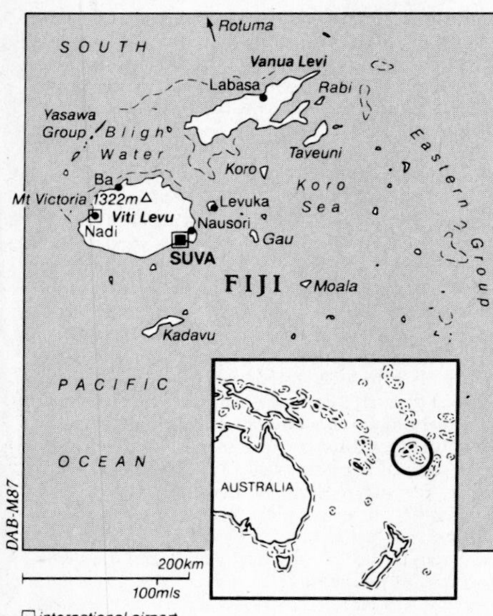

Location: South Pacific; Melanesia.

Fiji Visitors Bureau
PO Box 92
Suva, Fiji
Tel: 302 433. Fax: 300 970. Telex: 2180.
Embassy of Fiji
34 Hyde Park Gate
London SW7 5BN
Tel: (071) 584 3661. Fax: (071) 584 2838. Telex: 22408.
Opening hours: 0930-1730 Monday to Friday.
Fiji Visitors Bureau
Suite 433, High Holborn House
52/54 High Holborn
London
WC1V 6RB
Tel: (071) 242 3131. Fax: (071) 242 2838. Telex: 23770.
British Embassy
PO Box 1355
Victoria House
47 Gladstone Road
Suva, Fiji
Tel: 311 033. Fax: 301 406. Telex: 2129 PRODROME FJ.
Fiji Embassy
Suite 240
2233 Wisconsin Avenue, NW
Washington, DC
20007
Tel: (202) 337 8320. Fax: (202) 337 1996. Telex: 4971930.
Fiji Visitors Bureau
577 West Century Boulevard
Los Angeles, CA
90045
Tel: (310) 568 1616. Telex: 759972.
Embassy of the United States of America
PO Box 218
31 Loftus Street
Suva, Fiji
Tel: 314 466. Fax: 300 081. Telex: 2255.
Fiji Embassy
Suite 750
130 Slater Street
Ottawa, Ontario
K1P 6E2
Tel: (613) 233 9252. Fax: (613) 594 8705.
Canadian Consulate
PO Box 2193
7th Floor, LICI Building
Butt Street
Suva, Fiji
Tel: 300 589. Fax: 300 296.

AREA: 18,333 sq km (7078 sq miles).
POPULATION: 735,985 (1989 estimate).
POPULATION DENSITY: 40.1 per sq km.
CAPITAL: Suva. **Population:** 69,665 (1986).
GEOGRAPHY: Fiji is located in the South Pacific, 3000km (1875 miles) west of Australia and about 1930km (1200 miles) south of the Equator. It comprises 322 islands, 105 of which are uninhabited (some are little more than rugged limestone islets or tiny coral atolls). The two largest are Viti Levu and Vanua Levu, extinct volcanoes rising abruptly from the sea. There are thousands of streams and small rivers in Fiji, largest being the Kioa River on Viti Levu, which is navigable for 128km (80 miles). Mt Victoria, also on Viti Levu, is the country's highest peak, at 1322m (4430ft).
LANGUAGE: The main languages are Fijian and Hindi. English is widely spoken.
RELIGION: Methodist and Hindu with Roman Catholic and Muslim minorities. A strictly fundamentalist Methodist version of Christianity is enshrined in and informs the Fijian Constitution.
TIME: GMT + 12.
ELECTRICITY: 240 volts AC, 50Hz. Larger hotels also have 110-volt razor sockets.
COMMUNICATIONS: Telephone: IDD is available. Country code: 679. International calls can be made from

hotels, or from the Fiji International Telecommunications (FINTEL) office in Victoria Parade in Suva. **Fax:** The FINTEL office in Victoria also offers fax services. Major hotels have facilities. **Telex/telegram:** Facilities are available at major hotels in Suva and at the Fiji International Telecommunication Ltd office on Victoria Parade. **Post:** Airmail to Europe takes up to 10 days. Post office hours: 0800-1630 Monday to Friday, 0800-1300 Saturday. **Press:** A number of newspapers published in Fijian and Hindi including the *Fiji Post* and the *Island Business*. The main English-language daily is the *Fiji Times*, which claims to be 'the first newspaper published in the world today' – a reference to Suva's position just to the west of the International Date Line. *Fiji Magic* is the tourist newspaper, which may be of interest to visitors.
BBC World Service and Voice of America frequencies: From time to time these change. See the section *How to Use this Book* for more information.

BBC:

MHz	17.10	15.36	9.740	7.150

Voice of America:

MHz	18.82	15.18	9.525	1.735

PASSPORT/VISA

Regulations and requirements may be subject to change at short notice, and you are advised to contact the appropriate diplomatic or consular authority before finalising travel arrangements. Details of these may be found at the head of this country's entry. Any numbers in the chart refer to the footnotes below.

	Passport Required?	Visa Required?	Return Ticket Required?
Full British	Yes	No	Yes
BVP	Not valid	-	-
Australian	Yes	No	Yes
Canadian	Yes	No	Yes
USA	Yes	No	Yes
Other EC	Yes	1	Yes
Japanese	Yes	No	Yes

PASSPORTS: Valid passport required by all. All passports must be valid for at least four months from the date of entry.
British Visitors Passport: Not accepted.
VISAS: Required by all except:
(a) nationals of countries shown in chart above;
(b) nationals of Commonwealth countries;
(c) [1] nationals of EC countries with the exception of Portugal (who *do* need visas);
(d) nationals of Argentina, Austria, Brazil, Finland, Iceland, Indonesia, Israel, Liechtenstein, Mexico, Norway, Paraguay, Peru, Philippines, South Korea, Sweden, Switzerland, Taiwan, Thailand, Tunisia, Turkey, Uraguay and Venezuela.
Types of visa: Single or Multiple entry. Cost depends on rate of exchange (currently £20 for a single entry and £40 for a multiple). Transit visas are not required if stay in Fiji does not exceed 3 hours, the visitor does not leave the airport and has confirmed onward tickets.
Validity: 30 days, but can be extended for an additional six months on application to Immigration Dept, Fiji.
Application to: Consulate (or Consular Section at Embassy). For addresses, see top of entry.
Application requirements: (a) Valid passport. (b) Application form(s). (c) 2 photos. (d) Sufficient funds to cover duration of stay. (e) Onward/return air ticket. (f) Fee.
Working days required: 3 for applications in person; postal applications take 2 weeks.
Temporary residence: Enquiries should be directed to the Embassy of Fiji or the Ministry of Home Affairs, Government Building, Suva, Fiji.

MONEY

Currency: Fijian Dollar (F$) = 100 cents. Notes are in denominations of F$20, 10, 5, 2 and 1. Coins are in denominations of 50, 20, 10, 5, 2 and 1 cents.
Currency exchange: Exchange facilities are available at the airport and at trading banks.
Credit cards: Access/Mastercard, American Express, Diners Club and Visa are accepted at a small number of establishments. Check with your credit card company for details of merchant acceptability and other services which may be available.
Exchange rate indicators: The following figures are included as a guide to the movements of the Fijian Dollar against Sterling and the US Dollar:

Date:	Aug '89	Oct '90	Mar '91	Oct '92
£1.00=	2.39	2.76	2.58	2.40
$1.00=	1.48	1.41	1.48	1.51

Currency restrictions: There are no restrictions on the import of foreign or local currency. Unspent local currency can be re-exchanged on departure up to the amount of foreign currency imported. The export of local currency is limited to F$100. The export of foreign currency as cash is limited to the equivalent of F$500.
Banking hours: 0930-1500 Monday to Thursday, 0930-1600 Friday.

DUTY FREE

The following items may be imported by people over 17 years of age into Fiji without incurring customs duty:
200 cigarettes or 250g of tobacco goods;
1 litre of spirits or 2 litres of wine or 2 litres of beer;
Goods to the value of F$150.
Prohibited items: All categories of firearms, ammunition and all narcotics. Fruit or plants may be confiscated on entry.

PUBLIC HOLIDAYS

Public holidays observed in Fiji are as follows:
Apr 9 '93 Good Friday. **Apr 12** Easter Monday. **Jun** Ratu Sir Lala Sukuna Day. **Jun** Queen's Birthday. **Jul 26** Constitution Day. **Aug 30** Birth of the Prophet. **Oct 11** Independence Day. **Oct/Nov** Diwali. **Nov 14** Birthday of the Prince of Wales. **Dec 25-26** Christmas. **Jan 1 '94** New Year's Day.
Note: Muslim festivals are timed according to local sightings of various phases of the moon and therefore dates can only be approximations.

HEALTH

Regulations and requirements may be subject to change at short notice, and you are advised to contact your doctor well in advance of your intended date of departure. Any numbers in the chart refer to the footnotes below.

	Special Precautions?	Certificate Required?
Yellow Fever	No	1
Cholera	No	-
Typhoid & Polio	Yes	-
Malaria	No	-
Food & Drink	2	-

[1]: A yellow fever vaccination certificate is required from travellers over one year of age arriving from infected areas.
[2]: Mains water is normally heavily chlorinated, and whilst relatively safe may cause mild abdominal upsets. Bottled water is available and is advised for the first few weeks of the stay. Milk is pasteurised and dairy products are safe for consumption. Local meat, poultry, seafood, fruit and vegetables are generally considered safe to eat.
Health care: The main hospitals are located in Suva, Sigatoka, Lautoka, Ba, Savusavu, Tavenuni, Labasa and Levuka, with clinics and medical representations elsewhere throughout the islands. Medical insurance recommended.

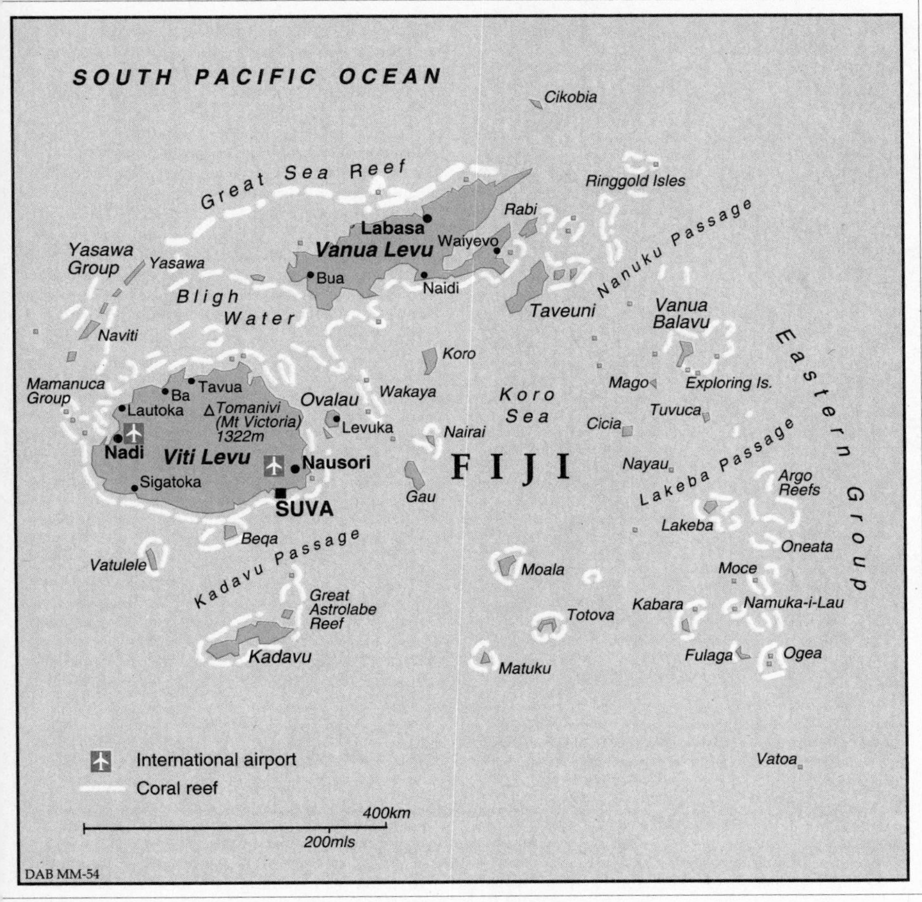

TRAVEL - International

AIR: *Air Pacific (FJ)* and *Polynesian Airways (PH)* are the main international airlines which serve Fiji. *Polynesian Airways* offer a 'Polypass' which allows the holder to fly anywhere on the airline's network: Sydney (Australia), Auckland (New Zealand), American Samoa, Cook Islands, Vanuatu, Western Samoa, New Caledonia, Fiji and, on payment of a supplement, Tahiti. The pass is valid for 30 days.
Approximate flight times: From *London* to Nadi is 27 hours 45 minutes (plus connection/stopover time).
From *Los Angeles* to Nadi is 11 hours.
From *Sydney* to Nadi is 3 hours 45 minutes.
International airports: *Nadi (NAN)* is 5km (3 miles) from the town of the same name. Airport facilities include a 24-hour, 7-day bank (BNZ); an outgoing duty-free shop; a bar; a restaurant; a left-luggage office; a post office and car hire.
Suva (SUV) is actually at Nausori, 21km (13 miles) from Suva. Nadi is where most international flights arrive, while Suva is the hub of the internal flight network. Buses and taxis are available at both airports.
Departure tax: F$10. Children under 16 years of age are exempt.
SEA: The international ports are Suva and Lautoka (Viti Levu). Passenger lines serving Fiji are *Polish Ocean, CTC, Cunard, Norwegian America, P&O, Princess Cruises, Royal Viking Line* and *Sitmar*. *Royal Interocean* is a cargo line that also carries passengers. There are regular sailings to Tuvalu, Kiribati, Western Samoa and Nauru.

TRAVEL - Internal

AIR: *Air Pacific (FJ)* operates shuttle services between Nadi and Suva (Nausori) and regular flights to Vanua Levu, Labasa and Taveuni. The flight time from Nadi to Suva is approximately 30 minutes. Tel: 386 444 (Suva)/72422 (Nadi).
Fiji Air operates from Suva to Coral Coast resorts,

Ovalau, Vatakoula, Bafour, Lakeba in the Lau group, Gau Island and Bua. A 'Discover Fiji' ticket is available which gives virtually unlimited flights (Rotuma and Funafuti in Tuvalu not included) for ten days. Tel: 301 524 (Suva)/72521 (Nadi). *Sunflower Air* operates four flights daily to Malololaitai (for Musket Cove and Plantation Village), and three daily to Pacific Harbour Resort. There are less frequent departures to Kadavu, Labasa, Tavenui and Savusavu. Tel: 73408 (Nadi).
Pacific Crown Aviation operates a helicopter out of Suva which is available for charter.
SEA: Government and local shipping companies operate freight and passenger services linking the outer islands. Cruises to offshore islands leave Nadi/Lautoka and Suva. A ferry goes back and forth regularly from Suva to Lambasa, and to Ovalau and Koro Island. Yachts and cabin cruisers are available for charter. Inter-island trips can take anything from a few hours to a few weeks, and are generally very inexpensive. In general, timetables are not posted. Persons wishing to travel about the islands in this way should enquire at the offices of one of the local shipping agents, being sure to confirm all arrangements with the captain once the vessel is in port. A number of roll-on-roll-off ferries now operate between the major islands, greatly reducing journey times. These boats have a capacity of between 300 and 500 passengers and have a full range of facilities, including bar, TV lounge and snack bar.
ROAD: There are about 3100km (1950 miles) of roads, 1100km (700 miles) of which are usable all year round. Traffic drives on the left. The approximate driving time from Nadi to Suva is three hours (on a tar-sealed road). The main roads on Viti Levu follow the coast, linking the main centres. **Bus:** Buses operate across Viti Levu and the other main islands between all towns and on suburban routes. Express air-conditioned buses operate between Suva and Nadi and between Suva and Lautoka. **Taxi:** Taxis are metered in towns. A fare table for long distances is required. **Car hire:** Car rental is available. **Documentation:** Foreign driving licence accepted.

ACCOMMODATION

HOTELS: There are a good number of luxury hotels, the majority of which are located in Nadi, Sigatoka, Douba, Suva, Raki Raki, Tavua and Lautaka and off Viti Levu at Savusavu and Ovalau. There are also many small, inexpensive hotels throughout the islnads. Increasing numbers of establishments are offering dormitory accommodation at cheap rates. Small resort islands include Beachcomber, Treasure, Castaway, Mana and Plantation Islands. A 5% hotel tax is levied on all hotel services charged to guests' accounts, including meals in hotel restaurants. For information contact the Fiji Visitors Bureau at the address above, or the Fiji Hotel Association, PO Box 13560, 42 Gorrie Street, Suva. Tel: 302 980. Fax: 300 331. (Listings of hotels, their cost and facilities can be supplied).
Grading: A star system is used to indicate the price range, as follows: **3-star** (deluxe price range), **2-star** (medium price range) and **1-star** (budget price range).
GUEST-HOUSES: These are known locally as *Budgetels* and are are clean, comfortable and most have a licensed bar, pool and restaurant, some are air-conditioned with kitchenettes. There is a youth hostel in Suva.

RESORTS & EXCURSIONS

There are many scenic and historic attractions in Fiji, including trips to copra, ginger, sugar cane and cocoa plantations. The capital, **Suva,** has many old shops and markets with various foods, artefacts, handicrafts and especially seafood. Places of historic interest include the *National Museum*, situated in the lush surrounds of *Thurston Gardens* next to *Government House* and the old *Parliament Buildings*. Other sites of interest on Fiji include the *Cultural Centre* at **Orchid Island,** just outside of Suva, the mysterious earthworks at **Tavenui** and the old colonial houses (situated around Fiji). The ethnic variety of Fiji society can be seen mainly in the towns (see *History & Government* section below). There are powerfully built Fijians dressed in wrap-around *sulus*, numerous Indians, men in Western clothes, women wearing colourful *saris* and a scattering of European, Chinese and other Pacific

FIJI	**HEALTH REGULATIONS**	**VISA REGULATIONS** Code-Link
GALILEO/WORLDSPAN	 TI-DFT/NAN/HE	 TI-DFT/NAN/VI
SABRE	 TIDFT/NAN/HE	TIDFT/NAN/VI

To access this information on your CRS, swipe the barcode with a light pen or type in the text under the barcode. For more information, see the introduction *How to Use This Book.*

Islanders. One tradition of both the Indians and Fijians is the practice of fire-walking. Fijian fire-walking has its origin in legend, while Indian fire-walking is done for religious reasons; although tourists can pay to see these ceremonies, the ritual remains a religious penance and not merely a tourist attraction. Cruises on large schooners or yachts to the different islands can be arranged, and tours around the main islands in comfortable coaches are also available. For the hardier, hiking in the mountains with dramatic views of the islands is another option.

SOCIAL PROFILE

FOOD & DRINK: International cuisine is available, but the local cooking is Fijian and Indian. Local dishes include *kakoda* (a marinated local fish steamed in coconut cream and lime), *raurau* (a taro leaf dish), *kassaua* (tapioca, often boiled, baked or grated and cooked in coconut cream with sugar and mashed bananas), and *duruka* (an unusual asparagus-like vegetable in season during April and May). Breadfruit is also common. Indian curries are served in all major hotels. A number of hotels and restaurants also serve the Fijian *lovo* feast of meats, fish, vegetables and fruit cooked in covered pits. Table service is normal, although some establishments offer buffet-style food at lunchtime. Hotels often serve meals to non-residents. **Drink:** A wide range of drinks are available. Local beers are *Carlton*, brewed in Suva, and *Fiji Bitter*, brewed in Lautoka. Local wines include *Meridan Moselle* and *Suvanna Moselle*. South Pacific Distilleries produce *Bounty Fiji Golden Rum, Old Club Whisky, Booth's Gin* and *Cossack Vodka*. Throughout Fiji the drinking of *yaqona* (pronounced Yanggona) or *kava* is common. In the past the drink was prepared by virgins, who chewed the root into a soft pulpy mass before adding water. It is made from the root of the pepper plant and the *yaqona* drinking ceremony is still important in the Fijian tradition, although it has also become a social drink. Bars and cocktail lounges have table and/or counter service. Only licensed restaurants, clubs and hotel bars can serve alcohol.
NIGHTLIFE: Major hotels and resorts have live bands and dancing during the evening. There are also a number of nightclubs with entertainment, especially in Suva. Cinemas show English-language and Indian films with programmes listed in the local newspapers. Most of Fiji's social life, however, is in private clubs and visitors can obtain temporary membership through hotels. Hotels offer Fijian entertainment *(mokeo)* on a rotation basis and details can be obtained from most hotel receptions.
SHOPPING: Favourite buys are filigree jewellery, wood carvings (such as *kava* bowls) and polished coconut shells, sea shells, woven work (such as mats, coasters, hats, fans and trays), tapa cloth and pearls. Most items are reasonably priced and bargaining is not a rule in shops. Some shopkeepers will give a discount with large purchases. Duty-free items are available and include cameras, televisions, watches, binoculars, clocks, lighters, hi-fi equipment, pewter, crystal and porcelain. **Shopping hours:** 0800-1700 Monday to Friday, half-day closing by some on Wednesdays and certain shops are open later on Fridays; 0800-1300 Saturday.

SPORT: Fishing: Fully equipped launches operate from the Beachcomber Travelodge, Fijian, Korolevu Beach and Regent of Fiji hotels. **Water-skiing** is also available. **Golf:** There are 18-hole courses in Suva and at Pacific Harbour. Nadi, Lautoka, Ba, Vatukaula, Nausori and Labasa have 9-hole courses. Private clubs welcome visitors if arrangements are made with the club secretary first. **Scuba diving & snorkelling:** The most popular diving area is Astrolabe Lagoon near Kadauu Island. Equipment can be hired at Tradewinds Marina, Suva, and at the Regent of Fiji Hotel and Mana Island Resort. **Surfing:** Dangerous reef waves prevent surfing in Fiji. **Horseriding:** Horses and equipment are available at several resorts. **Spectator sports:** From May to October **rugby, football, hockey** and **netball** are the main sports. The **cricket** and **tennis** seasons begin after October.
SPECIAL EVENTS: The following is a selection of the major festivals and other special events celebrated annually in Fiji. For a complete list, contact the Fiji Visitors Bureau.
Jul *Bula Festival*, Nadi. **Aug** *Hibiscus Festival*, Suva. **Sep** *Sugar Festival*, Lautoka. **Oct/Nov** *Diwali* (Festival of Lights).
SOCIAL CONVENTIONS: Fijians are a very welcoming, hospitable people and visitors should not be afraid to accept hospitality. Normal courtesies should be observed when visiting someone's home. Informal casual wear is widely acceptable. Swimsuits are acceptable on the beach and around swimming pools, but should not be worn in towns. Smoking is only restricted where specified. **Tipping:** Only necessary for very special services and then only a small tip is needed.

BUSINESS PROFILE

ECONOMY: The economy is largely agricultural, with sugar as the main product, although tourism is rapidly increasing in importance. Together, these make up about 90% of Fiji's foreign export earnings, although tourism has been damaged somewhat by the political upheaval since 1987. Copra, once the second most important product, has been overtaken by gold, fish and timber. Low-grade copper deposits have been discovered, though it is not clear whether or not these will be exploited. There are a number of light industrial enterprises producing goods such as cement, paint, cigarettes, biscuits, flour, nails, barbed wire, furniture, matches and footwear mainly for domestic consumption. The Government is also looking to attract manufacturers for export by offering tax incentives: textiles have started to develop under this regime and it is hoped that shipping services (repair yards, boatbuilding) as well as the timber industry will develop along the same lines. In the past, trade and commerce in Fiji have been dominated by the Indian population, many of whom are now trying to leave the country; the expiry in 1991 of many Indian leases on sugarcane production is one of several factors causing unease. Fiji's largest trading partners are Australia, New Zealand, Japan, the US and the UK.
BUSINESS: Lightweight or tropical suits are acceptable. **Office hours:** 0800-1630 Monday to Friday (some businesses close half an hour earlier on Fridays).
COMMERCIAL INFORMATION: The following organisation can offer advice: Suva Chamber of Commerce, PO Box 337, 7th Floor, Honson Building, Thomson Street, Suva. Tel: 211 327. Fax: 300 475.

HISTORY & GOVERNMENT

HISTORY: The indigenous islanders were first introduced to Europeans in the mid-17th century, taking in an assortment of roving traders, missionaries and shipwrecked sailors. As the rivalry of the European imperial powers spread to the Pacific during the late 19th century, Fiji fell under British control. The British brought in a large number of workers from India to develop a plantation economy. By the 1960s Indian descendants formed the majority community on the islands, leading to racial tensions between them and the indigenous Fijians. In the elections of April 1987, Indians won a majority in Parliament for the first time. This was the trigger for an army coup d'état, headed by Colonel Sitiveni Rabuka, to ensure the preservation of native Fijian rights. Colonel Rabuka declared himself head of an interim military government, pending a new constitution. Constitutional reforms were discussed and approved by the Great Council of Chiefs, which comprises the country's hereditary leaders, after which negotiations began in September 1987 involving leaders of all parties. This state of affairs was still unacceptable to Rabuka, who led another coup at the end of that month removing several key aides. Since the second coup, Fijian politics have been dominated by three men: Rabuka, the former Governor-General Ratu Sir Penaia Ganilau and a former Prime Minister, Ratu Sir Kamisese Mara. Ganilau resigned the

governorship at the end of 1987, but almost immediately assumed the post of President under the interim constitution which established Fiji as a republic for the first time. Mara again became Prime Minister. Both Ganilau and Mara still hold these posts, while Rabuka initially became Home Affairs minister, but returned within a year or so to his military duties. The resignation of the Governor led to Fiji withdrawing from the Commonwealth at the Commonwealth Summit in Vancouver, although there are plans to re-apply for membership once a new constitution has been implemented. Apart from Papua New Guinea, other countries were slow to recognise the new regime. Fiji has gradually acquired some international legitimacy, if only through its de facto control of the country, but has been repeatedly criticised for its allegedly discriminatory policies against non-Fijians. Ethnic Fijians are in the majority for the first time since 1945, according to recent government statistics, but at the price of large-scale emigration, particularly from the Indian community, with consequent ill effects on the Fijian economy as commercial and professional expertise drains from the country. During 1991, the economy was put under further strain by a dispute between sugar farmers and the Government over levels of payment. There were several brief strikes to which the Government responded with draconian anti-strike decrees. The first elections under the new constitution were held in 1992 and brought to power a coalition dominated by the principal ethnic Fijian party, Soqosoqo ni Vakavulewa ni Taukei (SVT). The SVT won 30 of the 37 'Fijian' seats in the 70-seat assembly and governs with the support of two independents and five MPs elected by 'other races' (mostly Europeans and Chinese). Sitiveni Rabuka was appointed Prime Minister by President Ganilau over his main rival, Josevata Kamikamica, also of the SVT, after securing the support of the ethnic Indian Fiji Labour Party. Labour Party support was, however, made conditional on a promise by Rabuka to review the constitution.

GOVERNMENT: The 1970 constitution was suspended in 1987, after the Rabuka coups. After a short period of rule under an interim constitution, a new constitution came into force in July 1990. It allows for a bicameral legislature comprising a 70-seat House of Representatives and a Senate of Chiefs with 34 appointed members. The seats in the House are divided along racial lines, with 37 seats to be elected by ethnic Fijians, 27 by Indians, and the remainder by others.

CLIMATE

Tropical. Southeast trade winds from May to October bring dry weather. The rainy season is from December to April.
Required clothing: Lightweight for summer, rainwear for the wet season.

SUVA Fiji (6m)

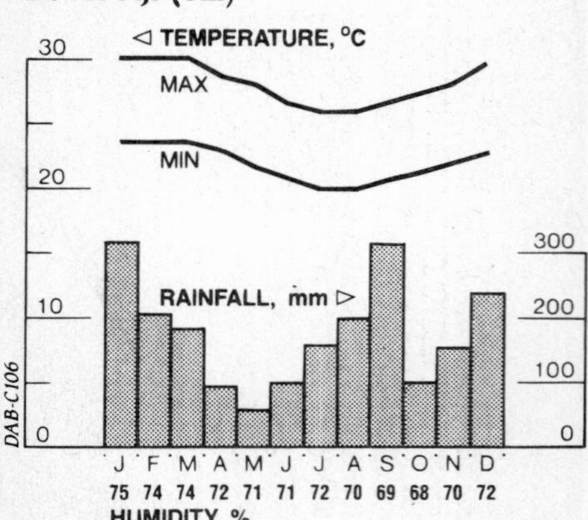

FINLAND

Location: Scandinavia, Europe.

Matkailun Edistämiskeskus (Finnish Tourist Board)
Töölönkatu 11
00100 Helsinki, Finland
Tel: (0) 403 0011. Fax: (0) 448 841.
Embassy of the Republic of Finland
38 Chesham Place
London SW1X 8HW
Tel: (071) 235 9531. Fax: (071) 235 3680. Telex: 24786 FINAMB G. Opening hours: 0830-1630 Monday to Friday (0900-1200 for visa applications).
Finnish Tourist Board
Queener House
66/68 Haymarket
London SW1Y 4RF
Tel: (071) 839 4048 *or* (071) 930 5871 (trade only). Fax: (071) 321 0696. Telex: 295960 FTBUK G. Opening hours: 0915-1200 and 1300-1715 Monday to Friday.
British Embassy
Itäinen puistotie 17
00140 Helsinki, Finland
Tel: (0) 661 293. Fax: (0) 661 342. Telex: 121122.
Consulates in: Kotka, Oulu (Uleåborg), Pori (Bjorneborg), Tampere (Tammerfors), Turku (Åbo), Vaasa (Vasa), Kuopio and Jyväskylä.
Embassy of the Republic of Finland
3216 New Mexico Avenue, NW
Washington, DC
20016
Tel: (202) 363 2430. Fax: (202) 363 8233. Telex: 248268.
Finnish Tourist Board
655 Third Avenue
New York, NY
10017
Tel: (212) 949 2333. Fax: (212) 983 5260. Telex: 620681 SCANDIA.
Embassy of the United States of America
Itäinen puistotie 14A
00140 Helsinki, Finland
Tel: (0) 171 931. Fax: (0) 174 681. Telex: 121644 USEMB SF.
Embassy of the Republic of Finland
Suite 850
55 Metcalfe Street
Ottawa, Ontario
K1P 6L5
Tel: (613) 236 2389. Fax: (613) 238 1474.
Finnish Tourist Board
Suite 604
1200 Bay Street
Toronto, Ontario
M5R 2A5
Tel: (416) 964 9159. Fax: (416) 964 1524.
Canadian Embassy
PO Box 779
P. Esplanadi 25B
00101 Helsinki 10, Finland
Tel: (0) 171 141. Fax: (0) 601 060. Telex: 121363.

AREA: 338,145 sq km (130,559 sq miles).
POPULATION: 4,998,478 (1990 estimate).
POPULATION DENSITY: 14.8 per sq km.
CAPITAL: Helsinki. **Population:** 490,629 (1990).
GEOGRAPHY: Finland is situated in Scandinavia at the far north of Europe. Bounded to the west by Sweden and the Gulf of Bothnia, to the north by Norway, to the east by the CIS and to the south by the Gulf of Finland, it is the fifth largest country in Europe. There are about 30,000 islands off the Finnish coast, mainly in the south and southwest, and 62,000 inland lakes, containing a further 98,000 islands. The Saimaa lake area is the largest inland water system in Europe. 10% of the total land area is water, and 65% forest, the country being situated almost entirely in the northern zone of a coniferous forest. In the south and southwest the forest is mainly pine, fir and birch. In Lapland, in the far north, trees become more sparse and are mainly dwarf birch. 8% of the land is cultivated.
LANGUAGE: The official language is Finnish, which is spoken by 93.6% of the population. Swedish is spoken by 6% of the population. About 1700 people speak Same (Lapp language). English is taught as the first foreign language from the age of eight.
RELIGION: 90% Lutheran, 10% others including Finnish Orthodox, Baptists, Methodists, Free Church, Roman Catholic, Jews and Muslims.
TIME: GMT + 2 (GMT + 3 in summer).
ELECTRICITY: 220 volts AC, 50Hz. Continental 2-pin plugs are standard.
COMMUNICATIONS: Telephone: Full IDD is available. Country code: 358. For international enquiries made from within Finland callers should dial 92020; tariff information is available on 92023. Local calls made in telephone boxes require F Mk1 or F Mk5 coins. **Fax:** Many hotels and businesses have fax facilities. Also available in larger post offices in Helsinki. **Telex/telegram:** There are telex services at the Central Post Office (see below for address). Telegrams can be left with the nearest post office or hotel desk. **Post:** Letters and postcards sent by airmail usually take about three days to reach destinations within Europe. Stamps are available from post offices, book and paper shops, stations and hotels. Visitors can have mail sent to them *Poste Restante*, Central Post Office, Mannerheimintie 11, Helsinki which is open 0800-2200 Monday to Saturday, 1100-2200 Sundays. Generally, post offices are open 0900-1700 Monday to Friday, closed Saturday. During winter many town offices are open 0900-1800. **Press:** There are over 90 daily newspapers including: *Uusi Suomi*, *Helsingin Sanomat*, *Ilta-Sanomat* and *Iltalehti*. *Suera* is a monthly illustrated news magazine and is one of several periodicals. *Kauppalehti* is one of the leading business newspapers. There are no English-language newspapers published in Finland.
BBC World Service and Voice of America frequencies: From time to time these change. See the section *How to Use this Book* for more information.

BBC:

MHz	15.57	9.410	6.195	3.955

Voice of America:

MHz	11.97	9.670	6.040	5.995

PASSPORT/VISA

Regulations and requirements may be subject to change at short notice, and you are advised to contact the appropriate diplomatic or consular authority before finalising travel arrangements. Details of these may be found at the head of this country's entry. Any numbers in the chart refer to the footnotes below.

	Passport Required?	Visa Required?	Return Ticket Required?
Full British	1	2	No
BVP	Valid	No	Yes
Australian	Yes	No	Yes
Canadian	Yes	No	Yes
USA	Yes	No	Yes
Other EC	1	No	Yes
Japanese	Yes	No	Yes

PASSPORTS: Valid passport required by all except the following nationals provided they hold a valid National ID card:
(a) Iceland, Norway and Sweden;
(b) **[1]** Belgium, Denmark, France (and overseas territories), Germany, Luxembourg, and the UK with BVP;
(c) Austria, Liechtenstein and Switzerland.
British Visitors Passport: Acceptable. The sum duration of trips to Finland, Norway, Denmark, Sweden and Iceland using a BVP must not exceed 3 months in any 6-month period.
VISAS: Required by all except:
(a) nationals shown on the chart above and under passports, but **[2]** holders of British Hong Kong passports *do* require a visa;
(b) nationals of Andorra, Argentina, Austria, Bahamas, Barbados, Belize, Bolivia, Botswana, Brazil, Chile, Colombia, Costa Rica, Côte d'Ivoire, Cuba, Cyprus, Czechoslovakia, Dominica, Dominican Republic, Ecuador, El Salvador, Fiji, Gambia, Grenada, Guatemala, Honduras, Hungary, Israel, Jamaica, Kenya, South Korea, Lesotho, Liechtenstein, Malawi, Malaysia, Malta, Mauritius, Mexico, Monaco, Namibia, New Zealand, Nicaragua, Niger, Panama, Peru, Poland, St Vincent & the Grenadines, San Marino, Seychelles, Singapore, Suriname, Swaziland, Switzerland, Tanzania, Trinidad & Tobago, Uganda, Uruguay, Vatican City and Zambia.
Visas are required for stays exceeding 3 months and for all who wish to work during their stay except nationals of Denmark, Iceland, Norway and Sweden.
Types of visa: Tourist, Transit and Business (free of charge).
Validity: 3 months for Tourist visa. Up to 5 days for Transit visa. Applications for renewal or extension should be made to the Embassy or Authorities in Finland.
Application to: Consulate (or Consular Section at Embassy). For addresses, see top of entry.
Application requirements: (a) Application form. (b) 2 passport-size photos. (c) Valid passport.
Working days required: 2-3 days. Some applications might be referred to the Finnish Ministry of the Interior. Allow 2-3 weeks.

FINLAND	HEALTH REGULATIONS	VISA REGULATIONS Code-Link
GALILEO/WORLDSPAN	 TI-DFT/HEL/HE	 TI-DFT/HEL/VI
SABRE	 TIDFT/HEL/HE	 TIDFT/HEL/VI

To access this information on your CRS, swipe the barcode with a light pen or type in the text under the barcode. For more information, see the introduction *How to Use This Book*.

Temporary residence: Apply to Finnish Embassy. Work permits and Residence permits should be arranged well in advance.
Note: Those wishing to visit the CIS from Finland are advised to obtain their visa in their country of origin; applications made in Helsinki take at least 8 weeks.

MONEY

Currency: Markka (F Mk) = 100 penniä. Notes are in denominations of F Mk1000, 500, 100, 50 and 10. Coins are in denominations of F Mk10, 5 and 1, and 50, 20 and 10 penniä.
Currency exchange: Foreign currency and travellers cheques can be exchanged in banks and currency exchange offices at ports, stations and airports.
Credit cards: Access/Mastercard, American Express, Diners Club and Visa enjoy wide acceptance. Check with your credit card company for details of merchant acceptability and other services which may be available. Up-to-date information is available in Helsinki on (0) 12511 *(American Express)*, (0) 694 7122 *(Diners Club)* or (0) 692 2439 (other cards).
Travellers cheques: American Express accepted throughout the country.
Exchange rate indicators: The following figures are included as a guide to the movements of the Markka against Sterling and the US Dollar:

Date:	Oct '89	Oct '90	Mar '91	Oct '92
£1.00=	6.78	7.01	7.03	7.71
$1.00=	4.29	3.6	4.04	4.86

Currency restrictions: Unrestricted import of local currency; export of local currency limited to F Mk500. Unrestricted import of foreign currency, but it must be declared on arrival; export up to declared amount allowed.
Banking hours: 0915-1615 Monday to Friday.

DUTY FREE

The following items may be imported into Finland by:
(a) Passengers aged 16 and over without incurring customs duty:
200 cigarettes or 250g of other tobacco products **[1]**;
Manufactured tobacco and cigarette rolling papers for making up to 200 cigarettes;
Non-commercial goods to a value of F Mk1500 **[2]**.
(b) Passengers aged 18 and over without incurring customs duty:
Cigarettes, tobacco products, cigarette rolling papers etc – as above;
Non-commercial goods – as above;
2 litres of beer and 2 litres of other mild alcoholic drinks (less than 21% by volume).
(c) Passengers aged 20 and over without incurring customs duty:
Cigarettes, tobacco products, cigarette rolling papers etc – as above;
Non-commercial goods – as above;
2 litres of beer and 2 litres of other mild alcoholic drinks (less than 21% by volume) or 2 litres of beer and 1 litre of strong alcoholic drinks.
Note: **[1]** 400 cigarettes or 500g of other tobacco products if arriving from outside Europe. **[2]** Goods may include foodstuffs up to a weight of 15kg, of which no more than 5kg should be edible fats (of which no more than 2.5kg should be butter).
Controlled items: The import and export of food, plants, medicines, firearms and works of art are subject to certain restrictions and formalities. In general, dogs and cats may be imported, provided they are accompanied by a certificate issued by a competent veterinary surgeon to the effect that 30 days prior to entry, and within the previous year, they have been vaccinated against rabies. The certificate must be in Finnish, Swedish, English or German. Dogs and cats from rabies-free countries (Sweden, Norway, Iceland, UK, Ireland, Australia and New Zealand) do not require a certificate if imported direct. The importation of drinks containing more than 60% alcohol by volume is prohibited. Consult the Finnish Tourist Board for further details.

PUBLIC HOLIDAYS

Public holidays observed in Finland are as follows:
Apr 9 '93 Good Friday. **Apr 12** Easter Monday. **Apr 30-May 1** May Eve and Day. **May 20** Ascension Day. **May 30** Whitsun. **Jun 25-26** Midsummer's Eve and Day Holiday. **Nov 6** All Saints' Day Holiday. **Dec 6** Independence Day. **Dec 24** Christmas Eve. **Dec 25** Christmas Day. **Dec 26** Boxing Day. **Jan 1 '94** New Year's Day. **Jan 6** Epiphany.
Note: Shops and offices usually close earlier on the eve of a public holiday.

HEALTH

Regulations and requirements may be subject to change at short notice, and you are advised to contact your doctor well in advance of your intended date of departure. Any numbers in the chart refer to the footnotes below.

	Special Precautions?	Certificate Required?
Yellow Fever	No	No
Cholera	No	No
Typhoid & Polio	No	-
Malaria	No	-
Food & Drink	No	-

Health care: There are no vaccination requirements for any international traveller. There is a Reciprocal Health Agreement with UK but, although consultation at a health centre is usually free, charges will be made for hospital and dental treatment, and prescribed medicines. Some of these charges may, however, be partially refunded by the Finnish Sickness Insurance Institute – enquire at a local office before leaving. For emergencies in Helsinki, dial 000; for other regions, enquire at hotels.

TRAVEL - International

AIR: The national airline of Finland is *Finnair (AY)*.
Approximate flight times: From *London* to Helsinki is 2 hours 55 minutes, from *Los Angeles* is 10 hours 35 minutes, from *New York* is 8 hours, from *Singapore* is 14 hours 5 minutes, from *Toronto* is 7 hours 45 minutes and from *Zurich* is 2 hours 55 minutes.
International airports: *Helsinki (HEL)* (Helsinki-Vantaa) is Finland's principal international airport, 20km (12 miles) north of the city (travel time – 25 minutes). Facilities include bank (0700-2300), duty-free shop, car rental, hotel, VIP lounge, a 24-hour electronic information system with four channels, conference rooms, restaurants, cafés and cafeteria bars. There are various charges for short- and long-term car parking. There is a coach service to city every 15 mins. A bus service runs two to four times an hour up until 2300. Taxi services are available. Some Helsinki hotels run courtesy coaches. The other international airports are *Jyväskylä (JYV)*, 21km (13 miles) from the city; *Kemi (KEM)*, 6km (4 miles) from the city; *Kokkola (KOK)*, 22km (14 miles) from the city; *Oulu (OUL)*, 15km (9 miles) from the city; *Rovaniemi (RVN)*, 10km (6 miles) from the city; *Tampere (TMP)*, 15km (9 miles) from the city; *Turku (TKU)*, 7km (4 miles) from the city; and *Vaasa* (VAA), 12km (7 miles) from the city.
SEA: *Finnjet-Silja Line* car ferry *GTS Finnjet* sails from Travemünde on the Baltic coast of Germany to Helsinki with further connections from Lübeck. Car ferries sail daily from Stockholm and other Swedish ports on the *Silja, Vaasalaivat-Vaasaferries* and *Viking* Lines. Other major ports are Turku, Naantali, Vaasa. Cruise lines with ships putting in to Finnish ports are *Royal Viking, Sally Line, Kristina Cruises, Eckerö Line, Birka Line, Jakob Line, KG Line, M/S Konstantin Simonov Cruises, Polferries, Saimaa Lines, Anedin Line, TUI Viking, CTC, Norwegian American* and *Lauro*.
RAIL: Rail-sea links from Hamburg, Copenhagen and Stockholm to Helsinki or Turku. There is a rail connection between Haparanda/Tornio in the north from Sweden, and daily trains to Moscow and St Petersburg.
ROAD: Most direct road routes include sea ferry links from Sweden or Germany, though there is a northern land link via northern Norway or Sweden to Finnish Lapland, which involves travel within the Arctic Circle. **Coaches:** There are coach services from many European cities, including direct services from London to Helsinki or Turku and Gothenburg with a sea link from Sweden. See below for information concerning *documentation* and *regulations*.

TRAVEL - Internal

AIR: There are 21 domestic airports in Finland. *Finnair* runs an excellent network of domestic services.
Cheap tickets: There are a variety of money-saving offers available. These include: *Finnair Holiday Ticket*, giving unlimited travel for 15 days (available to non-residents of Finland), which is available before departure to those who have a ticket for Finland; *Family discount* (1 full fare plus 25-75% discounts for other members); *Group discounts* which vary between 15% and 35%, depending on the size of the group; *Senior citizen's discounts* giving 50% discount (with some restrictions) for persons over 65; *Youth reduction* giving 50% discount (with some restrictions) for persons aged 12-23.
There are special 'Midnight Sun' return flights to Rovaniemi between June 15 and July 15. Contact Finlandia (for address, see below) or the Finnish Tourist Board for further information.
RIVER/LAKE: Traffic on the inland waterways is serviced by lake steamers and motor vessels. There is a wide choice of routes and distances. Popular routes are the 'Silver Line' between Hämeenlinna and Tampere; the 'Poet's Way' between Tampere and Virrat, and the Saimaa Lake routes. There are regular services also on Lake Päijänne and Lake Inari. On Lake Pielinen there are regular services, also by car ferry. Overnight accommodation in small cabins and meals and refreshments are available on lake steamers.
RAIL: There is 6000km (3700 miles) of rail network with modern rolling stock. Rail travel is cheap and efficient. In 1990 a fast train with a maximum speed of 140kmph (90mph) was introduced. Seat reservations are required for 'EP' express trains. Main rail connections run car-sleeper trains. Seats can be booked for a small extra charge. Tickets are valid for one month. Return fares are exactly double the price of a single fare.
Cheap fares: Special tickets offering discounts are available including: *Group tickets* (minimum of 3 people), giving 20/50% discount, valid for one month; *Finnrail pass*, giving unlimited travel for 8, 15 or 22 days, first or second class; *Finnish Senior Citizen's Rail Card*, which can be bought at any Finnish rail station entitles the holder to a 50% discount; *Scanrail Card*, valid for 21 days for travel in the Scandanavian countries with reductions of 25/50% for young people according to age; *Interrail Ticket*, valid in Finland as well as the rest of Europe; *Eurail Passes* are also accepted.
For further details and reservations contact the Finnish Tourist Board, or Finlandia Travel Agency, 223 Regent Street, London W1R 7DR. Tel: (071) 409 7334. Fax: (071) 409 7733.
ROAD: There are 75,000km (46,000 miles) of road. The main roads are passable at all times and are surfaced with asphalt or oil and sand. There are weight restrictions on traffic from April to May in southern Finland, and from May to early June in northern Finland. Traffic drives on the right in Finland. Horn-blowing is frowned upon. In some areas warnings of elk, deer and reindeer crossing will be posted. Drivers involved in an elk or reindeer collision should report the event to the Police immediately. Better still, they should take care to avoid collisions as there is not much difference between the consequences of a car/elk (etc) collision and a car/car collision. **Bus:** This is an excellent means of transport. There are more than 300 express services daily from Helsinki and connections can be made to the most remote and isolated parts of the country. In Lapland, buses are the major means of surface travel. Bus stations have restaurants and shops. Baggage left at one station is dispatched to its destination, even when change of bus and different bus companies are involved. One child under four is carried free (children 4-11 years pay half fare). Seats for coaches can be reserved in advance by paying the full fare and reservation fee. Timetables are widely available. **Cheap fares:** Group tickets are sold for groups travelling at least 75km (46 miles) and including at least four persons. Group discount is 20% for groups of five-nine people and 30% for larger groups. A family reduction is given with at least three paying members travelling together. The State post office also runs a bus service with routes that serve the rural areas. **Taxi:** Available in every city and from airports or major hotels, taxi drivers are not tipped. **Car hire:** Cars can be rented in Helsinki and other places. Normally, the hiring party should be at least 19-25 years of age and have at least one year's driving experience. The rates usually include oil, maintenance, liability and insurance, but no petrol. A few caravans are for hire. **Regulations:** Seat belts must be worn by the driver and all front seat passengers over 15. Outside of towns car headlights must be kept on at all times. In towns they must be used in dim, dark or rainy conditions. Cars towing caravans may not exceed 80kmph (50mph). Cars and caravans must have the same tyres. Studded tyres are allowed from October 1 to April 30 or when weather conditions are appropriate. During December to January snow tyres are recommended for vehicles under 3.5 tonnes. It is possible to hire tyres. Further information can be obtained from *Autoliitto* (Automobile and Touring Club of Finland), Kansakoulukatu 10, 00100 Helsinki. Tel: (0) 694 0022. Fax: (0) 693 2578. Telex: 124839 AUTOCLUB SF. If involved in an accident, immediately contact the Finnish Motor Insurer's Bureau *(Liikennevakuutusyhdistys)*, Bulevardi 28, 00120 Helsinki. Tel: (0) 19251. **Documentation:** UK driving licence or International Driving Permit and insurance required.
URBAN: Efficient and integrated bus, metro and tramway services, suburban rail lines and ferry services to Suomenlinna Islands are operated in Helsinki. A common fares system applies to all the modes (including the ferries) with a zonal flat fare and free transfer between services. Multi-trip tickets are sold in advance, as are var-

ious passes. The peninsular location of the city has led to an emphasis on public transport. The number 3 tram passes most of the main tourist attractions – a free brochure in English is available for those who wish to take the trip. **Helsinki Card:** This is available for one, two or three days. Once purchased, it gives free travel on public transport and free entry to about 50 museums and other sights in the city. Enquire at the Tourist Board for prices and further details.

JOURNEY TIMES: The following chart gives approximate journey times (in hours and minutes) from Helsinki to other major cities/towns in Finland.

	Air	Road	Rail
Tampere	0.35	2.50	2.15
Turku	0.30	2.40	2.16
Rovaniemi	1.15	-	12.00

ACCOMMODATION

HOTELS: Most Finnish hotels and motels have all modern conveniences. They are quite new and invariably have saunas and often a swimming pool. The price level varies from district to district, being higher in Helsinki and some areas of Lapland.

Many hotels and motels usually include breakfast in their rates. The service fee is usually included in the bill and is 15% of the room rate, for meals and drinks it is 14% on weekdays and 15% on Friday evenings, Saturdays, Sundays, holidays and the eve of holidays.

Advance reservations are advisable in the summer months (users of the Finncheque system should see below). Details of hotels are listed in the brochure *Hotels, Motels and Hostels in Finland*, available from Finnish Tourist Board offices. See also their publication *Finland Handbook* which gives, among other invaluable information, full details of accommodation in Finland and addresses of booking agencies.

A hotel cheque system called Finncheque offers the opportunity to travel from hotel to hotel in summer. There are 160 hotels in 80 locations to choose from. Only the first night can be reserved in advance. Reservations to next hotel are free of charge. Finncheques are personal and are available from accredited agents abroad, and in the UK from the Finlandia Travel Agency, 223 Regent Street, London W1R 7DR. Tel: (071) 409 7334. Fax: (071) 409 7733.

Accommodation at reduced rates is often possible at weekends, especially for groups and during weekends. Reductions are also possible for guests participating in special schemes run by hotel chains throughout Scandinavia. The *Finland Handbook* gives details. The *Finnish Hotel, Restaurant and Cafeteria Association* (tel: (0) 176 455; fax: (0) 171 430) and the *Hotel and Restaurant Council* (tel: (0) 632 488; fax: (0) 632 813) are at Merimiehenkatu 29, 00150 Helsinki. **Children:** If an extra bed is required for a child there is a supplementary charge. No charge is made for children under 15 if an extra bed is not required. **Summer hotels:** During summer (June 1 to August 31), when the universities are closed, the living quarters of the students become available to tourists. These are modern and clean and become the 'summer hotels' of Finland. They are located around the country in major cities. The price level of summer hotels is less than that of regular hotels. **Grading:** There is a hotel grading scheme linked to the Finncheque system. For *Category I* and *II* hotels (the former being the more expensive) the price includes accommodation in a double room, breakfast and service. For *Category III* hotels the price includes a self-service or packed lunch.

GUEST-HOUSES: A *gasthaus* in Finland is usually a privately-run family business. It is generally a small hotel with dining facilities for 20-50 people. In country areas the term may describe a restaurant with some accommodation available. Finlandia Hotels, Merimiehenkatu 29, 00150 Helsinki. Tel (0) 176 322. Fax: (0) 176 619. Telex: 123959. Bed & breakfast accommodation ranges from rooms in main buildings to cottages and outbuildings. There is no charge for children under 4, and there are discounts of 50% for children aged 4-12. For further information contact: Lomarengas ry, Malminkaari 23, 00700 Helsinki. Tel: (0) 3516 1321. Fax: (0) 3516 1370.

FARMHOUSE HOLIDAYS: More than 150 farmhouses take guests on a bed & breakfast and full or half-board board basis. They are in rural settings and almost always close to water. The guest rooms may be without modern conveniences, but are clean and there is usually a bathroom in the house. Some farms also have individual cottages for full board guests, or apartments with kitchen, fridge and electric stove for those wishing to cater for themselves. The guests can join the farm family for meals, take a sauna twice a week, row, fish, walk in the forests or join in the work of the farm. Full-board rates include two hotel meals, coffee twice a day and a sauna twice a week, children 50-75% reduction. The majority of farms are in central and eastern Finland, some on the coast and in the Åland Islands. **Grading:** Farmhouses are graded on a scale from 1 to 5 stars.

5-star: These are similar to 4-star, but separate facilities are available to each family.

4-star: These are farms where guest facilities are well furnished. Buildings and surroundings have been designed with the guest in mind and recreational opportunities are provided. WCs and showers are provided with a maximum of eight users per unit.

3-star: These are working farms with dedicated facilities for vacationing guests. Furnishings and decor are good. WCs and showers are in the same building with a maximum of ten users per unit.

2-star: These are primarily working farms. However, attention has been given to the comfort of guest facilities. WCs and showers are in the same building or in a separate service building.

1-star: These are very basic. There is usually electricity and heating. There will be either an outhouse or a WC and shower in a separate building.

SELF-CATERING: There are over 200 Holiday Villages in Finland, many in the luxury class with all modern conveniences. These villages consist of self-contained first-class bungalows by a lake and offer varied leisure activities, such as fishing, rowing, hiking and swimming. The best villages are open all the year round and can be used as a base for winter holidays and skiing. Some of the villages also have hotels and restaurants. Those in the top price bracket have several rooms, TV and all modern conveniences.

There are also about 5000 individually owned holiday cottages for hire, ranging from the humblest fishing hut on the coast or in the archipelago to the luxury villas of the inland lakes. They are all furnished and have cooking utensils, crockery and bed-linen as well as fuel for heating, cooking and lighting and in many cases a sauna and a boat. Most cottages inland are near a farm where the tourist can buy food. Reductions are available out of season. Enquire at tourist offices for details.

Grading: Only some of the holiday organisations have classifications. Where they exist they are as follows:

5-star: Cottage with at least 2 bedrooms, sitting room, kitchen, sauna (with dressing room), shower and toilet. Electricity and every modern convenience. Living space is at least 24 sq metres. Private rowing boat.

4-star: Cottage with at least 2 bedrooms, sitting room, kitchen, sauna, shower and toilet. Electricity. Living space is at least 24 sq metres. Private rowing boat.
3-star: Cottage with at least a bedroom, sitting room/kitchen or kitchenette, sauna, shower and toilet/privy. Electricity. Living space is at least 24 sq metres. Private rowing boat.
2-star: Cottage with at least sitting room, bed alcove, cooking facilities, well, sauna (own or shared) and privy. Living space is at least 12 sq metres. One rowing boat for two cottages at most.
1-star: Cottage with sitting room, cooking facilities, well, sauna (own or shared), shower and private section in jointly-used privy. Living space is at least 12 sq metres. Rowing boat available.
YOUTH HOSTELS: There are about 160 youth hostels in Finland. Many of them are only open in the summer from June 10 to August 15, and about 50 of them are also open in winter. Some of the hostels are in empty educational establishments, with accommodation and fairly large rooms, but a lot of them also offer 'family rooms'. The hostels do not in general provide food, but coffee and refreshments are available at most and some have self-service kitchens. There are no age restrictions and motorists may use the hostels. Sheets can be hired. All youth hostels accept Finncheques. For more information contact: The Finnish Youth Hostel Association, Yrjönkatu 38B, 00100 Helsinki. Tel: (0) 694 0377. Fax: (0) 693 1349. Telex: 122192 SUMHO SF.
Grading: Youth hostels are classified into three categories according to their facilities. The **3-star** category 'Finnhostels' provide facilities for courses and conferences. **2-** and **1-star** hostels meet basic international requirements.
CAMPING/CARAVANNING: There are about 350 campsites in Finland. The majority have cooking facilities, kiosks and canteens where food, cigarettes and sweets can be bought. Campsites are generally along waterways, within easy reach of the main roads and towns. Camping anywhere other than in official campsites is forbidden without special permission from the landowner. The camping season starts in late May or early June and ends in late August or early September. In southern Finland it is possible to sleep under canvas for about three months and in the north for about two months. Most campsites have indoor accommodation, camping cottages, and holiday cottages suitable for family accommodation. Prices depend on the classification of the campsite and are charged for a family, ie children, two adults, car, tent and trailer. The charge includes the basic facilities such as cooking, washing etc. If a camper has an international camping card (FICC) he does not require a national camping card. Further details are given in the booklet *Finland, Camping and Youth Hostels* available at Finnish Tourist Board Offices. Information, Camping Department, PO Box 776, Mikonkatu 25, 00101 Helsinki. Tel: (0) 170 868. Fax: (0) 654 358. Telex: 122619 FTATA SF.
Grading: The standard of sites varies and they are classified into the following three grades:
3-star: Covered cooking area, fire lighting area, main drainage, toilets, washroom with hot water, washing and ironing facilities, play and ball areas, site guarded on a 24-hour basis.
2-star: Covered cooking area, fire lighting area, main drainage, toilets, washing and washing-up facilities, showers, play area, site guarded at night.
1-star: Covered cooking area, fire lighting area, main drainage, toilets, washing-up facilities.

RESORTS & EXCURSIONS

Over the country as a whole there are marked differences in climate and landscape, with corresponding regional variations in traditions, culture and food. Seasonal variations are particularly marked in the north; in Lapland, for instance, the winter sports season lasts until May, and the midnight sun shines night and day for the whole of June and part of July. Autumn is also worth seeing, for in September the first frosts produce the vivid colours of 'Ruska'. In South Finland spring comes earlier and summer is longer. At Midsummer daylight lasts for nineteen hours and in summer there are generally many hours of warm sun.

Helsinki Metropolitan Area

There are about 770,000 inhabitants in the Helsinki Metropolitan Area, making it the most densely populated region in Finland. The area comprises four towns, **Helsinki** the capital, **Espoo**, **Vantaa** and **Kauniainen**. However, only half of the 800 sq km (300 sq miles) that it occupies is actually developed. The rest consists of parks, forests, shoreline, and lakes with almost a feeling of the countryside. In many places there are historical sights – old manors and churches – as well as buildings by the best-known of Finnish architects including *Dipoli Hall* at the *Helsinki University of Technology* in **Otaniemi**, an internationally acknowledged 20th-century masterpiece.
Resorts: Espoo, Helsinki, Vantaa.

Finnish Archipelago and Åland Islands

Finland is surrounded in the south, southwest and west by the *Baltic*, the *Gulf of Finland* and the *Gulf of Bothnia*. The coastline is extremely indented and its total length is 4600km (2760 miles). Around the coast is a vast archipelago of thousands of islands of varying sizes.
The coast and archipelago are largely composed of granite rocks, either grey or red, but nowhere do they rise very high. In many places there are long unspoiled sandy beaches. There are no tides to speak of, so the appearance of the seashore does not differ much from the lakeshores. In addition the seawater is not very salty as very little water of high salt content passes through the Danish straits, and the many rivers as well as the rainfall contribute more water to the Baltic than is lost by evaporation. A special feature of the Baltic is that the land is constantly rising from the sea, as much as 9mm a year in the narrow part of the Gulf of Bothnia, a long-term result of the end of the Ice Age. The archipelago can be explored by local cruises from many coastal towns.
Southwest Finland and the Åland Islands are the warmest part of the country and more deciduous trees grow here. Fruit and vegetables are extensively cultivated and 20% of the country's fields are here.
For historical reasons a large proportion of the Swedish speaking population of Finland lives in this region and is concentrated in the Åland Islands, the **Turku archipelago** and on the south coast. The region is often spoken of as the cradle of Finnish civilisation and the area has a larger concentration of granite churches and manors than elsewhere.
Resorts: Ekenäs, Hamina, Hanko, Hyvinkää, Hämeelinna, Kotka, Kouvola, Kuusankoski, Lohja, Mariehamn and Åland Islands, Naantali, Pargas, Pori, Porvoo, Rauma, Riihimäki, Turku, Uusikaupunki.

Finnish Lakeland

The majority of Finland's 180,000 lakes are situated between the coastal area of about 100km (60 miles) in width and the eastern frontier. The lakes are a veritable maze with their profusion of bays, headlands and islands. Sometimes they open out into broader waters. They are linked to each other by rivers, straits and canals forming waterways which in former times were a principal means of communication. Nowadays they are attractive routes for the tourist. As the lakes are usually shallow and the surrounding land is not high the water soon becomes warm in summer. A very large number of summer festivals of all kinds take place in the lakeland area, often in beautiful country settings.

Western Lakeland

Jyväskylä, Tampere, Lahti, Hämeenlinna region. This area comprises two major waterways, the oldest of which, the Finnish *Silverline* runs between Hämeenlinna, birthplace of Sibelius, and Tampere, through fertile agricultural lands with a fairly dense population. Lahti, a winter sports centre, lies at one end of *Lake Päijänne* where the land is higher and steep rocky cliffs rise to as much as 200 metres (650ft). At the other end is Jyväskylä, famous for its modern architecture.

Eastern Lakeland

The eastern region is dominated by *Lake Saimaa*, a vast area of water with a profusion of interconnected lakes. Dotted over their surface are no less than 33,000 islands and the shoreline is 50,000km (80,000 miles) long. A network of waterways leads from one to the other of the lively Savo towns such as **Savonlinna** with its medieval *Olavinlinna Castle*, the best preserved in Scandinavia and **Kuopio** known for its food speciality 'kalakukko'.

Forest Finland

The remoteness of Forest Finland has meant that the beauty of the wild, vast forests, rivers and lakes has remained unspoiled. It is a popular area for canoe and hiking trips, and rapid-shooting.
Northern Karelia, the southernmost part of Forest Finland, lies in the 'bulge' to the east of *Lake Pielinen*. The *Koli Heights* (347m, 1138ft), the highest point in Northern Karelia, overlook the lake. A large percentage of the Finnish Greek Orthodox population lives in Karelia, and the region has preserved its own special character, customs and food. One speciality is known far beyond the region, the 'Karjalan piirakka', Karelian pasty. *Kainuu*, the district round *Lake Oulujärvi*, is very wild and beautiful with vast forests, marshes, deep lakes and rapids. **Vuokatti**, near Sotkamo village, specialises in cross-country skiing. At *Olavinlinna Castle*, the Savonlinna Opera Festival is held annually in July. In addition to operas performed to international standards, there are a number of musical concerts.
Resorts: Iisalmi, Imatra, Joensuu, Jyväskylä, Kajaani, Kuopio, Lahti, Lappeenranta, Lieksa, Mikkeli, Nurmes, Outokumpu, Savonlinna, Tampere, Valkeakoski, Varkaus.

Ostrobothnia

The west coast area of Ostrobothnia with its long sandy beaches (of which the dunes of *Kalajoki* are the best known), is an agricultural region with a sunny climate and less rain than elsewhere. There are islands between **Vaasa** and **Kokkola** with old fishermen's villages. **Hailuoto Island** with its interesting fauna, can be reached by ferry from **Oulu**, the area's chief commercial and university centre.
Picturesque old wooden houses are still a living part of the coastal towns. Traditions are maintained in many local festivals where 'Pelimannit' play music handed down from father to son. A number of Swedish-speaking Finns live on the coast. **Seinäjoki** has administrative buildings designed by Alvar Aalto. 80km (130 miles) southeast of Seinäjoki is *Ähtäri Wildlife Park*.
The region just south of the Arctic Circle along the eastern frontier is centred round **Kuusamo**. In *Oulanka National Park* rivers with rapids run through gorge-like valleys. Seine fishing takes place on *Lake Kitkajärvi*. In summer there are numerous hiking routes. *Ruka Fell* is a popular winter sports centre.
Resorts: Jakobstad, Kokkola, Oulu, Raahe, Seinäjoki, Vaasa.

Lapland

Finnish Lapland is a place for those who wish to enjoy the peace and quiet of a remote area either in the comfort of first-class accommodation out in the wilds or in more primitive conditions. Lapland can offer gastronomic delights such as salmon and reindeer prepared in many ways, and the rare golden cloudberry. It is a very large area of 100,000 sq km (38,000 sq miles). Between the many rivers are vast uninhabited areas and swamps. In the valleys pine and spruce grow, but the most northerly regions are treeless tundra or low fell birch scrub. Many fells have gently rounded treeless tops.
There are only four towns in the province: **Rovaniemi** (the provincial capital), **Kemijärvi**, **Tornio** and **Kemi**. The whole of the rest of Lapland is a very sparsely populated area with a density of only slightly over two persons per sq km. Of the 200,000 inhabitants, about 3900 are Lapps and 600 Skolt Lapps, the latter belonging to the Orthodox church. About 200,000 reindeer roam freely on the fells. They are the property of 5800 different owners. There are reindeer round-ups from September to January. Special reindeer-driving competitions take place in March with participants from all over Lapland.
As regards scenery and communications, Lapland can be roughly divided into two areas: Eastern and Western Lapland.

Eastern Lapland

Suomutunturi, on the Arctic Circle, is a well-known winter sports centre, as are also **Pyhätunturi** and **Luostotunturi** and **Saariselkä Fells**. At **Porttikoski** and

Simo there are traditional lumberjack competitions in summer. Further north **Tankavaara** is a gold-panning centre. **Inari** village lies on the third largest lake in Finland, *Lake Inari* with 3000 islands, on one of which there is an old Lapp sacrificial palace. The *Sami Museum* is devoted to the history of the Lapps. In the wilds lies *Pielppajärvi Church*. The *River Lemmenjoki* flows into *Lake Inari* and is another well-known gold-panning region. The *Lemmenjoki National Park* has marked routes for hikers.

Western Lapland

The scenery differs from Eastern Lapland and the ground is higher. The fells rise in bare and impressive ranges. Among the best known are *Yllästunturi*, *Olostunturi* and *Pallastunturi*. All of them are winter sports centres but are attractive also at other seasons, especially for hiking. *Haltia Fell*, the highest in Finland, 1300m (4265ft) and *Saana Fell*, 1029m (3376ft), lie on the border between Finland, Norway and Sweden. In the north is the Lapp village of **Hetta**, scene of colourful festivities on Lady Day in March.

Resorts: Kemi, Kemijärvi, Rovaniemi, Tornio.

Winter Sports

Skiing is the main activity in the Finnish winter. All over the country there are marked and often illuminated ski tracks of varying length and difficulty setting out from near the centre of towns. The tracks lead through the forest and over snow to covered frozen lakes and the sea. **Cross-country skiing** can be enjoyed in south and central Finland up to the end of March. In Lapland the season lasts to the end of May and then there are 14-16 hours of sunshine. Winter begins in earnest when the snow comes to stay, that is, in Lapland at the end of October and elsewhere in November and December. By the end of winter in the north and northeast the snow is about 70cm (30 inches) deep. Avalanches are rare even in the fells. The lakes and ground freeze in Lapland in October and elsewhere in November or December. The coastal waters freeze in December. The temperature eventually falls well below zero but it does not feel unbearably cold because the air is dry. Finnish buildings are constructed to keep in the warmth with insulated walls, double windows and efficient central heating. Winter weather seldom affects transport, either by land or in the air, so services run according to timetables. Sea connections are easily maintained by the use of powerful ice-breakers.

By January the days are getting longer and the pace increases so that by April there are well over 12 hours of daylight even in Helsinki, and the sun is warm. The snow starts to melt at the beginning of March and in Lapland at the beginning of April. In South Finland the ground is clear of snow by April and in North Finland by May. The ice disappears in South Finland by the beginning of May and in North Finland by the end of May.

Skiing Centres: *The North* – Pallastunturi, Saariselkä, Olostunturi, Yllästunturi, Rovaniemi; *The Centre* – Suommu, Ruka, Isosyöte, Vuokatti, Ruuponsaari, Koli, Summassaari, Ahtäri, Jyväskylä, Ruka Fell, Joutsa; *The South* – Ellivuori, Messilä, Hyvinkää, Lahti.

SOCIAL PROFILE

FOOD & DRINK: Potatoes, meat, fish, milk, butter and rye bread are the traditional mainstays of the Finnish diet but food in Finland has been greatly influenced both by Western (French and Swedish) and Eastern (Russian) cooking. Tourists can rely on excellent fresh fish dishes on menus. Examples are pike, trout, perch, whitefish, salmon and Baltic herring. All are in abundance most of the year. Crayfish (a Finnish speciality) is available from July to August. One should also try reindeer meat, smoked or in other forms. Regional dishes include also *kalakukko*, a kind of fish and pork pie, baked in a rye flour crust, and *karjalan piirakka*, a pasty of rye flour stuffed with rice pudding or potato and eaten with egg butter. Various kinds of thick soups are also popular. In restaurants *(ravintola)* the menu is Continental with several Finnish specialities. Restaurant prices are moderate if the set menu is chosen. Most restaurants have a special menu for children, or other half-price meals. Inexpensive lunches are served at places called *kahvila* and *baari* (the latter is not necessarily a licensed bar). Information about **gourmet trails** may be obtained from Finnish Tourist Board offices; two are planned – for east and west Finland. The trails have been designed so that both can be covered in two to four days. Visitors on the trails will visit a variety of eating places from large chain hotels to inns and farmhouses, with the emphasis on the smaller, more personal places. Additionally in Lapland *Lappi à la carte* consists of three gourmet routes. An English route map with details is available from the Tourist Board. **Drink:** Restaurants are divided into two classes: those serving all kinds of alcohol and those serving only beers and wines. Waiter service is common although there are many self-service snack bars. Bars and cafés may have table and/or counter service and all internationally known beverages are available. The Finnish berry liqueurs, *mesimarja* (arctic bramble), *lakka* (cloudberry), and *polar* (cranberry), as well as the Finnish vodka (usually served ice cold with meals), are well worth trying. Finnish beer (grades III and IV A), is of a high quality and mild beers are served in most coffee bars. There are strict laws against drinking and driving. In restaurants beer is served from 0900 and other liquor from 1100. All alcohol is served until half an hour before the restaurant closes. Nightclubs are open to serve drinks until 0200 or 0300. Service begins at 1100 and continues until the restaurant closes. The age limit for drinking is 18 years, but consumers must be 20 before they can buy the stronger alcoholic beverages.

Restaurant classification: Prices for alcohol vary according to the restaurants classification.

E: Elite price category.
G: General price category.
S: Self-service price category.
A: Fully licensed.
B: Licensed for beer and wine.

SHOPPING: Finnish handicrafts, jewellery, handwoven *ryijy* rugs, furniture, glassware, porcelain, ceramics, furs and textiles are amongst the many Finnish specialities.

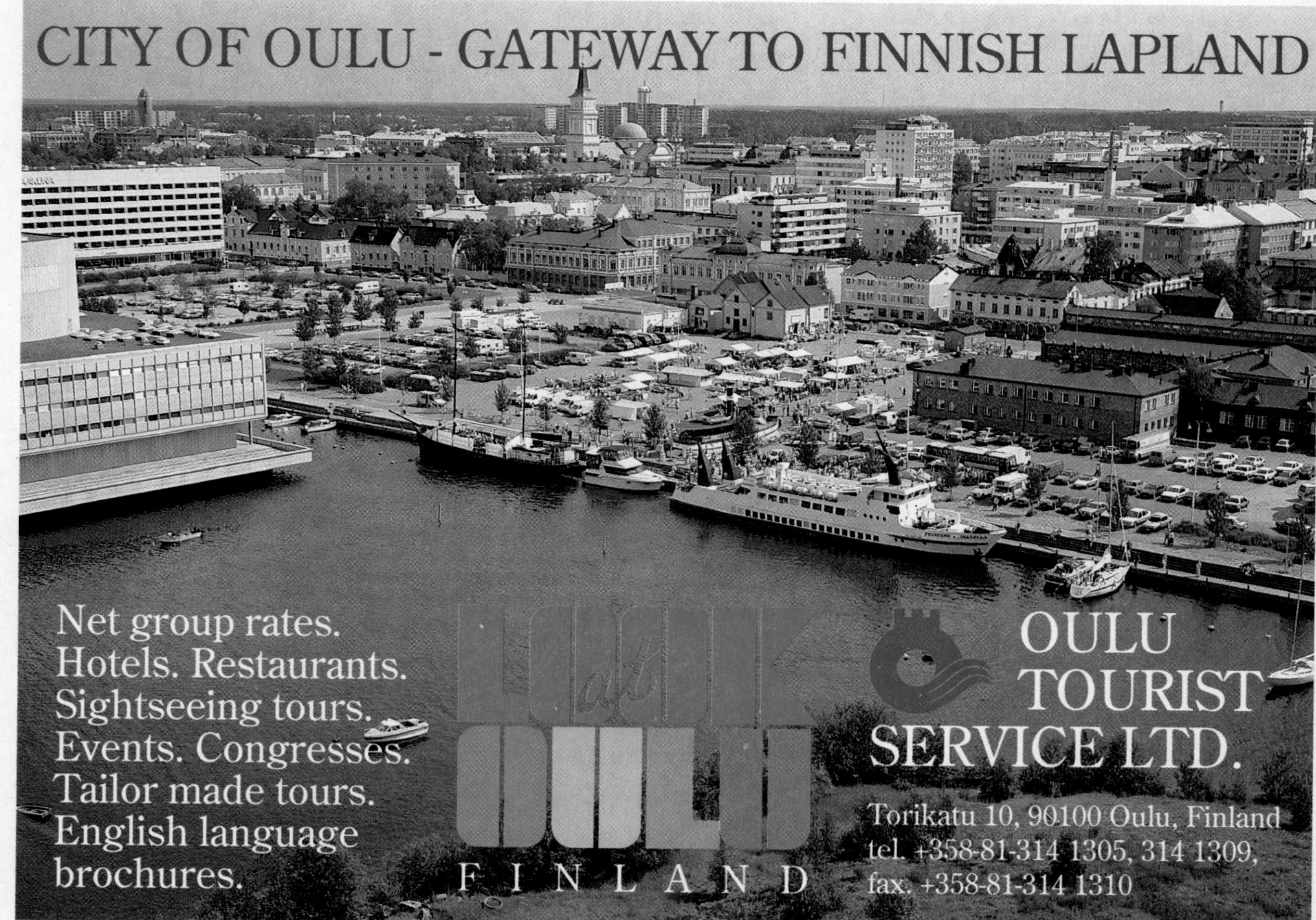

Excellent supermarkets and self-service shops can be found all over the country. Helsinki railway station has the first underground shopping centre in the country, where the shops are open from 0800 until 2200 (Sundays and holidays 1200 until 2200). At the Katajanokka boat harbour there is a shop selling glass, china, wooden articles and textiles. **Duty free:** Anyone permanently resident outside Scandinavia can claim back purchase tax at the time of departure. Repayment can be made (on presentation of a special cheque provided by the retailer) at the following gateways: Helsinki, Turku, Tampere, Mariehamn, Vaasa and Rovaniemi airports; on board ferries and ships operated by *Silja Line*, *Viking Line*, *Vaasaferries* and *Polferries*; and at the main checkpoints on the land borders with Sweden, Norway and the CIS. For further information on tax-free shopping contact: OY Finland Tax Free Shopping FTS AB, Yrjönkatu 29D, 00100 Helsinki. Tel: (0) 693 2433. **Shopping hours:** 0900-2000 Monday to Friday, 0900-1600 Saturday.

SPORT: Riding, hiking, golf, tennis, squash, archery and **gold panning** are all available. **Tennis:** It is estimated that one person in 20 in Finland plays tennis. There are over 1300 (mostly clay) outdoor courts and 350 indoor courts in the country. Many tourist centres have a court of their own. It can be difficult to hire equipment, so visitors are advised to bring their own. Many centres offer tennis courses lasting from three to seven days. Packages include accommodation and insurance. **Golf:** The main golf season runs from May to October, although in Kerimäki (and perhaps in other areas) the visitor is invited to play snow golf in winter. There are both 9- and 18-hole golf courses with most of the best being in the region of Helsinki. **Skiing:** The peak season in south and central Finland is from January to March. Ski centres in this region include Ellivuori in Vammala, Lahti, Joutsa, Kuopio, Lieksa and Saarijärvi. These centres offer *après-ski* entertainment as well. In Lapland the ski season lasts from late autumn to April, the most popular time being March and April. (See *Winter Sports* section in *Resorts & Excursion*.) **Cycling** is very good and bicycle races are popular. Ready-planned cycle routes are available, some of which follow old country roads whilst others follow the special cycle lanes in various cities. Along planned routes campsites, hostels and other forms of accommodation are available. Cycles can be hired from a variety of outlets including campsites, hotels, holiday villages, hotels, hostels and tourist information offices. Local tourist offices can provide details. **Fishing** takes place both in the sea and in the many inland lakes and waterways. The sea round Finland has a low salt content with the result that those fishing in the coastal region can catch both sea and freshwater fish in the same area. Foreign visitors over 18 years are required to purchase a general fishing licence (valid for one year) for all areas of Finland apart from the Åland Islands. This is obtainable from postal bank offices and from post offices. In addition permission from owners of fishing waters must be obtained. Some northern municipalities have their own fishing licences. **Watersports:** There are plenty of opportunities for **swimming, boating, canoeing, water-skiing** and **windsurfing**. There are about 26 water-skiing clubs in the Finnish Water-ski Association, about 30 windsurfing clubs, and boats may be hired at campsites, holiday villages and hotels. **Diving:** There are no commercial dive centres in Finland, but, in spite of the relatively low temperatures, the clear waters and absence of dangerous currents and poisonous fauna and flora along the south and southwest coast of Finland make the area ideal for the prepared diver; those who are interested should contact the Finnish Sport Divers' Association, Radiokatu 20, 00240 Helsinki. Tel: (0) 158 2258. Fax: (0) 158 2516. Telex: 121797 SVUL SF. **Boating:** Only experienced sailors with up-to-date charts (which are readily available) should navigate the Finnish archipelago in which there are many hidden rocks. A number of sailing courses are run by sailing schools approved by the Finnish Yachting Association. Instruction is given in Finnish but many instructors speak English, German or Swedish. Further information can be obtained from the Finnish Yachting Association, Radiokatu 20, 00240 Helsinki. Tel: (0) 1581. Fax: (0) 158 2369. Telex: 121797 SVUL SF. Lake cruises from a few hours to a couple of days can be taken from June to August using vessels ranging from romantic steamers to modern hydrofoils. **Canoeing:** The best canoeing waters are among the Finnish lakes which are linked in long chains by short channels with strong currents. In remote areas it is advisable to take a guide. Coastal canoeing is generally safe, but only the most experienced canoeists should attempt a sea-going trip. City tourist offices can supply ready-planned canoeing routes. All canoeists should use charts of the coastal regions and inland waterways. Further information can be obtained from the Finnish Canoe Association, Radiokatu 20, 00240 Helsinki. Tel: (0) 158 2363. Fax: (0) 145 237. Telex: 121797 SVUL SF. **Survival courses:** These are available in Kotka in February and March (where there are three tours each for a maximum of 15 people) and in Sotkamo from mid-August to the end of October (4-day survival courses for 4-12 people). The Kotka course, taking place in mid-winter, is the tougher and, although insurance is included in the price, participants are recommended to take out additional insurance.

SPECIAL EVENTS: The following is a selection of the major festivals and special events celebrated in Finland during 1993-94. For a complete list, contact the Finnish Tourist Board.

Apr 12 '93 *Kallavesj Boating Exhibition*, Kuopio. **May 21-23** *Gardening Fair*, Riihimäki. **Jun 21-8** *Jyväskyla Arts Festival*, Jyväskyla. **Jun 28-Jul 4** *Joensuu Song Festival*, Joensuu. **Jun 30-Jul 30** *Savonlinna Opera Festival*, Savonlinna. **Jul** *Lahti Organ Festival*. **Jul-Aug** *Arctic Canoe Race*, Kilpisjärvi-Tornio. **Aug 6-15** *Turku Music Festival*, Turku. **Aug 8-15** *Goldpanning World Festival*. **Aug 25-Sep 12** *Helskini Festival*, Helsinki. **Mar 11 '94** *Mountain Living Fair*.

SOCIAL CONVENTIONS: Handshaking is customary. Normal courtesies should be observed. It is customary for the guest to refrain from drinking until the host or hostess toasts their health with a 'skol'. Casual dress is acceptable. Black tie will usually be specified when required. Finns appear sometimes to be a bit reserved and visitors should not feel alarmed if there is a lack of small talk during the first half hour or so. **Tipping:** 15% service charge included in the bill in hotels. Restaurants and bars have 14% service charge on weekdays and 15% on weekends and holidays. The obligatory cloakroom or doorman fee is usually clearly indicated. Taxi drivers, washroom attendants, hairdressers are not tipped.

BUSINESS PROFILE

ECONOMY: Finland is a highly industrialised country, producing a wide range of industrial and consumer goods. Timber and related industries form the backbone of the economy, accounting for 40% of all Finnish exports, but the country is consequently vulnerable to fluctuations in the world market prices and demand levels for timber, paper, and finished products such as furniture. Agriculture is relatively important by the standards of most European industrialised economies, despite the country's climatic and geographical conditions which allow a very short growing season, giving Finland virtual self-sufficiency in basic foodstuffs such as grains, dairy products and root crops. The largest industrial sector is engineering, and although traditional 'metal bashing' industries have been in a strong position by world standards, there has nonetheless been a decline which threw Finland into an unprecedented recession at the turn of the 1990s. Industry is heavily dependent on imported components, which should merit increased attention from British firms. Paper, chemicals, woodworking, metal ores and textiles are Finland's other major export industries. Apart from engineering products, consumer goods are the country's main imported products. Through its geographical position and political neutrality, Finland has enjoyed the benefits of trade with both East and West, and is well placed to take up new opportunities in Eastern Europe and the CIS. Finland is also a member of the European Free Trade Association (EFTA), the trading bloc for Western European countries outside the EC, which now has a trade agreement with the EC. The country's major trading partners are Germany, the CIS and neighbouring Sweden. The value of the markka has now been pegged to that of the European Currency Unit.

BUSINESS: Businessmen are expected to dress smartly. Most Finnish business people speak English and/or German. Finnish is a complex language related to Hungarian and Estonian; details of available courses may be obtained from the Council for the Instruction of Finnish for Foreigners, Pohjoisranta 4 A 4, 00170 Helsinki. Local tourist boards and travel agents will be able to assist in finding translation services. Punctuality is essential for business and social occasions. Calling cards are common. Best months for business visits are February to May and October to December.

Office hours: 0800-1615 Monday to Friday.

COMMERCIAL INFORMATION: The following organisation can offer advice: Keskuskauppakamari (Finnish Central Chamber of Commerce), PO Box 1000, Fabianinkatu 14, 00101 Helsinki. Tel: (0) 650 133. Fax: (0) 650 303. Telex: 123814.

CONFERENCES/CONVENTIONS: Finland is among the world's top 20 conference destinations. In addition to conference centres and hotels there are cruise ships offering conference facilities. Information may be obtained from Helsinki-Finland Congress Bureau, Fabianinkatu 4 B 11, 00130 Helsinki. Tel: (0) 170 688. Fax: (0) 654 705. Telex: 125651 HFCB SF. In addition there are several Finnish congress organisers and travel agencies with congress departments. The Finnish Tourist Board can supply details.

HISTORY & GOVERNMENT

HISTORY: Most of the inhabitants of Finland are descended from a nomadic tribe that moved eastward across Russia, and settled around the time the Christian era began. The Lapps in the north arrived and settled a little earlier. Hunting, fishing and agriculture were the main pursuits of the people, but by AD1000 fur trading with surrounding countries had become a significant element in the economy. Thereafter the history of Finland has been closely linked with the competing interests of Sweden and Russia. A treaty in 1523 gave Russia a part of Karelia and in 1154 Eric IX of Sweden annexed the rest of Finland, although it was not until 1362 that Finland was granted the full rights of a Swedish province. By 1721 Russia controlled the whole of Karelia and in 1808 during the Napoleonic Wars gained total control of the country. In 1917, Finland was an autonomous region within the Russian Empire but, in the aftermath of the Bolshevik Revolution, Finland declared independence which the new Soviet government accepted after brief efforts to re-assert control. Further fighting between the two took place on the fringes of the Second World War between 1939 and 1941. Under a formal peace treaty signed in 1947, the Finns agreed to cede territory to the then USSR and pay reparation. The existence of a Pact of Friendship, Co-operation and Mutual Assistance between the two countries have led to the term 'Finlandisation'. However, since the visit of President Gorbachev in 1989, during which he formally accepted Finland's independence and neutrality, the word has no longer been a dirty one: indeed, it has been viewed as a possible model for emerging countries such as the Baltic states. The focus in recent years has been economic and environmental, from which both countries stand to gain substantial benefits. Domestic politics have been dominated by the Social Democratic Party (SDP) and the Centre Party (KP), which have led a long series of coalition governments and presided over the evolution of a centrist consensus in Finnish political life. In recent years, the only change in the political landscape has been caused by the emergence of the right-wing National Coalition Party (Kokoomus), which is now the second largest party after the SDP in the Eduskunta. Since the most recent elections in 1987, Finland has been governed by a 4-party coalition led by the SDP and Kokoomus while the Presidency (an important executive post) is held by the SDP-affiliated Dr Mauno Koivisto. The Government announced in December 1991 that it intended to apply for EC membership, overriding popular concern that membership would violate Finland's traditional political neutrality. As a member of EFTA, Finland has trade preferences through the EC/EFTA European Trade Area. The schedule envisages detailed negotiations during 1993 and a referendum in 1994 before full membership comes into effect in 1995. President Koivisto has declared that Finland is prepared to meet any obligations incumbent under the Maastricht treaty.

GOVERNMENT: The constitution allows for a President, who is Head of State, and a single-chamber assembly. The President is elected by direct popular vote for six years, while the 200-strong Parliament is elected every four years.

CLIMATE

Temperate climate, but with considerable temperature variations (see below). Summer is warm with relatively mild weather in spring and autumn. Winter, which lasts from November to mid-March, is very cold. In the north (see the chart for Sodankyla), the snow cover lasts from mid-October until mid May, but in the brief Arctic summer there may be up to sixteen hours of sunshine a day. Rainfall is distributed throughout the year with snow in winter, but the low humidity often has the effect of making it seem warmer than the temperature would indicate (even in Lapland, the temperature can rise to over 30°C). During warm weather, gnats and mosquitos can be a hazard, particularly in the north of the country. Bring a good supply of insect repellant. The *Midnight Twilight* season lasts for two months in the north during winter.

Required clothing: Light to mediumweights in warmer months. Medium to heavyweights in winter, with particularly warm clothing needed for the Arctic north. Waterproofing is essential throughout the year.

HELSINKI Finland (45m)

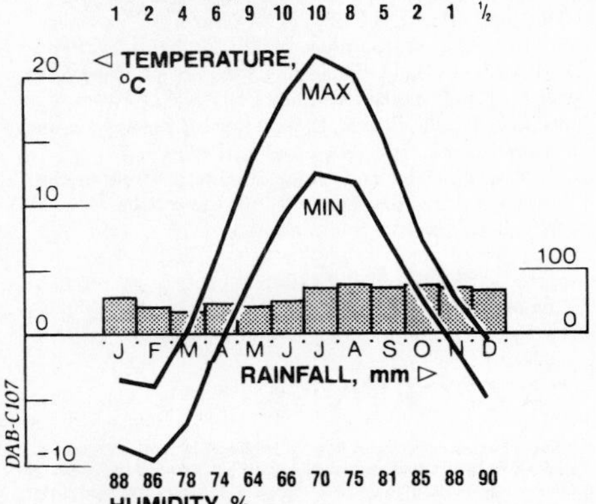

SODANKYLA Finland (178m)

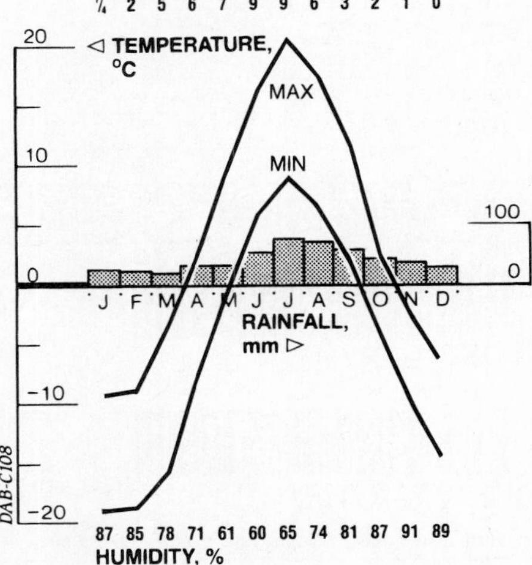

□ *international airport*

Location: Western Europe.

Note: For information on Overseas Departments, Overseas Territories and Overseas Collectivités Territoriales, please consult the section on *French Overseas Possessions* below (after the entry for French Guiana).

Maison de la France (Tourist Information Agency)
8 avenue de l'Opéra
75001 Paris, France
Tel: (1) 42 96 10 23. Fax: (1) 42 86 08 94. Telex: 214260.

Direction des Industries Touristiques
2 rue Linois
75740 Paris, Cedex 15
France
Tel: (1) 45 75 62 16. Fax: (1) 45 79 90 20. Telex: 870974.

Embassy of the French Republic
58 Knightsbridge
London SW1X 7JT
Tel: (071) 235 8080. Fax: (071) 259 6498. Telex: 261905 FRALON.

French Consulate General (Visa Section)
PO Box 57
6a Cromwell Place
London SW7 2JN
Tel: (0898) 200 289 (recorded information). Telex: 924153. Opening hours: 0900-1130 (and 1600-1630 for visa collection only) Monday to Friday (except French and British national holidays).

French Embassy (Cultural Section)
23 Cromwell Road
London SW7 2DQ
Tel: (071) 581 5292. Fax: (071) 823 8665. Opening hours: 0900-1300 Monday to Friday and 0930-1730 Wednesday.

French Embassy (Commercial Section)
21-24 Grosvenor Place
London SW1X 7HU
Tel: (071) 235 7080. Fax: (071) 235 8598. Telex: 263093 COMATL. Opening hours: 0830-1800 Monday to Friday.

French Government Tourist Office
178 Piccadilly
London W1V 0AL
Tel: (071) 499 6911 (recorded message). Fax: (071) 493 6594. Telex: 21902. Opening hours: 0900-1700 Monday to Friday.

Western Loire Tourist Board
375 Upper Richmond Road West
London SW14 7NX
Tel: (081) 392 1580. Fax: (081) 392 1318. Opening

hours: 0930-1800 Monday to Friday.

British Embassy
35 rue du Faubourg St Honoré
75383 Paris, Cedex 08
France
Tel: (1) 42 66 91 42. Fax: (1) 42 66 95 90. Telex: 650264.
Consulates in: Bordeaux, Lille, Calais, Boulogne-sur-Mer, Cherbourg, Dunkerque, Lyon, Marseille, Perpignan, Paris, Ajaccio (Corsica), Le Havre, Nantes, Nice, St Malo-Dinard, Toulouse, Cayenne (French Guiana), Martinique (Fort de France), Guadeloupe (Pointe à Pitre) and Réunion.

Embassy of the French Republic
4101 Reservoir Road, NW
Washington, DC
20007
Tel: (202) 944 6000. Fax: (202) 944 6072. *or* (202) 944 6200 (Consular Section).
Consulates in: Boston, Chicago, Detroit, Houston, Los Angeles, New Orleans, New York, San Francisco and Washington.

Embassy of the United States of America
2 avenue Gabriel
75008 Paris Cedex 08
France
Tel: (1) 42 61 80 75 *or* 42 96 12 02. Fax: (1) 42 66 97 83. Telex: 650221.
Consulates in: Bordeaux, Lyon, Marseille, Martinique and Strasbourg.

Embassy of the French Republic
42 Sussex Drive
Ottawa, Ontario
K1M 2C9
Tel: (613) 232 1795. Fax: (613) 232 4302. Telex: 0533564.
Consulates in: Chicoutimi, Edmonton, Halifax, Moncton, Montréal, North Sydney, Québec, Regina, St John's, Saskatoon, Sudbury, Toronto, Vancouver, Victoria, Whitehorse and Winnipeg.

French Government Tourist Office
Suite 490, 1981 McGill College
Montréal, Québec
H3A 2W9
Tel: (514) 288 4264. Fax: (514) 845 4868.

Canadian Embassy
35 avenue Montaigne
75008 Paris, France
Tel: (1) 47 23 01 01. Fax: (1) 47 23 56 28. Telex: 651806.
Consulates in: Lyon, St Pierre (St Pierre et Miquelon), Strasbourg and Toulouse.

AREA: 543,965 sq km (210,026 sq miles).
POPULATION: 56,614,493 (1990).
POPULATION DENSITY: 104.1 per sq km.
CAPITAL: Paris. **Population:** 2,152,423 (1990).
GEOGRAPHY: France, the largest country in Europe, is bounded to the north by the English Channel (*La Manche*), the northeast by Belgium and Luxembourg, the east by Germany, Switzerland and Italy, the south by the Mediterranean (with Monaco as a coastal enclave between Nice and the Italian frontier), the southwest by Spain and Andorra, and the west by the Atlantic Ocean. The island of Corsica, southeast of Nice, is made up of two *Départements*. The country offers a spectacular variety of scenery, from the mountain ranges of the Alps and Pyrénées to the attractive river valleys of the Loire, Rhône and Dordogne and the flatter countryside in Normandy and on the Atlantic coast. The country has some 2900km (1800 miles) of coastline.
LANGUAGE: French is the official language, but there are many regional dialects. Basque is spoken as a first language by some people in the southwest, and Breton by some in Brittany. Many people, particularly those connected with tourism in the major areas, will speak at least some English.
RELIGION: Approx 90% Roman Catholic with a Protestant minority. Almost every religion has at least some adherents.
TIME: GMT + 1 (GMT + 2 in summer).
ELECTRICITY: 220 volts AC, 50Hz. 2-pin plugs are widely used; adaptors recommended. Old hotels may still use 110 volts.
COMMUNICATIONS: Telephone: Full IDD is available. Country code: 33; (1) for Paris. The old *jeton* telephone boxes (where the discs are purchased over the counter at bars, railway stations, etc) have now been almost entirely phased out. Card-only telephones are becoming increasingly common, the pre-paid cards being purchased from post offices or *Tabacs*. International calls are cheaper from France between 2230-0800 Monday to Friday, and from 1400 Saturday to 0800 Monday. Calls can be received from all phone boxes showing the sign of a blue bell. **Fax:** Services are widely available; many hotels have facilities. **Telex:** There are public telex offices at 7 place de la Bourse and 7 rue Feydeau, 75002 Paris, which are open 24 hours a day, and telex facilities in the central post offices of most major towns, or in the offices of private companies, who will require an international telex credit card to charge the cost. The country code for telex is 42F. **Post:** Stamps can be purchased at post offices and *Tabacs*. Post normally takes a couple of days to reach its destination, within Europe. Post office opening hours: 0800-1900 Monday to Friday, 0800-1200 Saturday. **Press:** There are many daily newspapers, the most prominent being *Le Monde, Libération, France-Soir* and *Le Figaro*. Outside the Ile-de-France, however, these newspapers are not nearly as popular as the provincial press.
BBC World Service and Voice of America frequencies: From time to time these change. See the section *How to Use this Book* for more information.

BBC:				
MHz	12.09	9.410	6.195	0.648
Voice of America:				
MHz	11.97	9.670	6.040	5.995

PASSPORT/VISA

Regulations and requirements may be subject to change at short notice, and you are advised to contact the appropriate diplomatic or consular authority before finalising travel arrangements. Details of these may be found at the head of this country's entry. Any numbers in the chart refer to the footnotes below.

	Passport Required?	Visa Required?	Return Ticket Required?
Full British	1	No	*
BVP	Valid	-	*
Australian	Yes	Yes	*
Canadian	Yes	No	*
USA	Yes	No	*
Other EC	2	No	*
Japanese	Yes	No	*

PASSPORTS: Valid passport required by all except:
(a) **[1]** nationals of the UK provided they are in possession of a British Visitors Passport or a 60-hour British Excursion Document;
(b) **[2]** nationals of Belgium, Germany, Italy, Luxembourg, The Netherlands and Spain provided they are in possession of a passport expired for a maximum of 5 years or a valid national ID card;
(c) nationals of Andorra, Liechtenstein, Monaco and Switzerland, provided they are in possession of a passport expired for a maximum of 5 years or a valid National ID card.
Note [*]: It is advised that passengers hold return or onward tickets although this is not an absolute requirement.
British Visitors Passport: A British Visitors Passport can be used for holidays or unpaid business trips to France (including Corsica). For further information, see the *Passport/Visa* section of the introduction at the beginning of the book.
VISAS: Required by all except:
(a) nationals of countries shown in the chart above;
(b) nationals of Andorra, Austria, Cyprus, Czechoslovakia, Denmark, Finland, Hungary, Iceland, South Korea, Liechtenstein, Malta, Monaco, New Zealand, Norway, Poland, San Marino, Sweden, Switzerland and Vatican City provided the stay does not exceed 3 months;
(c) people of Czechoslovakian, Hungarian or Polish origin do not require a visa for a period of up to 3 months provided they hold a relevant travel document.
Note: British citizens who have retained their Commonwealth passports may require a visa. Check with the visa section of the Consulate for details.
Types of visa: Transit, cost £7.20; Short-stay single or Multiple entry, cost £24; stays for over 90 days, cost £72. Prices alter with the fluctuation of the exchange rate, so check for the exact price before travelling.
Note: Payment for visas may only be made using cash.
Validity: Transit visa valid for 1-5 days, excluding day of arrival; Short-stay visas valid for up to 3 months. For procedure regarding renewal, apply to French Consulate.
Application to: Consulate (or Consulate Section at Embassy). For addresses, see top of entry.
Application requirements: (a) Valid Passport. (b) Application form. (c) Photographs. (d) Return ticket to country of residence. (e) In certain cases travellers may require evidence of hotel reservations, business appointments, invitation from relatives, and means of support.
Note: Postal applications are *not* acceptable.
Working days required: For most nationals, 36 hours. However, nationals of Eastern European countries must allow 30 days, and nationals of Middle Eastern countries, or those with refugee travel documents, should allow 2 months.
Temporary residence: A Work Permit may often have to be obtained in France. For full details enquire at the French Consulate.

MONEY

Currency: French Franc (FFr) = 100 centimes. Notes are in denominations of FFr500, 200, 100, 50 and 10. Coins are in denominations of FFr100, 10, 5, 2 and 1, and 50, 20, 10, 5 and 1 centimes.
Currency exchange: Some first-class hotels are authorised to exchange foreign currency. Also look for the

FRANCE	**HEALTH REGULATIONS**	**VISA REGULATIONS** Code-Link
GALILEO/WORLDSPAN	 TI-DFT/PAR/HE	TI-DFT/PAR/VI
SABRE	 TIDFT/PAR/HE	 TIDFT/PAR/VI

To access this information on your CRS, swipe the barcode with a light pen or type in the text under the barcode. For more information, see the introduction *How to Use This Book*.

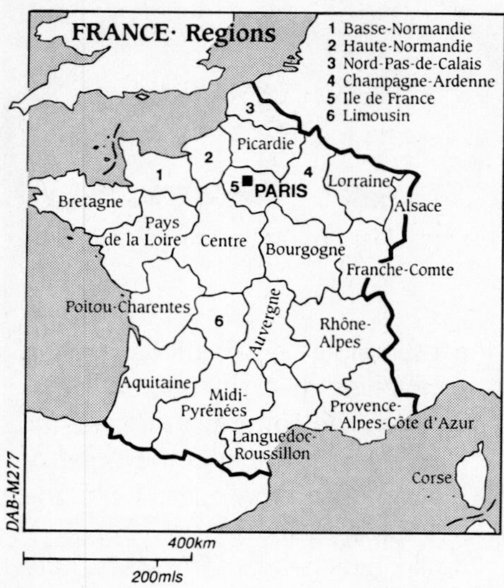

French equivalent of the Trustee Savings Bank, 'Crédit Mutuel' or 'Crédit Agricole', which have longer opening hours. Shops and hotels are prohibited from accepting foreign currency by law. Many UK banks offer differing exchange rates depending on the denominations of French currency being bought or sold. Travellers should check with their banks for details and current rates.

Credit cards: American Express, Diners Club and Visa are widely accepted. Check with your credit card company for details of merchant acceptability and other services which may be available.

Travellers cheques are accepted almost everywhere.

Exchange rate indicators: The following figures are included as a guide to the movements of the French Franc against Sterling and the US Dollar:

Date:	Oct '89	Oct '90	Oct '91	Oct '92
£1.00=	10.10	9.97	9.92	8.28
$1.00=	6.39	5.10	5.72	5.21

Currency restrictions: The import and export of of local and foreign currency is unrestricted. Amounts over FFr50,000 have to be declared.

Banking hours: 0900-1200 and 1400-1600 Monday to Friday. Some banks close on Monday. Banks close early (1200) on the day before a bank holiday; in rare cases, they may also close for all or part of the day after.

DUTY FREE

The following goods may be imported into France without incurring customs duty by:

(a) Passengers over 17 years of age entering from countries outside the EC:

200 cigarettes or 50 cigars or 100 cigarillos or 250g of tobacco;
1 litre of spirits of more than 22 degrees proof or 2 litres of alcoholic beverage up to 22 degrees proof;
2 litres of wine;
50g of perfume and 250ml of toilet water;
Other goods to the value of FFr300 (FFr150 per person under 15 years of age).

(b) Passengers over 17 years of age entering from an EC country:

300 cigarettes or 75 cigars or 150 cigarillos or 400g of tobacco;
1.5 litres of spirits of more than 22 degrees proof or 3 litres of spirits or sparkling wine up to 22 degrees proof;
5 litres of wine;
75g of perfume and 0.375 litres of toilet water;
Other goods to the value of FFr4200 (FFr1100 per person under 15 years of age).

(c) Passengers over 17 years of age entering from an EC country with duty-paid goods (as of January 1993):

800 cigarettes and 400 cigarillos and 200 cigars and 1kg of tobacco;
90 litres of wine (including up to 60 litres of sparkling wine);
10 litres of spirits;
20 litres of intermediate products (such as fortified wine);
110 litres of beer.

Prohibited items: Gold objects, other than personal jewellery below 500g in weight.

PUBLIC HOLIDAYS

Public holidays observed in France are as follows:

Apr 12 '93 Easter Monday. **May 1** Labour Day. **May 8** Liberation Day. **May 20** Ascension Day. **May 31** Whit Monday. **Jul 14** National Day, Fall of the Bastille. **Aug 15** Assumption. **Nov 1** All Saints' Day. **Nov 11** Remembrance Day. **Dec 25** Christmas Day. **Jan 1 '94** New Year's Day.

Note: In France the months of July and August are traditionally when the French take their holidays. For this reason the less touristic parts of France are quiet during these months, while coastal resorts are very crowded.

HEALTH

Regulations and requirements may be subject to change at short notice, and you are advised to contact your doctor well in advance of your intended date of departure. Any numbers in the chart refer to the footnotes below.

	Special Precautions?	Certificate Required?
Yellow Fever	No	No
Cholera	No	No
Typhoid & Polio	No	-
Malaria	No	-
Food & Drink	No	-

Rabies is present. For those at high risk, vaccination before arrival should be considered. If you are bitten abroad seek medical advice without delay. For more information consult the *Health* section at the back of the book.

Health care: There is a Reciprocal Health Agreement with the UK. On presentation of Form E111 at an office of the *Caisse Primaires D'Assurance Maladie* (Sickness Insurance Office), UK citizens are entitled to a refund of 70-80% of charges incurred for dental and medical (including hospital) treatments and prescribed medicines. The standard of medical facilities and practitioners in France is very high but so are the fees, and health insurance is recommended – even for UK citizens: a lot of paperwork is involved in obtaining refunds.

TRAVEL - International

AIR: The national airlines are: *Air France (AF)*, *Air Inter (IT)* and *UTA (UT)*.

Approximate flight times: From *London* to Paris is 1 hour 5 minutes; to Nice and Marseille is 2 hours.
From *Los Angeles* to Paris is 15 hours 5 minutes.
From *New York* to Paris is 8 hours (3 hours 45 minutes by Concorde).
From *Singapore* to Paris is 15 hours 5 minutes.
From *Sydney* to Paris is 25 hours 5 minutes.

International airports (for scheduled flights):

Paris-Charles de Gaulle (PAR/CDG) is 23km (14.5 miles) northeast of the city. There is a coach to the city every 15 minutes up to 2300. Buses and trains run to Paris Gare du Nord or Châtelet every 15-20 minutes up to 2350. There are taxis to the city. Duty-free facilities are available.

Paris-Orly (PAR/ORY) is 15km (9 miles) south of the city. Coaches run to the city every 20 minutes, buses every 15 minutes to Place Denfert Rochereau (travel time – 25 minutes) from outside Orly Ouest. Taxis are available. Hotel courtesy coaches run to Hilton Orly and PLM Orly. *RER/SNCF Orly-Rail* trains run every 15 minutes from 0530 to 2330 (travel time – 40 minutes).

Bordeaux (Merignac) *(BOD)* is 12km (7.3 miles) west of the city. There are coaches, buses and taxis to the city. Duty-free facilities are available.

Lille (Lesquin) *(LIL)* is 15km (9 miles) southeast of the city. Coaches are available to the city, as well as taxis. Duty-free facilities are also available.

Lyon (Lyon/Satolas) *(LYS)* is 30km (19 miles) east of the city. Coaches or taxis are available to the city. Duty-free facilities are also available.

Marseille (Marseille-Marignane) *(MRS)* is 25km (15.5 miles) northwest of the city. Coach service only departs to the city. Duty-free facilities are available.

Nice (Nice-Côte d'Azur) *(NCE)* is 7km (4 miles) west of the city. Coach to the city departs every 15-30 minutes until 2315. Bus No 9/10 every 20 minutes until 2000. Taxis to the city are available, as are duty-free facilities.

Toulouse (Blagnac) *(TLS)* is 7km (4 miles) northwest of the city. Coaches to the city depart every 45 minutes (24-hour service). Taxis are available to the city.

There are also small airports with some international flights at Biarritz, Caen, Deauville (St Gatien), Le Havre, Montpellier, Morlaix, Nantes, Rennes and Quimper.

SEA: The following companies run regular cross-channel ferries: *Brittany Ferries* from Plymouth to Roscoff and from Portsmouth to St Malo; *Commodore Shipping Services* from Jersey to St Malo; *Condor Hydrofoil* from Jersey, Guernsey, Sark and Alderney to St Malo; *Emeraude Ferries* from Jersey to St Malo; *Hoverspeed* from Dover to Boulogne and Calais, with train and coach to Paris; *Sally Line* from Ramsgate to Dunkirk; *Sealink* from Dover and Folkestone to Calais, Dover to Dunkirk, Folkestone to Boulogne and Newhaven to Dieppe; and *P&O* from Dover to Boulogne and Calais, and Portsmouth and Southampton to Calais, Cherbourg and Le Havre. These companies offer a variety of promotional fares and inclusive holidays for short breaks and shopping trips.

Passenger and roll-on/roll-off ferry links to and from North Africa and Sardinia are provided by the *Société Nationale Maritime Corse-Mediterranée (SNCM)* (see below in *Travel – Internal*).

RAIL: For cross-channel services see above.

International trains and through coaches run from the channel ports and Paris to destinations throughout Europe. For up-to-date routes and timetables contact *French Railways (SNCF)* or (in the UK) *British Rail International*. There is also a special bargain-price ticket combining air and rail travel. Flights depart from one of 16 airports in the UK and Ireland to Paris, and then on to a choice of 3000 destinations in France by train. Further information on these tickets can be obtained through *Air France* or *French Railways*.

ROAD: There are numerous and excellent road links with all neighbouring countries. See above for **car ferry** information. See below for information concerning **documentation** and **traffic regulations.**

The following companies run regular **coach** services to France from the UK: *Eurolines* and *National Express/Riviera Express*.

TRAVEL - Internal

AIR: *Air Inter* is the national domestic airline flying between Paris (from both Orly and Charles de Gaulle airports) and 45 cities and towns. It also connects regional airports including those in Corsica with those on the mainland. Details of all internal flights are available from *Air France*.

Note: *Air Inter's* 'Horaires et Tarifs' gives all flight information, as well as travel arrangements to and from all airports. Details of independent airlines may be obtained from the French Government Tourist Office.

SEA/RIVER: There are almost 9000km (5600 miles) of navigable waterways in metropolitan France, and all of these present excellent opportunities for holidays. Cruising boats may be chartered with or without crews, ranging in size from the smallest cabin cruiser up to converted commercial barges *(péniches)*, which can accommodate up to 24 people and require a crew of eight. Hotel boats, large converted barges with accommodation and restaurant, are also available in some areas, and a wide choice of price and comfort is available. For further information, contact the national or regional tourist board.

The main canal areas are the North (north and northeast of Paris) where most of the navigable rivers are connected with canals; the Seine (from Auxerre to Le Havre, but sharing space with commercial traffic); the East, where the Rhine and Moselle and their tributaries are connected by canals; in Burgundy, where the Sâone and many old and beautiful canals crisscross the region; the Rhône (a pilot is recommended below Avignon); the Midi (including the Canal du Midi, connecting the Atlantic with the Mediterranean); and Brittany and the Loire on the rivers Vilaine, Loire, Mayenne and Sarthe and the connecting canals. Each of these beautiful waterways offer a magnificent variety of scenery, a means of visiting many historic towns, villages and sites and, because of the slow pace (8kmph/5mph), an opportunity to learn much about rural France.

State-run car ferries known as *'BACs'* connect the larger islands on the Atlantic coast with the mainland; they also sail regularly across the mouth of the Gironde. The island of Corsica is served by passenger and roll-on/roll-off ferries operated by the *Société Nationale Maritime Corse-Mediterranée (SNCM)*, 61 boulevard des Dames, 13002 Marseille. Tel: 91 56 32 00. Telex: 440068. Services run from Marseille and Nice to Ajaccio, Propriano and Bastiá on the island.

RAIL: *French Railways (SNCF)* operate a nationwide network with 34,600km (21,500 miles) of line, over 12,000km (7500 miles) of which has been electrified. *TGV (Train à Grande Vitesse)* is the fastest train in the world, running on new high-speed lines from Paris to Brittany and southwest France at 300kmph (186mph) and to Lyon and the southeast at 270kmph (168mph). The *SNCF* is divided into five systems (East, North, West, Southeast and Southwest). The transport in and around Paris is the responsibility of a separate body, the *RATP* at 48 Quai Râpée, 75012 Paris. Tel: (1) 43 46 14 14 (general information). This provides a fully integrated bus, rail and métro network for the capital.

Tickets bought abroad: There is a range of special tickets on offer to foreign visitors, which usually have to be bought before entering France; some, such as the *France Rail'n'Drive Pass*, are only available in North America; others are unique to Australia and New Zealand. There are also special European *Rail and Drive* packages. The *France Railpass* gives the holder free travel on any four days within a period of fifteen days, or nine days within any one month; it is only sold outside France. Contact

LILLE GRAND PALAIS

EXPOSITIONS - CONGRES - SPECTACLES

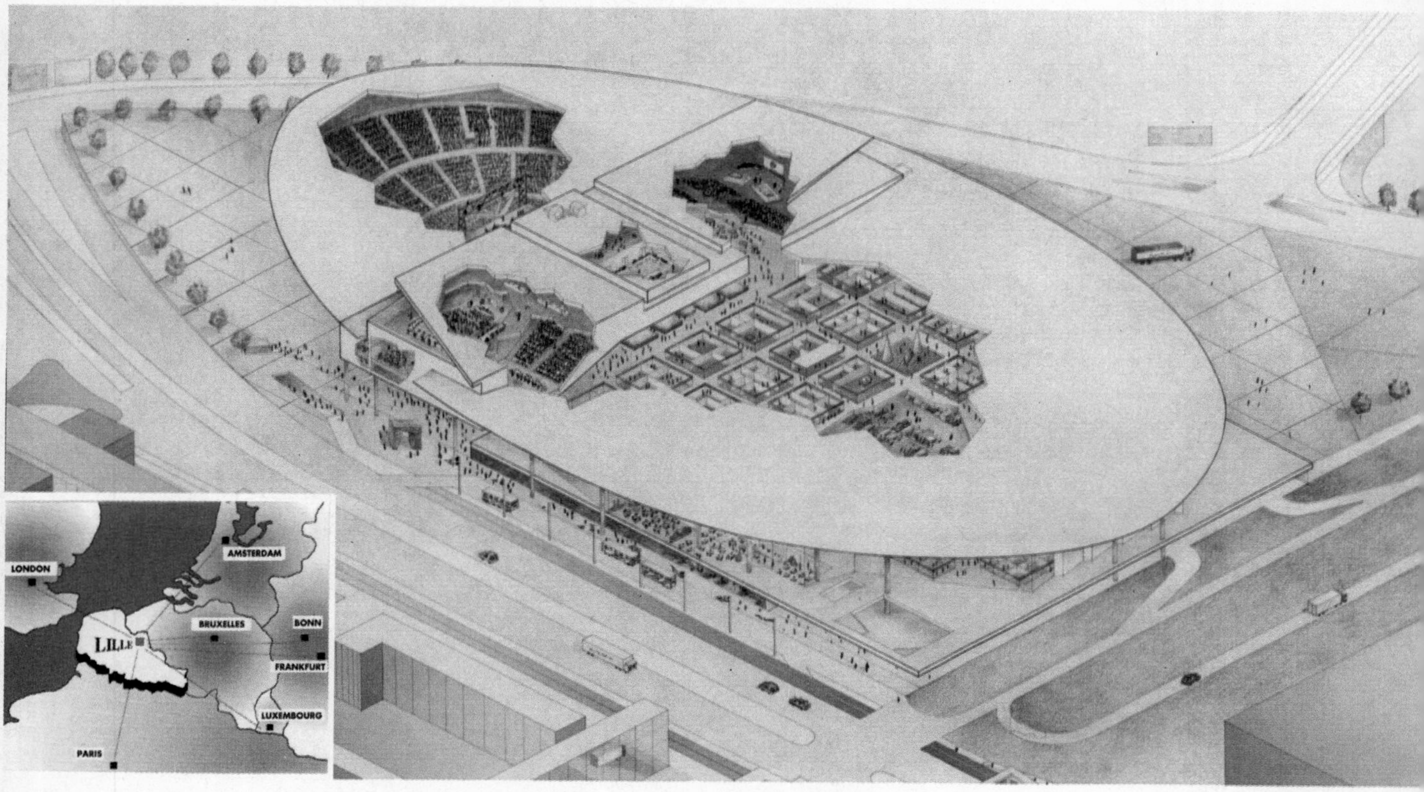

WELCOME TO LILLE
BIENVENUE A LILLE
WILLKOMMEN IN LILLE

As early as Spring 1994, LILLE GRAND PALAIS will be offering you a place for meetings, conferences, exhibitions, shows..., in short, a place for exchanges that is a true reflection of the European ambitions of the Lille metropolis and its region.

Made to measure for Europe, LILLE GRAND PALAIS will satisfy the most exacting demands.

Within easy reach of 3 european capitals, LILLE GRAND PALAIS will be the jewel awaited by the whole city of Lille, already adorned with its Flemish architecture, its many museums and art galleries, its rich pedestrian precincts with lively street cafes, its reputable restaurants and its numerous quality hotels.

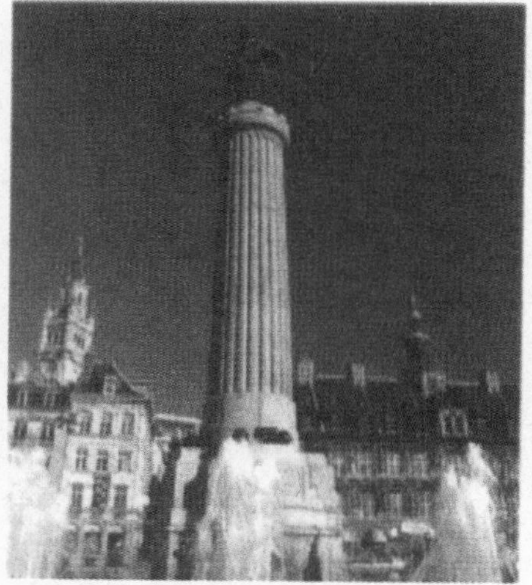

Photo D. RAPAICH

Working with you, to help you efficiently, an accomplished team of professionals will delight in sharing with you their passion for excellence and their taste for challenge.

Contact :
Mr Patrick MARNOT
LILLE GRAND PALAIS
48 rue des Canonniers
59800 Lille
France
tel: 33 20 74 04 00
fax: 33 20 74 85 57

SNCF for details. Holders of the ticket are also entitled to reduced car hire rates at over 200 railway stations, a reduced entrance fee to a large number of historic buildings, a free return ticket from the Paris airports to the city centre, travel concessions on the Paris métro and buses, and reduced prices for many other services and facilities. In addition, holders of this ticket do not need to pay supplements applied to Trans Europe-Expresses (TEEs) and some TGVs. It does not, however, include seat reservation charges (compulsory on TEE and TGV trains) and supplements for sleeping accommodation.

Tickets bought in France: It is important to validate (*composter*) tickets bought in France by using the orange automatic date-stamping machine at the platform entrance.

Note: There are various different kinds of tickets (including Family and Young Person's Tickets) offering reductions which can usually be bought in France. In general, the fares charged will depend on what day of the week and what time of the day one is travelling; timetables giving further details are available from *SNCF* offices.

The Blue, White and Red Tariff Calendar: The *French Railways'* tariff calendar is colour-coded; the colour of a particular period can affect the price of your ticket. The system of special fares, reductions, restrictions and so on is complex, as one would expect from such a highly sophisticated railway network. Enquire at *SNCF* offices for more details. The following breakdown of the tariff is included as a guide:

Blue (Off-peak): Normally 1200 Monday to 1200 Friday, and 1200 Saturday to 1500 Sunday.

White (Standard): Normally 1200 Friday to 1200 Saturday and 1500 Sunday to 1200 Monday, plus some public holidays.

Red (Peak): About 20 days in the year when no reduction is available. Apply to *French Railways* in London or any *SNCF* station for details.

Motorail (car sleeper) services are operated from Boulogne, Calais, Dieppe and Paris to all main holiday areas in both summer and winter. Motorail information and booking from *French Railways* (address above).

Ancillary services include coach tours and excursions throughout France, self-drive car hire and bicycle hire.

Skiing holidays: *SNCF*, in association with The French Association of Resorts Sportsgoods Retailers (AFMASS), organise skiing holidays. Packages marketed only in France, contact *SNCF* on arrival.

For all services: Full information is available from *French Railways (SNCF)*. In the UK, timetables, fares, information and bookings can also be obtained through principal British Rail Travel Centres. There is an English-language telephone information service in Paris. Tel: (1) 05 02 50 50.

ROAD: France has over 6000km (3728 miles) of motorways (*autoroutes*), some of which are free whilst others are toll roads (*autoroutes à péage*). Prices vary depending on the route, and caravans are extra. There are more than 28,000km of national roads (*routes nationales*). Motorways bear the prefix 'A' and national roads 'N'. Minor roads (marked in yellow on the Michelin roadmaps) are maintained by the *Départements* rather than by the Government and are classed as 'D' roads. It is a good idea to avoid travelling any distance by road on the last few days of July/first few days of August and the last few days of August/first few days of September, as during this time the bulk of the holiday travel takes place, and the roads can be jammed for miles. A sign bearing the words *Sans Plomb* at a petrol service station indicates that it sells unleaded petrol. The *Bison Futé* map provides practical information and is available from the French Government Tourist Office.

Bus: There are very few long-distance bus services in France apart from *Europabus*, about which information may be obtained from national British Rail Travel Centres. Local services outside the towns and cities are generally adequate. Information and timetables are only available locally.

Car hire: A list of agencies can be obtained at local tourist offices (Syndicats d'Initiative or Offices de Tourisme). Fly-drive arrangements are available through all major airlines. *French Railways* also offer reduced train/car-hire rates. Their 'France Vacances' pass offers free car hire to first-class passengers.

Caravans may be imported for stays of up to six months. There are special requirements for cars towing caravans which must be observed. Contact the French Government Tourist Office for details.

Regulations: The minimum age for driving is 18. It is forbidden to exceed 90kmph (56mph) within one year of passing a driving test. Speed limits are 60kmph (37mph) in built-up areas, 90kmph (56mph), outside built-up areas, 110kmph (68mph) on dual carriageways separated by a central reservation, and 130kmph (81mph) on motorways. Visitors who have held a driving licence for under one year may *not* travel faster than 90kmph (56mph) or any lower speed limit. Seat belts must be worn by all front seat passengers. Under-tens may not travel in the front seat. A red warning triangle must be carried for use in the event of a breakdown. All headlamp beams must be adjusted for right-hand drive and UK drivers are advised to apply a yellow covering to their headlamps (available from any AA or motoring shop). Snowchains are widely available, for hire or to buy. The police in France can and do fine motorists on the spot for driving offences such as speeding. Random breath tests for drinking and driving are used.

Priorité à droite: Particularly in built-up areas, the driver *must* give way to anyone coming out of a side-turning on the right. The *priorité* rule no longer applies at many roundabouts – the driver should now give way to cars which are already on the roundabout with the sign *vous n'avez pas la priorité*. Watch for signs and exercise great caution. All roads of any significance outside built-up areas have right of way, known as *Passage Protégé*, and will normally be marked by signs consisting either of an 'X' on a triangular background with the words 'Passage Protégé' underneath, or a broad arrow, or a yellow diamond. For further details on driving in France, a booklet called *Welcome on the French Motorways* is available free from French Government Tourist Offices.

Documentation: A national driving licence is acceptable. EC nationals taking their own cars to France are *strongly advised* to obtain a Green Card. Without it, insurance cover is limited to the minimum legal cover in France; the Green Card tops this up to the level of cover provided by the car owner's domestic policy. The car's registration documents must also be carried.

URBAN: Urban public transport is excellent. There are comprehensive bus systems in all the larger towns. There are also tramways, trolleybuses and a métro in Marseille; trolleybuses, a métro and a funicular in Lyon; and the world's first automated driverless train in Lille (where there is also a tramway). There are tramway services in St Etienne and Nantes and trolleybuses in Grenoble, Limoges and Nancy. The systems are easy to use, with pre-purchase tickets and passes. Good publicity material and maps are usually available.

Paris has the best urban transport network in the world.
Métro: The dense network in the central area makes the métro the ideal way to get about in Paris. When chang-

ing trains, look for the *Correspondances* sign on the platform. As each line is identified by the names of its termini, one should know the final destination of the train one wishes to catch and then follow the appropriate signs; *Direction – Créteil*, for example, would be the sign to follow for stations between *Balard* and *Créteil* when travelling from west to east. Each line also has a number, which is seldom used to identify it. There are maps on station platforms, and inside the trains. Buy a carnet of ten tickets rather than buying each singly. However long the journey and however many changes, one flat-fare ticket will suffice each time, except on the suburban portion of certain lines. First trains leave at about 0500, last trains at about 0030. A *Paris Visite* allows unlimited travel on most forms of public transport in Paris for a period of three to five consecutive days.

Rail: *RER* (fast suburban services). *Line A:* St Germain-en-Laye to Boissy-St Leger or Marne-la-Vallée; *Line B:* Remy-les-Chevreuse to Roissy via Chatelet-les-Halles and the Gare du Nord; *Line C:* Gare d'Orleans-Austerlitz to Versailles. These lines are divided into fare stages and fares vary according to distance, except within the metropolitan area where the same system applies as on the métro. There is also an extensive network of conventional suburban services run by the state *SNCF* rail system, with fare structure and ticketing integrated with the other modes of public transport.

Bus: The same tickets are used as on the métro, but bus routes are divided into fare stages *(sections)*. Inside Paris, one ticket covers up to two fare stages and two cover two or three stages or more. The first bus leaves at 0600 and the last bus at 2100, except on certain lines which run until 0030. Timetables are posted up at bus stops and in bus shelters. Fares and tickets have been standardised with those of private operators in the suburban areas. 2- to 4- or 7-day passes *(Billets de Tourisme)* entitle you to any number of journeys for the corresponding number of days on all Paris bus and métro lines (first-class on métro and *RER/RATP*), with the exception of minibuses, special bus services, and *RER/SNCF* lines. Available in Paris from RATP Tourist Offices at 53 quai des Grands-Augustins (tel: (1) 40 46 41 41), and place de la Madeleine (VIA International, tel: (1) 42 05 12 10) or from 50 of the métro stations, all seven main-line railway stations and certain banks. *Carte Orange* monthly passes (for which a passport-size photograph is required) is valid for any number of journeys for a calendar month within a given radius on Paris buses, métro and *RER*, suburban *(SNCF)* railways and some suburban buses *(RATP)*. These are available at any Paris or suburban railway or métro station, Paris bus stations and certain specially licensed shops. Children under four years of age travel free on buses and underground, while children between four and 12 travel half-price.

Taxi: Day and night rates are shown inside each cab. There are extra charges on journeys to and from race-courses, stations and airports and for luggage.

Private car: In the centre of Paris there are parking meters; otherwise parking time is restricted *(zone bleue)*. Car parks charging a fee are plentiful all over Paris and on the outskirts.

ACCOMMODATION

HOTELS: Room and all meals, ie full-board or 'pension' terms, are usually offered for a stay of three days or longer. Half board or 'demi-pension' (room, breakfast and one meal) terms are usually available outside the peak holiday period. They are not expensive but adhere to strict standards of comfort. Hotels charge around 30% extra for a third bed in a double room. For children under 12, many chains will provide another bed in the room of the parents free. *Logis de France* are small or medium-sized, inexpensive and often family-run hotels which provide good, clean, basic and comfortable accommodation with a restaurant attached. They publish a guide listing all the hotels and the amenities offered. *Relais-Châteaux* are châteaux hotels. Further information can be obtained from the Fédération Nationale de l'Industrie Hôtelière, 22 rue d'Anjou, 75008 Paris. Tel: (1) 42 65 04 61. Fax: (1) 47 42 15 20.

Paris: Hotel bookings can be made in person through tourist offices at stations or at the Central Information Bureau, 127 avenue des Champs-Elysées, 75008 Paris. Tel: (1) 47 23 61 72. Further information on hotels and other accommodation in France is available through the Fédération Nationale des Logis de France, 83 avenue d'Italie, 75013 Paris. Tel: (1) 45 84 83 84. Fax: (1) 44 24 08 74. Telex: 203030. **Guides:** The *Michelin Guides* to France are extremely useful, with up-to-date prices, opening dates and town plans. *Hotels de Tourism* publish an annual directory of its members available from the French Government Tourist Office. An official guide to all French graded hotels is available, as well as regional lists, the *Logis de France* guide and various chain/association guides from the French Government Tourist Office and bookshops. The Tourist Office publishes guides to hotels in Paris and the Ile-de-France, available free of charge.

Grading: *Hotels de Tourisme* are officially graded into five categories according to the quality of the accommodation, as are also the *Motels de Tourisme*. Gradings, which are fixed by government regulation and checked by the Préfecture of the Départements, are as follows:
4-star L: Luxury. **4-star:** Deluxe. **3-star:** First class. **2-star:** Standard. **1-star:** Budget.
Logis de France are subject to a specific code usually above basic requirements for their grade and are inspected regularly to ensure that they conform to the standards laid down.

SELF-CATERING: *Gîtes de France* are holiday homes (often old farmhouses) in the country, all of which conform to standards regulated by the non-profitmaking National Federation. Over 1500 *gîtes* have been reserved for the British section of the *Gîtes de France*. Annual membership gives access to full booking service including ferry crossings at reduced rates, overnight hotel bookings and fully illustrated handbook. The London booking service will confirm any booking within two weeks. Full information in the UK from *Gîtes de France* (Farm Holidays in France Ltd), 178-180 Piccadilly, London W1V 9BD. Tel: (071) 493 3480.
Villas, Houses and Apartments Rental: Villas and houses can be rented on the spot. Local *Syndicats d'Initiative* can supply a complete list or addresses of local rental agencies. Tourists staying in France for over a month may prefer to live in an apartment, rather than in a hotel. For information about apartments to rent apply to: Fédération Nationale des Agents Immobiliers (FNAIM) in Paris. Tel: (1) 42 93 61 24.

CHATEAUX HOLIDAYS: An association, *Château-Accueil*, publishes a list of châteaux offering accommodation suitable for families. Contact the Tourist Office for further information.

CAMPING/CARAVANNING: There are 7000 campsites throughout France. A few have tents and caravans for hire. Prices vary according to location, season and facilities. All graded campsites will provide water, toilet and washing facilities. Touring caravans may be imported for stays of up to six consecutive months. There are 100 British companies offering camping holidays in France. The French Government Tourist Office has a full list of tour operators who run all types of tours, including camping and special interest holidays.

The following camping and caravan site is open throughout the year in Paris: Paris-Ouest Bois de Boulogne, route du Bord de l'Eau, 75016 Paris. Tel: (1) 45 87 70 00.

Note: Cars towing caravans are not allowed to drive within the boundaries of the *Périphérique* (the Paris ring road).

YOUTH HOSTELS: There are hundreds of these in France, offering young people very simple accommodation at very low prices. There are hostels in all major towns. Stays are usually limited to three or four nights or a week in Paris. Hostels are open to all members of the National Youth Hostel Association upon presentation of a membership card. Lists are available from national youth hostelling organisations.

RESORTS & EXCURSIONS

Tourism is an industry of considerable importance in France and anything more than the briefest sketch of her many attractions is beyond the scope of this book. This section has been divided into a number of sub-sections by region, each containing basic descriptions of regional cuisine, culture, history and scenery: Paris & Ile-de-France; Brittany; Normandy; Nord, Pas de Calais & Picardy; Champagne & Ardennes; Lorraine, Vosges & Alsace; Burgundy & Franche-Comté; Auvergne & Limousin; Val de Loire; Western Loire; Aquitaine & Poitou-Charentes; Languedoc-Roussillon; Rhône/Savoie & Dauphiny; Midi-Pyrénées; Côte d'Azur & Provence; Corsica.

Note: The enclave of Monaco has its own entry in the *World Travel Guide*, as do the French Overseas Departments and many of the other French overseas possessions; see the contents pages for details.

Paris & Ile-de-France

Paris is one of the world's great cities and is easy to negotiate even on the first visit. The *périphérique* and *boulevard circulaire* ring roads enclose a core of 105 sq km (40 sq miles) which is small enough to walk across in an afternoon. There is an extensive (and cheap) métro network, now augmented by an efficient rapid transit system (the *RER*). The ring roads roughly follow the line of the 19th-century city walls and within them are most of the well-known sights, shops and entertainments. There are more than 80 museums and perhaps 200 art galleries in Paris. Beyond the ring roads is an industrial and commercial belt, then a broad ring of suburbs, mostly of recent construction.

Central Paris contains fine architecture from every episode in a long and rich history (including the present) together with every amenity known to science and every entertainment yet devised. The oldest neighbourhood is the **Ile-de-la-Cité**, an island on a bend in the Seine where the *Parisii*, a Celtic tribe, settled in about the 3rd century BC. The river was an effective defensive moat

and the *Parisii* dominated the area for several centuries before being displaced by the Romans in about 52BC. The island is today dominated by the magnificent cathedral of *Notre-Dame*. Beneath it is the *Crypte Archéologique*, housing well-mounted displays of Paris' early history. Having sacked the Celtic city, the Gallo-Romans abandoned the island and settled on the heights along the **Rive Gauche** (Left Bank), in the area now known as the *Latin Quarter* (Boulevards St Michel and St Germain). The naming of this district owes nothing to the Roman city: when the university was moved from the *Cité* to the left bank in the 13th century, Latin was the common language among the 10,000 students who gathered there from all over the known world. The *Latin Quarter* remains the focus of most student activity (the *Sorbonne* is here) and there are many fine book shops and commercial art galleries. The *Cluny Museum* houses some of the finest medieval European tapestries to be found anywhere, including 'The Field of the Cloth of Gold'. At the western end of the Boulevard St Germain is the *Orsay Museum*, a superb collection of 19th- and early 20th-century art located in a beautifully reconstructed railroad station.

Other Left Bank attractions include the *Panthéon*, the basilica of *St Séverin*, the *Palais* and *Jardin de Luxembourg*, the *Hôtel des Invalides* (containing Napoleon's tomb), the *Musée Rodin* and *St Germain-des-Prés*. Continuing westwards from the Quai d'Orsay past the *Eiffel Tower* and across the Seine onto the Right Bank, the visitor encounters a collection of museums and galleries known as the *Trocadero*, a popular meeting place for young Parisians. A short walk to the north is the *Place Charles de Gaulle*, known to Parisians as the *Etoile* and to tourists as the site of the *Arc de Triomphe*. It is also at the western end of that most elegant of avenues, the **Champs-Elysées** (Elysian Fields), justly famous for its cafés, commercial art galleries and sumptuous shops. At the other end of the avenue, the powerful axis is continued by the *Place de la Concorde*, the *Jardin des Tuileries* (where model sailing boats may be rented by the hour) and finally the Louvre.

The *Palais du Louvre* is currently being rebuilt and reorganised, but much of the fabulous collection remains open to the public. The most controversial addition to the old palace, a pyramid with 666 panes of glass, was almost as famous as the gallery itself long before completion. Everybody in Paris has an opinion about it; the consensus seems to be that the number of panes, matching the Biblical Number of the Beast, is somehow appropriate. North of the Louvre are the *Palais Royal*, the *Madeleine* and *l'Opéra*. To the east is *Les Halles*, a shopping and commercial complex built on the site of the old meat market. It is at the intersection of several Métro lines and is a good starting point for a tour of the city. There are scores of restaurants in the maze of small streets around Les Halles; every culinary style is practised at prices to suit every pocket. Further east, beyond the Boulevard Sebastopol, is another controversial newcomer, the Post-Modern *Georges Pompidou Centre of Modern Art* (also known as the *Beaubourg*). It provides a steady stream of surprises in its temporary exhibition spaces (which, informally, include the pavement outside, where lively and often bizarre street performers gather) and houses a permanent collection of 20th-century art. The *Centre Pompidou* is Paris' premier tourist attraction, having surpassed the Eiffel Tower in popularity in its first year. East again, in the Marais district, are the *Carnavalet* and *Picasso Museums*, housed in magnificent town houses dating from the 16th and 18th centuries respectively.

One of the best-known districts in Paris is **Montmartre**, which stands on a hill overlooking the Right Bank. A funicular railway operates on the steepest part of the hill, below *Sacré-Coeur*. Local entrepreneurs have long capitalised on Montmartre's romantic reputation as an artist's colony and if visitors today are disappointed to find it a well-run tourist attraction, they should bear in mind that it has been exactly that since it first climbed out of poverty in the 1890s. The legend of Montmartre as a dissolute cradle of talent was carefully stage-managed by Toulouse-Lautrec and others to fill their pockets and it rapidly transformed a notorious slum into an equally notorious circus. An earlier Montmartre legend concerns St Denis. After his martyrdom, he is said to have walked headless down the hill. The world's first gothic cathedral, *St Denis*, was constructed on the spot where he collapsed. Just north of **Belleville** (a working class district that produced Edith Piaf and Maurice Chevalier) at *La Villete*, is one of Paris' newer attractions, the *City of Science and Technology*. The most modern presentation techniques are used to illustrate both the history and the possible future of man's inventiveness; season tickets are available. One of the great pleasures of Paris is the great number of sidewalk cafés, now glass-enclosed in wintertime, which extends people-watching to a year-round sport in any part of the town. There are as many Vietnamese and Chinese restaurants as there are French cafés. North African eating places also abound, and dozens of American Tex-Mex eateries are scattered throughout the city. Bric-a-brac or *brocante* is found in a number of flea markets (*marché aux puces*) on the outskirts of town, notably at the Porte de Clignancourt. There are several antique centres (*Louvre des Antiquaires*, *Village Suisse* etc) where genuine antique furniture and other objects are on sale. Amongst the larger department stores are the Printemps and the Galeries Lafayette near the Opéra, the Bazaar Hôtel de Ville and the Samaritaine on the Right Bank and the Bon Marché on the Left Bank. The remains of the great forests of the **Ile-de-France** (the area surrounding Paris) can still be seen at the magnificent châteaux of *Versailles*, *Rambouillet* and *Fontainebleau* on the outskirts of Paris.

La Carte is a pass providing free admission to about 60 national and municipal museums in the Paris area. Visitors should note that most museums are closed for public holidays and for one day in the working week, usually Monday or Tuesday. Admission is half price on Sundays; concessions are available for those under 25 and persons over 65 years. The tourist office can supply details.

Brittany

Brittany comprises the *départements* of Côtes-du-Nord, Finistère, Ille-et-Villaine and Morbihan. Fishing has long been the most important industry and the rocky Atlantic coastline, high tides and strong, treacherous currents demand high standards of seamanship. At Finistère (*finis terrea* or Land's End) the Atlantic swell can drive spouts of water up to 30m (100ft) into the air. The coastal scenery is particularly spectacular at *Pointe du Raz* and *Perros-Guirec*. The Gaulois arrived on the peninsular in about 600BC. Little is known about their way of life or why they constructed the countless stone monuments to be found throughout Brittany – cromlechs, altars, menhirs and dolmans (**Carnac** is the supreme example of this). They were displaced by the Romans during the reign of Julius Caesar, who, in turn, were displaced by Celts arriving from Britain in AD460. The Celts named their new land Brittanica Minor and divided it into the coastal area, *l'Ar Mor* (the country of the sea), and the inland highlands, *l'Ar Coat* (the country of the woods). The two areas in Brittany are still referred to as **l'Amor** and **l'Argoat.** The Celts were master stonemasons, as may be seen by the many surviving *calvaires*, elaborately carved stone crosses. Brittany emerged from the Dark Ages as an independent duchy. A series of royal marriages eventually brought Brittany into France and by 1532 the perpetual union of the Duchy of Brittany with France was proclaimed. Despite its rugged coastline, it is possible to enjoy a conventional beach holiday in Brittany. The Emerald Coast, a region of northern Brittany centred on **Dinard**, has many fine bathing beaches. The beach resorts are often named after little-known saints: *St Enogat, St Laumore, St Brill, St Jacut, St Cast*, etc. There are also bathing beaches in the bay of St Brieuc, including **Val André, Etables** and **St Quay**. Brittany's main attractions are her wild beauty and the unique Breton culture. In general, coastal areas have retained a more characteristically Breton way of life than the hills inland. Elaborate Breton headresses are still worn in some parts, the style varying slightly from village to village. Breton religious processions and the ceremonies of the *pardons* that take place in a number of communities at various times of the year may have changed little since Celtic times. In the region around **Plouha** many of the inhabitants still speak Breton, a language evolved from Celtic dialects. The coast from **Paimpol** consists of colossal chunks of rock, perilous to shipping, as the many lighthouses suggest. The very pleasant villages and beaches of **Perros-Guirec, Trégastel** or **Trébeurden** contrast with the wild and rocky shoreline.

Near the base of the peninsula, at Aber Vrac'h and Aber Benoit, the ocean is caught and churned up in deep, winding chasms penetrating far inland. Further along the coast is the huge and sprawling port of Brest, possessing one of Europe's finest natural harbours which has a 13th-century castle. The canal running from Brest to Nantes makes a very pleasant journey either by hired boat or walking or on horseback, although not all of the route is navigable by water. The interior consists of wooded hills and farms, buttes with fine views, short rivers and narrow valleys. Many of the so-called mountains are merely undulating verdant dunes, barely 300m (1000ft) high. They are, nonetheless, remnants of the oldest mountain chain on the planet. Breton architecture is perhaps more humble than in other parts of France, being more akin to that of a village in England or Wales. Inland, there are several impressive castles and many walled towns and villages. The churches are small and simple. For the most part, Brittany benefits from the warmth of the Gulf Stream all year round, but the tourist season runs from June to September. The countryside blazes with flowers in the spring, attracting many varieties of birdlife. The city of Rennes, the ancient capital of Brittany, is a good base from which to explore the highlands; sights include the Palais de Justice, the castle, the Musée des Beaux-Arts and the Musée de Bretagne, which seeks to preserve and foster all things Breton. Some of Brittany's most productive farms are close to the northern shore. Fertilized with seaweed, they produce fine potatoes, cabbage, cauliflower, artichokes, peas, string beans and strawberries. The quality of locally produced ingredients lends itself to the simple Breton cuisine, which brings out natural flavours rather than concealing them with elaborate sauces. Raw shellfish (including oysters), lobster, lamb and partridge are particularly good. The salt meadows of lower Brittany add a distinctive flavour to Breton livestock and game. Crêpes (pancakes) are a regional speciality and there are two distinct varieties: a sweet dessert crêpe served with sugar, honey, jam, jelly or a combination (eg suzette); and the savoury sarrasin variety, made from buckwheat flour and served with eggs, cheese, bacon or a combination of several of these (the crêpe is folded over the ingredients and reheated). They can be bought ready-made in the local shops. Little or no cheese is produced in Brittany, but some of the finest butter in the world comes from here – it is slightly salted, unlike the butter from the other regions of France. Cider is frequently drunk with food, as well as wine. The popular wine, Muscadet, comes from the extreme southern point of Brittany, at the head of the Loire Estuary, near Nantes. It is a dry, fruity white wine that goes very well with shellfish, especially oysters.

Normandy

Normandy contains five *départements*: Seine Maritime, Calvados, Manche, Eure and Orne, all but the last two touching on the sea. Its southern border is the *River Couesnon* which has, over the years, shifted its course as it flows over almost flat country, gradually moving south of **Mont-Saint-Michel,** one of Europe's best-known architectural curiosities. Mont-Saint-Michel and its bay are on the Natural and Cultural World Heritage List drawn up by UNESCO. The tides are phenomenal. At their peak, there is a difference of about 15m (50ft) between the ebb and the flow, the height of a 5-storey building. The sands in the bay are flat and, when the tides are at their highest, the sea runs in over a distance of some 24km (15 miles) forming a wave about 70cm (2ft) deep. The sandbank changes from tide to tide and if the legend of the sea entering the bay at the speed of a galloping horse is perhaps a slight exaggeration, the danger of quicksand is real enough. The present *Abbey of Saint-Michel* was built in the 8th century by Bishop Aubert; his skull bears the mark of the finger of Saint Michel, the archangel Michael. **Cabourg** is the Balbec in Proust's novels. De Maupassant and Flaubert included Norman scenes in their novels and Monet, Sisley and Pissaro painted scenes of the coast and the countryside. **Deauville** – beach, casino, golf course and race track – is the social capital of the area. **Bayeux** is worth a visit for the fantastic tapestry – there is nothing like it in the world. The landing beaches and Second World War battlefields are remembered by excellent small museums in **Arromanches** (the landings), and **Bayeux** (battle of Normandy). There is also a 'peace museum' in **Caen**, with its beautiful Romanesque church and ruins of an enormous castle, founded by William the Conqueror. Other monuments worth visiting include the 14th-century *Church of St Etienne*, the *Church of St Pierre* (Renaissance) and the *Abbaye aux Dames*. There is also a museum of local crafts from the Gallo-Roman period to the present.

The cross-Channel terminus and port of **Dieppe** has attractive winding streets and a 15th-century castle, housing the *Musée de Dieppe*. There are some beautiful châteaux in Normandy, particularly along the route between Paris and Rouen. They include the *Boury-en-Vexin, Bizy at Vernon, Gaillon, Gaillard-les-Andelys, Vascoeuil* and *Martinville*. Along the same route are found a number of other sites classed *monument historique*; the *Claude Monet House* and garden in **Giverny**, the *Abbey de Martemer* (Lisors) and the village of **Lyon-la-Fôret**. All of these are worth a detour. The ancient capital of **Rouen** has restored ancient streets and houses, including the *Vieille Maison* of 1466 and the *place du Vieux-Marché*, where Jeanne d'Arc was burnt in 1432. There is a magnificent 13th-century cathedral, (the subject of a series of paintings by Monet) as well as many fine museums and churches, including *St Ouen* and *St Maclou*. The cloister of *St Maclou* was a cemetery for victims of the Great Plague. Normandy is a land of farmers and fishermen and is one of the finest gastronomic regions of France. Here is produced the finest butter in the world, a thick fresh cream and excellent cheeses, including the world-famous *Camembert, Pont l'Evêque* and *Liverot*. Both crustaceans and saltwater fish abound; *sole Normande* is one of the great dishes known to the gastronomic world. There is also lobster from Barfleur, shrimp from Cherbourg and oysters from Dive-sur-Mur. Inland one finds ducks from Rouen and Nantes, lamb from the salt meadows near Mont-Saint-Michel, cream from Isigny, chicken and veal from the Cotentin, and cider and calvados (applejack) from the Pays d'Auge.

Nord, Pas de Calais & Picardy

Northern France is made up of the *départements* of Nord/Pas de Calais (French Flanders) and Somme-Oise Aisne (Picardy).

Amiens, the principal town of Picardy, has a beautiful 13th-century cathedral, which is one of the largest in France. The choirstalls are unique. **Beauvais** is famous for its Gothic *Cathedral of St Pierre* (incorporating a 9th-century Carolingian church) which would have been the biggest Gothic church in the world, if it had been completed. Its 13th-century stained glass windows are particularly impressive. There is also a fine musuem of tapestry.

Compiègne is famous for its *Royal Palace*, which has been a retreat for the French aristocracy from the 14th century onwards and where Napoleon himself lived with his second wife, Marie-Louise. There are over a thousand rooms within the palace and the bedrooms of Napoleon and his wife, preserved with their original decorations, are well worth viewing for their ostentatiously lavish style. Surrounding the town and palace is the *Forest of Compiègne*, where the 1918 Armistice was signed, and which has been a hunting ground for the aristocracy for hundreds of years – a wander through its dark and tranquil interior is an exceptionally pleasant experience. The town also has a fine *Hôtel de Ville* and a *Carriage Museum* is attached to the Palace.

The château of **Chantilly** now houses the *Musée Condé* and there are impressive Baroque gardens to walk around, as well as a 17th-century stable with a 'live' *Horse Museum*. The town of **Arras**, on the *River Scarpe*, has beautiful 13th- and 14th-century houses and the lovely *Abbey of Saint Waast*. There are pretty old towns at **Hesdin** and **Montreuil** (with its ramparts and citadel). **Boulogne** is best entered by way of the lower town with the 13th-century ramparts of the upper town in the background; the castle next to the basilica of *Notre Dame* is impressive.

Le Touquet is a pleasant all-year-round coastal resort town with 10km (6 miles) of sandy beaches. The port of **Calais**, of great strategic importance in the Middle Ages, is today noted for the manufacture of tulle and lace, as well as being a cross-Channel ferry terminus. Nearby, the village of **Sangatte** is rapidly becoming a significant site. It is here that the French end of the Channel tunnel is being excavated. The diggings are well underway, just as they are across the Channel at Shakespeare Cliffs in Kent. When the tunnel is completed in 1993, high-speed trains will connect this entrance with Paris, Lille and Brussels. For the first time in history, travellers between the continent and London will be carried, comfortably and swiftly, without a transfer (Paris to London in four hours). The digging is attracting an unexpected stream of tourists all year round.

The further north one goes, the more beer is drunk and used in the kitchen, especially in soup and *ragoûts*. Wild rabbit is cooked with prunes or grapes. There is also a thick Flemish soup called *hochepot* which, literally, has everything in it but the kitchen sink. The cuisine is often, not surprisingly, sea-based – *matelotes* of conger eel and *caudière* (fish soup). Shellfish known as *coques*, 'the poor man's oyster', are popular too. The *marolles* cheese from Picardy is made from whole milk, salted and washed down with beer. Flanders, although it has a very short coastline, has many herring dishes, *croquelots* or *bouffis*, which are lightly salted and smoked. *Harengs salés* and *harengs fumés* are famous and known locally as *gendarmes* ('policemen').

Champagne & Ardennes

The chalky and rolling fields of Champagne might have remained unsung and unvisited, had it not been for an accident of history. Towards the end of the 17th century a blind monk, tending the bottles of mediocre wine in the cellars of his abbey at Hautviliers, discovered that cork made a fine stopper for aging his wine. After the first fermentation, cork kept air, the enemy of aging wine, from his brew. But it also trapped the carbon dioxide in the bottle and when he pulled the cork it 'popped'. At that moment, some say, the world changed for the better. 'I am drinking the stars,' he is said to have murmured as he took the first sip of champagne the world had ever known. This northeastern slice of France is composed of the *départements* of Ardennes, Marne, Aube and Haute Marne. On these rolling plains many of the great battles of European history have been fought, including many in the First and Second World Wars. The Ardennes was once known as the 'woody country' where Charlemagne hunted deer, wild boar, small birds and game in the now vanished forests. The area has three main waterways: the *Seine*, the *Aube* and the *Marne*. The **Marne Valley** between Ferté-sous-Jouarre and Epernay is one of the prettiest in France. Forests of beech, birch, oak and elm cover the high ground, vines and fruit trees sprawl across the slopes and corn and sunflowers wave in the little protected valleys. The valleys form a long fresh and green oasis, dotted with red-roofed villages. In 496 Clovis, the first king of France, was baptised in the cathedral in **Rheims.** From Louis VII to Charles X, the kings of France made it a point of honour to be crowned in the city where the history of the country really began. Rheims and its cathedral have been destroyed, razed, and rebuilt many times over the centuries. The *Church of St Rémi*, even older than the cathedral, is half Romanesque, half Gothic in style. The most remarkable feature is its great size, comparable to that of Notre Dame de Paris. Beneath the town and its suburbs there are endless caves for champagne. **Epernay** is the real capital of champagne, the drink. Here, 115km (72 miles) of underground galleries in the chalk beneath the city store the wine for the delicate operations required to make champagne. These include the blending of vintages, one of the most important tasks in the creation of champagne. It is left to age for at least three years. Aside from champagne as the world knows it, there is an excellent *blanc de blanc champagne nature*, an unbubbly white wine with a slight bite and many of the characteristics of champagne. The perfect Gothic style of the cathedral of *St Etienne* in **Châlons-sur-Marne** has preserved the pure lines of its 12th-century tower. Nearby, the little town of **St Ménéhould,** almost destroyed in 1940, has contributed to the gastronomic world recipes for pigs' feet and carp, but historically it is known for the fact that the postmaster, in 1791, recognised Louis XVI fleeing from Paris with his family and reported him.

Before the annexation of Franche-Comté and Lorraine, **Langres** was a fortified town. Its Gallo-Roman monuments, its 15th- and 17th-century mansions and its religious architecture make it well worth a visit. **Troyes,** ancient capital of the Champagne area, has a beautifully preserved city centre with a gothic cathedral, dozens of churches and 15th-century houses and a system of boulevards shaped like a champagne cork. The city also boasts the *Musée d'Art Moderne* in the old Bishops' Palace – a private collection of modern art, including works by Bonnard, Degas and Gauguin.

There are beautiful lakes in the Champagne-Ardenne region, the largest being *Lac du Der-Chantecoq*. The *Fôret d'Orient* has a famous bird sanctuary. There is no school of cooking founded on the use of champagne, but locally there are a few interesting dishes that include the wine. **Châlons-sur-Marne** has a dish that involves cooking chicken in champagne. It goes well in a sauce for the local trout; kidneys and pike have also been fried in champagne. In the Spring of 1992, the Marne-le-Vallée region introduced a thoroughly new concept to Europe – the **Euro Disney Resort** – a complete vacation destination located 32km (20 miles) from Paris. The site has an area of 1943 hectares (5000 acres), one-fifth of the size of Paris, and includes hotels, restaurants, a campground, shops, a golf course and has as its star attraction the *Euro Disneyland Theme Park*. Inspired by previous theme parks, Euro Disneyland features all the famous Disney characters plus some new attractions especially produced to blend with its European home. The site is easily accessible by motorway, regional rail services (with high-speed services from 1994) and by air. Euro Disney lies between two major international airports: *Roissy-Charles-de-Gaulle* and *Orly*.

Lorraine, Vosges & Alsace

This part of France is made up of two historic territories, *Alsace* and *Lorraine*, in which there are six *départements*: Vosges, Meurthe-et-Moselle, Meuse, Moselle, Bas-Rhin, Haut-Rhin and the territory of Belfort. These territories have seesawed from French to German control during conflicts between the two countries for centuries. The major cities of the area are Strasbourg, Metz, Nancy and Colmar. **Strasbourg,** by far the largest and most important, has been for centuries what its name suggests: A city on a highway – the highway being the east–west trade (and invasion) route and the north–south river commerce. Today it is the headquarters of the Council of Europe, but it is rich in historic monuments and architecture and possesses a magnificent cathedral. **Metz,** a Gallo-Romaine city, is situated in a strategic position as a defence point and is also a crossroads of trade routes. It contains some elegant medieval walls, arches and public buildings, but its pride is the *Cathedral of St Etienne*. **Nancy** is best known for its perfectly proportioned *Place Stanislas*, gracefully surrounded with elegant wrought-iron gages. The history of Lorraine is excellently documented in the town's museum. A visit to **Colmar** can be a pleasant glimpse into the Middle Ages, and it is one of the most agreeable cities in Alsace, as well as being capital of the Alsatian wine country. The narrow, winding, cobbled streets are flanked by half-timbered houses, painstakingly restored by the burghers of the city. The 13th-century *Dominican Convent of Unterlinden*, now a museum, contains some important works from the 15th and 16th centuries.

Steer-yourself boats are readily available for canal cruising in a number of locations. There are also regularly scheduled *Rhine* river and canal tours daily all summer; several hotel boats ply these waterways as well. Sightseeing helicopters and balloons make regular flights, weather permitting. Several sentimentally ancient steam trains make regular circuits including **Rosheim/Ottrat** (on the wine trail); at **Andolsheim** a steam train runs along the *canal d'Alsace* between Cernay and Soultz.

Throughout Alsace there are artisans' workshops, including glass and wood painting at **Wimmenau** and pottery in **Betschdorf** where studios and shops are open to the public. Organised walking tours that include overnight stops and meals *en route* are arranged from Colmar and **Mulhouse.** Bicycle trails are marked along the Rhine where rental bicycles are readily available. **Belfort,** a major fortress town since the 17th century, commands the *Belfort gap*, or *Burgundy gate*, between the *Vosges* and the *Jura* mountains. Dominating the routes from Germany and Switzerland, it became famous during the Franco-Prussian war of 1870-71 when it withstood a 108-day

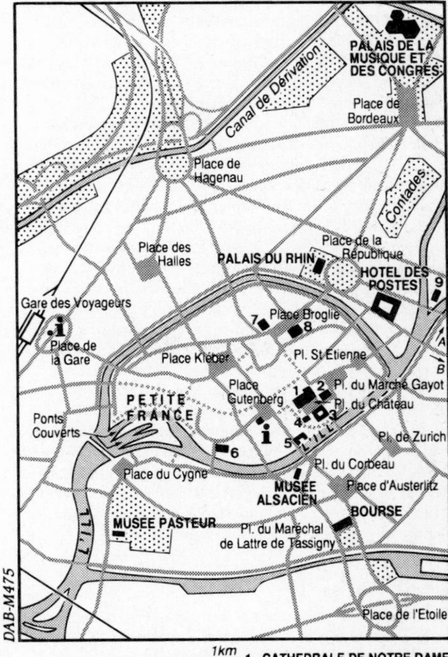

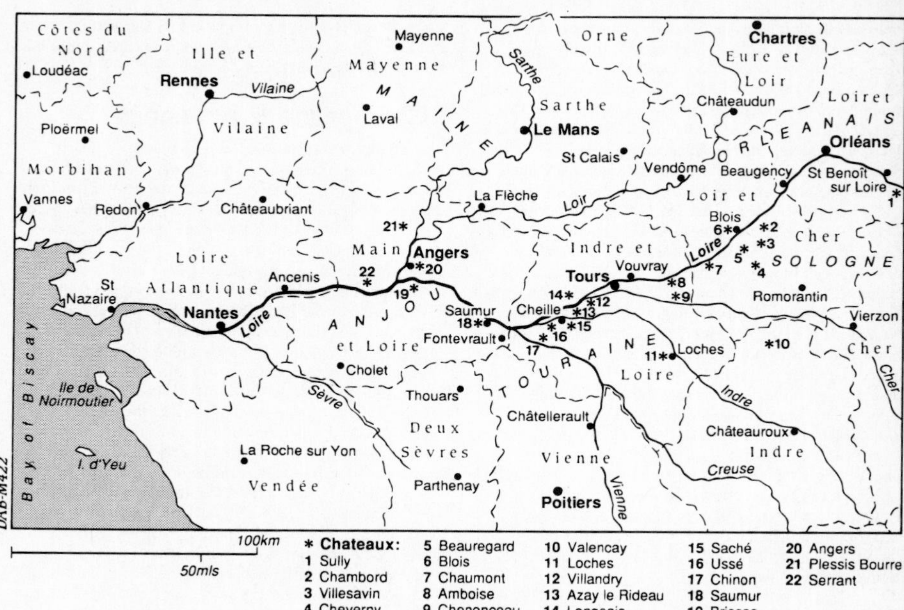

siege. This is commemorated by a huge stone statue, the *Lion of Belfort*, by Bartholdi, the creator of the Statue of Liberty. The *route de vin* lies between the Rhine and a low range of pine-covered mountains called the **Vosges**. The flat, peaceful plain is covered with orchards and vineyards. Lovely, rural villages dot the landscape, their church spires piercing the horizon. The wines of Alsace have a long history, the Alsatian grapes being planted before the arrival of the Romans. It has never been clearly understood where they originated; unlike other French wines, these depend more on grape type than soil or processing. Almost exclusively white with a fruity and dry flavour, they make an excellent accompaniment to the local food. Beer also goes well with Alsatian food and as might be expected, good beer is brewed in both the Alsace and the Lorraine areas. There are famous and popular mineral water sources in **Contrexeville** and **Vittel** (also a spa town). They were well known and appreciated by the Romans and today are the most popular in France. One of the food specialities of Alsace is *truite bleu*, blue trout, which is simply boiled so fresh as to be almost alive when tossed into the water. The swift rivers provide gamey trout and they can be fished by visitors if permits are obtained (at any city hall). The cooking is peppery and hearty and quite unlike that of any other French region. *Munster*, a strong winter cheese, is usually served with caraway seeds. Lorraine and Alsatian tarts are made with the excellent local fruits: *mirabelles* (small yellow plums), cherries, pears etc. Each of these fruits also makes a world-renowned *eau-de-vie*, a strong white alcohol liqueur which is drunk as a digestive after a heavy meal. Lorraine is famous for *quiche lorraine* made only in the classical manner: with cream, eggs and bacon. Nancy has a *boudin* (blood sausage), although this is found in all parts of France.

Burgundy & Franche-Comté

Burgundy begins near **Auxerre,** a small medieval town with a beautiful Gothic cathedral, and extends southward to the hills of Beaujolais just north of Lyon. The *départements* are the Yonne, Côte d'Or, Nièvre and the Saône-et-Loire. Driving through this region, one seems to be traversing a huge *carte des vins*: Mersault, Volnay, Beaune, Aloxe Corton, Nuits-Saint-Georges, Vosne-Romanée and Gevrey-Chambertin. This vast domain of great wines was for 600 years an independent kingdom, at times as strong as France itself, enjoying its heydey in the 15th century. Throughout a stormy history, however, Burgundy's vineyards survived thanks in large part to the knowledge, diligence and good taste of its monks. Several of the orders owned extensive vineyards throughout the region, among them the Knights of Malta, Carthusians, Carmelites and, most importantly, the Benedictines and Cistercians. As a result the 210km (130-mile) length of Burgundy is peppered with abbeys, monasteries and a score of fine Romanesque churches, notably in *Fontenay, Vézelay, Tournus* and *Cluny*. There are also many fortified châteaux. **Dijon**, an important political and religous centre during Burgundy's heyday in the 15th century, has several fine museums and art galleries, as well as the *Palais des Ducs*, once the home of the Dukes of Burgundy. There are also elegant restored town houses to be visited, dating from the 15th to the 18th century, and a 13th-century cathedral. The towns of **Sens** and **Macon** both possess fine churches dating from the 12th century. The region of Franche-Comté is shaped like a fat boomerang and is made up of the *départements* of Doubs, Jura and Haute Saône. The high French Jura mountains (rising in steps from 245-11,785m/800-5850ft) run north to south along the French-Swiss border. To the west is the forested Jura plateau, the vine-clad hills and eventually the fertile plain of northern Bresse, called the *Finage*. The heights and valleys of the Jura are readily accessible and, in the summertime, beautifully green, providing pasture land for the many milk cows used in the production of one of the great mountain cheeses: *Comté*. There are many lovely (and romantically named) rivers in this region – Semouse, Allance, Gugeotte, Lanterne, Barquotte, Durgeon, Colombine, Dougeonne, Rigotte and Romaine (named by Julius Caesar). They weave and twist, now and then disappearing underground to reappear again some miles away. All these physical characteristics combine to make Franche-Comté an excellent region for summer vacations and winter sports.

Val de Loire

The 'centre' of France from Chartres to Châteauroux and from Tours to Bourges includes the *départements* of Eure-et-Loir, Loiret, Loir-et-Cher, Indre, Indre-et-Loire and Cher. The Central Loire includes the famous *Châteaux* country, perhaps the region most visited by foreign tourists to France. Through it flows a part of the Loire River, the longest river in France, and considered to be its most capricious, often reducing to a mere trickle of water in a bed of sand. It has been called a 'useless' great river, because it drives no turbines or mill wheels and offers few navigable waterways. It could be said that the Loire serves only beauty and each of its tributaries has its own character. The *Cher* is a quiet, slow-moving river, flowing calmly through grassy meadows and mature forests. The château of **Chenonceaux** stands quite literally *on* the river; a working mill in the early medieval period when the Cher flowed more vigorously, it was transformed into perhaps the most graceful of all French châteaux, its court rooms running clear from one bank to the other on a row of delicate arches. Chenonceaux's development owed much to a succession of beautiful and powerful noblewomen, and its charm is of an undeniably feminine nature. The *Indre* is a river of calm reflections. Lilies abound and weeping willows sway on its banks. The château at **Azay-le-Rideau** was designed to make full use of these qualities and stands beside several small man-made lakes, each reflecting a different aspect of the building. Water is moved to and from the river and between the lakes through a series of gurgling channels. The water gardens and its reflections of the intricately carved exterior more than compensate for the rather dull interior. The *Vienne* is essentially a broad stream. It glides gracefully beneath the weathered walls of old **Chinon**, where several important chapters in French history were acted out. The château of **Blois**, which is one of the finest architecturally speaking, is certainly the most interesting in terms of history. It stands in the centre of the ancient town of the same name, towering over the battered stone houses clustered beneath its walls. **Chambord**, several miles south of the Loire, is the most substantial of the great châteaux. Standing in a moat in the centre of a vast lawn bordered by forests, the body of the building possesses a majestic symmetry. In contrast, the roofscape is a mad jumble of eccentric chimneys and apartments. Some have attributed the bizarre double-helix staircase to Leonardo da Vinci. The five châteaux described in outline above are generally ranked highest amongst the Loire châteaux and form the core of most organised tours. There are, of course, dozens more that can be visited and it is even possible to stay overnight in several. Contact the Tourist Office for more information. The Loire Valley is very warm and crowded with tourists in summer.

Besides châteaux, there is much else of interest in the Val de Loire and surrounding districts. There are magnificent 13th-century cathedrals in **Chartres** and **Tours**, as well as abbeys and mansions and charming riverside towns and villages.

Other places of outstanding interest include **Orléans**, famous for its associations with Jeanne d'Arc, with a beautiful cathedral, the *Musée des Beaux Arts* and 16th-century *Hôtel de Ville;* and **Bourges**, a 15th-century town, complete with maisons and museums and the *Cathedral of St Etienne*. The charming little town of **Loches**, southeast of Tours, has a fine château and an interesting walled medieval quarter. It was in the heartland of the **Touraine** where the true cuisine of France developed (Touraine was given the name 'the garden of France').

Western Loire

The region of the Western Loire comprises the *départements* of Loire-Atlantique, the Vendée, Maine et Loire, Sarthe and Mayenne. The Vendée and the Loire Atlantique share a beautiful and wild coastline with Brittany. There are 305km (190 miles) of sandy beaches. Inland, the mild climate makes for beautiful mature pastures, often prettified further by clumps of wild camelias and roses.

In the Western Loire, **La Baule**, a summer resort with a fine, seemingly endless beach, is a pleasant village with winding streets and giant pines, excellent hotels, restaurants and a casino. It has an unusually mild mini-climate and is exceptionally warm for the region. **Le Mans**, famous for its racetrack, is an historic old town built on a hill overlooking the west bank of the *Sarthe*. The 12th-century choir in the *Cathedral of Saint-Julian* is one of the most remarkable in France. The magnificent 13th- and 14th-century stained glass is also impressive. Most of the Sarthe Valley consists of beautifully wooded hills, divided by the thick hedges that are seasonally draped with wild roses, honeysuckle, or large juicy blackberries. In May or early June the apple and pear blossoms blend with the hawthorn; the orchards are in bloom and the fields and forests are rich and green. These two months are most attractive and the weather at that time is usually favourable; the autumn is less dry but as a rule usually remains pleasant through October.

Nantes on the coast of the Loire Atlantique, is a thriving commercial and industrial centre. There is a medieval castle, which also houses the *Musée d'Art Populaire*, a display of Breton costumes; a 15th-century cathedral; and a naval museum. Upstream from Nantes, the town of **Angers** contains some spectacular tapestries. In the castle can be seen 'St John's Vision of the Apocalypse' (14th century) and in the *Hôpital St Jean*, Jean Lurcat's 'Chant du Monde' (20th century). The Hôpital itself is very beautiful and there are several museums and art galleries in the town worth a visit, as well as the magnificent castle/fortress and the cathedral.

The regional cuisine has the advantages of excellent vineyards, an abundance and variety of fish from the Loire and its tributaries, plentiful butter and cheese, fruits and vegetables and easily available game from the forests. In general, the wines of the Loire all have a clean refreshing taste that makes them ideal for light lunches or as an *apéritif*.

Rhône, Savoie & Dauphiny

This region includes the French Alps and their foothills, and the vast long valleys of the Rhône and Saône rivers. The *départements* are Loire, Rhône, Ain, Ardèche, Drôme, Isère, Savoie and Haute-Savoie.

Lyon, in the deepest part of the Rhône valley, has a proud gastronomic tradition. As France's second city, Lyon is a major cultural, artistic, financial and industrial centre, with international festivals and trade fairs. The *Cathedral of St Jean* is well worth a visit, as are the Roman remains of the city, and the *Musée de la Civilisation Gallo-Romaine*. The French Alps stretch across Savoie and Dauphiny on the border with Italy. Napoleon came this way after escaping from Elba in 1815. Landing with 100 men near Cannes, he intended to march along the coast to Marseille and up the Rhône Valley to Lyon and Paris, but he received reports that the population on that route was hostile and was forced

instead to head inland through the mountains. They reached Gap (150kms/93 miles from the coast) in four days, Grenoble a few days after and arrived in Paris (1152kms/715 miles from Cannes) in 20 days with a large and loyal army in tow. It is possible to retrace his route, which passes through much beautiful scenery; each stopping place is clearly marked. The Alps have demanded much of France's engineers and some of the roads and railways are themselves tourist attractions. Notable examples include the 9km (6-mile) steam locomotive run from La Rochette to Poncharra (about 40km (24 miles) from Grenoble); and the 32km (19-mile) track (electrified in 1903) from Saint-Georges-de-Commiers to la Mira (again near Grenoble), with 133 curves, 18 tunnels and 12 viaducts. As in most mountainous regions of the world, white-water boating *(randonnées nautiques)* can be enjoyed on many of the Alpine rivers. Hiking is popular and well organized, utilizing the GR (*grandes randonées* or main trails) maps that show where the official marked trails pass. The rivers racing from the Alpine heights into the Rhône provide a great deal of electrical power and good opportunities for trout fishing. The *Fédération des associations agrée de Pêche et de Pisciculture de la Drôme* in Valence can lead a fisherman to the right spot (HQ in Valence, but branches in 36 cities). Skiing, however, is the principle sport in the French Alps. The best skiing is found, for the most part, west of Grenoble and south of Lake Geneva. All the resorts are well-equipped, provide warm, comfortable lodgings and good food. Some specialise in skiing the year round, but almost all have summer seasons with facilities such as golf courses, tennis courts, swimming pools and natural lakes. At the lake resort of **Annecy**, there is an unusual *Bell Museum* with a very fine restaurant attached; international festivals of gastronomy are held throughout the year. Savoie hosted the Winter Olympics in 1992.

Aquitaine & Poitou-Charentes

This area of sunshine and Atlantic air in the southwest of France includes the *départements* of Deux Sèvres, Vienne, Charente-Maritime, Charente, Gironde, Dordogne, Lot-et-Garonne, Landes and Pyrénées Atlantiques, the latter on the Spanish border. The coastline has 270km (170 miles) of beaches and the 30km (20 miles) or so from **Hossegor** to **Hendaye** fall within the Basque area and offer some of the best surfing in Europe.
North of Bordeaux the region of Guyenne is sometimes referred to as 'west-centre' as if it were a clearly defined part of France, yet a diversity of landscapes and an extraordinary mixing and mingling of races exists here – Celts, Iberians, Dutch and Anglo Saxons, to name a few. The linguistic frontier between the *langue d'oie* and *langue d'oc* runs between **Poitiers** (former capital of the Duchy of Aquitaine) and **Limoges**, creating a dialect which developed from both. These people have in common the great north–south highway, the important line of communication between the Parisian basin and the Aquitaine basin. Throughout the centuries it was the route of many invaders: Romans, Visigoths, Alemanni, Huns, Arabs, Normans, English, Huguenots and Catholics all moved along it. **Biarritz** and **Bayonne** are both resorts on the Aquitaine/Basque coast, close to the Spanish border. Biarritz has been famous as a cosmopolitan spa-town since the 19th century, when it was popular with European aristocracy. There are several sheltered beaches, as well as a casino. Bayonne, a few kilometres up the coast but slightly inland, is a typical Basque town which is worth a visit. There is a 13th-century cathedral and two museums (one of them devoted to Basque culture).
Bordeaux is on the *Garonne River* just above where it joins the Dordogne, the two streams forming an estuary called the *Gironde* which forms a natural sheltered inland harbour. It is flanked on both sides by vineyards as far as the eye can see. The combination of great wines and great wealth made Bordeaux one of the gastronomic cities of France and the city offers an impressive sight from the stone bridge with 17 arches that crowns the enormous golden horn which forms the harbour. The second largest city of France in area, the fourth in population, the fifth port, it was described by Victor Hugo with the words: 'Take Versailles, add Antwerp to it, and you have Bordeaux'. Its magnificent geographical position and unsurpassed vineyards belie Hugo's simplification. The city is the commercial and cultural centre for all of the southwest. South of Bordeaux along the coast is a strip of long sandy beaches backed by lagoons, some communicating with the sea, some shut off from it. Just at the back of this is the **Landes**, covered with growths of scrubby pine. Here in the marshes the shepherds walk on stilts. The hilly region between the *Adour* and Garonne rivers comprises the inland part of Gascony, first known as *Aquitania Propria* and later as *Novem Populena*. It was inhabited by Vascones, or Basques who, since prehistoric times, had lived in this area and south of the Pyrénées. In the south the Basque language has survived to this day, but the northern part of the area became known as Vasconia and then **Gascony**, a name made famous by the swashbuckling Gascons of literature; Cyrano de Bergerac, d'Artagnan of 'The Three Musketeers' and *le vert gallant* – Henri IV. In the centre of Gascony is the old countship of **Armagnac** which, like Cognac, provides the world with a magnificent brandy that bears the name of the region. The difference between the two stems from several factors: the type of grape used, the soil, the climate, the method of distilling the wine and the variety of wood used in the maturing casks. Armagnac is still made by local artisans and small farmers. The quality and taste varies much more than Cognac, but it inevitably retains its fine flavour.
The **Dordogne** (and neighbouring Lot) is the area where traces of prehistoric (Cro-Magnon) man abound. The *Dordogne River* itself, one of the most beautiful of all French rivers, flows swiftly through the region, its banks crowded with old castles and walled towns. In **Montignac** the fabulous painted caves of *Lascaux* are reproduced in the exact proportions and colours of the original, a few miles away. The reproduction was necessary as the original deteriorated rapidly when exposed to the heat and humidity of visitors. A highly interesting and informative museum and zoo of prehistoric artefacts and animals has been created in *le Thot* a few miles from Agen. The area around **Perigueux** is a country of rivers and castles – very different from those on the Loire as these are older and, for the most part, fortified defence points against medieval invaders. There are facilities for renting horse and gypsy wagons (*roulotte à chevaux*) for slow-moving tours of the region. Along with hiking treks, river boating and bicycling tours, it offers a relaxed way to explore this beautiful land.
It is possible in Aquitaine and Poitou-Charentes to find pleasant hotels and *auberges* for an overnight or few days' stay. They range from *gîtes* and *chambre d'hôtes* – a farm bed & breakfast programme – to châteaux hôtels with elegant restaurants. There are no less than 150 *chambres d'hôtes* stopovers in the Poitou-Charentes region alone, including many on the coast, near beaches and pleasure ports. The area of Poitou-Charentes has lovely mature woodland and an attractive coast where oysters are cultivated. The *Charente-Maritime* is known as 'the Jade Coast', with **Royan** to the south (a fine modern resort with 8 miles of fine sand beaches) and **La Rochelle** to the north. The rivers of the region offer quiet scenic walks or boating trips. The centre of the *département* of Charente, amid low, rolling hills covered with copses of trees and vineyards, is a little town of only 22,000 inhabitants whose name is known all over the world. Here, in an area of some 150,000 acres, the only brandy that can be called *Cognac* is produced. Use of the name is forbidden for brandy which is made elsewhere or from other than one of the seven officially accepted varieties of grape. The *Valois Château*, located here, was the birthplace of Francis I. The ancient port of **La Rochelle**, from which many pioneers left to explore the new world, is today a popular vacation and sailing port.
Close by, the offshore islands of **Oléron** and **Ré** are both connected to the mainland by bridges.

Languedoc-Roussillon

The combined territories of Languedoc and Roussillon include five *départements*: Aude, Gard, Hérault, Lozère and Pyrénées-Oriental. The area has been French since the 13th century and the name *languedoc* comes from *lang d'oc* or language in which 'yes' is *oc* (as opposed to *langue d'oie* the language in which 'yes' is *oui*). This ancient language is still heard throughout the south of France, on both sides of the Rhône. The Mediterranean coast between **Perpignan** (the ancient capital of the Kings of Majorca) and **Montpellier** now has one of the most modern holiday complexes in Europe, including the resorts of **La Grande Motte, Port Leucate** and **Port Bacarès**. More wine is produced in Languedoc-Roussillon than any other place in the world. The vineyards, started in the Roman era and producing red, white and rosé wine, begin in the **Narbonne** area, run past **Béziers** (the wine marketing centre for the region) and on to **Montpellier.** Once an important seaport which imported spices (its name derives from 'the Mount of Spice Merchants'), the city is an important intellectual and university centre with five fine museums, impressive 17th- and 18th-century architecture and a superb summer music festival. There are a great variety of other attractions in this warm southland. The Roman (and some Gallic) ruins are often magnificent; the *Maison Carré, Diana's Temple* and the *Roman Arena* in **Nîmes**, the Rome of the Gauls, are among the finest examples of Greco-Roman architecture to be found today. The 2000-year-old *Pont de Gard* is one of man's greatest architectural accomplishments and certainly worth a special trip. There is the medieval city of **Aigues-Mortes** which would still be recognizable to St Louis and his crusaders, for it was from here they embarked for the east; and the crenelated walled city of **Carcassonne** and towers of **Uzès** are unmissable.
The *canal du Midi*, ideal for steer-yourself canalling, is a tranquil waterway, largely abandoned by commerce, that connects the Atlantic with the Mediterranean. It runs through the sleepy village of **Castelnaudary**, famous for its *cassoulet*, past the citadel of Carcassonne and on through Montpellier.

Auvergne & Limousin

West of the Rhône are the volcanic highlands of the **Massif Central**, historically known as Auvergne and consisting today of the *départements* of Haute-Loire, Cantal, Pay-de-Dôme and Allier. The Limousin region to the west comprises Haute-Vienne, Creuse and Corrèze. Architecturally, Auvergne is rich in châteaux and churches (especially in the Allier and Loire gorges) and is noted for its colourful, rich and mysterious nature. The *National Park* here offers magnificent walking country – a land of water, mountains, plains and extinct volcanoes (the Cantal crater may once have been 30km/20 miles wide). There are ten spa resorts within its boundaries, as well as many lakes, rivers and forests. The high plateaux of *Combrailles, Forez* and *Bourbonnais* are very beautiful.
Clermont-Ferrand, which is the political and economic nucleus for the whole of the Massif Central, is a lively and sprawling town and the birthplace of the Michelin tyre empire. Much of the town's architecture (especially in the older parts of the Clermont area) is black, because of the local black volcanic rock. There is a 13th-century Gothic cathedral and a 14th-century Romanesque basilica, as well as several museums. The town makes a very good base for exploring the beautiful areas around it. There are plenty of good hôtels, *gîtes d'hôtes*, and *gîtes de France* throughout the region. The cuisine is splendid, including *cornet de Murat* (pastries), *pounti*, *truffades* and the St Nectaire cheeses.
The 2000-year-old regional capital of Limousin, **Limoges**, is an important rail and route crossroad, famous for the production of an extremely fine porcelain. The nearby city of **Aubusson** is noted for its tapestries (a local tradition dating back to the 8th century). Both cities are also famous for their enamel.

Midi-Pyrénées

The Midi-Pyrénées area, with its magnificent mountain scenery, lies between Aquitaine to the west and Languedoc-Roussillon to the east. It encompasses part of the Causses, the high plateau country and most of Gascony. Included in it are the *départements* of Lot, Aveyron, Tarn-et-Garonne, Tarn, Gers, Haut-Garonne, Ariège and Haute Pyrénées. This is a land of plains dotted with hillocks, sandy stretches, moors and pine woods, desolate plateaux cleft by magical grottoes, and little valleys covered with impenetrable forests. The northeastern section is a rough, mountainous land, known as the *Rouergue*. It is situated on the frontier of Aquitaine, formed by the plateau of the *Causse*, where game and wild birds feed on the thyme and juniper growing wild in the chalky soil. As a result, these little animals and birds develop a delicious and individual flavour. The principal town, **Rodez**, is severe and beautiful. The crenelated summit of its red tower, one of the marvels of French Gothic architecture, rises above a confusion of narrow streets and small squares. From here there are views of the high plateaus beyond the Aveyron, a majestically stark landscape of granite outcrops and steep ravines. The villages and farmhouses, built of local rock, often mimic the rock formations to the extent that they are all but invisible to outsiders.
To the southeast is **Millau**, gateway to the Tarn gorges, and to the south lies **Roquefort** with its windy caves that store the famous ewe's-milk cheese. These damp cold winds are the secret that has created the 'cheese of kings and the king of cheeses'. **Auch** was the ancient metropole of the Roman *Novem Populena*, one of the most important towns in Gaul, long rivalling *Burdigala* (Bordeaux) in importance. The cathedral has two Jesuit towers, choirstalls carved in solid oak and a 16th-century stained glass window. The people of Auch have erected a statue to *le vrai d'Artagnan* ('the real d'Artagnan'), the famous Gascon musketeer immortalised by Dumas. **Cahor**, situated on a peninsula formed by the *River Lot*, has a famous bridge, *Pont Valentré*, with its six pointed arches and three defensive towers rising 40m (130ft) above the river. It is the most magnificent fortified river span that has survived in Europe and was begun in 1308. Legend has it that the construction work was plagued with problems and the bridge still remained unfinished after 50 years. Then one of the architects made a pact with the devil and the bridge was finished without another hitch. A small figure of the devil is still visible on the central tower. A fine, very dark

red wine bears the name *Cahors*. It is made from grapes of the Amina variety brought in from Italy in Roman times. **Toulouse**, one of the most interesting cities of France, is an agricultural market centre, an important university town, an aero-research centre and one of the great cities of French art (it has seven fine museums). After the Middle Ages the stone quarries in the region were exhausted so the city was built with a soft red brick which seems to absorb the light. As a result it is called the *Ville Rose* and is described as 'pink in the light of dawn, red in broad daylight and mauve by twilight'. There are many beautiful public buildings and private dwellings, like the 16th-century Renaissance *Hotel d'Assezat* and one known as the *Capitole*, presently used for a city hall. The finest Romanesque church in southern France is here. The first Gothic church west of the Rhône was built in Toulouse, the *Church of the Jacobins*; and the first Dominican monastery was founded in Toulouse by Saint Dominic himself. Toulouse is a vibrant city with much activity, with its long rue Alsace-Lorraine being its axis. It is here in the early evenings that Toulousians and visitors alike sit for an apéritif at one of the large sidewalk cafés. The region was an important part of the Roman Empire, subjected for 800 years to Arabic influence (the Moors holding substantial parts of Spain just across the Pyrénées) and the cuisine has therefore developed from both Roman and Arabic. Toulouse sausage, a long fat soft sausage whose filling must be chopped by hand, is one of the ingredients of the local *cassoulet* as well as a very popular dish in its own right. **Albi** is another red-brick city, smaller but no less interesting than Toulouse, located on the *River Tarn*. The first extraordinary thing about Albi is its brick church. Albi was the centre of violent religious wars (the Albigenaise Heretics resisted the Catholic crusaders for decades). The mammoth red-brick *Cathedral of Sainte Cécile*, towering above all the other buildings of the town, was built as a fortress to protect the cruel bishop who imposed the church on the populace. Inside is a vast hall, subdivided by exquisite stonework embellished with statues. The nearby 13th-century *Palace of the Archbishop* (also fortified) is now a musuem containing the largest single collection of the works of Toulouse-Lautrec. The town of **Lourdes** has acted as a magnet for the sick in need of miracle cures, ever since the visions of Bernadette Soubirous in the mid-19th century. Apart from the famous grotto, there is a castle and a museum.

Côte d'Azur & Provence

The *Côte d'Azur*, or French Riviera, is in the *département* of the Alpes-Maritimes. It runs along the coast from the Italian border, through Monaco, and continues to a point just beyond Cannes and reaches 50 or more km (30 miles) northward into the steep slopes of the Alps, connecting the balmy coastal weather with the ideal ski resorts of the lower Alps. This part of the Mediterranean coast has more visitors each year during July and August than any other part of France, although many of the summer visitors are French. The two most famous French resorts, Cannes and Nice, are to be found here and the area is generally accepted as one of the most beautiful resort spots in the world. It well deserves its immense popularity – with artists (Matisse, Picasso, Chagall and Dufy) as well as tourists. The palm trees, blue sea, beautiful beaches, sparkling cities and villages with their splendid residences against the backdrop of the high green mountains have impressed visitors since the 18th century when the crochety doctor-cum-novelist, Tobias Smollet, paid a visit and described it in his *Travels in France and Italy*. The weather is wonderful with long, hot and sunny summers. There is plenty of diversion here, especially in the spring, summer and early autumn months. The coastal resort towns include **Cannes**, made popular as a resort by Lord Brougham in the 19th century when, because of a plague in Nice, he was forced to stop here; **Nice**, itself, the largest metropolis on the coast, a thriving commercial city as well as a year-round resort (the annual carnival and battle of roses perhaps date back to 350BC); **Napoule Plage**, a small and exclusive resort with several sandy beaches, a marina and a splendid view of the rolling green Maure Mountains; **Golfe-Juan**, now a popular resort town with many expensive mansions and hotels; **Juan-les-Pins**, with a neat harbour, beaches and pine forests in the hills which protect the village from the winds in both summer and winter; **Antibes** and **Cap d'Antibes**, very popular but expensive resorts; **Villefranche-sur-Mer**, a deep-water port which has been used by pleasure yachts and navies for centuries; **St-Jean-Cap-Ferrat**, an exclusive and expensive resort consisting of great private mansions and seaside estates; **Beaulieu**, much less exclusive, yet a fine resort town; **Menton** (near the Principality of Monaco), once a fishing village and citrus-fruit-producing area, now a pleasant vacation resort. The Côte d'Azur is an extraordinary playground with every kind of amusement. There are excellent museums, historic places dating from the pre-Christian era to the present day, hills, mountains, lakes and rivers, gorges and alpine skiing trails. The entire area has a generous supply of good, comfortable hotels as well as luxury châteaux, restaurants with every sort of food, and good drinking bars everywhere. One of the greatest museums in the world, the *Maeght Foundation*, is located in St-Paul-de-Vence. Picasso, Braque, Matisse and Léger museums also exist and there is plenty of beautiful foothill countryside to explore. Resorts further along the coast from Cannes include **St Tropez**, a terribly crowded and hard to reach fashionable village; **Port Grimaud**, the first of the custom-built 'fishing village' resorts (and now old enough to look almost like the real thing); **Ste Maxime**, a fashionable but crowded resort with fine beaches and harbour; **Fréjus**, which was a port when the Greeks were settling in the Mediterranean basin 'like frogs around a pond' and which is less fashionable than most of its neighbours; **St Raphael**, at one time a Roman resort, and now a comfortable middle-class vacation town. Spectacular weather is one of the major attractions of *Provence*, whose *départements* comprise Hautes Alpes, Alpes de Hautes Provence, Var, Vaucluse and Bouches du Rhône. The deep blue skies of summer are seldom clouded, although there is some rain in spring and fall. The only inhospitable element is the mistral, a wind that sometimes roars down the Rhône Valley, often unrelenting for three or four days. When the Romans arrived in Gaul, they were so delighted with the climate of the Bouches du Rhône that they made it a province rather than a colony, which was more usual.

The varied flora that have taken root in this land have given it the hues of pewter, bronze, dark green and fresh green. The sun has baked the dwellings to shades of ochre and rose while the deep red soil has provided tiles that remain red, defying the searing rays of the Midi sunshine. The towns, their architecture, stones and tiles all blend subtly throughout Provence with the majestic plane trees in the streets and squares. Their long heavy trunks of mottled greys and the graceful vaulting of the heavily leafed branches create a peculiar atmosphere not found anywhere else. These are the principal adornment of most of the cities, market towns and villages, generously bestowing a deep blue shade on the inhabitants, the mossy fountains, café terraces, games of *pétanque* and

kibitzers alike. The eras of Greek and Roman domination of Provence have left monuments scattered across the countryside. They include walled hill towns, triumphal arches, theatres, colosseums, arenas, bridges and aquaducts. Christianity brought the *Palace of the Popes* in **Avignon**, many churches and hundreds of roadside shrines or 'oratories' which have given the name *oradour* to many communities along the Rhône.

Christian art of the highest quality is scattered throughout the area from *Notre-Dame-des-Doms* in Avignon to *Notre-Dame-du-Bourg* in **Digne** in the centre of the lower alps. The pilgrims throughout the territory built wonderful churches typified by graceful semi-circular arches, round rose windows, statues of Christ surrounded by evangelists, saints, the damned in chains, and processions of the faithful. These are carved in stone so worn by the sun and wind they almost have the quality of flesh.

Many of the towns and villages are marked by a fortified castle and watchtower to guard against the coming of the Saracens, the Corsairs of the Rhône and marauding bands. For this was the invasion route, by land from the north and by sea from the south. *Tarascon, Beauclair, Villeneuve, Gourdon, Entrevaux, Sisteron* and many others had their 'close' and tower situated high above the river or overlooking the sea. **Marseille** was founded by the Greeks (they called it Massalia) and used as a base for their colonisation of the Rhône Valley. Today, it is France's most important commercial port on the Mediterranean and consequently is of a primarily industrial nature. Nonetheless, there are sites of interest to the conventionally minded tourist – the old port, the hilltop church of *Notre-Dame-de-la-Garde*, many fine restaurants (especially for seafood), several museums, Le Corbusier's *Unité d'Habitation*, the *Hospice de la Vieille Charité* and, of course, the *Château d'If*, one of the most notorious of France's historic island fortresses.

Vast oil refineries and depots dominate the sparsely populated salt flats and marshes to the north and west of the city, but the land is not yet dead. It is the perfect habitat for several species of birds found in few other places in western Europe, including bustards and nightjars. On the far side of the Rhône is the marshy area known as the **Camargue**, long used for the breeding of beef cattle and horses, for the evaporation of sea water to make salt, and more recently for growing rice. The cattle breeders, or cowboys, are armed with lances instead of lassos. Vast flocks of waterbirds nest here in a national bird reserve, among them pink flamingos and snow-white egrets.

When, in 123BC, Consul Sextias Calvinus established a camp beside some warm springs in the broad lower Rhône valley, it was named Aquae Sextiae – today known as **Aix-en-Provence.** The many olive trees found throughout Provence provide a popular fruit and one of the important staples of the local cuisine, a fine olive oil used extensively in the cooking of local food. Garlic, though not exclusively associated with Provence, is used more here than in any other part of France. It is sometimes called 'the truffle of Provence'. A third element, tomato, seems to get into most of the delicious Provençal concoctions as well. The cooking here varies from region to region. In the Camargue a characteristic dish is *estouffade de boeuf*. Marseille is noted for a dish called *pieds et paquets* ('feet and packages') which consists of sheeps' tripe stuffed with salt pork and cooked overnight in white wine with onions, garlic and parsley. *Tripe á la Niçoise* is similar, but none the less individual. Perhaps the most typical dish and one found in most parts of Provence is *tomates provençales*, a heavenly concoction with all the Provençal specialities: olive oil, garlic and parsley baked in and on a tomato. This combination can also be applied to courgettes (zucchini) and aubergines (egg plant). All of these vegetables, along with sweet peppers, are found in the most famous Provençal vegetable *ragoût* known, for some long lost reason, as *ratatouille*, this too being well laced with garlic and of course cooked in olive oil. Mayonnaise, also, well mixed with Provençal garlic, becomes *aioli*, which is served with boiled vegetables and/or fish. Quail, thrush, trout and crayfish were, not so long ago, the mainstays of the Provençal table, but stocks have declined and these dishes are now rarely served. *Gigot* (leg of lamb) is a more common local speciality. Surviving into the era of *nouvelle cuisine* and still the pride of the Provençal coast is the famous fish stew called *bouillabaisse*. Like *cassoulet* in Languedoc there are several versions, each claiming to be the 'authentic' one. The ingredients are not vastly different – having to do with the amount of saffron or the inclusion or exclusion of certain fish.

Few wines are grown in Provence, although some are quite good, especially those originating in the Lubéron. The four districts that have been granted recognition are best known for their rosé wines: *Cassis, Bandol, Bellet* and *la Palette*. They are all on the coast, except la Palette which is near Aix.

Corsica

The island of Corsica is made up of two French *départements*: Haute Corse (upper Corsica) and Corse du Sud (south Corsica). The 8720 sq km (3367 sq miles) are inhabited by not many more than 250,000 people. It is one of the very few places left in Europe that is not invaded by campers and trailers during the vacation season and its charm lies in this unspoiled and rugged atmosphere. The name Corsica, or *Corse*, is a modernisation of *Korsai*, believed to be a Phoenician word meaning 'covered with forests'. The Phoenician Greeks landed here 560 years before the Christian era to disturb inhabitants who had probably originated in Liguria. From that time on, Corsica has been fought for, or over, creating a bloody history probably unparalleled for such a small area. The Greeks were followed by the Romans, then the Vandals, Byzantines, Moors and Lombards. In 1768 Genoa sold Corsica to France and its 2500 years of disputed ownership ended. In spite of its extensive and colourful history it is of course best known as the birthplace of Napoléon Bonaparte. The island has been described as 'a mountain in the sea', for when approached by sea that is exactly what it looks like. A strange land, the mountains rise abruptly from the western shore where the coast is indescribably beautiful with a series of capes and isolated beachless bays; along its entire length rock and water meet with savage impact. The coastline, unfolded, is about 992km (620 miles) long. Corsica consists of heaths, forests, granite, snow, sand beaches and orange trees. This combination has produced a strange, fiery, lucidly intellectual and music-loving race of people, both superstitious and pious at the same time. The interior is quite undeveloped, with mountains, and dry scrubby land overgrown with brush called *maquis* (from the local *maccia* which means 'brush'). A dry wilderness of hardy shrubs – arbutus, mastic, thorn, myrtle, juniper, rosemary, rock rose, agave, pistachio, fennel, heather, wild mint and ashphodel, 'the flower of hell'. During the German occupation of France (1940-44) resistance fighters were given the name *maquis* from the association of the wild country in which they hid, much as the savage backlands of Corsica provided at one time comparatively safe shelter for the island bandits. There is a desolate grandeur about the *maquis*, while on the other hand the rugged beauty of Corsica's magnificent mountain scenery is anything but desolate.

A considerable amount of forested area remains, although since discovered by the Greeks it has been frequently raided for its fine, straight and tall *laricio* pine that seems to thrive only here. They have been known to grow as high as 60m (200ft), perfect for use as masts and are still used as such. Corsica is also rich in cork oaks, chestnuts and olives. There is a *Regional Nature Conservation Park* on the island. North of the eastern plain are the lowlands, principally olive groves, known as *La Balagne*, the hinterland of Calvi and l'Ile Rousse. To the south is the dazzling white city of **Ajaccio**, full of Napoleonic memorabilia. The town runs in a semicircle on the calm bay, set against a backdrop of wooded hills. At the foot of the cape at the northern end of the island is the commercial, but none the less picturesque, town of **Bastia**, with its historic citadel towering over the headland. The old town has preserved its streets in the form of steps connected by vaulted passages, converging on the *Vieux port*. The port itself, with a polyglot population, is busy all year round. A little further north, the terraced *St Nicholas Beach*, shaded by palm trees and covered with parasols and café tables, separates the old port from the new. The new port, just beyond, is the real commercial port of the island. Corsican cuisine is essentially simple, with the sea providing the most dependable

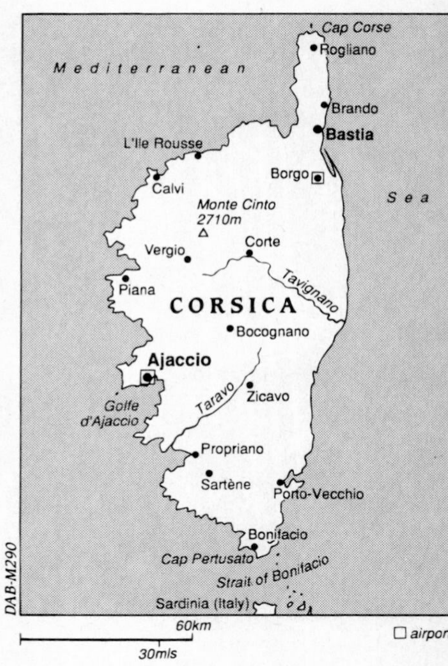

source of food, including its famous lobster. Freshwater fish abound in the interior and, as is to be expected, the *maquis* is game country. The aromatic herbs and berries add a particularly piquant flavour to the meat. Among the game available, *sanglier* and *marcassin* – young and older wild boar – turn up in season either roasted, stewed in a *daube* of red wine, or with a highly spiced local sauce *pibronata*. Sheep and goats are plentiful. Pigs, fed on chestnuts, are common at the Corsican table and they make an unusually flavoured ham. The extremes of the Corsican climate limit the variety of vegetables available. The Corsicans like hot and strong flavours that use even more herbs than are used in Provence. They like to shock with hot peppers and strong spices. A fish soup called *dziminu*, much like *bouillabaise* but much hotter, is made with peppers and pimentos. Inland freshwater fish is usually grilled and the local eels, called *capone*, are cut up and grilled on a spit over a charcoal fire. A peppered and smoked ham, called *prizzutu*, resembles the Italian *prosciutto*, but with chestnut flavour added. A favourite between-meal snack is *figatelli*, a sausage made of dried and spiced pork with liver. Placed between slices of a special bread, these are grilled over a wood fire. Red wine is available in abundance, but white and rosé are also produced on the island.

SOCIAL PROFILE

FOOD & DRINK: With the exception of China, France has a more varied and developed cuisine than any other country. There is almost complete unanimity of opinion that French food is the best in the Western world. The vegetables, cheese, butter and fruit eaten in a French restaurant are usually fresh, although with the mushrooming of cafeterias and fast-food establishments, quality is no longer always reliable. The simple, delicious cooking for which France is famous is found in the old-fashioned bistro and restaurant. There are two distinct styles of eating in France. One is of course 'gastronomy' *(haute cuisine)*, widely known and honoured as a cult with rituals, rules and taboos. It is rarely practised in daily life, partly because of the cost and the time which must be devoted to it. The other is family-style cooking, often just as delicious as its celebrated counterpart. It is the style of cooking experienced daily by the majority of French people and is the result of a carefully maintained family tradition.

Almost all restaurants offer two types of meal: *à la carte* (extensive choice for each course and more expensive) and *le menu* (a set meal at a fixed price with dishes selected from the full *à la carte* menu). At simple restaurants the same cutlery will be used for all courses. The tourist office publishes a guide to restaurants in Paris and the Ile-de-France. Many restaurants close for a month during the summer, and one day a week. It is always wise to check that a restaurant is open, particularly on a Sunday. Costs are not necessarily high. Generally speaking, mealtimes in France are strictly observed. Lunch is as a rule served from noon to 1330, dinner usually from 2000 to 2130, but the larger the city the later the dining hour.

Dishes include *tournedos* (small steaks ringed with

bacon), *châteaubriand, entrecôte* (rib steak) served with *béarnaise* (delicate sauce with egg base), *gigot de pre-salé* (leg of lamb roasted or broiled) served with *flageolets* (light green beans) or *pommes dauphines* (deep-fried mashed potato puffs). Other dishes include *brochettes* (combinations of cubed meat or seafood on skewers, alternating with mushrooms, onions or tomatoes) or *ratatouille niçoise* (stew of courgettes, tomatoes and aubergines braised with garlic in olive oil); *pot-au-feu* (beef boiled with vegetables and served with coarse salt) and *blanquette de veau* (veal stew with mushrooms in a white wine/cream sauce). In the north of France (Nord/Pas de Calais and Picardy) fish and shellfish are the star features in menus – oysters, *moules* (mussels), *coques* (cockles) and *crevettes* (shrimps) are extremely popular. In Picardy duck pâtés and *Fficelle picardy* (ham and mushroom pancake) are popular. In the Champagne-Ardenne region there are the hams of Rheims and de Sanglier (wild boar). Among the fish specialities in this area are *écrevisses* (crayfish) and *brochets* (pike). Alsace and Lorraine are the lands of *choucroute* and *kugelhof* (oven-baked buns), *quiche lorraine* and *tarte flambée* (onion tart). Spicy and distinctive sauces are the hallmark of Breton food, and shellfish is a speciality of the region, particularly *homard à l'americaine* (lobster with cream sauce). Lyon, the main city of the Rhône Valley, is the heartland of French cuisine, though the food is often more rich than elaborate. A speciality of this area is *quenelles de brochet* (pounded pike formed into sausage shapes and usually served with a rich crayfish sauce). Bordeaux rivals Lyon as gastronomic capital of France. Aquitaine cuisine is based on goosefat. A reference to 'Perigord' will indicate a dish containing truffles. Basque chickens are specially reared. In the Pyrénées, especially around Toulouse, you will find salmon and *cassoulet*, a hearty dish with beans and preserved meat. General de Gaulle once asked, with a certain amount of pride, how it was possible to rule a country which produced 365 different kinds of cheese; some of the better known are Camembert, Brie, Roquefort, Reblochon and blue cheeses from Auvergne and Bresse. Desserts include: *soufflé grand-marnier, oeufs à la neige* (meringues floating on custard), *mille feuilles* (layers of flaky pastry and custard cream), *Paris-Brest* (a large puff-pastry with hazelnut cream), *ganache* (chocolate cream biscuit) and fruit tarts and flans.

For more information on the specialities from the various regions of France, consult the regional entries above.

Drink: Countless books have been written on the subject of French wine, and space does not not here permit any major addition to the vast corpus of literature, which ranges from the scientific and learned to the emotional and anecdotal. Wine is by far the most popular alcoholic drink in France, and the choice will vary according to region. Cheap wine (*vin ordinaire*), worth a try at FFr4 upwards, can be either very palatable or undrinkable, but there is no certain way of establishing which this is likely to be before drinking. Wines are classified into AC (*Appellation Controllée*), VDQS (*Vin delimité de qualité superieure*), *Vin de Pays* and *Vin de Table*. There are several wine-producing regions in the country; some of the more notable are Bordeaux, Burgundy, Loire, Rhône and Champagne. In elegant restaurants the wine list will be separate from the main menu, but in less opulent establishments will be printed on the back or along the side of the *carte*. The waiter will usually be glad to advise an appropriate choice. In expensive restaurants this will be handled by a *sommelier* or wine steward. If in doubt, try the house wine; this will usually be less expensive and will always be the owner's pride. Coffee is always served after the meal (not with the desert), and will always be black, in small cups, unless a *café au lait* (or *à crème*) is requested. The bill (*l'addition*) will not be presented until it is asked for, even if clients sit and talk for half an hour after they have finished eating. Liqueurs such as Chartreuse, Framboise and Genepi (an unusual liqueur made from a local aromatic plant) are available. Many of these liqueurs, such as *eau de vie* and *calvados* (applejack) are very strong and should be treated with respect, particularly after a few glasses of wine. A good rule of thumb is to look around and see what the locals are drinking. Spirit measures are usually doubles unless a *baby* is specifically asked for. There is also a huge variety of aperitifs available. A typically French drink is *pastis*, such as Ricard and Pernod. The region of Nord Pas de Calais and Picardy does not produce wine, but brews beer and cider. Alsace is said to brew the best beer in France but fruity white wines, such as Riesling, Traminer and Sylvaner, and fine fruit liqueurs, such as Kirsch and Framboise, are produced in this area. The wines from the Champagne region of the Montagne de Reims district are firm and delicate (Vevenay Verzy), or full bodied and fully flavoured (Bouzy and Ambonnay). The legal age for drinking alcohol in a bar/café is 18. Minors are allowed to go into bars if accompanied by an adult but they will not be served alcohol. Hours of opening depend on the proprietor but generally bars in major towns and resorts are open throughout the day; some may still be open at 0200. Smaller towns tend to shut earlier. There are also all-night bars and cafés.

NIGHTLIFE: In Paris nightclubs and discos there is sometimes no entry fee although drinks are more expensive. Alternatively, the entrance price sometimes includes a *consommation* of one drink. As an alternative to a nightclub, there are many late-night bars. Tourist offices publish an annual and monthly diary of events available free of charge. Several guides are also available which give information about entertainments and sightseeing in the capital. Some of the best are *Pariscope, 7 à Paris, Officiel des Spectacles* and the English-language *Passion*. In the provinces the French generally spend the night eating and drinking, although in the more popular tourist areas there will be discos and dances. All weekend festivals in summer in the rural areas are a good form of evening entertainment. There are over 130 public casinos in the country.

SHOPPING: Special purchases include laces, crystal glass, cheeses, coffee, and, of course, wines, spirits and liqueurs. Arques, the home of Crystal D'Arques, is situated between St Omer and Calais, *en route* to most southern destinations. Lille, the main town of French Flanders, is known for its textiles, particularly fine lace. Most towns have fruit and vegetable markets on Saturdays. Hypermarkets, enormous supermarkets which sell everything from foodstuffs and clothes to hi-fi equipment and furniture, are widespread in France. They tend to be situated just outside a town and all have parking facilities. **Shopping hours**: Department Stores are open 0900-1830/1930 Monday to Saturday. Food shops are open 0700-1830/1930. Some food shops (particularly bakers) are open on Sunday mornings, in which case they will probably close on Mondays. Many shops close all day or half-day Monday. Hypermarkets are normally open until 2100 or 2200. Most towns have a fruit/vegetable market on Saturday.

SPORT: Almost every kind of sport, for spectators and participants, is available in the country, ranging from the thrills and passion of an international **rugby** match to a quiet game of **boules** in a sleepy village square. **Tennis** facilities are widespread, although they may be reasonably expensive. **Riding** is very popular. **Golf** courses are becoming common, particularly in the south. Game **shooting** permits are required from local *gendarmerie*. **Horseracing** is a popular spectator sport, as are rugby (played to highest standards) and **football**. **Sailing** and **boating** is available in the English Channel, Bay of Biscay, Riviera and major rivers (Loire, Rhône, Sâone). Cruising boats may be rented on the Rhône, Canal du Midi and Burgundy Canal. Yachts proliferate, especially in the south. There are thousands of miles of carefully marked **hiking** trails in France. They are known as Sentiers de Grande Randonnée, and are generally marked on maps. **Winter sports:** The French and Swiss Alps contain some of the best **ski resorts** in the world. There are over 480km (300 miles) of ski *piste*, over 150 ski lifts, innumerable ski schools and quality resort facilities. All the major resorts offer skiing package holidays. The season runs from early December to the end of April. The height of the season is during February and March, as is reflected in the higher prices. (See *Resorts & Excursions* for further details.) The French Government Tourist Office will also be able to supply a wide range of literature on this subject.

SPECIAL EVENTS: The following is a selection of the major festivals and other special events celebrated during 1993 in France. For a complete list, contact the French Government Tourist Office which publishes a handbook giving full details of the wide range of festivals and special events in France during 1993/4; free copies are available on request.

Apr 29-May 9 '93 *Foire de Paris*. **May 13-24** *Cannes Film Festival*. **May 24-Jun 6** *Rolland Garros International Tennis Tournament*, Paris. **Jun 11-20** *Paris Air Show*. **Jun 19-20*** *Le Mans* (24-hour motor race). **July** *Aix-en-Provence Festival*. **Jul 3-25** *Tour de France; Avignon Festival*. **Jul 4** *Grand Prix de France*, Magny-Cours Circuit. **Jul 14** *Bastille Day*. **Mid-Jul to beg of Aug** *Lorient Celtic Festival*. **Aug-Oct (1st Sunday)** *Grand Prix de l'Arc de Triomphe* (horse races), Paris.

Note [*]: Throughout the year there are several motor racing events in Le Mans, as well as trade fairs in various parts of the country; there are also many local festivals and fairs (which usually preserve their original agricultural purpose).

SOCIAL CONVENTIONS: Handshaking and, more familiarly, kissing both cheeks, are the usual form of greeting. The form of personal address is simply *Monsieur* or *Madame* without a surname and it may take time to get on first-name terms. At more formal dinners it is the most important guest or host who gives the signal to start eating. Meal times are often a long, leisurely experience. Casual wear is common but the French are renowned for their stylish sportswear and dress sense. Social functions, some clubs, casinos and exclusive restaurants warrant more formal attire. Evening wear is normally specified where required. Topless sunbathing is tolerated on most beaches but naturism is restricted to certain beaches – local tourist offices will advise where these are. Smoking is prohibited on public transport and in cinemas and theatres. Tobacconists display a red sign in the form of a double cone, usually located in cafés. A limited choice of brands can be found in restaurants and bars. **Tipping:** 12-15% service charge is normally added to the bill in hotels, restaurants and bars, but it is customary to leave small change with the payment; more if the service has been exceptional. Other services such as washroom attendants, beauticians, hairdressers and cinema ushers. Taxi drivers expect 10-15% of the meter fare.

BUSINESS PROFILE

ECONOMY: France has the fourth strongest capitalist economy in the world, after the USA, Japan and Germany. It has a wide industrial and commercial base, covering everything from agriculture to light and heavy industrial concerns, the most advanced technology and a burgeoning service sector. France is Western Europe's leading agricultural nation with over half of the country's land area devoted to farming. Wheat is the most important crop; maize, sugar beet and barley are also produced in large quantities. The country is self-sufficient in these (which are produced in sufficient surplus for major exports) and the majority of other common crops. The livestock industry is also expanding rapidly. As is well known, France is one of the world's leading wine producers. Despite criticism from some quarters (not least Britain) that French agriculture is inefficient, the sector has regularly turned in good profit margins and a sound export performance. With the emergence of newly industrialised countries, especially the 'Tiger economies' of the Pacific basin, France's share of the world market for industrial products has declined in recent years. Nonetheless, French companies retain a strong presence in many industries, particularly steel, motor vehicles, aircraft, mechanical and electrical engineering, textiles, chemicals and food processing. In advanced industrial sectors, France has a nuclear power industry sufficiently large to meet over half of the country's energy requirements (coal mining, once important, is in terminal decline), and is a world leader in computing and telecommunications. Service industries have not developed as far as in Britain with the exception of tourism, which has long been a major foreign currency earner, although the financial services industry has undergone rapid growth in the last few years. The Government has initiated a programme of privatisation to slim down the country's large industrial public sector. Oil and finance companies (including some of the banks nationalised in the 1980s) have been sold off, although the programme as a whole is not as aggressive or widespread as in Britain. France was a founder member of the European Community and has benefited greatly from its participation.

BUSINESS: Business people should wear conservative clothes. Prior appointments are expected and the use of calling cards usual. While a knowledge of French is a distinct advantage in business dealings, it is considered impolite to start a conversation in French and then have to revert to English. Business meetings tend to be formal and business decisions are only taken after lengthy discussion with many facts and figures to back up sales presentation. Business entertaining is usually in restaurants. Avoid mid-July to mid-September for business visits. **Office hours:** Generally 0900-1200 and 1400-1800 Monday to Friday.

COMMERCIAL INFORMATION: The following organisations can offer advice: Chambre de Commerce et d'Industrie de Paris, 27 avenue de Friedland, 75382 Paris, Cedex 08. Tel: (1) 42 89 70 00. Fax: (1) 42 89 78 68. Telex: 650100; *or*

Franco-British Chamber of Commerce, 10 rue de Longchamps, 75016 Paris. Tel. (1) 44 05 32 88. Fax: (1) 44 05 32 99.

CONFERENCES/CONVENTIONS: Paris is the world's leading conference city (in 1986 it hosted 358 conventions), with the total amount of seating available (over 100,000 seats) exceeding that of any rival city. Also in demand are the Riviera towns of Nice and Cannes (the Acropolis Centre in Nice being the largest single venue in Europe); other centres are Lyon,

Strasbourg and Marseille. The Business Travel Club (CFTAR) is a government-sponsored association of cities, departments, hotels, convention centres and other organisations interested in providing meeting facilities and incentives; it has over 80 members. Enquiries should be made through the French Government Tourist Office, which in several cities has a special department for business travel; these include London, Frankfurt, Düsseldorf, Milan, Madrid and Chicago.

HISTORY & GOVERNMENT

HISTORY: After the disintegration of the Roman Empire in the 5th century, Gaul was settled by Germanic peoples from the east. After the collapse of the Visigothic Merovingian kingdom, Gaul in the 8th and 9th centuries became the heart of Charlemagne's Frankish empire, which stretched from the Pyrénées to the Baltic. During the following centuries the area under the control of the French kings gradually increased, although it was not until the reign of Louis VI (1108-1137) that royal authority became more than an empty theory in some areas of France, whose rulers were his vassals in name only. Among the most powerful of these were the Dukes of Normandy who had, by the mid-12th century, acquired England and western France. In 1328, however, the direct line of the Capetian royal house became extinct: one of the claimants to the throne was Edward III of England. The resulting intermittent conflict, known as the Hundred Years' War, was not resolved until the final English defeat in 1453. The period of French recovery is associated with the reign of the astute Louis XI (1460-1483): by the time of his death the area of France was much as it is today. During the late 15th and 16th centuries, France was again distracted by foreign adventures, including the Italian Wars and several other grandiose pan-European schemes initiated by François I; and internal troubles (the Wars of Religion). This latter conflict was ended by the accession of the gifted Henry IV, a Protestant-turned-Catholic. Henry was assassinated in 1610, but his work of building up the power of the French state was continued under the administrations firstly of Cardinals Richelieu and Mazarin and subsequently the long reign of the 'sun king', Louis XIV (1643-1715), by which time the country had replaced Spain as the major European power. The 18th century was a period of great colonial expansion, and France again became involved in conflicts with England, this time over their possessions in the New World. The reign of Louis XV (1715-74), was in general a time of great prosperity in France but the age also witnessed a widening gap between rich and poor. The inequality of the taxation system (in particular the aristocratic and clerical exemption from the *taille*), the lack of political representation for the increasingly wealthy middle class and the inefficiency and profligacy of central government were but three of the underlying causes of the French Revolution of 1789, possibly the most significant event in European history, which overthrew Louis XVI. One of the great issues, the equality of the individual before the law, proved a decisive and divisive issue in Europe countries for the next century. Despite this, it was essentially a bourgeois revolution, as soon became apparent from the composition of the new government, based on an elected single chamber with the King as a near-impotent head of state. The government of the last years of the 18th century was deeply unstable, unpopular and impoverished, and was overthrown in 1799 by a rising army commander named Napoleon Bonaparte. After five years as consul, Napoleon was declared Emperor and embarked on a military campaign to establish a French empire in Europe. Defeat at Trafalgar at the hands of Nelson in 1805 left the sea in the hands of the British, but on land Napoleon scored a series of stunning victories in the next seven years to defeat the Prussians, Austrians and Russians. By 1812 the French empire extended beyond France to take in northwest Italy and the Low Countries, while the Confederation of the Rhine, Switzerland, Spain and the Grand Duchy of Warsaw were dependent states. Napoleon's fortunes went into decline after the ill-fated invasion of Russia in April 1812 in which 600,000 men – the largest army ever assembled – were driven back westwards six months later. Napoleon was forced into exile, his armies and empire dismantled by the Austrians and British. A final fling in 1815, was put down at the Battle of Waterloo. The monarchy was restored and remained until the uprising of 1848 led by radical students and workers. Although the insurrection was crushed within a few months the monarchy was again overthrown and the Second Republic declared. Four years later the army intervened and instituted the Second Empire with Louis Napoleon (a descendent of the first Emperor Napoleon) as emperor, seizing dictatorial power. The Second Empire (1852-1870) further expanded France's colonial possessions, while at home the repression was eased during the 1860s; in 1870 the regime obtained a popular mandate by referendum. France now faced a new enemy in the emerging power of Germany. The Franco-Prussian War of 1870-71 ended in defeat for the French and the annexation of Alsace-Lorraine by the Germans. The Third Republic, which was established in France after 1871, maintained an uneasy peace with its new powerful neighbour and sought succour in the *Entente Cordiale* with Britain. As events proved, the elaborate diplomatic designs of the late 19th and early 20th century in Europe were too fragile to guarantee peaceful co-existence in Europe. The interlocking network of treaties and alliances finally collapsed in August 1914 following the assassination of Grand Duke Ferdinand in Serbia. France recovered Alsace-Lorraine as a result of The Treaty of Versailles and introduced a new electoral system – still under the Third Republic – based on proportional representation. The inter-war years saw the election of a series of socialist governments and an increasing preoccupation with Germany and the deteriorating European situation. After the German invasion of Poland in 1939, France declared war on Germany. The Third Republic collapsed with the German invasion of 1940, when the notorious Vichy government capitulated and the country endured four years of Nazi occupation. In 1946 the Fourth Republic was established, but brought to an end in 1958 as a result of the Algerian crisis. The Fifth Republic has lasted from 1958 up until the present day. This constitution is characterised by the strong executive powers vested in the presidency, typified by the first holder of the office, General de Gaulle, the wartime leader of the anti-Nazi government in exile. The Fifth Republic was almost overthrown in 1968 by a radical alliance of students and industrial workers. By way of reaction, conservative presidents and centre-right majorities in the National Assembly governed France throughout the 1970s. In 1981, the Socialist François Mitterand won the presidential election, the first time the party's candidate had been victorious. In May 1988, he was re-elected for a second 7-year term. Under 'Ton-ton' (Uncle) Mitterand the French have pursued their customary activist and occasionally maverick foreign policy. There have been several military interventions in Africa, a counter-insurgency campaign in New Caledonia, and a historically based involvement in Lebanon. In 1991, the French also contributed a sizeable military force to the Gulf War allies. France's major foreign commitment, however, is to the European Community, and especially relations with Germany which may be considered the driving force behind the EC's progress towards economic and political harmonisation. The reunification of its powerful neighbour has, however, been viewed with equanimity in Paris. Back at home, Mitterand is looking to shore up the position of his Socialist Party prior to the next assembly elections in March 1993 and presidential poll in 1995. The appointment of a woman Prime Minister, Edith Cresson, in May 1991, was seen as an astute move; unfortunately, within months Madame Cresson had become, according to a series of opinion polls, the most unpopular premier in the history of the Fifth republic. Amid protests by farmers at Government and EC agricultural policy and a wave of strikes and industrial disputes in the public sector, Madame Cresson was forced to resign at the end of March 1992. President Mitterrand had to cast around for a successor. His first choice, the European Commission President Jacques Delors, turned the job down. Mitterand eventually settled on finance minister Pierre Bérégovoy. The new premier has had some success in arresting the recession which has threatened the French economy from the middle of 1991 but has failed to quell the more restive sections of the workforce. The Government also had to cope with a strong cross-party movement against French ratification of the Maastricht Treaty which sets out the next phase of EC integration. The vote, in October 1992, went narrowly in favour. The French government's desire not to upset its powerful farming lobby lie behind the continuing failure to reach a settlement at the Uruguay round of talks on GATT (General Agreement on Tariffs and Trade). Failure to resolve the outstanding conflict (which is mainly between the US and the EC) could have very serious consequences for the world economy.

GOVERNMENT: The President – who has considerable executive as well as coercive power – is elected by direct popular vote for a 7-year term. Legislative power is held by a bicameral parliament. The President is currently François Mitterand.

CLIMATE

A temperate climate in the north; northeastern areas have a more continental climate with warm summers and colder winters. Rainfall is distributed throughout the year with some snow likely in winter. The Jura Mountains have an alpine climate. Lorraine, sheltered by bordering hills, has a relatively mild climate.

Mediterranean climate in the south; mountains are cooler with heavy snows in winter.

The Atlantic influences the climate of the western coastal areas from the Loire to the Basque region; the weather is temperate and relatively mild with rainfall distributed throughout the year. Summers can be very hot and sunny. Inland areas are also mild and the French slopes of the Pyrénées are reputed for their sunshine record.

Mediterranean climate exists on the Riviera, Provence and Roussillon. Weather in the French Alps is variable. Continental weather is present in Auvergne, Burgundy and Rhône Valley. Very strong winds (such as the *Mistral*) can occur throughout the entire region.

Required clothing: European, according to season.

PARIS France (52m)

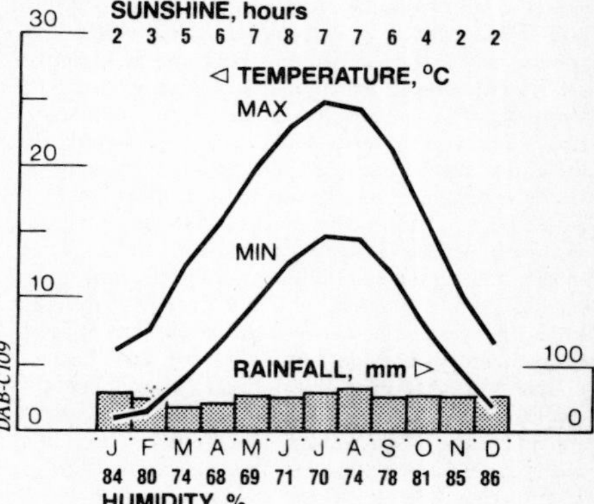

GRENOBLE France (223m)

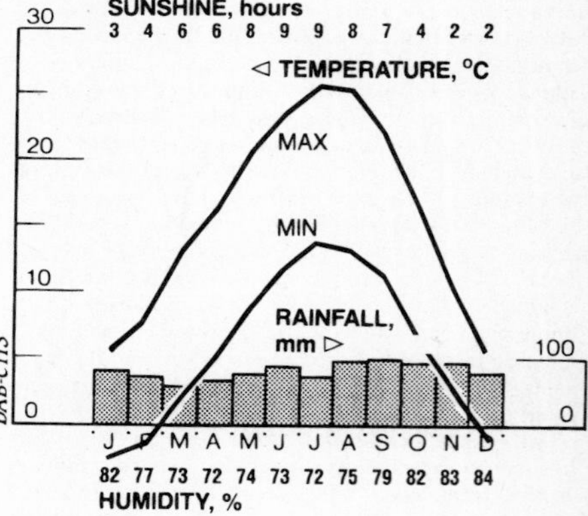

STRASBOURG France (149m)

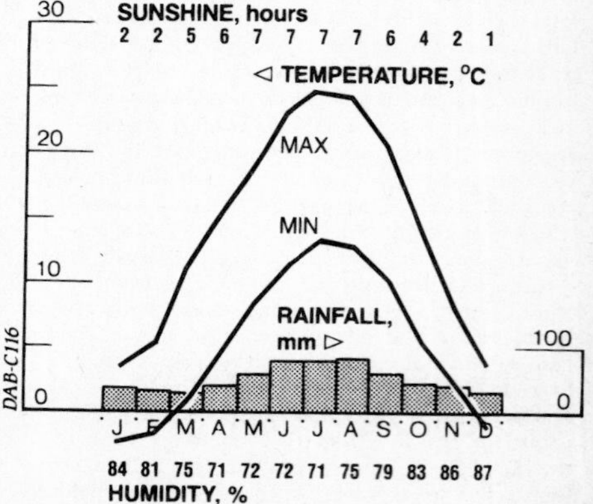

NICE France (5m)

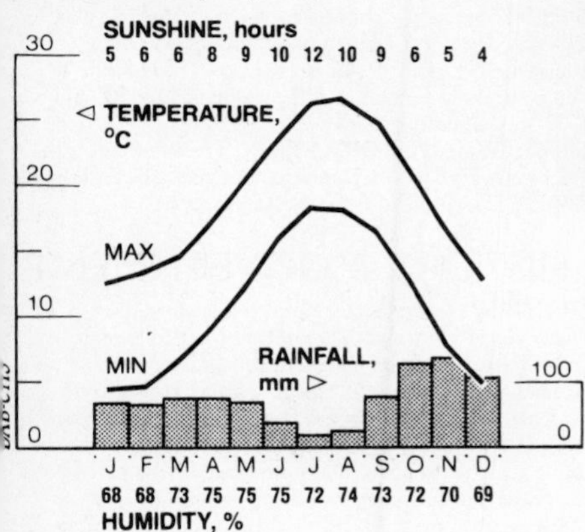

BORDEAUX France (47m)

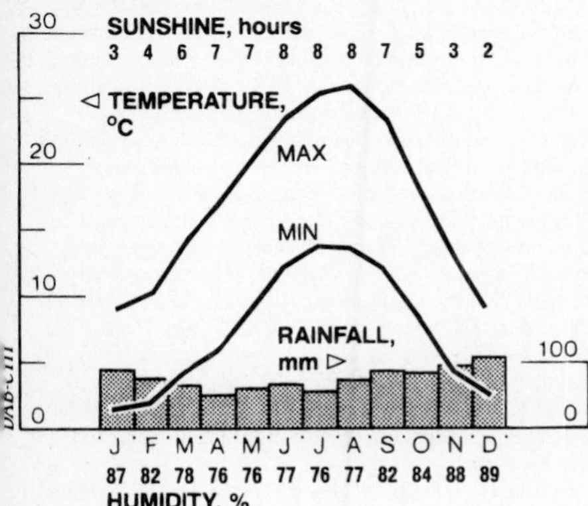

CHERBOURG France (8m)

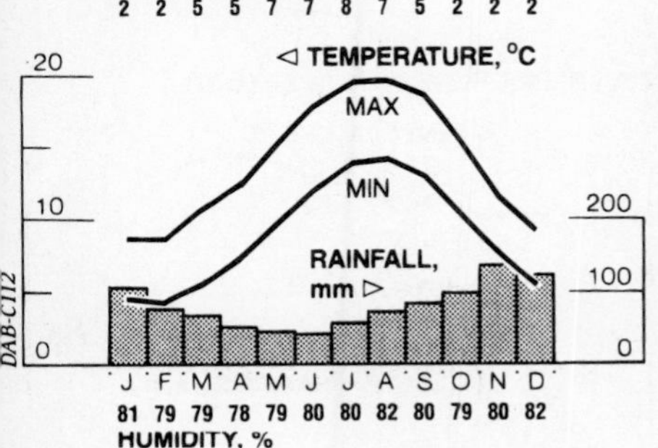

LYON France (200m)

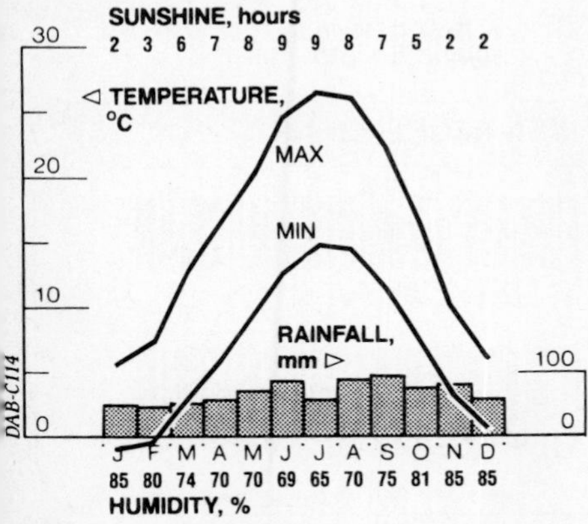

FRENCH GUIANA

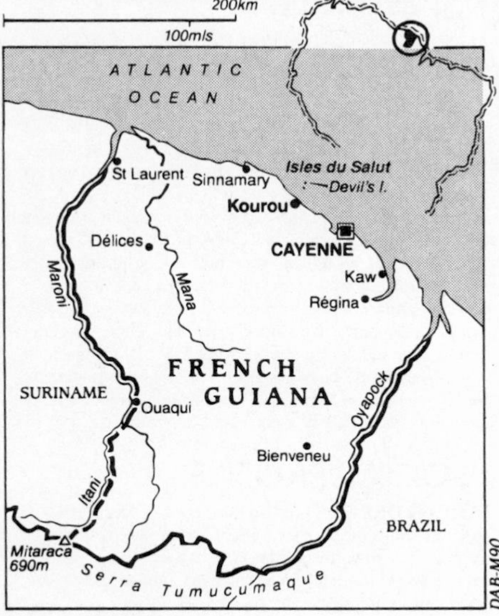

□ international airport

Location: South America, northeast coast.

Délegation Régionale du Tourisme pour la Guyane
BP 7008
97307 Cayenne, French Guiana
Tel: 318 491. Fax: 305 222. Telex: 910532.
French Guiana Tourist Bureau
26 rue du 4 Septembre
75002 Paris, France
Tel: (1) 42 68 11 07. Telex: 282445.
French Consulate General
21 Cromwell Road
London SW7 2DQ
Tel: (071) 581 5292. Fax: (071) 823 8665.
British Consulate
16 avenue Président
Monnerville
Cayenne, French Guiana
Tel: 311 034. Fax: 304 094. Telex: NCH 910365 FG.

AREA: 90,000 sq km (34,750 sq miles).
POPULATION: 114,808 (1990).
POPULATION DENSITY: 0.8 per sq km.
CAPITAL: Cayenne. **Population:** 41,637 (1990).
GEOGRAPHY: French Guiana is situated on the northeast coast of South America and is bordered by Brazil to the south and the east and by Suriname to the west. The southern *Serra Tumucumaque* is part of the eastern frontier, whilst the rest is formed by the River Clapoque. Suriname is to the west along the River Macromi-Itani and to the north is the Atlantic coastline. Along the coast runs a belt of flat marshy land behind which the land rises to higher slopes and plains or savannah. The interior is comprised of equatorial jungle. Off the rugged coast lie the Iles du Salut and Devil's Islands. Cayenne, the capital and chief port, is on the island of the same name at the mouth of the Cayenne River.
LANGUAGE: The official language is French, though most of the population speak a Creole *patois*. English is widely spoken.
RELIGION: Roman Catholic.
TIME: GMT - 3.
ELECTRICITY: 220/127 volts AC, 50Hz.
COMMUNICATIONS: Telephone: IDD available. Country code: 594. Calls out of French Guiana must be made through the international operator. **Fax:** Facilities are just starting to be introduced; check for availability. **Telex:** There are facilities in Cayenne. **Press:** The daily newspapers include *France Guyane* and *La Presse de Guyane*. There are no English-language newspapers.
BBC World Service and Voice of America frequencies: From time to time these change. See the section *How to Use this Book* for more information.

BBC:				
MHz	17.72	11.78	9.590	5.975
Voice of America:				
MHz	15.21	11.74	9.815	6.030

PASSPORT/VISA

Regulations and requirements may be subject to change at short notice, and you are advised to contact the appropriate diplomatic or consular authority before finalising travel arrangements. Details of these may be found at the head of this country's entry. Any numbers in the chart refer to the footnotes below.

	Passport Required?	Visa Required?	Return Ticket Required?
Full British	Yes	No	Yes
BVP	Not valid	-	-
Australian	Yes	Yes	Yes
Canadian	No/2	No/4	Yes
USA	No/2	No/4	Yes
Other EC	1	No/3	Yes
Japanese	No/2	No/4	Yes

Note: Regulations are liable to change at short notice and travellers are advised to check before departure.
PASSPORTS: Valid passport required by all except:
(a) [1] nationals of Belgium, France, Germany, Greece, Italy, Luxembourg, The Netherlands, Portugal and Spain with ID or a passport that has expired within the past 5 years (other EC nationals *do* require a passport);
(b) nationals of Monaco;
(c) [2] nationals of Canada, Japan and the USA providing they are in possession of documents proving identity, are staying for less than 3 months and are travelling as *bona fide* tourists.
British Visitors Passport: Not accepted.
VISAS: Required by all except nationals of:
(a) [3] EC countries (for visits up to 3 months);
(b) Andorra, Austria, Cyprus, Czechoslovakia, Hungary, Liechtenstein, Malta, Monaco, New Zealand, Norway, Poland, San Marino, Switzerland and the Vatican City;
(c) [4] Canada, Japan and the US, providing that the length of visit does not exceed 90 days, and that proof of identity can be produced.
Types of visa: Tourist or Business.
Temporary residence: Apply to French Consulate or Embassy.
Validity: Assessed on individual requirements.
Application to: French Consulate (or Consular Section at French Embassy). For addresses, see *France* entry above.
Application requirements: (a) 3 completed application forms. (b) 3 photos. (c) Travel documentation. (d) Evidence of means of support.
Working days required: Visas are usually issued on the same day, but there can be a delay of up to 1 month depending on the applicant's nationality.

MONEY

Currency: French Franc (FFr) = 100 centimes. Banknotes are in denominations of FFr500, 200, 100, 50 and 20. Coins are in denominations of FFr10, 5, 2 and 1, and 50, 20, 10 and 5 centimes.
Currency exchange: The Banque de la Guyane will exchange money (not on Saturdays). There are no exchange facilities at the airport.
Credit cards: Credit cards are not generally accepted, but check with your credit card company for details of merchant acceptability and other services which may be available.
Travellers cheques: These are only accepted in a few places in Cayenne and Kourou.
Currency exchange rates: As for France.
Currency restrictions: As for France.
Banking hours: 0745-1130 and 1500-1700 Monday to Friday.

DUTY FREE

As for France.

PUBLIC HOLIDAYS

Public holidays observed in French Guiana are as follows:
Apr 9-12 '93 Easter. **May 1** Labour Day. **May 20** Ascension Day. **May 31** Whit Monday. **Jul 14** National

Day. **Nov 11** Armistice Day. **Dec 25** Christmas Day. **Jan 1 '94** New Year's Day. **Feb/Mar*** Lenten Carnival.
Note: [*] Check with the Tourist Bureau or Consulate for exact dates.

HEALTH

Regulations and requirements may be subject to change at short notice, and you are advised to contact your doctor well in advance of your intended date of departure. Any numbers in the chart refer to the footnotes below.

	Special Precautions?	Certificate Required?
Yellow Fever	Yes	1
Cholera	No	No
Typhoid & Polio	Yes	-
Malaria	2	-
Food & Drink	3	-

[1]: A yellow fever vaccination certificate is required from travellers over one year of age coming from all countries.
[2]: Malaria risk, predominantly in the malignant *falciparum* form, exists throughout the year throughout French Guiana. Resistance to chloroquine has been reported.
[3]: Mains water is normally heavily chlorinated, and whilst relatively safe, may cause mild abdominal upsets. Bottled water is available and is advised for the first few weeks of the stay. Drinking water outside main cities and towns is likely to be contaminated and sterilisation is considered essential. Milk is unpasteurised and should be boiled. Powdered or tinned milk is available and is advised, but make sure that it is reconstituted with pure water. Avoid dairy products which are likely to have been made from unboiled milk. Local meat, poultry, seafood, fruit and vegetables are generally considered safe to eat.
Rabies is present. For those at high risk vaccination before arrival should be considered. If you are bitten abroad seek medical advice without delay. For more information consult the *Health* section at the back of the book.
Health care: There are medical facilities in Cayenne but very little elsewhere. Full health insurance is essential.

TRAVEL - International

AIR: French Guiana's national airline is *Air Guyane*, though is does only offer interal services.
Approximate flight time: From *London* to Cayenne is 11 hours 30 minutes.
International airport: *Cayenne (CAY)* (Rochambeau), 17km (11 miles) southwest of the city. Taxi to city, or hotel courtesy coaches are available. Limited facilities at the airport include currency exchange and car rental.
SEA: Cayenne is a regular port of call for ships of *Compagnie Generale Maritime* (France).
ROAD: A road runs along the coast from Guyana through Suriname to French Guiana, but it is impassable during the rainy season. At present, rebel activity in Eastern Suriname has cut off this route. There is an all-weather road connecting Cayenne with St Laurent and it is possible to drive from Paramaibo to Cayenne. The Cayenne district is served by a good road system. See below *documentation*.

TRAVEL - Internal

AIR: *Air Guyane* serves the interior of the country from Cayenne. Bookings may be made via *Air France (AF)*.
SEA/RIVER: There are numerous coastal and river transport services. Contact local authorities for information.
ROAD: Road along coast from Cayenne to Kourou and beyond, but travel can be difficult during rainy season.
Bus: Services operate along coast. **Taxi:** Available in Cayenne. **Car hire:** Available at airport or Cayenne.
Documentation: An International Driving Permit is recommended, although it is not legally required.

ACCOMMODATION

HOTELS: Since French Guiana was chosen as a site for European space development, a number of well-appointed air-conditioned hotels have been built. Cayenne, Kourou, Saint Laurent du Maroni and Mairipasoula all offer adequate, comfortable accommodation, but prices are higher than in Guyana or Suriname.
CAMPING/CARAVANNING: Inland camping only, sleeping on hammocks strung from the walls of a *carbet* (a jungle version of a shack).

RESORTS & EXCURSIONS

Cayenne: The capital and chief port. Points of interest include the Jesuit-built residence of the Prefect in the *Place de Grenoble*, the *Canal Laussant* (built in 1777), and the *Botanical Gardens*. There are also bathing beaches, the best of which is *Montjoly*.
Kourou: The main *French Space Centre* was built here which makes Kourou something of a European enclave. There are several restaurants and two good hotels. Tourist attractions include bathing, fishing and the *Sporting and Aero Club*.
Iles du Salut: These islands include the notorious *'Devil's Island'* where political prisoners were held. There is a hotel (an ex-mess hall for the prison warders) on **Isle Royale.**
Haut-Maroni and Haut-Oyapoc: Visits to Amerindian villages in these areas are restricted; permission must be obtained from the Préfecture in **Cayenne** before arrival in the country.

SOCIAL PROFILE

FOOD & DRINK: There is a fairly good selection of restaurants and hotel dining rooms offering a number of different cuisines. The majority of them are in Cayenne although French and Continental, Vietnamese, Chinese, Creole and Indonesian restaurants can be found elsewhere.
NIGHTLIFE: There are nightclubs in Cayenne, Kourou and St Laurent du Maroni. Cayenne also has cinemas featuring French-language films. A cinema can also be found in Kourou.
SHOPPING: Within the past few years a great many new boutiques have opened offering a wide range of merchandise. Good buys are basketry, hammocks, pottery, wood sculpture and gold jewellery.
SPORT: Fishing: Sea fishing is good from rocks; canoes are also available. **Swimming:** Safe around Ile de Cayenne and some hotels have pools. **Water-skiing:** Facilities are available for water-skiing in Cayenne. **Tennis:** There are courts in Cayenne and some hotels have courts. **Pioneering/hiking:** There are river trips and treks into the interior and jungle shelters are available for overnight stops. A special permit is necessary from the Préfecture in Cayenne.
SOCIAL CONVENTIONS: Conservative casual wear is suitable almost everywhere. On beaches, modest beachwear is preferred. Normal social courtesies should be adhered to.
Tipping: In hotels and restaurants a 10% tip is usual. Taxi drivers are not tipped.

BUSINESS PROFILE

ECONOMY: French Guiana's economy is heavily dependent on that of France itself, especially for imports of food and manufactured goods. It also receives large injections of development aid. Most of the workforce is engaged in the agricultural sector, principally forestry and fisheries. The country has valuable reserves of timber, but these have yet to be exploited fully because of lack of investment and poor infrastructure, especially roads. The development of mineral resources, which are thought to be present in commercially significant quantities, suffers from the same considerations. Tourism is similarly affected but has shown steady growth. One notable asset, acquired by virtue of French Guiana's geographical position near the Equator, is the European Space Agency satellite launch facility at Kourou which has brought some economic benefits to the country. French Guiana has a vast trade imbalance, with exports exceeding imports by a factor of 12. Other than France (which controls 60% of the export business to French Guiana), Trinidad and Tobago, the United States, Germany and Japan are the country's major trading partners. Trade with the UK is insignificant.
BUSINESS: Lightweight suits are required. English will be understood by practically everyone, although a working knowledge of French may be of assistance. The best time to visit is August to September. **Office hours:** 0800-1300 and 1500-1800 Monday to Friday.
COMMERCIAL INFORMATION: The following organisation can offer advice: Chambre de Commerce de la Guyane, BP49, 97321 Cayenne. Tel: 303 000. Telex: 910537.

HISTORY & GOVERNMENT

HISTORY: French Guiana was first discovered by Europeans in 1496, and the French first settled there in 1604. There have been numerous changes in control of the area, alternating between France, England, Holland and Portugal, and the territory was finally confirmed as French in 1817. The colony enjoyed a brief period of prosperity in the 1850s when gold was discovered, but otherwise has been in decline. French Guiana was finally given Overseas Department status in 1946. In the 1970s, demonstrations about the economic situation and French neglect of the area led to the detention of trade unionists and pro-independence politicians. The improvements promised in 1975 largely failed to materialise, but in 1982-83 reforms were introduced and some decentralisation took place. Local affairs are now dealt with by the Regional Council. The President of the Regional Council, Georges Othily, is French Guiana's single representative in the French Senate. Othily beat an incumbent member of the Parti Socialiste Guyanais, which has long been the strongest political party and is allied to its French namesake. The Gaullist Rassemblement pour la République is also well represented. Beyond the violent activities of some extremist groups, there is little pressure for full independence from France, and Paris has made it repeatedly clear that it will not countenance any change in French Guiana's status for the time being. The French government is becoming increasingly worried about the implications for French Guiana of the political instability in neighbouring Suriname. The Kourou space centre and satellite launch complex (see *Economy*, above) are now major strategic assets for the French.
GOVERNMENT: As an Overseas Department, French Guiana is represented by one member of the Senate and one member of the National Assembly in France. Locally, there is a 19-member General Council which assists an appointed Prefect, and the 31-member Regional Council. Both are elected for a 6-year term by universal adult suffrage.

CLIMATE

Tropical. Dry season is August to December; rainy season is January to June. Hot all year round, with cooler nights.
Required clothing: Tropical lightweights and rainwear.

CAYENNE French Guiana (6m)

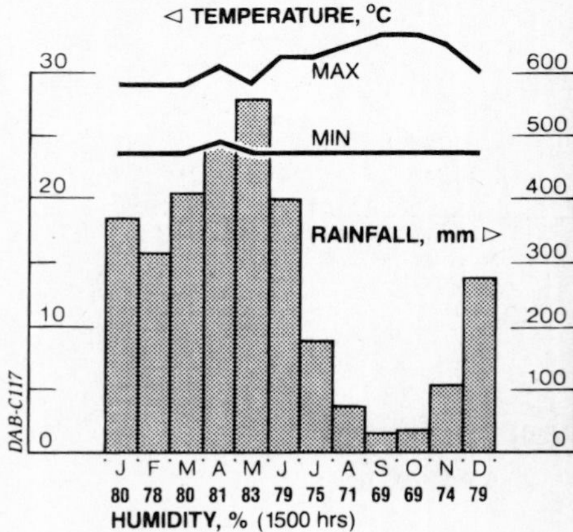

FRENCH GUIANA	HEALTH REGULATIONS	VISA REGULATIONS
GALILEO/WORLDSPAN	TI-DFT/CAY/HE	TI-DFT/CAY/VI
SABRE	TIDFT/CAY/HE	TIDFT/CAY/VI

Code-Link

To access this information on your CRS, swipe the barcode with a light pen or type in the text under the barcode. For more information, see the introduction *How to Use This Book*.

FRENCH OVERSEAS POSSESSIONS

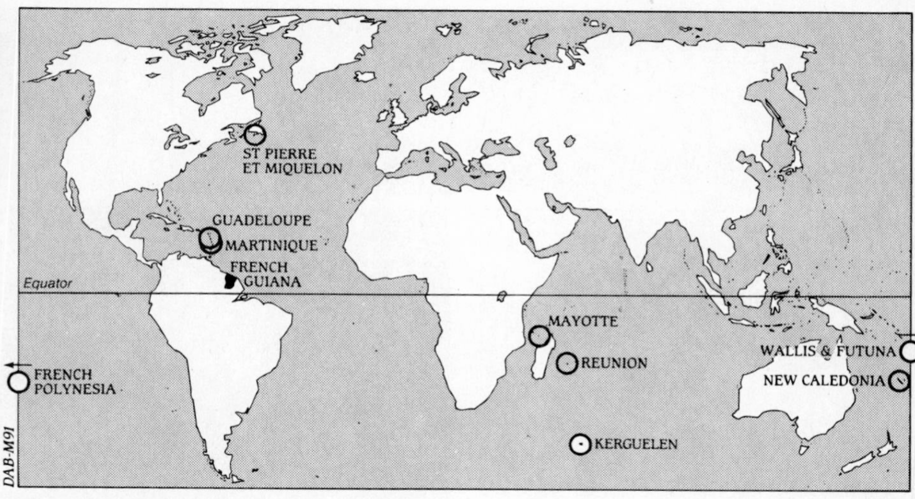

Note: Scattered throughout the world are several French *Départments*, *Territories* and *Collectivités Territoriales*. Most of these have their own sections in the *World Travel Guide*, but basic information is given for the others. Further information on all of the Possessions can be obtained from the **Agence Régionale du Tourisme**, BP 4274, rue du 11 Novembre, 97500 Saint Pierre. Tel: 412 384. Fax: 412 222 *or* 413 355. Telex: 914437; *or* the **French Government Tourist Office**, 178 Piccadilly, London W1V 0AL. Tel: (071) 499 6911 (recorded information). Fax: (071) 493 6594. Telex 21902; *or* the **French Embassy**, 58 Knightsbridge, London SW1X 7JT. Tel: (071) 235 8080. Fax: (071) 259 6498. Telex: 261905 FRALON; *or* the **Ministry of Overseas Departments and Territories,** 27 rue Oudinot, 75700 Paris. Tel: (1) 47 83 01 23.

FRENCH OVERSEAS DEPARTMENTS

There are four *départements d'outre-mer*, each one an integral part of the French Republic. Despite the greater autonomy achieved with the formation of their own individual Regional Councils in 1974, each French Overseas Department still returns elected representatives to the Senate and National Assembly in Paris, as well as to the European Parliament in Strasbourg.

GUADELOUPE and **MARTINIQUE** are in the Caribbean (also including the islands of St Martin and St Barthelemy); see the separately listed entries for these further on in the *World Travel Guide*.

FRENCH GUIANA is on the northwest coast of South America; see the separately listed entry above.

REUNION is in the Indian Ocean; see the separately listed entry further on in the *World Travel Guide*.

FRENCH OVERSEAS TERRITORIES

Like the French Overseas Departments above, the four *territoires d'outre-mer* are integral parts of the French Republic. However, each one is administered by an appointed representative of the French Government, and the level of autonomy is restricted.

FRENCH POLYNESIA is in the central South Pacific; see the separately listed entry below.

FRENCH SOUTHERN & ANTARCTIC TERRITORIES consist of a thin slice of the Antarctic mainland and a few small islands. The total area is 439,797 sq km (169,805 sq miles). The territory is used mainly for scientific purposes, although fishing in the area is important.

NEW CALEDONIA is in the South Pacific, east of Australia; see the separately listed entry further on in the *World Travel Guide*.

WALLIS AND FUTUNA ISLANDS
Location: Southwest Pacific between Fiji, Tuvalu and Western Samoa. **Area:** 274 sq km (106 sq miles). **Population:** 13,705 (1990). **Population Density:** 50 per sq km. **Capital:** Mata-Utu (Wallis Island). **Population:** 815 (1983). **Religion:** Roman Catholic. **Health:** Vaccinations against typhoid, tetanus and paratyphoid are advised. There is a hospital in the capital. **Travel:** The main airport (Hihifo) is on Wallis Island, 5km (3 miles) from Mata-Utu. Approximate flight time from London is 29 hours. There is also an airport in Futuna in Alo in the southeastern part of the island. *Air Calédonie (New Caledonia)* is the main airline serving the Islands. There is a weekly flight from Wallis Island to Nouméa (New Caledonia), and a thrice-weekly service from Wallis to Futuna. Boat services operate from New Caledonia and between the islands. Minibus services operate on Futuna and car hire is available. However, the only surfaced roads are in Mata-Utu. **Accommodation:** There are a small number of hotels on the islands; contact the **Maison de la France** (Tourist Information Agency), 8 avenue de l'Opéra, 75001 Paris. Tel: (1) 42 96 10 23; *or* the **French Government Tourist Office** (see above) for details of booking accommodation and other information.

OVERSEAS COLLECTIVITÉS TERRITORIALES

The administration of the two *collectivités territoriales* shares aspects of both the above categories: an integral part of the French Republic, they are administered by an appointed representative of the French Government, and yet at the same time they return elected representatives to the Senate and National Assembly in Paris, as well as to the European Parliament in Strasbourg.

MAYOTTE is part of the Comoros archipelago off the northwest corner of Madagascar. The island is claimed by the Federal Republic of the Comoros (which unilaterally declared independence from France in 1975), although residents have maintained that they wish to retain their close links with France. Various attempts have been made by international organisations, including the United Nations, to resolve the situation, although both the islanders and the French Government are in favour of maintaining Mayotte's special status. An airport and a deep-water port are being built, aided by French funding, with the intention of developing a tourist industry; completion is expected. **Area:** 374 sq km (144 sq miles). **Population:** 94,410 (1991). **Capital:** Dzaoudzi. **Population:** 5865 (1985). **Health:** There are no vaccination requirements for any international traveller, although precautions against malaria are advised. Only bottled water should be drunk. **Travel:** The main airport is *Pamandzi* on the island of the same name; services are available from Paris, the Comoros Islands and Réunion. There is a regular boat service to Mayotte, and there are approximately 110km (70 miles) of tarred roads on the island. **Accommodation:** There are a small number of hotels on the islands; contact the **Maison de la France** (Tourist Information Agency) for details of booking accommodation, and for other information contact the **Office du Tourisme de Mayotte,** 10 rue de Presbourg, 75116 Paris. Tel: (1) 45 01 28 30; *or* the **French Government Tourist Office** at the address above.

ST PIERRE ET MIQUELON comprises a group of small islands which lie off the southern coast of Newfoundland. Previously enjoying Departmental status, the islands have since 1955 been a part of the *collectivités territoriales*, partly as a result of a dispute with Canada over fishing and mineral rights in the area. **Area:** 242 sq km (93 sq miles). **Population:** 6392 (1990). **Capital:** Saint Pierre. **Population:** 5683 (1990); almost all of the population live in the capital or elsewhere on the small island of the same name. **Country dialling code:** 508. **Health:** No special precautions are required. **Travel:** The islands' airport is *Saint Pierre* which has international flights from Paris via Montréal or Halifax (stopovers are generally not permitted). The main airlines serving Saint Pierre are *Air Saint Pierre* and *Atlantic Airways*. Boat services operate between the islands and to Canada. Buses, taxis and hired cars are available. **Accommodation:** Hotels and guest-houses are available on the island; for details of booking accommodation and other information contact the **Agence Régionale du Tourisme,** BP 4274, rue du 11 Novembre, 97500 Saint Pierre. Tel: 412 384. Fax: 412 222 *or* 413 355. Telex: 914437. Information can also be obtained from the **French Government Tourist Office;** for address, see top of entry.

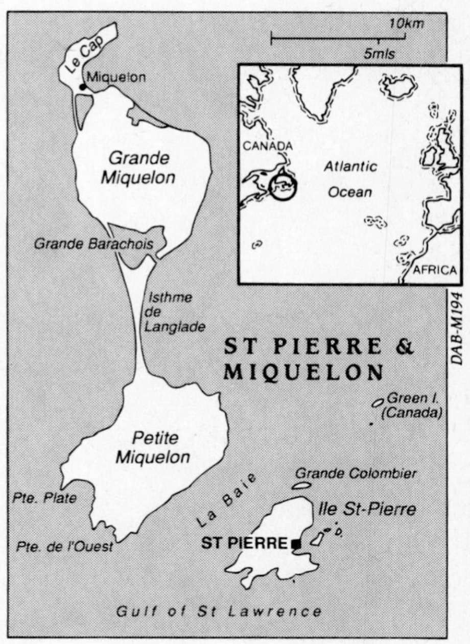

FRENCH POLYNESIA

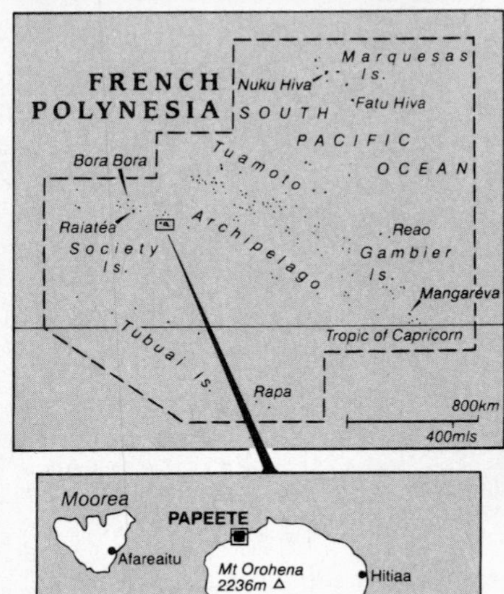

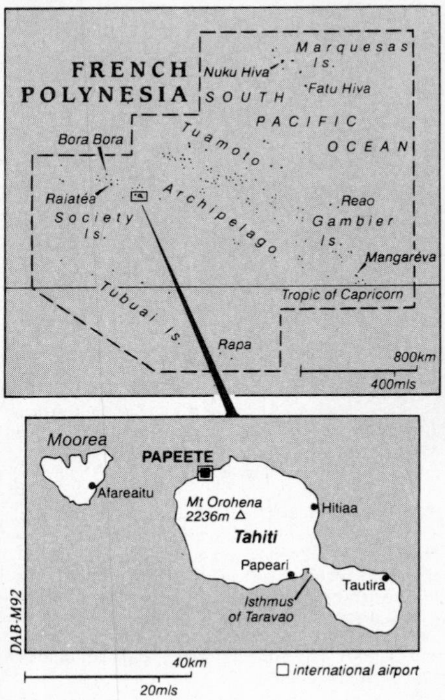

Location: South Pacific.

Diplomatic representation: French Polynesia is a French Overseas Territory; addresses of French Embassies, Consulates and Tourist Offices may be found in the *France* section above.

Office de Promotion et d'Animation Touristiques de Tahiti et ses Iles (OPATTI)
BP 65, Fare Manihini
boulevard Pomare
Papeete, Tahiti
Tel: 429 626. Fax: 436 619. Telex: 254.

Syndicat d'Initiative de la Polynésie Française
BP 326, Papeete, Tahiti
Tel: 438 535.

British Consulate
BP 1064
Propriété Boubée
route Tuterai Tane
Pirae
Papeete, Tahiti
Tel: 428 457 *or* 424 355. Fax: 410 847. Telex: 537 FP PTE.

Tahiti Tourist Promotion Board
Suite 1108
9841 Airport Boulevard
Los Angeles, CA
90045
Tel: (213) 649 2884. Fax: (213) 649 3825. Telex: 4971603.

AREA: 4000 sq km (1544 sq miles).
POPULATION: 199,031 (1991 estimate).
POPULATION DENSITY: 49.8 per sq km.
CAPITAL: Papeete (Tahiti Island). **Population:** 23,496 (1983).
GEOGRAPHY: French Polynesia comprises 130 islands divided into five archipelagos. The Windward and Leeward Islands, collectively called the Society Archipelago, are mountainous with coastal plains. Tahiti, the largest of the Windward group, is dominated by Mt Orohena at 2236m (7337ft) and Mt Aorai at 2068m (6786ft). Moorea lies next to Tahiti, a picturesque volcanic island with white sand beaches. The Leeward Islands to the west are generally lower in altitude. The largest islands are Raiatea and Bora Bora. Tuamotu Archipelago comprises 80 coral atolls, located 298km (185 miles) east of Tahiti. The Marquesas Islands lie 1497km (930 miles) northeast of Tahiti and are made up of two clusters of volcanic islands divided into a southern and northern group. The grass-covered Austral Islands south of Tahiti are scattered in a chain from east to west over a distance of 499km (310 miles).
LANGUAGE: The official languages are Tahitian and French. Other Polynesian languages are spoken by the indigenous population. English is widely understood, mainly by islanders accustomed to dealing with foreign visitors.
RELIGION: Protestant 55%; Catholic 24%.
TIME: GMT - 9 Gambier Islands; GMT - 9.5 Marquesas Islands; GMT - 10 Society Archipelago, Tubuai Islands, Tuamotu Archipelago (except Gambier Islands), Tahiti.
ELECTRICITY: 220 volts AC, 60Hz.
COMMUNICATIONS: Telephone: IDD is available. Country code: 689. **Fax:** Some hotels and the post offices have facilities. **Telex/telegram:** Facilities are limited to Papeete and Uturoa (Raiatea). All calls out of French Polynesia must be made via the international operator. Telex and telegrams can be sent from the post office on Boulevard Pomare, Papeete. **Post:** The post office hours are: 0700-1800 Monday to Friday (restricted service in the afternoon) and 0800-100 on weekends. Airmail to Europe takes up to two weeks. **Press:** There is an English-language weekly, the *Tahiti Sun Press*.
BBC World Service and Voice of America frequencies: From time to time these change. See the section *How to Use this Book* for more information.

BBC:				
MHz	17.10	15.36	9.740	7.150
Voice of America:				
MHz	18.82	15.18	9.525	1.735

PASSPORT/VISA

Regulations and requirements may be subject to change at short notice, and you are advised to contact the appropriate diplomatic or consular authority before finalising travel arrangements. Details of these may be found at the head of this country's entry. Any numbers in the chart refer to the footnotes below.

	Passport Required?	Visa Required?	Return Ticket Required?
Full British	Yes	No	Yes
BVP	Not valid	-	-
Australian	Yes	Yes	Yes
Canadian	Yes	No	Yes
USA	Yes	No	Yes
Other EC	1	No	Yes
Japanese	Yes	No	Yes

PASSPORTS: Valid passport required by all except [1] nationals of France being holders of national Identity Card or a passport expired less than 5 years.
British Visitors Passport: Not accepted.
VISAS: Required by all except:
(a) nationals of EC countries (no limit of stay for nationals of France), Canada, Japan and the USA for a stay of up to 3 months;
(b) nationals of Andorra, Austria, Cook Islands (if New Zealand passport holders), Cyprus, Finland, Iceland, South Korea, Liechtenstein, Malta, Monaco, New Zealand, Norway, San Marino, Sweden, Switzerland and Vatican City for stays of up to 1 month;
(c) nationals of Czechoslovakia, Hungary and Poland.
Note: (a) Visa requirements for other nationals wishing to visit Polynesia are subject to frequent change at short notice and travellers should contact the French Consulate General for up-to-date information. (b) Visas are not required by transit passengers who do not leave the airport. (c) Onward or return tickets must be held by all passengers.

Types of visa: Tourist and Transit (cost and validity on application).
Application to: French Consulate General. For address, see top of *France* entry.
Application requirements: (a) 3 forms. (b) 3 photos. (c) Onward ticket.
Working days required: Usually one day, although up to 1 month depending on nationality of applicant.
Temporary residence: Contact French Consulate General (or Consular Section at Embassy). For addresses, see *France* entry above.

MONEY

Currency: French Pacific Franc (CFP Fr) = 100 centimes. Notes are in denominations of CFP Fr5000, 1000, 500 and 100. Coins are in denominations of CFP Fr100, 50, 20, 10, 5, 2 and 1, and 50 centimes. French Polynesia is part of the French Monetary Area.
Currency exchange: Exchange facilities are available at the airport, major banks and at authorised hotels and shops in Papeete.
Credit cards: American Express is the most widely accepted, while Visa, Diners Club and Access/Mastercard have more limited use. Check with your credit card company for details of merchant acceptability and other services which may be available.
Travellers cheques: The recommended means of importing foreign currency.
Exchange rate indicators: The following figures are included as a guide to the movements of the French Pacific Franc against Sterling and the US Dollar:

Date:	Oct '89	Oct '90	Apr '91	Oct '92
£1.00=	180.00	177.00	180.00	150.00
$1.00=	113.99	90.60	103.51	94.52

Currency restrictions: As for France.
Banking hours: 0745-1530 Monday to Friday.

DUTY FREE

The following items may be imported into French Polynesia without incurring customs duty:
200 cigarettes or 100 cigarillos or 50 cigars or 250g of tobacco;
1 litre of spirits over 22% and 2 litres of still wine (for passengers over 17 years of age);
50g of perfume and 250ml of toilet water;
Goods up to a value of CFP Fr5000 (CFP Fr2500 for passengers up to 15 years of age).
Note: (a) Plants, cats, dogs, dangerous goods and drugs may not be imported. (b) All baggage coming from Brazil, Samoa and Fiji is collected for compulsory fumigation on arrival in Papeete; allow two hours.

PUBLIC HOLIDAYS

Public holidays observed in French Polynesia are as follows:
Apr 12 '93 Easter Monday. **May 3** Labour Day Holiday. **May 10** Liberation Day Holiday. **May 20** Ascension Day. **May 31** Whit Monday. **Jul 14*** Bastille/National Day. **Nov 11** Armistice Day. **Dec 25-26** Christmas. **Jan 1 '94** New Year's Day.
Note [*]: Celebrations continue for up to ten days.

HEALTH

Regulations and requirements may be subject to change at short notice, and you are advised to contact your doctor well in advance of your intended date of departure. Any numbers in the chart refer to the footnotes below.

	Special Precautions?	Certificate Required?
Yellow Fever	No	1
Cholera	No	No
Typhoid & Polio	Yes	-
Malaria	No	-
Food & Drink	2	-

[1]: A yellow fever vaccination certificate is required from travellers over one year of age coming from infected areas.
[2]: Mains water is normally chlorinated, and whilst relatively safe may cause mild abdominal upsets. Bottled water is available and is advised for the first few weeks of the stay. Drinking water outside main cities and towns may be contaminated and sterilisation is advisable. Milk is pasteurised and dairy products are safe for consumption. Local meat, poultry, seafood, fruit and vegetables are generally considered safe to eat.

Health care: Private medical insurance is recommended. There are about 30 hospitals and 140 doctors in French Polynesia.

TRAVEL - International

AIR: French Polynesia is served by *Air France (AF)*, *Qantas (QF)*, *Air New Zealand (NZ)* and *Hawaiian Airlines (HA)* for longhaul international flights. *Polynesian Airlines (PH)* operate within the Pacific region and offer a 'Polypass' which allows the holder to fly anywhere on the airline's network: Sydney (Australia), Auckland (New Zealand), Western Samoa, American Samoa, Cook Islands, Vanuatu, New Caledonia, Fiji and, on payment of a supplement, Tahiti. The pass is valid for 30 days.
Approximate flight times: From Papeete to *Auckland* is 5 hours 35 minutes, to *Honolulu* is 7 hours, to *London* 20 hours, to *Los Angeles* is 8 hours 15 minutes, to *New York* is 16 hours and to *Sydney* is 9 hours 35 minutes.
International airport: *Papeete (PPT)* (Faaa), on Tahiti, is 6.5km (4 miles) from the city (travel time – 15 minutes). Airport facilities include bank/bureau de change, duty-free shop, bar (0200-2200), restaurant (0800-1500), tourist information (24 hours) and car hire. Taxis are available.
SEA: International port is Papeete on Tahiti, served by *Sitmar*, *Cunard*, *Holland America*, *Norwegian America* and *Chandris*. Cruise ships include *Swedish America* and *Royal Viking*.

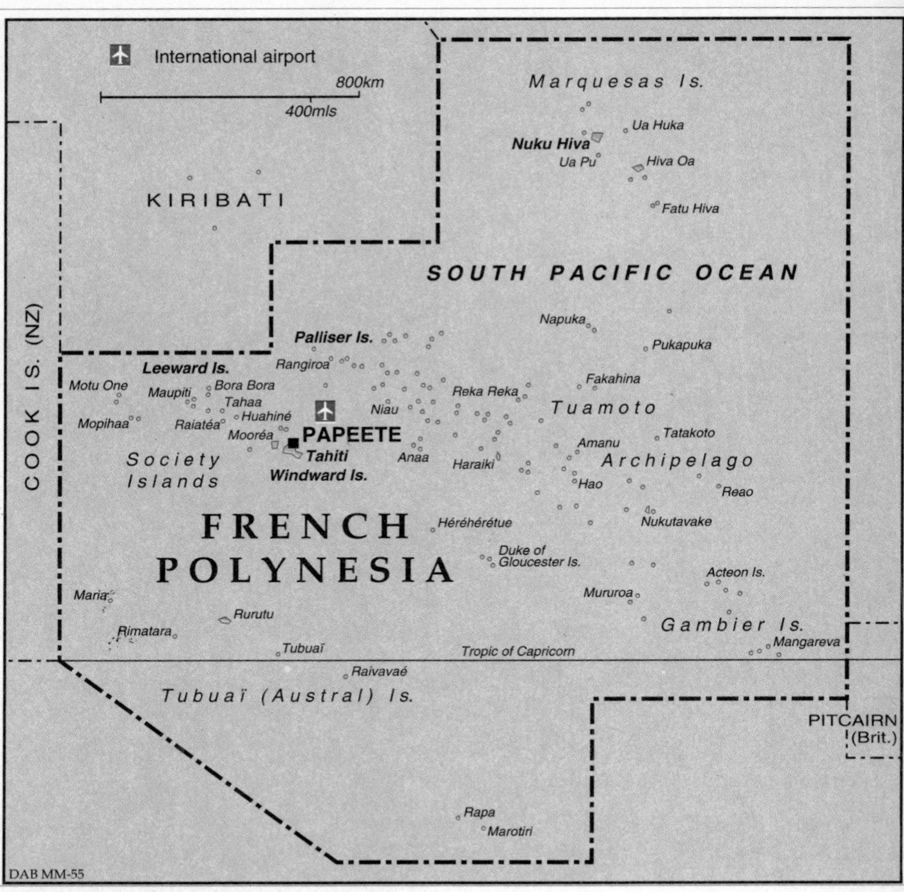

TRAVEL - Internal

AIR: Domestic flights run by *Air Tahiti (VT)* connect Tahiti with neighbouring islands (Moorea, Huahine, Raiatea, Bora Bora, Maupiti) and remote archipelagos (Tuamotu, Rangiroa, Naniti, Matauia, Anaa, Austral Islands of Runitu and Tubuai, Marquesas Islands of Hiva Oa and Ua Hivea).
SEA: There are inter-island connections on the many copra boats and schooners that make regular trips throughout the islands. Daily connections between Papeete, Moorea, Huahine, Raiatea, and Bora Bora.
ROAD: Bus: Basic buses, known as *trucks*, offer an inexpensive method of travel. They leave from the central market in Papeete town centre travelling to all destinations. No schedule is operated. **Taxis:** Available in Tahiti, Moorea, Bora Bora, Huahine and Raiatea. *Roll's Tahiti* offers a chauffeur-driven Silver Shadow Rolls Royce or a Daimler Double-Six for city shopping tours, sunset cruise with champagne, airport transfers, etc. **Car hire:** Major and local agencies including *Hertz*, *Budget Rent-a-car* and *Avis* rent cars in main islands. **Documentation:** National driving licence will be sufficient.

ACCOMMODATION

HOTELS: Accommodation varies from air-conditioned, carpeted, deluxe rooms with telephones and room service, to thatched-roofed bungalows (Tahitian *pensiones* where the bathroom is shared and may be outdoors with cold showers). In the outer islands, resort hotels normally have individual gardens and over-water bungalows and rooms, many built of bamboo, with shows and dance bands. There is a youth hostel in Papeete with 14 rooms (tel: 426 802); a youth hostel or student card is required. It is possible to rent a room in a family home through the Tourist Board (OPATTI) for a more genuine experience.

RESORTS & EXCURSIONS

Papeete, the capital of **Tahiti,** has in recent years been transformed into a bustling city, very much at variance with the traditional 'haere maru' (take it easy) attitude of the rest of the country. It is, however, still an attractive and colourful port set in magnificent scenery. To the west of the capital is *Venus Point*, where the first Europeans set foot on the island in 1767. It is overlooked by *Mount Orohena*, the highest point on the island. The Papeete public market, *Le Marché*, is open from 0500-1800 all week, but really comes to life on Sunday mornings. Flowers, spices, fabrics and fresh produce are on offer.
The surrounding area is characterised by its spectacular tropical scenery, banana groves, plantations and flowers. Places to see include the *Blowhole of Arahoho*, which throws water skywards; the *Faarumai* and *Vaipahi waterfalls;* the *Paul Gauguin Museum* and *Botanical Gardens* in **Papeari**; the 'marae' (open-air temple) of *Maheietea*, *Marae Grotto* and *Arahurahu*. The *Lagoonarium de Tahiti* offers four fish parks (including a shark pen) and an amazing underwater display (0900-1800 daily); admission is free.
Moorea, 17km (11 miles) from Tahiti, and connected to it by a 45-minute ferry service or 7-minute flight, is an island with a simpler and more rustic lifestyle and yet offers plenty of entertainment for the tourist, including traditional-style nightlife. Dominated by volcanic peaks, it also has dazzling white sand beaches and clear lagoons ideal for swimming, diving and

FRENCH POLYNESIA	HEALTH REGULATIONS	VISA REGULATIONS
		Code-Link
GALILEO/WORLDSPAN	TI-DFT/PPT/HE	TI-DFT/PPT/VI
SABRE	TIDFT/PPT/HE	TIDFT/PPT/VI

To access this information on your CRS, swipe the barcode with a light pen or type in the text under the barcode. For more information, see the introduction *How to Use This Book*.

snorkelling. Excursions include a visit to the beautiful *Opunohu Valley*, an ancient dwelling place, uninhabited for a century and a half, with 500 ancient structures including temples or *marae*, some of which have been restored. *La Belvedere* is a lookout spot from where the best view of the island may be had.
Tetiaroa, recently opened to the public and accessible only by air, is an important seabird sanctuary.
The **Leeward Islands, Huahine, Raiatea** and **Tahaa** are ancient and unspoilt islands, all less than an hour from Tahiti by plane or ferry. **Huahine**, to the north-west of Tahiti, comprises Huahine-Nui (big Huahine) and Huahine-Iti (little Huahine) which are linked by a narrow isthmus. Sheltered by the surrounding coral reef, the coastal waters and lagoons are good for encountering the local aquatic life. The archaeological site near *Maeva Village* is well worth a visit. **Raiatea** is the second largest island of French Polynesia, 193km (120 miles) from Tahiti, and is the administrative centre for the Leeward Islands. In former times, the island was known as Havai'i, the royal and cultural centre of the region. The ideal conditions make the island a year-round destination for sailing and fishing enthusiasts. The 'Vanilla Island' of **Tahaa** is surrounded by the same reef as Raiatea, and offers a tranquil and relaxed lifestyle as tourism is only starting here. The breeze constantly carries the aroma of vanilla, for the island's numerous vanilla plantations.
Bora Bora is 45 minutes from Tahiti by plane. Excursions include visits to the small villages outside the main town of **Vaitape** and climbs up the two mountains of *Otemanu* and *Pahia*. There are many opportunities for watersports such as deep-sea fishing, trips by glass-bottomed boat around the lagoons, scuba diving, snorkelling and swimming on a nearby 'motu' (small sandy atoll within the reef of Bora Bora). In common with so many other Polynesian islands, Bora Bora has many ancient temples. There are good hotels on the island.
The **Tuamotu** group of islands are largely uninhabited. There are air and ferry links between Tahiti and several of the more popular islands, including **Rangiroa**, which has facilities for all forms of watersports, mostly organised through the *Kia Ora* hotel.
The **Marquesas Islands** are less well-known among tourists, and as yet they have no first-class hotels. Paul Gauguin is buried on **Hiva Oa,** and on **Ua Huka** it is possible to go horseriding between the numerous valleys. The islands are four hours from Tahiti by plane.
The **Austral Islands** have a generally cooler climate than the rest of French Polynesia. The mutineers of the 'Bounty' attempted to make a settlement on *Tubuai* in 1789. Accommodation is plentiful in the form of bungalows on or near the beach.
Note: Most excursions, sightseeing trips and other leisure activities can be organised by hotels on the islands.

SOCIAL PROFILE

FOOD & DRINK: All the classified hotels have good restaurants. French, Italian, Chinese and Vietnamese food is served, as well as the Polynesian specialities; Papeete is noted for French and Chinese cuisine. Tahitian food can be found in some hotels. Popular dishes include smoked breadfruit, mountain bananas, *fafa* (spinach) served with young suckling pig, *poisson cru* (marinated fish), or *poe* (starchy pudding made of papaya, mango and banana). *Trucks* or lunch wagons parked on the waterfront sell steak, chips, chicken, *poisson cru brochettes* and *shish kebabs* (barbecued veal hearts). **Drink:** A full range of alcoholic drinks is widely available.
NIGHTLIFE: Papeete is full of life in the evenings with restaurants and nightclubs. Most hotels feature Tahitian dance shows, bands and other traditional entertainment.
SHOPPING: Facilities are concentrated in Papeete. Special purchases include Marquesan woodcarvings, dancing costumes, shell jewellery, Tahitian perfumes, *Monoi Tiare Tahiti* (coconut oil scented with Tahiti's national flower), vanilla beans and brightly patterned *pareu* fabrics that make the traditional Tahitian *pareo*. **Shopping hours:** 0730-1700 Monday to Friday, 0730-1100 Saturday. Tourist shops are open until late. Lunch breaks vary.
SPORT: Fishing: Fully equipped deep-sea fishing boats are available for charter at *Tahiti Actinautic.The Haura (Marlin) Club* is a member of the International Game Fishing Association. Other holiday villages and hotels can arrange trips. **Golf:** There is an 18-hole golf course at Atimanono. Hourly and day-long **horse-riding** tours can be arranged through *Club Equestre de Tahiti* and *Centre de Tourisme Equestre de Tahiti*, both at the Hippodrome, Pirae, Tahiti. **Watersports:** Equipment for **skindiving** can be hired, as can charter

boats to take divers to the best areas. Further details are available from the Tourist Office. To supplement the numerous sandy beaches and clear lagoons, there is an Olympic-size swimming pool at boulevard Pomare, Papeete, as well as pools at many hotels. **Tennis:** Courts are available at *Fautaua Tennis Club*, which offers temporary membership to visitors. Many of the island hotels have courts and some are available to non-residents. **Sailing:** The largest yachting organisation is the *Yacht Club de Tahiti*. Waters around the islands are ideal for small craft and several clubs and hotels hire outcraft. *Club Alpin* in Arue provides information and assistance for **climbing** Mt Aorai, with a shelter at 1798m (5900ft), Mt Orohena and Mt Diademe. **Spectator sports: Football** is popular throughout the islands and can be seen almost anywhere. Fautaua stadium near Papeete is a major venue on Sunday afternoons. Tahitian-style **horseracing** can be seen at the Hippodrome in Pirae. Races are held 12-15 times a year. Other scheduled spectator sports include **archery, cycling, boxing, canoeing, sailing** and **track events**.

SPECIAL EVENTS: The biggest festival is *Heiva I Tahiti* (akin to Bastille Day), starting on around Jul 14 and continuing for about ten days. There are many feasting, dancing and sporting events for which enthusiastic crowds of local inhabitants and tourists gather. The *Annual Tree Festival* takes place in October, each year with a different theme. Of great importance is also the *Festival of Tiare*, when the white Gardenia Taitensis is woven into frangrant tiaras. Other festivals of note include *New Year's Day* celebrations (including *Chinese New Year*), and various *Flower and Handicraft Festivals* and *Island Beauty Contests*.

SOCIAL CONVENTIONS: The basic lifestyle of the islands is represented by the simple Tahitian *fares* built of bamboo with *pandanus* roofs. Local women dress in bright *pareos* and men in the male equivalent, but casual dress is expected of the visitor. Traditional dances are still performed mostly in hotels, with Western dance styles mainly in tourist centres. Normal social courtesies are important. **Tipping:** Not practised, since it is contrary to the Tahitian idea of hospitality.

BUSINESS PROFILE

ECONOMY: The traditional Polynesian economy was agricultural (coconuts and vanilla) with, more recently, black pearls and shark meat joining the main products. The continuing use of Polynesia as a nuclear testing zone by the French has been – in economic terms anyway – something of a mixed blessing. When the test programme was in its infancy and expanding, there was a significant demand for construction labour and ancilliary services for the French military personnel who accompanied the missile systems. Although the French are still present, demand for local labour has declined and redundant workers no longer have the agricultural skills of earlier generations, resulting in high unemployment. Despite the nuclear facilities, tourism has grown quickly to the point where it is vital for economic survival, especially that of Tahiti, which is the largest of the island group. Nonetheless, imports exceed exports by a factor of ten, so that considerable aid is needed from the French (in exchange, essentially, for the test sites) to balance the country's finances. France dominates the islands' trade; the US is the other important trade partner.

BUSINESS: Informal in atmosphere. Literature will be in French, but English is understood in some business circles, particularly those connected with tourism. **Office hours:** 0730-1700 Monday to Friday.

COMMERCIAL INFORMATION: The following organisation can offer advice: Chambre de Commerce et d'Industrie de Polynésie Française, BP 118, rue Docteur Cassiau, Papeete. Tel: 420 344. Fax: 435 184. Telex: 274.

HISTORY & GOVERNMENT

HISTORY: The first Europeans to arrive on the island groups were 16th-century Spanish and Portuguese explorers. The British, notably Captain Cook and later Captain Bligh (of 'HMS Bounty' notoriety), and the French took over the islands in the 18th century. Tahiti, the largest island in French Polynesia, was made a French protectorate in 1842 and a colony in 1880. The other islands were annexed by the turn of the century. This status quo remained until 1957, when Polynesia was made an Overseas Territory. A revised constitution, introduced in 1977, ceded greater autonomy. Although a majority of the islanders appear to favour full independence, there is a substantial and powerful minority which opposes it. Moreover, the French government wishes to hold onto the territory in order to carry out its atomic testing programme. This has been the subject of considerable international controversy in recent years, which has been firmly resisted by Paris. The issue is an important one in French Polynesia's domestic politics which have been dominated in recent years by the centre-right Tahoeraa Huiraatira (TH) party, led by Gaston Flosse, which is allied to the French Gaullist Rassemblement pour la République and broadly supports continuing French rule and nuclear testing. Tahoeraa Huiraatira has won both of the last two elections for the Territorial Assembly in 1986 and 1991, and now leads a 2-party coalition with the centrist Aia Api (New Republic) party. The Flosse government is principally concerned with economic matters, and is seeking to arrest the islands' declining indigenous trades and reduce dependence on French support. However, there are also signs of growing local resistance to tourist development, the major growth industry of recent years which offers the best short-term prospect for a self-supporting economy.
GOVERNMENT: The Overseas Territory of French Polynesia is an integral part of France, and the French government is represented by a High Commissioner. The islands have enjoyed limited internal autonomy since July 1977, with a Territorial Assembly elected by universal adult suffrage for a 5-year term. The High Commissioner, however, retains sole responsibility for foreign affairs, defence and the judicial system.

CLIMATE

Temperate, but cooled by sea breezes. Two main seasons: humid (hot and wet) from December to February, cool and dry from March to November.
Required clothing: Lightweight cottons and linens are worn, with a warm wrap for cooler evenings. Rainwear is advisable.

PAPEETE French Polynesia (92m)

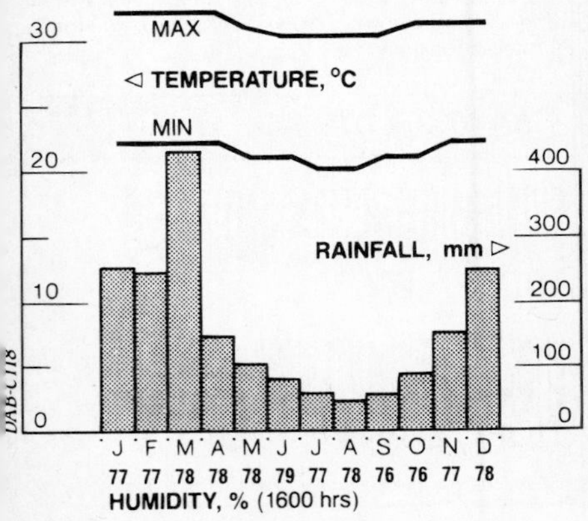

GABON

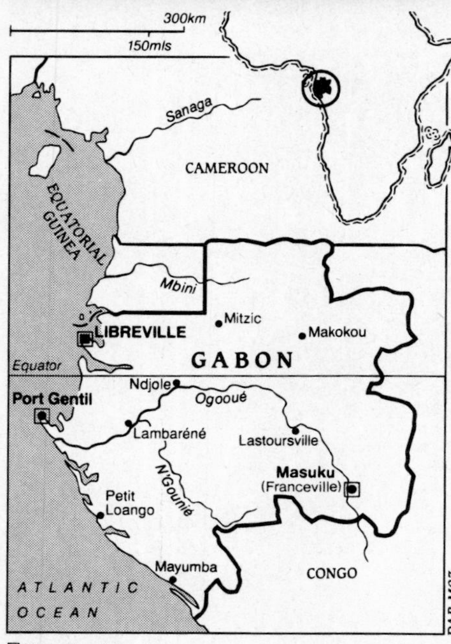

□ international airport

Location: West Coast of Central Africa.

Office National Gabonais du Tourisme
PO Box 161
Libreville, Gabon
Tel: 722 182.

Embassy of the Gabonese Republic
27 Elvaston Place
London SW7 5NL
Tel: (071) 823 9986. Fax: (071) 584 0047. Telex: 919418. Opening hours: 0900-1500 Monday to Friday.

British diplomatic and commercial representation: The British Embassy in Gabon closed in July 1991. The West African Department of the Foreign & Commonwealth Office is currently handling consular and commercial enquiries for Gabon. Tel: (071) 270 2516.

Embassy of the Gabonese Republic
2034 20th Street, NW
Washington, DC
20009
Tel: (202) 797 1000.

Embassy of the United States of America
BP 4000
boulevard de la Mer
Libreville, Gabon
Tel: 762 003/4. Fax: 745 507. Telex: 5250 GO.

Embassy of the Gabonese Republic
4 Range Road
Ottawa, Ontario
K1N 8J5
Tel: (613) 232 5301/2. Fax: (613) 232 6916. Telex: 053-4295.

Canadian Embassy
PO Box 4037
Libreville, Gabon
Tel: 743 464 *or* 743465. Fax: 743 466. Telex: 5527 GO.

AREA: 267,667 sq km (103,347 sq miles).
POPULATION: 1,206, 000 (1985 estimate).
POPULATION DENSITY: 4.5 per sq km.
CAPITAL: Libreville. **Population:** 352,000 (1988).
GEOGRAPHY: Gabon is bordered to the west by the Atlantic Ocean, to the north by Equatorial Guinea and Cameroon, and to the east and south by the Congo Republic. The 800km- (500 miles) long sandy coastal strip is a series of palm-fringed bays, lagoons and estuaries. The lush tropical vegetation (which covers about 82% of the interior) gives way in parts to the savannah. There are many rivers and they remain the main communication routes along which settlements have grown. Of the 40 or so Bantu tribes, the largest are the Fang, Eshira, Mbele and Okande. Only a small percentage of native Gabonese live in the towns, as the population is concentrated in the coastal areas and the villages along the banks of the many rivers, following a more traditional rural style of life.
LANGUAGE: The official language is French. The principle African language is Fang. Eshira is spoken by a tenth of the population. Bantu dialects spoken include Bapounou and Miene.
RELIGION: About 75% Christian, the remainder are Muslim and Animist religions.
TIME: GMT + 1.
ELECTRICITY: 220 volts AC, 50Hz.
COMMUNICATIONS: Telephone: IDD is available. Country code: 241. No area codes required. **Telex:** Facilities are available at the main post office in Libreville and major hotels. **Post:** Airmail from Gabon takes at least a week to Europe. Urgent letters should be sent by special delivery to ensure their safe arrival. Post office opening hours are 0800-1200 and 1430-1800 Monday to Friday. **Press:** There are two dailies, the *Gabon-Matin* and *L'Union*. There are several periodicals, published mainly on the topics of the Government and the economy. Official bulletins are published in French, and have limited circulations.
BBC World Service and Voice of America frequencies: From time to time these change. See the section *How to Use this Book* for more information.

BBC:				
MHz	25.75	17.88	15.40	7.105
Voice of America:				
MHz	21.49	15.60	9.525	6.035

PASSPORT/VISA

Regulations and requirements may be subject to change at short notice, and you are advised to contact the appropriate diplomatic or consular authority before finalising travel arrangements. Details of these may be found at the head of this country's entry. Any numbers in the chart refer to the footnotes below.

	Passport Required?	Visa Required?	Return Ticket Required?
Full British	Yes	Yes	Yes
BVP	Not valid	-	-
Australian	Yes	Yes	Yes
Canadian	Yes	Yes	Yes
USA	Yes	Yes	Yes
Other EC	Yes	1	Yes
Japanese	Yes	Yes	Yes

Prohibited entry: Nationals of Angola, Cape Verde, Cuba, Ghana, Guinea-Buissau, Haiti, Israel, Sao Tomé & Principe and South Africa will be refused entry, but may travel for transit purposes.
PASSPORTS: Valid passport required by all except nationals of Cameroon, Central African Republic, Chad, Congo and Equatorial Guinea, who must have a return ticket and national ID card or passport (expired for less than 5 years).
British Visitors Passport: Not accepted.
VISAS: Required by all except:
(a) [1] nationals of Germany (all other EC nationals *do* require a visa);
(b) nationals of Cameroon, Central African Republic, Chad, Congo, Côte d'Ivoire, Senegal and Togo.
Types of visa: Visitors and Transit. Cost: £20.
Validity: *Visitors:* 3 months. *Transit:* not required by those who continue their journey to a third country by the same or connecting aircraft within 24 hours. Tickets must be held with reserved seats and other documents for their onward journey.
Application to: Consulate (or Consular Section at Embassy). For addresses, see top of entry.
Application requirements: *Business visa:* Letter from company. *Tourist visa:* (a) 3 photographs. (b) 3 forms. (c) Fee.
Working days required: 2-4 weeks. Postal applications must include a registered SAE.

MONEY

Currency: CFA Franc (CFA Fr) = 100 centimes. Notes occur in denominations of CFA Fr10,000, 5000, 1000, 500 and 100 (the smallest of these is not negotiable in the UK). Coins are in denominations of CFA Fr100, 50, 25, 10, 5, 2 and 1.
Currency exchange: Gabon is part of the French Monetary Area and the CFA Franc is legal tender in all other former French Equatorial African countries (Chad, Congo, Central African Republic, Cameroon and Equatorial Guinea).
Credit cards: Limited use of Visa, American Express and Access/Mastercard. Diners Club more widely accepted, however in general the use of credit cards in Gabon remains relatively limited. Check with your credit card company for merchant acceptability and other facilities which may be available.
Travellers cheques: French Franc cheques are more readily converted than those in Sterling.
Exchange rate indicators: The following figures are included as a guide to the movements of the CFA Franc against Sterling and the US Dollar:

Date:	Oct '89	Oct '90	Oct '91	Oct '92
£1.00=	505.13	498.38	496.13	413.75
$1.00=	319.91	255.12	285.87	260.71

Currency restrictions: Import of foreign and local currency is unlimited, subject to declaration. Export of local currency is limited to CFA Fr250,000. Export of foreign currency is limited to the amount declared on arrival.
Banking hours: 0730-1130 and 1430-1630 Monday to Friday.

DUTY FREE

The following goods may be imported into Gabon by persons of 17 and over without incurring customs duty:
200 cigarettes or 50 cigars or 250g of tobacco (females – cigarettes only);
2 litres of alcoholic beverage;
50g of perfume;
Gifts up to CFA Fr5000.
Controlled items: Guns and ammunition require a police permit.

PUBLIC HOLIDAYS

Public holidays observed in Gabon are as follows:
Mar 12 '93 Renovation Day. **Mar 25** Eid al-Fitr (End of Ramadan). **Apr 12** Easter Monday. **May 1** Labour Day. **May 31** Whit Monday. **Jun 1** Eid al-Adha, (Feast of the Sacrifice). **Aug 17** Independence Day. **Aug 30** Mouloud, (Prophet's Birthday). **Dec 25-26** Christmas. **Jan 1 '94** New Year's Day. **Mar 12** Renovation Day. **Mar** Start of Eid al-Fitr (End of Ramadan).
Note: Muslim festivals are timed according to local sightings of various phases of the Moon and the dates given above are approximations. During the lunar month of Ramadan that precedes Eid al-Fitr, Muslims fast during the day and feast at night and normal business patterns may be interrupted. Some disruption may continue into Eid al-Fitr itself. Eid al-Fitr and Eid al-Adha may last anything from two to ten days, depending on the region. For more information see the section *World of Islam* at the back of the book.

GABON | **HEALTH REGULATIONS** | **VISA REGULATIONS** | Code-Link

GALILEO/WORLDSPAN

TI-DFT/LBV/HE

TI-DFT/LBV/VI

SABRE

TIDFT/LBV/HE

TIDFT/LBV/VI

To access this information on your CRS, swipe the barcode with a light pen or type in the text under the barcode. For more information, see the introduction *How to Use This Book.*

HEALTH

Regulations and requirements may be subject to change at short notice, and you are advised to contact your doctor well in advance of your intended date of departure. Any numbers in the chart refer to the footnotes below.

	Special Precautions?	Certificate Required?
Yellow Fever	Yes	1
Cholera	Yes	2
Typhoid & Polio	Yes	-
Malaria	3	-
Food & Drink	4	-

[1]: A yellow fever vaccination certificate is required from all travellers over one year of age.
[2]: Following WHO guidelines issued in 1973, a cholera vaccination certificate is not a condition of entry to Gabon. However, cholera is a serious risk in this country and precautions are essential. Up-to-date advice should be sought before deciding whether these precautions should include vaccination as medical opinion is divided over its effectiveness. See the *Health* section at the back of the book.
[3]: Malaria risk, predominantly in the malignant *falciparum* form, exists all the year throughout the country. Resistance to chloroquine has been reported.
[4]: All water should be regarded as being potentially contaminated. Water used for drinking, brushing teeth or making ice should have first been boiled or otherwise sterilised. Milk is unpasteurised and should be boiled. Powdered or tinned milk is available and is advised, but make sure that it is reconstituted with pure water. Avoid dairy products which are likely to have been made from unboiled milk. Only eat well-cooked meat and fish, preferably served hot. Pork, salad and mayonnaise may carry increased risk. Vegetables should be cooked and fruit peeled.
Bilharzia (schistosomiasis) is present. Avoid swimming and paddling in fresh water. Swimming pools which are well-chlorinated and maintained are safe.
Rabies is present. For those at high risk, vaccination before arrival should be considered. If you are bitten abroad seek medical advice without delay. For more information consult the *Health* section at the back of the book.
Health care: Travellers in rural areas should take own first-aid kit with anti-tetanus and anti-venom serums. Medical facilities are limited. Full health insurance is essential.

TRAVEL - International

AIR: Gabon's national airline is *Air Gabon (GN)*.
Approximate flight time: From *London* to Libreville is 10 hours 30 minutes.
International airport: *Libreville (LBV)* is 12km (7 miles) north of the city (travel time – 10 minutes). Airport facilities include bureaux de change (0830-1130, 1430-1730), shops (0800-2400), tourist information (open during operational hours), car rental (*Avis, Europcar, Hertz* and *Eurafrique*), hotel reservation desk and duty-free shops. Taxis are available.
There are also local airports at *Franceville* and *Port Gentil (POG)*.
SEA: Freighters with passenger cabins call at Libreville, Port Gentil and Moanda from Genoa, Marseille and other European ports.
ROAD: The main roads to Gabon from Yaounde (Cameroon) and Brazzaville (Congo) are not well maintained.

TRAVEL - Internal

AIR: There are nearly 200 airstrips. *Air Gabon* is the domestic airline and operates regular flights from Libreville, Oyem, Mitzic and other cities.
SEA: There are ferries and river barges running for example from Lambarene to Port Gentil and Libreville to Port Gentil.
RAIL: The *Trans-Gabon Railway* connects Libreville with Ndjole (five times a week), Booue and Franceville, with extensions under construction to Belinga in the north. It is necessary to book in advance, or the fare will be double if bought on the train.
ROAD: There are nearly 5000km (3100 miles) of road, but only 500km (310 miles) are tarred. Most of the country is impenetrable rain forest and the roads are generally of a poor standard. Road travelling in the rainy season is inadvisable. There is no road connection between the second largest city of Port Gentil and Libreville, or any other part of the country. **Bus:** Inter-urban travel is mainly by minibus or pick-up truck. Daily minibus services run from Libreville to Lambarene, Mouila, Oyem and Bitam (the last two usually involving night stops). Seats for these and other less frequent routes can be obtained from a broker, *Gabon Cars*, in Libreville. This is not, however, normally necessary for the main routes as seats will be readily available in the 'bus station' near the central market 0600-0800. There are also conventional buses on the Mouila route and other services out of Mouila. **Car hire:** Cars may be hired from main hotels and airports. **Documentation:** International Driving Permit advised and international insurance required.
URBAN: There are extensive shared taxis. There are bus services in Port Gentil and Franceville, and shared taxis in other centres. Taxi rates vary according to the time of day.

ACCOMMODATION

HOTELS: There are five high-class hotels in Libreville and also first-class hotels in Port Gentil, Franceville, Mouila, Lambarene, Oyem, Koulamoutou, Makokou and Tchibanga but, like most of the accommodation in Gabon, they are expensive. Tourist facilities, including comfortable accommodation, are being expanded throughout the country, especially along the coast and in towns close to the National Parks. There are hotels in other major cities and towns. These hotels will accept most major credit cards. For further information contact: Direction Generale de l'Hôtellerie et du Contrôle des Hotels, PO Box 403, Libreville. Tel: 738 380.
CAMPING: Free but limited. Use with caution.

RESORTS & EXCURSIONS

The main cities in Gabon are **Libreville, Port Gentil, Lambarene, Moanda, Oyem, Mouila and Franceville.**
Libreville is a lively and charming capital, beside the ocean, its white buildings contrasting with the green of the nearby equatorial forest. Sights include the art-craft village and the *National Museum*, which contains some of the most beautiful woodcarvings in Africa, especially the indigenous Fang style of carving which influenced Picasso's figures and busts. A visitor may also see the delightful *Peyrie Gardens*, in the heart of the city; the popular quarters of *Akebe* and *Nombakele*, the harbour, the *Cathedral of St Michel* (whose facade is covered with mosaics and woodcarvings) and the *Mount Bouet Market*. There are city tours conducted in French.
Elsewhere: A route winds through a forest of giant trees from Libreville to **Cape Esterias,** where the rocks abound with sea urchins, oysters and lobsters. Bathing from beautiful sandy beaches can be enjoyed in this area. It is possible to go to the *Kinguele Falls* on *M'Bei River* or to **Lambarene,** the town made famous by Doctor Schweitzer. His hospital is open to visitors and a tour on *Evaro Lake* can be organised. Adventure trips are available down the rapids of the **Okanda** region. Further south, the villages of **M'Bigou** and **Eteke** are famous for their local crafts and gold mines and, to the west, the enchanting **Mayumba** set between sea and lake. Eastwards, the region of **Bateke Plateau** comprises savannah and forest galleries, and tumultuous rivers spanned by liana bridges, such as the one at **Poubara.** Game and wildlife include forest elephants, buffaloes, sitatunga, river hogs, gorillas, panthers, crocodiles, monkeys and parrots. For the deep-sea fishermen, shark, barracuda, tarpon, scad, tuna and ray can be found. In the **Sette-Cama, Iguela** and **N'Dende** zones, visitors going on safari can hire guides experienced in tracking and approaching the game. For those armed only with camera and cine-camera, there is the *Lope* reserve and two national parks, *Wonga-Wongue* and *Moukalaba*.

SOCIAL PROFILE

FOOD & DRINK: Most hotels and restaurants serve French and continental-style food and are expensive. Gabonese food is distinctive and delicious, but not always readily available, as many restaurants are Senegalese, Cameroonian and Congolese restaurants. **Drink:** Licensing hours are similar to those in France.
NIGHTLIFE: There are nightclubs in Libreville with music and bars. Food is often served, although this can be expensive. There are also casinos at the *Inter-Continental Hotel* and the *Meridien Rendama Hotel*.
SHOPPING: In Libreville there are two bustling markets at Akebe-Plaine, Nkembo and Mon-Bouet. Stone carvings can be bought on the outskirts of both, fashioned by a group of carvers who have adapted traditional skills for the tourist market. Crafts from local villages can also be bought from stalls in the streets or from the villagers themselves. African (Fang) mask carvings, figurines, clay pots and traditional musical instruments can also be bought. **Shopping hours:** 0800-1200 and 1500-1900 Monday to Saturday. Some shops close on Monday.
SPORT: Swimming: Although a few hotels have pools the beaches on the Atlantic coast offer ideal bathing conditions. **Water-skiing:** Port Gentil at the mouth of the River Ogooue and Libreville have beaches with facilities for water-skiing and other **watersports.** Mayumba in the south and Cap Esterias, 35km (22 miles) from Libreville is a popular watersports centre at weekends. **Skindiving:** Perroquet and Pointe Denis both offer good skindiving. **Tennis:** Courts available in Libreville and Port Gentil. **Safaris:** Trips can be made to the Okanda National Park and other parks in the savannah region, all of which are rich in wildlife. Details obtained can be obtained from the Tourist Office in Gabon. **Fishing:** Many of the rivers offer excellent fishing; equipment can be hired at Port Gentil. Fish abound in Gabonese rivers and lakes, but the fishermen can find the largest variety along the coast and in the numerous lagoons located at the mouth of Ogooue.
SOCIAL CONVENTIONS: Dance, song, poetry and myths remain an important part of traditional Gabonese life. **Photography:** It is absolutely forbidden to photograph military installations. In general, permission to photograph anything should be requested first, to prevent misunderstandings.
Tipping: Should be 10%-15% unless service is included in the bill.

BUSINESS PROFILE

ECONOMY: Oil reserves and mineral deposits have allowed Gabon to develop into one of Africa's most successful economies. There is a small manufacturing base engaged in oil refining and the production of plywood, paints, varnishes and detergents, dry batteries, cement, cigarettes and textiles. Future growth in this sector is likely to be limited by a shortage of skilled labour, high costs and inadequate infrastructure. The main economic priority at present is agriculture; Gabon produces coffee, sugar cane, rubber and some crops. Efforts are under way to stimulate growth in these and other industries, notably fishing which is much under-exploited. The other sector with potential is the timber industry, since Gabon has considerable afforested areas. Gabon is a member of the Central African economic and customs union, UDEAC and of the CFA Franc Zone. Gabon has a large balance of payments surplus, and oil contributes 80% of export earnings. The potential for future growth is considerable, although recent setbacks, principally falling raw material prices, have forced the Government to accept an IMF-financed Structural Adjustment Programme. A joint debt-relief programme has been arranged with neighbouring Cameroon and Congo. Manufactured goods, transport equipment and foodstuffs are the main imports. The country's main trading partners are in the industrialised West, with France the largest followed by the USA, Japan and Germany.
BUSINESS: Tropical suits are required. French is the principal language used in business circles translators and interpreters are available through the Embassy. Strong business ties remain with France despite competition from the USA and Japan. **Office hours:** 0730-1200 and 1430-1800 Monday to Friday.
COMMERCIAL INFORMATION: The following organisations can offer advice: Chambre de

Commerce, d'Agriculture, d'Industrie et des Mines du Gabon, BP 2234, Libreville, Gabon. Tel: 722 064. Telex: 5554.
CONFERENCES/CONVENTIONS: Further information can be obtained from the Comité National des Fêtes et Conferences (COMINAFC), PO Box 882, Libreville. Tel: 761 766.

HISTORY & GOVERNMENT

HISTORY: The oldest human artefacts to have been discovered in Gabon are stone spearheads, which date back to 7000BC, but little more is known about Gabonese prehistory, the earliest of the present inhabitants being the Pygmies. From AD1100 onwards various Bantu tribes began migrating into the area. It was during this period of migration, which continued for several centuries, that the Portuguese discovered Gabon in 1472. Thereafter, Gabon was primarily of interest to the Dutch, French and British, who negotiated with the coastal tribes for slaves and ivory from the interior. The slave trade ceased in the middle of the 19th century, but not before it had destroyed the social inter-relationships of the tribes it affected. Land on either side of the Gabon River was annexed peacefully to the French during the mid-19th century as a province of French Equitorial Africa. The Republic of Gabon moved peacefully into independence in 1960 after a 3-year period of internal self-government. A French-style constitution was adopted the following year and Léon M'Ba became Gabon's first President. After seven years of stormy pluralism, the ruling Parti Démocratique Gabonais (PDG) declared Gabon a one-party state, but retained broadly pro-Western policies. President Omar Bongo, who succeeded M'Ba on the latter's death in 1967, has maintained these, which include close relations with the French: Gabon is France's principal supplier of uranium and a number of other strategic minerals. French troops were on hand in June 1990 to crush a rebellion led by industrial workers. Since the beginning of 1990, the Bongo government has almost completed the transformation, under way throughout much of Africa, from a one-party state to a pluralistic political system. The 120-seat elected national assembly is dominated by the PDG, which now has 66 seats with the remainder divided between 6 opposition parties, of which the most important are the Parti Gabonais du Progres (19 seats) and the Rassemblement des Bûcherons (17 seats). Casimir Oye Mba, the former head of the transitional administration, took over the premiership in November 1990, and was reappointed at the head of a new government, PDG-controlled with some minor party participation, in June 1991. A multi-party presidential election is due to be held in December 1993.
GOVERNMENT: A new constitution was adopted in March 1991 under which an executive President and 120-seat national assembly are elected for a 5-year term. The President appoints a Council of Ministers headed by a Prime Minister.

CLIMATE

Equatorial with high humidity. The dry season is from mid-May to mid-September, and the main rainy season is from February to April/May. Trade winds blow in the dry season.
Required clothing: Lightweight tropical, with raincoats advised during the rainy season.

LIBREVILLE Gabon (12m)

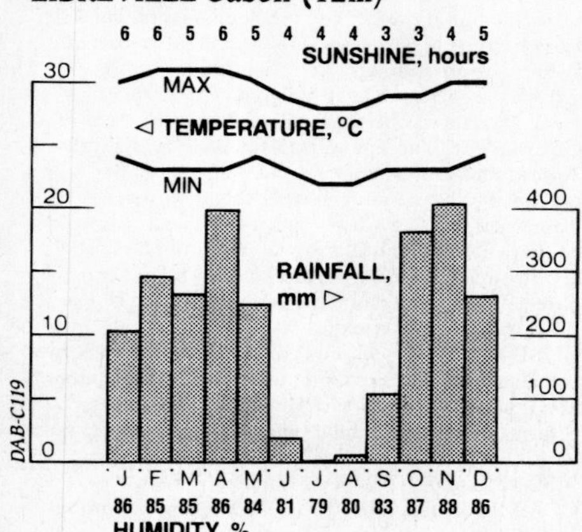

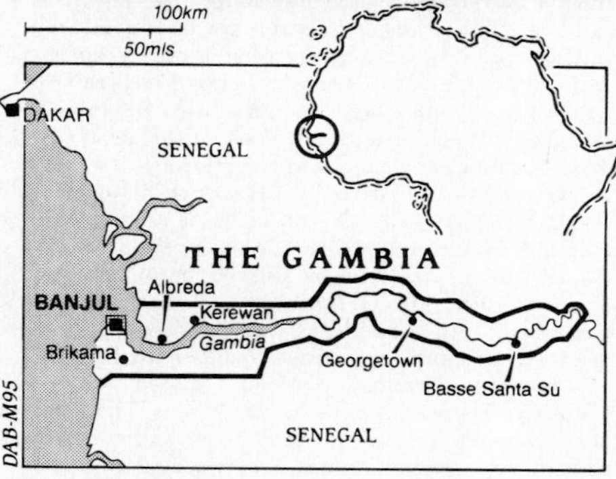

□ international airport

Location: West Africa.

Ministry of Information and Tourism
The Quadrangle
Banjul, The Gambia
Tel: 28496. Telex: 2204.
High Commission of the Republic of The Gambia
57 Kensington Court
London W8 5DG
Tel: (071) 937 6316/7/8. Telex: 911857.
Gambia National Tourist Office
Address as for High Commission.
Opening hours: 0930-1700 Monday to Thursday, 0900-1300 Friday.
British High Commission
PO Box 507
48 Atlantic Road
Fajara
Banjul, The Gambia
Tel: 95133. Fax: 96134. Telex: 2211.
Embassy of the Republic of The Gambia
Suite 720
1030 15th Street, NW
Washington, DC
20005
Tel: (202) 842 1356/9. Fax:(202) 842 2073. Telex: 204791.
Embassy of the United States of America
PO Box 19
Kairaba Avenue
Fajara, Banjul
The Gambia
Tel: 92856 *or* 92859 *or* 92789. Fax: 92475.
Consulate of The Republic of Gambia
Suite 300
363 St François Xavier Street
Montréal, Québec
H27 3P9
Tel: (514) 849 2885. Telex: 0525266.
Canadian High Commission to The Gambia
c/o Canadian Embassy
PO Box 3373
Dakar, Senegal

AREA: 11,295 sq km (4361 sq miles).
POPULATION: 800,000 (1988 estimate).
POPULATION DENSITY: 70.8 per sq km.
CAPITAL: Banjul. **Population:** 47,000 (1986).
GEOGRAPHY: The Gambia is situated on the Atlantic coast at the bulge of Africa. The country consists of a thin ribbon of land, at no point wider than 50km (30 miles), running east-west on both banks of the River Gambia. The Gambia is bounded to the west by the Atlantic Ocean and on all other sides by Senegal. It is also the smallest and westernmost African nation. The country mainly consists of a low plateau which decreases in height as it nears the Atlantic coast. The plain is broken in a few places by low flat-topped hills and by the river and its tributaries. The area extending from MacCarthy Island, where Georgetown is located, to the eastern end of the country is enclosed by low rocky hills. The coast and river banks are backed mainly by mangrove swamps, while the lower part of the river has steep red ironstone banks which are covered with tropical forest and bamboo. Away from the river the landscape consists of wooded, park-like savannah, with large areas covered by a variety of trees such as mahogany, rosewood, oil palm and rubber. On the coast the river meets the Atlantic with impressive sand cliffs and 50km (30 miles) of broad, unspoiled beaches, palm-fringed and strewn with shells. These silver sand beaches are one of The Gambia's main attractions for visitors seeking an escape from the European winter.
LANGUAGE: The official language is English. Local languages are Mandinka, Fula, Wollof, Jola and Serahule.
RELIGION: Over 80% Muslim, with the remainder holding either Christian or Animist beliefs.
TIME: GMT.
ELECTRICITY: 220 volts AC, 50Hz. Plugs are either round 3-pin or square 3-pin (15 or 13 amps).
COMMUNICATIONS: Telephone: IDD is available. Country code: 220. The country has an automatic telephone-system. **Fax:** There are nine GAMTEL offices in Banjul offering this service, some on a 24-hour basis. **Telex/telegram:** Services are run by GAMTEL, Cameron Street, Banjul. There are several GAMTEL branches in Banjul with telex stations. **Post:** Post office hours: 0800-1300 Monday to Friday, 0800-1100 Saturday. **Press:** Newspapers are English-language and include *The Gambia Weekly* (which appears every Friday), *The Nation, The Gambia Times* and *Gambia Onwards.*
BBC World Service and Voice of America frequencies: From time to time these change. See the section *How to Use this Book* for more information.

BBC:				
MHz	21.71	15.07	11.86	6.005
Voice of America:				
MHz	21.49	15.60	9.525	6.035

PASSPORT/VISA

Regulations and requirements may be subject to change at short notice, and you are advised to contact the appropriate diplomatic or consular authority before finalising travel arrangements. Details of these may be found at the head of this country's entry. Any numbers in the chart refer to the footnotes below.

	Passport Required?	Visa Required?	Return Ticket Required?
Full British	Yes	1	Yes
BVP	Not valid	-	-
Australian	Yes	No	Yes
Canadian	Yes	No	Yes
USA	Yes	Yes	Yes
Other EC	Yes	1	Yes
Japanese	Yes	Yes	Yes

PASSPORTS: Valid passport required by all.
British Visitors Passport: Not acceptable.
VISAS: Required by all except:
(a) those referred to in the chart above;
(b) nationals of Commonwealth countries;
(c) nationals of Benin, Burkina Faso, Côte d'Ivoire, Guinea Republic, Guinea-Bissau, Mali, Mauritania, Niger, Senegal and Togo;
(d) [1] nationals of Belgium, Denmark, Germany, Greece, Italy, Ireland, Luxembourg, The Netherlands, Spain and the UK (for the purposes of tourism only) for visits of up to 3 months;
(e) nationals of Finland, Iceland, Norway, San Marino, Sweden, Tunisia, Turkey and Uruguay for visits of up to 3 months.
Types of visa: Tourist and Business visas are £6. Collective visas are obtainable for organised groups.
Validity: Normally 90 days.
Application to: Consulate (or Consular Section at Embassy or High Commission). For address, see top of entry.
Application requirements: (a) Valid passport. (b) 2 application forms. (c) 2 photos.
Working days required: Often within 24 hours. Postal applications need recorded, stamped, self-addressed envelope.
Temporary residence: Refer enquiries to Gambian Embassy or High Commission.

MONEY

Currency: Gambian Dalasi (Di) = 100 bututs. Notes are in denominations of Di50, 25, 10, 5 and 1. Coins are in denominations of Di1, and 50, 25, 10, 5 and 1 bututs.
Credit cards: Access and Visa both have limited acceptance. Check with your credit card company for

details of merchant acceptability and other services which may be available.
Travellers cheques: US Dollar and Sterling travellers cheques are equally acceptable.
Exchange rate indicators: The following figures are included as a guide to the movements of the Dalasi against Sterling and the US Dollar:

Date:	Oct '89	Oct '90	Oct '91	Oct '92
£1.00=	12.25	15.47	16.35	13.13
$1.00=	7.76	7.92	9.42	8.27

Currency restrictions: The thriving black market for hard currency is officially discouraged, and visitors must complete a currency declaration form on arrival. Currency from Algeria, Ghana, Guinea, Mali, Morocco, Nigeria, Sierra Leone and Tunisia is neither accepted nor exchanged. There are no restrictions on the import of other foreign currencies; export is limited to the amount imported. CFA Francs are accepted. Local currency may be difficult to exchange outside the country.
Banking hours: 0800-1330 Monday to Thursday, 0800-1200 Friday.

DUTY FREE

The following goods may be imported into The Gambia without incurring customs duty:
200 cigarettes or 50 cigars or 250g of tobacco (or mixed to the same total quantity);
1 litre of spirits;
1 litre of beer or wine;
Goods up to a value of Di1000.

PUBLIC HOLIDAYS

Public holidays observed in The Gambia are as follows:
Mar 25 '93 Start of Eid al-Fitr. **Apr 9-12** Easter. **May 1** Labour Day. **Jun 1** Start of Eid al-Adha. **Aug 15** Assumption. **Aug 30** Mouloud (Birthday of the Prophet). **Dec 25** Christmas. **Jan 1 '94** New Year's Day. **Feb 18** Independence Day. **Mar** Start of Eid al-Fitr.
Note: Muslim festivals are timed according to local sightings of various phases of the Moon and the dates given above are approximations. During the lunar month of Ramadan that precedes Eid al-Fitr, Muslims fast during the day and feast at night and normal business patterns may be interrupted. Many restaurants are closed during the day and there are restrictions on smoking and drinking. Some disruption may continue into Eid al-Fitr itself. Eid al-Fitr and Eid al-Adha may last anything from two to ten days, depending on the region. For more information see the section *World of Islam* at the back of the book.

HEALTH

Regulations and requirements may be subject to change at short notice, and you are advised to contact your doctor well in advance of your intended date of departure. Any numbers in the chart refer to the footnotes below.

	Special Precautions?	Certificate Required?
Yellow Fever	Yes	1
Cholera	Yes	2
Typhoid & Polio	Yes	-
Malaria	3/Yes	-
Food & Drink	4/Yes	-

[1]: A yellow fever vaccination certificate is required from all travellers over one year of age arriving from endemic or infected areas.
[2]: Following WHO guidelines issued in 1973, a cholera vaccination certificate is no longer a condition of entry to The Gambia. However, cholera is a serious risk in this country and precautions are essential. Up-to-date advice should be sought before deciding whether these precautions should include vaccination as medical opinion is divided over its effectiveness. See the *Health* section at the back of the book.
[3]: Malaria risk, predominantly in the malignant *falciparum* form, exists throughout the year throughout the country. Chloroquine resistance has been reported. Travellers should consult their doctors for medical advice.
[4]: All water should be regarded as being potentially contaminated. Water used for drinking, brushing teeth or making ice should have first been boiled or otherwise sterilised. Milk is unpasteurised and should be boiled. Powdered or tinned milk is available and is advised, but make sure that it is reconstituted with pure water. Avoid dairy products which are likely to have been made from local milk. Only eat well-cooked meat and fish, preferably served hot. Pork, salad and mayonnaise may carry increased risk. Vegetables should be cooked and fruit peeled.
Bilharzia (schistosomiasis) is present. Avoid swimming and paddling in fresh water. Swimming pools which are well-chlorinated and maintained are safe.
Rabies is present. For those at high risk vaccination before arrival should be considered. If you are bitten abroad seek medical advice without delay. For more information consult the *Health* section at the back of the book.
Health care: Visitors are advised to bring good supplies of sun-screen lotion, insect repellent and anti-stomach upset medicines; all of these may be needed and they can prove expensive or, in some cases, impossible to buy in The Gambia. The Government provides both therapeutic and preventative medical and health services, and plays a dominant role in health services. There are two government-run hospitals: one in Banjul, the Royal Victoria Hospital, with children's and maternity wards; and the other at Bansang (Bansang Hospital), which is located about 320km (200 miles) up river. Other medical facilities run by the Government include Alatentu (a leprosy hospital), an infirmary, a mental hospital and a tuberculosis sanatorium. The Medical Research Centre at Fajara (opposite the British High Commission) provides good facilities as well. Maternal and child-welfare services have been extended to most parts of the country.
Health insurance is advised.

TRAVEL - International

AIR: The main airlines to serve the Gambia are *British Airways (BA)* and *Sabena (SN)*. The Gambia's national airline is *Gambian Airways (GM)*, head office in Banjul.
International flight time: From *London* to Banjul is approximately 5 hours 30 minutes (direct).
International airport: *Banjul (BJL)* (Yundum International) is 29km (18 miles) southwest of the city. Taxis are available to the city. During 1989, NASA upgraded airport facilities and it is now an emergency space shuttle landing site.
Departure tax: Gambian passport holders, Di35. Other passengers including non-Gambian residents, Di7.
SEA: Passenger accommodation on cargo boats sailing regularly from Liverpool, London and other European ports (eight to ten days) run by *West African Conference Lines*, which include *Elder Dempster*, *Palm Line*, *Guinea Gulf*, *Nigerian National*, *Black Star* and *Hoegh Lines*. There are two sailings a month. Cruise ships also call at Banjul. Around 400 or more craft dock at its port annually.
ROAD: Banjul can be reached by road from Dakar by the Trans-Gambia Highway, a distance of 480km (300 miles), which crosses the River Gambia by ferry between Farafenni and Mansa Konko as there is no bridge over the Gambia River. An alternative crossing is the car ferry between Barra Point and Banjul, reducing the journey to 320km (200 miles). Government buses also make the trip between The Gambia and Senegal, via Barra to Koalack and Dakar; there is also a high-class coach service.

TRAVEL - Internal

RIVER: The River Gambia provides excellent connections to all parts of the country. The ferry from Barra Point to Banjul runs every two hours in either direction and takes about 30 minutes. There is also a weekly ferry from Banjul to Basse, 390km (240 miles) away; the journey takes about a day and the length of stay at intermediate stops varies.
ROAD: There are slightly over 3000km (2000 miles) of roads in the country, about 450km (280 miles) of which are paved. Roads in and around Banjul are mostly bituminised, but unsealed roads often become impassable in the rainy season. Road construction programmes include the new link from Banjul to Serrekunda and the proposed link from Lamin Koto to Passimas. **Collective taxis:** These can be hired from Barra to Dakar. It is advisable to settle taxi fares in advance. **Car hire:** This is possible, check with company for details before travelling. **Documentation:** An International Driving Permit will be accepted for a period of three months. A valid UK licence can be used for a short visit.

ACCOMMODATION

HOTELS: Several Gambian hotels are geared primarily to package tours. Accommodation is often booked up in the tourist season (November to May), and confirmation of advance booking should be sought. Most of the hotels are self-contained complexes set in spacious gardens and will generally cater for most tourist needs. Bedrooms will not always be air-conditioned. For further information, contact the Gambian National Tourist Office (address at top of entry).
The number of hotels has increased greatly in recent years and is expected to continue; in 1967 there were only two hotels with a total of 52 beds, whereas now there are over 20 with 4500 beds, both in Banjul and along the coast. 75% of establishments belong to the Gambia Hotel Association which can be contacted c/o The Atlantic Hotel, PO Box 296, Marina Parade, Banjul, The Gambia. Tel: 28601/6. Fax: 27861. Telex: GV 2250.

RESORTS & EXCURSIONS

The Gambia is Africa's smallest nation, but nonetheless offers landscapes and attractions of great diversity – broad, sandy beaches on the Atlantic, lush tropical forests, swamps and marshes and large areas of wooded savannah.

Banjul & The Coast

The *River Gambia* is several miles wide at its mouth near **Cape St Mary**. It narrows to 5km (3 miles) at Banjul (known as Bathurst in pre-independence days), which is situated on **St Mary's Island** and has a deep sheltered harbour. **Banjul** is the only sizeable town in the country and is the seat of government. There is an interesting *National Museum*. The area around *MacCarthy Square* has a colonial atmosphere, with pleasant 19th-century architecture. Nearby is the craft market. Souvenirs can also be bought at *bengdulalu* (singular: *bengdula*) near the Wadner Beach, Sunwing and Fajara hotels, at the Senegambia Hotel and at Kotu beach. *Bengdula* in the Mandinka language means a 'meeting place' and is a shopping area consisting of African-style stalls, usually built near hotels.

GAMBIA | **HEALTH REGULATIONS** | **VISA REGULATIONS** | Code-Link

GALILEO/WORLDSPAN

TI-DFT/BJL/HE

TI-DFT/BJL/VI

SABRE

TIDFT/BJL/HE

TIDFT/BJL/VI

To access this information on your CRS, swipe the barcode with a light pen or type in the text under the barcode. For more information, see the introduction *How to Use This Book.*

Local handicrafts of a large variety can be bought at *bengdulalu*. The Atlantic coast to the south of Banjul boasts some of the finest beaches in all Africa with no less than 15 hotels in the **Banjul**, **Kombo** and **St Mary** area. They are served by the international airport at **Yundum**, a few miles from the capital.

The River Gambia

This is the dominant feature of the country and is the major method of transportation and irrigation as well as providing opportunities for fishing, boating and sailing. A cruise up the River Gambia is highly recommended. Most remarkable is the abundance and variety of birdlife along the shores. Particularly well worth visiting is the *Abuko Nature Reserve*, which has crocodiles, monkeys, birds and antelope. Details of cruises can be found on hotel noticeboards. Banjul is the starting point for coach and river trips to all parts of the country and coastline. The whole river and the numerous creeks (known locally as *bolongs*) which join it, are fascinating to the bird lover and the student of nature.

THE RIVER MOUTH: *Fort Bullen* at **Barra Point** was built by the British 200 years ago to cover the approaches to Banjul and the river, succeeding *James Island Fortress* (destroyed by the French) as the main point of defence in the colony. It can be reached by direct ferry from the capital. **Oyster Creek** is the centre of an area of creeks and waterways which can be visited from Banjul.

UPRIVER FROM BANJUL: Albreda was the main French trading post before they withdrew from The Gambia. Nearby is the historic village of **Juffure,** home of the ancestors of black American writer Alex Haley, author of 'Roots'. Visitors who want to see more of the countryside may cross by ferry from Banjul to Barra and travel by road to Juffure and Albreda (the journey lasts about 50 minutes), and then by canoe to **James Island** in the calm waters of the River Gambia. **Tendaba** is a new holiday centre, 160km (100 miles) from Banjul by river or road. Further upriver, the fascinating circles of standing stones around **Wassau** have now been identified as burial grounds more than 1200 years old. **Georgetown** was the 'second city' of colonial days, and is still the administrative and trading centre of the region. **Basse Santa Su** is the major trading centre for the upper reaches of the Gambia River. Handsome trading houses built at the turn of the century can be seen there. By the riverside at **Perai Tenda** can be found a multitude of abandoned shops formerly operated by European, Gambian and Lebanese merchants in the days when upriver commerce offered substantial profits for private traders. **Sutukoba** was once a thriving trading town and the ancient Portuguese entrepot for goods from the interior of the continent.

SOCIAL PROFILE

FOOD & DRINK: Western food is available at most tourist hotels and restaurants, and some also serve Gambian food. Recommended dishes include *benachin* (also called 'Jollof Rice', a mixture of spiced meat and rice with tomato puree and vegetables), *base nyebe* (rich stew of chicken or beef with green beans and other vegetables), *chere* (steamed millet flour balls) *domodah* (meat stewed in groundnut puree and served with rice), *plasas* (meat and smoked fish cooked in palm oil with green vegetables) served with *fu-fu* or mashed *cassava churq-gerteh* (a sweet porridge consisting of pounded groundnuts, rice and milk). Local fruits like mangoes, bananas, grapefruit, papayas and oranges are delicious and are available in the markets. **Drink:** A good selection of spirits, beers and wines is available. Local fresh fruit juice is delicious.

NIGHTLIFE: In general the nightlife is subdued, although there are nightclubs in Banjul, Farjara, Bakau and Serrekunda. Gambian ballet, drumming, dancing and fire-eating displays are organised at a hotel every week.

SHOPPING: Souvenirs can be bought in Banjul at the craft market across from MacCarthy Square and at *bengdulalu* (see *Resorts & Excursions* above). One of the most popular purchases is the *Gambishirt*, made of printed and embroidered cotton cloth, mostly in bright colours. Some of the souvenirs are gaudy, others exceedingly attractive. Woodcarvings, beaded belts, silver and gold jewellery, and ladies handbags are also popular items. Other West African handicrafts made of straw, beads, leather, cloth or metal can be purchased here. **Shopping hours:** 0900-1200 and 1400-1700 Monday to Thursday, and from 0900-1300 Friday and Saturday.

SPORT: Swimming: The estuary of the River Gambia on the Atlantic coast provides miles of magnificent beaches with warm seas throughout the year. Caution is necessary due to strong currents, but the beach at Cape St Mary is safe for both children and adults. **Watersports:** Atlantic resorts cater for **windsurfing** and **surfing. Fishing:** Both sea and river fishing is good all year, particularly line fishing from the beaches. Several sport fishing boats are available for sea angling trips. **Sailing:** The Gambia Sailing Club at Banjul welcomes visitors. A notable event is the race to Dog Island; in addition, regattas are organised on special occasions. **Golf:** The Banjul Golf Club has an 18-hole golf course at Fajara near the Atlantic coast. International meetings are organised every year. **Wrestling:** The traditional national sport; contests can be watched in most towns and villages. **Birdwatching:** Very popular in The Gambia; the country has one of largest number of bird species per square mile in the world. **Tennis** courts are available at some hotels, while details of the location of other courts are available from the Tourist Information Office or most hotel receptions. Tennis clubs include The Cedar Club near Serekunda and the Reform Club in Banjul. *Bouts* (a traditional sport) can be seen on most weekends in Banjul and its suburbs, Serekunda and Bakau. Inter-club **cricket** is played in league matches organised by the Gambia Cricket Association which also organises international matches. A league **football** championship is organised by the Gambia Football Association.

SPECIAL EVENTS: There are big celebrations at Christmas, and also during the Muslim festivals of *Tabaski* and *Koriteh*, but dance or acrobatic street shows can be seen at any time of the year.

SOCIAL CONVENTIONS: Handshaking is a common form of greeting; 'Nanga def' ('How are you?') is the traditional greeting. Gambians are extremely friendly and welcoming and visitors should not be afraid to accept their hospitality. Many Gambians are Muslim and their religious customs and beliefs should be respected by guests; however most understand the English customs and language. Visitors should remember that the right hand only should be used for the giving or receiving of food or objects. Casual wear is suitable although beachwear should only be worn on the beach or at the poolside. Only the very top-class dining rooms encourage guests to dress for dinner. Despite the effects of tourism, traditional culture in music, dancing and craftsmanship still flourishes in the many villages on both banks of the River Gambia. **Tipping:** 10% service charge is sometimes included in hotel and restaurant bills.

BUSINESS PROFILE

ECONOMY: The economy of The Gambia is almost entirely agricultural, with groundnuts (in the form of nuts, oil and cattle cake) accounting for well over 90% of total exports. Agriculture, forestry and fishing provide a living for 85% of the people and contribute about 59% of the Gross Domestic Product, whereas the industrial sector contributes less than 3%. In the past few years the tourist industry has grown rapidly, and is the most dynamic sector of the economy; the number of tourists has grown from 660 in 1965 to over 25,000 in 1975 and to nearly 112,986 in 1988/9, contributing 10% of the GDP. Another big cash earner is the Gambia Port Authority. There is great potential in the fisheries sector, and the Government, with United Nations Development Programme (UNDP) assistance, is encouraging improved methods and the modernisation of boats. General policy is concerned with trying to broaden the economic base, and there is much excitement about the results of recent seismic surveys which indicate the presence of oil and gas deposits. The Gambia is a member of the Economic Community of West African States (ECOWAS).

BUSINESS: Businessmen wear jackets and ties for business meetings. A personal approach is important in Gambian business circles. Punctuality is appreciated and it is advisable to take calling cards, although their use is not widespread. **Office hours:** 0900-1600 Monday to Thursday, and from 0900-1200 Friday and Saturday.

COMMERCIAL INFORMATION: The following organisation can offer advice: Gambia Chamber of Commerce and Industry, PO Box 33, 78 Wellington Street, Banjul, The Gambia. Tel: 27042 *or* 29761.

HISTORY & GOVERNMENT

HISTORY: The River Gambia was known to the Carthaginians in the 5th century BC, and subsequently the area became part of several successive African empires. During the colonial period, several European powers contested for ownership of the river and the rich trade which it carried. Britain eventually gained control of the mouth and lower reaches of the river, thereby establishing an enclave in the surrounding French territories of Senegal, a useful base from which to launch attacks on French trading settlements. The Gambia was Britain's first and last colony, being colonised in 1765 (although until 1843 it was united with Sierra Leone) and gaining independence 200 years later in February 1965.

The country became a republic in April 1970 and it is now part of the Commonwealth. The Gambia has enjoyed a high degree of stability since independence, being the only former British West Africa territory not to have experienced a successful military coup, and is consequently regarded as one of the most stable countries in West Africa, if not the whole of the continent. Nonetheless, the failed coup which took place in 1981 had a profound effect on Gambian politics. Immediately after the restoration of the legitimate government, which took place with the help of Senegalese (and a small number of British) troops, a confederation of Senegal and The Gambia was announced under the leadership of President Diouf of Senegal with President Jawara as his deputy. The intention was to harmonise the two countries' political, economic and defence policies as a preparatory step towards full unification.

The project was aborted in 1989, although very close links between the two countries remain despite the divorce. In the last two years, The Gambia has been involved in repeated efforts to find a political settlement in strife-torn Liberia and committed troops to the ECOWAS Monitoring Group which operates there in a peacekeeping capacity. President Jawara was confirmed in office for a further term at elections held on May 12, 1992.

GOVERNMENT: The legislature is unicameral with 49 members. The President (Sir Dawda Jawara since 1972) is elected for a 5-year term. The Confederation has a Council of Ministers and a 60-seat Confederal Legislative Assembly, which meets twice a year.

CLIMATE

The Gambia is generally recognised to have the most agreeable climate in West Africa. The weather is subtropical with distinct dry and rainy seasons. From mid-November to mid-May coastal areas are dry, while the rainy season lasts from June to October. Inland the cool season is shorter and daytime temperatures are very high between March and June. Sunny periods occur on most days even in the rains.

Required clothing: Lightweight for January to April and rainwear from June to October. Synthetic fabrics are not useful in the rainy season.

BANJUL The Gambia (27m)

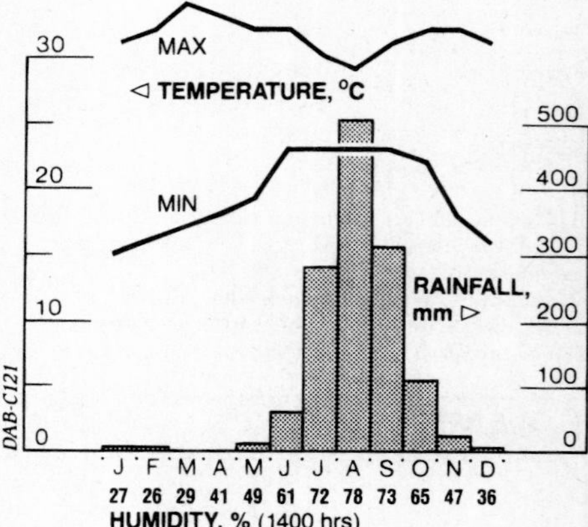

TEMPERATURE CONVERSIONS
-20 -10 0°C 10 20 30 40
0 10 20 30°F40 50 60 70 80 90 100
RAINFALL CONVERSIONS 0mm 200 400 600 800
0in 5 10 15 20 25 30

GERMANY (FEDERAL REPUBLIC OF)

Location: Western/Central Europe.

Deutsche Zentrale für Tourismus e.V. (DZT)
Beethovenstrasse 69
W-6000 Frankfurt/M 1
Federal Republic of Germany
Tel: (69) 75720. Fax: (69) 751 903.

Embassy of the Federal Republic of Germany
23 Belgrave Square
1 Chesham Place
London SW1X 8PZ
Tel: (071) 824 1300. Fax: (071) 235 0609.
Consulate: Tel: (071) 235 0165 (recorded information on visas). Fax: (071) 235 0609. Opening hours: 0900-1200 Monday to Friday.
Consulates also in: Manchester (tel: (061) 237 5255) *and* Edinburgh (tel: (031) 337 2323).

German National Tourist Office
Nightingale House
65 Curzon Street
London W1Y 7PE
Tel: (071) 495 3990 (general enquiries) *or* (071) 495 0081 (trade only). Fax: (071) 495 6129. Opening hours: 1000-1700 Monday to Friday.

British Embassy
Friedrich-Ebert-Allee 77
W-5300 Bonn 1
Federal Republic of Germany
Tel: (228) 234 061. Fax: (228) 234 070. Telex: 886887.
Consulates in: Düsseldorf, Frankfurt, Hamburg, Bremen, Nuremberg, Freiburg, Hannover, Munich, Stuttgart, Kiel and Berlin.

Embassy of the Federal Republic of Germany
4645 Reservoir Road, NW
Washington, DC
20007-1998
Tel: (202) 298 4000. Fax: (202) 298 4249. Telex: 248321.
Consulates in: Atlanta, Boston, Chicago, Detroit, Houston, Los Angeles, Miami, New Orleans, New York (tel: (212) 308 8700) and San Francisco.

German National Tourist Office
33rd Floor
747 Third Avenue
New York, NY 10017
Tel: (212) 308 3300. Fax: (212) 688 1322. Telex: 49572363.

Embassy of the United States of America
Deichmanns Aue 29
W-5300 Bonn 2
Federal Republic of Germany
Tel: (228) 339-1. Fax: (228) 339-2663. Telex: 885452.

Embassy of the Federal Republic of Germany
1 Waverley Street
Ottawa, Ontario
K2P 0T8
Tel: (613) 232 1101/2/3/4/5. Fax: (613) 594 9330. Telex: 0534226.
Consulates in: Calgary, Edmonton, Halifax, Kitchener, Montréal, Regina, St John's, Toronto, Vancouver and Winnipeg.

German National Tourist Office
Suite 604
North Tower
175 Bloor Street East
Toronto, Ontario
M4W 3R8
Tel: (416) 968 1570. Fax: (416) 968 1986.

Canadian Embassy
Friedrich-Wilhelm-Strasse 18
W-5300 Bonn 1
Federal Republic of Germany
Tel: (228) 231 061. Fax: (228) 230 857. Telex: 886421.
Consulates in: Berlin, Düsseldorf and Munich.

AREA: 356,945 sq km (137,817 sq miles).
POPULATION: 79,670,000 (1990).
POPULATION DENSITY: 223 per sq km.
CAPITAL: Berlin. **Population:** 3,409,000.
Administrative Capital: Bonn. **Population:** 282,190. The move of the administration to Berlin should be completed by the end of 1998. However, eight ministries are to remain in Bonn, therefore creating two administrative capitals.
GEOGRAPHY: The Federal Republic of Germany shares frontiers with Austria, Belgium, the Czech Republic, Denmark, France, Luxembourg, The Netherlands, Poland and Switzerland. The northwest of the country has a coastline on the North Sea with islands known for their health resorts, while the Baltic coastline in the northeast stretches from the Danish to the Polish border. The country is divided into 16 states *(Bundesländer)* including the formerly divided city of Berlin. The landscape is exceedingly varied, with the Rhine, Bavaria and the Black Forest being probably the three most famous features of western Germany. In eastern Germany the country is lake-studded with undulating lowlands which give way to the hills and mountains of the Lausitzer Bergland, the Saxon Hills in the Elbe Valley and the Erzgebirge, whilst the once divided areas of the Thuringian and Harz ranges in the central part of the country are now whole regions again. River basins extend over a large percentage of the eastern part of Germany, the most important being the Elbe, Saale, Havel, Spree and Oder. Northern Germany includes the states of Lower Saxony (Niedersachsen), Schleswig-Holstein, Mecklenburg-West Pomerania and the city states of Bremen and Hamburg. The western area of the country consists of the Rhineland, the industrial sprawl of the Ruhr, Westphalia (Westfalen), Hesse (Hessen), the Rhineland Palatinate (Rheinland-Pfalz) and the Saarland. In the southern area of the country are the two largest states, Baden-Württemberg and Bavaria (Bayern), which contain the Black Forest (Schwarzwald), Lake Constance (Bodensee) and the Bavarian Alps. Munich (München), Stuttgart and Nuremberg (Nürnberg) are the major cities. The eastern part of the country is made up of the states of Thuringia, Saxony, Brandenburg, Saxony-Anhalt and Berlin. The major cities in eastern Germany are Dresden, Leipzig, Erfurt, Halle, Potsdam, Schwerin and Rostock. Apart from Leipzig and Rostock these are all also recently reconstituted state-capitals.
LANGUAGE: German. English is widely spoken and french is also spoken, particularly in the Saarland. Whereas in the north of Schleswig-Holstein, Danish is spoken by the Danish minority and taught in schools. Regional dialects often differ markedly from standard German.
RELIGION: Approximately 51% Protestant, 36% Roman Catholic and other non-Christian denominations.
TIME: GMT + 1 (GMT + 2 in summer).
ELECTRICITY: 220 volts AC, 50Hz.
COMMUNICATIONS: Telephone: Full IDD is available. Country code: 49. National and international calls can be made from coin- or card-operated telephone booths. There are already 2200 card-operated public telephones in the new eastern states. Calls can be made from post offices. Cheap rate applies from between 1800-0800 Monday to Friday and all day Saturday and Sunday. **Fax:** Facilities are increasingly available in east Germany. **Telex:** Fully automatic telex and telecommunications services are available throughout the country. Telegrams can be sent during opening hours from all post offices. Public telex facilities are available at Fernmeldeamt 1, Winterfeldstrasse 21, W-1000 Berlin 62; and Presshaus 1, Heussallee 2-10, W-5300 Bonn. **Post:** Stamps are available from hotels, slot machines and post offices. A 4-figure postal code is used on all internal addresses, preceded with 'W-' for western Germany and 'O-' for eastern Germany. This will change in May 1993 with the introduction of new 5-digit postal codes nationwide; the prefixes of 'O' and 'W' will then become redundant. *Poste Restante* mail should be addressed as follows: recipient's name, Postlagernd, Hauptpostamt, post code, name of town. Post office hours: 0900-1800 Monday to Friday and 0900-1200 Saturday. Smaller branches may close for lunch. **Press:** Newspapers are free of government control. The most influential dailies include *Süddeutsche Zeitung*, *Die Welt* and the *Frankfurter Allgemeine Zeitung*. The most widely read of the weekly papers are *Der Spiegel* and *Die Zeit*. Some new or revamped newspapers, such as *Super* and *Berliner Kurier*, have emerged out of eastern Germany and are competing well with western German papers. There are no English-language papers printed in the country.
BBC World Service and Voice of America frequencies: From time to time these change. See the section *How to Use this Book* for more information.

BBC:

MHz	12.10	9.410	6.195	3.955

A service is also available on 648kHz and 198kHz (0100-0500 GMT). A service for Greater Berlin is available on 90.2FM.

Voice of America:

MHz	11.97	9.670	6.040	5.995

PASSPORT/VISA

Regulations and requirements may be subject to change at short notice, and you are advised to contact the appropriate diplomatic or consular authority before finalising travel arrangements. Details of these may be found at the head of this country's entry. Any numbers in the chart refer to the footnotes below.

	Passport Required?	Visa Required?	Return Ticket Required?
Full British	1	No	No
BVP	Valid	No	No
Australian	Yes	No	Yes
Canadian	Yes	No	Yes
USA	Yes	No	Yes
Other EC	2	No	No
Japanese	Yes	No	Yes

GERMANY | **HEALTH REGULATIONS** | **VISA REGULATIONS** | Code-Link

GALILEO/WORLDSPAN

TI-DFT/FRA/HE

TI-DFT/FRA/VI

SABRE

TIDFT/FRA/HE

TIDFT/FRA/VI

To access this information on your CRS, swipe the barcode with a light pen or type in the text under the barcode. For more information, see the introduction *How to Use This Book*.

PASSPORTS: Valid passport required by all except:
(a) [1] nationals of the UK holding a BVP;
(b) [2] holders of national ID cards issued to nationals of Austria, Belgium, Denmark, Finland, France, Greece, Iceland, Ireland, Italy, Liechtenstein, Luxembourg, Malta, Monaco, The Netherlands, Norway, San Marino, Spain and Switzerland.
Note: (a) Nationals of *all* countries arriving in the Federal Republic of Germany wishing to take up employment must be in possession of a full passport. (b) Holders of British passports with the endorsement *British Citizen*, and holders of British passports issued before January 1, 1983, with the endorsement '*Holder has the right of abode in the United Kingdom*' may enter without a visa. Holders of other British passports may require a visa and should consult the Embassy before making any travel arrangements.
British Visitors Passport: Valid. A BVP can be used for holidays or unpaid business trips of up to 3 months.
VISAS: Required by all except:
(a) nationals of countries referred to on the chart above;
(b) nationals of countries also referred to above under passport exemptions;
(c) nationals of Andorra, Argentina, Benin, Bolivia, Brazil, Brunei, Burkina Faso, Chile, Colombia, Costa Rica, Côte d'Ivoire, Croatia, Cyprus, Czechoslovakia, Ecuador, El Salvador, Finland, Guadeloupe, Guam, Guatemala, Honduras, Hungary, Iceland, Israel, Jamaica, Kenya, South Korea, Liechtenstein, Macau, Malawi, Malaysia, Malta, Martinique, Mexico, Monaco, Nepal, New Caledonia, New Zealand, Niger, Norway, Panama, Paraguay, Peru, Poland, Puerto Rico, San Marino, Singapore, Slovenia, Sweden, Switzerland, Togo, Uruguay, Vatican City, Venezuela and Yugoslavia.
Nationals of other countries, including children under 16 years of age, require a visa.
Types of visa: Entry, £8. Transit, £2.80. Residence, enquire at Embassy for details.
Validity: *Entry:* normally up to 3 months (see also *Working days required* below). *Transit:* 12 hours.
Application to: Consulate (or Consular Section at Embassy). For addresses, see top of entry.
Application requirements: (a) 2 application forms. (b) Photos. (c) Proof of adequate means of support during stay. (d) Proof of medical insurance.
Working days required: For UK residents applying in the UK, visas will normally be issued within 24 hours. If the stay is likely to be for more than 3 months, applications should be made at least 6 weeks in advance of the intended date of departure. Visa applications by non-residents have to be referred to the German Embassy in the applicant's home country, and may take up to 8 weeks to be issued.
Temporary residence: Residence permits may be obtained from the Aliens Office of the local council in Germany, no later than 3 months after entry. Nationals of EC and EFTA countries and the USA may apply for a residence permit after entry.
Work permits: British citizens have the right to look for work or to take up a job previously obtained in the Federal Republic of Germany without a work permit. A residence permit must, however, be obtained for stays of over 3 months (see above). A booklet, *Residence and Work in Germany*, is obtainable from the Embassy.

MONEY

Currency: Deutsche Mark (DM) = 100 Pfennigs. Notes are in denominations of DM1000, 500, 200, 100, 50, 20, 10 and 5. Coins are in denominations of DM5, 2 and 1, and 50, 10, 5, 2 and 1 Pfennigs.
Credit cards: All credit cards are accepted. Check with your credit card company for details of merchant acceptability and other services which may be available.
Eurocheques are accepted up to a value of DM400. They can be exchanged in building societies, banks and post offices.
Travellers cheques: These can be changed at banks, post offices, railway stations, travel bureaux and hotels. Generally they provide the best rate of exchange.
Exchange rate indicators: The following figures are included as a guide to the movements of the Deutsche Mark against Sterling and the US Dollar:

Date:	Oct '89	Oct '90	Oct '91	Oct '92
£1.00=	2.97	2.97	2.91	2.44
$1.00=	1.88	1.52	1.68	1.54

Currency restrictions: There are no restrictions on the import or export of either local or foreign currency.
Banking hours: In the west: 0830-1300 and 1430-1600 Monday to Friday; open to 1730 Thursdays in the main cities. In the east: 0800-1200 Monday to Friday, plus 1430-1730 Tuesday and Thursday.

DUTY FREE

The following goods may be imported into the Federal Republic of Germany without incurring customs duty by:
(a) Visitors residing in an EC country:
300 cigarettes or 150 cigarillos or 75 cigars or 400g of tobacco;
1.5 litres of spirits with an alcohol content exceeding 22% by volume or 3 litres of spirits or liqueurs with an alcohol content not exceeding 22% by volume or 3 litres of sparkling wine or liqueur wine;
5 litres of any other wine;
1000g of coffee or 400g of coffee extract or essence;
200g of tea or 80g of tea extract or essence;
75g of perfume and 375ml of toilet water;
Personal goods (including foodstuffs) to the value of DM1235, of which no more than DM115 worth may originate from non-EC states.

(b) Visitors residing in a non-EC country:
200 cigarettes or 100 cigarillos or 50 cigars or 250g of tobacco;
1 litre of spirits with an alcohol content exceeding 22% by volume or 2 litres of spirits or liqueurs with an alcohol content not exceeding 22% by volume or 2 litres of sparkling or liqueur wine;
2 litres of any other wine;
500g of coffee or 200g of coffee extract or essence;
100g of tea or 40g of tea extract or essence;
50g of perfume and 0.25 litre of toilet water;
Personal goods to the value of DM115.
(c) Visitors entering from an EC Country with duty-paid goods (as of January 1993):
800 cigarettes and 400 cigarillos and 200 cigars and 1kg of tobacco;
90 litres of wine (including up to 60 litres of sparkling wine);
10 litres of spirits;
20 litres of intermediate products (such as fortified wine);
110 litres of beer.
Note: (a) In the case of goods purchased in a tax/duty-free shop, only the regulations for imports from non-EC countries apply; exemption from duty is conditional upon the goods being carried in the traveller's personal luggage. (b) The tobacco and alcohol allowances are granted only to those over 17 years, and the coffee allowances only to those over 15. (c) Wine in excess of the above allowances imported for personal consumption and valued at less than DM250 will be taxed at an overall rate of 15%; this includes 14% import turnover tax.

PUBLIC HOLIDAYS

Public holidays observed in the Federal Republic of Germany are as follows:
Apr 9-12 '93 Easter. **May 1** Labour Day. **May 20** Ascension Day. **May 31** Whit Monday. **Jun 10** Corpus Christi [1]. **Aug 15** Ascension of the Virgin Mary [2]. **Oct 3** Day of Unity. **Oct 31** Day of Reformation [4]. **Nov 1** All Saints' Day [1]. **Nov 17** Day of Prayer and Repentance. **Dec 25-26** Christmas. **Jan 1 '94** New Year's Day. **Jan 6** Epiphany [3].
Note: (a) In addition, Carnival (Rose) Monday, which is not an official public holiday, is celebrated on Feb 14, '94. (b) The holidays indicated with footnotes are Roman Catholic feast days and are celebrated only in the areas indicated: [1] Baden-Württemberg, Hesse, Saarland, North Rhine-Westphalia, Rhineland-Palatinate and Catholic areas of Bavaria only; [2] Saarland and Roman Catholic areas of Bavaria only; [3] Baden-Württemberg and Bavaria only. (c) [4] Eastern states only.

HEALTH

Regulations and requirements may be subject to change at short notice, and you are advised to contact your doctor well in advance of your intended date of departure. Any numbers in the chart refer to the footnotes below.

	Special Precautions?	Certificate Required?
Yellow Fever	No	No
Cholera	No	No
Typhoid & Polio	No	-
Malaria	No	-
Food & Drink	1	-

[1]: Tap water is considered safe to drink. Milk is pasteurised and dairy products are safe for consumption. Local meat, poultry, seafood, fruit and vegetables are generally considered safe to eat.
Rabies is present; look out for 'Tollwut' signs. For those at high risk, vaccination before arrival should be considered. If you are bitten abroad seek medical advice without delay. For more information consult the *Health* section at the back of the book.
Health care: There is a Reciprocal Health Agreement with the UK. On presentation of the form E111 (see the *Health* section at the back of the book), UK citizens are entitled to free medical and dental treatment. Prescribed medicines and hospital treatment must be paid for. Private insurance is recommended for specialist medical treatment outside the German National Health Service, which can be very expensive.
Surgery hours are generally 1000-1200 and 1600-1800 (not Wednesday afternoons, Saturday or Sunday). The emergency telephone number is 112; additionally, there is an emergency call-out service out of surgery hours (1800-0700). Chemists open 0900-1800 Monday to Friday and Saturday morning.
There are 250 officially recognised medical spas and watering places with modern equipment providing therapeutic treatment and recreational facilities for visitors seeking rest and relaxation. A list of the spas and health resorts and various treatments can be ordered from the German National Tourist Office or directly from Deutschen Bäderverband e.V. (German Spas Association), Schumannstrasse 111, W-5300 Bonn 1. Tel: (228) 262 010.

TRAVEL - International

AIR: The national airline is *Lufthansa (LH)*.
Approximate flight times: From *London* to Hamburg, Bremen or Hannover is 1 hour 20 minutes; to Cologne/Bonn is 1 hour 10 minutes; to Frankfurt/M is 1 hour 25 minutes; to Nuremberg is 2 hours 30 minutes (with one stop); and to Munich is 1 hour 40 minutes.
From *Los Angeles* to Frankfurt/M is 14 hours 50 minutes.
From *New York* to Frankfurt/M is 8 hours 20 minutes.
From *Singapore* to Frankfurt/M is 14 hours 5 minutes.
From *Sydney* to Frankfurt/M is 24 hours 55 minutes.
International airports: *Berlin-Tegel (BER)* (Otto Lilienthal) is 8km (5 miles) northwest of the city (travel time – 20 minutes). Airport facilities include duty-free shop, bank/bureau de change, post office (0630-2100), restaurant (0600-2045), shops, tourist information, hotel reservation and car hire. A bus no 109 goes to the city every 10 minutes from 0500-2400; return is from Bahnhof Zoo or Budapester Strasse. There is a 24-hour taxi service and a bus service every thirty minutes from *Berlin Tegel* airport to east Berlin *Schönefeld* airport.
Berlin-Schönefeld (SXF) is 20km (12 miles) southeast of the city (travel time – 1 hour). Airport facilities include duty-free shop, bank/bureau de change (0800-2200), post office, restaurant (0600-1000, 1100-2200), hotel reservation, tourist information and car hire. S-Bahn no S9 departs to the city (*Westkreuz*) via Alexanderplatz and Bahnhof Zoo; also S10 (*Ostkreuz*) runs via Oranienburg. Further connections with the regional train services R1, R2 and R12 are available at the same tariff as the S-Bahn. A bus no 171 runs between U-Bahn Station Rudow (Line 7) and the airport. 24-hour taxi service is available to the city.
Berlin-Tempelhof is 6km (4 miles) southeast of the city centre (travel time – 20 minutes). Airport facilities include duty-free shop, other shops and car hire. Bus no 119 departs every 5-10 minutes to the city. The underground lines 6 and 7 run every 5-10 minutes (travel time – 15 minutes). Taxis are available.
Leipzig/Halle (LEJ) is 20km (12 miles) northwest of the city (travel time – 30 minutes). Coach departs to the city every 30 minutes, 0700-1700 and at 1830, 1900 and 2000. Return is from the main railway station and major hotels. 24-hour taxi services are available to the city. Airport facilities include duty-free shop, conference centre, bank (0800-1800), tourist information and restaurant (0800-2100).

Dresden (DRS) (Klotsche) is 10km (6 miles) from Dresden (travel time – 25 minutes). Daily bus services are available to the city.
Bremen (BRE) (Neuenland) is 3km (2 miles) from the city (travel time – 20 minutes). There is a duty-free shop (0900-1630), bureau de change (0630-1930), conference centre, car hire and hotel reservation. Tram no 5 takes approximately 12 minutes to the city centre. Services run every 5-15 minutes Monday to Saturday, and every 15-30 minutes on Sundays. There is a 24-hour taxi service.
Cologne (Köln/Bonn) (CGN) (Wahn) is 14km (9 miles) southeast of Cologne, and 21km (13 miles) northeast of Bonn (travel time – 25 and 35 minutes respectively). There is a duty-free shop, tourist information, conference centre, car hire, restaurant, bar, bank/building society and shops. Bus no 170 goes to Cologne every 20 minutes (0600-2245). An express bus no 670 goes to Bonn every 30 minutes from 0650-2245, returning from Stadthaltestelle am Hauptbahnhof (bus station near the main railway station) from 0550-2140. There is a 24-hour taxi service at the airport.
Düsseldorf (DUS) (Lohausen) is 13km (8.5 miles) north of the city. There is a duty-free shop. A train goes to the city every 20 minutes from 0530-2330 (the airport station is under the arrival hall). Return is from Hauptbahnhof (main railway station) every 30 minutes from 0500-2309. An S-Bahn connection (S7) and bus no 727 are available as well. Taxis run a 24-hour service to Düsseldorf.
Frankfurt/M (FRA) (Rhein/Main) is 12km (7 miles) southwest of the city. Facilities include duty-free shops, banks, restaurants, bars, shops, tourist information, Airport Conference Centre (32 conference rooms) and car hire. Travel to and from the city is by buses no 61 and 62 every 20 minutes from 0500-2300, returning from Hauptbahnhof. Lines S14 (every 20 minutes) and S15 (every 10 minutes) go to the city from 0415-0044 (the station is underneath the arrival hall). S-Bahn S14 also goes directly to Mainz and Wiesbaden (travel time – 40 minutes). The airport has its own Intercity train station which also offers international services (Switzerland, Austria and Hungary). The Lufthansa Courtesy Airport Bus connects with Mannheim (travel time – 1 hour) and Wiesbaden (travel time – 1 hour). There is a 24-hour taxi service to Frankfurt.
Hamburg (HAM) (Hamburg-Fuhlsbüttel) is 12km (7.5 miles) north of the city centre (travel time – 25 minutes). There is a duty-free shop. Coaches go to the city every 20 minutes from 0600-2300, returning from Zentral Omnibus Bahnhof Kirchenallee. Bus numbers 109, 31 (Express) and 606 (nightbus) go to the city every 20 minutes (hourly throughout the night) from 0500-2400, returning from Hauptbahnhof and Stephansplatz. Express bus service runs to Ohlsdorf station (travel time – 9 minutes). A 24-hour taxi service is available.
Hannover (HAJ) (Langenhagen) is 11km (7 miles) north of the city (travel time – 30 minutes). There is a duty-free shop. *British Airways* and *Lufthansa* flights go to London. Bus no 609 goes to the city every 25 minutes from 0600-2200, returning from the city air terminal at the main railway station (Ernst-August-Platz). A 24-hour taxi service runs to Hannover.
Munich (MUC) (Franz Joseph Strauß) is 28.5km (18 miles) northeast of the city (travel time – 38 minutes). Facilities include duty-free shop, restaurants, post office, banks, conference centre, car hire and bars. Direct link with the S-Bahn S8 runs every 20 minutes from Hauptbahnhof. The Airport City Bus runs every 20 minutes to the Hauptbahnhof (0710-2050); further bus services are available. The lines S3 and S6 running to the city offer interchange with underground, bus and tram services. Another airport bus goes 10 times a day to Augsburg.
Münster-Osnabrück (MSR) is 25km (16 miles) from the city. There is a duty-free shop. Buses go to Münster (travel time – 30 minutes) and Osnabrück (travel time – 35 minutes). Taxis take 40 minutes.
Nuremberg (NUE) is 7km (4.5 miles) north of the city centre. There is a duty-free shop. The Airport Express runs every 30 minutes to the Hauptbahnhof 0500-2300 (return between 0530-2330). There is a 24-hour taxi service. Bus no 32 goes to Thon with interchanging bus no 30 to Erlangen (travel time – 20 minutes). There is a direct bus link from the airport to Erlangen (20 minutes).
Saarbrücken (SCN) (Ensheim) is 16km (10 miles) from the city centre. There is an hourly bus service to the city and taxis are also available.
Stuttgart (STR) (Echterdingen) is 14km (9 miles) south of the city (travel time – 35 minutes). There is a duty-free shop. Express bus connection (Line A) goes direct to the main station every 30 minutes from 0625-2325. Return is from the city Air Terminal from 0525-2255. An S-Bahn will be available from early 1993. There is a 24-hour taxi service to Stuttgart.
Inter-airport link: Düsseldorf, Cologne/Bonn and Frankfurt/M are linked by the *Lufthansa Airport Express*. Meals and drinks are served to passengers and are included in the fare. Luggage can be cleared for the next stage of the journey.
SEA: The following shipping lines serve routes to Germany:
Scandinavian Seaways: Harwich/Hamburg.
Sealink: Harwich–Hook of Holland, Dover–Calais, Folkestone–Boulogne, Newhaven–Dieppe.
P&O European Ferries: Felixstowe–Zeebrugge, Dover–Calais, Portsmouth–Le Havre, Portsmouth–Cherbourg, Dover–Boulogne, Dover–Ostend.
Olau Line: Sheerness–Flushing (Holland).
North Sea Ferries: Hull–Rotterdam, Hull–Zeebrugge.
Sally Line: Ramsgate–Dunkirk.
Hovercraft: Dover–Boulogne/Calais.
Ferry connections also exist from the Federal Republic to Norway, Denmark, Sweden, Finland, the Russian Federation and Lithuania.
RAIL: Routes from London are from London Victoria via Dover and Ostend, or London Liverpool Street to Hook of Holland via Harwich. Travel time to Cologne/Bonn is around 10 hours.
There are excellent connections between the Federal Republic of Germany and other main European cities. For more information, contact German Rail in London. Tel: (071) 233 6554.
ROAD: The Federal Republic is connected to all surrounding countries by a first-class network of motorways and trunk roads. Regular coach services to the Federal Republic of Germany from the UK are operated at present by *Eurolines* (tel: (071) 730 0202) to Berlin, Cologne, Frankfurt, Dortmund, Hannover and Munich; and by *Transline* (tel: (0708) 864 911). In every major city there are *Mitfahrerzentralen* (car sharing agencies) which offer shared car travelling to all European cities on the basis of shared costs; an agency fee is charged.
See below for information on **documentation** and **traffic regulations.**

TRAVEL - Internal

AIR: Internal services are operated by *Lufthansa* and several regional airlines. Frankfurt is the focal point of internal air services and all airports in the Federal Republic can be reached in an average of 50 minutes flying time. There are several airports in the country apart from those listed above which offer internal air services. Helgoland, Sylt and some other Friesian Islands are served by seasonal services operated by regional airlines or air taxi services. Connections by air are run daily from Berlin, Bremen, Cologne/Bonn, Düsseldorf, Frankfurt/Main, Hamburg, Hannover, Munich, Nuremberg, Stuttgart and Westerland/Sylt (summer only).
The majority of western airports offer several flights a week to Leipzig and Dresden.
SEA/RIVER: Regular scheduled boat services operate on most rivers, lakes and coastal waters, including the Danube, Main, Moselle, Rhine, Neckar and the Weser, and also on Lakes Ammer See, Chiemsee, Königssee and Constance. Ferry services are operated on Kiel Fjord and from Cuxhaven to Helgoland and to the East and North Frisian Islands as well as to Scandinavian destinations. Besides these scheduled services, special excursions are available on all navigable waters. The *KD German Rhine Line* covers the Rhine and Moselle rivers, and has 27 comfortable ships which operate daily from Easter to late October. Tours with entertainment on board and excursions are arranged as well as cruises between The Netherlands and Switzerland. *Hapag/Lloyd* operates cruises of 7-20 days from Bremerhaven, Hamburg and Kiel in summer. Lake Constance (Europe's third largest inland lake) is served by regular steamers, pleasure boats and car ferries between the German, Swiss and Austrian shores. A 15-day 'Holiday Ticket' is available for travel on any of five days on scheduled services on the Obersee and Überlingen parts of the lake, as well as certain other boats. This covers rail and bus lines, and on the remaining ten days entitles the holder to 50% reductions on the fares of the same services.
RAIL: Note: The information that follows applies largely to western Germany. Rail services are at present less frequent in eastern Germany, though modernisation programmes are underway. For latest information leaflets contact German Rail or the German National Tourist Office.
With a railway network as complex, modern and sophisticated as that in the western part of the Federal Republic of Germany, it is obviously impossible to give all the details of the main routes, facilities, timetables, fares and reductions which are available. Details of up-to-date prices, and where they can be bought, can be found in the DB companion brochure, *Travel Planner*, available from German Rail or the Tourist Office. The following section gives brief descriptions of the major special fares and tickets which are currently on offer. Some of these can only be obtained in the Federal Republic. Other new schemes, or modifications to existing ones, may be introduced in the future.
The *Deutsche Bundesbahn* (DB), German Federal Railways, and the *Deutsche Reichsbahn* (DR) in the East operate some 32,684 passenger trains each day over a 40,800km (25,500-mile) network and many international through services. The network does not radiate around the capital as the federal structure provides an integrated system to serve the main regional centres. At present the Eastern system is undergoing extensive modernisation programmes involving track improvement, signalling and rolling stock. The introduction of the new high-speed *InterCity Express*, travelling at 280kmph (175mph), reduced travel times between the major centres immensely. The service is operating hourly only on some connections at the moment; a supplement is payable. The extensive InterCity network (300 trains per day) connects the major centres at hourly intervals, and ensures swift interchange between trains. A supplement of £2.90 (DM8 when bought from the ticket collector) is also charged for 1st or 2nd class on *Intercity* and *Eurocity* trains. Smaller towns are linked by the 26 InterRegio lines at 2-hour intervals. Supplementing the system of

these longer-distance trains are several commuter networks in larger cities. **Facilities and services:** Buffet cars with some seating for light refreshments and drinks are provided on InterRegio (IR) trains. Most *InterCity* and *EuroCity* trains carry a 48-seat restaurant, offering a menu and drinks throughout the journey. The newer generation *InterCity Express* trains combine both of the above-mentioned facilities, offering a selection of snacks and menu in their restaurant cars. First-class passengers are provided with 'at-your-seat' service. The *InterCity Express* also provides a service car with conference compartment, 2-card telephones and fully equipped office (photocopier, fax etc). **Sleeping cars:** Many have showers, and air-conditioning is provided on most long-distance overnight trains. Beds are bookable in advance. Some trains provide couchettes instead. Sleeping-car attendants serve refreshments. Seat reservations can be made for all long-distance trains well in advance. When reserving a seat on an **Intercity** train you can specify to be in a *Grossraumwagen*, which is a carriage with adjustable seats and without compartments, or an *Abteilwagen*, which is made up of compartments. **Bicycle hire:** At over 200 stations in areas suited for cycle tours, the DB operates a bike hire service (ticket holders have special reduced rates). **Mountain railways:** Cable cars, chairlifts or cogwheel railways serve all popular mountain sites.

Saverticket: Available for a return journey on one weekend or within one month.

Supersaverticket: Available for a return journey on a Saturday or within one month (not valid on Fridays, Sundays and during the rush hour).

EURO DOMINO: These tickets replace the *German Rail Pass* (GRP) and the *German Youth Rail Pass* of German Rail DB previously available in Europe. As from January 1, 1993, both will only be on sale in non-European countries. *EURO DOMINO*-tickets, which enable holders to make flexible travel arrangements, are available in 19 European countries. They have to be bought in the country of residence for which a valid passport or other form of ID has to be shown. First- and second-class tickets are available for travellers over 26 years of age; for passengers under 26, only second-class is available. The tickets are valid for 5 days within a month. They also entitle holders to a discount of 25% on rail travel in the country of origin or in all countries which comply with the system. Children between 4-12 years pay half and get a 50% discount, children under four travel free. The German variety of the ED-ticket is valid on the complete network of the DB and DR, all *InterCity* trains including the *InterCity Express*, can be used without paying a supplement. Motorail is exempt. Where seat reservation is required, a reduced fee is charged; the usual rates apply for couchette and sleeping-cars.

Inter-Rail: Available to those under 26. Covers rail travel in the whole of Europe for one month.

Tramper Monthly Ticket: Available to all persons under 23 and to all students under 27. It is valid for a month, and gives unlimited free use of all rail services in the Federal Republic of Germany. A passport and a loose passport-size photo are needed when purchasing one. These tickets are available in Germany only.

Rail Europ Senior (RES) Card: This offers considerable savings (up to 30%) on rail travel in the Federal Republic of Germany for men over 65 and women over 60. The card is available from British Rail travel centres and major railway stations. It is valid for one year. This card is superseding the old Senior Citizen's Railcard, and although some reductions on journeys to the continent will still be available to persons holding Senior Citizen's Railcards, it will be necessary to obtain a new Senior Card to get the full benefit of the new scheme.

Motorail: The German Federal Railway has a fully integrated motorail network, connecting with the rest of the European motorail network. Trains run mostly during the summer and at other holiday periods; most have sleeper, couchette and restaurant/buffet cars.

ROAD: The western part of the Federal Republic of Germany is covered by a modern network of motorways (*Autobahnen*) extending over 10,500km (6563 miles). There are over 487,000km (303,000 miles) of roads in all, and every part of the country can be reached by motorists. Lead-free petrol is obtainable everywhere, although there may be hold-ups at eastern petrol stations. The breakdown service of the ADAC is available in the western and eastern part of the country, though in the new states the *Auto Club Europa (ACE)* and the *Allgemeine Deutsche Motorsportverband (ADMV)* also provide a service. Help is given free of charge to members of affiliated motoring organisations, such as the AA, and only parts have to be paid for. Breakdown services, including a helicopter rescue service, are operated by the *ADAC* (German automobile association). In the event of a breakdown, use emergency telephones located along the motorway. When using these telephones ask expressly for road service assistance ('Strassenwachthilfe'). In almost all cases, the number to dial for emergency services is 110 (sometimes 115 in the eastern states, depending on the area). The tourist office publishes the booklet *Autobahn-Service* giving information on all the facilities and services available on the motorways throughout the country.

Note: Although motorways in eastern Germany are of a reasonable standard, many secondary roads are still poorly surfaced and in a state of disrepair. It will take time before they are brought up to Western standards.

Bus: Buses serve villages and small towns, especially those without railway stations. Operated by the Post or by German Railways, they only tend to run between or to small places and there are few long-distance services. *Europabus/Deutsche Touring* runs services on special scenic routes such as the *Romantic Road* (Wiesbaden/Frankfurt to Munich/Füssen) and the *Road of the Castles* between Mannheim/Heidelberg to Rothenburg and Nuremberg.

Taxis: These are available everywhere in town and country. Watch out for waiting-period charges and surcharges. All taxis are metered.

Car hire: Self-drive cars are available at most towns and at over 40 railway stations. Chauffeur-driven cars are available in all large towns. Rates depend on the type of car. Some firms offer weekly rates including unlimited mileage. VAT at 14% is payable on all rental charges. On request, cars will be supplied at airports, stations and hotels. It may be difficult to use credit cards at petrol stations.
Several airlines, including *Lufthansa*, offer 'Fly-drive'. Contact the National Tourist Office for details.

Motoring organisations: The *Allgemeiner Deutscher Automobil Club* (ADAC) based in Munich, and the *Automobilclub von Deutschland* (AvD) based in Frankfurt have offices at all major frontier crossings and in the larger towns. They will be able to assist foreign motorists, particularly those belonging to affiliated motoring organisations. They also publish maps and guidebooks which are available at their offices. ADAC operates an emergency service to relay radio messages to motorists. In both winter and summer there are constant radio reports on road conditions and traffic. They will also rent snow chains.

Regulations: Traffic signs are international. Speed limits

in western Germany are 50kmph (31mph) in built-up areas and 100kmph (62mph) on all roads outside built-up areas. Motorways *(Autobahnen)* and dual carriageways have a recommended speed limit of 130kmph (81mph). From January 1, 1993, speed limits in eastern Germany are the same as in the western part of the country though the actual road condition does not always allow for it. Restrictions are indicated where applicable. Children under 12 must not travel in the front seats. Seat belts must be worn in the front and back. All visitors' cars must display vehicle nationality plates. Fines can be imposed for running out of petrol on a motorway. The warning triangle is compulsory. There is a total alcohol ban when driving in eastern Germany. There are plans to introduce a nationwide alcohol limit of 0.5% (in western Germany it is presently 0.8%).
Documentation: Foreign travellers may drive their cars for up to one year if in possession of a national licence or International Driving Permit and car registration papers. EC nationals taking their own cars are strongly advised to obtain a Green Card. Without it, insurance cover is limited to the minimum legal cover; the Green Card tops this up to the level of cover provided by the car owner's domestic policy.
URBAN: Good public transport services exist in all towns. All urban areas have bus services, and these are supplemented in a number of larger cities by underground and suburban railway trains. In many towns, block tickets for several journeys can be purchased at reduced rates and unlimited daily travel tickets are available. In many larger cities tickets for your local transport journey have to be purchased from ticket machines before you board the suburban train *(S-Bahn)*, underground *(U-Bahn)*, bus or tram. There are numerous sophisticated vending machines which service all the main boarding points and a wide range of relevant maps and leaflets are available to travellers. Although there is often no conductor on trams and underground trains, inspections are frequent and passengers without valid tickets will be fined on the spot.
Berlin: The city's excellent public transport includes an extensive network of buses, underground and S-Bahn which is supplemented by the regional services of the Deutsche Reichsbahn. In the eastern part of the city, tram services and the ferries of the Berliner Verkehrs-Betriebe, BVG (Berlin Public Transport) in conjunction with east Berlin's 'White Fleet' provide further services. The underground lines 1 and 9 run a 24-hour service Friday night to Saturday and Saturday night to Sunday. The Berlin-Ticket is valid for 24 hours for unlimited travel on bus, underground, S-Bahn and the BVG ferries (DM12, DM6 with discount). The special BVG-excursions coaches are exempt. Holders of the Combined Day-Ticket (DM22; DM11 with discount) enjoy unlimited travel with bus, underground and S-Bahn as well as on the complete ferry network of either organisation. A spec ial Weekly Ticket with a validity of 7 days costs DM30 (only at Bahnhof Zoo). Further details are availalbe from the information desks of the BVG.
Note: Pedestrians should be aware that it is an offence to cross a road when the pedestrian crossing lights are red, even if there is no traffic on the road. On-the-spot fines for offenders are common.
JOURNEY TIMES:
(1) The following chart gives approximate journey times (in hours and minutes) from **Berlin** to other major cities and towns in the Federal Republic of Germany.

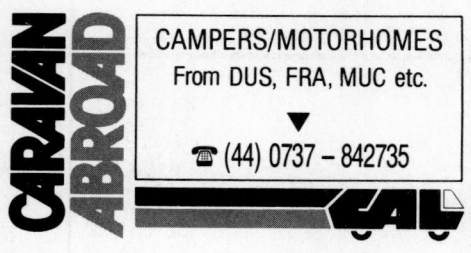

	Air	Road	Rail
Hamburg	0.45	4.00	4.45
Cologne	1.05	7.00	7.10
Frankfurt/M	1.10	6.30	8.00
Munich	1.20	7.00	10.10
Dresden	-	2.30	3.00
Leipzig	-	2.00	2.30
Erfurt	-	4.30	5.00
Rostock	-	2.30	3.00

(2) The following chart gives approximate journey times (in hours and minutes) from **Bonn** to other major cities and towns in the Federal Republic of Germany.

	Air	Road	Rail	River
Hamburg	0.55	4.00	4.30	-
Hannover	-	3.00	3.15	-
Frankfurt	0.40	2.20	2.00	a
Düsseldorf	-	1.00	0.45	-
Cologne	b	0.20	0.15	0.40
Stuttgart	0.50	4.00	3.30	-
Munich	1.00	7.00	6.00	-
Berlin	1.05	8.00	8.00	-
Leipzig	-	7.00	9.00	-
Dresden	1.45	8.00	13.00	-

[a]: There is a hydrofoil service (not daily) between Cologne and Mainz via Koblenz and Bonn which takes about 3 hours 30 minutes.
[b]: Cologne and Bonn share the same airport; see the *Air* section in *Travel – International* above for details.
Note: All the above times are average times by the fastest and most direct route; by motorways in the case of road journeys, and by the quickest hydrofoil service for the time by river. The slow boat from Bonn to Cologne, for instance, takes three hours.

ACCOMMODATION

HOTELS: There is a good selection of hotels in the Federal Republic of Germany and comprehensive guides can be found at the German National Tourist Office. They can also provide the German Hotel Association Guide, published by the Deutscher Hotel- und Gaststättenverband (DEHOGA), Kronprinzenstrasse 46, W-5300 Bonn 2. Tel: (228) 820 080. Fax: (228) 820 0846. Telex: 885489. This association counts some 50% of establishments offering accommodation in western Germany among its membership and can supply further information on accommodation in the Federal Republic. Some hotels are situated in old castles, palaces and monasteries. Alongside these are modern, comfortable hotels and well-planned and purpose-built premises. Examples of accommodation for a family on holiday is a country inn offering bed, breakfast and meal. More demanding visitors are also well catered for with medium to luxury hotels. The German hotel trade is extremely well-equipped with facilities from swimming pools and saunas to exercise gyms. When touring in the country with no fixed itinerary, it is obviously often difficult to make reservations in advance. Watch out for *Zimmer Frei* (Rooms to Let) notices by the roadside, or go to the local Tourist Office (usually called *Verkehrsamt*). Try to get to the town where you want to stay the night by 1600, particularly in summer. **Grading:** (The following information applies to western Germany only). Hotels are not graded as such, but every establishment offering accommodation falls into a particular category which stipulates rigid criteria regarding facilities offered. The categories are as follows:
Hotel: Must be accessible to all persons; must provide accommodation and at least one restaurant for guests and non-guests. It must also have a number of rooms for common use by all residents such as a lounge etc. 27% of establishments fall into this category.
Gasthof: A 'Gasthof' (inn) must provide the same facilities as a hotel except for the common rooms such as a lounge etc. 30% of establishments fall into this category.
Pension: A 'Pension' must provide accommodation and food only for guests. It does not have to provide a restaurant for non-residents nor does it have to provide any common rooms. 16% of establishments fall into this category.
Hotel garni: Provides accommodation and breakfast only for guests. 27% of establishments fall into this category.
HOTELS IN EASTERN GERMANY: In the eastern part of the country visitors still generally stay at the Interhotels or in small private hotels, which at present are part of an extensive modernisation programme. Generally, the increasing demand puts further strain on the limited bed capacity.
SELF-CATERING: All-in self-catering deals are available that include sea travel to a German or other Channel port, and accommodation at the resort. The latter might be in anything from a farmhouse to a castle. Details are available from The German National Tourist Office.
YOUTH HOSTELS: There are 640 youth hostels throughout both eastern and western Germany. They are open to members of any Youth Hostel Association affiliated to the International Youth Hostel Association. Membership can be obtained from the YHA or *Deutsches Jugendherbergswerk* (German Youth Hostel Organisation), Postfach 1455, Bismarckstrasse 8, W-4930 Detmold. Tel: (5231) 7401-0. Reservation is advised during the high season (and throughout the year in major cities).
FARMHOUSES: The booklet *Urlaub auf dem Bauernhof* (*Holidays at the Farm*) is published in conjunction with the German Agricultural Society and can be obtained from *Agratour GmbH*, Eschborner Landstrasse 122, W-6000 Frankfurt/M 1. Tel: (69) 247 88419-0/91. Regional guides on most tourist regions can also be obtained from the Tourist Office. All afore-mentioned booklets are published in German only. A basic knowledge of German will be required for such a holiday. A catalogue with addresses in the whole of the country, including 2000 addresses in the eastern part, can be ordered from Landschriftenverlag GmbH Bonn, Zentrale für den Landurlaub, Heerstrasse 73, W-5300 Bonn 1. Tel: (228) 631 284/5. It costs DM15 and is published annually in December.
CAMPING/CARAVANNING: There are well over 2500 campsites in the Federal Republic of Germany. They are generally open from April to October, but 400 sites, mostly in winter sports areas, stay open in the winter and have all necessary facilities. (Campsites in the eastern part of the country are of a very basic standard.) The permission of the proprietor and/or the local police must always be sought before camp is pitched anywhere other than a recognised campsite. It is not normally possible to make advance reservations on campsites. A free map/folder giving details of several hundred selected campsites throughout the country is available from German National Tourist Board. The German Camping Club publishes a camping guide of the best sites in Germany; contact Deutscher Camping-Club (DCC), Mandlstrasse 28, W-8000 München 40. Tel: (89) 334 021. The *AA Guide to Camping and Caravanning on the Continent* lists nearly 2000 European campsites, including a large section on Germany.
HISTORIC HOLIDAYS: Information about holidays in castles, stately mansions and historic hostelries may be obtained by contacting the National Tourist Office or by writing to Gast im Schloss e.V., Geschäftsstelle D49-10, Postfach 120620, W-6800 Mannheim. Tel: (621) 126 620.

RESORTS & EXCURSIONS

Situated at the crossroads of Europe, the scenery of the Federal Republic of Germany is enormously varied and includes sandy beaches, towering mountains, forests, lakes and settlements ranging from medieval villages to some of Europe's greatest cities. Every region offers different foods and a wide range of wines and local beers. The country is divided into 16 states *(Bundesländer)*. The north includes the North Sea coast and the East Friesian islands, Schleswig-Holstein, the city-states of Hamburg and Bremen as well as the Weser-valley, Lüneburg Heath and the Harz Mountains. The central western area of the country consists of the Rhineland region, the industrial sprawl of the Ruhr, the varied landscapes of Westphalia, the wine region Rhineland Palatinate, the Saarland and the state of Hesse with its fairytale scenic road. The Black Forest can be found in the south and is part of the state of Baden-Württemberg. Areas of touristic interest in this state include the Neckar Valley, Swabia and Lake Constance. Munich (München) is the capital of Bavaria. The main tourist regions are the Bavarian Forest to the east with the first German Nationalpark near the border with the Czech Republic, Franconia to the north, Upper Bavaria and the Alps to the south and the Allgäu region. Bavaria is the most popular tourist destination for nationals and visitors. The Baltic coast with its resorts is the most popular holiday region in the east, followed by the Thuringian Forest, the northern lake district, Saxon Hills, the Harz Mountains and the Zittauer Gebirge. More detailed information on the various regions and cities in Federal Republic of Germany follows.

North Germany

Undiscovered by many holidaymakers, the northern region, although relatively flat, offers pleasant scenery with gently rolling hills, lake country and fine sandy beaches and dunes in the state of Schleswig-Holstein.
Hamburg is the second largest city in the Federal Republic of Germany with a population of 1.6 million people. It is a city-state, forming with Lübeck, Bremen and Rostock the ancient *Hanseatic League* of ports, and Hamburgers have always been extremely proud of their independence. A first impression can be gained on a sightseeing tour, starting at the Hauptbahnhof. The Baroque *Church of St Michaelis* (Der Michel), the *Town Hall* with its distinctive green roof, the elegant *Hanseviertel*, the *Alster Arcade* and the Alster Lake (separated in *Binnenalster* and *Aussenalster*), the biggest lake inside a city in Europe, all are symbols of the city. Museums of interest include the domed Hamburg Art Gallery (*Kunsthalle*), the *Historical Museum*, the *Decorative Arts and Crafts Museum* and the *Altonaer Museum*. Hamburg is equally well-endowed with theatres including the Hamburg State Opera (*Hamburgische Staatsoper*), the German Theatre (*Deutsche Schauspielhaus*) and the North German dialect *(plattdeutsch)* theatre, the *Ohnsorgtheater*. In the heart of the city is the *Planten un Blomen* park near the Congress Centrum Hamburg, which is renowned for its fountain displays during the summer; in the evenings at 2200 the display is accompanied by music (classical,

popular) and changing coloured lights. On a visit during daylight hours to the park, the *Television Tower* should not be missed. With the lift (DM5) to the top platform, visitors can enjoy a view of the city from above, the harbour, the northern districts and the surrounding countryside. Just below is a restaurant which turns full circle in the course of an hour enabling every vantage point to be enjoyed at the diners' leisure. Not far from the Television Tower, next to the Feldstraße underground station, the large *Dom* funfair takes place several times a year. From Feldstraße it is not far to the famous St Pauli district which includes the notorious *Reeperbahn*. After dark this area comes alive – though is might be different if the FC St Pauli football team is playing at home – with neon lights, music, crowds, theatres (it is here that the German production of *Cats* was staged) and doormen trying to attract people into their establishments. After a long night the night owls meet at 0630 on the *Fischmarkt*, where not only fish straight from the cutter is for sale, but fresh fruit, vegetables and bread. A trip through the Harbour is also an experience and a wide range of tours is available. Hamburg enjoys unrivalled shopping facilities with pedestrian shopping streets, elegant arcades, fine department stores and street cafés concentrated in the area between the main railway station and the *Gänsemarkt*. Refuge from a hectic day's shopping can be sought by hiring a rowing boat or a paddle boat (a security has to be left) and exploring the Alster and the intricate network of canals (Hamburg has more bridges than Venice) which extend throughout the city. On Sundays a stroll on the banks of the River Elbe is a favourite pastime and the numerous cafés and restaurants make sure that nobody overdoes the walking.

Bremen, also a city-state with over half a million inhabitants, is the oldest German maritime city, having been a market town since AD965. The oldest buildings are clustered around the market like the Gothic *Rathaus* (1405-1410). In front of it stands the *Roland*, the statue of an medieval knight and symbol of the city. The extensive pedestrian zone includes a sculpture of the *Bremer Stadtmusikanten*, made famous in the fairy tale by Grimm. Also part of this is the *Schnoorviertel*, a district which retained its medieval charm with narrow cobbled streets, now housing art galleries and exclusive shops. In **Schleswig-Holstein** is Germany's 'Little Switzerland' and the dukedom of Lauenburg, an area of quiet meadows and wooded hills. Glistening among them are the blue waters of innumerable lakes and fjords reaching deep into the interior of this state. A trip could also include visits to tiny undiscovered towns such as **Ratzeburg** and **Mölln** or to one of a string of Baltic resorts such as **Timmendorfer Strand, Grömitz, Damp 2000** and **Schönhagen,** whose golden, sandy beaches attract crowds of visitors every summer. **Lübeck,** whose picturesque oval-shaped old town, ringed by water, still has many reminders of the city's political and commercial golden age in the Middle Ages, claims the title of the most beautiful town of Northern Germany. The *Holsten Gate*, the Rathaus and the many examples of northern red-brick town houses are part of the historic heritage. In 1993 the historic town centre is to become a car-free zone.

Flensburg, the most northerly town in the Federal Republic, has architecture dating back to the 16th century and for many years of its history was part of Denmark. Just south of Flensburg is **Kappeln an der Schlei**, a picturesque small town between the Fjord and the Baltic. Every hour during the summer the traffic comes to a halt when the rotating bridge allows sail and fishing boats to pass. At the beginning of the season in May the *Heringstage* lures visitors to taste the town's speciality: herring. Along the Schlei lies the old Viking town of *Haithabu* – the interesting museum is well worth a visit. Further south, still on Schleswig-Holstein's east coast, is the state's capital **Kiel.** It is a modern city with a large university, and is located on the Nord-Ostsee (Kiel) Canal which connects the North Sea with the Baltic. Annually in June yachting and sailing enthusiasts flock to the *Kieler Woche*. Currently the main yachting centre of the Federal Republic of Germany, it offers excellent facilities.

East Friesland consists of a wide plain interspersed by ranges of tree-covered hills known for their health resorts and modern spa facilities, as well as their fine sandy beaches. The car-free East Frisian Islands also offer relaxed health holidays. Sea air and scenery along the coast guarantee a happy and restful holiday atmosphere. In contrast is **Lower Saxony** with its large nature reserve between the rivers Elbe and Aller. The countryside comprises moorlands with wide expanses of heather, grazing sheep, clumps of green birch trees and junipers. Of interest in this area are the half-timbered houses of **Celle** and **Lüneburg**. Further west is the town of **Oldenburg**, the economic and cultural centre of the region between the Ems and the Weser; to the north is the spa town of **Wilhelmshaven**, which has as its speciality relaxing and therapeutic mud baths. It is also the starting point for many tours along the East Friesland coast and the offlying islands.

Westphalia extends from the Rhine to the Weser Valley. For many, Westphalia conjures up images of the industrial Ruhr Valley, but the region is also one of outstanding natural beauty, historical interest and moated castles. Areas of particular interest include the **Teutoburger Forest** with its nature reserves; **Münsterland,** with the ancient episcopal *See of Münster* (whose attractions include the Gothic *Town Hall* where the Peace of Westphalia, which brought to an end the horrors of the Thirty Years' War, was signed in 1648); and the **Sauerland Region**, a peaceful area of lakes, forests and hills, providing good skiing in the winter and beautiful walking country at any time of the year.

South of Münster is the industrial area of the **Ruhr**. Made up of several large cities all merging into each other to form one enormous conurbation, the *Ruhrgebiet* is, despite its heavily industrial character, a vibrant centre of culture with many museums, theatres, art galleries and opera houses and the area also has a large number of parks providing refuges from the industrial landscape. The older buildings, surviving or restored, as well as other occasional examples are reminders of the days when the cities were only small towns, separated by fields and open rolling countryside. The main cities of the Ruhr are (going west to east): **Krefeld; Duisburg**, Germany's largest internal port; **Mühlheim; Essen**, in the heart of the region; **Bochum**; and **Dortmund**, centre of Germany's brewing industry. South of the Ruhr and bordering the beautiful Siegerland and Sauerland regions is **Wuppertal,** which, stretched out along its own valley, is home to a unique suspension railway urban transit system, the *Schwebebahn*.

The state capital of Lower Saxony, Hannover, hosts the renowned Hannover Trade Fair. The 'Big City in the Park' is also an important internal crossroads with interesting sights. Attractions include the *Herrenhausen Castle* and the *Royal Gardens of the Duke Georg von Calenberg*. The annual music and theatre festival which is performed on open-air stages within the garden, attracts many visitors each summer. The city also has a 14th-century market church, the *Marienkirche*, several museums and a 15th-century town hall.

Romantic Germany can be found in the **Weser Valley**,

where there are fairytale towns such as **Hameln** (Hamlyn), famed for the tale of the Pied Piper. A play about the infamous piper is re-enacted during the summer months every Sunday at noon. The town has several buildings in Weser Renaissance style.

The Rhineland

The Rhineland is Germany's oldest cultural centre. Names such as Cologne, Aachen and Mainz are synonymous with soaring Gothic architecture and with the history and lives of many of the great names of Western Europe. However, the area consists of more than a mere series of riverside towns. Here too are the vast plains of the Lower Rhine farmlands, the crater lakes of the **Eifel Hills,** the **Bergisches Land** with its lakes and *Altenberg Cathedral* and the **Seven Mountains.** Visitors are attracted to the Rhineland and the **Moselle Valley** not only for their beauty and romanticism, but also for the convivial atmosphere engendered by wine and song, after all 'Rhineland is Wineland'. Like most of its tributaries, the Rhine is lined with vineyards wherever the slopes face the sun. Alternating with the vineyards are extensive orchards which, in spring, are heavy with blossom. The **Ahr Valley** is particularly famous for its red wine; nearby is the famous **Nürburgring** racing circuit. **Trier**, the oldest German town close to the Luxembourg border, is situated on the River Moselle. The city houses the most important Roman ruins north of the Alps. Following the River Moselle eastwards towards Koblenz are several towns well-known among wine connoisseurs – **Bernkastel-Kues, Kröv, Beilstein** and **Cochem.** The Rhine Valley between Cologne and Mainz is world famous for its wines and wine festivals during the autumn. The Rhine Gorge's numerous castles include *Stolzenfels*, *Marksburg Castle*, *Rheinfels* at **St Goar** and the *Schönburg Castle* at **Oberwesel.** Along the Cologne–Mainz route the *KD German Rhine Line* operates boats between Good Friday and the end of October enabling the passenger to enjoy the view of both sides of the river with vineyards and picturesque villages lining the banks. The main cities on the Rhine, from north to south, are as follows:

Düsseldorf is one of the great cities of the German industrialised north, an important commercial and cultural centre and the capital of the state of North Rhine-Westphalia (Nordrhein-Westfalen); the city in fact developed over 700 years from a small fishing village at the mouth of the Düssel River to become the country's leading foreign trade centre. The city is an extremely prosperous city with a fine opera house as well as many concert halls, galleries and art exhibitions. There are over 20 theatres and 17 museums, including the *State Art Gallery of North Rhine-Westphalia*, the *Kunsthalle* (City Exhibition Hall) and the late Baroque *Benrath Palace*.

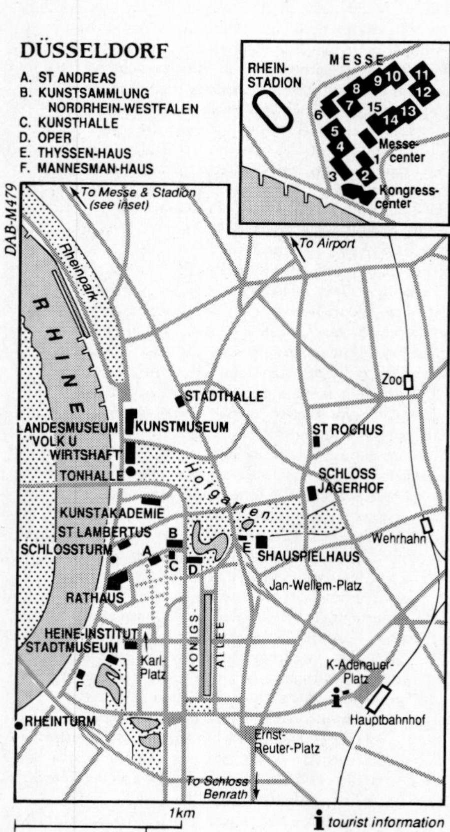

The major exhibition centre is to the north of Hofgarten, which has been staging trade fairs since the time of Napoleon. The heart of the city is the *Königsallee* or 'Kö', a wide boulevard bisected by a waterway and lined with trees, cafés, fashionable shops and modern shopping arcades. Nearby are the botanical gardens, the *Hofgarten*, the Baroque *Jägerhof Castle* and the state legislature. Other attractions include the remains of the 13th-century castle, *St Lambertus Church*, the rebuilt 16th-century *Town Hall*, *Castle Benrath* in southern Düsseldorf and the many gardens and lakes both in the city and in the suburbs.

Cologne (Köln) is an old Roman city and an important cultural and commercial centre holding many trade fairs each year. Attractions include the *Cathedral of St Peter and St Mary* (13th-19th century); the golden reliquary of the Three Magi; Roman remains with a Dionysian mosaic, praetorium, water conduits and catacombs; Romanesque churches of *St Pantaleon*, *St George*, *St Apostein*, *St Gereon* and *St Kunibert*, Gothic churches of *St Andreas* and the *Minoritenkirche* and *Antoniterkirche;* medieval city wall and the *Roman-Germanic Museum*. Several examples of Roman art have been preserved, among them the Dionysosmosaic, the *Praetorium*, the sewage system and the catacombs. The *Wallraf-Richartz Museum* (paintings) is located in a controversial modern building next to the main railway station and the river. Worth a visit is the *Schnütgen Museum* (medieval ecclesiastical art); the zoo; and the *Rhine Park* with 'dancing fountains'. The city is a major starting point for boat trips on the Rhine. It also has a famous carnival. The *Altstadt* (old town) has been lovingly reconstructed and can be enjoyed on foot as can the extensive pedestrian shopping zone.

Aachen (Aix-La-Chapelle), a beautiful spa town and the old capital city of the empire of Charlemagne, is not actually on the Rhine, being situated about 50km (30 miles) west of Cologne. It is actually located at the border of three countries – the Federal Republic, Belgium and The Netherlands – and a short distance from the city is a point where you can stand in all three countries at once. Attractions in Aachen include the *Cathedral;* Charlemagne's marble throne; the *Octagonal Chapel;* the *Town Hall* built between 1333 and 1370 on the ruins of the imperial palace, with Coronation Hall and Charlemagne frescoes; *Suermondt Museum* (paintings, sculptures); and the elegant fountains of sulphorous water, bearing witness to the spa status of the city. In July, an international riding, jumping and driving tournament occurs.

The over 2000-year-old university town and longstanding federal capital **Bonn** will become the second capital of the country, even when the move of 10 ministries to Berlin is complete, as the Parliament and some administration is to remain. South of the actual city is the former spa of Bad Godesberg, which is now part of Bonn. It is also the embassy district and offers a good selection of international restaurants and shops. Attractions include the *Cathedral* (11-13th centuries) and cloisters; *Kreuzberg Chapel*, approached by a flight of 'holy steps'; *Schwarzrheindorf Church* (two storied: 1151); *Town Hall* (1737) and market square; art collections in the *Godesburg* (1210); *Redoute* (1792); *Poppelsdorf Palace* (1715-40) and botanic garden; the *Beethoven Museum* in the house where he was born, and much general theatrical and musical activity associated with the life and work of the great composer; *Pützchens Market* (September); *University* (1725) and *Hofgarten*. Excursions can be made from Bonn to the *Siebengebirge* (Seven Hills), the *Ahr Valley*, *Brühl Castle* and the *Nürburgring*. The city also has many parkland areas, such as the *Kottenforst*, *Venusberg* and *Rhine Promenade*. Keeping with old tradition, the beginning of May sees the *Festival of the Burning Rhine*.

Koblenz is situated at the confluence of the Rhine and the Moselle. From the *Ehrenbreitstein Fortress* (1816-32) the visitor has a spectacular view over the *Deutsches Eck Monument* to German unity and the Rhine and Moselle rivers. Other attractions include *Monastery Church* (12th and 13th centuries); former *Electors' Palace; Collegiate Church of St Florin* (12th century with 14th-century chancel); *Church of Our Lady* (12th century with 15th-century chancel). Ehrenbreitstein also houses a *Beethoven Museum*.

Trier on the Moselle is, as its name indicates, not on the Rhine but on its tributary, the Moselle. It is situated on the Luxembourg frontier about 100km (60 miles) south-west of Koblenz. It is the oldest city in Germany, a Roman imperial capital in the 3rd and 4th centuries AD, and has been declared a UNESCO World Heritage site. Attractions include *The Porta Nigra* (city gate, 2nd century); *Roman Baths; Basilica; Amphitheatre; Cathedral* (4th century); Gothic *Church of Our Lady*; *Simeonstift* with 11th-century cloisters; *Church of St Matthew* (Apostle's grave); *Church of St Paulinus* (designed by Balthasar Neumann); *Regional Museum; Episcopal Museum; Municipal Museum; Municipal Library* (with notable manuscripts); and the house where Karl Marx was born.

Mainz is the capital of the Rhineland Palatinate, a university town and episcopal see dating back 2000 years, situated on the rivers Rhine and Main. Attractions include the international museum of printing *(Gutenberg Museum)*; the 1000-year-old *Cathedral; Electors' Palace; Roman Jupiter Column* (AD67); *'Sparkling Hock' Museum; Citadel* with monument to the general Nero Claudius Drusus; old half-timbered houses; *Mainzer Fassenacht* (carnival); and the *Wine Market* (late August and early September). The sunny slopes of the Rhinegau Hills is the centre of one of the world's most famous wine-producing regions.

Central Germany

East of the Rhineland Palatinate lies the state of **Hesse**, the capital city of which is Wiesbaden. The northern part of Hesse – *Kurhesse Waldeck* – boasts lakes, forests and state-recognised health resorts. Hesse is also known for its many rural villages with half-timbered houses and their old customs are observed to this day. The *German Fairy Tale Road* leads through some of these towns. **Schwalmstadt, the** home of 'Little Red Riding Hood', is a town where people still wear traditional costumes to church on Sundays and at folk festivals. In the Reinhardswald, *Sababurg* – now a castle-hotel – inspired the Brothers Grimm to write the 'Sleeping Beauty' story. The **Lahn**, a tributary of the Rhine, is much visited for romantic scenery in *Nassau*, *Wetzlar*, *Limburg* and at the *Schaumburg Castle*. Also on this river is the old university town of **Marburg** which attracts visitors from all over the world.

Wiesbaden is the capital of the state of Hesse. It is an international spa and congress centre in the Taunus and on the Rhine; the spas specialise in the treatment of rheumatism. Attractions include the *Kurhaus* and casino; the *Wilhelmstrasse*, with elegant shops and cafés; *Hesse State Theatre*; the *Neroberg* (245m/804ft, with high rack railway); the *Greek Chapel;* international riding and jumping championships in the grounds of *Biebrich Palace* at Whitsun; boat trips on the Rhine; and woodland walks.

Darmstadt is situated a few miles to the east of the Rhine. Attractions include the Palace (16th and 17th centuries); *Prince George Palace* (18th century) with porcelain collection; *Regional Museum; Luisenplatz* with Ludwigsäule; artists' colony on *Mathildenhöhe; 'Wedding Tower'* and *Russian Chapel; National Theatre* on the Marienplatz; and *Kranichstein Hunting Lodge* with hunting museum and hotel.

The city of **Frankfurt am Main** is a major financial, commercial and industrial centre situated at the crossroads of Germany. Its soaring skyline has led to the nickname of 'Mainhattan'. Although almost all of the city was destroyed in 1944, many of the buildings in the Old Town have been carefully restored. The *Römer*, the town hall and crowning place of the German emperors since 1562, has been rebuilt from scratch. There are, however, some survivals, including part of the cathedral and the 13th-century chapel that once adjoined *Frederick Barbarossa's Palace*. In the *City Museum* there is a perfect scale model of the old

FRANKFURT am Main

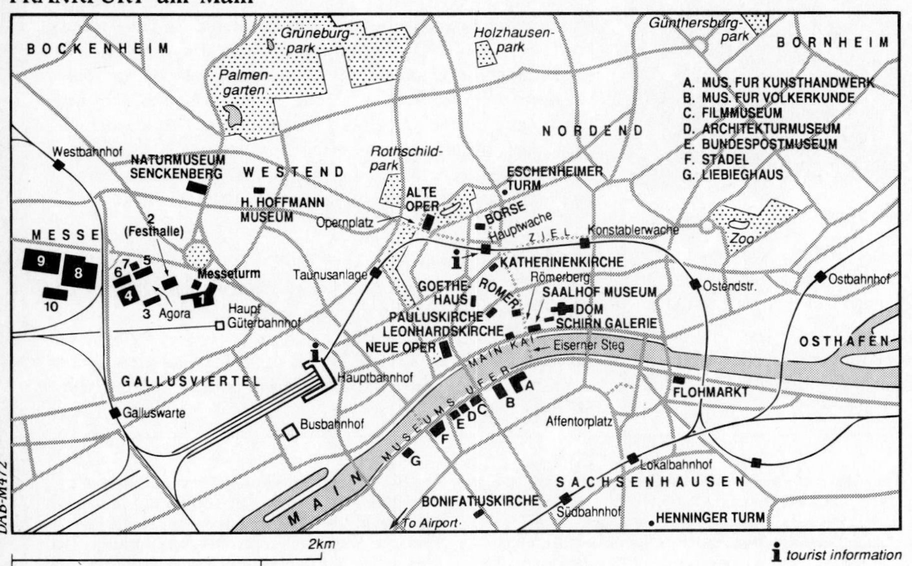

town, and also the astonishing city silver. The stark *Paulus Church* was home to the first German parliament in 1848. Other attractions elsewhere in the city include the zoo, the birthplace of Goethe, the *Opera House*, the suburbs of *Sachsenhausen* and *Höchst*, both formerly towns in their own right, and the *Messe*, the exhibition halls complex. Art enthusiasts should pay a visit to the *Natural History Museum* with its extensive Städel paintings.

Further south is the rolling hill country of the **Odenwald**, a region rich in legend and folklore and renowned for its hiking facilities. The western slopes are traversed by the Bergstrasse. The region is noted for its particularly mild climate which enables the cultivation of a wide range of flowers and fruit. The Odenwald can be explored by way of two routes; the *Nibelungenstrasse* and the *Siegfriedstrasse*. Places worth visiting include **Erbach,** which has a Baroque palace and a medieval watchtower; the resort of **Lindenfels;** and the spa town of **Bad König.** Northwest of Frankfurt and north of Wiesbaden is the wooded hill country of the **Taunus**, a ski centre during the winter. Resorts here include the old town of **Oberursel,** the spa town of **Bad Homburg** and, nearby, the preserved Roman fort of **Saalburg,** situated on the line which marked the old frontier of the Roman Empire. Northeast of Frankfurt is the Baroque town of **Fulda,** gateway to the Rhön region. Some of the buildings here date back to the 9th century. Further north is **Kassel,** home of the *Grimm Brothers Museum*, and the *Wilhelmshöhe Palace* with its magnificent grounds.

The Southwest

The two southern states of the Federal Republic of Germany are also the largest; **Bavaria** and **Baden-Württemburg**.

In the north of **Baden-Württemberg** is the *Neckar Valley*. The most famous place on the river is Germany's oldest university town, **Heidelberg,** which is dominated by the ruins of its famous 14th-century castle. For many the city personifies the era of Romanticism. Other attractions include the 'Giant Cask' in the cellar holding 220,000 litres (48,422 gallons); in the summer, evening serenade concerts in the castle courtyard; *Apothecaries' Museum; Church of the Holy Ghost; St Peter's Church; Karlstor Gate;* and wine taverns. The castle there remains partly Renaissance, partly Gothic and Baroque in style, serenade concerts are played during the summer in the Schloßhof. Vineyards are located along the Neckar Valley, around castles such as *Gutenberg, Hornberg* and *Hirschhorn,* which offer splendid views across the landscape. To the east of Heidelberg, another scenic route begins, the 280km-long (175-miles) *Road of the Castles,* going to Nuremberg in Bavaria. This route follows the river branching off at **Heilbronn** continuing east to medieval places in Bavaria such as **Rothenburg** and **Ansbach** in Bavaria. Further to the south is the *Swabian Jura,* the limestone plateau between the Black Forest and Europe's longest river, the Danube. Places to visit include the *Hohenzollern Castle* near **Hechingen,** *Beuren Abbey* and the *Bären Caves.* Picturesque towns are **Urach** and **Kirchheim unter Teck.** Albert Einstein's birthplace, **Ulm,** houses the world's tallest cathedral spire (160m/528ft). Following the road from Ulm one reaches **Reutlingen** and **Blaubeuren** with a fine abbey which is well worth a visit. Another remarkable Baroque church can be found at **Zwiefalten.** In the southwestern corner of the state, the Rhine acts as a natural border between France and Germany and there lies the **Black Forest**. Walking enthusiasts will enjoy the air filtered by the large pine tree forests, the mountainous scenery and the beautifully situated lakes in the south such as *Titisee* and *Schluchsee.* The Black Forest is well known for its mineral springs whose healing powers were first recognised by the Romans. Its chief spa, **Baden-Baden,** was the summer capital of Europe during the last century. Travellers still flock to this delightful town to 'take the waters', which may be inhaled as a vapour, bathed in or simply drunk. Fortified by the water's therapeutic powers, one can take advantage of the town's many sporting facilities. For the less energetic, the evening could be spent playing roulette or baccarat, in a casino which Marlene Dietrich herself regarded as the most elegant in the world. Other attractions include the Baroque *Kleine Theater, National Art Gallery,* ruins of the *Roman Baths*, the *Margravial Palace* (museum), 15th-century *Collegiate Church, Russian Church, Romanian Chapel,* parks and gardens, *Lichtentaler Allee*, tennis, riding, 18-hole golf course, winter sports, international horseracing weeks at Iffezheim and a modern congress hall. There are also many charming villages and resorts in the surrounding area that are well worth visiting, principally **Freudenstadt,** which claims to have more hours of sunshine than any other German town, and **Triberg,** with its waterfalls and swimming pool surrounded by evergreens. The other main towns and cities in the region not mentioned above are as follows:

Mannheim is a commercial, industrial and cultural centre on the confluence of the rivers Rhine and Neckar. Attractions include the former *Electors' Palace*, now the university; *Municipal Art Gallery; Reiss Museum* in the old arsenal; the old *Town Hall* and *Market Square;* and the *National (Schiller) Theatre.*

Saarbrücken is mainly a modern industrial city, the capital of the Saarland, situated about 140km (90 miles) west of Mannheim on the French frontier. Attractions include the *Church of St Ludwig and Ludwigsplatz* (1762-75); *Collegiate Church of St Arnual* (13th and 14th centuries); palace with grounds and Gothic church; and a Franco-German garden with a miniature town (Gullivers Miniature World).

Stuttgart is the capital of Baden-Württemberg. Often referred to as 'the largest village in Europe', Stuttgart is a green and open city surrounded by trees and vineyards with only a quarter of its area built on. Two of its major industries are the manufacture of Mercedes cars and the publishing industry. Attractions include the modern *Staatsgalerie;* the *Prinzenbau* and *Alte Kanzlei* on the *Schillerplatz* ; the *Neues Schloss*, a vast palace which served as the residence for the Kings of Württemberg and has been painstakingly restored since 1945; *Württemberg Regional Museum; Daimler-Benz Automobile Museum;* 15th-century *Collegiate Church; TV Tower* (193m/633ft high); *Killesberg Park; Ludwigsburg Palace; Wilhelma Zoo;* botanical gardens; theatre (ballet); and mineral-water swimming pools. The Stuttgart Ballet and the Stuttgart Chamber Orchestra are renowned the world over.

Freiburg is the capital of the Black Forest, an archepiscopal see and an old university town. The Gothic *Cathedral* (12th-15th centuries) has a magnificent tower (116m) and is accepted as an architectural masterpiece. Other attractions include the historic red *'Kaufhaus'* on the Cathedral Square (1550); *Augustinian Museum;* Germany's oldest inn, the *Roten Bären;* and many excellent wine taverns. The city is noted for its trout and game dishes and because of several ecological experiments it was named the Green Capital of Germany. The nearby *Schauinsland Mountain* (1284m/4213ft) can be reached by cable-car. Nearby **Todtnauberg** in the Upper Black Forest is the highest situated resort in the Black Forest (1006m/3300ft) and a perfect observation point is the *Belchen* summit nearby. The highest mountain is the *Feldberg* whose slopes are frequented during the winter season by skiers and winter sports enthusiasts.

Konstanz is a German university and cathedral town on the *Bodensee* (Lake Constance) which marks the border between Austria, Switzerland and the Federal Republic. Konstanz is a frontier anomaly, a German town on the Swiss side of the lake, completely surrounded by Swiss territory except for a strip on the waterfront. Attractions include the *Konzilsgebäude* (14th century); Renaissance *Town Hall* (16th century); historic old *Insel Hotel* (14th century); *Barbarossa-Haus* (12th century); *Hus-Haus* (15th century); and the old town fortifications *Rheintorturm, Pulverturm* and *Schnetztor.* The town has theatres, concert halls, a

casino, and hosts an international music festival as well as the *Seenachtfest*, a lake festival. *Reichenau*, an island with a famous monastery, and the island of *Mainau* make an interesting day trip.
The Bavarian town of **Lindau** is a former free imperial city on an island in Lake Constance. It has a medieval town centre and an old *Town Hall* (1422-35). Other attractions include *Brigand's Tower*, *Mang Tower*, *Cavazzen House* (art collection), *Heidenmauer Wall*, *St Peter's* with Holbein frescoes; harbour entry (old lighthouse); international casino; and boat trips. Opposite the town of Konstanz is **Meersburg,** an old town with a 7th-century castle. As an area Lake Constance is the focal point of a delightful holiday district, rich in art treasures and facilities for outdoor activities.
Ulm is famous above all for its soaring Gothic *Cathedral* (768 steps in the 161m/528ft tower; choir stalls by J. Syrlin). Other attractions include the beautiful *Town Hall* with famous ornamental clock; *Corn Exchange* (1594); *Schuhaus* (1536); *Schwörhaus* (1613); old fishermen's quarter with city wall and *Metzgerturm* (tower); *Wiblingen Monastery*, Baroque library; *Museum of Bread;* and the *Municipal Museum* with local works of art.
Heilbronn is a former imperial city, surrounded by vineyards and situated on the Road of the Castles. The Renaissance *Town Hall* has an outside staircase, clock, gable and artistic clock. Other attractions include the 16th-century *Käthchen House* and the Gothic *Kilian Church* with the 62m-high tower (1513-29). The town is also a good base for excursions into the *Neckar Valley*.
Tübingen, south of Stuttgart, is a world-famous romantic university town on the River Neckar. The old town centre is undamaged. Attractions include the *Castle of the Count Palatine* (1078); late Gothic *Collegiate Church* (1470) with royal burial place; *Market Square* with *Town Hall* (1453); picturesque Neckar front; *Hölderlin Tower;* site of former student lock-up (1514); old and new lecture theatres *(Aula);* memorials to Johannes Kepler, Hegel, Schelling, Hölderlin, Mörike, Hauff and Uhland who studied at the theological seminar of the university.

Bavaria

Bavaria consists of four main tourist areas: the *Bavarian Forest and East Bavaria*; *Swabia* and the *Allgäu* in the southwest; *Upper Bavaria* with the German part of the Alps in the south and *Franconia*, the northern region of Bavaria.
The various landscapes feature towering mountains, lakes, forests and many resorts.
In the **Upper Bavaria** region the best-known places include **Garmisch-Partenkirchen, Berchtesgaden, Mittenwald** and **Oberammergau,** home of the Passion Play. One of the most spectacular feasts of architecture that epitomises the fairytale landscape of Bavaria is *Neuschwanstein Castle*, built by Ludwig II of Bavaria. Constructed on the ridge of a mountain valley surrounded by snowcapped peaks, it is a vision from fairyland while at night it changes into the perfect home for Count Dracula.
The vast **Bavarian Forest** can be found in the eastern part of Bavaria bordering the Czech Republic, and site of the first national park. This still unspoiled and peaceful region offers much for those who enjoy outdoor activities and especially walking. Old historic towns such as the Three River Town of **Passau** and the 2000-year-old **Regensburg** provide interesting contrasts to the nature reserves and the *German National Park*. Numerous art treasures can be found in the northern part of Bavaria – the **Franconia** region. Its main attractions include medieval and historic old towns such as **Coburg,** home of Prince Albert; the cathedral town of **Bamberg; Bayreuth,** which stages an annual *Wagner Opera Festival;* and **Würzburg,** with its world-famous Baroque palace, set on the river Main amongst the Franconian vineyards. **Nuremberg** (Nürnberg), the main city in this region, is a modern metropolis and yet the centre of the town has retained its traditional style. The many valleys, forests, lakes and castles of the Swiss Franconian area and the *Fichtel Mountains*, combined with the nature reserves in the *Altmühl Valley*, make Franconia an ideal holiday centre.
Connecting the northern area of Bavaria with the south is the most famous of all the German scenic roads – the *Romantic Road*. The towns along the way give visitors an excellent insight into the region's history, art and culture. Places of particular interest are the afore-mentioned **Würzburg;** medieval **Rothenburg, Dinkelsbühl** and **Nördlingen; Augsburg,** founded in 15BC by the Romans; the pilgrimage *Wieskirche Church* in the meadows; *Steingaden Abbey* and the most popular sight of *Neuschwanstein Castle* near the village of **Schwangau.**
The main towns and cities in Bavaria are as follows:
The Bavarian capital **Munich** (München) is the third largest German city with 1.2 million inhabitants and a major international artistic and business centre. The 800-year-old city is renowned for its numerous interesting museums and several fine Baroque and Renaissance churches. The *Alte Pinakothek* is home to the largest collection of Rubens paintings in the world; directly opposite is the *Neue Pinakothek* with a collection of modern paintings. The *German Museum* (natural science and technology) with planetarium and a life-size coal mine is also interesting for children. Worth a visit is the *Lenbach Gallery* in the impressive villa of the Munich 'Painter Viscount'. Only a short walk away is the *Glyptothek* on the Königsplatz, housing Greek and Roman sculptures. Other attractions include the *Royal Palace* and *Royal Treasury; Bavarian National Museum* and others; the *Church of Our Lady*, the *Theatinerkirche* and *Asamkirche;* and the *Church of St Michael*. The *Marienplatz* is surrounded by the New and Old Town Hall and the restored *Mariensäule*. Every day at 1100 a large group watches the carillion depicting the Schäfflertanz. Site of the 1972 Olympic Games, the facilities are now used by the residents of the city. The *Olympia Park* with its stadium and the 300m (1000ft) tower are now used as a recreational area. Munich is also the setting for the most famous of all German events, the *Oktoberfest* beer festival. This has its origins in 1810 when Crown Prince Ludwig of Bavaria married Princess Therese von Sachsen-Hildburghausen. The people liked the festival so much that it became a regular feature and now takes place annually for two weeks – the first Sunday in October is always the last day of the festival. The nine Munich breweries all have their own beertents, serving their beer exclusively. The city has many famous beer cellars, including the *Hofbräuhaus* and the *Mathäser Bierstadt*, the largest in the world. The district of *Schwabing* has been the city's artists' colony since the 1920s and is still recommended for its good shopping, cafés, small theatres and stalls along the Leopoldstrasse. An escape from the city is offered by the *Englischer Garten*, one of the largest parks in Europe. Right in the middle stands the Chinese Tower surrounded by typical beer gardens. The many theatres include the *National Theatre* (opera house), the Rococo theatre built by Cuvilliés and the *Schauspielhaus* (playhouse). The *Nymphenburg Palace* is home to a portait gallery and a famous collection of china. The *Fasching* (carnival) season reaches its peak during February with several balls and other festivities; but the *Auer Dult*, a funfair and flea market takes place three times a year.
The old city of the Fuggers **Augsburg,** founded in AD15 by the Romans, lies northwest of Munich and was once the financial centre of Europe. It was here, in 1555, that the

Peace Treaty was signed which halted the German religious conflicts during the Reformation. It also boasts the oldest council housing in the world, dating back to 1519. Other attractions include the *Cathedral* (807 Romanesque/1320 Gothic) with 12th-century stained-glass windows and 11th-century bronze door; *St Ulrich's Church* (16th century); *St Anna's Church* (Luther memorial 16th century); *Town Hall* (1615); *Perlach Tower*, Baroque fountain (16/17th centuries); *Arsenal; Fugger Palace* (16th century); *City Gates* (14-16th centuries); *Fuggerei* (1519); *Schaezler Palace* and Rococo banquet hall (18th century) with German Baroque gallery and Old German gallery with paintings by Holbein and Dürer; *Maximilian Museum; Roman Museum;* and *Mozart House*.

Bamberg is an old imperial town and bishopric, built on seven hills, with many medieval and Baroque buildings. Attractions include the *Imperial Cathedral* (13th century) with famous 'Bamberger Reiter' sculpture, reliefs, royal tombs and Veit Stoss altar; the old *Town Hall;* picturesque fishermen's dwellings *('Little Venice'); Old Royal Palace, New Palace* (picture gallery) and rose garden; and *Michaelsberg Monastery*.

Bayreuth is mainly famous for its *Wagner Opera Festival* which takes place every year from late July to August. Other attractions, many of which are connected with the life and works of the composer, include the *Festival Theatre* (1872-1876), *Wahnfried House* (Wagner's home, now a museum), *Wagner Memorial* ('Chiming Museum'), *Freemasons' Museum*, Wagner's grave in the Court Gardens; former residence of the Margrave; *Opera House* (larges European Baroque stage), *Ermitage* (park); and the parish church. The city is also a convenient base for excursions into the *Fichtel Mountains, Oberpfälzer Woods* and the 'Franconian Switzerland'.

Nuremberg (Nürnberg) is a mainly modern city which has, nevertheless, managed to retain much of its medieval centre. The *Church of St Lawrence* and the *Church of St Sebald* are built in the typical red sandstone of the region. Attractions include the *Imperial Castle;* the *City Wall* (over 5km/3 miles long) with 46 watchtowers; *Dürer's house; Museum of Toys; Fembohaus* (municipal museum); *Germanic National Museum; Museum of Transport;* 'Old Nürnberg', a guild hall; *Town Hall;* the *'Schöne Brunnen' fountain; Church of Our Lady* (with mechanical clock) and the zoo (dolphin pool). The international toy fair and the famous Christmas Fair, *Christkindlmarkt*, also attract many visitors.

Passau is situated at the confluence of the Danube, the Inn and the Ilz. Attractions include the Baroque *Cathedral* with the world's largest church organ; *Bishop's Palace* with Rococo staircase; *Oberhaus* and *Niederhaus* fortresses (13th-14th centuries); and Inn quay with Italian architecture.

Regensburg is about 80km (50 miles) northeast of Munich, a city which can trace its roots back to the 1st century AD. Attractions of the old epicscopal city include the *Cathedral* (famous 'Regensburger Domspatzen' choir); *St Emmeram's Church* (crypts, tombs); the *'Scottish Church'* (Romanesque portal); *Old Chapel; Palace Niedermünster* (excavations); *Porta Praetoria* (North Gate); 12th-century stone bridge; *Old Town Hall* with the Imperial Chamber; fine patrician residences; palace of the princes of Thurn and Taxis; and museums.

The old Franconian imperial town **Rothenburg o.d.T.** is famous for its well-preserved medieval atmosphere. It is possible to walk along its two miles of encircling walls with over 30 gates and towers, overlooking the magnificent patrician houses. Other attractions include the *Town Hall* (16th-17th centuries); *Church of St Jacob* with altar by Riemenschneider (circa 1500); the *Plönlein;* 'Meistertrunk' clock; extensive network of footpaths; and traditional medieval inns.

The northern Bavarian town **Würzburg**, about halfway between Frankfurt and Nuremberg, nestles between vineyards famous for their *Bocksbeutel* (specially formed bottle). The *Festung Marienberg* (fortress) offers a spectacular view over the city and its numerous spires. Walking across the 15th-century *Old Main Bridge*, with statues of the Franconian apostles of Lilian, Totnan and Kolonat, the view is dominated by the imposing Romanesque *Cathedral*. Attractions include the *Mainfränkisches Museum*, housed in the former arsenal with examples of the work of Riemenschneider (1460-1531) and the *Marienkirche*, built in AD706 and one of the oldest churches in the country. The Baroque Castle-Palace *(Residenz)*, designed by Balthasar Neumann taking Versailles as a model, is supposedly one of the most elaborate buildings of the country. Candlelit Mozart concerts take place during the summer months in the *Emperor's Hall* and the *Hofgarten*. The grand staircase with the painting by Tiepolo here is regarded as one of the finest examples of the Baroque style in Europe. The *Käppele*, another Baroque building, was also designed by Balthasar Neumann. The town library and the tourist information found a home in the *Haus zum Falken* (Falcon House), which has an impressive Rococo façade. Relaxation and diversion from sightseeing are provided by the numerous wine bars – the *Stachel* (thorn) was built in 1413 – cafés and restaurants. Nearly the whole of the city centre is a pedestrian zone, only disturbed by the way of public transport, the trams.

Berlin

Berlin is the largest city in Germany. It is also the country's capital and the future seat of Government. The move of several ministries is to be completed by 1998. Its location at the heart of central Europe and the disappearance of the Iron Curtain are sure to mean that its importance in Europe can only increase, while its location within Germany is liable to shift the country's centre of gravity eastwards. Since November 1989 when the Wall came down, nearly 100 streets have been reconnected, disused 'ghost' stations on the underground and overground suburban railways have sprung back to life and the watchtowers, dogs and barbed wire that divided the city, the country and indeed the continent for 28 years have virtually disappeared; nevertheless the two parts of the city remain very different places. Although this is largely due to the economic contrast between west and east, the two halves of the city have never been of a uniform character. The east contains the densely populated, urban proletarian quarters of **Mitte, Pankow, Prenzlauer Berg** and **Friedrichshain** which inspired the theatre of Erwin Piscator and Bertold Brecht, although west Berlin also had its 'red' quarters like the Wedding, Neukölln and Kreuzberg (Kreuzberg is currently known for its pubs and the high proportion of Turkish nationals whose shops dominate the streets). In comparison, the green and leafy areas of **Charlottenburg** and **Zehlendorf** exude a more bourgeois atmosphere. After the city was occupied by the four post-war victorious powers, the two halves diverged even more as West Berliners broke away from their past and embraced the idea of a new, intensely Western, americanised city. At the same time their fellow citizens in the east chose instead to retain what remained of the old Berlin. It is for this reason that the eastern half of the city arguably gives a more accurate image of what Berlin was like in the 20s and 30s, although you have to move slightly away from the city centre with its awkward juxtaposition of ponderous Prussian monuments and monolithic post-war social-realist architecture, in order to find the quarters that, despite wartime destruction followed by decades of decay, nevertheless retain a vestige of the atmosphere of the pre-war capital.

Alexanderplatz, immortalised in Alfred Döblin's 1929 novel *Berlin Alexanderplatz*, was one of the main centres of the old 1920s Berlin as well as of post-war East Berlin. It is likely with time to re-emerge as an important focal point in the newly united city, although through relentless modernisation it has changed character completely and is now a bustling if faceless area of cafés, hotels and the 119ft-high Television Tower (*Fernsehturm*) which dominates the skyline of the city. The oldest church in Berlin, the *Nikolai Church* (13th century), lent its name to the surrounding district, the Nikolaiviertel. This part of the city is an example for well-planned city restoration; it suffered tremendously during the war and was rebuilt partly with historic details, partly with modern façades on the occasion of the 750th Anniversary of Berlin. Sweeping westwards away from Alexanderplatz is **Unter den Linden**, which Friedrich the Great saw as the centrepiece of his royal capital and which changed from one of the premier thoroughfares of the old unified city to the showpiece of the German Democratic Republic, lined with restored monumental buildings and diplomatic delegations to the former capital of the GDR. However, for nearly thirty years it was in fact a dead-end, a monumental avenue cut off by the Wall. At its western end, the *Brandenburg Gate* (Brandenburger Tor) has been the supreme symbol of the city of Berlin (and even of elusive German nationhood) since its completion in 1791. Situated just within the old boundaries of East Berlin the view of the Brandenburg Gate from the West was for nearly 30 years obscured by the Wall which ran directly in front of it and as such it became an eloquent symbol of post-war European division. Now, for the first time since 1961, it is accessible from both East and West and is perhaps the most potent evocation of the peaceful revolution of 1989. The deceptively benign-looking *Berlin Wall* has all but gone and walkers and cyclists now roam along what was so recently known as the *Todesstreifen* or *Death Strip*. Quite a few tourists were able to buy 'their' own piece of the Mauer, other parts can now be seen in several museums.

Berlin is not just an industrial city but also a cultural and scientific capital with several universities. It houses three opera houses, 53 theatres and more than 100 cinemas. East Berlin has a rich array of museums, most of which can be found on *Museumsinsel* (Museum Island) in a fork of the *River Spree*. The most famous is the *Pergamon Museum* which houses works of classical antiquity such as the *Pergamon Altar*, and art of the Near East, Islam and the Orient. Among the many museums in the west are the *Ägyptisches Museum* (Egyptian Museum) at Charlottenburg, which contains the world famous bust of Queen Nefertiti; the museums at **Dahlem** housing the major part of the Prussian State art collections; and the *Berlin Museum* in the old Supreme Court Building in Kreuzberg. The restored *Martin-Gropius-Bau* houses changing art exhibitions and the Berlin Gallery, with exhibits of the Jewish collection of the Berlin Museum and a 20th-century exhibition. Nearby is the **Prince Albrecht Area** which is to become an international monument and reminder, as the building of the Gestapo, later the *Reichssicherheitshauptamt*, stood here. The exhibition entitled *Topography of Terror* documents this part of the history. The planned *Kulturforum* is to be constructed next to the *National Gallery* (designed by van der Rohe), the Philharmonic, the Chamber Music Hall and other museums, and will be developed as a cultural centre for the city.

One of the major cultural attractions of the eastern part of Berlin is the *Deutsche Staatsoper* staging highly impressive performances in a superbly refurbished classical setting. However, with the demise of the German Democratic Republic, subsidies are no longer guaranteed and the Opera's future is uncertain as ticket prices are forced to

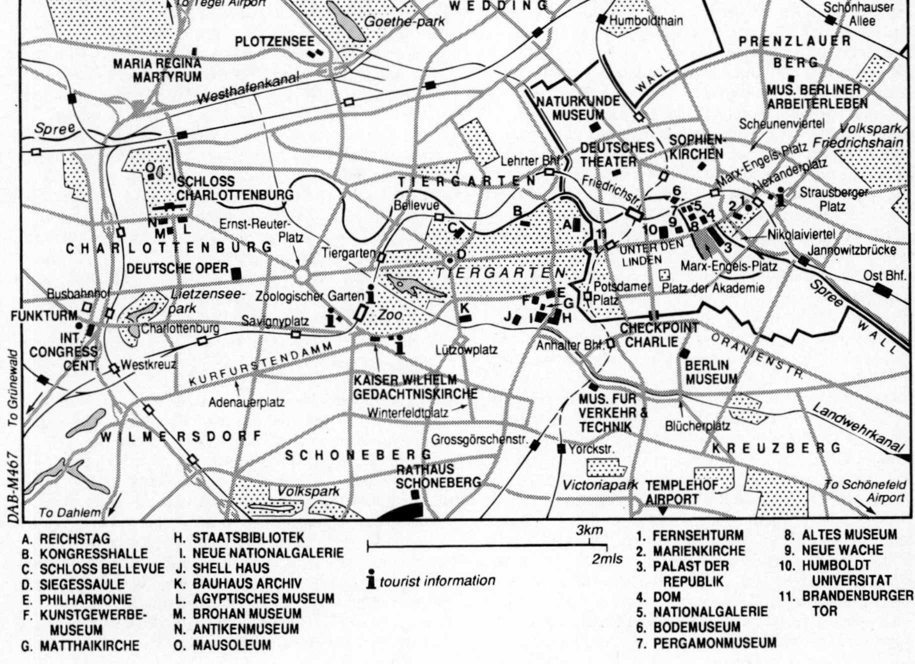

conform to market rates. Nevertheless, Berlin's cultural scene will no doubt continue to draw visitors from all over the world. The arguably finest concert hall is part of the *Schauspielhaus Berlin*, designed by the famous architect Karl Friedrich Schinkel. At 1200, 1500 and 1900 visitors can enjoy the carillion of the tower of the *French Cathedral*. Other attractions are as diverse as the *Berlin Festival* in September, the *Jazz Festival* in the autumn, the *Berlinale* in February, the Philharmonic Concerts and the thriving 'alternative' theatre.

Venturing west from the Opera along **Unter den Linden** and through the *Tiergarten* the visitor will eventually arrive at the heart of West Berlin, the *Kurfürstendamm*, popularly referred to as the 'Ku'damm'. As with so many features of this once divided city it is all too easy to attribute symbolic significance to the 'Ku'damm', for in a sense it is the embodiment of the glitzy materialistic West and of the differences created by the two systems which co-existed in Berlin for 40 years. Pulsating with traffic and people 24 hours a day and lined with cafés and shops, despite unification it still seems a thousand miles away from the bleak Alexanderplatz in the other half of the city. After taking time to sit in a café for a while and watch the crowds go by, strolling eastwards along the *Ku'damm* one will come to the *Kaiser-Wilhelm-Gedächtniskirche*. Preserved as a ruin after the destruction of the Second World War it is a stark reminder of the city's suffering from bombardment and its post-war rebirth. Not far from here also are the *Europa Center*, containing shops, nightlife and a rooftop café with a splendid view of the whole city, and the world-renowned department store, the *KaDeWe* (short for *Kaufhaus des Westens*). Other attractions of the western half of the city include: the *Siegesäule* (Victory Column), built at the order of Kaiser Wilhelm I two years after victory in the Franco-Prussian War of 1871; the *Tiergarten*, an English-style park in the heart of the city; and the *Kreuzberg* quarter, whose tenement buildings are home to a flourishing alternative culture and a large Turkish community. The *Reichstag*, reconstructed after 1945 and containing a fascinating exhibition, *Fragen an die Deutsche Geschichte* (Questioning German History), is to undergo another round of modernisation before the ministries can move in. *Schloss Charlottenburg*, the splendid Baroque and Rococo palace of Friedrich the Great, was the former summer home of the king outside Berlin. The Palace Park is ideal for long walks. The *Gedenkstätte Plötzensee* is a memorial to the 2500 members of the resistance who were executed here and generally to the German resistance during the Nazi reign. Since the 1920s when the city immortalised by Christopher Isherwood in *Goodbye to Berlin* enjoyed a reputation for decadence and radicalism which attracted people from all over Europe, Berlin has been known for its vibrant, flamboyant nightlife. This was fostered after the forming of the Federal Republic as, cut off from the rest of the country, West Berlin continued to attract and nurture an alternative culture, a radical political awareness and an adventurous creativity. Several alternative projects have gained more and more attention, among them the old *UFA-Factory* with cinema, circus, café, bakers and more, and the *Ökodorf e.V.* (centre and meeting place for people involved in ecological activities). Another of those is the first women-only hotel *artemisia* in Europe. Although Sally Bowles and her like may no longer be found revelling through the night in a smoke-filled cabaret on the Tauentzien, West Berlin is still a city that is open 24 hours a day with an unrivalled range of nightclubs, bars, restaurants, cabarets and *Kneipen* (pubs), catering for every taste and budget. There are excellent twice-monthly listings guides, *Prinz*, *Tip* and *Zitty*, as well as *Oxmox* (monthly), giving details of everything going on in the city, including East Berlin. Published on alternate weeks, they are available from any news kiosk. Diversion from the city life can be easily found as the city boundaries include numerous recreational areas, such as the *Pfaueninsel* (peacock island), now a nature reserve; the *Spanauer* and *Tegler Forests* and the *Grunewald*. The *People's Park Friederichshain* in the eastern part of the city is simultaneously the largest and oldest park in east Berlin.

Mecklenburg-West Pomerania

The state of **Mecklenburg-West Pomerania** contains the longest stretch of the Baltic coast in Germany. The northeast city of **Neubrandenburg** on Lake Tollense is an example of a well-preserved medieval city with a city wall, moat and towers. The city centre is surrounded by a circular city wall with four city gates, three moats and several *Wiekhäuser* (fortifications). The university and old *Hanseatic* town of **Rostock** lies on the Baltic coast. The university was founded in 1419 and was the first university in Northern Europe. Attractions in the city include the elegant burghers' houses in *Thälmann Square*, the 15th-century *Town Hall*, the late Gothic *Marien Church* with its 15th-century Astronomical Clock and baroque organ and the district of *Warnemünde* with its fishing harbour. The city was somewhat of a showpiece for the regime of the former GDR and has monumental housing complexes which are now home to many of the city's problems.

Greifswald, a small university town east of Rostock, has original 15th-century burghers' houses and part of a medieval fishing village. Birthplace of the famous German painter Caspar David Friedrich, the city's aspect was radically altered in the post-war period through the construction of new residential areas and industrial zones. The White Fleet of passenger boats serves all the coastal ports, and calls at **Hiddensee Island**, an island with no cars or streets and a large protected bird colony. The island of **Rügen**, with its nature reserve and famous chalk cliffs, is the largest island in Germany and is a popular holiday destination. From here there are connecting ferries to the Republic of Lithuania in the eastern Baltic region.

Schwerin was founded in 1160 and is still a charming town today. *Schwerin Castle*, on the lake of the same name and surrounded by a terraced garden crossed by a canal, was for many decades the Residence of the Dukes of Mecklenburg and is one of the finest examples of German Gothic architecture. In the historic old quarter of the city is the well-preserved Gothic *Cathedral*, the *Town Hall* and an interesting *Museum* with collections of French, German and Dutch paintings from the 17th, 18th and 19th centuries.

March of Brandenburg

Graphically described by the 19th-century German writer Theodore Fontane, the area of the **March of Brandenburg** that surrounds Berlin is a region of birch and pine forests and open horizons. The picturesque **Spreewald** lies south of Berlin and offers numerous waterways to be explored by boat and tranquil hamlets such as **Bückchen** to be discovered. Flat-bottomed barge is still the main means of transport in the heart of this region, as it has been for centuries. At **Lehde** there is a museum of original houses and farm buildings, complete with interiors. There are also several examples of the culture of the *Sorben*, a resident slavic minority.

Potsdam, although lacking many of its former attractions, has preserved several 18th-century buildings. The city also boasts three extensive parks, the *Neuen Garten* with the marble palace (closed for modernisation) and *Schloss Cecilienhof* (the Potsdam Conference took place here), the

Babelsberg (park designed by the Prince of Pückler-Muskau) and naturally *Sanssouci* containing a gilded tea-house, and *Sanssouci Palace*, built on the instructions of Frederick the Great by Knobelsdorff. This, the favourite palace of Frederick the Great, is definitely a must for every visitor. The picture gallery next door to the palace contains many old masters. The *Dutch Quarter* of the city should also not be missed.

Traces of Frederick the Great are also to be found at **Rheinsberg,** which was immortalised by Kurt Tucholsky's tale of the same name. The beautifully situated castle is to become a museum. The **Schorfheide** is an area of forest north of Berlin. Beavers, otters and eagles have claimed this picturesque area as their own. In the centre of this landscape of birches and pines lies the *Werbellin Lake*. Any visit to the region should also include a visit to the former Cistercian monastery of *Chorin*, where in the summer concerts are staged.

Saxony, Saxony-Anhalt and Thuringia

Magdeburg, an industrial town to the southwest of Berlin, contains the statue of the Magdeburg Knight, a cathedral dating from AD955 and the *Monastery of Our Lady*. The attractive town of **Quedlinburg**, 55km (34 miles) southwest of Magdeburg, has many 16th-century half-timbered houses such as the *Finkenherd* and a Renaissance *Town Hall* that have been restored to their original condition. Among the towering scenery of the **Harz Mountains**, a region ideal for walking and winter sports holidays and dotted with villages noted for their attractive carved timber-fronted houses, lies the town of **Wernigerode** whose castle and 16th-century town hall endow it with a fairytale air. There is a museum of church relics here. On a walk the visitor can see half-timbered houses of 6 centuries, among them the *Crooked House*. **Stolberg** is often described as the 'Pearl of the South Harz region' and contains characteristic half-timbered houses and a *Town Hall* dating back to 1492 which contains no inner staircase. Just to the south lies the city of **Halle**, where Martin Luther often preached in the *Marienkirche* in the *Market Square* . Handel was born in this city in 1685, and is commemorated by an annual festival. One of the most famous Reformation towns is nearby **Wittenberg**, where Martin Luther nailed his '95 Theses Against Indulgences' to the door of the castle church in 1517. Numerous magnificent buildings from the 16th-century, *Luther's House*, the *Melanchton House*, the *Castle Church* and the buildings of the former *University* bear witness to the town's historical significance.

South of Halle lies the historic town of **Naumburg** with its beautiful late Romanesque/early Gothic *Cathedral of St Peter and St Paul*. A trip from here into the old Hanseatic towns of **Salzwedel**, **Stendal** and **Tangermünde** to see the medieval fortifications is especially recommended.

Thuringia lies between Saxony and Hesse. The wooded heights and slate mountains of the *Thuringian Forest* make this region an ideal area for walking. The most famous route for hiking is the *Rennsteig* which stretches for over 168km (105 miles). The entire region of the Rennsteig is a protected zone and is therefore immune to any industrial or urban development. The walker will come across many rare plants and birds such as the capercaillie and the black grouse. A flourishing craft industry and winter sports facilities centred in **Suhl** are further attractions which draw visitors to the region. **Eisenach**, the birthplace of Johann Sebastian Bach, contains the oldest *Town Gate* in Thuringia and the Romanesque *Nikolai Church*. The town is dominated by the *Wartburg Castle* where Martin Luther sought refuge and translated the New Testament into German.

The southern 1000-year-old town of **Weimar** was home of many great men, including Luther, Bach, Liszt, Wagner and Schiller. A great cultural centre of the past, the city experienced its golden age in the 18th and 19th century. Goethe lived here for 50 years and was a major influence as a civil servant, theatre director and poet. Goethe's house is now the *National Museum*. Literature enthusiasts should not miss the Goethe and Schiller Archive. Bach was Court Organist and Court Concertmaster, Liszt and Richard Strauss were each director of music. There is documentation of their private and public lives kept in hotels and museums in the town. A gruesome museum commemorates the nearby site of **Buchenwald** concentration camp. Other noteworthy sites in the region are **Gera** with its Renaissance *Town Hall* and fine *Burghers' Houses*, the old university town of **Jena**, the castle ruins at **Friedrichsroda**, imperial city **Nordhausen** with its late Gothic *Cathedral* and Renaissance *Town Hall*, the picturesque town of **Mühlhausen,** and **Erfurt** with its well-preserved town centre which is on the UNESCO list of monuments.

Saxony, too, has much to offer the visitor. To the southeast of Halle lies **Leipzig**, a city with a fascinating history. Lenin printed the first issues of his Marxist newspaper here. Lessing, Jean Paul Sartre and Goethe all studied at the university. Leipzig is a town of music and books, 38 publishers have their houses here. It is the birthplace of Wagner, and Bach was choirmaster at *St Thomas' Church* between 1723 and 1750 (St Thomas' Church has been completely restored, as has the 16th-century *Town Hall*). Johann Sebastian Bach's church choir still exists, and is of an excellent standard, as is the city's *Gewandhaus* Orchestra. The old *University* (1407), the famous *Auerbach Cellar* and the *Kaffeebaum*, the most famous of the city's pubs, are further attractions in the city. Today Leipzig is known throughout the World for its international trade fairs.

To the southeast of Leipzig, in Southern Saxony, are **Meissen** and Dresden. Meissen is the oldest china manufacturing town in Europe, famous for its fine Meissen china. Visitors may still see round the factory. When wandering through the narrow streets and alleyways of the city the visitor will feel transported back to a former age. The *Albrechtsburg Cathedral* (1485) and the *Bishop's Castle* tower above the city. Meissen is also the centre of a wine-growing region.

With over half a million inhabitants **Dresden** is one of the largest towns in southeast Germany. Its heyday was in the 17th and 18th centuries when August the Strong and subsequently his son August III ruled Saxony. The most famous building in the city is the restored *Zwinger Palace*, which contains many old masters in its picture gallery, among them the Sistine Madonna by Raphael. Dresden was often referred to as 'Florence on the Elbe' until allied bombings destroyed so much of the Baroque magnificence of the city in the Second World War. However, some of the finest buildings, such as the Catholic *Hofkirche*, the *Palace Church*, the *Semper Opera* and the *Green Vault* treasure chamber of the Saxon Princes, either survived the bombings or have been restored in the intervening period, while the ruins of the *Frauenkirche* are a constant reminder of the horror unleashed on the city in 1944. Other attractions include the *Arsenal*, which has a vast collection of armour and weapons from the Middle Ages to the present day, the fountains in the *Pragerstrasse*, the old market, the Philharmonic Orchestra and the *Kreuz* Choir.

The **Erzgebirge** region near Dresden forms the border with the Czech Republic. Its mountainous wooded landscape makes it ideal for walkers in the summer and skiiers in the winter. **Sächsische Schweiz** *(Saxon Switzerland)*,

the sandstone mountain range with its unique cliff formations, is visited every year by tourists from all over Germany and is to become a National Park. **Chemnitz** (formerly Karl-Marx-Stadt) is a grim, polluted industrial city and is the main town in the region. It was heavily destroyed during the war and only a few of the historic buildings remain. These are the *Old Town Hall* (16th century) and the 800-year-old *Red Tower*; others are **Freiberg**, **Kuchwald**, with its open-air theatre, and **Seiten** with its toy museum. **Zwickau** is the birthplace of Robert Schumann and is home to a late Gothic *Cathedral*, a *Town Hall* dating back to 1403 and numerous old burghers' houses.

The Dresden and Cottbus districts contain the minority **Sorbs**, descendants of a 6th-century slavic people. Sorb-language newpapers and broadcasts combine with teaching in local schools to retain the Sorb culture.

SOCIAL PROFILE

FOOD & DRINK: The main meal of the day in Germany tends to be lunch with a light snack eaten at about seven in the evening. Breakfast served in homes and hotels usually consists of a boiled egg, bread rolls with jam, honey, cold cuts and cheese slices. Available from snack bars, butcher shops, bakers and cafés are grilled, fried or boiled sausages *(Bratwurst)* with a crusty bread roll or potato salad (costing approximately DM6, depending on facilities). There are also bread rolls filled with all kinds of sausage slices, hot meat filling (such as *Leberkäse*), pickled herring, gherkins and onion rings or cheese. In bakeries, Strudel with the traditional apple filling, a variety of fruits and cream cheese, is available. There is also an astonishingly wide variety of breads. A set menu meal (available from DM20) in a simple *gasthof* or café usually includes three courses: a soup is the most popular starter. The main meal consists of vegetables or a salad, potatoes, meat and gravy. For puddings there is often a sweet such as a *blancmange*, fruit or ice cream. Restaurants often serve either beer or wine. Cakes and pastries are normally reserved for the afternoon with *Kaffee und Kuchen* ('coffee and cakes') taken at home or in a café. Cafés serving *Kaffee und Kuchen* are not only to be found in cities, towns and villages but also at or near popular excursion and tourist spots. International speciality restaurants such as Chinese, Greek, Turkish and others can be found everywhere in the western part of the country. Waiter or waitress service is normal although self-service restaurants are available. Bakeries and dairy shops specialise in lighter meals if preferred. The choice and service in restaurants in eastern Germany varies greatly and is, in many cases, not comparable to Western standards.

Local regional specialities cover an enormous range:

Frankfurt and Hesse: *Rippchen mit Sauerkraut* (spare ribs) and of course *Frankfurter* sausages and *Ochsenbrust* with green sauce, *Zwiebelkuchen* (pastry filled with onions) and *Frankfurter Kranz* cream cake.

Westphalia and Northern Rhineland: *Rheinischer Sauerbraten* (beef marinaded in onions, sultanas, pimento, etc), *Reibekuchen* (potato fritters), *Pfeffer-Potthast* (spiced beef with bay leaves) and *Moselhecht* (Moselle pike with creamy cheese sauce). Westphalia is also famous for its smoked ham, sausages and bread such as *Pumpernickel.*

Stuttgart and Baden: *Schlachtplatte* (sauerkraut, liver sausage and boiled pork). A variety of pastas are served such as *Maultaschen* (a type of ravioli) and *Spätzle* (noodles), as well as *Eingemachtes Kalbfleisch* (veal stew with white sauce and capers) and *Schwarzwälder Kirschtorte* (Black Forest gateau).

Munich and Bavaria: *Leberkäs* (pork and beef loaf), as well as a variety of dumplings, *Spanferkel* (suckling pig), the famous *Weisswurst* (white sausages), *Strudel*, *Leberknödelsuppe* (liver dumplings soup), *Nürnberger Lebkuchen* (gingerbread) and from the same town grilled *Rostbratwurst* sausages.

Hamburg and Northern Germany: *Hamburger Aalsuppe* (eel/lobster/crayfish soup), *Labskaus* (hotpot with fried eggs), *Rote Grütze* mit Sahne oder Vanillesosse (fruit compote served with cream or custard), smoked eel, *Rumtopf* (fruit marinaded in rum), Lübecker marzipan, *Heidschnuckenbraten* (Lüneburg Heath mutton), fish with green sauce, *Bauernfrühstück* (omelette with fried potatoes, tomatos and onions) and bread rolls filled with fish or prawns as a snack.

Bremen: *Kohl und Pinkel* (kale and spare ribs), *Matjes Hering* (white herring), eel soup and *Hannoversches Blindhuhn* (hotpot with bacon, potatoes, vegetables and fruit).

Berlin: *Eisbein mit Sauerkraut* (leg of pork) and mashed potatoes, *Bouletten* (meat balls), *Kartoffelpuffer* (potatoe fritters), *Eierpfannkuchen* (pancakes), *Berliner Pfannkuchen* (doughnut), and *Berliner Weisse mit Schuss* (beer with a dash of something – usually raspberry syrup).

March of Brandenburg: *Teltower Rübchen* (swedes), *Mohnprielen* and *Mohnstriezel* (pastries with poppy seeds), *Morchelgerichte* (a mushroom dish), Oder crabs, *Eberswalder Spritzkuchen* (doughnuts), *Schwarzsauer mit Backpflaumen und Klößen* (black pudding with prunes and dumplings).

Saxony: *Leipziger Allerlei* (vegetables in white sauce), *Dresdner Stollen* (German christmas cake), *Speckkuchen* (pastry filled with bacon).

Saxony-Anhalt: *Lehm und Stroh* (sauerkraut with mushy peas), *Köhlersuppe* (croutons, suet, onions and mushrooms), *Speckkuchen mit Eiern und Kümmel* (pastry filled with bacon, served with eggs and caraway seeds). *Zerbster Brägenwurst* (sausage) with Bitterbier. *Baumkuchen* (literally tree cake, the thin layers of pastry are like the rings of trees).

Thuringia: *Thüringer Rostbratwürste* (grilled sausages), *Hefeplinsen* (pancakes with raisins) with sugar or jam. Apple, plum, poppy seed, cream cheese or onion crumbles. Numerous mushroom dishes, these are called *Schwämm.*

Mecklenburg-West Pomerania: *Plum'n un Klüt* (plums and dumplings), *Spickbost* (smoked goose breast).

Drink: Bars can either have table service and/or counter service, although customers will often find that the drinks bought are simply marked down on a beer mat to be paid for on leaving. The legal age for drinking alcohol in a bar or café is 18. Minors are allowed to go into a bar if accompanied by an adult but they will not be served alcohol. Opening hours depend on the proprietor but generally bars in major towns and resorts are open all day and close around midnight or later. Exceptions are Berlin and Hamburg where every pub can open for 24 hours. The national drink is **beer** in its many forms. Regional flavours vary from light *pilsner*-type lagers to heavy stouts. Two of particular note are *Bayrisches G'frornes* (frozen beer) from Bavaria and *Mumme* (bittersweet beer without hops) to be found in Hannover.

German **wines** are among the finest in the world. Some of the most famous are grown in the Rhine and the Moselle Valley but also in the Ahr region, Nahe, Franconia and Baden area. Try *Äppelwoi* (cider) in Frankfurt, *Cannstatter* (white wine) in Stuttgart, *Kirschwasser* (cherry schnapps) in Baden, and *Würzburger* (dry white wine) in Würzburg.

NIGHTLIFE: In all larger towns and cities in western Germany and also in the major eastern cities visitors will have the choice between theatre, opera (Hamburger Staatsoper, Deutsche Oper Berlin and the National Theatre in Munich are some of the most famous names), nightclubs, bars with live music and discos catering for every taste. Berlin, in particular, is famous for its large

Share in the Celebration

Join us for our 250th anniversary season

Music Director Kurt Masur

The Great Hall of the Gewandhaus Leipzig

For further information please contact:

Gewandhaus
zu Leipzig
Augustusplatz 8
O-7010 Leipzig
Germany

Tel. 49-341-7132326
Fax: 49-341-2117167

selection of after-hours venues. Traditional folk music is found mostly in rural areas. There are *Bierkellers* in the south and wine is drunk in small wine cellars in the Rhineland Palatinate, Franconia and Baden region.
SHOPPING: Special purchases include precision optical equipment such as binoculars and cameras, porcelain, handmade crystal, silver, steelware, Solingen knives, leatherwear, sports equipment, toys from Nuremberg and Bavarian *Loden* cloth. Special purchases in eastern Germany include musical instruments, wooden carved toys from the Erzgebirge Mountains, and Meissen china (the workshops in Meissen are open to the public).
Shopping hours: 0800/0900-1800/1830 Monday to Wednesday and Friday; 0900-2030 Thursdays and 0900-1330 Saturday. On the first Saturday of each month shops are open until 1600 and closed 1300-1500 in smaller towns.
SPORT: The Federal Republic of Germany has extensive sports facilities with a sports field or stadium in all larger towns. League **football** matches take place on Saturday afternoons. International matches also take place from time to time: the national team are the current world champions, as well as having been runners-up in the two previous World Cups in 1982 and 1986. **Race courses** can be found at Baden-Baden, Hamburg, Munich and Frankfurt. **Horseriding** is very popular and hotels with riding facilities are located in all tourist regions. National centres are Verden and Warendorf (National Stud). There are over 200 major **golf** courses. The northern coastline and the extensive rivers and lakes provide **sailing, swimming** and both sea and river **fishing**. A fishing permit is needed (cost approx. DM15 a day). Fishing is particularly good on inland waterways; fishing and sailing are also popular at the Bay of Lietzow on the Baltic coast. The Baltic coast has many beaches. All resorts and larger towns in the Federal Republic of Germany have swimming pools. **Winter sport** resorts are mainly in the Suhl area in the south of the country. The main resort is Oberhof, which offers excellent **ski-jumping** and **tobogganing**. **Skiing:** In Bavaria, skiing is available at resorts such as *Garmisch-Partenkirchen*, *Berchtesgaden*, *Oberstdorf*, *Inzell*, *Reit im Winkl*, as well as in the southern mountains. Other areas are the Harz Mountains, the Black Forest and the Bavarian Forest. The season runs from November to April. **Curling** is especially popular in Upper Bavaria. Other popular sports include **tennis, squash** and **windsurfing**. **Ice hockey** and **skating** are both popular. **Cycling** is increasingly popular and cycling paths ensure that even in cities cycling is a safe form of transport. Push-bikes are available from certain railway stations for hire and a list of these railway stations is available through DB or GNTO. Organised holidays can be booked through: *Rotalis Reisen per Rad*, W-8011 Baldham near München (tel: (08106) 7175) and other organisations. Enquire at the Tourist office. **Walking areas:** The Harz Mountains, Black Forest and the Bavarian Forest are some of the best. The network of marked trails amounts to 132,000km (82,500 miles) and also in the eastern states enthusiasts can find new trails. The District of Templin in the March of Brandenburg provides 480km (300 miles) of paths. The Deutsche Alpenverein (German Alps Club) maintains several huts in the Alps and the other ranges. It also organises tours and courses in **rock climbing**. The Saxon Hills between Dresden and Bad Schandau, with more than 1000 prepared routes, provide good training for aspiring climbers. Excellent possiblities can also be found in Oberhof.
SPECIAL EVENTS: Hundreds of annual festivals are celebrated throughout the country and full details can be obtained from the Tourist Board. The following list is a selection of those events celebrated in 1993/4:
Mar 9-13 '93 *Leipzig Spring Fair*, Leipzig. **Mar 12-Jun 6** *Pablo Picasso*, Munich (exhibition). **Apr 3-26** *Frühjahrs-Dippemess*, Frankfurt (funfair). **Apr 18-May 2** *Ice Hockey World Championships*, Munich. **End of Apr** *Tree Blossom Festival*, Werder, March of Brandenburg. **Apr 23-May 1** *Film Festival*, Dresden. **Apr 23-Oct 17** *Internationale Gartenbauausstellung*, Stuttgart (horticultural show). **Apr 30** *Walpurgisnacht*, throughout the Harz. **May 1** *Burning Rhine*, Bonn. **May 20-Jun 13** *Musikfestspiele*, Semperoper, Dresden. **Jun 26-Jul 18** *Princely Wedding Pageant*, Landshut. **Jun 12-27** *Theater Festival*, Munich. **Jul 3-19** *Kiliani-Volksfest*, Würzburg (funfair). **Jul 7** *Burning Rhine*, Rüdesheim. **Jul 31-Aug 27** *Richard-Wagner-Festspiele*, Bayreuth. **Aug 14** *Burning Rhine*, Koblenz. **Early Sep** *Wine and Sausage Market*, Bad Dürkheim. **Sep 18** *Rhine in Flames*, St Goarshausen. **Sep 25-Oct 10** *Cannstatter Volksfest*, Stuttgart (funfair). **Oct 16-31** *Freimarkt*, Bremen (funfair). **Early Nov-early Dec** *Winter Dom*, Hamburg (funfair). **Nov 26-Dec 24** *Christkindlmarkt*, Nürnberg. **Feb 14 '94** *Rose Monday Parades* in Cologne, Mainz and Düsseldorf.
The old Hanseatic town of Lübeck celebrates its 850th Anniversary in 1993 with numerous events throughout the year; Münster celebrates its 1200th Anniversary and Potsdam its 1000th Anniversary. The state of Lower Saxony recreates the Romanesque era in 1993 with the theme *Wege in the Romanik* (Introduction to the Romanesque era), starting in spring with the opening of the exhibition *Romanesque Era in Lower Saxony* in the Dankwarderode Fortress (Braunschweig).
A complete list is available from the Tourist Office.
SOCIAL CONVENTIONS: Handshaking is customary. Normal courtesies should be observed and it is common to be offered food and refreshment when visiting someone's home. When eating a meal it is considered impolite to leave your left hand on your lap when using your right hand for soup, etc. Your left hand should rest lightly on the table. Before eating it is normal to say *Guten Appetit* to the other people at the table to which the correct reply is *Ebenfalls*. It is customary to present the hostess with unwrapped flowers (according to tradition, one should always give an uneven number and it is worth noting that red roses are exclusively a lover's gift). Courtesy dictates that when entering a shop, restaurant or even a bus you should utter a greeting such as *Guten Tag* (or *Grüss Gott* in Bavaria) before saying what it is that you want; to leave without saying *Auf Wiedersehen* can also cause offence. Similarly, when making a telephone call, asking for the person you want to speak to without stating first who you are is considered rude.
Casual wear is widely acceptable, but more formal dress is required for some restaurants, the opera, theatre, casinos and important social functions. Evening wear is worn when requested. Smoking is prohibited where notified and on public transport and in some public buildings. Visitors should be prepared for an early start to the day with shops, businesses, schools, etc opening at 0800 or earlier. It is very common practice to take a mid-afternoon stroll on Sunday, so that town and city centres at this time are often very animated places, in stark comparison with Saturday afternoons when, due to early closing of the shops, town centres can seem almost deserted (see *Shopping* above). **Tipping:** Service charge on hotel bills. Restaurant bills in the west include 10% service charge. It is also customary to tip taxi drivers, hairdressers and cloakroom attendants.

BUSINESS PROFILE

ECONOMY: From the ruins of the Third Reich, both parts of divided post-war Germany emerged over the next two decades as the economic powerhouses of their respective European blocs. The unified German economy is now the third most productive in the world with a GDP of US$1.6 trillion (£850 billion). The bulk of this achievement was in the West (the pre-unification Federal Republic), where it is still referred to as the 'Wirtschaftwunder' (economic miracle). The Western economy is essentially industrial, with large chemical and car manufacturing plants, mechanical, electrical and electronic engineering, and rapidly growing advanced technology and service sectors in computing, biotechnology, information processing and media. The East's (former Democratic Republic's) economy never dominated COMECON – the Soviet bloc Council for Mutual Economic Assistance – in the way that the West did the EC: the CIS economy overshadowed all of its East European neighbours. However, the East did achieve the highest growth and per capita income within the bloc, and developed major trading links both within and outside COMECON. Lacking raw materials, the core of its trade exchanged manufactured goods for Polish coal and Soviet oil and gas but, by the time of reunification, 30% of East German trade was conducted outside the bloc. Its geographical position and special relationship with West Germany, coupled with a strong industrial base, drove this process. Although the East was undoubtedly economically successful by Eastern European standards, reunification illustrated starkly, almost brutally, how far Eastern Europe had fallen behind the West. Optimists, particularly among the old FRG's political leadership, declared brightly that West German industry would smoothly sweep up the more efficient and modern industries in the East while a large injection of corporate investment from the same quarter would account for any excess or redundant capacity in the GDR economy. Western business executives were far more sceptical. While they appreciated the new market opportunities, they concluded that demand in the East could be met by increasing their existing production levels and shipping the goods eastwards rather than 'greenfield' investment or purchasing ailing, incompatible and costly GDR industries. There have been some notable exceptions to this trend: Volkswagen took under their wing the manufacturers of the legendary Trabant motor car, but most of the inward investment has been in relatively underdeveloped service industries such as media, advertising and management services. Though welcome, this is inadequate. Eastern economic development cannot be based on services alone; some industrial base is necessary. The Bonn government also hoped that the instant conversion of the GDR's Ostmark into Deutschmarks at the artificial rate of one-to-one (as against a true market rate of between 5 and 10 Ostmarks to DM1) would stimulate the eastern economy by putting more money into eastern pockets. Unfortunately, the newly affluent eastern consumers showed more interest in buying imported goods than home-grown ones. Most economic analysts believe that the currency conversion and other decisions were serious misjudgements conceived during the heady rush towards unification. By 1991, it was clear that the Eastern economy, were it standing alone, would collapse. Output had fallen to 35% of pre-unification levels and unemployment and workers on 'zero short-time working' (effectively redundancy on full pay) accounted for half the workforce. The economy as a whole has weathered the global recession of the early 1990s fairly well. Growth has slowed but is still occurring. There is confidence that the underlying strength of the economy is such that the East will eventually be pulled up to approximate economic parity with the West, perhaps over the space of a decade. However, many policy planners are becoming seriously worried about the cost of this mammoth enterprise. Perhaps DM150 billion has been pumped into the east since 1989. Unfortunately very little has gone into tangible investment; the majority has been spent on unemployment benefit and social welfare. A 12-month 7.5% surcharge on income tax has lightened the load to some extent but the tax is politically unsustainable over any length of time. Severe spending cuts are being prepared for the budget later in 1992 and the *Bundesregierung* (Federal Government) has resisted pressure from other European governments to cut interest rates (so that they can reduce their own). German trade with Eastern Europe has grown relatively quickly compared to other routes; otherwise no change in German trade patterns should be expected. The main UK exports are office and data-processing equipment, electrical goods and machinery, and oil; vehicles and various types of machinery comprise the bulk of UK imports.
BUSINESS: Business people are expected to dress smartly. English is spoken by many local business people, but it is an advantage to have a working knowledge of German, or an interpreter. Appointments should be made well in advance, particularly in the summer. Appointments may be suggested slightly earlier in the day than is often the custom in Britain. Once made, appointment times should be strictly adhered to. Some firms may close early on Friday afternoons. Always use titles such as *Herr Doktor*, or *Frau Doktor* when addressing business contacts. Punctuality is essential for business visits. **Office hours:** 0800-1600 Monday to Friday.
COMMERCIAL INFORMATION: The following organisations can offer advice: Deutscher Industrie- und Handelstag (Association of German Chambers of Industry and Commerce), Adenauerallee 148, W-5300 Bonn 1. Tel: (228) 104-0. Fax: (228) 104-158. Telex: 886805; *or*
German Chamber of Industry and Commerce, 16 Buckingham Gate, London SW1E 6LB. Tel: (071) 233 5656. Fax: (071) 233 7835.
The first affiliates 69 Chambers of Industry and Commerce. There are also Chambers of Industry and Commerce in all major German towns and a regional Chamber of Commerce for each of the states. The above organisation also has branch offices in most major western European capitals.
BUSINESS IN THE FORMER GDR: 45 years of central planning have left the economy of what is now the eastern half of the Federal Republic of Germany in a weak state with numerous uneconomic companies, a lack of essential investment in up-to-date technology and distorted markets (see *Economy* section above). However, together with the EC Commission, the German government is attempting to encourage investment in the eastern half of the country in order to expedite the reconstruction (*Wiederaufbau*) of the economy there and to raise material conditions to the same high standards of western Germany. To this end the Government has set up investment incentives which, they stress, are available on equal terms to both German and foreign investors alike and the European Recovery Programme Fund (formerly the Marshall Fund) has been extended to cover what was previously the German Democratic Republic. Information about the various schemes is available from the Department of Trade and Industry in London *or* from the various banks administering the incentive programmes for the Federal Government. They are as follows:
European Recovery Programme (Berliner Industrie Bank), Landeckerstraße 2, W-1000 Berlin 33.
Tel: (30) 820 030. Fax: (30) 824 3003.
Bank for Reconstruction (Kreditanstalt für Wiederaufbau), Palmengartenstraße 5-9, W-6000 Frankfurt/M 1. European Recovery Programme credits for modernisation, effluent treatment and clean-air programmes plus its own investment credit scheme.

LUDWIG-MAXIMILIANS-UNIVERSITY MUNICH

Faculty of Medicine, Dean: Prof. Dr. Dr. h. c. Klaus Peter

KLINIKUM GROSSHADERN

Marchioninistr. 15
D-8000 München 70
Tel. 0 89 / 70 95 - 1
Fax 0 89 / 700 44 18

Department	Head
Anesthesiology	Prof. Dr. Dr. h. c. Klaus Peter
Cardiosurgery	Prof. Dr. Bruno Reichart
Gynecology and Obstetrics	Prof. Dr. Hermann Hepp
Internal Medicine	
Clinic I	Prof. Dr. Gerhard Riecker
Clinic II	Prof. Dr. Gustav Paumgartner
Clinic III	Prof. Dr. Wolfgang Wilmanns
Neurology	Prof. Dr. Thomas Brandt
Neurosurgery	Prof. Dr. Hans-Jürgen Reulen
Orthopaedic Surgery	Prof. Dr. H. J. Refior
Otorhinolaryngology	Prof. Dr. Ernst Kastenbauer
Physical Medicine and Rehabilitation	Prof. Dr. Edward Senn
Surgery	Prof. Dr. F. W. Schildberg
Urology	Prof. Dr. Alfons Hofstetter
Radiology and Radiotherapy	Prof. Dr. Dr. h. c. Josef Lissner
Clinical Chemistry	Prof. Dr. Dietrich Seidel

KLINIKUM INNENSTADT

Ziemssenstr. 1
D-8000 München 2
Tel. 0 89 / 51 60 - 1
Fax 0 89 / 51 60 - 51 99

Department	Head
Children's Hospital	Prof. Dr. H. B. Hadorn, Prof. Dr. Dietrich Reinhardt
Pediatric Surgery	Prof. Dr. Ingolf Joppich
Dentistry/Oral Surgery	Prof. Dr. Dr. D. Schlegel, Prof. Dr. Reinhard Hickel Prof. Dr. W. Gernet, Prof. Dr. Ingrid Rudzki-Janson
Dermatology	Prof. Dr. Gerd Plewig
Gynecology and Obstetrics	Prof. Dr. Günther Kindermann
Internal Medicine	Prof. Dr. Peter C. Scriba, Prof. Dr. Detlef Schlöndorff
Infection & Tropical Disease	Prof. Dr. Thomas Löscher
Occupational Medicine	Prof. Dr. Günter Fruhmann
Ophthalmology	Prof. Dr. Otto-Erich Lund
Psychiatry	Prof. Dr. Hanns Hippius
Surgery	Prof. Dr. Leonhard Schweiberer
Forensic Medicine	Prof. Dr. Wolfgang Eisenmenger
Immunology	Prof. Dr. Gert Riethmüller
Microbiology	Prof. Dr. G. Ruckdeschel (komm.)

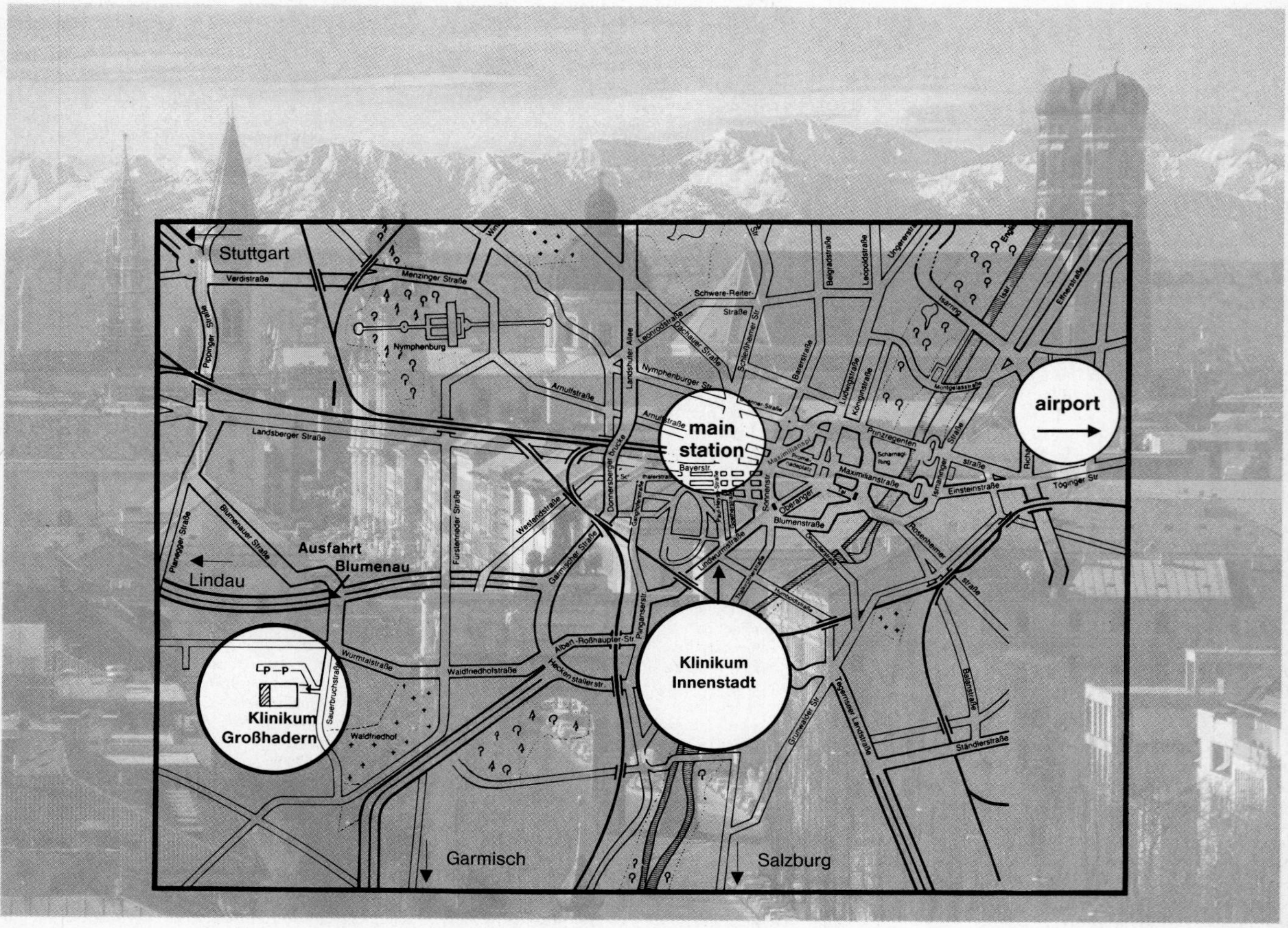

Tel: (69) 7431-0. Fax: (69) 7431-2944.
German Equalisation Bank (Deutsche Ausgleichsbank), Wielandstraße 4, W-5300 Bonn 2. European Recovery Programme credits for start-ups, waste management and energy-saving programmes plus its own investment credit scheme.
National Consulates in the Federal Republic of Germany can also advise potential investors (addresses at the beginning of the entry).

CONFERENCES/CONVENTIONS: The western part of Germany can offer a highly developed and well-equipped network of conference destinations. For information contact the German Convention Bureau, Lyoner Strasse 20, W-6000 Frankfurt/M 71. Tel: (69) 666 7083/4. Fax: (69) 666 6085.
Founded in 1973 the Bureau is a nonprofit-making organisation sponsored by Germany's major convention cities, hotels, travel agents and carriers, as well as the country's leading travel and tourist associations, including the German National Tourist Board, Lufthansa and the German Federal Railways.
Note: Outside Berlin and Leipzig, a city which has for years played host to an important annual trade fair, there are at present only limited facilities for meetings in eastern Germany. It is likely to be some considerable time until facilities in the east match those of western Germany. Contact the German Convention Bureau or the Tourist Office for more information.

HISTORY & GOVERNMENT

HISTORY: The rich and complex history of what is now Germany is inseparable from that of central and western Europe from the 5th century onwards. It is often said that the Germanic tribes destroyed the Roman empire, but the Visigoths, Ostrogoths and Franks who settled in western Europe after the deposition of the Emperor Romulus in AD476 were anxious to perpetuate, at least in some of its aspects, a system which they both admired and found administratively convenient. Indeed, it was a Frank, Charlemagne, who revived the Roman Empire in the West in AD800, thus being the first to unite what is now Germany together with the area of France and northern Italy, albeit only for the 40 years of his own reign and that of his son, Louis the Pious. The division of Charlemagne's empire was confirmed by the Treaty of Verdun (AD843), as a result of which much of what is now Germany passed to Louis' son, Louis the German. During the next 80 years, Germany fragmented into five large duchies (Saxony, Bavaria, Franconia, Lorranie and Swabia), whose dukes managed to establish a *de facto* hereditary tenure. The 10th century witnessed a growth in the power of central authority under the leadership of the House of Saxony, while in the 11th century and early 12th century, under the Salian dynasty, the power of the crown was in many ways at its height. In 1152, following a disputed succession and a civil war, the dynamic Frederick Barbarossa acceded to the throne: he is one of the most significant figures in German history. Frederick, his son Henry VI and his grandson Frederick II made prodigious attempts to revive the reality of royal power in Germany and Italy, but the task proved impossible and by the late 13th century the country was seething with civil war. This period saw the emergence for the first time of the House of Habsburg. Temporarily deposed by other dynasties during the next 150 years, Albert V of Habsburg re-established his clan's ascendancy in 1438. The Habsburgs were to rule the Empire, with only a brief interruption, until 1806. By this time Germany had dissolved into a patchwork of over 300 states, some no more than a town or castle, and increasingly the Habsburg Emperors derived their power and influence from their extensive family lands. In 1519, Charles V became Emperor, uniting by his dynastic connections Spain, the Low Countries, Naples, Sicily, Burgundy, the Holy Roman Empire and all the Spanish possessions in the New World. Germany, in common with much of the rest of Europe, was riven by the Reformation at this time, despite Charles V's attempts to impose a religious solution by force. The impossibility of holding together such a large empire was recognised by Charles himself, and on his abdication in 1556 the imperial office and the Habsburg lands passed to his brother Ferdinand I. Sporadic warfare against the Turks continued, but a more serious catastrophe was the complex, interlocking series of struggles known to history as the Thirty Years War (1618-1648), during which many of Europe's disputes were fought out on German soil. One of the results of the Peace of Westphalia in 1648 was the emergence of the previously minor state of Brandenburg-Prussia as a major power; the territorial gains were built upon by a series of cunning and ruthless rulers and, by the early 18th century, the new kingdom was the scourge of other European states, the Habsburg Empire not least. Frederick the Great is the king most strongly associated with the growth of Prussian militarism. By the time the moribund Holy Roman Empire – not inaccurately described by a contemporary as being 'neither holy, nor Roman, nor an empire' – was formally abolished by Napoleon in 1806 (by which time the Habsburgs had already assumed the title of Emperor of Austria), much of its northern and eastern parts had already been absorbed by Prussia. After 1815 the German Confederation was established with 39 states. German unification continued apace throughout the century, the most significant figure being Count (later Prince) von Bismarck, Chancellor under Emperor Wilhelm I. Various wars, both offensive and defensive, were fought with other European states, the most notable being the Franco-Prussian War (1870-71), and an increasingly complex web of treaties and diplomacy (including the Dual and Triple Alliances of 1878 and 1892) grew up, which for a time contained the equally increasingly ambitious policies of the major European states and their empires. It was a revolt in Serbia which finally shattered the illusion of European security, precipitating a complex chain of events which led to the First World War. After 1918 a democratic constitution was adopted, but political instability and severe economic problems assisted the rise of the National Socialists under Adolf Hitler during the 1930s. Hitler sought to reverse the perceived humiliation imposed by the 1919 Versailles Treaty (the political settlement at the end of the First World War) by initiating a major rearmament programme which no other European power seemed inclined to challenge. Hitler then set about creating the Third Reich, first by merger (Anschluss) with Austria, then annexation of the Czech Sudetenland, followed by the then Czechoslovakia itself. When Hitler threatened Poland, Britain and France then drew the line: from there, it was a short route to the Second World War. After six years of global warfare, at an estimated cost of 60 million lives, the German army was defeated in 1945 by the Allied armies of the United States, the USSR, Britain and others. This produced the post-war division of Europe into Western and Soviet spheres of influence. Germany was divided into two parts: the eastern, Soviet-controlled portion became the German Democratic Republic; the western part emerged to become the Federal Republic of Germany. The city of Berlin, which lay within the GDR, was itself divided into Allied and Soviet-controlled zones. East Berlin became the capital of the GDR while the isolated West Berlin was attached to the Federal Republic. The Federal Republic was established in September 1949, under the supervision of the three Western allied powers – the United States, Britain and France. Federal politics adopted the familiar pattern of Social Democratic (SPD) and centre-right Christian Democrat (CDU), parties typical of most of Western Europe. The dominant political figure of the era was Konrad Adenauer, Chancellor between 1949 and 1963. Adenauer and his economics minister Ludwig Erhard were the principal architects of the country's phenomenal economic growth after 1945. A major foundation of this was the European Coal and Steel Community, under which the Federal Republic and France, together with several smaller neighbours, established a free trade area in these products. This was the basis of the European Economic Community, which was formally established by the 1957 Rome Treaty. The Christian Democrats remained in power until 1972, at which point the SPD took control of the Bundestag under the leadership of Willi Brandt. Brandt resigned in 1974 and was replaced by Helmut Schmidt. Brandt initiated the *Ostpolitik* under which peaceful co-operation became the centrepiece of relations with the DDR; it was conceived as an alternative to the sterility of the Cold War. The Soviets had sponsored the creation of the GDR in October 1949 and granted formal independence to the country five years later. During the 1950s, the GDR embarked on a full-scale programme of socialist development complete with wholesale agricultural reform and breakneck industrial construction. Popular discontent with some of the policies culminated in a series of uprisings throughout the decade – notably in 1953 – which were put down forcefully. Political power in the GDR was vested in the sole hands of the Sozialistische Einheitspartei Deutschlands (SED – Socialist Unity Party), an amalgam of leftist and pre-war anti-fascist parties dominated by the Communist Party. Walter Ulbricht was succeeded as Party First Secretary in 1971 by Erich Honecker, who remained in the post almost until the end of the GDR. As with the Federal Republic, relations with the 'other' Germany dominated the political agenda in the GDR. *Ostpolitik* was continued by Brandt's successor, Helmut Schmidt, and by the government which took office after the SPD lost its overall majority at the 1980 election. This was a coalition of the SPD and the small centrist Free Democrats, then led by Hans-Dietrich Genscher, who became the Federal Republic's Foreign Minister for the next 12 years. The coalition collapsed in 1982 after which the Free Democrats promptly switched sides and teamed up with the right-wing Christian Democrats (CDU) under Helmut Kohl. Two general elections later, in 1992, Kohl is still Chancellor, but now of a unified Germany. The dramatic process of unification began with the accession of Gorbachev in Moscow and accelerated after mid-1989. During September 1989, 50,000 East Germans had left for the West, the majority via Hungary which, to Honecker's intense annoyance, had all but abandoned travel restrictions to the West. Honecker was then removed from office, just days after Gorbachev had visited the country. Honecker's immediate replacement, Egon Krenz, struggled in vain to find a political solution. Amid massive daily demonstrations in the GDR's major cities, the Politburo, the Berlin Wall and the SED leadership fell in turn between the beginning of November 1989 and the end of the year. The GDR acquired its only non-Communist President, the liberal democrat Manfred Gerlach. The first free election for a national GDR leadership was held in March 1990, and victory went to the centre-right Alliance for Germany coalition led by Lothar de Mazière and firmly backed by Chancellor Kohl and the CDU. The Party for Democratic Socialism – the SED as was – took a respectable third place, behind the Social Democrats. The major issue at the polls was not unification itself – which was seen as more or less inevitable – but the timing of it. Kohl and the CDU read the electorate's mind better in promoting union as quickly as possible, contrasting with the comparatively gradual, cautious approach of the other parties. The decision on unification was not, of course, exclusively one for the Germans: the agreement of the wartime allies was required. The West presented no problems. Washington was enthusiastic, while Paris and London were lukewarm but in no way obstructive. Real difficulty was expected, however, from the Soviet Union, whose nuclear delivery systems and 300,000 plus troops in the GDR were a cornerstone of Soviet defence strategy. Moreover, how would Germany fit into the existing European security structure? The Western powers were adamant that a unified Germany should belong to NATO; the Soviets firmly insisted on its neutrality. In the event, a settlement was reached more easily than anyone dared hope. The terms were: all Soviet forces to withdraw; Germany to belong to NATO, and NATO forces currently stationed in the Federal Republic could stay (other than those whose removal was agreed during the on-going negotiations on European conventional forces). 1994 is the date set for completion of the Soviet (now CIS) withdrawal. The cash offer of several billion Marks to offset relocation costs of Soviet troops rendered the agreement somewhat more palatable to the Soviets although, in truth, they had little alternative, holding precious few cards with which to negotiate. Besides which, the Warsaw Pact was on the point of disintegrating. NATO will not find its new acquisition an easy proposition, however. With the Russians gone, opinion throughout the NATO countries is increasingly sceptical of the need to maintain costly garrisons in Germany; hawkish assertions of the vital contribution to European security sound increasingly hollow. The new Germany, with nearly 80 million people and twice the GNP of the EC's next largest member, will ultimately dominate the Community. And one of the persisting anomalies of modern Germany may be resolved: that its economic power has not nearly been matched by its international political influence. The political complexion of united Germany's government was decided at national elections on December 3, 1990: as expected, Chancellor Kohl won a comfortable majority in the Bundestag. The major problem facing Kohl's third administration has been the state of the eastern economy, which turned out to be in much worse condition than even the most pessimistic analyses had surmised (see *Economy*). Optimists both within and outside the country were hoping that this would be no more than an unpleasant interlude in the continuing German miracle play. The sceptics have proved to have been more prescient: unemployment has rocketed in the east, as many enterprises fold in the face of competition from the west. Chancellor Kohl's apparently impregnable position has suffered accordingly as the SPD has scored a number of notable local electoral victories. There has been some friction within Kohl's Christian Democrats, particularly between eastern and western representatives. This came to a head in the summer of 1992 with a cross-party proposal to form an 'East German Movement' which has attracted support from ex-East Premier de Mazière, his CDU colleague and former Eastern Interior Minister Peter-Michael Diestel and Gregor Gysi of the PDS (ex-communists). They aim to reverse the widespread perception that the East has been 'degraded and excluded' from the Western-dominated political system. If the situation within the CDU deteriorates much further, Chancellor Kohl may find his own position seriously undermined. He has also lost a stalwart minister in Hans-Dietrich Genscher who resigned in 1992. His replacement, Klaus Kinkel, although not the first choice, is thought to be a good selection.

GOVERNMENT: The present constitution dates from May 1949, the Federal Republic of Germany being formally established four months later. The country is a parliamentary democracy with a bicameral legislature (Bundesrat and Bundestag, with 68 and 663 members respectively). Executive authority lies with the Federal government, led by the Federal Chancellor. The Federal President is the constitutional Head of State. Each of the states has its own legislature with power to pass laws on all matters not expressly reserved for the competence of the Federal Government. The former German Democratic Republic has been absorbed into this system, adding five Länder to the total.

CLIMATE

Temperate throughout the country with warm summers and cold winters, but prolonged periods of frost or snow are rare. Rain falls throughout the year.
Required clothing: European clothes with light- to medium-weights in summer, medium- to heavy-weights in winter. Waterproofing is needed throughout the year.

BERLIN Fed. Rep. of Germany (51m)

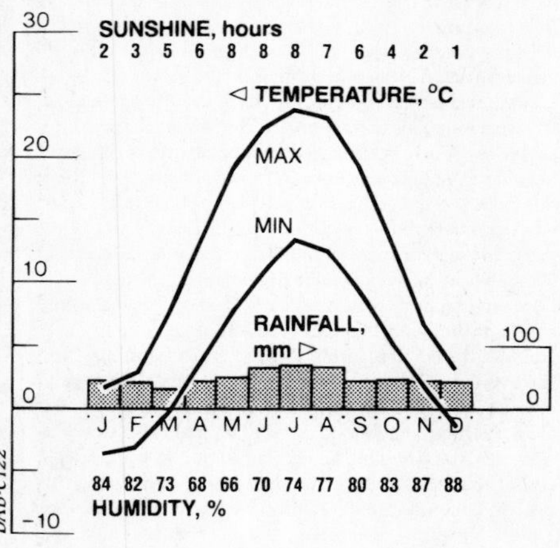

FRANKFURT Fed. Rep. of Germany (103m)

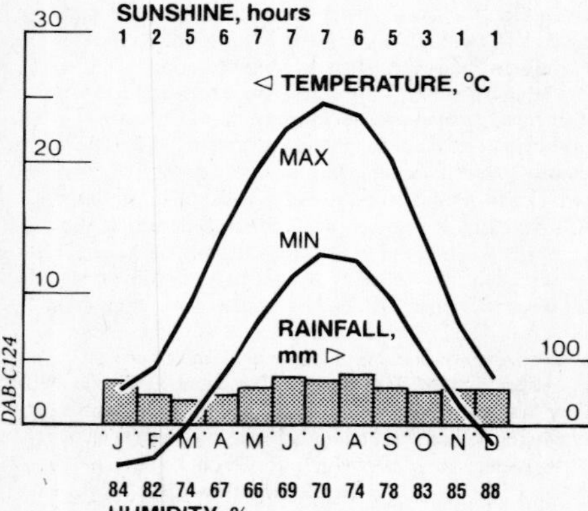

MUNICH Fed. Rep. of Germany (527m)

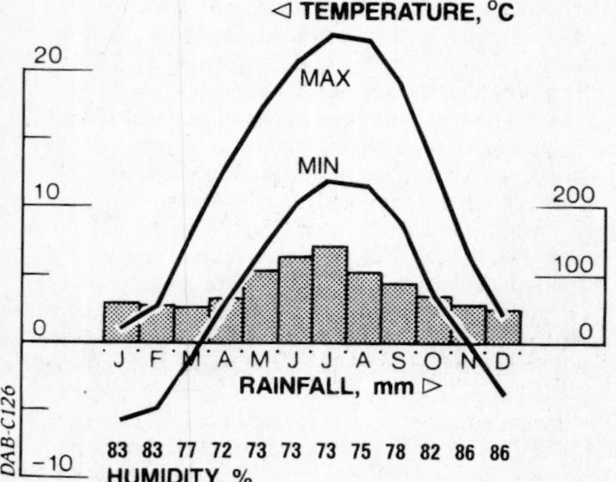

GHANA

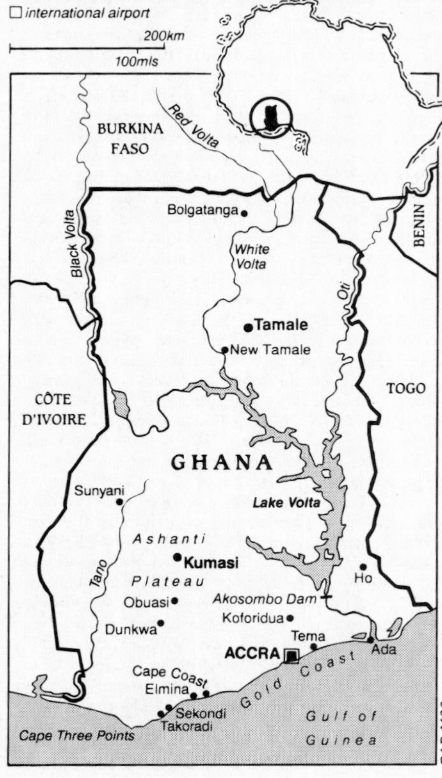

Location: West Africa.

Ghana Tourist Board
Ministry of Trade and Tourism
First Floor, PO Box 3106
Accra, Ghana
Tel: (21) 665 441. Telex: 2714.

Ghana High Commission (Education and Visas)
104 Highgate Hill
London N6 5HE
Tel: (081) 342 8686. Fax: (081) 342 8566/70. Telex: 21370 TIMBO D.

Ghana High Commission (Tourist Information)
102 Park Street
London W1Y 3RJ
Tel: (071) 493 4901. Fax: (071) 493 9923. Telex: 23934.

British High Commission
PO Box 296
Osu Link, off Gamel Abdul Nasser Avenue
Accra, Ghana
Tel: (21) 221 665 *or* 221 715 *or* 221 738 *or* 221 745. Fax: (21) 224 572. Telex: 2323 UKREP GH.

Embassy of the Republic of Ghana
3512 International Drive, NW
Washington, DC 20008
Tel: (202) 686 4520. Fax: (202) 686 4527.

Ghana Permanent Mission to the United Nations
(for visas and tourist information)
19 East 47th Street
New York, NY 10017
Tel: (212) 832 1300.

Embassy of the United States of America
PO Box 194
Ring Road East
Accra, Ghana
Tel: (21) 775 348/9 *or* 775 297/8. Fax: (21) 776 008. Telex: 2579 EMBUSA GH.

Embassy of the Republic of Ghana
1 Clemow Avenue
Ottawa, Ontario
K1S 2A9
Tel: (613) 236 0871/2/3. Fax: (613) 236 0874.

Canadian Embassy
PO Box 1639
42 Independence Avenue
Accra, Ghana
Tel: (21) 773 791. Fax: (21) 773 792. Telex: 2024.

AREA: 238,537 sq km (92,100 sq miles).
POPULATION: 15,028 (1990 estimate).
POPULATION DENSITY: 63 per sq km.
CAPITAL: Accra. **Population:** 867,459 (1984).
GEOGRAPHY: Ghana is situated in Africa and is a rectangular- shaped country bounded to the north by Burkina Faso, the east by Togo, the south by the Atlantic Ocean and the west by the Côte d'Ivoire. A narrow grassy plain stretches inland from the coast, widening in the east, while the south and west are covered by dense rainforest. To the north are forested hills beyond which is dry savannah and open woodland. In the far north is a plateau averaging 500m (1600ft) in height. In the east the Akuapim Togo hills run inland from the coast along the Togo border. The Black and White Volta rivers enter Ghana from Burkina Faso merging into the largest man-made lake in the world, Lake Volta. Ghana's coastline is dotted with sandy palm-fringed beaches and lagoons.
LANGUAGE: The official language is English. Local African languages are widely spoken, including Twi, Fante, Ga and Ewe.
RELIGION: Christian, Muslim and traditional beliefs. All forms of religion have a strong influence on Ghanaian life.
TIME: GMT.
ELECTRICITY: 220 volts AC, 50Hz; usually 3-pin plugs. Single phase, 3-phase plugs are used in larger buildings. Light bulbs are of the bayonet type.
COMMUNICATIONS: Telephone: IDD service to major cities. Country code: 233. Calls made from Ghana to Europe may be subject to delays of up to 48 hours. The internal telephone system is generally limited to Accra; there are few services outside the capital. Those that do exist are extremely unreliable; a rehabilitation and modernisation scheme is underway. **Fax:** There is a 24-hour fax service in Accra. **Telex/telegram:** Service from Post & Telecommunications Corporation, High Street, Accra and Stewart Avenue, Kumasi. There are three charge rates. **Post:** Airmail letters to Europe may take two weeks or more to arrive. **Press:** Daily newspapers are in English and include *The Ghanaian Times*, *The People's Daily Graphic* and *The Pioneer*.
BBC World Service and Voice of America frequencies: From time to time these change. See the section *How to Use this Book* for more information.

BBC:

MHz	17.79	15.40	12.09	9.600

Voice of America:

MHz	21.49	15.60	9.525	6.035

PASSPORT/VISA

Regulations and requirements may be subject to change at short notice, and you are advised to contact the appropriate diplomatic or consular authority before finalising travel arrangements. Details of these may be found at the head of this country's entry. Any numbers in the chart refer to the footnotes below.

	Passport Required?	Visa Required?	Return Ticket Required?
Full British	Yes	Yes	Yes
BVP	Not valid	-	-
Australian	Yes	Yes	Yes
Canadian	Yes	Yes	Yes
USA	Yes	Yes	Yes
Other EC	Yes	Yes	Yes
Japanese	Yes	Yes	Yes

PASSPORTS: Valid passport required by all except nationals of Benin, Burkina Faso, Cape Verde Islands, Côte d'Ivoire, Gambia, Guinea Republic, Guinea-Bissau, Liberia, Mali, Mauritania, Niger, Nigeria, Senegal, Sierra Leone and Togo.
British Visitors Passport: Not acceptable.
VISAS: Required by all except nationals of Benin, Burkina Faso, Cape Verde Islands, Côte d'Ivoire, Gambia, Guinea Republic, Guinea-Bissau, Mali, Mauritania, Niger, Nigeria, Senegal, Sierra Leone and Togo.
An *Entry Visa* is required for all non-Commonwealth nationals not mentioned above. An *Entry Permit* is required for all Commonwealth nationals.
Cost: All visas (including Transit visas) and permits cost £30; Multiple visas cost £60.
Validity: Valid for 3 months from the date of issue. However, length of stay is at the discretion of airport officials and only one month is guaranteed. Visas may be extended when in Ghana.
Application to: Consulate (or Consular Section at Embassy or High Commission). For address, see top of entry.
Application requirements: *British and Commonwealth nationals:* (a) Valid passport. (b) 4 Entry Permit application forms to be completed. (c) Evidence of return ticket and/or a letter of guarantee from a company in

support of the application (the letter should explain the nature of business the applicant will be conducting in Ghana). (d) 4 passport photos. *Non-Commonwealth nationals:* (a) Valid passport. (b) 4 application forms. (c) 4 passport photos.
Working days required: 2.
Note: Business travellers involved in diamond or scrap metal industries must have their applications referred to Accra and should allow a month for processing.
Temporary residence: Application with sufficient notice to be made to High Commission or Embassy.

MONEY

Currency: Cedi (C) = 100 pesewas. Notes are in denominations of C500, 200, 100, 50, 10, 5, 2 and 1. Coins are in denominations of C5 and 1; and 50, 20, 10, 5, 2.5, 1 and 0.5 pesewas.
Currency exchange: The Ghanaian Cedi is pegged to the US Dollar but, as indicated in the exchange rate indicators below, it has been subject to frequent devaluations. Foreign currency must be exchanged with authorised dealers only (any bank in Ghana and certain hotels).
Credit cards: Limited use of Diners Club, Visa and Access/Mastercard. Check with your credit card company for details of merchant acceptability and other services which may be available.
Exchange rate indicators: The following figures are included as a guide to the movements of the Cedi against Sterling and the US Dollar:

Date:	Oct '89	Oct '90	Oct '91	Oct '92
£1.00=	454.78	662.41	651.37	773.08
$1.00=	288.01	339.09	375.32	487.14

Currency restrictions: Free import of foreign currency, subject to declaration (on exchange control form T5 which must be retained to record transactions). Export of foreign currency is limited to the amount declared on import. The import and export of local currency is limited to C3000 and should be recorded in passport. Unused local currency can be re-exchanged on proof of authorised exchange, and visitors are advised to retain all currency exchange receipts.
Banking hours: 0830-1400 Monday to Thursday and 0830-1500 Friday. A few city branches are open from 0830-1200 on Saturdays.

DUTY FREE

The following goods may be imported into Ghana by persons aged 16 and over without incurring customs duty:
400 cigarettes or 100 cigars or 1lb of tobacco;
1 litre of spirits and 1 litre of wine;
200g of perfume;
Toiletries and small food items.
Prohibited items: Animals; firearms; ammunition; explosives; machines for duplicating keys; condensed, evaporated or dried milk and mercury.

PUBLIC HOLIDAYS

Public holidays observed in Ghana are as follows:
Mar 6 '93 Independence Day. **Apr 9-12** Easter. **May 1** Labour Day. **Jun 5** Anniversary of the 1979 coup. **Jul 1** Republic Day. **Dec 25-26** Christmas. **Dec 31** Revolution Day. **Jan 1 '94** New Year's Day. **Mar 6** Independence Day.

HEALTH

Regulations and requirements may be subject to change at short notice, and you are advised to contact your doctor well in advance of your intended date of departure. Any numbers in the chart refer to the footnotes below.

	Special Precautions?	Certificate Required?
Yellow Fever	Yes	1
Cholera	Yes	2
Typhoid & Polio	Yes	-
Malaria	3	-
Food & Drink	4	-

[1]: A yellow fever vaccination certificate is required by all.
[2]: A cholera vaccination certificate is required if com-

GHANA	HEALTH REGULATIONS	VISA REGULATIONS
GALILEO/WORLDSPAN	 TI-DFT/ACC/HE	 TI-DFT/ACC/VI
SABRE	  TIDFT/ACC/HE	 TIDFT/ACC/VI

Code-Link

To access this information on your CRS, swipe the barcode with a light pen or type in the text under the barcode. For more information, see the introduction *How to Use This Book.*

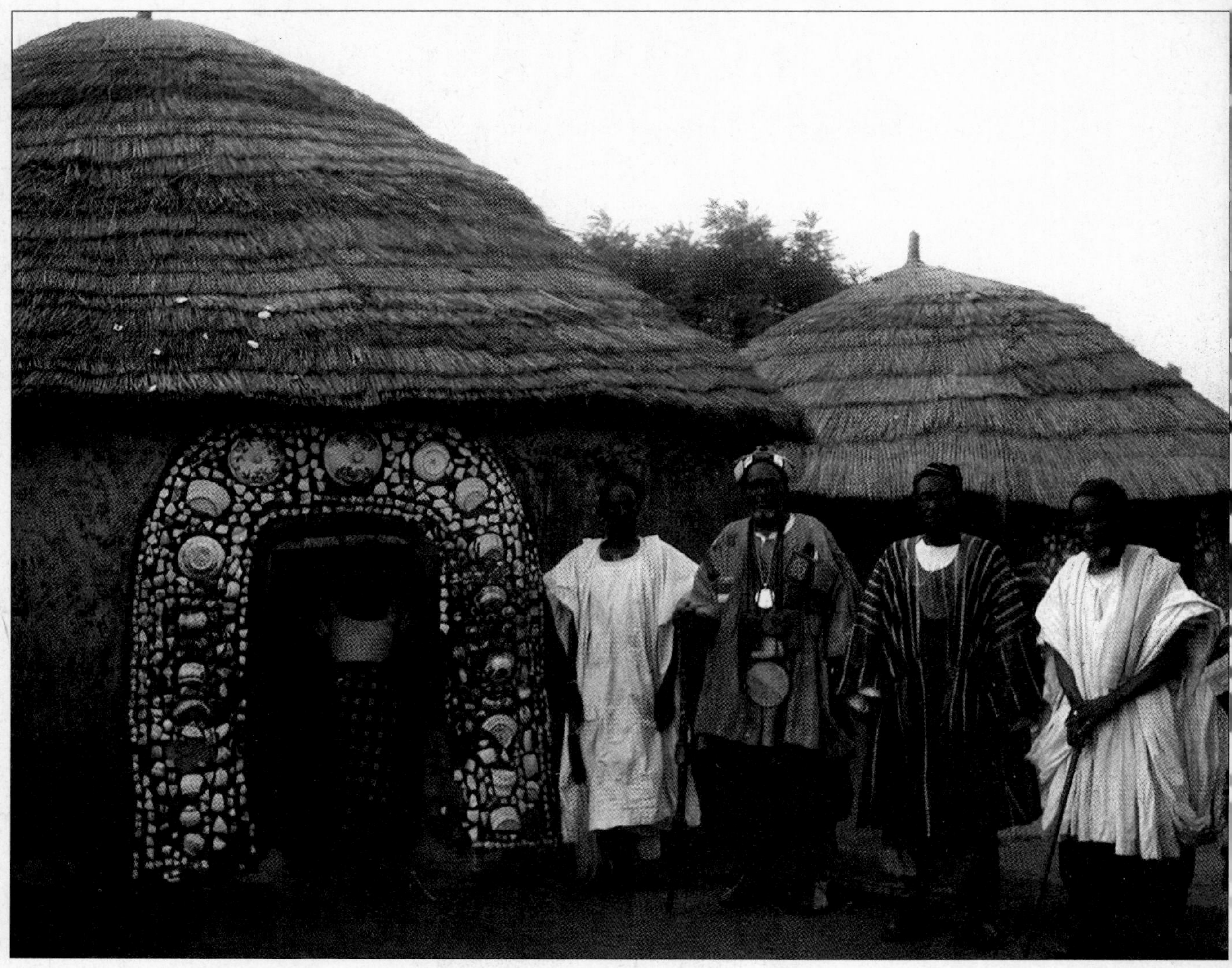

ing from an infected or endemic area, and vaccination is strongly recommended. Cholera is a serious risk in this country and precautions are essential. See the *Health* section at the back of the book.

[3]: Malaria risk, predominantly in the malignant *falciparum* form, exists all year throughout the country. Vaccination is recommended.

[4]: All water should be regarded as being potentially contaminated. Water used for drinking, brushing teeth or making ice should have first been boiled or otherwise sterilised. Milk is unpasteurised and should be boiled. Powdered or tinned milk is available and is advised, but make sure that it is reconstituted with pure water. Avoid dairy products which are likely to have been made from local milk. Only eat well-cooked meat and fish, preferably served hot. Pork, salad and mayonnaise may carry increased risk. Vegetables should be cooked and fruit peeled.

Bilharzia (schistosomiasis) is present. Avoid swimming and paddling in fresh water. Swimming pools which are well-chlorinated and maintained are safe.

Rabies is present. For those at high risk, vaccination before arrival should be considered. If you are bitten abroad seek medical advice without delay. For more information consult the *Health* section at the back of the book.

Health care: Health insurance is advised. Medical facilities exist in all the regional capitals as well as in most towns and villages.

TRAVEL - International

AIR: Ghana's national airline is *Ghana Airways (GH)*. It provides flights from Accra to London three times a week, to Dusseldorf twice a week and to Rome once a week. Other airlines flying to Accra include *Aeroflot, Air Afrique, Balkan, British Airways, Egypt Air, Ethiopian Airlines, KLM, Nigeria* and *Swissair*.

Approximate flight time: From *London* to Accra is 6 hours 30 minutes.

International airport: *Accra 'Kotoka' (ACC)*, 10km (6 miles) north of Accra (travel time – 20 minutes). Coaches depart to the city every hour from 0600-2400. Return is from Holy Trinity Cathedral and various hotels. Taxis to the city are also available. Work has started on upgrading the airport.

Departure tax: US$10.

SEA: Ghana has two deep-water ports, one at Takoradi, the other at Tema.

ROAD: A coast road links Lagos, Cotonou and Lomé to Accra. The best internal road from Abidjan (Côte d'Ivoire) runs inland through Kumasi. The road from Burkina Faso crosses the border at Navrongo. Long-distance taxis operate between Ghana and neighbouring countries. See below for information on documentation.

TRAVEL - Internal

AIR: There are domestic airports in Kumasi, Tamale and Sunyani.

RAIL: The rail network is limited to a 1000km (600-mile) loop by the coast connecting the cities Accra, Takoradi and Kumasi and several intervening towns. Trains run at least twice a day on all three legs of this triangle. There are two classes of ticket. Passenger cars are not air-conditioned.

ROAD: There are almost 32,000km (21,000 miles) of roads in Ghana of which 6000km (3700 miles) are paved. **Car hire:** Available from *Hertz/Avis* and local agencies but extremely expensive, whether with or without driver. **Coaches:** State-run coach services connect all major towns. **Documentation:** An International Driving Permit is recommended, although it is not legally required. A British driving licence is valid for 90 days.

URBAN: Two major road improvement projects are underway in Accra and Kumasi as an attempt to improve traffic flow in these cities. Accra has extensive bus services operated by the City Transport Authority, although more than half of the journeys are operated by private services which run small buses *(Moto-way)*, minibuses *(Tro-Tro)* – of which there are 120,000 – and wooden-body trucks *(Mammy Wagons)*. There are over 300,000 conventional taxis. Drivers do not generally expect tips.

ACCOMMODATION

HOTELS: Many hotels are run by the State Hotels Corporation and they are generally of a run-down standard. There are hotels, both private and state-owned, in all the regional capitals – Kumasi, Takoradi, Cape Coast, Sunyani, Koforidua, Bolgatanga, Tamale, Ho and Akosombo. It is advisable to book in advance. The hotels are supplemented by 'Catering Rest Houses' which are administrated by the Government. These generally provide basic accommodation and a restaurant and are of variable standard. There are also motels at Mole National Park on the western coast at Cape Coast and Elmina, and around the big cities. All the above are listed in the official guidebook available from the Ghana Tourist Board in Accra (address above). **Grading:** International hotels in Accra, Kumasi, and Takoradi offer the equivalent of 4-star facilities although there is no formal grading system in Ghana.

REST HOUSES: In more remote regions a combination of privately owned and state-sponsored 'Rest Houses' offer accommodation. These establishments are frequently self-catering and may provide little more than a bed, a few cooking utensils and a charcoal burner, and may well have no washing or toilet facilities.

HOST-BASED VISITS: In the past it has been possible to obtain accommodation in outlying villages by negotiating with the Headman. A new venture, *Insight Travel*, offers visitors the opportunity of staying with Ghanaians and sharing village activities such as working on the family farm, learning local music or dance, and participating in community events. Excursions can also be arranged. All hosts (who come from a variety of backgrounds including business, teaching and government service) have homes in or around Kumasi in the Ashanti region of Ghana. Holidays are organised in conjunction with *Adehye Tours* in Ghana. In the UK contact the Africa Travel Centre, 4 Medway Court, Leigh Street, London WC1H 9QX. Tel: (071) 387 1211; *or* Insight Travel, 6 Norton Road, Garstang, Preston, Lancashire PR3 1JY. Tel: (0995) 606095. Fax: (0995) 602124. Costs of holidays are usually around £500 per person, plus flight.

CAMPING: Camping in national parks is encouraged, but

only for the very adventurous, as it can be dangerous. In game reserves visitors must be accompanied by an armed guide.

RESORTS & EXCURSIONS

For the purposes of this guide, the country has been divided into three regions: Greater Accra, Kumasi Ashanti and the West Coast. This does not necessarily reflect administrative or tribal boundaries.

Greater Accra Region

Accra: The *National Museum* has a large collection of Ghanaian art as well as a poignant reminder of the country's turbulent recent history; a statue of the man who brought Ghana to independence in 1957, Kwame Nkrumah, has its arms cut off.
Aburi: 38km (24 miles) to the north of Accra in the *Akwapim Hills. The Sanatorium* (now a rest house) built there in the 19th century is indicative of the refreshing climate. The *Botanical Gardens*, planted by British naturalists in colonial days, has a comprehensive array of subtropical plants and trees.
Shai Hills Game Reserve: A comparatively small reserve some 50km (30 miles) by road from Accra. Horses may be hired here to explore the park.
Ada: A popular resort at the mouth of the *Volta* where many Ghanaians have holiday bungalows; a vacation village is under construction. Swimming is safe in the river mouth. Anglers have the opportunity to catch barracuda and Nile perch. Nearby are the salt marshes of the *Songow Lagoon*, famous for their birdlife.

Kumasi Ashanti Region

Kumasi is the historic capital of the Ashanti civilisation, where ruins of the *Maryha Palace* and the *Royal Mausoleum* burnt down by Lord Baden-Powell may be examined. The *Cultural Centre* is a complex comprising a museum, library and outdoor auditorium largely devoted to the Ashanti. There is also a *'Living Museum'*, a farm and reconstituted village, where craftsmen such as potters, goldsmiths and sculptors can be seen at work using traditional methods. Of particular interest are weavers making the vividly coloured Kente cloth, the ceremonial dress of the region.
Owabi Wildlife Sanctuary: To the west, close to Kumasi. Further to the northeast is the *Boufom Wildlife Sanctuary* containing the spectacular *Banfabiri Falls*. To the south is the pleasant gold mining city of **Obuasi**.
Akosombo: Originally built to house construction workers when the Volta River was dammed to form the largest man-made sheet of water on earth, Akosombo is now developing as a holiday centre, particularly for watersports. The waterway stretches for two thirds of the length of the country. A round trip on the car ferry to **Kete-Kachi** takes a day; alternatively one can take the 3 day trip to the northern capital of **New Tamale** at the head of the lake. There are facilities for sailing, water-skiing and other watersports.
Mole National Park: The best equipped of the reservations in Ghana. The visitor can go either on foot or hire a Land Rover but must always be accompanied by a guide. Routes are planned to take in species of antelope, monkeys, buffalo, warthog, and, more rarely, lions and elephants, which have been introduced into the region. Unlike many African game reserves the visitor is allowed to camp, and explore the area at will, rather than being confined to a car on a set route. Modern tourist facilities exist at the entrance to the Park; these include a motel with restaurant, swimming pool, night club and banking facilities.

West Coast

At **Dixcove** there is an enjoyable fish market and a 17th-century British fort. Nearby **Busua** is a tropical beach with palms and with spectacular Atlantic breakers; however, as with much of the Ghanaian coast, swimming is unsafe due to the treacherous undertow of the waves. In this area there are to be found small rocky inlets which are safe for swimming. **Elmina** ('the mine'): The first Portuguese settlement in Ghana; contains an intact 15th-century fort. This resort is popular with Ghanaians.
Cape Coast and Takoradi: Both bear evidence of colonial times; Cape Coast was the first British settlement and is dominated by the ruined castle, once used to house slaves before shipping them to the Americas.

SOCIAL PROFILE

FOOD & DRINK: International food is available in most large hotels and many restaurants serve a range of local traditional foods. On the coast prawns and other seafood are popular. Dishes include traditional soups (palmnut, groundnut), *Kontomere* and *Okro* (stews) accompanied by *fufu* (pounded Cassava), *kenkey* or *gari*. In Accra there are also restaurants serving Middle Eastern, Chinese, French and other European cuisine. **Drink:** Local beer, which is similar to lager, is readily available. Spirits are available in special stores which stock luxury items and only accept foreign currency. These are run by the Government.
NIGHTLIFE: In Accra and other major centres there are nightclubs with western popular music and Afro beat.
SHOPPING: The availability of all commodities is sporadic. Artefacts from the Ashanti region and northern Ghana can be bought along with attractive handmade gold and silver jewellery. Modern and old African art are also available (although prices are expensive), in particular Ashanti stools and brass weights formerly used to measure gold. In all the northern markets, earthenware pots, leatherwork, locally woven shirts and *Bolgatanga* baskets woven from multi-coloured raffia are sold. **Shopping hours:** 0800-1200 and 1400-1730 Monday, Tuesday, Thursday and Friday; 0800-1300 Wednesday and Saturday.
SPORT: Golf: There are courses at Mole National Park, Accra and Kumasi. **Watersports:** For those in search of **sailing** or **water-skiing** there are a number of centres with good facilities particularly on Lake Volta, where there is a yacht club at Akosombo, and at Ada on the mouth of the Volta. Another exhilarating experience is to be taken out over the surf in a local fishing boat. Although Ghana's coast offers miles of sandy beaches, bathing can be dangerous. Near Accra there are three **swimming** pools within yards of the surf. Ada, at the mouth of the Volta, also offers safe swimming with less risk of bilharzia, but it is not advised to swim upstream. **Spectator sports:** Ghanaians are keen **footballers, tennis players** and **boxers**. Another popular sport is **horseracing** at the Accra racecourse every Saturday.
SPECIAL EVENTS: Ghanaian festivals are well worth seeing with drumming, dancing and feasting. Every part of the country has its own annual festivals for the affirmation of tribal values, the remembrance of ancestors and past leaders, and the purification of the state in preparation for another year. The most impressive national celebrations are on the following days:
Mar 6 '93 *Independence Day*, Accra. **Jun 5** *Anniversary of the 1979 Uprising*, Accra.
SOCIAL CONVENTIONS: Ghanaians should always be addressed by their formal titles unless specifically requested otherwise. Handshaking is the usual form of greeting. **Tipping:** When a service charge is not included a 10% tip is usual.

BUSINESS PROFILE

ECONOMY: Agriculture occupies most of the working population, while mining for diamonds and other minerals is a major employer and an important foreign currency earner. The fishing industry developed significantly during the 1980s, with a relatively modern fleet replacing traditional canoe fishing. However, the economy has suffered throughout the last decade from the low world price for cocoa, the principal cash crop. Similarly, the oil industry has been depressed for the same reason, although the steady growth in production has avoided any loss of earnings. Ghana is a member of the Economic Community of West African States. During the last few years it has also been a test bed for a new kind of economic development programme arranged and supervised by the International Monetary Fund (IMF) and the World Bank. Termed the Structural Adjustment Programme, it involves measures to liberalise the economy, remove trade barriers and state intervention in industry and maintain firm budgetary control. Although similar to previous IMF/World Bank packages in content, it has the benefit for developing countries of being stretched over a longer period and is thus less drastic in its impact. It is generally considered to have been a success in Ghana and has since been applied elsewhere. The rural economy has especially benefited: this has contributed to Ghana's present self-sufficiency in food. The UK is the largest trading partner, accounting for 20% of Ghana's exports and nearly 30% of imports. Ghana received $600 million in multi- and bilateral aid in 1989 of which the UK contributed £30 million directly. Nigeria, the US, Germany, Japan and The Netherlands are other important trading partners.
BUSINESS: Appointments are customary and visitors should always be punctual for meetings. Best time for business visits is from September to April. **Office hours:** 0800-1200 and 1400-1700 Monday to Friday, 0830-1200 Saturday.
COMMERCIAL INFORMATION: The following organisation can offer advice: Ghana National Chamber of Commerce, PO Box 2325, Accra. Tel: (21) 662 427. Fax: (21) 662 210. Telex: 2687.

HISTORY & GOVERNMENT

HISTORY: The modern state of Ghana covers part of what used to be home to the powerful Ashanti kingdom, which fought a series of wars against British colonists during the 19th century. The kingdom was not fully suppressed until 1901, when it was annexed into the existing Gold Coast colony, one of the British West African settlements. Neighbouring British Togoland was put under Gold Coast administration two decades later. This colonial combine became the first African state to achieve full independence from Britain in 1957. Ghana's first post-independence ruler, Kwame Nkrumah, was the pioneer of 'African socialism' which advocates the application of the ideas of European socialism modified to take account of the particular circumstances of the Africans. Nkrumah initially sought a prominent role in the Non-Aligned Movement, but during the early 1960s gradually developed close ties with the Soviet bloc. Behind the Government's active foreign policy and radical image, however, the country was increasingly wracked by mismanagement and corruption. In 1966, for these reasons, Nkrumah was overthrown by a military coup. A pattern of fledgling civilian governments aborted by the intervention of the armed forces has dogged Ghana ever since. The leading figure in Ghanaian politics today is Flight-Lieutenant Jerry Rawlings, orchestrator of coups in 1979 and 1981 and the country's current Head of State. The Government's policies are broadly left-of-centre, though not especially hardline, and an economic development programme designed by the IMF has been conscientiously implemented (see *Trading Brief* above). Recent political developments include a gradual move towards political pluralism. Local elections were held during 1988 and multi-party elections for the presidency were held in November 1992. Rawlings, representing the national democratic Congress, was victorious with 58% of the vote, comfortably beating four other candidates. Legislative elections are due in mid-December 1992. Abroad, Ghana's relations with its immediate neighbours are not good. To the north, relations with Burkina Faso have been poor since the death of Rawlings' close friend Thomas Sankara. To the east, mutual accusations of destabilisation have been made by the Governments of Ghana and Togo. Ghanaian troops have played a major role in the ECOWAS peacekeeping force in Liberia, not least to try and protect Ghanaian nationals, several thousand of whom were reportedly held hostage at one stage by one of the rebel factions.
GOVERNMENT: Under the provisions of a new constitution accepted by referendum in April 1992, the President and a new National Assembly will be elected. The constitution is in the process of being implemented.

CLIMATE

A tropical climate, hot and humid in the north and in the forest land of Ashanti and southwest plains. Rainy season is April to July. On the coast there is no real seasonal change.
Required clothing: Tropical lightweight clothing. Sunglasses essential.

ACCRA Ghana (65m)

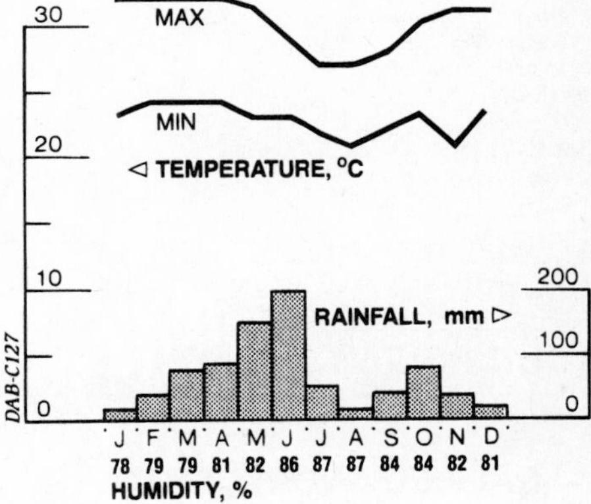

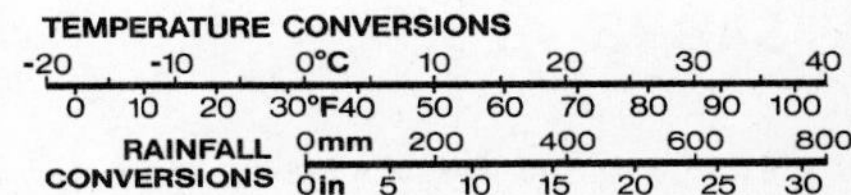

GIBRALTAR

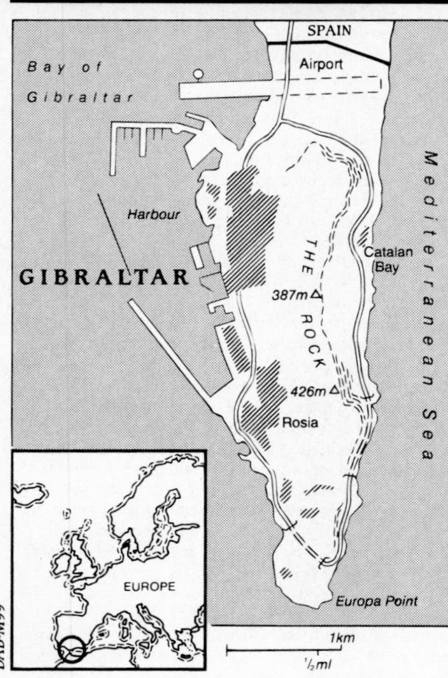

Location: Western entrance to the Mediterranean, southern tip of Europe.

Diplomatic representation: Gibraltar's foreign affairs are handled by the UK Foreign and Commonwealth Office, King Charles Street, London SW1A 2AH. Tel: (071) 270 3000. All other enquiries to Gibraltar Information Bureau.

British Passport Office
Clive House
70-78 Petty France
London SW1 9HD
Tel: (071) 271 8552/8.

Gibraltar Tourism Agency Ltd
PO Box 303
Cathedral Square
Gibraltar
Tel: 76400. Fax: 79980. Telex: 2223 GK.

Gibraltar Information Bureau
Arundel Great Court
179 The Strand
London WC2R 1EH
Tel: (071) 836 0777. Fax: (071) 240 6612. Telex: 266303. Opening hours: 0900-1730 Monday to Friday.

Gibraltar Information Bureau
710 Madison Offices
1155 15th Street, NW
Washington, DC
20005
Tel: (202) 452 1108. Fax: (202) 872 8543.

AREA: 5.6 sq km (2.16 sq miles).
POPULATION: 30,861 (1990 official estimate).
POPULATION DENSITY: 5510.9 per sq km.
CAPITAL: Gibraltar.
GEOGRAPHY: Gibraltar is a large promontory of jurassic limestone, situated in the western entrance to the Mediterranean. The 5km-long Rock contains 143 caves, over 48km (30 miles) of road and as many miles of tunnels. The highest point of the Rock is 425m (1400ft) above sea level. An internal self-governing British Crown Colony, Gibraltar has given its name to the Bay and the Straits which it overlooks. Spain is to the north and west and Morocco is 26km (16 miles) to the south.
LANGUAGE: English and Spanish are the official languages.
RELIGION: 77% Roman Catholic, with Church of England, Church of Scotland, Jewish, Hindu and other minorities.
TIME: GMT + 1 (GMT + 2 in summer).
ELECTRICITY: 220/240 volts AC, 50Hz.
COMMUNICATIONS: Telephone: IDD is available. Country code: 350. **Fax:** Facilities are available in some hotels. **Telex/telegram:** Enquire for both at Gibtel, 60 Main Street, or after office hours at Mount Pleasant, 25 South Barracks Road. There are two telex offices. **Post:** Airmail delivery to the UK takes between one and five days. Airmail flights are usually daily. There is a *Poste Restante* facility at the main post office in Main Street. Post office hours: 0900-1515 Monday to Friday (0900-1700 in winter), and 1000-1300 on Saturdays. **Press:** Newspapers are in English; most are published weekly. *The Gibraltar Chronicle* (est. 1801) is the only daily.
BBC World Service and Voice of America frequencies: From time to time these change. See the section *How to Use this Book* for more information.

BBC:				
MHz	15.07	12.09	9.410	6.195
Voice of America:				
MHz	11.97	9.670	6.040	5.995

PASSPORT/VISA

Regulations and requirements may be subject to change at short notice, and you are advised to contact the appropriate diplomatic or consular authority before finalising travel arrangements. Details of these may be found at the head of this country's entry. Any numbers in the chart refer to the footnotes below.

	Passport Required?	Visa Required?	Return Ticket Required?
Full British	1	No	No
BVP	Valid	-	-
Australian	Yes	No	No
Canadian	Yes	No	No
USA	Yes	No	No
Other EC	2	No	No
Japanese	Yes	No	No

PASSPORTS: Required by all except:
(a) **[1]** British nationals, provided they are in possession of a BVP.
(b) **[2]** EC nationals in possession of an identity card (with the exception of nationals of Spain and Portugal who *do* require a passport).
British Visitors Passport: Acceptable, but visitors cannot take excursions into Morocco unless in possession of a full passport.
VISAS: Required by nationals of Afghanistan, Albania, Algeria, Angola, Argentina, Bangladesh, Benin, Bhutan, Bulgaria, Central African Republic, Chad, China, Comoros, Congo, Cuba, Czechoslovakia, Djibouti, Egypt, Equatorial Guinea, Ethiopia, Gabon, Ghana, Guinea Republic, Guinea-Bissau, Haiti, Hungary, Indonesia, India, Iran, Iraq, Jordan, North Korea, Laos, Lebanon, Liberia, Libya, Madagascar, Mali, Mauritania, Mongolia, Morocco, Mozambique, Myanmar, Nepal, Nigeria, Pakistan, Philippines, Poland, Romania, Rwanda, Sao Tomé & Princípe, Saudi Arabia, Senegal, Somalia, Sri Lanka, Sudan, Syria, Taiwan, Thailand, Togo, Tunisia, Turkey, Uganda, US Pacific Trust Territories, USSR, Vietnam, Yemen and Zaire. Contact the Foreign and Commonwealth Office for latest information.
Applications to: Any British visa issuing post abroad or in the UK or the visa section of the British Passport Office in London (address above).
Note: All nationals who require a visa to enter the UK need a separate visa to enter Gibraltar.
Temporary residence: Persons must obtain prior permission from the Government of Gibraltar if wishing to work. (Nationals of EC countries are exempted.)

MONEY

Currency: Gibraltar uses the pound Sterling. Gib£1 = 100 new pence. The Gibraltar government issues bank notes of Gib£50, 20, 10, 5 and 1 for local use only. Coinage is the UK coinage. All UK notes are also accepted. All international travellers cheques and credit cards are accepted. UK Postcheques are accepted in post offices, but not Girobank cheques. Tourists from the UK are strongly advised to change their unspent Gibraltar pounds into UK pound notes at parity in Gibraltar before departure; UK banks charge for exchanging the Gibraltar Pound.
Banking hours: 0900-1530 Monday to Thursday, 0900-1530 and 1630-1800 Friday.

DUTY FREE

The following goods may be taken into Gibraltar without incurring Customs duty:
200 cigarettes or 100 cigarillos or 50 cigars or 250g of tobacco;
2 litres of fortified or sparkling wine or 1 litre of spirits, liqueurs and cordials or 2 litres of still wine;
50g of perfume and 0.25 litre of toilet water;
Goods to a total value of £32.

PUBLIC HOLIDAYS

Public holidays observed in Gibraltar are as follows:
Apr 9-12 '93 Easter. **May 3** May Day. **May 31** Spring Bank Holiday. **Jun 14** Queen's Official Birthday. **Aug 30** Late Summer Bank Holiday. **Dec 27-28** Christmas Holiday. **Jan 1 '94** New Year's Day. **Mar 8** Commonwealth Day.

HEALTH

Regulations and requirements may be subject to change at short notice, and you are advised to contact your doctor well in advance of your intended date of departure. Any numbers in the chart refer to the footnotes below.

	Special Precautions?	Certificate Required?
Yellow Fever	No	No
Cholera	No	No
Typhoid & Polio	No	-
Malaria	No	-
Food & Drink	1	-

[1]: Mains water is normally chlorinated, and whilst relatively safe may cause mild abdominal upsets. Bottled water is available and is advised for the first few weeks of the stay. Milk is pasteurised and dairy products are safe for consumption. Local meat, poultry, seafood, fruit and vegetables are generally considered safe to eat.
Health care: Gibraltar is a British Crown Colony and UK citizens, on presentation of a UK passport, are entitled to free treatment in public wards at St Bernard's Hospital and at Casemates Health Centre. (Other EC nationals are similarly entitled on presentation of form E111.) Medical treatment elsewhere and prescribed med-

GIBRALTAR | **HEALTH REGULATIONS** | **VISA REGULATIONS** | Code-Link

GALILEO/WORLDSPAN

TI-DFT/GIB/HE

TI-DFT/GIB/VI

SABRE

TIDFT/GIB/HE

TIDFT/GIB/VI

To access this information on your CRS, swipe the barcode with a light pen or type in the text under the barcode. For more information, see the introduction *How to Use This Book*.

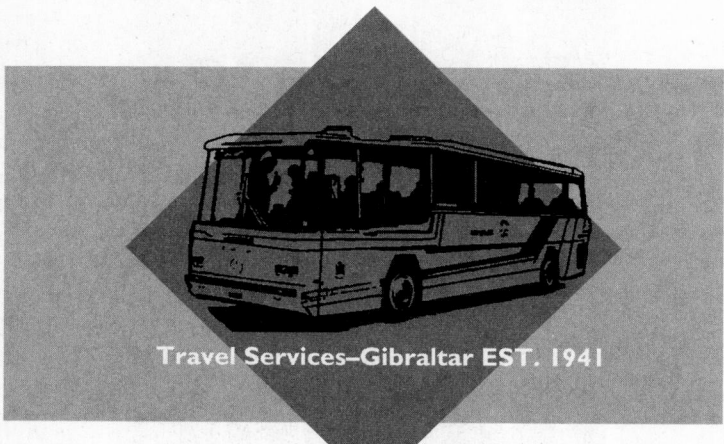

icines must be paid for. Dental treatment must also be paid for but extractions are undertaken for only a nominal charge at St Bernard's Hospital during normal weekday working hours.
Note: Passengers travelling from Gibraltar to Spain or Morocco are advised to refer to the *Health* entry for those countries.

TRAVEL - International

AIR: *GB Airways (GT)* operates direct services to Gibraltar from Europe and Africa.
Approximate flight time: From *London* to Gibraltar is 2 hours 45 minutes.
International airport: *Gibraltar (GIB)* (North Front) is 2km (1.6 miles) north of the town centre. A bus to the centre departs every 15 minutes from 0900-2130. Return is from the Market Place bus stop. Taxis and courtesy coaches are available. There are duty-free facilities.
SEA: International cruises are run by *CTC, P&O, BI, Polish Ocean, Costa, Norwegian American, Norwegian Cruises/Union Lloyd* and *TVI Cruises*. There is a regular ferry service to Tangier, Morocco.
ROAD: The only international land access is the frontier with Spain at La Linea. There are no caravanning or camping facilities, and sleeping in vehicles is not permitted.

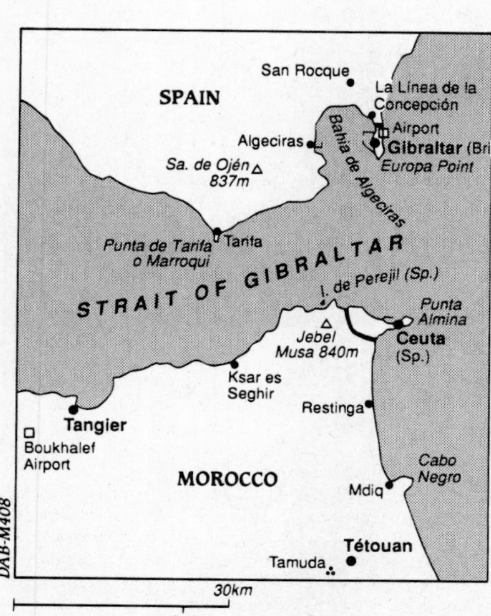

TRAVEL - Internal

ROAD: Traffic drives on the right. **Bus:** There are good local bus services operating at frequent intervals. **Taxi:** There are plenty of taxis and the driver is required by law to carry and produce on demand a copy of the taxi fares.
Car hire: Both self-drive and chauffeur-driven cars are available. Touring outside Gibraltar can also be arranged.
Documentation: Third Party insurance is compulsory. A UK driving licence is accepted.
JOURNEY TIMES: The following chart gives approximate journey times (in hours and minutes) from Gibraltar to major foreign cities:

	Air	Road	Rail	Sea
London	2.45	-	-	-
Tangier	0.20	-	-	1.00
Malaga	-	3.00	-	-
Madrid	-	12.00	10.00	-

ACCOMMODATION

HOTELS: Hotels range from luxury establishments with lounges, terrace shops, bars and swimming pools to more modest hotels. Summer rates are in force from April 1 to October 31. More information may be obtained from the Gibraltar Information Bureau on request.
SELF-CATERING: There is one wholly self-catering hotel, the Gibraltar Beach Hotel.
CAMPING: Camping is not permitted; however beach tents or beach umbrellas may be rented from villagers at Catalan Bay. These will include two deck chairs. Tent supplies and space for pitching on, however, is limited and it is advisable to book well in advance. Tents can only be used during the day.

RESORTS & EXCURSIONS

The town of Gibraltar is an 18th-century British Regency town built on a 15th-century Spanish town which was, in turn, built on a 12th-century Moorish town. The principal tourist sites and places of interest are:
St Michael's Cave, situated 300m (1000ft) above sea level, was known to the Romans for its spectacular stalactites and stalagmites. It is part of a complex series of interlinked caves including *Leonora's Cave* and *Lower St Michael's Cave*. Today it is used for concerts and ballet.
The *Upper Galleries*, hewn by hand from the Rock in 1782, house old cannon and tableaux evoking the Great Siege (1779-1783).
The *Apes' Den* is the home of the famous Barbary Apes, which are in fact not apes but tail-less macaque monkeys.
The *Gibraltar Museum* contains caveman tools and ornaments excavated from the Rock's caves, including a replica of the Gibraltar Skull, the first Neanderthal skull found in Europe (1848). There are also exhibits from the Phoenician, Greek, Roman, Moorish, Spanish, and British periods of the Rock's history; a comprehensive collection of prints and lithographs; a collection of weapons, 1727-1800; a large-scale model of the Rock made in 1865; and displays of fauna and flora. The museum itself was built above a fine, complete 14th-century *Moorish Bath House*.
Other sites of interest are: the 14th-century keep of the much-rebuilt *Moorish Castle*; the *Shrine of Our Lady of Europe*, a mosque before conversion to a Christian chapel in 1462, housing the 15th-century image of the Patroness of Gibraltar; the ancient *Nun's Well*, a Moorish cistern; *Parson's Lodge Battery* (1865), above Rosia Bay; *The Rock Buster*, an 100-ton gun; the 18th-century *Garrison Library*; *Trafalgar Cemetery*; *Alameda Gardens*; *Europa Point*, just 26km (16 miles) from Africa; the almost complete *city walls*, dating in part from the Moorish occupation.
Some popular tourist activities in Gibraltar are: the *cable-car trip* to the top of the Rock, stopping at the apes' den on the way up; the *Convent*, residence of the Governor, and formerly a 16th-century Franciscan Monastic house; the *Guided Walking Tour of Places of Worship*, Wednesdays at 1000, including visits to Gibraltar's two cathedrals, a synagogue, the Garrison chapel, the Presbyterian church and the Methodist chapel – all

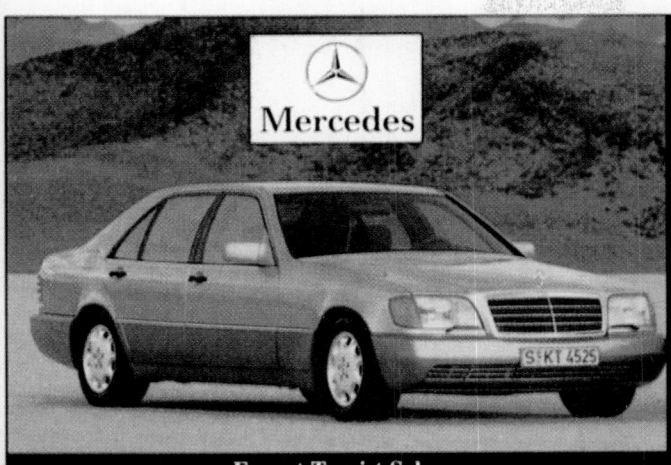

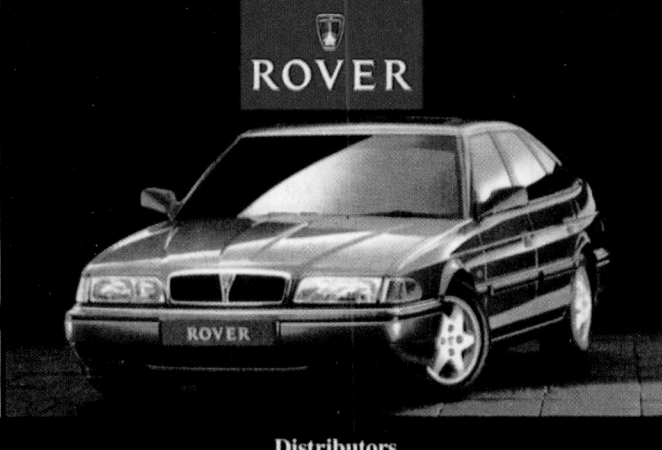

buildings of historic interest; the *guided walking tour* around the city walls, every Friday at 1030; and the *Mediterranean Steps Walk* which starts at O'Hara's *Battery* (the highest point in Gibraltar), snakes down the eastern cliff and around the southern slopes to the western side of the Rock.

Gibraltar has five beaches. On the east side are *Eastern Beach*, *Catalan Bay* and, towards the south, *Sandy Bay*, where the Rock is very sheer and parking difficult. *Little Bay*, a pebble beach, and *Camp Bay/Keys Promenade* are on the western coast.

Day trips to Ronda, Malaga and Jerez in Andalucia, Spain can be arranged from Gibraltar, as can day trips by air to Tangier and other Moroccan cities (see the entry for *Spain* below for further information on Andalucia). The Gibraltar Tourism Agency is in Cathedral Square. The staff will advise on tours and excursions and where to buy tickets.

SOCIAL PROFILE

FOOD & DRINK: There are bars and bistros throughout the town, and at the Marina, operating under Mediterranean licensing hours and selling British beer. Restaurants cover the whole range, from the highly sophisticated to simple or fast-food establishments. Gibraltar's geographical location and its history as a British colony means that it can offer a large selection of British dishes as well as French, Spanish, American, Moroccan, Italian, Chinese and Indian cuisine. **Drink:** Spirits and tobacco are substantially cheaper than in the UK for identical brands. All types of alcoholic drinks are served, including draught beer (served at the *Gibraltar Arms*).

NIGHTLIFE: Gibraltar has a number of discos and nightspots open until the early hours of the morning. The Casino complex includes a restaurant, nightclub, roof restaurant (summer) and gaming rooms, and is open from 0900 to the early hours.

SHOPPING: All goods are sold in Gibraltar at reduced-tax prices, and free of VAT. The majority of shops are in or near Main Street. Silk, linen, jewellery, perfumes, carvings, radios, leatherwork, electronic and photographic equipment, cashmere and watches can be bought. **Shopping hours:** 1000-1900 Monday to Friday and 1000-1300 Saturday.

SPORT: Many forms of **watersports** are available in Gibraltar. Pier **fishing** facilities are available and there are charter boats for hire, although deep-sea fishing (for blue shark and swordfish) is not always available at short notice. For a more leisurely sport, go on a boat trip to see and photograph the dolphins in the Bay. **Scuba diving** is a growing sport. There is also **parasailing** and **water-skiing**.
SPECIAL EVENTS: The following is a selection of major festivals and other special events celebrated in Gibraltar during 1993/4. For a complete list with exact dates, contact the Gibraltar Information Bureau.
May '93 *Annual Flower Show*. **Jun** *International Festival of Music and Performing Arts*. **Sep** *Battle of Britain Ceremony*. **Oct** *Trafalgar Day Ceremony*. **Nov-Dec** *Gibraltar Annual Drama Festival*.
SOCIAL CONVENTIONS: Gibraltar is a strongly traditional society with an attractive blend of British and Mediterranean customs. **Tipping:** Normally 10-15%.

BUSINESS PROFILE

ECONOMY: The main sources of income are the British armed forces who have bases and ship repair and docking facilities on the Rock. Tourism and offshore financial services are the other principal earners. The construction industry is also important. The economy is affected to a large extent by the state of relations with Spain and, in particular, the level of border crossings. At present, these are almost wholly unrestricted with the result that many native Gibraltarians work in Spain and a significant number of Spaniards have jobs on the Rock. The UK is naturally the largest source of imports. Gibraltar is not an exporter as such but earns foreign exchange through re-export, mainly into Spain.
BUSINESS: English is normally used for business, but Spanish may be used for business connected with Spain. **Office hours:** 0900-1300 and 1500-1800 Monday to Friday. **Government Department hours:** Generally 0845-1315 and 1415-1730 Monday to Thursday, and 0845-1315 and 1415-1715 Friday; but hours vary according to department and season.
COMMERCIAL INFORMATION: The following organisation can offer advice: Gibraltar Chamber of Commerce, PO Box 29, Suite 11, Don House, 30-38 Main Street. Tel: 78376. Fax: 78403. Telex: 2151.
Information is also available from the Gibraltar Information Bureau.
CONFERENCES/CONVENTIONS: Maximum seating at present is for 700 persons, though facilities at hotels for conferences and conventions continue to be developed and, from February 1992, Europort Gibraltar, an 82,000 sq m (212,000 sq ft) financial complex, will offer extensive office and conference facilities. St Michael's Cave (see *Resorts & Excursions* above) offers an absolutely unique and scenic meetings' location. Contact the Gibraltar Information Bureau for further information.

HISTORY & GOVERNMENT

HISTORY: Gibraltar derives its name from Tariq Ibn Zeyad (Gibel Tariq – Tarik's Mountain), who led the 8th-century conquest of Spain by a combined force of Arabs and Berbers crossing from Africa. Gibraltar's unusual status was not acquired until almost 1000 years later, long after the Islamic invaders had been driven out, as a consequence of the 1713 Treaty of Utrecht which brought to an end the War of the Spanish Succession and gave the territory to Britain. The British interpretation of the treaty, moreover, holds that the territory was ceded to them indefinitely. The presence of a foreign-owned mini-state on the Spanish mainland has been an irritant in Anglo-Spanish relations ever since. The Spanish dictator Franco launched a campaign in 1963 through the United Nations to reclaim Gibraltar, adding to the pressure by closing the border and severing telephone links. Despite a more flexible and amicable attitude on the part of the Spanish since the death of Franco in 1975 (the border was finally opened in 1985), there has been little movement on the basic issue of sovereignty. The Gibraltarians have been equally unyielding in their attachment to Britain. Trilateral co-operation between the UK, Spain and Gibraltar has steadily improved in the security field and will necessarily be strengthened as the EC's common border plan comes into operation. There has been some shifting of ground in Madrid as regards the constitutional future of Gibraltar: premier Felipe González has suggested to the British some form of joint authority. However, the general election in Gibraltar in January 1992, which returned Bossano with a large majority, strengthens the hand of those on the Rock who prefer outright independence although, in public statements, Bossano remains vague about his intentions.
GOVERNMENT: Gibraltar is a British Crown Colony, where the Queen is represented locally by a Governor-General and Commander-in-Chief, Admiral Sir Derek Reffell, as Head of State. The Chief Minister, currently Mr Joseph Bossano, presides over the Council of Ministers which administers domestic affairs. fifteen of the 17-member House of Assembly are elected to represent the population's local interests. The ex-officio members are the Attorney General and the Financial and Development Secretary. Britain is responsible for defence and foreign affairs.

CLIMATE

Warm throughout the year, with hot summers and mild winters with no snow. Summer (May to September) can be very hot and humid. **Required clothing:** Lightweight for summer and medium-weight for winter months.

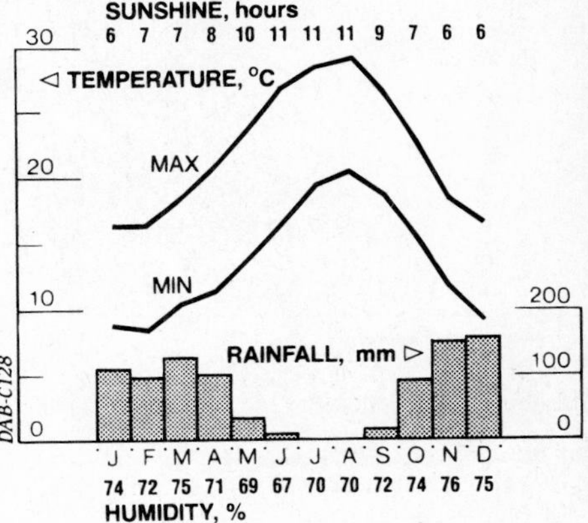

□ international airport

Location: Southeast Europe.

Ellinikos Organismos Tourismou (EOT)
(Greek National Tourist Board)
Odos Amerikis 2B
105 64 Athens, Greece
Tel: (1) 322 3111. Fax: (1) 322 4148. Telex: 215832.

Embassy of the Hellenic Republic
1a Holland Park
London W11 3TP
Tel: (071) 221 6467. Fax: (071) 229 8040. Telex: 266751. Opening hours: 0930-1230, 1400-1500 Monday to Friday.

National Tourist Organisation of Greece (GNTO)
4 Conduit Street
London W1R ODJ
Tel: (071) 734 5997. Fax: (071) 287 1369. Telex: 21122 GR TOUR G. Opening hours: 0930-1730 Monday to Thursday, 0930-1630 Friday.

British Embassy
Odos Ploutarchou 1
106 75 Athens,
Greece
Tel: (1) 723 6211. Fax: (1) 724 1872. Telex: 216440 LION GR.
Consulates in: Crete, Corfu, Patras, Rhodes, Salonika, Samos, Syros and Volos.

Embassy of the Hellenic Republic
2221 Massachusetts Avenue, NW
Washington, DC
20008
Tel: (202) 939 5800. Fax: (202) 939 5824.
Consulates in: Atlanta, Boston, Chicago, New Orleans, New York (tel: (212) 988 5500) and San Francisco.

National Tourist Organisation of Greece
645 Fifth Avenue
New York, NY
10022
Tel: (212) 421 5777.

Embassy of the United States of America
Leoforos Vassilissis Sofias 91
106 60 Athens, Greece
Tel: (1) 721 2951. Fax: (1) 646 3450. Telex: 215548.

Greek Embassy
76-80 MacLaren Street
Ottawa, Ontario
K2P 0K6
Tel: (613) 238 6271. Fax: (613) 238 6273.

Greek National Tourist Organisation
Main Level
1300 Bay Street
Toronto, Ontario
M5R 3K8
Tel: (416) 968 2220. Fax: 968 6533. Telex: 06218604.

Canadian Embassy
Odos Ioannou Ghennadiou 4
115 21 Athens, Greece
Tel: (1) 723 9511. Fax: (1) 724 7123.

AREA: 131,957 sq km (50,949 sq miles).
POPULATION: 10,269,074 (1991 estimate).
POPULATION DENSITY: 77.8 per sq km.
CAPITAL: Athens. **Population:** 885,737 (1981).
GEOGRAPHY: Greece is situated on the Mediterranean, and is bordered to the north by Albania, Yugoslavia and Bulgaria, and to the east by Turkey. To the east is the Aegean Sea, and to the west the Ionian Sea. The mainland consists of the following regions: Central Greece, Peloponnese, Thessaly (east/central), Epirus (west), Macedonia (north/northwest), and Thrace (northwest). Euboea, the second largest of the Greek islands, lying to the northeast of the central region, is also considered to be part of the mainland region. The Peloponnese peninsula is separated from the northern mainland by the isthmus of Corinth. The northern mainland is dissected by high mountains (such as the Pindus) that extend southwards towards a landscape of fertile plains, pine-forested uplands and craggy, scrub-covered foothills. The islands account for one-fifth of the land area of the country. The majority are thickly clustered in the Aegean between the Greek and Turkish coasts. The Ionian Islands are the exception; they are scattered along the west coast in the Ionian Sea. The Aegean archipelago includes the Dodecanese, lying off the Turkish coast, of which Rhodes is the best known; the Northeast Aegean group, including Lemnos, Lesbos, Chios, Samos and Ikaria; the Sporades, off the central mainland; and the Cyclades, 39 islands of which only 24 are inhabited. Crete, the largest island, is not included in any formal grouping.
For fuller descriptions of these regions and islands, see below under *Resorts & Excursions*.
LANGUAGE: Greek (Demotiki is now the official language for both conversation and the written word). Most people connected with tourism will speak at least some English, German, Italian, or French.
RELIGION: 97% Greek Orthodox; Muslim and Roman Catholic minorities.
TIME: GMT + 2 (GMT + 3 in summer).
ELECTRICITY: 220 volts AC, 50Hz.
COMMUNICATIONS: Telephone: IDD is available throughout the mainland and islands. Country code: 30, followed by (1) for Athens, (31) for Thessaloniki, (81) for Heraklion and (661) for Corfu. For IDD access from within Greece, call 00. **Fax:** Main post offices and large hotels have facilities. **Telex/telegram:** There are telex/telegram facilities in main post offices and large hotels in all Greek cities and the major islands. **Post:** All letters, postcards, newspapers and periodicals will automatically be sent by airmail. There are *Poste Restante* facilities at most post offices throughout the country. Advance notice is required at all Athens branches except for the central office in Eolou Street. A passport must be shown on collection. Post office hours: 0800-1400 Monday to Friday and 0800-1330 Saturday. **Press:** There are 18 daily newspapers in Athens including *Eleftheros Typos*, *Ta Nea* and *Eleftherotyia*. *Athens News* and *Greece Today* are both published daily in English.
BBC World Service and Voice of America frequencies: From time to time these change. See the section *How to Use this Book* for more information.
BBC:

MHz	17.64	15.07	9.410	6.180

A service for the Greek islands is available on 1323kHz/226.7m.
Voice of America:

MHz	9.670	6.040	5.995	1.197

A service is also available on 792kHz/379m.

PASSPORT/VISA

Regulations and requirements may be subject to change at short notice, and you are advised to contact the appropriate diplomatic or consular authority before finalising travel arrangements. Details of these may be found at the head of this country's entry. Any numbers in the chart refer to the footnotes below.

	Passport Required?	Visa Required?	Return Ticket Required?
Full British	Yes	No/2	No
BVP	Valid	No	No
Australian	Yes	No	No
Canadian	Yes	No	No
USA	Yes	No	No
Other EC	I	No	No
Japanese	Yes	No	No

PASSPORTS: Valid passport required by all except:
[1] nationals of Austria, Belgium, France, Germany, Italy, Luxembourg and the UK provided they hold a valid ID card (or BVP) for a stay of up to three months.
British Visitors Passport: Valid.
VISAS: Required by all except:
(a) nationals of the countries referred to in the chart above for a period of up to 3 months (including **[2]** holders of British passports with the exception of citizens of Hong Kong who should see (d) below;
(b) nationals of Andorra, Antigua & Barbuda, Argentina, Austria, Bahamas, Barbados, Belgium, Cyprus, Czechoslovakia, Ecuador, Finland, Gambia, Germany, Hungary, Iceland, Israel, Italy, Liechtenstein, Malta, Mexico, Monaco, New Zealand, Nicaragua, Norway, San Marino, South Korea, Sweden, Switzerland and Zimbabwe for a period of up to 3 months;
(c) nationals of Brazil, Chile, Dominican Republic, Peru, Portugal, Seychelles, South Africa, Tanzania and Uruguay for a period of up to 2 months;
(d) nationals of Hong Kong for a period of up to 1 month.
Note: Nationals of Bahrain, Kuwait and Qatar can obtain a visa upon arrival.
Types of visa: Tourist and Transit. Cost varies according to nationality.
Validity: Up to 3 months, depending on nationality. Transit visas are valid for up to 4 days.
Application to: Visa section, Embassy in London. For address, see top of entry.
Application requirements: Personal applications only: (a) Application form with stamped addressed envelope. (b) Sufficient funds to cover stay. (c) Fee. (d) Passport.
Working days required: 1 day.
Temporary residence: Apply to the Aliens Department in Athens, 173 Alexandras Avenue, 155 22 Athens. Tel: 646 8103. Ext 379. **Important note:** Persons arriving in and departing from Greece on a charter flight risk having the return portion of their ticket invalidated by the authorities if, at any time during their stay, they leave Greece and remain overnight or longer in another country.

MONEY

Currency: Drachma (Dr). Notes are in denominations of Dr5000, 1000, 500, 100 and 50. Coins are in denominations of Dr50, 20,10, 5, 2 and 1.
Currency exchange: Foreign currencies and travellers cheques can be exchanged at all banks, saving banks and exchange counters. Exchange rates can fluctuate from one bank to another. Many UK banks offer differing exchange rates depending on the denominations of Greek currency being bought or sold. Check with banks for details and current rates. Generally banks in Greece charge a commission of 2% with a minimum of Dr50 and a maximum of Dr4500 on the encashment of travellers cheques.
Credit cards: Diners Club, Visa, American Express, Access/Mastercard and other major credit cards are widely accepted (although less so in petrol stations). Check with your credit card company for details of merchant acceptability and other services which may be available.
Travellers cheques: All major currencies are widely accepted.
Exchange rate indicators: The following figures are included as a guide to the movements of the Drachma against Sterling and the US Dollar:

Date:	Oct '89	Oct '90	Oct '91	Oct '92
£1.00=	263.7	298.6	324.92	315.52
$1.00=	167.0	152.9	187.22	198.82

Currency restrictions: Import of foreign currency is free, subject to declaration of amounts greater than US$1000. Export of foreign currency is limited to the amount declared on import. The import of local currency is limited to Dr100,000 and the export to Dr20,000.
Banking hours: 0800-1400 Monday to Friday. Many banks on larger islands stay open in the afternoon and some during the evening to offer currency exchange facilities during the tourist season. The GNTO bureau in Athens can give full details.

DUTY FREE

The following goods may be imported into Greece without incurring customs duty by:
(a) Passengers from EC countries:
300 cigarettes or 75 cigars or 150 cigarillos or 400g of tobacco;
1.5 litres of alcoholic beverages or 5 litres of liquers, still and sparkling wines;
75g of perfume and 0.375 litres of eau de cologne;
1000g of coffee or 400g of coffee extract;
200g of tea or 80g of tea extract;
Gifts up to a total value of Dr137,000 provided no single item has a value of over Dr77,500 (children under 15 are allowed up to Dr34,000).
(b) Passengers from other countries:
200 cigarettes or 50 cigars or 100 cigarillos or 250g of tobacco;
1 litre of alcoholic beverage or 2 litres of wine;

50g of perfume and 0.25 litre of eau de cologne;
500g of coffee or 200g of coffee extract;
100g of tea or 40g of tea extract;
Gifts up to a total value of Dr10,500 (children under 15 are allowed up to Dr5500).
(c) Passengers entering from an EC country with duty-paid goods (as of January (1993):
800 cigarettes and 400 cigarillos and 200 cigars and 1kg of tobacco;
90 litres of wine (including up to 60 litres of sparkling wine);
10 litres of spirits;
20 litres of intermediate products (such as fortified wine);
110 litres of beer.
Restricted entry: It is forbidden to bring in plants with soil and windsurfboards (unless a Greek national residing in Greece guarantees it will be re-exported).
Note: It is forbidden to export antiquities without the express permission of the Archaeological Service in Athens. Those who ignore this will be prosecuted.

PUBLIC HOLIDAYS

Public holidays observed in Greece are as follows:
Mar 1 '93 Shrove Monday. **Mar 25** Independence Day. **Apr 16** Good Friday. **Apr 18** Easter Sunday. **Apr 19** Easter Monday. **May 1** Labour Day. **Jun 7** Holy Spirit Day. **Aug 15** Assumption. **Oct 28** Ohi Day. **Dec 25** Christmas Day. **Dec 26** St Stephen's Day. **Jan 1 '94** New Year's Day. **Jan 6** Epiphany. **Mar** Shrove Tuesday.

HEALTH

Regulations and requirements may be subject to change at short notice, and you are advised to contact your doctor well in advance of your intended date of departure. Any numbers in the chart refer to the footnotes below.

	Special Precautions?	Certificate Required?
Yellow Fever	No	1
Cholera	No	No
Typhoid & Polio	No	-
Malaria	No	-
Food & Drink	2	-

[1]: A yellow fever vaccination certificate is required from travellers over six months of age coming from infected areas.
[2]: Mains water is normally chlorinated, and whilst relatively safe may cause mild abdominal upsets. Bottled water is available and is advised for the first few weeks of the stay. Milk is pasteurised and dairy products are safe for consumption. Local meat, poultry, seafood, fruit and vegetables are generally considered safe to eat.
Rabies is present. For those at high risk, vaccination before arrival should be considered. If you are bitten abroad seek medical advice without delay. For more information consult the *Health* section at the back of the book.
Health care: There is a Reciprocal Health Agreement with the UK, but it is poorly implemented and it is essential to take out holiday insurance. Refunds for medical treatment are theoretically available from the Greek Social Insurance Foundation on presentation of form E111 (see *Health* at the back of the book). Chemists can diagnose and supply drugs. There are often long waits for treatment at public hospitals. Hospital facilities on outlying islands are sometimes sparse, although many ambulances without adequate facilities have air ambulance backup.

TRAVEL - International

AIR: Greece's national airline is *Olympic Airways (OA)*.
Approximate flight times: From *London* to Athens is 3 hours 15 minutes; to Rhodes is 3 hours 45 minutes; to Corfu is 3 hours 5 minutes; to Heraklion is 3 hours 45 minutes; and to Skiathos is 3 hours 20 minutes.
From *Los Angeles* to Athens is 20 hours 35 minutes.
From *New York* to Athens is 11 hours 10 minutes.
From *Singapore* to Athens is 11 hours 25 minutes.
From *Sydney* to Athens is 22 hours 5 minutes.
International airports: *Athens (ATH)* (Hellinikon) is 10km (6 miles) from the city. Regular bus and taxi services are available to the city. Taxis charge extra for baggage. Airport facilities include a duty-free shop, car hire (*Avis, Budget, Hertz, Inter-rent*), 24-hour bank and exchange services, bar and restaurant facilities.
Heraklion (HER) (Crete) is 5km (3 miles) from the city. Bus and taxi services are available. Airport facilities include a cafeteria and a duty-free shop.
Thessaloniki (SKG) (Micra) is 16km (10 miles) from the city. Regular coach and taxi services are available. There is a duty-free shop, cafeteria and bar.
Corfu (CFU) (Kerkyra) is 3km (2 miles) from the city. Regular coach and taxi services are available. There is a duty-free shop, cafeteria and bar.
Rhodes (RHO) (Paradisi) is 16km (10 miles) from the city. Coach and taxi services are available. Airport facilities include a duty-free shop, car hire (*Avis, Rent-a-car*), bank and exchange services, cafe and a 24-hour bar.
There are also international airports at Alexandroupolis (AXD), Ioannina (IOA), Kos (KGS), Mykonos (JMK), Paros (PAS), Salonika (SKG), Skiathos (JSI) and Thira (JTR), most of which predominately serve summer traffic.
SEA: The major Greek ports are Piraeus, Thessaloniki and Volos, Igoumenitsa, Heraklion, Corfu, Patras and Rhodes. Shipping and ferry boat lines link these ports with Egypt, Italy, Cyprus, Syria, Yugoslavia, Israel and Russia. Greek ports are used by a number of cruise lines including *Epirotiki, K Lines, Carpas Cruises, Costa, Chandris, Mediterranean Passenger Services, Med Sun Lines, Royal Cruise Line, Sun Line* and *Swan Hellenic*. The GNTO can give full details.
A car ferry links the Italian ports of Brindisi and Ancona with Patras and Piraeus. There are services from Igonmenitsa to Ancona, Bari and Brindisi; Heraklion to Ancona and Brindisi; Corfu to Ancona, Bari, Brindisi; Rhodes to Ancona. During the summer months there are also services between Ithaca to Brindisi and Cephalonia to Brindisi. A subsidiary of *DFDS* operates a scheduled car ferry service from Alexandria (Egypt) via Heraklion to Patras and on to Ancona.
RAIL: The national railway company is *Hellenic State Railways (OSE)*. The following continental rail services run from London to Athens:
Acropolis Express: London–Paris–Milan–Trieste–Belgrade*–Athens.
Hellas Express: London–Amsterdam–Cologne–Bonn –Stuttgart –Munich–Salzburg–Zagreb*–Belgrade*–Nis –Athens.
Interail tickets, for those aged 26 and under, include rail travel within Greece, but a supplement will be added for couchettes; the ticket does not include the cost of ferries between other countries or islands, but certain shipping lines offer a discount to ticket holders. Check with the companies concerned for details.
ROAD: It is possible to ferry cars across to one of the major ports of entry or to enter overland. Points of overland entry are Evzoni and Niki in Yugoslavia,* 550km (341 miles) from Athens, or Promohonas in Bulgaria, 736km (457 miles) from Athens. From Yugoslavia the route is via Italy (Trieste), Austria (Graz), and Belgrade. The journey from northern France to Athens is over 3200km (2000 miles). For car ferry information, see entry on **Sea** above. **Bus:** There are routes from Athens via Thessaloniki to Sofia, Paris, Dortmund and Istanbul. Information and bookings from terminals in Athens at 6 Sina Street; 1 Karolou Street, and 17 Filellinon Street; also at Thessaloniki rail station. See below for information on **documentation** and **traffic regulations.**
Note [*]: At the time of writing, due to the present situation of war in **Yugoslavia**, it is extremely unwise and dangerous to take any route through Yugoslavia. Consult the tourist office for advice on alternative routes.

TRAVEL - Internal

AIR: *Olympic Airways (OA)* have their own terminal (Athens West) and fly from Athens to Kerkira (Corfu), Heraklion, Chania (Crete), Thessaloniki, Rhodes, Samos, Mykonos, Santorini, Lemnos, Milos, Cephalonia, Zakinthos, Mitilini, Skiathos, Aktion, Alexandroupolis, Chios, Kassos, Kastoria, Kavala, Cos, Kozani, Kithira, Ioannis, Larissa and Paros; from Rhodes to Karpathos and to Kassos.
SEA: It is both cheap and easy to travel around the islands. There are ferry services on many routes, with sailings most frequent during the summer. Tickets can be bought from the shipping lines' offices located around the quaysides. In major ports the larger lines have offices in the city centre. There are three classes of ticket which offer varying degrees of comfort; couchette cabins can be booked for the longer voyages or those wishing to avoid the sun. Most ships have restaurant facilities. During high season it is wise to buy tickets well in advance, as inter-island travel is very popular.
Ferry routes: From **Piraeus** there are regular sailings to the following (figures in brackets are approximate journey times in hours and minutes, although journey lengths vary according to whether the ferry reaches its destination using a direct route or stops at islands in between Piraeus and its final port of call):
Agios Kirikos (Ikaria) (8 hrs); Agios Nikolaos (Crete) (1330); Amorgos (Cyclades); Anafi (Cyclades) (1840); Astipalaia (Dodecanese) (13 hrs); Chalki (Halki) (Dodecanese) (3030); Chania (Crete) (12 hrs); Chios (11 hrs); Donoussa (Cyclades) (1030-2615); Elafonissos (10 hrs); Folegandros (Cyclades) (12 hrs); Geraka (Peloponnese); Gytheion (Peloponnese) (17 hrs); Heraklia (Iraklia) (Cyclades) (1540-2100); Heraklion (Crete) (12 hrs); Santorini (Cyclades) (1130); Ios (Cyclades) (11 hrs); Kalymnos (Dodecanese) (12 hrs); Karlovassi (Samos) (10 hrs); Karpathos (Dodecanese) (26 hrs); Kassos (Dodecanese) (2330); Kimolos (Cyclades) (8 hrs); Kythira (Peleponnese) (0945); Kythnos (Cyclades) (4 hrs); Cos (Dodecanese) (14 hrs); Koufonissia (Cyclades) (1430-2300); Leros (Dodecanese) (10 hrs); Milos (Cyclades) (8 hrs); Monemvassia (Peloponnese) (6 hrs); Mykonos (Cyclades) (0530); Mitilini (14 hrs); Naxos (Cyclades) (8 hrs); Neapolis (Peloponnese) (0825); Nissiros (Dodecanese) (2230); Paros (Cyclades) (7 hrs); Patmos (Dodecanese) (8 hrs); Portokagio (Peloponnese) (0630); Rhodes (18 hrs); Samos (Vathi) (12 hrs); Santorini (Thera) (Cyclades) (12 hrs); Schinoussa (Cyclades) (1520-2300); Serifos (Cyclades) (5 hrs); Sifnos (Cyclades) (0530); Sikinos (Cyclades) (1030); Sitia (Crete) (14 hrs); Symi (Dodecanese) (2630); Syros (Cyclades) (0430); Thessaloniki (8 hrs); Tilos (Dodecanese) (29 hrs); Tinos (Cyclades) (0445); and Vathi (Samos) (12 hrs). Check sailing times either with individual lines, the National Tourist Organisation of Greece, or in Piraeus upon arrival in Greece.
There are also services from **Piraeus** or **Zea** to the Saronic Gulf: Aegina, Methana, Poros, Hydra (Idra), Ermioni, Porto-Heli and Spetses; and also to Leonidio, Monemvassia, Nauplia, Neapolis-Kithira, Tolo and Tiros. Local services from **Rafina** (near Athens) to Gavrion (Andros), Karistos (Euboea), Marmari (Euboea), Mesta (Chios), Mykonos, Naxos, Paros, Syros and Tinos.
Other routes include Agia Marina–Nea Styra; Perama–Salamis; Rio–Antirio; Aedipsos–Arkitsa; Eretria–Oropos; Glifa–Agiokambos; Patras–Ithaca; Patras–Sami; Patras–Corfu; Patras–Paxi; Preveza–Aktion; Igoumenitsa–Corfu; Corfu–Paxi; Kyllini–Zante; Kyllini–Cephalonia (Poros); Kavala–Thassos (Limenas); Kavala–Thassos (Prinos); Keramoti–Thassos; and Alexandroupolis–Samothrace.
A **hydrofoil** service (the 'Flying Dolphins') offer a fast and efficient service from Piraeus, travelling throughout the islands. Although this is slightly more expensive than travelling by ferry, journey times are cut drastically. There are also fast hydrofoil services from Zea Marina, Lavrio, Agios Konstandinos, Volos, Kimi (Euboea), Thessaloniki and Gytheion. Numerous types of yachts

GREECE	HEALTH REGULATIONS	VISA REGULATIONS Code-Link
GALILEO/WORLDSPAN	 TI-DFT/ATH/HE	TI-DFT/ATH/VI
SABRE	TIDFT/ATH/HE	 TIDFT/ATH/VI

To access this information on your CRS, swipe the barcode with a light pen or type in the text under the barcode. For more information, see the introduction *How to Use This Book*.

and sailing vessels can be chartered or hired with or without crews. 'Flotilla holidays' are popular, and the GNTO has a full list of companies running this type of holiday.
RAIL: North: Regular daily trains from Athens to Thessaloniki, Thebes, Livadia, Paleofarsala, Larissa, Plati, Edessa, Florina, Seres, Drama, Komotini, Halkida and Alexandroupolis (connections from Thessaloniki and Larissa). **South:** Athens to Corinth, Xylokastra, Patras, Mycenae, Olympia, Argos, Tripoli, Megalopolis and Kalamata.
Cheap fares: 20% rebate on return fares. Touring cards lasting 10, 20 and 30 days entitle the holder to unlimited travel on trains (2nd class) and on *CH* buses for a reduced cost (further reductions for groups). Prices depend on the number of passengers and duration of validity. Other reductions available include *Senior Passes* (for national transport: see below), *Interail Senior* and *Junior Cards*, and, for passengers residing outside Europe, *Eurailpass* and *Eurail* Youth Pass cards.
Senior cards: Valid for one year. Entitle passengers to: (a) 50% reduction on rail travel and *CH* buses. (b) Five single journeys free of charge, provided dates do not coincide with *either* the ten days before and after Easter *or* the ten days before and after Christmas. There are further reductions for groups.
For further information on the above schemes, contact the GNTO.
Train information: 1-3 Karolou Street, Athens (tel: (01) 524 0647/8) or G. Sina Street, Athens (tel: (01) 362 4402).
ROAD: Greece has a good road network on the whole. Examples of some distances from Athens: to Thessaloniki 511km (318 miles); to Corinth 85km (53 miles); to Igoumenitsa 587km (365 miles); to Delphi 165km (103 miles). **Bus:** Buses link Athens and all main towns in Attica, Northern Greece and the Peloponnese. Service on the islands depends on demand, and timetables should be checked carefully; some islands do not allow any kind of motorised transport, islanders use boats, or donkeys and carts to travel around; these are also worth finding out about. Fares are cheap. *Hellenic State Railways (OSE)* run services to northern Greece from the Karolou Street terminus and to the Peloponnese from the Sina Street station.
Bus information: For information on buses from Athens to the provinces, enquire at Terminal A, 100, Kifissou Street, Athens *or* Terminal B, 260, Liossion Street, Athens.
Taxi: Rates are per km and are very reasonable, with extra charge for fares to/from stations, ports and airports. Taxis run on a share basis, so do not be surprised if the taxi picks up other passengers for the journey. There is an additional charge from 0100-0600, with double fare from 0200-0400.
Car hire: Most car hire firms operate throughout Greece. For details contact the GNTO.
Regulations: The minimum age for driving is 17. Children under 10 must sit in the back seat. Seat belts must be worn. There are fines for breaking traffic regulations. The maximum speed limit is 100kmph (60 mph) on motorways, 80kmph (49 mph) outside built-up areas, and 50 kmph (31mph) in built-up areas. There are slightly different speed limits for motorbikes. It is illegal to carry spare petrol in the vehicle.
Documentation: A national driving licence is acceptable for EC nationals. EC nationals taking their own cars to Greece *must* obtain a Green Card, to top up the insurance cover to that provided by the car owner's domestic policy. It is no longer a legal requirement for visits of less than three months, but without it, insurance cover is limited to the minimum legal cover in Greece. Don't forget the car registration documents. Nationals of non-EC countries should contact the *ELPA*. *ELPA* (Grecian Automobile Touring Club) has organised a **road assistance** service on main roads, conditions of which have vastly improved. Contact: ELPA, 2-4 Messogion Avenue, 115 27 Athens. Tel: (1) 779 1615, or in an emergency 104 *or* 174. There are good repair shops in big towns and petrol is easily obtainable.
JOURNEY TIMES: The following chart gives approximate journey times (in hours and minutes) from Athens to other major cities and islands in Greece.

	Air	Road	Sea
Corfu	0.50	11.00	14.00
Crete	0.50	-	12.00
Mykonos	0.45	-	5.5
Rhodes	0.55	-	14.00
Thessaloniki	0.50	8.00	-
Thira	0.40	-	12.00

Note: The journey time by road to Corfu includes a sea crossing from Patras.

ACCOMMODATION

HOTELS: Reservations can be made through the *Hotel Chamber* at 6 Aristidou Street, Athens, or by writing directly to the hotels. The range of hotels can vary greatly both among the islands and on the mainland, from high class on larger islands and mainland to small seasonal chalets. Booking for the high season is essential. *Xenia* hotels are owned and often run by the GNTO. Small family hotels are a friendly alternative to the hotel chains. The Panhellenic Hotel Hoteliers Association has branches in Athens, Heraklion, Rhodes Town, Corfu Town and Thessaloniki. The Hellenic Chamber of Hotels is responsible for all hotels in Greece and can be contacted at 24 Stadiou Street, Athens 105 64, Greece. Tel: (1) 323 6641 *or* 323 3501. Fax: (1) 322 5449. Telex: 214269. **Grading:** Hotels are all officially classified as Luxury or rated on a scale from A to E. The category denotes what facilities must be offered and the price range that the hotelier is allowed to charge.
SELF-CATERING: Furnished rooms in private houses, service flats, apartments and villas are available. All types of accommodation can be arranged through tour operators in this country. The GNTO can provide a full and up-to-date list on request. **Grading:** As for hotels.
TRADITIONAL SETTLEMENTS: There are traditional settlements and hostels on Makrinitsa (Pilion), Vizitsa (Pilion), Milies (Pilion), Ia (Santorini), Mesta (Chios), Psara Island, Areopolis (Mani), Vathia (Mani), Papingo (Epirus), Koriskades (Central Greece), Monemvassia (Peloponnese) and Gythion (Peloponnese) which offer single, double or triple bedrooms with shower, or a 4-bed house. **Grading:** As for hotels.
CAMPING/CARAVANNING: There is a wide network of official campsites. For details contact the GNTO. It is not permitted to camp anywhere except registered sites.
YOUTH HOSTELS: Hostels in Athens can be found at 57, Kypselis Street, Athinia. Tel: (1) 822 5860, and at 20 Kallipoleos Street, Viron. There are 25 others throughout the country.
Note: Tourist police in the main tourist destinations of Greece are specially trained to assist visitors with accommodation, maps, timetables, details of places to visit or special events. All wear flag badges denoting which language(s) they are able to speak; do not hesitate to ask for help.

RESORTS & EXCURSIONS

For the purposes of clarity, information on *Resorts & Excursions* within Greece has been divided into 13 regional sections. These do not necessarily reflect administrative boundaries.
Note: Some of the beaches and seas of Greece are host to the threatened Loggerhead Turtle and the Monk Seal; visitors who find themselves in areas where they breed should keep their distance, behave quietly (this includes car noise), avoid leaving rubbish which may be dangerous (for example turtles may die after eating plastic bags which they mistake for jellyfish) and at night avoid showing lights.

Central Greece

Athens is in the region of Attica, which is characterised by calm beaches, and the pinewoods and thyme-covered slopes of Mount *Parnes*, *Hymettus* and *Pentelico*. The city of Athens is dominated by the flat-topped hill of the **Acropolis,** site of the 2400-year-old **Parthenon,** one of the most famous classical monuments in the world (which is beautifully lit at night by a mass of coloured lights), the *Theatre of Dionysius*, the *Doric Temple of Heiphaistos*, the *Roman Forum*, *Hadrian's Arch*, and the waterclock of Andronikos Kyrrhestes, commonly known as the *Tower of the Winds*. On the far side of the Acropolis is the restored *Odeon of Herod Atticus*, a superb theatre in which the open-air plays of the International Athens Festival are held from June to September. In the centre of Athens there are modern shops, restaurants, international-class hotels and nightclubs. The old quarter of the town, **Plaka**, which spreads around the Acropolis, provides a picturesque contrast with its famed flea market, small tavernas, craft shops and narrow winding alleys.
Piraeus, lying at the innermost point of the *Saronic Gulf* just outside Athens, is the main port of the town. From here ferries leave regularly for the islands and other points along the coast. An electric train service connects Athens and Piraeus.
SOUTHWARDS ALONG THE WEST COASTLINE: The **Apollo Beach** is one of the best developed tourist areas, stretching from **Piraeus** as far as **Cape Sounio** at the southern tip of the promontory. Marinas, well-appointed swimming beaches, small bays, modern hotel complexes, rented flats, numerous tavernas which specialise in fish foods, luxury-class restaurants and nightclubs are all attractions of the area.
Resorts (and their distance from Athens) include: *Paelo Faliro* (8km/5 miles), *Alimos* (11km/7 miles), *Glifada* (17km/11 miles), *Voula* (18.5km/11.5 miles), *Kavouri* (23km/14 miles), *Vouliagmeni* (24km/15 miles), *Vouliagmeni Lake* (a natural lake with medicinal waters, set in beautiful surroundings) (26km/16 miles), *Varkiza* (28km/17 miles), *Lagonissi* (40km/25 miles), *Anavissos* (51km/32 miles), and *Cape Sounio* (69km/43 miles).
Cape Sounio is a towering promontory which dominates the landscape for miles around. Here the superb ruins of the *Temple of Poseidon*, surrounded by steep access paths, crown the cape.
NORTHWARDS AROUND THE GULF OF CORINTH: Kineta (55km/34 miles from Athens), a coastal resort with an extensive beach, lies on the *Saronic Gulf* and can be reached on the Old Corinth road. **Porto Germeno** (73km/45 miles from Athens), **Psatha** (67km/42 miles) and **Alepohori** (61km/38 miles) are typical Attic villages, set in thick pinewoods, bordering on the *Gulf of Corinth*. Sheltered bays provide excellent swimming. Accommodation is available and there are numerous restaurants specialising in fish dishes. Further north, near the main road from Athens to Delphi, lie the southern slopes of **Mount Parnassus**, which towers 2457m (8061ft) over the Gulf of Corinth. Here the land forms a natural stone amphitheatre which houses the *Sanctuary of Apollo*, one of the most famous archaeological sites in Greece. **Delphi** (176km/109 miles from Athens) can be reached by road through Boeotia via Levadia and Arachova. This is the site of the famous Oracle, where rulers of Greece came for many centuries for political and moral guidance. The centre of the complex of temples is the *Doric Temple of Apollo* dating from the 4th century BC. *The Delphi Museum* contains the superb statue of the Charioteer, circa 475BC. **Itea**, ancient Chalkion, lies on the northern coast of the Corinthian Gulf. There is an excellent beach that skirts the olive trees and a good road leads to **Kira** where the remains of the ancient pier can still be seen at the bottom of the sea. Good bathing spots in **Phokida** include *Itea, Kira, Galaxidi, Eratini*, and the small islands of **Trizonia** and **Ai-Gianis.**
THE EAST COAST OF ATTICA: Stretching from **Cape Sounio** to **Skala Oropou**, there are a succession of resorts, set amid pine woods. These include (all distances are from Athens) *Lavrio* (52km/32 miles), *Porto Rafti* (38km/24 miles), *Loutsa* (30km/19 miles), *Rafina* (28km/17 miles), *Mati* (29km/18 miles), *Agios Andreas* (31km/19 miles), *Nea Makri* (33km/21 miles), *Schinias* (44km/27 miles), *Agia Marina* (47km/29 miles), and *Agii Apostoli* (44km/27 miles). In general there is a wide choice of hotels, rooms to rent, restaurants and tavernas.
THE SARONIC GULF ISLANDS: The Saronic Gulf stretches from the Attica coastline to the Peloponnese shores. The best known islands here are **Aegina, Salamis, Methana, Poros, Hydra, Spetses, Dokos, Spetsopoula** and the islets of **Angistri** and **Moni.** The Gulf is served by passenger ships, car ferries and fast-sailing hydrofoils. Passenger ships sail from the central harbour at **Piraeus** for Aegina, Methana, Poros, Hermione (Eermioni), Hydra and Spetses, while car ferries sail to Aegina, Methana and Poros. Special timetables cover small motorship sailings to **Agia Marina** and **Souvala** on the island of Aegina. Further information can be obtained from Piraeus Central Port Authority. Tel: (Piraeus) 452 0910. Fast hydrofoil services supplement steamer services. For Aegina, sailings are from the central harbour at Piraeus. For Methana, Poros, Hydra, Hermione, Porto-Heli, Spetses, Leonidio, Nauplia, Kythera, Neapolis and Monemvassia, sailings are from the Zea Marina, close to Piraeus. A local Piraeus bus connects the terminus with Zea Marina. One-day cruises to the islands of Aegina, Poros and Hydra leave daily throughout the year from Flisvos Marina at Paleo Faliro.
Salamis, close to Piraeus, enjoys a frequent shuttle service by motor sailing vessels, *caiques*, from nearby Piraeus and from **Perama** across the Straits. The island has good roads and a network of bus and taxi services. At **Eandio** there are the remains of ancient Telamon. Sandy beaches are at **Kaki Vigla, Moulki, Kanakia** and **Peristeria.** There are no large hotels.
Aegina (Egina) is a favourite among holidaymakers for its excellent beaches, clear seas and fine climate. The terrain is flat and cycling is popular. Other means of transport are buses, taxis and horsedrawn carriages. There are beauty spots and beaches at **Plakakia, Agia Marina, Faros** and **Marathonas. Angistri** and **Moni** are two small wooded islands which offer opportunities for excursions.
Methana, jutting out from the Peloponnese peninsula, is renowned for its medieval springs at Methana town

ATHENS

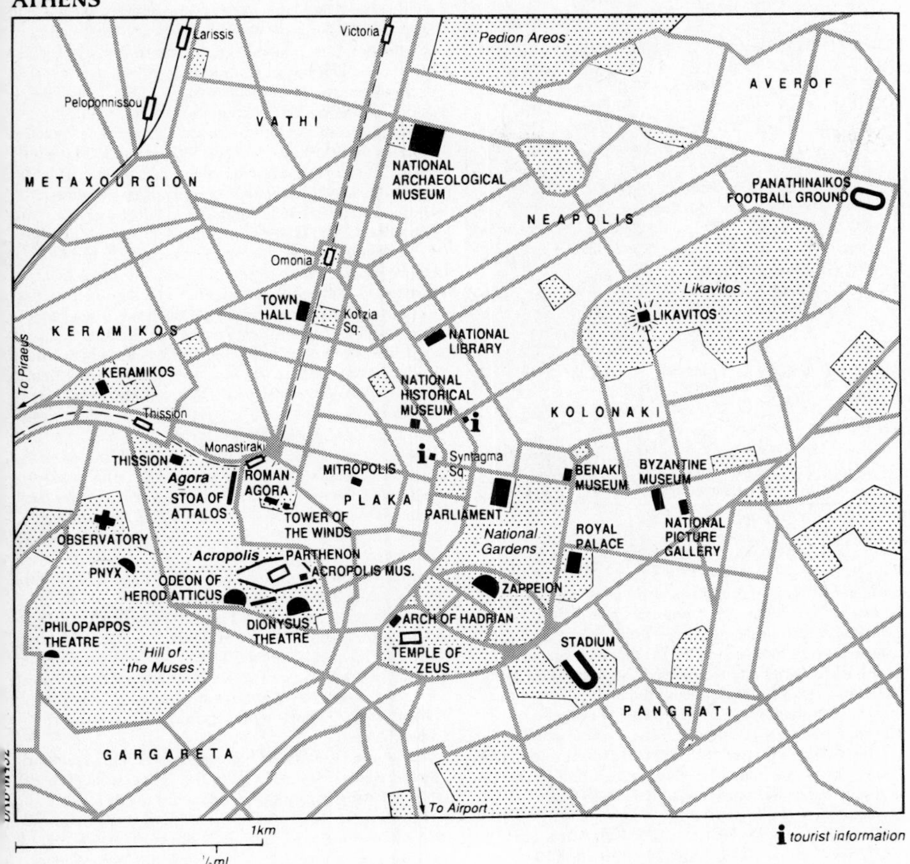

and modernised hydrotherapy installations run by the National Tourist Organisation. Methana attracts a large number of visitors every year.

Poros is a thickly wooded island lying just off the Peloponnesian mainland township of **Galatas**. It is made up of two islands, linked by a narrow neck of land: **Calavria** and **Sphaeria** on which the town of Poros is built. Ferries leave for the mainland where there is a famous lemon grove and the remains of ancient Trizina, the legendary birthplace of Theseus. Sandy beaches, at **Askeli** and **Neorio**, are also accessible by ferry.

Hydra is a cosmopolitan island offering an active nightlife. Beaches are at **Kamina, Molos, Palamida, Bisti** and **Mandraki** and the sea cave of *Bariami* has been converted into a swimming pool; many beaches are more easily reached by boat. The island does not allow any motorised transport. There is only a small number of hotel rooms and most visitors hire or own their accommodation. A large (closed) monastery is centred at the highest point of the island.

Spetses lies at the southern extremity of the Saronic Gulf. It has long been a holiday resort and has good hotels and entertainment facilities. Seaside resorts include *Zogeria, Agia Marina, Agia Anangiri* and *Agia Pasaskevi*.

The Peloponnese

Corinth is the most convenient starting point for a tour of the seven provinces of the **Peloponnese**, separated from central Greece by the *Canal of Corinth*. **Corinth** was once a city state rival of Athens and a powerful maritime state. The old town of Corinth, destroyed by earthquake in 1858, was built up only to be destroyed again in 1928. The modern city, despite its beautiful location, is unremarkable. 8km (5 miles) away, on the northern slopes of *Akorinthos Mountain*, are the ruins of ancient Corinth, the capital of Roman Greece, where well-preserved Roman remains and the columns of the temple of Apollo are still to be seen. South of Corinth lies the impressive open-air theatre of Epidaurus, which offers performances at weekends during the Epidaurus Festival from July to August. Other archaeological sites in the area include the famous *Lion Gate* at **Mycenae** where it is possible to stay overnight in the pavilion; the ancient temple, theatre and sanctuary at **Argos**; and the *Heraion* near the village of **Perahora.** There are museums at Corinth, **Nauplia** and **Epidaurus.**

WEST AND SOUTHWEST FROM CORINTH: From Corinth the coast road passes the villages of **Vrahati, Kokkoni** and **Kiato** before it reaches the popular coastal resort of **Xylokastra**, where there is a magnificent view of the *Parnassus* and *Elikon* mountains. After the *Kiato Bridge*, a road leads high into the mountains and the extensive fir forests round **Goura**. Another mountain road leads inland from **Xylokastra** to the cool alpine climate of **Trikala** at *Mount Zira*, the main ski centre of the south.

WESTERN PELOPONNESE: Scores of bays and sandy beaches deck the coastline. Several beaches, including *Katakolo* and *Agios Andreas* (to the west of Pirgos) and *Kourouta* and *Kyllini* (to the north), offer modern amenities. **Patras** is a thriving commercial and industrial centre, the third most important town in Greece and its main western port. Distinctive for its arcaded streets, Patras is also a pleasant seaside resort with some good hotels. It is an ideal base for visitors to the region. West of Patras is Lapas and, further south, are *Kourouta* and *Palouki* beaches, connected by a daily bus to **Amaliada**.

At **Kyllini** there are mineral springs, hydropathic installations and a number of new hotels. With a public beach, it is a lively resort as well as a spa. East of Patras there are beaches at **Psathopirgos, Lambiri, Longos, Selianitika, Kounoupeli** and **Kalogria.** A tiny train climbs up the *Vouraikos Gorge* from **Diakofto** to **Kalavanta**. Other resorts include *Vartholomio, Niko Leika* (Egio), *Lakopetra*, and *Metoni*. A road runs 77km (48 miles) southeast of Patras through superb mountain scenery to **Kalavrita**. **Olympia**, the original site of the games where the flame is still lit, can be reached by the mountain road from Kalavrita. At Olympia, there are the ruins of Atlas, a museum of the *Olympic Games* and two archaeological museums. Olympia can be reached (a) by car along the coast of **Ahaia** or from **Tripoli** in the central Peloponnese – both of the drives are very interesting, so one may try the 334km (208-mile) coast route via Patras and Pirgos one way, returning via Tripoli; (b) by train (Athens–Patras–Pirgos–Olympia). From Olympia the road turns east and follows the Alfios River through the wild Arcadian Mountains. There is a spa at **Loutra**. The road becomes hair-raising with a sheer drop of 300m (1000ft) after **Isounda**, and should only be attempted by the adventurous. The main road from Olympia to Tripoli is less treacherous, going down from the mountains to the plain of Tripoli. At **Bassae** is the well-preserved temple of the Epicurian Apollo. At **Kaifa** there is a hot-spring resort built on an island in the middle of the lake. The picturesque coast of the western Peloponnese offers plenty of opportunities for swimming. Between Kyllini and Kiparissia, the beaches at **Kastro, Loutra Kyllinis, Kourouta, Skafidia, Katakolo, Kaifa** and **Kiparissia** are popular.

SOUTHEAST OF CORINTH: There are beaches at **Loutraki**, a well-known resort with restaurants, modern shops, hotels and cinemas; at *Nea Kios* near **Argos**; *Assini Kosta* in the south and *Tolo*. On the southern tip of the promontory, southeast of Corinth, is the resort of **Porto-Heli**, which has attractive beaches, some quite unspoilt, and good swimming. With a good road network – making trips to interesting places such as **Nauplia** and **Epidaurus** convenient – ample hotel accommodation, and many opportunities for sea sports, Porto-Heli is a popular summer resort. There is a sea connection between Porto-Heli and the Saronic Gulf Islands and a ferry from the island of Spetses. On the east coast **Nafplio** is a well-preserved Venetian town which overlooks a lovely bay.

SOUTHERN PELOPONNESE: The once powerful city state of **Sparta** is notorious in ancient history for the austerity of its regime, but it is now a provincial town with parks, broad avenues and a pleasant atmosphere. At **Mystra**, 4km (2.5 miles) away, lie the ruins of a Byzantine city and, to the north, are the *Taigetos* and *Parnon* mountains. South of Sparta, the port of **Githio** is a good starting point for exploring the Mani area. There are caves with underground lakes and rivers at **Glifada** and **Alepotripa** in the Diros region. The island of **Kythera** (Kithira) lies 14 nautical miles off **Kavo Maleas** on the southernmost tip of the Peloponnese. Ships dock at **Agia Pelagia** near a beautiful stretch of coastline and bathing beach. The capital, Kythera, 30km (19 miles) south, is easily reached on the main roadway which crosses the island. It is a neat hamlet, built on a hillside overlooking the sea, which is crowned by a Venetian castle. **Kapsali** is the main harbour. Other resorts include *Anarnti, Areopolis, Gytheion, Monemvassia* and *Mystra*.

Euboea

The island of **Euboea** (or **Evia**) is the second largest in Greece after Crete. A main highway and ferry boats from several terminals connect this island, of great natural beauty and scenic variety, to the mainland. Euboea is brisk with tourist traffic, but there are still many peaceful and unspoilt villages. There are large fertile valleys, sandy beaches, organised bathing facilities, secluded coves and wooded mountainsides, ideal for climbing. Resorts include *Halkida, Malakonta, Lefkanti, Kambos, Amarinthos, Almiropotamos, Marmari, Honeftiko, Limni, Agiokambos, Edipsos, Agios Georgios, Nea Stira, Karistos, Kimi* and *Rovies*.

On the other side of the Northern Euboean Gulf is the prefecture of **Fthiotida** with mountains, valleys, rivers, numerous medicinal springs, woodland, and sandy beaches. There are some excellent beaches at **Kamena Vourla**, one of the best-known and most frequented spas. **Skala** also has fine bathing beaches and, west of **Lamia**, the capital of the region, is the *Ipati Spa* with modern hydrotherapy facilities.

Winter sports enthusiasts should visit the *Mount Parnassus Winter Sports Resort*, 27km (17 miles) from **Arachova** and 17km (11 miles) from **Amfiklia**. The Greek National Tourist Organisation (GNTO) installations are located at **Fterolaka** and at **Kelaria**, at an altitude of 1600–2250m (5250–7380ft). The centre is open daily from December to April between 0900-1600 hours. In **Gerondovrahos**, at an altitude of 1800m (5910ft) on *Mount Parnassus*, there is a ski centre run by the Athenian Ski Club.

Other resorts include *Agios Konstandinos, Arkitsa* and *Livanates*.

Thessaly

The fertile plain of **Thessaly** in Central Greece is surrounded by *Mount Pindus, Olympus, Pelion, Orthrys, Ossa* and *Agrapha*. The *River Pinios*, flowing down from the western slopes of the Pindus, cuts Thessaly in two and, passing through the valley of **Tempi**, meets the sea.

Olympus, home of the immortal gods and land of the Centaurs, is only one of the many places in Thessaly where relics of ancient Greece can be seen and, on the western edge of the plain of Thessaly, just as the Pindus range begins to form, there are 24 perpendicular rocks on which Byzantine monks built their monastic community, the *Meteora*, about 600 years ago.

Nearby resorts include *Agiokambos, Elati, Kalambaka, Kardista, Larissa, Neraida, Smokovo* and *Trikala*.

At the northernmost point of *Pagassitikos Bay* is the port of **Volos**, traditionally the launching place of Jason and the Argonauts in their search for the Golden Fleece. There are several seaside villages along the *Pagasitic*

Gulf, including **Agria**, 7km (4 miles) southeast of Volos. Northeast of Volos, there are hill villages and seaside towns on the Aegean; notably **Portaria, Makrinitsa, Hania, Zagora, Horefto, Ai-Gianis** and **Tsangarada.** Other coastal resorts include *Afissos, Agios Loanis, Agios Lavrendis, Alikes, Kala Nera, Milies, Vizitsa* (where there are traditional mansions, some of which are being renovated by the National Tourist Board of Greece as guest-houses), *Tri Keri, Nea Anhialos, Platania, Milopotapos.* There are winter sports centres on *Mount Pelion*.

Epirus

Epirus, the northwest corner of the Greek peninsula, is the most mountainous region in Greece. **Parga** lies 77km (48 miles) from **Preveza** and 90km (56 miles) from Arta. It is a small, picturesque town built in a semi-circle round the bay. Flanked by small inlets, coves, sandy beaches and islets, Parga is surrounded by wooded hills. Going north out of **Janene,** the road leads through the **Vikos Gorge**, the canyon formed by the *River Aoos*, which houses 46 pretty villages, known as the **Zagorokozia.** The Gorge is set in the *Vikos-Aoos National Park*, where the small villages of **Micro** and **Mega Papingo** are also located.

There are resorts at *Arta, Dodoni, Igoumenitsa, Janene, Katrossikia, Metsovo, Plataria, Preveza* and *Skamneli.* Roman ruins can be seen at *Nikopolis, Kassopi, Messopotamos* and *Dodoni.*

Macedonia

Macedonia stands slightly apart from the rest of the country. Part of Greece for little more than two generations, its scenery and climate have more in common with the adjoining Balkans. Though bitterly cold in winter, this is still a particularly beautiful part of Greece, rich in historical monuments and archaeological sites. In the area around **Florina**, are the lakes including the dramatic *Prespa* basin. **Grevena**, in the southern part of Macedonia, is mountainous, with the **Pindus** range rising to the west and the **Hassia** range to the north. The unspoilt villages in the area are ideal for those in search of peace and quiet. **Platamonas,** on the west coast, is a popular summer resort, with camping grounds and supervised swimming beaches.

Other northern resorts include *Aridea, Gianitsa, Edessa, Skidra, Drossopigi, Nermfeon* and *Kastoria.* In the south, there are more resorts at *Perivoli, Kozani, Neapolis Petrana, Ptolemaida, Siatista, Kato Vermion, Naoussa* and *Veria.* Coastal resorts include *Katerini, Korinos, Lertokana, Litokoro, Makrigialos, Methoni, Paralia* and *Plaka.* One of Greece's largest sports centres is at **Kato Vermio** (Seli), near **Naoussa.**

Thessaloniki is the second largest city in Greece. A modern coastal town, it contains much Byzantine art as well as churches and museums including the superb *Archaelogical Museum.* The neighbouring villages and suburbs offer good walks and cafés, but beaches are often unclean. There are many historical sites in Thessaloniki, including the *Arch of Galerius* built in AD 297; ruins of the *Roman agora* (which are still being excavated), Roman market, theatre and Roman baths; **Exedra** close to the *Egnatian Way;* **Nymphaion**, the circular building whose cisterns now serve as the chapel of *Agios Ioannis Prodromis;* the *Rotunda* and the fine churches including the 8th-century *Ayia Sofia.* The newly-restored and striking *White Tower* affords an excellent view.

Northeast of Thessaloniki is the mountainous and wooded peninsula of **Halkidiki** (Chalcidice), the highlight of eastern Macedonia. There are numerous archaeological sites, including the *Temple of Zeus Ammon* on the shore at **Kalithea** and the ruins of ancient *Olynthos* on **Kassandra**. The countryside, with pinewoods and olive groves, is ideal for peaceful walks. Kassandra and **Sithonia** shelter the north's best beaches and are both fast-growing holiday destinations. Here also is the religious community of *Mount Athos*, which can only be visited by men with a special permit. No women are allowed in. This is issued by the Ministry of Foreign Affairs (tel: (01) 361 0581) or by the Ministry of Northern Greece, Directorate of Civil Affairs at Odus El Venizelou 48, Thessaloniki. (tel: 031) 264 321. Overnight stays are forbidden for those without proven religious or scientific interests in the area.

In east Macedonia, on the road from **Drama** to **Kavala**, lies **Philippi.** Named after the father of Alexander the Great, it is known to be the site of the defeat of Caesar's murderers, Brutus and Cassius, by Octavius in 42BC, and of the first recorded preaching of St Paul in Greece. Today it is one of Macedonia's most extensive archaeological sites.

Thassos lies off the coast of eastern Macedonia. It is thickly wooded with plane, oak, cedar and olive groves. Thassos has good beaches for swimming and fishing at **Makriamos, Arhangelos, Agios Ioannis, Limenas, Potos** and **Pefkari.** The islet of **Thassopoula** just offshore can be reached by caique. On the north shore is the capital, **Limenas,** which has a museum. There are archaeological sites nearby including the *Temple of Pythian Apollo*, the agora, the theatres and the *Choregic Monument* set inside the sanctuary of Dionysus. **Thassos** can be reached by ferry from Keramoti or Kavala on the mainland.

Kavala is a modern, commercial seaside port which still retains many traditional features, particularly in the town centre. There are hotels, beaches, museums, restaurants and tavernas as well as an aqueduct and Byzantine citadel. Boats can be hired for fishing, water-skiing and sailing. Popular sandy beaches are at **Kalamitsa, Batis** and **Toska,** and secluded ones at **Iraklitsa** and **Peramos**. There are also some little-known stalactite and stalagmite caves and many archaeological sites nearby. **Mount Pangaion** is a good area for hunting and climbing.

Thrace

Going east from Macedonia the villages become more oriental in style. **Xanthi** is an attractive small town clinging to the hilly sides of the *Eskeje Remma Valley*. Southwest of Xanthi is **Avdira.** Nearby **Lagos**, built on the narrow strip of land in the lagoon is rich in wildfowl. One of the best northern beaches is 8km (5 miles) east of **Fanari.** The main road dips down to the coast before going inland again to **Komotini**, further east, then follows the coast via **Nia Hili** to **Alexandroupolis**, which has an archaeological museum of local finds. North from here is **Soufli**, famous for its silks.

The Ionian Islands

The Ionian Islands lie off the west coast of mainland Greece. Comparatively isolated from each other in the past, each of the six islands has developed differently.

Corfu (Kerkira) is the northernmost island of Western Greece. Its natural beauty has led to a degree of commercialisation. The capital, also called Corfu, has two small harbours with large Venetian fortresses. With Italian, French and English influences evident in its architecture, Corfu is a typical Ionian island town. It is made up of wide avenues and large squares, among them the graceful *Spianada* or Esplanade, cobbled alleyways, arches and colonnades. Recommended sights are the *Archaeological Museum*, which houses finds from local archaeological excavations; the *Museum of Asiatic Art;* the *Town Hall*, a splendid example of Venetian architecture (built in 1663); the 12th-century Byzantine *Church of St Jason and Sosipater* and the *Church of Saint Spyridon.* Good roads lead out of Corfu town to excellent harbours suitable for swimming and fishing, such as **Roda, Kassiopi** and **Douloura,** and to traditional inland villages such as **Ano Korakiana, Ano Garouna, Doukades, Agii Douli** and **Pelekas** where, from the top of its rocky hill, the sunset can be superb. In the region of Pelekas lies *Ropa's Meadow* (Livaditou Ropa), Corfu's excellent golf course. On the western side of the island the roads thread their way through olive and orange groves, pine trees and cypresses. Resorts on Corfu include *Kanoni*, where a narrow causeway leads to the *Monastery of Vlaherni; Perama; Benitses; Moraitika; Messongi; Dassia; Gouvia; Gastouri* and the museum palace *The Achilleion*, partly converted into a casino; *Ipsos* and *Paleokastritsa.*

Paxi, as yet undeveloped, is the smallest of the Ionians and has quiet sandy beaches, bays, rocky promontories and caves. Dense grapevines and olive groves cover the island. The main resort is *Giaios* (or Paxi), on the east coast. Excursions can be made to **Andipaxi,** a tiny island 3 miles to the south of Paxi.

Levkas (Lefkada), joined by a narrow strip of land to the Greek mainland, is a green and fertile island which is surrounded by many islets. Excursions, involving some mountain climbing, can be made in the centre of Levkas, near the *Stavrota Mountain.* There is good swimming and fishing in the villages of **Agios Nikitas** on the northwestern coast, **Ligia** on the southeastern coast or **Vassiliki** (which is also popular with windsurfers) on the southwestern coast.

Cephalonia (Kefalonia) has beaches at **Makri** and **Plati, Yialos, Skala, Fiskardo** and in the Palli district close to the *Monastery of Kepourio.* The mountainous scenery (including the 1600-metre *Mount Enos*) is dramatic and the island has a good network of roads. At **Assos** there is a castle and in the capital, **Argostoli**, an *Archaeological Museum* and *Folk Art Museum.*

Ithaca (Ithaki) is close to Cephalonia, and is well known for being the island home of the great Odysseus, hero of the Trojan war. The small and mountainous island is renowned for its coves. **Vathi**, the capital, is small, and its white houses fan out in a mounting semi-circle at one end of the bay. There are beaches at **Kuoni**, south of Frikies, and from here there is a road going to *Loizos' cave*, where traces of the worship of Artemis, Hera and Athena have been found.

Zante (Zakinthos) is the southernmost island in the Ionian group. Zante is also the name of the capital, where in the town museum there are Ionian historic treasures. In the southeast is the huge bay of *Laganas*, where there are numerous hotels and restaurants and lively nightlife. There are more sandy beaches at *Argassi, Alikes* and *Tsilivi*, 3km (2 miles) from the town of Zante.

Crete

The largest and most southerly Greek island, Crete is rich in historical remains and scenic variety. Along the northern shores there are modern resorts. Alongside lie the scattered remains of older civilizations – Minoan palaces, Byzantine churches, Venetian castles and sites of more recent struggles. Crete is divided into four prefectures – **Chanea** (Hania), **Rethymnon** (Rethimno), **Heraklion** (Iraklion) and **Agios Nikolaos** – and has a good road network and regular communications.

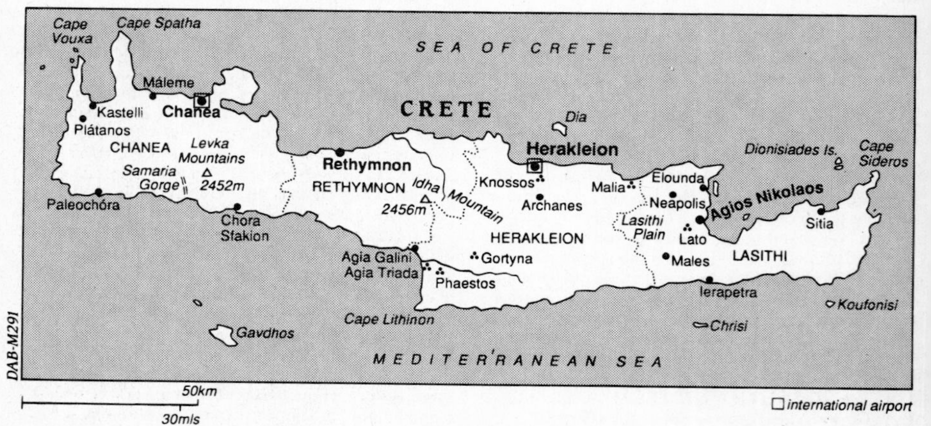

Heraklion, the largest and busiest town on the island, has a variety of nightlife and sightseeing to offer. In the prefecture of Heraklion are three of the most important Minoan centres – *Knossos, Phaestos* and *Malia*. Crete is well known as the setting for the battle between Theseus and the Minotaur, and the ruins of Knossos are popularly held to be the site of the labyrinth.
East of Heraklion is **Agios Nikolaos**, one of the best-known holiday resorts on the island. As a result it is very crowded in the high season. Much of the east coast of Crete has been developed specifically as a tourist area and is a popular target for package tours. The prefecture of Rethymnon combines the gentle scenery of the northern and southern coastlines with the precipitous gorges of the *Idi* and *White Mountains*. The main town, **Rethymnon**, on the northern coast, is an hour and a half's bus ride west from the airport. There is a well-preserved Venetian fort behind the harbour and, like the other large towns on the north coast, Venetian influence is apparent in the architecture.
In the Lasithi region, **Elounda** and **Ierapetra** are the most developed resorts and, at the western end of the island, is the fertile region of Chanea (Xania). **Chanea**, the main town, has a mixture of modern, neo-classical and Venetian architecture. Places to visit are the popular seaside resorts of *Plátanos, Máeme* and *Kolimbari;* the freshwater springs at **Falarsana**; and the *Samaria Gorge*, the longest in Europe.
Other resorts include *Agia Galini, Agia Mannia, Agia Plagia, Amnissos, Amoudara, Chanea, Elounda, Gouves, Heraklion, Kokini Hani, Limenas Hersonissou, Malia, Seteia* and *Stalida*.

The Dodecanese

This cluster of 12 islands lies to the southeast of the Greek mainland. Distances between the islands are fairly small, so visitors can easily hop from one to another, swapping, say, the relative sophistication of **Rhodes** and **Cos** for the calmer and simpler life on **Tilos** or **Astipalaia.**
Rhodes is one of the most popular and best-developed islands in the Mediterranean. It offers international-class hotels, varied nightlife, sports facilities and duty-free shopping. It has 370km (230 miles) of coastline and a good, well-surfaced road network. Bus services bring most of the towns and villages within easy reach of the capital. Travel agents organise daily sightseeing trips to the archaeological sites and beauty spots. Rhodes is 267 nautical miles from Piraeus and is connected by boat services. Rhodes airport is international and there are daily direct flights from Athens. The main town, also called Rhodes, lies on the very northern tip of the island. It is made up of two distinct parts, the new town and the old town which stands within the walls of the medieval fortress. The 15th-century *Knight's Hospital* is now an archaeological museum which houses the celebrated Aphrodite of Rhodes. The *Palace of the Grand Masters* also has a splendid collection. 2km (1.2 miles) to the west of Rhodes town lies the *Acropolis* of ancient Rhodes. Many impressive ruins can still be seen, including the *Temple of Apollo* and a theatre and stadium, which date back to the 2nd century BC.
At **Filerimos**, 15km (9miles) from Rhodes, lie the ruins of ancient **Ialisos**. The view from the Acropolis is spectacular. Ancient **Kameiros**, 25km (16 miles) southwest of Ialisos, is one of the few archaeological sites in Greece where many buildings and monuments from the Hellenistic period can still be seen.
56km (35 miles) to the southeast of Rhodes is *Lindos*, with its well-preserved remains scattered on the ancient Acropolis.
There are resorts at *Faliraki, Ixia, Kalithea, Kremasti, Afandou Golf, Ialisos, Kritinia, Lindos* and *Profitis Elias*.
Rhodes is a favourite for sports enthusiasts: there is good fishing at **Lindos, Kameiros** and **Genadi** and there are facilities for water-skiing, sailing, tennis, basketball and golf at sports grounds and clubs all over the island.
Conducted tours: By coach – half-day: daily tour of the town, excursions to **Lindos, Kamiros, Ialisos, Butterfly Valley** and 'Rhodes By Night' which includes an evening meal and folk dances; whole day: tour of Byzantine antiquities.
Cruises: There is a whole-day cruise along the east coast of Rhodes to **Simi** and **Panormitis** and conducted tours to **Cos, Halki, Tilos, Nissiros** and **Patmos.**
Excursions by air: To Athens, Nauplia, Epidaurus, Corinth (2 days), Heraklion (museum), Knossos, Phaestos, Gortys and Agia Triada (3 days).
Inter-island connections by air: Flights are available between Rhodes and Cos, Karpathos, Heraklion (Crete), Mykonos, Thera (Santorini) and Kassos.
Cos (Kos) is a fertile island with a mild climate, sandy beaches (some of which have black volcanic sand) and ample hotel accommodation. Most places of historical and sightseeing interest lie within the pretty main town of the same name, and its immediate surroundings, and can be easily visited on foot or by hiring a bicycle. The *Plane Tree of Hippocrates*, a massive tree with a trunk 12m (39ft) in circumference, is near here, as is the castle of the *Knights of St John*, an impressive example of medieval defensive architecture with its double wall and moat; an ancient agora with remains of Greek buildings of the 4th to 2nd centuries BC; the *Temple of Dionysius*; the *Odeon;* a restored Roman villa with mosaic decorations; some Roman Baths; and a *Gymnasium* of the Hellenistic period (2nd century BC) with a restored colonnade of Xytos. The beaches towards **Lambi**, to the north of Cos, and towards **Agios Fokas**, to the south, are being developed. Places to visit include **Asfendiou, Kardamena, Pili,** the old fortress at **Palio Pili**, the fishing villages of **Marmari** and **Mastihari, Kefalos** with its pleasant beach and *Palatia* where ruins of *Astipalaia*, the ancient capital of Cos, survive.
Other resorts include *Antimahia, Lambi Milos Lappa* and *Psalidi*.
There are frequent daily flights to the mainland, and frequent connections by ship to Piraeus. Local steamship lines link Cos with Rhodes and Kalimnos and with Nissiros.
Conducted Tours: There is a daily coach tour of the island.
Cruises: There are day cruises to **Kalymnos, Nissiros** (with a visit to its volcano), **Patmos** (with a visit to the monastery and *Grotto of St John the Baptist*) and to **Pserimos** and its splendid swimming beach.
Patmos lies 140 nautical miles from Piraeus, with which it is connected by steamship services. It is also linked with the Dodecanese group of islands by an inter-island boat service. The nearby isles of **Fourni, Lipsi** and **Leros** are easily accessible from Patmos. The island, a place of pilgrimage, is dominated by the massive and formidable *Monastery of St John the Divine* in **Hora**. The 'sacred grotto', where St John received and dictated 'Revelations', is enshrined in the *Church of the Apocalypse*, just below the Monastery. Hora, the island capital, lies 2km (1.2 miles) away from the port of **Skala** and can be reached by bus or taxi. It is an extraordinary sight: whitewashed houses arranged along maze-like alleys too narrow for cars, clustered around the base of the monastery. Patmos has fine beaches at *Grikos, Meloi, Netia, Diakofit* and around *Kambos Bay*, which can be reached by motor launch or by car from Skala. Excursions to the monasteries of *Panagia Apolou* and *Panagia Geranou* are particularly pleasant.
Kalymnos lies 180 nautical miles from Piraeus, with which it is connected by regular steamship services. An inter-island boat service also links Kalymnos with other islands of the Dodecanese. Rocky and barren on the whole, Kalymnos is famous for its sponge fishing – a tradition which is expressed in many folk songs and local dances. Along the west coast of the island there are several resorts, including *Linaria, Mirties* and *Massouri*. Excursions can be made to the stalagmite and stalactite *Grotto of Spilia Kefalas* (35 minutes by motor launch); to the health springs at **Therma** (1km/0.6 miles to the south of the Kalymnos town); and to **Horio,** the old capital which stands below the medieval castle. Near Horio are the remains of the Franco-Byzantine fortress, *Pera-Kastro*, and the traces of the *Church of Christ of Jerusalem*, built towards the end of the 4th century AD. To the southwest lie the monasteries of *Evangelistria* and *Agia Ekaterini*, both of which have guest-houses. There are boat trips to the nearby isles of **Telendos** and **Pserimos**, ideal for swimming and fishing.
Simi, a predominantly rocky island, lies 235 nautical miles from Piraeus and 25 nautical miles from Rhodes. The steamship line that serves the rest of the Dodecanese calls at Simi. The beach at **Pedi** is good for swimming and the bays of *Nanou, Marathoundas* and *Niborio* can be reached by motor launch. Nearby are the deserted islands of **Seskli** and **Nemo,** ideal for fishing.
Karpathos is a mountainous island with fertile valleys and plains. Piraeus lies 227 nautical miles away while Rhodes, with which it is connected by steamship and summer flights, is only 89 nautical miles away. The island capital, **Pigadia**, lies in a wide, curving bay on the east coast. Its small port of **Possi** is a natural harbour and there are good beaches nearby. Transport is provided by buses and taxis while motor launches serve the coastal areas. Attractive spots are *Aperi, Volada, Mirtonas, Othos, Messohori* and its beautiful bathing beach, *Agia Marina*, the fishing port **Finiki,** and **Arkassa.** The northern part of Karpathos is dominated by the densely forested mountain of *Profitis Ilias* (1140m/3740ft). From the small harbour of **Diafani,** on the northern coast, a road will take you to **Olimbos,** a charming village where ancient traditions and customs are very much alive. Excursions can be made to the northern headland of Karpathos and the tiny isle of **Saria,** where the remains of the ancient city of **Nissiros** can be seen (access is by motor launch from Diafani), and to *Kira-Panagia*, a picturesque bay with a fine beach and monastery.
Leros, a mountainous but extensively cultivated island, lies 169 nautical miles from Piraeus. Excursions can be made to the coastal villages of **Agia Marina, Koukouli, Kithoni, Panagies, Blefouti, Gourna, Lepida** and **Temenia.** Traces of the island's past glory include the Franco-Byzantine fort overlooking the capital town, **Platanos**, and the ruins of the Byzantine castle on *Mount Kasteli*, to the northwest. **Leros** is ideal for fishing and small craft can be hired. Laki, one of the largest natural harbours in the Mediterranean, lies 3km (2 miles) from Platanos. The villages of Leros can be reached by taxi along well-paved roads. Old customs and traditions also survive on Leros: the celebrations at Carnival time are reminiscent of the ancient Dionysian festivities.
Tilos, lying 290 nautical miles from Piraeus and only 49 nautical miles northwest of Rhodes, is an island neglected by tourists. It is a hilly island with many isolated and unspoilt beaches. Its few inhabitants live at **Livadia**, a natural port, and at **Megalo Horio** which is crowned by a medieval castle. There are good bathing beaches at *Livadia, Agios Antonios* and *Plaka*. Mules and donkeys are the major forms of transport. Almost all coastal regions offer splendid fishing and boats are available for hire.
Nissiros is connected with Piraeus (200 nautical miles) and Rhodes (60 nautical miles) by regular steamship service. Only 42 sq km (16 sq miles) in area, Nissiros seems larger, due to the massive but inactive volcano which towers over the island. The capital, **Mandraki,** is built below the medieval castle and *Monastery of Panagia Spiliani*. 8km (5 miles) southwest of Mandraki lie the remains of the ancient Acropolis with its Pelasgian walls, still well preserved in many places. The fishing village of **Pali** has a good beach where there is excellent swimming.
Halki, a small hilly island with many unspoilt beaches, lies 302 nautical miles from Piraeus and 35 nautical miles from Rhodes. The steamship line, which serves all the small islands of the Dodecanese, calls at Halki. There are no cars or buses on this peaceful island but horses and small motorboats can be hired. The small population of Halki busies itself with fishing and sponge diving. The capital, **Niborio**, is built in tiers, and from the midst of its squat white houses rises the tall bell-tower of **Agios Nikolaos.** Nissiros's best bathing beach is nearby.
Kastelorizo (Megisti), the easternmost of the islands in the Aegean Sea, is a mere 9 sq km (6 sq miles) in area. It is connected to nearby Rhodes by a twice-weekly boat. Above the houses, on a high rock, rises an old castle which the Knights of St John reconstructed in the 14th century. The fascinating *Grotto of Parasta*, which can be reached by boat, is to the southeast of the island. There are beaches next to the harbour at **Agios Stefanos** and on the uninhabited isle of **Agios Georgios** (10 minutes by motorboat).
Astipalaia, mountainous but fertile, has a coastline 110km (68 miles) long, indented with beautiful bays. It can be reached from Piraeus, 165 nautical miles away, by the steamship line which links the Dodecanese.
Astipalaia offers peace and quiet. The capital, also called Astipalaia, is dominated by its Franco-Byzantine castle. The most beautiful parts of the island are **Livadi** and **Maltezana** where there are fine sandy beaches.
Kassos lies between Crete and Karpathos from which it is separated by only 3 nautical miles. Piraeus is 215 nautical miles away and Rhodes 94 nautical miles. Like all the small islands in the Dodecanese group it is served by an inter-island steamship line. **Emborios,** the port, and **Fri,**

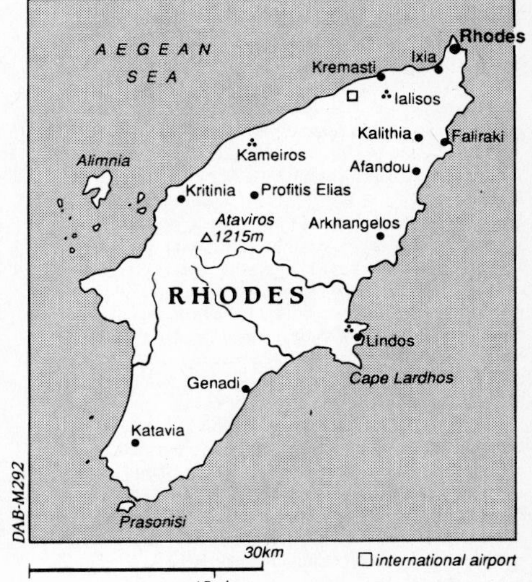

the principal town, are picturesque. **Selai,** a cave to the west of the village of **Agia Marina,** is filled with stalactites of various formations. Nearby there are remains of an ancient wall. Non-asphalt roads and country paths lead to pretty villages such as **Panagia, Arvanitohori** and **Poli.** The isle of **Armathia** can be reached by boat.
Climate: In the summer months (June to September) the temperature averages between 77-87°F. In the winter (October to May) the temperature normally averages between 53-63°F.

Northeast Aegean Islands

This group of islands, fairly widely scattered in the waters of the northeast Aegean, includes **Chios** (Hios), **Samos, Lesbos** (Lesvos), **Lemnos** (Limnos), **Ikaria** and the smaller islets around them.
Lemnos, 188 nautical miles from Piraeus, is still relatively unknown to the main tourist stream. **Mirina,** its capital, is built over the ancient city of the same name and has a museum housing exhibits from the island's history. There is a swimming beach nearby. At **Nea Koutali,** pinewoods reach down to the sea. Exactly opposite Nea Koutali, on the eastern shore of the large bay, is **Moudros,** a charming town with attractive houses, a stately church and good beaches. Shellfish and strong local wine are specialities. Lemnos is linked to Athens and Thessaloniki by air, and to Kimi, Agios Efstratios, Kavala, Samonthraki, Alexandroupolis, Mitilini, Thessaloniki, Agios Konstantinos and the islands of the Sporades and the Dodecanese by steamer service.
Lesbos is 118 nautical miles from Piraeus and is the largest island in this group, with vast olive groves, shady pine woods, good beaches and picturesque monasteries. The capital, **Mitilini,** has a bathing beach with good facilities at *Tzamakia*. There are other beaches at **Vateron, Petra, Skala Eftalou, Agios Issidoros** (pebble beach) and along the *Gulf of Kaloni* on the east coast of the island. At **Loutra Thermis** there are therapeutic springs which have been known since antiquity.
Mithimna, or Molivos, in the north of the island, is a meeting place for artists from all over the world.
Lesbos is linked to Athens by air and to Piraeus, Thessaloniki, Moudania, Leros, Cos, Kalimnos, Patmos, Rhodes, Skiathos, Samos, Chios, Lemnos, Agios Efstratios and Agios Konstantinos by steamer service.
Chios (Hios), 153 nautical miles from Piraeus, is dominated by two mountains, the *Profitis Elias* and *Oros*. The capital town Chios lies on the eastern shore, very close to the coastline of Turkish Ionia. The port has a dual character – the old waterfront with its small, distempered houses and numerous fishing smacks, and the new quays behind which stand modern buildings and busy patisseries. The archaeological museum, located behind the quay warehouses, contains interesting exhibits. There is also a museum of modern Greek sculpture and the fine churches of *Agios Issidoros* and *Agios Andreas*. There are good beaches at **Karfa, Marmaro, Nago, Pandorikias, Langada** and **Emborios** (black pebbles) and near the *Monastery of Agia Markella*. Villages in the south of the island still have a medieval appearance. The village of **Mesta** is one of the traditional settlements which the National Tourist Organization has turned into small guest-houses. A medieval settlement, it has suffered little damage and change in the course of centuries. The port serving Mesta is **Passalimani,** a small fishing village, where there are rooms to let. Small vessels from Chios sail to the historic island of **Psara** with its unfrequented beaches, rich fishing grounds and the *Kimissis Theotokou Monastery*. The one port and village on the island has a guest-house. Small vessels also sail to the **Inoussai Islands,** another secluded refuge with sandy beaches and small tavernas.
Chios is linked to Athens by air and to Piraeus by ferryboat. Steamer services also operate from Thessaloniki, the Dodecanese and Sporades, but on a less frequent schedule. There are also connections with Lemnos, Ikaria, Samos, Kavala and Crete. Mesta is linked with Rafina.
Samos, 174 nautical miles from Piraeus, is a land of forested hills, olive groves, vineyards and meadows. Samos, the island's capital, has undergone extensive development but has retained many elegant buildings and museums. A short road links the port area with **Vathi,** the old quarter built on the slopes of the red clay hills behind the port. From Samos town a good asphalt road runs the length of the island's coast to **Karlovassi,** passing the beaches at **Kokan, Tsarmadou, Aviakia, Darlovossi** (pebble) and **Potami,** 2km (1.2 miles) beyond. To the west are the beaches at **Votsalakia** and **Hrissi Amnos,** probably the best on the island. There are well-appointed beaches at **Psili Ammos** and **Possidonion,** on the south east coast, at **Gangos** and along the *Cape of Kotsika*. Close to the eastern shore lie the islets of **Agios Nikolaos, Prassonissi** and **Vareloudi,** excellent for snorkel fishing.
There are flights to Samos from Athens and a regular steamer service from Piraeus. Steamer services also operate from Thessaloniki, Kavala, Agios Efstratios, Chios, Kalymnos, Cos, Lemnos, Leros, Mudania, Mitilini, Patmos, Rhodes, Chalki, Karpathos, Kassos, Anafi, Santorini, Milos and Folegandros, but on a less frequent schedule. There are also sailings twice or three times a week for the islet of Fourni.
Ikaria is 143 nautical miles from Pireaus and lies between Samos and Andros. The southern side of the island is steep and rocky but the northern shore is lined with good bathing beaches. The main port and capital is **Agios Kirikos.** There are thick pinewoods, streams and a sandy beach at **Armenistis** and a spa at **Therma.** At **Therma Lefkadas** there are hot medicinal springs. Motor boats can be chartered to **Fanari,** on the northeastern corner of the island, and to the small island of **Fourni,** famous for its lobsters, *raki*, honey and an exceptional sandy beach. There is a Piraeus-Ikaria steamer service but, as an alternative, fly to Samos and from there pick up the steamer service to Ikaria.

The Sporades

Across the waters from the eastern coast of mainland Greece are the four islands of the Sporades – **Skiathos, Skopelos, Alonissos** and **Skyros**. The islands are becoming very popular and it is advisable to book early, especially in the high season. In addition to hotels there are villas and rooms to rent from individual families. A list of private lodgings can be obtained from the local tourist police.
Skiathos is 41 nautical miles from the town of **Volos.** The island is green and idyllic, with 70 sandy inlets, several bays and three harbours. Its highest wooded summit rises to 438m (1437ft). Nine smaller islands surround Skiathos. Two of these, the**Tsougries,** lie across the main harbour, offering safe anchorage to boats and a small marina for yachts. The main town, also called Skiathos, was built in 1830 on two low hills. It is the hub of the tourist summer season, with several hotels, villas and rooms to let. There is a good road which hugs the southern coast with its many bays, linking the town with *Koukounaries*, the famous pine grove. Another way to get around Skiathos is by motor launch. They run at regular intervals to the more popular beaches for a moderate fare. There are also motorboats for hire. The nights in Skiathos are especially lively, with tavernas, bars, and discotheques. There are beaches at **Koukounaries, Mandraki, Lalaria** (pebble beach) and **Agia Eleni.** Worth visiting is the ancient walled town of **Kastro,** northeast of Skiathos town. Skiathos has many facilities for tourists including a marina with a supply station, a medical centre, tourist police and a garage for light car-repairs.
Skopelos is 58 nautical miles from Volos. The island has small bays, golden sands and slopes covered with olive trees, churches and monasteries. The main town of Skopelo, a seaport with narrow cobbled streets and a sandy beach, is quieter than Skiathos. There are beaches which have shallow and safe waters for children at *Stafylos Cove;* at **Limnonari** – to which you cross by boat from **Agnondas;** at **Panormos,** a wind-protected bay; at **Milia** and **Elios;** and at **Loutraki,** the *Glossa port*. For those who prefer shingle beaches, there is *Agios Konstandinos*. The *Tripiti Grotto* is also worth visiting.
Alonissos is 62 nautical miles from Volos. The centre of the island has been submerged, leaving two small islets and several smaller ones still. A rock mass called *Psathoura*, where there are several grottos with stalactites, is all that remains of ancienti Alonissos. With only 10km (6 miles) of roads on Alonissos, the best way of getting about is by motorboat, sharing the fare. These ply between the islands and beaches and excursion sites. The beaches at **Kokkinokastro,** 30 minutes by caique from the small port of **Patitri,** *Palavodimos*, *Steni Vala*, *Ai-Nikolas* and *Kalamakia* offer excellent bathing. On some of the surrounding, virtually uninhabited isles there are isolated, good beaches but no amenities. There are guest-houses and rooms to rent as well as bungalows and small hotels. Other services include a medical centre, port authority, customs, police and motorboat rentals for fishing trips and excursions. *Cyclop's Cave*, decorated with stalactites and stalagmites, is to be found on the island of **Gioura. Psathoura** has remains of an ancient city, most of which are submerged. Divers will see traces of streets, houses and windows in shallow waters. When the sea is calm they can be seen from the surface.
Skyros (Skiros) is 25 nautical miles from Kimi, in Euboea, and 118 nautical miles from Piraeus. The island's main port is **Linaria** and there are beaches nearby at *Magazia*, *Molos* and *Girismati*. The more distant beaches of *Ahili*, *Aspi*, *Kalamitsa*, *Pefkos*, *Atsitsa*, *Tris Boukes* and *Aherounes* also offer good bathing and can be reached by car. However, only the road to **Ahili, Aspi** and **Aherounes** is asphalt. *Atsitsa* and *Pefkos* are more islolated beaches. In most places there are small tavernas by the sea and, in summer, cruises round the island with small boats are organised.
Climate: In the summer months (June to September) the temperature averages between 73-80°F. In the winter (October to May) the temperature averages between 50-68°F.

The Cyclades

Kea (Tzia), 42 nautical miles from Piraeus, is dotted with small, cultivated valleys, sandy beaches, fruit orchards, clusters of whitewashed houses, quaint villages and a large number of churches. A short distance inland from the port of **Korissia** lies **Hora,** with its 15 churches and elegant archways. Several windmills, chapels and notable monasteries are scattered around the island's countryside. One is the famous *Convent of Panagia Kastriani*, overlooking *Otzia Bay*. Archaeological sites include one close to the *Vourkari* fishing hamlet. At **Koundouro** and **Pisses** there are good swimming beaches.
Kythnos (Kithnos) is 54 nautical miles from Piraeus. A small island, its harsh landscape is softened by the dashes of green provided by vineyards and fig trees. It has two harbours, **Loutra** and **Merihas,** both sheltered anchorages. Clinging to the barren hillside is **Hora** (this is the name usually given to the main township or head village) also known as **Messaria.** White Cycladic cottages, churches with frescoes and icons and the spontaneous hospitality of the islanders combine to make Kythnos increasingly popular with visitors in search of beauty and quiet. Loutra gets its name from the well-known warm medicinal springs in the area. Sites worth visiting include the monasteries of *Panagia tou Nikou* and *Panagia tis Kanalas*.
Serifos is 70 nautical miles from Piraeus. Ships calling at the island anchor at **Livadi** which is surrounded by gardens and orchards. From here the road climbs up to Hora where flagstones pave the narrow alleys, lined by typically Cycladic houses and churches. Higher still stands the old Venetian fortress. Attractive beaches are to be found at **Mega Livadi** and **Koutalas.**
Sifnos is 82 sq km (52 sq miles) in area. An attractive drive inland from the port of **Kamares** leads to the capital **Apollonia,** which echoes back to the time the god Apollo was worshipped there. In the modern town, many houses retain their distinctive Cycladic character. There are a number of notable churches and a folkloric museum. The medieval atmosphere in the old capital, **Kastro,** is striking. There is an archaeological collection in the *Roman Catholic Cathedral*. The villages of **Artemonas** and **Exambela** are built on gently undulating hills amid picturesque windmills. It is estimated that there are 365 churches and chapels on Sifnos. Monasteries such as those of *Ai Yanni tou Moungou*, *Agios Symeon*, *Ai Lia* and *Panagia Hrissopigi* are of interest.
Kimolos, 88 nautical miles from Piraeus, is an island of white chalk cliffs. Ships call at the harbour of **Pstahi.** In the capital, Kimolos, houses are smothered with flowers and the streets are laid with decorated flagstones. The indented coastline is lined with fine, sandy beaches. There are hot natural springs at **Prassa,** and a submerged city off the coast at **Koftou** is of archaeological interest.
Milos is 82 nautical miles from Piraeus. This beautiful island is inseparably associated with Venus, the goddess of love. **Adamas,** on the eastern shore, is the island's port. The icons of the *Church of Agia Trias* there are noteworthy. **Plaka,** the island's typically Cycladic capital, is overlooked by the remains of a Frankish castle and the 13th-century Byzantine *Church of Thalassistra*. The *Archaeological Museum* houses ceramics from the island dating back to the 6th millenium BC, and the *Folkloric Museum* contains examples of popular art. There are extensive early Christian catacombs near the small village of **Tripiti.** Attractive swimming beaches include those at **Chivadolimni, Pollonia** and **Adamas** and excursions can be made in small craft to the *Glaronissia;* to volcanic islets with remarkable caves and crystalline rocks; to the Sykia sea-cave with its gaily coloured sea bed; and to the islet of **Andimilos.**
Andros is 85 nautical miles from Piraeus. The island is green with pine-clad hills, olive groves and vineyards. Its port is **Gavrion** and its capital **Andros,** an attractive town with numerous mansions in the neo-classical style, hotels, clubs, a noteworthy maritime museum, as well as an archaeological museum with ceramics from ancient Agora and a rich collection of finds from the excavations on the island, dating back to the Geometric, Classical and Hellenistic Periods. There are fine swimming beaches all over the island, including *Gavrion*, *Batsi*, *Nimborio* and *Korthion*. At **Paleopolis** there are remains of ancient walls, a theatre and stadium. The *Panachrantou Monastery* at **Falika** and the Byzantine *Church of Taxiarchon* in **Messaria** are worth a visit. *Apikia* is well-known for its mineral springs.
Tinos, 86 nautical miles from Piraeus, is a focus of pilgrimages celebrating the Annunciation (March 25) and

the Dormition (August 15) when thousands of pilgrims flock to this sacred island to attend celebrations in honour of the Virgin Mary at the marble *Church of the Evangelistria*. There is also a *Byzantine Museum*, and an archaeological museum, exhibiting finds from the ancient temples of Poseidon and Amphitrite. Buses connect the villages with the town of Tinos. The island's fine beaches include *Agios Fokas* and *Kionia*, very close to the town, and **Kolibithra,** on the northern coast. At **Kionia** there are also traces of ancient settlements.
Syros (Siros) is 80 nautical miles from Piraeus, lying at the heart of the Cycladic complex. Its capital and main port **Ermoupolis** is also the capital of the Cyclades. It has many notable buildings in the neo-classical style, such as the town hall and the customs house, as well as a fine theatre, spacious public squares and impressive churches. Upper Syros retains a strong medieval flavour with city walls, narrow cobbled streets and arcades.
Mykonos (Mikonos) is 95 nautical miles from Piraeus. Renowned for its many windmills, catching the brisk 'meltemi' breezes, this barren island is a very popular holiday resort. Mykonos town comprises a modern harbour, whitewashed alleys, churches in the distinctive local style, shops selling local arts and crafts, small tavernas, cafés and discotheques. The *Paraportiani Church* near the quay is considered to be an architectural masterpiece. The *Archaeological Museum* exhibits finds excavated from the necropolis on the nearby islet of **Rineia.** There is also a *Museum of Popular Art*. Interesting excursions can be made to the monasteries of *Agios Panteleimon*, close to **Hora,** and the *Tourliani Monastery* at **Ano Mera.** Beaches range from cosmopolitan to secluded, and include *Agios Stefanos, Kalafatis, Platis Yialos* and *Ornos*. The best beaches, however, are on the south side of the island and can be reached by caique from Plati Yialos. They are *Paradise*, *Super Paradise*, *Agrari* and *Elia*. From Mykonos, there is a boat service to the sacred island of **Delos.**
Delos (Dilos) was a sacred island in ancient times, and is said to have been the birthplace of Apollo and Artemis. The island has many archaeological sites, such as the *Lions Way* and the three temples of Apollo. A museum exhibits Archaic, Classical, Hellenistic and Roman sculptures, including the *Archaic Sphinx of the Naxians* and *Acroteria* (Victories) from the temple of the Athenians.
Paros is 90 nautical miles from Piraeus. The island's hinterland has undulating hills that contain the famous Parian marble. **Parikia**, the island's capital and main port, is built on the site of the ancient city. It is the custom on the island to have doors and windows open in the houses as a sign of welcome to strangers visiting the island. A narrow, stone-paved alley leads to one of the most impressive shrines in Christendom, the *Ekatondapiliani* or Katapoliani church. At **Kolimbithres** the rugged coast forms inlets with golden sands. There are attractive swimming beaches at **Drios, Alikes** and **Piso Livadi.** Of the island's monasteries *Zoodohos Pigi Longovarda* and *Christou Tou Dassous* are the most significant.
Antiparos is separated from Paros by a narrow channel. The main attraction on this small island is its famous cave with stalactites; this can be reached by pack animals which carry visitors from the beach. There are many deserted beaches.
Thira (Santorini) is 127 nautical miles from Piraeus. Vast geological upheavals gave this Cycladic island its unique form – a steep plateau with sheer cliffs which rises from the sea. Because of its height and shape, there is often a warm romantic wind that blows through the island. A funicular railway, pack mules or donkeys carry visitors up from the harbour of **Skala** to the island's capital Thira, a picturesque town with twisting alleys, arcades, a museum and an old Frankish quarter. It is also a good vantage point from which to view the **Kamenes**, two jet black volcanic islets in the bay that can be visited by light craft, as can **Therasia** (Thirassia), the second largest island of the Santorini group. There are some interesting archaeological remains in Ancient Thira which has witnessed the passage of Phoenicians, Dorians, Romans and Byzantines. There are remains of a cluster of houses, a market place, baths, theatres, temples, tombs and early Christian relics. **Akrotiri** is also of great interest for the relics of the Minoan civilisation which have been excavated there. The *Monastery of Profitas Ilias* on the island's summit and the swimming beaches of *Perissa* and *Kamazi* are other attractions.
Naxos, 106 nautical miles from Piraeus, is the largest and most fertile island in the Cyclades group. Everywhere lies evidence of the island's long history: the *Temple of Apollo;* the immense gateway on the tiny islet of **Palatia**, linked to the main island by a causeway; Mycenaean tombs; a museum; remains of a Mycenaean settlement at **Grotta** (Cave); a castle; and historical churches. The village of **Halki** has a medieval fortress and several Byzantine churches. From Naxos town the road leads inland to the village of **Sangri** from where one can visit the famous *Himaros Tower*, one of the best-preserved monuments of the Hellenistic period. There are many sandy beaches, such as at **Apollonas, Kastraki, Vigla** and **Agios Georgios.**
Ios, 114 nautical miles from Piraeus, is an extremely popular and busy island. Close to the small harbour of **Ormos,** where fishing smacks and yachts anchor, lies the attractive swimming beach of *Yalos*; other pleasant beaches are at *Koumbaras*, *Manganavi* and *Psathi*.
Amorgos, where the cities of Minoa, Arkesini and Aegiali once flourished, has several ruins of archaeological interest. There is a harbour in **Katapola** and, in **Hora,** whitewashed houses are built up a rocky slope. In the same area lies **Panagia Exohoriani** where a fiesta is held on August 15 every year. At **Plakoto** there are remains of an ancient tower and of a temple. There are good beaches at **Agios Panteleimon, Kato Akrotiri, Agia Anna** and **Agia Paraskevi.**
Sikinos-Folegandros: These two islands lie fairly close to Ios and are attractive for their genuine island life and solitude. **Hora** is the only sizeable village on Sikinos. Its cottages are built in the distinctive island style along narrow alleys and there is a fine cathedral church. Attractions include the castle and *Hrissopigi Monastery* which is built like a fortress. There is a good swimming beach at **Spillia.**
Folegandros is an island of wild beauty, rugged and barren. There are some sandy beaches tucked away among the rocks, such as at **Karavostassi** on the southeastern coast of the island. **Panagia** has an interesting church and at **Hrissospilia** there is a cave with stalactites, stalagmites and ancient ruins.
Anafi, the most southerly of the Cycladic group of islands, has a rocky shoreline with many creeks. There are several smaller, attractive islands which people in search of the 'genuine article' are gradually discovering. **Schinoussa** with its extremely picturesque, tiny harbour; *Mersinia* or *Donoussa* with its superb sandy beaches; and the Koufonissia group of **Keros** and **Heraklia** – all of them are very modest in size and provide peaceful anchorages.

SOCIAL PROFILE

FOOD & DRINK: Restaurant and taverna food tends to be very simple, rarely involving sauces but with full use of local olive oil and charcoal grills. Dishes like *Dolmades* (stuffed vine leaves), *Moussaka*, *Kebabs* and *Avgolemono* (soup) can be found everywhere. *Taramosalata* and a variety of seafood dishes, especially squid *(Kalamari)* or octopus, are excellent. Salads are made with the local cheese *(Fetta)* and fresh olive oil. Olives are cheap and plentiful. All restaurants have a standard menu which includes the availability and price of each dish. A good proportion of the restaurants will serve international dishes. Hours are normally 1200-1500 for lunch and 2100-2400 for dinner. Waiter service is usual. **Drink:** One of the best-known Greek drinks is *Retsina* wine, made with pine-needle resin. Local spirits include *Ouzo*, an aniseed-based clear spirit to which water is added. Local brandy is sharp and fiery. Greek coffee is served thick and strong, and sugared according to taste. Greek beer is a light *Pilsner* type. Visitors may be required to pay for each drink if seated some way from the bar. **Opening hours** vary according to the region and local laws.
NIGHTLIFE: This is centred in main towns and resorts with concerts and discotheques.
SHOPPING: Special purchases include lace, metalwork, pottery, garments and knitwear, furs, rugs, leather goods, local wines and spirits. Athens is the centre for luxury goods and local handicrafts. The flea markets in Monastiraki and Plaka, below the Acropolis, are all crowded in high season. **Note:** There is a temptation to buy fake antiques, especially archaeological items. It is in fact illegal to export any item of real antiquity.
Shopping hours: These vary according to the season and location, but a rough guide follows: 0830-1500 Monday, Wednesday and Saturday; 0830-1400 and 1730-2030 Tuesday, Thursday and Friday.
Note: Most holiday resort shops stay open late in the evening
SPORT: Athens has one **golf** club, the Glifada Golfcourse & Club. There are also clubs on Rhodes, Corfu and Halkidiki. There are several **tennis** clubs. There are **horseriding** clubs in Attica, Thessaloniki and Corfu. Those who wish to shoot in Greece must have a special licence. **Mountaineering** is becoming increasingly popular and there is scope for **hill walking** and **climbing**. There are over 7000 Karstic cave formations in the country, the majority in Crete. **Skiing** centres are open December to March in a number of areas. Contact the GNTO for details. **Watersports:** There are excellent facilities along all coastlines of the mainland and particularly in the islands. Most major hotels can help with arrangements. **Scuba diving:** The use of breathing apparatus is prohibited in many areas: check with Port Authorities. For a full list of areas where scuba diving is permitted, contact the GNTO. **Fishing:** Greek waters offer good fishing, particularly during the summer and autumn. Boats and equipment can be found in most villages. Ask at Amateur Anglers and Maritime Sports Club (Akti Moutspoulou, Piraeus).
SPECIAL EVENTS: The following is a selection of the major annual festivals and special events celebrated in Greece during 1993/4. For a complete list, contact the GNTO.
Mar '93 *Carnival* (marks the beginning of Lent with celebrations throughout the country), particularly in Naoussa, Veria, Kozani, Skyros, Chios, Galaxidi and Thebes. **Apr** *Holy Week* (religious processions and ceremonies throughout the country). **Late Jun-Sep** *Athens Festival* (opera, ballet, classical and contemporary music at the magnificent amphitheatre of Epidaurus); *Patras Festival* (ancient and modern drama, ballet, and concerts). **Late Jun-Aug** *Epidavros Festival* (classical drama at the Lycabettus Theatre). **Jul and Aug** *Philippi Festival* (ancient drama, ballet, and concerts); *Wine Festival*, Dafni (near Athens). **Aug** *Epirotika Festival*, Janene; *Hippokraetia Festival*, Cos. **Late Aug-late Sep** *Wine Festival*, Rethymnon (Crete).
SOCIAL CONVENTIONS: Visitors to Greece will find the Greeks to be well aware of a strong historical and cultural heritage. Traditions and customs differ throughout Greece, but overall a strong sense of unity prevails. The Greek Orthodox Church has a strong traditional influence on the Greek way of life, especially in more rural areas. The throwing back of the head is a negative gesture. Dress is generally casual. Smoking is prohibited on public transport and in public buildings. **Tipping:** 15% is usual.

BUSINESS PROFILE

ECONOMY: Traditionally agricultural, accession to the European Community gave a new impetus to the Greek economy, particularly the industrial sectors of textiles, clothing and shoes, cement, mining and metals, chemicals, steel and processed agricultural products. Tourism, the most important service industry, has boomed during the 1980s and is expected to continue growing during the 1990s. Greek enterprises have consistently found difficulty penetrating European markets, however, because of the comparatively small scale of the majority of businesses. The country produces large quantities of wheat, barley, maize, tobacco and fruit for export. By EC standards Greece is both poor and underdeveloped (over 50% of the working population work the land – a very high proportion by EC standards) but it experienced rapid growth during the 1970s which continued, albeit at a slower rate, through the 1980s. The EC takes about 50% of all Greek exports and supplies 40% of imports. Outside the Community, Saudi Arabia (oil), Japan and the US are the country's major trading partners. Large EC loans have been provided in the last couple of years to keep the economy solvent. There have been several disputes between the Greek government and the European Commission over the terms of repayment, but until the Government's ambitious privatisation programme gets under way, the Treasury will probably not be able to lighten the debt burden. Much debate has surrounded a unique sale, proposed by the Government, of 35 of Greece's 2500-odd offshore islands: the Government hopes to raise $10 million by enticing the wealthy of the world with the privilege of island ownership which was previously afforded only to Greek shipping magnates. But the Government will have to find more lucrative items to sell in order to make a serious impact on the 1991 budget deficit of $1.6 billion. By the middle of 1992, a comprehensive programme of sales had been drawn up and the large industrial holding companies are likely to be among the first to go. Public utilities are also due for disposal: of these, the telecommunications operator HTO is the most attractive and lucrative.
BUSINESS: Formal suits are expected. French, German and English are often spoken as well as Greek.
COMMERCIAL INFORMATION: The following organisation can offer advice: Athens Chamber of Commerce, Odos Akademias 7, 106 71 Athens. Tel: (1) 360 4815. Telex: 215707.
CONFERENCES/CONVENTIONS: Enquiries can be made to the GNTO.

HISTORY & GOVERNMENT

HISTORY: Greece was the birthplace of European civilisation. The period from 700BC saw the rise of the great city states of Athens, Corinth and Sparta, frequently engaged in long struggles for supremacy, and uniting only when faced with the common threat of invasion by the Persian Empire. The zenith was reached in the 5th century BC when Athens became the cultural and artistic centre of the Mediterranean, producing magnificent works of architecture, sculpture, drama and literature. Athens lost her empire through a mutually suicidal struggle with her arch rival Sparta. The nation was then forcibly united under Alexander the Great. After defeating the sagging military might of Persia in a number of major battles, the expansion of the Empire spread Greek influence through the East as far as India and through Egypt. The Empire fragmented after Alexander's death in 323BC, and the fall of the Greek hegemony was completed when the country came under the sway of Rome. Under Constantine the Empire gained a new capital in Constantinople, and Greece continued under the sway of the Eastern Empire when the Empire divided. The Byzantines were, however, unable effectively to defend all of their empire from invaders and only occasionally did Greece enjoy the security of effective Imperial rule. The major beneficiaries of this were the Venetians, who increased their influence in Greece and other parts of the empire. Byzantium finally fell to the Turks in 1453, although the process of conquest was already well under way by the end of the 14th century. For the next 350 years, Greece was part of the Ottoman Empire. Many attempts were made to shake off the yoke of the Ottomans, such as the rising of 1770 which was supported by Catherine the Great. After a bitter War of Independence from 1821, a free state was declared in 1829. The effective consolidation was a gradual process, the last territory to be handed back being the Dodecanese Islands in 1945. Until 1967, Greece was a monarchy but the country then endured the rule of the Colonels. After their fall in 1974, elections gave the New Democracy Party a majority. A subsequent referendum rejected the idea of a return to monarchical rule. From 1981 to 1989 the country was ruled by the socialist PASOK party under Andreas Papandreou. PASOK lost the first of two elections in 1989 following a series of scandals. Neither poll was conclusive and a caretaker government was installed until another round of voting in April 1990. On this occasion New Democracy emerged once again as the largest single party with sufficient seats to form a majority government headed by party leader Constantine Mitzotakis. The Mitzotakis government has made a few adjustments to Greek foreign policy, in concert with the changing political environment in Europe. Most attention is devoted to the EC. Renewed efforts have been made to resolve the Cyprus dispute, assisted by some easing of the tension between Greece and Turkey. It is now the countries to the north that are causing most concern in Athens. Yugoslavia is engulfed by civil war, with a danger that the southern province of Macedonia, which borders on Greece, could become embroiled. Macedonia is seeking recognition of its independence under that name, a proposal which has successfully been blocked by Athens in the EC. And in keeping with the general European trend, Greece has also moved away from its former close relations with Serbia. The volatile situation in Albania, which has led several thousand Albanians to cross the border into Greece (before being repatriated), is also worrying the Athens government.

GOVERNMENT: Greece is a unicameral parliamentary democracy. The parliament has 300 members and is elected for a 4-year term. The Prime Minister is the leader of the largest party. The President is Head of State but has no executive powers.

CLIMATE

Greece has a warm Mediterranean climate. In summer, dry hot days are often relieved by stiff breezes, especially in the north and coastal areas. Athens can be stiflingly hot, so visitors should allow time to acclimatise. The evenings are cool. Winters are mild in the south but much colder in the north. November to March is the rainy season.

Required clothing: Lightweight clothes during summer months, including protection from the midday sun. Light sweaters are needed for evenings. Rainproof wear is advised for autumn. Winter months can be quite cold, especially in the northern mainland, so normal winter wear will be required.

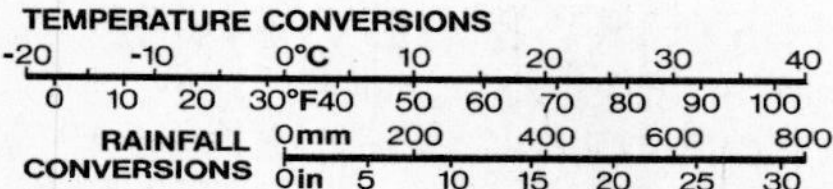

NAXOS Greece (3m)

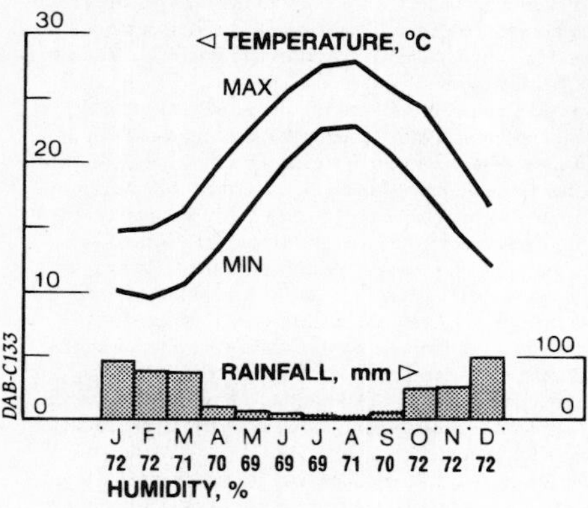

THESSALONIKI Greece (2m)

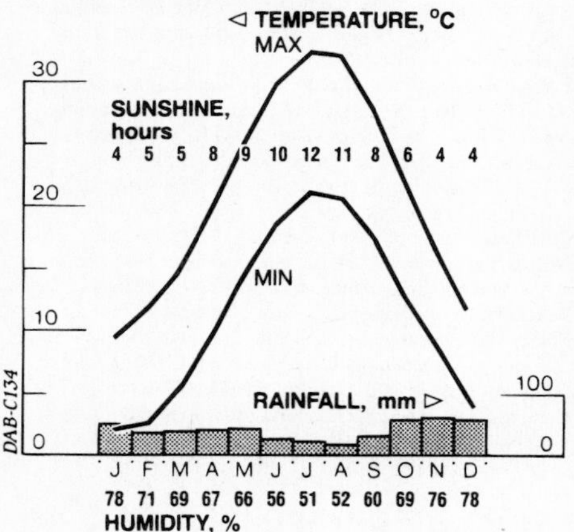

CORFU Greece (25m)

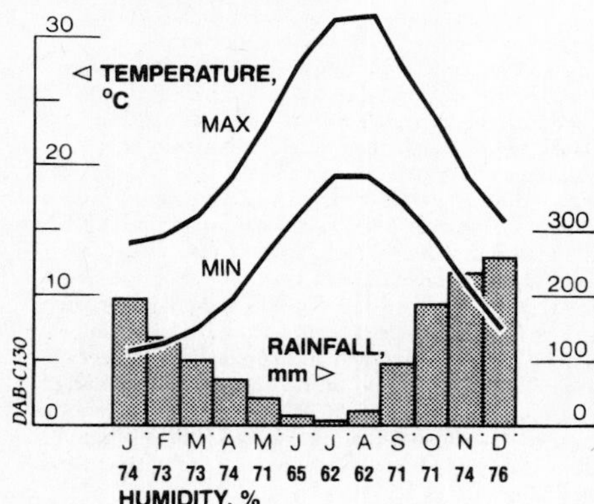

ATHENS Greece (107m)

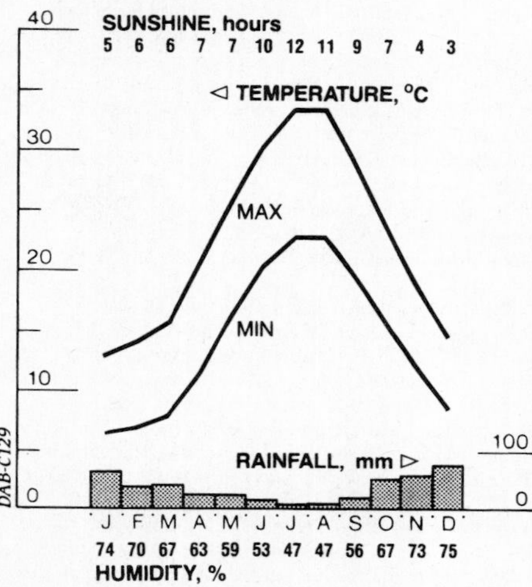

GREENLAND

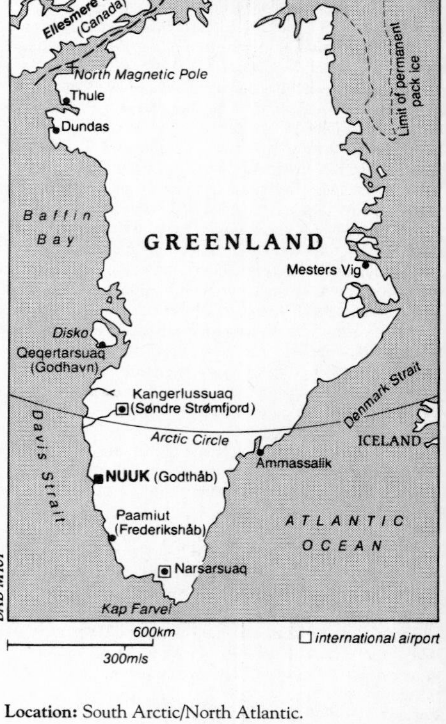

Location: South Arctic/North Atlantic.

Important note: The Arctic weather conditions in Greenland may cause delays and interruptions in transport services or changes to planned itineraries. In some cases, this may result in additional hotel accommodation or helicopter/ship transportation costs. Such expenses *must* be paid by the traveller at the time. Tour operators and airlines are unable to accept responsibilities for expenses resulting in any such delays, but tour companies will normally be able to give refunds for services, transport, accommodation etc which were paid for in advance, but which they were not able to provide. These refunds, where applicable, will only be made after the end of the trip. It is, therefore, very important to retain all unused vouchers or tickets. *It is strongly recommended that travellers take as much money as possible with them in order to cover expenses which may arise as a result of unforeseen delays.*

KNTK (The Tourist Associations of Greenland)
PO Box 116
DK-3922 Nanortalik, Greenland
Tel: 33441. Fax: 33442.
There are tourist offices in Kangerlussuaq/Sdr, Strømfjord, Narsarsuaq and most towns in Greenland.

Greenland Tourism A/S
PO Box 1552
DK-3900 Nuuk, Greenland
Tel: 22888. Fax: 22877.

Greenland Tourism A/S
Box 2151
52 Pilestraede
DK-1016 Copenhagen K, Denmark

For Diplomatic Representation, see **Royal Danish Embassies** in the entry for *Denmark.*

Danish Tourist Board
169-173 Regent Street
London W1A 2LT
Tel: (071) 734 2637. Fax: (071) 494 2170. Opening hours: 0900-1700 Monday to Friday.

British Honorary Consulate
PO Box 1073
Royal Greenland
Vestervig 45
DK-3900 Nuuk, Greenland
Tel: 24422. Fax: 22409. Telex: 90437 PROGHB GD.

Grønlands Hjemmestyre
(Greenland Home Rule Government)
PO Box 1015
DK-3900 Nuuk, Greenland

Tel: 23000. Fax: 25002. Telex: 90613.
For tourist information, see the **Danish Tourist Board** in *New York* and *Toronto* in the entry on **Denmark.**

AREA: 2,175,600 sq km (840,000 sq miles).
POPULATION: 55,533 (1991 estimate).
POPULATION DENSITY: 0.025 per sq km.
CAPITAL: Nuuk (Previously called Godthåb).
Population: 12,657 (1991).
GEOGRAPHY: Greenland is the world's biggest island (if Australia is counted as a continent). The surrounding seas are either permanently frozen or chilled by the mainly cold currents caused by the meeting of the Arctic and the North Atlantic Oceans. The inland area is covered with ice, stretching 2500km (1500 miles) north-south and 1000km (600 miles) east-west. In the centre, the ice can be up to 3km (2 miles) thick. The ice-free coastal region, which is sometimes as wide as 200km (120 miles), covers a total of 341,700 sq km (131,900 sq miles), and is where all of the population is to be found. This region is intersected by deep fjords which connect the inland ice area with the sea. The midnight sun can be seen north of the Arctic Circle; the further north one is, the more the midnight sun will be in evidence. The arctic night in the winter results in a continuous twilight and, in the far north of the country, complete darkness. The Northern Lights can be seen during the autumn and winter months.
LANGUAGE: The official languages are Greenlandic, an Inuit (Eskimo) language and Danish. Greenlanders connected with tourism will normally speak at least some English.
RELIGION: Church of Greenland (part of the Protestant Church of Denmark) and Danish. There is a Roman Catholic church in Nuuk.
TIME: East Greenland/Mesters Vig: GMT (summer and winter).
Scoresby Sound: GMT - 1 (GMT in summer).
Ammassalik and west coast: GMT - 3 (GMT - 2 in summer).
Thule area: GMT - 4 (summer and winter).
ELECTRICITY: 220 volts AC, 50Hz.
COMMUNICATIONS: Telephone: IDD is available. Country code: 299. There are no area codes. There are no telephone boxes in Greenland, but calls can be made from hotels. **Telegram:** All towns have a telegraph station. **Post:** Greenland produces its own stamps which are popular among collectors. Post from Greenland takes about four to five days to reach Europe. Post office hours: 0900-1500 Monday to Friday. **Press:** There are no daily newspapers in Greenland, but there are two weekly and one monthly publications.
BBC World Service and Voice of America frequencies: From time to time these change. See the section *How to Use this Book* for more information.

BBC:				
MHz	12.10	9.410	6.195	3.955
Voice of America:				
MHz	11.97	9.670	6.040	5.995

PASSPORT/VISA

Regulations and requirements may be subject to change at short notice, and you are advised to contact the appropriate diplomatic or consular authority before finalising travel arrangements. Details of these may be found at the head of this country's entry. Any numbers in the chart refer to the footnotes below.

	Passport Required?	Visa Required?	Return Ticket Required?
Full British	1	2	No
BVP	Valid	No	No
Australian	Yes	No	Yes
Canadian	Yes	No	Yes
USA	Yes	No	Yes
Other EC	1	No	No
Japanese	Yes	No	Yes

PASSPORTS: Valid passport required by all except:
(a) **[1]** nationals of Belgium, Denmark, France, Germany, Italy, Luxembourg and The Netherlands in possession of a national identity card, and nationals of the UK in possession of a BVP (other EC nationals *do* require a passport);
(b) nationals of Austria, Liechtenstein and Switzerland in possession of a national identity card;
(c) nationals of Finland, Iceland, Norway and Sweden in possession of identification papers provided travel does not include any non-Scandinavian countries.
British Visitors Passport: Valid for nationals of the UK.
VISAS: Required by all except:
(a) **[2]** nationals of the UK with the exception of holders of passports described as 'British Protected Person' or with endorsement 'holder is subject to control under the Immigration Act 1971' or 'the Commonwealth Immigration Act' (holders of these types of British passport *will* need visas). Note that nationals whose country of origin is Bangladesh, Ghana, India, Nigeria, Pakistan or Sri Lanka will need an 'exempt' stamp from UK immigration authorities, in addition to an 'indefinite stay' stamp.
(b) nationals of other countries referred to in the chart above;
(c) nationals of Andorra, Argentina, Australia, Austria, Bahamas, Barbados, Belize, Benin, Bolivia, Botswana, Brazil, Brunei, Canada, Chile, Colombia, Costa Rica, Côte d'Ivoire, Croatia, Cyprus, Czechoslovakia, Dominica, Dominican Republic, Ecuador, El Salvador, Fiji, Finland, Gambia, Grenada, Guatemala, Guyana, Honduras, Hungary, Iceland, Israel, Jamaica, Kenya, Kiribati, South Korea, Lesotho, Liechtenstein, Malawi, Malaysia, Malta, Mauritius, Mexico, Monaco, Namibia, New Zealand, Nicaragua, Niger, Norway, Panama, Paraguay, Peru, Poland, St Lucia, St Vincent & the Grenadines, San Marino, Seychelles, Sierra Leone, Singapore, Slovenia, Solomon Islands, Suriname, Swaziland, Sweden, Switzerland, Tanzania, Thailand, Togo, Trinidad & Tobago, Tunisia, Tuvalu, Uganda, Uruguay, Vatican City, Venezuela, Yugoslavia, Zambia and Zimbabwe.
Types of visa: Tourist, Business and Transit. Cost: £14 for Tourist; for Transit some free reciprocal arrangements exist.
Validity: Tourist and Business visas are normally valid for up to 3 months from date of arrival.
Application to: Danish Consulate (or Visa Section at Embassy). For address, see top of entry. Specify that a visa for Denmark and Greenland is required.
Application requirements: (a) Valid passport. (b) 2 application forms. (c) 2 photographs.
Personal applications should be made to the visa office 0930-1300 Monday to Friday. Postal applicants should enclose a stamped, self-addressed and registered envelope and payment by crossed postal order. Telephone enquiries should be made between 0900-1000 and from 1500-1600. There are special facilities for business travellers, who should phone for details.
Working days required: 6-8 weeks.
Temporary residence: Persons wishing to stay in Greenland for more than 3 months should make their application *in their home country* well in advance of their intended date of departure.
Note: The regulations are the same as for Denmark (see the *Passport/Visa* section for Denmark above). Special permits are, however, necessary for persons wishing to visit the military zone around Thule. Danish nationals should apply to the Ministry of Greenland in Copenhagen.

MONEY

Currency: Danish Krone (DKr) = 100 øre. Notes are in denominations of DKr1000, 500, 100 and 50. Coins are in denominations of DKr20, 10, 5 and 1, and 50 and 25 øre.
Currency exchange: Cheques drawn on Danish banks or on Eurocheque cards can be cashed at banks. Travellers cheques and cash can also be exchanged. There are two Greenland banks, *Nuna Bank* (PO Box 1031, Skibshavnsvej 33, DK-3900 Nuuk) and *Grønlandsbanken* (PO Box 1033, DK-3900 Nuuk). *KNI* represents the banks in other towns and villages.
Note: There is no banking service in Søndre Strømfjord at present.
Credit cards: Limited use of American Express and Diners Club. Credit cards are not widely accepted; check with your credit card company for merchant acceptability and other facilities which may be available.
Travellers cheques: Cheques in major currencies may be exchanged as indicated above.
Exchange rate indicators: The following figures are included as a guide to the movements of the Danish Krone against Sterling and the US Dollar:

Date:	Oct '89	Oct '90	Oct '91	Oct '92
£1.00=	11.61	11.36	11.24	9.36
$1.00=	7.35	5.81	6.48	5.89

Currency restrictions: None.
Banking hours: 0900-1500 Monday to Wednesday and Friday; 0930-1800 Thursday.

DUTY FREE

The following goods may be imported into Greenland without incurring customs duty:
200 cigarettes or 250g of tobacco and 200 cigarette papers (travellers must be over 15);
1 litre of spirits or 2 litres of fortified wine and 2 litres of ordinary wine (travellers must be over 18).
These goods must be carried by the traveller personally.
Prohibited items: Pistols, fully or semi-automatic weapons, narcotics and live animals. Hunting rifles require a licence; apply to the carrying airline.

PUBLIC HOLIDAYS

Public holidays observed in Greenland are as follows:
Apr 9-12 '93 Easter. **May 7** General Prayer Day. **May 20** Ascension Day. **May 31** Whit Monday. **Jun 5** Constitution Day. **Jun 21** National Day. **Dec 25-26** Christmas. **Jan 1 '94** New Year's Day.

HEALTH

Regulations and requirements may be subject to change at short notice, and you are advised to contact your doctor well in advance of your intended date of departure. Any numbers in the chart refer to the footnotes below.

	Special Precautions?	Certificate Required?
Yellow Fever	No	No
Cholera	No	No
Typhoid & Polio	No	-
Malaria	No	-
Food & Drink	No	-

Rabies is present. For those at high risk, vaccination before arrival should be considered. If you are bitten abroad seek medical advice without delay. For more information consult the *Health* section at the back of the book.
Health care: No vaccinations or certificates are required for entry into Greenland. There are hospitals and dentists in all towns. Although medical services are generally free, medical insurance is advisable, particularly as charges are made for dental treatment.
Travellers are advised to bring their own medicines and prescribed drugs, as these can often be difficult to obtain in Greenland.

TRAVEL - International

AIR: Flying to Greenland by scheduled services will usually involve a stopover in Iceland or Denmark; contact SAS or *Greenlandair* for further details.
Approximate flight time: From *London* to Greenland is 5 hours 30 minutes (including stopover in Copenhagen).
International airports: There are international airports at: *Søndre Strømfjord (SFJ)*, served from Copenhagen by SAS; *Narsarsunq (UAK)*, served from Copenhagen by *Greenlandair* and from Iceland by *Icelandair;*

GREENLAND | **HEALTH REGULATIONS** | **VISA REGULATIONS** | Code-Link

GALILEO/WORLDSPAN

TI-DFT/SFJ/HE

TI-DFT/SFJ/VI

SABRE

TIDFT/SFJ/HE

TIDFT/SFJ/VI

To access this information on your CRS, swipe the barcode with a light pen or type in the text under the barcode. For more information, see the introduction *How to Use This Book.*

Kulusuk, served from Iceland by *Icelandair*;
Ilulissat, served from Iceland by *Icelandair* and *Greenlandair*;
Nuuk, served from Iceland by *Greenlandair* and from Canada/Frobisher Bay by *First Air*.
Services are generally more frequent during the summer months. Connections can then be made to other parts of the country.
Note: By far the most common, and recommended, method of visiting Greenland is with a tour operator. Stories of people travelling independently and subsequently finding themselves in trouble are not uncommon. Only travellers already familiar with the country are advised to make the journey by themselves.

TRAVEL - Internal

AIR: Local services are operated by *Grønlandsfly (GL)* using both planes and helicopters. Contact PO Box 1012, 3900 Nuuk. Tel: 28888. Fax: 27288. Telex: 90602. The frequency of departure on all routes is variable, and it is advisable to make reservations well in advance. Reservations made outside Greenland will take some time to confirm.
SEA: Between May and January, *KNI* boats operate services along the west coast. In addition, all villages are served by local boats connecting them with the nearest town, but space may be limited. Boats in some towns may be available for hire, with a skipper.
RAIL/ROAD: There are no railways in Greenland and no roads suitable for travelling from town to town. Air and seacraft are the most practical means of travel for the inexperienced visitor.
DOG SLEDGES: In Sisimiut, Aasiaat, Ilulissat and Ammassalik, dog sledges can be hired by the day, or for longer periods. **Warning:** Attractive animals though they are, it is important to remember that sledge dogs are usually only semi-tame. This is just one reason why dog sledges should be given right of way at all times. Take particular care, as they are almost totally silent.
JOURNEY TIMES: The following chart gives approximate journey times (in hours and minutes) from Nuuk to other major cities/towns in the country:

	Air	Water
Disko Bay	2.5	48
South Greenland	1.5	48
East Greenland	3	

ACCOMMODATION

HOTELS: There are hotels in the major towns, but only those in Ammassalik, Ilulissat, Maniitsoq, Narsarsuaq, Narsaq, Nuuk, Qasigiannguit, Qaqortoq, Sisimiut, Strømfjord and Ummannaq approach European standards. There is no public accommodation in Upernavik, Thule or Scoresbysund. All reservations should be made in advance; contact Greenland Tourism or the Danish Tourist Board for telephone and telex numbers. For further information on accommodation, contact the CHR (Association of Hotels and Restaurants in Greenland), PO Box 73, DK-3900 Nuuk. Tel: 21500. Fax: 24340.
YOUTH HOSTELS: Youth hostel accommodation is available in Narsarsuaq, Narsaq, Julianehab, Godthab and Jakobshavn. Elsewhere in South Greenland it is possible to stay overnight in mountain huts. Contact local tourist office.
CAMPING: There are no official campsites, but most places have specific areas for tent-pitching. Camping is permitted everywhere except on ruins and on cultivated land in South Greenland.

RESORTS & EXCURSIONS

Organised excursions can be arranged from every town in Greenland, and especially **Nuuk, Narsaq, Ilulissat, Sisimiut** and **Narsarsuaq.** For information on all-inclusive tours/package tours, hiking and hotels, contact Greenland Tourism or the Danish Tourist Board for a list of tour operators.
Greenland is not a country for those seeking an average, ordinary holiday. The scenery, which, together with the clear air and the general sense of space and freedom, constitutes the chief attraction; it is always remarkable and often breathtakingly spectacular. Excursions may be made on foot, by boat, by plane, by helicopter or by dog sledge according to the season and the terrain.
Mountain walking: Guides are advisable for mountain walking, but not always available. Mountain huts are often available, particularly in the region of the *Narsaq* and *Qaqortoq* peninsulas and *Vatnahverfi*. Walking tours in the central western coastal area can be organised by contacting Greenland Travel PO Box 130 DK-1004 Copenhagen K. Group tours, usually with a guide, are operated by a number of tour-operators. Enquire with Greenland Tourist Service.
Main Tourist Centres: Nuuk, the capital, has a population of 10,500, and is overlooked by *Sermitsiaq Mountain*. One of the major attractions is the *Greenland National Museum*. It is situated near the entrance to a large fjiord complex with steep mountains, lush valleys and a few small villages.
Narsarsuaq and **Qagsiarsuk** in Southern Greenland was the area first settled by the Viking Eric the Red 1000 years ago. Many ruins from this epoch of Greenland's history still survive.
Ilulissat (Jakobshavn) in West Greenland (Disco Bay) has many modern as well as traditional buildings, and is surrounded by exceptionally spectacular scenery. Knud Rasmussen's house is worth a visit. Motor-trips to nearby trading stations can sometimes be arranged.
Julianehab is the largest town in South Greenland and the area's administrative centre. The town has several houses of historical interest and a museum. Excursions can be arranged by the local tourist office.
Narsaq tourist office also arranges regular excursions.
The area between **Søndre Strømfjord** and **Sisimiut** is very suitable for walking in summer and for dog sledge expeditions in winter. Cross country skiing can also be arranged.
There is a small *Inuit* (Eskimo) museum at **Qaqortoq,** which includes an exact copy of a turf-built house.
There are minor local museums in most towns. The country also has many ruins of old Norse settlements and Eskimo houses. For further details, contact tour operators, The Danish Tourist Board or the local Tourist Offices in Greenland.
Note: No finds may be removed from ancient monuments, which are all protected areas.

SOCIAL PROFILE

FOOD & DRINK: Most hotels have restaurants of a good standard, where Danish food and Greenland specialities are served. Reindeer meat (caribou), musk ox, fowl, shrimps and fish are the most popular local food. Prices are similar to Denmark.
SHOPPING: The range of goods available is similar to that in an ordinary Danish provincial town, but prices are in general slightly higher. Special purchases include bone and soapstone carvings, skin products and beadwork. The Greenland Home Rule Administration can provide information on claiming tax back on items purchased in Greenland. **Shopping hours:** 0900-1730 Monday to Friday; 0830-1300 Saturday. These will vary from region to region.
SPORT: During the summer period anglers come to Greenland for the superb Arctic **fishing** in the rivers and fjords. **Hunting** permits can be obtained from the police-stations and **fishing** permits from the local tourist offices. Persons hunting or fishing without a licence are liable to a fine and confiscation of equipment. Persons interested should contact the local tourist offices for detailed information. **Mountaineering** or **glacier scaling** can be performed by experienced mountaineers and skiiers, while actual expeditions need a permit from the Danish Polar Centre, Hausergade 3, DK-1128 Copenhagen K. The country also offers excellent opportunities for those interested in activities such as **geology, botany** and **ornithology.** Maps of the coastal area (scale 1:250,000) can be purchased from the Kort og Matrikelstyrelsen, Proviantgaarden, Rigsdagsgaarden 7, DK-1218, Copenhagen K.
Photography: A UV or skylight filter and a lens shade should always be used. In winter, the camera must be polar-oiled. It is advisable to bring your own films. Film cannot be developed in Greenland.
SPECIAL EVENTS: The return of the sun after the arctic night is celebrated in North Greenland. In Ilulissat, this takes place around 13th January. At Easter time dog sledge races take place in several North Greenland towns. Every summer there is a sheepfarmers' show in the south.
SOCIAL CONVENTIONS: Life is generally conducted at a more relaxed pace than is usual in Northern Europe, as exemplified by the frequent use of the word *imaqa* – 'maybe'. Until recently, foreign visitors were very rare. The name of the country in Greenlandic is *Kalaallit Nunaat*, meaning 'Land of the People'. **Photography:** Throughout the country there is a ban on taking photographs inside churches or church halls during services. **Tipping:** Service charge is usually added to the bill. Tips are not expected.

BUSINESS PROFILE

ECONOMY: Fish and fish products, and especially shrimps, are the territory's most valuable exports. Greenland withdrew from the European Community in February 1985 over the issue of fisheries policy. EC member states retain the right to fish within the declared exclusion zone in exchange for a cash payment of around US$25 million per annum. Although there are plans to develop the island's mineral deposits of iron ore, uranium, zinc, lead and coal, the economy ultimately depends on large subsidies from the Danish central government. Denmark retained a monopoly on trade with Greenland until 1950 and continues to dominate its trading patterns. The KNI – the Royal Greenland Trade Department – organises transport, supplies and production in the country. Germany, Norway, the US and France are the other significant trading partners.
BUSINESS: Suits should be worn. A knowledge of Danish is extremely useful. **Office hours:** 0900-1500 Monday to Friday.
CONFERENCES/CONVENTIONS: For information on conferences/conventions, contact Greenland Travel, PO Box 130, DK-1004 Copenhagen K, Denmark. Tel: (45 33) 131 011. Fax: (45 33) 138 592.

HISTORY & GOVERNMENT

HISTORY: Greenland first came under the rule of Denmark in the late 14th century, and became an integral part of the Danish realm in 1953. A nationalist movement led to the formation of the Siumut, a left-wing political party, during the mid-1970s following Greenland's vote against the Danish decision to seek membership of the EC. A referendum in 1979 approved home rule within the Kingdom of Denmark, with about 75% voting in favour of internal autonomy, defence and foreign policy remaining in the hands of Denmark. Subsequently, a new 21-member parliament was set up, recently expanded to between 23 and 26 seats depending on the proportions of votes cast for each party. In 1982, in another referendum, the population voted by a narrow majority to leave the EC, which they had joined as part of Denmark in 1972. Greenland is now an overseas territory in association with the EC. Another source of conflict between Greenland and Denmark has been the presence of a major American military radar facility (part of the Defence Early Warning network) at Thule in the north. Residents claim that it attracts the attention of potential adversaries and is now, given the end of the Cold War, redundant. Campaigners also claim the installation operates in violation of the 1972 Anti-Ballistic Missile treaty. For their part, the Danes maintain that their obligations as a NATO member imply that the facility must stay. Thule has also had a major effect on Greenland's domestic politics: an argument between parties over proposed modernisation of the complex brought down Greenland's coalition government in March 1987.
GOVERNMENT: The two parties at odds – the left-wing nationalist Siumit and the centrist Inuit Ataqatigiit – are the territory's principal political forces.

CLIMATE

Greenland has an Arctic climate, but owing to the size of the country there are great variations in the weather. As the climate graph below shows, winters can be severe and the summers comparatively mild, particularly in areas which are sheltered from the prevailing winds.
Precipitation, mostly snow, is moderately heavy around the coast. The north of the country, and much of the interior, enjoys true Arctic weather, with the temperature only rising above freezing for brief periods in the summer.
Note: Conditions in all parts of the country can become hazardous when there is a combination of a low temperature and a strong wind. Local advice concerning weather conditions should be followed very carefully. Nevertheless, the summer months are suitable for a wide range of outdoor activities.
Required clothing: Good quality wind- and waterproof clothes, warm jerseys and moulded sole shoes at all times of the year; also some slightly thinner clothes – it is important to be able to change clothing during a day's climbing as temperatures can vary greatly during one day.
Sunglasses and protective sun lotion are strongly advised. Extra warm clothes are necessary for those contemplating dog-sledge expeditions. Extra clothes are not always available for hire in Greenland.

NUUK Greenland (20m)

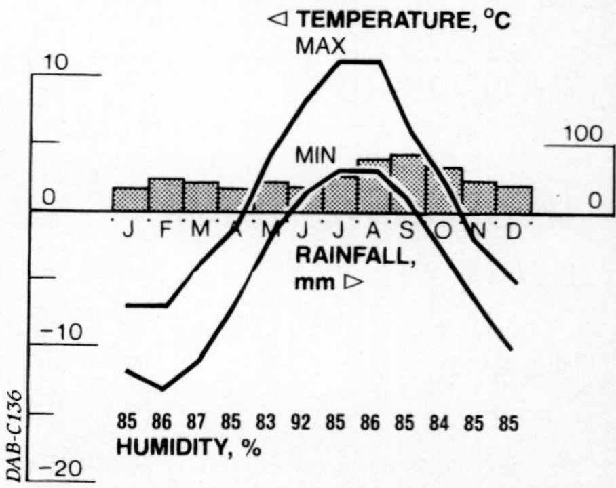

GRENADA

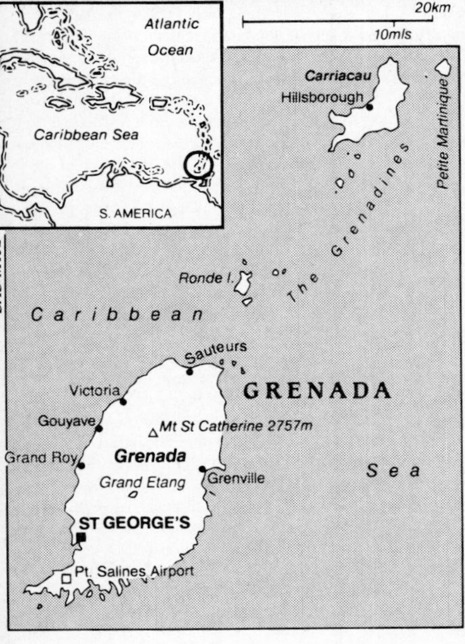

Location: Caribbean, Windward Islands.

Grenada Board of Tourism
PO Box 293
The Carenage
St George's, Grenada
Tel: 2279 *or* 2001. Fax: 6637. Telex: 3422 MINTCA GA.
Grenada High Commission
1 Collingham Gardens
London SW5 0HW
Tel: (071) 373 7800/8/9. Fax: (071) 370 7040. Telex: 889183 GRECOM G. Opening hours: 0930-1330 and 1430-1730 Monday to Friday.
Grenada Board of Tourism
Address as above
Tel: (071) 370 5164/5. Fax: (071) 370 7040. Telex: 889183. Opening hours: 0930-1730.
British High Commission
14 Church Street
St George's, Grenada
Tel: 440 3222 *or* 440 3536. Fax: 440 4939. Telex: 3419 UKREP GA.
Embassy of Grenada
1701 New Hampshire Avenue, NW
Washington, DC 20009
Tel: (202) 265 2561.
Grenada Board of Tourism
Suite 900D
820 2nd Avenue
New York, NY 10017
Tel: (212) 687 9554. Fax: (212) 573 9731.
Embassy of the United States of America
PO Box 54
Point Salines
St George's, Grenada
Tel: 1731. Fax: 4820.
Consulate General of Grenada
Suite 820
439 University Avenue
Toronto, Ontario
M5G 1Y8
Tel: (416) 595 1343.
Grenada Board of Tourism
Address as above
Tel: (416) 595 1339. Fax: (416) 565 8278.
The Canadian High Commission to Grenada
c/o The Canadian High Commission
PO Box 404
Bridgetown, Barbados.

AREA: 344.5 sq km (133 sq miles).
POPULATION: 93,000 (1991 estimate).
POPULATION DENSITY: 290.3 per sq km.
CAPITAL: St George's. **Population:** 7500 (1980 estimate).
GEOGRAPHY: Grenada is located in the Caribbean. The island is of volcanic origin and is divided by a central mountain range. It is the most southerly of the Windward Islands. Agriculture is based on nutmeg, cocoa, sugar cane and bananas. Tropical rainforests, gorges and the stunning beauty of dormant volcanoes make this a fascinating and diverse landscape with some of the finest beaches in the world. Carriacou and some of the other small islands of the Grenadines are also part of Grenada.
LANGUAGE: English.
RELIGION: Christian: Roman Catholic 64%, Anglican 22%, Methodist 3%, Seventh Day Adventists 3%.
TIME: GMT - 4.
ELECTRICITY: 220/240 volts AC, 50Hz.
COMMUNICATIONS: Telephone: Full IDD service. Country code: 1 809. No area codes are in use. **Fax:** Cable and Wireless provide a service in St George's.
Telex/telegram: International Cable & Wireless (West Indies) Limited offer telegraphic and telex services from 0700-1900 on weekdays, and 0700-1000 and 1600-1800 on public holidays and Sundays. **Post:** The post office in St George's is open 0800-1600 Monday to Friday and 0800-1200 Saturday. **Press:** All newspapers are printed weekly in English. They include *The Grenadian Voice, The Grenada Guardian* and *The Informer.*
BBC World Service and Voice of America frequencies: From time to time these change. See the section *How to Use this Book* for more information.

BBC:				
MHz	17.84	15.22	9.915	6.195
Voice of America:				
MHz	15.21	11.70	6.130	0.930

PASSPORT/VISA

Regulations and requirements may be subject to change at short notice, and you are advised to contact the appropriate diplomatic or consular authority before finalising travel arrangements. Details of these may be found at the head of this country's entry. Any numbers in the chart refer to the footnotes below.

	Passport Required?	Visa Required?	Return Ticket Required?
Full British	No	No	Yes
BVP	Not valid/1	-	-
Australian	Yes	No	Yes
Canadian	No	No	Yes
USA	No	No	Yes
Other EC	Yes	2	Yes
Japanese	Yes	No	Yes

Restricted entry: Nationals of South Africa wishing to go to Grenada should apply direct to Grenada providing full details with their application.
PASSPORTS: Valid passport required by all except:
(a) nationals of Canada, the UK and the USA in possession of two forms of valid ID (eg driving licence, birth certificate or electoral registration, one of which must have a photo) for stays of up to 3 months;
(b) nationals of the Commonwealth of Dominica, St Vincent & the Grenadines and St Lucia, with acceptable identification.
British Visitors Passport: [1] Not officially accepted. Although the immigration authorities of this country may in certain circumstances accept British Visitors Passports for persons arriving for holidays or unpaid business trips of up to three months, travellers are reminded that no formal agreement exists to this effect and the situation may, therefore, change at short notice. In addition, UK nationals using a BVP and returning to the UK from a country with which no such formal agreement exists may be subject to delays and interrogation by UK immigration.
VISAS: Required by all except:
(a) those who continue their journey to a third destination within 14 days, providing they hold an onward ticket;
(b) **[2]** nationals of EC countries (with the exception of nationals of the Republic of Ireland who *do* require visas);
(c) nationals of Antigua & Barbuda, Australia, Bahamas, Bangladesh, Barbados, Belize, Bermuda, Botswana, Brunei, Canada, Cayman Islands, Christmas Islands, Cocos Islands, Dominica, Fiji, Finland, Gambia, Ghana, Guyana, Iceland, India, Israel, Jamaica, Japan, Kenya, Kiribati, South Korea, Lesotho, Liechtenstein, Malawi, Malaysia, Maldives, Malta, Mauritius, Nauru, New Zealand, Nigeria, Norway, Papua New Guinea, St Kitts & Nevis, St Lucia, St Vincent & the Grenadines, Western Samoa, San Marino, Seychelles, Sierra Leone, Singapore, Solomon Islands, Sri Lanka, Swaziland, Sweden, Switzerland, Tanzania, Tonga, Trinidad & Tobago, Tuvalu, Uganda, USA, Vanuatu, Venezuela, Zambia and Zimbabwe.
Types of visa: Tourist and Business. Cost: £8.
Validity: Up to 3 months.
Application to: Consulate (or Consular Section at Embassy or High Commission) well in advance of intended day of departure. For addresses, see top of entry.
Application requirements: (a) Valid passport. (b) Completed application forms. (c) 2 passport-size photographs. (d) Fee payable by cash or postal order. (e) Stamped self-addressed envelope. (f) Business letters from contact for Business visas.

MONEY

Currency: Eastern Caribbean Dollar (EC$) = 100 cents. Notes are in denominations of EC$100, 20, 5 and 1. Coins are in denominations of EC$1 and 50, 25, 10, 5, 2 and 1 cents.
Currency exchange: The Grenada National Bank, The Grenada Co-operative Bank, Barclays Bank International, The Royal Bank of Canada, Grenada Bank of Commerce and The Bank of Nova Scotia are all found on the island.
Credit cards: American Express and Visa are widely accepted, whereas Access/Mastercard and Diners Club acceptance is less common. Some shops and car hire companies may not accept credit cards. Check with your credit card company for details of merchant acceptability and other services which may be available.
Travellers cheques: Widely accepted.
Exchange rate indicators: The following figures are included as a guide to the movements of the Eastern Caribbean Dollar against Sterling and the US Dollar:

Date:	Oct '89	Oct '90	Oct '91	Oct '92
£1.00=	4.26	5.27	4.69	4.27
$1.00=	*2.70	*2.70	*2.70	*2.70

Note [*]: The Eastern Caribbean Dollar is tied to the US Dollar.
Currency restrictions: Free import of local currency, subject to declaration. Export limited to amount declared on import.
Banking hours: 0800-1400 Monday to Thursday, 0800-1300 and 1430-1700 Friday.

DUTY FREE

The following goods may be imported into Grenada without incurring customs duty:
200 cigarettes or 50 cigars or 250g of tobacco;
1 quart wine or spirits;
A reasonable amount of perfume.

PUBLIC HOLIDAYS

Public holidays observed in Grenada are as follows:
Apr 9 '93 Good Friday. **Apr 12** Easter Monday. **May 1** Labour Day. **May 31** Whit Monday. **Jun 10** Corpus Christi. **Aug 2** Emancipation Day/August Holiday. **Aug 9** Carnival Monday. **Aug 10** Carnival Tuesday. **Oct 25** Thanksgiving Day. **Dec 25-26** Christmas. **Jan 1 '94** New Year's Day. **Feb 7** Independence Day.

HEALTH

Regulations and requirements may be subject to change at short notice, and you are advised to contact your doctor well in advance of your intended date of departure. Any numbers in the chart refer to the footnotes below.

	Special Precautions?	Certificate Required?
Yellow Fever	No	1
Cholera	No	No
Typhoid & Polio	Yes	-
Malaria	No	-
Food & Drink	2	-

[1]: A yellow fever vaccination certificate is required from all travellers over one year of age coming from infected areas.
[2]: Mains water is normally chlorinated and relatively safe. Bottled water is available. Milk is pasteurised and dairy products are safe for consumption. Local meat, poultry, seafood, fruit and vegetables are generally considered safe to eat.
Health care: Medical facilities are adequate. Health insurance is advised.

TRAVEL - International

AIR: The main airlines to serve Grenada are *American Airlines (AA), LIAT (LI), British Airways (BA)* and *BWIA International (BW)* which offer connections with Grenada from other Caribbean islands.
Approximate flight times: From Grenada to *London* (via Barbados) is 9 hours, to *Los Angeles* is 9 hours and to *New York* is 5 hours.
International airport: *Point Salines (GRN)* airport is close to St George's, and there are taxis operating between the airport and the capital. Facilities include duty-free and handicraft shops, snack bars and boutiques.
Departure tax: EC$35 on all departures.
SEA: St George's, considered the most picturesque port in the Caribbean, is port of call for many cruise lines,

including *Cunard, Costa, TUI Cruises, Royal Viking* and CTC. *Geest Lines* sail from England via Barbados, stopping at St Vincent and St Lucia or Dominica on the return trip. 70% (197,775) of tourist arrivals are cruise-ship passengers. Inter-island schooners sail to Carriacou, Petit Martinique and Isle de Ronde up to four times weekly. Check at a local tourist office for times and fares.

TRAVEL - Internal

SEA: Grenada has a very large fleet of charter yachts, from large professional vessels to smaller bare-boat charters. Round-island trips are very popular. Arrangements can be made via the Tourist Board in Grenada.
ROAD: Roads are narrow and winding. Driving follows British customs, and traffic drives on the left. **Taxi:** Taxis are the most efficient means of transport. **Bus:** Buses are cheap but slow. **Car hire:** A large range of vehicles is available (from limousines to mini-mokes) in St George's or St Andrew's. Credit cards are not always accepted by car hire companies. **Documentation:** A temporary licence to drive (costing approximately EC$60) is available from local authorities on presentation of a valid British or Northern Ireland driving licence. An International Driving Permit is recommended, although it is not legally required.
JOURNEY TIMES: The following chart gives approximate journey times (in hours and minutes) from St George's to other major cities/islands in Grenada.

	Air	Road	Sea
Grenville	-	0.35	-
Carriacou	0.20	-	3.30

ACCOMMODATION

HOTELS: Grenada offers a variety of modern, luxurious hotels. Pre-booking is essential. An 8% service charge and 7.5% government tax is added to all room prices. Contact the National Tourist Office for details and exact price listings. There is also a Grenada Hotel Association at Ross Point Inn, St George's, Grenada. Tel: 444 1353. Fax: 444 4847. **Tipping:** 10% service charge and 8% Government tax is added to all hotel bills.
GUEST-HOUSES: There are a few guest-houses, some of which offer self-catering facilities.
SELF-CATERING: There is a growing number of apartments and villas available for rent. Contact the Grenada Board of Tourism for details.

RESORTS & EXCURSIONS

St George's: *The Carenage*, a picturesque inner harbour with 18th-century warehouses and restaurants, the botanical gardens, the zoo and *Fort George* (built by the French in 1705) are all worth a visit. See also the outer harbour, *St Andrew's Presbyterian Church* and *Fort Frederick*.
Spice Country: On the way here, north from the capital, you pass through some of the prettiest fishing villages on the island. Hidden among the red roofs of **Gouyave** is the factory where spices are sorted, dried and milled. The *Dougaldston Estate* is a traditional plantation in the centre of the nutmeg and cocoa growing region.
Sauteurs/Morne des Sauteurs: From these rocks the last of the island's Carib Indians plummeted to their deaths in 1650.
Levera Bay & Grande Anse: Two of the island's best beaches.
Grand Etang: Extinct volcano cradling a beautiful 30-acre blue lake.
Annandale Falls: A 15m (50ft) cascade that flows into a mountain stream.
Carriacou: In 'the Grenadines of Grenada', a yachtsman's paradise.

SOCIAL PROFILE

FOOD & DRINK: Local specialities include seafood and vegetables, *calaloo soup*, crabs, conches *(lambi)* and avocado ice-cream. Most hotels and restaurants offer fully international cuisine, serving a large variety of tropical fish and English, Continental, American and exotic West Indian food. **Drink:** A local company supply a wide variety of local fruit juices and nectars. The local rum and beer, *Carib*, is excellent. Bars are stocked with most popular wines and spirits, including various brands of whisky, rum, and brandy. In past times casks containing Grenadian rum were stamped with the words 'Georgius Rex Old Grenada', the acronym GROG formed from these words is said to be the origin of the navy word 'grog'.
NIGHTLIFE: Based in hotels, with discos, organised shows and cabarets.
SHOPPING: Special purchases include spices, straw goods, printed cottons and other fabrics. There are a number of duty-free shops selling quality goods from all over the world. **Shopping hours:** 0800-1600 Monday to Friday, 0800-1200 Saturday.
SPORT: Golf and tennis: Both available either independently or through hotels. **Watersports:** Equipment for all watersports is available. **Yachting:** Yachting is extremely popular. A number of major yacht races and regattas are held throughout the year. A variety of small and large craft may be rented. Contact the Grenada Board of Tourism for details. **Fishing:** A major fishing tournament is held in January.
SPECIAL EVENTS: There are several yachting and fishing events throughout the year; in addition, public holidays are usually accompanied by some form of special event or celebration. For full details of events taking place during 1993/1994, contact the Grenada Board of Tourism.
SOCIAL CONVENTIONS: Local culture reflects the island's history of British and French colonial rule and, of course, the African cultures imported with the slaves – African influence is especially noticeable on the island of Carriacou in their Big Drum and in Grenada with the Shango dance. The Roman Catholic Church also exerts a strong influence on the way of life. Local people are generally friendly and courteous. Dress is casual and informal but beachware is not welcome in town.

BUSINESS PROFILE

ECONOMY: The Grenadian economy is predominantly agricultural and centred on the production of spices. The principal exports are nutmeg, cocoa, bananas and sugar cane. Earnings from all these products have varied substantially according to fluctuations in the world market. Repeated attempts to broaden the base of the economy – by, for example, developing the fishing industry, have failed to yield dividends. Local industry is minimal and has scarcely expanded at all since the mid-1980s. The most important single economic activity is tourism, and this too has stagnated. Grenada relies on extensive foreign aid from the US, the UK, Canada and the European Community. The UK and US are the island's main trading partners.
BUSINESS: All correspondence and trade literature is in English. **Office hours:** 0800-1200 and 1300-1600 Monday to Friday.
COMMERCIAL INFORMATION: The following organisation can offer advice: Grenada Chamber of Industry and Commerce, PO Box 129, Decaul Building, Mount Gay, St George's. Tel: 2937. Fax: 6627. Telex: 3469.
CONFERENCES/CONVENTIONS: Eight hotels offer facilities, seating from 25-300 persons. The Grenada Board of Tourism Office can supply details.

HISTORY & GOVERNMENT

HISTORY: For a small island, Grenada has had an especially turbulent history. The earliest known inhabitants were peaceful Arawak inhabitants, but they were overrun by warlike (and cannibalistic) Caribs some time before AD1300. The first serious attempt at settlement by Europeans was in 1609, but the Caribs resisted fiercely and it wasn't until 1650 that the French were able to claim the island. It remained a French colony until taken by the British in 1783. Grenada was an important centre in the slave trade between Africa and the sugar plantations of the West Indies. With the emancipation of slaves and the disintegration of the plantation system, the majority of islanders came to depend on a few local industries and their own smallholdings. Radical politics have been a hallmark of Grenadian society since the early 1950s when trade union organisation, promoted by Eric Gairy, a firebrand ex-teacher, took root among the workforce. Gairy ultimately led Grenada into independence from Britain in February 1974, and subsequently won three elections for the premiership. Not all were content with Gairy's regime, and among his opponents was the New JEWEL Movement (Joint Endeavour for Welfare, Education and Liberation), a group of mainly young, educated left-wingers led by Maurice Bishop. In the spring of 1979, the NJM deposed Gairy in a bloodless coup. The US believed that the NJM was determined to turn Grenada into a mini-Cuba and from 1980 onwards increased political pressure against the Government. How to respond to this, and other questions, split the NJM leadership, and led to the military coup of October 1983 in which Bishop was killed. The coup provided a pretext for the US invasion and the restoration of the pre-NJM system of government under the tutelage of the Americans. Four existing political parties allied to form the New National Party (NNP) under the leadership of the veteran politician Herbert Blaize to keep out Eric Gairy who was still on the scene. At the general election in December 1984, the NNP won handsomely. At the latest poll in March 1990, the National Democratic Congress (NDC), a party formed in 1987 when opposition parties merged, was elected to govern under the premiership of Mr Nicholas Braithwaite. Grenada is one of the four members of the Organisation of Eastern Caribbean States which are beginning moves towards political and economic integration: other island states in the Caribbean are strongly opposed to such moves but its proponents feel that it is essential to safeguard the economic future of the region. It seems more likely than not that others will join in due course. At the most recent polls held in March 1990, no single party achieved an overall majority but the National Democratic Congress, formed in 1987 from the ashes of Eric Gairy's GULP (Grenada United Labour Party) and two other centre-left groupings, was able to form a government with support from smaller parties.
GOVERNMENT: The Prime Minister, currently Nicholas Braithwaite, presides over a Cabinet of seven ministers. The Head of State is the British monarch, HM Queen Elizabeth II.

CLIMATE

Tropical. The dry season runs from February to May. The rainy season runs from June to December.
Required clothing: Tropical lightweights and cool summer clothing.

KINGSTOWN St Vincent

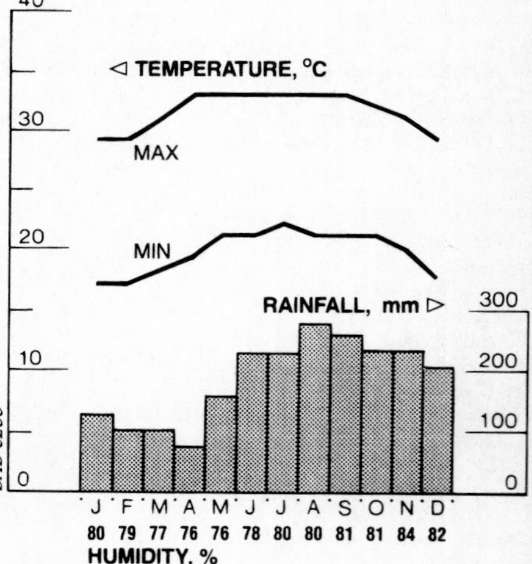

GRENADA | **HEALTH REGULATIONS** | **VISA REGULATIONS** | Code-Link

	HEALTH REGULATIONS	VISA REGULATIONS
GALILEO/WORLDSPAN	TI-DFT/GND/HE	TI-DFT/GND/VI
SABRE	TIDFT/GND/HE	TIDFT/GND/VI

To access this information on your CRS, swipe the barcode with a light pen or type in the text under the barcode. For more information, see the introduction *How to Use This Book.*

GUADELOUPE

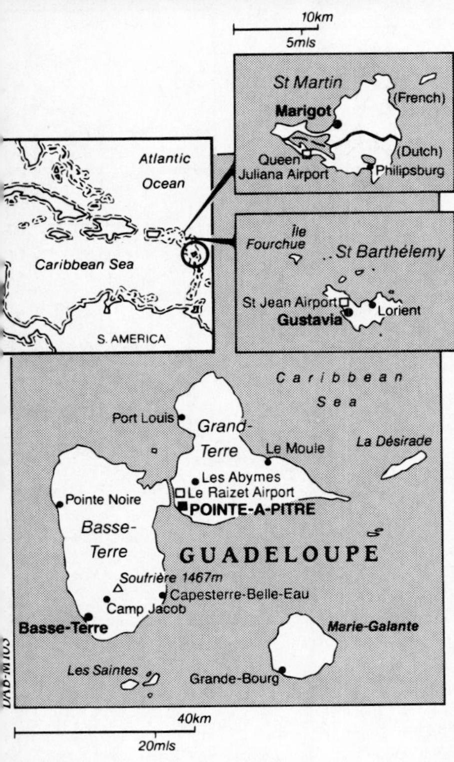

Location: Caribbean, at the arc of the Leeward group of islands of the Lesser Antilles.

Office du Tourisme
BP 1099, 5 square de la Banque
97181 Pointe-à-Pitre
Guadeloupe
Tel: 820 930. Fax: 838 922. Telex: 919715.

Embassy of the French Republic
58 Knightsbridge
London SW1X 7JT
Tel: (071) 235 8080.

French Consulate General (Visas)
PO Box 57
6a Cromwell Place
London SW7 2JN
Tel: (071) 581 5292 *or* (0898) 200 289. Telex: 924153 FRELON. Opening hours: 0900-1200 (and 1600-1630 for visa collection only) Monday to Friday (except French and British national holidays).

French Government Tourist Office
178 Piccadilly
London W1V 0AL
Tel: (071) 499 6911 (recorded message) *or* (071) 493 6594. Fax: (071) 493 6594. Telex: 21902. Opening hours: 0900-1700 Monday to Friday.

British Consulate
BP 2041, Zone Industrielle de Jarry
97192 Pointe-à-Pitre Cedex, Guadeloupe
Tel: 266 429. Telex: OUVRE 019779 GL.

Embassy of the French Republic
4101 Reservoir Road, NW
Washington, DC 20007
Tel: (202) 944 6000 *or* 944 6200 (Consular section). Fax: (202) 944 6072.

Embassy of the French Republic
42 Sussex Drive
Ottawa, Ontario K1M 2C9
Tel: (613) 232 1795. Fax: (613) 232 4302. Telex: 0533564.

French Government Tourist Office
Suite 490, 1981 McGill College
Montréal, Quebec, H3A 2W9
Tel: (514) 288 4264. Fax: (514) 845 4868.

AREA: Total: 1780 sq km (687 sq miles). **Basse-Terre:** 839 sq km (324 sq miles). **Grand-Terre:** 564 sq km (218 sq miles). **Marie-Galante:** 150 sq km (58 sq miles). **La Désirade:** 29.7 sq km (11.5 sq miles). **Les Saintes:** 13.9 sq km (5.4 sq miles). **St Barthélemy:** 95 sq km (37 sq miles). **St Martin** (which shares the island with St Maarten, part of the Netherland Antilles): 88 sq km (34 sq miles).
POPULATION: 386,988 (1990 estimate).
POPULATION DENSITY: 217.4 per sq km.
CAPITAL: Basse-Terre (administrative). **Population:** 14,107 (1989 estimate). Pointe-à-Pitre, on Grande Terre (commercial centre). **Population:** 26,083 (1989 estimate).
GEOGRAPHY: Guadeloupe comprises Guadeloupe proper (Basse-Terre), Grande Terre (separated from Basse-Terre by a narrow sea channel) and five smaller islands. Basse-Terre has a rough volcanic relief whilst Grande Terre is flat and chalky. All the islands have beautiful white- or black-sand palm-fringed beaches. There are also many lush mountainous areas with stunning and unspoiled tropical scenery.
LANGUAGE: The official language is French. The *lingua franca* is Creole *patois* and English is also widely spoken.
TIME: GMT - 4.
RELIGION: The majority are Roman Catholic, with a minority of predominantly Evangelical protestant groups.
ELECTRICITY: 110 or 220 volts AC, 50Hz.
COMMUNICATIONS: Telephone: IDD is available. Country code: 590. Good internal network. There are no area codes. **Telex:** Facilities available in the capital. **Post:** Airmail takes a week to reach Europe. **Press:** Newspapers are all in French. The main daily is *France Antilles*.
BBC World Service and Voice of America frequencies: From time to time these change. See the section *How to Use this Book* for more information.

BBC:				
MHz	17.84	15.22	9.915	6.195
Voice of America:				
MHz	15.21	11.70	6.130	0.930

PASSPORT/VISA

Regulations and requirements may be subject to change at short notice, and you are advised to contact the appropriate diplomatic or consular authority before finalising travel arrangements. Details of these may be found at the head of this country's entry. Any numbers in the chart refer to the footnotes below.

	Passport Required?	Visa Required?	Return Ticket Required?
Full British	Yes	No	Yes
BVP	Not valid	-	-
Australian	Yes	Yes	Yes
Canadian	Yes	No	Yes
USA	Yes	No	Yes
Other EC	Yes	No	Yes
Japanese	Yes	No	Yes

PASSPORTS: Required by all.
British Visitors Passports: Not accepted.
VISAS: Required by all except:
(a) nationals of countries as shown above;
(b) nationals of Andorra, Austria, Cyprus, Finland, Liechtenstein, Malta, Monaco, Norway, San Marino, Sweden, Switzerland and Vatican City.
Types of visa: Please refer to the Guadeloupe Section of a French Embassy.
Validity: Up to 3 months.
Application to: Guadeloupe Section of a French Embassy.
Application requirements: (a) 3 application forms. (b) 3 photos. (c) Evidence of return ticket. (d) Valid passport.
Working days required: Visas issued the same day.

MONEY

Currency: French Franc (FFr) = 100 centimes. Notes are in the denominations of FFr500, 200, 100, 50, and 20. Coins are in the denominations of FFr10, 5, 2 and 1, and 20, 10, and 5 centimes.
Credit cards: Access/Mastercard (limited), Diners Club, American Express and Visa are accepted. Check with your credit card company for details of merchant acceptability and other services which may be available.
Travellers cheques are accepted in most places, and may qualify for discount on luxury items. US and Canadian dollars are also accepted in some places.
Exchange rate indicators: The following figures are included as a guide to the movements of the French Franc against Sterling and the US Dollar:

Date:	**Oct '89**	**Oct '90**	**Oct '91**	**Oct '92**
£1.00=	10.10	9.97	9.92	8.28
$1.00=	6.39	5.10	5.72	5.21

Currency restrictions: As for France.

DUTY FREE

Guadeloupe is an Overseas Department of France, and the duty-free allowances are therefore the same as for France.

PUBLIC HOLIDAYS

Public holidays observed in Guadeloupe are as follows:
Apr 9 '93 Good Friday. **Apr 12** Easter Monday. **May 1** Labour Day. **May 20** Ascension Day. **May 31** Whit Monday. **Jul 14** National Day. **Jul 21** Victor Schoëlcher Day. **Nov 11** Armistice Day. **Dec 25** Christmas Day. **Jan 1 '94** New Year's Day. **Jan 6** Epiphany. **Feb/Mar*** Lenten Carnival.
Note [*]: Check with Tourist Board for the exact date.

HEALTH

Regulations and requirements may be subject to change at short notice, and you are advised to contact your doctor well in advance of your intended date of departure. Any numbers in the chart refer to the footnotes below.

	Special Precautions?	Certificate Required?
Yellow Fever	No	1
Cholera	No	No
Typhoid & Polio	Yes	-
Malaria	No	-
Food & Drink	2	-

[1]: A yellow fever vaccination certificate is required by travellers over one year of age arriving from an infected or endemic zone.
[2]: Mains water is chlorinated and whilst relatively safe, may cause mild abdominal upsets. Bottled water is available and is advised for the first few weeks of stay. Drinking water outside main cities and towns may be contaminated and sterilisation is advised. Milk is pasteurised and dairy products are safe for consumption. Local meat, poultry, seafoods and fruit are generally considered safe to eat.
Bilharzia (Schistosomiasis) is present. Avoid swimming and paddling in fresh water. Swimming pools, which are well maintained and chlorinated, are safe.

TRAVEL - International

AIR: Guadeloupe's national airline is *Air Guadeloupe*.
Approximate flight times: From Guadeloupe to *London* is 12 hours 40 minutes (including a stopover time of one hour in Paris), to *Los Angeles* is 9 hours and to *New York* is 6 hours.

GUADELOUPE | **HEALTH REGULATIONS** | **VISA REGULATIONS** | Code-Link

TI-DFT/PTP/VI

To access this information on your CRS, swipe the barcode with a light pen or type in the text under the barcode. For more information, see the introduction *How to Use This Book*.

International airport: *Point-à-Pitre (PTP)* (Raizet), 3km (2 miles) from Point-à-Pitre.
SEA: Guadeloupe is a point of call following international cruise liners: *Chandris, Holland America, Royal Caribbean, Cunard, Sun Line, Sitmar, TUI Cruises* and *Princess Cruises*. Many ships ply between Guadeloupe and Martinique, and also connect with Miami and San Juan.

TRAVEL - Internal

AIR: *LIAT, Air Antilles , Air Guadeloupe, Windward Island Airlines* and *BWIA* connect Guadeloupe with the smaller islands in the group. *Air France* also offers a limited inter-island service. There are domestic airports on the islands of Marie-Galante, La Désirade and Saint-Barthélemy.
SEA: Regular ferry services ply around the islands.
ROAD: There is a good public **bus** service, **taxi** services and many **car and van rental** companies. **Documentation:** National driving licence is sufficient, but at least one year's driving experience is required. An International Driving Licence is advised.

ACCOMMODATION

HOTELS: There is a good selection of hotels on Guadeloupe, ranging from first-class beach resorts to country inns. The accommodation on the outlying islands can be interesting, but may be very basic. At present there are over 3000 rooms throughout the group. The tax on hotel rates is 5-7% rising to 20-30% in the high season (mid-December to mid-April). The Relais de la Guadelope provides a central booking service. **Grading:** 3-/4-star hotels offer sporting and cultural activities in addition to board and lodging. There are also two particular categories of hotel Hibiscus (H) and Alamandas (A). Hibiscus hotels are 2- or 3-star establishments usually run as a family affair. Alamandas hotels are sophisticated 1- or 2-star establishments. Many hotels in the Caribbean offer accommodation according to one of a number of plans: **FAP** is Full American Plan; room with all meals (including afternoon tea, supper etc). **AP** is American Plan; room with three meals. **MAP** is Modified American Plan; breakfast and dinner included with the price of the room, plus in some places British-style afternoon tea. **CP** is Continental Plan; room and breakfast only. **EP** is European Plan; room only.
SELF-CATERING: Villas and Cottages may be rented. Obtain further information from the tourist office.

RESORTS & EXCURSIONS

Point-à-Pitre, the commercial capital of Guadeloupe, is a gracious town with a pleasant square at its core, the *Place de la Victoire*, which is surrounded by a busy market and, further out, the docks. It is an active, lively port with many narrow streets worth exploring. The *Pavillion d'Exposition de Bergevin* and the *Centre Cultural Remy Nainsouta* are two museums well worth a visit. On **Basse-Terre**, *Saint Marie de Capesterre* where Columbus landed should be visited, as should the Hindu temple to its south. The small town of **Trois Rivières** has a collection of Indian relics which could be visited on the way to the *National Park* near **St Claude**. This 74,000-acre park, of great natural beauty, is situated at the base of *La Soufrière*, an inactive volcano. The town of **Basse-Terre** itself is a beautiful old French colonial town, situated at the foot of La Soufrière. The *St Charles Fort* is of French military architecture, built in 1605 and now restored into a museum. The cathedral and market place are also worth seeing. At *Fort Fleur de L'Epée* on **Grand-terre** there are some fascinating underground caves and to the north of these the old sugar town of **Sainte Anne** should not be missed. The other islands of **Marie-Galante, La Désirade** and **Les Saintes** are visited less frequently and are best suited to the resourceful traveller. La Désirade, quiet and undeveloped, is known for its seafood. Les Saintes are a string of tiny islands, only two of which are inhabited, **Terre-de-Haut** and **Terre-de-Bas.** These have a selection of modestly priced hotels. Marie-Galante has a number of good hotels and beaches. Its old and crumbling mills are reminders of its history as a major sugar plantation.

SOCIAL PROFILE

FOOD & DRINK: Predominantly seafood, cooked in many French, Creole, African, Hindu or South-East Asian styles. Dishes include lobster, turtle, red snapper, conch and sea urchin. Island specialities include stuffed crab, stewed conch, roast wild goat, jugged rabbit and broiled dove. The spicy flavour of Creole cuisine should not be missed. The more formal restaurants will require appropriate dress. **Drinks** include a great supply of French wines, Champagnes, liqueurs and local rum. A local speciality, *Rum Punch* (a brew of rum, lime, bitter and syrup), is a must. There are no licensing restrictions.
NIGHTLIFE: There are plenty of restaurants, bars and discotheques, with displays of local dancing and music. The famous dance of the island is called the *Biguine*.
SHOPPING: Worthwhile purchases are French imports, including perfume, wine, liqueurs and lalique crystal. Local items include fine-flavoured rum, straw goods, bamboo hats, voodoo dolls, and objects of aromatic Vetevier root. Travellers cheques give a 20% discount in some shops. **Shopping hours:** 0830-1300 and 1500-1800 Monday to Friday; 0830-1300 Saturday.
SPORT: All **watersports** are available somewhere on Guadeloupe, but they may be less well developed than on some of the other Caribbean islands. The **swimming** and the **snorkelling** are excellent, as is the **fishing** (including deep-sea, harpoon fishing). Some of the beaches are for nude and topless sunbathing. **Small-boat sailing** is popular as well as **water-skiing. Tennis, golf** (at the famous 18-hole course of Saint-Françoise, at Le Méridien hotel, designed by R. Trent Jones), **horseriding, hiking** and **mountain climbing** are all possibilities.
SPECIAL EVENTS: There are many local festivals and special events, both Roman Catholic and Creole. For details contact the French Tourist Board.
SOCIAL CONVENTIONS: The atmosphere is relaxed and informal. Casual dress is accepted everywhere, but formal dress is needed for dining out and in nightclubs. **Tipping:** 10% is normal.

BUSINESS PROFILE

ECONOMY: Guadeloupe's economy is relatively diverse by regional standards – with agriculture, light industry and tourism – but remains heavily dependent on French aid. Sugar has been the principal export earner, but both production and revenues have declined during the 1980s. Bananas have now replaced sugar as the main export product. Coffee, cocoa and vanilla are the other important cash crops. Tourism is a fast-growing sector, although it has suffered from a general downturn in the Caribbean and from the effects of hurricanes. France supplies most of the island's imports and takes three-quarters of its exports.
BUSINESS: Lightweight suits, safari suits, and shirt and tie are recommended for business meetings. Best times to visit are January to March and June to September. Much of the island's business is connected to France. **Office hours:** 0800-1700 Monday to Friday, 0800-1200 Saturday.
COMMERCIAL INFORMATION: The following organisation can offer advice: Chambre de Commerce et d'Industrie de Pointe-à-Pitre, BP 64, rue F. Eboué, 97152 Pointe-à-Pitre. Tel: 900 808. Fax: 902 187. Telex: 919780.

HISTORY & GOVERNMENT

HISTORY: Guadeloupe was discovered by Columbus in 1493. French colonies were established in 1635. The British made brief attempts to occupy the islands during the 18th and the 19th centuries, but the islands have always remained under French control. In 1946 the islands were given the status of Overseas Departments and as a result of President Mitterand's decentralisation policies, Guadeloupe became an administrative region and is represented in the French national assembly by four deputies: two Socialists and one apiece from the Communists and the Gaullist RPR. All four major parties maintain branches on the island. The General Council, which handles Guadeloupe's internal affairs and whose powers have been recently augmented, has a left majority although the RPR is the largest single party with 15 of the 41 seats. Of particular importance to the future development of Guadeloupe is a recent report by the Ministry of Overseas Departments recommending significant changes to improve social and economic conditions on the island.
GOVERNMENT: The government Commissioner on Guadeloupe represents France and the island sends three representatives to the National Assembly in Paris. There is a General Council and a Regional Council which administers the islands. There are also General Councils and Regional Councils for the local affairs of the Antilles.

CLIMATE

Warm weather throughout the year. The main rainy season is from June to October. Brief showers can, however, occur at any time. The humidity can be very high.
Required clothing: Lightweights and waterproofs.

CAMP JACOB Guadeloupe (533m)

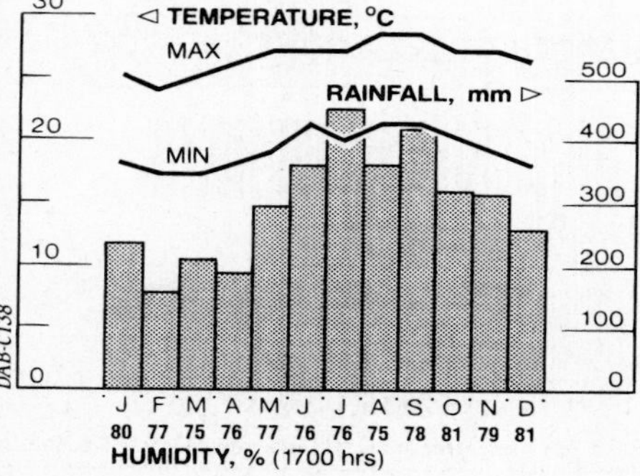

GUATEMALA

□ *international airport*

Location: Central America.

Note: The recent history of Guatemala is one of extreme political unrest. Travel anywhere outside major commercial centres is not recommended.

Guatemala Tourist Commission
7a Avenida 1-17
Centro Cívico
Zona 4, Guatemala City
Guatemala
Tel: (2) 311 333. Fax: (2) 318 893. Telex: 5532.
Embassy of the Republic of Guatemala
13 Fawcett Street
London
SW10 9HN
Tel: (071) 351 3042. Fax: (071) 376 5708. Telex: 926556.
British Embassy
7th Floor, Edificio Centro Financerio
Tower Two, 7a Avenida 5-10
Zona 4, Guatemala City
Guatemala
Tel: (2) 321 601/2/4. Fax: (2) 341 904. Telex: 5686 BRITON GU.
Embassy of the Republic of Guatemala
2220 R Street, NW
Washington, DC 20008
Tel: (202) 745 4952/3/4. Fax: (202) 745 1908. Telex: 361499.
Embassy of the United States of America
Avenida La Reforma 7-01
Zona 10, Guatemala City
Guatemala
Tel: (2) 311 541/55.
Embassy of the Republic of Guatemala
Suite 504
885 Meadowlands Drive
Ottawa, Ontario
K2C 3N2
Tel: (613) 224 4322 *or* 224 4780 (Consular section). Fax: (613) 224 4434.
Guatemala Tourist Commission (INGUAT)
SACA Information Centre
72 McGill Street
Toronto, Ontario
M5B 1H2
Tel: (416) 348 8597. Fax: (416) 348 8597.
Canadian Embassy
Galerías España
6th Floor, 7 Avenida 11-59
Zona 9, Guatemala City
Guatemala
Tel: 321 411/3/7/8 *or* 321 426/8. Fax: 321 419. Telex: 5206.

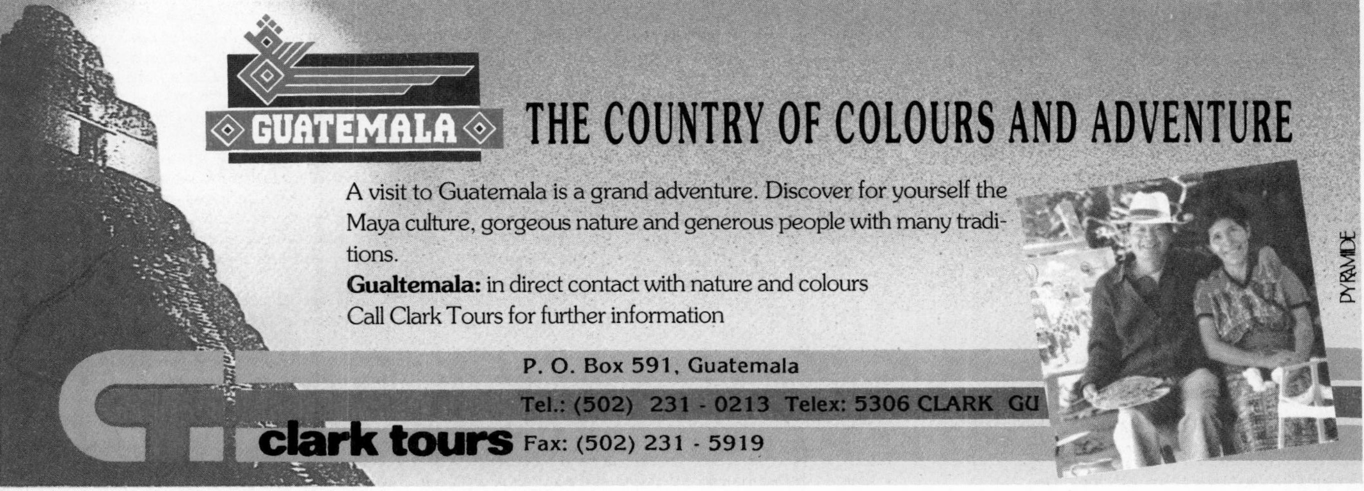

AREA: 108,889 sq km (42,042 sq miles).
POPULATION: 9,453,953 (1991 estimate).
POPULATION DENSITY: 86.8 per sq km.
CAPITAL: Guatemala City. **Population:** 1,095,677 (1991).
GEOGRAPHY: Guatemala is located in Central America and shares borders with Mexico, Belize, Honduras and El Salvador. The landscape is predominantly mountainous and heavily forested. A string of volcanoes rises above the southern highlands along the Pacific, three of which are still active. Within this volcanic area are basins of varying sizes which hold the majority of the country's population. The region is drained by rivers flowing into both the Pacific and the Caribbean. One basin west of the capital has no river outlet and thus has formed Lake Atitlán, which is ringed by volcanoes. To the northwest, bordering on Belize and Mexico, lies the low undulating tableland of El Petén, 36,300 sq km (14,000 sq miles) of almost inaccessible wilderness covered with dense hardwood forest. This area covers approximately one-third of the national territory, yet contains only 40,000 people.
LANGUAGE: The official language is Spanish. English is widely spoken in Guatemala City. Over 20 indigenous languages are also spoken.
RELIGION: Mostly Roman Catholic and about 25% Protestant.
TIME: GMT - 6.
ELECTRICITY: 110 volts AC, 60Hz. There are some regional variations.
COMMUNICATIONS: Telephone: IDD is available. Country code: 502. Telephone calls to Europe are slightly cheaper between 1900 and 0700. **Fax:** Some hotels have facilities. **Telex/telegram:** Telex facilities are available in Guatemala City; local telegrams can be sent from the central post office. Urgent telegrams are charged at double the ordinary rate. **Post:** Airmail to Europe takes from 6 to 12 days. **Press:** All newspapers are in Spanish. Publications include *El Gráfico*, *Prensa Libra* and *La Hora*.
BBC World Service and Voice of America frequencies: From time to time these change. See the section *How to Use this Book* for more information.

BBC:				
MHz	17.84	15.22	9.590	7.325
Voice of America:				
MHz	15.21	11.58	9.775	5.995

PASSPORT/VISA

Regulations and requirements may be subject to change at short notice, and you are advised to contact the appropriate diplomatic or consular authority before finalising travel arrangements. Details of these may be found at the head of this country's entry. Any numbers in the chart refer to the footnotes below.

	Passport Required?	Visa Required?	Return Ticket Required?
Full British	Yes	No	Yes
BVP	Not valid	-	-
Australian	Yes	Yes	Yes
Canadian	Yes	Yes	Yes
USA	Yes	Yes	Yes
Other EC	Yes	1	Yes
Japanese	Yes	No	Yes

Restricted entry: Nationals from the following countries require special authorisation from the Department of Immigration in Guatemala prior to applying for a visa: Afghanistan, Albania, Angola, Algeria, Bangladesh, Benin, Bhutan, Bolivia, Botswana, Bulgaria, Cambodia, Central African Republic, CIS, China, Colombia, Congo, Cuba, Czechoslovakia, Djibouti, Dominican Republic, Ecuador, Ethiopia, Germany, Guyana, Hong Kong, Hungary, India, Iran, Iraq, Jordan, Kenya, North Korea, Laos, Lebanon, Libya, Malawi, Mali, Mongolia, Myanmar, Namibia, Nepal, Oman, Pakistan, Peru, Poland, Romania, Rwanda, Somalia, Sudan, Suriname, Sri Lanka, Tanzania, Tunisia, Uganda, Vietnam, Yemen, Yugoslavia and Zaire.
Details of passport, profession, purpose of travel, family or business contact in Guatemala, return ticket and evidence of means of support are all required. Enquire at Consulate (or Consular Section at Embassy) for further details, as the specified nationalities may be subject to change at short notice.
Authorisation will take three to four weeks. Cost: £6.
PASSPORTS: Required by all.
British Visitors Passport: Not accepted.
VISAS: Required by all except:
(a) [1] nationals of EC countries (other than Greece, Ireland and Portugal who *do* need visas);
(b) nationals of Argentina, Austria, Belize, Ecuador, Finland, Israel, Japan, Norway, Sweden, Switzerland and Vatican City;
(c) nationals of Costa Rica, El Salvador, Honduras, Nicaragua and Uruguay, for stays not exceeding 30 days.
Note: Nationals of Canada, Mexico, USA and the UK entering Guatemala by air do not need a visa. They will be issued with a Tourist card at Guatemala airport.
Types of visa: Visitors (tourist) and Business. Both valid for 30 days from date of entry, but must be used within 30 days of issue. Fee £7.
Application to: Guatemalan Consulate (or Consular Section at Embassy). For address, see top of entry.
Application requirements: *For Tourist visa:* (a) 1 application form. (b) 1 photo. (c) Valid passport. *For Business visa:* (a) 2 application forms. (b) 2 photos. (c) Letter from applicant's company in duplicate.
Working days required: 1.

MONEY

Currency: Quetzal (Q) = 100 centavos. Notes are in denominations of Q100, 50, 20, 10, 5 and 1, and 50 centavos. Coins are in denominations of 25, 10, 5 and 1 centavos.
Currency exchange: From November 1989 the exchange rate ceased to be fixed. It may be difficult to negotiate notes which are torn.
Credit cards: Visa and American Express are accepted, whilst Diners Club and Access/Mastercard have a more limited acceptance. Check with your credit card company for details of merchant acceptability and other services which may be available.
Travellers cheques: Accepted by most banks and most good hotels, though the visitor may experience the occasional problem. Travellers cheques in US Dollars are recommended.
Exchange rate indicators: The following figures are included as a guide to the movements of the Quetzal against Sterling and the US Dollar (official rates):

Date:	Oct '89	Oct '90	Oct '91	Oct '92
£1.00=	4.50	11.03	8.70	8.33
$1.00=	2.85	5.65	5.01	5.25

Currency exchange: There are no restrictions on the import or export of either local or foreign currency.
Banking hours: 0900-1500 Monday to Friday.

DUTY FREE

The following goods may be imported by persons over 18 years of age into Guatemala without incurring customs duty:
80 cigarettes or 3.5 oz of tobacco;
1.5 litres (2 bottles) of alcohol (opened);
2 bottles of perfume (opened).

PUBLIC HOLIDAYS

Public holidays observed in Guatemala are as follows:
Apr 9-12 '93 Easter. **May 1** Labour Day. **Jun 30** Anniversary of the Revolution. **Aug 15** Assumption (Guatemala City only). **Sep 15** Independence Day. **Oct 12** Columbus Day. **Oct 20** Revolution Day. **Nov 1** All Saints' Day. **Dec 24** Christmas Eve. **Dec 25** Christmas Day. **Dec 31** New Year's Eve. **Jan 1 '94** New Year's Day. **Jan 6** Epiphany.

HEALTH

Regulations and requirements may be subject to change at short notice, and you are advised to contact your doctor well in advance of your intended date of departure. Any numbers in the chart refer to the footnotes below.

	Special Precautions?	Certificate Required?
Yellow Fever	No	1
Cholera	No	No
Typhoid & Polio	Yes	-
Malaria	2	-
Food & Drink	3	-

[1]: A yellow fever vaccination certificate is required from travellers over one year of age coming from countries with infected areas. Nationals of The Guinea Republic and Nigeria who do not present such a certificate will be subject to five days quarantine.
[2]: Malaria risk exists throughout the year below 1500m in *departamentos* of: Alta Verapaz, Baja Verapaz, Chimaltenango, El Petén, El Quiché, Huehuetenango, Izabal, San Marcos, Santa Rosa and Sololá.
[3]: All water should be regarded as being potentially contaminated. Water used for drinking, brushing teeth or making ice should have first been boiled or otherwise sterilised. Milk is unpasteurised and should be boiled. Powdered or tinned milk is available and is advised, but make sure that it is reconstituted with pure water. Avoid dairy products which are likely to have been made from local milk. Only eat well-cooked meat and fish, preferably served hot. Pork, salad and mayonnaise may carry increased risk. Vegetables should be cooked and fruit peeled.
Rabies is present. For those at high risk, vaccination before arrival should be considered. If you are bitten abroad seek medical advice without delay. For more information consult the *Health* section at the back of the book.
Altitude sickness may be experienced in higher places, and exertion should be avoided.
Hepatitis inoculation is highly recommended.
Health care: There are good medical facilities in Guatemala City, but insurance is strongly advised.

TRAVEL - International

AIR: Guatemala's national airline is *Aviateca (GU)*.
Approximate flight times: From Guatemala to *London* is 8 hours (plus stopover time in Miami or Madrid), to *Los Angeles* is 6 hours and to *New York* is 7 hours.
International airport: *Guatemala City (GUA)* (La Aurora), 7km (4 miles) south of the city. A bus to the city runs every 30 minutes. Taxi services to Guatemala City are available. Airport facilities include car hire, vaccination centre, duty-free shop, bar, buffet, restaurant, bank, tourist information, telephones and exchange bureaux.
Departure tax: Q20 is levied on all international flights.
SEA: There are several international passenger services from North America, the Far East and Europe to Santo Tomás in Mexico. Cargo services run to the Pacific ports of San José and Champerico. There are also seven direct lines linking Guatemala with the Far East.
RAIL: There is a daily rail link between the Pacific and Caribbean coasts from Guatemala City to Puerto Barrios, and a daily link via Mazatenango from Guatemala City to Mexico (although an overnight stay is necessary at the border). No meals are served on these trains.
ROAD: The Inter-American Highway runs through Guatemala from Mexico in the North and El Salvador in the South. **Bus:** There are bus services from Mexico and El Salvador, Nicaragua, Costa Rica and Panama. The route south is liable to disruption due to the deteriorating political situation in this part of Central America. Border crossings can be subject to considerable delays. The buses used by some companies are comfortable and air-conditioned, but it is vital to book as far in advance as possible *for every stage of the journey*.
See below for information on **documentation**.

TRAVEL - Internal

AIR: Air transport is by far the most efficient means of internal travel since there are over 380 airstrips. *Aviateca (GU)*, *Aeroquetzal* and *Aerovias* run daily flights from Guatemala City to Petén. Private charter flights are available.
ROAD: There is an extensive road network but less than a third of the roads are all-weather. Many of the roads are made from volcanic ash, and therefore very muddy during the rains. There are, however, about 13,000km (8000 miles) of first- and second-class roads in the country with paved highways from Guatemala City to the principal towns in the interior and to both the Atlantic and Pacific ports. **Bus:** The network of regular bus services between major towns is cheap but crowded. **Car hire:** *Hertz* (tel: 311 711), *Avis* (tel: 310 017), *Europcar International* (tel: 318 365) and local firms exists in Guatemala City. Rates are low, but insurance is extra. It is also possible to hire motorcycles. **Taxi:** Flat rate for short or long run within city although prices tend to be expensive. Cars can also be hired by the hour. Vehicles must be summoned by phone as they do not cruise for hire. There are ranks at the main international hotels. Tipping is discretionary (5-10%). **Documentation:** A local licence will be issued on production of visitor's own national driving licence.
URBAN: Guatemala City and major towns have limited, but cheap and regular, bus services.

ACCOMMODATION

HOTELS: There are many hotels in Guatemala City to suit every pocket and taste. Antigua (the capital until largely destroyed by earthquakes in 1773, a fate which also befell the present capital in 1976) also has a good choice of hotels. Puerto Barrios, Chichicastenango, Quetzaltenango, Panajachel (near Lake Atitlán) and Coban also have a reasonable selection of hotels, although elsewhere accommodation is more limited. Throughout the country standards are inconsistent. Most hotels charge a 17% room tax. Registered hotels are required to display room rates; the Tourist Office in Guatemala City will deal with complaints. **Tipping:** 10-15% is normal in hotels where service has not been included.
PENSIONS/GUEST-HOUSES: Most large towns have guest/boarding houses offering inexpensive accommodation.
CAMPING: There are campsites throughout the country although facilities are basic. A popular excursion is to stay overnight on camping grounds on the still-active Pacaya volcano to see the glow of the ashes and lava from the volcano's eruptions. Around Lake Atitlán camping is permitted only in designated areas.

RESORTS & EXCURSIONS

Guatemala City and its environs: The city lies on an attractive site at the edge of a plateau cut by deep ravines. The old quarter with its low colonial houses is situated in the northern part of the city. A Plaza called *Parque Central* lies at its heart and is bordered by the *National Palace*, the *Cathedral*, the *National Library* and an arcade of shops. In the south of the city, close to the airport and the national racecourse, is *Parque La Aurora*, which contains the zoo, the *Archaeological Museum* and the *Handicrafts Museum*. Churches to visit include the cathedral, *Cerro de Carmen*, *La Merced*, *Santo Domingo*, *Santuario Expiatorio*, *Las Capuchinas*, *Santa Rosa* and *Capilla de Yurrita*.
Outside Guatemala City is **Antigua**, a beautifully situated town which was, before its destruction in an earthquake, considered to be the most splendid in Central America. Monuments that survived include the *Plaza de Armas*, the *Cathedral*, the *University of San Carlos* and the *San Francisco Church*.
Three nearby volcanoes, *Volcán de Agua*, *Volcán de Acatenango* and *Volcán de Fuego*, all offer incomparable views of the city and surrounding countryside.
On the route to Guatemala City: Quirigua is remarkable for its memorials of the ancient Mayan Empire while **Zacapa**, **Chiquimula** and **Esquipular** have some of the finest colonial churches in the Americas.
Caribbean coast: The port of **Puerto Barrias** has the nearby beach of *Escobar* to recommend it. Inland from here is *Lake Izabal* which has the Spanish fort of *San Felipe* and is a reserve for some of the earth's rarest mammals.
San José: The country's second largest port where fishing and swimming are available. An interesting journey can be taken through the *Chiquimula canal* by launch from the old Spanish port of *Iztapa*, which is now a bathing resort.
Lake Atitlán: One of the most beautiful lakes in the world, surrounded by purple highlands and olive-green mountains and with over a dozen villages on its shores. Visitors can stay at or near **Panajachel**. Water-skiing, swimming and boating are all available.
Western Guatemala: Totonicapán is a thriving industrial town whose local pottery is for sale throughout the country. Its market is considered to be one of the cheapest here. **Momostenango** is the centre for blanket weaving.
Quezaltenango: The most important city in Western Guatemala, set amongst a group of high mountains and volcanoes. It is a modern city, but it also has narrow colonial streets, broad avenues, fine public buildings and a magnificent plaza.
Flores: Lies in the heart of the Petén forests, built on an island in the middle of the beautiful *Lake Petén*.
Itza: *Tikal*, the great Mayan ruins of vast temples and public buildings. One needs at least two days to see them all.
Sayaxche: A good centre for visiting the Petén, whether your interest is in wildlife or Mayan ruins. The best of the latter are *Seibal*, *Itzan*, *Dos Pilas*, *Yaxha* and *Uaxactun*.

SOCIAL PROFILE

FOOD & DRINK: There is a variety of restaurants and cafés serving a wide selection of cooking styles including American, Argentine, Chinese, German, Italian, Mexican and Spanish. Fast-food chains also have outlets here and there are many continental style cafés. The visitor should note that food varies in price rather than quality.
NIGHTLIFE: In Guatemala City in particular there are nightclubs and discotheques with modern music and dance. Guatemala is the home of *marimba* music which can be heard at several venues. In the cities the *marimba* is a huge elaborate xylophone with large drum sticks played by from four to nine players. In rural areas the sounding boxes are made of different shaped gourds *(marimbas de tecomates)*. There are also theatres and numerous plays in English and other cultural performances. Films with English and Spanish subtitles are often shown in major towns.
SHOPPING: Special purchases include textiles, handicrafts, jewellery, jade carvings, leather goods, ceramics and basketry. Markets are best for local products and bargaining is necessary. Coban is the cheapest place to buy silverware. **Shopping hours:** 0800-1800 Monday to Saturday.
SPORT: Swimming: North of the capital is the Parque Minerva where there are two swimming pools. There are pools at Ciudad Olímpica, and *Baños del Sur* has large hot baths in Guatemala City and some hotels. **Bowling:** 10-pin bowling and billiards can be played at Bolerama 0-61, Zona 4 in the city. **Basketball/Baseball:** Courts at the Parque Minerva. **Golf:** There is an 18-hole golf course at the Guatemala Country Club, 8km (5 miles) from the city. **Tennis** can be played at the Guatemala Lawn Tennis Club and the Mayan Club.
SOCIAL CONVENTIONS: Guatemala is the most populated of the Central American republics and is the only one which is predominantly Indian, although the Spanish have had a strong influence on the way of life. Full names should be used when addressing acquaintances, particularly in business. Dress is conservative and casual wear is suitable except in the smartest dining rooms and clubs.
Tipping: 10-15% is normal in restaurants where service has not been included.

BUSINESS PROFILE

ECONOMY: Coffee is the leading export in this largely agricultural economy, accounting for about one-third of foreign earnings. Other major crops are sugar cane, bananas, cardamom and cotton. Guatemala boasts the largest manufacturing sector in Central America, producing processed foods, textiles, paper, pharmaceuticals and rubber goods. Oil deposits, first discovered in the mid-1970s, are being exploited by American concerns but the country remains a marginal producer and continues to rely heavily on imported oil. Poor weather and the civil war have disrupted economic development during the last two decades, although Guatemala has received solid support from the United States and international institutions such as the Inter-American Development Bank and the IMF. The US is substantially Guatemala's largest trading partner, followed by El Salvador, Honduras, Mexico and some EC countries, notably Germany and Italy.
BUSINESS: Guatemalan businessmen tend to be rather formal and conservative. Normal courtesies should be observed and appointments should be made. Punctuality is appreciated and calling cards can be useful. **Office hours:** 0800-1800 Monday to Friday, 0800-1200 Saturday.
COMMERCIAL INFORMATION: The following organisation can offer advice: Cámara de Comercio de Guatemala (Chamber of Commerce), 10a Calle 3-80, Zona 1, Guatemala City. Tel: (2) 826 81/2/3. Fax: (2) 514 197. Telex: 5478.

HISTORY & GOVERNMENT

HISTORY: Guatemala was one of the territories overrun by the Spanish conquistador Cortes in the 17th century. Pressure on their empire during the early 19th century forced the Spanish to concede independence

GUATEMALA | **HEALTH REGULATIONS** | **VISA REGULATIONS** | Code-Link

GALILEO/WORLDSPAN

TI-DFT/GUA/HE

TI-DFT/GUA/VI

SABRE

TIDFT/GUA/HE

TIDFT/GUA/VI

To access this information on your CRS, swipe the barcode with a light pen or type in the text under the barcode. For more information, see the introduction *How to Use This Book*.

to their American colonies, principally Mexico, into which Guatemala was briefly incorporated in 1822. Subsequent plans to fuse the countries of the Central American isthmus were equally short-lived. Guatemala enjoyed comparative stability, punctuated by brief periods of upheaval, under a series of dictators who were content to keep the country under a quasi-feudal regime underpinned by a small clique of land-owning families. The government of Colonel Arbenz Guzman attempted various land reforms in the early 1950s, but was overthrown by a US-backed invasion led by military opponents of Arbenz. The country then slid into a state of almost perpetual civil war between a series of right-wing military governments and various leftist guerrilla movements and although Guatemala has completed a successful transition from military to civilian government, the military retain considerable political power. In May 1985 Guatemala's new constitution was promulgated and, in June, General Victores announced that elections for the presidency, the National Congress and 331 mayoralities would be held later in the year. Vinicio Cerezo secured 68% of the votes cast in the presidential poll, and his party, the Partido Democracia Cristiana Guatemalteca (PDCG) formed the majority party in the new National Congress as well as winning the majority of mayoralities. Despite an inauspicious tenure, the Cerezo administration not only remained in office for its full term of five years, but handed over to another civilian government. At the 1990 poll, Jorge Serrano, an independent businessman of an evangelical bent, was the victor. Serrano's role model is the Peruvian leader Alberto Fujimori, some of whose policies he has adopted. These include the formation of a coalition government along with free-market economics with particular emphasis on attracting foreign investment. On the security front, President Serrano has brought the guerrillas to the negotiating table, overcoming military opposition, although the subsequent talks have repeatedly stalled. Abroad, the main issue facing the country is the dispute with neighbouring Belize, over which Guatemala has territorial claims: since diplomatic relations with Britain (the former colonial power) were restored in 1987, protracted negotiations were held on and off for four years until 1991, when the Guatemalans finally accepted the principle of Belizean sovereignty. Although Guatemala has not dropped its territorial claim, a political settlement is now a distinct possibility. The Guatemalans have acquired access to Belizean maritime facilities as part of the deal. The oft-ignored plight of Guatemala's indigenous Indian poulation was unexpectedly recognised in 1992 with the award of the Nobel Peace Prize to the human rights campaigner Rigoberta Menchu.
GOVERNMENT: Under the 1986 constitution, legislative power is vested in a single-chamber elected assembly with 100 members elected every five years. The President, also elected every five years, holds executive power.

CLIMATE

Guatemala's climate varies according to altitude. The coastal regions and the northeast are hot throughout the year, while the highlands have a much more temperate climate. The rainy season is from June to October, and the rest of the year is quite dry. Temperatures fall sharply at night.
Required clothing: Lightweight tropicals. Jacket or light woollens for night.

GUATEMALA CITY (1300m)

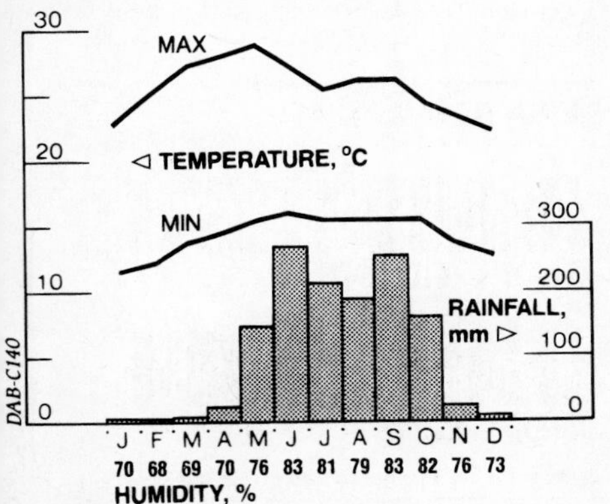

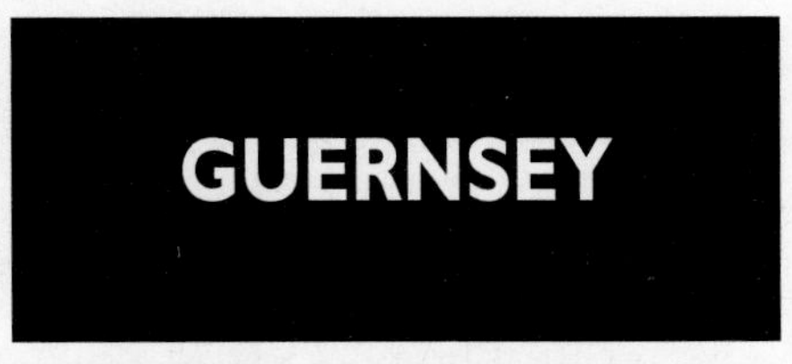

GUERNSEY

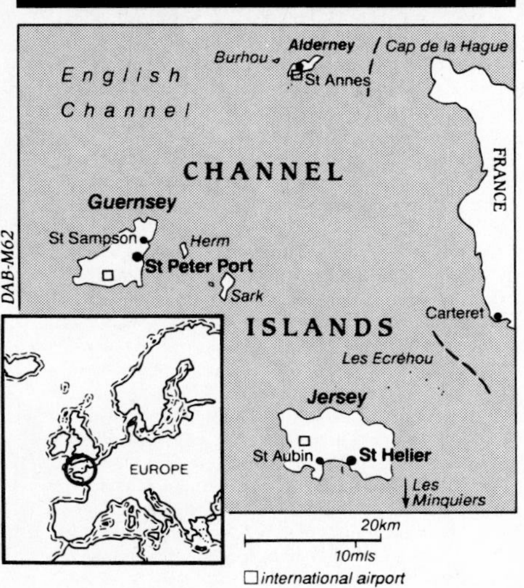

Location: English Channel, off the northern coast of France.

Guernsey Tourist Office
PO Box 23
White Rock
St Peter Port
Guernsey, Channel Islands
Tel: 726 611. Fax: 721 246. Telex: 4191612.

AREA: 65 sq km (25 sq miles).
POPULATION: 58,000.
POPULATION DENSITY: 892.3 per sq km.
CAPITAL: St Peter Port.
GEOGRAPHY: Guernsey is situated in the Gulf of St Malo, 50km (30 miles) from the coast of France and 130km (80 miles) from the south coast of England. The cliffs on the south coast rise to 80m (270ft), from which the land slopes away gradually to the north. Guernsey is an ideal centre for excursions to the other Channel Islands and France.
LANGUAGE: English is the official language. Norman *patois* is spoken in some parishes.
RELIGION: Church of England, Baptist, Congregational and Methodist.
TIME: GMT (GMT + 1 from March to October).
ELECTRICITY: 240 volts AC, 50Hz.
COMMUNICATIONS: Telephone: To telephone Guernsey from the UK the STD code is 0481; calls from overseas must be made using the UK country code 44. **Post:** Only Guernsey stamps will be accepted on outgoing mail. The main post office is at Smith Street, St Peter Port. Post boxes are painted blue. **Press:** The local newspapers are *The Guernsey Evening Press* (daily except Sunday) and *The Weekender*. English, French, German, Dutch and Italian newspapers are also available at newsagents.

PASSPORT/VISA

Regulations and requirements may be subject to change at short notice, and you are advised to contact the appropriate diplomatic or consular authority before finalising travel arrangements. Details of these may be found at the head of this country's entry. Any numbers in the chart refer to the footnotes below.

	Passport Required?	Visa Required?	Return Ticket Required?
Full British	1	No	No
BVP	Valid	No	No
Australian	Yes	No	No
Canadian	Yes	No	No
USA	Yes	No	No
Other EC	1/2	No	No
Japanese	Yes	No	No

PASSPORTS: Valid passport required by all except:
(a) [1] British citizens and nationals of the Irish Republic who travel between their own country and Guernsey;
(b) [2] nationals of EC countries holding national identity cards;
(c) nationals of Austria, Liechtenstein, Monaco and Switzerland holding national identity cards (for up to 6 months).
Note: If travel is via France (or any other country), the entry requirements for that country will have to be satisfied.
British Visitors Passport: Acceptable but not required unless a British passport holder is travelling on to a country other than the UK or the Republic of Ireland.

MONEY

Currency: Pound Sterling (£) = 100 pence. Notes are in denominations of £50, 20, 10, 5 and 1. Coins are in denominations of £1, and 50, 20, 10, 5, 2 and 1 pence. On September 30, 1992, a new 10-pence coin was introduced. In 1990 a new smaller 5 pence came into circulation; the old 5-pence piece is no longer legal tender. All UK notes and coins are legal tender, and circulate with the Channel Islands issue. Note that Channel Islands notes and coins are not accepted in the UK, although they can be reconverted at parity in UK banks.
Currency exchange: Foreign currencies can be exchanged at bureaux de change, in banks and at many hotels.
Credit cards: Access/Mastercard, American Express, Diners Club and Visa are all widely accepted. Check with your credit card company for details of merchant acceptability and other services which may be available.
Travellers cheques can be exchanged.
Exchange rates: The following is included as a guide to the movement of Sterling against the US Dollar:

Date:	Oct '89	Oct '90	Oct '91	Oct '92
$1.00=	0.63	0.51	0.57	0.63

Banking hours: 0930-1530 Monday to Friday. Some banks are open later on weekdays and on Saturday morning.

DUTY FREE

The Channel Islands are largely a duty-free zone. The following goods may be exported *from* Guernsey without incurring customs duty in the UK:
200 cigarettes or 50 cigars or 250g of tobacco;
1 litre of alcoholic beverages if over 22% proof or 2 litres of sparkling or fortified wines;
2 litres of still table wine;
50g (0.6 litre) of perfume and 250ml of toilet water;
Other goods to a value of £32.
For import allowances into Guernsey, see the entry for the United Kingdom.
Quarantine: There is a total ban on the importation of animals other than from the UK or other Channel Islands.

PUBLIC HOLIDAYS

Public holidays observed in Guernsey are as follows:
Apr 9 '93 Good Friday. **Apr 12** Easter Monday. **May 3** May Day. **May 9** Liberation Day (commemorating the arrival of the British Forces to the Island at the end of World War Two). **May 31** Spring Bank Holiday. **Aug 30** Late Summer Bank Holiday. **Dec 25** Christmas Day. **Dec 26** Boxing Day. **Jan 1 '94** New Year's Day.

HEALTH

Regulations and requirements may be subject to change at short notice, and you are advised to contact your doctor well in advance of your intended date of departure. Any numbers in the chart refer to the footnotes below.

	Special Precautions?	Certificate Required?
Yellow Fever	No	No
Cholera	No	No
Typhoid & Polio	No	-
Malaria	No	-
Food & Drink	No	-

Health care: Guernsey has a large hospital (Princess Elizabeth Hospital) and many medical and dental practices. There is a Reciprocal Health Agreement with the UK (Guernsey is a Crown Dependency and not strictly part of the UK). On presentation of proof of residence in the UK (driving licence, NHS card, etc), UK citizens are entitled to free hospital and other medical treatment, free emergency dental treatment and free travel by ambulance; most prescribed medicines must be paid for. Medical insurance is recommended.

TRAVEL - International

AIR: Approximate flight time: From *London* to Guernsey is 45 minutes.
International airport: *Guernsey (GCI)*, 5km (3 miles) from St Peter Port (travel time – 20 minutes). Bus and

ST PETER PORT

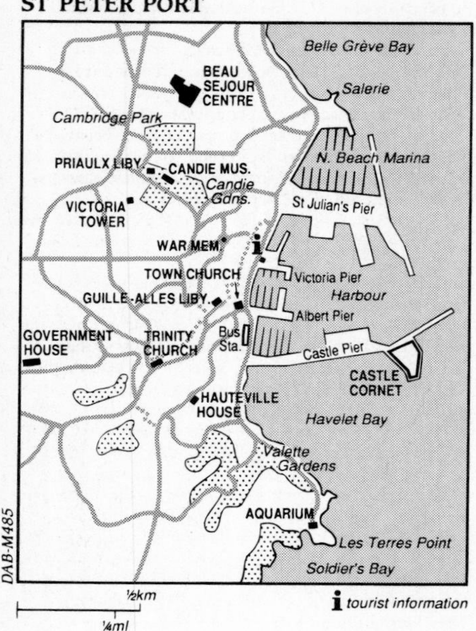

taxi services are available to the town.

Guernsey can be reached all year round from various locations on mainland Britain, Dinard and Cherbourg, and during the summer from Amsterdam, Dortmund, Dusseldorf, Frankfurt, Hamburg, Paderborn/Lippstadt, Paris, Stuttgart and Zurich.

SEA: *British Channel Island Ferries* have daily sailings from Poole, Dorset (limited timetable in winter). *Condor Hydrofoil* operates seasonal services from Weymouth and St Malo. Services from France include *Seafox*, operating from Dielette, and *Emeraude Lines* operating from St Malo, Portbail, Carteret, St Quay Portrieux and Granville. Day excursions are available daily to Herm and Sark by boat. Inter-island services are also available from *Aurigny Air Services* and *Condor Hydrofoil*.

TRAVEL - Internal

ROAD: A comprehensive bus service serves all parts of the island. A variety of island tours are also available during the summer. **Car hire:** There are many car hire companies available on Guernsey, with rates that compare favourably with the UK. There is an unlimited mileage allowance. Coach hire for large parties is also available. **Bicycle hire:** Available from various firms for daily or weekly hire. **Regulations:** Driving is on the left. Maximum speed limit is 56kmph (35mph). Parking is free, although time limits are imposed. If these are exceeded, a fine of £10 is charged. **Documentation:** A full national driving licence is required.

JOURNEY TIMES: The following chart gives approximate journey times (in hours and minutes) from St Peter Port, Guernsey to the neighbouring Channel Islands.

	Air	Sea
Alderney	0.15	-
Herm Island	-	0.20
Jersey	0.15	1.00
Sark Island	-	0.40

ACCOMMODATION

A full colour brochure of all accommodation is available from the Guernsey Tourist Office (address at top of entry). The Guernsey government has a scheme for the compulsory inspection and grading of hotels to ensure standards of accommodation are maintained and improved.

HOTELS: A large selection of well-maintained hotels, offering facilities for the single or group visitor, is available. Over 91% of the rooms have en suite facilities. All have at least a washbasin and hot and cold running water in all rooms. Advance booking is advisable during the summer period. For the brochure mentioned above contact the Guernsey Tourist Office or the Guernsey Hotel and Tourism Association. **Grading:** All hotels are graded, being given a number of Crowns (with 5 Crowns given as the highest grade) according to the facilities offered. Some registered hotels have either not been awarded any Crowns or are awaiting their assessment.

5 Crowns: All bedrooms contain a fixed bath and WC en suite; most offer central heating, indoor or outdoor swimming pool, baby listening service, special diets, special rates and are open throughout the year.

4 Crowns: All bedrooms contain a fixed bath or shower and WC en suite; many offer central heating, indoor or outdoor swimming pool, baby listening service, special diets, special rates and are open throughout the year.

3 Crowns: 75% of rooms must contain a fixed bath or shower and WC en suite; several offer all or some of the following: central heating, indoor or outdoor swimming pool, baby listening service, special diets, special rates and are open throughout the year.

2 Crowns: 50% of rooms must contain a fixed bath or shower and WC en suite; several offer all or some of the following: central heating, indoor or outdoor swimming pool, baby listening service, special diets, special rates and are open throughout the year.

1 Crown: 25% of rooms must contain a fixed bath or shower and WC en suite; some may offer the following: central heating, indoor or outdoor swimming pool, baby listening service, special diets, special rates and are open throughout the year.

For more information contact the Guernsey Hotel and Tourism Association (GHATA), c/o Guernsey Chamber of Commerce, States Arcade, Market Street, St Peter Port. Tel: 713 583.

GUEST-HOUSES: These are normally family-run establishments, providing a good standard of accommodation in a homely atmosphere. This can be based on full-board, half-board or bed & breakfast, according to the visitor's requirements. A number of these have residential liquor licences. **Grading:** All are graded from A to D, with A being the highest.

SELF-CATERING: Units are graded from A to C according to size, number of persons accommodated, standards and amenities offered.

CAMPING: There are five official campsites at various locations around the island. Full details are available from the Tourist Office. Visitors are not permitted to bring caravans into Guernsey.

RESORTS & EXCURSIONS

St Peter Port is an attractive harbour town with narrow streets leading uphill from the sea. It has all the character of a traditional fishing village, complete with boats bobbing about in the harbour. The town church has a 12th-century chancel, a 15th-century south chapel and the interior dates back to 1886. Just above the *French Halles* is the *Guille-Alles Library*. The *Island Museum* at **Candie** won 'Museum of the Year' award in 1979 (open 1030-1730 daily).

Nearby *Castle Cornet* overlooks the harbour. Built during the reign of King Stephen, it has been the scene of many historic battles and bears the military stamp of many eras, from Norman times through to the Nazi occupation during the Second World War. The castle also contains the *Royal Guernsey Militia Museum*, a *Maritime Museum* and attractive gardens (open 1030-1730 daily, April to October). *Hauteville House*, on the south side of St Peter Port at the top of the hill, was the home of French writer Victor Hugo from 1855-1870. The French coast can be seen from the window of his study, and it was here that he wrote *The Toilers of the Sea*. Hugo's statue stands in *Candie Gardens*, which is also the location of the oak he planted, now a symbol of European unity. The miniature botanical gardens also contain subtropical plants, trees and shrubs, all grown in the open.

The *Dolmens* (tombs of prehistoric tribes) are also worth seeing, with examples scattered around the island. Among the more notable are *Déhus Dolmen*, near the yacht marina in the **Vale**, *La Varde Dolmen* at the Pembroke end of **L'Ancresse Common**, *Le Creux Faies* at **L'Erée**, and *La Catioroc*, on a mound overlooking **Perelle Bay** (said to be a former meeting place for Guernsey witches).

Among the castles are *Ivy Castle* near **Le Bouet**, a Norman stronghold built before the Norman Conquest of England, and *Vale Castle* at **St Sampson's**, whose origins are lost in time, where a Russian garrison was stationed circa 1805. There are fortifications at *Fort Pezerie*, *Fort Grey*, *Fort Saumerez* and *Fort George*. Martello Towers are to be found scattered around the island.

Few of the fortifications made by the Nazis remain, most of these being on the cliffs. The underground hospital at **St Andrews** is the largest German structure in the Channel Islands, and this is now a tourist attraction. The *Occupation Museum* at the **Forest** contains many relics and a glimpse into life during the Nazi occupation.

The cliffs around the island make a pleasant walk, and lead to many bays, most of which are suitable for bathing and accessible from the cliffs. Inland one finds many pleasant walks. The *Water Lanes* leading to the shore are also worth seeing, particularly at **Moulin Huet** and **Petit Bôt**. The *Chapel* at **Les Vauxbelets** is the smallest church in the world, with space for a priest and a congregation of two.

SOCIAL PROFILE

FOOD & DRINK: Guernsey is famous for its food and the island has a wide variety of restaurants ranging from traditional French and English cuisine to Italian, Indian and Chinese. The local speciality is shellfish, with freshly caught lobsters, crabs and scallops forming the basis of many dishes. Table service is normal in restaurants, with counter service in bars. There are two self-service restaurants in St Peter Port. **Drink:** A wide variety of alcoholic beverages is available and spirits, beers and wines are relatively cheap compared to the mainland. Eating out is also excellent value for money because there is no VAT. Bars may open between 1030 and 2345 daily except Sunday.

NIGHTLIFE: Discotheques are located in various parts of the island, whilst live music and cabarets are organised by some hotels during the summer season. The Beau Sejour Leisure Centre at St Peter Port contains a cinema, theatre, bars and café.

SHOPPING: There is no VAT but a Guernsey Bailiwick tax is imposed on certain goods such as spirits, wines, beers and tobacco. Prices of luxury goods are relatively cheaper than in the UK, although the overall cost of foodstuffs is higher. Special purchases include Guernsey's local pottery and crafts. **Shopping hours:** 0900-1730 Monday to Saturday. Early closing is on Thursday, although most shops will stay open. Some shops open in the evening during summer months.

SPORT: The Beau Sejour Leisure Centre caters for a wide variety of sports, including **tennis**, **squash**, **swimming**, **badminton**, **bowls**, five-a-side **football**, **roller skating**, **keep-fit** classes and **snooker**. **Windsurfing** boards are available for hire from Cobo and L'Ancresse Bays. The Island has an 18-hole **golf** course; **horseriding**, **go-karting**, **sailing**, **flying** and **fishing** (including wreck fishing) are also available.

SPECIAL EVENTS: Below are a selection of special events in Guernsey. For full details of special events and festivals celebrated during 1993/94, please contact the Guernsey Tourist Office.

Apr 27-29 '93 *Guernsey Festival of Food and Wine*. **Apr 30-May 3** *Jazz Weekend*. **May 9** *Liberation Day*. **Jun 19-26** *International Dance Festival*. **Jun 20** *Hash House Harriers Half Marathon*. **Jun 27-Jul 3** *Square Dance Festival*. **Jul 5** *Viaer Marchi* (Traditional Guernsey Evening). **Jul 7** *Harbour Carnival*. **Jul 24** *National Hill Climb*. **Aug 6-9** *Folk Festival*. **Aug 7** *Rocquaine Regatta*. **Aug 11-12** *South Agricultural Show*. **Aug 18-19** *West Agricultural Show*. **Aug 25-26** *North Agricultural Show* (Battle of Flowers). **Sep 2-8** *International Power Boat Week*. **Sep 10-12** *Guernsey Lily Amateur Film Festival*. **Sep 13** *Guernsey Longcourse*

GUERNSEY — **HEALTH REGULATIONS** — **VISA REGULATIONS** — Code-Link

GALILEO/WORLDSPAN

TI-DFT/GCI/HE

TI-DFT/GCI/VI

SABRE

TIDFT/GCI/HE

TIDFT/GCI/VI

To access this information on your CRS, swipe the barcode with a light pen or type in the text under the barcode. For more information, see the introduction *How to Use This Book*.

Triathlon. **Sep 13-19** *Battle of Britain Week.* **Sep 25-Oct 23** *Guernsey Festival.* **Oct 1-3** *Air Rally.* **Oct 17-23** *Chess Festival.*

SOCIAL CONVENTIONS: Handshaking is the customary form of greeting and normal social courtesies should be observed when visiting someone's home. It is not usual to start eating until everyone is served. If invited to someone's home a small present such as flowers or chocolates is appreciated. Casual wear is acceptable in most places. Smoking is not allowed on buses. **Tipping:** 10-12% is normal, except where a service charge is included.

BUSINESS PROFILE

ECONOMY: Finance, tourism and agriculture are the main contributors to Guernsey's buoyant economy. The island has gradually been developed as an offshore financial centre: several London merchant banks are now incorporated here to take advantage of tight disclosure laws and low taxes. Flowers and tomatoes are the main exporters, and internationally renowned.

BUSINESS: Business people are generally expected to dress smartly, with a suit and tie for men. Appointments should be made and calling cards are customary. Business is conducted in English. **Office hours:** 0900-1700 Monday to Friday.

COMMERCIAL INFORMATION: The following organisation can offer advice: Guernsey Chamber of Commerce, States Arcade, Market Street, St Peter Port, Guernsey. Tel: 727 483. Telex: 4191445.

CONFERENCES & CONVENTIONS: Approximately 100 conferences are held in Guernsey each year, with the total number of delegates being between 10,000 and 12,000 per annum; the maximum recommended conference size is 750. Organisers can obtain advice from the Conference Manager at the Guernsey Tourist Office (address at beginning of entry).

HISTORY & GOVERNMENT

HISTORY: In the 11th century, the Channel Islands *(les Isles Normandes)*, of which Guernsey is one, were part of the Duchy of Normandy. When William, Duke of Normandy, conquered England the Channel Islands were incorporated into the combined realm of England and Normandy. One hundred and forty years later, King John of England lost mainland Normandy to the French but the Channel Islands stayed loyal to England. The French made many subsequent attempts over the ensuing centuries to capture the islands, all of which were repelled. The Germans were more successful, albeit briefly, during the Second World War when many of the island's population were evacuated to England. Guernsey has long enjoyed a large degree of internal self-government, developing its own legal and political institutions. The British Government is responsible for Guernsey's external relations.

GOVERNMENT: The British monarch is head of state, represented locally by a Lieutenant-Governor. Internal affairs are governed by the island's parliament, the States of Deliberation. The 'States', as it is commonly known, has 57 members divided into four groups: 12 *conseillers* chosen from an electoral college; 33 deputies elected directly by universal suffrage; 10 representatives of the *douzaines* or parish councils; and 2 representatives from the small neighbouring island of Alderney.

CLIMATE

The most popular holiday season is from Easter to October, with temperatures averaging 20-21°C. These months give an average of 200 and 260 hours of sunshine. Rainfall is mainly during the cooler months. The sea is 17°C on average during the summer.

Required clothing: Normal beach and holiday wear for summer, with some warmer clothing as there are often sea breezes. Warm winter wear and rainwear are advised.

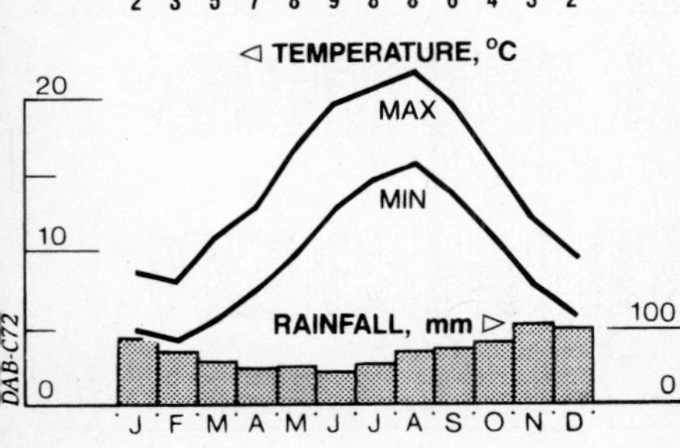

GUINEA REPUBLIC

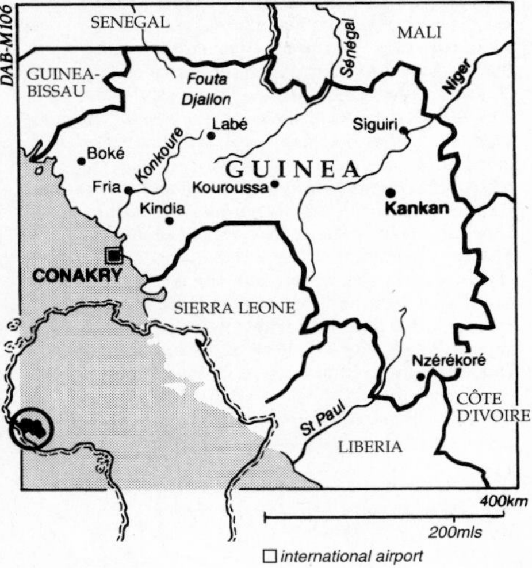

Location: West Africa.

Secrétariat d'Etat au Tourisme et à l'Hôtellerie
BP 1304
square des Martyrs
Conakry, Guinea
Tel: 442 606.

Embassy of the Republic of Guinea
51 rue de la Faisanderie
75016 Paris
France
Tel: (1) 47 04 81 48. Telex: 648497.

British Consulate
BP 834
Conakry, Guinea
Tel: 461 734 *or* 465 361 *or* 443 442. Fax: 444 215. Telex: 22294.

Embassy of the Republic of Guinea
2112 Leroy Place, NW
Washington, DC
20008
Tel: (202) 483 9420. Telex: 49606982.

Embassy of the United States of America
BP 603
2d boulevard and 9th Avenue
Conakry, Guinea Republic
Tel: 441 520/1/2/3/4. Fax: 441 522.

Embassy of the Republic of Guinea
483 Wilbrod Street
Ottawa, Ontario
K1N 6N1
Tel: (613) 232 1133/4/5. Fax: (613) 230 7560. Telex: 0534304.

Canadian Embassy
PO Box 99
Corniche Sud, Coleah
Conakry, Guinea Republic
Tel: 463 626. Fax: 444 236. Telex: 2170.

AREA: 245,857 sq km (94,926 sq miles).
POPULATION: 5,071,000 (1988 estimate).
POPULATION DENSITY: 20.6 per sq km.
CAPITAL: Conakry. **Population:** 656,000 (1983).

GEOGRAPHY: The Republic of Guinea is located in West Africa and bounded to the northwest by Guinea-Bissau, the north by Senegal and Mali, the east by Côte d'Ivoire, the south by Liberia and the southwest by Sierra Leone. Guinea's many rivers supply water to much of West Africa. The River Niger flows north from the southern highlands into Mali before turning south again through Niger and Nigeria. The coastal plain is made up of mangrove swamps, while inland are the Fouta Djalon hills which form several distinct ranges and plateaux over the whole of western Guinea. In the northeast, savannah plains of the Sahel region stretch into Mali. To the south are mountains known as the Guinea Highlands.

LANGUAGE: French is the official language. Susu, Malinké and Fula are local languages.

RELIGION: Muslim, Animist and Christian. The majority (approx 75%) of the population are Muslim.

TIME: GMT.

ELECTRICITY: 220 volts, 50Hz.

COMMUNICATIONS: Telephone: IDD service is available. Country code: 224. **Telex:** There are facilities at the *Hotel de l'Indépéndence* and *Grand Hotel de l'Unité*. **Post:** There are numerous post offices in the capital. **Press:** The weekly newspaper is the *Horoya*. Two official publications, *Journal Official de Guinée* and *Le Travailleur de Guinée*, are published in French.

BBC World Service and Voice of America frequencies: From time to time these change. See the section *How to Use this Book* for more information.

BBC:

MHz	21.71	15.07	11.86	6.005

Voice of America:

MHz	21.49	15.60	9.525	6.035

PASSPORT/VISA

Regulations and requirements may be subject to change at short notice, and you are advised to contact the appropriate diplomatic or consular authority before finalising travel arrangements. Details of these may be found at the head of this country's entry. Any numbers in the chart refer to the footnotes below.

	Passport Required?	Visa Required?	Return Ticket Required?
Full British	Yes	Yes	Yes
BVP	Not valid	-	-
Australian	Yes	Yes	Yes
Canadian	Yes	Yes	Yes
USA	Yes	Yes	Yes
Other EC	Yes	Yes	Yes
Japanese	Yes	Yes	Yes

Restricted entry: Journalists may visit the Republic of Guinea by Government invitation only.

PASSPORTS: Valid passport required by all.

British Visitors Passport: Not accepted.

VISAS: Required by all except nationals of Algeria, Benin, Cape Verde, Côte d'Ivoire, Cuba, Egypt, Gambia, Ghana, Guinea-Bissau, Liberia, Mali, Mauritania, Morocco, Niger, Nigeria, Romania, Senegal, Sierra Leone, Togo and Tunisia.

Types of visa: Tourist, Business and Transit. Transit visas are not required by those continuing their journey by the same aircraft and not leaving the airport.

Application to: Embassy (or Consular Section at Embassy). For addresses, see top of entry.

Application requirements: (a) 2 application forms. (b) 2 passport-size photographs. (c) Passport (has still to be valid for six months after intended length of stay).

Working days required: 5 weeks.

MONEY

Currency: Guinea Franc (FG) = 100 centimes. The currency is equivalent to the CFA Franc but remains independent from it. Notes are in denominations of FG5000, 1000, 500, 100, 50 and 25.

Currency exchange: Hotels will accept some foreign currencies in payment.

Credit cards: Limited use of Access/Mastercard. Check with your credit card company for details of merchant acceptability and other services which may be available.

Exchange rate indicators: The following figures are included as a guide to the movements of the Guinea Franc against Sterling and the US Dollar:

Date:	Oct '89	Oct '90	Oct '91	Oct '92
£1.00=	474.30	585.45*	521.25*	1284.64
$1.00=	300.37	299.69*	300.35*	809.48

Note [*]: The rate given is the public transaction rate.

Currency restrictions: Import or export of local currency is prohibited. Import of foreign currency is unlimited but must be declared on arrival; export is limited to the amount declared on arrival.

Banking hours: 0830-1230 and 1430-1700 Monday to Friday.

DUTY FREE

The following goods may be imported into Guinea without incurring customs duty:
1000 cigarettes or 250 cigars or 1kg of tobacco;
1 bottle of alcohol (opened);
A reasonable amount of perfume.

PUBLIC HOLIDAYS

Public holidays observed in Guinea are as follows:
Mar 25 '93 Eid al-Fitr, end of Ramadan. **Apr 12** Easter Monday. **May 1** Labour Day. **Aug 27** Anniversary of Women's Revolt. **Aug 30** Mouloud (Prophet's Birthday). **Sep 28** Referendum Day. **Oct 2** Republic Day. **Nov 1**

All Saints' Day. **Nov 22** Day of 1970 Invasion. **Dec 25** Christmas Day. **Jan 1 '94** New Year's Day. **Mar** Start of Eid al-Fitr.
Note: Muslim festivals are timed according to local sightings of various phases of the Moon and the dates given above are approximations. During the lunar month of Ramadan that precedes Eid al-Fitr, Muslims fast during the day and feast at night and normal business patterns may be interrupted. Many restaurants are closed during the day and there may be restrictions on smoking and drinking. Some disruption may continue into Eid al-Fitr itself. Eid al-Fitr may last anything from two to ten days, depending on the region. For more information see the section *World of Islam* at the back of the book.

HEALTH

Regulations and requirements may be subject to change at short notice, and you are advised to contact your doctor well in advance of your intended date of departure. Any numbers in the chart refer to the footnotes below.

	Special Precautions?	Certificate Required?
Yellow Fever	Yes	1
Cholera	Yes	2
Typhoid & Polio	Yes	-
Malaria	Yes/3	-
Food & Drink	4	-

[1]: A yellow fever vaccination certificate is required from travellers over one year of age coming from infected areas.
[2]: Following WHO guidelines issued in 1973, a cholera vaccination certificate is no longer a condition of entry to Guinea. However, cholera is a serious risk in this country and precautions are essential. Up-to-date advice should be sought before deciding whether these precautions should include vaccination as medical opinion is divided over its effectiveness. See the *Health* section at the back of the book.
[3]: A malaria risk, predominantly in the malignant *falciparum* form, exists all year throughout the country. Resistance to chloroquine has been reported.
[4]: All water should be regarded as being potentially contaminated. Water used for drinking, brushing teeth or making ice should have first been boiled or otherwise sterilised. Only eat well-cooked meat and fish, preferably served hot. Pork, salad and mayonnaise may carry increased risk. Vegetables should be cooked and fruit peeled.
Rabies is present. For those at high risk, vaccination before arrival should be considered. If you are bitten abroad seek medical advice without delay. For more information consult the *Health* section at the back of the book.
Bilharzia (schistosomiasis) is present. Avoid swimming and paddling in fresh water. Swimming pools which are well-chlorinated and maintained are safe.
Meningitis, hepatitis, filariasis and *onchocerciasis* (river blindness) can occur.
Health care: Health insurance is essential. There are rudimentary medical, dental and optical facilities in Conakry.

TRAVEL - International

AIR: Guinea's national airline is *Air Guinée (GI)*. There are regular air connections with Guinea-Bissau, Nigeria, Congo, Ghana, Morocco, Gambia, France and Belgium.
Approximate flight time: From *London* to Conakry is 9 hours (including stopover time in Paris or Brussels of up to 3 hours).
International airport: *Conakry (CKY)*, 13km (8 miles) southwest of the city. Taxis are available to the city.
Departure tax: FG9000. African destinations – FG4800.
SEA: The principal shipping lines calling at Conakry are *Lloyd Triestino, DSS Line (UK)* and *Polish Ocean Lines*.
ROAD: Roads link Freetown (Sierra Leone) with Conakry and with Ganta on the Liberian border; and Bamako (Mali) with Siguiri and Kankan. Roads from Liberia and Mali can be difficult. Buses operate from Tambacomda (Senegal) and Bamako (Mali). See also *Travel – Internal* below.

TRAVEL - Internal

AIR: *Air Guinée* operates internal services to some of the main towns, such as Conakry, Labé, Kankan, Boké, Kissidougou, Macenta, Nzérékoré and Siguiri.
Departure tax: FG3000 for all domestic flights.
RAIL: A twice-weekly passenger service connects Conakry, Kindia and Kankan. There are also five trains a week between Port Kamsar and Sangaredi. There is a limited buffet service. In general, rail travel is not recommended.
ROAD: Roads are in poor condition and little used, and the minor roads are overgrown with bush. However, improvements are currently under way. Travel by road is often impossible in the rainy season (May-Oct). The roads between Conakry (via Kindia) and Kissidougou and from Boké to Kamsar are both metalled, as is the road to Freetown. **Taxis** are available, although fares should be negotiated in advance. **Documentation:** International Driving Permit required.
URBAN: Buses and taxis operate cheaply within Conakry. It is not necessary to tip taxi drivers.

ACCOMMODATION

HOTELS: In Conakry there are a few highly priced hotels of an adequate standard. Kankan also has a few hotels. Accommodation should be booked well in advance with written confirmation.
RESTHOUSES: These are available in most of the major towns; enquire locally.
CAMPING: Not allowed in Guinea.

RESORTS & EXCURSIONS

In 1958, when it declared independence from France, Guinea became an isolated and secretive country. However, after the death of the dictator Sekou Touré in 1984, Guinea began, slowly, to allow tourists through its once stubbornly closed doors. Yet it is still one of the least visited countries in Africa and can be difficult, despite declarations to the contrary, to acquire visas.
Guinea's main attraction to tourists is its relatively undisturbed countryside. Its landscape varies from mountains to plains and from savannahs to forests, and the three great rivers of West Africa – the Gambia, the Senegal and the Niger – all originate here. The **Fouta Djalon** highlands are well known for their picturesque hills, offering superb views, and the rolling valleys and waterfalls, which are all presided over by the mostly Muslim population of Fula herders and farmers. In the eastern part of Guinea lie many historical towns with echoes and remnants of medieval empires. In the south is the **Guinée Forestière,** a highland area of rainforest and old pre-Islamic tribes.
The capital, **Conakry,** is located on the island of Tumbo and is connected to the Kaloum Peninsula by a 300m-long pier. The city is well laid-out, its alleys shaded by mangrove and coconut palm trees. The *Cathedral*, built in the 1930s and located in the town centre, is well worth viewing. There is also a *National Museum*. The *Kakimbon Caves* in the village of **Ratoma,** now a suburb of Conakry, are the source of many interesting legends and are bestowed with great religious signficance by the local Baga people. The **Iles de Los,** off the Kaloum Peninsula, are well recommended as a tourist destination and are easily accessible from Conakry. About 150km (93 miles) outside Conakry is the picturesque *Le Voile de la Marée*, nestled at the bottom of a 70m-high rock from which the River Sabende plunges, amidst lush vegetation, into a deep pond. In **Pita,** located between Dalaba and Labé, can be found the *Kinkon Falls*, which are 150m of rushing water.
There are no national parks in Guinea, but wildlife can best be seen in the northeast savannahs between the Tinkisso River and the Mali border, in the foothills of the Fouta Djalon and in the southeast.

SOCIAL PROFILE

FOOD & DRINK: Restaurants, except in the capital where Western-style food is available, generally serve local dishes including *jollof rice*, stuffed chicken with groundnuts, and fish dishes. These are usually served with rice and may be spicy. Staples are cassava, yams and maize. Guineans are fond of very hot maize soup, served from calabashes. **Drink:** Main hotels, mostly in the capital, have reasonable restaurants where a wide variety of alcoholic beverages are served, including good West African brands of beer. This is also available in local bars.
NIGHTLIFE: Although there are theatres, nightclubs and cinemas, Guineans prefer to make their own entertainment. In the streets people can often be seen gathered together to dance, sing and play traditional musical instruments or home-made guitars. Conakry is a dynamic centre for music and the singing of the Kindia people is particularly beautiful.
SHOPPING: Although department stores in the major cities are poorly stocked, local markets sell a unique display of goods. Special purchases include brightly coloured, distinctive Guinean clothes, wood carvings, leather rugs in bold black-and-white designs, skins, metal jewellery, locally produced records, calabashes and jewellery. **Shopping hours:** 0900-1800 Monday to Saturday.
SPORT: In Landreah is the 28 September Stadium where a number of sporting events are held. **Football** is the most popular sport and the national team is more than competent. **Swimming:** There are one or two beaches on the Los Island (which lies just off the coast near Conakry), but currents can be strong and swimmers are advised to exercise care and follow local advice.
SOCIAL CONVENTIONS: Although Muslim customs are less strict than in the Arab world, beliefs and traditions should be respected by tourists. Casual dress is acceptable. **Photography:** A permit (applied for in advance) has to be obtained from the Ministère de l'Intérieur et de la Securité. **Tipping:** A 5% service charge will usually be included in the bill.

BUSINESS PROFILE

ECONOMY: Most of the population is engaged in subsistence agriculture. Until 1984 the economy functioned under centralised state control. The regime which took over has endeavoured to decentralise economic control and production which, apart from agriculture, is concentrated in mining. Guinea has substantial reserves of bauxite – which accounts for over 90% of export earnings – and diamonds which suffered from low world demand during the late 1970s and early 1980s, but the sector has now recovered. The country's natural resources have helped to secure extensive foreign aid to bolster the economy: this previously derived from the then Soviet Union but now comes largely from Western donors. Guinea has also benefitted from growing regional co-operation: Cameroon, for example, processes much of the bauxite ore to produce aluminium. Guinea is a member of both the Mano River Union (with Liberia and Sierra Leone) and of the Gambia River Development Organisation (with Gambia and Senegal). France is the major importer in Guinea and the USA is the destination for 20% of the country's exports.
BUSINESS: Appointments should be made in

GUINEA REPUBLIC	HEALTH REGULATIONS	VISA REGULATIONS (Code-Link)
GALILEO/WORLDSPAN	TI-DFT/CKY/HE	TI-DFT/CKY/VI
SABRE	TIDFT/CKY/HE	TIDFT/CKY/VI

To access this information on your CRS, swipe the barcode with a light pen or type in the text under the barcode. For more information, see the introduction *How to Use This Book*.

advance. Tropical-weight suits and ties are worn by some business visitors, but these are not essential. A knowledge of French is advisable. **Office hours:** 0800-1630 Monday to Thursday; 0800-1300 Friday.
COMMERCIAL INFORMATION: The following organisation can offer advice: Chambre de Commerce, d'Industrie et d'Agriculture de Guinée, BP 545, Conakry. Tel: 444 495. Telex: 609.

HISTORY & GOVERNMENT

HISTORY: The division between Guinea Republic and Guinea-Bissau dates from a Franco-Portuguese agreement of 1886, one of many concluded in West Africa to settle the competing claims of European colonialists. Guinea was the only French protectorate which refused to join the French Community upon independence in 1958, when the French handed power to the Parti Democratique de Guinée. This became the sole legitimate political party and pursued a policy of socialist revolution. By 1983, the regime's unpopularity was such that an estimated two million people (a quarter of the population) had fled the country. In March 1984 the ruler of Guinea since independence, President Sekou Touré, died and the army immediately seized power in a bloodless coup. The new leader was Col. Lansana Conté, who remained as President until yielding to the collective presidency of the CTRN (see below) in January 1992 prior to the holding of presidential elections. In foreign policy, the Conté government immediately set about improving political and economic links with its West African neighbours. Guinea also sought to reduce French influence by diversifying links with the European Community (a vital export market). During 1989, the regime unveiled plans for a gradual move towards democratic government, but the original timetable was too slow and vague to forestall civil unrest, which escalated during 1990 until firmly repressed. A new Constitution (see below) was put to national referendum in December 1990 and accepted by a large majority.
GOVERNMENT: The 1982 Constitution was suspended after the 1984 coup, but a new one (the *Loi Fundamentale*) was not introduced until 1990. Under its provisions, a joint military-civilian body, the Comité Transitoire de Redressement National (CTRN, Transitional Committee for National Recovery), whose task is to supervise the transition to political plurality and elected government, was implemented. The CTRN has a deadline of 1995 by which to complete its work.

CLIMATE

The climate is tropical and humid with a wet and a dry season. Wet season lasts from May to October; dry season lasts from November to April.
Required clothing: Tropical or washable cottons throughout the year. A light raincoat or umbrella is needed during the rainy season.

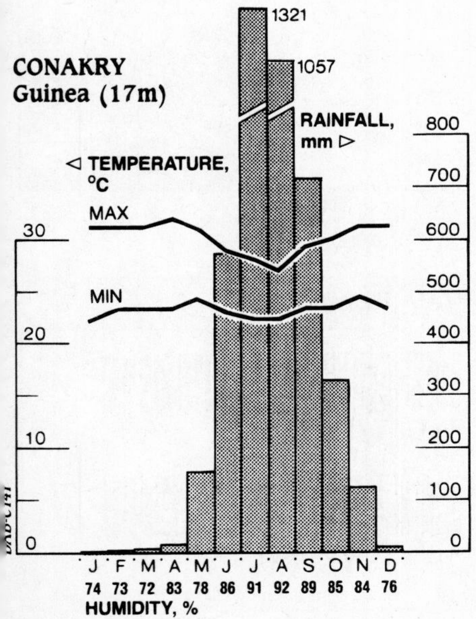

Location: West Africa.

Centro de Informação e Turismo
CP 294
Bissau, Guinea-Bissau.
Consulate General of the Republic of Guinea-Bissau
8 Palace Gate
London W8 4RP
Tel: (071) 589 5253. Fax: (071) 589 9590. Opening hours: 1000-1300 Monday to Thursday.
Embassy of the Republic of Guinea-Bissau
Rua de Alconene 17-17A
1400 Lisbon
Portugal
Tel: (1) 615 371/2/3. Telex: 14326.
British Consulate
Mavegro International
CP 100
Bissau, Guinea-Bissau
Tel: 211 529. Telex: 259 MAVEGRO BI.
Embassy of the Republic of Guinea-Bissau
Mezzanine Suite
918 16th Street, NW
Washington, DC
20006
Tel: (202) 872 4222. Fax: (202) 872 4226.
Embassy of the United States of America
Avenida Domingos Ramos
1067 Bissau Cedex, Guinea-Bissau
Tel: 201 139 *or* 201 145 *or* 201 113. Fax: 201 159.
Honorary Consulate of the Republic of Guinea-Bissau
Suite 900
2075 University Street
Montréal, Québec
H3A 2L1
Tel: (514) 848 0769.

AREA: 36,125 sq km (13,948 sq miles).
POPULATION: 943,000 (1989 estimate).
POPULATION DENSITY: 26.1 per sq km.
CAPITAL: Bissau. **Population:** 943,000 (1989).
GEOGRAPHY: Guinea-Bissau (formerly Portuguese Guinea) is located in West Africa, and is bounded to the north by Senegal and to the south by the Guinea Republic. It encompasses the adjacent Bijagós Islands and the island of Bolama. The country rises from a coastal plain broken up by numerous inlets through a transitional plateau to mountains on the border with Guinea. Thick forest and mangrove swamp cover the area nearest the Atlantic Ocean. Savannah covers the inland areas.
LANGUAGE: Official language is Portuguese. The majority of the population speak Guinean Creole. Balante and Fulani languages are also spoken.
RELIGION: 30% Muslim, 66% Animist, 4% Christian.
TIME: GMT.
ELECTRICITY: Limited electricity supply on 220 volts AC, 50Hz.
COMMUNICATIONS: Telephone: IDD available. Country code: 245. **Telex:** Facilities are available at the main post office in Bissau. International Telex code: BI.
Press: There are no English-language papers. *Nô Pintcha* and *Voz da Guiné* are published daily.
BBC World Service and Voice of America frequencies: From time to time these change. See the section *How to Use this Book* for more information.

BBC:				
MHz	21.71	15.07	11.86	6.005
Voice of America:				
MHz	21.49	15.60	9.525	6.035

PASSPORT/VISA

Regulations and requirements may be subject to change at short notice, and you are advised to contact the appropriate diplomatic or consular authority before finalising travel arrangements. Details of these may be found at the head of this country's entry. Any numbers in the chart refer to the footnotes below.

	Passport Required?	Visa Required?	Return Ticket Required?
Full British	Yes	Yes	Yes
BVP	Not valid	-	-
Australian	Yes	Yes	Yes
Canadian	Yes	Yes	Yes
USA	Yes	Yes	Yes
Other EC	Yes	Yes	Yes
Japanese	Yes	Yes	Yes

PASSPORTS: Valid passport required by all.
British Visitors Passport: Not accepted.
VISAS: Required by all except nationals of Benin, Burkina Faso, Cape Verde, Côte d'Ivoire, Cuba, Gambia, Ghana, Guinea, Liberia, Mali, Mauritania, Niger, Nigeria, Senegal, Sierra Leone and Togo. Visas can be extended in Bissau Central Police Station. Contact Embassy for details.
Application to: Consulate (or Consular Section at Embassy). For addresses, see top of entry.
Application requirements: (a) 2 completed application forms. (b) 2 photos. (c) Passport.
Working days required: Applications should be made 1 day in advance; same day if applying in the UK.

MONEY

Currency: Guinea-Bissau Peso (GBP) = 100 centavos. Notes are in denominations of GBP500, 100 and 50. Coins are in denominations of GBP20, 10, 5, 2.5 and 1, and 50, 20, 10 and 5 centavos.
Credit cards: Limited use of Access in the capital, but check with your credit card company for details of merchant acceptability and other services which may be available.
Travellers cheques: These can be cashed at any bank. There is a fixed rate of commission on all transactions.
Exchange rate indicators: The following figures are included as a guide to the movements of the Guinea-Bissau Peso against Sterling and the US Dollar:

Date:	**Oct '89**	**Oct '90**	**Oct '91**	**Oct '92**
£1.00=	**1027.65**	**1268.47**	**1129.37**	**7907.50**
$1.00=	**650.82**	**649.33**	**650.75**	**4982.67**

Currency restrictions: Import and export of local currency is prohibited. There are no restrictions on the import of foreign currency, export is limited to the amount declared on arrival.
Banking hours: 0730-1000 Monday to Friday.

DUTY FREE

The following goods can be imported into Guinea-Bissau without incurring customs duty:
A reasonable quantity of tobacco products and perfume in opened bottles.
Prohibited items: Alcohol.

PUBLIC HOLIDAYS

Public holidays observed in Guinea-Bissau are as follows:
Mar 25 '93 Korité (End of Ramadan). **May 1** Labour Day. **Jun 1** Tabaski (Feast of the Sacrifice). **Aug 3** Anniversary of the Killing of Pidjiguiti. **Sep 24** National Day. **Nov 14** Anniversary of the Movement of Re-adjustment. **Dec 25** Christmas Day. **Jan 1 '94** New Year's Day. **Jan 20** Death of Amílcar Cabral. **Mar** Korité (End of Ramadan).
Note: Muslim festivals are timed according to local sightings of various phases of the Moon and the dates given above are approximations. During the lunar month of Ramadan that precedes Korité, Muslims fast during the day and feast at night and normal business patterns may be interrupted. Many restaurants are closed during the day and there may be restrictions on smoking and drinking. Some disruption may continue into Korité itself. Korité and Tabaski may last anything from two to ten days, depending on the region. For more information see the section *World of Islam* at the back of the book.

HEALTH

Regulations and requirements may be subject to change at short notice, and you are advised to contact your doctor well in advance of your intended date of departure. Any numbers in the chart refer to the footnotes below.

	Special Precautions?	Certificate Required?
Yellow Fever	Yes	1
Cholera	Yes	2
Typhoid & Polio	Yes	-
Malaria	3	-
Food & Drink	4	-

[1]: A yellow fever vaccination certificate is required from travellers over one year of age coming from infected areas and from the following countries: all mainland African countries lying wholly or in part between 20°N and 20°S except Sudan, Cameroon, Malawi, Namibia, Botswana and Zimbabwe; and – in Latin America – Bolivia, Brazil, Colombia, Ecuador, French Guiana, Guyana, Panama, Peru, Suriname and Venezuela.
[2]: Following WHO guidelines issued in 1973, a cholera vaccination certificate is no longer a condition of entry to the Guinea Republic. However, cholera is a serious risk in this country and precautions are essential. Up-to-date advice should be sought before deciding whether these precautions should include vaccination as medical opinion is divided over its effectiveness. See the *Health* section at the back of the book.
[3]: Malaria risk, predominantly in the malignant *falciparum* form, exists all year throughout the country. Resistance to chloroquine has been reported.
[4]: All water should be regarded as being potentially contaminated. Water used for drinking, brushing teeth or making ice should have first been boiled or otherwise sterilised. Only eat well-cooked meat and fish, preferably served hot. Pork, salad and mayonnaise may carry increased risk. Vegetables should be cooked and fruit peeled.
Rabies is present. For those at high risk, vaccination before arrival should be considered. If you are bitten abroad seek medical advice without delay. For more information consult the *Health* section at the back of the book.
Bilharzia (schistosomiasis) is present. Avoid swimming and paddling in fresh water. Swimming pools which are well-chlorinated and maintained are safe. *Meningitis*, *hepatitis*, *filariasis* and *onchocerciasis* (river blindness) can occur.
Health care: Health insurance is essential.

TRAVEL - International

Guinea-Bissau's national airline is *Transportes Aéreos da Guiné Bissau*. Other airlines that fly direct to Bissau include *TAP Air Portugal (TP)*, *EAS (Europe Aero Service)* and *Aeroflot (SU)*.
Approximate flight time: From *London* to Bissau is 10 hours 20 minutes (including stopover of 1 hour 30 minutes, often in Lisbon). There are daily flights from Lisbon to Bissau.
International airport: *Bissau (BXO)* (Bissalanca), 11km (7 miles) from the city (travel time – 30 minutes). Taxi service is available to the city.
Departure tax: US$8-US$12, depending on destination.
SEA/RIVER: Ferries running between coastal and inland ports form an important part of the transport system, especially as roads are often impassable (see *Sea/River* in *Travel – Internal* below). The main port is Bissau. This and four inland ports are currently being expanded and upgraded. A new commercial river port is planned at N'Pungda.
ROAD: Travellers should check that overland entry is allowed before embarking (the usual route of entry is by plane from Conakry in the Guinea Republic); entry from Senegal is not recommended. New roads are planned to link Guinea-Bissau with several neighbouring states.

TRAVEL - Internal

AIR: There are 60 small airfields. The national airline provides internal flights, including the outlying islands.
SEA/RIVER: Most towns are accessible by ship. Riverboats can reach almost all areas; there are ferries from Bissau to Bolama (often irregular due to tides) and Bissau to Bafata, calling at smaller towns en route. Coast-hopping ferries go from the north coast to Bissau.
ROAD: There are more than 3000km (1850 miles) of roads, one-fifth tarred and a similar proportion improved for all-weather use. Improvements are planned. There are local and long-distance **taxis** and **buses** (the latter offer limited services). **Documentation:** An International Driving Permit is recommended, although it is not legally required. A temporary driving licence is available from local authorities on presentation of a valid British driving licence.

ACCOMMODATION

HOTELS: Several new hotels include the 4-star Sheraton in North Bissau with 175 rooms and the 24 Septembre Hotel. There is also a brand new leisure hotel on the island of Maio that can be reached by ferry from Bissau, and another hotel is being built in the north on the beach of Varella. Guinea-Bissau also offers some small, inexpensive hotels. Accommodation should be booked in advance. Tariffs are liable to change at any time, therefore confirmation of booking is essential.
CAMPING: There are no designated campsites and camping is not recommended.

RESORTS & EXCURSIONS

Until recently, Guinea-Bissau was well off the tourist route, but efforts have been made to encourage visitors to this beautiful country.
The capital, **Bissau,** is a pleasant town of about 50,000 people. The *Museum of African Artefacts* is well worth a visit.
Bolama, the original capital of Guinea-Bissau, is now a rather attractive ruin, and the island is worth seeing, with good beaches. **Bubaque** is another island of interest. All the coastal islands are unspoiled.

SOCIAL PROFILE

FOOD & DRINK: Guinea-Bissau's few small hotels offer cheap excellent food including *jollof rice*, chicken and fish dishes. Staples are cassava, yams and maize.
SHOPPING: Locally made artefacts and carvings can be found in the markets. There are also some modern shops in Bissau. **Shopping hours:** 0730-1000 Monday to Friday.
SPORT: Swimming: Seas are warm and offer good bathing and swimming. However, bathers should not venture out of their depth in some parts as currents can be strong. **Fishing:** Some of the rivers and the sea offer excellent fishing, although facilities have not been developed.
SOCIAL CONVENTIONS: Casual wear is widely accepted. Social customs should be respected, particularly in Muslim areas. **Tipping:** 10% is an acceptable amount, although not encouraged.

BUSINESS PROFILE

ECONOMY: Rice is the staple food in this poor, largely subsistence economy. The main cash crops are groundnuts, cashews and palm kernels. Timber is the only significant industry. Cotton production is being developed with EC assistance; a sugar complex is planned and the fishing industry has been earmarked for major expansion. The possible exploitation of oil and bauxite deposits is being considered. In the short term, it seems little can be done to lighten the country's massive foreign debt. Guinea-Bissau will continue to rely on large quantities of foreign aid, of which it is among the highest per capita recipients in the world. France, Portugal, Italy and Thailand are Guinea-Bissau's largest trading partners.
BUSINESS: Businessmen wear safari suits (bush jackets without a tie). A knowledge of Portugese is useful as only few executives speak English. Visits during Ramadan should be avoided.
COMMERCIAL INFORMATION: For further information contact: Associacio Commercial e Industrial e Agricola da Guiné-Bissau.

HISTORY & GOVERNMENT

HISTORY: Guinea-Bissau emerged from the Portuguese-occupied stretch of West Africa after the agreement of 1886 with the French which fixed colonial boundaries in the region. Like other Portuguese colonies, Guinea-Bissau suffered a protracted war of independence between 1963 and 1974, led on the rebel side by Amílcar Cabral, a highly respected figure inside the country. In 1974 a military coup in Portugal, itself partly the result of heavy losses sustained by the Portuguese army in Guinea-Bissau, brought about the sudden withdrawal of the colonial authorities. In September that year, Portugal formally recognised the independence of Guinea-Bissau. The emancipation of women has played a major part in the programme of rebuilding the culture of Guinea-Bissau since the War of Independence. Polygamy is officially discouraged and legal reforms have been made to protect women's rights. Concerted campaigns against illiteracy and the very high infant mortality rate have met with only limited success due to the lack of human and economic resources. The Portuguese colonisation of Guinea-Bissau has left its mark on buildings, language and the economy. The president and leader of the PAIGC, who has held office since 1978, is João Vieira, formerly chief of the armed forces. During the 1980s, Vieira's government managed a steady improvement in relations with the former colonial power, Portugal, and other EC nations, particularly France. The principal motive has been economic, since Guinea-Bissau is very poor, but it has paid political dividends in the form of diplomatic support from Europe. This is in spite of a patchy record of repression of political dissent (as shown by the steady stream of defections by regime members to Portugal). On the whole, the Vieira government has worked hard to improve its country's fortunes under demanding circumstances. The Government has recently followed the continental trend and made provision for multi-party legislative and presidential elections.
GOVERNMENT: The post-independence government has consistently pursued socialist policies under the direction of the Partido Africano da Independência da Guiné e Cabo Verde (PAIGC), the sole legitimate political party. A new constitution adopted in 1984 maintained the hegemony of the PAIGC. A series of constitutional amendments in 1991 have made provision for multi-party elections for the National Assembly and Presidency.

CLIMATE

The climate is tropical, with a wet season from May to November. The dry season is from December to April, with hot winds from the interior. Humidity is high from July to September.
Required clothing: Tropical lightweight cotton clothes and raincoat for the rainy season.

BISSAU Guinea Bissau

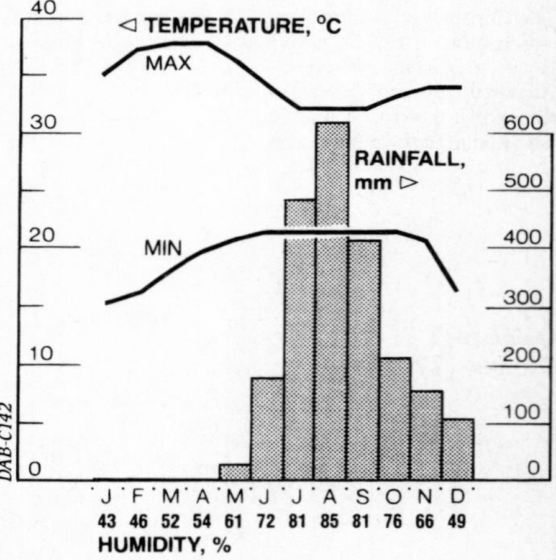

GUINEA-BISSAU	HEALTH REGULATIONS	VISA REGULATIONS
GALILEO/WORLDSPAN	TI-DFT/BXO/HE	TI-DFT/BXO/VI
SABRE	TIDFT/BXO/HE	TIDFT/BXO/VI

Code-Link

To access this information on your CRS, swipe the barcode with a light pen or type in the text under the barcode. For more information, see the introduction *How to Use This Book*.

GUYANA

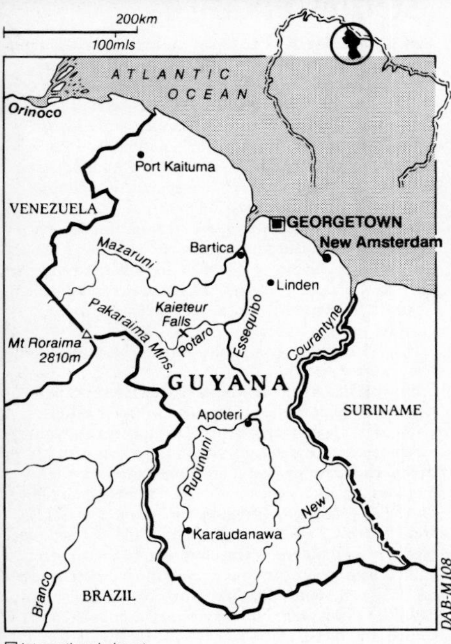

☐ *international airport*

Location: South America, northeast coast.

Guyana Overland Tours
PO Box 10173
48 Prince's and Russell Streets
Charlestown
Georgetown, Guyana
Tel: (2) 69876.

High Commission for the Co-operative Republic of Guyana
3 Palace Court
London W2 4LP
Tel: (071) 229 7684-8. Fax: (071) 727 9809. Telex: 23945.
Opening hours: 0930-1730 Monday to Friday (except national and British holidays); 0930–1430 Monday to Friday (visas).

British High Commisson
PO Box 10849
44 Main Street
Georgetown, Guyana
Tel: (2) 65881/4. Fax: (2) 53555. Telex: 2221 UKREP GY.

Embassy of the Co-operative Republic of Guyana
2490 Tracy Place, NW
Washington, DC
20008
Tel: (202) 265 6900. Telex: 64170.

Consulate General of the Co-operative Republic of Guyana
622 Third Avenue
New York, NY
10017
Tel: (212) 527 3215.

Embassy of the United States of America
PO Box 10507
99-100 Young and Duke Streets
Kingston
Georgetown, Guyana
Tel: (2) 54900-9. Fax: (2) 58497. Telex: 2213 AMEMSY GY.

High Commission for the Co-operative Republic of Guyana
Suite 309, 151 Slater Street
Ottawa, Ontario
K1P 5H3
Tel: (613) 235 7249/7240. Fax: (613) 235 1447. Telex: 0533684.
Consulate in Toronto.

Canadian High Commission
PO Box 10880
High and Young Streets
Georgetown, Guyana
Tel: (2) 72081/5 *or* 58337. Fax: (2) 58380. Telex: 2215.

AREA: 214,969 sq km (83,000 sq miles).
POPULATION: 811,000 (1988 estimate).
POPULATION DENSITY: 3.8 per sq km.
CAPITAL: Georgetown. **Population:** 72,049 (1976).
GEOGRAPHY: Guyana lies in the northeast of South America, bordered by Venezuela to the west, Suriname to the southeast and Brazil to the south. It is bordered by the Atlantic Ocean to the north and east. The word 'Guiana' (the original spelling) means 'land of many waters' and the name was well chosen for there are over 1600km (965 miles) of navigable rivers in the country. The interior is either high savannah uplands (such as those along the Venezuelan border, called the *Rupununi*, and the *Kanaku Mountains* in the far southwest), or thick, hilly jungle and forest, which occupy over 85% of the country's area. The narrow coastal belt contains the vast majority of the population, and produces the major cash crop, sugar, and the major subsistence crop, rice. One of the most spectacular sights to be seen in the interior is the towering Kaieteur Falls along the Potaro River, five times the height of Niagara. The country has 322km (206 miles) of coastline. Nearly 25% of the population lives in or near Georgetown.
LANGUAGE: English is the official language but Hindi, Urdu and Amerindian are also spoken.
RELIGION: 50% Christian, 35% Hindu, less than 10% Muslim.
TIME: GMT - 3.
ELECTRICITY: 110 volts AC, 60Hz.
COMMUNICATIONS: Telephone: IDD is available to main towns and cities. Country code: 592. **Fax:** Facilities are available at the Guyana Telephone and Telegraph Company and the Bank of Guyana Building in Georgetown. **Telex/telegram:** Available at The Guyana Telephone and Telegraph Company and Bank of Guyana Building. Certain hotels also have facilities. **Press:** The daily state-owned newspaper is *The Guyana Chronicle*. The independent *Stabroek News* is published every day except Monday.
BBC World Service and Voice of America frequencies: From time to time these change. See the section *How to Use this Book* for more information.

BBC:				
MHz	15.22	9.915	7.325	6.195
Voice of America:				
MHz	15.21	11.58	9.775	5.995

PASSPORT/VISA

Regulations and requirements may be subject to change at short notice, and you are advised to contact the appropriate diplomatic or consular authority before finalising travel arrangements. Details of these may be found at the head of this country's entry. Any numbers in the chart refer to the footnotes below.

	Passport Required?	Visa Required?	Return Ticket Required?
Full British	Yes	Yes	Yes
BVP	Not valid	-	-
Australian	Yes	Yes	Yes
Canadian	Yes	Yes	Yes
USA	Yes	Yes	Yes
Other EC	Yes	Yes	Yes
Japanese	Yes	Yes	Yes

PASSPORTS: Valid passport required by all.
British Visitors Passport: Not acceptable.
VISAS: Required by all except:
(a) persons of Guyanese birth with foreign passports providing passport clearly indicates place of birth or they have other satisfactory documentary evidence;
(b) nationals of the CARICOM countries, ie Antigua & Barbuda, Bahamas, Barbados, Belize, Dominica, Grenada, Jamaica, Montserrat, St Kitts & Nevis, St Lucia, St Vincent & the Grenadines, Suriname and Trinidad & Tobago, provided they hold onward or return tickets and sufficient funds for duration of stay.
Types of visa: Single- and Multiple-entry; Transit. Entry fees vary according to nationality of applicant, since they are charged on a reciprocal basis; £20 Single-entry, £44 Multiple-entry for UK passport holders.
Validity: Visas are valid for 3 months from date of issue. Length of stay and extension is at the discretion of the Immigration Office.
Application to: Consulate (or Consular Section at Embassy or High Commission). For addresses, see top of entry.
Application requirements: (a) Application form. (b) 2 photos. (c) Sufficient funds to cover length of stay. (d) Passport, valid for at least 6 months prior to travel. (e) Business letter or letter of invitation.
Working days required: Applicants should contact Embassy or High Commission at least one week in advance of travel to Guyana, although it may only take 2 days to process.
Temporary residence: Permission must be obtained from Minister of Home Affairs, Guyana.

MONEY

Currency: Guyana Dollar (Guy$) = 100 cents. Notes are in denominations of Guy$100, 20, 10, 5 and 1. Coins are in denominations of 50, 25, 10, 5 and 1 cents. Due to the rate of inflation most transactions involve notes only.
Currency exchange: Banks offer exchange facilities, but the bureaucratic procedures for changing money can be protracted, owing to the strict financial control regulations prevailing in the country.
Credit cards: American Express, Visa, Access/Mastercard and Diners Club enjoy limited acceptance (eg at the Forte Crest and Tower hotels). Check with your credit card company for details of merchant acceptability and other services which may be available.
Travellers cheques: The exchanging of these can lead to great complications, and for this reason they are not recommended for those who may wish to change money in a hurry.
Exchange rate indicators: The following figures are included as a guide to the movements of the Guyana Dollar against Sterling and the US Dollar:

Date:	**Oct '89**	**Oct '90**	**Oct '91**	**Oct '92**
£1.00=	47.26	87.02	220.66	198.46
$1.00=	29.93	45.00	127.14	125.06

Currency restrictions: The import or export of foreign currency over the equivalent of US$10,000 must be declared. The Guyanese Dollar is not negotiable abroad.
Banking hours: 0800-1200 Monday to Thursday; 0800-1200 and 1530-1700 Friday.

DUTY FREE

The following goods can be imported (by persons over 16 years of age) into Guyana without incurring customs duty:
200 cigarettes or 50 cigars or 225g tobacco;
Spirits not exceeding 570ml;
Wine not exceeding 570ml;
A reasonable amount of perfume.

PUBLIC HOLIDAYS

Public holidays observed in Guyana are as follows:
Mar 25 '93 Eid al-Fitr, end of Ramadan. **Apr 9** Good Friday. **Apr 12** Easter Monday. **May 1** Labour Day. **May**

GUYANA	HEALTH REGULATIONS	VISA REGULATIONS Code-Link
GALILEO/WORLDSPAN	TI-DFT/GEO/HE	TI-DFT/GEO/VI
SABRE	TIDFT/GEO/HE	TIDFT/GEO/VI

To access this information on your CRS, swipe the barcode with a light pen or type in the text under the barcode. For more information, see the introduction *How to Use This Book*.

3 Indian Heritage Day Holiday. **Jun 1** Eid al-Adha, Feast of the Sacrifice. **Jun 28** Caribbean Day. **Aug 2** Freedom Day. **Aug 30** Yum an-Nabi (Prophet's Birthday). **Oct/Nov** Deepavali (Divali). **Dec 25-26** Christmas. **Jan 1 '94** New Year's Day. **Feb 23** Republic Day. **Mar** Start of Eid al-Fitr.

Note: (a) Muslim festivals are timed according to local sightings of various phases of the Moon and the dates given above are approximations. During the lunar month of Ramadan that precedes Eid al-Fitr, Muslims fast during the day and feast at night and normal business patterns may be interrupted. Many restaurants are closed during the day and there may be restrictions on smoking and drinking. Some disruption may continue into Eid al-Fitr itself. Eid al-Fitr and Eid al-Adha may last anything from two to ten days, depending on the region. For more information see the section *World of Islam* at the back of the book. (b) Hindu festivals are declared according to local astronomical observations and it is only possible to forecast the month of their occurrence.

HEALTH

Regulations and requirements may be subject to change at short notice, and you are advised to contact your doctor well in advance of your intended date of departure. Any numbers in the chart refer to the footnotes below.

	Special Precautions?	Certificate Required?
Yellow Fever	Yes	1
Cholera	No	-
Typhoid & Polio	Yes	-
Malaria	2	-
Food & Drink	3	-

[1]: A yellow fever vaccination certificate is required from travellers coming from infected areas and from the following countries: Angola, Belize, Benin, Bolivia, Brazil, Burkina Faso, Burundi, Cameroon, Central African Republic, Chad, Colombia, Congo, Costa Rica, Côte d'Ivoire, Ecuador, French Guiana, Gabon, Gambia, Ghana, Guatemala, Guinea, Guinea-Bissau, Honduras, Kenya, Liberia, Mali, Nicaragua, Niger, Nigeria, Panama, Peru, Rwanda, São Tome e Príncipe, Senegal, Sierra Leone, Somalia, Suriname, Togo, Uganda, Venezuela, Tanzania and Zaïre.

[2]: Malaria risk exists throughout the year in the North West Region and areas along the Pomeroon River. Chloroquine-resistant *falciparum* is reported. **Note:** Sleeping under a mosquito net is recommended, especially in Georgetown, as are insect repellants.

[3]: Mains water is normally chlorinated in main cities, and whilst relatively safe may cause mild abdominal upsets. Bottled water is available and is advised for the first few weeks of the stay. Milk is unpasteurised and should be boiled. Powdered or tinned milk is available and is advised, but make sure that it is reconstituted with pure water. Avoid dairy products which are likely to have been made from unboiled milk. Local meat, poultry, seafood, fruit and vegetables are generally considered safe to eat.

Health care: Health insurance is recommended. Hospital treatment in Georgetown is free, but a doctor will charge for an appointment.

TRAVEL - International

AIR: Guyana's national airline is *Guyana Airways Corporation* (GY).

Approximate flight time: From *London* to Guyana is 10 hours (via Port of Spain – no direct flights).

International airport: *Georgetown (GEO)* (Timehri) is 28km (17 miles) from the city (travel time – 35 minutes). Coach to the city is available. An irregular and crowded bus service to the city is also available. Taxis meet every plane. There are duty-free facilities at Georgetown Airport but the opening hours are erratic. The bank is open 0800-1400.

Departure tax: Guy$1000 is levied on all international departures; transit passengers and children under 7 years of age are exempt.

SEA: The *Royal Netherlands Line* sails every two weeks from Europe and New York or New Orleans. Numerous schooners sail between Guyana and the Caribbean islands, but schedules are erratic. For details contact local ports. Up to 12 passengers are carried by cargo vessels run by the *Royal Netherlands Steamship Company* which ply from London, Southampton and Liverpool to Georgetown.

Following recent improvements in relations with Suriname, a ferry service across the Berbice River now links the two countries.

RAIL: There are no passenger rail services.

ROAD: International road links are currently limited to a short stretch across the Brazilian border as far as Lethem. The only reliable link from there to Georgetown is by air. There are plans to extend the road from Linden as far as the Brazilian border and to establish a car ferry service across the Corentyne River to Suriname. It is uncertain if there is a reliable route to Venezuela.

See below for information on **documentation**.

TRAVEL - Internal

AIR: The only reliable means of travelling into the interior is by air. *Guyana Airways Corporation* operate scheduled services between Georgetown and other main centres. Flights to the Kaieteur Falls are run once a week by *Guyana Airways Corporation*, but there can be problems securing a reservation, and the schedule leaves little time for sightseeing. Group charters are the most practical arrangement. The charter of Bretton Norman Islander airplanes is available from *Guyana Aviation Group*, Georgetown Airport. *Guyana Overland Tours* run a 6-day trip on the first Tuesday of every month for groups of ten or more, but require at least one month's notice.

SEA/RIVER: Guyana has almost 1000km (600 miles) of navigable inland waterways, the most notable being the Mazaruni, Essequibo, Potaro, Demerara and Berbice rivers. Government steamers communicate with the interior up the Essequibo and Berbice rivers, but services can be irregular due to flooding and rapids. The Government also runs a coast-hopping service from Georgetown to several northern ports. Smaller craft operate where there is sufficient demand throughout the country.

RAIL: Mining concerns operate railways, but there are no scheduled passenger services.

ROAD: All-weather roads are concentrated in the eastern coastal strip, although there is now a road inland as far as Linden and there are plans to extend it as far as the Brazilian border. The coastal road linking Georgetown, Rossignol, New Amsterdam and Crabwood Creek (Corentyne) is fairly good. Because of Guyana's many rivers, most journeys of more than a few miles outside the capital will involve ferries and the attendant delays. **Bus:** Georgetown's Stabroek market is the terminus for buses operated by the *Guyana Transport Company*. These are regular but generally crowded. Areas served: Linden, Timehri (international airport) and Patentia (all hourly), Rossignol (11 a day) and Parika (15 a day). Services from Vreed en Hoop to Parika operate in conjunction with the passenger ferry service across the Demerara to Georgetown; services from New Amsterdam to Crabwood Creek operate in conjunction with ferries across the Berbice River. Rival 'tapir' minibuses also operate on some of the routes. There are a number of up-country bus links, some run by the mining companies. Bush buses to Isano, Mahdia and Tumatumari are run weekly by the *Transport and Harbours Department*, connecting with the steamer at Bartica. **Taxi:** It is advisable to travel by taxi at night. Vehicles are plentiful. There is a standard fare for inner-city travel; night fares are extra. For longer trips, fares should be agreed before departure. A 10% tip is usual in taxis. **Car hire:** Limited availability from local firms in Georgetown. **Note:** There are often serious petrol shortages in Guyana, which can make travelling long distances by car hazardous. **Documentation:** Foreign licence or International Driving Permit accepted.

ACCOMMODATION

HOTELS: There are some good hotels in Georgetown, of which the Forte Crest Hotel conforms to international standards. Others of a reasonable standard include the Tower Hotel, the Park Hotel and the Woodbine Hotel. There are no high-season charges. As power-cuts are commonplace, it is advisable for visitors to take a torch with them.

GUEST-HOUSES: Ranch, by invitation only.

CAMPING/CARAVANNING: There are no camping facilities.

RESORTS & EXCURSIONS

Georgetown: The 19th-century wooden houses supported on stilts and charming green boulevards laid out along the lines of the old Dutch canals give the capital a unique character. Some of the more impressive wooden buildings dating from the colonial past include the city hall, *St George's Cathedral*, the *Law Courts* and the *President's Residence*. The *Botanical Gardens*, which cover 120 acres, have a fine collection of palms, orchids and lotus lilies; nearby is the new *Cultural Centre* which contains what is probably the best theatre in the Caribbean. Also worth visiting is the *Natural History Museum*, which contains an up-to-date display of all aspects of Guyanese life and culture.

Bartica: At the junction of the Essequibo and Mazaruni rivers is the 'take-off' town for the gold and diamond fields, *Kaieteur Falls* and the rest of the interior. Kaieteur Falls is particularly recommended; situated on the Potaro River, it ranks with Niagara, Victoria and Iquazu in majesty and beauty. It lies within the *Kaiteur National Park*, which also contains a wide variety of wildlife.

SOCIAL PROFILE

FOOD & DRINK: The food in hotels and restaurants reflects the range of influences on Guyanan society. From India came curries, especially mutton, prawn or chicken, and Africa contributed dishes such as *foo-foo* (plantains made into cakes) and *metemgee* (edows, yams, cassava and plantains cooked in coconut milk and grated white of coconut). Portuguese garlic pork and Amerindian pepperpot are specialities. On the menus of most restaurants one may find chicken, pork and steak and, most of the time, shrimp. The best Chinese food in the country can be found in Georgetown. **Drink:** It is best to drink bottled water in Guyana. Local rum, known as Demerara rum, is well worth trying, while the local beer is *Banks* from Guyana.

NIGHTLIFE: There are numerous nightclubs and bars in Georgetown.

SHOPPING: Stabroek Market in Georgetown has local straw hats, baskets, clay goblets and jewellery. Other shops sell Amerindian bows and arrows, hammocks, pottery and salad bowls. Government-run shops sell magnificent jewellery, utilising local gold, silver, precious and semi-precious stones. Prices are very low for the quality of goods. **Shopping hours:** 0800-1130 and 1300-1600 Monday to Friday; 0800-1130 Saturday. **Note:** It is absolutely essential to ensure that receipts and correct documentation are retained, otherwise visitors may experience difficulty when clearing customs.

SPORT: Cricket and **hockey** are both popular, and the Bourda is one of the most attractive cricket grounds in the West Indies. **Shooting:** Night hunting from boats is often a feature of coastal river fishing, and small local deer and capybara are often encountered. Licence for use of firearms and ammunition must be requested one month before arrival. Tourists are permitted to bring in only one firearm. **Riding:** There is a pony club in Georgetown and horses are available at Manari Ranch in the Rupununi Savannahs. **Fishing:** The rivers and the interior abound in game fish, the best known of which is the man-eating piranha (called locally *perai*). The most sought after by the sportsman is the *lucanni*, a fish similar to the large-mouth bass. Most of the interior rivers are difficult for the more casual visitor to get to, but those who book in advance can take a few hours' flight to the largest fresh water fish in the world, the *arapaima*, weighing about 113kg (250lbs). Some of the coastal rivers within reach of Georgetown are also good for fishing, although it is wise to stay overnight in the fishing grounds, as the best are 4-5 hours' drive from the city. Fishing licences are required.

SOCIAL CONVENTIONS: In Georgetown it is wise to exercise care when travelling after dark and to avoid obtrusive displays of wealth. Address colleagues and business acquaintances as either 'Mr' or 'Comrade', eg Comrade John Brown, although using the surname only is also acceptable. Hospitality is important to the Guyanese and it is quite common for the visitor to be invited to their homes. Informal wear is widely acceptable, but men should avoid wearing shorts. Formal dress is usual in smarter dining rooms and for important social functions. **Tipping:** 10% at hotels and restaurants.

BUSINESS PROFILE

ECONOMY: Apart from agriculture – which allows Guyana self-sufficiency in sugar, rice, vegetables, fruit, meat and poultry – bauxite mining is the main economic activity in Guyana. Bauxite, sugar cane and rice are Guyana's largest exports. Gold and diamonds are the other important mining industries. Forests cover 80% of the land area, but timber has yet to assume any great economic importance. The economy has recovered from near-total collapse in 1982 with the benefit of large amounts of foreign aid under bilateral arrangements and from multinational sources including the International Monetary Fund. The UK, the USA, Canada and Germany are Guyana's main export markets. Guyana's $220-million annual import bill is shared between the USA (30%), the UK (13%), Japan (4.5%), Trinidad &Tobago, Indonesia and others. Guyana is a founder member of CARICOM, the Caribbean economic union.

BUSINESS: Businessmen need only shirts and light-

weight trousers for most business meetings. Appointments should be made and punctuality is appreciated. Calling cards are useful. The pace of business and general attitudes are very Caribbean-orientated. It is, however, wise to bear in mind that the country is very much part of South America, the ties with the Caribbean being more a hangover from British colonial days than a reflection of Guyanese popular consciousness. **Office hours:** 0800-1130 and 1300-1630 Monday to Friday.
COMMERCIAL INFORMATION: The following organisation can offer advice: Georgetown Chamber of Commerce and Industry, PO Box 10110, 156 Waterloo Street, Cummingsburg, Georgetown. Tel: (2) 56451.

HISTORY & GOVERNMENT

HISTORY: The original inhabitants were the American Indians who mainly live semi-nomadic lives in the rainforests and savannah. In the towns live a large number of blacks descended from African slaves or migrants from the islands of the Caribbean. With the abolition of slavery in 1834 the plantation owners had to import labourers from India. Indians now form the largest racial group, living mostly in the agricultural areas, particularly Demerara. Other immigrants were the Americans, Europeans (mainly Portuguese, British and Dutch) and the Chinese. The country was originally formed from countries ceded by the Dutch to the British, who named it British Guyana. The urban/rural split between the Africans and Asians is reflected in the main divisions between Guyana's two main political parties – the People's Progressive Party, which draws the Indian support, and the People's National Congress, formed in 1957 after a split from the once-unified PPP. The PNC under Forbes Burnham won every election – albeit against regular allegations of fraud – from 1966 until Burnham's death in 1985. At this point Burnham's deputy, Desmond Hoyte, took office. Hoyte held onto office until September 1992 when elections postponed from the previous year ousted him in favour of the veteran leftist politician Cheddi Jagan. Abroad, Guyana has a number of unresolved border disputes with its neighbours, Venezuela and Suriname. The Guyana-Venezuela dispute has been referred to UN mediation, while a joint commission has been established to look at the border issue with Suriname. Another issue which has become of particular concern to the Guyanese is the environment: Guyana is vulnerable to flooding of its littoral plain, which is vital economically, and small fluctuations in the regional climate could have devastating effects.
GOVERNMENT: Under the constitution, adopted in 1980, legislative power is held by the unicameral National Assembly which has 65 members. Executive power is held by the President, who leads the majority party in the Assembly. The President appoints and leads a Cabinet of Ministers responsible to parliament.

CLIMATE

Guyana's climate is warm and tropical throughout the year. The rainfall is generally high for most of the year, as is the humidity. November to January and April to July are the rainy seasons, while in coastal areas the climate is tempered by sea breezes.
Required clothing: Tropical-weight clothes for the rainy seasons and lightweight, cotton tropical wear for February to March and August to October.

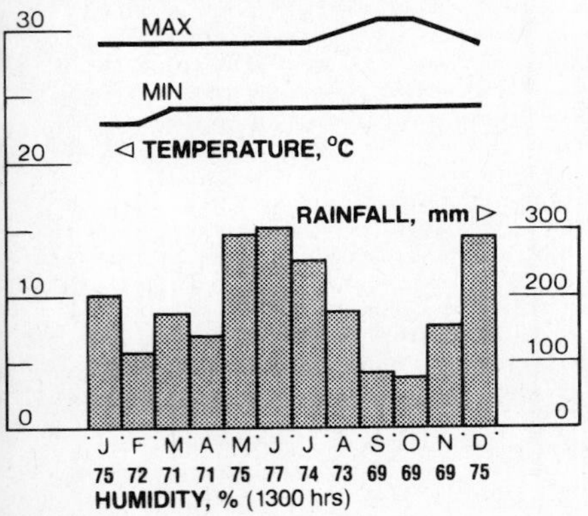

Location: Caribbean; island of Hispaniola.

Office National du Tourisme d'Haiti
avenue Marie-Jeanne
Port-au-Prince, Haiti
Tel: 225 400. Telex: 20206.
Embassy of the Republic of Haiti
BP 25
160a avenue Louise
1050 Brussels, Belgium
Tel: (2) 649 7381. Fax: (2) 649 6247.
British Consulate
PO Box 1302
Hotel Montana
Port-au-Prince, Haiti
Tel: 73969. Fax: 74048. Telex: 2030259.
Embassy of the Republic of Haiti
2311 Massachusetts Avenue, NW
Washington, DC
20008
Tel: (202) 332 4090/1/2. Fax : (202) 745 7215. Telex: 440202.
General Consulate of Haiti
60 East 42nd Street
New York, NY
10017
Tel: (212) 697 9767.
Embassy of the United States of America
BP 1761
boulevard Harry Truman
Port-au-Prince, Haiti
Tel: 220 200. Fax: 239 007.
Embassy of the Republic of Haiti
Suite 212
Place de Ville
Tower B
112 Kent Street
Ottawa, Ontario
K1P 5P2
Tel: (613) 238 1628/9. Fax: (613) 238 2986.
Canadian Embassy
BP 826
Edifice Banque Nova Scotia
route de Delmas
Port-au-Prince, Haiti
Tel: 223 358. Fax: 223 872. Telex: 20069.

AREA: 27,750 sq km (10,714 sq miles).
POPULATION: 6,486,000 (1990 estimate).
POPULATION DENSITY: 233.7 per sq km.
CAPITAL: Port-au-Prince. **Population:** 738,342 (1984).
GEOGRAPHY: Haiti is situated in the Caribbean and comprises the forested mountainous western end of the island of Hispaniola, which it shares with the Dominican Republic. Its area includes the Ile de la Gonâve, in the Gulf of the same name; among other islands is La Tortue off the north peninsula. Haiti's coastline is dotted with magnificent beaches, between which stretches lush sub-tropical vegetation, even covering the slopes which lead down to the shore. Port-au-Prince is a magnificent natural harbour at the end of a deep horseshoe bay.
LANGUAGE: The official language is French. Local *patois* and English are widely spoken in tourist areas.
RELIGION: Roman Catholic with Protestant minorities. Voodooism (an African religion) is still found in Haiti, despite the largely Christian population. Considered by some to be 'black magic', voodooism is a folk religion, manifested by a series of complex ritual drawings, songs and dances.
TIME: GMT - 5 (GMT - 4 April to October).
ELECTRICITY: 110 volts AC, 60Hz.
COMMUNICATIONS: Telephone: IDD available. Country code 509; there are no area codes. The internal service is reasonable. **Telex:** International telex facilities are available at main hotels and at offices of TELECO. **Post:** Airmail to Europe takes up to a week. The main post office in Port-au-Prince, Cité de l'Exposition, is in Place d'Italie. Post office hours: 0800-2000 Monday to Friday and 0830-1200 Saturdays. Letters posted after 0900 will not be despatched until the following work day. **Press:** The four main dailies are *Le Matin*, *Le Nouvelliste* and *Panaroma*.
BBC World Service and Voice of America frequencies: From time to time these change. See the section *How to Use this Book* for more information.

BBC:

MHz	17.84	15.22	9.915	6.195

Voice of America:

MHz	21.49	15.60	9.525	6.035

PASSPORT/VISA

Regulations and requirements may be subject to change at short notice, and you are advised to contact the appropriate diplomatic or consular authority before finalising travel arrangements. Details of these may be found at the head of this country's entry. Any numbers in the chart refer to the footnotes below.

	Passport Required?	Visa Required?	Return Ticket Required?
Full British	Yes	1	Yes
BVP	Not valid	-	-
Australian	Yes	Yes	Yes
Canadian	No	No	Yes
USA	No	No	Yes
Other EC	Yes	2	Yes
Japanese	Yes	Yes	Yes

PASSPORTS: Valid passport required by all except nationals of Canada and the USA holding proof of citizenship (birth certificate, etc) for a stay of up to 30 days.
British Visitors Passport: Not accepted.
VISAS: Required by all except:
(a) **[1]** nationals of the UK holding passports that indicate right of abode in the UK (ie holders of British Commonwealth passports *may* require visas);
(b) nationals of Argentina, Austria, Israel, Liechtenstein, Monaco, Norway, South Korea, Sweden and Switzerland for a stay not exceeding 90 days;
(c) **[2]** nationals of Belgium, Denmark, Germany, Luxembourg and The Netherlands (holders of Dutch passport issued in Suriname *need* a visa) for a stay not exceeding 90 days (other EC nationals *do* require a visa);
(d) nationals of USA and Canada for a stay of up to 90 days
(e) travellers in transit who do not leave the airport.
Note: National of France, Italy and Spain may obtain visas on arrival.
Types of visa: Tourist, Business and Transit. Fee: £3.40.
Validity: 3 months. For a stay of 90 day,s return or onward tickets are needed.
Application to: Consulate (or Consular Section at Embassy). For addresses, see top of entry.
Application requirements: (a) 2 photos. (b) Valid passport. (c) Fee. (d) Letter of confirmation from company for Business visa.
Temporary residence: Contact Embassy of the Republic of Haiti.
Note: A Government *Head Tax* of US$20 is levied on all non-residents who are leaving Haiti after a stay of more than 72 hours.

MONEY

Currency: Gourde (Gde) = 100 centimes. Notes are in denominations of Gde500, 250, 100, 50, 10, 5, 2 and 1. Coins are in denominations of 50, 20, 10 and 5 centimes. US currency also circulates (the Gourde is tied to the US Dollar).
Currency exchange: US Dollars are accepted and exchanged everywhere. Other foreign currencies are accepted for exchange only by some banks.

Credit cards: American Express is widely accepted; Diners Club has more limited use. Check with your credit card company for details of merchant acceptability and other services which may be available.
Travellers cheques: Accepted by most major shops and banks.
Exchange rate indicators: The following figures are included as a guide to the movements of the Gourde against Sterling and the US Dollar:

Date:	Oct '89	Oct '90	Oct '91	Oct '92
£1.00=	7.90	9.76	8.69	16.64
$1.00=	5.00	4.99	5.00	10.48

Currency restrictions: There are no restrictions on the import and export of foreign or local currency.
Banking hours: 0900-1300 Monday to Friday.

DUTY FREE

The following goods can be imported into Haiti without incurring customs duty:
200 cigarettes or 50 cigars or 250g of tobacco;
1 litre of spirits;
Small quantity of perfume or toilet water for personal use.
In addition, Haitian nationals and foreign residents may bring in for their personal use new goods with a total value not exceeding US$200.
Prohibited goods: Coffee, matches, methylated spirits, pork, all meat products from Brazil and the Dominican Republic, drugs and firearms (except sporting rifles with prior permission).

PUBLIC HOLIDAYS

Public holidays observed in Haiti are as follows:
Apr 9 '93 Easter. **Apr 14** Pan-American Day/Bastilla's Day. **May 1** Labour Day. **May 18** Flag Day. **May 22** National Sovereignty. **Aug 15** Assumption. **Sep 15** Independence Day. **Oct 24** United Nations Day. **Nov 2** All Souls' Day (half-day). **Nov 18** Army Day. **Dec 5** Discovery Day. **Dec 25** Christmas Day. **Jan 1 '94** Independence Day. **Jan 2** Heroes of Independence Day. **Feb 15** Shrove Tuesday.

HEALTH

Regulations and requirements may be subject to change at short notice, and you are advised to contact your doctor well in advance of your intended date of departure. Any numbers in the chart refer to the footnotes below.

	Special Precautions?	Certificate Required?
Yellow Fever	No	1
Cholera	No	No
Typhoid & Polio	Yes	-
Malaria	2	-
Food & Drink	3	-

[1]: A yellow fever vaccination certificate is required from travellers coming from infected areas.
[2]: Malaria risk, in the malignant *falciparum* form, exists throughout the year below 300m in suburban and rural areas. Malaria prophylaxis is highly recommended.
[3]: All water should be regarded as being potentially contaminated. Water used for drinking, brushing teeth or making ice should have first been boiled or otherwise sterilised. Milk is unpasteurised and should be boiled. Powdered or tinned milk is available and is advised, but make sure that it is reconstituted with pure water. Avoid dairy products which are likely to have been made from local milk. Only eat well-cooked meat and fish, preferably served hot. Pork, salad and mayonnaise may carry increased risk. Vegetables should be cooked and fruit peeled.
Rabies is present. For those at high risk, vaccination before arrival should be considered. If you are bitten abroad seek medical advice without delay. For more information consult the *Health* section at the back of the book.
Health care: Health insurance is recommended. Medical facilities are fairly good. The local herb tea is said to be good for stomach upsets.

TRAVEL - International

AIR: Approximate flight times: From Port-au-Prince to *London* is 8 hours, to *Los Angeles* is 9 hours, to *New York* is 5 hours and to *Singapore* is 33 hours (with good connections). There are good connections with the USA, the West Indies and France.
International airport: *Port-au-Prince (PAP)* (Mais Gaté) is 13km (8 miles) east of the city (travel time – 25 minutes). There is a snack bar, duty-free shop, bank, bar and car hire facilities. Taxis are available to the city.
Departure tax: US$15; transit passengers and children under two years of age are exempt.
SEA: Cap Haïtien and Port-au-Prince are both ports of call for a number of cruise lines: *Norwegian American, Royal Caribbean, Commodore Cruise/Cosmos* and *Holland America.*

TRAVEL - Internal

AIR: There are scheduled routes between Port-au-Prince and Cap Haïtien; and Port-au-Prince and Santo Domingo. Reservations should be double checked as delays and cancellations are common. Planes may be chartered.
SEA: Sailing trips can be arranged from Port-au-Prince to beaches around the island, including glass-bottomed boat trips over Sand Cay Reef.
RAIL: There is no rail system.
ROAD: During the 1980s all-weather roads have been constructed from Port-au-Prince to Cap Haïtien and Jacmel. **Bus:** Services depart from Port-au-Prince to Cap Haïtien, Jacmel, Jérémie, Hinche, Les Cayes and Port de Paix on an unscheduled basis. **Taxi:** Station wagons *(camionettes)* run between Port-au-Prince and Petionville, as well as some other towns. Tipping is unnecessary. **Car hire:** Available independently in Port-au-Prince and Petionville, or through hotels and the airport. Petrol can be very scarce outside Port-au-Prince. All hired cars' registration numbers begin with 'L'. **Documentation:** Some foreign driving licences are acceptable for up to three months, after which a local permit is necessary. However, most will need an International Driving Permit.
URBAN: Bus: *Tap-taps,* which run within Port-au-Prince with a standard rate for any journey, are colourful but crowded. **Taxi:** Unmetered, with fixed route prices, otherwise fares agreed in advance. Taxi licence plates begin with the letter 'P'. Shared taxis *(publiques)* are the cheapest form of taxi service in the towns. Drivers can be hired for tours by the hour or the day with price negotiated.

ACCOMMODATION

Accommodation is limited in Haiti. Existing facilities include modest small inns, guest-houses and palatial-style hotels. The majority of accommodation is in Port-au-Prince and Petionville, while the beach hotels are north of the capital on the road to St Marc or west towards Petit Gonâve. Accommodation is also to be found in Cap Haïtien, Jacmel, the Gonâve Bay area, Les Cayes and the Petit-Gonâve beach area. Swimming pools and air-conditioning are essential in central hotels where the heat can become severe. All resorts offer substantial reductions between April 16 and December 15. A 10% service charge and 5% room tax will be added to all hotel bills. For more information contact: Association Hotelière et Touristique d'Haiti, c/o Hotel Montana, BP 2562, rue F Cardozo, route de Pétionville, Port-au-Prince. Tel: 227 507. Telex: 20493.
Note: It is vital to make reservations well in advance for the Carnival period.

RESORTS & EXCURSIONS

The capital, **Port-au-Prince,** is a bustling city with a population of over half a million. Places to visit include the busy *Iron Market,* the two Cathedrals, the *Museum of Haitian Art,* the *Statue of the Unknown Slave,* the *Gingerbread Houses* and the *Defly Mansion.* The hillside suburb of *Petionville* offers a calmer respite and some of the city's best dining, gallery-hopping and nightlife.
Cap Haïtien and the North Coast: On Christmas Eve 1492, Columbus ran aground on the north coast of Hispaniola near the present-day site of *Cap Haïtien.* The wreck of the Santa Maria lies nearby. Today, communications in the region are more convenient, and Cap Haïtien is only 40 minutes by plane from the capital. The town nestles at the foot of lush green mountains and is surrounded by several fine beaches. The *Citadelle* is not to be missed – a remarkable fortress in the mountains, 40km (25 miles) south of Cap Haïtien – the nearby ruins of *Sans Souci Palace.* A half-hour drive leads to the village of **Milot,** gateway to the Citadelle and site of the palace ruins. Versailles was the model for *Sans Souci,* and the ruins still suggest a link.
Jacmel and the South Coast: With the completion of a well-marked road over the mountains several years ago, the drive to Jacmel is now a pleasant two hours or less through breathtaking scenery. There are several beaches in this region. High in the mountains south of the capital is the town of **Kenscoff,** much favoured by Haitians as a summer resort.

SOCIAL PROFILE

FOOD & DRINK: The French cuisine is authentic and the Creole specialities combine French, tropical and African influences. Dishes include Guinea hen with sour orange sauce, *tassot de dinde* (dried turkey), *grillot* (fried island pork), *diri et djondjon* (rice and black mushrooms), *riz et pois* (rice and kidney beans), *langouste flambé* (flaming local lobster), *ti malice* (sauce of onions and herbs), *piment oiseau* (hot sauce) and *grillot et banane pese* (pork chops and island bananas). Sweets include sweet potato pudding, mango pie, fresh coconut ice cream, cashew nuts and island fruits. French wine is available in the better restaurants. The island drink is rum and the best is probably 'Barbancourt', made by a branch of Haiti's oldest family of rum and brandy distillers.
NIGHTLIFE: There is plenty of choice ranging from casinos to African drum music and modern Western music and dance. There is something happening in at least one major hotel every evening with the main attraction being folkloric groups and voodoo performances. On Saturday nights *bamboche,* a peasant-style dance, can be seen in one of the open-air dance halls. Hotels can give further up-to-date information on local nightlife.
SHOPPING: Bargaining at the Iron Market is recommended where good and bad quality local items can be bought, including carvings, printed fabrics, leather work, paintings (particularly in the naif style, for which Haiti is famous), straw hats, seed necklaces and jewellery, cigars and foodstuffs. Port-au-Prince has a good selection of shops and boutiques selling a wide range of local and imported items. Bargaining is an accepted practice.
Shopping hours: 0800-1200 and 1300-1600 Monday to Friday; 0800-1200 Saturday.
SPORT: Watersports: Kyona and Ibo beaches (Ibo is on Cacique Isle) are best for **swimming, snorkelling, spear-fishing, sailing, boomba racing** in native dugout canoes and **water-skiing. Fishing:** La Gonave is a popular location for fishermen. **Hunting:** Best season is from October to April, especially for duck shooting, when there are 63 varieties gathered on Haiti's lakes and étangs (ponds). Permission to bring firearms into Haiti is necessary and can be obtained from the Chief of Army, Grand Quartier General, Port-au-Prince, Haiti. **Golf:** There is a 9-hole course at the Petionville Club. **Tennis** courts at Petionville Club, El Rancho, Ibo Beach, Ibo Lake, Kaloa Beach, Royal Haitian hotels, Habitation Le Clerc and at the Club Med in Montraus. **Spectator sports: Football** is the favourite national sport, followed by **basketball. Cockfighting** can be seen every Saturday and Sunday in the circular Gaguere. There are also many informal cockfights throughout the island.
SPECIAL EVENTS: The principal annual festivals are the *Carnival,* held throughout Haiti three days before Ash Wednesday; the *Ra Ra,* held in Leogane from Ash Wednesday to Easter; and the *Pan American Discovery Day* celebrations held on December 5 to celebrate Columbus' landfall on the north coast. For a complete list of carnivals and festivals held during 1993/4 contact the Haiti National Tourist Board.
SOCIAL CONVENTIONS: Informal wear is acceptable, although scanty beachwear should be confined to the beach or poolside. Only the most elegant dining rooms encourage guests to dress for dinner. **Tipping:** 10% service charge is added to hotel and restaurant bills. Taxi drivers do not expect tips.

BUSINESS PROFILE

ECONOMY: Haiti's average income is the lowest in the Western hemisphere by a considerable margin (US$360 per annum, 1987 figures) and exacerbated by vast disparities between the incomes of rich and poor. The World Bank estimates that 85% of the people live at below the absolute poverty line. Two-thirds of the employed population work in agriculture, mainly in the coffee plantations which generate 25% of Haiti's export earnings. Sugar cane, sweet potatoes, cocoa and sisal are also grown for export. Coffee earnings suffered from droughts during the 1980s and the collapse in the world price. Market factors also affected receipts from bauxite mining, another key economic sector which at one stage ground to a complete halt. Tourism, once promising, has all but vanished. Haiti relies for most of its finance on overseas aid, particularly from the United States, although the Americans have occasionally proved reluctant to give money which simply disappears with monotonous regularity: the fall of the sickeningly corrupt Duvalier dynasty has improved the situation somewhat, but not as much as hoped for. Industry cannot develop to any great extent until some semblance of an infrastructure has been built. The bulk of Haiti's trade takes place with the USA.
BUSINESS: It is usual to wear a suit for initial or formal calls. The British Trade Correspondent can put visitors in touch with a reliable English-French translator if required. Business visitors are generally entertained to lunch or dinner by their agents or important customers and should return invitations either at their hotel or a restaurant. Best time to visit is November to March. **Office hours:** 0700-1600 Monday to Friday.
COMMERCIAL INFORMATION: The following organisation can offer advice: Chambre de Commerce et d'Industrie de Haiti, Boîte Postale 982, Port-au-Prince. Tel: 222 475. Fax: 220 281.

HISTORY & GOVERNMENT

HISTORY: First discovered by Columbus and colonised in the 17th century by the French, Haiti gained independence in 1804 (seceding from the neighbouring Dominican Republic) after a 12-year uprising by African-descended slaves. During the rest of the 19th century, Haiti was under the control of a succession of dictators, none of whom had the wherewithal to resolve the conflict between the mulattoes, who held political power, and negroes. America took control early in the 20th century, sending troops in at one stage to support the regime. After 30 years as a US protectorate, Haiti returned to indigenous rule. Elections in 1957 brought to power Dr Francis Duvalier, a country physician, who presided over one of the world's most authoritarian regimes. With the help of a private militia known as the Tontons Macoutes (the Creole phrase for 'Bogeymen'), political dissent was systematically eradicated and opponents jailed or murdered. The traditional Voodoo religion was widely abused in order to intimidate critics. Duvalier (commonly known as 'Papa Doc') died in 1971, handing the leadership over to his son Jean Claude ('Baby Doc') who ruled the country for the next 15 years in the same manner as his father. Half-hearted efforts – such as the elections in which all opposition candidates were arrested on polling day – were made to present a more acceptable face to the outside world, primarily in order to secure foreign aid. Despite the constant attentions of the Tontons, political opposition continued to grow, crucially within the army; in the spring of 1986 these elements finally turned against the regime and forced Duvalier's flight from the country. A succession of military governments followed before Haiti started the transition to civilian rule. Presidential elections were held in mid-December 1990 under the supervision of the United Nations and brought to the presidency the radical priest Jean-Bertrand Aristide. Aristide faced a formidable task in attempting to rebuild his shattered country. Overseas aid was forthcoming, but many Western donors were wary of Aristide's radical credentials despite the overwhelming public support which he enjoyed. Nine months later, army chief Brigadier-General Raoul Cedras siezed power in a military coup. Aristide was exiled. A delegation from the OAS made repeated unsuccessful attempts to negotiate with the Cedras junta, while applying diplomatic pressure and arranging economic sanctions. In June 1992, with the talks going nowhere, the army announced the creation of a 'government of national consensus' with Marc Bazin, one of the presidential candidates defeated by Aristide, at its head. A conservative seen as a representative of the country's rich elite, Bazin's appointment was duly ratified by the lower house of parliament. International recognition continues to elude the Government, with only the Vatican having recognised it. The trade embargo appears now to have little effect upon the regime.
GOVERNMENT: Haiti is formally governed according to the terms of the Constitution promulgated in 1987 which allows for a bicameral legislature (a 77-member Chamber of Deputies and 27-member Senate), and for legislative and presidential elections. The present regime has not yet pronounced upon the country's constitutional future.

CLIMATE

Tropical, with intermittent rain throughout the year. Much cooler temperatures exist in hill resorts and there is a high coastal humidity.
Required clothing: Tropical lightweights with rainwear and warm clothing for hill regions.

PORT AU PRINCE Haiti (37m)

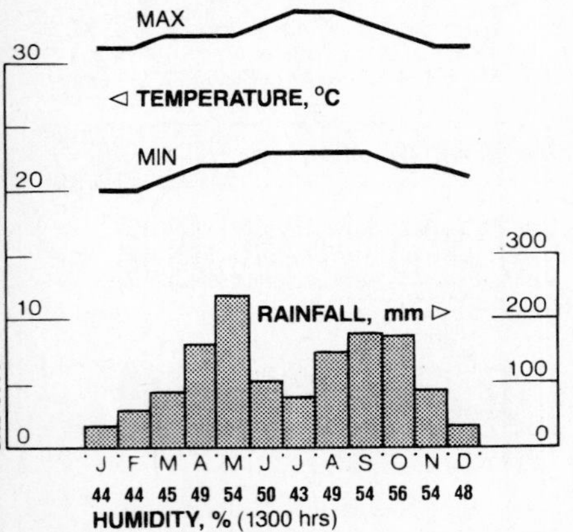

Location: Central America.

Note: Due to the uncertain political situation in Nicaragua, it is not advisable to travel to the Mosquitia region in the east of Honduras.

Instituto Hondureño de Turismo
Apartado Postal 3261
Centro Guanacaste
Barrio Guanacaste
Tegucigalpa
Honduras, CA
Tel: 226 618 *or* 381 475. Fax: 382 102.
Embassy of the Republic of Honduras *and* **Consulate General**
115 Gloucester Place
London W1H 3PJ
Tel: (071) 486 4880. Fax: (071) 486 4880 (outside office hours). Office hours: 1000-1600 Monday to Friday.
British Embassy
Apartado Postal 290
Edificio Palmira, 3er Piso
Colonia Palmira
Tegucigalpa
Honduras, CA
Tel: 325 429 *or* 320 612 *or* 320 618. Fax: 325 480. Telex: 1234 PRODROME HO.
British Consulate
Apartado Postal 298
Terminales de Puerto Cortes
San Pedro Sula
Honduras, CA
Tel: 542 600. Telex: 5513
Embassy of the Republic of Honduras
3007 Tilden Street, NW
Washington, DC
20008
Tel: (202) 966 7702 *or* 966 2604 *or* 966 5008 *or* 4596.
Fax: (202) 966 9751.
Embassy of the United States of America
Unit 2924
Avenido La Paz
Tegucigalpa
Honduras, CA
Tel: 323 120. Fax: 320 027.
Embassy of the Republic of Honduras
Suite 300-A
151 Slater Street
Ottawa, Ontario
K1P 5H3
Tel: (613) 233 8900. Fax: (613) 232 0193.
Consulates in: Montréal, Québec, Toronto and Vancouver.
Consulate of Canada
Apartado Postal 174C
Edificio Comercial Los Castonos, 6° Piso
Boulevard Morazan
Tegucigalpa
Honduras, CA
Tel: 314 548 *or* 314 538. Fax: 315 793. Telex: 1683 DOMCAN HO.

AREA: 112,088 sq km (43,277 sq miles).
POPULATION: 4,915,900 (1991 estimate).
POPULATION DENSITY: 43.9 per sq km.
CAPITAL: Tegucigalpa, DC. **Population:** 670,100 (1991).
GEOGRAPHY: Honduras shares borders in the southeast with Nicaragua, in the west with Guatemala, and in the southwest with El Salvador. To the north lies the Caribbean and to the south the Pacific Ocean. In the interior of the country is a central mountain system running from east to west, cut by rivers flowing into both the Caribbean and Pacific. The lowlands in the south form a plain along the Pacific coast. The Gulf of Fonseca in the southwest contains many islands which have volcanic peaks. The large fertile valleys of the northern Caribbean lowlands are cultivated with banana plantations. However, large areas of land in Honduras are unsuitable for cultivation, and communications tend to be difficult. The majority of the population lives in the western half of the country, while the second largest concentration of people is in the Cortés area which extends northwards from Lake Yojoa towards the Caribbean.
LANGUAGE: Official language is Spanish. English is widely spoken by the West Indian settlers in the north and on the Bay Islands off the Caribbean coast.
RELIGION: Roman Catholic majority; Evangelist and Mormon.
TIME: GMT - 6.
ELECTRICITY: 110/220 volts AC, 60Hz.
COMMUNICATIONS: Telephone: Services between Honduras and western Europe are available. IDD available. Country code: 504. **Fax:** Empresa Hondureña de Telecomunicaciones (HONDUTEL) offer a service.
Telex/telegram: Ordinary and letter telegrams (min 22 words) may be sent. A telex service is operated by HONDUTEL and the Tropical Radio Company. **Post:** Airmail to western Europe takes between four and seven days. Post office hours: 0800-1200 and 1400-1800 Monday to Saturday. **Press:** Daily newspapers are in Spanish, and include *El Heraldo, La Prensa, La Tribuna* and *ElTiempo*. The weekly *Honduras This Week* is published in English.
BBC World Service and Voice of America frequencies: From time to time these change. See the section *How to Use this Book* for more information.

BBC:				
MHz	17.84	15.22	9.590	7.325
Voice of America:				
MHz	15.21	11.74	9.815	6.030

PASSPORT/VISA

Regulations and requirements may be subject to change at short notice, and you are advised to contact the appropriate diplomatic or consular authority before finalising travel arrangements. Details of these may be found at the head of this country's entry. Any numbers in the chart refer to the footnotes below.

	Passport Required?	Visa Required?	Return Ticket Required?
Full British	Yes	No	Yes
BVP	Not valid	-	-
Australian	Yes	No	Yes
Canadian	Yes	No	Yes
USA	Yes	No	Yes
Other EC	Yes	No	Yes
Japanese	Yes	No	Yes

PASSPORTS: Valid passport required by all.
British Visitors Passport: Not accepted.
VISAS: Required by all travelling on business. For other purposes, required by all except:
(a) nationals mentioned in the chart above;
(b) nationals of Finland, Guatemala, New Zealand, Norway, Panama, Sweden and Switzerland;
(c) those in transit continuing their journey within 48 hours.
Types of visa: Business and Tourist visas; cost approximately £10.
Validity: Up to 1 month.
Application to: Consulate (or Consular Section at Embassy). For addresses, see top of entry.
Application requirements: (a) Valid passport. (b) 1 photo. (c) Completed form. (d) Business letters where applicable.
Exit permit: Required by all visitors staying longer than 90 days.

MONEY

Currency: Lempira (L) = 100 centavos. Notes are in denominations of L100, 50, 20, 10, 5, 2 and 1. Coins are in denominations of 50, 20, 10, 5, 2 and 1 centavos. A *real* is one-eighth of a Lempira, and is used colloquially, though there is no such coin.

Currency exchange: Sterling cannot normally be exchanged, even in banks; visitors should therefore take US Dollar travellers cheques.
Credit cards: Access/Mastercard, American Express, Diners Club and Visa are accepted. Check with your credit card company for details of merchant acceptability and other services which may be available.
Travellers cheques: Normally accepted by Banco De Ahorro Hondureno. All other banks will only cash travellers cheques which are accredited to them (but not for US currency).
Exchange rate indicators: The following figures are included as a guide to the movements of the Lempira against Sterling and the US Dollar:

Date:	Oct '89	Oct '90	Oct '91	Oct '92
£1.00=	3.15	11.42	9.24	9.36
$1.00=	*2.00	5.85	5.32	5.89

Note [*]: Official rates; for free market rates, add 5-25%. The exchange rate, which was pegged to the dollar, has been allowed to float since 1990.
Currency restrictions: No restrictions on import, but US Dollars must be declared. No restrictions on export of foreign currency except US Dollars up to the amount declared. All visitors are required to import a minimum of US$100.
Banking hours: 0900-1500 Monday to Friday.

DUTY FREE

The following goods may be imported into Honduras without incurring customs duty:
200 cigarettes or 100 cigars or 1lb of tobacco;
2 bottles of alcoholic beverage;
Reasonable amount of perfume for personal use;
Gifts up to a total value of US$50.

PUBLIC HOLIDAYS

Public holidays observed in Honduras are as follows:
Apr 14 '93 Day of Americas. **Apr 8** Maundy Thursday. **Apr 9** Good Friday. **May 1** Labour Day. **Sep 15** Independence Day. **Oct 3** Birth of General Morazán. **Oct 12** Discovery of America Day. **Oct 21** Armed Forces Day. **Dec 25** Christmas Day. **Dec 31** New Year's Eve. **Jan 1 '94** New Year's Day.

HEALTH

Regulations and requirements may be subject to change at short notice, and you are advised to contact your doctor well in advance of your intended date of departure. Any numbers in the chart refer to the footnotes below.

	Special Precautions?	Certificate Required?
Yellow Fever	Yes	1
Cholera	Yes	-
Typhoid & Polio	Yes	-
Malaria	2	-
Food & Drink	3	-

[1]: A yellow fever vaccination certificate is required of all travellers coming from infected areas.
[2]: Malaria risk, in the benign *vivax* form, exists throughout the year in Departments of Atlántida, Choluteca, Colón, Cortés, Gracias a Dios, Olancho, Islas de la Bahía, Valle and Yoro; especially in rural areas.
[3]: All water should be regarded as being potentially contaminated. Water used for drinking, brushing teeth or making ice should first be boiled or otherwise sterilised. Milk is unpasteurised in rural areas and should be boiled. Powdered or tinned milk is available and is advised, but make sure that it is reconstituted with pure water. Avoid dairy products which are likely to have been made from unboiled milk. Only eat well-cooked meat and fish, preferably served hot. Pork, salad and mayonnaise may carry increased risk. Vegetables should be cooked and fruit peeled.
Rabies is present. For those at high risk, vaccination before arrival should be considered. If you are bitten abroad seek medical advice without delay. For more information consult the *Health* section at the back of the book.
Health care: Health insurance is recommended. There are hospitals in Tegucigalpa and all the large towns. Mosquito nets are recommended for coastal areas.

TRAVEL - International

AIR: The national airline of Honduras is *SAHSA (Servicios Aéreos de Honduras)*. A sales tax of 10% is payable on international bookings for tickets issued in Honduras.
Approximate flight times: From *London* to Honduras is 12 hours 30 minutes. (There are no direct flights from London; connections generally via Miami or Houston.) From *New York* to Honduras is 8 hours.
International airport: *Tegucigalpa (TGU)* (Toncontin), 7km (4 miles) southeast of the city. Airport facilities include bar, restaurant, duty-free shop, bank, post office, vaccination centre and car hire.
There are also local airports at San Pedro Sula (SAP) (Dr Ramón Villeda Morales), Islas de la Bahía (ROA) and at La Ceiba (LCE) (Goloson).
Departure tax: US$20 levied on all passengers over 12 years.
SEA: The principal ports on the Atlantic and Caribbean coastline are Puerto Cortés, Tela, La Ceiba and Trujillo. The principal ports on the Pacific coastline are Amapala and El Henecan. Sailings to Puerto Cortés from Europe are frequent. Ships operated by *Harrison line*, *Carol Line*, *Cie Generale Transatlantique*, *Hapag Lloyd*, *The Royal Netherlands Steamship Company* and vessels owned or charted by the *United Fruit Company* and *Standard Fruit Company* sometimes have limited passenger accommodation.
RAIL: There are no rail services between Honduras and neighbouring countries.
ROAD: Road routes run from El Salvador and Nicaragua via the Pan-American Highway, and from Guatemala on the Western Highway. Visas must be obtained before the journey is undertaken. Border crossings can be fraught with delay. **Bus:** The *Ticabus* company runs international services to all Central American capitals, but these comfortable coaches are often booked days in advance.

TRAVEL - Internal

AIR: Local airlines (*SAHSA*, *Aéreoservicios* and *Islena Airline*) operate daily services which link Tegucigalpa and other principal towns. *Islena Airline* runs services to Utila, the cheapest Bay Island (off the Caribbean coast). Apart from Tegucigalpa, the main airports are *Dr Ramon Villeda Morales Airport*, 17km (11 miles) from the centre of San Pedro Sula, and the airport at La Ceiba. Over 30 smaller airfields handle light aircraft and commercial aviation. There is a hospitals and airport tax of 2.5% on domestic journeys for tickets issued in Honduras.
SEA: Ferries operate between ports on the Atlantic, Pacific and Caribbean coastlines. For details contact local port authorities. There are sailings from La Ceiba and Puerto Cortés to the Bay Islands several times a week. Arrangements must be made with local boat owners.
RAIL: There are only three railways, confined to the northern coastal region and mainly used for transport between banana plantations.
ROAD: There is a total of 11,790km (7369 miles) of roads of which 8364km (5228 miles) are all-weather, and 2383km (1489 miles) are paved. However, internal air transport is much more convenient for business visitors. An all-weather road exists from Tegucigalpa to San Pedro Sula, Puerto Cortés, La Ceiba and towns along the Caribbean coast, as well as to the towns around the Gulf of Fonseca in the south. **Bus:** Local lines run regular services to most large towns, but the services are well used and booking in advance is essential. On the whole the services are very cheap. **Taxi** are not metered, and run on a flat rate within cities. For other journeys fares should be agreed before starting journey. **Car hire:** Self-drive cars are available at the airport. **Documentation:** Both international or foreign driving licences are accepted.
JOURNEY TIMES: The following chart gives approximate journey times (in hours and minutes) from Tegucigalpa to other major cities/towns in Honduras.

	Air	Road
Comayagua	-	1.00
Siguatepeque	-	2.30
San Pedro S.	0.25	3.30
Choluteca	-	2.30
La Ceiba	0.35	5.00
Bay Islands	0.40	*7.00
Sta Rosa de Copan	-	6.00
Puerto Cortes	-	4.00

Note [*]: Includes sea crossing of 2 hours.

ACCOMMODATION

HOTELS: Reasonable hotels are available in both Tegucigalpa and San Pedro Sula (where the rates are lower, but standards equivalent to those in the capital are maintained). Elsewhere both rates and standards of comfort are somewhat lower. The Instituto Hondureño de Turismo (address at beginning of entry) can supply lists of hotels with accommodation details. For further information contact the Honduran Hotel Association, Edificio Midence Soto, 12° No 1214, Tegucigalpa, DC. Tel: 370 982. **Grading:** Hotels are split into three categories (upper, middle and lower) according to standard.

RESORTS & EXCURSIONS

Tegucigalpa, the capital, was originally founded as a mining camp in 1524. Unlike so many of Central America's cities, Tegucigalpa has never been subjected to the disasters of earthquake or fire and so retains many traditional features. Visitors to the capital should plan to visit the city's impressive parks, particularly *Concordia* where models of Copan's Mayan architecture are displayed, and the *United Nations Park* for a spectacular view of the city. Recommended also is a visit to neighbouring *Comayagua*, former capital of Honduras and now a colonial masterpiece of cobbled streets, tiny plazas and white-washed homes.
The Caribbean Coast: Two coastal towns are important to tourists and commercial visitors:
La Ceiba, which lies at the foot of the towering 1500m (5000ft) **Pico Bonito,** still a major banana port, now looks to tourism as a future major industry. There are good hotels and beaches, and a new international airport, one of the city's major assets.
Trujillo was once a thriving port and the old capital of colonial Honduras. Trujillo today offers many old Spanish buildings, a fascinating pirate history and superb tropical beaches. New resorts and subdivisions are now opening in the Trujillo area.
Bay Islands: 50km (30 miles) off the Caribbean coast of Honduras lies the exotic archipelago of the Bay Islands. Consisting of three major islands (Roatan, Guanaja and Utila) and several smaller islands, the Bay Islands have a history that spans the ancient Mayan civilisation, early Spanish exploration, colonial buccaneers and the British Empire. **Roatan** and **Guanaja** are hilly, tropical islands, protected by a great coral reef which provides fine skindiving. **Utila** offers wide expanses of sandy beach and is ringed by tiny palm tree cays.
San Pedro Sula: Fast-growing banana, sugar manufacturing and distribution centre for the entire north coast. Today San Pedro Sula boasts a new airport, first-class hotels and several excellent restaurants.
Copán: The ancient city of Copán is 171km (106

HONDURAS | **HEALTH REGULATIONS** | **VISA REGULATIONS** | Code-Link

GALILEO/WORLDSPAN

TI-DFT/TGU/HE

TI-DFT/TGU/VI

SABRE

TIDFT/TGU/HE

TIDFT/TGU/VI

To access this information on your CRS, swipe the barcode with a light pen or type in the text under the barcode. For more information, see the introduction *How to Use This Book*.

miles) from San Pedro Sula. *The Copán Ruins Archaeological Park* in Western Honduras is the best remaining testament to the culture of the Mayan Indians. Among the best of the ruins are the magnificent *Acropolis* composed of courts and temples, the *Great Plaza*, a huge amphitheatre, and the *Court of the Hieroglyphic Stairway*. Near the *Great Acropolis* recent archaeological work brought to light invaluable excavations.

SOCIAL PROFILE

FOOD & DRINK: There is a wide variety of restaurants and bars in Tegucigalpa and the main cities. Typical dishes include *Curiles* (seafood), *tortillas*, *frijoles*, *enchiladas*, *tamales*, *de elote* (corn tamales), *nacatamales*, *tapado*, *yuca con chicharron* and *mondongo*. Typical tropical fruits include mangoes, papayas, pineapples, avocados and bananas.
NIGHTLIFE: There are cinemas and some discotheques in the main cities.
SHOPPING: Local craftsmanship is excellent and inexpensive. Typical items include woodcarvings, cigars, leather goods, straw hats and bags, seed necklaces and baskets. **Shopping hours:** 0830-1130 and 1330-1730 Monday to Saturday.
SPORT: Fishing: There is good fishing on both coasts and Lake Yojoa offers some of the best bass fishing in the world. **Scuba/snorkelling:** Excellent diving in the clear waters of the Bay Islands with coral and tropical fish. Some hotels include rental of equipment in price. **Golf:** An increasingly popular sport, with courses available in most major populated areas. **Swimming:** Safe swimming on both sea boards where beautiful sandy beaches can be found. **Spectator sports: Football** is the most popular national sport followed closely by **baseball**. Others include **basketball, boxing** and **bowling.**
SPECIAL EVENTS: The following special events are celebrated in Honduras during 1993, for further information contact the Embassy.
Mar 20-Apr 23 '93 *Holy Week*. **Apr** *Pine Festival*. **May (3rd Saturday)** *Great National Carnival*. **Jun 29** *St Peter*. **Jul 22-29** *Potatoes Festival*. **Aug (last Saturday)** *Carnival of Maize*. **Sep 14-20** *Civic Week*. **Oct 17** *Fish Festival*. **Dec 8** *Our Lady of Concepcion*. **Dec 12** *Our Lady of Guadaloupe*.
SOCIAL CONVENTIONS: There are strong Spanish influences, but the majority of the population are Mestizo, mainly leading an agricultural way of life with a low standard of living. Many rural communities can still be found living a relatively unchanged, traditional lifestyle. Normal social courtesies should be observed. It is customary for a guest at dinner or someone's home to send flowers to the hostess, either before or afterwards. Conservative casual wear is widely acceptable with dress tending to be less conservative in coastal areas. Beachwear and shorts should not be worn away from the beach or poolside. Men need to wear dinner jackets for formal social occasions. Hotels, restaurants and shops included a 7% sales tax on all purchases. **Tipping:** Service is included in most restaurant bills. In hotels, cafeterias and restaurants 10-15% of the bill is customary where service is not included. Porters and cabdrivers get a tip when helping with the luggage (L0.50 to L1).

BUSINESS PROFILE

ECONOMY: Honduras relies on agriculture and timber. The main agricultural products are bananas, beans, coffee, cotton, maize, rice, sorghum and sugar; there is some dairy and beef farming. Apart from wood and wood products, light industries produce a variety of consumer goods. Both sectors have experienced difficulties during the 1980s, with export earnings especially badly hit by low world prices and slack demand within the Central American Common Market of which Honduras is a member. The economy is propped up to a large degree by various forms of American-sponsored aid – both direct and multilateral (through the IMF, Inter-American Development Bank and others) – as the country became increasingly militarised under American prompting. Mining of zinc, lead, copper, gold and silver are growing, but as yet contribute a small proportion of gross domestic product. The USA is responsible for slightly over half of all Honduran trade.
BUSINESS: It is customary to address a professional person by his or her title, particularly on first meeting or during early acquaintance. Business people are generally expected to dress smartly and some dining rooms require men to wear a jacket. There are very few local interpreter or translation services available. Though many businessmen throughout the country also speak English, correspondence should be in Spanish. **Office hours:** 0800-1200 and 1400-1700 Monday to Friday, 0800-1100 Saturday.
COMMERCIAL INFORMATION: The following organisations can offer advice:
Federación de Cámaras de Comercio e Industrias de Honduras (FEDECAMARA), Apartado Postal 3444, Boulevard Centroamércia, Tegucigalpa. Tel: 328 110. Fax: 312 049 Telex: 1537; *or*
Cámara de Comercio e Industrias de Cortés, Apartado Postal 14, 17a Avenida, 10a y 12a Calle, San Pedro Sula. Tel: 530 761.

HISTORY & GOVERNMENT

HISTORY: Christopher Columbus landed on the Honduran coast in 1502. Twenty years later, Spanish troops under the conquistador Cortés occupied the territory. When Spain's Central American empire was dissolved 300 years later, Honduras was grouped into an ill-fated United Provinces of Central America. Subsequent efforts to unify the region eased the way for the gradual domination of the whole isthmus by the United States. Recent Honduran politics have revolved around the land reform issue. The army, which has on the whole supported the major landowners who oppose any redistribution, has controlled the Government for most of the last 40 years. Honduras' defence policy is in some ways closely allied with the US, especially in relation to the 'Contra' war in Nicaragua, and the Americans have made a considerable military commitment to Honduras since 1980. In August 1989 the Hondurans were the key to a successfully concluded peace agreement under which the Nicaraguan Contra forces would be demobilised. The agreement, pushed through despite American coolness and outright objections from the Contras themselves (who were not a party to the discussions), was partly the result of Honduran weariness with the extensive militarisation of their country. With the Contra issue settled, the Honduran government could now concentrate on its major problem of the collapsing economy, which is the key issue for the country's new President, Rafael Leonardo Callejas of the Partido Naçional, who won the most recent presidential elections held in November 1989. An IMF-backed programme has led to considerable hardship for much of the population, but has been rewarded by the IMF with continuing loans for the country. The Government has also taken some minor measures to address the country's appalling human rights record.
GOVERNMENT: Under the provisions of the 1982 constitution, a civilian executive President is elected by universal suffrage every four years. This post is presently held by Rafael Callejas. There are also 4-yearly elections for the 130-seat National Assembly.

CLIMATE

The climate is tropical, with cooler, more temperate weather in the mountains. The north coast is very hot with rain throughout the year, and though the offshore breezes temper the climate, the sun is very strong. The dry season is from November to April and the wet season runs from May to October. Humidity figures are not available.
Required clothing: Lightweight cottons and linens; warmer clothes are recommended between November and February and in the mountains. Waterproofs are needed for the wet season.

TEGUCIGALPA Honduras (1007m)

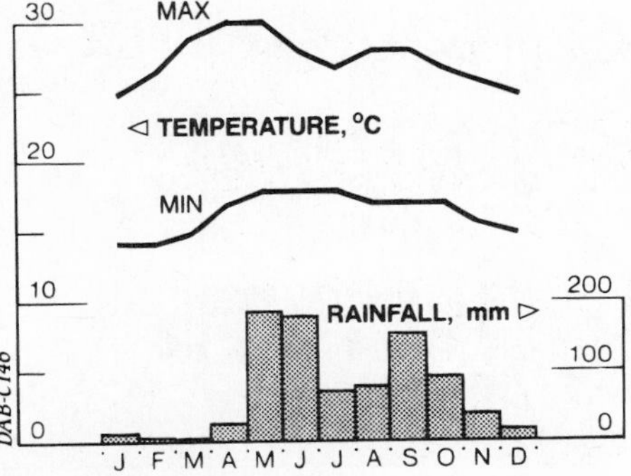

Location: Far East.

Hong Kong Tourist Association
Head Office
35th Floor, Jardine House
1 Connaught Place
Hong Kong
Tel: 801 7111. Fax: 810 4877.
Hong Kong Government Office
6 Grafton Street
London W1X 3LB
Tel: (071) 499 9821. Fax: (071) 493 1964. Opening hours: 0930-1300 and 1400-1730 Monday to Friday.
Hong Kong Tourist Association
125 Pall Mall
London SW1Y 5EA
Tel: (071) 930 4775. Fax: (071) 930 4777. Opening hours: 0930-1730 Monday to Friday.
UK Passport Office
Clive House
70-78 Petty France
London SW1
Tel: (071) 279 3434.
British Trade Commission
9th Floor
Bank of America Tower
12 Harcourt Road
Hong Kong
Tel: 523 0176. Fax: 845 2870. Telex: 73031 UK TRADE HX.
Hong Kong Tourist Association
5th Floor, 590 Fifth Avenue
New York, NY
10036-4706
Tel: (212) 869 5008/9.
Hong Kong Tourist Association
Suite 909
347 Bay Street
Toronto, Ontario
M5H 2R7
Tel: (416) 366 2389. Fax: (416) 366 1098.

AREA: 1075 sq km (415 sq miles).
POPULATION: 5,822,500 (1991 estimate).
POPULATION DENSITY: 5416.3 per sq km.
GEOGRAPHY: Hong Kong is located in the Far East, just south of the tropic of Cancer. Hong Kong Island is 32km (20 miles) east of the mouth of Pearl River and 135km (84 miles) southeast of Canton. It is separated from the mainland by a good natural harbour. Hong Kong Island was ceded to Britain by the Treaty of Nanking (1842); and the Kowloon Peninsula (south of Boundary Street and Stonecutters Island) by the Convention of Peking (1860). The area of Boundary Street to Shenzhen River and 235 islands, now known as the New Territories, were leased to Britain in 1898 for a period of 99 years. New Territories (plus 235 islands) comprises 891 sq km (380 sq miles). Shortage

of land suitable for development has led to reclamation from the sea, principally from the seafronts of Hong Kong Island and Kowloon.

LANGUAGE: Cantonese is the most widely spoken, but English is spoken by many, particularly in business circles. Chinese is the official language. English-speaking policemen have a red flash on their shoulder lapels.

RELIGION: Buddhist, Confucian, Taoist, with Christian and Muslim minorities, but there are also places of worship for most other religious groups.

TIME: GMT + 8.

ELECTRICITY: 200 volts AC, 50Hz.

COMMUNICATIONS: Telecommunications services in Hong Kong are as sophisticated and varied as one might expect in an advanced Western-style economy (including radio-paging and viewdata) and the following list is not exhaustive. **Telephone:** Directory Enquiries is computerised. For directory enquiries, dial 1081 (English) or 1083 (Chinese). Full IDD is available. Country code: 852. Local public telephone calls cost HK$1. **Fax:** Hong Kong Telecommunications Ltd and the post office provide services. Bureaufax and international services are also available. **Telex/telegram:** Public telex facilities are available on Hong Kong Island at the Hong Kong Telecommunications office , New Mercury House, 22 Fenwick Street, Wanchai, and Hermes House, Middle Road, Kowloon and at larger hotels. **Post:** Regular postal services are available. Airmail to Europe takes three to five days. *Poste Restante* facilities are available. Post office hours: 0800-1800 Monday to Friday; 0800-1400 Saturday. **Press:** English-language dailies include *Asian Wall Street Journal, Hong Kong Standard, International Herald Tribune* and *South China Morning Post.*

BBC World Service and Voice of America frequencies: From time to time these change. See the section *How to Use this Book* for more information.

BBC:

MHz	6.750			

Voice of America:

MHz	15.43	11.72	5.985	1.143

PASSPORT/VISA

Regulations and requirements may be subject to change at short notice, and you are advised to contact the appropriate diplomatic or consular authority before finalising travel arrangements. Details of these may be found at the head of this country's entry. Any numbers in the chart refer to the footnotes below.

	Passport Required?	Visa Required?	Return Ticket Required?
Full British	Yes	No/1	Yes
BVP	Not valid	-	-
Australian	Yes	No/2	Yes
Canadian	Yes	No/2	Yes
USA	Yes	No/3	Yes
Other EC	Yes	No/3/4	Yes
Japanese	Yes	No/3	Yes

PASSPORTS: Valid passport required by all.

British Visitors Passport: Not acceptable.

Note: Since October 1980, all visitors to Hong Kong must carry some form of official identification *at all times*. For UK visitors this should be a valid passport. The police make random checks and those without identification are liable to face prosecution.

VISAS: Required by all except:

(a) **[1]** British passport holders for visits not exceeding 12 months;

(b) **[2]** nationals of Australia, Canada and other Commonwealth countries (*except* nationals of Bangladesh and Pakistan – only 1 month) for visits not exceeding 3 months;

(c) **[3]** nationals of Germany, Greece, Japan and USA, for visits not exceeding 1 month;

(d) **[4]** nationals of Belgium, Denmark, France, Ireland, Italy, Luxembourg, The Netherlands, Portugal and Spain for visits not exceeding 3 months;

(e) nationals of Andorra, Austria, Brazil, Chile, Colombia, Ecuador, Fiji, Israel, Liechtenstein, Monaco, Norway, San Marino, Sweden, Switzerland and Turkey for visits not exceeding 3 months;

(f) nationals of Argentina, Costa Rica (except holders of a provisional passport who *do* require a visa), Dominican Republic, El Salvador, Finland, Guatemala, Honduras, Iceland, Mexico, Morocco, Nepal, Nicaragua, Panama, Paraguay, Peru, Tunisia, Uruguay and Venezuela for visits not exceeding 1 month;

(g) nationals of Algeria, Angola, Bahrain, Benin, Bhutan, Bolivia, Bosnia-Hercegovina, Burkina Faso, Burundi, Cameroon, Cape Verde, Central African Republic, Chad, Comoros, Congo, Côte d'Ivoire, Croatia, Djibouti, Egypt, Equatorial Guinea, Estonia, Ethiopia, Federated States of Micronesia, Gabon, Guinea Republic, Guinea-Bissau, Haiti, Indonesia, Jordan, Kuwait, Latvia, Liberia, Lithuania, Madagascar, Mali, Mauritania, Mozambique, Niger, Oman, Philippines, Qatar, Marshall Islands, São Tomé e Príncipe, Saudi Arabia, Senegal, Slovenia, South Africa, Suriname, Thailand, Togo, United Arab Emirates, Vatican City, Yemen, Yugoslavia and Zaïre for visits not exceeding 14 days;

(h) nationals of Djibouti, Myanmar (Burma), Namibia, Poland, South Korea and Sudan for visits not exceeding 7 days.

Note: Nationals of countries which formerly comprised the Eastern Bloc, and Afghanistan, Cambodia, China, CIS, Cuba, Iran, Iraq, North Korea, Laos, Lebanon, Libya, Mongolia, Somalia, Syria, Taiwan and Vietnam, require visas. For clarification or further information, consult the Hong Kong Immigration Department or their booklet *Do you need a Visa for Hong Kong?* (also available from the Hong Kong Government Office in London).

Application to: British Consulate (or Consular Section at British Embassy or High Commission) or, if applying in the UK, the UK Passport Office.

MONEY

Currency: Hong Kong Dollar (HK$) = 100 cents. Notes are in denominations of HK$1000, 500, 100, 50, 20 and 10. Coins are in denominations of HK$5, 2 and 1, and 50, 20, 10 and 5 cents.

Currency exchange: Foreign currency can be changed in banks, hotels, money-changers and shops.

Credit cards: Access/Mastercard, American Express, Diners Club and Visa are widely accepted. Check with your credit card company for details of merchant acceptability and other services which may be available.

Travellers cheques: Accepted almost everywhere.

Exchange rate indicators: The following figures are included as a guide to the movements of the Hong Kong Dollar against Sterling and the US Dollar:

Date:	Oct '89	Oct '90	Oct '91	Oct '92
£1.00=	12.31	15.13	13.44	12.26
$1.00=	7.80	7.74	7.74	7.73

Currency restrictions: There no restrictions on the import or export of either local or foreign currency.

Banking hours: 0900-1630 Monday to Friday and 0900-1330 Saturday.

DUTY FREE

The following goods may be imported into Hong Kong without incurring customs duty:

200 cigarettes or 50 cigars or 250g of tobacco;

1 litre bottle of wine or spirits;

60ml perfume.

Note: (a) If arriving from Macau, duty-free imports for Macau residents are limited to half the above cigarette, cigar and tobacco allowance. (b) Aircraft crew and passengers in direct transit via Hong Kong are limited to 20 cigarettes *or* 2 oz of pipe tobacco. (c) The import of animals is strictly controlled. (d) Firearms must be declared upon entry and handed into custody until departure. (e) Non-prescribed drugs may not be brought in without doctor's certificate of use.

PUBLIC HOLIDAYS

Public holidays observed in Hong Kong are as follows:
Apr 5 '93 Ching Ming Festival. **Apr 9-12** Easter. **Jun 12-14** Queen's Official Birthday. **Jun 24** Tuen Ng (Dragon Boat Festival). **Aug 28** Last Saturday in August. **Aug 30** Liberation Day. **Oct 1** Day following Mid-Autumn Festival. **Oct 23** Chung Yeung Festival. **Dec 25-27** Christmas. **Jan 1 '94** New Year. **Jan 22-25** Lunar New Year.

Note: Some of the above dates are provisional only. Travellers should confirm them closer to the time of their visit.

HEALTH

Regulations and requirements may be subject to change at short notice, and you are advised to contact your doctor well in advance of your intended date of departure. Any numbers in the chart refer to the footnotes below.

	Special Precautions?	Certificate Required?
Yellow Fever	No	No
Cholera	No	No
Typhoid & Polio	Yes	-
Malaria	1	-
Food & Drink	2	-

[1]: There may be an occasional risk of malaria in rural areas.

[2]: All water direct from government mains in Hong Kong exceeds the United Nations World Health Organisation standards and is fit for drinking. However, all hotels also provide bottled water in guest rooms. Milk is pasteurised and dairy products are safe for consumption. Local meat, poultry, seafood, fruit and vegetables are generally considered safe to eat. Only eat well-cooked meat and fish, preferably served hot. Pork, salad and mayonnaise may carry increased risk. Vegetables should be cooked and fruit peeled.

Health care: There is a Reciprocal Health Agreement with the UK, but it is of a limited nature. On presentation of a valid passport *and* an NHS card, free emergency treatment is available at certain hospitals and clinics. Small charges are made for all other services and treatment. All visitors are advised to take out private health insurance. Hotels have a list of government-accredited doctors. First-class Western medicine is practised. Excellent dental care is available.

TRAVEL - International

AIR: The main airline to serve Hong Kong is *Cathay Pacific (CX).*

Approximate flight times: From Hong Kong to *London* is 13 hours 35 minutes, to *Los Angeles* is 16 hours 25 minutes, to *New York* is 18 hours 45 minutes, to *Singapore* is 3 hours 30 minutes and to *Sydney* is 7 hours 40 minutes.

International airport: *Hong Kong International* (Kai Tak) is 7.5km (4.5 miles) from central Hong Kong. Airport facilities include an outgoing duty-free shop, a wide range of car hire companies, banks, and 24-hour bars and restaurants. All the above are open 0600-2400. Airbus A1 runs (circular route) to Kowloon (journey time – 20 minutes); Airbus A2 runs to central Hong Kong every 15 minutes; Airbus A3 (circular route) runs to Causeway Bay (journey time – 30 minutes); taxis are plentiful.

Departure tax: Adults pay HK$150; children under 12 are free. Only Hong Kong currency is accepted.

HONG KONG — **HEALTH REGULATIONS** — **VISA REGULATIONS** — Code-Link

GALILEO/WORLDSPAN

TI-DFT/HKG/HE

TI-DFT/HKG/VI

SABRE

TIDFT/HKG/HE

TIDFT/HKG/VI

To access this information on your CRS, swipe the barcode with a light pen or type in the text under the barcode. For more information, see the introduction *How to Use This Book.*

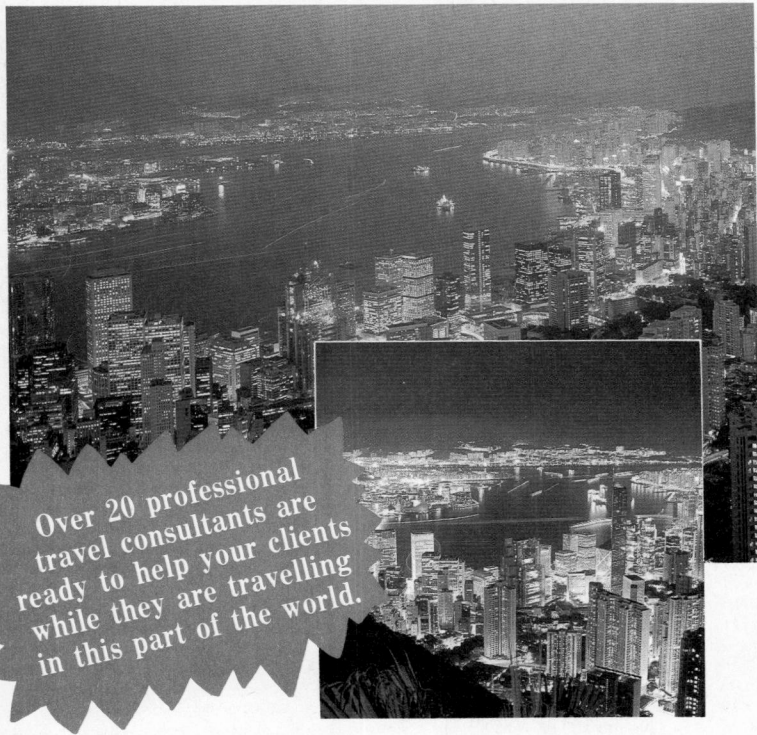

SEA: Lines serving the port of Hong Kong are as follows: *Norwegian America, Royal Viking, CTC, Sitmar* and *Lindblad Travel.* Hovercrafts link Hong Kong with China; there are also a number of ships sailing to major Chinese ports, although these are less frequent. Enquire locally for details.
Travel to Macau: Journey times: by jetfoil – 55 mins; by hydrofoil – 75 minutes. See also the section on *Macau* below.
RAIL: The *Kowloon–Canton Railway (KCR)* operates a service jointly with *Chinese Railways* from Kowloon to Canton, four times a day; first-class only with restaurant car. However, there are also local KCR trains running regularly (every 3–20 minutes) to Lo Wu, the last stop before the Chinese border. It is possible to then cross the border to Shenzhen, the first city in China over the border. To go as far as Lo Wu, it is necessary to hold a visa for China, otherwise it is only possible to get to Sheung Shui.

TRAVEL - Internal

SEA: Cross-harbour passenger services (shortest route 7-10 minutes) are operated by *Star Ferries* (sailing every five minutes) from 0630-2330. There are frequent passenger and vehicle services on other cross-harbour routes. *Wallah wallahs* (small motorboats) provide 24-hour service. The outlying islands are served daily by ferries and hydrofoils. However, the opening of the Cross Harbour Tunnel means that *wallah wallahs* are decreasing in popularity.
Tours of the harbour and to Aberdeen and Yaumatei typhoon shelters are available by *Watertours* junks, and visits are possible to outlying islands by public ferry services.
RAIL/METRO: *Mass Transit Railway (MTR)* has four lines and provides a cross-harbour link. It is more expensive than the ferry, but quicker, particularly if you are travelling further into Kowloon than Tsimshatsui. An MTR Tourist Ticket is available, valid for HK$25 worth of travel. If you are staying for a week or more it is worth getting a $50 or $200 ticket, which will provide travel up to that value. They are more convenient than buying a ticket each time you travel, and also work out slightly cheaper. The only other railway line in the colony is the Kowloon–Canton (KCR) line which has 13 stations within Hong Kong. Trains run between 0552-0012.
ROAD: Traffic drives on the left. **Bus** routes run throughout the territory, with cross-harbour routes via the tunnel. These, however, are often very crowded. Air-conditioned coaches operate along certain Hong Kong and Kowloon routes. Maxicabs, however, operate on fixed routes without fixed stops. **Minibuses** can pick up passengers and stop on request except at regular bus stops and other restricted areas. **Trams:** Only available on Hong Kong Island. Peak Tram on the Island is a cable tramway to the upper terminus on Victoria Peak, 400m (1300ft) high. **Taxis** are plentiful in Hong Kong and Kowloon. Extra charge (HK$20) for the Cross Harbour Tunnel. Red taxis serve Hong Kong Island and Kowloon, green ones the New Territories, and blue ones Lantau Island. Many drivers speak a little English, but it is wise to get your destination written in Chinese characters. **Rickshaws** are gradually disappearing and are now purely a tourist attraction. It is advisable to agree the fare in advance.
Car hire: A wide selection of self-drive and chauffeur-driven cars is available, although car hire is not that popular in Hong Kong. **Documentation:** An International Driving Permit is recommended, although it is not legally required. A valid national licence is accepted for up to 12 months. Minimum age is 18 years. Third Party insurance is compulsory.
JOURNEY TIMES: The following chart gives approximate journey times (in hours and minutes) from the Hong Kong Island terminals to main tourist districts and outlying islands.

	Road	Metro	Sea
Kai Tak	0.35	-	-
Kowloon	0.20	0.04	0.10
Causeway Bay	0.10	-	-
Lantau Is.	-	-	1.00
Aberdeen	0.20	-	-
Cheung Chau	-	-	1.00

ACCOMMODATION

HOTELS: There is an excellent selection of hotels, but due to intensifying interest on the part of visitors wanting to see the colony before it reverts to Chinese control, hotels are becoming increasingly booked up. Advance booking is strongly advised, especially in the peak periods March to April and October to November. Since 1988 there have been 19 hotels and 9000 new rooms opened and by 1995 there will be an estimated 35,494 rooms. Consequently the high occupancy rates and premium prices will be a thing of the past. Guest-house and hostel accommodation is also available. 10% service charge and 5% Government tax are added to the bill. Many hotels are members of the Hong Kong Tourist Association (address at top of entry). 75 hotels belong to the Hong Kong Hotels Association, 508-511 Silvercord Tower II, 30 Canton Road, Kowloon. Tel: 375 3838. Fax: 375 7676.
Grading: Though there is no grading structure as such, hotel members of the HKTA fall into one of four categories: **High Tariff A Hotels** (17 members); **High Tariff B Hotels** (26 members); **Medium Tariff Hotels** (31 members); **Hostels/Guest-houses** (10 members).
SELF-CATERING: Resort houses on the outlying islands can be hired.
CAMPING/CARAVANNING: Permitted in the countryside, though permission is required within the Country Park protection area.
YOUTH HOSTELS: There are four main YMCA/YWCAs in Hong Kong. The YMCA in Kowloon is at 41 Salisbury Road, Tsim Sha Tsui, Kowloon. Tel: 369 2211. For details contact the tourist office. There are numerous youth hostels in Hong Kong, all of which are outside the city. Contact Hong Kong Youth Hostels Association Ltd, Room 225-226, Block 19, Shek Kip Mei Estate, Sham Shuipo, Kowloon. Tel: 788 1638.

RESORTS & EXCURSIONS

Hong Kong is a major tourist destination as well as being one of the world's major business centres. This tax-free, bustling port and commercial centre has many luxury hotels and lesser hostelries which are used as bases to explore Hong Kong, the New Territories and the many small islands. Transportation is modern and well organised and most tours and sightseeing trips are completed in time for the tourist to be back in Hong Kong the same day to enjoy the nightlife. A tour of the New Territories takes about six hours, one of Hong Kong Island about four. Other popular excursions include sport and recreation tours and night tours, such as a dinner cruise and a tram tour with cocktails served. Contact

HONG KONG: Central & Wan Chai

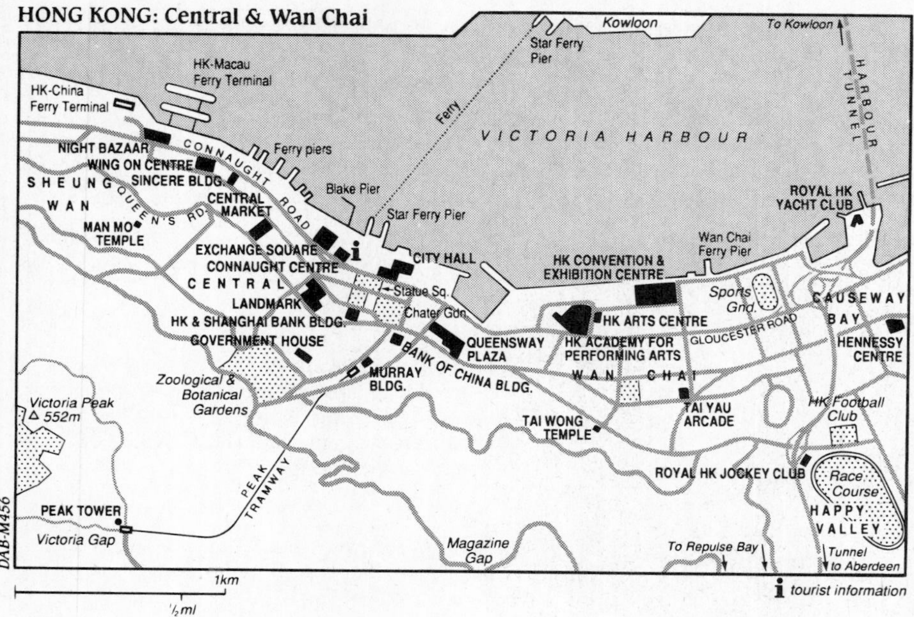

the Tourist Association in London, or in Hong Kong (addresses and phone numbers above) for further details. Places worth visiting include: *Sung Dynasty Village* – a re-creation of a 1000-year-old Chinese village; *Tsimshatsui* – shops, restaurants and a space museum in a vast complex; nightly planetarium 'sky shows'; the harbour and its magnificent skyline (tours of the harbour can be made by junk); *The Peak* – take a tram to the 'top' of Hong Kong Island for exceptional views and the Chinese Peak Tower Village at its upper terminus with restaurant and coffee shop; the night markets; *Ocean Park*, with performing dolphins and killer whales; the floating restaurants; *Repulse Bay*, with the *Tin Hau Temple* overlooking the beach; *Stanley Market;* the New Territories countryside, tranquil rural beauty near the Chinese border; the Chinese markets; *Miu Fat Monastery, Ching Chung Koon* and many other splendid Chinese temples; the fishing villages; *Sea Ranch* – a luxury resort and country club with beaches on Lantau Island; the splendid *Po Lin Monastery,* also on **Lantau Island.** Many of the islands have delightful beaches to escape the hubbub of the city – *Lantau, Lamma* and *Cheung Chau* are just three of these.

Special Interest Tours: A wide variety of these are available, and the Hong Kong Tourist Association provides a booklet giving details.

SOCIAL PROFILE

FOOD & DRINK: Hong Kong is one of the great centres for international cooking. Apart from Chinese food, which is superb, there are also many Indian, Vietnamese, Filipino, Singapore/Malaysian and Thai restaurants. It is the home of authentic Chinese food from all the regions of China, which may be sampled on a sampan in Causeway Bay, on a floating restaurant at Aberdeen, in a Kowloon restaurant, in a street market or at a deluxe hotel. Hotels serve European and Chinese food but there are also restaurants serving every type of local cuisine. In fact there is a complex of 27 restaurants called simply **Food Street** near the Excelsior Hotel, where you can eat the specialities of China, Japan and Europe.

HONG KONG: Kowloon

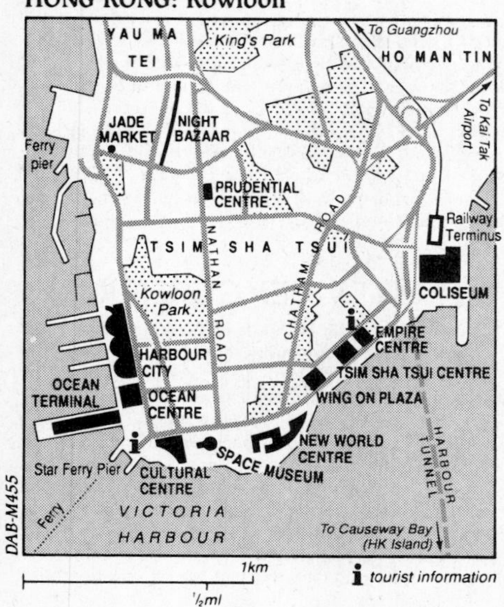

Hong Kong Island and Kowloon abound in restaurants serving many varieties of Chinese and European food. All leading hotels have excellent restaurants featuring dishes of various nations and most have coffee shops serving light meals. Restaurants serving snacks are increasingly popular. There are no licensing hours.

Chinese regional variations on food include Cantonese, Northern (Peking), Chiu Chow (Swatow), Shanghai, Sichuan and Hakka. Cantonese is based on parboiling, steaming and quick stir-frying to retain natural juices and flavours. The food is not salty or greasy and seafoods are prepared especially well, usually served with steamed rice. Specialities include *Dim Sum* (savoury snacks, usually steamed and served in bamboo baskets on trolleys). These include *Cha siu bao* (barbecue pork bun), *Har gau* (steamed shrimp dumplings) and *Shiu mai* (steamed and minced pork with shrimp). The emphasis in Northern food is on bread and noodles, deep-frying and spicy sauces. Specialities include *Peking duck* and hotpot dishes. Shanghainese food is diced or shredded, stewed in soya or fried in sesame oil with pots of peppers and garlic. *Chiu Chow* is served with rich sauces and Hakka food is generally simple in style with baked chicken in salt among the best dishes. Sichuan food is hot and spicy with plenty of chillies. A speciality is barbecued meat. **Drink:** The Chinese do not usually order a drink before dinner. Popular Chinese wines and spirits are *Zhian Jing* (a rice wine served hot like *Sake*), *Liang hua pei* (potent plum brandy), *Kaolian* (a whisky) and *Mao toi*. Popular beers are the locally brewed *San Miguel* and *Tsingtao* (from China) with imported beverages widely available.

NIGHTLIFE: There are many nightclubs, discotheques, hostess clubs, theatres and cinemas. Cultural concerts, plays and exhibitions can be seen at Hong Kong's City Hall which also has a dining room, ballroom and cocktail lounge. The Hong Kong Cultural Centre includes a 2100 seater Concert Hall, 1750-seat Grand Theatre, a studio theatre with 300-500 seats and restaurants, bars and other facilities, has become the major venue for cultural concerts, plays and operas. Hong Kong Art Centre in Wanchai supplements the City Hall's entertainment with culture in the form of Chinese opera, puppet shows, recitals and concerts. American, European, Chinese and Japanese films with subtitles are shown at a number of good air-conditioned cinemas. Two daily papers, the *Hong Kong Standard* and the *South China Morning Post*, contain details of entertainment. An unusual event to watch is night horseracing held on Wednesday nights from September to May. For further details contact the Hong Kong Tourist Association.

SHOPPING: Whether one is shopping in modern air-conditioned arcades or more traditional street markets, the range of goods available in Hong Kong is vast. Many famous name shops have opened in Hong Kong, bringing the latest styles in great variety. Places that display the HKTA sign (Hong Kong Tourist Association) are the best guarantee of satisfaction. Bargaining is practised in the smaller shops and side stalls only. There are excellent markets in Stanley on Hong Kong Island, which is in a beautiful setting in a small village on the coast, and in Temple Street, Kowloon, which is a night market. Tailoring is first class. Except for a few items such as liquor and perfume, Hong Kong is a duty-free port. **Shopping hours:** Hong Kong Island (Central & Western): 1000-1800 (1000-2000 along Queen's Road). Hong Kong Island (Causeway Bay & Wanchai): 1000-2130. Kowloon (Tsin Sha Tsui & Yan Ma Tei): 1000-1930. Kowloon (Mongkok): 1000-2100. Many shops are open on Sunday.

SPORT: Spectator sports are **soccer, rugby** and **cricket. Jogging** facilities are provided by some hotels. The Clinic at Adventis Hospital holds jogging sessions every Sunday. There are also good facilities for **squash, golf, tennis, hiking, riding, bowling** and **ice skating,** as well as health centre facilities available. There are over 30 highly acclaimed beaches throughout the territory. Excellent **skindiving, water-skiing** and **sailing** are available. **Horserace** meetings, at which vast sums of money change hands, are held from September to May on Saturday or Sunday afternoons and Wednesday evenings. The two main **racecourses** are at Happy Valley (Hong Kong Island) and Shatin (New Territories). For details contact the Royal Hong Kong Jockey Club. There are also many massage parlours, although these vary in respectability.

SPECIAL EVENTS: The following is a selection of the major festivals and special events celebrated in Hong Kong during 1993/1994. For a complete list, with exact dates, contact the Tourist Association.
Mar 12-28 '93 *Hong Kong Food Festival.* **Apr 5** *Ching Ming Festival.* **May** *Cheung Chau Bun Festival.* **Jun 24** *Dragon Boat Festival.* **Jun 3-4** *International Dragon Boat Races.* **Aug 31** *Hungry Ghosts Festival.* **Sep 30** *Mid-Autumn Festival.* **Oct 23** *Chung Yeung Festival.* **Dec 22** *Winter Solstice.* **Feb 10 '94** *Chinese New Year.* **Feb 24** *Spring Lantern Festival.*

Note: A festival in Hong Kong is a major event on a scale hardly understood in the West. During Chinese New Year festivities, there is total disruption of everyday life.

SOCIAL CONVENTIONS: Handshaking is the common form of greeting. In Hong Kong the family name comes first, so Wong Man Ying would be addressed as Mr Wong. Most entertaining takes place in restaurants rather than in private homes. Usually informal and normal courtesies should be observed when visiting someone's home. During a meal a toast is often drunk saying *Yum Sing* at each course. There may be up to 12 courses served in a meal, and although it is not considered an insult to eat sparingly, a good appetite is always appreciated and it is best to taste every dish. It is customary to invite the host to a return dinner. Informal wear is acceptable. Some restaurants and social functions often warrant formal attire. Smoking is widely acceptable and only prohibited where specified. **Tipping:** Most hotels and restaurants add 10% service charge. An additional 5% gratuity is expected and small tips for taxi-drivers, doormen and washroom attendants.

BUSINESS PROFILE

ECONOMY: Under the terms of the Sino-British agreement, Hong Kong's existing economic system will be preserved for at least 50 years. Hong Kong has the archetypal 'Tiger economy', the appellation now afforded to the fast-growing economies of the Pacific Basin. Its mainstays are light manufacturing industry, financial services and shipping, the latter assisted by Hong Kong's fine natural port. The manufacturing sector has thriving textile and consumer electronics industries, employing almost half the workforce and producing three-quarters of Hong Kong's export income. The colony is also the world's leading producer of children's toys. The economy suffered some loss of business confidence both in the wake of the 1984 Sino-British agreement and the events of June 1989 in the People's Republic. The growth rate, which averaged 8% in the 1980s, slipped to between 2-3% at the beginning of the 1990s, with inflation hitting double

figures, but the economy remains vibrant and has received a substantial boost from the recently announced airport construction project. Hong Kong is the world's 11th largest trading economy and its major trading partner is China, followed by Japan, Taiwan, the UK and the USA. Declining trade with the USA in recent years has been offset by growth in European markets, especially Germany. The best guarantor of Hong Kong's economic future is the continuing prosperity of the Special Economic Zones in southern China which are Hong Kong's immediate neighbours. Provided the status of these Zones is maintained, Hong Kong will be more or less merged into them: as one Hong Kong businessman put it, 'the border will effectively move north' to the northern boundaries of the Special Economic Zones.

BUSINESS: Business people are generally expected to dress smartly. Local business people are usually extremely hospitable. Appointments should be made in advance and punctuality is appreciated. Business cards are widely used with a Chinese translation on the reverse. Most top hotels provide business centres for visiting business people, with typing, duplication, translation and other services. **Office hours:** 0900-1300 and 1400-1700 Monday to Friday; 0900-1230 Saturday. Some Chinese offices open earlier than 0930 and close later than 1700.

COMMERCIAL INFORMATION: The following organisation can offer advice: Hong Kong General Chamber of Commerce, PO Box 852, United Centre, 22nd Floor, 95 Queensway, Hong Kong. Tel: 529 9229. Fax: 527 9843. Telex: 83535.

CONFERENCES/CONVENTIONS: The Hong Kong Convention and Incentive Travel Bureau is a division of the Hong Kong Tourist Association (address at top of entry) which specialises in promoting Hong Kong as a leading venue with a special East/West position; it publishes lavish and detailed brochures showcasing the region for conference and incentive planners, together with a glossy catalogue of promotional material and a directory of associations and societies in Hong Kong. There were 245 association conferences, 57 exhibitions, 315 corporate meetings and 517 incentive group meetings in 1991, mostly with participants from the Pacific Basin (including the USA); Europe, the UK and Germany also figured significantly. There are venues with seating for up to 12,500 persons. For further information contact the Hong Kong Convention and Incentive Travel Bureau Office (see listing for the Tourist Association in Hong Kong).

HISTORY & GOVERNMENT

HISTORY: Hong Kong came under British administration as a direct result of the Opium Wars of the last century. When peace terms were drawn up in 1841 at the Treaty of Nanking, the Emperor of China agreed that Britain should have an insular trading base, but the name of the island was left blank until ratification in the following year, by which time Hong Kong was already a thriving British-run harbour. The Kowloon peninsula was ceded under the Convention of Peking in 1860, and in 1898 the New Territories were leased from China for 99 years. The British have maintained full control over Hong Kong since then, apart from a 4-year period during the Second World War when the territory was occupied by the Japanese. Under the agreement signed by the British and Chinese governments in December 1984, the colony will revert to control of the People's Republic of China in June 1997. Despite misgivings in some quarters about the lack of British consultation with the Hong Kong people and over the true nature of Chinese intentions, the transition seems likely to pass off without serious difficulty. However, the behaviour of the Chinese authorities against the Tiananmen Square demonstrators in the summer of 1989 led many Hong Kong residents to reconsider their long-term futures in the territory after 1997. Their prospects of entering the UK, however, depend on whether they qualify among the 50,000 Hong Kong citizens plus dependants who will be granted right of residency in the UK. Not all would-be emigrants want to go to Britain and many have secured other foreign passports. While these people are looking to get out, another, more unfortunate group, has been seeking desperately to get in. These are the estimated 60,000 'boat people' who fled to Hong Kong from Vietnam during the mid- and late 1980s. The Hong Kong authorities interned the great majority of them in camps prior to repatriation. The main point of contention between the British and Chinese governments is democratic representation. Under the colonial regime, democratic representation had historically been kept to a minimum; the British now appear to be seeking to widen the representative base of the partially-elected Legislative Council, in the teeth of resistance from Beijing which says that the matter is closed and, besides, any measures taken now will be reversed after 1997. The main pressure on Hong Kong's last Governor (probably), former Conservative MP Chris Patten, comes from United Democrats of Hong Kong, led by Martin Lee, a particular *bête noire* of Beijing. Patten took over from Sir David Wilson as Governor in 1992. As well as the issues of representation, he will also have to shepherd Hong Kong's new international airport to near-completion. Everybody agrees a new airport is needed: the problem, however, concerns the finance. Budgeted at HK$1 billion (£700 million), the package put together by the Hong Kong government met immediate objections from the Chinese, who had complained that it would drain the territory's coffers. A settlement was reached in the summer of 1991, under which the Chinese agreed to let the project go ahead, but they extracted considerable political capital in the process and an agreement permitting Chinese representatives to sit on the airport committee: the first time that China has been directly represented on a Hong Kong government body. China's main instrument on the ground is the New China News Agency which functions as a *de facto* embassy. Despite the bluster from Beijing about 'subversion' and the scepticism in Hong Kong regarding the integrity of any Chinese promises, China's leaders are well aware that their interests in Hong Kong – through which China earns two-thirds of its foreign exchange and numerous other economic benefits – will not be best served by alienating those who have brought the territory its continuing prosperity.

GOVERNMENT: Hong Kong is currently administered by a British Governor-General, who appoints an Executive Council and 60 members of a Legislative Council, which has 7 official members (civil servants and the British military commander), 3 ex-officio members, 18 appointed members and 32 elected members (18 members elected by the electoral college; 14 members elected by 9 'functional constituencies' – elite groups such as doctors, lawyers and architects).

CLIMATE

Hong Kong experiences four distinct seasons, with the climate influenced in winter by the north/northeast monsoon and in summer by the south/southwest monsoon. Summers are very hot, with the rainy season running from June to August. Spring and autumn are warm with occasional rain and cooler evenings. Winter can be cold, but most days are mild. There is a risk of typhoons from July to September.

Required clothing: Lightweight cottons and linens are worn during warmer months, with warmer clothes for spring and autumn evenings. It should be noted that even during the hottest weather, a jacket or pullover will be required for the sometimes fierce air-conditioning indoors. Warm mediumweights are best during winter. Waterproofing is advisable during summer rains.

HONG KONG (33m)

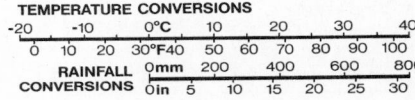

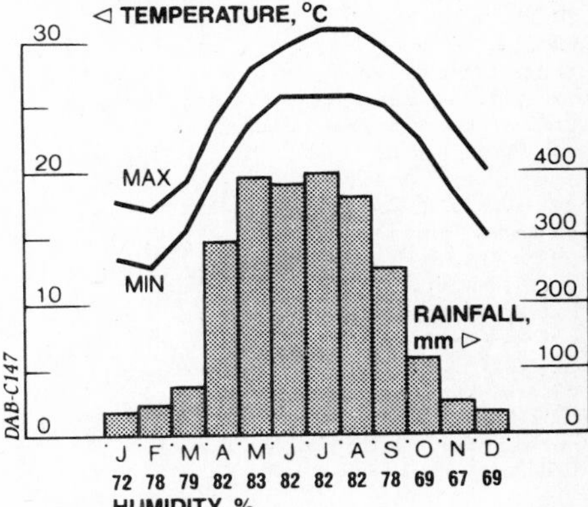

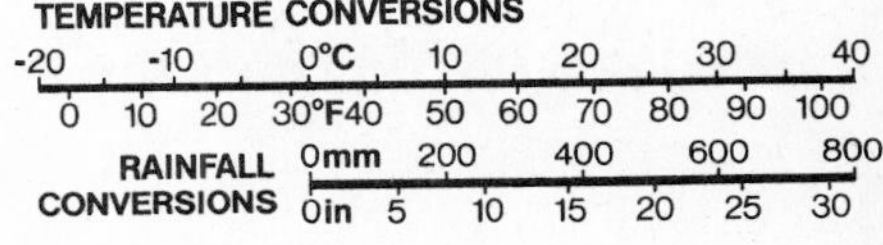

TEMPERATURE CONVERSIONS
-20 -10 0°C 10 20 30 40
0 10 20 30°F40 50 60 70 80 90 100
RAINFALL CONVERSIONS
0mm 200 400 600 800
0in 5 10 15 20 25 30

Location: Central Europe.

Országos Idegenforgalmi Hivatal (OIH)
(Hungarian Tourist Board)
Vigadó u. 6
1051 Budapest, Hungary
Tel: (1) 118 0750. Fax: (1) 118 5241. Telex: 225182.
Idegenforgalmi, Beszerzési, Utazási és Szallitási Rt. (IBUSZ)
(Hungarian Travel Agency)
Felszabadulás tér 5
1364 Budapest, Hungary
Tel: (1) 118 1120. Fax: (1) 117 7723. Telex: 224976.
Embassy of the Hungarian Republic
35 Eaton Place
London SW1X 8BY
Tel: (071) 235 4048 *or* 235 7191 *or* 235 2664. Fax: (071) 823 1348.
Consulate: Tel: (071) 235 2664. Opening hours: 1000-1230 Monday to Friday.
Danube Travel Agency (General agent for IBUSZ)
6 Conduit Street
London W1R 9TG
Tel: (071) 493 0263. Fax: (071) 493 6963. Telex: 23541.
Opening hours: 0930-1700 Monday to Friday.
British Embassy
Harmincad Ucta 6
Budapest V, Hungary
Tel: (1) 118 2888. Fax: (1) 118 0907. Telex: 224527.
Embassy of the Hungarian Republic
3910 Shoemaker Street, NW
Washington, DC 20008
Tel: (202) 362 6730. Fax: (202) 966 8135.
Hungarian Travel Company
(North American Division)
Suite 1104, One Parker Plaza
Fort Lee, NJ
07024
Tel: (201) 592 8585. Fax: (201) 592 8736. Telex: 428187.
Embassy of the United States of America
Unit 25402
Szabadság tér 12
1054 Budapest V, Hungary
Tel: (1) 112 6450. Fax: (1) 132 8934. Telex: 224222.
Embassy of the Hungarian Republic
7 Delaware Avenue
Ottawa, Ontario
K2P 0Z2
Tel: (613) 232 1711 *or* 232 1549. Fax: (613) 232 5620.
Consulate: Tel: (613) 232 3209.
Consulates in: Montréal, Toronto, Vancouver and Calgary.
Canadian Embassy
Budakeszi ut. 32
1121 Budapest, Hungary
Tel: (1) 176 7312 *or* 176 7512 *or* 176 7711/2. Fax: (1) 176 7689. Telex: 224588.

AREA: 93,033 sq km (35,920 sq miles).
POPULATION: 10,375,300 (1990 estimate).
POPULATION DENSITY: 111.5 per sq km.
CAPITAL: Budapest. **Population:** 2,016,132 (1990).
GEOGRAPHY: Hungary is situated in central Europe, sharing borders to the north with Slovakia, to the northeast with the CIS, to the east with Romania, to the south with Croatia and Yugoslavia and to the west with Austria and Slovenia. There are several ranges of hills, chiefly in the north and west. The Great Plain *(Nagyalfold)* stretches east from the Danube to the foothills of the Carpathian Mountains in the CIS, to the mountains of Transylvania in Romania, and south to the Fruska Gora range in Croatia. Lake Balaton is the largest unbroken stretch of inland water in central Europe.
LANGUAGE: Hungarian (Magyar) is the official language. German is widely spoken. Some English and French is spoken, mainly in western Hungary.
RELIGION: 65% Roman Catholic, 20% Protestant. Eastern Orthodox and Jewish. No official national religion.
TIME: GMT + 1 (GMT + 2 in summer).
ELECTRICITY: 220 volts AC, 50Hz.
COMMUNICATIONS: Telephone: IDD available. Country code: 36. For long-distance calls dial 06. Local public telephones are operated by a Ft5 coin. Red phones are for international calls. **Telex:** Facilities available from major hotels and main post office in Budapest, Petőfi Sándor Utca (0700-2100). **Post:** Airmail takes three days to one week to reach European destinations. In addition to the main post office, the offices at West and East railway stations in Budapest are open 24 hours a day. Stamps are available from tobacconists as well as post offices. Post office hours: 0800-1800 Monday to Friday, 0800-1400 Saturday. **Press:** In 1988 censorship laws were relaxed and since 1989 private ownership of publications has been permitted. National dailies include *Népszabadság, Magyar Hirlap* and *Népszava.* There is an English-language newspaper, the *Daily News.*
BBC World Service and Voice of America frequencies: From time to time these change. See the section *How to Use this Book* for more information.

BBC:				
MHz	15.57	12.09	9.410	6.195
Voice of America:				
MHz	9.670	6.040	5.995	1.197

PASSPORT/VISA

Regulations and requirements may be subject to change at short notice, and you are advised to contact the appropriate diplomatic or consular authority before finalising travel arrangements. Details of these may be found at the head of this country's entry. Any numbers in the chart refer to the footnotes below.

	Passport Required?	Visa Required?	Return Ticket Required?
Full British	Yes	No	No
BVP	Not valid	-	-
Australian	Yes	Yes	No
Canadian	Yes	No	No
USA	Yes	No	No
Other EC	Yes	No	No
Japanese	Yes	Yes	No

PASSPORTS: Valid passport required by all. All passports must be valid for at least 6 months.
British Visitors Passport: Not acceptable.
VISAS: Required by all except:
(a) [1] nationals of European countries and the CIS (nationals of Albania and Turkey *do* require a visa);
(b) nationals of USA and Canada;
(c) nationals of Argentina, Chile, Costa Rica, Cuba, Nicaragua and Uruguay;
(d) nationals of Seychelles, Mongolia and South Korea.
Types of visa: Single-entry Tourist, Transit or Business (£12 plus pre-paid registered envelope); Double-transit or Double-entry (£24); Multiple-entry visa (£40).
Validity: *Entry visa* (tourist, business) – valid for 30-day stay within 6 months of the date of issue. *Transit visa* – valid for 48-hour stay within 6 months from date of issue. *Multiple-entry visa* – valid for multiple entries into Hungary within 6 months from the date of issue.
Application to: Consulate (or Consular Section at Embassy). For addresses, see top of entry. Visas are not issued at road border points or at Budapest Airport.
Application requirements: (a) 2-4 passport-size photos. (b) Valid passport. (c) Completed visa application form. (d) Fee (£2 per passport for postal applications; no fee, normally, if applicant is travelling with Danube Travel). (e) Written invitation from Hungary if Business visa. (f) Nationals of Turkey and all other countries in Asia and Africa also need to submit their return ticket (whether for air or rail).
Working days required: A visa may be obtained 48 hours after approval. Postal applications should be accompanied by a stamped, self-addressed, registered envelope.
Note: Within 48 hours of arrival visitors who stay for more than 30 days must register with the police (hotels will handle this); if staying in a private residence there is no requirement to register.

MONEY

Currency: Forint (Ft) = 100 fillér. Notes are in denominations of Ft5000, 1000, 500, 100, 50 and 20. Coins are in denominations of Ft20, 10, 5, 2 and 1, and 50, 20 and 10 fillér. A large number of commemorative coins in circulation are legal tender.
Currency exchange: Currency can be exchanged at hotels, banks, airports, railway stations, travel agencies and some restaurants. Retain all exchange receipts, as it is illegal to change money on the black market.
Credit cards: Access/Mastercard, American Express, Diners Club and Visa are accepted. Check with your credit card company for details of merchant acceptability and other services which may be available.
Travellers cheques: Widely accepted in stores and banks.
Exchange rate indicators: The following figures are included as a guide to the movements of the Forint against Sterling and the US Dollar:

Date:	Oct '89	Oct '90	Oct '91	Oct '92
£1.00=	96.28	120.80	130.73	125.90
$1.00=	60.97	61.84	75.32	79.33

Currency restrictions: Import and export of local currency is limited to Ft100 *(check with Embassy or local banks before departure).* Unlimited import of foreign currency, provided the amount is declared. Export of foreign currency is limited to the amount declared on import; there is no compulsory money exchange. Hungarian currency can be exchanged for up to 50% of the officially exchanged sum (but not more than US$100) at any authorised office or branch of the National Savings Bank.
Banking hours: 0900-1400 Monday to Friday and 0900-1200 Saturday.

DUTY FREE

The following goods may be imported into Hungary by persons over 16 years of age without incurring customs duty:
250 cigarettes or 50 cigars or 250g of tobacco;
1 litre of alcoholic beverage and 2 litres of wine;
250g of perfume;
Gifts to the value of Ft5000.

HUNGARY | **HEALTH REGULATIONS** | **VISA REGULATIONS** | Code-Link

GALILEO/WORLDSPAN

TI-DFT/BUD/HE

TI-DFT/BUD/VI

SABRE

TIDFT/BUD/HE

TIDFT/BUD/VI

To access this information on your CRS, swipe the barcode with a light pen or type in the text under the barcode. For more information, see the introduction *How to Use This Book.*

PUBLIC HOLIDAYS

Public holidays observed in Hungary are as follows:
Mar 15 '93 Anniversary of 1848 uprising against Austrian rule. **Apr 12** Easter Monday. **May 1** Labour Day. **Aug 20** Constitution Day. **Oct 23** Day of Proclamation of the Republic. **Dec 25-26** Christmas. **Jan 1 '94** New Year's Day. **Mar 15** Anniversary of the 1848 uprising against Austrian rule.

HEALTH

Regulations and requirements may be subject to change at short notice, and you are advised to contact your doctor well in advance of your intended date of departure. Any numbers in the chart refer to the footnotes below.

	Special Precautions?	Certificate Required?
Yellow Fever	No	No
Cholera	No	No
Typhoid & Polio	No	-
Malaria	No	-
Food & Drink	1	-

[1]: Mains water is normally chlorinated, and whilst relatively safe may cause mild abdominal upsets. Bottled water is available and is advised for the first few weeks of the stay. Milk is pasteurised and dairy products are safe for consumption. Local meat, poultry, seafood, fruit and vegetables are generally considered safe to eat.
Rabies is present. For those at high risk, vaccination before arrival should be considered. If you are bitten abroad seek medical advice without delay. For more information consult the *Health* section at the back of the book.
Health care: There is a Reciprocal Health Agreement with the UK. On presentation of a UK passport, treatment is free at hospitals, 'poly-clinics' and doctor's surgeries. For emergencies, call 04. Charges will be made for dental and ophthalmic treatment and for prescribed medicines. For an emergency dental service, call 330 189. Chemists are open in the capital from 0800-1000. There are chemists with a 24-hour emergency service open in every district.

TRAVEL - International

AIR: The national airline is *Malév (MA)*, operating flights to 37 cities.
Approximate flight time: From Budapest to *London* is 2 hours 40 minutes.
International airport: *Budapest Ferihegy (BUD)*, 16km (10 miles) from the city (travel time – 30 minutes). There are now two terminals, one of which is used exclusively by *Malév, Air France* and *Lufthansa*. Facilities include a duty-free shop, florist, newsagent, restaurant and bar, bureaux de change, banks, tourist information centre, gift shop, post office (November-March: 0800-1600; April-October: 0800-1930). Regular coach and bus services are available to the city. Taxis are available at all times. The major car-hire companies are represented.
RIVER: From April 4 to October 1 there is a daily hydrofoil service between Vienna and Budapest (except Sundays). There is also a daily hovercraft service from April to October. 20kg of luggage may be carried free of charge.
RAIL: Links with the rest of Europe are good and there are three international trains daily to Budapest. Inter-Rail, Eurotrain and RES concessions are valid on the Hungarian State Railways *(MAV)*. Between Dresden and Budapest there is a car transport system. The *Orient Express* offers a good route from Paris overnight via Stuttgart, Munich and Vienna, reaching Budapest at 2030. There are first- and second-class day carriages from Paris through to Budapest and also first- and second-class sleeping cars on four days a week with a dining car from Stuttgart.
The *Wiener Waltzer* from Basel travels via Zurich, Salzburg and Vienna to Budapest, arriving at 1430. First- and second-class day carriages run from Basel through to Budapest and both sleeping cars and couchettes (the latter second-class only) as far as Vienna. There is a mini-bar service in Switzerland and Austria, and a dining car in Hungary.
The most convenient route from London is via Dover/Ostend joining *Ostend/Vienna* Express with sleeping cars and couchettes to Vienna.
Note: In general, travellers leaving Hungary by train must pay their fare in convertible currency. Most generally recognised international concessionary tickets are accepted in Hungary; contact *MAV* for details. Seat reservations are strongly advised for all services.
Luggage allowances: 35kg for adults, 15kg for children.
ROAD: Route via The Netherlands, Belgium and Austria and from Vienna via the E5 Transcontinental Highway which passes near Bratislava (Slovak Republic). Bus connections are available from Austria, the CIS, Croatia, the Czech Republic, Germany, Italy, Poland, the Slovak Republic and Slovenia.

TRAVEL - Internal

AIR: Internal air services are operated by *Danube Air* which flies from *Budaors Airport*, 16km (10 miles) from the centre of Budapest. 6-, 8-, 10- and 14-seater turbo-prop and jet aircraft are used and the service connects the capital with about 12 towns and cities throughout Hungary.
RIVER/LAKE: There are regular services on the Danube and Lake Balaton from spring to late autumn. *MAHART* and the *Budapest Travel Company (BKV)* also operate ferries in the city centre, the Roman Embankment *(Római Part)* and at some crossing points.
Ferry services on the Danube, suitable for cars and buses, operate hourly between Esztergom and Párkány (Sturovo) throughout the year (except for when the river is frozen) daily 0800-1800.
On Lake Balaton, a ferry operates during the summer at 40-minute intervals daily between Tihanyrév and Szántódrév 0620-2400; at other times of the year the service runs 0630-1930.
RAIL: Services are operated by *MAV*. Tel: (1) 122 0660. All main cities are linked by efficient services but facilities are often inadequate. Supplements are payable on express trains. Reservations for express trains are recommended, particularly in summer. Tickets can be bought 60 days in advance on domestic railway lines, as can seat reservations.
Cheap fares: Concessions are available for groups (minimum of six persons) and for pensioners (55 years for women, 60 for men). Balaton and Tourist Season Tickets (7-10 days) are also available. Contact *MAV* for details.
ROAD: There are eight arterial roads in the country: all but the M8 start from central Budapest. No tolls are charged. From Budapest the two main highways are the M1 from Györ to Vienna and the M7 along Lake Balaton. The M3 connects Budapest with eastern Hungary. Generally the road system is good. **Bus:** Budapest is linked with major provincial towns. Tickets are available from Volán long-distance bus terminal, Budapest, and at IBUSZ and Volán offices throughout the country. A bus season ticket is also available. **Car hire:** Rental cars are available at *Ferihegy Airport* or at IUBSZ, Volán, Express and Budapest Tourist offices as well as at major hotels. **Regulations:** Speed limits are 60kmph (37mph) in built-up areas, 80kmph (50mph) on main roads, 100kmph (62mph) on highways and 120kmph (75mph) on motorways. Seat belts are compulsory. Petrol stations are infrequent and there are no special tourist petrol coupons. There is a total alcohol ban when driving; severe fines are imposed for infringements. **Breakdowns:** The Hungarian Automobile Club (Helpline tel: (1) 169 3714) operates a breakdown service on main roads at weekends and a 24-hour service on motorways. **Documentation:** International Driving Permit and Green Card insurance necessary.
URBAN: There is good public transport in all the main towns in Hungary. The capital Budapest has bus, trolleybus, tramway, suburban railway *(HEV)*, a 3-line metro and boat services. The metro has ticket barriers at all stations. The bus-trolleybus-tramway system has pre-purchase flat fares with ticket puncher on board. Day passes are available for all the transport modes in the city. Trams and buses generally run from about 0430-2300. Some night services also operate. The metro runs from 0430-2310 and stations can be identified by a large 'M'. There is also a cogwheel railway (Városmajor–Széchenyi Hill), a *Pioneers' Railway* (Hüvösvölgy–Széchenyi Hill), a chairlift and a funicular. There are tramways in some of the other towns, or else good bus services. Day

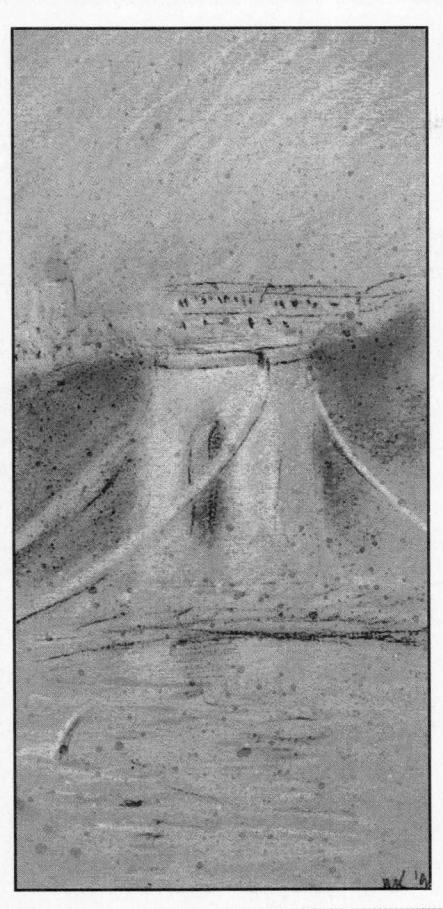

passes are available in Budapest.

JOURNEY TIMES: The following chart gives approximate journey times (in hours and minutes) from Budapest to other major cities/towns in Hungary.

	Road	Rail
Sopron	3.30	3.25
Miskolc	3.00	2.20
Pécs	3.00	3.00
Szeged	2.00	2.20
Szentendre	0.30	0.40
Lake Balaton	2.00	2.15

ACCOMMODATION

HOTELS: In all classes of hotel, visitors from the West can expect to be made very welcome and service will usually be friendly and smooth. In addition to hotels, there are Tourist Hostels, which provide simple accommodation usually in rooms with four or more beds. **Grading:** Hungarian hotels are classified by use of a star rating system. **5-** and **4-star** hotels are luxury class and are generally extremely comfortable. **3-star** hotels are comfortable but less luxurious and offer good value for money. **2-** and **1-star** hotels are generally adequate and clean.

GUEST-HOUSES: Available almost everywhere. Paying-guest accommodation is an inexpensive and excellent way of getting to know the people. Renting often includes bathroom but not breakfast. Such accommodation can be booked through tourist offices once in Hungary or via Danube Travel (address above). Applications should be made well in advance.

SELF-CATERING: Bungalows with two rooms, fully equipped, can be rented at a large number of resorts. Full details and rates can be obtained from tourist offices in Hungary or Danube Travel.

CAMPING/CARAVANNING: Camping is forbidden except in the specially designated areas. Booking at: Hungaro-Camping Ltd, Kalvin Sq 9, Budapest 1091, or through travel agencies. Most of the sites cater only for campers bringing in their own equipment. Caravans are permitted on sites that have power points; a parking charge is made. Young people between six and 16 pay half price and there is no charge for children under the age of six. **Grading:** There are four categories of site, designated **I, II, III** and **IV**, according to the amenities provided, and most are open from May to September.

YOUTH HOSTELS: There are ten in Budapest and 14 in other towns. Hostels are open all day and beds cost around US$6. Contact: Express Youth and Student Travel Bureau, V Szabadság tér 16, Budapest 1395. Tel: (1) 131 7777.

RESORTS & EXCURSIONS

The country has, for convenience, been divided into five regions.

Budapest & the Danube

The capital city of **Budapest,** situated on one of the most beautiful areas of the Danube, is made up of two parts – *Buda* and *Pest*. The former is the older, more graceful part, with cobbled streets and medieval buildings; the latter is the commercial centre. The capital is a lively city which has long been a haven for writers, artists and musicians. In the *Buda* section can be found *Gellert Hill* which gives a wonderful view of the city, river and mountains; on the hill is the *'Citadella'*, a stone fort. *The Royal Palace*, bombed during the Second World War and now reconstructed, houses the *National Gallery* with collections of fine Gothic sculpture and modern Hungarian art (including many paintings by Mihaly Munkácsy), and the *Historical Museum of Budapest*, containing archaeological remains of the old city, and furnishings, glass and ceramics from the 15th century. Also in the Buda region is the *Fisherman's Bastion* – so called because it was the duty of the fishermen of the city to protect the northern side of the Royal Palace during the Middle Ages – and *Matthias Church* with its multicoloured tiled roof.

On the *Pest* side are the *Parliament;* the *Hungarian National Museum*, containing remarkable treasures including the oldest skull yet found in Europe and Liszt's gold baton; the *Belvárosi Templom*, Hungary's oldest church, dating back to the 12th century; the *Museum of Fine Arts* housing European paintings; the *Ethnographic Museum* and *Margaret Island*, connected to both Buda and Pest by a bridge. The whole island is a park with a sports stadium, swimming pool, spas, a rose garden and fountains. Budapest has about a hundred hot springs; one is in the city zoo, much to the delight of the local hippo population who breed there very successfully.

Upstream from Budapest is *Szentendre*, an old Serbian market town where the Hungarian painter Károly Ferenczy did most of his work; there is a museum named after him containing historical, archaeological and ethnographic collections as well as paintings. The *Serbian Museum for Ecclesiastical History* contains many fine examples of ecclesiastical art from the 14th to the 18th centuries. There are many good exhibitions in

BUDAPEST

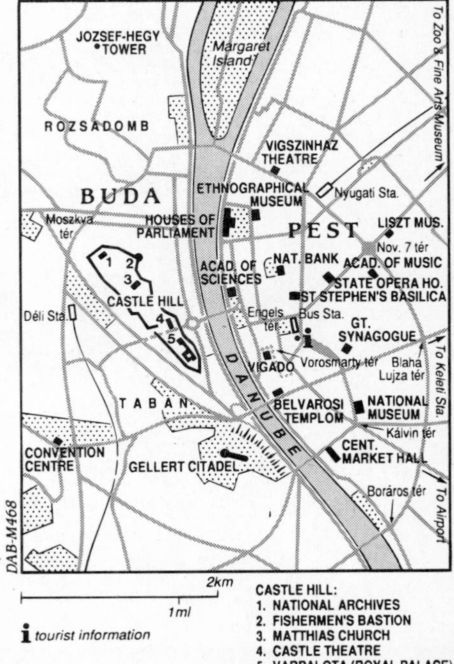

the city, particularly of the ceramics of Marigt Kovács.
Visegrád, a few miles further upriver, was once a royal stronghold, but is now a tourist resort. The 15th-century summer palace has been excavated and restored. The *King Matthias Museum* housed in a Baroque mansion displays many archaeological discoveries.
Esztergom was originally a Roman outpost; it later became the residence of Magyar kings in the 12th and 13th centuries. The *Cathedral*, the *Museum of the Stronghold of Esztergom* and the *Christian Museum of Esztergom*, containing some of Hungary's finest art collections, are worth visiting.

Lake Balaton & the West

The lake is a popular holiday region, not least because of its sandy beaches and shallow waters, with an average depth of only 3.5m (11ft). The surrounding countryside consists mainly of fertile plains dotted with old villages. Further west, towards the Austrian border, the terrain becomes more hilly and forested.
Székesfehérvár, between the lake and Budapest, has a 17th-century *Town Hall* in the Baroque style, as well as the *Zichy Palace* and the *Garden of Ruins* – an open-air museum.
Siófok, on the south shore of the lake, has some of the sandiest beaches and best facilities for tourists.
Keszthely is a pleasant old town containing the *Georgikon*, founded in the 18th century, the first agricultural college in Europe; the *Helikon Library*; and the *Balaton Museum*.
Balatonfüred is a well-known health resort with 11 medicinal springs.
Veszprém, 10km (6 miles) north of *Lake Balaton*, built on five hills, is a pretty town with cobbled streets. It is the home of the *Var Museum*, an *Episcopal Palace* and the 15th-century *Gizella Chapel*.
Further west, the main towns are **Szombathely** (which claims to be the oldest town in Hungary) and **Zalaegerszeg.** Szombathely has superb examples of Romanesque stonework.
Sopron, close to the Austrian frontier, is built on its old Roman foundations, and reminders of the region's history are still very much in evidence. Among the sights here are the *Fire Tower*, the *Liszt Museum* and the ancient quarry at **Fertörákos.**
Nearby is the spa town of **Balf** and the Baroque castle of *Fertöd*, recently restored to its original condition. Two other towns worth visiting in this region are the walled town of **Köszeg,** and the riverside town of **Györ,** on the main Budapest–Vienna highway. About 18km (11 miles) southeast of Györ is the ancient hilltop monastery of *Pannonhalma*, with a library containing over a quarter of a million books.

The Great Plain Area

This region covers more than half the country, and contains thousands of acres of vineyards, orchards and farmland.
Kecskemét, 85km (53 miles) southeast of the capital, is the home town of the composer Zoltán Kodály. Although an industrial town in many respects, it still has some fine examples of peasant architecture, and of crafts in the *Naive Artists and Katona Jozsef Museum*. There is an artists' colony, and it is also a centre for folk music. Outside the town is the *Kiskunság National Park* with the *Shepherd Museum* showing how animals and people lived in earlier times.
Szeged is the economic and cultural centre of this region. It is famed for its Festival of Opera, Drama and Ballet held in July and August. Here too is Hungary's finest Greek Orthodox (Serbian) church.
Baja is a small, picturesque town on the banks of both the Danube and Sugovica rivers. It has many small islands, some old churches and an artists' colony.

Southern Hungary

Pécs, the main town of this region, contains much architecture dating back to the Middle Ages. The area was also colonised by the Romans, and there are many archaeological sites and museums containing relics from this period; in addition, the Turkish conquest of Hungary during the 16th century has left Pécs, like so many other Hungarian cities, with many glorious examples of Ottoman architecture. Principal amongst these is the *Mosque of Pasha Hassan Yakovali*.
Mohács, on the Danube, was the site of the battle in 1526 at which the Turks gained control of Hungary. The battlefield has now been turned into a memorial park.
Kalocsa is a town of museums where many aspects of Hungarian folklore are preserved. South of Kalocsa is the *Forest of Gemenc*, a government-protected nature reserve and the home of many varieties of plant and animal life.

The Northern Highlands

Miskolc, Hungary's second biggest city, is situated near the Slovak border. Primarily industrial, the city has nevertheless several points of interest, including medieval architecture and the warren of man-made caves in the *Avas Hills* near the city centre. Nearby are the beautiful *Bükk Mountains*.

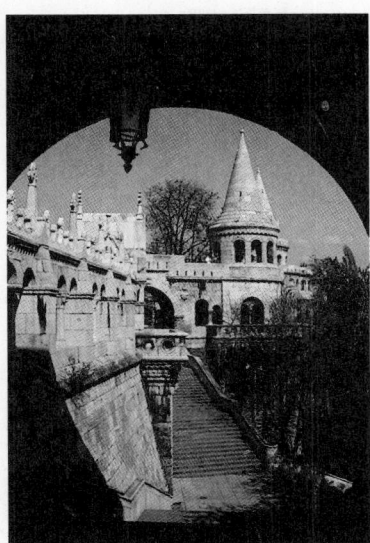

Eger, one of the country's oldest cities, has nearly 200 historical monuments, including the *Minaret*.
Due east of Miskolc is **Tokaj,** the centre of the most famous wine-producing region of the country. Halfway between Tokaj and the Slovak border is the spectacular castle of *Sárospatak*, one of Hungary's greatest historical monuments.

SOCIAL PROFILE

FOOD & DRINK: There is a good range of restaurants. Table service is common, although there are many inexpensive self-service restaurants. A typical menu offers two or three courses at inexpensive rates. Fine dairy and pastry shops *(cukrászda)* offer light meals. Specialities include *halászlé* (fish soups) with pasta and Goulash *gulyás* soup. Western goulash is called *pörkölt* or *tokány*. Stuffed vegetables, sweet cakes, *gundel palacsinta* (pancake) and pastries are also popular. **Drink:** *Eszpresszó* coffee bars and *Drink* bars offer refreshments. *Gerbeaud's* is probably Budapest's most famous coffee-house. *Tokaji* (strong dessert wine) or Bull's Blood (strong red wine) are recommended. *Pálinka* or *Barack* (apricot brandy) is a typical liqueur. Imported beers and soft drinks are also available. There are no licensing hours, but the legal age for drinking in a bar is 18 years. Minors are allowed to go into bars but will not be served alcohol.
NIGHTLIFE: Budapest has many nightclubs, bars and discos. There is a casino in the Budapest Hilton, and one on the river in front of the Forum. Cinemas in major towns show many English films. During summer months the popular Lake Balaton resort has a lively nightlife. Western Hungary in particular has a lot of very good wine cellars. Visitors would do well to search out traditional folk music and dancing, as the gypsy music which is so common in bars is not considered the 'true' folk tradition of the country. The magnificent Budapest Opera House stages regular performances, and seats are (by Western standards) exceedingly cheap.
SHOPPING: Special purchases include embroideries, Herend and Zsolnay porcelain, and national dolls. **Shopping hours:** 1000-1800 Monday to Friday, 1000-1300 Saturday. Food shops are open from 0700-1900 Monday to Friday and 0700-1400 Saturday.
SPORT: Details of **hunting** seasons and licences are available from: Mavad Uri Utca 39, Budapest I. Holidays for **horseriding** enthusiasts, including cross-country tours and a stay on a stud farm, are available from IBUSZ Hobby and Horseriding Dept, tel: (1) 118 2916; or Danube Travel in London. **Sailing and rowing** are available on Lake Balaton and the Danube. Details from IBUSZ. **Skiing** is popular in the Buda Hills, near Budapest, centred on Szabadsághegy. **Ice skating** is another popular winter sport, especially on Lake Balaton when the lake is frozen over in mid-winter.
SPECIAL EVENTS: The following is a selection of some of the major festivals and special events celebrated annually in Hungary. For a complete list, contact Danube Travel.
Mar *Budapest Spring Festival.* **Jun** *Hortobágy Equestrian Days.* **Jun-Jul** *Sopron Early Music Days.* **Jul** *Pécs Summer Theatre Festival; Szentendre Summer Festival; Debrecen Jazz Days.* **Aug** *Grand Prix; St Stephen's Day.* **Sep** *Budapest Arts Weeks and Contemporary Music Festival.*
There are also International Trade Fairs in May and September. The many music and folklore festivals normally take place from July to August.
SOCIAL CONVENTIONS: Most Hungarians enjoy modern music and dance, although older people still preserve their old traditions and culture, particularly in small villages. Handshaking is customary. Both Christian name and surname should be used. Normal courtesies should be observed. At a meal, toasts are usually made and should be returned. A useful word is *egészségünkre* (pronounced Ay-gash-ay-gun-gre), meaning 'your health'. Very few people speak English outside hotels and big restaurants and consequently they are unable to help visitors much. A knowledge of German is very useful. Gifts are acceptable for hosts as a token of thanks, particularly when invited for a meal. Casual wear is acceptable in most places, with the exception of expensive restaurants and bars. Formal attire should be worn for important social functions, but it is not common practice to specify dress on invitations. Smoking is prohibited on public transport in towns and public buildings. You may smoke on long-distance trains. **Photography:** Military installations should not be photographed; other restrictions will be signposted. **Tipping:** Not obligatory, although 10-15% is normal for most services.

BUSINESS PROFILE

ECONOMY: Before the political upheaval in Central and Eastern Europe during 1989, Hungary had gone furthest of all the socialist bloc countries in decentralising and deregulating the economy. Although this

If You Are In Budapest, Hungary . . .

H-1025 Budapest, Vérhalom u. 17
Tel: (00-36-1) 1150-287. Fax: (00-36-1) 1155-481.

Our Hotel is situated in the most beautiful part of the capital on Rose-Hill surrounded by a 2-hectare green park. Most of the rooms overlook the Danube. The hotel consists of 228 rooms. Each room has a bathroom and toilet and, as well as TV set, telephone, radio and minibar. There are 7 closed garages under the house and 56 parking places .

There is a large hall – with all required technical equipment – for conferences, meetings, receptions and three smaller rooms (each for 40 persons) for discussions, courses etc, at your disposal. On the fifth floor can be found the Pub and on the sixth the restaurant which offers you spectacular views of the town. On the ground floor there is a small souvenir shop and a bar with music. In our bar while listening to music and having fun you can enjoy the unique panoramic view of the capital.

Hotel Rózsadomb (Rose Hill) Is Waiting For You.

228 ROOMS WITH BATHROOM, TV, PHONE, MINI-BAR, SCENIC PANORAMIC VIEWS, BEAUTIFUL GARDENS, IDEAL PARKING FACILITIES, ARRANGING CONVENTION, TRAININGS, RECEPTIONS, RESTAURANTS, BAR, SEPERATE HALLS, MODERATE PRICES, 36 (100.DM) FOR TWO WITH BREAKFAST

A PART OF AMERICA IN THE HEART OF BUDAPEST

In the heart of the city, near the Houses of Parliament, you may find a little America when you call Getz Travel.

Experienced, well-trained English speaking staff will be delighted to look after your travel arrangements. Just call them and your ticket will be delivered to your office at no extra cost.

The Agency is using American Airlines' SABRE reservation system which is considered the best in the industry. Getz Travel is the fastest growing agency in Budapest serving the business community.

Getz International Travel Agency Ltd. 1055 Budapest, Falk Miksa utca 5

Tel: 1120-649. Fax: 1121-014

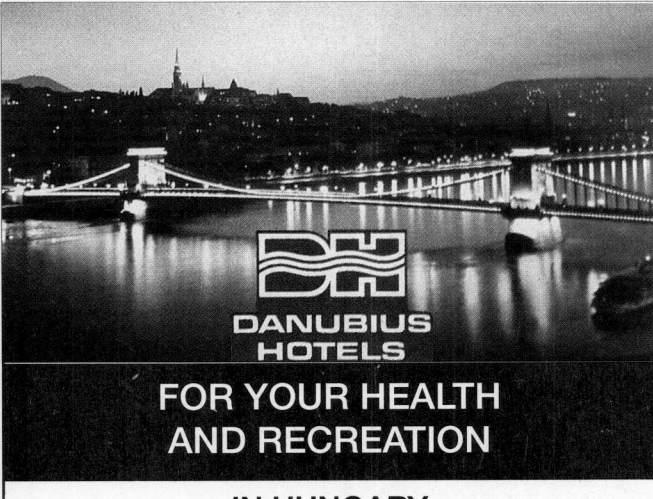

brought considerable dividends in the form of constant economic growth and ready availability of foodstuffs and consumer goods, it allowed the Government to build up a large overseas debt and stimulated unprecedented price inflation, which has steadily risen since the end of socialist government and now stands at around 35%. Hungary is poor in natural resources other than bauxite, natural gas, and some oil. For this reason, it relies especially heavily on foreign trade which, according to Government information, accounts for half of gross national product – an extraordinarily high proportion. Hungary has a fairly well-developed industrial economy concentrated in chemicals, plastics, pharmaceuticals, fertilisers, computers and telecommunications, mining, construction and aluminium (from the bauxite deposits). The country has also traditionally been an exporter of agricultural produce, particularly fruit and vegetables, maize and wheat, sugar beet, potatoes and livestock. The Government has earmarked this sector for attention in future economic development, with one eye on the future membership of the European Community. Hungary has eschewed the 'big bang' road to capitalism and opted for a more gradual transition to a market economy. Price controls have largely been removed and a programme of privatisation is under way, starting with the retail and property sectors. The private commercial sector and capital markets are developing steadily. Hungary has adopted a different approach to privatisation from its neighbours: while they have used voucher systems to transfer state assets directly to the population, Hungary is looking for 'real' owners – either indigenous enterprises, foreign companies or joint ventures – to take over the 2000 major industrial enterprises. The programme expects to have disposed of half of these by 1994. Before 1989, Hungary's trade patterns were dominated by barter exchange with the Soviet Union under which Soviet raw materials were exchanged for Hungarian manufactured goods. The CIS is still an important trading partner, but 35% of Hungarian trade is now with the European Community. Austria is also an important trading partner.

BUSINESS: Business people are expected to dress smartly. Local business people are generally friendly and hospitable and it is usual for visitors to be invited to lunch or dinner in a restaurant. Business cards are

widely distributed and visitors are well advised to have a supply available in Hungarian. Best months for business visits are September to May. Appointments should always be made. Interpreter and translation services may be booked through IBUSZ; contact the Danube Travel Agency in London for details (see above for address). **Office hours:** 0830-1700 Monday to Friday.

COMMERCIAL INFORMATION: The following organisation can offer advice: Magyar Gazdasági Kamara (Hungarian Chamber of Commerce), PO Box 106, H-1389 Budapest. Tel: (1) 153 3333. Fax: (1) 153 1285. Telex: 224745.

HISTORY & GOVERNMENT

HISTORY: During the 9th century, Finno-Ugriar nomads came into Hungary via South Russia, settling down in the latter half of the 10th century. The Arpád dynasty ruled until the end of the 13th century when Hungary was devastated by a Mongol invasion. Matthias Corvinus subsequently re-established Hungary as the leading power in Central Europe, also developing Magyar arts and literature. His successor, Laszló II, undid his work within a few years, and Hungary fell under Turkish sovereignty during the 16th century, re-establishing independence after the Thirty Years War. Hungary formed an alliance with Austria and was ruled by a Magyar aristocracy. It remained an essentially feudal state until 1914 (under monarchic and republican regimes), with an antiquated social system (by European standards) which was not fully dismantled until after the Second World War. Hungary sided with Nazi Germany during the War until 1944, when German troops occupied the country and the Hungarians sought to break the alliance. The Germans in turn were driven out by the Russians in January 1945. By 1949, Hungary had become a Soviet-style socialist state, a member of the Warsaw Pact and a People's Republic. The ruling Hungarian Socialist Workers' Party was riven by factional splits between pro-Soviet hardliners and the more liberally inclined group around Imre Nagy. The dispute came to a head in 1956 when hardliners led by Janos Kádár overthrew premier Imre Nagy with the support of Soviet army units. Despite its origins, the Hungarian regime had by the 1970s become the most liberal of all Soviet bloc systems. This was largely a result of the introduction in 1968 of the 'New Economic Mechanism' which allowed a significant role to be taken by private enterprise and the market in the Hungarian economy. Expressions of political opposition were not as ruthlessly suppressed as elsewhere in Eastern Europe. The HSWP nonetheless maintained a firm grip on the country's political and economic life. During the 1980s the political situation relaxed still further as Kádár's influence over the Government was gradually reduced. He was removed from the ruling Politburo in 1988 and Hungary began the transition to a pluralistic political system. When elections were held in two rounds in the spring of 1990, it was the relatively new opposition umbrella group, the centre-right Hungarian Democratic Forum, which took 165 seats in the new 386-seat assembly followed by the Alliance of Free Democrats, the Smallholders' Party and the Socialist Party (the restyled HSWP). The Hungarian Democratic Forum leads a coalition government with József Antall as Hungary's new Prime Minister. Hungary's transition to a market economy has been rather easier than that of its central European neighbours. Closer links with the EC – including hoped-for associate membership – are a key aspect of Hungarian foreign policy, which is otherwise geared to growing concerns about regional instability. The Hungarian government is concerned not to antagonise Serbia because of the large ethnic Hungarian minority (numbering around 400,000) in the quasi-autonomous region of Vojvodina. Similar considerations govern Hungary's relations with Romania where 1.7 million Hungarians live, mostly in Transylvania, and its attitude on the break-up of Czechoslovakia (10% of the Slovak Republic's population is Hungarian). There is also a large Hungarian community in the Ukraine. In total, 25% of all Hungarians live outside their mother country.

GOVERNMENT: Legislative power is held by the 386-seat National Assembly which is elected for four years. The Council of Ministers, the highest executive organ, is elected by the Assembly on the advice of the President. The President is also elected by the National Assembly for a 4-year term, and may serve two terms.

CLIMATE

There are four seasons, with a very warm summer from June to August. Spring and autumn are mild, while winters are very cold. Rainfall is distributed throughout the year with snowfalls in winter.

Required clothing: Lightweights are worn in summer and warmer clothes in spring and autumn. Medium to heavyweights are worn during winter. Waterproofing is advisable throughout the year.

BUDAPEST Hungary (120m)

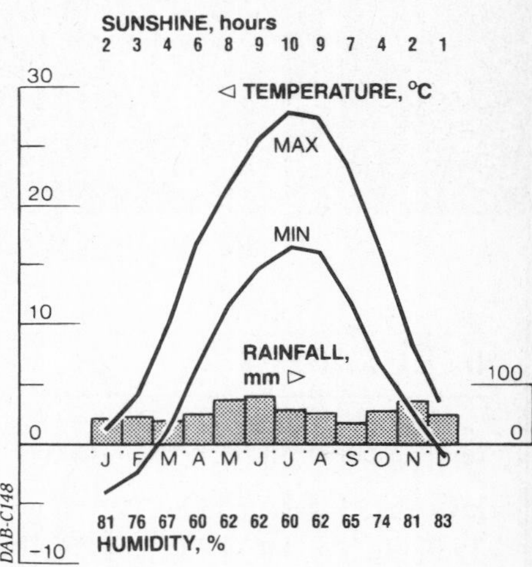

TEMPERATURE CONVERSIONS
-20 -10 0°C 10 20 30 40
0 10 20 30°F40 50 60 70 80 90 100
RAINFALL CONVERSIONS 0mm 200 400 600 800
0in 5 10 15 20 25 30

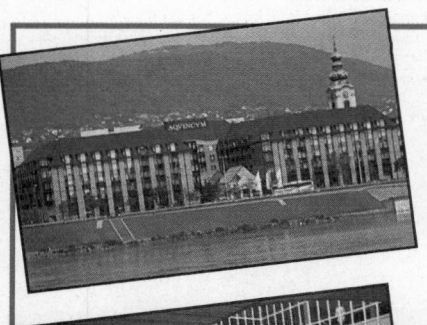

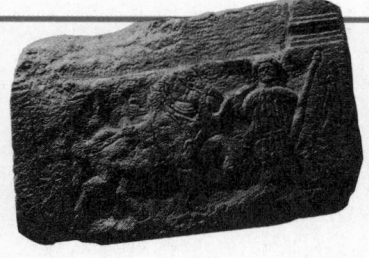

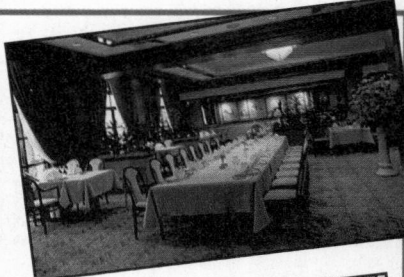

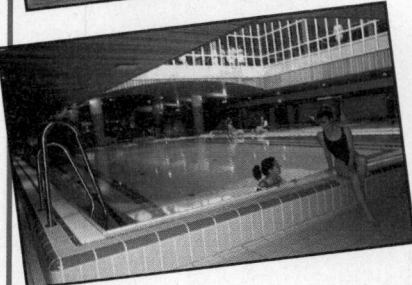

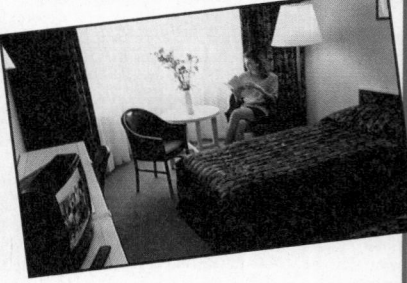

ICELAND

Location: North Atlantic, close to Arctic circle.

Iceland Tourist Board
Gimli Lækjargata 3
101 Reykjavík
Iceland
Tel: (1) 27488. Fax: (1) 624 749. Telex: 27488.

Embassy of the Republic of Iceland
1 Eaton Terrace
London
SW1W 8EY
Tel: (071) 730 5131/2. Fax: (071) 730 1683. Telex: 918226. Opening hours: 0900-1600 Monday to Friday.

Iceland Tourist Bureau/Iceland Air
172 Tottenham Court Road
London
W1P 9LG
Tel: (071) 388 5346. Fax: (071) 387 5711. Telex: 23689. Opening hours: 0900-1700 Monday to Friday.

British Embassy
PO Box 460
Laufásvegur 49
121 Reykjavík
Iceland
Tel: (1) 15883/4. Fax: (1) 27940. Telex: 2037 UKREYK IS.

British Vice-Consulate
Glerargata 26
Akureyri
Iceland
Tel: (6) 21165.

Embassy of the Republic of Iceland
2022 Connecticut Avenue, NW
Washington, DC
20008
Tel: (202) 265 6653/4/5. Fax: (202) 265 6656.
Consulates in: Atlanta, Bayamon (Puerto Rico), Boston, Chicago, Dallas, Detroit, Harrisburg, Houston, Dallas, Los Angeles, Miami, Minneapolis, New York (tel: (212) 686 4100), Portland, San Francisco, Seattle and Tallahassee.

Iceland Tourist Board
655 Third Avenue
New York, NY
10017
Tel: (212) 949 2333.

Embassy of the United States of America
PO Box 40
Laufásvegur 21
Reyjkavík, Iceland
Tel: (1) 29100. Fax: (1) 29139. Telex: 3044.

Consulate General of the Republic of Iceland
Suite 700
116 Lisgar Street
Ottawa, Ontario
K2P 0C2
Tel: (613) 238 5064 *or* 238 7412.
Consulates in: Calgary, Edmonton, Halifax, Montréal, Regina, St John's, Toronto, Vancouver and Winnipeg.

Consulate General of Canada
PO Box 8094
Sudurlandsbraut 10
108 Reykjavík, Iceland
Tel: (1) 680 820. Telex: 94014879.

AREA: 103,000 sq km (39,769 sq miles).
POPULATION: 255,708 (1990 estimate).
POPULATION DENSITY: 2.5 per sq km.
CAPITAL: Reykjavík. **Population:** 97,569 (1990 estimate).
GEOGRAPHY: Iceland is a large island in the North Atlantic close to the Arctic Circle and includes islands to the north and south. The landscape is wild, rugged and colourful with black lava, red sulphur, hot blue geysers, grey and white rivers with waterfalls and green valleys. Iceland's coastline is richly indented with bays and fjords, and its varied and dramatically rugged land has a total surface area of slightly under 104,000 sq km (40,000 sq miles). The whole of the central highland plateau of the island is a beautiful but barren and uninhabitable moonscape; so much so that the first American astronauts were sent there for pre-mission training. Five-sixths of the area of Iceland is uninhabited, the population being concentrated on the coast, in the valleys and in the plains of the south-west and southeast of the country. More than half the population live in or around Reykjavík, the capital. Iceland is one of the most active volcanic countries in the world. Hekla, in the south of Iceland, is the most famous and magnificent volcano of them all. It has erupted no fewer than 16 times since Iceland was settled, and throughout the Middle Ages was considered by European clergymen as one of the gateways to Hell itself. Another volcano, Snæfellsnes, fired Jules Verne's imagination to use its crater as the point of entry for his epic tale *Journey to the Centre of the Earth.* Iceland's highest and most extensive glacier is Vatnajokull at 8500 sq km (3300 sq miles), the largest in Europe.
LANGUAGE: The official language is Icelandic. English (which is taught in schools) and Danish are widely spoken.
RELIGION: Lutheran, with a Catholic minority.
TIME: GMT.
ELECTRICITY: 220 volts AC, 50Hz. Plug fittings are normally 2-pin with round section pins 4mm in diameter with centres 2cm apart. Lamp fittings are screw-type. Almost all the power is generated by thermal hydro-electric stations.
COMMUNICATIONS: Telephone: Full IDD service is available. Country code: 354. International calls can be made from public phones, which are found in the main towns. **Fax:** Public facilities are available at the main telephone headquarters in Austurvoll Square and in most hotels and offices. **Telex/telegram:** Telexes can be sent from post offices as well as from some major hotels and the telecommunications centre in Austurvoll Square (open daily). There is a 24-hour telegram service from the Telegraph Office in Reykjavík. **Post:** There is an efficient airmail service to Europe. Post offices are open 0830-1630 Monday to Friday. The post office in the Central Bus Station is open until 1930 on weekdays and on Saturdays from 0800-1500. **Press:** The most popular newspapers are *Morgunbladid, DV* and *Tíminn.* There are no English-language dailies printed in Iceland, but an English-language magazine, *News from Iceland,* is available.
BBC World Service and Voice of America frequencies: From time to time these change. See the section *How to Use this Book* for more information.

BBC:				
MHz	12.10	9.410	6.195	3.955
Voice of America:				
MHz	11.97	9.670	6.040	5.995

PASSPORT/VISA

Regulations and requirements may be subject to change at short notice, and you are advised to contact the appropriate diplomatic or consular authority before finalising travel arrangements. Details of these may be found at the head of this country's entry. Any numbers in the chart refer to the footnotes below.

	Passport Required?	Visa Required?	Return Ticket Required?
Full British	1	No	Yes
BVP	Valid	No	Yes
Australian	Yes	No	Yes
Canadian	Yes	No	Yes
USA	Yes	No	Yes
Other EC	1	No	Yes
Japanese	Yes	No	Yes

PASSPORTS: **[1]** Valid passport required by all except:
(a) nationals of the UK in possession of a valid BVP;
(b) nationals of Denmark, Finland, Iceland, Norway and Sweden travelling between those countries;
(c) nationals of Austria, Belgium, France, Germany, Italy, Liechtenstein, Luxembourg, The Netherlands and Switzerland provided travelling as tourists and holding a valid national ID card.
British Visitors Passport: Acceptable. A BVP is valid for holidays or unpaid business trips to Iceland for a period not exceeding 3 months. Trips to Iceland, Denmark, Norway, Sweden or Finland must add up to less than 3 months in any 9-month period.
VISAS: Required by all except:
(a) nationals of countries referred to on the chart above;
(b) nationals of Scandinavian countries;
(c) nationals of Anguilla, Antigua & Barbuda, Austria, Bahamas, Barbados, Belize, Bermuda, Botswana, Brazil, Brunei, Cayman Islands, Chile, Cyprus, Czechoslovakia, Dominica, Falkland Islands, Fiji, Gambia, Gibraltar, Grenada, Guyana, Hong Kong, Hungary, Israel, Jamaica, Kiribati, South Korea, Lesotho, Liechtenstein, Malawi, Malaysia, Malta, Mexico, Mauritius, Monaco, Montserrat, New Zealand, Romania, St Helena, St Kitts & Nevis, St Lucia, St Vincent & the Grenadines, San Marino, Seychelles, Singapore, Solomon Islands, Swaziland, Switzerland, Tanzania, Trinidad & Tobago, Turks & Caicos Islands, Tuvalu, British Virgin Islands, Uruguay, Vanuatu, Vatican City and Yugoslavia, for a stay of up to 3 months.
Types of visa: Entry; cost £10.
Validity: Up to 3 months. For extensions apply to nearest police authority in Iceland.
Application to: Consulate (or Consular Section at Embassy). For addresses, see top of entry.
Application requirements: (a) Completed visa application form. (b) 2 photos. (c) Valid passport. (d) Return or onward ticket to a country to which the applicant has a legal right of entry. (e) For

ICELAND | **HEALTH REGULATIONS** | **VISA REGULATIONS** | Code-Link

GALILEO/WORLDSPAN

TI-DFT/REK/HE

TI-DFT/REK/VI

SABRE

TIDFT/REK/HE

TIDFT/REK/VI

To access this information on your CRS, swipe the barcode with a light pen or type in the text under the barcode. For more information, see the introduction *How to Use This Book.*

postal applications, a stamped self-addressed envelope.
Working days required: Minimum 5 days by post or personal visit.
Temporary residence: Enquire at Icelandic Embassy.

MONEY

Currency: Iceland Krona (IKr) = 100 aurar. Notes are in denominations of IKr5000, 1000, 500 and 100. Coins are in denominations of IKr50, 10, 5 and 1, and 50 and 10 aurar.
Credit cards: Visa, Access/Mastercard, Diners Club and American Express are widely accepted. Check with your credit card company for details of merchant acceptability and other services which may be available.
Travellers cheques: Widely used.
Exchange rate indicators: The following figures are included as a guide to the movements of the Krona against Sterling and the US Dollar:

Date:	Oct '89	Oct '90	Oct '91	Oct '92
£1.00=	97.60	107.70	103.3	91.45
$1.00=	61.81	55.13	59.52	57.63

Currency restrictions: There is no limit to the import of foreign and local currency. The export of local currency is limited to IKr17,000. The export of foreign currency is limited to the amount imported.
Banking hours: 0915-1600 Monday to Friday.

DUTY FREE

The following goods may be imported into Iceland by passengers over 16 years of age without incurring customs duty:
200 cigarettes or 250g of tobacco;
*1 litre of spirits and 1 litre of wine (under 21% proof) or 1 litre of spirits and 6 litres of beer (8 litres of Icelandic beer);**
Imported food to the retail value of IKr4000 or to 3kg.
Note: All fishing equipment must be disinfected and a veterinary certificate obtained within seven days of arrival. [*] Only for passengers of 20 years of age and over.
Prohibited items: Drugs, firearms and uncooked meats.

PUBLIC HOLIDAYS

Public holidays observed in Iceland are as follows:
Apr 2 '93 First Day of Summer. **Apr 8** Maundy Thursday. **Apr 9** Good Friday. **Apr 11** Easter Sunday. **Apr 12** Easter Monday. **May 1** Labour Day. **May 20** Ascension. **May 30** Whit Sunday. **May 31** Whit Monday. **Jun 17** National Day. **Aug 2** Workers' Holiday. **Dec 24** Christmas Eve (half day). **Dec 25** Christmas Day. **Dec 26** Boxing Day. **Dec 31** New Year's Eve (half day). **Jan 1 '94** New Year's Day.

HEALTH

Regulations and requirements may be subject to change at short notice, and you are advised to contact your doctor well in advance of your intended date of departure. Any numbers in the chart refer to the footnotes below.

	Special Precautions?	Certificate Required?
Yellow Fever	No	No
Cholera	No	No
Typhoid & Polio	No	-
Malaria	No	-
Food & Drink	No	-

Health care: All hospitals have excellent standards of medical service. There is a Reciprocal Health Agreement with the UK. On presentation of a UK passport or NHS card, all in-patient treatment at hospitals and emergency dental treatment for children aged 6-15 is free. Other medical and dental treatment, prescribed medicines, and travel by ambulance must be paid for.

TRAVEL - InternationaL

AIR: The national airline is *Icelandair (FI)*.
Approximate flight times: From Iceland to *London* is 2 hours 50 minutes and to *Glasgow* is 2 hours 10 minutes.
International airport: *Keflavik (REK)*, 45km (28 miles) southwest of Reykjavík (travel time – 45 minutes). Airport facilities include bus services, departing after the arrival of each flight; taxi services; a duty-free shop selling a wide range of goods, including Icelandic handmade items such as sweaters; banking and

exchange facilities, open on arrival of all scheduled services; restaurants and bars open 0700-2300 and car hire (*Icelandair*) offices. (For further details on car hire, see the *Road* section below.)
There are international flights from major European and North American destinations, although some of these operate only seasonally. Flights are operated to the Faroe Islands and Greenland during the summer months. For further details, contact *Icelandair*.
SEA: The *Smyril Line* of Torshaven in the Faroe Islands operates a weekly passenger and car ferry service in summer from the Faroe Islands to Seydisfjordur on the east coast of Iceland, to Lerwick in the Shetlands, to Bergen, Norway and to Hanstholm, Denmark. There is a *P&O* ferry service from Iceland to the Shetlands and an overnight stay there may be necessary. Full details are available from *Regent Holidays* (tel: (0272) 211 711).

TRAVEL - Internal

AIR: *Icelandair (FI)* runs domestic services throughout the island to ten major destinations which link with regional carriers in the west, north and east of the country. There are 12 local airports. *Icelandair* also offers a variety of special air packages for the internal traveller. These include *Air Rover*, *Air/Bus Rover* and *Fly as you please*. For further details contact the local office.
SEA: Ferry services serve all coastal ports in summer, although weather curtails timetables in winter. There is a regular passenger/car ferry service between Reykjavik and Akranes.
RAIL: There is no railway system in Iceland.
ROAD: Roads serve all settlements. The 12,000km (7500 miles) of roads are mostly gravel rather than tarred. **Bus:** Services are efficient and cheap, connecting all parts of the island during the summer. In winter, buses operate to a limited number of destinations. Holiday tickets (*Omnibus Passport*) and *Air/Bus Rovers* are valid for unlimited travel by scheduled bus services; also *Full-Circle Passports* are available, valid for circular trips around Iceland (without any time limit). **Taxi:** Available from all hotels and airports. **Car hire:** Car rental services are available from Reykjavík, Akureyri and many other towns. **Note:** Drivers who are used to reliable, well-surfaced roads and regular road markings should think twice before hiring self-drive cars in Iceland, particularly if they are going to be driving away from the main centres.
Documentation: Drivers must be over 20 years of age. An International Driving Permit is recommended, although it is not legally required. A temporary licence to drive is available from local authorities on presentation of a valid British or Northern Ireland driving licence.
JOURNEY TIMES: The following chart gives approximate journey times (in hours and minutes) from Reykjavík to other major cities/towns in Iceland.

	Air	Road	Sea
Isafjordur	0.50	10.00	-
Saudakrokur	0.45	4.30	-
Akureyri	0.55	6.00	-
Husavik	1.00	7.00	-
Höfn	0.65	9.30	-
Westman Is.	0.30	*1.00	6.00
Egilsstadir	0.70	14.00	-

Note [*]: To Thorlakshofn, then sea crossing.

ACCOMMODATION

HOTELS: These are not classified but most have rooms with private bathroom or shower, telephone, radio and TV on request. The more expensive ones also have hairdressers, shops and beauty parlours. Hotel or hostel accommodation is available in most areas (other than the interior, which is largely uninhabited). A brochure is obtainable from the Icelandic Hotel and Restaurant Association, Gardastraeti 42, 101 Reykjavík. Tel: (1) 27410 *or* 621410. Fax: (1) 27478.
PENSIONS & GUEST-HOUSES: These are available in the larger towns. Rooms are also available in private houses with breakfast included in the cost.
FARMHOUSE HOLIDAYS: Fairly widely available; contact the Iceland Tourist Bureau for details. Full board (three meals daily) is included. Reductions are available for children.
CAMPING/CARAVANNING: The inhospitable interior and unpredictable weather do not lend themselves to favourable camping conditions. The best method is to exploit the interior using the coastal ports as a base rather than camping outside the towns. The best-equipped camping grounds are to be found in Reykjavík, Husafell, Isafjordur, Varmahlid, Akureyri, Myvatn, Eglisstadir, Laugarvatn, Thingvellire, Jokulsargljufur and Skaftafell. In some places camping is restricted to certain specially marked areas, while elsewhere camping is generally free. Campers, however, must request permission from the local farmer to camp on any fenced and/or cultivated land.
YOUTH HOSTELS: Youth hostels are open in Reykjavík, Leirubakki, Fljotsdalur, Vestmannaeyjar, Reynisbrekka, Hofn in Hornafjordur, Stafafell, Berunes, Seydisfjordur, Husey, Akureyri, Blonduos, Isafjordur and Breidavik. Many country hostels provide overnight accommodation for travellers bringing their own sleeping bags or bedrolls for a fee. In uninhabited areas there are a number of huts, owned by the touring club of Iceland, where travellers can stay overnight. They must observe regulations posted in the huts and bring their own sleeping bags and food. Groups travelling with the club always have priority over others. For more information, contact the Icelandic Youth Hostel Association, Laufásvegur 41, Reykjavík. Tel: (1) 38110.

RESORTS & EXCURSIONS

Only the coastal regions of Iceland are inhabited. Probably the best way to enjoy the tourist attractions is to take one of the coach tours which are arranged all over the island and use the coastal towns as a base. The main fjord areas are in the far northwest and southeast while along the southern coastline are sandy beaches, farmlands, waterfalls and glaciers. The central region consists of spectacular highland plateaux, volcanoes, glaciers and mountains. Waterfalls abound in Iceland and, with the many glacial streams and rivers in the country, some are the largest in Europe. *Gullfoss* – the 'Golden Waterfall' – near **Geysir**, is always a favourite visit for tourists.
Reykjavík and the South: Reykjavík is the world's most northerly capital (although Nuuk in Greenland runs a close second). It is set on a broad bay, surrounded by mountains, and is in an area of geothermal hot springs providing it with a natural central heating system and pollution-free environment. It is a busy city of around 90,000 inhabitants and has a combination of old-fashioned wooden architecture and very modern buildings. There are nightclubs, art galleries and museums. Flights can be booked to visit the **Westman Islands** off the south coast, and **Heimay**, where a recent volcanic eruption partially destroyed the town. Also there are trips to the hot springs and geysers of the area. *Reykjavík Excursions* operate daily excursions from the capital throughout the southwest part of Iceland as well as city sightseeing tours and special itineraries.
The Western Fjords: There are coach trips from Reykjavík to visit the small fishing villages and towns along the fjord in the northwest: **Kroksfardarnes, Holmavik, Korksfjaroarnes, Orlygshofn** and **Isafjordur.** The road climbs over mountain passes between each new fjord, stopping at Iceland's only whaling station, the *Museum of Farm Implements and Fishing Equipment* between Orlygshofn and Isafjordur and the *Dynjandi Waterfall*. Accommodation on these trips is in community centres and schools for those with sleeping bags. (For further information, contact Isafjordur Tourist Office. Tel: (4) 3557 *or* 3457.)
The Central Highlands: A number of Icelandic tour companies operate 'Safaris' in specially constructed overland buses into the mountainous interior. These are camping tours, and tents are provided. Sleeping bags can be bought or rented. Also recommended are warm clothing, hiking shoes, rubber boots and swim suits for bathing in the warm pools. The tours go through lava beds, sandy deserts and rivers, passing

glacial lakes with floating icebergs, glaciers, vast ice-fields, mountain ranges, crevasses and extinct volcanoes, and the *Skaftafell National Park*.
Akureyri and the North: Akureyri is the country's second most important town and is the commercial centre of a mainly agricultural region. There are museums of folklore and natural history in the town itself and coach tours to visit *Lake Myvatn*, an important bird sanctuary with many rare species, surrounded by lava formations, volcanoes and craters. *Nordair* offers a midnight sun trip flight to **Grimsey**, an offshore island which is within the Arctic Circle. Other places within easy reach of Akureyri include **Dimmuborgir,** the *Dettifoss* and *Godafoss* waterfalls and the *Myvatn* district, where there are hot pools for bathing. The temperature of some of these pools has risen recently making them uncomfortable for bathing, but others are still usable.
Höfn and the Southeast: This is an area of increasing tourist development. From Hofn, a fishing village on the southeast coast, sightseeing trips leave for *Jokullon*, a river lake at the mouth of the largest glacier in Europe, *Vatnajokull*. A journey over the glacier in a heated snowmobile is possible. Hofn also has horseriding facilities.

SOCIAL PROFILE

FOOD & DRINK: Icelandic food in general is based on fish and lamb, as well as owing much to Scandinavian and European influences. The salmon of Iceland is a great delicacy, served in many forms, one of the most popular being *graflax*, a form of marination. Fishing is Iceland's most important export, accounting for some 80% of the country's gross national product. There is also a heavy emphasis on vegetables grown in greenhouses heated by the natural steam from geysers. Specialities include *hangikjot* (smoked lamb), *hardfiskur* (dried fish), *skyr* (curds) and Icelandic *sild* (herring and salmon). There have been some welcome additions to the selection of eating places in Reykjavík and there is now a small but attractive choice of restaurants to cater for all pockets with new tourist menus. **Drink:** Bars have table and/or counter service, and will serve coffee as well as alcohol. In coffee shops you pay for the first cup; you help yourself to subsequent cups. There is a wide selection of European spirits and wines but no alcoholic beer on sale in Iceland. *Brennivin* (a potent variation of aquavit made from potatoes) is a local drink.
NIGHTLIFE: Nightclubs and cinemas exist in major centres. Leading theatres are the National Theatre and the Reykjavík Idno Theatre, closed in summer, but during the tourist season there is an attractive light entertainment show in English called 'Light Nights' with traditional Icelandic stories and folk songs. The Iceland Symphony Orchestra gives concerts every two weeks at the University Theatre during the season September to June.
SHOPPING: Fluffy, earth-coloured *Lopi* wool blankets and coats, jackets, hats and handknits are synonymous with Iceland. Several local potters handthrow earthenware containers in natural colours. Crushed lava is a common addition to highly glazed ceramic pieces which are popular as souvenirs. The duty-free shop at Keflavik Airport sells all of these products, as does the Iceland Tourist Bureau souvenir shop in Reyjkavík. **Shopping hours:** 0900-1800 Monday to Friday and 0900-1300/1600 Saturday.
SPORT: Ornithology: Lake Myvatn in northern Iceland is apparently the most fertile spot on the globe at that latitude and is a favourite breeding ground for many species of birdlife, particularly waterfowl. **Fishing:** The salmon fishing in Iceland is widely regarded as being among the best in world. Trout and charr may also be caught. There are many opportunities for **walking holidays** and **natural history tours;** enquire at the Tourist Bureau. **Pony trekking** holidays rely on the services of the sure-footed Icelandic horse, a descendant of the original Viking horse brought over from Norway over 1100 years ago. **Swimming** is very popular in Iceland – surprisingly mostly outdoors – since there are many natural and man-made pools, heated by geothermal springs, a natural phenomenon common in Iceland. In fact the word 'geyser' was derived from the Icelandic word *Geysir*, which is the name of Iceland's famous spouting hot spring in the southwest of the country. The main spectator sports are **soccer, handball, basketball** and **field athletics.**
SPECIAL EVENTS: The following is a selection of the major festivals and special events celebrated in Iceland during 1993/4. For a complete list, contact the Iceland Tourist Bureau.
Mar 3-28 '93 *Art from the Faroe Islands*, Reykjavík. **Mar 17-20** *The Nordic Film Festival*, Reykjavík. **Apr 24-Jun 6** *Borealis VI* (art exhibition), Reykjavík. **Jun-Aug** *Icelandic Summer Exhibitions*, Reykjavík. **Jun 4-31** *Hafnarfjöröur Art Festival*, Hafnarfjöröur. **Jun 6** *Seafarer's Day*, Reykjavík and all Icelandic fishing ports. **Jun 17** *National Day*, Nationwide celebrations with parades, competitions and entertainment. **Jun 18-Aug 30** *Light Nights* (theatre presentations on Icelandic sagas and legends in English), Reykjavík. **Jul 30-Aug 2** *Westman Island Festival*. **Aug 15** *Hólahátio Celebrations*, Hjaltadal. **Aug 28-Oct 3** *The Nordic House's Anniversay Exhibition*, Reykjavík. **Sep** *Annual Sheep and Horse Round-up*.
SOCIAL CONVENTIONS: Visitors will find Iceland is a classless society with a strong literary tradition. Handshaking is the normal form of greeting. An Icelander is called by his first name because his surname is made up of his father's christian name plus 'son' or 'daughter' (eg John, the son of Magnus, would be called John Magnusson, while John's sister, Mary, would be known as Mary Magnusdottír). People are addressed as *Fru* (Mrs); and *Herra* (Mr). Visitors will often be invited to homes especially if on business and normal courtesies should be observed. Icelanders pay careful attention to their appearance and, as for most Western countries, casual wear is widely acceptable although unsuitable for smart and social functions. **Tipping:** Service charges are included in most bills and extra tips are not expected.

BUSINESS PROFILE

ECONOMY: Iceland is short of indigenous raw materials and thus relies heavily on foreign trade to keep its relatively successful economy ticking over. Exports of goods and services account for over one-third of gross national product. The largest proportion of these derive from fisheries and related products such as fishmeal and oil. The economy is thus particularly susceptible to fluctuating world prices in this commodity and maintains a broad fisheries exclusion zone (200 miles) to protect its earnings. Other sources of revenue come from sale of minerals such as aluminium, ferro-silicon, cement and nitrates used in fertilisers. Light industry is developing steadily and producing knitwear, blankets, textiles and paint. The major problem in the economy of recent years has been the fall-out from the wholesale liberalisation of trade with the European Community and the European Free Trade Association, the grouping of non-EC European countries of which Iceland is a member, which left some local companies unable to compete in some products such as furniture and household goods. The EC and EFTA agreed the creation of a free-trade zone, the European Economic Area, in October 1991. Iceland's principal import suppliers are, in order of importance, Germany, Denmark, Norway and Britain. Britain, the USA and Germany are the country's main export markets.
BUSINESS: Business people are expected to dress smartly. Local business people are conservative but very friendly and most speak English. Previous appointments are not generally necessary, but visits between May and September should be planned in advance as many local business people travel abroad at this time. The telephone directory is listed by Christian name. **Office hours:** 0900-1700 Monday to Friday. Most offices are closed on Saturday. Some firms close down completely for an annual 3-week holiday; this is usually in July.
COMMERCIAL INFORMATION: The following organisation can offer advice: Verzlunarrád Islands (Chamber of Commerce), Hús verslunarinnar (House of Commerce), 103 Reykjavík. Tel: (1) 83088. Fax: (1) 686 564. Telex: 2316.
CONFERENCES/CONVENTIONS: There are several large hotels in Reykjavík equipped for conferences and business meetings, while smaller conferences may be held at venues outside the capital. The Iceland Tourist Bureau can organise events; there are also private contractors. For more information contact the Tourist Bureau direct.

HISTORY & GOVERNMENT

HISTORY: Settled by the Norse seafarers in the 9th century, Iceland subsequently became part of the Danish territory. The origins of democracy in Iceland may be found at Thingvellir, about an hour's drive from Reykjavík, where the original Viking settlers turned a cliff wall into a natural amphitheatre. This makes the Icelandic parliament the oldest still surviving in the world. The island was granted its own constitution in the 1840s and in 1918 it achieved self-government. Iceland became an independent republic in 1944. Icelandic politics display the customary western European spectrum of political parties, although a notable feature is the influence of women, both within the main parties (Independents, Progressives, Social Democrats) and in their own right through the Women's Alliance, which currently holds six of the 63 seats in the Althing. Iceland also boasts a woman President, Vigdís Finbogadóttir, who has been elected for three consecutive terms since 1980. Coalitions have been the order of the day in the Althing without exception since 1959. These were of a broadly centre-right persuasion until the mid-1970s, since when the left has dominated. At the general election in April 1991, the Independence Party emerged as the largest grouping in the Althing with 26 seats and formed a coalition administration with the 10-seat SDP. Icelandic foreign policy is dominated by two factors: fishing and relations with the Atlantic powers. Iceland is a member of NATO, the Nordic Council and of the Council of Europe. It has, however, historically eschewed membership of the European Community, partly because of its Scandanavian links and partly because of its fisheries policy, which clashes with the EC regime of stock management by quotas. Iceland did, however, join the European Free Trade Area (EFTA) in 1970, and hence the European Economic Area, the alliance of the EC and EFTA. On the issue of whaling, Iceland has been among those objecting to the International Whaling Commission's ban: in 1992, the Government withdrew from the IWC.
GOVERNMENT: Executive power is vested in the President and government, while legislative authority is in the President and Althing (parliament) jointly.

CLIMATE

Iceland's climate is tempered by the Gulf Stream. Summers are mild and winters rather cold. The colourful *Aurora Borealis* (Northern Lights) appear from the end of August. From the end of May to the beginning of August, there are nearly 24 hours of perpetual daylight in Reykjavík, while in the northern part of the country the sun barely sets at all. Winds can be strong and gusty at times and there is the occasional dust storm in the interior. Snow is not as common as the name of the country would seem to suggest, and in any case does not lie for long in Reykjavík; it is only in north Iceland that skiing conditions are reasonably certain. However, the weather is very changeable at all times of the year, and in Reykjavík there may be rain, sunshine, drizzle and snow in the same day. As a popular Icelandic saying has it: 'Iceland doesn't have a climate – only weather.' However, one thing is certain at all times of year: the air is clean and pollution-free, with no smog.
Required clothing: Lightweights in warmer months, with extra woollens for walking and the cooler evenings. Medium- to heavy-weights are advised in winter. Waterproofing is recommended throughout the year.

REYKJAVIK Iceland (18m)

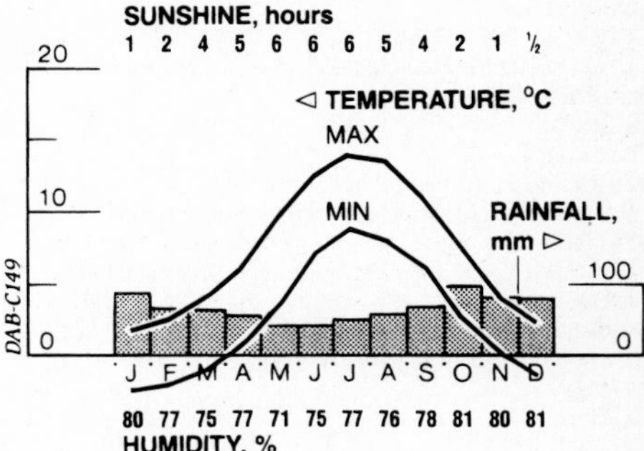

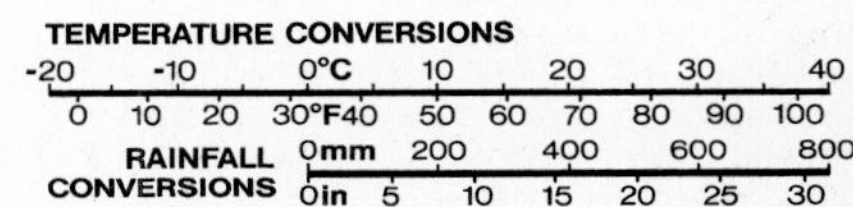

INDIA

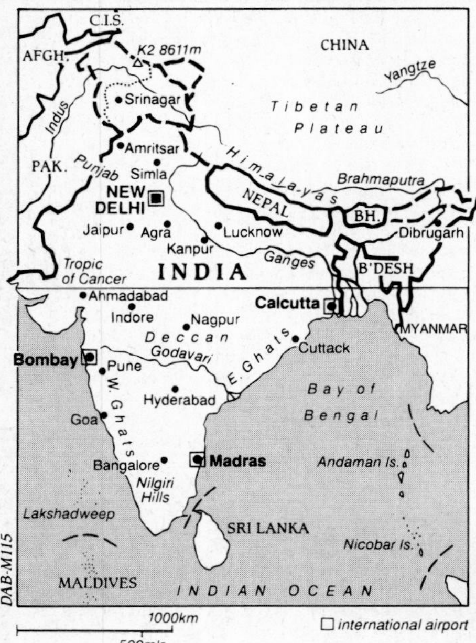

Location: Indian sub-continent.

Department of Tourism of the Government of India
Ministry of Civil Aviation and Tourism
Transport Bhavan
1 Parliament Street
New Delhi 110 001, India
Tel: (11) 371 17890 *or* (11) 371 4114. Fax: (11) 371 0518. Telex: 3166527.
Office of the High Commissioner for India
India House
Aldwych
London WC2B 4NA
Tel: (071) 836 8484. Fax: (071) 836 4331. Telex: 263581.
Visas: Tel: (071) 240 2084 *or* (071) 836 0990. Opening hours: 0930-1300 and 1400-1730 Monday to Friday (0930-1300 for visa application, and 1630-1730 for collection).
Government of India Tourist Office
7 Cork Street
London W1X 1PB
Tel: (071) 437 3677. Fax: (071) 494 1048.
Opening hours: 0930-1300 and 1400-1800 Monday to Friday.
British Embassy
Shanti Path
Chanakyapuri
New Delhi 110 021, India
Tel: (11) 600 651. Fax: (11) 687 2028. Telex: 03182065.
British High Commission
Shanti Path
Chanakyapuri
New Delhi 211 100, India
Tel: (11) 601 371. Fax: (11) 609 940. Telex: 3165125 BHC IN.
Deputy High Commissions in: Bombay, Calcutta and Madras.
Embassy of India
2107 Massachusetts Avenue, NW
Washington, DC
20008
Tel: (202) 939 7000. Fax: (202) 939 7027.
Government of India Tourist Office
Room 1530, Rockefeller Plaza
North Mezzanine
New York, NY
10112
Tel: (212) 586 4901/2/3. Fax: (212) 582 3274.
Embassy of the United States of America
Shanti Path
Chanakyapuri
New Delhi 110 021, India
Tel: (11) 600 651. Fax: (11) 687 2028 *or* 687 2391.
Telex: 3165269.
Consulates in: Bombay, Calcutta and Madras.
High Commission for India
10 Springfield Road
Ottawa, Ontario
K1M 1C9
Tel: (613) 744 3751/2/3. Fax: (613) 744 0913. Telex: 0534172.
Consulates in: Toronto and Vancouver.
India Government Tourist Office
Suite 1003
60 Bloor Street West
Toronto, Ontario
M4W 3B8
Tel: (416) 962 3787/8. Fax: (416) 962 6279.
Canadian High Commission
PO Box 5207
7/8 Shantipath
Chanakyapuri
New Delhi 110 021, India
Tel: (11) 687 6500. Fax: (11) 687 6579. Telex: 03172363.
Consulate in Bombay.

AREA: 3,287,262 sq km (1,269,218 sq miles).
POPULATION: 843,930,861 (1991).
POPULATION DENSITY: 256.7 per sq km.
CAPITAL: New Delhi. **Population:** 8,375,188 (1991).
GEOGRAPHY: India shares borders to the northwest with Pakistan, to the north with China, Nepal and Bhutan, and to the east with Bangladesh and Myanmar. To the west lies the Arabian sea, to the east the Bay of Bengal and to the south the Indian Ocean. Sri Lanka lies off the southeast coast, and the Maldives off the southwest coast. The far northeastern states and territories are all but separated from the rest of India by Bangladesh as it extends northwards from the Bay of Bengal towards Bhutan. The Himalayan mountain range to the north and the Indus River (west) and Ganga River (east) form a physical barrier between India and the rest of Asia. The country can be divided into five regions: Western, Central, Northern (including Kashmir and Rajasthan), Eastern and Southern.
LANGUAGE: The national language is Hindi, in the Devanagri script. The States are free to decide their own regional languages for internal administration and education. There are 14 official languages in India.

CIS
CHINA
AFGHANISTAN
PAKISTAN
Tibet
NEPAL
BHUTAN
BANGLADESH
SRI LANKA
MALDIVES
Arabian Sea
Bay of Bengal
INDIAN OCEAN
International boundary
State boundary
International airport
Major port of entry
Tourist centre
Other important place
National highway
Main railway
Miles
300
Kilometres
400
JAMMU AND KASHMIR
HIMACHAL PRADESH
PUNJAB
HARYANA
RAJASTHAN
UTTAR PRADESH
GUJARAT
MADHYA PRADESH
BIHAR
WEST BENGAL
ORISSA
MAHARASHTRA
ANDHRA PRADESH
KARNATAKA
TAMIL NADU
KERALA
ASSAM
MEGHALAYA
NAGALAND
MANIPUR
MIZORAM
TRIPURA
ARUNACHAL PRA
SIKKIM
LAKSHADWEEP (India)
ANDAMA AND NICOBAR (India)
DADRA AND NAGAR HAVELI
DIU (Goa, Daman & Diu)
DAMAN
GOA (Goa, Daman & Diu)
SRINAGAR
DELHI
CHANDIGARH
SIMLA
JAIPUR
LUCKNOW
PATNA
GANGTOK
DISPUR
SHILLONG
KOHIMA
IMPHAL
AIZAWL
AGARTALA
ITANAGAR
CALCUTTA
BHUBANESWAR
BHOPAL
GANDHINAGAR
BOMBAY
SILVASSA
PANAJI
HYDERABAD
BANGALORE
MADRAS
TRIVANDRUM
PORT BLAIR
KATHMANDU
THIMPU
DHAKA
COLOMBO
Tourist Regions
NORTH
EAST
WEST
SOUTH
DELHI
CALCUTTA
BOMBAY
MADRAS

Hindi and Urdu are widely spoken in the North. English is widely used, especially in commerce.
RELIGION: 83.5% Hindu, 10.7% Muslim, 1.8% Sikh, 2.6% Christian, 0.7% Buddhist, 0.7% others.
TIME: GMT + 5.30.
ELECTRICITY: 220 volts AC, 50Hz is usual. Some areas have a DC supply. Plugs used are of the round 2- and 3-pin type.
COMMUNICATIONS: Telephone: IDD service is available to a number of cities in India. Otherwise calls must be placed through the international operator. Country code: 91. **Fax:** Facilities are available in most 5-star hotels and some offices of the Overseas Communication Service in large cities. **Telex/telegram:** International 24-hour service from large hotels and telegraphic offices in major cities. **Post:** Airmail service to Europe takes up to a week. Stamps are often sold at hotels. **Press:** There are numerous local dailies published in several languages. Many newspapers are in English, the most important include *The Times of India*, *Indian Express*, *The Hindu* and *The Statesman*.
BBC World Service and Voice of America frequencies: From time to time these change. See the section *How to Use this Book* for more information.

BBC:

MHz	15.31	11.95	9.740	9.580

A service is also available on 1413kHz.

Voice of America:

MHz	21.49	15.60	9.525	6.035

PASSPORT/VISA

Regulations and requirements may be subject to change at short notice, and you are advised to contact the appropriate diplomatic or consular authority before finalising travel arrangements. Details of these may be found at the head of this country's entry. Any numbers in the chart refer to the footnotes below.

	Passport Required?	Visa Required?	Return Ticket Required?
Full British	Yes	Yes	No
BVP	Not valid	-	-
Australian	Yes	Yes	No
Canadian	Yes	Yes	No
USA	Yes	Yes	No
Other EC	Yes	Yes	No
Japanese	Yes	Yes	No

Note: Admission will be refused to nationals of Afghanistan whose documents show they have boarded in Pakistan. Admission will also be refused to holders of British passports who have been forcibly deported (this includes persons of Indian origin); they will be deported from India on their arrival flight.
PASSPORTS: Valid passport required by all.
British Visitors Passport: Not acceptable.
VISAS: Required by all except nationals of Bhutan and Nepal, who may enter for up to 3 months providing the visit is not for business.
Types of visa: Tourist, Business and Transit. Prices vary according to length and purpose of stay. (Travellers should consult High Commission or Embassy for details.) With the exception of citizens of Afghanistan, China, Iran and South Africa, Transit visas are not required for passengers whose tickets show they intend to continue their journey from the airport, providing they do not leave the airport, and providing they continue their journey within 72 hours (24 hours if travelling via Bombay). Nationals of Pakistan must travel via Amritsar, Delhi or Bombay airports, continuing their journey the same day and they are not allowed to leave the airport. Nationals of Bangladesh may require a visa if they have to leave the airport for a connecting flight. Restricted Area Permits are needed to visit some areas (see *Restricted and protected areas* below).
Validity: Tourist – up to one month; Business – up to one year.
Application to: Consulate (or Consular Section at High Commission or Embassy). For addresses, see top of entry.
Application requirements: (a) Sufficient funds to cover duration of stay. (b) Business visa applicants should present letter from company. (c) Valid passport. (d) 3 passport photos.
Note: Postal applications should enclose payment in postal orders only.
Working days required: Personal visits, 2 days; by post, 4 to 5 weeks.
Temporary residence: Prior permission should be sought before entry into India.
Restricted and protected areas: Certain parts of the country have been designated protected areas and others restricted areas. Visitors to any of these areas must have a special permit and in some cases prior government authorisation. *Passengers are strongly advised to check with the Government of India Tourist Office (GITO) for up-to-date information before departure.*
The following areas are currently restricted to travellers: The States/Union Territories of Arunachal Pradesh, Assam (except Kaziranga National Park), Meghalaya, Mizoram, Nagaland, Sikkim Tripura, the Andaman and Nicobar Islands (except Port Blair municipal area, Havelock Island, Long Island, Neid Island, Mayabunder, Diglipur and Rangat, where night halt is allowed, and Jolly Buoy, South Cinque, Red Skin, Mount Harriet and Madhurban, where only day visits are allowed), Lakshadweep Islands and Bangaram Island.

MONEY

Currency: Rupee (RS) = 100 paise. Notes are in denominations of RS500, 100, 50, 20, 10, 5, 2 and 1. Coins are in denominations of RS2 and 1, and 50, 25, 20, 10 and 5 paise.
Currency exchange: Currency can only be changed at banks or authorised money changers.
Credit cards: Access/Mastercard, American Express, Diners Club and Visa are accepted. Check with your credit card company for details of merchant acceptability and other services which may be available.
Travellers cheques are widely accepted and may be changed at banks.
Exchange rate indicators: The following figures are included as a guide to the movements of the Rupee against Sterling and the US Dollar:

Date:	Oct '89	Oct '90	Oct '91	Oct '92
£1.00=	26.74	35.50	44.70	45.00
$1.00 =	16.93	20.20	25.75	28.36

Currency restrictions: Import and export of local currency is prohibited, except for Rupee travellers cheques. Foreign currency may be exported up to the amount imported and declared. All foreign currency must be declared on arrival if value over US$1000, and when exchanged the currency declaration form should be endorsed, or a certificate issued. The form and certificates must be produced on departure to enable reconversion into foreign currency. Changing money with unauthorised money changers is not, therefore, advisable.
Banking hours: 1000-1400 Monday to Friday, and 1000-1200 Saturdays.

DUTY FREE

The following goods may be imported into India by passengers over 17 years of age without incurring customs duty:
200 cigarettes or 50 cigars or 250g of tobacco;
0.95 litres of alcoholic beverage;
0.25 litres of toilet water;
Goods for personal use or gifts to a value of RS600 (foreign passport holders) or RS2600 (Indian passport holders).
Prohibited items: Narcotics, plants, gold and silver bullion and coins not in current use are prohibited.

PUBLIC HOLIDAYS

Public holidays observed in India are as follows:
Mar 8 '93 Holi. **Mar 25** Eid al-Fitr. **Apr 1** Ramnavami. **Apr 5** Mahavira Jayanti. **Apr 9** Good Friday. **May 6** Buddha Purnira. **Jun 1** Eid al-Zuha. **Jul 1** Muharram. **Aug 15** Independence Day. **Aug 30** Thiru Onam Day. **Sep 19** Ganesh Chaturthi. **Oct 2** Mahatma Gandhi's Birthday. **Oct 24** Vijaya Dasami; Dussehra. **Nov 13** Deepavali (Diwali). **Nov 29** Guru Nanak's Birthday. **Dec 25** Christmas Day. **Jan 1 '94** New Year's Day. **Jan 26** Republic Day. **Feb 6** Guru Ravidas' Birthday. **Feb 19** Mahasivaratri. **Feb/Mar** Eid al-Fitr. **Mar 8** Holi.
Notes: (a) In addition to the above there are numerous festivals and fairs which are also observed in some states as holidays, the dates of which change from year to year. For more details contact the Indian Tourist Office. See also under the heading *Special Events* in the *Social Profile* section. (b) Muslim festivals are timed according to local sightings of various phases of the Moon and the dates given above are approximations. During the lunar month of Ramadan that precedes Eid al-Fitr, Muslims fast during

INDIA	HEALTH REGULATIONS	VISA REGULATIONS Code-Link
GALILEO/WORLDSPAN	 TI-DFT/DEL/HE	TI-DFT/DEL/VI
SABRE	TIDFT/DEL/HE	 TIDFT/DEL/VI

To access this information on your CRS, swipe the barcode with a light pen or type in the text under the barcode. For more information, see the introduction *How to Use This Book*.

the day and feast at night and normal business patterns may be interrupted. Many restaurants are closed during the day and there may be restrictions on smoking and drinking. For more information see *World of Islam* at the back of the book.

HEALTH

Regulations and requirements may be subject to change at short notice, and you are advised to contact your doctor well in advance of your intended date of departure. Any numbers in the chart refer to the footnotes below.

	Special Precautions?	Certificate Required?
Yellow Fever	Yes	1
Cholera	Yes	2
Typhoid & Polio	Yes	-
Malaria	3	-
Food & Drink	4	-

[1]: Any person (including infants over six months old) arriving by air or sea without a yellow fever certificate is detained in isolation for a period up to 6 days if arriving within 6 days of departure from or transit through an infected area (30 days if travelling by ship).
[2]: Travellers proceeding to countries that impose restrictions for arrivals from India or from an infected area in India on account of cholera are required to possess a certificate. An inoculation against cholera is recommended.
[3]: Malaria risk exists, mainly in the benign *vivax* form, throughout the year in the whole country excluding parts of the States of Himachal Pradesh, Jammu and Kashmir, and Sikkim. High resistance to chloroquine is reported in the malignant *falciparum* form.
[4]: All water should be regarded as being potentially contaminated. Water used for drinking, brushing teeth or making ice should have first been boiled or otherwise sterilised. Milk is unpasteurised and should be boiled. Powdered or tinned milk is available and is advised, but make sure that it is reconstituted with pure water. Avoid dairy products which are likely to have been made from unboiled milk. Only eat well-cooked meat and fish, preferably served hot. Pork, salad and mayonnaise may carry increased risk. Vegetables should be cooked and fruit peeled.
Rabies is present. For those at high risk, vaccination before arrival should be considered. If you are bitten abroad seek medical advice without delay. For more information consult the *Health* section at the back of the book.
Health care: It is advisable to bring specific medicines from the UK. There are state-operated facilities in all towns and cities and private consultants and specialists in urban areas. In Sikkim, there are four district hospitals at Singtam, Gyalshing, Namchi and Mangan and one central hospital at Gangtok supplemented by small dispensaries and centres.
On leaving India: Visitors leaving for countries which impose health restrictions on arrivals from India are required to be in possession of a valid certificate of inoculation and vaccination. There is no health check-up of passengers leaving by air or sea.

TRAVEL - International

AIR: India's national airline is *Air India (AI)*.
Approximate flight times: From *London* to Delhi is 9 hours, to Calcutta 12 hours, to Madras 12 hours 30 minutes and to Bombay 9 hours.
From *Los Angeles* to Delhi is 25 hours 30 minutes.
From *New York* to Delhi is 18 hours.
From *Singapore* to Delhi is 5 hours.
From *Sydney* to Delhi is 10 hours.
International airports: *Bombay (BOM)* is 29km (18 miles) north of the city (travel time – 40 minutes). There is a coach to the *Air India* office and major hotels. Taxi services go to the city. Taxi fares have fixed rates from the airport to the city. Public transport is also available in the form of the *EATS* bus service and local buses. Other facilities include a retiring room for passengers in transit and a child care lounge.
Calcutta (CCU) is 13km (11 miles) northeast of the city (travel time – 60 minutes). There is a 24-hour coach service to *Indian Airlines* city office and major hotels. A bus goes every 10 minutes 0530-2200. Taxi services go to the city. There is a 24-hour post office, bars, duty-free shops and restaurants available.
Delhi (DEL) (Indira Ghandi International) is 16km (10 miles) from the city (travel time – 45 minutes). There are coach, bus and taxi services to the city. There are 24-hour duty-free shops and restaurants.
Madras (MAA) is 18km (14 miles) southwest of the city (travel time – 40 minutes). A coach meets all flight arrivals 0900-2300. There is a train every 20-30 minutes 0500-

2300. Bus no 18A runs every 25 minutes 0500-2200. Taxi services go to the city.
Airport facilities: All the above airports have money exchange facilities, tourist information offices and hotel reservation services.
Note: *Ahmedabad Airport* is being upgraded as an international airport.
Departure tax: RS150 is levied against passengers (including infants) to Afghanistan, Bangladesh, Bhutan, Burma, the Maldives, Nepal, Pakistan and Sri Lanka, and RS300 to all other countries.
SEA: The main passenger ports are Bombay, Calcutta, Cochin, Madras, Calicut, Panaji (Goa) and Rameswaram. Indian ports are also served by several international shipping companies and several cruise lines. There are, however, no regular passenger liners operating to South-East Asia.
RAIL: Note: This section gives details of the major overland routes to neighbouring countries (where frontiers are open); in most cases these will involve road as well as rail travel. Details should be checked with the GITO as they may be subject to change.
Connections to Pakistan are currently only possible between Amritsar and Lahore. Permission to travel through Punjab must be obtained.
The most practical and popular route to Nepal is by train to Raxaul (Bihar) and then by bus to Kathmandu; also, by train to Nautanwa (UP) and then by bus to Kathmandu/Pokhara, or Bhairawa to Lumbibi for Pokhara. It is also possible to make the crossing from Darjeeling by bus to Kathmandu across the southern lowlands.
The best way of reaching Bhutan is by train to Siliguri, then bus to Phuntsholing. There is also an airlink from Calcutta to Paro by *Druk Air*.
To Bangladesh, the best route is Calcutta to Bangaon (West Bengal) by train, rickshaw across the border to Benapol, with connections via Khulna or Jessore to Dhaka. Another route is from Darjeeling via Siliguri, then train or bus from Jalpaiguri to Haldibari.
Currently no land frontiers are open between India and Myanmar or the People's Republic of China.
ROAD: Of late, the overland route from Europe to India has become very popular, but travellers should have accurate information about border crossings, visa requirements and political situations en route. Several 'adventure holiday' companies arrange overland tours and buses to India. For information on overland routes to neighbouring countries, please consult the *Rail* section above. For information on required **documentation**, see the *Road* section below.

TRAVEL - Internal

AIR: The domestic airline is *Indian Airlines*. The network connects over 70 cities. *Indian Airlines* also operate regular flights to the neighbouring countries of Pakistan, Nepal, Bangladesh, Sri Lanka, Afghanistan, the Maldives, Singapore and Bangkok.
Special fares: There are various special *Indian Airlines* fares available to foreign nationals and Indian nationals residing abroad. All are available throughout the year, and may be purchased either abroad or in India, where payment is made in a foreign convertible currency (such as US Dollars or Sterling). With the exception of the Youth Fare India (see below), discounts of 90% are available for children under two years, and of 50% for children between two and 12. Full details of all the special fares are contained in the *See India Travel Schemes* brochure, available from the GITO. A summary of each is given below.
Discover India costs US$400 and is valid for 21 days from first flight, offering unlimited economy-class travel on all domestic *Indian Airlines* services. No stop may be visited more than once, except for transfer.
Youth Fare India is valid for 120 days, offering a 25% discount on the normal US Dollar fare. It is available to those aged between 12 and 30 at the commencement of travel for journeys on economy/executive class of domestic air services and Indo-Nepal services.
South India Excursion is valid for 21 days from the first flight on *Indian Airlines*, offering economy-class (up to 30% off the normal US Dollar fare) travel between any or all of the south India stations of Madras, Trichi, Madurai, Trivandrum, Cochin, Coimbatore and Bangalore. For individual passengers, this fare must be combined with fares from the Maldives or Sri Lanka to India via Madras, Tiruchirapalli or Trivandrum.
India Wonderfares (North, South, East and West) cost US$200 and are valid for seven days, offering economy-class travel between main centres in India. No town may be visited more than once, except for transfer.
SEA/RIVER: There are ferries from Calcutta and Madras to Port Blair in the Andaman Islands, and from Cochin and Calicut to the Lakshadweep Islands. Services are often seasonal, and are generally suspended during the monsoon.
One particularly attractive boat journey is the 'backwaters' excursion in the vicinity of Cochin in Kerala.
Several local tours are available.
RAIL: The Indian internal railway system is the largest in Asia and second largest in the world. There are 60,900km (37,850 miles) of track, over 7000 stations and over 11,000 locomotives, including 5000 steam engines. Rail travel is relatively inexpensive. Express services link all the main cities and local services link most other parts of the country. Buses connect with trains to serve parts of the country not on the rail network.
Special fares: There is a special **Indrail Pass** consisting of a single non-transferable, non-refundable ticket which enables a visitor to travel on any train without restriction within the period of validity. It is sold only to foreign nationals and Indians residing abroad holding a valid passport, and replaces all other concessional tickets. Payment is accepted only in foreign currency (US$ or Sterling). Children between 5-12 years of age are entitled to a **Child Indrail Pass,** and pay roughly half the normal fare. Children under five years of age travel free. The normal free *baggage allowances* are 70kg air-conditioned class, 50kg first-class/AC Chair Car and 35kg second-class. **Child Indrail Pass** holders are entitled to half the above allowance. Holders of an **Indrail Pass** are exempted from all reservation fees, sleeping car charges, express train meal charges and other costs. *Validity:* A ticket can be used within one year of its issue. Validity period is from the date of commencement of first journey up to midnight of the date on which validity expires. The ticket must be used within one year of its issue. *Advance reservation* is essential, particularly on overnight journeys, arranged through travel agents. Reservations are on a first-come-first-served basis. For individuals or small groups a 2/3-month notice should suffice; during summer months a longer period is desirable to ensure reservations for the entire itinerary. Reservations can be made up to 360 days in advance. **Indrail** passes can be reserved and booked in the UK from *SD Enterprises*. Tel: (081) 903 3411.
Palace on Wheels: Expensively decorated Edwardian-style luxury steam train. Each coach consists of saloon, four sleeping compartments with upper and lower berth, bathroom, shower, toilet and small kitchen. Room service is available. There is a dining car, a bar, an observation car and a fully equipped first-aid centre. Tariff includes cost of travel; full catering; elephant, camel and boat rides; conducted sightseeing tours; and entrance fees.
Itinerary: Delhi; Jaipur; Udaipur; Jaisalmer; Jodhpur; Bharatpur; Agra; Delhi.
Bookings: Several tour operators/travel agents organise escorted tour facilities which includes the *Palace on Wheels*.
ROAD: An extensive network of **bus** services connects all parts of the country, and is particularly useful for the mountainous regions where there are no rail services. Details of routes may be obtained from the local tourist office. **Tourist cars:** There are a large number of chauffeur-driven tourist cars (some air-conditioned) available in important tourist centres of India. These unmetered tourist cars run at a slightly higher rate than the ordinary taxis, and are approved by GITO. Self-drive cars are not generally available.
Documentation: A 'Carnet de Passage' with full insurance and green card are required. An International Driving Permit is recommended. A temporary licence to drive is available from local authorities on presentation of a valid national driving licence. Traffic drives on the left.
URBAN: *Taxis* and *auto rickshaws* are available in large cities and fares are charged by the kilometre. They do not always have meters but where they do, insist on the meter being flagged in your presence. Fares change from time to time and therefore do not always conform to the reading on the meter, but drivers should always have a copy of the latest fare chart available for inspection. Most visitors prefer not to take public transport. For those interested, *Bombay Electric Supply & Transport (BEST)* is one of the best public transport operators in India, but the visitor taking one of their buses should beware of pickpockets and avoid the rush hour. The train service is also good.
JOURNEY TIMES: The following chart gives approximate journey times from Delhi to other major cities/towns in India.

	Air	Road	Rail	Sea
Bombay	1.50	28.00	17.30a	-
Calcutta	2.00	30.00	18.00b	-
Madras	3.00	45.00	32.00	-
Hyd'bad	1.55	40.00	24.00	-

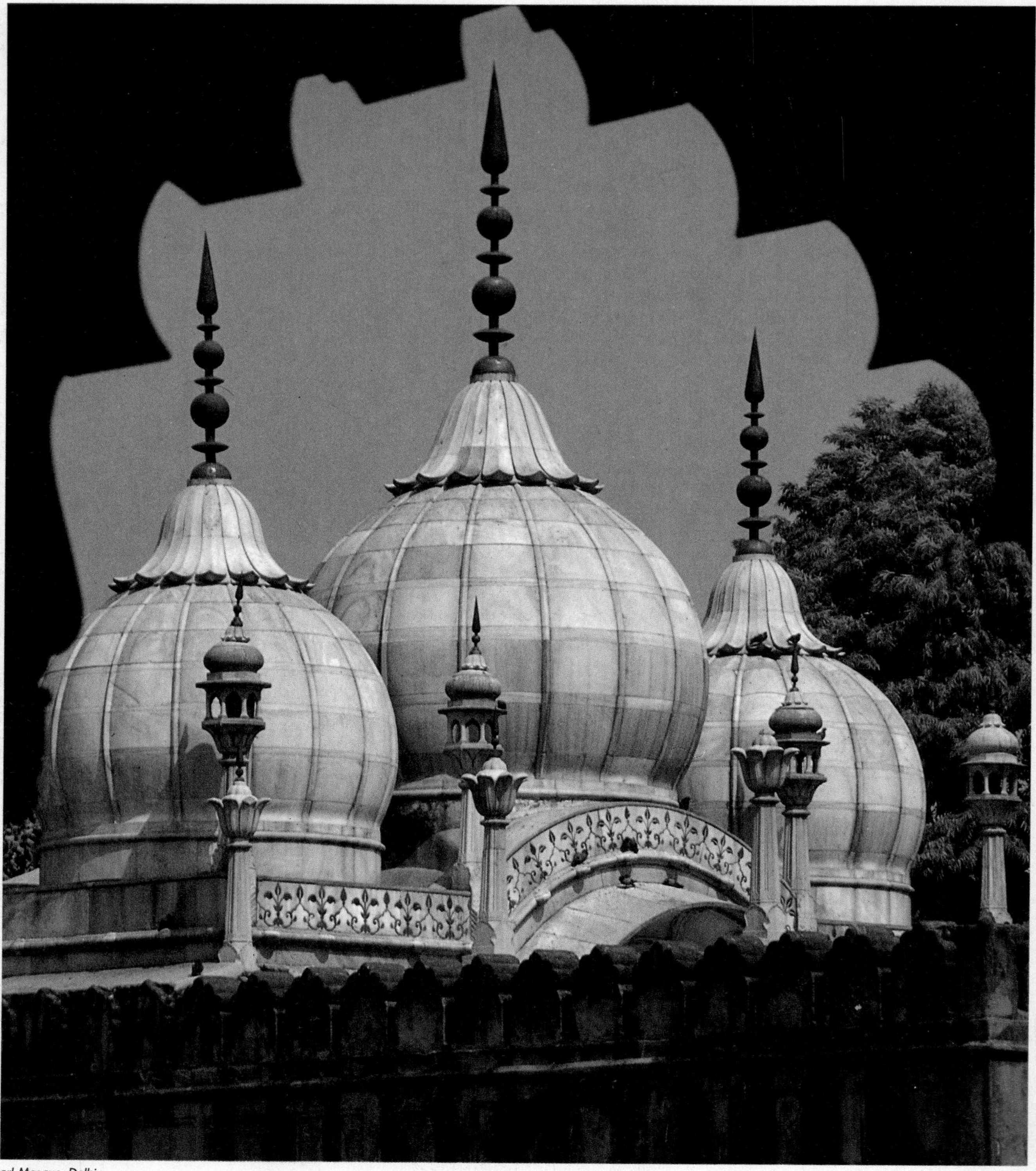

Pearl Mosque, Delhi

Agra	0.40	4.30	3.15	-
Jaipur	0.40	6.00	5.15	-
Jammu	1.50	14.45	16.00	-
Triv'rum	5.00c	62.00	60.00	-
Patna	1.30	22.00	16.00	-
Port Blair	5.05c	-	-	d

[a] Time by express (not daily); normal train takes 23 hours. **[b]** Time by express (not daily); normal train takes 25 hours. **[c]** Does not include stopover in Madras. **[d]** Boat journey from Madras takes 3 to 4 days.

Note: Further information (including route maps, times of express trains and more detailed journey-time charts) may be found in the official *India* brochure, available free from the Government of India Tourist Office.

ACCOMMODATION

For all sections, contact the GITO for detailed information.

HOTELS: Modern Western-style hotels are available in all large cities and at popular tourist centres. Usually they offer a choice of first-class Western and Indian cuisine. Hotel charges in India are moderate compared to those in many other countries. A 10% service charge and a 7-20% 'luxury tax' is normally added to bills.

A full list of *Government Approved Hotels, Palace Hotels* and *ITDC (Ashok) Travellers' Lodges* is available from the Government of India Tourist Office. **Grading:** Hotels range from **5-star deluxe, 5-** and **4-star** hotels, which are fully air-conditioned with all luxury features, **3-star** hotels, which are functional and have air-conditioned rooms, to **2-** and **1-star** hotels, which offer basic amenities.

TOURIST BUNGALOWS: There are tourist bungalows (known as holiday homes in Maharashtra and Gujarat, and tourist lodges in West Bengal) at almost every tourist centre in the country, under the control of the respective State Government Tourist Development Corporation, except in the metropolitan cities of Delhi, Calcutta, Madras, Bombay and Bangalore. These include a clean single, double and family room, most with a bath and general canteen.

At holiday homes and certain tourist cottages there are kitchen facilities. Bookings should be made (a deposit will be required) with the managing director of the respective corporation, or with the manager of the bungalow.

HOUSEBOATS: These are peculiar to Srinagar. Moored on the banks of the river Jhelum and the Dal and Nagin lakes, they range from 24-38m (79-125ft) in length and 3-6m (10-20ft) in width. There are two living rooms, two or three bedrooms, bathrooms, and hot and cold running water. The boats have every comfort and are sumptuously furnished with all modern amenities: electricity, crockery, cutlery, radios and decks for bathing. Smaller boats can be punted about and moored at different places. Each house-boat has a paddle boat for crossings and an attached kitchen-boat which also serves as quarters for the staff. Reductions are available for children and, in the lower two categories, for lodging only. **Grading:** There are four categories: **deluxe, A, B** and **C**.

CAMPSITES are to be found throughout India. Full addresses may be obtained from the GITO or the YMCA Tourist Association, Cum Programme Centre, Jai Singh Rd, New Delhi 110 001. Tel: (11) 311 915. Telex: 62547.

YOUTH HOSTELS: These provide a convenient and cheap base for organised tours, trekking, hiking or mountaineering. The Department of Tourism has set up 16 hostels, spread throughout every region, ideally placed for exploring both the plains and the hill stations. Each has a capacity for about 40 beds or more, segregated roughly half and half into male and female dormitories. Beds with mattresses, bedsheets, blankets, wardrobe with locks, electric light points, member kitchen with pots and pans and parking areas are available at each hostel.

RESORTS & EXCURSIONS

India has a rich history and the palaces, temples and great cities of its ancient cultures cannot fail to grip the imagination. In the spring particularly, the big cities come alive with concerts, plays, parties and exhibitions. Among the most spectacular hill stations (mountain resorts which make ideal destinations in summer) are **Simla** (once the Imperial summer capital), **Mussoorie, Ranikhet** and **Nainital** (within reach of Delhi), and Calcutta's magnificent resort, **Darjeeling** – which offers a glimpse of *Mount Everest* and a breathtaking view of the whole *Kanchenjunga* range. Along the fabled coasts of **Malabar** and **Coromandel**, sandy beaches stretch unspoiled for miles. Skiing is possible in the silent snow-bound heights of *Gulmarg* and *Kufri* in the Himalayas.

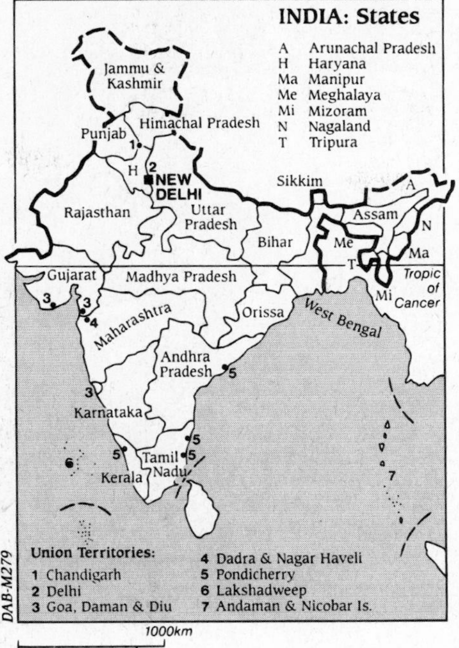

The North

Delhi has two parts: **New Delhi**, India's capital and the seat of government, is a 20th-century city, offering wide tree-lined boulevards, spacious parks and the distinctive style of Lutyen's architectural design; 'Old' **Delhi**, on the other hand, is a city several centuries old, teeming with narrow winding streets, temples, mosques and bazaars. Notable sites are the *Red Fort* and the nearby *Jama Masjid* (India's largest mosque) and the *Qutab Minar's* soaring tower. Delhi attracts the finest musicians and dancers offering an ideal opportunity to hear the *sitar*, *sarod* and the subtle rhythm of the *tabla*, and to see an enthralling variety of dance forms, each with its own costumes and elaborate language of gestures. Theatres and cinemas show films from all over India, and the city has some of the country's finest restaurants offering many styles of regional cuisine.

Delhi lies at the apex of the *'Golden Triangle'* – an area filled with ancient sites and monuments. In the southwest lies **Agra**, city of the fabled *Taj Mahal*. This magnificent mausoleum was built by Shah Jahan, who was later imprisoned by his own son in the nearby *Red Fort*. Other important landmarks are *Akbar's Palace*, the *Jahangir Mahal*, and *Mussumman Burj*, an octagonal tower, and the *Pearl Mosque*. Nearby is **Fatehpur Sikri,** the town Akabar built as his new capital but abandoned after only a few years. This town is now no more than a ghost town. The southwestern pivot of the triangle is **Jaipur**, gateway to the desert state of Rajasthan. Known as the 'Pink City' because of the distinctive colour of its buildings, Jaipur is a town of broad, open avenues and many palaces. The *Amber Palace*, just outside the city is particularly beautiful. To the southwest is **Udaipur**, famed for its *Lake Palace Hotel*, built on an island in the lake, while to the north, in the centre of the Rajasthan desert, is **Jodhpur**, with its colourful, winding lanes and towering fortress. **Jaisalmer** is a charming oasis town, once a resting place on the old caravan route to Persia. Among its attractions are the camel treks out into the surrounding desert.

To the south of the 'Golden Triangle' is the huge state of Madhya Pradesh. Its greatest attractions lie close to the northern frontier. Less than 160km (100 miles) from Agra is the great ruined fortress at **Gwalior.** To the east lies **Khajuraho** with its famous temples and friezes of sensuously depicted figures – a must for any visitor.

To the east of Delhi is the state of Uttar Pradesh, through which flows the sacred *River Ganges*. Built along its bank is **Varanasi,** India's religious centre, from where the dead are cremated in the open or floated down river. The town itself is a maze of winding streets, filled with pilgrims, wandering holy men and priests giving offerings to the gods.

Less than 320km (200 miles) to the north of Delhi is **Simla**, the greatest of all hill stations, surrounded by finely scented pine forests and the rich beauty of the *Kulu Valley*.

In the far north, reaching into Central Asia, is the extensive mountain region of **Kashmir**, an area long established as a popular summer resort, and the valley of the *River Jhelum*. The gateway to the region is **Jammu**, a town surrounded by lakes and hills. The temples of *Rambireshwar* and *Raghunath* number among its most impressive sights. Jammu is the railhead for **Srinagar**, the ancient capital of Kashmir, and favourite resort of the Mughal emperors. It was they who built the many waterways and gardens around *Lake Dal*, complementing the natural beauty of the area. Among the attractions are the houseboats where visitors can live on the lakes surrounded by scenery so beautiful it is known as 'paradise on earth'.

Srinagar is also a convenient base for trips to **Gulmarg** and **Pahalgam.** Gulmarg offers fine trout fishing, and enjoys the distinction of having the highest golf course in the world. From here there are good views of *Nanga Parbat*, one of the highest mountains in the world. It is well placed as a starting point for treks into the hills and mountains. *Pahalgam* is another popular hill resort and base for pilgrimages to the sacred cave of *Amar Nath*.

More exotic, though less accessible, is the region of Ladakh, beyond the Kashmir Valley. It is a mountainous land of many temples and has much in common with Tibet. The capital, **Leh**, is situated high in the Karakouram mountain range, through which passed the old silk route from China to India and Europe.

The West

The principal metropolis of Western India is **Bombay**, the capital of the state of **Maharashtra,** a bustling port and commercial centre, with plate-glass skyscrapers and modern industry jostling alongside bazaars and the hectic streetlife. Many of the country's films are made in the famous Bombay studios. The city also boasts one of the finest race tracks in India, the Mahalaxmi course. There is a pleasant seafront with a palm-lined promenade and attractive beaches such as *Juhu*, *Versova*, *Marve*, *Madh* and *Manori*. On the waterfront is Bombay's most famous landmark, the *Gateway to India*, from where boats leave on the 10km (6-mile) journey across the busy harbour to the **Elephanta Island**. The island is famous for the 8th-century cave temples, on whose walls are large rock carvings, the finest of which is the 3-faced *Maheshmurti*, the great Lord.

To the north lies the state of **Gujarat,** famous for its silks, as the birthplace of Mahatma Gandhi, and as the last refuge of the Asian lion, found deep in the *Gir Forest*. **Ahmadabad**, in the east of the state, is the principal textile city of India, producing silks which are famous throughout the world. Ahmadabad is also the site of *Sabarmati Ashram*, founded by Mahatma Gandhi, from where his ideology of non-violence is still promoted. Gandhi's birthplace is some 320km (200 miles) to the west, in the fishing village of **Porbandar**.

To the east of Bombay is **Aurangabad**, the starting point for visits to two of the world's most famous rock-cut temples. The Buddhist cave temples at **Ajanta** date back at least 2000 years. Cut into the steep face of a deep rock gorge, the 30 caves contain exquisite paintings depicting daily life at that time.

The caves at **Ellora** depict religious stories and are Hindu, Buddhist and Jain in origin. The *Temple of Kailasa* is the biggest cut out monolith temple in the world. Southeast of Bombay are several fine hill stations, notably **Matheran** with its narrow gauge trains, **Mahabaleshwar** and **Pune** with its peaceful *Bund Gardens*.

Further to the south lies **Goa.** The 100km- (60-mile) long coastline offers some of the finest beaches in the subcontinent. Goa was Portuguese until 1961, and there is also a charming blend of Latin and Indian cultures. **Panaji**, the state capital, is one of the most relaxed and elegant of India's cities. The town is dominated by the huge *Cathedral of the Immaculate Conception*, but the shops, bars and pleasant streets are its main attraction. 'Old Goa', only a bus ride away from Panaji, displays a bewildering variety of architectural styles. Buildings of note include the *Basilica* and the *Convent and Church of St Francis of Assisi*. In nearby **Ponda** is the 400-year-old *Temple of Shri Mangesh*, which is said to be the oldest Hindu shrine.

Accommodation in the region includes the luxury resort of **Aguada**, the Taj holiday village and the Aguada hermitage. There are also good, simple hotels and cottages for rent in villages along the coastline, notably **Calangute, Baya** and **Colva.**

Goa also has several wildlife sanctuaries, including *Bondla* in the hills of western *Ghats*, where wild boar and sambar can be seen in their natural habitat. The region is famous for its food – an array of dishes, both Indian and Portuguese – as well as for its colourful festivals, including the spectacular Carnival held on the three days leading up to Ash Wednesday.

The South

The south is the part of India least affected by incursions of foreign cultures through the centuries. It is here that Indian heritage has survived in its purest form.

The regional capital is **Madras**, India's fourth largest city. Madras is the cradle of the ancient Dravidian civilisation, one of the oldest articulate cultures in the world. It is also home of the classical style of Indian dancing and a notable centre of temple sculpture art. Sprawling over 130 sq km (50 sq miles), the metropolis has few tall buildings and enjoys the relaxed ambience of a market town rather than the bustle of a huge city. From *Madras Lighthouse* there is a fine view of the city that includes many churches which tell of the city's strong Christian influence, first introduced in AD78 when the apostle St Thomas was martyred here.

Madras, however, is largely a commercial city and the centre of the area's rail, air and road networks, and serves as a good starting point from which to explore the south. Within the region are several important religious centres, notably **Kanchipuram**, which has an abundance of temples, and whose striking *gopurams,* or gateways, are decorated with sculptures of gods and goddesses. Inland is **Madurai**, with a large and bustling temple, and **Thanjavur**. Also worth visiting is **Tiruchirapalli,** which has a fortress built atop a strange boulder-shaped hill that dominates the town.

Further south, along the coast, is **Pondicherry**, an attractive town with a distinctive French style, and beyond, **Rameswarum**, the ferry link to Sri Lanka.

To the west lies the state of **Kerala,** where many of India's major coastal resorts are to be found. Among the finest is **Kovalam**, offering unspoilt beaches and a new complex of modern amenities, including luxury bungalows and a 5-storey hotel with swimming pool. Only a few miles away is **Trivandrum**, the state capital with its famous *Padmanabhaswamy Temple*. Further inland is the *Periyar Game Sanctuary* which has a rich and varied wildlife. Other resorts include *Cranganorre*, *Alleppey* and *Cochin*.

Further to the north is the state of **Karnataka,** which has fine, unexplored beaches at **Karwar**, **Mahe** and **Udipi**. The state's capital is **Bangalore**, an affluent city which is the centre of electronics and engineering industries, but has many charming parks and gardens. To the southwest lies **Mysore**, where incense is manufactured, and where you can stay in the *Lalitha Mahal Hotel*, previously the home of a Maharaja.

Karnataka has a number of important religious and historical sites, including the ruins at **Hampi** to the north of Bangalore, and the vast statue of Lord Bahubali at *Sravanabelagola*, north of Mysore.

To the east of Karnataka is the state of Andhra Pradesh, with its capital at **Hyderabad,** offering a well-stocked one-man museum. 220km (350 miles) to the east is **Visakhapatnam**, India's fourth largest port.

Far away to the east across the Bay of Bengal are the **Andaman Islands**, a lushly forested archipelago which has exotic plant life and a wide variety of corals and tropical fish, making it a major attraction for snorkelling enthusiasts. The islands' capital, **Port Blair,** can be reached from Madras and Calcutta by boat or air.

The East

The largest city in India and hub of the east is **Calcutta**. Established as a British trading post in the 17th century, it grew rapidly into a vibrant centre. Its colonial heritage is reflected in the buildings of Chowringhee Street and Clive Street, now Jawaharlal Nehru Road and Netaji Subhash Road. The city is filled with life and energy. It is a major business centre and offers fine markets and bazaars. It is also the centre of much of the country's creative and intellectual activity, including the sub-continent's finest film-makers. Central Calcutta is best viewed from the *Maidan*, the central area of parkland where early morning *yoga* sessions take place. The city's *Indian Museum* is one of the finest in Asia. Other attractions include the white marble *Victoria Memorial*, the *Octherlony Institute* and the headquarters of the Rama Krishna movement. Across the river are the *Kali Temple of Dakshineshwasar* and the *Botanical Gardens*.

To the west is the state of **Bihar,** with the religious centre of **Bodhgaya,** a sacred place for both Hindus and Buddhists. To the south, in the state of **Orissa,** are three temple cities. Foremost is **Bhubaneswar**, a town in which there once stood no less than 7000 temples, 500 of which have survived. Largest of these is the great *Lingaraja Temple*, dedicated to Lord Shiva. A short journey away to the south of Bhubaneswar lies **Puri**, one of the four holiest cities in India, now being developed as a beach resort. In June and July Puri stages one of India's most spectacular festivals, the *Rath Yatra* or 'Car Festival', at which pilgrims pay homage to images of gods drawn on massive wooden chariots. A short distance along the coast to the north is **Konarak**, known for its 'Black Pagoda' – a huge solitary temple to the sun god in the form of a chariot drawn by horses. The sculpture has a sensuous nature similar to that of Khajuraho, and is counted amongst the finest in India.

To the north of Calcutta is one of the great railway journeys of the world, the 'Toy Train' to **Darjeeling**. The last part of the line runs through jungle, tea gardens and pine forests. Darjeeling straddles a mountain slope which drops steeply to the valley below, and commands fine views of *Kanchenjunga* (8586m/28,169ft), the third highest mountain in the world. It is the headquarters of the Indian Mountaineering Institute, as well as the birthplace of Sherpa Tenzing. It is also a world-renowned tea-growing centre.

A bus journey of two and a half hours takes one to **Kalimpong**, a bazaar town at the foot of the Himalayas. From here a number of treks can be made to places offering fine panoramas of the mountains.

Further north is the mountain state of **Sikkim**. The capital, **Gangtok**, lies in the southwest. The main activity for visitors is trekking, although it is still in its infancy and facilities are minimal. At the moment travel for non-Indian residents is limited. Trekking is allowed only to groups, while individuals may only visit **Gangtok**, **Rumtek** and **Phodom**. The nearest railheads are Darjeeling and Silguri, on the slow but spectacular line of India's northeast frontier railway.

Even further to the east are the states of **Assam** and **Meghalaya.** Assam is famous for tea and wildlife reserves, and can be reached from the state capital of **Gauhati**. The tiger reserve of *Manas* is also rich in other varieties of wildlife, while in **Kaziranga** it is possible to see the one-horned rhinoceros of India.

Shillong, the capital of Meghalaya, is the home of the Khasi people. The region is filled with pine groves, waterfalls and brooks and is described as the 'Scotland of the East'.

Beach Resorts

India's coast has some of the most beautiful beaches in the world. Below are listed both well-known resorts, such as Goa, and several intriguing lesser-known beaches. Hotel facilities and accommodation are also indicated. Further information may be obtained by consulting other sections in *Resorts & Excursions* above.

Major beaches include:

Goa: Calangute, Baga Beach, Colva Beach. *5-star hotels with private beaches:* Fort Aguada Beach Resort, Oberoi Bogmalo Beach and Cidade de Goa. It has reasonably priced hotels, tourist cottages, a tourist resort and youth hostels.

Bombay: Juhu Beach. 5-star hotel complex. Crowded.

Kovalam: Ashok Beach resort. 5-star hotel complex, including beach cottages, Halcyon Castle and Kovalam Palace Hotel. Hotel Samudra, Kerala Tourism Development Corporation, is reasonably priced.

Madras Region: Fisherman's Cove at **Covelong** beach resort; shore cottages by the shore temples at **Mamallapuram**. Mamallapuram beach resort.

Puri: 3- and 4-star hotels, tourist bungalows, youth hostels. Major Hindu pilgrim centre.

Lesser known beaches include:

Gujarat: Tithal, Ubhrat, Hajira, Diu (UT), Daman (UT), Chorwad, Dahanu and Dwarka. Cheap hotels, holidays homes. **Maharashtra:** Off Bombay: Madh, Marve and Manori. Cheap hotels: Murud Janjira. Holiday homes: Erangal. **Goa:** Karwar, Ankola, Gokarna, Honnavar and Bhatkal. **Karnataka:** Ullal (smaller beach resort, Summer Sands, cottages), Udupi (Hindu pilgrim centre), Mahe (UT) and Mangalore. **Kerala:** Cannanore, Quilon, Varkala. **Tamil Nadu:** Kanya Kumari, Tiruchendur, Rameswaram, Karikal (UT) and Pondicherry (UT). **Andhra Pradesh:** Maipadu, Machilipatnam, Mangiripundi and Bheemunipatnam. **Orissa:** Golpalpur on Sea, Oberoi Hotel, tourist bungalows. **West Bengal:** Digha – reasonably priced hotels, tourist bungalows.

Note: UT = Union Territory.

Hill Stations

Hill stations have long been popular among Indians and foreign visitors alike for providing a relaxing and salubrious retreat from the heat of the plains. Further information on some of the places mentioned here may be found by consulting other sections in *Resorts & Excursions* above.

The most popular include:

Kashmir: Leh in Ladakh, Srinagar, Pahalgam, Gulmarg for lakes, houseboats, good hotels, tourist reception centres. **Himachal Pradesh:** Simla (various types of hotels, tourist bungalows), nearby Kufri (winter sports centre, skating rink, snow skiing facilities), Kulu, Manali (reasonably priced hotels, log huts, travellers lodges and tourist bungalows). **Uttar Pradesh:** Nainital boasts a lake boat club, Almora, Ranikhet (reasonably priced hotels, tourist bungalows, clubs, youth hostels), Mussoorie, Ropeway (hotels and tourist bungalows). **West Bengal:** Darjeeling, RA, Kalimpong for mountaineering. **Meghalaya:** Shillong. **Sikkim:** Gangkok (RA, hotels). **Tamil Nadu:** Ootacamund, Udagamandalam, Kodaikanal, Silvery Lake – hotels, tourist bungalows.

Lesser known hill stations include:

Himachal Pradesh: Dalhousie, Dharamsala, Nahan, Paonta Saheb, Keylong, Chamba and Kangra. **Kashmir:** Sonamarg, Batote. **Uttar Pradesh:** Dehra Dun, Lansdown. **West Bengal:** Mirik. **Madhya Pradesh:** Pachmarhi. **Maharashtra:** Mahabaleshwar, Panchgani, Panhala, Matheran, Lonavla and Khandala. **Gujarat:** Saputara. **Rajasthan:** Mount Abu. **Tamil Nadu:** Yercaud, Coonoor, Kotagiri. **Kerala:** Ponmundi, Munnar. **Karnataka:** Mercara. **Andhra Pradesh:** Horseley Hills. **Meghalaya:** Shillong. **Bihar:** Netarhat.

Trekking

Trekking conjures up visions of the spectacular northern and eastern Himalayas, the mist-strewn Western Ghats or the blue tranquillity of the Nilgiri Hills. India is the ideal destination for a trekking holiday, offering everything from short and easy excursions to the long challenges of the snowy peaks. Trekking requires the stamina to walk long hours and the mental agility to adapt to a spectacular and ever-changing landscape.

The highest mountain range on earth – the Himalayas – form 3500km (2200 miles) of India's northern and eastern frontiers. The spectacle of the snow-capped peaks, glaciers, pine-forested slopes, rivers and lush meadows of wild flowers cannot be equalled. Peninsular India offers natural beauty of another kind, clothed in green woodland and fragrant orchards.

Below is a description of the most important trekking areas in India, and also a section devoted to general trekking information and sources of further information.

JAMMU & KASHMIR: Jammu & Kashmir is India's northernmost state, and the one which is best-known for trekking. It is an extravagantly beautiful land of flower-spangled meadows, wild orchards, spectacular coniferous forests, icy mountain peaks and clear streams and rivers. The capital, **Srinagar**, is the base for many treks, notably to the blue Zabarwan Hills and Shankaracharya Hill.

The three other main bases in Jammu & Kashmir are **Pahlagam** (100km, 62 miles from Srinigar) in the *Lidder Valley*, the base for treks to sacred *Amarnath, Aru, Lidderwat* and the glacial lakes of *Tarsar* and *Tulian;* **Gulmarg** (51km, 32 miles from Srinagar), from where treks can be made to the crystal tarns of *Apharwat* and *Alpather*, the upland lakes of **Vishansar** and **Gangabal** and the *Thajiwas Glacier;* and **Sonamarg**, in the *Sindh Valley*, the base for treks into the surrounding mountains. Srinagar is also the roadhead for trips into the arid plateau of *Ladakh*, a country of perpetual drought, the home of wild asses and yaks and with high ranges that have some of the largest glaciers in the world outside the polar regions. **Leh**, the divisional capital, lies on an ancient silk route and is the base for spectacular treks across this remarkable landscape.

Further south, excellent trekking may be had in the vicinity of Jammu, the railhead to the *Kashmir Valley*. The three main centres are **Kishtwar**, **Doda** and **Poonch**.

HIMACHAL PRADESH: The landscape of this province ranges from the barren rocks and raging torrents of the valleys of *Spiti* and *Lahaul* in the north to the southern orchard country of *Kangra* and *Chamba*. Treks from **Manali** include the *Bhaga River* to **Keylong**, and then on to the *Bara Shigri* glacier or over the *Baralacha Pass* to Leh (see above). **Kullu**, in the centre of the province, is set in a narrow valley between the towering Himalayas and the *River Beas*, and is famous for its temples and religious festivals. Treks from here traverse terraced paddy fields and on to remoter regions of snow and ice. The view from the *Rohtang Pass* is particularly spectacular. The town of **Dharamsala**, in the *Kangra Valley*

area, is the base for treks into the *Bharmaur Valley* over the *Indrahar Pass*, and on to other still higher passes beyond. **Chamba**, situated on a mountain above the *Ravi River*, is named after the fragrant trees which flourish around its richly carved temples. Treks from the nearby town of **Dalhousie** lead to the glacial lake of *Khajjiar* and to the passes of *Sach* and *Chini*. **Shimla,** once the summer capital of the British, is a high hill station and the base for treks into *Kullu Valley* via *Jalori Pass* and on to the Kalpur and Kinnaur valleys.

GARHWAL: Set high in the *Garhwal Himalayas*, this region (which is sometimes referred to as the Uttarakhand) abounds in myths and legends of the Indian Gods. It is also where the source of the life-giving 'Ganga' is to be found; indeed, many of the great rivers of northern India have their headwaters in this land of lush valleys and towering snow-ridged peaks. **Mussoorie**, a hill station much used by the British to escape the searing heat of the plains, is an excellent base for treks into the *Gangotri* and *Yamounotri* valleys. The source of the Ganga at **Gaumukh** can also be reached from here. Another hill station, **Rishikesh**, is situated just north of the sacred city of **Hardwar**, and is the base for treks to another holy shrine, *Badrinath*. A particularly rewarding stop en route to Badrinath is the breathtaking *Valley of Flowers*, which is in full bloom in August. Other destinations include *Hemkund Lake*, *Mandakini Valley* and *Kedarnath*, one of the twelve Jyotirlings of Lord Shiva with a beautiful temple.

KUMAON: This region, which stretches from the Himalayas in the north to the green foothills of Terai and Bhabar in the south, consists of the three northeastern Himalayan districts of Uttar Pradesh, all of which are particularly rich in wildlife. One of the major trekking centres is **Almora**, an ideal base for treks into pine and rhododendron forests with dramatic views of stark, snow-capped mountains. The *Pindiri Glacier* and the valley of *Someshwar* can be reached from here. Another base is **Nanital**, a charming, orchard-rich hill station. It is the base for short treks to **Bhimtal**, **Khurpatal** and *Binayak Forest*. **Ranikhet**, with a magnificent view of the central Himalayas, is the base for treks to **Kausani.** The view from here is one of the most spectacular in India, and inspired Mahatma Gandhi to pen his commentary on the Gita-Anashakti Yoga.

DARJEELING AND SIKKIM: Dominated by the five summits of mighty *Kanchenjunga*, the Darjeeling and Sikkim area of the Eastern Himalayas is also a region of gentle hills and dales, pine forests, turquoise lakes and burbling streams. One of the best ways of arriving in the area is by the 'toy train' from New Jalpaiguri. The town of **Darjeeling** is the home of the Everest climber Tenzing Norgay and also of the Himalayan Mountaineering Institute, and is the base for both low- and high-level treks. Destinations include *Tiger Hill* (offering a breathtaking view of the Himalayas), and the peaks of *Phalut*, *Sandakphu*, *Singalila* and *Tanglu*. To the north, Sikkim is a wonderland of ferns and flowers, birds and butterflies, orchids and bamboos, forests of cherry, oak and pine, all set among sweetly flowing rivers, terraced paddy fields and blazing rhododendrons. Deep in the interior are Sikkim's famous monasteries, their white prayer flags fluttering against a deep blue sky. The capital is **Gantok**, a convenient base for treks into the mysterious north and east of the region, to sacred *Yaksum*, *Pemayangtse* and the mountains near **Bakkhim** and **Dzongri**.

ARAVALLI HILLS: The Aravallis, remnants of the oldest mountain range in the sub-continent, resemble outcroppings of rocks rather than mountains and are virtually barren except for thorny acacias and date palm groves found near the oases. The main resort in the region, *Mount Abu*, stands on an isolated plateau surrounded by rich green forest. A variety of one-day treks are available from here, all of which afford the opportunity to visit some of the remarkable temples in the region, notably *Arbuda Devi Temple*, carved out of the rock face and offering spectacular views across the hills. **Guru Shikhar, Gaumukh** and *Achalgarh Fort* can all be reached during one-day treks from Mount Abu.

SATPURA RANGE: This range straddles central India and forms the northern border of the *Deccan*. The main hill station is **Pachmarhi,** a beautiful resort of green forest glades and deep ravines overlooking red sandstone hills. Short treks can be had from here to the *Mahadeo* and *Dhupgarh* peaks.

WESTERN GHATS: The Western Ghats run parallel to the west coast of India from the River Tapti to the southernmost tip of the sub-continent. The mountains are lush and thickly forested and although they cannot claim to have the awesome majesty of the great Himalayas the region has many features of great natural beauty. The hill station of **Mahabaleshwar**, in the north of the range, is the highest in the area and is considered an ideal base for trekkers. Other popular bases and trekking destinations include **Lonavala**, **Khandala**, **Matheran** and **Bhor Ghat**, a picturesque region of waterfalls, lakes and woods. Further south in Karnataka is **Coorg**, perched on a green hilltop and surrounded by mountainous countryside. **Madikeri** is a take-off point for treks in this region. The *Upper Palani* hills in Tamil Nadu are an offshoot of the Ghats, covered in rolling downs and coarse grass. **Kodaikanal** is the attractive base for two short treks to *Pilar Rock* and *Green Valley View*. **Courtallam**, also in Tamil Nadu, is surrounded by dense vegetation and coffee and spice plantations; rich in wildlife, it is also one of the most beautiful areas of the Western Ghats.

NILGIRIS: The gentle heights of southern India, a world away from the daunting Himalayas, are friendly and approachable with treks made simple by moderate altitudes and a pleasant climate. Sometimes known as the *Blue Mountains* because of their lilac hue, they are noted for their orange orchards, tea gardens, wooded slopes and tranquil lakes. There are three major trekking centres here: **Ootacamund** (popularly known as Ooty) is the base for walks to the *Wenlock Downs*, the *Kalahatti Falls* and *Mudumali Game Sanctuary*; **Coonor**, conveniently situated for *Drogg's Peak* and *Lamb's Rock*; and **Kotagiri**, the oldest of the three, whose sheltered position enables it to offer many shaded treks to explore the tranquillity of the Nilgiris.

GENERAL TREKKING INFORMATION: Essential equipment: Tent, sleeping bag, foam/inflatable mattress, rucksack, umbrella (doubles as a walking stick), sun-hat, dark glasses, toilet requirements. **Clothing:** Wind-proof jacket, down jacket, trousers, shirts, woollen pullover, woollen underwear (for high altitudes), and gloves. **Footwear:** Be sure to take a light, flexible and comfortable pair of trekking boots (two pairs should be taken for longer treks) and at least three pairs of woollen socks. Use talc to keep feet dry. **First-aid kit:** Sterilised cotton wool, bandages, antiseptic ointment, water purification tablets, pills etc for common ailments (such as cough, cold, headache, stomach ache etc), eye lotion, anti-sunburn cream, a hot stimulant for emergencies, and morphia salt tablets to avoid cramps. **Miscellaneous:** Torch, thermos/water bottle, insect repellant, mirror, cold cream, lip-salve, walking stick, spare boot laces, sewing kit, tinned and dehydrated food. **Food & accommodation:** Board and lodging accommodation is available on all trekking routes. **Permits:** No system of issuing Trekking Permits exists in India. Trekkers are, however, reminded that it is forbidden to enter Restricted and Protected Areas without the correct documentation. Please consult the Tourist Office before departure or local tourist offices on arrival in India to ascertain what restrictions may apply and what documentation may be required. **Season:** This varies from region to region; check with the Tourist Office for further information. In general, the season runs from April to June and September to November. It is possible to undertake treks in the valleys of Lahaul, Pangi and Zanskar and in Ladakh during the rainy season (June to August), as these areas receive minimal precipitation.

Mountaineering: Permission for mountaineering *must* be obtained from the Indian Mountaineering Foundation, Anand Niketan, Beneto Juarez Road, New Delhi, ND 110 021.

Wildlife

The Indian peninsula is a continent in itself, the geographical diversity of which has resulted in a vast range of wildlife, with over 350 species of mammals and 1200 species of birds in the country. Each region has something special to offer: the **hangul** is restricted to the valley of Kashmir in northern India, the **rhino** is found in isolated pockets along the Brahmaputra River in the east, the **black langur** in the Western Ghats, and Western India is the home of the last remaining **Asiatic lions**. Two of India's most impressive animals, the **Bengal** (or Indian) **tiger** and the **Asiatic elephant** are still found in most regions, though their population has shrunk drastically.

Most of India's wildlife finds refuge in over 200 sanctuaries and parks around the country. The following list refers to some of the more important of these. Accommodation often needs to be booked in advance, either by direct application or through the local State TDC or the controlling authority of the respective park. The GITO produces a map *(Wildlife – India)* which contains fuller details on these points.

NORTHERN INDIA

Dachigam Wildlife Sanctuary (Kashmir): Broad valley; mountain slopes; rare hangul deer, black and brown bear, leopard; heronry.

Govind Sagar Bird Sanctuary (Himachal Pradesh). Bird sanctuary with crane, duck, goose and teal.

Corbett National Park (Uttar Pradesh): Himalayan foothills near Dhikala; Sal forest and plains; tiger, elephant, leopard and rich birdlife. Excellent fishing in Ramganga River.

Dudhwa National Park (Uttar Pradesh): Nepal border; tiger, sloth bear and panther.

Flower Valley National Park (Uttar Pradesh): When in bloom this 'roof garden' at 3500m (11500ft) is a glorious blaze of colour. Permits are required to enter.

Sariska National Park (Rajasthan): About 200km (125 miles) from Delhi. Forest and open plains; sambar (largest Indian deer), cheetal (spotted deer), nilgai (Indian antelope), black buck, leopard and tiger; good night-viewing.

Ranthambhor (Sawai Madhopur – Rajasthan): Hill forest, plains and lakes; sambar, chinkara (Indian gazelle), tiger, sloth bear, crocodiles and migratory water-birds.

Bharatpur National Park (Keoloadeo Ghana Bird Sanctuary) (Rajasthan): India's most outstanding bird sanctuary; many indigenous water-birds; huge migration from Siberia and China; crane, goose, stork, heron, snakes, birds etc.

Bandhavgarh National Park (Madhya Pradesh). Situated in the Vindhyan Mountains, this park has a wide variety of wildlife including panther, sambar and gaur.

Kanha National Park (Madhya Pradesh): Sal forest and grassland; only home of barasingha (swamp deer), tiger, cheetal and gaur.

Shivpuri National Park (Madhya Pradesh): Open forest and lake; chinkara, chowsingha (4-horned antelope), nilgai, tiger, leopard and water-birds.

EASTERN INDIA

Kaziranga National Park (Assam): Elephant grass and swamps; one-horned Indian rhinoceros, water buffalo, tiger, leopard, elephant, deer and rich birdlife. Elephant transport is available within the park.

Manas Wildlife Sanctuary (Assam): On the Bhutan border, rainforest, grassland and river banks; rhino, water buffalo, tiger, elephant, golden langur and water-birds; fishing permitted.

Palamau Tiger Reserve (Bihar): Rolling, forested hills; tiger, leopard, elephant, sambar, jungle cat, rhesus macaque (monkey) and occasionally wolf.

Hazaribagh National Park (Bihar): Sal forested hills; sambar, nilgai, cheetal, tiger, leopard and occasionally muntjac (larger barking deer).

Sundarbans Tiger Reserve (West Bengal): Mangrove forests; tiger, fishing cat, deer, crocodile, dolphin and rich birdlife. Transport: access and travel by chartered boat.

Jaldapara Wildlife Sanctuary (West Bengal): Tropical forest and grassland; rhino, elephant and rich birdlife.

Similipal Tiger Reserve (Orissa): Immense Sal forest; tiger, elephant, leopard, sambar, cheetal, muntjac and chevrotain.

SOUTHERN INDIA

Periyar Wildlife Sanctuary (Kerala): Large artificial lake; elephant, gaur, wild dog, black langur, otters, tortoises and rich birdlife including hornbill and fishing owl. Viewing by boat.

Vedanthangal Water Birds Sanctuary (Tamil Nadu): One of the most spectacular breeding grounds in India. Cormorants, herons, storks, pelicans, grebes and many others.

Point Calimere Bird Sanctuary (Tamil Nadu): Particularly noted for flamingo, also for heron, teal, curlew and plover, black buck and wild pig.

Pulicat Bird Sanctuary (Andhra Pradesh): Flamingo, grey pelican, heron and tern.

Dandeli National Park (Karnataka): Park with bison, panther, tiger and sambar. Easily accessible from Goa.

Jawahar National Park (includes **Bandipur** and **Nagarhole** National Parks (Karnataka), and the Wildlife Sanctuaries of **Mudumalai** (Tamil Nadu) and **Wayanad** (Kerala): Extensive mixed forest; largest elephant population in India, leopard, gaur, sambar, muntjac and giant squirrel. Birds include racquet-tailed drongo, trogon and barbet.

WESTERN INDIA

Krishnagiri Upavan National Park (Maharashtra): Formerly known as Borivli, this park protects an important scenic area close to Bombay. Kanheri Caves and Vihar, Tulsi and Powai lakes; water-birds and smaller types of wildlife. Lion Safari Park nearby.

Tadoba National Park (Maharashtra): Teak forests and lake; tiger, leopard, nilgai and gaur. Viewing by night.

Sasan Gir National Park (Gujarat): Forested plains and lake; only home of Asiatic Lion, sambar, chowsingha, nilgai, leopard, chinkara and wild boar.

Nal Sarovar Bird Sanctuary (Gujarat): Lake; migratory water-birds; indigenous birds include flamingo.

Little Rann of Kutch Wildlife Sanctuary (Gujarat): Desert; herds of khur (Indian wild ass), wolf and caracal.

Velavadar National Park (Gujarat): New Delta grasslands; large concentration of black buck.

SOCIAL PROFILE

FOOD & DRINK: The unforgettable aroma of India is not just the heavy scent of jasmine and roses on the warm air. It is also the fragrance of spices so important to Indian cooking – especially to preparing curry. The word 'curry' is an English derivative of *kari*, meaning spice sauce, but curry does not, in India, come as a powder. It is the subtle and delicate blending of spices such as turmeric, cardamom, ginger, coriander, nutmeg and poppy seed. Like an artist's palette of oil paints, the Indian cook has some 25 spices (freshly ground as required) with which to mix the recognised combinations or *masalas*. Many of these spices are also noted for their medicinal properties. They, like the basic ingredient, vary from region to region.

Although not all Hindus are vegetarians, vegetable dishes are more common than in Europe, particularly in southern India. Broadly speaking, meat dishes are more common in the north, notably, *Rogan Josh* (curried lamb), *Gushtaba* (spicy meat balls in yoghurt) and the delicious *Biryani* (chicken or lamb in orange-flavoured rice, sprinkled with sugar and rose water). Mughlai cuisine is rich, creamy, deliciously spiced and liberally sprinkled with nuts and saffron. The ever-popular *Tandoori* cooking (chicken, meat or fish marinated in herbs and baked in a clay oven) and kebabs are also northern cuisine. In the south, curries are mainly vegetable and inclined to be hotter. Specialities to look out for are *Bhujia* (vegetable curry), *Dosa*, *Idli* and *Samba* (rice pancakes, dumplings with pickles, and vegetable and lentil curry), and *Raitas* (yoghurt with grated cucumber and mint). Coconut is a major ingredient of southern Indian cooking. On the west coast there is a wide choice of fish and shellfish: Bombay duck (curried or fried bombloe fish) and *pomfret* (Indian salmon) are just two. Another speciality is the Parsi *Dhan Sak* (lamb or chicken cooked with curried lentils) and *Vindaloo* (vinegar marinade). Fish is also a feature of Bengali cooking as in *Dahi Maach* (curried fish in yoghurt flavoured with turmeric and ginger) and *Malai* (curried prawn with coconut). One regional distinction is that, whereas in the south rice is the staple food, in the north this is supplemented and sometimes substituted by a wide range of flat breads, such as *Pooris*, *Chapatis* and *Nan*. Common throughout India is *Dhal* (crushed lentil soup with various additional vegetables), and *Dhai*, the curd or yoghurt which accompanies the curry. Besides being tasty, it is a good 'cooler'; more effective than liquids when things get too hot.

Sweets are principally milk-based puddings, pastries and pancakes. Available throughout India is *Kulfi*, the Indian ice cream, *Rasgullas* (cream cheese balls flavoured with rose water), *Gulab Jamuns* (flour, yoghurt and ground almonds), and *Jalebi* (pancakes in syrup). Besides a splendid choice of sweets and sweetmeats, there is an abundance of fruit, both tropical – mangoes, pomegranates and melons – and temperate – apricots, apples and strawberries. Western confectionery is available in major centres. It is common to finish the meal by chewing *Pan* as a digestive. Pan is a betel leaf in which are wrapped spices such as aniseed and cardamom.

Besides the main dishes, there are also countless irresistible snacks available on every street corner, such as *Samosa*, *Fritters*, *Dosa* and *Vada*. For the more conservative visitor, Western cooking can always be found. Indeed, the best styles of cooking from throughout the world can be experienced in the major centres in India.

Drink: Tea is India's favourite drink and many of the varieties are famous the world over. It will often come ready brewed with milk and sugar unless 'tray tea' is specified. Coffee is increasingly popular. *Nimbu Pani* (lemon drink), *Lassi* (iced buttermilk) and coconut milk straight from the nut are cool and refreshing.

Restaurants have table service and, depending on area and establishment, will serve alcohol with meals. Most Western-style hotels have licensed bars. Visitors will be issued All India Liquor Permits on request by Indian Embassies, Missions or Tourist Offices or from the Tourist Office in London. Currently, only Gujarat and Tamil Nadu impose prohibition, but this may change; check with the Tourist Office for up-to-date information. In almost all big cities in India certain days in the week are observed as dry days when the sale of liquor is not permitted. Tourists may check with the nearest local tourist office for the prohibition laws/rules prevailing in any given state where they happen to be travelling or intend to travel.

Soft drinks (usually sweet) and bottled water are widely available, as are Western alcoholic drinks. Indian beer and gin are comparable with the world's best, and are not expensive.

NIGHTLIFE: India has generally little nightlife as the term is understood in the west, although in major cities a few Western-style shows, clubs and discos are being developed. In most places the main attraction will be cultural shows featuring performances of Indian dance and music. The Indian film industry is the largest in the world, now producing three times as many full-length feature films as the United States. Bombay and Calcutta are the country's two Hollywoods. Almost every large town will have a cinema, some of which will show films in English. Music and dancing are an important part of Indian cinema, combining with many other influences to produce a rich variety of film art. Larger cities may have theatres staging productions of English-language plays.

SHOPPING: Indian crafts have been perfected over the centuries, from traditions and techniques passed on from generation to generation. Each region has its own specialities, each town its own local craftspeople and its own particular skills. Silks, spices, jewellery and many other Indian products have long been famous and widely sought; merchants would travel thousands of miles, enduring the hardships and privations of the long journey, in order to make their purchases. Nowadays, the marketplaces of the sub-continent are only eight hours away, and for fabrics, silverware, carpets, leatherwork and antiques, India is a shopper's paradise. Bargaining is expected, and the visitor can check for reasonable prices at state-run emporiums. **Fabrics:** One of India's main industries, its silks, cottons, and wools rank amongst the best in the world. Of the *silks*, the brocades from Varanasi are among the most famous; other major centres include Patna, Murshidabad, Kanchipuram and Surat. Rajasthan *cotton* with its famous 'tie and dye' design is usually brilliantly colourful, while Madras cotton is known for its attractive 'bleeding' effect after a few washes. Throughout the country may be found the 'himroo' cloth, a mixture of silk and cotton, often decorated with patterns. Kashmir sells beautiful *woollens*, particularly shawls. **Carpets:** India has one of the world's largest carpet industries, and many examples of this ancient and beautiful craft can be seen in museums throughout the world. Kashmir has a long history of carpet-making, influenced by the Persians. Pure wool and woven wool and silk carpets are exquisitely made, and though fairly expensive, they are marked up sharply by the time they reach the west. Each region will have its own speciality; one such are the distinctive, brightly coloured Tibetan rugs, available mainly in Darjeeling. **Clothes:** Clothes are cheap to buy, and can be tailor-made in some shops, usually very quickly. Cloths include silks, cottons, *himroos*, brocades, chiffons and *chingnons*. **Jewellery:** This is traditionally heavy (particularly *kundan* from Rajasthan) and stunningly elaborate. Indian silverwork is world-famous. Gems can be bought and mounted. Apart from diamonds, other stones include lapis lazuli, Indian star rubies, star sapphires, moonstones and aquamarine. Hyderabad is one of the world's leading centres for pearls. **Handicrafts and leatherwork:** Once again, each area will have its own speciality; the range includes fine bronzes, brasswork (often inlaid with silver), canework and pottery. Papier maché is a characteristic Kashmir product, some decorated with gold leaf. Marble and alabaster inlay work, such as chess sets and ornamental plates, are a speciality of Agra. Good leatherwork buys include open Indian sandals and slippers. **Woodwork:** Sandalwood carvings from Karnataka, rosewood from Kerala and Madras, Indian walnut from Kashmir. **Other buys:** Foods such as pickles, spices and Indian tea, and perfumes, soap, handmade paper, Orissan playing cards and musical instruments.

Shopping hours: 0930-1800 Monday to Saturday in most large stores.

Note: It is forbidden to export antiques and art objects

over 100 years old, animal skins or objects made from skins.
SPORTS: A wide range of activities is available in India, ranging from watching **horseracing** at Calcutta to **fishing** in Kashmir, and from **golf** to **polo.** The great Indian sport, though, is **cricket**. Interest in the game reaches almost fever pitch, particularly during the winter test season when the country's national team are in action in all the major cities. Club matches can also be seen in almost every town. **Skiing** is fast becoming a popular sport, and facilities are offered by some resorts in the north of the country (including Gulmarg and Kufri), set in some of the most beautiful mountain landscape in the world. **River running** is another young sport in India; the snow-fed mountain rivers of the northern Himalayas place them among the best regions in the world for this sport. **Camel safaris** can be taken in the Thar desert and range from one to 15 days' duration; an ideal way to visit this fascinating region. Delhi is the country's centre for **rock climbing**, also available in the Aravalli Hills and the Western Ghats. **Hang gliding, ballooning** and **gliding** are also becoming more widely available for those who wish to obtain a bird's-eye view of some of the landscape. **Motor rallying** is an excellent sport for participants and spectators alike. The most notable, and demanding, event is the *Himalayan Car Rally*. Most large hotels have swimming pools, and there are facilities for a wide range of **watersports** including **sailing, rowing** and **water-skiing** at seaside resorts. The Andaman Islands in particular are noted for their **scuba diving. Fishing** is also available, particularly in the Kangra Valley and Simla, in Darjeeling and Orissa and throughout the Himalayas. Tackle can often be hired from local fishing authorities. Check with the local tourist office for details of seasons and licences. **Golf** enthusiasts will find many courses open to visitors throughout India; enquire at major hotels for details of temporary membership. *Calcutta Amateur Golf Championships* attract large numbers of serious golfers in the east; the standards are high, and for those interested, temporary membership is available from the Royal Calcutta Golf Club. Srinagar and Gulmarg have good courses and hold tournaments in the spring and autumn. The course at Shillong is widely regarded as being one of the most beautiful in the world. Other participating sports include **horseriding** in hill stations and **tennis** and **squash**, available in hotels and private clubs. Spectator sports include **football**, interest in which is increasing, while **polo** and **hockey** are sports at which the Indians have long excelled, winning many Olympic Gold medals. For information on **trekking**, see the section above.
SPECIAL EVENTS: Below is a selection from the hundreds of Indian festivals celebrated throughout the year. Public holidays are indicated PH. All the festivals are nationwide unless otherwise stated.
January/February
Sankranti/Pongal (mainly Tamil Nadu, Andhra Pradesh and Karnataka): 3 days, colourful Tamil harvest festival. **Republic Day** (PH): Establishment of Republic 26th January 1950. Grand Military Parade and Procession of dancers (Delhi). **Basanta Panchami** (mainly in the Eastern region): Hindu, dedicated to Saraswati the beautiful Goddess of Learning. Women wear yellow saris. **Floating Festival** (Madurai): Birthday of local 17th-century ruler; elaborately illuminated barge carrying decorated temple deities at the Mariamman Teppakulam Pool amid chanting hymns.
February/March
Eid al-Fitr: Ramadan Eid, Muslim. Celebration to mark the end of the month of Ramadan. **Shivratri:** Solemn worship of Hindu deity, Lord Shiva. Fasting and chanting. Special celebrations at Chidambaram, Kalahasti, Khajuraho, Varanasi and Bombay. **Holi** (mainly northern): Popularly called the festival of colours. **Advent of Spring:** Lively, with much throwing of coloured water and powders. **Carnival** (Goa): Mainly three days during Lent. Unique celebrations at this carnival. **Easter** (PH): Good Friday/Easter Sunday. **Kumbh Mela:** The oldest and most important of the Hindu festivals. It takes place every three years, at one of the four great holy cities; Nasik in Maharashtra, Ujjain (MP), Prayag (Allahabad) and Hardwar (both in UP). It is attended by millions of pilgrims who take a holy dip in the sacred Ganges River.
April/May
Ramnavami: Birth of Rama, incarnation of Vishnu. No processions. Plays and folk theatres. **Mahavira Jayanti:** Jain festival; birth of Mahavira, the 24th and last Tirthankara. **Vaisakhi** (Northern India, West Bengal and Tamil Nadu): Hindu Solar New Year. Bhangra dancing. Women wear yellow saris. **Pooram** (Trichur): New Moon. Spectacular sight of large number of elephants carrying ceremonial umbrellas around the temple; midnight firework display. **Meenakshi Kalyanam** (Madurai): Marriage of Meenakshi with Lord Shiva. Colourful temple festival. Deities borne by colossal chariot. 10-day festival. **Fair** (Rajasthan): Urs Ajmer Sharif. Ajmer, six days. Religious, cultural and commercial extravaganza dedicated to the Sufi. Music; no procession.
June/July
Eid al-Zuha: Bakri Eid, Muslim. The most celebrated Islamic festival in India, commemorating the sacrifice of Abraham. **Muharram:** Muslim. Commemoration of Imam Hussain's martyrdom. Tiger dancers lead processions of colourful replicas of martyr's tomb. Colourful, particularly at Lucknow. **Rath Yatra** (Mainly Orissa): Greatest temple festival in honour of Lord Jagannah (Lord of the Universe). Three colossal chariots drawn from Puri temple by thousands of pilgrims. Similar festivals, on a smaller scale, take place at Ramnagar (near Varanasi), Berampore (near Calcutta) and Jagannathpur (near Ranchi).
July/August
Teej (Rajasthan, particularly Jaipur): Procession of the Goddess Parvati to welcome monsoon; elephants, camels, dancers etc. Women wear green saris. Colourful. **Raksha Bandhan** (Northern and western India): Legendary re-enactment, girls tie rakhis or talismans to men's wrists. Colourful build up. **Naga Panchami** (Mainly Jodphur, Rajasthan and Maharashtra): Dedicated to the green thousand-headed mythical serpent called Sesha. The day is also observed in many other parts of Western and Eastern India. **Amarnath Yatra:** Hindu. Lidder Valley, Kashmir at full moon. Pilgrims visit the place where Lord Shiva explained the secret of salvation to his consort Parvati.
August/September
Independence Day (15 August) (PH): Prime Minister delivers address from Delhi's Red Fort. **Janmashtami** (Particularly Agra, Bombay and Mathura): Lord Krishna's Birthday. **Onam:** Kerala's Harvest Festival; spectacular snake boat races in many parts of Kerala. **Ganesh Chaturthi** (mainly Pune, Orissa, Bombay and Madras): Dedicated to elephant-headed God Ganesh. Giant models of the deity processed and immersed in water. Colourful, and particularly worth visiting on the Day of Immersion at Bombay.
September/October
Dussehra: The most popular festival in the country, celebrated in different ways in different parts of the country. In the north and particularly in Delhi (where it is known as

Ram Lila), plays and music recall the life of Rama; in Kulu, the festival is also very colourfully celebrated. In Bengal and many parts of Eastern India it is known as Durga Puja, and in the South as Navaratri. **Fair, Himachal Pradesh:** Kulu Valley, to coincide with Dussehra (ten days). **Gandhi Jayanti** (National PH): Mahatma Gandhi's Birthday. No processions. **Gurpurab** (mainly in northern India): Anniversaries of ten gurus, spiritual teachers or preceptors of Sikhism. No processions.

November

Diwali: One of the most lively and colourful festivals in India. In some regions it marks the start of the Hindu New Year. In Eastern India, the goddess Kali is particularly worshipped; elsewhere, it is Lakshmi, the goddess of prosperity, who is venerated. Everywhere there are magnificent illuminations and fireworks. **Bihar:** Largest cattle fair in the world; one month Sonepur, Patna; on banks of the Ganges. **Guru Nanak Jayanti:** Guru Nanak's Birthday, the founder of Sikhism. **Pushkar Mela** (Pushkar, near Ajmer, Rajasthan): Important and colourful. Camel and cattle fair, attended by Rajputs from miles around. Camel races and acrobatics etc.

December

Christmas Day (PH): Most exuberantly celebrated in Goa, Bombay and Tamil Nadu.

Note: Besides the above festivals there are hundreds of festivals and fairs which are of regional significance, celebrated with equal pomp and colour. The most authentic of these are the following: The Temple Festivals in South India, a list of which is often available at GITOs. Festivals at Ladakh in Kashmir. Festivals in Rajasthan; a visitor will be unlucky to visit Rajasthan at a time when a festival of some kind is not either in progress or about to take place.

Music Festivals

There are also a large number of music festivals throughout the year, including:

Jan *Sangeet Natak Akademi*, New Delhi; *Tyagaraja Tiruvayyaru*, near Thanjavur. **Mar** *Shankar Lal*, New Delhi. **Aug** *Vishnu Digambar*, New Delhi. **Sep** *Bhatkhande*, Lucknow. **Oct** *Sadarang*, Calcutta. **Nov** *Sur-Singar*, Bombay. **Dec** *Tansen Gwalior*; *Music Academy*, Madras; *Shanmukhananda; The Music, Dance and Drama Festival*, Bombay.

The visitor may also be lucky enough to witness dancing at a village festival or a private wedding.

Note: Hindu festivals are declared according to local astronomical observations and it is only possible to forecast the month of their occurrence.

SOCIAL CONVENTIONS: The Indian greeting is to fold the hands and tilt the head forward to *namasthe*. Indian women prefer not to shake hands. All visitors are asked to remove footwear when entering places of religious worship. The majority of Indians remove their footwear when entering their houses, and the visitor should follow suit accordingly. Because of strict religious and social customs, visitors must show particular respect for traditions when visiting someone's home. Many Hindus are vegetarian and many, especially women, do not drink alcohol. Sikhs and Parsees do not smoke and it is important for guests to follow all local customs. Small gifts are acceptable as tokens of gratitude for hospitality. Women are expected to dress with sobriety. Trousers, short skirts or tight clothing should not be worn, since this will generally only attract unwelcome attention. Business people are not expected to dress formally except for meetings and social functions. Trained English-speaking guides are available at fixed charges at all important tourist centres. French, Italian, Spanish, German, Russian and Japanese speaking guides are available in some cities. Consult the nearest GITO. Unapproved guides are not permitted to enter protected monuments, and tourists are therefore advised to ask for the services of guides who carry a certificate issued by the Department of Tourism. **Photography:** Formalities are mainly in regard to protected monuments and the wildlife sanctuaries. Special permission of the Archaeological Survey of India, New Delhi, must be sought for use of tripod and artificial light to photograph archaeological monuments, and photographs of the wildlife sanctuaries are allowed on payment of a prescribed fee which varies from one sanctuary to another. Contact the nearest GITO. **Tipping:** It is usual to tip porters (20-25 paise per bag) and waiters, guides and drivers 10% where service is not included.

BUSINESS PROFILE

ECONOMY: India is a country of astonishing poverty coupled with a comparatively well-developed industrial economy which has invested much in advanced technology initiatives such as digital communications and space research. The country rates in the top dozen in the world by Gross National Product and is one of the highest in terms of investing national wealth in industrial projects. Roughly two-thirds of the population are involved in agriculture, both subsistence – mainly cereals – and cash crops, including tea, rubber, coffee, cotton, jute, sugar, oilseeds and tobacco. The agricultural sector has been severely affected, however, by frequent droughts during the 1980s and early 1990s, particularly as harvests depend almost entirely on the annual monsoon. India has some oil deposits which are now playing a growing role in the economy as well as assisting the balance of payments deficit, which constantly hampers the country's economic development. India's industrial base has expanded greatly in the last two decades with major developments in heavy engineering – especially transport equipment, a major export earner – iron and steel, chemicals and electronics. The 1990 Gulf crisis caused significant damage to the Indian economy through the loss of two of its most important trading partners, the increase in the price of imported oil, the loss of remittances from Indian workers in both Iraq and Kuwait and their return home, which put a sudden strain on the labour market. In 1992, serious drought has emerged as the major obstacle to economic growth while political difficulties have prevented the Rao government from tackling the public sector. Japan and the CIS are India's major trading partners among a wide range of significant bilateral links stretching from Australia and the Pacific Basin through Western Europe to the United States, Canada and Brazil.

BUSINESS: English is widely used in commercial circles, so there is little need for interpreter and translation services. Business cards are usually exchanged. All weights and measures should be expressed in metric terms. Indian businessmen welcome visitors and are very hospitable. Entertaining usually takes place in private clubs. The best months for business visits are October to March, and accommodation should be booked in advance. **Office hours:** 0930-1730 Monday to Friday.

COMMERCIAL INFORMATION: The following organisations can offer advice:

Associated Chambers of Commerce and Industry of India (ASSOCHAM), 2nd Floor, Allahabad Bank Building, 17 Parliament Street, New Delhi 110 001. Tel: (11) 310 704. Fax: (11) 312 193. Telex: 3161754; *or*

Federation of Indian Chambers of Commerce and Industry, Federation House, Tansen Marg, New Delhi 110 001. Tel: (11) 331 9251. Telex: 3162521.

CONFERENCES/CONVENTIONS: The main congress and exhibition centres in the country are Delhi, Bombay, Calcutta, Madras, Srinagar, Agra, Jaipur, Udaipur, Varanasi, Bhubeneswar, Hyderabad, Bangalore and Panaji. In addition, top-class hotels and auditoria with convention and conference facilities are found throughout the country. *Air India, Indian Airlines* and leading hoteliers and travel agents are members of the International Congress and Conference Association (ICCA) and together they provide all the services required for an international event, including the organising of pre- and post-conference tours. There are two particularly useful booklets which give information on India in general, and in particular on conference facilities, called *Conventionally Yours* and *India: an Unusual Environment for Meetings*, available from the GITO. For further information contact the India Convention and Promotion Bureau (ICPB), Ashok Hotel, Chanakyapuri, New Delhi. Tel/Fax: (11) 687 3612. Telex: 03165647.

HISTORY & GOVERNMENT

HISTORY: Indian civilisation can be traced back to at least 2500BC, although the ancient civilisations did not encompass the whole of India as we know it today. The first known civilisation settled along the Indus River (notably Harappa and Mohenjo-Daro) in what is now Pakistan. This, however, collapsed around 1500BC. Between 521 and 486BC, under Darius, this area became part of the Persian Empire. Alexander the Great arrived in India in 326BC, but did not venture beyond the boundaries of the Persian Empire, which only covered the north. India's two great religions, Hinduism and Buddhism, had already been developed. Various dynasties followed, the last of which was the Gupta Empire (AD319-606). The invasion of the White Huns brought all this to an end, and northern India became fragmented, not being unified again until the coming of the Muslims. During this time the south had been trading by sea with the Romans and Egyptians. The Muslims made their presence felt after AD600, but this was mainly in the north. Under the Mogul Empire (1526-1738) the Hindus and Muslims became allied, but there were always certain tensions. The Marathas gradually built up their influence, defeating the Moguls at the Battle of Panipat in 1761. The Maratha Empire continued until the British East India Company took over at the beginning of the 19th century, after several years' struggling with both the French and the Marathas. The indigenous campaign for independence began with the formation of the Indian National Congress in 1885, but it made little progress until after the end of the First World War, when Mahatma Gandhi led the

Congress and began the policy of noncooperation with the British. The colonial authorities were gradually persuaded that reforms were needed, but the Congress itself was split on a key issue: the Muslims, under Mohammed Ali Jinnah, claimed a separate homeland in provinces such as the Punjab and Bengal, where they formed a majority of the population, but Gandhi wanted India as a unified state. Jinnah's view, supported by the last Governor-General, Earl Mountbatten, prevailed and in August 1947 the independent states of India and Pakistan came into being. Since this time India has been a democratic republic, the first proper elections taking place in 1951, and Hindu law has been modernised to a great extent, eradicating many of the old inequalities. Nonetheless the caste system, which assigns an individual to a particular stratum in society from birth, has proved resilient to reform. India has also developed a broadly secular polity and has for the most part been free of violent religious strife (although there are dangerous signs that this may be changing). Indian politics have been dominated since independence by the Nehru family: Jawaharlal ('Pandit') was the first Prime Minister; then came his daughter, Indira Gandhi (one of the modern world's first woman leaders); and finally her son, Rajiv. Their political power has been exercised through the Congress Party, which has governed India for most of the time since independence. The party has been known as Congress (I) following a split in the original Congress during the 1970s. Mrs Ghandi held office in several different Parliaments until October 1984, when she was assassinated by Sikh members of her personal bodyguard. Rajiv Ghandi took over immediately afterwards. Successive governments during the 1980s have been dogged by the various manifestations of civil strife and a series of challenging foreign policy problems. Of these the most taxing was the Indian military intervention in the intercommunal conflict in Sri Lanka, where, in 1987, the Indian army became involved in a peace-keeping capacity for two years. This role as regional 'policeman' was also exemplified in late 1988 when Indian forces were instrumental in overthrowing an abortive invasion attempt in the Maldives. It is relations with Pakistan, however, that will always tend to dominate India's foreign policy agenda. Relations between the two have varied between chilly and war. The division of East and West Pakistan in 1971 into the contemporary states of Bangladesh and Pakistan followed decisive military and political intervention by the Indian government. Since then, the border dispute between India and Pakistan in the Kashmir region – which dates back to the division between the two countries at independence – has occasionally erupted into armed conflict. The last twelve months have seen an increase in tension in the region. India is currently led by a veteran senior figure and former foreign minister, P V Narasimha Rao, who was selected by the Congress (I) party after the assassination of Rajiv Ghandi in May 1991 by Tamil separatists while campaigning in the south. The election Rajiv was working on was held a few weeks later and the Congress (I) Party came out with just enough seats to form a government. The Rao government has concentrated in the early stages on the economy, aiming to cut Government spending and trim India's huge public sector. Abroad, Delhi has made efforts to improve relations with Peking and taken advantage of the current chill between the USA and Pakistan (see *Pakistan*) to improve relations with Washington. The Foreign Ministry is also worried by developments in the CIS, with whom India was traditionally close.

GOVERNMENT: India is a federal republic with certain powers reserved to the 25 states. There are seven Union Territories (Andaman and Nicobar Islands; Chandigarh; Dadra and Nagar Haveli; Delhi; Goa, Daman and Diu; Lakshadweep; and Pondicherry), which are governed from Delhi. Central government is bicameral parliament and cabinet. The Head of State is the President (presently Ramaswamy Venkataraman) and the executive power is vested in the Prime Minister (presently P. V. Narasimha Rao).

CLIMATE

Hot tropical weather with variations from region to region. Coolest weather lasts from November to mid-March, with cool, fresh mornings and evenings and dry, sunny days. Really hot weather, when it is dry, dusty and unpleasant, is between April and June. Monsoon rains occur in most regions in summer between June and September.

Western Himalayas: Srinagar is best from March to October; July to August can be unpleasant; cold and damp in winter. Simla is higher and therefore colder in winter and places like Pahalgam, Gulmarg and Manali are usually under several feet of snow (December to March) and temperatures in Ladakh can be extremely cold. The road to Leh is open from June to October.

Required clothing: Lightweight to mediumweights are advised from March to October, with warmer clothes for the winter. The weather is subject to rapid changes in the mountains, therefore it is important to carry suitable equipment to allow for these. Waterproofing is advisable.

Northern Plains: Extreme climate, warm inland from April to mid-June falling to almost freezing at night in winter, between November and February. Summers hot with monsoons between June and September.

Required clothing: Lightweight cottons and linens in summer with warmer clothes in winter and on cooler evenings. Waterproofing is essential during monsoons.

Central India: Madhya Pradesh State escapes the very worst of the hot season, but monsoons are heavy between July and September. Temperatures fall at night in winter.

Required clothing: Lightweights are worn most of the year with warmer clothes during evenings, particularly in winter. Waterproofed clothing is advised during monsoon rains.

Western India: November to February is most comfortable, although evenings can be fairly cold. Summers can be extremely hot with monsoon rainfall between mid-June and mid-September.

Required clothing: Lightweight cottons and linens are worn most of the year with warmer clothes for cooler winters, and waterproofing is essential during the monsoon.

Southwest: The most pleasant weather is from November to March. Monsoon rains fall between late April and July. Summer temperatures are not as high as Northern India, although humidity is extreme. There are cooling breezes on the coast. Inland, Mysore and Bijapur have pleasant climates with relatively low rainfall.

Required clothing: Lightweights are worn all year with warmer clothes for cooler evenings, particularly in winter. Waterproofing is advised during the monsoon.

Southeast: Tamil Nadu experiences a northeast monsoon between October and December and temperatures and humidity are high all year. Hills can be cold in winter. Hyderabad is hot, but less humid in summer and much cooler in winter.

Required clothing: Lightweight cottons and linens. Waterproofing is necessary during the monsoon. Warmer clothes are worn in the winter, particularly in the hills.

Northeast: March to June and September to November are the driest and most pleasant periods. The rest of the year has extremely heavy monsoon rainfall and it is recommended that the area is avoided.

Required clothing: Lightweight cottons and linens. Waterproofing is advisable throughout the year and essential in monsoons, usually from mid-June to mid-October. Warmer clothes are useful for cooler evenings.

BOMBAY India (11m)

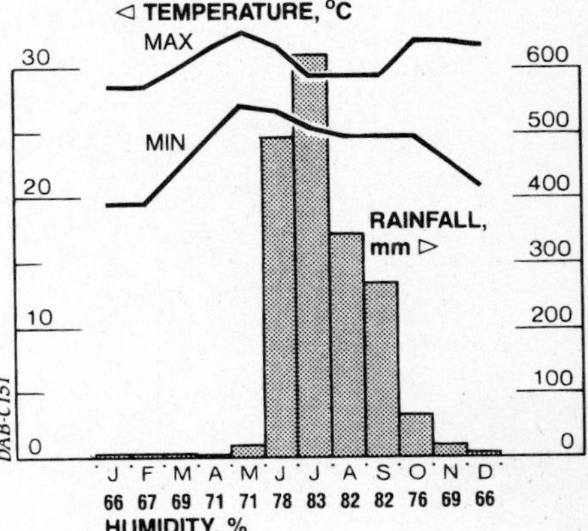

DELHI India (218m)

◁ TEMPERATURE, °C

MAX

MIN

RAINFALL, mm ▷

J F M A M J J A S O N D

57 51 36 27 28 45 67 72 62 44 41 56

HUMIDITY, %

DAB-C150

HYDERABAD India (542m)

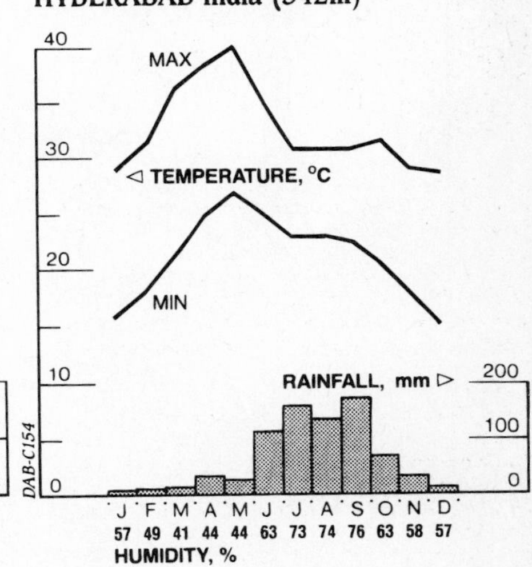

MADRAS India (16m)

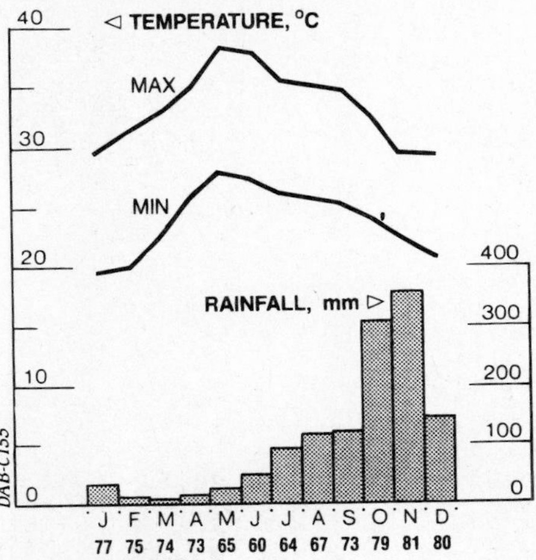

CALCUTTA India (6m)

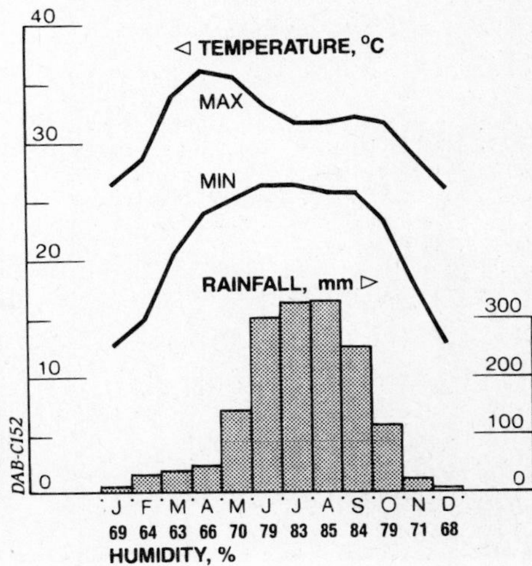

INDONESIA

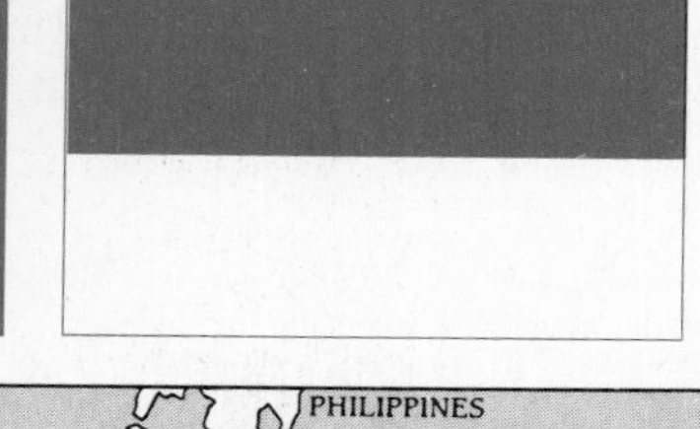

*East Timor incorporated into Indonesia July 1976

□ international airport

Location: South East Asia.

Dewan Pariwisata Indonesia (Tourist Board)
81 Jalan Kramat Raya
Jakarta 10450, Indonesia
Tel: (21) 310 3088. Telex: 45625.

Embassy of the Republic of Indonesia
38 Grosvenor Square
London W1X 9AD
Tel: (071) 499 7661. Fax: (071) 491 4993. Telex: 28284 INDONEG. Opening hours: 1000-1300 and 1430-1600 Monday to Friday.

Indonesia Tourist Board
3/4 Hanover Street
London W1R 9HH
Tel: (071) 493 0334. Fax: (071) 493 1747.

Indonesia Tourist Promotion Office for West Europe
Wiesenhüttenstrasse 17
W-6000 Frankfurt/M 1
Germany
Tel: (69) 233 677. Fax: (69) 230 840. Telex: 418986 ITPOD.

Garuda Indonesia (National Airline)
35 Duke Street
London W1M 5DF
Tel: (071) 486 3011 (reservations). Fax: (071) 224 3971. Telex: 8954225.

British Embassy
Jalan MH Thamrin 75
Jakarta 10310, Indonesia
Tel: (21) 330 904. Fax: (21) 321 824. Telex: 61166.
Consulates in: Medan and Surabaya.

Embassy of the Republic of Indonesia
2020 Massachusetts Avenue, NW
Washington DC
20036
Tel: (202) 775 5200. Fax: (202) 775 5316.

Consulate General of Indonesia
5 East 68th Street
New York , NY
10021
Tel: (212) 879 0600 (visas and tourist information).

Indonesian Tourist Promotion Office
3457 Wilshire Boulevard
Los Angeles, CA
90010
Tel: (213) 387 2078. Fax: (213) 380 4876.
Also deals with enquiries from Canada.

Embassy of the United States of America
PO Box 1
Medan Merdeka Selatan 5
Jakarta, Indonesia
Tel: (21) 360 360. Fax: (21) 386 2258. Telex: 44218.
Consulates in: Medan and Surabaya.

Embassy of the Republic of Indonesia
287 MacLaren Street
Ottawa, Ontario
K2P 0L9
Tel: (613) 236 7403. Fax: (613) 563 2858.
Consulates in: Toronto, Vancouver and Edmonton.

Canadian Embassy
PO Box 1052
5th Floor, WISMA Metropolitan
Jalan Jendral Sudirman
Jakarta 10010, Indonesia
Tel: (21) 510 709. Fax: (21) 571 2251. Telex: 65131.

AREA: 1,919,443 sq km (741,101 sq miles).
POPULATION: 179,136,110 (1989 estimate, including East Timor).
POPULATION DENSITY: 93.3 per sq km.
CAPITAL: Jakarta (Java). **Population:** 7,347,800 (1983 estimate).
GEOGRAPHY: Indonesia is made up of six main islands, Sumatra, Java, Sulawesi, Bali, Kalimantan (part of the island of Borneo) and Irian Jaya (the western half of New Guinea), and 30 smaller archipelagos, in total 13,677 islands. 3000 of these islands are inhabited and stretch over 4828km (3000 miles), most lying in a volcanic belt with more than 300 volcanoes, the great majority of which are extinct. The landscape varies from island to island, ranging from high mountains and plateaux to coastal lowlands and alluvial belts.
LANGUAGE: Bahasa Indonesian (a variant of Malay)

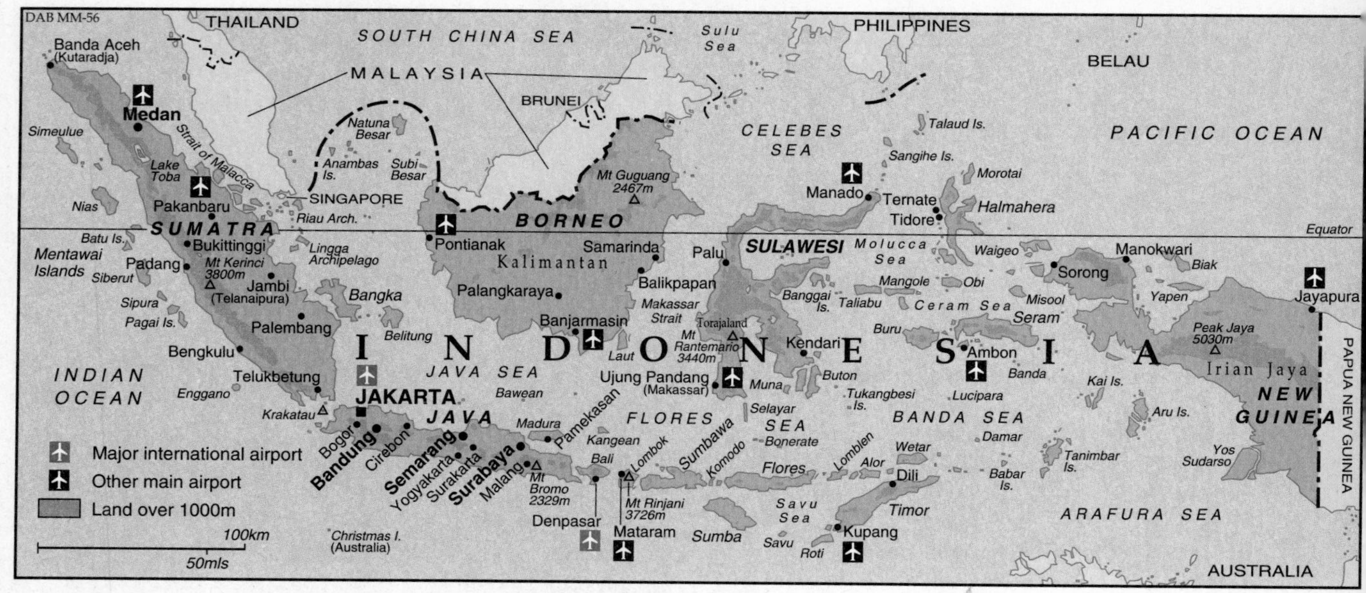

is the national language, but each ethnic group has its own language, and altogether more than 250 dialects are spoken. The older generation still speak Dutch as a second language, but a large number of younger people now speak some English.

RELIGION: There is a Muslim majority of about 87%, with Christian, Hindu (mainly in Bali) and Buddhist minorities. Animist beliefs are held in remote areas.

TIME: Indonesia spans three time zones:

Bangka, Billiton, Java, West and Middle Kalimantan, Madura and Sumatra: GMT + 7.

Bali, Flores, South and East Kalimantan, Lombok, Sulawesi, Sumba, Sumbawa and Timor: GMT + 8.

Aru, Irian Jaya, Kai, Moluccas and Tanimbar: GMT + 9.

ELECTRICITY: Generally 110 volts AC, 50Hz, but 220 volts AC, 50Hz, in some areas, including Jakarta; 220-volt supplies are gradually superseding 110-volt supplies.

COMMUNICATIONS: Telephone: IDD available to main cities. Country code: 62 (followed by 22 for Bandung, 21 for Jakarta, 61 for Medan, and 31 for Surabaya). **Telex/telegram:** Public telex facilities are operated from the Directorate General for Post and Communications in Jakarta (24 hours), and also from some major hotels and at the chief telegraphic offices in Semarang, Yogjakarta, Surabaya and Denpasar. Telegrams can be sent from any telegraphic office: in Jakarta facilities are available 24 hours a day, but services outside Jakarta are less efficient. **Post:** Airmail to Europe takes up to ten days. Internal mail is fast and generally reliable by the express service (Pos KILAT), but mail to the outer islands can be subject to considerable delays. **Press:** There are several English-language newspapers in Jakarta and on the other islands, notably *The Indonesian Times*, *Indonesian Observer* and *The Jakarta Post*.

BBC World Service and Voice of America frequencies: From time to time these change. See the section *How to Use this Book* for more information.

BBC:				
MHz	17.83	11.95	9.740	6.195
Voice of America:				
MHz	18.82	15.18	9.525	1.735

PASSPORT/VISA

Regulations and requirements may be subject to change at short notice, and you are advised to contact the appropriate diplomatic or consular authority before finalising travel arrangements. Details of these may be found at the head of this country's entry. Any numbers in the chart refer to the footnotes below.

	Passport Required?	Visa Required?	Return Ticket Required?
Full British	Yes	No	Yes
BVP	Not valid	-	-
Australian	Yes	1	Yes
Canadian	Yes	No	Yes
USA	Yes	No	Yes
Other EC	Yes	2	Yes
Japanese	Yes	No	Yes

Restricted entry: Portuguese nationals will be refused entry under all circumstances; nationals of South Africa and Israel require special permission.

PASSPORTS: Valid passport required by all; expiry date must be at least 6 months after date of entry.

British Visitors Passport: Not acceptable.

VISAS: Tourist visas are required by all except the following, providing stay does not exceed 60 days:

(a) nationals of countries referred to in the chart above;

(b) **[1]** Australian nationals (other than journalists, who *do* require visas);

(c) **[2]** nationals of EC countries with the exception of Portugal (see *Restricted entry* above);

(d) nationals of Argentina, Austria, Brazil, Brunei, Chile, Finland, Iceland, South Korea, Liechtenstein, Malaysia, Malta, Mexico, New Zealand, Norway, Philippines, Singapore, Sweden, Switzerland, Taiwan, Thailand, Venezuela and Yugoslavia;

(e) nationals of any country (except South Africa) travelling to Indonesia for conference purposes who have documentary proof of approval from the Indonesian government (also valid for tourist purposes).

Note: (a) All business visitors and all those visiting relatives or friends (ie not staying in a hotel) require a Business or Social visa, whatever their nationality. (b) All tourists wishing to stay longer than 30 days must obtain visas in advance of visit. (c) All children travelling with parents who require visas must also have visas, even if travelling on their parents' passports. (d) Travellers in transit may remain in the airport for up to 8 hours without a Transit visa.

Types of visa: Tourist (£6), Business (£10 for 4 weeks, £22 for 5 weeks), Social (cost as for Business) and Transit (£6). Business and Social visas are free to those not needing Tourist visas (as listed above). Re-entry permit visas cost £19.

Validity: Tourist – 2 months; Business and Social – 3 months.

Application to: Consulate (or Consular Section at Embassy). For addresses, see top of entry. Visas will not be issued on arrival.

Application requirements: (a) Passport valid for at least 6 months after entry date. (b) Application form. (c) 3 photos. (d) Sufficient funds to cover duration of stay. (e) Onward or return tickets, which may be purchased at point of entry.

Working days required: Minimum 3, for applications made by post or in person.

Temporary residence: Application to be made to the Consular Department at the Indonesian Embassy.

Note: People wishing to travel to Irian Jaya must obtain a special permit from the State Police Headquarters in Jakarta or regional police headquarters. Issue of the permit may take two days.

Gateways: Entry and exit must be made from one of the following ports: *Air:* Polonia, Batu Besar, Simpang Tiga, Tabing, Soekarno Hatta International, Halim Perdanakusuma, Ngurah Rai, Sam Ratulangie, Pattimura, Mokmar, Pontianak and Kupang. *Sea:* Belawan, Batu Ampar, Tanjung Emas, Tanjung Priok, Tanjung Perak, Benoa, Padang Bai, Pattimura, Ambon, Bitung and Sempang Tiga.

MONEY

Currency: Rupiah (Rp) = 100 sen. Notes are in denominations of Rp10,000, 5000, 1000, 500 and 100. Coins are in denominations of Rp100, 50, 25, 10 and 5.

Currency exchange: Though in the main centres for tourism there should be no difficulty exchanging major currencies, problems may occur elsewhere. The best currency for exchange purposes is the US Dollar.

Credit cards: Access/Mastercard, American Express, and Visa are accepted. Check with your credit card company for details of merchant acceptability and other services which may be available.

Travellers cheques: Limited merchant acceptance but can be easily exchanged at banks and larger hotels.

Exchange rate indicators: The following figures are included as a guide to the movements of the Rupiah against Sterling and the US Dollar:

Date:	Oct '89	Oct '90	Oct '91	Oct '92
£1.00=	2877	3676	3435	3318
$1.00=	1822	1882	1979	2091

Currency restrictions: There are no restrictions on the import or export of foreign currency. The import and export of local currency is limited to Rp50,000, which must be declared. Local currency may be exchanged on departure.

Banking hours: 0800/0830-1200/1400 Monday to Saturday.

DUTY FREE

The following goods may be imported into Indonesia by travellers over 18 years of age without incurring customs duty:

(a) For a 1-week stay:

200 cigarettes or 50 cigars or 100g of tobacco;
Less than 2 litres of alcohol (opened);
A reasonable amount of perfume;
Gifts up to the value of US$100.

(b) For a 2-week stay:

400 cigarettes or 100 cigars or 200g of tobacco;
Alcohol, perfume and gifts as above.

(c) For a stay of more than two weeks:

600 cigarettes or 150 cigars or 300g of tobacco;
Alcohol, perfume and gifts as above.

Note: Cameras and jewellery must be declared on arrival. It is prohibited to import weapons, ammunition, non-prescribed drugs, television sets, Chinese publications and medicines, and pornography.

PUBLIC HOLIDAYS

Public holidays observed in Indonesia are as follows:
Mar 25 '93 Eid al-Fitr (End of Ramadan). **Apr 9** Good Friday. **May 20** Ascension Day. **Jun 1** Eid al-Adha (Feast of the Sacrifice). **Jun 21** Muharram (Islamic New Year). **Aug 17** Indonesian National Day. **Aug 30** Mouloud (Prophet's Birthday). **Dec 25** Christmas Day. **Jan 1 '94** New Year's Day. **Mar** Start of Eid al-Fitr.

Note: (a) Muslim festivals are timed according to local sightings of various phases of the Moon and the dates given above are approximations. During the lunar month of Ramadan that precedes Eid al-Fitr, Muslims fast during the day and feast at night and normal business patterns may be interrupted. Many restaurants are closed during the day and there may be restrictions on smoking and drinking. Some disruption may continue into Eid al-Fitr itself. Eid al-Fitr and Eid al-Adha may last anything from two to ten days, depending on the region. For more information see the section *World of Islam* at the back of the book. (b) There are also Buddhist festivals timed according to phases of the moon.

HEALTH

Regulations and requirements may be subject to change at short notice, and you are advised to contact your doctor well in advance of your intended date of departure. Any numbers in the chart refer to the footnotes below.

	Special Precautions?	Certificate Required?
Yellow Fever	No	1
Cholera	Yes	2
Typhoid & Polio	Yes	-
Malaria	3	-
Food & Drink	4	-

[1]: A yellow fever vaccination certificate is required from travellers coming from infected areas and from those countries that have in the past been classified as endemic or infected areas.
[2]: Following WHO guidelines issued in 1973, a cholera vaccination certificate is no longer a condition of entry to Indonesia. However, cholera is a serious risk in this country and precautions are essential. Up-to-date advice should be sought before deciding whether these precautions should include vaccination as medical opinion is divided over its effectiveness. See the *Health* section at the back of the book.
[3]: Malaria risk in the malignant *falciparum* form throughout the year everywhere except parts of Java-Bali, Jakarta municipality and other big cities. The existing form is reported to be 'highly resistant' to chloroquine and 'resistant' to sulfadoxine/pyrimethane.
[4]: All water should be regarded as being a potential health risk. Water used for drinking, brushing teeth or making ice should have first been boiled or otherwise sterilised. Milk is unpasteurised and should be boiled. Powdered or tinned milk is available and is advised, but make sure that it is reconstituted with pure water. Avoid dairy products which are likely to have been made from local milk. Only eat well-cooked meat and fish, preferably served hot. Pork, salad and mayonnaise may carry increased risk. Vegetables should be cooked and fruit peeled.
Rabies is present. For those at high risk, vaccination before arrival should be considered. If you are bitten abroad seek medical advice without delay. For more information consult the *Health* section at the back of the book.
Bilharzia (schistosomiasis) is present in central Sulawesi. Avoid swimming and paddling in fresh water. Swimming pools which are well-chlorinated and maintained are safe.
Health care: Health insurance, to include emergency repatriation cover, is advised.

TRAVEL - International

Note: For a list of the air and sea ports which may be used to enter and exit Indonesia, see the end of the *Passport/Visa* section above.
AIR: Indonesia's national airline is *Garuda Indonesia* (GA).
Approximate flight times: From *London* to Jakarta is 20 hours 20 minutes and to Bali is 22 hours 15 minutes (with a good connection in Jakarta). From *Los Angeles* to Jakarta is 24 hours 20 minutes. From *New York* to Jakarta is 30 hours via Europe or 31 hours via Los Angeles. From *Singapore* to Jakarta is 1 hour 35 minutes. From *Sydney* to Jakarta is 7 hours 55 minutes.
International airports: *Jakarta (CGK)* (Soekarno-Hatta) is 20km (12 miles) northwest of the city (travel time – 45 minutes). A bus goes to the city every 30 minutes 0630-2100. Buses leave Jakarta from Gambir railway station and from Rawamangun and Blok M bus stations. Taxis are also available to the city centre at a cost of approx Rp12,000. Airport facilities include banks/bureaux de change, a post office, duty-free shops, gift shops, restaurants, snack bars (all open 1 hour before and after flights), car rental *(Hertz)* and 24-hour medical/vaccination facilities. A regular bus shuttle goes to Jakarta's second airport, *Halim Perdana Kusuma (HLP)*, 13km (8 miles) southeast of the city (travel time – 45 minutes).
Denpasar (DPS) (Ngurah Rai), 13km (8 miles) south of the city, is the main airport on Bali (travel time to city – 15 minutes). A bus goes to the city every 5 minutes 0400-2000. Return is from Jegal bus station, Imam Bonjal Street. Taxis are available to the city and to Kuta, Logian, Sanur and Nusadua. There are duty-free facilities at the airport.
Departure tax: This is levied on all passengers. From Jakarta and Denpasar the tax for international depar-

INDONESIA	**HEALTH REGULATIONS**	**VISA REGULATIONS** Code-Link
GALILEO/WORLDSPAN	TI-DFT/CGK/HE	TI-DFT/CGK/VI
SABRE	TIDFT/CGK/HE	TIDFT/CGK/VI

To access this information on your CRS, swipe the barcode with a light pen or type in the text under the barcode. For more information, see the introduction *How to Use This Book*.

tures is Rp15,000; for domestic flights it is Rp3500.
SEA: International ports are Belawan (Sumatra), Denpasar (Bali), Tanjung Priok (Java), Padang Bay (Bali), Surabaya (Java) and Tandjung Pinang.
Passenger lines: CTC, *Cunard*, *Dominion Far East*, *Lindblad*, *Norwegian American*, *Pacific International*, *P&O*, *Royal Viking*, *Sitmar* and *Windjammer Cruises*.
Cargo/passenger lines: *American President Lines*, *Austasia*, *Ben Shipping*, *Golden Line*, *Lykes*, *Polish Ocean* and *Royal Interocean*.
RAIL: There is a daily sea and rail service between Belawan and Penang (West Malaysia) operated by *National Railroad of Indonesia*.
ROAD: Indonesia's international land borders are between Kalimantan and the Malaysian states of Sarawak and Saba on the island of Borneo, and Irian Jaya and Papua New Guinea. There are no road links with Saba and the few (poorly maintained) roads to Sarawak are not recognised as gateways to Indonesia. Access through the forests of Papua New Guinea is virtually impossible (assuming it were allowed).

TRAVEL - Internal

AIR: Indonesia has a good internal air system linking most of the larger towns to Jakarta. *Kemayoran*, Jakarta's domestic airport, is 3km (1.8 miles) from the city. Domestic operators include *Bouraq Indonesia Airlines*, *Garuda Indonesia*, *Merpati Nusantara Airlines* and *Sempati*.
Visit Indonesia Air Pass: This gives access to varying numbers of cities depending on the ticket bought. Contact *Garuda Indonesia* for prices and further information.
SEA: Sailings available to Sumatra, Sulawesi and Kalimantan. Ferries between Ketapangan, Java, Gilimanuta and Bali depart regularly.
RAIL: There is a total of nearly 7000km (4350 miles) of track on Sumatra, Madura and Java. In Sumatra trains connect Belawan, Medan and Tanjong Balai/Rantu Prapet (two or three trains daily) in the north, and Palembang and Panjang (three trains daily) in the south. An extensive rail network runs throughout Java. The *Bima Express*, which has sleeping and restaurant cars, links Jakarta and Surabaya; there are also other express services. There are three classes of travel, but first class exists only on principal expresses. There is some air-conditioned accommodation.
ROAD: There are over 219,000km (136,875 miles) of roads in the country, of which about 13,000km (8125 miles) are main or national roads and 200km (125 miles) are motorway. There are good road communications within Java and to a lesser extent on Bali and Sumatra. The other islands have a poor road system, although conditions are improving with tourism becoming more important. **Bus:** There are regular services between most towns. Bus trips can be made from Jakarta to Bali (two days). Indonesia is the land of *jam karet* (literally 'rubber time') and complicated journeys involving more than a single change should not be attempted in a day. Bus fares are about the same as third-class rail. Vehicles can be extremely crowded. The crew includes three conductors who also act as touts. There are 'Bis Malam' night-buses on a number of routes, running in competition with the railways. Pre-booking is essential. **Taxi:** Available in all cities. All taxis are metered. Outside Jakarta, the *bajaj*, a bicycle rickshaw, can be hired by the journey or by the hour. **Car hire:** Available with local agents. Traffic drives on the left. **Documentation:** An International Driving Permit is required.
URBAN: Jakarta is the only city with an established conventional bus service of any size. Double-deckers are operated. In Jakarta and other major towns the *helecak*, a motorised rickshaw, offers cheaper transport than taxis. Fares should be bargained for. As well as taxis, there are also *bajajs*, pedicabs and other minibus-type services.

ACCOMMODATION

HOTELS: International hotels are found only in major towns and tourist areas. Several of these have business centres with a variety of services. High hotel taxes are charged (10% service, plus 10% government tax). Resort hotels on Bali vary from international class, luxury hotels to beach cottages along the shore. Most hotels have pools and can supply most leisure equipment. **Grading:** All hotels are graded according to facilities.

RESORTS & EXCURSIONS

For the purposes of this section the country has been divided into the main tourist areas, these being: Java, Sulawesi, Sumatra, Eastern Indonesia, Bali and Lombok.

Java

The capital city of **Jakarta** offers sightseeing from the colonial Dutch and British periods, with many fine colonial-style buildings and the recently restored 'old quarter'. The *National Monument* towers 140m (450ft) above the Merdeka Square and is crowned with a 'flame' plated in pure gold. The *Central Museum* has a fine ethnological collection including statues dating from the pre-Hindu era. Worth visiting is the *Portuguese Church*, completed by the Dutch in 1695, which houses a magnificent and immense Dutch pump organ. The modern *Istiqlal Mosque* in the city centre is one of the largest in the world. There is an antiques market on Jalan Surabaya and numerous batik factories in the Karet area which are worth a visit. Throughout the island, puppet shows are staged, in which traditional *wayang gotek* and *wayang Kulit* marionettes act out stories based on well-known legends; performances can sometimes last all night. 13km (8 miles) from Yogyakarta is the **Prambana** temple complex, built in honour of the Hindu gods Shiva, Brahma and Vishnu, which includes the 10th-century *Temple of Loro Jonggrang* and said to be the most perfectly proportioned Hindu temple in Indonesia. At the temple there are also open-air performances of Ramayana ballet which involve

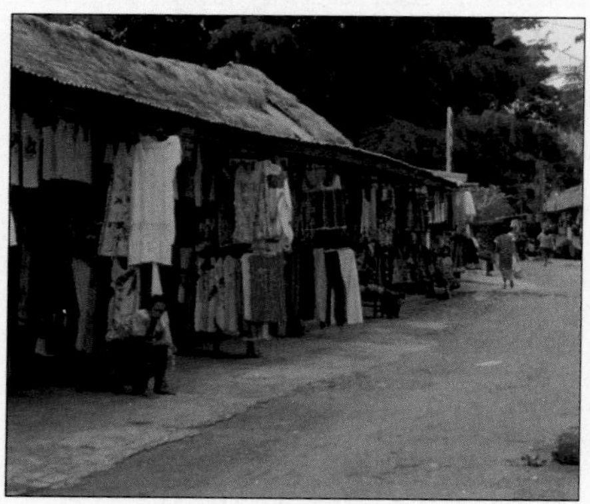

hundreds of dancers, singers and *gamelan* musicians. Perched on a hill to the west of Yogyakarta is **Borobudur**, probably the largest Buddhist sanctuary in the world, which contains more than 5km (3 miles) of relief carvings. The *Royal Mangkunegaran Palace* in Surakarta is now used as a museum and has displays of dance ornaments, jewellery and 19th-century carriages used for royal occasions. *Madiun* has Java's one and only cockfighting arena; fights take place on Thursday afternoons. **Mount Bromo** in the east of Java is still very active and horseback treks to the crater's edge can be made from nearby Surabaya. During August and September **Madura** is a venue for a series of bullock races which culminate in a 48-hour non-stop carnival celebration in the town of **Pamekasan.**

Sulawesi

Unofficially known as 'Orchid Island', Sulawesi is a land of high mountains, misty valleys and lakes. In the south is *Bantimurung Nature Reserve* which has thousands of exotic butterflies. The island has numerous geysers and hot springs, the most celebrated of which are at Makule, Karumengan, Lahendong, Kinilow and Leilem. **Torajaland** is known as the 'Land of the Heavenly Kings' and its people are noted for their richly-ornamented houses and custom of burying the dead in vertical cliff-side tombs. **Ujung Pandang,** formerly Makassar, is celebrated for the *Pinsa Harbour* where wooden schooners of the famous Buganese seafarers are moored. **Fort Rotterdam**, built by Sultan Ala in 1660 to protect the town from pirates, is now being restored. Racing is a popular island activity; there is horse racing and bullock racing and at *Ranomuut* there are races with traditional horse-drawn carts *(bendi)*.

Sumatra

Sumatra is the second-largest island in Indonesia, sitting astride the Equator, with a volcanic mountain range, hot springs, unexplored jungle and vast plantations. There are many reserves established to protect the indigenous wildlife from extinction. *Mount Loeser Reserve*, *Bengkulu* and *Gedung Wani* organise supervised safaris enabling visitors to see at close hand tigers, elephants, tapirs and rhinos. *Lake Toba*, once a volcanic crater, is 900m (3000ft) above sea level and has an inhabited island in the middle. *Lingga* village near **Medan** is a traditional Karonese settlement with stilted wooden houses which have changed little through the centuries. At **Bukkitinggi** is the old fortress of *Fort de Kock* and nearby a zoo, market, a renovated rice barn and the *Bundo Kandung Museum*. The best beaches are on the east coast.

Eastern Indonesia

Indonesia is made up of almost 14,000 islands. The wildest and least visited of these are in the east, gathered in two great archipelagos north and south of the treacherous Banda Sea.
MOLUCCAN ARCHIPELAGO: Also known as the Maluku Archipelago, it is made up of one thousand islands, many uninhabited and the rest so isolated from each other and (since the decline of the Spice Trade) from the outside world that each has its own culture and very often its own language.
Halmahera is the largest island in the Moluccan group and one of the most diverse. On the coast are relic populations of all the great powers who competed for domination of the Spice Trade – Arabs, Gujuratis, Malays, Portuguese and Dutch – whilst inland the people speak a unique language that has little or nothing in common even with other unique, but related, languages on the more remote islands. **Morotai,** to the north, was the site of a Japanese air base during World War II, but is now engaged in the production of copra and cocoa products. **Ternate** and **Tidore**, tiny volcanic islands off the west coast of Halmahera, were once the world's most important source of cloves and consequently amassed far more wealth and power than their size would seem to merit. The Sultanate of Ternate was an independent military power of considerable muscle before the arrival of the Portuguese, exerting influence over much of South-East Asia. Both islands are littered with the remains of this and the equally strident Colonial era and draw more tourists than their larger neighbour. Further south, **Ambon** was another important centre of the clove trade and has over 40 old Dutch fortresses dating from the early 17th century. **Banda**, in the middle of the Banda Sea, is often referred to as the original 'Spice Island' and is famous as a nutmeg-growing centre.
NUSA TENGARRA ARCHIPELAGO: Nusa Penida was at one time a penal colony but now attracts visitors to its dramatic seascapes and beaches. **Komodo** is home of the world's largest and rarest species of monitor lizard, while **Sumba** is noted for its beautiful 'Ikat' cloth. The islands north of **Timor** – including Solor, Lembata, Adonara, Alor, Wetar and Pantar – are rarely visited by tourists; there are many old fortresses on the islands and from here seafarers used to set sail on whale hunts. Timor itself is out of bounds to tourists because of the bloody and protracted war with separatists in the east of the island. The cultures on **Roti, Ndau** and **Sawu** have apparently changed little since the Bronze Age, yet the islands' inhabitants are renowned as musicians and palm weavers. The **Terawangan Islands** are a small group with beautiful

beaches and coral gardens. **Lucipara** has excellent waters for snorkeling. **Kangean, Tenggaya, Bone Rate** and **Tukang Besi** are a group of isolated atolls in the Flores and Banda seas epitomising everyone's idea of a tropical paradise.

IRIAN JAYA: The western part of the island of New Guinea, this is one of the last great unexplored areas of the world. Even today, visiting ships are often greeted by flotillas of warriors in war canoes. All those intending to visit Irian Jaya must obtain special permits from State Police Headquarters in Jakarta.

Bali

The landscape of Bali, 'Island of the Gods', is made up of volcanic mountains, lakes and rivers, terraced ricefields, giant banyans and palm groves and, on the coast, bays ringed with white sandy beaches. The island lies a short distance from the eastern coast of Java, across the Strait of Bali. Although its total area is only 2095 sq km (1309 sq miles) the island supports a population of approximately two and a half million. Unlike the rest of Indonesia, the predominant religious faith is Hinduism, though in a special form known as 'Agama-Hindu'. Stretching east to west across the island is a volcanic chain of mountains, dominated by the mighty **Gunung Agung** (Holy Mountain) whose conical peak soars more than 3170m (10,400ft) into the sky. North of the mountains, where the fertility of the terrain permits, is an area devoted to the production of vegetables and copra. The fertile rice-growing region lies on the central plains. The tourist areas are in the south, around **Sanur Beach** and at **Kuta**, which lies on the other side of a narrow isthmus.

The island has thousands of temples – the exact number has never been counted – ranging from the great 'Holy Temple' at **Besakih** to small village places of worship. Of the many festivals, most are held twice a year and involve splendid processions, dances and daily offerings of food and flowers made to the gods. Cremations are also held in great style, though their cost is often almost prohibitive for the average Balinese family.

Denpasar is the island's capital. Sights include the *Museum*, a new art centre and the internationally recognised *Konservatori Kerawitan*, one of the major centres of Balinese dancing. The *Sea Temple of Tanah Lot* on the west coast (a short drive from Kediri) is one of the most breathtaking sights of Bali. *Goa Gajah* (Elephant Cave) near Bedulu is a huge cavern with an entrance carved in a fantastic design of demoniacal shapes, animals and plants, crowned by a monstrous gargoyle-like head. The *Holy Springs of Tampaksiring* are believed to possess curative properties and attract thousands of visitors each year.

Serangan Island is also known as Turtle Island because of the turtles kept there in special pens. The island lies south of Sanur and can be reached by sail boat or, at low tide, on foot. Every six months the island becomes the scene of a great thanksgiving ceremony in which tens of thousands take part.

The sacred monkey forest at **Sangeh** is a forest reserve which, as well as being the home of a variety of exotic apes, also has a temple. **Penelokan** is a splendid vantage point for views of the black lava streams from *Mount Batur*. It is also possible to sail across the nearby *Lake Batur* to Trunyan for a closer look at the crater. North of Kintamani, at an altitude of 1745m (5725ft), lies the highest temple on the island, *Penulisan*. *Pura Besakih*, a temple which dates back originally to the 10th century, stands high on the volcanic slopes of Gunung Agung. Nowadays, it is a massive complex of more than 30 temples, and the setting for great ceremonial splendour on festival days. **Padangbai** is a beautiful tropical coastal village, where lush vegetation backs a curving stretch of white, sandy beach. It is also the island's port of call for giant cruise liners. *Goa Lawah* lives up to its name ('bat cave' in the local tongue), a safe and holy haven for thousands of bats which line every inch of space on its walls and roof. Non bat-lovers should avoid moonlight strolls in the area, as the animals leave for food sorties at night. *Kusambe* is a fishing village with a black sand beach. *Lake Bratan* is reached via a winding road from Budugul. The shimmering cool beauty of the lake and its pine forested hillsides is an unusual sight in a tropical landscape.

Lombok

15 minutes flight (or a ferry trip) away is Lombok, an unspoilt island whose name means 'chilli pepper'. Its area is 1285 sq km (803 sq miles). The island possesses one of the highest volcanic mountains in the Indonesian archipelago, *Mount Rindjani*, whose cloud-piercing peak soars to 3745m (12,290ft). The population of about 750,000 is a mixture of Islamic Sasaks, Hindu Balinese and others of Malay origin. The two main towns are **Mataram**, the capital, and the busy port of **Ampenan**; both are interesting to explore. The south coast is rocky. The west, with shimmering rice terraces, banana and coconut groves and fertile plains, looks like an extension of Bali. The east is dry, barren and desert-like in appearance. The north, the region dominated by Mount Rindjani, offers thick forests and dramatic vistas. There are also some glorious beaches, some of white sand, others, such as those near Ampenan, of black sand.

At **Narmada**, reached by an excellent east-west highway, is a huge complex of palace dwellings, complete with a well containing 'rejuvenating waters', built for a former Balinese king. At Pamenang you can hire a boat and go skindiving, entering a clear-water world of brilliantly coloured coral and inquisitive tropical fish.

Indonesian Culture

Dancing is considered an art, encouraged and practised from very early childhood. The extensive repertoire is based on ancient legends and stories from religious epics. Performances are given in village halls and squares, and also in many of the leading hotels by professional touring groups. The dances vary enormously, both in style and number of performers. Some of the more notable are the *Legong*, a slow, graceful dance of divine nymphs; the *Baris*, a fast moving, noisy demonstration of male, warlike behaviour; and the *Jauk*, a riveting solo offering by a masked and richly costumed demon. Many consider the most dramatic of all to be the famous *Cecak* (Monkey Dance) which calls for 100 or more very agile participants.

Art centres: The village of *Ubud* is the centre of Bali's considerable art colony and contains the galleries of the most successful painters, including those of artists of foreign extraction who have settled on the island. Set in a hilltop garden is the *Museam Puri Lukistan* (Palace of Fine Arts) with its fine display of sculpture and paintings in both old and contemporary styles. *Kamasan*, near Klungkung, is another centre, but the painting style of the artists is predominantly *wayang* (highly stylised). Other artistic centres include *Celuk* (gold and silver working), *Denpassar* (woodworking and painting) and *Batubulan* (stone carving).

SOCIAL PROFILE

FOOD & DRINK: Almost every type of international cuisine is available in Jakarta, the most popular being Chinese, French, Italian, Japanese and Korean. Indonesia's spices make its local cuisine unique. Specialities include: *rijstafel* (an Indonesian-Dutch concoction consisting of a variety of meats, fish, vegetables and curries), *sate* (chunks of beef,

fish, pork, chicken or lamb cooked on hot coals and dipped in a sauce of peanuts), *sate ajam* (broiled, skewered marinated chicken), *ajam ungkap* (Central Java; deep-fried, marinated chicken), *sate lileh* (Bali; broiled, skewered fish sticks), *ikan acar kuning* (Jakarta; lightly marinated fried fish served in a sauce of pickled spices and palm sugar), *soto* (a soup dish with dumpling, chicken and vegetables), *gado-gado* (Java; a salad of raw and cooked vegetables with peanut and coconut milk sauce), *babi guling* (Bali; roast suckling pig) and *opor ajam* (boiled chicken in coconut milk and light spices). Indonesians like their food highly spiced and the visitor should beware. In particular look out for the tiny, fiery hot, red and green peppers often included in salads and vegetable dishes. A feature of Jakarta are the many *warungs* (street stalls). Each specialises in its own dish or drink, but the traveller is probably best advised not to try them without the advice of an Indonesian resident. There are restaurants in the hotels which, along with many others, serve European, Chinese and Indian food.
NIGHTLIFE: Jakarta nightclubs feature international singers and bands and are open until 0400 during weekends. Jakarta has over 40 cinemas and some English-language and subtitled films are shown. There are also casinos, and theatres providing cultural performances. Many of the larger hotels, particularly in Bali, put on dance shows accompanied by the uniquely Indonesian Gamelan Orchestras. Throughout the year many local moonlight festivals occur; tourists should check locally. Indonesian puppets are world famous and shows for visitors are staged in various locations.
SHOPPING: Favourite buys are batik cloth, woodcarvings and sculpture, silverwork, woven baskets and hats, bamboo articles, krises (small daggers), paintings and woven cloth. At small shops bartering might be necessary. **Shopping hours:** 0830-2000 Monday to Saturday. Some shops open Sunday.
SPORT: Golf: There are golf courses at the major tourist destinations. **Skating:** There is an ice-skating rink at Jalan Pintu Gelora VII, Senayan. **Watersports:** The Putri Skindiving Centre, Tanjung Priok, can organise trips and rents out equipment. Swimming is safe at the beaches and many hotels have pools. **Horseriding:** The Jakarta International Saddle Club maintains a complex of sports facilities where riding lessons are available. **Spectator sports:** Horseraces are held every Sunday afternoon at Pulo Mas, JLJ Ahmed Yani. Jai Alai (a form of Basque Pelota) is played daily at Hailai Jaya Ancol, Bina Ria, Tanjung Priok. Chinese shadow boxing competitions can be watched at Loka Sari and JL Mangga Besar. There are fully equipped watersports centres on Java, one at '1000 Islands' north of Jakarta, another at Surabaya.
SPECIAL EVENTS: There are a number of festivals which take place during the year, the dates of which often vary according to the Hindu or Buddhist calendars. Bali stages some magnificent festivals all year round. Festival calendars can be obtained on arrival. The Sultan's birthday in mid-December is celebrated by a fair and festival in Yogyakarta, Java. Some of the more important events throughout the year are listed below (for exact dates contact the tourist office):
Feb *Pasola Jousting Tournament*, Sumba Island; *Nyale Festival*, South Lombok. **Mar-Apr** *Maleman Sriwedari*, a month-long traditional night fair, Central Java. **Apr** *Mappanre Tasi Ceremony*, South Kalimantan. **May** *Jakarta Festival*. **Jun** *Paper Kite Festival*, Pangandaran Beach. **Jun-Jul** *Bali Arts Festival*; *Lake Toba Festival*, North Sumatra. **Jul** *Bunaken Festival*, North Sulawesi; *Tabuik*, West Sumatra; *Art Festival*, Banda Aceh; *Art Festival*, South Sulawesi; *Tabot*, Bengkulu. **Jul-Aug** *Darwin, Australia to Ambon Yacht Competition*, Ambon. **Aug** *Bidar Canoe Race*, South Sumatra; *Pacu Jalur*, Riau; *The Lake of Poso Festival*, Central Sulawesi. **Sep** *Grebeg Maulid*, Yogykarta; *Erau Festival*, East Kalimantan. **Nov** *Kesodo Ritual Ceremony*, East Java.
SOCIAL CONVENTIONS: Indonesia encompasses no fewer than 250 separate languages and dialects, many of them as different from each other as Welsh is from English. Since independence many have developed a strong sense of national pride, and maintain traditions of dance, painting, woodcarving and stone-carving. Social courtesies are often fairly formal. In particular, when drink or food is served, it should not be touched until the host invites the guest to do so. Never pass or accept anything with the left hand. Indonesians are polite and will extend endless courtesies to foreigners whom they trust and like. When invited home a gift is appreciated (as long as it is given with the right hand). Informality is normal, but a few smart establishments encourage guests to dress for dinner. Safari suits are acceptable on formal occasions and for business wear. Muslim customs, especially those concerning female clothes, should be observed. **Tipping:** Not compulsory. 10% is customary except where a service charge is included in the bill. Porters expect Rp500 per bag.

BUSINESS PROFILE

ECONOMY: Oil and gas are the backbone of the Indonesian economy, providing half of both domestic product and export earnings. Revenues are now set to decline steadily and the Government is seeking to broaden the country's economic base. The country has immense potential with reserves of tin, bauxite, nickel, copper and gold; it is also one of the world's leading producers of rubber and a major source of tea and coffee. The manufacturing industry is growing steadily and has now become a significant export earner in its own right. Two-thirds of the land is covered by forest but the Government has banned further commercial logging operations. Japan is the country's major trading partner, supplying manufactured goods in exchange for raw materials. The pattern of trade with the United States, Singapore and Germany is similar.
BUSINESS: Business dealings should be conducted through an agent and tend to be slow. Visiting cards are widely used. Literature should be in English, but prices should be quoted in US Dollars as well as Sterling. **Office hours:** 0700/0900-1500/1700 Monday to Friday. Some offices open on Saturday mornings. **Government office hours:** 0800-1500 Monday to Thursday, 0800-1130 Friday and 0800-1200 Saturday.
COMMERCIAL INFORMATION: The following organisation can offer advice: Kamar Dagang dan Industri Indonesia (KADIN) (Indonesian Chamber of Commerce and Industry), 3rd-5th Floors, Chandra Building, Jalan M H Thamrin 20, Jakarta 10350. Tel: (21) 324 000. Fax: (21) 310 6098. Telex: 61262.

HISTORY & GOVERNMENT

HISTORY: For almost a thousand years, Indonesia has been involved in maritime trade, resulting in a wide range of religious, cultural and ethnic influences. The Chinese were among the first to trade with the islands, followed by Hindu and Buddhist merchants from India. In the 9th century, Arab and Malay seafarers introduced the Islamic faith, with European ideas and beliefs arriving much later. From 1814 until the Japanese invasion during World War II, Indonesia's people and resources were subjected to the autocratic Dutch rule. When finally Indonesia proclaimed its independence in 1945, the country had literally been stripped of many of its natural riches and little had been built by the colonial powers in return. In addition to the massive task of developing this incipient nation, Indonesia also had to overcome suspicious minorities and rivalries among their dozens of tribes and ethnic groups. The leaders chose as their national motto the phrase *Bhineka Tunggal Ika*, meaning 'unity in diversity'. The country's first President, Dr Sukarno, had been a prominent figure in the independence movement since the 1920s. The Sukarno government's foreign policy had two main elements: an active role in the new and relatively vibrant Non-Aligned Movement; and a close relationship with China, recently taken over by the Communists and consequently the key regional power outside the control of the Western powers. The domestic agenda always dominated, however, and in its efforts to hold the country together and hold on to power, the regime became increasingly repressive and corrupt. Economic difficulties further fuelled the growth of the opposition, in particular the powerful Indonesian Communist Party (PKI). In September 1965, a coup was launched by sections of the army with full PKI support. The immediate political struggle, which the Government eventually won, was one of the closest in recent history. The army chief of staff, General Suharto, backed Sukarno, and saved the regime. Between 400,000 and 1 million died in the aftermath of the coup. In March 1967, Suharto took over the Presidency, which he holds to this day. Under the Suharto government, the army holds ultimate political power while a technocrat class runs the country day-to-day. The regime has brought Indonesia comparative peace, stability and steady economic growth. Manifestations of Muslim fundamentalism – Indonesia is the world's largest Muslim country – are rigorously con-

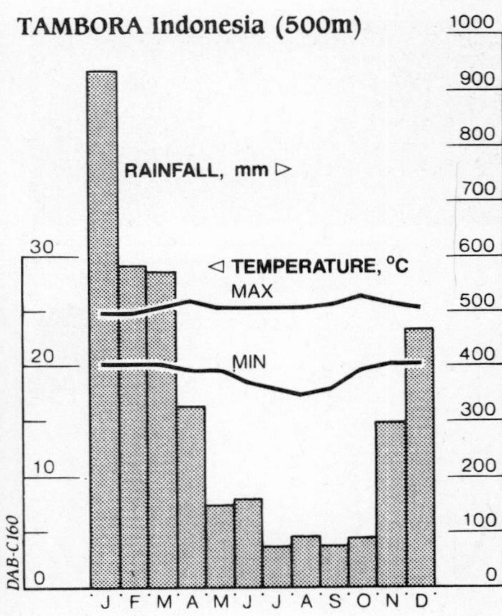

trolled by the Government: both Sukarno and Suharto have adhered consistently to a policy of allowing religious diversity as a guarantor of social stability, although attempts to formally enshrine this in an official doctrine of Pancsila were dropped and the Government has since introduced various pro-Islamic policies. Jakarta faces rebellions in some parts of its sprawling territory. The most prominent of these is East Timor. Vacated suddenly in 1975 by the Portuguese, whose colony it had been, East Timor enjoyed just a few days of independence before Indonesian troops invaded and claimed the territory as Indonesia's 27th province. In the counter-insurgency campaign which followed, the Indonesian army killed over one hundred thousand East Timor inhabitants during their pursuit of the pro-independence guerrillas of FRETILIN (Frente Revolucionário de Este Timor Independente). Although FRETILIN is still active, the Indonesian army controls most of the territory, and recent incidents such as the brutal massacre of unarmed pro-independence demonstrators in the capital Dili in November 1991 show that the army intends to maintain a firm grip on the territory. Elsewhere, Aceh in northern Sumatra and the Melanesians of Irian Jaya have both risen up in the past few years in opposition to the Government's economic development and population policies. Although Indonesia is a long-standing member of the Non-Aligned Movement, Suharto has steadily tilted his country towards the West in recent years, and joined the pro-western ASEAN bloc (Association of South East Asian Nations). Relations between Indonesia and China (with whom Sukarno was previously friendly) and with the then Soviet Union improved greatly from the mid-1980s onwards. National Assembly elections in June 1992 saw the government-backed Golkar party returned once again with 67% of the vote, a small drop from the 73% which it attracted at the previous poll in 1987. The main opposition parties, the United Development Party (PPP) and the Democratic Party of Indonesia (DPI) won 17% and 15% respectively.

GOVERNMENT: Power essentially lies with the President and his advisers, who have a secure base in the armed forces. The Indonesian parliament is bicameral, consisting of the People's Congress (MPR) and the People's Representative Assembly (DPR), each elected for 5-year terms. The government-sponsored Sekber Golkar party holds a majority in each chamber.

CLIMATE

Tropical climate varying from area to area. The Eastern monsoon brings the driest weather (June to September). The Western monsoon brings the main rains (December to March). Rainstorms occur all year. Higher regions are cooler.

Required clothing: Lightweights with rainwear. Warmer clothes are needed for cool evenings and upland areas.

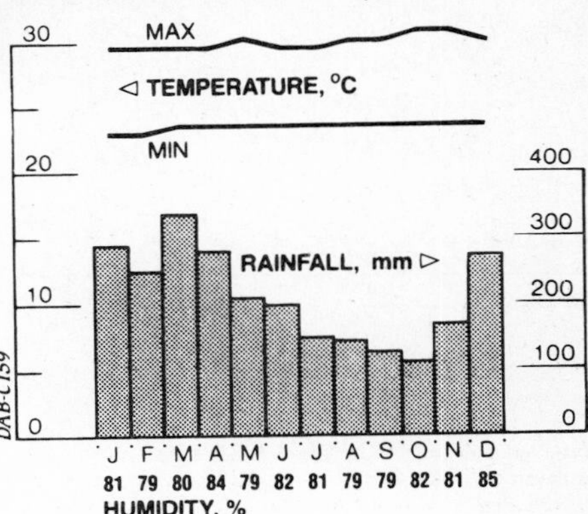

BALIKPAPAN Indonesia (7m)

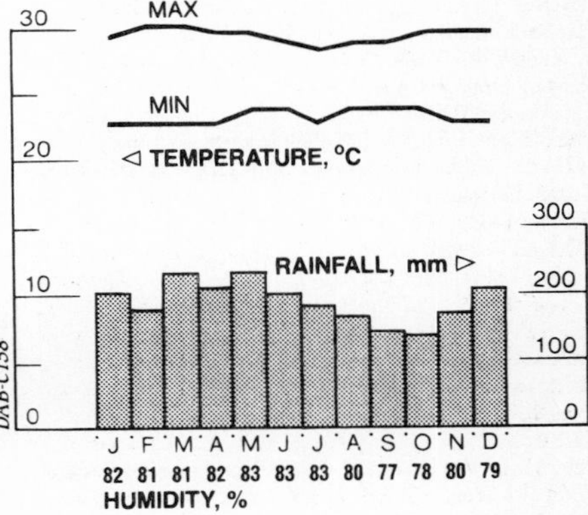

JAKARTA Indonesia (8m)

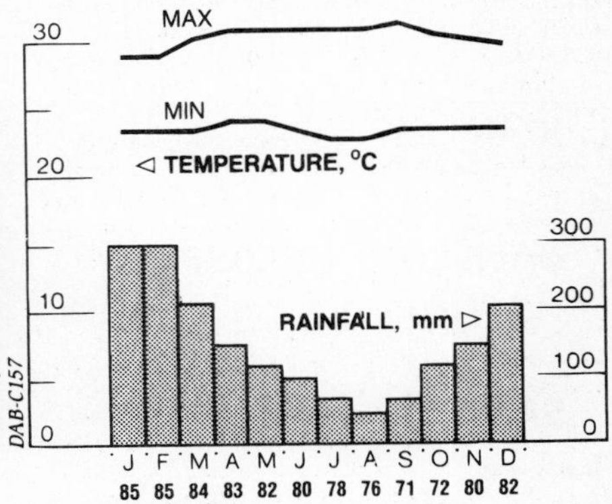

IRAN

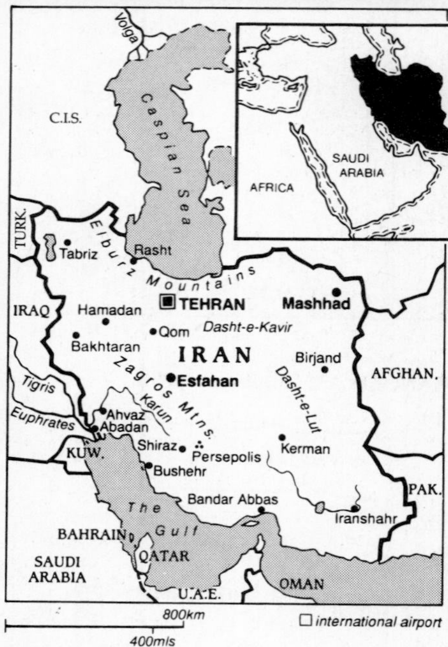

Location: Middle East.

Iran National Tourist Organisation (INTO)
boulevard Elisabeth II
Tehran, Iran
Tel: (21) 624 019 *or* 626 428.

Embassy of the Islamic Republic of Iran
27 Prince's Gate
London SW7 1PX
Tel: (071) 584 8101. Fax: (071) 589 4440. Telex: 23998 IRAN GB.

Iranian Consulate
50 Kensington Court
Kensington High Street
London W8 5DB
Tel: (071) 937 5225 *or* 795 4949 (for visa enquiries). Fax: (071) 938 1615. Opening hours: 0900-1200 Monday to Friday.

British Embassy
PO Box 11365-4474
143 Ferdowsi Avenue
Tehran 11344, Iran
Tel: (21) 675 011 (7 lines). Fax: (21) 678 021. Telex: 212493 PROD IR.

Embassy of the Islamic Republic of Iran
245 Metcalfe Street
Ottawa, Ontario
K2P 2K2
Tel: (613) 235 4726 *or* 233 4726 (Consular section). Fax: (613) 232 5712.

Canadian Embassy
PO Box 11365-4647
57 Shahid Javad-e-Sarfaraz
Ostad-Motahari Avenue
Tehran, Iran
Tel: (21) 622 623. Fax: (21) 623 202. Telex: 212337 MCAN IR.

AREA: 1,648,000 sq km (636,296 sq miles).
POPULATION: 54,203,000 (1989 estimate).
POPULATION DENSITY: 32.9 per sq km.
CAPITAL: Tehran. **Population:** 6,042,548 (1986).
GEOGRAPHY: Iran is located in the Middle East, bounded to the north by the CIS and the Caspian Sea, the east by Afghanistan and Pakistan, the south by the Persian Gulf and the Gulf of Oman, and the west by Iraq and Turkey. The centre and east of the country is largely barren undulating desert, punctured by *qanats* (irrigation canals) and green oases, but there are mountainous regions in the west along the Turkish and Iraqi borders and in the north where the Elburz Mountains rise steeply from a fertile belt around the Caspian Sea.
LANGUAGE: Persian *(Farsi)* is the most widely spoken language, Arabic is spoken in Khuzistan in the southwest and Turkish in the northwest around Tabriz. English, French and (to a lesser extent) German is spoken by many businessmen and officials.
RELIGION: Predominantly Islamic; mostly Shi'ite, with a minority of Sunnis. The 1976 census recorded 300,000 Christians, 80,000 Jews and 30,000 Zoroastrians.
TIME: GMT + 3.5.
ELECTRICITY: 220 volts AC, 50Hz.
COMMUNICATIONS: Telephone: IDD service available. Country code: 98. Telephone booths are yellow. **Telex/telegram:** Facilities are available at the Central Telegraph Office, Meydan Sepah, Tehran. There are three rates of charge. There are also telex facilities at the major hotels. **Post:** Airmail to Europe can take at least two weeks. The Central Post Office in Tehran is on Sepah Avenue. Post boxes are yellow. Stamps can be bought at some cigarette kiosks. Post office hours: Generally 0730-1400 Saturday to Thursday, but some main post offices stay open until 1900. **Press:** Officially the press is free, but in practice it is highly censored. The main English-language daily is the *Tehran Times*.
BBC World Service and Voice of America frequencies: From time to time these change. See the section *How to Use this Book* for more information.

BBC:				
MHz	17.64	15.57	11.76	7.160
Voice of America:				
MHz	9.670	6.040	5.995	1.260

PASSPORT/VISA

Regulations and requirements may be subject to change at short notice, and you are advised to contact the appropriate diplomatic or consular authority before finalising travel arrangements. Details of these may be found at the head of this country's entry. Any numbers in the chart refer to the footnotes below.

	Passport Required?	Visa Required?	Return Ticket Required?
Full British	Yes	Yes	Yes
BVP	Not valid	-	-
Australian	Yes	Yes	Yes
Canadian	Yes	Yes	Yes
USA	Yes	Yes	Yes
Other EC	Yes	Yes	Yes
Japanese	Yes	No	Yes

Entry restrictions: Nationals of Israel, Jordan and Morocco will be refused entry under all circumstances. Women judged to be dressed immodestly will be refused entry.
PASSPORTS: Valid passport required by all.
British Visitors Passport: Not acceptable.
VISAS: Required by all except nationals of Turkey and Yugoslavia (for a stay not exceeding 3 months).
Types of visa: Entry, Transit and Business. Fee varies according to nationality of applicant and type of visa.
Note: (a) A visa cannot be issued for passports which have a validity of less than 6 months. (b) All foreigners must register with the police within 48 hours of arrival. (c) Exit permits required by all (often included with visa).
Validity: Entry visa: up to 3 months from the date of authorisation. Transit visa: maximum of 10 days. Applications for renewal or extension should be made to the Iranian Embassy.
Application to: Consulate (or Consular Section at Embassy). For addresses, see top of entry.
Application requirements: (a) 2 completed application forms. (b) 3 photos. (c) Stamped self-addressed envelope, if passport sent by post. (d) Fee. (e) Holders of British passports applying for a Transit visa must provide a letter of recommendation from the British Foreign and Commonwealth Office in London. All other nationals must provide a similar letter from the appropriate Embassy. (f) Applicants for a Business visa must have the authorisation of the Iranian Ministry of Foreign Affairs (to be obtained via business associates in Iran).
Other requirements: A return ticket must be purchased before travelling to Iran. Those buying their outward ticket from Iran should provide a letter from an Iranian bank indicating that the equivalent in currency of the cost of the ticket has been exchanged.
Working days required: Business visa: 1 week. Others: 4 weeks.
Temporary residence: All foreigners wishing to stay for more than 3 months must obtain a residence permit. Application must be made within 8 days of arrival to Police Headquarters or the Ministry of Foreign Affairs in Tehran.

MONEY

Currency: Iranian Rial (RL) = 100 dinars. Notes are in denominations of RL10,000, 5000, 2000, 1000, 500, 200 and 100. Coins are in denominations of RL50, 20, 10, 5, 2 and 1.
Exchange rate indicators: The following figures are included as a guide to the movements of the Iranian Rial against Sterling and the US Dollar:

Date:	**Oct '89**	**Oct '90**	**Oct '91**	**Oct '92**
£1.00=	**116.90**	**126.90**	**115.80**	**104.15**
$1.00=	**74.03**	**64.96**	**66.72**	**65.63**

Currency restrictions: There are no restrictions on the import of foreign currency if declared on arrival (there is a special form). Export of foreign currency is up to the limit imported and declared. Import of local currency is up to RL20,000. Export of local currency is up to RL5000. Any amount larger than this requires authorisation from the Central Bank. With one exception, all the Iranian banks were nationalised in June 1979. The number of foreign banks has fallen dramatically since the Revolution, but there are still around 30 in operation. Foreign visitors must convert the equivalent of US$300 into Rials.
Banking hours: 0730-1330 Saturday to Wednesday, 0800-1230 Thursday. Closed Friday.

DUTY FREE

The following goods may be imported into Iran without incurring customs duty:
200 cigarettes or equivalent in tobacco products;
A reasonable quantity of perfume for personal use;
Gifts on which the import duty/tax would not exceed RL11,150.
Prohibited items: Alcohol, narcotics, guns and ammunition, aerial photo cameras, radio apparatus, fashion magazines and filmed, recorded or printed material carrying views contrary to those held by the current regime.

PUBLIC HOLIDAYS

Public holidays observed in Iran are as follows:
Mar 20 '93 Oil Nationalisation Day. **Mar 21-24** Now Ruz (Iranian New Year). **Mar 25** Eid al-Fitr (End of Ramadan). **Apr 1** Islamic Republic Day. **Apr 2** Revolution Day. **Jun 1** Eid al-Adha (Feast of the Sacrifice). **Jun 9** Ashoura. **Jul 14** Martyrdom of Imam Ali. **Aug 30** Mouloud (Prophet's Birthday). **Jan 20 '94** Leilat al-Meiraj (Ascension of Muhammad). **Feb 11**

IRAN	HEALTH REGULATIONS	VISA REGULATIONS	Code-Link
GALILEO/WORLDSPAN	 TI-DFT/THR/HE	TI-DFT/THR/VI	
SABRE	 TIDFT/THR/HE	 TIDFT/THR/VI	

To access this information on your CRS, swipe the barcode with a light pen or type in the text under the barcode. For more information, see the introduction *How to Use This Book.*

National Day (Fall of the Shah).
Note: Muslim festivals are timed according to local sightings of various phases of the Moon and the dates given above are approximations. During the lunar month of Ramadan that precedes Eid al-Fitr, Muslims fast during the day and feast at night and normal business patterns may be interrupted. Many restaurants are closed during the day and there may be restrictions on smoking and drinking. Some disruption may continue into Eid al-Fitr itself. Eid al-Fitr and Eid al-Adha may last anything from two to ten days, depending on the region. For more information see the section *World of Islam* at the back of the book.

HEALTH

Regulations and requirements may be subject to change at short notice, and you are advised to contact your doctor well in advance of your intended date of departure. Any numbers in the chart refer to the footnotes below.

	Special Precautions?	Certificate Required?
Yellow Fever	No	1
Cholera	No	No
Typhoid & Polio	Yes	-
Malaria	2	-
Food & Drink	3	-

[1]: A yellow fever vaccination certificate is required from travellers over one year of age coming from infected areas. Former endemic zones are considered to be infected.
[2]: Malaria risk, mainly in the benign *vivax* form, exists from March through November in Sistan-Baluchestan and Hormozgan provinces, the southern parts of Fars, Kohgiluyeh-Boyar, Lorestan, and Chahar Mahal-Bakhtiari governates, and the north of Khuzestan. Resistance to chloroquine has been reported in the malignant *falciparum* strain.
[3]: Mains water is normally chlorinated, and whilst relatively safe may cause mild abdominal upsets. Bottled water is available and is advised for the first few weeks of the stay. Pasteurised milk is available; unpasteurised milk should be boiled. Powdered or tinned milk is available and is advised, but make sure that it is reconstituted with pure water. Avoid dairy products which are likely to have been made from local milk. Only eat well-cooked meat and fish, preferably served hot. Salad and mayonnaise may carry increased risk. Vegetables should be cooked and fruit peeled.
Rabies is present. For those at high risk, vaccination before arrival should be considered. If you are bitten abroad seek medical advice without delay. For more information consult the *Health* section at the back of the book.
Bilharzia (schistosomiasis) is present in southwestern Iran. Avoid swimming and paddling in stagnant fresh water. Swimming pools which are well-chlorinated and maintained are safe.
Health care: Health facilities are limited outside Tehran. Medical insurance is essential.

TRAVEL - International

AIR: Iran's national airline is *Iran Air (IR)*.
Approximate flight time: From *London* to Tehran is 8 hours 5 minutes.
International airport: *Tehran (THR)* (Mehrabad) is 11km (7 miles) west of the city. Airline buses are available to the city for a fare of RL10 (travel time – 30 minutes). Taxis are also available to the city centre for approx. RL1200 (travel time – 30-45 minutes). Airport facilities include a 24-hour bank, 24-hour post office, 24-hour restaurant, snack bar, 24-hour duty-free shop, gift shops, 24-hour tourist information, first aid/vaccination facilities.
Departure tax: RL1500 for foreigners, RL1000 for nationals. Transit passengers remaining in the airport and children under two years of age are exempt.
SEA: The main port was Khorramshahr, but this is now totally destroyed from the war with Iraq. Bandar Abbas and Bandar Anzelli are still in use as ports. *P&O* connect Iranian ports with Persian Gulf States and Karachi.
RAIL: Sleeping cars run once-weekly from Moscow through to Tehran. The *Qom-Zahedan Line*, when completed, will link Europe with India, but the through train from Turkey to Tehran is currently suspended. Contact Embassy or *Iranian State Railways* (see below) for details.
ROAD: No reliable international through road links. There are various routes possible from Turkey and Pakistan, but these are not recommended. Cars can also be put on boats at Venice or Brindisi and picked up at Ezmir. For details of political conditions governing access, contact the Embassy. See below for information on required **documentation**.

TRAVEL - Internal

AIR: *Iran Air* runs services to Tehran, Tabriz, Isfahan, Shiraz, Mashhad, Khorramshahr, Zahedan and other major cities. *Aseman Air* also runs services to the major cities. The vast size of Iran makes internal flights the most practical method of transport.
Departure tax: RL1000 on all departures.
RAIL: The Trans-Iranian Railway is of relatively recent construction, being started in 1938. The main line links Bandar-e Khomaini at the bottom of the Persian Gulf to Bandar-e Torkman at the southeast of the Caspian Sea through Ahvaz, Dorud, Arak, Qom, Tehran and Sari. Several other lines connect from remote provinces. Frontier stations are Razi (for Turkey), Djolfa (for the CIS) and Kerman (for bus link with Pakistan). There are many areas in the mountains and the desert which can only be reached by rail. However, rail links are at present uncertain.
Rail services are operated by *Iranian State Railways*, Tehran. Tel: (021) 6114/5. Telex: 213103. There are some air-conditioned trains, also sleeping and dining cars on many trains. Daily services run on all routes. There are slightly over 4560km (2830 miles) of rail track in the country; several new lines are under construction and others are being extended.
ROAD: The road network is extensive, with more than 33,000km (20,500 miles) of paved roads and 456km (283 miles) of motorways, but the quality is unreliable. The two main roads, the A1 and A2 (not wholly completed as yet), link the Iraqi and Pakistani borders and the Afghanistani and Turkish borders. **Bus:** Widespread, cheap and comfortable, although services tend to be erratic. **Taxi:** Available in all cities. The Urban Taxis (orange or blue) will carry several passengers at a time and are much cheaper than the private taxis which only carry one person. Group taxis for up to ten people are available for intercity travel. Prices are negotiated beforehand and tipping is not necessary. **Car hire:** Available in most cities and from airports. **Documentation:** An International Driving Licence is required. Personal insurance is also required. Traffic drives on the right. All motorists entering Iran must possess a *Carnet de Passage en Douane* or pay a large deposit.
URBAN: Tehran has an extensive bus system, including double-deckers. Tickets are bought in advance at kiosks. Plans for a 4-line metro were suspended after the 1979 revolution, and construction did not recommence until 1986.
JOURNEY TIMES: The following chart gives approximate journey times (in hours and minutes) from Tehran to other major cities/towns in Iran.

	Air	Road	Rail
Ahvaz	1.30	17.00	19.00
B. Abbas	1.55	28.00	-
Esfahan	1.00	8.00	9.00
Kerman	1.30	20.00	18.00
Mashhad	1.30	14.00	15.00
Shiraz	1.30	15.00	-
Tabriz	1.20	12.00	11.00

ACCOMMODATION

HOTELS: A number of hotels are available and there is a fair range of accommodation. The fact that a hotel bears the name of an internationally known chain does not necessarily imply any current management connection. Student accommodation is available in small hotels. Schools and private houses also offer accommodation.
CAMPING/CARAVANNING: There are limited camping facilities and off-site camping is discouraged. Registration with the police is required if camping.

RESORTS & EXCURSIONS

Tehran, the capital, is essentially a modern city, but the best of the old has been preserved. The *Sepahsalar Mosque* has eight minarets, from which the city can be viewed. The *Bazaar* (open every day except Fridays and religious holidays) is one of the world's largest. An endless maze of vaulted alleys, everything from fine carpets to silver and copper ware to exotic aromatic spices can be found here. There is a separate section for each trade practised and craftsmen can be seen at their work. Museums include the *Archaeological* (open 0900-1200 and 1300-1600 daily, 0800-1100 Friday; closed Tuesdays), *Ethnological* (open 0800-1500 daily; closed Thursday and Friday), *Contemporary Art* (open 0900-1200 and 1300-1600 daily; closed Monday), *Glass and Ceramics* (open 0900-1200 and 1300-1600 daily; closed Monday), *Decorative Art* (open 0900-1200 and 1300-1600 daily; closed Monday) and *National Art* (open 0800-1600 daily; closed Thursday and Friday). More traditional towns, such as **Rey, Varamin, Qazvin** and **Shemshak**, are within easy reach of Tehran.
The area of **Azerbaijan** borders Turkey, Iraq and the CIS. It is a region of mountains, fertile valleys and the great salt lake of *Rezaiyeh*. The town of **Tabriz** is the country's second largest city, with a ruined but restored fine Blue mosque built in 1465. The covered *Qaisariyeh Bazaar* dates back to the 15th century. About 22km (14 miles) from the salt lake is the town of **Rezaiyeh,** which claims to be the birthplace of Zoroaster. Other towns worth visiting include **Ardebil, Astara, Bandar, Enzeki** and **Rasht.**
The Golden Triangle is the name popularly given to the region enclosed by the ancient cities of **Hamadan, Kermanshahan** and **Khorrambabad**. This is a part of Iran which is particularly rich in historical associations; for many centuries the *Silk Route* passed through the pleasant rolling countryside of the region, and there are several indications of settlements dating back over 6000 years. **Hamadan** was the summer capital of the Persian Emperors, although one of the few easily visible signs of the city's antiquity is the *Stone Lion*, dating back to the time of Alexander. **Kermanshahan** is a good base for visiting the *Taghe Bostan Grottoes*, which have several excellent bas-relief carvings. The site of the *Seleucid Temple of Artemis* is in **Kangavar;** it consists of massive fallen columns and is now being reconstructed.
Isfahan is the former capital of Persia. The city's most remarkable feature is its magnificent central square which is roughly seven times larger than San Marco in Venice. The mosques, palaces, bridges and gardens also deserve a visit. The *Friday Mosque* (Masjid-e Jomeh) is one of Iran's finest buildings. The *Shaikh Lotfullah Mosque* is famous for the stalactite effect of its northern entrance. There are also several good bazaars.
Shiraz is the capital of the **Fars Province**, and another of the country's ancient cities. Several of the buildings date back to the 9th century, and there are several excellent parks and gardens. 50km (30 miles) away is **Persepolis,** famous for the *Ceremonial Seat of Darius*, built on an enormous platform carved out of the Kuhe Rahmat.
Khorasan is a large province in the east where a great revival of learning occurred in the early Middle Ages.
Mashhad, a former trading post on the Silk Route, is the capital of the region.
The city of **Kerman** in the southern desert region has several stunning mosques and a ruined citadel.

SOCIAL PROFILE

FOOD & DRINK: Rice is the staple food and the Iranians cook it superbly. Dishes include *chelo khoresh* (rice topped with vegetables and meat in a nut sauce), *polo chele* (pilau rice), *polo sabzi* (pilau rice cooked with fresh herbs), *polo chirin* (sweet-sour saffron-coloured rice with raisins, almonds and orange), *adas polo* (rice, lentils and meat), *morgh polo* (chicken and pilau rice), *chelo kababs* (rice with skewered meats cooked over charcoal), *kofte* (minced meat formed into meatballs), *kofte gusht* (meatloaf), *abgusht* (thick stew), *khoreshe badinjan* (mutton and aubergine stew), *mast-o-khier* (cold yoghurt-based soup flavoured with mint, chopped cucumber and raisins) and *dolmeh* (stuffed aubergine, courgettes or peppers). Most Iranian meals are eaten with a spoon and fork, but visitors may choose a Western dish and eat with a knife and fork. **Drink:** Fruit and vegetable juices are popular, as are sparkling mineral waters. Tea is also popular and drunk in the many tea-houses *(ghahve khane)*. The consumption of alcohol is strictly forbidden.
SHOPPING: While the shops offer a wide selection of quality goods, local items can be bought in the many bazaars. Purchases include hand-carved, inlaid woodwork; carpets; rugs; silks; leather goods; mats; tablecloths; gold; silver; glass and ceramics. Bargaining is customary.
SPORT: Water-skiing facilities are available at the Karadj Dam near Tehran. Hotel **swimming** pools are open to non-residents and an entrance fee is charged. Some hotels have **tennis** courts and instruction is available at the Amjadieh Sports Centre in Tehran. There are several **horseriding** clubs, particularly in Tehran. There is an 18-hole **golf** course in Tehran affiliated to the Hilton Hotel on Valiye Asr Avenue. **Skiing:** The skiing season is from January to March in the Elburz Mountains. Resorts include Abe Ali, 62km (38 miles) east of Tehran; the Noor Slope, 71km (44 miles) from the capital; Shemshak, 59km (37 miles) from Tehran, and Dizine near the town of Gatchsar. Equipment for hire and all the usual winter sports facilities are available. **Hunting** licences are needed and safaris can often be organised through the hotel and the Tehran-based safari company. **Fishing:** Many streams are well stocked with trout including the Djaje-Rud, the Karadje and the Lar. The dammed lakes of the Karadje and the Sefid Rud are also filled with fish. **Horseracing** meetings are held at the Park-e-Mellat, Tehran. **Polo** matches are played at the polo grounds on the Karadj road out of Tehran.

SOCIAL CONVENTIONS: Feelings about certain countries (such as America and the UK) run high, so the visitor should avoid contentious subjects. The westernisation of the Iranian way of life has been arrested since the fall of the Shah, and Koranic law exercises a much more traditional influence over much of the populace. In general, Western influences are now discouraged. Handshaking is customary, but not with members of the opposite sex. Visitors should address hosts by their surname or title. Iranians are very hospitable and like to entertain. It is also customary to be offered tea, and guests are expected to accept such offers of hospitality. Because of Islamic customs, dress should be conservative and discreet, especially women's. Businessmen are expected to wear a suit and more formal attire is also needed in smart dining rooms and for important social functions. During Ramadan, smoking, eating and drinking in public is prohibited between sunrise and sunset; however facilities are always available in major hotels. **Tipping:** In large hotels, a 10-15% service charge is added to the bill. In restaurants *(chelokababis)* it is usual to leave some small change. Tipping is not expected in tea-houses or small hotels.

BUSINESS PROFILE

ECONOMY: The economy is undergoing major reconstruction after the phenomenal damage resulting from the war with Iraq. With the ruinous drain on resources – both financial and human – at an end, the country can now concentrate on rebuilding what was one of the region's most prosperous economies. Iran's wealth comes from oil, and has thus been affected by the low world price throughout the latter part of the 1980s as well as the heavy demand from the military, exacerbated by an international arms embargo which forced Iran's weapons buyers into black market deals at grossly inflated prices. The agricultural sector is important for the numbers of people that it employs, but it has performed poorly in recent years and Iran has to import large quantities of foodstuffs. This has contributed to the present high level of inflation, unofficially estimated at around 100%. The Rial has also declined sharply in value in the last ten years, further increasing the cost of imported goods. One of the most urgent problems facing the regime is how to arrest the steady decline in living standards that the country has experienced since the revolution. Difficult relations with the West have led the Iranian government to try to diversify its trading links: one beneficiary of this was the CIS, which signed a series of major deals with Iranian corporations. The Government's long-term plans call for a diversification of the economy, reducing the dependence on oil – 20% of which is sold to Japan – in favour of agriculture and light industry. Iran now faces its most severe economic test for many years: upon its performance the future stability of the country may rest.
BUSINESS: Most Iranian businessmen speak English and are polite and conservative in manner and expect an appropriate response from visitors. Exchanging calling cards is normally restricted to senior people. Appointments should be made and punctuality is expected for business meetings. Business gifts are quite acceptable.
Office hours: 0800-1400 Saturday to Wednesday, 0800-1200 Thursday.
COMMERCIAL INFORMATION: The following organisation can offer advice: Iran Chamber of Commerce, Industries and Mines, 254 Taleghani Avenue, Tehran, Iran. Tel: (21) 836 031. Fax: (21) 825 111. Telex: 213382.

HISTORY & GOVERNMENT

HISTORY: In 1925, after a period of political instability, Reza Khan was proclaimed Shah, replacing the previous incumbent, a member of the Qajar dynasty. Reza Khan was forced to abdicate in favour of his son (Reza Pahlavi) in 1941. By the early 1960s, the new Shah had established his control of the country, and Iran experienced a period of economic growth (mainly based on the oil industry), supported by several Western powers, notably the United States. The Shah's rule became increasingly brutal, and by the late 1970s the growing discontent found expression in the fundamentalist preachings of the exiled religious leader Ayatollah Khomeini. By January 1979, the Shah found his position to be untenable and left the country. The effects of the Revolution were not confined to Iran. The American hostage crisis in 1980-81, which so bedevilled President Jimmy Carter's last year in office and which arguably cost him the 1980 election, provoked considerable anti-Iranian feeling in the West. The example of the Iranian revolution has inspired Shi'ite Muslims throughout Asia and North Africa. Often excluded from political power by the more numerous Sunnis, Shi'ites today are increasingly assertive politically, and many governments of Islamic nations have needed to modify their political and social policies. The balance of power in Lebanon and Sudan, to name but two countries, has been fundamentally altered as a result, and several other regimes are very nervous indeed. The protracted war with neighbouring Iraq was brought to a close in August 1988. It placed a considerable drain on the country, and claimed hundreds of thousands of lives. The period since the war has seen the rise to power of the former Majlis speaker, Hasemi Rafsanjani, and he assumed the Presidency after the death of Ayatollah Khomeini. Rafsanjani is not a 'moderate' as such: the key difference with the other main faction led by Interior Minister Mohtasheri is over the issue of 'exporting' the Islamic revolution elsewhere. Rafsanjani believes the project to be too costly politically, and probably not viable. He retains the support of the middle classes, who appreciate the relatively relaxed social regime that followed Khomeini's death, and of the bazaars, the essential crucible of Iranian politics from where the movement against the Shah began. But Rafsanjani is constrained in his options by continuing pressure from the fundamentalists who have kept a firm grip on the mosques. Their continuing influence is apparent from the confirmation of the *fatwa* (death sentence) against Salman Rushdie, author of the *Satanic Verses*, which has soured relations with Britain. However, diplomatic links were restored in October 1990 as part of a package to secure the release of the Western hostages held in Lebanon by pro-Iranian Hezbollah guerrillas. Since then, the fundamentalists lost ground in the Majlis elections, but have kept the pressure up on Rafsanjani with a series of organised riots and probably a number of bomb attacks. The Government has also sought an improvement of relations with the CIS, which has produced dividends in arms supplies and manufactured goods. Late 1990 brought Iran some much-needed luck in the form of the Gulf crisis, of which it is probably the greatest single beneficiary. Its great regional rival, Iraq, is now the subject of international disfavour. With the recent influx of refugees from both southern and northern Iraq, adding to the existing exile population of Kurds, Iraqis and Afghans, Iran now hosts the largest number of refugees of any country in the world. There is a possibility that diplomatic relations, now restored with most of Western Europe, may be resumed with the USA. There is concern in Western capitals, however, about a recent arms buying spree by the Iranians.
GOVERNMENT: Legislative power is vested in the Islamic Consultative Assembly (Majlis), with 270 members. The chief executive is the President, and both are elected by universal adult suffrage for a 4-year term. A 12-member Council of Guardians ensures that legislation is in accordance with the constitution and Islamic precepts. The elections, however, are not entirely free: of the 50 candidates who stood for the presidency in 1985, only three were considered fit to run.

CLIMATE

Dry and hot in summer, harsh in winter. Low annual rainfall.
Required clothing: Tropical attire is worn from April to October. Mediumweight clothing is advised from November to March.

TEHRAN Iran (1220m)

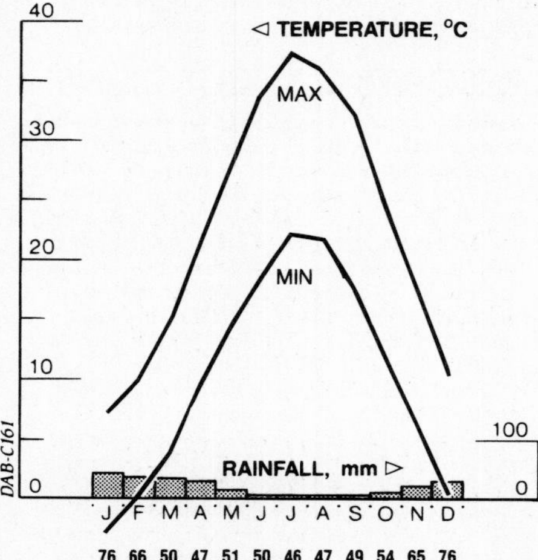

IRAQ

international airport

Location: Middle East.

Note: Due to the current uncertain situation, visitors to Iraq are advised to seek advice from the Foreign Office (or exterior affairs department of their country) before travelling. Visits to Iraq have been discouraged by virtually all governments; sanctions are still being applied by UN members. Much of what follows reflects the situation as it was before the Gulf War. It is presented in the hope that, when current issues are fully resolved, it will again prove to be useful.

Embassy of the Republic of Iraq
21 Queen's Gate
London SW7 5JG
Tel: (071) 584 7141/6. Fax: (071) 584 7716. Telex: 918752. Opening hours: 0900-1530 Monday to Friday.
Iraqi Airways
4 Lower Regent Street
London SW1Y 4PE
Tel: (071) 930 1155/7. Fax: (071) 839 8559. Telex: 27128 IRAQI G.
Presently closed.
British Embassy
Zukak 12
Mahala 218
Hay al-Khelood
Baghdad, Iraq
Tel: (1) 537 2121/5. Telex: 213414 PRODRM K.
Presently closed due to the political situation.
Republic of Iraq Interests Section
c/o Embassy of Algeria
1801 P Street, NW
Washington, DC
20036
Tel: (202) 483 7500. Fax: (202) 462 5066.
Embassy of the United States of America
PO Box 2447
929/7/57 Hay Babel
Masba
Alwiyah
Baghdad, Iraq
Tel: (1) 719 6138/9 *or* 719 3791 *or* 718 1840. Telex: 212287 USINT IK.
Presently closed due to the political situation.
Embassy of the Republic of Iraq
215 McLeod Street
Ottawa, Ontario
K2P 0Z8
Tel: (613) 236 9177/8. Fax: (613) 567 1101.
Presently closed due to the political situation.
Canadian Embassy
PO Box 323

Hay Al-Mansour
Mahalla 609
Street 1, House 33
Baghdad, Iraq
Tel: (1) 542 1459/1932/1933. Telex: 212486 DMCAN IK.
Presently closed due to the political situation.

AREA: 438,317 sq km (169,235 sq miles).
POPULATION: 17,250,000 (1988 estimate).
POPULATION DENSITY: 39.4 per sq km.
CAPITAL: Baghdad. **Population:** 3,844,608 (1987).
GEOGRAPHY: Iraq shares borders with Turkey, Iran, the Gulf of Oman, Kuwait, Saudi Arabia, Jordan and Syria. There is also a neutral zone between Iraq and Saudi Arabia administered jointly by the two countries. Iraq's portion covers 3522 sq km (1360 sq miles). The country's main topographical features are the two rivers, the Tigris and the Euphrates, which flow from the Turkish and Syrian borders in the north to the Gulf in the south. The northeast is mountainous, while in the west the country is arid desert. The land surrounding the two rivers is fertile plain, but the lack of effective irrigation has resulted in flooding and areas of marshland.
LANGUAGE: 80% Arabic, 15% Kurdish.
RELIGION: 45% Sunni Muslim, 50% Shi'ite Muslim, with Druze and Christian minorities.
TIME: GMT + 3 (GMT + 4 in summer).
ELECTRICITY: 220 volts AC, 50Hz. Various 2- and 3-pin plugs are in use.
COMMUNICATIONS: Telephone: IDD service is available. Country code: 964. **Telex/telegram:** Facilities in Baghdad. Telegrams and telex messages can be sent from the telegraph office next to the post office in Rashid Street. Services are also available at major hotels. There is a 20% surcharge on telex tariffs. **Post:** Airmail between Europe and Iraq usually takes five to ten days, but can take longer. Avoid using surface mail. **Press:** Newspapers published in Arabic include *Ath-Thawra*, *Al-Iraq* and *Riyadhi*. Periodicals are also published. The main English-language daily is the *Baghdad Observer*.
BBC World Service and Voice of America frequencies: From time to time these change. See the section *How to Use this Book* for more information.

BBC:

MHz	15.07	11.76	9.740	9.410

A service is also available on 1413kHz and 702kHz (0100-0500 GMT).

Voice of America:

MHz	9.670	6.040	5.995	1.260

PASSPORT/VISA

Regulations and requirements may be subject to change at short notice, and you are advised to contact the appropriate diplomatic or consular authority before finalising travel arrangements. Details of these may be found at the head of this country's entry. Any numbers in the chart refer to the footnotes below.

	Passport Required?	Visa Required?	Return Ticket Required?
Full British	Yes	Yes	Yes
BVP	Not valid	-	-
Australian	Yes	Yes	Yes
Canadian	Yes	Yes	Yes
USA	Yes	Yes	Yes
Other EC	Yes	Yes	Yes
Japanese	Yes	Yes	Yes

Note: The Embassy is currently issuing visas, although applications in the first instance have to be referred by telex to Baghdad. However, the Foreign Office advises people not to travel to Iraq at the present time.
Entry restrictions: Holders of passports containing Israeli or South African visas will be refused entry.
PASSPORTS: Required by all; must be valid for at least 3 months from date of issue of visa.
British Visitors Passport: Not acceptable.
VISAS: Required by all except nationals of Jordan (including Palestinians with Jordanian passports).
Types of visa and validity: *Business* (visits by invitation only): 3 months duration. *Transit:* required only if intending to leave the airport or if the stay in the airport will exceed 6 hours. *Tourist* visas are extremely difficult to acquire at the present time. Prices are available on application (£39 for visa plus £30 telex fee for UK nationals). Visas should be applied for before entry into Iraq.
Application to: Consulate (or Consular Section at Embassy). For addresses, see top of entry.
Application requirements: (a) Valid passport. (b) 2 passport-size photos. (c) 2 application forms. (d) Fee.
Working days required: One week from receipt of approval from Baghdad (which may take 1 month or more).
Exit permits: (a) Nationals of countries not belonging to the Arab League who wish to stay longer than 14 days or beyond the validity of their visa must obtain an *Arrival Notice* from the Directorate of Residents in Sa'adoun Street, Baghdad, within 14 days of arrival. Applicants must present a letter of support from their sponsors (usually a government office) and 2 photographs. The *Arrival Notice* obviates the need for an *Exit Permit* unless the visit will exceed 30 days, in which case the applicant must obtain a further letter of support and possibly a *Residence Permit* (which itself will only be issued on presentation of a *Work Permit*). Heavy fines are imposed on those not adhering to these requirements and offenders may encounter great difficulty in leaving Iraq. (b) Nationals of Arab League countries must obtain an *Arab Affairs Card* from an Arab Affairs Office within 14 days of arrival. This also obviates the need for an *Exit Permit*.

MONEY

Currency: Iraqi Dinar (ID) = 20 dirhams = 1000 fils. Notes are in denominations of ID10, 5 and 1 dinars, and 500 and 250 fils. Coins are in denominations of ID1, and 100, 50, 25, 10, 5 and 1 fils. A large number of commemorative coins has also been minted, some for everyday circulation, others for collectors. The Iraqi Dinar is pegged to the US Dollar.
Credit cards: These are not generally accepted.
Travellers cheques: These are not generally accepted.
Note: Foreign currency can be used at special duty-free shops in Baghdad up to a value of US$200. To obtain this concession, goods must be purchased within 20 days of arrival and passports must be produced.
Exchange rate indicators: The following figures are included as a guide to the movements of the Iraqi Dinar against Sterling and the US Dollar:

Date:	Oct '89	Oct '90	Oct '91	Oct '92
£1.00=	0.50	0.61	0.59	0.59
$1.00=	0.31	0.31	0.34	0.37

Currency restrictions: Import of local currency is allowed up to ID500. Import of foreign currency is unlimited, providing a declaration is made on arrival. However, Israeli currency is prohibited. Export of local currency is limited to ID25. Foreign currency export is restricted to the amount imported and declared.
Banking hours: 0800-1200 Saturday to Wednesday, 0800-1100 Thursday. Banks close at 1000 during the Ramadan religious festival.

DUTY FREE

The following goods may be imported into Iraq without incurring customs duty:
200 cigarettes or 50 cigars or 250g tobacco;
1 litre of wine or spirits;
500ml of perfume (2 small opened bottles);
Other goods to the value of ID100, less the value of the above items.
Note: The import of typewriters as personal baggage is prohibited.

PUBLIC HOLIDAYS

Public holidays observed in Iraq are as follows:
Mar 25 '93 Eid al-Fitr (End of Ramadan). **Jun 1** Eid al-Adha (Feast of the Sacrifice). **Jun 21** Islamic New Year. **Jun 30** Ashoura. **Jul 14** Republic Day (Anniversary of the 1968 coup). **Aug 30** Mouloud (Prophet's Birthday). **Jan 1 '94** New Year's Day. **Jan 6** Army Day. **Jan 20** Leilat al-Meiraj. **Feb 8** 14 Ramadan Revolution (Anniversary of the 1963 coup). **Mar** Start of Eid al-Fitr.
Note: Muslim festivals are timed according to local sightings of various phases of the Moon and the dates given above are approximations. During the lunar month of Ramadan that precedes Eid al-Fitr, Muslims fast during the day and feast at night and normal business patterns may be interrupted. Many restaurants are closed during the day and there may be restrictions on smoking and drinking. Some disruption may continue into Eid al-Fitr itself. Eid al-Fitr and Eid al-Adha may last anything from two to ten days, depending on the region. For more information see the section *World of Islam* at the back of the book.

HEALTH

Regulations and requirements may be subject to change at short notice, and you are advised to contact your doctor well in advance of your intended date of departure. Any numbers in the chart refer to the footnotes below.

	Special Precautions?	Certificate Required?
Yellow Fever	No	1
Cholera	Yes	2
Typhoid & Polio	Yes	-
Malaria	3	-
Food & Drink	4	-

[1]: A yellow fever vaccination certificate is required from travellers coming from infected areas.
[2]: Following WHO guidelines issued in 1973, a cholera vaccination certificate is not a condition of entry to Iraq. However, cholera is a serious risk in this country and precautions are essential. Up-to-date advice should be sought before deciding whether these precautions should include vaccination as medical opinion is divided over its effectiveness. See the *Health* section at the back of the book.
[3]: Malaria risk is almost entirely in the benign *vivax* form and exists from May to November below 1500m (4920ft) in some areas in the north (Arbil and Nineveh provinces).
[4]: All water should be regarded as being potentially contaminated. Water used for drinking, brushing teeth or making ice should have first been boiled or otherwise sterilised. Milk is unpasteurised and should be boiled. Powdered or tinned milk is available and is advised, but make sure that it is reconstituted with pure water. Avoid dairy products which are likely to have been made from unboiled milk. Only eat well-cooked meat and fish, preferably served hot. Pork, salad and mayonnaise may carry increased risk. Vegetables should be cooked and fruit peeled.
Note: All nationals entering Iraq for a period of five days or more are required to take an HIV blood test within the initial five days of entering the country. The hospitals in Baghdad designated to carry out the test and issue the certificate are Al Kindi, Al Kerama and Al Kadhimiya. Outside Baghdad, centres for preventative medicine in the governates should be approached. A

IRAQ | **HEALTH REGULATIONS** | **VISA REGULATIONS** | Code-Link

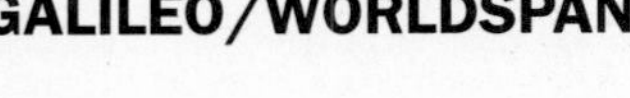
GALILEO/WORLDSPAN

TI-DFT/BGW/HE

TI-DFT/BGW/VI

SABRE

TIDFT/BGW/HE

TIDFT/BGW/VI

To access this information on your CRS, swipe the barcode with a light pen or type in the text under the barcode. For more information, see the introduction *How to Use This Book*.

medical certificate issued by Health Authorities outside Iraq is not valid and a fine of £500 will be incurred if this rule is not adhered to. People are advised to take their own syringes. Tour groups are able to show HIV test certificates issued in their own country.
Bilharzia (schistosomiasis) is present. Avoid swimming and paddling in fresh water. Swimming pools which are well-chlorinated and maintained are safe.
Rabies is present. For those at high risk, vaccination before arrival should be considered. If you are bitten abroad seek medical advice without delay. For more information consult the *Health* section at the back of the book.
Health care: Health insurance including emergency repatriation cover is essential. Medical and dental facilities in major centres are good.

TRAVEL - International

Note: At present, all air travel into Iraq is prohibited due to UN sanctions held against Iraq. The following information is given with regard to conditions before the Gulf War with the intention that it may prove useful should sanctions be lifted and flights to Iraq resumed. The closest airport is Amman Airport in Jordan, from which there is a 15-hour air-conditioned coach ride into Baghdad. However, this journey is best made during the day and in a convoy, as the route passes through some reportedly dangerous territories within Iraq.
AIR: Iraq's national airline is *Iraqi Airways (IA)*.
Approximate flight time: From *London* to Baghdad is 6 hours.
International airport: *Baghdad (BGW)* (Saddam International) is 18km (11 miles) south of the city (travel time – 20 minutes). Coach service is available to the city and returns from Damascus Street (100 minutes before flight departure). Taxi services go to the city with rates negotiable for shared taxis. There is a surcharge after 2200 hours. Airport facilities include 24-hour banks, bureaux de change, post office, duty-free shops, bars, restaurants, snack bar, shops and first aid. Car rental is also available at the airport.
Departure tax: ID10; children under 12 years are exempt.
SEA: At present, all ports in Iraq are closed. Before the Gulf War, *Polish Ocean Lines* operated two routes: Amsterdam–Hamburg–Gdynia–Dubai; and Kuwait–Basra.
RAIL: No services are running at present on the route into Iraq from Turkey and Syria.
ROAD: At present, only the borders from Turkey and Jordan are open to road travel. Before the Gulf War, principal international routes ran through Turkey, Syria and Jordan. Work on the Express Highway, an attempt to link Iraq with Kuwait, Syria and Jordan, has been suspended for the time being. Contact the Embassy for up-to-date political conditions and border details.

TRAVEL - Internal

AIR: At the present time, there are no aircraft whatsoever allowed into Baghdad. However, before sanctions there were regular flights between Baghdad, Basra and Mosul.
RAIL: Rail services are operated by the *State Enterprise for Iraqi Railways*. Tel: (1) 53 73 00 11. Telex: 212272. The country has over 2400km (1500 miles) of track, most of which is standard gauge. A further 300km (200 miles) or so is under construction. The principal route is from the Syrian border at Tel-Kotchek to Mosul, Baghdad and Basra. Trains also run from Baghdad to Kirkuk and Arbil. A service operates three times daily between Baghdad and Basra. Some sleeping cars, restaurants and air-conditioned accommodation are available.
Note: Many tracks were destroyed during the fighting and it is uncertain if any passenger services are running at all. Contact *State Enterprise for Iraqi Railways* for up-to-date information.
ROAD: There are 25,000km (15,500 miles) of road. Principal routes are from Baghdad to Kirkuk, Arbil, Nineveh and Zakho; Baghdad to the Jordanian frontier; Baghdad to Kanaquin (the Iranian border); Baghdad to Hilla and Kerbela; and Baghdad to Basra and Safwan (Kuwait border). **Bus:** Services run from Baghdad and other main cities. **Taxi:** Services are available both in cities and for transit. Fares should be negotiated in advance. Metered taxis charge twice the amount shown on the meter. Tipping is not necessary. **Car hire:** Available at the airport and in Baghdad. **Documentation:** International Driving Permit required. Third Party insurance is necessary.
URBAN: Baghdad has an extensive bus system with double-deckers, and also private minibuses and shared taxis. Bus tickets should be pre-purchased at kiosks. A metro is under construction.

ACCOMMODATION

HOTELS: Mainly for business travellers. Modern hotel accommodation is limited and bookings should be made in advance. All prices are set by the Government for high-class hotels. Small hotels are also available for low budgets, but with a lower standard of facilities. Hotel bills are payable in foreign currency. A 10% service charge is usually added to the bill.

RESORTS & EXCURSIONS

Note: Many areas have suffered serious damage from the Gulf War and infrastructures once intact may be found to be severely damaged or missing altogether.
BAGHDAD & ENVIRONS: In the capital, there is a striking contrast between new buildings and shabbier back streets. The Government aims to preserve the city's Islamic character by protecting the ruins of historic buildings such as the *Ike Abbasid Palace*. Long-established markets still trade. The museums of *Iraqi Folklore* and *Modern Art* are well worth visiting. The *River Tigris* is a central feature of the city.
Towns and excursions: South of the capital is **Babylon,** the great city once ruled by the Semitic King Hammirabi. The city, and particularly the famous *Hanging Gardens*, are now being restored.
NORTHERN/KURDISH REGION: Mountainous and forested area. **Note:** Enormous friction between the Government and the Kurds, who wish to establish an autonomous Kurdish state, makes travel in this region inadvisable at present. Check with the Embassy for the current situation.
Towns and excursions: Kirkuk has assumed importance since the discovery of oil. It is famous for 'Eternal Fires', the endless burning of gas seepage. **Mosul** is the main northern town with the 13th-century *Palace of Qara Sariai* and the old *Mosque of Nabi Jirjis*. *Ninevah* is an ancient and rich archaeological site near Mosul. **Arbil** is probably the oldest continuously inhabited city in the world.

SOCIAL PROFILE

FOOD & DRINK: Restaurants serve both Middle Eastern and European dishes. Popular Iraqi dishes are *kubba* (a wheat preparation known as *borghul* is mixed with minced meat and moulded around nuts, sultanas, spices, parsley and onion, then boiled), *dolma* (vine leaves, cabbage, lettuce, onions, aubergine, marrow or cucumbers stuffed with rice, meat and spices), *tikka* (small chunks of mutton on skewers grilled on a charcoal fire), *quozi* (small lamb boiled whole and grilled, stuffed with rice, minced meat and spices and served on rice) and *masgouf* (fish from the Tigris, cooked on the river bank). Waiter service is usual.
Drink: There is strict adherence to Islamic laws on the consumption of alcohol, which is available within the limits of religious laws. However, a permit for alcohol may be necessary. Effectively this means at international hotels only. Most hotels have bars with counter/table service. Certain hotels prohibit the consumption of alcohol by visitors. During the lunar month of Ramadan smoking and drinking in public is not permitted.
NIGHTLIFE: Baghdad has nightclubs with cabaret, music and dancing, as do other main towns. There are also cinemas, theatres and bars.
SHOPPING: The long-established town markets sell copperware, silver, spices, carpets and brightly coloured rugs. In Baghdad the copper market is a centre of noisy activity with coppersmiths beating their pots into shape. **Shopping hours:** 0830-1300 and 1700-1900 Saturday to Thursday.
SOCIAL CONVENTIONS: Due to a long and varied history, Iraq is a culturally rich country. Today traditional Islamic culture predominates, with Koranic law playing an active role in the day-to-day life of the country, and visitors should be careful to respect this and act accordingly. Visitors should always address their hosts by full name and title. Traditional Arab hospitality is followed as a rule, in accordance with religious law. Conservative and discreet dress should be worn in observance of local Islamic laws.
Photography: The execution of journalist Farzad Bazoft exemplifies the need for extreme caution when photographing anything of a sensitive nature. This includes photographs of local people (the Muslim religion does not allow the representation of human or animal images in any form); and also any government installations, buildings or indeed anything else that may be considered off-limits to visitors. If in any doubt, do not take a photo. **Tipping:** Normal limit is 10-15%. Taxi drivers need not be tipped since the fare is agreed before the journey.

BUSINESS PROFILE

ECONOMY: The Iran-Iraq War brought a halt to many years of steady development of the Iraqi economy fuelled by oil revenues from Iraq's major export commodity. Agriculture continues to employ most of the population, however, which has shown gradual improvement as government finance has assisted modernisation of farming with large irrigation schemes and mechanisation. The Government also used oil revenues to develop light industry on an import substitution principle, concentrating in recent years on textiles, chemicals and foodstuffs. Before the Gulf War, oil accounted for over 95% of export earnings, which came chiefly from Brazil, Japan, Spain, Turkey, the former Yugoslavia and Italy. Under the terms of the UN embargo imposed in the autumn of 1990, no trade whatsoever is permitted between Iraq and UN member states. Iraq now faces a poor economic situation with much of its oil industry and infrastructure destroyed by coalition bombing prior to the counter-invasion of Kuwait and later in January 1993 in response to non-compliance with the UN. It has an enormous overseas debt which it has little chance of ever meeting. It will be many years before Iraq will be able to reach the state of development which it had achieved by the mid-1980s, although it is proceeding apace with reconstruction. At present the UN embargo is still in force.
BUSINESS: Formal courtesies are common and expected. Visiting cards are regularly exchanged and these are often printed in Arabic and English. Meetings may not always be on a person-to-person basis and it is often difficult to confine items to the business in progress as many topics may be discussed in order to assess the character of colleagues or traders. **Office hours:** 0800-1400 Saturday to Wednesday, 0800-1300 Thursday. Friday is the weekly day of rest when offices tend to be closed.
COMMERCIAL INFORMATION: Under normal circumstances the following organisation can offer advice: Federation of Iraqi Chambers of Commerce, Mustansir Street, Baghdad. Tel: (1) 888 6111.

HISTORY & GOVERNMENT

HISTORY: In antiquity Iraq was at the heart of the Sumerian and Babylonian Empires. The Caliphate had control of the territory during the late 12th and early 13th century before they were dislodged by the advancing Mongols. At the end of the 14th century, Iraq and Azerbaijan to the north (now part of the CIS) were conquered and subsumed into the empire ruled by Timur (also known as Tamerlane). The Turks were the next imperial invaders, ruling from the early 1500s until the collapse of the Ottoman Empire at the end of the First World War. In 1920 Iraq was placed under a League of Nations mandate, administered by the British, whose forces had occupied most of the country. The Hashemite Amir Faisal ibn Hussain, brother of the new ruler of neighbouring Jordan, Abdallah, was proclaimed King in 1921. (The two monarchs were chosen by the British as a reward for Hashemite support in the war against the Turks.) The country acheived independence in 1932 but British forces intervened once again in 1941 to prevent a pro-Nazi coup. British troops were withdrawn in 1947, and the sole remaining foreign military presence, a British airbase, was closed in 1959. The previous year, the Hashemite dynasty had been overthrown by a group of radical army officers led by Brigadier Abdul al-Karim Kassem. Inspired by the example of Gamal Abdel Nasser in Egypt, the new regime failed to consolidate its position, however, and relied on a precarious coalition of forces which quickly disintegrated. After Kassem was killed in 1963 during a further coup, Colonel Abdul Salem Muhammed Aref set up a new government. Iraq declared war on Israel at the outbreak of the Six-Day War in June 1967, although Iraqi forces were not engaged. In 1968, Iraq's final coup in recent history brought to power the Ba'ath Party. Ba'ath ideology espouses pan-Arabism, socialism and resistance from foreign interference, although many political scientists have noted its similarity to European fascism. Ba'athism was originally brought into Iraq from Syria during the 1950s by merchants and traders and grew quickly within Iraq. As it did so, however, the Syrian and Iraqi strains grew apart from one another and by the end of the 1960s were dis-

tinctly hostile. As time has passed, relations between Iraq and Syria have merely deteriorated. (The alacrity with which Syria joined the anti-Iraqi coalition led by the USA in 1990 was clear evidence of this process.) In July 1979, the top leadership of the Ba'ath party underwent a reshuffle, with the former Vice-Chairman of the Revolutionary Command Council, the supreme ruling body, emerging on top of the pack. Thus began the regime of Saddam Hussein, President and Ba'ath Party leader. As Iraqi leader, Saddam's main objectives have been to establish his country as the undisputed leader of the Arab world and to overcome the Arabs' two principal enemies in the Middle East: Iran and Israel. A close relationship with the Soviet Union was built up, both to provide superpower backing and a reliable supply of arms on credit. Saddam had reached the top at a time of escalating tension between Iran and Iraq. Iran appeared to be in chaos following the Islamic revolution which overthrew the Shah. The Iraqis perceived a good opportunity to resume a long-running territorial dispute over the Shatt al-Arab waterway which feeds the Gulf and divides the two countries. The Iraqis abrogated a settlement of the dispute reached in 1975 and launched a full-scale invasion of Iran in September 1980. Despite support of one kind or another from almost every major state, including the Americans, the Iraqis failed to win the decisive military victory they had hoped for and the war degenerated into a war of attrition horribly similar to the First World War. The fighting lasted until August 1988 with Iraq having made some minor territorial gains. Saddam Hussein duly proclaimed a great 'victory'. But the war had other, more important consequences for the country. In the course of the war, Iraq had built up a large indigenous military industrial complex which was capable of producing not only basic armaments but chemical and biological weapons, the missile systems to deliver these, and considerable progress towards a nuclear device. By contrast, the civil economy, including the all-important oil industry, was crippled and the exchequer had incurred an enormous foreign debt, estimated at between US$60 and US$80 billion. Most of this was owed to Saudi Arabia and Kuwait. The Kuwaitis, small and worryingly close to Iran, had contributed the most, but far from buying the sheikhdom peace of mind, it became a source of friction. This and other disputes, plus a historical territorial claim, combined to provide Saddam with a pretext for the invasion and occupation of Kuwait on August 1, 1990. Saddam guessed that the reaction from the West would be noisy but ineffectual. Elsewhere, he guessed that Arab governments would mostly rally round, or at least not denounce the invasion, and that the Soviets, preoccupied by their own domestic situation and with several thousand military advisers in Iraq, would give little trouble. All were reasonable assumptions but consistently wrong. In the hours after the invasion, in an impressive feat of telephone diplomacy, US President Bush assembled a formidable anti-Iraqi coalition of Western states, Japan, the Soviet Union and, most importantly, several key Arab nations, including Egypt, Syria and Saudi Arabia. China was prevailed upon not to be obstructive. Only Jordan, Yemen and the Palestine Liberation Organisation backed Iraq. Within days, the United Nations Security Council had passed a resolution implementing total mandatory economic sanctions against Iraq, and a multinational military task force was in the process of being assembled en route to Saudi Arabia with the objectives of (a) deterring possible Iraqi aggression against Saudi Arabia, and (b) removing the Iraqis from Kuwait by force should sanctions and diplomatic pressure fail to work. The Americans provided the largest military contingent; the British, French, Egyptians, Syrians and Saudis also sent sizeable forces; many other countries supplied token units; still others, including the Germans, Japanese and the Kuwaitis themselves, offered financial contributions to defray the expenses of the enterprise. At the end of November, the UN Security Council passed a further resolution which implicitly authorised military action after January 15, 1991. Within hours of the passage of the deadline, the coalition unleashed a month-long aerial onslaught against Iraqi military emplacements and strategic installations in Kuwait and Iraq itself. Coalition ground forces then launched a full-scale counter-invasion of Kuwait and southern Iraq at the end of February. Iraqi resistance was little more than token and after just four days of the ground war, the coalition called a truce. The focus of attention now switched to the internal situation in Iraq itself. The predominately Shi'ite population of southern Iraq and the Kurds in the north immediately staged a dual-pronged armed rebellion against the remnants of the Iraqi army. The Iraqi remnants, it transpired, were rather more substantial than had been thought and both parties were quickly defeated by the army's superior firepower. The result was a terrible human tragedy as Kurdish and Shi'ite civilians, barely protected by their lightly armed guerrilla forces, fled to the mountains of the north or the marshes of the southeast. Western troops later marked out 'safe havens' for the Kurds within Iraq, expelling Iraqi armed forces which had previously occupied them, and in 1992 imposed restrictions on Iraqi aircraft movements in the south, where a war of attrition against the Shi'ites continues. In the north, the Iraqis have imposed an economic blockade on the Kurdish-controlled region. Kurdish politicians have held a series of inconclusive negotiations with Baghdad to find a political settlement. The Kurds are also under pressure from Turkey who are pursuing a counter-insurgency campaign into Iraq against separatist Kurdish guerrillas in southeast Turkey. The security situation aside, the regime has been most concerned with the economy: basic services such as electricity and water were resumed and it is clear that the Iraqis have managed to bring much material into the country despite the sanctions regime. In Iraq itself, UN teams have been scouring the country seeking out Saddam's weapons of mass destruction and associated facilities such as storage depots and assembly plants. However due to Saddam Hussein's lack of cooperation with UN regulations, hostilities re-opened in January 1993 with the bombing of Iraqi military-related installations by a UN coalition of American, British and French forces. At the time of writing, however, it appears that the inauguration of US President Clinton has induced a more conciliatory attitude on the part of Saddam Hussein which may result in a fresh diplomatic approach.As for the stability of Saddam's position, all his abundant survival instincts are evidently intact, supported by the vast and still functioning security apparatus. There were apparently well-founded reports of an attempted coup in May 1992, involving at least two Republican Guard units, which was put down. For all his well-documented misjudgements and brutal behaviour, Saddam is still grudgingly accepted both inside Iraq and abroad as probably the only person who can hold the country together. Despite all his attempts to redraw the geopolitical map of the Middle East, it is ironically the purported stability of the region that is the best guarantor of Saddam's survival. The prospect of a 'Balkanised' Iraq is an anathema to Washington.
GOVERNMENT: Since 1970, the supreme political body is the 9-member Revolutionary Command Council (RCC). Its chairman is President Saddam Hussein. The National Assembly consists of 250 delegates, with the Arab Ba'ath Socialist Party holding 73% of the seats. The other main group is the Progressive National Patriotic Front. The Assembly is supposed to be elected every four years by universal adult suffrage, but no election has been held since 1980.

CLIMATE

Summers are very hot and dry. Winters are warm with some rain.
Required clothing: Very lightweight for summer and jacket or sweater for evenings in winter.

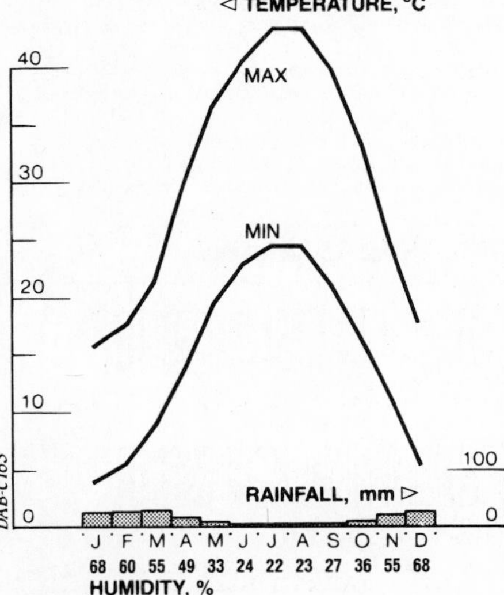

Location: Europe, off the west coast of Britain.

Bord Fáilte Eireann
Baggot Street Bridge
Dublin 2, Ireland
Tel: (1) 765 871. Fax: (1) 764 760. Telex: 93755.

Embassy of the Republic of Ireland
17 Grosvenor Place
London SW1X 7HR
Tel: (071) 235 2171. Fax: (071) 245 6961. Telex: 916104.
Passport and Visa Section: Tel: (071) 245 9033. Fax: (071) 493 9065.

Irish Tourist Board/Bord Fáilte
150 New Bond Street
London W1Y 0HD
Tel: (071) 493 3201. Fax: (071) 493 9065. Telex: 266410. Opening hours: 0915-1715 Monday to Thursday and 0915-1700 Friday.

British Embassy
31-33 Merrion Road
Dublin 4, Ireland
Tel: (1) 269 5211. Fax: (1) 283 8423. Telex: 93717.

Embassy of the Republic of Ireland
2234 Massachusetts Avenue, NW
Washington, DC
20008
Tel: (202) 462 3939. Fax: (202) 232 5993. Telex: 64160.
Consulates in: Boston, Chicago, New York (tel: (212) 319 2555) and San Francisco.

Irish Tourist Board
757 Third Avenue
New York, NY
10017
Tel: (212) 418 0800 (general enquiries) *or* (800) 223 6470 (travel agents).

Embassy of the United States of America
42 Elgin Road
Ballsbridge
Dublin 4, Ireland
Tel: (1) 688 777. Fax: (1) 689 946.

Embassy of the Republic of Ireland
170 Metcalfe Street
Ottawa, Ontario
K2P 1P3
Tel: (613) 233 6281. Fax: (613) 233 5835.

Irish Tourist Board
Suite 1150
160 Bloor Street
Toronto, Ontario
M4W 1B9
Tel: (416) 929 2777. Fax: (416) 929 6783.

Canadian Embassy
65 St Stephen's Green
Dublin 2, Ireland
Tel: (1) 781 988. Fax: (1) 781 285. Telex: 93803.

AREA: 70,283 sq km (27,136 sq miles).
POPULATION: 3,523,401 (1991).
POPULATION DENSITY: 50.1 per sq km.
CAPITAL: Dublin. **Population:** 920,956 (1986).
GEOGRAPHY: The Republic of Ireland lies on the North Atlantic Ocean to the west and is separated from Britain by the Irish Sea to the east. The northeastern part of the island (Northern Ireland) is part of the United Kingdom. The country has a central plain surrounded by a rim of mountains and hills offering some of the most varied and unspoilt scenery in Europe – quiet sandy beaches, semi-tropical bays warmed by the Gulf Stream, and rugged cliffs make up the 5600km (3500 miles) of coastline.
LANGUAGE: Irish (Gaelic) is the official language, spoken by about 55,000 people (mostly in the west). The majority speak English.
RELIGION: Roman Catholic 95%, Protestant 5%.
TIME: GMT.
ELECTRICITY: 220 volts AC, 50Hz.
COMMUNICATIONS: Telephone: IDD is available. Country code: 353 followed by the area code, omitting the initial zero. **Note:** From April 1, 1993 some Dublin phone numbers will change. Numbers beginning with 2 or 4 will be prefixed with 8 and those beginning with 95/98 will be prefixed with 2. **Fax:** Many hotels have facilities. **Telex:** Telex services are fully automatic to the UK and Europe and are available from main post offices and hotels. **Post:** Irish postage stamps must be used on letters posted in the Republic. Post offices are open from 0900-1730/1800 Monday to Friday and 1900-1300 Saturday. Sub-post offices close at 1300 on one day of the week. The central post office is in O'Connell Street, Dublin, and open from 0800-2000 Monday to Friday for all business (1900 for parcels); 0800-2300 for sale of postage stamps, acceptance of telegrams, registered letters and express letters. Sundays and public holidays: 0900-1100 for sale of stamps, acceptance of telegrams, registered letters and express letters; 0900-2000 for *Poste Restante* correspondence. **Press:** There are six daily newspapers published in Dublin including *The Irish Times*, the *Evening Press*, *Evening Herald* and the *Irish Independent*; and two in Cork. British dailies and Sunday papers are available.
BBC World Service and Voice of America frequencies: From time to time these change. See the section *How to Use this Book* for more information.

BBC:				
MHz	12.10	9.750	6.195	3.955
Voice of America:				
MHz	11.97	9.670	6.040	5.995

PASSPORT/VISA

Regulations and requirements may be subject to change at short notice, and you are advised to contact the appropriate diplomatic or consular authority before finalising travel arrangements. Details of these may be found at the head of this country's entry. Any numbers in the chart refer to the footnotes below.

	Passport Required?	Visa Required?	Return Ticket Required?
Full British	No/1	No	Yes
BVP	2	-	-
Australian	Yes	No	Yes
Canadian	Yes	No	Yes
USA	Yes	No	Yes
Other EC	1	No	Yes
Japanese	Yes	No	Yes

PASSPORTS: Valid passport required by all except:
(a) [1] nationals of Belgium, France, Germany, Luxembourg and The Netherlands provided they hold a valid national ID card. For UK nationals, see *British Visitors Passport* below. (Other EC nationals *do* require a passport.)
(b) nationals of Liechtenstein, Monaco and Switzerland, provided they hold a valid ID card.
British Visitors Passport: [2] Accepted, although there is in fact no passport control between Great Britain and Northern Ireland and the Irish Republic. Passengers in transit through the UK are advised to hold onward or return tickets beyond Ireland to destinations outside the UK.
VISAS: Required by all except:
(a) nationals of the countries referred to in the chart above;
(b) nationals of Andorra, Argentina, Austria, Bahamas, Barbados, Botswana, Brazil, Chile, Costa Rica, Cyprus, Czechoslovakia, Ecuador, El Salvador, Fiji, Finland, Gambia, Grenada, Guatemala, Guyana, Honduras, Hong Kong (if holding a British passport), Hungary, Iceland, Israel, Jamaica, Kenya, South Korea, Lesotho, Malawi, Malaysia, Malta, Mauritius, Mexico, Nauru, New Zealand, Nicaragua, Norway, Panama, Paraguay, Portugal, San Marino, Sierra Leone, Singapore, South Africa, Swaziland, Sweden, Tanzania, Tonga, Trinidad & Tobago, Uganda, Uruguay, Vatican City, Venezuela, Western Samoa, Yugoslavia, Zambia and Zimbabwe.
Types of visa: Various categories, enquire at Embassy. Fee varies according to nationality and purpose of travel.
Application to: Consulate (or Consular Section at Embassy). For address, see top of entry.
Application requirements: (a) 1 completed application form. (b) Fee. (c) Letters to substantiate purpose of visit. (d) Return ticket (advisable but not essential).

MONEY

Currency: Irish Punt (IR£) = 100 pence. Notes are in denominations of IR£100, 50, 20, 10 and 5. Coins are in denominations of IR£1, and 50, 20, 10, 5, 2 and 1 pence.
Credit cards: Access/Mastercard, American Express, Diners Club and Visa are all widely accepted. Check with your credit card company for details of merchant acceptability and other services which may be available.
Travellers cheques: Accepted throughout Ireland.
Exchange rate indicators: The following figures are included as a guide to the movements of the Irish Punt against Sterling and the US dollar:

Date:	Oct '89	Oct '90	Oct '91	Oct '92
£1.00=	1.11	1.11	1.09	0.93
$1.00=	0.70	0.57	0.63	0.59

Currency restrictions: No restrictions on import of local or foreign currencies. Export is limited to IR£150, or the equivalent of IR£1200 in foreign currency. Any more than this can be changed into travellers cheques which can then be freely exported. Non-residents can export any foreign currency up to the amount imported and declared.
Banking hours: 1000-1230 and 1330-1500 Monday to Friday. In Dublin, banks stay open until 1700 on Thursdays; there will also be one late opening night in other parts of the country, but the day will vary.

DUTY FREE

The following goods may be imported without incurring customs duty, as long as the items have *not* been bought in duty-free shops, thus avoiding tax:
(a) Goods obtained duty- and tax paid in the EC:
*300 cigarettes or 150 cigarillos or 75 cigars or 400g of tobacco;**
*1.5 litres of spirits (more than 22% volume) or 3 litres of other alcoholic beverages, including sparkling or fortified wine plus 5 litres of table wine;**
75g of perfume and 0.375 litres of toilet water;
Goods up to the value of IR£302 (IR£77 per person for visitors under 15 years of age) with no one item exceeding IR£65 in value.
(b) Goods obtained duty- and/or tax-free in the EC, or duty- and tax-free on a ship or aircraft, or goods obtained outside the EC:
*200 cigarettes or 100 cigarillos or 50 cigars or 250g of smoking tobacco;**
*1 litre of spirits (more than 22% volume) or 2 litres of other alcoholic beverages, including sparkling or fortified wine, plus 2 litres of table wine**;
50g of perfume and 0.25 litres of toilet water;
Goods to value of IR£34 (IR£17 for passengers under 15 years old).
Note [*]: Tobacco and alcoholic beverages are only available to passengers over 17 years of age.

PUBLIC HOLIDAYS

Public holidays observed in the Republic of Ireland are as follows:
Mar 17 '93 St Patrick's Day. **Apr 9** Good Friday. **Apr 12** Easter Monday. **Apr 20** Bank Holiday. **Jun 7** Bank Holiday. **Aug 2** Bank Holiday. **Oct 25** Bank Holiday. **Dec 25** Christmas Day. **Dec 26** Boxing Day. **Jan 1 '94** New Year's Day. **Mar 17** St Patrick's Day.

HEALTH

Regulations and requirements may be subject to change at short notice, and you are advised to contact your doctor well in advance of your intended date of departure. Any numbers in the chart refer to the footnotes below.

	Special Precautions?	Certificate Required?
Yellow Fever	No	No
Cholera	No	No
Typhoid & Polio	No	-
Malaria	No	-
Food & Drink	No	-

Health care: There is a Reciprocal Health Agreement with the UK. All prescribed medicines, and dental and medical treatment, are normally free (hospital treatment in public wards of health service hospitals is free if arranged through a doctor). Local Health Boards arrange consultations with doctors and dentists. No documents are required to take advantage of the agreement but visitors should make it clear before treatment that they wish to be treated under the EC's social security regulations; it may be necessary to complete a simple statement to this effect.

TRAVEL - International

AIR: The Republic of Ireland's national airline is *Aer Lingus (EI)*.
Approximate flight time: From Dublin to London is 50 minutes. There are a wide range of promotional air fares to Ireland from main cities in Britain. An ever increasing number of airlines connect regional UK airports with Ireland.
International airports: *Dublin Airport* (DUB), 11km (7 miles) north of the city. The 41A city bus leaves Abbey Street every ten minutes (travel time – 25 minutes). Airport express coach departs to the city bus station every 20 mins. Taxis are available to the city centre. Airport facilities include airside duty-free shop, car hire, bank/exchange, bar, restaurant, tourist information centre and chemist. Opening hours vary throughout the year with the majority of facilities open until 2100.
Shannon Airport (SNN), 26km (16 miles) west of Limerick (travel time – 25 minutes). Bus services are available to and from both Limerick and Clare, approximately every hour. Daily express coach travels between Limerick and Shannon and between Galway and Shannon. Taxi service is available to Limerick. Airport facilities include outgoing duty-free shop, bank/bureau de change, bar, restaurant and Tourist Information Centre.

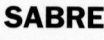

IRELAND	HEALTH REGULATIONS	VISA REGULATIONS Code-Link
GALILEO/WORLDSPAN	 TI-DFT/DUB/HE	 TI-DFT/DUB/VI
SABRE	 TIDFT/DUB/HE	 TIDFT/DUB/VI

To access this information on your CRS, swipe the barcode with a light pen or type in the text under the barcode. For more information, see the introduction *How to Use This Book.*

Cork Airport (ORK), 8km (5 miles) southwest of the city (travel time – 25 minutes). Buses travel between the city centre and airport. Taxis are available to the city centre. Airport facilities include outgoing duty-free shop, car hire, bar and restaurant. Facilities are open during operational hours.

Knock/Connaught Airport (NOC) (Horan International), 11km (7 miles) north of Claremorris (Co Mayo) receives international flights from the UK only. Bus and taxi services are available to Claremorris, from where onward rail and bus connections are available to the rest of the country. Airport facilities include duty-free shop, bar, restaurant and car hire (pre-booking advised).

Galway/Corrib Airport, 6.5km (4 miles) northeast of Galway City. Airport facilities include hotel and guesthouse accommodation, bar, duty-free shop, exchange bureau and café. Taxi rank and car hire at scheduled flight times only.

SEA: Ferry routes from the UK are: Cairnryan and Stranraer to Larne (Northern Ireland) (2 hours 20 minutes); Douglas (Isle of Man) to Dublin (4 hours); Holyhead (Isle of Anglesey) to Dublin (3 hours 50 minutes) and Dun Laoghaire (3 hours 30 minutes); Fishguard to Rosslare (3 hours 30 minutes); Swansea to Cork (10 hours, May to September only); Pembroke to Rosslare (4 hours 15 minutes). There are also ferries from Le Havre and Cherbourg in France to Rosslare and from Le Havre to Cork.

B&I Line, Sealink Stena Line, Swansea-Cork Ferries and *P&O Ferries* all operate regular car ferry sailings to Ireland.

RAIL: Rail links serve Ireland from all the above ferry ports, as well as from Northern Ireland.

TRAVEL - Internal

AIR: *Aer Lingus* (as well as several other carriers) operate services throughout the country. Charter flights are also available. The Aran Islands are served by *Aer Aran* (from Galway).

Domestic airports: *Waterford* (WAT), 9km (6 miles) from the city centre. Bus and taxi services are available into Waterford. Car hire is also available (pre-booking advised).

Galway (GWY), approximately 8km (5 miles) from the city centre. Bus and taxi services available into Galway centre.

Sligo (SXL), 8km (5 miles) from Sligo Town. Bus and taxi services are available into Sligo. Essential facilities only.

Carrickfinn (CFN) in Co Donegal. Essential facilities only. Taxis need prior booking.

Kerry (Farranfore) (KIR) in Co Kerry, 19km (12 miles) from both Killarney and Tralee. Taxi services available to both these towns and to the nearby railway station. Car hire is also available.

As well as the airports listed above (and in *Travel – International*), there are also various small licensed airstrips which receive passenger services; enquire at the Irish Tourist Board for details of operators and routes.

SEA: Ferry services run to the various west coast islands. Enquire locally.

RAIL: Rail services in the Republic are owned by *Iarnród Eireann (Irish Rail)*, and express trains run between the main cities. There are two classes of accommodation, with restaurant and buffet cars on some trains. Unlimited travel tickets for specific periods are available under schemes such as *Rambler* (Republic only) and *Overlander* (all-Ireland). The *Eurorail* card system is valid in Ireland.

ROAD: The network links all parts of Ireland; road signs are international. Traffic drives on the left. **Bus:** Internal bus services are run by *Bus Eireann* (Irish Bus) which has a nationwide network of buses serving all the major cities and most towns and villages outside the Dublin area. Bus services in remote areas are infrequent. An 'Expressway' coach network complements rail services. The central bus station is in Store Street, Dublin. Unlimited travel *CIE* tickets can also cover bus routes. **Coach tours:** Many companies offer completely escorted coach tours, varying in length and itinerary. Full-day and half-day guided tours are organised from the larger towns and cities. These run from May to October. Full details are available from *CIE* Tours International office. **Car hire:** Available from all air and sea ports as well as major hotels. All international hire companies are represented in Ireland, as well as local operators. Age requirements vary from 21 to 75 years. A full licence from the driver's home country is required, and the driver will normally be required to have had at least two years' experience. **Taxis:** Service is available in major cities. Cruising taxis are infrequent. Places to get taxis are hotels, rail and bus stations or at taxi stands. **Bicycle hire:** Ask for a Tourist Board leaflet. **Documentation:** EC nationals taking cars into the Republic require: motor registration book (or owner's authority in writing); full EC driving licence or International Driving Permit; nationality coding stickers; insurance cover valid for the Republic. A *Green Card is strongly recommended, as without it insurance cover is limited to the minimum legal requirement in Ireland* – the Green

Card tops this up to the cover provided by the visitor's domestic policy.
URBAN: Extensive bus services operate in Dublin. There is a new, fast suburban rail service (DART), connecting Howth and Bray, including a link to Dun Laoghaire (the ferry port). The *Dublin Explorer* ticket is valid for four days on all Dublin buses and DART suburban trains. This ticket may not be used before 0945 hrs, but there are no evening restrictions.
JOURNEY TIMES: The following chart gives approximate journey times (in hours and minutes) from Dublin to other major cities/towns in the country.

	Air	Road	Rail
Cork	0.40	4.30	3.15
Galway	0.35	4.00	3.00
Limerick	-	3.30	3.00
Shannon A'port	0.35	-	-
Waterford	0.30	3.00	2.40
Kilkenny	-	2.00	1.45
Killarney	-	5.30	3.30

ACCOMMODATION

There are many forms of accommodation in Ireland, ranging from hotels and guest-houses to farmhouses, town and country homes, holiday hostels, youth hostels, holiday centres and self-catering. Prices vary according to location, type of accommodation, facilities and season. The official Tourist Board guide to accommodation in hotels, guest-houses, town and country homes and farmhouses is available, price £4. For details apply to Bord Fáilte (Irish Tourist Board), address at top of entry.
HOTELS: There are 668 hotels inspected, approved and graded by Bord Fáilte and prices are fixed by the Tourist Board. Most hotels belong to the Irish Hotels Federation, 13 Northbrook Road, Dublin 6, Ireland. Tel: (1) 976 459. Fax: (1) 974 613.
Grading: The Irish Tourist Board register and grade hotels as follows:
A* Top grade of hotel. All rooms have a private bathroom, many have suites. Dining facilities include top class à la carte.
A All provide a high standard of comfort and service. With few exceptions, all have private bathrooms.
B* Medium-priced. Comfortable accommodation and good service. Majority have private bathrooms.
B Likely to be family operated with a limited but satisfactory standard of food and comfort. Some rooms will have a private bathroom.
C Hotels that are clean and comfortable with satisfactory accommodation and service.
GUEST-HOUSES: Guest-houses are smaller, more intimate establishments often under family management. There are over 209 guest-houses registered and inspected by the Irish Tourist Board. These range from converted country houses to purpose-built accommodation. Meals range from bed and breakfast to full board. The minimum number of bedrooms is five and the availability of meals is not a requirement.
Grading: The Irish Tourist Board register and grade guest-houses as follows:
A Guest-houses which provide a very high standard of comfort and personal service. In most cases Grade A guest-houses provide a good quality evening meal, hot and cold running water in all bedrooms, and some premises have rooms with private baths.
B* Guest-houses which provide a high standard of comfort and personal service. Hot and cold running water in all bedrooms. Some premises have rooms with private baths.
B Guest-houses that are well furnished offering very comfortable accommodation with limited, but good standard of food and service. Hot and cold running water in all bedrooms.
C Guest-houses that are clean and comfortable. Hot and cold running water in all bedrooms. Adequate bathroom and toilet facilities.
Ungraded premises: Hotels and guest-houses not sufficiently long in operation are left ungraded.
FARMHOUSES/TOWN & COUNTRY HOMES: There are 2853 town or country homes and 517 farmhouses offering bed & breakfast on a daily or weekly basis with other meals often provided.
Irish Homes: This informal type of accommodation gives you the opportunity to share in the life of an Irish family in an urban or country setting. They may live in a Georgian residence, a modern bungalow or a traditional cottage. A farmhouse holiday again gives scope for meeting the people and is especially suitable for children. You can forget about city life and enjoy the everyday life of the farm. Either way you will have a relaxing and friendly holiday.
All homes and farmhouses that have been inspected and approved by the Irish Tourist Board are listed in the official guide, available from the Tourist Board. In addition to this, the Town and Country Homes Association and *Fáilte Tuaithe* (pronounced Foil-tya Too-ha), the Irish Farmhouse Association, produce their own annual guides to their members' houses. These are also available from the Irish Tourist Board in Britain and from tourist information offices throughout Ireland. For more information contact: Fáilte Tuaithe (Irish Farm Holidays), Ashton Grove, Knockraha, Co Cork. Tel: (21) 821 537. Fax: (21) 821 007; or the Town and Country Homes Association, Killeadan, Bundoran Road, Ballyshannon, Co Donegal. Tel: (72) 51377. Fax: (72) 51207. Telex: 40060.
SELF-CATERING: There are over 2507 self-catering establishments scattered throughout Ireland, listed by the Irish Tourist Board. Self-catering holidays are available for those who like to come and go as they please without any restrictions. There is self-catering accommodation to suit all tastes, including houses, self-contained apartments, cottages and caravans. There are even traditional-style thatched cottages which are fully equipped and located in carefully selected beauty spots.
CAMPING/CARAVANNING: Ireland's caravan and camping parks are inspected by the Irish Tourist Board. Those that meet minimum requirements are identified by a special sign and listed in an official guide which shows the facilities at each park. Firms offering touring caravans, tents and camping equipment for hire are included in the listing. There are 125 caravan and campsites. The majority are open from May to September.
YOUTH HOSTELS: 48 youth hostels are operated by *An Oige* (the Irish Youth Hostel Association), 39 Mountjoy Square, Dublin 1. Tel: (1) 363 111/364 749. Fax: (1) 365 807. Telex: 32988. They provide simple dormitory accommodation with comfortable beds and facilities for cooking one's own meals. Usage is confined to members of *An Oige* or other youth organisations affiliated to the International Youth Hostel Federation. Non-members can buy stamps at hostels entitling them to further hostel use.
HOLIDAY HOSTELS: 11 registered holiday hostels offer privately owned accommodation at reasonable prices. Dormitory-style sleeping accommodation and/or private bedrooms are available. Some provide meals, others breakfast only. For further information contact: Irish Budget Hostels, Doolin Village, Co Clare. Tel: (65) 74006. Fax: (65) 74421.
HOLIDAY CENTRES: These centres offer a comprehensive holiday with a wide variety of amenities and facilities including self-catering units, indoor heated swimming pool and restaurant facilities. The centres are registered with the Irish Tourist Board.

RESORTS & EXCURSIONS

Ireland's coastline is 2200km (3500 miles) long, offering an astonishing variety of scenery and conditions, from the long, gently sloping strands of the east coast to the wild rocky headlands of the west. There are a number of well-equipped, popular resorts, but Ireland is still unspoilt by over-commercialisation. The majority of resorts – including some of the loveliest – are peaceful, unpretentious places ideal for family holidays. Some of the most spectacular beaches are uncrowded, even at the height of summer. Indeed, the whole country is noted for its relaxed pace of life. Amongst the many attractions are the many pre-Christian sites dotted all over the country. There are over 50 Tourist Information Offices throughout the country who will be able to offer help, advice and suggestions regarding all aspects of holidays and travel in their regions. Offices are normally open from 0900 to 1800 Monday to Friday and 0900 to 1300 Saturdays, but these may vary according to local custom and circumstance. Offices at seaports and airports will generally keep extended hours during the summer months.
REGIONS: For the purposes of this survey the country has been divided into the following four regions:
The East Coast: Counties Dublin, Louth, Meath, Kildare, Wicklow, Wexford, Carlow, Waterford and Kilkenny.
The Southwest: Counties Cork, Kerry, Clare, Limerick and Tipperary.
The West: Counties Galway, Mayo, Sligo, Leitrim and Donegal.
The Lakelands: Counties Monaghan, Cavan, Longford, Westmeath, Roscommon, Offaly and Laois.

The East Coast (including Dublin)

This coast was, owing to its geographical situation, the region which felt most strongly the effects of colonisation, both by the Vikings from the 9th century onwards and by the English after the Anglo-Norman invasion of 1170. It is a rich and varied area with woods, beaches, cliffs, stately homes and ruined castles.
Dublin, the capital city of Ireland, is spread over the broad valley of the *River Liffey* around Dublin Bay in a great sweep of coast from the rocky brow of **Howth** in the north to the headland of **Dalkey** in the south, and sheltered by the *Wicklow Hills*. In addition to its imposing public buildings, Dublin is particularly rich in architecture of the 18th century with fine Georgian mansions, wide streets and spacious squares. There are fashionable shopping centres and a range of cultural and sporting entertainments. From the city it is just a short journey to the *Dublin Mountains* or to one of the beaches.
There are many public parks in Dublin, the most famous of which being *Phoenix Park* at the western edge of the city. Originally priory land, it became a royal deer park in the 17th century and is now famous as the scene of the murder of two British parliament officials in 1882 by an organisation called the 'Invincibles'. The park is also noted for the Viceroy Lodge and a 200ft obelisk erected in tribute to the Duke of Wellington in 1817. The park, with a circumference of seven miles, has a network of roads and many quiet walks running through it. There is a zoo near the main entrance and an area known as *The Fifteen Acres* (but actually covering about 200), once the old duelling grounds, but now used as playing fields. At the northern end of the park is the Phoenix Park Racecourse.
A full programme of sightseeing tours of Dublin (all year) and surrounding areas (in summer) is operated by *Bus Eireann*. Walking tours or 'Tourist Trails' are signposted in the city centre. These tours are contained in a special booklet giving maps and background information on points of interest along the routes and details of approved Dublin and national guides; for details of these and the many evening entertainments, see the daily newspapers or enquire at the Tourist Information Office.
Housed in the west wing of Leinster House, *The National Gallery* has over 2000 paintings and a collection of Irish antiquities from the Stone Age to medieval times. The most famous exhibits include the 8th-century Ardagh Chalice and Tara Brooch and the 12th-century Cross of Cong. There is also a room devoted to the Easter Rising and War of Independence. Other museums worth visiting include the *Dublin Civic Museum*; the *Municipal Gallery of Modern Art*; the *National Library of Ireland* and the *Royal Irish Academy Library*. *Trinity College Library* houses the 8th-century Book of Kells and the finest collection of early illuminated manuscripts in Ireland.
Trinity College is the city's most famous landmark. Founded by Elizabeth I in 1591, it is noted for its cobbled stone quadrangles and imposing grey college buildings.
Dublin Castle, the seat of British administration from the 12th century to the 1920s, can be found on high ground west of Dame Street and *Christ Church Cathedral*, one of the city's finest historical buildings, located at the end of Lord Edward Street.
Dublin has facilities for most major sports. The national hurling and Gaelic football finals (September) and the Dublin Horse Show (July/August) are outstanding among the city's sporting events. There is horseracing at two suburban courses and at other venues within easy reach,

DUBLIN

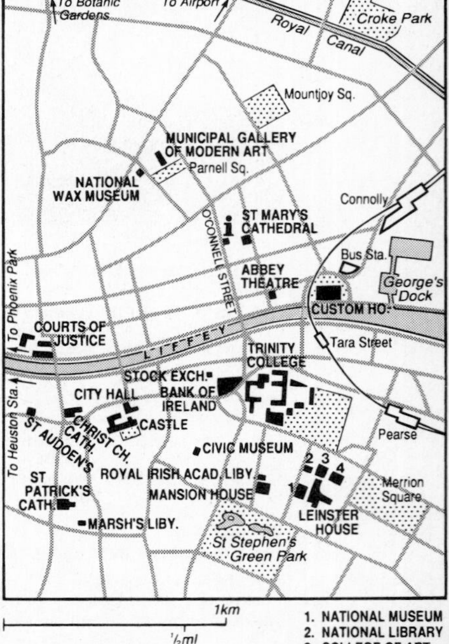

rugby at Landsdowne Road and greyhound racing for most of the year on six evenings a week at one of the two Dublin tracks. The golfer has about 30 excellent courses to choose from. Sea bathing is available at nearby resorts, and there are municipal indoor heated pools in the city and suburbs.

Theatre is always available in Dublin. The principal theatres are the *Abbey*, *Peacock*, *Gate*, *Gaiety*, *Olympia* and *New Eblana*. During the summer the Gaiety and the Olympia provide a season of variety and revue with well-known Irish and visiting artists, and occasional weeks of light opera and drama presented by first-class managements. The Gate is concerned mainly with producing the internationally recognised classics, and has a special feeling for the work of Irish writers of sophisticated comedy – such as Goldsmith, Sheridan, Wilde and Shaw. The Eblana is a small theatre which has been acclaimed for its productions of modern plays.

The National Theatre of Ireland is the Abbey, where the programme consists almost entirely of new plays by Irish authors interspersed with revivals from the repertoire, which includes Yeats, Synge, O'Casey, Bouccicault, Behan and Beckett. In the same building, the smaller *Peacock Theatre* provides the Abbey Players with an opportunity for experimental work.

The shows of *Lambert Mews Theatre* are directed and produced by the famous Lambert puppeteers. The theatre seats 100 people and is 10km (6 miles) from the city centre. Performances are nightly with two matinées weekly for children.

All these theatres perform Monday to Saturday; bookings should be made in advance.

The *Projects Arts Centre* presents drama, poetry readings and recitals at lunchtime and in the evening. These are very popular with student visitors (open also on Sundays).

The *National Concert Hall*, Earl's Fort Terrace, provides high-quality concerts throughout the year.

Meath and **Louth** (the smallest of the 32 counties), between Dublin and the border, are lush and wooded counties with many fine beaches and, particularly in Louth, rugged cliffs rising out of the sea. The *Cooley Peninsula* in Louth has a beautiful coastline and is the setting of one of the oldest legends of Irish literature, the Táin Bó Cuailnge (the Cattle Raid of Cooley). Meath contains the greatest wealth of historical remains in the country including *Tara*, the seat of Celtic Ireland, 10th-century High Crosses, and the largest Norman fortress in Ireland at *Trim*. **Wicklow,** south of the capital, is known as 'the Garden of Ireland'. It is also rich in stately homes and in reminders of Ireland's early medieval Christian heritage. In the hinterland of County Wicklow and County Dublin are the *Wicklow Mountains*. Further south from Wicklow is **Wexford,** also a fertile farming region, surrounded by hills and rivers and is famous for its Opera Festival. **Ardmore** is a charming resort with an extensive sandy beach. There is a medieval cathedral and round tower with spectacular views over Ardmore bay. **Tramore** is a busy seaside resort with a 3-mile beach and excellent entertainment facilities. **Dunmore East** has a picturesque harbour, headlands, cliffs and coves.

EXCURSIONS: **Newgrange, Dowth** and **Knowth** are the most important of the group of around 40 Stone Age monuments known as the Brú Na Bóinne. These burial chambers, known as passage graves, predate the pyramids. The *Cooley Peninsula* (Louth) is good for hill walks. In the Dublin environs *Howth Castle* and *Malahide Castle*, **Dun Laoghaire** (pronounced 'Dun Leary'), **Russborough** and *Castletown House* and the Archbishop's ruined castle at **Swords** are all worth seeing. **Waterford** is a city with two cathedrals, exhibitions in the city hall and some interesting glassworks. The burial place of Richard Strongbow and his Irish wife Eva can be found here. A short distance from the city is the village of **Passage East,** where Richard landed in 1170, an event which was to bind together the fortunes of England and Ireland.

RESORTS: The eastern seaboard has some 400km (250 miles) of fine, silvery sand beaches running from the Mountains of Mourne to the port of Waterford. **Duncannon** is a pleasant holiday town with a good strand and a rocky coast to the south. There is good walking and little traffic to the end of the peninsula. The area is ideal for those looking for isolated spots. The two finest sandy beaches are *Booley Strand* and *Dollar Bay*. **Fethard-on-Sea** is a quiet village on Hook Peninsula with a good beach. **Rosslare** is best known for its 6-mile beach backed by dunes and pleasant countryside. **Curracloe** has a very long beach backed by interesting countryside. **Kilmuckridge** is known for its excellent beach with fine sand backed by *Old World Village*. **Blackwater** is a picturesque village with a sandy beach. **Ballymoney** is situated three miles north of Courtown. There is a good beach backed by dunes here. **Arklow,** a seaport town, has safe bathing from fine sandy beaches at *North and South Strands*. *Johnstown Strand* and *Ennereilly Strand* are also good bathing places. It has an amusement centre with swimming pool. **Brittas Bay** has an excellent beach of fine sand. **Dun Laoghaire** is a large, residential town with bathing, yachting, etc. There is a beach at *Seapoint* and outdoor pool open from May-August. The famous 'Forty-Foot' swimming place is at **Sandycove.** The beach at *Sandycove Harbour* is also popular. **Howth** is a fishing village. There is good bathing from *Balscadden Beach* (shingle) and *Claremont Strand* (sand). **Ireland's Eye,** a little island one mile offshore, has some delightful bathing coves. There is also an old stone church here on the site of a 6th-century monastery and an 18th-century Martello tower. **Portmarnock:** Popular seaside resort with an excellent beach. **Malahide:** Popular seaside area with a good sandy beach. **Skerries** is a well-known North Dublin bathing place with a good beach and islands rocks of that name. **Balbriggan** is a coastal town with a good beach. **Blackrock** in County Louth has a wide shallow beach and no cliffs. **Carlingford** has a small shingle and sand beach on *Carlingford Lough*. Nearby is the scenic village of **Omeath** with a shingle beach. **Donabate** has a ruined castle and safe sandy beaches and leads to **Lambay Island,** the scene of the first Viking raid in 795. **Rush:** Seaside resort with safe sandy beaches. **Clogher Head** has outstanding views of the Mountains of Mourne and Skerries. There is also a wide sandy beach safe for bathing. **Ardmore** is a charming resort with an extensive sandy beach. **Tramore** has a 3-mile beach and excellent entertainment facilities. **Dunmore East** has an attractive harbour, headlands, cliffs and coves.

The West Coast

The western and northwestern counties (Galway, Mayo, Sligo, Leitrim and Donegal) are the least anglicised part of the country, a land of thatched cottages and peat fires, limestone plains and steep craggy cliffs, and of **Connemara,** a region of stark beauty which has long fired the imaginations of writers, poets and painters. The area is dominated by two spectacular mountain ranges, the *Twelve Bens* and *Maam Turks*. The northwest in particular consists of a rugged landscape of steep cliffs, often overlooking lonely islands, interspersed with sandy beaches. Inland the scenery is varied, ranging from the bleak mountains of **Donegal** to the lakes of **Leitrim.** The landscape is broken up by fertile valleys and dotted with ancient churches, prehistoric tombs and crumbling ruins. In County **Mayo,** the upland stretches from Lough Corrib and Killary Harbour in the south to the Mullet Peninsula in Killala Bay in the north. Traditional Ireland is very much in evidence here and the scenery is spectacular. The *Holy Mountain of Croagh Patrick* forms a mysterious conical shape and dominates the surrounding countryside for miles. The mountain is the place where St Patrick reputedly threw the reptiles out of Ireland and is now a place of pilgrimage; many thousands of people climb the mountain every year. There are spectacular views from the mountain and on a good day the Twelve Bens mountain range and Achill Island can be seen. **Achill** is the largest off the Irish coast and has a beautiful 2-km beach with fantastic rock formations at one end. The poet W B Yeats was a native of County **Sligo,** and his writings – which are commemorated annually in Sligo – provide the most eloquent and lyrical descriptions of this part of the country, with its mountains, lakes and golden coastal scenery. Yeats is buried in Drumcliff churchyard. Sligo is also, however, an area of outstanding archaeological interest. In the *Bricklieve Mountains* (at **Carrowkeel,** northwest of Ballinafad) is a Stone Age passage-grave cemetery. The *Stone of Cu* is a vast megalithic tomb to be found north of *Lough Gill* near **Fermoyle**. Cormac MacAirt, famous King of Ireland, was reputedly born and raised by a she-wolf in the *Caves of Kesh* in **Keshcorran Hill.**

The city of **Galway**, itself containing many examples of English, Spanish and French-influenced architecture, makes a convenient starting point for explorations in the west.

EXCURSIONS: The **Aran Islands** – Inishmore, Inishmaan and Inisheer – are accessible by air or boat from Galway, or short boat crossing from *Rossaveal.* They are Gaelic speaking and distinctive for the limestone rock similar to that found on the The Burren. Some of the earliest surviving examples of prehistoric fortifications are to be found here, together with many early Christian monastic settlements and a *Folk Museum*. The West Coast is a particularly beautiful area of the country. **Westport**, one of the most attractive towns in the area is unusual in that it was planned by the architect James Wyatt in the late 18th-century, and its most famous attraction is *Westport House*, a superb stately home situated by a lake. 4000 acres of Connemara have been designated as a national park. The principal attractions in this area include the *Maam Turk Mountains; Kylemore Abbey* and *Lough Mask Abbey*. Lough Mask House was notorious as the former home of one Captain Boycott, a man so unpopular with his tenants that nobody could work with him – hence the word 'boycott'. Between Lough Corrib and Lough Mask is Cong, where the film 'The Quiet Man' was filmed. It is also the site of *The Cross of Cong*, a 12th-century Celtic cross made for Cong Abbey, a ruined Augustian Abbey also dating back to the 12th century. **Inishmurray Island,** four miles offshore has a 6th-century monastery and some well-preserved early Christian gravestones. W B Yeats was buried in the grounds of the 19th-century church **Drumcliff**, once a monastic settlement founded by St Colomba, a stone's throw from **Benbulben**, one of the most spectacular mountians in the country. Standing at 1730ft, the mountain changes its face as you walk around it. *Lissadell House*, a typical aristocratic country home of the last century, is famous for its associations with Yeats.

RESORTS: The **Aran Islands:** Long sandy beaches at **Kilmurvey, Killeaney** and **Kilronan. Inisheer:** Fine sandy beaches. **Spiddal:** Four safe sandy beaches near Spiddal. **Inverin:** Seven sandy beaches within three miles. **Carraroe:** Four sandy beaches nearby. **Lettermore:** *Lettercallow Beach* and other small sandy beaches within driving distance. **Lettermullen:** Coral beach two miles from Lettermullen and a mile-long sandy beach at **Dynish** (three miles). **Carna:** Long sandy beaches at **Callowfeanish, Mweenish** and **Moyrus.** Short sandy beach at **Ardmore. Roundstone:** Fine strands at **Gurteen,** *Dog's Bay*, *Murvey Beach*, *Dolin Beach*, *Bunowen Beach*, *Aillebrack Beach*, *Dunloughan Beach*, *Mannin Beach* and *Coral Beach* composed of fragments of coraline with smooth rocks. **Cleggan:** Six safe sandy beaches close by, two within walking distance. **Clifden:** Holiday resort, excellent beaches close to town and at **Leagaun** (seven miles). **Letterfrack:** Safe bathing at **Renvyle, Tullybeg** and **Lettergesh. Salthill:** Popular resort with many holiday amenities and good strands within two miles. **Kinvara:** 3.5-mile-long sandy beach *Traught Strand*. **Achill Island:** Safe sandy beaches at **Keel, Dooagh, Keem** and **Dugort. Ballina:** Long sandy beaches at *Bertragh*, *Carrowmore-Lackan*, *Ross Strand* and *Bunatrahir Strand*. **Belmullet:** Nine safe sandy beaches within easy driving distance. **Mulrany:** Good bathing strand. **Louisburgh:** 2-mile beach at *Old Head* and five more sandy beaches within driving distance. **Westport:** Bathing at **Bertra, Lecanvey** and **Kilsallagh. Lahinch:** Popular resort for bathing. Entertainment centre. Good recreational facilities. **Spanish Point:** A good sandy beach situated two miles west of **Milltown Malbay.** Recreational facilities. **Doolin:** Small village with thriving folk music events and a small sandy beach. **Silver Strand:** At **Freagh,** two miles north of Milltown Malbay, is a good, safe bathing place. **Kilkee:** Lovely resort built around a semi-circular bay; excellent bathing facilities; recreational facilities include golf, skindiving and sea fishing. **Moville:** Family resort by the shores of *Lough Foyle* on the *Inishowen Peninsula*. Fine coastal scenery. **Greencastle:** On Lough Foyle, three miles from Moville; good bathing beach. **Culdaff:** Secluded resort with a fine beach. Many beaches and cliffs along the coast. **Malin/Malin Head:** Four miles north of **Cardonagh,** Malin Head is nine miles further on. Malin Head is the most northerly point of Ireland affording superb coastal views. **Ballyliffen:** Secluded resort in beautiful surroundings. Bathing on the *Pollan Strand*. **Clonmany:** Village between hills and the sea. Fine coastal scenery. **Buncrana:** Well-developed holiday resort; fine scenery and recreational facilities. **Rathmullan:** Good bathing beach on the shore of *Lough Swilly*. **Portsalon:** On western shore of Lough Swilly near *Fanad Head*. Bathing, fine cliff scenery. **Rosapenna:** Between Carrigart and Downings on *Rosguill Peninsula*. Ideal centre from which to tour. **Downings:** Quiet little resort with superb beaches and coastal scenery. **Carrigart:** On *Mulroy Bay* at foot of Rosguill Peninsula; beach surrounded by sandhills. **Dunfanaghy:** Well-equipped resort at *Sheephaven Bay*; splendid cliff scenery at *Horn Head*. **Portnablagh:** 1.5 miles from Dunfanaghy; excellent beach and bathing facilities; also beach at Marble Hill. **Gortahork:** Irish-speaking village under *Muckish Mountain*; departure point for *Tory Island*. **Derrybeg:** Secluded little resort with fine coastal scenery. **Bunbeg:** Peaceful resort sheltered by cliffs, within easy reach of many beauty spots; excellent sea bathing. **Burtonport:** Sheltered harbour; ideal for boating trips to nearby islands; rugged, rocky scenery. Strand at **Keadue** (three miles). **Aranmore Island:** three miles from mainland on rugged and complex coastline; cliff scenery, sea caves, bathing; may be reached by boat from **Burtonport. Dungloe:** Interesting geological curiosities; bathing in *Mahory Bay*. **Maas:** Conveniently situated between **Narin** and **Glenties;** ideal centre from which to tour the 'Highlands of Donegal'. **Narin** and **Portnoo:** Overlooking lovely *Gweebarra Bay;* magnificent strand at Narin. **Rosbeg:** On the rugged shore of *Dawros Bay;* excellent beach and pleasant scenery. **Ardara:** Charming resort situated in a deep valley on *Loughros Mor Bay*; good touring centre. **Malinmore:** Pretty holiday resort with strand seven miles west of Carrick; impressive cliff scenery. **Carrick:** Ideal centre for boating and climbing; startling panoramic views from *Slieve League* seacliff (1973ft). **Killybegs:** Fine natural harbour; fish-curing centre. **Inver:** On mouth of *Eany River* (Mountcharles – 4 miles); good beach and bathing. **Mountcharles:** Overlooking *Donegal Bay* with charming scenery; sandy beach nearby. **Rossnowlagh:** Situated on Donegal Bay with excellent strand backed by gentle hills. **Bundoran:** One of Ireland's chief seaside resorts; on southern shore of Donegal Bay; lovely strand and all holiday amenities. **Mullaghmore:** Sheltered little resorts with superb bathing beach; sandhills. **Rosses Point:** Mainly noted for its championship golf course; fine strand. **Strandhill:** Popular resort at the foot of *Knocknarea Mountain*. **Enniscrone:** Popular family resort; excellent beach, surf bathing, salt-water baths.

The Southwest

The counties of the southwest (Clare, Cork, Kerry, Limerick and Tipperary) comprise all of the ancient Kingdom of Munster and part of Connaught. This region includes the *River Shannon*, an area of great natural beauty and excellent fishing, countless lakes (including Lough Derg), ranges of rugged mountains such as the *Knockmealdowns*, the *Galtees*, and rich fertile plains, as well as a staggering variety of historical and prehistoric remains.

EXCURSIONS: The Burren, a vast limestone plain, of great interest to botanists and archaeologists; hundreds of castles, ranging from the immaculate to the dilapidated; **Limerick**, Ireland's fourth-largest city, with Georgian buildings; the 13th-century *King John's Castle* and the 12th-century *St Mary's Cathedral; Bunratty Castle*, a few miles from Limerick, with its famous folk museum and medieval-style banquets; **Cashel**, one of the most important historical sites in the country; the beautiful countryside of the **Dingle Peninsula**, the westernmost point of Europe; the 'Ring of Kerry' road, taking in such places as **Killorglin** (with the Puck Fair in August), **Killarney, Valentia,** *Lough Currane*, the *Staigue Fort* and the *Standing Stones* at the *Shrubberies* near **Kenmare;** *Blarney Castle* and the *Blarney Stone*, near Cork; the city of **Cork** with *St Fin Barre's Cathedral*, **Fota Island** on the edge of the city, the old town, many churches, museums and art galleries; many quiet towns ringed with hills, such as **Bandon** and **Macroom; Tralee,** an attractive town with a good shopping centre and annual international 'Rose of Tralee' festival, and a good base for excursions to the west coast.

RESORTS: Beal: Long sandy beach on the Shannon estuary near **Ballybunion,** a leading holiday resort. Fine stretch of sand fronts the town. Affords good and safe bathing. Good sporting and recreational facilities. **Ballyheigue:** Quiet village, miles of sandy beach on a low lying peninsula. **Cloghane:** Fine beach situated beneath the eastern slopes of *Brandon Mountain*. **Ballyferriter/Dunquin:** Magnificent scenery of sandy coves among rocky cliffs overlooking the **Blasket Islands. Ventry:** Long safe sandy beach five miles from Dingle**. Inch:** 4-mile strand on *Dingle Peninsula*. **Ballymona:** Sandy beach three miles from **Ballycotton. Glenbeigh:** Two miles from Glenbeigh is *Rossdbeigh Strand*. Extensive sandy beach. Good bathing. **Valentia Island:** Situated less than a quarter of a mile offshore. Striking cliff scenery. Bathing and good sea fishing. Bridge from **Portmagee. Beginish Island:** In *Valentia Harbour;* has a fine strand. **Ballinskelligs:** Fine strand just outside the village. Attractions include boating, bathing, fishing and lovely coastal scenery. **Waterville:** Good sandy beaches near the village. **Reenore:** Sandy beach within a few miles of Waterville. **Kells:** Pleasant sandy cove within easy reach of Waterville. **Castlecove:** Sandy beach situated amid rugged romantic scenery. **Sneem:** Fifteen minutes drive to safe sandy beaches. **Parknasilla:** Good bathing in nearby coves. Boating facilities. **Tahilla:** Secluded village in *Coongar Harbour*. **Kenmare:** Beautifully situated. Good bathing. **Ballydonegan:** Fine beach with good bathing. **Castletownbere:** Sheltered harbour. Small shingle beach nearby. **Glengariff:** Pleasant coastal resort. **Ballylickey:** Secluded sea inlet; fine scenery. **Bantry:** Well situated, sheltered by a background of hills. **Kilcrohane:** Secluded spot on *Dunmanus Bay*. **Ahakista:** Good bathing at coves and little strands nearby. **Barleycove:** Fine sandy beach. **Crookhaven:** Charming harbour. **Goleen:** Secluded sandy beach. **Schull:** Sea and mountain scenery. Excellent for bathing, boating and rambling. **Ballydehob:** Small village with a quaint harbour. **Baltimore:** Shingle beach. Sailing and boat trips. **Castletownshend:** Pretty village in a secluded haven. **Union Hall:** Quaint fishing village. Shingle beach. **Glandore:** Attractive little resort popular for bathing. **Rosscarbery:** Quiet spot for a holiday. Good bathing. **Owenahincha Strand:** A favoured bathing place near Rosscarbery. **Castlefreke:** Safe sandy beaches in the area of Castlefreke. **Inchadoney:** Situated three miles from Clonakilty. Offers good bathing from a sandy beach. **Clonakilty:** Many good places for swimming within easy reach of here, such as *Harbour View*, *Broad Strand*, *Inchadoney*, *Dooneen*, *Long Strand*, *Dunworley* and *Dunneycove*. **Courtmacsherry:** A favourite seaside resort. Attractions include bathing, boating and tennis. **Garrettstown Strand:** Sandy beach. **Kinsale:** Good bathing nearby at *Summer Cove*. **Oysterhaven:** Small pebble beach. **Inch:** Fine sheltered sandy beach. **Ballycotton:** Fishing harbour. **Garryvoe:** Quiet spot with a fine stretch of sand. **Youghal:** Popular resort. Five miles of sandy beach. **Crosshaven:** Popular seaside resort.

The Lakelands

The Lakelands (Monaghan, Cavan, Longford, Westmeath, Roscommon, Offaly and Laois) are to be found in central Ireland, and the landscape ranges from fertile limestone plains and brown peat bogs to gently rolling hills and towering mountains which slope down to winding wooded valleys, moorlands and glens. Many of the counties can point to a turbulent past, owing to their geographical situation on the frontiers of the *Pale* (the area around Dublin) which made them a battleground for the recurring conflicts between the Irish clans and their English rulers. Nowadays, this mainly agricultural part of the country is considerably more peaceful, although Ireland's colourful, tempestuous and often tragic past is recalled here as elsewhere in the country in song, poetry, myths and legends, and history. There are also several more concrete reminders, in the buildings and ruins which are dotted across the landscape, ranging from prehistoric burial mounds to 19th-century manor houses.

EXCURSIONS: *Dun a Ri Forest Park*, **Kingscourt;** *Killykeen Forest Park* and *Cuilcagh Mountain* (Cavan), source of the Shannon; *The Rock of Dunamase* and *Emo Court Gardens* near **Portlaoise;** old monastic settlement at **Fore,** and *Athlone Castle*, Co Westmeath; Goldsmith Country, Co Longford; Patrick Kavanagh Country, Co Monaghan; *Birr Castle* and old monastery at **Clonmacnois,** Co Offaly; *Lough Key Forest Park* and *Boyle Abbey* (both near Boyle), and *Roscommon Castle*, Co Roscommon; the city of **Kilkenny,** with its castle, museums, cathedral, a perfect Tudor merchant's house, and many other survivals from the city's influential past; the ruins of *Jerpoint Abbey* near **Thomastown;** *Dunmore Cave; Carton House* at **Maynooth** (Kildare), and the obelisk *Connolly's Folly* nearby; *White's Castle* at **Athy,** overlooking the *River Barrow;* the many lakes and rivers, offering possibilities for boating, fishing or merely a beautiful setting for a relaxing holiday.

SOCIAL PROFILE

FOOD & DRINK: Ireland is a farming country noted for its meat, bacon, poultry and dairy produce. The surrounding sea, inland lakes and rivers offer fresh fish including salmon, trout, lobster, Dublin Bay prawns, oysters (served with Guinness and wholemeal bread), mussels and periwinkles. Dublin has a wide selection of restaurants and eating places to suit every pocket, as do the other major towns. Table and self service are both common. The most typical Irish dishes will usually be found in a country restaurant, and include corned beef and carrots, boiled bacon and cabbage and Irish stew. Other local delicacies are *crubeens* (pigs trotters), *col-cannon* (a mixture of potatoes and cabbage cooked together) and soda bread and soufflé made with *carrageen* (a variety of seaweed). Visitors should note that 'tea' is often almost a full meal with sandwiches and cakes.
Pubs are sometimes called 'lounges' or 'bars' and there is often a worded sign outside the premises rather than the traditional painted boards found in Britain. Pubs and bars have counter service. The measure used in Ireland for spirits is larger than that used in Britain – an Irish double is equal to a triple in Britain.
Irish coffee is popular (a strong glass of black coffee, brown sugar and whiskey with cream). Almost any drink is imported but the two most internationally distinctive products are *whiskey* (spelt with an 'e') and *stout*. Irish whiskey has a uniquely characteristic flavour and is matured in a wooden barrel for a minimum of seven years. Amongst the most popular brands are *Jamesons* and *John Powers Gold Label*, but others include *Paddy*, *Tullamore Dew*, *Old Bushmills*, *Middleton*, *Reserve* and *Hewitts*. Certainly as popular as whiskey is *stout* which is bottled or served from the tap. *Guinness*, one of the most famous, popular and distinctive drinks in the world, is found everywhere and *Murphy's* is almost as widely available. One of the most popular of lighter ales is *Smithwick's* or *Harp Lager*, also available everywhere. Liqueurs such as *Irish Mist* and *Bailey's* are both made from a base of Irish whiskey.
Licensing hours are 1030-2300 (to 2330 in summertime) and to 2300 Sunday all year round. Holy Hour has been abolished. All bars close 1430-1630 Sundays.
NIGHTLIFE: Most towns have discos or dancehalls and many bars and pubs have live music and folk-singing, with professional ballad singers and groups who are often highly accomplished. Medieval castle banquets (such as those at Bunratty Castle) are very popular with visitors and there is a good choice of theatres and cinemas.
SHOPPING: Special purchases include handwoven tweed, hand-crocheted woollens and cottons, sheepskin goods, gold and silver jewellery, Aran knitwear, linen, pottery, Irish crystal and basketry. **Shopping hours:** 0900-1730/1800 Monday to Saturday. Many towns have late night opening until 2000/2100 Thursday or Friday and smaller towns may have one early closing day a week.
Note: It is possible to claim 'cashback' on goods bought in Ireland on leaving the country. For further information, contact: The Revenue Commissioners (VAT Section), Castle House, South Great Georges Street, Dublin 2. Tel: (1) 729 777, ext 2440/1/2/3.
SPORT: The national sports are **Gaelic football** and **hurling**. There are 200 **golf** courses run by the Golfing Union of Ireland, and many people come to Ireland specifically for a golfing holiday, where the course rates are relatively cheap compared with the UK. The courses are set both by the sea and inland, nearly half are 18-hole. Ample hotel and guest-house accommodation is available adjacent to most courses. Many of the larger hotels have **tennis** courts. **Equestrianism** is one of the principal tourist attractions of Ireland and facilities for **horseriding** are found all over the country. A full list of stables and riding holidays is available from the Irish Tourist Board. **Racecourses:** The principal racecourses are at Phoenix Park, Leopardstown, Fairyhouse (Irish Grand National every year), The Curragh (Irish Sweeps Derby) and Punchestown (also an international cross-country and 3-day event riding course). **Football:** Although club football in Ireland is not of the highest standard, the national team has prospered considerably in recent years, reaching the quarter-finals of the 1990 World Cup. **Fishing:** Ireland has some of the best fishing of any country in the world, being blessed with uncounted miles of rivers and streams and over 5500km (3500 miles) of coastline. **Freshwater angling:** There is no closed season but March to October are the most suitable months for bream, rudd, roach, dace and perch. **Sea angling:** Permits and licences are not required. A day's boat fishing excursion can be organised. A wide range of fishing exists, from piers, rocks, in the surf or from boats. The Atlantic is particularly challenging, offering its own rewards for the angler who wishes to explore. **Game fishing:** Generally the brown trout season is from mid-February or March until September 30. A licence is required for game fishing. Open salmon season is January 1 to September 7, according to district. A licence is essential, and generally a permit is also required. The best sea trout period is from June to September 30 and until October 12 in some areas. Salmon licences/permits also cover sea trout.

SPECIAL EVENTS: The following are some of the main festivals in Ireland during 1993/4. For full details contact the Irish Tourist Board:
Apr 18-20 '93 *Irish Dancing World Championships.* **Jun 10-19** *GPA Music in Great Irish Houses.* **Aug 3-7** *Dublin Film Festival.* **Aug 10-12** *August Puck Fair*, Killorglin. **Aug 11-13** *Clarenbridge Oyster Festival*, Clarenbridge, Co Galway. **Aug 19** *Connemara Pony Show.* **Aug 20-26** *Rose of Tralee International Festival.* **Aug 21-29** *Kilkenny Arts Week.* **Aug 23-26** *Galway Oyster Festival*, Galway. **Sep 18-Oct 3** *Waterford International Festival of Light Opera*, Waterford. **Oct 7-10** *17th International Gourmet Festival*, Kinsale. **Oct 22-25** *Cork Jazz Festival.* **Oct 4-16** *Dublin Theatre Festival.* **Oct 14-31** *Wexford Opera Festival.*
SOCIAL CONVENTIONS: The Irish are gregarious people, and everywhere animated 'crack' (talk) can be heard. Oscar Fingal O'Flahertie Wills (better known as Oscar Wilde) once claimed: 'We are the greatest talkers since the Greeks'. Close community contact is very much part of the Irish way of life and almost everywhere there is an intimate small-town atmosphere. Visitors will find the people very friendly and welcoming no matter where one finds oneself in the country. A meal in an Irish home is usually a substantial affair and guests will eat well. Dinner is at midday and the evening meal is known as tea. Even in cities there is less formal wear than in most European countries and casual dress is widely acceptable as in keeping with a largely agricultural community. Women, however, often dress up for smart restaurants and social functions. Handshaking is usual, and modes of address will often be informal. Smoking is acceptable unless otherwise stated. **Tipping:** The customary tip in Ireland is 10-12%. Many hotels and restaurants add this in the form of a service charge indicated on the menu or bill. It is not customary to tip in bars unless you have table service when a small tip is advised. Tipping porters, taxi drivers, hairdressers etc is customary but not obligatory.

BUSINESS PROFILE

ECONOMY: Ireland was not industrialised to the same degree as the rest of Europe, and only in the last few years has agriculture been overtaken as the largest single contributor to national product. Agriculture remains a key sector, however, and the Government is seeking to consolidate its role within the economy by modernisation and expansion of food processing industries. Ireland's recent industrial development has been achieved by a deliberate policy of promoting export-led and advanced technology businesses, partly by offering attractive packages for foreign investors. Textiles, chemicals and electronics have performed particularly strongly. Promising oil and gas deposits have been located off the southern coast. Trade is dominated by the UK, which provides half of total imports and takes 40% of Ireland's exports. One major benefit of EC membership for Ireland, however, is that it has proved able to diversify its trade patterns.
BUSINESS: Business people should wear formal clothes for meetings. Local business people are very friendly and an informal business approach is most successful. However, it is advisable to make prior appointments and to allow enough time to complete business matters. Avoid business visits in the first week of May, during July, August and at Christmas or New Year.
COMMERCIAL INFORMATION: The following organisation can offer advice: Chambers of Commerce of Ireland, 7 Clare Street, Dublin 2. Tel: (1) 612 888. Fax: (1) 766 043. Telex: 90716.
CONFERENCES/CONVENTIONS: For more information contact the Irish Tourist Board or the Convention Bureau of Ireland, Bord Fáilte, Baggot Street Bridge, Dublin 2. Tel: (1) 765 871. Fax: (1) 764 760.

HISTORY & GOVERNMENT

HISTORY: The history of Ireland is, by any standard, a troubled and often tragic one. The two most enduring features of it are the unswerving commitment to Catholicism on the part of the majority of the population, the origins of which can be traced back to the pioneering monastic orders of the 5th and 6th centuries; and the continual state of limbo (from the 1170s onwards) in which it lived out its relationship with the English state, never so fully conquered that it absorbed the culture and way of life of its larger neighbour. There followed after the monastic age a long struggle against the Viking invaders who sought to use Ireland as a base for trade with continental Europe. The Vikings built heavily fortified ports to defend themselves, thereby laying the foundations of some of Ireland's major cities such as Dublin, Limerick and Waterford. The Irish chieftains had limited success in dislodging the Norse, but an often uneasy *modus vivendi* was reached involving the fortified towns and rapidly shifting alliances of the 50-odd states throughout the rest of the country. Most of these rulers had the ambition of establishing an overlordship (and the title of 'High King '), which existed as a pretext and almost unattainable goal in the numerous conflicts of the period. It was one such war, in the 1160s, which resulted in the involvement of the English. Richard of Clare, Earl of Pembroke (nicknamed Strongbow), was invited by one chief to support his claims, but instead Strongbow conquered almost the entire country with only a tiny force of archers and mounted knights in 1169-70. A stream of Norman families moved across the Irish Sea, effectively colonising the country and coming into conflict with the Irish tribal system. Repeated and largely unsuccessful efforts from the 14th century onwards were made to bring the island under control. The turbulent and increasingly polarised political life of Ireland took a new and bitter twist after the English Civil War, when the Irish rose in favour of the deposed monarchy in 1649. The victorious Oliver Cromwell led an army across the Irish Sea and the rebellion was ruthlessly put down. Over the next few years all Catholic land was expropriated and given to a new wave of Protestant immigrants. The subsequent Act of Union, passed in 1801, incorporated the whole of Ireland, along with England, Scotland and Wales, into the United Kingdom. However, the grossly inadequate response of the Government to the potato famine of 1845-6, which decimated the Irish population through death or emigration, highlighted its lack of interest in the welfare of the Irish people. Various independence movements pursued an almost continuous struggle against the Government until Home Rule was granted in 1920. The Easter Rising of 1916, centred on the Main Post Office in Dublin, is a particular landmark in the fight for independence. The terms of independence stipulated that Ireland be partitioned into two parts. The reason was that in the northern provinces, where most Protestants had settled three centuries earlier, there was fierce opposition to the prospect of being ruled by a Government drawn from the country's Catholic majority. Six of the nine counties of the historic province of Ulster therefore remained in the United Kingdom. The other 26 counties became the Irish Free State. The ensuing Civil War in the south between supporters and opponents of the agreement gave rise to the country's two main political parties, Fianna Fáil and Fine Gael. In 1937 the Irish Free State was given full sovereignty within the Commonwealth, a new constitution having been adopted, and remaining links with Britain dissolved. In 1949 the 26 counties became a Republic and formal ties with the Commonwealth were ended. Since the 1970s, Ireland has been governed alternately by Fianna Fáil and a coalition of Fine Gael and the smaller Labour Party. In 1989, Charles Haughey (head of the largest single party, Fianna Fáil) detected an opportunity to secure an absolute majority in the Dail, which eluded him on each of the previous three occasions that he has been elected Taioseach. The electorate were not persuaded of the virtues of this situation and returned yet another coalition government, this time linking Fianna Fáil with half a dozen TDs (elected representatives) of the Progressive Democrats, formed after a split within Fianna Fáil in 1985. That year saw the signing of the landmark Anglo-Irish Accord, which allowed Dublin consultative status over the future political development of the north, with which the Irish government has been deeply concerned since the current phase of the 'Troubles' began in 1969. Political progress on this issue remains nonetheless painfully slow, but the Anglo-Irish Agreement does at least recognise that Dublin's attitude is crucial to a political settlement. Ireland has proved an enthusiastic EC member, especially in comparision to Britain, since joining in 1973. Haughey finally left office in January 1992, forced out by a seemingly unending series of political scandals. His successor, former Finance Minister Albert Reynolds, was Taioseach for less than a year before his coalition partners pulled out and forced a general election. With coalition government inevitable, negotiations have centred on the Labour Party, whose leader Dick Spring, is favourite for the Taioseach's job. (Although three Dail votes after, the three party leaders Albert Reynolds (FF), John Bruton (FG) and Spring were all rejected by TDs.) The most likely outcome at the moment appears to be a Fianna Fáil/Labour coalition. Whatever the complexion of the new government, it will have to cope with a social upheaval which is challenging the prevailing morality of the Catholic Church, particularly over the issues of divorce and abortion. The arguments promise to be long and bitter.

GOVERNMENT: Since 1949 Ireland has been a republic with a bicameral legislature: the Dáil (pronounced 'Doyle') has 166 members and is directly elected by universal adult suffrage every five years; the 60-strong Senate has 49 directly elected members with the balance made up of political appointees. Executive power is vested in the Taioseach (pronounced 'Teashock', equivalent to Prime Minister) who presides over a Cabinet of Ministers. The Cabinet is responsible to the Dáil for its actions.

CLIMATE

The temperate climate is due to mild southwesterly winds and the Gulf Stream. Summers are warm, while temperatures during winter are much cooler. Spring and autumn are very mild. Rain falls all year.

Required clothing: Lightweights during summer with warmer mediumweights for the winter. Rainwear is advisable throughout the year.

DUBLIN Ireland (68m)

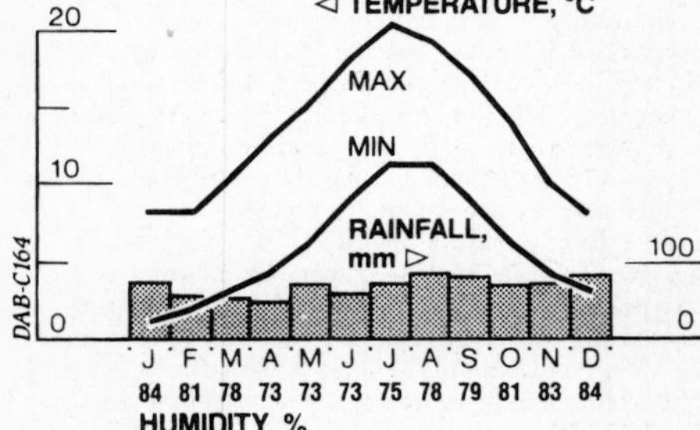

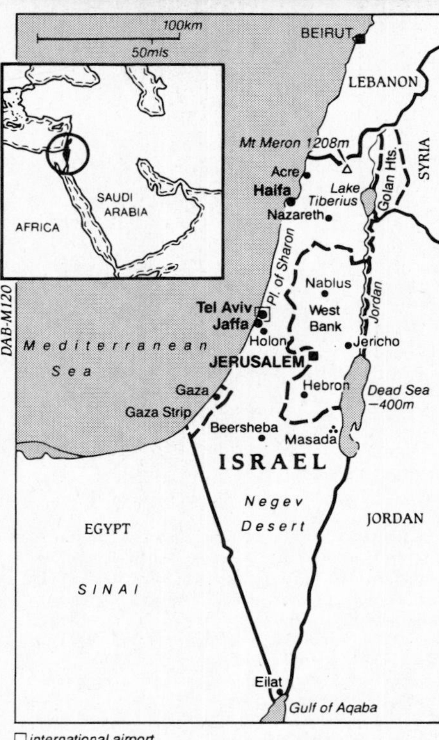

□ *international airport*

Location: Eastern Mediterranean.

Ministry of Tourism
PO Box 1018
24 King George Street
Jerusalem 91000, Israel
Tel: (2) 237 311. Fax: (2) 382 148. Telex: 26115.

Embassy of Israel
2 Palace Green
London W8 4QB
Tel: (071) 957 9500. Fax: (071) 957 9555. Opening hours: 1000-1300 Monday to Thursday, 1000-1200 Friday (Visa Section).
The Embassy is closed to the public.

Israel Government Tourist Office
18 Great Marlborough Street
London W1V 1AF
Tel: (071) 434 3651. Fax: (071) 437 0527. Telex: 27467. Opening hours: 1100-1400 Monday to Thursday (0900-1700 for telephone enquiries), 0900-1500 Friday (for telephone enquiries only).

British Embassy
192 Rehov Hayarkon
Tel Aviv 63405, Israel
Tel: (3) 524 9171/8. Fax: (3) 291 699. Telex: 33559 PRODR IL.
Consulates in: Eilat and Jerusalem.

Embassy of Israel
3514 International Drive, NW
Washington, DC
20008
Tel: (202) 364 5500. Fax: (202) 364 5610.
Consulates in: Atlanta, Boston, Chicago, Houston, Los Angeles, Miami, New York, Philadelphia and San Francisco.

Israel Government Tourist Office
19th Floor, 350 Fifth Avenue
New York, NY
10118
Tel: (212) 560 0650 *or* 560 0721/2. Fax: (212) 629 4368. Telex: 23423021.

Embassy of the United States of America
PO Box 100
71 Rehov Hayarkon
Tel Aviv 63903, Israel
Tel: (3) 517 4338. Fax: (3) 663 449. Telex: 33376 *or* 371386.

Embassy of Israel
Suite 1005
50 O'Connor Street
Ottawa, Ontario
K1P 6L2
Tel: (613) 237 6450. Fax: (613) 237 8865.
Consulates in: Montréal and Toronto.

Israel Government Tourist Office
Suite 700
180 Bloor Street West
Toronto, Ontario
M5S 2V6
Tel: (416) 964 3784. Fax: (416) 961 3962.

Canadian Embassy
PO Box 6410
220 Rehov Hayarkon
Tel Aviv 61063, Israel
Tel: (3) 527 2929. Fax: (3) 527 2333. Telex: 341293 CANAD IL.

AREA: 21,946 sq km (8,473 sq miles), including East Jerusalem.
POPULATION: 4,476,800 (1988 estimate).
POPULATION DENSITY: 204 per sq km.
CAPITAL: Jerusalem. **Population:** 493,500 (1988). This figure includes East Jerusalem.
GEOGRAPHY: Israel is on the Eastern Mediterranean, bordered by Lebanon and Syria to the north, Jordan to the east, and Egypt to the south and west. The country stretches southwards through the Negev Desert to Eilat, a resort town on the Red Sea. The fertile Plain of Sharon runs along the coast, while inland, parallel to the coast, is a range of hills and uplands with fertile valleys to the west and arid desert to the east. The Great Rift Valley begins beyond the sources of the River Jordan and extends south through the Dead Sea (the lowest point in the world), and south again into the Red Sea, continuing on into Eastern Africa.
LANGUAGE: Hebrew and Arabic are the official languages. English is spoken in most places and French, Spanish, German, Yiddish, Russian, Polish and Hungarian are widely used.
RELIGION: Jewish (82%), Muslim (14%), with Christian minorities.
TIME: GMT + 2 (GMT + 3 in summer).
ELECTRICITY: 220 volts AC, 50Hz. 3-pin plugs are standard; if needed, adaptors can be purchased in Israel.
COMMUNICATIONS: Telephone: Full IDD service. Country code: 972. Local telephone directories are in Hebrew, but there is a special English-language version for tourists. **Fax:** This service is available at most 4- and 5-star hotels. Fax is increasingly used by Israeli business people. **Telex/telegram:** Ordinary telex facilities are available to guests in most deluxe hotels in Jerusalem and Tel Aviv and in main post offices. **Post:** Airmail to Europe takes up to a week. There are *Poste Restante* facilities in Jerusalem and Tel Aviv. Post office hours: 0830-1230 and 1530-1830 Sunday to Thursday, 0800-1330 Wednesday and 0800-1200 Friday. All post offices are closed on Shabbat (Saturday) and holy days, although central telegraph offices are open throughout the year. **Press:** The main dailies are *Davar*, *Ha'aretz*, *Yediot Aharonoth* and *Ma'ariv*. Newspapers are printed in a variety of languages, including English. Political and religious affiliations are common. The English-language daily is the *Jerusalem Post*.
BBC World Service and Voice of America frequencies: From time to time these change. See the section *How to Use this Book* for more information.

BBC:				
MHz	15.07	11.76	1.323	0.639
Voice of America:				
MHz	9.670	6.040	5.995	1.260

PASSPORT/VISA

Regulations and requirements may be subject to change at short notice, and you are advised to contact the appropriate diplomatic or consular authority before finalising travel arrangements. Details of these may be found at the head of this country's entry. Any numbers in the chart refer to the footnotes below.

	Passport Required?	Visa Required?	Return Ticket Required?
Full British	Yes	Yes	Yes
BVP	Not valid	-	-
Australian	Yes	2	Yes
Canadian	Yes	2	Yes
USA	Yes	2	Yes
Other EC	Yes	1/3	Yes
Japanese	Yes	Yes	Yes

PASSPORTS: Valid passport required by all. They must be valid for a minimum of six months after the intended

date of departure.
British Visitors Passport: Not accepted.
VISAS: Required by all. Nationals of the following countries will be issued visas free of charge on arrival (which will *not* be entered on passport if so requested):
(a) [1] EC countries (*except* Germany if born before January 1, 1928, and Portugal who *do* require pre-arranged visas);
(b) [2] Australia, Canada and the USA;
(c) Argentina, Aruba, Austria, Bahamas, Barbados, Bolivia, Brazil, Central African Republic, Chile, Colombia, Costa Rica, Cyprus, Dominican Republic, Ecuador, El Salvador, Fiji, Finland, Guatemala, Haiti, Hong Kong, Hungary, Iceland, Jamaica, Japan, Lesotho, Liechtenstein, Malawi, Maldives, Mauritius, Mexico, Netherlands Antilles, New Zealand, Norway, Paraguay, Philippines, San Marino, St Kitts & Nevis, South Africa, Suriname, Swaziland, Sweden, Switzerland, Trinidad & Tobago, Uruguay and Yugoslavia.
Nationals of the following countries may obtain visas on arrival but must pay the standard fee:
[3] South Korea and Spain.
All other nationals must obtain visas prior to arrival, which *will* normally be entered in the passport, and must pay the standard fee.
Types of visa: Tourist/Entry: £8 plus £1 for postage. Transit visas are not required by those who continue their journey within 24 hours by the same or connecting flights. Passengers are allowed to leave the airport.
Validity: Maximum is normally 3 months.
Application to: Consulate (or Consular Section at Embassy). For addresses, see top of entry.
Application requirements: (a) Application form. (b) Photo. (c) Return ticket.
Working days required: Depends on nationality.
Temporary residence: Apply to the Ministry of the Interior in Israel.
Note: As a concession to travellers intending to travel at a later date to countries inimical to Israel, entry stamps will, on request, be entered only on the entry form AL-17 and not on the passport. This facility is not available to those required to obtain their Israeli visas in advance.

MONEY

Currency: New Israel Shekel (SK) = 100 new agorot (singular, agora). Notes are in denominations of SK100, 50, 10, 5 and 1. Coins are in denominations of SK1, and 50, 10, 5 agorot, and 1 agora.
Currency exchange: Foreign currency can only be exchanged at authorised banks and hotels. It is advisable to leave Israel with the minimum of Israeli currency. US Dollars, Sterling and Irish Punts are widely accepted. Payments of certain local taxes may be avoided by paying in foreign currency.
Credit cards: All major credit cards are accepted.
Travellers cheques: These are widely accepted.
Exchange rate indicators: The following figures are included as a guide to the movements of the New Israel Shekel against Sterling and the US Dollar.

Date:	Oct '89	Oct '90	Oct '91	Oct '92
£1.00=	3.24	3.93	4.14	3.97
$1.00=	2.05	2.01	2.38	2.50

Currency restrictions: Visitors may import unlimited amounts of local and foreign currency. For non-residents, export of local currency is limited to SK500, whilst foreign currency export is limited to an amount no greater than that imported. Foreign currency exchanged on arrival may be re-converted up to a maximum value of US$3000 or equivalent on the presentation of exchange receipts. These regulations are for non-residents only; residents should enquire at an Israel Government Tourist Office. Certain foreign currency regulations apply to travellers intending to enter Israel by land; they should seek advice before embarking.
Banking hours: 0830-1230 and 1600-1800 Sunday, Tuesday and Thursday; 0830-1200 Friday and 0830-1230 Wednesday and Monday.

DUTY FREE

The following goods may be imported into Israel by persons aged 17 years and over without incurring customs duty:
250 cigarettes or 250g of tobacco products;
1 litre of spirits;
2 litres of wine;
250ml of eau de cologne or perfume;
Gifts up to the value of US$125.
Note: Flowers, plants and seeds may not be imported without prior permission. Fresh meat may not be imported.

PUBLIC HOLIDAYS

Public holidays observed in Israel are as follows:
Mar 3 '93 Purim. **Apr 6-12** Pesah (Passover). **Apr 26** Yom Ha'Atzmaut (Israel Independence Day). **May 19** Jerusalem Liberation Day. **May 26** Shavu'ot (Pentecost). **Jul 27** Tisha B'av (9th of Av Fast). **Sep 16-17** Rosh Hashana (New Year). **Sep 25** Yom Kippur (Day of Atonement). **Sep 30** Sukkot (Tabernacles). **Oct 7** Simchat Torah (Rejoicing of the Law). **Dec 9-16** Hanukkah (Feast of Lights). **Jan 27 '94** Tu B'Shevat (Arbor Day). **Feb 25** Purim. **Mar 27-Apr 3** Pesah (Passover).
Note: Jewish festivals commence on the evenings of the dates given above. Only the first and last days of Passover and Sukkot are officially recognised as national holidays, but there may be some disruption on intermediate dates; many shops and businesses will open, but close early. The Jewish religious day is Saturday – *Shabbat* – and begins at nightfall on Friday until nightfall on Saturday. Most public services and shops close early on Friday as a result. Muslim and Christian holidays are also observed by the respective populations. Thus, depending on the district, the day of rest falls on Friday, Saturday or Sunday.

HEALTH

Regulations and requirements may be subject to change at short notice, and you are advised to contact your doctor well in advance of your intended date of departure. Any numbers in the chart refer to the footnotes below.

	Special Precautions?	Certificate Required?
Yellow Fever	No	No
Cholera	No	No
Typhoid & Polio	Yes	-
Malaria	No	-
Food & Drink	1	-

[1]: Mains water is normally chlorinated, and whilst relatively safe may cause mild abdominal upsets. Bottled water is available and is advised for the first few weeks of the stay. Drinking water outside main cities and towns may be contaminated and sterilisation is advisable. Milk is pasteurised and dairy products are safe for consumption. Local meat, poultry, seafood, fruit and vegetables are generally considered safe to eat.
Rabies is present. For those at high risk, vaccination before arrival should be considered. If you are bitten abroad seek medical advice without delay. For more information consult the *Health* section at the back of the book.
Health care: Israel has excellent medical facilities and tourists may go to all emergency departments and first-aid centres. Health centres are marked by the red Star of David on a white background. Medical insurance is recommended.

TRAVEL - International

Note: Entry stamps will, on request, be entered only on the entry form AL-17 and not on the passport. This facility is not available to those required to obtain their Israeli visas in advance (see *Passport/Visa* section above for details).
AIR: Israel's national airline is *El Al Israel Airlines (LY)*.
Approximate flight times: From *London* to Tel Aviv and to Eilat is 5 hours. From *Los Angeles* to Tel Aviv is 17 hours 35 minutes. From *New York* to Tel Aviv is 12 hours 55 minutes. From *Singapore* to Tel Aviv is 10 hours 55 minutes. From *Sydney* to Tel Aviv is 14 hours 35 minutes.
International airport: *Tel Aviv (TLV)* (Ben Gurion International) is 14km (9 miles) from the city. There is a coach every 15 minutes to Tel Aviv and bus number 475 goes to the city. There is also a taxi service. The *El Al* airline bus goes to the airport terminal in Tel Aviv. Departure depends on *El Al* arrivals. Duty-free facilities are available.
Departure tax: From Ben Gurion (except to Egypt) US$12; to Egypt US$11; from Eilat and Jerusalem US$6; from Rafiah SK21.50; from Nitzana SK5.50; from Taba SK12.70. Children under two years are exempt.
SEA: Principal international passenger ports are Haifa and Ashdod. There are regular sailings of car/passenger ferries from Greece and Cyprus and cargo/passenger services from the USA (New York, Galveston) run by *Prudential Lines* and *Lykes Lines* to Haifa and Ashdod. Cruise lines run to Haifa from Venice and other Mediterranean ports. The *Grimaldi/Siosa Lines* run a service from Alexandria to Ashdod.
ROAD: There is now a regular daily coach service from Cairo to Israel. On the whole, road access to Israel is extremely limited. It is possible to travel from Jordan to the West Bank via the Allenby Bridge near Jericho, although travellers may be required to stop and be checked at any point. A return crossing is allowed if starting from the Jordanian side, but those crossing from the West Bank may not subsequently re-enter Israel by the same route. Access is not allowed to any of the other Arab counties. Contact the Israeli Tourist Office for further details.

TRAVEL - Internal

AIR: A comprehensive service linking Tel Aviv with Eilat and all major cities is run by *Arkia/Israel Inland Airways (IZ)*.
SEA/LAKE: Ferries run across the Sea of Galilee (Lake Kinnerit) from Tiberias on the west side to En Gev kibbutz on the eastern shore. Coastal ferries supply all ports. For details contact local port authorities.
RAIL: Passenger trains run between Jerusalem and Tel Aviv, Haifa and Nahariyya, with an hourly service between Tel Aviv and Haifa. There is one-class travel, and reservable accommodation in forced-air ventilated cars is available on some trains. All services are suspended on religious holidays, and between sunset on Friday and sunset on Saturday (*Shabbat*).
ROAD: An excellent system of roads connects all towns. Distance by road from Jerusalem to other cities are as follows: Tel Aviv 63km (39 miles), Tiberias 155km (97 miles), Eilat 310km (194 miles), Netanta 93km (58 miles), Dead Sea 104km (65 miles), Zefat 192km (120 miles) and Haifa 158km (99 miles). **Bus:** Two national bus systems, run by the *Egged* and *DAN* co-operatives, provide extensive services. The service is fast and efficient as well as cheap. With a few exceptions, services are suspended on religious holidays, and between sunset on Friday and sunset on Saturday (Shabbar). **Taxi:** Services are either run by companies or by individuals. There are both shared taxis (*sheruts*) and ordinary taxis. Taxi drivers are required by law to operate the meter. **Car hire:** Available in major cities. Hire fees and petrol are not cheap, and taxis are recommended for short journeys only. **Documentation:** Full driving licence and insurance are required. An International Driving Permit is recommended, although it is not legally required.
Note: Israeli drivers are obliged to pick up soldiers who are hitch-hiking in preference to civilians.
URBAN: *DAN* and *Egged* provide good local bus services in the main towns. Taxis are available.

ISRAEL	HEALTH REGULATIONS	VISA REGULATIONS Code-Link
GALILEO/WORLDSPAN	 TI-DFT/TLV/HE	TI-DFT/TLV/VI
SABRE	 TIDFT/TLV/HE	 TIDFT/TLV/VI

To access this information on your CRS, swipe the barcode with a light pen or type in the text under the barcode. For more information, see the introduction *How to Use This Book*.

ACCOMMODATION

From small, simple guest-houses to 5-star deluxe hotels, Israel offers a wide choice and high standards of accommodation. For a holiday with a difference, unique to Israel, there are *kibbutz country inns* in all parts of the country where one can find relaxed informality in delightful rural surroundings. Kibbutz Fly-Drive holidays are very popular and so are discovery tours by air-conditioned coach, staying at different hotels and kibbutzim to see the whole country.

HOTELS: There are over 300 hotels listed for visitors by the Ministry of Tourism. Prices vary according to grade and season. It is best to book months in advance for Israel's high season (April to October) and for religious holiday seasons. 258 hotels are members of the Israel Hotel Association, 29 Ha'mered Street, Tel Aviv 68125. Tel: (3) 650 131. Fax: (3) 510 0197. Telex: 371273 CIHA. **Grading:** The Ministry of Tourism introduced a grading system in 1988, but this was abolished on Jan 1 1992 until further notice. However, hotels will be evaluated according to facilities and services they offer, rates and location.

HOLIDAY/RECREATION VILLAGES: Located on the Mediterranean or the Red Sea Gulf, these villages provide accommodation usually in the form of small 2-bed cabins and bungalows. The standard fittings often include full air-conditioning and facilities. Most are only open between April and October and the emphasis is on casual living.

SELF-CATERING: Apartments and individual rooms are available on a rental basis throughout the country.

KIBBUTZ GUEST-HOUSES: All are clean and comfortable with modern dining rooms. Most have swimming pools (though it is wise to check that this is open to visitors) and provide a valuable insight into the style and aims of kibbutz life. Approximately 26 out of the 265 kibbutzim have these guest-houses and each is located in a rural or scenic part of the country which is usually open all year. Further information is available from the Tourist Office. **Grading:** Standards vary between 3 and 4 stars and costs are dependent on the grade of accommodation.

CHRISTIAN HOSPICES: Throughout the country some 30 Christian hospices (operated by a variety of denominations) provide rooms and board at low rates. Although preference is given to pilgrimage groups, most will accommodate general tourists. They vary greatly in size and standards but all offer tourists basic accommodation in situations where hotels are full. Details are available from the Tourist Office.

CAMPING/CARAVANNING: The fine climate means Israel is a good country for camping, with campsites providing a touring base for each region. They offer full sanitary facilities, electric current, a restaurant and/or store, telephone, postal services, first-aid facilities, shaded picnic and camp-fire areas and day and night watchmen. They can be reached by bus but all are open to cars and caravans. Most have tents and cabins, as well as a wide range of equipment for hire. All sites have swimming facilities either on-site or within easy reach. Hitch-hiking for campers is easy and popular, but one must compete for places with Army personnel, who have priority over citizens. For further information, contact the Tourist Office or Project 67, 10 Hatton Gardens, London EC1N 8AH. Tel: (071) 831 7626.

YOUTH HOSTELS: Hostels in Israel can be dormitory, family bungalows, huts or modern cubicles and they are scattered all over the country in both urban and rural areas. For further details write to the YHA or the IYHA, PO Box 1075, 3 Dorot Rishonim Street, Jerusalem 91009. Tel: (2) 252 706. Fax: (2) 250 676. Information is also available from the Tourist Office.

RESORTS & EXCURSIONS

Israel is a remarkable, fascinating and controversial country. For many it is, above all, the Holy Land. Religious attractions include the walk along the Via Dolorosa to the *Church of the Holy Sepulchre* in **Jerusalem** (the Holy City and cradle of Judaism, Christianity and Islam); the *Church of the Nativity* in **Bethlehem** and the *Church of the Annunciation* in **Nazareth**; the serenity of **Galilee** and the ride across the *River Jordan*, the river in which Jesus was baptised; and **Jericho,** one of the oldest cities in the world.

Tel Aviv: An exciting city offering commerce, culture and sandy beaches. The biggest attraction is the *Israeli Philharmonic Orchestra*. There are also several museums and the bustling *Carmel Flea Market*. In 1950, **Jaffa** was united with Tel Aviv; situated a mile from the city, this is one of the oldest ports in the world. It has archaeological finds reaching back to the 3rd century BC, a beach, a lively nightlife in *Old Jaffa* and a flea market.

Jerusalem: For Jews, Christians and Muslims, this is one of the the most revered cities on earth. Attractions also exist for the more secular: everything from religious emblems and relics of antiquity to modern items of interest. Religious tours are available from West Jerusalem which include *Mount Zion* and the *Tomb of David*. Other sites are the *Tomb of Judges*, the memorial to the six million Jews who died in the Holocaust, and *Mea Shearim* ('the hundred gates'). In East Jerusalem visitors may follow the *Way of the Cross*, enter the *Church of the Holy Sepulchre*, and see the *Wailing Wall*, the *Dome of the Rock* and the Jaffa and Damascus gates.

Excursions: Three important excursions are to the *Hill of Rachel*, *En Karem* and *Abu Ghaush*.

The Negev: This area, once largely desert, is now being irrigated and farmed in a settlement movement started by, amongst others, David Ben Gurion. **Be'er Sheeva** and **Dimona** are both of interest, but **Eilat**, in particular, is the place for visitors. Eilat is the best-equipped seaside resort in the Middle East, and a paradise for underwater enthusiasts.

There are several attractive places in the coastal region; these include **Ashkelon** with the *National Park*, the *Sharon Valley* with its orange groves, historic **Caesarea,** and **En Hod**, the artists' village.

Haifa: Israel's leading seaport is both an industrial town and an ancient fortress. It is lively and interesting and provides a good starting point for visits to Galilee.

Galilee: Places of interest are the *Sea of Galilee* itself, Nazareth – now an Arab town – the *Bet She'arim Catacombs*, **Megiddo, Tiberias** and the *Mount of Beatitudes*. The Tourist Office, together with a consortium of interested parties, is actively promoting Galilee as a tourist destination. Emphasis is being placed on the environment, sports, culture, history and health, with spa resorts (which have been used since Roman times) especially featured. The *Museum of Mediterranean Archaeology* celebrates many finds in the region.

The West Bank: In this troubled area are to be found **Bethlehem, Hebron, Jericho, Nablus** and **Samaria**. Consult with the Embassy or the Tourist Office before making any definite plans for visiting this area.

SOCIAL PROFILE

FOOD & DRINK: Restaurants in Israel offer a combination of Oriental and Western cuisine, in addition to the local dishes. Some restaurants are expensive, though a high price does not necessarily mean a high standard. Table service is usual. There are many snack bars. Restaurants, bars and cafés catering to tourists must have menus in two languages (Hebrew plus French or English). Israeli cuisine is essentially a combination of Oriental and Western cuisine, plus an additional distinct flavour brought by the many and varied nationalities which make up the Israelis. Dishes such as Hungarian *goulash*, Russian *borsht*, Viennese *schnitzel* or German *braten* are found next to Oriental items such as *falafel*, *humus*, *tahini*, *shashlik*, *kebabs* and Turkish coffee, as well as traditional Jewish dishes such as *gefilte* fish, chopped liver and chicken soup.

Kosher food: The Hebrew word *kosher* means food conforming to Jewish religious dietary laws. Pork and shellfish are officially prohibited, but it is possible to find them on many menus. Milk, cream or cheese may not be served together with meat in the same meal.

Drink: The wines of Israel range from light white to dry red and sweet rosé. There is also a good choice of local brandies and liqueurs. Liqueurs include *Hard Nut* (a walnut concoction of Eliaz winery), *Sabra* (chocolate and orange) and *Arak* (an anise drink). Israeli beers are *Maccabee*, *OK* and *Gold Star*. A centre for liqueurs is the monastery at Latrun on the road between Jerusalem and Tel Aviv.

NIGHTLIFE: There are nightclubs and discotheques in most towns. Tel Aviv has a wealth of entertainment to divert the visitor and there are rock, jazz, folk and pop music clubs in all the main cities and resorts. Israeli folklore and dance shows can be seen everywhere, especially in the kibbutzim. The Israeli Philharmonic Orchestra can be heard at the Binynei Haooma Hall in Jerusalem during the winter. A summer attraction is the *Israel Festival of International Music* and arts events. Cinema is popular in Israel and many cinemas screen three daily shows of international and local films (all Hebrew films are subtitled in English and French). Tickets for all events and even films can be bought in advance from ticket agencies and sometimes from hotels and tourist offices.

ARTS & CULTURE: There are art galleries all over Israel, with colonies of artists in the village of En Hod on Mount Carmel near Haifa, at Zefat and in Jaffa. Every large town has its museum; the *Israel Museum* in Jerusalem housing the Dead Sea Scrolls and the *Museum of the Diaspora* at Tel Aviv are internationally famous and too good to miss.

SHOPPING: There is a wide choice for shoppers in Israel; and in certain shops, especially in Arab markets, visitors can, and should, bargain. Tourists who buy leather goods at shops listed by the Ministry of Industry, Trade and Tourism and pay for them in foreign currency are exempt from VAT and receive a 25% discount on leather goods if these are delivered to them at the port of departure. Special purchases include jewellery, diamonds and other precious stones, ceramics, embroidery, glassware, wines, religious articles and holy books. 'Cashback' on duty-free items can be claimed from the Department of Customs, 32 Agron Street, Jerusalem 944190.

Shopping hours: 0900-1900 Sunday to Thursday, some shops close 1300-1600; 0900-1300 Friday. Remember that the shopping facilities are both Israeli and Arabic, and are therefore governed by two different sets of opening hours and methods of business. Jewish stores observe closing time near sunset on Friday evenings before *Shabbat* (Saturday) and Arabic stores close on Friday. It takes a while to realise that Sunday is a normal working day unlike in Western countries. For shoppers, the Jewish stores are therefore open on Friday, Arab markets on Saturday and both are open on Sundays when Christian stores close. Shops in the hotels are often open until midnight.

SPORT: Among annual sports events are the *Tel Aviv Marathon* and the *Kinereth Swimming Gala*. **Football, basketball** and **tennis** are popular. Many hotels have **tennis** courts, and there is a fine 18-hole **golf** course at Caesarea. **Horseriding** is available throughout the country. **Bicycling** and **skiing** are popular too. There are excellent facilities at kibbutz sportsgrounds and in cities.

Winter sports: To many people's surprise there is a full skiing season at Mount Hermon, on the northern border.

Water sports: Swimming, surfing, sailing, water-skiing, yachting and **fishing** are all available. All the large hotels have swimming pools. **Skindiving** and **aqualung diving** are especially popular in Eilat on the Red Sea coast with an excellent underwater observatory descending to the floor of the coral reef near the town. Eilat is a particularly good destination for winter sun for visitors from Western Europe.

Note: The Red Sea coastline has been designated a preservation area and any tourists found with 'souvenirs' such as coral will suffer severe fines from both the Israeli and Egyptian authorities.

SPECIAL EVENTS: In Bethlehem each Christmas there are Catholic, Protestant and Orthodox church services from December 24 to January 6. In Jerusalem, the Crucifixion and Resurrection of Christ are celebrated each Easter. The following is a selection of some of the other major festivals and special events celebrated during 1993 in Israel. For a complete list, contact the Israeli Government Tourist Office.

Mar-Apr '93 *Dead Sea Blues and Souls Festival*. **Apr** *The 5th Jerusalem International Judaica Fair; En Gev Festival*. **Apr 18-24** *16th Jerusalem International Book Fair*. **May 2-21** *Israel Festival*, Jerusalem. **Jun** *Student Film Festival*, Tel Aviv; *International Harmonica Festival; 34th International Chess Games*. **Jun-Jul** *International Music Festival*, Netanya. **Jul** *Israeli Folkdance Festival*, Karmiel; *Hebrew Song Festival*, Arad. **Jul 6-8** *International Folklore Festival*, Haifa. **Jul-Aug** *17th 'Zimriya' World Assembly of Choirs*, Jerusalem. **Aug 3-14** *Khutzot Hayotzer Arts & Crafts Fair*, Jerusalem. **Sep 29-Oct 7** *Feast of Tabernacles* (Christian Festival). **Dec** *Liturgica '93*, Jerusalem.

SOCIAL CONVENTIONS: Usually very informal, but in keeping with European style of hospitality. Visitors should observe normal courtesies when visiting someone's home and should not be afraid to ask questions about the country as most Israelis are happy to talk about their homeland, religion and politics. Often the expression *shalom* is used, which means 'peace' and is used instead of hello and goodbye. Dress is casual, but in Christian, Muslim and Jewish holy places modest attire is worn. For places such as the Western Wall visitors are given a cardboard hat to respect the religious importance of the site. Business people are expected to dress smartly, while plush restaurants, nightclubs and hotel dining rooms may require guests to dress for dinner. Formal evening wear is usually specified on invitations. It is considered a violation of the *Shabbat* (Saturday) to smoke in certain restaurants and many hotels. There is usually a sign to remind the visitor, and to disregard this warning would be regarded as discourteous to Orthodox Jews.

Tipping: Tipping in Israel is less evident than in many other countries. A 10% service charge is added to restaurant, café and hotel bills by law, which is distributed among the staff.

BUSINESS PROFILE

ECONOMY: Israel has a diverse and sophisticated manufacturing economy which in many respects rivals that of Western Europe. Agriculture is relatively small – about 5% of national product – with citrus fruit as the main commodity and export earner. The industrial sector is concentrated in engineering, aircraft, electronics, chemicals, construction materials, textiles and food processing. Mining is also small but is set to expand, with production of potash and bromine. There is a small indigenous oil industry. The infrastructure is well-developed and tourism, in which there has been considerable investment, is growing slowly but steadily. However, Israel suffers from a lack of natural resources, resulting in a large import bill, and very heavy defence expenditure. Offsetting that is a vast aid package from the United States, probably worth around US$5 billion per annum. The Labour government elected in 1992 is also likely to benefit from a US$10 billion loan provision to finance housing resettlement. The economy has recovered from its major difficulties during the 1980s, which culminated in 1000% inflation and the almost total collapse of the shekel, but growth is sluggish and any improvement in economic performance has been hampered by an inefficient state sector. A privatisation programme of some form is likely to be implemented in the near future, if the opposition of Israel's powerful union movement can be overcome. Telecommunications, shipping and chemicals are prime candidates for being sold off. The USA is Israel's largest export market, followed by the UK.

BUSINESS: Business can be frustrating, as in many instances it is difficult to get a positive reply to a straight question. However, perseverance will pay off. Appointments are usual, as is the use of business cards. Israelis tend not to be punctual and it is not uncommon to be kept waiting for as long as half an hour. Normal courtesies should be observed, although business meetings tend to be less formal than in Britain. **Office hours:** 0800-1300 and 1500-1800 Sunday to Thursday (Nov-May) and 0730-1430 Sunday to Thursday (Jun-Oct). Some offices are open half-day Friday.

COMMERCIAL INFORMATION: The following organisation can offer advice: Federation of Israeli Chambers of Commerce, PO Box 20027, 84 Hahashmonaim Street, Tel Aviv 67011. Tel: (3) 561 2444. Fax: (3) 561 2614. Telex: 33484 CHCOM IL.

CONFERENCES/CONVENTIONS: The Ministry of Tourism brochure *Picture a Perfect Convention* states that 'about two thousand years ago, some of the greatest conventions were held near Tiberias where it was recorded that five thousand were amply catered for'. Israel's record as a contemporary international conference centre began in 1963, and the country now attracts about 150 international meetings a year with 50,000 delegates; scientific and academic meetings account for about half the meetings, though religious and sporting events are on the increase. In 1991, more than 60% of meetings were held in Jerusalem. Apart from hotels and the convention centres in Jerusalem and Tel Aviv, opportunities exist to hold meetings in kibbutzim. For further information contact: International Conventions Division, Ministry of Tourism, PO Box 1018, Jerusalem 91009. Tel: (2) 237 311. Fax: (2) 254 226. Telex: 25218.

HISTORY & GOVERNMENT

HISTORY: The history of Israel may be traced back to 2000BC, though the earliest recorded event derives from the era of Moses (around 1300BC) when elements of the tribes of Israel escaped to Palestine from serfdom in the eastern Nile delta. Once established there, the Jewish people maintained control of much of Palestine, despite occasional clashes with the neighbouring Assyrians and Philistines, until overrun by the Greek conqueror Alexander the Great in the 4th century BC. By AD100 the country was under direct Roman rule. Palestine was subsequently occupied by Arabs, then retaken by the armies of the First Crusade (1096-1100). The Christians established several states, including the Kingdom of Jerusalem, which survived until the fall of Acre in 1291, although after the battle of Hattin in 1187, Jerusalem was no longer a permanent part of it. After 1291 the area fell under the domination of the Mamelukes and subsequently the Ottoman Empire, while the Jews were dispersed over Europe, Asia, Africa and later throughout the rest of the world. Few countries today lack a community descended from Jewish settlers. The Zionist movement emerged in the 19th century with the aim of re-establishing a separate Jewish nation in Palestine, building on a common sense of identity of the scattered Jewish communities and the insecurity caused by frequent persecution. The aspirations of the Zionist movement were ultimately recognised by the British government in the Balfour Declaration of 1917, which followed Britain's occupation of Palestine after defeating the Turks in the Middle East during the First World War. The Balfour Declaration formed the basis of the 1920 mandate granted by the League of Nations which acceded to British rule over the territory. The mandate laid the foundations of the modern Arab-Israeli conflict as the British struggled to balance their commitment to the Jews against the rights of the indigenous Arab population. After the Second World War and the appalling slaughter of Jews in Hitler's concentration camps, the United Nations favoured the creation of a separate Jewish state carved out of Arab Palestine. The Arabs refused to accept this, but the imminent expiry of the mandate and pressure from Jewish immigrants, many of whom had moved to Palestine after the war, forced the British to withdraw. The Jewish leaders inaugurated the State of Israel in May 1948, bringing an immediate conflict with the Arab population which escalated into full-scale war. Although neighbouring Arab states, notably Jordan, intervened on the Arab side, the Israelis took control of and held about three-quarters of Palestine. The remainder – the largely Arab-peopled area between Jerusalem and the River Jordan commonly described today as the 'West Bank' – was occupied by the Jordanian army. Since the Six Day War of 1967, in which Israel defeated a combined force from several Arab countries, the West Bank has been occupied by the Israelis; similar territorial losses were suffered by the Egyptians in the Sinai Peninsula and Gaza Strip, and by the Syrians in the Golan Heights. Efforts to recover these in the 1973 Yom Kippur War were repulsed by Israel. Since then, the only progress towards a lasting Arab-Israeli settlement has been the Camp David Accord between Israel and Egypt signed in 1979. The Accord included not only a peace treaty but provisions for the return of occupied land to Egypt (which has been effected) and for a transition to autonomous rule for West Bank Palestinians (which has not). Since the end of 1987, Palestinian activists have wound down the armed struggle in place of a more generalised campaign of civil disobedience, street disturbances and strikes known under the collective rubric of *al-intifada* (the Uprising). This has been coupled with a diplomatic offensive by the exiled PLO leadership which has borne some dividends, particularly after unconditional PLO acceptance of UN resolutions 242 and 338 which implicitly recognise Israel's right to exist.

The latest phase of the saga dates from the end of the 1991 Gulf War. The Bush administration had made a definite commitment to finding a regional settlement as part of its pre-Gulf War diplomacy. Persuading the Israelis to turn up, however, was not easy but the sudden influx of Soviet Jewry to Israel provided a unique opportunity. Ever short of money, the Israelis lodged a request with the USA for a US$10-billion loan guarantee to facilitate the resettlement process. Bush agreed, subject to Israeli participation in a US-Soviet sponsored peace conference involving the Israelis and representatives of the key Arab players. The Israelis denounced the condition as blackmail and 'anti-semitic' and called on Congress (heavily influenced as ever by the powerful Jewish lobby) to block the Bush proposal. The administration stood its ground; the Israelis agreed to turn up. The format for the conference, the first phase of which was held in Madrid at the beginning of November 1991, was designed by US Secretary of State James Baker. Delegations from Israel, Syria, Lebanon and Jordan attended. The Jordanian delegation included a number of Palestinians unconnected – at Israeli insistence – with the PLO. The Israelis did, however, turn a blind eye to the fact that the Palestinians were heavily influenced by an 'advisory' team which did include PLO members and guided the official Palestinian delegation throughout. Substantive discussions progressed slowly at the early sessions in late 1991 and the first months of 1992, and revolved around the construction of a mutually acceptable formula for Palestinian autonomy. With the Israelis in a relatively intransigent frame of mind, the only real achievement of this phase of the talks was that it built up enough momentum to carry through to another round. A major sticking point was, and continues to be, Israeli settlement of the occupied territories. By the spring of 1992, suspicion had arisen on the Arab side that the Israelis under Shamir were dragging out the negotiations to put as many settlements on the ground as possible before reaching any agreement; this was later admitted by Shamir. All parties needed to wait for the result of the forthcoming Israeli general election. The campaign preceding the poll at the end of June was one of the most bitter in Israeli history. Shamir led for the ruling Likud bloc while the leadership of Likud's main rival, the Labour Party, had been wrested from Shimon Peres by Yitzhak Rabin, one of the last of Israel's soldier-politicians who was Defence Minister at the time of the Six Day War, premier in the mid-1970s and Defence Minister in the national unity government of the mid-1980s. The Labour Party and its allies won a comfortable victory. Labour (44 seats), Meretz (13), the orthodox religious party Shas (7) and two Arab-based parties (2 each) make up the ruling coalition, led by Rabin, which has a majority of 13 in the Knesset. Rabin quickly outlined his proposals for an Arab-Israeli settlement. The main provisions are a halt on investment in settlements 'not essential to Israeli security' – which was sufficient to unlock the stalled American loan guarantee – and elections for a representative Palestinian assembly to administer the occupied territories. (Likud prepared to concede only municipal elections.) On the Palestinian side, although *al-intifada* is running out of steam, there are dangerous splits emerging, especially in the occupied territories where the Islamist-inspired Hamas organisation, which rejects compromise with the Israelis, is gaining support. And the Syrians have still not shown any inclination to reach an accord unless the Golan Heights are handed back, which they will not be. Once the Israeli elections were over, a few rounds of talks were held before the American presidential election again put the process on ice. It will resume in earnest in 1993.

GOVERNMENT: Israel has a parliamentary system of government, with a single chamber, the Knesset, elected every four years by universal adult suffrage. The Knesset passes legislation and appoints a president as Head of State. Executive power rests with the Cabinet, led by the Prime Minister, which takes office after a vote of confidence from the Knesset.

CLIMATE

Mediterranean, with a pleasant spring and autumn. Winters in the north can be cool. Rain in winter is widespread, particularly in Jerusalem. Snow is rare. Summers can be very hot, especially in the south. The Red Sea resort of Eilat has a good climate for beach holidays all the year round.

Required clothing: Lightweight cottons and linens for warmer months are required. Mediumweights are recommended for winters, although on the Red Sea coast they are unlikely to be necessary during the day.

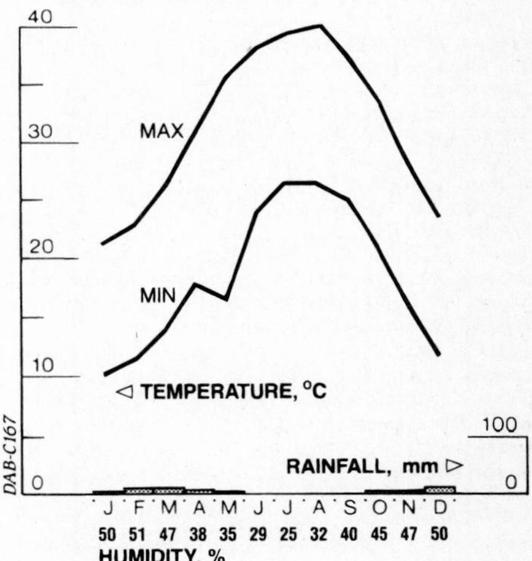

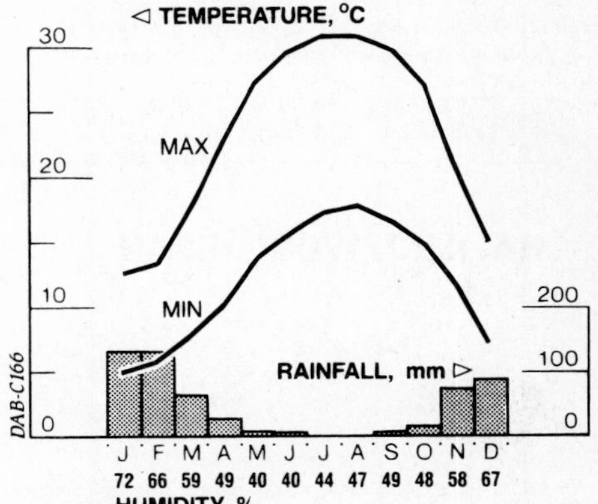

Location: Western Europe.

Ente Nazionale Italiano per il Turismo (ENIT)
Via Marghera 2
00185 Roma, Italy
Tel: (6) 49711. Fax: (6) 446 3379 *or* 446 9907. Telex: 621314/8.

Embassy of the Italian Republic
14 Three Kings Yard
Davies Street
London W1Y 2EH
Tel: (071) 629 8200. Fax: (071) 629 8200. Telex: 23520 ITADIPG.

Italian Consulate
38 Eaton Place
London SW1 8AN
Tel: (071) 235 9371 *or* 259 6322 (for recorded visa information). Fax: (071) 823 1609. Telex: 8950932. Opening hours: 0900-1200 Monday to Friday.

Italian State Tourist Office (ENIT)
1 Princes Street
London W1R 8AY
Tel: (071) 408 1254. Fax: (071) 493 6695. Telex: 22402 ENIT GBG. Opening hours: 0930-1700 Monday to Friday.

British Embassy
Via XX Settembre 80A
00187 Roma, Italy
Tel: (6) 482 5551 *or* 482 5441. Fax: (6) 487 3324. Telex: 626119 BREMB I.
Consulates in: Florence, Milan, Turin, Trieste, Genoa, Venice, Naples, Brindisi and Bari.

Embassy of the Italian Republic
1601 Fuller Street, NW
Washington, DC
20009
Tel: (202) 328 5500. Fax: (202) 462 3605. Telex: 64461.
Consulates in: Boston, Chicago, Detroit, Houston, Los Angeles, Newark, New Orleans, New York (tel: (212) 737 9100), Philadelphia and San Francisco.

Italian State Tourist Office (ENIT)
Suite 1565
630 Fifth Avenue
New York, NY
10111
Tel: (212) 245 4961 *or* 245 4822. Fax: (212) 586 9249. Telex: 236024.

Embassy of the United States of America
Via Vittorio Veneto 119A
00187 Roma, Italy
Tel: (6) 46741. Telex: 622322 AMBRMA.

Embassy of the Italian Republic
11th Floor
275 Slater Street
Ottawa, Ontario
K1P 5H9
Tel: (613) 232 2401/2/3. Fax: (613) 233 1484. Telex: 610056.

Italian State Office (ENIT)
Suite 1914
1 place de Ville Marie
Montréal, Québec
H3B 3M9
Tel: (514) 866 7669. Fax: (514) 392 1429. Telex: 525607.

Canadian Embassy
Via GB de Rossi 27
01161 Roma, Italy
Tel: (6) 841 5341. Fax: (6) 884 8752.

AREA: 301,277 sq km (116,324 sq miles).
POPULATION: 57,576,429 (1989 estimate).
POPULATION DENSITY: 191.1 per sq km.
CAPITAL: Rome. **Population:** 2,803,931 (1989).
GEOGRAPHY: Italy is situated in Europe and attached in the north to the European mainland. To the north the Alps separate Italy from France, Switzerland, Austria and Slovenia.
Northern Italy: The Alpine regions, the Po Plain and the Ligurian-Etruscan Appennines. Piemonte and Val d'Aosta contain some of the highest mountains in Europe and are good areas for winter sports. Many rivers flow down from the mountains towards the Po Basin, passing through the beautiful Italian Lake District (Maggiore, Como, Garda). The Po Basin, which extends as far south as the bare slopes of the Appennines, is covered with gravel terraces and rich alluvial soil and has long been one of Italy's most prosperous regions. To the east, where the River Po flows into the Adriatic Sea, the plains are little higher than the river itself; artificial (and occasionally natural) embankments prevent flooding.
Central Italy: The northern part of the Italian penin sula. Tuscany (Toscana) has a diverse landscape with snow-capped mountains (the Tuscan Appennines), lush countryside, hills and a long sandy coastline with offshore islands. Le Marche, lying between the Appennines and the Adriatic coast, is a region of mountains, rivers and small fertile plains. The even more mountainous *regioni* (administrative districts) of Abruzzo and Molise are bordered by Marche to the north and Puglia to the south, and are separated from the Tyrrhenian Sea and to the west by Lazio and Campania. Umbria is known as the 'green heart of Italy', hilly with broad plains, olive groves and pines. Further south lies Rome, Italy's capital and largest city. Within its precincts is the Vatican City (see separate entry on *Vatican City*).
Southern Italy: Campania consists of flat coastal plains and low mountains, stretching from Baia Domizia to the Bay of Naples and along a rocky coast to the Calabria border. Inland, the Appennines are lower, mellowing into the rolling countryside around Sorrento. The islands of Capri, Ischia and Procida in the Tyrrhenian Sea are also part of Campania. The south is wilder than the north, with mile upon mile of olive trees, cool forests and rolling hills. Puglia, the 'heel of the boot', is a landscape of volcanic hills and isolated marshes. Calabria, the 'toe', is heavily forested and thinly populated. The Calabrian hills are home to bears and wolves.
The Islands: Sicily (Sicilia), visible across a 3km (2-mile) strait from mainland Italy, is fertile but mountainous with volcanoes (including the famous landmark of Mount Etna) and lava fields, and several offshore islands. Sardinia (Sardegna) has a mountainous landscape, fine sandy beaches and rocky offshore islands.
For more information on each region, see the *Resorts & Excursions* section below.
LANGUAGE: Italian is the official language. Dialects are spoken in different regions. German and Ladin are spoken in the South Tyrol region (bordering Austria). French is spoken in all the border areas from the Riviera to the area north of Milan (border with France and Switzerland). Slovenian is spoken in the provinces bordering Slovenia. English, German and French are also spoken in the biggest cities and resorts by people connected with tourism.
RELIGION: Roman Catholic with Protestant minorities.
TIME: GMT + 1 (GMT + 2 in summer).
ELECTRICITY: 220 volts AC, 50Hz.
COMMUNICATIONS: Telephone: Full IDD service available. Country code: 39 (followed by 6 for Rome, 2 for Milan, 11 for Turin, 81 for Naples, 41 for Venice and 55 for Florence). Telephone kiosks accept Lit100 and Lit200 coins, as well as *gettoni*, tokens which are available at tobacconists and bars. There are some card phones, and phonecards can be purchased at post offices, tobacconists and certain newsagents. **Fax:** Some hotels have facilities. **Telex/telegram:** Telex facilities are available at the main post offices. Telex code: 43. *Italcable* operates services abroad, transmitting messages by cable or radio. Both internal and overseas telegrams may be dictated over the telephone. **Post:** The Italian postal system tends to be subject to delays. Letters between Italy and European destinationsusually take a week to ten days to arrive. Letters intended for *Poste Restante* collection should be addressed to Fermo Posta and the town. Stamps are sold in post offices and tobacconists. Post office hours: 0800/0830-1200/1230 and 1400/1430-1730/1800 Monday to Friday; Saturday mornings only. **Press:** The main towns publish a weekly booklet with entertainment programmes, sports events, restaurants, nightclubs etc. A daily English-language newspaper, *Daily American*, is published in Rome. Among the most important Italian dailies are *La Stampa* (Turin), *Corriere della Sera* (Milan), *La Repubblica* (Rome), *Il Messaggero* (Rome), *Il Giorno* (Milan) and *Il Giornale* (Milan).
BBC World Service and Voice of America frequencies: From time to time these change. See the section How to Use this Book for more information.

BBC:

MHz	15.57	12.10	7.325	6.195

Voice of America:

MHz	11.97	9.670	6.040	5.995

PASSPORT/VISA

Regulations and requirements may be subject to change at short notice, and you are advised to contact the appropriate diplomatic or consular authority before finalising travel arrangements. Details of these may be found at the head of this country's entry. Any numbers in the chart refer to the footnotes below.

	Passport Required?	Visa Required?	Return Ticket Required?
Full British	I	No	No
BVP	Valid	-	-
Australian	Yes	No	No
Canadian	Yes	No	No
USA	Yes	No	No
Other EC	I	No	No
Japanese	Yes	No	No

ITALY | **HEALTH REGULATIONS** | **VISA REGULATIONS** | Code-Link

GALILEO/WORLDSPAN

TI-DFT/ROM/HE

TI-DFT/ROM/VI

SABRE

TIDFT/ROM/HE

TIDFT/ROM/VI

To access this information on your CRS, swipe the barcode with a light pen or type in the text under the barcode. For more information, see the introduction *How to Use This Book.*

Note: The regulations stated below also apply to San Marino and Vatican City.
PASSPORTS: Valid passport required by all except:
(a) [1] nationals of Belgium, France, Germany, Greece, Luxembourg, The Netherlands, Portugal and Spain if carrying a valid national ID card, and the UK if carrying a British Visitors Passport;
(b) nationals of Austria, Liechtenstein, Malta, Monaco, San Marino and Switzerland if carrying valid national ID cards.
British Visitors Passport: A British Visitors Passport can be used for holidays or unpaid business trips of up to 3 months to Italy.
VISAS: Required by all except:
(a) nationals of countries referred to in the chart above for stays not exceeding 3 months;
(b) nationals of Andorra, Argentina, Austria, Barbados, Benin, Bolivia, Brazil, Chile, Colombia, Costa Rica, Côte d'Ivoire, Cyprus, Dominican Republic, Ecuador, El Salvador, Fiji, Finland, Guatemala, Guyana, Honduras, Hong Kong (British nationals), Hungary, Iceland, Jamaica, Kenya, Kuwait, Liechtenstein, Malaysia, Maldives, Malta, Mexico, Monaco, New Zealand, Niger, Norway, Paraguay, Peru, San Marino, Singapore, Sweden, Switzerland, Togo, Trinidad & Tobago, Uganda, Uruguay, Vatican City, Western Samoa and Yugoslavia for stays not exceeding 3 months;
(c) nationals of Venezuela for visits not exceeding 2 months;
(d) nationals of Czechoslovakia, Israel, Poland, South Korea and Lesotho for stays not exceeding 1 month.
Transit visas: Not required by those continuing their journey to a third country by the same or connecting aircraft, or by those who continue their journey to a third country within 48 hours from the same airport at which they arrive. Tickets with reserved seats and valid documents for onward travel must be held. This facility is not available to stateless persons and nationals of Afghanistan, Angola, Cape Verde, Guinea-Bissau, Iran, North Korea, Mongolia, Mozambique, São Tomé, Taiwan, Vietnam and Zimbabwe.
Types of visa: *Transit:* applicants must present their passports endorsed with the visa of the countries beyond Italy which they intend to visit and rail/air tickets as evidence of the continuation of their journey. *Entry visa:* tourist or business. Details from the Italian Consulate. No visas for multiple entries can be issued. Cost: £12.
Validity: 1 month from date of issue with some exceptions.
Application to: Consulate (or Consular Section at Embassy). For addresses, see top of entry. Postal applications are not acceptable.
Application requirements: (a) Passport which has been valid for at least three months. (b) Completed application form. (c) Return ticket. (d) 1 passport-size photograph. (e) Proof of financial means. (f) Where applicable, a letter from sponsoring company in Italy; a work reference; a letter from school, college or university. (g) Where applicable, marriage certificate showing proof of marriage to an EC national.
Stateless persons and holders of travel documents must present 4 forms and 4 photographs.
Working days required: 1.
Note: In the UK, current visa requirements are held on an automatic 'dial & listen' service. Tel: (071) 259 6322.

MONEY

Currency: Italian Lira (Lit). Notes are in denominations of Lit100,000, 50,000, 10,000, 5000, 2000 and 1000. Coins are in denominations of Lit500, 200, 100, 50 and 20. There is a plan to introduce a 'new Lira' worth 1000 times the present currency, but no firm date has been established for this at the time of writing.
Currency exchange: Travellers cheques, cheques and foreign money can be changed at banks, railway stations and airports, and very often at main hotels (generally at a less convenient rate). Many UK banks offer differing exchange rates depending on the denominations of Italian currency being bought or sold. Check with banks for details and current rates.
Credit cards: Access/Mastercard, Diners Club and Visa are widely accepted. Check with your credit card company for merchant acceptability and other facilities which may be available.
Travellers cheques are accepted almost everywhere.
Exchange rate indicators: The following figures are included as a guide to the movements of the Lira against Sterling and the US Dollar:

Date:	Oct '89	Oct '90	Oct '91	Oct '92
£1.00=	2182	2230	2178	2108
$1.00=	1382	1142	1255	1329

Currency restrictions: Check with the bank before departure. Import and export of both foreign and local currency is limited to Lit20,000,000. If it is intended to import or export amounts greater than this, the amount imported should be declared and validated on form V2 on arrival.
Banking hours: These vary from city to city but, in general, 0830-1330 and 1500-1600 Monday to Friday.

DUTY FREE

The following goods may be imported into Italy without incurring customs duty by:
(a) residents of European countries travelling from an EC country:
300 cigarettes or 75 cigars or 150 cigarillos or 400g of tobacco;
1.5 litres of spirits (over 22% volume) or 3 litres of fortified or sparkling wine;
75g (90cc/3 fl oz) of perfume and 375cc (13 fl oz) of toilet water;
750g of coffee or 300g of coffee extract;
150g of tea or 60g of tea extract;
Goods to the value of Lit418,000.
(b) residents of European countries travelling from a non-European country:
200 cigarettes or 50 cigars or 100 cigarillos or 250g of tobacco;
750ml of spirits (over 22% volume) or 2 litres of alcoholic beverages (not over 22% volume);
50g (60cc/2fl oz) of perfume and 250mls of toilet water;
500g of coffee or 200g of coffee extract;
100g of tea or 40g of tea extract;
Goods to the value of Lit167,000.
(c) other passengers:
400 cigarettes or 100 cigars or 200 cigarillos or 500g of tobacco;
Goods to the value of Lit67,000;
Alcohol and other allowances are as for passengers travelling from non-European countries above.
(d) visitors over 17 years of age arriving from EC countries with duty-paid goods (as from January 1993):
800 cigarettes and 400 cigarillos and 200 cigars and 1kg of tobacco;
90 litres of wine (including up to 40 litres of sparkling wine):
10 litres of spirits;
20 litres of spirits;
20 litres of intermediate products (such as fortified wine);
110 litres of beer.

PUBLIC HOLIDAYS

Public holidays observed in Italy are as follows:
Apr 12 '93 Easter Monday. **Apr 25** Liberation Day. **May 1** Labour Day. **Aug 15** Assumption. **Nov 1** All Saints' Day. **Nov 5** National Unity Day. **Dec 8** Immaculate Conception. **Dec 25** Christmas. **Dec 26** Boxing Day. **Jan 1 '94** New Year's Day. **Jan 6** Epiphany.
In addition, local feast days are held in honour of town patron saints, generally without closure of shops and offices. These include:
Turin/Genoa/Florence: Jun 24 (St John the Baptist). **Milan:** Dec 7 (St Ambrose). **Siena:** Palio Horserace. **Venice:** Apr 25 (St Mark). **Bologna:** Oct 4 (St Petronius). **Naples:** Sep 19 (St Gennaro). **Bari:** Dec 6 (St Nicholas). **Palermo:** Jul 15 (St Rosalia). **Rome:** Jun 29 (St Peter).

HEALTH

Regulations and requirements may be subject to change at short notice, and you are advised to contact your doctor well in advance of your intended date of departure. Any numbers in the chart refer to the footnotes below.

	Special Precautions?	Certificate Required?
Yellow Fever	No	No
Cholera	No	No
Typhoid & Polio	No	-
Malaria	No	-
Food & Drink	1	-

[1]: Water precautions are only necessary for short stays in rural areas. The inscription 'Acqua Non Potabile' means water is not drinkable. Bottled water is available and is advised for the first few weeks of the stay. Milk is pasteurised and dairy products are safe for consumption. Local meat, poultry, seafood, fruit and vegetables are considered safe to eat.
Rabies is present. For those at high risk, vaccination before arrival should be considered. If you are bitten abroad seek medical advice without delay. For more information consult the *Health* section at the back of the book.
Health care: A Reciprocal Health Agreement with the rest of the EC allows free dental and medical (including hospital) treatment on presentation of form E111; prescribed medicines must be paid for. Insurance is advised for specialist treatment. Italy is well endowed with health spas, some famous as far back as the Roman era. The most important and best-equipped health resorts in Italy are Abano Terme and Montegrotto Terme (Veneto), Acqui Terme (Piemonte), Chianciano and Montecatini Terme (Tuscany), Fiuggi (Lazio), Porretta Terme and Salsomaggiore Terme (Emilia-Romagna), Sciacca (Sicilia) and Sirmione (Lombardia). At Merano (Alto Adige) it is possible to have a special 'grape treatment' where the main element in the diet is grapes.

TRAVEL - International

AIR: Italy's national airline is *Alitalia (AZ)*.
Approximate flight times: From Rome to *London* is 2 hours 30 minutes, to *Los Angeles* is 15 hours 35 minutes, to *New York* is 9 hours 45 minutes, to *Singapore* is 13 hours 55 minutes and to *Sydney* is 24 hours 50 minutes.
International airports: *Rome (ROM)* (Leonardo da Vinci or Fiumicino), 35km (22 miles) southwest of the city (travel time – 50 minutes). Taxis available to the city (45-70 minutes). Airport facilities: outgoing duty-free (0800-2230), car hire (0700-2200), bank/exchange (0700-2200), bar/restaurant (0700-2230).
Bologna (BLQ) (Borgo Panigale), 6km (4 miles) northwest of the city (travel time – 20 minutes). Good airport facilities. Buses are available to the city.
Catania (CTA) (Fontanarossa), 7km (4.5 miles) from the city.
Genoa (GOA) (Cristoforo Colombo, Sestri), 7km (4.5 miles) west of the city (travel time – 25 minutes). Duty-free facilities. Buses are available to the city.
Milan (MIL) (Linate), 10km (6 miles) east of the city (travel time – 25 minutes). Taxis are available to the city (travel time – 40/60 minutes). Airport facilities: outgoing duty-free facilities, car hire, bank/exchange and bar/restaurant.
Milan (MIL) (Malpensa), 46km (29 miles) northwest of the city (travel time – 80 minutes).
Naples (NAP) (Capodichino), 7km (4.5 miles) north of the city (travel time – 35 minutes). Duty-free facilities.
Pisa (PSA) (Galileo Galilei), 2km (1.5 miles) south of the city (travel time – 10 minutes). Duty-free facilities.
Note: People travelling to Florence can fly to Pisa and then take the new train service directly from Pisa Airport to Florence, which takes one hour. The rail station in Pisa is practically inside the airport. Rail services connect with arrivals and departures of all international flights and major domestic services.
Palermo (PMO) (Punta Raisi), 32km (20 miles) west of the city (travel time – 25 minutes).
Turin (TRN) (Caselle), 16km (10 miles) northwest of the city (travel time – 35 minutes).
Venice (VCE) (Marco Polo), 13km (8 miles) northwest of the city (travel time – 20 minutes).
SEA: International sailings to Italy run from Greece, Egypt, Libya, South America, the Far East, Malta, Spain, France and Tunisia. For details contact shipping agents direct or consult the *Travellers' Handbook*, available from the Italian State Tourist Office.
RAIL: The main rail connections from London (Victoria) and Paris to Italy are:
Palatino (Paris/Rome). Couchettes and sleeping cars only.
Naples Express (Paris, Turin, Genoa, Pisa, Rome, Naples).
Simplon Express (Paris, Lausanne, Brigue, Domodossola, Milan, Venice, Trieste).
Italia Express (Calais, Lille, Strasbourg, Basle, Milan,

Bologna, Florence, Rome).
Many other European trains have through-coaches to the main Italian cities.
ROAD: Road routes from the UK to Italy run through France, Austria, Switzerland and Slovenia and most routes use the tunnels under the Alps and Appennines.
Cars: Italian Railways run regular daily services called 'autotreno' to convey cars, especially during the summer holiday season: Milan–Genoa–Naples–Villa San Giovanni; Bologna–Naples–Villa San Giovanni. These services operate from special railway stations and are generally bookable at the departure station. Owners must travel on the same train. The documents required are the log-book, valid driving licence with Italian translation, Green Card insurance and national identity plate fixed to the rear of the vehicle. For information on routes contact the Italian State Tourist Office.
Coaches: *Euroways* is a consortium of three international travel companies: *Wallace Arnold* in the United Kingdom, *VIA* in France and *SITA* in Italy. They jointly run a luxury coach service from the UK to Italy on the following route: London, Dover, Paris, Mont Blanc, Aosta, Turin, Genoa, Milan, Venice, Bologna, Florence and Rome. The route involves changing in Paris (arrival – 1730, departure – 1830). A coach leaving at 0830 from London Victoria Coach Station arrives in Italy the following day, with the following approximate arrival times (depending on route taken from Paris): Turin (0830), Genoa (1130), Milan (1130), Venice (1400), Bologna (1130), Florence (1600) and Rome (1900). The service runs on Monday from March to December, more frequently in the summer months.
See below for information on required **documentation** and **traffic regulations.**

TRAVEL - Internal

AIR: *Alitalia (AZ)* and other airlines run services to all the major cities. There are over 30 airports. For details contact the airlines or the Italian State Tourist Office.
SEA: Italy's principal ports are Venice, Genoa, La Spezia, Civitavecchia, Naples, Messina, Cagliari, Bari, Pescara, Ancona, Trieste, Palermo, Catania, Livorno and Brindisi. A number of car and passenger ferries operate throughout the year linking Italian ports.
Ferries: Regular boat and hydrofoil services run to the Islands of Capri, Elba, Giglio, Sardegna (Sardinia), Sicilia (Sicily) and the Aeolian Islands. There are also some links along the coast.
RAIL: There are over 20,000km (12,400 miles) of track in the country, of which slightly over half is electrified. The *Italian State Railways (FS)* (tel: (6) 84901; fax: (6) 883 1108; telex: 622345) runs a nationwide network at very reasonable fares, calculated on the distance travelled, and there are a number of excellent reductions. These include the *Travel at Will* ticket which gives unlimited travel on all rail services including TEE and 'Rapido' trains, without payment of the supplementary charges which normally apply. Tickets on express trains should be booked in advance.
Children aged between 4-11 pay half the adult rate.
First- and second-class travel is available on most services. Regional timetables (including some bus links) are generally on sale at station bookstalls.
In addition to FS, there are also several local railway companies, most of whom run short-distance trains on narrow-gauge track. On Sicily, frequent services run from Palermo and Catania/Siracusa to mainland destinations via the Messina train ferries. There are also local trains which run from Palermo to Agrigento and Catania. On Sardinia, several daily trains run from Cagliari to Porto Torres and Olbia.
ROAD: There are nearly 300,000km (185,500 miles) of roads in Italy, including 6000km (3700 miles) of motorway which link all parts of the country. Tolls are charged at varying distances and scales, except for the Napoli-Reggio Calabria stretch which is toll-free. Secondary roads are also excellent and require no tolls. Road signs are international. Many petrol stations are closed between 1200 and 1500. You are advised to check locally about exact opening times.
Traffic regulations: Speed limits are 50kmph (30mph) in urban areas, 80/90kmph (50/60mph) on country roads, 130kmph (80mph) on motorways (110kmph or 70mph on weekends). Undipped headlights are prohibited in towns and cities, but are compulsory when passing through tunnels. All vehicles must carry a red warning triangle, available at border posts. **Note:** Fines for speeding and other driving offences are on the spot and particularly heavy.
Breakdown service: In case of breakdown on any Italian road, dial 116 at the nearest telephone box. Tell the operator where you are, your plate number and type of car and the nearest ACI Office will be informed for immediate assistance.
Customs regulations: Visitors must carry their log-book, which must either be in their name as owner or must have the owner's written permission to drive the vehicle. Customs documents for the temporary importation of motor vehicles (also aircraft and pleasure-boats) have been abolished.
Bus: Good coach services run between towns and cities and there are also extensive local buses, including good services on Sicily and Sardinia. In more remote areas, buses will usually connect with rail services.
Taxi: Taxi services are available in and between all cities.
Car hire: Self-drive hire is available in most cities and resorts. Many international and Italian firms operate this service with different rates and conditions. With the larger firms it is possible to book from other countries through the car hire companies, their agents or through the air companies. Generally, small local firms offer cheaper rates, but cars can only be booked locally. Many car rental agencies have booths at the airport or information in hotels. *Avis* has offices in Rome at Via Tiburtina (tel: (6) 470 1400), *Hertz* are at Ciampino Airport (tel: (6) 724 0095), and *Europcar* at Via Lombardia 7 (tel: (6) 465 802). Many special-rate fly/drive deals are available for Italy.
Documentation: Visitors must either carry an international green card for their car or motor vehicle (also for boats) or other insurance. A British driving licence is valid in Italy but must be accompanied by a translation obtainable free of charge from the RAC, AA, ACI frontier and provincial offices or the Italian State Tourist Office. Motorcycles no longer require customs documents, but refer to the customs regulations above. A driving licence or a motorcycle driving licence is required for motorcycles over 50cc. Passengers are required by law to wear seat belts.
URBAN: All the big towns and cities (Rome, Milan, Naples, Turin, Genoa, Venice) have good public transport networks.
Metro: In Rome there are two underground lines – Metropolitana A from Via Ottaviano via Termini station to Via Anagnina, and Metropolitana B between Termini station and Exhibition City (EUR) (Via Laurentina). Both day and monthly passes are available. Milan also has a metro service, with tickets usable on both metro and bus, and there are plans to construct one in Turin.
Tram: There is a 28km (17-mile) network consisting of eight routes in Rome; Milan, Naples and Turin also have tram services.
Bus: Services operate in all main cities and towns; in Rome, the network is extensive and complements the metro and tram systems. The fares structure is integrated between the various modes. Buy a flat-fare ticket or a weekly pass in advance from a roadside or station machine. Information is available from the ATAC booth in front of the Termini station. Trolley buses also run in a number of other towns. In larger cities fares are generally pre-purchased from machines or shops. Bus fares – generally at a standard rate per run – can be bought in packets of five or multiples and are fed into a stamping machine on boarding the bus.
Taxis: Available in most towns and cities. In Rome they are relatively expensive, with extra charges for night service, luggage and taxis called by telephone. All charges are listed on a rate card displayed in the cab with an English translation. Taxis can only be hailed at strategically located stands or by telephone. Avoid taxis that are not metered. 8-10% tip is expected by taxi drivers and this is sometimes added to the fare for foreigners.
City tours: *Rome:* run by many travel agencies, these tours allow first-time visitors to get a general impression of the main sights and enables them to plan further sightseeing. Information is available from the Italian State Tourist Office. Horse carriages are available in Rome. Charges are high. In *Venice*, privately hired boats and gondolas are available, as well as a public ferry service.
JOURNEY TIMES: The following chart gives approximate journey times (in hours and minutes) from Rome to other major cities/towns in Italy.

	Air	Road	Rail
Florence	0.45	2.30	2.30
Milan	0.65	6.00	6.00
Venice	0.65	6.00	6.30
Naples	0.45	2.00	2.30
Palermo	0.60	10.00	14.30
Cagliari	0.55	-	-

ACCOMMODATION

HOTELS: There are about 40,000 hotels throughout the country. Every hotel has its fixed charges agreed with the provincial tourist board. Charges vary according to class, season, services available and locality. The Italian State Tourist Office publishes every year the offical list of all Italian hotels and pensions (*Annuario Alberghi*) which can be consulted through your travel agent or the Italian State Tourist Office. In all hotels and pensions service charges are included in the rates. VAT (IVA in Italy) operates in all hotels at 10% (19% in deluxe hotels) on room charges only.
Visitors are now required by law to obtain an official receipt when staying at hotels. Rome is well provided with hotels, but it is advisable to book in advance. Rates are high with added extras. To obtain complete prices, ask for quotations of inclusive rates. Cheap hotels, which usually provide basic board (room plus shower), offer an economical form of accommodation throughout Italy, and there is a wide choice in the cities. Again, especially in the main cities, it is wise to book in advance (bookings should always be made through travel agents or hotel representatives). There are many regional hotel associations in Italy; the principal national organisation is FAIAT (Federazione delle Associazioni Italiane Alberghi e Turismo), Via Toscana 1, 00187 Roma. Tel: (6) 474 1151/2/3. Fax: (6) 463 004. Telex: 613116.
Grading: Hotels are graded on a scale of **1** to **5 stars.**
MOTELS: Located on motorways and main roads. The two biggest chains are AGIP or ACI.
FARMHOUSE HOLIDAYS: These are organised through AGRITURIST, whose head office is based at Corso Vittorio Emanuele 101, Roma. Tel: (6) 651 2342.
SELF-CATERING: Villas, flats and chalets are available for rent at most Italian resorts. Information is available through daily newspapers and agencies in the UK and from the Italian State Tourist Office or Tourist Office *(Azienda Autonoma di Soggiorno)* of the locality concerned. The latter are also able to advise about boarding with Italian families.
TOURIST VILLAGES: These consist of bungalows and apartments, usually built in or near popular resorts. The bungalows vary in size, but usually accommodate four people and have restaurant facilities.
CAMPING/CARAVANNING: Camping is very popular in Italy. The local Tourist Office in the nearest town will give information and particulars of the most suitable sites. On the larger campsites it is possible to rent tents/caravans. There are over 1600 campsites and full details of the sites can be obtained in the publication *Campeggi e Villaggi Turistici In Italia*, published by the Touring Club Italiano and Federcampeggio. An abridged list of sites with location map, *Carta d'Italia Parchi Campeggio*, can be obtained free of charge by writing to Centro Internazionale Prenotazione, Federcampeggio, Casella Postale 23, 50041 Calenzano (Firenze). Tel: (55) 882 391. Telex: 570397. The Italian State Tourist Office may also be able to supply information.
The tariffs at Italian campsites vary according to the area and the type of campsite. There are discounts for members of the AIT, FICC and FIA. Usually there is no charge for children under three years of age. The Touring Club Italiano offers camping sites already equipped with fixed tents, restaurants, etc. For details write to TCI, Corso Italia 10, 20122 Milano. Tel: (2) 85261. Fax: (2) 852 6362. Telex: 321160. To book places in advance on campsites belonging to the International Campsite Booking Centre it is necessary to write to Centro Internazionale Prenotazioni Campeggio, Casella Postale 23, 50041 Calenzano (Firenze), asking for the list of the campsites with the booking form.
Mountain Huts: It is possible to rent a hut in the mountains from the Club Alpino Italiano, Via Foscolo 3, Milan tel: (2) 802 1554 *or* (0) 805 7519. The cost for one night varies from Lit4000 to Lit7000. There is a 20% increase between December 1 and April 30.
YOUTH HOSTELS: There are 52 youth hostels run by the Italian Youth Hostels Association (*Associazione Italiana Alberghi per la Gioventù*) throughout Italy. Listing and opening dates can be obtained from the Italian State Tourist Office. In Rome, the head office is at: Via Cavour 44, 00184 Roma. Tel: (6) 462 342. Fax: (6) 474 1256. Telex: 622404. During the summer season, in the major cities, reservations are essential and must be applied for direct to the hostel at least 15 days in advance, specifying dates and numbers. There are also student hostels in several towns.

RESORTS & EXCURSIONS

For ease and speed of reference, the country has been divided into the following areas: Northern Italy (including the cities of Turin, Milan, Venice, Bologna, Genoa, Trieste and Vicenza); Central Italy (including the cities of Florence, Pisa, Ancona, Perugia, Rome, Pescara and Campobasso); Southern Italy (including the cities of Naples, Bari, Potenza and Catanzaro, as well as the resort towns in the Bay of Naples); and The Islands (Sicily and Sardinia). Main holiday resorts are included in each section, as well as important religious sites, business centres and a brief mention of the region's art history.

Northern Italy

(Administrative *Regioni:* Valle d'Aosta, Piedmont, Lombardy, Liguria, Trentino-Alto Adige, Veneto, Emilia-Romagna and Friuli-Venezia Giulia.)

VALLE D'AOSTA: A ruggedly scenic region at the foot of Europe's highest mountains – Mont Blanc, Monte Rosa, Cervino (Matterhorn) and Gran Paradiso – bordering France and Switzerland. Valle d'Aosta is politically autonomous and to some extent culturally distinct from the rest of Italy; French is spoken as a first language by most of the inhabitants. The picturesque ruins of countless castles and other fortifications testify to the region's immense strategic significance before the era of air travel, it being the gateway to two of the most important routes through the Alps, the Little and Great St Bernard Passes. Tourism, wine-growing, pasturing and iron-working are the major industries.

Aosta, the principal city, has many well-preserved Roman and medieval buildings. It was founded in the first century by the Emperor Augustus as a settlement *(colonia)* for discharged soldiers of the elite Pretorian Guard. The massive Roman city walls are almost complete and, within them, the old town retains the grid-iron street plan characteristic of all such military townships. Two impressive gateways, the *Porta Pretoria*, formed the main entrance into the old Roman town and a medieval noble family lived in its tower, which now houses temporary exhibitions. Further ancient Roman sites include the *Teatro Romano*, where theatrical presentations are still shown on a platform overlooking the old theatre; *Arco di Augusto*, erected in 25BC to honour the Emperor Augustus (for whom the city is named – Aosta being a corruption of Augustus); the *Forum* and the still well-intact *Roman Bridge*, which once arched gracefully over the River Buthier, now entirely dried up.

There are several fine ski resorts in the area (see below under *Ski Resorts*), most notably **Courmayeur** and **Breuil-Cervinia**.

Ibexes may be seen in the **Gran Paradiso National Park**, a popular destination for hill-walkers and climbers.

The *Mont Blanc Tunnel* has largely superseded the St Bernard Passes as a major overland freight route.

PIEDMONT: The densely populated Upper Po Basin is the site of Italy's most important heavy industries, a vast plain pinned to the earth by gargantuan factories and held flat by a harness of motorways. By contrast, the mountains to the west, on the border with France, are sparsely populated and have a wholly pastoral economy. To the north is *Lake Maggiore*, the most elegant of the North Italian lakes and popular since Roman times as a retreat for city-dwellers.

The best-known **wines** of this region are *Barolo*, Italy's most celebrated red, and *Asti Spumante*, a sparkling white. *Barolo* wine is produced in the hills surrounding the town of **Alba,** where there are a number of wine musuems. Alba itself is one of the region's most interesting towns, with medieval towers, Baroque and Renaissance architecture and cobbled streets full of specialist delicatessans and shops. The most exciting time to visit is during the month of October, when the *October Festival* (involving a donkey race and displays of medieval pageantry) and the *Truffle Festival* are celebrated. *Asti Spumante* is produced just outside the town of **Asti,** a normally quiet little town, except during the month of September when it holds its annual *Palio* and comes suddenly alive with street banquets, medieval markets, an historic 14th-century parade and a bare-backed horse race around the arena of *Campo del Palio*.

Torino (Turin) is the largest city in the region and the fourth-largest in the country. For the first few decades of this century, it was the automobile capital of the world. It was here that the Futurists became so excited with the potential of mechanised transport that they declared Time dead – henceforth, they declared, everything would be measured in terms of speed alone. The city remains the focus of Italy's automobile industry. *Fiat* offer guided tours of their headquarters, where a full-scale test track may be found on the roof. Turin does, of course, add up to far more than an infatuation with motor cars. The inhabitants boast that, with its broad, tree-lined avenues flanked by tall, handsome townhouses, it is *La Parigi d'Italia*, the Italian Paris. Uptown Turin is centred on the main shopping street, *Via Roma*, which links the city's favourite square, the *Piazza San Carlo*, with its most dramatic building, the baroque *Palazzo Madama*, which houses the *Museum of Ancient Art*, one of several nationally important museums in the city. The Turin Shroud may be viewed in the 15th-century white marble Cathedral.

LOMBARDY: A prosperous region with fertile soil, a temperate climate and, for the tourist, the spectacular lakes *Como*, *Garda*, *Maggiore* (shared with Piedmont) and *Lugano*. As in Piedmont, the *Po Valley* is the site of much heavy industry. High mountains in the north, marking Italy's frontier with Switzerland, provide excellent skiing and climbing. Lombardy's most famous culinary inventions are *minestrone* soup and *osso buco* – literally ox knuckles.

Milan is Italy's most sophisticated city, a financial and commercial centre of world importance and a rival to Paris in the spheres of modern art and fashion. Its international character is marked by a concentration of skyscrapers found nowhere else in Italy, contrasting and competing with the landmarks of historic Milan, but built in the same boastful spirit of civic pride that, 500 years ago, gave the city its splendid Gothic *Duomo*. Even today, this is the world's second-largest church, yet despite its size, it creates an impression of delicate and ethereal beauty due to its pale colour and the fine intricate carving that covers its exterior. The whole fabric of the city – its many palaces, piazzas and churches – speaks of centuries of continuous prosperity. The *Castello Sforzesco*, in the west of the city, is a massive fortified castle, begun by the Viscontis and finished by the Sforzas. It was the political and social bastion of the ruling Sforzas during Milan's peak as a political/cultural centre and many Renaissance elite were entertained in its luxurious domains. Its court artists included Leonardo da Vinci and Bramante and it now houses a number of museums. Leonardo da Vinci's famous fresco, *The Last Supper*, may be viewed at the convent of *Santa Maria della Grazie*. The *Teatro della Scala* remains the undisputed world capital of opera and is well worth viewing for its magnificent opulence.

Just south of Milan is the town of **Pavia**, the ancient capital known as 'the city of 100 towers'. One of these, the *Torre Civica*, suddenly collapsed in 1989, killing four people. The town also has many interesting churches, including the Renaissance *Duomo*, thought to have been worked on by Bramante and da Vinci; the Romanesque *San Michele*, with an elaborately carved facade; and the 12th-century *San Pietro in Ciel d'Oro*, with a magnificent 14th-century altarpiece. The *Broletto*, Pavia's medieval town hall, and the 14th-century *Castello*, housing an art gallery, archaeology museum and sculpture museum, are also worth visiting. Though sedate and resting in an air of dusty elegance by day, Pavia bursts into life at night when its people come out for their evening promenade and the streets seem to buzz with activity.

The *Certosa di Pavia*, 10km outside of town, is a monastery famous for its lavish design. Originating as the family mausoleum of the Visconti family, it was later finished by the Sforzas and became the dwellings for a Carthusian order of monks sworn to deep contemplation and for whom speech is forbidden. However, a chosen few are allowed to give visitors a guided tour and tell the story behind their palatial surroundings.

Cremona, the birthplace of the Stradivarius violin, is a charming haven of historic architecture. A walk around the medieval *Piazza del Comune* offers various architectural treats: the *Torazzo*, one of Italy's tallest medieval towers; the *Duomo*, with its magnificent astrological clock; and the *Loggia dei Militia*, the former headquarters of the town's medieval army. There are also two interesting museums: the *Museo Strativariano*, housing a plethora of Stradivarius musical instruments, and the *Museo Civico*, with more Stadivari and some interesting bits and pieces belonging to Garibaldi.

Mantua was another Lombardy bastion of the ruling dynasties of the Viscontis and Sforzas. It is also the birthplace of a number of renowned Italians, ranging from Virgil (a statue of whom overlooks the square facing the *Broletto*, the medieval town hall) to Tazio Nuvolone, one of Italy's most famous racing drivers (for whom there is a small museum dedicated to his accomplishments). Its churches, *Sant'Andrea* (designed by Alberti and the burial place of Mantua's famous court painter, Mantegna) and the Baroque *Duomo* in the *Piazza Sordello* are both important works of architecture. However, the most famous sites of Mantua are its two palaces: *The Palazzo Ducale* and *The Palazzo del Te*. The Palazzo Ducale, once the largest in Europe, was the home of the Gonzagas family, and has a number of impressive paintings by artists such as Rubens and Mantegna. The Palazzo del Te was built as a Renaissance pleasure palace for Frederico Gonzaga (known as a playboy) and his mistress, Isabella. The decorations by Giulio Romano are outstanding and well worth viewing.

Bergamo, nestled at the foot of the Bergamese Alps, is made up of two cities – the old and once Venetian-ruled *Bergamo Alta* (upper Bergamo) and the modern *Bergamo Bassa* (lower Bergamo). The old city is well appreciated for its ancient Venetian fortifications, palaces, towers and churches, including the 12th-century *Palazzo della Ragione*, the *Torre del Comune*, the *Duomo of Bergamo*, *Colleoni Chapel* and the *Church of Santa Maria Maggiore*. The modern city's main attraction is the *Accademia Carrara*, one of Italy's largest art collections, with paintings by Canaletto, Botticelli, Mantegna, Carpaccio, Bellini and Lotto, amongst others. The two cities are connected by a funicular.

The great northern **lakes** lie in a series of long, deep valleys running down onto the plains from the Alps. Lake Garda is perhaps the wildest and most spectacular, Como the prettiest and Maggiore the most elegant (and popular). Lake Lugano lies for the most part in Switzerland.

Resorts on *Lake Maggiore* include: Pallanza (where the Villa Taranto has a fine botanical garden), Stresa, Arona, Intra and Orta; on *Lake Como*: Cadenabbia, Cernobbio, Bellagio, Tremezzo and Menaggio; and on *Lake Garda*: Limone, Sirmione, Desenzano and Gardone.

The major **mountain resorts**, winter and summer, are Livigno (duty-free area), Madesimo, Stelvio, Santa Caterina Valfurva, Bormio, Aprica and Chiesa.

LIGURIA: Two hundred miles of rocky, wooded coastline running from France to Tuscany, where the Italian 'boot' begins. This is the *Riviera*, Italy's answer to the Côte d'Azur, and there are ample facilities for tourists even in the smallest of ports. The coastal hills are less developed.

Genoa, capital of Liguria, has long been an important commercial and military port. Columbus and Garibaldi, the great Italian patriot, were born nearby. The medieval district of the city holds many treasures, such as the *Porta Soprana* (the old stone entrance gate to the city), the *Church of Sant'Agostino* (next to the Museo dell'Architectura e Scultura Ligure), the beautiful *Church of San Donato*, the 12th-century *Church of Santa Maria di Castello* and the Gothic *Cattedrale di San Lorenzo*. Outside the medieval district, *Via Garibaldi*, where many of the city's richest inhabitants built their palaces, is a beautiful walk, with *Palazzo Podesta*, *Palazzo Bianco* (now an art gallery with paintings by Van Dyck and Rubens) and the magnificently decorated *Palazzo Rosso* (adjacent to Palazzo Bianco and housing paintings by Titian, Caravaggio and Durer). A tour (once daily in the afternoon) around the Genoa harbour is available, and the city is also recommended for its excellent shopping opportunities.

Ligurian **resorts** are very popular with holidaymakers. **Portofino** is one of the best known, with its small picturesque harbour full of sleek pleasure yachts, luxury clothes shops, its romantic villas owned by the rich and famous perched on the hillside and the *Castello di San Giorgio*, sitting high up on a promontory with magnificent views of the Portofino harbour and bay. The beach at **Santa Margherita Ligure,** just 5km (3 miles) south of Portofino, is an excellent place to swim, with an almost fairytale swimmer's-eye view of the surrounding cliffs and villas from the warm and crystal-clear aquamarine water. Nearby **Rapallo,** 8km (5 miles) south of Portofino, is a less fashionable but more reasonable town to stay in and is recommended for those seeking a more lively alternative to the quieter and more exclusive resorts of Portofino and Santa Margherita. Other resorts in this region include Ventimiglia, San Remo, Diano Marina, Alassio, Pietra Ligure, Spotorno, Sestri Levante, Lerici and the Cinque Terre, five relatively unspoilt fishing villages.

TRENTINO & ALTO ADIGE: These wholly mountainous regions on the Swiss border straddle the valley of the River Isarco, which flows from the *Brenner Pass* down into Lake Garda. Germanic and Italian cultures blend here to the extent that, towards the north, German is increasingly found as the first language. *The Dolomites* to the east are a range of distinctively craggy mountains, isolated to such an extent from both Italy and Switzerland that in the more remote valleys the inhabi-

VENICE

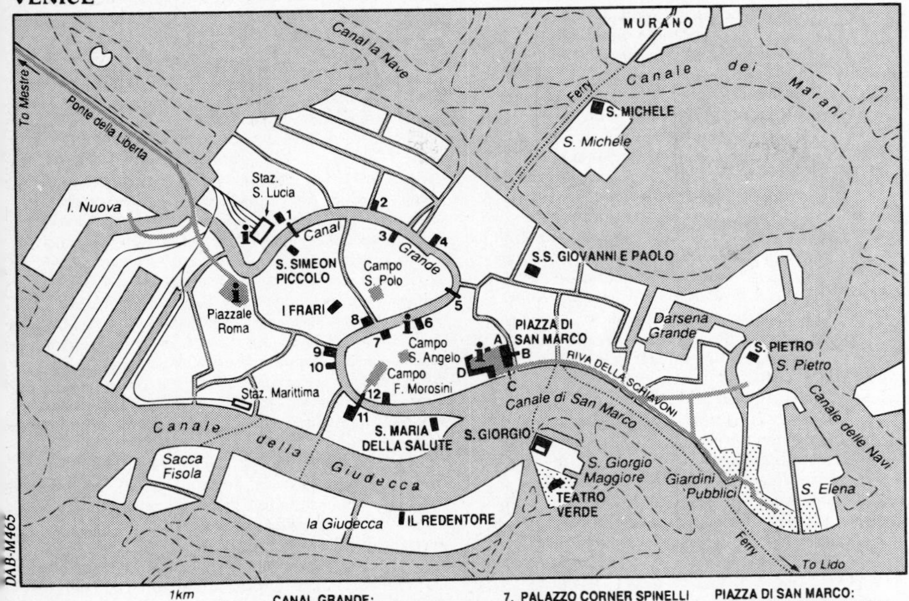

CANAL GRANDE:
1. SCALZI & PONTE DEGLI SCALZI
2. PALAZZO VENDRAMIN CALERGI
3. PALAZZO PESARO
4. CA D'ORO
5. PONTE DI RIALTO
6. PALAZZO GRIMANI
7. PALAZZO CORNER SPINELLI
8. PALAZZO PISANI
9. CA' FOSCARI (UNIVERSITA)
10. PALAZZO CA' REZZONICO
11. GALLERIE & PONTE DELL'ACCADEMIA
12. CA' CORNER

PIAZZA DI SAN MARCO:
A. BASILICA DI SAN MARCO
B. PONTE DEI SOSPIRI (BRIDGE OF SIGHS)
C. PALAZZO DUCALE
D. MUSEO CORRER & CAMPANILE DI SAN MARCO

tants speak Ladin, an ancient Romance language not much different from Latin.

Trento is the principal town of Trentino and is worth visiting for its wealth of art works, gathered by the dynasty of princes who ruled the area from the 10th-18th centuries. Many of these artistic acquisitions are viewable in the town's museums, which include the *Castello di Buonconsiglio*, *Museo Provinciale d'Arte* and the *Museo Diocesano Trentino*.

Bolzano is the principal town of Alto Aldige, further north. A somewhat austere commercial town, it appears as an unlikely portal to one of the most extraordinary panoramic drives in Italy – the mountain route through the Dolomites to Cortina d'Ampezzo called *La Grande Strada delle Dolomiti*. Upon entering the *Val d'Ega*, at the beginning of the route, the scenery is suddenly lush with foliage and rocks as the light seeps artistically through the forest trees. About 20km (12 miles) from the beginning of the route is *Lake Carezza*, an extraordinarily beautiful limpid pool of bright green water reflecting the trees and mountains around it. This is just the beginning of an unrelentingly awe-inspiring passage through The Dolomites and its small alpine towns, ski resorts and endless panoramas of craggy peaks and tree-clad mountainsides.

One of the most famous mountain resorts and the second largest town in this region is **Merano,** 28km (17 miles) north of Bolzano. Popular for its spas, thermal waters and moderate climate (the temperature tends to remain above freezing all winter, despite its close proximity to a range of snow-laden ski slopes), it is also visually rewarding, with extensive landscaped gardens and a charming mixture of architectural styles from Gothic to Art Nouveau. Other **mountain resorts** in the region include Solda, Selva di Val Gardena, Santa Cristina, Oritsei, Corvara, Bressanone, Brunico, Vipiteno, Madonna di Campiglio, Canazei, Moena, Pozza di Fassa, San Martino di Castrozza and Riva, which lies at the top of Lake Garda.

VENETO: The *Lower Po Valley*, the eastern bank of Lake Garda and the eastern Dolomites, occupying what was once the Republic of Venice.

Venezia (Venice) stands on an island in a lagoon at the northern end of the Adriatic Sea, a position which gave it unique economic and defensive advantages over its trading rivals. Much of the wealth generated was, of course, invested in the construction of monuments to the glory of both God and the merchants, and Venice must be counted as one of the highlights of any tour of Italy. The city's main monuments – the *Doge's Palace*, *St Mark's Square* and the *Bridge of Sighs* – have gained fame through the innumerable paintings representing them, not least by such artists as Canaletto, but the whole city is in many ways a work of art. Away from the main thoroughfares, it is characterised by little canals, small squares (often containing remarkable Gothic churches) and above all, since it contains no motor traffic, by serenity – the city's ancient name was 'La Serenissima'. One of the most evocative representations of Venice must be in Thomas Mann's book, *Death in Venice*.

Note: The causeway linking the city with the mainland can become very clogged with traffic. Although there is a large car park on the island, it is often easier to park at one of several near the north end of the causeway and continue by foot, bus or taxi; there are also trains connecting with boats.

The Venetian aristocracy built many villas in the surrounding countryside; some, including the *Villa Pisani* at **Stra** and the *Villa Valmarana* at **Vicenza,** are open to the public.

Popular **Adriatic resorts** include Lido di Iesolo, Bibione and Caorle.

The city of **Padua** is famous for the great *Basilica of St Antony;* St Antony himself was buried here and it is an important pilgrimage site. The city also contains works by Giotto (Scrovegni Chapel frescoes) and Donatello. Nearby, **Abano** and **Montegrotto** provide fully equipped thermal establishments for the treatment of many rheumatic complaints.

Vicenza is the birthplace of Andrea Palladio, whose published analyses of ancient architecture did much to spread the Renaissance throughout Europe. His buildings here include the *Basilica Palladiana* and the *Palazzo Chiericatai*.

Verona, historically associated, among other things, with Shakespeare *(Romeo and Juliet* and *The Two Gentlemen of Verona)* contains a well-preserved *Roman Arena* (operas are staged there in summer), and the lovely but austere *Church of San Zeno*. This graceful city is surrounded by a river and there are many beautiful bridges, as well as exquisite churches, charming squares and bustling markets.

Cortina d'Ampezzo is Italy's best-known (but not most challenging) ski resort. The Winter Olympics were held here in 1956. It makes a fine base for exploring The Dolomites in summer.

EMILIA ROMAGNA: A region of gentle hills between the *River Po* and the *Appennines*. As elsewhere in the Po Basin, intensive agriculture is pursued alongside heavy industry.

Bologna is one of the oldest cities in Italy and the site of Europe's oldest university. Often overlooked as a tourist destination, it nevertheless possesses a distinctive charm, due largely to the imaginative use of brickwork. Arcades flanking many of the streets add to the appeal. Notable buildings include the *Cathedral of San Pietro*, the huge Gothic *Church of San Petronio*, numerous palaces and the *Leaning Towers* of the *Piazza di Porta Ravegnana*. The city is also the home of Bolognese meat sauce and the Bologna sausage.

Parma boasts a fine Romanesque cathedral and baptistry, and an opera house with strong connections with Verdi, who lived at nearby **Sant'Agata.**

Italy's most celebrated poet, Dante, is buried at **Ravenna**, the ancient capital of the western Roman Empire during its decline under Gothic and Byzantine domination. The city's former importance is marked by the profusion of extravagant mosaics found in its many Romanesque buildings. The *International School of Mosaics* at Ravenna is open to foreigners.

Faenza (known to the French as 'Faience') is famed for its majolica pottery. This craft has enjoyed a resurgence in recent years under the direction of the *Faenza International Institute of Ceramics*.

Other cities in Emilia-Romagna include **Modena** and **Ferrara**, both with many fine palaces associated with the Este family; and **Reggio**, the old provincial capital.

Adriatic resorts include Rimini, Riccione, Cattolica, Milano, Marittima and Cesenatico, all within easy reach of the tiny Republic of San Marino (see entry on *San Marino*).

FRIULI-VENEZIA GIULIA: A region in the north-eastern corner of Italy bordering Austria and Slovenia. It has changed hands many times over the centuries and Friulian society is a complex mix of cultures. Half of the population speak Friulian, a language closely allied to ancient Latin.

In the 18th century, the Austrian Emperors commissioned the construction of a deep-water port at **Trieste** and so ended Venice's long domination of the Adriatic Sea. The port has remained the most important in the area and, following the collapse of the Austro-Hungarian Empire after the First World War, was ceded to Italy. This arrangement was not finally formalised until 1962, when a long-running border dispute with the then Yugoslavia was settled with the aid of the United Nations. Although there are several Roman remains (most notably the 2nd-century Theatre), the most prominent buildings are no older than the port.

The coast west of Trieste has some excellent **beach resorts.** Sistiana, Duino, Lignano and Grado are among the most popular.

Inland are **Udine** and **Pordenone**, agricultural centres on the fertile Friuli plain. Further north are the foothills of the eastern *Dolomites* and the *Julian Alps* (part of Slovenia) where ski resorts are now being developed. The road from Udine to Villach in Austria is an important overland freight route; it winds up the dramatic valley of the *Isonzo*, a river rendered an astonishing shade of blue by minerals leached from the Julian Alps.

SKI RESORTS: The majority of the Italian ski resorts are in the Alps and in The Dolomites, although there are also a few in the Appennines and it is possible to ski along the slopes of *Mount Etna* in Sicily (see relevant sections below). The following examples all have hotels, boarding houses and/or self-catering and are equipped with first-class lift systems. For further details, contact the Italian State Tourist Office in London, tour operators or travel agents.

Valle d'Aosta: Cervinia, Courmayeur, Chamois, Gressoney, La Thuille, Pila, Valtournenche.

Piedmonte: Bardonecchia, Claviere, Limone-Piemonte, Macugnaga, Sauze d'Oulx, Sestriere, Sportinia.

Lombardy: Aprica, Bormio, Chiesa di Valmalenco, Foppolo, Livigno, Madesimo, Ponte di Legno, Santa Caterina di Valfurva, Tonale.

Trentino: Andalo, Canazei, Madonna di Campiglio, Marilleva, Pozza di Fassa, San Martino di Castrozza.

Alto Adige (Südtirol): Alpi di Siusi (Seiseralm), Campo Tures (Sand in Taufers), Colfosco (Kolfuschg), Corvara in Badia (Kurfar), Crontour area (in ten localities), including Brunico (Bruneck) and San Vigilio di Marebbe (St Vigil in Enneberg), Dobbiaco (Toblach), Nova Levante (Welschnofen), Ortisei (St Ulrich), Passo Stelvio (Stilfserjoch) (only summer skiing), Renon (Ritten), San Candido (Innichen), Santa Cristina Valgardena (St Christina), Selva di Val Gardena (Wolkenstein), Val Senales (Schnalstal).

Friuli-Venezia Giulia: Piancavallo, Sella Nevea.

Veneto: Alleghe, Arabba, Ravascletto, Cortina d'Ampezzo, Falcade.

Central Italy

(Administrative *Regioni:* Tuscany, Marche, Umbria, Abruzzi, Molise and Lazio.)

TUSCANY: This fertile region lies between the northern Appennines and the Mediterranean Sea. The landscape of Tuscany is typically one of vine-covered hills, cypress woods, fields of sunflowers and remote hilltop villages. *Chianti*, the best-known Italian **wine**, is made here. There are a number of **volcanic spas**, most notably *Montecatini*, *Bagni di Lucca*, *Casciana Terme* and *Chianciano*.

Florence (Firenze), the principal Tuscan city, is the world's most celebrated storehouse of Renaissance art and architecture. Set on the banks of the *Arno* below the wooded foothills of the Appennines, this beautiful city has long been the focus of Italian arts and letters. Dante, Boccaccio, Petrarch, Giotto, Leonardo da Vinci, Michelangelo, Brunelleschi, Alberti, Donatello, Botticelli, Vasari and Angelico are among those associated with establishing the pre-eminence of the city. Brunelleschi's revolutionary design for the dome of the *Cathedral of Santa Maria del Fiore* is generally accepted as the first expression of Renaissance ideas in architecture. This dome still dominates the city's roofscape, just as the great

FLORENCE

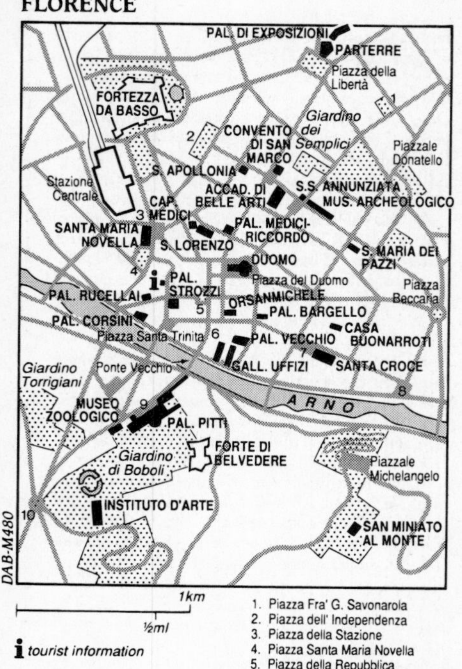

Piazza del Duomo at its feet dominates life at street level. The square is ringed with cafés and is a popular meeting point. Between there and the river are many of the best-loved palaces – including *Palazzo Strozzi, Palazzo Corsini, Palazzo Rucellai, Palazzo Vecchio* and the *Uffizi Gallery* – whilst close by to the north are the churches of *Santa Maria Novella* and *San Lorenzo* (by Brunelleschi, Michelangelo and others), and the *Palazzo Medici-Ricccordi*. The *Palazzo Pitti* and the *Boboli Gardens* are just across the river (via the Ponte Vecchio). All in all, it is an astonishing concentration of superb buildings, many of them housing fabulous collections of paintings and sculpture.

The *Uffizi Gallery* houses the most celebrated collection – indeed it claims to hold the finest collections of paintings anywhere in the world. Examples of work start from the transition period when Europe was emerging from the Middle Ages, largely represented by religious paintings and icons (notably by Lorenzo Monaco, Giottino and Gentile da Fabriano), through the highpoint of the Renaissance to the early 18th century. Some of the most famous paintings of each period are in the Uffizi, such as Botticelli's *Birth Of Venus*, Leonardo da Vinci's *Annunciation*, Michelangelo's *Holy Family*, Titian's *Urbino Venus* and Caravaggio's *Young Bacchus*. One of the most striking paintings is the *Medusa* by Caravaggio.

Michelangelo's famous statue of David may be viewed at the *Accademia di Belle Arti* near the University.

Siena's most prosperous era pre-dated the Renaissance and consequently much of the fabric of the city is in the older Gothic and Romanesque styles. There is a fine Gothic and Romanesque *Cathedral* built in stunning black and white marble with a magnificent interior (visitors dressed inappropriately, ie in short skirts, shorts or skimpy shirts, will be denied entry). The *Piazzo del Campo*, overlooked by the giant *campanile* of the *Palazzo Pubblico*, is possibly the most complete Gothic piazza in Italy. The city is an important religious centre, being the birthplace of St Catherine, and there is a church here devoted to her worship. The 700-year-old university holds a summer school in Italian. Siena is probably most famous for its *Palios*, bare-backed horse races which take place every year on July 2 and August 16 around the huge *Campo* in the centre of Siena. It has been a special event since the 14th century and attracts crowds from all over the world.

Pisa, north of Siena, is famous for its *Leaning Tower*, a free-standing *campanile* or bell tower associated with the 11th-century Gothic *Cathedral* nearby. Near the *Quadrilateral* is the *Campo Santo Cemetery*. Built in the 13th century to enclose earth brought from Jerusalem, it is a unique colonnaded quadrangle in the Tuscan Gothic style.

Other towns of note in Tuscany include **Lucca**, famous for its one hundred churches and robust city walls; **San Gimignano,** known as the 'city of beautiful towers' and one of the best-preserved medieval towns in Italy; **Volterra,** another beautifully preserved medieval town perched on a hilltop; **Livorno** (Leghorn), the principal commercial port; and **Carrara**, where high-grade white marble has been quarried since Etruscan times.

The coast of Tuscany offers many sandy beaches. Popular **beach resorts** include Viareggio, Forte dei Marmi, Lido di Camaiore, Marina di Pietrasanta, Marina di Massa, Tirrenia, Castiglione della Pescaia, San Vincenzo, Castiglioncello, Quercianella, Porto Santo Stefano, Porto Ercole, Ansedonia and Talamone.

The **Tuscan Archipelago** is a group of scattered islands lying between Tuscany and Corsica. The best known are Elba and Giglio. There are regular hydrofoil and ferry links with mainland ports. **Elba** is 17.5km (28 miles) long and 7.5km (12 miles) wide, and can be reached by steamer or hydrofoil from *Piombino*. Famous for being the place where Napolean was exiled, the island is well worth a visit, with lovely beaches and campsites shaded by pines. Napoleon's two homes can be visited: one, the *Palazzina Napoleonica dei Mulini*, which he created out of two windmills, situated near the *Forte della Stella*, **Portoferraio** and the other, 6km away, the *Villa Napoleonica di San Martino*, which he set up as his country seat. Near to this villa is the *Pinacoteca Foresiana*, a neo-classical art gallery built in 1851.

MARCHE: A mountainous agricultural region on the central Adriatic coast south of San Marino.

Ancona, the regional capital and largest town in the region, is an important naval and commercial port with several well-preserved Roman remains such as the *Arco di Traiano* and the *Resti di Anfiteatro Romano*.

Urbino was once Italy's greatest seat of learning and is now a pleasant Renaissance hilltown, its skyline a soaring vista of domes and towers. Also the birthplace of Raphael, several of his works may be viewed in the art gallery at the *Ducal Palace*, along with works by Piero della Francesca and Titian. Raphael's childhood home is also open for viewing.

Loreto is said to be the site of the house in which Jesus was born and attracts many pilgrims from around the world. According to legend, the house was moved from Nazareth in the 13th century to protect it from marauding Muslims. Angels carried it first to the Balkans then on to Loreto; the journey took four years. The house is enclosed in the elaborate Gothic *Sanctuaria della Santa Casa*. The *Madonna of Loreto* was elected patron saint of airmen in 1920.

Popular **beach resorts** include Gabicce, Pesaro (Rossini's birthplace), Fano, Senigallia, Civitanova, San Benedetto del Tronto, Porto Recanati and Porto Potenza Picena. As elsewhere on the Adriatic coast, beach resorts tend to be highly organised, with tables and sun loungers laid out in neat lines (often very close together). More informal beaches may be found below the spectacular Costa Conero cliffs a few miles south of Ancona.

UMBRIA: A mountainous inland region between Tuscany and Marche. There is very little industry here and few towns of any great size. The principal agricultural products are corn, olives, sugar beet, tobacco, wine and wool.

Perugia, the region's capital, has been continuously inhabited for more than 25 centuries and contains many Etruscan and Roman remains, with well-preserved buildings reflecting every era in the subsequent development of Italian architecture. Particularly notable are the ancient Etruscan city walls. *L'Università per Stranieri* offers courses for foreigners wishing to study Italian language and civilisation.

Assisi is a picturesque medieval hilltown to the east of Perugia. Famous as the home of St Francis, founder of the Franciscan Order of monks, it attracts many tourists. The life of St Francis is commemorated in 28 frescoes by Giotto in the *Basilica di San Francesco*, Italy's earliest Gothic church.

Arezzo, set on a hillside, has both a strong modern and medieval aspect. *The Medici Fortress* and the *Cathedral*, built in the 13th-16th centuries, stand majestically on the hilltop overlooking the modern part of town which sits on the plain below. The *Piazza Grande* is a wonderful medieval square with an old well in the centre, surrounded by impressive historic buildings on all sides: the *Palazzetto della Fraternità*, the *Church of Santa Maria della Pieve* and *Loggiato del Vasari* (once the residence of Vasari, art historian and patron of many of Italy's most famous painters). The *Basilica di San Francesco* contains the famous frescoes of Piero della Francesca, *Story of the Cross*. Amidst all this history, the city still thrives today and is now the centre of the antique trade.

Other important Umbrian towns include **Spoleto**, host to an annual festival of music, drama and dance; **Orvieto**, perched dramatically on a volcanic outcrop rising from the Umbrian lowlands; and **Città di Castello,** mountain stronghold of the Vitelli family.

ABRUZZI: This region encompasses the highest parts of the great Appennine chain. The northern mountains are generally too desolate for agriculture and much of the land is sparsely populated. A **ski resort** has been built in the limestone massif of *Gran Sasso*. The southern uplands are covered with a great forest of beech, which has been designated a national park. Marsican brown bears (unique to Italy), wolves, chamois and eagles may be seen here.

L'Aquila, the principal city, contains an imposing castle.

Celano is an interesting town, dominated by a turreted castle whose fortified walls provide a walkway around the castle offering picturesque views over the surrounding hilly countryside. The rest of the town appears to be thriving with active and trendy young people which projects a surprising contrast to the staid medieval architecture.

Tagliocozzo, named after the Greek muse of Theatre, appears at first sight to be just like any other town until one discovers the old Renaissance square with its 14th-15th century houses and lantern-lit alleys twisting around behind it. A stroll through this area at night is a remarkable experience, thick with a medieval atmosphere that verges on the eerie.

The main **Adriatic resorts** are Giulianova, Silvi Marina, Francavilla and Montesilvano. Pescara is, as its name implies, primarily a fishing port.

MOLISE: One of the poorest parts of mainland Italy, this area is mountainous with poor soil and a scattered population. It does, however, possess its own rugged beauty. The Matese mountain range is still the haven of wolves and

ROME

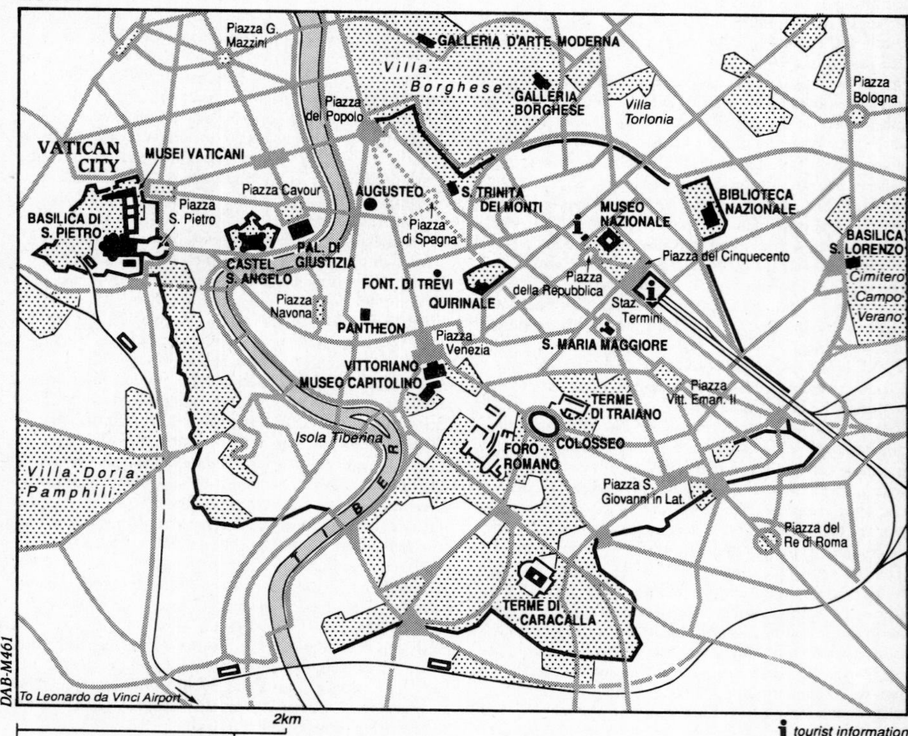

various birds of prey. It also offers some excellent skiing resorts and tends not to be as overcrowded as some of Italy's other skiing areas. The winter sports centre of **Campitello Matese** is well recommended and for those looking for a quiet place to retreat after a day's skiing, the town of **San Massimo** is an excellent place to stay, with its peaceful lamplitstreets and hospitable people. The largest cities in the region are the industrial towns of **Isernia** and **Campobasso**. The only Adriatic resort of any size is *Vasto*.

LAZIO: On the western side of the Italian 'boot', this is a region of volcanic hills, lakes and fine beaches. Half the population live in Rome, the Italian capital. The wines of this region include *Frascati*.

Rome is an extraordinary city – innumerable remarkable buildings of all ages, from pre-Christian to the present day; broad sunny streets, outrageous traffic, calm courtyards, fabulous fountains – even to list the major attractions would be beyond the scope of this book (but don't miss the *Piazza Navona* or the *Trevi Fountain*). The ruins of the *Roman Arena* have a haunting beauty. *St Peter's Basilica* is within the boundaries of the Vatican City, which is a separate state: see separate entry in the *World Travel Guide*. Rome hosts several international trade fairs in June.

Inland from Rome are the hill towns known as the *Castelli Romani*, where Romans go for Sunday excursions. **Tivoli,** just 40km east of Rome, was once the haven of the rich, first in Roman times and later during the Renaissance. It is well-known for its magnificent villas and gardens, such as the *Villa d'Este*, *Villa Gregoriana* and, just outside of Tivoli, the *Villa Adriana*.

Frascati, only 20km south of Rome, is famous for its *Frascati* wine, a light, delicate, dry white wine which has an international reputation. The town itself is very pleasant, emerging elegantly out of the surrounding verdant forestland. Many of the town's restaurants specialise in the local wine, and it is also widely available in all the local shops. Other hill resorts include **Genzano, Castel Gandolfo** and **Rocca di Papa.**

The unwelcome presence of malarial mosquitoes in the coastal marshes that once stretched the length of Lazio prevented settlement on any scale. The marshes have now been drained and this quiet, gentle coastline can now be enjoyed without risk. **Ostia**, the ancient port of Rome, is now a well-organised beach resort. **Terracina,** further south, is a resort with miles of soft, white sand beach. The town itself is also interesting, with the modern quarter offering plenty of shops, as well as restaurants with outdoor seating dotted gingerly around its attractive squares. The old part of town, located higher up on the hill, is full of children playing nonchalantly amidst the crumbling ruins of ancient buildings, with the old *Duomo* presiding over all this activity with an unpreturbed and dignified air. The Duomo is well worth a visit, as is the Roman *Temple of Jupiter Anxurus*, believed to have been built in the 1st century BC. Located on the very top of the hill overlooking the sea, it is a perfect place, either by day or night, to view the town of Terracina and the entire bay spreading around on either side.

One of the most popular resorts among the locals is **Sperlonga,** south of Terracina. The beach there is among the most beautiful in the region and the town itself is reminiscent of a Greek island village. Getting around town can be hard work, though rewarding. Seemingly endless steps wind up and around through white arches and vaulted ceilings only to suddenly break open with a spectacular vista of the sea and cliffs. Down below, on the far end of the beach, is a romantic-looking grotto beside the remains of the *Villa of Tiberius*. 30km (20 miles) offshore is the unspoilt island of **Ponza.**

Other resorts in the area include *Anzio* (site of the Allied landing), *Sabaudia* and *San Felice Circeo*.

Civitavecchia is an important naval and merchant port; there are also regular sailings to Sardinia.

Southern Italy

(Administrative *Regioni:* Campania, Puglia, Basilicata, Calabria.)

CAMPANIA: Called *Campania Felix* ('blessed country') by the Romans because of its fertile soil, mild climate and (by Southern Italian standards) plentiful water. Wine, citrus fruits, tobacco, wheat and vegetables are grown.

Naples, the third largest Italian city, occupies one of the most beautiful natural settings of any city in Europe. Above it is the bare cone of *Mount Vesuvius*, an active volcano, and beside it the broad sweep of the *Bay of Naples* and the *Tyrrhennian Sea*. The city itself is a mad jumble of tenements and traffic, street vendors and crumbling palaces.

A toll road leads most of the way up to the summit of **Vesuvius** (it is the local Lover's Lane); the final few hundred yards involve an energetic scramble up a bare pumice track. The viewing platform is right on the rim of the caldera and provides a dizzying view of both the steam-filled abyss and the whole of the Bay of Naples. Nearby, the remains of **Pompeii** and **Herculaneum**, engulfed in the great eruption of AD79, are a unique record of how ordinary Romans lived their daily lives. Moulds of people and animals found extraordinarily well-preserved, buried under the burning ash, can be seen at Pompeii, and the decoration in some of the excavated villas is amazingly intact, including numerous wall paintings of gods and humans in scenes ranging from the heroic to the erotic.

The city of **Caserta** was the country seat of the Kings of Naples. The Baroque *Royal Palace* owes much to Versailles. There are imposing Greek temples at **Paestum**.

The peninsula just south of Naples is one of the most popular regions in Italy for holidaymakers, especially those in search of sun and sand. But the added bonus for many is the extraordinary beauty of the region: sheer craggy cliffs rise dramatically over the shimmering blue-green Mediterranean waters, and everywhere there are breathtaking views of hills and sea. History and culture are also present in abundance and it is easy to understand the persistent attraction of the area for visitors.

Sorrento, located on the north side of the peninsula, has attracted artists for centuries. Wagner, Nietzsche and Gorky have spent some time here and Ibsen wrote *The Ghosts* while in Sorrento (the town does possess a somewhat haunted quality at night, with dimly but artistically lit ruins just visible in the depths of its plunging forested gorges). The *Museo Correale* in Sorrento has Roman relics and some furniture, paintings and porcelain belonging to the Correale family, but the outside part of the museum is by far the more interesting, with a walk through gardens and vineyards to a promontory overlooking the bay offering a spectacular view of the harbour and the surrounding towns and cliffs. Sorrento is also the closest link to the island of **Capri,** just off the coast (links are also available from Positano, Amalfi and Naples). Ferries and hydrofoils leave from the harbour throughout the day, arriving at the *Marina Grande*. Boats are then available from here to Capri's main tourist attraction, the *Blue Grotto*. Other sites worth seeing include the *Villa Tiberio*, built as the Roman Emperor Tiberius's retirement villa on the island and notorious for the pursuit of various pleasures with took place inside its once luxurious walls. Now reduced to an organised rubble of stones, it takes some imagining, but the views are superb and almost worth the strenuous 45-minute walk up the hill. The *Garden of Augustus*, south of the town of Capri, is pretty, but often crowded with tourists. From here there is access to a 'beach' down a dizzyingly winding road where visitors are permitted to swim off the rocks of this wild shore.

Ischia, another island in the Bay of Naples, is easily accessible from Sorrento or from Naples. Although larger than Capri, it is not quite so popular with tourists, but well-visited by the locals who appreciate it more for its calm and scenic beauty.

Amalfi, situated in the middle of the south side of the peninsula, is perhaps the most well-known of the region's resort towns. However, the town still has an authentic air about it, despite its popularity with tourists. The mostly Romanesque *Duomo* with its 13th-century bell tower, located in the main square, looks entirely untouched by the contemporary hustle and bustle around it. The *Cloister of Paradise*, just to the right of the Cathedral, also makes good viewing. There are some excellent restaurants and the local wine, *Sammarco*, bottled in Amalfi, is superb and inexpensive.

Perched high above Amalfi, 'closer to the sky than the seashore', as André Gide wrote, is the former independent republic of **Ravello.** It is from here that on a clear day the most spectacular views of the Amalfi Coast can be had, above all from the *Villa Cimbrone* where marble statues line a belvedere that is perched on the very edge of the cliff 1100ft up.

Positano, about 25 km along the coast from Amalfi, is a small exclusive resort of great beauty. Heaped high above the coast its brightly painted houses and bougainvillea have inspired a thousand picture postcards and draw crowds of visitors every summer.

Other Campanian resorts include Maiori, Vietri sul Mare and Palinuro.

PUGLIA (Apulia): A southeastern region encompassing the forested crags of the *Gargano spur*, the mostly flat *Salentine peninsula* (the 'heel' of Italy) and, between them, the *Murge*, a limestone plateau riddled with caves (notably at **Castellana**). With the exception of **Bari** and **Taranto**, both large industrial ports, the Apulian economy is wholly agricultural. The main products are tobacco, grapes, vegetables, almonds and olives.

Puglia was important in Roman times as the gateway to the eastern Mediterranean. The port of **Brindisi**, now eclipsed by Bari in commercial terms, was the terminus of the *Via Appia*, along which Eastern produce was conveyed to Rome and beyond. The *Museo Archeologico Provinciale* houses many relics from this prosperous era. Virgil died in Brindisi in 19BC.

On the *Murge* plateau between **Alberobello** and **Selva di Fasano,** the countryside is littered with thousands of extraordinary stone dwellings known as *trulli*. Circular with conical roofs (also of stone), they are similar to the more famous *nuraghi* of Sardinia.

At the northern end of the plateau is a unique octagonal castle, the *Castella del Monte*, built as a hunting lodge in the 13th century by the Holy Roman Emperor Frederick II (the self-styled *Stupor Mundi*, 'Wonder of the World'). Nearby, at **Canosa di Puglia,** are the extensive remains of the important Roman town of *Canusium*.

The convent of *Santa Maria delle Grazie* in **San Giovanni Rotondo** is an important pilgrimage site because of its connections with Padre Pio da Petralcina.

There are fine **beaches** on the Adriatic coast between Barletta and Bari.

BASILICATA (Lucania): A remote and mainly mountainous region between Puglia and Calabria. It is heavily forested in the north around *Monte Vulture*, a large extinct volcano; elsewhere, the hills are flinty and barren. Many rivers flow down from the southern Appennines into the *Gulf of Taranto*, irrigating the fertile coastal plain behind **Metaponto** (birthplace of Pythagoras). The population is small.

The principal town, **Potenza**, was almost entirely rebuilt after a severe earthquake in 1857, only to suffer a similar scale of destruction in the Second World War.

CALABRIA: The toe of the 'boot', a spectacularly beautiful region of high mountains, dense forests and relatively empty beaches. Chestnut, beech, oak and pine cover almost half of Calabria and are a rich hunting ground for mushroom enthusiasts. *Porcini* (boletus edulis), fresh, dried and pickled, therefore adorn the shelves of all the speciality shops of the region. Higher up in the mountains the land only sustains light grazing, but the meadows are abloom with a multitude of wild flowers each spring. It is only on isolated patches of reclaimed land on the marshy coast that agriculture is possible and consequently the inhabitants are amongst the poorest in Italy. They are further tormented by frequent earthquakes. Some wolves still survive in the mountains, particularly in the central Sila Massifs. **Catanzaro**, **Cotenza** and **Reggio**, on the straits of Messina, are the major towns. The best beaches are on the west coast. A typical and especially picturesque little town is **Tropea,** built on the rocks above the Tyrrhenian Sea, with a high street that is at its most busy in the evening and ends abruptly at a panorama platform above the beach. A multitude of shy cats slink through the cobbled alleys undisturbed at siesta time; and secluded sandy coves among outcrops of rock alternate with long stretches of beach as far as the eye can see. The beaches on the east coast of Calabria are rockier and more rugged but even better for undisturbed beach adventures – especially during the often already very warm months of Mai and June.

The Islands

(Sicily and Sardinia.)

SICILIA: Strategically situated between Italy and North Africa and with fertile soil and rich coastal fishing grounds, Sicily has suffered an almost continuous round of invasion for as long as history has been recorded. The Greeks, Carthaginians, Romans, Byzantines, Arabs, Normans, Angevins, Aragonese, Bourbons and, most recently, the Germans (and the Allies) during the Second World War – all have left their mark on this unique island, the most populous in the Mediterranean. The economy is based on the production of citrus fruit, almonds, olives, vegetables, wine (including *Marsala*), wheat and beans, together with mining, fishing (anchovies, tuna, cuttlefish and swordfish) and the raising of sheep and goats.

The capital, **Palermo**, is a splendid city in a grand style, opulent, vital, full of remarkable architecture, particularly Norman and Baroque. Notable buildings include the *Martorana, Santa Maria di Gesu, San Giuseppe dei Teatini* and *San Cataldo* churches, the cathedral and the *Palazzo dei Normanni*. The catacombs at the *Capuchin Monastery* contain thousands of mummified bodies.

Syracuse is said to possess the best natural harbour in Italy. The old town stands on a small island just off the coast and contains many historic buildings. Archimedes lived and died here.

Catania is a spacious city dating mostly from the 18th century, having been rebuilt following a succession of earthquakes. Europe's largest and most active volcano, **Mount Etna**, stands nearby and with its fine beaches

the city attracts many tourists.
Taormina, further up the coast, is an immensely pretty resort town. Perched on a cliff within sight of Mount Etna, it has fine beaches, a well-preserved Greek theatre, a castle and a cathedral.
Messina, a busy port with a deep natural harbour, was almost entirely destroyed by an earthquake in 1908. The cathedral is an exact replica of that destroyed in the 1908 calamity, which was built in the 11th century by King Roger.
Sicily is littered with the remains of successive invading cultures and a full listing of important sites is beyond the scope of this book. The following is a representative selection of sites and buildings: the Norman cathedral at **Monreale**, containing an acre and a half of dazzling mosaics; the numerous Greek remains at **Agrigénto** said to be better preserved than any in Greece itself; the Greek theatre at **Syracuse**; the vast *Temple of Apollo* at **Selinunte**; and the Byzantine cliff dwellings at *Cava d'Ispica* near **Modica**. Popular **seaside resorts** include *Cefalù* (near Palermo), *Mondello*, *Acitrezza*, *Acireale*, *Taormina* (see above) and *Tindari*. There are extensive sandy beaches on the southern coast.
Many attractive small islands surround Sicily, offering excellent facilities for **underwater fishing.** Accommodation is generally simple (although there are some excellent hotels). These islands are the **Lipari Group** (*Lipari* itself, *Vulcano*, *Panarea* and *Stromboli*), *Ustica*, *Favignana*, *Levanzo*, *Marettimo*, *Pantelleria* and *Lampedusa*.
SARDINIA (Sardegna): This is the second largest island in the Mediterranean. Much of Sardinia away from the coasts is an almost lunar landscape of crags and chasms and is largely uninhabited. In recent years, there has been much investment in tourist infrastructure, particularly in the northern area known as the

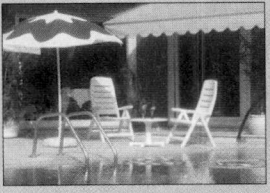

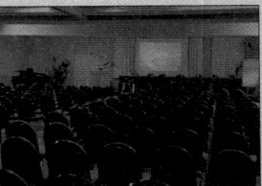

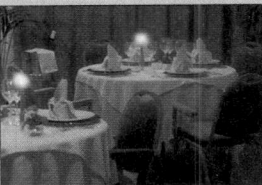

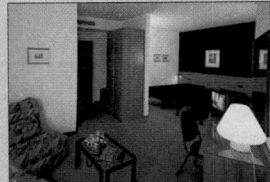

Costa Smeralda and on the west coast near Alghera. This is the only region in Italy without motorways. The Sardinian language is closer to Latin than is modern Italian.
Cagliari, the capital, stands in a marshy valley at the south of the island. It was founded by the Phoenicians and subsequently expanded by the Romans, who knew it as *Carales*. It is today a busy commercial port and site of most of the island's heavy industry.
The only other towns of any size are **Sassari**, in the northwest near the resort area around Alghero; **Nuoro**, an agricultural town on the edge of the central massif, a good base from which to explore the interior; and **Olbia**, a fishing port and car ferry terminus on the edge of the Costa Smeralda.
There are numerous Bronze Age remains throughout the islands, the best known being the *nuraghi* – circular (sometimes conical) stone dwellings. The largest collection of these may be found at **Su Nuraxi**, about 80km (50 miles) north of Cagliari.
Beach resorts include Santa Margherita di Pula, Alghero, Santa Teresa, Porto Cervo, Capo Boi and the island of La Maddalena.

SOCIAL PROFILE

FOOD & DRINK: Table service is most common in restaurants and bars. There are no licensing laws.
Pasta plays a substantial part in Italian recipes, but nearly all regions have developed their own special dishes. Examples of dishes from each region are listed below. Italy has over 20 major wine regions, from Val d'Aosta on the French border to Sicily and Sardinia in the south. **Drink:** Wines are named after grape varieties or after their village or area of origin. The most widespread is the *Chianti* group of vineyards, governed by the *Chianti Classico* quality controls (denoted by a black cockerel on the neck of each bottle). The Chianti area is the only area in Italy with such quality controls. *Denominazione di origine controllata* wines come from officially recognised wine-growing areas (similar to Appellation Controllé in France), while wines designated *Denominazione controllata e garantita* are wines of fine quality. Vermouths from Piemonte vary from dry and light pink to dark-coloured and sweet. Aperitifs such as *Campari* and *Punt e Mes* are excellent appetisers, while Italian liqueurs include *Strega*, *Galliano*, *Amaretto* and *Sambuca*. Examples of wine from each region are listed below.
***Rome*: Food:** *abbacchio* (suckling lamb in white wine flavoured with rosemary), *cannelloni* (pasta stuffed with meat, calves' brains, spinach, egg and cheese), *broccoli romani* (broccoli in white wine), *salsa romana* (sweet-sour brown sauce with raisins, chestnut and lentil purée served with game) and *gnocchi alla romana* (semolina dumplings). Of Rome's cheeses the best include *mozzarella*, *caciotta romana* (semi-hard, sweet sheep cheese), *pecorino* (hard, sharp sheep's milk cheese) and *gorgonzola*. **Wines:** Frascati, Albano, Grottaferrata, Velletri, Montefiascone, and Marino (whites); Marino, Cesanese and Piglio (reds).
***Piemonte* and *Val d'Aosta*: Food:** *fonduta* (a hot dip with Fontina cheese, milk and egg yolks sprinkled with truffles and white pepper), *lepre piemontese* (hare cooked in Barbera wine and sprinkled with herbs and bitter chocolate), *zabaglione* (hot dessert with beaten egg and Marsala wine). **Wines:** Barolo, Barbera, Barbaresco, Gattinara and Grignolino.
***Lombardia*: Food:** *risotto alla milanese* (rice with saffron and white wine), *zuppa pavese* (tasty clear soup with poached eggs), *minestrone* (thick soup with chopped vegetables), *osso buco* (shin of veal cooked in tomato sauce served with rice), *panettone* (Christmas cake with sultanas and candied fruit). **Wines:** Valtellina, Sassella, Grumello and Inferno.
***Trentino* and *Alto Adige*: Food:** some excellent sausages and hams come from these regions. **Wines:** Lago di Caldaro and Santa Maddalena.
***Veneto*: Food:** *fegato alla ceneziana* (calves' liver thinly sliced and cooked in butter with onions), *baccalà alla vicentina* (salt cod simmered in milk), *radicchio rosso di treviso* (wild red chicory with a bitter taste). **Wines:** Soave, Bardolino and Valpolicella.
***Friuli-Venezia Giulia*: Food:** *pasta e fagioli* (pasta and beans), *prosciutto di San Daniele* (raw ham). **Wines:** Tokai, Malvasia, Pinot Bianco and Pinot Grigio (whites); Merlot, Cabernet and Pinot Nero (reds).
***Liguria*: Food:** *pesto* (sauce made of basil, garlic, pine nuts and *pecorino* cheese with pasta), *cima genovese* (cold veal stuffed with calves' brains, onions and herbs), *pandolce* (sweet cake with orange flavour). **Wine:** Sciacchettra.
***Emilia-Romagna*: Food:** *parmigiano* (parmesan cheese), *prosciutto di Parma* (Parma ham), *pasta con salsa bolognese* (sauce of meat, cheese and tomato served with pasta), *vitello alla bolognese* (veal cutlet cooked with Parma ham and cheese), *cotechino e zampone* (pigs' trotters stuffed with pork and sausages). **Wines:** Lambrusco, Albana, Trebbiano and Sangiovese.
***Toscana*: Food:** *bistecca alla fiorentina* (thick T-bone steak grilled over charcoal, sprinkled with freshly ground black pepper and olive oil), *minestrone alla fiorentina* (tasty vegetable soup with slices of country bread), *pappardelle alla lepre* (pasta with hare sauce), *tortina di carciofi* (baked artichoke pie), *cinghiale di maremma* (wild boar from Maremma region near Grosseto) with dishes of ham, sausages and steaks. Sweets include *panforte di Siena* (confection of honey, candied fruits, almonds and cloves), *castagnaccio* (chestnut cake with nuts and sultanas) and *ricciarelli* (delicate biscuit of honey and almonds from Siena). **Wines:** Chianti, Vernaccia, Aleatic and Brunello di Montalcino.
***Marche*: Food:** *brodetto* (many varieties of fish on toast, garnished with carrot, celery, tomato, laurel tips and white wine), *pasticciata* (pasta baked in oven, a method preferred by Marches). **Wine:** Verdicchio.
***Abruzzo-Molise*: Food:** the favourite pasta in this region is known as *maccheroni alla chitarra* because it is cut in thin strips. Desserts include *parrozzo* (rich chocolate cake) and *zeppole* (sweetened pasta). **Wines:** Cerasolo di Abruzzo, Montepulciano (reds); Trebbiano (dry white). The district is also home of a strong liqueur known as *Centerbe*.
***Umbria*: Food:** Truffles, spaghetti, *porchetta alla perugina* (suckling pig), *carne ai capperi e acciughe* (veal with caper and herb sauce) and good-quality local sausages, salami and *prosciutto* famous throughout Italy. **Wine:** Orvieto (white, sweet or dry).
***Campania*: Food:** *pizza* (the culinary pride of Campania) served in a great variety of recipes, *bistecca alla pizzaiola* (steak with sauce made from tomatoes, garlic and oregano), *sfogliatelle* (sweet ricotta cheese turnovers) and *mozzarella* cheese (originally made with buffalo milk). **Wines** come from the islands of Capri and Ischia.
***Puglia*: Food:** *coniglio ai capperi* (rabbit cooked with capers) and *ostriche* (fresh oysters baked with bread crumbs). **Wines:** Sansevero, Santo Stefano, Aleatico di Puglia.
***Calabria and Basilicata*: Food:** *sagne chine* (lasagne with artichoke and meat balls), *zuppa di cipolle* (onion soup with Italian brandy), *sarde* (fresh sardines with olive oil and oregano), *alici al limone* (fresh anchovies baked with lemon juice), *melanzane Sott'Olio* (pickled aubergines), *mostaccioli* (chocolate biscuits) or *cannariculi* (fried honey biscuits). **Wines:** Agliatico, Cirò.
***Sicily*: Food:** *pesce spada* (swordfish stuffed with brandy, mozzarella and herbs, grilled on charcoal), *pasta con le sarde* (pasta with fresh sardines), *caponata* (rich dish of olives, anchovies and aubergines), *pizza siciliana* (pizza with olives and capers) and *triglie alla siciliana* (grilled mullet with orange peel and white wine). Excellent sweets are *cassata* (ice cream of various flavours with candied fruit and bitter chocolate) and *frutti di marturana* (marzipan fruits). **Wines:** Regaleali, Corvo di Salaparuta (both red and white, a highly aromatic wine ideal for fish), Marsala.
***Sardinia*: Food:** the coastline offers a wide selection of fish, including lobster which is served in soup, stews and grills. Main dishes include *burrida* (fish stew with dogfish and skate) and *calamaretti alla sarda* (stuffed baby squid). **Wines:** Vernaccia, Cannonau, Piani, Oliena and Malvasia.
NIGHTLIFE: Nightclubs, discos, restaurants and bars with floorshows and dancing can be found in most major towns and tourist resorts. In the capital, English-language films can be found at the Pasquine Cinema, *Vicolo della Paglia*, just off Santa Maria in Trastevere. Restaurants and cafés throughout Italy will invariably have tables outside: in Rome the *Massimo D'Azeglio* is a hotel restaurant famous for its classic food. Open-air concerts in summer are organised by the *Opera House* and the *Academy of St Cecilia*, while there is open-air theatre at the *Baths of Caracalla*. Jazz, rock, folk and country music can all be heard at various venues.
SHOPPING: Many Italian products are world-famous for their style and quality. Care should be taken when buying antiques since Italy is renowned for skilled imitators. Prices are generally fixed and bargaining is not general practice, although a discount may be given on a large purchase. Florence, Milan and Rome are famous as important fashion centres, but smaller towns also offer good scope for shopping. It is advisable to avoid hawkers or sellers on the beaches. Some places are known for particular products, eg Como (Lombardia) for silk, Prato (Tuscany) for textiles, Empoli (Tuscany) for the production of bottles and glasses in green glass, Deruta (Umbria) and Faenza (Emilia-Romagna) for pottery, Carrara (Tuscany) for marble. Torre Annunziata (Campania) and Alghero (Sardinia) are centres for handicraft products in coral, and in several parts of Sardinia business cards and writing paper made of cork are produced. Cremona (Valle d'Aosta) is famous for its handmade violins. Castelfidardo (Marche) is famous for its accordion factories, and for its production of guitars and organs. Two small towns concentrate on producing their speciality: Valenza (Piemonte), which has a large number of goldsmith artisans, and Sulmona (Abruzzo), which produces 'confetti', sugar-coated almonds used all over Italy for wedding celebrations. Vietri sul Mare (Campania) is one of the most important centres of ceramic paving-tiles, and Ravenna (Emilia-Romagna) is famous for mosaics. Main shopping areas are listed below.
Rome offers a wide choice of shops and markets. Every shop in the fashionable Via Condotti–Via Sistina area offers a choice of styles, colours and designs rarely matched, but at very high prices. Equally expensive are shops along Via Vittorio Veneto, a street famous for its outdoor cafés. Old books and prints can be bought from bookstalls of Piazza Borghese. Rome's flea market is at Porta Portese in Trastevere on Sunday mornings, selling everything from second-hand shoes to 'genuine antiques'.
Milan's industrial wealth is reflected in the chic, elegant shops of Via Montenapoleone. Prices tend to be higher than in other major cities.
Venice is still famous for its glassware, and there is a great deal of both good and bad glass; that made on the island of Murano, where there are also art dealers and skilful goldsmiths, has a reputation for quality. Venetian lace is also exquisite and expensive; however, most of the lace sold is no longer made locally (only lace made on the island of Burano may properly be called Venetian lace).
Florence boasts some of the finest goldsmiths, selling from shops largely concentrated along both sides of the Ponte Vecchio bridge. Florentine jewellery has a particular quality of satin finish called *satinato*. Much filigree jewellery can also be found. Cameos are another speciality of Florence, carved from exotic shells.
Southern Italy: In the south there are still families handmaking the same local products as their ancestors: pottery and carpets in each region; filigree jewellery and products of wrought iron and brass in Abruzzo; products in wood in Calabria; corals and cameos in Campania; a variety of textiles, including tablecloths, in Sicily and Sardinia. In Cagliari it is possible to find artistic copies of bronze statuettes from the Nuraghe period of the Sardinian Bronze Age. In the larger towns such as Naples, Bari, Reggio, Calabria, Palermo and Cagliari there are elegant shops with a whole range of Italian products. Many smaller towns have outdoor markets, but souvenirs sold at there are sometimes of very low quality, probably mass-produced elsewhere.
Shopping hours: 0900-1300 and 1600-1930 Monday to Saturday, with some variations in Northern Italy where the lunch break is shorter and the shops close earlier. Food shops are often closed on Wednesday afternoons.
SPORT: Football is the most popular spectator sport (the national team won the World Cup in 1934, 1938 and 1982 and hosted the 1990 event, in which they finished third). Other popular sports are **cycling** (the *Giro d'Italia* is the most famous cycling race through Italy); **motor racing**, held at the Monza autodrome near Milan (Lombardia); **sailing, motorboat racing** and **riding. Golf:** There are first-class golf courses all over Italy, from Lombardia and Trentino in the north, through Tuscany (near Florence) and Lazio (near Rome), down to Calabria and Sardinia where the golf season is very long due to the mild climate. There are thousands of **tennis** courts (both covered and in the open-air) in the big towns and tourist resorts. Bocce **bowls** is as traditional in Italy as it is in France, especially in small villages where it is played on Sundays after High Mass. **Fishing** can be enjoyed in the rivers in Northern Italy or in the open sea, where it is possible to rent a boat with or without fishermen. Divers and underwater fishermen will find their paradise in Sardinia and Sicily, around the Tremiti Islands (Puglia) in the Adriatic, or along the coasts of Tuscany and Liguria, where equipment can be hired. The **winter sports** resorts are expanding throughout, in the Alpine regions in places such as Cervinia and Courmayeur in Val d'Aosta, Claviere and Sauze d'Oulx in Piemonte, Aprica and Bormio in Lombardia, Alpi di Siusi, Cortina d'Ampezzo, Marilleva and Selva di Valgardena in The Dolomites (Trentino–Alto Adige–Veneto), and in Central Italy, in resorts such as Abetone (Tuscany), Campo Imperatore in Lazio, and in several places in Abruzzo, down to Mount Etna in Sicily. **Equestrian:** One of Rome's most prestigious events is its international horse show held in May. There is also flat racing starting in February at the Capanelle track. Each of the three seasons lasts two months, the second starting in May and the third in September. Trotting races take place at the Villa Gloria track in February, June to November. Genoa has frequent **yachting** regattas, as does Santa Margherita Ligura, where a canoe regatta is also held in July for small boat-handlers.
SPECIAL EVENTS: Traditional festivals are celebrated in most towns and villages in commemoration of local historical or religious events, the most notable and spectacular being the following:
Agrigento: Folklore. Almond Blossom Festival (February).
Ascoli Piceno: Joust of the Quintana. Historical pageant with over 1000 people (annually the first Sunday in August).
Arezzo: Joust of the Saracen with armoured knights, dating from the 13th century (annually the first Sunday in September).

Assisi: Celebration of the Holy Week (Easter Week). Music and Song contest (annually the first Saturday and Sunday in May).
Bari: 'Sagra di San Nicola', historical procession in costume (May 7-8).
Cagliari: 'Sagra di Sant'Efisio', one of the biggest and most colourful processions in the world (May 1).
Florence: 'Scoppio del Carro', Explosion of the Cart in the Cathedral Square, annually on Easter Sunday; and 'Gioco del Calcio', 16th-century football match in medieval costumes (June 24 and 28).
Foligno: Revival of a 17th-century joust with 600 knights in costumes (second Sunday in September).
Gubbio: 'Festa dei Ceri', procession of local costumes (May 15).
Lucca: 'Luminaria di Santa Croce'. Illuminations and procession (September 14).
Marostica: Human Chess Game (every year on the second weekend in September).
Naples: 'Festa di San'Gennaro', gathering in the Cathedral to pray for the liquefaction of the Saint's blood.
Nuoro: Festival of the Redeemer (last week in August).
Oristano: 'Sa Sartiglia', medieval procession and jousting (Carnival Time).
Piana Degli Albanesi (Palermo): Celebration of Epiphany according to Byzantine rite (January 6). Also Easter celebrations (Easter Sunday).
Pisa: Historical regatta and illuminations (June 16-17).
Rome: Epiphany Fair (January 6). 'Festa de'Noantri' (July 16-24).
Sansepolcro (Arezzo): 'Palio dei Balestrieri', medieval contest (Second Sunday in September).
Sassari: Traditional procession of over 3000 people, the Cavalcata Sarda (annually the first Sunday in May).
Siena: Bare-back horserace (July 2 and August 16).
Venice: 'Carnevale' (February). Procession of gondolas (July 16-17). 'Il Redentore', historical regatta (annually the first Sunday in September).
Viareggio: 'Carnevale' (February).
Viterbo: Procession of the 'Macchina di Santa Rosa', commemorating the transport of the Saint's body to the Church of Santa Rosa (September 3).
SOCIAL CONVENTIONS: The social structure is heavily influenced by the Roman Catholic church and, generally speaking, family ties are stronger than in most other countries in Western Europe. Normal social courtesies should be observed. Dress is casual in most places, though beachwear should be confined to the beach. Conservative clothes are expected when visiting religious buildings and smaller, traditional communities. Formal wear is usually indicated on invitations. Smoking is prohibited in some public buildings, transport and cinemas. Visitors are warned to take precautions against theft, particularly in the cities. **Tipping:** Service charges and state taxes are included in all hotel bills. It is customary to give the waiter or waitress 10% in addition.

BUSINESS PROFILE

ECONOMY: The Italian economy performed well during the late 1980s, to the point where Italy can legitimately claim *il sorpasso*, the overtaking of Britain in per capita Gross Domestic Product. Entering the 1990s, there are signs of significant economic difficulties, exemplified by the Government's inability to control the vast public sector deficit. Traditionally agricultural, Italy industrialised rapidly after 1945, particularly in manufacturing and engineering, to the point where only 12% of the population is now engaged in agriculture. The majority of these live in the south of Italy, which is substantially poorer than the centre and north of the country. The role of a group of large state holding companies was vital in ensuring economic growth, although it is now widely felt that these have outlived their usefulness and should be broken up. (The collapse of one of these, Efim, in July 1992, has badly dented financial confidence.) However, it is the decline of the dynamic small and medium-sized business sector that is causing most concern amongst economic analysts.
Nonetheless, Italy's achievements have been remarkable, all the more so given the lack of any natural resources. All the country's oil and many of its raw materials must be imported. The economy thus relies heavily on the export of manufactured goods to pay for these, particularly of industrial machinery, vehicles, aircraft, chemicals, electronics, textiles and clothing. The tourism industry has also steadily grown in importance. Main trading partners are EC countries, Latin America, the USA, Canada, Saudi Arabia, the CIS and Libya.
BUSINESS: A knowledge of Italian is a distinct advantage. Prior appointments are essential. Remember that ministries and most public offices close at 1345 and, except by special appointment, it is not possible to see officials in the afternoon. Milan, Turin and Genoa form the industrial triangle of Italy; Bologna, Florence, Padua, Rome, Verona and Vicenza also have important business centres. In all the above cities major trade fairs take place throughout the year. See under the relevant city sections in *Resorts & Excursions*. **Office hours:** 0900-1300 and 1400-1800 Monday to Friday.
COMMERCIAL INFORMATION: The following organisation can offer advice: Unione Italiana delle Camere di Commercio, Industria, Artigianato e Agricoltura (Italian Union of Chambers of Commerce, Industry, Crafts and Agriculture), Piazza Sallustio 21, 00187 Roma. Tel: (6) 47041. Telex: 622327.
CONFERENCES/CONVENTIONS: There are many hotels with facilities. Further information can be obtained from the national conference organisation: ItalCongressi, Largo Virgilio Testa 23, 00144 Roma. Tel: (6) 592 2545. Fax: (6) 592 2649. Telex: 624688.

HISTORY & GOVERNMENT

HISTORY: Although Italy has only been unified since 1861, the rich and complex history of the peninsula has, perhaps more than that of any other country, influenced the course of European development, particularly in the fields of culture and political thought. The most important early settlers in the area, which was later to be known as Italy, were the Etruscans, who had established settlements in northern Italy by the 6th century BC. By the 3rd century BC, the city state of Rome, having subdued most of the peninsula, was intent on extending its influence elsewhere. At its greatest extent the Empire (so called after 30BC) made the Mediterranean a Roman lake and for several centuries conferred on its inhabitants the benefits of the *Pax Romana*: culture (mainly Hellenic in origin), law, relative peace and comparative prosperity. By the 5th century, however, internal discord and external pressures resulted in the disintegration of the empires, although the Germanic peoples who assumed the rule of Italy, at first as representatives of the Eastern Emperor in Constantinople, were more concerned with the continuity of the Roman way of life than has often been supposed. From AD493 the Ostrogothic kingdom of Theodoric maintained the unity of Italy, but the region was reconquered by Justinian (AD535-53). By the late 6th century, however, settlers from northern Europe had established a kingdom in Lombardy and before long Italy had fragmented into a dozen or so states. For the next thousand years the exceedingly complex history of Italy can be seen in terms of a northern region (dominated by the Holy Roman Empire, the Papacy and the growing power of the city states) and a southern region (dominated first by the vestiges of Byzantine power, and later by the Muslims and then the Normans and their successors such as the Angevins, the Aragonese and the Bourbons). Charlemagne gained control of northern Italy in the late 8th century, and for the rest of the medieval period his successors made repeated and largely unsuccessful attempts to recreate the imperial power in the region. The 11th century saw the rise of the independent city states of Florence, Genoa, Milan and particularly Venice, all of which pursued an independent policy and soon began to wield a commercial and political importance out of all proportion to their size. In the south, Sicily was taken by the Muslims in the 9th century, but then fell to the Normans in 1059 who soon established control over most of the southern part of the peninsula. In the 12th century the kingdom was one of the greatest centres of culture in Europe, particularly under Roger II. Briefly reunited by marriage to the Hohenstaufen empire of Henry VI and Frederick II between 1189 and 1268, Naples and Sicily were then ruled respectively by the houses of Anjou and Aragon until the latter reunited the region in 1442. The popes played a leading role in the tortuous diplomacy of 15th-century Italy. The period witnessed arguably the greatest ever flowering of art and culture (the Italian Renaissance), associated with writers such as Machiavelli, Aristio and Guicciardini and notable patrons such as the Medici and several popes supporting a wealth of artists including Fra Angelico, Raphael, Botticelli and, greatest of all, Michelangelo and Leonardo da Vinci. Politically, the 16th century represented a victory for Spanish over French influence in Italy, and the Habsburgs established themselves particularly strongly in Milan, Naples and Sicily. Many of the smaller states changed hands on numerous occasions during the following two centuries, and although the large city states maintained their independence, their power was in general on the wane. The Enlightenment of the 18th century found particularly strong expression in the Kingdom of Naples and Sicily (by now ruled by the Bourbons), but elsewhere centralised power was largely absent. Opposition to Habsburg was led by Garibaldi and the house of Savoy (also Kings of Sardinia since 1720), and by 1861 the ruling princes of northern and central Italy had been deposed and Victor Emmanuel II became the first king of Italy, with Florence as the capital. The full annexation of Venice and Rome was not completed for another ten years. Italy's colonial conquests were limited (largely due to the failure of the Ethiopian campaigns) and the rulers enjoyed more success in their efforts to consolidate their own position at home, despite the considerable distractions of the various complex struggles in the Balkans. Despite being neutral in 1914, Italy joined the Allies in the following year and made some territorial gains in the peace which followed the First World War. The inter-war years were dominated by economic problems, further attempts at expansion and the rise of the Fascists under Mussolini. Italy supported Hitler's Germany in 1939, but after the surrender of Italian forces and the arrest of Mussolini in 1943, the new government backed the Allies for the remainder of the Second World War. King Victor Emmanuel III abdicated in 1946 and a Republic was proclaimed; since that time the country has been dominated by the Christian Democrats, although there have been many governmental coalitions. Elections rarely produce dramatic changes in Italy. The Christian Democrat Party (DC) has been the dominant power in each of the 51 governments since the war, although during the 1980s the premiership has been held by politicians from other smaller parties. However, the almost traditional instability of the Italian government seems to have little impact on the Italians as a nation. The Communist Party (PCI), the largest in Western Europe with just under 30% of the Italian vote, has dominated the opposition. The PCI has recently undergone a major revision of its political strategy, renouncing Marxism in an apparent attempt to improve its electoral appeal. The latest general election, held in April 1992, again produced an inconclusive result. It was left to the traditional parties to try and put together a government. This process was even more tortuous than usual, compounded by the need to find a new head of state as well. This position was filled at the 15th attempt at the end of May when the Christian Democrats proposed a veteran party figure, Luigi Scalfaro, who proved acceptable to the restyled PCI, the Partito Democratico della Sinistra (PDS, Democratic Party of the Left). Scalfaro's first task was to supervise the formation of a new government. An amenable Socialist Party (PSI) figure was found in the form of the respected law professor Giuliano Amato. The 51st premier enjoyed the significant advantage of being one of the few senior PSI figures untainted by the latest corruption scandal to break over Italy, involving the payment of large bribes to politicians by construction companies in exchange for public works contracts. This scandal, substantial even by Italian standards, and the upsurge during the summer of 1992 of Mafia violence, with the murder of two of Italy's most famous investigating magistrates, has brought Italy to something of a social and moral crisis. As the economy goes into recession, the common view that politics don't really matter because the economy will look after itself is being replaced by serious soul-searching about the nature of Italian public life. That the Mafia, in its various guises, continues to grow and operate with impunity under the protection of a coterie of corrupt politicians and administrators, is seen as an indictment of the fabric of Italian society. The Italian system of proportional representation, which often gives excessive power to small parties which hold the balance of votes, is coming under increasing scrutiny as a major problem. Italy has important foreign concerns, arising from its membership of the European Community and its proximity to the Balkans. The arrival of thousands of Albanian 'boat people' during 1991 was an illustration of the consequences of instability in that region. For the same reason, Italy also has an interest in the civil war in the former Yugoslavia, although it does have the luxury of being relatively insulated by Slovenia. The Italian government's efforts to assist a settlement have been focussed in the European Community, where it has also been a relative keen supporter of the Maastricht process of European integration.
GOVERNMENT: The legislature is bicameral and members are elected on a basis of proportional representation by universal suffrage. A Council of Ministers has executive power, appointed by the

President (who is Head of State, elected by an electoral college and representatives from each region in Italy) and responsible to the Parliament.

CLIMATE

Summer is hot, especially in the south. Spring and autumn are mild with fine, sunny weather. Winter in the south is much drier and warmer than in northern and central areas. Mountain regions are colder with heavy winter snowfalls.

Required clothing: Lightweight cottons and linens are worn during the summer, except in the mountains. Lightweight to mediumweights are worn in the south during winter, while warmer clothes are worn elsewhere. Alpine wear is advised for winter mountain resorts.

ROME Italy (46m)

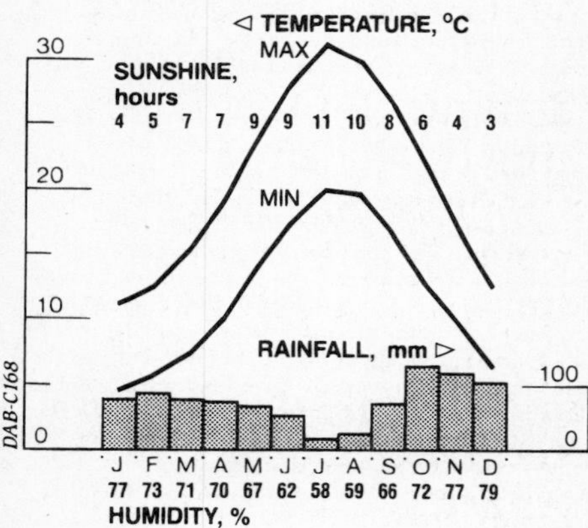

MILAN Italy (147m)

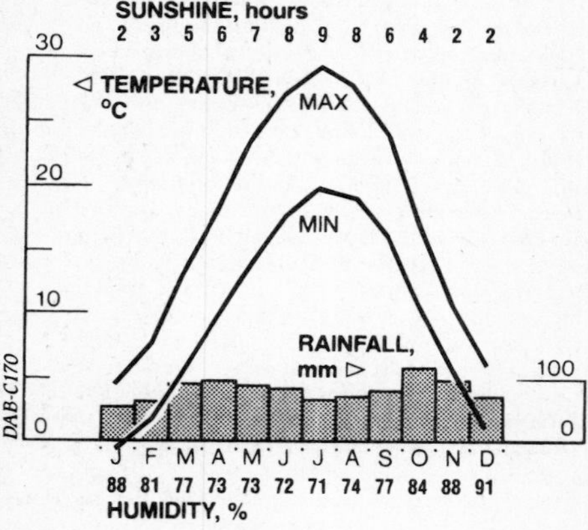

PALERMO Sicily (71m)

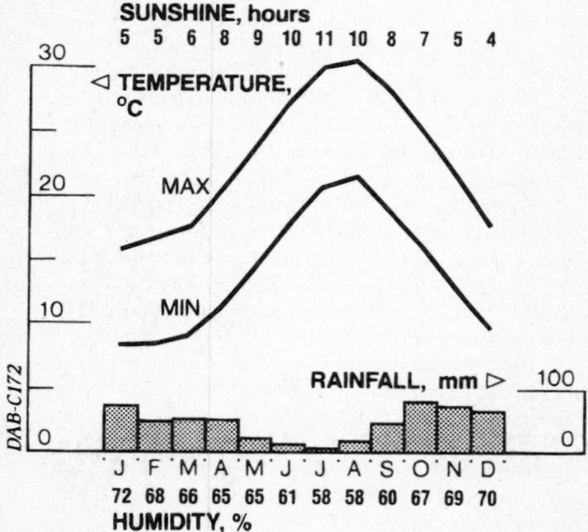

JAMAICA

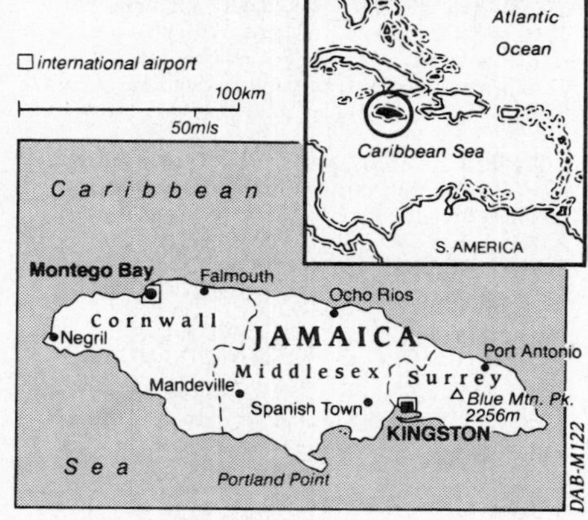

Location: Caribbean.

Jamaica Tourist Board
PO Box 360
21 Dominica Drive
Kingston 5, Jamaica
Tel: 929 9200. Fax: 929 9375. Telex: 2140.

Jamaica High Commission
1-2 Prince Consort Road
London SW7 2BZ
Tel: (071) 823 9911. Fax: (071) 589 5154. Telex: 263304.

Jamaica Tourist Board
Address as above.
Tel: (071) 224 0505. Fax: (071) 224 0551. Telex: 295510.
Opening hours: 0930-1730 Monday to Friday.

British High Commission
PO Box 575
Trafalgar Road
Kingston 10, Jamaica
Tel: 926 9050. Fax: 929 7868. Telex: 2110.

Jamaican Embassy
Suite 355
1850 K Street, NW
Washington, DC
20006
Tel: (202) 452 0660. Fax: (202) 452 0081. Telex: 64352.

Jamaica Consulate General
10th Floor, 866 Second Avenue
New York, NY
10017
Tel: (212) 935 9000.

Tourist Board
Address as above
Tel: (212) 688 7650. Fax: (212) 759 5012.

Embassy of the United States of America
3rd Floor, Jamaica Mutual Life Centre
2 Oxford Road
Kingston 5, Jamaica
Tel: 929 4850. Fax: 926 6743.

Jamaican High Commission
Suite 402
275 Slater Street
Ottawa, Ontario
K1P 5H9
Tel: (613) 233 9311/9314. Fax: (613) 233 0611.

Jamaica Tourist Board
Suite 616
One Eglinton Avenue
Toronto, Ontario
M4P 3A1
Tel: (416) 482 7850. Fax: (416) 482 1730.

Canadian High Commission
PO Box 1500
Mutual Security Bank Building
30 Knutsford Boulevard
Kingston 5, Jamaica
Tel: 926 1500-7. Fax: 926 1702. Telex: 2130 BEAVER JA.

AREA: 10,991 sq km (4244 sq miles).
POPULATION: 2,415,100 (1990 estimate).
POPULATION DENSITY: 219.7 per sq km.
CAPITAL: Kingston. **Population:** 661,600 (1989 estimate).
GEOGRAPHY: Jamaica is the third largest island in the West Indies, a narrow outcrop of a submerged mountain range. The island is crossed by a range of mountains reaching 2256m (7402ft) at the Blue Mountain Peak in the east and descending towards the west with a series of spurs and forested gullies running north and south. Most of the best beaches are on the north and west coasts. The island's luxuriant tropical and subtropical vegetation is probably unsurpassed anywhere in the Caribbean.
LANGUAGE: Official language is English. Local *patois* is also spoken.
RELIGION: Protestant majority (Anglican, Baptist and Methodist) with Roman Catholic, Jewish, Muslim, Hindu and Bahai communities. Rastafarianism, a religion based on belief in the divinity of the late Emperor of Ethiopia, Haile Selassie (Ras Tafari), is also widely practised.
TIME: GMT - 5 (GMT- 6 in summer).
ELECTRICITY: 110 volts AC, 50Hz, single phase, with American 2-pin plug standard, but many hotels offer, in addition, 220 volts AC, 50Hz, single phase, from 3-pin sockets.
COMMUNICATIONS: Telephone: Full IDD is available. Country code: 1809. There are no area codes. **Fax:** This service is available from 0700-1000 every day at the *Jamintel* office in Kingston. Widely available in most hotels and offices. **Telex/telegram:** Facilities for sending telex and telegrams are widely available. Telex facilities at the British High Commission may be used in emergencies. **Post:** Airmail to Europe takes up to four days. Post office hours: 0830-1630 Monday to Friday. **Press:** Daily papers are *The Daily Gleaner*, *The Star* and *The Jamaica Herald*.
BBC World Service and Voice of America frequencies: From time to time these change. See the section *How to Use this Book* for more information.

BBC:				
MHz	17.84	15.22	9.915	5.975
Voice of America:				
MHz	15.21	11.70	6.130	0.930

PASSPORT/VISA

Regulations and requirements may be subject to change at short notice, and you are advised to contact the appropriate diplomatic or consular authority before finalising travel arrangements. Details of these may be found at the head of this country's entry. Any numbers in the chart refer to the footnotes below.

	Passport Required?	Visa Required?	Return Ticket Required?
Full British	Yes	No	Yes
BVP	Not valid/2	-	-
Australian	Yes	No	Yes
Canadian	1	No	Yes
USA	1	No	Yes
Other EC	Yes	No	Yes
Japanese	Yes	No	Yes

PASSPORTS: [1] Valid passport required by all except for residents and nationals of the USA and Canada entering Jamaica from either the USA or Canada who hold a valid national ID. If entering from other countries, they do require a passport.
British Visitors Passport: [2] Not accepted. Although the immigration authorities of this country may in certain circumstances accept British Visitors Passports for persons arriving for holidays or unpaid business trips of up to 3 months, travellers arc reminded that no formal agreement exists to this effect and the situation may, therefore, change at short notice. In addition, UK nationals using a BVP and returning to the UK from a country with which no such formal agreement exists may be subject to delays and interrogation by UK immigration.
VISAS: Required by all except:
(a) nationals of EC countries (nationals of the UK and Ireland for period of 6 months; nationals of Denmark, Italy, Luxembourg, The Netherlands, Belgium and Germany for a period not exceeding 3 months; nationals of France, Greece, Portugal and Spain for a period not exceeding 30 days);
(b) nationals of Commonwealth countries;
(c) nationals of the USA (including Virgin Islands and Puerto Rico) for stays not exceeding 6 months;
(d) nationals of Austria, Finland, Iceland, Israel, Leichtenstein, Mexico, Norway, San Marino, Sweden, Switzerland and Turkey for stays not exceeding 3 months;
(f) nationals of Argentina, Brazil, Chile, Costa Rica, Ecuador, Japan and Uruguay for stays not exceeding 30 days;
(e) nationals of Venezuela for stays not exceeding 14 days.

SuperClubs

The Gold Standard Of All-Inclusive Vacations

GRAND LIDO®
NEGRIL

The ultimate all-inclusive vacation that features a 147' private luxury yacht, 24 hour room service and even complimentary valet, dry cleaning, manicures and pedicures.

HEDONISM II®
NEGRIL

This is the first vacation for mind, body, spirit and soul where the pleasure truly comes in many forms.

COUPLES®
JAMAICA & ST. LUCIA

The original holiday created for romantics by romantics where the couple finds its rightful place in the sun.

RUNAWAY BAY

The terrific-terrific, Jamaica-Jamaica vacation brings you the time of your life with Jamaica's best Scuba, golf and tennis academies, fun, entertainment and more.

Boscobel Beach®
JAMAICA

The first all-inclusive holiday for the whole family where children under 14 sharing their parents' room stay, eat and play completely free.

A SuperClubs holiday is the freedom of choice to design your own holiday day by day as you see fit. You can go all day and all night. Or you can do nothing but listen to the edict of your own whim.

SuperClubs provide everything for one all-inclusive price - sports, fabulous food, entertainment, bar drinks, exquisite rooms. Even cigarettes are complimentary, and there's no tipping.

Holiday Feature Inclusions	Grand Lido Negril	Hedonism II	Couples, Jamaica	Couples, St. Lucia	Jamaica-Jamaica	Boscobel Beach
All Meals	•	•	•	•	•	•
Wine with lunch & dinner	•	•	•	•	•	•
Bar drinks and cigarettes	•	•	•	•	•	•
Scuba	•	•	•	•	•	•
Waterskiing	•	•	•	•		•
Windsurfing	•	•	•	•	•	•
Sailing	•	•	•	•	•	•
Snorkelling	•	•	•	•	•	•
Water polo	•	•	•	•	•	•
Swimming pool	•	•	•	•	•	•
Nude beach	•	•	•		•	
Cruises	•			•	•	
Jacuzzis	•	•	•	•	•	•
Golf			•		•	•
A/C Squash courts		•	•			
Horse riding	•	•	•	•	•	
Tennis	•	•	•	•	•	•
Bicycles		•	•	•	•	•
Exercise gym	•	•	•	•	•	•
Volleyball	•	•	•	•	•	•
Aerobics	•	•	•	•	•	•
Arts & Crafts		•	•	•	•	•
Indoor games room	•	•	•	•	•	•
Live entertainment	•	•	•	•	•	•
Disco	•	•			•	•
Piano bar	•	•	•	•	•	•
Excursions			•	•	•	•
Airport transfers	•	•	•	•	•	•
Hotel taxes	•	•	•	•	•	•
No tipping	•	•	•	•	•	•
Adults only	•	•	•	•	•	
Children welcome						•

For further information call SuperClubs in the UK: 0992-447420. Fax: 0992-468064.
Rawdon House, Victorian Wing, High Street, Hoddesdon, Herts, EN11 8TE

Provided that the above have a valid passport, evidence of sufficient funds and a return or outward bound ticket for their next destination.
Note: Except for persons in certain categories, a Work Permit is required for a business visit. The Consulate (or Consular Section at Embassy or High Commission) can advise.
Types of visa: Entry visa; Transit visa. Cost of visas vary – enquire on application.
Application to: Consulate (or Consular Section at Embassy or High Commission). For addresses, see top of entry.
Application requirements: (a) 2 photos. (b) Valid passport. (c) Completed application form(s). (d) Fee.
Working days required: 48 hours, but some applications are referred to Immigration authorities in Kingston, for which time should be allowed when applying for visa.
Temporary residence: Enquire at Embassy.

MONEY

Currency: Jamaican Dollar (J$) = 100 cents. Notes are in denominations of J$100, 50, 20, 10, 5, 2 and 1. Coins are in denominations of J$1 and 50, 25, 20, 10, 5 and 1 cents.
Currency exchange: Visitors should change money only at airport bureaux, banks or hotels.
Credit cards: Access/Mastercard, American Express, Diners Club and Visa are all widely accepted. Check with your credit card company for details of merchant acceptability and other services which may be available.
Travellers cheques: US Dollar cheques are recommended. Eurocheques are now accepted by all commercial banks.
Exchange rate indicators: The following figures are included as a guide to the movements of the Jamaican Dollar against Sterling and the US Dollar:

Date:	Oct '89	Oct '90	Oct '91	Oct '92
£1.00=	8.86	14.51	27.45	35.07
$1.00=	5.47	7.68	15.81	22.10

Currency restrictions: Free import and export of foreign currency is allowed, subject to declaration. The import and export of local currency is limited to J$20. It is prohibited to import local currency for non-residents.
All hotel bills, car rental and duty-free bills must be paid for in Jamaican currency.
Banking hours: 0900-1400 Monday to Thursday and 0900-1500 Friday.

DUTY FREE

The following goods may be imported into Jamaica without incurring customs duty:
200 cigarettes or 50 cigars or 250g tobacco;
1 litre of spirits;
1 litre of wine;
12fl oz of toilet water;
150g of perfume;
Gifts to the value of J$1000 during each 6-month period.
Prohibited items: Explosives, firearms, dangerous drugs, meat, fresh fruit, coffee, honey or vegetables cannot be brought into Jamaica. Cats and dogs are also prohibited unless arriving directly from the UK, having been born and bred there, carrying a certificate from the Ministry of Agriculture, Fisheries and Food (Hook Rise, Tolworth, Surbiton, Surrey) and if a permit for their import has been obtained from the Ministry of Agriculture, Hope Gardens, Kingston 6.

PUBLIC HOLIDAYS

Public holidays observed in Jamaica are as follows:
Apr 4 '93 Ash Wednesday. **Apr 9** Good Friday. **Apr 12** Easter Monday. **May 23** Labour Day. **Aug 2** Independence Day. **Oct 19** National Heroes Day. **Dec 25-26** Christmas. **Jan 1 '94** New Year's Day.

HEALTH

Regulations and requirements may be subject to change at short notice, and you are advised to contact your doctor well in advance of your intended date of departure. Any numbers in the chart refer to the footnotes below.

	Special Precautions?	Certificate Required?
Yellow Fever	No	1
Cholera	No	No
Typhoid & Polio	Yes	-
Malaria	No	-
Food & Drink	2	-

JAMAICA	**HEALTH REGULATIONS**	**VISA REGULATIONS**
GALILEO/WORLDSPAN	 TI-DFT/KIN/HE	 TI-DFT/KIN/VI
SABRE	 TIDFT/KIN/HE	 TIDFT/KIN/VI

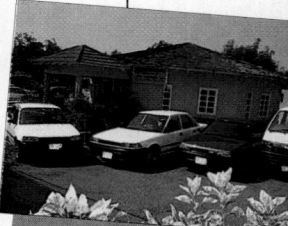

Code-Link

To access this information on your CRS, swipe the barcode with a light pen or type in the text under the barcode. For more information, see the introduction *How to Use This Book*.

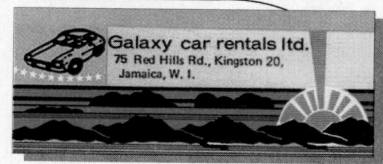

[1]: A yellow fever vaccination certificate is required from travellers over one year of age coming from infected areas.
[2]: Mains water is normally chlorinated, and whilst relatively safe may cause mild abdominal upsets. Bottled water is available. Milk is pasteurised and dairy products are safe for consumption. Local meat, poultry, seafood, fruit and vegetables are generally considered safe to eat.
Health care: Health insurance is recommended. There are 30 government-controlled hospitals.

TRAVEL - International

AIR: Jamaica's national airline is *Air Jamaica (JM)*.
Approximate flight times: From Kingston or Montego Bay to *London* is 10 hours (direct flight), to *Los Angeles* is 8 hours 40 minutes, to *New York* is 5 hours and to *Singapore* is 33 hours.
International airports: *Norman Manley International (KIN)* (Kingston) is 17.5km (11 miles) southeast of the city. Coach, bus and taxis to city. Duty-free facilities are available.
Montego Bay (MBJ) (International) is 3km (2 miles) north of the city. Duty-free facilities are available.
Trans Jamaica Airlines (JQ) runs shuttle services between the airports.
Departure tax: J$200 for all passengers over two years of age, except for those in transit.
SEA: Both Montego Bay and Ocho Rios are ports of call for the following cruise lines: *Royal Viking*, *Royal Caribbean*, *Norwegian Caribbean*, *Carnival Cruise*, *Costa Lines*, *Sun Line* and *Holland America*. Two ships, the *Regent Sea* and the *Britanis*, start their cruises from Montego Bay. Other passenger/freight lines *(Geest)* sail from North, South and Central American ports. *Lauro Lines* sail to Kingston from the Mediterranean.

TRAVEL - Internal

AIR: *Trans Jamaica Airlines (JQ)* runs services to and from Kingston, Montego Bay, Port Antonio, Mandeville, Ocho Rios and Negril. During the winter season there are frequent daily flights, as well as shuttle flights between the two major airports.
SEA: There are a number of local operators running yacht tours around the island, as well as cruises. Boats and yachts can also be hired on a daily or weekly basis. Contact Tourist Board for details.
RAIL: A diesel service runs twice daily between Kingston and Montego Bay. The total network extends to almost 340km (211 miles) and is an enjoyable way to see the interior of the island.
ROAD: There is a 17,000km (11,000 miles) road network, one-third tarred. **Bus:** Reliable service in Kingston and Montego Bay; less reliable for trans-island travel. Coach and minibus tours are bookable at most hotels. **Taxi:** Not all taxis are metered, so it is best to check standard charges prior to embarkation on journey. 10% tip is usual. **Car hire:** Most major towns, as well as airports, have rental facilities, both local and international. Rental can also be arranged via hotels. Traffic in Jamaica drives on the left. **Documentation:** A full British driving licence is valid for up to a year.
URBAN: Kingston's public conventional bus services have deteriorated due to operational and engineering problems, and most transport in the capital is now by private minibus.
JOURNEY TIMES: The following chart gives approximate journey times (in hours and minutes) from Montego Bay to other major cities/towns in Jamaica.

	Air	Road	Rail
Kingston	0.30	3.00	4.00
Negril	0.20	1.30	-
Ocho Rios	0.30	2.00	-
Port Antonio	0.40	4.30	-

ACCOMMODATION

HOTELS: There are over 144 hotels and guest-houses throughout the island; all are subject to 10% general consumption tax and must be paid for in Jamaican currency. 90% of all hotels belong to the Jamaica Hotel & Tourist Association, 2 Ardene Road, Kingston 10. Tel: 926 3635/6. Fax: 929 1054.
Grading: Hotels are government-controlled in four categories: **A, B, C** and **D**. The categories are based on rates charged. Many of the hotels offer accommodation according to one of a number of 'Plans' widely used in the Caribbean; these include *Modified American Plan* (MAP) which consists of room, breakfast and dinner and *European Plan* (EP) which consists of room only.
SELF-CATERING: There are over 837 cottages for rent on the island. Information is available from the Jamaica Tourist Board. The properties range from small apartments to houses with several bedrooms. Some tour operators can arrange villa accommodation including car rental and tours, as well as travel to and from the villa. Information is also available from the Jamaican Association of Villas & Apartments Ltd (JAVA), PO Box 298, Pineapple Place, Ocho Rios, St Ann. Tel: 974 2508.
CAMPING/CARAVANNING: The island has many campsites, including the well-known Strawberry Fields, which offers all types of facilities, including the hiring of tents and ancillary equipment.

RESORTS & EXCURSIONS

Jamaica is a tropical island of lush green vegetation, waterfalls and dazzling white beaches. Columbus was in the habit of declaring that each new island he chanced upon was more beautiful than the last, but he seems to have maintained a lifelong enthusiasm for the beauty of Jamaica, despite having been marooned there for a year on his last voyage. One of the larger islands of the Caribbean, it offers excellent tourist facilities and superb beaches and scenery. For purposes of this guide the main resorts in Jamaica have been divided into the following sections: Montego Bay (including the northwest coast resort of Negril); the North Coast Beach Resorts (including Falmouth, Ocho Rios and Port Antonio); and Kingston and the South (including Mandeville and Spanish Town).

Montego Bay

One of the world's great seaside resorts, **Montego Bay** (or Mo'Bay, as it is more colloquially called) is the capital of Jamaican tourism and market town for a large part of western Jamaica. Dating back to 1492, Montego Bay is Jamaica's second largest city and one of the most modern in the Caribbean. From *Gloucester* and *Kent Avenues* there is a superb view onto the clear Caribbean waters – the main tourist attraction – and the long reef protecting the bay. Most of the hotels are found on a strip of coastline about a mile and a half long. There are three main beaches: *Doctor's Cave Beach* (so named because it was once owned by a Dr McCatty and had a cave that has since eroded away) which has beautiful white sand, and where the exceptionally clear water is believed to be fed by mineral springs; *Walter Fletcher Beach*, nearest the centre and a short walk from the Upper Deck Hotel; and *Cornwall Beach*, which is a few yards from the local Tourist Board Office. A short way inland from the Bay is *Rose Hall*, a restored Great House on a sugar plantation.
Rocklands Feeding Station is home to some of the most exotic birds in the world, such as the mango hummingbird, orange quit and the national bird of Jamaica, the Doctor Bird. Visitors are allowed to feed the birds at certain times of the day.
The *Governor's Coach* is a 65km (40-mile) diesel train ride through thick mountain forests into the interior, passing through banana and coconut plantations and *Ipswich Caves* (a series of deep limestone recesses) to the sugar estate of the famous *Appleton Rum Factory* and **Catadupa**, where shirts and dresses are made to measure.
Negril is 80km (50 miles) west of Montego Bay and has a beach stretching for 11km (7 miles) which offers sailing, water-skiing, deep-sea fishing, scuba diving, parasailing and windsurfing. First coming to attention as an artists' centre and, later, as a focus of 'alternative' culture in the 1960s, it is becoming increasingly popular as a holiday destination which, perhaps untypically, seems likely to preserve much of its original character – indeed, the law requires all buildings to be of modest proportions. Along the street, entrepreneurial Jamaicans sell a variety of craft goods from the many shanty-like shops in Negril. There is also a hectic nightlife in the many clubs that have, over the years, proliferated along the beach. *Rick's Café* is a favourite haunt both for Jamaicans and visitors; located at **West Point**, which is as far west as Jamaica goes, it is famous as the place from which to observe the sun going down.

North Coast Resorts

Falmouth: A delightful harbour resort, 42km (26 miles) from Montego Bay. From here one can visit **Rafters Village** for rafting on the *Martha Brae*, and a fascinating crocodile farm called *Jamaica Swamp Safaris*. There is also a plantation mansion, *Greenwood Great House*, once owned by the Barrett Brownings. The *Church of St Paul* offers Sunday services, where visitors can listen to the choir singing.
Ocho Rios lies roughly 108km (67 miles) east of Montego Bay. The name is said to have come from the old Spanish word for *roaring river*, or, in modern Spanish, *eight rivers*. Ocho Rios was once a sleepy fishing village, and although there are now resort facilities, international hotels and restaurants offering a variety of cuisines, the town has kept something of the sleepy atmosphere of small-town Jamaica. One of the most stunning sights in Jamaica is *Dunn's River Falls*, a crystal water stairway which leads to the nearby Botanical gardens. Ocho Rios is known as the garden-lover's paradise, and the *Shaw Park Botanical Gardens* exhibit the fascinating variety of the area's exotic flora, for which the town is celebrated. Not surprisingly, two of the most popular tours available are to working plantations at *Brimmer Hall* and *Prospect* where sugar, bananas and spices are still grown and harvested using many of the traditional skills handed down through generations.
Any sightseeing itinerary should include a drive along *Fern Gully*, a road running along an old riverbed that

winds through a 6.5km (4-mile) valley of ferns. Another tour is the *Jamaica Night on the White River*, a canoe ride up the torchlit river to the sound of drums. Dinner and open bar is available on the riverbank (Sunday evenings). *Columbus Park*, at **Discovery Bay**, commemorates Columbus's arrival in Jamaica with a museum and 24-hour open-air park exhibiting relics of Jamaican history. Other tours include *Runaway Bay*, which has fine beaches, excellent scuba diving and horseriding; and the *Runaway Caves* nearby, which offers a boat ride 35m (120ft) below ground on a lake in the limestone *Green Grotto*.

Port Antonio, one of the Caribbean's most beautiful bays, is surrounded by the *Blue Mountains*. The town dates back to the 16th century, and sights include *Mitchell's Folly*, a 2-storey mansion built by the American millionaire Dan Mitchell in 1905, and the ruins of a 60-room *Great House*. The surrounding sea is rich in game fish, with blue marlin as the great prize (there is an annual Blue Marlin Tournament run alongside the Jamaican International Fishing Tournament in Port Antonio every autumn); there are also kingfish, yellowtail, wahoo and bonito. The island's most palatial homes are nestled in the foothills. Rafting is available on the *Rio Grande*, comprising 2-hour trips on 2-passenger bamboo rafts, which begin high in the *Blue Mountains* at **Berrydale,** sail past plantations of bananas and sugar cane, and end up at *Rafter's Rest* restaurant at *Margaret's Bay*. The scenic *Somerset Falls* nearby is a popular picnic spot. Beaches in the Port Antonio area include *San San* and *Boston* (where the Jamaican 'jerk pork' is found), while the *Blue Lagoon* is a salt-water cove offering fishing, swimming and water-skiing and is considered one of the finest coves in the Caribbean.

Kingston and the South

Kingston is Jamaica's capital city and cultural centre. With the largest natural harbour in the Caribbean (and seventh largest in the world), Kingston is also an industrial centre where Georgian architecture mixes with modern office blocks while, on the outskirts, spreading suburbs house the hundreds of thousands who increasingly work in the city. Although most tourists head for the beaches and resorts, Kingston has much to offer in the way of sightseeing.

The *National Gallery of Art* has a colourful display of modern art and is recommended. *Hope Botanical Gardens* contain a wide variety of trees and plants, and are particularly famous for orchids. A band plays here on Sunday afternoons. There is a *Crafts Market* on King Street and the *Port Royal*, on top of the peninsula bordering *Kingston Harbour*, is a museum to the time when Kingston was known as the 'richest and wickedest city on earth' under the domination of Captain Morgan and his buccaneers. The *White Marl Arawak Museum* is also worth visiting; here one can see artefacts and relics of the ancient culture of the Arawak Indians. The grounds of the *University of the West Indies*, built on what was once a sugar plantation, are open to the public. *Caymanas Park* is a popular racetrack, where one can bet on the horses every Wednesday and Saturday and on public holidays. The *Caymanas Golf Course* hosts the Jamaica Open and Pro-Am, held every November. Polo is played nearby every weekend.

Spanish Town, a short drive to the west of Kingston, is the former capital of Jamaica. The *Spanish Town Square* is said to be one of the finest examples of Georgian architecture in the Western Hemisphere. The Spanish *Cathedral of St Jago de la Vega* is the oldest in the West Indies.

Mandeville: Summer capital amid beautiful gardens and fruits, Mandeville is in the middle of Jamaica's citrus industry, 600m (2000ft) above sea level and the highest town on the island. Mandeville offers cool relief from the heat of the coast, and has a golf course and tennis and horseriding facilities. The town is the centre of the bauxite industry, and as such is a good starting point for trips to the surrounding areas.

On the south coast are *Milk River Spa*, the world's most radioactive mineral bath with waters at a temperature of 33°C; *Lover's Leap* in the Santa Cruz Mountains, a sheer 180m (60ft) cliff overhanging the sea; *Treasure Beach* and the resort of *Bluefields*.

SOCIAL PROFILE

FOOD & DRINK: Jamaican food is full of fire and spice, taking advantage of pungent spices and peppers. Jamaican dishes include 'rice and peas' (a tasty dish with no peas at all but with kidney beans, white rice, coconut milk, scallions and coconut oil). Another dish is salt fish (dried cod) and *ackee* (the exotic cooked fruit of the ackee tree), curried goat and rice (spicy and strong), Jamaican pepperpot soup (salt pork, salt beef, *okra* and Indian kale known as *callaloo)*, chicken fricassé Jamaican-style (a rich chicken stew with carrots, scallions, yams, onions, tomatoes and peppers prepared in unrefined coconut oil) and roast suckling pig (a 3-month-old piglet which is boned and stuffed with rice, peppers, diced yam and thyme mixed with shredded coconut and corn meal). *Patties* are the staple snack of Jamaica (pastries filled with ground beef and breadcrumbs) and can be found everywhere, but vary in price and filling. Waiter service is usually available in catering establishments. **Drink:** Jamaican rum is world-famous, especially *Gold Label* and *Appleton*. *Rumona* is a delicious rum cordial. *Red Stripe* beer is excellent, as is *Tia Maria* (a Blue Mountain coffee and chocolate liqueur). Fresh fruit juice is also recommended, as is Blue Mountain coffee, an excellent variety. Bars have table and/or counter service. There are no licensing hours and alcohol can be bought all day.

NIGHTLIFE: At larger resort hotels small bands and occasional guitar-carrying *calypso* singers can be heard. Folkloric shows are held and steel bands often play. At least once a week there is a torchlit, steel-band show with limbo dancing and fire-eating demonstrations. There are also discotheques, nightclubs and jazz music. Native to Jamaica is *Reggae* music and dancing. The Jamaica Tourist Board arranges 'Meet the People' evenings in various scenic locations through the island. Contact the Tourist Office in Kingston, Montego Bay, Port Antonio or Ocho Rios.

SHOPPING: Special purchases are locally made items and duty-free bargains. Crafts include hand-loomed fabrics, embroidery, silk screening, woodcarvings, oil paintings, woven straw items and sandalmaking. Custom-made rugs and reproductions of pewter and china from the ruins of the ancient submerged city of Port Royal can be bought in the In-Craft workshop. At *Highgate Village* in the mountains, Quakers run a workshop specialising in wicker and wood furniture, floor mats and other tropical furnishings. Jamaican rum, the *Rumona* liqueur (the world's only rum-based liqueur, hard to find outside the island) and *Ian Sangsters Rum Cream* are unique purchases. Other local specialities are *Pepper Jellies*, jams and spices. There are shops offering facilities for 'in-bond' shopping which allows visitors to purchase a range of international goods free of tax or duty at very competitive prices. These goods are sealed (hence the 'bond') and because goods are tax or duty free can only be opened once away from Jamaican waters or territory. All goods must be paid for in Jamaican currency. **Shopping hours:** 0900-1700 Monday to Friday. Some shops close half day Wednesday in Kingston, and on Thursday in the rest of the island.

SPORT: Watersports: Many hotels have **swimming** pools and beaches. The best beaches for bathing are mainly on the northern coast. **Surfing** is also best on the north coast, east of Port Antonio, where long lines of breakers roll into Boston Bay. Clear waters, coral reefs, shipwrecks, sponge forests, submerged caves and fish offer interesting underwater exploring. **Diving** shops are equipped for rentals and offer guided **snorkel** and **scuba** trips. There are also a number of clubs and centres offering instruction and equipment. Most beach hotels have sunfish, sailfish and/or windsurfboards for hire. To charter larger boats contact the Royal Jamaica Yacht Club. Facilities for **water-skiing** are offered at most beach hotels and at the Kingston Ski Club at Morgan's Harbour. **Fishing:** Fresh- and sea-water fishing are popular. Mountain mullet, hognose mullet, drummer and small snook are caught in rivers. **Deep-sea fishing** charters can be arranged through hotels in main resorts. **Spearfishing** is permitted among the reefs. No licence is needed. Entry forms are available for the Blue Marlin Tournament competition held in Port Antonio during September. **Tennis:** There are plenty of courts and most hotels without their own court have access to those nearby. **Golf:** Jamaica has developed some of the Caribbean's most beautiful and challenging golf courses. Montego Bay is the best area and it is not necessary to be resident at a hotel to play on its three courses. **Horseriding:** Some stables for horseriding are open all year, others run schedules during the winter season and most arrangements can be made through hotels. The Chukka Cove Riding Centre at Runaway Bay offers tuition, polo and accommodation. **Cricket** is the national pastime and matches are played from January to August in Sabina Park, Kingston and other locations throughout the island. Probably the second most popular sport is **football**, which is played throughout the year. **Polo** has a tradition going back over a century; matches are played all year round in Kingston. Matches at Kingston and at Drax Hall, near Ocho Rios, are played every week. **Horseraces** are held at Caymanas Race Track, Kingston.

SPECIAL EVENTS: The following is a selection of the major festivals and other special events celebrated annually in Jamaica during 1993/4. For a complete list, contact the Jamaica Tourist Board.

Mar '93 *JAMI Awards* (local music industry awards), Kingston. **Apr** *Carnival*, Kingston; *The Annual Red Stripe International Horse Show & Gymkhana*, Ocho Rios. **May** *Jamaica International Hot Air Balloon Festival and Air Show*, Montpelier. **Jun** *Ikebana International Show* (exhibition). **Jul** *Jamaica Festival Contest and Exhibition Finals*. **Aug** *Reggae Sunsplash* (world's leading reggae stars perform in concerts and at special beach parties), Montego Bay. **Aug 2** *Jamaica Festival Grand Gala*, Kingston. **Sep** *Montego Bay Blue Marlin Tournament*. **Oct** *Port Antonio Blure Marlin Tournament*. **Nov** *Harmony Hall Art Exhibiton*, Ocho Rios. **Dec** *Johnnie Walker World Championships of Golf '93*, Montego Bay. **Feb 6 '94** *Bob Marley's Birthday Bash*.

Throughout the year there are also fishing, equestrian, golf, tennis, fashion, musical and horticultural events.

SOCIAL CONVENTIONS: Handshaking is the customary form of greeting. Normal codes of practice should be observed when visiting someone's home. Jamaicans are generally very hospitable and guests will usually be encouraged to stay for a meal. In these instances a small gift is appreciated. Casual wear is suitable during the day, but shorts and swimsuits must be confined to beaches and poolsides. Evening dress varies from very casual in Negril to quite formal during the season in other resorts, where some hotels and restaurants require men to wear jackets and ties at dinner. In the summer people dress up less. As tourism is a major industry in Jamaica, the visitor is well catered for, and hotel and restaurant staff are generally friendly and efficient. Outside Kingston the pace of life is relaxed and people are welcoming and hospitable. Music and African culture are very apparent, as are old British colonial influences. Signs can be seen on the island claiming 'Jah lives', Jah being the name given to God by the Rastafarians. Possession of marijuana may lead to imprisonment and deportation. Above all the visitor must not try to smuggle it out of the country since the authorities are aware of all the tricks. **Tipping:** Most Jamaican hotels and restaurants add a service charge of 10%. Otherwise 10-15% is expected. Chambermaids, waiters, hotel bellboys and airport porters all expect tips. Taxi drivers receive 10% of the fare.

BUSINESS PROFILE

ECONOMY: Jamaica is the world's largest producer of bauxite and alumina, and the economy has suffered during the 1980s as a result of the low world price and falling demand for the ores. Decisions by the mines' owners, a group of American multinationals, to scale down the level of operations precipitated a major row with the Government which subsequently took control of one of the mines and re-opened it. Tourism has become the major source of foreign exchange and has grown rapidly despite the impact of several hurricanes. Agriculture (principally sugar cane, bananas, coffee and cocoa) has maintained a steady position in the economy, and improved efficiency and production methods offset by climatic conditions and the state of the world markets. Manufacturing is expanding steadily, with cement, textiles, tobacco and other consumer goods among the products. The current Manley government has embarked on a familiar course of privatisation of state-owned enterprises and tight budgetary controls implemented with IMF support. The USA dominates Jamaica's trade, providing half the country's imports and taking over 30% of exports.

BUSINESS: Business people should wear a 'shirtjac' (bush jacket without a tie), known locally as a *kareba*. Usual formalities are required and appointments and business cards are normal. All trade samples now need an import licence which can be obtained from the Trade Administration Department, PO Box 25, The Office Centre, 12 Ocean Boulevard, Kingston. Tel: 922 1840. Samples of non-commercial value are allowed into the country without a licence prior to arrival, although it may still be necessary to visit the office of the Trade Administrator to exchange the licence copy for a clearance copy which the customs authorities demand before clearing the goods. **Office hours:** 0830-1630/1700 Monday to Friday.

COMMERCIAL INFORMATION: The following organisation can offer advice: Jamaica Chamber of Commerce and Associated Chambers of Commerce of Jamaica, PO Box 172, 7-8 East Parade, Kingston. Tel: 922 0150. Fax: 924 9056.

Dunn's River Falls, Ocho Rios

CONFERENCES/CONVENTIONS: The Jamaican Conference Centre in Kingston was opened by HM Queen Elizabeth II in 1983. There are also several hotels in Jamaica with dedicated conference facilities. Seating is available for up to 1000 persons at some centres. The Jamaican Tourist Board (address at top of entry) can supply information.

HISTORY & GOVERNMENT

HISTORY: Initially occupied by the Spanish, then the British in 1655, Jamaica soon became the most important of the British Caribbean slaving colonies. Within 100 years, virtually the whole island had been divided up into large plantations owned by absentee landlords and worked by forced labour imported from West Africa. After the abolition of slavery in 1834, Jamaica became relatively prosperous under orthodox colonial rule until the early 20th century when a spate of natural disasters, compounded by the depression of the 1930s, put the economy into decline. The 1930s also saw the rise of black political activity and trade union organisation, forming in the process the rivalries which characterise modern Jamaican politics. Since independence in 1962, the political arena has been dominated by the struggle between the right-wing Jamaican Labour Party (JLP) and the leftist Peoples National Party (PNP). The JLP held power throughout the 1960s, but lost the national election of 1972 to the PNP under the leadership of Michael Manley, whose father Norman had founded the party. Despite growing economic difficulties, Manley and the PNP were returned to office in 1976 with an increased majority. The next three years brought no improvement in the economy and political violence increased alarmingly, as a result of which the PNP was defeated and the JLP under Edward Seaga formed the next government. Seaga adopted a pro-American stance in economic and foreign affairs, loosening controls on foreign investment in Jamaica and contributing troops to the American-led invasion of Grenada in 1983. Manley was eventually returned to power in 1989. During its current term of office the Manley government has dropped much of the PNP's previous radical agenda, maintaining free market economic policies and almost going out its way to keep on good terms with the USA. Jamaica has also sought closer co-operation with its fellow Caribbean states, particularly at an economic level. A major issue for Jamaica is the rising tide of crime-related and political violence. Despite entreaties from the leaders of both main political parties, the violence shows no sign of abating. Apart from the damage which this is doing to the country's social and political fabric, it is likely to have a bad effect on the economy, negating much of the work which has been put into stimulating its recent growth. This problem must now be confronted by Manley's successor. In poor health, Manley retired in early 1992 and was replaced by his former deputy, P J Patterson.

GOVERNMENT: The Head of State is the British monarch, represented by a Governor-General who has nominal and rarely used powers. The 60-member House of Representatives, which is responsible for legislation, is elected every five years by universal suffrage. An upper house, the Senate, has 21 appointees to ratify legislation.

CLIMATE

Tropical all year. The rainy months are May and October, but showers may occur at any time. Cooler evenings.

Required clothing: Lightweight cottons and linens; light woollens are advised for evenings. Avoid synthetics.

KINGSTON Jamaica (34m)

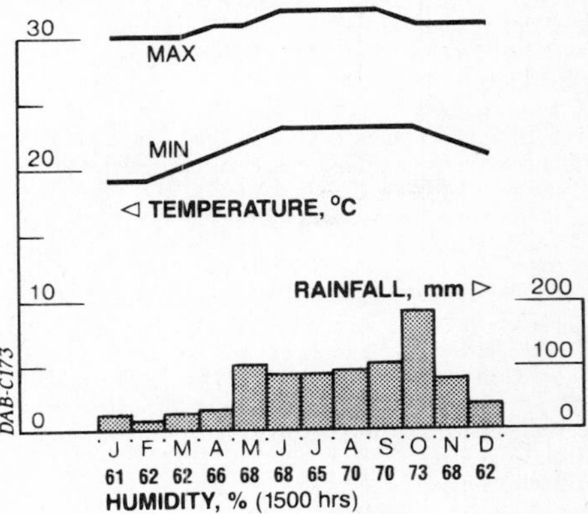

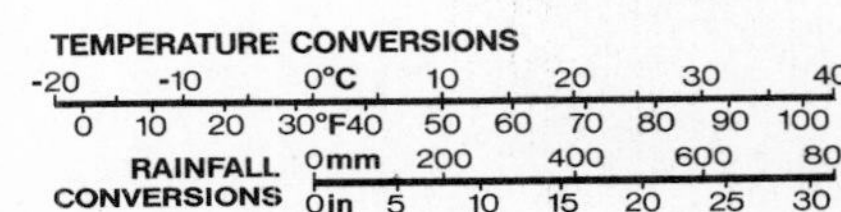

JAPAN

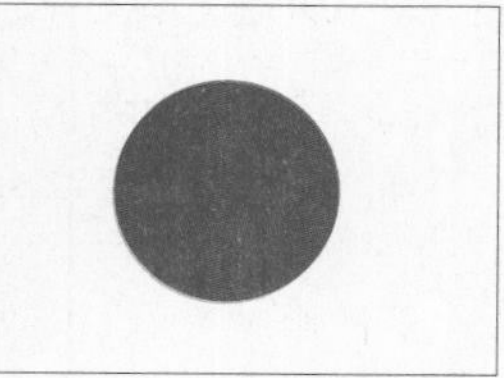

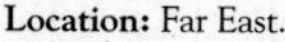

Location: Far East.

Japan National Tourist Organisation
Tokyo Kotsu Kaikan Building
2-10-1 Yuraku-cho
Chiyoda-ku
Tokyo, Japan
Tel: (3) 32 16 19 01. Telex: 24132.

Embassy of Japan
101-104 Piccadilly
London W1V 9FN
Tel: (071) 465 6500. Fax: (071) 491 9348. Opening hours: 0930-1230 and 1430-1630 Monday to Friday.
Consulate in: Edinburgh (tel: (031) 225 4777).

Japan Trade Centre
Leconfield House
Curzon Street
London W1Y 7FB
Tel: (071) 493 7226.

Japan National Tourist Organisation
167 Regent Street
London W1R 7FD
Tel: (071) 734 9638 *or* 734 9639. Fax: (071) 734 4290. Opening hours: 0930-1730 Monday to Friday.

British Embassy
No 1 Ichiban-cho
Chiyoda-ku
Tokyo 102, Japan
Tel: (3) 32 65 55 11. Fax: (3) 52 75 31 64. Telex: 22755.
Consulates in: Osaka, Hiroshima, Fukuoka and Nagoya.

Embassy of Japan
2520 Massachusetts Avenue, NW
Washington, DC
20008
Tel: (202) 939 6700. Fax: (202) 328 2187. Telex: 904017.
Consulates in: Agana, Anchorage, Atlanta, Boston, Chicago, Honolulu, Houston, Kansas City, Los Angeles, New Orleans, New York (tel: (212) 371 8222), Portland, Saipan, San Francisco and Seattle.

Japan National Tourist Organisation
Rockefeller Plaza
630 5th Avenue
New York, NY
10111
Tel: (212) 757 5640. Fax: (212) 307 6754. Telex: 424273 JNTO.

Embassy of the United States of America
PO Box 258
Unit 45004
10-1, Akasaka 1-chome
Minato-ku
Tokyo 107, Japan
Tel: (3) 32 24 50 00. Fax: (3) 35 05 18 62.
Consulates in: Okinawa, Osaka-Kobe, Sapporo and Fukuoka.

Embassy of Japan
255 Sussex Drive
Ottawa, Ontario
K1N 9E6
Tel: (613) 236 8541. Fax: (613) 563 9047.
Consulates in: Edmonton, Halifax, Montréal, Regina, St John's, Toronto, Vancouver and Winnipeg.

Japan National Tourist Organisation
165 University Avenue
Toronto, Ontario
M5H 3B8
Tel: (416) 366 7140. Fax: (416) 366 4530.

Canadian Embassy
3-38 Akasaka 7-chome
Minato-ku
Tokyo 107, Japan
Tel: (3) 34 08 21 01/8. Fax: (3) 34 79 53 20. Telex: 22218 DOMCAN J.

AREA: 377,815 sq km (145,875 sq miles).
POPULATION: 123,156,678 (1991).
POPULATION DENSITY: 325.9 per sq km.
CAPITAL: Tokyo. **Population:** 11,631,901 (1991).
GEOGRAPHY: Japan is separated from the Asian mainland by 160km (100 miles) of sea. About 80% of the country is covered by hills and mountains, a number of which are active or inactive volcanoes. A series of mountain ranges run from northern Hokkaido to southern Kyushu. The Japanese Alps (the most prominent range) run in a north-south direction through central Honshu. The highest mountain is Mount Fuji at 3776m (12,388ft). Lowlands and plains are small and scattered, mostly lying along the coast and composed of alluvial lowlands and diluvial uplands. Largest is Kanto Plain in the Tokyo Bay region. The coastline is very long in relation to the land area, and has very varied features. The deeply indented bays with good natural harbours tend to be adjacent to mountainous terrain.
LANGUAGE: Japanese. Some English is spoken in major cities.
RELIGION: Shintoist and Buddhist (most Japanese follow both religions) with a Christian minority.
TIME: GMT + 9.
ELECTRICITY: 100 volts AC, 60Hz in the west (Osaka). 100 volts AC, 50Hz in eastern Japan and Tokyo. Plugs are flat 2-pin with screw-type light bulbs.

COMMUNICATIONS: Telephone: Full IDD service. Country code: 81. International calls can be made from the KDD (International Telephone and Telegraph Centre) 3-2-5 Kasumigaseki, Chiyoda-ku. International calls can also be placed from hotels. **Fax:** Sending and receiving can be arranged at any hour at major hotels. KDD (Kokusai Denshin Denwa Co Ltd) offers facilities in Tokyo, Osaka, Yokohama and Nagoya.
Telex/telegram: Telex booths are available at main post offices and main offices of Kokusai Denshin Denwa Co Ltd and Nippon Denshin Denwa Kaisha. Telegrams can be sent from the main hotels and from the above companies, also from larger post offices in major cities. Two rates are available. Overseas telegrams can also be sent from the central post office in Tokyo until midnight.
Post: Letters can be taken to the central post office in front of Tokyo Station, which provides English speaking personnel. Airmail to Europe takes four to six days to arrive. All post offices have *Poste Restante* facilities, and will hold mail for up to ten days. Post office hours: 0900-1700 Monday to Friday, 0900-1200 Saturday. **Press:** The English-language daily newspapers in Tokyo include *The Asahi Evening News*, *The Daily Yomiuri*, *The Japan Times* and *The Mainichi Daily News*.
BBC World Service and Voice of America frequencies: From time to time these change. See the section *How to Use this Book* for more information.

BBC:				
MHz	21.72	15.28	9.570	7.180
Voice of America:				
MHz	15.43	11.72	5.985	1.143

PASSPORT/VISA

Regulations and requirements may be subject to change at short notice, and you are advised to contact the appropriate diplomatic or consular authority before finalising travel arrangements. Details of these may be found at the head of this country's entry. Any numbers in the chart refer to the footnotes below.

	Passport Required?	Visa Required?	Return Ticket Required?
Full British	Yes	No/1	Yes
BVP	Not valid	-	-
Australian	Yes	Yes	Yes
Canadian	Yes	No/2	Yes
USA	Yes	No/2	Yes
Other EC	Yes	No/1/2	Yes
Japanese	-	-	-

PASSPORTS: Valid passport required by all.
Note: The Japanese authorities do not recognise: (a) Chinese residents of Taiwan; (b) passports issued by the Democratic People's Republic of Korea; (c) collective passports issued to groups of passengers (other than those issued to a family travelling together); (d) tourists, whether or not they hold a visa, who do not possess visible means of support for tourism, onward or return tickets and other documents for their next destination. Such people may be refused entry.
British Visitors Passport: Not accepted.
VISAS: Required by all except:
(a) **[1]** nationals of Germany, Ireland and United Kingdom for a stay not exceeding 6 months;
(b) **[2]** nationals of Belgium, Canada, Denmark, France, Greece, Italy, Luxembourg, The Netherlands, Portugal, Spain and the USA (diplomatic passport holders *do* require a visa) for a stay not exceeding 3 months;
(c) nationals of Argentina, Bahamas, Barbados, Chile, Colombia, Costa Rica, Cyprus, Dominican Republic, El Salvador, Finland, Guatemala, Honduras, Iceland, Israel, Lesotho, Malaysia, Malta, Mauritius, New Zealand, Norway, Peru (diplomatic passport holders *do* need a visa), San Marino, Singapore, Suriname, Sweden, Tunisia, Turkey, Uruguay and Yugoslavia for a stay not exceeding 3 months;
(d) nationals of Austria, Liechtenstein, Mexico (diplomatic passport holders *do* need a visa) and Switzerland for a stay not exceeding 6 months;
(e) nationals of Brunei for a stay not exceeding 14 days.
Types of visa: Business (cost varies); Transit; Tourist. Prices depend on nature of intended visit: for example, UK and Irish nationals would not normally require a visa, but for long stays or for working visits UK nationals pay £4.90, Indian nationals £3.60; visas for all other nationals usually cost £12.90. Contact the Consulate (or Consular Section at Embassy) for further details.
Validity: Depends on a variety of conditions, including nationality and purpose of visit. Enquire at the Consulate (or Consular Section at Embassy) for further details.
Application to: Consulate (or Consular Section at Embassy). For addresses, see top of entry.
Application requirements: (a) Passport. (b) Completed

JAPAN | **HEALTH REGULATIONS** | **VISA REGULATIONS** | Code-Link

GALILEO/WORLDSPAN

TI-DFT/TYO/HE

TI-DFT/TYO/VI

SABRE

TIDFT/TYO/HE

TIDFT/TYO/VI

To access this information on your CRS, swipe the barcode with a light pen or type in the text under the barcode. For more information, see the introduction *How to Use This Book*.

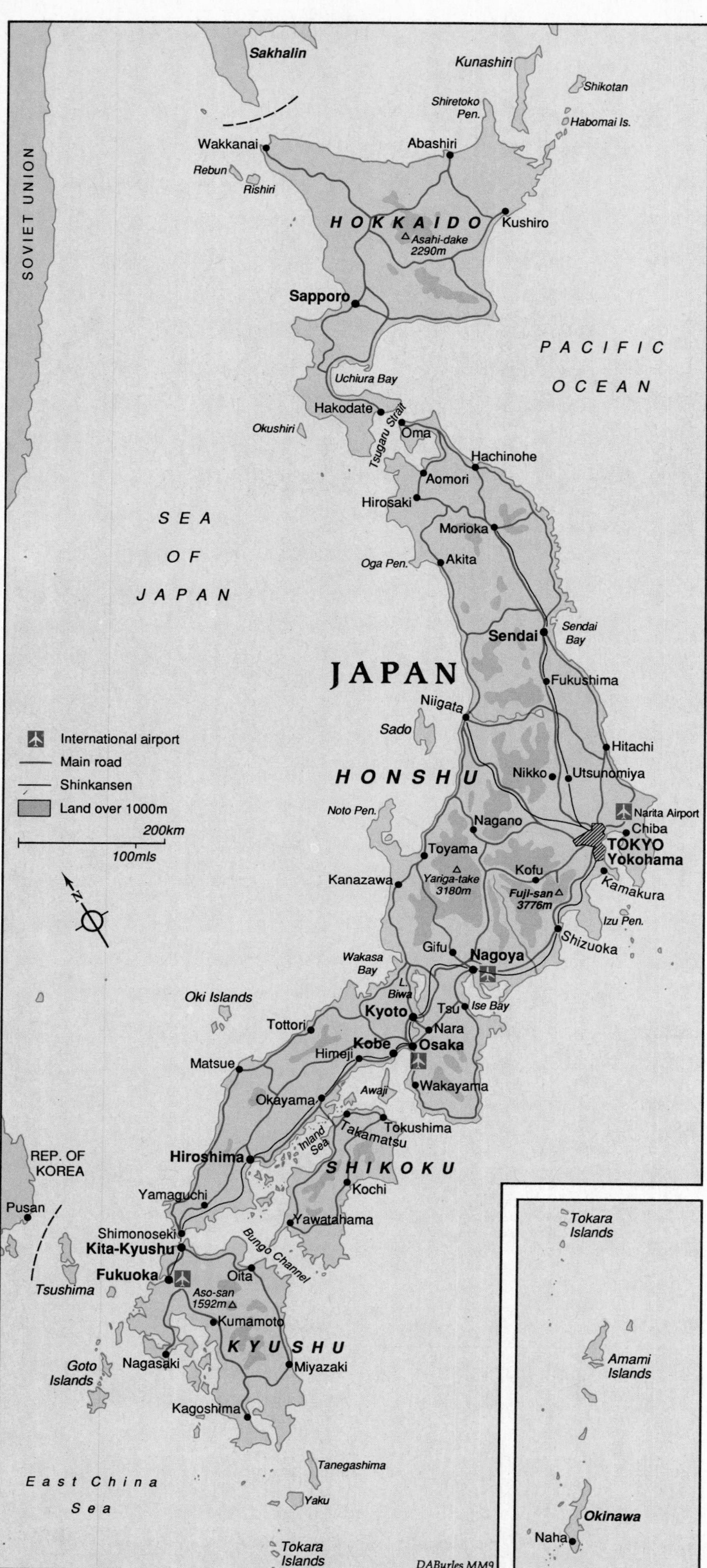

application form. (c) 1 passport-size photograph. (d) Return air/sea ticket or copy. (e) A letter of introduction (for business visas).

Note: Nationals of Communist and Middle Eastern countries must submit 2 completed visa application forms and 2 photos.

Working days required: 7 days.

MONEY

Currency: Japanese Yen (¥) = 100 sen. Notes are in denominations of ¥10,000, 5000 and 1000. Coins are in denominations of ¥500, 100, 50, 10, 5 and 1.

Currency exchange: All money must be exchanged at an authorised bank or money changer.

Credit cards: Visa, Diners Club, American Express, Access/Mastercard and other major credit cards are widely used. Check with your credit card company for merchant acceptability and for other facilities which may be available.

Travellers cheques: These can be exchanged at major banks and larger hotels.

Exchange rate indicators: The following figures are included as a guide to the movements of the Japanese Yen against Sterling and the US Dollar:

Date:	Oct '89	Oct '90	Oct '91	Oct '92
£1.00=	225.25	250.25	224.50	193.50
$1.00=	142.65	128.10	129.36	121.93

Currency restrictions: Import of local currency is unrestricted; export is limited to ¥5,000,000. There are no restrictions on the import or export of foreign currency.

Banking hours: 0900-1500 Monday to Friday.

DUTY FREE

The following goods may be imported into Japan without incurring customs duty:

400 cigarettes or 100 cigars or 500g of tobacco;
3 bottles (approx 760cc each) of spirits;
2oz perfume;
Gifts up to the value of ¥200,000.

Note: Tobacco and alcohol allowances are for those aged 20 or over. Oral declaration is necessary on arrival at Customs.

Prohibited items: Guns, pornograhy and narcotic drugs.

PUBLIC HOLIDAYS

Public holidays in Japan are as follows:

Apr 29 '93 Greenery Day. **May 3** Constitution Memorial Day. **May 5** Children's Day. **Sep 15** Respect for the Aged Day. **Sep 23/24** Autumnal Equinox Day. **Oct 10** Health Sports Day. **Nov 3** Culture Day. **Nov 23** Labour Thanksgiving Day. **Dec 23** Birthday of the Emperor. **Jan 1 '94** New Year's Day. **Jan 15** Coming of Age Day. **Feb 11** National Foundation Day. **Mar 21/20** Vernal Equinox Day.

Note: (a) If a holiday falls on a Sunday, the following day is treated as a holiday. (b) Over the New Year, almost all shops are closed January 1-3.

HEALTH

Regulations and requirements may be subject to change at short notice, and you are advised to contact your doctor well in advance of your intended date of departure. Any numbers in the chart refer to the footnotes below.

	Special Precautions?	Certificate Required?
Yellow Fever	No	No
Cholera	No	No
Typhoid & Polio	Yes	-
Malaria	No	-
Food & Drink	No	-

Health care: Health insurance is *strongly* recommended. The International Association for Medical Assistance to Travellers provides English-speaking doctors. There are hospitals in major cities such as Tokyo, Osaka, Kyoto, Kobe, Hiroshima and Okinawa.

TRAVEL - International

AIR: Japan's largest airline is *Japan Air Lines (JL)*.

Approximate flight times: From *Anchorage* to Tokyo is 7 hours 20 minutes. From *Hong Kong* to Osaka is 3 hours. From *London* to Tokyo is 11 hours 30 minutes on a non-stop flight (stopover can add a further 5 or 6 hours) and to Osaka is 15 hours. From *New York* to Tokyo is 14 hours. From *Los Angeles* to Tokyo is 10 hours. From *Singapore* to Tokyo is 7 hours 30 minutes. From *Sydney* to Tokyo is 10 hours.

International airports: *New Tokyo International Airport (TYO)* (Narita City) is 66km (41 miles) northeast of Tokyo (travel time – 1 hour 10 minutes). There is a bus

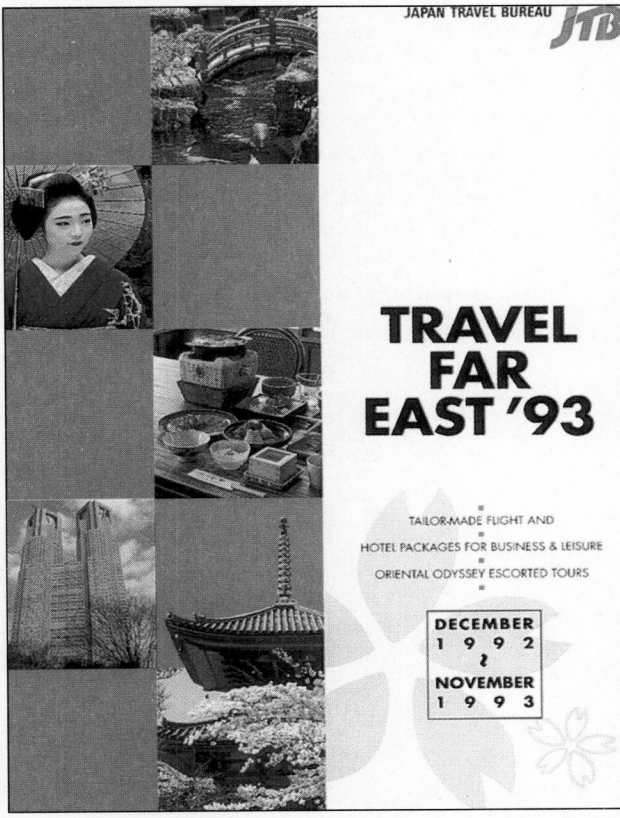

to the city air terminal every 10 minutes from 0700-2400 then taxi to hotels (bus tickets are bought in the terminal). The journey from Tokyo City Air Terminal, located at Hakozaki, Nihombashi, to Tokyo Central Station takes 15 minutes by bus or taxi. There is a coach to major hotels every 20-50 minutes, 0700-2100. JR Narita Express line runs from Narita station terminal located beneath the airport to Tokyo station (53 mins, ¥2890), Shinjuku (80 mins, ¥3050), Yokohama (90 mins, ¥4100) every hour and every half-hour at busy periods from 0745-2145. Keisei 'Skyliner Train' also runs from the airport terminal to Keisei Ueno Station (60 mins, ¥1630) from 0750-2200. There are taxis to the city, with a surcharge after 2200 (60-70 minutes). Airport facilities include an outgoing duty-free shop, bank/exchange from 0900-2400 and car hire: *Nippon Renter Car*.

A second Terminal opened on December 6, 1992, with its own Japan Railways and Keisei Line station in the basement. There is also a free shuttle bus connecting both terminals every 10-15 minutes (travel time – 10 minutes). The Terminal itself consists of a main and a satellite building connected by a fully automated shuttle.

Osaka International (OSA) (Itami) is 20km (12 miles) northwest of Osaka. There is a bus to the city every 20 minutes from 0800-2120 (travel time – 30 minutes). Return is from the coach terminal, Umeda, and there are pick-ups at major hotels from 0620-2020. A train goes to the city every 15 minutes from 0432-2350. Return is from Hankyu railway station, Umeda (train to Hotarugaike station) from 0500-0007. There are buses to the city every 20 minutes from 0808-2130. Return is from Osaka bus station, Maru Building, every 10 minutes from 0612-2012. Taxis to the city impose a surcharge after 2200. Airport facilities include an outgoing duty-free shop, car hire, bank/exchange and bar/restaurant.

Fukuoka International (FUK) is 25 minutes travel time from Fukuoka City. Airport facilities include an outgoing duty-free shop, car hire, bank/exchange and bar/restaurant.

Nagoya International (NGO) has flights to Hong Kong, Seoul, Bangkok, Singapore, Honolulu, Taipei, Brisbane, Melbourne and Sydney.

Departure tax: ¥2000 is levied at *New Tokyo International Airport*. None at other airports.

SEA: Japan is easily accessible by sea, and passenger ships include the major ports on their schedules. The *Royal Viking Line's* world cruise puts in at Kobe and there are also cruises between the Japanese islands en route to Shanghai and Hong Kong. The *Pearl of Scandinavia* leaves from Kobe on a cruise along the coast of China.

RAIL: The Trans-Siberian route to Japan is an interesting and very well-organised, if lengthy, trip. Connections can be made daily from London (Liverpool Street) via Harwich or London (Victoria) via Dover through Europe to Moscow. There are sleeping cars four times a week from Hook of Holland to Moscow, and twice a week from Ostend to Moscow. The route from Moscow can be either by air, train and boat or train and boat via Khabarovsk and Nakhodka (a port east of Vladivostok) to Yokohama.

TRAVEL - Internal

AIR: Services are run by *Japan Airlines (JL)*, *All Nippon Airways (NH)* and *TOA Domestic Airlines (JD)*. Japanese Airlines provides English-speaking hostesses and ground staff and links major cities, whereas the others serve similar routes and smaller towns.

Tokyo's domestic airport is *Haneda*. A monorail service runs from Hamamatsu-cho to Haneda. International flights from Haneda are made via Japan's international airports, see above. Main routes are Tokyo/Sapporo; Tokyo/Fukuoka; Tokyo/Osaka; and Tokyo/Naha. Tickets can be purchased at automatic machines at *Tokyo International Airport's* domestic departure counter and at *Osaka International Airport*.

RAIL: Japan's rail network is one of the best in the world, and is widely used for both business and pleasure. Very frequent services run on the main routes. *Shinkansen*, the 'Bullet Trains', are the fastest, with compartments for wheelchair passengers, diners and buffet cars. Supplements are payable on the three classes of express train and in 'Green' (first-class) cars of principal trains, for which reservations must be made.

Japan Rail Pass: An economical pass for foreign tourists, which must be purchased before you arrive in Japan can be obtained from *Japan Airlines* (*JL* users only), Japan Travel Bureau, Miki Travel, Nippon Travel Agency, Tokyu Travel Europe and Kintetsu International Express. It can also be used on JR buses and JR ferries.

Hotel reservation tickets can also be bought with bullet-train tickets. See the *Japan Rail Pass* brochure available from the Tourist Board. Express and 'limited express' trains are best for intercity.

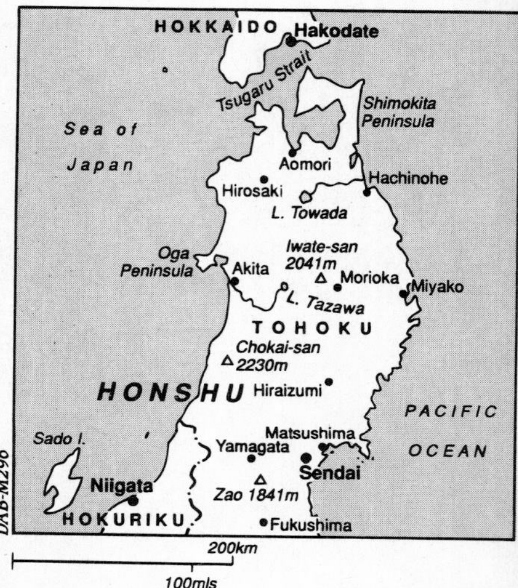

ROAD: Driving around Japan is not recommended: it can be daunting, as there are few English road signs and the roads are crowded. Traffic in cities is congested and driving in urban areas is to be avoided. Driving is on the left. The Keiyo Highway, Tohoku Expressway, Tomei Expressway and the Meishin Expressway link Japan's major Pacific coastal cities, passing through excellent scenery. **Documentation:** An International Driving Permit is required.

URBAN: Public transport is well developed, efficient and crowded. The **underground** systems and privately-run suburban rail services, which serve all the main cities, are very convenient but best avoided in rush hours. **Buses** can be confusing and are best used with someone who knows the system. Otherwise get exact details of your destination from your hotel. Fares systems are highly automated, particularly rail and underground, but passes may be available. On buses, payment may be made on leaving. Tokyo has a very large public transport network of buses, tramways, two underground systems and half a dozen private railways. The underground, tramway and bus services, run by the Tokyo Transportation Bureau, have a flat central area fare and stage fares elsewhere. Books of tickets can be bought. The Eidan underground is a bigger seven-line system.

Taxis: There is a minimum charge for the first 2km (1.2 miles) and there is a time charge in slow traffic. It is advisable for the visitor to have prepared in advance the name and address of his destination in Japanese writing together with the name of some nearby landmark; a map may also help. Hotels can help with this.

JOURNEY TIMES: The following chart gives approximate journey times (in hours and minutes) from Tokyo to other major cities/towns in the country.

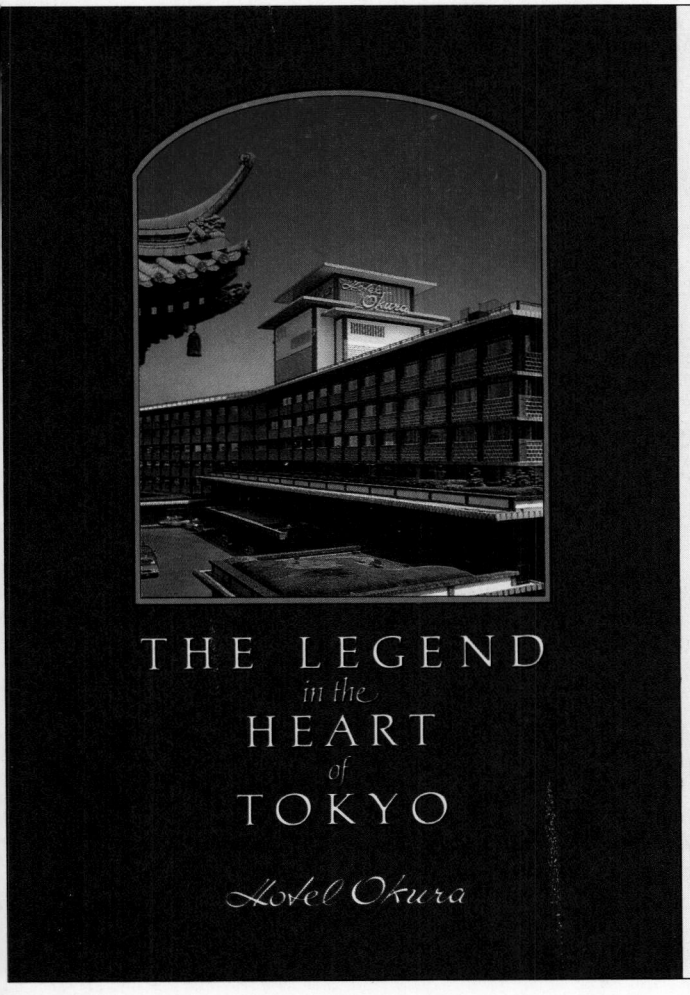

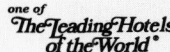

	Air	Road	Rail	Sea
Nagoya	-	4.00	2.00	-
Kagoshima	1.50	26.00	10.00	48.00
Fukuoka	1.45	13.00	6.30	-
Nagasaki	1.55	18.00	9.00	-
Okinawa	2.30	-	-	60.00
Osaka	1.00	6.00	3.15	-
Sapporo	1.25	-	15.00	-

ACCOMMODATION

HOTELS: Hotels are 'Western' or 'Japanese' style, sometimes both. Western is much like any modern American or European hotel. Japanese style is comfortable and provides an exciting new experience; for instance, in some hotels the Japanese tea ceremony is demonstrated. Many non-obligatory extras are available. Service charges of 10-15% and taxes of 3% (6% if hotel charge exceeds ¥10,000 per night) are added to the bill. **Grading:** No accommodation grading system operates in Japan. For further information contact the Japan Hotel Association, Shin Otemachi Building, 2-2-1 Otemachi, Chiyoda-ku, Toyko 100. Tel: (3) 32 79 27 06. Fax: (3) 32 74 53 75; *or* The Japan Tourist Hotel Association, Kokusai Kanko Kaikan, 8-3 Marunouchi 1-chrome, Chiyoda-ku, Toyko 100. Tel: (3) 32 31 53 30. Fax: (3) 32 01 55 68.

GUEST-HOUSES: Staying at a *ryokan*, a traditional inn, is one of the real delights of Japan. Japanese-style inns are rarely cheaper than their Western-style equivalents; usually, however, breakfast and dinner – generally Japanese dishes – are included in the overnight rates. Full facilities are provided. No shoes are worn in the house as slippers are provided. Small gifts or 5% may be given with bill.

YOUTH HOSTELS: There are many Youth Hostels throughout Japan. Contact Japan Youth Hostels Inc, Hoken Kaikan, 1-2 Sadohara-cho, 1-Chome, Ichigaya, Shinjuku, Tokyo 162. Tel: (3) 32 69 58 31.

RESORTS & EXCURSIONS

Japan is a chain of mountainous islands lying off the coasts of China and, in the far north of Hokkaido, of the CIS. Much of the land is unsuitable for agriculture and remains as forest. The coastline is indented with numerous bays and inlets.

Tokyo: There is much to see in the capital: the *Emperor's Palace* with its grounds set out as a park; *Ginza*, the shopping and entertainment area; *Shinjuku*, the western quarter with a national park, the *Botanical Garden* and the *Meiji Shrine*. There is a thriving nightlife: clubs, theatres, music and food from all over the world.

From Tokyo visitors can go to see the *Boso Peninsula* and **Shirahama** with its fine beaches; **Narita**, a pilgrimage centre; **Mito**, particularly in February when it is covered with plum blossoms; **Mashiko**, the bonsai and pottery centre; **Bonsai Village**; **Ogawa-machi**, the home of paper making and most of all **Nikko** which, set in a national park, and with splendid temples and mausoleums, is one of the most visited sites in the country.

Fuji-Hakone-Izu: This area, which contains *Mount Fuji*, Japan's highest mountain, is one of great appeal to the visitor. Attractions include *Fuji Five Lakes* and a hot spring resort, **Hakone**; swimming and boating and facilities for skating, hiking, fishing and camping are available.

Japanese Alps: These mountains, in the centre of **Honshu Island,** are popular with both native and foreign climbers.

Nagoya is one of the major industrial cities, as well as

TOKYO

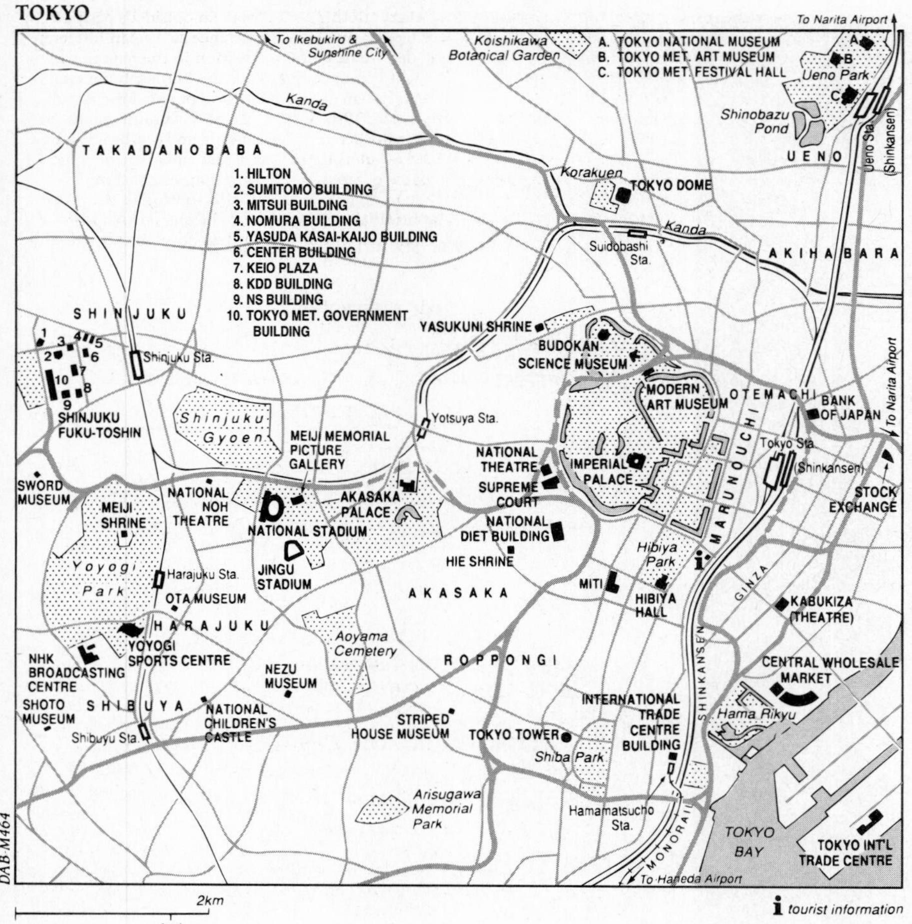

being a centre for traditional handicrafts. It is within easy reach of the Alps and the *Ise-Shima National Park*. **Kyoto** was founded in AD794 as a ceremonial capital built in the classical Chinese style. It is best seen on foot. Visitors can stroll round the temples, palaces and shrines, see the Zen headquarters and walk through the quiet streets with their workshops of the textile weavers.

Nara dates back from the earliest days of the Japanese people. It draws a million visitors a year to see its traditional house, the 5-storey pagoda of *Kofuku-ji*, its ancient statues and ceremonial buildings and its famous *Great Buddha Hall* – the largest wooden structure in the world – and the world's largest bronze statue, that of Buddha.

Nagasaki is said to be Japan's first international city. There is the *Peace Park* to see, as well as *Glover House* (the site of 'Madame Butterfly'), the *Chinese Temple*, the *Spectacles Bridge*, the *Suwa Shrine*, the hot springs and *Mount Aso*, the largest active volcano in the world.

SOCIAL PROFILE

FOOD & DRINK: Japanese cuisine, now popular in the west, involves very sensitive flavours, fresh crisp vegetables and an absence of richness. Specialities include *teriyaki* (marinated beef grilled in oil), *sukiyaki* (thin slices of beef, bean curd and vegetables cooked in soy sauce and then dipped in egg), *tempura* (deep fried seafood and vegetables), *sushi* (slices of raw seafood placed on lightly-vinegared rice balls – very refreshing and not as gruesome as it sounds), and *sashimi* (slices of raw seafood dipped in soy sauce). The best place to try these is a *Kaiten* (sushi bar), where many varieties pass the customer on a conveyor belt allowing complete choice over which delicacies to try. Fine Oriental food (Korean – very hot – and Chinese) is served in restaurants. Western dishes in expensive places are good but cheaper restaurants tend to be disappointing. Restaurants have table service and in many places it is customary to remove footwear. **Drink:** *Sake*, hot rice wine is strong and distinctively fresh-tasting. *Shochu*, a strong aquavit, is an acquired taste. Japanese wines are worth trying once, and beer – similar to lager – is recommended. Popular brands are *Kirin*, *Sapporo*, *Suntory* and *Asahi*. Waiter service is common in bars. The Japanese are very fond of original Scotch Whisky, but this is both very expensive and highly sought after; therefore Japanese versions of this drink are often consumed. There are no licensing hours. Drinking is subject to long-standing rituals of politeness. The hostess will pour a drink for the visitor, and will insist on the visitor's glass being full. The host will also appreciate the visitor pouring drinks for him but it is bad manners for a visitor to pour one for himself.

NIGHTLIFE: Abundant cinemas, bars, coffee shops and night clubs. In the summer the rooftop beer gardens are busy and street cafés are becoming popular. Some clubs have hostesses who expect to be bought drinks and snacks. In bigger night clubs and bars a basic hostess charge is levied. However, there are thousands of other bars and clubs. In Tokyo there are concerts almost every night where several symphony orchestras perform, as do soloists and ensembles. Foreign opera companies, ballet companies and orchestras visit Japan all year round. Tickets should be bought in advance because shows are quickly sold out. *Play Guides* ticket offices are situated in major department stores. *Karaoke* bars are a very popular form of entertainment (or embarrassment!) in Japan and are well worth a visit.

SHOPPING: A blend of Oriental goods and Western sales techniques confront the shopper, particularly at the big department stores, which are more like exhibitions than shops. Playgrounds for children are available. Special purchases: *kimonos*, *mingei* (local crafts including kites and folk toys); *Kyoto* silks, fans, screens, dolls; religious articles such as *Shinto* and Buddhist artefacts; paper lanterns; hi-fi equipment, cameras, televisions and other electronic equipment. **Tax exemptions** are available on presentation of passport. Bargaining is not usual. **Shopping hours:** 1000-1900.

SPORT: A great variety of sports are available. **Sumo**, ceremonial wrestling, and **judo** are Japan's national sports, drawing huge crowds. There are opportunities for the visitor to purchase a costume and learn some of the techniques. Classes are for men and women and in most large schools English is spoken. **Kendo**, Japanese fencing, is spectacular and practised in numerous clubs and college halls. **Baseball** is the favourite team sport with the season lasting almost all year round. There are day and night games and tickets are reasonably priced and widely available. **Golf** is very popular with businessmen and there are excellent courses in and around Tokyo. It is expensive, as in most countries, and there are some courses where membership is required or it is only possible to play by invitation.

SPECIAL EVENTS: A large number of festivals are celebrated in Japan throughout the year in different parts of the country. Some are hugely spectacular, others are religiously orientated. The following are a selection of annual events and festivals. For full details of events in 1993/4, contact the Japan National Tourist Organisation.

May 9-23 '93 *Sumo Tournaments*, Tokyo. **May 15** *Aoi Matsuri* (Hollyhock Festival of Shimogamo and Kamigamo Shrines), Kyoto. **May 17-18** *Toshogu Haru-no-Taisai* (procession of people dressed in samurai costume), Nikko City. **Jun 15** *Chagu-Chagu Umakko* (procession of horses), Moriaka City. **Jul 4-18** *Sumo Tournaments*, Nagoya. **Jul 16-17** *Gion Matsuri*, Yasaka Shrine, Kyoto. **Jul 24-25** *Tenjin Matsuri*, Tenmangu Shrine, Osaka. **Aug 5-7** *Kanto*, Akita City. **Aug 8** *Nebuta Matsuri*, Aomori; *Tanabata Matsuri* (elaborate and colourful paper displays), Sendai City. **Aug 12-15** *Awa Odori* (with singing and dancing in the streets). **Sep** *Sumo Tournaments*, Tokyo. **Oct 7-9** *Kunchi Festival*, Nagasaki. **Oct 22** *Jidai Matsuri* (Festival of Eras, commemorating the founding of Kyoto), Heian Shrine, Kyoto. **Jan 1 '94** *Festival of the Festivals* (celebrating New Year's Day); *Toka Ebisu Festival* (with prayers offered to the god of business), Osaka; *Sumo Tournaments*, Tokyo. **Feb** *Bean*

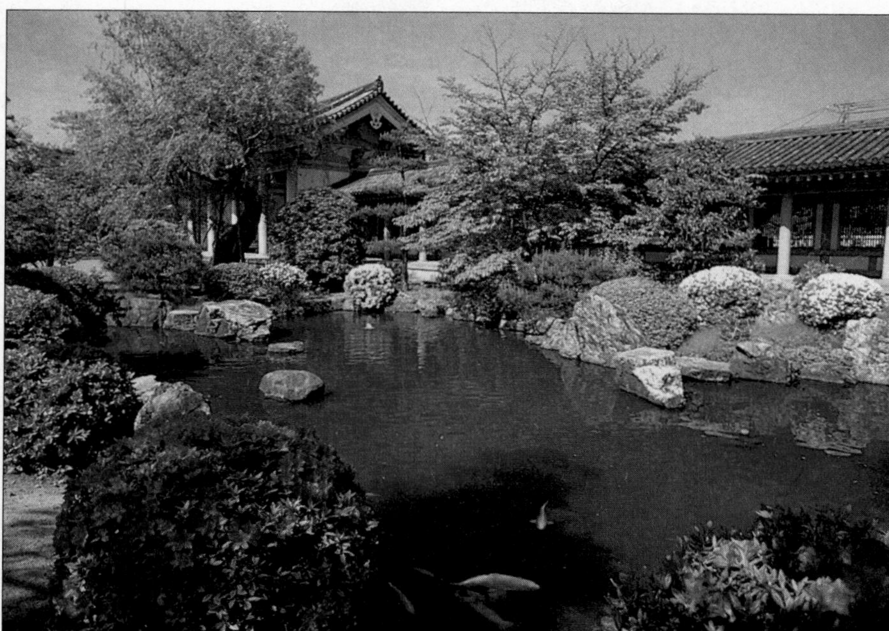

Throwing Festival (marking the end of winter). **Feb 3-14** *Alpine World Ski Championships*, Morioka. **Feb 5-11** *Snow Festival*, Sapporo. **Mar** *Sumo Tournaments*, Osaka. **Mar 3** *Hinamatsuri* (Doll Festival).

SOCIAL CONVENTIONS: Japanese manners and customs are vastly different from those of western people. A strict code of behaviour and politeness is recognised and followed by almost all Japanese. However, they are aware of the difference between themselves and the West and therefore do not expect visitors to be familiar with all their customs but expect them to behave formally and politely. A straightforward refusal does not form part of Japanese etiquette, in fact the word 'no' does not exist in the Japanese vocabulary. A vague 'yes' does not really mean 'yes' but the visitor may be comforted to know that confusion caused by non-committal replies occurs between the Japanese themselves. Entertaining guests at home is not as customary as in the West, as it is an enterprise not taken lightly and the full red-carpet treatment is given. Japanese men are also sensitive lest their wives be embarrassed and feel that their hospitality is inadequate by Western standards; for instance, by the inconvenience to a foreign guest of the custom of sitting on the floor. Bowing is the customary greeting but handshaking is becoming more common for business meetings with Westerners. The suffix *san* should be used when addressing all men and women; for instance Mr Yamada would be addressed as Yamada-san. When entering a Japanese home or restaurant it is customary to remove shoes. Table manners are very important, although the Japanese host will be very tolerant towards a visitor. However, it is best if visitors familiarise themselves with basic table etiquette and use chopsticks. It is customary for a guest to bring a small gift when visiting someone's home. Exchange of gifts is also a common business practice and may take the form of souvenir items such as company pens, ties or high quality spirits. Smoking is only restricted where notified. **Tipping:** Tips are never expected; where a visitor wishes to show particular appreciation of a service, money should not be given in the form of loose change but rather as a small financial gift. Special printed envelopes can be bought for financial gifts of this type.

BUSINESS PROFILE

ECONOMY: Japan is the economic phenomenon of the late 20th century: Japan's Gross National Product ranks second in the world after the United States. A variety of factors have contributed to the country's current prevailing success. A wholly modern economy built up following the devastation of the Second World War was not hampered, in the manner of the American and some European economies, by a large defence commitment. Judicious application of import controls is coupled with a uniquely aggressive export drive orchestrated by the powerful Ministry of International Trade and Industry (MITI), while an exceptionally high savings ratio in proportion to net earnings has fuelled a consistently high level of industrial investment in manufacturing industries which have honed the process of cutting overheads down to a fine art. Finally, the structure of the Japanese domestic economy revolves around a series of large multi-product corporations serviced with components and raw materials by a plethora of small firms with low overheads and labour costs (a function increasingly met by the 'Tiger' economies of the Pacific Basin: Singapore, South Korea, Taiwan and Hong Kong), and using a distribution system which foreign companies complain is especially restrictive. The result is a US$3000 billion Gross National Product and an annual trade surplus of US$100 billion. Manufactured goods are the strongest sector, particularly vehicles and electronic goods, although traditional industries such as coal mining, ship building and steel are also profitable. The only sector which does not measure up to Western standards at present is agriculture which is inefficient and heavily protected by the Government, partly as a result of the vagaries of the Japanese electoral system. Rice farming, for instance, is one of a variety of issues behind the apparently serious trade row between Japan and the United States: the USA alleges rice imports are being unfairly restricted to protect Japanese farmers. Conversely, there have been many occasions of Western nations complaining about the 'dumping' of cheap Japanese goods in already saturated markets. The newest and fastest growing sector of the Japanese economy is financial services – despite the sharp decline since 1990, the Tokyo Stock Exchange is the largest in the world in terms of the value of shares traded – and, here again, American and European companies complain of discrimination (such as the exclusion of British market-makers from the Tokyo market). These routine allegations cannot disguise the massive success of the post-war Japanese economy, especially given the almost total lack of raw materials (particularly oil). The USA has a 20% share of Japan's US$150 billion (1982 figures) import market, followed by Korea and Indonesia (5.5%), Australia, China, Taiwan and Saudi Arabia (5%). The emphasis in Japanese trade is slowly switching from manufactured goods to exports of services and 'invisibles' (such as finance and insurance). Overseas investments are growing rapidly, particularly in property: property prices within Japan itself are reaching astronomical levels and a crash in the domestic market was widely forecast in 1991. This duly occurred and triggered economic slowdown in 1992, although most observers think this is unlikely to be serious or long-lasting. Japan's trade surplus continues to set new records, to which MITI has responded with a commitment to spend US$1 billion in 1992/93 promoting imports.

BUSINESS: A large supply of visiting cards printed in English and Japanese is essential. Cards can be quickly printed on arrival with Japanese translation on the reverse side. Appointments should be made in advance, and, because of the formality, visits should consist of more than a few days. Punctuality is important. Business discussions are often preceded by tea and are usually very formal. **Office hours:** 0900-1700 Monday to Friday.

COMMERCIAL INFORMATION: The following organisations can offer advice: Nippon Shoko Kaigi-sho, (Japan Chamber of Commerce and Industry), 2-2, 3-chome, Marunouchi, Chiyoda-ku, Tokyo. Tel: (3) 32 83 78 51. Fax: (3) 32 11 48 59; *or*

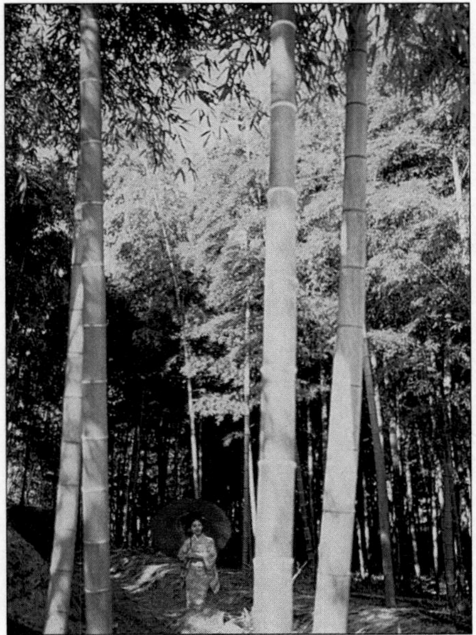

Japanese Chamber of Commerce, 2nd Floor, Salisbury House, 29 Finsbury Circus, London EC2M 5QQ. Tel: (071) 628 0069. Fax: (071) 628 0248.

CONFERENCES/CONVENTIONS: The Japan Convention Bureau is a division of the Japan National Tourist Organisation (address at top of entry); its *Convention Planner's Guide to Japan* lists 25 cities with conference facilities including Tokyo, Kyoto, Osaka, Yokohama, Hiroshima and Nagasaki. In 1991 there were 1244 international meetings in Japan with 61,123 participating foreign delegates. During that year, Kyoto proved to be the most favourite meeting destination for the second consecutive year, hosting 209 conventions. For further information contact the Japan Convention Bureau, 2-10-1 Yurakucho, Chiyoda-ku, Toyko 100. Tel: (3) 32 16 29 05. Fax: (3) 32 14 76 80.

HISTORY & GOVERNMENT

HISTORY: Until the late 16th century Japan was governed by a group of feudal barons, most of whose energies were devoted to warring amongst themselves. External threats, such as attempted Mongol invasions in the late 13th century, nonetheless served to unite the various factions against the common enemy and create a latent national consciousness which emerged gradually over the next 300 years. The actual unification of Japan began during the *Tokugawa* period 1600-1868, during which a national administrative hierarchy was forged from the family structures of the ruling class. During this period the *shogun*, a powerful warlord, retained supreme executive power. One of the hallmarks of this period from an outsider's perspective was Japan's unyielding resistance to foreign influence; and despite its powerful position in the region, which brought it into contact with the European imperial powers, Japan conducted a kind of anti-foreign policy. In the late 19th century, as the *Tokugawa* regime eventually declined into inertia and profligacy, a new breed of rulers took control and embarked on a programme of rapid industrialisation, establishing a Western-style system of administration in the process. Executive power reverted to the emperor. Japan's imperial ambitions in East Asia developed during this period, exemplified by the occupation of Korea in 1905 after the defeat of its main imperial rival, Russia, in a war which had begun the previous year. The Japanese took little active part in the First World War, despite a formal declaration of war on Germany, but Japanese factories produced munitions and supplies for the allies throughout. In the 1920s and 1930s, Japan resumed its expansionist regional policies, with China as the main target. Coming up against the British, who had substantial political and economic interests in China, it contributed to the subsequent alliance with Germany in the Second World War. Between 1938 and 1941 Japan's forces occupied China and South-East Asia, expelling the British from Singapore, Malaysia and Hong Kong. The American entry into the war turned the balance against the Japanese, who were slowly pushed back over the following four years, finally surrendering after the nuclear attacks on Hiroshima and Nagasaki. Japan was occupied by American troops, and in 1946, the Americans imposed the constitution that governs Japan today. The main political party, the Liberal Democratic Party, was formed in 1955 from a coalition of centre-right groups and has held power ever since, taking slightly under 50% of the vote at successive elections. Japan's political activity and prominence abroad does not yet match the external influence enjoyed by its economy. The LDP's monopoly of power has been shaken since 1989 by a succession of financial and other scandals which now threaten to undermine the Japanese political system: ossified and endemically corrupt as it is, that would probably be no bad thing. The main opposition, the Socialist Party, led by Japan's leading woman politician Takako Doi, has made some inroads into the overwhelming LDP majority but has not yet seriously threatened it. Japan acquired a new Emperor in 1989 when Akihito suceeded his father Hirohito. The role and status of the Emperor is a sensitive issue in modern Japan. Despite the Americans' best efforts, Hirohito was never fully rehabilitated because of his knowledge of Japanese war crimes; Akihito represents a new generation of Emperor whom observers of royalty expect to adopt the style of European monarchs rather than the inaccessible demi-god status of his predecessors. As for his country, Akihito's 'descent to mortality' should coincide with Japan's assumption of a profile in the international community more consistent with its economic muscle, although several instances during the early 1990s suggest that this may be some time in coming. The Japanese contribution to the anti-Iraqi coalition was exclusively financial: the sum proffered, totalling US$4 billion, was provided, or so it appeared in some Western capitals, somewhat reluctantly. The American-drafted constitution imposed upon Japan after 1945 forbade the deployment of Japanese military personnel outside the country (but see below). Nor has Tokyo's foreign policy been outstandingly successful elsewhere: Japan proved to be the exception to the Soviet Union's trail-blazing diplomacy from the mid-1980s onwards. The reason is a territorial dispute over ownership of the Northern Territories (as the Japanese refer to them), known as the Kurile Islands by the Russian Federation, under whose jurisdiction the islands fall. The island lie off the northern coast of Hokkaido amid rich fishing grounds and perhaps large mineral deposits. To the west, the development of Japanese relations with the European Community are broadly governed by a declaration of intent on future political and economic co-operation made at a mini-summit between representatives of the two in 1991. Trade imbalance and access to markets are the main issues of contention between the two but the divisions are not yet as pronounced as those between the US and Japan. The area where Japan has made most progress in its own backyard of East Asia, where memories of Japan's brutal occupation are gradually fading (though they are still an important political consideration): awkward bilateral relations, such as those with the Koreans – both North and South – have undergone notable improvement. Japan now invests more in the Pacific Basin region than in the United States and under the new world order, Japan is assuming the principal role in guaranteeing regional security. In June

1992, after nearly two years of fractious debate, the Diet passed a law permitting Japanese troops to be stationed overseas. Rigorous conditions upon their deployment essentially limit them to peacekeeping functions. Relations with China continue to be particularly sensitive, a legacy of the Japanese occupation during the 1930s and 40s, despite formal normalisation in 1972. Back at home, Toshiiki Kaifu was unceremoniously dumped in mid-1991; three of five main LDP faction leaders emerged to claim the premiership. All led factions of roughly equal size, and the nomination turned on the support of Shin Manemaru, the party 'godfather' without whose sanction nothing happened (he has now departed, a victim of a financial scandal). The victor was Kiichi Miyazawa, a former Finance Ministry official and deputy premier who, at 72, was taking his last shot at the top job. Miyazawa has found himself presiding over what is, by post-war standards, an unprecedented economic crisis. The stock market has halved in value since 1990 and property prices have fallen sharply, pushing a number of banks and financial institutions, who hold many of their assets in those forms, into debt. GDP growth has slowed, and overseas investment has declined from the record levels of two years ago. Most, but not all, Japan-watchers believe that the downturn is strictly temporary and ephemeral; however, there is a growing school of thought which interprets recent economic indicators as portending a protracted recession, followed by banking collapse and global trade wars, to which the government will be unable to respond adequately.

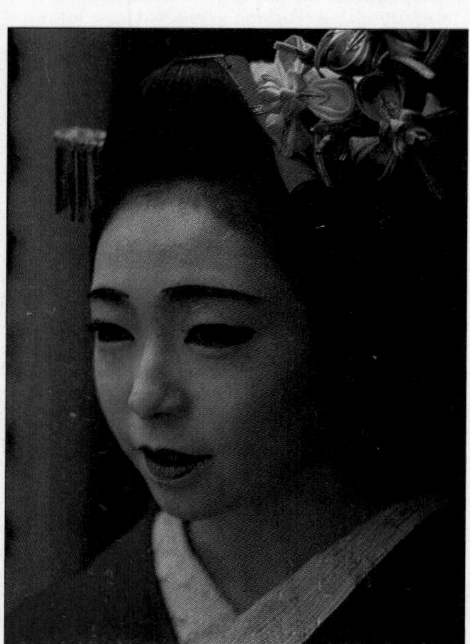

GOVERNMENT: The Japanese parliament, the *Diet*, has an upper and lower house with 252 and 511 members respectively, elected for 6- and 4-year terms respectively. The Diet approves the appointment of a Prime Minister who holds executive power with the assistance of a Cabinet of Ministers; the appointment of the Prime Minister is formally entrusted to the Emperor, who is Head of State although constitutionally impotent.

CLIMATE

Except for the Hokkaido area and the subtropical Okinawa region, the weather is in general mostly temperate, with four seasons. Winters are cool and sunny in the south, cold and sunny around Tokyo (which occasionally has snow), and very cold around Hokkaido, which is covered in snow for up to four months a year. Summer, between June and September, ranges from warm to very hot, while spring and autumn are generally mild throughout the country. Rain falls throughout the year but June and early July is the main rainy season. Hokkaido, however, is much drier than the Tokyo area. Rainfall is intermittent with sunshine. Typhoons are only likely to occur in September or October but rarely last more than a day.

Required clothing: Lightweight cottons and linens are required throughout summer in most areas. There is much less rainfall than western Europe. Light to mediumweights during spring and autumn; medium to heavyweights for winter months according to region. Much warmer clothes will be needed in the mountains all year round.

NAGASAKI Japan (27m)

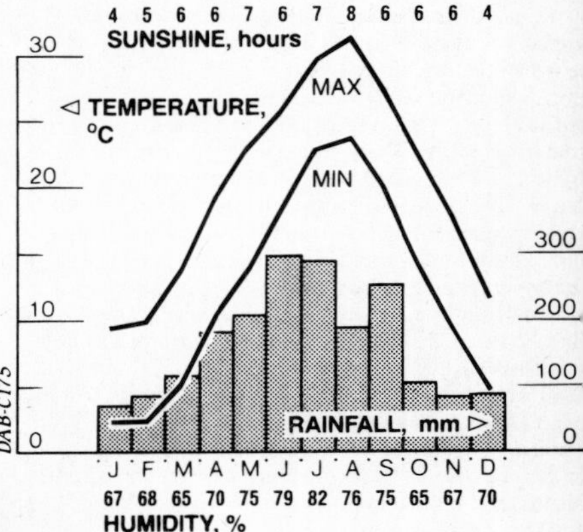

SAPPORO Japan (17m)

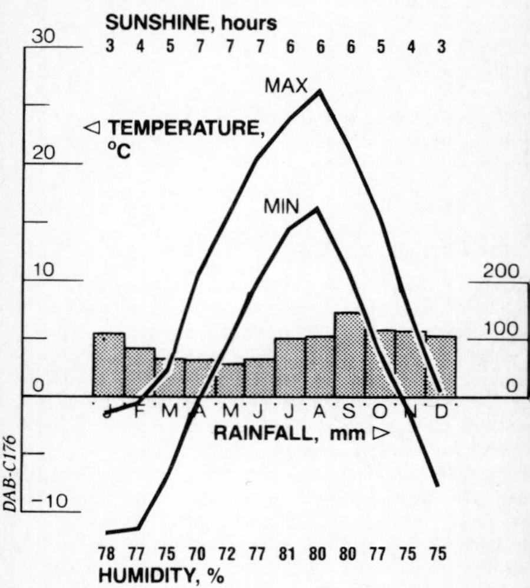

TOKYO Japan (4m)

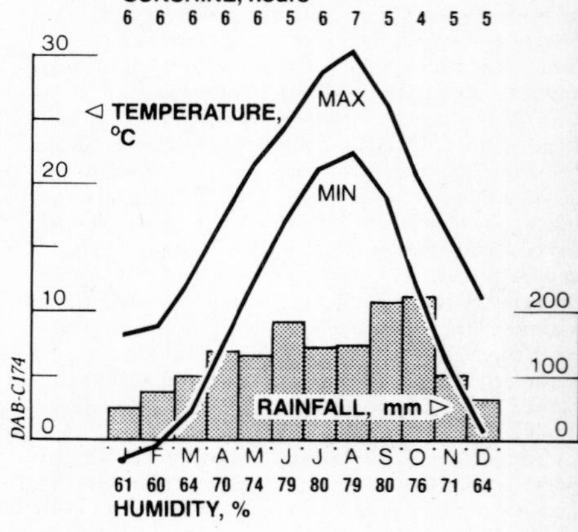

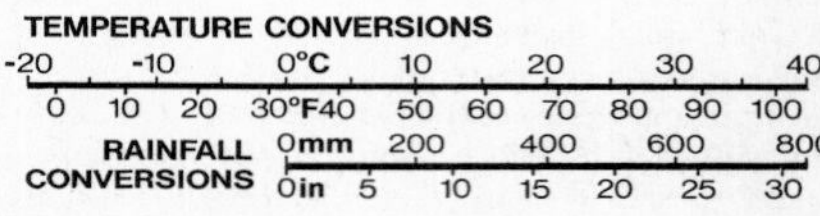

JERSEY

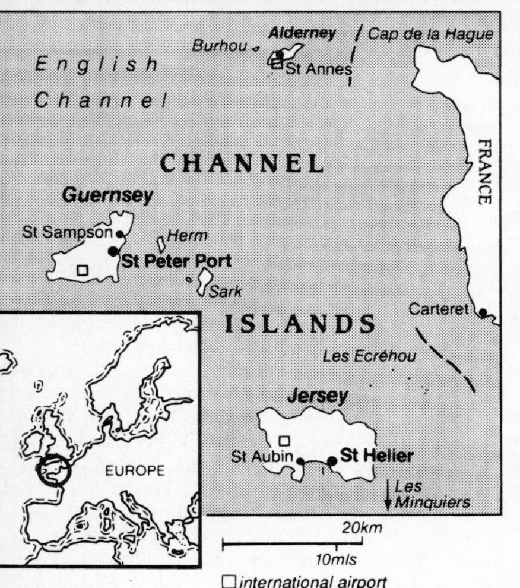

Location: English Channel (off the north French coast).

Jersey Tourism
Liberation Square
St Helier, Jersey JE1 1BB
Tel: 78000. Fax: 35569. Telex: 4192223.

Jersey Tourism (London Marketing Consultant and Public Relations Office)
Wordsmith Marketing and Public Relations
38 Dover Street
London W1X 3RB
Tel: (071) 493 5278. Fax: (071) 491 1565.

AREA: 116.2 sq km (44.8 sq miles).
POPULATION: 82,809 (1989).
POPULATION DENSITY: 712.6 per sq km.
CAPITAL: St Helier. **Population:** 28,123 (1991).
GEOGRAPHY: Jersey is the largest of the Channel Islands, lying approximately 170km (100 miles) south of the coast of England and 23km (14 miles) from the coast of Normandy in France. The island is roughly 14.5km (9 miles) by 8km (5 miles). It slopes from north to south and often appears to visitors to be largely composed of pink granite. Jersey has over 20 bays, many small harbours and magnificent beaches bathed by the warm waters of the Gulf Stream. The sunshine record for the British Isles has been held by Jersey for the past 30 years, with an average of over 1900 hours.
LANGUAGE: English is commonly used. A dialect of Norman-French is still spoken by some people.
RELIGION: Each of Jersey's parishes has its own Anglican church, but some parishes, particularly St Helier, have been sub-divided to provide more than one centre for Church of England worship. There are 12 Roman Catholic and 18 Methodist churches, and also a wide range of Free churches.
TIME: GMT (GMT +1 in summer, March to September).
ELECTRICITY: 240 volts AC, 50Hz.
COMMUNICATIONS: Telephone: STD code to Jersey from UK is 0534, from elsewhere dial UK code then 534. Calls to the UK and many other countries may be made from all public telephones and from most hotels and guest-houses. **Fax:** Facilities are available for business guests in a few hotels and at fax bureaux in St Helier. **Telex:** Facilities are available at larger hotels. **Post:** There is a standard one-price rate to the UK, which is in general as good as first-class UK service, although the prices are lower than UK second class. There is also one rate for internal mail. UK stamps are not valid in Jersey. The main post office is in Broad Street, St Helier. Post office hours: 0900-1730 Monday to Friday, 0900-1230 Saturday. **Press:** Newspapers published in Jersey are the *Freestyle Weekly*, *Jersey Evening Post* and *Jersey Weekly Post*.

PASSPORT/VISA

Regulations and requirements may be subject to change at short notice, and you are advised to contact the appropriate diplomatic or consular authority before finalising travel arrangements. Details of these may be found at the head of this country's entry. Any numbers in the chart refer to the footnotes below.

	Passport Required?	Visa Required?	Return Ticket Required?
Full British	No/1	No	No
BVP	Valid	-	-
Australian	Yes	No	No
Canadian	Yes	No	No
USA	Yes	No	No
Other EC	2	No	No
Japanese	Yes	No	No

PASSPORTS: Valid passport required by all except:
(a) [1] British citizens and nationals of the Republic of Ireland who travel between their own country and Jersey;
(b) [2] nationals of EC countries holding national identity cards;
(c) nationals of Austria, Liechtenstein, Monaco and Switzerland holding British Visitors Card and national ID card (up to 6 months).
Note: If travel is via France (or any other country) the entry requirements for that country will have to be satisfied.
British Visitors Passport: Acceptable but not required unless a British passport holder is travelling to a country other than the UK or the Republic of Ireland.

MONEY

Currency: Pound Sterling (£) = 100 pence. Notes are in denominations of £50, 20, 10, 5 and 1. Coins are in denominations of £1 and 50, 20, 10, 5, 2 and 1 pence. On September 30, 1992 a new 10 pence coin was introduced. In 1990 a new smaller 5-pence piece came into circulation; the old 5-pence piece is no longer legal tender. All UK notes and coins are legal tender, and circulate with the Channel Isles issue. Note that Channel Islands notes and coins are not accepted in the UK, although notes can be reconverted at parity in UK banks.
Currency exchange: Money can be exchanged at bureaux de change, in banks and at many hotels.
Credit cards: Access/Mastercard, American Express, Diners Club and Visa are all widely accepted. Check with your credit card company for details of merchant acceptability and other services which may be available.
Travellers cheques: These are widely accepted.
Exchange rates: The following is included as a guide to the movement of Sterling against the US Dollar:

Date:	**Oct '89**	**Oct '90**	**Oct '91**	**Oct '92**
$1.00=	**0.63**	**0.51**	**0.58**	**0.63**

Currency restrictions: There are no currency restrictions.
Banking hours: 0930-1530 Monday to Friday. Some banks are open on Saturday morning.

DUTY FREE

The Channel Islands are a low duty zone. The following goods may be exported *from* Jersey without incurring customs duty in the UK:
200 cigarettes or 50 cigars or 250g of tobacco (double allowance if living outside the UK);
1 litre of alcoholic beverage if over 38.8% proof or 2 litres if under 38.8% proof or 4 litres wine (2 sparkling and 2 still);
50g (2 fl oz) perfume and 250ml toilet water;
Other goods to a value of £32.
Note: (a) For import allowances into Jersey, see the entry for the United Kingdom. (b) There is a total ban on the importation of animals other than from the UK or other Channel Islands.

PUBLIC HOLIDAYS

Public holidays observed on Jersey are as follows:
Apr 9 '93 Good Friday. **Apr 12** Easter Monday. **May 3** May Day Holiday. **May 9** Liberation Day. **May 31** Spring Bank Holiday. **Aug 30** Late Summer Holiday. **Dec 25** Christmas Day. **Dec 26** Boxing Day. **Jan 1 '94** New Year's Day.

HEALTH

Regulations and requirements may be subject to change at short notice, and you are advised to contact your doctor well in advance of your intended date of departure. Any numbers in the chart refer to the footnotes below.

	Special Precautions?	Certificate Required?
Yellow Fever	No	No
Cholera	No	No
Typhoid & Polio	No	-
Malaria	No	-
Food & Drink	No	-

Health care: There is a Reciprocal Health Agreement with the UK. On presenting proof of UK residence (driving licence, NHS card, etc) free in- and out-patient treatment is available at the General Hospital, Gloucester Street, St Helier (tel: 59000). The agreement does not cover the costs of medical treatment at a doctor's surgery (but there is a free GP-style surgery most mornings at the General Hospital), prescribed medicines, or dental treatment, but travel by ambulance is free. Despite the agreement, private medical insurance is advised for UK residents on long visits in case emergency repatriation is necessary and to cover the cost of prescribed medicines and dental treatment. All visitors should bring the name and address of their family doctor in the event of a serious accident or illness.

TRAVEL

AIR: Approximate flight time: From *London* to Jersey is 40 minutes.
International airport: *St Peters' (JER)* is 8km (5 miles) from St Helier. Facilities include a bureau de change, low tariff shopping, restaurant and bar, and provision for the disabled. Taxis are available and the local bus to town goes every 15 minutes.
SEA: From England: There is a *British Channel Island Ferries* night and daytime car/passenger ferry sailing from Poole (May/September) and a night only winter schedule. There are two *Condor* hydrofoils offering a daily service from Weymouth during the tourist season, taking 3 hours and 30 minutes.
From France: St Malo: Car-only crossing is provided by *Commodore Travel/Morvan Fils*, car/passenger ferries by *Emeraude Ferries*, hydrofoil crossing by *Condor/Morvan Fils*,

JERSEY	**HEALTH REGULATIONS**	**VISA REGULATIONS**
GALILEO/WORLDSPAN	TI-DFT/JER/HE	TI-DFT/JER/VI
SABRE	TIDFT/JER/HE	 TIDFT/JER/VI

Code-Link

To access this information on your CRS, swipe the barcode with a light pen or type in the text under the barcode. For more information, see the introduction *How to Use This Book*.

and crossing by 'vedettes' (200-capacity ferries) by *Vedettes Blanches* and *Vedettes Armoricaines*. From Granville, Port Bail and Carteret, passenger ferries are provided by *Vedettes Vertes Granvillaises*, *Vedettes Armoricaines*, *SMCJ*, *Nord Sud Voyages*, *Jersey Ferries* and *Vedettes Blanches*.

Visitors bringing speedboats, surfboards or sailboards into Jersey *must* register at the Harbour Office on arrival. Third Party insurance is required.

ROAD: There are over 800km (500 miles) of roads and lanes criss-crossing the island. **Buses** operate throughout the island; the network centres on the bus and coach station at Weighbridge, St Helier. **Car hire** is generally very cheap, and so is petrol. There are over 35 car hire firms, mostly in St Helier. Persons wishing to hire a car must (a) be over 20 years of age; (b) have had a full licence for at least one year; and (c) have a valid full licence with no endorsements or disqualifications for dangerous or driving over the alcohol limit within the previous five years. **Bicycle hire** is available from eight firms in St Helier, one in St Ouen and one in Millbrook. **Motorcycles** and **mopeds** can also be hired – there are ten firms in St Helier. Crash helmets must be worn. Addresses and telephone numbers of all these companies can be obtained from the tourist office. **Documentation:** Visitors who wish to bring their own car must have a valid certificate of insurance or an international green card, and a valid driving licence. Nationality plates must be displayed. **Motor caravans** and **trailers** may *not* be imported. There is a speed limit of 40kmph (25mph) or 30kmph (19mph) in built-up areas, which is reduced in some places to 20kmph (12mph).

ACCOMMODATION

The booklet *Jersey 1993* available from the tourist office (see top of entry), gives comprehensive information on all forms of accommodation on the island. Short-break and longer-stay holidays are available throughout the year. The most popular season is from May until September.

HOTELS: The official accommodation list is obtainable from the Jersey Hotel and Guest House Association, 60 Stopford Road, St Helier, Jersey JR2 4LB. Tel: 21421. **Grading:** Jersey has its own hotel and guest-house grading scheme. Hotels are graded from **1** to **5 suns** and guest-houses are graded from **1** to **3 diamonds**. The greater the number of suns or diamonds, the higher the grade achieved. All hotels are inspected and graded annually. *Disabled Visitors:* The Maison des Landes, St Ouen, Jersey JE3 2AE (tel: 481 683) offers accommodation for up to 40 disabled visitors and family/friends. It is open between early April and late October.

GUEST-HOUSES: There are over 230 guest-houses on the island, some offering bed, breakfast and evening meals, others just bed & breakfast. Despite the large number of establishments, advance booking is recommended as many guest-houses are not open throughout the whole year. **Grading:** See *Hotels* above.

HOLIDAY VILLAGES: There are two holiday villages on the island: Jersey Holiday Village, Portelet Bay. Tel: 45555 *or* 47302 (no facilities for children under three); and Pontins Ltd, Holiday Village, Plémont Bay, St Ouen, Jersey JB3 2BD. Tel: 81873 (no facilities for children under six).

SELF-CATERING: There is limited self-catering accommodation registered with the Tourism Department. Premises taking less than six people do not have to register and are not inspected. This type of accommodation is available through a number of handling agents.

Furnished flats, bungalows, chalets and villas are not generally available, owing to the acute shortage of housing for permanent residents. Some units do, however, become available at various times and advertisements can be placed in the local newspaper. Contact the *Jersey Evening Post*, Advertisement Department, PO Box 582, Five Oaks, St Saviour, Jersey JE4 8XQ. Tel: 73333. Fax: 79681. Telex: 4192644.

CAMPING/CARAVANNING: Camping is only permitted on recognised campsites, of which there are six. Due to limited capacity, advance booking is essential. There are no caravan sites on Jersey.

HOSTELS: Enquiries for accommodation for organised parties should be made to Aquila Methodist Youth Hostel, 1 Great Union Road, St Helier, Jersey. Tel: 23722. Half-board accommodation for parties of 10-80 persons (boys, girls or mixed parties) are catered for; open July and August.

ST HELIER

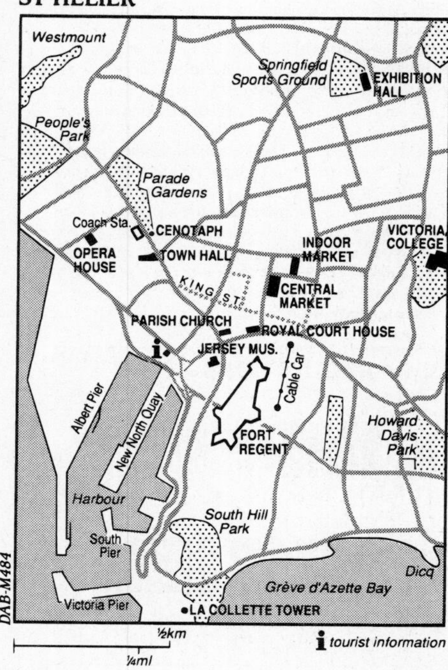

RESORTS & EXCURSIONS

St Helier, the capital and by far the biggest town on the island, is overlooked by two fortifications. *Elizabeth Castle* is built on an island on the bay, and can be reached at low tide. This fortress withstood the army of Oliver Cromwell for seven weeks in 1651, and was used by the occupying Germans during the last war. *Fort Regent* is built on an outcrop above the town. It has recently been converted into a leisure complex with sports and conference facilities. There is an aquarium, a postal museum, a funfair, swimming pools and a wide variety of indoor sporting facilities, while the castle's ramparts give excellent views across the town and the bay. Also worth a visit is the *Jersey Museum* at Pier Road.

The best shopping area in the town is to be found in the King Street–Queen Street precinct area. Most luxury goods are less expensive than in the UK, as Jersey, although not tax free, has low duties on items such as alcohol, cigarettes, perfume, cosmetics and electrical goods.

The North (St Ouen, St Mary, St John, Trinity): The main beaches in this region are those at *Plémont*, with a sheltered bay, rock pools and caves; *Grde Lecq*, reached by a road that runs through a wooded valley; *Bonne Nuit Bay*, a peaceful harbour with a small beach nestling behind a huge headland; *Bouley Bay*, particularly popular with sub-aqua enthusiasts and anglers; and *Rozel*, on the northeast coast, a fishing harbour with an old fort and a small sandy beach. The coast of France can be seen on a clear day.

The *Jersey Zoological Park*, in **Trinity,** is the headquarters of the Jersey Wildlife Preservation Trust, founded by Gerald Durrell. The Trust is a sanctuary for many endangered species of animals, and a visit to the zoo is strongly recommended. More wildlife can be encountered at the *Carnation Nursery and Butterfly Farm* in **St Mary,** home of hundreds of rare and exotic butterflies. *La Mare Vineyards*, close to **Devil's Hole**, has vineyards set in the grounds of an 18th-century farmhouse. There are displays from the local cider industry and homemade products are on sale.

The West (St Ouen, St Peter, St Brelade): The west coast consists almost entirely of one 8km (5-mile) beach on *St Ouen's Bay*. The area is very good for surfers, but is only suitable for strong swimmers.

There are many traditional crafts practised in this part of the island, and many of the workshops can be visited and the products purchased; these include decorative candles at *Portinfer* (St Ouen), local pottery and leatherwork at *L'Etacq* (St Ouen) and stone-ground flour from locally grown corn at *Le Moulin de Quetival*, St Peter's Valley. The grounds of the fine old *St Ouen Manor* are occasionally open to the public. In **St Peter's Village** is a motor museum, adjoining an old German bunker, which houses a collection of veteran and vintage cars, motorcycles, military vehicles and a Jersey steam railway exhibition. There is also a museum in **St Ouen,** displaying floats entered in the well-known *Battle of the Flowers*, a local festival held each year on the second Thursday in August.

The South (St Brelade, St Peter, St Lawrence, St Helier, St Saviour, St Clement): The main beaches in this region are those at *St Clement's Bay*, with several rock pools and sandy gullies; *St Aubin's Bay*, a 5km (3-mile) stretch of sand curving round from St Aubin to the capital; *Portelet*, a secluded sandy bay; *St Brelade's Bay*, widely regarded as one of the most beautiful beaches on the island, ideal for windsurfing and water-skiing; and *Beauport*, a small bay to the west of St Brelade flanked by towering rocks of pink granite. *Howard Davies Park* in **St Saviour** is one of the most attractive of Jersey's public gardens with many subtropical trees and shrubs which flourish in the mild climate. In the **St Lawrence** parish, St Peter's Valley, is the *German Military Underground Hospital*, which has several reminders of Jersey's occupation during the Second World War. There are many displays of photographs and documents, and a collection of firearms, daggers and memorabilia.

The East (St Martin, Grouville): The two main beaches in this region cover almost the whole of the eastern coast, and are separated by the promontory of Petit Portelet. To the north of this is *St Catherine's Bay*, popular with anglers, and the tiny village of **Anne Port.** Further south is the *Royal Bay of Grouville* dominated by a magnificent castle, *Mont Orgueil*, which overlooks the small port of Gorey. The town is famous for its pottery and visits around the workshop can be arranged. Inland at *La Hougue Bie* in Grouville, a museum housed in a massive neolithic tomb dating back 5000 years has exhibitions on the agriculture, archaeology, geology and history of the island.

Probably the best way of seeing the island is to walk or cycle round it. The north has the highest land and the most rugged scenery, but gentler walks are possible inland and in the south. One suggested route follows the line of the old Jersey Railway – now a traffic-free public path – which runs from St Aubin to the lighthouse at **Corbière** on the island's southwestern tip.

SOCIAL PROFILE

FOOD & DRINK: Jersey has an excellent range of restaurants to cater for every taste. Seafood is very popular and a wide selection of home-grown produce is available. The island has an enviable reputation for good cuisine whether in small pubs, wine bars or high-class restaurants. **Licensing hours:** 0900-2300 Monday to Saturday, 1100-1300 and 1630-2300 Sundays.

SHOPPING: The Island is a low duty area and there is no VAT. As well as St Helier (where there are two covered markets), there are shopping areas such as Red Houses, St Brelade and Gorey, St Martin. Luxury items such as spirits, cigarettes, jewellery and perfumes are popular buys. Local products such as knitwear, pottery, woodcrafts and even flowers are good value.

Shopping hours: 0930-1730 Monday to Saturday; some shops close early on Thursday afternoons.
SPORT: There are facilities for most sports, particularly watersports such as surfing, windsurfing, water-skiing, fishing, sailing and sub-aqua. **Swimming** is a popular leisure activity, and there are many bays and beaches offering excellent bathing (see above *Resorts & Excursions*). Bathers should beware, however, as Jersey has some of the largest tidal movements in the world, with as much as 12km (40ft) between low and high tide causing very strong currents. Some beaches are patrolled by beach guards and have safe areas marked with warning flags. On the western coast (St Ouen's Bay), the strong waves can also prove hazardous. There are open-air swimming pools at Havre de Pas and West Park, and two at Fort Regent. **Surfing:** The best area is around St Ouen Bay. There are surfing schools and equipment hire facilities at the Watersplash and the Sands and year-round professional tuition at El Tico. **Sub aqua:** The waters around the island support a rich and varied marine life and there are good facilities for divers. **Boat dives, skindiving** and equipment hire are available from Watersports or the Underwater Centre at Bouley Bay. **Windsurfing** races are held every Sunday during the summer, and there are several schools including the Jersey Wind & Water Windsurfer Schools at St Aubin and St Brelade's Bay, Longbeach Windsurfing & Boating Centre, the Sands and the Watersplash. **Water-skiing:** Facilities and tuition are available at La Haule, St Aubin's Bay and St Brelade's Bay. **Yachting:** There are two sailing clubs on the island: The Royal Channel Islands Yacht Club, St Aubin and The St Helier Yacht Club. There is also a **canoeing** school in St Helier. There are two 18-hole **golf** courses: La Moye, St Brelade and Royal Jersey, plus two 9-hole courses, one at Grd'Azette and the other at Five Mile Road, St Ouen. Booking is advisable. Jersey holds its own Open Championship every year which is attended by many well-known European professional golfers. **Tennis:** There are courts at Caesarean Tennis Club and at Grd'Azette. **Horseriding:** Several schools provide tuition and escorted hacks. **Squash:** Temporary membership of the island's two clubs is available; contact Jersey Squash Club and the Lido Squash and Social Club. There are also courts at the Fort Regent Leisure Centre. **Angling** is very popular, particularly during the summer, and there are a number of sea-fishing clubs who run shore and boat festivals during the summer. Boating and fishing trips operate from St Helier. *Warning:* Fishing from rocks should not be attempted until the visitor has obtained information about local tides, currents and weather conditions. Fly fishing is available at the Val de la Mer and the St Catherine Reservoirs; temporary membership can be obtained.
SPECIAL EVENTS: The following is a selection of the major festivals and other special events celebrated in Jersey in 1993. For a complete list, contact the Tourist Office.
Apr 9-12 '93 *Jersey Easter Hockey Festival.* **Apr 22-25** *Jersey Jazz Festival.* **May** *Jersey Petanque Open Competition; Jersey Rowing Club Spring Regatta.* **May 7-9** *39th International Air Rally.* **May 12-22** *Good Food Festival.* **May 12-13** *Salon Culinaire.* **May 17-21** *Italian Festival Week.* **May 28-31** *Helier Morris Men Weekend of Dance.* **Jun 7-13** *Portuguese Festival Week.* **Jun 17-20** *Jersey European Open Golf Tournament.* **Jun 21-26** *Irish Festival Week.* **Jul** *Sark to Jersey Rowing Race.* **Jul 12-17** *Jersey Floral Island Festival.* **Aug 12** *Battle of Flowers.* **Aug 22-29** *Jersey Beach Festival.* **Sep 16** *Battle of Britain Air Display.* **Sep 17-20** *Folk and Blues Festival.* **Oct** *Royal Jersey Golf Club Pro-Am Championship.* **Oct 1-17** *Festival France.* **Oct 17-20** *Jersey Country Music Festival.* **Oct 24-28** *Festival of Darts.* **Nov 6-7** *Bar Billiard League – British Open Championships.* **Nov 7** *Diet Coke Jersey Half Marathon.*
SOCIAL CONVENTIONS: Similar to the rest of the UK, with French influences. **Tipping:** In general, this follows UK practice.

BUSINESS PROFILE

ECONOMY: Although agriculture is still important as a source of employment and prestige – Jersey cows are renowned throughout the world – offshore banking and tourism produce more for the economy: the former because of the island's exemption from the UK tax system and the latter through continental influence and a friendly climate.
BUSINESS: Business people are generally expected to dress smartly (suits are usual). Appointments should be made and the exchange of business cards is customary. A knowledge of English is essential. **Office hours:** 0900/0930-1700/1730 Monday to Friday.
COMMERCIAL INFORMATION: The following organisation can offer advice: Jersey Chamber of Commerce, 19 Royal Square, St Helier, JE2 4WA. Tel: 24536. Fax: 34942.
CONFERENCES/CONVENTIONS: Jersey plays host each year to a large number of conferences; the main period is from October to May. For further information, contact the Conference Bureau, Jersey Tourism, Liberation Square, St Helier, JE1 1BB. Tel: 78000. Fax: 35569.

HISTORY & GOVERNMENT

HISTORY: Jersey has been inhabited for many thousands of years, as can be seen from the neolithic tomb at La Hougue Bie. It was the Normans who made the greatest impact on the Channel Islands, annexing them to the Duchy of Normandy during the 10th century. When William of Normandy gained the English crown in 1066, the Channel Islands became part of the Anglo-Norman realm, and they were the only part of it to be retained after the loss of Normandy in 1205. As a mark of his gratitude for their loyalty, King John granted Jersey its own constitution; this has been ratified by every successive monarch and the connection between the island and the English throne is expressed in the flag, which contains a crest surmounted by the Plantagenet crown. Jersey has, like its neighbours, been at various times a haven for smugglers and pirates, and also vulnerable to attack due to its proximity to France, so often Britain's enemy. The islanders fought off French invasions on many occasions, particularly during the 14th and 15th centuries. One of the most serious threats, led by the Baron de Rullecourt, was eventually defeated in 1781. The Channel Islands were occupied by the Germans during the Second World War. The mixture of languages – English, French and Norman French – reflects the history of the island. Jersey has jealously guarded its independence since the war, although this has been principally manifested by the promotion of offshore finance and rigid controls on rights of residency.
GOVERNMENT: Jersey is not part of the United Kingdom, but is a direct dependency of the British crown with its own legislative and taxation systems which are an intriguing blend of Norman and English. The Jersey States Assembly, one of the oldest legislative bodies in the world, is composed of 12 Constables, 12 Senators and 29 Deputies (none of whom receives any remuneration for their services), as well as several non-voting officials, some of whom are appointed by the crown. The island's laws are subject to ratification by the Privy Council, although this is little more than a formality.

CLIMATE

The most popular holiday season is from May until the end of September, with temperatures averaging 20-21°C. Rainfall averages 33 inches a year, most of which falls during the cooler months. Sea temperatures average over 17°C in deep water during the summer.
Required clothing: Normal beach and holiday wear for summer, with a jersey or similar as there are often sea breezes. Warm winter wear and rainwear advised.

ST HELIER Jersey (9m)

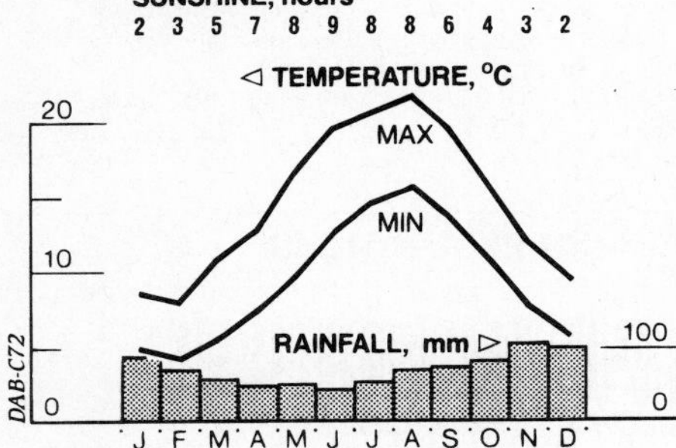

TEMPERATURE CONVERSIONS
-20 -10 0°C 10 20 30 40
0 10 20 30°F40 50 60 70 80 90 100
RAINFALL CONVERSIONS 0mm 200 400 600 800
0in 5 10 15 20 25 30

Location: Middle East.

Ministry of Tourism
PO Box 224
Amman, Jordan
Tel: (6) 642 311. Fax: (6) 648 465. Telex: 21741.
Embassy of the Hashemite Kingdom of Jordan
6 Upper Phillimore Gardens
London W8 7HB
Tel: (071) 937 3685. Telex: 919338. Opening hours: 1000-1500 Monday to Friday.
Royal Jordanian Airlines/Tourist Information
211 Regent Street
London W1R 7DD
Tel: (071) 437 9465. Fax: (071) 494 0433. Telex: 24330.
British Embassy
PO Box 87
Abdoun
Amman, Jordan
Tel: (6) 823 100. Fax: (6) 813 759. Telex: 22209 PRODROM JO.
Embassy of the Hashemite Kingdom of Jordan
Consular Section
3504 International Drive, NW
Washington, DC
20008
Tel: (202) 966 2664. Fax: (202) 966 3110. Telex: 64113.
Embassy of the United States of America
PO Box 354
Jabal
Amman, Jordan
Tel: (6) 644 371. Telex: 21510.
Jordan Information Bureau
2319 Wyoming Avenue, NW
Washington, DC
20006
Tel: (202) 265 1606.
Royal Jordanian Airlines
18th Floor
535 Fifth Avenue
New York, NY
10017
Tel: (212) 949 0050.
Embassy of the Hashemite Kingdom of Jordan
Suite 701
100 Bronson Avenue
Ottawa, Ontario
K1N 6R4
Tel: (613) 238 8090. Fax: (613) 232 3341. Telex: 0534583.
Jordan Tourist Information Office
c/o Royal Jordan

Suite 738
1801 McGill College
Montréal, Québec
H3A 2N4
Tel: (514) 288 1655

Canadian Embassy
PO Box 815403
Pearl of Shmeisani Building
Shmeisani,
Amman, Jordan
Tel: (6) 666 124. Fax: (6) 689 227. Telex: 23080.

AREA: 97,740 sq km (37,738 sq miles).
POPULATION: 4,009,000 (1990 estimate). Of these, an estimated 2,796,100 live on the East Bank of the River Jordan (1986 figures), the remainder live on the West Bank which is occupied by Israel. About half a million people in East Jordan are classified as Palestinian refugees and are maintained by the United Nations Relief and Works Agency. Another quarter of a million people are reckoned to have been displaced by the events of 1967.
POPULATION DENSITY: 41 per sq km.
CAPITAL: Amman. **Population:** 1,160,000 (1986).
GEOGRAPHY: Jordan shares borders with Israel, Syria, Iraq and Saudi Arabia. The Dead Sea is to the northwest and the Gulf of Aqaba to the southwest. A high plateau extends 324km (201 miles) from Syria to Ras en Naqeb in the south with the capital of Amman at a height of 800m (2625ft). Northwest of the capital are undulating hills, some forested, others cultivated. The Dead Sea depression, 400m (1300ft) below sea level in the west is the lowest point on earth. The River Jordan connects the Dead Sea with Lake Tiberius (in Israel). To the west of the Jordan is the occupied West Bank. The east of the country is mainly desert. Jordan has a tiny stretch of Red Sea coast, centred on Aqaba.
LANGUAGE: Arabic is the official language. English and some French are also spoken.
RELIGION: Over 80% Sunni Muslim, with Christian and Shi'ite Muslim minorities.
TIME: GMT + 2.
ELECTRICITY: 220 volts AC, 50Hz. Lamp sockets are screw-type, and there is a wide range of wall sockets.
COMMUNICATIONS: Telephone: IDD service is available within cities, with direct dialling to most countries. Country code: 962 (followed by 6 for Amman). There is no telephone connection to Israel from Jordan. **Fax:** Use of fax is increasing. Most good hotels have facilities. **Telex/telegram:** Public telex facilities are available at leading hotels. The overseas telegram service is reasonably good. Telegrams may be sent from the Central Telegraph Office; Post Office, 1st Circle, Jebel Amman; Post Office, Jordan Intercontinental, Jebel Amman; or from major hotels and post offices. **Post:** Packages should be left opened for customs officials. Airmail to Europe takes three to five days. For a higher charge there is a rapid service guaranteeing delivery within 24 hours to around 22 countries. Post office opening hours: 0800-1800 Saturday to Thursday, closed Friday (except for the downtown post office on Prince Mohammed Street in Amman which is open on Fridays). **Press:** The English-language newspapers are *The Jordan Times* (daily) and *The Star* (weekly).
BBC World Service and Voice of America frequencies: From time to time these change. See the section *How to Use this Book* for more information.

BBC:				
MHz	21.47	15.57	11.76	1.323
Voice of America:				
MHz	11.97	9.670	6.040	5.995

PASSPORT/VISA

Regulations and requirements may be subject to change at short notice, and you are advised to contact the appropriate diplomatic or consular authority before finalising travel arrangements. Details of these may be found at the head of this country's entry. Any numbers in the chart refer to the footnotes below.

	Passport Required?	Visa Required?	Return Ticket Required?
Full British	Yes	Yes	No
BVP	Not valid	-	-
Australian	Yes	Yes	No
Canadian	Yes	Yes	No
USA	Yes	Yes	No
Other EC	Yes	Yes	No
Japanese	Yes	Yes	No

Restricted entry and transit: Holders of Israeli passports or visas, valid or otherwise, will be refused entry. South African passport holders will also be refused entry. Entry will be refused to nationals of Bangladesh, India, Pakistan, Sri Lanka and Turkey who have valid visas but who have failed to obtain prior approval from the Ministry of the Interior.
PASSPORTS: Valid passport required by all.
British Visitors Passport: Not acceptable.
VISAS: Required by all except nationals of Bahrain, Egypt, Iraq, Kuwait, Oman, Saudi Arabia, Syria, the United Arab Emirates and Yemen. Nationals of certain countries – including all Western European countries, the USA, Canada, Australia, New Zealand and Japan – coming from another Arab country can obtain Transit visas on arrival at the airport in Jordan. Those arriving in Jordan overland directly from occupied territories must hold a visa for Jordan. This must be obtained from a representation of Jordan abroad. (Not applicable to nationals of Bangladesh, India, Pakistan, Sri Lanka and Turkey, who are required to seek prior approval from the Ministry of the Interior, as well as holding a visa.)
Types of visa: Transit, Tourist, Student – £21 (single entry valid for 3 months); Transit, Tourist, Student – £42 (multiple entry valid for 3 months); Business – £22 (single entry valid for 3 months); Business – £42 (multiple entry valid for one year).
Visa fees are not payable by groups of five people or more whose journey has been arranged through a travel agent and who intend to stay in Jordan for at least 4 nights.
Validity: *Tourist:* 3 months. *Business:* 3 months or 1 year.
Application to: Consulate (or Consular Section of Embassy). For addresses, see top of entry.
Application requirements: (a) Completed application form. (b) Passport valid for at least 6 months. (c) 1 photo. (d) Stamped self-addressed envelope if applying by post. (e) Fee. (f) Company letter for a business visa.
Working days required: 2 days, if applying in person. Allow a few days for postal applications.
Temporary residence: Apply to Embassy.

MONEY

Currency: Dinar (JD) = 1000 fils. Notes are in denominations of JD20, 10, 5, and 1, and 500 fils. Coins are in denominations of 250, 100, 50, 25, 20, 10, 5 and 1 fils.
Credit cards: American Express and Visa are widely accepted, whilst Access/Mastercard and Diners Club have more limited use. Check with your credit card company for details of merchant acceptability and other services which may be available.
Travellers cheques: Those issued by UK banks are accepted by licensed banks and money changers.
Exchange rate indicators: The following figures are included as a guide to the movements of the Dinar against Sterling and the US Dollar:

Date:	Oct '89	Oct '90	Oct '91	Oct '92
£1.00=	1.06	1.27	1.18	1.09
$1.00=	0.67	0.65	0.68	0.68

Currency restrictions: The import of both local and foreign currency is unrestricted provided that it is declared. Export of local currency is limited to JD300. Export of foreign currency is limited to the amount imported and declared on arrival.
Note: Israeli currency is prohibited.
Banking hours: 0830-1230 and 1530-1730 Saturday to Thursday. Hours for Ramadan are from 0830-1000, although some banks open in the afternoon.

DUTY FREE

The following goods may be imported into Jordan without incurring customs duty:
200 cigarettes or 25 cigars or 200g of tobacco;
2 bottles of wine or 1 bottle of spirits;
A reasonable amount of perfume for personal use;
Gifts up to the value of JD50 or the equivalent to US$150.

PUBLIC HOLIDAYS

Public holidays observed in Jordan are as follows:
Mar 22 '93 Arab League Day. **Mar 25** Start of Eid al-Fitr. **May 25** Independence Day. **Jun 1** Eid al-Adha (Feast of the Sacrifice). **Jun 21** Islamic New Year. **Aug 11** King Hussein's Accession. **Aug 30** Mouloud (Birth of the Prophet). **Nov 14** King Hussein's Birthday. **Jan 15 '94** Arbour Day. **Jan 21** Leilat al-Meiraj. **Mar 22** Arab League Day. **Mar** Start of Eid al-Fitr.
Note: (a) Christmas and Easter holidays are only observed by Christian businesses. (b) Muslim festivals are timed according to local sightings of various phases of the Moon and the dates given above are approximations. During the lunar month of Ramadan that precedes Eid al-Fitr, Muslims fast during the day and feast at night and normal business patterns may be interrupted. Many restaurants are closed during the day and there may be restrictions on smoking and drinking. Some disruption may continue into Eid al-Fitr itself. Eid al-Fitr and Eid al-Adha may last anything from two to ten days, depending on the region. For more information see the section *World of Islam* at the back of the book.

HEALTH

Regulations and requirements may be subject to change at short notice, and you are advised to contact your doctor well in advance of your intended date of departure. Any numbers in the chart refer to the footnotes below.

	Special Precautions?	Certificate Required?
Yellow Fever	No	1
Cholera	Yes	2
Typhoid & Polio	Yes	-
Malaria	No	-
Food & Drink	3	-

[1]: A yellow fever vaccination certificate is required from travellers over one year of age coming from infected areas.
[2]: Following WHO guidelines issued in 1973, a cholera vaccination certificate is not a condition of entry to Jordan. However, cholera is a risk in this country and precautions are essential. Up-to-date advice should be sought before deciding whether these precautions should include a vaccination as medical opinion is divided over its effectiveness. See the *Health* section at the back of the book.
[3]: Water used for drinking, brushing teeth or making ice should have first been boiled or otherwise sterilised. Milk is unpasteurised and should be boiled. Powdered or tinned milk is available and is advised, but make sure that it is reconstituted with pure water. Food and water in rural areas may carry increased risk – special care should be taken with dairy products and salad. Ensure that meat and fish are thoroughly cooked. Peel all fruit. *Rabies* is present. For those at high risk, vaccination before arrival should be considered. If you are bitten

JORDAN | **HEALTH REGULATIONS** | **VISA REGULATIONS** | Code-Link

GALILEO/WORLDSPAN

TI-DFT/AMM/HE

TI-DFT/AMM/VI

SABRE

TIDFT/AMM/HE

TIDFT/AMM/VI

To access this information on your CRS, swipe the barcode with a light pen or type in the text under the barcode. For more information, see the introduction *How to Use This Book*.

abroad seek medical advice without delay. For more information consult the *Health* section at the back of the book.
Health care: Health insurance is recommended. There are excellent hospitals in large towns and cities, with clinics in many villages.

TRAVEL –International

AIR: The national airline is *Royal Jordanian Airlines (RJ)*.
Approximate flight time: From *London* to Amman is 5 hours 30 minutes.
International airport: *Queen Alia International (AMM)* is 32km (20 miles) southeast of the capital, to which it is connected by a good highway (travel time – 30 minutes). There is a regular bus service, and taxis are also available. There are duty-free facilities.
The previous international airport, situated 5km (3 miles) northeast of the city, is now only used for charter flights.
Departure tax: JD10 for individual tourists; JD25 for Jordanian nationals on international departures. Passengers in transit are exempt.
SEA: The only port is Aqaba, which is on the cruise itineraries for *Neptune*, *Royal Viking Sea* and *Navarino*. *Medlink* sails from Yugoslavia twice weekly. *Fayez* sails from Saudi Arabia and Egypt. Sea tax payable of JD5.
Car and passenger ferries: Aqaba to Suez and Aqaba to Nueibe. There is a weekly passenger service to Suez and Jeddah. Contact *Telestar Maritime Agency*.
RAIL: No scheduled international services, but there are tracks to Syria.
ROAD: Routes are via Syria and Turkey through Ramtha, 115km (70 miles) north of Amman (driving time from Damascus is four hours, plus up to three hours delay at the frontier). There is a shared taxi service from Amman to Damascus. Multi-entry visas may be needed. A coach service runs from Damascus to Irbid or Amman. Public buses/coaches run from Amman to Damascus and Baghdad daily, as well as to Allenby Bridge for the crossing to the occupied West Bank. To cross, permission is required – apply to the Ministry of the Interior, Amman. The granting of permission is usually routine, but allow three full working days. Road tax payable of JD3.
See below for information on **documentation**.

TRAVEL–Internal

AIR: *Royal Jordanian Airlines* operate regular flights to Aqaba. It is also possible to hire executive jets and helicopters.
RAIL: There is no longer a reliable public railway service.
ROAD: Main roads are good (there are nearly 3000km/1900 miles of paved roads in the country), but desert tracks should be avoided. It is important to make sure that the vehicle is in good repair if travelling on minor roads or tracks. Take plenty of water and follow local advice carefully. In case of breakdown, contact the Automobile Association. **Bus:** Services are efficient and cheap. *JETT* bus company (tel: (6) 664 146) operates services from Amman to other towns and cities in the country. Daily services to Aqaba and Petra. **Taxi:** Shared taxi service to all towns on fixed routes, also available for private hire. Shared taxis to Petra should be booked in advance owing to demand.
Car hire: *Avis* and four national companies operate services, available also from hotels and travel agents. Drivers are available for the day.
Note: When using routes which go near the Israeli border (and even when sailing or swimming in the Red Sea without a guide) the traveller should always have all papers in order and within reach.
Documentation: An International Driving Permit is required. Visitors are not allowed to drive a vehicle with normal Jordanian plates unless they have a Jordanian driving licence.
URBAN: There are conventional buses and extensive fixed-route 'Servis' shared taxis in Amman. The 'Servis' are licensed, with a standard fares scale, but there are no fixed pick-up or set-down points. Vehicles often fill up at central or outer terminal points and then run non-stop.

ACCOMMODATION

HOTELS: There are several high standard hotels in Amman and Aqaba where alcoholic drinks can be served at all times. Hotels are fully booked during business periods so booking in advance is advised. Winter and summer rates are the same. All rates are subject to 20% tax and service. **Grading:** Hotels are graded from **5-** to **1-star**. 5- and 4-star hotels have discotheques and nightclubs with live music, but no elaborate floorshows.

RESORTS & EXCURSIONS

Due to Jordan's small size any destination within the country may be reached by road from the capital, Amman, in a day.

Amman

Amman, the capital since 1921, contains about a third of the population. It is built on seven hills which form natural focal points in this otherwise straggling city. Tortuous roads wind between the square white houses which cluster together on the hillsides. With extensive modern building projects, Amman is now very well equipped with excellent hotels and tourist facilities, especially in the *Jabal* (hill) areas. The central *souk* is a colourful example of the markets abounding in Jordan. Remains from Roman, Greek and Ottoman Turk occupations are dotted around the city, the main attraction being the Roman amphitheatre from the 2nd century AD in the centre of the city. There is also the (Jebel el Qalat) Citadel which houses the *Archaeological Museum*; the *National Gallery of Fine Arts* and *Popular Museum of Costume and Jewellery*. Amman is very well sited for excursions to the other parts of the country.

North of Amman

Jerash is less than one hour's drive from Amman through the lovely hills of ancient **Gilead**. A magnificent Greco-Roman city on an ancient site, beautifully preserved by the desert sands, Jerash is justly famous for the *Triumphal Arch*, the *Hippodrome*, the great elliptical forum, the theatres, baths and gateways, the Roman bridge and the wide street of columns which leads to the *Temple of Artemis*. *Son et Lumière* programmes run in four different languages (French, English, German and Arabic). Other languages can be catered for upon request. Cost: JD1 per person. For information on festivals in Jerash, see *Special Events* in the *Social Profile* section below.
Irbid, which is 77km (49 miles) from Amman, is a city of Roman tombs and statues, and narrow streets with close-packed shops and arched entrances. **Umm Qais** in the far north of the country, the Biblical *'Gadara'*, dominates the area round *Lake Tiberias* (Sea of Galilee). Once a city favoured by the Romans for its hot springs and theatres, it had declined to a small village by the time of the Islamic conquests. Its ruins, however, are still impressive: the *Acropolis* built in 218BC, the forum, the colonnaded street with still-visible chariot tracks and the *Nymphaeum* and remains of a large basilica. Returning along the northwest border from Umm Qais to Jerash through the luxuriant scenery of the *Jordan River Valley*, one can visit the town of **Al Hammeh**, in sight of the Israeli-occupied *Golan Heights*, a town known for its hot springs and mineral waters; and **Pella**, once a city of the *Roman Decapolis*, now being excavated, and the hilltop castle of *Qalaat al-Rabadh* built by the Arabs in defence against the crusaders. The scenery in this surprisingly fertile part of Jordan is often very beautiful, especially in the spring when the Jordan Valley and surrounding area is covered in a profusion of flowers.

East of Amman

Towards **Azraq** and beyond is the vast desert which makes up so much of Jordan. Within this arid landscape are the fertile oases of the *Shaumari* and *Azraq Wetland Parks*, now run with the help of the World Wildlife Fund. Wild animals once native to Jordan, such as the oryx and gazelle, are being re-introduced, while the Wetlands are visited by thousands of migratory birds each year. The *Shaumari* was opened in October 1983 in an attempt to protect the country's dwindling oryx population. There are plans to open a further ten wildlife reserves which will cover more than 4100 sq km (1580 sq miles). The project is being organised by the Jordanian Royal Society for the Conservation of Nature, a body which has recently stepped up its efforts to protect the country's wildlife and to prevent pollution affecting the very busy port of Aqaba. Severe fines are imposed on anyone contravening Jordan's strict laws on these matters.
Also in the east are the desert *Umayyad castles* (Qasr) of *Amra* and *Al-Kharanah*. Built as hunting lodges and to protect caravan routes they are well preserved with frescoes and beautiful vaulted rooms.

West of Amman

Salt, once the Biblical *'Gilead'*, is a now a small town set in a fertile landscape, retaining much of its old character as a former leading city of *Transjordan*. Filled with the character, sights, sounds and aromas of an old Arab town with its narrow *souk*, its innumerable flights of steps, its donkeys and coffee houses, it has a tolerant, friendly, oriental atmosphere. 24km (15 miles) from Amman is *Iraq al-Amir*, the only Hellenistic palace still to be seen in the Middle East.

South of Amman

The Dead Sea, 392m (1286ft) below sea level and the lowest point on earth, glistens by day and night in an eerie, dry landscape. The Biblical cities of Sodom and Gomorrah are thought to be beneath its waters. Supporting no life and having no outlet, even the non-swimmer can float freely in the rich salt water. The Dead Sea at the end of the *River Jordan* is the natural barrier between Jordan and the occupied West Bank.
There are three routes from Amman to Aqaba, the most picturesque being *The King's Highway*, the whole length of which is dotted with places of interest.
Madaba and nearby *Mount Nebo*, where Moses is said to have struck the rock, were both flourishing Byzantine towns and have churches and beautifully preserved mosaics. In Madaba there are also ancient maps of 6th-century Palestine, a museum and an old family carpet-making industry which uses ancient looms. Off the Highway is **Mukawir**, a small village near the ruins of Machaerus of Herod Antipas, where Salome danced. From the summit of nearby *Qasr al-Meshneque*, where St John was beheaded, is a magnificent view of the Dead Sea, and sometimes even of Jerusalem and the *Mount of Olives*. Nearby *Zarqa Main* has hot mineral-water springs. Rugged scenery characterises this area; deep gorges, waterfalls, white rocks, small oases, birds and wild flowers. Further south on the Highway is **Kerak**, a beautiful medieval town surrounded by high walls and with a castle. Other places of historical, scenic or religious interest along the route before Petra include **Mutah** and **Mazar**, **Tafila**, **Edomite Qasr Buseirah** and the magnificent crusader hill fortress, *Shaubek castle*.
Petra is one of the wonders of the Middle-Eastern world: a gigantic natural amphitheatre hidden in the rocks out of which a delicately coloured city with immense facades has been carved; it was lost for hundreds of years and only rediscovered in 1812. The temples and caves of Petra rest high up above a chasm, with huge white rocks forming the *Bab*, or gate, of the *Siq*, the narrow entrance which towers over 21m (70ft) high. Until recently the rock caves were still inhabited by Bedu. Most of this unique city was built by the Nabatean Arabs in the 6th and 5th centuries BC as an important link in the caravan routes. It was added to by the Romans who carved out a huge theatre and, possibly, the spectacular classical facade of the *Khazneh* (treasury). Away from the road, it is only possible to reach Petra on horseback. This city of rock stairs, rock streets, rock-carved tombs and dwellings and temples has among its other attractions the *Qasr al-Bint* castle shrine and the *Al-Habis* caves and museums; while a short distance away from the more commercialised site of Petra is *Al-Barid* where a number of tombs lie in solitude and tranquillity among the rocks. There is a resthouse in Petra built against the rock wall near the beginning of the *Siq*, where it is advisable to book early in season, but is bitterly cold in winter. The Petra Forum Hotel also offers accommodation. The last stop south before Aqaba is *Wadi Rum*, about five hours from Amman by road. A Beau Geste-type fort run by the colourful Desert Patrol (Camel Corps), it was built to defend the valley in a great plain of escarpments and desert wilderness, and is a place strongly associated with T E Lawrence (Lawrence of Arabia). Many Bedu, of a tribe thought to be descended from Mohammed, still live in the valley in tents. Some tours will arrange trips into the desert to stay with a bedouin tribe or camping in the valley, a round trip being 97km (60 miles).
Aqaba: At the northeast end of the *Gulf of Aqaba* is Jordan's only port, and can be reached from Amman by road or air. It has grown considerably over the past few years, both as a port and as a tourist centre, due in part to its excellent beach and watersports facilities, 5-star hotels, and its low humidity and hot climate. The town has a variety of small shops and several good restaurants, and it leaves most of the other tourist facilities to be provided for by the hotels. These include windsurfing, scuba diving, sailing and fishing. Most hotels have swimming pools, and will offer continental and some traditional cuisine. Some provide business and conference facilities and excursions to Amman, Petra and Wadi Rum. A year-round resort, Aqaba boasts some of the best coral-reef diving and snorkelling sites in the world, often very close to shore, in water which rarely falls below 20°C.

SOCIAL PROFILE

FOOD & DRINK: The cuisine varies although most restaurants have a mixed menu which includes both Arabic and European dishes. Dishes include *Meze* (small starters such as *humus*, *fool*, *kube* and *tabouleh*); a variety of *Kebabs; Mahshi Waraq 'inab* (vine leaves stuffed with rice, minced meat and spices); *musakhan* (chicken in olive oil and onion sauce roasted on Arab bread); and the Jordanian speciality *mensaf* (stewed lamb in a yogurt sauce served on a bed of rice), a dish which is normally eaten with the hand. **Drink:** Drinking Arabic coffee is a ritual. Local beer and wine are available, as are imported beverages. There are no licensing laws. During Ramadan drinking and smoking in public is forbidden between sunrise and sunset.
NIGHTLIFE: There are nightclubs, theatres and cinemas in Amman, while some other major towns have cinemas.
SHOPPING: Every town will have a *souk* (market), and there are also many good craft and jewellery shops. There is a particularly good gold and jewellery market in Amman. Special items include: Hebron glass, mother-of-pearl boxes, pottery, backgammon sets, embroidered table cloths, jewelled rosaries and worry beads, nativity sets made of olive wood, leather hassocks, old and new brass and copper items, kaftans hand-embroidered with silver and gold thread. **Shopping hours:** 0900-1300 and 1530-1830 Sunday to Thursday (closed Fridays).
SPORT: Aqaba, on the shores of the Gulf of Aqaba (Red Sea), offers **swimming**, **boating**, **scuba diving** and **water-skiing**. There is a diving centre at Aqaba, but diving is limited to experienced divers with licences. It is forbidden to remove coral or shells, or to use harpoon guns and fishing spears. There are public swimming pools at the Hussein Youth City and various hotels in Amman. The Dead Sea is another popular area. In Amman, the Hussein Youth City has **tennis** courts as does the YMCA and several hotels. **Football** and **squash** are also available in Amman.
SPECIAL EVENTS: There are two major festivals every year in Jordan: The *Jerash Festival for Culture and Arts* takes place every August during a 2-week period and includes daily performances by Jordanian, Arab and international folklore troupes and performing artists. There is also the *Aqaba Water Sports Festival* in mid-November which includes international-class competition in water-skiing and other aquatic sports.
SOCIAL CONVENTIONS: Handshaking is the customary form of greeting. Jordanians are proud of their Arab culture, and hospitality here is a matter of great importance. Visitors are made to feel very welcome and Jordanians are happy to act as hosts and guides, and keen to inform the tourists about their traditions and culture. Islam always plays an important role in society and it is essential that Muslim beliefs are respected (see *World of Islam* section at the back of the book). Arabic coffee will normally be served continuously during social occasions. To signal that no more is wanted, slightly twist the cup when handing it back, otherwise it will be refilled. A small gift is quite acceptable in return for hospitality. Women are expected to dress modestly and beachwear must only be worn on the beach or poolside. **Photography:** It is polite to ask permission to take photographs of people and livestock, and in some places photography is forbidden. **Tipping:** 10-12% service charge is generally added in hotels and restaurants and extra tips are discretionary. Porters' and drivers' tips are about 8%.

BUSINESS PROFILE

ECONOMY: Jordan's agricultural sector has never recovered from the loss of the West Bank after the 1967 Middle East war, which deprived Jordan of 80% of its fruit-growing area and a proportionate amount of export revenue. Tomatoes, citrus fruit, cucumbers, water melons, aubergines and wheat are the principal commodities grown in the remaining, mostly desert area. The country's political stability – an unusual asset in the volatile Middle East – has ensured Jordan a steady flow of foreign aid which now underpins the economy. Industry, mostly light, has grown steadily along with tourism. The main industries are phosphate mining and potash extraction from the Dead Sea area. Other commercial enterprises include paints, plastics and cement. The ongoing search for exploitable oil deposits, unsuccessful thus far, continues. Jordan's £1-billion import bill derives from products from (in descending order) Iraq, the USA, the UK, Japan and Germany.
BUSINESS: English is widely spoken in business circles. Avoid Friday appointments. A good supply of visiting cards is essential. Formality in dress is important and for men a suit and tie should be worn for business meetings. **Office hours:** 0800-1400 Saturday to Thursday (Government offices); 0900-1700 Saturday, Wednesday and Thursday (other offices).
COMMERCIAL INFORMATION: The following organisation can offer advice: Amman Chamber of Commerce, PO Box 287, Amman. Tel: (6) 666 151. Telex: 21543.

HISTORY & GOVERNMENT

HISTORY: Modern Jordan comprises territory on the east and west banks of the River Jordan (the West Bank, formerly part of Palestine, is currently occupied by Israel). The East Bank, once part of the Turkish Ottoman empire, was known as Transjordan to the British, who occupied it in 1917. Like neighbouring Palestine, Transjordan came under a League of Nations mandate under which the British maintained control. The mandate ceased in 1946, at which point Transjordan attained full independence under the present constitution. The country came under the rule of King Abdullah ibn Hussein, a member of the Arabian Hashemite dynasty who had held the position of Emir since the 1920s. When King Abdullah was assassinated in 1951, the crown passed to his son Hussein ibn Talal. King Hussein assumed the throne in 1952 and has ruled the country ever since. Jordanian history and politics since independence have been dominated by the Palestinian issue and relations with Israel. When war broke out in 1948 between the newly declared state of Israel and the Palestinians, backed by the forces from neighbouring Arab countries, the Jordanian army occupied a 6000-sq-km area of Palestine bounded by the West Bank of the River Jordan. Until a major change in Jordanian policy in 1988, the West Bank comprised three of Jordan's eight provinces, while over half of the Jordanian population claimed Palestinian origin. Relations between King Hussein and the Palestinians were difficult from the very start: his father was murdered by a Palestinian extremist. Jordan lost the West Bank after the Six-Day War of 1967, and gained the thousands of Palestinian refugees who fled across the Jordan. Many of them joined one of the myriad of guerrilla groups organised under the umbrella title of the Palestine Liberation Organisation. (The modern PLO is a coalition of seven main factions, the largest of which is Al-Fatah headed by the PLO's overall leader Yasser Arafat.) Hussein ultimately came to feel that they constituted a major threat to his authority and in September 1970, he deployed the Jordanian army to expel them. In 1973, Israel again defeated a combined Arab force, including a small Jordanian contingent, in the Yom Kippur war: Jordan lost no territory on this occasion. Throughout the late 1970s and early 1980s Jordan pulled back from regional politics to concentrate more on domestic matters. After 1967, political power in Jordan had been concentrated fully in the hands of the King and his Council of Ministers while elections had been postponed indefinitely. The National Assembly had met only to pass a handful of constitutional amendments which formally sanctioned the King's powers. In 1984 Hussein initiated a gradual liberalisation of the political system: the National Assembly was recalled for its first full session for 17 years. The Jordanians continued to seek a resolution of the Palestinian problem, then in conjunction with an initiative of the Reagan administration, but were frustrated by a claimed lack of movement on the Isreali side. In 1987 the Intifada lead, in July the following year, to a surprise decision by Hussein to cede the residual Jordanian interest in the internal affairs of the occupied West Bank (notably financing public services such as education). Following the disposal of the West Bank, the National Assembly was again dissolved while a new electoral law was drawn up. Elections for the 80-seat House of Representatives were held in November 1989. Although political parties are officially banned – and have been since 1966 – Islamic parties were allowed to organise discretely. As elsewhere in the Arab world, Jordan has seen a sudden growth of Islamic fundamentalism. In the event, Palestinian and nationalist candidates probably won 7 seats (the absence of parties means that calculating affiliations is somewhat error-prone); the Islamic parties and their independent supporters took 30-35 seats; a handful of leftists and anti-corruption candidates got in; and the remainder – just under half – were won by supporters of the Government. The major problem facing the Jordanian government was the state of the economy. Increases in the prices of basic goods had led to riots early in 1990. The parlous condition of the economy was exacerbated later in the year by the onset of the Gulf crisis and UN sanctions against Iraq. (Jordan was a major transhipment route for goods destined for Iraq.) In the summer of 1992, the services of the pro-Iraqi Prime Minister Mudar Badran were dispensed with and a new premier of Palestinian extraction, Taher Masri, was appointed in June 1991: part of his brief was to improve the democratic credentials of the regime by introducing laws legalising the creation of political parties and guaranteeing press freedom. Masri's appointment was also valuable in putting together the joint Jordanian-Palestinian team for the lateast round of Middle East peace talks, which began in October 1991 in Madrid. This was essential because Israel would not accept a single Palestinian delegation and firmly stipulated that they could only be represented as part of a joint delegation. There has been greater optimism in Jordan about the outcome of the talks since the election of the Labour government in Israel, but the King will still have to cope with influential Muslim fundamentalist opinion, which remains implacably opposed to any accommodation with Israel In November 1992 at a crucial stage in the talks, the fundamentalists, who had been excluded from the Government, were able to force Masri's resignation. Masri's replacement was Sharif Zeid bin Shaker, a senior adviser to King Hussein, who has the tacit support of the fundamentalists. Although Sharif Zeid quickly reassured key foreign governments that there will be no change of policy on the talks, there is uncertainty about future Jordanian positions given that the new premier must rely upon fundamentalist support and may be obliged to bring a few of their number into cabinet ranks. Jordanian participation in the talks has led to an improvement in relations with the USA, Saudi Arabia and the Gulf states and, in particular, to the resumption of US aid payments to Jordan.
GOVERNMENT: Jordan is a constitutional monarchy with a bicameral legislature. The House of Representatives has 80 members elected by universal adult suffrage for a 4-year term. The second chamber, the House of Notables, has 30 members appointed by the King for an 8-year term. Executive power is held by the King, who governs with the assistance of a Council of Ministers. The current Prime Minister is Sharif Zeid bin Shaker. Until 1988, the Israeli-occupied West Bank was considered to comprise three of Jordan's eight administrative provinces.

CLIMATE

Hot and dry summers with cool evenings. The Jordan Valley below sea level is warm during winter and extremely hot in summer. Rain falls between November and March in colder months.
Required clothing: Lightweight cottons and linens are advised between May and September. Warmer clothes are necessary for winter and cool summer evenings. Rainwear is needed from November to April.

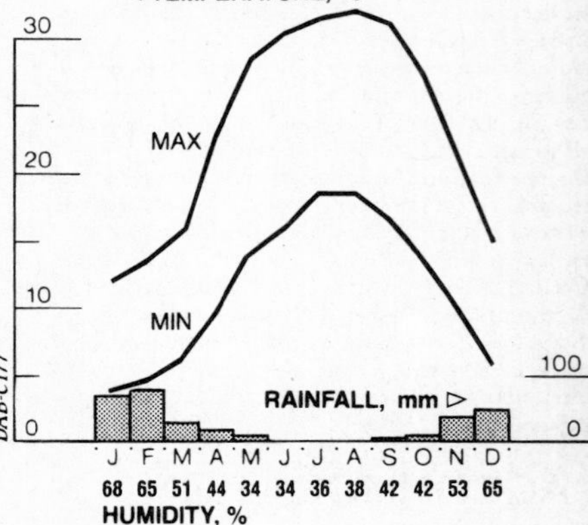

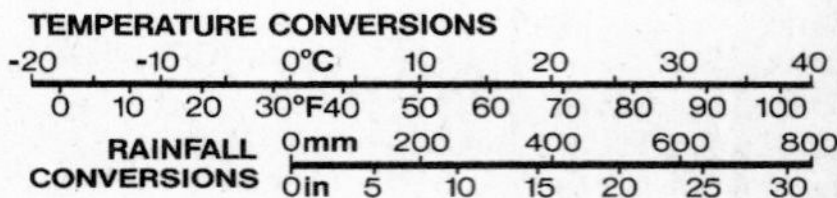

KENYA

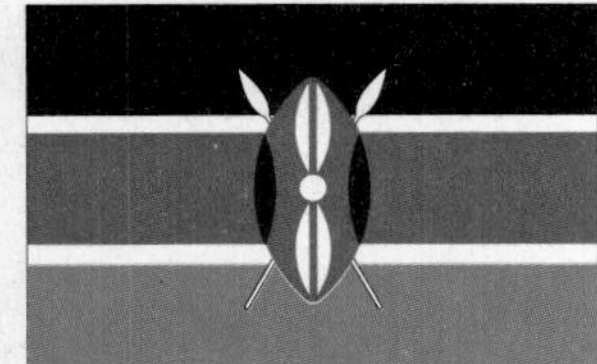

Location: East Africa.

Kenya Tourist Development Corporation
PO Box 42013
Nairobi, Kenya
Tel: (2) 330 820. Telex: 23009.

Kenya High Commission
45 Portland Place
London W1N 4AS
Tel: (071) 636 2371/2/3/4/5. Fax: (071) 323 6717. Telex: 262551. Opening hours: 0900-1300 and 1400-1700 Monday to Friday.

Kenya Tourist Office
25 Brook's Mews
off Davies Street
Mayfair
London W1Y 1LG
Tel: (071) 355 3144. Fax: (071) 323 6717. Telex: 262551. Opening hours: 0900-1700 Monday to Friday.

British High Commission
PO Box 30465
Bruce House
Standard Street
Nairobi, Kenya
Tel: (2) 335 944. Fax: (2) 333 196. Telex: 22219 UKREP.
Consulate in: Mombasa.

Embassy of the Republic of Kenya
2249 R Street, NW
Washington, DC
20008
Tel: (202) 387 6101.

Kenya Tourist Office
424 Madison Avenue
New York, NY
10017
Tel: (212) 486 1300. Fax: (212) 688 0911. Telex: 204427 KCNY UR.

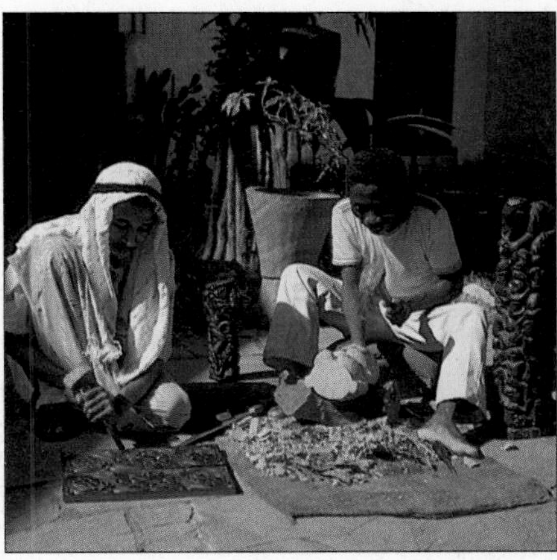

Embassy of the United States of America
PO Box 30137
Unit 64100
corner of Moi and Hailé Sélassie Avenues
Nairobi, Kenya
Tel: (2) 334 141. Fax: (2) 340 838. Telex: 22964.
Consulate in: Mombasa.

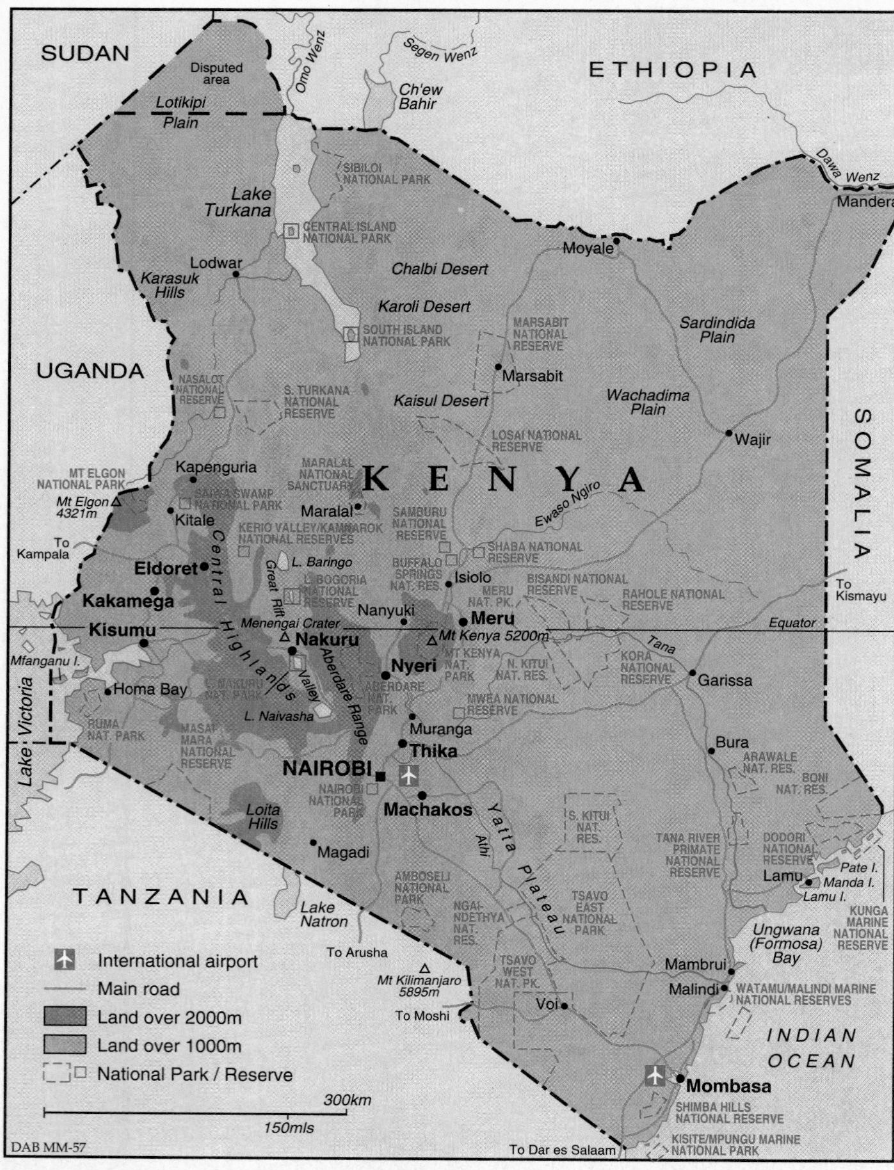

High Commission of the Republic of Kenya
415 Laurier Avenue East
Ottawa, Ontario
K1N 6R4
Tel: (613) 563 1773/4/5/6. Fax: (613) 233 6599.
Canadian High Commission
PO Box 30481
Comcraft House
Hailé Sélassie Avenue
Nairobi, Kenya
Tel: (2) 214 804. Fax: (2) 226 987. Telex: 22198 DOMCAN.

AREA: 580,367 sq km (224,081 sq miles).
POPULATION: 24,870,000 (1989 estimate).
POPULATION DENSITY: 42.9 per sq km.
CAPITAL: Nairobi. **Population:** 1,162,189 (1985).
GEOGRAPHY: Kenya shares borders with Ethiopia in the north, Sudan in the northwest, Uganda in the west, Tanzania in the south, and the Somali Republic in the northeast. To the east lies the Indian Ocean. The country is divided into four regions: the arid deserts of the north, the savannah lands of the south, the fertile lowlands along the coast and around the shores of Lake Victoria, and highlands in the west, where the capital Nairobi is situated. Northwest of Nairobi runs the Rift Valley, containing the town of Nakuru and Aberdare National Park, overlooked by Mount Kenya (5200m, 17,000ft), which also has a national park. In the far northwest is Lake Turkana (formerly Lake Rudolph). Kenya is a multi-tribal society and has a diverse pattern of tribes; in the north live Somalis and the nomadic Hamitic peoples (Turkana, Rendille and Samburu), in the south and eastern lowlands are Kamba and Masai cattle herders and the Nilotic Luo live around Lake Victoria. The largest tribe is the Kikuyu who live in the central highlands and have traditionally been the dominant tribe in commerce and politics, although this is now shifting. There are many other smaller tribes and although Kenya emphasises nationalism, tribal and cultural identity is evident. A small European settler population remains in the highlands, involved in farming and commerce.
LANGUAGE: Kiswahili is the national and English is the official language. Kikuyu and Luo are also widely spoken.
RELIGION: Mostly traditional, and about 25% Christian, 6% Muslim.
TIME: GMT + 3.
ELECTRICITY: 220/240 volts AC, 50Hz. Plugs are UK-type round 2-pin or flat 3-pin. Bayonet-type light sockets.
COMMUNICATIONS: Telephone: IDD service is available to the main cities. Country code: 254 (followed by 2 for Nairobi, 11 for Mombasa and 37 for Nakuru). **Fax:** This service is available to the public at the main post office and the Kenyatta International Conference Centre in Nairobi, and at some major hotels in Nairobi and Mombasa. **Telex/telegram:** Telex facilities are available at Nairobi General Post Office. New Stanley and Hilton Hotels have facilities for their guests. Overseas telegrams can be sent from all post and telegraphic offices and private telephones. Nairobi GPO is open 24 hours. **Post:** Airmail to Europe takes up to four days, and the service is generally reliable. Post offices are open 0800-1700 Monday to Friday and 0800-1300 Saturday. **Press:** The main dailies include *Daily Nation*, *Kenya Times* and *The Standard*. Nairobi is the main publishing centre.
BBC World Service and Voice of America frequencies: From time to time these change. See the section *How to Use this Book* for more information.

BBC:				
MHz	21.47	17.88	15.42	9.630
Voice of America:				
MHz	21.49	15.60	9.525	6.035

PASSPORT/VISA

Regulations and requirements may be subject to change at short notice, and you are advised to contact the appropriate diplomatic or consular authority before finalising travel arrangements. Details of these may be found at the head of this country's entry. Any numbers in the chart refer to the footnotes below.

	Passport Required?	Visa Required?	Return Ticket Required?
Full British	Yes	No	Yes
BVP	Not valid	-	-
Australian	Yes	Yes	Yes
Canadian	Yes	No	Yes
USA	Yes	Yes	Yes
Other EC	Yes	1	Yes
Japanese	Yes	Yes	Yes

PASSPORTS: Valid passport required by all.
British Visitors Passport: Not acceptable.
VISAS: Required by all except:
(a) nationals of the UK;
(b) [1] nationals of Denmark, Germany, Ireland, Italy and Spain (all other EC nationals *do* require a visa);
(c) nationals of Ethiopia, Finland, Namibia, Norway, San Marino, Sweden, Turkey and Uruguay;
(d) nationals of the following Commonwealth countries: Antigua & Barbuda, Bahamas, Bangladesh, Barbados, Bermuda, Botswana, Canada, Cyprus, Dominica, Gambia, Ghana, Grenada, Jamaica, Kiribati, Lesotho, Malawi, Malaysia, Maldives, Malta, Mauritius, Nauru, Papua New Guinea, St Kitt's & Nevis, St Lucia, St Vincent & the Grenadines, Seychelles, Sierra Leone, Singapore, Solomon Islands, Swaziland, Tanzania, Tonga, Trinidad & Tobago, Turks & Caicos Islands, Tuvalu, Uganda, Vanuatu, Western Samoa, Zambia and Zimbabwe.
Note: Travellers needing a visa are advised to acquire one before their journey; a visitor's pass is available to those without a visa on arrival, but a deposit of £250 refundable upon departure may be required before a pass is issued.

KENYA | **HEALTH REGULATIONS** | **VISA REGULATIONS** | Code-Link

GALILEO/WORLDSPAN
TI-DFT/NBO/HE

TI-DFT/NBO/VI

SABRE

TIDFT/NBO/HE

TIDFT/NBO/VI

To access this information on your CRS, swipe the barcode with a light pen or type in the text under the barcode. For more information, see the introduction *How to Use This Book*.

[1]: A yellow fever vaccination certificate is required from travellers over one year of age arriving from infected areas; those countries formerly classified as endemic zones are considered to be still infected by the Kenyan authorities.
[2]: Following WHO guidelines issued in 1973, a cholera vaccination certificate is no longer a condition of entry to Kenya. However, cholera is a serious risk in this country and precautions are essential. Up-to-date advice should be sought before deciding whether these precautions should include vaccination, as medical opinion is divided over its effectiveness. See the *Health* section at the back of the book.
[3]: Malaria risk exists throughout the year in the whole country. There is usually less risk in Nairobi and in the highlands (above 2500m) of the Central, Rift Valley, Eastern, Nyanza and Western Provinces. The predominant *falciparum* strain has been reported as 'highly resistant' to chloroquine and 'resistant' to sulfadoxine/pyrimethamine.
[4]: Mains water is normally chlorinated, and whilst relatively safe may cause mild abdominal upsets. Bottled water is available and is advised for the first few weeks of the stay. Drinking water outside main cities and towns is likely to be contaminated and sterilisation is considered essential. Milk is pasteurised and dairy products are safe for consumption. Local meat, poultry, seafood, fruit and vegetables are generally considered safe to eat.
Bilharzia (schistosomiasis) is present. Avoid swimming and paddling in fresh water. Swimming pools which are well-chlorinated and maintained are safe.
Health care: Health insurance is essential. *East African Flying Doctor Services* have introduced special Tourist Membership which guarantees that any member injured or ill while on safari can call on a flying doctor for free air transport.
Note: There is a risk of contracting *AIDS* if the necessary precautions are not taken. It is advisable to take a kit of sterilised needles for any possible injections needed.
Rabies is present. For those at high risk, vaccination before arrival should be considered. If you are bitten abroad seek medical advice without delay. For more information consult the *Health* section at the back of the book.

Types of visa: Entry and Transit. Cost – £6 for most nationals for standard visas.
Validity: Up to 3 months. Renewals or extensions can be made at Immigration in Nyayo House, Uhuru Highway, Nairobi.
Application to: Consulate (or Consular Section at Embassy or High Commission). For addresses, see top of entry.
Application requirements: (a) Valid passport. (b) Completed application form. (c) Fee. (d) 2 photos for referrable visas only.
Working days required: Consult Embassy or High Commission. The length of time it takes to process the application depends on whether or not it has to be referred to Nairobi. Otherwise 24 hours.
Temporary residence: Apply to Principal Immigration Officer, PO Box 30191, Nairobi, Kenya.

MONEY

Currency: Kenyan Shilling (KSh) = 100 cents. Notes are in denominations of KSh500, 100, 50, 20 and 10. Coins are in denominations of KSh5 and 1, and 50, 10 and 5 cents.
Currency exchange: Currency can be exchanged at the major banks, some of which are more co-operative than others. Black market transactions are common, but inadvisable.
Credit cards: Access/Mastercard, American Express, Diners Club and Visa are all widely accepted. Check with your credit card company for details of merchant acceptability and other services which may be available.
Travellers cheques: These can be changed at banks.
Note: Tanzanian and Ugandan currencies are only negotiable if in the form of travellers cheques.
Exchange rate indicators: The following figures are included as a guide to the movements of the Kenyan Shilling against Sterling and the US Dollar:

Date:	Oct '89	Oct '90	Oct '91	Oct '92
£1.00=	34.50	44.80	49.40	55.12
$1.00=	21.84	22.93	28.46	34.73

Currency restrictions: The import and export of local currency is prohibited. Free import of foreign currency is allowed provided declared. Foreign currency may be exported up to either the equivalent of KhS5000 or the amount declared on arrival. There is no limit placed on travellers cheques and letters of credit.
Banking hours: 0900-1400 Monday to Friday; 0900-1100 on the first and last Saturday of each month. The airport banks are open until midnight every day. Banks on the coast close half an hour earlier. National and international banks have branches in Mombasa, Nairobi, Kisumu, Thika, Eldoret, Kericho, Nyeri and in most other major towns.

DUTY FREE

The following goods may be imported by passengers over 16 years of age into Kenya without incurring customs duty:
200 cigarettes or 225g of tobacco;
1 bottle of spirits or wine;
1 pint of perfume.
Note: Firearms and ammunition require a police permit. Gold, diamonds and wildlife skins or game trophies not authorised by a Kenyan government department are prohibited.

PUBLIC HOLIDAYS

Public holidays observed in Kenya are as follows:
Mar 25 '93 Eid al-Fitr (End of Ramadan). **Apr 9** Good Friday. **Apr 12** Easter Monday. **May 1** Labour Day. **Jun 1** Madaraka Day and Eid al-Adha, Feast of the Sacrifice. **Oct 11** Moi Day. **Oct 20** Kenyatta Day. **Dec 13** Jamhuri Day. **Dec 25-26** Christmas. **Jan 1 '94** New Year's Day. **Mar** Eid al-Fitr.
Note: (a) Holidays falling on a Sunday are observed the following Monday.
(b) Muslim festivals are timed according to local sightings of various phases of the Moon and the dates given above are approximations. During the lunar month of Ramadan that precedes Eid al-Fitr, Muslims fast during the day and feast at night and normal business patterns may be interrupted. Many restaurants are closed during the day and there may be restrictions on smoking and drinking. Some disruption may continue into Eid al-Fitr itself. It may last anything from two to ten days, depending on the region. For more information see the section *World of Islam* at the back of the book.

HEALTH

Regulations and requirements may be subject to change at short notice, and you are advised to contact your doctor well in advance of your intended date of departure. Any numbers in the chart refer to the footnotes below.

	Special Precautions?	Certificate Required?
Yellow Fever	No	1
Cholera	2	2
Typhoid & Polio	Yes	-
Malaria	3	-
Food & Drink	4	-

TRAVEL - International

AIR: Kenya's national airline is *Kenya Airways (KQ)*.
Approximate flight times: From Nairobi to *London* is 8 hours; to *New York* is 17 hours 30 minutes; to *Los Angeles* is 20 hours; to *Singapore* is 13 hours and to *Sydney* is 25 hours.
International airports: *Nairobi (NBO)* (Jomo Kenyatta International) is 13km (8 miles) southeast of the city. Bus number 34 runs every 30 minutes from 0630-2100 (travel time – 30 minutes). Taxis are also available to the city. Airport facilities include an outgoing duty-free shop, 24-hour bank/exchange services, post office (0800-1700 Monday to Friday), restaurant/bar and car hire from a range of international companies.
Mombasa (MBA) (Moi International) is 13km (8 miles) west of the city. There is a regular bus service by *Kenya Airways* to their city centre office in Mombasa (travel time – 15 minutes). Taxis are available. Airport facilities include an outgoing duty-free shop, bank (0500-1400), restaurant/bar, 24-hour tourist information and car hire from a range of international companies.
Note: Immigration procedures in Kenyan airports are likely to be extremely slow, so it is wise to arrive early.
Departure tax: US$20.
SEA/LAKE: A regular international passenger service operates between Mombasa, the Seychelles and Bombay. Short-distance ships sail between Mombasa, Dar-es-Salaam and Zanzibar. The ports in the Lake Victoria passenger service include Port Victoria/Kisumu, Homa Bay and Mfangano. Passenger and cruise lines that run to Kenya are as follows: *TFC Tours*, *Polish Ocean*, *Hellenic Lines* (from the USA and Red Sea), *Moore/McCormack (USA)*, *Lykes Lines* and *Norwegian American*.
Ferries in Lake Victoria connect Kisumu in Kenya to Mwanza, Musoma and Bukoba in Tanzania. Fares are paid for in the port of embarkation currency. It is also possible to get ferries from Mombasa to Pemba and Zanzibar in Tanzania, and also to Chiamboni in Somalia. Enquire locally for details.
RAIL: The through train services to Uganda and Tanzania are currently suspended, but a thrice-weekly train runs to the frontier from where there are onward connections by taxi.
ROAD: Kenya can be entered by road from all neighbouring countries, *although some routes may be inadvisable due to uncertain political conditions*. Check with the Foreign Office if in doubt.
Travel from Somalia is generally via Liboi, where a change of bus will be required. The route from Sudan is currently not recommended due to the civil war in the

south. The main crossing points from Tanzania are at Namanga and Lunga Lunga, with smaller posts at Isebania and Taveta. Some direct coach services operate. From Uganda there are crossing points at Malaba and Buisa. Note that at Malaba the Kenyan and Ugandan customs posts are about 1km apart and no transport between them is available. For all road frontier crossings, it is advisable to contact the Kenya AA (PO Box 40087, Nairobi) prior to departure from country of origin for up-to-date information concerning insurance requirements and conditions.
Note: For their own safety when travelling overland through the northeastern province of Kenya, travellers are advised to contact the Tourist Development Corporation (see above) for advice. Four-wheel drive vehicles are recommended for travel in this region.

TRAVEL - Internal

AIR: *Kenya Airways* operates an extensive network of flights, which includes scheduled services to Mombasa, Malindi, Lamu Island, Kisumu (on the shore of Lake Victoria) and inclusive tours to the game parks and the coast from Nairobi. There are also private airlines such as *Caspair* operating light aircraft to small air strips. Planes can also be chartered and are useful for transportation into game parks.
Departure tax: KSh50 on all domestic flights.
SEA: Local ferries run between Mombasa, Malindi and Lamu. For details contact local authorities and tour operators.
RAIL: *Kenya Railways Corporation* runs passenger trains between Mombasa and Nairobi; trains generally leave in the evening and arrive the following morning after a journey of about 13-14 hours. There are also branches connecting Taveta and Kisumu to the passenger network. There is a daily train in each direction on the Nairobi–Kisumu route, and also an overnight service (travel time – approx 14 hours). Trains are sometimes delayed, but most of the rolling stock is modern and comfortable, and most trains have restaurant cars. There are three classes: first class is excellent, with 2-berth compartments, wardrobe etc; second class is more basic but comfortable; third is basic. The dining car service on the Nairobi–Mombasa route is very highly regarded. Sleeping compartments should be booked in advance.
ROAD: Traffic drives on the left. All major roads are now tarred and many of the others have been improved, particularly in the southwest, although vast areas of the north still suffer from very poor communications. Care should be taken when leaving trunk roads as the surfaces of the lesser roads vary greatly in quality, particularly during the rainy season. There are petrol stations on most highways. The Kilifi Bridge linking Mombasa to Malindi has opened, serving as an alternative to the Kilifi ferry, and easing traffic flows to the northern circuit.
Bus: There is a network of regular buses and shared minibuses *(Matatu)*; the fares do not vary greatly, but buses tend to be the safer method of transport. All bus companies are privately run. In some towns the different bus services and the *Matatu* share the same terminus.
Taxi: Kenya is very well served by long-distance taxis, carrying up to seven passengers. The best services are between the capital and Mombasa and Nakuru. Taxis and minibuses are a convenient method of travel on the coast. **Car hire:** Self-drive and chauffeur-driven cars may be hired from a number of travel agents in Nairobi, Mombasa and Malindi. This can be expensive, and rates – particularly the mileage charges – can vary a good deal. Only 4-wheel-drive cars should be considered.
Tours and safaris: Many tour companies in Nairobi offer package arrangements for visits to the game parks and other attractions. *Rhino Safaris* offer a fleet of over 100 safari vehicles to all the game parks and reserves. Before booking it is very important to know exactly what the all-in price provides. **Documentation:** British or foreign driving licences are accepted for up to 90 days, but this must be endorsed in Kenya at a local police station. Visitors bringing in vehicles with registration other than Ugandan or Tanzanian must obtain an 'International Circulation Permit' from the Licensing Officer in Nairobi. This will be issued free of charge on production of a permit of customs duty receipt and a certificate of insurance. An International Driving Permit is strongly recommended, although it is not legally required. For further details, apply to the Registrar of Motor Vehicles in Nairobi.
URBAN: Nairobi and Mombasa have efficient bus systems. Only single tickets are sold (by conductors). There are also unregulated *Matatu*, 12- to 25-seat light pick-ups and minibuses. These are often severely overloaded and recklessly driven and therefore should be used with caution. *Kenatco* runs a fleet of taxis and these are usually very reliable. The older yellow-band taxis do not have meters, so fares should be agreed in advance. A 10% tip is expected. Taxis cannot be hailed in the street.

JOURNEY TIMES: The following chart gives approximate journey times (in hours and minutes) from Nairobi to other major cities/towns in Kenya.

	Air	Road	Rail
Kisumu	1.05	7.00	14.00
Malindi	0.45	8.00	-
Mombasa	1.00	6.00	14.00
Lamu	1.30	13.00	-
Diani	1.30	7.00	-
Nakuru	0.30	3.00	5.00
Eldoret	1.15	7.00	9.00
Masai Mara	0.30	5.00	-
Amboseli	0.30	3.00	-

ACCOMMODATION

HOTELS: Many of Nairobi's hotels are up to top international standards, and some of them are very much in the colonial style. Cheaper hotels are also available. Hotel bills must be paid in foreign currency, or in Kenyan Shillings drawn from an external, a shipping or an airline account. **Grading:** Accommodation in Kenya is divided into groups: town hotels, vacation hotels, lodges and country hotels. Within each group, grading is according to amenities and variety of facilities. The rating is subject to the fulfilment of strict requirements concerning technical equipment, comfort, services, sanitation and security.
CAMPING/CARAVANNING: There are no restrictions on camping in Kenya. Visitors should be aware that camping in remote regions can be dangerous due to wild animals and to *shifta* (armed bandits); the latter are a hazard particularly in the far north. A list of licensed tented camps is available from the Tourist Office or the press section of the High Commission.
YOUTH HOSTELS: There are youth hostels in all major towns. For further information, contact the Youth Office in Nairobi. Tel: (2) 723 012.

RESORTS & EXCURSIONS

For the purposes of this guide, Kenya has been divided into three regions: Central Highlands, The Coast and National Parks.

Central Highlands

Nairobi: The 'Green City in the Sun' is an attractive city with wide tree-lined streets and spacious parkland suburbs. Its pleasant aspect together with canny investment in facilities such as the *Kenyatta Conference Centre* have made Nairobi an important centre for international business and conference activities. However, despite the capital's clean and smart appearance, urban crime (as in most big cities) is on the increase and visitors are advised to take precautions as they would take in any other cosmopolitan centre in the world (this would include avoiding certain areas, especially at night – some travellers advise against walking alone through *Uhuru Park* at any time). There is a full range of shopping opportunities, from purpose-built American-style malls to rickety African markets, and a great variety of restaurants and nightclubs. The *African Heritage Café*, Banda Street, serves traditional African meals. The *Thorn Tree Café* at the New Stanley Hotel is an open-air café and a good place to meet fellow visitors. The *New Supreme* and *Minar* serve top-quality Indian food and there is a good choice of international food at all hotels. The *Carnivore* serves barbecued wild game. There are open-air swimming pools at the *Serena*, *Boulevard* and *Jacaranda* hotels – non-residents may pay to swim. Other places of interest in or near Nairobi include: *Bomas of Kenya*, a short distance outside the city centre, where displays of traditional dancing are put on for visitors; *Kenya National Museum* with its particularly good ethnographic exhibits; The *Snake Park*, opposite the museum, houses snakes indigenous to East Africa and a few from other parts of the world; adjacent to the Snake Park is a collection of traditional mud and thatch huts and granaries containing tools characteristic of different tribes. *Nairobi National Park* is just 8km (5 miles) from Nairobi city centre yet still seems a savage and lonely place during the week (carloads of city-dwellers invade at the weekend). It was Kenya's first national park and today looks much as it does in the early photographs – wild, undulating pasture dotted with every kind of East African plain-dwelling animal except elephants. Visits can be arranged through the *Hilton Hotel*. At the gates to the park is the *Animal Orphanage* where young, sick and wounded animals are cared for.
Lake Naivasha is an hour's drive from the capital. It is known for the abundance and variety of its birdlife and spectacular views. There are opportunities for rock climbing.
Nanyuki, at the foot of *Mount Kenya*, provides a starting point both for climbers and safaris.
Nakuru is situated in the *Rift Valley* about 230km (140 miles) west of Nairobi. It has the feel of a frontier town. *Lake Nakuru National Park* was once said to be home to half the world's total population of pink flamingoes, and even today visitors in winter will encounter these ungainly birds in awesome numbers. Many less spectacu-

lar birds can also be seen. Baboons often sport on the lake's western cliffs. *Menengai Crater*, an extinct volcano, stands nearby. 50km (30 miles) to the north of Nakuru, along a fairly good road, is *Lake Baringo*, smaller than Lake Nakuru, but with the same variety of birdlife. There is a permanent tented camp on the island at its centre, where boats may be hired to cruise through the reeds at the lake's northern end, a habitat rich in water fowl, egrets, giant herons and fishing eagles.
Kisumu on *Lake Victoria* is a commercial centre linked by road to the capital. Visits can be made to *Mount Elgon National Park*, famous for its mountain flowers and fauna.

The Coast

Mombasa: The second largest city in Kenya, 500km (300 miles) from Nairobi. Until the ascendancy of the Western powers in the Indian Ocean, Mombasa was second only to Zanzibar as a centre for trade with Arabia, India, and the Far East – slaves and ivory were exchanged for spices and small goods, and later for gold dollars. Mombasa is still an important port, prospering from its position at the head of the only railway into the Kenyan interior, but visitors are likely to find the rakish grey forms of foreign warships to be more typical of modern Mombasa than the flotillas of Arab dhows that still collect in the *Old Harbour*. Mombasa is the headquarters for Kenya's coastal tourist trade, but has none of the fine beaches to be found to the north and south. There are, however, several places of interest: The *Old Town* retains a strongly Arab flavour, with narrow, crowded streets and street vendors selling all manner of local and imported craftwork; *Fort Jesus*, built by the Portuguese in 1593 and taken by the Omani Arabs in 1698 after a 33-month seige, is now a museum and worth visiting (0830-1830 every day of the year); *Biashara Street* is probably the best place to go to buy kikoi and khanga cloths; the *Old Harbour* is an interesting place for early morning and late afternoon strolls, and is often filled with sailing dhows from the Yemen and Persian Gulf; *The Ivory Room* off Treasury Square is now permanently closed. The *Tourist Office* is on Moi Avenue near the Giant Tusks (0800-1200 and 1400-1630 Monday to Friday and 0800-1200 Saturday). Staff are very helpful.
Malindi, 125km (80 miles) north of Mombasa, contains the *Malindi and Watamu Marine National Parks* where one can see fish through a glass-bottomed boat or take part in snorkelling or skindiving. Close to Watamu is a ruined city (now the *Gedi National Park*) which dates from the 13th century and is very well preserved. The little village of **Mambrui**, north of Malindi, is also worth a visit.
Lamu Island, 200km (125 miles) north of Malindi, is an exceptionally beautiful place with fine white sandy beaches, sailing dhows and a fascinating town. No motorised vehicles are allowed on the island and the streets are so narrow that donkeys and hand-carts are the only vehicles that can negotiate them. There are many mosques and fine old Arab houses with impressive carved wooden doors. Other attractions in the city include the *Hindu Temple* in Mwagogo Road, off Treasury Square, and the bazaars. Fishing trips may be taken by dhow and day trips to the 14th- and 15th-century ruins on the nearby islands of **Pate** and **Manda** can be arranged with local boat owners. On the Prophet's Birthday there is a week-long festival, with dancing, singing and other celebrations. Many Muslims come to Lamu from all along the coast to enjoy this celebration. The best time to visit the island is outside the main tourist season (April-November).
The South Coast, protected by its coral reef, is famous for its beautiful and safe beaches. Resorts include Likoni, Tiwi, Diani Beach and Shimoni.
The North Coast is famous for such resorts as Bamburi Beach, Kenya Beach, Watamu Beach and Casuarina Beach.

National Parks

Kenya's national parks and game reserves have long been famous for their variety and wealth of flora and fauna. That they have remained Africa's foremost areas of accessible wilderness is due to a vigorous campaign of preservation and management mounted since the 1960s with increasing success by the Kenyan government. Whilst drought and overgrazing have destroyed some regions and there is still conflict between tribal interests and wildlife preservation, the Government fully recognises that Kenya's future prosperity may depend on maintaining its remarkable natural heritage.
One-tenth of all land in Kenya is designated as national parkland. Forty parks and reserves cover all habitats from desert to mountain forest, and there are even two marine parks in the Indian Ocean. Tourist facilities are extremely good. There are many organised safaris, but those with the time and money may choose to hire their own vehicle and camping equipment. Day trips by balloon are becoming a very popular way to view game, especially in the Masai Mara Game Reserve, and it is advisable to book well in advance.

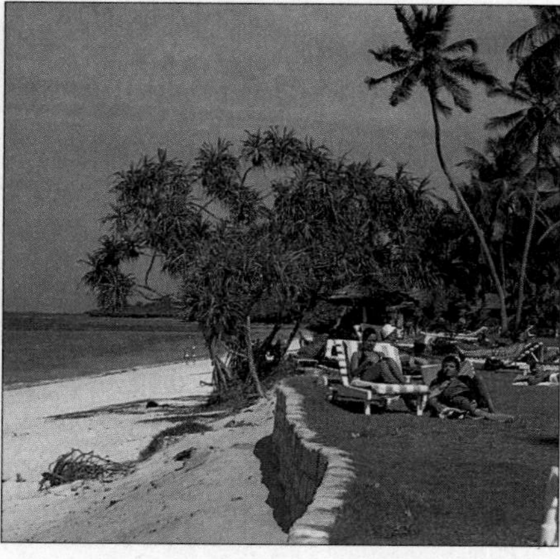

Some smaller parks are described in the preceding sections covering the Central Highlands and the Coast. The following is a selection of the better-known parks.
Aberdare National Park: A closely wooded mountain range rising to over 4000m (13,000ft), adjacent to Mount Kenya. It is possible to see **elephants, rhinos,** rare forest **antelopes** such as the **bongo** and **dik-dik, leopards, lions** and **monkeys.** However, the dense vegetation and misty alpine climate hides most wildlife from the inexpert observer, the exceptions being **giant forest pigs, baboons** and **buffaloes,** which often sleep or feed beside the many dirt tracks. Most visitors prefer to watch for animals from the comfort of the park's two lodges, *Treetops* and the *Ark*, both built on platforms overlooking clearings which are floodlit at night. On the higher slopes, giant alpine plants sprout from an almost perpetual fog. There are many waterfalls, the greatest being *Guru Falls* which drops over 300m (1000ft).
Amboseli National Park: A small park by Kenyan standards, covering just under 400 sq km (155 sq miles) at the centre of the border with Tanzania, 220km (140 miles) from Nairobi. The fine view it affords of snow-capped *Mount Kilimanjaro*, Africa's highest mountain (5895m/19,340ft), brings many visitors, but the park itself has seen better days. The once-lush savannah is now largely a dust-bowl and most animals have retreated into areas of scrub forest and marshland.
Masai Mara National Reserve: 390km (240 miles) from Nairobi in the southwest corner of the country, this reserve is a slice of Africa as seen by Hollywood – a vast rolling plain beneath the Mara escarpment striped black once a year by millions of **wildebeeste** and **zebra** migrating north from the Serengeti plains in neighbouring Tanzania. Continually harried by predators, thick columns of exhausted animals eventually converge at one spot on the *Mara River* and wait nervously to cross. A panic anywhere within the herd is transmitted flank-to-flank until it reaches those by the river, who fall twenty feet into water already bloodied and bobbing with bloated carcasses. The inelegant beasts must swim past **crocodiles, hippos** and flapping **vultures** to join the sparse but growing herd on the other side. The stench is unimaginable and this spectacle is probable best seen from one of three balloons operating from *Grosvenor's Camp*. During the migration season (July/August), the reserve's resident **lions** lounge prominently in the sun, fat and seemingly placid, and apparently indifferent to tourists. Other animals to be seen, at any time of the year, include **elephants, cheetahs, baboons, gazelles, giraffes, jackals, hyenas, water buffaloes, ostriches** and several types of **antelope.** There are 13 tented camps and

two lodges *(Mara Serena Lodge* and *Keekorok Lodge)* in the reserve. Grosvenor's Camp, with its own airstrip, is the largest and best-equipped. A luxury hotel stands on the escarpment just outside the reserve and gives fine views over the plain. Masai tribespeople live on the reserve's fringes. They are often keen to sell traditional bead necklaces and decorated gourds to tourists, or to pose for tourist cameras in return for a small fee.
Meru National Park: 400km (250 miles) from Nairobi, this features Kenya's only colony of **white rhinos.** It remains one of the more unspoilt parks.
Mount Kenya National Park: 600 sq km (230 sq miles) of forest and bare rock straddling the equator, all above 1800m (6000ft), rising to over 5000m (17,000ft) in the year-round snow fields at the mountain's peak. The ascent is very beautiful and may be climbed without special equipment, but it is advisable to take time so as to avoid altitude sickness. Climbers should be accompanied by a guide. Porters are also available and there are huts to stay in along the way. Plenty of warm clothes are required as well as your own food supplies. A *Rockclimber's Guide to Mount Kenya and Mount Kilimanjaro* can be bought from the Mountain Club of Kenya, PO Box 45741, Nairobi (tel: (2) 501 747). The mountain is one of the last haunts of the **black leopard** and the **black and white colobus monkey.** Lord Baden-Powell is buried nearby in **Nyeri.**
Samburu Game Park: An area of semi-desert halfway between Nairobi and *Lake Turkana* that provides a rare chance to see the **oryx, gerenuk, reticulated giraffe** and **Grevy's zebra. Ostriches** and **elephants** are easily spotted in this open habitat. There are two lodges, *Samburu Lodge* and *River Lodge*, both of which hang out bait to attract leopards for the guests to study whilst sitting at the bar. The park takes its name from the Samburu people, distantly related to the Masai.
Tsavo National Park: At 21,000 sq km (8,000 sq miles), it is Kenya's largest park by far, but much of it is closed to the public. Despite a drastic fall in the **elephant** population in the 1970s (caused by over-stocking), there are still many large herds. Much of the land is open savannah and bush woodland inhabited by **buffaloes,** a few **rhinos, lions, antelopes, gazelles, giraffes** and **zebras. Crocodiles** and **hippos** can be seen at *Mzima Springs* in the west of the park.
Lake Turkana (formerly Lake Rudolph): There are several parks and reserves in the far north of Kenya, gathered around Lake Turkana. This extraordinary lake, running for several hundred miles through windswept and largely uninhabited deserts, contains many unique species of fish and marine plants and has recently gained a reputation as a fishing resort. Several lodges have sprung up on the eastern shore to cater for this trade and consequently general tourism is expected to increase. Despite the harsh climate, many of Kenya's better-known animals manage to survive here, as do the tiny people of the El Molo tribe, who fish the eastern waters. There are two large volcanic islands in the lake. The flooded crater of the southernmost island has a resident population of unnaturally **large crocodiles.** The lake is subject to violent storms, which disturb algae to produce remarkable colour changes in the water.

SOCIAL PROFILE

FOOD & DRINK: Kenya's national dishes appear on most hotel menus. The country's beef, chicken, lamb and pork are outstandingly good, as are the wide variety of tropical fruits. Local trout, Nile perch and lobster, shrimps and Mombasa oysters are included on menus in season. Indian and Middle Eastern food is available in most areas. Some game-park lodges serve game, including buffalo steaks marinaded in local liqueurs and berries, often garnished with wild honey and cream. Most Kenyans eat maize, beans and maize meal. At the small 'hotelis', *chai* (tea boiled with milk and sugar) and *mandazi* (doughnuts) are popular. There is a wide range of restaurants in Nairobi and Mombasa, otherwise hotels in smaller towns offer restaurant service. **Drink:** Locally brewed beer (*Tusker* and *White Cap*) and bottled sodas may be found throughout the country. *Kenya Cane* (spirit distilled from sugar cane) and *Kenya Gold* (a coffee liqueur) are produced in Kenya. Traditional beer made with honey *uki* and locally made spirit distilled from maize (*Changaa*) may sometimes be found.
NIGHTLIFE: Most of the major hotels in Nairobi and the tourist resorts have dancing with live bands or discotheques each evening. There are also a few nightclubs with an African flavour. There is a large selection of cinemas in Nairobi which show mainly American, British and European films.
SHOPPING: *Khanga*, *kitenge* and *kikoi* cloths may be bought in markets and the Bishara Streets of Nairobi and Mombasa. There is a particularly good co-operative shop in Machakos which sells *kiondos*, bags dyed with natural dyes and with strong leather straps. Makonde carvings

are sold throughout the country, and young Kamba and Masai men sell carvings and necklaces on the beaches of the south coast. **Shopping hours:** 0830-1230 and 1400-1630 Monday to Saturday. **Note:** The sale of souvenirs made of wildlife skins (this includes reptiles) is forbidden.

SPORT: Tennis, squash, bowls, horseriding and **polo** are all popular sports. Kenya also has good **athletics** facilities and the Kenyans have a fine record in world competitions. Sports clubs accept visitors. **Watersports: Sailing, water-skiing, swimming** and **surfing** are popular in the coastal resorts both north and south of Mombasa; these include Malindi, Nyali, Bamburi, Shanzu, Kikambala and Kilifi. These resorts have fine sandy beaches and there are several coral reefs. Trout **fishing** in the lakes is particularly good between November and March.

SPECIAL EVENTS: The following is a selection of special events celebrated annually in Kenya. For a complete list, contact the Tourist Office.

Apr (Easter Period) *Kenya Safari Rally*. **Apr** *Kenya Domestic Tourism Exhibition*. **May/Jun** *Kenya Schools Music Festival*. **Sep** *Mombasa National Show*. **Sep 9-Oct 3** *Nairobi International Show* (organised by the Agricultural Society of Kenya, featuring all aspects of Kenyan business and industry).

SOCIAL CONVENTIONS: Western European habits prevail throughout Kenya as a result of British influences in the country. Kenyans are generally very friendly. Dress is informal, and casual lightweight clothes are accepted for all but the smartest social occasions. **Tipping:** A KSh10 tip is usual except where a service charge has been made, when any additional amount is at the visitor's discretion.

BUSINESS PROFILE

ECONOMY: The Kenyan economy is largely agricultural: 85% of the population work on the land. The main cash crops are tea and coffee, both of which were severely affected by the droughts of the 1980s. Kenya is one of the few African countries with a significant dairy industry. Apart from tea and coffee, petroleum products are Kenya's main export, although the country is also a major importer of crude oil. Manufactured goods account for the rest of Kenya's imports, which come mostly from the United Kingdom, Germany and Japan. The UK and Germany, along with neighbouring Uganda, are Kenya's main export markets. Kenya is the third-largest recipient of British aid in the world and the largest in Africa. Much of this is direct financial assistance to ease Kenya's short-term balance of payments problems. Kenya has reached agreement with the IMF on a Structural Adjustment Programme (similar to many negotiated in the Third World) that should increase commercial opportunities in the country. Kenya has been one of Africa's strongest economies, with average growth of 5% in the late 1980s, and the economic outlook is fairly good provided the problems of an overweight public sector, rising inflation and unemployment are tackled. A speedy resolution of the current political uncertainty is also necessary.

BUSINESS: Lightweight suits are recommended for all occasions. Prior appointments are necessary. Although Kiswahili is the national language, English is the official language and is widely spoken. **Office hours:** 0800-1300 and 1400-1700 Monday to Friday, 0830-1200 Saturday. In Mombasa, offices usually open and close half an hour earlier.

COMMERCIAL INFORMATION: The following organisations can offer advice: Kenya National Chamber of Commerce and Industry, PO Box 47024, Ufanisi House, Hailé Sélassie Avenue, Nairobi. Tel: (2) 334 413; *or* Investment Promotion Centre, PO Box 55704, Nairobi. Tel: (2) 221 401. Telex: 25460.

CONFERENCES/CONVENTIONS: The Kenyatta International Conference Centre is in Nairobi.

HISTORY & GOVERNMENT

HISTORY: Excavations in Kenya suggest that the region is the cradle of humanity, the home some 3.25 million years ago of *Homo habilis*, from whom *Homo sapiens* descended. What is certain is that, in more recent times, Kenya was the settling place of a huge number of tribes from all over the continent, with a long history of migration, settlement and conflict. During the following centuries, the region became prosperous on the profits of trade, and also as an entrepôt for commerce from the Indian Ocean. The Portuguese arrived in the early 16th century, and having wrested control of the area's trade from the Arabs, absorbed Kenya into their commercial empire. By 1720 they had been driven out by the Arabs, and for the next two centuries the region was largely ruled by Omani dynasties from Arabia. During the 1820s, a local power struggle led to the British being invited into the region by the Mazrui dynasty, and by the middle of the century both the British and the Germans were competing for control of the coast and its hinterland during the second great colonial period. By the 1890s the threat of the Masai tribesmen had, by a mixture of diplomacy and war, largely been neutralised, and the British were able to penetrate into the highlands. The Mombasa to Uganda railway line was constructed at this time, and Nairobi owes its present importance to the fact that it was a convenient staging point on the edge of the highlands. It soon became the headquarters of the British administration. By the early 20th century, the fertile lands to the north were attracting a large number of white settlers led by Lord Delamere who came into conflict with the local population. Many tribes, such as the Masai and the Kikuyu, were displaced. The movement for territorial, economic and political rights soon found an able leader in Jomo Kenyatta, who spent much of the 1930s and 1940s in Europe pressing the case for his cause. After World War II, this gathered pace. The main organisation opposing colonial rule was the Kenya African Union (KAU), which came increasingly into violent conflict with the European settlers. The fight for independence was a difficult and sometimes bloody affair, particularly the 3-year guerrilla war mounted during the 1950s by the nationalist Land Freedom Army (better known as the Mau Mau) against the British colonial authorities. Kenya was nonetheless an early beneficiary of Harold Macmillan's 'winds of change' policy towards Africa. The main nationalist party, the Kenyan African National Union (KANU), led by Kenyatta, took power on Independence Day in December 1963, despite British efforts to sponsor an alternative. During the 1980s Kenyan politics were dominated by the struggle between moderate and radical factions within the ruling KANU party. The moderates, led by Tom Mboya (assassinated in 1969) and Kenyatta's eventual successor, Daniel Arap Moi, consistently held the upper hand. Moi used an ill-conceived coup attempt in 1982, apparently organised by a shadowy organisation known as Mwakenya, to consolidate his grip. Opposition parties, which had been just tolerated up to that point, were banned outright thereafter. In recent years, the Kenyan government has come under increasing pressure, particularly from its Western aid donors, to liberalise the political regime preparatory to introducing multi-party democracy. The main opposition movement, the Forum for the Restoration of Democracy (FORD), though split, posed a major threat to Moi's hold on power. The two factions, FORD-Kenya, led by ex-vice president Oginga Odinga, and FORD-Asili, headed by former cabinet minister Kenneth Matiba, had their opportunity before the voters on December 7, 1992, but Moi won a disputed poll. FORD-Kenya aimed to attract votes from Kenya's two largest tribal blocs, the Kikuyu and the Luo, both of whom are thought to have been alienated from Moi by the dominance of the government by members of the President's own Kalenjin tribe.

GOVERNMENT: Kenya's legislature is the 188-member National Assembly, elected every five years by universal adult suffrage from a slate of candidates put up by the Kenyan African National Union. The President is also directly elected for five years.

CLIMATE

The coastal areas are tropical, but tempered by monsoon winds. The lowlands are hot but mainly dry, while the highlands are more temperate with four seasons. Nairobi has a very pleasant climate throughout the year due to its altitude. Near Lake Victoria the temperatures are much higher and rainfall can be heavy.

Required clothing: Lightweight cottons and linens with rainwear are advised for the coast and lakeside. Warmer clothing is needed in June and July and for the cooler mornings on the coast. Lightweights are needed for much of the year in the highlands. Rainwear is advisable between March and June and October and December.

NAIROBI Kenya (1798m)

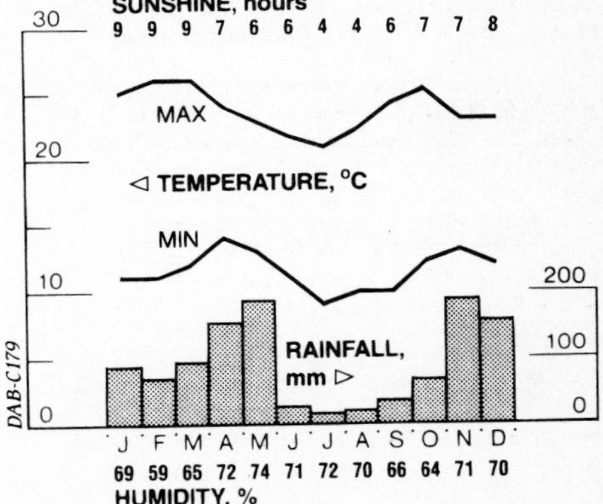

KIRIBATI

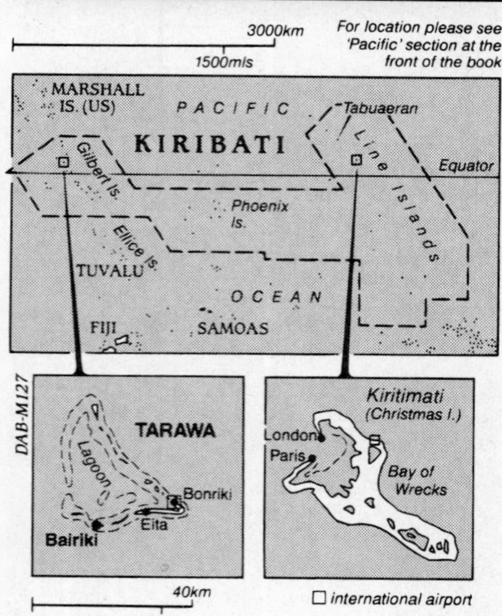

Location: South Pacific, Micronesia.

Kiribati Visitors Bureau
PO Box 261
Bikenibeu, Bairiki
Tarawa, Kiribati
Tel: 28287/8. Fax: 26193. Telex: 77039.

Consulate of Kiribati
Faith House
7 Tufton Street
London SW1P 3QN
Tel: (071) 222 6952. Fax: (071) 976 7180.

Commonwealth Information Centre
Commonwealth Institute
230 Kensington High Street
London W8 6NQ
Tel: (071) 603 4535. Fax: (071) 602 7374. Telex: 8955822.
Provides general information on Kiribati.

British High Commission
PO Box 61
Bairiki
Tarawa, Kiribati
Tel: 21327. Fax: 21488. Telex: 77050 UKREP KI.

Canadian High Commission
PO Box 12049
61 Molesworth Street
Wellington, New Zealand
Tel: (4) 473 9577. Fax: (4) 471 2082. Telex: NZ3577.

AREA: 861 sq km (332 sq miles).
POPULATION: 72,298 (1990).
POPULATION DENSITY: 89.2 per sq km.
CAPITAL: Tarawa. **Population:** 28,802 (1990).
GEOGRAPHY: Kiribati (pronounced 'Kiribass', formerly the Gilbert Islands) consists of three groups in the central Pacific: Kiribati (including Banaba, formerly Ocean Island), the Line Islands and the Phoenix Islands. The 33 islands, scattered across two million square miles of the central Pacific, are low-lying coral atolls with coastal lagoons. The exception is Banaba, which is a coral formation rising to 80m (265ft). The soil is generally poor, apart from Banaba, and rainfall variable. Coconut palms and pandanus trees comprise the main vegetation. There are no hills or streams throughout the group. Water is obtained from storage tanks or wells.
LANGUAGE: I-Kiribati and English.
RELIGION: Gilbert Islands Protestant Church and Roman Catholic.
TIME: GMT + 12, except as follows:
Canton Island, Enderbury Island: GMT - 11;
Christmas Island: GMT - 10.
ELECTRICITY: 240 volts AC, 50Hz.
COMMUNICATIONS: The Government provides radio and postal services to all inhabited islands.
Telephone: IDD available throughout urban Tarawa. Country code: 686. Radio telephone calls can be arranged to most outer islands. **Fax:** This is available at the local Telecoms Office. **Telex/telegram:** Available in Betio 0800-1900 daily and on outer islands from 0800-1600 Monday to Friday. Telegrams may take several days to reach Europe. **Post:** Airmail to Europe takes up to two weeks. There is a weekly postal service for overseas mail. Post offices open 0800-1230 and 1330-1615 Monday to Friday. **Press:** The weekly paper is *Te Uekera*, in English and I-Kiribati.
BBC World Service and Voice of America frequencies: From time to time these change. See the section *How to Use this Book* for more information.

BBC:				
MHz	17.10	15.36	9.740	7.150
Voice of America:				
MHz	18.82	15.18	9.525	1.735

PASSPORT/VISA

Regulations and requirements may be subject to change at short notice, and you are advised to contact the appropriate diplomatic or consular authority before finalising travel arrangements. Details of these may be found at the head of this country's entry. Any numbers in the chart refer to the footnotes below.

	Passport Required?	Visa Required?	Return Ticket Required?
Full British	Yes	1	Yes
BVP	Not valid	-	-
Australian	Yes	Yes	Yes
Canadian	Yes	No	Yes
USA	Yes	No	Yes
Other EC	Yes	1	Yes
Japanese	Yes	Yes	Yes

PASSPORTS: Required by all.
British Visitors Passport: Not accepted.
VISAS: Required by all except:
(a) [1] nationals of Denmark, Spain and the UK (excluding Northern Ireland). All other EC nationals *do* require a visa;
(b) nationals of Antigua & Barbuda, Bahamas, Barbados, Bermuda, Botswana, British Virgin Islands, Canada, Cayman Islands, Cook Islands, Cyprus, Ecuador, Falkland Islands, Fiji, Gibraltar, Grenada, Guam, Guyana, Hong Kong, Iceland, Jamaica, Kenya, Lesotho, Malaysia, Malta, Montserrat, New Zealand, Niue, Norway, The Philippines, St Kitts & Nevis, St Lucia, Samoa (American), Western Samoa, San Marino, Seychelles, Sierra Leone, Singapore, Solomon Islands, Sweden, Switzerland, Tonga, Trinidad & Tobago, Tunisia, Turks & Caicos Islands, Tuvalu, Uruguay, USA, Vanuatu and Zimbabwe.
Note: (a) Maximum period of stay without a visa for nationals of the above list varies from country to country. Enquire at passport office for details. (b) Nationals of some countries require references along with their visas. Check details with the Consulate (or the Consular Section at the Embassy or High Commission).
Types of visa: *Transit:* not required by travellers holding valid documents and tickets for return or onward travel, and providing they do not leave the airport. *Business and Tourist visas:* £8 plus £3 referral fee.
Application to: Ministry of Foreign Affairs in Kiribati or any British Consulate. For addresses, see top of this entry and the top of the *United Kingdom* entry.
Application requirements: Completed forms and appropriate letters from company/sponsors if on business.
Temporary residence: Apply to: Office of the President, PO Box 68, Bairiki, Tarawa, Kiribati.

MONEY

Currency: Australian Dollar (A$) = 100 cents. Notes are in denominations of A$100, 50, 20, 10, 5 and 2. Coins are in denominations of A$1, and 50, 20, 10, 5, 2 and 1 cents.
Currency exchange: US Dollars may be exchanged for local currency at the Bank of Kiribati Ltd or local hotels.
Credit cards: Not accepted.
Travellers cheques: Accepted in hotels, some shops and at the Bank of Kiribati Ltd.
Exchange rate indicators: The following figures are included as a guide to the movements of the Australian Dollar against Sterling and the US Dollar:

Date:	Oct '89	Oct '90	Oct '91	Oct '92
£1.00=	2.08	2.27	2.18	2.22
$1.00=	1.28	1.20	1.25	1.40

Currency restrictions: There are no restrictions on the import or export of either foreign or local currency.
Banking hours: 0900-1400 Monday to Friday.

DUTY FREE

The following goods may be imported into Kiribati without incurring customs duty:
200 cigarettes or 50 cigars or 225g tobacco;
1 litre of spirits and 1 litre of wine (for persons over 21 years of age);
A reasonable amount of perfume for personal use.

PUBLIC HOLIDAYS

Public holidays observed in Kiribati are as follows:
Apr 9-12 '93 Easter. **Jul 12** Independence Day. **Aug 4** Youth Day. **Dec 25-26** Christmas. **Jan 1 '94** New Year.

HEALTH

Regulations and requirements may be subject to change at short notice, and you are advised to contact your doctor well in advance of your intended date of departure. Any numbers in the chart refer to the footnotes below.

	Special Precautions?	Certificate Required?
Yellow Fever	No	1
Cholera	No	No
Typhoid & Polio	Yes	-
Malaria	No	-
Food & Drink	2	-

[1]: A yellow fever vaccination certificate is required from travellers over one year of age coming from infected areas.
[2]: All water should be regarded as a potential health risk. Water used for drinking, brushing teeth or making ice should have first been boiled or otherwise sterilised. Only eat well-cooked meat and fish, preferably served hot. Pork, salad and mayonnaise may carry increased risk. Vegetables should be cooked and fruit peeled.
Health care: Health insurance is recommended. Tungaru Central Hospital on Tarawa provides medical

KIRIBATI	HEALTH REGULATIONS	VISA REGULATIONS
GALILEO/WORLDSPAN	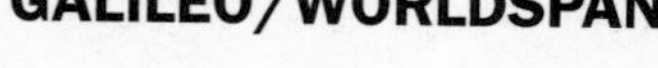 TI-DFT/TRW/HE	 TI-DFT/TRW/VI
SABRE	 TIDFT/TRW/HE	 TIDFT/TRW/VI

Code-Link

To access this information on your CRS, swipe the barcode with a light pen or type in the text under the barcode. For more information, see the introduction *How to Use This Book*.

service to all the islands. Government dispensaries on all islands are equipped to handle minor ailments and injuries.

TRAVEL - International

AIR: Kiribati is mainly served by *Air Nauru (ON)* and *Air Marshall Islands*. The national airline, *Air Tungaru (VK)*, flies to Hawaii (Honolulu) and Fiji.
Approximate flight time: From *London* to Tarawa via Sydney and Nauru is 30 hours 30 minutes (excluding stopover time).
International airports: *Tarawa (TRW)* and *Christmas Island (CXI)*.
SEA: International ports are Tarawa, Banaba and Christmas Island, all served by the following cargo lines: *Pacific Forum Line, Bank Line, Daiwa Line, Tanker Ship (McDonald Hamilton)* and *China Navigation Co*.

TRAVEL - Internal

AIR: *Air Tungaru (VK)* operates an internal scheduled service to nearly all outer islands linking them with Tarawa.
ROAD: Driving is on the left. All-weather roads are limited to urban Tarawa and Christmas Island. **Bus:** Available on urban Tarawa only. **Taxi:** Available on urban Tarawa only. **Car hire:** Available on urban Tarawa and Christmas Island only. **Documentation:** International Driving Permit required.

ACCOMMODATION

HOTELS: There are four hotels in Kiribati, on Tarawa, Christmas Island and Abemama.
RESTHOUSES: Inexpensive resthouses can be found on all the other islands, for example Otintai, Tarawa; Robert Louis Stevenson, Abemama; Captain Cook, Christmas Island. However, cooking facilities are limited and visitors should take what they need with them. Prices for accommodation in resthouses vary considerably.

RESORTS & EXCURSIONS

There are few tours available in Kiribati. However, visits to Second World War battlegrounds and natural history expeditions with studies of the birdlife (large colonies of which live on Christmas Island) are available. There are also trips to see outrigger canoe races and dancing contests. Excellent facilities exist in Kiribati for snorkelling and deep-sea fishing or simply sunbathing on one of the many beaches. Visitors are always welcome in the *maneaba*, a traditional community meeting house, where they may enjoy traditional dancing, singing and storytelling – local culture is still the dominant influence in these islands.

SOCIAL PROFILE

FOOD & DRINK: There are few restaurants in Kiribati as tourism has not yet become a main source of income. They are mainly situated in the larger towns and include the M'Aneaba restaurant at Aantebuku and the Otintai Hotel dining room, both on Tarawa. Local specialities in the southern islands of Kiribati include the boiled fruit of *pandanus* (screwpine), sliced thinly and spread with coconut cream. A Kiribati delicacy is *palu sami*, which is coconut cream with sliced onion and curry powder, wrapped in taro leaves and pressure cooked in an earth-oven packed with seaweed. It can be eaten on its own or served with roast pork or chicken. As in many of the islands of the South Pacific, there is a tendency amongst local people to regard imported canned products as luxuries.
NIGHTLIFE: There are 'Island Nights' which feature traditional Polynesian music and dancing, film shows and feasts in *Maneabas* (local meeting houses) which can be found throughout the islands.
SHOPPING: Handicrafts include baskets, table mats, fans and cups made from pandanus leaves, coconut leaves and coconut shell. Sea-shell necklaces are popular, as are models of Gilbertese canoes and houses. A prized item is the Kiribati shark-tooth sword made of polished coconut wood with shark teeth, filed to razor sharpness, lashed to the two edges. These days, most examples are modern reproductions. **Shopping hours:** 0800-1200 and 1400-1800 Monday to Friday, and 0800-1200 Saturday.
SPORT: Hotels offer **canoeing, fishing** and **snorkelling** facilities. **Birdwatching** is popular, especially on Christmas Island where millions of birds swarm everywhere. Game fishing on Christmas Island is also becoming popular. A fishing licence is unnecessary and charters are easily available. **Swimming:** Numerous beaches offer safe bathing.
SOCIAL CONVENTIONS: Like the other Pacific islanders, the people are very friendly and hospitable and retain much of their traditional culture and lifestyle. In this casual atmosphere European customs still prevail alongside local traditions. Although in official correspondence the western convention of signing names with initials is adopted, it is more polite (and customary) to address people by their first name. **Tipping:** Not expected.

BUSINESS PROFILE

ECONOMY: The end of phosphate mining in Kiribati had a devastating effect on the economy given that the commodity was the major export earner (accounting for 85% of revenue). Coconuts are the principal agricultural product: agriculture as a whole is limited by the poor quality of the soil. Fishing, especially tuna, is the other major economic activity. Despite reasonable earnings from all these, Kiribati is heavily dependent on foreign aid to meet an annual balance of payments deficit approaching A$20 million. Most trade takes place with Australia, New Zealand, the UK, Japan, the USA, Papua New Guinea and Fiji.
BUSINESS: Shirt and smart trousers or skirt will suffice most of the time; ties need only be worn for smart occasions. **Office hours:** 0800-1230 and 1330-1615 Monday to Friday.

HISTORY & GOVERNMENT

HISTORY: There are indications of prehistoric migrations from South-East Asia, but the present inhabitants of Kiribati descend mainly from a Samoan influx during the 13th to 15th centuries. Following European discovery, Kiribati came into contact with other Pacific islanders and the Chinese; traces of this intermixing remain in both the population and culture. Village government in Kiribati continues in the pre-colonial mode. In 1892, Kiribati became part of the British colony of the Gilbert and Ellice islands, and was administered by the West Pacific High Commission in Fiji. The islands were occupied by the Japanese during the Second World War, site of some of the fiercest fighting between Japan and the United States. The transition to independence began in 1963 with the formation of legislative and executive councils under the supervision of a British Governor-General, who took over the functions previously exercised by the High Commissioner. The Legislative Council later evolved into the Maneaba ni Maungatabu (see below). In 1975, the Ellice Islands seceded from the main group to form the separate territory of Tuvalu. The remaining Gilbert Islands, plus a few smaller islands which the colonial authorities had tacked onto the group, became the independent republic of Kiribati in July 1979. Ieremia Tabai, a veteran of Kiribati politics, won the first three post-independence elections, held in 1982, 1983 and 1987. Constitutional restraints meant that he had to stand down at the election held in late 1991, but he continues to exert considerable influence on the government. His successor is his former Vice President, Teatao Teannaki. A particular feature of Kiribati politics is the dearth of political parties. There were in fact none at all – presidential and assembly candidates stood as independents – until 1985. That September, the Christian Democratic Party was formed by Harry Tong, runner-up to Tabai in the 1983 election. The 1985 deal with the then Soviet Union, providing access to Kiribati waters for Soviet fishing vessels, provoked strong opposition from Western powers and from some quarters within Kiribati itself; the agreement was ratified nonetheless by the Maneaba, although it lapsed 12 months later after a dispute over the licence fee. **GOVERNMENT:** Kiribati has a unicameral chamber legislature, Maneaba ni Maungatabu, with 36 members elected for four years by universal adult suffrage. The Beretitenti (President) is head of both state and government, and is also directly elected. The President appoints a Cabinet from the incumbent members of the Maneaba, with which he shares executive power.

CLIMATE

Maritime equatorial in the central islands of the group. The islands to the north and south are more tropical. The trade winds blow between March and October, making this the most pleasant time of the year, while the highest rainfall (December to March) is concentrated on the northern islands. November to February is more wet and humid than the rest of the year.
Required clothing: Light cottons and waterproof clothing are advised from December to March. Bikinis should not be worn except on the beach.

TABUAERAN Kiribati (6m)

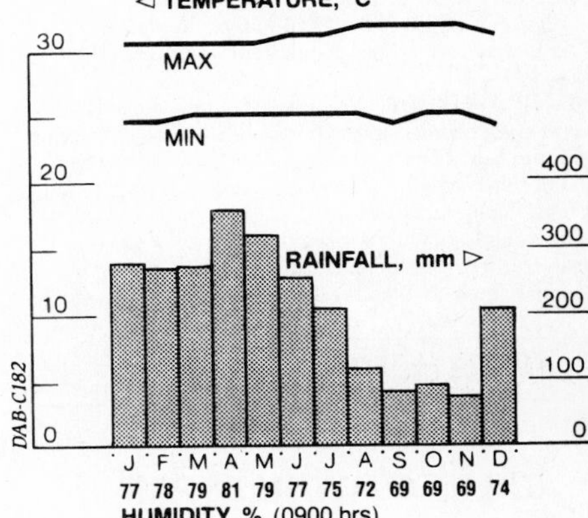

TEMPERATURE CONVERSIONS
-20 -10 0°C 10 20 30 40
0 10 20 30°F40 50 60 70 80 90 100
RAINFALL CONVERSIONS 0mm 200 400 600 800
0in 5 10 15 20 25 30

KOREA (DEMOCRATIC PEOPLE'S REPUBLIC OF)

Location: Far East.

Ryohaengsa (Korea International Travel Company)
Central District
Pyongyang, DPR Korea
Tel: 22331. Fax: 817 607. Telex: 5998.
Kumgangsan International Tourist Company
Central District
Pyongyang, DPR Korea
Tel: 31562.
General Delegation of the DPR of Korea
104 boulevard Bineau
92200 Neuilly-sur-Seine, France
Tel: (1) 47 45 17 97. Fax: (1) 47 38 12 50. Telex: 615021F.
There is no diplomatic mission in the UK. For information contact:
Regent Holidays
15 John Street
Bristol BS1 2HR
Tel: (0272) 211 711. Fax: (0272) 254 866. Telex: 444606. Opening hours: 0900-1730 Monday to Friday (an appointment may be necessary).

AREA: 120,538 sq km (46,540 sq miles).
POPULATION: 21,773,000 (1990 estimate).
POPULATION DENSITY: 180.6 per sq km.
CAPITAL: Pyongyang. **Population:** 2,000,000 (1986 estimate).
GEOGRAPHY: The Democratic People's Republic of Korea shares borders in the north with China, in the east with the Sea of Japan, in the west with the Yellow Sea and in the south with the demilitarised zone (separating it from the Republic of Korea). Most of the land consists of hills and low mountains and only a small area is cultivable. Intensive water and soil conservation programmes, including land reclamation from the sea, are given high priority. The eastern coast is rocky and steep with mountains rising from the water and this area contains most of the river waterways.
LANGUAGE: Korean.
RELIGION: There is no official religion, but Buddhism is practised by a sizeable minority and there are also Christian and Chundo Kyo minorities.
TIME: GMT + 9.
ELECTRICITY: 110/220 volts AC, 60Hz.
COMMUNICATIONS: Telephone: No IDD service is available and there is a very sparse internal network. **Telex/telegram:** Services available in all Pyongyang hotels. **Post:** Services are extremely slow and limited outside the capital. Airmail takes about ten days to reach Europe. Post office hours: 0900-2100 every day. **Press:** Major daily newspapers include *Rodong Shinmun*, *Minju Choson* and *Pyongyang Shinmun*. There are no English-language newspapers.
BBC World Service and Voice of America frequencies: From time to time these change. See the section *How to Use this Book* for more information.

BBC:				
MHz	21.72	15.28	11.96	7.180
Voice of America:				
MHz	15.43	11.72	5.985	1.143

PASSPORT/VISA

Regulations and requirements may be subject to change at short notice, and you are advised to contact the appropriate diplomatic or consular authority before finalising travel arrangements. Details of these may be found at the head of this country's entry. Any numbers in the chart refer to the footnotes below.

	Passport Required?	Visa Required?	Return Ticket Required?
Full British	Yes	Yes	Yes
BVP	Not valid	-	-
Australian	Yes	Yes	Yes
Canadian	Yes	Yes	Yes
USA	Yes	Yes	Yes
Other EC	Yes	Yes	Yes
Japanese	Yes	Yes	Yes

PASSPORTS: Valid passport required by all.
British Visitors Passport: Not accepted.
VISAS: Required by all.
Applications to: Consular Section of the General Delegation of the DPR Korea in France (address see above). Applications should be made well in advance. Tourists can generally only enter as part of a group sanctioned by the Korean Tourist Bureau. It is only possible to travel as an individual if the whole tour itinerary is pre-booked. UK agents for the Korean Tourist Bureau are Regent Holidays (address at top of entry).

MONEY

Currency: Won (NKW) = 100 jon. Notes are in denominations of NKW100, 50, 10, 5 and 1. Coins are in denominations of 50, 10, 5 and 1 jon.
Exchange rate indicators: The following figures are included as a guide to the movements of the Won against Sterling and the US Dollar:

Date:	Oct '89	Oct '90	Oct '91	Oct '92
£1.00=	1.53	1.89	1.68	3.40
$1.00=	0.97	0.97	0.97	2.14

Currency restrictions: Import and export of local currency is prohibited. There are no restrictions on foreign currency, but the amount must be declared.

DUTY FREE

The following goods may be imported into the Democratic People's Republic of Korea without incurring customs duty:
A reasonable amount of tobacco and alcoholic beverages.
Prohibited items: Binoculars, wireless sets, arms, ammunition, explosives, drugs, plants and seeds. Animals and all groceries require valid certificates of entry.

PUBLIC HOLIDAYS

Public holidays observed in the Democratic People's Republic of Korea are as follows:
Mar 8 '93 International Women's Day. **Apr 15** Kim Il Sung's Birthday. **May 1** May Day. **Aug 15** Anniversary of Liberation. **Sep 9** Independence Day. **Oct 10** Anniversary of the foundation of the Korean Workers' Party. **Dec 27** Anniversary of the Constitution. **Jan 1 '94** New Year's Day. **Feb 16** Kim Jong Il's Birthday. **Mar 8** International Women's Day.

HEALTH

Regulations and requirements may be subject to change at short notice, and you are advised to contact your doctor well in advance of your intended date of departure. Any numbers in the chart refer to the footnotes below.

	Special Precautions?	Certificate Required?
Yellow Fever	No	No
Cholera	Yes	1
Typhoid & Polio	Yes	-
Malaria	No	-
Food & Drink	2	-

[1]: Following WHO guidelines issued in 1973, a cholera vaccination certificate is not a condition of entry to the Democratic People's Republic of Korea. However, cholera is a risk in this country and precautions are essential. Up-to-date advice should be sought before deciding whether these precautions should include a vaccination, as medical opinion is divided over its effectiveness. See the *Health* section at the back of the book.
[2]: All water should be regarded as a potential health risk. Water used for drinking, brushing teeth or making ice should have first been boiled or otherwise sterilised. Milk is unpasteurised and should be boiled. Powdered or tinned milk is available and is advised, but make sure that it is reconstituted with pure water. Avoid dairy products which are likely to have been made from unboiled milk. Only eat well-cooked meat and fish, preferably served hot. Pork, salad and mayonnaise may carry increased risk. Vegetables should be cooked and fruit peeled.
Rabies is present. For those at high risk, vaccination before arrival should be considered. If you are bitten abroad seek medical advice without delay. For more information consult the *Health* section at the back of the book.
Health care: Health insurance is essential.

TRAVEL - International

AIR: The main airlines serving the Democratic People's Republic of Korea are *Civil Aviation Company (JS)*, *Aeroflot Russian International Airlines*, and *Civil Aviation Administration of China (CA)*.
Approximate flight time: From *London* to Pyongyang is 16 hours.
International airport: *Pyongyang (FNJ)* (Sunan) is 30km (18.5 miles) from the city (travel time – 45 minutes).
SEA: Main international ports are Chongjin, Hungnam, Haeju, Najin, Wonsan and Nampo, the port of Pyongyang.
RAIL: A through-train from Pyongyang to Beijing runs four times a week and there is also a thrice-weekly sleeping car through to Moscow. There are no routes to the Republic of Korea.
ROAD: There are roads from Dandong, Lu-ta, Liaoyang, Jilin and Changchun in China and Vladivostock in the Russian Federation, but foreigners are only permitted to enter the country by rail or by air.

NORTH KOREA	**HEALTH REGULATIONS**	**VISA REGULATIONS** Code-Link
GALILEO/WORLDSPAN	 TI-DFT/FNJ/HE	TI-DFT/FNJ/VI
SABRE	 TIDFT/FNJ/HE	TIDFT/FNJ/VI

To access this information on your CRS, swipe the barcode with a light pen or type in the text under the barcode. For more information, see the introduction *How to Use This Book*.

TRAVEL - Internal

AIR: There are flights from Pyongyang, Hambeing and Chongjin, although foreigners are not allowed to use these.
RAIL: The extensive rail network built by the Japanese during the Second World War has been broken by the separation of north and south Korea, but the main passenger routes run from Pyongyang to Sinuiji, Haeju and Chongjin. Service, however, is slow.
ROAD: The quality of major roads is good; many are dual carriageways. There are no buses between cities.
URBAN: Pyongyang has a 4-line metro and regular bus services.
JOURNEY TIMES: The following chart gives approximate journey times (in hours and minutes) from Pyongyang to other major cities/towns in the DPR of Korea.

	Road	Rail
Diamond Mt	10.00	-
Kaesong	8.00	6.00
Nampo	1.30	8.00

ACCOMMODATION

Pyongyang has five first-class hotels where foreigners stay, although groups cannot know in advance which one will be used. All other towns have one first-class hotel for use by groups.

RESORTS & EXCURSIONS

It is impossible to avoid the looming figure of Kim Il Sung, and nowhere more so than in the museums. The *Gates of Pyongyang* are worth seeing, and *Morangborg Park* and *Taesongsan Recreation Ground* (with its fairground attractions) offer relaxation. An industrial plant will almost certainly form part of the visitor's itinerary. Beyond the capital, Kim Il Sung's birthplace is a national shrine and there are also, at **Kaesong** (six hours from the capital by train), treasures from Korea's imperial history. For the (mainly communist) 13th World Festival of Youth and Students in 1989 a 150,000-seat stadium was built in Pyongyang. The object of constructing this and other facilities was to rival the Olympic Games which had been held in Seoul (Republic of Korea) the previous year.

SOCIAL PROFILE

FOOD & DRINK: Reasonable restaurants can be found in the main towns and cooking is usually based on the staple food, rice. In hotels and restaurants it is better to stick to the Korean, Chinese or Japanese items on the menu as experience of Western and Russian cooking is limited. Eating out is arranged by the guide. Those drinking alcohol should be discreet.
NIGHTLIFE: A night at the revolutionary opera provides a unique experience. There are also circuses and musical events of a high quality.
SPORT: As mentioned in *Resorts & Excursions* above, in 1989 the country hosted the 13th World Festival of Youth and Students with a consequent expansion of sports facilities around the capital.
SOCIAL CONVENTIONS: Discretion and a low political profile are advised. **Tipping:** Not practised.

BUSINESS PROFILE

ECONOMY: The Democratic People's Republic of Korea has a Soviet-style command economy based on heavy industry. The country has rich mineral deposits, including most of the major base metals, as well as gold, silver and tungsten. Since the main industrial infrastructure was developed in the 1950s, development resources have gradually been shifted to light industry and latterly concentrated on automation and modernisation. Most trade is conducted with the CIS, Japan and China, where a number of joint industrial ventures have been set up. Trade with the West is low but is slowly rising (Western Europe in total accounts for about 5%). Korea has yet to adopt any of the political or economic reforms which have swept Eastern Europe, nor does it seem likely to do so as long as the current leadership retains power. However, the North faces severe economic difficulties in the short-term, following the loss of a large number of key export markets, particularly parts of the CIS, which will compound what has been an almost total lack of growth. The North's economic planners will inevitably start to look to the South, which long ago outstripped the North on economic performance (despite a dearth of raw materials, the South's GDP, with twice the population, is six to eight times that of the North).
BUSINESS: Suits are required. Business transactions will take place outside the office, generally in the evening, as visitors are not allowed to enter offices.
COMMERCIAL INFORMATION: The following organisation can offer advice: Korean Committee for the Promotion of International Trade, Central District, Pyongyang.

HISTORY & GOVERNMENT

HISTORY: Once a unified country with an independent monarchy, Korea came under strong Japanese influence in the latter part of the 19th century. Japanese forces occupied the country in 1905 and formally annexed it five years later, deposing the emperor in the process. Korea remained under Japanese control until the end of the Second World War when the Japanese were driven out by Soviet and American forces. In a manner similar to post-war Germany, Korea was divided into military occupation zones along the 38th parallel (line of latitude). The then Soviet Union withdrew from the North in 1948, having overseen the creation of a Democratic People's Republic and ensured the pre-eminence of the communist Korean Workers' Party in the country's political life. The North aspired to reunify Korea under communist rule and in 1950, supported by the Chinese communists who had taken power the previous year, invaded the South. American and other allied forces joined the South to repel the invasion. After three years of bitter fighting, the existing division was restored and an armistice signed between the two Koreas. Since then, relations between North and South have been at best cool. Recent diplomatic activity on the part of the Democratic People's Republic of Korea (DPRK), along with public relations exercises, such as the reuniting of families split by the war, suggest a more conciliatory attitude from the North in the future. The DPRK has been firmly ruled since 1948 by Kim Il Sung, 'The Great Leader', as the head of KWP. His son, Kim Jong Il, 'The Dear Leader', is evidently being groomed for his future succession. Regimented to an extraordinary degree and all but hermetically sealed from the outside world, North Korea has been guided by the tenets of *juche*, Kim Il Sung's idiosyncratic philosophical cocktail of Stalinist orthodoxy, nationalism and religious mysticism. The population know next to nothing of the outside world: the danger of contaminating radio and television broadcasts (which caused so much trouble in, for instance, Albania) has been averted by electronic doctoring of available equipment. Nonetheless, since 1970, the DPRK has for the most part maintained a steady policy of trying to improve relations with the South, leading eventually to reunification, a goal which Kim Il Sung has formally decreed for his country. The rapprochement, such as it is, has been uniquely tortuous, but external factors have served to force the pace in the last few years. The end of the Cold War has removed, on the one hand, an ideological cornerstone of the North–South confrontation and, on the other, the strategic basis for superpower backing of either side. The upheaval in the Soviet Union had a profound impact upon the North Korean leadership, whose basic geopolitical strategy since the civil war had been to play the two communist giants, China and the Soviet Union, off against each other. Seoul's forging of diplomatic relations with Moscow and its former allies in Eastern Europe was a major blow to the North Koreans, one of a series which they have endured on the international stage during the last 12 months. Pyongyang's efforts to improve its bilateral relations in the region have been held up by international concern over its nuclear programme: despite having signed the 1972 Nuclear Non-Proliferation Treaty, the North Koreans had until early 1992 refused to open their nuclear facilities to international inspection unless the American nuclear inventory in the South (whose existence the Adenies) was also removed. Heavy pressure from Moscow, Beijing and elsewhere influenced a change of heart. By contrast, in September 1991, representatives from both North and South Korea appeared among five new delegations (the others were from the Baltic states) at the United Nations General Assembly. The North had previously insisted that Korea should only join the UN as a single entity under northern leadership and its attendance marks a major concession by Pyongyang. The pace of convergence was maintained with the signing in December of a non-aggression pact between the two governments. Changes in Europe and East Asia have also had a profound economic impact upon the North Koreans. Not only have several key export markets been lost, but the South, which long ago outstripped the North in economic performance, is being courted by Moscow, who are very keen to improve trade links. Irrespective of the logic and aspirations of the two Koreas, unification will almost certainly have to wait until the demise of Kim Il Sung. Most Korea-watchers doubt whether his son and heir will be able to exert the same grip over the country.
GOVERNMENT: The country is ruled by the Korean Workers' Party. The popularly elected Supreme People's Assembly is constitutionally the highest organ of the State, but real power lies with the Standing Committee of the Political Committee of the Party Central Committee, chaired by Kim II Sung.

CLIMATE

Moderate with four distinct seasons. The hottest time is July to August, which is also the rainy season; coldest is from December to January. Spring and autumn are mild and mainly dry.
Required clothing: Lightweight cottons and linens are worn during the summer. Light- to mediumweights are advised in the spring and autumn, and medium- to heavy-weights in the winter. Waterproofing is advisable during the rainy season.

PYONGYANG DPR of Korea (27m)

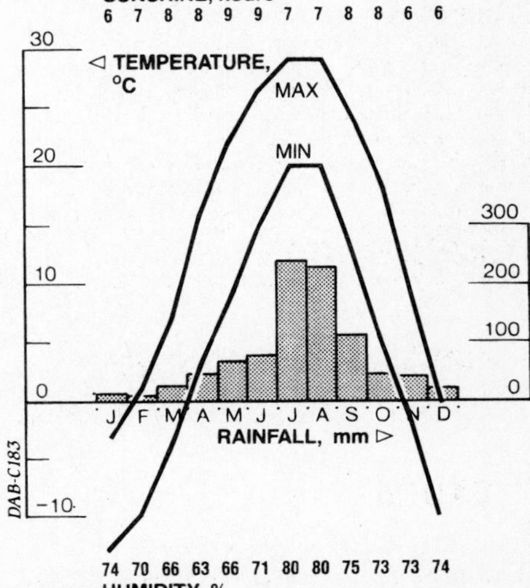

KOREA (REPUBLIC OF)

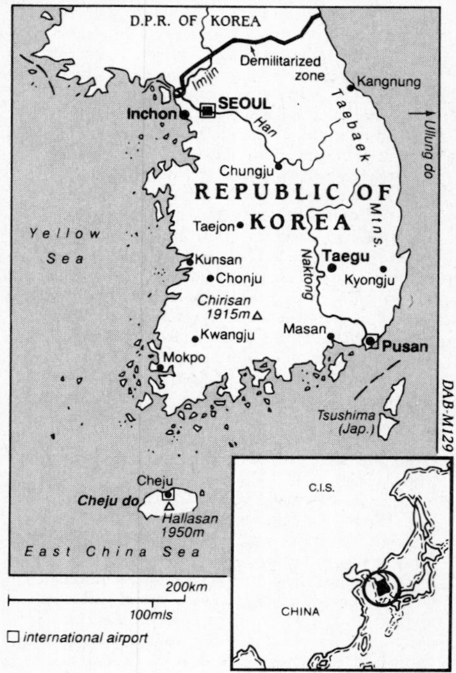

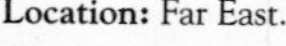

Location: Far East.

Korea National Tourism Corporation
KNTC Building
PO Box 903
10 Da-dong
Chung-ku
Seoul 100, Republic of Korea
Tel: (2) 757 6030. Fax: (2) 757 5997. Telex: 28555.

Embassy of the Republic of Korea
4 Palace Gate
London W8 5NF
Tel: (071) 581 0247. Fax: (071) 589 9134. Telex: 919620.
Opening hours: 0930-1730 Monday to Friday. *Visa Section:* 1000-1200 and 1400-1600 Monday to Friday.

Korea National Tourism Corporation
2nd Floor, Vogue House
1 Hanover Square
London W1R 9RD
Tel: (071) 408 1591. Fax: (071) 491 2302.

Note: The KNTC can also offer advice and information on conference facilities in the Republic of Korea.

British Embassy
4 Chung-dong
Chung-ku
Seoul 100, Republic of Korea
Tel: (2) 735 7341. Fax: (2) 733 8368. Telex: 27320.

British Consulate
PO Box 75
12th Floor, Yoochang Building 25-2
4-Ka Chungang-Dong
Chung-Ku
Pusan, Republic of Korea
Tel: (51) 463 0041/4630. Telex: 53323 HYOPSUNG.

Embassy of the Republic of Korea
2370 Massachusetts Avenue, NW
Washington, DC
20008
Tel: (202) 939 5600. Fax: (202) 797 0595.

Korean Consulate General
460 Park Avenue
New York, NY
10022
Tel: (212) 752 1700. Fax: (212) 371 1086.

Korea National Tourism Corporation
7th Floor
2 Executive Drive
Fort Lee, NJ
07024
Tel: (201) 585 0909.

Embassy of the United States of America
Unit 15550
82 Sejong-Ro
Chongro-ku
Seoul 96205-0001, Republic of Korea
Tel: (2) 732 2601. Fax: (2) 738 8845.
Consulate in: Pusan (tel: (51) 246 7791).

Embassy of the Republic of Korea
5th Floor
151 Slater Street
Ottawa, Ontario
K1P 5H3
Tel: (613) 232 1715/6/7. Fax: (613) 232 0928.
Consulates in: Montréal, Toronto and Vancouver.

Korea National Tourism Corporation
Suite 406
480 University Avenue
Toronto, Ontario
M5G 1V2
Tel: (416) 348 9056. Fax: (416) 348 9058.

Canadian Embassy
PO Box 6299
10th Floor, Kolon Building
45 Mugyo-dong, Chung-ku
Seoul 100-170, Republic of Korea
Tel: (2) 753 2605/6. Fax: (2) 755 0686. Telex: 27425.

Todamsambong Peak

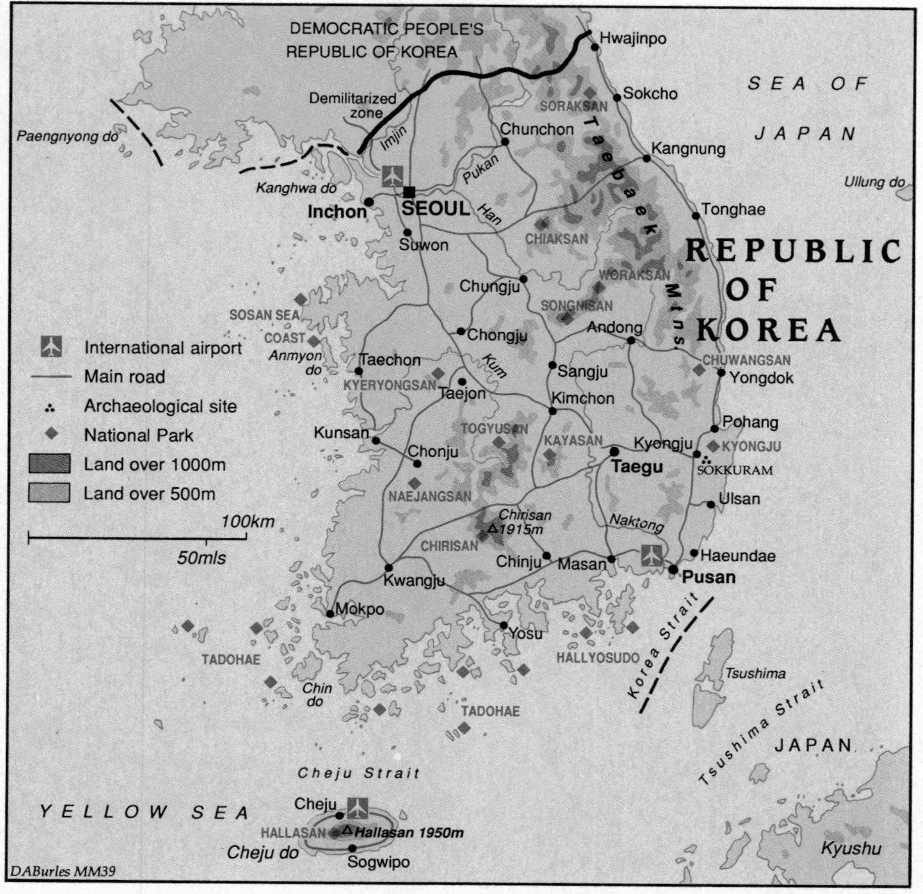

AREA: 99,222 sq km (38,310 sq miles), excluding demilitarised zone.
POPULATION: 43,268,301 (1991 estimate).
POPULATION DENSITY: 436.1 per sq km.
CAPITAL: Seoul. **Population:** 10,627,790 (1990).
GEOGRAPHY: The Republic of Korea (South Korea) shares borders to the north with the demilitarised zone (separating it from the Democratic People's Republic of Korea), to the east with the Sea of Japan, to the south with the Korea Strait (separating it from Japan) and to the west with the Yellow Sea. There are many islands, bays and peninsulas in the Korea Strait. The volcanic island of Cheju lies off the southwest coast. Most of the country consists of hills and mountains and the 30% of flat plain contains the majority of the population and cultivation. Most rivers rise in the mountains to the east, flowing west and south to the Yellow Sea. The Naktong River flows into the Korea Strait near the southern port of Pusan. The eastern coast is rocky and steep with mountains rising from the sea.
LANGUAGE: Korean.
RELIGION: Mahayana Buddhism with a large Christian minority. Also Confucianism, Daoism and Chundo Kyo.
TIME: GMT + 9.
ELECTRICITY: 110 and 220 volts AC, 60Hz. Policy is to phase out the 110-volt supply.
COMMUNICATIONS: Telephone: IDD is available to Seoul and other major cities. Country code: 82. **Fax:** This service is available at major hotels and business centres. **Telex/telegram:** There is a service at all main hotels. Korea International Telecommunications Services at 1, Choong-ro, Chung-gu, Seoul provide a 24-hour public service. **Post:** Airmail to Europe takes up to ten days. Post offices open 0900-1700 Monday to Friday and 0900-1300 Saturday. **Press:** English-language national dailies are *The Korea Herald* and *The Korea Times*.
BBC World Service and Voice of America frequencies: From time to time these change. See the section *How to Use this Book* for more information.

BBC:				
MHz	21.72	15.28	9.570	7.180
Voice of America:				
MHz	15.43	11.72	5.985	1.143

PASSPORT/VISA

Regulations and requirements may be subject to change at short notice, and you are advised to contact the appropriate diplomatic or consular authority before finalising travel arrangements. Details of these may be found at the head of this country's entry. Any numbers in the chart refer to the footnotes below.

	Passport Required?	Visa Required?	Return Ticket Required?
Full British	Yes	1	No
BVP	Not valid	-	-
Australian	Yes	2	Yes
Canadian	Yes	2	Yes
USA	Yes	2	Yes
Other EC	Yes	1	Yes
Japanese	Yes	Yes	Yes

Restricted entry: Holders of passports containing valid or expired visas for North Korea or any other evidence of having visited that country will be refused entry or transit permission.

PASSPORTS: Valid passport required by all.
British Visitors Passport: Not acceptable.
VISAS: Required by all except:
(a) [1] nationals of Belgium, France, Greece, Luxembourg and The Netherlands for stays of up to 3 months; nationals of Denmark, Germany, Ireland, Spain and the UK for stays of 2 months, extendable to 3 months; nationals of Italy and Portugal for stays of up to 2 months;
(b) nationals of Austria, Bangladesh, Barbados, Colombia, Costa Rica, Dominica, Finland, Iceland, Liberia, Malaysia, Mexico, Norway, Pakistan, Peru, Singapore, Sweden, Switzerland, Thailand and Turkey for stays of up to 3 months;
(c) nationals of Lesotho and Suriname for stays of up to 2 months;
(d) nationals of Tunisia for stays of up to 1 month;
(e) [2] nationals of all other non-Communist countries are allowed to stay for a maximum of 15 days without a visa if they hold a confirmed onward ticket.
Note: There are visa exemptions for the following categories: business, touristic visits, meetings, medical treatment, lectures, games and contests, performances, location shots and cultural exchange. For full details, contact the Embassy (or Consular Section at Embassy).
Types of visa: Tourist, Transit and Business: £9.30.
Validity: Up to 3 months from the date of issue.
Application to: Consulate (or Consular Section at Embassy). For addresses, see top of entry.
Application requirements: (a) Passport with at least 6 months remaining validity. (b) Completed application form. (c) Photo. (d) £9.30 fee, payable by company cheque or postal order only. (e) Business letters where appropriate. (f) Copy of green card if US permanent resident. (g) Stamped, self-addressed envelope if applying by post. Please allow a further week for return of documents.
Working days required: 2-3 days (short stay); 4-8 weeks (work and residence).
Temporary residence: Applications for a residence certificate or for a stay of more than 90 days should be made to the Immigration Office in Seoul. Tel: (2) 503 7010.

MONEY

Currency: Won (SKW). Notes are in denominations of SKW10,000, 5000 and 1000. Coins are in denominations of SKW500, 100, 50, 10, 5 and 1. A larger denomination, the Chon *(jeon)*, valued at SKW1000, is also in use, but only on cheques, banker's orders, etc.
Credit cards: Diners Club, Visa, American Express and Access/Mastercard are widely accepted, but check with your credit card company for details of merchant acceptability and other services which may be available.
Travellers cheques: Accepted, but may be difficult to change in smaller towns.
Exchange rate indicators: The following figures are included as a guide to the movements of the Won against Sterling and the US Dollar:

Date:	Oct '89	Oct '90	Oct '91	Oct '92
£1.00=	1077	1408	1300	1265
$1.00=	682	721	749	797

Currency restrictions: There are restrictions on the import of both local and foreign currency; check with the Embassy for current allowances. All currency must be declared on arrival, and if greater than US$5000, must be entered on a Foreign Exchange Record. Export of local currency is limited to US$5000 equivalent; export of foreign currency is limited to the amount declared on arrival.
Banking hours: 0930-1630 Monday to Friday, and 0930-1330 Saturday.

DUTY FREE

The following goods may be imported into the Republic of Korea without incurring customs duty:
400 cigarettes, 50 cigars, 200g pipe tobacco (total quantity not exceeding 500g);

SOUTH KOREA | **HEALTH REGULATIONS** | **VISA REGULATIONS**

GALILEO/WORLDSPAN

TI-DFT/SEL/HE

TI-DFT/SEL/VI

SABRE

TIDFT/SEL/HE

TIDFT/SEL/VI

To access this information on your CRS, swipe the barcode with a light pen or type in the text under the barcode. For more information, see the introduction *How to Use This Book*.

2 bottles (total 1520cc) of alcohol;
2oz of perfume;
Gifts up to SKW300,000.
Note: It is prohibited to bring the following articles into the country: any printed material, films or phonograph records considered by the authorities to be subversive or harmful to national security or public interests; any firearms, explosives or other weapons; textile fabrics in excess of 5 sq metres (6 sq yards); more than five foreign phonograph records; radio equipment and any animals or plants prohibited by the relevant regulations.

PUBLIC HOLIDAYS

Public holidays observed in the Republic of Korea are as follows:
Mar 1 '93 Independence Movement Day. **Apr 5** Arbor Day. **Apr 28** Buddha's Birthday. **May 5** Children's Day. **Jun 6** Memorial Day. **Jul 17** Constitution Day. **Aug 15** Liberation Day. **Sep 29-Oct 1** Thanksgiving Day. **Oct 3** National Foundation Day. **Dec 25** Christmas Day. **Jan 1-2 '94** New Year. **Jan 22-24** Lunar New Year. **Mar 1** Independence Movement Day.

HEALTH

Regulations and requirements may be subject to change at short notice, and you are advised to contact your doctor well in advance of your intended date of departure. Any numbers in the chart refer to the footnotes below.

	Special Precautions?	Certificate Required?
Yellow Fever	No	-
Cholera	Yes	1
Typhoid & Polio	Yes	-
Malaria	No	-
Food & Drink	2	-

[1]: Following WHO guidelines issued in 1973, a cholera vaccination certificate is not a condition of entry to the Republic of Korea. However, cholera is a risk in this country and precautions are essential. Up-to-date advice should be sought before deciding whether these precautions should include a vaccination, as medical opinion is divided over its effectiveness. See the *Health* section at the back of the book.
[2]: Mains water is normally chlorinated, and whilst relatively safe may cause mild abdominal upsets. Bottled water is available and is advised for the first few weeks of the stay. Milk is unpasteurised and should be boiled. Powdered or tinned milk is available and is advised, but make sure that it is reconstituted with pure water. Avoid dairy products which are likely to have been made from unboiled milk. Only eat well-cooked meat and fish, preferably served hot. Pork, salad and mayonnaise may carry increased risk. Vegetables should be cooked and fruit peeled.
Japanese encephalitis is transmitted by mosquitoes between June and the end of October in rural areas. A vaccine is available, and travellers are advised to consult their doctor prior to departure.
HIV/AIDS: People wishing to stay in the Republic of Korea for more than three months must supply a certificate showing they have tested HIV negative, issued within one month before their arrival.
Health care: Health insurance is recommended. There are facilities in all tourist areas, and hotels will recommend a local doctor.

Popchusa Temple

TRAVEL - International

AIR: The Republic of Korea's national airline is *Korean Air (KE)*.
Approximate flight times: From *London* to Seoul is 12 hours; add 1 hour if flying to any other main city.
From *New York* to Seoul is 17 hours 40 minutes (including stopover in Anchorage).
From *Los Angeles* to Seoul is 10 hours and 30 minutes.
From *Sydney* to Seoul is 9 hours.
International airports: *Seoul (SEL)* (Kimpo) is 26km (16 miles) from the city. Coaches depart to the city every 8 minutes 0530-2140 (travel time – 50 minutes). Buses depart every 5 minutes. Taxis to the city are also available. Airport facilities: currency exchange, pharmacy, children's restroom, post office, gift shop, duty-free shop, car hire, local products shop and restaurant.
Pusan (PUS) (Kim Hae) is 27km (17 miles) from Pusan in the far south. The airport receives flights from Tokyo, Osaka and Fukuoka. There are bus, coach and taxi services to the town. Airport facilities: currency exchange, post office, duty-free shop, snack bar, gift shop, restaurant, travel information service and car hire.
Cheju (CJU) (Cheju). Buses and coaches are available to the town. Airport facilities: currency exchange, post office, duty-free shop, snack bar, gift shop and travel information service.
Departure tax: SKW7200, payable at the airport.
SEA: International ports are Pusan (in the far south) and Inchon (due west of Seoul). Passenger lines are *Pukwan Ferry* and *Orient Overseas Lines*. Cargo/passenger lines include *American Mail* and *American President*. Crossings from Japan can be made via *Pukwan* ferry (Pusan–Shimonoseki). Three weekly trips from the USA are offered by *Lykes Lines* and *American President Lines*. *Knutsen Lines* run services from Australia.
RAIL/ROAD: There are no rail or road links with the Democratic People's Republic of Korea across the Republic of Korea's only land frontier. However, this may change in the near future as the border is to be opened gradually, starting with foreign visitors travelling in organised groups.

TRAVEL - Internal

AIR: *Korean Air (KE)* runs frequent services between Seoul and Pusan, Taegu, Cheju, Ulsan and Kwangu.
SEA: A steamer service runs along the scenic south coast between Mokpo and Pusan twice daily. A hydrofoil service links Pusan and Yosu via Ch'ungmu, five times a day *(Angel Line)*. Ferries connect Pusan with Cheju Do Island once a day. Car ferries run three times a week.
RAIL: *Korean National Railroads* connect major destinations. Super-express trains operate on Seoul–Mokpo, Seoul–Pusan (twice weekly), Seoul–Chongju and Seoul–Kyongju routes. Some have air-conditioning and restaurant cars. A supplement is payable for better quality accommodation on some trains. Station signs in English are common and English translations of timetables are usually available.
ROAD: The network extends over more than 50,000km (32,000 miles) of roads; half of it is paved. Excellent motorways link all major cities, but minor roads are often badly maintained. **Bus:** Local and express buses are inexpensive, though local buses within cities are often crowded and make no allowances for English-speakers. Air-conditioned super-express buses, operating in competition with trains, connect major cities and are to be recommended for their comfort, while towns and villages are linked by local bus services. **Taxi:** Cheap and a good way to travel. **Car hire:** Available from some hotels and travel agents. *Hertz* in Seoul operates 200 cars. *Cheju Rent-a-Car* operates 30 cars. **Documentation:** International Driving Permit required.
URBAN: Seoul has underground and suburban railways and well-developed bus services, all of which are very crowded. Taxis are widely available. Good bus services also operate in other cities.
JOURNEY TIMES: The following chart gives approximate journey times (in hours and minutes) from Seoul to other major cities/towns in the Republic of Korea:

	Air	Road	Rail
Pusan	0.50	5.30	4.10
Taegu	0.40	3.50	4.10
Kwangju	0.50	3.55	6.00
Ulsan	0.50	4.40	4.00
Chinju	1.10	5.20	6.30
Cheju	0.55	-	-
Kyongju	-	4.40	3.30

Traditional Wedding Procession

Hyang-wonjong Pavilion

Additional times: From Pusan to Cheju by sea is 11 hours. From Mokpo to Cheju by sea is 5 hours 30 minutes. From Pusan to Kyongju is 1 hour by road and 40 minutes by rail.

ACCOMMODATION

HOTELS: There are many modern tourist hotels in the major cities and tourist areas. All of these are registered with the Government. Most rooms have private baths, and heating and cooling systems. Facilities in most tourist hotels include dining rooms, convention halls, bars, souvenir shops, cocktail lounges, barber and beauty shops and recreation areas. **Grading:** All registered hotels are classified according to their standard and quality of service. The Rose of Sharon, the national flower of Korea, is used as a symbol of quality and hotels range from 5 Sharons (deluxe) to 2 Sharons (third class).
YOGWANS: These are Korean inns; very reasonable and considered by many travellers as the 'only place to stay'. Sleeping arrangements consist of a small mattress and a firm pillow on the *ondol*, the hot floor-heating system which is traditional in Korea. There are also Western-style rooms. For further information contact Korea Hotels & Accommodation Association. Tel: (2) 631 9868.
SELF-CATERING: Cottages are available for rent at seaside resorts, but fees are high and few services are provided.
CAMPING: Campsites are located throughout the country. Contact the Tourism Corporation for details.
YOUTH HOSTELS: At present there are 20 youth hostels in Korea, mainly located in Seoul, Kyongju, Pusan, Puyo, Sokcho and vicinities. For more information and reservations contact the Korean Youth Hostel Association, 27 Supyo-dong, Ghung-gu, Seoul. Tel: (2) 266 2896.

RESORTS & EXCURSIONS

Most visitors to Korea start their tours in **Seoul**, the capital, which has recovered from the devastation of the Korean War to become a bustling and sophisticated commercial centre. There are, however, still many glimpses of its past, including royal palaces, markets, museums and traces of the ancient walls. Seoul has been the nation's capital since 1394 and is still laid out in the traditional square pattern adopted by many Chinese cities. The city was encircled by 16km (10 miles) of high walls, and when it was threatened all nine gates were closed. Four of the gates still remain.
A whole-day tour of ancient and modern Seoul includes a visit to *Changdokkung Palace*, which has been used for royal functions since the 17th century. The main gate to the palace is believed to be the oldest in Seoul. Adjoining the palace are the *Secret Gardens*, a picturesque area of lakes and woodland which was once a retreat for members of the royal family.
Toksukung Palace was once a royal villa, but is now a *Museum of Modern Arts*, while *Kyongbokkung Palace*, which dates back to 1394, was burned during the Japanese invasion of 1592 and was left in ruins until 1868, when it was rebuilt. The grounds house many of Korea's most historic stone pagodas and monuments. The *Great South Gate of Seoul*, called Namdaemun, is regarded as Korea's foremost national treasure. It was built in 1448, but had to be repaired after the Korean War.
Seoul's *Pagoda Park* commemorates the spot where the Korean Declaration of Independence was proclaimed in 1919; the park was designed as a setting for the huge *Wongak-sa Pagoda*, built of marble and granite. A good viewpoint is *Namsan Mountain* in the middle of the city. On the top is the *Seoul Tower*, a new TV transmitter with an observation deck which has spectacular views extending west to Inchon. Other spots for city sightseeing include the *Octagonal Pagoda*, built in 1348, and the *East Gate Market Place*.

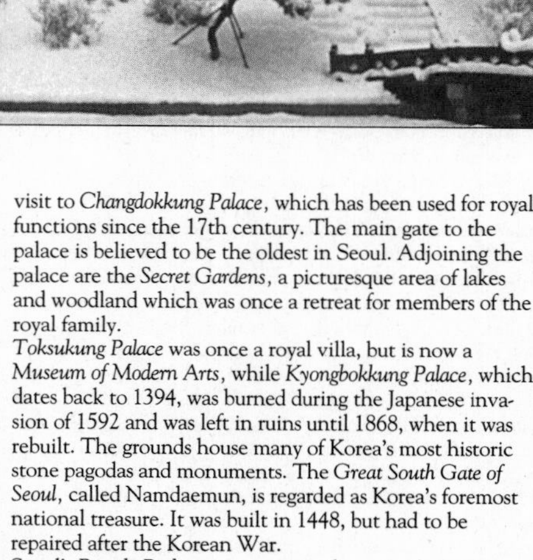

Songsan Ilch'ulbong Peak

50km (30 miles) south of Seoul is the Korean Folk Village of **Suwon**. The village is a real, live and functioning rural community out of a past era where artefacts and dress are authentic, where craftsmen can be observed at their trades and where folk dances and other traditional Korean entertainments and customs are performed daily.
Another popular touring area is centred on **Kyongju** on the southeast coast about 320km (200 miles) from Seoul. It is an area rich with the relics of Korea's history and culture and was named by UNESCO as one of the world's ten most important historic city sites. It was the capital of the Shilla Dynasty from 57BC to AD935 and at that time was one of the six largest cities in the world. Kyongju is Korea's best-known centre of ancient history and crafts and the city has many temples, royal tombs and monuments and what is regarded as the finest pre-modern astronomic observatory in Asia, probably one of the oldest structures of its kind in the world. The local branch of the *National Museum* has thousands of relics of the Shilla era, including gold crowns and girdles, jewellery, ceramics and weapons. Just outside the town is the *Pulguksa Temple*, one of Korea's most important Buddhist sites. Many of the structures here date back to AD751, but some of the wooden buildings have been rebuilt many times over the centuries. Nearby is the *Sokkuram Grotto*, with its huge granite Buddha. The *Onung* or Five Tombs complex is believed to be the burial place of the first Shilla king, his queen, and three later monarchs. Within easy reach of Kyongju is the *Bomun Lake Resort*, a complex of hotels, a convention centre, golf course, marina and shopping centre.
In the south of Korea is **Pusan**, the country's largest seaport. The area has two important beach resorts, *Haeundae* and *Songjong*. **Haeundae** is probably the most popular resort in the area and has a long, sandy beach with a good range of hotels and restaurants. There are also medicinal hot springs. Another hot-spring resort is *Tongnae;* nearby is *Kumgang Park* which boasts some unusual rock formations and historic relics, including a pagoda and several temples.
An up-and-coming tourist area is **Cheju Island**, a 1-hour flight from Seoul and only 40 minutes from Pusan. Different in many ways from the Korean mainland, its volcanic origin gives a distinct landscape dominated by *Mount Halla*, Korea's highest mountain at 1950m (6400ft).
Striking contrasts in scenery are part of any tour on **Cheju Island,** which might include visits to *Samsonghyol Caves*, the *Grotto of the Serpent* and the *Dragon Pool*. A

SIGHTS AND SOUNDS OF THE WORLD

Over 100 countries across five continents will proudly exhibit their unique cultural and aesthetic elements, from colourful street parades and electrifying laser shows to traditional handicraft displays.

A truly international forum of cultural exchange which provides an opportunity to rediscover the origins of cultural traditions awaits the visitor at **Taejon EXPO '93.**

TRADITIONAL AND MODERN SCIENCE AND TECHNOLOGY COME TOGETHER

Mankind's scientific achievements throughout civilization will come together at Taejon EXPO '93, displaying our infinite capacity of imagination . . . A journey without end, but one with a distinct destination.

The first domestically-produced magnetic-levitated train, pollution-free electric vehicles, solar-powered cars, recreations of ancient rockets and the famous iron-clad solar-powered turtle ship, ground surveillance airship, flight simulations, the first non-slit 365-degree multi-slide vision, high-definition television – all will converge for a dynamic demonstration and application of state-of-the-art technology in Taejon, destined to stimulate scientific interest and appreciation among visitors. Be a part of this scientific and technological adventure at **Taejon EXPO '93.**

HARMONY BETWEEN SCIENCE AND NATURE

Since ancient times, Koreans have held a profound reverence towards nature. Development and stability, as the classical thinkers once wrote, can be realised through harmony with nature.

As the first international exposition to address the charter of the Rio Environmental Summit, Taejon EXPO '93 will bring this living philosophy to new heights by presenting improved methods of resources recycling and conservation as well as introducing new technologies for environmental protection. If you want to make this world a greener place, we invite you to **Taejon EXPO '93.**

● Accommodation in Taejon

Hotels in Taejon

Hotels in Taejon	No. of rooms	Tel No. 82+42+ No.
Hotel Riviera Yusong ★★★★	173	823 2111
Yusong Hotel ★★★★	192	822 0811
Tourist Hotel Picasso ★★★★	65	627 3001/10
Hotel Hongin ★★★★	58	822 2000
Kyungwon Tourist Hotel ★★★★	81	534 8877
Hotel Adria ★★★★	80	824 0211
Daelim Hotel ★★★	67	255 2161/7
Princess Tourist Hotel ★★★	52	823 9900/1
Joongang Hotel ★★★	59	253 8801/4
Prince Hotel ★★★	31	253 5853/4
Family Hotel ★★★	31	255 4083/90
Mugunghwa Hotel ★★★	64	822 1233/6
Taejon Hotel ★★★	52	253 8131/9
Munhwa Hotel ★★★	42	256 7000
Life Hotel ★★★	32	253 5337/40
Dongyang Hotel ★★★	32	627 0011/5
New Seoul Hotel ★★★	52	252 8161
Lucky Hotel ★★★	30	526 9481/4
Hotspring Tourist Hotel ★★	64	820 8888
Yusong Royal Tourist Hotel ★★	58	822 0720
Hanil Tourist Hotel ★★	30	283 4401/5
TOTAL 21	**1,345**	

Over 4,600 rooms in Taejon alone, our wide range of new and comfortable accommodation awaits you in Korea, all priced at surprisingly reasonable costs. Wherever you stay, you will experience the world-renowned hospitality that only Koreans can provide.

For more information, please call (82-2) 551-4858, Fax (82-2) 551 4822.

Pulguksa Temple

full-day tour of the island takes in visits to tangerine orchards, the *Chongbang Waterfalls*, a model farm village and *Songsanilchulbong Park*. The mountainous terrain of Korea's **East Coast** provides breathtaking scenery, a blaze of colour in autumn and the setting for winter sports with a modern, fully equipped ski centre. There are plenty of touring opportunities along this 390km (240-mile) stretch of coastline, from the popular beach of *Hwajinpo* down to Pusan in the south. The mountains run down to the sea, but are interspersed by a series of long, sandy beaches, harbours and small fishing villages. Three national parks – **Soraksan, Odaesan** and **Chuwangsan** – have been designated and all are accessible from a new coastal highway opened in 1978. In the Soraksan National Park, **Sorakdong Village** has been developed as a tourist resort village and is the starting point for climbing trails; nearby is the *Sinhung-sa Temple*, first built in AD645, but reconstructed in the 17th century. A cable car runs between Sorakdong Village and the *Kwongumsong Fortress*, parts of which date back to 57BC. In the same area is the city of **Sokch'o**, a major fishing port, and nearby is the newly developed *Choksan Hot Springs* resort.

SOCIAL PROFILE

FOOD & DRINK: Korea has its own cuisine, quite different from Chinese or Japanese. Rice is the staple food and a typical Korean meal consists of rice, soup, rice water and 8 to 20 side dishes of vegetables, fish, poultry, eggs, bean-curd and sea plants. Most Korean soups and side dishes are heavily laced with red pepper. Dishes include *kimchi* (highly spiced pickle of Chinese cabbage or white radish with turnips, onions, salt, fish, chestnuts and red pepper), soups (based on beef, pork, oxtail, other meat, fish, chicken and cabbage, almost all spiced), *pulgogi* (marinated, charcoal-broiled beef barbecue), *Genghis Khan* (thin slices of beef and vegetables boiled at the table) or *sinsollo* (meat, fish, eggs and vegetables such as chestnuts and pinenuts cooked in a brazier chafing dish at the table). Other examples of local cuisine are *sanjok* (strips of steak with onions and mushrooms), *kalbichim* (steamed beef ribs), fresh abalone and shrimps (from Cheju Island, served with mustard, soy or chilli sauces) and Korean seaweed (prized throughout East Asia). There is waiter as well as counter service. Most major hotels will offer a selection of restaurants, serving Korean, Japanese and Chinese cuisine or more Western-style food. **Drink:** Local drinks are mostly made from fermented rice or wheat and include *jungjong* (expensive variant of rice wine), *soju* (like vodka and made from potatoes or grain) or *yakju/takju* (cloudy and light tan-coloured) known together as *makkoli*. Korean beers are *Crown* and *OB*. *Ginseng* wine is strong and sweet, similar to brandy, but varies in taste according to the basic ingredient used. The most common type of drinking establishment is the *Suljip* (wine bar), but there are also beer houses serving well-known European brands.
NIGHTLIFE: Seoul has a growing number of nightclubs, cabarets, restaurants, theatres and beer halls. There are also many cinemas. Operas, concerts and recitals can be seen at the National Theatre and performances of Korean classical music, dances and plays can be seen at Korea House and the Drama Centre. For daily listings of events consult Korea's two English-language papers. Licensed casinos operate at various locations throughout the country.
SHOPPING: Favourite buys to look for are hand-tailored clothes, sweaters (plain, embroidered or beaded), silks, brocades, handbags, leatherwork, gold jewellery, topaz, amethyst, amber, jade and silver, ginseng, paintings, costume dolls, musical instruments, brassware, lacquerware, wood carvings, baskets, scrolls and screens. Prices are fixed in department stores, but may be negotiated in arcades and markets. Major cities have 'Foreigners' Duty Free shops where people can use foreign currency with a valid passport. Hotels will be able to tell guests the location. **Shopping hours:** 1030-1930 Monday to Friday. Smaller shops open earlier and close late.
SPORT: Climbing: The Korea National Park has excellent climbs at Mount Pukhan, Seoul, Mount Sorak on the East Coast and Mount Halla and Cheju Island. **Shooting:** There is pheasant shooting on Cheju Island between November and February. **Skiing:** Principle resorts are the Yongpyong Ski Resort (Dragon Valley International Ski Resort) at Tackwallyong Area and Chonmasan Ski Resort near Seoul. Modern facilities, lifts, accommodation and equipment are available in several areas. **Swimming:** Major hotels have swimming pools and there are fine beaches along the coast and lakes in the resorts. There are large outdoor pools at Walker Hill Resort. **Horseracing:** The horseracing season in Seoul starts in June at Tuksom Track, eight miles from the downtown area. **Fishing** is regarded as a major leisure activity, as Korea is surrounded by sea on three sides and has many reservoirs and streams. **T'aekwondo** is the main martial art practised in Korea.
SPECIAL EVENTS: The most significant festival is Buddha's Birthday in which the 'Feast of Lanterns' is performed in Korea's streets. Of great importance are the annual village rituals which are nationally recognised. At these festivals, mountain spirits, great generals and royalty of the past are remembered and celebrated, as well as festivals of prayer for a good harvest. All the festivals are characterised by processions, by masked and costumed local people, music, dancing, battles and sports to recreate the original historic event or to conjure up good spirits. Some major festivals and other events for 1993 are listed below, but contact the Korea National Tourism Corporation for more details and exact dates. 1994 has been declared 'Visit Korea Year' and there will be several festivals to celebrate the 600th Anniversary of Seoul being the capital of Korea. **Apr '93** *King Tanjong Memorial Festival*, Yongwol; *Loop Battle Festival*, Seoul; *Cherry Blossom Festival*, Chinhae; *Ritual of Unsan* (honouring mountain spirits and legendary leaders), Unsan-myon. **May** *Royal Shrine Rites*, Seoul; *Memorial Festival for King Sejong*, Yoju; *Arangje Festival*, Miryang; *Chinnam Festival*, Yosu. **Jun** *Tano Harvest Prayer Festival*, Kangnung. **Aug 7-Nov 7** *Taejon Expo '93*. **Sep** *Sokchonje*, *Confucian Festival*, Seoul; *Paekche Cultural Festival*, Puyo. **Oct** *Mount Soraksan Festival*, Kangwon-do; *Cultural Festival*, Yoju; *Shilla Cultural Festival*, Kyongju; *Halla Cultural Festival*, Cheju Island. There are numerous other festivals and ceremonies in October. **Nov** *Kaech'on Art Festival*, Chinju.
SOCIAL CONVENTIONS: Shoes should be removed before entering a Korean home. Entertainment is usually lavish and Koreans may sometimes be offended if their hospitality is refused. Customs are similar to those in the West. Small gifts are customary and traditional etiquette requires the use of the right hand for giving and receiving. Dress should be casual and practical clothes are suitable. The rural population wear traditional costume. For men it is the *hanbok*, a short jacket, loose trousers and *kat* – a tall, dark hat with round brim. Women wear a *chima-jeogon*, a very loose, unfitted dress of silk with a *chogori*, a small jacket resembling a bolero with long sleeves. **Tipping:** Though not a Korean custom, most hotels and other tourist facilities add a 10% service charge to bills. Taxi drivers are not tipped unless they help with the luggage.

Hongdo Island

BUSINESS PROFILE

ECONOMY: Korea is one of the so-called 'Tiger economies' of the Pacific Rim, which have undergone rapid growth and industrialisation since the 1960s and have forged a major presence in world export markets. Korea's strength is in four areas: shipbuilding, steel, consumer electronics (of which Korea is the world's eighth-largest producer) and construction. Korean companies have established a major presence in the world construction industry, providing a major source of 'invisible earnings'. This has produced one of the world's highest economic growth rates during the last decade. The early 1990s have brought worries about overheating, and as inflation and the trade deficit have increased rapidly, the Government is hoping to engineer a gradual slowdown. An important economic issue in the 90s will be whether the family-owned commercial groups, the *chaebol* who are the heart and soul of

Downtown Seoul

the Korean economy, will be able to reform themselves to adjust to the demands of a mature industrial economy. Furthermore, pressure will grow on the Korean government to liberalise its trading and financial systems to allow greater foreign involvement in the economy. Compared with the north, which has extensive coal and mineral deposits, the South is relatively poor in natural resources, although there have been recent offshore discoveries of natural gas which should help to reduce South Korea's dependence on imported energy. Economic factors have played a central role in the evolving political situation in the region, underpinning the rapprochement between Seoul and Moscow, and may be decisive in the future of divided Korea itself (see *History*). The United States and Japan are South Korea's main trading partners, but export growth during the 1990s is likely to be driven by the country's newer trading relationships, in particular the CIS and the People's Republic of China.

BUSINESS: Businessmen are expected to wear a suit and tie. English is widely spoken in commercial and official circles. Prior appointments are necessary and business cards are widely used. The use of the right hand when giving and receiving particularly applies to business cards. Best months for business visits are February to June. **Office hours:** 0830-1800 Monday to Friday; 0900-1300 Saturday.

COMMERCIAL INFORMATION: The following organisations can offer advice: Korean Chamber of Commerce and Industry (KCCI), PO Box 25, 45 4-ka, Namdaemun-no, Chung-ku, Seoul 100. Tel: (2) 757 0757. Fax: (2) 757 9475. Telex: 25728; *or*

Korea Trade Centre, Ground Floor, Vincent House, Vincent Square, London SW1P 2NB. Tel: (071) 834 5082. Fax: (071) 630 5233. Telex: 22375 KOTRA.

CONFERENCES/CONVENTIONS: The new Korea Exhibition Centre (KOEX) in Seoul opened in 1988, forming part of the World Trade Centre. Tel: (2) 553 7907/8. Fax: (2) 557 5784. Between 1981 and 1990 the average annual growth rate of the Korean convention industry registered about 11% in terms of events and 33% in participants. In 1990, 220 international events were held throughout the country. The Korea Convention and Co-ordinating Committee (c/o Korea National Tourism Corporation, 10 Ta-dong, Chung-gu, Seoul; tel: (2) 757 6030; fax: (2) 757 5997) can also offer advice and information on meeting facilities in the Republic of Korea.

HISTORY & GOVERNMENT

HISTORY: The first records of the country date back to the 1st century AD, when the first native kingdoms were formed. Before this the area was settled by Chinese groups. The country became unified in the 7th century; however it was not until the late 14th century that, under the Yi dynasty, Korea entered a period of outstanding cultural achievement. At the turn of the 16th century, Korea was invaded by Japan and, later, the Manchus, after which the country fell under Chinese influence. Korea was then annexed to Japan in 1910. At the end of the Second World War, the country was divided along latitude 38 degrees North (the 38th parallel). War broke out between the two forces in 1950; an armistice was signed in 1953. For the next three decades, locked into opposing Cold War blocs, the two Koreas went their separate ways. South Korea developed a successful capitalist economy, but manifestly failed to evolve a comparable political system. Until the early 1980s, South Korea was governed by a series of dictatorships, both civilian and military, under which political dissent led to imprisonment. The country's political leaders, with their powerbase in the monopoly Democratic Justice Party, realised at this point that some relaxation of the existing tight political controls was necessary. The question, as ever, was how far to go and how fast. In 1981 martial law was lifted. Within five years, a powerful parliamentary opposition had emerged in the form of the New Korea Democratic Party (NKDP), led by the veteran dissident Kim Dae-Jung. Protests at the slow, sometimes non-existent pace of reform continued nonetheless. University students were especially prominent in the opposition movement, with frequent protests and occupations which sometimes became violent. The students' role was crucial: unlike the West where student protest has often been decried by the population at large, South Korea's student movement, the *Chondaehyop*, is widely supported by ordinary people who feel it able to articulate their complaints and desires. By now, the regime was also being challenged by South Korea's burgeoning labour movement, which had emerged with the country's rapid industrialisation. The combination was a potent one and in 1987 launched its greatest challenge yet to the regime. With the eyes of the world on South Korea because of the Olympics, the Government was terrified of any disruption and duly announced the holding of multi-party elections under a reformed constitution in which the elected assembly was granted much-augmented powers. A new government was formed in February 1988 by the Democratic Justice Party, which had been victorious at the polls, with Roh Tae Woo as President. The National Assembly now boasted three opposition parties: the NKDP had metamorphosed into the Reunification Democratic Party. None of the four enjoyed an overall majority in the Assembly until February 1990 when, in a surprise move, three of the four parties merged, including the Democratic Justice Party which had monopolised Korean politics for so long. The new formation, the Democratic Liberal Party, enjoyed a healthy majority over Kim Dae-Jung's PDP (now the Democratic Party) which was left out in the cold. President Roh's term of office comes to an end in February 1993 after elections at the end of 1992. All that is certain is that the next occupant of the presidential Blue House will be called President Kim: either Kim Young Sam, the DLP favourite, or the veteran opposition politician Kim Dae-Jung. Whoever inaugurates the Seventh Republic in 1993 will have to deal with the unification issue. Both sides have moved cautiously but, in spite of the vast legacy of antagonism and mistrust and the wide and growing political and economic divergence, there is ever more contact and co-operation between the two Koreas. Policy makers in Seoul have watched closely the process of German reunification (dozens of 'study teams' have been sent to the Federal Republic) and taken a number of lessons from the process. The main one is that rapid unification would be severely disruptive and so costly – around US$30-50 billion annually – as to threaten the South with bankruptcy. There is also a vast political and psychological gulf between the two Koreas which cannot be rapidly bridged. With the blessing of the main regional powers, China, Japan, and the CIS, plus the USA, Korean officals are now suggesting that unification might be completed by 2020. The appearance of delegations from both North and South at the United Nations General Assembly in September 1991 was a diplomatic victory for the South. Further progress was made at the end of the year with the signing in December of a non-aggression pact and a treaty banning nuclear weapons between the two governments. The North aside, the principal concern for Roh's successor will be cooling the overheating in the South Korean economy (see *Economy*).

GOVERNMENT: The President is Head of State and elected for a single term of seven years by an Electoral College of 5278 members. The College in turn is directly elected by universal adult suffrage. The President governs with the assistance of an appointed Cabinet of Ministers. Legislation is the responsibility of the unicameral National Assembly. Two-thirds of the Assembly's 284 members are popularly elected for a 4-year term; the remaining seats are distributed among the parties represented.

CLIMATE

Moderate climate with four seasons. The hottest part of the year is during the rainy season between July and August, and the coldest is December and January. Spring and autumn are mild and mainly dry.

Required clothing: Lightweight cottons and linens are worn during summer, with light- to mediumweights in spring and autumn. Medium- to heavyweights are advised during the winter.

PUSAN Rep. of Korea (69m)

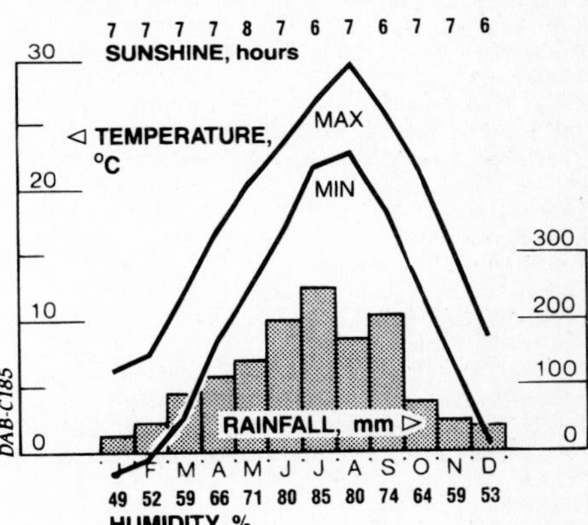

SEOUL Rep. of Korea (86m)

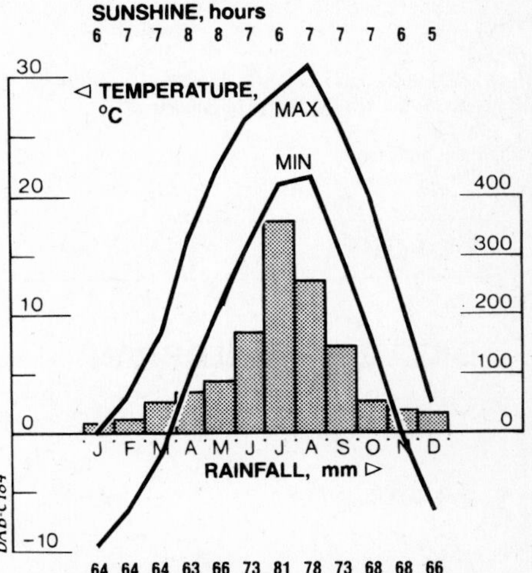

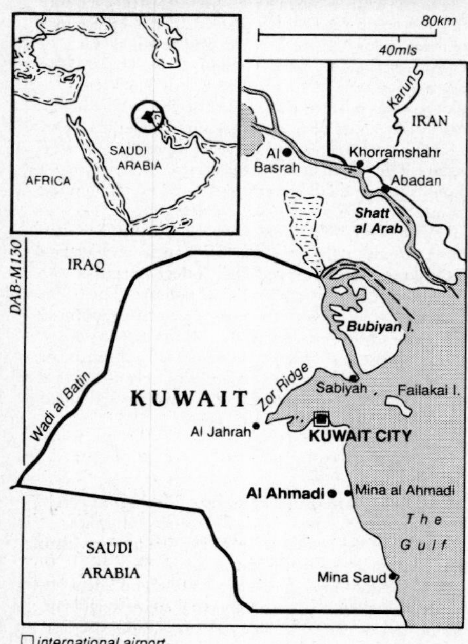

□ *international airport*

Location: Middle East.

Department of Tourism
Ministry of Information
PO Box 193
13002 Safat
Kuwait City, Kuwait
Tel: 243 6644. Fax: 242 9758. Telex: 44041.
Touristic Enterprise Company of Kuwait
PO Box 23310
13094 Safat
Kuwait City, Kuwait
Tel: 564 4621. Telex: 22801.
Embassy of the State of Kuwait
45-46 Queen's Gate
London SW7 5HR
Tel: (071) 589 4533 (ask for press office for tourist information). Fax: (071) 589 2978 *or* 255 3990 (press office). Telex: 261017. Opening hours: 0930-1300 and 1400-1600 Monday to Friday; 0930-1230 Monday to Friday. (Visa section).
British Embassy
PO Box 2
Arabian Gulf Street
13001 Safat
Kuwait City, Kuwait
Tel: 243 2047. Fax: 240 7395. Telex: 44614.
Embassy of the State of Kuwait
2940 Tilden Street, NW
Washington, DC
20008
Tel: (202) 966 0702. Fax: (202) 364 2868.
Embassy of the United States of America
PO Box 77
Arabian Gulf Street
13001 Safat
Kuwait City, Kuwait
Tel: 242 4151. Fax: 244 2855. Telex: 2039 HILTELS KT.
Honorary Consulate of the State of Kuwait
1510 Walkley Road
Ottawa, Ontario
K1V 6P5
Tel: (613) 731 3242.
Canadian Embassy
PO Box 25281
13113 Safat
Kuwait City, Kuwait
Tel: 256 3025. Fax: 256 4167. Telex: 23549.

AREA: 17,818 sq km (6880 sq miles).
POPULATION: 2,142,600, of whom 1,316,014 are non-Kuwaiti (1990 estimate).
POPULATION DENSITY: 120.3 per sq km.
CAPITAL: Kuwait City. **Population:** 44,335 (1985).
GEOGRAPHY: Kuwait shares borders with Iraq and Saudi Arabia. To the southeast lies the Persian Gulf, where Kuwait has sovereignty over nine small islands. The landscape is predominantly desert plateau with a lower, more fertile coastal belt.
LANGUAGE: Arabic, but English is widely understood, especially in commerce and industry.
RELIGION: 95% Muslim, with Christian and Hindu minorities.
TIME: GMT + 3.
ELECTRICITY: 240 volts AC, 50Hz, single phase. UK-type flat 3-pin plugs are used.
COMMUNICATIONS: Telephone: Full IDD is available. Country code: 965. **Fax:** Several hotels have facilities. **Telex/telegram:** Telex facilities are available at main hotels or the central post office (24 hours). 24-hour telegram services are available at the Ministry of Post and Telegraph Offices, Abdullah Al Salem Square, Kuwait City, but must be handed to the post office (opening hours: 0700-2359 Saturday to Wednesday, 0700-1200 Thursday). **Post:** Airmail to Europe takes about five days. **Press:** The English-language newspapers are the *Arab Times* and the *Kuwait Times*. Although remaining loyal to the Royal family, the press enjoys a fair degree of freedom.
BBC World Service frequencies: From time to time these change. See the section *How to Use this Book* for more information.
BBC:

MHz	15.07	12.10	9.670	6.180

A service is also available on 1413kHz and 702kHz (0100-0500 GMT).

PASSPORT/VISA

Regulations and requirements may be subject to change at short notice, and you are advised to contact the appropriate diplomatic or consular authority before finalising travel arrangements. Details of these may be found at the head of this country's entry. Any numbers in the chart refer to the footnotes below.

	Passport Required?	Visa Required?	Return Ticket Required?
Full British	Yes	Yes	No
BVP	Not valid	-	-
Australian	Yes	Yes	No
Canadian	Yes	Yes	No
USA	Yes	Yes	No
Other EC	Yes	Yes	No
Japanese	Yes	Yes	No

Restricted entry: Holders of Israeli passports and holders of passports containing valid or expired visas for Israel or any other evidence of having visited the country will be refused entry or transit permission.
PASSPORTS: Valid passport required by all.
British Visitors Passport: Not acceptable.
VISAS: Required by all except nationals of Bahrain, Oman, Qatar, Saudi Arabia and the United Arab Emirates.
Types of visa: Visa and Transit visa; Entry Permit. Transit visas are not required if passengers hold onward tickets and do not leave the airport. Full visas are generally only required by those intending (and invited) to take up employment. UK nationals visiting for up to a month will – usually – only need an entry permit (effectively a short-stay visa). However, it is advisable to check with the Embassy well in advance if an entry permit will be sufficient as applications for full visas can take some time. Entry permits are issued free of charge.
Cost: The fee for a full visa depends on the applicant's nationality (nationals of Italy, Norway, Sweden, Turkey, the UK and the USA are exempt).
Note: Visas and entry permits are only issued to business visitors on the invitation of a contact in Kuwait.
Validity: *Entry permit:* 1 month from date of entry. *Visa:* Enquire at Consulate.
Application to: Consulate (or Consular Section at Embassy). For addresses, see top of entry.
Application requirements: *Entry permit*: (a) Valid passport. (b) 2 completed application forms (originals, not photocopies). (c) 2 photos. (d) Covering letter from visitor's company. (e) Fax or other confirmation from sponsor/contact in Kuwait. (f) Registered, self-addressed envelope. *Visa:* As above, plus: (g) 'No Objection Certificate' from the Kuwaiti Ministry of the Interior (must be obtained before application can proceed). (h) Fee (where applicable).
Working days required: 24 hours (plus, for Visa applications, up to a month for obtaining the NOC).
Temporary residence: Enquire at Embassy. Note that 'British Citizens' who wish to take up employment will require instead (or eventually) a *residence permit*. This must be obtained before arrival in Kuwait as it is not possible to transfer status from 'visitor' to 'temporary resident' without first returning to the UK.

MONEY

Currency: Kuwait Dinar (KD) = 1000 fils. Notes are in denominations of KD20, 10, 5 and 1, and 500 and 250 fils. Coins are in denominations of 100, 50, 20, 10, 5 and 1 fils.
Credit cards: Access/Mastercard, Diners Club, Visa and American Express are accepted. Check with your credit card company for details of merchant acceptability and other services which may be available.
Travellers cheques: Widely accepted.
Exchange rate indicators: The following figures are included as a guide to the movements of the Kuwait Dinar against Sterling and the US Dollar:

Date:	Oct '89	Oct '90	Oct '91	Oct '92
£1.00=	0.50	*	0.50	0.47
$1.00=	0.30	*	0.29	0.30

Note:* Figures unavailable.
Currency restrictions: There are no restrictions on import or export apart from gold bullion, which must be declared.
Banking hours: 0800-1200 Saturday to Thursday.

DUTY FREE

The following goods may be imported into Kuwait without incurring customs duty:
500 cigarettes or 907g of tobacco.
Prohibited items: All alcoholic or narcotic imports are strictly prohibited; also, pork products and goods of Israeli or South African origin. Penalties for attempting to smuggle restricted items are severe.

PUBLIC HOLIDAYS

Public holidays observed in Kuwait are as follows:
Mar 25 '93 Start of Eid al-Fitr (End of Ramadan). **Jun 1** Eid al-Adha (Feast of the Sacrifice). **Jun 21** Islamic

KUWAIT | **HEALTH REGULATIONS** | **VISA REGULATIONS** | Code-Link

GALILEO/WORLDSPAN

TI-DFT/KWI/HE

TI-DFT/KWI/VI

SABRE

TIDFT/KWI/HE

TIDFT/KWI/VI

To access this information on your CRS, swipe the barcode with a light pen or type in the text under the barcode. For more information, see the introduction *How to Use This Book*.

New Year. **Aug 30** Birth of the Prophet. **Jan 1 '94** New Year's Day. **Jan 24** Leilat al-Meiraj. **Feb** Ramadan begins. **Feb 25-26** Kuwaiti National Day. **Mar** Eid al-Fitr (End of Ramadan).
Note: Muslim festivals are timed according to local sightings of various phases of the Moon and the dates given above are approximations. During the lunar month of Ramadan that precedes Eid al-Fitr, Muslims fast during the day and feast at night and normal business patterns may be interrupted. Many restaurants are closed during the day and there may be restrictions on smoking and drinking. Some disruption may continue into Eid al-Fitr itself. Eid al-Fitr and Eid al-Adha may last anything from two to ten days, depending on the region. For more information see the section *World of Islam* at the back of the book.

HEALTH

Regulations and requirements may be subject to change at short notice, and you are advised to contact your doctor well in advance of your intended date of departure. Any numbers in the chart refer to the footnotes below.

	Special Precautions?	Certificate Required?
Yellow Fever	No	No
Cholera	Yes	1
Typhoid & Polio	Yes	-
Malaria	No	-
Food & Drink	2	-

[1]: Following WHO guidelines issued in 1973, a cholera vaccination certificate is no longer a condition of entry to Kuwait. However, cholera is a risk in this country and precautions are essential. Up-to-date advice should be sought before deciding whether these precautions should include vaccination as medical opinion is divided over its effectiveness. See the *Health* section at the back of the book.
[2]: Mains water is normally chlorinated, and whilst relatively safe may cause mild abdominal upsets. Bottled water is available and is advised for the first few weeks of the stay. Milk is pasteurised and dairy products are safe for consumption. Local meat, poultry, seafood, fruit and vegetables are generally considered safe to eat.
Health care: Medical insurance is essential. Both private and government health services are available.

TRAVEL - International

AIR: Kuwait's national airline is *Kuwait Air (KU)*.
Approximate flight times: From Kuwait to *London* is 6 hours, to *New York* is 13 hours, to *Los Angeles* is 19 hours, to *Singapore* is 11 hours 30 minutes and to *Sydney* is 17 hours.
International airport: *Kuwait (KWI)*, 16km (10 miles) south of Kuwait City (travel time – 25 minutes). Reliable transport to and from the city, including bus (travel time – 30 minutes) departing every 45 minutes from 0600-2300 and taxi service. Tel: 433 4499 (24-hour flight information). Facilities include restaurants, shops, cafeteria, bank/bureaux de change, car rental (*Al Mulla, Avis, Budget* and *Europcar*), conference room and post office.
Departure tax: KD2 for international departures.
SEA: More than 30 shipping lines call regularly at Kuwait City, Kuwait's major port. Most traffic is commercial.
ROAD: There are excellent road links with Saudi Arabia and Iraq and hence on to Syria and Jordan. There are two preferred routes from the Mediterranean: Tripoli–Homs–Baghdad–Basra–Kuwait and Beirut–Damascus–Amman–Kuwait. The latter route follows the Trans-Arabian Pipeline (TAP line) through Saudi Arabia; the former runs across the Syrian desert. **Note:** Due to the current political and military situation in both Lebanon and southern Iraq, it is wise to check with the Embassy before selecting a route.

TRAVEL - Internal

SEA: Dhows and other small craft may be chartered for trips to the offshore islands.
ROAD: There is a good road network only between cities. **Bus:** *Kuwait Transport Company* operates a nationwide service which is both reliable and inexpensive. **Taxis:** These are recognisable by red licence plates and may be hired by the day, in which case fares should be agreed beforehand. Shared taxis are also available. Taxis can be phoned and this service is popular and reliable. A standard rate is applicable in most taxis, but those in hotel ranks are more expensive. Tipping is not expected. **Car hire:** Self-drive is available. If you produce an International Driving Permit, the rental company, within five days, will produce a temporary local licence, valid for one month.
Documentation: International Driving Permit required. A temporary driving licence is available from local authorities on presentation of a valid British or Northern Ireland driving licence. Insurance must be arranged with the Gulf Insurance Company or the Kuwait Insurance Company.

ACCOMMODATION

There is a good selection of high standard hotels. Accommodation is generally expensive. Visitors are advised to make reservations well in advance. All rates are subject to a 15% service charge.
Note: Many hotels suffered damage and looting in the Gulf War, but Kuwait has been busy making reparations and most establishments, including the main hotels, have now re-opened. Not all of the parks have been repaired and many museums have not re-opened.

RESORTS & EXCURSIONS

Kuwait City is a bustling metropolis of high-rise office buildings, luxury hotels, wide boulevards and well-tended parks and gardens. Its seaport is used by oil tankers and cargo ships and many pleasure craft. Its most dominant landmark is *Kuwait Towers*, and its oldest is *Seif Palace*, built in 1896, whose interior has a lot of original Islamic mosaic tilework, though these suffered badly during the Iraqi occupation. The *Kuwait Museum* was also stripped of many artefacts and has not yet re-opened.
Excursions: Failakai Island: A port with many old dhows which can be reached by boat. There are also some Bronze Age and Greek archaeological sites well worth viewing. **Al Jahra:** where traditional-style *Boums* and *Sambuks* (boats) are still built, although nowadays vessels are destined to work as pleasure boats rather than pearl fishing or trading vessels. *Mina Al Ahmadi:* Oil port with immense jetties for supertanker traffic.

SOCIAL PROFILE

FOOD & DRINK: There is a good choice of restaurants serving a wide choice of international and Arab cuisine and prices are reasonable. In restaurants, waiter service is the norm. Although most Arabs eat with their right hand, knives and forks are usually provided. **Note:** Alcohol is totally prohibited in Kuwait.
NIGHTLIFE: Several cinemas in Kuwait City show recent films. Two theatres often put on very good amateur productions. There is also a selection of nightclubs.
SHOPPING: All the basic and most luxury goods are available in boutiques or small general stores in Kuwait City. **Shopping hours:** 0830-1230 Saturday to Thursday, 1530-2030 Friday.
SPORT: Swimming, sailing, scuba diving and **powerboating** (especially popular in Kuwait) are available. **Horseriding** clubs flourish in the winter. There are numerous **tennis** courts in the capital, usually owned by hotels. **Football** is popular.
SOCIAL CONVENTIONS: Handshaking is the customary form of greeting. It is unlikely that a visitor will be invited to a Kuwaiti's home, as entertaining is usually conducted in a hotel or restaurant. A small gift promoting the company, or representing one's native country, is always welcome. As far as dress is concerned, the visitor will notice that Kuwaitis wear the national dress of long white *dishdashes* and white headcloths, and that most women wear *yashmaks*. In respect of this, it is important for women to dress modestly according to Islamic law. It is not acceptable for men to wear shorts in public or to go shirtless. All other Islamic rules and customs must be respected. Any user of narcotics can expect to receive a sentence of up to five years imprisonment, plus a heavy fine. 'No Smoking' signs are posted in many shops. It is greatly appreciated if visitors learn at least a few words of Arabic. **Tipping:** A service charge of 15% is usually added to bills in hotels, restaurants and clubs. Otherwise 10% is acceptable.

BUSINESS PROFILE

ECONOMY: Kuwait's considerable wealth is the result of the country's vast oil deposits: Kuwait possesses between 15% and 20% of the world's total known reserves. Oil now accounts for about 70% of domestic output, reflecting the Government's strategy of diversifying the economy as far as possible since oil production has steadily declined from its peak in 1972. The Government has eschewed heavy industrial projects in favour of light manufacturing industries such as paper and cement. There is a small fishing industry and a little agriculture. Before the Gulf War, transit trade with Iraq was also an important source of income. The most important non-petroleum sector, however, is overseas investment. This is controlled by the somewhat secretive Kuwait Investment Office, which has acquired major holdings in a number of large Western corporations (including British Petroleum, which the Kuwaitis were controversially forced to reduce in 1987 on instructions from the British government). The yearly income from KIO investments is at least as large as the country's US$6-billion annual receipts from oil. 90% of Kuwait's export earnings are derived from oil, with Japan, The Netherlands and Italy as the main markets. The principal exporters to Kuwait are, in descending order of value: Japan, the USA, Germany and the UK, which has cornered about 10% of the market. Reconstruction contracts have temporarily boosted the volume of trade between Kuwait and the West.
BUSINESS: Men are expected to wear suits and ties for business and formal social occasions. English is widely spoken in business circles although a few words or phrases of Arabic are always well received. Visiting cards are widely used. Some of the bigger hotels have translation and bilingual secretarial services. **Office hours:** *Winter*: 0800-1300 and 1600-2000 Saturday to Thursday. *Summer*: 0800-1300 and 1500-1900 Saturday to Wednesday.
COMMERCIAL INFORMATION: The following organisation can offer advice: Kuwait Chamber of Commerce and Industry, PO Box 775, Chamber's Building, Ali as-Salem Street, 13008 Safat, Kuwait City. Tel: 243 3854. Fax: 243 3858. Telex: 22198.

HISTORY & GOVERNMENT

HISTORY: The area which became Kuwait was part of the Turkish Ottoman empire from the 16th century until the latter part of the 19th century when the As-Sabah family, which now rules Kuwait, took control of local administration and steered the country into a semi-autonomous position. However, fearing that the Turks would try to reassert their control, the Kuwaitis made an agreement with the British allowing for British control of Kuwaiti foreign affairs in exchange for British military protection. This danger passed with the collapse of the Ottoman empire at the end of the First World War, although Kuwait remained a British protectorate until 1961, when the country was granted full independence. Sheikh Abdullah assumed the position of head of state, adopting the title of Emir. The large revenues from oil production allowed independent Kuwait to build up its economic infrastructure and institute educational and social welfare programmes. Surrounded by three major Middle Eastern powers – Iran, Iraq and Saudi Arabia – Kuwait moved cautiously in foreign affairs and has also been a key member of the Organisation of Petroleum Exporting Countries (OPEC). Relations with Iran were poor throughout the 1980s. Concern about Iran was, however, comparatively misplaced as the real threat to the country – as is now all too clear – came from Iraq. Iraqi territorial claims over Kuwait date back to Kuwaiti independence. Kuwait had been seriously threatened by Iraq in 1961, but was deterred by British military intervention. In 1990, no such assistance was available. Kuwait had given firm backing to the Iraqis during the Iran-Iraq war, loaning some US$40-60 billion to Baghdad (in what was unkindly dubbed 'cheque-book diplomacy'). The Saudis also lent substantial sums to Iraq, but with the crucial difference that they did not seriously expect to have it repaid. The Kuwaitis were less compromising and repeatedly insisted that the money be returned. This dispute compounded by other oil-related factors prompted the invasion. When the Iraqis crossed the border on August 1, meeting minimal resistance, the Emir, accompanied by members of his family and senior officials, escaped down the motorway towards the western Saudi town of Taif with just hours to spare. The country which Sheikh Jaber and his entourage left behind was rapidly incorporated into Iraq as its '19th province' and then systematically dismantled. Literally everything that was not nailed down was shipped back to Iraq. Nine months later the Kuwaitis recovered their country by virtue of an American-led UN-backed multinational military force which drove the Iraqis out. After a period of euphoria, the Kuwaitis were confronted with the aftermath of the war and the need to address a number of difficult questions. The infrastructure and oil-fields were almost completely destroyed by the Iraqis. The task of capping the oil wells, blown up by the retreating Iraqis, was fortunately completed far quicker than had been originally scheduled: the last fire was put out in November 1991. Putting the economy back on its feet will demand much time and effort, but is far from insurmountable: the Kuwaitis are not short of money. A far more awkward problem for the As-Sabah family is the future government of Kuwait and their role in it. While in exile, the Emir made a commitment to restore the 1962 constitution, which provides for the elections of a National Assembly and greatly limits the power of the ruling family. The Assembly was suspended in 1976 by the Emir on the grounds that it was 'not acting in the best interests of the state'; it was recalled in 1981 and suspended again in 1986. When the Emir returned to Kuwait in March 1991, he immediately declared a 3-month period of martial law. The Kuwaiti authorities also imposed stricter conditions on citizenship and staunched the influx of foreign nationals who had previously worked in Kuwait in large numbers, at one stage making up half the population. The number of people resident in Kuwait is now half of its pre-war level. Some months after his return, after concerted domestic and international pressure, the Emir announced that elections to the consultative assembly would be held in October 1992. Opponents of the regime took over 30 of the 50 seats, forcing their way into the Government for the first time, although the As-Sabahs continue to hold on to the key ministries. Kuwait signed a 10-year defence co-operation deal in September 1991 allowing Washington to maintain supply depots, training facilities and access to ports and airfields. The USA is discussing similar agreements with the other members of the Gulf Co-operation Council which will, it is hoped, form the basis of a regional security structure. The Kuwaitis are also negotiating an analogous deal with the British. Such agreements are felt essential in view of the unchanging attitude towards Kuwait in Baghdad: on several occasions during 1992, senior Iraqis have spoken publicly of the necessity of unification between Iraq and Kuwait and the return of the wayward '19th province' to the bosom of the motherland.

GOVERNMENT: The Emir, who is selected by and from members of the ruling As-Sabah family, holds exclusive executive power. The Emir appoints a Prime Minister and a Cabinet of Ministers. Legislative power is vested in a unicameral National Assembly with 50 elected members who serve for four years. Only adult males are permitted to vote. Political parties are banned.

CLIMATE

Kuwait shares European weather patterns but is hotter and drier. Summers (April to October) are hot and humid with very little rain. Winters (November to March) are cool with limited rain. Springs are cool and pleasant.

Required clothing: Tropical lightweights for summer and warmer mediumweights for cooler winter climate.

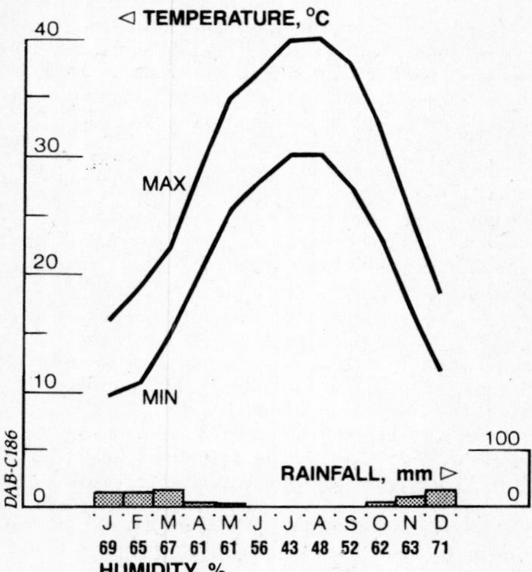

LAOS

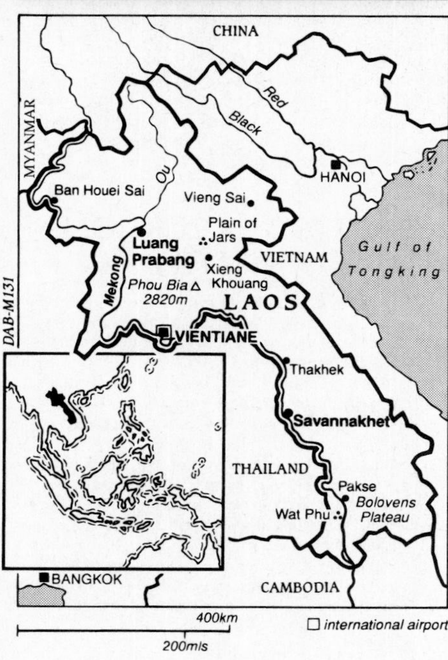

Location: South-East Asia.

National Tourism Department
Ministry of Trade and Tourism
BP 3556
Vientiane, Laos
Tel: 3254. Fax: 5025. Telex: 4343.

Embassy of the Lao People's Democratic Republic
74 avenue Raymond Poincaré
75116 Paris, France
Tel: (1) 45 53 02 98 *or* 45 53 70 47. Fax: (1) 47 27 57 89. Telex: 610711.
Opening hours: 0900-1230 and 1400-1700 Monday to Friday. *Visa Section:* 0900-1230 Monday to Friday.

Orbitours Pty Ltd
GPO Box 3309
7th Floor, Dymocks Building
428 George Street
Sydney, NSW 2001
Australia
Tel: (2) 221 7322. Tel (toll-free): (0 800) 89 2006 (UK) *or* (1 800) 235 5895 (USA). Fax: (2) 221 7425. Telex: AA127081.

The British Embassy in Bangkok, Thailand, deals with enquiries relating to Laos.

Embassy of the Lao People's Democratic Republic
2222 S Street, NW
Washington, DC
20008
Tel: (202) 332 6416/7. Telex: 904061.
Also deals with enquiries from Canada.

Embassy of the United States of America
BP 114
rue Bartholonie
Vientiane, Laos
Tel: 2220. Fax: 4675.

The Canadian Embassy in Bangkok, Thailand, deals with enquiries relating to Laos.

AREA: 236,800 sq km (91,400 sq miles).
POPULATION: 4,139,000 (1990 estimate).
POPULATION DENSITY: 17.5 per sq km.
CAPITAL: Vientiane. **Population:** 377,409 (1985).
GEOGRAPHY: Laos is a landlocked country bordered to the north by China, to the east by Vietnam, to the south by Cambodia and to the west by Thailand and Myanmar. Apart from the Mekong River plains along the border of Thailand, the country is mountainous, particularly in the north, and in places is densely forested.
LANGUAGE: Laotian. French, Vietnamese and some English are also spoken. Tribal languages, such as Meo, are also spoken.
RELIGION: The Laos-Lum (Valley Laos) people follow the Hinayana (Theravada) form of Buddhism. The religion of the Laos-Theung (Laos of the mountain tops) ranges from traditional Confucianism to Animism and Christianity.
TIME: GMT + 7.
ELECTRICITY: 220 volts AC, 50Hz.
COMMUNICATIONS: Telephone: Restricted IDD available. Country code: 856. Telephone link with Bangkok. Contact Embassy for details of telecommunications facilities. **Press:** English-language dailies in Laos include the *Vientiane May*.
BBC World Service and Voice of America frequencies: From time to time these change. See the section *How to Use this Book* for more information.

BBC:				
MHz	11.96	11.75	9.740	6.195
Voice of America:				
MHz	15.43	11.72	5.985	1.143

PASSPORT/VISA

Regulations and requirements may be subject to change at short notice, and you are advised to contact the appropriate diplomatic or consular authority before finalising travel arrangements. Details of these may be found at the head of this country's entry. Any numbers in the chart refer to the footnotes below.

	Passport Required?	Visa Required?	Return Ticket Required?
Full British	Yes	Yes	Yes
BVP	Not valid	-	-
Australian	Yes	Yes	Yes
Canadian	Yes	Yes	Yes
USA	Yes	Yes	Yes
Other EC	Yes	Yes	Yes
Japanese	Yes	Yes	Yes

PASSPORTS: Required by all.
British Visitors Passport: Not accepted.
VISAS: Required by all. *Transit visas* are not required for passengers who continue their onward journey by the same aircraft, provided that they hold tickets with reserved seats and documents necessary for entry to their destination. This facility applies to all nationals. A 7-day Transit visa can be obtained in Hanoi for only US$10. *Business visas* require an invitation from a corresponding organisation in Laos. *Tourist visas* are obtainable only through certain tour operators and in Bangkok for US$100, valid for 2 weeks.
Application to: Consulate (or Consular Section at Embassy). For addresses, see top of entry.
Application requirements: (a) 2 photos. (b) 2 forms. (c) Permission from the Ministry of Foreign Affairs, Vientiane. (d) Letter from sponsor for business application.
Working days required: Applications should be made as far in advance as possible.

MONEY

Currency: Laotian New Kip (Kp) = 100 cents (at). Notes are in denominations of Kp50, 20, 10, 5 and 1.
Currency Exchange: Thai and US currency is widely accepted in shops, markets and hotels in Vientiane and Luang Prabang.
Credit cards: Credit cards are not accepted.
Travellers cheques: Limited acceptance.
Exchange rate indicators: The following figures are included as a guide to the movements of the Laotian New Kip against Sterling and the US Dollar:

Date:	Oct '90	Mar '91	Oct '91	Oct '92
£1.00=	1386	1214	1216	1130.77
$1.00=	709	698	701	712.52

Currency restrictions: No restrictions on the import or export of foreign currency, although banks will only accept Thai Bahts, Pounds Sterling or US Dollars. The import and export of local currency is prohibited.
Banking hours: *Winter:* 0830-1130 and 1400-1500 Monday to Saturday. *Summer* (Mar 1 to Sep 30): 0800-1200 and 1330-1630 Monday to Saturday.

DUTY FREE

The following goods may be imported into Laos **from countries not bordering Laos** without incurring customs duty:
500 cigarettes or 100 cigars or 500g of tobacco;
1 bottle of alcohol;
2 bottles of wine;
Perfume for personal use.

PUBLIC HOLIDAYS

Public holidays observed in Laos are as follows:
Apr 13-15 '93 Lao New Year (Water Festival). **May 1** Labour Day. **Aug/Sep** Buddhist Memorial Day. **Dec 2** National Day. **Jan 1 '94** New Year's Day.

HEALTH

Regulations and requirements may be subject to change at short notice, and you are advised to contact your doctor well in advance of your intended date of departure. Any numbers in the chart refer to the footnotes below.

	Special Precautions?	Certificate Required?
Yellow Fever	No	1
Cholera	Yes	2
Typhoid & Polio	Yes	-
Malaria	Yes/3	-
Food & Drink	Yes/4	-

[1]: A yellow fever vaccination certificate is required from travellers coming from infected areas.
[2]: Following WHO guidelines issued in 1973, a cholera vaccination certificate is not a condition of entry to Laos. However, cholera is a serious risk in this country and precautions are essential. Up-to-date advice should be sought before deciding whether these precautions should include vaccination, as medical opinion is divided over its effectiveness. See the *Health* section at the back of the book.
[3]: *Malaria* risk exists throughout the year in the whole country, except Vientiane. The malignant *falciparum* form is prevalent and is reported to be 'highly resistant' to chloroquine.
[4]: All water should be regarded as being potentially contaminated. Water used for drinking, brushing teeth or making ice should have first been boiled or otherwise sterilised. Milk is unpasteurised and should be boiled. Powdered or tinned milk is available and is advised, but make sure that it is reconstituted with pure water. Avoid dairy products which are likely to have been made from unboiled milk. Only eat well-cooked meat and fish, preferably served hot. Pork, salad and mayonnaise may carry increased risk. Vegetables should be cooked and fruit peeled.
Rabies is present. For those at high risk, vaccination before arrival should be considered. If you are bitten abroad seek medical advice without delay. For more information consult the *Health* section at the back of the book.
Health care: Health insurance is essential.

TRAVEL - International

Note: *Vientiane Airport* and the river ferry from Nong Khai are the only gateways into Laos. **Diethelm Travel** of Bangkok and **Orbitours** in Sydney can organise trips to order (within the limitations imposed by restrictions on travellers) into Laos from Bangkok.
AIR: The national airline of Laos is *Lao International (QV)*. *Del Chang*, a US-owned company, joined with *Lao Aviation* in 1991 to form *Lao International* and now has international routes from Vientiane to Hanoi, Bangkok, Phnom Penh and Ho Chi Minh City.
International airport: *Vientiane (VTE)* (Wattay) is 4km (2.5 miles) from the city (travel time – 20 minutes).
Departure tax: US$5; children under two years are exempt.
RAIL: There are no railways in Laos, but the Thai system stretches from Bangkok via Nakhon Ratchasima to Nong Khai on the Lao/Thailand border. A ferry links the Laotian side of the Mekong, 19km (12 miles) east of Vientiane every day except Sunday.
ROAD: There are road links with Vietnam and Cambodia but these cannot be used by foreign visitors.

TRAVEL - Internal

Note: Travel outside the capital is severely restricted for foreigners.
AIR: Domestic air services run from Vientiane to Luang Prabang, Pakse and Savannakhet.
RIVER: The Mekong and other rivers are a vital part of the country's transportation system.
RAIL: There are no internal rail services.
ROAD: Many of the roads have been paved in recent years, including the main highway from the Thai border at Savannakhet to the Vietnamese border. However, few main roads are suitable for all-weather driving. There is no permissible road access to the south of Vientiane and most roads outside the province are of poor quality and dangerous (drivers are known to have been set upon by bandits). Permission to travel by road outside the capital is difficult to obtain. In the north of the country there is a road link between Vientiane and Luang Prabang, and from Vientiane to Nam Dong and Tran Ninh. **Bus** services link only a few major towns. **Car hire** arrangements can be made through hotels. **Documentation:** International Driving Permit recommended, although it is not legally required.
URBAN: Taxis are available in Vientiane, but may only operate along fixed routes similar to those of the urban buses.

ACCOMMODATION

HOTELS: There are 12 hotels in Vientiane, but facilities are sparse elsewhere. Local village hostels are available, but with few amenities. For more details of prices and location contact the Embassy.
CAMPING: There are no facilities for camping in Laos.

RESORTS & EXCURSIONS

Until 1988, when 500 visitors arrived, Western tourists were not allowed access to Laos, but a steady increase is now anticipated. Most Laotian monuments are Buddhist, but many structures show the influence of the French upon the country, not least the *Monument des Morts* in **Vientiane** which bears a striking, if somewhat rococo, similarity to the Arc de Triomphe in Paris. Visitors will find Vientiane to be an extremely laid-back city for a national capital. 25km (15 miles) from the capital is the stone garden of *Xieng Khuane*. In the royal palace at **Luang Prabang**, the former capital of Laos, there is fine artwork, and the visitor can see gifts made to former kings. Nearby, the *Phousi* in the town centre is a huge rock which visitors can ascend for a panoramic view of the river. Several interesting excursions along the *Mekong River* are possible from Luang Prabang, including a visit to the *Pak Ou Caves* where a profusion of statues of Buddha may be seen. **Wat Xieng Khwan,** in Vientiane province near the ferry port to Thailand, has an extraordinary temple.

SOCIAL PROFILE

FOOD & DRINK: Rice, expecially the glutinous variety, is the staple food and dishes will be Indo-Chinese in flavour and presentation. Lao food can be found on the stalls in the markets. There are several fairly good French restaurants in Vientiane, catering mainly for the diplomatic community. Baguettes and croissants are normally eaten for breakfast. **Drink:** Rice whisky *lao lao* is popular and there are two brands available. The beer is also worth a try.
SHOPPING: The markets in Vientiane and Luang Prabang (about 40 minutes by air from Vientiane) are worth a visit. The traveller can buy silk, silver jewellery and handmade shirts. Although the majority of shops have fixed prices, bartering is still advisable for antiques and other art objects. **Shopping hours:** 0800-1200 and 1400-1700 Monday to Friday; 0800-1200 Saturday.
SPECIAL EVENTS: The majority of festivals are linked to Buddhist holidays. The following occur annually:
Apr *Pi Mai* (celebrations for the new lunar year). **May** *Visakha Bu-saa* (Buddha's birth, enlightenment and death). **Aug/Sep** *Haw Khao Padap Din* (Festival of the Dead); *Boat Races*, Luang Prabang. **Nov** *That Luang Festival* (processions of monks receiving alms and floral votives; fireworks and music), Vientiane. **Dec/Jan** *Bun Pha Wet* (the life of Prince Vessantara is recited). **Feb** *Magha Puja* (anniversary of a speech held by Buddha); *Tet* and *Chinese New Year*.
SOCIAL CONVENTIONS: Religious beliefs should be respected. Do not point with your feet as these are regarded as the lowest part of the body. Lao people should not be touched on the head. Handshaking is not that usual, Lao people greet each other with their palms together and a slight bowing of the head. Avoid all topics of politics and related subjects in conversation. **Tipping:** Practised modestly in hotels and restaurants.

BUSINESS PROFILE

ECONOMY: Laos is one of the world's poorest countries, and its predominantly agricultural economy has been unable to operate at much above subsistence level since the mid-1970s. The country has considerable though largely untapped reserves of tin, lead and zinc, as well as iron ore, coal and timber. Laos has a large balance of payments deficit, once financed by the United States but now supported by the CIS. The Laotian economy, whose problems are compounded by a shortage of skilled labour and foreign exchange, depends also on East European and Vietnamese support and lately from certain Western countries, principally Sweden and Japan. Rice, both highland and lowland varieties, is the main crop grown, but others include maize, cassava, pulses, groundnuts, fruits, sugar cane and tobacco. The small-scale manufacturing industries include beer and cigarette production. The CIS is Laos's largest trading partner by a considerable margin.
BUSINESS: Punctuality is appreciated. Lightweight suits, shirt and tie should be worn. English is not spoken by all officials and a knowledge of French will be useful. Business cards should have a Laotian translation on the reverse. Best time to visit is during the dry season, from November to April. **Office hours:** 0800-1200 and 1400-1700 Monday to Friday; 0800-1200 Saturday.
COMMERCIAL INFORMATION: The following organisations can offer advice: Lao National Chamber of Commerce and Industry, BP 1163, Vientiane. Tel: 3171; *or*
Société de Commerce Lao, BP 278, 43-47 avenue Lane Xang, Vientiane. Tel: 2944. Fax: 5753. Telex: 4318.

HISTORY & GOVERNMENT

HISTORY: Originally known as *Lanxang* (the land of a million elephants), Laos was part of French Indo-China, with full independence being attained in 1953 under the rule of King Sisavang Vong. The monarchy was opposed by former nationalist guerrillas organised into the Laotian Patriotic Front (LPP) whose fighters, the Pathet Lao, formed an alliance with the Viet Minh (later Viet Cong) nationalists in neighbouring Vietnam, to expel the residual French, and later to counter American influence in the region and the regimes supported by them. Despite repeated efforts, both before and after the communist takeover in 1975, the Chinese failed to exert any significant influence

LAOS	HEALTH REGULATIONS	VISA REGULATIONS (Code-Link)
GALILEO/WORLDSPAN	TI-DFT/VTE/HE	TI-DFT/VTE/VI
SABRE	 TIDFT/VTE/HE	TIDFT/VTE/VI

To access this information on your CRS, swipe the barcode with a light pen or type in the text under the barcode. For more information, see the introduction *How to Use This Book*.

over the country; indeed, after 1975 Laos became dependent on military and economic assistance from Vietnam, China's enemy. In the late 1980s, however, tension between China and Laos at last began to ease: diplomatic relations (which had been severed in the late 1970s) were restored in December 1987, and cultural and bilateral trade agreements signed. Relations with Thailand and with the West have followed a similar pattern. Since 1988 there has been greatly expanded commercial contacts between Thailand and Laos and the political relationship has much improved. The dominant political figures in Laos since independence have been the veteran General Secretary of the Lao People's Revolutionary Party (whose armed wing is the Pathet Lao) Kaysone Phomvihane, and Prince Souphanouvong (the 'Red Prince'). Constitutional reform, introducing political pluralism and economic liberalisation, is in progress, although the Pathet Lao will retain monopoly control of political power in the short term. A recent shake-up of the Laotian leadership saw Kaysone Phomvihane assume the post of President, while he himself was replaced by Defence Minister General Khamtai Siphandon. The changes may allow a new role in the country's political life for the main opposition movements, the right-wing pro-royalist United Lao National Liberation Front and the United Front for the National Liberation of the Lao People, whose activities during the 1980s have been confined to armed rebellion from bases among the tribes of the northern hills.

GOVERNMENT: Laos was declared a republic in 1975 by the National Congress of People's Representatives. Under the current regime, the Congress appoints a President as Head of State and a Council of Ministers, led by the Prime Minister, which nominally holds executive power. The effective political power in Laos, however, is the 7-strong Politburo of the Laotian Peoples' Revolutionary Party, the successor of the Laotian Patriotic Front.

CLIMATE

The temperature varies according to altitude, with cooler weather in the highlands. Throughout most of the country the climate is hot and tropical, with the rainy season between May and October when temperatures are at their highest. The dry season runs from November to April.

Required clothing: Tropicals and washable cottons are worn all year. Rainwear is essential during the rainy season.

VIENTIANE Laos (162m)

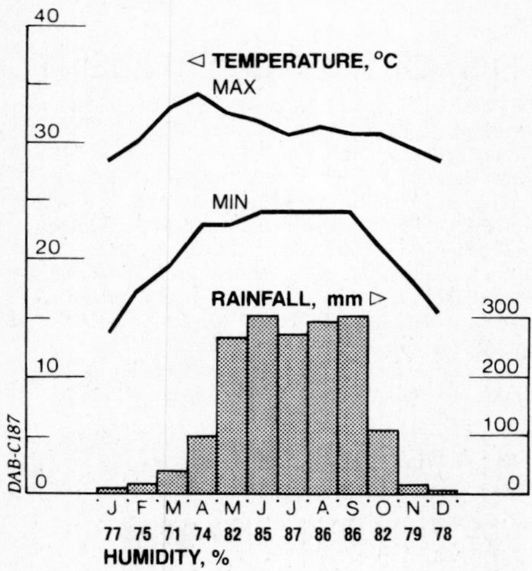

TEMPERATURE CONVERSIONS
-20 -10 0°C 10 20 30 40
0 10 20 30°F40 50 60 70 80 90 100
RAINFALL CONVERSIONS 0mm 200 400 600 800
0in 5 10 15 20 25 30

LATVIA

☐ *international airport*

Location: Northern Europe.

Latvian Tourist Office
Brivibas bulvaris 36
226170 Riga, Latvia
Tel: (2) 229 945. Fax: (2) 284 572.

Latvian Embassy
72 Queensborough Terrace
London W2 3SP
Tel: (071) 727 1698. Fax: (071) 221 9740.

British Embassy
3rd Floor
Elizabetes Iela 2
226010 Riga, Latvia
Tel: (2) 883 0113 *or* 320 737 *or* 325 287. Fax: (2) 883 0112. Telex: 1445166.

Latvian Embassy
4325 17th Street, NW
Washington, DC
20011
Tel: (202) 726 8213/4. Fax: (202) 726 6785.

Embassy of the United States of America
Raina bulvaris 7
226050 Riga, Latvia
Tel: (2) 220 502 *or* (35849) 311 348 (cellular link). Fax: (35849) 314 665 (cellular link).

Consulate General of Latvia
19th Floor
700 Bay Street
Toronto, Ontario
M5G 1Z6
Tel: (416) 408 2540. Fax: (416) 289 3857.

Canadian Embassy to Latvia
Canadian Embassy
PO Box 16129
S-10323 Stockholm
Sweden
Tel: (8) 237 920.

AREA: 64,589 sq km (24,938 sq miles).
POPULATION: 2,686,000 (1991 estimate).
POPULATION DENSITY: 41.6 per sq km.
CAPITAL: Riga. **Population:** 916,500 (1990).
GEOGRAPHY: Latvia is situated on the Baltic coast and borders Estonia in the north, Lithuania in the south, the Russian Republic in the east and Belarus in the southeast. The coastal plain is mostly flat, but inland to the east the land is hilly with forests and lakes. There are about 12,000 rivers in Latvia, the biggest being the River Daugava. The ports of Riga and Ventspils never freeze over during the winter.
LANGUAGE: Latvian is the official language. It is an Indo-European, non-Slavic and non-Germanic language and is similar only to Lithuanian. Russian and, increasingly, English are widely spoken. German and Swedish are also understood.
RELIGION: Predominantly Protestant (Lutheran) with Roman Catholics in the East of the country. There is also a Russian Orthodox minority.
TIME: GMT + 2 (GMT + 3 in summer).
ELECTRICITY: 220 volts AC, 50Hz. European-style 2-pin plugs are in use.
COMMUNICATIONS: Telephone: IDD is available. Country code: 7 013 (dial 2 for Riga). Directory enquiries is 09. Two American telecommunications companies and *Swedish Telecom* are currently competing for the contract to update the Latvian telephone system. **Fax/telex:** Facilities are available in the Main Post Office in Riga (address see below). **Telegram:** For services from public phones, dial 06. There is also service at the hotel service bureau. **Post:** The Main Post Office is at Brivibas bulvaris 21. Tel: 224 155 *or* 213 381. Post to Western Europe takes up to six days. **Press:** Newspapers are published in Latvian and Russian. *Atmoda (Awakening)* appears once a month in English and *Baltija* magazine appears three times a year in English, Russian, German and Latvian. *The Baltic Observer* is an English-language paper published weekly.
BBC World Service and Voice of America frequencies: From time to time these change. See the section *How to Use this Book* for more information.

BBC:				
MHz	12.10	9.410	7.120	3.955
Voice of America:				
MHz	11.97	9.670	6.040	5.995

PASSPORT/VISA

Regulations and requirements may be subject to change at short notice, and you are advised to contact the appropriate diplomatic or consular authority before finalising travel arrangements. Details of these may be found at the head of this country's entry. Any numbers in the chart refer to the footnotes below.

	Passport Required?	Visa Required?	Return Ticket Required?
Full British	Yes	Yes/1	Yes
BVP	Not valid	-	-
Australian	Yes	Yes/1	Yes
Canadian	Yes	Yes/1	Yes
USA	Yes	Yes/1	Yes
Other EC	Yes	Yes/1	Yes
Japanese	Yes	Yes/1	Yes

PASSPORT: Required by all.
British Visitors Passport: Not accepted.
VISAS: [1] Required by all. Visas can be obtained at the airport in Riga, by USA, British and most European nationals, but it is advisable to get them in advance from the Embassy. A Latvian visa is also valid for the other Baltic States.
Note: Visa regulations are liable to change. It is advisable to contact the Latvian Embassy (addresses above) at least three weeks before travelling for the latest information.
Types of visa: Business and Tourist. Cost: £7 if applying in person, £10 by post (with the exception of USA nationals for whom visas are free).
Validity: *Business:* 6 months. *Tourist:* 3 months. Specify Single- or Multiple-entry on application.
Application to: Embassy (or Consular Section of Embassy). For addresses, see top of entry.
Application requirements: (a) Valid passport. (b) 1 completed application form. (c) 1 passport-size photo. (d) A letter from sponsoring company/organisation in Latvia is helpful for Business visas, but not essential.
Working days required: *Personal visits:* Same-day collection for morning applications (visa section opens at 1100). In an emergency, visas can be issued immediately. *Postal applications:* By return post whenever possible.

MONEY

Currency: The new Latvian currency, the Lat, is under preparation but is unlikely to be introduced until the beginning of 1993. A stopgap currency, the Latvian Rouble, was introduced on July 20, 1992. The Russian rouble is no longer accepted in shops and hotels, but can be exchanged at local bureaux for 1 Latvian Rouble = 100 Russian Roubles. The current rate is 1 Latvian Rouble = £1.50, but the unoffical exchange rate is anything up to £1 = 220 Latvian Roubles. Check with the Embassy for the latest currency information before travelling.
Currency exchange: The banking system is presently being developed, but several bureaux de change have opened in hotels, post offices and train stations. These tend to close at 1600. The most convenient currencies to change are the German DM and the US$ in small denominations.
Credit cards: Only accepted on a very limited basis by hotels and some petrol stations. Check with your credit card company for details of merchant acceptability and other services which may be available.
Currency restrictions: The import and export of the Rouble

s prohibited. There is no limit on foreign currency import-
d, subject to declaration. Export is restricted to the amount eclared.

DUTY FREE

The following goods may be imported into Latvia without ncurring customs duty by travellers of 16 years or older:
litre of spirits and 2 litres of wine;
'50 cigarettes or 250g tobacco.

PUBLIC HOLIDAYS

'ublic holidays observed in Latvia are as follows:
Apr 9 '93 Good Friday. **Apr 12** Easter Monday. **May 1** Aay Day. **Jun 23-24** St John's Day. **Nov 18** National Day. **Dec 25-26** Christmas. **Dec 31** New Year's Eve. **Jan** **'94** New Year's Day.

HEALTH

Regulations and requirements may be subject to change at short notice, and ou are advised to contact your doctor well in advance of your intended date f departure. Any numbers in the chart refer to the footnotes below.

	Special Precautions?	Certificate Required?
Yellow Fever	No	No
Cholera	No	No
Typhoid & Polio	No	-
Malaria	No	-
Food & Drink	1	-

1]: All tap water should be regarded as potentially contaminated, particularly in Riga. Water used for drinking, brushing teeth or making ice should have first been boiled or otherwise sterilised.

Rabies is present. For those at high risk, vaccination before arrival should be considered. If you are bitten abroad seek medical advice without delay.

Health care: Health insurance is advised. Ordinary medicaments such as plasters, aspirin, etc are practically unavailable, therefore it is wise to buy these before travelling.

TRAVEL - International

AIR: Latvia's national airline is *Baltic Intenatinal Airlines* and offers twice-weekly flights from Düsseldorf via Frankfurt/M to Riga. Other airlines to serve Riga are *Austrian Airlines*, *Hamburg Airlines*, SAS and *Lufthansa*.

There are indirect flights to the Latvian capital via Moscow, Copenhagen, Stockholm and Helsinki from all major European cities. *Hamburg Airlines* operates direct charter flights from Hambvurg via Berlin to Riga twice a week. *Lufthansa* has direct service form Frankfurt/M to Riga five times a week. *Aeroflot Russian International Airline (RIA)* offers connections twice weekly to Vienna as well as connections to Zurich (either via Copenhagen or Moscow).

Approximate flight times: From *Frankfurt/M* to Riga 2 hours 30 minutes; from London 5 houts 30 minutes (via Helsinki) and from New York approximately 14 hours (via Helsinki).

International airport: *Riga (RIX)* (Spilva) is located 7km (11 miles) from the city.

SEA: There are ferry connections from Riga to Rostock and Keil, as well as from Stockholm with the *Baltic Express Line*. Several shipping lines run cruises on the Baltic Sea calling at Riga.

RAIL: Latvia has a reasonably well-developed rail network. There are links with neighbouring Belarus and with Estonia to the north and Lithuania to the south. The main route into western Europe runs form Riga to Berlin via Warsaw and Vilnius.

ROAD: The road network is relatively well-developed and there are good routes through to Belarus and to the neighbouring two Baltic republics. Entry by car is possible from Finland and the Russian Federation, Poland and Belarus or Lithuania. Border posts Poland and Lithuania: Ogrodniki–Lazdijai; Poland and Belarus: Terespol–Brest.

TRAVEL - Internal

RAIL: Latvia's reasonably well-developed rail network includes routes from Riga to all other major towns in the country. The Railway Terminal is Stacijas lauk. For information about trains, call 007.

ROAD: There are good connections to all parts of the country from Riga. Since independence, petrol shortages have dramatically increased and drivers should expect delays at the petrol pumps. Diesel and normal 4-star petrol are readily available, though lead-free petrol can only be obtained at two petrol stations in Riga (Pernavas Iela 28 and Brivibas Iela 386) and at one station at the M12 near Panevezvys. **Buses** are a better form of transport than trains in Latvia. The Central Bus Station is at Pragas Iela 1. **Car hire:** Available through hotels, reservation recommended. Drivers can also be hired. **Traffic regulations:** Seat belts must be worn. Speed limits on country lanes are 80kmph (50mph) and in cities 50kmph (32mph). **Documentation:** European nationals should be in possession of the new European Driving Licence.

URBAN: Taxis in Riga are cheap, but prices are rising due to petrol shortages. All parts of the city can also be reached by bus. Tickets for buses, trams and trolley buses can be bought in advance from kiosks.

ACCOMMODATION

HOTELS: Due to the present level of bed-capacity, early reservation is absolutely necessary. Since independence there has been a scramble from Western firms to turn the old state-run hotels into modern Western-standard enterprises. Five of the 13 main hotels in Riga are currently already being renovated in joint ventures with Western firms. In December 1991, the only first-class hotel in Latvia, the *Hotel de Rome*, opened offering high levels of comfort in its 90 rooms with mini-bar, colour TV, radio and telephone. It also has several shops and conference rooms. Many more such joint ventures with firms from all over western Europe and the United States will ensure that the standard of accommodation in Latvia rapidly reaches western European levels. Outside Riga, which for the time being is the main location of the current expansion in hotel accommodation, Latvia enjoys a good range of modest accommodation, left over from the pre-independence days, including large hotels and smaller pension-type establishments. A star-grading system is to be introduced at some time in the future. For more details contact the Latvian Embassy or the Tourist office (addresses at beginning of entry).

PRIVATE HOMES: A good way to meet local people and to get a feel for everyday life is to stay in a private home. For more details contact Inroads Inc, PO Box 3197, Merrifield, VA 22116-3197, USA. Tel: (616) 383 0178.

RESORTS & EXCURSIONS

Riga, situated on a sandy plain 15km from the mouth of the River Daugava, is the capital of Latvia and is one of the most beautiful of the Baltic cities. The old quarter contains a remarkable diversity of architectural styles and this feature is perhaps best epitomised by the *Dome Cathedral*. Begun in 1201, the building has been added to throughout the centuries, resulting in a fascinating blend of Romanesque, Gothic, Renaissance, Baroque and classical styles. The cathedral's organ, with nearly 7000 pipes, is recognised as one of the world's greatest musical instruments and concerts are regularly performed here. The numerous other historical buildings in Riga bear witness to Latvia's chequered history. Since its restoration after the First World War the old quarter of the city has been a protected area. The one surviving town gate is the so-called *Sweden Gate*, whilst the symbol of Riga, the 137m-high tower of the *Petrus Church*, towers above the city. The *Johannis Church* of the former Dominican monastery was built in the 14th century and is one of several interesting churches in this former episcopal seat. Most of the structure dates back to the 15th century and was constructed in a mixture of Romanesque and Gothic styles. At the end of the 18th century, Katharina II built the *Peter and Paul Church* north of the castle. Merchants' houses from the Middle Ages such as the *Three Brothers* and the 24 warehouses in the old quarter are also picturesque examples of Latvian architecture. The residence of Peter I near the cathedral has been dramatically altered and rebuilt. Riga has several museums including the *Historical Museum of Latvia* (founded in 1896), housed in the castle, and the *Latvian Museum of Medicine*, as well as two art galleries – the *Museum of Foreign Art* which contains Flemish masterpieces and the state *Art Gallery of Latvia*. In central Riga the *Freedom Monument (Brivibas Piemineklis)* is a very significant site for Latvians. Built in 1935, the monument is a striking obelisk crowned by a female figure with upstretched arms holding three stars which represent the three major areas of Latvia: Kurzeme, Vidzeme and Latgale.

Not far from the city is the open-air *Latvian Ethnographic Museum* where farm buildings from all over the Republic dating back to between the 16th and 19th centuries are displayed.

Several kilometres from Riga is the seaside health resort of **Jurmala**. Attractions include ten miles of pines and dunes and its renowned sanatoria. Another Latvian health resort is **Sigulda**. Situated on the picturesque banks of the *River Gauja*, the town has been established since the 13th century and attractions here include the ruins of the castle and local caves.

The most important Baroque building is the Palace in **Pilsrundale**, about 77km (123 miles) south of Riga, near the Lithuanian border. This fine summer residence was designed by the Italian architect Rastrelli who was responsible for the Winter Palace in St Petersburg. The attached park is excellent for long walks. Nature enthusiasts will enjoy the rich flora and fauna in the regions of *Kurzeme*, *Vidzeme* and *Latgale*, which are also a favourite with hikers. Throughout the country, the landscape is dotted with picturesque villages such as **Cesis, Kuldiga, Talsi** and **Bauska** where life generally follows a very relaxed pace.

SOCIAL PROFILE

FOOD & DRINK: Hors d'oeuvres are very good and often the best part of the meal. Local specialities include *kotletes* (meat patties), *skabu kapostu zupa* (cabbage soup), *Alexander Torte* (raspberry- or cranberry-filled pastry strips), smoked fish, including salmon and trout, *kvass* (lemonade-honey drink), *piragi* (pastry filled with bacon and onions) and Sorrel soup with boiled pork, onions, potatoes and barley. The best restaurant is *Lido*, on Lacplesa Iela. **Drink:** Riga's *Black Balsam* is a thick, black alcoholic liquid which has been produced since 1700. The exact recipe is a closely guarded secret, but some of the ingredients include ginger, oak bark, bitter orange

LATVIA	HEALTH REGULATIONS	VISA REGULATIONS Code-Link
GALILEO/WORLDSPAN	TI-DFT/RIX/HE	TI-DFT/RIX/VI
SABRE	 TIDFT/RIX/HE	TIDFT/RIX/VI

To access this information on your CRS, swipe the barcode with a light pen or type in the text under the barcode. For more information, see the introduction *How to Use This Book*.

peels and cognac. There are several local beers including the dark beer *Bauskas Tumsais* and the pale *Gaisais*. *Jever Bar* and the bar of the *Hotel Ridzene* are good places to drink.
NIGHTLIFE: Riga has a range of restaurants, bars and cafés.
SHOPPING: Amber is a good buy in all three Baltic Republics. Other purchases include folk art, wickerwork and earthenware.
SPECIAL EVENTS: *John's Night*, the summer solstice on June 23-24, is the main festival celebrated in Latvia. Beer is brewed specially for the event and a special cheese is prepared. People wear wreaths of flowers and greenery and spend the night around the bonfire where summer solstice songs are sung. Other events celebrated in 1993 include:
Feb 21-Mar 1 '93 *Riga Cathedral* (international boys' choir festival). **Apr** *Baltic Theatre Spring*. **Apr 12-20** *Symposium of Documentaries of the Baltics*, Riga. **Jul 2-4** *21st Latvian Singer Festival* and *11th Latvian Dance Festival*. For a complete list contact the Embassy (for addresses, see beginning of entry).
SOCIAL CONVENTIONS: Handshaking is customary. Normal courtesies should be observed. Western cigarettes are a welcome gift to Latvian smokers. The Latvians are somewhat reserved and formal, but nevertheless very hospitable. They are proud of their culture and their national heritage and visitors should take care to respect this sense of national identity. **Tipping:** Taxi fares and restaurant bills include a tip. Tipping is usually expected, but it is wise to maintain a sense of proportion, bearing in mind that the value of US$1 is the equivalent to about one-third of one month's salary (see *Money* above).

BUSINESS PROFILE

ECONOMY: The Latvian economy before the Second World War was dominated by light industry. After 1945, heavy industry was introduced leaving a legacy of extensive pollution which the Latvians are committed to cleaning up. With few raw materials, Latvia is dependent on producing manufactured goods from imported materials. Key industries include vehicle and railway rolling stock manufacture, electronics, fertilisers and chemicals, timber and light machinery. Dairy farming, fishing and timber are important in the agricultural sector. The infrastructure is, in common with the other Baltic states, comparatively well-developed. Latvia faces a major problem with electricity supply. It is hoping to buy one billion KwH from Lithuania, which has the only nuclear power plant in the Baltics. Estonia has announced that this year it will provide only 40% of the electricity supplied to Latvia last year. Latvia currently produces 50% of its consumption. About 60% of its domestic production comes from three hydroelectric plants on the River Daugava. The Government has initiated economic reforms to bring in a market economy and encourage foreign investment although it faces serious short-term difficulties arising from lack of raw materials, particularly oil, and the disruption of old trading links with the former Soviet Union. Latvia was admitted to the European Bank for Reconstruction and Development in December 1991. By the beginning of 1993, Latvia is expected to have introduced its own currency, the Lat, and have joined the International Monetary Fund.
BUSINESS: Business cards are exchanged. Appointments should be arranged in advance. In general, business is conducted in a fairly formal manner and old Soviet ways persist. **Office hours:** 0830-1830 Monday to Friday.
COMMERCIAL INFORMATION: The following organisations can offer advice: Chamber of Commerce, Brivibas bulvaris 21, 226189 Riga. Tel: (2) 228 036 *or* 332 205. Fax: (2) 332 276. Telex: 161111; *or*
Department of Foreign Economic Relations, 36 Brivibas Boulevard, 226269, Riga. Tel: (2) 288 656. Fax: (2) 284 572.

HISTORY & GOVERNMENT

HISTORY: The largest of the three Baltic republics, Latvia has, like Estonia to the north and Lithuania to the south, been an important trading centre and strategic pawn in the Baltic region. The various Latvian tribes functioned under local self-government until the end of the 13th century when the territory was conquered by the German Teutonic Knights. Latvia was subject to sporadic invasions by the Poles and the Swedish until the 18th century when Russia under Peter the Great emerged as a major European power. By 1795 the entire Latvian territory was under Russian control. The Bolshevik revolution of 1917 heralded the end of Russian suzerainty; this was decided at the 1918 Treaty of Brest-Litovsk under which Russia was obliged to cede its Baltic territories. The Bolsheviks invaded Latvia the following year, but were driven out by a joint Latvian-German force. The Treaty of Versailles then forced the Germans to leave allowing the Latvians to assert their independence for the first time for over 600 years. The Second World War again threatened the country, however, with foreign domination and in 1940 the Russians again took over. Latvia had, that same year, signed a bilateral non-aggression pact with the Germans and a pact with Moscow. The Russians were driven out by the Nazi invasion of the Soviet Union in 1941, but returned three years later, after which Latvia was incorporated into the Soviet Union along with Estonia and Lithuania. Campaigning for democracy and independence did not begin in earnest until October 1988 with the formation of the Popular Front of Latvia. In contrast with neighbouring Estonia, the Latvian Communist Party adopted an anti-reform stance and called for the establishment of presidential rule (by decree). At elections to the Supreme Soviet in March 1990, the main opposition movement, the Popular Front of Latvia (LTF), won a convincing victory by taking 131 of the 201 seats. Most of the remainder were won by an alliance of the Communist party and the Russophone anti-independence grouping, Interfront. The new Supreme Soviet thereupon adopted a series of resolutions to prepare the transition to full independence. At this point, President Gorbachev declared these resolutions null and void, and an alliance of Latvian communists and the military began a campaign of propaganda and harassment against the new Latvian government. The crisis came to a head in January 1991 when a 'Committee of Public Salvation' led by the Latvian Communist Party's First Secretary, Alfred Rubiks, sought to take over the republic. This coup was defeated. Latvia's independence was finally secured in August 1991 after the attempted coup in Moscow which also failed, but undermined Gorbachev's position. In common with the other Baltic Republics, Latvia's independence was quickly recognised internationally, and by the USSR State Council at the beginning of September 1991. Days later, the country was readmitted to the United Nations. Latvia is gradually assuming the trappings of an independent country. At the end of July 1992, the Soviet rouble was replaced by the 'Latvian Rouble' which will be the legal tender until the introduction of a new currency, the Lat, due to be introduced in early 1993. Latvia can expect a spell of economic difficulty as it adjusts to life outside the old Soviet system, particularly the lack of raw materials such as petroleum, but the Government is pressing ahead with reforms to introduce a market economy and encourage foreign investment.
GOVERNMENT: The current, interim constitution of Latvia comprises a number of clauses drawn from the 1922 constitution, which was annulled after the Soviet occupation in 1940. A new constitution is presently being drafted. Under current arrangements, legislative powers are vested in the elected 201-member Supreme Council. The Head of State, the President, chairs the Council. The Supreme Council appoints a Council of Ministers, headed by a Prime Minister who holds executive authority.

CLIMATE

Temperate climate, but with considerable temperature variations. Summer is warm with relatively mild weather in spring and autumn. Winter, which lasts from November to mid-March, can be very cold. Rainfall is distributed throughout the year with the heaviest rainfall in August. Snowfall is common in the winter months.

RIGA Latvia (3m)

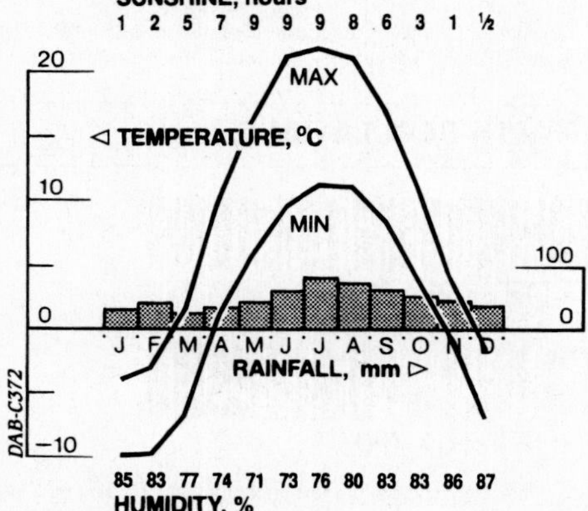

LEBANON

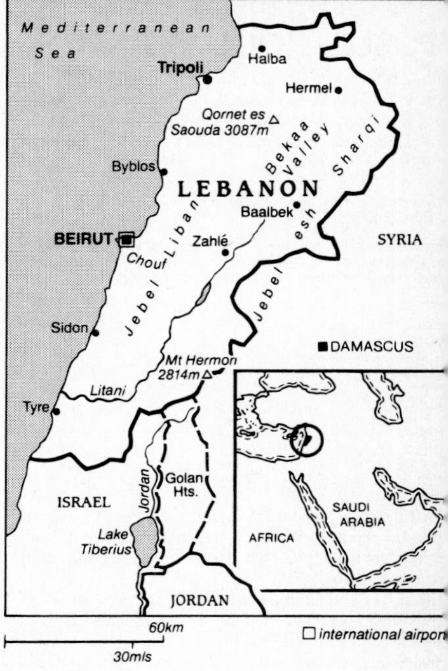

Location: Middle East.

Note: Due to the conflict in the Lebanon it is advisable to check with either the Foreign Office or a Lebanese Embassy before travelling.

National Council of Tourism in Lebanon (CNTL)
PO Box 11-5344
Central Bank Street
Beirut, Lebanon
Tel: (1) 864 532. Telex: 20898.
Embassy of the Republic of Lebanon
21 Kensington Palace Gardens
London W8 4QM
Tel: (071) 229 7265. Fax: (071) 243 1699. Telex: 262048. Opening hours: 0900-1230 Monday to Friday.
Lebanese Consular Section
15 Palace Gardens Mews
London W8 4QQ
Tel: (071) 727 6696. Fax: (071) 243 1699. Telex: 262048. Opening hours: 0930-1230 Monday to Friday.
Lebanese Tourist & Information Office
90 Piccadilly
London W1V 9HB
Tel: (071) 409 2031.
British Embassy
East Beirut:
PO Box 60180
Middle East Airlines Building
Tripoli Autostrade
Jal el Dib
East Beirut, Lebanon
Tel: (1) 417 007 *or* 410 596 *or* 416 112. Telex: 44104 PRODROM LE.
West Beirut:
Shamma Building, Raouché
Ras Beirut, Lebanon
Tel: (1) 812 849 *or* 812 851 *or* 804 929. Telex: 20465 PRODROM LE.
Consulate in: Tripoli.
Embassy of the Republic of Lebanon
2560 28th Street, NW
Washington, DC
20008
Tel: (202) 939 6300. Fax: (202) 939 6324.
Lebanese Consulate
9 East 76th Street
New York, NY
10021
Tel: (212) 744 7905.
Embassy of the United States of America
avenue de Paris
Immeuble Ali Reza

Beirut, Lebanon
Telex: 20280.
Embassy of Lebanon
640 Lyon Street
Ottawa, Ontario
K1S 3Z5
Tel: (613) 236 5825. Fax: (613) 232 1609.
Consulate in: Montréal.
Canadian Embassy to Lebanon
Canadian Embassy
PO Box 3394
Damascus, Syria
Tel: (11) 236 851 *or* 236 892. Fax: (11) 228 034. Telex: 412422 CANADA SY.

AREA: 10,452 sq km (4,036 sq miles).
POPULATION: 2,897,000 (1988 estimate).
POPULATION DENSITY: 277.2 per sq km.
CAPITAL: Beirut. **Population:** 1,200,000 (1991 estimate).
GEOGRAPHY: Lebanon shares borders to the north and east with Syria, and to the south with Israel, while to the west lies the Mediterranean. It is a mountainous country and between the two parallel mountain ranges of Jebel Liban and Jebel esh Shargi lies the fertile Bekaa Valley. Approximately one-half of the country lies at an altitude of over 900m (3000ft). Into this small country is packed such a variety of scenery that there are few places to equal it in beauty and choice. The famous cedar trees grow high in the mountains, while the lower slopes bear grapes, apricots, plums, peaches, figs, olives and barley, often on terraces painstakingly cut out from the mountainsides. On the coastal plain, citrus fruit, bananas and vegetables are cultivated, with radishes and beans grown in tiny patches.
LANGUAGE: The official language is Arabic. French is the second most commonly used language and English is also spoken, especially in business circles. Kurdish and Armenian are spoken by a small percentage of the population.
RELIGION: 57% Muslim (Shi'ite majority), 42% Christian (mostly Roman Catholic) and 1% others including Jewish.
TIME: GMT + 2 (GMT + 3 in summer).
ELECTRICITY: 110/220 volts AC, 50Hz. Subject to fluctuation and blackouts.
COMMUNICATIONS: Telephone: IDD is available. Country code: 961. **Telex:** International facilities available. Contact Embassy for details. **Post:** Service to Europe usually takes four days, to the USA five or six days. **Press:** There are a number of English-language dailies. Most newspapers are in Arabic or French. The papers tend to have strong political affiliations.
BBC World Service and Voice of America frequencies: From time to time these change. See the section *How to Use this Book* for more information.

BBC:				
MHz	21.47	15.57	11.76	1.323
Voice of America:				
MHz	9.670	6.040	5.995	1.260

PASSPORT/VISA

Regulations and requirements may be subject to change at short notice, and you are advised to contact the appropriate diplomatic or consular authority before finalising travel arrangements. Details of these may be found at the head of this country's entry. Any numbers in the chart refer to the footnotes below.

	Passport Required?	Visa Required?	Return Ticket Required?
Full British	Yes	Yes	Yes
BVP	Not valid	-	-
Australian	Yes	Yes	Yes
Canadian	Yes	Yes	Yes
USA	Yes	Yes	Yes
Other EC	Yes	Yes	Yes
Japanese	Yes	Yes	Yes

Restricted entry: Passports containing a visa for Israel, valid or expired, used or unused, are not valid for travel to Lebanon.
PASSPORTS: Valid passport required by all except nationals of Syria arriving from their country with a valid national ID. Passports must be valid for at least 6 months beyond the estimated duration of stay in Lebanon.
British Visitors Passport: Not acceptable.
VISAS: Required by all except nationals of Syria.
Types of visa: Transit, Visitor and Employment; Single entry – £12, Multiple entry – £24. Business and Employment visas are not being issued by the Embassy unless agreed by both the Ministry of Labour and the Sûreté Générale in Beirut. Tourist visas are not being issued at present.
Validity: Visitors visas are generally valid for between 2 weeks and 3 months and are renewable on request when in the country. Transit visas are valid for between 24 hours and 2 weeks.
Application to: Consulate (or Consular Section at Embassy). For addresses, see top of entry.
Application requirements: *Business visas:* (a) Valid passport. (b) Invitation telex from Lebanese company host to Embassy in London. (c) Letter from applicant's company in the UK. (d) 2 completed application forms. (e) 2 photos. (f) Fee.
Working days required: At the present time applications require approval from Beirut, so allow 6-8 weeks.
Temporary residence: Formalities for temporary residence will be arranged in Lebanon.

MONEY

Currency: Lebanese Pound (L£) = 100 piastres. Notes are in denominations of L£1000, 500, 250, 100, 50, 25, 10, 5 and 1. Coins are in denominations of L£1, and 50, 25, 10, 5, 2.5 and 1 piastres.
Credit cards: Limited acceptance of Access/Mastercard, Diners Club and Visa. Check with your credit card company for details of merchant acceptability and other services which may be available.
Travellers cheques: Limited acceptance.
Exchange rate indicators: The following figures are included as a guide to the movements of the Lebanese Pound against Sterling and the US Dollar:

Date:	Oct '89	Oct '90	Oct '91	Oct '92
£1.00=	745.33	1544.8	1543.3	3189.6
$1.00=	472.03	790.8	889.2	2009.8

Currency restrictions: There are no restrictions on the import or export of foreign or local currency.
Banking hours: 0830-1230 Monday to Saturday.

DUTY FREE

The following goods may be imported into Lebanon without incurring customs duty:
*200 cigarettes or 200g cigars or 200g of tobacco;**
1 litre of alcohol;
60g of perfume.
Note [*]: From June to October some visitors may be allowed *500 cigarettes or 500g of tobacco.* A valid import licence is required for any arms or ammunition.

PUBLIC HOLIDAYS

Public holidays observed in Lebanon are as follows:
Mar 22 '93 Arab League Anniversary. **Mar 25** Start of Eid al-Fitr. **Apr 12** Easter (Western Church). **Apr 16-19** Easter (Eastern Church). **May 20** Ascension Day (Western Church). **Jun 1** Start of Eid al-Adha. **Jun 21** Islamic New Year. **Jun 30** Ashoura. **Aug 15** Assumption Day. **Aug 30** Mouloud, Birth of Mohammed. **Nov 1** All Saints' Day. **Nov 22** Independence Day. **Dec 25** Christmas Day. **Dec 31** Evacuation Day. **Jan 1 '94** New Year's Day. **Jan 21** Leilat al-Meiraj. **Feb 9** Feast of St Marron. **Mar** Eid al-Fitr. **Mar 22** Arab League Anniversary.
Note: Muslim festivals are timed according to local sightings of various phases of the Moon and the dates given above are approximations. During the lunar month of Ramadan that precedes Eid al-Fitr, Muslims fast during the day and feast at night and normal business patterns may be interrupted. Many restaurants are closed during the day and there may be restrictions on smoking and drinking. Some disruption may continue into Eid al-Fitr itself. Eid al-Fitr and Eid al-Adha may last anything from two to ten days, depending on the region. For more information see the section *World of Islam* at the back of the book.

HEALTH

Regulations and requirements may be subject to change at short notice, and you are advised to contact your doctor well in advance of your intended date of departure. Any numbers in the chart refer to the footnotes below.

	Special Precautions?	Certificate Required?
Yellow Fever	No	1
Cholera	Yes	2
Typhoid & Polio	Yes	-
Malaria	No	-
Food & Drink	3	-

[1]: A yellow fever vaccination certificate is required from travellers arriving from infected areas.
[2]: Following WHO guidelines issued in 1973, a cholera vaccination certificate is not a condition of entry to Lebanon. However, cholera is a risk in this country and precautions are essential. Up-to-date advice should be sought before deciding whether these precautions should include vaccination, as medical opinion is divided over its effectiveness. See the *Health* section at the back of the book.
[3]: Mains water is normally chlorinated, and whilst relatively safe may cause mild abdominal upsets. Bottled water is available and is advised for the first few weeks of the stay. Drinking water outside main towns and cities is likely to be contaminated and sterilisation is considered essential. Milk is pasteurised and dairy products are safe for consumption. Local meat, poultry, seafood, fruit and vegetables are generally considered safe to eat.
Rabies is present. For those at high risk, vaccination before arrival should be considered. If you are bitten abroad seek medical advice without delay. For more information consult the *Health* section at the back of the book.
Health care: Health insurance is essential.

TRAVEL - International

AIR: The national airline is *Middle East Airlines – Air Liban (ME)*.
Approximate flight time: From *London* to Beirut is 5 hours 5 minutes.
International airport: *Beirut International (BEY)* (Khaldeh) is 16km (10 miles) south of the city (travel time – 20 minutes). Duty-free facilities are available. Bus and yellow taxi services are available to the city.
Departure tax: L£35,000 for business class, L£50,000 for first-class passengers and L£25,000 for economy class.
SEA: Main international ports are Beirut, Tripoli, Jounieh, Tyre and Sidon. No cruise ships put in at any of the Lebanese ports.
RAIL: There are no passenger services operating at present.
ROAD: Best international routes are via Turkey and Aleppo/Homs and Lattaguieh in Syria along the north/south coastal road, and also the Beirut/Damascus trunk road. Bus services are available from Europe. For details contact the Embassy. Communications are often disrupted due to the unstable political situation. Refer to the Embassy for travel advice.

LEBANON	HEALTH REGULATIONS	VISA REGULATIONS Code-Link
GALILEO/WORLDSPAN	TI-DFT/BEY/HE	 TI-DFT/BEY/VI
SABRE	 TIDFT/BEY/HE	 TIDFT/BEY/VI

To access this information on your CRS, swipe the barcode with a light pen or type in the text under the barcode. For more information, see the introduction *How to Use This Book*.

TRAVEL - Internal

AIR: *Middle East Airlines – Air Liban (ME)* run internal flights to major cities.
SEA: Ports are served by coastal passenger ferries. For details contact the Embassy.
ROAD: Bus: Intercity buses run by private companies are cheap and efficient, but not comfortable. Services can be disrupted. **Taxi:** Intercity taxis operate throughout Beirut and Lebanon. Travel is normally shared. Prices are negotiated in advance. Town taxis have red licence plates, and an official tariff. There is a surcharge of 50% after 2200. **Car hire:** Self-drive cars are available, but chauffeur-driven vehicles are recommended. Check with the Tourist & Information Office. **Documentation:** An International Driving Permit is recommended, although it is not legally required. A temporary licence to drive is available from local authorities on presentation of a valid British or Northern Ireland driving licence. Green Card insurance is required. **Note:** Road travel can be dangerous due to the political situation.
URBAN: In Beirut, private shared taxis have provided the only public transport since normal bus services were suspended in 1975. They only operate during daylight hours.

ACCOMMODATION

Note: All accommodation rates are subject to a 15% service charge.
HOTELS: Hotels are available to suit all budgets, but the availability of accommodation is unpredictable due to the unstable political situation within Lebanon, with many hotels closed. Check reservations very carefully through Lebanese representatives at home before departing. Winter and summer rates are the same. The volatile situation means that all rates may be subject to considerable variation. **Grading:** Hotels are classified from **1** to **4 stars** (**A** and **B** within each class).
GUEST-HOUSES: Local hostels are available in coastal villages with reasonable prices. There are youth hostels in major towns.
SELF-CATERING: Furnished and other apartments are available for rent.
CAMPING/CARAVANNING: Youth Centre (part of the National Tourism Council) provides information on campsites, cheap rooms, youth hostels and work camps.

RESORTS & EXCURSIONS

Beirut is at the crossing of three continents. It is a city of many sects, a fact which has contributed to the country's recent tragic history of violence. Despite this, life in many parts of the city continues in a surprisingly calm fashion, with shoppers in the streets and sunbathers on beaches. The city is deeply divided; the most obvious manifestation of this is the 'Green Line' which separates Muslim West Beirut from the Christian East. People commute daily from east to west, but rarely after sunset do they cross the no-man's land. Strange and surreal, on good days one can drive to popular mountain resorts; on bad days no one ventures out. Its seafront location boasts beaches, clifftops, restaurants and, until recently, theatres and a dazzling variety of shopping possibilities.
Tripoli, the country's second city, still retains much of its provincial charm. There are two parts – the port area and the city proper – which are divided by acres of fragrant orange plantations.
Sidon is a city with a sea castle built of stones from Roman remains and it offers well-stocked markets.
Tyre is out of bounds to ordinary citizens, but it is well worth persisting with the local authorities to see the remains of the ancient city which are immense and very impressive. The chariot-racing arena has been perfectly preserved.
Byblos is reputed to be the oldest town in the world, with Phoenician, Egyptian and Byzantine influences much apparent. Fishing boats and pleasure craft ply the harbour.
Beiteddine, in the *Chouf Mountains*, is the site of the palace built by the Amir Bishir in the 19th century. The courtyard and state rooms are well worth a visit.
Baalbek contains one of the best-preserved temple areas of the Roman world still in existence. It is, in fact, a complex of several temples behind which soar the columns of the *Temple of Jupiter*.

SOCIAL PROFILE

FOOD & DRINK: In Beirut there is every kind of restaurant: French, Italian, German, Austrian, Scandinavian, Greek, Chinese, Japanese, American, Indian, Malaysian, Spanish and Filipino. Good Arab food is available everywhere. A dish unique to Lebanon is *kibbe*, made of lamb or fish pounded to a fine paste, with burghol or cracked wheat, and served raw or baked in flat trays or rolled into balls and fried. Also recommended is the traditional Lebanese *maza*, a range of up to 40 small dishes served as hors d'oeuvres with *arak*. Main courses are likely to include Lebanese staple ingredients of vegetables, rice and mutton. *Lahm mishwi* (pieces of mutton with onions, peppers and tomato) is popular. Other typical dishes are *tabbouli, houmos* and *mtabbal*. Lebanese palates also favour pastries with local varieties of baked doughs flavoured with nuts, cream and syrup. A meal is always concluded with a wide range of fruits including melon, apples, oranges, persimmon, tangerines, cactus fruit, grapes and figs. Table service is the norm in restaurants. **Drink:** Bars have table and/or counter service. Although many Lebanese are Muslim, alcohol is not prohibited.
NIGHTLIFE: Nightclubs spice the evenings in Beirut (although many have now been closed) and mountain resorts. Entertainment ranges from solo guitarists to orchestras and floor shows. Some British-type pubs can be found in Beirut. There are many cinemas presenting the latest films from all over the world. The *Casino du Liban* in Maameltain earns its international reputation with its lavish gambling halls, luxurious restaurants and cabaret.
SHOPPING: Lebanon's traditional *souks* or markets are found all over the country offering decorative and precious handmade items at very low prices. Special purchases include traditional pottery and glassware, as well as cutlery made of tempered steel or copper with ram or buffalo bone handles shaped in the form of beautiful and colourful birds' heads. Brass and copper goods include braziers, bowls, fluted jugs, ashtrays, swords and doorstops, all attractively designed and hand-engraved. Cloth, silk and wool kaftans, *abayas* (embroidered nightwear) and table linen are popular, as are handworked gold and silver. Shops sell the latest Western goods including clothes, cosmetics, furniture and electrical appliances.
SPORT: Watersports: The Mediterranean coast offers **swimming, scuba diving, snorkelling, water-skiing** and **sailing** all year. Many beaches offer full facilities and most have guest memberships and fresh-water pools to supplement the sea. Boats may be rented by **anglers** along the coast, but most local anglers prefer to fish in the deep waters by the shore. **Winter sports:** Mountain resorts such as The Lebanon Cedars, Farayam, Laklouk and Karrat Bakish offer excellent accommodation and winter sports facilities. **Golf:** The Golf Club of Lebanon has a 9-hole (par 72) course available to visitors on application for guest membership (details from hotel or Tourist Police). **Tennis:** There is a wide selection of tennis courts in major towns and resorts. **Horseriding:** Lebanon's Equestrian Federation now includes six riding clubs with excellent Arab horses available. **Spectator sports:** Numerous local clubs play **football** all year, ranging from small playing fields to national competitions.
SOCIAL CONVENTIONS: Handshaking is the normal form of greeting. Many Lebanese are Muslim and their traditions and customs should be respected. It is acceptable to give a small gift, particularly if invited home for a meal. As far as dress is concerned, casual dress is suitable for daytime wear, except in main towns where dress tends to be rather formal. Smarter hotels and restaurants often require guests to dress for dinner. Smoking is common and acceptable unless specified otherwise. **Tipping:** Service is generally included in hotel and restaurant bills and it is not necessary to tip taxi-drivers.

BUSINESS PROFILE

ECONOMY: Before the onset of the ruinous civil war in the mid-1970s, Beirut was the major financial and commercial centre for the Middle East. The economy is now dependent on sizeable injections of foreign aid. The banking and financial services sector, although far from flourishing, has shown remarkable resilience. Transit trade, long an important source of earnings for the Lebanese economy, has been all but wiped out because of the fighting. A relatively small proportion of the population – about a quarter – are engaged in agriculture, producing citrus fruit, olives and cereals. Some light industries continue to operate on a sufficient scale to sustain an export economy, with textiles, pharmaceuticals and jewellery as the main products. Saudi Arabia is the principal market for Lebanese exports, while the EC countries – particularly Italy and France – are the main suppliers of the country's imports.
BUSINESS: Business people usually wear a jacket and tie. English is spoken by many local business people and normal courtesies are observed. Appointments and business cards are used. Best months for business visits are October to December and February to June. **Office hours:** *June to October:* 0800-1300 Monday to Saturday; *November to May:* 0830-1230 and 1500-1800 Monday to Friday, and 0830-1230 Saturday.
COMMERCIAL INFORMATION: The following organisation can offer advice: Beirut Chamber of Commerce and Industry, PO Box 11-1801, Sanayeh, Beirut. Tel: (1) 349 530. Fax: (1) 865 802. Telex: 42241.

HISTORY & GOVERNMENT

HISTORY: Lebanon differs from the rest of the Middle East in having mountains and a relative abundance of water. The mountains have, over the course of history, provided an inaccessible haven for tribes and religious groups escaping from repression and persecution in other parts of the Middle East. The principal groupings in the Middle East are: the Maronites, Christians who, uniquely among Eastern Christians, maintained links with and secured support from their co-religionists in Europe; the Shi'ite Muslims, who arrived in Lebanon to escape persecution from the Sunni majority elsewhere in Islam; and the Druze, a heretical Muslim sect founded in the 10th century. The colonial powers that subsequently occupied Lebanon – the Ottoman Turks and the French – were content to leave these sects more or less to themselves. The Turks took control of the area in the 16th century during the major expansion of the Ottoman Empire and remained there until the end of the First World War. With the dissolution of that empire, the French were granted a League of Nations mandate to administer Lebanon until independence in 1941. From that time the disparate communities cohabited in relative peace with political power divided between Christians, Shi'ite and Sunni Muslims. Under this set-up, Lebanon developed a thriving economy based on providing business services – banking and finance, transport and trade facilities – for other countries in the region. This situation prevailed until the 1970s when the Palestine Liberation Organisation (PLO), whose headquarters had been expelled from Jordan in 1971, set up shop in Lebanon with the tacit agreement of the Lebanese. The influx of a large new community with a powerful armed wing upset the relatively fragile political balance in Lebanon. The PLO's presence ultimately led to the Israeli invasion of Lebanon in 1982. By then Lebanon had been engulfed in a 6-year-old civil war between right-wing Christian militias (the Falange and later the forces led by General Michel Aoun) and a coalition of Muslim and Palestinian forces. After the war began in 1976, Beirut was split across the 'Green Line' dividing the city between the Christian-dominated east of the city and the Muslim west. Central government all but broke down, despite repeated attempts to find some kind of political solution. The Israeli invasion succeeded in driving most of the Palestinian guerrillas out of Lebanon, but failed in its principal political objective of installing a Christian-dominated government in power. The Israeli occupation earned Tel Aviv much international criticism although, following the election of a coalition government in Tel Aviv, the Israelis withdrew in early 1985 to a self-declared security zone in the south (which remains to this day) controlled by the IDF (Israeli Defence Forces) and their local allies, the South Lebanon Army, led by General Antoine Lahad. Israel was not the only foreign power which had been drawn into the Lebanese imbroglio: a 5000-strong French, Italian and American peace-keeping force landed in Beirut in mid-1983 to try to keep the rival factions apart. They withdrew nine months later after a series of suicide bomb attacks by radicals from the Hezbollah movement which killed 250 US Marines. Hezbollah, the 'Party of God', was a new player on the scene, composed of fundamentalist Shi'ites and backed by Iran. It quickly emerged as a major influence on the balance of forces in Lebanon and assumed the brunt of the fighting against the Israelis and the South Lebanon Army in the south. In Beirut, they initiated a campaign of kidnapping Westerners to gain political leverage over Western governments and the release of their own people held in South Lebanon, Israel and further afield. With Israel and the West out of the picture in most of Lebanon by 1985, attention turned to the Syrians once again. Participants themselves as well as ringmasters, the Syrians had their own agenda for Lebanon: to put an end to Christian Maronite political dominance;

ınd to prevent the PLO from re-establishing any significant presence in the country. After four years of political stagnation, a new phase opened up in November 1989 with the election of a new National Assembly and of René Doawad to the presidency. Doawad asked the veteran Muslim politician, Salim el-Hoss, to try and form a government. Just a few weeks into his presidency, however, Doawad was assassinated in Beirut. He was succeeded by Elias Hrawi, who became one of the troika – Prime Minister Salim el-Hoss and the speaker of the parliament, Hussein Hussein were the others – which, with Syrian backing, ed the official administration in the Muslim areas of Lebanon. Militant Christians, led by General Michel Aoun, refused to accept Syrian hegemony and continued fighting. The Syrians were unable to bring their full military clout to bear – because of American resistance – until the Iraqi invasion of Kuwait. The Americans now wanted Syrian support for the multinational force assembled to expel Saddam from Kuwait, in exchange for which the Syrians got a free hand in Lebanon. General Aoun's forces were quickly crushed. By the end of 1991 the Syrians were in control of Beirut and most of the north and centre of the country, apart from an enclave under the control of the Christian Lebanese Forces militia. To the south, a more confused picture persisted. The Druze, some Palestinians, and two Muslim militias (Amal and Hezbollah) occupied their assorted patches, while the very south of the country bordering on Israel remained incorporated into the Israelis' 'security zone', controlled by the South Lebanese Army and the Israelis themselves. Here, fighting continued between the Israelis and their allies, on one side, and certain Muslim groups, principally the radicals of Hezbollah. The Western hostages held by Hezbollah and other radical groups – including all the Britons and Americans – were eventually released as part of a complex exchange package. International attention is now focused on the latest attempt to solve the Arab-Israeli dispute in which Lebanon has been participating. The Lebanese delegation tends to follow the Syrian line; it also seeks to use the forum to push for an Israeli withdrawal from the southern part of the country. A general election was held in Lebanon in August 1992. Christian groups boycotted it, a decision they now appear to regret, while the Muslims, including Hezbollah, now have complete control of the Parliament.

GOVERNMENT: The 1926 Constitution allows for the election of a National Assembly of 99 members every four years. At elections in 1989 René Doawad was elected President, but assassinated within weeks of taking office. His replacement was Elias Hrawi, who has held office to date. The current Prime Minister is Rafiq Hariri.

CLIMATE

There are four seasons. Summer (June to September) is hot on the coast and cooler in the mountains. Spring and autumn are warm and pleasant. Winter (December to mid-March) is mostly rainy, with snow in the mountains.

Required clothing: Lightweight cottons and linens are worn during warmer months. Warmer clothes are advised during the winter, along with rainwear. Heavier clothing is advised in the mountains.

BEIRUT Lebanon (34m)

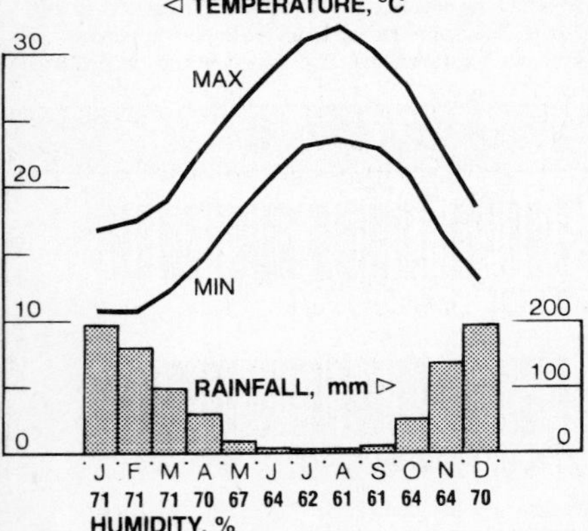

LESOTHO

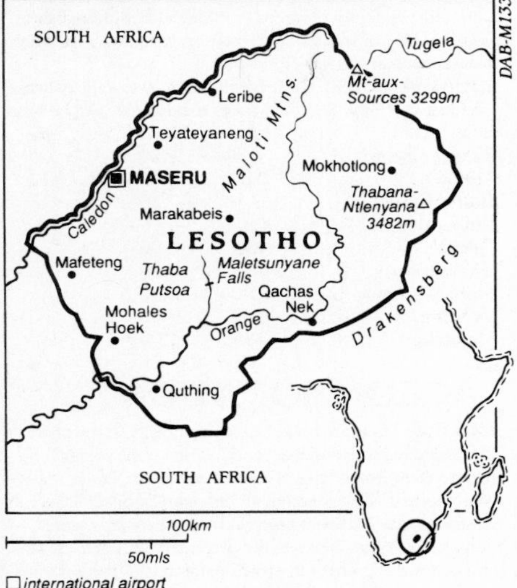

Location: Southern Africa.

Lesotho National Tourist Board
PO Box 1378
Maseru 100, Lesotho
Tel: 323 760 *or* 322 896 (information). Fax: 310 108.
Telex: 4280 LO.

High Commission for the Kingdom of Lesotho
10 Collingham Road
London SW5 0NR
Tel: (071) 373 8581/2. Fax: (071) 835 2097. Telex: 262995. Opening hours: 0900-1600 Monday to Friday.

British High Commission
PO Box Ms 521
Maseru 100, Lesotho
Tel: 313 961. Fax: 310 120. Telex: 4343 LO.

Embassy of the Kingdom of Lesotho
2511 Massachusetts Avenue, NW
Washington, DC 20008
Tel: (202) 797 5533/4/5/6. Fax: (202) 234 6815.

Embassy of the United States of America
PO Box 333
Maseru 100, Lesotho
Tel: 312 666. Fax: 310 116. Telex: 4506 LO.

High Commission for the Kingdom of Lesotho
202 Clemow Avenue
Ottawa, Ontario K1S 2B4
Tel: (613) 236 9449 *or* 236 0960. Fax: (613) 238 3341.
Consulates in: Montréal and Vancouver.

Canadian High Commission
Private Bag A-325
5 Orpen Road
Maseru 100, Lesotho
Tel: 324 189. Fax: 310 113. Telex: 4371 CMHMC LO.

AREA: 30,355 sq km (11,720 sq miles).
POPULATION: 1,619,000 (1987 estimate).
POPULATION DENSITY: 53.3 per sq km.
CAPITAL: Maseru. **Population:** 109,382 (1986).
GEOGRAPHY: Lesotho is a landlocked country surrounded on all sides by South Africa. It is a mountainous kingdom situated at the highest part of the Drakensberg escarpment on the eastern rim of the South African plateau. Its mountainous terrain is cut by countless valleys and ravines making it a country of great beauty. To the west the land descends through a foothill zone of rolling hills to a lowland belt along the border where two-thirds of the population live. Three large rivers, the Orange, the Caledon and the Tugela, rise in the mountains.
LANGUAGE: Sesotho and English.
RELIGION: 70% Catholic, 30% Lesotho Evangelical and Anglican.
TIME: GMT + 2.
ELECTRICITY: 250 volts AC, 50Hz.
COMMUNICATIONS: Telephone: IDD is available to some cities. Country code: 266 (no area codes). There is a limited internal telephone network. **Telex/telegram:** Limited facilities exist in main post offices and hotels. For charges contact High Commission or Embassy. **Post:** Post offices are generally open 0800-1300 and 1400-1630 Monday to Friday, 0800-1300 Saturday. **Press:** *Lesotho Today* is the major English newspaper.

BBC World Service and Voice of America frequencies: From time to time these change. See the section *How to Use this Book* for more information.

BBC:				
MHz	6.190	3.255	1.197	0.902
Voice of America:				
MHz	21.49	15.60	9.525	6.035

PASSPORT/VISA

Regulations and requirements may be subject to change at short notice, and you are advised to contact the appropriate diplomatic or consular authority before finalising travel arrangements. Details of these may be found at the head of this country's entry. Any numbers in the chart refer to the footnotes below.

	Passport Required?	Visa Required?	Return Ticket Required?
Full British	Yes	1	Yes
BVP	Not valid	-	-
Australian	Yes	No	Yes
Canadian	Yes	No	Yes
USA	Yes	No	Yes
Other EC	Yes	2	Yes
Japanese	Yes	No	No

Note: Visitors travelling via South Africa will need to comply with South African passport/visa regulations.
PASSPORTS: Required by all.
British Visitors Passport: Not accepted.
VISAS: Required by all except:
(a) [1] holders of British passports in which they are described as British subjects being 'Citizen of the United Kingdom and Colonies' (except nationals of India and Nigeria who *do* need visas);
(b) [2] nationals of Denmark, Germany, Greece, Ireland and Italy (other EC nationals *do* need visas);
(c) nationals of Australia, Canada, Japan and the USA;
(d) nationals of Bahamas, Bangladesh, Barbados, Botswana, Cyprus, Dominica, Fiji, Finland, Gambia, Ghana, Grenada, Guyana, Iceland, Israel, Jamaica, Kenya, Kiribati, South Korea, Madagascar, Malawi, Malaysia, Malta, Mauritius, Nauru, New Zealand, Norway, Papua New Guinea, Western Samoa, San Marino, Seychelles, Sierra Leone, Singapore, Solomon Islands, Sri Lanka, St Lucia, St Vincent & the Grenadines, South Africa, Swaziland, Sweden, Tanzania, Tonga, Trinidad & Tobago, Tuvalu, Uganda, Zambia, Zimbabwe (including holders of an unexpired Rhodesian passport) and holders of Taiwan passports.
Types of visa: Tourist, Business and Transit. Cost: Single-entry £5, Multiple-entry £10.
Validity: Up to 3 months.
Application to: Consulate (or Consular Section at Embassy or High Commission). For addresses, see top of entry.
Application requirements: (a) 2 application forms. (b) 2 photos. (c) Return ticket. (d) Business sponsor's letter for Business visa.
Working days required: 1.
Temporary residence: Apply to the Ministry of the Interior, Maseru. Enquire at Embassy for details.

MONEY

Currency: Loti (Lo) = 100 lisente. Notes are in denominations of Lo50, 20, 10, 5 and 1. Coins are in denominations of Lo1, and 50, 20, 10, 5, 2 and 1 lisente. The plural of 'Loti' is 'Maloti'. The South African Rand is accepted as legal currency on a par with the Loti.
Credit cards: Limited acceptance of Visa, Access/Mastercard and Diners Club. Check with your credit card company for details of merchant acceptability and other services which may be available.
Travellers cheques: Limited use outside the capital.
Exchange rate indicators: The following figures are included as a guide to the movements of the Loti against Sterling and the US Dollar:

Date:	Oct '89	Oct '90	Oct '91	Oct '92
£1.00=	4.27	4.94	4.89	4.68
$1.00=	2.70	2.53	2.81	2.95

Currency restrictions: The import and export of currency is not restricted, but must be done in consultation with a bank.
Banking hours: 0830-1300 Monday to Friday and 0830-1100 Saturday.

DUTY FREE

The following goods may be imported into Lesotho without incurring customs duty:
400 cigarettes and 50 cigars and 250g of tobacco;

1 litre of alcohol;
Perfume not exceeding 300ml.
Note: No alcohol may be imported by nationals of South Africa. Sporting equipment may be imported as part of passenger's luggage.

PUBLIC HOLIDAYS

Public holidays observed in Lesotho are as follows:
Mar 12 '93 Moshoeshoe's Day. **Apr 9-12** Easter. **May 20** Ascension Day. **Jul 1** Family Day. **Jul 17** King's Birthday. **Oct 4** Independence Day. **Oct 7** National Sports Day. **Dec 25** Christmas Day. **Dec 26** Boxing Day. **Jan 1 '94** New Year's Day. **Jan 28** Anniversary of the overthrow of Chief Jonathan's Government. **Mar 12** Moshoeshoe's Day.

HEALTH

Regulations and requirements may be subject to change at short notice, and you are advised to contact your doctor well in advance of your intended date of departure. Any numbers in the chart refer to the footnotes below.

	Special Precautions?	Certificate Required?
Yellow Fever	Yes	1
Cholera	Yes	-
Typhoid & Polio	Yes	-
Malaria	No	-
Food & Drink	2	-

[1]: Yellow fever vaccination certificate required of travellers arriving from infected areas.
[2]: Tap water is considered safe to drink. However, drinking water outside main cities and towns may be contaminated and sterilisation is advisable. Milk is pasteurised and dairy products are safe for consumption. Local meat, poultry, seafood, fruit and vegetables are generally considered safe to eat.
Rabies is present. For those at high risk, vaccination before arrival should be considered. If you are bitten abroad seek medical advice without delay. For more information consult the *Health* section at the back of the book.
Bilharzia (schistosomiasis) is present. Avoid swimming and paddling in fresh water. Swimming pools which are well-chlorinated and maintained are safe.
Health care: Health insurance is recommended.
Note: Since the most practical way to reach Lesotho is to go through South Africa, it will also be necessary to conform to South African health regulations.

TRAVEL - International

AIR: Lesotho's national airline is *Lesotho Airways Corporation*.
Approximate flight time: From *London* to Maseru is 14 hours (including 2 hours for stopover).
International airport: *Maseru (MSU)* (Moshoeshoe I International) is 18km (11 miles) south of Maseru. Buses go to the city (travel time – 35 minutes). Airport facilities include bank (1200-1400); bureau de change (0700-1800 Tuesday and Friday); post office, bars, restaurants, duty-free shops, left luggage and flight information (all open 0700-1800 in winter, 0730-1730 in summer) and car rental (*Avis* and *Hertz*).
Departure tax: Lo10. Transit passengers and children under five years of age are exempt.
RAIL: The South African railway network has a link to Maseru. The 26km (16-mile) journey from Maseru to Marseilles Junction on the South African mainline railway network takes about an hour.
ROAD: Routes exist to the west and south from South Africa. There are three major road links to South Africa: at Maseru Bridge (0600-2200), at Ficksburg Bridge in the north (0600-2000) and at Van Rooyen's Gate in the south (0600-2000). Other crossing points exist, but the road surfaces are less good. All of these are open by 0800, but some close as early as 1600.
See below for **documentation** information.

TRAVEL - Internal

AIR: There are regular charter flights for tourists within Lesotho connecting the main towns.
ROAD: The road system is underdeveloped, and few roads are paved. The main road which runs through the towns around the western and southern borders is tarred, but other roads can be impassable during the rainy season. There are **minibuses** in the lowlands. **Documentation:** International Driving Permit recommended. National driving licences are normally valid, providing that they are either in English or accompanied by a certified translation. Enquire at the High Commission or Embassy for details.
JOURNEY TIMES: The following chart gives journey times (in hours and minutes) from Maseru to other towns in Lesotho.

	Air	Road
Teyateyaneng	-	0.20
Leribe	0.20	1.00
Butha-Buthe	-	1.30
Mokhotlong	0.35	7.00
Qacha's Nek	0.45	8.00
Thabatseka	0.25	5.00
Mohale's Hoek	0.20	1.30
Quthing	0.30	3.00
Mafeteng	0.15	1.00

ACCOMMODATION

HOTELS: There are hotels of varying quality in the main towns and mountain lodges giving access to the wilder regions. New hotels have been built at Maseru, Leribe and Masionokang. Two government hotels are at Sehlabathele in the east and in Makones near Quthing (open dry season only) providing accommodation but not food. There are several hotels in Maseru of international standard. Further information can be obtained from the Hotel, Liquor and Tourism Association, Private Bag A84, Maseru 100. Fax: 310 158. Telex: 4333 LO.
LODGES: Commercial concerns have built several lodges providing bungalow accommodation.
YOUTH HOSTELS: Current information can be obtained from the Youth Hostel Association, PO Box 970, Maseru. Tel: 311 969.

RESORTS & EXCURSIONS

Maseru is the obvious stepping-off point for a holiday. There are local highlights to visit such as the historical cemetery and the fascinating architecture of the *King's Palace* and the *Prime Minister's Residence*. From Maseru you can take many day trips, either independently or by luxury motor coach, visiting surrounding points of interest.
Near Maseru, the *Ha Khotso bushmen rock paintings* are well worth a visit. Also nearby is *Thaba Bosiu*, a flat-topped hill where the Basotho made a last heroic stand against the Boers. Many of their chiefs are buried here. The *Outward Bound Centre* in Lesotho is situated at **Thaba Patsoa** in the foothills of the *Malutis*. Half a million Rand have been spent on the camp, equipment and transport. The staff are skilled instructors using teaching techniques perfected in the Outward Bound's 33 centres throughout the world. Outward Bound is a concept of providing young people with the opportunity of encountering the more rugged aspects of nature and extending their own physical and mental capacities. Courses include rock-climbing, mountaineering, canoeing, sailing, camping and riding. For more information contact the Outward Bound Association, PO Box 367, Leribe 300, Lesotho. Tel: (11) 659 0524 (in Johannesburg).
Pony trekking: At the moment three treks are offered, two of them covering the great falls at *Ribaneng, Ketane* and *Maletsunyane*, the latter being particularly noteworthy as it is the highest single-drop fall in southern Africa. There is a choice of return once **Semonkong** has been reached between flying back to Maseru on the fourth day or continuing the pony ride for another two days to the *Ha Ramabanta*, where motor transport will be available for the return to Maseru. The other route is the *Molimo Nthuse* circular trip, starting at the *Molimo Nthuse* ('God Help Me') *Lodge* (the actual base for the *Basotho Pony Trekking Centre*) and going over *Thaba Putsoa* ('Blue Mountain') Pass to reach *Ha Markabei-Senqunyane Lodge* on the second day. The return trip via **Molikaliko** and *Qiloane Falls* reaches Molimo Nthuse from a different direction on the fifth day. Unlike the three falls of the first trip, Qiloane is a wide fall with several smaller drops. Overnight stops are usually made in the rural areas in the huts of the remote Basotho where a taste of real Basotho life is experienced. All the routes pass through magnificent countryside. **The South:** The southern region of Lesotho is being promoted for tourism, with hotels at **Moyeni, Mohale's Hoek** and the new building of the *Orange River Hotel* which has facilities for swimming, horseriding, canoeing, mountain climbing and hiking. Worth visiting in the district are the *Metlejoeng Caves*, 2km (1.2 miles) south of Mahale's Hoek; the dinosaur footprints at **Maphutseng** and **Moyeni;** the *Masitise Cave House* and the petrified forest on the mountain of *Taaba-Ts'oeu*. In the southeast, in the border region between Transkei and South Africa, is one of the most beautiful parts of Lesotho. It is ideal for trekking. Places of most interest include **Ramanbanta, Semonkong** (where the *Maletsunyane Waterfalls* are to be found), the **Sehlabathebe National Park** and the **Mont aux Sources National Park.**

SOCIAL PROFILE

FOOD & DRINK: The main hotels in Maseru serve international foods, but there are also some interesting places to dine in the main towns. Hotels and restaurants in Lesotho cater for all nationalities. There are *halal* foods and seafood. Cooking styles include French, Italian and Continental, with Chinese dishes at the China Garden Restaurant in Maseru. Much food has to be imported from South Africa, but freshwater fish is in abundant supply. **Drink:** Good beer is widely available and better establishments will have a good choice of beers, spirits and wines.
NIGHTLIFE: Some hotels and restaurants have live entertainment. There are also several cinemas in Maseru and there are casinos at the two major international hotels.
SHOPPING: There are many handicraft shops and centres selling items including Lesotho's famous conical hats; grass-woven articles (mats, brooms and baskets); pottery; wool and mohair rugs; tapestries and other textiles; rock painting reproductions; traditional seed, clay bead and porcupine quill jewellery; silver and gold; copper work (particularly chess sets of African design) and ebony items. **Shopping hours:** 0800-1700 Monday to Friday and 0800-1300 Saturday.
SPORT: Fishing: Lesotho's dams and rivers contain local and imported fish. Brown and rainbow trout and carp provide satisfying sport for anglers. **Riding/climbing:** Pony trekking and mountain climbing are popular and ideal ways of seeing the rugged beauty of the land. **Birdwatching:** As many as 279 species of birds have been recorded and keen birdwatchers should take a trip along the Mountain Road to see birds rare to southern Africa. **Swimming:** Bilharzia-free rivers and lakes and hotel pools are available for bathing. **Tennis:** Maseru has high-standard tennis courts at the Maseru Club. **Golf:** There are 9-hole golf courses. **Spectator sports: Horseracing** is a popular sport and meetings take place throughout the country. **Football** is Lesotho's national game and matches are played most Saturdays and Sundays.
SOCIAL CONVENTIONS: If spending some time in rural villages, it is polite to inform the Head Chief. It is likely that he will be very helpful. Normal social courtesies and a friendly, warm approach will be greatly appreciated. Dress should be practical and casual but, particularly in Muslim areas, all customs should be respected (including those regarding modesty in dress). Religion plays an important part in daily life. **Photography:** Photographs must not be taken of the following: the palace, police establishments, government offices, the airport or monetary authority buildings. **Tipping:** 10% is normal in restaurants and hotels.

BUSINESS PROFILE

ECONOMY: 80% of the population are engaged in agriculture; farming maize, wheat and other crops. Nonetheless, over half the country's food must be imported from South Africa. Wool, mohair and hides are important exports. Prospects for the embryonic diamond industry were dashed

LESOTHO | **HEALTH REGULATIONS** | **VISA REGULATIONS** | Code-Link

GALILEO/WORLDSPAN

TI-DFT/MSU/HE

TI-DFT/MSU/VI

SABRE

TIDFT/MSU/HE

TIDFT/MSU/VI

To access this information on your CRS, swipe the barcode with a light pen or type in the text under the barcode. For more information, see the introduction *How to Use This Book*.

by the slump in world demand in the early 1980s, since when foreign visitors to Lesotho's many casinos have become the country's principal source of foreign exchange. Tourism is growing in importance, while Lesotho's government has regularly sought both foreign aid – particularly for infrastructure programmes – and, more recently, capital investment from the Far East which Lesotho hopes to attract by promoting the country as a source of cheap labour and an export platform for the region. South Africa, which exercises something of a stranglehold over the economy, is Lesotho's major trading partner: the Southern African Customs Union provides over 95% of the country's imports.
BUSINESS: Lightweight suit, shirt and tie should be worn for business meetings. English will be spoken by most business people. Usual business formalities should be observed, but expect a casual atmosphere and pace. **Office hours:** 0800-1300 and 1400-1630 Monday to Friday, 0800-1300 Saturday. **Government office hours:** 0800-1245 and 1400-1630 Monday to Friday.
COMMERCIAL INFORMATION: The following organisation can offer advice: Lesotho Chamber of Commerce and Industry, PO Box 79, Maseru 100. Tel: 323 482.

HISTORY & GOVERNMENT

HISTORY: The Basotho only emerged as a nation around 1820 when Moshoeshoe the Great gathered the remnants of tribes scattered by Zulu and Matabele raids and established a stronghold at Butha-Buthe, and later on the mountain of Thaba-Bosiu, about 30km (20 miles) from what is now Maseru. In 1868, Moshoeshoe placed himself and his people under the protection of the British government. The Kingdom of Lesotho under King Moshoeshoe II became independent in 1966. The nation is an amalgamation of mainly Sesotho-speaking people with some 20% originally of Nguni descent, and the rest comprising San, Griqua, Indian and Europeans who have become naturalised Basotho with a strong cultural tradition. Since independence, Lesotho's politics have been dominated by the Basutoland National Party (BNP), a conservatively inclined party favouring a policy of accommodation with South Africa, led by Chief Leabua Jonathan. His autocratic style of rule drew strong opposition, both political and paramilitary, in the form of the Lesotho Liberation Army, which allegedly has South African support. On January 20, 1986, Chief Jonathan was overthrown in a coup by Major General J M Lekhanya. Although the South African government has vehemently denied any involvement, the new regime proved more amenable to South African regional security policies. In any event, Lesotho's political options were constrained by South Africa: Pretoria's closure of the border during 1983, which precipitated severe food shortages within Lesotho, was a telling reminder of South African power. Lekhanya clashed on several occasions with King Moshoeshoe, but in 1991 Lekhanya was himself overthrown by a group of army officers. The new leader, Elias Rameama, has promised a future return to civilian rule. Moreover, the King, in exile in London, has been permitted to return to the country and resume his reign at the beginning of August.
GOVERNMENT: The monarch, King Moshoeshoe II, is Head of State with no formal political powers. After 1970, when Chief Jonathan abandoned the constitution after losing the national election, the country was governed by an appointed Cabinet of Ministers. The new constitution, adopted in 1983, allows for a National Assembly of 60 members – of whom not less than two-thirds must be popularly elected – and a Senate of tribal chiefs and appointees of the monarch.

CLIMATE

Temperate climate with well-marked seasons. Summer is the rainy season. Snow occurs in the highlands from May to September. The hottest period is from January to February. Lesotho is a land of blue skies and more than 300 days of sun.
Required clothing: During the summer, lightweight cottons. In winter, medium to heavyweight clothes are advised. Waterproofing is necessary during the rainy season.

MOKHOTLONG Lesotho (2375m)

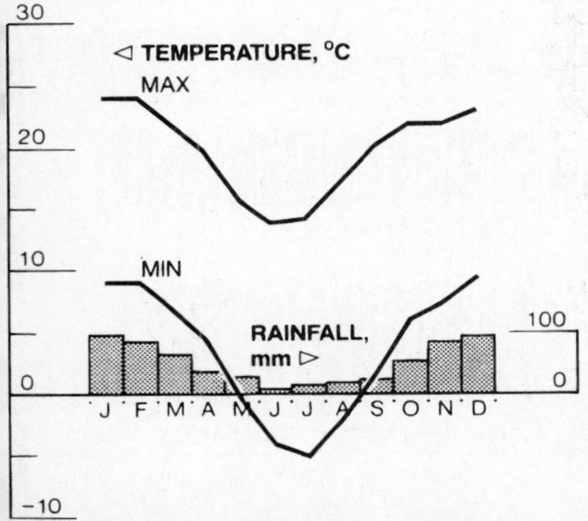

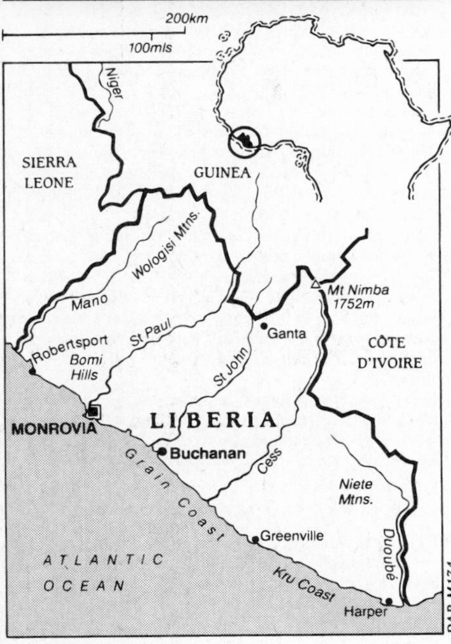

□ international airport

Location: West Africa.

Note: The British Embassy in Liberia has been closed since March 1991. The High Commission in Sierra Leone is responsible for monitoring developments in Liberia.

Bureau of Tourism
Sinkor
Monrovia, Liberia.
Tel: 224 984.
Embassy of the Republic of Liberia
2 Pembridge Place
London W2 4XB
Tel: (071) 221 1036. Opening hours: 0900-1530 Monday to Friday.
British Embassy
PO Box 120
Mamba Point
Monrovia, Liberia
Tel: 221 491. Telex: 44287.
British High Commission
Standard Chartered Bank of Sierra Leone Ltd
Lightfoot Boston Street
Freetown, Sierra Leone
Tel: (22) 223 961. Telex: 3235.
Embassy of the Republic of Liberia
5201 16th Street, NW
Washington, DC 20011
Tel: (202) 291 0761.
Embassy of the United States of America
PO Box 98
111 United Nations Drive
Mamba Point
Monrovia, Liberia
Tel: 222 994.
Embassy of the Republic of Liberia
Suite 2600, 160 Elgin Street
Ottawa, Ontario
K1N 8S3
Tel: (613) 232 1711. Fax: (613) 563 9869.
Consulates in: Montréal and Rexdale.
Consulate of Canada
PO Box 53
EXCHEM Compound
Harbel, Liberia.
Tel: 721 086 *or* 223 903. Telex: 44299 EXCHEM L1.

AREA: 97,754 sq km (37,743 sq miles).
POPULATION: 2,607,000 (1990 estimate).
POPULATION DENSITY: 26.7 per sq km.
CAPITAL: Monrovia. **Population:** 421,058 (1984).
GEOGRAPHY: Liberia borders Sierra Leone, Guinea and Côte d'Ivoire. The Atlantic coastline to the west is 560km (348 miles) long, of which over half is sandy beach. Lying parallel to the shore are three distinct belts. The low coastal belt is well watered by shallow lagoons, tidal creeks and mangrove swamps, behind which rises a gently undulating plateau, 500-800m (1640-2625ft) high, partly covered with dense forests. Inland and to the north is the mountain region which includes Mount Nimba 1752m (5748ft) and Waulo Mountain 1400m (4593ft). About half the country's population are rural dwellers.
LANGUAGE: English is the official language. The main African languages are Bassa, Kpelle and Kru.
RELIGION: Officially a Christian state; Islam is practised in the north and traditional beliefs exist throughout the country.
TIME: GMT.
ELECTRICITY: 110 volts AC, 60Hz.
COMMUNICATIONS: Telephone: IDD service to some cities. Country code: 231 (no area codes). The internal network in Monrovia is gradually being extended over the country. **Telex/telegram:** Cable communication with Europe and USA via Dakar, but not with West Africa. **Post:** Airmail to Europe takes 5-12 days. **Press:** The Liberian press is in the English-language, with four main papers: *The Daily Observer*, *Mirror*, *Sunday Express* and *The New Liberian*.
BBC World Service and Voice of America frequencies: From time to time these change. See the section *How to Use this Book* for more information.

BBC:				
MHz	21.71	15.07	11.86	6.005
Voice of America:				
MHz	11.97	9.670	6.040	5.995

PASSPORT/VISA

Regulations and requirements may be subject to change at short notice, and you are advised to contact the appropriate diplomatic or consular authority before finalising travel arrangements. Details of these may be found at the head of this country's entry. Any numbers in the chart refer to the footnotes below.

	Passport Required?	Visa Required?	Return Ticket Required?
Full British	Yes	Yes	Yes
BVP	Not valid	-	-
Australian	Yes	Yes	Yes
Canadian	Yes	Yes	Yes
USA	Yes	Yes	Yes
Other EC	Yes	Yes	Yes
Japanese	Yes	Yes	Yes

Restricted entry: No entry for 'white' South African passport holders, unless transiting directly in the same aircraft without leaving the airport.
PASSPORTS: Valid passport required by all.
British Visitors Passport: Not acceptable.
VISAS: Required by all except nationals of Benin, Burkina Faso, Cape Verde, Côte d'Ivoire, Gambia, Ghana, Guinea Republic, Guinea-Bissau, South Korea, Mali, Mauritania, Niger, Nigeria, Senegal, Sierra Leone and Togo.
Types of visa: Tourist, Business and Resident. Most EC nationals pay £20; UK citizens pay £20.
Validity: Valid for 60 days from date of issue.
Application to: Consulate (or Consular Section at Embassy). For addresses, see top of entry.
Application requirements: (a) Completed application form in duplicate, with photograph attached to each form. (b) Valid passport. (c) Onward ticket. (d) International yellow fever inoculation certificate.
Working days required: 1.
Temporary residence: Application should be made prior to arrival to the Ministry of Foreign Affairs, Monrovia.
Note: All visitors holding a visa issued abroad and intending to stay in Liberia for more than 15 days must report within 48 hours of their arrival to: The Immigration Office, Broad Street, Monrovia. Two passport photographs must be submitted.

MONEY

Currency: Liberian Dollar (L$) = 100 cents. The currency is pegged to the US Dollar (L$1 = US$1) and US Dollar notes are in circulation in the following denominations: US$20, 10, 5, 2 and 1 as legal tender. Coins are in denominations of L$5 and 1, and 50, 25, 10, 5 and 1 cents.
Credit cards: The use of Access/Mastercard and Diners Club is limited. Check with credit card company for

details of merchant acceptability and other services which may be available.

Exchange rate indicators: The following figures are included as a guide to the movements of the Liberian Dollar against Sterling and the US Dollar:

Date:	Oct '89	Oct '90	Oct '91	Oct '92
£1.00=	1.58	1.96	1.74	1.59
$1.00=	1.00	1.00	1.00	1.00

Currency restrictions: There are no restrictions on import or export of local or foreign currency.

Banking hours: 0900-1200 Monday to Thursday, and 0800-1400 Friday. Bank of Monrovia, Tubman Boulevard, Sinkor, is also open 0800-1100 Saturdays.

DUTY FREE

The following goods may be imported into Liberia without incurring customs duty:

200 cigarettes or 25 cigars or 250g tobacco products;
1 litre of alcoholic beverage;
100g (4 fl oz) of perfume;
Goods to the value of US$125.

PUBLIC HOLIDAYS

Public holidays observed in Liberia are as follows:

Mar 12 '93 Decoration Day. **Mar 15** J J Robert's Birthday. **Apr 9** Good Friday. **Apr 11** Fast and Prayer Day. **Apr 12** National Redemption Day. **May 14** National Unification Day. **Jul 26** Independence Day. **Aug 24** Flag Day. **Nov 6** Thanksgiving Day. **Nov 12** National Memorial Day. **Nov 29** President Trubman's Birthday. **Dec 25** Christmas Day. **Jan 1 '94** New Year's Day. **Feb 11** Armed Forces Day. **Mar 12** Decoraton Day. **Mar 15** J J Robert's Birthday.

HEALTH

Regulations and requirements may be subject to change at short notice, and you are advised to contact your doctor well in advance of your intended date of departure. Any numbers in the chart refer to the footnotes below.

	Special Precautions?	Certificate Required?
Yellow Fever	Yes	1
Cholera	Yes	2
Typhoid & Polio	Yes	-
Malaria	3	-
Food & Drink	4	-

[1]: A yellow fever vaccination certificate is required from all travellers over one year of age. Note that the certificate must be presented with all visa applications.

[2]: Following WHO guidelines issued in 1973, a cholera vaccination certificate is not a condition of entry to Liberia. However, cholera is a serious risk in this country and precautions are essential. Up-to-date advice should be sought before deciding whether these precautions should include vaccination, as medical opinion is divided over its effectiveness. See the *Health* section at the back of the book.

[3]: Malaria risk, predominantly in the malignant *falciparum* form, exists all year throughout the country. High resistance to chloroquine and resistance to sulfadoxine-pyrimethamine has been reported.

[4]: All water should be regarded as being potentially contaminated. Water used for drinking, brushing teeth or making ice should have first been boiled or otherwise sterilised. Milk is unpasteurised and should be boiled. Powdered or tinned milk is available and is advised, but make sure that it is reconstituted with pure water. Avoid dairy products which are likely to have been made from unboiled milk. Only eat well-cooked meat and fish, preferably served hot. Pork, salad and mayonnaise may carry increased risk. Vegetables should be cooked and fruit peeled.

Rabies is present. For those at high risk, vaccination before arrival should be considered. If you are bitten abroad seek medical advice without delay. For more information consult the *Health* section at the back of the book.

Bilharzia (schistosomiasis) is present. Avoid swimming and paddling in fresh water. Swimming pools which are well-chlorinated and maintained are safe.

Health care: Chemists are well supplied with European and American medicines. There are good private physicians as well as clinics and hospitals. Medical insurance is essential.

TRAVEL - International

AIR: Liberia's national airline is *Air Liberia (NL)*. Other main airlines servicing Liberia include *Ethiopian Airlines*, *Aeroflot* and *Zambia Airways*.

Approximate flight time: From *London* to Monrovia is 9 hours 40 minutes.

International airport: *Monrovia (MLW)* (Robertsfield International) is 60km (38 miles) southeast of the city. There are bus services and taxis to and from the city. Airport facilities include restaurant, bar, duty-free shop, post office and gift shops. Some West African airlines land at *Spriggs Payne Airport* which is in the city itself.

Departure tax: L$20 must be paid by all passengers embarking for destinations abroad, except children under 12 years and those transiting within 24 hours.

SEA: There are unscheduled freighter services with passenger accommodation from European ports. The main Liberian ports are Monrovia, Buchanan, Greenville, Harper and Robertsport. The port in Monrovia is presently being expanded.

ROAD: Best routes to Liberia are through Guinea, Sierra Leone and Côte d'Ivoire, but they are impassable during the rainy season. The northeastern route to Sierra Leone (via Kolahun and Kailahun) is currently closed.

TRAVEL - Internal

AIR: *Air Liberia (NL)* operates regular services from Monrovia to major towns. There are 60 airfields for small aircraft.

SEA/RIVER: There is a passenger service between Monrovia and Buchanan. Unscheduled coastal steamers may sometimes take passengers. Small craft are used for local transportation on Liberia's many rivers. **Canoe safaris:** Between December and March, the Liberian Forest Development Authority arranges canoe trips upriver from Greenville, a small seaport 200km (125 miles) southeast of Monrovia.

RAIL: Three lines run inland from the coast. All are primarily used for the transport of mining produce from the interior, but the privately-owned *LAMCO* line operates a daily passenger/freight service from Buchanan to Yekepa, near the border with Côte d'Ivoire and Guinea.

ROAD: Difficulties in bypassing lagoons and bridging river estuaries often result in long detours and delays along the coast. Main roads are from Monrovia to Buchanan and from Monrovia to Sanniquellie with branches to Ganta and Harper. Many of the smaller roads are still untarred. Vehicle transport is limited. **Bus:** Primitive bus services between main towns may be available. **Car hire:** Self-drive or chauffeured cars may be hired from Monrovia. **Documentation:** An International Driving Permit is recommended, although it is not legally required. A temporary licence to drive is available from local authorities on presentation of a valid British or Northern Ireland driving licence and is valid for up to 30 days.

URBAN: A minibus service operates in Monrovia. Taxis are available and tipping is unnecessary.

ACCOMMODATION

HOTELS: Hotel accommodation can be quite expensive, but not extortionate by international standards. It is advisable to book well in advance, whatever the category of accommodation. There are a few air-conditioned hotels of international standard and a range of inexpensive hotels and motels. The top hotels charge from US$60 a night. Hotels in the mid-range charge from US$25-35 and tend to be on the sleazy side.

GUEST-HOUSES: There are several mission guest-houses with both cooking and laundry facilities about 4km from the centre. Prices are from L$10 night.

CAMPING: There are no official sites; camping is free. Use caution.

YOUTH HOSTELS: The YMCA is cheap, but often full, and is located on the corner of Broad and McDonald Street.

RESORTS & EXCURSIONS

Monrovia, the capital, is a sprawling city on the coast divided by inlets, lagoons and rocky headlands. The city has several nightclubs, restaurants and bars, centred on the area around Gurley Street. There are several good sandy beaches near the capital. **Providence Island,** where the first settlers from the USA arrived in the early 19th century, has a museum which records both this event and the indigenous arts and crafts of the region. 80km (50 miles) from the capital is *Lake Piso*, ideal for swimming, fishing and watersports. Conducted tours of the *Firestone Rubber Plantation*, one of the largest in the world, make an interesting day excursion, situated only 50km (30 miles) from Monrovia. There are several museums and cultural centres outside the capital; contact the Embassy information departments for further details. Some of the country's most beautiful beaches can be found at **Robertsport.**

The most evocative description of Liberia can be found in Graham Greene's *Journey without Maps*, an account of his overland trip across the country in 1935. Although it can now hardly pretend to be an up-to-date guide book, the descriptions and the atmosphere of the country it creates – particularly when dealing with the mysterious and jungle-rich interior – make the book a valuable and entertaining introduction for anyone planning to visit the country.

SOCIAL PROFILE

FOOD & DRINK: Liberia's hotels, motels and restaurants serve a variety of American, European, Asian and African dishes, as well as the more predictable fare of hotel dining rooms. Here, as well as in the smaller towns of the north and east, the visitor should enjoy sampling some of the more unusual West African foods in 'Cookhouses' which serve rice with traditional Liberian dishes. **Drink:** Liberia produces a lot of its own brands of alcoholic drink, which are readily available – some of the beers are excellent; wines and imported beverages are also available.

NIGHTLIFE: In Monrovia, nightlife is extensive with dozens of crowded nightclubs, discotheques and bars open until the early hours. Most of the nightlife centres are on Gurley Street. Providence Island has a bandstand and an amphitheatre where performances of traditional African music and dance are staged.

SHOPPING: Monrovia's sidestreets are crowded with tailors selling brightly coloured tie-dyed and embroidered cloth which they will make up immediately into African or European styles. Monrovia offers the shopper elegant boutiques and shops as well as modern, air-conditioned supermarkets which compete with old-fashioned stores. Liberian handicrafts include carvings in sapwood, camwood, ebony and mahogany, stone items, soapstone carvings (such as fertility symbols from the Kissi), ritual masks, metal jewellery and figurines and reed dolls of the Loma. **Shopping hours:** 0800-1300 and 1500-1800 Monday to Saturday.

SPORT: Swimming and **boating** are popular at the many sandy beaches. These include Bernard's Beach, Elwa Beach, Kenema Beach, Kendaje Beach, Sugar Beach, Cedar Beach, Cooper's Beach and Caesar's Beach, all of which charge a small entrance fee. Lake Piso is also ideal for swimming and other watersports. **Skindiving:** Season from December to May, when the sea is at its clearest. **Angling:** There is good fishing in the Saint Paul and Mesurado rivers, along the coast and at Lake Piso, where there are traditional fishing villages. **Tennis and golf:** There are various private clubs. **Horseriding:** There is a riding club in Monrovia. **Football** is the Liberian national sport.

SOCIAL CONVENTIONS: In Muslim areas the visitor should respect the conventions of dress and the food laws, since failure to do so will be taken as an insult. Dress is casual and must be practical, but smarter dress will be expected in hotel dining rooms and for important social functions. The visitor should be aware that the cost of living is high.

LIBERIA | **HEALTH REGULATIONS** | **VISA REGULATIONS** | Code-Link

GALILEO/WORLDSPAN

TI-DFT/MLW/HE

TI-DFT/MLW/VI

SABRE

TIDFT/MLW/HE

TIDFT/MLW/VI

To access this information on your CRS, swipe the barcode with a light pen or type in the text under the barcode. For more information, see the introduction *How to Use This Book.*

Sending flowers or chocolates to hosts is inappropriate and a letter of thanks is all that is required. **Tipping:** There is no need to tip taxi drivers, but other tips are normally 50 cents.

BUSINESS PROFILE

ECONOMY: Liberia's economic development was fuelled by substantial American investment, with the result that much of the economy is under US control. 70% of the population work the land, producing rice as the staple food and palm oil, coffee and cocoa as cash crops. Rubber, however, is the major agricultural earner. The country's major trading commodity is iron ore, which was at one time responsible for 75% of export earnings, but has since declined to about 50% with the fall in world demand for steel. The Government's efforts during the 1980s to diversify Liberia's economic base did attract some light manufacturing concerns, producing cement and other building materials, soap, shoes, umbrellas and other consumer products. Germany, Korea and Italy are Liberia's main foreign customers; Norway, Korea and Singapore are the leading importers into the country. The civil war has, however, inflicted considerable damage on Liberia's economy and trade volumes have fallen drastically. The country will take many years to recover.
BUSINESS: Business dress is informal – normally a safari suit or a shirt and tie is acceptable. The language used in business circles is English. **Office hours:** 0800-1200 and 1400-1600 Monday to Friday.
COMMERCIAL INFORMATION: The following organisation can offer advice: Liberia Chamber of Commerce, PO Box 92, Monrovia. Tel: 223 738. Telex: 44211.

HISTORY & GOVERNMENT

HISTORY: Prior to the 19th century the region now known as Liberia was inhabited by tribes originating from the Sudan. These tribes fall into three main groupings: the Kru group, who have a seafaring tradition; the Mande-speaking group, who have a rich and influential reservoir of tribal traditions; and a third grouping with a farming tradition. Modern Liberia came into existence as a result of negotiations conducted between local rulers and the representatives of settlers from the United States, mostly freed negro slaves who were encouraged to resettle in the lands of their forebears and were aided by various philanthropic organisations in America. They controlled Liberia almost exclusively for over a hundred years from the early 19th century. For many years, the colonial powers refused to recognise the new state, and it was not until 1847 that the country was formally able to proclaim itself an independent republic – the first in Africa. This state of affairs did not, unfortunately, produce even the limited material and commercial benefits that colonialism conferred on other parts of the continent, and the settlers, hampered largely by a lack of capital and foreign investment, were never able to develop the kind of economic base that would make them as independent in practice as they were in name. Large sections of the country's territory were ceded to the colonies of Britain and France during the 19th and early 20th centuries. Since 1926, the date of the Firestone Concession, Liberia has cultivated close ties with the United States. The aim of Government policy, through intermarriage between members of the various communities, has been to develop a national consciousness in a unified segment of society whose members can no longer trace their origins. Traditional cultural values, however, are strong, being transmitted mainly through powerful secret societies. Urban culture is a mixture of 19th-century American, traditional African and contemporary American and Western European customs and values. Liberia was ruled by elected civilian governments until a right-wing military coup in 1980, during which President William Tolbert was assassinated. A People's Redemption Council, led by Master-Sergeant Samuel Doe, then took power. In January 1986, Doe became President. Doe proved to be solidly pro-Western in both domestic and foreign policy, though his regime was not wholly stable. A number of coup attempts and a worsening economic situation led the Doe government to adopt increasingly repressive measures to maintain its position. The United States, to which Liberia is especially close, voiced rare criticism of economic mismanagement, alleging corruption and electoral fraud. Late in 1989, severe communal violence broke out after an apparent failed coup attempt. The army attacked villages suspected of harbouring the rebels while thousands of people fled across the border into neighbouring Côte d'Ivoire. As the fighting continued, it became clear that three distinct factions were engaged in a national power-struggle: forces loyal to Doe, and two mutually opposed rebel groups led by Charles Taylor and Prince Yormie Johnson. Taylor, a former Doe aide, and Johnson had started their campaign under the same banner, the National Patriotic Front of Liberia (NPFL). At the end of 1989, the Front guerrilla army, numbering no more than a few hundred incredibly ill-armed men (slings, bows and arrows were more in evidence than guns), crossed the border from Côte d'Ivoire and raided a few small towns. Doe in Monrovia over-reacted and despatched two battalions north to engage the rebels. However, their brutal behaviour towards the local population provided the Front with a sizeable flood of recruits. Desertions from the army also helped to swell the rebel forces and instil some professional soldiery. The main fighting between Doe's troops and the Taylor/Johnson axis took place during the spring and summer of 1990. Two factors defined the political character of the civil war. One was the tribal division between the Krahn, to which Doe and most of his adherents belonged, and the Gio and Mano people, who had felt the brunt of the army's indiscipline earlier in the year and who consequently formed the bulk of the rebel forces. The second was the split between Taylor and Johnson, which occurred in February, after which their followers spent as much time fighting each other as Doe. Nonetheless, Doe was steadily pushed back until, by mid-August, he was holed up in the presidential palace with only his Israeli-trained personal security regiment remaining with him. Taylor's forces controlled most of the countryside, while Johnson's militarily superior forces held the capital and surrounding area. On September 9, Doe was formally deposed and then shot and killed under uncertain circumstances. Johnson assumed the presidency temporarily during September, since when it has passed through several hands. The present incumbent, Amos Sawyer, has managed to pacify some parts of the country, largely with the assistance of a Nigerian-led peace-keeping force from ECOWAS (the Economic Community of West African States). ECOWAS has also been deeply involved in the search for a political settlement, having sponsored a series of negotiations between the rival parties and providing a multinational peace-keeping force. The Americans, meanwhile, who have a major strategic interest in the country, have yet to make any overt intervention, but are keeping a worried vigil. Taylor and his NPFL guerrillas have kept up the fight, launching occasional assaults against ECOWAS units, but their forces are dwindling despite occasional recruitment drives across the border in Sierra Leone. Taylor has also been fighting the Sierra Leonean army, a conflict which triggered the change of government in that country in April 1992. By the middle of the year, ECOWAS were evidently tiring of trying to bring the warring factions together and threatened to impose economic sanctions against Liberia if they persisted in obstructing the latest peace plan.
GOVERNMENT: The People's Redemption Council was dissolved in 1983 in preparation for a return to civilian rule. A new constitution was approved by referendum in July 1984, followed by elections in October 1985. The dual-chamber National Assembly has a 26-member Senate and a 64-member House of Representatives. The President is directly elected by universal adult suffrage for a 6-year term.

CLIMATE

Hot, tropical climate with little variation in temperature. The wet season runs from May to October. The dry *Harmattan* wind blows from December to March, making the coastal belt particularly arid.
Required clothing: Lightweight cottons and linens are worn throughout the year, with waterproofing advised during the wet season.

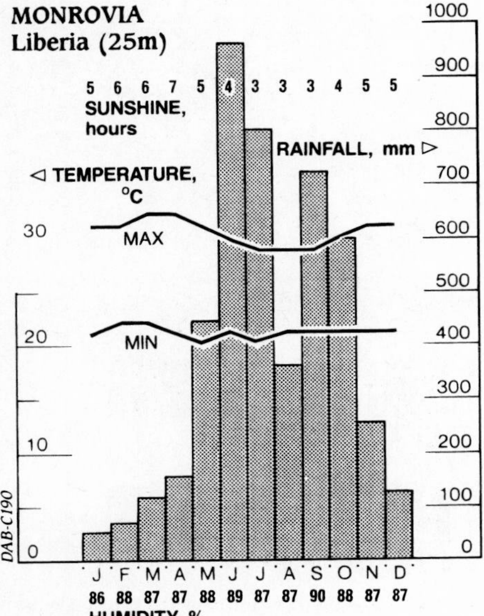

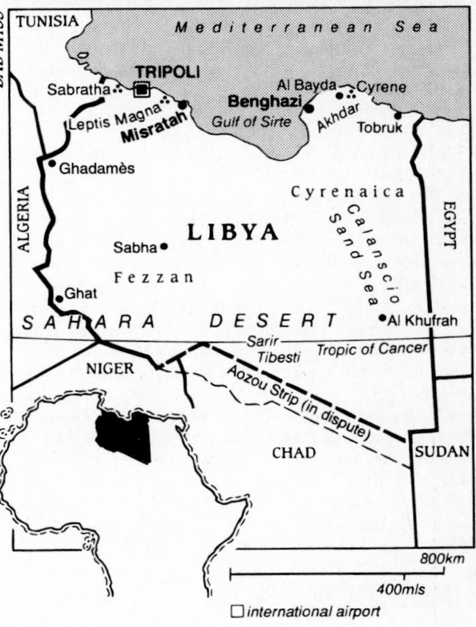

Location: North Africa.

Note: The Socialist People's Libyan Arab Great Jamahiriya does not currently maintain embassies in the United States of America or in the United Kingdom and it is generally very difficult to get a visa as a tourist. This situation is not likely to change in the immediate future.

Department of Tourism and Fairs
PO Box 891
Sharia Omar Mukhtar
Tripoli, Libya
Tel: (21) 32255. Telex: 20179.
Libyan Interests Section
c/o Royal Embassy of Saudi Arabia
119 Harley Street, London W1
Tel: (071) 486 8387. Fax: (071) 224 6349. Telex: 266767.
Libyan People's Bureau
2 rue Charles Lamoureux
75116 Paris, France
Tel: (1) 47 04 71 60. Telex: 620643. Opening hours: 0900-1500 Monday to Friday.
British Interests Section
c/o Embassy of the Italian Republic
PO Box 4206
Sharia Uahran 1
Tripoli, Libya
Tel: (21) 31191. Telex: 20296.
Libyan Interests Section
c/o Embassy of the United Arab Emirates
Suite 740
600 New Hampshire Avenue, NW
Washington, DC
20037
Tel: (202) 338 6500.
Embassy of the Socialist People's Libyan Arab Jamahiriya
c/o Permanent Mission of the Socialist People's Libyan Arab Jamahiriya to the United Nations
309-315 East 48th Street
New York, NY
10017
Tel: (212) 752 5775.

AREA: 1,775,500 sq km (685,524 sq miles).
POPULATION: 3,773,000 (1988 estimate).
POPULATION DENSITY: 2.1 per sq km.
CAPITAL: Tripoli. **Population:** 990,697 (1984).
GEOGRAPHY: Libya consists mostly of huge areas of desert. It shares borders with Tunisia and Algeria in the west, and Egypt in the east, while the Sahara extends across the southern frontiers with Niger, Chad and the Sudan. There are almost 2000km (1250 miles) of

Mediterranean coast, with a low plain extending from the Tunisian border to the Jebel Akhdar (Green Mountain) area in the east. Inland the terrain becomes more hilly. Agriculture has developed mainly on the coast between Zuara and Misurata in the west and from Marsa Susa to Benghazi in the east. In the uplands of the old province of Cyrenaica and on Jebel Akhdar the vegetation is more lush. With the exception of the 'Sand Sea' of the Sarir Calanscio, and the Saharan mountains of the Sarir Tibesti, there are oases scattered throughout the country.

LANGUAGE: Arabic (which must be used for all official purposes), with some English or Italian. English is normally understood by people working in hotels, restaurants and shops.

RELIGION: Muslim (Sunni).

TIME: GMT+ 1 (GMT + 2 in summer).

ELECTRICITY: 150/220 volts AC, 50Hz. All services may be intermittently disrupted by power cuts.

COMMUNICATIONS: Telephone: IDD service is available. Country code: 218. **Telex:** Telex services are available at the larger hotels. **Post:** Postal services are available in all main towns, but services are generally poor and erratic, and mail may be subject to censorship. Airmail to Europe takes approximately two weeks. **Press:** There are several newspapers and periodicals, but none are published in English. The main dailies are *Arraid* and *El Balag*.

BBC World Service and Voice of America frequencies: From time to time these change. See the section *How to Use this Book* for more information.

BBC:

MHz	21.47	17.64	15.07	9.410

Voice of America:

MHz	11.97	9.670	6.040	5.995

PASSPORT/VISA

Regulations and requirements may be subject to change at short notice, and you are advised to contact the appropriate diplomatic or consular authority before finalising travel arrangements. Details of these may be found at the head of this country's entry. Any numbers in the chart refer to the footnotes below.

	Passport Required?	Visa Required?	Return Ticket Required?
Full British	Yes	Yes	Yes
BVP	Not valid	-	-
Australian	Yes	Yes	Yes
Canadian	Yes	Yes	Yes
USA	Yes	Yes/1	Yes
Other EC	Yes	Yes/2	Yes
Japanese	Yes	Yes	Yes

Restricted entry and transit: Holders of Israeli or South African passports, or holders of passports containing a valid or expired visa for either country, will be refused entry or transit. All passports are formally inspected.

PASSPORTS: Valid passport required by all except holders of Palestinian identity documents and national identity cards issued to nationals of the following countries: Algeria, Bahrain, Egypt, Iraq, Jordan, Kuwait, Lebanon, Mauritania, Morocco, Oman, Qatar, Saudi Arabia, Somalia, Sudan, Syria, Tunisia, United Arab Emirates and Yemen.

British Visitors Passport: Not accepted.

VISAS: Required by all except nationals of Algeria, Malta and Mauritania who must hold a *No Objection Certificate* or return tickets.

Note: (a) At time of going to press, no visas were being issued in the United Kingdom. Enquiries for visa applications should generally be addressed to any of Libya's diplomatic representatives in the relevant country or abroad (such as the Libyan People's Bureau in Paris; address at top of entry). (b) Business visitors should be sponsored by a Libyan company who will organise the issue of a Business visa for them. (c) All travellers in possession of a Tourist or Visitor's visa will be refused entry if they do not possess at least US$500 or equivalent. (d) A translation in Arabic of the first two pages of the visitor's passport must accompany each visa application. (e) **[1]** US nationals and their families do not require a visa if sponsored by a Libyan company. (f) **[2]** Nationals of Germany must obtain their visas in Bonn. (g) Pakistan nationals must have both a re-entry and a permanent visa.

MONEY

Currency: Libyan Dinar (LD) = 1000 dirhams. Notes are in denominations of LD10, 5 and 1, and 500 and 250 dirhams. Coins are in denominations of 100, 50, 20, 10, 5 and 1 dirhams.

Credit cards: Limited acceptance of Diners Club and Visa. Check with credit card company for details of merchant acceptability and other services which may be available.

Travellers cheques: Use of these is common.

Exchange rate indicators: The following figures are included as a guide to the movements of the Libyan Dinar against Sterling and the US Dollar:

Date:	Oct '89	Oct '90	Oct '91	Oct '92
£1.00=	0.48	0.52	0.49	0.44
$1.00=	0.30	0.27	0.28	0.28

Currency restrictions: Free import of foreign currency, subject to declaration. Export of foreign currency limited to the amount declared on import. The import and export of local currency is limited to LD20.

Banking hours: 0800-1200 Saturday to Wednesday (winter); 0800-1200 Saturday to Thursday and 1600-1700 Saturday and Wednesday (summer).

DUTY FREE

The following goods may be imported into Libya without incurring customs duty:

200 cigarettes or 25 cigars;

A reasonable amount of perfume.

Prohibited items: All alcohol is prohibited, as is the import of any kind of food. All goods made in Israel or manufactured by companies that do business with Israel are prohibited. For a full list of prohibited items contact the nearest Libyan diplomatic representative.

PUBLIC HOLIDAYS

Public holidays observed in Libya are as follows:

Mar 25 '93 Start of Eid al-Fitr. **Mar 28** British Evacuation Day. **Jun 1** Eid al-Adha, Feast of the Sacrifice. **Jun 11** Evacuation Day. **Jun 21** Islamic New Year. **Jun 30** Ashoura. **Aug 30** Mouloud (Prophet's Birthday). **Sep 1** Revolution Day. **Oct 7** Evacuation Day. **Jan 20 '94** Leilat al-Meiraj. **Mar** Eid al-Fitr. **Mar 28** British Evacuation Day.

Note: Muslim festivals are timed according to local sightings of various phases of the Moon and the dates given above are approximations. During the lunar month of Ramadan that precedes Eid al-Fitr, Muslims fast during the day and feast at night and normal business patterns may be interrupted. Many restaurants are closed during the day and there may be restrictions on smoking and drinking. Some disruption may continue into Eid al-Fitr itself. Eid al-Fitr and Eid al-Adha may last anything from two to ten days, depending on the region. For more information see the section *World of Islam* at the back of the book.

HEALTH

Regulations and requirements may be subject to change at short notice, and you are advised to contact your doctor well in advance of your intended date of departure. Any numbers in the chart refer to the footnotes below.

	Special Precautions?	Certificate Required?
Yellow Fever	Yes	1
Cholera	Yes	2
Typhoid & Polio	Yes	-
Malaria	3	-
Food & Drink	4	-

[1]: A yellow fever vaccination certificate is required from travellers over one year of age arriving from infected areas.

[2]: Following WHO guidelines issued in 1973, a cholera vaccination certificate is not a condition of entry to Libya. However, cholera is a risk in this country and precautions are essential. Up-to-date advice should be sought before deciding whether these precautions should include vaccination, as medical opinion is divided over its effectiveness. See the *Health* section at the back of the book.

[3]: A very limited malaria risk exists in two small areas in the southwest of the country from February to August.

[4]: Mains water is normally chlorinated, and whilst relatively safe may cause mild abdominal upsets. Bottled water is available and is advised for the first few weeks of the stay. Drinking water outside main cities and towns is likely to be contaminated and sterilisation is considered essential. Milk is unpasteurised and should be boiled. Powdered or tinned milk is available and is advised, but make sure that it is reconstituted with pure water. Avoid dairy products which are likely to have been made from unboiled milk. Only eat well-cooked meat and fish, preferably served hot. Salad and mayonnaise may carry increased risk. Vegetables should be cooked and fruit peeled.

Rabies is present. For those at high risk, vaccination before arrival should be considered. If you are bitten abroad seek medical advice without delay. For more information consult the *Health* section at the back of the book.

Bilharzia (schistosomiasis) is present. Avoid swimming and paddling in fresh water. Swimming pools which are well-chlorinated and maintained are safe.

Health care: Medical facilities outside the main cities are limited. Full health insurance is recommended.

TRAVEL - International

AIR: Libya's national airline is *Jamahiriya Libyan Arab Airlines (LN)*.

Approximate flight time: From *London* to Tripoli is 6 hours (including stopover time).

International airport: *Tripoli International (TIP)* is 35km (21 miles) south of the city (travel time – 40 minutes). Bus and taxi services are available to the city.

Benina International (BEN) is 29km (18 miles) from Benghazi city centre.

Sebha (SEB) is 11km (7 miles) from the town.

SEA: The main ports are as-Sider, Benghazi, Mersa Brega, Misurata and Tripoli. A new port is presently being built at Darna. Several shipping lines operate services from Europe to Libya. A car ferry operated by the Libyan government shipping line sails regularly from Tripoli to Malta and several Italian ports. Italian lines of *Grimaldi* and *Tirrenia* run similar services from Genoa and Naples to Tripoli and Benghazi.

RAIL: There is no passenger rail system.

ROAD: Main routes to Libya are from Tunisia, Algeria, Niger, Chad and Egypt. The border with Egypt has been re-opened, although the most commonly used route is via Tunisia.

TRAVEL - Internal

AIR: *Jamahiriya Libyan Arab Airlines (LN)* provide fast and frequent internal services between Tripoli, Benghazi, Sabha, Al Bayda, Mersa Brega, Tobruk, Misrafah, Ghadamès and Al Khufrah. They also offer an hourly shuttle between Tripoli and Benghazi.

ROAD: The main through road follows the coast from west to east. Main roads are Al Qaddahia–Sebha, Sabha–Ghat, Tripoli–Sabha, Agedabia–Al Khufrah, Garian–Jefren, Tarhouna–Homs, Mersa Susa–Ras, Hilal–Derna and Tobruk–Jaghboub. Since 1969, signposts other than those in Arabic script have been prohibited; signs and house numbers are, in any case, rare outside the main towns. Petrol is available throughout Libya, and is currently about half the price of that in

LIBYA | **HEALTH REGULATIONS** | **VISA REGULATIONS** | Code-Link

GALILEO/WORLDSPAN

TI-DFT/TIP/HE

TI-DFT/TIP/VI

SABRE

TIDFT/TIP/HE

TIDFT/TIP/VI

To access this information on your CRS, swipe the barcode with a light pen or type in the text under the barcode. For more information, see the introduction *How to Use This Book*.

Britain. There are no reliable town maps. Spare parts are often difficult to obtain: in particular, automatic transmissions can prove almost impossible to repair. The quality of servicing is generally poor by European standards, as is the standard of driving. **Bus & taxi:** There is a bus service between Tripoli and Benghazi. A minibus service operates from Benghazi to Tobruk. Taxi fares should be agreed in advance. **Car rental:** Self-drive cars are available in Tripoli and Benghazi. **Documentation:** National driving licence valid for three months. Afterwards, a Libyan licence must be obtained.
URBAN: A substantial publicly owned bus system operates in Tripoli. Fares are charged on a 3-zone basis. There is a similar system in operation in Benghazi. Services are generally irregular and overcrowded.

ACCOMMODATION

HOTELS: Tripoli and Benghazi have comfortable modern hotels, such as the Grand, Kasr Libya, Libya Palace and Marhaba in Tripoli, and the Kasr al Jazeera and Omar Khayam in Benghazi. Elsewhere there are hotels in Al Bayda, Cyrene (Shahat), Ghadamès, Homs, Sabha, Tobruk and Derna.

RESORTS & EXCURSIONS

The old city in **Tripoli** is a typically picturesque North African jumble of narrow alleyways; photographers are advised not to take pictures of the port. Historical towns worth visiting include **Leptis Magna** which is 120km (75 miles) east of Tripoli, **Cyrene** which is 245km (150 miles) east of Benghazi, **Sabratha** which is 75km (45 miles) west of Tripoli and **Ghadamès**, the 'Pearl of the Desert', which is 800km (500 miles) south of Tripoli, connected by air.

SOCIAL PROFILE

FOOD & DRINK: Since alcohol was banned by the Government in 1969 many restaurants have closed, and those remaining are very expensive. Hotel restaurants, although not particularly good, are therefore often the only eating places. Most restaurants have table service, and although food is traditionally eaten with the right hand only, knives and forks will generally be available. There are no bars.
NIGHTLIFE: All nightclubs have been closed. There are several cinemas in major towns, some showing foreign films. There are no theatres or concert halls.
SHOPPING: *Souks* in the main towns are the workplaces of many weavers, copper-, gold- and silversmiths and leatherworkers. There are numerous other stalls selling a variety of items including spices, metal engravings and various pieces of jewellery.
SPORT: There are good beaches for **swimming** away from the municipal beaches of Tripoli and Benghazi. Facilities for **tennis, golf** and **10-pin bowling** are available in the major cities. Spectator sports include **football** and **horseracing**.
SOCIAL CONVENTIONS: Life in Libya is regulated fairly strictly along socialist/Islamic principles; in general Arab courtesies and social customs prevail and should be respected. Women do not generally attend typical Arab gatherings. See also the *World of Islam* section at the back of the book. In religious buildings and small towns women should dress modestly. Beachwear must only be worn on the beach. Smoking is common and codes of practice concerning smoking are the same as in Europe. **Photography:** Taking photographs of public buildings is prohibited and permission should be sought before taking a person's photograph as, interpreted strictly, the religion of Islam does not allow the human image to be depicted. **Tipping:** A tip of 10-20% is usually included in hotel and restaurant bills. Porters are tipped, but taxi drivers are not.

BUSINESS PROFILE

ECONOMY: 95% of Libya's export earnings come from oil, which has enabled the Qathafi government to finance substantial military expenditure and build up the country's economic infrastructure. The fluctuations in oil prices are thus a major problem for the state's economic planners, who are uncertain as to what revenues will be available from one year to the next. Revenues in 1973 were around US$4 billion, rising to US$21 billion in 1980, but falling to US$5 billion by 1987. Libya now has a substantial external debt, the servicing of which imposes further demands on finance. The domestic economy, previously buoyant, is now showing signs of strain. Nonetheless, sufficient funds were found to complete (in 1991) a major irrigation project – the largest of its type in the world – which will bring water to previously arid areas. The Government has relaxed the previously tight restrictions on private ownership and foreign investment in an effort to stimulate the economy. Libya was a prime mover behind the formation of the Union of the Arab Maghreb. Qathafi has tried similar alliances in the past, mostly out of a desire to promote Pan-Arabism, but on this occasion, economic considerations seem to be more important. Italy and Germany are Libya's major trading partners.
BUSINESS: Shirt sleeves are acceptable business wear in hot weather. Suits and ties are worn for more formal occasions. Most business dealings take place with state organisations and English is often understood. It is, however, government policy for official documents to be in Arabic (or translated into Arabic) and for official business to be conducted in Arabic. Business persons need to be fully prepared for this. Appointments are necessary and business cards are useful, though not widely used. Hours for businesses and Government offices fluctuate considerably, but the working day starts early. **Office hours:** Generally 0700-1400.
COMMERCIAL INFORMATION: The following organisation can offer advice: Tripoli Chamber of Commerce, Industry and Agriculture, PO Box 2321, Sharia al-Fatah September, Tripoli. Tel: (21) 33755. Telex: 20181.

HISTORY & GOVERNMENT

HISTORY: From the 8th century BC onwards (when the region was settled by the Phoenicians) Libya has been conquered and settled several times over. Its archaeological heritage includes both Greek and Roman remains. Present-day Libyans descend almost entirely from the Arabian incursion of the 11th century AD, with a few black Africans from the south and indigenous Berbers in the west. Though traditionally the rural people have been nomadic shepherds, since the discovery of oil there has been a drift into the towns. Once one of Italy's few colonies, Libya was occupied by the British and French during the Second World War. Under United Nations direction, the country was granted full independence in 1951. King Idris became Head of State, pursuing a broadly pro-Western foreign policy while keeping up cordial relations with other Arab states. During the 1950s and 1960s, major discoveries of oil, with consequent benefits for state finances, greatly improved the economic prospects of the country. In 1969, the military coup occurred which not only radically altered Libyan politics, but brought the country to world attention. The coup was the last of the wave of Nasserite revolutions which had swept the Arab world over the previous years. The country was taken over by a Revolutionary Command Council, led by Colonel Muammar al-Qathafi. After several unsuccessful attempts to forge the Pan-Arab unity that had eluded other adherents of Nasser's political philosophy, Qathafi embarked on the *Green Revolution*, a process which transformed Libya from top to bottom into a state where all local and regional administration was devolved to a set of representative congresses and committees. The objective was the creation of a *Jamahiriya* (see below). An Islamic code of justice, less severe than those since adopted by Muslim fundamentalist regimes, was introduced and still operates. Qathafi's takeover was not immediately opposed by Western governments, who were used to Nasserite rhetoric and believed that in practice an accommodation could be reached with the new regime. The turning point came in 1973 with the nationalisation of the oil industry, including the Libyan operations of foreign multinationals, followed by the oil crisis of the same year in which Libya played a key role. Since then Libya – and Qathafi especially – has become a particular bugbear of the West, due to Qathafi's uncompromising revolutionary stance and idealistic behaviour, and the Libyan government's alleged political and practical support for a variety of revolutionary and terrorist groups. More recently the Libyan policy of murdering exiled opponents of the regime has worsened relations still further. The former Soviet Union, once Libya's principal arms supplier, found Qathafi no easier to deal with than did the British or Americans. Despite regular external efforts to destabilise it, the regime faces little internal opposition: the Libyan people have obtained real material benefits under Qathafi and take a certain pride in the fact that their previously anonymous country is the subject of regular world attention and even military attack from the United States. If there is any threat to Qathafi, it is likely to come from radical elements in the armed forces rather than the somewhat disorganised array of pro-Western opponents in exile in the United States, Western Europe and Egypt. Nevertheless, the United States has made frequent efforts to topple him, as shown most spectacularly in the bombing of Tripoli in 1986, although Qathafi managed to turn it into a propaganda victory. Libya has subsequently pursued a more quiescent foreign policy, although there has been rumoured backing of one faction in the Liberian civil war and of opponents of the Sudanese military government. Diplomatic relations with Egypt have been resumed after a long freeze; the road between the two countries has been re-opened and Qathafi visited Cairo at President Mubarak's personal invitation in October 1991. Libya is a member of the Union of the Arab Maghreb, formed in February 1989 and conceived as a political and economic bloc analogous to the European Community. Relations with the West have experienced little improvement, however, despite a diplomatic offensive by Tripoli during 1990 and 1991. Despite the urging of its Mediterranean members, the EC has refused to lift economic sanctions against Libya. In November 1991, Britain and the USA publicly accused Libyan intelligence of being responsible for the bombing of an airborne American airliner over the Scottish town of Lockerbie in December 1988. This is a complicated story, with many unexplained and contradictory features, but the unequivocal blaming of Libya for the attack quickly reduced the argument to a simple matter of whether or not the Libyans would hand over two named suspects for trial in either the United States or Scotland. When the Libyans did not comply, the Western powers secured the endorsement of the UN Security Council to impose limited economic sanctions against Libya. Recent attempts to resolve the dispute have revolved around the delivery of the two suspects to a neutral third country, but at the moment it seems that nothing short of full compliance will satisfy London and Washington. The Lockerbie dispute has stalled Qathafi's efforts to rehabilitate Libya – by, for example, providing details to the British of Libyan support for the IRA – and gain international respectability. For reasons that remain somewhat obscure, Qathafi has renounced Pan-Arabism, after years of support, as well as 'terrorism'. The never-ending twists and turns in Libyan policy mean that as long as Qathafi is at the helm, foreign governments will never be entirely trusting.
GOVERNMENT: Since 1977 Libya has officially been a *Jamahiriya* – a 'state of the masses' – in which all political power is devolved to a network of local and regional People's Committees, Basic Peoples' Congresses and Revolutionary Committees. Muammar al-Qathafi holds the title of Leader of the Revolution and, despite the formal structure of government, retains an effective power of veto and, along with his colleagues in the Revolutionary Command Council (as was), keeps control over defence and foreign policy.

CLIMATE

Mediterranean climate with almost constant sun and little rainfall (November to February). Summers are hot and winters mild with cooler evenings. The desert has hot days and cold nights.
Required clothing: Lightweights are worn, with warmer clothes needed for winter days by the coast and cold desert nights. Rainwear is advisable during winter in the coastal zone.

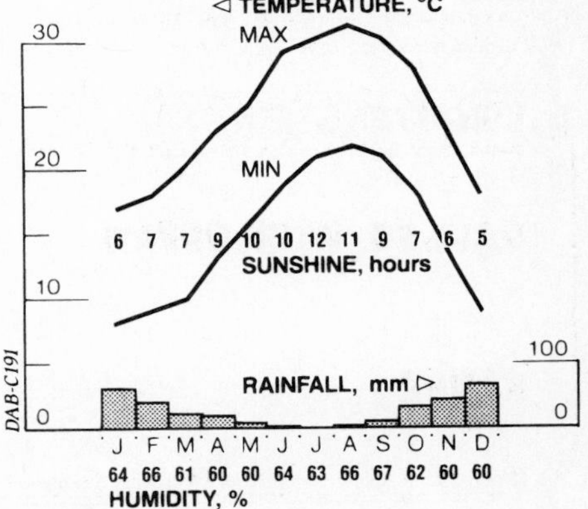

LIECHTENSTEIN

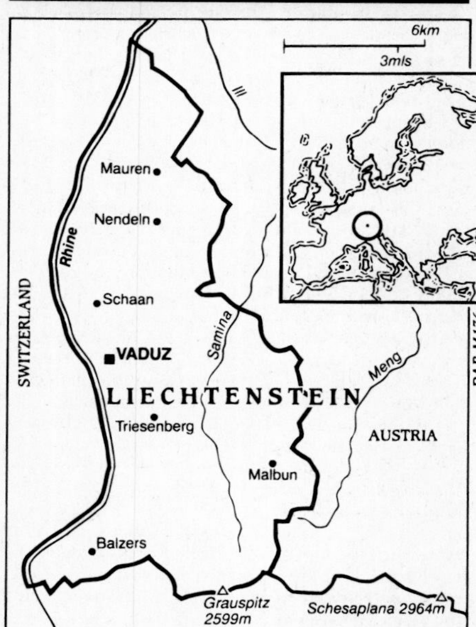

Location: Western Europe.

Note: Liechtenstein maintains very few overseas missions and is generally represented by Switzerland. Addresses of Swiss missions may be found in the *Switzerland* entry below.

Liechtenstein National Tourist Office
Postfach 139
Kirchstrasse 10
FL-9490 Vaduz
Liechtenstein
Tel: 232 1443. Fax: 232 0806. Telex: 889488.

Swiss National Tourist Office
Swiss Centre
Swiss Court
London W1V 8EE
Tel: (071) 734 1921 (general enquiries) *or* (071) 734 4577 (trade only). Fax: (071) 437 4577. Opening hours: 0900-1700 Monday to Friday.

British Consulate General
Dufourstrasse 56
CH-8008 Zurich
Switzerland
Tel: (1) 261 15 20. Fax: (1) 252 83 51. Telex: 816467 UKZUR CH.
Deals with enquiries relating to Liechtenstein.

Consulate General of the United States of America
Zollikerstrasse 141
CH-8008 Zurich
Switzerland
Tel: (1) 422 2566. Fax: (1) 383 9814. Telex: 816830.
Deals with enquiries relating to Liechtenstein.

Canadian Embassy
PO Box 3000
Kirchenfeldstrasse 88
CH-3005 Berne
Switzerland
Tel: (31) 446 381/5. Fax: (31) 447 315. Telex: 911308.
Deals with enquiries relating to Liechtenstein.

AREA: 160 sq km (61.8 sq miles).
POPULATION: 29,400 (1991 estimate).
POPULATION DENSITY: 183.8 per sq km.
CAPITAL: Vaduz. **Population:** 5000 (1991).
GEOGRAPHY: Liechtenstein shares borders with Austria and Switzerland and lies between the upper reaches of the Rhine Valley and the Austrian Alps. The principality is noted for its fine vineyards.
LANGUAGE: German; a dialect of Alemannish is widely spoken. English is also spoken.
RELIGION: Christian, predominantly Roman Catholic.
TIME: GMT + 1 (GMT + 2 in summer).
ELECTRICITY: 220 volts AC, 50Hz.
COMMUNICATIONS: Telephone: Full IDD service. Country code: 41 75. **Fax:** Most hotels have facilities. **Telex/telegram:** Telecommunications are available from post offices and hotels. Service is reliable and efficient. **Post:** Post office opening hours 0800-1200 and 1400-1800 Monday to Friday (0800-1800 Monday to Friday and 0800-1100 Saturday in Vaduz), and 0800-1200 Saturday. No extra charge is made for letters sent by airmail within Europe. Post to European destinations takes three to four days. **Press:** There are two daily newspapers, *Liechtensteiner Vaterland* and *Liechtensteiner Volksblatt*. Neither is printed in English.
BBC World Service and Voice of America frequencies: From time to time these change. See the section *How to Use this Book* for more information.

BBC:

MHz	15.57	12.09	9.750	6.195

A service is also available on 648kHz and 198kHz (0100-0500 GMT).

Voice of America:

MHz	9.670	6.040	5.995	1.197

PASSPORT/VISA

The passport and visa requirements for persons visiting Liechtenstein are the same as for Switzerland. For further details, see the entry *Switzerland* below.

MONEY

Currency: Swiss Franc (SFr) = 100 centimes. Notes are in denominations of SFr1000, 500, 100, 50, 20 and 10. Coins are in denominations of SFr5, 2 and 1, and 50, 20, 10 and 5 centimes. The principality of Liechtenstein belongs to the Swiss monetary area.
Credit cards: All major credit cards are accepted, American Express being particularly useful.
Travellers cheques: Widely accepted.
Exchange rate indicators: The following figures are included as a guide to the movements of the Swiss Franc against Sterling and the US Dollar:

Date:	Oct '89	Oct '90	Oct '91	Oct '92
£1.00=	2.60	2.52	2.55	2.17
$1.00=	1.65	1.29	1.47	1.37

Currency restrictions: There are no restrictions on the import and export of either local or foreign currency.
Banking hours: 0800-1200 and 1330-1630 Monday to Friday.

DUTY FREE

The customs regulations for persons visiting Liechtenstein are the same as for Switzerland. For further details, see the entry *Switzerland* below.

PUBLIC HOLIDAYS

Public holidays observed in Liechtenstein are as follows:
Mar 19 '93 St Joseph's Day. **Apr 9** Good Friday. **Apr 12** Easter Monday. **May 1** Labour Day. **May 20** Ascension. **May 31** Whit Monday. **Jun 10** Corpus Christi. **Aug 15** National Holiday. **Sep 8** Nativity of the Virgin Mary. **Nov 1** All Saints' Day. **Dec 8** Immaculate Conception. **Dec 25** Christmas. **Jan 1 '94** New Year's Day. **Jan 6** Epiphany. **Feb 15** Shrove Tuesday. **Mar 19** St Joseph's Day.

HEALTH

Regulations and requirements may be subject to change at short notice, ar you are advised to contact your doctor well in advance of your intended da of departure. Any numbers in the chart refer to the footnotes below.

	Special Precautions?	Certificate Required?
Yellow Fever	No	No
Cholera	No	No
Typhoid & Polio	No	-
Malaria	No	-
Food & Drink	No	-

Rabies is present. For those at high risk, vaccination before arrival should be considered. If you are bitten abroad seek medical advice without delay. For more information consult the *Health* section at the back of the book.
Health care: Health insurance is recommended. Medical facilities are scarce, but of a high standard.

TRAVEL

AIR: Approximate flight time: From *London* to Zurich is 1 hour 30 minutes. For further details see entry for *Switzerland*.
International airport: The nearest international airport (anc the most convenient for travel from the UK) is *Zurich (Kloten)*, at a distance of approximately 120km (73 miles). Travel to Liechtenstein can then be continued by rail, bus o road. An autoroute connects Zurich with Liechtenstein (firs exit: Balzers). Cars can be hired through agencies at the airport for this journey, and in Liechtenstein.
RAIL: The best rail access is via the Swiss border stations at Buchs (SG) or Sargans (easier and closer when coming from Zurich) or the Austrian station at Feldkirch. All are well served by express trains and connected with Vaduz by bus. From Buchs it takes only 15 minutes by bus or 10 minutes by taxi.
ROAD: An autoroute (N13) runs along Liechtenstein's Rhine frontier to Lake Constance, Austria and Germany in the north, and southwards past Chur towards St Moritz. To the west there are autoroutes to Zurich, Bern and Basel. **Bus:** Local buses operate between all 11 villages, and to the Liechtenstein alpine area. **Documentation:** A national driving licence is sufficient.
JOURNEY TIMES: The following chart gives approximate journey times (in hours and minutes) from Vaduz to major cities in Europe.

	Road	Rail
Zurich	1.30	1.30
Geneva	4.00	6.00
Munich	3.00	4.30
Frankfurt/M	5.30	7.30
Milan	3.30	5.00
Paris	10.00	9.00

ACCOMMODATION

HOTELS/GUEST-HOUSES: Until recently, with few notable exceptions, the best hotels (although none of deluxe standard) were in or near Vaduz, but new establishments have now been built along the Rhine Valley and among the mountains. There are 47 hotels and guest-houses in Liechtenstein, with approximately 1400 beds in total. Eight hotels have an indoor swimming pool. In the alpine region, there are around 50 chalets and other self-catering establishments. About 150 establishments belong to the Liechtensteiner Gastgewerbeverband, Hotel Kulm, Dorfzentrum, FL-9497 Triesenberg. Tel: 262 8777. Fax: 268 2861.
INNS: A Liechtenstein speciality is the mountain inn. All are at least 1200m (4000ft) up, but easily accessible by car. They are ideal for those seeking peace and quiet and clean air. Some of these inns have recently been enlarged and modernised.
ALPINE HUTS: There are alpine huts at Gafadura, 1428m (4284ft) high, which accommodate 550 and at Bettlerjoch Pfälzer-Hütte, 2111m (6333ft) high, which accommodates 100.

LIECHTENSTEIN | **HEALTH REGULATIONS** | **VISA REGULATIONS** | Code-Link

GALILEO/WORLDSPAN

TI-DFT/ZRH/HE

TI-DFT/ZRH/VI

SABRE

TIDFT/ZRH/HE

TIDFT/ZRH/VI

To access this information on your CRS, swipe the barcode with a light pen or type in the text under the barcode. For more information, see the introduction *How to Use This Book*.

CAMPSITES: Mittagspitze, FL-9495 Triesen (tel: 392 2686 or 392 3677; fax: 392 3680) and Bendern, FL-9487 Bendern (tel: 373 1211).
HOLIDAY APARTMENTS/CHALETS: Contact the local tourist office in Malbun, Triesenberg or Vaduz for information.
YOUTH HOSTELS: Liechtenstein's only youth hostel is between Schaan and Vaduz, 500m (150ft) away from the main road. It has sleeping accommodation for 96 (12 rooms with 6 beds, 4 rooms with 4 beds and 4 rooms with 2 beds).

RESORTS & EXCURSIONS

The Principality of Liechtenstein covers both lowlands – including part of the fertile Rhine Valley and the steep western slope of the Three Sisters massif – and mountains. The latter are in the eastern part of the country and are accessible through three high valleys, the best known being that of Malbun, Liechtenstein's premier ski resort (see below).
RESORTS: Vaduz, Triesen, Balzers, Triesenberg, Planken, Schaan, Eschen, Mauren, Gamprin, Schellenberg, Ruggell, Malbun Steg.
The **winter sports** area is concentrated around Malbun at 1600m (5250ft) and Steg at 1300m (4250ft). At Malbun there are two chair lifts, four ski lifts and a natural ice rink. Steg has become famous for its popular cross-country skiing loop with three distances – 4km, 6km, 10.5km – which is also equipped for use at night. Steg also has a ski lift and sledge-run.
EXCURSIONS: In summer, hikers and ramblers may wish to explore Liechtenstein's vineyards, forests and nature reserves. The principality's mountains attract climbers of all abilities. For the less energetic, there are several sites of interest to the tourist. In the capital, **Vaduz**, visit the *Art Collection of the Principality*, *Postage Stamp Museum* and the *National Library*. The *National Museum* in Vaduz is temporarily closed for renovation, but may re-open by the end of 1993. There are local museums in **Triesenberg, Balzers** and **Schaan**. Also worth a visit are the theatre at **Schaan**; the *Gutenberg Castle* and *St Peter's Chapel* at **Balzers**; the *St Mamerten* and *Maria Chapels* and the old part of the village in **Triesen**; Roman excavations and the *St Maria zum Trost Chapel* in **Schaan**; the *Chapel of St Joseph* in **Planken**; Roman excavations at **Eschen-Nendeln**; parish churches in **Mauren, Bendern** and **Ruggell**; and the ruins of the upper and lower **Burg Schellenberg**.

SOCIAL PROFILE

FOOD & DRINK: Waiter service is normal in restaurants, cafés and bars. The cuisine is Swiss with Austrian overtones and there are a good number of restaurants. **Drink:** Some extremely good wines are produced in Liechtenstein, particularly *Vaduzer* (red wine). All internationally known beverages are obtainable. There are strict laws against drinking and driving.
NIGHTLIFE: There are cinemas at Vaduz and Balzers. Dancers congregate at the Maschlina-Bar in Triesen; Tiffany in Eschen; Derby in Schaanwald; Roxy, Trailer and Römerkeller at Balzers and Turna in Malbun.
SHOPPING: Prices and the range of goods are the same as Switzerland. Apart from the usual souvenirs, there are attractive dolls in local costumes, handmade ceramics, pottery, and Liechtenstein postage stamps. **Shopping hours:** Generally 0800-1200 and 1330-1630 Monday to Friday, and 0800-1600 Saturday. From April to October souvenir stores in Vaduz are open on Sundays and holidays.
SPORT: Several hotels have indoor **swimming** pools. **Bowling** is a popular sport, catered for in several hotels. **Winter sports:** Excellent facilities. Main resorts include Malbun and Steg. Malbun is gaining popularity on the international **skiing** circuit for its varied facilities, and is a particularly good resort for beginners. Steg has particularly good **cross-country skiing**. In the summer, all the resorts are good starting points for **walking** tours. Gaflei at 1500m (4920ft) is the starting point for the *Fürstensteig*, a path along the high ridge dividing the Rhine and Samina valleys.
SPECIAL EVENTS: The following are the two most important special events to be celebrated in Liechtenstein in 1993. For a list of all festivals scheduled for 1993/4, contact the Swiss Tourist Board.
Jul 4-24 '93 *International Master Courses in Music*, with various concerts, Vaduz. **Aug 15** *National Holiday Celebrations* (with fireworks), Vaduz.
SOCIAL CONVENTIONS: These are the same as those for the rest of northwest Europe. Regulations concerning smoking are becoming increasingly strict. **Tipping:** 15% service charge will be included in most bills, but additional tips for extra services are expected. Taxis will indicate if service has not been included. Tipping of servants in private houses is expected.

BUSINESS PROFILE

ECONOMY: Manufacturing industry has developed rapidly since the Second World War, before which the economy was predominantly agricultural. Metals, machine tools and precision instruments form the bulk of Liechtenstein's exports. These used to be sent out through Switzerland, which handles Liechtenstein's external interests on behalf of the Government, but an increasing number of firms are now exporting directly from Liechtenstein. The fastest-growing sector of the economy is in financial services: 25,000 foreign corporations have taken advantage of the strict laws on banking secrecy to establish nominee companies which pay no tax on either incomes or profits. The country's authorities have realised, however, that they will need to introduce monitoring mechanisms in the near future to bring Liechtenstein into line with other Western European states, including Switzerland. With a very small domestic market, Liechtenstein has a large balance of payments surplus. Liechtenstein joined the European Free Trade Area (EFTA) in 1991. Exports are divided between other EFTA members, the EC and other countries.
BUSINESS: Personal visits and the following of all business formalities are very important. Times to avoid business visits are over Easter, the second half of July and August, and the week before Christmas. **Office hours:** Generally 0800-1200 and 1400-1800 Monday to Friday. Often, however, lunchtime is shorter and closing is therefore earlier.
COMMERCIAL INFORMATION: The following organisation can offer advice: Liechtenstein Industrie- und Handelskammer (Chamber of Industry and Commerce), Postfach 232, Josef Rheinberger-Strasse 11, FL-9490 Vaduz. Tel: 232 2744. Fax: 233 1503.
CONFERENCES/CONVENTIONS: Although there is no conference asssociation in Liechtenstein a number of hotels have conference facilities and can organise conventions: *Löwen and Schlössle* in Vaduz, *Meierhof* in Triesen, *Kulm* in Triesenberg, *Gorfion* and *Malbuner-Hof* in Malbun/Triesenberg.

HISTORY & GOVERNMENT

HISTORY: The last remnant of the Holy Roman Empire, the pocket-size Principality of Liechtenstein is a prosperous, independent, hereditary monarchy. Liechtenstein's ruler of 51 years, until his death in November 1989, was His Highness Franz Joseph II. His son and heir, Prince Hans Adam (now His Highness Hans Adam II) was granted all the Regency's executive powers in 1984. The country is united with Switzerland in a Customs Union and represented by Switzerland abroad. The population shares German-Swiss traditions, values, social courtesies and behaviour, but remain proud of their independent status. From 1928 until 1970 the Progressive Citizens' Party (FPB) was the dominant political party in the country before the Fatherland Party (VU) took power in the 1970 election. The VU has held a majority in the Landtag, the Liechtenstein parliament, since then. Women, who make up two-thirds of the electorate, were debarred from voting until 1984, and were able to vote for the first time in the election of 1986. For the following election, held in March 1989, the number of seats in the Landtag was increased from 15 to 25, and the VU achieved a majority of just one seat. As a member of the European Free Trade Association (EFTA), Liechtenstein is due to join the European Economic Area creating a free trade area from the combined membership of the European Community and EFTA.
GOVERNMENT: The single-chamber assembly, the *Landtag*, has 25 members elected every four years by proportional representation. The Sovereign is Head of State.

CLIMATE

The climate is temperate, with warm, wet summers and cool to cold winters.
Required clothing: Mediumweights with some lightweight clothing is advised for summer. Heavyweights are worn in winter. Waterproofing is needed throughout the year.

ZURICH Switzerland (569m)

SUNSHINE, hours
1 3 5 6 7 7 8 7 6 3 2 1
TEMPERATURE, °C
MAX
MIN
RAINFALL, mm
J F M A M J J A S O N D
81 77 71 66 66 66 67 69 74 78 82 83
HUMIDITY, %
DAB-C298

LITHUANIA

Location: Northern Europe.

The Lithuania Travel Company
Ukmerges 20
232600 Vilnius, Lithuania
Tel: (122) 356 526. Fax: (122) 356 270.
Embassy of the Republic of Lithuania
17 Essex Villas
London W8 7BP
Tel: (071) 938 2481. Fax: (071) 938 3329. Opening hours: 1000-1730 Monday to Friday.
Lithuania House
2 Ladbroke Gardens
London W11 2PT
Tel: (071) 727 2470. Fax: (071) 992 8456. Opening hours: 1130-1430 and 1700-2300 Monday to Friday.
British Embassy
2 Antakalnio Gatve
2055 Vilnius 55, Lithuania
Tel: (122) 222 070/1. Fax: (122) 357 579 or (010 871) 144 5164 (satellite link). Telex: 1445165.
Embassy of the Republic of Lithuania
2622 16th Street, NW
Washington, DC
20009
Tel: (202) 234 5860 or 234 2639. Fax: (202) 328 0466.
Embassy of the United States of America
Akmenu 6
232600 Vilnius, Lithuania
Tel: (122) 222 724. Fax: (122) 222 779.
Lithuania falls under the jurisdiction of the Canadian Embassy in Stockholm, Sweden.

AREA: 65,200 sq km (25,173 sq miles).
POPULATION: 3,739,000 (1991 estimate).
POPULATION DENSITY: 57.3 per sq km.
CAPITAL: Vilnius. **Population:** 592,500 (1990).
GEOGRAPHY: Lithuania is situated on the Baltic coast and borders Latvia in the north, the Kaliningrad region of the CIS and Poland in the southwest and Belarus in the southeast. The geometrical centre of Europe lies in Eastern Lithuania near the village of Bernotai, 25km (40 miles) north of Vilnius. The landscape alternates between lowland plains and hilly uplands and has a dense, intricate network of rivers, including the Nemunas and the Neris. 1.5% of the country's territory is made up of lakes, the majority of which lie in the north of the Baltic highlands and include Lake Druksiai and Lake Tauragnas.
LANGUAGE: Lithuanian is the official language. Lithuanian has a large number of dialects for such a small territory, including High Lithuanian (*Aukstaiciai*) and Low Lithuanian (*Zemaiciai*). Since independence the indiscriminate use of Russian can cause offence. English should be used if unsure.
RELIGION: Predominantly Roman Catholic with a minority of Evangelical Lutherans and Evangelical Reformists.

TIME: GMT + 2 (GMT + 3 in summer).
ELECTRICITY: 220 volts AC, 50Hz. European 2-pin plugs are in use.
COMMUNICATIONS: Telephone: IDD is available. IDD code: 70 (122 for Vilnius). **Fax:** A fax service is available at the Foreign Tourists Service Bureau at the Hotel Lietuva, Ukmerges 20, Vilnius. Tel: (122) 356 074. **Post:** Post to Western Europe takes up to six days. The central post office is at Gedimino pr. 7, Vilnius. Tel: (122) 616 614. **Press:** Newspapers are published in Lithuanian and some in Russian or Polish. The major dailies are *Lietuvos Rytas, Respublika* and *Valstieciu laikrastis. The Baltic Independent* is an English-language weekly covering Estonia, Latvia and Lithuania. For subscriptions, write to: 150 Cranbrook Road, Parkstone, Poole, Dorset BH12 3JB. Tel: (0202) 741 727. Fax: (0202) 715 066.
BBC World Service and Voice of America frequencies: From time to time these change. See the section *How to Use this Book* for more information.

BBC:				
MHz	12.10	9.410	7.120	3.955
Voice of America:				
MHz	11.97	9.670	6.040	5.995

PASSPORT/VISA

Regulations and requirements may be subject to change at short notice, and you are advised to contact the appropriate diplomatic or consular authority before finalising travel arrangements. Details of these may be found at the head of this country's entry. Any numbers in the chart refer to the footnotes below.

	Passport Required?	Visa Required?	Return Ticket Required?
Full British	Yes	No	Yes
BVP	Not valid	-	-
Australian	Yes	Yes	Yes
Canadian	Yes	Yes	Yes
USA	Yes	Yes	Yes
Other EC	Yes	1	Yes
Japanese	Yes	Yes	Yes

PASSPORT: Required by all.
British Visitors Passport: Not accepted.
VISA: The situation is still changing regarding visa requirements. At present, a visa is required by all except:
(a) **[1]** nationals of Denmark and the UK (other EC nationals *do* need a visa);
(b) nationals of Bulgaria, the CIS, Czech Republic, Estonia, Hungary, Latvia, Poland and Slovak Republic.
However, when travelling on a direct flight or sea crossing, a 7-day visa will be issued for a higher fee upon entry. Visas issued for Lithuania are also valid for Estonia and Latvia. For the latest information contact the Embassy *at least 3 weeks* before travelling.
Note: Nationals of countries where Lithuanian as yet has no representation can obtain a visa upon entry without paying the higher fee.
Types of visa: Single- and Multiple-entry.
Validity: *Single-entry:* 1 month; *Multiple-entry:* 1 year. Cost – £10.
Application to: Consulate (or Consular Section of Embassy). For addresses, see top of entry.
Application requirements: (a) Passport. (b) 2 passport-size photos. (c) 2 completed application forms. (d) Letter stating reason of travel and length of stay. (e) Fee. (f) If applying by post, stamped self-addressed envelope.
Working days required: 3 days. Visas can be obtained in 1 day at a cost of £20.

MONEY

Currency: Currently a transition currency, the Talonas, is in circulation. The Talonas is at parity with the Rouble. A Lithuanian currency is due to be introduced in 1993: **Lita = 100 centu.** Coins are in denominations of 5, 2 and 1 Litas and 50, 20 and 10 centu.
Currency exchange: Currency can be exchanged at the Hotel Lietuva, Ukmerges 20, Vilnius (tel: (122) 356 074), where daily exchange rates are posted. Currency can also be exchanged in Kaunus and Klaipeda.
Currency restrictions: The import of foreign currency is unlimited, but must be declared on arrival. The export is limited to the amount declared.

DUTY FREE

The following goods may be imported into Lithuania without incurring customs duty:
1 litre of spirits or 2 litres of wine;
250 cigarettes or 250g tobacco.

PUBLIC HOLIDAYS

Public holidays observed in Lithuania are as follows:
Apr 12 '93 Easter Monday. **May 2** Mothers' Day. **Jul 6** Anniversary of Mindaugas Coronation (Day of Statehood). **Nov 1** All Saints' Day. **Dec 25-26** Christmas. **Jan 1 '94** New Year's Day. **Feb 16** Restoration of Lithuanian Statehood (1918).

HEALTH

Regulations and requirements may be subject to change at short notice, and you are advised to contact your doctor well in advance of your intended date of departure. Any numbers in the chart refer to the footnotes below.

	Special Precautions?	Certificate Required?
Yellow Fever	No	No
Cholera	No	No
Typhoid & Polio	No	-
Malaria	No	-
Food & Drink	No	-

Rabies is present. For those at high risk, vaccination before arrival should be considered. If you are bitten abroad seek medical advice without delay. For more information consult the *Health* section at the back of the book.
Health care: Health insurance is recommended. In the event of an accident tourists were previously entitled to free medical aid, though as the health sector is currently restructured this can not now be guaranteed.

TRAVEL - International

AIR: The national airline is *Lithuanian Airlines (TE)*. Other airlines offering connections to Vilnius are *Lufthansa* (three times a week via Frankfurt/M) and *Hamburg Airlines* (twice a week from Hamburg via Berlin). *Austrian Airlines* has two direct and two indirect flights a week from Vienna (via Copenhagen). *Swiss Air* flies twice a week non-stop from Zurich.
Approximate flight times: From *London* to Vilnius takes 4 hours 30 minutes (via Frankfurt/M) and from *Berlin* takes 2 hours 30 minutes.
International airport: *Vilnius Airport (VNO)* is situated approximately 10km (6 miles) from the city centre.
SEA: There is a daily ferry service from Mukran near Saßnitz on the island of Rügen (Germany) to Klaipeda on the Baltic coast of Lithuania. The journey takes approximately 20 hours and reservations are recommended. For further information, contact *Deutsche Seereederei Rostock (DSR)*, Saßnitz on Rügen (tel: (38392) 45221). Klaipeda is the only naturally ice-free port on the Baltic coast other than Kaliningrad and other sea routes link the town with 200 foreign ports.
RAIL: Lithuania has a well-developed rail network and Vilnius is the focal point for rail connections in the region. Major routes go to Riga (Latvia), Minsk (Belarus) and Kaliningrad (Russian Federation). There are also direct links to Grodno (Belarus) and Warsaw (Poland). A daily sleeper train connects Berlin-Lichtenberg with Vilnius via Warsaw and Grodno.
ROAD: Lithuania has a good network of roads connecting the country with all the neighbouring republics. The border points are as follows: Terespol (Poland)–Brest (Belarus) and Ogrodniki (Poland)–Lazdijai (Lithuania).

TRAVEL - Internal

AIR: There are domestic airports at Kaunus, Palanga and Siauliai.
RAIL: There are good connections from Vilnius to Kaunus and to other major centres in the country.
ROAD: There are reasonable road connections from Vilnius to all other major towns within Lithuania. Foreign currency and credit cards are accepted at petrol stations, though fuel shortages are not uncommon. Lead-free petrol is available at Marijampolè at the M12. **Car hire:** Self-drive cars can be arranged through several national and, increasingly, international firms. **Traffic regulations:** Seat belts must be worn. The speed limit on country lanes is 80kmph and 50kmph inside towns. **Documentation:** European nationals should be in possession of the new European driving licence.
URBAN: Public transport in urban districts includes buses and trolley-buses, which run from 0600-0100. Transport coupons are bought at news kiosks before boarding either the bus or trolley-bus. **Taxis** display green illuminated signs and can be hailed in the street or found at taxi ranks. Private taxis display checkered signs.

ACCOMMODATION

HOTELS: Since independence, Western-style hotels and motels are being built in Lithuania in cooperation with foreign firms. Several joint ventures with American and European partners will provide accommodation with Western-style comfort. Modernisation and renovation programmes are presently concentrated in the capital. The 3-star *Hotel Lietuva* has 400 rooms and is near the city centre. Meanwhile Vilnius and the other major centres in the country enjoy an adequate range of good accommodation including large hotels and smaller pensions. A star grading system is in force. For more details contact Lithuania House or the Lithuanian Travel Company (see addresses at the beginning of this entry).
CAMPING: A campsite is to be opened at Traikai near Vilnius.

RESORTS & EXCURSIONS

The historic city of **Vilnius** is the capital of Lithuania. Surrounded on three sides by wooded hills and divided in two by the *River Neris*, the ancient and modern centre of the city lies on the southern or left bank of the river. Unlike Tallinn and Riga in the other Baltic republics, Vilnius is not of Germanic origin, although like these other cities it has a large old quarter which is gradually being restored. The architecture is a mix of various western European styles although Italian influences predominate. The heart of the capital is the beautiful and spacious *Gediminas Square*, the main feature of which is the *Cathedral*

LITHUANIA	**HEALTH REGULATIONS**	**VISA REGULATIONS** Code-Link
 **GALILEO/WORLDSPAN**	 TI-DFT/KUN/HE	 TI-DFT/KUN/VI
SABRE	 TIDFT/KUN/HE	 TIDFT/KUN/VI

To access this information on your CRS, swipe the barcode with a light pen or type in the text under the barcode. For more information, see the introduction *How to Use This Book*.

built in the Classical style. Although this was for years used as a picture gallery, it was returned three years ago to the Roman Catholic Church. Another interesting church is the *St Peter and St Paul* which houses the body of St Casimir, one of the most revered of Lithuania's princes. Any itinerary of the city should include the historic *University of Vilnius*, which was founded in the 16th century, the Golden Age in the city's history. Granted its charter in 1579, the university is among the oldest universities in Europe and has a distinctly Renaissance feel with its inner courtyards and arcades. To enjoy a view of the whole city visitors should climb the tower of *Gediminas Castle*. High on a hill in the centre of the city it rises above Vilnius and is the symbol of the Lithuanian capital.
About 25km (18 miles) from Vilnius lies **Trakai**, an ancient capital of Lithuania. Situated on the shore of the picturesque *Lake Galve*, on which boat rides are available, the city has a castle dating from the 14th century. To the west of Vilnius lies the industrial and cultural centre of **Kaunas**, Lithuania's second city. Also known as the 'city of museums' it boasts, amongst others, the *Museum of Devil's Sculptures* and a memorial to those who suffered during the Nazi occupation. Kaunas also numbers three theatres, some 11th-century castle ruins and the old *City Hall* among its attractions. Other places of interest in Lithuania include the small riverside resort of **Druskininkai** situated 135km (84 miles) from Vilnius and the small town of **Rumsiskes**, 80km from Vilnius, with its open-air museum exhibiting farmhouses from all the various regions of the country. Popular seaside resorts include **Palanga** and **Kursiu Nerija,** which are famous for their clean beaches and natural sand dunes, while not far away to the south lies the city of **Klaipeda**, an important seaport as well as the main centre for ferry connections from Lithuania. The two main centres in the north of the country are **Siauliai**, an important industrial city, and **Panevezys** with its famous *Drama Theatre*.

SOCIAL PROFILE

FOOD & DRINK: Hors d'oeuvres are very good and often the best part of the meal. Local specialities include *skilandis* (a snack meat), *salti barsciai* (cold soup), *oepelinai* (dumplings), *vedarai* (potato sausage) and *zeppelins* (made from grated potatoes with minced meat inside). Braised goose stuffed with apples and plums is also a Baltic speciality.
NIGHTLIFE: Opera and ballet are staged in the city at the Vienuolio Theatre.
SHOPPING: Amber, linen goods and local crafts are good buys.
SPORT: Lithuania has extensive sporting facilities including the 15,000-seat *Zalgiris* stadium in Vilnius and facilities for **swimming, football, handball, basketball, tennis** and **ice hockey**.
SPECIAL EVENTS: There are a number of special events in Lithuania. The following is a list of Days to Remember in 1993:
Mar 4 '93 *St Casimir Day* (Patron of Lithuania). **Mar 11** *Independence Day*. **May 2** *International Labour Day*. **May 7** *Press Day*. **Jun 14** *Mourning and Hope Day*. **Jun 24** *Jonine's* (John's) *Day*. **Jul 15** *Battle of Tannenberg Day*. **Aug 23** *Black Ribbon Day*. **Sep 23** *Remembrance Day*. **Sep 8** *Vytautas Coronation Day; St Mary's Birthday*. **Nov 2** *Day for Commemorating the Dead*. **Nov 23** *Soldiers' Day*. **Dec 10** *Human Rights Day*.
For further information, please contact Lithuania House (for address, see top of entry).
SOCIAL CONVENTIONS: Handshaking is customary. Normal courtesies should be observed. The Lithuanians are proud of their culture and their national heritage and visitors should take care to respect this sense of national identity. **Tipping:** Taxi fares and restaurant bills include a tip.

BUSINESS PROFILE

ECONOMY: Lithuania has historically been the least developed of the Baltic republics with a smaller industrial base and greater dependence on agriculture. Electrical, electronic and optical goods and light machinery are the main industrial products. Food-processing is also an important industry, with an ample supply of agricultural products from Lithuania's own farming and fisheries sector. Lacking any raw materials, Lithuania is totally dependent on imported fuel and energy, a fact which the Kremlin exploited during the economic sanctions imposed in 1989/90. Lithuania's other economic asset is the Baltic's only naturally ice-free port (other than Kaliningrad). Lithuania has agreed, along with nine other countries bordering on the Baltic, to establish a regional co-operation organisation, the Council of Baltic Sea States. The Government has embarked on a series of reforms to introduce a market economy and liberalise foreign trade, although in the early stages extensive government intervention is likely to be needed to ensure the supply of essential goods and maintain economic stability.
BUSINESS: Business is conducted in a fairly formal manner and a smart appearance is important. Appointments should be made in advance. German and French are the most commonly used languages for international commerce, although a knowledge of English is not unusual. **Office hours:** 0900-1800 Monday to Friday.
COMMERCIAL INFORMATION: The following organisations can offer advice: Chamber of Commerce and Industry of the Republic of Lithuania, Algirdo 31, 232600 Vilnius. Tel: (122) 661 450. Fax: (122) 661 550. Telex: 261114; *or*
LITIMPEKS (Lithuanian foreign trade company), Verkiu 37, 232600 Vilnius. Tel: (122) 355 616. Fax: (122) 354 047.

HISTORY & GOVERNMENT

HISTORY: The Lithuanians, along with the Letts and ancient Prussians, are closely related historically to the Slavs. The first recorded Lithuanian state was created in 1293 by an alliance of tribes to meet the threat of the German Knights advancing from the east. Under Grand Duke Gediminas, who is recognised as the founder of Lithuania, the territory was extended during the 14th century southwards to take in Minsk and later as far as the Black Sea. At the Union of Lublin in 1569, a full-scale merger between Lithuania and Poland took place, but the next 150 years showed it was insufficient to protect Lithuania from the territorial ambitions of other regional powers. At the end of the 18th century, Poland was carved up and occupied in successive partitions. Russia took possession of Lithuania in 1795 and held on to it until the early 20th century. The Russians were driven out by the German army in 1915 and, after the Bolshevik revolution brought an end to Russian involvement in the First World War, Lithuania declared independence. In 1921 Lithuania joined the League of Nations. Although the Lithuanians had settled their differences with the Russians, temporarily at least, the Poles continued to occupy Vilnius, the Lithuanian capital, in defiance of Allied demarcation which had awarded the city to the Lithuanians. The capital of the new state was therefore established at Kaunas. The Lithuanian constitution promulgated in 1922 declared Lithuania to be a parliamentary republic with the Sejm as the legislative organ. However, a military coup in December 1926 brought Antanas Smetona to power at the head of an authoritarian regime backed by the nationalist Tautininku movement. The status of Lithuania was again altered following the Nazi-Soviet Pact of 1939, whose secret protocols allowed for a Soviet takeover of all three Baltic republics: Lithuania was occupied by the German Army in 1941 until its re-annexation by the Soviets three years later. The republic underwent some industrialisation and immigration of ethnic Russians between the 1950s and the mid-1980s, though not on the scale experienced by Estonia or Latvia. By the time Mikhail Gorbachev came to power in the Kremlin in 1985, the population still comprised 80-90% ethnic Lithuanians. Pressure for political and economic reform in Lithuania was spearheaded by the Lithuanian Reform Movement, Sajudis, which put forward a programme of democratic and national rights coupled with support for an independent Lithuania. The Lithuanian Communist Party was split between Sajudis supporters – who won a majority on the Lithuanian Supreme Soviet at elections in February/March 1990 – and those who backed the Moscow position asserting the supremacy of the centre. The haste with which the Lithuanians moved to enact their programme (in contrast with the more cautious approach adopted by Estonia and Latvia) provoked the Kremlin into implementing economic sanctions against Lithuania in April 1990: specifically, blocking essential fuel supplies. The embargo lasted until June when the Sajudis leader and chairman of the Supreme Soviet (now effectively the Lithuanian parliament), Vytautas Landsbergis, announced a suspension of the independence declaration. In January 1991, Landsbergis declared that the suspension of independence was at an end. Moscow despatched special forces troops to take control of radio, television and other key installations. The troops were only partially successful and were faced by a mass popular mobilisation, called by Landsbergis. An uneasy stand-off persisted throughout the first half of 1991, punctuated by a referendum on independence which won 90% support, until the failure of the August coup in Moscow which brought an effective end to Soviet government. Lithuanian independence followed immediately, unopposed and by default. The country was internationally recognised and rapidly gained admission to the United Nations, the Conference on Security and Co-operation in Europe and the European Bank for Reconstruction and Development. An attempt to implement price rises at the beginnning of 1991 had already led to the resignation of Lithuania's first Prime Minister, the charismatic Kazimiera Prunskiene, replaced by Gediminas Vagnorius. The transition to a full market economy has now begun. The new government's foreign policy is dominated by relations with its two large neighbours, Russia and Poland. The long-running border dispute with Poland was settled with the signing of a friendship and co-operation treaty in January 1992, and a commitment by Lithuania to safeguard the position of its ethnic Polish minority. Economic problems contributed to the unpopularity of the Government which was surprisingly thrown out at the general election of October 1992 with a return to power for the ex-communist democratic Labour Party. Party leader Algirdas Brazauskas is Lithuainia's new President.
GOVERNMENT: Under the Fundamental Law adopted in March 1990, legislative authority rests with the popularly elected Supreme Council of 141 members. The Head of State chairs the Council and is elected by the body for no more than two terms of fiv years. The Council also elects a Council of Ministers, headed by the Prime Minister, to whom executive powers are granted.

CLIMATE

Temperate climate, but with considerable temperature variations. Summer is warm with relatively mild weather in spring and autumn. Winter, which lasts from November to mid-March, can be very cold. Rainfall is distributed throughout the year with the heaviest rainfall in August. Heavy snowfalls are common in the winter months.

VILNIUS Lithuania (75m)

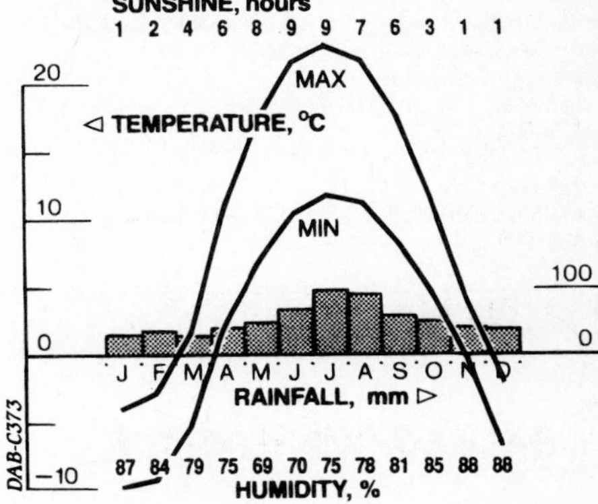

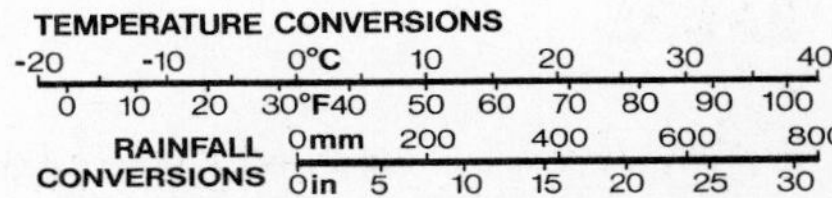

LUXEMBOURG

□ international airport

Location: Western Europe.

Office National du Tourisme
BP 1001, 77 rue d'Anvers
1010 Luxembourg-Ville
Tel: 40 08 08. Fax: 40 47 48. Telex: 2715 ONTOUR.
Embassy of the Grand Duchy of Luxembourg
27 Wilton Crescent
London SW1X 8SD
Tel: (071) 235 6961. Fax: (071) 235 9734. Telex: 28120 AMBLUX. Opening hours: 0900-1300 and 1400-1700 Monday to Friday.
Luxembourg Tourist Office
122 Regent Street
London W1R 5FE
Tel: (071) 434 2800. Fax: (071) 734 1205. Telex: 94016933 LUXT. Opening hours: 0900-1700 Monday to Friday.
British Embassy
BP 874
14 boulevard Roosevelt
L-2018 Luxembourg-Ville
Tel: 22 98 64/5/6. Fax: 22 98 67. Telex: 3443 PRODROLU.
Embassy of the Grand Duchy of Luxembourg
2200 Massachusetts Avenue, NW
Washington, DC
20008
Tel: (202) 265 4171. Fax: (202) 328 8270. Telex: 64130.
Consulates in: Atlanta, Chicago, Fort Worth, Kansas City (Missouri), Los Angeles, Miami, Middletown, New Orleans, New York, Mountain View, Pittsburgh, San Francisco, Seattle and Youngstown.
Luxembourg National Tourist Office
801 Second Avenue
New York, NY
10017
Tel: (212) 370 9850. Fax: (212) 922 1685. Telex: 125778 *or* 620241.

Embassy of the United States of America
22 boulevard E. Servais
2535 Luxembourg-Ville
Tel: 46 01 23. Fax: 46 14 01.
Luxembourg Consulate
3877 Draper Avenue
Montréal, Québec H4A 2N9
Tel: (514) 489 6052.
Consulates also in: Calgary and Vancouver.

AREA: 2586 sq km (999 sq miles).
POPULATION: 384,400 (1990 estimate).
POPULATION DENSITY: 148.6 per sq km.
CAPITAL: Luxembourg-Ville. **Population:** 75,377 (1991).
GEOGRAPHY: Luxembourg shares borders to the north and west with Belgium, to the south with France and to the east with Germany. One-third of the country is made up of the hills and forests of the Ardennes, while the rest is wooded farmland. In the southeast is the rich wine-growing valley of Moselle.
LANGUAGE: The official language is a German-Moselle-Frankish dialect. However, the commercial language, and that of the press, is German. French is also used for administrative purposes. Many Luxembourgers also speak English.
RELIGION: 97% Roman Catholic, 1.2% Protestant, 1.8% others.
TIME: GMT + 1 (GMT + 2 in summer).
ELECTRICITY: 220 volts AC, 50Hz.
COMMUNICATIONS: Telephone: Full IDD is available. Country code: 352 (no area codes). International phones have a yellow sign showing a telephone dial with a receiver in the centre. **Fax:** There is a fax booth at the Luxembourg-Ville main post office. Faxes may be sent to a central number (49 11 75) for delivery by express mail within Luxembourg. **Telegram/telex:** There are facilities at the post office at 25 rue Aldringen, Luxembourg-Ville, and in all major towns. Hotels often allow guests to use their facilities. **Post:** Post to European destinations takes two to four days. There are *Poste Restante* facilities throughout the country. Prospective recipients must first register for a PO Box. Mail will be held for up to one month. Post office hours are generally 0800-1200 and 1330-1700 Monday to Friday. The Luxembourg-Ville main office is open 0700-1900. Smaller offices may open for only a few hours. Telephone 49911 for details. **Press:** There is one English-language newspaper, *The News Digest*. The daily with the highest circulation is the *Luxemburger Wort – La Voix du Luxembourg*.
BBC World Service and Voice of America frequencies: From time to time these change. See the section *How to Use this Book* for more information.

BBC:

MHz	12.10	9.750	6.195	3.955

A service is also available on 648kHz and 198kHz (0100-0500 GMT).

Voice of America:

MHz	11.97	9.670	6.040	5.995

PASSPORT/VISA

Regulations and requirements may be subject to change at short notice, and you are advised to contact the appropriate diplomatic or consular authority before finalising travel arrangements. Details of these may be found at the head of this country's entry. Any numbers in the chart refer to the footnotes below.

	Passport Required?	Visa Required?	Return Ticket Required?
Full British	1	No	Yes
BVP	Valid	-	-
Australian	Yes	No	Yes
Canadian	Yes	No	Yes
USA	Yes	No	Yes
Other EC	1	No	Yes
Japanese	Yes	No	Yes

Note: Proof of adequate finances and return or onward ticket (and visa for country of next destination if needed) are required for all visitors.
PASSPORTS: A valid passport is required by all except:
(a) [1] nationals of EC countries who hold a valid national ID card or, if UK citizens, a BVP;
(b) nationals of Andorra, Austria, Liechtenstein, Malta, Monaco, San Marino and Switzerland, providing they hold a valid national ID card.
British Visitors Passport: A British Visitors Passport is valid for holidays or unpaid business trips to Luxembourg; children under 16 cannot, however, go on their brother's or sister's passport. For further information, see the *Passport/Visa* section of the *Introduction* at the beginning of the book.
Note: 60-hour ID cards are *not* acceptable; in certain circumstances (enquire at Consulate) expired passports may be acceptable as ID cards; and where full national passports are required, they must be valid for at least 3 months after the last day of the intended visit.
VISAS: Required by all except:
(a) nationals of countries referred to in the above chart;
(b) nationals of those countries listed under passport exemptions above;
(c) nationals of Argentina, Australia, Brazil, Brunei, Burkina Faso, Chile, Costa Rica, Cyprus, Czechoslovakia, Ecuador, El Salvador, Finland, Guatemala, Honduras, Hungary, Iceland, Israel, Jamaica, South Korea, Malawi, Malaysia, Mexico, New Zealand, Nicaragua, Niger, Norway, Panama, Paraguay, Poland, Singapore, Sweden, Togo, Uruguay, Vatican City and Venezuela.
Note: Nationals of all republics of the former Yugoslavia now need a visa to enter Liechtenstein.
Types of visa: Tourist and Transit.
Cost and validity: *Tourist visa:* £21 for a stay of up to 1 month; £28 for a stay of up to 3 months; £34 for a stay of up to 12 months or multiple visits. *Transit visa:* £9. Transit visas are valid only for such stops as are necessary for transit; 3 days maximum stay.
Note: As visas will normally be valid for all 3 Benelux countries (Belgium, The Netherlands and Luxembourg), passports or travel documents must also be valid for all 3 countries.
Application to: Consulate (or Consular Section at Embassy). For addresses, see top of entry.
Application requirements: (a) Completed application form. (b) Registered self-addressed envelope for return of visas. (c) 1 photo. (d) Relevant passport or travel document. (e) Fee. (f) Signed declaration stating that visa holder agrees to abide by terms of visa.
Note that in some cases 5 forms and 3 photos will be required. Enquire at Consulate (or Consular Section at Embassy) for further details.
Working days required: Usually within 24 hours or by return of post. Some applications can take up to 3 weeks, including Arab, Chinese, Ghanaian, Mauritian, Pakistani, South African and Sri Lankan and all republics of former Yugoslavia (as well as non-resident Indian and Bangladeshi).
Temporary residence: Enquire about special application procedures at Embassy.

MONEY

Currency: Luxembourg Franc (LFr) = 100 centimes. Notes are in denominations of LFr5000, 1000 and 100. LFr50 and 20 notes have been taken out of circulation. Coins are in denominations of LFr50, 20, 5 and 1, and 25 centimes. The Luxembourg Franc is on a par with the Belgian Franc. However, Luxembourg Francs are not always legal tender in Belgium, whereas Belgian Francs are always accepted in Luxembourg.
Credit cards: Access/Mastercard, American Express, Visa and Diners Club are all widely accepted. Check with your credit card company for details of merchant acceptability and other services which may be available.

LUXEMBOURG | **HEALTH REGULATIONS** | **VISA REGULATIONS** | Code-Link

GALILEO/WORLDSPAN

TI-DFT/LUX/HE

TI-DFT/LUX/VI

SABRE

TIDFT/LUX/HE

TIDFT/LUX/VI

To access this information on your CRS, swipe the barcode with a light pen or type in the text under the barcode. For more information, see the introduction *How to Use This Book*.

Travellers cheques: Widely accepted.
Exchange rate indicators: The following figures are included as a guide to the movements of the Luxembourg Franc against Sterling and the US Dollar:

Date:	Oct '89	Oct '90	Oct '91	Oct '92
£1.00=	62.60	61.25	60.10	50.20
$1.00=	39.65	31.35	34.63	31.63

Currency restrictions: There are no restrictions on the import and export of either local or foreign currency.
Banking hours: Generally 0900-1200 and 1400-1400 Monday to Friday, but may vary greatly.

DUTY FREE

The following goods may be imported into Luxembourg without incurring customs duty by:
(a) travellers arriving from EC countries:
*300 cigarettes or 75 cigars or 150 cigarillos or 400g of tobacco products;**
*1.5 litres of alcohol over 22% proof or 3 litres of alcohol not over 22% proof or 3 litres of sparkling wine;**
*5 litres of table wine;**
1000g of coffee or 400g of coffee extract/essence;
200g of tea or 80g of tea extract/essence;
75g of perfume and 375ml of toilet water;
Other goods to the value of LFr25,000 (LFr6400 for passengers under 15 years of age).
(b) travellers arriving from other European countries and from outside Europe:
*200 cigarettes or 50 cigars or 100 cigarillos or 250g of tobacco products;**
*1 litre of alcohol over 22% proof or 2 litres of alcohol not over 22% proof or 2 litres of sparkling wine;**
*2 litres of table wine;**
50g of perfume and 250ml of toilet water;
500g of coffee or 200g of coffee extract/essence;
100g of tea or 40g of tea extract/essence;
Other goods to the value of LFr2000 (LFr1000 for passengers under 15 years of age).
(c) travellers over 17 years of age arriving from EC countries with duty-paid goods (as of January 1993).
800 cigarettes and 400 cigarillos and 200 cigars and 1kg of tobacco;
90 litres of wine (including up to 60 litres of sparkling wine);
10 litres of spirits;
20 litres of intermediate produ cts (such as fortified wine);
110 litres of beer.
Note [*]: Alcohol and tobacco products are only available to passengers of 17 years of age or over.

PUBLIC HOLIDAYS

Public holidays observed in Luxembourg are as follows:
Apr 12 '93 Easter Monday. **May 1** Labour Day. **May 20** Ascension Day. **May 31** Whit Monday. **Jun 23** National Day. **Aug 15** Assumption Day. **Nov 1** All Saints' Day. **Dec 25** Christmas Day. **Dec 26** St Stephen's Day. **Jan 1 '94** New Year's Day.
Note: A maximum of two official public holidays falling on a Sunday may be deferred to the following Monday. Confirm with the National Tourist Office.

HEALTH

Regulations and requirements may be subject to change at short notice, and you are advised to contact your doctor well in advance of your intended date of departure. Any numbers in the chart refer to the footnotes below.

	Special Precautions?	Certificate Required?
Yellow Fever	No	No
Cholera	No	No
Typhoid & Polio	No	-
Malaria	No	-
Food & Drink	1	-

[1]: Tap water is considered safe to drink. Milk is pasteurised and dairy products are safe for consumption. Local meat, poultry, seafood, fruit and vegetables are generally considered safe to eat.
Rabies is present. For those at high risk, vaccination before arrival should be considered. If you are bitten abroad seek medical advice without delay. For more information consult the *Health* section at the back of the book.
Health care: There are Reciprocal Health Agreements with all other EC member states. UK citizens should obtain form E111 from the Department of Health before travelling. This entitles them to free hospital treatment and a partial refund of other medical and dental treatments. Refunds are paid by the *Caisse National d'Assurance Maladie des Ouvriers*.

TRAVEL - International

AIR: Luxembourg's national airline is *Luxair (LG)*.
Approximate flight time: From *London* to Luxembourg is 1 hour.
International airport: *Luxembourg (LUX)* (Findel) is 7km (4.5 miles) northeast of the city. Airport facilities include an outgoing duty-free shop, car hire (0800-1900), bank/exchange facilities (0800-1230 and 1330-1900) and a tourist information office (1000-1800). Travel time from the airport to the city centre is approximately 20 minutes. Coaches depart for the city every 50 minutes from 0605-2245; returning coaches depart from the city's air terminus at platform 5, Place de la Gare, from 0535-2230. Bus number 9 departs for the city every 40 minutes from 0520-2312; returning buses depart from Neudorf bus station, Place de la Gare, from 0503-2250. Taxis are available.
RAIL: The direct daily rail connection *London*–Victoria–Ostend–Brussels–*Luxembourg* takes about 11 hours if the crossing is by ferry; if the crossing is by jetfoil, the journey takes 8 hours 30 minutes. There are direct train links with principal cities in neighbouring countries. Inter-Rail and Eurailpass are valid.
ROAD: Luxembourg is easily reached from the UK via Belgium or France within a day. Luxembourg-Ville is about 320km (200 miles) from Ostend, and 420km (260 miles) from Boulogne or Calais. Either way, the quickest route is to take the motorway to Brussels then head south through Namur along the E411.
See below for information on **documentation** and **traffic regulations**.

TRAVEL - Internal

RAIL: The efficient rail service is run by *CFL* and is fully integrated with the bus network. Reductions are offered for weekend and holiday return tickets. *CFL* rail services and *CFL/CRL* buses in Luxembourg are covered by the 'Benelux Tourrail' railpass covering Belgium, The Netherlands and Luxembourg. This gives unlimited travel on any five days within a 17-day period throughout the year. There are also single-day tickets which give unlimited travel on all trains/buses, which cost LFr120, and concessions for old age pensioners. *Rail/Coach Rover Tickets* are valid for both networks.
ROAD: As in the rest of Western Europe, there is an excellent network of roads and motorways in Luxembourg. **Bus:** Cross-country buses are punctual and operate between all major towns. **Taxi:** Taxis are metered. There is a minimum charge and a 10% surcharge is applied from 2200-0600. Taxis are plentiful but cannot be hailed in the street. A 15% tip is usual for taxi drivers. **Car hire:** All the main agencies operate in Luxembourg. **Traffic regulations:** The minimum age for driving is 17. It is obligatory to carry LFr600 at all times for the payment of fines; there are stiff drinking/driving spot fines. The wearing of seat belts is compulsory in the front seat and in the back, where seat belts are fitted. Children under 10 years of age must travel on back seats. Motorcyclists must use dipped beam even by day. The speed limit is 60kmph (37mph) in built-up areas, 90kmph (56mph) outside built-up areas, and 120kmph (74mph) on motorways. For more details, contact Automobile Club du Grand-Duché de Luxembourg, 54 Rte de Longwy, Bertrange, Luxembourg-Helfenterbruck. Tel: 45 00 45.
Documentation: Third Party insurance is necessary. A Green Card is not obligatory but is *strongly recommended*. Without it, visitors have only the minimum legal cover in Luxembourg (if they have motor insurance at home). The Green Card tops this up to the level of cover provided by the visitor's domestic policy. A valid national driving licence is sufficient.
URBAN: Luxembourg-Ville has municipal bus services, for which single-journey flat-fare tickets may be purchased; 10-journey tickets are also available, but must be purchased in advance.
JOURNEY TIMES: The following chart gives approximate journey times (in hours and minutes) from Luxembourg-Ville to other major cities/towns in Europe:

	Air	Road	Rail
Amsterdam	0.45	5.30	6.30
Brussels	0.45	2.00	2.30
Frankfurt/M	0.50	2.30	3.30
Paris	1.00	4.00	4.00
London	1.00	*8.00	**8.00
Zurich	1.20	5.00	5.00

Note: [*] Including ferry crossing (via Calais); [**] jetfoil crossing via Ostend.

ACCOMMODATION

HOTELS: For information on hotels in Luxembourg contact the Luxembourg National Tourist Office (which can supply a free national guide) *or* the National Hotel Association to which all hotels in the Grand Duchy belong. Contact: Horesca (Hotel Association), 9 rue des Trévires, L-1025 Bonnevoie. Tel: 48 71 65. Fax: 48 71 56. **Grading:** Luxembourg has a wide range of hotels and has recently adopted the *Benelux* system of classification, in which the standard of the accommodation is indicated by a row of 3-pointed stars from the highest (five stars) to the minimum (one star). However, membership of this scheme is voluntary, and at present only approximately a quarter of hotels have been classified. There may be first-class hotels, therefore, which do not have a classification. *Benelux* star ratings follow the following criteria:
5-star (H5): This is a new category signifying luxury hotel. There are two establishments in this category.
4-star (H4): First-class hotels. 80% of rooms have private bath. Other amenities include night reception and room service. 15% of graded hotels in Luxembourg belong to this category. There are 32 in this category.
3-star (H3): Half of the rooms have private bath. Other amenities include day reception. 29% of graded hotels in Luxembourg belong to this category. There are 49 in this category.
2-star (H2): A quarter of rooms have private bath. Other amenities include a bar. 9% of graded hotels in Luxembourg belong to this category. There are 29 hotels in this grouping.
1-star (H1): Simple hotel. No private baths, but hot and cold water in rooms. Breakfast available. 12% of graded hotels in Luxembourg belong to this category.
HOLIDAY APARTMENTS: A number of holiday flats and chalets are available throughout the country. A free pamphlet giving location and facilities is published by the National Tourist Office.
RESTHOUSES: The *Gîtes d'Etape Luxembourgeois* maintain a series of resthouses and vacation homes throughout the country. Married people are not admitted except as group leaders. For information apply to 'Gîtes d'Etape Luxembourgeois' at 29 rue Michel, Welter, L-2730 Luxembourg-Ville. Tel: 97 21 72.
CAMPING: There are over 120 campsites throughout the country. According to government regulations, campsites are ranged in three different categories and the tariff in each camp is shown at the entrance. The National Tourist Office publishes a free, comprehensive brochure giving all relevant information concerning campsites.
YOUTH HOSTELS: There are youth hostels at Beaufort, Bourglinster, Echternach, Ettelbruck, Grevenmacher, Hollenfels, Lultzhausen, Luxembourg-Ville, Vianden and Wiltz. A *Youth Hostel Guide* may be obtained free of charge from the National Tourist Office in London *or* the Luxembourg Youth Hostels Association, 18 place d'Armes, L-2013 Luxembourg-Ville. Tel: 25588. Fax: 463 987.

RESORTS & EXCURSIONS

Resorts: Luxembourg, Clervaux, Diekirch, Echternach, Esch-sur-Sûre, Remich, Vianden, Wiltz and Mondorf-les-Bains (which has recently been completely revamped with a sports and leisure centre).
Excursions: Museum of Natural History and the Museum of History and Art in *Luxembourg State Museum;* tumulus at **Bill/Mersch**; Roman palace at **Echternach**; *Trevirian Oppidum* (1st century) at **Titelberg**; Gallo-Roman rural sanctuary at **Steinsel;** *Gallo-Roman Villa* at **Mersch**; castles at **Beaufort, Larochette, Bourscheid** and **Vianden**; chair lift, castle and wild boar sanctuary at Vianden; and the *Germano-Luxembourg Natural Park* (daily tours by coach from Luxembourg-Ville bus station).

SOCIAL PROFILE

FOOD & DRINK: Luxembourg cooking combines German heartiness with Franco-Belgian finesse. Local dishes include *carré de porc fumé* (smoked pork and broad beans or sauerkraut – of Teutonic origin), *cochon de lait en gelée* (jellied suckling pig) and *jambon d'Ardennes* (famous smoked Ardennes ham). The preparation of trout, pike and crayfish is excellent, as are the pastries and cakes. *Tarte aux quetsches* is recommended. Delicious desserts are prepared with local liqueurs and some restaurants will make *omelette soufflée au kirsch*. A dash of *quetsch*, *mirabelle* or *kirsch* will be added to babas or fruit cups. Most aspects of restaurants and bars are similar to the rest of Europe. **Drink:** Luxembourg's white Moselle wines resemble those of the Rhine, but are drier than the fruitier wines of the French Moselle. Beer is another speciality and is a traditional industry. Best-known brands are *Mousel, Bofferding, Diekirch, Funck* and *Simon*. There are also many local liqueurs and strong spirits such as *Eau de vie* (45/50% alcohol). The minimum

age for drinking in bars is 17, and anyone younger than 17 must be accompanied by an adult to cafés and bars. Hours are generally from 0700-2400 (weekdays) and until 0300 (weekends and public holidays). Nightclubs are generally open until 0300.
SHOPPING: Special purchases include beautiful porcelain and crystal. Villeroy and Boch crystal factories in Septfontaines are open to visitors. A regional speciality is earthenware pottery from Nospelt, where in August there is a fortnight's exhibition of local work. **Shopping hours:** 0900-1200 and 1400-1800 (closed Monday morning). Some shops open during lunch.
SPORT: Although small, Luxembourg offers the tourist opportunities for **walking tours, riding, tennis** and **golf**, and some **rock climbing, boating** and **water-skiing. Hunting** permits, valid for five days only, are granted to foreigners non-resident in the Grand Duchy and **fishing** licences are issued by the District Commissioners of Luxembourg, Diekirch and Grevenmacher, as well as by different communal administrations.
SPECIAL EVENTS: The following are bank holidays celebrated in 1993. For a complete list of special events contact the National Tourist Office.
Feb 22 '93 *Carnival Monday*. **Sep** *Local Fête* and *Biergerdag*, Luxembourg-Ville. **Nov 2** *All Souls' Day*.
SOCIAL CONVENTIONS: Handshaking is the normal greeting. The code of practice for visiting someone's home is similar to other western European countries: it is acceptable to give gifts if invited for a meal. Casual dress is widely acceptable, but some dining rooms, clubs and social functions will demand formal attire. Evening wear, black tie (for men) is usually specified on invitation if required. Smoking is prohibited where notified and is becoming increasingly unacceptable. **Tipping:** Bills generally include service, but a rounding up is often given. Taxi drivers expect 15% of meter charge.

BUSINESS PROFILE

ECONOMY: Even by Western European standards, Luxembourg is a prosperous country with a high standard of living and virtually no unemployment. Two very different industries – banking and steel – are the mainstays of the economy. Domestically produced iron ore was used for the steel industry until 1981, when mining ceased, since when the steel industry has relied on imported raw materials; nonetheless, having weathered the global downturn in demand for steel and other crises in the industry, this is likely to remain an important economic sector for the time being. Banking is less important as an employer, but more valuable now in its contribution to GNP. The Government is coming under international pressure, however, to relax its strict laws on banking secrecy which have proved so valuable in attracting bankers to the country. The Government will act on this in order to harmonise Luxembourg practice with the rest of the EC, but it has also reinforced a general perception within Luxembourg that the country has replaced over-dependence on steel with over-dependence on financial services (Luxembourg is a major insurance centre as well). With this in mind, the Government is encouraging new industries to set up or develop indigenously in Luxembourg: construction and audio-visual equipment are the most promising candidates at present. Chemicals have performed steadily. Luxembourg also has a healthy agricultural sector which produces potatoes, barley, oats, wheat and fruit. The economy has long been linked with that of Belgium through the Belgo-Luxembourg Economic Union, established in 1921, through a 1958 Treaty of Economic Union, and latterly through the European Community, with whom Luxembourg conducts most of its foreign trade.
BUSINESS: Business persons are expected to wear suits. It is advisable to make prior appointments and business cards are often used. Avoid business visits during Christmas and New Year, Easter week and July and August. **Office hours:** Generally 0830-1200 and 1400-1800 Monday to Friday.
COMMERCIAL INFORMATION: The following organisations can offer advice: British Chamber of Commerce for Belgium and Luxembourg, Britannia House, 30 rue Joseph II, B-1040 Brussels, Belgium. Tel: (2) 219 9000. Fax: (2) 217 6763. Telex: 22703 BRITEM; *or*
Chamber of Commerce, 7 rue Alcide de Gasperi, L-2981 Luxembourg-Kirchberg. Tel: 43 58 53. Fax: 43 83 26. Telex: 60174.
CONFERENCES/CONVENTIONS: The location of the Grand Duchy of Luxembourg at the heart of the EC ensures its status as one of the most popular destinations for conferences and conventions in western Europe. The number of nights spent in Luxembourg for meetings purposes exceeded 5500 in 1988 and this figure is likely to increase steadily in years to come. For further information contact: Luxembourg Congrès, Centre Arsenal, boulevard Royal, L-2420 Luxembourg. Tel: 46 34 34. Fax: 47 40 11.

HISTORY & GOVERNMENT

HISTORY: Luxembourg has historically experienced commercial prosperity as well as regular military incursions and occupations. Having survived the jurisdiction of the old Holy Roman Empire – three of whose rulers in the 14th and 15th centuries were from the House of Luxembourg – Luxembourg owes its continued existence to a mixture of good fortune and good diplomacy, which has prevented it from being permanently absorbed into the territories of its larger neighbours. By the time that Luxembourg's independence was finally confirmed in 1867, however, the Grand Duchy was left with such a tiny territory that its people had to look across its borders for economic survival. This has resulted in a cosmopolitan attitude, which has survived to the present day and is exemplified not only by the fact that the country has the highest percentage of foreigners of any EC country, but also by the trilingual ability of its people. Luxembourg was a founder member of the European Community (having formed close economic ties with The Netherlands and Belgium) and was host to the European Parliament until its move to a permanent site in Brussels in 1989. Luxembourg is in the mainstream on the current EC issues of monetary union, social policy and immigration. Domestic politics are typical of Western European nations, with Christian Democrat and Socialist parties and a centrist Parti Démocratique represented in the national assembly. These have recently been joined by environmentalists. The most recent elections to the Chamber of Deputies, held in 1989, returned a coalition government involving the centre-left Parti Chrétien Social (PCS) for the third consecutive occasion. The PCS, whose leader Jacques Santer is Prime Minister, governs in partnership with Parti Ouvrier Socialiste Luxembourgeois.
GOVERNMENT: The Grand Duchy of Luxembourg is a hereditary and constitutional monarchy. The Unicameral Chamber of Deputies has legislative power, members of which are elected by universal adult suffrage for five years. Executive power is formally in the hands of the Grand Duke, but is in practice wielded by the Council of Ministers. The Prime Minister is currently Jacques Santer, who is also Governor of the IMF – leader of the Parti Chrétien-Social.

CLIMATE

Warm weather from May to September and snow likely during winter months. The north, the Ardennes region, tends to be wetter than the south.
Required clothing: European; waterproofs are advisable at all times of the year.

LUXEMBOURG CITY (334m)

SUNSHINE, hours
2 3 5 6 7 7 7 6 5 3 2 1
◁ TEMPERATURE, °C
20
MAX
MIN
10
RAINFALL, mm ▷
100
0
0
J F M A M J J A S O N D
89 85 76 72 73 75 75 77 80 86 90 93
HUMIDITY, %
DAB-C193

TEMPERATURE CONVERSIONS
-20 -10 0°C 10 20 30 40
0 10 20 30°F40 50 60 70 80 90 100
RAINFALL CONVERSIONS
0mm 200 400 600 800
0in 5 10 15 20 25 30

MACAU

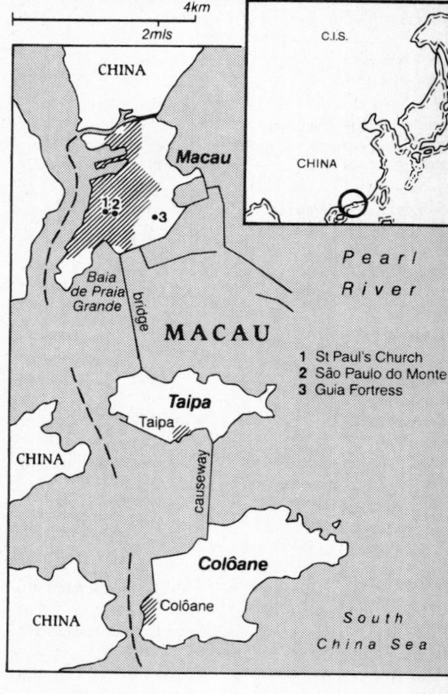

Location: South China coast.

Direcção dos Serviços de Turismo
(Macau Government Tourist Office)
CP 3006
Edificio Ritz
Largo do Senado 9
Macau
Tel: 77218 *or* 375 156 *or* 315 566. Fax: 510 104. Telex: 88338 TURIS OM.
Embassy of the Portuguese Republic
11 Belgrave Square
London SW1X 8PP
Tel: (071) 235 5331/4. Fax: (071) 245 1287. Telex: 28484. Opening hours: 1000-1300 and 1400-1700 Monday to Friday.
Portuguese Consulate General
Silver City House
62 Brompton Road
London SW3 1BJ
Tel: (071) 581 3598. Fax: (071) 581 3085. Telex: 8950154. Opening hours: 0900-1330 Monday to Friday.
Macau Tourist Information Bureau
6 Sherlock Mews
Paddington Street
London W1M 3RH
Tel: (071) 224 3390. Fax: (071) 224 0601. Opening hours: 1030-1730 Monday to Friday.
The British Trade Commission in Hong Kong deals with enquiries relating to Macau from UK citizens (for address, see Hong Kong entry).
Macau Tourist Information Bureau
Suite 316
70a Greenwich Avenue
New York, NY 10011
Tel: (212) 206 6828. Fax: (212) 924 0882.
Macau Tourist Information Bureau
PO Box 1860
3133 Lake Hollywood Drive
Los Angeles, CA 90068
Tel: (213) 851 3402. Fax: (213) 851 3684. Telex: 910-3214604.
Macau Tourist Information Bureau
Western Canada:
Suite 305
1530 West 8th Avenue
Vancouver, British Columbia
V6J 1T5
Tel: (604) 736 1095. Fax: (604) 736 7761.
Eastern Canada:
5059 Yonge Street
North York, Ontario

M2N 5P2
Tel: (416) 733 8786. Fax: (416) 221 5227.
Canadian Embassy to Macau
Office of the Commission for Canada
PO Box 11142
8 Connaught Place
Hong Kong
Tel: 810 6736. Fax: 810 4321.

AREA: 17.32 sq km (6.69 sq miles).
POPULATION: 452,300 (1989).
POPULATION DENSITY: 26,120 per sq km.
CAPITAL: Macau.
GEOGRAPHY: Macau is situated on a tiny peninsula at the mouth of the Pearl River and is linked to mainland China by a narrow isthmus, the Ferreira do Amaral. The territory also includes the islands of Taipa and Colôane, which are linked to the peninsula by a causeway and a bridge. The landscape is essentially flat, with seven small hills.
LANGUAGE: The official languages are Portuguese and Chinese (Cantonese). English is widely spoken by those engaged in trade, tourism and commerce.
RELIGION: Roman Catholic, Buddhism, Daoism and Confucianism.
TIME: GMT + 8.
ELECTRICITY: Usually 220 volts AC, but older establishments use 110 volts AC; 50Hz.
COMMUNICATIONS: Telephone: IDD service is available. Country code: 853. International facilities are available at the General Post Office at Leal Senado Square, Macau City, and the Central Post Offices in Taipa and Coloane. **Fax:** Hotels have fax facilities. **Telex/telegram:** Services available at larger hotels and telecommunication offices, as well as all pay-phones. **Post:** Airmail to Europe takes three to five days. **Press:** Newspapers are in Portuguese or Chinese. The only English-language papers are the monthly *Macau Travel Talk* and the biennial *Macau Image*.
BBC World Service and Voice of America frequencies: From time to time these change. See the section *How to Use this Book* for more information.

BBC:				
MHz	15.36	11.96	9.740	9.570
Voice of America:				
MHz	17.74	11.76	7.275	1.575

PASSPORT/VISA

Regulations and requirements may be subject to change at short notice, and you are advised to contact the appropriate diplomatic or consular authority before finalising travel arrangements. Details of these may be found at the head of this country's entry. Any numbers in the chart refer to the footnotes below.

	Passport Required?	Visa Required?	Return Ticket Required?
Full British	Yes	No	No
BVP	Not valid	-	-
Australian	Yes	No	No
Canadian	Yes	No	No
USA	Yes	No	No
Other EC	Yes	No	No
Japanese	Yes	No	No

PASSPORTS: Valid passport required by all.
British Visitors Passport: Not acceptable.
VISAS: Visas may be obtained on arrival in Macau. However, nationals of countries which do not maintain diplomatic relations with Portugal *must* obtain their visas in advance from Portuguese Consulates overseas, and may not obtain them on arrival in Macau. Visas are required by all except:
(a) nationals of EC countries;
(b) nationals of Australia, Canada, Japan and the USA;
(c) nationals of Austria, Brazil, South Korea, Malaysia, New Zealand, Norway, Philippines, Singapore, Sweden, Switzerland and Thailand;
(d) residents of Hong Kong who are British and Commonwealth subjects, for a stay not exceeding 20 days; residents of Hong Kong who are nationals of other countries do not require visas if staying less than 3 days;
(e) Chinese residents holding Hong Kong identity cards or re-entry permits, or holders of a British passport endorsed 'British subject' are allowed a 3-month stay.
Note: For (a)-(c) above, visas will be required if intending to stay more than 20 days.
Types of visa: Tourist and Business. Cost: *Individual* – HK$175; *Family* – HK$320; HK$80 for children under 12; *Group* HK$80 per person for bona fide groups of 15 persons or more.
Validity: 20 days. Can be extended by one month at no charge on application to the immigration office.
Application to: Consulate (or Consular Section at Embassy). For addresses, see top of entry.
Application requirements: (a) 2 application forms. (b) 2 photos. (c) Valid passport. (d) Return or onward ticket. (e) Alien Registration or Green Card. (f) Company letter of responsibility for those travelling on business.
Working days required: Visas can normally be issued the same day.
Temporary residence: Enquire at Information Bureau.

MONEY

Currency: Pataca (MOP) = 100 avos. Notes are in denominations of MOP1000, 500, 100, 50, 10 and 5. Coins are in denominations of MOP5 and 1, and 50, 20 and 10 avos.
Credit cards: Access/Mastercard and Visa are accepted. Check with credit card company for details of merchant acceptability and other services which may be available.
Travellers cheques: These may be exchanged at banks, licensed money changers and at many hotels.
Exchange rate indicators: The following figures are included as a guide to the movements of the Pataca against Sterling and the US Dollar:

Date:	Oct '89	Oct '90	Oct '91	Oct '92
£1.00=	12.75	15.63	13.90	12.63
$1.00=	8.07	8.00	8.01	7.96

Note: The Pataca is loosely pegged to the Hong Kong Dollar.
Currency restrictions: There are no restrictions on the import or export of either local or foreign currency.
Banking hours: 0930-1600 Monday to Friday, and 0930-1200 Saturday.

DUTY FREE

The following goods may be imported into Macau without incurring customs duty:
A reasonable amount of tobacco, alcohol and perfume for personal use.
Prohibited items: Drugs and firearms.
Note: There is a 5% duty on the import of electrical appliances and equipment. There are no export duties, but as travel is almost invariably via Hong Kong, the relevant Hong Kong import/export regulations must be observed. See the *Hong Kong* entry earlier in the *World Travel Guide*.

PUBLIC HOLIDAYS

Public holidays observed in Macau are as follows:
Apr 5 '93 Ching Ming Festival. **Apr 9** Good Friday. **Apr 11** Easter. **Apr 25** Anniversary of the Portuguese Revolution. **May 1** Labour Day. **Jun 10** Camoens/Portuguese Communities Day. **Jun 24** Dragon Boat Festival Day and Feast of St John the Baptist. **Oct 1** Day following Chinese Mid-Autumn Festival and National Day of the People's Republic of China. **Oct 5** Portugese Republic Day. **Oct 23** Festival of Ancestors. **Nov 2** All Souls' Day. **Dec 1** Restoration of Independence. **Dec 8** Feast of the Immaculate Conception. **Dec 22** Winter Solstice. **Dec 24-25** Christmas. **Jan 1 '94** New Year's Day. **Feb 10** Chinese New Year.

HEALTH

Regulations and requirements may be subject to change at short notice, and you are advised to contact your doctor well in advance of your intended date of departure. Any numbers in the chart refer to the footnotes below.

	Special Precautions?	Certificate Required?
Yellow Fever	No	No
Cholera	No	No
Typhoid & Polio	No	-
Malaria	No	-
Food & Drink	1	-

[1]: All water should be regarded as being potentially contaminated. Water used for drinking, brushing teeth or making ice should have first been boiled or otherwise sterilised. Milk is unpasteurised and should be boiled. Powdered or tinned milk is available and is advised, but make sure that it is reconstituted with pure water. Avoid dairy products which are likely to have been made from unboiled milk. Only eat well-cooked meat and fish, preferably served hot. Pork, salad and mayonnaise may carry increased risk. Vegetables should be cooked and fruit peeled.
Health care: Health insurance is recommended. There are good medical facilities, and religious orders or hotels will also give assistance.

TRAVEL - International

AIR: There is no airport in Macau, although there are plans to complete one early in 1995. Most transport is via Hong Kong. There are also plans for a national airline named *Macau International Airlines* which will begin services as soon as the airport is in operation.
Approximate flight time: From *London* to Hong Kong is 18 hours; for other flight times, see *Hong Kong* entry.
Helicopter services, run by *East Asia Airlines*, operate daily flights in two 8-seat Bell 222 helicopters (travel time – 20 minutes). Cost: HK$830 (weekdays), HK$930 (weekends and public holidays).
Departure tax: MOP20.
SEA: A ferry service operates 24 hours a day between Macau and Kaohsiung, Taiwan. The *Macmosa* departs from Macau each Tuesday and Saturday morning arriving 24 hours later; departure from Kaohsiung is on Sunday and Wednesday afternoons. Onward travel to China can be arranged. The journey time to Hong Kong by jumbo-catamaran is about 70 minutes and by high-speed ferry is 90 minutes. Further information is available from: *Hong Kong Ferries* (formerly Sealink), Central Harbour Services Pier, Pier Road, Central, Hong Kong. Tel: 542 3081. Fax: 854 3847. Telex: 81340 HYFCO HX; *or*
Hong Kong Hi-Speed Ferries Limited, 13th Floor, V. Heun Building, 138 Queen's Road, Central, Hong Kong. Tel: 815 3043. Fax: 543 0324. Telex: 89846 HKFPF HX.
The **baggage allowance** is currently 20kg per person on high-speed ferries. In general, luggage is limited to hand-carried items. Tour operators can arrange luggage-handling where required.
Jetfoils operate a 24-hour service and take about 55 minutes from Hong Kong. Bookings for groups can be made directly by contacting any of the following: *Far East Hydrofoil Co Ltd.* Tel: 859 3333. Fax: 858 1014. Telex: 74200 SEDAM HX; *or*
Hong Kong Macau Hydrofoil Co Ltd. Tel: 559 9255 *or* 521 8302. Fax: 810 0952. Telex: 74493 HMHCO HX.
Departure tax: Passengers embarking at Hong Kong for Macau must pay HK$22 per person, and HK$20 on departure from Macau.

TRAVEL - Internal

ROAD: There is a bridge to Taipa Island, with plans to construct a second bridge carrying a 4-lane highway from the international airport (currently under construction in the Pearl River estuary) to the Macau-China border at Gongbei.

MACAU | **HEALTH REGULATIONS** | **VISA REGULATIONS** | Code-Link

GALILEO/WORLDSPAN

TI-DFT/QMP/HE

TI-DFT/QMP/VI

SABRE

TIDFT/QMP/HE

TIDFT/QMP/VI

To access this information on your CRS, swipe the barcode with a light pen or type in the text under the barcode. For more information, see the introduction *How to Use This Book*.

Bus: There are five bus routes in the city. No 3 runs from the ferry terminal to the city centre. Bus services operate daily to the islands. First buses run from about 0700, the last at about midnight (but the last to the islands leaves at about 2300).
Car hire: For information and bookings contact: *Macau Mokes Group Ltd*, Avenida Marciano Baptista, Macau. Tel: 378 851. Fax: 555 433. Telex: 88251 MBC OM; *or Avis Rent-A-Car*, Mandarin Oriental, Macau. Tel: 336 789 *or* 567 888 ext. 3004. Fax: 314 112. **Taxi:** Most taxis are black with a cream-coloured top. Rickshaws and pedicabs, bicycles with a 2-seater section at the back, are also available for hire. Prices should be agreed in advance. It is worth remembering that many of the attractions in Macau are located on hilltops, beyond the reach of even the strongest-legged pedicab driver. Chauffeur-driven limousines are also available.
Documentation: An International Driving Permit is not required for drivers from the UK.

ACCOMMODATION

There are various types of accommodation, with the full range from first-class to economy-class hotels, plus inns, villa-apartments housed in new buildings, and older colonial hotels. At weekends the hotels, villas and inns are usually full, so it is wise to make a reservation. There are presently about 6000 hotel rooms in Macau. Most hotels are air-conditioned and have a private bath. A 10% service charge is added to hotel bills plus a 5% Government tax. For further information, contact The Macau Hotels Association, c/o Pousada de Sao Tiago, Avenida da Republica, Macau. Tel: 378 111. Fax: 522 170. Telex: 88376 TIAGO OM.

RESORTS & EXCURSIONS

MACAU: The most famous sight in Macau is probably the ruins of the *Church of St Paul's*, originally built in 1602 and rebuilt in 1835 after a disastrous typhoon. The Jesuit citadel of *São Paulo do Monte* is almost directly in the centre of Macau. It forms the strong central point of the old city wall, and was instrumental in preventing the Dutch from conquering the city in 1622. The 17th-century *Guia Fortress* stands on the highest point in Macau; its lighthouse is the oldest on the China coast. The complex of temples known as *Kun Iam Tong* dates from the time of the Ming dynasty, about 400 years ago, and contains, amongst other works of art, a small statue of Marco Polo. The oldest Chinese temple in the country is that of the *Goddess A-Ma*, and dates back at least six centuries. It has some excellent multi-coloured bas-relief stone carvings. The finest expression of Portuguese architecture is probably the *Leal Senado*, the Senate Chamber. The *Public Library*, off the main staircase, and the main chamber itself are well worth a visit. The *Sun Yat Sen Memorial Home*, the former residence of the Revolutionary leader who overthrew the Ching Dynasty in 1910, is now a museum. It is open every day except Tuesdays between 1000 and 1300, and also between 1500 and 1700 at weekends. *São Domingo's Church*, built in the 17th century, is one of the most beautiful religious buildings in Macau. Other churches of interest include those of *Santo Agostinho*, *São Jose* and *S Lourenco*. *Monuments* of note in the country include those in honour of Jorge Alvares and Vasco da Gama. The *Chinese Garden of Lou Lim Ioc* is also well worth a visit.
TAIPA: The island of Taipa is known for its firework factories. It also contains several small Buddhist temples and some old Portuguese buildings.
COLOANE: Colôane has several beaches, as well as woods and hills. It has interesting Chinese Temples, the *Chapel of St Francis Xavier* and a traditional junk-building yard near the village.

SOCIAL PROFILE

FOOD & DRINK: Most restaurants have table service. Hotels, inns and restaurants offer a wide variety of food. They specialise in Portuguese dishes, but also offer cuisine from China, Japan, Korea and Indonesia. Local Macau food is spicy, a unique combination of Chinese and Portuguese cooking methods. Dishes include *bacalhau* (cod served baked, grilled, stewed or boiled), *caldo verde* and *sopa a alentejana* (rich soups with vegetables, meat and olive oil), 'African chicken' (grilled with hot spices), *galinha a portuguesa* (chicken baked with potatoes, onions, eggs and saffron – the appearance of curry without the spice), *minche* (minced meat with fried potato and onion), Macau sole (fried fish is usually served with salad) and *feijoados* (from Brazil, stews of kidney beans, pork, potatoes, cabbage and spicy sausage). The speciality of *dim sum* (Chinese savoury snacks steamed and served in bamboo baskets on trollies) includes *cha siu bao* (steamed pork dumplings), *har gau* (steamed shrimp dumplings) and *shui mai* (steamed and minced pork with shrimp). **Drink:** Bars have table and/or counter service. Alcohol is easily obtainable. There are no licensing laws. All restaurants offer a variety of Portuguese red and white wines and sparkling *vinho verde*, as well as port and brandy, all at low prices.
NIGHTLIFE: Most of the nightlife is centred on the hotels, many of which have nightclubs with cabaret, Portuguese folk dancing, lively dance bands, discotheques, international menus and bars. In summer there are several open-air *esplanadas* serving soft drinks around the square in front of Hotel Lisboa. Gambling is a big attraction for visitors to Macau and the casinos are open 24 hours, providing famous entertainers, baccarat, blackjack, roulette and Chinese games like *fantan* and *dai-siu* (big and small). There are also *keno* and one-armed bandits (called 'hungry tigers' in Macau).
SHOPPING: Macau's most popular buys remain jewellery (particularly gold), Chinese antiques, porcelain, pottery, electric gadgetry, cameras, watches and beading work. They are available at duty-free prices because Macau is a free port and no sales tax is charged. Bargaining is expected on many items. Other popular buys are Chinese herbs and medicines, dried seafood (such as sharks' fins), abalone, Chinese and Macau pastries, and locally made knitwear from stalls. When purchasing antiques, gold and jewellery, it is advisable to patronise shops recommended by the Goldsmiths' and Jewellers' Association and the Macau Government Tourist Office (who publish a shopping guide). A warranty and a receipt should be asked for when buying jewellery, gold, cameras, watches and electrical goods. **Shopping hours:** Generally 1000-2000 Monday to Saturday. Some shops may be closed on the first of every month.
SPORT: Greyhound **racing** takes place at the Canidrome on Av General Castelo Branco on Tuesdays, Thursdays, weekends and Hong Kong public holidays from 8pm. The Far East's gala motorcycle and Formula III car racing event, the Macau Grand Prix, is held during the third week in November. The Macau Jockey Club organises flat races at its track on the island of Taipa. Courts and equipment are available for **badminton** and **tennis** on request in advance from the Macau Government Tourist Office. A **bowling** centre with four lanes is located on the ground floor of Hotel Lisboa. **Squash** courts are available at the Oriental Macau and Royal Hotels. **Swimming** pools are found in major hotels like the Hyatt Regency, Lisboa, Pousada de S Tiago, Pousada de Coloane, Royal, Oriental Macau and Estoril. Public pools are also available in Macau and Coloane Island.
SPECIAL EVENTS: The Macau Tourist Information Bureau and Government Tourist Office can supply details of the many festivals celebrated in Macau. Some of the 1993/94 events are listed below. Festivals which are also official public holidays are listed in the *Public Holidays* section above.
Apr 14 '93 *A-Ma Festival*. **May 13** *Procession of Our Lady of Fatima*. **May 28** *Feast of the Bathing of Lord Buddha; Feast of the Drunken Dragon* and *Tam Kong Festival*. **Jun 7** *International Dragon Boat Festival*. **Sep 11, 19, 26** *International Fireworks Festival*. **Sep 30** *Mid-Autumn Festival*. **Oct 5** *International Fireworks Festival*. **Mid-Oct** *Macau International Music Festival*. **Nov** *Macau Grand Prix; Macau Marathon*.
SOCIAL CONVENTIONS: Entertaining generally takes place in restaurants and public places. It is rare to be invited to a private home, unless the person is wealthy. Spirits are standard gifts in return for hospitality. Apart from formal occasions in restaurants and nightclubs, casual wear is acceptable. **Tipping:** A 10% service charge will be added to most hotel and restaurant bills, but a small tip should also be left.

BUSINESS PROFILE

ECONOMY: Macau has long been an important international distribution outlet for many Chinese products and in this way is fairly similar to Hong Kong. It has an active manufacturing and exporting sector whose main products are textiles, toys, optics, rubber, china, furniture and footwear. Macau is increasingly famous for its gambling facilities and tourism has now developed as a major source of income. China, Hong Kong and the USA are the territory's major trading partners.
BUSINESS: Business people are expected to dress smartly. Calling cards are essential, appointments should be made in advance and punctuality is appreciated. The Macau Business Centre (PO Box 138, Ground Floor, Edificio Ribeiro, tel: 373 379 *or* 511 631 *or* 323 598; fax: 511 631; telex: 88251 MBC OM) offers secretarial and supporting services, meeting rooms, microphones, tape recorders, video tape and telex.
COMMERCIAL INFORMATION: The following organisation can offer advice: Associação Comercial de Macau, Fifth Floor, Edificio ACM, Rua de Xangai 175, Macau. Tel: 572 042. Fax: 594 513. Telex: 88229.
CONFERENCES/CONVENTIONS: There are three major meetings venues: the Jai Alai Stadium (with seating for up to 5000), the Forum (a multi-purpose complex with seating for up to 4000) and the University of East Asia conference centre (with seating for up to 764). Several hotels also have facilities, and support services can be provided by the Macau Business Centre (see above). For information contact the Macau Government Tourist Office in Macau (see address above).

HISTORY & GOVERNMENT

HISTORY: Macau was officially founded in 1557 during the great era of Portuguese overseas exploration initiated by Prince Henry the Navigator. Macau soon became the major entrepôt between the East and Europe; as a result, several other colonial powers, notably the Dutch, made repeated attempts to conquer the province. During the early 17th century, when the Portuguese were fighting a protracted war of independence against the Spanish (who then ruled Portugal), the Dutch tried on no less than four occasions to gain control of Macau, but were repulsed each time. After the House of Braganza regained control of Portugal from the Spanish Habsburgs in 1640, Macau was granted the official title of *Cidade do Nome de Deus, de Macau, Não há outra mais Leal* (City of the Name of God, Macau, There is None More Loyal). In 1670 Macau was confirmed as a Portuguese possession by the Chinese. Macau went into decline as a regional trading centre from the early 19th century, when the British, the most recent colonial power in the region, began to settle along the Chinese coast, and in 1841 occupied the island of Hong Kong. This deep-water port attracted larger ships and trade began to shift to the British Crown Colony. With its trading monopoly thus broken, for a while Macau became little more than a summer residence for the traders from Canton, who found the province a salubrious and relaxing retreat from the Cantonese noise and bustle. Macau was held under firm Portuguese control until the leftist military coup in 1974 which overthrew the Caetano dictatorship. The new regime immediately instituted a new colonial policy under which all remaining territories would undergo a rapid transition to full independence – in some cases, over as little as 12 months. Macau demanded more delicate handling because of the Chinese interest, although there was no time constraint comparable to Hong Kong's 1997 deadline. In 1976, the Lisbon government redefined Macau as a 'Special Territory' and granted a large measure of administrative and economic independence. In 1985, following the Hong Kong example, the Portuguese announced the opening of negotiations with Beijing on the transfer of sovereignty to the People's Republic. The final settlement, which was ratified in January 1988, provides for a handover in 1999 after which Macau will, like Hong Kong, become a 'Special Administrative Region' within China. The Portuguese have enjoyed a rather easier time than the British, not least because all Macau's citizens have been offered Portuguese passports (a practicable proposition, given the population of under half a million). However, their legacy to the territory is a less creditable one: the economy is stagnant; the bureaucracy ossified and corrupt. Compared with Hong Kong, the Chinese will find it less awkward to deal with but also less stimulating.
GOVERNMENT: Macau is a Special Territory of Portugal. The Governor holds executive power in all matters except foreign affairs, which remains the responsibility of the President of Portugal. There is a Legislative Assembly of 23 members, 16 of whom are elected, whilst the others are appointed by the Governor. The Portuguese government has negotiated a provisional agreement for the transfer of power to the Chinese, progress being spurred by the talks between neighbouring Hong Kong and China, although with less urgency.

CLIMATE

Subtropical climate with very hot summers and a rainy period during the summer months. Most rain occurs in the afternoon. Winds can reach gale force, and typhoons are not unknown.
Required clothing: Lightweight cottons and linens are advised during warmer months, with warmer clothing for spring and autumn evenings. Warmer clothes are worn during the winter. Waterproofing is advisable.

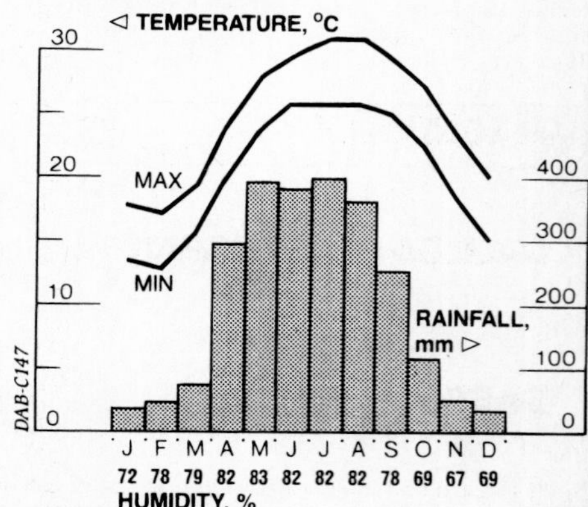

THE FORMER YUGOSLAV REPUBLIC OF MACEDONIA

Location: Ex-Yugoslav republic; southeastern Europe.

Note: The United Nations and other international organisations declined to recognise the independent Republic of Macedonia in January 1992, publicly reconfirming this decision a number of times. The nearest UK, USA and Canadian embassies are in Belgrade, whose authorities do not recognise the Republic of Macedonia.

Ministry of Foreign Relations
Dame Gruev bb
91000 Skopje
Macedonia
Tel: (91) 236 311.
ECGD (Country Policy Desk)
Tel: (071) 512 7000.
FCO (Yugoslav Desk)
Tel: (071) 270 3000.
Embassy of Yugoslavia
5-7 Lexham Gardens
London W8 5JJ
Tel: (071) 370 6105/9. Fax: (071) 370 3838. Telex: 928542. Opening hours (for visa applications): 1000-1300 Monday to Friday.
Macedonia Steel Ltd
c/o Macedonia Information Office
Kingsway House
103 Kingsway
London WC2B 6QX
Tel: (071) 405 5812. Fax: (071) 831 1577. Telex: 268314. Opening hours: 0900-1700 Monday to Friday.
Note: The sole UK outlet for various Macedonian business interests, and also the contact point for the Association of Macedonians in Britain, this company office is also willing to act as a channel to facilitate contact with government ministries, banks and enterprises in Macedonia.
Embassy of Yugoslavia
2410 California Avenue, NW
Washington, DC
20008
Tel: (202) 462 6566. Fax: (202) 797 9663.
Consulates in: Chicago, Cleveland, New York (tel: (212) 838 2300), Pittsburgh and San Francisco.
Macedonian World Congress
PO Box 2826
Ormond Beach, FL 32175-2826
Tel: (904) 676 2466. Fax: (904) 676 2462.
Embassy of Yugoslavia
17 Blackburn Avenue
Ottawa, Ontario
K1N 8A2
Tel: (613) 233 6289. Fax: (613) 233 7850.
Consulates in: Montréal, Toronto and Vancouver.

AREA: 25,713 sq km (9928 sq miles), or 10% of the territory of the former Yugoslav federation (its fourth largest republic).
Note: The ex-Yugoslav republic of 'Macedonia' is only one of three areas of the historical region of 'Macedonia', which includes Pirin Macedonia (Bulgaria) and Aegean Macedonia (Greece), with a total area of 66,600 sq km (25,700 sq miles), most of which is in Greece.
POPULATION: 2,033,964 (1991), or 9% of the total population of the former Yugoslav federation (its fourth most populous republic).
Note: Macedonia contains the majority of people claiming to be 'Macedonians', whose existence as a separate nation is denied in both Bulgaria and Greece (similarly in Albania and Serbia).
POPULATION DENSITY: 79.1 per sq km.
CAPITAL: Skopje. **Population:** 563,000 (1991).
GEOGRAPHY: Roughly rectangular in shape, and on the strategic Vardar valley north–south communications route, Macedonia is landlocked, bordering Serbia to the north, Albania to the west, Greece to the south and Bulgaria to the east.
LANGUAGE: Under the new unitary constitution of November 1991, Macedonian is the official language (using the Cyrillic alphabet and being akin to Bulgarian). Albanian, Turkish, Roma and Serbo-Croat are also used by ethnic groups.
RELIGION: Eastern Orthodox Macedonians of internationally unrecognised autocephalous status approximately 64.6%, Muslim Albanians 21%, Muslim Turks 5% and Serbian Orthodox Serbs 2.1%. As elsewhere in the former Yugoslav federation, local politics are now strongly divided along national confessional lines.
Note: As the Albanians did not co-operate with the 1991 census, the figure given for their share of the population is a contested estimate, with the true figure more like 30% of the total.
TIME: GMT + 1 (GMT + 2 from March to September).
ELECTRICITY: 220 volts Ac, 50Hz.
COMMUNICATIONS: Telecommunications/Post: Still internationally IDD-connected as part of the former Yugoslav federation. Country code: 38. All telecommunications services, as well as the post, are generally working normally, although uncertainty still surrounds all future international connections via Serbia and Greece, whose respective authorities subjected Macedonia to an ongoing economic blockade in 1992. **Press:** The two main daily newspapers, both printed in Skopje, are *Nova Makedonija* and *Vecer*. **TV/Radio:** The state TV-radio station, *RTS*, broadcasts in Macedonian, Albanian and Turkish. The Ministry of Information acts as the state news agency, periodically producing material in English for international distribution.
BBC World Service and Voice of America frequencies: From time to time these change. See the section *How to Use this Book* for more information.

BBC:				
MHz	15.070	12.095	9.410	6.180
Voice of America:				
MHz	9.670	6.040	5.995	1.260

PASSPORT/VISA

Regulations and requirements may be subject to change at short notice, and you are advised to contact the appropriate diplomatic or consular authority before finalising travel arrangements. Details of these may be found at the head of this country's entry. Any numbers in the chart refer to the footnotes below.

	Passport Required?	Visa Required?	Return Ticket Required?
Full British	1	No	No
BVP	Valid	-	-
Australian	Yes	No	No
Canadian	Yes	No	No
USA	Yes	No	No
Other EC	Yes	2	No
Japanese	Yes	No	No

Note: Due to the current political situation, entry requirements are liable to change at short notice. It is advisable to contact an embassy for up-to-the-minute information (see addresses at top of entry).
Restricted entry: Visas will not be granted to nationals of South Africa.
PASSPORTS: [1] Valid passport required by all with the exception of nationals of the UK entering as tourists and in possession of a valid British Visitors Passport (see below). Entry is allowed for up to 90 days.
British Visitors Passport: Acceptable for holidays or unpaid business trips. A stay beyond 90 days will require permission from the local authorities.
VISAS: Required by:
(a) [2] nationals of Greece;
(b) nationals of Afghanistan, Albania, Bangladesh, Ghana, Iran, Lebanon, Nigeria, Pakistan, the Philippines, Sri Lanka and Turkey.
Types of visas: Single entry/single exit: £4.50. Double entry/double exit: £9. Transit visas, valid for 7 days (to be used within 6 months of issue): £4.50 for single entry and £9 for double entry. Transit visas are not required, however, by those holding tickets with confirmed onward reservations within 24 hours and who do not leave the airport.
Validity: Where they are required, visas are valid for 6 months from date of issue and cannot be postdated.
Application to: Consulate (or Consular Section at Embassy). For addresses, see top of entry.
Application requirements: (a) Application form. (b) Valid passport. (c) Self-addressed, postage-paid, registered envelope for return of passport and documents. (d) Fee payable to Embassy in cash or by postal order (cheques will only be accepted from travel agencies, firms and companies).
Note: Nationals who require visas may, on entry, be expected to state that they have at least US$150 per person and day for their intended stay in Yugoslavia, and may be asked to produce a return ticket.
Working days required: Visas are issued immediately to personal callers. Postal applications for passport holders takes 7 days.
Temporary residence: Enquire at Embassy. Visas can be extended if local authorities are contacted within 7 days of arrival.

PUBLIC HOLIDAYS

Public holidays observed in Macedonia are as follows:
May 1-2 '93 Labour Days. **May 24** Culture Day. **Jul 4** Veterans' Day. **Aug 2** Bank Holiday. **Oct 11** Bank Holiday. **Nov 29-30** Republic Days. **Jan 1-2 '94** New Year.

MONEY

Currency: Yugoslav Dinar (YuD) = 100 paras. Still relying on former Yugoslav Dinars in circulation, the Skopje government does not have the resources to issue a new currency, although a new Macedonian Denar is planned

MACEDONIA | **HEALTH REGULATIONS** | **VISA REGULATIONS** | Code-Link

GALILEO/WORLDSPAN

TI-DFT/SKP/HE

TI-DFT/SKP/VI

SABRE

TIDFT/SKP/HE

TIDFT/SKP/VI

To access this information on your CRS, swipe the barcode with a light pen or type in the text under the barcode. For more information, see the introduction *How to Use This Book*.

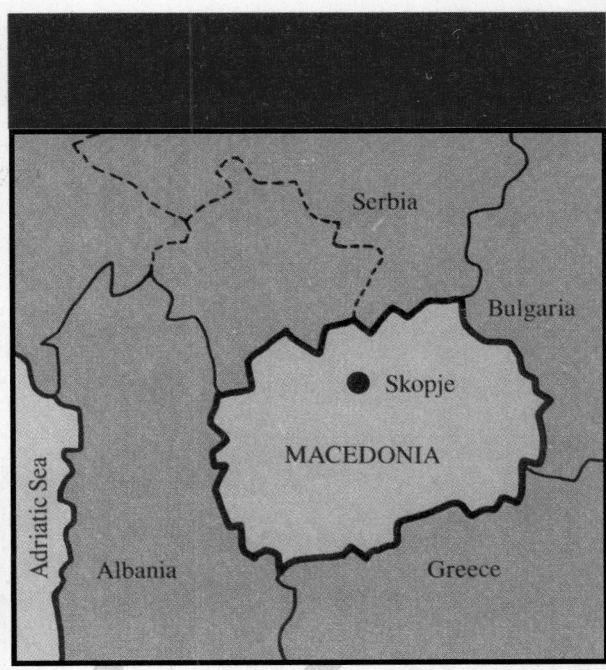

CALLING FOR LOVE

Let me tell you about love,
about a special kind of love.
This love has many rivers – but not too big,
many fields – but not too big,
high mountains – but not so very big,
towns and villages – but not too big.
This love has air: in winter it cuts like a knife
and crunches,
and in summer it clings to the skin and burns.
This love has certain scents: of plums and
watermelons,
of peaches, grapes and wine,
the yellow powder of seasoned tobacco
and the black seeds of poppies.
It has lakes: not many – one special,
which fills your imagination
and breaks the laws of your dreams.
There you can drink the dew,
but the land is the dew, too,
so you cannot swallow it
and cannot return it,
it is in the flow to the heart
and, doodling, discovers the geography of
its being
in a small southern land in Europe.
Where are there places like this place?
Where are there wines – white, red,
like these wines?
How similar is it to other places,
and how different?
You arrive among hills and dales,
swim in love's rivers and lakes,
doze among flowers in mountain pastures
and dream of love brushing
your closed eyelids,
trying to open them
and show you the secret of its being.
You open your eyes, search – and discover
you are close to a special kind of love!

GORDANA MIHAILOVA BOSNAKOSKA, WRITER, SKOPJE, MACEDONIA

later in 1992 or 1993. As of July 1992, local hyper-inflation was running at the rate of over 200% per month.
Currency exchange: As elsewhere in the ex-Yugoslav republics, the only true repositries of value and real mediums of exchange locally are the DM and the US$ (the Pound Sterling is rarely used or seen in the republic). *Emigré* hard currency remittances are reportedly of considerable local importance, although few of these resources ever enter the official banking system.
Exchange rate indicators: The following figures are included as a guide to the movements of the Yugoslav Dinar against Sterling and the US Dollar:

Date:	Nov '89	Oct '90	Oct '91	Oct '92
£1.00=	113,000.70	20.98*	37.89	325.00
$1.00=	72,413.14	10.74*	21.83	204.79

Note [*]: On January 1, 1990, Yugoslavia launched its new currency at DM1 = YuD7, £1 = YuD19 and US$1 = YuD12.

TRAVEL – International

AIR: The national airline is *Palair Macedonian Airlines*. It offers connections to the USA, Canada and Australia.
Note: Because of the civil war to the north, and the Greco-Serbian economic blockade of the republic, normal use of the main north–south road and rail routes through and beyond Macedonia is no longer possible, with extensive delays on both borders with Serbia and Greece. The main routes to Albania and Bulgaria are operating more or less normally.

TRAVEL – Internal

AIR: The Belgrade–Skopje–Ohrid air service, formerly run by *JAT*, is no longer operating at present. The new national airline *Palair Macedonian Airlines* runs domestic services.
RAIL/ROAD: All the main internal road and rail services are operating normally, with links from Skopje to *Kumanovo* in the north, to *Teluvo* in the west, to *Stip* in the east and to *Tilov, Velco, Prilep* and *Bitola* in the south.
Note: The local situation is very changeable and the advice of the FCO's travel advice unit should be sought prior to any visit. For up-to-date information on the situation, tel: (071) 270 4129.

ACCOMMODATION

HOTELS: Macedonia has no Deluxe/A-class hotels. There are B-class hotels in Skopje and the Ohrid Lake tourist area on the border with Albania and Greece.

RESORTS & EXCURSIONS

Macedonia is a parched, harsher land in summer compared to other countries in this region. Greek, Turkish and Bulgarian influences are strong. Macedonia is also noted for its icons and frescoes. **Bitola**, 5km (3 miles) from the Greek border, has the nearby ruins of the Greek city of *Heraclea*. **Ohrid** on *Lake Ohrid* contains the *Church of St Sophia*, said to be the most elaborate medieval monument in Macedonia. The *Church of St Clement* has some wonderfully coloured frescoes. **Skopje**, Macedonia's capital, was badly damaged in an earthquake in 1963. Despite this there are interesting sights – a magnificent medieval footbridge spanning the *River Vardar*, the *Mustafa Pasha mosque*, the 15th-century *Daut Pasha Turkish bath* and the *Church of St Panteleimon*.

SOCIAL PROFILE

FOOD & DRINK: Macedonian dishes show big Turkish and Greek influences. Different varieties of kebabs can be found almost everywhere as can dishes such as *musaka* (aubergines and potatoes baked in layers with minced meat). A national speciality are *gravce na tavce* (beans in a skillet) and the delicious Ohrid trout.
SOCIAL CONVENTIONS: Handshaking is the common practice on introduction. Local business protocol is fairly informal, but things go very slowly or not at all due to the local bureaucracy and the more recent general socio-economic collapse in the republic.
SPECIAL EVENTS: The *Ohrid Folklore Festival* is celebrated annually during July and August.

BUSINESS PROFILE

ECONOMY: The poorest and least economically developed of the former Yugoslav republics, Macedonia accounted for an inconsequential 5.6% of Yugoslavia's GDP in 1990-91 (around US$3 billion), with a GDP per capita of around US$1400 (US$1200 less than the all-Yugoslav average). A predominantly agricultural economy with few natural resources, Macedonia was formerly the most dependent of the poorer Yugoslav republics on federal subsidies from the richer north for its economic development. These ended in 1991, when the old Yugoslav market also disappeared, thereby bringing about a virtual collapse of the local industrial sector, which consisted mainly of capital goods. In addition, there have been local attempts to bring about an internationally recognised independence, which prompted the Belgrade government to renounce responsibility for the former republic's foreign debt. This was followed, in 1992, by a devastating Greco-Serbian economic blockade, which brought the republic to the point of complete socio-economic collapse as of July 1992. Lack of international recognition (other than by Bulgaria and Turkey) means that Macedonia cannot as yet obtain any foreign economic assistance other than emergency humanitarian aid. Even with recognition and some help from official government and multilateral agency sources, the republic has very poor future economic prospects. The only substantive local economic asset is tobacco, but its largely high tar classification had made it increasingly unviable in EC markets, even before the foreign blockade made such exports impossible. More promising in the longer term are the hard currency remittances of the 150,000 or more *émigré* Macedonians in Western Europe and North America (plus another 200,000 in Australia), but even here chronic political uncertainty is preventing anything but the most minimal repatriation of the considerable resources reportedly involved. UK economic links with Macedonia are reportedly marginal.
BUSINESS: Suits and ties are correct attire for men, with skirt, blouse and tights the accepted attire for women. Compared to the northern ex-Yugoslav republics, English and German are not so widely used as second languages. **Office hours:** 0700/0800-1500/1600 Monday to Friday.
COMMERCIAL INFORMATION: The following organisations can offer advice: National Bank of Macedonia, Kompleks Banki bb, 91000 Skopje. Tel: (91) 230 111; *or* Chamber of Economy of Macedonia, Ivo. R. Lola 25, 91000 Skopje. Tel: (91) 229 211.

HISTORY & GOVERNMENT

HISTORY: An ancient, strategically important and much-contested territory, the historical region known

as Macedonia was variously controlled by the Greeks, Romans, Bulgarians, Byzantines, Serbs and Ottoman Turks, who conquered the area in 1371, and kept it until the 19th century. Then, as Turkish power declined, Macedonia once again became a bone of contention between its various neighbours and their respective superpower allies. In 1893, the Internal Macedonian Revolutionary Organisation (IMRO) was founded to promote independence. In 1912-13, the Balkan Wars drove the Turks out of the area, and it was carved up between Serbia and Greece, with Bulgaria retaining only a small part. Vardar Macedonia became part of the new 'Kingdom of Serbs, Croats and Slovenes' in 1918 ('Yugoslavia' from 1929). This caused much anti-Serbian resentment locally during the inter-war period, when the IMRO was also used as a terrorist organisation against Belgrade by Bulgaria, which again occupied the area under German direction during the Second World War. In 1945, the area became a constituent republic of the new communist Yugoslav federation, which the Serbs opposed. Thereafter a new 'Macedonian' nation was created, but this was never accepted as being legitimate by any of the republic's neighbours. In December 1990, following the collapse of communism in Yugoslavia, Macedonia held its first multi-party elections for the 120-seat national assembly, the *Sobranje*. The results, from a very low turn-out, were inconclusive. A new version of the Internal Macedonian Revolutionary Organisation (IMRO) took the most seats (37), followed by the former communist Social Democratic League of Macedonia (SDLM), the ethnic Albanian Party of Democratic Prosperity (PDP), and the Liberal Party of Macedonia (LPM). With the SDLM's Kiro Gligorov as President, a number of unstable coalition governments followed. In October 1991, IMRO joined the opposition leaving its smaller allies to run a minority administration. Concommitantly, Yugoslavia dissolved into civil war, thereby forcing all the ethnic Macedonian political parties, but not the PDP (which wants to reunify the Albanian-dominated areas of western Macedonia with Albania), to speak out for an independent Macedonia.
Macedonia's quest for international recognition, along with Croatia, Slovenia and Bosnia-Hercegovina, has run up against fierce objections from Greece, which feels that Skopje's use of the title 'Macedonia' implies a territorial claim against Aegean Macedonia in Greece. (The ancient name 'Paeonia' is one preferred alternative.) In January 1992, when the EC formally recognised Croatia and Slovenia, recognition of Macedonia was duly vetoed by Greece; UN and other international recognition has similarly been stalled. The Skopje government's other principal objective of securing economic stability has also proved elusive.
GOVERNMENT: Legislative power rests with the elected 120-seat National Assembly, the Sobranje. Executive authority is wielded by the State President and Council of Ministers.

CLIMATE

Mostly a landlocked country, Macedonia has a pronounced continental climate, with very cold winters and hot summers.
Required clothing: Mediumweight clothing and warm overcoats in winter; lightweight clothing and raincoats required for the summer.

The Government of Greece has asked publishers to point out that the term 'Macedonia' to denote the former Yugoslav Republic of Macedonia has not been recognised by the UN or the EC as the state's official name.

Any references to 'Macedonia' in this context, in this or any section of the *World Travel Guide*, are for convenience, and not designed to imply a recognition of this term by any of the countries represented in the publication.

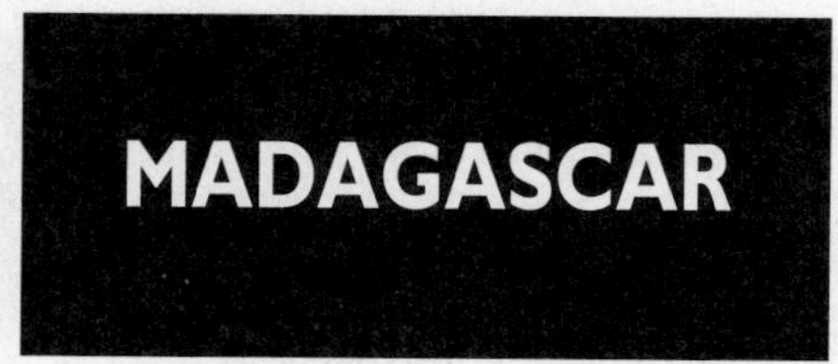

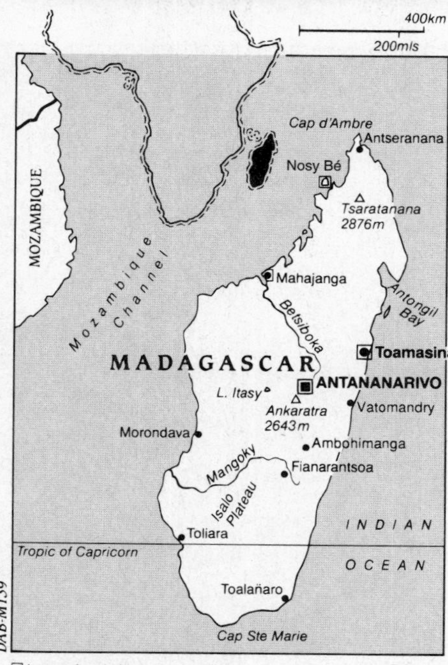

□ international airport

Location: Indian Ocean, 500km (300 miles) off the coast of Mozambique.

Direction du Tourisme de Madagascar
BP 610
Tsimbazaza
101 Antananarivo, Madagascar
Tel: (2) 26298. Fax: (2) 26719. Telex: 26298.
Consulate of the Democratic Republic of Madagascar
16 Lanark Mansions
Pennard Road
London W12 8DT
Tel: (081) 746 0133. Fax: (081) 746 0134. Opening hours: 0900-1300 Monday to Friday.
British Embassy
BP 167
Première Etage, Immeuble 'Ny Havana'
Cité de 67 Ha
101 Antananarivo, Madagascar
Tel: (2) 27749. Fax: (2) 26690. Telex: 22459 PRODRO MG.
Embassy of the Democratic Republic of Madagascar
2374 Massachusetts Avenue, NW
Washington, DC
20008
Tel: (202) 265 5525.
Embassy of the United States of America
BP 620
14-16 rue Rainitovo
Antsahavola
101 Antananarivo, Madagascar
Tel: (2) 21257. Fax: (2) 34539. Telex: 22202.
Embassy of the Democratic Republic of Madagascar
282 Somerset Street West
Ottawa, Ontario
K2P 0J6
Tel: (613) 563 2506 *or* 563 2438. Fax: (613) 231 3261.
Canadian Embassy to Madagascar
The Canadian High Commission
PO Box 1022
Dar-es-Salaam, Tanzania
Tel: (51) 46000. Fax: (51) 46005. Telex: 41015.

AREA: 587,041 sq km (226,658 sq miles).
POPULATION: 11,197,000 (1990 estimate).
POPULATION DENSITY: 19.1 per sq km.
CAPITAL: Antananarivo (formerly Tananarive).
Population: 900,000 (1990).
GEOGRAPHY: Madagascar, the fourth largest island in the world, lies in the Indian Ocean off the coast of Mozambique. It includes several much smaller islands. A central chain of high mountains, the Hauts Plateaux, occupies more than half of the main island and is responsible for the marked differences – ethnically, climatically and scenically – between the east and west coasts. The narrow strip of lowlands on the east coast, settled from the 6th century by Polynesian seafarers, is largely covered by dense rainforests, whereas the broader west coast landscape, once covered by dry deciduous forests, is now mostly savannah. The east coast receives the monsoon and, on both coasts, the climate is wetter towards the north. The southern tip of the island is semi-desert, with great forests of cactus-like plants. The capital, Antananarivo, is high up in the Hauts Plateaux near the island's centre. Much of Madagascar's flora and fauna is unique to the island. There are 3000 endemic species of butterfly; the many endemic species of lemurs fill the niches occupied elsewhere by animals as varied as racoons, monkeys, marmots, bush babies, sloths and even (though this variant is now extinct) bears; there is a similar diversity of reptiles, amphibians and birds (especially ducks), and also at all levels of plant life.
LANGUAGE: The official languages are Malagasy (which is related to Indonesian) and French. Hova and other dialects are also spoken. Very little English is spoken.
RELIGION: 51% follow Animist beliefs, about 43% Christian; remainder Muslim.
TIME: GMT + 3.
ELECTRICITY: Mostly 220 volts AC, also 110 volts and 380 volts AC; 50Hz. Plugs are generally 2-pin.
COMMUNICATIONS: Telephone: IDD is available to major towns. Country code: 261. **Telex/telegram:** Telex services are available at the telecommunications centre and the Colbert and Hilton Hotels in the capital. The main post office *(PTT)* in Antananarivo offers a 24-hour telegram transmission service. **Post:** The *Poste Restante* facilities at main post offices are the most reliable option. Airmail to Europe takes at least seven days and surface mail three to four months. **Press:** There are no English-language newspapers; seven dailies are published in French and/or Malagasy.
BBC World Service and Voice of America frequencies: From time to time these change. See the section *How to Use this Book* for more information.

BBC:				
MHz	21.47	11.94	6.005	3.255
Voice of America:				
MHz	21.49	15.60	9.525	6.035

PASSPORT/VISA

Regulations and requirements may be subject to change at short notice, and you are advised to contact the appropriate diplomatic or consular authority before finalising travel arrangements. Details of these may be found at the head of this country's entry. Any numbers in the chart refer to the footnotes below.

	Passport Required?	Visa Required?	Return Ticket Required?
Full British	Yes	Yes	Yes
BVP	Not valid	-	-
Australian	Yes	Yes	Yes
Canadian	Yes	Yes	Yes
USA	Yes	Yes	Yes
Other EC	Yes	Yes	Yes
Japanese	Yes	Yes	Yes

PASSPORTS: Valid passport required by all.
British Visitors Passport: Not acceptable.
VISAS: Required by all.
Types of visa: Business and Tourist. A transit visa is not required by those who continue their journey to a third country by the same or first connecting aircraft within 24 hours, provided that tickets and documents are held for their onward journey and they do not leave the airport. Business visas cost £45 (2 entries cost £55). Tourist visas cost £30 (2 entries cost £40).
Validity: Visas are issued for the duration of 30 or 90 days and are valid for 6 months from date of issue.
Application to: Consulate (or Consular Section at Embassy. For addresses, see top of entry.
Application requirements: (a) Passport. (b) 1 application form. (c) 5 photos. (d) Letter of recommendation on company headed notepaper if requesting business visa. (e) Return ticket or confirmation of booking from travel agent. (f) Add 70p for recorded postage per passport to visa fees if applying by post.
Working days required: Same day for applications in person, 10 days by post.

MONEY

Currency: Malagasy Franc (MGFr) = 100 centimes. Notes are in denominations of MGFr10,000, 5000, 1000 and 500. Coins are in denominations of MGFr100, 50,

20, 10, 5, 2 and 1.
Credit cards: Visa, American Express, Access/ Mastercard and Diners Club are accepted at the capital's Colbert and Hilton hotels. These and other cards have limited use elsewhere in the country. Check with your credit card company for details of merchant acceptability and other services which may be available.
Travellers cheques: These can be exchanged in banks and major hotels.
Exchange rate indicators: The following figures are included as a guide to the movements of the Malgasy Franc against Sterling and the US Dollar:

Date:	Oct '89	Oct '90	Oct '91	Oct '92
£1.00=	2314	2429	2200	2726
$1.00=	1465	1243	1267	1718

Currency restrictions: The import and export of local currency is prohibited. Foreign currencies are unrestricted provided they are declared on import and the exported amounts do not exceed the declaration. Unspent MGFr may not be reconverted into foreign currency for export. These regulations are for foreign tourists; businessmen should enquire at a Malagasy Consulate.
Banking hours: 0800-1100 and 1400-1600 Monday-Friday.

DUTY FREE

The following goods can be imported into Madagascar without incurring customs duty:
500 cigarettes or 25 cigars or 500g of tobacco;
1 bottle of alcoholic beverage.

PUBLIC HOLIDAYS

Public holidays observed in Madagascar are as follows:
Mar 29 '93 Commemoration of the 1947 Rebellion. **Apr 9** Good Friday. **Apr 12** Easter Monday. **May 1** Labour Day. **May 20** Ascension. **May 31** Whitsun. **Jun 26** Independence Day. **Nov 1** All Saints' Day. **Dec 25** Christmas. **Dec 30** Anniversary of the Democratic Republic of Madagascar. **Jan 1 '94** New Year's Day. **Mar 29** Commemoration of the 1947 Rebellion.

HEALTH

Regulations and requirements may be subject to change at short notice, and you are advised to contact your doctor well in advance of your intended date of departure. Any numbers in the chart refer to the footnotes below.

	Special Precautions?	Certificate Required?
Yellow Fever	Yes	1
Cholera	Yes	2
Typhoid & Polio	Yes	-
Malaria	3	-
Food & Drink	4	-

[1]: A yellow fever vaccination certificate is required from travellers arriving from, or having passed through, an area considered by the Malagasy authorities to be infected; enquire at Embassy.
[2]: A cholera vaccination certificate is recommended for travellers arriving from, or having passed through, an area considered by the Malagasy authorities to be infected; enquire at Embassy. See the *Health* section at the back of the book.
[3]: Malaria risk, predominantly in the malignant *falciparum* form, exists all year throughout the country and is highest in coastal areas. Resistance to chloroquine has been reported.
[4]: All water should be regarded as being potentially contaminated. Water used for drinking, brushing teeth or making ice should have first been boiled or otherwise sterilised. Milk is unpasteurised and should be boiled. Powdered or tinned milk is available and is advised, but make sure that it is reconstituted with pure water. Avoid dairy products which are likely to have been made from unboiled milk. Only eat well-cooked meat and fish, preferably served hot. Pork, salad and mayonnaise may carry increased risk. Vegetables should be cooked and fruit peeled.
Rabies is present. For those at high risk, vaccination before arrival should be considered. If you are bitten abroad seek medical advice without delay. For more information consult the *Health* section at the back of the book.
Bilharzia (schistosomiasis) is present. Avoid swimming and paddling in fresh water. Swimming pools which are well-chlorinated and maintained are safe.
Hepatitis is endemic and precautions are advised.
Health care: Health insurance is strongly recommended; it should include cover for emergency repatriation. It is highly recommended that visitors bring medication for stomach upset.

TRAVEL - International

AIR: Madagascar's national airline is *Air Madagascar (MD).*
Approximate flight time: From *London* to Antananarivo is 13 hours 50 minutes (including connection at Paris). There are regular flights from Madagascar to Réunion, Mauritius, Kenya, Tanzania, the Comoros and the Seychelles.
International airports: *Antananarivo (TNR)*, 17km (11 miles) from the city. Airport facilities include restaurant and currency exchange. It is linked by a regular bus service to the *Air Madagascar* office and the Hilton Hotel (the centre for Madagascar Airtours). Taxis asking special higher rates are also available at the airport.
Also: *Nosy Bé* (links with the Seychelles), *Mahajanga* (East Africa and the Comoro Islands), *Toamasina* (Mauritius and Reunion islands); and *Arivonimamo* (international standby airport), 45km (28 miles) from the capital.
Departure tax: MGFr30,000 on most international flights; MGFr21,000 for flights within the region (passengers in transit are exempt).
SEA: International tour operators promote Madagascar as a stopping place on extended cruises of the Indian and western Pacific Oceans. Expensive private cruises can be arranged from the USA and Europe. Toamasina is the main port.

TRAVEL - Internal

AIR: Most of Madagascar can be reached by air (there are more than 100 airfields), the exceptions being a few towns in the central highlands. *Air Madagascar's* 'Air Tourist Pass' is available and allows unlimited travel for certain periods.
Departure tax: MGFr9000 for domestic flights.
SEA/RIVER/CANAL: Madagascar has a strong maritime tradition and there are many coastal transport services. Rapids render many of the rivers unnavigable; the *Direction du Tourisme* can organise small-boat safaris on the Betsiboka and the Tsiribihina. The Pangalanes Canal runs for almost 600km (370 miles) along the east coast. Much of it is currently too clogged with silt for commercial traffic; the *Direction du Tourisme* can arrange sailing holidays.
RAIL: There are passenger rail services from the east coast port of Toamasina via Antananarivo to Antsirabe (branch line to Lake Alaotra); and from Manakara, also on the east coast, to Fianarantsoa. The northern line is to be extended. The southern line passes through spectacular rainforests. First-class carriages are air-conditioned. Light refreshments are sometimes available. One or two trains run daily on each route.
ROAD: The road network is in need of repair. Tarred roads of varying quality link the main towns in the central highlands and continue to the most populous parts of the east and northwest coasts. There are three main routes, from Antananarivo to Majungo (RN4), to Toamasina (RN2) and to Fianarantsoa (RN7). There are isolated sections of tarred road elsewhere, but dirt tracks are more normal. Many roads are impassable in the rainy season (November to March). In 1988, the World Bank approved a US$140m loan to rehabilitate the network.
Bus: A flat fare is charged, irrespective of the distance travelled. Services can be unreliable. **Taxi:** Flat fares apply except in Antananarivo and Fianarantsoa, where fare is calculated according to whether the ride is confined to the 'lower town' or goes on to the 'upper town'. There are two types of taxi: the *Taxi-be*, which is quick and comfortable, and the *Taxi-brousse* (bush taxi), which is cheaper, slower, makes more stops and generally operates on cross-country routes. Fares should be agreed in advance and tipping is unnecessary. **Rickshaw:** The *pousse-pousse* takes passengers except where traffic or gradient makes it impractical. Prices are not controlled and vary according to distance. **Stagecoach:** A few covered wagons continue to take passengers in Antananarivo.
Car hire: This is not widespread and car-hire agencies can only be found in the main tourist towns. It is advisable to make enquiries in advance about insurance requirements for car hire. **Motor-bike hire:** Available through Club Double M, Androhibe, BP 1398, 101 Antananarivo. Tel: (2) 42392. Telex: 22577 CLUB MM MG. **Documentation:** National driving licence is all that is required.

ACCOMMODATION

HOTELS: Since hotel development is in its early stages, some areas are better served than others, notably the capital Antananarivo, Nosy Bé and Toamasina. However, recent projects aimed at increasing the number of international-standard establishments have led to the opening of national tourism centres where good to medium standard accommodation is now available at moderate prices. As well as classified or classifiable accommodation, group and youth lodging is available. European-style accommodation is scarce outside the larger towns, and those visiting remote areas should travel with an open mind. Enquiries should be addressed to the Tourism Office in Antananarivo or *Air Madagascar* agencies. The *Guide to Madagascar* by Hilary Bradt provides excellent information on hotels and is available through the Madagascan Consulate in the UK or through bookshops. **Grading:** Hotels are classified with from **1** to **5 stars** (5-star being equivalent to an international standard of about 3 stars); a secondary system of **ravinala** (travellers' palms) is used for more 'rustic' accommodation. More Information is available from the Groupement des Associations et des Sydicats du Tourisme de Madagascar (GAST), BP 465, 41, Lalana Ratsimilaho, Ambatonakanga, Antananarivo. Tel: (2) 22230 *or* 27680. Fax: (2) 34901. Telex: 22478.

RESORTS & EXCURSIONS

The *Direction du Tourisme* (address at top of entry) offers a wide range of tours, some lasting as long as a month.
Note: Those who intend to make their own arrangements should be aware that bandits operate in certain highland regions and that the terrain and climate make surface travel exceedingly difficult (and often impossible) throughout much of the country for much of the year.

The Central Highlands

The capital and several other important towns are situated in the central section of the *Hauts Plateaux*, the chain of rugged, ravine-riven mountains that run from north to south down the centre of Madagascar.
Antananarivo, often abbreviated to *Tana*, is built on three levels. Dominating the city is the *Queen's Palace* and associated Royal Village or *Rova*. Now a national monument (opening: 0900-1200 and 1400-1700), it was once the residency of the Merina dynasty which, in the 19th century, united all Madagascar for the first time. On the lowest level is the market of Analakely. The *Zuma Market*, claimed to be the second-largest in the world and certainly worth a visit, is busiest on Fridays. The *Tsimbazaza Zoological and Botanical Garden* is open 0800-1100 and 1400-1700 Thursdays, Sundays and holidays.

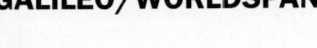

MADAGASCAR | **HEALTH REGULATIONS** | **VISA REGULATIONS** | Code-Link

GALILEO/WORLDSPAN

TI-DFT/TNR/HE

TI-DFT/TNR/VI

SABRE

TIDFT/TNR/HE

TIDFT/TNR/VI

To access this information on your CRS, swipe the barcode with a light pen or type in the text under the barcode. For more information, see the introduction *How to Use This Book*.

The Tourist Information Office is nearby. It is wise not to wander too far after dark.
Ambohimanga, the birthplace of the Malagasy state, is 20km (12 miles) from the capital. Known variously as 'the blue city', 'the holy city' and 'the forbidden city', it is surrounded by forests. The citadel was an important Merina stronghold and retains several structures associated with their ceremonies. Its main gate is an enormous stone disc; 40 men were needed to roll it into position. Ancestor worship may be witnessed on Sundays.
Mantasoa, 80km (50 miles) from the capital, is a popular spot for picnics. The area was landscaped for the Merina queens by a ship-wrecked Frenchman and includes an artificial lake, pine forests and Madagascar's first industrial park.
Ampefy, 90km (60 miles) from the capital, is a volcanic region with spectacular waterfalls and geysers. Dams are used here to catch eels.
Perinet, 140km (90 miles) from the capital, is a nature reserve, home of the *indri* (a tail-less lemur) and many species of orchid. Also known as *Andasibe*.
Antsirabe, 170km (110 miles) from the capital, is a thermal spa and Madagascar's main industrial centre. The volcanic hills surrounding the town are dotted with crater lakes. Madagascar's second-highest mountain, *Tsiafajovona*, may be seen to the west of the road from Antananarivo.

The North

The lush north is dominated by two great mountains. *Tsarantanana*, at 2880m (9450ft) the island's highest, is covered with the giant ferns and lichens peculiar to high altitude rainforests. *Montagne d'Arbre* (1500m/4900ft) is a national park and is famous for its orchids and lemurs. The monsoon falls in the north between December and March.
Mahajanga, a provincial capital, stands at the mouth of Madagascar's largest river, the *Betsiboka*. The road to the capital is open between July and October. Boats depart for Nosy Bé and several other islands. The beach here is said to be free of sharks. The island's finest grottoes are at **Anjohibe**, 90km (60 miles) inland. There is a nature reserve at **Ankarafantsika**.
Nosy Bé is Madagascar's most important holiday resort. An island surrounded by smaller islands lying off the northwest coast, it is one hour by air from the capital. Exotic perfume plants such as ylang-ylang, vanilla (Madagascar is the world's largest producer), lemon grass and patchouli are grown here. The main town is **Hell-Ville**. Nearby, there is a ruined 17th-century Indian village.
Antsiranana (formerly Diégo Suarez) is a cosmopolitan seaport overlooking a beautiful gulf at the northernmost tip of the island. It is a provincial capital. There are many lakes, waterfalls and grottoes in the rainforests above the port. Wildlife includes lemurs, crocodiles and orchids. Permission to visit the national park at Montagne d'Arbre nearby must be obtained from the *Ministère des Eaux et Forêts*, which has an office in the town. Boats may be taken to Nosy Bé. There is a good sandy beach at **Ramena**, but sharks may be a problem. The road southwards to the capital is only open between July and October.
Ile Ste-Marie (Nosy Boraha) lies off the east coast, 150km (90 miles) north of Toamasina. Its dense vegetation and the difficulty of navigating the lagoons which surround it made it an ideal base for pirates and, later, a colony for convicts. There are many clove plantations and several historic sites, including Madagascar's oldest Catholic church.
Toamasina, on the northeast coast, is the country's main port and a provincial capital. It is an 8-hour drive from Antananarivo and, like the capital, it has several busy markets, including the *Bazaar Be*. 11km (7 miles) north of the town are the *Ivolina Gardens*, containing every kind of vegetable species from the eastern forests and many varieties of animal life.
Vatomandry, further south, is a very popular beach resort even though the sharks prevent swimming.

The South

The arid south is noted for its many remarkable species of cactus- and baobab-like plants and for the highly developed funerary art of its inhabitants, past and present.
Fianarantsoa, a provincial capital, is an important centre for wine and rice production and a good base for exploring the southern highlands. Places to visit in the surrounding mountains include **Amabalavao**, said to be the 'home of the departed', where *antemore* paper and *lamba aridrano* silk are made; nearby **Ambondrome** and **Ifandana** crags, where the revered bones of exhumed ancestors may be seen (the latter was the site of a mass suicide in 1811); **Ambositra** and the neighbouring **Zafimaniny** villages, where intricate marquetry products are made; the **Isalo National Park**, situated in a chain of sandstone mountains (camping is possible but it can only be reached by 4-wheel drive or on foot with a guide); and **Ranomafana**, a thermal spa.
Mananjary is a popular beach resort on the east coast (but not for sea-bathing because of sharks).
Taolanaro (formerly Fort Dauphin) in the southeast corner of the island, is the site of the first French settlement. Parts of the 17th-century fort remain. The city and surrounding area is famous for its seafood and for its orchids and carnivorous pitcher plants, which can be seen at the *Mandona Agricultural Centre* at **Sainte-Luce Bay**.

The West

Western Madagascar was once covered with deciduous forests, but is now mostly savannah. The economy is based around the *zebu*, a species of ox introduced to the island in the 8th century by settlers from South-East Asia.
Toliara, a provincial capital on the southwest coast, has excellent bathing beaches and opportunities for skindiving, fishing, sailing and other watersports.

SOCIAL PROFILE

FOOD & DRINK: In Madagascar eating well means eating a lot. Malagasy cooking is based on a large serving of rice with a dressing of sauces, meat, vegetables and seasoning. Dishes include *ro* (a mixture of herbs and leaves with rice); beef and pork marinaded in vinegar, water and oil, then cooked with leaves and vegetables, onion and pickles and seasoned with pimento; *ravitoto* (meat and leaves cooked together); *ramazava* (leaves, pieces of beef and pork browned in oil); *vary amid 'anana* (rice, leaves or herbs, meat and sometimes shrimps) often eaten with *kitoza* (long slices of smoked, cured or fried meat). The people of Madagascar enjoy very hot food and often serve dishes with hot peppers. **Drink:** The choice of beverages is limited. The national wine is acceptable. Malagasy drinks include *litchel* (an aperitif made from litchis), *betsa* (fermented alcohol) and *toaka gasy* (distilled from cane sugar and rice) and 'Three Horseshoes' lager. Non-alcoholic drinks include *ranon 'apango* or *rano vda* (made from burnt rice) and local mineral waters.
NIGHTLIFE: There are a few discotheques, sometimes with bands and solo musicians. Casinos can be found at Antananarivo, Toamasina and on Nosy Bé. Most main towns have cinemas and theatres, and touring theatre groups perform local plays throughout the country. Traditional dance troupes can also be seen.
SHOPPING: Handicrafts include *lamba* (traditional squares of cloth in various designs and woven materials); *zafimaniny* marquetry, which is applied to furniture, chessboards and boxes; silverwork such as *mahafaly* crosses and *vangavanga* bracelets; jewellery made from shells and precious stones; items woven from reeds, raffia and straw; *antemore* paper decorated with dried flowers; and embroidery. All products incorporating Malagasy flora or fauna (including dried flowers) require export permits. Shoppers should make sure that they obtain this at the time of purchase; they should also be aware that many items on sale (including tortoise-shell products) have been manufactured illegally and may not be taken out of the country, with or without a permit. **Shopping hours:** 0800-1200 and 1400-1800 Monday to Saturday.
SPORT: Tennis: There are courts in most main towns. **Golf:** Facilities at Tana. **Watersports:** Many towns have municipal pools. Sea-bathing along the east coast is not advised due to sharks. Main **diving** centres are Nosy Bé (with its neighbouring islands, Tanikely, Nosy Mitsio and Nosy Radama), Nosy Lava, Toliara and Ile Ste-Marie (Nosy Boraha). **Water-skiing** and **sailing** centres are located at Ambohibao (Lake Mantasoa), Antsiralse (on Andraikiba Lake) and Ramona. **Trekking:** The *Direction du Tourisme* can organise a variety of trekking and hiking trips in many different parts of the country. They are generally designed to cater for specific interest groups – speleologists, mineralogists, ethnologists, ornithologists, those who wish to see rare orchids or lemurs, etc. Pony-trekking is also possible. **Spectator sports:** There are numerous **football** pitches and during the dry season it has been known to use rice fields as pitches. **Basketball** and **volleyball** are exceedingly popular and covered stadiums have been built.
SPECIAL EVENTS: There are many customary events and celebrations (see *Social Conventions* below), especially in rural areas. *Mphira gasy* (Malagasy singers) sing and dance theatrically in groups recounting a story and presenting its moral; typically a performance lasts from 30 minutes to an hour. The rice harvest is celebrated in many places. September 1993 heralds the First International Trade Fair, to be held in Antananarivo.
SOCIAL CONVENTIONS: Visitors to Madagascar remark on the welcoming nature of the people, though some unprepared Westerners may be irritated by their relaxed attitude to time (public forms of transport, for example, won't generally move until they're full – no matter how long it takes to fill the last seat). Dress is casual, except for the very smartest hotel and restaurant functions. Entertaining is done in restaurants and bars, and a good degree of acquaintance is necessary before being invited to a family home. Outside major towns, the people are poor but very hospitable. However, to offer money for lodging could be construed as an insult, therefore it is advisable to offer a contribution to the host towards the next family or village festival, which should be warmly received (MGFr1500 per person per night without food and MGFr2500 per person including food is an acceptable contribution). It is also advisable to give MGFr1000 to the village headman. Respect should be paid to the many local taboos (*fady*) – but as these vary from region to region this is not easy and very often the best that a traveller can do is show that his intentions are honourable; however, it is clear that advice should be sought before approaching tombs and graves. It remains the practice in some regions (though it is becoming increasingly rare due to the enormous cost) to invite an ancestor to a village celebration, disinterring the body so that the ancestor may attend physically, and later re-interring the body with new shrouds; this traditional observance (known as *famadihana*) amply demonstrates the continuing hold of traditional beliefs. Visitors invited to such an occasion should consider it a great honour.
Photography: Do not photograph military or police establishments. **Tipping:** Tipping is not customary, although waiters expect 10% of the bill. In European-style hotels and restaurants the French system of tipping is followed. One should also tip in Chinese and Vietnamese establishments.

BUSINESS PROFILE

ECONOMY: Madagascar's overwhelmingly agricultural economy relies heavily on coffee production to earn foreign exchange. Vanilla, cloves, sisal, cocoa and butter beans are the island's other important cash crops exported in quantity. Rice and cassava are produced primarily for domestic staple consumption. Fishing is one industry underdeveloped thus far: the Government, which exercises extensive control over the economy, is hoping to improve its performance. The country has appreciable mineral deposits of chromium ore and other materials, including uranium and bauxite, but these are scattered and fairly inaccessible and the Government has found exploitation to be uneconomic. About 17% of the Gross National Product derives from the manufacturing industry, mainly textiles and food processing. Madagascar's once dire balance of payments problem was alleviated during the 1980s under IMF tutelage, but the country still depends on loans and aid from the EC (especially France) and the World Bank. France accounts for about 30% of all Madagascar's trade; the USA and the CIS are other important trading partners. More recently, the Government has been looking at ways of exploiting Madagascar's other prominent asset: its abundance of exotic wildlife. Tourism has obvious development potential, but there is also the possibility of devising some kind of 'debt for nature' scheme analogous to the support programmes set up in South America to protect the rainforests.
BUSINESS: Tropical lightweight suits are appropriate wear. If arranged far enough in advance, the Embassy can arrange interpreters for business meetings.
COMMERCIAL INFORMATION: The following organisation can offer advice: Fédération des Chambres de Commerce, d'Industrie et d'Agriculture de Madagascar, BP 166, 20 rue Colbert, 101 Antananarivo. Tel: (2) 21567.

HISTORY & GOVERNMENT

HISTORY: According to local legend, the island was first inhabited by the Vazimba, a race of white pygmies. These people, if they existed, were displaced by successive waves of Polynesian migrants from the Malayo-Indonesian archipelago, which began as early as the 6th century AD. The settlers brought with them the zebu (a humped ox) and South-East Asian crops, along with methods of cultivation: parts of Madagascar, especially in the south, still retain a strong South-East Asian flavour. In the 9th century, Madagascar was an important trading power in the western Indian Ocean. Bantu tribes from mainland Africa later settled on the west coast. The island was unified under one ruler for the first time in the early 19th century. The Merina dynasty, who established the modern capital, ruled until 1896, when they were overthrown by a French military force. The French introduced cash crops to their new colony. In 1948 the Malagasy people sought to re-establish their independence through armed insurrection. They were unsuccessful, but the uprising paved the way or independence, which came in 1960. Philibert Tsirana's PSD party ruled with the support of France and the people of the coastal regions until 1972, when highland agitation against French influence prompted the Army Chief of Staff, Major-General Ramanantsoa, to assume executive power for the purpose of pursuing a more nationalistic policy. Three years later the military government resigned after selecting Lt-Commander Didier Ratsiraka as Head of State. A gradual civilianisation of the Government culminated in 1977 with elections to the National People's Assembly, which were won by the sole legal party, *Avant-garde de la Révolution Malgache* (AREMA). A left-wing splinter party, the *Mouvement National pour l'Indépendence de Madagascar* (MONIMA) was allowed to contest the 1983 presidential elections, but President Ratsiraka was re-elected. Elections scheduled for 1988 were postponed. In February 1989, Gen Rakotoarijaona resigned after ten years as Prime Minister. His controversial replacement was Col Ramahatra, a highlander who claims descent from the Merina Queens. His appointment has reopened a long-standing rift between the highland and lowland (coastal) clans and allowed disparate lowland opposition groups – ranging from Christian Democrats to old-style Maoists – to put aside their feuds and unite against highland/Merina factions in the Government. However, President Ratsiraka is allied to neither camp and has generally enjoyed the consistent support of the French since they managed to persuade him to drop his initial attachment to Marxism in the 1970s. At the most recent elections, held in May 1989, Ratsiraka's AREMA party took 120 of the 137 seats in the National Assembly. In the latter part of 1991, however, the Government has been seriously threatened by widespread civil unrest. The army, which has killed hundreds of protestors, is divided, but an influential section of it, supported by the French, wants to see the back of Ratsiraka. After resisting at first the entreaties of the opposition leadership – a collection of churchmen and retired military figures – Ratsiraka reached agreement with them at the end of October 1991 on the installation of an 18-month transitional administration led by himself.

GOVERNMENT: The President, elected by universal adult suffrage every seven years, wields executive power. Legislative power is held by the 137-member National People's Assembly, elected by universal adult suffrage every five years. The President is also Head of State and Chairman of the Supreme Revolutionary Council, an advisory body, and he elects the Prime Minister and, guided by the Assembly, the Council of Ministers.

CLIMATE

Hot and subtropical climate, colder in the mountains. Rainy season: November to March. Dry season: April to October. The south and west regions are hot and dry. Monsoons bring storms and cyclones to the east and north from December to March. The mountains, including Antananarivo, are warm and thundery from November to April and dry, cool and windy the rest of the year.

Required clothing: Lightweights are worn during the summer on high central plateaus and throughout the year in the north and south. Warmer clothes are advised during evenings and winter in mountainous areas. Rainwear is advisable.

TOAMASINA Madagascar (5m)

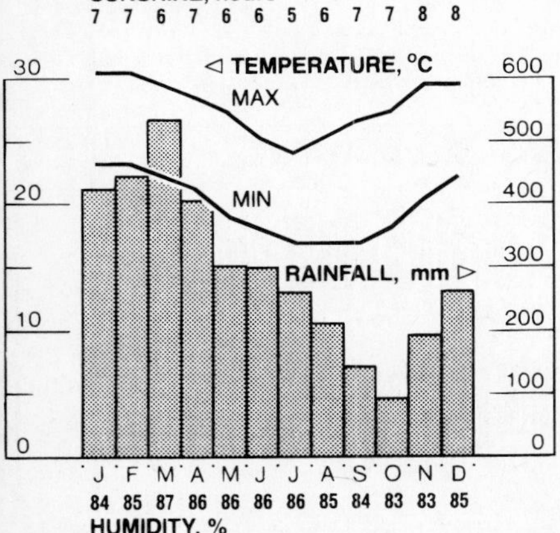

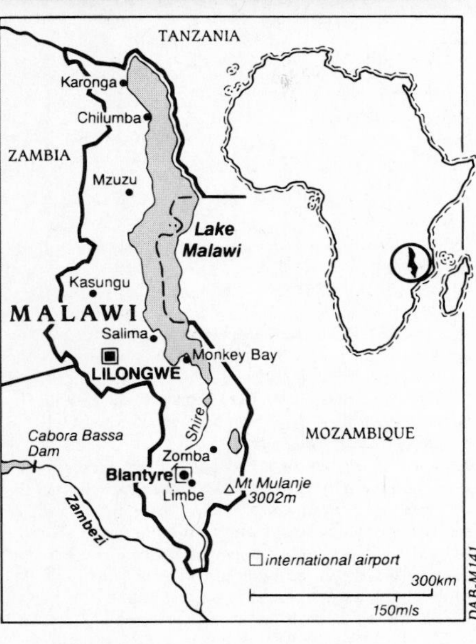

Location: Southeast Africa.

Department of Tourism
PO Box 402
Blantyre, Malawi
Tel: 620 300. Fax: 620 947. Telex: 44645.

High Commission for the Republic of Malawi *and* **Tourist Office**
33 Grosvenor Street
London W1X 0DE
Tel: (071) 491 4172/7. Fax: (071) 491 9916. Telex: 263308. Opening hours: 0930-1300 and 1400-1700 Monday to Friday.

British High Commission
PO Box 30042
Social Club
Lilongwe 3, Malawi
Tel: 780 669. Fax: 782 657. Telex: 44727 UK REPLI MI.

Embassy of the Republic of Malawi
2408 Massachusetts Avenue, NW
Washington, DC
20008
Tel: (202) 797 1007. Fax: (202) 265 0976.

Embassy of the United States of America
PO Box 30016
Area 40, Flat 18
Lilongwe 3, Malawi
Tel: 783 166. Fax: 780 471. Telex: 44627.

High Commission for Malawi
7 Clemlow Avenue
Ottawa, Ontario
K1S 2A9
Tel: (613) 236 8931. Fax: (613) 236 1054.
Consulates in: Montréal and Toronto.

Canadian High Commission
PO Box 1257
Lilongwe, Malawi
Tel: 723 732. Fax: 721 553. Telex: 45386 CAN PRO.

AREA: 118,484 sq km (45,747 sq miles).
POPULATION: 8,556,000 (1991 estimate).
POPULATION DENSITY: 72.2 per sq km.
CAPITAL: Lilongwe. **Population:** 233,973 including suburbs (1987). (Although Blantyre, with a population of 331,588, is the largest city in the country.)
GEOGRAPHY: Malawi shares borders to the north and northeast with Tanzania, to the south, east and southwest with Mozambique and to the north and northwest with Zambia. Lake Malawi, the third largest lake in Africa, is the dominant feature of the country, forming the eastern boundary with Tanzania and Mozambique. The scenery varies in the different regions: the Northern Region is mountainous, the highest peaks reaching to over 3000m (985ft), with the rolling Nyika Plateau, rugged escarpments, valleys and the thickly forested slopes of the Viphya Plateau. The Central Region is mainly a plateau, over 1000m (3300ft) high, with fine upland scenery. This is the country's main agricultural area. The Southern Region is low-lying with the 2100m-(6890ft) high Zomba Plateau south of Lake Malawi and the huge, isolated Mulanje Massif in the southeast. The variety of landscape, and the wildlife it supports, makes this relatively unspoilt country particularly attractive to visitors.
LANGUAGE: The official language is English. Chichewa is widely spoken and is regarded as the national language especially by Malawi's largest single ethnic group, the Chewa, who live along the lakeshore and on the plains. The Tonga live mainly in the Northern Region, as far as Usisya, and speak Chi Tonga. The Tumbuka-Henga live mostly between Mzimba and Karonga, while even further north live the Ngonde, who also have their own language.
RELIGION: Animist with Christian, Hindu and Muslim minorities. Along the southern lakeshore the Yao culture groups, a number of whom are Muslim, predominate (they are also found at Salima and Nkhotakota in the Central Region along with the Ngoni – the *Ngoma* is their spectacular war dance). The Ngonde are a predominantly Christian group.
TIME: GMT + 2.
ELECTRICITY: 230/240 volts AC, 50Hz. A variety of plugs are in use, most modern buildings using square 3-pin plugs.
COMMUNICATIONS: Telephone: IDD is available. Country code: 265 (no area codes). **Fax:** Bureaux offering public fax services have recently opened in Blantyre and Zomba. **Telex/telegram:** Bureaux offering public telex services have recently opened in Blantyre and Zomba. Public facilities for sending telegrams exist at the main post office. **Post:** Letters take about ten days to reach Europe by airmail. Post offices are generally open 0730-1200 and 1300-1700 Monday to Friday. Post offices in some of the larger towns may be open 0900-1000 Sundays, but only to sell stamps or to accept telegrams. **Press:** The two main newspapers are *The Daily Times* (Monday to Friday) and *The Malawi News* (Saturday).
BBC World Service and Voice of America frequencies: From time to time these change. See the section *How to Use this Book* for more information.

BBC:				
MHz	21.47	11.94	6.190	3.255
Voice of America:				
MHz	21.49	15.60	9.525	6.035

PASSPORT/VISA

Regulations and requirements may be subject to change at short notice, and you are advised to contact the appropriate diplomatic or consular authority before finalising travel arrangements. Details of these may be found at the head of this country's entry. Any numbers in the chart refer to the footnotes below.

	Passport Required?	Visa Required?	Return Ticket Required?
Full British	Yes	No	Yes
BVP	Not valid	-	-
Australian	Yes	No	Yes
Canadian	Yes	No	Yes
USA	Yes	No	Yes
Other EC	Yes	1	Yes
Japanese	Yes	Yes	Yes

Entry restrictions: Men with very long hair will be denied entry. Women may not wear trousers and should ensure that skirts and dresses cover their knees. (Dress restrictions do not apply if in transit or at lakeside resorts, game reserves, national parks, Zomba Plateau and Mount Mulanje.)
PASSPORTS: Valid passport required by all.
British Visitors Passport: Not acceptable.
VISAS: Required by all except:
(a) nationals of countries as shown in the chart above;
(b) [1] nationals of Belgium, Denmark, Germany, Republic of Ireland, Luxembourg, The Netherlands and Portugal (nationals of other EC countries *do* need visas);
(c) nationals of Antigua & Barbuda, Bahamas, Bangladesh, Barbados, Belize, Botswana, Brunei, Cyprus, Dominica, Fiji, Finland, Gambia, Ghana, Grenada, Guyana, Iceland, Jamaica, Kenya, Kiribati, Lesotho, Malaysia, Maldives, Malta, Mauritius, Mozambique, Nauru, New Zealand, Nigeria, Norway, Papua New Guinea, San Marino, Seychelles, Sierra Leone, Singapore, Solomon Islands, South Africa, Sri Lanka, St Kitts & Nevis, St Lucia, St Vincent & the Grenadines, Swaziland, Sweden, Tanzania, Tonga, Trinidad & Tobago, Tuvalu, Uganda, Vanuatu, Western Samoa, Zambia and Zimbabwe.
Types of visa: Tourist (3-month, 6-month and 12-

month) and Transit. Cost varies according to nationality of visitor and the strength of the Kwacha. The Transit visa is valid for 3 days, but is not usually required of Western or Commonwealth visitors.
Validity: Upon entry into Malawi a 3-month Tourist visa is granted, subject to certain conditions. Extensions will not normally be granted in Malawi.
Application to: Consulate (or Consular Section at Embassy or High Commission); for addresses, see top of entry. Alternatively, contact the Deputy Chief Immigration Officer (address below).
Application requirements: (a) 2 application forms. (b) 2 photos. (c) Fee (variable). (d) Valid passport. (e) Onward ticket. (f) Proof of means of support during residence in country. (g) Letter from company/sponsor where required.
Working days required: 5.
Temporary residence: Application should be made prior to arrival. Contact the Deputy Chief Immigration Officer, PO Box 331, Blantyre, Malawi.

MONEY

Currency: Kwacha (Mk) = 100 tambala. Notes are in denominations of Mk50, 20, 10, 5 and 1. Coins are in denominations of 50, 20, 10, 5, 2 and 1 tambala.
Currency exchange: Lesser-known currencies will be difficult to exchange in Malawi.
Credit cards: Acceptance of credit cards is limited, but in the capital and main hotels Access/Mastercard, Diners Club and American Express, can be used. Check with your credit card company for details of merchant acceptability and other services which may be available.
Travellers cheques and major currencies, including US Dollars and Sterling, can be exchanged in banks, hotels and other institutions. In remote areas, the Treasury Office of Local District Commissioners offices will cash cheques.
Exchange rate indicators: The following figures are included as a guide to the movements of the Kwacha against Sterling and the US Dollar:

Date:	Oct '89	Oct '90	Oct '91	Oct '92
£1.00=	4.42	5.05	4.82	6.51
$1.00=	2.80	2.59	2.77	4.10

Currency restrictions: Import and export of local currency up to Mk20 is allowed. Import of foreign currency is unlimited if declared. Export of foreign currency is allowed up to the limit declared on entry.
Banking hours: 0800-1300 Monday to Friday.

DUTY FREE

The following goods may be imported into Malawi without incurring customs duty:
200 cigarettes or 250g of tobacco in any form;
*1 litre of spirits or 1 litre of beer or 1 litre of wine;**
250ml of toilet water;
50g of perfume.
Note [*]: Alcoholic goods are only available to passengers 16 years of age or older.
Prohibited items: The import of firearms is prohibited unless a permit has been bought in advance from the Registrar of Firearms, Box 41, Zomba.

PUBLIC HOLIDAYS

Public holidays observed in Malawi are as follows:
Mar 3 '93 Martyr's Day. **Apr 9-12** Easter. **May 14** Kamuzu Day, Birthday of President Banda. **Jul 6** Republic Day. **Oct 17** Mothers' Day. **Dec 21** National Tree Planting Day. **Dec 25** Christmas Day. **Dec 26** Boxing Day. **Jan 1 '94** New Year's Day. **Mar 3** Martyr's Day.
Note: If a public holiday falls on a Saturday, the previous day will be a holiday; if on a Sunday the next day will be the holiday. Ad hoc public holidays or extensions may also be declared by the President, sometimes at short notice.

HEALTH

Regulations and requirements may be subject to change at short notice, and you are advised to contact your doctor well in advance of your intended date of departure. Any numbers in the chart refer to the footnotes below.

	Special Precautions?	Certificate Required?
Yellow Fever	No	1
Cholera	Yes	2
Typhoid & Polio	Yes	-
Malaria	3	-
Food & Drink	4	-

[1]: A yellow fever vaccination certificate is required from travellers arriving from infected areas.
[2]: Following WHO guidelines issued in 1973, a cholera vaccination certificate is not a condition of entry to Malawi. However, cholera is a risk in this country and precautions are essential. Up-to-date advice should be sought before deciding whether these precautions should include vaccination, as medical opinion is divided over its effectiveness. See the *Health* section at the back of the book.
[3]: Malaria risk exists all year throughout the country. The predominant *falciparum* (malignant) strain is reported to be 'highly resistant' to chloroquine and 'resistant' to sulfadoxine/pyrimethamine.
[4]: All water should be regarded as being potentially contaminated. Water used for drinking, brushing teeth or making ice should have first been boiled or otherwise sterilised. Milk is unpasteurised and should be boiled. Powdered or tinned milk is available and is advised, but make sure that it is reconstituted with pure water. Avoid dairy products which are likely to have been made from unboiled milk. Only eat well-cooked meat and fish, preferably served hot. Pork, salad and mayonnaise may carry increased risk. Vegetables should be cooked and fruit peeled.
Rabies is present. For those at high risk, vaccination before arrival should be considered. If you are bitten abroad seek medical advice without delay. For more information consult the *Health* section at the back of the book.
Bilharzia (schistosomiasis) is present, but Lake Malawi is entirely safe. Avoid swimming and paddling in slow-moving fresh water elsewhere. Swimming pools which are well-chlorinated and maintained are safe.
Health care: Health insurance is essential. It is advisable to take personal medical supplies.

TRAVEL - International

AIR: Malawi's national airline is *Air Malawi (QM)*.
Approximate flight time: From *London* to Lilongwe is 12 hours 10 minutes (including 1 hour in Harare). There are also connections between Malawi and Kenya, Mauritius, South Africa and Zimbabwe.
International airports: *Lilongwe (LLW)*, Kamuzu International, is 22km (13.6 miles) from the city. Taxi services are available to the city from the airport. Airport facilities include a duty-free shop, post office, car hire (*Hertz* and *SS Rent-a-Car*), bank/exchange (0730-2100), restaurant (0600-2200) and bar (0730-2200).
Blantyre (BLZ), Chileka, is 18km (11 miles) from the city. There is a coach service to the city. Airport facilities include car hire (*Hertz* and *SS Rent-a-Car*), restaurant and bar (0730-2000).
Departure tax: A passenger service charge of US$20 is levied on all international flights. This must be paid in US currency. Malawi passport holders can pay in local currency (Mk40). There is no tax on internal travel.
RAIL: There are two international rail links, both with Mozambique, connecting with the seaports of Beira and Nacala. The latter was recently re-opened after being closed by sabotage for four years during the war in Mozambique. There are plans to extend the internal network from the present terminus at Mchinji across the border to Zambia.
ROAD: There are roads linking Malawi with all surrounding countries.

TRAVEL - Internal

AIR: The air network (*Air Malawi*) links Blantyre and Lilongwe with local airports at Mzuzu and Karonga. In addition, planes are available for charter, thereby giving access to the many small airports in the country; contact *Capital Air Services Ltd.*
SEA: Cruises on Lake Malawi's shores are run by local steamer services. Food and cabins are available. For details contact the local authorities. *Malawi Railways* operate boat services on the lake from the railhead at Chipoka.
RAIL: *Malawi Railways* operate the only two lines in the country. The main route (see map) connects Mchinji, Lilongwe, Salima, Chipoka, Blantyre, Limbe and Nsanje to the Mozambique port of Beira. The other line branches off to the east at Mkaya, south of Balaka, passing through Liwonde on the way to the Mozambique border. Passenger services are regular, but slow and expensive. Trains have three classes, restaurant and sleeping cars. For further information contact Malawi Railways, PO Box 5144, Limbe. Tel: 640 844. Telex: 44810.
ROAD: There are over 11,500km (7200 miles) of roads in the country. All major and most secondary roads are all-weather. The main north–south highway to Karonga is now sealed. **Bus:** There is a good bus system, including an express service, connecting main towns. The journey from Mzuzu to Karonga is particularly spectacular. Luxury coaches operate Blantyre–Zomba–Lilongwe. **Car hire:** This is available in major towns. Cars should be reserved well in advance as they are in big demand. Chaffeur-driven cars are also available. **Documentation:** Nationals of certain countries, including the UK, do not require an International Driving Permit. A national driving licence is sufficient.
URBAN: Bus: Double-decker buses are available in Blantyre and Lilongwe and there is a regular bus service in all major cities. **Taxi:** Taxis are in short supply and cannot be hailed on the street. For taxi services in Blantyre: tel: 636 402. Taxi drivers expect a 30-tambala tip.

ACCOMMODATION

HOTELS: In the main centres there are excellent hotels, the most sophisticated being in Blantyre and Lilongwe. In addition there are some excellent lodge-style hotels in the main tourist resorts.
RESTHOUSES: Clean and comfortable resthouses are operated by the Department of Tourism. All have bathrooms and cooking facilities, although guests generally have to provide their own food.
CAMPING: There are a few developed sites, some of which offer superb lake or mountain views. Campsites can be found throughout the country. The camping season is a long one with the dry weather lasting from April to November. Facilities at all the sites include water, toilets and shade.

RESORTS & EXCURSIONS

For convenience, the country has been divided into four sections: North, Central, South and Lake Malawi. There is also a section giving information on the Wildlife Reserves and National Parks in Malawi.

MALAWI | **HEALTH REGULATIONS** | **VISA REGULATIONS** | Code-Link

GALILEO/WORLDSPAN

TI-DFT/LLW/HE

TI-DFT/LLW/VI

SABRE

TIDFT/LLW/HE

TIDFT/LLW/VI

To access this information on your CRS, swipe the barcode with a light pen or type in the text under the barcode. For more information, see the introduction *How to Use This Book*.

The Northern Region

The road from Kasungu to Mzuzu, the least visited centre of the northern region, crosses the rolling grasslands of the Viphya Plateau. Further north towards the *Livingstonia Mission* is the Livingstonia escarpment and the *Manchewe Falls*, which are approached along the escarpment road made up of 22 hairpin bends. The Manchewe Falls are a spectacular sight, set amidst magnificent scenery. There is a museum in Livingstonia. The region has recently become more popular with visitors, and there is now a first-class hotel at **Mzuzu,** which caters for visitors to local beauty spots such as *Nyika National Park* and *Nkhata Bay*.

Lake Malawi

Stretching from the northeastern-most tip of Malawi to **Mangochi** in the south is the massive **Lake Malawi**. The surface area of the lake covers nearly 24,000 sq km (15,000 square miles), and lies in the deep, trough-like rift valley which runs the length of the country. The shores of the lake are generally sandy, and the water itself is free of bilharzia. Crocodiles (the scourge of African lakes) have been effectively eliminated from main resort areas. There are no tides or currents. Most of the hotels provide pleasure craft enabling visitors to enjoy water-skiing, sailing, fishing or windsurfing. For tropical fish enthusiasts and snorkellers, Lake Malawi is an underwater paradise. It is now known to contain more species of fish than any other lake in the world; over 350 at the latest count. Some of the rarest tropical fish in the world are unique to the lake, which is also the home of fish eagles, black eagles, several varieties of kingfishers, terns and many other birds.

Likoma Island in the middle of the lake is worth a visit – there are excellent swimming facilities off the beaches and a very interesting *Anglican Cathedral* up the hill.

One of the best ways of seeing Lake Malawi is to cruise in the 630-ton *Ilala II*, the lake's mini-liner which travels between *Monkey Bay* (north of Club Makokola) and **Karonga** in the north of the country. The 1052km (654-mile) voyage gives the passenger the opportunity to visit lake ports and to view the spectacular mountain scenery. March to May are the calmest months for the 'Lake Cruise', and regular scheduled voyages are made from Friday to the Wednesday of the following week. The heavy demand for cabins on the *Ilala II* during the holiday season means that advanced payment and bookings are essential.

Cape Maclear, near Monkey Bay, is worth a visit – there is a pebble beach and warm lake-water to swim in.

Thumbi Island is a nature reserve offshore from the bay.

Nkhata Bay is quiet and deserted.

Nkhotakota was once the centre of the slave trade in southern Africa. It is also one of Africa's oldest market towns.

The Central Region

Salima is the main lakeshore resort of the central region, offering excellent tourist facilities and a campsite.

Lizard Island, near Salima, is a nature reserve, and home to many varieties of lizard and eagle.

Due west of Salima, across a large fertile plain, is the new capital city of **Lilongwe**. Situated on the crossroads of the agriculturally rich central region, Lilongwe replaced Zomba as Malawi's capital. It is a modern city of imaginative architecture in an unspoiled garden setting. North of the capital is the 2000 sq km (770 sq miles) **Kasungu National Park** – a vast area of undulating woods and grassland teeming with wildlife (see below). Northwest of Lilongwe is the country's main tobacco-growing area.

The Southern Region

Blantyre, the commercial centre of the southern region, was established at the end of the last century. It is really two cities; Blantyre and **Limbe**, about 7km (4 miles) apart, and separated by an industrial zone. The *National Museum* is halfway between Blantyre and Limbe, off the main road.

Southwest of Blantyre is **Lengwe,** the smallest of the country's national parks (see below). 60km (35 miles) north of Blantyre is the university town of **Zomba**, the country's former capital, which has an excellent market. Nearby is *Zomba Mountain*, sparkling with waterfalls and trout streams, bluegum plantations and rare plants, particularly orchids. Its foothills shelter one of Africa's loveliest golf courses, situated among streams, tiny waterfalls, trees and rock formations. Also in the region is *Chingwe's Hole*, reputed to be too deep to measure.

To the southeast are large tea estates, out of which rises the magnificent **Mulanje Massif**, a huge block of mountains of more than 640 sq km (250 sq miles) rising to over 3000m (9850ft) at its highest point at **Sapitwa**. For the tourist, Mulanje offers a wide scope of activities, from rock climbing and mountain walking, to the more leisurely pursuit of trout fishing. Most areas of the massif are accessible by either paths or firebreaks. A number of well-tended forestry huts provide suitable bases for exploring the grassy uplands, forests and numerous summits. The normal time for visiting Mulanje is from April to December, although many visitors enjoy the dramatic effects of the heavy rains which fall for the rest of the year.

Woodcarving from local cedar is available in the villages at the base of the massif.

National Parks

Malawi has five main National Parks open to visitors: **Nyika National Park** is situated in the north of the northern region and is open to visitors throughout the year. It covers most of the Nyika Plateau, which lies at an altitude of 2000-3000m (1250-1850ft). The rolling grassland is broken by deep valleys and occasional patches of evergreen, natural forest and bubbling streams. Nyika is known to sustain many rare birds, butterflies, game and a multitude of flowers. *Chelinda Camp*, set high up on the edge of a pine forest and overlooking a trout-filled dam, provides accommodation in comfortable cottages with log fires. The *Chowo Forest*, located near **Chelinda**, is excellent for walking. It is one of the last areas of natural forest left in the park.

Kasungu National Park, situated in the northwest of the central region 112km (68 miles) from Lilongwe, consists of some 2000 sq km (772 sq miles) of woodland. The Park is best known for its elephants, which appear in the early morning and evening to drink from *dambos* or river channels. The grasslands support large herds of buffalo, and occasionally rhino appear. Less common are the elusive cheetahs, leopards and lions, which occasionally appear for a few days. Other animals include the sable antelope, zebra, kudu and reedbuck. Kasungu is usually open from the beginning of May until the end of December. Accommodation is available at the *Lifupa Wildlife Lodge*, a complex of thatched rondavel cottages with a restaurant, day camp, swimming pool and basic provisions.

Lengwe National Park, in the southwest corner of the southern region, is only 130 sq km (80 sq miles). This park has the distinction of being the farthest place north where the rare, shy Nyala antelope is found. This beautiful animal may be seen, often in large numbers, together with Livingstone's Suni, one of the smallest species of antelope, and the equally rare Blue or Samango monkey. Other game include bushbuck, kudu, hartebeest, impala, warthog and duiker. Visitors may view game at close quarters from concealed hides. The best time of day for this is first thing in the morning. Limited accommodation is available at *Lengwe Game Camp*.

Liwonde National Park, situated on the flat plain of the Shire Valley, stretches from *Lake Malombe* in the north to Liwonde township in the south. Boats are available for trips through reed swamps, where hippo, elephants and waterbuck come to drink. When travelling by road, woodland and grassland animals such as sable antelope, kudu, duiker and baboon can also be seen. An aquatic bird sanctuary has been developed, home to a variety of birdlife including egrets, herons, ducks, geese, kingfishers and nesting cormorants. The park is closed from November to May. In the near future, camping and self-catering facilities will be available. There are also plans for the introduction of boat trips from one of the hotels on the southern tip of Lake Malawi to Liwonde Barrage and back. Enquire at the Tourist Office for up-to-date details of these developments.

Lake Malawi National Park, on the southern and central parts of the lake, is the most recent of Malawi's parks, established in 1980. Tropical fish, which can be viewed with the use of scuba equipment and masks, are a speciality of the park, while further inland klipspringer, bushbuck and vervet monkeys may be seen. Access to the park is easy throughout the year. There are camping facilities and plans to build other accommodation, including a modern hotel, in the near future. There are also good hotels at *Nkopola Lodge* and *Club Makokola*. Enquire at the Tourist Office for further details.

In addition to the National Parks there are a number of other reserves, sanctuaries and protected areas where there are no facilities at present for visitors. The **Majete Game Reserve,** about 65km (40 miles) to the north of Lengwe, is less accessible and less well provided for, but has a large number of animals including hippos, elephants and big cats. Southeast of Lengwe is the **Mwabvi Game Reserve,** which has a small number of black rhino, impala, zebra and sable. Others include the **Nkhotakota Game Reserve** in the Central Region, **Lizard Island** near Salima, **Lilongwe Nature Sanctuary** in the capital itself, and **Michiru Mountain Park** near Blantyre, which offers some of the best birdwatching in the area.

SOCIAL PROFILE

FOOD & DRINK: Fresh fish from Lake Malawi is the country's speciality, *chambo* (Tilapia fish) being the main lake delicacy. There are trout from streams on the Zomba, Mulanje and Nyika plateaux. Hotel restaurants and many of those in the cities are of a very high standard. They offer a wide choice of excellent food including *haute cuisine*, the unique *Lake Malawi* dishes and the best Malawi beef. Poultry and dairy produce are plentiful and tropical fruits are abundant in season. The local beer is very good and imported beer and soft drinks are widely available. Wine is imported from major wine-producing countries.

SHOPPING: Malawi produces a variety of colourful arts and crafts. Items are invariably handmade and there is no mass production of curios aimed specifically at the tourist market. Purchases include woodcarvings, wood and cane furniture, soapstone carvings, decorated wooden articles, colourful textiles, pottery, beadwork, cane and raffia items. Traditional musical instruments are also sold throughout Malawi.

Shopping hours: 0800-1700 Monday to Saturday.

SPORT: Fishing: Lake Malawi offers excellent fishing, particularly on the southern shores in April when anglers take part in the tackle tournament organised by the Angling Society. A popular collecting point for anglers is Mangochi, roughly 190km (120 miles) from Blantyre, while Boadzulu Island, Nkopola Lodge and White Rock are also good spots. Boats should be arranged in advance from lakeshore hotels. Catches include lake yellow fish, lake salmon and lake tiger. River mouths in the Salima area, the Kapichira Falls on the Shire, and Nyika and Zomba Plateaux are also excellent bases for fishermen. Visitors should contact the Angling Society at PO Box 744, Blantyre, for further information. **Mountaineering:** *Mount Mulanje*, rising to a majestic height of 3000m (9850ft), is the highest mountain in central Africa and has proven to be an irresistible lure to climbers. The mountain includes the longest sheer rock face in Africa, as well as some less challenging trekking along mountain paths. A 2- to 6-day tour is recommended, and there are huts available for hire. *Dedza* in the Central Region offers challenging slopes, as do *Michiru Ndirande* and *Chiradzulu* near Blantyre. In the north, 1- to 6-day wilderness trails are available to walkers along the grassland of the *Nyika Plateau*. Guides and porters are available; visitors must, however, supply their own camping equipment. **Golf:** There are seven golf courses in Malawi, most are 9-hole courses with alternate tees to provide 18 holes. Green and caddy fees are very reasonable. **Watersports:** Swimming, water-skiing and sailing are all popular in Lake Malawi. **Horseriding** is also available.

SPECIAL EVENTS: Dance plays a part in most ceremonies in Malawi, an important dance being the *Gule Wamkulu* with its heavily carved masks, feathers and skin paint. It is performed by the Chewa and Mang'anja, and this and other national dances can be seen at *Kamuzu Day Celebrations* on May 14, or at the annual *Malawi Republic Day* national celebrations on July 6.

SOCIAL CONVENTIONS: Visitors are particularly requested to observe local customs in styles of dress. In Malawi it is illegal for a woman to appear in public in a dress that does not cover the knees, or to wear trousers. Short dresses and trousers may, however, be worn at some holiday resorts and trousers may be worn in some of the national parks, game and forest reserves. For men, long hair (below collar) is frowned upon, although dress restrictions are being relaxed.

Tipping: Most tourist hotels and restaurants have a 10% service charge added to the bill and tipping is only really necessary for extra services.

BUSINESS PROFILE

ECONOMY: The economy is almost entirely agricultural, with both subsistence and cash crops including tobacco, sugar, tea and maize being farmed. Despite being self-sufficient in food, Malawi ran up a vast balance of payments deficit during the 1980s and is now heavily dependent on foreign aid, both bilateral and from the World Bank. The situation has now been made worse by the drought currently affecting the country (Malawi had largely escaped the effects of previous spells).

Manufacturing industry is small as yet and concentrated in light industrial import substitution projects such as textiles, agricultural implements and processed foodstuffs. The UK is Malawi's most important trading partner, taking one-third of the country's exports and providing 15% of Malawi's imports. South Africa, Japan, Germany and The Netherlands are Malawi's other important trading partners.

BUSINESS: Suits or a jacket and tie are suitable for business meetings in cities. Similar to the European system, appointments should generally be made and calling cards are used. Offices tend to open early in Malawi. Best months for business visits are May to July and September to November. **Office hours:** 0730-1700 Monday to Friday.

COMMERCIAL INFORMATION: The following organisation can offer advice: The Associated Chambers of Commerce and Industry of Malawi, PO Box 258, Chichiri Trade Fair Grounds, Blantyre. Tel: 671 988. Fax: 671 147. Telex: 43992.

CONFERENCES/CONVENTIONS: Malawi's only dedicated conference centre is the Kwacha International Conference Centre in Blantyre, with seating for up to 500 persons. Details of this and hotels with conference facilities can be obtained from the Department of Tourism.

HISTORY & GOVERNMENT

HISTORY: Formerly Nyasaland, Malawi was once named *Maravi*, or 'reflected light', perhaps referring to the brilliant glitter on Lake Malawi as the sun shines over it. The shores of Lake Malawi have been inhabited for thousands of years, and recent archaeological excavations have revealed evidence of settlements dating back to the late Stone and Iron Ages. The majority of the present population descend from Bantu tribes (ancestors of the present Chewa, Nyanja, Lomwe, Yao, Tumbuka, Sena, Tonga, Ngoni and Ngonde tribes) who arrived in the region some time before the first Arab slave traders and Portuguese explorers. British colonial settlers and missionaries, men such as the famous Dr David Livingstone, moved into the area in the late 1850s. With the growth of commerce and expanding plantations of successful cash crops, Malawians migrated towards settlers' estates in search of work. Colonial domination became inevitable, and in 1891 the British declared the country the British protectorate of Nyasaland. In 1953 the British federated Nyasaland with Northern and Southern Rhodesia (now Zambia and Zimbabwe), but Nyasaland seceded in 1963, following elections which gave Dr Hastings Kamuzu Banda's Malawi Congress Party (MCP) a majority in the Legislative Council. In 1964, Nyasaland became independent as Malawi, and two years later Dr Banda declared it a republic and a one-party state. Membership of the Malawi Congress Party is compulsory for all citizens: it is impossible, for example, to buy food in a market without producing a party card. In 1971 Dr Banda became President for Life. He has since retained a firm grip on the country and acted vigorously to repress any opposition. In 1979, he publicly admitted having sent a letter bomb to the exiled leader of the Socialist League of Malawi, Dr Attati Mpakati, who was later assassinated in 1983. The founders of the Malawi Freedom Movement, Orton and Vera Chirwa, were arrested in 1981 and have been detained ever since on grounds of 'conspiracy'. More recently, the Malawian trades union leader Chakufwa Chihana was arrested immediately on his return from Zambia, where he had espoused the cause of democracy in Malawi, and detained on grounds of 'sedition'. Of all the countries of Southern Africa, Malawi has enjoyed the closest relations with South Africa. It is the only one which maintained an embassy in Pretoria before 1990 and whose head of state visited the country (Banda went there in 1971). Malawi refused, however, to recognise the South African 'homelands' as independent. Malawi's relations with its black-ruled neighbours have been patchy. Banda remained neutral during the independence struggles of the 1970s in Angola, Mozambique and Zimbabwe. Since then, Malawi has become involved in the civil war in Mozambique between the ruling FRELIMO movement and RENAMO (Mozambique National Resistance) which has driven almost one million refugees into Malawi from Mozambique. RENAMO was initially sponsored by the Rhodesians, then taken over by the South Africans after 1980. Mozambique accused Malawi of providing bases and support to RENAMO during the 1980s; Malawi denied the accusation and in 1986 countered that Mozambique and Zimbabwe had hatched a plot to overthrow the Banda government. Relations between the Malawian and Mozambican governments improved in the late 1980s; Malawian troops helped defend vital rail links against attack and Malawi itself suffered a series of assaults by RENAMO. Malawi will be glad of the Mozambican political settlement that appears to have been reached in 1992 which will hopefully allow most of the refugees to go home. Banda must now address the growing domestic political crisis which became apparent at national elections in June 1992. The surprise was not the result – all candidates belonged to the MCP – but the turnout, which independent observers reckoned to be an unprecedented low figure of 40-50%. Domestic opposition – 'meat for the crocodiles' according to Banda – has become gradually more outspoken, notably the Democratic Alliance, although they still fear 'massive repression'. For the moment their safety is, at least partially, guaranteed by action on the part of Malawi's foreign aid donors who have been, since the end of the Cold War, less prepared to turn a blind eye to Banda's excesses. At the last meeting of the Paris Club of donors in May 1992, Malawi was refused development aid and granted £95-million humanitarian aid to alleviate the effects of drought and the refugee influx (Banda had asked for £150 million). The Club has made it clear to Banda that the provision of future aid will be dependent on the results of a human rights 'audit' to be carried out in November. The regime will also be expected to move towards representative democracy. This may be a task for Banda's successor (Banda himself is in his 90s). The front-runner at present is Banda's right-hand man, Minister of State John Tembo, in whose hands much of the day-to-day running of the country now rests.

GOVERNMENT: The President is Head of State and holds all executive powers. Legislative authority is vested in the unicameral National Assembly with 112 members, elected from the ranks of the Malawi Congress Party for a 5-year term.

CLIMATE

Varies from cool in the highlands to warm around Lake Malawi. Winter (May to July) is dry and nights can be cold, particularly in the highlands. The rainy season runs from November to March. Around Lake Malawi the climate is particularly dry with cooling breezes.

Required clothing: Lightweights are worn all year around Lake Malawi, with warmer clothes advised in the mountains, particularly during winter and on chilly evenings elsewhere. Waterproofing is advisable.

LILONGWE Malawi (1134m)

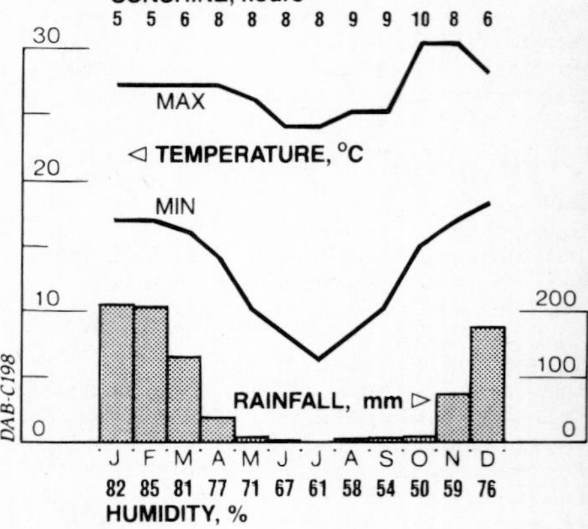

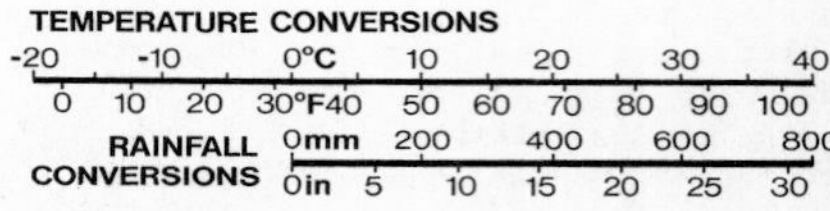

MALAYSIA

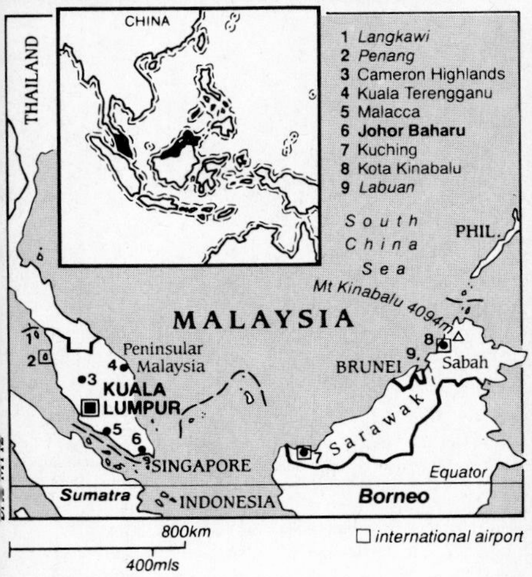

Location: South-East Asia.

Malaysia Tourism Promotion Board
24-27th Floors, Menara Dato' Onn
Putra World Trade Centre
45 Jalan Tun Ismail
50480 Kuala Lumpur, Malaysia
Tel: (3) 293 5188. Fax: (3) 293 5884. Telex: 30093 MTDCKL MA.

High Commission for the Federation of Malaysia
45 Belgrave Square
London
SW1X 8QT
Tel: (071) 235 8033. Fax: (071) 235 5161. Telex: 262550. Opening hours: 0900-1700 Monday to Friday.

Malaysia Tourism Promotion Board
57 Trafalgar Square
London
WC2N 5DU
Tel: (071) 930 7932. Fax: (071) 930 9015. Telex: 51299659.

British High Commission
185 Jalan Ampang
50450 Kuala Lumpur, Malaysia
Tel: (3) 248 2122 *or* 248 7122 (Consular section). Fax: (3) 248 0880. Telex: 35225 UKREP MA.
Honorary British Representatives in: Kuching, Kota Kinabalu, Penang, Johore Baru and Miri.

Embassy of the Federation of Malaysia (Visa Section)
2401 Massachusetts Avenue, NW
Washington, DC
20008
Tel: (202) 328 2700. Fax: (202) 483 7661. Telex: 440119.

Malaysia Tourism Promotion Board
Suite 804
818 West Seventh Street
Los Angeles, CA
90017
Tel: (213) 689 9702. Fax: (213) 689 1530. Telex: 6714719 MTIC UW.

Embassy of the United States of America
PO Box 10035
376 Jalan Tun Razak
50700 Kuala Lumpur, Malaysia
Tel: (3) 248 9011. Fax: (3) 243 5207. Telex: 32956.

High Commission for the Federation of Malaysia
60 Boteler Street
Ottawa, Ontario
K1N 8Y7
Tel: (613) 237 5182. Fax: (613) 237 4852. Telex: 053-3064.
Consulate in: Toronto.

Malaysia Tourist Information Centre
830 Burrard Street
Vancouver, British Columbia
V6Z 2K4
Tel: (604) 689 8899. Fax: (604) 689 8804.

Canadian High Commission
PO Box 10990
7th Floor, Plaza MBF
172 Jalan Ampang
50732 Kuala Lumpur, Malaysia
Tel: (3) 261 2000. Fax: (3) 261 3428. Telex: 30269.

AREA: 329,758 sq km (127,320 sq miles).
POPULATION: 17,755,900 (1990).
POPULATION DENSITY: 53.8 per sq km.
CAPITAL: Kuala Lumpur. **Population:** 1,158,200 (1991).
GEOGRAPHY: Malaysia is situated in central South-East Asia, bordering on Thailand in the North, with Singapore and Indonesia to the South and the Philippines to the East. It is composed of Peninsular Malaysia and the states of Sabah and Sarawak on the north coast of the island of Borneo, 650-950km (404-600 miles) across the South China Sea. Peninsular Malaysia is an area of forested mountain ranges running from north to south, on either side of which are low-lying coastal plains. The coastline extends some 1900km (1200 miles). The west coast consists of mangrove swamps and mudflats which separate into bays and inlets. In the west, the plains have been cleared and cultivated, while the unsheltered east coast consists of tranquil beaches backed by dense jungle. Sarawak has alluvial and, in places, swampy coastal plains with rivers penetrating the jungle-covered hills and mountains of the interior. Sabah has a narrow coastal plain which gives way to mountains and jungle. Mount Kinabalu, at 4101m (13,455ft) is the highest peak in Malaysia. The major islands are Langkawi (a group of 99 islands), Penang, and Pangkor, off the west coast; and Tioman, Redang, Kapas, Perhentian and Rawa off the east coast.
LANGUAGE: Bahasa Malaysia is the national and official language, but English is widely spoken. Other languages are Chinese (Mandarin), Iban and Tamil.
RELIGION: 53% Muslim, 19% Buddhist. The remainder are Taoist, Confucianist, Hindu and Animist.
TIME: GMT + 8.
ELECTRICITY: 220 volts AC, 50Hz. Square 3-pin plugs and bayonet-type light fittings are generally used.
COMMUNICATIONS: Telephones: IDD service is available. Country code: 60. Public coin-operated phones can be found in many areas, such as supermarkets and post offices. Local calls cost 10 sen. Telephone Card public phones can be found throughout the country. These can be purchased at airports, petrol stations and some shops for amounts ranging from R3-R50. There are presently two types – Kadfon and Unicard – and these can only be used in their appropriate marked phone-booths. **Fax:** Fax centres for public use are located in the main post offices of all large towns. Most main hotels also have facilities. **Telegram/telex:** Public telex facilities are available 24 hours at Telegraph Office, Jalan Raja Chulan, Kuala Lumpur, and most main hotels. Telegrams can be sent from any telegraph office. **Post:** There are post offices in the commercial centre of all towns, open 0800-1700 Monday to Saturday. **Press:** The English-language dailies printed in Peninsular Malaysia are the *National Echo, Business Times, Malay Mail, New Straits Times* and *The Star*. There are also several English-language Sunday newspapers and periodicals. *The Borneo Bulletin*, published in Brunei, also circulates. There are many printed in other languages and several in two or three languages.
BBC World Service frequencies: From time to time these change. See the section *How to Use this Book* for more information.

BBC:				
MHz	**15.36**	**9.740**	**6.195**	**3.915**

PASSPORT/VISA

Regulations and requirements may be subject to change at short notice, and you are advised to contact the appropriate diplomatic or consular authority before finalising travel arrangements. Details of these may be found at the head of this country's entry. Any numbers in the chart refer to the footnotes below.

	Passport Required?	Visa Required?	Return Ticket Required?
Full British	Yes	No/1	Yes
BVP	Not valid	-	-
Australian	Yes	No/1	Yes
Canadian	Yes	No/1	Yes
USA	Yes	No/1	Yes
Other EC	Yes	No/1	Yes
Japanese	Yes	No/1	Yes

Restricted entry: Passports issued by Israel are not recognised by the Malaysian government. Those of scruffy appearance will be denied entry.
PASSPORTS: A valid passport or other travel document recognised by the Malaysian Government is required by all. The former should be valid for at least 6 months beyond the intended stay in Malaysia and the latter should be endorsed with a valid re-entry permit. All visitors must also have proof of adequate funds and an onward or return sea or air ticket.
British Visitors Passport: Not accepted.
VISAS: Most visitors (including all nationals of countries listed in the chart) do not require a visa to enter Malaysia if the period is less than a month and the purpose of the visit is business or social (see below for more detailed requirements). However, [1] all visitors require a **Visit Pass**. This will be issued at the port of entry if the visitor is travelling for business or tourism, or for a social visit; those travelling for other purposes should apply in advance of their visit. The length of stay granted by the Visit Pass is at the discretion of the Immigration authorities. Those issued with a Visit Pass for tourism or a social visit may not subsequently take up employment or engage in any business or professional activity during their stay in Malaysia.
In addition to the visit pass, **visas** are required at all times by nationals of Taiwan, and holders of a Hong Kong Certificate of Identity, and by all others except:
(a) holders of full British passports and Commonwealth and British Protected Persons (other than holders of Indian and Sri Lankan passports who *do* need a visa) who can prove that they may return to their country of origin, visiting Malaysia for any purpose;
(b) nationals of Liechenstein, The Netherlands, San Marino and Switzerland for whatever purpose or period of stay;
(c) nationals with full passports issued by Austria, Belgium, Denmark, Finland, Germany, Czechoslovakia, Iceland, Italy, Japan, Luxembourg, Norway, South Korea, Sweden, Tunisia, and USA do not require a visa for a social/business visit for a period of 3 months;
(d) nationals of Algeria, Bahrain, Jordan, Kuwait, Lebanon, Egypt, Morocco, Oman, Qatar, Saudi Arabia, Turkey, UAE and Yemen for a business/social visit for a period of 3 months;
(e) nationals of Afganistan, Iran, Iraq, Libya and Syria for a visit of 2 weeks;
(f) nationals of Albania, Bulgaria, Romania for 1 week;
(g) members of ASEAN countries, ie Indonesia, Philippines, Thailand, Singapore, for a 1-month visit.
Validity: The permitted length of stay is entered on the visit pass at the time it is issued and is at the discretion of the issuer. Extensions are possible. The cost of visas varies according to nationality.
Application and inquiries to: Immigration (or Consular Section at Embassy or High Commission). For addresses, see top of entry.

MALAYSIA | **HEALTH REGULATIONS** | **VISA REGULATIONS** | Code-Link

GALILEO/WORLDSPAN

TI-DFT/KUL/HE

TI-DFT/KUL/VI

SABRE

TIDFT/KUL/HE

TIDFT/KUL/VI

To access this information on your CRS, swipe the barcode with a light pen or type in the text under the barcode. For more information, see the introduction *How to Use This Book*.

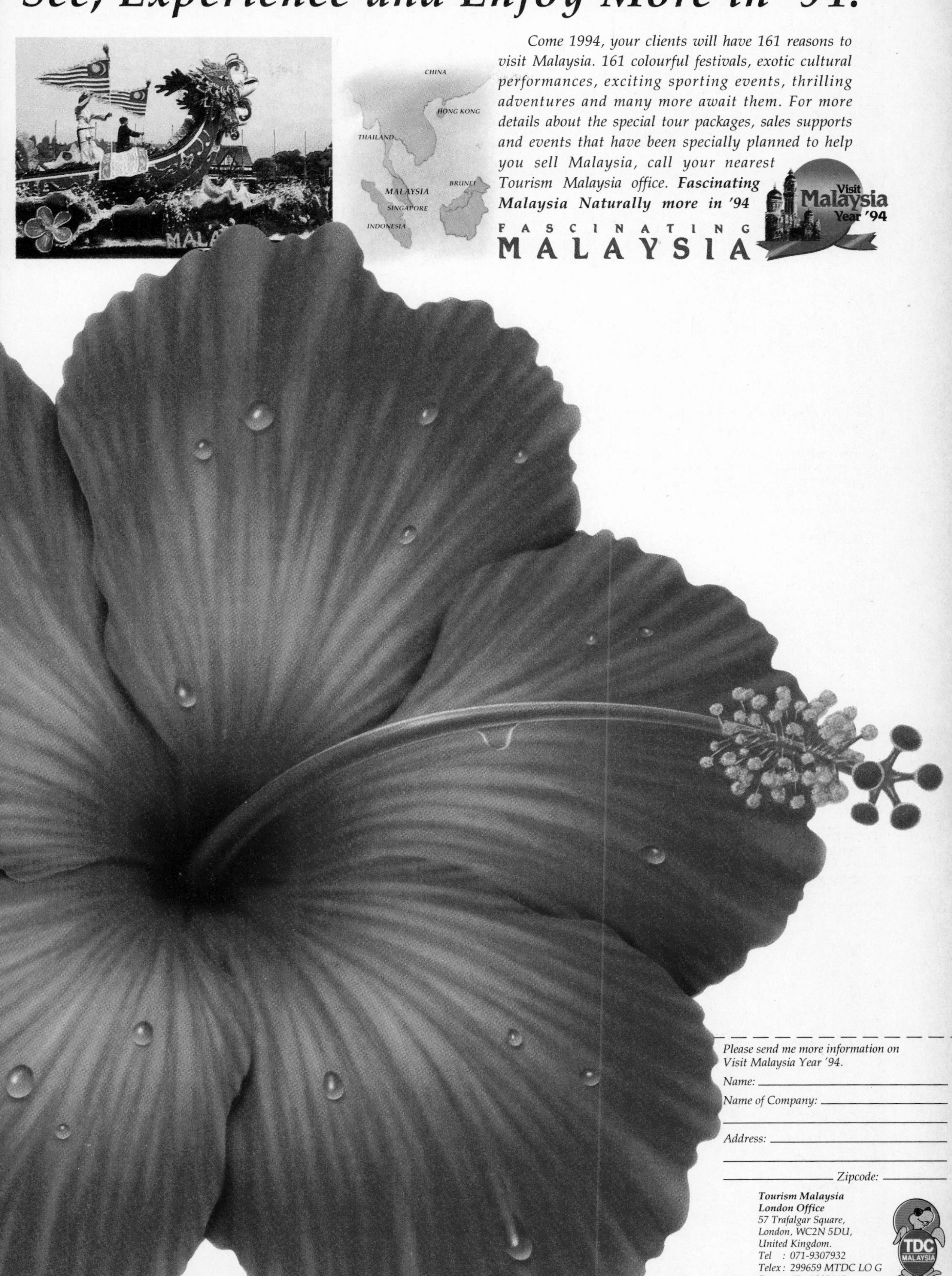
See, Experience and Enjoy More in '94.
Come 1994, your clients will have 161 reasons to visit Malaysia. 161 colourful festivals, exotic cultural performances, exciting sporting events, thrilling adventures and many more await them. For more details about the special tour packages, sales supports and events that have been specially planned to help you sell Malaysia, call your nearest Tourism Malaysia office. Fascinating Malaysia Naturally more in '94
CHINA
HONG KONG
THAILAND
MALAYSIA
SINGAPORE
BRUNEI
INDONESIA
FASCINATING MALAYSIA
Visit Malaysia Year '94
Please send me more information on Visit Malaysia Year '94.
Name:
Name of Company:
Address:
Zipcode:
Tourism Malaysia
London Office
57 Trafalgar Square,
London, WC2N 5DU,
United Kingdom.
Tel : 071-9307932
Telex: 299659 MTDC LO G
Fax : 071-9309015
TDC MALAYSIA

Application requirements: (a) Photo. (b) Fee. (c) Completed form.
Working days: 2.
Temporary residence: Contact the Immigration Attaché at an Embassy or High Commission. Those wishing to take up employment should have their prospective employers contact the Malaysianisation Secretariat in Kuala Lumpur.

MONEY

Currency: Ringgit (R) = 100 sen. Notes are in denominations of R1000, 500, 100, 50, 20, 10, 5 and 1. Coins are in denominations of R1, and 50, 20, 10, 5 and 1 sen. There are also a large number of commemorative coins in various denominations which are legal tender. The Ringgit is often referred to as the Malaysian Dollar.
Credit cards: Visa, Access/Mastercard, Diners Club and American Express are accepted. Check with your credit card company for details of merchant acceptability and other services which may be available.
Travellers cheques: Accepted by all banks, hotels and large department stores.
Exchange rate indicators: The following figures are included as a guide to the movements of the Ringgit against Sterling and the US Dollar:

Date:	Oct '89	Oct '90	Oct '91	Oct '92
£1.00=	4.25	5.26	4.76	3.98
$1.00=	2.69	2.69	2.74	2.50

Currency restrictions: There are no restrictions on the import or export of either local or foreign currency by visitors (except Israeli currency).
Banking hours: Banks are open by 1000 (by 0800 in Sabah), and close at 1500. Banks in Sabah generally break for lunch (1200-1400). Saturday opening times are usually 0930-1130.

DUTY FREE

The following goods may be imported into Malaysia without incurring customs duty:
200 cigarettes or 50 cigars or 225g of tobacco;
1 litre of spirits or wine or malt liquor;
Perfumes in opened bottles to the value of R200;
Gifts and souvenirs not exceeding a total value of R200.
Controlled & prohibited items: Visitors must declare valuables and may have to pay a deposit. It is prohibited to import goods from Israel as well as non-prescribed drugs, weapons and pornography. Drug-smuggling carries the death penalty.

PUBLIC HOLIDAYS

Public holidays observed in Malaysia are as follows:
Mar 25-26 '93 Hari Raya Puasa (End of Ramadan). **May 1** Labour Day. **May 6** Vesak Day. **Jun 1** Hari Raya Haji (Feast of the Sacrifice). **Jun 5** King's Birthday. **Aug 30** Mouloud (Prophet's Birthday). **Aug 31** Independence Day. **Nov 13** Deepavali. **Dec 25** Christmas Day. **Jan 23-24 '94** Chinese New Year. **Mar** Hari Raya Puasa (End of Ramadan).
Note: (a) Should a holiday fall on a Sunday, or a declared public holiday, it will be observed on the next working day. (b) In addition to the above, there are a number of State holidays, celebrated in particular areas only. For more information contact the Tourist Development Corporation of Malaysia. (c) Muslim festivals are not widely celebrated in Sabah, Sarawak or Labuan Federal Territory. Elsewhere, they are timed according to local sightings of various phases of the Moon and the dates given above (for Hari Raya Puasa, Hari Raya Haji and Mouloud) are approximations. During the lunar month of Ramadan that precedes Hari Raya Puasa (Eid al-Fitr), Muslims fast during the day and feast at night and normal business patterns may be interrupted. Many restaurants are closed during the day and there may be restrictions on smoking and drinking. Some disruption may continue into Hari Raya Puasa (Eid al-Fitr) itself. Hari Raya Puasa and Hari Raya Haji (Eid al-Adha) may last anything from two to ten days, depending on the region. For more information see the section *World of Islam* at the back of the book. (d) Hindu festivals are declared according to local astronomical observations and it is only possible to forecast the month of their occurrence. They are not widely celebrated in Sabah or Sarawak.

HEALTH

Regulations and requirements may be subject to change at short notice, and you are advised to contact your doctor well in advance of your intended date of departure. Any numbers in the chart refer to the footnotes below.

	Special Precautions?	Certificate Required?
Yellow Fever	No	1
Cholera	Yes	2
Typhoid & Polio	Yes	-
Malaria	3	-
Food & Drink	4	-

[1]: A yellow fever vaccination certificate is required from travellers over one year of age coming from infected areas. Those countries formerly classified as endemic are considered by the Malaysian authorities to be infected areas.
[2]: Following WHO guidelines issued in 1973, a cholera vaccination certificate is not a condition of entry to Malaysia. However, cholera is a risk in this country and precautions are essential. Up-to-date advice should be sought before deciding whether these precautions should include vaccination, as medical opinion is divided over its effectiveness. See the *Health* section at the back of the book.
[3]: Malaria risk exists only in small foci in isolated inland regions below 1700m (5577ft). Urban and coastal areas are generally safe, the exception being Sabah where there is a risk, predominantly in the malignant *falciparum* form, throughout the year. The *falciparum* strain is reported to be 'highly resistant' to chloroquine and 'resistant' to sulfadoxine/pyrimethamine.
[4]: All water should be regarded as being potentially contaminated. Water used for drinking, brushing teeth or making ice should have first been boiled or otherwise sterilised. Milk is unpasteurised and should be boiled. Powdered or tinned milk is available and is advised, but make sure that it is reconstituted with pure water. Avoid dairy products which are likely to have been made from unboiled milk. Only eat well-cooked meat and fish, preferably served hot. Pork, salad and mayonnaise may carry increased risk. Vegetables should be cooked and fruit peeled.
Note: It is generally considered safe to drink water straight from the tap; however, the above advice is left unchanged as it reflects the caution taken by many visitors unused to the Malaysian way of life and no authority is absolutely clear on this matter.
Rabies is present. For those at high risk, vaccination before arrival should be considered. If you are bitten abroad seek medical advice without delay. For more information consult the *Health* section at the back of the book.
Health care: Health insurance is recommended. Hospitals are found in all the main cities and can deal with all major needs. Smaller towns and rural areas have travelling dispensaries. In an emergency, dial 999.

TRAVEL - International

AIR: The national airline is *Malaysia Airlines (MAS)*.
Approximate flight time: From *London* to Kuala Lumpur is 12 hours.
International airports: *Kuala Lumpur* (Subang International) (KUL) is 22.5km (14 miles) west of the

city (travel time – 35 minutes). A bus goes to the city (Jalan Sultan Mohammed Bus Terminal) every 30 minutes. A taxi to the city centre is available. Fare coupons are available from a counter in the terminal. Airport facilities include an incoming and outgoing duty-free shop, bank/exchange, post office, restaurant and bar, and several car-hire firms, all open 0900-2300.

Penang (Bayan Lepas) (PEN) is 16km (10 miles) from Georgetown, capital of this small island off the northwest coast of the peninsula. Though not receiving as many international flights as Kuala Lumpur, there are connections from the UK via Hong Kong, Singapore or Bangkok. Airport facilities include an incoming and outgoing duty-free shop, restaurant and bar, bank and exchange and several car-hire firms, all open 0900-2200.

Kota Kinabalu (BKI) is 6.5km (4 miles) from the city. Situated on the northern coast of Sabah state (the north-eastern part of Borneo Island), this airport is the international gateway to East Malaysia (Sabah and Sarawak) and receives international flights from all over the world. Connections from the UK go via Singapore, Hong Kong and via Kuala Lumpur. Airport facilities include bank/exchange facilities and restaurant and bar, all open 0900-2200.

Kuching (KCH) is 11km (7 miles) from the city. Situated in the west of Sarawak on the island of Borneo, the airport receives a limited number of international flights.

Departure tax: R20 for international departures, including to Brunei and Singapore.

SEA: The major international ports are Georgetown (Penang), Port Kelang (for Kuala Lumpur) and, in East Malaysia (for Sabah and Sarawak), Kota Kinabalu, Lahad Datu, Sandakan, Tawau, Labuan Island and Kuching. There are two new ports under development in Sarawak: Bintulu and Pending Point. Shipping lines with passenger services to Malaysia include *Blue Funnel*, *P&O* and *Straits Shipping*. Cargo/Passenger lines are *Austasia*, *Knutsen*, *Lykes*, *Neptune Orient*, *Orient Overseas* and *Straits Shipping*.

RAIL: Through services operate to and from Singapore via Kuala Lumpur and Butterworth to Bangkok daily.

ROAD: Peninsular Malaysia is linked by good roads to Thailand and (via a causeway) to Singapore. Road connections between the two eastern states, Sarawak and Sabah, and their neighbours on Borneo, Brunei and the Indonesian state of Kalimantan are fairly good.

TRAVEL - Internal

AIR: *Malaysia Airlines (MAS)* serves numerous commercial airports in Peninsular Malaysia. In East Malaysia, MAS, backed by *Pelangi Air* crisscross both Sabah and Sarawak and also fly to Brunei. *Singapore Airlines*, *Royal Brunei* and *Thai International* operate flights to certain Malaysian destinations. Plans are underway for the further development of several airports, including Kuala Lumpur. There are many other small airstrips also in use.

Departure tax: R5 is collected at all airports.

SEA/RIVER: Coastal ferries sail frequently between Penang and Butterworth and there is a scheduled passenger service linking Port Kelang with both Sarawak and Sabah. Small rivercraft often provide the most practical means of getting about in east Malaysia, even in the towns, and they are the only way to reach the more isolated settlements (unless one has access to a helicopter). Boats may easily be chartered and river buses and taxis are plentiful.

RAIL: *Malayan Railways* operates nearly 2092km (1300 miles) of line. The fast daytime 'Rakyat Express' runs from Singapore to Butterworth. Express trains are modern, and some have sleeping berths and buffet cars. There is also some air-conditioned and first-class accommodation. East Malaysia has one railway line; it runs along the coast from Kota Kinabalu (Sabah), then inland up a steep jungle valley to the small town of Tenom. Other than this line, there are two main lines operated for a passenger service. One runs along the west coast and from Singapore which runs northwards to Kuala Lumpur and Butterworth, meeting the Thai railways at the border. The other line separates from the west coast line at the town of Gemas and takes a northeastern route to Kota Bharu and Tenom. There are no rail services in Sarawak.

Special tickets: 10-day and 30-day tickets are available, giving unlimited travel on all trains through Peninsular Malaysia and Singapore except the 'Rakyat Express' and the 'Mesra Express'. Enquire at the Malaysia Tourism Promotion Board for further details.

ROAD: Most roads in the Peninsular states are paved and signs leading to the various destinations are well placed and clear. **Buses:** Local bus networks are extensive; there are almost 1000 routes, with regular services in and between all principal cities. Four-wheel drive buses are used in rural areas of Sabah and Sarawak.

Minibuses: Available in the city areas. **Trishaw:** These are inexpensive for short trips. Pre-arrange the price.

Taxis: These and shared taxis are a fast means of intertown travel, but delays may be encountered whilst drivers get their passenger load before moving off. There is a 50% surcharge for fares between midnight and 0600 and an extra R1 is charged for taxis booked by phone. Taxi coupons providing fixed prices to specific destinations can be purchased at the Kuala Lumpur railway station and the airport. **Car hire:** This is available through several agencies. Some agencies provide cars on an unlimited-mileage basis. Cars with driver are also available.

Documentation: An International Driving Licence is required. A national driving licence is sufficient for UK nationals, but has to be endorsed by the Registrar of Motor Vehicles in Malaysia.

URBAN: Parking in the centre of Kuala Lumpur and other towns is restricted to spaces for which a charge is made and a receipt is given. Public transport services in Kuala Lumpur are provided by conventional buses and by 'Bas Mini' fixed-route minibuses, taxis and pedi-cabs (trishaws) licensed by the Government. Bus fares vary, but the 'Bas Mini' rates are flat. These are used for shorter journeys, and tend to be crowded. A mono-rail system in Kuala Lumpur was completed in 1992.

JOURNEY TIMES: The following chart gives approximate journey times (in hours and minutes) from Kuala Lumpur to other major centres in Malaysia.

	Air	Road	Rail
Ipoh	0.30	3.00	4.30
Penang	0.45	6.00	9.30
Alur Setar	0.45	7.00	7.30
Kuantan	0.35	4.00	-
Johor Baharu	0.35	5.00	6.00
Singapore	0.45	6.00	7.00

ACCOMMODATION

HOTELS: Malaysia has many hotels of luxury and economy class. It is necessary to book well in advance, especially at Easter, Midsummer and Christmas when the Malaysians take their holidays in the popular resorts, notably Penang, Langkawi and the Highlands. The more basic hotels have little in the way of modern washing or bathing facilities, often only a water trough instead of a bath or shower. There is no formal classification system. Government tax of 5% and service charge of 10% are added to bills. Tips are only expected (on the basis of good service) for room service and porterage. Laundry service is available in most hotels. For further information, contact the Malaysian Association of Hotels, c/o Langkawi Holiday Villa, Pulau Langkawi, Kedah. Tel: (3) 262 2922. Fax: (3) 262 2937. Telex: MA31345.

GOVERNMENT RESTHOUSES: These are subsidised, moderately priced hotels. They are basic, but always clean and comfortable, with full facilities and usually good restaurants. As they are primarily travelling inns they tend to fill up quickly, so it is advisable to telephone and reserve a room.

CAMPING: There are camping facilities in the Taman Negara or national park. Here jungle lodges provide tents, camp beds, pressure lamps and mosquito nets for trips into the rainforests.

YOUTH HOSTELS: There are not many of these, but they are very cheap. Accommodation is in dormitories and meals can be arranged. Visitors must register at the hostel from 1700-2000. Hostels are to be found in Cameron Highlands, Kuala Lumpur, Kuantan, Malacca, Penang and Port Dickson. The Kuala Lumpur International Youth Hostel is at 21 Jalan Kampung Attap, 50460 Kuala Lumpur. Further details can be obtained from the Youth Hostel Association or the Tourist Development Corporation.

RESORTS & EXCURSIONS

For the purpose of this section the country has been divided into five regions: Kuala Lumpur, Malacca and the Southwest; Penang, Langkawi and the Pangkor Islands; the Hill Resorts; the East Coast; and Sabah and Sarawak.

Kuala Lumpur, Malacca and the Southwest

This is the most developed and densely populated region of the country. This is also where the most important historical remains are found.

Malaysia's capital city and main international gateway, **Kuala Lumpur**, was founded in the 1890s, and its architecture reflects a cosmopolitan mix of Malay, Chinese, Indian and European cultures. Primarily a business and commercial centre, the city has much to offer the leisure visitor. The *Tasek Perdana Lake Gardens* are one of the city's most well-known natural landmarks, a popular spot for picnics and walking. Boats may be hired. Within the gardens are *Parliament House* and the *National Monument*. Close by is the *National Museum* which houses many historical exhibits. Near the railway station is the *National Mosque* surrounded by lawns ornamented with fountains. Nearby is the old Chinese temple of *Chan See Yuen* and the colourful Indian temple of *Sri Mahamariaman*. At the recently developed 50-year-old *Central Market*, local craftsmen can be seen at work, local food savoured at hawker stalls, and cultural and musical performances enjoyed. The *Batu Caves* lie a few miles to the north of the city. These large natural caves, reached by 272 steps, house the Hindu shrine of Lord Subramaniam. Nearby is the *Museum Cave*, a fascinating display of brightly coloured statues and murals from Hindu

mythology. *Templar Park*, 22km (14 miles) north of Kuala Lumpur, is a well-preserved tract of primary rain-forest which is rich in scenic beauty. Jungle paths, swimming lagoons and waterfalls all lie within the park boundaries. Malaysia's latest agricultural park, located Cherakah at Shah Alam, Selangor, has a large playing area with premises for skateboarders and rollerskaters.

Petaling Jaya, midway between the airport and Kuala Lumpur, was intended as a dormitory town, but has now become a major centre in its own right. It has international hotels, restaurants and nightlife and is close to four excellent golf courses.

Port Dickson is on the coast, about one and a half hour's travelling time from Kuala Lumpur. Malaysians flock here from the city at weekends, but with 18km (11 miles) of beach there is always plenty of room. The bays are ideal for all kinds of watersports and fishing and there are facilities for water-skiing, motor cruising and deep-sea fishing.

Port Kelang, further to the north, is Malaysia's main port, famous for its fish restaurants specialising in steamed crabs, fried prawns and shark's fins.

The city of **Malacca** is two hours by road from Kuala Lumpur. Founded in the early 15th century, Malacca remains predominantly a Chinese community, although there are many reminders of periods under Portuguese, Dutch and British rule; some of these can be seen in the Malacca museum. Architectural remains include the *Cheng Hoon Teng Temple* in the centre of the city, the gateway of the *A Formosa* Portuguese fortress, *St Paul's Church* with the grave of St Xavier, the *Stadthuys*, the Dutch *Christ Church* and the *Tranquerah Mosque*, one of the oldest in the country. There are several international hotels in Malacca, augmented by a fully equipped resort complex 12km (7 miles) outside the city.

The journey south from Malacca to Johor Baharu and thence Singapore passes through **Muar** and **Batu Pahat.**

Penang, Langkawi & Pangkor

The island of **Penang**, described as the 'Pearl of the Orient', lies just off the northwest coast of Peninsular Malaysia. Recently a network of expanded tourist facilities has been created. As well as being a particularly beautiful tropical island of palm trees and sandy beaches, it is also the main international gateway to northern Malaysia. It was the natural harbour which first attracted the British to Penang in the late 18th century, and the port is still one of the most important in the country. There is a regular ferry service between the island and the town of Butterworth on the mainland. The third-longest bridge in the world links Penang to the mainland.

Georgetown, the island's one town, is made up of Malay, Chinese, Thai, Indian and European cultures. The main shopping is on Campbell Street and Canarvon Street. Worth visiting are *Khoo Kongsi*, an old Chinese clan house, *Fort Cornwallis*, a British 18th-century fortress, *Penang Museum and Art Gallery* and the many churches, temples and mosques found throughout the town.

For those who want a single-centre holiday, Penang is a good choice, enabling the visitor to see something of Malaysian life in the town and small villages, as well as offering some of the most beautiful beaches in the country. Some of the most attractive beaches are situated along *Batu Feringgi* on the north coast. The island's main hotels are along this strip, although new international hotels have recently appeared close to the airport and also in Georgetown.

Penang has more than just beaches; one of the most unusual attractions is the *Snake Temple*, which swarms with venomous snakes, but visitors will be relieved to know that they are heavily drugged with incense. In the centre of the island is *Penang Hill*; the 700m (2300ft) summit, where there is a delightful small hotel which is gained by a funicular railway and offers splendid views and leisure walks.

More than 100km (60 miles) north of Penang lie the 99 islands, many of which are just outcrops of coral, that make up **Langkawi.** The largest, Langkawi Island, is the only one with sophisticated tourist facilities (it has been declared a free port and duty-free shopping is available). It is currently enjoying something of a building boom, with several international hotels under construction. There is already a fully equipped resort complex. The island's many coves, lagoons and inlets make it ideal for all kinds of watersports such as swimming, sailing, fishing and scuba diving. Horseriding and golf are also available. Travel to Langkawi is by air from Kuala Lumpur, Penang and Alor Star or by road and sea.

Unspoilt, seldom-visited **Pangkor Island,** about 100km (60 miles) south of Penang (and half an hour by ferry from Lumut), has recently gained popularity as a result of two new international hotels. Innumerable bays boast excellent sandy beaches and all kinds of watersports. Pangkor has no air links.

The Hill Resorts

Dotted about the mountain range which runs down the spine of Malaysia are several hill resorts. All are situated more than 1400m (4500ft) above sea level and offer cool, pleasant weather after the humidity of the plain and the cities.

Less than one hour by road from Kuala Lumpur is **Genting Highlands,** which boasts Malaysia's only casino (passports required). Genting Highlands can also be reached by regular helicopter service from Kuala Lumpur. Facilities include four hotels, golf courses with a magnificent clubhouse, an artificial lake, a health and sports centre, and an indoor swimming pool. **Fraser Hill,** set in lush jungle 100km (60 miles) north of Kuala Lumpur, is popular with both holidaymakers and golf enthusiasts. A wide range of other sports are available. There is also a self-contained township, self-catering bungalows and an international standard hotel. A daily shuttle ser-

vice operates between the Merlin Hotel and Fraser Hill. Still further north, about four hours from Kuala Lumpur, is **Cameron Highlands.** This, one of the best-known mountain resorts in Asia, consists of three separate townships: **Brinchang, Tanah Rata** and **Ringlet.** An international standard hotel and many bungalows are set around a golf course in lush green surroundings. Tennis, squash, badminton, jungle walks and swimming are available. From here visit **Gunung Brinchang** at 2064m (6773ft) above sea level, the highest inhabited point in Peninsular Malaysia and therefore a magnificent viewpoint.

The East Coast

This part of the country contains many of the finest beaches, including some of the least spoilt in southern Asia. In effect, the whole east coast is one huge beach, backed by jungle. The region, which covers two-thirds of Peninsular Malaysia, comprises the states of Kelantan, Terengganu, Pahang and Johor, as well as the islands of Tioman and Rawa. It is served by daily *MAS* services from Kuala Lumpur into Kota Baharu, Kuantan and Kuala Terengganu and from Penang into Kota Baharu. Air-conditioned coaches connect from most major towns in the country to the east coast resorts, though clients should be reminded that travel by road is sometimes impossible during the monsoons.

Kuantan, the state capital of Pahang, is fast gaining popularity as a beach resort. The region around Kuantan is also well known for village festivals and for the craft of weaving pandanus leaves into mats, hats and baskets. Woodcarving and batik are also traditional crafts in this part of the country.

Asia's first Club Mediteranée holiday village is in **Cherating**, about 45km (30 miles) north of Kuantan. Also in the region is Malaysia's answer to Loch Ness, *Lake Chini*, in whose waters mythological monsters are said to lurk, guarding the entrance to a legendary sunken city.

In the north of the state is Malaysia's largest national park, **Taman Negara.** Surrounded by the world's oldest tropical forest (supposedly 130 million years old), the park has remained virtually untouched and is a favourite haunt for outdoor enthusiasts, especially bird-watchers. The journey to the park headquarters involves travel by train, road and a 3-hour boat ride. Accommodation is modest and limited, and clients are advised to make early reservations.

The island of **Tioman,** in the South China Sea off the coast of Pahang, will be familiar to fans of the film 'South Pacific', as it was here that the film-makers found their mythical Bali Hai. Tioman is the largest of a group of 64

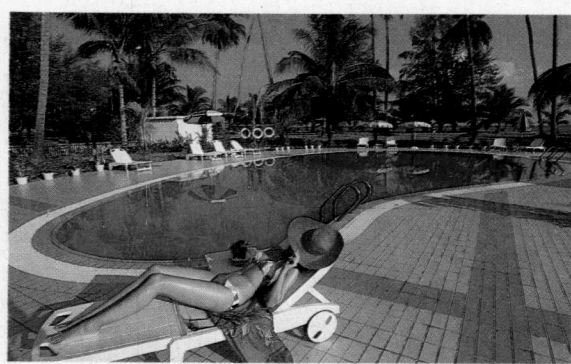

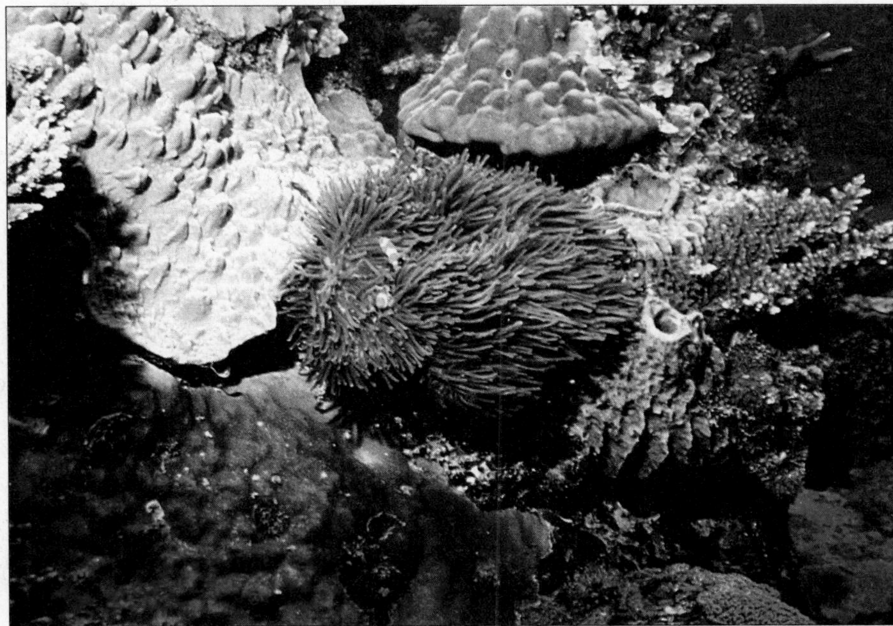

›lcanic islands and a must for deep-sea diving enthusi-ts. The islands are accessible by boat from Mersing or y helicopter or light aircraft from Mersing, Kuala umpur or Singapore.

he state of **Terengganu** has 225km (140 miles) of white ındy beaches. Swimming and all forms of watersports e favourite pastimes. There are several turtle-breeding eaches; at *Rantau Abang*, the Visitor Centre can arrange r guests to watch giant turtles laying their eggs.

ordering Thailand in the north is the state of Kelantan, hose capital **Kota Baharu** is a colourful, vibrant city. he beaches here are clean and unspoilt and the sea leal for swimming, diving and fishing. The state is nowned for its many cultural festivals, some of which e unique to the region. *Puja Umur* (the birthday of the ultan) is celebrated with a week-long festival, beginning ith a parade in Kota Baharu. A form of art unique to elantan is the *Ma'yong*, a combination of ballet, opera, mantic drama and comedy, originally a form of court ntertainment. Shadow play, top-spinning and kite flying e also to be seen.

ɔhor Baharu, in the southern state of Johor, is Ialaysia's southernmost gateway, and also the road and ail gateway from Singapore via a 1.5km (1-mile) cause-ay that connects the island to Peninsular Malaysia. laces of interest include *Johor Lama*, the seat of the ɔhor Sultanate after eviction from Malacca; the *Kota inggi Waterfalls*; the *Ayer Hitam* ceramic works; *Muar*, ımous throughout the country for its ghazal music and ance-inducing Kuda Kepang dances; the rubber and alm-oil plantations; and **Desaru**, Johor's newest beach esort. Desaru boasts unspoilt beaches and jungle. All inds of sports are played here, from swimming, canoeing nd snorkelling to pony riding and jungle trekking. here are also plans to develop a second 18-hole golf ourse. Accommodation is in Malaysian-style chalets and otels, and campers are also welcome.

Sabah & Sarawak

)espite being separated from Peninsular Malaysia (Sabah y 950km/600 miles and Sarawak by 650km/404 miles) y the South China Sea, Sabah and Sarawak can be eached by direct flights from Kuala Lumpur and ingapore.

abah, known as 'The Land Below The Wind', is home f the world's oldest jungles and one of South-East Asia's ighest peaks, *Mount Kinabalu*. A large part of the ascent an be made by road, but the final part must be climbed y foot. The region also offers excellent opportunities for xpeditions and technical rock climbing. Contact the ark Warden, PO Box 626, Kota Kinabalu. Tel: (88) 211 81. The **Mount Kinabalu National Park** is famous for ontaining over 500 species of birds and over 800 species f orchids. Overnight accommodation is available.

Kota Kinabalu, the capital and main gateway, is a new ity built upon the ruins of Jesselton, which was badly lamaged during the Second World War, and designed round the gold-domed *State Mosque*. From *Signal Hill* here is a good view of the city.

ust south of Kota Kinabalu is the resort of **Tanjung Aru,** where the recently opened beach complex has been lesigned with both business traveller and holidaymaker in mind. As well as conference and meeting facilities, there is also a ferry shuttle service into the town.

Tuaran is half an hour's drive from Kota Kinabalu. The road runs through lush valleys, forested hills and rubber plantations. The town has a good *'Tamu'* (market).

Sandakan, nearly 400km (250 miles) from Kota Kinabalu, is the old capital of Borneo. 24km (15 miles) from the town is the *Sepilok Sanctuary*, home of the 'wild men of Borneo', the world's largest orangutan population.

The **Tenom** region can be reached from Kota Kinabalu by Sabah's only railway line. A spectacular and thrilling experience, it follows the *Padas River* up through narrow jungle gorges in the *Crocker Range*. Tenom town is renowned for its style of longhouse building, unchanged through centuries, and traditional songs and dances performed there.

The state of **Sarawak** occupies the northwest coastal region of the island of Borneo. Most people who live in Sarawak use the intricate network of waterways to get about. Visitors are encouraged to do so too, although taxis and hire cars are available in the larger towns for those who prefer more conventional means of transport.

Kuching, on the banks of the River Sarawak, is the financial and commercial centre of the state, as well as being a gateway to a huge area of dense tropical rainforest and mountain ranges. Villages on stilts still cling precariously to the river banks. A visit to the *Sarawak Museum* affords valuable insights into the history, wildlife and anthropology of Borneo.

Overnight excursions can be made up the *Skrang River*, with accommodation provided in longhouses. There are also downriver trips to **Santubong,** an ancient trading post on the coast.

The **Bako National Park,** covering an area of approximately 26 sq km (10 sq miles), has interesting wildlife and vegetation, including carnivorous plants, long-nosed monkeys and Sambar deer. Excursions are organised from Kuching.

Other excursions, often via Miri, can be made to the *Niah Caves,* which show evidence of human existence dating back to 5000BC. The caves are also valued for their guano and bird's nests, the latter being used to make soup. Many of the caves – and some are more easily accessible than others – may be visited with a guide.

Excursions to the independent Sultanate of **Brunei** can also be made (see the separate country entry above).

SOCIAL PROFILE

FOOD & DRINK: In multi-racial Malaysia, every type of cooking from South-East Asia can be tasted. Malay food concentrates on subtleties of taste using a blend of spices, ginger, coconut milk and peanuts. *Sambals* (a paste of ground chilli, onion and tamarind) is often used as a side dish. *Blachan* (a dried shrimp paste) is used in many dishes and *ikan bilis* (tiny sun-dried fish) are eaten with drinks. Popular Malay dishes include *satay* which consists of a variety of meats, especially chicken, barbecued on small skewers with a dipping sauce of spicy peanuts and a salad of cucumber, onion and compressed rice cakes. The best sauce often takes several hours to prepare to attain its subtle flavour. *Gula Malacca* (a firm sago pudding in palm sugar sauce) is also served in restaurants. There are many regional types of Chinese cooking including Cantonese, Peking, Hakka, Sichuan and Taiwanese. Indian food is also popular, with curries ranging from mild to very hot indeed. Vegetarian food, chutneys and Indian breads are also available. Indonesian cuisine also combines the use of dried seafoods and spiced vegetables with the Japanese method of preparation with fresh ingredients cooked to retain the natural flavour. Japanese-style seafood such as *siakaiu beef* (grilled at the table), *tempura* (deep-fried seafood) and *sashimi* (raw fish with salad) are excellent. Korean and Thai food are available in restaurants. Amongst Malaysia's exotic fruits are starfruit, durian, guavas, mangos, mangosteen and pomelos. Western food is served throughout the country, particularly in major hotels which have continental menus and international coffee shops. Table service is normal, and in Chinese restaurants chopsticks are customary. Indian and Malay food is eaten with the fingers.

Drink: Although the country is largely Islamic, alcohol is available. Local beers such as *Tiger* and *Anchor* are recommended and also the famous *Singapore Gin Sling*.

NIGHTLIFE: Kuala Lumpur has a selection of reputable nightclubs and discotheques, most belonging to the big hotels. Penang is also lively at night, larger hotels having cocktail lounges, dining, dancing and cultural shows. There are night markets in most towns, including both Kuala Lumpur and Penang Chinatown. Malay and Chinese films often have English subtitles and there are also English films. The national lottery and Malaysia's only casino at Genting Highlands are Government approved and visitors are not supposed to gamble elsewhere. *Keno* and Chinese *Tai Sai*, roulette, baccarat, french bull and blackjack are played at the casino. Dress is relatively formal and you must be over 21.

SHOPPING: Shopping in Malaysia ranges from exclusive department stores to street markets. Bargaining is expected in the markets, unless fixed prices are displayed. The islands of Labuan and Langkawi are duty-free zones. Cameras, pens, watches, cosmetics, perfume and electronic goods are available duty-free throughout Malaysia. Malaysian speciality goods include pewterware, silverware and brassware; batik; jewellery; pottery and *songket*. Enquire at Malaysian Royal Customs and Excise about claiming cashback on duty free. **Shopping hours:** Most shops keep their own opening hours, usually within the range of 0900-2200.

SPORT: Malaysia has many unusual sports, including **Gasing-top spinning** (called *Main Gasing*) using tops fashioned from hardwood and delicately balanced with lead. **Wau-kite flying** is a traditional pastime. **Sepak Takraw** is a game like volleyball, played with a ball made of rattan strips. Players may use their heads, knees and feet but not their hands. **Car racing:** Held at Batu Tiga track near Kuala Lumpur. **Golf:** There are more than 40 golf clubs. The Malaysian Open Golf Championships, held each March, attract top professionals. **Horseracing:** Held in Ipoh, Kuala Lumpur and Penang. **Hunting:** Big-game hunting is regulated by Federal Game Wardens who issue necessary licenses. Guides, trackers and porters must be recruited locally. The importation of arms must be arranged through the Malaysia Police Department. For further information write to Chief Game Warden, MATIC, 109 Jalan Ampang, 50450 Kuala Lumpur. Tel: (3) 243 4929. **Karate:** More than 150 karate training centres offer regular training sessions under black-belt instructors six days a week. Visitors are welcome to receive free karate training for one week in any of the centres. A list can be obtained from the Chief Instructor, Karate Budokan International, Jalan Jubilee, Kuala Lumpur. **Yacht races:** These are held every Sunday at Port Dickson, about 95km (60 miles) from Kuala Lumpur.

SPECIAL EVENTS: Some of the strangest and most colourful festivals in the world are held in Malaysia, many of which are linked with state or regional public holidays. *Chinese New Year* is a major festival wherein the Lion Dance is performed, gifts are exchanged, visits to the temples are made and 'open houses' are held for the welcoming of friends and relatives. Children are given *ang-pows* – money placed in bright red envelopes. In October/November, the Indian community celebrates *Deepavali* or the 'Festival of Lights'. Hindu homes are decorated with candles and oil lamps for 'open house'. In November the Chinese celebrate the *Nine Emperor God's Festival*, in which volunteers are put into a trance before their cheeks are pierced by long skewers. The Indian population holds a similar event in February. Both festivals are held in towns where there is a sizeable Indian or Chinese community. For a list of special events from 1993/4, contact the Malaysia Tourism Promotion Board.

▼ *»Rebans« Trommler*

SOCIAL CONVENTIONS: Malaysia's population is a mixture of diverse cultures and characters. In general, the racial groups integrate, but keep to their individual traditions and lifestyles. Malays still form more than half of the total population and lead a calm life governed by the authority of elders and a strong sense of respect and etiquette. The Indian, Pakistani and Sri Lankan members of the population originally came to Malaysia to take up positions in the civil service, police and local government departments, as well as in the new rubber plantations, but many are now among the professional classes. European influences (Dutch, British and Portuguese in particular) are also very marked in Malaysia, although the European section of the population is now small. As far as greetings are concerned, the Malaysian equivalent of 'hello' is the Muslim 'peace be with you'. Malay men are addressed *Encik* (pronounced Enchik) with or without the name; Malay women should be called *Cik* (pronounced Che) if they are single and *Puan* if they are married. Chinese and Indians usually use Western forms of address. Hospitality is always warm, lavish and informal. Visitors should follow Malaysian example and respect religious beliefs, such as taking off footwear at the door and wearing appropriate clothing. Dress should be informal, but not over-casual. Within towns, smoking has now become the subject of government disapproval and fines are levied in a number of public places, such as cinemas, theatres and libraries. **Tipping:** 10% service charge and 5% Government tax are commonly included in bills. Taxi drivers are not tipped.

BUSINESS PROFILE

ECONOMY: The Malaysian economy is centred on the production of a number of key commodities: crude oil, palm oil, tin and rubber, of which Malaysia is the world's largest producer. These four items account for over 65% of Malaysia's export earnings. Despite the spectacular decline in the prices of tin and oil during the 1980s, Malaysia coped unusually well with the global recession of the late 1980s. Timber production, another important industry, has also been cut back through conservation measures. The Government has embarked upon an economic development strategy which has targeted particular industries for development: as well as those which are dependent on the country's natural resources, electronics transport equipment, machinery, steel and textiles have been selected to broaden Malaysia's economic base. Manufacturing now accounts for over a quarter of Gross National Product. Japan, which exchanges finished products for raw materials – particularly oil and gas – is Malaysia's largest trading partner, followed by the USA and Singapore. The rapid growth of the 1980s, averaging 7-8% per annum, will have to be curtailed somewhat during the early 1990s to avoid 'overheating' in the form of high inflation and an explosion of the country's current account deficit.

BUSINESS: Suits or safari suits are acceptable for business meetings. Business visitors should remember that the Malay population is predominantly Muslim and religious customs should be respected and normal courtesies observed, eg appointments, punctuality and calling cards. **Office hours** vary between Peninsular Malaysia and East Malaysia. In general most offices are open by 0830 and close between 1600 and 1730. Almost all close for an hour between 1200 and 1400. Most close at 1200 Saturday.

COMMERCIAL INFORMATION: The following organisations can offer advice: National Chamber of Commerce and Industry of Malaysia, Tower Plaza Pekeliling, Jalan Tun Razak, 50400 Kuala Lumpur. Tel: (3) 442 9871. Fax: (3) 441 6043. Telex: 33642; *or* Malaysian International Chamber of Commerce and Industry, PO Box 10192, 10th Floor, Wisma Damansara, Jalan Semantan, 50706 Kuala Lumpur. Tel: (3) 254 2677. Fax: (3) 255 4946.

CONFERENCES/CONVENTIONS: Many conferences and conventions are held in Malaysia each year. Apart from the dedicated facilities at the Putra World Trade Centre in Kuala Lumpur, many hotels have facilities. Further information can be obtained from the Malaysia Tourism Promotion Board, Convention Promotion Division, 24th-27th Floor, Menara Dato' Onn, Putra World Trade Centre, 45 Jalan Tun Ismail, 50480 Kuala Lumpur. Tel: (3) 293 5188. Fax: (3) 293 0207. Telex: 30093 MA.

HISTORY & GOVERNMENT

HISTORY: The region now known as Malaysia was first mentioned in Chinese and Sanskrit records of the 7th and 8th centuries. In subsequent centuries the area was under the influence of Thai and Indonesian

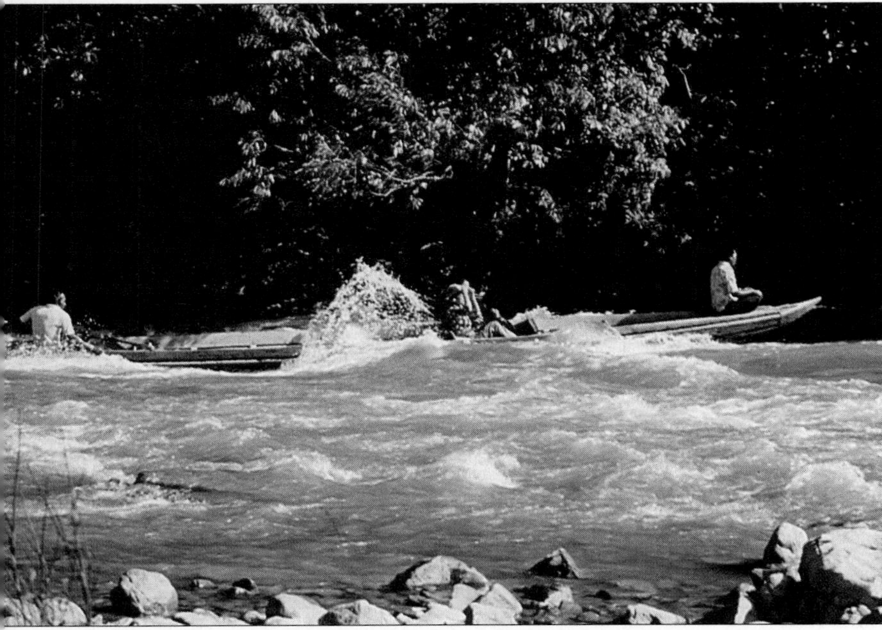

empires until, in the 15th century, it became a centre of Islamic influence centred on Malacca. Colonised by the British in the 19th century, the 11 separate states of Peninsular Malaysia fell to the Japanese during the Second World War. In 1946, as British Protectorates, they were united in the Malayan Union, which became the Federation of Malaya in 1948. In the same year, communist guerrillas launched an armed independence struggle which continued until 1960, although Malaya became independent (within the Commonwealth) in 1957. In 1963 the Federation of Malaya merged with Singapore and the former British colonies of Sarawak and Sabah (North Borneo) to form Malaysia. The Prime Minister of Malaya since independence, Tunku Abdul Rahman became Prime Minister of Malaysia. In 1965 Singapore seceded. Five years later, following serious rioting aimed at the economically influential Chinese community, Rahman resigned and was succeeded by Tunku Abdul Razak who created a National Front party (NF), now a 10-party coalition dominated by the United Malays National Organisation (UMNO). The Front won the 1982 general election convincingly under the leadership of Datuk Seri Dr Mahathir Mohammad. Mahathir has orchestrated a change in Malaysian foreign policy since the late 1980s. Previously a stalwart of the pro-Western ASEAN bloc (Association of South-East Asian Nations), Malaysia has now established diplomatic relations with its communist-run neighbours, including Vietnam. Also in 1989, Malaysia hosted the biennial Commonwealth conference, which improved the country's image, even though the conference was dogged, as ever, by arguments over South Africa. Malaysia also has a stake, along with five other countries (China, Vietnam, Taiwan, the Philippines and Brunei), in one of the region's main outstanding territorial disputes, the possibly mineral-rich Spratly Islands. On the domestic front, Mahathir sought a fresh mandate from the electorate by announcing a snap election in October 1990. His principal opponent was his former Cabinet colleague Tunku Razaleigh Hamzah. Although a close election was expected, Mahathir won a crushing victory. Razaleigh's apparent support, based on opposition to Mahathir's increasingly autocratic style of government, simply evaporated. Despite the defeat, Razaleigh's party, entitled Semangat '46 (Spirit of '46), is firmly established as a major player in Malaysian politics. There are also slightly ominous signs of friction between ethnic Malays and the Chinese community (now about one-third of the population). Mahathir has stated that he has no intention of standing down before the expiry of his current term of office in 1995 and, although his health is poor, he is unlikely to face a serious challenge while continuing to deliver economic success to Malaysia. There are no clear pointers to his successor, although observers have noted the rapid rise of Malaysia's new Finance Minister, Anwar Ibrahim.

GOVERNMENT: Malaysia has a complex federal political system, with much power still in the hands of nine hereditary sultans, who elect the Head of State (entitled HM the Yang di-Pertuan Agong) every five years from among their number. The head of government is the Prime Minister.

CLIMATE

Tropical without extremely high temperatures. Days are very warm, while nights are fairly cool. The main rainy season in the east runs between November and February, while August is the wettest period on the west coast. East Malaysia has heavy rains (November to February) in Sabah and in Sarawak. However, it is difficult to standardise the country's climate, as rainfall differs on the east and west coasts according to the prevailing monsoon winds (northeast or southwest).

Required clothing: Lightweight cottons and linens are worn throughout the year. Waterproofing is advisable all year.

CAMERON HIGHLANDS Malaysia (1448m)

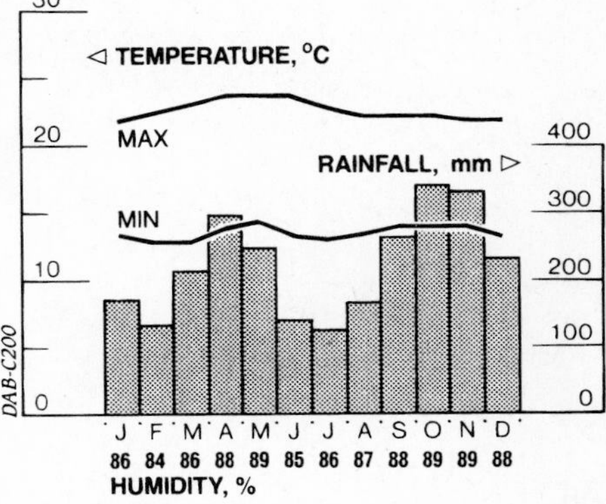

LABUAN Malaysia (18m)

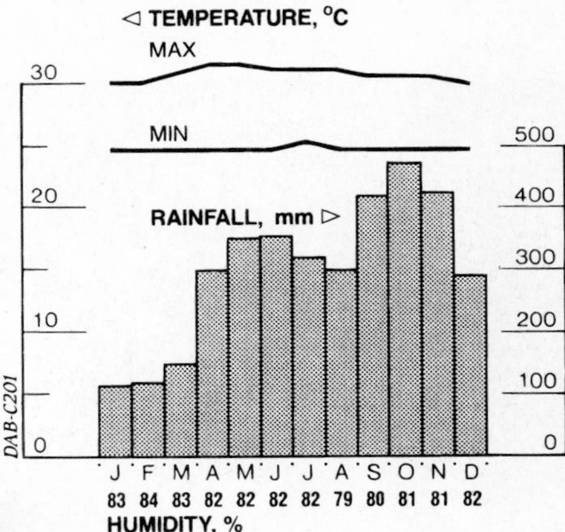

PENANG Malaysia (5m)

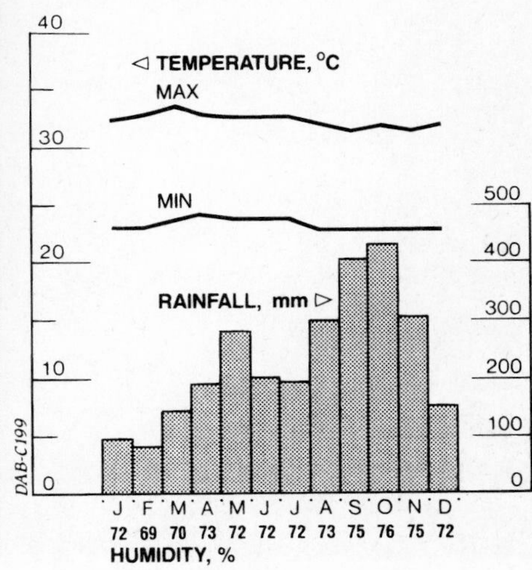

MALDIVES REPUBLIC

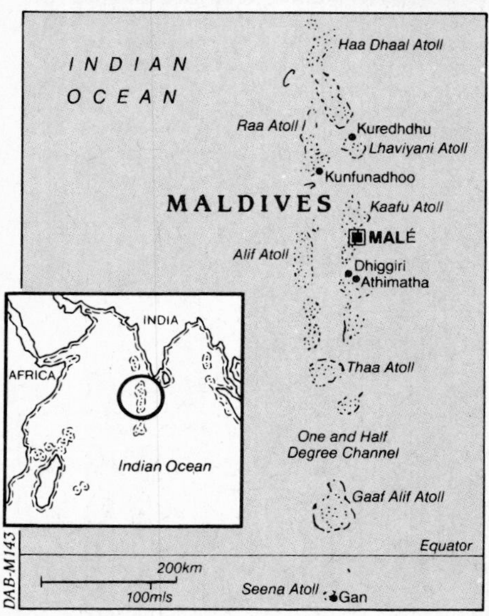

Location: A group of islands in the Indian Ocean, 500km (300 miles) southwest of the southern tip of India.

Diplomatic representation: The Republic of Maldives does not maintain embassies in the United Kingdom, Canada or the United States of America. The Maldives fall under the jurisdiction of the relevant High Commission or Embassy in Colombo, Sri Lanka.

Ministry of Trade and Industries
Ghaazee Building
Ameer Ahmed Magu
Malé 20-05
Maldives
Tel: 323 279. Fax: 325 218. Telex: 77076.

Ministry of Tourism
Ghaazee Building
Ameer Ahmed Magu
Malé 20-05
Maldives
Tel: 323 224/6/8. Fax: 322 512. Telex: 66019 TOURISM MF.

Tourist Information Unit
Marine Drive North
Malé 20-05
Maldives
Tel: 325 528.

Honorary Tourism Representative for the Maldives Republic in the UK
Maldive Travel
3 Esher House
11 Edith Terrace
London
SW10 0TH
Tel: (071) 352 2246 *or* 351 9351. Fax: (071) 351 3382. Telex: 941 3686 MAGIC G.

Maldives Mission
Suite 800C
820 Second Avenue
New York, NY
10017
Tel: (212) 599 6195. Fax: (212) 972 3970. Telex: 0960945 UNSOPAC NYK.

AREA: 302 sq km (117 sq miles).
POPULATION: 213,215 (1990).
POPULATION DENSITY: 706 per sq km.
CAPITAL: Malé. **Population:** 55,130 (1990).
GEOGRAPHY: The Maldives Republic is located 500km (300 miles) southwest of the southern tip of India and consists of about 1190 low-lying coral islands, of which only 200 are inhabited. Most of the inhabited islands are covered by lush tropical vegetation and palm trees, while the numerous uninhabited islands, some of which are mere sand spits or coral tips, are covered in shrubs. Each island is surrounded by a reef enclosing a shallow lagoon. Hundreds of these islands together with other coral growth form an atoll, surrounding a lagoon. All the islands are low-lying, none more than two metres above sea level. The majority of the indigenous population do not mix with the tourist visitors, with the exception of those involved with tourism in the resorts and Malé.
LANGUAGE: The national language is Dhivehi. English is spoken on Malé and resort islands.
RELIGION: The indigenous population is almost entirely Sunni Muslim.
TIME: GMT + 5.
ELECTRICITY: 220 volts AC, 50Hz. Round-pin plugs.
COMMUNICATIONS: Telephone: IDD is available. Country code: 960. **Fax:** Services are available in Malé and the resorts. **Telex/telegram:** Telecommunications in the Maldives are good – telex and telegram services are available to and from anywhere in the world from the Cable & Wireless Office in Malé, Dhiraagu and the resorts. **Post:** Airmail to Europe takes about a week. Post office hours: 0730-1330 and 1600-1750 Saturday to Thursday. **Press:** Fortnightly English newspapers include *The Maldives News Bulletin* and *Spectrum*. Information about local events is widely available on all the resort islands.

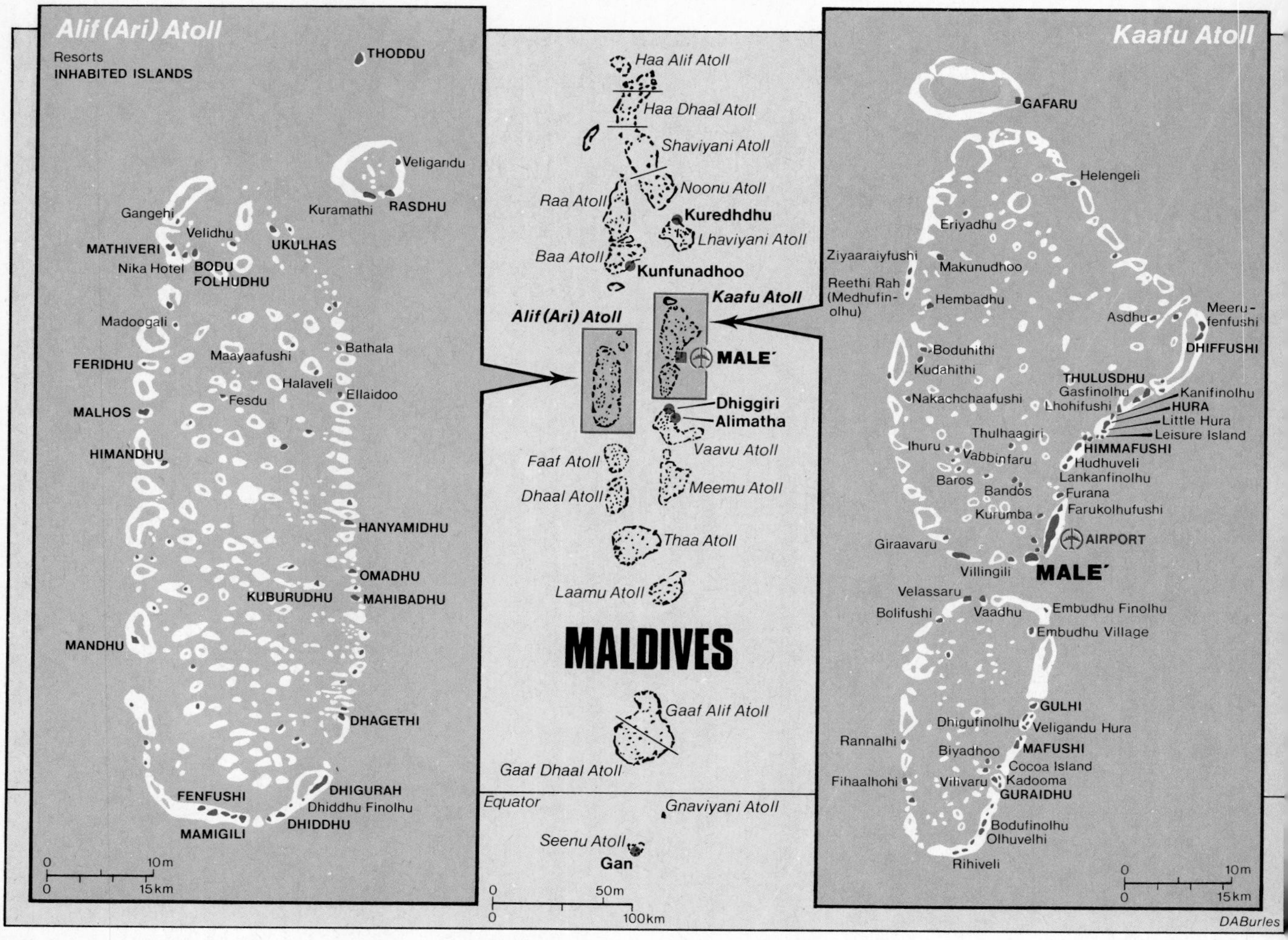

Alif (Ari) Atoll
Resorts
INHABITED ISLANDS
THODDU
Veligandu
RASDHU
Kuramathi
Gangehi
Velidhu
MATHIVERI
UKULHAS
Nika Hotel
BODU FOLHUDHU
Madoogali
Bathala
Maayaafushi
FERIDHU
Halaveli
Fesdu
Ellaidoo
MALHOS
HIMANDHU
HANYAMIDHU
OMADHU
KUBURUDHU
MAHIBADHU
MANDHU
DHAGETHI
DHIGURAH
FENFUSHI
Dhiddhu Finolhu
DHIDDHU
MAMIGILI
0 10m
0 15km

Haa Alif Atoll
Haa Dhaal Atoll
Shaviyani Atoll
Noonu Atoll
Raa Atoll
Kuredhdhu
Lhaviyani Atoll
Baa Atoll
Kunfunadhoo
Kaafu Atoll
Alif (Ari) Atoll
MALE'
Dhiggiri
Alimatha
Vaavu Atoll
Faaf Atoll
Meemu Atoll
Dhaal Atoll
Thaa Atoll
Laamu Atoll
MALDIVES
Gaaf Alif Atoll
Gaaf Dhaal Atoll
Equator
Gnaviyani Atoll
Seenu Atoll
Gan
0 50m
0 100km

Kaafu Atoll
GAFARU
Helengeli
Eriyadhu
Ziyaaraiyfushi
Makunudhoo
Reethi Rah (Medhufinolhu)
Hembadhu
Asdhu
Meeru-fenfushi
DHIFFUSHI
Boduhithi
Kudahithi
THULUSDHU
Gasfinolhu
Kanifinolhu
Nakachchaafushi
Lhohifushi
HURA
Little Hura
Leisure Island
Thulhaagiri
HIMMAFUSHI
Ihuru
Vabbinfaru
Hudhuveli
Baros
Lankanfinolhu
Bandos
Furana
Kurumba
Farukolhufushi
AIRPORT
Giraavaru
Villingili
MALE'
Velassaru
Bolifushi
Vaadhu
Embudhu Finolhu
Embudhu Village
GULHI
Dhigufinolhu
Veligandu Hura
Rannalhi
Biyadhoo
MAFUSHI
Cocoa Island
Fihaalhohi
Vilivaru
Kadooma
GURAIDHU
Bodufinolhu
Olhuvelhi
Rihiveli
0 10m
0 15km
DABurles

BBC World Service frequencies: From time to time these change. See the section *How to Use this Book* for more information.

BBC:

MHz	15.31	11.96	9.740	6.180

A service is also available on 1413kHz.

PASSPORT/VISA

Regulations and requirements may be subject to change at short notice, and you are advised to contact the appropriate diplomatic or consular authority before finalising travel arrangements. Details of these may be found at the head of this country's entry. Any numbers in the chart refer to the footnotes below.

	Passport Required?	Visa Required?	Return Ticket Required?
Full British	Yes	1	Yes
BVP	Not valid	-	-
Australian	Yes	1	Yes
Canadian	Yes	1	Yes
USA	Yes	1	Yes
Other EC	Yes	1	Yes
Japanese	Yes	1	Yes

Restricted entry: The Republic of Maldives refuses entry to nationals of Israel.

PASSPORTS: Valid passport required by all.
British Visitors Passport: Not accepted.
VISAS: [1] Required by all. Visas are valid for 30 days and will be issued on arrival at Malé airport free of charge. Visas may be extended on payment of a small fee. Nationals of India, Italy, Pakistan and Bangladesh will be issued a visa valid for 90 days. No photographs are required.
Note: Foreigners who enter the Maldives must be in possession of US$10 minimum per day of stay. This does not include those entering through a tourist agency or on recruitment.

MONEY

Currency: Maldivian Rufiya (MRF) = 100 laris. Notes are in denominations of MRF500, 100, 50, 20, 10, 5 and 2. Coins are in denominations of MRF1, and 50, 25, 10, 5, 2 and 1 laris.
Credit cards: Most major island resorts will accept American Express, Visa, Mastercard, Eurocard and Diners Club. Arrangements vary from island to island, and it is advisable to check with your credit company for details of merchant acceptability and other facilities which may be available.
Exchange rate indicators: The following figures are included as a guide to the movement of the Maldivian Rufiya against Sterling and the US Dollar:

Date:	Oct '89	Oct '90	Oct '91	Oct '92
£1.00=	14.25	18.92	17.67	18.21
$1.00=	9.02	9.67	10.19	11.48

Currency restrictions: There are no restrictions on import or export, but non-residents should declare all imports exceeding MRF150,000 in order to facilitate re-export. Tourist transactions must be conducted in local currency.
Banking hours: 0900-1300 Sunday to Thursday.

DUTY FREE

The following goods may be imported into the Maldives without incurring customs duty:
200 cigarettes or 50 cigars or 250g of tobacco;
A reasonable number of gifts.
Note: (a) Alcoholic beverages, pornographic literature, goods of Israeli origin, idols of worship or drugs may not be imported. The export of coral and tortoiseshell, except in the form of ornaments, is forbidden (the government has banned the killing of turtles). (b) Malé has a large duty-free shopping complex where various items of merchandise may be purchased at reasonable prices.

PUBLIC HOLIDAYS

Public holidays observed in the Maldives Republic are as follows:
Mar 25 '93 Start of Eid al-Fitr. **Jun 1** Start of Eid al-

MALDIVES REPUBLIC | **HEALTH REGULATIONS** | **VISA REGULATIONS** | Code-Link

GALILEO/WORLDSPAN

TI-DFT/MLE/HE

TI-DFT/MLE/VI

SABRE

TIDFT/MLE/HE

TIDFT/MLE/VI

To access this information on your CRS, swipe the barcode with a light pen or type in the text under the barcode. For more information, see the introduction *How to Use This Book*.

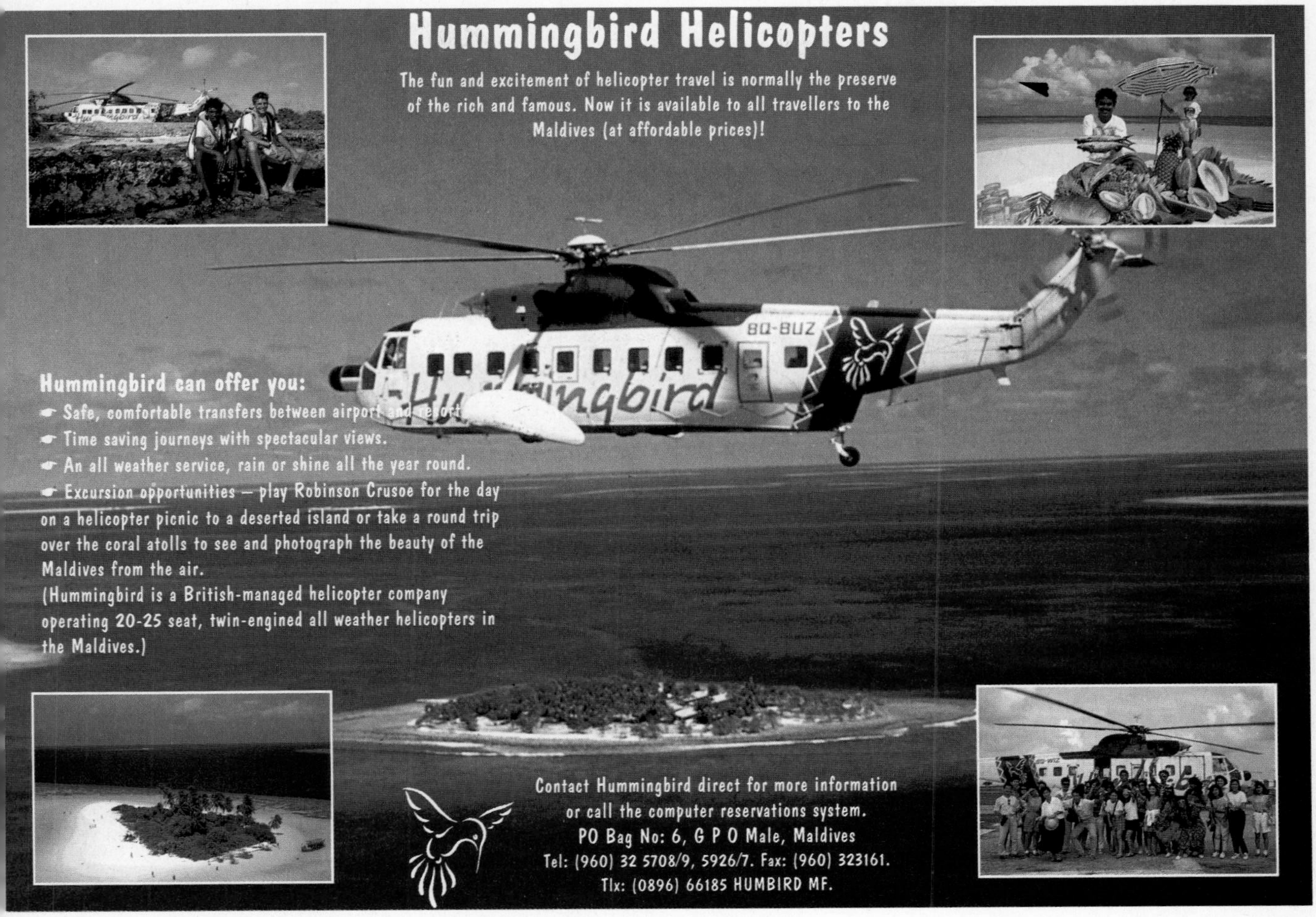

Adha. **Jun 21** Islamic New Year. **Jul 26** Independence Day. **Aug 30** Mouloud (Birth of the Prophet). **Nov 3** Victory Day. **Nov 11** Republic Day. **Dec 10** Fisheries' Day. **Jan 1 '94** New Year's Day. **Jan 7** National Day. **Mar** Start of Eid al-Fitr.

Note: (a) Some holidays are celebrated according to the Islamic calendar and others are public or government holidays. (b) Muslim festivals are timed according to local sightings of various phases of the Moon and the dates given above are approximations. During the lunar month of Ramadan that precedes Eid al-Fitr, Muslims fast during the day and feast at night and normal business patterns may be interrupted. Many restaurants are closed during the day and there may be restrictions on drinking. Some disruption may continue into Eid al-Fitr itself, although this is generally unlikely to affect life on the resort islands. Eid al-Fitr and Eid al-Adha may last anything from two to ten days, depending on the region. For more information see the section *World of Islam* at the back of the book.

HEALTH

Regulations and requirements may be subject to change at short notice, and you are advised to contact your doctor well in advance of your intended date of departure. Any numbers in the chart refer to the footnotes below.

	Special Precautions?	Certificate Required?
Yellow Fever	Yes	1
Cholera	Yes	2
Typhoid & Polio	Yes	-
Malaria	3	-
Food & Drink	4	-

[1]: A yellow fever vaccination certificate is required from travellers arriving from infected areas.

[2]: Following WHO guidelines issued in 1973, a cholera vaccination certificate is not a condition of entry to the Maldives. However, cholera is a risk in this country and precautions are essential. Up-to-date advice should be sought before deciding whether these precautions should include vaccination as medical opinion is divided over its effectiveness. See the *Health* section at the back of the book.

[3]: Malaria is disappearing; the last two indigenous cases were reported in 1983.

[4]: All water other than that provided in restaurants and in thermos flasks in hotel rooms should be regarded as a potential health risk. Rain water and desalinated water is provided for drinking in some resorts. Water of uncertain origin used for drinking, brushing teeth or making ice should have first been boiled or otherwise sterilised. Milk is unpasteurised and should be boiled. Powdered or tinned milk is available and is advised, but make sure that it is reconstituted with pure water. Avoid dairy products which are likely to have been made from unboiled milk. Only eat well-cooked meat and fish, preferably served hot. Salad and mayonnaise may carry increased risk. Vegetables should be cooked and fruit peeled.

Rabies is present. For those at high risk, vaccination before arrival should be considered. If you are bitten abroad seek medical advice without delay. For more

information consult the *Health* section at the back of the book.
Health care: There is a hospital on Malé and first-aid facilities are available on the main resort islands. Health insurance is recommended.

TRAVEL - International

AIR: The national airline is *Air Maldives*, although it does not operate international services. Direct flights are operated from a number of countries in the region (such as India, Singapore, Sri Lanka and the United Arab Emirates) and also from Europe.
Approximate flight time: From *London* to Malé is 11 hours (excluding stopover).
International airport: *Malé International (MLE)* on Hulule Island is 2km (1.2 miles) from the town. Boats from the various island resorts meet each arriving plane to take visitors to their respective accommodation. If an advance booking has been made, representatives of the resorts will receive tourists at the airport and will take care of all onward transport arrangements.
Departure tax: US$7.

TRAVEL - Internal

AIR: Internal air services are operated by *Air Maldives*, linking Malé with Kadhdhoo and Gan. There are also services to Hanimaadhoo in the north, although these islands will not be on most visitors' itineraries.
Hummingbird, a new company, operates a helicopter service around the Maldives; the transfer from the airport to the resort islands may be an optional extra on your tour. The service is also available for trips around the islands during your stay. To contact *Hummingbird* in Malé: Hummingbird Helicopters (Maldives) Pvt Ltd, Luxwood 2, Marine Drive-H, PO Bag 6, Malé 20-02. Tel: 325 708. Fax: 323 161. Telex: 66185.
SEA: Visitors generally remain on their resort island for duration of stay, although island-hopping trips by ferries are widely available. Local charter boats are also easily available for hire. The indigenous inhabitants, however, live a parochial life and tend to visit only Malé, and even then irregularly.
ROAD: Travel on individual islands does not present any problem since few of them take longer than half an hour to cross on foot.

ACCOMMODATION

HOTELS: There are three hotels on Malé and one on Gan; there are also 36 guest-houses on Malé and rooms in private homes, although most visitors stay on resort islands. There are no **guest-houses** or **self-catering** facilities on any of the resort islands. For more information contact Maldives Association of the Tourism Industry (MATI). Tel: 323 080. Fax: 322 678. Telex: 66024.
RESORTS: There are 63 resorts which vary from extravagantly luxurious to fairly simple.
Accommodation almost invariably consists of thatch-roofed coral cabanas with en-suite facilities. The rooms are fan-cooled although some have air-conditioning and/or a refrigerator. Many resort groups have recently installed desalination plants to provide clean tap water. The resorts are fully integral communities with sport and leisure facilities, restaurants and bars and, in some cases, a shop and/or disco. No island has more than one resort and these range in size from six to 130 units with most having between 30 and 50 units. Different islands tend to attract different nationalities.

RESORTS & EXCURSIONS

For a long time, the Maldives Republic was one of the best-kept secrets in the world; a beautiful string of low-lying coral islands in the Indian Ocean, a paradise for scuba divers, watersport enthusiasts and sunseekers alike. All of these attractions are still very much in evidence, but in recent years the tourism potential of the country has been developed in the form of a large number of island resorts. Several tour operators have added the Maldives to their programmes, and since the introduction of direct flights from Europe the islands have become an increasingly popular longhaul destination.
The Maldives consist of 19 atolls, about 1190 islands in all, most of them uninhabited. Most of the resorts are to be found in **Malé (Kaafu) Atoll**. A few are found in **Vaavu**, **Baa** and **Lhaviyani**. **Alifu (Ari) Atoll** has been declared the new Tourism Zone of the Maldives and work to upgrade and build new resorts is progressing in this area. All resorts offer night fishing trips, superb snorkelling and windsurfing, and most have facilities for scuba diving, dhoni sailing, water-skiing and volleyball. Some offer other sporting facilities, including badminton and tennis.
The following section describes some of the major resort islands in the Maldives; further information can be obtained from the UK Tourism Representative (see top of entry for address), from tour operators or by contacting the island resort direct; see the *Resort Directory* below for a full list of resorts and their telex numbers.
The capital of the Maldives is **Malé**, situated on the island of the same name close to the airport on the southern point of the North Malé Atoll. Although accommodation is available, very few foreign visitors stay in the capital; even those doing business normally stay in one of the nearby resort islands and travel to Malé by boat. Most islands provide boat services to the capital at least once a week (a small charge is usually made). The capital also has several shops which sell examples of local handicrafts and imported goods. Other attractions include the *National Museum* and the gold-domed *Mosque*.

Kaafu Atoll – North

The following section describes some of the major resorts in the Kaafu Atoll (also known as the North and South Malé Atolls). See the map for location, and the *Resort Directory* below for a full list of resorts and telex numbers.
Baros is about 450m (1500ft) long and 180m (600ft) wide, and this oval-shaped island is located approximately one hour by boat from the airport. One side of the island is full of corals, within 3-6m (10-20ft) of the shallow beach, perfect for snorkelling and diving lessons, whilst the other side is a superb beach ideal for swimming and water-skiing.
East of Baros is the island of **Bandos**, one of the larger resorts whose accommodation consists of well-furnished beach houses. There is a particularly good diving school; one of the attractions is a dive down to the aptly-named *Shark Point*.
The island of **Vaadhu,** on the north tip of the South Malé Atoll and about 10 minutes by boat from the airport, also has a fully equipped diving school. There are 33 cabana-style rooms whose features include freshwater showers, and which reflect the high level of capital investment which has been made in the resort.

Hudhuveli, situated on the east side of the North Malé Atoll is, like Bandos and Vaadhu, operated by Deen's Orchid Agency. It is a modern beach resort with single unit bungalows with straw roofing and fresh-water showers.

Ihuru is a small island, exceedingly beautiful and much photographed. The accommodation consists of simple bungalows with a total of 58 beds.

Kurumba: This tiny island, where accommodation was recently completely renovated, covers an area of half a square mile and is 20 minutes by boat from the airport and 30 minutes from Malé. Most watersports can be arranged, including scuba diving; the colourful fish in the lagoon will eat out of your hand.

Nakatchafushi boasts the country's largest lagoon, and is perhaps one of the most photographed of all the islands. Located on the western side of the Malé Atoll, it is 24km (15 miles) from the airport, a journey time of approximately 90 minutes. The lagoon is perfect for watersports and a long strip of sand at the western end of the island is a haven for beach-combers.

Furana is a resort within easy reach of the airport. The resort's deep lagoon makes it a favourite base for visiting 'yachties'.

Makunudhoo: It is a 2-hour voyage from the airport to this island, one of the most expensive resorts and one which is renowned for its food. The Swiss-run island probably provides the best anchorage of any resort and always has yachts for charter. It is protected on all sides by a beautiful lagoon. The accommodation consists of individual thatched bungalows situated in coconut groves leading down to the beach.

Kanifinolhu (Kani) is on the eastern edge of the atoll. The seas around the island boast some of the best inside reefs in the country, and the protection provided by the external reef makes diving possible even in the roughest conditions. The style of the accommodation is influenced by local and oriental design and some rooms have air-conditioning. The island has a desalination plant for fresh water.

Farukolufushi and **Thulhagiri** are two recently redesigned and renovated Club Med properties which are both, especially the former, close to the airport. Both have superb facilities for watersports. Thulhagiri has one windsurfing board for every twin-bedded room and a swimming pool.

Other highly regarded North Malé resorts are **Boduhithi** and the neighbouring **Kudahithi** and, closer to the airport, **Lhohifushi** which has a beautiful lagoon and a wide range of watersport facilities. Kudahithi, the most expensive resort in the Maldives, has only six units; excellent for small, private groups.

Kaafu Atoll – South

Still in the Malé (Kaafu) Atoll, but to the south of the airport, are a further score of resorts. Notable among these are **Biyadoo** and **Villivaru** which are 30km (20 miles) from the airport. Both are owned and managed by the Taj group from India. Biyadoo is the closest thing in the Maldives to an international resort and guests might even be invited to dress for dinner. Villivaru is not quite so upmarket. The nearby **Cocoa Island** has only 12 two-storey thatched huts, all of which are beautifully furnished. Private groups can rent the entire resort.

To the north of Cocoa Island are the 'twin' islands of **Veligandu Huraa (Veli)** and **Dhigufinolhu**, connected by a causeway across the lagoon. The latter is the more lively of the two, with more rooms and more in the way of entertainment: Veli has individual bungalows and a more intimate atmosphere. They are only a gentle stroll away from each other should one feel the need for a change of mood.

North of Cocoa Island is **Kandoomaafushi**, where flowering shrubs surround chalet-style accommodation. Trips can be arranged to the nearby fishing village.

Bodufinolhu (Fun Island) is located on the eastern reef of the South Malé Atoll. It is ringed with a massive lagoon and connected to two uninhabited islets which can be reached on foot at low tide. All rooms are on the beachfront with en-suite bathrooms, air-conditioning, IDD telephones and hot and cold desalinated water.

Other Atolls

Most of the resorts are to be found in the North and South Malé Atolls, but there are also several others, most in the northern island groups (see map).

Resorts in the **Alifu (Ari) Atoll,** which is to the west of Malé, include **Kuramathi**, a relatively large island which has first-class facilities and offers an excellent beach, superb diving, windsurfing, water-skiing, parasailing and night fishing. **Nika Island** is a small, away-from-it-all, up-market, 15-room resort offering clients the choice of three excellent restaurants and some of the most comfortable boats in the Maldives. **Fesdu** is situated in the heart of the atoll rather than on the periphery. Accommodation consists of 45 thatched round-houses, all of which are close to the beach. **Angaga**, also in Ari Atoll, is a recently opened resort. It is small, impressively constructed in traditional Maldivian style and with air-conditioned rooms and fresh hot and cold water. Other resorts include **Halaveli**, **Bathala**, **Ellaidoo**, **Machchafushi**, **Gangehi**, **Madoogali** and **Mayaafushi**; several others are under construction.

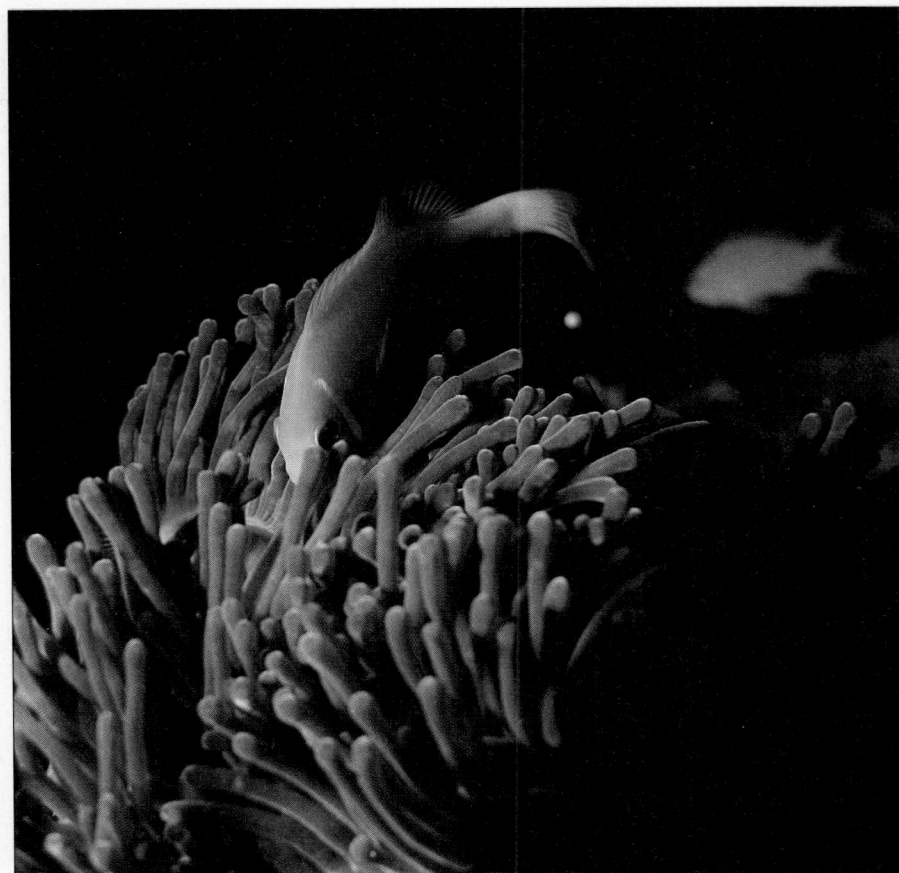

To the south is the **Vaavu Atoll** with some of the best diving in the entire archipelago. A well-established, long-popular resort, especially among visiting Italians, is the 54-bungalow **Alimatha**.
To the north is **Laviyanai Atoll** with the fairly simple 25-cabana **Kuredu** resort, essentially a spot for the besotted diver.
The **Baa Atoll** is about 130km (80 miles) north-west of the capital, one of the few places where traditional arts and crafts are still practised. The atoll has one resort, **Kunfundau**, with 50 beds.
Most tourism is in the northern atolls, but **Seenu**, the southernmost atoll of the archipelago (situated south of the equator) is known to many as the site of a former RAF staging post in **Gan**. The potential of the infrastructure here far surpasses that on other islands and many attempts have been made to develop Gan into a large, international tourist resort and to adapt the airport for receiving international wide-bodied jets. There is a regular, heavily-booked domestic flight between Malé and Gan operated by *Maldive Airways;* helicopter services may also be available. Check locally for more information.

SOCIAL PROFILE

FOOD & DRINK: Malé, the capital, has a few simple restaurants which serve local and Indian food. On the other islands there are no restaurants other than those run by the resort. Cuisine is international, with all foodstuffs other than seafood imported. The fish is magnificent. Curries and oriental buffets are widely available. **Drinks:** There is a good range of alcoholic and non-alcoholic drink, reflecting the demands of the visitors. There are a few local cocktails, including *The Maldive Lady*, a powerful and delicious concoction, the composition varying from bar to bar and island to island.
Note: All bars are situated in island communities or in hotels on Malé. All accept cash, but normally add orders onto the total bill. Locals do not drink at all, and all alcoholic consumption by visitors takes place in bars, hotels or resort communities.
NIGHTLIFE: There is little or no organised nightlife, though most resorts have informal discotheques around the bar areas, sometimes featuring live bands playing either traditional or Western music. Beach parties and barbecues are also popular. On some evenings many resorts have cultural shows and some show videos.
SHOPPING: Local purchases include sea shells (only when bought in official shops; they may *not* be removed from the beach or from the sea), lacquered wooden boxes and reed mats. There are strict prohibitions against the export of any type of coral. **Shopping hours:** 0800-2300 Saturday to Thursday. Shops officially shut in deference to Muslim prayer times five times a day (the most important being the evening prayer at 1800) for 15 minutes; however, this rule is not always strictly adhered to in the tourist areas away from the capital.
SPORT: **Scuba diving** and **windsurfing** facilities with fully qualified multi-lingual instructors are available at all resorts. Night **dives** are arranged. The underwater life is rated among the best in the world. Some resorts have glass-bottomed boats. All resorts have **water-skiing** facilities and some have catamarans for hire. **Fishing** trips, either by day or by night, are popular and readily arranged. Those at night will usually end with a barbecue at the resort with the day's catch being cooked and eaten. A few resorts have facilities for sports such as **tennis, football, volleyball** and **badminton**.
SOCIAL CONVENTIONS: Dress is informal, but locals, who are Muslim, will be offended by nudity or scanty clothing in public places, and the Government rigidly enforces these standards. Handshaking is the most common form of greeting. Hospitality as such is non-existent, even on Malé. The indigenous population not involved in the tourist trade lives in isolated island communities maintaining almost total privacy. A large number of locals smoke, and there are no restrictions on smoking in public, even during Ramadan. **Tipping:** This is officially discouraged.

BUSINESS PROFILE

ECONOMY: The bulk of the population live in a subsistence economy based around fishing and coconuts. There is very little cultivable land. Fishing and shipping are the most important components of the economy, and the Maldives have suffered from the shipping recession of the 1980s. Tourism, an important source of foreign exchange, has recently been slightly affected by the communal strife in nearby Sri Lanka, traditionally the main embarkation point for the Maldives, but the recent inauguration of direct flights from Europe is expected to overcome this problem. Many of the 63 resort islands currently in operation have in recent years made considerable investment in infrastructure such as desalination plants, refurbished accommodation, generators and air-conditioning, and there is every sign that this sector of the economy will continue to thrive in the forseeable future. The islands received a major setback in May 1991 when monsoon and abnormal tidal waters caused considerable damage throughout the archipelago.
BUSINESS: Since the islands import almost everything, business potential is high, but only on Malé. Business appointments are only loosely adhered to, and all business practices are extremely informal. Most business takes place during the morning. **Office hours:** 0730-1330 Saturday to Thursday. Friday is the official rest day.
COMMERCIAL INFORMATION: The following organisation can offer advice: State Trading Organisation, STO Building, 7 Haveeree Higun, Malé 20-02. Tel: 323 652. Fax: 325 218. Telex: 66006.

HISTORY & GOVERNMENT

HISTORY: The Dihevin, as the islanders are called, are a mixed people of Aryan, Negroid, Sinhalese, Dravidian and Arab descent. The Maldive Islands became a British Protectorate, with an elected Sultan as Head of State, in 1887. The islands became a Republic, briefly, in 1953-54 and achieved full independence as a Sultanate in 1965. Three years later, the Republic of the Maldive Islands was re-established and Ibrahim Nasir, Prime Minister since 1954, became President. In 1978, President Nasir decided against a third term as President, and was succeeded by Maumoon Abdul Gayoom. In 1985, the Maldives was a founder member of the South Asian Association for Regional Co-operation and hosted the fifth regional summit in 1991. An attempted coup, successfully put down with the aid of Indian troops, occurred in late 1988. During 1990, efforts were made to improve political and economic relations with India under the guidance of the India Maldives Joint Commission on Economic and Technical Co-operation. Global climatic changes have also been a cause of concern to the low-lying island, and the Maldives hosted an international conference on the subject in 1989. In 1990 increasing criticism of the country's oligarchic political regime was met by President Gayoom's decision to devolve certain presidential powers and introduce a package of reforms. The President then established an anti-corruption board in April 1991 to head off further criticism of public life in the Maldives.
GOVERNMENT: President Gayoom was re-elected for a third term as President in 1988. The legislature, or Majlis, has 48 members. Forty are elected by universal suffrage for a 5-year term (two from Malé and two from each of the 19 atolls); the remaining eight are presidential appointees. Outside the capital, however, considerable power is exercised by the atoll chiefs (*Verins*), who are appointed by the President.

CLIMATE

The Maldives have a hot tropical climate. There are two monsoons, the southwest monsoon from May to October, and the northeast monsoon from November to April. Generally the southwest monsoon brings more wind and rain in June and July. The temperature rarely falls below 25°C, even during the night. The best time to visit is November to Easter.
Required clothing: Lightweight cottons and linens throughout the year. Light rainwear is advisable during the monsoon season.

MALE Maldives

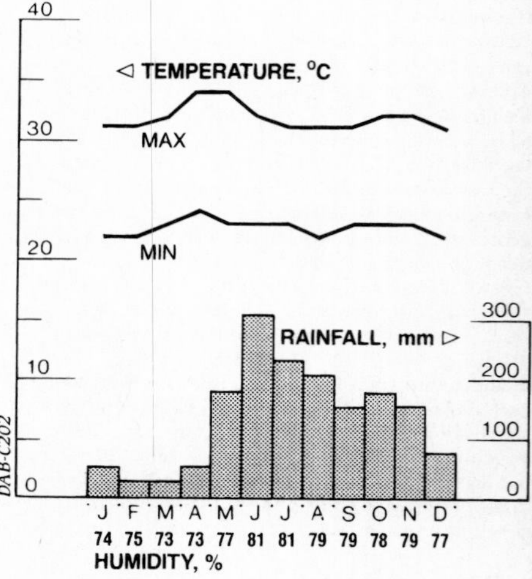

TEMPERATURE CONVERSIONS
-20 -10 0°C 10 20 30 40
0 10 20 30°F40 50 60 70 80 90 100

RAINFALL CONVERSIONS
0mm 200 400 600 800
0in 5 10 15 20 25 30

MALI

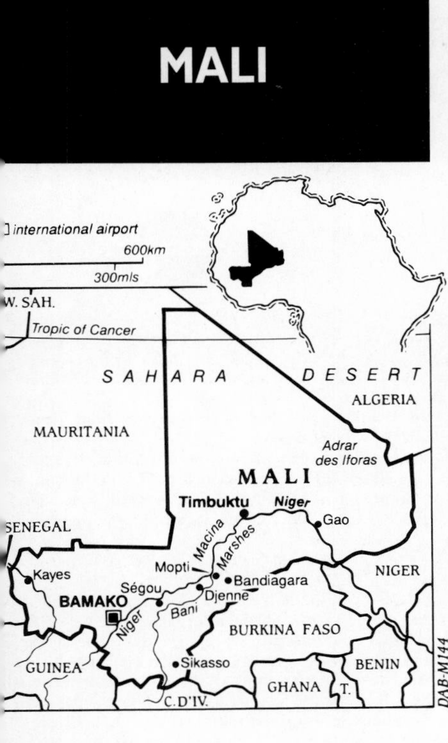

Location: Central West Africa.

Société Malienne d'Exploitation des Ressources Touristiques (SMERT)
BP 222
place de la République
Bamako, Mali
Tel: 225 942. Telex: 2433.

Embassy of the Republic of Mali
487 avenue Molière
B-1060 Brussels, Belgium
Tel: (2) 345 7432 *or* 345 7589. Fax: (2) 344 5700. Telex: 22508. Opening hours: 0900-1300 and 1400-1630 Monday to Friday.

British Consulate
BP 2069
Bamako, Mali
Tel: 222 064.

Embassy of the Republic of Mali
2130 R Street, NW
Washington, DC
20008
Tel: (202) 332 2249 *or* 939 8950.

Embassy of the United States of America
BP 34
rue Rochester NY et rue Mohamed V
Bamako, Mali
Tel: 225 470. Fax: 228 059. Telex: 2248 AMEMB MJ.

Embassy of the Republic of Mali
50 Goulburn Avenue
Ottawa, Ontario
K1N 8C8
Tel: (613) 232 1501 *or* 232 3264. Fax: (613) 232 7429.
Consulates in: Montréal and Toronto.

Canadian Embassy
PO Box 198
Bamako, Mali
Tel: 222 236. Fax: 224 362. Telex: 2530.

AREA: 1,240,192 sq km (478,841 sq miles).
POPULATION: 8,156,000 (1990 estimate).
POPULATION DENSITY: 6.6 per sq km.
CAPITAL: Bamako. **Population:** 740,000 (1984).
GEOGRAPHY: Mali is a landlocked republic, sharing borders with Mauritania, Algeria, Burkina Faso, Côte d'Ivoire, Guinea, Niger and Senegal. It is a vast land of flat plains fed by two major rivers, the Senegal on its western edge and the great River Niger. On its journey north the Niger converges with the River Bani, and forms a rich inland delta, the marshlands of the Macina, stretching for some 450km (280 miles) along the river's length, in some places 200km (124 miles) wide. The central part of the country is arid grazing land, called the Sahel, which has suffered great drought. At Timbuktu the Niger reaches the desert and here it turns first to the east, then to the southeast at Bourem, where it heads for the ocean. In the desert, near the Algerian and Niger borders in the northeast, the Adrar des Iforas Massif rises 800m (2625ft). The north of the country is true desert except for the few oases along the ancient trans-Sahara camel routes. Tuaregs still live around these oases and camel routes. Further south live the Peulh cattle-raising nomads. The majority of the population lives in the savannah region in the south. The peoples of this region comprise Songhai, Malinke, Senoufou, Dogon and the Bambara (the largest ethnic group).
LANGUAGE: The official language is French. Local languages include Bambara, Senoufou, Sarakolle, Tuareg and Arabic.
RELIGION: Muslim, with Christian and Animist minorities.
TIME: GMT.
ELECTRICITY: 220 volts AC, 50Hz in Bamako. Larger towns in Mali have their own locally generated supply.
COMMUNICATIONS: Telephone: Limited IDD service. Country code: 223. Manual exchanges and operator service in the provinces, which can prove unreliable. **Telex:** Telexes can be sent from the Central Telex Office in Bamako and main hotels. **Post:** International post limited to main towns and central post office. Airmail to Europe takes approximately two weeks. For further details contact the Embassy. **Press:** There are no English-language newspapers. The only daily, *L'Essor*, is published in French.
BBC World Service and Voice of America frequencies: From time to time these change. See the section *How to Use this Book* for more information.

BBC:				
MHz	17.79	15.07	15.04	9.410
Voice of America:				
MHz	21.49	15.60	9.525	6.035

PASSPORT/VISA

Regulations and requirements may be subject to change at short notice, and you are advised to contact the appropriate diplomatic or consular authority before finalising travel arrangements. Details of these may be found at the head of this country's entry. Any numbers in the chart refer to the footnotes below.

	Passport Required?	Visa Required?	Return Ticket Required?
Full British	Yes	Yes	Yes
BVP	Not valid	-	-
Australian	Yes	Yes	Yes
Canadian	Yes	Yes	Yes
USA	Yes	Yes	Yes
Other EC	Yes	Yes	Yes
Japanese	Yes	Yes	Yes

PASSPORTS: Valid passport required by all except nationals of Algeria, Benin, Burkina Faso, Cameroon, Chad, Côte d'Ivoire, Gambia, Guinea, Niger, Nigeria, Senegal, Togo and Tunisia in possession of valid ID or a passport expired for not more than 5 years.
British Visitors Passport: Not acceptable.
VISAS: Required by all except nationals of Mauritania and Morocco and those referred to under passport exemptions above.
Types of visa: Tourist, Transit and Business. Cost: BFr1030 per person plus BFr200 postal charges.
Validity: One month from the date of entry, although visas can be extended in Mali, either in Bamako at the Immigration Service or at any police station. Visas may be obtained up to 6 months in advance of travelling to Mali.
Application to: Consulate (or Consular Section at Embassy). For addresses, see top of entry.
Application requirements: (a) 2 application forms. (b) 2 photos. (c) Stamped self-addressed envelope. (d) If application is for Business visa, 2 documents of attestation. (e) Fee payment must be made in cash.
Working days required: Allow one week if applying by post; 24 hours if applying in person.
Temporary residence: Enquire at Embassy.

MONEY

Currency: CFA Franc (CFA Fr) = 100 centimes. Notes are in denominations of CFA Fr10,000, 5000, 1000, 500 and 100. Coins are in denominations of CFA Fr100, 50, 25, 10, 5. Mali is part of the French Franc zone and the CFA Franc is pegged to the French Franc at fixed parity.
Currency exchange: Possible at main banks in Bamako, but plenty of time should be allowed, as changing money at a bank can be a slow process. French Franc notes are sometimes accepted in cash transactions. In 1984 the Mali Franc was abolished and replaced by the CFA Franc (CFA Fr1 = 2 Mali Francs).
Credit cards: Limited use of Diners Club and Access/Mastercard. Check with your credit card company for details of merchant acceptability and other services which may be available.
Travellers cheques: Can be exchanged at banks.
Exchange rate indicators: The following figures are included as a guide to the movements of the CFA Franc against Sterling and the US Dollar:

Date:	Oct '89	Oct '90	Oct '91	Oct '92
£1.00=	505.13	498.38	496.12	413.75
$1.00=	319.90	255.12	285.87	260.71

Currency restrictions: The import and export of local currency is unlimited. The import of foreign currency is unlimited provided it is declared, whilst export is limited to bank notes up to a value of CFA Fr25,000.
Banking hours: 0730-1500 Monday to Thursday, 0730-1230 Friday.

DUTY FREE

The following items may be imported into Mali without incurring customs duty:
1000 cigarettes or 250 cigars or 2kg of tobacco;
A reasonable amount of alcoholic beverage and perfume in open bottles for personal use.
Note: Cameras and films must be declared.

PUBLIC HOLIDAYS

Public holidays observed in Mali are as follows:
Mar 25 '93 Korité (End of Ramadan). **Apr 12** Easter Monday. **May 1** Labour Day. **May 25** Africa Day. **Jun 1** Tabaski (Feast of the Sacrifice). **Aug 30** Mouloud (Birth of the Prophet). **Sep 22** Independence Day. **Sep 29** Baptism of the Prophet. **Nov 19** Anniversary of the 1968 Coup. **Dec 25** Christmas Day. **Jan 1 '94** New Year's Day. **Jan 20** Armed Forces Day. **Mar** Start of Korité.
Note: Muslim festivals are timed according to local sightings of various phases of the Moon and the dates given above are approximations. During the lunar month of Ramadan that precedes Korité (Eid al-Fitr), Muslims fast during the day and feast at night and normal business patterns may be interrupted. Many restaurants are closed during the day and there may be restrictions on smoking and drinking. Some disruption may continue into Korité itself. Korité and Tabaski (Eid al-Adha) may last anything from two to ten days, depending on the region. For more information see the section *World of Islam* at the back of the book.

HEALTH

Regulations and requirements may be subject to change at short notice, and you are advised to contact your doctor well in advance of your intended date of departure. Any numbers in the chart refer to the footnotes below.

	Special Precautions?	Certificate Required?
Yellow Fever	Yes	1
Cholera	Yes	2
Typhoid & Polio	Yes	-
Malaria	3	-
Food & Drink	4	-

[1]: A yellow fever vaccination certificate is required by all travellers over one year old arriving from all countries.
[2]: Following WHO guidelines issued in 1973, a cholera vaccination certificate is not a condition of entry to Mali. However, cholera is a serious risk in this country and precautions are essential. Up-to-date advice should be sought before deciding whether these precautions should include vaccination, as medical opinion is divided over its effectiveness. See the *Health* section at the back of the book.
[3]: Malaria, mainly in the malignant *falciparum* form, is present all year throughout the country. Resistance to chloroquine has been reported.
[4]: All water should be regarded as being potentially contaminated. Water used for drinking, brushing teeth or making ice should have first been boiled or otherwise sterilised. Milk is unpasteurised and should be boiled. Powdered or tinned milk is available and is advised, but make sure that it is reconstituted with pure water. Avoid dairy products which are likely to have been made from unboiled milk. Only eat well-cooked meat and fish, preferably served hot. Pork, salad and mayonnaise may carry increased risk. Vegetables should be cooked and fruit peeled.
Rabies is present. For those at high risk, vaccination before arrival should be considered. If you are bitten abroad seek medical advice without delay. For more information con-

sult the *Health* section at the back of the book.
Bilharzia (schistosomiasis) is present. Avoid swimming and paddling in fresh water. Swimming pools which are well-chlorinated and maintained are safe.
Health care: Health insurance is essential. There are 3500 hospital beds. There is one doctor for every 26,000 inhabitants.

TRAVEL - International

AIR: Mali's national airline is *Air Mali (MY)*.
Approximate flight time: From *London* to Bamako is 11 hours (including stopover in Brussels or Paris).
International airport: *Bamako (BKO)* is 15km (9 miles) from the city (travel time – 20 minutes). A bus service into the city is available.
Departure tax: CFA Fr3500; for destinations in Africa CFA Fr2500.
RAIL: There is a twice-weekly service from Bamako to Dakar (Senegal) which has air-conditioning, sleeper facilities and restaurant cars. It will also carry cars. There are plans to extend rail links into Guinea.
ROAD: The best road connections are from Côte d'Ivoire and Burkina Faso. The remote and desolate trans-Saharan route from Algeria is hazardous. There are also road links with Senegal and Guinea. The all-weather road follows the Niger as far as Niamey (Niger). **Bus:** Services operate from Kankan (Guinea) to Bamako, as well as from Bobo Dioulasso (Burkina Faso) to Segou and Mopti, and Niamey (Niger) to Gao.

TRAVEL - Internal

AIR: Some domestic flights are provided by *Tombouctou Air Service* and light aircraft can be chartered from the *Société des Transports Aériens (STA)*.
RIVER: Between July and December there are weekly services between Bamako and Gao via Timbuktu along the River Niger. However, because of drought in the Sahel desert, services are sometimes suspended. The journey is approximately 1300km (800 miles) and takes five or six days. Between December and March travel is only possible between Mopti and Gao. Food is available on the boats and first-class cabins can be booked in advance. Motorised and non-motorised *pirogues* are available for hire between Timbuktu and Mopti. Following the completion of the Manantali Dam in 1988, work is continuing to improve the navigability of the River Senegal.
RAIL: There is a daily service from Bamako to Kayes, en route to Dakar on the Senegal coast. There are two trains, one Malian and one Senegalese – the Senegalese train is far superior, with air-conditioning and buffet car. The railway line is Mali's most important method of transport, over and above the road link. There is also a daily service from Bamako to Koulikoro.
ROAD: Roads in Mali range from moderate to very bad. The main road runs from Sikasso in the south to Bamako, and to Mopti and Gao. Between Mopti and Gao travel can be difficult during the rains, when the Niger, at its confluence with the Bani, splits into a network of channels, and floods its banks to form the marshlands of the *Macina*. **Bus:** Services run between the main towns. **Documentation:** International Driving Permit recommended, although not legally required.
Note: Off the main roads you should travel in convoy and take a complete set of spare parts.
URBAN: Taxi: Collective taxis in cities are very cheap. The taxis charge standard fare regardless of the distance travelled. Tipping is not expected.

ACCOMMODATION

HOTELS: Only Bamako has hotels that meet international standards, but other main towns have hotels of an adequate standard and some have air-conditioning. Accommodation tends to be expensive and difficult to obtain at short notice – advance booking is recommended.
LODGES: There are a number of *campements* in the **National Park of La Boucle du Baoule.** The reserve is 120km (75 miles) from Bamako.

RESORTS & EXCURSIONS

Bamako, the capital, is a modern town which is the educational and cultural centre of Mali. The main places of interest are the markets, the *Botanical Gardens*, the zoo and the craft centre.
Djenne is known as the 'Jewel of the Niger'. Founded in 1250, it has a beautiful mosque and it is one of the oldest trading towns along the trans-Saharan caravan routes. *Old Djenne* was founded around 250BC and is located about 5km (3 miles) from Djenne.
Mopti is at the confluence of the Bani and the Niger and is built on three islands joined by dykes. There is another fine mosque here.
Southeast of Mopti is to be found the Bandiagara country, peopled by the Dogons, whose ancient beliefs have been largely untouched by Islam. The Dogon villages are extremely unique and picturesque and visitors should treat villagers with respect.
Timbuktu is a name which has passed into English vernacular as a byword for inaccessibility and remoteness. It is, however, neither of these things due to the magnificent camel caravans (some of them comprised of over 3000 animals) which arrive every year from the Taoudenni salt mines to distribute their produce throughout the Sahel. By the 15th century, Timbuktu was the centre of a lucrative trade in salt and gold, straddling the trans-Saharan caravan routes, as well as being a great centre of Islamic learning. Much of this ancient city is in decay, but it is the site of many beautiful mosques (*Djingerebur*, *Sankore* and *Sidi Yahaya* for example) and tombs, some dating back to the 14th century.
Gao is another ancient city which had its heyday in the 15th century. Gao houses the mosque of *Kankan Moussa* and the tombs of the Askia dynasty. There are also two excellent markets. The city has recently undergone much urban development.
San and **Ségou** are both interesting towns worth a visit. The **National Park of La Boucle de Baoule** contains an array of southern Sahalian species of wildlife, including giraffe, leopard, lion, elephant, buffalo and hippo.

SOCIAL PROFILE

FOOD & DRINK: Several of the hotels, notably the Hôtel de l'Amitié, have restaurant and bar facilities of international standard, serving international cuisine, and most towns have small restaurants serving local and North African dishes. A particular Malian speciality is *La Capitaine Sangha*, a kind of Nile perch served with hot chilli sauce, whole fried bananas and rice. There is a limited choice of restaurants. These are open to non-residents, but the visitor is also advised to try the local and North African foods found in small restaurants in town. **Drink:** Alcohol is available in bars (with very late opening hours), but since the majority are Muslim there is a good range of fresh fruit juices. Most people tend to drink fruit juice rather than alcohol. Malian tamarind and guava juices, drunk in tall glasses full of ice, are delicious.
NIGHTLIFE: Bamako has a good selection of nightclubs with music and dancing.
SHOPPING: Traditional crafts range from the striking masks of the Bambara, Dogon and Malinko peoples, to woodcarvings, woven cloth and mats, gold and silver jewellery and copperware. Excellent pottery is made in the Segou region, while Timbuktu is a good centre for iron and copper articles, including swords, daggers and traditional household utensils.
SPORT: In Bamako, Omni-Sport, a Soviet-built sports complex, has a **swimming** pool and good facilities for a large number of sports.
SOCIAL CONVENTIONS: Proud of their glorious past, these people consider their poverty less important than their rich traditions. They are dignified and reserved and though they may appear aloof and distant, they are not hostile and will gracefully welcome visitors into their homes. Visitors must remember that this is a Muslim country and the religious customs and beliefs of the people should be respected. Modesty in dress, particularly for women, is essential. **Tipping:** A 10% tip is customary in restaurants and bars, but is not normal for taxi drivers. Porters receive CFA Fr100 per piece of luggage.

BUSINESS & SOCIAL

ECONOMY: The economy of Mali, one of the poorest countries in the world, is almost entirely agricultural even though less than 2% of the land is, or indeed can be, cultivated. The people are engaged in raising livestock and growing subsistence crops such as millet, sorghum, maize and, increasingly, rice. In a

MALI	HEALTH REGULATIONS	VISA REGULATIONS Code-Link
GALILEO/WORLDSPAN	 TI-DFT/BKO/HE	 TI-DFT/BKO/VI
SABRE	 TIDFT/BKO/HE	 TIDFT/BKO/VI

To access this information on your CRS, swipe the barcode with a light pen or type in the text under the barcode. For more information, see the introduction *How to Use This Book*.

good season, enough is produced for some export business. Otherwise, exports rely on cash crops, principally cotton and groundnuts; fruit and vegetables are exported to Europe. Indeed, despite poor rainfall, Mali has produced agricultural surpluses two years running. There is no significant industry and virtually all non-agricultural products have to be imported. Large aid grants and loans assist Mali to balance its budget and develop aspects of its economy. The new government has introduced decentralising and liberalisation measures as conditions for international support. It is also hoping to develop the tourist industry, as well as mining to exploit recently discovered deposits of phosphates, bauxite, manganese and uranium to add to the growing quantities of salt, limestone and gold. France is Mali's major trading partner, providing a quarter of imports and taking a similar proportion of exports.

BUSINESS: The forms of address are those of France, eg *Monsieur le Directeur*. Lightweight or tropical suit and tie are advised for only the smartest meetings. Otherwise, a light, open-neck shirt is worn. It is essential to be able to speak French for business purposes.

Office hours: 0730-1430 Monday to Thursday and Saturday, 0730-1230 Friday.

COMMERCIAL INFORMATION: The following organisation can offer advice: Chambre de Commerce et d'Industrie du Mali, BP 46, place de la Liberté, Bamako. Tel: 225 036. Telex: 2435.

HISTORY & GOVERNMENT

HISTORY: Once one of the great centres of Islamic culture and wealth, Mali (which is among the continent's most ancient states outside of North Africa) owed much of its reputation by the 15th century to its situation as a major trading centre and tax levier on the trans-Saharan route. The whole Niger trading area declined in influence and power as the European maritime nations began to trade directly with the primary suppliers, and the trans-Saharan routes fell into obscurity. Mali became part of French West Africa in the 19th century. In 1960, together with what is now Senegal, it achieved independence as the Federation of Mali, although Senegal seceded after a few weeks. The first President of the resulting Republic of Mali was Modibo Keita, who severed ties with France and developed strong links with the USSR. In 1967, however, hyper-inflation forced Mali to rejoin the Franc Zone. In 1968, a military coup overthrew Keita and power was assumed by the Military Committee for National Liberation (CMLN) under Lieutenant (later General) Moussa Traoré. In 1976 Traoré formed the sole legal political party, the Union Democratique du Peuple Malien (UDPM), and began a slow civilianisation of the administration.

Frequent reshuffles and rapid personnel turnovers indicated the insecurity of the Traoré regime which was the target of several attempted coups during its 23-year term. It was finally brought down in March 1991. Another army officer, Lieutenant-Colonel Amadou Toumani Touré, assumed power at the head of the Conseil National de Réconciliation (CNR, National Reconciliation Council). Under pressure from France, the new regime has organised a national conference to discuss a new constitution and has provisionally set down a framework for elections and the withdrawal of the army from politics early in 1992. The other pressing issue facing Touré is the Tuareg question. The Tuareg are nomadic people whose traditional territory spans eastern Mali, western Niger and the northern part of Burkina Faso. The collapse of the Tuareg's livestock-based economy through drought has caused growing tension between the Tuareg and the rest of the Malian population. The agreed schedule for the introduction of representative government was met and presidential elections were held in April 1992. The victor was university professor Alpha Oumar Konare, who won a comfortable majority, although only 20% of the electorate turned out to vote. Konare appointed ex-banker Younoussi Touré as Prime Minister.

GOVERNMENT: A new constitution allowing for presidential elections was introduced in 1992 after the overthrow of the military dictatorship by the Conseil National de Réconciliation and approved by a national referendum. Executive power rests with the President of the Republic who is elected for a five-year term. The President appoints a Prime Minister who, in turn, appoints a Council of Ministers. A 129-member national assembly, also elected for five years, holds legislative powers.

CLIMATE

Three main seasons which vary according to latitude. Rainy season runs between June and October, diminishing further north. The cooler season (October to February) is followed by extremely hot, dry weather until June.

Required clothing: Lightweight cottons and linens are worn throughout most of the year, though warmer clothing is needed between November and February. Waterproofing is advised during the rainy season.

BAMAKO Mali (340m)

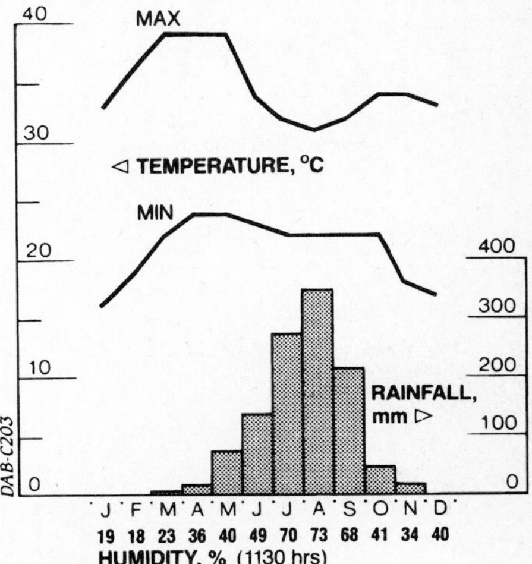

MALTA

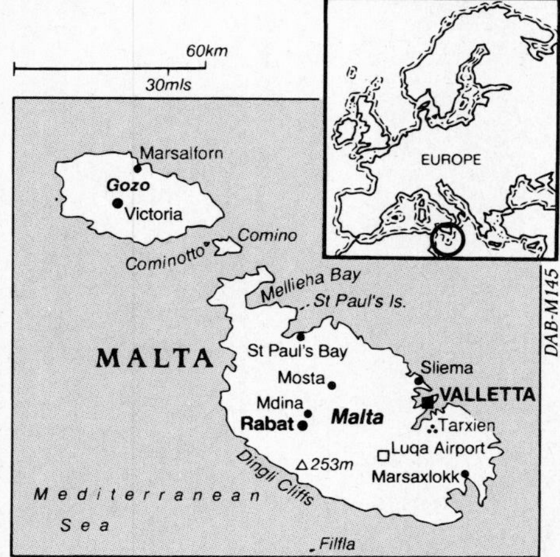

Location: Mediterranean, south of Sicily.

National Tourism Organisation (NTOM)
280 Republic Street
Valletta, Malta
Tel: 224 444. Fax: 220 401. Telex: 1105 HOL MW.

High Commission for the Republic of Malta
16 Kensington Square
London W8 5HH
Tel: (071) 938 1712/6. Fax: (071) 837 8664 *or* 937 0979. Telex: 261102 MLT LDN G. Opening hours: 1000-1300 and 1400-1600 Monday to Friday.

Malta National Tourist Office
Suite 300
Mappin House
4 Winsley Street
London
W1N 7AR
Tel: (071) 323 0506. Fax: (071) 323 9154.

British High Commission
PO Box 506
7 St Anne Street
Floriana
Valletta, Malta
Tel: 233 134-8. Fax: 622 001. Telex: 1249 UKREP MW.

Embassy of the Republic of Malta
2017 Connecticut Avenue, NW
Washington, DC
20008
Tel: (202) 462 3611/2. Fax: (202) 387 5470. Telex: 62431.
Consulates in: Boston, Carnegie, Detroit, Houston, Los Angeles, New York, St Paul, St Louis and San Francisco.

Embassy of the United States of America
PO Box 535
2nd Floor, Development House
St Anne Street
Floriana
Valletta,
Malta
Tel/Fax: 240 424/5 *or* 243 216/7 *or* 243 653 *or* 223 654.

Consulate General of the Republic of Malta
Suite 305
1 St John's Road
Toronto, Ontario
M6P 4C7
Tel: (416) 767 4902 *or* 767 2901. Fax: (416) 767 0563. Telex: 06984767.
Consulates in: Montréal and St John's.

Consulate of Canada
Demajo House
103 Archbishop Street
Valletta,
Malta
Tel: 233 121. Fax: 235 145. Telex: 1278 OJAMED MW.

AREA: 316 sq km (122 sq miles).
POPULATION: 373,000 (1990 estimate).
POPULATION DENSITY: 1180.4 per sq km.
CAPITAL: Valletta. **Population:** 9210 (1988 estimate).
GEOGRAPHY: The Maltese archipelago is situated in the middle of the Mediterranean, the largest inhabited island, Malta, lying 93km (58 miles) south of Sicily and 290km (180 miles) from North Africa. Gozo and

Some of Malta's most beautiful Cathedrals are underwater

From the thyme-covered cliffs of the south western coast, which rise as high as 800 feet, to the rich golden sands of tiny, sculptured coves, the bells of innumerable 'Festas' call the faithful to worship.

But beneath the clear, azure blue waters that wash the coastlines, lies a

"Luzzus" the famous Maltese fishing boats

veritable honeycomb of caves and caverns.

Here, the divers glide through vermilion reefs, a chorus of Damsel fish swirling in their wake, as the eerie underwater glow from phosphorescent rock lights their path like a beacon.

Ta'Pinu Basilica, Gozo. One of the 365 churches on the islands of Malta.

Suddenly, they will find themselves in a vast, underwater cathedral, the rays of the sun burning through the natural windows.

The water is warm and inviting, and so clean and clear that a kaleidoscope of colour greets your every glance.

As the sun begins to set, the multi-coloured fish of the night create a silent firework display between the crumbling maritime wrecks that whisper of ancient adventures; and along the coastline, the lights sparkle from honeyed sandstone villages, as rich red wine toasts another day.

Tomorrow, the bright colours of the windsurfers will vie for attention with the thousands of tiny, coloured boats, their painted eyes warding off the devil.

But how could there be evil in such a place, where belongings remain where you left them, and doors swing open at a touch? Here, there is only the natural heartbeat of life, raised but to dance and celebrate another Saint's Day, or perhaps

Casino de Malte in St. Julian's.

to ride the wheel of fortune in the elegant Casino.

Some travel thousands of miles to experience such a life. The wise travel three hours to the islands of Malta.

ITALY
GOZO
COMINO
VALLETTA
MALTA
MEDITERRANEAN SEA
NORTH AFRICA

I have to know more about Malta. I am particularly interested in (tick relevant boxes):–

- ☐ Historical Sites and Architecture
- ☐ Yearly Calendar of Events
- ☐ Watersports and Diving ☐ Gozo
- ☐ Quality Accommodation

Name ____________________

Address ____________________

____

____

____________________ Postcode __________

Send to the Malta National Tourist Office, Mappin House, Suite 300, 4 Winsley Street, London W1N 7AR. Tel: **071-323 0506**

AIR MALTA

THE ISLANDS OF MALTA
Explore 6,000 Years of Civilisation.

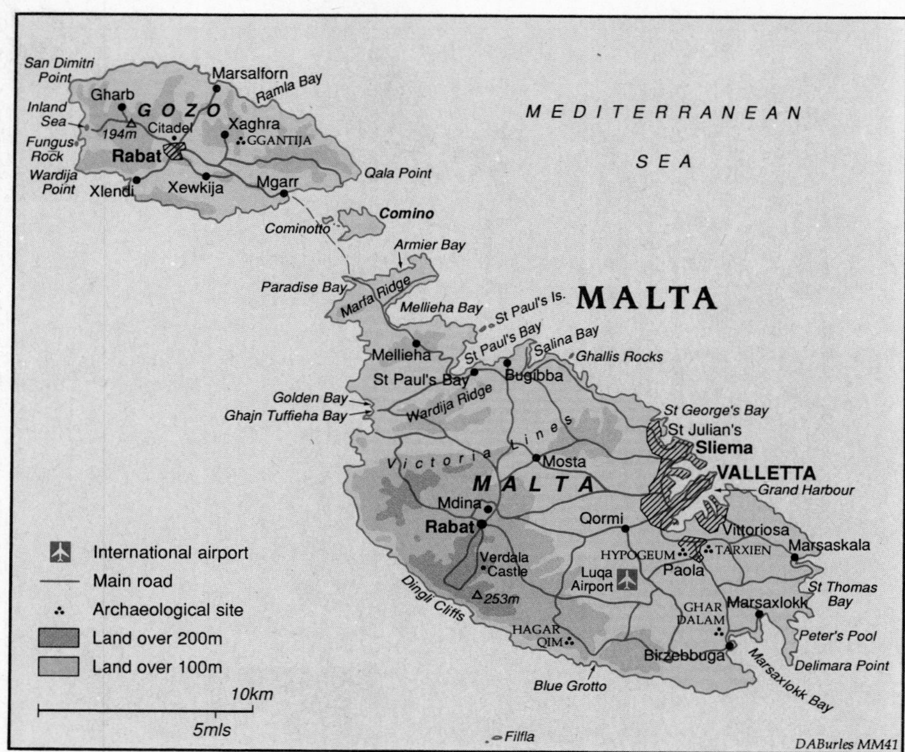

Comino are the only other inhabited islands. The landscape of all three is characterised by low hills with terraced fields. Malta has no mountains or rivers. Its coastline is indented with harbours, bays, creeks, sandy beaches and rocky coves. Gozo is connected to Malta by ferry and is more thickly vegetated, with many flat-topped hills and craggy cliffs. Comino, the smallest island, is connected to Malta and Gozo by ferry and is very sparsely populated.

LANGUAGE: Maltese (a Semitic language) and English are the official languages. Italian is also widely spoken.

RELIGION: Roman Catholic.

TIME: GMT + 1 (GMT+ 2 in summer).

ELECTRICITY: 240 volts AC, 50Hz. There is no standardisation of electrical fittings, although the 13-amp square-pin socket and plug seem to be gaining in popularity.

COMMUNICATIONS: Telephone: IDD is available from the following locations: Main Telegraph Office, St Georges Road, St Julian's (24-hour service); branch office, South Street, Valletta (0800-1900 Monday to Saturday); Luqa Airport (0700-1900 daily); Bisazza Street, Sliema (0800-1300 Monday to Friday in summer, 0800-1200 and 1300-1600 rest of year), Gozo (0730-2100 daily). Country code: 356. There are no area codes. Local calls can be made from numerous red phone boxes found all over the island. **Fax:** Telemalta Corporation provides an international service through its offices and branches. **Telex/telegram:** Both can be sent from Telemalta Corporation, St Georges Road, St Julian's. **Post:** Good postal services within the island. **Press:** The two Maltese dailies are *L'Orizzont* and *In-Nazzjon Taghna*. The only daily English-language newspaper published on the island is *The Times*.

BBC World Service and Voice of America frequencies: From time to time these change. See the section *How to Use this Book* for more information.

BBC:

MHz	15.07	12.10	7.325	6.195

Voice of America:

MHz	11.97	9.670	6.040	5.995

PASSPORT/VISA

Regulations and requirements may be subject to change at short notice, and you are advised to contact the appropriate diplomatic or consular authority before finalising travel arrangements. Details of these may be found at the head of this country's entry. Any numbers in the chart refer to the footnotes below.

	Passport Required?	Visa Required?	Return Ticket Required?
Full British	1	No	Yes
BVP	Valid	-	-
Australian	Yes	No	Yes
Canadian	Yes	No	Yes
USA	Yes	No	Yes
Other EC	1	No	Yes
Japanese	Yes	No	Yes

PASSPORTS: [1] Valid passport required by all except nationals of EC member countries in possession of valid ID who are visiting as tourists for no more than 3 months.

British Visitors Passport: Valid for stays of up to 3 months for holidays or unpaid business trips.

VISAS: Required by all except:

(a) nationals of countries listed in the chart above;

(b) nationals of Commonwealth countries (except nationals of Bangladesh, Ghana, Nigeria, Indian and Sri Lanka who *do* need a visa to enter Malta);

(c) nationals of Algeria, Argentina, Austria, Croatia, Egypt, Finland, Iceland, Kuwait, Libya, Liechtenstein, Monaco, Morocco, Norway, Poland, San Marino, Saudi Arabia, Slovenia, Sweden, Switzerland, Tunisia, Turkey, Uruguay, Vatican City and Yugoslavia;

(d) holders of Hungarian passports, who may stay for up to 30 days.

Types of visa: Tourist and Business. Cost – £5.40 plus £2 for telex clearance by authorities in Malta. Single visas only.

Validity: 3 months. For renewal or extension apply to the High Commission or Embassy.

Application to: Consulate (or Consular Section at Embassy or High Commission). For addresses, see top of entry.

Application requirements: (a) 3 application forms. (b) 2 photos. To be handed in at the High Commission or Embassy.

Working days required: 15 days, postal or personal.

Temporary residence: Apply to Principal Immigration Officer, Immigration Office, Police Headquarters, Floriana, Malta.

MONEY

Currency: Maltese Lira (M£) = 100 cents = 1000 mils. Notes are in denominations of M£20, 10, 5, and 2. Coins are in denominations of M£1, and 50, 25, 10, 5, 2 and 1 cents, and 5, 3 and 2 mils. A number of gold and silver coins are also minted.

Currency exchange: Money can be changed at banks, some hotels, and larger shops and restaurants.

Credit cards: Access/Mastercard, American Express, Diners Club and Visa are accepted. Check with your credit card company for details of merchant acceptability and other services which may be available.

Travellers cheques: Exchanged in the normal authorised institutions.

Exchange rate indicators: The following figures are included as a guide to the movements of the Maltese Lira against Sterling and the US Dollar:

Date:	Oct '89	Oct '90	Oct '91	Oct '92
£1.00=	0.55	0.58	0.53	0.51
$1.00=	0.35	0.30	0.31	0.32

Currency restrictions: The import of local currency is limited to M£50. Import and export of foreign currency, up to the amount declared on import, is free subject to declaration. The export of local currency is limited to M£25.

Banking hours: 0800-1200 Monday to Thursday, 0800-1200 and 1430-1600 Friday; 0800-1130 Saturday.

DUTY FREE

The following items may be imported into Malta without incurring customs duty:

200 cigarettes or 50 cigars or 100 cigarillos or 250g tobacco;
1 litre spirits;
1 litre wine;
10ml perfume;
125ml toilet water.

Note: It is advisable to declare any larger or unusual items of electrical equipment you are bringing into the island (such as video cameras, portable televisions or video recorders), as this will prevent duty being levied on these items when leaving the country.

Restricted entry: Pets are not allowed into Malta without prior approval of the Director of Agriculture and Fisheries. Pets imported from the UK have to go into quarantine for 3 weeks. All dogs and cats must be vaccinated against rabies at least 20 days before they are imported.

PUBLIC HOLIDAYS

Public holidays observed in Malta are as follows:
Mar 19 '93 St Joseph's Day. **Mar 31** Freedom Day. **Apr 9** Good Friday. **May 1** May Day. **Jun 7** Memorial of the 1919 Riot. **Jun 29** St Peter and St Paul. **Aug 15** Assumption. **Sep 8** Our Lady of the Victories Day. **Sep 21** Independence Day. **Dec 8** Immaculate Conception. **Dec 13** Republic Day. **Dec 25** Christmas Day. **Jan 1 '94** New Year's Day. **Feb 10** St Paul's Shipwreck. **Mar 19** St Joseph's Day. **Mar 31** Freedom Day.

MALTA	HEALTH REGULATIONS	VISA REGULATIONS (Code-Link)
GALILEO/WORLDSPAN	 TI-DFT/MLA/HE	 TI-DFT/MLA/VI
SABRE	 TIDFT/MLA/HE	 TIDFT/MLA/VI

To access this information on your CRS, swipe the barcode with a light pen or type in the text under the barcode. For more information, see the introduction *How to Use This Book*.

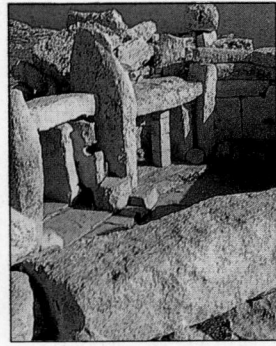

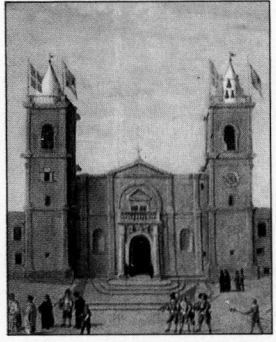

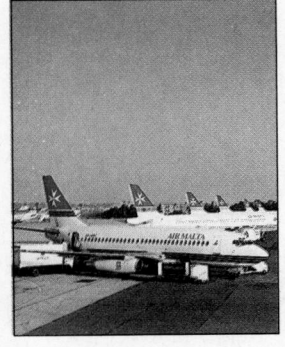

HEALTH

Regulations and requirements may be subject to change at short notice, and you are advised to contact your doctor well in advance of your intended date of departure. Any numbers in the chart refer to the footnotes below.

	Special Precautions?	Certificate Required?
Yellow Fever	No	1
Cholera	No	2
Typhoid & Polio	No	-
Malaria	No	-
Food & Drink	3	-

[1]: A yellow fever vaccination certificate is required from travellers over nine months of age arriving from infected areas. If indicated on epidemiological grounds, infants under nine months of age are subject to isolation or surveillance if arriving from an infected area.
[2]: A cholera vaccination certificate may be required from travellers arriving from infected areas.
[3]: Mains water is normally chlorinated, and whilst safe may cause mild abdominal upsets. Bottled water is available and is advised for the first few weeks of the stay. Milk is pasteurised and dairy products are safe for consumption. Local meat, poultry, seafood, fruit and vegetables are generally considered safe to eat.
Health care: UK passport-holders staying less than 30 days will receive emergency hospital treatment only at a state-run hospital. The principal hospitals are St Luke's, Gwardamanga in Malta and Craig Hospital in Gozo. Health insurance is advised.

TRAVEL - International

AIR: Malta's national airline is *Air Malta (KM)*.
Approximate flight time: From *London* to Luqa is 3 hours.
International airport: *Luqa*, 8km (5 miles) southeast of Valletta (travel time – 15 minutes). Buses 32, 33, 34 and 35 go every 30 minutes from 0600-2100 to and from Valletta City Gate. There is a full taxi service to all parts of Malta, with fares regulated by meter. Airport facilities include an outgoing duty-free shop, car hire, bank, currency exchange and restaurant/bar. All facilities are open 24 hours. A new terminal with an annual capacity of 2.5 million passengers is due to open.
SEA: The main ports are Grand Harbour, Marsaxlokk and Mgarr/Gozo. The Gozo Channel Company operates a service between Malta and Catania (Sicily) from April to September. There are links at Catania with Tripoli and Benghazi.
A new high-speed (45 knots) **catamaran** service now operates between Malta and Sicily twice a week. The service operates to several Sicilian ports.

TRAVEL - Internal

AIR: There is a helicopter service operating during the summer months between Malta and Gozo. A quick alternative to the ferry service, it runs eight times a day and takes only five minutes.
SEA: A passenger car ferry operates several times daily between Cirkewwa in Malta and Mgarr in Gozo, with connections to Comino. Crossing time is about 20 minutes. For further information, contact the *Gozo Channel Company*, Hay Wharf, Sa Maison in Malta.
In addition, a new hovercraft service is now in operation between Malta and Gozo. The first boat leaves Gozo at 0700 and the last one leaves Malta at 2030. This service is for passengers only. The fare is M£2 in peak season and M£1 off-peak.
ROAD: Driving is on the left. Speed limit is 64kmph (39mph). **Bus:** Good local services operate from Luqa, Valletta, Sa Maison and Victoria (Gozo) to all towns. **Taxi:** Identifiable by their all-white livery and red number plates and are under meter charge at government-controlled prices. **Car hire:** A number of car hire firms offer self-drive cars. Both *Hertz* and *Avis* have

desks at the airport. Rates on Malta are among the cheapest in Europe. **Documentation:** Full national driving licence is needed.

ACCOMMODATION

Accommodation in Malta is provided in hotels, holiday complexes, guest-houses, hostels or self-catering flats. Many hotels offer substantial reductions, particularly during the off season. **Grading:** There is a star classification standard for all hotels in the Maltese islands, introduced by the Secretariat for Tourism and the Hotels and Catering Establishments Board. All classified hotels are thoroughly inspected before their star grading is allocated and are regularly inspected to ensure that standards are maintained. Gradings range from 1- to 5-star, indicating the level of standards, facilities and services offered by the hotel. Gradings are as follows:

5-star: Superior standard, fully air-conditioned accommodation; all rooms with private bath and shower; telephone, radio and TV; room service on a 24-hour basis; bar; restaurant and coffee shop; lounge area; dancing facilities; pool and sports facilities; 24-hour reception; laundry, pressing and dry-cleaning; shops and hairdresser.

4-star: High standard, fully air-conditioned accommodation; all rooms with private bath or shower and internal or external telephone and radio; room service from breakfast time to midnight; bar; restaurant; pool or service beach facilities; 24-hour reception; laundry, pressing and dry-cleaning; lounge; shops, including hairdresser.

3-star: Good accommodation; all rooms with private bath or shower and internal or external telephone; bar and restaurant facilities; lounge area; 24-hour reception; laundry, pressing and dry-cleaning service.

2-star: Modest accommodation; at least 20% of rooms have private bath or shower; all rooms with wash basin and mirror; at least breakfast facilities are offered; telephone or service bell in all rooms; front office service during the day and at least porter service during the night.

1-star: Small hotel with simple accommodation; at least common bath and toilet facilities are available; all rooms with wash basin and mirror; at least breakfast facilities are offered; front office service during the day and at least porter service during the night.

RESORTS & EXCURSIONS

The Maltese islands, situated almost at the centre of the Mediterranean, offer the attraction of clear blue waters, secluded bays and sandy beaches while, in the towns, medieval walled citadels and splendid baroque churches and palaces reflect the rich history of the islands.

Malta

Valletta: The town was built at the end of the 16th century by the Knights of St John as the island's new capital, and, more importantly, as a fortress commanding an impregnable position over the peninsula. The city developed around what is now Republic Street, Old Bakery Street and Merchants Street, the latter containing some of the finest examples of Maltese-style baroque architecture in the islands. The *Co-Cathedral of St John's* has an austere exterior, but the interior is a sumptuous mixture of gilded tracery, marble mosaic floors and a lapis lazuli altar behind which is a remarkable marble group of the Baptism of Christ. The painting by Caravaggio of the beheading of St John is in the Oratory. The *Grand Master's Palace* in Republic Street was built 500 years ago as the abode of the Grand Master of the Order of St John, and contains a series of paintings depicting the great siege of 1565, painted by a pupil of Michelangelo, and a group of tapestries originally designed for Louis XIV. The palace also houses an armoury which has one of the best collections in existence. The *Manoel Theatre*, named after one of the most popular Grand Masters, is the second-oldest theatre in Europe and stages performances of opera, theatre, music and ballet between October and May. The *National Museum of Fine Art*, housed in an 18th-century palace, has a collection of furniture, paintings and treasures connected with the Knights of St John. The church of *Our Lady of Victories*, built in 1566, is the oldest church in Valletta and was built to commemorate the victory over the Turks. At the nearby Auberge de Provence is the *National Museum of Archaeology*, which has exhibits from the area dating back to prehistory. The town also has a bustling market in the Floriana suburb on Sunday mornings and another one in front of the Co-Cathedral of St John's from Monday to Saturday.

Within close proximity to Paola are the archaeological sites of *Tarxien*, with its neolithic temple; *Hypogeum*, a complex of ancient underground burial chambers on three levels dating back 3000 years; and *Ghar Dalam* (Dark Cave) where the remains of now extinct birds and animals such as dwarf hippos and elephants have been found.

Sliema lies on the *Grand Harbour* facing Valletta. It is a large, modern cosmopolitan town bustling with hotels, shops, cafés, cinemas, restaurants, bars,

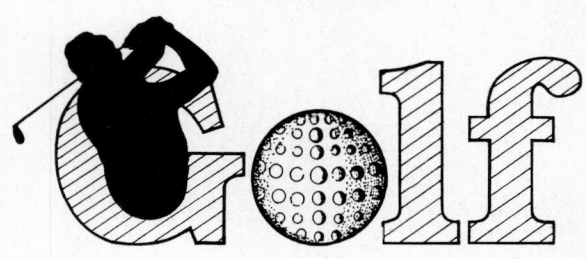

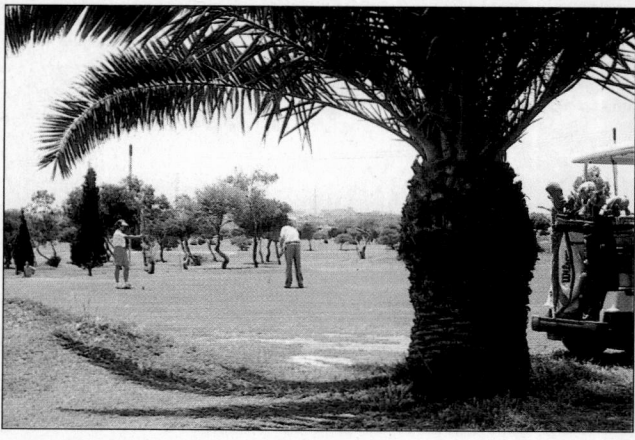

clubs and discos. The shoreline here is rocky, but is nevertheless good for bathing.

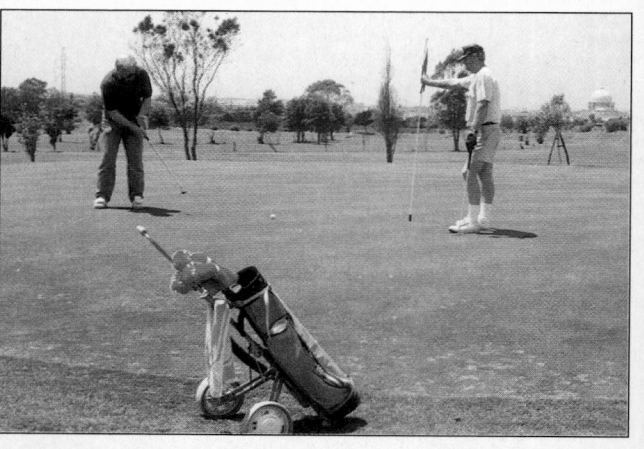

Mdina is perched on a high plateau towering over the rest of the island. It was once Malta's capital and the citadel is one of the finest surviving examples of a medieval walled city. The town is entered by a stone drawbridge which leads to a maze of narrow streets, lined with churches, monasteries and palaces, connected by tiny piazzas. Of particular interest is the Norman-style *Palazzo Faisan* which has a collection of antique weapons and pottery, a cathedral, and a museum that still houses a magnificent collection of art treasures, survivals from the sacking which the town suffered at the hands of the French in the 18th century. From *Bastion Square* the visitor has a breathtaking view of the surrounding fields and villages, and also of *St Paul's Bay*.

Rabat has many fine baroque churches, *St Paul's* and *St Agatha's catacombs* and the *Roman Villa*. There are many interesting walks within close proximity to the town, such as the *Chadwick Lake, Dingli Cliffs* and *Verdala Castle* overlooking *Buskett Gardens*, the only wooded area in Malta.

On the southwest shore is the *Blue Grotto* where, legend reports, sirens bewitched seafarers with their songs. Four caves reflect the brilliant colours of the corals and minerals in the limestone. The most spectacular is Blue Grotto itself, which is best viewed in the early morning with a calm sea. Buses run to the caves from Valletta.

Marsaxlokk, **Birzebbugia** and **Marsacala** are typical Maltese fishing communities, sprawled along the coves and inlets at the southernmost tip of Malta. Fishing nets and colourfully painted boats crowd the waterfronts, and each day's fresh catch can be eaten at the family-run tavernas. Also at Marsaxlokk is the recently discovered *Temple of Juno* which was originally used by the Greeks as a place of worship to the goddess of fertility.

The most popular beach area is along the north coast where sandy beaches are plentiful and the clear waters here are ideal for sailing, skindiving and water-skiing. The best beaches are at *Paradise Bay, Golden Bay, Mellieha Bay, Armier Bay* and *Ghajn Tuffieha Bay*, all of which are very popular during the summer and pleasantly quiet during spring.

Gozo

Gozo is the sister island and the second-largest of the archipelago. The landscape consists of flat-topped hills, steep valleys and rugged cliffs and villas that nestle among *peach, lemon, olive* and *orange* groves. In spring the island comes ablaze with the flowering *hibiscus, oleander, mimosa* and *bougainvillaea*. Some of the local crafts (lace and knitwear) are sold from the doorways of houses and on the street.

The capital of Gozo is **Victoria** (formerly Rabat), built by the Arabs on *Castle Hill*, which offers the visitor panoramic views of the whole island. The cathedral has no dome, but inside a trompe l'oeil painting on its ceiling gives the illusion of a dome. There is also a cathedral museum.

The *Museum of Archaeology* contains Roman remains from a shipwreck on the island and items excavated from the neolithic temple at **Ggantija.**

Other places of interest on Gozo include the *Citadel* ('Gran Castello'), with its historic bastions and old houses (one of them set up as a folk museum). There are alabaster caves at **Xaghra**, with stalactites and stalagmites. These underground caves are known as *Xerri's Grotto* and *Ninu's Grotto*. The basilica at *Ta'Pinu*, near the village of **Gharb**, is one of the most beautiful of Maltese churches and an official Vatican place of pilgrimage. **Xewkija** is a small town with a beautiful new church, built round the old parish church of *St John the Baptist*.

The waters surrounding the island are unpolluted and crystal clear. The most important beaches are *I-Qawra*, better known as the inland sea, with a secluded pebbly bathing pool, crystal clear water and sheer cliffs; an unspoilt sandy beach known as *Ir-Ramla l-Hamra* and *Xlendi Bay*. In summer there are numerous festivals with fireworks and horseracing in the streets. **Marsalforn** is a fishing village on the north coast which has become one of Gozo's most popular seaside resorts.

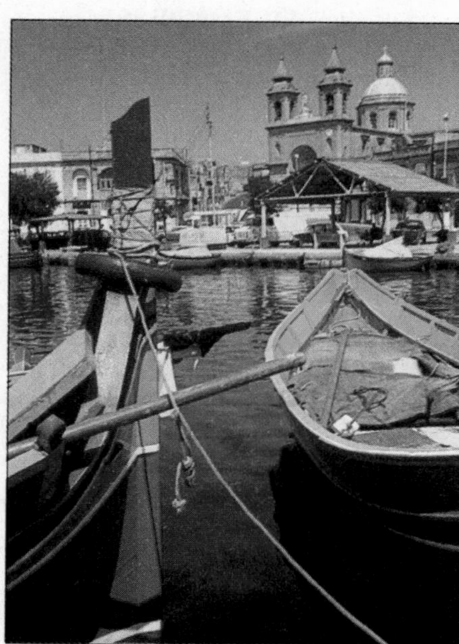

Comino

The island of **Comino**, thick with wild herbs (particularly *cumin*), lies between Malta and Gozo and is inhabited by probably no more than a dozen farmers. Paths which wind through the unusual rock formations provide the only communication links and the island is ideal for anyone seeking a very quiet holiday. A few sandy coves and small bays, such as 'Blue Lagoon' are the main attractions.

SOCIAL PROFILE

FOOD & DRINK: There is a very good choice of restaurants and cafés from deluxe to fast food (hamburgers and fish & chips) including Chinese, fish and beachside tavernas and bars. Table service is normal, but many bars and cafés have table and/or counter service. Local dishes include *lampuki pie, bragoli* and *fenek* (rabbit cooked in wine). Pork and fish dishes are recommended and vegetables are excellent. The best Maltese fruits are oranges and grapes; also delicious are strawberries, melons, mulberries, tangerines, pomegranates and figs. **Drink:** Maltese beer is excellent, and foreign beers are also available. There is a wide variety of good and inexpensive Maltese wine and foreign wines and spirits. Licensing hours of bars, restaurants and cafés are usually 0900-0100 and beyond, although alcohol can only be bought before 0100. Most hotel bars close between 1300 and 1600 and then reopen after 1800.

NIGHTLIFE: There are several discotheques. **Roulette**, **baccarat**, **black jack** and **boule** can be played at the palatial 'Dragonara' casino, St Julian's. The Manoel Theatre is one of the oldest in Europe. Cinemas show many English and Italian films.
SHOPPING: Special purchases include Malta weave, pottery, glass, ceramics, dolls, copper and brass items. Malta is renowned for its gold and silver filigree work and handmade lace. **Shopping hours:** 0900-1300 and 1600-1900 Monday to Saturday.
SPORT: Rowing regattas are held frequently from April to November; these take place in the Grand Harbour during April and September. The Valletta Yacht Club is at Couvre Port, Manoel Island, in Marsamxetto Harbour (temporary members accepted). **Golf:** There is an 18-hole golf course at the Marsa Sports Club which also has facilities for tennis, squash, cricket, polo and horseracing. **Underwater sports** meetings are organised by the Federation of Underwater Activities. Ideal conditions exist in Malta for scuba diving and snorkelling. **Bowling:** There is a 10-pin bowling centre at Msida. **Swimming:** Most large hotels have their own swimming pool and bathing is safe everywhere around the islands. **Windsurfing** has become a very popular sport and many hotels and beach establishments offer equipment. **Spectator sports: Football** is very popular and matches are played at the Stadium, Ta'Qali and at the Marsa Stadium from September to June. **Waterpolo:** National waterpolo competitions are held during summer. Matches are played at the National Swimming Pool, Marsascala. A summer league takes place at various waterpolo clubs. **Horseraces** are held all Sunday afternoons at the Marsa National Racecourse from the end of October to the middle of May. **Clay Pigeon/Skeet shooting:** This is a popular sport in Malta with regular practice-sessions and competitions on Sunday mornings.
SPECIAL EVENTS: The Malta National Tourist Office can supply full details of events taking place in Malta in 1993/1994. The following list is a selection of events:
Mar 11-14 '93 *Boat Fair*, Naxxar. **Mar 25-28** *Travel and Tourism Fair*, Naxxar. **Apr 9-12** *Good Friday/Easter Pageants*. **Apr 14-18** *Green Week*, Naxxar. **May 2** *Feast of St Publius* (starting the summer festa season). **Mid-May** *The Annual Flower, Fruit and Vegetable and Potplant Show*, Attard. **May 25-29** *5th Games for the Small States of Europe*. **May-Sep** *Festa Season*. **Jun 19** *Il-Bandu* (banner parades, horses and pageants), Rabat and Mdina. **Jun 29** *Feast of St Peter and St Paul* (including folk dancing and singing). **Mid-Jul to Mid-Aug** *Maltafest* (a month of cultural activities with the participation of local and foreign artists). **Aug 15** *Pageant* (commemorating the lifting of the Siege in 1942). **Sep 7** *Great Siege of 1565*, Vittoriosa Square. **Sep 8** *Our Lady of Victories Day* (including a regatta and boat races in the Grand Harbour). **Sep 21** *Independence celebrations*. **Oct-May** *Theatre Season* (including music, drama and ballet), Manoel Theatre, Valletta. **Nov 14-19** *5th International Choir Festival*. **Nov 24-27** *XXXII Golden Knight International Amateur Film and Video Fesitval*. **Dec 13** *Republic Day*. **Dec 20-Jan 2 '94** *Christmas Festivities*. **Feb** *Carnival* (with masks, costumes and an impressive parade), Valletta.
SOCIAL CONVENTIONS: The usual European courtesies are expected, but the visitor should also bear in mind the tremendous importance of Roman Catholicism; if visiting a church, for instance, modest dress covering the shoulders and legs will be expected. Smoking is prohibited on public transport and in some public buildings, including cinemas. **Tipping:** 10% is expected in hotels and restaurants when not included in the bill. Tip taxi drivers 10%.

BUSINESS PROFILE

ECONOMY: For many years the British naval dockyards were the mainstay of the Maltese economy. The decision to close them in 1958 forced the Government to devise a comprehensive economic policy for the islands. The docks were nationalised in 1973 and converted to operate as a commercial shipyard, engaged in both shipbuilding and repair, which remains a key source of income despite the recent world recession in merchant shipping. The light industry sector began to develop from the early 1960s onwards and now boasts such varied industries as textiles and clothing (the most important), plastics, printing, electronic components and electrical equipment. Agriculture has maintained a steady and important role in the economy, with grapes, potatoes and onions the principal products, many of which are exported. Tourism is a valuable source of foreign exchange. Lacking significant raw materials, Malta

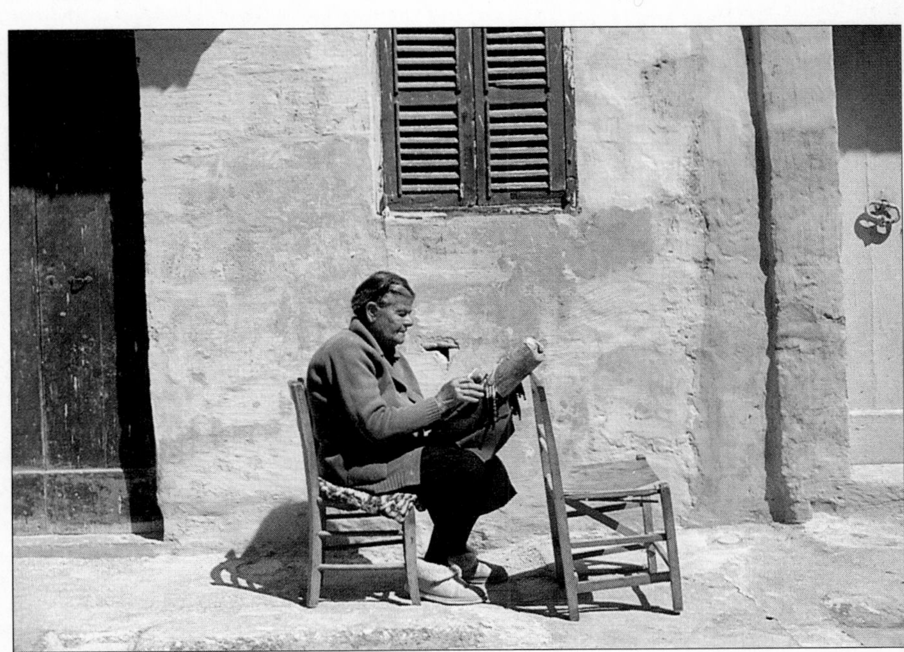

must import most of its requirements, particularly oil, the bulk of which comes from Libya, leaving the country with a continuous balance of payments deficit. Italy is the largest trading partner, followed by Germany and the United Kingdom.

BUSINESS: English is widely spoken in business circles and, on the whole, Maltese business people have a conservative approach to business protocol. Punctuality is expected and appreciated and dress must be smart. The best months for business visits are October to May. **Office hours:** 0830-1245 and 1430-1730 Monday to Friday, 0830-1200 Saturday. Some smaller offices close 1300-1600, opening again later.

COMMERCIAL INFORMATION: The following organisation can offer advice: Chamber of Commerce, Exchange Buildings, Republic Street, Valletta 05. Tel: 247 233. Fax: 245 223. Telex: 740.

CONFERENCES/CONVENTIONS: The Malta National Tourist Office can loan a free promotional video to conference and incentive organisers and are happy to assist with all initial enquiries.

HISTORY & GOVERNMENT

HISTORY: Malta's situation in the central Mediterranean has made it an important strategic base since the earliest days of navigation. The first civilisation to leave any significant remains flourished in the 3rd millenium BC, building many megalithic temples; later the island was occupied by the Phoenicians, the Carthaginians and the Romans. Christianity arrived early, in about AD60, when St Paul was shipwrecked off the coast, and the religion rapidly established itself. On the partition of the Roman Empire, Malta passed under the control of Constantinople. Arab attacks during the 8th and 9th centuries culminated in the surrender of the islands to the governor of Muslim Sicily in 870, but by the end of the following century the Normans had reconquered Sicily, and Malta passed back to Christian control in 1090. The Norman rule of the 12th century witnessed a great expansion of trade and a flowering of the arts and sciences, reflecting the splendours of Sicily itself, but the death of the last Hautville king in 1194 ushered in a period of confusion. Prosperity alternated with internal chaos for the rest of the Middle Ages, as the island repeatedly became caught up in the great dynastic struggles of the Mediterranean. The Hohenstaufer (mainly Frederick II), the Angevins, the Aragonnese, the Venetians, the Genoese, the Papacy, the Kings of France and the Arabs all, at various times, attempted to gain control of Malta. Not until the 16th century, when Malta, together with Sicily, became part of the vast empire of Charles V, did political stability return, and in 1530 Charles recognised the strategic value of the islands for Christendom by granting them to the Knights of St John. For the next 250 years Malta was a bulwark against Turkish ambitions in Europe, notably in 1565 when, against overwhelming odds, the island was successfully defended. Napoleon briefly held Malta in the last three years of the 18th century, but a British-backed rebellion forced him to retreat and the British ruled for the next 181 years. The most famous episode in Malta's recent history was the heroic defence of the island during the Second World War for which the nation was awarded the George Cross. In 1956 a referendum came down heavily in favour of full integration with Britain, a policy then backed by the governing Maltese Labour Party (MLP) under Dom Mintoff. Successive rounds of talks failed, and by 1961 independence was sought by both the major political parties, the other being the conservative Nationalist Party then led by Dr Borg Olivier. Independence was achieved in 1964, and Dr Borg Olivier became Prime Minister. Mintoff's MLP won the 1971 elections and began to pursue a policy of neutrality, reaching treaties with Libya (including, in 1984, a 5-year military co-operation agreement), Italy and the then USSR, amongst other states. In 1979 the British military base was closed. In May 1987, 16 years of MLP rule came to an end and Dr Edward Fenech Adami of the Nationalist Party became Prime Minister. Close contacts with Libya continue, but relationships with Western governments have improved. The centre-right government had followed the general European pattern of liberalising the economy. The major political issue in the immediate future will be Malta's application to join the European Community: some considerable diplomatic legwork will be needed before the Maltese government has any hope of entry.

GOVERNMENT: Malta's Head of State is a largely ceremonial President, and executive power is held by the Cabinet, chosen from the unicameral legislature, the House of Representatives, elected every five years.

CLIMATE

Warm most of the year. The hottest months are between July and September, but the heat is tempered by cooling sea breezes. Rain falls for very short periods, mainly in the cooler winter months.

Required clothing: Lightweight cottons and linens are worn between March and September, although warmer clothes may occasionally be necessary in spring and autumn and on cooler evenings. A light raincoat is advisable for winter.

VALLETTA Malta (70m)

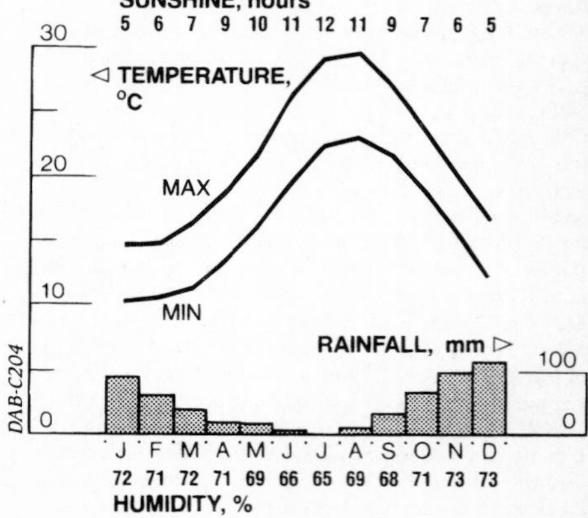

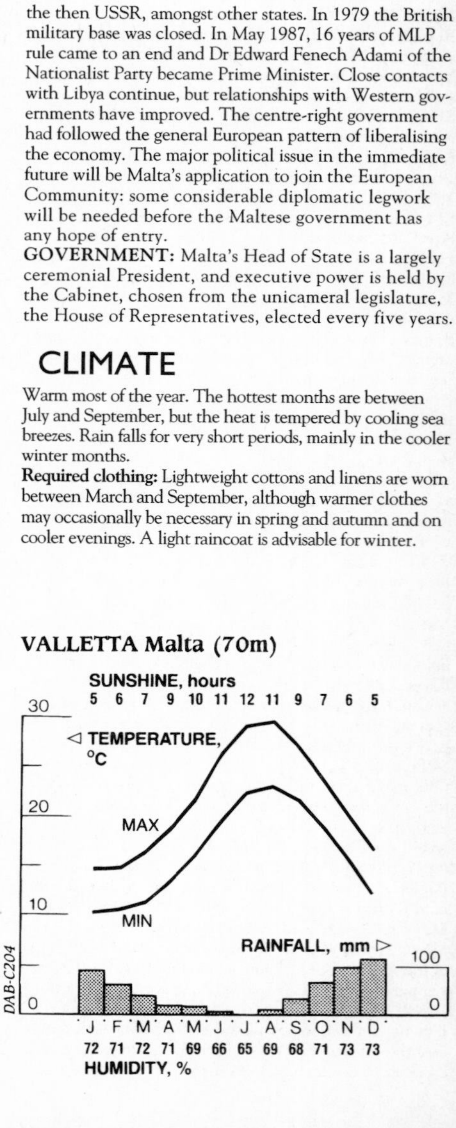

MARTINIQUE

Location: Caribbean; northernmost of the Windward group of islands.

Diplomatic representation: Martinique is an Overseas Department of the Republic of France. Addresses of French Embassies, Consulates and Tourist Offices may be found in the *France* entry earlier in the *World Travel Guide*. For more detailed tourist information, contact:

Office du Tourisme
BP 520
Pavillon du Tourisme
boulevard Alfassa
97206 Fort-de-France
Martinique
Tel: 637 960. Fax: 736 693. Telex: 912678.

Délégation Regionale au Tourisme
41 rue Gabriel Péri
97200 Fort-de-France
Martinique
Tel: 631 861.

British Consulate
route du Phare
97200 Fort-de-France
Martinique
Tel: 615 630. Fax: 613 389. Telex: 912729 MR.

Consulate General of the United States of America
BP 561
14 rue Blenac
97206 Fort-de-France
Martinique
Tel: 631 303. Fax: 602 080. Telex: 912670 *or* 912315 MR.

Martinique Tourist Office
Suite 480
1981 McGill College
Montréal, Québec
H3A 2W9
Tel: (514) 844 8566. Fax: (514) 844 8901.

AREA: 1100 sq km (424.7 sq miles).
POPULATION: 359,572 (1990).
POPULATION DENSITY: 326.9 per sq km.
CAPITAL: Fort-de-France. **Population:** 101,540 (1990).
GEOGRAPHY: The French Overseas Department of Martinique, a volcanic and picturesque island, is the northernmost of the Windward Caribbean group. The island is noticeably more rocky than those of the Leeward group, with beaches (of fine black or white or peppered sand) surrounded by sugar, palm, banana and pineapple plantations. Christopher Columbus called it 'the most beautiful country in the world' and, before he named it in honour of St Martin, it was called *Madidina* ('island of flowers') by the native population.
LANGUAGE: The official language is French; the main local dialect is Creole.
RELIGION: The majority of the population are Roman Catholic.
TIME: GMT - 4.
ELECTRICITY: 220/380 volts AC, 50Hz.
COMMUNICATIONS: Telephone: IDD is available. Country code: 596. Other islands can only be reached through the international operator. There are both payphones and cardphones on the island. *Télécartes* (phonecards) are sold at the PTT Office in rue Antoine Siger, Fort-de-France. There are only card phones at the airport. **Telex:** There are reasonable public telex facilities available in the main hotels. **Post:** Letters to Europe must be sent by airmail from the main post offices and take about a week to reach Europe. Post offices are open 0700-1800 Monday to Friday, and Saturday mornings. **Press:** Newspapers are in French and vary in their political bias. The main daily is *France Antilles*.
BBC World Service and Voice of America frequencies: From time to time these change. See the section *How to Use this Book* for more information.

BBC:				
MHz	17.72	11.78	9.915	5.965
Voice of America:				
MHz	15.21	11.70	6.130	0.930

PASSPORT/VISA

Regulations and requirements may be subject to change at short notice, and you are advised to contact the appropriate diplomatic or consular authority before finalising travel arrangements. Details of these may be found at the head of this country's entry. Any numbers in the chart refer to the footnotes below.

	Passport Required?	Visa Required?	Return Ticket Required?
Full British	Yes	No	Yes
BVP	Not valid	-	-
Australian	Yes	2	Yes
Canadian	Yes	No	Yes
USA	Yes	No	Yes
Other EC	1	No	Yes
Japanese	Yes	No	Yes

PASSPORTS: Required by all except the following nationals who have a passport which has expired for not more than 5 years, or a valid national ID card:
(a) **[1]** nationals of France, Germany, Greece, Italy, Luxembourg, Monaco, The Netherlands, Portugal and Spain (all other EC nationals *do* need passports);
(b) nationals of Canada, Japan and the USA.
British Visitors Passport: Not accepted.
VISAS: Required by all except:
(a) nationals of countries as shown in the chart above and nationals of countries mentioned under *Passports;*
(b) **[2]** nationals of Australia can enter with a French visa;
(c) nationals of Andorra, Austria, Finland, Liechtenstein, Monaco, Norway, San Marino, Sweden, Switzerland and Vatican City;
(d) nationals of Antigua & Barbuda, Bahamas, Bangladesh, Barbados, Belize, Botswana, Cyprus, Dominica, Gambia, Ghana, Grenada, Guyana, India, Jamaica, Kenya, Kiribati, Lesotho, Malawi, Malaysia, Maldives, Malta, Mauritius, Nauru, New Zealand, Nigeria, Pakistan, Papua New Guinea, St Kitts & Nevis, St Lucia, St Vincent & the Grenadines, Seychelles, Sierra Leone, Solomon Islands, Sri Lanka, Swaziland, Tanzania, Tonga, Trinidad & Tobago, Tuvalu, Uganda, Vanuatu, Western Samoa, Zambia and Zimbabwe;
(e) nationals of the following countries travelling on a French visa: Algeria, Argentina, Benin, Bolivia, Brunei, Burkina Faso, Central African Republic, Colombia, Congo, El Salvador, Guatemala, Israel, Mali, Mauritania, Mexico, Morocco, Niger, Singapore, Uruguay, Venezuela and Yugoslavia.
Validity: Up to 3 months.
Application to: Martinique section of French Consulate.
Application requirements: (a) 3 application forms. (b) 3 photos. (c) Evidence of return ticket. (d) Valid passport.
Working days required: Visas issued on the same day.

MONEY

Currency: French Franc (FFr) = 100 centimes. Notes are in denominations of FFr500, 200, 100, 50 and 20. Coins are in denominations of FFr10, 5, 2 and 1, and 50, 20, 10 and 5 centimes.
Currency exchange: US and Canadian Dollars are widely accepted.
Credit cards: Access/Mastercard (limited), Diners Club, American Express and Visa are accepted. Check with your credit card company for details of merchant acceptability and other services which may be available.
Travellers cheques: Accepted in most places, and may qualify for discounts on luxury items.
Exchange rate indicators: The following figures are included as a guide to the movements of the French Franc against Sterling and the US Dollar:

Date:	Oct '89	Oct '90	Oct '91	Oct '92
£1.00=	10.10	9.97	9.92	8.28
$1.00=	6.40	5.10	5.71	5.21

Currency restrictions: As for France.

DUTY FREE

The island of Martinique is an Overseas Department of France, and therefore duty-free allowances are the same as those for France.

PUBLIC HOLIDAYS

Public holidays observed in Martinique are as follows:
Apr 9-12 '93 Easter. **May 1** Labour Day. **May 20** Ascension Day. **May 31** Whit Monday. **Jul 14** National Day. **Nov 11** Armistice Day. **Dec 25** Christmas Day. **Jan 1 '94** New Year's Day.

HEALTH

Regulations and requirements may be subject to change at short notice, and you are advised to contact your doctor well in advance of your intended date of departure. Any numbers in the chart refer to the footnotes below.

	Special Precautions?	Certificate Required?
Yellow Fever	No	1
Cholera	No	No
Typhoid & Polio	Yes	-
Malaria	No	-
Food & Drink	2	-

[1]: A yellow fever vaccination certificate is required from travellers over one year of age arriving from infected areas.
[2]: Mains water is normally chlorinated, and whilst relatively safe may cause mild abdominal upsets. Bottled water is available and is advised for the first few weeks of the stay. Drinking water outside main cities and towns may be contaminated and sterilisation is advisable. Milk is pasteurised and dairy products are safe for consumption. Local meat, poultry, seafood, fruit and vegetables are generally considered safe to eat.
Bilharzia (schistosomiasis) is present. Avoid swimming and paddling in fresh water. Swimming pools which are well-chlorinated and maintained are safe.
Tuberculosis is still present in Martinique. Consult your doctor for advice on inoculation before departure.
Health care: A Reciprocal Health Agreement exists between France and the UK. However, the benefits which go with this agreement may not be fully available for Martinique. Check with your doctor before departure. Martinique has 14 hospitals.

TRAVEL - International

AIR: Martinique's national airline is *Air Martinique (NN)*.
Approximate flight times: From *London* to Martinique is 12 hours (including an average stopover time of 1 hour in Paris); from *Los Angeles* is 9 hours; from *New York* is 6 hours and from *Singapore* is 33 hours.
International airport: *Fort de France* (Lamentin) is 15km (9 miles) from the city. Airport facilities include restaurant, shops and car hire. *LIAT*, *Air Antilles*, *Air Guadeloupe*, *BWIA* and *Air France* offer flights from Fort-de-France to many other Caribbean islands.
SEA: Martinique is a point of call for the following international cruise lines: *Chandris*, *Holland America*, *Royal Caribbean*, *Cunard*, *Sun Line*, *Sitmar*, *TUI Cruises* and *Princess Cruises*. There are ships plying the Caribbean between Martinique and Guadeloupe and others sail from Miami and San Juan. There are also regular ferry services around the islands.

TRAVEL - Internal

AIR: Aeroplanes and helicopters may be chartered from *Air Martinique*.
SEA: Scheduled ferries ply between Fort-de-France, Pointe du Boit and Anse Mitan.
ROAD: The road system is well-developed and surfaced. **Buses** provide a limited service. **Taxis** are government-controlled, plentiful and reasonably cheap if shared. There is a surcharge at night. Martinique has a system of communal taxis. **Car hire:** The island has excellent car-rental facilities. 50cc **mopeds** do not need a licence and can be hired from TS Auto, 38 route de Ste Thérèse,

Fort-de-France. Tel: 633 305. **Bicycles** can also be hired. **Documentation:** An International Driving Permit is recommended, but a national driving licence is sufficient, provided the driver has at least one year's experience.

ACCOMMODATION

HOTELS: There is a good selection of hotels on Martinique. 10% service is charged, sometimes with other Government taxes added. There is a *Relais de la Martinique*, an association of small hotels and guest-houses offering special reservation and tour facilities. Hotels range from deluxe, to medium- and low-priced. For further information contact the tourist office.
SELF-CATERING: *Gîtes* (furnished apartments or bungalows) are widely available. For rental, contact the Association pour le Tourisme en Espace Rural, Relais des Gîtes de France, BP 1122, Maison du Tourisme Vert, 9 boulevard du Général-de-Gaulle, 97248 Fort-de-France Cédex. Tel: 736 792.

RESORTS & EXCURSIONS

The terrain of Martinique varies from the high mountains of the north and centre to the rolling hills around Fort-de-France and the safe, sheltered harbours of the lower west coast. **Mont Pelée,** the 1430m (4700ft) volcanic mountain in the north, last erupted in 1902 (in a unique explosion which literally ripped the summit off), destroying the city of St-Pierre and its entire 30,000 population. (Only a prisoner, Auguste Ciparis, survived – who was subsequently pardoned and ended his days as a fairground exhibit in America.) The remains of St-Pierre are now a tourist attraction. Photomurals are on display in the *Musée Volcanologique*.
The region is being developed as a natural park and leisure area. Near **Carbet,** where Columbus landed on his fourth voyage in 1502, is the restored plantation of **Leyritz,** which is now visited by many tourists. The *Centre d'Art Paul Gauguin* may be found in Carbet itself. North of this region is **Pointe du Boit,** Martinique's major resort area.
Fort-de-France, the island's capital, is a town of winding streets and colourful markets. In the centre of the town is the park of *La Savanne*. A statue in La Savanne square commemorates Napoleon's Empress Josephine, a native of Martinique, whose home, *La Pagerie*, is one of the main tourist attractions. **Les Trois-Ilets** (Josephine's birthplace) are situated across the bay from Fort-de-France.
The *Musée Departmental* has remains of the predominantly Arawak and Carib Indian prehistory of the island. There is an interesting *Caribbean Arts Centre*. Martinique has ten small museums celebrating aspects of the island's culture and history including the Empress Josephine's connection with the island, the eruption of Pelée, the rum trade and dolls made from local materials.
Ste Anne, La Diamant and **Les Anses d'Arlets** have some of the island's best bathing beaches. *HMS Diamond Rock*, 4km (2.5 miles) off Diamant, is a rock which was designated a man-of-war by the British during the Napoleonic wars and rates a 12-gun salute from passing British warships.

SOCIAL PROFILE

FOOD & DRINK: French influences and seafood includes lobster, turtle, red snapper, conch and sea urchin. Islands' specialities include stuffed crab, stewed conch, roast wild goat, jugged rabbit and broiled local dove. *Colombo* is goat, chicken, pork or lamb in a thick curry sauce. Creole cuisine is also widely available and is an original combination of French, Indian and African traditions seasoned with exotic spices. Meals are ended with exotic fruit.
Drink: There is a a great supply of French wines, champagne, liqueurs and local rum. Local specialities are *ti punch*, a brew of rum, lime juice, bitters and syrup, *shrub*, a Christmas liqueur consisting of rum and orange peel and *planteur*, made from rum and fruit juice. Guava, soursop, passionfruit, mandarin and sugar-cane juice are all common. There are no licensing restrictions.
NIGHTLIFE: There are plenty of restaurants, bars, discotheques, and displays of local dancing and music. The *Ballet Martiniquais* is one of the world's most prestigious traditional ballet companies. Limbo dancers and steelbands are often laid on at hotels in the evenings. The local guide, *Choubouloute*, contains information on local entertainment and is sold in newsagents for FFr5.
SHOPPING: French imports are worthwhile purchases, especially wines, liqueurs and lalique crystal. Local items include rum, straw goods, bamboo hats, voodoo dolls, baskets and objects of aromatic vetiver roots. A discount of 20% is given if payment is made by travellers cheques in some tourist shops. **Shopping hours:** 0830-1300 and 1500-1800 Monday to Friday.
SPORT: Watersports: Swimming, water-skiing, smallboat sailing, snorkelling and spearfishing are available at many coastal resorts. **Tennis:** There are courts at many large hotels. Visitors can obtain temporary membership and play at night as well as during the day. For further information, contact La Ligue Regional de Tennis, Petit Manoir, Lamentin. Tel: 510 800. **Horseriding** is a very enjoyable way to see Martinique's lovely countryside. **Golf:** There is an 18-hole golf course at Trois-Ilets. There is also **horseracing** at the Carère track at Lamentin. **Hiking** and **mountain-climbing** are also catered for.
SPECIAL EVENTS: From January 1 to Lent every weekend is celebrated by a carnival, culminating in the festivities on *Ash Wednesday*. The main carnival takes place in the beginning of February for *Mardi Gras*, when everyone dresses up in fantastic costume and parade the streets. On Ash Wednesday, 'devils' clad in black and white form a procession, lamenting the death of Vaval. At *Easter*, children fly coloured kites. Dances originating in Africa are a feature of these events. The *Béguine* is a famous dance from this part of the world. *Gommier races* (with enormous rectangular sailing boats with colourful sails and teams of oarsmen) are a wonderful sight at festivals from July to January.
SOCIAL CONVENTIONS: The atmosphere is generally relaxed and informal. Casual dress is acceptable everywhere, but formal attire is needed for dining out and nightclubs. **Tipping:** 10% is acceptable.

BUSINESS PROFILE

ECONOMY: The economy relies almost exclusively on tourism and agriculture. Sugar cane and bananas are the main crops, both of which have suffered severely from the series of hurricanes which devastated much of the Caribbean during the 1980s and also seriously affected the tourist infrastructure. Tourism has been in decline due to global recession and political instability on the island. The Government is trying to encourage diversification in the economy, by promoting other crops among farmers on the one hand and providing incentives for small businesses and light industry on the other. These have yet to fill the gaps left by the decline of traditional economic sectors, however. France accounts for over 75% of Martinique's foreign trade, with the remainder of the import market captured by the major EC economies and the United States. There is considerable trepidation on the island about the likely effects of the Single European Market and the fierce economic competition which this is likely to bring.
BUSINESS: Lightweight suits and Safari suits are recommended. The best time to visit is January to March and June to September. Much of the island's business is connected with France. **Office hours:** 0830-1300 and 1500-1800 Monday to Friday, 0830-1300 Saturday.
COMMERCIAL INFORMATION: The following organisation can offer advice: Chambre de Commerce et d'Industrie de la Martinique, 50-56 rue Ernest Deproge, Fort-de-France. Tel: 552 800. Fax: 606 668. Telex: 912633.

HISTORY & GOVERNMENT

HISTORY: Prior to the discovery of Martinique by Columbus in 1493, the islands were inhabited by Arawak and Carib Indians. There was no real European interest in the island until French colonies were established in 1635. Though the British made brief attempts to occupy the island during the 18th and 19th centuries, it has remained under French control ever since (along with Guadeloupe). Slavery was abolished in 1848, and in the late 19th century, tens of thousands of immigrant workers arrived from India to replace the slave workforce on the plantations. In 1946, both islands of the French Antilles were given the status of Overseas Departments. There was little political movement until 1974 when Martinique, along with Guadeloupe and French Guiana, was given regional status entailing some local political and economic autonomy. This was increased in 1982 and 1983 with measures introduced by President Mitterrand in a package of decentralisation policies. Most affairs, with the major exception of defence and security, are now broadly under local control. The main problem for the Government is the economy, which has had little investment or development, other than in tourism which is declining: unemployment is high and rising; younger people now emigrate as a matter of course. French government policy seeks to stress the importance of developing economic and political links with other Caribbean nations. At the most recent poll, held in October 1990, the Union of the Left (a coalition of three parties) took a third of the vote and 14 of the 41 council seats and now governs in an alliance with smaller parties. Camille Darsières was elected to the Presidency of the Council.
GOVERNMENT: The government Commissioner on Martinique represents France, and the island sends four representatives to the French National Assembly and two to the Senate. The General Council and the Regional Council administer the island's local affairs.

CLIMATE

Warm weather throughout the year, with the main rainy season occurring in the autumn. However, showers can occur at any time, but they are usually brief. Cooler in the upland areas.
Required clothing: Lightweight, with waterproof wear advised for the rainy season.

FORT DE FRANCE Martinique (144m)

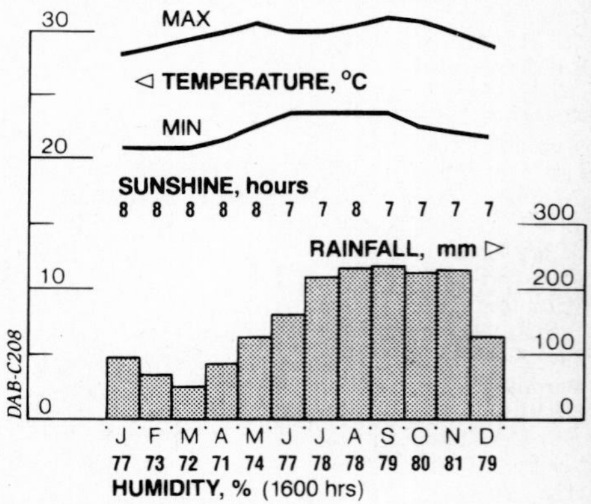

MARTINIQUE	HEALTH REGULATIONS	VISA REGULATIONS
GALILEO/WORLDSPAN	TI-DFT/FDF/HE	TI-DFT/FDF/VI
SABRE	TIDFT/FDF/HE	 TIDFT/FDF/VI

Code-Link

To access this information on your CRS, swipe the barcode with a light pen or type in the text under the barcode. For more information, see the introduction *How to Use This Book*.

MAURITANIA

Location: West Africa.

Société Mauritanienne de Tourisme et d'Hôtellerie (SMTH)
BP 552
Nouakchott, Mauritania
Tel: 53351.

Honorary Consulate of the Islamic Republic of Mauritania
140 Bow Common Lane
London E3 4BH
Tel: (081) 980 4382. Fax: (081) 556 6032.

Embassy of the Islamic Republic of Mauritania
5 rue de Montévidéo
75116 Paris, France
Tel: (1) 45 04 88 54. Telex: 620506.

British Embassy in Morocco handles all enquiries relating to Mauritania.

Embassy of the Islamic Republic of Mauritania
2129 Leroy Place, NW
Washington, DC
20008
Tel: (202) 232 5700.

Embassy of the United States of America
BP 222
Nouakchott, Mauritania
Tel: 52660/3. Fax: 51592. Telex: 5558.

The Permanent Mission of the Islamic Republic of Mauritania
9 E 77th Street
New York, NY
10021
Tel: (212) 737 7780. Fax: (212) 472 3314. Telex: 311352.
Also deals with enquiries from Canada.

The Canadian Embassy in Dakar, Senegal, handles all enquiries relating to Mauritania.

AREA: 1,030,700 sq km (397,950 sq miles).
POPULATION: 1,969,000 (1990 estimate.).
POPULATION DENSITY: 1.9 per sq km.
CAPITAL: Nouakchott. **Population:** 450,000 (1986).
GEOGRAPHY: Mauritania is bordered by Algeria, Mali, Western Sahara (Sahrawi Arab Democratic Republic) and Senegal. To the west lies the Atlantic Ocean. Mauritania consists mainly of the vast Saharan plain of sand and scrub. Most of this area is a sea of sand dunes, but in places the land rises to rocky plateaux with deep ravines leaving isolated peaks. The Adrar plateau in the central region rises to 500m (1640ft) and the Tagant further south to 600m (1970ft). The area is scattered with towns, small villages and oases. The northern bank of the Senegal River, which forms the country's southern border, is the only area in the country with any degree of permanent vegetation and it supports a wide variety of wildlife.
LANGUAGE: The official languages are Arabic and French. The Moors of Arab/Berber stock, speaking Hassaniya dialects of Arabic, comprise the majority of the people. Other dialects include Soninke, Pulaar and Wolof. English is rarely spoken.
RELIGION: Islam is the official religion. Despite ethnic and cultural differences among Mauritanians, they are all bound by a common Muslim attachment to the Malekite sect.
TIME: GMT.
ELECTRICITY: 127/220 volts AC, 50Hz. Round 2-pin plugs are normal.
COMMUNICATIONS: Telephone: IDD is available in Nouakchott and Nouadhibou. Country code: 222 (no area codes). **Telex:** Nouakchott and Nouadhibou have telex facilities. **Post:** International postal facilities are limited to main cities. Airmail to Europe takes approximately two weeks. **Press:** Newspapers are in French and Arabic. The only daily is *Ach-Chaab*.
BBC World Service and Voice of America frequencies: From time to time these change. See the section *How to Use this Book* for more information.

BBC:				
MHz	21.71	15.07	11.86	6.005
Voice of America:				
MHz	21.49	15.60	9.525	6.035

PASSPORT/VISA

Regulations and requirements may be subject to change at short notice, and you are advised to contact the appropriate diplomatic or consular authority before finalising travel arrangements. Details of these may be found at the head of this country's entry. Any numbers in the chart refer to the footnotes below.

	Passport Required?	Visa Required?	Return Ticket Required?
Full British	Yes	Yes	Yes
BVP	Not valid	-	-
Australian	Yes	Yes	Yes
Canadian	Yes	Yes	Yes
USA	Yes	Yes	Yes
Other EC	1	2	Yes
Japanese	Yes	Yes	Yes

PASSPORTS: Valid passports required by all except:
(a) **[1]** nationals of Italy;
(b) nationals of Burkina Faso, Cameroon, Central African Republic, Chad, Congo, Côte d'Ivoire, Gabon, Gambia, Guinea Republic, Madagascar, Mali, Niger, Senegal and Sierra Leone, who may enter on a national identity card or passport which has expired no longer than 5 years.
British Visitors Passport: Not accepted.
VISAS: Required by all except:
(a) **[2]** nationals of France and Italy;
(b) nationals of Burkina Faso, Cameroon, Cape Verde, Central African Republic, Chad, Congo, Côte d'Ivoire, Gabon, Gambia, Ghana, Guinea Republic, Guinea-Bissau, Liberia, Madagascar, Mali, Niger, Nigeria, Romania, Senegal, Sierra Leone, Togo and Tunisia;
(c) members of the League of Arab States (see *International Organisations* at the beginning of the book for a full list).
Types of visa: Tourist or Business (valid for 1 month). Cost: FFr112. Visitors intending to stay for more than one month should apply to the local immigration office on arrival.
Transit: A visa is not required for passengers arriving by air and continuing to a third country within 24 hours, by the same or connecting aircraft, provided they hold tickets with reserved seats, and other documents for their onward journey, and do not leave the airport.
Application to: Consulate (or Consular Section at Embassy). For addresses, see top of entry. The Honorary Consulate in London does *not* issue visas.
Application requirements: (a) 3 forms. (b) 3 photos. (c) Fee. (d) Yellow fever vaccination certificate. (e) Evidence of return ticket *or* sufficient currency for the length of stay. (f) Company letter for Business visas. Stamped, self-addressed envelope if applying by post.
Working days required: 3.

MONEY

Currency: Mauritanian Ougiya (U) = 5 khoums. Notes are in denominations of U1000, 500, 200 and 100. Coins are in denominations of U20, 10, 5 and 1, and 1 khoum.
Credit cards: Not accepted.
Travellers cheques: Limited use.
Exchange rate indicators: The following figures are included as a guide to the movements of the Ougiya against Sterling and the US Dollar:

Date:	Oct '89	Oct '90	Oct '91	Oct '92
£1.00=	132.20	158.21	147.67	168.22
$1.00=	83.73	80.99	85.08	105.99

Currency restrictions: The import and export of local currency is prohibited. There is no restriction on the import of foreign currency provided the amount is declared on arrival. The balance of foreign currency not spent but declared on entry may be exported, but the import declaration must be produced.
Banking hours: 0700-1500 Sunday to Thursday.

DUTY FREE

The following items can be imported into Mauritania by persons over 18 years of age without incurring customs duty:
200 cigarettes or 25 cigars or 450g of tobacco (females – cigarettes only);
50g of perfume.

PUBLIC HOLIDAYS

Public holidays observed in Mauritania are as follows:
Mar 25 '93 Korité (End of Ramadan). **May 1** Labour Day. **May 25** African Liberation Day (Anniversary of the OAU's foundation). **Jun 1** Tabaski (Feast of the Sacrifice). **Jun 21** Islamic New Year. **Aug 30** Mouloud (Prophet's Birthday). **Nov 28** National Day. **Jan 1 '94** New Year's Day. **Jan 20** Leilat al-Meiraj. **Mar** Korité.
Note: Muslim festivals are timed according to local sightings of various phases of the Moon and the dates given above are approximations. During the lunar month of Ramadan that precedes Korité (Eid al-Fitr), Muslims fast during the day and feast at night and normal business patterns may be interrupted. Many restaurants are closed during the day and there may be restrictions on smoking and drinking. Some disruption may continue into Korité itself. Korité and Tabaski (Eid al-Adha) may last anything from two to ten days, depending on the region. For more information see the section *World of Islam* at the back of the book.

HEALTH

Regulations and requirements may be subject to change at short notice, and you are advised to contact your doctor well in advance of your intended date of departure. Any numbers in the chart refer to the footnotes below.

	Special Precautions?	Certificate Required?
Yellow Fever	Yes	1
Cholera	Yes	2
Typhoid & Polio	Yes	-
Malaria	3	-
Food & Drink	4	-

[1]: A yellow fever vaccination certificate is required from all travellers over one year of age, except travellers arriving from a non-infected area and staying less than two weeks in the country.
[2]: Following WHO guidelines issued in 1973, a cholera vaccination certificate is not a condition of entry to Mauritania. However, cholera is a serious risk in this country and precautions are essential. Up-to-date advice should be sought before deciding whether these precautions should include vaccination, as medical opinion is divided over its effectiveness. See the *Health* section at the back of the book.
[3]: Malaria risk, mainly in the benign *vivax* form, exists throughout the year except in the following northern areas: Dakhlet-Nouadhibou, Inchiri, Adrar and Tiris-Zemour.
[4]: All water should be regarded as being potentially contaminated. Water used for drinking, brushing teeth or making ice should have first been boiled or otherwise sterilised. Milk is unpasteurised and should be boiled. Powdered or tinned milk is available and is advised, but make sure it is reconstituted with pure water. Avoid dairy products which are likely to have been made from unboiled milk. Only eat well-cooked meat and fish, preferably served hot. Pork, salad and mayonnaise may carry increased risk. Vegetables should be cooked and fruit peeled.
Rabies is present. For those at high risk, vaccination before arrival should be considered. If you are bitten abroad seek medical advice without delay. For more information consult the *Health* section at the back of the book.
Bilharzia (schistosomiasis) is present. Avoid swimming and paddling in fresh water. Swimming pools which are well-chlorinated and maintained are safe.
Health care: Medical facilities are very limited. The hospital in the capital has 450 beds; there are fewer than 100 other beds elsewhere. Health insurance, to include cover for emergency repatriation, is essential.

TRAVEL - International

AIR: Mauritania's national airline is *Air Mauritanie (MR)*.
Approximate flight time: From *London* to Nouakchott is 7 hours (via Paris).
International airports: *Nouakchott (NKC)* is 4km (2.5 miles) east of the city (travel time – 20 minutes). Taxis are available to the city.
Nouadhibou (NDB) airport is 4km (2.5 miles) from the city. Taxis are available to the city.
SEA: The principal port is Nouadhibou and there is a small port at Nouakchott, while St Louis in Senegal also serves Mauritania.
RAIL: A line from Nouadhibou to F'Derik is primarily for hauling iron ore for export. The ore trains do, however, include a passenger coach which provides a daily return service.
ROAD: The most reliable way into Mauritania overland is from Senegal. From Dakar, the journey to Nouakchott is along a 575km (360-mile) tarred road. The River Senegal has to be crossed by ferry at Rosso. A service operates 0730-1200 and 1500-1800 daily. There is also a paved road from Mali. Travellers intending to drive into Mauritania from the north should contact the nearest Mauritanian diplomatic mission for an assessment of political conditions in the Western Sahara; the *Route du Mauritanie* via Algeria and Senegal is out of service.

TRAVEL - Internal

AIR: *Air Mauritanie (MR)* operates internal flights between Nouakchott and the main towns. At present there are two daily connecting flights between Nouadhibou and Nouakchott.
RAIL: The only line runs between Nouadhibou and Zouerate and serves the ore mines. Services are free but journeys are long and arduous and not recommended.
ROAD: There are adequate roads linking Nouakchott with Rosso in the south of the country, Néma in the southeast and Akjoujt in the north. A paved highway, namely *La Route de l'Espoir*, runs east from Nouakchott to Mali. All other routes are sand tracks necessitating the use of 4-wheel drive vehicles. In some regions during and after the rainy season roads may become impassable. Similarly, in the dry season tracks can be obscured by drifting sand; a guide is highly recommended if not essential. **Car hire:** Available in Nouakchott, Nouadhibou and Atar. Four-wheel drive vehicles with a driver can be hired and are recommended, but they are very expensive. **Documentation:** An International Driving Permit is recommended, although it is not legally required.
Note: Never attempt any desert journey without a full set of spare parts and essential safety equipment. The *Secretariat Generale à l'Artinasat et au Tourisme* in Nouakchott can give further information and advice on road travel.
URBAN: Taxis are very expensive in the towns (Nouakchott and Nouadhibou) but plentiful. Fares are set, not metered, and a small tip is expected.

ACCOMMODATION

HOTELS: Hotel accommodation is very limited in Mauritania and visitors are advised to book well in advance. The larger hotels in Nouakchott are very comfortable and have air-conditioning, but even in the capital accommodation is limited and expensive. Bills normally include service and local tax. For more information contact the tourist and hotel association (address at beginning of entry).
RESTHOUSES: There are numerous government resthouses throughout the country, bookable through the *Secretariat Generale à l'Artinasat et au Tourisme*.

RESORTS & EXCURSIONS

Much of the land is dry and inhospitable. There are also political and military impediments to travel, mainly concerning the Moroccan adventure in Western Sahara.
Nouakchott: The capital of Mauritania is a new city created in 1960. It lies near the sea in a flat landscape of low dunes scattered with thorn bushes, on a site adjoining an old Moorish settlement, the Ksar. The modern buildings maintain the traditional Berber style of architecture. The following places are worth visiting: the *Plage du Wharf*, the mosque, the *Ksar* and its market, the African market and the camel market, the crafts centre, the *Maison de la Culture* and the carpet factory.
Nouadhibou: A growing port and centre of the fishing industry, Nouadhibou is situated on a peninsula at the northern end of the *Bay of Levrier*. Inland, the landscape is empty desert.
The Coast: Mauritania's coast is essentially an 800km-(500-mile) long sandy beach, all but devoid of vegetation, but supporting an astonishingly large and varied population of birds. The waters are equally rich in fish and consequently, despite the shortage of fresh water, some coastal stretches are inhabited by man. One tribe, halfway between Nouakchott and Nouadhibou, survives through a symbiotic relationship with wild dolphins: the marine mammals drive fish towards the shore, the tribesmen swim out with nets, and both get their share. Japanese and CIS trawlers are rapidly depleting offshore fish stocks.
Adrar Region: It is important to check on conditions for travel before setting out for this region as government permission may be necessary. The Adrar is a spectacular massif of pink and brown plateaux gilded with dunes and intersected by deep canyons sheltering palm groves. It lies in the north central part of the country, and begins about 320km (200 miles) northeast of Nouakchott. **Atar**, capital of the region, is an oasis lying on the route of salt caravans. It is the market centre for the nomads of northern Mauritania and has an old quarter, the Ksar, with flat-roofed houses and a fine palm grove. The oasis of **Azoughui** was the *Almoravid* capital in the 11th and 12th centuries, and remains of fortified buildings from this period can still be seen. A whole day excursion from Atar leads over the breathtaking mountain pass of *Homogjar* to **Chinguetti**, a holy city of Islam, founded in the 13th century, which has a medieval mosque and a library housing ancient manuscripts. Much of the old town is disappearing under the encroaching drifts of sand.
Afollé and Assaba: It is worth making a tour of the Afollé and Assaba regions, south and southeast of the Tagant, via **Kiffa, Tamchakett** and **Ayoun el Atrous,** to the wild plateaux of **El Agher.** The interesting archaeological sites include *Koumbi Saleh*, once capital of the Ghana Empire, 70km (45 miles) from Timbedra along a good track. Near Tamchakett is **Tagdawst,** which has been identified as *Aoudaghost*, ancient capital of a Berber empire. **Oualata** lies 100km (60 miles) from **Néma** at the end of a desert track, and was at one time one of the greatest caravan entrepôts of the Sahara. A fortified medieval town built in terraces up a rocky peak, it has for centuries been a place of refuge for scholars and has a fine library. The Muslim cemetery of **Tirzet** is nearby.

SOCIAL PROFILE

FOOD & DRINK: A limited number of hotel restaurants in the capital serve Western food, but restaurants serve more traditional fare; the local dishes, based on millet, can be delicious and inexpensive. Mauritanian food includes *mechoui* (whole roast lamb), dates, spiced fish and rice with vegetables, fish balls, dried fish, dried meat and *couscous*. **Drink:** Consumption of alcohol is prohibited by the Islamic faith, but alcoholic beverages may be found in hotel bars. *Zrig* (camel's milk) is a common drink, as is sweet mint tea.
SHOPPING: Handicrafts such as dyed leather cushions and some engraved silver items, rugs and woodcarvings can be bought on the open market. A fine selection of silver jewellery, daggers, wood and silver chests and carpets can be bought in the crafts centre in Nouakchott. Unique to the Tagant region are neolithic arrowheads, awls and pottery, while at Boutilimit in the south is a Marabout centre (Institute of High Islamic Studies) where fine carpets of goat and camel hair are made. **Shopping hours:** 0800-1200 and 1400-1900 Saturday to Thursday; 0800-1200 and 1530/1600-1900 during *hivernage* (the rainy season from June to November).
SPORT: Deep-sea **fishing** facilities are available at Nouakchott. At La Guera across the Cap Blanc peninsula fishermen rent out sailing boats for fishing. The Senegal River also has good fishing.
SOCIAL CONVENTIONS: Islam has been the major influence in this country since the 7th and 8th centuries and visitors should respect the religious laws and customs. Dress for women should be of utmost modesty. Nearly all the population have traditionally been nomadic herdsmen. The bulk of the population is divided into the Bidan (55%) and the Harattin (20%), with Negroes concentrated in the Senegal River area. Class and tribal differences tend to be contiguous.
Tipping: 12-15% is normal.

BUSINESS PROFILE

ECONOMY: Successive years of drought have turned once fertile land to desert, and heavy losses of livestock have led most of the nomadic population to find employment in the towns. Agricultural production takes place mainly in the south on the Senegal River where the land is irrigated. Vegetables, millet, rice and dates are the main crops, and the Government is concentrating its resources on improving the agricultural produce in this area. The most important industry is the exploitation of iron ore in the north of the country which is undergoing a major expansion. Copper mining has been suspended due to lack of competitiveness (a result of the low world price) but may resume in the near future. Mauritania, which remains an exceptionally poor country, relies on a great deal of foreign aid, most of which comes from the Arab countries. Japan and the southern EC countries are Mauritania's main export markets, while the major exporters to the country are France (30%) and Spain (26%), followed by Germany, The Netherlands and the USA. The present government has embarked on a programme on an IMF-supervised structural adjustment programme which seeks to foster private enterprise and reform state-owned commercial concerns, especially the banking system which was close to disintegration. Mauritania is a member of the Economic Community of West African States (ECOWAS) and the Union of the Arab Maghreb.
BUSINESS: Use forms of address as for France, eg *Monsieur le Directeur*. It is essential that businessmen have a sound knowledge of French, as very few executives speak English. **Office hours:** 0800-1500 Saturday to Wednesday; 0800-1300 Thursday.
COMMERCIAL INFORMATION: The following organisation can offer advice: Chambre de Commerce, d'Agriculture, d'Elevage, d'Industrie et des Mines de Mauritanie, BP 215, Nouakchott. Tel: 52214. Telex: 581.

HISTORY & GOVERNMENT

HISTORY: Mauritania lies across one of the great trans-Saharan trade routes. The empire of Ghana, based in southeast Mauritania, originally dominated the area; then, for over 500 years up to 1674 when the Arabs defeated them, the Almoravid dynasty controlled the trade in gold, slaves and salt. Various

MAURITANIA	HEALTH REGULATIONS	VISA REGULATIONS Code-Link
GALILEO/WORLDSPAN	 TI-DFT/NKC/HE	TI-DFT/NKC/VI
SABRE	TIDFT/NKC/HE	 TIDFT/NKC/VI

To access this information on your CRS, swipe the barcode with a light pen or type in the text under the barcode. For more information, see the introduction *How to Use This Book*.

European navigators made fitful contacts with the region, but French domination of the region was only established in the late 19th and early 20th centuries. Mauritania achieved full independence from France in 1960. Since the mid-1970s the country has been locked in conflict with its two northern neighbours, Algeria and Morocco, concerning the future of Western Sahara (formerly Spanish Sahara) which was ceded jointly to Morocco and Mauritania by Spain in 1975. The main opposition to the 1975 settlement came from the Polisario Front, who demanded self-determination for Western Sahara (and achieved recognition by the UN as the Sahrawi Arab Democratic Republic). Mauritania is a member of the Union of the Arab Maghreb, the North African political and economic union formed in February 1989 with Morocco, Libya, Tunisia and Algeria. To the south, a border dispute broke out between Mauritania and Senegal over agricultural rights later in 1989. In 1990, President Taya removed several Muslim hardliners from the Government indicating a more relaxed policy towards dissent within the country and calmer relations with Mauritania's non-Muslim neighbours. At the end of January 1992, Mauritania staged its first multi-candidate presidential election since independence. The principal challenger to the incumbent and favourite President Taya was Ahmed Ould Daddah. With strong support from the southern part of the country, Daddah registered 32% in the provisional result against Taya's 60%. Although there was appreciable malpractice, the result is likely to stand. In the national assembly elections, which were boycotted by the six principal opposition parties, Taya's Democratic and Social Republican Party won 67 of the 79 seats in the lower house and 36 out of 56 in the senate. Taya was inaugurated as President in April, and appointed a civilian Prime Minister, Sidi Mohamed Ould Boubacar.
GOVERNMENT: The latest constitution, which allows for a multi-party political system, was introduced in July 1991 after approval in a national referendum. Executive power rests with the President, elected by universal suffrage, for a 6-year term. The bicameral legislature, also popularly elected, comprises a 79-seat national assembly (elected for five years) and a 56-member senate with a 6-year mandate. The President appoints a Prime Minister who is head of the Government.

CLIMATE

Most of the country is hot and dry with practically no rain. In the south, however, rainfall is higher with a rainy season which runs from July to September. The coast is tempered by trade winds and is mild with the exception of the hot Nouakchott region (where the rainy season begins a month later). Deserts are cooler and windy in March and April.
Required clothing: Lightweight cottons and linens, with a warm wrap for cool evenings. Waterproofing is necessary for the rainy season.

NOUAKCHOTT Mauritania (21m)

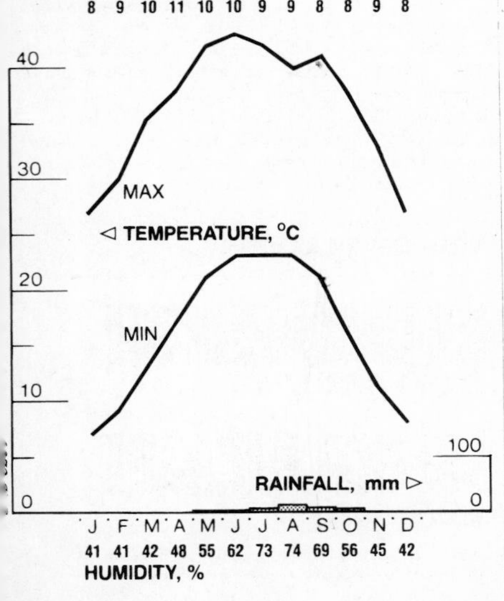

MAURITIUS

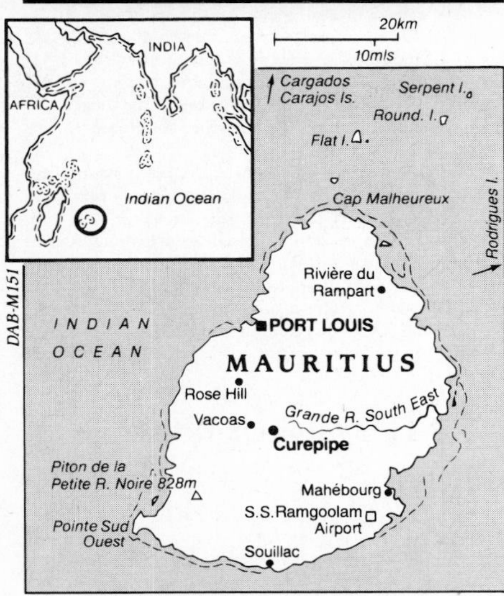

Location: Indian Ocean, off southeast coast of Africa; due east of Madagascar.

Mauritius Government Tourist Office
Emmanuel Anquetil Building
Jules Koenig Street
Port Louis, Mauritius
Tel: 201 1703. Fax: 212 5142. Telex: 4249 EXTERN IW.
Mauritius High Commission
32/33 Elvaston Place
London SW7 5NW
Tel: (071) 581 0294. Fax: (071) 823 8437. Telex: 917772. Opening hours: 0930-1300 and 1400-1700 Monday to Friday.
Mauritius Government Tourist Office
32 Elvaston Place
London SW7 5NW
Tel: (071) 584 3666. Fax: (071) 225 1135. Opening hours: 0930-1700 Monday to Thursday and 0930-1630 Friday.
British High Commission
PO Box 186
Curepipe
King George V Avenue
Floréal, Mauritius
Tel: 686 5795/6/7/8/9. Fax: 686 5792. Telex: 4266 UKREP IW.
Embassy of Mauritius
Suite 134, Van Ness Centre
4301 Connecticut Avenue, NW
Washington, DC
20008
Tel: (202) 244 1491. Fax: (202) 966 0983. Telex: 64362.
Also deals with enquiries from Canada.
Mauritius Tourist Information Service
15 Penn Plaza
415 Seventh Avenue
New York, NY
10001
Tel: (212) 239 8350. Fax: (212) 695 3018. Telex: 9102509815.
Embassy of the United States of America
4th Floor, Rogers House
President John F Kennedy Street
Port Louis, Mauritius
Tel: 208 2347. Fax: 208 9534.
Canadian High Commission
PO Box 1022
38 Mirambo Street
Dar-es-Salaam, Tanzania
Tel: (51) 46000 *or* 46011. Fax: (51) 46005. Telex: 41015.
Also deals with enquiries relating to Mauritius.

AREA: 2040 sq km (788 sq miles).
POPULATION: 1,053,400 (1990 estimate).
POPULATION DENSITY: 516 per sq km.
CAPITAL: Port Louis. **Population:** 136,323 (1985 estimate).
GEOGRAPHY: Mauritius is in the Indian Ocean 2000km (1200 miles) off the southeastern coast of Africa, due east of Madagascar. The island-state stands on what was once a land bridge between Asia and Africa called the Mascarene Archipelago. From the coast the land rises to form a broad fertile plain on which sugar cane flourishes. Some 500km (300 miles) east is Rodrigues Island, while northeast is Cargados Carajos Shoals and 900km (560 miles) to the north is Agalega.
LANGUAGE: English is the official language. The most widely spoken languages are Creole, Hindi and Bhojpuri. French, Urdu, Arabic and Chinese are also spoken. In the 1983 census 13 different language groups were specifically identified, with Creole and Hindi speakers accounting for about half the population.
RELIGION: 51% Hindu, 31% Christian, 16% Muslim.
TIME: GMT + 4.
ELECTRICITY: 220/240 volts AC, 50Hz. UK-type 3-pin plugs are commonly used in hotels.
COMMUNICATIONS: Telephone: IDD is available. Country code: 230. There are no area codes. There are a limited number of public telephone booths, mainly at the airport and in major hotels. **Fax:** Some hotels have facilities. **Telex/telegram:** Messages can be sent from the Mauritius Telecommunications Service offices at Cassis and Port Louis. There are also public facilities at Overseas Telecoms Services Ltd, Rogers House, President John F Kennedy Street, Port Louis. **Post:** Airmail to Europe usually takes five days, four to six weeks by sea. Post office hours are generally 0900-1100 and 1200-1600 Monday to Friday, and 0800-1100 Saturday. **Press:** Of the seven daily newspapers, two are published in Chinese and the remainder in French and English. *L'Express* and *The Sun* have the highest circulation.
BBC World Service and Voice of America frequencies: From time to time these change. See the section *How to Use this Book* for more information.

BBC:				
MHz	25.75	17.88	11.73	6.005
Voice of America:				
MHz	21.49	15.60	9.525	6.035

PASSPORT/VISA

Regulations and requirements may be subject to change at short notice, and you are advised to contact the appropriate diplomatic or consular authority before finalising travel arrangements. Details of these may be found at the head of this country's entry. Any numbers in the chart refer to the footnotes below.

	Passport Required?	Visa Required?	Return Ticket Required?
Full British	Yes	No	Yes
BVP	Not valid	-	-
Australian	Yes	No	Yes
Canadian	Yes	No	Yes
USA	Yes	No	Yes
Other EC	Yes	No	Yes
Japanese	Yes	No	Yes

Restricted entry: Holders of passports issued by the governments of Taiwan, Turkish Cyprus or the South African 'homelands' of Bophuthatswana, Ciskei, Transkei and Venda can only enter with a special permit obtained from the Passport and Immigration Officer (for address, see below).
PASSPORTS: Required by all. The passport has to be valid for at least six months.
British Visitors Passport: Not acceptable.
VISAS: Required by all except:
(a) nationals referred to in the chart above;
(b) nationals of Commonwealth countries for stays of up to 3 months (but nationals of Sri Lanka *do* require a visa);
(c) nationals of Austria, Bahrain, Finland, Iceland, Israel, Norway, Qatar, Sweden, Switzerland and Turkey for stays of up to 3 months.
(d) nationals of Kuwait, Monaco, Oman, San Marino, Saudi Arabia, Tunisia, United Arab Emirates and Vatican City can obtain a 15-day visa upon arrival.
Note: Nationals of South Africa should contact the Embassy for the latest regulations.
Types of visa: Tourist and Business; both are obtainable free of charge. Visas are not required by passengers in transit providing they continue their journey to a third country within 72 hours.
Validity: Tourist and Business visas are normally valid for up to 3 months. Applications for extension should be made to the relevant authority (see below).
Application to: Consulate (or Consular Section at Embassy or High Commission). For addresses, see top of entry.
Application requirements: (a) Valid passport. (b) Photos. (c) Proof of means of support during stay.
Working days required: Varies according to

nationality of applicant.
Temporary residence: Residence permits are issued by the Passport and Immigration Officer, Passport and Immigration Office, Line Barracks, Port Louis, Mauritius. Work permits are necessary for those taking up employment.

MONEY

Currency: Mauritian Rupee (MRe) = 100 cents. Notes are in denominations of MRe1000, 500, 200, 100, 50, 20, 10 and 5. Coins are in denominations of MRe5 and 1, and 50, 20, 10, 5, 2 and 1 cents.
Credit cards: Access/Mastercard, Visa, Diners Club and American Express are widely accepted. Check with your credit card company for details of merchant acceptability and other services which may be available.
Travellers cheques: May be exchanged at banks, hotels and authorised dealers.
Exchange rate indicators: The following figures are included as a guide to the movements of the Mauritian Rupee against Sterling and the US Dollar:

Date	Oct '89	Oct '90	Oct '91	Oct '92
£1.00=	24.59	27.40	27.46	26.97
$1.00=	15.57	14.03	15.82	15.73

Currency restrictions: Import of foreign currency is unlimited, subject to declaration, whilst export is limited to the amount declared on import. Import of local currency is limited to MRe700, export to MRe350.
Banking hours: 0930-1400 Monday to Friday, 0930-1130 Saturday (except for Bank of Mauritius).

DUTY FREE

The following goods may be imported into Mauritius by persons over 16 years of age without incurring customs duty:
250g of tobacco products;
2 litres of wine, ale or beer and 1 litre of spirits;
250ml of toilet water and up to 100ml of perfume for personal use.

PUBLIC HOLIDAYS

Public holidays observed in Mauritius are as follows:
Mar 12 '93 Independence /Republic Day. **Mar 24** Ougadi. **Mar 25** Eid al-Fitr (End of Ramadan). **Apr 9** Good Friday. **May 1** Labour Day. **Sep 20** Ganesh Chaturti. **Nov 1** All Saints' Day. **Nov 13** Divali. **Dec 25** Christmas Day. **Jan 1-2 '94** New Year. **Jan** Chinese Spring Festival. **Feb*** Cavadee *and* Maha Shivaratree. **Mar 12** Independence Day. **Mar** Start of Eid al-Fitr. **Mar/Apr*** Ougadi.
Note: [*] Enquire at the Tourist Office for exact dates. (a) There is a diversity of cultures in Mauritius, each with its own holidays. (b) Muslim festivals are timed according to local sightings of various phases of the Moon and the dates given above are approximations. During the lunar month of Ramadan that precedes Eid al-Fitr, Muslims fast during the day and feast at night and normal business patterns may be interrupted. Some disruption may continue into Eid al-Fitr itself. Eid al-Fitr and Eid al-Adha may last anything from two to ten days, depending on the town or region. For more information, see the section *World of Islam* at the back of the book. (c) Hindu and Chinese festivals are declared according to local astronomical observations and it is often only possible to forecast the approximate time of their occurrence.

HEALTH

Regulations and requirements may be subject to change at short notice, and you are advised to contact your doctor well in advance of your intended date of departure. Any numbers in the chart refer to the footnotes below.

	Special Precautions?	Certificate Required?
Yellow Fever	No	1
Cholera	No	No
Typhoid & Polio	No	-
Malaria	2	-
Food & Drink	3	-

[1]: A yellow fever vaccination certificate is required of travellers over one year of age arriving from infected areas. The Mauritius government considers those countries and areas classified as yellow fever endemic to be infected.
[2]: Malaria risk, exclusively in the benign *vivax* form, exists throughout the year in northern rural areas apart from Rodrigues Island.
[3]: Water used for drinking should have first been boiled or otherwise sterilised. Bottled water is readily available. Milk is unpasteurised and should be boiled. Powdered or tinned milk is available and is advised, but make sure that it is reconstituted with pure water. Avoid dairy products which are likely to have been made from unboiled milk. Vegetables should be cooked and fruit peeled.
Bilharzia (schistosomiasis) is present. Avoid swimming and paddling in fresh water. Swimming pools which are well-chlorinated and maintained are safe.
Health care: Public medical facilities are numerous and of a high standard and there are several private clinics. All treatment at state-run hospitals is free for Mauritians and certain minor treatment may be free for visitors (check with Embassy or High Commission). Nonetheless, health insurance is advised.

TRAVEL - International

AIR: The national airline of Mauritius is *Air Mauritius (MK)*.
Approximate flight time: From *London* to Mauritius is 11 hours 30 minutes (non-stop).
International airport: *Mauritius (MRU)* (Sir Seewoosagur Ramgoolam) is 48km (30 miles) southeast of Port Louis (travel time – 40 minutes). Airport facilities include duty-free shopping, banking facilities, snack bar, post office, shops and car hire (*Avis, Europcar, Hertz* and *White Sand Tours*). There are bus and taxi services to the city.
Departure tax: MRe100. Passengers transiting within 48 hours and children under two years of age are exempt.
SEA: Port Louis is the main port. It is primarily commercial (sugar exports, general imports) but there is a limited passenger service to Réunion and Rodrigues Island.

TRAVEL - Internal

AIR: *Air Mauritius* operates daily flights connecting Plaisance Airport and Rodrigues Island.
SEA: Regular sailings to Rodrigues Island from Port Louis. Contact: *Rogers & Co,* PO Box 605, President John F Kennedy Street, Port Louis. Tel: 208 6801. Telex: 4312.
ROAD: There is a good network of sealed roads covering the island. Traffic drives on the left. **Bus:** There are excellent and numerous bus services to all parts of the island. **Taxis** have white registration plates with black figures. As they are not metered, fares should be negotiated in advance (with return mileage included). Taxi drivers do not expect a tip. **Car hire:** There are numerous car-hire firms. **Documentation:** International Driving Permit recommended, although a foreign licence is accepted. A temporary driving licence is available from local authorities on presentation of a valid British or Northern Ireland driving licence.
URBAN: Bus and taxi services are available in urban areas.
JOURNEY TIMES: The following chart gives approximate journey times (in hours and minutes) from Port Louis to other major cities/towns in Mauritius.

	Road
Curepipe	0.20
Plaisance	1.00
Grand Bay	0.30
St Geran	1.00
Touessrok	1.00
Souillac	1.00

ACCOMMODATION

There is an abundance of hotels throughout the island and a number of smaller family holiday bungalows. From June to September reservations should be made in advance. For more information contact the Tourist Office at the address above or the Association des Hôteliers et Restaurateurs Ile Maurice, c/o Mauritius Employers Federation, Cerne House, Chaussée, Port Louis. Tel: 212 1599 *or* 212 4298 *or* 212 4012.

RESORTS & EXCURSIONS

Port Louis: Capital and main port of Mauritius, the city was founded by the French Governor, Mahé de Labourdonnais, in 1736. The harbour is sheltered by a semi-circle of mountains. The city has plenty of character, and in some quarters signs of its past elegance are still evident. Off the main square, the palm-lined *Place d'Armes*, there are some particularly fine French colonial buildings, especially *Government House* (18th century) and the *Municipal Theatre*, built around the same time. There are two cathedrals, Protestant and Catholic, a fine *Supreme Court Building*, some 18th-century barracks and the *Natural History Museum* (exhibiting Mauritius's most famous bird, the extinct Dodo). On the outskirts of the city, at the foot of the mountains, is the *Champ de Mars*, originally laid out by the French for military parades, and now a race-course. The best views of the race-course, city and harbour are from a splendid boulevard called *Edward VII Avenue*, and from *Fort Adelaide*, a citadel fortified in the time of William IV. South of Port Louis is *Le Reduit*, the French colonial residence of the President of Mauritius, set in magnificent gardens. Other places of interest include the *Jummah Mosque* in Royal Street and the *Chinese Pagoda*.
Curepipe: The island's main residential town provides good shops and restaurants. Between Curepipe and Vacoas is the spectacular *Trou aux Cerfs*, an extinct crater 85m (280ft) deep and more than 180m (600ft) wide, from the rim of which an extensive view of the island can be seen.
Pamplemousses Gardens: The gardens are known to naturalists throughout the world for their large collection of indigenous and exotic plants, including the *Giant Victoria Regia* lily and many species of palm trees. Of particular interest is the talipot palm, which is said to flower once every 100 years and then die. There are also tortoises here, some of them over 100 years old.
Rochester Falls: Water cascades over spectacular rock formations. Spectacular joints have been formed by the contraction of lava due to sudden cooling. The falls are near **Souillac** and can be reached by a road which crosses a sugar plantation that is open to visitors.
Grand Bassin: Within a short distance of Mare Longue and resting in the crater of an extinct volcano, this is one of the island's two natural lakes. It is a place of pilgrimage for a large number of Mauritians of the Hindu faith.
Plaine Champagne: The highest part of the central plateau (740m/2430ft), from where there is a superb view of the *Rivière Noire Mountains* and the sea lining the horizon. The forest-clad slopes of Rivière Noire contain some fine specimens of indigenous timber and interesting plants peculiar to the island. For the keen birdwatcher, the mountains are the habitat of most of the remaining indigenous species.
Chamarel: A twisting metalled road leads from *Case Noyale* village to Chamarel. This is a mound of undulating land of contrasting layers of colour, and the patches of blue, green, red and yellow earth are believed to be the result of weathering. The nearby *Chamarel Waterfall* emerges from the moors and primeval vegetation and is startlingly beautiful.
Casela Bird Park: This park, set in the district of Rivière Noire, stretches over 20 acres of land and contains more than 140 varieties, amounting to 2500 birds. Specimens from the five continents may be seen there,

MAURITIUS	HEALTH REGULATIONS	VISA REGULATIONS Code-Link
GALILEO/WORLDSPAN	 TI-DFT/MRU/HE	TI-DFT/MRU/VI
SABRE	TIDFT/MRU/HE	 TIDFT/MRU/VI

To access this information on your CRS, swipe the barcode with a light pen or type in the text under the barcode. For more information, see the introduction *How to Use This Book*.

but the main attraction is the Mauritian Pink Pigeon, which is one of the rarest birds in the world. Other attractions are the fish ponds, tortoises, monkeys, orchids (seasonal), and the overall scenery which has a peaceful atmosphere created by the trees, streams and small cascades.

Aquarium: Facing the calm water of the lagoon between *Pointe aux Piments* and *Trou aux Biches* is the Aquarium populated by 200 species of fish, invertebrates, live coral and sponges, all originating from the waters around the island. An open-circuit sea-water cycle of one million litres runs through the 36 tanks everyday. The Aquarium offers a unique opportunity to admire the colourful treasures of the Indian Ocean.

La Vanille Crocodile Park: Near *Rivière des Anguilles*, in the wild south, this is a farm breeding Nile crocodiles imported from Madagascar. The site offers a vast park with a nature walk through luxuriant forest studded with freshwater springs. A small zoo of animals found in the wild in Mauritius is also located here.

Domaine des Grands Bois: On the 2000 acres of this magnificent park visitors can watch the rich fauna in a lush exotic setting. Ebony, eucalyptus, palm trees and wild orchids provide the backdrop for stags, deer, monkeys and other wildlife.

Domaine Les Pailles: This nature park nestling at the foot of a mountain range covers an area of 3000 acres. Among the attractions are a replica of a sugar mill and an old rum distillery as well as interesting animal life. Drives through the park in Land Rovers or horse-drawn carriges are also possible.

Beaches

Tamarin: Lying in the shadow of the Rivière Mountains, Tamarin has a fine lagoon which is split in two by the Rivière Noire estuary. The bathing at this point is a big attraction and amenities are provided for exciting surfing in the big ocean swells.

Grand Baie: The northern coastline beyond Baie du Tombeau has many delightful beaches: *Pointe aux Piments*, famous for its underwater scenery; *Trou aux Biches*, with its fringe of *filaos* (casuarina) and coconut palms and its splendid Hindu temple; then further up the coast *Choisy*, one of the most popular beaches on the island, offering facilities for safe bathing, sailing, windsurfing and water-skiing; and finally the coastline curves into Grand Baie itself, the main centre for yachting, water-skiing, windsurfing and many other sports.

Péreybère: This delightful little cove is midway on the coast road between Grand Baie and Cap Malheureux. The deep clear, blue water makes it one of the very best bathing places on the whole island.

Cap Malheureux: This is a fishing village in the extreme north with a magnificent view of *Flat Island, Round Island* and *Gunner's Quoin*, islands of volcanic origin, rising from the sparkling light-green sea.

Grand Gaube: Further along the coast is another charming fishing village where fishermen have earned a well-deserved reputation for their skill in the making of sailing craft and of deep-sea fishing.

Roches Noires/Poste Lafayette: These are both favoured seaside resorts, especially in the hotter months, because of the fresh prevailing winds that blow almost all the year round from the sea.

Belle Mare: A beautiful white sandy beach with fine bathing. The coast, with its white sweep of sands at *Palmar* and *Trou d'Eau Douce*, stretches out lazily to Grand Port, a quaint little village by the sea. There the beach narrows and the road follows the coastline closely to **Mahébourg.** *Pointe d'Esny*, the adjoining white sandy beach with its string of bungalows, leads to Blue Bay.

Blue Bay: In a semi-circle of *filao* trees is one of the finest bathing spots on the island. Situated on the southeast coast, not far from Mahébourg, Blue Bay offers a fine stretch of white sandy beach, and a deep, clear, light-blue bathing pool. There is also scope for yachting and windsurfing.

SOCIAL PROFILE

FOOD & DRINK: Waiter service is normal in restaurants and bars. Standards of cuisine, whether French, Creole, Indian, Chinese or English, are generally very high but fruit, meat, vegetables and even fresh seafood are often in short supply and restaurants must often depend on imports. Specialities include venison (in season), *camarons* (freshwater prawns) in hot sauces, octopus, creole fish, fresh pineapple with chilli sauce, and rice with curry. **Drink:** Rum and beer are staple beverages for Mauritians but there is good imported wine, mineral water, *alouda* (almond drink) and fresh coconut milk.

NIGHTLIFE: In some towns and in Grand Bay there are discotheques and nightclubs with music and dancing. In the Chinese quarter of Port Louis is a Chinese casino. Rivière Noire is a Creole fishermen's district where *sega* dancing is especially lively on Saturday nights. *Sega* troupes give performances at most hotels. Gamblers are lavishly catered for; casinos in the island's hotels are amongst the island's attractions.

SHOPPING: The Central Market in Port Louis is full of beautifully displayed goods, including fruit, vegetables, spices, fish, meat and handicrafts. Island crafts include jewellery, Chinese and Indian jade, silks, basketry and pottery. There is no duty on textile products. Shop signs may be in English, French or Chinese. **Shopping hours:** *Port Louis*: 0900-1700 Monday to Friday, 0900-1200 Saturday. *Curepipe, Rose Hill, Quatre Bornes*: 0900-1800 Monday to Wednesday and Friday to Saturday, 0900-1200 Thursday and Sunday.

SPORT: Swimming: Beaches, lagoons and inlets around the coast offer plenty of opportunity for safe bathing (see above under *Resorts & Excursions*), supplemented by hotel swimming pools. **Skindiving:** Grand Baie, north of Pamplemousses Gardens, is a popular beach for skindiving. **Fishing:** There is good coastal and inland fishing around the island. **Horseracing:** The Hippodrome at the Champ de Mars has meetings at the weekends between May and October.

SPECIAL EVENTS: With origins in three continents and three major religions there is a great diversity of religious and cultural festivals. The following is only a selection. For a complete list and for exact dates of the following in 1993/1994, enquire at the Government Tourist Office.

Mar '93 *Ougadi*. **Sep** *Father Laval* (festival of a saint who had healing powers); *Ganesh Chaturti*. **Sep** *Muhurram* (Islamic procession). **Nov** *Divali* (a colourful Hindu festival). **Jan/Feb '94** *Cavadee* (Hindu festival). **Feb** *Chinese Spring Festival*. **Feb/Mar** *Maha Shivaratree* (Hindu celebration in honour of Shiva). **Dates to be announced:** *Holi* (a very enjoyable Hindu festival); *Chinese Dragon Festival* (similar to the Hong Kong celebration).

SOCIAL CONVENTIONS: Handshaking is the customary form of greeting. Visitors should respect the traditions of their hosts, particularly when visiting a private house. The type of hospitality the visitor receives is determined by the religion and social customs of the host, which are closely related. It is appropriate to give a gift as a small token of appreciation if invited for a meal. Dress is normally informal although men will need to wear a suit for particularly formal occasions. **Tipping:** 10% is usual in most hotels and restaurants.

BUSINESS PROFILE

ECONOMY: Until recently, the Mauritian economy was based on the production and export of sugar. The only other cash crops of any significance are tobacco and tea. During the late 1970s, the economy experienced considerable difficulties owing to a combination of poor sugar harvests and low world prices for the commodity aggravated by the general effects of world recession. Earlier in the decade, Mauritius had established an Export Processing Zone, which produced manufactured goods specifically for export using large quantities of raw materials by attracting foreign investment into the country on favourable terms. With the sugar price failing to recover in the 1980s, this strategy began to pay off as Mauritius' balance of payments improved. Textiles are the key industry in the Export Zone, although there has been recent diversification into other manufactured goods such as consumer electronics and electrical devices. France, the United States, Hong Kong, the UK and South Africa are the country's largest trading partners. The Government's latest initiative proposes the establishment of offshore financial and banking facilities on the island. As there is hardly a small island nation worldwide which does not try to do the same, it remains to be seen how Mauritius fares against the myriad competition. Mauritius is a member of the Indian Ocean Commission, which seeks to promote regional economic co-operation.
BUSINESS: Safari suits are often worn in business circles. Appointments should be made. English is widely understood in the business community. **Office hours:** 0900-1600 Monday to Friday and 0900-1200 Saturday.
COMMERCIAL INFORMATION: The following organisation can offer advice: Mauritius Chamber of Commerce and Industry, 3 Royal Street, Port Louis. Tel: 208 3301. Fax: 208 0076. Telex: 4277.

HISTORY & GOVERNMENT

HISTORY: Formerly a French possession, Mauritius and its neighbouring islands were captured by the British in 1810. An electoral system based on the Westminster model was introduced in the late 1950s, and Dr (later Sir) Seewoosagur Ramgoolam's Labour Party came to power. In 1968 independence was achieved, but the British kept a number of smaller islands, including Diego Garcia with its important naval base which today is leased to and occupied by the Americans. Post-independence politics have been dominated by Ramgoolam, and by the two principal figures of the Mauritian left, French-born Paul Bérenger and (later Sir) Aneerood Jugnauth. The charismatic Bérenger is a dramatic contrast to the cautious, pragmatic Jugnauth, and the focus of the Mauritian political scene has often been the personal and political clash between the two. Both rose to prominence in the Mouvement Militant Mauricien (MMM) which emerged as the principal opposition to Ramgoolam's coalition governments of the late 1960s and 1970s. These administrations were dominated by Ramgoolam's own Mauritian Labour Party (MLP) and the Parti Mauricien Social Démocratique (PMSD) led by Gaëtan Duval. Growing disillusionment with Ramgoolam brought the MMM to power, in alliance with the Parti Socialiste Mauricien, at the 1982 general election with a landslide victory. Political disagreement and personality clashes characterised the administration and the Government was fortunate to struggle through most of its term. Jugnauth had by now left the MMM to form the Mouvement Socialiste Mauricien (MSM) and fought the 1987 election campaign in alliance with the Labour Party and the Social democrats. The 3-party alliance won the poll. The coalition dissolved in 1990 and a new alliance between the MMM and Jugnauth's ruling MSM was formed to fight the 1991 election: the strategy proved a success and a MSM/MMM government was elected. The domestic policies of successive governments have followed orthodox social democratic lines with a mixed economy and state-sponsored welfare systems. Mauritian foreign policy has been notable for its promotion of links with South Africa – at a time when that country was still an international pariah – particularly for trade and investment. The other important overseas issue has concerned the status of Diego Garcia (see above). The current position is that the British government has agreed to abandon its claim to the atoll when the present lease to the USA expires in 2016. Mauritius may then negotiate directly with the Americans over its future. The outcome depends on the requirements of US global strategy at the time.
GOVERNMENT: Under constitutional amendments which came into effect in March 1992, Mauritius is now a republic. Legislative power rests with the unicameral 62-seat National Assembly, which is elected by universal suffrage for a 5-year term. (Eight additional members are also appointed from among the defeated candidates to ensure an ethnic balance in the assembly.) The National Assembly elects the President of the Republic who is Head of State. The President appoints the Prime Minister from the assembly and other ministers on the recommendation of the Prime Minister.

CLIMATE

Warm coastal climate (particularly January to April). Temperatures are slightly lower with more rain inland on the plateau around Curepipe. Tropical storms are likely in the cyclone season which runs from December to March. Sea breezes blow all year, especially on the east coast.
Required clothing: Lightweights for summer, with warmer clothing being needed for the winter evenings.

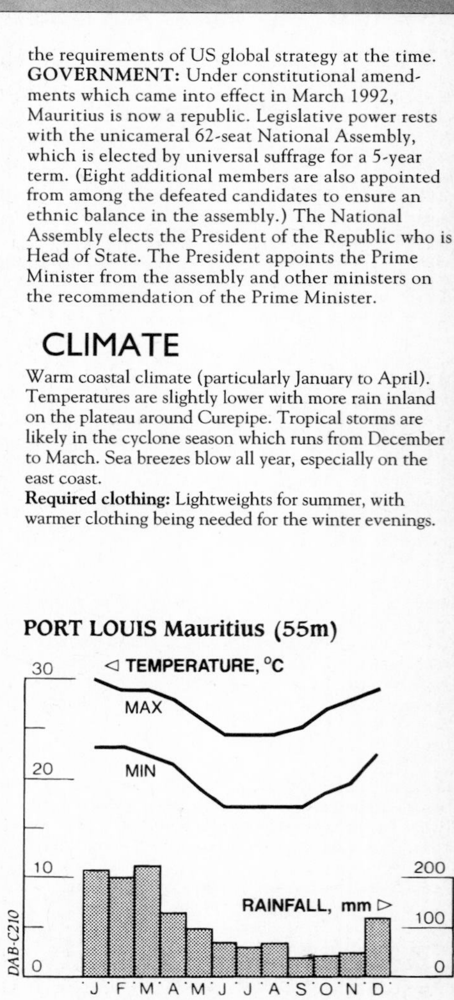

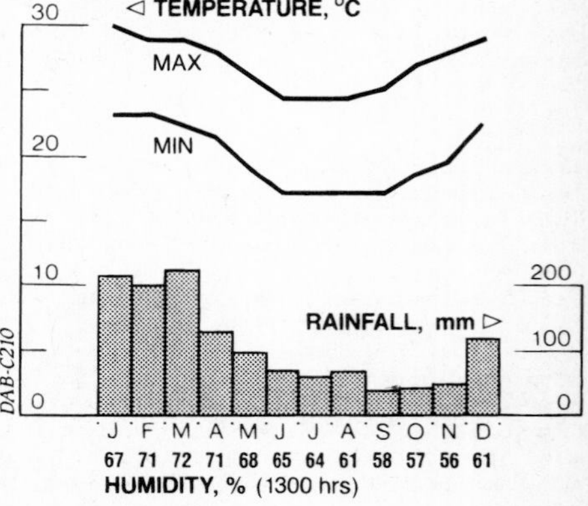

MEXICO

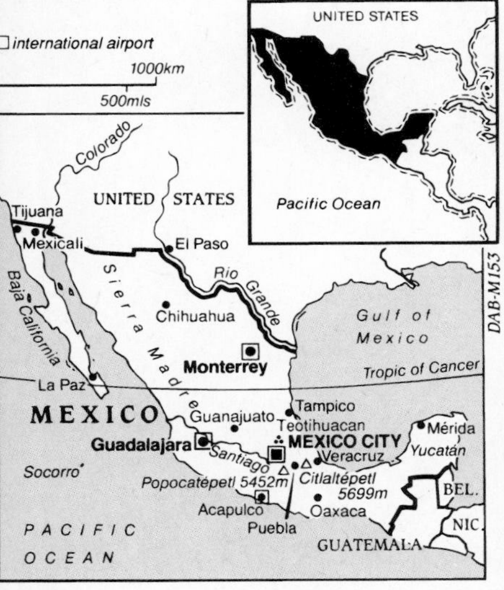

Location: Southern North America.

Fondo Nacional de Fomento al Turismo (FONATUR)
17th Floor
Insurgentes Sur 800
Colonia del Valle
03100 México DF, Mexico
Tel: (5) 687 2697. Telex: 1777636.

Embassy of the United Mexican States
42 Hertford Street
Mayfair
London W1Y 7TF
Tel: (071) 499 8586 *or* 235 6393 (Visa section). Fax: (071) 495 4035. Opening hours: 0930-1300 and 1500-1600 Monday to Friday (0900-1400 Monday to Friday during August); recorded information outside these hours.

Mexican Tourist Office
60/61 Trafalgar Square
London WC2N 5DS
Tel: (071) 734 1058. Fax: (071) 930 9202.

British Embassy
Apartado 96 bis
Río Lerma 71
Colonia Cuauhtémoc
06500 México DF
Mexico
Tel: (5) 207 2089. Fax: (5) 207 7672. Telex: 1773093.
Consulates in: Mexico City, Acapulco, Ciudad Juárez, Guadalajara, Mérida, Monterrey, Tampico and Veracruz.

Embassy of the United Mexican States
1911 Pennsylvania Avenue, NW
Washington, DC
20006
Tel: (202) 728 1600. Fax: (202) 234 7739. Telex: 248459.

Mexican Government Tourism Office
Suite 10002
405 Park Avenue
New York, NY
10022
Tel: (212) 755 7261.

Embassy of the United States of America
Paseo de la Reforma 305
Colonia Cuauhtémoc
06500 México DF, Mexico
Tel: (5) 211 0042. Fax: (5) 511 9980. Telex: 1773091.
Consulates in: Ciudad Juarez, Guadalajara, Monterrey, Tijuana, Hermosillo, Matamoros, Mazatlán, Mérida and Nuevo Laredo.

Embassy of the United Mexican States
Suite 1800
130 Albert Street
Ottawa, Ontario
K1P 5G4
Tel: (613) 233 8988 *or* 233 9272 *or* 233 9917. Fax: (613) 235 9123.
Consulates in: Montréal, Québec, Toronto and Vancouver.

Mexican Government Tourism Office
Suite 1801
2 Bloor Street West
Toronto, Ontario
M4W 3E2
Tel: (416) 925 0704. Fax: (416) 925 6061.

Canadian Embassy
Apartado Postal 105-05
Calle Schiller 529 (Rincon del Bosque)
Colonia Polanco
11580 México DF, Mexico
Tel: (5) 254 3288. Fax: (5) 545 1769 *or* 255 0353 *or* 254 8654. Telex: 1771191.
Consulates in: Acapulco, Cancún, Guadalajara, Mazatlán, Oaxaca, Puerto Vallarta and Tijuana.

AREA: 1,958,201 sq km (756,066 sq miles).
POPULATION: 81,140,922 (1990).
POPULATION DENSITY: 41.4 per sq km.
CAPITAL: Mexico City. **Population:** 8,236,960 (1990).
GEOGRAPHY: Mexico is at the southern extremity of North America and is bounded in the north by the USA, northwest by the Gulf of California, west by the Pacific, south by Guatemala and Belize, and east by the Gulf of Mexico and the Caribbean. Mexico's geographical features range from swamp to desert, and from tropical low-

Mitla

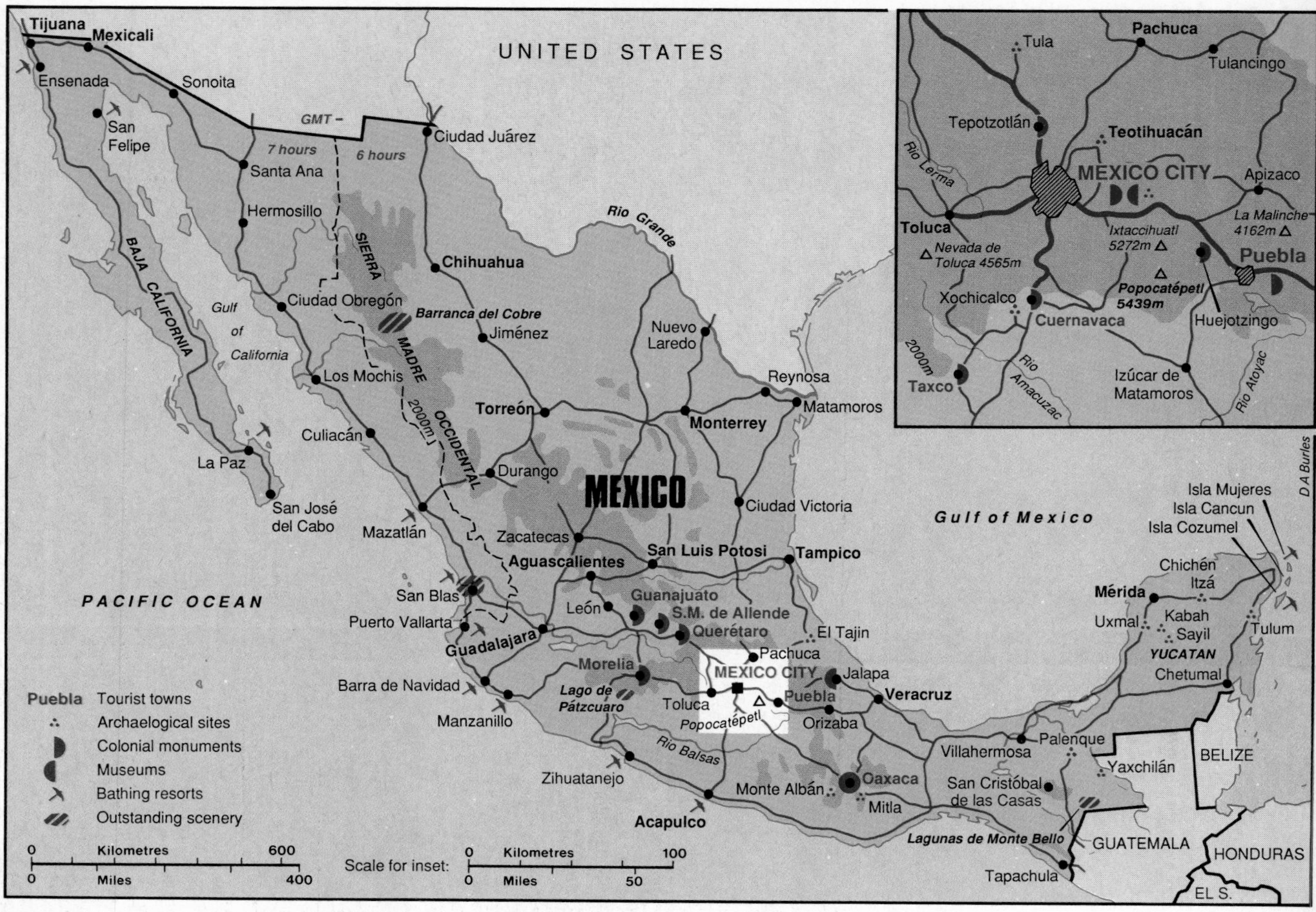

land jungle to high alpine vegetation. Over half the country has an altitude above 1000m (3300ft). The central land mass is a plateau flanked by ranges of mountains to the east and west that lie roughly parallel to the coast. The northern area of this plateau is arid and thinly populated, and occupies 40% of the total area of Mexico. The southern area is crossed by a range of volcanic mountains running from Cape Corrientes in the west through the Valley of Mexico to Veracruz in the east, and includes the magnificent volcanoes of Orizaba, Popocatépetl, Ixtaccíhuatl, Nevado de Toluca, Matlalcueyetl and Cofre de Perote. This is the heart of Mexico and where almost half of the population lives. To the south the land falls away to the sparsely populated Isthmus of Tehuantepec whose slopes and flatlands support both commercial and subsistence agriculture. In the east the Gulf Coast and the Yucatán peninsula are flat and receive over 75% of Mexico's rain. The most productive agricultural region in Mexico is the northwest, while the Gulf Coast produces most of Mexico's oil and sulphur. Along the northwest coast, opposite the peninsula of Baja California, and to the southeast along the coast of Bahía de Campeche and the Yucatán peninsula, the lowlands are swampy with coastal lagoons.

LANGUAGE: Spanish is the official language. English is widely spoken.

RELIGION: 97% Roman Catholic.

TIME: Mexico spans three different time zones:

South, Central and Eastern Mexico: GMT - 6 (Central Standard Time).

Nayarit, Sonora, Sinaloa and Baja California Sur: GMT - 7 (Mountain Time).

Baja California Norte: GMT - 8 (Pacific Time).

Daylight saving is operated during summer months; clocks are put forward by one hour.

ELECTRICITY: 110 volts AC, 60Hz. US 2-pin (flat) plugs are usual.

COMMUNICATIONS: Telephone: IDD is available. Country code: 52. Long-distance calls are very expensive. **Fax:** Major hotels have facilities. **Telex/telegram:** International telex facilities are available at a number of hotels in Mexico City and in Acapulco, Chihuahua, Guadalajara, Mérida, Monterrey, Puebla, Tampico and Veracruz. The telegraphic system is run by *Telegrafos Nacionales* and telegrams should be handed in to their offices. In Mexico the main office for international telegrams is at Balderas y Colón, Mexico 1 DF. **Post:** Airmail to Europe takes about six days. Surface mail is slow. Within the capital there is an immediate delivery (*Entrega Inmediata*) service, which usually takes two or three days. **Press:** The major daily newspapers published in Spanish are *Excélsior, La Universal, La Journada, Uno Más Uno* and *El Dia*. The English-language daily is *The News*.

BBC World Service and Voice of America frequencies: From time to time these change. See the section *How to Use this Book* for more information.

BBC:				
MHz	17.840	15.220	9.590	7.325
Voice of America:				
MHz	15.21	11.74	9.815	6.030

PASSPORT/VISA

Regulations and requirements may be subject to change at short notice, and you are advised to contact the appropriate diplomatic or consular authority before finalising travel arrangements. Details of these may be found at the head of this country's entry. Any numbers in the chart refer to the footnotes below.

	Passport Required?	Visa Required?	Return Ticket Required?
Full British	Yes	No	No
BVP	Not valid	-	-
Australian	Yes	No	No
Canadian	No/1	No	No
USA	No/1	No	No
Other EC	Yes	3	2
Japanese	Yes	No	No

Note: No brief account of the complex Mexican Passport/Visa regulations is likely to be fully successful. Readers are advised to use the following for general guidance, but to check on the requirements that specifically apply to them with the appropriate Consulate (or Consular Section at Embassy). Non-compliance with visa regulations will result in fines and transportation (at the carrier's expense) to the visitor's country of origin.

PASSPORTS: Valid passport required by all except [1] USA and Canadian citizens who can present a birth certificate or other acceptable national ID.

Note: [2] Nationals of Greece must possess a return ticket; other EC nationals are exempt.

British Visitors Passport: Not accepted.

MEXICO	**HEALTH REGULATIONS**	**VISA REGULATIONS** Code-Link
GALILEO/WORLDSPAN	 TI-DFT/MEX/HE	TI-DFT/MEX/VI
SABRE	 TIDFT/MEX/HE	TIDFT/MEX/VI

To access this information on your CRS, swipe the barcode with a light pen or type in the text under the barcode. For more information, see the introduction *How to Use This Book*.

MEXICO

Where the Renaissance went after it left Europe.

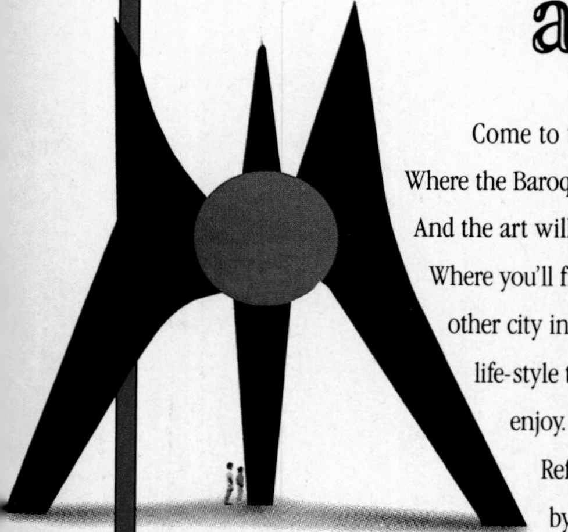

Come to the city touched by magic. Where the Baroque cathedrals are works of art. And the art will touch your very soul. Where you'll find more museums than any other city in the world. And sample a grand life-style that few cities in the world still enjoy. Come stroll the Paseo de la Reforma—a Boulevard designed by Emperor Maximilian himself. Explore the Zona Rosa's cobblestone streets, sidewalk cafes and boutiques. Behold the magnificent muraled walls of the oldest university on the continent. Ride flower-laden gondolas down the canals of Xochimilco. Come to the city where everyone goes home richer. And where you can treasure not only the beauty of Europe's Golden Age, but of Mexico's. Come visit the city where the Renaissance still flourishes. Come to Mexico City.

For information call your travel agent or write to: Mexico City Dist. Center, P.O. Box 4070, Woodland Hills, CA 91365-4070.

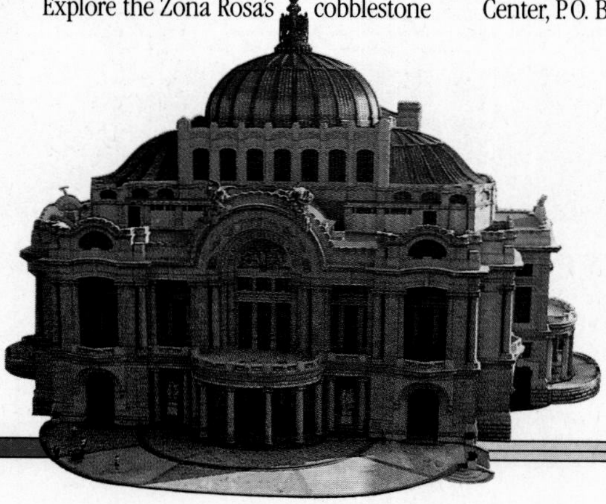

You'll find art from centuries past and well into the future.

Visit a breathtaking palace overflowing with sonatas, concertos, Tamayo's and Siqueiros'.

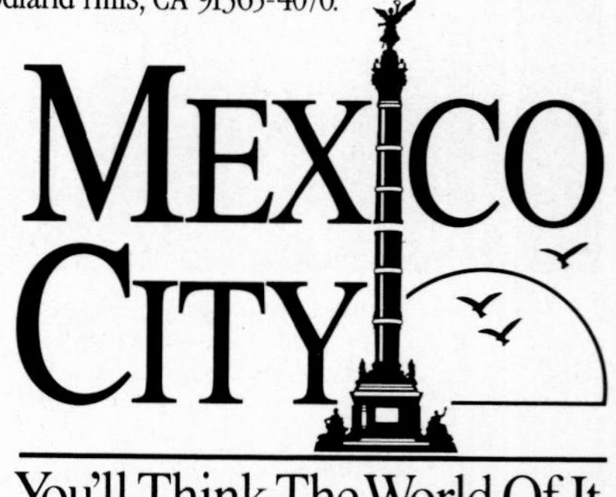

ote: Minors (ie under 18 years of age) travelling with one rent or *unaccompanied* to Mexico require both parents' nsent certified by a public notary or an authorisation gned by the parents at the Mexican Consulate in person, entifying themselves with their passports. It is necessary at the non-travelling parents sign or provide such authosation.

OURIST CARDS: Available *only* to people entering exico on holiday, for reasons of health, or to engage in ientific, artistic or sporting activities which are neither munerative nor lucrative. *The Consular office retains the ght to request further evidence of the applicant's intention to sit Mexico as a tourist whenever such intention has not been tablished to the Consul's satisfaction.* The same right applies ith regard to evidence of the applicant's financial means sustain him/herself while in Mexico.

ationals of the following countries can apply for a ourist Card:

) **[3]** EC nationals (except nationals of France who *do* eed a visa);

) Australia, Canada, Japan and the USA;

:) Austria, Chile, Finland, Iceland, Israel, Liechtenstein, lonaco, New Zealand, Norway, Singapore, Sweden and witzerland.

or requirements and regulations relevant to other nationlities, contact the Mexican Embassy.

USINESS CARDS: Available to people entering lexico on business: ie to promote sales, visit associates, rmalise contract arrangements, make investments, perrm market research, seek representatives and purchase oods for export, etc. It is *not* for those engaging in activies of a technical nature, employment or work of any kind. usiness Cards are valid for multiple entry.

Nationals of the following countries can apply for a Business Card:

a) **[3]** EC nationals (except nationals of Portugal and pain). Nationals of France, Greece, Italy and Luxembourg *lso* need a visa stamped in their passports;

b) Argentina, Bahamas*, Belize, Bolivia*, Brazil*, Chile*, Colombia*, Costa Rica*, Ecuador, El Salvador, Guatemala*, Honduras*, Jamaica*, Nicaragua*, Portugal*, Venezuela*, Romania and the Yugoslav Republics only if ermanent residents in the UK;

c) Australia*, Canada, Japan and the USA*;

d) Austria, Finland, Liechtenstein, Monaco*, New ealand*, Norway, Panama*, Paraguay*, Peru*, Sweden, witzerland and Uruguay.

For requirements and regulations relevant to other nationalties, contact the Mexican Embassy.

Note [*]: In addition, these nationals also require a visa tamped in their passport.

TECHNICIAN CARDS: Available to persons entering or technical purposes such as advice, repair or installation of nachinery or computer programmes, training etc. Technician Cards are valid for multiple entry.

Nationals of the following countries can apply for a Technician Card:

(a) **[3]** EC nationals (except nationals of Ireland, Luxembourg, Portugal and Spain). Nationals of Belgium, France, Greece and Italy *also* need a visa stamped in their passport;

(b) Australia*, Canada, Japan* and the USA*;

(c) Austria*, CIS*, Czechoslovakia*, Finland*, Hungary*, Iceland*, Israel*, New Zealand*, Norway, Poland*, Sweden and Switzerland*.

For requirements and regulations relevant to other nationalities, contact the Mexican Embassy.

Note [*]: In addition, these nationals also require a visa stamped in their passport.

Validity: The period is specified on the individual Card (usually 30 or 90 days; 6 months for nationals of Canada, the UK and the USA, renewable for a further 6 months in Mexico). *Tourist Cards:* Valid for one entry only. *Business Cards:* From the date of issue the holder has 90 days to enter Mexico; the Card is valid for 30 days. *Technician Cards:* From the date of issue the holder has 90 days to enter Mexico and, from the date of entry, may remain for up to 30 days. Applicants for Technician Cards who have a letter of sponsorship from a Mexican company will receive a Multiple-entry Card valid for 1 year.

Applications to: Consulate (or Consular Section at Embassy) or authorised airlines flying Mexican routes. For addresses, see top of entry.

Application requirements: In some cases a personal application will be required (although in general this does not apply to tourists).

Tourist Cards: (a) Passport with a minimum of 6 months validity. (b) Covering letter with date of entry and departure. (c) Return air ticket, sufficient funds for period of stay, application form and 3 passport-size photos for nationals of Greece.

Business Cards: (a) Valid passport. (b) Completed application form. (c) Company letter stating nature of business, companies to be visited and financial responsibility for applicant's fees and salary. (d) 2 recent, identical photos. (e) Fee. (f) A letter from the applicant's national chamber of commerce if staying longer than 30 days.

Technician Cards: (a) Passport with a minimum of 1 year's validity. (b) Completed application form. (c) Letter from the Mexican firm stating specific purpose of the visit and requesting applicant's services. (d) 2 recent, identical photos. (e) Fee.

Notes: (a) All postal applications have to be accompanied by a stamped, self-addressed envelope for recorded or registered delivery. (b) An International Certificate of Vaccination against Cholera is required for travellers arriving within 2 weeks of visiting an infected area.

Cost: Tourist Cards are free; Business and Technician Cards vary.

Working days required: Personal – 2 days; postal – 1 week.

VISAS: Available for all except holders of a Tourist card or visa-replacing document. Applications should be accompanied by submission of the following to the Embassy: (a) Passport. (b) 2 photos. (c) Proof of return ticket. (d) Fee.

Note: Non-compliance with visa regulations will result in fines and transportation at carrier's expense to country of origin.

Temporary residence: Apply to Mexican Embassy.

Chacmool

MONEY

Currency: Peso (Mex$) = 100 centavos. Notes are in denominations of Mex$100, 50, 20, 10, 5, 2 and 1. Coins are in denominations of Mex$5 and 1, and 50, 10 and 5 centavos.

Currency exchange: The exchange rate of the Mexican Peso against Sterling and other hard currencies has, in recent years, been subject to considerable fluctuation (see table below).

Credit cards: American Express, Diners Club, Visa and Access/Mastercard are widely accepted.

Travellers cheques: Travellers cheques or letters of credit in US Dollars issued by well-known banks or travel organisations are readily negotiable in banks and hotels. Sterling travellers cheques are not readily negotiable except at head offices of banks in the capital, and may be subject to a considerable discount.

Exchange rate indicators: The following figures are included as a guide to the movements of the Mexican Peso against Sterling and the US Dollar (free-market rates):

Date:	Oct '89	Oct '90	Oct '91	Oct '92
£1.00=	4107	5688	5315	4922
$1.00=	2601	2912	3062	3101

Currency restrictions: Local currency may be imported up to Mex$5000; the import of foreign currency is unlimited provided declared. Foreign currency may be exported up to the amount imported and declared; local currency may be exported up to Mex$5000. The export of gold coins is prohibited.

Banking hours: 0900-1330 Monday to Friday; some banks are open on Saturday afternoon.

DUTY FREE

The following goods may be imported into Mexico by persons over 18 years of age without incurring customs duty:

400 cigarettes or 2 boxes of cigars or a reasonable quantity of pipe tobacco;
3 bottles of wine or spirits;
A reasonable amount of perfume or toilet water;
1 stills camera, 1 portable film or video camera and up to 12 unexposed rolls of film or video cassettes for each camera;
A reasonable amount of personal and electrical goods;
Various objects with the value of up to US$300 or the equivalent.

PUBLIC HOLIDAYS

Public holidays observed in Mexico are as follows:
Mar 21 '93 Birth of Benito Juárez. **Apr 9-12** Easter. **May 1** Labour Day. **May 5** Anniversary of Battle of Puebla. **Sep 16** Independence Day. **Oct 12** Discovery of America. **Nov 2** All Souls' Day [1]. **Nov 20** Anniversary of the Mexican Revolution of 1910. **Dec 12** Day of Our Lady of Guadalupe [1]. **Dec 24-25** Christmas. **Jan 1 '94** New Year's Day. **Feb 5** Constitution Day. **Mar 21** Birth of Benito Juárez.

Note: (a) **[1]** Not official holidays, but widely celebrated. (b) In addition there are many local holidays. For details, contact the Mexican Tourist Office.

HEALTH

Regulations and requirements may be subject to change at short notice, and you are advised to contact your doctor well in advance of your intended date of departure. Any numbers in the chart refer to the footnotes below.

	Special Precautions?	Certificate Required?
Yellow Fever	No	1
Cholera	Yes	2
Typhoid & Polio	Yes	-
Malaria	3	-
Food & Drink	4	-

[1]: Yellow fever vaccination certificate is required from travellers over six months of age arriving from infected areas.

[2]: An International Certificate of Vaccination against Cholera is required of all travellers arriving within two weeks of having visited an infected area. Cholera is a serious risk in this country and precautions are essential. Up-to-date advice should be sought before deciding wheter these precautions should include vaccination, as medical opinion is divided over its effectiveness. See the *Health* section at the back of the book.

[3]: Malaria risk, predominantly in the benign *vivax* form, exists in rural areas of the following States (in decreasing order of importance): Oaxaca, Chiapas, Guerrero, Campeche, Quintana Roo, Sinaloa, Michoacán, Nayarit, Colima and Tabasco. Foci of the *falciparum* strain exist mainly in Chiapas.

[4]: All water should be regarded as being potentially contaminated. Water used for drinking, brushing teeth or making ice should have first been boiled or otherwise sterilised. Milk is unpasteurised and should be boiled. Powdered or tinned milk is available and is advised, but make sure that it is reconstituted with pure water. Avoid dairy products which are likely to have been made from

unboiled milk. Only eat well-cooked meat and fish, preferably served hot. Pork, salad and mayonnaise may carry increased risk. Vegetables should be cooked and fruit peeled.
Rabies is present. For those at high risk, vaccination before arrival should be considered. If you are bitten abroad seek medical advice without delay. For more information consult the *Health* section at the back of the book.
Health care: Health insurance is recommended. Medical facilities are very good and there are both private and state-organised hospitals, doctors, clinics and chemists. Medicines are often available without prescriptions and pharmacists are permitted to diagnose and treat minor ailments. Due to the high altitude of Mexico City, the visitor may take some time to acclimatise to the atmosphere, particularly since its geographical location results in an accumulation of smog. The levels of pollution in Mexico City are extremely high, and are considered a health threat, so caution should be taken.

TRAVEL - International

AIR: Mexico's national airlines are *Aerovias de Mexico (AM)* and *Mexicana (MX)*.
Approximate flight times: From Mexico City to *London* is 12 hours 20 minutes; to *Los Angeles* is 5 hours 20 minutes; to *New York* is 5 hours; to *Singapore* is 22 hours 45 minutes and to *Sydney* is 19 hours.
International airports: *Mexico City (MEX)* (Benito Juárez) is 15km (8 miles) south of the city. Buses run to the city every 15 minutes from 0600-2200 for a fare of Mex$3 (travel time – 35 minutes). Return is from Camino Real Hotel, Reforma Street from 0600-2200. Metro trains depart to the city every 20 minutes. The airport metro station is 20 minutes walk from the airport terminal. Hotel courtesy coach is available to the Airport Holiday Inn. Taxis are also available for approximately Mex$10 (travel time – 20 minutes). Airport facilities include duty-free facilities (0600-2400), restaurants (0700-2400), 24-hour bank/bureau de change, 24-hour bar, 24-hour snack bar, chemist (0500-2200), 24-hour shops, tourist information (0600-2300), 24-hour left luggage, post office (0800-1900), first aid (with vaccinations for cholera and yellow fever available) and car rental (*Avis, Dollar* and *National*).
Guadalajara (GDL) (Miguel Hidalgo) is 20km (12 miles) southeast of the city (travel time – 30 minutes). Airport facilities include restaurant, bar, snack bar, bank, post office and shops. Coaches depart to the city every 10 minutes (0500-2400). Hotel courtesy coaches are available to Camino Real, El Tapatio, Holiday Inn and Sheraton hotels.
Acapulco (ACA) (General Juan N Alvarez) is 26km (16 miles) southeast of the city (travel time – 30 minutes). Airport facilities include restaurant, bank, post office and car hire. Coaches run to the city. Return is from Las Hamacas Hotel. Taxi services are available to the city, with a surcharge after 2200.
Monterrey (MRY) (General Mariano Escobero) is 24km (15 miles) northeast of the city (travel time – 45 minutes). Airport facilities include restaurant, bar, bank, post office, shops and car hire. Coach and taxi services run to the city.
Departure tax: Airports levy departure taxes of about US$14 for international flights and US$4 for domestic flights.
SEA: The major cruise ports in Mexico are Cozumel, Acapulco, Tampico, Zihuatanejo/Ixtapa, Manzanillo, Puerto Vallarta and Mazatlán. Regular passenger ships run from the USA, South America and Australia. Principal shipping lines are *Polish Ocean Lines, P&O* and *Fred Olsen Lines*.
RAIL: Railway connections with Mexico can be made from any city in the USA or Canada. All trains are provided with pullman sleepers, restaurant cars, lounge observation and club cars. Most trains are air-conditioned.
ROAD: Main points of entry from the USA are Mexicali from San Diego; Nogales from Phoenix/Tucson; El Paso/Ciudad Juárez from Tucson and Alberquerque; Eagle Pass/Piedras Negras from Del Río, San Angelo and El Pas; Laredo/Nuevo Laredo from Houston, San Antonia and Del Río; and Brownsville/Matamoros from Houston and Galveston. From Guatemala there are two main roads into Mexico. The Pan American Highway crosses into Mexico from Guatemala and continues through Central America and South America.
See below for information on **documentation**.

TRAVEL - Internal

AIR: There is an excellent network of daily scheduled services between principal commercial centres operated by *Aerovias de México* and *Mexicana*. Many of these smaller airports will also have capacity for large planes and some international flights. Flights between Mexico City and Guadalajara take about 55 minutes and Mexico City to Monterrey about 75 minutes.
SEA: Steamer ferries operate regularly between Mazatlán and La Paz (Baja California) daily; between Guaymas and Santa Rosalia, across the Gulf of California; between La Paz and Topolobampo three or four times weekly; and from Puerto Vallarta to Cabo San Lucas twice weekly. Some west coast cruises include Pacific ports such as Mazatlán, Puerto Vallarta and Acapulco.
RAIL: Mexico has a good railway network and trains link all the main towns in the country. However, most people travel by bus since it is considerably faster and provides a more extensive service.
ROAD: Mexico's road network extends to almost 235,000km (146,000 miles), of which slightly less than half is paved. A toll is charged for use of the expressways, which are managed by *Caminos y Puentes Federales de Ingresos y Servicios Conexos*. Rest areas at toll sites also provide ambulance and breakdown services. An organisation known as 'Angeles Verdes' (Green Angels) provides breakdown assistance to tourists on the highways free of charge except for petrol, oil and spare parts. **Bus:** Mexico is linked by an excellent and very economical bus system. There are first-class and deluxe coaches as well as ordinary buses. Central bus terminals in major cities provide service and information on fares and schedules. **Car hire:** Self-drive cars are available at airports, city centres and resorts.
Documentation: Foreign driving licence or International Driving Permit accepted. It is suggested that you insure your vehicle; there are some short-term policies available at very reasonable rates in Mexico.
URBAN: There is an excellent and cheap metro system in Mexico City with frequent trains and flat fares. However, it is often crowded and some familiarity with the city is necessary to use it successfully. The metro opens at 0500 Monday to Saturday and 0700 Sunday. There is also a small tramway network, and extensive bus and trolleybus services. The latter system has recently been modernised, and also has a flat fare. There is a state-run bus and trolleybus service in Guadalajara, with trolleybuses running in tunnels, and also extensive private bus services. **Taxis:** Four different types of taxi operate in Mexico City. Yellow and white taxis (usually Volkswagens) are metered, as are orange taxis (*Sitio*), which are available at taxi-

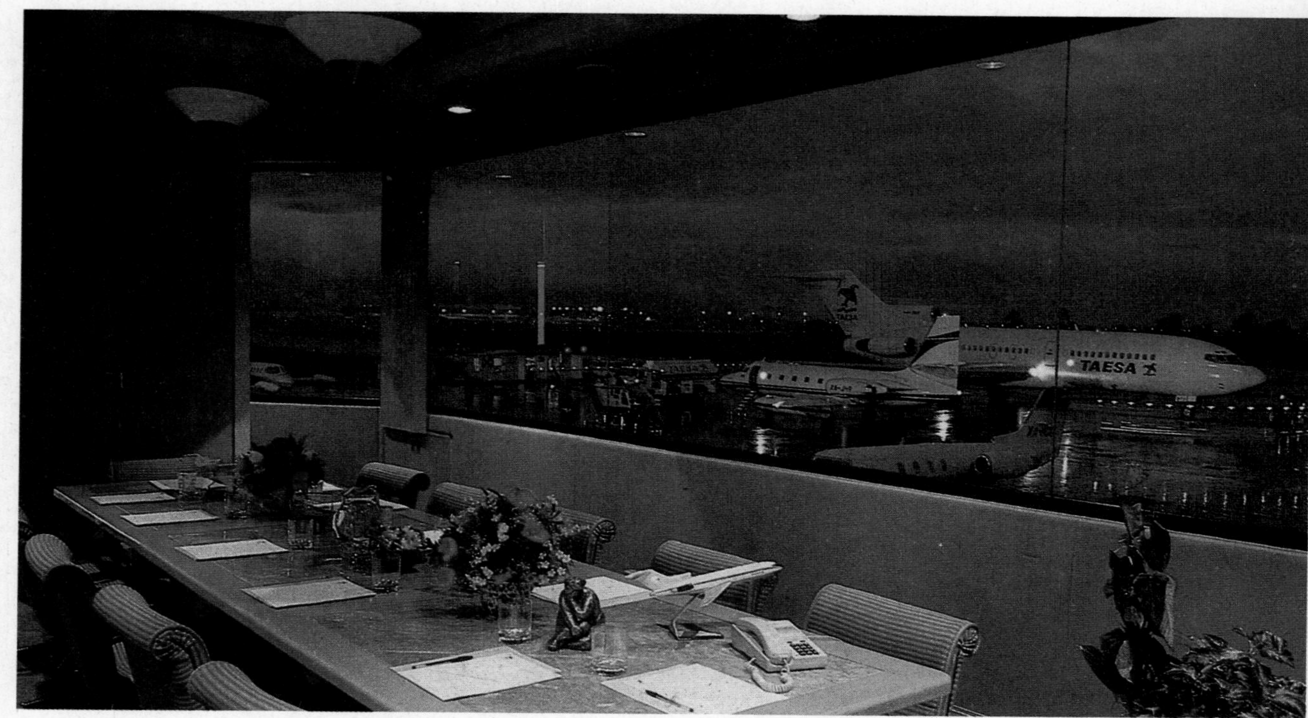

Ing. Carlos Hank Rhon
Chairman of the Board
Cap. Alberto Abed
President
Act. Carlos Rivera
Executive Vice-President Marketing and Corporate Planing
Rafael Montero
Executive Vice-President Charter Division
Cap. Steve Wilson
Executive Vice-President Private Aviation Division
Paul Fisher
Executive Vice-President Sheduled Flight Division
Marco Antonio Baeza
Executive Vice-President Advertising, Promotion and Public Relation
Karla Nagel
Promotion Manager

Head Office and Administration
(525) 2270727
Domestic and Internacional Reservations
(525) 705 61 64
Zone "c" of hangares 27 Aeropuerto Internacional • México City 15620
República Mexicana
Lada sin costo 91-800-70127

New York Sales Office
500 5th Ave. suite 424, New York N.Y. 10110
Tel. (2129 398 1360) Fax: (212) 398 91 69
U.S.A. HAWAII y Puerto Rico
Toll-Free 1 800 32 TAESA

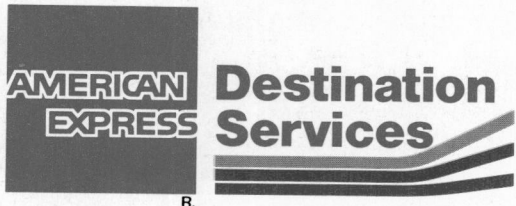

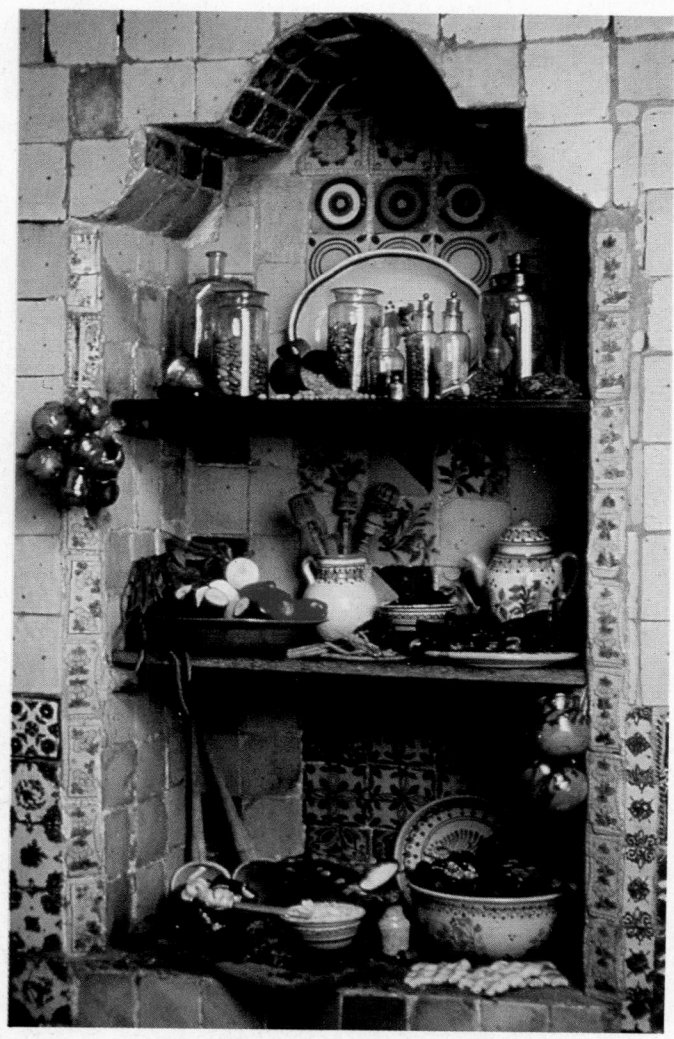

ands. These charge slightly more, and it is advisable agree the fare before starting the journey. *Turismo* xis with English-speaking drivers are available outde main hotels. They are not metered and fares ould be agreed before starting journey. *Peseros* reen and white) are shared taxis travelling on fixed utes, for which fares are charged according to the stance travelled. Tipping is not compulsory for any the taxi services.

JOURNEY TIMES: The following chart gives approximate journey times (in hours and minutes) from Mexico ity to other major cities/towns in Mexico.

	Air	Road	Rail
capulco	0.35	6.00	-
ancún	2.15	30.00	-
axaca	0.15	10.00	12.00
hihuahua	2.15	34.00	40.00
uerto Vallarta	1.55	14.00	-
uadalajara	0.55	9.00	12.00
ijuana	2.45	36.00	-

ACCOMMODATION

HOTELS: The enormous growth of tourism in Mexico reflected in the wide range of hotels from the modrn, elegant and expensive to the clean and modest. here are a variety of chain hotels throughout Mexico s well as 'dude' ranches, thermal spas and resorts that eature specific facilities. Reservations should be conrmed by hotels in writing at the time of booking as otel tariffs are liable to alteration at any time; it is specially important to make reservations when travelng in the high season. There is a wide range of prices vith plenty of choice throughout the country; every otel is required to display officially approved rate chedules, but the visitor should note that most rates o not include meals. There are also a number of more nodest **guest-houses** (*casas de huespedes*). Information an be obtained from the Mexican Hotel and Motel Association, CP 11590, Thiers 83, Colonia Anzures, México DF. Tel: (5) 250 1054 *or* 531 7813. **Grading:** Mexico operates a 5-star grading system similar to that n Europe, with an additional *Gran Turismo* category. All hotels are covered. The criteria for inclusion in ach of the six grades are as follows:

Gran Turismo: 108 prerequisites including central airconditioning, satellite dish and minimum floor area of 32 sq metres (105 sq ft). Shopping area and additional quality services also required.

5-star: 96-101 prerequisites including room service 16 hours a day and minimum floor area of 28 sq metres (92 sq ft). Restaurant, cafeteria, nightclub, commercial areas, good hygiene and security is also required.

4-star: 71-76 prerequisites including adequate furniture and minimum floor area of 25 sq metres (82 sq ft). Some commercial areas and a good standard of maintenance is also required.

3-star: 47-52 prerequisites including adequate furniture and minimum floor area of 21.5 sq metres (71 sq ft). Restaurant, cafeteria, ceiling fan and some complimentary service required.

2-star: 33-37 prerequisites including adequate furniture and minimum floor area of 19 sq metres (62 sq ft). Standards for hygiene and security should be met. First-aid facilities are required.

1-star: 24-27 prerequisites including adequate furniture and minimum floor area of 15 sq metres (49 sq ft). Standards for guests' comfort should be met.

CAMPING: The national parks in Mexico are officially the only areas where no permits or fees are required for camping and hiking. Camping is allowed anywhere within the park areas. Further information can be obtained from the Ministry of Tourism or the National Park Headquarters, Nezahualcoyotl 109, México 1 DF. Tel: (5) 352 8249. Most camping, however, is outside national parks, the most popular regions being the west coast and Baja California. The western Pacific coast has excellent caravan 'hookups' while Baja California is far more informal and isolated. The number of caravan parks along Mexico's major motorways is growing, and there is no difficulty in locating places to park.

RESORTS & EXCURSIONS

Mexico, rich in reminders of ancient civilisations, is also a modern developing nation. Temples and cathedrals contrast with futuristic buildings, motorways and fully equipped beach resorts. Mexico City, one of the world's largest cities, has one of the world's largest universities. Elsewhere, elements of the ancient and colonial cultures persist in aspects of rural life. Fetes and festivals are celebrated with enthusiasm, and the markets in towns and villages are lively and colourful.

Mexico City

The capital of Mexico stands at an altitude of 2240m (7350ft) beneath two snow-capped volcanoes, *Popocatépetl* and *Iztaccíhuatl*. The city features broad avenues, fashionable residential quarters, parks and gardens, palaces, popular street markets and lively squares. Sights include *The Zócalo*, the capital's largest and oldest square; on one side of it stands the *Cathedral*, begun in 1573 and completed in the 19th century. The *National Palace*, built in 1692 on the ruins of the Palace of Montezuma, is now the office of the President of the Republic. *Plaza de las Tres Culturas* celebrates the three major cultures that have shaped Mexico: here are Aztec ruins, a 17th-century Colonial church built in the Baroque style and several fine late 20th-century buildings. The *Basilica of Nuestra Señora De Guadalupe*, a shrine built on a spot where the Virgin is said to have appeared to the Indian Juan Diego in 1531, is a major pilgrimage centre. Built in 1976, it has a capacity of 10,000 inside plus another 25,000 outside when the 70 surrounding portals are opened. *Chapultepec Park* is the site of a castle which houses the *National Museum of History* and the *National Museum of Anthropology*, holding displays of archaeological treasures from every era and all parts of Mexico. The floating gardens of *Xochimilco* and the fashionable street of *Paseo de la Reforma* are also worth a visit. The *Polyforum de Siqueiros*, built to an exciting design by David Alfaro Siqueiros, is a huge exhibition centre with plenty of space for dancing and theatrical performances. The *Ciudad Universitaria*, located in *Pedregal Square*, is another fine example of modern Mexican architecture. The complex includes a stadium with capacity for 100,000 spectators.

DAY EXCURSIONS FROM MEXICO CITY: **Teotihuacan**, the 'City of the Gods', 48km (30 miles) northeast of Mexico City, was built about 2000 years ago. Well worth a visit are the *Pyramids of the Sun and Moon*, the Citadel with the *Temple of Quetzacoatl* (the plumed serpent) and the *Palace of Quetzalpapalotl* (the plumed butterfly), all found in a mile-long stretch called the Avenue of the Dead. **Tula**, 95km (59 miles) north of Mexico City, is the former capital of the Toltec empire. It is renowned for its *Atlantes*, several high columns depicting warriors, and its particularly attractive squares and flower gardens. Other places of interest include the *Palacio de Cortés* and a 16th-century church. **Cuernavaca**, 85km (53 miles) from the capital, is built around two large squares. On one stands the *Palacio de Cortés* (built in 1538), now a museum containing frescoes

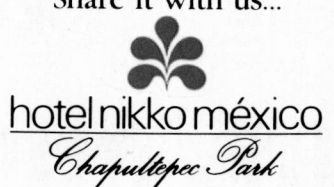

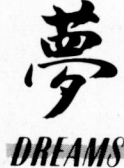

by Diego Rivera. The cathedral dates from the 16th century. The town also contains the 18th-century *Borda Gardens* and the Indian market which sells *huaraches* (sandals) and leather goods. Articles made of straw are sold too. **Xochicalco,** 40km (25 miles) south of Cuernavaca, is one of the country's most interesting ceremonial centres, especially noted for its *Building of the Plumed Serpent.*.

Tepotzotlán, 43km (27 miles) from the capital, is notable for its Churrigueresque Baroque church, the facade of which is decorated with more than 300 sculptures. The convent, dating from the 16th century, has monumental buttresses. On a hill nearby there is an Aztec shrine dedicated to the god of feasting and drinking where annually, on September 8, a fete is held which features Aztec dancing and the performance of an Aztec play. In the town itself, in the third week of December, a different kind of performance takes place. The experiences of Mexican pilgrims en route to Bethlehem are edifyingly enacted in *pastorellas*.

Toluca, 66km (41 miles) from the capital, lies in a valley dominated by the snowcapped *Nevado de Toluca,* an extinct volcano (its two craters are known as the Sun and the Moon). As well as a fine market, the town has two interesting museums, dedicated to archaeology and to folk art. Nearby are the Indian villages of *Tenancingo, Metepec* and *Chiconcuac*. Five miles north of Toluca is *Calixtlahuaca,* an Aztec site of archaeological interest where a circular pyramid is dedicated to the god of wind.

Taxco, 160km (100 miles) from Mexico City, has also been classed as a national monument. The town's fortune was made from the silver mines. The selling of silverware and jewellery is a thriving local trade. As well as numerous interesting narrow cobbled streets, the *Church of Santa Prisca* is a jewel of Baroque architecture, with a *reredos* decorated with gold leaf and a wealth of statues and ornaments. Residences of the colonial period include the *Casa Humboldt, Casa de Borda* and *Casa de Figueroa*. The *Cacahuamilpa Caves* are to the north of Taxco.

Nestling in the foothills of the Sierra Madre is **Puebla.** Capital of the state of the same name, it can be reached by a 96km (60-mile) drive southwest from Mexico City. It is famous for its colonial architecture with glazed tiles, which cover most of the church domes and house walls, and for the skilled craftsmen who produce them. Sights include the *Cathedral* (one of the largest and oldest in Mexico), the *Church of Santo Domingo* and the *Chapel of the Rosary*. The Cathedral has 14 chapels and is built of blue-grey stone, whilst a feature of the Church of Santo Domingo is its goldleaf ornamentation. The *Casa del Alfenique* displays craftware and regional costumes. From Puebla it is possible to see the volcanoes of *Popocatepetl, Ixtaccihuatl* and *Pico de Orizaba*.

Acolman, 39km (24 miles) north of the capital on the road to Teotihuacan, is gathered about a convent founded in the 16th century by an Augustinian order.

Cholula, 124km (77 miles) from Mexico City, is a pre-Hispanic religious centre containing more than 400 shrines and temples; today there are over 350 churches, many built on the ruins of former places of worship. The *Pyramid of Tepanapa* is the largest of all Mexican pyramids; on the top of it stands the *Sanctuary of Nuestra Señora de los Remedios*. The 49 domes of the *Capilla Real* (Royal Chapel) give it the appearance of a mosque. Also worth a visit is *San Francisco Acatepec,* a church 6km (3.5 miles) from Cholula. The town is noted for its fiestas which include Moor and Christian dances on August 15 and Indian dances on September 8, the fete of the *Virgen de los Remedios*.

Ixtapan de la Sal, 80km (50 miles) from Toluca, is a picturesque village with excellent hot springs and spa facilities.

Valle de Bravo, 80km (50 miles) southwest of Toluca is a resort town at an elevation of 1869m (6135ft) set amid pines on a large lake.

Central Mexico and Colonial Cities

The central highlands, benefitting from a milder climate, constitute the most populous region of Mexico. Many of the colonial cities include a unique blend of indigenous and Spanish culture; these historic centres have remained virtually intact since the time of the conquest. The conquistadores built picturesque villages, depicting the old Spain, near the silver mines. Today, the main attractions of this region are the architecture, vast panoramic views, a large variety of handicrafts and exciting regional cuisines.

One of the most popular circuits is the one following the so-called *Independence Route*, starting from Mexico City, going north, towards Querétaro, San Miguel Allende, Guanajuato, Morelia, Patzcuaro and Guadalajara. Another circuit not to be missed starts in Guadalajara, again going north, to Aguascalientes, Zacatecas and San Luis Potosi.

Guadalajara, capital of Jalisco, has a quaint colonial atmosphere, despite being the agricultural, commercial and industrial centre of the western highlands. Horsedrawn carriages may be hired and band concerts are frequently staged in the plazas. The local music is the 'mariachi', so-named because it was often used at weddings. A feature of this music is the distinctive trumpet playing, and the gaudy costumes of the male and female singers. The *Cathedral* has 11 altars, 30 columns and an extensive art collection. There are also many parks: the *Parque Agua Azul* ('Blue Water') is noteworthy for its forest-like atmosphere and variety of entertainments; the *Parque des las Armas* is where the boys and girls of the town flirtatiously serenade each other; and around the Cathedral there are two parks, the *Parque de los Laureles* and the *Parque de la Revolución*. The *Plaza de Rotunda* contains columns and statues in honour of Jalisco's past heroes; the *Plaza Libertad* has a market with a wide range of locally produced goods. During the annual October Festival, horsemanship can be seen at the *charreada* (rodeo) and bullfighting. The famous 'Mexican Hat Dance' originated in this area, locally it is called '*Jarabe Tapati*'.

Guanajuato is on Mexico's famous 'Independence Route', a road 1400m (875 miles) in length, along which can be traced Mexico's historic struggle for independence. The town preserves a genuine colonial charm in places such as *Hidalgo*, an underground street, the *Governor's Palace*, the *Juarez Theatre*, the *University*, the *Basilica of Nuestra Señora de Guanajuato* and the *Valenciana Church*. The parish *Church of Dolores Hidalgo* is of great significance, being the place where in 1810 Father Miguel Hidalgo raised the 'Grito de Dolore', the cry of rebellion against the Spanish when, with 80,000 armed supporters, he commenced the independence struggle.

The aristocrat among the colonial cities is **Morelia,** a city halfway between the capital and Guadalajara. Apart from a few modern buildings, the city retains its atmosphere of the old Spain. The *Plaza de los Martires* forms the centre of the city, flanked on one side by the *Cathedral*, bearing an unusual pink stone façade, with its 200ft high tower. Sights not to be missed include the *College of San Nicolas* (founded 1540), the *Church of Santa Rosa* and the impressive *Aqueduct* built in 1790 to carry water into the city. Between November and February, visitors should go to the *Monarch Butterfly Refuge* near Angangueo, near Morelia. Each year these butterflies migrate from Canada and the USA to a mountain bordering the state of Michoacan in Mexico.

Patzcuaro, situated in the Tarascan Indian country, is

Cholula-Puebla, 'El Sagrario'

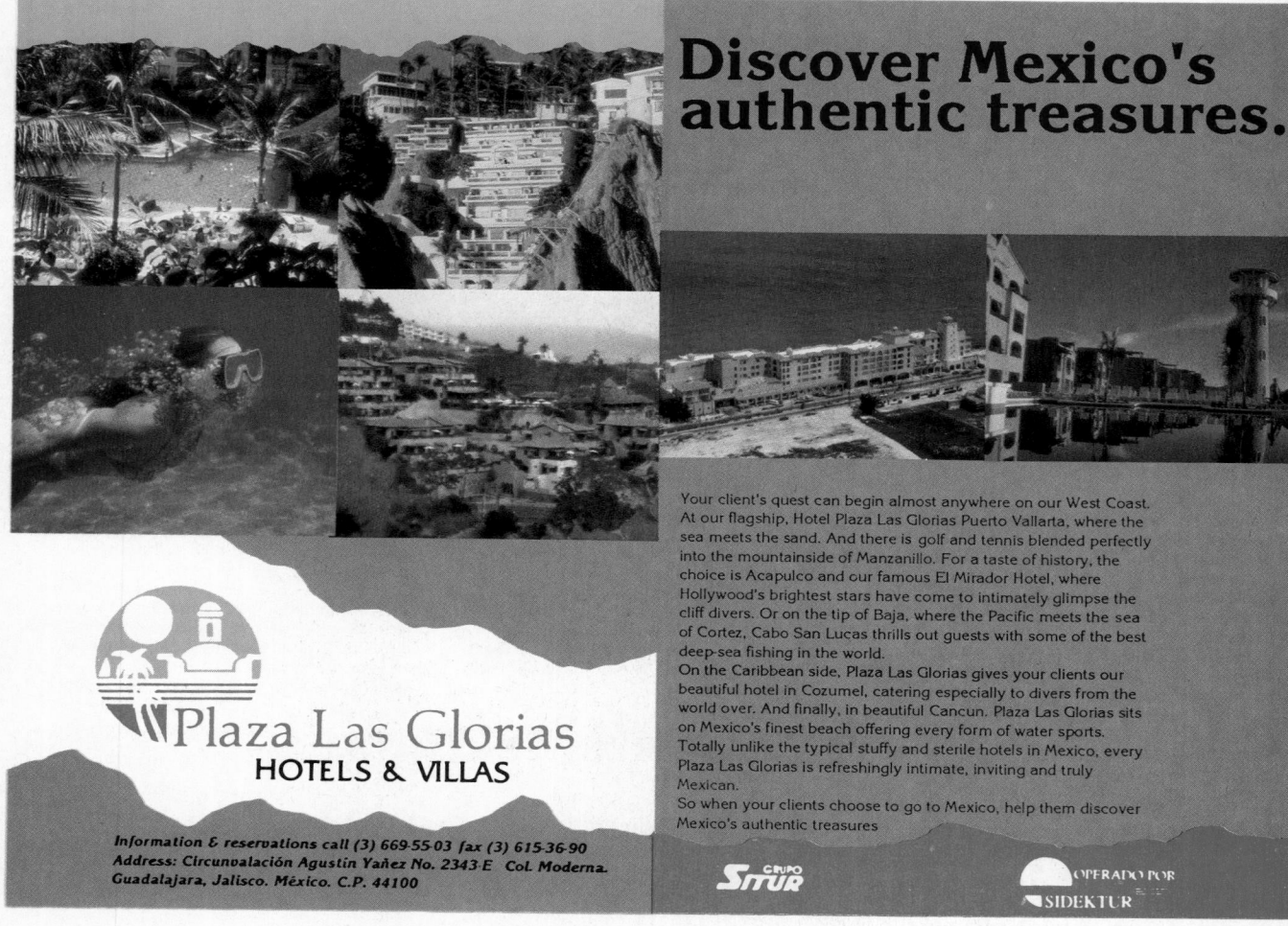

best known for butterfly net fishing for whitefish. Every Friday morning the plaza is covered with numerous market stalls, offering ceramics, woodcarvings, copper and woven goods, laquerware and even furniture for sale. The Day of the Dead on November 2 is celebrated in **Janitzio** as nowhere else in Mexico.

Querétaro is where the Emperor Maximilian was captured, tried and executed and where the present Mexican constitution was drawn up in 1917. A former San Franciscan monastery is now a local museum, whilst the San Agustin monastery has become the *Federal Palace*. The mansion of the Marquis Villa del Aguila, who ordered the building of the town's aqueduct, is in the *Plaza de la Independencia*. The town has excellent hotels and restaurants.

San Miguel de Allende, founded by a Franciscan friar in 1542, is now classed as a national monument. It is a place of narrow, cobbled streets and squares lined with trees. The houses and patios have elegant colonial architecture and the town is a fitting location for the *Allende Institute*, a school of fine arts named after a hero of the revolution whose name was also added to the name of the town. In 1880 the Indian master mason, Ceferino Gutierez, applied the tools of his trade to the architecture of the *Parroquia de San Miguel*. Its Franciscan starkness was transformed into Gothic. The *Casa de los Perros* (House of Dogs) has sculptured dogs on its balcony. The annual *Posadas* at Christmas-time is one of the fiestas for which the town is noted.

Aguascalientes has belonged to the Kingdom of Nueva Galicia since 1535. It was a stopping place for travellers on the silver route during the 18th century. Many of the baroque buildings from this period still remain; the most interesting are the temples of Guadalupe, Encino, San Marcos, San Diego and San José de la Merced; also worth visiting are the government and municipal palaces, the *House of Culture* and *Excedra*, and the Ionian column marking the centre of Mexico.

The state capital of **San Luis Potosi**, 351km (218 miles) northeast of Guadalajara, is the centre of a rich mining and agricultural area. Featured throughout the city are the many colourful, glazed tiles found on churches, plazas and streets, such as the *Church of San Francisco* with its blue-and-white tiled dome and a suspended glass boat in the transept; *Carmen*, at the Plaza Morelos, with a tiled dome and intricate façade and *Iglesia de San Miguelito* in the old part of the city. Other sites include the *Palacio de Gobierno* (1770), housing paintings of former governors, and the colonial treasury, the *Antigua Caja Real* (1767).

Zacatecas was founded by the Spanish in 1546; at that time the nearby silver mines were among the richest in the country. Much of the revenue was sent to Spain, but much remained to finance the fine cathedrals and palaces. The *Convent of Guadalupe* houses one of the largest art collections of the Americas and is also an important place for pilgrimages.

Northern Mexico

The north is mostly desert, a vast, high, windswept plateau flanked by the Occidental and Oriental chains of the *Sierra Madre*. Most of the population is gathered in several large cities and on the coasts; parts of the plateau are used for agriculture, but much of the north bears little trace of man.

Chihuahua, capital of the state of the same name (Mexico's largest), is an important industrial and commercial centre. There are, however, many charming edifices dating from the Colonial era, including the 18th-century *Cathedral*, the *Government Palace*, the *City Hall* and *Quinta Luz*, which is the *Villa Museum* (containing Pancho Villa memorabilia). There is also a monument to the *División del Norte of Doroteo Arango* (Pancho Villa in the unfamiliar guise of his real name). Entertainments include bullfights, dog and horseraces, nightclubs and restaurants.

In the state of Chihuahua, **Ciudad Juárez** has a commercial and cultural centre with modern buildings based on traditional styles of architecture. The handicrafts section includes sarapes (blankets) and glassware, both of which can be seen being made. In the town there are bullfights, and horse and greyhound racing, along with a full nightlife. Restaurants serve international and Mexican cuisine.

The remarkable *Copper Canyon Railway* passes through Chihuahua on its way from Ojinaga on the Rio Grande to the Gulf of California. Admired by engineers for the bravura with which its constructors overcame massive technical problems, it may also be enjoyed by tourists as the best way of seeing the canyons, mesas and bare peaks of the Sierra Madre Occidental. The view at the *Barranca del Cobre*, where the *Urique River* has cut a 3660m- (12,000ft) deep chasm through the mountains, is said to surpass anything the Grand Canyon can offer. The journey lasts about 13 hours.

Monterrey is Mexico's industrial powerhouse, standing beneath the highest peaks of the Sierra Madre Oriental in a setting of great natural beauty. The remnants of Monterrey's more tranquil past (the *Cathedral*, the *Palacio del Gobierno*, the *Obispado*) compete with its present-day pre-occupations.

Tijuana claims to be 'the world's most visited city', receiving more than 20 million visitors every year, many of them day-trippers from California. With San Diego just a few miles away across the border, it is the land gateway to and from the USA, thriving on the sale of souvenirs.

Baja California

Baja California is a peninsula 1100km (700 miles) long that extends south from Tijuana into the Pacific Ocean. It comprises two states, Baja California Norte and Baja California Sur. The enclosed Gulf is rich in marine life and offers excellent opportunities for experienced divers and anglers (although the currents are treacherous). The estuary of the *Colorado River* lies at the top of the Gulf; only a trickle of fresh water now reaches the sea, most having been diverted for agriculture far upstream. The Pacific coast of the peninsula is an important breeding ground for whales. The interior is mountainous desert, for the most part waterless and inhabited by only the hardiest plants and animals.

Cabo San Lucas and **San Jose del Cabo** are the main tourist destinations, offering miles of excellent beaches. At Cabo San Lucas on the tip of the peninsula, 260km (162 miles) from La Paz, seals may often be seen.

Mexicali is the capital of Baja California Norte. It provides a base for those who wish to explore the surrounding mountains and countryside of Rumorosa.

La Paz, the capital of Baja California Sur, is in a bay on the Gulf of California. Watersports and deep-sea angling are well catered for. The beaches of *Las Hamacas*, *Palmeira*, *El Coromuel* and *Puerto Balandra* provide excellent bases for swimmers and skindivers; the waters are calm and clear. Fish and seafood figure prominently on the menus of the local restaurants.

Southern Mexico

The states of **Guerrero, Oaxaca, Chiapas** and **Tabasco** form the junction between North and Central America. Here, where the two Sierra Madre chains merge before continuing south towards the Andes, the deserts give way to highland forests and lowland jungles, and the

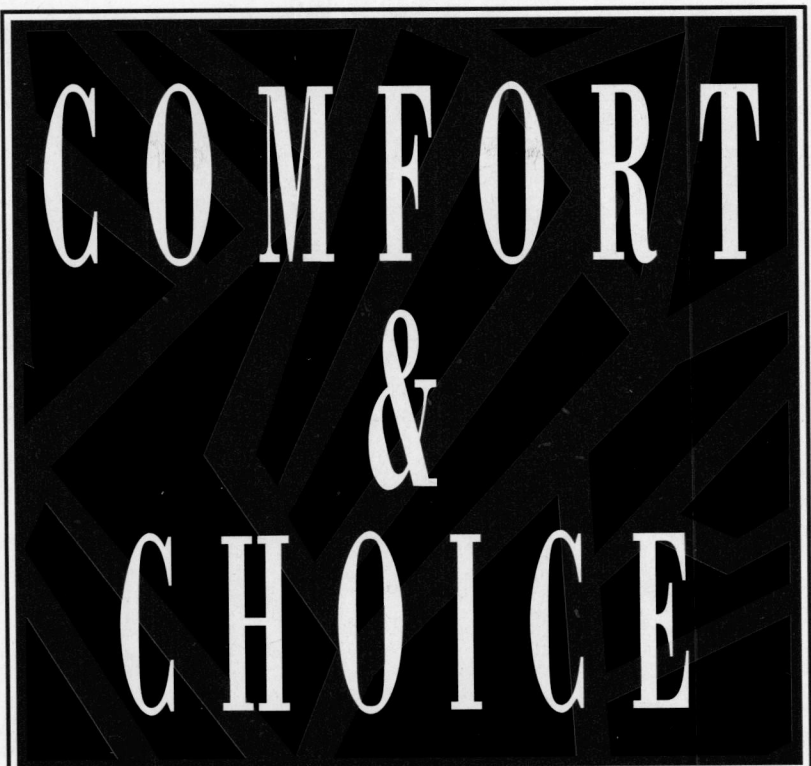

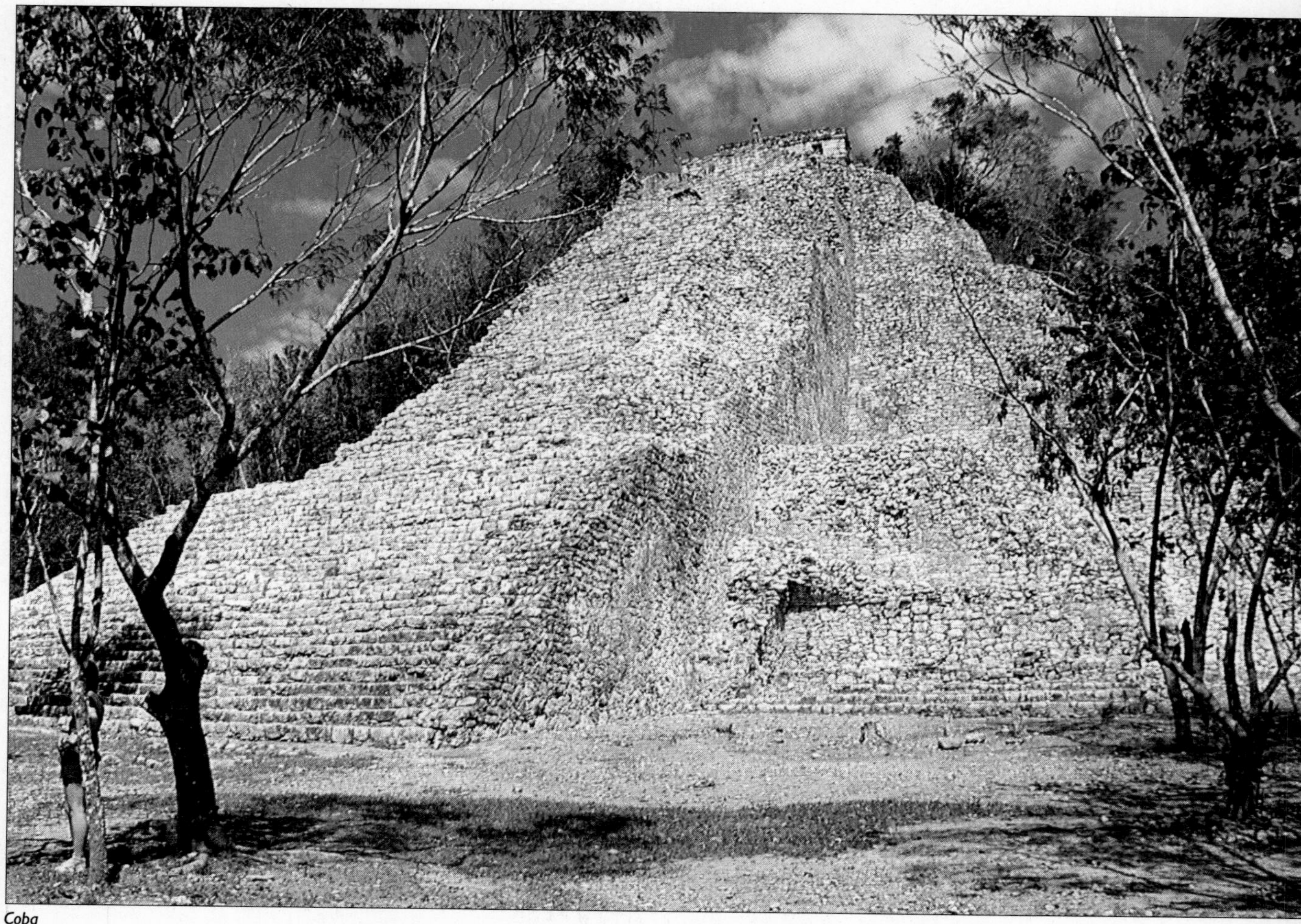

Coba

mean annual temperature is 70°F and more. Acapulco attracts the most visitors (see below), but there is much else to delight the more adventurous tourist. As elsewhere in Mexico, there are many picturesque and charming hilltop towns. There are lagoons on both coasts and many beautiful lakes high up in the mountains.

Oaxaca, or the 'Jade City', features pleasant gardens, an archaeological museum, arcade-fringed squares and several fine churches, including the fortress-like *Santo Domingo* which dates back to the 17th century. The inside of the church is decorated with a profusion of colourful Baroque ornaments, statues and altars. Adjacent to the Santo Domingo is a monastery. In the *Zocalo*, a square with many arcades and cafés, an orchestra gives free concerts twice a week, and there are always street musicians improvising on their marimbas. The cathedral in this square was commenced in the 16th century and completed two centuries later. Hand-woven and hand-embroidered clothing, gold jewellery and shiny black pottery can be purchased at the market on Saturdays. The *Archaeological Museum* has a collection of Zapotec and Mixtec artefacts in gold, jade, silver, turquoise and quartz. In the *Church of la Soledad* there is the statue of the Virgin of la Soledad, patron saint of the town to whom many miracles are ascribed.

Mitla, 45km (28 miles) from Oaxaca, features numerous Mixtec remains, including the *Hall of Columns* and the *Column of Life* which visitors are invited to grasp if they wish to determine how long they will live. The *Frisel Museum* is in Mitla.

Monte Albán, 14km (9 miles) from Oaxaca, was a sacred city in prehistoric times and the religious centre of the Zapotec culture, which flourished 2000 years ago. The remarkable *Central Plaza*, the *Ball Court* and many of the tombs are open to the public. Aldous Huxley wrote that 'Monte Albán is the work of men who knew their architectural business consummately well.' The town covers an area of 38 sq km (15 sq miles). Day trips by bus are available at Oaxaca.

Tuxlta Gutierrez is the state capital of Chiapas and the home of Mexico's famed *Marimba* music. Set in a thriving coffee-growing region, it is a good base to explore the nearby villages where life has changed little since prehispanic times. A short drive away is the impressive **Sumidero Canyon.** Mountain peaks surround the 1829m (6000ft) drop along the 42km (26-mile) rift and are an impressive sight.

San Cristobal de las Casas was founded 1528 by Diego de Mazariegos as the colonial capital of the region. At an altitude of 2195m (7200ft) the 2-hour drive from Tuxlta Gutierrez involves a rapid temperature change. The city itself holds an abundance of interesting architecture, as well as paintings and sculptures of the colonial period. During the year, several festivals are held here, making it an important gathering spot for the indigenous craftsmen. It is also known as a centre for writers, musicians and poets.

The capital of Yucatán State is **Mérida**, the 'White City', founded in 1542 on the site of an ancient Mayan town. Its streets are lined with laurel trees and its parks bursting with colourful flowers. There is much to keep the tourist here, including a fine cathedral, the *Casa de Montejo*, and a museum of archaeology, but above all it is a good base for excursions.

Mayan World

More than 3000 years ago in the diverse landscape of what is now Guatemala, Belize, Western Honduras and part of El Salvador as well as the Mexican states of Yucatán, Quintana Roo, Campeche, Chiapas and Tabasco, emerged a highly sophisticated civilisation, the Mayas.

This variety of landscape was also matched by the abundance of flora and fauna unrivalled anywhere else in the continent. Birdlife, especially, seems to abound, including toucans, parrots and macaws, hummingbirds and others. The lowland rainforest of Chiapos, Campeche and Quintana Roo is home to such exotic wildlife as ocelots, margays, whitetail deer, anteaters, peccaries, tapirs, howler and spider monkeys and jaguars, the largest wildcats in the Americas. The upland cloud-forests are home to the multicoloured guacamayas as well as the resplendent and elusive quetzal, an emerald-coloured bird with trailing feathers once considered sacred by the ancient Mayas. The coast also supports a wealth of birdlife, as well as alligators and manatee, a rare aquatic animal distantly related to the elephant, can be found in the coastal lagoons. The Wildlife Reserve of Contoy Island is the resting and nesting place for hundreds of migrant and resident birds. Even the underwater world can offer a richness of species such as marlin, snapper, grouper, bonito, wahoo, shrimp, lobster, octopus and sailfish, and the beaches are important nesting places for sea turtles during the summer months.

At the height of their development (AD250-900) the Mayans built extraordinary temples and ceremonial centres, many of which are now engulfed within the rainforest. Among the most important archaeological sites to be found in this region are Palenque and Bonampak (Chiapas); La Venta and Comacalco (Tabasco); Edzna, Chicanna and Becan (Campeche); Chichén-Itzá and Uxmal (Yucatán) and Tulum and Coba (Quintana Roo).

Nestled in the foothills at the edge of the Chiapas rainforest lies **Palenque**. This small but important Mayan site is one of the most aesthetically appealing sites of the Mayan world, with its exquisite stucco façades. The *Temple of Inscriptions* (above the crypt of a Maya king), the *Multileveled Palace* and the *Temple of the Count* are not to be missed. It is easily reached in a couple of hours drive from Villahermosa or San Cristobal de las Casas.

The site of **Bonampak**, 150km (90 miles) southeast of Palenque, is famous for the finest Mayan murals ever to be discovered. Housed in the *Temple of Frescoes*, the multicoloured murals depict scenes of Mayan warfare, sacrifice and celebration.

The museum park of **Parque-Museo La Venta** not only boasts one of the few extensive collections of Olmec artefacts, but it is also the only archaeological site ever to be completely transplanted. The original Olmec city of La Venta (15,000BC) was situated on the island of Tonala and featured, among other exceptional sculptures, the colossal human heads that now characterise the Olmec civilisation. Originally evacuated in 1925, it was moved to **Villahermosa** in the 1970s due to the fear that nearby oil drilling would damage the site. The museum park contains 30 Olmec sculptures set in a botanical garden.

About 67km (42 miles) from Villahermosa is **Comacalco**. This archaeological site of the Maya civilisation dates back to the late classic period (AD500-900). Some of the structures resemble those at Palenque though they are still unique in the region. All the buildings here are made from bricks rather than the stone used elsewhere. In fact, Comacalco means 'in the house of bricks'. Sights not to be missed are the *Great Acropolis* with its detailed stucco masks and the small museum.

Edzna, 65km (40 miles) southeast of Campeche, dates back to 300BC. Besides the Chenes-style architecture, visitors can also see an extensive network of canals, reservoirs and waterholes. Attractions include the *Great Acropolis*, the *Small Acropolis*, the *Platform of the Knives*, the *Ball Court*, the *Temple of Stone Masks* and

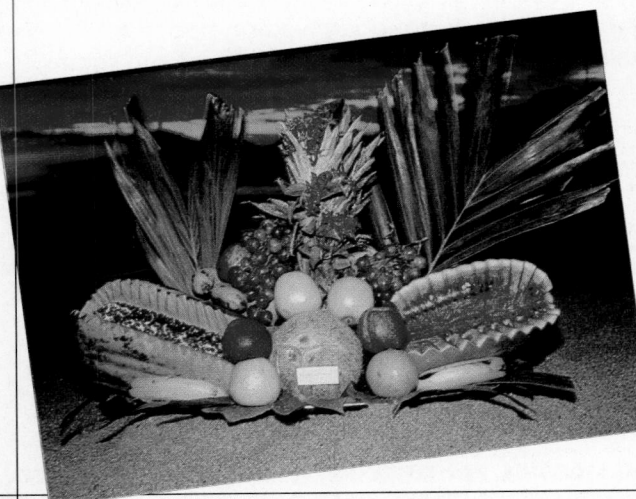

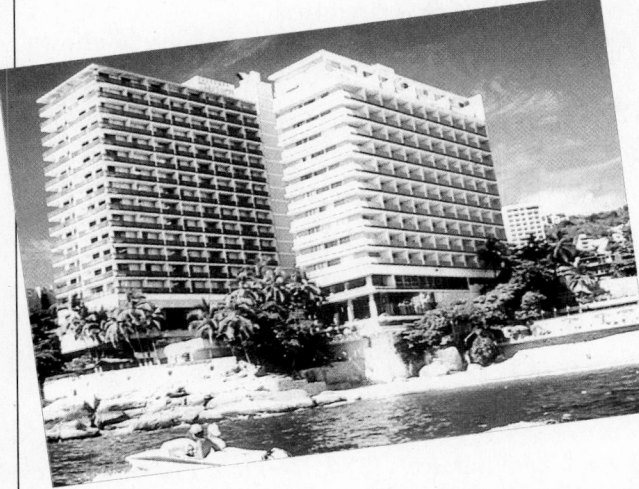

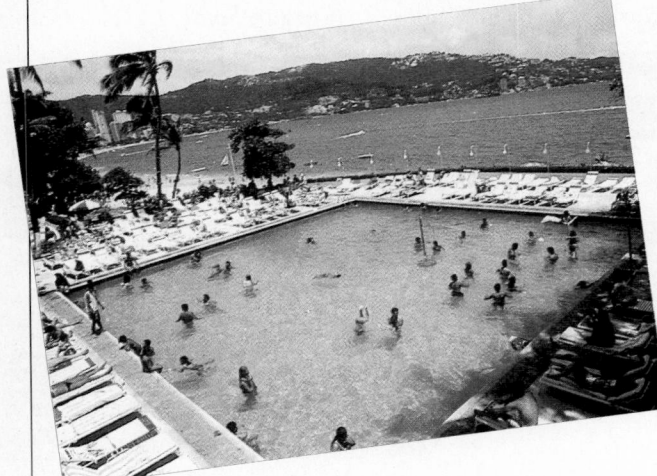

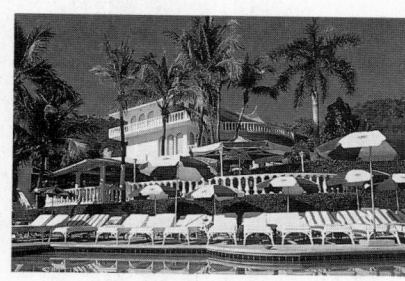

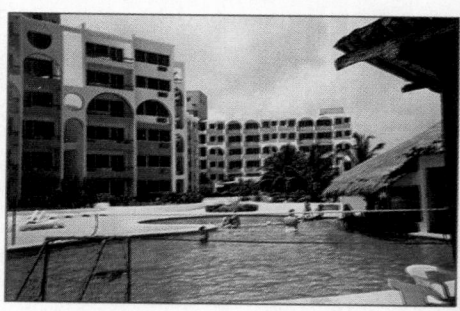

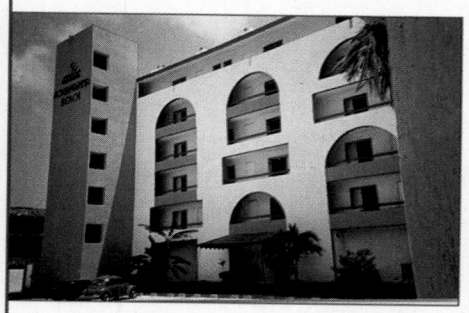

the *Nohochna*.
The famous archaeological and World Heritage site of **Chichén-Itzá**, 120km (75 miles) east of Mérida, contains the *Pyramid of Kukulcan (El Castillo)*, where one can find the 'Red tiger with jade eyes'. During the spring and autumn equinox (March 21-22 and September 21-22), huge crowds gather to see a unique spectacle, when shadows create the illusion of a serpent descending the northern staircase. Of interest are also the snaking columns of the *Temple of the Warriors*, a ball court in perfect condition, *El Caracol* (the observatory), the *Caves of Balankanche* and the *Sacred Cenote* (where bejewelled young girls were thrown into the well as sacrifices to the rain god Chac).
The elaborate stucco work and detailed façades of **Uxmal**, 80km (50 miles) south of Mérida, have led to a comparison of the city with Rome. Among the fine stonework are notably the entwined serpents in the *Nun's Quadrangle*, the *House of Pigeons* and the *Ball Court*. Other attractions include the *Pyramid of the Magician* and the *Governor's Palace*.
The walled fortress of **Tulum**, 131km (78 miles) south of Cancún, has been described as one of the most dramatic sites of the prehispanic world. Perched atop rugged cliffs on the coast, this last outpost of the Mayan civilization commands a breathtaking view of the Caribbean. Settlement here dates from AD900-1500 and sights include the *Temple of the Descending God*, *El Castillo* and the *Temple of the Frescoes*.
Coba, 38km (24 miles) north of Tulum, is possibly the largest archaeological site on the Yucatán peninsula. This town, set among dense jungle and marshlands and including four lakes, dates from the classical period and is believed to have been occupied during the time of the conquest. The most significant groupings of sites are the *Coba Group*, *Las Pinturas*, the *Macanxoc Group*, the *Crossroad Pyramid* and the *Chumuc Mul Group*. It also houses the tallest structure in Yucatán, the *Nohoch Mul Pyramid*.

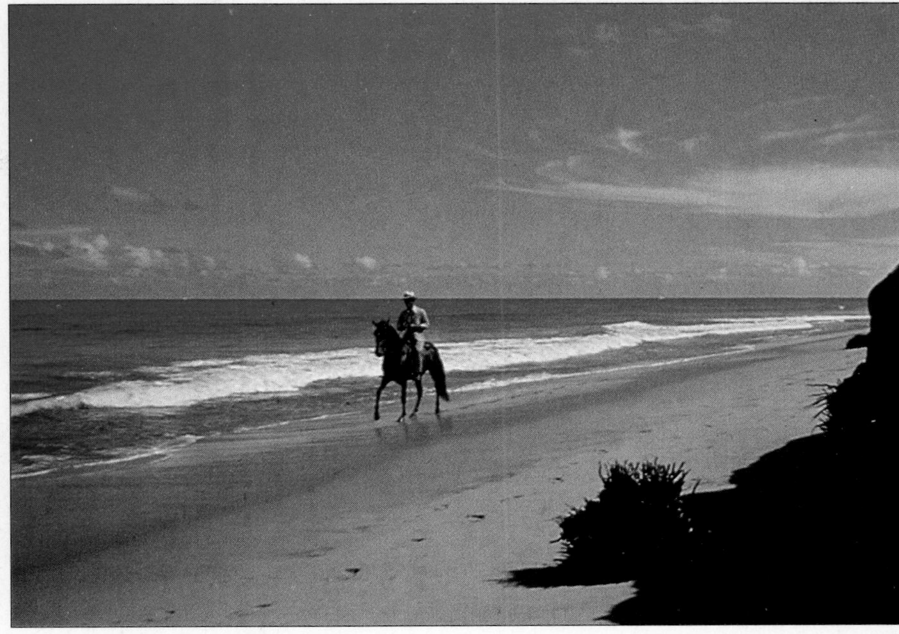

Beach Resorts

PACIFIC COAST: Acapulco, situated on Acapulco Bay, is probably the most famous beach resort in Mexico. The town stretches for over 16km (10 miles) round the bay. It has many beaches as well as numerous top-class hotels. The *malecón* (seaside promenade) runs along the beaches. There is a square in the centre of the old town to the west of the Bay. This lively and fashionable resort offers skindiving, angling, parachute sailing, water-skiing, golf, tennis, riding and the unique spectacle of the Quebrada divers. The waters of the bay are famous for their calmness and safety, though the beach of *La Condesa* has rougher waters and a good surf for those who want it. The two beaches nearest the centre of the town are *Playa Caleta* and *Playa Calatella*; the sun on these is considered to be at its best in the morning. The late afternoon sun is thought to be best on *Playa Hornos*, which is further around the bay to the east. Scuba-diving lessons can be arranged if wanted. Nearby is **Roqueta Island**, visited regularly by glass-bottomed boats from which the underwater image of the Virgin of Guadalupe can be seen. The island itself is popular for family trips.
Fort San Diego, in the middle of the town, is where the last battle of the Mexican War of Independence was fought. Admission is free but it is closed on Thursdays.
Behind the town of Acapulco rise the *Sierra Madre Mountains*, a favourite location for photographers who relish the multi-verdant greenery, the rocky cliffs and the breathtaking views over the bay.
16km (10 miles) away is **Pie de la Costa** which has a lagoon and several large beaches. The surf is risky.
Ixtapa-Zihuatanejo, to the north of Acapulco, is a new resort complex with moorings for yachts and a golf course.
Manzanillo, a major seaport, has recently become an important resort. The emphasis is on watersports, but the spacious beaches afford good swimming. Fishing is of a world-class standard.
Mazatlán, famed as an angling centre, also has numerous beaches and facilities for surfing, skindiving, tennis, golf, riding and shooting. The name of the town means 'Place of the Stag' in the Nahuatl language, an indication of the town's longstanding association with sporting activities. The *malecón*, which runs along the beachfront, is disguised by a variety of names, being named Avenida Camaron in the north and then proceeding through a number of name changes till it becomes Olas Atlas in the south. In the evening strollers promenade along this beachfront among the *arañas* (covered carts), 4-wheeled carriages and 3-wheeled taxis. The *Mirador* is a tower on the *malecón* from which divers give a spectacular display twice a day. 'El Faro' on the promontory of Cerro del Creston is one of the highest lighthouses in the world. There are direct flights from Los Angeles as well as from numerous Mexican cities and a ferry crosses regularly from La Paz in Baja California. The island of *Mexcaltitan* nearby is said to be the original home of the Aztecs.
Puerto Vallarta is the largest town in the immense Bahía de Banderas resort area (1 hour 10 minutes by air from Mexico City). It is situated on the *Bahía de Banderos Bay*, which is the largest natural bay in Mexico. There are a hundred miles of coastline with many sandy beaches and facilities for parasailing, shooting, scuba diving, sailboarding, fishing, golf and tennis. Boat trips provide opportunities to explore the coast. For the visitor who would relish the experience of journeying in a dugout canoe there is the chance to visit **Yelapa**, a Polynesian-style village which cannot be visited in any other way. The mountains behind the bay may be explored on horseback. 'Charreadas', uniquely Mexican rodeos, are held at certain times of the year. Amongst the smaller resorts are **San Blas, Barra de Navidad, Zihuatanejo, Puerto Escondido** and **Puerto Angel**.
CARIBBEAN COAST: Cozumel, Cancún and **Isla Mujeres** are island resorts off the Yucatán Peninsula. Only recently developed for tourism, they offer sun, sand and sea in a wild and beautiful tropical setting. The seafood is particularly good. Giant turtles come ashore to breed on Isla Mujeres.
Veracruz is a lively seaport, with excellent seafood cuisine – the visitor will particularly enjoy carnival time in this easy-going city.

SOCIAL PROFILE

FOOD & DRINK: Self-service (fast food) is available but table-service is usual. Bars have table- and/or counter-service. There are laws relating to minors and licensing on civic holidays. Mexican cuisine is delicious and varied; there are many specialities, such as *turkey mole*, a sauce containing a score of ingredients including several sorts of chilli, tomatoes, peanuts, chocolate, almonds, onions and garlic. Another sauce, *guacamole*, incorporates avocado pears, red peppers, onions and tomatoes, and often accompanies turkey, chicken, with *tortillas* (pancakes made with maize). There are also *enchiladas*, *tacos* (maize pancakes served with pork, chicken, vegetables or cheese and chilli) and *tamales*. Every region of Mexico has its own cuisine. International cuisine is available at most hotels in the larger cities, and at most restaurants. There is a wide variety of exotic fruits such as papayas, mangoes, guavas, *zapotes*, pineapples, *mameyes* and *tunas* (juicy prickly pears, fruit of the cactus). **Drink:** Imported spirits are expensive, local spirits probably give better value for money; the best buys are rum and gin. European aperitifs are produced in Mexico and are of excellent quality; and, of course, there is *tequila* (made from *maguey*, a variety of cactus). It is traditionally drunk neat with a pinch of salt and a bite of lemon, and makes excellent cocktails. Mexico's coffee liqueur, *kahlúa*, is world famous. *Hidalgo*, *Domecq* and *Derrasola* are good Mexican white wines, whilst *Los Reyes* and *Calafia* are excellent reds. All the big supermarkets sell spirits, beer and wine.
NIGHTLIFE: With a range of settings from panoramic restaurants to intimate bars, Mexico City offers excellent music and assorted cuisine, with some of the best bars and restaurants located in hotels. Nightlife is very vibrant and exciting and features a large variety of top name entertainers, international shows, jazz groups, rock groups, traditional Mexican music and dancing, Spanish Flamenco dancers and gypsy violins. Worth seeing is the impressive light show, with accompanying sound show at the archaeological site of Teotihuacan. The history and mythology of this ancient civilization are re-created through a gorgeous display of coloured lights, poetic dialogue and music. The season runs from October to May.
SHOPPING: Good buys include silverware, ceramics and locally made pottery, woven wool blankets *(sarapes)*, brightly coloured scarves in wool or silk *(rebozos)*, richly embroidered charro hats, straw work, blown glass, embossed leather, hard and semi-precious stones, gold and silver jewellery, finely pleated men's shirts in cotton voile *(guayaberas)*, white dresses embroidered with multi-coloured flowers *(huipiles)*, which are sold in the markets, and hammocks. The best shopping is in Mexico City, Cuernavaca, Taxco, San Miguel de Allende, Acapulco, Guadalajara, Oaxaca, Mérida and Campeche. **Shopping hours:** 0900-2000 Monday to Saturday (Mexico City) and 0900-1400 and 1600-2000 Monday to Friday (rest of the country).
SPORTS: Horseriding: Horses and professional guides are available in major towns and resorts. **Tennis:** Almost all major resorts have tennis courts and there are complexes which include luxury accommodation at Cancún on the Caribbean coast and at Manzanillo, Ixtapa and Puerto Vallarta on the Pacific coast. Acapulco, however, remains the tennis capital, with almost perfect weather from October through to June. **Golf:** Although many of Mexico's best golf courses are part of private clubs or resort hotel complexes, some of them allow visitors, particularly in the tourist resorts. **Swimming:** Major city hotels and most hotel resorts have swimming pools and some towns have public baths. Both seaboards have warm waters ideal for bathing and there are many resorts, the most famous of which is Acapulco. **Water-skiing:** Acapulco has particularly good facilities, but other resorts also have equipment for hire, including speed-boats. **Surfing/parasailing:** Surfing can be enjoyed on the pacific breakers and parasailing is another exciting sport. **Scuba diving/snorkelling:** Diving is particularly popular in the clear waters of Cozumel and Cancún, although equipment can be hired in most major coastal resorts. **Sailing/windsurfing:** The Gulf, Caribbean and Pacific coasts and mountain lakes offer excellent sailing. Most resort hotels will rent small sailing boats to guests. Windsurfing has become extremely popular. For further information write to the Mexican Sailing Federation, 13th Floor, Balderas 36, Mexico City. **Fishing:** Mexico's coast offers some of the best deep-sea fishing in the world. Every major port has charter boats and fishing gear for hire and even the smallest fishing village is likely to have at least one fishing boat for hire. Freshwater fishing is also allowed in lakes, lagoons, dams and rivers. Regulations vary according to season. A Mexican fishing permit is obtainable, free of charge, from the local game

or fish warden, the office of the Captain of the Port, or any local office of the Secretary of Commerce. Anglers may request more information from the Secretaria de Pesca, Permisos de Pesca Deportiva, Baja California 252, 06100 México DF. **Spectator sports: Football** is played every Sunday at noon and Thursday night throughout the year at the Aztec Stadium in Mexico City and at other locations throughout the country. The Mexican **baseball** league begins in April and in the capital games can be seen almost daily since there are two home teams. **Jai alai** is a very fast game of Basque *pelota* played with a small ball and straw rackets and can be watched at Fronton courts in Acapulco, Tijuana and Mexico City. **Horseraces** are held four times a week at The Hippodrome de las Americanas in Mexico City and Tijuana (October and September).

SPECIAL EVENTS: Mexicans celebrate more than 120 fetes and festivals in a year, some of them religious, others secular, national or local. Most provide occasion for music, dancing, processions and fireworks. The following is a selection of the major festivals and other special events celebrated annually in Mexico. For a complete list, contact the Mexican Tourist Office.

Apr '93 *International Horse Fair*, Texcoco. **Apr-May** *San Marcos National Fair*, Aquascalientes. **May** *Holy Cross Day* (celebrated by construction workers), nationwide. **Jun** *Corpus Christi* (special events varying regionally), nationwide. **Jul (last two Mondays)** *Guelaguetza* (votive cultural event dating back to pre-Columbian times), Oaxaca. **Aug** *Eve of the Feast of the Assumption of the Virgin Mary* (streets carpeted in designs of flower-petals and coloured sawdust, and a midnight procession), Huamantla (Tlaxcala). **Sep-Oct** *Coronation of the Regional Festivities Queen* (and several other celebrations), San Miguel de Allende (Guanajuato). **Oct** *October Festivals*, Guadalajara. **Dec** *National Silver Fair*, Taxco; *Festival of the Radishes* (local farmers compete to produce the best or biggest radish, others make radish carvings and exhibit them), Oaxaca. **Jan 6 '94** *Feast of the Epiphany* (the 'Three Kings' bring gifts to Mexican children), nationwide. **Feb (third week)** *Mardi Gras*, nationwide. **Mar** *Fair* (in celebration of Benito Juarez's birthday), Gelatao (Oaxaca).

SOCIAL CONVENTIONS: Handshaking is the most common form of greeting. Casual sportswear is acceptable for daytime dress throughout the country. At beach resorts dress is very informal for men and women and nowhere are men expected to wear ties. In Mexico City, however, dress tends to be smart in elegant restaurants and hotel dining rooms. Smoking is unrestricted except where notified. Mexicans regard relationships and friendships as the most important thing in life next to religion and they are not afraid to show their emotions. A large Mexican family always seems to find room for one more and a visitor who becomes friends with a Mexican will invariably be made part of the family. Visitors should always remember that local customs and traditions are important. **Tipping:** Service charges are rarely added to hotel, restaurant or bar bills and many of the staff depend on tips for their livelihood. 15% is expected and 20% if the service has been very good. Airport porterage is charged at the equivalent of US$1 per bag.

BUSINESS PROFILE

ECONOMY: Agriculture is the main economic sector although it is relatively weak in terms of efficiency and productivity. The main crops produced for export are coffee, tomatoes, fruit and vegetables. Although practically anything can be grown in Mexico, only one-sixth of the land is suitable for cultivation. Improving the efficiency of Mexican farming is a high priority for the Government. The source of most of Mexico's wealth in recent years is its considerable oil deposits. Mexico is the world's fourth largest producer of crude oil, and oil products now account for one-third of total export earnings. Other mineral deposits include silver, bismuth, arsenic and antimony and smaller deposits of sulphur, lead, zinc and cadmium. Production has been limited over the years, however, by inadequate investment. The country's oil revenues have for the most part been used to finance a successful industrialisation programme. Car assembly, steel, textiles, food processing and breweries are the main industries, all of which have developed rapidly since the 1960s so that Mexico is now self-sufficient in almost all semi-manufactured goods. The United States dominate Mexico's trade, providing 70% of the country's imports (US$14.5 billion) and taking slightly under 70% (US$18 billion) of its exports. The Mexican economy is expected to receive a powerful boost following the signing of the North American Free Trade Area (NAFTA) agreement with the USA and Canada (subject to ratification by the US Congress). The deal, signed after 14 months of complex negotiations, arose from an initiative by Mexico's President Salinas. Despite the apparent imbalance of bringing together two members of G7 with a Third World economy, the prospects for the new common market, which rivals the EC in population and net output, are almost unanimously thought to be good for all parties, but especially Mexico. Provisional independent forecasts expect NAFTA to generate 600,000 jobs in Mexico and boost US-Mexican trade by US$24 billion by 1995. Japan, Germany and Spain are Mexico's other important trading partners. Britain is the largest foreign investor in Mexico after the USA.

BUSINESS: English is widely spoken in business circles although it is preferable for the visitor to be able to speak Spanish. Letters written in Spanish should be replied to in Spanish. Business wear is formal. Mexicans attach much importance to courtesy and the use of titles. Prior appointments are necessary and if in doubt about a correct title it is advisable to use *licenciado* in place of *señor*. Best months for business visits are January to June and September to November. Avoid the two weeks before and after Christmas and Easter. **Office hours:** Vary considerably; usually 0800-1500 Monday to Friday.

COMMERCIAL INFORMATION: The following organisation can offer advice: Confederacíon de Cámaras Nacionales de Comercio, Servicios y Turismo (CONCANACO), Apartado 113 bis, 2° y 3°, Balderas 144, Centro Cuauhtémoc, 06079 México DF. Tel: (5) 709 1559. Fax: (5) 709 1152. Telex: 1777318.

CONFERENCES/CONVENTIONS: The meetings, conventions, exhibitions and incentives planner's kit issued by the Mexican Ministry of Tourism lists over 70 convention venues in Mexico City, Acapulco, Taxco, Morelia, Puerto Vallarta, Ixtapa, Guadalajara, Mazatlán, Cancún and Mérida. Taxco, Acapulco, Morelia and Cancún have dedicated centres, the largest of which, in Acapulco, can seat up to 8000 people. The national association is the Convention and Visitors' Council, Donato Guerra 25, Esq, Reforma 42, 06048 México DF. Tel: (5) 566 0457 *or* 592 2677, ext 1017. Fax: (5) 592 3403.

HISTORY & GOVERNMENT

HISTORY: Mexico has an ancient and fascinating history. It begins with the Olmec civilisation in around 1500BC, which reached its height about 1200BC. Olmec (meaning 'people from the rubber country') were an advanced culture in religion, architecture and mathematical systems.

The earliest known date was recorded by them in 31BC, according to our present calendars. By AD500, two great cities had emerged, Teotihuacan (with a population of approximately 200,000) and Cholula, a religious centre near Puebla which survived until the Spanish Conquest in 1521. The height of Mayan civilisation was reached between AD600-900. The Toltecs, whose capital was Tula, were the predominant civilisation of this time. Known for their fine architecture, elegant speech and intellectual pursuits, they were the ancestors of the famous Aztecs who were thriving at the time Columbus arrived in the New World in 1492. In 1519, a Spaniard named Hernan Cortés arrived from Cuba with a crew of 550 sailors and explorers and settled just north of today's city of Veracruz. By this time the Aztec empire controlled vast territories from the Yucatán peninsula to the Pacific, with over 370 individual nations under their authority. Ruling from their capital city, Tenochtitlan, the Aztecs demanded heavy tribute from their subjects, which may have caused some to side with Cortés in his attack on the Aztecs. The other factor on Cortés' side was the lucky coincidence that 1519 was the exact year when legend had it that the Aztec god, Quetzalcoatl, had promised his followers he would return – from the east – and so Cortés was mistaken for a god. After two years of fighting and great loss of life on both sides, the Aztecs were defeated under their final ruler, Cuauhtemoc. After being conquered by Spain, Mexico achieved independence after the wars of 1810-21. In 1824 a constitution was adopted and Mexico's first President, Guadalupe Victoria, was inaugurated and both Britain and the USA officially recognised the Republic of Mexico. But stability was short-lived. In 1847, Mexico was forced to cede half of its territory to the USA. In 1861, Benito Juarez, a Zapotec Indian from the state of Oaxaca, was elected President. Faced with overwhelming debts (mainly owed to France, Spain and Britain), Juarez announced a 2-year moratorium on payment of foreign debts. The French Emperor Napoleon III sent an army to Veracruz to enforce his claim to payment. A series of civil wars and conflicts with European governments and the USA punctuated the next 30 years. However, Juarez was elected to a third term and is now considered among Mexico's most popular leaders, having come from a humble background and instituting such welcome changes as a total reform of the education system (making primary school attendance free and obligatory) and completing a railroad from Mexico City to Veracruz. Afterwards, the dictatorship of Porfirio Díaz (between 1876 and 1910) brought an autocratic stability to the Republic. Several revolutions and coups followed before the egalitarian 1917 Constitution was introduced which led to the accession of the Partido Revolucionario Institucional (Institutional Revolutionary Party, PRI), which created an effective one-party state within the framework of an elective democracy, and has managed to hold on to power ever since. The PRI was effectively unchallenged until the mid-1970s, when opposition parties managed to build up strong bases of support. Although they have yet to wrest any more than the odd provincial governorship from PRI hands, electoral occasions are no longer the *faits accomplis* of old. Since the 1960s, Mexico has developed a largely oil-based economy. This resulted from the nationalisation in 1938 of all reserves and all extraction and refining infrastructure owned and operated by British and American oil concerns. The state oil company, PEMEX, is Mexico's largest commercial concern and its employees, the 'petroleros', are considered an industrial elite. Under the government of Lopez Portillo, who was eelcted Presdient in 1976, the country was brought to the verge of bankruptcy by the negotiation of enormous foreign loans, totalling US$80 billion, borrowed against future oil revenues to finance a massive programme of economic and social development. Corruption and mismanagement, coupled with a collapse in the oil price during that period, precipitated a major political crisis in 1982. This was handled by Lopez Portilo's successor, Miguel de la Madrid, who implemented economic reforms and anti-corruption measures, but achieved only limited success in the face of entrenched vested interests. Carlos Salinas de Gortari, who won the next round in 1988, has had more success. This election was significant for the challenge to the PRI by the Frente Democrático Nacional (FDN) led by a disillusioned ex-PRI apparatchik, Cuauhtémoc Cardenas, but the PRI managed to hold on under dubious circumstances; dislike of Cardenas' leftist platform ensured that international complaints were muted. The new government's declared priorities were economic reform and a renegotiation of the foreign debt – by now around US$100 billion. The programme met with widespread opposition, manifested by strikes in the public sector the following year but it was widely praised in Western capitals and dubbed 'Cactus Thatcherism'. The essential features of the programme were: a reduction in public spending; a large devaluation of the Mexican peso (around 20%); a programme of privatisation (although PEMEX is probably immune for the time being); reform of the tax system; and the removal of import controls and tariff reductions. The move towards a liberal trading regime has included Mexico's application to join GATT (the General Agreement on Tariffs and Trade) and the instigation by Salinas of a free-trade treaty with the United States and Canada, creating a North American economic bloc. The details of the North American Free Trade Area were settled between the three governments in August 1992 after 14 months of negotiation. For Mexico, which in principle stands to benefit most from NAFTA, there follows a year or so of tense waiting while the deal is ratified by the US Congress and the Canadian Parliament. The Salinas government has also improved its standing in Washington by cracking down on drug trafficking. Popular as all this may be overseas, Mexicans have seen little benefit as yet. Living standards have fallen sharply under Salinas. The PRI lost a provincial election in Baja California in the northwest for the first time in 50 years: the right-wing Partido Accíon Nacional (PAN, National Action Party) was victorious here. However, congressional elections in August 1991 confirmed the enduring popularity of the PRI which won 60% of the vote and hence an absolute majority in the Chamber of Deputies. Since the collapse of the Communist Party of the Soviet Union, the PRI holds the record for being the longest-serving ruling party in the world: the party has been in office, in one or other manifestation, since 1929.

GOVERNMENT: Mexico is a Federal Republic with 31 states and one Federal District. The bicameral National Congress is elected by universal adult suffrage. The 64 members of the Senate (two per state plus two for the Federal District) serve for a term of six years. The 500-seat Chamber of Deputies consists of members elected for three years, 300 from single member constituencies with the remaining 200 allocated to minority parties on the basis of proportional representation. The President, who appoints a Cabinet, has executive power and serves a term congruent with that of the Senate. Each state has its own Governor and elected Chamber of Deputies.

CLIMATE

Climate varies according to altitude. Coastal areas and lowlands (*terra caliente*) are hot and steamy with high humidity, while the central plateau is temperate even in winter. The climate of the inland highlands is mostly mild, but sharp changes in temperatures occur between day and night. The cold lands (*terra fría*) lie above 2000m (6600ft). Rainfall varies greatly from region to region. Only the Sierra Madre Oriental, the Isthmus of Tehuantepec and the state of Chiapas in the far south receive any appreciable amount of rain during the year, with the wet season running between June and September. All other areas have rainless seasons, while the northern and central areas of the central plateau are dry and arid. There is some snow in the north in winter. The dry season runs from October to May.

Required clothing: Lightweight clothes in summer and mediumweights for winter. Rainwear is advised for the mountains in winter.

ACAPULCO Mexico (3m)

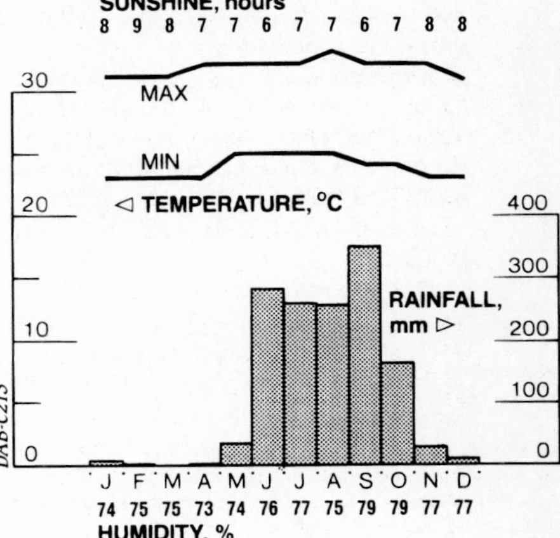

LA PAZ Mexico (18m)

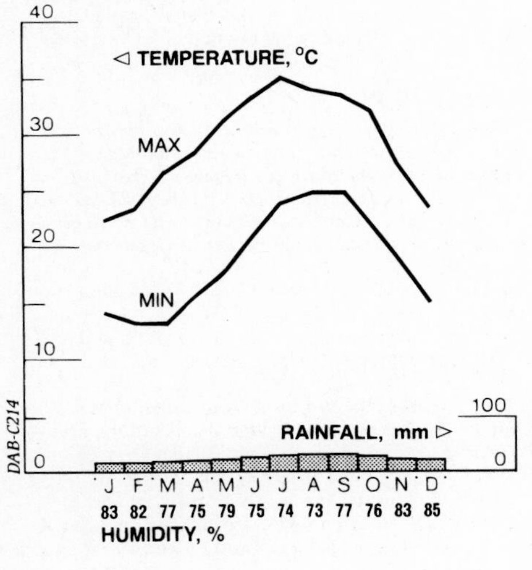

MEXICO CITY (2485m)

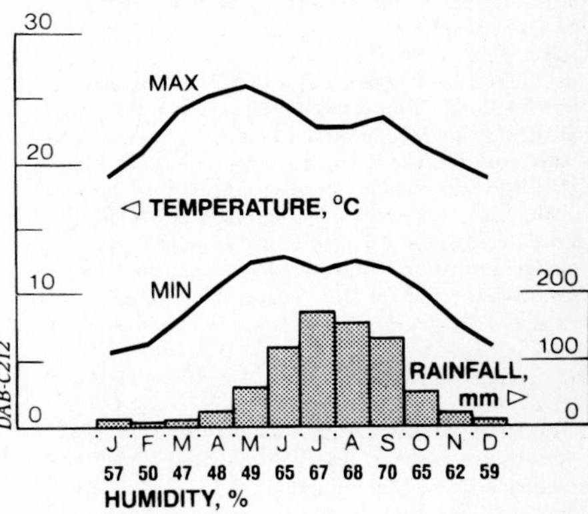

MERIDA Mexico (22m)

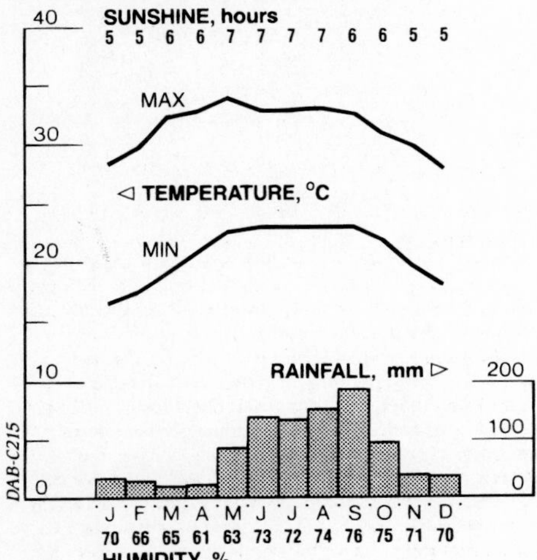

MONTERREY Mexico (534m)

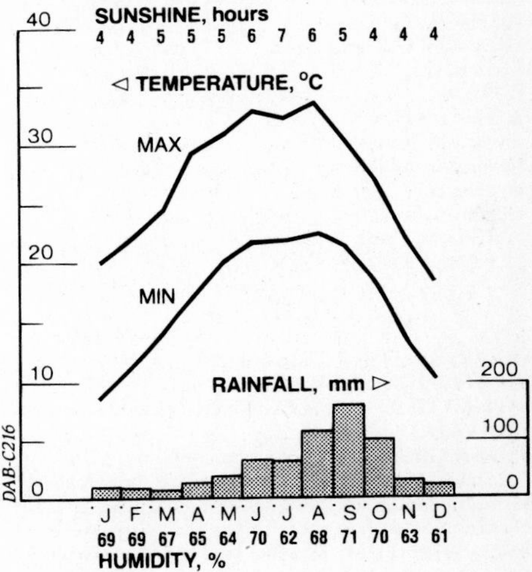

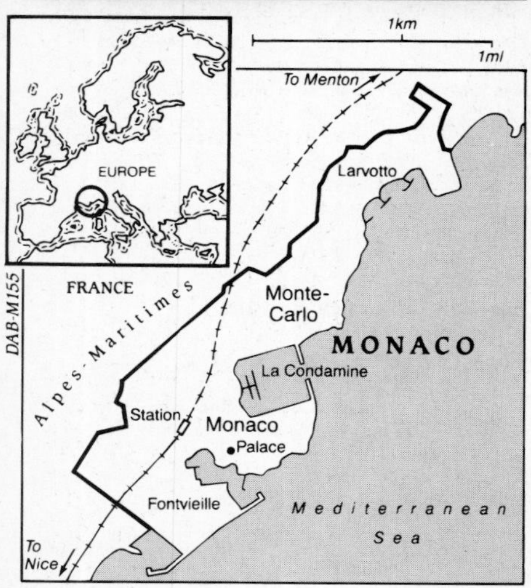

Location: Western Europe.

Direction du Tourisme et des Congrès de la Principauté de Monaco
2A boulevard des Moulins
98030 Monte Carlo, Monaco
Tel: 308 701. Fax: 509 280. Telex: 469760 MC.

Monaco Embassy *and* **Consulate General**
4 Cromwell Place
London SW7 2JE
Tel: (071) 225 2679. Fax: (071) 581 8161. Opening hours: 1000-1230 and 1400-1700 Monday to Friday.

Monaco Government Tourist & Convention Office
3-18 Chelsea Garden Market
Chelsea Harbour
London SW10 0XE
Tel: (071) 352 9962. Fax: (071) 352 2103. Opening hours: 0900-1700 Monday to Friday.

British Consulate General
24 avenue du Prado
13006 Marseille, France
Tel: 91 53 43 32. Fax: 91 37 47 06. Telex: 420307.

Consulate General of the Principality of Monaco *and* **Monaco Government Tourist and Convention Office**
845 Third Avenue
New York, NY
10022
Tel: (212) 759 5227. Fax: (212) 754 9320. Telex: 424253.
Consulates in: Boston, Chicago, Dallas, Delray Beach, Honolulu, Los Angeles, New Orleans, Philadelphia and San Francisco.

Consulate General of the United States of America
12 boulevard Paul Peytral
13286 Marseille Cedex, France
Tel: 91 54 92 00. Fax: 91 55 09 47.

Consulate General of the Principality of Monaco
14th Floor
1800 McGill College Avenue
Montréal, Québec
H3A 3K9
Tel: (514) 849 0589.
Consulate in: Vancouver.

Canadian Consulate
Immeubles Les Ligures
2 Honoré Labande
98000 Monte Carlo, Monaco
Tel: 92 16 14 15.

AREA: 1.95 sq km (0.75 sq mile).
POPULATION: 29,876 (1990).
POPULATION DENSITY: 15,321 per sq km.
CAPITAL: Monaco-Ville.
GEOGRAPHY: Monaco is second only to the Vatican as the smallest independent state in Europe. Set on the Mediterranean coast of France just a few miles from the Italian border, the principality is a constitutional monarchy and relies largely on foreign currency for an economic base. Its principal industry is tourism. The country is a narrow ribbon of coastline backed by the Alpes Maritimes foothills, creating a natural amphitheatre overlooking the sea, with the population centred in four districts. Monaco-Ville is set on a rocky promontory dominating the coast. The Palace is the home of the Grimaldi family, the oldest ruling house in Europe. Monaco-Ville also boasts a fine Romanesque cathedral among its other attractions. La Condamine is the area around the Port, while Monte Carlo is the main centre for business and entertainment. Fontvieille has been set aside as an area for new light industrial and residential development.
LANGUAGE: French. Monégasque (a mixture of French Provençal and Italian Ligurian), English and Italian are also spoken. Native Monégasques make up only a minority of Monaco's population.
RELIGION: Roman Catholic (Monaco has a Catholic Bishop) with Anglican minorities.
TIME: GMT + 1.
ELECTRICITY: 220 volts AC, 50Hz. Round 2-pin plugs are in use.
COMMUNICATIONS: Telephone: Full IDD is available. Country code: 33 93. **Fax:** Some hotels have facilities. **Telex/telegram:** Available at hotels and post offices. Telephones and telegraphic services are open daily 0800-2100 at the main post office (see below). **Post:** Same rates as France. The main post office is at The Scala Palace, Beaumarchais Square. Opening hours: 0800-1900 Monday to Friday and 0800-1200 Saturday. There are special Monégasque stamps. **Press:** The *Journal de Monaco* is published weekly. French newspapers are widely available, as are English books and magazines.
BBC World Service and Voice of America frequencies: From time to time these change. See the section *How to Use this Book* for more information.

BBC:				
MHz	15.07	12.10	7.325	6.195
Voice of America:				
MHz	11.97	9.670	6.040	5.995

PASSPORT/VISA

The passport and visa requirements for persons visiting Monaco are the same as for France. For further details, see the entry for *France* earlier in the *World Travel Guide.*

MONEY

Currency: French Franc. See the entry for *France* for details of exchange rate, currency restrictions, etc.
Credit cards: Access/Mastercard, American Express, Crédit Agricole, Diners Club and Visa are widely accepted. Check with your credit card company for details of merchant acceptability and other services which may be available.
Banking hours: 0900-1200 and 1400-1630 Monday to Friday.

PUBLIC HOLIDAYS

Public holidays observed in Monaco are as follows:
Apr 12 '93 Easter Monday. **May 1** Labour Day. **May 20** Ascension Day. **Jun 31** Whit Monday. **Jun 13** Corpus Christi. **Aug 15** Assumption. **Nov 1** All Saints' Day. **Nov 19** Monaco National Day. **Dec 8** Immaculate Conception. **Dec 25-26** Christmas. **Jan 1 '94** New Year's Day. **Jan 27** Saint-Dévote Day.

HEALTH

Regulations and requirements may be subject to change at short notice, and you are advised to contact your doctor well in advance of your intended date of departure. Any numbers in the chart refer to the footnotes below.

	Special Precautions?	Certificate Required?
Yellow Fever	No	No
Cholera	No	No
Typhoid & Polio	No	-
Malaria	No	-
Food & Drink	1	-

[1]: Mains water is normally chlorinated, and whilst relatively safe may cause mild abdominal upsets. Bottled water is available and is advised for the first few weeks of the stay. Milk is pasteurised and dairy products are safe for consumption. Local meat, poultry, seafood, fruit and vegetables are generally considered safe to eat.
Rabies is present. For those at high risk, vaccination before arrival should be considered. If you are bitten abroad seek medical advice without delay. For more information consult the *Health* section at the back of the book.

Health care: Health insurance is recommended. There are high standards of medical care.

TRAVEL

AIR: There is no airport in Monaco. Helicopter services run by *Héli-Air Monaco* link the principality with the nearest airport, *Nice* (Nice-Cote d'Azur), 22km (14 miles) from Monaco. The journey takes 6 minutes. *Héli-Air* also serves points along the Côte d'Azur and in Italy. Taxis or special buses are available from place d'Armes, place du Casino, Tourist Office, Hotel Mirabeau and Hotel Beach Plaza. For more information contact: Héli-Air Monaco, Monaco Heliport, Quartier de Fontvieille, 98000 Monaco. Tel: 92 05 00 00. Fax: 303 789. Telex: 479343 ELIAIR.
RAIL: An extensive train service runs through the principality to all neighbouring towns, with connections at Marseille onto high-speed *TGV* trains to Paris. There are also daily and overnight through trains. The *SNCF Métrazur* summer service runs every 30 minutes, stopping at all towns on the Côte d'Azur between Cannes and the Italian frontier at Menton, including Monaco. For passenger information, tel: 875 050.
ROAD: Cannes and Nice are 50km (31 miles) and 18km (11 miles) west of Monaco. The French/Italian border and Menton are 12km (7 miles) and 9km (6 miles) east of Monaco. No formalities are required to cross the frontier between France and the Principality of Monaco. **Coach:** There is a direct service connecting Nice airport with Monaco airport. For passenger information, tel: 213 083. **Bus:** There are good connections with the surrounding areas, with the following regular services:
Nice: Seaside route with stops at Cap d'Ail, Eze-sur-Mer, Beaulieu-sur-Mer and Villefranche-sur-Mer. Service from 0600-2100 approximately every 30 minutes. Middle Corniche route with stops at Cap d'Ail, Eze-Village and Col de Villefranche. Services from 0600-1815 (2000 Saturday and Sunday) approximately every hour.
Menton: Seaside route with stops in Roquebrune and Cap-Martin (service from 0530-2100) approximately every 30 minutes.
Service to Saint Roman/Rocher de Monaco, Jardin Exotique/Rocher de Monaco, Gare SNCF/Larvotto Beach and Rocher de Monaco/Parking Touristique Fontvieille. Buses run approximately every five minutes between Monaco-Ville and the Casino, every ten minutes towards St Roman or the Jardin Exotique and between the Railway Station and beaches (Larvotto). **Taxis:** Available from Allée des Bouligrins, Monaco-Monte Carlo Railway Station and avenue Princesse Grace. Surcharge after 2200. **Documentation:** As for France, a national driving licence will suffice.
JOURNEY TIMES: The following chart gives approximate journey times (in hours and minutes) from Monaco to a selection of other cities in Europe.

	Air	Road	Rail	Sea
London	1.45	-	-	-
Paris	1.15	-	-	-
Nice	*0.06	0.45	0.30	0.20
Menton	-	0.35	0.25	-
Geneva	0.50	3.30	4.00	-
Rome	1.00	-	-	-

Note [*]: Time by helicopter – see above under **Air**.

ACCOMMODATION

HOTELS: Some of the most luxurious hotels and conference facilities are centred in Monaco, and all are equipped with extensive modern amenities. In 1989 there were 245,146 overnight visitors in the principality. For further information, please contact The Tourist Office (Direction du Tourisme et des Congrès de la Principauté de Monaco). **Grading:** Hotels in Monaco are graded in a 1-, 2-, 3-, 4- and 4-star deluxe system. The principality has over 20 hotels, one of which is in the 4-star deluxe category and six of which are in the 4-star category.
SELF-CATERING: Apartments are available to let. For further details contact Utoring Diffusion, 44 boulevard d'Italie, Monte Carlo. Tel: 30 30 79.

RESORTS & EXCURSIONS

Monaco forms an enclave into the French Departement of the Alpes Maritimes. The narrow ribbon of coastline is backed by the mountains, which form a natural protective barrier. This area creates a natural amphitheatre. From the heights of the *Tête de Chien* or Mont Agel, or from lower down from the Moyenne-Corniche at the level of the entrance to the *Jardin Exotique,* there are a number of panoramic viewpoints looking out over exceptional scenery. The ancestral Rocher and the promontory of Spélugues bor-

under the harbour where pleasure boats are moored. The rock of Monaco has a medieval air. It is a city of bright, clean streets which converge on the *Prince's Palace Square*, where there are museums, boutiques and restaurants.
Monaco-Ville: *The Prince's Palace*: Changing of the Guard daily at 1155. *The State Apartments in the Prince's Palace*: Open daily 0930-1230 and 1400-1830 July to September. *Palace Museum* (Napoleonic souvenirs and Palace archives): Open daily (except Monday) 0900-1130 and 1400-1730 October to June; 0930-1200 and 1400-1830 July to September. *The Oceanographic Museum and Aquarium*: Open daily 0930-1900 October to May; 0900-1900 June and September; 0900-2100 July to August. *Historial des Princes de Monaco* (Waxworks Museum): Open daily 0900-1800.
Monaco: *Exotic Garden – Grottoes – Museum of Prehistoric Anthropology*: Open daily 0900-1800 October to April; 0900-1900 May to September. *Zoological Gardens*: Open daily 1400-1900 October to June (except Tuesday and Friday); 1000-1200 and 1400-1800 Sundays and official holidays; 1000-1130 and 1330-1815 July to September.
Monte Carlo: *National Museum* – 'Automatons and Dolls of Yesterday' – Sculptures in the Rose-Garden: Open daily 1000-1215 and 1430-1830. *Casino* (minimum age for entrance is 21): Gambling rooms, open daily from 1000. Private gambling rooms, open daily from 1600. *SBM/Loews Casino* (minimum age for entrance is 21): Gambling rooms, open from 1600 Monday to Friday and from 1300 Saturday and Sunday.
Monte Carlo Bord de Mer: Situated next to the Bas-Moulins and Larvotto areas, and until recently sparsely developed. The creation of this new district was made possible by re-routing railway tracks underground. The development has a beach, restaurants, snack bar and shops.
Larvotto, in the East of Monaco, has extensive sporting facilities at the prestigious Monte Carlo Sporting and Sea Clubs where there are restaurants and a double-sized swimming pool.
Note: For a description of the area of France surrounding Monaco, see the *Southeast* section of the entry for *France* earlier in the *World Travel Guide*.

The Casino, Monte Carlo

SOCIAL PROFILE

FOOD & DRINK: Restaurants in Monaco offer a wide choice of food. Service and standards are excellent. Cuisine is similar to France, with some delicious local specialities. There are many restaurants and bars with late opening hours. Specialities include: *barbaguian*, a type of pastry filled with rice and pumpkin; *fougasse*, fragrant orange flower water pastries decorated with nuts, almonds and aniseed; *socca*, chickpea flour pancakes; *stocafi*, dried cod cooked in a tomato sauce.
NIGHTLIFE: The world-famous Monte Carlo Casino is a perennial attraction. The building also houses the Casino Cabaret and the *Salle Garnier*, the delightful gilded Opera House offering a winter season of ballet, opera and music. There are further gambling venues in the Loews Monte Carlo Hotel and the Monte Carlo Sporting Club. There are also numerous nightclubs, cinemas, discotheques and variety shows.
SHOPPING: Monégasque products include perfume, ceramics, clothing, hosiery, shoes, books, jewellery and embroidery. Handcrafted items are sold at Boutique du Rocher, a charity of the late Princess Grace. Monégasque stamps are highly prized by collectors. **Shopping hours:** 0900-1200 and 1500-1700 Monday to Saturday.
SPORT: Golf: The Monte Carlo Golf Club has an undulating course where tournaments are regularly staged. There is also a miniature golf course. **Tennis/squash:** The Monte Carlo Country Club has excellent tennis and squash facilities, and is the venue for international tennis championships which attract big-name tennis stars. **Swimming:** Bathing in the sea is safe (if often crowded), and in addition to hotel swimming pools there are several heated sea water pools open throughout the year. **Sailing:** The Yacht Club de Monaco offers sailing lessons during July and August and the harbour also has facilities. **Watersports:** Monaco has facilities for water-skiing, skindiving, parasailing and windsurfing. **Spectator sports:** In late May the famous *Monaco Grand Prix Formula One* race takes place through the narrow winding streets. In addition to the above, there are also a number of health spas and beauty centres in Monaco.
SPECIAL EVENTS: The following is a selection of festivals and events taking place in Monaco in the period 1993/4. In addition to the following, there are musical events throughout the year. For further information concerning events and festivals please contact the Government Tourist & Convention Office (address at the top of this entry).
Mar 14 '93 *Variety Shows*. **Mar 20** *Le Bal de la Rose*. **Apr 1-4** *Monte Carlo Magical Grand Prix*. **Apr 10-16** *Monte Carlo Spring Arts Festival*. **Apr 17-25** *Monte Carlo International Tennis Championships*. **May 12** *Music Awards*. **May 20-23** *Formula One Grand Prix*. **Jun 9-Jul 1** *International Award of Contemporary Art Exhibition*. **Jun 30-Jul 3** *Open Golf Tournament*. **Jul 31-Aug 15** *International Biennial Exhibition of Antique Dealers, Jewellers and Art Galleries*. **Aug 3-7** *International Fireworks Festival*. **Aug 4-8** *Concerts at the Prince's Palace*. **Aug 6** *Monégasque Red Cross Gala*. **Aug 23-Sep 1** *International Festival of Amateur Theatre*. **Oct 21-23** *Baroque Music Season*. **Nov 18-19** *Monégasque National Holiday*.
SOCIAL CONVENTIONS: Casual wear is acceptable for daytime and dress is the same as for the rest of the French Riviera. Smart restaurants, dining rooms, clubs and the Casino's private rooms require more formal attire. Smoking during meals is frowned upon. Handshaking and, more familiarly, kissing both cheeks, are accepted forms of greeting. **Tipping:** Hotel and restaurant bills generally include a 15% service charge; however, where this is not added it is customary to leave a 15% tip. Taxi drivers are usually tipped 15% of the fare.

BUSINESS PROFILE

ECONOMY: The heart of the economy is banking, insurance and tourism. The financial sector accounts for just over one-third of non-industrial turnover. The property business is also thriving after a downturn early in the 1980s which coincided with the global recession. Construction and light industry – pharmaceuticals, plastics and electronics – are the other important productive sectors. Almost all the principality's external trade is conducted with France. 'Offshore banking' has been hampered by French restrictions on foreign exchange movements, but these should be eased after the introduction of EC regulations at the end of 1992.
BUSINESS: A suit should be worn and prior appointments are necessary. Business meetings are formal. It is considered impolite to begin a conversation in French and then revert to English. **Office hours:** 0900-1200 and 1400-1700 Monday to Friday.
COMMERCIAL INFORMATION: The following organisation can offer advice: Conseil Economique (consultative organisation dealing with all aspects of the national economy), 8 rue Louis Notari, 98000 Monte Carlo. Tel: 302 082.
CONFERENCES/CONVENTIONS: There is a full range of facilities at the Convention Centre and Auditorium (built on land reclaimed from the sea), including technical support and exhibition areas. The

MONACO	HEALTH REGULATIONS	VISA REGULATIONS
GALILEO/WORLDSPAN	 TI-DFT/MCM/HE	 TI-DFT/MCM/VI
SABRE	TIDFT/MCM/HE	 TIDFT/MCM/VI

Code-Link

To access this information on your CRS, swipe the barcode with a light pen or type in the text under the barcode. For more information, see the introduction *How to Use This Book*.

The Oceanographic Museum

International Conference Centre (with a capacity for up to 450 persons) also has support facilities and has recently been refurbished. Six other venues are listed in the Monte Carlo brochure. A new Cultural and Exhibition Centre is planned for 1996. From 1978 to 1989 Monaco hosted over 2500 events, with 389 held in 1989; during this 12-year period the number per annum more than doubled. Further information can be obtained from the Monaco Government Tourist and Convention Authority, 2A boulevard des Moulins, 98030 Monte Carlo. Tel: 308 701 *or* 506 088. Fax: 509 280. Telex: 469760.

HISTORY & GOVERNMENT

HISTORY: The history of Monaco is inseparable from that of the House of Grimaldi. Originally of Genoese extraction, the Grimaldis rose to prominence during the 12th century, when one member of the family became ambassador both to the court of the German Emperor Frederick II (Barbarossa) and to that of his Byzantine counterpart, Manuel Commenus. In the late 13th century, however, with the Holy Roman Empire riven with internal strife, the Grimaldi family were forced to take refuge in Provençe. It was François Grimaldi who in 1297 led a group of partisans into the fortress of Monaco, which has been ruled by the family ever since, the Grimaldis preserving their independence through a mixture of good luck and cunning diplomacy. At various times, they were to be found allied with almost every power in the region, particularly during the Italian Wars in the late 15th and early 16th centuries when Monaco's geographical position left them ideally placed to either help or hinder the repeated and largely unsuccessful attempts by the kings of France to conquer the peninsula. This Machiavellian approach – indeed, Machiavelli himself was in Monaco in the early 16th century to sign a treaty on behalf of Florence – paid dividends in 1612 when Honoré II was granted the title of prince by the French crown. He signed a treaty of friendship with France, and the principality remained independent from that time on, despite a brief interruption during the French Revolution. The family's motto – 'Deo Juvante' (With God's Help) – provides another possible explanation for the survival of this tiny country. The centre of Monte Carlo was created in the latter part of the 19th century, largely at the initiative of Prince Charles III. Monaco became an independent state under French protection in 1861. The first constitution, introduced in 1911, was overhauled in 1962 when legislative authority was vested jointly in the Prince and the elected National Council. At the last election in 1988, all 18 seats on the Council were taken by the National and Democratic Union, perpetuating the monopoly which it secured in both previous polls in 1978 and 1983. The principality's two opposition parties – one liberal, one communist – are all but dormant.

GOVERNMENT: Currently the government of the principality is under the supreme authority of Prince Rainier III, and is exercised by a Minister of State assisted by three Government Councillors. The Monégasque electorate elects the Conseil National and the Conseil Communal.

CLIMATE

Monaco has a mild climate throughout the year, the hottest months being July and August, and the coolest being January and February. Rain mostly falls during the cooler winter months and there is an average of only 60 days' rain per year.

Required clothing: Lightweights are worn, with a warm wrap for cooler summer evenings. Light to mediumweights are advised for winter

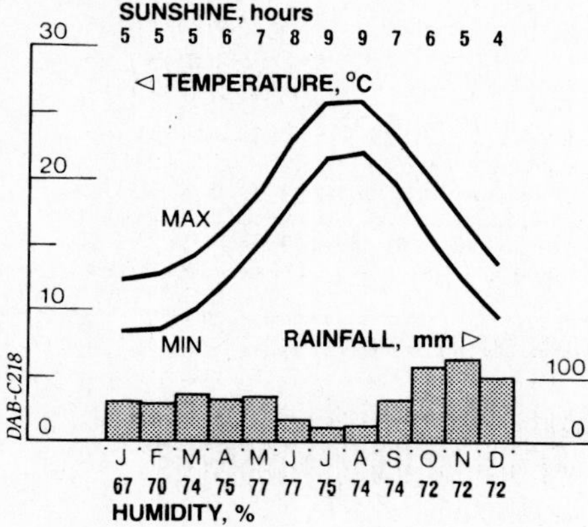

TEMPERATURE CONVERSIONS
-20 -10 0°C 10 20 30 40
0 10 20 30°F40 50 60 70 80 90 100
RAINFALL CONVERSIONS 0mm 200 400 600 800
0in 5 10 15 20 25 30

MONGOLIA

☐ *international airport*

Location: Central Asia.

Mongolian National Tourism Organisation
Ulan Bator
Mongolia
Tel: 20163.

Juulchin Foreign Tourism Corporation
Huv'sgalchdyn Gudamzh
Ulan Bator 11
Mongolia
Tel: 20246. Telex: 232 ZHUUL MH.

Mongolian Embassy
7 Kensington Court
London W8 5DL
Tel: (071) 937 0150. Fax: (071) 937 1117. Telex: 28849.
Opening hours: 1000-1230 Monday to Friday.

British Embassy
PO Box 703
30 Enkh Taivny Gudamzh
Ulan Bator 13
Mongolia
Tel: 51033/4.

Embassy of Mongolia
10201 Iron Gate Road
Potomac, MD 20854
Tel: (301) 983 1962. Fax: (301) 983 2140.
Also deals with enquiries from Canada.

Embassy of the United States of America
Ulan Bator, Mongolia.

Canadian Embassy to Mongolia:
Canadian Embassy
23 Starokonyushenny Pereulok
Moscow 121002
Russian Federation
Tel: (095) 241 1111 *or* 241 5070. Fax: (095) 241 4400.
Telex: 413401 DMCAN SU.

AREA: 1,565,000 sq km (604,250 sq miles).
POPULATION: 2,156,300 (1992).
POPULATION DENSITY: 1.4 per sq km.
CAPITAL: Ulan Bator. **Population:** 575,000 (1991).
GEOGRAPHY: Mongolia has a 3000km (1864-mile) border with the CIS in the north and a 4670km (2901-mile) border with China in the south. From north to south it can be divided into four areas: mountain-forest steppe, mountain steppe and, in the extreme south, semi-desert and desert (the latter being about 3% of the entire territory). The majority of the country has a high elevation, with the principal mountains concentrated in the west. The highest point is peak Nairamdal in the Altai Mountains at 4370m (14,337ft). The lowest point, Lake Khoch Nuur in the east, lies at 560m (1820ft). There are several hundred lakes in the country and numerous rivers, of which the Zabkhan is the longest at 1300km (800 miles).
LANGUAGE: Mongolian Khalkha is the official language. There are also many Mongolian dialects.
RELIGION: Buddhist Lamaism is the main religion. Also Shamanism.

TIME: GMT + 8 (GMT + 9 in summer).
ELECTRICITY: 220 volts AC, 60Hz.
COMMUNICATIONS: Telephone: There are a limited number of telephones. No IDD service is available and international calls must be booked through the international operator. For a Mercury line dial 0109 761. **Fax:** Service began in December 1990. **Telex:** Limited facilities available in Ulan Bator. **Post:** Airmail to Europe takes up to two weeks. There is a DHL service in Ulan Bator. **Press:** There are no English-language papers published in Mongolia. The main newspapers include *Ardyn Erkh, Ardchilal* and *Ug.*
BBC World Service and Voice of America frequencies: From time to time these change. See the section *How to Use this Book* for more information.

BBC:				
MHz	21.72	15.36	11.96	7.180
Voice of America:				
MHz	17.74	11.76	7.275	1.575

PASSPORT/VISA

Regulations and requirements may be subject to change at short notice, and you are advised to contact the appropriate diplomatic or consular authority before finalising travel arrangements. Details of these may be found at the head of this country's entry. Any numbers in the chart refer to the footnotes below.

	Passport Required?	Visa Required?	Return Ticket Required?
Full British	Yes	Yes	Yes
BVP	Not valid	-	-
Australian	Yes	Yes	Yes
Canadian	Yes	Yes	Yes
USA	Yes	Yes	Yes
Other EC	Yes	Yes	Yes
Japanese	Yes	Yes	Yes

PASSPORTS: Valid passport required by all.
British Visitors Passport: Not accepted.
VISAS: Required by all.
Types of visa: Tourist or Business. Visas may be obtained through Juulchin and other travel agencies. A group visa in the name of the tour leader is valid for all tourists on the list attached – providing relevant details (nationality, sex, date of birth, passport numbers, and dates of issue and expiry) are given at the time of application (a group consists of 6-25 persons). Tourist and Business visas cost £14 in the UK. Tourist visas are also required for stopovers.
Validity: Any length of time is considered.
Application to: Travel agencies arranging travel to Mongolia, or from Mongolian Embassies in London, New York, New Delhi, Tokyo, Paris, Geneva, Brussels and Bonn.
Application requirements: (a) Valid passport. (b) 1 photo. (c) Confirmation and approval for the intended visit from Juulchin, the foreign tourism corporation and other agents. (d) A registered, stamped and self-addressed envelope is required for postal applications.
Working days required: 7. However, Transit visas may be obtained in 2 days.
Temporary residence/work permit: Enquire at the Mongolian Embassy.

MONEY

Currency: Tugrik (Tug) = 100 mongos. Notes are in denominations of Tug100, 50, 20, 10, 5, 3 and 1. Coins are in denominations of Tug1, and 50, 20, 15, 10, 5, 2 and 1 mongos.
Currency exchange: Official organisations authorised to exchange foreign currency include commercial banks in Ulan Bator and exchange bureaus at certain hotels.
Credit cards: These are not accepted.
Travellers cheques: Midland Bank and Thomas Cook (UK) travellers cheques are accepted.
Exchange rate indicators: The following figures are included as a guide to the movements of the Tugrik against Sterling and the US Dollar:

Date:	Oct '89	Oct '90	Oct '91	Oct '92
£1.00=	5.31	6.55	72.97	63.26
$1.00=	3.36	3.35	42.40	39.86

Currency restrictions: The import and export of local currency is prohibited. There is no limit on the amount of foreign currency imported but it must be declared. Foreign currency may be exported up to the amount imported and declared.
Banking hours: 1000-1500 Monday ro Friday.

DUTY FREE

The following goods may be imported into Mongolia without incurring customs duty:
A reasonable amount of tobacco;
A reasonable amount of alcoholic beverages;
Goods to the value of Tug50,000.
Prohibited items: Guns, weapons and ammunition without special permission; explosive items; radioactive substances; narcotics; pornographic publications; any publications, records, films and drawings against Mongolia; research materials; paleontological and archeological findings; collections of various plants and their seeds; birds and wild or domestic animals; wool, raw skins, hides and furs without permission from the appropriate authorities.
Note: (a) Every tourist must fill in a customs declaration which should be retained until departure. This allows for the free import and re-export of articles intended for personal use for the duration of stay. (b) Goods to the value of Tug20,000 are allowed to be exported from Mongolia.

PUBLIC HOLIDAYS

Public holidays observed in Mongolia are as follows:
Mar 8 '93 International Women's Day. **Jul 11-13** National Days. **Nov 26** Constitution Day. **Jan 1 '94** New Year. **Feb*** Tsagaan Sar (Mongolian Lunar New Year).
Note [*]: 2-day public holiday; check with the Mongolian National Tourism Organisation for exact dates.

HEALTH

Regulations and requirements may be subject to change at short notice, and you are advised to contact your doctor well in advance of your intended date of departure. Any numbers in the chart refer to the footnotes below.

	Special Precautions?	Certificate Required?
Yellow Fever	No	1
Cholera	No	2
Typhoid & Polio	Yes	-
Malaria	No	-
Food & Drink	3	-

[1]: Yellow fever certificates are required by all travellers except pregnant women and children under nine months.
[2]: A vaccination for cholera is required.
[3]: All water should be regarded as being potentially contaminated. Water used for drinking, brushing teeth or making ice should have first been boiled or otherwise sterilised. Milk is unpasteurised and should be boiled. Powdered or tinned milk is available and is advised, but make sure that it is reconstituted with pure water. Avoid dairy products which are likely to have been made from unboiled milk. Only eat well-cooked meat and fish, preferably served hot. Pork, salad and mayonnaise may carry increased risk. Vegetables should be cooked and fruit peeled.
Rabies is present. For those at high risk, vaccination before arrival should be considered. If you are bitten abroad seek medical advice without delay. For more information consult the *Health* section at the back of the book.
A *smallpox* vaccination is also required.
Vaccination against *Hepatitis* A is also advised.
Health care: There are almost 23,000 hospital beds and more than 5000 doctors. Health insurance is recommended.

TRAVEL - International

AIR: Mongolia's national airline is *Air Mongol (Mongolian Civil Air Transport or MIAT) (OM).*
Approximate flight time: From *London* to Ulan Bator is 14 hours including stopovers.
International airport: *Ulan Bator (ULN)* (Buyant Ukha) is 15km (9 miles) from the city.
RAIL: Ulan Bator is linked to the CIS and China by the *Trans-Mongolian Railway*. An express train runs once a week between Moscow, Ulan Bator and Beijing. Trains on international routes have sleeping and restaurant cars. There are also two other weekly trains from Ulan Bator to Beijing.
ROAD: There are several international road links; the principal route is via Irkutsk (East Siberia) to Ulan Bator.

TRAVEL - Internal

AIR: Internal flights are operated by *Air Mongol*. This is the recommended means of travelling to remote areas.
RAIL: There are 1600km (1000 miles) of track. The main line runs from north to south: Sühbaatar–Darhan–Ulan Bator–Saynshand. Branch lines serve the principal industrial regions.
ROAD: Paved roads are to be found only in or near major cities. **Bus:** There are bus services between towns, but the roads are mostly unpaved. **Car hire:** Available through Juulchin. Jeeps, camels or horses are available for hunters, trekkers and special interest travellers.
JOURNEY TIMES: The following chart gives approximate journey times (in hours and minutes) from Ulan Bator to other major cities/towns in Mongolia.

	Air	Road
Erdenet	3.00	-
Gobi Desert	1.30	-
Gurran Naur	1.30	-
Khujurt	0.45	-
Korum	1.00	-
Terelj		1.00

ACCOMMODATION

HOTELS: There are hotels in most major centres, particularly in Ulan Bator, Erdenet and Darhan. These provide full board, daily excursions and entrance fees to museums and the services of a guide or interpreter. Accommodation can be arranged through the National Tourist Organisation, Juulchin, in Ulan Bator. **Grading:** Deluxe, semi-deluxe, first-class and tourist are the four categories of Mongolian hotels.
RESORT SPAS: There is limited accommodation for visitors. Prices are available on request.
CAMPING: At Terelj there is a tourist camp where the visitor can take the opportunity to live in a Mongolian *yurt*. There is also a country tourist camp at Khujirt which is open from May to October.

RESORTS & EXCURSIONS

The capital **Ulan Bator** is the country's political, commercial and cultural centre. There are many museums in the city, the largest being the *State Central Museum*. The paleontological section has a magnificent display of the skeletons of giant dinosaurs. Others include the *Fine Arts Museum* and

MONGOLIA | **HEALTH REGULATIONS** | **VISA REGULATIONS** | Code-Link

GALILEO/WORLDSPAN

TI-DFT/ULN/HE

TI-DFT/ULN/VI

SABRE

TIDFT/ULN/HE

TIDFT/ULN/VI

To access this information on your CRS, swipe the barcode with a light pen or type in the text under the barcode. For more information, see the introduction *How to Use This Book*.

the *Museum of Revolution*. There are also many Buddhist temple museums and the still-functioning *Gandan Monastery*. Ulan Bator also has several theatres and theatre groups, such as the *State Opera and Ballet Theatre*, the *State Drama Theatre* and the *Folk Song and Dance Ensemble*. The Ulan Bator *State Public Library* has a unique collection of 11th-century Sanskrit manuscripts. Travel outside the capital must usually be by prior arrangement. Every province has its own museums containing examples of local culture. The most popular tour takes the visitor to the **Gobi Desert,** the habitat of several rare animals, including Bactrian wild camels, snow leopards, Przhevalsky horses and Gobi bears. Coaches take parties to country tourist camps, the nearest to Ulan Bator is **Terelj,** 85km (50 miles) from the capital, where the *Gorki Mountains*, the *Tortoise Rock* and *Orkhon's Waterfall* may be seen. **Khangal** is a mountainous region with 40 hot-water springs renowned for their curing properties. Another therapeutic spring can be found in **Khujirt,** site of the ruins of the world-renowned *Kharkhorin*, capital of the Great Mongolian Empire of the 13th century.

SOCIAL PROFILE

FOOD & DRINK: Meat is the basis of the diet, primarily beef and mutton. Fish is also beginning to be widely available. **Drink:** Mongolian vodka is excellent, as is the beer (though expensive). However, hot and cold beverages are included with all meals, with liquors available at an additional cost.
NIGHTLIFE: There are evening performances at the State Opera and Ballet Theatre, State Drama Theatre and Puppet Theatre; the Folk Song and Dance Ensemble and People's Army Song and Dance Ensemble are in the capital. Other major towns also have theatres. Circus entertainment is also very popular.
SHOPPING: In Ulan Bator there are many duty-free shops where convertible currencies are accepted. In all other shops, local currency must be used. The best buys include wines, cashmere garments, camel wool blankets, national costumes, boots, jewellery, carpets, books and records.
SPORT: An increasing number of sports facilities are being developed and most major towns have organised sporting events. Traditional sports include **horseracing, wrestling** and **archery,** which are all ancient and highly skilled contests with complex traditional rules.
SPECIAL EVENTS: 1993 sees the 831th birthday of Genghis Khan and the 72nd anniversary of the People's Revolution in July. For full details of events in 1993/4 contact the Mongolian National Tourism Organisation.
SOCIAL CONVENTIONS: Religious customs should be respected. **Tipping:** Not customary.

BUSINESS PROFILE

ECONOMY: The vast bulk of the working population is engaged in animal herding. Industrial activity is dominated by food, hides and wool processing, and is concentrated around Ulan Bator. Coal mining takes place mostly at the major fields of Darhan and Choibalsan; there are other important mineral deposits of flouspar, tungsten, tin, gold and lead. Textiles and light engineering complete Mongolia's main economic activities. A deterioration in relations with China since the early 1970s led to a downturn in the economy, but in recent years both industrial output and grain production have risen somewhat. The Government is seeking to develop the economy by concentrating on the infrastructure and the introduction of a new metal-working sector. In 1984 some 80% of Mongolia's trade was with the then USSR, and most of the remainder was with other Eastern European countries. From 1990 onwards, in common with its fellow members of COMECON, the Soviet bloc economic and trading union, Mongolia entered a period of major political and economic liberalisation. In particular the Government introduced a crash programme of privatisation which aims to transfer 80% of the economy into private hands through a scheme under which the people are allocated vouchers which they convert into stocks of their choice as enterprises come on to the market. Begun in 1990, 20% of the vouchers had been converted by July 1992 and the Government expects the process to be completed by the end of 1993. The upheaval in the Soviet Union caused great concern in Mongolia: relations with the former superpower have deteriorated seriously and the new government has so far proved unable to reach agreement with Moscow on future trade relations. This has led to severe shortages of raw materials and a consequent decline in output. Industrial production is between 50-80% below 1990 levels; exports were halved in 1991. As for future prospects, the Japanese and other East Asian nations are better placed to exploit any new opportunities. However, remote and impoverished as Mongolia is, it faces an uphill struggle to improve its economic lot.
BUSINESS: Suits are recommended: mediumweight for summer, and heavyweight for winter. Translator services should be arranged prior to departure to Mongolia. **Office hours:** 0900-1800 Monday to Friday and 0900-1500 Saturday.
COMMERCIAL INFORMATION: The following organisation can offer advice: Mongolian Chamber of Commerce and Industry, 336 Huv'sgalchdyn Örgön Chölöö, Ulan Bator 11. Tel: 24620. Telex: 79336.
CONFERENCES/CONVENTIONS: For further information contact The Chamber of Commerce and Industry (for address, see above).

HISTORY & GOVERNMENT

HISTORY: A united Mongolian state was first established in the 13th century under the leadership of Temujin (Genghis Khan). His armies, and those of his successors, devoured Asia and Eastern Europe and threatened to engulf Western Europe as well. In the 17th century the region became the Chinese province of Outer Mongolia. Mongolian independence was achieved, with Russian support, in 1911. China attempted to reassert its rule following the Russian Revolution of 1917 but was beaten back in 1921, with Soviet help. A short-lived restoration of the traditional feudal Buddhist monarchy was followed in 1924 by the declaration of a People's Republic, under the Mongolian People's Revolutionary Party (MPRP). China finally recognised Mongolian independence in 1946. Foreign affairs are dominated by Mongolia's close relationship with the CIS. The USSR's decision, in 1988, to withdraw a significant proportion of the 50,000 troops previously stationed there, greatly eased tension in the region. It also helped to lay the groundwork for the 1989 Sino-Soviet summit and a rapprochement between China and the then USSR. Early in 1990, Mongolia followed its fellow COMECON members, bowing to similar political pressures, when the Communist Party ceded its monopoly of political power and promised multi-party elections within months. Jambyn Batmönh, who had assumed the office of President in 1984 (taking over from Yumjaagiyn Tsedenbal, leader for 30 years) resigned – along with the entire Politburo – to be replaced by Punsalmaagiyn Ochirbat. At the election in July 1990, the MPRP (Communist Party) attained a large majority, with a handful of seats won by opposition candidates from the Mongolian Democratic Party. Dashiyn Byambasüren from the MPRP's reformist wing was appointed to the post of Prime Minister. The Government has committed itself to transforming Mongolia into a market economy, but the government which was managing this delicate process was overcome by the problems in January 1992 and resigned. Its successor, more strongly influenced by non-communist elements, has made slow progress.
GOVERNMENT: From 1925 until 1990, the Mongolian People's Revolutionary Party (Communist Party) was the only legal party, dominating the 430-member legislature (the People's Great Hural) as well as all other aspects of society. In March 1990, the leading role of the Party was erased from the Constitution in preparation for multi-party elections. A new constitution took effect in February 1992 which renders Mongolia a democratic parliamentary state with an independent judiciary and guarantees on basic human rights.

CLIMATE

A cool climate with short, mild summers and long, severe winters (October to April). Some rain falls during summer and there is snow during winter.
Required clothing: Mediumweights are worn during summer, with very warm heavyweights advised for winter.

ULAN BATOR Mongolia (1325m)

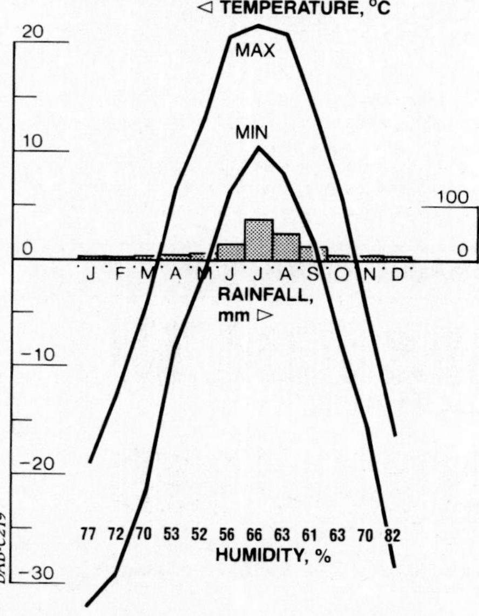

MONTSERRAT

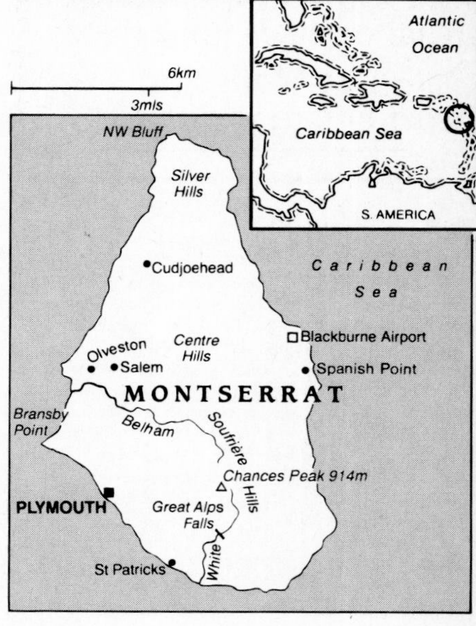

Location: Leeward Islands, Caribbean.

Department of Tourism
PO Box 7
Church Road
Plymouth, Montserrat
Tel: 2230. Fax: 7430.
High Commission for Eastern Carribbean States
10 Kensington Court
London W8 5BL
Tel: (071) 937 9522. Fax: (071) 937 5514.
Windotel (for tourist information)
3 Epirus Road
London SW6 7UJ
Tel: (071) 730 7144. Fax: (071) 938 4793.
Caribbean Tourism Association
20 East 46th Street
New York, NY
10017-2417
Tel: (212) 682 0435. Fax: (212) 697 4258.
High Commission for the Countries of the Organisation of Eastern Caribbean States
Suite 1610, Tower B
112 Kent Street
Place de Ville
Ottawa, Ontario
K1P 5P2
Tel: (613) 236 8952. Fax: (613) 236 3042. Telex: 0534476.
Melaine Communications Group Inc (for tourist information)
33 Niagara Street
Toronto, Ontario
M5V 1C2
Tel: (416) 362 3900/1. Fax: (416) 362 9841.

AREA: 102 sq km (39.5 sq miles).
POPULATION: 11,900 (1987 estimate).
POPULATION DENSITY: 116.7 per sq km.
CAPITAL: Plymouth. **Population:** 1478.
GEOGRAPHY: Montserrat is one of the Leeward Islands group in the Caribbean. It is a volcanic island with black sandy beaches and lush tropical vegetation. There are three main volcanic mountains on the island and Chance's Peak is its highest point at 915m (3002ft). The crater of Galways Soufrière can be reached by road and the more energetic can see the hot springs and high mountain pools. The Great Alps Waterfall is one of the most spectacular sights in the West Indies.
LANGUAGE: English.
RELIGION: Roman Catholic, Anglicans, Methodist and other Christian denominations.
TIME: GMT - 4.
ELECTRICITY: 120/220 volts AC, 60Hz.

COMMUNICATIONS: Telephone: Full IDD is available. Country code: 491. **Fax/telex/telegram:** Cable & Wireless (WI) Ltd runs international links from Plymouth. **Post:** Main post office in Plymouth open 0815-1555 Monday, Tuesday, Thursday and Friday, and 0815-1125 Wednesday and Saturday. **Press:** All newspapers are in English and are published weekly or twice-weekly.

BBC World Service and Voice of America frequencies: From time to time these change. See the section *How to Use this Book* for more information.

BBC:				
MHz	**17.72**	**11.78**	**9.915**	**5.965**
Voice of America:				
MHz	**15.21**	**11.70**	**6.130**	**0.930**

PASSPORT/VISA

Regulations and requirements may be subject to change at short notice, and you are advised to contact the appropriate diplomatic or consular authority before finalising travel arrangements. Details of these may be found at the head of this country's entry. Any numbers in the chart refer to the footnotes below.

	Passport Required?	Visa Required?	Return Ticket Required?
Full British	No/1	No	Yes
BVP	Not valid	-	-
Australian	No/2	No	Yes
Canadian	No/1	No	Yes
USA	No/1	No	Yes
Other EC	No/2	No/3	Yes
Japanese	No/2	No	Yes

PASSPORTS: Valid passports are required by all except:
(a) **[1]** nationals of Canada, the USA and the UK may enter as tourists with a valid national ID card or other form of identity for a maximum stay of 6 months;
(b) **[2]** all other nationals provided they enter as tourists for a maximum stay of 14 days.

British Visitors Passport: Not accepted. Although the immigration authorities of this country may in certain circumstances accept British Visitors Passports for persons arriving for holidays or unpaid business trips of up to 3 months, travellers are reminded that no formal agreement exists to this effect and the situation may, therefore, change at short notice. In addition, UK nationals using a BVP and returning to the UK from a country with which no such formal agreement exists may be subject to delays and interrogation by UK immigration.

VISAS: Required by all except:
(a) nationals of countries mentioned in chart above;
(b) nationals of Commonwealth countries;
(c) **[3]** nationals of EC countries (nationals of Ireland and Portugal *do* require visas if their stay exceeds 14 days and if entering on business);
(d) nationals of Fiji, Iceland, Liechtenstein, Norway, San Marino, Sweden and Tunisia.

Note: Other nationals do not require a passport or visa provided they enter as tourists and continue their journey to a third country within 14 days. This facility does not extend to nationals of Afghanistan, Albania, Angola, Argentina, Bulgaria, China, the CIS, Cuba, Czechoslovakia, Hungary, North Korea, Mongolia, Romania, Syria, Vietnam and Yugoslavia who *do* need a visa and a passport at all times.

Types of visa: Tourist and Transit (cost depends on nationality).

Validity: Depends on nationality.

Application to: Consulate (or Consular Section at High Commission). For addresses, see top of entry.

Application requirements: Enquiries to The Chief Immigration Officer, Government Head Office, Plymouth, Monserrat.

Working days required: Enquire at High Commission.

Note: All passengers must hold a return or onward ticket to a country to which they have a legal right of entry and sufficient funds to cover the period of their stay. Passengers not in possession of a return or onward ticket may be required to leave a deposit on arrival. Passengers not complying with any of the entry regulations listed above may be deported.

Temporary residence: Enquire at High Commission.

MONEY

Currency: East Caribbean Dollar (EC$) = 100 cents. Notes are in denominations of EC$100, 20, 10 and 5. Coins are in denominations of 25, 10, 5, 2 and 1 cents.

Currency exchange: There are three banks in Montserrat.

Credit cards: Visa is widely accepted. Check with your credit card company for details of merchant acceptability and other services which may be available.

Travellers cheques: Accepted in tourist areas and by selected merchants.

Exchange rate indicators: The following figures are included as a guide to the movements of the East Caribbean Dollar against Sterling and the US Dollar:

Date:	**Oct '89**	**Oct '90**	**Oct '91**	**Oct '92**
£1.00=	**4.27**	**5.27**	**4.69**	**4.27**
$1.00=	***2.70**	***2.70**	***2.70**	***2.70**

Note [*]: The Eastern Caribbean Dollar is tied to the US Dollar.

Currency restrictions: There are no restrictions on the import of local or foreign currency if declared. Export of local and foreign currency is limited to the amount imported and declared. Any foreign currency exported is subject to a 1.75% levy.

Banking hours: 0800-1500 Monday, Tuesday and Thursday; 0800-1300 Wednesday; 0800-1700 Friday and 0830-1230 Saturday.

DUTY FREE

The following goods may be imported into Montserrat without incurring customs duty:
*200 cigarettes or 50 cigars;**
*Wines and spirits not exceeding 1.14 litres;**
168g (6oz) of perfume;
Gifts up to value of EC$250.

Note [*]: Tobacco products and alcoholic beverages are only available to passengers 17 years of age or over.

Prohibited items: The importation of all firearms is strictly prohibited.

PUBLIC HOLIDAYS

Public holidays observed in Montserrat are as follows:
Mar 17 '93 St Patrick's Day. **Apr 9** Good Friday. **Apr 12** Easter Monday. **May 3** Labour Day. **May 31** Whit Monday. **Jun 12** Queen's Official Birthday. **Aug 2** August Monday. **Nov 23** Liberation Day. **Dec 25** Christmas Day. **Dec 27** Boxing Day. **Dec 31** Festival Day. **Jan 1 '94** New Year's Day. **Mar 17** St Patrick's Day.

HEALTH

Regulations and requirements may be subject to change at short notice, and you are advised to contact your doctor well in advance of your intended date of departure. Any numbers in the chart refer to the footnotes below.

	Special Precautions?	Certificate Required?
Yellow Fever	No	1
Cholera	2	-
Typhoid & Polio	Yes	-
Malaria	No	-
Food & Drink	3	-

[1]: A yellow fever vaccination certificate is required of travellers over one year of age coming from infected areas.

[2]: Following WHO guidelines issued in 1973, a cholera vaccination certificate is not a condition of entry to Montserrat. However, cholera is a serious risk in this country and precautions are essential. Up-to-date advice should be sought before deciding whether these precautions should include vaccination as medical opinion is divided over its effectiveness. See the *Health* section at the back of the book.

[3]: Mains water is normally chlorinated, and whilst relatively safe may cause mild abdominal upsets. Bottled water is available and is advised for the first few weeks of the stay. Milk is pasteurised and dairy products are safe for consumption. Local meat, poultry, seafood, fruit and vegetables are generally considered safe to eat.

Bilharzia (schistosomiasis) is present. Avoid swimming and paddling in fresh water. Swimming pools which are well-chlorinated and maintained are safe.

Health care: The general hospital has 70 beds and there are eight doctors on the island. There is a Reciprocal Health Agreement with the UK, but it is of a limited nature. On presentation of proof of UK residence, free treatment is available at the general hospital and at state-run clinics to those aged over 65 and under 16. Dental treatment is also free for school-age children. Private health insurance is recommended.

TRAVEL - International

AIR: The nearest international gateway is Antigua.

Approximate flight times: From *London* to Montserrat is 10 hours, including an hour's stopover in Antigua; from *Los Angeles* is 9 hours; from *New York* is 6 hours; and from *Singapore* is 33 hours.

International airport: *Plymouth (PLH)* (Blackburne) is 17km (11 miles) from the city (travel time – 20 minutes). Airport facilities include restaurant, bar and shops. Taxis run to Plymouth (costing about US$11) and resort hotels.

Departure tax: An airport tax of US$6 or equivalent is levied on all international departures. Children under 12 and passengers transiting within 24 hours are exempt.

SEA: *Holland America* runs cruises from Miami to Montserrat.

TRAVEL - Internal

SEA: Charter yachts are available. The main harbour is at Plymouth. A new jetty and port facilities are currently under construction. For visiting craft there is a yacht club and several marinas.

ROAD: There are good road networks to all towns. Montserrat has 185km (115 miles) of well-paved roads, but driving can be difficult for those not used to winding mountain roads. **Bus:** There are many sightseeing buses. Scheduled buses come hourly. **Taxis:** There are fixed rates for standard journeys. Drivers can act as guides and a number of different tours can be arranged. **Car hire:** This is available at the airport, in Plymouth, or via hotel. A car (with or without driver) is often included in the price of accommodation.

Documentation: A valid foreign licence can be used to purchase a temporary licence at either the airport or Plymouth police station.

ACCOMMODATION

HOTELS: These are generally small, with personal service. Rates are more expensive in the winter than in the summer. Some hotels have cottages as well as a selection of rooms. Maid, babysitting and laundry services can be arranged. A 7% Government tax, usually with a 10% service charge, is added to all bills. **Grading:** There are too few hotels for any grading system to be very significant. Hotels in Montserrat, like many others in the Caribbean, offer accommodation according to one of a number of plans:

FAP (Full American Plan): Room with all meals (including afternoon tea, supper etc).

AP (American Plan): Room with three meals.

MAP (Modified American Plan): Breakfast and dinner included with the price of the room plus, in some places,

MONTSERRAT | **HEALTH REGULATIONS** | **VISA REGULATIONS** | Code-Link

GALILEO/WORLDSPAN

TI-DFT/MNI/HE

TI-DFT/MNI/VI

SABRE

TIDFT/MNI/HE

TIDFT/MNI/VI

To access this information on your CRS, swipe the barcode with a light pen or type in the text under the barcode. For more information, see the introduction *How to Use This Book*.

British-style afternoon tea.
CP (Continental Plan): Room and breakfast only.
EP (European Plan): Room only.
SELF-CATERING: Villas and apartments are available throughout the island, bookable direct or through the Montserrat Tourist Board. All accommodation booking must be confirmed with a 20% deposit. A service charge of 10% is added on all accommodation bills.

RESORTS & EXCURSIONS

When Irish settlers arrived in Montserrat during the 17th-18th centuries (from other islands in the Caribbean, from the colony of Virginia and as prisoners of Oliver Cromwell) they nicknamed it *The Emerald Isle* because of the lush green giant ferns and forests climbing the sides of Montserrat's two volcanoes. Place names like *Galway Estates*, *Cork Hill* and *St Patricks* (not to mention *Potato Hill)* still bear witness to the Irish influence. For the purposes of this guide Montserrat has been divided into two regions: The Coast (where most towns and resorts are to be found) and Inland (where the volcanic natural features of the island can be explored).

The Coast

The capital, **Plymouth**, is a small settlement of about 3500 people which still has a very 'British' atmosphere. Places of interest include the *Government House* and the 18th-century Anglican *Church of St Anthony*. 300m (1000ft) above the town is the 18th-century *Old Fort* on St George's Hill. The *Dutchers Studio* in **Olveston** is worth a visit. There are also the *Galways Estates* ruins with artefacts of the old sugar industry, and the *Bransby Point* fortifications with restored cannon. *Rendezvous Bay* contains the only white (coral) sand beach in Montserrat; sand in the other bays is of volcanic origin and may be grey or black. Several bays offer excellent opportunities for snorkelling and a variety of watersports; others are totally undeveloped (though plans for some of them exist, and those who like their scenery untouched should make the most of current opportunities). *Sport* in the *Social Profile* section gives further information about watersports and sports in general.
Montserrat's national bird, the *icterus oberi* (a species of oriole), can be seen at *Woodlands* or *Bamboo Forest* areas.

Inland

The interior of Montserrat has several places of interest, though they are not always easy to get to and a pair of good walking shoes is recommended; however, those energetic enough to trek past sulphurous springs and vents to get to a waterfall (and some warm bathing beneath it), climb mountains and scramble down into dormant volcanoes will be amply rewarded by the scenery en route and the magnificent views. The best view of the island is from the summit of the 900m (3000ft) *Chance Peak;* reaching it involves a stiff 1- to 2-hour climb; there are steps along the way to help the traveller. The small lake at the summit may or may not contain a mermaid, but only those who get there will have any chance of finding out. If she is there, legend says that whoever grabs her comb and makes it down to the sea before being caught by her companion, the diamond serpent (there's always a catch), gets her treasure. Taking children (but not the very young) to some other places is easier, but it is often advisable to take a guide, as paths are not smooth and assistance will be appreciated along some of the rougher stretches.
A quarter of an hour's drive from the capital the route to the *Great Alps Waterfall* commences; after leaving the cars, visitors take a path (following roughly the course of the White River, crossing it a few times) through the underbrush (called 'land of the prickly bush' for a good reason) and into lush green woods where a stream plummets from 20m (70ft) down into a pool.
An expedition into the mouth of *Galways Soufrière* is a must for those fascinated by the sulphurous hubbling and bubbling of a volcano. Those who get to the car park and want to try something else can take a walk to the *Bamboo Forest* (three hours there and back).

SOCIAL PROFILE

FOOD & DRINK: There are restaurants in the main towns, as well as hotel dining rooms. The island specialities are fresh seafood and *mountain chicken* – not actually chicken, but the leg from a local species of large frog (Dominica is the only other island where these frogs can be found). Barbecues are popular and other local dishes include pumpkin soup, goat water, aubergine patties, salt fish, crêpes and dishes made from abundant local fruits. *Dasheen* and other local vegetables are served in most hotels. Waiter service is normal. **Drink:** Most bars serve imported beers, spirits and wines. Rum is the local drink often served in punch or cocktails. The local rum punch liqueur is *Perks Punch*.
NIGHTLIFE: Some hotels arrange live entertainment with local music and dance. Barbecues are very popular. Further information can usually be found in hotels.
SHOPPING: Locally made items include jewellery, needlework, ceramics, glassware and some interesting artefacts made from coconut. Clothing, tablecovers and soft items may be purchased from a government-run boutique. Plymouth really comes alive on market days, with hawkers of tropical produce and handmade items. **Shopping hours:** 0800-1200 and 1300-1600 Monday, Tuesday and Thursday; 0800-1200 Wednesday and Saturday; 0800-1200 and 1300-1700 Friday.
SPORT: Golf: Visitors can play at the 11-hole Belham River Valley course, which is arranged to be playable as two 9-hole golf courses. **Hiking:** A popular destination for hikers is Galways Soufrière. **Swimming:** Most hotels and villas have their own swimming pools. Beaches are of 'black' volcanic sand. East coast beaches are picturesque, but dangerous for swimmers. **Scuba diving/snorkelling:** The surrounding waters are excellent for scuba diving. Equipment may be rented or purchased on the island. Snorkelling equipment is available at the Vue Pointe Hotel. Hotels can arrange professional instruction. **Sailing:** Montserrat has a yacht club. **Tennis:** The Vue Pointe Hotel has tennis courts open to visitors. **Fishing:** Sea-fishing trips can be organised through hotels. **Cricket** is popular and matches are played from February to June.
SPECIAL EVENTS: Carnival celebrations take place at Christmas and up to the New Year. *St Patrick's Day* is particularly celebrated in St Patrick's village. Other events for 1993 include:
Apr 12 '93 *Easter Monday Round the Island Relay Race*. **May 3** *Fishing Tournament*. **Oct** *Mountain Bike Competition*.
SOCIAL CONVENTIONS: Casual clothes are acceptable. Beachwear should be confined to the beach or poolside. The lifestyle is generally peaceful, combining many English influences with West Indian. The people are usually friendly and relaxed. All visitors are made welcome. **Tipping:** Service charge and Government tax is added to restaurant and hotel bills.

BUSINESS PROFILE

ECONOMY: The island's main economic activity is agriculture, which performs well below its potential, though its output is perfectly adequate and reasonably efficient. The main crops are cotton, and fruit and vegetables including peppers and limes. The Government is aiming for eventual self-sufficiency in agricultural produce: the emphasis has been on livestock in recent years which has shown promising development. Tourism is the other important economic sector, contributing about one-quarter of the Gross National Product. There is little industry apart from food processing and textiles whose export performance has improved sharply with improved access to North American markets. 'Offshore' financial services, an increasingly common feature of small Caribbean economies, are expected to grow over the next few years. The Government is hoping that the recent clean-up and introduction of stricter regulations will improve Montserrat's tarnished image. The island's main trading partner is the United States, which takes 90% of Montserrat's exports and provides 30% of imports. The rest of Montserrat's trade takes place with fellow members of CARICOM, the Caribbean trading bloc, and the United Kingdom.
BUSINESS: A short or long-sleeved shirt or safari suit is suitable for most business visits. **Office hours:** 0800-1200 and 1300-1600 Monday to Friday.
COMMERCIAL INFORMATION: The following organisation can offer advice: Montserrat Chamber of Commerce and Industry, PO Box 384, Marine Drive, Plymouth. Tel: 3640. Fax: 4660.
CONFERENCES/CONVENTIONS: Up to 125 persons can be seated at the largest venue, where extra rooms and back-up facilities are available. Contact the Montserrat Tourist Board for further details.

HISTORY & GOVERNMENT

HISTORY: Arawak and Carib Indians were the first residents of Alliouagana, 'land of the prickly bush,' until Christopher Columbus claimed it for Spain in 1493, whereupon he named the island Santa Maria de Montserrat. It was not until 1632 that the British colonised the island, which is still a British dependency. The actual settlers were mainly of Irish Catholic origin, who appreciated the presence of an Atlantic Ocean between them and Oliver Cromwell. Irish surnames among the present population reflect this history. Between 1871 and 1956 the island was administered as part of the Federal Colony of the Leeward Islands. In 1960 the British created a constitution, while retaining executive power in the hands of an Administrator (retitled Governor in 1971). Two parties initially vied for control of the Legislative Council: the Progressive Democrats (PDP), who were in power from 1973-78, and the People's Liberation Movement (PLM), who have been in office ever since, winning the 1978, 1983 and 1987 general elections. The PLM leader, John Osborne, has been Chief Minister since 1978. Since 1987 the pair have been joined by the National Development Party (NDP), formed by PDP dissidents and business interests. Several efforts to forge an alliance between the NDP and the Progressive Democrats strong enough to unseat the PLM have failed. At the most recent election in September 1991, the victor was the newly-formed National Progressive Party, which took four seats; its leader Reuben Meade became Chief Minister. The PLM and the NDP won one seat each and the remaining seat fell to an independent candidate. The dominant political issue on the island is independence. There is not thought to be enough widespread support for it among the population, although Osborne was a long-standing proponent of it. The main argument levelled against it is that Montserrat would be unable to survive economically. Osborne seemed determined to press ahead in the late 1980s, but his plan was scuppered by the massive destruction caused by Hurricane Hugo in 1989. This left the country more dependent than ever on the performance of its financial services sector, which has been under something of a cloud in recent years following a major police investigation (conducted by Scotland Yard detectives) which led to several prosecutions and the de-registration of a number of banks. The independence issue is now apparently in abeyance. A promised referendum for 1990 was postponed; no new date has been set. The banking sector has, meanwhile, undergone an overhaul: legislation approved by the Legislative Council in December 1991 imposed far more stringent controls on the 'offshore' financial sector. In August 1992, Osborne and one of his former ministers, Noel Tuitt, were charged with corruption.
GOVERNMENT: Under the 1960 Constitution, the Governor, who is appointed by the British monarch, is responsible for defence, external affairs and internal security. The Governor is President of the 7-member executive Council. The Legislative Council has 12 members: a Speaker, 2 official members, 2 nominees and 7 elected representatives.

CLIMATE

The climate is subtropical, tempered by trade winds. There is little climatic variation throughout the year. The heaviest rainfall occurs during the summer months; however, the heavy cloudbursts serve to refresh the atmosphere and once they are over the sun reappears.
Required clothing: Tropical lightweights are worn, with light woollens for cooler evenings. A light raincoat or an umbrella is useful.

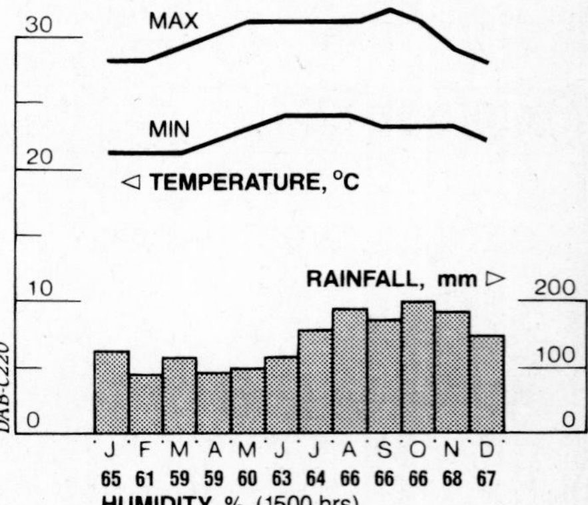

MOROCCO

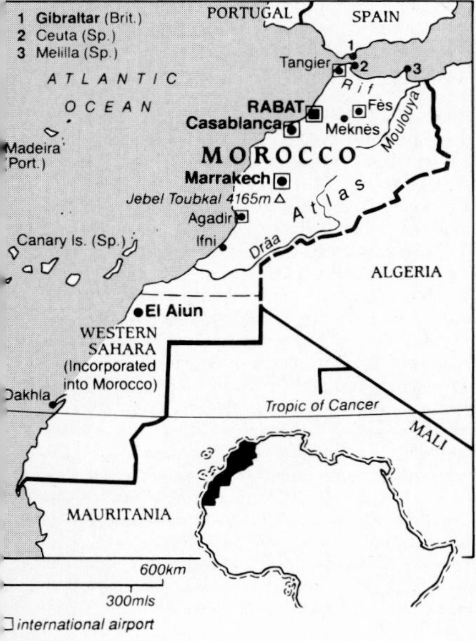

Location: North Africa.

Office National Marocain de Tourisme
Angle avenue Al Abtal
Zankat Oved Fes
Rabat, Morocco
Tel: (7) 775 171. Fax: (7) 777 437. Telex: 31933.

Embassy of the Kingdom of Morocco
49 Queen's Gate Gardens
London SW7 5NE
Tel: (071) 581 5001. Fax: (071) 225 3862. Telex: 28389.
Opening hours: 0930-1700 Monday to Friday.

Moroccan Consulate
Diamond House
97-99 Praed Street
London W2 1NT
Tel: (071) 724 0719. Fax: (071) 225 3862. Opening hours: 1000-1300 Monday to Friday.

Moroccan National Tourist Office
205 Regent Street
London W1R 7DE
Tel: (071) 437 0073/4. Fax: (071) 734 8172. Telex: 262213. Opening hours: 0900-1700 Monday to Friday.

British Embassy
BP 45
17 boulevard de la Tour Hassan
Rabat, Morocco
Tel: (7) 720 905/6 *or* 731 403/4. Fax: (7) 720 906. Telex: 31022.
Consulates in: Casablanca, Tangier and Agadir.

Embassy of the Kingdom of Morocco
1601 21st Street, NW
Washington, DC
20009
Tel: (202) 462 7979-82. Fax: (202) 265 0161. Telex: 248378.

Moroccan National Tourist Office
20 East 46th Street
New York, NY
10017
Tel: (212) 557 2520.

Embassy of the United States of America
BP 003
2 avenue de Marrakech
Rabat, Morocco
Tel: (7) 762 265. Fax: (7) 765 661. Telex: 31005 M.
Consulate in: Casablanca.

Embassy of the Kingdom of Morocco
38 Range Road
Ottawa, Ontario
K1N 8J4
Tel: (613) 236 7391/2. Fax: (613) 236 6164.
Consulates in: Montréal and Vancouver.

Moroccan National Tourist Office
Suite 1460
2001 rue Université
Montréal, Québec
H3A 2A6
Tel: (514) 842 8111/2. Fax: (514) 842 5316.

Canadian Embassy
CP 709
13 bis, rue Jaafar As-Sadik
Rabat-Agdal, Morocco
Tel: (7) 772 880. Fax: (7) 772 887. Telex: 31964.

AREA: 710,850 sq km (274,461 sq miles). This includes the disputed territory of the Western Sahara, which covers 252,120 sq km (97,344 sq miles).
POPULATION: 25,208,000 (1990).
POPULATION DENSITY: 35.5 per sq km (excluding Western Sahara).
CAPITAL: Rabat. **Population:** 1,472,000 (1990).
GEOGRAPHY: Morocco is located on the westernmost tip of North Africa, bordering Algeria to the east,

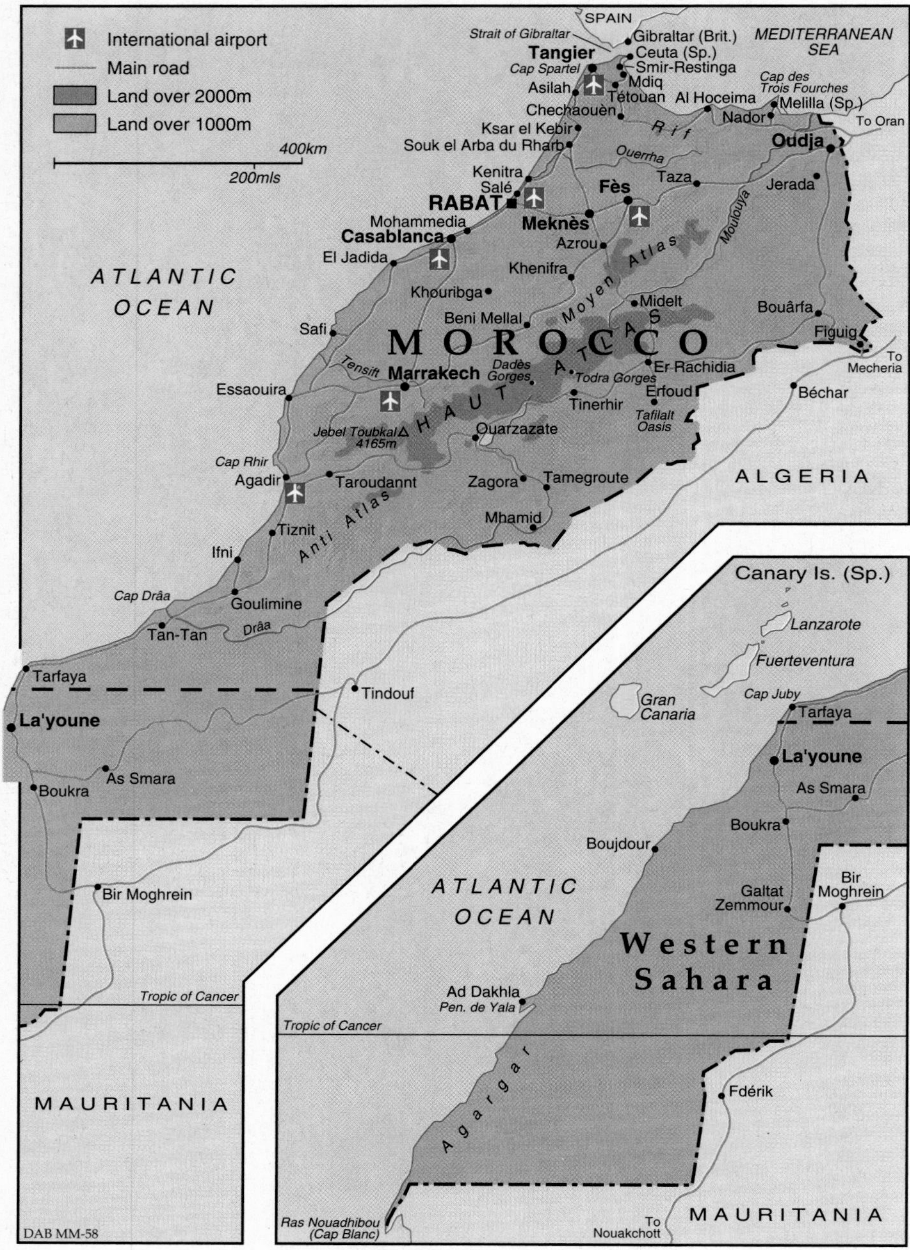

Mauritania to the southeast and the disputed territory of the Western Sahara (Sahrawi Arab Democratic Republic) to the south. Running through the middle of the country is the Atlas mountain range, which leads to the fertile plains and sandy beaches of the Atlantic coast. The Middle Atlas range sweeps up from the south, rising to over 3000m (9850ft), covered with woodlands of pine, oak and cedar, open pastureland and small lakes. The Rif Mountains run along the north coast. The ports of Ceuta (Sebta) and Melilla on the north coast are administered by Spain.

LANGUAGE: The official language is Arabic, but some Berber is spoken. French is widely spoken throughout the country, except in the northern regions where Spanish is more predominant. English is also understood, particularly in the North and around Agadir.

RELIGION: Predominantly Muslim with Jewish and Christian minorities. Morocco's population and culture stems from a cross section of origins, including Berbers, Arabs, Moors and Jews.

TIME: GMT (GMT + 1 in summer).

ELECTRICITY: 110-127 volts AC, 50Hz is most common, but 220 volts is standard for new installations.

COMMUNICATIONS: Telephone: IDD is available. Country code: 212. **Fax:** This is available in major hotels. **Telex/telegram:** There are telex facilities available in most of Morocco's major hotels. Telegram facilities are available throughout the country at main post offices. **Post:** Airmail to Europe takes up to one week and can be unreliable. **Press:** Daily newspapers are published in French and Arabic. The main publications are *Le Matin*, *L'Opinion* and *Al Alam*.

BBC World Service and Voice of America frequencies: From time to time these change. See the section *How to Use this Book* for more information.

BBC:				
MHz	21.71	15.07	12.10	9.410
Voice of America:				
MHz	11.97	9.670	6.040	5.995

PASSPORT/VISA

Regulations and requirements may be subject to change at short notice, and you are advised to contact the appropriate diplomatic or consular authority before finalising travel arrangements. Details of these may be found at the head of this country's entry. Any numbers in the chart refer to the footnotes below.

	Passport Required?	Visa Required?	Return Ticket Required?
Full British	Yes	No	Yes
BVP	Not valid	-	-
Australian	Yes	No	Yes
Canadian	Yes	No	Yes
USA	Yes	No	Yes
Other EC	Yes	1	Yes
Japanese	Yes	No	Yes

Restricted entry: Israeli passport holders are prohibited from entering Morocco. This also applies to people of untidy appearance who do not comply with requirements regarding general appearance and clothing.

PASSPORTS: Valid passport required by all. Nationals of Austria, Denmark, Finland, France, Germany, Iceland, Norway, Spain, Sweden and Switzerland who travel as an organised group can also enter with their national ID cards or other passport-replacing documents.

British Visitors Passport: Not accepted.

VISAS: Required by all except:

(a) nationals of countries as shown above;

(b) [1] nationals of Denmark, France, Germany, Greece, Ireland, Italy, Spain and the UK (other EC nationals *do* require a visa);

(c) nationals of Commonwealth countries;

(d) nationals of Algeria, Andorra, Argentina, Austria, Bahrain, Brazil, Chile, Congo, Côte d'Ivoire, Finland, Guinea, Iceland, Indonesia, Kuwait, Liberia, Libya, Liechtenstein, Mali, Malta, Mexico, Monaco, New Zealand, Niger, Norway, Oman, Peru, Philippines, Qatar Romania, Saudi Arabia, Senegal, Sweden, Switzerland, Tunisia, Turkey, United Arab Emirates, Venezuela and Yugoslavia.

Types of visa: *Single-entry visa* – £4.50; *Double-entry visa* – £7.20 (these prices may fluctuate in accordance with the Moroccan Dirham/Pound Sterling exchange rate); *Transit visa* is free of charge.

Validity: Entry visas are valid for 3 months; visitors wishing to stay longer should apply to the police within 15 days of arrival (except for nationals of France and Spain who may stay for an unlimited period provided they report to the police within 3 months). For other visa queries contact the Embassy.

Application to: Consulate (or Consular Section at Embassy). For addresses, see top of entry.

Application requirements: (a) 4 completed application forms. (b) 4 photos. (c) Valid passport (valid for more than 6 months on date of entry into Morocco). (d) Fee. (e) Sufficient funds for length of stay.

Working days required: Application forms are sent to Morocco for clearance and so it is advisable to apply well in advance of intended travel date.

MONEY

Currency: Moroccan Dirham (DH) = 100 centimes. Notes are in denominations of DH200, 100, 50, 10 and 5. Coins are in denominations of DH5 and 1, and 50, 20, 10 and 5 centimes.

Credit cards: Some credit cards are accepted. Check with your credit card company for details of merchant acceptability and other services which may be available.

Exchange rate indicators: The following figures are included as a guide to the movement of the Moroccan Dirham against Sterling and the US Dollar:

Date:	Oct '89	Oct '90	Oct '91	Oct '92
£1.00=	13.60	15.86	15.01	13.22
$1.00=	8.61	8.11	8.65	8.33

Currency restrictions: The import and export of local currency is prohibited; all local currency must be reconverted prior to departure. The import and export of foreign currency is unlimited. Upon production of bank vouchers, half the Moroccan currency purchased during a visitor's stay may be re-exchanged for foreign currency (subject to some limitations).

Banking hours: 0830-1100 and 1430-1630 Monday to Friday (winter); 0800-1400 Monday to Friday (summer). These hours may vary during Ramadan.

DUTY FREE

The following goods may be imported into Morocco without incurring customs duty:

200 cigarettes or 50 cigars or 400g of tobacco;
1 litre of spirits and 1 litre of wine;
250ml of perfume.

PUBLIC HOLIDAYS

Public holidays observed in Morocco are as follows: **Mar 3 '93** Feast of the Throne. **Mar 25** Eid al-Seghir (Eid al-Fitr, end of Ramadan). **May 1** Labour Day. **Jun 1** Eid el-Kebir (Eid al-Adha, feast of the sacrifice). **Jun 21** Islamic New Year. **Jun 30** Ashoura. **Aug 14** Oued ed-Dahab Day. **Aug 30** Mouloud (Prophet's Birthday). **Nov 6** Anniversary of the Green March. **Nov 18** Independence Day. **Jan 1 '94** New Year's Day. **Mar 3** Feast of the Throne. **Mar** Eid al-Seghir (Eid al-Fitr, end of Ramadan).

Note: Muslim festivals are timed according to local sightings of various phases of the Moon and the dates given above are approximations. During the lunar month of Ramadan that precedes Eid el-Seghir (Eid al-Fitr), Muslims fast during the day and feast at night and normal business patterns may be interrupted. Some disruption may continue into Eid el-Seghir itself. Eid el-Seghir and Eid el-Kebir (Eid al-Adha) may last anything from two to ten days, depending on the region. For more information see the section *World of Islam* at the back of the book.

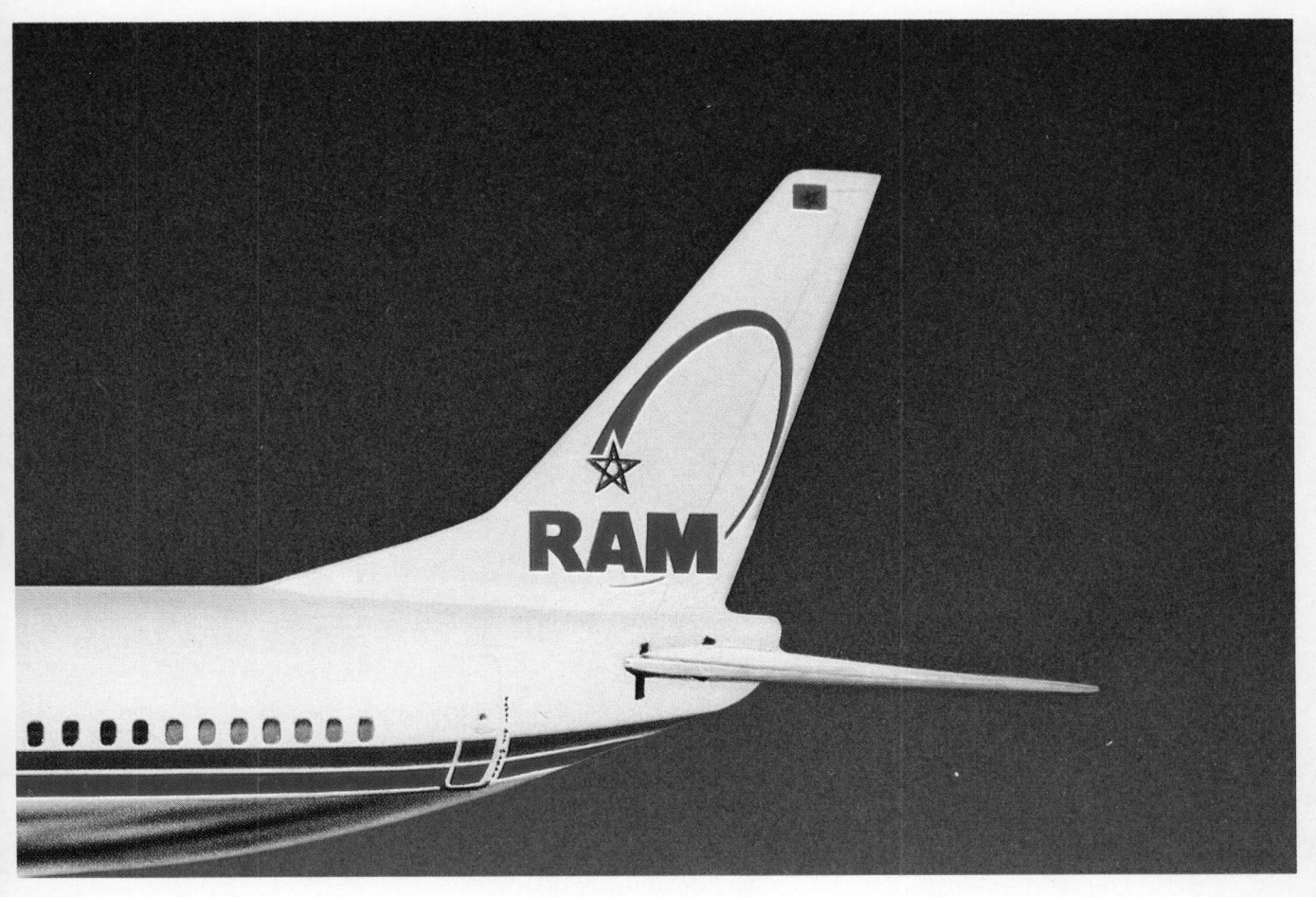

MOROCCO

Morocco – a fascinating mix of African, Islamic, Arab, Berber and European cultures. As well as the four Imperial Cities of Fez, Meknes, Marrakech and Rabat, natural attractions range from the Atlantic and Mediterranean beaches to the remote austerity of the High Atlas and Rif mountains.

Morocco is traversed by four distinct mountain ranges, the Rif, Middle Atlas, High Atlas and Anti-Atlas. Interspersed in and between these lie fertile plateaux and plains, while to the south the agriculture peters out into the forbidding wastes of the Sahara.

Islam is the predominant religion, and has been since the 8th century. Its importance in both cultural and social terms, combined with the alternating French and Spanish domination during certain periods, provide the very essence and the heart of this country. Everywhere one visits the epic scale of the past is writ large in total contrast to, but in harmony with, the bustling modernity of major cities. It is this unique combination which makes Morocco so utterly fascinating, so alluring and so mysterious.

Morocco is a relatively conservative society, retaining its centuries-old traditions. This is one of the major contributory factors to Morocco's growing recognition as a first class and diverse tourism destination. Indeed, tourism is one of the country's most buoyant economic sectors.

So much to experience, so many different swirling visions of dramatic history, of awesome natural splendour, of cultural diversity. The Imperial Cities – Rabat, Fes, Marrakech and Meknes – have all at one time been the capital, and each has its own unique atmosphere and

style. Cosmopolitan Tangier, once a free port, welcomes travellers at the gateway of the Mediterranean and the Atlantic. Relax in one of the many beach resorts, tee off at one of the spectacular golf courses, or take up the challenge of the ski slopes of the Middle and High Atlas. And still, after all these pleasures, there is the mystery and allure of the South: a land of sand dunes and rocky escarpments dotted with Berber castles and ancient fortified villages; in places, as at Dades Gorge, rent apart by awesome ravines hewn from the ancient rock by sparkling rivers; now encrusted with oases and palm groves; now shimmering under the delicate coral shades of a desert sunset. All these and so many other wonders await you, easily accessible in a country with a modern transport infrastructure and a range of accommodation facilities second to none.

Morocco the magical, Morocco the magnificent, Morocco the mysterious – whatever *you* want Morocco to be, it is waiting for you.

CONFERENCE & INCENTIVE

Morocco – the perfect destination for your conference or incentive trip. Moroccan hotels offer a sophisticated range of facilities for international meetings with a diversity of environments, making them an ideal destination for all. Nowhere is the legendary hospitality more exemplified than in the quality, style and courtesy of the major venues for both meeting and incentive travellers. Every wish can be catered for. Sports and leisure facilities at the major hotels are unrivalled. International golf courses, flying clubs, equestrian centres, ski resorts and sun-drenched beaches are often only a short journey away. Hunting, shooting and fishing aquire a new meaning when you are stalking wild boar in the Atlas Mountains, or casting for trout in sparkling mountain steams. And for the truly adventurous, expeditions to the deep south can easily be arranged. The following hotels offer the highest standard in conference facilities and activities for business travellers.

MARRAKECH

La Mamounia

A sumptuous palace with 228 rooms and suites, renovated in 1986 in Moorish and Art-deco styles, lying between the new and old towns in a 7-acre garden beside ancient city walls. There is a grill room, several restaurants, a poolside buffet and five bars, and a wide range of facilities. The ballroom seats 400 plenary style, but can be divided into three smaller rooms. There are in addition two further meeting rooms and a fully-equipped business centre.

Hotels Es Saadi

Set in the city's residential area, the hotel has a gourmet restaurant and a pool-side snack-bar. Together with 150 rooms and suites, sauna, exercise and massage facilities are available, as well as shops and a casino. There are also two tennis clay courts and a golf practice area. The main plenary room seats 170 for conferences and 100 banquet-style: the Winter Garden seats up to 70 people. Two other rooms have space for 20 to 30 delegates.

Hotel Mansour Eddahbi

This Pullman hotel, opened in 1989, has outstanding conference facilities. The main banqueting hall holds 1800, while a smaller theatre seats 500. There are 403 rooms and 38 suites equipped with the latest facilities which, together with six restaurants, shops, nightclubs, fitness club and pool, make it the ideal conference location.

Imperial Borj

This modern hotel is ideal for smaller groups, with a 300-seater conference centre. There are 187 rooms and 20 suites, three restaurants and a swimming pool.

Palais de Congres

Marrakech houses a superb Convention Centre with conference area, a spacious banqueting hall and the smaller Ambassador Suite. There are two golf courses nearby while the newly completed Les Jardins de La Palmeraie has been sculpted out of the terrain with water hazards and bunkers. The ski slopes of the Atlas Mountains at Oukaimeden are 45 minutes away (season Dec-Apr). Organised mountain trekking arranged all year round.

FEZ

Palais Jamai

Overlooking the old medina, surrounded by Andalucian gardens, the hotel has two restaurants and pool buffet. Leisure facilities include tennis courts, Turkish bath, massage, and golf and horseriding nearby. There are 99 rooms, 15 apartments and five Royal Suites. Business facilities include two conference rooms and AV equipment.

CASABLANCA

Royal Mansour

Recently renovated, this city-centre hotel is noted for its numerous restaurant and bar services. As well as 182 rooms and 23 suites there are well-equipped conference rooms and a professionally staffed business centre.

Sheraton

The ballroom of this sophisticated hotel seats 400, while there are four smaller meeting rooms. 306 rooms, including 22 suites and a Royal suite, are superbly furnished. Facilities include four restaurants, three bars and a nightclub. A swimming pool, squash and fitness centre with sauna, jacuzzi and massage parlour provide relaxation.

Hyatt Regency

Near the city centre and 30 minutes from the airport, one of the attractions is the Hollywood-evoking Bar Casablanca and the Black House Club. The main conference and banqueting room accommodates 800-plus and can be divided. 171 rooms and 59 suites are beautifully designed and furnished. The Mohammedia Golf course is nearby.

RABAT

Hyatt Regency

Two hundred and twenty luxurious rooms located close to the Royal dar Es Salam course and only ten minutes from downtown Rabat. Its ballroom seats 1100 and is complemented with business centre and meeting rooms. Several restaurants, a fitness centre with pool, four clay tennis courts, a driving range and nearby beach make it a top location whether for business or pleasure.

AGADIR

Europahotel Safir

This hotel is ideal for incentive groups: the Europahotel Safir is well positioned for a wide range of beach activities. Numerous sporting activities such as golf are also available.

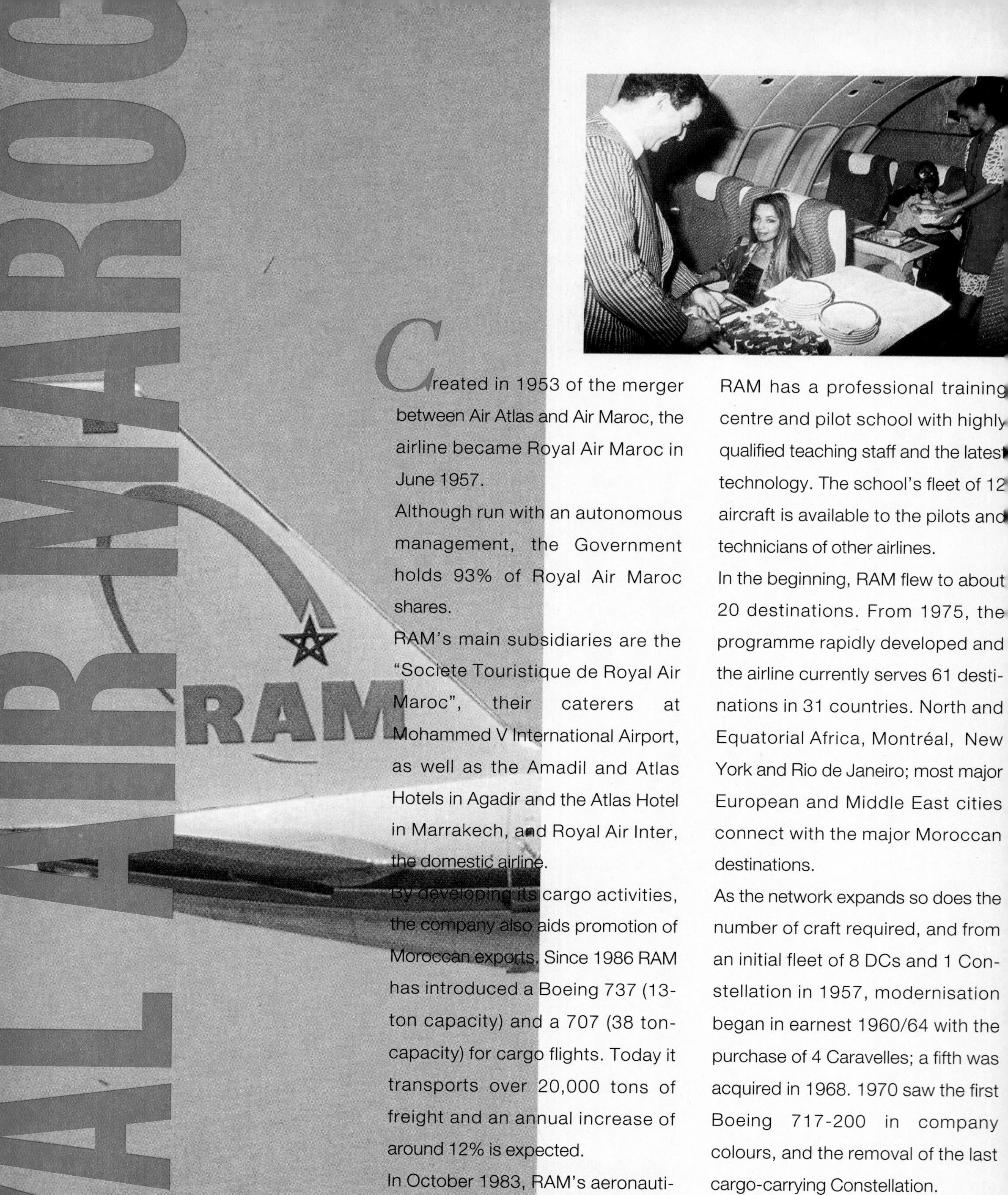

Created in 1953 of the merger between Air Atlas and Air Maroc, the airline became Royal Air Maroc in June 1957.

Although run with an autonomous management, the Government holds 93% of Royal Air Maroc shares.

RAM's main subsidiaries are the "Societe Touristique de Royal Air Maroc", their caterers at Mohammed V International Airport, as well as the Amadil and Atlas Hotels in Agadir and the Atlas Hotel in Marrakech, and Royal Air Inter, the domestic airline.

By developing its cargo activities, the company also aids promotion of Moroccan exports. Since 1986 RAM has introduced a Boeing 737 (13-ton capacity) and a 707 (38 ton-capacity) for cargo flights. Today it transports over 20,000 tons of freight and an annual increase of around 12% is expected.

In October 1983, RAM's aeronautical workshops attained their FAA accreditation, testifying an equivalent standard to the USA. This is due to the highly qualified personnel of whom 750 are specialised technicians and to a sophisticated infrastructure.

RAM has a professional training centre and pilot school with highly qualified teaching staff and the latest technology. The school's fleet of 12 aircraft is available to the pilots and technicians of other airlines.

In the beginning, RAM flew to about 20 destinations. From 1975, the programme rapidly developed and the airline currently serves 61 destinations in 31 countries. North and Equatorial Africa, Montréal, New York and Rio de Janeiro; most major European and Middle East cities connect with the major Moroccan destinations.

As the network expands so does the number of craft required, and from an initial fleet of 8 DCs and 1 Constellation in 1957, modernisation began in earnest 1960/64 with the purchase of 4 Caravelles; a fifth was acquired in 1968. 1970 saw the first Boeing 717-200 in company colours, and the removal of the last cargo-carrying Constellation.

RAM chose the Boeing 737 in 1975 to replace the Caravelles, and the next year two 707s were purchased. Two 747s were then added, and in 1986 the company acquired two 757s.

Services from London Heathrow to

The RAM fleet now consists of the following:
1 Boeing 747-200; 1 747-SP;
8 727s (6 advanced);
2 707-320Cs; 7 737-400 & 500s
7 737-200s of which two are cargo convertible;
2 757-200s; 2 Fokker 27s;
3 ATR-42s.
A further 10 737-400s and 500s are now on order.

Tangier, Casablanca, Agadir and Marrakech on a daily basis with three direct flights to Casablanca, three direct flights to Tangier and one direct flight to Marrakech and with easy connections to up to 18 cities throughout Morocco. An important recent development is the $525-million order for 12 Boeing 737s, bringing the total number of new-generation 737s in the fleet to 22. Royal Air Maroc was the first African or Middle Eastern airline to introduce 737-400s and 737-500s back in 1990, while 727-200s have been deployed since 1970. The order demonstrates the airline's continuing commitment to fleet renewal on medium-range airplanes. Mohamad Mekouar, President and Director General of Royal Air Maroc, sees this exciting development as 'underlining our confidence in the future traffic growth between Europe and Morocco.'

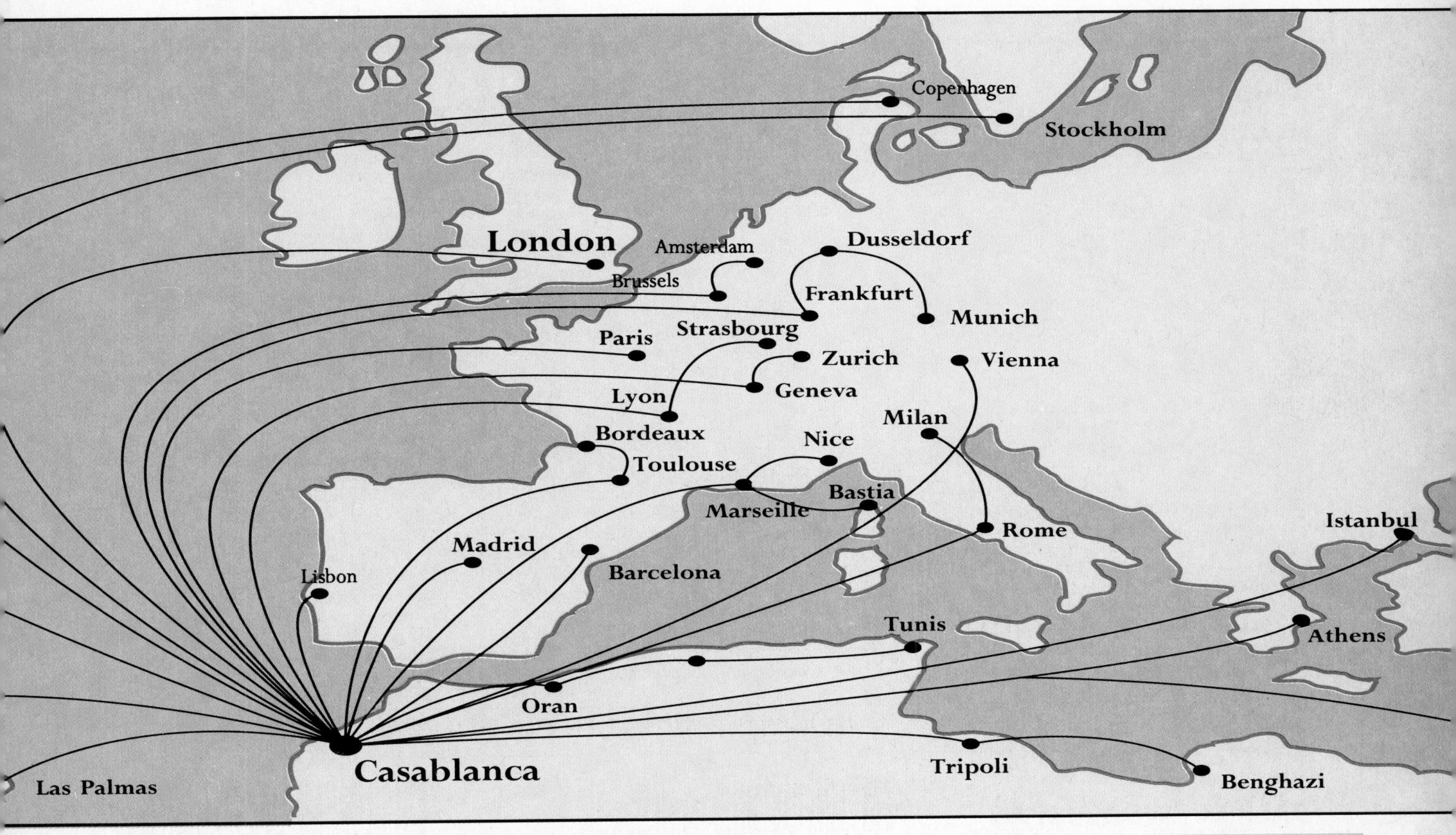

Copenhagen
Stockholm
London
Amsterdam
Dusseldorf
Brussels
Frankfurt
Munich
Paris
Strasbourg
Zurich
Vienna
Geneva
Lyon
Milan
Bordeaux
Nice
Toulouse
Bastia
Marseille
Istanbul
Rome
Madrid
Barcelona
Lisbon
Tunis
Athens
Oran
Casablanca
Tripoli
Benghazi
Las Palmas

For further information contact: Royal Air Maroc
Moroccan International Airlines. 205 Regent Street,
London W1R 7DE.
Tel: 071 439 8854. Fax: 071 287 0127.

HEALTH

Regulations and requirements may be subject to change at short notice, and you are advised to contact your doctor well in advance of your intended date of departure. Any numbers in the chart refer to the footnotes below.

	Special Precautions?	Certificate Required?
Yellow Fever	No	No
Cholera	No	No
Typhoid & Polio	Yes	-
Malaria	1	-
Food & Drink	2	

[1]: A minimal malaria risk, exclusively in the benign *vivax* form, exists from May to October in rural areas of the following provinces: El Kelâa, Chefchaouèn, Settat, Kénifa and Khémisset.

[2]: Mains water is normally chlorinated, and whilst relatively safe may cause mild abdominal upsets. Bottled water is available and is advised for the first few weeks of the stay. Drinking water outside main cities and towns may be contaminated and sterilisation is advisable. Milk is unpasteurised and should be boiled. Powdered or tinned milk is available and is advised, but make sure that it is reconstituted with pure water. Avoid dairy products which are likely to have been made from unboiled milk. Only eat well-cooked meat and fish, preferably served hot. Pork, salad and mayonnaise may carry increased risk. Vegetables should be cooked and fruit peeled.

Rabies is present. For those at high risk, vaccination before arrival should be considered. If you are bitten abroad seek medical advice without delay. For more information consult the *Health* section at the back of the book.

Bilharzia (schistosomiasis) is present in small foci. Avoid swimming and paddling in fresh water. Swimming pools which are well-chlorinated and maintained are safe.

Health care: There are good medical facilities in all main cities, including emergency pharmacies (sometimes in the Town Hall) outside normal opening hours. Government hospitals provide free or minimal charge emergency treatment. Full health insurance is essential.

TRAVEL - International

AIR: Morocco's national airline is *Royal Air Maroc (AT)*.

Approximate flight times: From London to *Rabat* is 3 hours and to *Tangier* is 2 hours 30 minutes.

International airports: *Casablanca (CAS)* (Mohammed V) is 30km (19 miles) south of the city (travel time – 35 minutes). Airport facilities include outgoing duty-free shop (closed after last arrival), post office, banking and exchange services (open for arrival and departure of planes), restaurant and bar (0800-2300) and car hire *(Hertz, Avis, Europcar, Intercar* and *Locoto)*. There are bus and taxi services into Casablanca and coach services available to Rabat.

Rabat (RBA) (Salé) is 10km (6 miles) northeast of the city (travel time – 15 minutes). Airport facilities include restaurant, snack bar, bank, post office, shops and car hire. Taxi service is available to the city.

Tangier (TNG) (Boukhalef Souahel) is 12km (7.5 miles) from the city (travel time – 20 minutes). Airport facilities include outgoing duty-free shop, banking and exchange facilities, restaurant and bar (0900-2100), car hire facilities *(Avis, Omnium, Starc-Hertz* and *Moroccan Holidays)*. Bus and taxi services are available into Tangier.

Agadir (AGA) (Inezgane) is 8km (5 miles) from the city (travel time – 15 minutes). Bus and taxi services go into the town. Airport facilities include banking and exchange, bar (no restaurant) and car hire *(Europcar, Hertz* and *Africa Car)*.

Fez (FEZ) (Sais) is 10km (6 miles) from the city (travel time – 10 minutes). Taxi service is available to the city.

Marrakech (RAK) (Menara) is 6km (4 miles) from the city. Taxi and bus services are available to the city. There are banking facilities at the airport.

SEA: Principal ports are Tangier, Casablanca and Ceuta. Lines serving these ports are *Transtour, Compañía Trasmediterránea, Limadet, Bland Line* (from Spain and Gibraltar), *Polish Ocean Lines* and *Nautilus* (from Spain and the USA) and *Comanav*.

Car/passenger ferries: There are cheap and regular car and passenger ferry links between southern Spain and Tangier and the Spanish enclaves on the north Moroccan coast. Most links are roll-on, roll-off car

MOROCCO	HEALTH REGULATIONS	VISA REGULATIONS
		Code-Link
GALILEO/WORLDSPAN	 TI-DFT/RBA/HE	 TI-DFT/RBA/VI
SABRE	 TIDFT/RBA/HE	 TIDFT/RBA/VI

To access this information on your CRS, swipe the barcode with a light pen or type in the text under the barcode. For more information, see the introduction *How to Use This Book*.

erries except where shown. The routes are from Algeciras to Ceuta (Sebta) (car ferry); Algeciras to Tangier (hydrofoil and car ferry); Tarifa to Tangier (hydrofoil only); Gibraltar to Tangier (hydrofoil and car ferry); Almería to Melilla (car ferry) and Málaga to Melilla (car ferry).

There are also car ferries between Sète on the French coast (between Béziers and Montpellier on the Golfe du Lyon) and Tangier run by *Compagnie Marocaine de Navigation*.

RAIL: The link from Oujda on the Algerian border has recently re-opened.

ROAD: The best road link is from southern Spain or France via passenger/car ferries (see above under *Sea*). There is also a road link on the north Algerian border.

TRAVEL - Internal

AIR: *Royal Air Maroc (AT)* operates regular services from Casablanca airport to Agadir, Al Hoceima, Dakhla, Fez, Marrakech, Ouarzazate, Oujda, Rabat, Tangier and Tetouan. There are discounts for those under 26 of up to 40%.

RAIL: The Moroccan rail system, though limited, runs regular and cheap services with first-class travel available. Rail fares are amongst the cheapest in the world. Trains are air-conditioned and sleeping cars and restaurant cars are available. The network runs from Oujda in the northeast to Casablanca on the west coast, Tangier on the north coast and Marrakech in the interior. The most useful route is from Fez to Rabat and Casablanca, with five daily and two overnight trains. There are also two daily trains and one overnight train (without sleepers) which run from Casablanca to Marrakech.

Cheap fares: The European Inter-Rail pass is valid in Morocco; holders may be entitled to a discount on the fare of a ferry ticket – check with the company concerned for details. Discounts of up to 30% are available for groups of more than ten. Seats can be reserved in advance for first- and second-class seats. Trains can also be chartered.

ROAD: The major Moroccan roads, particularly those covering the north and northwest of the country, are all-weather highways. In the interior, south of the High Atlas Mountains, road travel becomes much more difficult, especially across the Atlas Mountains in winter.

Coach: The main centres are connected by a wide variety of coach services, many of which are privately run. The two largest firms are *CTM* (covering the whole country) and *SATAS* (between Casablanca, Agadir and south of Agadir). **Bus:** Connections between most major towns and villages are regular and frequent, although buses can be very crowded and it may be wise to buy tickets well in advance and arrive well before departure to secure a seat. The price of tickets is very low, especially with some of the smaller local bus companies. It is customary to tip the guard for loading luggage. For charter purposes, air-conditioned motor coaches are available from several companies. **Taxi:** Those available in major towns, the *petits taxis*, are metered (see below under *Urban*). Other larger taxis, usually Mercedes cars, are used for travel to areas outside towns. These can be shared, but fares should be agreed before departure. **Car hire:** *Avis* and *Hertz* can be delivered to Gibraltar or Tangier from London. Major hire companies have offices in Tangier, Casablanca and Agadir. Car hire is generally expensive. **Documentation:** Foreign driving licences are accepted, as well as International Driving Licences. Third Party insurance is required. A Green Card is also necessary. Insurance can be arranged locally.

URBAN: There are extensive bus services in Casablanca and other main towns. Pre-purchase tickets are sold. Urban area *petits taxis* are plentiful and have metered fares. Taxi drivers expect a 10% tip.

CHRIS LAWRENCE

JOURNEY TIMES: The following chart gives approximate journey times (in hours and minutes) from Casablanca to other major cities/towns in Morocco.

	Air	Road	Rail
Rabat	0.30	1.30	1.00
Marrakech	*0.40	4.00	4.00
Agadir	*0.55	9.00	-
Fez	*0.40	5.00	5.00
Meknes	-	2.30	3.30
Tangier	*0.50	7.00	6.00
Oujda	*1.05	12.00	12.00
Laayoune	1.30	20.00	-
Errachidia	1.35	12.00	-

Note: [*] These represent times by the main air link from Casablanca.

ACCOMMODATION

HOTELS: Morocco has 100,000 hotel beds. In all sizeable centres there is quite a wide choice. The upper end of the market is represented by internationally known hotels in most main towns. For more information contact the Fédération Nationale de l'Industrie Hôtelière, 11 rue Caporal Beaux, Casablanca. Tel: (2) 319 083. Telex: 21857. **Grading:** Hotels are rated from **1 star** to **5 stars.**
SELF-CATERING: Self-catering apartments are available in Agadir, Marrakech and Tangier. Full details are available from the National Tourist Office.
CAMPING/CARAVANNING: There are established campsites with good facilities in many parts of Morocco. Full details are available in a brochure from the National Tourist Office.
YOUTH HOSTELS: There are hostels in Asni, Azrou, Casablanca, Fez, Ifrane, Meknes and Rabat. Up-to-date information is available from the Union Marocaine des Auberges de Jeunesse, 6 Place Amiral Phillibert, Casablanca. Tel: (2) 220 551.

RESORTS & EXCURSIONS

For the purpose of this guide Morocco has been divided into three parts: Imperial Cities, The Coast and The South.

Imperial Cities

Fez, Marrakech, Meknes and Rabat are known as the Imperial Cities, each having been the country's capital at some time during its history.
Rabat, the present capital of Morocco, was founded in the 12th century. It is a town of trees and flowers, and many monumental gateways, including the *Gate of the Ambassadors* and the *Oudaias Kasbah Gate*. There is a good selection of hotels and numerous pavement cafés. The nearby Mamora forest and the many beaches are popular tourist attractions, particularly during the summer.
Other attractions include *Tour Hassan*, the grandiose minaret of a vast, uncompleted 12th-century mosque; the *Mohammed V Mausoleum*, an outstanding example of traditional Moroccan architecture; the *Royal Palace*; the *Chellah*, with superb monuments, delightful gardens and Roman ruins; the *Oudaias*; the *National Museum of Handicrafts* and the antique Moorish café. The battlements surrounding the old town, and part of the new city, date from the mid-12th century. Also worth a visit is **Salé,** Rabat's twin city, at the opposite side of the river, believed to have been founded in the 11th century.
Meknes is protected by 16km (25 miles) of battlements, flanked by towers and bastions. The city reflects the power and the constructive genius of King Moulay Ismail, a contemporary of Louis XIV, who ruled the country for 55 years. The *Michlifen* and *Djebel Habri* are two ski resorts above Meknes. The city boasts a wonderful *souk* (market).
Fez is the most ancient and impressive of the imperial cities. Built in the 8th century it has more history and mystery than anywhere else in Morocco. Officially encompassing two cities – El Bali and Jadid – Fez is famous for the *Nejjarine Square* and *Fountain*, the *Er Rsif* and *Andalous* mosques, the *Royal Palace*, the *Kasbah* and *Karaouine University*, which is older than Oxford University. The market in Fez is one of the largest in the world. Here one can buy almost anything.
The valley of *Ouergha* to the north is famed for its *souks* and Morocco's most celebrated gathering of riders, which is said to have been attended by Pope Sylvester II prior to his accession in AD999 and resulted in him introducing Arab mathematics to Europe. Other attractions are the *Karaouine Mosque* and *Mesbahai Medersa*, an old school, remarkable for its traditional architecture and late afternoon auctions in the *Kissaria*, the shopping area.
Founded in 1062, **Marrakech** was once the capital of an empire which stretched from Toledo to Senegal. It is a city of labyrinthine alleyways, secluded palaces, museums, mosques and markets. The city's gardens are still supplied with water from 11th-century underground irrigation canals. Other attractions include *Djemmaa-el-Fna*, the city square where dancers, fortunetellers, acrobats and storytellers perform; *Koutoubia*, the 12th-century minaret which is as tall as the towers of Notre Dame; the *Ben Youssef Medersa* with its mosaics, marbles and carved woodwork; the sumptuous *Bahia Palace;* the beautiful *Saadian Tombs* housing the remains of rulers of the Saadian dynasty; the *Menara and Aquedal gardens*; the famed camel market and a horse-drawn carriage ride, at sunset, around the seven and a half miles of the old city.
An hour's drive from Marrakech is **Oukaimeden,** Morocco's best ski resort. This trip can be combined with a visit to **Ourika** (which has a donkey market) and **Asni.** The latter is an excellent base for visiting *Mount Toubkai*, Morocco's highest mountain, set in spectacular countryside.

CHRIS LAWRENCE

The Coast

The Mediterranean Coast between Tangier and Nador has a string of creeks, bays, sheltered beaches and cliffs along the Mediterranean shore, ideal for swimming, boating and fishing. *Al Hoceima, M'Diq, Taifor* and *Smir/Restinga* are all new resorts, offering a wide variety of accommodation, from luxury hotels to well-situated bungalows.
The Atlantic coast is often rocky, with some long stretches of fine sand and calm bays.
Tangier, gateway to Africa, is the country's most cosmopolitan town, a place where – surviving from the days when Tangier was a free port – the street signs are in three languages; in fact, no less than 12 nations have occupied the city at one time or another since the 5th century. The city has a picturesque and active market called the *Grand Socco*. Other places worth visiting include the *Mendoubia Gardens*, the *Sidi Bounabib Mosque*, the *Moulay Ismail Mosque* and the *Merinid College*. Excursions in the region include visits to the mountain town of **Chechaouen,** the fishing village of **Asilah** and the *Caves of Hercules* at **Cape Spartel.**
Also on the Atlantic coast is the newer city of **Casablanca**. Founded at the beginning of the century, it is the country's principal commercial town, the second-largest town in Africa and one of the continent's biggest ports.
Agadir is a modern holiday city with superb beaches, excellent resort hotels and self-catering accommodation, which offers all types of sports activities. From here there are excursions to the towns of **Taroudant, Tiznit, Tafraout, Goulimine, Essaouira** and, of course, the famous Marrakech.
Mohammedia and *El Jadida* are two other resorts in this region. The latter has an old 'Portuguese quarter', including the *Church of Assumption*, an enormous underground *Cistern*, the 'Gate on the Sea' and fortifications.

The South

The South is a region rich in folklore and spectacular scenery, dotted with small oasis villages and quiet towns surrounded by orchards and olive groves. **Erfoud** is the centre for excursions to the oasis of *Tafilalet*, kept green and fertile by the underground waters of the Ziz and the Rheris. **Er Rachidia** is the provincial capital of the Tafilalet region, and has a bustling market on the main

CHRIS LAWRENCE

square. On the road between Er Rachidia and Erfoud are the 'Blue Springs' at Meski and the natural amphitheatre of *Cirque de Jaffar* near **Midelt. Tinerhir**, once a garrison of the French Foreign Legion, is worth visiting for its kasbahs. Near Tinerhir is the outstanding scenery of the *Dades* and *Todra* gorges.

Ouarzazate: Of particular interest is the kasbah of *Taourirt*, the *Museum of Arts and Crafts* and the *Carpet Weavers' Co-operative Shop*.

Zagora: From the top of the Djebel Zagora there is a spectacular view of the *Draa Valley* and desert. 18km (11 miles) away from Zagora is the oasis of **Tamergroute** which has a library containing some of the earliest Arabic manuscripts, written nine centuries ago on gazelle skins. They are on display at the *Zaouia Nasseria*. Nearby, **Mhamid** and its palm groves are at the gates of the great sand desert. South of Agadir, the pink kasbahs of **Tafraoute** perch on spurs of rock, their facades often painted with strange designs in white or ochre.

Goulimine is the site of the *Blue Men's souk*, held each weekend. A camel market also takes place once a week, on Saturdays.

SOCIAL PROFILE

FOOD & DRINK: Morocco's traditional *haute cuisine* dishes are excellent and good value for money. They are often exceedingly elaborate, based on a diet of meat and sweet pastries. Typical specialities include: *harira*, a rich soup, and *bastilla*, a pigeon-meat pastry made from dozens of different layers of thick flaky dough. *Couscous*, a dish based on savoury semolina that can be combined with egg, chicken, lamb or vegetables, is a staple Moroccan dish. *Touajen* are stews, often rich and fragrant, using marinaded lamb or chicken. *Hout* is a fish version of the same stew, while *djaja mahamara* is chicken stuffed with almond, semolina and raisins. Also popular are *mchoui*, pit-roasted mutton, and *kab-el-ghzal*, almond pastries. Hotel restaurants usually serve French cuisine. Restaurants offer a good selection of food, including typical Moroccan dishes, French, Italian or Spanish meals. The 3-course fixed menus are not expensive. Many of the souks have stalls selling kebabs *(brochettes)* often served with a spicy sauce. Most restaurants have waiter service. **Drink:** The national drink is mint tea made with green tea, fresh mint and sugar. Coffee is made very strong, except at breakfast. Bars can have either waiter or counter service. Laws on alcohol are fairly liberal (for non-Muslim visitors) and bars in most tourist areas stay open late. Wines, beers and spirits are widely available. Locally produced wines, beers and mineral waters are excellent and good value, but imported drinks tend to be expensive.

NIGHTLIFE: Morocco offers a variety of entertainment from casinos, discotheques, restaurants and nightclubs, often with belly dancing. There are modern nightclubs in all the cities and resorts around the country. There are casinos in Marrakech and Mohammedia. Traditional Moroccan entertainment, such as folk dancing, can be seen in every town. In the *Djemmaa-el-Fna*, the market square outside the old city of Marrakech, all types of performers, from acrobats and folk dancers to snake-charmers and fortunetellers, turn out all day, every day, and with foodstalls, bric-a-brac stands and souvenir stalls, provide a dazzling spectacle for the visitor.

SHOPPING: The co-operative shops of Moroccan craftsmen, *coopartim*, operate under state control selling local handicrafts at fixed prices and issue an authenticity receipt or a certificate of origin for customs when exporting. *Souks* are also worthwhile places to visit for local products. Special buys are leather, tanned and dyed in Fez; copperware; silver; silk or cotton garments; and wool rugs, carpets and blankets. Bargaining is essential, and good buys generally work out at around a third of asking price. In the south there are Berber carpet auctions, especially in Marrakech, Taroudant and Tiznit. You will need a guide to make the best of these occasions. **Shopping hours:** Generally 0830-1230 and 1400-1830 Monday to Saturday (0830-1200 and 1400-1900 Monday to Saturday in Tangier), but some shops in Medinas *(souks)* may open on Sundays and many shops close on Fridays.

SPORT: Swimming: Sandy beaches offer safe bathing, although the Atlantic can be cold even in summer. Mohammedia, Agadir, El Jadida, Oualidia, Safi and Essaouira are all good bathing resorts. The Mediterranean coast is now being developed and newly built resort villages offer superb swimming and diving. **Fishing** permits are necessary for trout streams, lakes and pike lakes, and are issued by the Waters and Forests Department or local clubs. Sea fishing trips can also be organised. **Hunting:** The Arboaua area offers wild boar, partridge, hare, mallard, quail and snipe during the season, which lasts from October to March. Hunting permits are available from the National Tourist Office, and a permit for the importation of hunting rifles can be issued on production of a valid national shooting permit and three photographs. **Golf:** There are courses at the Dar es Salaam Club in Rabat, Mohammedia, Tangier Country Club, Casablanca's Royal Golf Anfa, Cabo Negro, Agadir and Marrakech. **Winter sports:** Ifrane in the Middle Atlas and Oukaimeder in the High Atlas offer skiing facilities. Mount Tidiquin in the Ketama district and Djebel Bou Volane in the Middle Atlas are popular areas for expedition-type skiing and walking trips (with few amenities). **Horseriding:** There are horseriding clubs in all major towns, notably Casablanca, Rabat, Marrakech, Agadir and Fez. Several clubs organise pony treks in the Middle Atlas.

SPECIAL EVENTS: The following events are celebrated annually in Morocco. For further information and specific dates, please contact the National Tourist Office (address at beginning of entry).

May '93 *Festival of Roses*, El Kelaa des M'Gouna. **Jun** *Camel Festival*, Gelmin; *Folklore Festival*, Marrakech. **Jul** *F M Festival of Music*, Marrakech. **Sep** *Imilchil Festival*, Tissa; *Folklore Festival*, Marrakech; *International Festival of Classical Music*, Marrakech; *Horse Festival*, Tissa. **Oct** *Festival of Dates*, Erfoud.

SOCIAL CONVENTIONS: Handshaking is the customary form of greeting. Many of the manners and social customs emulate French manners, particularly amongst the middle class. The visitor may find, in some social situations, that patience, a good temper and firmness will pay dividends. Often visitors may find themselves the centre of unsolicited attention. In towns, young boys after money will be eager to point out the way, sell goods or simply charge for a photograph, while unofficial guides will always be offering advice or services. The visitor should be courteous but wary of the latter. Normal social courtesies should be observed in someone's home. Casual wear is widely acceptable, although swimsuits and shorts should be confined to the beach or poolside. Smoking is widespread and it is customary to offer cigarettes.

Tipping: Service charges are usually included in hotel bills; it is customary to tip hairdressers, cinema usherettes and waiters between DH1 and DH2.

BUSINESS PROFILE

ECONOMY: Agriculture employs most of the working population, the principal crops being cereals, citrus fruits and vegetables. Morocco is the world's largest exporter of phosphate rock and has other considerable mineral assets, including iron ore, coal, lead, zinc, cobalt, copper, silver and manganese. The main components of the manufacturing sector are food-processing, textiles and leather goods production. Tourism and remittances from Moroccan workers abroad are other major sources of revenue. The economy ran into some difficulty during the early 1980s due to the high cost of imported oil – Morocco has no deposits of its own – and of servicing its

CHRIS LAWRENCE

external debt. Debt rescheduling, falling oil prices and better harvests have since improved its economic position and Morocco is starting to benefit from one of the best infrastructures on the African continent. The country's economic performance is still vulnerable to the effects of a high birth rate, unemployment and an inefficient public sector, although the settlement of the war in Western Sahara should lift some of the public expenditure burden. The Government has introduced a series of IMF-sponsored reforms, including trade liberalisation and public expenditure cuts, in exchange for successive assitance programmes. The King has expressed his desire for Morocco to join the European Community, but this is a somewhat fanciful notion and the country must be content with membership of the Union of the Arab Maghreb. Morocco's main trading partner is France, followed by other EC countries. Spain, Germany and the USA are Morocco's main import suppliers.

BUSINESS: Business people should be of a smart appearance, although a suit is not necessary in very hot weather. Appointments should be made in advance. Negotiations often involve a great deal of bargaining and a visitor should expect to deal with a number of people. **Office hours:** *Winter* (September to July except Ramadan): 0830-1200 and 1430-1800 or later; *Ramadan* (see *Public Holidays*): 0900-1500/1600; *Summer* (July to early September): 0800-1500/1600, though many revert to winter hours.

COMMERCIAL INFORMATION: The following organisation can offer advice: La Fédération des Chambres de Commerce et d'Industrie du Maroc, 6 rue d'Erfoud, Rabat-Agdal. Tel: (7) 767 078. Fax: (7) 767 076. Telex: 36662.

CONFERENCES/CONVENTIONS: The Pullman Conference Centre in Marrakech provides meeting facilities for up to 5000 people. Further information can be obtained from Pullman Hotels in London at Resinter, c/o Novotel Hotel, 1 Shortlands, London W6 8DR. Tel: (071) 724 1000.

HISTORY & GOVERNMENT

HISTORY: Formerly divided between French and Spanish colonies, Morocco became independent in 1956, although Spain retained (and retains) claims over some areas, most of which were ceded to Morocco over the next 13 years. Morocco's first Head of State was Sultan Mohammad V, who later changed his title to King, and was succeeded on his death in 1961 by his son, Hassan II. Internal unity has been maintained since 1974 by the existence of external challenges around the disputed former Spanish Sahara area. Initially these revolved around conflicts with Spain and Mauritania but, since 1976, Morocco's main enemies have been the guerrillas of the Polisario Front and their Saharan government in exile, the Sahrawi Arab Democratic Republic, based in Algeria. Hassan began a dialogue with the Polisario Front in the late 1980s which produced a ceasefire early in September 1991. A referendum in Western Sahara to determine the status of the region has been postponed indefinitely. Internal opposition to Hassan is provided by the left-wing Union Socialiste des Forces Populaires (USFP) and radical Islamic groups (although the tide of Islamic fundamentalism which has swept the rest of North Africa has failed to make much headway in Morocco). Parliamentary elections were held in August 1992; the bulk of the seats were won by moderate supporters of the regime. Hassan has sought to strengthen ties with the European Community, although a Moroccan suggestion that the country might apply for membership has been dismissed by the Community. Morocco was a founder member of the Union of the Arab Maghreb; the links fostered by the Union between Morocco and Algeria were important in settling the Saharan conflict. In 1990, Morocco contributed a small troop detachment to UN coalition fighting Iraqi forces in the Gulf.

GOVERNMENT: King Hassan has retained executive power and control over the Chamber of Representatives (via a series of right-wing/centre coalitions, alternating with direct rule by the King), despite a number of coup and assassination attempts, and intermittent civil unrest.

CHRIS LAWRENCE

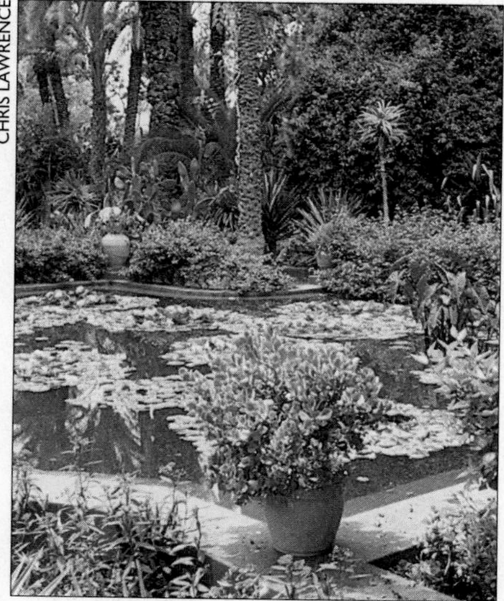

CLIMATE

The climate varies from area to area. The coast has a warm, Mediterranean climate tempered on the eastern coast by southwest trade winds. Inland areas have a hotter, drier, continental climate. In the south of the country the weather is very hot and dry throughout most of the year, with the nights coolest in the months of December and January. Rain falls from November to March in coastal areas. Mostly dry with high temperatures in summer. Cooler climate in the mountains. Marrakech and Agadir enjoy a average temperature of 21°C in the winter.

Required clothing: Lightweight cottons and linens are worn during summer, with warm mediumweights for the evenings during winter and in the mountains. Waterproofing is advisable in the wet season, particularly on the coast and in the mountains

RABAT Morocco (75m)

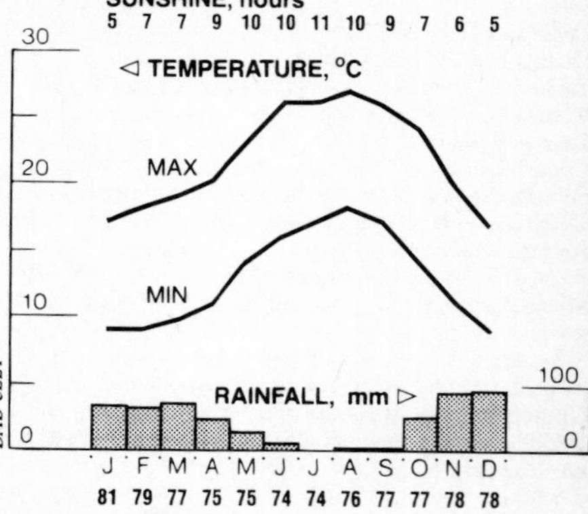

AGADIR Morocco (48m)

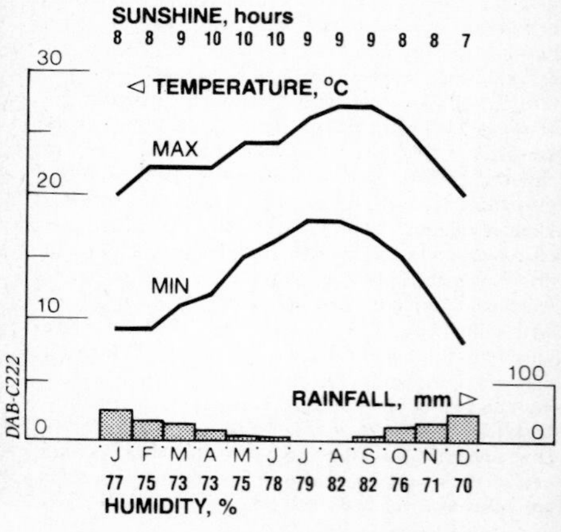

MOZAMBIQUE

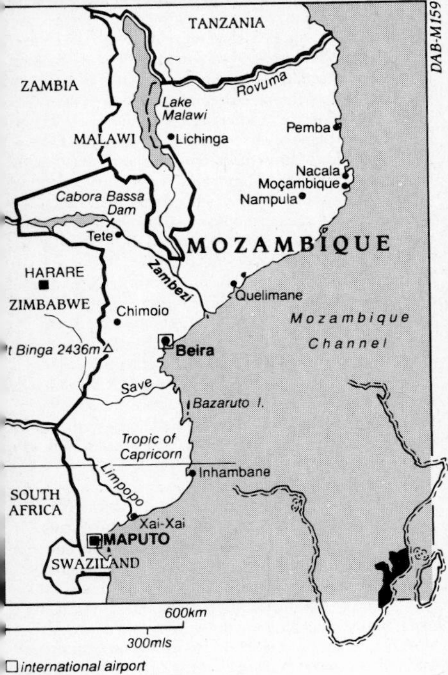

Location: Southeast Africa.

Note: Despite the recent peace agreement, unrest in Mozambique still affects the country and great care should be taken at all times. In general, the greatest risks are in the north and the least in major towns and cities.

Empresa Nacional de Turismo (ENT) (Mozambique National Tourism Company)
Caixa Postal 614
Avenida 25 de Setembro 1211
Maputo, Mozambique
Tel: (1) 25011. Fax: (1) 421 795. Telex: 6303.
Embassy of the Republic of Mozambique
21 Fitzroy Square
London W1P 5HJ
Tel: (071) 383 3800. Fax: (071) 383 3801. Telex: 342681 MOZEM G. Opening hours: 0900-1700 Monday to Friday; visa enquiries 0900-1300.
Embassy of the Republic of Mozambique
Avenida de Berna 7
Lisbon 1000, Portugal
Tel: (1) 771 747. Fax: (1) 771 747. Telex: 13641.
British Embassy
Caixa Postal 55
Avenida Vladimir I Lénine 310
Maputo, Mozambique
Tel: (1) 420 111. Telex: 6265.
Embassy of the Republic of Mozambique
Suite 570
1990 M Street, NW
Washington, DC 20036
Tel: (202) 293 7146. Fax: (202) 235 0245. Telex: 248530.
Also deals with enquirires from Canada.
Embassy of the United States of America
Caixa Postal 783
Maputo, Mozambique
Tel: (1) 492 797.
Canadian Embassy
PO Box 1578
4th Floor, Room 4
22 Joaquim Lapa
Maputo, Mozambique
Tel: (1) 420 818. Fax: (1) 74169. Telex: 6684 ACDI MO.

AREA: 799,380 sq km (308,641 sq miles).
POPULATION: 15,656,000 (1990 estimate).
POPULATION DENSITY: 19.6 per sq km.
CAPITAL: Maputo. **Population:** 1,006,765 (1987 estimate).
GEOGRAPHY: Mozambique borders Tanzania to the north, Zambia to the northwest, Zimbabwe to the west, and South Africa and Swaziland to the south. To the east lies the Indian Ocean and a coastline of nearly 2500km (1550 miles) with beaches bordered by lagoons, coral reefs and strings of islands. Behind the coastline a vast low plateau rising towards mountains in the west and north accounts for nearly half the area of Mozambique. The landscape of the plateau is savannah – more or less dry and open woodlands with tracts of short grass steppe. The western and northern highlands are patched with forest. The Zambezi is the largest and most important of the 25 main rivers which flow through Mozambique into the Indian Ocean. The major concentrations of population (comprising many different tribal groups) are along the coast and in the fertile and relatively productive river valleys, notably in Zambezia and Gaza provinces. The Makua-Lomwe, who belong to the Central Bantu, live mainly in the area north of Zambezia, Nampula, Niassa and Cabo Delgado provinces. The Thonga, who are the predominant race in the southern lowlands, provide a great deal of the labour for the South African mines. In the Inhambane coastal district are the Chopi and Tonga, while in the central area are the Shona. The Makonde inhabit the far north. Mestizos and Asians live in the main populated area along the coast and in the more fertile river valleys.
LANGUAGE: Portuguese is the official language. Many local African languages, such as Shangaan, Ronga and Muchope, are also spoken.
RELIGION: Christian (mainly Roman Catholic), Muslim and Hindu. Many also follow traditional beliefs.
TIME: GMT + 2.
ELECTRICITY: 220 volts AC, 50Hz.
COMMUNICATIONS: Telephone: IDD is available. Country code: 258. **Telex/telegram:** Connections are via South Africa to international telecommunications network. Reliable telex service in Maputo and Beira. Internal communications exist between most major towns. **Post:** Postal services are available in main centres. Airmail to Europe usually takes five to seven days, but sometimes takes longer. **Press:** There are no English-language newspapers published in Mozambique. The daily papers are *Notícias* and *Diário de Moçambique*.
BBC World Service and Voice of America frequencies: From time to time these change. See the section *How to Use this Book* for more information.

BBC:				
MHz	25.75	17.88	11.94	6.005
Voice of America:				
MHz	21.49	15.60	9.525	6.035

PASSPORT/VISA

Regulations and requirements may be subject to change at short notice, and you are advised to contact the appropriate diplomatic or consular authority before finalising travel arrangements. Details of these may be found at the head of this country's entry. Any numbers in the chart refer to the footnotes below.

	Passport Required?	Visa Required?	Return Ticket Required?
Full British	Yes	Yes	Yes
BVP	Not valid	-	-
Australian	Yes	Yes	Yes
Canadian	Yes	Yes	Yes
USA	Yes	Yes	Yes
Other EC	Yes	Yes	Yes
Japanese	Yes	Yes	Yes

PASSPORTS: Valid passport required by all.
British Visitors Passport: Not accepted.
VISAS: Required by all.
Types of visa: Tourist, Transit or Business; cost £15.
Validity: 1 month (extendable in Mozambique).
Application to: Mozambique Embassies or Consulates *or* Ministerio de Negocias Estrangeiros, CP 290, Maputo. Telex: 6418; *or*
Direccao de Nacional de Migraco, Avenue Ho Chi Minh, Maputo. Telex: 6254; *or*
Empresa Nacional de Turismo (address and telex above).
Note: A visa can sometimes be obtained through a contact living in Mozambique.
Application requirements: (a) Official application form. (b) 3 passport photos. (c) Passport number. (d) Tourists need to be part of an approved package tour.
Working days required: Applicants should apply well in advance as normally approval from Maputo will be required.
Temporary residence: Apply to Embassy of Republic of Mozambique in Portugal (for address, see above).

MONEY

Currency: Mozambique Metical (M) = 100 centavos. Notes are in denominations of M10,000, 5000, 1000, 500, 100 and 50. Coins are in denominations of M20, 10, 5, 2.5 and 1, and 50, 20 and 10 centavos.
Exchange rate indicators: The following figures are included as a guide to the movements of the Metical against Sterling and the US Dollar:

Date:	Nov '88	Oct '90	Oct '91	Oct '92
£1.00=	1151.26	1277.45	3071.97	4310.43
$1.00=	626.71	809.25	1770.08	2716.09

Currency restrictions: Import and export of local currency is prohibited. Free import of foreign currency is allowed, subject to declaration. Export of foreign currency is limited to the amount declared on import.
Banking hours: 0730-1115 Monday to Friday.

DUTY FREE

The following goods may be imported into Mozambique without incurring customs duty:
200 cigarettes or 250g of tobacco;
500ml of spirits;
A reasonable quantity of perfume (opened).
Controlled items: Narcotics are prohibited. Firearms require a permit.

PUBLIC HOLIDAYS

Public holidays observed in Mozambique are as follows:
Apr 7 '93 Women's Day. **May 1** Labour Day. **Jun 25** Independence and Foundation of FRELIMO Day. **Sep 7** Victory Day. **Sep 25** Armed Forces Day. **Dec 25** Family Day. **Jan 1 '94** New Year's Day. **Feb 3** Heroes' Day.

HEALTH

Regulations and requirements may be subject to change at short notice, and you are advised to contact your doctor well in advance of your intended date of departure. Any numbers in the chart refer to the footnotes below.

	Special Precautions?	Certificate Required?
Yellow Fever	No	1
Cholera	Yes	2
Typhoid & Polio	Yes	-
Malaria	3	-
Food & Drink	4	-

[1]: A yellow fever vaccination certificate is required of travellers over one year of age coming from infected areas.
[2]: Following WHO guidelines issued in 1973, a cholera vaccination certificate is not a condition of entry to Mozambique. However, cholera is a serious risk in this country and precautions are essential. Up-to-date advice should be sought before deciding whether these precautions should include vaccination, as medical opinion is divided over its effectiveness. See the *Health* section at the back of the book.
[3]: Malaria risk exists throughout the year in the whole country. The predominant *falciparum* strain is reported to be 'highly resistant' to chloroquine.
[4]: All water should be regarded as being potentially contaminated. Water used for drinking, brushing teeth or making ice should have first been boiled or otherwise sterilised. Milk is unpasteurised and should be boiled. Powdered or tinned milk is available and is advised, but make sure that it is reconstituted with pure water. Avoid dairy products which are likely to have been made from unboiled milk. Only eat well-cooked meat and fish, preferably served hot. Pork, salad and mayonnaise may carry increased risk. Vegetables should be cooked and fruit peeled.
Rabies is present. For those at high risk, vaccination before arrival should be considered. If you are bitten abroad seek medical advice without delay. For more information consult the *Health* section at the back of the book.
Bilharzia (schistosomiasis) is present. Avoid swimming and paddling in fresh water. Swimming pools which are well-chlorinated and maintained are safe.
Health care: Full health insurance is essential. Medical facilities are scarce and of a poor standard. Many rural health centres were forced to close during the conflict with the MNR rebels. There is one doctor per 44,000 inhabitants.

TRAVEL - International

AIR: Mozambique's national airline is *LAM-Linhas Aéreas de Moçambique (TM)*.
Approximate flight time: From *London* to Maputo is 14 hours, including stopover in Johannesburg.
International airports: *Maputo (MPM)* (Mavalane) is 8km (5 miles) north of the city (travel time – 20 minutes). Airport facilities include restaurant, bar, snack bar and post office. Taxis are rarely available at the airport and the visitor should arrange for someone to meet them if possible. Flight information, tel: (1) 465 025/34, ext 345.
Beira (BEW) is 13km (8 miles) from the city (travel time – 15 minutes). Beira only receives flights from Continental Europe, other African countries and America. Airport facilities include restaurant, shops and a post office.
Departure tax: US$20.
SEA: British, European, American, Japanese and South

African cargo vessels call at Maputo and Beira, but there are no regular passenger services.
RAIL: A train runs six times a week from Johannesburg to the Mozambique border at Komatipoort where there is a connection (not guaranteed) to Maputo. There are no connections at present between Harare and Beira or Harare and Maputo, as the border crossings are closed; railway connections to Zimbabwe are being rehabilitated. There are connections from Malawi to Beira (though the border may still have to be crossed on foot) and to Nacala.
Note: The political situation makes rail travel unreliable.
ROAD: There are good road links with all neighbouring countries except Tanzania. For entry requirements and routes for border crossing, contact the Embassy.

TRAVEL - Internal

AIR: There are flights linking Maputo with Blantyre, Inhambane, Beira, Quelimane, Tete, Lichinga, Nampula and Pemba. Flights depart from Maputo between 0500 and 0730 and are subject to seasonal alterations. Air taxi services are also available, and are the safest means of transport outside the main cities due to the fighting within the country.
Departure tax: US$10.
RAIL: There is no rail connection between Maputo and Beira. There is a rail link between Beira and Tete and lines from the towns of Mozambique and Nacala, via the junction at Monapo, to Nampula and Lichinga. Trains also run from Maputo to Goba and Ressano Garcia, and northwards on the line to Zimbabwe. Most trains have three classes, but there are few sleepers and no dining or air-conditioned cars. For seats and sleepers it is necessary to book in advance. All train services are at present liable to be disrupted.
ROAD: Tarred roads connect Maputo with Beira and Beira with Tete. **Bus:** There are regular services covering most of the country. It is essential to carry food and water on long journeys. There are frequent controls to check papers, especially in the north and near the border with Zimbabwe. Bus travel is the cheapest form of transport in the country. **Taxi:** Rarely available outside Maputo. **Car hire:** There are only one or two car-hire firms and rental cars are difficult to obtain. Only hard currency is accepted. **Documentation:** International Driving Permit required.
Note: Owing to fighting within Mozambique, travel by road outside the capital is currently inadvisable.
URBAN: Bus services in Maputo are being improved with the introduction of new vehicles, and there are now fairly extensive services. Taxis are metered but hard to find. Taxi drivers expect a 10% tip.

ACCOMMODATION

HOTELS: Hotels of international standard are found in the cities of Maputo and Beira, and accommodation is adequate in smaller towns. Prices are available on request.
GUEST-HOUSES: It is possible to rent holiday cottages, bungalows and *rondavels* cheaply.
CAMPING/CARAVANNING: There are campsites along the beaches, and a rest camp with a restaurant in Gorongosa Game Park. Camping is also permitted at various Catholic and Protestant missions in the country.

RESORTS & EXCURSIONS

The country is slowly opening to tourism, but so far only package tours are permitted. Casual visitors are not allowed. **Beira** has lovely beaches and is the base for trips to *Gorongosa National Park*. Other beaches are *Ponta do Ouro*, *Malagane* (in the south), **Inhaca Island** (near Maputo), **Inhambane** with its beach resort of *Tofo* (about 400km or 250 miles north of the capital), *Xai-Xai*, *San Martino do Bilene* and *Chonguene*. The museum in **Maputo** houses paintings and sculptures by well-known local artists. The gallery in the Ministry of Labour building is also worth a visit, as is the market. **Moçambique** is a fascinating town, full of 17th- and 18th-century buildings. Regions that are being developed as tourist resorts include the **Bazaruto Archipelago**, an excellent game-fishing area, and the islands of **Santa Carolina** and **Zalala**, north of Beira.

NATIONAL PARKS: The **Gorongosa National Park** is open from the beginning of May to the end of October. Visits can be booked through the LAM office in Maputo. Access is provided by an airstrip at Chitengo. Guides and cars are available inside the park. The **Maputo Elephant Park** is on the right bank of the Maputo River. The **Marromeu National Park** is at the mouth of the Zambesi River.

SOCIAL PROFILE

FOOD & DRINK: The cuisine is mainly Portuguese with Far Eastern influences. Specialities are *piri-piri* chicken, shellfish, including Delagoa Bay prawns (which are grilled and served with *piri-piri* sauce), *matapa* (sauce of ground peanuts and cassava leaves) with rice or *wusa* (stiff maize porridge). There are restaurants in main towns and hotels.
NIGHTLIFE: There are a number of nightclubs in Maputo which offer music and dancing. The style of music varies from typical Mozambican ballads to Western pop music. Most major towns have cinemas.
SHOPPING: Special purchases include basketwork, reed mats, woodcarvings, masks, printed cloth and leather articles. **Shopping hours:** 0830-1300 and 1500-1830 Tuesday to Saturday. On Mondays shops are closed in the mornings and open 1400-1830 in the afternoons.
SPORT: Fishing: There is good fishing for marlin, barracuda, sailfish and swordfish. Notable resorts are Inhaca Island near Maputo, the Bazarutoto Archipelago and Mozambique Island. **Swimming:** There are many safe beaches and lagoons with safe bathing; however, there is a danger of occasional sharks in the warm Indian Ocean. Many hotels have pools. **Skindiving:** Some resorts have facilities and excellent clear waters full of underwater sights for the skin-diver to explore. Zavora's coral reef is outstanding.
SPECIAL EVENTS: For details of events in 1993/1994 contact the Mozambique National Tourism Company.
SOCIAL CONVENTIONS: Shaking hands is the customary form of greeting. The courtesies of address customary in Portugal and other Latin countries are still observed. Casual wear is acceptable. Formal dress is seldom required. **Tipping:** 10% is customary, although it is discouraged in hotels.

BUSINESS PROFILE

ECONOMY: The departure of Portuguese personnel, who made up most of the skilled workforce immediately after independence, and the subsequent debilitating civil war has devastated the Mozambiquan economy. The industrial base, which has never been extensive, is very weak. Those light industries still functioning include food-processing, textiles, brewing, cement and fertilizer production. Heavy industry and mining have the potential for major development but demand a more substantial infrastructure than the Government can sustain. Agriculture, which employs 90% of the working population, contributes little beyond subsistence level, and during the 1980s has been further worsened by recurrent drought. Cash crops include cashew nuts, tea, sugar, sisal, cotton, copra, oil seeds and some citrus fruit. Mozambique consequently depends heavily on large injections of foreign aid. The generally parlous state of the economy has shown some signs of improvement, as the Economic Recovery Plan instituted in 1987 starts to take effect. USA, Singapore and Zimbabwe are Mozambique's most important trading partners. The political settlement reached in August will allow the long task of reconstruction to begin. The all-important Beira and Limpopo rail corridors have been open for some months under a local cease-fire agreement and foreign investment has been picking up.
BUSINESS: Safari suits are advised for the hot season, while lightweight suits or jackets should be worn for the rest of the year. Prior appointments are recommended. There are few translation facilities available in Maputo, though it is usually possible to find someone in business circles who can help. January is the main holiday month, so this should be avoided for business trips. **Office hours:** 0800-1200 and 1400-1700 Monday to Friday, 0800-1200 Saturday.
COMMERCIAL INFORMATION: The following organisation can offer advice: Câmara de Comércio de Moçambique, CP 1836, Rua Mateus Sansão Mutemba 452, Maputo. Tel: (1) 491 970. Telex: 6498.

HISTORY & GOVERNMENT

HISTORY: Records of Arabs and Indians trading with populations in the region exist from the 10th century. From the 15th century onwards, Portuguese influence gradually displaced the Arabs and Indians in the trading system. Mozambique became a Portuguese colony in the 19th century and an overseas province in 1951. Nationalist groups began to form in the 1960s and negotiations on the country's independence began in earnest in 1974, after the coup in Portugal. Mozambique became independent in 1975, and the FRELIMO liberation movement took power. The FRELIMO leader Samora Machel was President from 1975 until his death in a plane crash in October 1986, initally following an orthodox Marxist programme while at the same time encouraging Western investment in the country, a delicate policy which he followed with a fair degree of success. Mozambique's desperate problems are largely the result of the 16-year civil war which has wracked the country. The National Resistance Movement (RENAMO), who are backed by South Africa and have contacts in the United States, have been fighting a guerrilla war against FRELIMO. Two peace treaties in 1984 and 1989 both broke down within months of their signing. In October 1991, after 18 months of Italian-brokered talks, a more provisional settlement was reached between RENAMO and FRELIMO under which both sides offered mutual guarantees on security. Further agreements confirming the settlement were reached in August and October 1992, following the first face-to-face meeting between President Chissano and RENAMO leader Alfonso Dhlakama. The terms of the settlement allow for elections within 12 months at which RENAMO will be able to campaign. RENAMO's position, despite its background as a terrorist organisation of the Rhodesian and South African security forces, is stronger than might be imagined. In several provinces the organisation has developed a genuine political base, yet despite the political and economic disintegration that has taken place during FRELIMO's rule, the movement retains widespread support within the country. The legacy of the 16-year-long civil war has been terrible for Mozambique. The population is cowed, brutalised and largely dependent on foreign aid. As if that were not enough, the country has been badly affected by the drought which has gripped the whole region.
GOVERNMENT: The President holds executive power and appoints and presides over a council of ministers, responsible to the People's Assembly.

CLIMATE

Inland is cooler than the coast and rainfall higher as the land rises, with most rain between January and March. Hottest and wettest season is October to March. From April to September the coast is warm and breezy.
Required clothing: Lightweight cottons and linens.

MAPUTO Mozambique (64m)

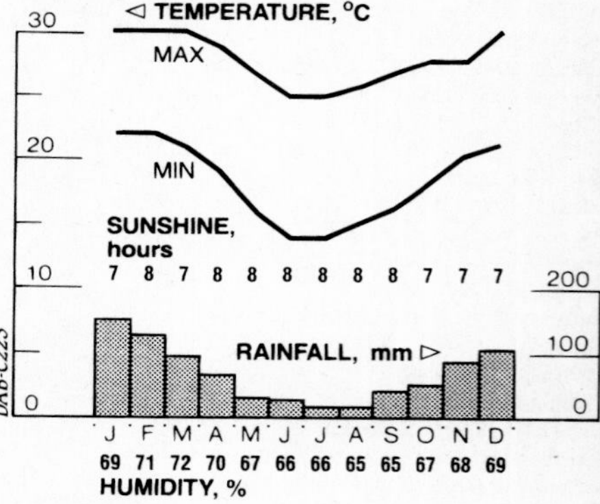

MOZAMBIQUE	HEALTH REGULATIONS	VISA REGULATIONS
GALILEO/WORLDSPAN	TI-DFT/MPM/HE	TI-DFT/MPM/VI
SABRE	TIDFT/MPM/HE	TIDFT/MPM/VI

Code-Link

To access this information on your CRS, swipe the barcode with a light pen or type in the text under the barcode. For more information, see the introduction *How to Use This Book*.

MYANMAR

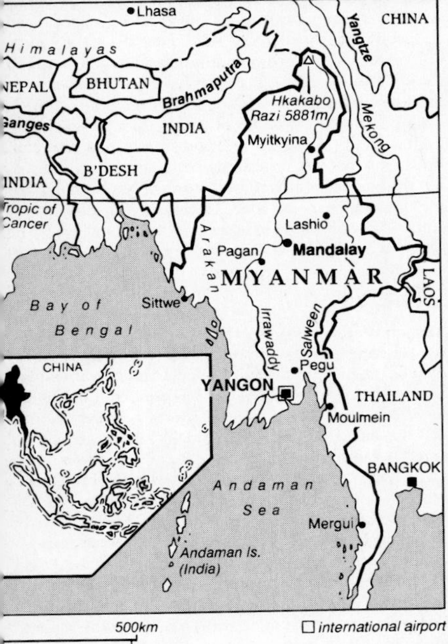

Location: South-East Asia.

Note: The Union of Myanmar, the name adopted by Burma in 1989, is now in general use. The old name continues to be used, but should not be used in official communications.

Myanmar Hotels and Tourism Services
PO Box 1398
77-91 Sule Pagoda Road
Yangon 11141, Myanmar
Tel: (1) 83363. Fax: (1) 89588. Telex: 21330 HOTOCO BM.

Myanmar Travel and Tours
77-79 Sule Pagoda Road
Yangon 11141, Myanmar
Tel: (1) 78376.
Fax and Telex numbers as above.

Embassy of the Union of Myanmar
19a Charles Street
Berkeley Square
London W1X 8ER
Tel: (071) 629 6966. Fax: (071) 629 4169. Telex: 267609 MYANMA G. Opening hours: 0930-1630 Monday to Friday.

Visa Section
Address as above.
Tel: (071) 499 8841. Opening hours: 1000-1300 Monday to Friday.

British Embassy
PO Box 638
80 Strand Road
Yangon, Myanmar
Tel: (1) 81700/2/3. Fax: (1) 89566. Telex: 21216 PRODRM BM.

Embassy of the Union of Myanmar
2300 S Street, NW
Washington, DC
20008
Tel: (202) 332 9044/5. Fax: (202) 332 9046. Telex: 248310.

Consulate General of the Union of Myanmar
Permanent Mission of Myanmar to the United Nations
135 East 36th Street
New York, NY
10016
Tel: (212) 685 2003. Fax: (212) 685 1561.

Embassy of the United States of America
PO Box 521
581 Merchant Street
Yangon, Myanmar
Tel: (1) 82055 *or* 82181. Fax: (1) 80409. Telex: 21230 AMBYGN BM.

Embassy of the Union of Myanmar
Suite 902, The Sandringham Apartments
85 Range Road
Ottawa, Ontario
K1N 8J6
Tel: (613) 232 6434/5 *or* 232 6446. Fax: (613) 232 6435.

Canadian Embassy to Myanmar:
c/o Canadian High Commission
PO Box 569
Dhaka, Bangladesh
Tel: (2) 883 639. Fax: (2) 883 043.

AREA: 676,552 sq km (261,218 sq miles).
POPULATION: 39,350,000 (1988 estimate).
POPULATION DENSITY: 58.2 per sq km.
CAPITAL: Yangon (Rangoon). **Population:** 2,513,023 (1983).
GEOGRAPHY: Myanmar is a diamond-shaped country extending 925km (575 miles) from east to west and 2100km (1300 miles) from north to south. It is bounded by China, Laos and Thailand in the east, and by Bangladesh, India and the Indian Ocean in the south and west. The Irrawaddy River runs through the centre of the country and fans out to form a delta on the south coast; Yangon stands beside one of its many mouths. North of the delta lies the Irrawaddy basin and central Myanmar, which is protected by a horseshoe of mountains rising to over 3000m (10,000ft), creating profound climatic effects. To the west are the Arakan, Chin and Naga Mountains and the Patkai Hills; the Kachin Hills are to the north; to the east lies the Shan Plateau, which extends to the Tenasserim coastal ranges. Intensive irrigated farming is practised throughout central Myanmar, and fruit, vegetables and citrus crops thrive on the Shan Plateau, but much of the land and mountains are covered by subtropical forest.
LANGUAGE: The official language is Burmese. There are over 100 distinct languages and dialects spoken in Myanmar. English is spoken in business circles.
RELIGION: 85% Theravada Buddhist. The remainder are Hindu, Muslim, Christian and Animist.
TIME: GMT + 6.30.
ELECTRICITY: 220/230 volts AC, 50Hz.
COMMUNICATIONS: Telephone: IDD is available to the main cities. Country code: 95. There is a limited public internal service. **Telex/telegram:** Telegrams may be sent from the Central Telegraph Office on Maha Bandoola Street and there are further facilities at the Post and Telecommunications Corporation in Yangon. Telex facilities are available to businessmen at main hotels but not to the public. **Post:** Service to Europe takes up to a week and letter forms are quicker than ordinary letters. To ensure despatch it is advisable to go personally to the post office to obtain a certificate of posting, for which a small fee is charged. **Press:** The English-language newspaper is *The Working People's Daily*.
BBC World Service and Voice of America frequencies: From time to time these change. See the section *How to Use this Book* for more information.

BBC:				
MHz	17.79	11.75	9.740	6.195
Voice of America:				
MHz	17.74	15.40	11.71	7.125

PASSPORT/VISA

Regulations and requirements may be subject to change at short notice, and you are advised to contact the appropriate diplomatic or consular authority before finalising travel arrangements. Details of these may be found at the head of this country's entry. Any numbers in the chart refer to the footnotes below.

	Passport Required?	Visa Required?	Return Ticket Required?
Full British	Yes	Yes	Yes
BVP	Not valid	-	-
Australian	Yes	Yes	Yes
Canadian	Yes	Yes	Yes
USA	Yes	Yes	Yes
Other EC	Yes	Yes	Yes
Japanese	Yes	Yes	Yes

Restricted entry: Holders of passports issued by North Korea and Taiwan are refused admission.
PASSPORTS: Valid passport required by all.
VISAS: Required by all. A separate visa is required for each child over 7 years of age even if travelling on their parent's passport.
Types of visa: Tourist (£10) and Business (£20).
Validity: Tourist visas are granted for a *maximum of 14 days stay* in Myanmar, but are valid for 3 months from the date of issue. For business purposes the visa, which must be obtained before entry, can be extended once in Myanmar.
Application to: Consulate (or Consular Section at Embassy). For addresses, see top of entry.
Application requirements: *Tourist Visa:* (a) 3 photos. (b) 2 application forms. (c) Air ticket to Myanmar or a letter from airline or travel agency concerned giving details of flights in and out of Yangon (land entry into Myanmar is not allowed). (d) Valid passport. *Business Visa:* (a) 3 application forms. (b) 3 photos. (c) Letter from sponsoring body, firm or department stating detailed reasons for the applicant's visit and the name of the Myanmar Government Department, Corporation or Agency to be contacted; the letter must state the precise nature of the business to be conducted and indicate the financial status of the applicant. (d) Valid passport.
Working days required: 24 hours (provided the Government's letter of permission has been submitted).
Exit permits: A *Report of Departure form D* is required by all persons holding entry or transit visas for stays exceeding 30 days. The permit must be acquired before booking passage.

MONEY

Currency: Kyat (Kt) = 100 pyas. Notes are in denominations of Kt200, 90, 45, 15, 10, 5 and 1. Coins are in denominations of Kt1, and 50, 25, 10, 5 and 1 pyas. Kt100,000 is known as a *lakh*, and Kt10 million as a *crore*. Kyat is pronounced like the English word 'chat'. To combat the black market and limit the financial power of dissident groups, currency denominations are occasionally declared invalid without prior notice. Limited refunds are usually allowed for certain sectors of the population.
Credit cards: These are not generally accepted, but check with your credit card company for details of merchant acceptability and other services which may be available.
Travellers cheques: Accepted.
Exchange rate indicators: The following figures are included as a guide to the movements of the Kyat against Sterling and the US Dollar:

Date:	**Oct '89**	**Oct '90**	**Oct '91**	**Oct '92**
£1.00=	10.78	11.58	10.72	11.31
$1.00=	6.83	5.93	6.18	7.13

Currency restrictions: The import and export of local currency is prohibited. There are no import limits on foreign currencies, but the amounts must be declared on entry and the declaration certificate kept safe – on departure, foreign currencies are checked with the amounts declared on entry. A minimum equivalent to US$100 must be exchanged on entry. Only a quarter of the foreign currency converted to Kyats during stay in Myanmar will be allowed to be re-converted on exit. There are regular customs checks at Yangon airport, aimed at curbing black-market activities; this makes it essential to keep all receipts in order to account for money spent while in the country.
Banking hours: 1000-1400 Monday to Friday.

DUTY FREE

The following goods may be taken into Myanmar by persons over 17 years of age without incurring customs duty:
400 cigarettes or 100 cigars or 250g tobacco;
1.136 litres of alcohol;
500ml of perfume or eau de cologne.
Prohibited items: Playing cards, gambling equipment and pornography.
Note: Travellers must obtain a permit from the Exchange Control Department to take jewellery totalling more than Kt250 in value out of Myanmar. All jewellery (including wedding rings) should be declared; failure to do so may result in visitors being refused permission to export it on departure.

PUBLIC HOLIDAYS

Public holidays observed in Myanmar are as follows:
Mar '93 Full Moon of Tabaung. **Mar 2** Peasants' Day. **Mar 27** Armed Forces Day. **Apr** Maha Thingyan-Water Festival. **Apr 17** Myanma New Year. **May** Full Moon of Kason. **May 1** Workers' Day. **Jun 1** Start of Eid al-Adha. **Jul 19** Martyrs' Day. **Aug** Full Moon of Waso. **Oct** Full Moon of Thadingyut. **Nov** Tazaungdaing Festival. **Dec 3** National Day. **Dec 25** Christmas Day. **Jan 4 '94** Independence Day. **Feb 12** Union Day. **Mar** Full Moon of Tabaung. **Mar 2** Peasants' Day. **Mar 27** Armed Forces Day.
Note: Buddhist holidays are determined according to lunar sightings, and dates given here are approximations only. Other festivals celebrated by minorities include the Hindu Devali festival in November; Islamic observance of Bakri Idd in late November; Christmas and Easter; and the Karen New Year in early January. For further information on holidays in 1993/94, contact the Embassy.

HEALTH

Regulations and requirements may be subject to change at short notice, and you are advised to contact your doctor well in advance of your intended date of departure. Any numbers in the chart refer to the footnotes below.

	Special Precautions?	Certificate Required?
Yellow Fever	Yes	1
Cholera	Yes	2
Typhoid & Polio	Yes	-
Malaria	3	-
Food & Drink	4	-

[1]: A yellow fever vaccination certificate is required from all travellers arriving from infected areas. Nationals and residents of Myanmar are required to possess certificates of vaccination on their departure to an infected area.
[2]: Following WHO guidelines issued in 1973, a cholera vaccination certificate is no longer a condition of entry to Myanmar. However, cholera is a serious risk in this country and precautions are essential. Up-to-date advice should be sought before deciding whether these precautions should include vaccination, as medical opinion is divided over its effectiveness. See the *Health* section at the back of the book.
[3]: Malaria risk (predominantly in the malignant *falciparum* form) below 1000m in the following areas: (a) throughout the year in Karen State; (b) from March to December in Chin, Kachin, Kayah, Mon, Rakhine and Shan States, in Pegu Division, and in Hlegu, Hmawbi and Taikkyi townships of Yangon; (c) from April to December in rural areas of Tenasserim Division; (d) from May to December in Irrawaddy Division and rural areas of Mandalay Division; (e) from June to November in rural areas of Magwe Division and in Sagaing Division. The *falciparum* strain is reported to be 'highly resistant' to chloroquine and 'resistant' to sulfadoxine/pyrimethamine.
[4]: All water should be regarded as being potentially contaminated. Water used for drinking, brushing teeth or making ice should have first been boiled or otherwise sterilised. Milk is unpasteurised and should be boiled. Powdered or tinned milk is available and is advised, but make sure that it is reconstituted with pure water. Avoid dairy products which are likely to have been made from unboiled milk. Only eat well-cooked meat and fish, preferably served hot. Pork, salad and mayonnaise may carry increased risk. Vegetables should be cooked and fruit peeled.
The WHO advises that foci of *plague* are present in Myanmar. Further information should be sought from the Department of Health or from any of the hospitals specialising in tropical diseases listed in the *Health* section at the back of the book.
Japanese encephalitis may be caught via mosquito bites, particularly in rural areas between June and October. A vaccine is available, and travellers are advised to consult their doctor prior to departure.
Rabies is present. For those at high risk, vaccination before arrival should be considered. If you are bitten abroad seek medical advice without delay. For more information consult the *Health* section at the back of the book.
Health care: Health insurance is strongly recommended. There are hospitals and clinics in cities and larger towns, and regional health centres in outlying areas. It is advisable to carry a remedy against minor enteric upsets.

TRAVEL - International

AIR: Myanmar's national airline is *Myanmar Airways (UB)*.
International airport: *Yangon (YGN)* (Mingaladon) is 19km (12 miles) from the city. Airport facilities include restaurant, bar, snack bar, bank, post office, duty-free shop and tourist information. Travel to the city is by taxi (not always available) or by bus number 9, departing every 15 minutes (travel time – 30 minutes). Bus number 9 returns from Merchant Street. In 1987 a 5-year project to upgrade facilities commenced.
Departure tax: US$6 or Kt15 is levied; children under 18 years of age and passengers in direct transit are exempt.
Note: Air travel is the only means of access into Myanmar.

TRAVEL - Internal

AIR: Air travel is the most efficient way of moving within Myanmar, but there is a rather limited schedule of flights. Internal security can restrict ease of movement. There are daily flights to most towns; charter flights are also available. There are over 50 airstrips in the country. For tickets and information, contact Myanmar Hotels and Tourism Services (address at top of entry).
Internal flight times: From Yangon to *Mandalay* is 2 hours 10 minutes; to *Pagan* is 1 hour 30 minutes; and to *Heho* is 1 hour 25 minutes.
SEA/RIVER: The best way of seeing Myanmar is by boat, particularly between Bhamo–Mandalay and Mandalay–Pagan. Myanmar has about 8000km (5000 miles) of navigable rivers. Local travel agents can arrange trips. It is generally necessary to provide own food.
Note: Delays are frequent, so allow plenty of time for boat travel.
RAIL: *Myanmar Railways* provides services on several routes, the principal line being Yangon to Mandalay (travel time – 12-14 hours). Overnight trains have sleeping cars. There is also a good service from Mandalay–Lashio–Myitkyina. The state-run railway has 4300km (2700 miles) of track and serves most of Myanmar. First class is available but, with the exception of the Yangon to Mandalay line, services are regularly afflicted with delays caused by climatic, technical and bureaucratic difficulties. Tickets must be purchased through Myanmar Hotels and Tourism Services, 24 hours in advance if possible; it is also worth travelling first class if possible. There are regular services from Yangon to Mandalay and from Yangon to Thazi. Combined rail/bus tickets are obtainable.
ROAD: There are long-distance **buses,** but these are not recommended due to their condition and the condition of the roads. There has been some modernisation of Myanmar's once antiquated vehicles. Japanese pick-up trucks run unscheduled services between large towns. **Bicycles** are available for hire.
Documentation: An International Driving Permit required. This must be presented to the police, who will endorse it or issue a visitor's licence.
URBAN: Yangon has a circular rail service. There is also an antiquated and over-crowded bus service in all cities. Yangon has blue government taxis with set fares. Unmetered 3- and 4-wheel taxis are available in cities, as are rickshaws; it is wise to pre-arrange fares.

ACCOMMODATION

HOTELS: Bookings should be made well in advance. Yangon only has 400 hotel beds. Contact the Hotels and Tourism Services. There are also hotels at the resorts of Sandoway, Taunggyi and Pagan. In general, advance booking is advisable, particularly from November to March. **Grading:** There is an increasing number of hotels, divided into three categories: luxury, first class and lower.
Visitors travelling away from the normal tourist routes should carry sleeping bags or blankets, as pagodas, temples and monasteries will usually only accommodate visitors for a night or two. Although reserved for state officials in many towns, inns will often accommodate travellers who have been granted official permission.

RESORTS & EXCURSIONS

Myanmar remains a fascinating land, all the more so because it has been virtually closed to the outside world since 1960. Magnificent stupas, temples and pagodas can be found throughout Upper and Lower Myanmar. Much of Upper and Lower Myanmar is out of bounds, owing to the civil war. Few coastal resorts have been opened to tourists, but Sunday round-trip flights are arranged by the Tourist Corporation to Napali and Sandoway beaches during the dry season. Other sports can be played at clubs in Yangon, but it is necessary to be a member or guest.
For the purpose of this guide, Myanmar has been divided into four regions: The South (including Yangon); Central Myanmar (including Pagan and Mandalay); The East and The Northwest.

The South

Yangon (or *Rangoon*), the capital, is a city of Buddhist temples, open-air markets, food stalls and ill-repaired colonial architecture. It has a population of over two million. Although most of the city has been built in the last hundred years, and although it suffered considerable damage during the Second World War, there are still several examples of a more ancient culture. These include the golden *Shwe Dagon Pagoda,* one of the most spectacular Buddhist shrines in Asia and reputedly 2500 years old (although rebuilt in 1769); the *Sule Pagoda*; the *Botataung Pagoda,* hollow inside with a mirrored maze; and the *Maha Pasan Guha* or 'Great Cave'.
Outside the capital, places worth visiting include the *Naga-Yone* enclosure near **Myinkaba,** with a Buddha figure entwined and protected by a huge cobra – a combination of Buddhism and Brahman astrology; *Kyaik Tyo* and its 'Golden Rock Pagoda', an 18ft shrine built on a gold-plated boulder atop a cliff; and **Pegu,** founded in 1573, with its golden *Shwemawdaw Pagoda* and market. Just northeast of Pegu is the *Shwethalyaung Buddha,* revered as one of the most beautiful and lifelike of reclining Buddhas, which was lost and totally overgrown by jungle after the destruction of Pegu in 1757. It was rediscovered in the British era, during the construction of the railway line.

Central Myanmar

Pagan is one of the greatest historical areas in the country. It is best seen at sunrise or sunset. More than 13,000 pagodas were once spread over this dry plain during the golden age of the 11 great kings (roughly 1044-1287); this came to an end with the threat of invasion by Kublai Khan from China, and this extraordinary area was abandoned. Now there are fewer than 3000 pagodas. The actual village of Pagan has a museum, market and places to eat and stay; within walking distance of Pagan, there are lacquerware workshops and an attractive temple. There are dozens of awe-inspiring open temples in the Pagan area (about 40 sq km), but places of special interest include the *Shwegugyi Temple,* built in 1311 and noted for its fine stucco carvings; the *Gawdawpalin Temple,* badly damaged in the 1975 earthquake, but still one of the most impressive of the Pagan temples; and the *Thatbyinnyu Temple,* which is the highest in Pagan.
Mandalay, the old royal city, is rich in palaces, stupas, temples and pagodas (although the city has suffered several bad fires which have destroyed some buildings), and is the main centre of Buddhism and Burmese arts. There are some excellent craft markets and there are thriving stone-carving workshops and gold-leaf industries. Taking its name from *Mandalay Hill* (rising about 240m to the northeast of the palace), the city was

UNION OF MYANMAR	HEALTH REGULATIONS	VISA REGULATIONS (Code-Link)
GALILEO/WORLDSPAN	 TI-DFT/RGN/HE	TI-DFT/RGN/VI
SABRE	TIDFT/RGN/HE	TIDFT/RGN/VI

To access this information on your CRS, swipe the barcode with a light pen or type in the text under the barcode. For more information, see the introduction *How to Use This Book.*

ounded by King Mindon in 1857, the old wooden alace buildings at Amarapura being moved and reconructed. Sights of interest include the huge *Shweyattaw uddha*, close to the hill, with its outstretched finger ointing towards the city; the *Eindawya Pagoda*, built 1847 and covered in gold leaf; the *Shwekyimyint agoda* containing the original Buddha image consecrated by Prince Minshinzaw during the Pagan period; nd the *Mahumuni Pagoda* or 'Great Pagoda', housing he famous and revered Mahumuni image. Covered in old leaf over the years by devout Buddhists, this image vas brought from Arakan in 1784, although it is hought to be much older. The base, moat and huge valls are virtually all that remain of the once stupenlous *Mandalay Palace*, which was an immense walled ity (mostly of timber construction) rather than a alace. It was burnt down in 1942. A large scale model gives an indication of what it must have been like. The *hwenandaw Kyaung Monastery* was at one time part of he palace complex and was used as an apartment by King Mindon and his chief queen. Like the palace, the wooden building was once beautifully gilded. There are ome extraordinary carved panels inside and also a hotograph of the *Atumashi Kyaung Monastery*, lestroyed by fire in 1890. The ruins can be seen to the outh of the *Kuthodaw Pagoda*, called 'the world's biggest book' because of the 729 marble slabs that surround the central pagoda – they are inscribed with the entire Buddhist canon.

The area around Mandalay contains several older, abandoned capital cities. **Sagaing** is easily accessible to the visitor, and contains interesting pagodas at *Tupayon*, *Aungmyelawka* and *Kaunghmudaw*. Sagaing was for a time the capital of an independent Shan kingdom. In the 15th century, **Ava** was chosen as the kingdom's new capital and it remained so until well into the 19th century, when the kingdom vanished; the old city walls can still be traced. **Mingun** (a pleasant river trip from Mandalay) possesses the famous *Mingun Bell*, supposedly the largest uncracked, hung bell in the world. It was cast in 1790 by King Bodawpaya to be hung in his giant pagoda, which was never finished, due to the king's death in 1819. The base of the pagoda alone is about 50m (165ft) high. **Amarapura,** south of Mandalay, was founded by Bodawpaya in 1783 and the city is famous for its cotton and silk weaving.

The East

This region of the country offers the visitor opportunities for walking and rock-climbing, and the various hill stations, such as *Kalaw*, provide a pine-forested escape from the heat and humidity of Yangon. The caves and lake at **Pindaya** are famous; the caves contain thousands of Buddha images. Near the village of **Ye-ngan** are the *Padah-Lin caves*, containing prehistoric paintings. *Inle Lake* on the Shan Plateau is famous for its floating gardens and leg-rowing fishermen. *Maymyo* is a charming British hill station further north, with attractive waterfalls and a pleasant climate because of its high altitude.

The Northwest

Difficult communications usually prevent tourists from visiting this largely tribal region. Many of Myanmar's minority peoples live here, including the famous 'giraffe women', who have copper or brass rings around their necks, wrists and ankles; new rings are added each year until the young girl is married.

SOCIAL PROFILE

FOOD & DRINK: The regional food is hot and spicy. Fish, rice, noodles and vegetables spiced with onions, ginger, garlic and chillies are the common local ingredients. Local dishes include *lethok son* (a sort of spicy vegetarian rice salad), *mohinga* (fish soup with noodles) and *oh-no khauk swe* (rice noodles, chicken and coconut milk). The avocados by Inle Lake are very good. Delicious fruits are available in the markets and food stalls appear on the corners of most large towns. Chinese and Indian cuisine is offered in many hotels and restaurants. **Drink:** Tea is a popular drink; the spices which are added to it can make your tongue turn bright red. Locally produced soft drinks are generally of poor quality and rather expensive. Coffee is not common. Locally produced beer, rum, whisky and gin are generally available.
NIGHTLIFE: Western-style nightlife is non-existent, although there are occasional performances in Yangon's three theatres. Cinemas are popular and seven of Yangon's 50 cinemas regularly show English-language films.
SPORT: Many Western sports are played. **Football** can be seen at Aung San Stadium in Yangon and on small fields throughout the country. The national game is **Chinglone;** its object is to keep a cane ball in the air for as long as possible using only feet and knees with teams of six players. Burmese **boxing** is another popular sport; it can appear extremely vicious to the uninitiated spectator.
SPECIAL EVENTS: The Buddhist calendar is full of festivals, many timed to coincide with the full moon. Any visitor would be unlucky not to be able to enjoy at least one during any stay. The Myanmar New Year, *Maha Thingyan*, takes place in mid-April and lasts for at least three days. Two other major festivals are *Thadingyut*, at the October full moon, and *Tazaungdaing*, in early November. The Buddhist Lent (July to October) is marked by three months' fasting and other religious observances.
SOCIAL CONVENTIONS: Handshaking is the normal form of greeting. Full names are used, preceded by *U* (pronounced *oo*) in the case of an older or well-respected man's name, *Aung* for younger men and *Ko* for adult males; a woman's name is preceded by *Daw*. Courtesy and respect for tradition and religion is expected; for instance, shoes and socks must be removed before entering any religious building and it is customary to remove shoes before entering a traditional home (in most modern residences this is no longer observed except in bedrooms). When sitting, avoid displaying the soles of the feet, as this is considered offensive. Small presents are acceptable and appreciated, although never expected. Shorts and mini-skirts should not be worn. **Tipping:** It is usual to give between 5% and 10% on hotel and restaurant bills. Taxi drivers do not expect a tip.

BUSINESS PROFILE

ECONOMY: A potentially rich country, Myanmar has all but stood still economically under the maladministration of the Burma Socialist Programme Party (now the National Unity Party). Agriculture, mainly livestock and fishing, is the largest single sector but continues to rely on traditional non-mechanised methods. Rice, generally the principal export earner, has diminished in importance in line with the continually depressed state of the world market. Teak is the country's other main export. Other crops include oil-seeds, sugar cane, cotton, jute and rubber. Myanmar has significant deposits of oil, tin, copper and coal, but has failed to exploit them fully, although there are current plans to institute major redevelopment of this sector. A wide range of manufactured goods are assembled locally but the majority are imported ready-made. Myanmar's economic development will continue to be stunted as long as its chronic foreign exchange problems continue: this has forced the Government and state-controlled trading agencies to arrange awkward barter deals. China, Japan and the 'Tiger' economies of the Pacific Basin (notably Singapore) are Myanmar's main trading partners.
BUSINESS: Lightweight suits recommended during the day; jackets needed for top-level meetings. Most commercial business transactions will be conducted in English. Business cards in Burmese script can be useful. The best time to visit is October to February. **Office hours:** 0930-1630 Monday to Friday.
COMMERCIAL INFORMATION: There are over 20 Government Corporations dealing with all aspects of business. The Inspection and Agency Corporation in Yangon promotes business with foreign companies.

HISTORY & GOVERNMENT

HISTORY: Burmans first settled in the area during the 9th century and by the 11th century, led by the Buddhist King Anawratha, had established a powerful kingdom. During the Mongol invasions the country was captured by Kublai Khan (1287) and subsequently Burma was divided. By the mid-18th century, a new dynasty was established under King Alaungpaya with its capital in Yangon. Burma was annexed to Britain as part of the Indian Empire in the 19th century; but in 1937 the country was granted separate dominion status. The independent Union of Burma came into formal existence in 1948, and in 1974 was named the Socialist Republic of the Union of Burma. In 1988, years of idiosyncratic policies, isolationism and chronic economic mismanagement by the then Burma Socialist Programme Party finally brought on a popular uprising, with students and Bhuddhist monks to the fore. A military coup in September, followed by the bloody suppression of the demonstrations, brought the political upheaval to a halt. Far from being deposed, the coup strengthened Ne Win's position within the country: the leader of the coup, General Saw Maung, and his senior staff are all known as long-standing supporters of the reclusive dictator. Ne Win has recently relinquished his official titles as leader of the nation, but he continues to exercise considerable influence over the running of the country. The principal internal opposition is led by ex-army General Tin Oo and the Western-educated liberal Aung Sang Suu Kyi, who is under house arrest. The major armed threat, however, is posed by a variety of border insurgencies. The largest of these groupings is the Karen tribe, whose ranks have been swelled by dissident students fleeing from the capital. In 1989 Burma became officially known as the Union of Myanmar. After the disturbances of 1988 and 1989, which were savagely put down with the loss of thousands of lives, the Government concluded that some political concessions were essential and announced that elections would be held. The main opposition movements campaigned under the banner of the National League for Democracy and won the election, which was held in May 1990, with around 80% of the seats in the national assembly. Despite the comprehensive victory, the Ne Win regime used elaborate delaying tactics and harrassment of opposition leaders to hold onto power, which it shows no sign of relinquishing. Outside the capital the army launched a new offensive in 1991 against the Karen guerrillas and their allies, who continue to operate from their stronghold on the Thai border. A government-in-exile has been established in their headquarters at Manerplaw as part of a political initiative to gain international support against the Government. The xenophobic Ne Win junta is clearly able to withstand considerable external pressure. If anything, its position has strengthened in the last 12 months: logging and drug trafficking in the parts of the border under government control have provided a major source of funds which has allowed the military to re-equip with the latest Chinese *material*.
GOVERNMENT: The 1974 constitution established an elected People's Assembly (the *Pyithu Hluttaw*), which in turn elected a State Council. These and other state organs were abolished following the 1988 coup and Myanmar is currently ruled by a State Law and Order Restoration Council.

CLIMATE

A monsoon climate with three main seasons. The hottest period is between February and May, with little or no rain. Rainy season exists from May to October and dry, cooler weather from October to February.
Required clothing: Lightweight cottons and linens throughout most of the year are required. Light raincoat or umbrella needed during rainy season. Warmer clothes are advised for coolest period and some evenings.

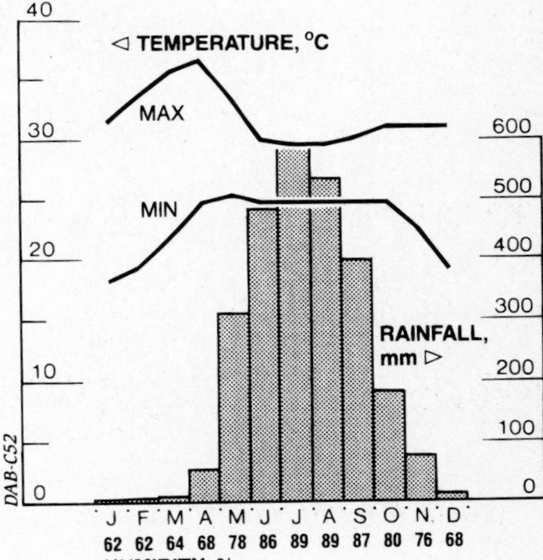

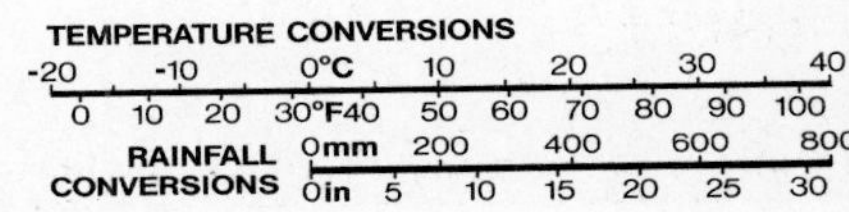

NAMIBIA

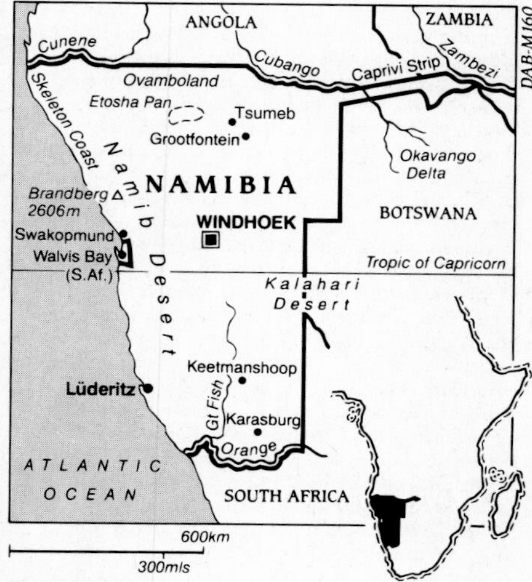

Location: Southwest Africa.

Note: Namibia gained independence on March 21, 1991 and some of the information included below (particularly the *Passport/Visa* and *Money* sections) may be subject to change at short notice. Visitors to Namibia should contact the High Commission or Embassy to obtain up-to-date information.

Ministry of Wildlife, Conservation and Tourism
Private Bag 13346
Windhoek 9000, Namibia
Tel: (61) 220 241. Fax: (61) 221 930.

High Commission for the Republic of Namibia
Centre Link
34 South Molton Street
London
W1Y 2BP
Tel: (071) 344 9706. Fax: (071) 409 7306. Telex: 262479. Opening hours: 0900-1700 Monday to Friday.

British High Commission
116 Leutwein Street
Windhoek 9000, Namibia
Tel: (61) 223 022. Fax: (61) 228 895.

Embassy of the Republic of Namibia
1605 New Hampshire Avenue, NW
Washington, DC
20009
Tel: (202) 986 0540. Fax: (202) 986 0443.

Embassy of the United States of America
PO Box 9890
Ausplan Building
14 Losen Street
Windhoek 9000, Namibia
Tel: (61) 221 601 *or* 222 675 *or* 222 680. Fax: (61) 229 792.

Canadian Embassy
PO Box 2147
111a Gloudina Street
Ludwigsdorf
Windhoek 9000, Namibia
Tel: (61) 222 941 *or* 222 966. Fax: (61) 224 204. Telex: 402 WK.

AREA: 824,292 sq km (318,261 sq miles).
POPULATION: 1,252,000 (1988 estimate).
POPULATION DENSITY: 1.5 per sq km.
CAPITAL: Windhoek. **Population:** 114,500 (1988 estimate).
GEOGRAPHY: Namibia (formerly known as South West Africa) is in southwest Africa. It is a large and mainly barren country sharing borders with Angola to

MARK VAN AARDT

The Spitzkoppe Mountain

Namibia
A VAST DIFFERENCE
Namibia Tourism:
Private Bag 13346, Windhoek Namibia. Tel: (010 26461) 284-2360. Fax: 22-1930.
Or: Namibia Verkehrsbüro, Postfach 2041, W-6380 Bad Homburg 3, Germany.
Tel: (06172) 406650/54, Fax: (06172) 406690.
LINTAS-NAMIBIA 93/2443

the north, Botswana to the east, South Africa to the south and, in the Caprivi Strip, a narrow panhandle of Namibian territory jutting from the northeast corner of the country, with Zambia and Zimbabwe. To the west is 1280km (795 miles) of some of the most desolate and lonely coastline in the world. The port of Walvis Bay, situated roughly halfway down Namibia's coast, is jointly administrated with South Africa. Along its entire length, the vast shifting sand dunes of the Namib Desert spread inland for 80-130km (50-80 miles). In the interior, the escarpment of a north–south plateau slopes away to the east and north into the vast interior sand basin of the Kalahari. In the far northwest the 66,000 sq km (25,500 sq miles) of the Kaokoveld Mountains run along the coast, while further inland lies the Etosha Pan (the giant of Namibia's saline lakes), a flat, lifeless, dry river bed, surrounded by grasslands and bush which support a large and varied wildlife. The Etosha Pan National Park & Game Reserve is one of the finest in Africa, in that it remains, to a large extent, free of man's influence.
LANGUAGE: English is the official language. Afrikaans, German, Herero and Owambo are also spoken.
RELIGION: Christian majority.
TIME: GMT + 2.
ELECTRICITY: 220/240 volts AC. Outlets are of the 3-pin type.
COMMUNICATIONS: Telephone: IDD is available. Country code: 264. **Fax:** Some hotels have facilities. **Telex/telegram:** Good facilities to all major centres. A telegraph service is available in every town. **Post:** Good postal service. Airmail to Europe takes from approximately four days to two weeks. **Press:** Newspapers are printed Monday to Friday. English-language dailies include *The Windhoek Advertiser* and *The Namibian*.
BBC World Service and Voice of America frequencies: From time to time these change. See the section *How to Use this Book* for more information.

BBC:				
MHz	25.75	17.88	11.94	6.005
Voice of America:				
MHz	21.49	15.60	9.525	6.035

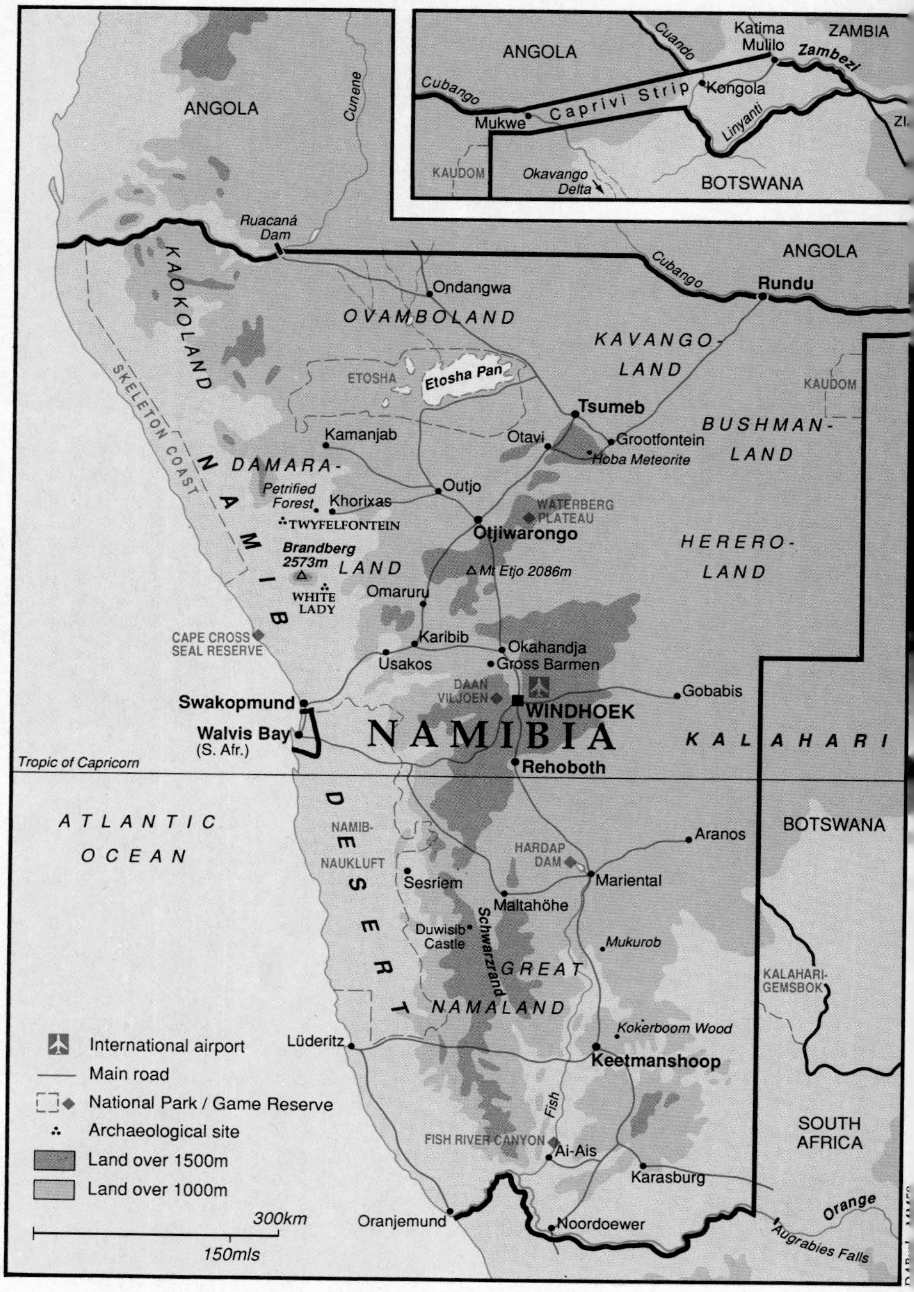

PASSPORT/VISA

Regulations and requirements may be subject to change at short notice, and you are advised to contact the appropriate diplomatic or consular authority before finalising travel arrangements. Details of these may be found at the head of this country's entry. Any numbers in the chart refer to the footnotes below.

	Passport Required?	Visa Required?	Return Ticket Required?
Full British	Yes	No	Yes
BVP	Not valid	-	-
Australian	Yes	Yes	Yes
Canadian	Yes	No	Yes
USA	Yes	No	Yes
Other EC	Yes	1	Yes
Japanese	Yes	No	Yes

PASSPORTS: Valid passport required by all.
British Visitors Passport: Not accepted.
VISAS: Required by all except nationals of the following for a stay of up to 3 months:
(a) [1] EC countries (nationals of Greece, Portugal and Spain *do* require a visa);
(b) Austria, CIS, Finland, Iceland, Liechtenstein, Norway, Sweden and Switzerland;
(c) Canada, Japan and the USA;
(d) Angola, Botswana, Mozambique, Tanzania, Singapore, South Africa, Zambia and Zimbabwe.
Types of Visa: Tourist and Business; visas are issued free.
Validity: 3 months.
Application to: Consulate (or Consular Section at High Commission or Embassy). For addresses, see at the top of entry.
Application requirements: (a) Valid passport. (b) Completed application form. (c) 2 photos. (d) Proof of adequate funds. (e) Company letter if on business.
Working days required: Variable. Apply as early as possible.
Temporary residence: Apply to the High Commission or Embassy (addresses at top of entry).

MONEY

Currency: South African Rand (R) = 100 cents. Notes are in denominations of R50, 20, 10 , 5 and 2. Coins are in denominations of R1, and 50, 20, 10, 5, 2 and 1 cents. The Namibian Dollar is to be introduced in 1993.
Credit cards: Access/Mastercard, American Express and Visa are accepted. Check with your credit card company for details of merchant acceptability and other services which may be available.
Exchange rate indicators: The following figures are included as a guide to the movements of the Rand against Sterling and the US Dollar:

Date:	Oct '89	Oct '90	Oct '91	Oct '92
£1.00=	4.27	4.94	4.89	4.68
$1.00=	2.70	2.53	2.81	2.95

Currency restrictions: All currency must be declared at port of entry. The import and export of local currency is limited to R500. The import of foreign currency is unlimited. Export is limited to the amount imported and declared on arrival.

NAMIBIA	HEALTH REGULATIONS	VISA REGULATIONS
GALILEO/WORLDSPAN	TI-DFT/WDH/HE	TI-DFT/WDH/VI
SABRE	TIDFT/WDH/HE	TIDFT/WDH/VI

Code-Link

To access this information on your CRS, swipe the barcode with a light pen or type in the text under the barcode. For more information, see the introduction *How to Use This Book*.

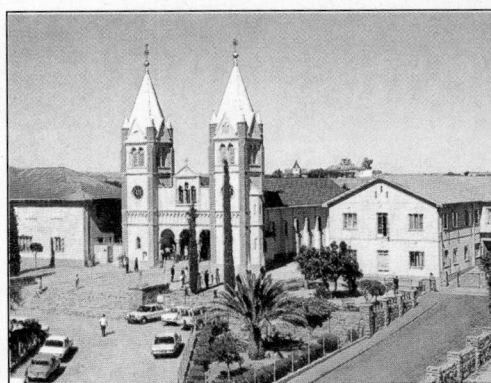

Banking hours: 0900-1530 Monday to Friday, 0830-1100 Saturday.

DUTY FREE

The following goods may be imported into Namibia by persons over 16 years of age without incurring customs duty:

400 cigarettes or 50 cigars or 250g of tobacco;
2 litres of wine and 1 litre of spirits;
50ml of perfume and 250ml of toilet water;
Gifts to the value of R500, but including value of imported duty-free items.

Controlled items: Firearms need a permit which should be issued by customs when entering the country.

PUBLIC HOLIDAYS

Public holidays observed in Namibia are as follows: **Mar 21 '93** Independence Day. **Apr 9-12** Easter. **May 1** Workers Day. **May 4** Casinga Day. **May 20** Ascension. **May 25** Africa Day. **Aug 26** Heroes' Day. **Oct 7** Day of Goodwill. **Dec 10** Human Rights Day. **Dec 25-26** Christmas. **Jan 1 '94** New Year's Day. **Mar 21** Independence Day.

HEALTH

Regulations and requirements may be subject to change at short notice, and you are advised to contact your doctor well in advance of your intended date of departure. Any numbers in the chart refer to the footnotes below.

	Special Precautions?	Certificate Required?
Yellow Fever	Yes	1
Cholera	No	No
Typhoid & Polio	Yes	-
Malaria	2	-
Food & Drink	3	-

[1]: A yellow fever vaccination certificate is required from travellers arriving from infected areas. Those countries or parts of countries that were included in the former endemic zone in Africa and South America are regarded by the Namibian authorities as infected. Travellers with scheduled airlines whose flights have originated outside areas regarded as infected but have passed through such areas in transit are not required to possess a certificate provided they have remained at the scheduled airport or in the adjacent town during transit. All passengers with unscheduled airlines whose flights originated or passed in transit through an infected area are required to possess a certificate.
The certificate is not insisted upon in the case of children under one year of age, but such infants may be subject to surveillance and they will not be allowed to proceed to Natal or to the Lowveld of the Transvaal in South Africa within six days of leaving any place or port within an infected area.
[2]: Malaria risk exists in the northern rural regions from November to May/June. The predominant *falciparum* strain is reported to be 'highly resistant' to chloroquine.
[3]: Mains water is normally chlorinated, and whilst relatively safe may cause mild abdominal upsets. Bottled water is available and is advised for the first few weeks of the stay. Drinking water outside main cities and towns may be contaminated and sterilisation is advisable. Milk is pasteurised

MARK VAN AARDT

Windhoek City from lookout point

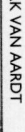

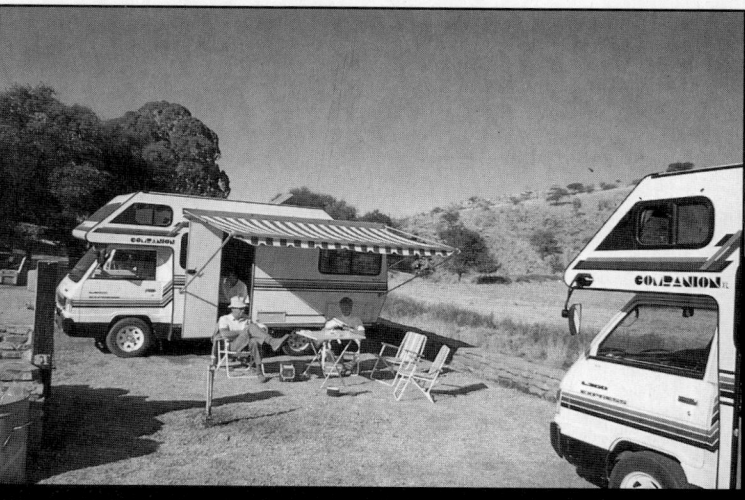

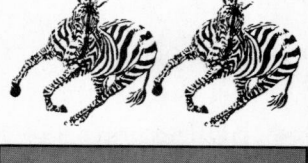

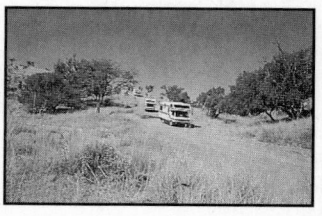

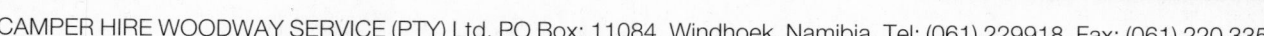

MARK VAN AARDT

Himba woman in Kaokoland

and dairy products are safe for consumption. Local meat, poultry, seafood, fruit and vegetables are generally considered safe to eat.
Rabies is present. For those at high risk, vaccination before arrival should be considered. If you are bitten abroad seek medical advice without delay. For more information consult the *Health* section at the back of the book.
Bilharzia (schistosomiasis) is present in Kavango and the Caprivi Strip. Avoid swimming and paddling in fresh water in these regions (also because of the presence of crocodiles). Swimming pools which are well chlorinated and maintained are safe.
Health care: Anti-bite serums for snakes and scorpions are advised. Health insurance is essential.

TRAVEL - International

AIR: Namibia's national airline is *Air Namibia (SW)*. *SAA* has landing rights.
Approximate flight time: From *London* to Windhoek is 18 hours (including a stopover of 2 hours and 35 minutes in Frankfurt).
International airport: *Windhoek (WDH)* is 42km (20 miles) from the city (travel time – 35 minutes). Airport facilities include restaurant, bar, snack bar, post office, currency exchange and car hire. A bus service to the city meets all flight arrivals. The return departs from the *SAA* terminus at the corner of Kaiser and Peter Müller Streets, 90 minutes before flight departure, with pick-ups at Safari Motel, Kalahari Sands and Continental hotels. Taxis to the city are also available.
SEA: There is a modern deep-water harbour at Walvis Bay which is jointly administered by South Africa and Namibia. There is also a small port at Lüderitz.
RAIL: The only cross-border line from South Africa runs up central Namibia through Windhoek to terminate at Grootfontein, with branches to Walvis Bay and Lüderitz.
ROAD: A tarred road runs from the south through Upington in South Africa to Karasburg. The untarred road from the east from Botswana to Gobabis is currently being upgraded as part of a new trans-Kalahari highway. The road from Luanda in Angola through Namibia to South Africa is tarred, but travel conditions can be very difficult due to military disputes.

TRAVEL - Internal

AIR: Flying is the quickest and often the most economical way to travel around the country. *Air Namibia* links all of the major towns in the territory.
RAIL: There are daily through services from Pretoria and Cape Town to Windhoek, via De Aar, Prieska, Upington, Karasburg and Keetmanshoop. First- and second-class, as well as restaurant cars are available on this route. Local passenger and goods trains run daily.
ROAD: Roads are generally fairly well maintained. There are 37,000km (23,000 miles) of gravel and 4400km (2700 miles) of all-weather roads. **Bus:** Services are not well developed and there is no transport except **taxis** in Windhoek. A luxury bus service exists between Windhoek and all major centres in Namibia and South Africa. **Car hire:** Self-drive cars are available at the airport and Windhoek city centre. **Documentation:** An International Driving Permit is required.

ACCOMMODATION

HOTELS: There are good quality hotels both in Windhoek and Swakopmund, and some scattered throughout the country. In Windhoek there is the 4-star Kalahari Sands hotel. 3-star hotels include the Safari Hotel in Windhoek, the Hansa Hotel in Swakopmund, the Mokuti Lodge at Etosha and the Canyon Hotel in Keetmanshoop. Hotel accommodation is limited and visitors are advised to book well in advance. For further information contact Han-Hotel Association, PO Box 950, Windhoek.
Grading: Hotels are classified on a scale of **1** to **4 stars.**
LODGES: In the Etosha Pan National Park and other game reserves there are well-equipped rest camps with comfortable accommodation. Further information from *Tasa-Tourism and Safari Association of Namibia*, PO Box 6850, Windhoek.
CAMPING: Some of the national parks have camping facilities, notably the Etosha Pan National Park & Game Reserve. There is also camping at Ai-Ais, a hot-spring area towards the South African border, Hardap Dam in the south, Gross Barmen near Okahandja, and Popa Falls in Kavango. There are also camping facilities at various places along the coast.

MARK VAN AARDT

Epupa Falls on the Kunene River, Kaokoland

MARK VAN AARDT

Elephants at Gemsbokvlakte, Etosha National Park

RESORTS & EXCURSIONS

Namibia's many attractions include ten national parks, under the control of the Department of Agriculture and Nature Conservation. Some of them are listed below.

Etosha National Park & Game Reserve, with its unique Pan, is certainly one of the most famous game sanctuaries in the world. There are vast stocks of wildlife, particularly elephants, lions, zebras, giraffes, springboks, kudus, gemsboks or oryxes, hyenas, jackals, leopards and cheetahs. It is open throughout the year. There are well-equipped camps with comfortable rondavel accommodation and camping facilities.

Kalahari Gemsbok National Park lies on the southeast corner of the *Kalahari Desert* and must be entered through South Africa. In the summer, the heat can be almost unbearable.

Fish River Canyon is in the south of the country and only second in dimensions to the Grand Canyon. Trips are best arranged from Keetsmanshoop. Situated on the Fish River is **Hardap Dam**.

Ai-Ais and **Gross Barmen** are hot-spring resorts and there are spectacular falls at **Augrabies**. The **Brandberg/Twyfelfontein** area has some very ancient rock paintings and a petrified forest and is sometimes known as *The White Lady*.

The Namib Desert appears more like the surface of the moon with its towering sand dunes (some of them 300m/1000ft high), and is believed to be the oldest desert in the world. **Namib Naukluft**, at 46,768 sq km (18,057 sq miles), is the fourth largest conservation area in the world. There are campsites in the Namib Desert at Sesriem and in the Naukluft. The **Skeleton Coast** is a strange desert shoreline with massive dunes and treacherous rocks, the name relating to the number of ships wrecked and lost in the vicinity. The delightful little seaside resort of **Swakopmund** is situated in the middle of Namibia's coastline. It is surrounded by desert and sea, and has several interesting buildings which date back to the time when Namibia was a German colony. **Lüderitz** is a small port in the southern Namib region, with much charm and atmosphere from bygone days of diamond prospecting.

Windhoek is the attractive capital of the country and surrounded by mountains. Like other towns in the country, it has several examples of German colonial architecture, including the *Christuskirche*, the *Alte Feste* and the *Tintenpalast* (Ink Palace), the former colonial administrative building.

MARK VAN AARDT

Eland at Chudob, Etosha National Park

SOCIAL PROFILE

FOOD & DRINK: Restaurants and cafés reflect the German influence on Namibia and most dining rooms offer a reasonable choice of local and continental cuisine. They are found mainly in the major cities. A speciality of Namibia is game in all variations; worth a try are *biltong* and *rauchfleisch* (smoked meat).

NIGHTLIFE: In the white area of Windhoek there are restaurants, German cafés, a cinema and a theatre.

SHOPPING: Windhoek has a selection of fashionable shops. Local crafts can be bought in some specialised shops and at the Windhoek Street Market, held every second Saturday. Good buys include diamonds and semi-precious stones, Herero dolls, hand-carved wooden objects, jewellery, *karosse* rugs, liqueur chocolates made in Windhoek and *swakara* garments. **Shopping hours:** 0830-1700 Monday to Friday, 0830-1300 Saturday.

SPORT: Northwest of Usakos, rising out of the Namib, is the 2000m (6562ft) Spitzkoppe where there is good **mountaineering**. Some of the coastal and river areas provide good opportunities for **fishing**. There are several **hiking** trails in the Fish River Canyon, the Waterberg Plateau Park, the Naukluft Mountains and the Ugab River.

SPECIAL EVENTS: The following is a selection of festivals during 1993/94. A complete list can be obtained from the Ministry of Wildlife, Conservation and Tourism (address see above).

Apr/May '93 *Carnival*, Windhoek. **Aug 26** *Herero Festival*. **Sep** *Trade Fair*, Windhoek. **Oct** *Oktoberfest*, Windhoek.

SOCIAL CONVENTIONS: Western customs prevail; normal courtesies should be shown when visiting someone's home. **Tipping:** 10% is customary.

BUSINESS PROFILE

ECONOMY: The newly independent Namibia has bright economic prospects. Mining has been the mainstay of the economy under South African control. Namibian mines produce diamonds, copper, lead, zinc and uranium – the Rossing uranium mine is the world's largest; the sector contributes about 35% of the national product. A smaller but nonetheless valuable proportion comes from agriculture and fisheries. Livestock dominates the agricultural sector, although a sizeable proportion of the population is engaged in subsistence farming of crops such as wheat, maize and millet. Agriculture is becoming increasingly difficult as the years pass and the desert encroaches on previously fertile soil. It has also been seriously damaged during the early 1990s by the drought afflicting the whole region. Namibia enjoys some of the richest fishing grounds in the world, although catches of pilchard – the main species in the area – have been depleted by excessive fishing.

Commercial shipping, a potentially lucrative business, is constrained by the refusal of the South Africans to cede Walvis Bay, the best deep-water port in Africa on the Atlantic side, to the Namibians, although since September 1991 it has come under joint administration. The problem facing the new government in managing the economy is how to meet the expectations of the poorer black population while not alienating the white-run multinational companies which control most of Namibian business. Most of the country's trade is with South Africa: raw materials are exported in exchange for manufactured goods. This pattern is likely to continue for the forseeable future although there will be some growth in trading links with other countries.

BUSINESS: Suits should be worn in winter, safari suits in summer. Prior appointments are necessary. English is widely spoken in business circles. The best times to visit are February to May and September to November. **Office hours:** 0730-1630/1700 Monday to Friday.

COMMERCIAL INFORMATION: The following organisation can offer advice: Chamber of Commerce and Industries of Namibia, PO Box 191, Third Floor, SWA Building Society Building, Windhoek 9000. Tel: (61) 222 000. Fax: (61) 33690.

MARK VAN AARDT

Quiver Tree Forest near Keetmanshoop, Southern Namibia

HISTORY & GOVERNMENT

HISTORY: Colonisation, first by the Germans and then by the South Africans, has destroyed many of Namibia's rich and diverse cultural traditions, but Namibia still retains a strong cultural character of its own and the people have retained their distinctive identities even though most of their original traditions now only survive in remote rural areas. The history of Namibia from the foundation of the United Nations in 1945 to Namibian independence in 1991 was dominated by the repeated refusal of the South African government to convert their League of Nations mandate to administer the country (which was granted after the First World War) into a UN trusteeship, or indeed to recognise that the UN, or any other organisation, had a legitimate interest in the region. In 1977 the five western members of the Security Council began negotiations aimed at bringing about the implementation of Resolution 385, providing for UN supervised elections. Progress was very slow, but in 1988, the South Africans and Cubans agreed to withdraw their troops from Angola (see *Angola* entry) as an essential preparatory step before a Namibia settlement, which quickly followed. Despite some initial problems with the demobilisation of SWAPO and the South African forces in Namibia, the peace process developed more or less as planned. Elections were held in November 1989, with SWAPO taking 57% of the votes, sufficient for an overall majority but less than the two-thirds for which the party was hoping to enable them to rewrite the UN-sponsored constitution. The main rival to SWAPO, the South African-backed Democratic Turnhalle Alliance led by Dirk Mudge, made a strong showing amongst whites and in areas populated by groups nervous of the Ovambo dominance of SWAPO. Although there have been some complaints about alleged inefficiency and corruption, SWAPO has clearly jettisoned its revoluntionary rhetoric, knowing that Namibia's future prosperity depends on overcoming the former divisions between different elements in the country. For that reason, as much as anything else, social transformation has been slow: in particular, the economy has remained largely in the hands of its previous white ownership. The continuing weakness of the opposition means, however, that SWAPO's position is probably not under threat. Negotiations with Pretoria over the status of Walvis Bay have continued. The South Africans have not conceded sovereignty over the port or the dozen offshore islands which Namibia also claims, but in September 1991 the two governments agreed to administer them jointly pending a final settlement.

GOVERNMENT: Under the Constitution which took effect upon independence in March 1990, executive authority rests with the President, who is directly elected for a five-year term. Legislative power is vested in the National Assembly with 78 members, 72 of whom are elected for five years while the remainder are presidential nominees.

CLIMATE

The cold Benguela current keeps the coast of the Namib Desert cool, damp and rain-free for most of the year with thick coastal fog. Inland all the rain falls in summer (October to April). Summer temperatures are high while the altitude means that nights are cool and winters are fairly cold.

Required clothing: Light cottons, with slightly heavier cottons or light woollens for evening. In inland areas, shoes are essential during the day as the ground is so hot.

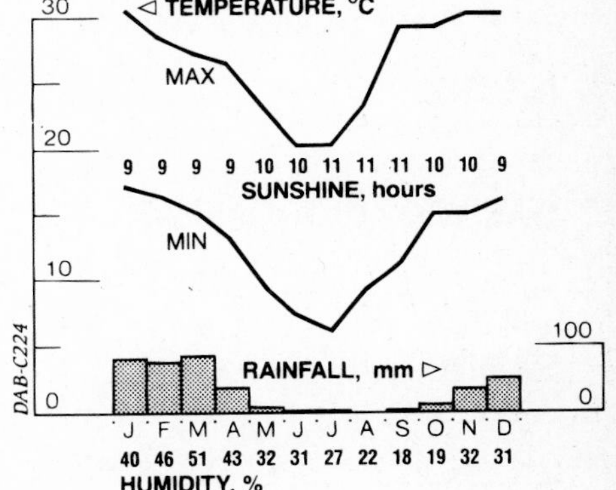

NAURU

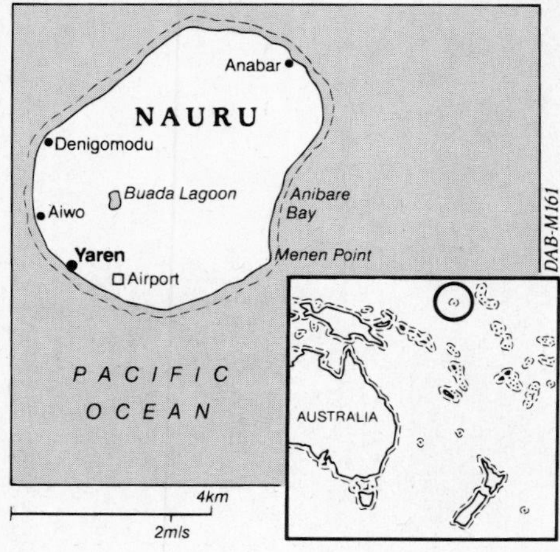

Location: South Pacific.

Air Nauru
Directorate of Civil Aviation
Government of Nauru Offices
Yaren, Republic of Nauru
Tel: 3310. Telex: 33081.
Nauru Government Office
3 Chesham Street
London SW1X 8ND
Tel: (071) 235 6911. Fax: (071) 235 7423. Opening hours: 0930-1700 Monday to Friday.
The British Embassy in Fiji deals with enquiries relating to Nauru:
British Embassy
PO Box 1355
Victoria House
47 Gladstone Road
Suva, Fiji
Tel: 311 033. Fax: 301 406. Telex: 2129.

AREA: 21.3 sq km (8.2 sq miles).
POPULATION: 9350 (1989 estimate).
POPULATION DENSITY: 439 per sq km (1989).
CAPITAL: Yaren District.
GEOGRAPHY: Nauru is an oval-shaped outcrop, situated in the South Pacific west of Kiribati, surrounded by a reef, which is exposed at low tide. There is no deep-water harbour on the island but offshore moorings are reputedly the deepest in the world. The island's beaches, interspersed by coral pinnacles, are bordered inland by a fertile coastal strip encircling the island. On the inner side of the fertile section there is a coral cliff which rises to a height of 60m (200ft). Above the cliff is an extensive plateau bearing high-grade phosphate which is infertile and unpopulated, with the exception of a small fringe around a shallow lagoon and a few bush-like trees. Mining operations, which have gutted the island, will probably cease by 1995 when the phosphates are exhausted and the island will have to be re-landscaped due to the disruption caused. A case before the International Court of Justice in The Hague seems likely to determine just what the former trustees of the island (Australia, New Zealand and the UK) will contribute to this prerequisite for reshaping the island's economy.
LANGUAGE: Nauruan and English.
RELIGION: Christian, mostly Nauruan Protestant Church.
TIME: GMT + 12.
ELECTRICITY: 110/240 volts AC, 50Hz.
COMMUNICATIONS: Telephone: IDD is available. Country code: 674. **Telex/telegram:** Facilities at Nauru Government Communications Office. **Post:** Airmail to Europe takes up to a week. **Press:** The main newspaper is *The Bulletin*, published fortnightly in Nauruan and English.
BBC World Service and Voice of America frequencies: From time to time these change. See the section *How to Use this Book* for more information.

BBC:				
MHz	17.10	15.36	9.740	7.150
Voice of America:				
MHz	18.82	15.18	9.525	1.735

PASSPORT/VISA

Regulations and requirements may be subject to change at short notice, and you are advised to contact the appropriate diplomatic or consular authority before finalising travel arrangements. Details of these may be found at the head of this country's entry. Any numbers in the chart refer to the footnotes below.

	Passport Required?	Visa Required?	Return Ticket Required?
Full British	Yes	Yes	Yes
BVP	Not valid	-	-
Australian	Yes	Yes	Yes
Canadian	Yes	Yes	Yes
USA	Yes	Yes	Yes
Other EC	Yes	Yes	Yes
Japanese	Yes	Yes	Yes

PASSPORTS: Valid passport required by all.
British Visitors Passport: Not accepted.
VISAS: Required by all except those in transit who continue their journey to a third country by the same or first connecting aircraft, provided they hold tickets with reserved seats and other documents for onward travel.
Types of visa: Visitor and Business. Both are free of charge.
Validity: Visas are limited to a maximum of 4 months' validity, but can be extended by applying to the principal Immigration Officer in Nauru.
Applications to: Principal Immigration Officer, Alf Itsimaera, Immigration Department. Tel: 3181. Fax: 3173.
Application requirements: There are no application forms. Write giving full name, date of birth, marital status, occupation, country of birth and nationality, name of country issuing passport and passport number and date of issue, purpose of visit, duration of intended stay, and means of arrival and departure with approximate dates. Applicants for Business visas require a letter from their sponsoring company.
Working days required: Applications have to be sent to Nauru so plenty of time should be allowed.
Temporary residence: Contact the Principal Immigration Officer in Naura.

MONEY

Currency: Australian Dollar (A$) = 100 cents. Notes are in denominations of A$100, 50, 20, 10, 5, 2 and 1. Coins are in denominations of A$1, and 50, 20, 10, 5, 2 and 1 cents.
Credit cards: American Express, Diners Club and Visa are accepted. Check with your credit card company for details of merchant acceptability and other services which may be available.
Exchange rate indicators: The following figures are included as a guide to the movements of the Australian Dollar against Sterling and the US Dollar:

Date:	Oct '89	Oct '90	Oct '91	Oct '92
£1.00=	2.01	2.46	2.18	2.22
$1.00=	1.27	1.26	1.25	1.40

Currency restrictions: There are no restrictions on the import or export of either local or foreign currency.

DUTY FREE

The following goods may be imported into Nauru without incurring customs duty:
400 cigarettes or 50 cigars or 450g of tobacco;
3 bottles of alcoholic beverage (if visitor is over 21 years of age);
A reasonable amount of perfume.
Prohibited items: Narcotics and firearms.
Note: Nauruan artefacts may not be exported without a licence.

PUBLIC HOLIDAYS

Public holidays observed in Nauru are as follows:
Apr 9-12 '93 Easter. **Oct 26** Angam Day. **Dec 25-26** Christmas. **Jan 1 '94** New Year's Day. **Jan 31** Independence Day.

HEALTH

Regulations and requirements may be subject to change at short notice, and you are advised to contact your doctor well in advance of your intended date of departure. Any numbers in the chart refer to the footnotes below.

	Special Precautions?	Certificate Required?
Yellow Fever	No	1
Cholera	No	No
Typhoid & Polio	Yes	-
Malaria	No	-
Food & Drink	2	-

[1]: A yellow fever vaccination certificate is required from travellers over one year of age coming from infected areas.
[2]: Mains water is normally chlorinated, and whilst relatively safe may cause mild abdominal upsets. Bottled water is available and is advised for the first few weeks of the stay. Drinking water outside main cities and towns may be contaminated and sterilisation is advisable. Local meat, poultry, seafood, fruit and vegetables are generally considered safe to eat.
Health care: Health insurance is recommended. Standards of health care are high.

TRAVEL - International

AIR: Nauru's national airline is *Air Nauru (ON)*.
Approximate flight time: From *London* to Nauru Island is 31 hours, including stopovers in Hong Kong, Manila, Koror and Guam.
International airport: *Nauru Island (INU)*.
Departure tax: A$10 per person on departure.
SEA: The international port is Nauru, served by *Nauru Pacific Line*, *Royal Shipping Co* and *Daiwa Navigation Co*. Main sealinks are with Australia, New Zealand and Japan. Coastal hazards force commercial vessels to moor some way offshore at what are reputed to be the deepest permanent anchorages in the world.

NAURU	**HEALTH REGULATIONS**	**VISA REGULATIONS** Code-Link
GALILEO/WORLDSPAN	TI-DFT/INU/HE	 TI-DFT/INU/VI
SABRE	 TIDFT/INU/HE	 TIDFT/INU/VI

To access this information on your CRS, swipe the barcode with a light pen or type in the text under the barcode. For more information, see the introduction *How to Use This Book*.

TRAVEL - Internal

RAIL: There are just over 5km (3 miles) of railway to serve the phosphate area.
ROAD: A sealed road, 19km (12 miles) long, circles the island and there are several miles of road running inland to Buada and the phosphate areas. Driving is on the left. **Buses** provide public transport. **Car hire** is available. **Documentation:** A national driving licence will suffice.

RESORTS & EXCURSIONS

Since the extensive phosphor fields were found in the 1900s, the island is still mainly used for the exploration of the natural fertilizer. The *Nauru Phosphate Corporation* is the largest employer. The population lives mainly at the coasts or on the shore of *Buada Lagoon*, the remainder of the island is used for phosphor extraction. Nauru is not a major tourist destination and there are only two hotels. One is situated on the west coast, nearby are restaurants and shops. The other is at *Anibare Bay*, on the sparsely populated east coast.

SOCIAL PROFILE

FOOD & DRINK: Most of the available food is canned, refined and imported. Fresh food is limited to a small amount of fish, and very occasionally beef. There are no local fruit or vegetables. The island is very well served with restaurants with a wide range of international dishes, but little is fresh. Most international brands of alcohol are available, but are quite expensive.
NIGHTLIFE: This mostly revolves around the dining rooms and bars. There is one cinema located in the southern part of the island.
SHOPPING: Service and goods at government shops tend to be of poor quality. The range of goods and standards at Chinese shops is better, but Nauru is not a shopper's paradise. Visitors should buy essential goods in advance. The absence of taxes means that electrical goods, cigarettes and alcohol are cheaper.
SPORT: The national game is Australian-rules **football**, which is played all through Saturday on the sports field just north of Location (on the western side of the island); there is no charge for spectators. Nearby are **tennis** and **volleyball** courts. **Snooker** can be played at the *East End Club*.
SOCIAL CONVENTIONS: The island has a casual atmosphere in which diplomacy and tact are always preferable to confrontation; European customs continue alongside local traditions. **Tipping:** Not generally practised.

BUSINESS PROFILE

ECONOMY: Nauru's economy depends almost entirely on the extraction and sale of phosphates, of which the Nauru Phosphate Corporation has a monopoly. Much of the revenue has been invested in long-term economic development programmes, anticipating the eventual exhaustion of the phosphate deposits which is expected in the mid-1990s. The island is, however, becoming increasingly important as a centre for offshore banking. There is some agriculture but it is limited by the lack of fertile land. There is no tourist industry. Almost all the island's revenue derives from phosphates; most imports of foodstuffs, consumer and capital goods come from New Zealand and Australia.
BUSINESS: Shirt and smart trousers or skirt will suffice; more formal wear is needed only for very special occasions. English and French are widely spoken. The best time to visit is May to October.
COMMERCIAL INFORMATION: The following organisation can offer advice: The Central Bank of Nauru, PO Box 289, Nauru. Tel: 3238. Fax: 3203. Telex: 33085.

HISTORY & GOVERNMENT

HISTORY: Nauru is one of the world's smallest and most remote sovereign states and was one of the many Pacific islands first settled centuries ago by the dauntless seafaring Polynesian and Melanesian explorers. It was allocated to Germany under the 1887 Anglo-German Convention, shortly before phosphate, the island's principal raw material, was discovered at the turn of the century. Nauru was captured by Australian forces in 1914 and continued under Australian rule (other than a period of Japanese occupation from 1942 to 1945) until independence was granted in 1968. A plan to evacuate the islanders in order to develop Nauru's remaining phosphate deposits precipitated the protest movement which eventually led to independence. Nauru has sought compensation from the British, Australian and New Zealand governments, but no agreement has been reached despite lengthy negotiations. Nauru's first Head of State was the Head Chief, Hammer DeRoburt, who managed to hold on to power for most of the time between independence and 1989. (In 1976, Parliament unseated DeRoburt after some members objected to his autocratic style, but he was re-elected two years later, winning further elections in 1980, 1983 and 1986.) His great political rival, Kennan Adeang, assumed office after DeRoburt's defeat in no-confidence motions on two occasions, but was deposed both times within weeks. In December 1989, Bernard Dowiyogo was elected President, beating DeRoburt by ten votes to six. DeRoburt retired and died in 1992. The most pressing issue for Nauru in the immediate future may be its physical existence: a recent UN report on the likely consequences of the 'greenhouse effect' has indicated that a rise in sea levels is probable and that some low-lying land areas are threatened with flooding
GOVERNMENT: The President of Nauru is elected by a unicameral Parliament, itself elected by universal adult suffrage every three years.

CLIMATE

A maritime, equatorial climate tempered by northeast trade winds from March to October. Wettest period is from December to March.
Required clothing: Lightweight cottons and linens with waterproofing all year.

NAURU (27m)

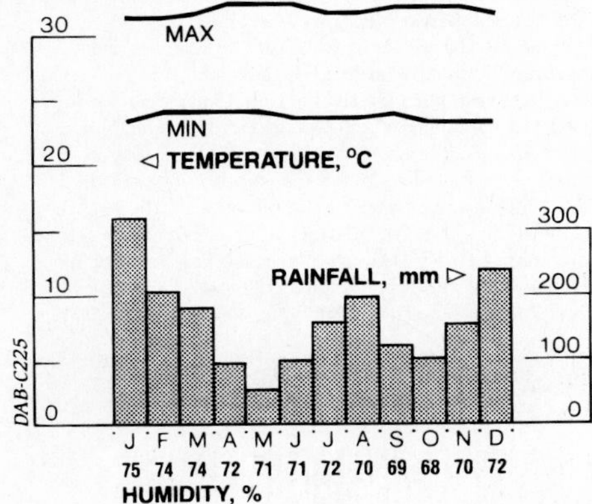

TEMPERATURE CONVERSIONS
-20 -10 0°C 10 20 30 40
0 10 20 30°F40 50 60 70 80 90 100
RAINFALL CONVERSIONS 0mm 200 400 600 800
0in 5 10 15 20 25 30

NEPAL

Location: Indian sub-continent.

Department of Tourism
HM Government of Nepal
Tripureshor
Kathmandu
Nepal
Tel: (1) 221 306.
Royal Nepalese Embassy
12a Kensington Palace Gardens
London
W8 4QU
Tel: (071) 229 1594 *or* 229 6231. Fax: (071) 792 9861. Telex: 261072. Opening hours: 0900-1300 and 1400-1730 Monday to Friday.
British Embassy
PO Box 106
Lainchaur
Kathmandu, Nepal
Tel: (1) 410 583. Fax: (1) 411 789. Telex: 2343 BRITEM NP.
Royal Nepalese Embassy
2131 Leroy Place, NW
Washington, DC
20008
Tel: (202) 667 4550. Fax: (202) 667 5534. Telex: 440085 EVER UI.
Embassy of the United States of America
Pani Pokhari
Kathmandu, Nepal
Tel: (1) 411 179. Fax: (1) 419 963. Telex: 2381.**Nepalese Consulate General**
Suite 202
820 2nd Avenue
New York, NY
10017
Tel: (212) 370 4188. Fax: (212) 953 2038.
Nepalese Consulate General
310 Dupont Street
Toronto, Ontario
M5R 1V9
Tel: (416) 968 7252.
The Canadian High Commission in India deals with enquiries relating to Nepal.
Canadian High Commission
PO Box 5207
New Delhi
India
Tel: (11) 687 6500. Fax: (11) 687 6579.

AREA: 147,181 sq km (56,827 sq miles).
POPULATION: 19,500,000 (1991 estimate).
POPULATION DENSITY: 125.3 per sq km.
CAPITAL: Kathmandu. **Population:** 235,160 (1981).
GEOGRAPHY: Nepal is a landlocked kingdom sharing borders with China (Tibet) to the north and northwest, and India to the west, south and east. The country can be divided into five zones: the Terai, the Siwaliks, the Mahabharat Lekh, the Midlands or Pahar and the Himalayas. The greater part of the

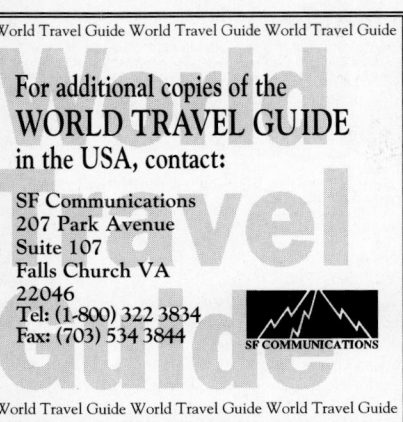

country lies on the southern slope of the Himalayas extending down from the highest peaks through hill country to the upper edge of the Ganges Plain. The hilly central area is crossed by the Lower Himalayas where there are eight of the highest peaks in the world, leading up to Mount Everest. Wildlife in Nepal includes tigers, leopards, gaur, elephants, buffalo and deer.
LANGUAGE: The official language is Nepali. Other languages include Maithir and Bhojpuri.
RELIGION: Mainly Hindu, with Buddhist and Muslim minorities.
TIME: GMT + 5.45.
ELECTRICITY: 220 volts AC, 50Hz. There are frequent power cuts.
COMMUNICATIONS: Telephone: IDD is available to Kathmandu only. All other calls go through the international operator. Country code: 977. The Telecommunication Office, Tripureshnawar, deals with telephone calls, cables and telexes. The International Telephone Office is open 1000-1700 Sunday to Friday, but international telephone connections are very difficult. **Fax:** Many travel agents and a few hotels have fax services. The Nepal Telecommunications Corporation booth at the airport has fax services. **Telex/telegram:** The Central Telegraph Office offers a 24-hour international telephone and telegram service seven days a week. **Post:** Postal services are available in most centres. Make sure that letters are hand cancelled at the post office (post boxes should not be used for important communications). Main hotels will also handle mail. Opening hours: the General Post Office in Kathmandu is open 1000-1700 (1600 in winter) Sunday to Friday. **Press:** English-language dailies are *The Commoner*, *The Motherland* and *The Rising Nepal*. *The International Herald Tribune*, *Time* and *Newsweek* can all be found in Kathmandu. *Himal* is a magazine published six times a year, devoted to environment issues throughout the Himalayas. At certain times of day there are radio and television news broadcasts in English.
BBC World Service and Voice of America frequencies: From time to time these change. See the section *How to Use this Book* for more information.

BBC:

MHz	15.31	11.96	9.740	6.180

A service is also available on 1413kHz.

Voice of America:

MHz	21.49	15.60	9.525	6.035

PASSPORT/VISA

Regulations and requirements may be subject to change at short notice, and you are advised to contact the appropriate diplomatic or consular authority before finalising travel arrangements. Details of these may be found at the head of this country's entry. Any numbers in the chart refer to the footnotes below.

	Passport Required?	Visa Required?	Return Ticket Required?
Full British	Yes	Yes	No
BVP	Not valid	-	-
Australian	Yes	Yes	No
Canadian	Yes	Yes	No
USA	Yes	Yes	No
Other EC	Yes	Yes	No
Japanese	Yes	Yes	No

PASSPORTS: Valid passport required by all except nationals of India.
British Visitors Passport: Not acceptable.
VISAS: Required by all except nationals of India.
Types of visa: Tourist – £15 per person. A 15-day visa can be obtained for US$20 at the airport. Business can be conducted on a Tourist visa.
Validity: Entry valid up to 3 months maximum (and with visa extension for no more than 4 months in one year), and valid for 30 days after entry. For full conditions on visa extension (including charges and conditions) contact Consulate (or Consular Section at Embassy). Visas can be extended in Nepal costing Rs80 for the second month, provided you have proof that you have exchanged US$15 per day of extension.
Application to: Consulate (or Consular Section at Embassy). For addresses, see top of entry.
Application requirements: (a) 1 completed application form. (b) Valid passport. (c) 1 photo. (d) Fee.
Working days required: 1 day for Tourist visas.

MONEY

Currency: Nepalese Rupee (Rs) = 100 paisa. Notes are in denominations of Rs1000, 500, 100, 50, 20, 10, 5, 2 and 1. Coins are in denominations of Rs1, and 50, 25, 10 and 5 paisa.
Currency exchange: It is illegal to exchange your currency with persons other than authorised dealers in foreign exchange. Obtain Foreign Exchange Encashment Receipts when changing currency and keep them, as these will help in many transactions, including getting visa extensions and trekking permits.
Credit cards: American Express is widely accepted, and Access/Mastercard and Visa have more limited use. Check with your credit card company for details of merchant acceptability and other services which may be available.
Travellers cheques: Accepted at banks and major hotels. If trekking, it is important to bear in mind that cash is needed.
Exchange rate indicators: The following figures are included as a guide to the movements of the Nepalese Rupee against Sterling and the US Dollar:

Date:	Oct '89	Oct '90	Oct '91	Oct '92
£1.00=	37.95	57.18	74.36	73.74
$1.00=	24.03	29.27	42.48	46.47

Currency restrictions: Import of local and Indian currency is prohibited. Foreign currency must be declared. Export of local currency is prohibited. Only 15% of the amount exchanged into local currency will be reconverted into foreign currency on departure and exchange receipts must be presented.
Banking hours: 1000-1450 Sunday to Thursday, 1000-1250 Friday. The Nepal Rastra Bank Exchange Counters at New Road, Kathmandu, are open 0800-2000.

DUTY FREE

The following goods may be imported into Nepal without incurring customs duty:
A reasonable quantity of tobacco, alcoholic beverage and perfume.
Note: (a) All baggage must be declared on arrival and departure. (b) There are limits on the importation of certain goods including cameras, videos and electronic goods. (c) Objects of archaeological or historical interest may not be exported; certain antique articles must be referred to the Department of Archaeology before export.

PUBLIC HOLIDAYS

Public holidays observed in Nepal are as follows:
Feb/Mar '93 Shivaratri (In Honour of Lord Shiva). **Mar** Holi Festival. **Mar 8** Nepalese Women's Day. **Apr** Navabarsha (New Year's Day). **Apr 10** Teachers' Day. **Apr/May** Baishakh Purnima (Birthday of Lord Buddha). **May/Jun** Indra Jatra (Festival of Rain God). **Sep/Oct (one week)** Durga Puja Festival. **Oct 24** UN Day. **Oct/Nov (three days)** Tihar (Festival of Lights). **Nov 7** Queen Aishworya's Birthday. **Nov 9** Constitution Day. **Dec 17** Mahendra Jayanti. **Dec 28** King Birendra's Birthday. **Jan 11 '94** Unity Day. **Jan 30** Martyrs' Day. **Feb/Mar** Shivaratri. **Feb 18** Tribhuvan Jayanti (King Tribhuvan's Birthday) and Rashtriya Prajatantra Divas (Democracy Day). **Mar** Holi Festival. **Mar 8** Nepalese Women's Day.

HEALTH

Regulations and requirements may be subject to change at short notice, and you are advised to contact your doctor well in advance of your intended date of departure. Any numbers in the chart refer to the footnotes below.

	Special Precautions?	Certificate Required?
Yellow Fever	No	1
Cholera	Yes	2
Typhoid & Polio	Yes	-
Malaria	3	-
Food & Drink	4	-

[1]: A yellow fever vaccination certificate is required of travellers coming from infected areas.
[2]: Following WHO guidelines issued in 1973, a cholera vaccination certificate is not a condition of entry to Nepal. However, cholera is a serious risk in this country and precautions are essential. Up-to-date advice should be sought before deciding whether these precautions should include vaccination, as medical opinion is divided over its effectiveness. See the *Health* section at the back of the book.
[3]: Malaria risk, mainly in the benign *vivax* form, exists throughout the year in rural areas of the Terai districts of Dhanukha, Mahotari, Sarlahi, Rautahat, Bara, Parsa, Rupendehi, Kapilvastu and especially along the Indian border. The malignant *falciparum* form has been reported to be 'resistant' to chloroquine.
[4]: All water should be regarded as being potentially contaminated. Water used for drinking, brushing teeth or making ice should have first been boiled or otherwise sterilised. Milk is unpasteurised and should be boiled. Powdered or tinned milk is available and is advised, but make sure that it is reconstituted with pure water. Avoid dairy products which are likely to have been made from unboiled milk. Only eat well-cooked meat and fish, preferably served hot. Pork, salad and mayonnaise may carry increased risk. Vegetables should be cooked and fruit peeled.
Rabies is present. For those at high risk, vaccination before arrival should be considered. If you are bitten abroad seek medical advice without delay. For more information consult the *Health* section at the back of the book.
Japanese encephalitis exists particularly in rural areas between June and October. A vaccine is available, and travellers are advised to consult their doctor prior to departure. It is transmitted by mosquitoes.
High altitude sickness is a hazard for trekkers, so it is important to be in good health before travelling. Advice can be obtained from the Himalayan Rescue Association near the Kathmandu Guest House, Thamel.
Health care: The most convenient hospital for visitor care is Patan Hospital in Lagankhel. Most hospitals have English-speaking staff and big hotels have doctors. Pharmacies in Kathmandu, mainly along New Road, offer a wide range of Western drugs at low prices. In Kathmandu you can get certain vaccinations free of charge at the Infectious Diseases Clinic. Full medical insurance is essential.

TRAVEL - International

AIR: Nepal's national airline is *Royal Air Nepal (RA)*.
Approximate flight time: From *London* to Kathmandu is 10 hours 15 minutes (not including stopover time).
International airport: *Kathmandu (KTM)* (Tribhuvan) is 6.5km (4 miles) east of the city (travel time – 20 minutes). A coach to the city meets all flight arrivals (0600-1800). Taxis to the city are available. There are full duty-free facilities at Kathmandu airport.
Departure tax: Rs450 for international flights.
RAIL: Two stretches of the Indian Railway Line run to the border with Nepal, where cycle-rickshaws are available for onward journeys.

NEPAL	HEALTH REGULATIONS	VISA REGULATIONS Code-Link
GALILEO/WORLDSPAN	   TI-DFT/KTM/HE	TI-DFT/KTM/VI
SABRE	 TIDFT/KTM/HE	  TIDFT/KTM/VI

To access this information on your CRS, swipe the barcode with a light pen or type in the text under the barcode. For more information, see the introduction *How to Use This Book.*

ROAD: There are 12 possible points of entry. New roads have been built linking Kathmandu with India and Tibet.

TRAVEL - Internal

AIR: There is a network of domestic flights linking major towns, radiating from Kathmandu. Many of these offer spectacular views across the mountains. Helicopters can be chartered from *Royal Nepal Airlines Corporation*.
RAIL: There are light- and narrow-gauge railways in Nepal.
ROAD: Road system is of unpredictable quality. **Bus:** There are services operated by the *Transport Corporation of Nepal* and also by private operators. **Car hire:** Cars can be hired from the *Hertz* representative and *Gorkha Travels*, or from the *Avis* representative and *Yeti Travels*, both in Kathmandu. Traffic drives on the left. Chauffeur-driven cars can only be hired in the Kathmandu Valley. **Documentation:** An International Driving Permit is valid in Nepal for 15 days. The minimum driving age is 18. A temporary licence to drive is available from local authorities on presentation of a valid national driving licence.
URBAN: There are bus services in the populous areas around Kathmandu, which include the neighbouring cities of Patan and Bhaktapur. A trolleybus route provides frequent journeys over the 11km (7-mile) Kathmandu–Bhaktapur road. Private minibuses feed the trolleybus route from nearby villages. On buses and trolleybuses belonging to the Transport Corporation of Nepal a 4-stage fare system applies, with colour-coded tickets issued by conductors. **Tempos:** These are metered 3-wheel scooters, which work out slightly cheaper than taxis. **Taxi:** Metered taxis are plentiful in Kathmandu; at night the meter reading plus 50% is standard. Private taxis are more expensive and fares should be agreed before departure. **Rickshaws** operate throughout the city. Fares should be negotiated in advance. **Bicycles and motorcycles:** These can be hired from bike-shops or hotels by the hour or by the day. Motorcyclists require a driving licence. Bicyclists should make sure they have a working bell.

ACCOMMODATION

HOTELS: Kathmandu has an increasing number of international-class hotels which are particularly busy during spring and autumn, when it is advisable to book well in advance. Comfortable hotels can also be found in Pokhara, and the Royal Chitwan National Park in the Terai Jungle. A Government tax is added to bills, which varies according to the star rating of the hotel.
LODGES: Besides the officially recognised hotels there are a number of lodges or hostels which in Kathmandu are located in the old part of the town, in the streets around the Durbar Square or in the Thamel district. The *Lukla Sherpa Cooperative* offers lodging to mountaineers in Sherpa country (PO Box 1338, Kathmandu), and accommodation at Paplu in the Sagarmatha zone can be provided by the *Hostellerier des Sherpas*, who can be contacted through *Great Himalaya Adventure*, Kantipath, Kathmandu.

RESORTS & EXCURSIONS

Nepal is known as the abode of the gods. For many years a secret, unknown country, it was in the 1950s faced with making a leap from the 11th century to modern times. Visited first by mountaineers and trekkers, it later became the haunt of hippies. In 1989 restrictions barring several areas to tourists were lifted.

Kathmandu

The capital is a magical place. In the centre is Durbar Square where there is a wonderful collection of temples and shrines, Buddhist and Hindu, used by the people as stalls from which they sell produce by day and as shelter for their animals by night, as well as places of worship. The old *Royal Palace* is in the square, as is the *Statue of Hanuman the Monkey-God*, clad in a red cloak. Here too is the house of the living goddess, Kumari, where a young girl lives from the age of about six to puberty, leaving her house only to attend to the daily supplications of her followers (which she receives sitting on a throne in the temple) and for the many festivals. Several involved rituals accompany her selection. Climbing upwards from the city one can reach the famous monkey temple.
Just 5km (3 miles) west of the city, below the Nagarjun Forest, are the *Balaju Water Gardens*, with a reclining statue of Lord Vishnu and a 22-headed sea-dragon fountain. 19km (12 miles) south of Kathmandu, and accessible by taxi, are the *Godavari Royal Botanical Gardens* housing trees, shrubs and beautiful orchids in an idyllic setting.

The Kathmandu Valley

Kathmandu was once one of three equal cities, the other two being **Patan** and **Bhaktapur**, each of which has its own Kumari (see above); other towns have Kumaris but of a lesser status. The *National Art Museum* in Bhaktapur, located in the old Malla Palace with its 55 windows, has unusual, colourful animal paintings on the second floor which are well worth viewing. Other museums in Bhaktapur are the *National Woodworking Museum*, showing fine examples of Newari woodcarving, and the *National Brass and Bronze Museum*, both in Dattatreya Square. Patan has the *Jawalakhel Zoo*, housing exotic South Asian animals.
West of Kathmandu is the amazing Buddhist *stupa* (temple) of *Swayambhunath*, with its large staring eyes. There are shrines for every purpose in the valley, such as the shrine of Ganesh the Elephant-God, reputed to bring good luck. There are four Ganesh temples in the valley, each a masterpiece of Nepalese architecture – one in Kathmandu's Durbar Square, one in **Chabahil**, one in **Chobar** and one near Bhaktapur. **Lumbini,** being the birthplace of Lord Buddha, is one of the world's most important pilgrimage sites.
The nearby **Royal Chitwan National Park** is a jungle overflowing with wildlife. There are many lodges here offering visitor accommodation, canoeing, white-water rafting and elephant rides. **Nagarkot Village,** situated on rice steppes in magnificent countryside, provides spectacular views of Mount Everest, mist permitting. The hill town of **Gorkha** is the ancestral home of the Shah dynasty and residence of the original Gurkha soldiers. There is a lively bazaar and the *Royal Trek to Pokhara* begins here. The secluded town of **Pokhara** lies 200km (125 miles) west of Kathmandu in the centre of Nepal on *Lake Phewa*. No other place in the world commands such a view of the Himalayas. It is a starting point for mountaineers and trekkers, and was at one time the home of JRR Tolkein.

The Mountains

One of the principal reasons for visiting Nepal must be either to see or to climb the mountains, especially **Mount Everest.** A number of local agents can arrange trips with guides into the mountains for a day. Climbing and mountain treks can also be arranged. Trekking permits are necessary for travel beyond Kathmandu or Pokhara and are issued by the Central Immigration Office. The trekking season is generally from September to May, but the best periods are October to December and March to April. The countryside is generally rugged and the trails are loose but, with a *qualified* guide (ie one obtained through a reputable agency) and other sensible precautions, trekking is normally a perfectly safe activity, offering by far the best way of viewing the spectacular countryside. Some agents can arrange flights in light aircraft over Mount Everest. Flights are also available from Jomosom and other locations west of the capital, flying over the spectacular *Annapurna* range.

SOCIAL PROFILE

FOOD & DRINK: Despite its isolation and the variety of its local produce, Nepal has not developed a distinctive style of cooking. An exception is *Newar* cuisine, which can be very elaborate and spicy. Most dishes here are regional Indian. Rice is the staple food. Dishes include *dal* (lentil soup), spiced vegetables, *chapatis* and *tsampa* (eaten by the hill people), a raw grain, ground and mixed with milk, tea or water. Sweets and spicy snacks include *jelabi, laddus* and *mukdals*. Regional dishes include *gurr*, a Sherpa dish of raw potatoes, pounded with spices, then grilled like pancakes on a hot, flat stone. Tibetan cooking includes *thukba* (thick soup) and *momos* (fried or boiled, stuffed ravioli). Meat includes goat, pork, chicken or buffalo, but beef is forbidden. There is a wide selection of restaurants in Kathmandu, although elsewhere the choice is limited. A 12% Government tax is added to bills. **Drink:** The national drink is *chiya* (tea brewed with milk, sugar and spices; in the mountains it is salted with yak butter). Another popular mountain drink is *chhang* (beer made from fermented barley, maize, rye or millet). *Arak* (potato alcohol) and *raksi* (wheat or rice spirit) are also drunk. Nepalese beer is available, as is good quality local rum, vodka and gin. Local whisky is not so palatable, but imported varieties are widely available.
NIGHTLIFE: Kathmandu has a few cinemas featuring mainly Indian films. For Western films see the programmes of the European and American cultural centres. Most people are asleep by 2200. Nightlife is fairly limited; a few temples and restaurants offer entertainment and some tourist hotels stage Nepalese folk dances and musical shows. There is a casino with baccarat, chemin de fer and roulette, open 24 hours a day, every day, at the Soaltee Oberoi Hotel.
SHOPPING: There are bargains for those careful to avoid fakes and the badly made souvenirs sold by unscrupulous traders. Popular buys include locally made clothes such as lopsided *topi* (caps), knitted mittens and socks, Tibetan dresses, woven shawls, Tibetan multicoloured jackets and men's diagonally fastened shirts; and *pashmin* (fine goats' wool blankets), *khukri* (the national knife), *saranghi* (a small, 4-stringed viola played with a horse-hair bow), Tibetan tea bowls, *papier mâché* dance masks, Buddhist statuettes and filigree ornaments, bamboo flutes and other folk objects. **Shopping hours:** 1000-1900 Sunday to Friday (some stay open on Saturday and holidays).
SPORT: Golf: The Royal Golf Club has a 9-hole course open to member-sponsored guests. **Tennis:** Several of Kathmandu's hotels have tennis courts open to non-residents for a small fee. Alternatively, contact the Tennis (HIT) Centre. **Fishing:** Terai rivers and valley lakes are often good fishing grounds for *asla* (snow trout) and *masheer*. The best months are February, March, October and November. Permits can be obtained from the National Parks and Wildlife Conservation Department in Banswar. **Swimming:** Several hotels in Kathmandu have pools open to non-residents. Caution is needed when swimming in mountain rivers; the larger lowland rivers are safer, but bathers should be wary of the occasional crocodile. **Horseriding:** Must be arranged in advance. The Nepal National Health & Sports Council will be able to provide information on a wide range of sporting activities available in the country.
SPECIAL EVENTS: Nepalese festivals fall into several categories. Most are performed in honour of the gods and goddesses, some mark the seasons or agricultural cycles, and others are simply family celebrations. The usual form of celebration is to take ritual baths in rivers or lakes, visit temples to offer worship, and feasting and ritual fasting. The festivals in Kathmandu Valley are the most rich and spectacular. For a list of special events and festivals in Nepal send a stamped, self-addressed envelope to the Embassy.
SOCIAL CONVENTIONS: Superstition and religion merge into one. As a foreigner, all visitors are 'polluted' and there are several customs associated with this attitude: never step over the feet of a person, always walk round; never offer food and drink which is 'polluted', in other words food that you have tasted or bitten; never offer or accept anything with the left hand, use the right or both hands. It is rude to point at a person or statue with a finger (or even with a foot). Shoes and footwear should be removed when entering houses or shrines. Kitchens and eating areas of houses should also not be entered with footwear, as the hearth of a home is sacred. Do not stand in front of a person who is eating as this means your feet will be next to his food; squat or sit by his side. Local *Chorten* are built to pacify local demons or dead persons and should be passed by in a clockwise direction, as should temples; the earth and universe revolve in this direction. Small flat stones with inscriptions and supplications next to the *Chorten* should not be removed as souvenirs; this is considered as sacrilege by the Nepalese. Avoid touching a Nepalese dressed all in white; his dress signifies a death in the family. Shaking hands is not a common form of greeting; the normal greeting is to press the palms together in a prayer-like gesture. A gift given to a host or hostess will probably be laid aside unopened; to open a parcel in the presence of a guest is considered uncivil. Casual wear is suitable except for the most formal meetings or social occasions. Bikinis, shorts, bare shoulders and backs may not be appreciated. Men only remove their shirts when bathing. Overt public displays of affection, especially near religious places, are inappropriate. Nepalese cities are generally safe, but take sensible precautions with personal possessions. **Photography:** Always ask permission first. In general it is allowed outside temples and at festivals, but not at religious ceremonies or inside temples; however, there is no hard and fast rule and the only way to be sure of not giving offence is to ask first and accept the answer. **Tipping:** Only usual in tourist hotels and restaurants. Taxi drivers need only be tipped when they have been particularly helpful. 10% is sufficient for all three services. Elsewhere tipping should be avoided.

BUSINESS PROFILE

ECONOMY: Nepal is one of the world's least developed countries, with the tenth-lowest per capita GNP (according to World Bank figures). Although most of the land is uncultivatable, 90% of the working population find employment in agriculture and forestry. Foodstuffs and live animals provide about 30% of Nepal's export earnings. The manufacturing sector is very small and concentrated in light industries such as construction materials, carpet-making and food-processing. The country has a considerable hydroelectric potential which would save Nepal from having to import much of its energy requirements, but it is as yet highly underdeveloped. The Government has a cherished hope of exporting hydroelectric power to northern India, where energy is in short supply, but the project is fraught with political difficulties. There is some mining of mica and small quantities of lignite, copper, coal and iron ore. The country runs a large trade deficit and relies on extensive amounts of foreign aid, especially food aid. India is the main trading partner, and the 15-month dispute resolved in June 1990 (see *History*) caused considerable damage to the Nepalese economy. The frontier with China has recently been opened and a trade agreement signed with the Chinese government.
BUSINESS: Tropical-weight suits or shirt and tie are recommended. Best time to visit is October to May. **Office hours:** 1000-1700 Sunday to Friday (summer), and 1000-1600 (winter).
COMMERCIAL INFORMATION: The following organisations can offer advice: Nepal Chamber of Commerce, PO Box 198, Chamber Bhavan, Kanti path, Kathmandu. Tel: (1) 222 890. Fax: 228 324. Telex: 2349; *or*
Federation of Nepalese Chambers of Commerce and Industry, PO Box 269, Tripureshor, Kathmandu. Tel: (1) 212 096. Telex: 2574.

HISTORY & GOVERNMENT

HISTORY: For most of its known history, Nepal was ruled by an hereditary king but, from the middle of the 19th century, hereditary prime ministers of the Rana family controlled the country. In 1951 the Ranas were overthrown and the monarchy restored under King Tribhuvan. Four years later he was succeeded by his son, King Mahendra. In 1959 Mahendra established a parliamentary constitution, and the ensuing elections were won by the Nepali Congress (led by B P Koirala) which had played a key role in the re-establishment of the monarchy. A year later, however, a royal coup led to the banning of all political parties and the establishment of a constitution based on the traditional village councils (the Panchayat system). Mahendra ruled until his death in 1972 when he was succeeded by his son Birendra, who is the current ruler. Following a referendum, in which the Panchayat regime was approved by a narrow majority, Birendra persevered with the system, assisted by censorship and repression where necessary. As serious opposition to the regime gathered strength through the 1980s, the King wavered in his response to the movement between more repressive measures and cosmetic administrative reforms designed to defuse the situation. In 1986, a member of the minority Newari community, Marich Man Singh Shrestha, became Prime Minster for the first time, holding the office until his dismissal and replacement by Lokendra Bahadur Chand in 1990. During 1990, growing public unrest brought the underlying political tension to the surface, and forced the King to make concessions on the introduction of representative government. Following negotiations between the Government and the newly legalised opposition parties – the Nepali Congress Party and the United Left Front – a draft constitution was promulgated in November 1990. General elections held in May 1991 gave the largest number of votes to the Congress Party (linked to the Indian party of the same name) which took 110 of the 205 seats in the new parliament. The United Marxist-Leninist Party, with 69 seats, is the largest opposition grouping. Birendra also moved to solve a crisis in Nepal's foreign policy, which arose from the expiry of a trade agreement with India. No new agreement could be reached and the border was closed by the Indians for over a year, threatening Nepal with economic crisis. The border has been re-opened now that the two governments have settled their differences. Relations with China have undergone steady improvement in the last few years, culminating in a week-long visit to Peking in 1992 by Nepalese Prime Minister Koirala.
GOVERNMENT: Nepal is a constitutional monarchy. Although rather more power has been vested in the monarch than is customary under such a system, the principal centre of legislative and executive power is the 205-seat 2-chamber parliament. Elections in May 1991 brought a government of the Nepali Congress Party to power under the leadership of Prime Minister Girija Prasad Koirala.

CLIMATE

Nepal's weather is generally predictable and pleasant. Summer and monsoon are from June to October. The remainder of the year is dry. Spring and autumn are the most pleasant seasons; winter temperatures drop to freezing with a high level of snowfall in the mountains.
Required clothing: Lightweight and tropical clothes with umbrella are advised for June to August. Between October and March lightweight clothes are worn in Kathmandu, with a coat for evenings and warm clothing for the mountains.

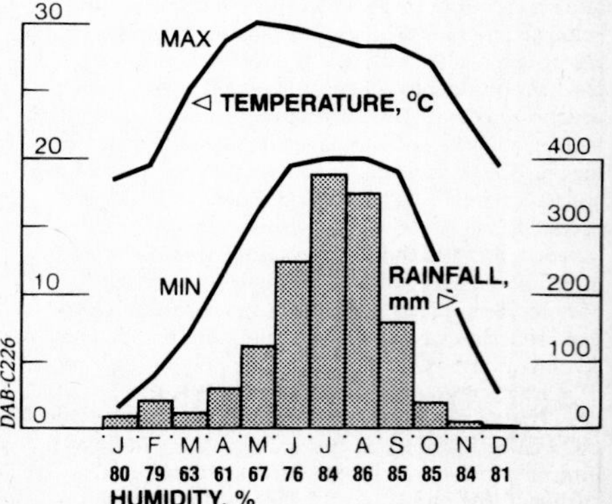

THE NETHERLANDS

Location: Northwest Europe.

Nederlands Bureau voor Toerisme
PO Box 458
2260 MG Leidschendam
The Netherlands
Tel: (70) 370 5705. Fax: (70) 320 1654. Telex: 32588.

Royal Netherlands Embassy
38 Hyde Park Gate
London SW7 5DP
Tel: (071) 584 5040. Fax: (071) 581 3450. Telex: 28812 NETEMB.
Consular Section: Tel: (071) 581 3458. Opening hours: 1000-1330 Monday to Friday.

Netherlands Board of Tourism
25-28 Buckingham Gate
London SW1E 6LD
Tel: (071) 931 0661. Fax: (071) 828 7941. Telex: 269005.

British Embassy
Lange Voorhout 10
2514 ED The Hague
The Netherlands
Tel: (70) 364 5800. Fax: (70) 360 3839. Telex: 31600 BEMB NL.

Royal Netherlands Embassy
4200 Linnean Avenue, NW
Washington, DC
20008
Tel: (202) 244 5300. Fax: (202) 362 3430.

Consulate General of the Netherlands
1 Rockefeller Plaza
New York, NY
10020
Tel: (212) 246 1429. Fax: (212) 333 3603.

Netherlands Board of Tourism
21st Floor
355 Lexington Avenue
New York, NY
10017
Tel: (212) 370 7367. Fax: (212) 370 9507.

Embassy of the United States of America
Box 1000
Lange Voorhout 102
2514 EJ The Hague
The Netherlands
Tel: (70) 310 9209. Fax: (70) 361 4688. Telex: 31016.

Royal Netherlands Embassy
3rd Floor
275 Slater Street
Ottawa, Ontario
K1P 5H9
Tel: (613) 237 5030. Fax: (613) 237 6471.

Netherlands Board of Tourism
Suite 710
25 Adelaide Street East
Toronto, Ontario
M5C 1Y2
Tel: (416) 363 1577. Fax: (416) 363 1470.

Canadian Embassy
Sophialaan 7
The Hague
The Netherlands
Tel: (70) 361 4111. Fax: (70) 356 1111. Telex: 31270.

AREA: 33,938 sq km (13,104 sq miles).
POPULATION: 15,064,586 (1991 estimate).
POPULATION DENSITY: 444 per sq km.
CAPITAL: Amsterdam. **Population:** 702,444 (1991).
SEAT OF GOVERNMENT: The Hague. **Population:** 444,242 (1991).
GEOGRAPHY: The Netherlands shares borders to the south with Belgium and the east with Germany, while the North Sea lies to the north and west. Large areas of The Netherlands have been reclaimed from the sea and consequently one-fifth of the country lies below sea level. The country is flat and level and is crisscrossed by rivers and canals. Areas reclaimed from the sea, known as *polders*, are extremely fertile. The landscape is broken by the forest of Arnhem, the bulb fields in the west, the lakes of central and northern areas, and coastal dunes which are among the most impressive in Europe.
LANGUAGE: Dutch. English is widely spoken and understood. French and German are also spoken.
RELIGION: 38% Roman Catholic, 30% Protestant; 26% do not profess any religion.
TIME: GMT + 1 (GMT + 2 in summer).
ELECTRICITY: 220 volts AC, 50Hz.
COMMUNICATIONS: Telephone: Full IDD is available. Country code: 31 (followed by 20 for Amsterdam, 10 for Rotterdam, 70 for The Hague). Telephone information given in French, English and German. The cheap rate is from 1800-0800 Monday to Friday and at the weekend. Calls can be made from public booths or post offices. Booths accept 25 cents, Gld1 and Gld2.5 coins or cards. These can be bought at post offices, VVV offices, and shops displaying the *PTT-telephone card* poster. **Fax:** Services are widely available and are also provided by some hotels. **Telex/telegram:** There are no major public telex offices, but there are facilities in main hotels. Telegram facilities are available at all main post offices; telegrams can also be sent directly from telephone kiosks. **Post:** Stamps are available from all post offices as well as from tobacconists and kiosks selling postcards and souvenirs. Mail takes approximately five days. Post offices are open 0830-1700 Monday to Friday. Some major post offices are open 0830-1200 Saturday. There are all-night post offices in Amsterdam (Niedwezijds Voorburgwal, behind the Royal Palace) and Rotterdam (Coolsingel). **Press:** The main dailies are *De Telegraaf, Algemeen Dagblad* and *De Volkskrant*. Foreign newspapers are widely available.
BBC World Service and Voice of America frequencies: From time to time these change. See the section *How to Use this Book* for more information.

BBC:

MHz	12.10	9.410	6.045	3.955

A service is also available on 648kHz and 198kHz (0100-0500 GMT).

Voice of America:

MHz	11.97	9.670	6.040	5.995

PASSPORT/VISA

Regulations and requirements may be subject to change at short notice, and you are advised to contact the appropriate diplomatic or consular authority before finalising travel arrangements. Details of these may be found at the head of this country's entry. Any numbers in the chart refer to the footnotes below.

	Passport Required?	Visa Required?	Return Ticket Required?
Full British	1	No	No/2
BVP	Valid	No	No/2
Australian	Yes	No	No/2
Canadian	Yes	No	No/2
USA	Yes	No	No/2
Other EC	1	No	No/2
Japanese	Yes	No	No/2

PASSPORTS: Valid passport required by all except the following with a valid identity card:
(a) [1] EC nationals (UK nationals require a British Visitors Passport);
(b) nationals of Andorra, Austria, Liechtenstein, Malta, Monaco, San Marino and Switzerland (with a valid identity card).
Where national passports are required, they must be valid for at least 3 months after the last day of the intended visit.
Note: [2] It is advisable to have a return ticket, but not obligatory. If visitor is not in possession of a return ticket, proof of sufficient means of support may be required.
British Visitors Passport: A BVP is valid for holidays or unpaid business trips of up to 3 months. Children under 16 years of age travelling to The Netherlands, Luxembourg or Belgium cannot do so on their brother's or sister's passport.
VISAS: Required by all except:
(a) nationals of countries referred to in the chart above;
(b) nationals of countries referred to above under passport exemptions;
(c) nationals of Argentina, Bermuda, Brazil, Brunei, Burkina Faso, Chile, Costa Rica, Cyprus, Czechoslovakia, Ecuador, El Salvador, Finland, Guatemala, Honduras, Hong Kong (British Passport holders only), Hungary, Iceland, Israel, Jamaica, South Korea, Malawi, Malaysia, Mexico, New Zealand, Nicaragua, Niger, Norway, Panama, Paraguay, Poland, Singapore, Sweden, Togo, Turkey (if resident in an EC country), Uruguay, Vatican City and Venezuela.
All visa exemptions are for stays of up to 3 months.
Nationals of all other countries require a visa.
Types of visa: Transit, Travel and Sojourn (for tourist or business purposes). Enquire at Consulate General for further details.
Benelux Visas can be issued by the Belgium, Luxembourg or Netherlands embassies abroad, valid for entry into all three countries. The visa number must begin with the letters BE, NE or LUX, to indicate which country the passenger will enter first. Passengers with this type of visa are strongly advised to be holding onward or return tickets, or proof of means of support.
Validity: Transit: 24 hours. Travel and Sojourn visas depend on duration of visit(s).
Application to: Consulate (or Consular Section at Embassy). For addresses, see top of entry.
Application requirements: (a) Completed application forms. (b) Valid passport. (c) Fee where applicable. (d) Photos (not needed for Transit visas).
The number of forms and photos required is dependent on the nationality of the applicant.
Working days required: Often within 24 hours, but can take up to 6 weeks for certain nationals (see entry for Luxembourg earlier in the *World Travel Guide*).
Temporary residence: Work permit and residence permit required if other than EC member. Enquire at the Embassy.

MONEY

Currency: Guilder (Gld) = 100 cents. Notes are in denominations of Gld1000, 250, 100, 50, 25 and 10. Coins are in denominations of Gld5, 2.5 and 1, and 25, 10 and 5 cents.
Currency exchange: Exchange offices are indicated by the letters GWK.
Credit cards: Access/Mastercard, American Express, Diners Club and Visa are accepted. Check with your credit card company for details of merchant acceptability and other services which may be available.
Travellers cheques: The easiest form of currency to exchange.
Exchange rate indicators: The following figures are included as a guide to the movements of the Guilder against Sterling and the US Dollar:

Date:	Oct '89	Oct '90	Oct '91	Oct '92
£1.00=	3.37	3.35	3.28	2.74
$1.00=	2.13	1.72	1.89	1.73

Currency restrictions: There are no restrictions on the import and export of either local or foreign currency.
Banking hours: 0900-1600 Monday to Friday.

DUTY FREE

The following goods may be imported into The Netherlands without incurring customs duty:
(a) European travellers from EC countries:
300 cigarettes or 75 cigars or 150 cigarillos or 400g of tobacco; [1]
1.5 litres of alcoholic beverages stronger than 22° proof or 3 litres of alcoholic beverages less than 22° proof or 5 litres of non-sparkling wine; [1]
8 litres of Luxembourg wine; [1]
75g of perfume;
3/8 litre of toilet water;
Other goods up to the value of Gld1400.
(b) Travellers arriving from EC countries with duty paid goods (as of January 1993):
800 cigarettes and 400 cigarillos and 200 cigars and 1kg tobacco; [1]
90 litres of wine including up to 60 litres of sparkling wine; [1]
10 litres of spirits and 20 litres of port or sherry and 110

litres of beer. [1]
(c) Travellers from non-EC European countries:
200 cigarettes or 50 cigars or 100 cigarillos or 250g of tobacco; [1]
1 litre of alcoholic beverages stronger than 22° proof or 2 litres less than 22° proof or 2 litres of liqueur wine; [1]
2 litres of wine; [1]
8 litres of non-sparkling Luxembourg wine; [1]
50g of perfume and 250ml of toilet water; [1]
Other goods to the value of Gld125.
(d) Travellers originating from outside Europe:
400 cigarettes or 100 cigars or 500g tobacco; [1]
Wine, spirits and perfume same as for non-EC European countries; [1]
Other goods to the value of Gld125.
[1]: These allowances are only for travellers aged 17 years and above.
Note: (a) Enquiries concerning current import regulations should be made to the Royal Netherlands Embassy in the country of departure, or to the national Chamber of Commerce. (b) Cats and dogs imported into The Netherlands from any countries other than Belgium or Luxembourg require a health certificate. The importation of psittacine birds (parrots or parrot-like birds) is limited to two per family, and a health certificate is required for each bird. The importation of monkeys is prohibited. For more information, contact the Agricultural Department at the Royal Netherlands Embassy.

PUBLIC HOLIDAYS

Public holidays observed in The Netherlands are as follows:
Apr 9 '93 Good Friday. **Apr 12** Easter Monday. **Apr 30** Queen's Day. **May 5** National Liberation Day. **May 20** Ascension Day. **May 31** Whit Monday. **Dec 25-26** Christmas. **Jan 1 '94** New Year's Day.

HEALTH

Regulations and requirements may be subject to change at short notice, and you are advised to contact your doctor well in advance of your intended date of departure. Any numbers in the chart refer to the footnotes below.

	Special Precautions?	Certificate Required?
Yellow Fever	No	No
Cholera	No	No
Typhoid & Polio	No	-
Malaria	No	-
Food & Drink	No	-

Rabies is present. For those at high risk, vaccination before arrival should be considered. If you are bitten abroad seek medical advice without delay. For more information consult the *Health* section at the back of the book.
Health care: The standard of health care (and other social services) is very high in The Netherlands. There is a Reciprocal Health Agreement with all other EC countries. On presentation of form E111 by UK residents (available from post offices or the Department of Health), all medical treatment, including hospital treatment, is free; prescribed medicines and dental treatment must, however, be paid for. *Emergency telephone numbers:* Amsterdam: 664 2111 (central doctors service) *or* (20) 622 2222 (police alarm number). Rotterdam: (10) 411 5504. The Hague: (70) 345 5300 (physicians' general information) *or* 346 9669 (physicians' night service). For police, fire or ambulance emergencies, dial 06-11 anywhere in the country.

TRAVEL - International

AIR: The Netherlands' national airline is *Royal Dutch Airlines (KLM)*.
Approximate flight times: From Amsterdam to *Belfast* is 1 hour 5 minutes; to *London* is 1 hour; to *Manchester* is 1 hour 5 minutes and to *New York* is 9 hours 45 minutes (including stopover in London).
International airports: Principally Amsterdam, with a small number of international flights also operated from Rotterdam, Eindhoven and Maastricht.
Amsterdam (AMS) (Schiphol) is 15km (9 miles) southwest of the city (travel time by train – 20 minutes). *KLM* buses provide a daily service from 0600-2400 departing every half-hour and stopping at the following hotels: Hotel Ibis; Amsterdam Hilton; Golden Tulip Barbizon; Centraal; Park Hotel and Apollo Hotel and return to Schiphol. Trains to Zuid station (Amsterdam South) run every 15 minutes from 0525-0015; return is from Zuid station, Parnassusweg/Minervalaan (via tram no 5 from the city centre) from 0545-0040. There is now a direct rail link between the airport and Amsterdam Central Station, with trains every 15 minutes and an all-night service. There is a service to the RAI Congress Centre every 15 minutes from 0525-0012. Return from RAI station (via tram no 4 from the city centre) from 0545-0040. Plentiful taxis are available to the city. Airport facilities: restaurants, outgoing duty-free shop, banks, car rental. Flight information: (20) 601 0966.
Rotterdam (RTM) (Zestienhoven) is 9km (5.5 miles) northwest of the city (travel time – 15 minutes). Bus no 33 departs every 30 minutes from 0700-1900. Return is from Central Station, Knisplein, from 0630-1830. Taxis to the city are also available. Airport facilities: restaurant, bank, outgoing duty-free shop, car rental. 24-hour flight information: (10) 446 0813.
Eindhoven (EIN) (Welschap) airport is 8km (5 miles) from the city. Coaches run every 15 minutes and taxis to the city are also available. Airport facilities: car rental, outgoing duty-free shop. Flight information: (40) 516 142.
Maastricht (MST) (Beek) airport is 8km (5 miles) from the city. Airport facilities: outgoing duty-free shop.
Groningen (GRQ) (Elede) airport is 9km (6 miles) from the city.
Enschede (ENS) (Twente) airport is 8km (5 miles) from the city.
SEA: Regular car and passenger ferries are operated from the UK to The Netherlands via the following routes and shipping lines: *North Sea Ferries:* Hull to Rotterdam (Europoort); travel time – 14 hours; 1 sailing nightly. *Olau Line UK Ltd:* Sheerness to Vlissingen; travel time – 7 hours (day), 8 hours 30 mins (night); 2 sailings daily. *Sealink:* Harwich to Hook of Holland; travel time – 7 hours 30 mins (day), 8 hours (night); 2 sailings daily. *Hoverspeed UK Ltd:* coach/hovercraft service from London to Amsterdam; travel time – 10 hours; 2 or 3 services daily.
Note: *North Sea Ferries* and *P&O* run services to The Netherlands via Belgium.
RAIL: Rail connections from London via either Harwich and Hook of Holland, or Dover and Ostend (boat or jetfoil). Information is available in the UK from any British Rail Travel Centre. There are direct links from Amsterdam to Paris, Brussels, Zürich, Frankfurt, Copenhagen and Luxembourg.
ROAD: The Netherlands are connected to the rest of Europe by a superb network of motorways. Although frontier formalities between The Netherlands and Germany and Belgium have now all but vanished, motorists – particularly on smaller roads – should be prepared to stop when asked to do so by a customs official.

TRAVEL - Internal

AIR: *KLM Cityhopper (HN)* operates between Amsterdam, Rotterdam, Groningen, Enschede, Maastricht and Eindhoven. Enquire at *KLM* offices or at the Board of Tourism for further information.
SEA: Ferry service to the Wadden Islands across the Ijsselmeer (former Zuyder Sea) and Scheldt Estuary. There is also a service to the Frisian Islands across the Waddenzee. *Boat Tours* run excursions from Amsterdam, Rotterdam, Utrecht, Arnhem, Groningen, Giethoorn, Delft and Maastricht.
RAIL: The highly developed rail network is efficient and cheap, and connects all towns. Both Intercity and local trains run at least half-hourly on all principal routes. Rail and bus timetables are integrated, and there is a common fare structure throughout the country.
Cheap fares: *Rail Rovers* are available for one, three or seven days. UK prices are as follows:

	1st Class	2nd Class
1 day:	£25.00	£17.00
3 days:	£31.00	£25.00
7 days:	£59.50	£39.50

Public Transport Link Rovers are issued in conjunction with *Rail Rovers*, costing an additional £2 for one day, and £7.50 for seven days. These cover unlimited travel on all public transport buses and trams in town and country, and on the metro system in Amsterdam and Rotterdam. *Benelux Tourrail Cards* are available for travel in the Netherlands, Belgium and Luxembourg. These allow unlimited travel for any five days in a 17-day period. Other deals include *Multi-Rovers, Family Rovers* and *Teenage Rovers*. Children under four years of age travel free on all journeys within The Netherlands. Children between 4-11 years travelling unaccompanied are entitled to a 40% reduction on the adult single or day-return fare. Those accompanied by an adult travel for Gld1. On international journeys, children aged 4-11 pay half of the adult fare on the Dutch rail section of the trip. Even greater savings are available on the *Child's Railrunner* tickets for children 4-11 years old travelling with a fare-paying adult (19 years or older), and includes up to three children travelling with any one adult. Contact the Railway Authority of any of the participating countries for prices and further information.
Inter-Rail passes are also valid in The Netherlands.
Any enquiries about rail travel, the purchase of *Rail Rover* tickets etc, in the UK should be addressed to: Netherlands Railways, 25-28 Buckingham Gate, London SW1E 6LD. Tel: (071) 630 1735. Fax: (071) 233 5832.
ROAD: Excellent road system. Visitors to The Netherlands may use credit cards when obtaining petrol. The motoring association in The Netherlands is the ANWB (Koninklijke Nederlandsche Toeristenbond), Wassenaarseweg 220, The Hague. Tel: (70) 314 1420.
Bus: Extensive regional bus networks exist. Long-distance coaches also operate between the cities, but costs are generally on a par with trains. **Taxi:** It is less usual to hail a taxi in the street in Holland. Taxis have an illuminated sign 'taxi' on the roof and there are taxi ranks at railway stations and at various other points in the cities. Taxis can also be phoned. Usually there are meters in the taxi showing the fare, including the tip. **Car hire:** Available from airports and main hotels. All European car-hire companies are represented. **Bicycle hire:** Bikes can be hired from all main railway stations, but must be returned to the station from which they are hired. A returnable deposit is required. **Regulations:** Driving is on the right. Drivers should be particularly aware of cyclists; often there are special cycle lanes. There is a chronic shortage of parking space in central Amsterdam, and the rush hours (0700-0900 and 1700-1900) should be avoided throughout the whole country. Parking fines are severe. Headlights should be dipped in built-up areas, but it is prohibited to use sidelights only. Children under 12 should not travel in the front seat. Seat belts are compulsory. Speed limits are 80kmph (49mph) on major roads, 120kmph (74mph) on motorways and 50kmph (31mph) in towns. **Documentation:** An International Driving Licence is not required, as long as a driving licence from the country of origin is held. Trailers and caravans are allowed in without documents. A Green Card is advisable, but not compulsory. Without it, drivers with motor insurance policies in their home country are granted only the minimum legal cover in The Netherlands; the Green Card tops this up to the level of cover provided by the driver's own policy.
URBAN: Public transport is very well developed in the cities and large towns. A *strippenkaart* national fares sys-

NETHERLANDS	HEALTH REGULATIONS	VISA REGULATIONS Code-Link
GALILEO/WORLDSPAN	 TI-DFT/AMS/HE	 TI-DFT/AMS/VI
SABRE	 TIDFT/AMS/HE	 TIDFT/AMS/VI

To access this information on your CRS, swipe the barcode with a light pen or type in the text under the barcode. For more information, see the introduction *How to Use This Book*.

tem exists. Strips of 15 tickets each are widely available at railway stations, post offices and some tourist offices. These are accepted anywhere in payment of standard zonal fares. There are also individual and multi-day tickets for the cities. For more detailed information on travel within Amsterdam, Rotterdam and The Hague, see below. All the towns and cities are well served by bus services; in addition, Utrecht has a tram service, and there are trolleybuses in Arnhem.

Amsterdam: Information: VVV (Amsterdam Tourist Office), Stationsplein 10 (opposite Central Station). Tel: (20) 626 6444. Opening hours: *Summer:* 0700-2230 Mon to Sun; *Winter:* normal office hours. Amsterdam has an extensive network of buses, trams and metro (*GVB*), with frequent services from early morning to about midnight. There are less frequent services throughout the night at a higher fare. Full information on services (including a map), day tickets and *strippenkaart* (strip-tickets) can be obtained from the GVB office in front of the Central Station (open every day 0700-2230) or the GVB Central Office at Prins Hendrikkade 108-114. The GVB is easy to use, and the tram system can be very useful, since it is not only good value (as are the buses and metro) but also enables reasonably quick travel even during the busiest periods of the day. *RAI Trade Fair Centre:* A 45-minute walk, a taxi ride, or the number 4 tram from the city centre. *Taxi:* Taxis are not generally hailed, but found at a limited number of ranks in the city centre. They can also be ordered by phone. *Car hire:* The major European firms, including *Hertz* and *Avis*, are represented. Cars can also be hired through most hotels.

Rotterdam: Information: VVV Rotterdam, Head Office, Coolsingel 67, Rotterdam. Tel: (10) 413 6000. Telex: 21228. The city has excellent bus and tram services, and a 2-line metro network. These work on a zonal system. Information is available from the Central Station. *Taxi:* Available from ranks or by phone. *Car hire:* The major European firms, including *Avis* and *Hertz*, are represented.

The Hague: Information: VVV Den Haag-Kantoor Winkelcentrum Babylon, Koningin Julianaplein 30. Tel: (70) 354 6200. The Hague has bus and tram services. Information is available from the Central Station, Koningin Julianaplein. *Taxi:* Available from ranks or by phone. *Car hire: Avis* and *Hertz* are represented.

JOURNEY TIMES: The following chart gives approximate journey times (in hours and minutes) from Amsterdam to other major cities in The Netherlands:

	Air	Road	Rail
The Hague	-	0.40	0.44
Rotterdam	-	1.00	1.00
Utrecht	-	0.25	0.30
Groningen	-	2.00	2.20
Arnhem	-	1.10	1.10
Maastricht	0.40	2.30	2.30
Vlissingen	-	2.00	2.45
Eindhoven	0.30	1.30	1.25
Breda	-	1.30	1.50

ACCOMMODATION

HOTELS: The Netherlands has a wide range of accommodation, from luxury hotels in big towns to modern motels along motorways. The Netherlands Reserverings Centrum (NRC) can make reservations throughout the country: Postbus 404, 2260 AK Leidschendam, The Netherlands. Tel: (70) 320 2611. Telex: 33755.

Grading: The Netherlands Board of Tourism issues a shield to all approved hotels by which they can be recognised. This must be affixed to the front of the hotel in a conspicuous position. Hotels which display this sign conform to the official standards set by Netherlands law on hotels and it protects the tourist and guarantees certain standards of quality. Some hotels are also graded according to the *Benelux* system in which standard is indicated by a row of 3-pointed stars from the highest (5-star) to the minimum (1-star). However, membership of this scheme is voluntary, and there may be first-class hotels which are not classified in this way. *Benelux* star ratings adhere to the following criteria:

5-star (H5): This is a new category signifying luxury hotel.

4-star (H4): First-class hotels. 80% of rooms have a private bath. Other amenities include night reception and room service.

3-star (H3): Half of the rooms have a private bath. Other amenities include day reception.

2-star (H2): A quarter of rooms have a private bath. Other amenities include a bar.

1-star (H1): Simple hotel. No private baths, but hot and cold water in rooms. Breakfast available.

Cat H: Hotel with minimal comfort.

Cat O: Simple accommodation.

GUEST-HOUSES: These are called *pensions* and rates vary. Book through local tourist offices.

SELF-CATERING: Farmhouses for groups can be booked months in advance via the local tourist offices. Holiday Chalets, especially in the relatively unknown parts of Zeeland, can be booked through the local tourist office. Bungalow parks throughout the country can be booked through the Netherlands Reservation Centre; see above.

CAMPING/CARAVANNING: There are some 2500 registered campsites in Holland. At only 500 are you able to book in advance, the others operate on a first-come, first-served basis. Off-site camping is not permitted. It is advisable to book in advance. Prices are fairly high and it is often far better value to stay more than one night. A list is available from the Board of Tourism.

YOUTH HOSTELS: Over 50 in various towns and villages. Information is available from Stiching Nederlandse Jeugdherberg Centrale, Prof. Tulpstraat 2-6, Amsterdam, The Netherlands.

RESORTS & EXCURSIONS

For the purposes of this survey, the country has been divided into seven regions: *Amsterdam* (including the province of Noord-Holland); *Rotterdam; The Hague* (including the province of Zuid-Holland); *Utrecht; The North* (the provinces of Friesland, Groningen and Drenthe); *The East* (the provinces of Flevoland, Overijssel and Gelderland); and *The South* (the provinces of Noord-Brabant, Zeeland and Limburg). There is also a brief section devoted to coastal resorts.

Amsterdam

Tourist Office Tel: (20) 626 6444. Fax: (20) 625 2869. Telex: 12324.

Amsterdam, which is the capital of The Netherlands though not its seat of government, is built around a concentric network of canals which are spanned by over 1000 bridges (one of the most attractive ways of viewing the city is a canal tour). Many of the city's houses date back to Holland's golden age in the 17th century; though each is individual, these houses, crowded against each other, have a characteristic narrow frontage, with four to six floors and a modest degree of ostentation most notable in the unique, ornamented gables. Excursions to diamond-cutting centres are available. The city contains

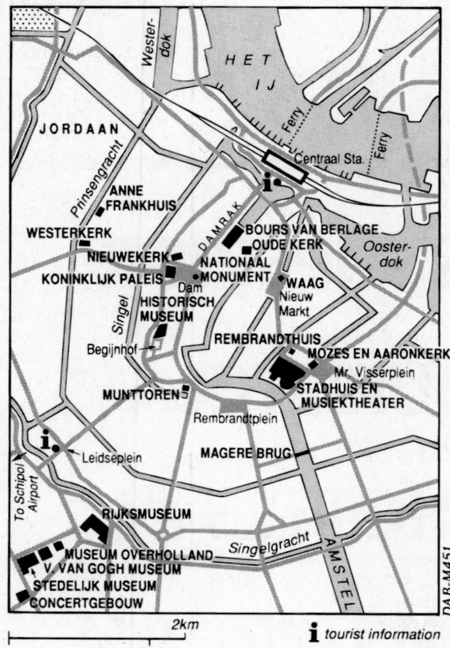

53 museums, 61 art galleries, 12 concert halls and 20 theatres; a special canal boat links 16 of the major museums. Outside Amsterdam, visitors can take the opportunity to see working windmills and examples of the region's traditional urban and village construction. There are annual events such as the Amsterdam Art Weeks and the Holland Festival.

It is possible to book a VVV approved guide/hostess in Amsterdam by contacting Guidor, c/o Netherlands Reservation Centre (address in the *Accommodation* section above).

SIGHTSEEING: A selection of some of the most popular sights follows:

Rijksmuseum: National museum with Dutch paintings dating from the 16th-19th century, including *The Nightwatch* by Rembrandt. To be found at Stadhouderskade 42. Opening hours: 1000-1700 Tuesday to Saturday, 1300-1700 Sunday and holidays, closed Mondays, January 1 and April 30

Anne Frank's House: Prinsengracht 263. Opening hours: 0900-1700 Monday to Saturday and 1000-1700 Sundays (winter); 0900-1900 Monday to Saturday and 1000-1900 Sundays (summer). Closed December 25, New Year's Day and Yom Kippur.

Vincent Van Gogh Museum: Paulus Potterstraat 7. Opening hours: 1000-1700 Tuesday to Saturday, 1300-1700 Sunday and holidays, closed Mondays and New Year's Day.

Museum Het Rembrandthuis: Jodenbreestraat 4-6. Opening hours: 1000-1700 Monday to Saturday, 1300-1700 Sunday and holidays, closed New Year's Day and February 17-21.

Stedelijk Museum (Museum of Modern Art): Paulus Potterstraat 13. Opening hours: 1100-1700 Monday to Sunday. Closed New Year's Day.

Other interesting places to visit include: The *Royal Palace;* the *Nieuwe Kerk;* the *Martelwerktuigenmuseum* (the Torture Museum), the *Munt Tower,* which looms over the floating flower market on the Singel canal; the open-air market at *Waterlooplein;* the *Begijnhof* (14th-century almshouses around a quiet courtyard); and bookshops in the *Oudemanhuispoort.*

NIGHTLIFE: Many of the nightclubs are concentrated in the Rembrantsplein–Leidseplein area. There is a weekly magazine, 'Amsterdam This Week', which will give you a good idea of the week's events and clubs worth visiting. Walletjes, the notorious 'red-light' district of the city, is on the east side of Damrak. Here and around Leidseplein are any number of bars and clubs, many with live music, from cabaret to modern jazz.

Concert halls/theatres: *Stadsschouwburg* (opera) and *Concertgebouw* (classical music, opera, ballet). Enquiries can be made through the VVV Theatre Booking Office situated on Stationsplein 10, Amsterdam, open 1000-1600 Monday to Saturday.

NOORD-HOLLAND: Tourist Office: As for Amsterdam (above).

The Amsterdam VVV publishes a booklet outlining over 15 excursions which highlight the Dutch image abroad (ie clogs, tulips, cheese and windmills). Day trips are available to **Alkmaar**, where there is a famous cheese market at Waagplein 1000-1200 from mid-April to mid-September every Friday; a frequent train service runs from Central Station. There is also a frequent bus service from Central Station to **Volendam** and **Marken**, both old fishing villages, largely built of wood. The former is predominantly Catholic, the latter Protestant.

Haarlem (20km or 12 miles west of Amsterdam) is a centre of Dutch tulip-growing and the surrounding countryside affords a fine view of the bulb fields from the end of March to mid-May; the town itself has a fine museum. Nearby are **Hoorn** and **Enkhuizen**, which are watersports centres; the casino at **Zandvoort** (5km or 3 miles west of Haarlem), also the site of the *Dutch Grand Prix;* and the *National Zuyder Zee Museum,* Wierdijk 18, Enkhuizen, an outdoor museum with ships and reconstructed houses etc, open from early April to mid-October, 1000-1700 Monday to Sunday (closed January 1st and December 25th-26th). There is a famous *Flower Auction* in **Aalsmeer**, Legmeerdijk 313; open 0730-1130 Monday to Friday. Near **Lisse**, 8km (5 miles) south of Haarlem, are the *Keukenhof Gardens,* which have a lily show in the last week; open from the end of March to mid-May, 0800-1930 Monday to Sunday. The *Frans Roozen Nurseries & Tulip Show* and the bulb fields can be visited at Vogelenzangweg 49; open 0800-1800 Monday to Sunday (April and May) and 0900-1700 Monday to Sunday (July to September). **Broek op Langedijk** has Europe's oldest vegetable auction hall with a large and interesting exhibition of land reclamation of the immediate area; open from May to September, 1000-1700 Monday to Friday, and for groups from April to September, Monday to Friday, by appointment only.

The Hague

Tourist Office. Tel: (70) 354 6200. Telex: 31490.

The Hague (Den Haag, officially 's-Gravenhage) is a cosmopolitan city which has over 60 foreign embassies and is the seat of the International Court of Justice, as well as being the capital of the province of Zuid-Holland. Although The Hague is the seat of government of The Netherlands, it is not, contrary to popular belief, the country's capital. The central part of the Old Town is the *Binnenhof,* an irregular group of buildings surrounding an open space. The seaside resort of **Scheveningen** (which has the country's only pier) is a nearby suburb.

SIGHTSEEING: A selection of some of the most popular sights follows.

Madurodam Miniature Town: Haringkade 175. Opening hours: 0900-2230 Monday to Sunday (March to May); 0900-2300 (June to August); 0900-2130 (September); 0900-1800 (October to January) (illuminated after dark).

Panorama Mesdag: Zeestraat 65B. Largest panoramic circular painting in the world, created by the artist Mesdag and others, famous for its perfect optical illusion. Opening hours: 1000-1700 Monday to Saturday, and 1200-1700 Sunday and holidays.

Antique Walk: VVV route including most of the 150 antique shops in The Hague – the detailed description and map are printed on the back of a reproduction 1614 print and are available from VVV information offices.

Parliament Buildings and Knight's Hall: Tel: (70) 364 6144. 13th-century buildings with regular tours and slide shows explaining the history of the Binnenhof. Opening hours: 1000-1600 Monday to Saturday (last guided tour 1555).

Royal Cabinet of Paintings: In the Mauritshuis at Korte Vijverberg 8. Tel: (70) 365 4779. Collection includes the *Anatomical Lesson of Dr Tulp* by Rembrandt, and other 17th-century Dutch works. Opening hours: 1000-1700 Tuesday to Saturday, 1100-1700 Sunday and holidays, closed January 1, April 30 and December 25.

Other interesting places to visit include: The *Huis ten Bosch Palace,* the *Puppet Museum,* the antique market at the *Lange Voorhout,* the *Duinoord* district built in the style of old Dutch architecture, the *Haagse Bos* wooded park, the 17th-century *Nieuwe Kork* and the *Royal Library.*

ZUID-HOLLAND: Tourist Office. Tel: (15) 126 100. 22km (14 miles) southeast of Rotterdam and about 45km (28 miles) southeast of The Hague is **Kinderdijk**, near Alblasserdam, where several windmills operate. They can be visited during the week. **Delft**, centre of the Dutch pottery industry and world famous for its blue hand-painted ceramics, is roughly midway between Rotterdam and The Hague. **Gouda**, 20km (12 miles) southeast of Rotterdam, is famous for its cheese market and the *Candlelight Festival* in December. The town centre is dominated by the massive late-Gothic *Town Hall.* Nearby is the old town of **Oudewater,** which has many beautiful gabled houses of the early 17th century. 12km (7 miles) northwest of Gouda is the town of **Boskoop,** renowned for its fruit trees; a visit during the blossom season is particularly recommended. **Dordrecht**, 15km (9 miles) southeast of Rotterdam and about 37km (23 miles) southeast of The Hague, was an important port until a flood in 1421 reduced the economic importance of the town. The museum in the city has a good collection of paintings from the 17th, 18th and 19th centuries, while the most striking building is probably the *Grote Kerk,* begun in about 1305. **Leiden** (20km or 12 miles northeast of The Hague, 40km or 25 miles north of Rotterdam), the birthplace of Rembrandt, was a famous weaving town during the Middle Ages, and played a large part in the wars of independence against Spain in the 16th century. The university was founded by William the Silent in 1575 in return for the city's loyalty. The Pilgrim Fathers lived here for ten years (1610-1620) and *The Pilgrim Fathers' Documentation Centre* in **Boisotkade** (Vliet 45) has many artefacts, records and paintings dating from the period of their stay in the city.

There are many **beach resorts** in this region of the country. Some of the major ones include Scheveningen, Katwijk aan Zee, Noordwijk aan Zee, Monster, Wassenaar, 's-Gravenzande, Wassenaar and Ter Heijde.

Rotterdam

Tourist Office. Tel: (10) 413 6000. Fax: (10) 413 0124. Telex: 21228.

Rotterdam is the world's largest port and is the hub of the Dutch economy; it deals mainly with containerised merchandise. Much of the city was obliterated during the Second World War, and only certain parts retain any of the old buildings. Historically, the city has been an important manufacturing centre since the 14th century, but its pre-eminence as a port dates only from the early 19th century.

SIGHTSEEING: A selection of some of the most popular sights follows.

Euromast & Space Tower: Parkhaven 20. The Observation Tower at 185m (605ft) is the highest point in Holland. Opening hours: Euromast – 1000-1800 daily (winter); 1000-2100 (summer). Space Tower – 1100-1600 daily (only open weekends in January-February).

Museumschip 'De Buffel': Leuvehaven. This is now part of the Maritime Museum. Tel: (6) 413 2680.

Museum Boymans van Beuningen: Mathenesserlaan 18-20. Tel: (6) 441 9400. A unique collection of paintings, sculptures and objets d'art. Opening hours: 1000-1700 Tuesday to Saturday, 1100-1700 Sunday and holidays, closed January 1 and April 30.

Harbour tours: Willemsplein. Tel: (6) 413 5400. Boat tours *(Spido)* through the harbour of Rotterdam, are available throughout the year. In the summer there are excursions to Europoort, the Delta Project and evening tours. There are also luxury motor cruisers for hire. A drive through the harbour of Rotterdam is also possible. The journey is one of between 100 and 150km (60 to 90 miles), and takes in almost every aspect of this massive harbour. The route passes wharves and warehouses, futuristic grain silos and unloading equipment, cranes and bridges, oil refineries, power stations and lighthouses, all of which create a skyline of awesome beauty, particularly at sunset. The docks, waterways, canals and ports-within-ports are interspersed with some surprising and apparently incongruous features; at one point the route passes a garden city built for shipyard workers, while further on there is a village and, at the harbour's westernmost point, a beach. A visit to Rotterdam harbour is recommended, even for someone with no interest in or knowledge of the arcana of grain silos or crude-oil terminals.

Blijdorp Zoo: Van Aersenlaan 49. Tel: (6) 464 731. An open-plan zoo, beautifully laid out, with a restaurant. Opening hours: 0900-1700 Monday to Sunday.

Museums: The municipal museums are open 1000-1700 Monday to Saturday, 1100-1700 Sunday and holidays. They are closed on January 1 and the Queen's Birthday (April 30).

Other interesting places to visit include: 17th-century houses in the *Delfshaven* quarter of the city; the *Pilgrimskerk;* collections of maps and seacharts at the *Delfshaven Old Town Hall;* many traditional workshops for pottery, watchmaking and woodturning.
NIGHTLIFE: The major concert venue is the *De Doelen Concert Hall* (classical music, plays), which has 2000 seats.

Utrecht

Tourist Office: Vredenburg 90, 3511 BD Utrecht. Tel: (6) 34 03 40 85. Fax: (30) 331 417.
The province of Utrecht in the very heart of The Netherlands, contains numerous country houses, estates and castles set in landscaped parks and beautiful woods. The city of Utrecht – the fourth largest in The Netherlands – is set on a slightly elevated tract of land (the *Geest),* a fact which, in a country vulnerable to flooding, has greatly aided the city's commercial development. It is one of the oldest cities in the country, the site being first settled by the Romans. During the Middle Ages, Utrecht was often an imperial residence, and the city's bishops regularly played an important role in the secular affairs of Europe. The city's prosperity allowed the construction of several beautiful churches, particularly the *Cathedral of St Michael* (13th century), *St Pieterskerk* and *St Janskerk* (both 11th century) and *St Jacobkerk* (12th century). Other buildings of note include the *House of the Teutonic Order,* the 14th-century *Huys Oudaen,* the *Hospice of St Bartholomew* and the *Neudeflat,* a more modern construction (built in the 1960s), but one which affords from its 15th-floor restaurant a superb view across the city. The city also has several museums, including the *Central Museum* (which has an excellent Department of Modern Art), the *Archiepiscopal Museum,* the *Railway Museum,* the *Archaeological Collection* and the *Municipal Museum.*
The countryside around Utrecht is very fertile and has much of the atmosphere of a very large garden. The town makes a convenient base for excursions into the Veluwe region in the province of Gelderland (see below under The East).
25km (16 miles) to the northeast of Utrecht is the town of **Amersfoort**, set in a region of heathland and forest. The old town is well preserved, one of the most attractive buildings being the *Church of St George.* 8km (5 miles) away is the town of **Soestdijk**, containing the *Royal Palace* and the beautiful parklands of the Queen Mother. Between Soestdijk and Hilversum is **Baarn**, a favourite summer resort among the Dutch.

The North

Tourist Offices. *Friesland* (tel: (58) 132 224) *Groningen* (tel: (50) 139 700) *Drenthe* (tel: (5920) 51777).
FRIESLAND: The province of Friesland in the northwest of the country has its own language and its own distinct culture. The marshlands along the North Sea coast contain much land that has been reclaimed from the sea. Friesian cattle are among the most famous inhabitants of this region, whose marshy soil does not permit intensive arable cultivation. The Friesian lake district in the southern part of the state centres on the town of **Sneek**. The region has many opportunities for watersports, particularly yachting. Near Sneek is the small town of **Bolsward,** which has a magnificent Renaissance *Town Hall.*
Leeuwarden, the capital of Friesland, has several old buildings and the *Friesian Museum,* probably the most important provincial museum in the country. 6km (4 miles) to the west is the village of **Marssum,** which has a 16th-century manor house. There are daily ferry connections with four of the Friesian Islands and a chain of museums on the Aldfaer's Erf Route. The Hollandse and Friesian Islands (Texel, Vlieland, Terschelling, Ameland and Schiermonnikoog), on which there are extensive bird sanctuaries and areas of outstanding natural beauty, lie north of the mainland. Accommodation and campsites are available.
GRONINGEN: The agricultural province of Groningen is known for its fortified country houses dating back to the 14th century. The provincial capital, **Groningen** is commercially the most important town in the north of The Netherlands, as well as being a major cultural centre. Groningen is an old Hanse town, and the centre of what has long been a fertile and prosperous region. The city suffered considerable damage during the Second World War, but many of the 16th-18th century buildings have now been restored.
DRENTHE: This is a province of extensive cycle paths, prehistoric monuments (particularly in the area of the village of **Havelte**) and Saxon villages. The region is almost entirely agricultural, much of the land being drained by the system of *venns* and *weiks.* The main town, **Assen**, set in an area of woodlands, was an insignificant village until the middle of the last century, and has no historical monuments. The *Provincial Museum* is, however, worth a visit. There are also several Megalithic tombs to be found south and southwest of the town.

The East

Tourist Offices. *Overijssel* (tel: (5490) 18767) *Gelderland* (tel: (85) 420 330) *Flevoland* (tel: (3200) 43444).
The wooded east consists of the provinces of Overijssel, Gelderland and Flevoland.
OVERIJSSEL: The province of Overijssel is a region of great variety. In the little town of **Giethoorn**, small canals take the place of streets, and all transport is by boat. At **Wanneperveen** there is a well-equipped watersports centre. The old Hanseatic towns of **Zwolle** and **Kampen** have splendid quays and historic buildings. There are bird sanctuaries along the *Ijsselmeer.*
GELDERLAND: This is The Netherland's most extensive province, stretching from the rivers of the south to the sand dunes of the north. Gelderland is often referred to as 'the back garden of the west'. **Arnhem** is the major city. It was heavily damaged in the Second World War; indeed, its important position on the Rhine has led to it being captured, stormed, occupied and generally mistreated on many occasions during its long history. The old part of the town has, however, been skilfully rebuilt. There is a large open-air museum near Arnhem showing a collection of old farms, mills, houses and workshops, all of which have been brought together to form a splendid park. Not far from the town centre there is a zoo and a safari park.
Nearby is the **Hoge Veluwe National Park**, an extensive sandy region and a popular tourist area, which contains a game reserve (in the south), and the *Kroller-Muller Art Gallery and Museum,* with many modern sculptures and paintings (including a Van Gogh collection). One ticket enables you to see all of this, and there are free bicycles available to cycle round the park. Gallery and museum opening hours: 1000-1700 Tuesday to Saturday, 1100-1700 Sunday and holidays (April to October); 1300-1700 daily (November to March). Sculpture park opening hours: 1000-1630 Tuesday to Saturday, 1100-1630 Sunday and holidays (April to October).
Almost all the old traditional villages have been converted into holiday resorts. There are no towns of any size in the Veluwe region.
FLEVOLAND: Much of Flevoland was drained for the first time in the 1950s and 1960s, and is in many ways a museum of geography; the southern part of the province is not yet completely ready for cultivation, and visitors can witness the various stages of agricultural preparation. **Lelystad** is the main town of the region, built to a controversial design in the 1960s. Part of the province has also been designated as an overspill area for Randstad Holland. Flevoland's 1100 sq km (425 sq miles) of land include many large bungalow parks, and also the **Flevohof** amusement park.

The South

Tourist Offices. *North Brabant* (tel: (76) 222 444 *Limburg* (tel: (4406) 13364) *Zeeland* (tel: (1184) 12345 *or* 19275).
NORTH BRABANT: This province consists mainly of a plain, rarely more than 30m (100ft) above sea level, and is mostly agricultural. The region is known for its carnival days in February and the *Oude Stijl Jazz Festival.* The capital of the province is the city of **'s-Hertogenbosch** (non-Dutch speaking visitors will welcome the use of 'Den Bosch' as a widely accepted abbreviation) situated at the centre of a region of flat pasture land which floods each winter. *St Jan's Cathedral* is the largest in the country; the provincial museum is also worth visiting. Other major cities in this large and comparatively densely populated province include **Eindhoven**, an industrial centre which has grown up in the last 100 years; **Breda**, an old city with many medieval buildings – it was here that the declaration was signed in 1566 which marked the start of the Dutch War of Independence; and **Tilburg**, an industrial centre which also has a large amusement and recreation park (to the north of the city) whose attractions include a haunted castle.
At **Europaweg, Kaatsheuvel,** is the *De Efteling Recreation and Adventure Park,* with approximately 50 attractions, including a large fairytale wood and a big dipper; open 1000-1800 Monday to Saturday from the end of March to mid-October.
At Museumpark 1, **Overloon,** is the *Dutch National War & Recreation Museum,* which includes displays of heavy armament in a park setting and other exhibits devoted to the history of World War II. Open 1000-1700 Monday to Sunday (early April to September); 1000-1800 Monday to Sunday (June to August); closed January 1, December 24-26 and December 31.
At Beekse Bergen 1, **Hilvarenbeek,** is the *De Beekse Bergen Safari Park.* Safari buses are available (continuous journey). Opening hours: 1000-1800 April to September; 1000-1630 October.
LIMBURG: The province of Limburg, the most southerly in the country, is bordered by both Belgium and Germany. The rolling hills covered with footpaths make this a good place of walking holidays among the woods and along the river banks and brooks. It is also famous for its cuisine. In the extreme south of the province is the city of **Maastricht**, and its position at the crossroads of three countries makes it ideal for excursions to such nearby cities as Aachen over the border in the Federal Republic of Germany. Maastricht itself is one of the oldest towns in the country, and its *Church of St Servatius* is the oldest in The Netherlands. The church treasury is well worth a visit. Further north is the town of **Roermond**, an important cultural and artistic centre dominated by the superb *Munsterkerk.*
ZEELAND: The province of Zeeland has several medieval harbour towns where some of the best seafood in Europe can be found. Most of the province lies below sea level and has been reclaimed from the sea. The region also includes several islands and peninsulas in the southwest Netherlands (Walcheren, Goeree-Overflakkee, Schouwen-Duiveland, Tholen, St Filipsland and North and South Beveland). The province has become renowned for a massive engineering project of flood barriers designed to protect the mainland and the results of reclamation from the devastating floods which periodically sweep the coastline. The countryside is intensively farmed. The capital of the province is **Middelburg**, a town which has been important since medieval times. The *Town Hall* is widely regarded as being one of the most attractive non-religious Gothic buildings in Europe. 8km (5 miles) to the north is the small town of **Veere** which retains many buildings from its golden age in the early 16th century. The North Sea port of **Flushing** (Vlissingen) is, for many British travellers arriving by boat, their first sight of The Netherlands. It is also the country's first town in another sense; in 1572 it became the first place to fly the free Dutch flag during the War of Independence.

The Coast

There are 280km (175 miles) of beaches and over 50 resorts in The Netherlands, almost all of which are easily accessible from Rotterdam, Amsterdam and The Hague. Large areas have been specially allocated for naturists and the beaches themselves are broad, sandy and gently sloping. There is surf along the coast, and those who wish to swim must be strong enough to withstand the hidden currents. Swimmers should obtain and follow local advice. In the high season, life guards are on duty along the more dangerous stretches of the coast.

SOCIAL PROFILE

FOOD & DRINK: There are few dishes which can be described as quintessentially Dutch, and those that do fall into this category are a far cry from the elaborate creations of French or Italian cuisine. Almost every large town, however, has a wide range of restaurants specialising in their own brands of international dishes including Chinese, Italian, French, Yugoslavian, Spanish, German, American and British. Indonesian cuisine, a result of the Dutch colonisation of the East Indies, with its use of spices and exotic ingredients, is particularly worth trying. A typical Dutch breakfast usually consists of several varieties of bread, thin slices of Dutch cheese, prepared meats and sausage, butter and jam or honey and often a boiled egg. A working lunch would be *koffietafel,* once again with breads, various cold cuts, cheese and conserves. There will often be a side dish of omelette, cottage pie or salad.
The most common daytime snack are *broodjes* (sandwiches) which can be filled with anything or everything, and are served in the ubiquitous sandwich bars – *broodjeswinkels.* Filled pancakes are also popular. Lightly salted 'green' herring can be bought from street stalls (they are held by the tail and slipped down into the throat). More substantial dishes are generally reserved by the Dutch themselves for the evening meal: *erwtensoep* (thick pea soup served with smoked sausage, cubes of bacon, pig's knuckle and brown or white bread), *groentensoep* (clear consommé with vegetables, vermicelli and meatballs), *hutspot* (potatoes, carrots and onions), *klapstuk* (an accompaniment of stewed lean beef), and *boerenkool met rookworst* (frost-crisped kale and potatoes served with smoked sausage). Seafood dishes are often excellent, particularly in Amsterdam or Rotterdam, and include *gebakken zeetong* (fried sole), *lekkerbekjes* (fried whiting), Royal imperial oysters, shrimps, mussels, lobster and eel (smoked, filleted and served on toast or stewed or fried). Favourite Dutch desserts include *flensjes* or *pannekoeken* (25 varieties of Dutch pancake), *wafels met slagroom*

(waffles with whipped cream), *poffertje* (small dough balls fried and dusted with sugar) and *spekkoek* (alternate layers of heavy buttered sponge and spices from Indonesia), which translated means 'bacon cake'. Coffee, tea, chocolate and fruit juice are drunk at breakfast. Restaurants usually have table service. Bars and cafés generally have the same, though some are self-service. Dress varies very much according to the type of establishment, and is therefore a matter of choice. **Drink:** The local spirit is *jenever* (Dutch gin), normally taken straight and chilled as a chaser with a glass of beer, but it is sometimes drunk with cola or vermouth; it comes in many varieties depending on spices used. Favoured brands are *Bols, Bokma, De Kuyper* and *Claeryn*. Dutch beer is excellent. It is a light, gassy *pils* type beer, always served chilled, generally in small (slightly under half-pint) glasses. The most popular brand in Amsterdam is *Amstel*. Imported beers are also available, as are many other alcoholic beverages. Dutch liqueurs are excellent and include *Curaçao, Triple Sec* (similar to Cointreau), *Parfait d'Amour* and Dutch-made versions of crème de menthe, apricot brandy and anisette. There are no licensing laws and drink can be bought all day. Bars open later and stay open until the early hours of the morning at weekends.
NIGHTLIFE: Large cities have sophisticated nightclubs and discos, but late opening bars and cafés are just as popular in provincial towns. There are theatres and cinemas in all major towns. Amsterdam is a cosmopolitan city, with lively nightlife, and some of the best jazz clubs in Europe (see *Resorts & Excursions* above). There are legal casinos in Amsterdam, Rotterdam, Zandvoort, Valkenburg and Scheveningen (which claims to have the largest in Europe); all have an age limit of over 18 (passports must be shown).
SHOPPING: Special purchases include Delft (between The Hague and Rotterdam) blue pottery and pottery from Makkum and Workum, costume dolls, silverware from Schoonhoven, glass and crystal from Leerdam and diamonds from Amsterdam. **Shopping hours:** 0900-1730/1800. Foodstores close on Saturday at 1600, other stores at 1700. Late closing is on Thursday or Friday. **Note:** Bulbs and plants may not be exported except by commercial growers, or by individuals with a health certificate from the Plant Disease Service.
SPORT: Football, athletics and **cycling** are the most popular national sports. **Tennis** courts and **golf** courses are available. For local information contact the Board of Tourism. **Sailing** on Loosdrechtse Plassen (South of Amsterdam) Friesland Lakes, Veerse Meer and the Ijsselmeer. Boats can be hired without difficulty in most places. Touring Holland's canals and rivers is popular. **Water-skiing** is not permitted on inland lakes. **Fishing** is popular throughout the country, but while no licence is needed for sea fishing, inland fishing licences are required and are available at local post offices.
SPECIAL EVENTS: The following list gives a selection of the major festivals and special events in The Netherlands during 1993/1994:
Mar 12-21 '93 *European Fine Art Fair*, Maastricht. **Mar 19-20** *Amsterdam Blues Festival*. **Mar 25-May 23** *Keukenhof* (flower festival), Lisse. **Apr-Sep** *Flower Parades*, in various towns in the bulb field region. **Apr 17-18** *Museum Weekend* (special events and free entry at over 800 museums across the country). **Apr 28-Jun 6** *World Press Photo Exhibition*, Nieuwe Kerk, Amsterdam. **Apr 30** *Queen's Day*. **May 20-23** *National Tug Day*. **May 23** *Books on the Dam*. **May 29-30** *Amsterdam Kite Festival*. **Jun 1-30** *Holland Festival*, Amsterdam. **Jun 13** *Amsterdam Canal Run*. **Jun 24-Jul 3** *World Roots Festival*. **Jun-Aug** *Vondelpark Open Air Theatre*. **Jun-Sep** *Town Halls in Holland*, Amsterdam. **Jul-Aug** *Skutsjesilen* (sailing barge races across the Fresian Lakes), Friesland. **Jul 20-23** *Nijmegen Four Day March*, Nijmegen. **Jul 8-11** *North Sea Jazz Festival*, The Hague. **Oct** *Delft Art and Antique Fair*, Het Prisenhof. **Oct** *Pro World Cup Windsurfing*, The Hague. **Mar '94** *European Fine Art Fair*, Maastricht. **Mar-May** *Keukenhof*, Lisse.
For more information on events and festivals held in The Netherlands in 1993/1994 contact the Press and Public Relations Officer at the Royal Netherlands Embassy, or the Netherlands Board of Tourism.
SOCIAL CONVENTIONS: It is customary to shake hands. English is spoken as a second language by many and is willingly used; many Dutch people will also speak German and French. Hospitality is very much the same as for the rest of Europe and America. It is customary to take a small gift if invited for a meal. Casual wear is widely acceptable. Men are expected to wear a suit for business and social functions. Formal wear may be required for smart restaurants, bars and clubs. Evening dress (black tie for men) is generally specified on invitation. **Tipping:** All hotels and restaurants include 15% service and VAT. It is customary to leave small change when paying a bill. One or two Guilders is usual for porters, doormen and taxi drivers. Hairdressers and barbers have inclusive service prices.

BUSINESS PROFILE

ECONOMY: The Netherlands has few natural resources other than natural gas and it relies mainly on exports of manufactured goods and agricultural products. After the United States, The Netherlands is the world's largest exporter of farm produce. Dairy products, meat, vegetables and flowers are the main products. Industry is well-developed with all kinds of heavy engineering, production of petrochemicals and plastics, pharmaceuticals, synthetic fibres and steel. There is a wide range of light industries, including the manufacturing of electronic goods, although the traditionally strong textiles sector is in decline. Most of The Netherlands' industry is concentrated in the Randstad, a small region – 5% of the total land area – bounded by the three main cities of Amsterdam, Rotterdam and The Hague. The country's economic prospects are good and The Netherlands has weathered the recession of the early 1990s well. The country has a strong base in new technological industries of computing, telecommunications and biotechnology. The main black spot on the economic front is the continuing excessive budget deficit, which the government must act to arrest before it damages future economic development. The bulk of The Netherlands' trade takes place inside the European Community. Germany is the largest single trading partner, responsible for about 25% of The Netherlands' imports and exports. Belgium/Luxembourg, France and the UK follow.
BUSINESS: Appointments are necessary and visiting cards are exchanged. The Dutch expect a certain standard of dress for business occasions. English is widely spoken. Best months for business visits are March to May and September to November. Practical information can be obtained from the Economic Information Service in The Hague (tel: (70) 379 8933). The majority of Dutch business people speak extremely good English, and promotional literature can be disseminated in English. However, interpreters can be booked through the Director of Congres Interpreters, at Prinsegracht 993 in Amsterdam (tel: (20) 625 2535). Translators can be booked through the United Dutch Translation Office, Keizersgracht 560-2, 1017 EM Amsterdam (tel: (20) 626 5889), or through The Netherlands Chamber of Commerce in the country of departure. (There are Netherlands-British Chambers of Commerce in London, Manchester and The Hague, and Netherlands-US Chambers of Commerce in New York and Chicago.) There are also many secretarial agencies in The Netherlands, such as International Secretaries, who will be able to supply short-term help to visiting business travellers. The principal venue for trade fairs is the RAI Exhibition Centre in Amsterdam. **Office hours:** 0830-1700 Monday to Friday.
COMMERCIAL INFORMATION: The following organisations can offer advice:
The Hague Chamber of Commerce and Industry, Konigskade 30, 2596 AA The Hague. Tel: (70) 379 5795. Fax: (70) 324 0684. Telex: 33003; *or*
Amsterdam Chamber of Commerce and Industry, De Ruyterkade 5, 1013 AA Amsterdam. Tel: (20) 523 6600. Fax: (20) 523 6677.
CONFERENCES/CONVENTIONS: The largest conference and exhibition centres are RAI in Amsterdam and the Jaarbeurs in Utrecht. There are smaller centres in The Hague, Rotterdam and Maastricht, as well as many hotels with facilities. The fourth-largest conference centre in The Netherlands is Noordwijk, where the largest hotel has a helipad; this small seaside town has won prizes for its clean beaches. Amsterdam and The Hague both have business centres. For further information contact The Netherlands Convention Bureau, Amsteldijk 166, 1079 LH Amsterdam. Tel: (20) 646 2580. Fax: (20) 644 5935. (See *Business* above for details of support services.)

HISTORY & GOVERNMENT

HISTORY: Since the early Middle Ages, the region of the Low Countries had established itself as one of the most prosperous parts of Europe but – paradoxically – also one of the most politically unstable. At various times the ambitions of both the Kings of France and the Holy Roman Emperors threatened to annexe the region, although neither were powerful enough to subdue the proud municipalities permanently which, largely as a result of the wool trade, had grown up during the medieval period. By the early 16th century, imperial influence had gained the upper hand, and the Low Countries had, partly through dynastic ties, become annexed to the far-flung empire of the Habsburgs. It was against their rule that the largely Protestant northern provinces of the Low Countries, led by William of Orange and Nassau, rebelled in 1568. The struggle for independence, which lasted until 1648, also saw a remarkable growth in Dutch seapower (a phenomenon never satisfactorily explained by historians) as many Spanish and Portuguese possessions in the New World and the Far East were seized. The 17th century, the so-called 'Golden Age', also witnessed a flowering of art and culture which placed the tiny but rich country at the forefront of European culture. In 1689, William III of Orange also became King of England, but the association was severed on his death in 1702. During the 18th century, the power of The Netherlands was on the wane, and in 1810 it was absorbed into Napoleon's empire. Subsequently, the whole area of the Low Countries was briefly reunited (1814-30). In 1848 the constitution was amended, giving the monarch only limited powers. The Netherlands took no part in the First World War, but suffered badly as a result of the Nazi invasion of 1940. Post-war Dutch diplomacy has concentrated on increasing European unity, and these efforts culminated in 1957 when The Netherlands became one of the six founder-members of the EC. In the second half of 1991, the Dutch held the Presidency of the EC and were responsible for organising the crucial summit at Maastricht in December 1991 which was set up to decide the future of EC integration in economic and monetary policy and other areas. Domestic politics have been dominated by the customary Western European blend of conservative and social democratic governments. At the most recent elections for the First (lower) Chamber, held in June 1989, the Christian Democrat CDA and the centrist VVD (People's Freedom and Democracy) formed a coalition with, by the smallest possible margin, a combined total of 38 of the 75 seats. In the Second (upper) Chamber, the CDA-VVD alliance holds 76 of 150 seats. The centre-left PvdA (Labour Party) is the largest opposition party in both chambers.
GOVERNMENT: The Netherlands is a constitutional monarchy with a bicameral multi-party legislature. The Prime Minister is Mr Ruud Lubbers (Christian Democrat Party) and the reigning monarch is Queen Beatrix.

CLIMATE

Mild, maritime climate. Summers are generally warm with changeable periods, but excessively hot weather is rare. Winters can be fairly cold with the possibility of some snow. Rainfall is prevalent all year.
Required clothing: European according to season with light to mediumweights worn in warmer months and medium to heavyweights in winter. Rainwear is advisable all year.

VLISSINGEN Netherlands (1m)

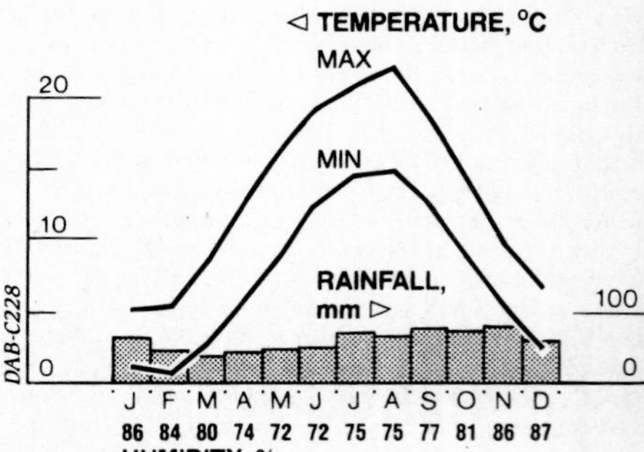

UTRECHT Netherlands (3m)

SUNSHINE, hours
2 2 4 5 7 7 6 6 5 3 2 1
◁ TEMPERATURE, °C
MAX
MIN
20
10
0
RAINFALL, mm ▷
100
0
J F M A M J J A S O N D
86 83 76 70 67 67 72 74 77 81 87 88
HUMIDITY, %
DAB-C227

NEW CALEDONIA

International airport

Location: South Pacific.

Diplomatic representation: New Caledonia is a French Overseas Territory; addresses of French Embassies, Consulates and Tourist Offices may be found in the *France* section above.

GIE Destination Nouvelle-Calédonie
BP 688
Immeuble Manhattan
39-41 rue de Verdun
Nouméa, New Caledonia
Tel: 272 632. Fax: 274 623. Telex: 3063 NM TOURISM.

AREA: 19,103 sq km (7376 sq miles).
POPULATION: 164,173 (1989).
POPULATION DENSITY: 8.6 per sq km.
CAPITAL: Nouméa. **Population:** 65,110 (1989).
GEOGRAPHY: New Caledonia (which has been a French Overseas Territory since 1958) is an island group off the northeast coast of Australia. Mountains run the entire length of the main island. On the western side the land is relatively flat and forested by gum trees. The east coast is more mountainous with beautiful seashores fringed by tropical plants. Crystalline serpentine rock covers more than half the island. About 48km (30 miles) southeastwards lies the Isle of Pines (Kunie), famed for its caves and grottoes containing stalactites and stalagmites. The Loyalty Group lies to the east of New Caledonia, the main islands being Ouvea, Lifou and Mare. The remaining islands are the Chesterfield Group, Hinter, Huon Group, Matthew and Walpole.
LANGUAGE: French is the official language, but Polynesian and Melanesian are also spoken. English is also widely spoken.
RELIGION: Roman Catholic, Protestant.
TIME: GMT + 11.
ELECTRICITY: 220 volts AC, 50Hz.
COMMUNICATIONS: Telephone: 80% automatic. IDD is available. Country code: 687. There is a 24-hour service for international calls. International calls are bookable at the Post Office (0730-1800) or through hotels. **Telex/telegram:** Telex facilities are available in most businesses and hotels. Central telex/telegram agency, rue Eugène Porcheron, Nouméa. **Post:** Airmail to Europe takes up to a week. The Post Office, located on rue Eugène Porcheron, is open 0715-1115 and 1200-1800. **Press:** Newspapers are published in French and include *Les Nouvelles Calédoniennes*.
BBC World Service and Voice of America frequencies: From time to time these change. See the section *How to Use this Book* for more information.

BBC:				
MHz	17.10	15.36	9.740	7.150
Voice of America:				
MHz	18.82	15.18	9.525	1.735

PASSPORT/VISA

Regulations and requirements may be subject to change at short notice, and you are advised to contact the appropriate diplomatic or consular authority before finalising travel arrangements. Details of these may be found at the head of this country's entry. Any numbers in the chart refer to the footnotes below.

	Passport Required?	Visa Required?	Return Ticket Required?
Full British	Yes	No	Yes
BVP	Not valid	-	-
Australian	Yes	Yes	Yes
Canadian	Yes	No	Yes
USA	Yes	No	Yes
Other EC	Yes/1	No	Yes
Japanese	Yes	No	Yes

PASSPORTS: Valid passport required by all, **[1]** except nationals of France carrying a national identity card or passport expired a maximum of five years.
British Visitors Passport: Not accepted.
VISAS: Required by all except:
(a) nationals of France for an unlimited period, other EC nationals for a stay not exceeding 3 months;
(b) nationals of Andorra, Austria, Cyprus, Finland, Iceland, Liechtenstein, Malta, Monaco, Norway, San Marino, Sweden, Switzerland and Turkey for a stay not exceeding 3 months;
(c) nationals of Canada, New Zealand, the USA and Japan for a stay not exceeding 1 month.
Note: Visa requirements for other nationals wishing to visit New Caledonia are subject to frequent change at short notice and travellers should contact the French Consulate General for up-to-date information.
Types of visa: Tourist and Transit.
Application to: French Consulate General. (see top of *France* entry).
Application requirements: (a) 3 completed application forms. (b) 3 photos. (c) Onward ticket.
Working days required: Usually 1 day, although up to 1 month depending on nationality of applicant.
Temporary residence: Contact French Consulate General (or Consular Section at Embassy).

MONEY

Currency: French Pacific Franc (CFP Fr) = 100 centimes. Notes are in denominations of CFP Fr5000, 1000, 500 and 100. Coins are in denominations of CFP Fr50, 20, 10, 5, 2, and 1 and 50 centimes. New Caledonia is part of the French Monetary Area.
Currency exchange: Exchange facilities are available at the airport and at trade banks.
Credit cards: American Express and Visa are widely accepted; Access/Mastercard and Diners Club have more limited use. Check with your credit card company for details of merchant acceptability.
Exchange rate indicators: The following figures are included as a guide to the movement of the French Pacific Franc against Sterling and the US Dollar:

Date:	Oct '89	Oct '90	Oct '91	Oct '92
£1.00=	180.0	177.0	179.4	150.0
$1.00=	114.0	90.61	103.4	94.52

Currency restrictions: Import and export restrictions for currency are the same as those for France (see above).
Banking hours: 0730-1545 Monday to Friday.

DUTY FREE

The following goods may be imported into New Caledonia without incurring customs duty:
200 cigarettes or 50 cigars or 250g of tobacco;
1 bottle of alcoholic beverage;
A reasonable amount of perfume for personal use.

PUBLIC HOLIDAYS

Public holidays observed in New Caledonia are as follows:
Apr 12 '93 Easter Monday. **May 3** For Labour Day. **May 7** For Liberation Day. **May 20** Ascension. **May 31** Whit Monday. **Jul 14** Fall of the Bastille. **Sep 24** New Caledonia Day. **Nov 11** Armistice Day. **Dec 25** Christmas Day. **Jan 1 '94** New Year's Day.

HEALTH

Regulations and requirements may be subject to change at short notice, and you are advised to contact your doctor well in advance of your intended date of departure. Any numbers in the chart refer to the footnotes below.

	Special Precautions?	Certificate Required?
Yellow Fever	No	1
Cholera	No	2
Typhoid & Polio	Yes	-
Malaria	No	-
Food & Drink	3	-

[1]: A yellow fever vaccination certificate is required from travellers over one year of age arriving from infected areas.
[2]: Travellers arriving from infected areas do not require vaccination and will not be given chemoprophylaxis. They are required, however, to fill out a form for use by the Health Service.
[3]: Mains water is normally chlorinated, and whilst relatively safe may cause mild abdominal upsets. Bottled water is available and is advised for the first few weeks of the stay. Drinking water outside main cities and towns may be contaminated and sterilisation is advisable. Milk is pasteurised and dairy products are safe for consumption. Local meat, poultry, seafood, fruit and vegetables are generally considered safe to eat.
Health care: Nouméa has one public hospital, three private clinics and an adequate selection of chemists. Hotels can generally recommend an English-speaking doctor or dentist. Insurance is recommended.

TRAVEL - International

AIR: New Caledonia's national airline is *Air Calédonie International (SB)*.
Approximate flight time: From *London* to Nouméa is 26 hours, including three stopovers, but this may increase to 30 hours, depending on the day of travel.
International airport: *Nouméa (NOU)* (La Tontouta), 48km (30 miles) from the city (travel time – 60 minutes). Airport facilities include post office (0700-1100 and 1200-1600), bureau de change, duty-free shops (available for scheduled flights), bar, restaurant and car rental (*Avis* and *Hertz*). Taxi and coach services to city.
SEA: International port is Nouméa, served by the following shipping lines: *Chandris, CTC, P&O, Princess Cruises, Sitmar* and *Polish Ocean Lines*.

TRAVEL - Internal

AIR: Domestic flights run by *Air Caledonie (TY)*, maintaining regular services from Nouméa to airfields on the island, and the other smaller islands. The principal local airport is *Magenta Airport*, 6km (4 miles) from Nouméa city centre. From here *Air Caledonie* operates regular flights to Touho (east coast), Kone, Koumac, Belep (west coast), and to the neighbouring Isle of Pines and the Loyalty Islands: Mare, Ouvea, Lifou and Tiga.
Charter flights: Light aircraft are available from *Air Caledonie* for charter; for further details contact *Air Caledonie*, Aviazur.
Approximate flight times: From Nouméa to *Kunie* (Isle of Pines) is 30 minutes; to *Lifou* is 50 minutes; to *Mare* is 50 minutes; to *Ouvea* is 45 minutes; to *Tiga* is 45 minutes; to *Koné* is 35 minutes; to *Touh* is 1 hour 5 minutes; to *Koumac* is 1 hour 40 minutes and to *Belep* is 2 hours 35 minutes.
SEA: There are regular sea links to the other smaller islands from Grande Terre. For details contact the local authorities.
ROAD: Traffic drives on the right. Limited road system.
Buses are available throughout the island. A mail bus makes a round trip of the island. **Taxi:** Charges are for time and distance. Surcharge after 1900 and on Sundays. **Car hire:** *Hertz, Avis, Budget* and *AB Location* and local *Mencar* all have representatives in the capital. Special vehicles (called 'Baby Cars') are available for hire 0600-1930.
Documentation: International or national driving permit is required.
JOURNEY TIMES: The following chart gives approximate journey times (in hours and minutes) from Nouméa to other major cities/towns in New Caledonia.

	Air	Road
Bourail	-	2.10
Hienghene	-	5.10
Koné	0.35	3.30
Poindimie	-	4.10
Thio	-	2.00
Tontouta	-	0.45
Touhó	1.05	4.40

ACCOMMODATION

There is a very good selection of accommodation available in New Caledonia with hotels, country inns and rural lodgings offering a range of standards and prices.
HOTELS: Mostly small and intimate. Prices range from moderate to expensive. Modern hotels have been built at Anse Vata and the Baie des Citrons and there is also new bungalow-style accommodation in remoter parts of the main island and in the outer islands. For further informtion contact: Union de l'Hôtellerie Touristique de Nouvelle Caledonie, c/o Kuendi Beach Mote, BP 404, Nouméa. Tel: 278 989. Fax: 276 033.
CAMPING: Permission should be sought from landowners before setting up camp.
YOUTH HOSTELS: Situated outside the city is a hostel with dormitories and communal facilities at reasonable rates. Non-YHA members are also accommodated.

RESORTS & EXCURSIONS

The following guide is divided into three sections on Grande Terre, and two further sections on other islands.

Grande Terre – Nouméa

Nouméa, the capital, overlooks one of the world's largest sheltered natural harbours. It is a busy little city with a population composed of many racial groups: French, Melanesian and Indonesian amongst others. Minibuses and *Le Petit Train* are probably the best ways of seeing the city and its suburbs. The centre of the network is the bus depot on the *Baie de la Moselle*. Attractions in the city include *St Joseph's Cathedral*, the *Berheim Library*, the market, many old colonial houses and the *Aquarium*, one of the world's leading centres of marine scientific research. Nearby, the *South Pacific Commission Building* houses a collection of native handicrafts from all over the South Seas. The *New Caledonia Museum* is open Tuesday to Saturday, and also contains many local handicrafts and ornaments. 4km (2.5 miles) from the capital is the *Botanical Park*, the home of over 700 species of animals.

Within easy reach of Nouméa is the *Amedée Lighthouse*, built during the reign of Napoleon III and shipped to New Caledonia in pieces. It is situated in a coral reef 18km (11 miles) from the capital. There are excellent opportunities for swimming and scuba diving in the lagoon.

East of the capital is *Mont-Doré*, a mountain surrounded by magnificent coastal scenery. On the way, stops can be made at the Melanesian village of **St Louis**, and the *Plum Lookout* for a spectacular view across the surrounding reef.

The Coast

The West Coast: 170km (105 miles) from Nouméa is **Bourail**, where there are many elaborate and beautiful caves and rock formations shaped by the Pacific breakers. Further north is the ancient site of *Koné*, where decorated pottery dating back to the 10th century BC has been discovered. From the town of **Koumac**, a new road has been constructed which loops round the top of the island. The scenery consists of pure white sand beaches and offshore atolls, backed by dense rainforest.

The East Coast: The new road takes one to *Hienghéne*, which has a lagoon surrounded by 120m (400ft) high black cliffs. **Poindimié**, the main town of the east coast, is further south. Nearby is **Touhó**, overlooked by a 500m (1640ft) peak. The region is dotted with old churches and Melanesian villages, forests, coconut palms and countless beautiful beaches. At the southern point of this coast is **Yaté**, a town surrounded by lakes, waterfalls and rich wooded countryside. Day trips are available from the capital.

The Isle of Pines

Discovered and named by Captain Cook in 1774, the Isle of Pines lies some 70km (45 miles) off the southeast coast of Grande Terre. This beautiful island has many white sand beaches and turquoise lagoons and is lush with rainforests, pines, orchids and ferns. Archaeological excavations have revealed settlements over 4000 years old. The island was also briefly used as a convict settlement during the 19th century and the giant ruins of the jail can still be seen, though now half-strangled by the dense vegetation. There are many rural lodges on the island which offer simple but excellent accommodation on or near the beaches. Day trips are available from Nouméa to **Vao**, the main town on the Isle of Pines.

The Loyalty Islands

This archipelago lies 100km (60 miles) off the east coast of New Caledonia, and is widely regarded as being superb for scuba diving and spear-fishing.

Maré Island, the furthest south, has an area of 650 sq km (250 sq miles). Most of the population live in the town of **Tadine**.

Lifou Island, the largest of the three with 1150 sq km (445 sq miles), has over 7000 inhabitants. The main town is **Chépénétié**.

Ouvea Island is 130 sq km (50 sq miles), but is rarely more than 3 or 4km (2 to 2.5 miles) wide. The lagoon is particularly rich in fish. Almost all of the population live in **Fayaové**.

SOCIAL PROFILE

FOOD & DRINK: The choice of eating-places and food on New Caledonia is excellent; costs vary from moderate to expensive. Fine food is a passion and *Cordon Bleu* cuisine is widely available. Gourmet restaurants and bistros serve French, Italian, Spanish, Indonesian, African and Chinese cooking. Dishes include Pacific spiny lobsters, prawns, crabs or mangrove oysters and salads of raw fish (marinated in lime juice). An island speciality is *bougna;* roast pig, fish or chicken wrapped in banana leaves and cooked on hot stones covered with sand. First-class delicatessens and grocers in Nouméa and at Anse Vata Beach provide a wide choice of picnic fare. Wine is imported from France and there is a very good selection.

NIGHTLIFE: There are discos and also a casino, the only one in the South Pacific, situated at Anse Beach. Nightclubs in Nouméa are lively with both European and local floorshows. There are also cinemas which show French films.

SHOPPING: In Nouméa boutiques sell fashionable French clothes, mainly casual but sometimes *haute couture*. Further purchases include luxury French goods such as perfume, jewellery and footwear, and silk scarves, sandals and handbags from Italy can also be found. Duty-free items are also sold. Local items include curios made of shells, coral, woodcarving, ceramics, hand-painted materials, aloha shirts, tapa cloth and records of Polynesian music. Discounts may be obtained in duty-free shops. **Shopping hours:** 0730-1100 and 1400-1800 Monday to Friday, 0730-1100 Saturday.

SPORT: Watersports: Scuba diving and **snorkelling** facilities provide compressors, tanks, wet suits, regulators and qualified instructors. For further details contact the Nauti Club, Kuto, Isle of Pines and the Amédeé Diving Club. Special facilities for **fishing** are available on Turtle Island. The coral barrier reef off the shore of Nouméa is excellent for underwater spearfishing. For further details contact The Spear Fishing Club in Nouméa. Fine beaches throughout the islands are supplemented by hotel pools and the Olympic-size **swimming** pool behind the Château Royal Casino is open daily. **Tennis:** On presentation of a tourist card, visitors can play tennis on the courts at Mont Coffyn Tennis Club; there are also courts at Chateau Royal Casino at Anse Vata beach. **Squash:** The new club at the Baie des Pêcheurs welcomes visitors. Equipment is available on the premises. **Riding:** Horses are kept at Club d'Etrier where visitors must be introduced by a member. Melanesian men and women wearing bright clothes play weekend **cricket** in the squares. Arrangements can be made in the capital for **hiking** trips into the interior.

SOCIAL CONVENTIONS: There is a casual atmosphere, and European customs still prevail alongside local traditions. Casual wear is the norm, but smart restaurants require a less casual style of dress. Long trousers are required for men at night in restaurants and clubs. Only the casino requires a jacket and tie. **Tipping:** There is no tipping.

BUSINESS PROFILE

ECONOMY: The mainstays of the country's economy are mining, fishing, tourism, forestry and agriculture. A certain amount of light industry is currently being developed. After Canada and the USA, New Caledonia is the world's largest producer of nickel. The economy is relatively prosperous, although recent economic growth has been inhibited by the low world price for nickel, which accounts for nearly 90% of export revenue. Standards of living are nonetheless fairly high. The agricultural sector produces cereals, fruit and vegetables, as well as copra and coffee for export. The country is an Associate Member of the EC. France is the largest trading partner, responsible for approximately half of all imports and exports.

BUSINESS: Appointments should be made. Business people generally work long hours and take long lunch breaks, but business lunches are rare as most businessmen go home at lunchtime. Prices should be quoted in French or French Pacific Francs. Best time to visit is May to October.

Office hours: 0730-1130 and 1400-1800 Monday to Frida 0730-1100 Saturday.

COMMERCIAL INFORMATION: The following organisation can offer advice: Chambre de Commerce et d'Industrie, BP M3, Nouméa Cedex. Tel: 272 551. Fax: 27 114. Telex: 3045.

HISTORY & GOVERNMENT

HISTORY: Discovered by Europeans in 1766, New Caledonia has been a French colony since 1853, and fought for the allies in both World Wars. It became a French Overseas Territory in 1946. From time to time, attempts have been made by the indigenous population to free themselves from French rule. The most serious of these was the *Canaque Revolt* of 1878 which was only put down after a guerrilla campaign lasting for more than a year. In recent years, intermittent conflicts have flared between the Melanesians and the French, reflecting the widely differing attitudes which exist towards the various plans for self-government. The majority of Kanaks (Melanesians) now support the FLNKS (National Kanak Socialist Liberation Front) created in 1984 and led, until his assassination in 1989, by the charismatic Jean-Marie Tjibaou. The French-descended settlers – *caldoches* – mostly back the Gaullist-linked RPCR. Both sides have adopted an uncompromising position on independence. The traditional bi-partisan approach between Gaullists and Socialists on colonial matters has broken down, although both parties recognise the strategic importance of the island for nuclear testing. In November 1988 there was a national referendum which approved an interim statute remodelling the New Caledonian constitution as from June 1989. The statute stipulates that the issue of territorial independence must be resolved by referendum before December 31 1998. New Caledonia is currently governed according to the provisions of a temporary constitution until a new permanent one is ready. Tjibaou has been succeeded as head of the FLNKS by Paul Neaoutyine.

GOVERNMENT: New Caledonia is part of the Republic of France and as such elects representatives to the French Parliament. In addition there are three Regional Assemblies Southern Region (32 members), Northern Region (15 members) and Loyalty Islands (7 members), which together form a Territorial Congress, headed by the High Commissioner. The High Commissioner is advised by an 8-member 'Consultative Committee' selected from leading figures on the island.

CLIMATE

Warm, subtropical climate. The cool season is from June to September and the hottest period from October to May. The main rains are between January and March. Climate is tempered by trade winds.

Required clothing: Lightweight cottons and linens are worn especially in the evenings. Rainwear is advisable.

NOUMEA New Caledonia (9m)

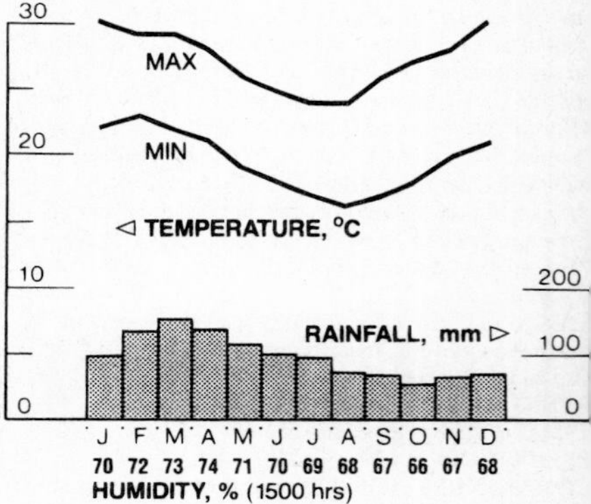

NEW CALEDONIA	HEALTH REGULATIONS	VISA REGULATIONS
GALILEO/WORLDSPAN	 TI-DFT/NOU/HE	 TI-DFT/NOU/VI
SABRE	TIDFT/NOU/HE	TIDFT/NOU/VI

Code-Link

To access this information on your CRS, swipe the barcode with a light pen or type in the text under the barcode. For more information, see the introduction *How to Use This Book*.

NEW ZEALAND

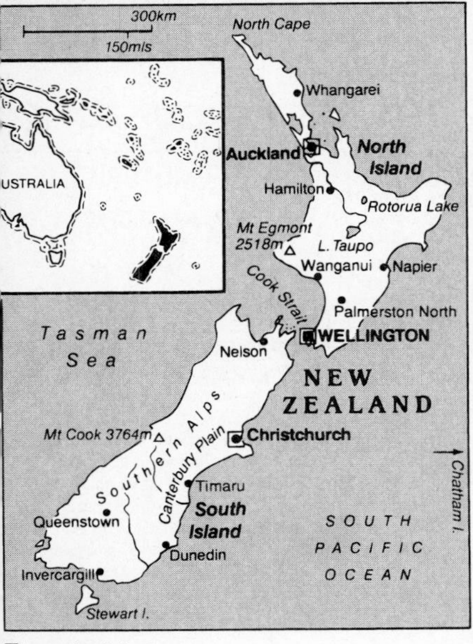

□ international airport

Location: South Pacific.

New Zealand Tourism Board
PO Box 95
256 Lambton Quay
Wellington, New Zealand
Tel: (4) 728 860. Fax: (4) 781 736.

New Zealand High Commission
New Zealand House
80 Haymarket
London SW1Y 4TQ
Tel: (071) 930 8422. Fax: (071) 839 4580. Telex: 24368.
Opening hours: 1000-1200 and 1400-1600 Monday to Friday.

New Zealand Tourism Board
New Zealand House
80 Haymarket
London SW1Y 4TQ
Tel: (071) 973 0360. Fax: (071) 839 8929. Opening hours: 1000-1200 and 1400-1600 Monday to Friday.

British High Commission
PO Box 1812
44 Hill Street
Wellington 1, New Zealand
Tel: (4) 726 049. Fax: (4) 711 974. Telex: 3325 UKREP NZ.
Consulates in: Auckland and Christchurch.

New Zealand Embassy
37 Observatory Circle, NW
Washington, DC
20008
Tel: (202) 328 4800. Fax: (202) 328 1441.
Consulate General in: Los Angeles. Tel: (213) 477 8241.

Embassy of the United States of America
PO Box 1190
29 Fitzherbert Terrace
Wellington, New Zealand
Tel: (4) 722 068. Fax: (4) 781 701.

New Zealand High Commission
Suite 727, Metropolitan House
99 Bank Street
Ottawa, Ontario
K1P 6G3
Tel: (613) 238 5991. Fax: (613) 238 5707.

New Zealand Tourism Board
Suite 1200
888 Dunsmuir Street
Vancouver, British Columbia
V6C 3K4
Tel: (604) 684 2117. Fax: (604) 684 1265.

Canadian High Commission
PO Box 12049
61 Molesworth Street
Wellington 1, New Zealand
Tel: (4) 739 577. Fax: (4) 712 082. Telex: 2377.

AREA: 267,844 sq km (103,415 sq miles).
POPULATION: 3,434, 950 (1991 estimate).
POPULATION DENSITY: 12.8 per sq km.
CAPITAL: Wellington. **Population:** 324,792 (1991 estimate). Auckland, with a population of 885,377 (1991 estimate) is the largest city in the country.
GEOGRAPHY: New Zealand is 1930km (1200 miles) southeast of Australia and consists of two major islands, the North Island (114,470 sq km/44,197 sq miles) and the South Island (150,660 sq km/58,170 sq miles) which are separated by Cook Strait. Stewart Island (1750 sq km/676 sq miles) is located immediately south of the South Island, and the Chatham Islands lie 675km (420 miles) to the southeast of the North Island. Going from north to south temperatures decrease. Compared to its huge neighbour Australia, New Zealand's three islands make up a country that is relatively small (about 20% more land mass than the British Isles). Two-thirds of the country is mountainous, a region of swift flowing rivers, deep alpine lakes and dense subtropical forest known as 'bush'. The country's largest city, Auckland, is situated on the peninsula which forms the northern part of North Island. The southern part of North Island is characterised by fertile coastal plains rising up to volcanic peaks. Around Rotorua, 240km (149 miles) south of Auckland, there is violent thermal activity in the form of geysers, pools of boiling mud, springs of hot mineral water, silica terraces, coloured craters and hissing fumaroles which make Rotorua a world-famous tourist attraction. The South Island is larger, although only about one-third of the population live there. The Southern Alps extend the whole length of the island, culminating in Mount Cook, the country's highest peak. In the same region are the Franz Josef and Fox glaciers.
There are also four Associated Territories: **The Cook Islands**, about 3500km (2175 miles) northeast of New Zealand; **Niue**, 920km (570 miles) west of the Cook Islands (area 260 sq km/100 sq miles); **Tokelau**, three atolls about 960km (600 miles) northwest of Niue (area 12 sq km/4 sq miles); and the **Ross Dependency**, which consists of over 700,000 sq km (270,270 sq miles) of the Antarctic.
LANGUAGE: The official languages are English and Maori.
RELIGION: 27% Anglican, 14% Roman Catholic and other Christian denominations.
TIME: GMT + 12 (GMT + 13 from the last week in March to the first week in October).
ELECTRICITY: 230 volts AC, 50Hz. Most hotels provide 110-volt AC sockets (rated at 20 watts) for electric razors only.
COMMUNICATIONS: Telephone: IDD is available. Country code: 64. **Fax:** Many hotels provide facilities. **Telegram/telex:** Telegrams can be sent from all post offices or telephoned through at any time. All main post offices and some hotels have public telex facilities. **Post:** Post offices are open 0900-1700 Monday to Friday. Airmail to Europe takes four to five days and to the USA three to ten days. **Press:** The English-language daily newspapers with the highest circulation include *New Zealand Herald*, *Auckland Star* and *Evening Post*.
BBC World Service and Voice of America frequencies: From time to time these change. See the section *How to Use this Book* for more information.

BBC:				
MHz	17.10	15.36	9.740	7.150
Voice of America:				
MHz	18.82	15.18	9.525	1.735

PASSPORT/VISA

Regulations and requirements may be subject to change at short notice, and you are advised to contact the appropriate diplomatic or consular authority before finalising travel arrangements. Details of these may be found at the head of this country's entry. Any numbers in the chart refer to the footnotes below.

	Passport Required?	Visa Required?	Return Ticket Required?
Full British	Yes	No	Yes
BVP	Not valid	-	-
Australian	Yes	No	No
Canadian	Yes	No	Yes
USA	Yes	No	Yes
Other EC	Yes	No	Yes
Japanese	Yes	No	Yes

PASSPORTS: Valid passport required by all. Citizens of countries whose governments are not recognised by New Zealand should check that their documentation is acceptable.
Validity: Passports should be valid for at least 3 months beyond the period of intended stay.
British Visitors Passport: Not acceptable.
VISAS: Required by all except:
(a) nationals of the UK and other British passport holders for visits of up to 6 months providing they have evidence of the right of abode;
(b) nationals of EC countries for visits up to 3 months, but note that Portuguese nationals *must* have right of residence in Portugal and French nationals *must* be residing in France (see *(d)* below);
(c) nationals of Austria, Canada, Finland, Iceland, Indonesia, Japan, Kiribati, Liechtenstein, Malaysia, Malta, Monaco, Nauru, Norway, Singapore, Sweden, Switzerland, Thailand, Tuvalu and the USA (except US Samoans, who *do* require a visa) for visits of up to 3 months;
(d) French citizens residing in Tahiti or New Caledonia for visits of up to 30 days.
Validity: Variable.
Application to: Consulate (or Consular Section at Embassy or Immigration Service at High Commission). For addresses, see top of entry.
Application requirements: (a) Application form(s). (b) 1 photo. (c) Valid passport. (d) Sufficient funds for duration of stay – NZ$1000 for each person for every month or NZ$400 if the accommodation is already paid for. (e) Onward ticket. (f) Company/sponsor letter for Business visas. (g) Fee.
Working days required: 21.
Temporary residence: Maximum 6 months stay.

MONEY

Currency: New Zealand Dollar (NZ$) = 100 cents. Notes are in denominations of NZ$100, 50, 20, 10 and 5. Coins are in denominations of NZ$2 and 1, and 50, 20, 10 and 5 cents.
Currency exchange: Exchange facilities are available throughout New Zealand.
Credit cards: Access/Mastercard, American Express, Diners Club and Visa are accepted. Check with your credit card company for details of merchant acceptability and other services which may be available.
Travellers cheques: Can be exchanged at official rates at trading banks and large hotels.
Exchange rate indicators: The following figures are included as a guide to the movements of the New Zealand Dollar against Sterling and the US Dollar:

Date:	**Oct '90**	**May '91**	**Oct '91**	**Oct '92**
£1.00	3.21	3.03	3.05	2.94
$1.00=	1.64	1.72	1.76	1.85

Currency restrictions: There are no restrictions on the import and export of foreign or local currency (except for cheques and money orders which require Reserve Bank consent).
Banking hours: 1000-1600 Monday to Friday.

DUTY FREE

The following items may be imported into New Zealand without incurring customs duty:
*200 cigarettes or 50 cigars or 250g tobacco or a mixture of up to 250g;**
*4.5 litres of wine or beer;**
*1.125 litres or 40oz spirits or liqueurs;**
A reasonable amount of perfume for personal use;
Goods to a total value of NZ$700.
Note: [*] For persons over 17 years of age.
Prohibited items: The New Zealand government publishes a full list of personal items allowed for import without incurring duty such as jewellery and photographic or sporting equipment (firearms, however, require a police permit). Visitors are advised not to take fruit or plant material with them.

PUBLIC HOLIDAYS

Public holidays observed in New Zealand are as follows: **Apr 9 '93** Good Friday. **Apr 12** Easter Monday. **Apr 25** ANZAC Day. **Jun 7** Queen's Official Birthday. **Oct 25** Labour Day. **Dec 25** Christmas Day. **Dec 26** Boxing Day. **Jan 1-2 '94** New Year. **Feb 6** Waitangi Day.
Note: Each province also observes its particular anniversary day as a holiday.

HEALTH

Regulations and requirements may be subject to change at short notice, and you are advised to contact your doctor well in advance of your intended date of departure. Any numbers in the chart refer to the footnotes below.

	Special Precautions?	Certificate Required?
Yellow Fever	No	No
Cholera	No	No
Typhoid & Polio	No	-
Malaria	No	-
Food & Drink	1	-

[1]: Tap water is considered safe to drink. Milk is pasteurised and dairy products are safe for consumption. Local meat, poultry, seafood, fruit and vegetables are generally considered safe to eat.
Health care: Medical facilities, both public and private, are of a high standard. There are no snakes or dangerous wild animals in New Zealand. Sandflies are prevalent in some cases, but these can be effectively countered with insect repellent. The only poisonous creature is the very rare Katipo spider. Should visitors need drugs or pharmaceutical supplies outside normal shopping hours they should refer to 'Urgent Pharmacies' in the local telephone directory for the location of the nearest pharmacy or check with their hotel.

TRAVEL - International

AIR: New Zealand's national airline is *Air New Zealand (NZ)*.
Approximate flight times: From *London* to Auckland is 28 hours, to Wellington 30 hours and to Christchurch 30 hours 30 minutes.
From *Los Angeles* to Auckland is 12 hours 45 minutes.
From *New York* to Auckland is 17 hours 45 minutes.
From *Singapore* to Auckland is 11 hours 15 minutes.
From *Sydney* to Auckland is 3 hours 20 minutes.
International airports: *Auckland (AKL)* (Mangere), 22.5km (14 miles) south of the city (travel time – 40 minutes). Coach service every 30 minutes on the hour and half-hour 0700-2300 to downtown terminal. Taxis are available to the city with surcharge after 2200 and at weekends. Airport facilities include outgoing duty-free shop with a full range of items, car hire *(Avis, Budget* and *Hertz)* and banking and exchange facilities open to cover the times of all international flights.
Christchurch (CHC) airport, 10km (6 miles) northwest of the city (travel time – 20 minutes). Bus no 24 runs every 30 minutes 0630-2200. Taxis are available to the city with surcharge after 2200. Airport facilities include outgoing duty-free shop with a full range of items, car hire *(Avis, Budget* and *Hertz)* and banking and exchange facilities open covering the times of all international flights.
Wellington (WLG) (Rongotai), 8km (5 miles) southeast of the city (travel time – 30 minutes). Coach service runs every 20 minutes 0600-2200. Taxis are available to the city with surcharge after 2200. Airport facilities include outgoing duty-free shop with a full range of items, car hire *(Avis* and *Hertz)* and banking and exchange facilities open to cover the times of all international flights.
Departure tax: NZ$20 for all flights out of Auckland and Wellington and NZ$16 for all flights out of Christchurch. Transit passengers and children under two years of age are exempt.
SEA: The principal ports are Auckland, Wellington, Lyttleton, Dunedin, Picton and Opua, which are served by the following shipping lines: *Ben Shipping, Blue Star, Port Royal Interocean, P&O* and *Sitmar*. *Polish Ocean Lines* sail from Europe, and *Farrell Lines* from the USA. Inter-island rail ferry service available between Wellington and Picton several times daily.

TRAVEL - Internal

AIR: *Air New Zealand (NZ), Mount Cook Airlines (NM)* and *Ansett New Zealand (ZQ)* operate domestic flights between the major airports (see above) as well as Palmerston North, Dunedin, Napier, Queenstown, Rotorua and 27 other airports throughout the two islands.
RAIL: There is a reliable but limited rail service on 5000km (3106 miles) of railway with many routes of great scenic attraction. Express services between Auckland and Wellington (daytime and overnight), Christchurch and Invercargill, Christchurch and Picton, Christchurch and Greymouth, and Wellington and Napier. There are dining cars on some trains, but there are no sleeping cars on overnight services. All services are one-class travel only.
Travel passes: Allow unlimited travel on *New Zealand Railways'* train, coach and ferry services.
ROAD: There are 96,000km (59,650 miles) of roads. Traffic drives on the left. **Bus:** There are regional bus networks which serve most parts of the country. **Coach:** Modern coaches operate scheduled services throughout the country. It is advisable to make reservations for seats. Contact an Intercity Travel Centre for details. A *Kiwi Coach Pass* is available for use on *Mt Cook Landliner Services* and other principal operators' services. It is advisable to make reservations for seats. Contact the Tourism Board for details. **Taxis:** There are metered taxis throughout the country. **Car hire:** Major international firms and local firms have offices at airports and most major cities and towns. The minimum age for driving a rented car is 21. **Documentation:** Domestic permits are accepted from the following states: Australia, Canada, Germany, Fiji, Namibia, The Netherlands, South Africa, Switzerland, the UK and the USA. Otherwise an International Driving Permit is required.
URBAN: Good local bus services are provided in the main towns; there are also trolleybuses in Wellington. Both Auckland and Wellington have zonal fares with pre-purchase tickets and day passes.
JOURNEY TIMES: The following chart gives approximate journey times (in hours and minutes) from Wellington to other major cities/towns in New Zealand.

	Air	Road	Rail	Sea
Auckland	1.00	9.00	10.00	-
Rotorua	1.15	3.30	6.00	-
Napier	1.00	6.30	6.00	-
N. Plymouth	1.00	8.30	-	-
Palmerston N.	0.30	2.30	2.30	-
Picton	0.30	-	-	3.00
Christchurch	0.45	*7.20	*5.20	-
Dunedin	1.20	*12.20	*11.20	-
Queenstown	2.05	*15.40	-	-
Bay of Islands	2.00	14.00	-	-
Nelson	0.20	6.00	-	-
Mt Cook	2.00	10.00	-	-
Glaciers (west coast)	§1.45	8.20	-	-

Notes: [*] Plus ferry crossing of 3 hours. [§] Plus 2.30 hours by road.

ACCOMMODATION

MOTELS & HOTELS: New Zealand has hotels and motels of international standard, moderately priced modern hotels, private hotels and guest-houses. Rates on the whole are cheaper in rural areas, while every city and town has low-cost motels or hotels. Low-cost motels have grown greatly in popularity in recent years, and most have a wide range of facilities; they offer self-catering, and account for 75% of the accommodation. Most belong to the Motel Association of New Zealand (Inc), PO Box 1697, Wellington. Tel: (4) 385 8011. Fax: (4) 385 0826. Some establishments belong to the Hotel Association of New Zealand, Austraus House, 36 Customs Street East, Auckland. Tel: (9) 795 624.
Disabled travellers: The Tourist Department can supply a publication, *New Zealand Access: Guide for the Less Mobile Traveller*, which lists suitable accommodation and facilities. **Grading:** New Zealand has no national system of grading hotels and motels although the New Zealand Tourism Board and the Automobile Association will introduce the star grading system by 1994. Until then, location, facilities and tariffs are generally a reliable indication of standard.
CAMPING/CARAVANNING: There are many sites throughout New Zealand. Rates and facilities vary considerably. It is advisable to make advance reservations during December to Easter. *New Zealand Motor Camps* offer communal washing, cooking and other facilities at main resorts. Visitors are required to provide their own tents and equipment at these camps, but equipment can be hired from a number of companies. Occupants are usually required to supply their own linen, blankets and cutlery. A number of companies can arrange motor camper rentals, with a range of fully equipped vehicles; full details can be obtained form the New Zealand Tourism Board.
FARM HOLIDAYS: The New Zealand Tourism Board can supply a list of host farms which can offer accommodation to visitors.
YOUTH HOSTELS: The Youth Hostel Association runs hostels throughout the country and in most towns, and reservations can be made in advance from December to March. The Association's address is PO Box 68149, Auckland. Tel: (9) 309 2802. Fax: (9) 373 5083. In the major cities there are alternative cheap forms of accommodation, for example backpackers hostels all over the country.

RESORTS & EXCURSIONS

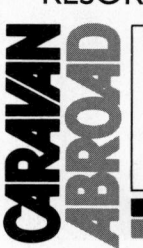

In order to simplify this section, the two main islands are described separately. However, North and South Islands may easily be incorporated into a single visit, as travel between the two, either by boat or plane, is quite straightforward (see the *Travel – Internal* section above). There is also a section on Niue, an island associated with New Zealand almost midway between Tonga and Samoa.

North Island

The visitor is most likely to arrive in New Zealand at its largest city, the business centre of **Auckland**. The city's low-rise buildings spread over the neighbouring low hills, and there is a fine harbour to explore. Recent developments include new restaurants along Parnell and Ponsonby Road. The city offers good shopping and a handsome university section, while an exploration of its suburbs is recommended – the beach and town of **Takapuna** just across the water, for example. Public transport is swift and cheap with a flat-fare system. The driver will often provide useful information.
The beaches of **Northland**, the peninsula stretching away from Auckland, are particularly popular with swimmers and sunbathers. There are many small beach settlements throughout the country, ideal for a quiet and relaxing holiday.
More photogenic than Auckland, although inclined to get poor weather, is **Wellington**, the capital city, with its new buildings grouped along a series of steep hillsides overlooking a deep harbour. A tightly populated city, it has many good shops and pedestrian streets, while several of its restaurants and hotels offer splendid views across to the nearby South Island. Wellington is the terminus for ferries and for trips to the islands in the straits.
Since the country is scattered with volcanoes, mostly extinct, it would be a great pity to miss the famous **Rotorua** which, along with the glow-worm caves of *Waitomo*, is probably one of the best-known tourist attractions in the country. Rotorua presents a good base for exploring the geysers and the large thermal zone of the North Island. There are also other areas of geyser activity in the region, one such is *Orakei Korako*, about 30 minutes from Rotorua. Rotorua is also a major centre of Maori culture and there is an arts centre where young Maoris continue the tradition of carving wood and stone. Souvenirs can be purchased, and visitors might also see the shy, nocturnal kiwi.
Besides Rotorua, four active volcanoes may also be vis-

NEW ZEALAND	HEALTH REGULATIONS	VISA REGULATIONS
GALILEO/WORLDSPAN	TI-DFT/WLG/HE	TI-DFT/WLG/VI
SABRE	TIDFT/WLG/HE	 TIDFT/WLG/VI

Code-Link

To access this information on your CRS, swipe the barcode with a light pen or type in the text under the barcode. For more information, see the introduction *How to Use This Book*.

ed in the North Island and other extinct volcanoes, ıch as *Mount Egmont* on the west coast, add a unique ote of exotic distinction to the country's scenery. Jnspoilt regions such as the *Coromandel Peninsula* will lso appeal to lovers of wild beauty. *Lake Taupo*, in the ery middle of the North Island, offers much sport for shing enthusiasts, and in the northeast coastal towns ıere are also good facilities for deep-sea fishing.

South Island

At **Nelson**, a small city on the coast, the visitor will ınd a garden town with spectacular beaches and a rowing arts community. There is an excellent choice f routes for exploring the natural beauty of the South sland and to take in such attractive towns as **Dunedin** nd **Invercargill**, both having strong Scottish roots nd still retaining the Celtic flavour.
On the edge of the Canterbury Plains is the 'Garden City' of **Christchurch**, which has some very English haracteristics. The *River Avon* flows through the centre f the city to the many old stone buildings and stately omes. The neo-Gothic Cathedral and its surrounding quare are the nucleus of the city, and other places of nterest include the *Old Canterbury University*, the *Canterbury Museum*, the *Chamber of Commerce Building*, *Riccarton House* and the *Provincial Council Buildings*. There are also many parks, gardens, galleries nd museums.
The mountain resort of **Queenstown** is a major centre or ski enthusiasts from all over the world. At warmer imes of the year it is a wonderful place for hiking, a astime well catered for all over the South Island, with plenty of tracks provided. The scenery of the South Island is extraordinary and much can be accomplished in a short time, but it would be a pity not to inger in such attractive small towns as **Arthur's Pass**, eached through a rainforest along narrow roads and past gushing waterfalls, or to view the mass of **Mount Cook**, and the exhilarating ski-plane rides.
There are also a number of national parks covering a total of 5.25 million acres, with scenery that includes forests, valleys, thermal areas, lakes, mountains, glaciers and coastal bays. Most have good facilities for the visitor. One of these is the **Abel Tasman Park** in the northwest which can be reached on foot, or better still by boat from the small town of **Kaiteriteri.** For nature enthusiasts such parks offer a rare opportunity to observe the wildlife, increasingly rare in the more populated areas where imported species, particularly birds, have driven out local creatures. Once the flat plains surrounding Christchurch were dotted with many species of the ostrich-like moas, but now they have been replaced with sheep, while the nation's symbol, the kiwi, is rarely seen in daylight and it is unlikely the visitor will see one outside a zoo. Nevertheless, the keen ornithologist will still be able to find many species in their natural habitat. New Zealand is also a haven for many rare plants, particularly ferns and heathers.

Niue

Niue is an isolated island of 259 sq km (100 sq miles) located 480km (298 miles) from Tonga and 560km (348 miles) from Western Samoa. Niue, a British protectorate in 1900, was formally annexed to New Zealand as part of the Cook Islands in 1901. In October 1974 Niue became the smallest self-governing state under the status of 'a self-governing country in free association with New Zealand'. This allows Niueans to retain New Zealand citizenship while maintaining self-government in their own country.
Most of the 2267 nationals (1989) descend from settlers from Tonga, Samoa and Fiji who arrived between AD 600-1000, and developed their own particular culture. Exchanges of money and food through the community's children form a major ritual, once a rite of passage expressing the power of the father through his skill in fishing and planting crops. Niuean children are still bestowed with gifts of money or handmade mats and cloths from their relatives upon coming of age. Girls also have their ears pierced and boys receive their first haircut.
Many other ceremonies and social events stem from the processing of food. One community ritual is based on the extraction of *nu pia* starch from arrowroot, which is used in traditional dishes and soups and often given as a gift. Another ritualised ceremony surrounds *ti* root, which is made into a sweet drink or eaten as a sweet with coconuts. Other popular foods include taro, kumara, coconuts, pawpaw, bananas, tomatoes, capsicum and many varieties of yam.
A tropical island bathed by southeast trade winds, Niue offers visitors many natural wonders and a superb climate with warm days and pleasantly cool

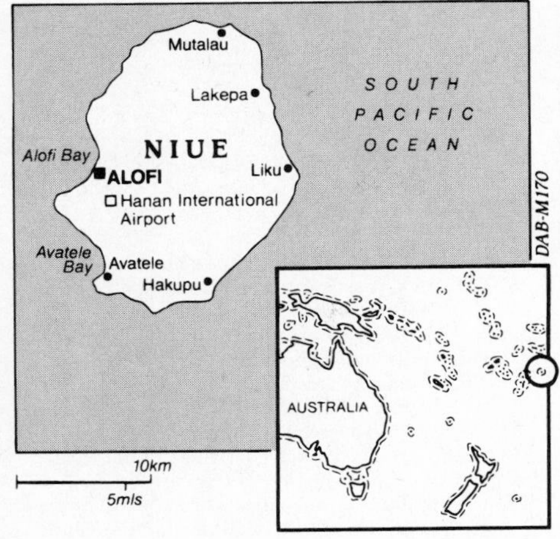

nights. It has some of the most undisturbed forests in the world, designated *tapu* areas by the locals, where no humans were allowed to set foot for centuries. Now all the *tapu* forests, except the one controlled by **Hakupu** village, are penetrable. These forests are full of lush undergrowth, coconut palms and some of the oldest ebony trees known. At the edge of the forest, the coast gives way to extraordinary coral outcrops. Forest walking and scuba diving/snorkelling, along with various types of fishing, are the visitors' favourite pastimes on this island. Recommended sites include national and maritime parks, the *Niue Cultural Centre* (exhibiting unique Niuean artefacts) and the *Womens' Town Club Hall*, with a craftshop featuring various handicrafts for sale. The *Niue Sports Club* provides regular entertainment, from bar/discos to nights of village dances. The *Niue Hotel and Sails Restaurant* features *Fiafia* nights. There are facilities for golf and tennis on the island and traditional Niuean cricket is the most popular spectator sport. Niuean women are especially regarded for the quality of their weaving, producing hats, baskets, handbags and mats from indigenous plants which make excellent buys for the visitor. The major festivals on the island are *Prayer Week* and *Takai Week*, celebrated in the first week of January, and the Constitutional Celebrations in October. *Samoa Air* provides weekly flights to Niue from Pago Pago, American Samoa, and *Niue Airlines* operates fortnightly services from Auckland, New Zealand.

SOCIAL PROFILE

FOOD & DRINK: New Zealand has a reputation as a leading producer of meat and dairy produce with lamb, beef and pork on most menus. Venison is also widely available as deer farming increases. Locally produced vegetables, such as *kumara* (a natural sweet potato), are good. There is also a wide range of fish available including snapper, grouper, John Dory and trout. Seasonal delicacies such as whitebait, oysters, crayfish, scallops and game birds are recommended. New Zealand's traditional dessert is *pavlova*, a large round cake with a meringue base, topped with fruit and cream. Many picnic areas with barbecue facilities are provided at roadside sites. Restaurants are usually informal except for very exclusive ones. Waiter service is normal, but self-service and fast-food chains are also available. Many restaurants invite the customer to 'BYO' (bring your own liquor). **Drink:** New Zealand boasts an excellent range of domestic wines and beers, some of which have won international awards. A wide range of domestic and imported wines, spirits and beers is available from hotel bars, bottle stores, wholesalers and wine shops. Bars have counter service and public bars are very informal. Lounge bars and 'house bars' (for hotel guests only) are sometimes more formal and occasionally have table service. The minimum drinking age in a bar is 20. There is some variation in licensing hours in major cities and some hotel bars open Sunday, providing a meal is eaten. In most hotels and taverns, licensing hours are 1100-2300 except Sunday.
NIGHTLIFE: New Zealand has an active and varied entertainment industry. Theatres offer good entertainment ranging from drama, comedy and musicals to pop concerts and shows. In large cities there are often professional performers or guest artistes from overseas. Visitors should check 'What's On' in local papers when touring. There are also cinemas and a small selection of nightclubs in larger cities.
SHOPPING: Special purchases include distinctive jewellery made from New Zealand *greenstone* (a kind of jade) and from the beautiful translucent *paua* shell. Maori arts and crafts are reflected in a number of items such as the carved greenstone *tiki* (a unique Maori charm) and intricate woodcarvings often inlaid with paua shell. Other items of note include woollen goods, travel rugs, lambswool rugs, leather and skin products. **Shopping hours:** Nearly all stores and shops are open 0900-1730 Monday to Friday and 1000-1300 Saturday. Some shops open until 2100 Thursdays/Fridays and some open Sundays. There are invariably extended hours in resort areas.
SPORT: Rugby and **netball** are the national sports, while **football, soccer** and **cricket** are also played. New Zealand enjoys a unique reputation as a country with virtually unlimited scope for outdoor recreation. There are many **golf** courses. **Skiing:** A major winter sport that is well catered for on the slopes of Mount Ruapehu in the North Island and the ski fields of Coronet Peak, Treble Cone and Mount Hutt in the South Island. **Hiking** tours are available throughout New Zealand, examples being the Milford Track, Routeburn Track, Hollyford Valley and Fjordland National Park. **Fishing:** The lakes and rivers of the Taupo and Rotorua districts are known for excellent trout fishing. Deep-sea fishing is good off the coastline of Northland (the peninsula north of Auckland in the North Island). The South Island offers good trout and salmon fishing. Tourists can buy special 1-month licences through the Tourism Board. **Lawn bowls:** A popular national sport played from September to April; most towns have greens. **Tennis:** Most towns and resorts have courts. **Swimming:** There are municipal and hotel swimming pools plus miles of safe coastline. **Other sports:** There is also **motor racing, greyhound racing, horseracing** (trotting, pacing and gallops), **athletics** and **sheep dog trials.** Details of all events appear in local papers.
SPECIAL EVENTS: Special events for 1993/1994 include:
Mar '93 *Bell Tea Horse of the Year Show*, Auckland. **Mar 6-7** *Auckland Port Festival.* **Mar 9-15** *National Lifesaving Champs*, New Plymouth. **Apr 3-11** *Bluff Oyster and Seafood Festival.* **Apr 3-12** *Royal Easter Show* (agriculture and farming show). **May 1** *Fletcher Challenge Rotorua Marathon*, Rotorua. **May 29-31** *New Zealand Gold Guitar Awards*, Gore. **Jun 17-19** *New Zealand National Agricultural Fieldays*, Hamilton. **Jul 12-18** *Queenstown Winter Festival.* **Oct 23-25** *Lifespan Mountains to Sea Multi-sport Event.* **Nov 18-21** *Trinity Garden Festival*, Auckland. **Dec 29-Jan 9 '94** *Asia Pacific Orienteering Carnival*, lower North Island. **Jan** *World Gliding Champs*, Oamaru. **Late Feb-March** *New Zealand International Festival of the Arts.* **May 11-14** *World Ploughing Contest*, Taieri.
For further details contact the New Zealand Tourism Board.
SOCIAL CONVENTIONS: Should a visitor be invited to a formal Maori occasion, the *hongi* (pressing of noses) is common. Casual dress is widely acceptable. New Zealanders are generally very relaxed and hospitable. Stiff formality is rarely appreciated and after introductions first names are generally used. Smoking is restricted where notified. **Tipping:** Service charges and taxes are not added to hotel or restaurant bills. Tips are not expected.

BUSINESS PROFILE

ECONOMY: Although New Zealand is primarily thought of as an agricultural country, this sector employs less than 10% of the workforce and contributes just 8% of GNP. Nonetheless, it remains an important source of export earnings, particularly from wool, meat and dairy products. There are significant natural resources, of which the energy-related, notably natural gas and coal, have been developed. There are some promising mineral deposits of titanium, gold, silver and sulphur which have yet to be exploited. From the late 1970s a new generation of industrial enterprises centred on these resources were established to replace the traditional industries (textiles, agricultural machinery and fertilisers) which were declining. From the mid-1980s to date, New Zealand has undergone the most radical economic transformation of any Western industrialised country, with extensive privatisation, the dismantling of many welfare systems, abolition of subsidies and tariff barriers and a plethora of corporate regulations. The results have been a while in coming, but New Zealand now boasts inflation which is the lowest in the OECD (the 24 main industrialised nations) and the lowest budget deficit for a decade. Most remarkable, according to a recent study of future

competitiveness, New Zealand now heads the OECD in this field, ahead of Japan, Denmark and Germany. Australia is New Zealand's largest trading partner, and the two governments have concentrated on establishing a completely free trading regime between them. There are plans for all tariff barriers and licensing procedures to be abolished by 1995. Japan, the United States and the UK are the other major trading partners. New Zealand played a prominent role during the closing stages of the Uruguay round of the General Agreement on Tariffs and Trade (GATT) as a member of the dozen-strong 'Cairns Group' of agricultural exporters who, in alliance with the United States, have endeavoured to force the European Community to get rid of their exceptionally high tariffs under the Common Agricultural Policy. The EC refused which, along with American prevarication over free trade in services (transport, telecommunications), caused a breakdown in the talks. This may have extremely serious consequences for New Zealand trade, which relies heavily on agricultural exports: the EC is the largest single overseas market.
BUSINESS: Business wear is generally conservative and both sexes tend toward tailored suits. Some businessmen dress in shorts and knee-length socks during summer, particularly in the North Island, but a suit is preferable for visitors. Appointments are necessary and punctuality is appreciated. Calling cards are usually exchanged. The business approach is fairly conservative and visitors should avoid the period from Christmas to the end of January. The best months for business visits are February to April and October to November. **Office hours:** 0900-1700 Monday to Friday.
COMMERCIAL INFORMATION: The following organisation can offer advice: Wellington Chamber of Commerce, Enterprise House, 3-9 Church Street, Wellington 1. Tel: (4) 722 725. Fax: (4) 711 767.
CONFERENCES/CONVENTIONS: The largest centres are in Auckland, Wellington and Christchurch. Many hotels also have facilities. There are over 20 regional convention bureaux in New Zealand, most of which are members of NZ Convention Association (Inc), PO Box 33-1202, Takapuna, Auckland. Tel: (9) 486 4128. Fax: (9) 486 4126. Also known as Conventions New Zealand.

HISTORY & GOVERNMENT

HISTORY: New Zealand was first settled at least 1000 years ago by the Polynesian Maoris, a well-ordered tribal society led by hereditary chiefs and a powerful priesthood. The first European arrival was the Dutchman Abel Tasman in 1642, but it was not until the voyages of Captain James Cook in 1769 and 1779 that the islands were charted and explored. British settlers began to emigrate after British sovereignty was established in 1840, and Wellington was founded soon afterwards. New Zealand was granted internal self-government in 1852, and the later years of the century saw a rapid growth in investment, communications and agricultural production. In 1893, New Zealand became the first country in the world to extend the vote to women. New Zealand became a Dominion in 1907, and its forces took part in both World Wars. The country is a member of the Commonwealth and also several other international organisations, including ANZUS, the Five Power Defence Agreement and the South Pacific Forum. Membership of of Western alliances was suspended, however, when Labour Prime Minister David Lange, elected in 1984, declared New Zealand nuclear-free and prevented US and British vessels which might be nuclear-powered or carrying nuclear weapons from entering New Zealand's ports. While these policies put the small country on the international stage, Lange's government was engaged in radical economic reform at home. The measures, engineered by Lange's Finance Minister, Roger Douglas, bore some resemblance to those implemented by the then British Prime Minister Margaret Thatcher, including tight restrictions on public spending and privatisation of state bodies. Lange eventually resigned at the beginning of August 1989, but his replacement as Prime Minister was not Douglas, as expected, but another of his Cabinet members, Geoffrey Palmer. Palmer himself resigned in early September 1990, just weeks before the scheduled general election at the end of October 1990. This was won by the opposition national Party which had been out of office for a decade. Labout faced up to its spell in opposition by appointing Mike Moore, a former foreign affairs and defence minister and a leading light of the younger generation of Labour Party politicians, as party leader. The National Party leader Jim Bolger assumed the premiership. The economic policies pursued by Labour had failed to yield the results expected after six years of frugality and the economy continued to struggling; nonetheless the new government continued with the same measures. It was 1992 before they began to bear fruit in the form of low inflation and a spurt of economic growth, although unemployment remains high and New Zealanders no longer enjoy the comprehensive welfare system of before. The Government is nervously watching last-minute efforts to save the Uruguay round of the GATT (General Agreement on Tariffs and Trade) talks, the breakdown of which could cause yet further damage to the economy. New Zealand has now reversed the 7-year-old Labour policy on visiting warships and is endeavouring to mend fences with its erstwhile ANZUS treaty partners. Its attitude towards French nuclear testing in the Pacific remains unchanged, and Wellington is leading the South Pacific opposition to French plans to resume testing. The French government imposed a temporary ban in April 1992 but dropped it after just four months. Past form suggests that Paris will not pay the slightest attention to New Zealand or the South Pacific Forum.
GOVERNMENT: The British monarch is the Head of State, represented by the Governor-General. Real power is held by the Executive Council, led by the Prime Minister.

CLIMATE

Subtropical in the North Island, temperate in the South Island. The North has no extremes of heat or cold, but winter can be quite cool in the South, with snow in the mountains. Rainfall is distributed evenly throughout the year.
Required clothing: Lightweight cottons and linens are worn in the North Island most of the year and in summer in the South Island. Mediumweights are worn during winter in the South Island. Rainwear is advisable throughout the year, and essential if visiting the rain forest areas in the South Island.

WELLINGTON New Zealand (126m)

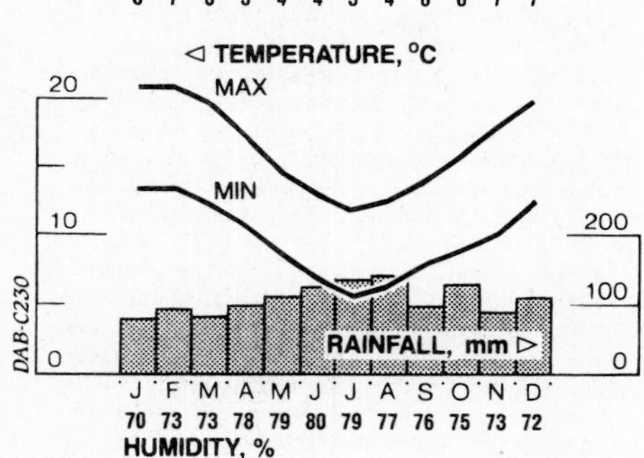

DUNEDIN New Zealand (2m)

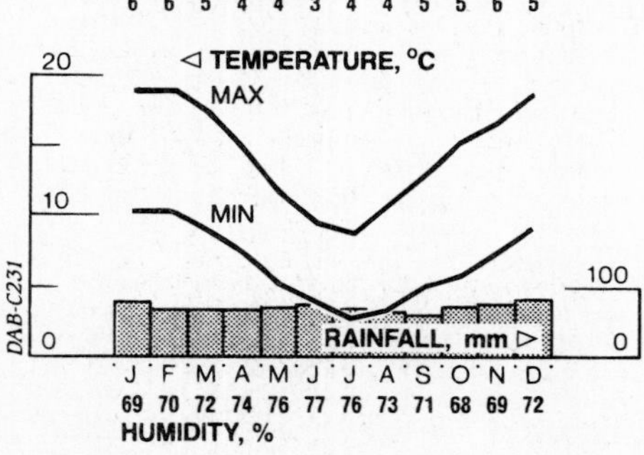

NICARAGUA

Location: Central America.

Note: It is *essential* to obtain up-to-date information from the British or Nicaraguan Embassies prior to finalising travel arrangements.

Instituto Nicaragüense de Turismo (Inturismo)
Apartado 122
Avenida Bolívar Sur
Managua, Nicaragua
Tel: (2) 25436. Fax: (2) 25314. Telex: 1299.
Embassy of the Republic of Nicaragua
8 Gloucester Road
London SW7 4PP
Tel: (071) 584 4365. Fax: (071) 823 8790. Telex: 269895. Opening hours: 0930-1330 Monday to Friday.
Consular Section: (071) 584 3231.
British Embassy
Apartado A-169
El Reparto 'Los Robles', Primera Etapa
Entrada principal de la Carretera de Masaya
4a Casa a Mano Derecha
Managua, Nicaragua
Tel: (2) 71112. Fax: (2) 73827. Telex: 2166 PRODROME NK.
Embassy of the Republic of Nicaragua
1627 New Hampshire Avenue, NW
Washington, DC
20009
Tel: (202) 939 6570. Fax: (202) 939 6542.
Embassy of the United States of America
Apartado 327
Km 4.5, Carretera Sur
Managua, Nicaragua
Tel: (2) 666 010.
Embassy of the Republic of Nicaragua
Suite 908
170 Laurier Avenue West
Ottawa, Ontario
K1P 5V5
Tel: (613) 234 9361/2. Fax: (613) 238 7666.
Canadian Embassy to Nicaragua:
c/o Canadian Embassy
Apartado Postal 10303
San José, Costa Rica
Tel: 230 446. Telex: 2179.

AREA: 120,254 sq km (46,430 sq miles).
POPULATION: 3,871,000 (1990 estimate).
POPULATION DENSITY: 32.2 per sq km.
CAPITAL: Managua. **Population:** 819,679 (1981 estimate).
GEOGRAPHY: Nicaragua borders Honduras to the north and Costa Rica to the south. To the east lies the Caribbean, and to the west the Pacific. In the north are

the Isabella mountains, while the country's main feature in the southwest is Lake Nicaragua, 148km (92 miles) long and about 55km (34 miles) at its widest. The island of Ometepe is the largest of the 310 islands on the lake. These islands have a reputation for great beauty, and are one of the country's main tourist attractions. Lake Managua is situated to the north. Volcanoes, including the famous Momotombo, protrude from the surrounding lowlands northwest of the lakes. The country's main rivers are the San Juan, the lower reaches of which form the border with Costa Rica, and the Rio Grande. The Corn Islands *(Islas del Maiz)* in the Caribbean are two small beautiful islands fringed with white coral and palms. They are very popular as holiday resorts with both Nicaraguans and tourists. The majority of Nicaragua's population live and work in the lowland between the Pacific and western shores of Lake Nicaragua, the southwestern shore of Lake Managua and the southwestern sides of the range of volcanoes. It is only in recent years that settlers have taken to coffee growing and cattle farming in the highlands around Matagalpa and Jinotega.
LANGUAGE: Spanish. Along the Mosquito Coast *(Costa de Mosquito)* there are English speaking communities in which African or mixed African and indigenous Indians predominate.
RELIGION: 85% Roman Catholic.
TIME: GMT - 6.
ELECTRICITY: 110 volts AC, 60Hz.
COMMUNICATIONS: Telephone: IDD is available. Country code: 505. **Telex/telegram:** Facilities in Managua. **Post:** Airmail to Europe takes up to two weeks. *Poste Restante* services are available in Managua. Post offices are open 0900-1730 Monday to Saturday. **Press:** All newspapers are in Spanish. The main publications are *Barricada* and *El Nuevo Diario*.
BBC World Service and Voice of America frequencies: From time to time these change. See the section *How to Use this Book* for more information.

BBC:				
MHz	17.72	11.78	9.590	5.975
Voice of America:				
MHz	15.21	11.74	9.815	6.030

PASSPORT/VISA

Regulations and requirements may be subject to change at short notice, and you are advised to contact the appropriate diplomatic or consular authority before finalising travel arrangements. Details of these may be found at the head of this country's entry. Any numbers in the chart refer to the footnotes below.

	Passport Required?	Visa Required?	Return Ticket Required?
Full British	Yes	No	Yes
BVP	Not valid	-	-
Australian	Yes	Yes	Yes
Canadian	Yes	Yes	Yes
USA	Yes	No	Yes
Other EC	Yes	1	Yes
Japanese	Yes	Yes	Yes

PASSPORTS: Valid passport, at least 6 months old (with a further 6 months to run), required by all.
British Visitors Passport: Not acceptable.
VISAS: Required by all except:
(a) nationals of Guatemala;
(b) nationals of the UK and Commonwealth countries being 'Citizens of the UK and Colonies.'
(b) [1] nationals of Belgium, Denmark, Greece, Ireland, Luxembourg, The Netherlands, Spain and the UK for stays of up to 90 days;
(c) nationals of Finland, Liechtenstein, Norway, Sweden, Switzerland and the USA for stays of up to 90 days;
(d) nationals of Hungary for stays of up to 30 days.
All the above exemptions apply to bona fide tourists only.
Types of visa: Tourist and Business. Cost: US$25.
Validity: Most Tourist visas are valid for 1 month.
Application to: Consulate (or Consular Section at Embassy). For addresses, see top of entry.
Application requirements: (a) Valid passport. (b) Completed application form. (c) 2 photos. (d) Fee of US$25. (e) Onward or return ticket. (f) Evidence of sufficient means (at least US$200) to cover expenses during stay.
Working days required: 48 hours.
Temporary residence: Enquire at Embassy.

MONEY

Currency: Nicaraguan Gold Córdoba (C) = 100 centavos. Notes are in denominations of (C)100, 50, 10, 20, 10, 5 and 1, and 50, 25, 10, 5 and 1 centavos.
Credit cards: Access/Mastercard and Diners Club are both accepted on a limited basis. Check with your credit card company for details of merchant acceptability and other services which may be available.
Travellers cheques: Accepted in a number of places, though it is advisable to have them in US Dollars.
Exchange rate indicators: The following figures are included as a guide to the movement of the Nicaraguan Gold Córdoba against Sterling and the US Dollar:

Date:	**Oct '91**	**Oct '92**
£1.00=	8.69	8.58
$1.00=	5.00	5.41

Note: Frequent adjustments to the traded value of the Córdoba and the various exchange systems that have been used make it impossible to make meaningful comparative assessments over successive years. The figures above represent the exchange rate for the Córdoba.
Currency restrictions: There are no restrictions on the import or export of currency.
Banking hours: 0830-1200 and 1400-1630 Monday to Friday; 0830-1130 Saturday.

DUTY FREE

The following items can be imported into Nicaragua without incurring customs duty:
200 cigarettes or 500g tobacco;
3 litres of spirits or wine;
1 bottle perfume or eau de cologne.
The import of the following goods is prohibited:
Canned meats and dairy products;
Medicines without an accompanying prescription;
Military uniforms;
Firearms not covered by the regulations governing the importation of firearms for sporting purposes (contact the Embassy for details).
The export of the following goods is prohibited:
Archaeological items;
Artefacts of historic or monetary value;
Food;
Medicines not accompanied by a prescription.

PUBLIC HOLIDAYS

Public holidays observed in Nicaragua are as follows:
Apr 8 '93 Maundy Thursday. **Apr 9** Good Friday. **May 1** Labour Day. **Jul 19** Liberation Day. **Aug 10** Managua Local Holiday. **Sep 14** Battle of San Jacinto. **Sep 15** Independence Day. **Dec 25** Christmas Day. **Jan 1 '94** New Year's Day.
Note: A considerable number of local holidays are also observed.

HEALTH

Regulations and requirements may be subject to change at short notice, and you are advised to contact your doctor well in advance of your intended date of departure. Any numbers in the chart refer to the footnotes below.

	Special Precautions?	Certificate Required?
Yellow Fever	No	1
Cholera	No	No
Typhoid & Polio	Yes	-
Malaria	2	-
Food & Drink	3	-

[1]: A yellow fever vaccination certificate is required from all travellers aged one year and over arriving from infected areas.
[2]: Major risk of malaria, predominantly in the benign *vivax* form, exists from June to December in rural areas as well as in the outskirts of the towns of Bluefields, Bonanza, Chinandega, León, Puerto Cabeza, Rosita and Siuna.
[3]: All water should be regarded as being potentially contaminated. Water used for drinking, brushing teeth or making ice should have first been boiled or otherwise sterilised. Milk is unpasteurised and should be boiled. Powdered or tinned milk is available and is advised, but make sure that it is reconstituted with pure water. Avoid dairy products which are likely to have been made from unboiled milk. Only eat well-cooked meat and fish, preferably served hot. Pork, salad and mayonnaise may carry increased risk. Vegetables should be cooked and fruit peeled.
Rabies is present. For those at high risk, vaccination before arrival should be considered. If you are bitten abroad seek medical advice without delay. For more information consult the *Health* section at the back of the book.
Health care: Medical insurance is essential.

TRAVEL - International

AIR: Nicaragua's national airline is *Lanica*.
Approximate flight time: From *London* to Managua is 20 hours 30 minutes including stopovers in Madrid and La Havana.
International airport: *Managua (MGA)* (Augusto Cesar Sandino) is 9km (5.5 miles) from the city (travel time – 15 minutes). Full duty free facilities are available. There is a bus every 10 minutes 0500-2200. A taxi service runs to the city.
Departure tax: US$10 on all departures.
SEA: Major ports are Corinto, Puerto Sandino, El Bluff and Puerto Cabezas which are served by shipping lines from Nicaragua, Central American, North American and European countries.
ROAD: The Pan-American Highway runs through Nicaragua via Esteli and Managua. There are daily bus services *(Ticabus)* between Managua and most Central American capitals. Tickets are sold up to five days in advance, and all border documentation must be completed before ticket is issued.

TRAVEL - Internal

SEA: A twice-weekly boat service runs between Bluefields and the Corn Islands. It is also possible to visit the 300 or so islands on Lake Nicaragua, which are very beautiful.
RAIL: There is only one railway, the *Ferro-Carril del Pacifico*, 349km (245 miles) long. A diesel service has increased both speed and comfort. Trains from Managua run two or three times daily to Leon, and four times daily to Granada. There is also a service between Leon and Rio Grande.
ROAD: Bus: There is a service to most large towns. Booking seats in Managua in advance is advisable.
Taxis: Available at airport or in Managua. Prices should be agreed before departure. A map of each area in the city determines taxi prices. **Car hire:** Available in Managua or at airport. This is the best way of travelling, as public transport is slow and overcrowded. Tarred roads to San Juan del Sur and Corinto. **Documentation:** National licences are only valid for 30 days.
URBAN: The bus and minibus services in Managua are cheap, but they can be both crowded and confusing.
JOURNEY TIMES: The following chart gives approximate journey times (in hours and minutes) from Managua to other major cities and towns in Nicaragua.

	Road
Granada	1.00
Masaya	0.30
Esteli	1.15

NICARAGUA | **HEALTH REGULATIONS** | **VISA REGULATIONS** | Code-Link

GALILEO/WORLDSPAN

TI-DFT/MGA/HE

TI-DFT/MGA/VI

SABRE

TIDFT/MGA/HE

TIDFT/MGA/VI

To access this information on your CRS, swipe the barcode with a light pen or type in the text under the barcode. For more information, see the introduction *How to Use This Book*.

Chinandega	1.30
Matagalpa	1.00
Jinotega	2.30
Rivas	1.30

ACCOMMODATION

Many of the hotels were destroyed in the earthquake of 1972, although new hotels are gradually being opened in Managua. Several have been built along the highway that bypasses the old part of the city, but there is still a shortage. A 10% tax is levied on all hotel bills. There are motels along the Pan-American Highway and modern resort hotels along the west coast, offering a good standard of accommodation. **Grading:** Hotels in Managua have been divided into three categories: upper, middle and lower, to provide an indication of price and standard.

RESORTS & EXCURSIONS

The Towns

Managua: The centre of the capital was completely destroyed by an earthquake in December 1972, and there was further severe damage during the civil wars of 1978-1979. The Government has now decided that it will rebuild the old centre, adding parks and recreational facilities. In the old centre of Managua one can still see examples of colonial architecture in the *National Palace* and the Cathedral.
Places of Interest: There are several volcanic crater lagoons in the environs of Managua, some of which have become centres of watersports and residential development and also have attractive boating, fishing and picnicking facilities. *Laguna de Xiloa* is the most popular of these lagoons. Boats can be hired on the shores of *Lake Managua* for visiting the still-smoking *Momotombo volcano* and the shore villages. A recreation centre has recently been built on the shores of the nearby *Tiscapa Lagoon*.
Leon: The 'intellectual' capital of Nicaragua, with a university, religious colleges, the largest cathedral in Central America and several colonial churches. There was heavy fighting here during the civil wars of 1978-1979 and much of it was damaged.
Granada: The third city of the republic lies at the foot of the *Mombacho volcano*. It has many beautiful buildings and has faithfully preserved its Castilian traditions. The cathedral has been rebuilt in neo-classical style. Also of interest are the *Church of La Merced*, the *Church of Jalteva* and the fortress-church of San Francisco.

The Beaches

There are several beaches on the Pacific Coast about an hour's drive from Managua. The nearest are *Pochomil* and *Masachapa*. A visit to the *El Velero* beach, where the sea is ideal for both surfing and swimming, is recommended. On the Caribbean coast there are a number of small ports, the most important of which is **Bluefields**. From here one can get a boat to the beautiful, coral-fringed **Corn Islands**, the larger of which is a popular Nicaraguan holiday resort with surfing and bathing facilities that make it ideal for tourists.

SOCIAL PROFILE

FOOD & DRINK: Restaurants, particularly in Managua, serve a variety of cooking styles including Spanish, Italian, French, Latin American and Chinese. Seafood is available as are imported beverages. Shortages occur in some areas. Vegetarian restaurants of the government-owned *Colectivo de Soja* may be found in several towns; the use of soya as an alternative to meat is encouraged. **Drink:** There are a number of cheap but good restaurants/bars *(coreders)* where beer, often the cheap local brand, is available. At the other end of the scale, the few plush hotels have sophisticated restaurant/bars with a choice of international cuisine and beverages.
NIGHTLIFE: Managua has several nightclubs, some offering live music. There are also cinemas with French, Spanish and English films. Tipitapa, a tourist resort on the shore of Lake Managua, has a casino.
SHOPPING: Local items include goldwork, embroidery, shoes and paintings. Traditional crafts are available, particularly in Masaya, at the handicrafts market. **Shopping hours:** 0800-1800 Monday to Friday and 0800-1200 Saturday.
SPORT: Watersports: Beaches on the Pacific coast offer safe **swimming** as do those on the Caribbean, including the popular Corn Islands. Often the better beaches have a small entrance charge. Many of the better hotels have pools open to non-residents. In the volcanic crater lagoons there is also safe swimming. Bathing in Lake Managua and Lake Nicaragua should be avoided due to contamination and sharks. Bathing is possible in the Laguna de Tiscapa. El Velero beach or Pochomil on the Pacific coast is ideal for **surfing** as are a number of other beaches along the west coast. **Other sports:** There are a number of good **fishing** spots on the country's waterways and sea shores. **Baseball** is the national game.
SPECIAL EVENTS: The following is a selection of festivals and other special events celebrated annually in Nicaragua. For a complete list of events in 1993/1994 contact the Tourist Office.
Easter *Fiesta*, Granada; *Holy Week Ceremonies*, Leon. **Aug** *Festival of Santo Domingo*, Managua; *Assumption of the Virgin (fiesta)*, Granada. **Dec** *Christmas Mummers and Masques Festival*, Granada.
SOCIAL CONVENTIONS: Dress is informal. Some women wear trousers. **Photography:** Avoid photographing military sites or personnel. **Tipping:** 10% of the bill is customary in hotels and restaurants. No tip is necessary for taxi-drivers but porters expect a small tip.

BUSINESS PROFILE

ECONOMY: Agriculture is the main economic activity, with cotton, coffee, sugar, bananas and meat as the principal exports. Although key industrial sectors were nationalised after the revolution in 1979, the greater proportion of the economy remains in private hands. The attitude of the United States has proved critical as far as the Nicaraguan economy has been concerned: the USA instituted a trade boycott, refused bilateral aid and blocked multilateral aid and loans from the World Bank and the Inter-American Development Bank, and financed the 'Contra' organisation which has wreaked havoc in Nicaragua's northern provinces. These factors compounded an already poor economic situation characterised by a large foreign debt, high inflation, excessive government spending (especially on defence) and a shortage of foreign exchange. The damage was somewhat alleviated, however, by the Nicaraguans' successful pursuit of new export markets in Europe, particularly Scandinavia, Eastern Europe, the former USSR and Canada. Some economic aid was also made available from these sources. The efforts of the United States were nothing against the effect of Hurricane Joan in 1988 which caused damage estimated at US$1 billion. The damage inflicted then has since been compounded by persistent drought. Mexico, Japan and other Central American countries are now Nicaragua's largest trading partners.
BUSINESS: Businessmen often wear sports shirts in hot weather but never shorts. A knowledge of Spanish is an advantage, though some business people speak English. Enquire at Embassy for interpreter services. Best time to visit is November to March. **Office hours:** 0800-1200 and 1430-1730 Monday to Friday and 0800-1300 Saturday.
COMMERCIAL INFORMATION: The following organisation can offer advice: Cámara de Comercio de Nicaragua, Apartado 135, Frente a Lotería Popular, C C Managua JR. Tel: (2) 70718.

HISTORY & GOVERNMENT

HISTORY: From the 16th century, Nicaragua was ruled by Spain. In 1838 the country achieved independence, albeit under growing United States influence. US troops were invited into the country in 1912, but were withdrawn in 1933, following a 6-year guerrilla struggle to evict them, led by Augusto César Sandino. The role of the US forces was taken up by the National Guard, led by General Anastasio Somoza Garcia, who seized power in 1935 and whose family ruled Nicaragua, in an increasingly despotic and corrupt manner, until 1979. In that year, after a 17-year guerrilla war, the last Somoza was overthrown by the Frente Sandinista de Liberación Nacional (FSLN). The 'Sandinistas' established a Junta of National Reconstruction, and began a programme of agrarian reform, nationalisation of industry, and massive health and literacy schemes. However, in 1981, following the election of Ronald Reagan as US President, the USA began a programme of destabilisation in Nicaragua, setting up the 'Contra' guerrilla forces in Honduras and mounting an economic boycott. The Contra war has caused severe problems for the FSLN government, and persistent attempts by neighbouring countries to establish a peace treaty foundered on US opposition until the 1989 agreement with Honduras. US aid to the Contras has now been severely cut. Following the recent agreement with Honduras, which was a considerable diplomatic coup for the Sandinistas, the US-backed war in Nicaragua seems almost over. Elections in February 1990 showed how much Sandinista popularity suffered during the years of turmoil and austerity. Violeta Chamorro, widow of the publisher Pedro Chamorro (who was killed by the Somoza regime), defeated Ortega when she stood on behalf of the combined opposition UNO Alliance representing 14 of the 21 opposition parties in Nicaragua. The Government's decision to bring an end to the negotiated cease-fire designed as a prelude to the electoral campaign drew widespread criticism while reflecting continued Contra military activity. Relations with the United States are obviously improved but surprising strains have appeared, mostly because of American neglect, particularly the failure to produce a large proportion of several hundred million dollars in promised aid. In the summer of 1992, the US Congress blocked a US$116 million aid package until land originally confiscated by the Sandinistas (and formerly owned by American interests) is handed back by the Government, and the Sandinistas' continuing influence over the police and the military is curtailed. Chamorro responded defiantly to the embargo, condemning American interference in Nicaraguan affairs. The resettlement plan for demobilised 'Contras' is proving difficult to implement, and there have been periodic bouts of fighting between rival claimants for certain plots of land. More significantly, during 1992, demobilised troops from both sides have united to protest against the Government's failure to provide free land, as promised, to ex-soldiers. In Managua, much of Chamorro's energy is consumed by holding together the fractious UNO coalition. The President herself has little to do with the day-to-day business of government, which is mostly in the hands of her son-in-law Antonio Oyanguren Lacayo and his deputy, Antonio Ibarra. Lacayo is at the centre of recent corruption allegations involving misuse of state bank funds and foreign aid.
GOVERNMENT: The President, who is elected for a six-year term, wields executive power assisted by a deputy and Cabinet of Ministers. Legislative power rests with the National Assembly, whose 92 members (reduced from 96 in 1990) are popularly elected by proportional representation.

CLIMATE

Tropical climate for most of the country. The dry season is from December to May, and the rainy season is from June to November. The northern mountain regions have a much cooler climate.
Required clothing: Lightweight cottons and linens are required throughout the year. Waterproofing is advisable particularly during the rainy season. Warmer clothes are advised for the northern mountains.

MANAGUA Nicaragua (56m)

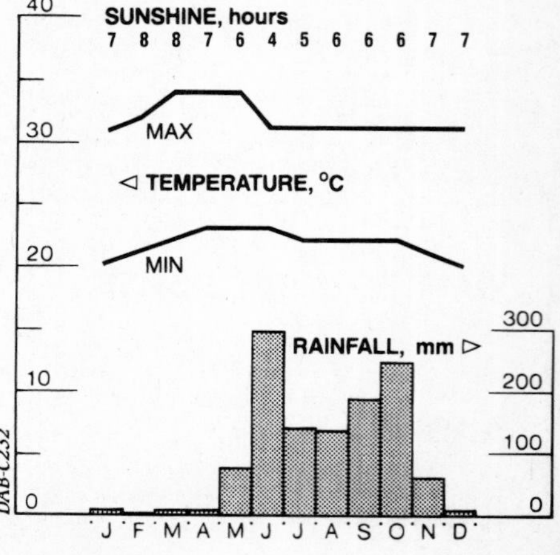

NIGER

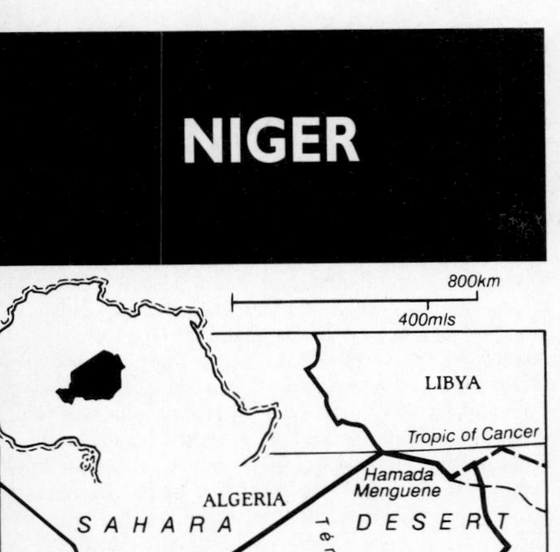

Location: Central Africa.

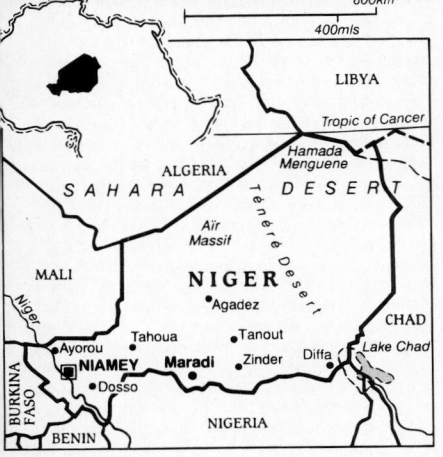

Office National du Tourisme (ONT)
BP 612
avenue du Président H Luebke
Niamey, Niger
Tel: 732 447. Telex: 5467.
Embassy of the Republic of Niger
154 rue du Longchamp
75116 Paris, France
Tel: (1) 45 04 80 60. Fax: (1) 45 04 62 26. Telex: 611080. Opening hours: 0900-1230 (applications) and 1430-1800 Monday to Friday.
Honorary British Vice-Consulate
BP 11168
Niamey, Niger
Tel: 732 015 *or* 732 539.
Embassy of the Republic of Niger
2204 R Street, NW
Washington, DC 20008
Tel: (202) 483 4224.
Embassy of the United States of America
BP 11201
rue des Ambassades
Niamey, Niger
Tel: 722 661-4. Telex: 5444 NI.
Embassy of the Republic of Niger
38 Blackburn Avenue
Ottawa, Ontario
K1N 8A2
Tel: (613) 232 4291/2/3. Fax: (613) 230 9808.
Consulate in: Montréal.
Canadian Embassy
PO Box 362
Sonara II Building
avenue du Premier Pont
Niamey, Niger
Tel: 733 686/7 *or* 733 758. Fax: 735 064. Telex: 5264.

AREA: 1,267,000 sq km (489,191 sq miles).
POPULATION: 7,249,596 (1988 estimate).
POPULATION DENSITY: 5.7 per sq km.
CAPITAL: Niamey. **Population:** 360,000 (1981 estimate).
GEOGRAPHY: Niger has borders with Libya and Algeria to the north, Chad to the east, Nigeria and Benin to the south, and Mali and Burkina Faso to the west. The capital, Niamey, stands on the north bank of the Niger River, and has long been a major trading centre on this important navigable waterway. The river meanders for 500km (300 miles) through the southwestern corner of the country. To the east is a band of semi-arid bush country along the border with Nigeria, shrinking by 20km (12 miles) every year as over-grazing claims more land for the *Ténéré Desert*, which already occupies over half of Niger. This desert is divided by a range of low mountains, *Aïr ou Azbine*, in the eastern foothills of which lies the city of Agadez. Surrounded by green valleys and hot springs amid semi-desert, this regional capital is still a major terminus for Saharan caravans. The desert to the west of the mountains is a stony plain hosting seasonal pastures; to the north and east are mostly vast expanses of sand. There is arable land beside Lake Chad in the extreme southeastern corner of the country. The Hausa people live along the border with Nigeria and most are farmers. The Songhai and Djerma people live in the Niger valley and exist by farming and fishing. The nomadic Fulani, who are a tall, fine-featured people, have spread all over the Sahel. The robed and veiled Tuaregs once dominated the southern cities; the few who remain are camel herders and caravanners on the Saharan routes. The Manga (or Kanun) live near Lake Chad and are well known for their colourful ceremonies in which pipes and drums accompany slow, stately dancing.
LANGUAGE: The official language is French. Also spoken are Hausa (by 60% of the population), Djerma, Manga, Zarma and Tuareg dialects.
RELIGION: 95% Muslim, 0.5% Christian, remainder Animist.
TIME: GMT + 1.
ELECTRICITY: 220/380 volts AC, 50Hz.
COMMUNICATIONS: Telephone: IDD is available. Country code: 227 (no area codes). **Telex/telegram:** Services are available from the Chief Telegraph Office, Niamey, some hotels and other telegraph offices. There are three rates of charge. **Post:** Airmail to Europe takes up to two weeks. Post offices are generally open 0730-1230 and 1530-1800. **Press:** All newspapers are published in French.
BBC World Service and Voice of America frequencies: From time to time these change. See the section *How to Use this Book* for more information.

BBC:				
MHz	15.10	17.79	15.40	9.410
Voice of America:				
MHz	21.49	15.60	9.525	6.035

PASSPORT/VISA

Regulations and requirements may be subject to change at short notice, and you are advised to contact the appropriate diplomatic or consular authority before finalising travel arrangements. Details of these may be found at the head of this country's entry. Any numbers in the chart refer to the footnotes below.

	Passport Required?	Visa Required?	Return Ticket Required?
Full British	Yes	No	Yes
BVP	Not valid	-	-
Australian	Yes	Yes	Yes
Canadian	Yes	Yes	Yes
USA	Yes	Yes	Yes
Other EC	Yes	1	Yes
Japanese	Yes	Yes	Yes

PASSPORTS: Valid passport required by all.
British Visitors Passport: Not accepted.
VISAS: Required by all except:
(a) **[1]** nationals of EC countries (except nationals of Greece, Ireland, Spain and Portugal, who *do* require visas);
(b) nationals of Benin, Burkina Faso, Cape Verde, Central African Republic, Chad, Congo, Côte d'Ivoire, Finland, Gambia, Ghana, Guinea, Guinea-Bissau, Liberia, Madagascar, Mali, Mauritania, Mauritius, Morocco, Nigeria, Norway, Senegal, Sierra Leone, Sweden, Togo and Tunisia.
All exemptions are for stays of up to 3 months.
Application to: Consulate (or Consular Section at Embassy). For addresses, see top of entry.
Application requirements: (a) 3 completed application forms. (b) 3 photos. (c) A return ticket or proof of sufficient funds to cover repatriation costs. (d) Visitors entering by road: bank letter stating to cover repatriation costs and proof of car insurance. (e) Letter of assurance not to take up employment while in Niger. (f) Postal applications should be accompanied by a stamped, self-addressed envelope.
Working days required: 24 hours.
Exit permit: Must be obtained from the Immigration Department in Niamey before departure.
Note: Passports must be presented to the police in each town where an overnight stay is intended. Passports are stamped at each town, so blank pages will be required. It is prohibited to travel by any route other than that stamped in the passport by the police.

MONEY

Currency: CFA Franc (CFA Fr) = 100 centimes. Notes are in denominations of CFA Fr10,000, 5000, 1000, 500 and 100. Coins are in denominations of CFA Fr100, 50, 25, 10, 5, 2 and 1.
Credit cards: Diners Club and Access/Mastercard are both accepted on a limited basis. Check with your credit card company for details of merchant acceptability and other services which may be available.
Travellers cheques: Accepted by hotels, restaurants, most shops and airline offices.
Exchange rate indicators: The following figures are included as a guide to the movements of the CFA Franc against Sterling and the US Dollar:

Date:	Oct '89	Oct '90	Oct '91	Oct '92
£1.00=	505.13	498.40	496.12	431.75
$1.00=	319.90	255.10	285.87	260.71

Currency restrictions: The import and export of foreign currency is unlimited. The import of local currency is unlimited. Export of local currency is limited to CFA Fr25,000.
Banking hours: 0800-1100 and 1600-1700 Monday to Friday.

DUTY FREE

The following items may be imported into Niger by passengers of 15 years of age or older without incurring customs duty:
200 cigarettes or 100 cigarillos or 25 cigars or 250g of tobacco;
1 litre of spirits.
Note: (a) A licence is required for sporting guns. Customs must authorise their temporary admission. (b) Digging up or attempting to export ancient artefacts is prohibited. (c) Pornography is prohibited. (d) Apparatus for transmission or reception needs special authorisation (as does photographic equipment, see *Photography* under *Social Conventions*). (e) Selling cars without permission is prohibited.

PUBLIC HOLIDAYS

Public holidays observed in Niger are as follows:
Mar 25 '93 Start of Eid al-Fitr. **Apr 12** Easter Monday. **Apr 15** Anniversary of the 1974 coup. **May 1** Labour Day. **Jun 1** Eid al-Adha. **Jun 21** Islamic New Year. **Aug 3** Independence Day. **Aug 30** Mouloud (Birth of the Prophet). **Dec 18** Republic Day. **Dec 25** Christmas. **Jan 1 '94** New Year's Day. **Mar** Start of Eid al-Fitr.
Note: (a) Muslim festivals are timed according to local sightings of various phases of the Moon and the dates given above are approximations. During the lunar month of Ramadan that precedes Eid al-Fitr, Muslims fast during the day and feast at night and normal business patterns may be interrupted. Many restaurants are closed during the day and there may be restrictions on smoking and drinking. Some disruption may continue into Eid al-Fitr itself. Eid al-Fitr and Eid al-Adha may last anything from two to ten days, depending on the region. For more information see the section *World of Islam* at the back of the book. (b) Niger's small Christian community also observes Easter, Whitsun, Ascension, Assumption, All Saints' Day and Christmas.

HEALTH

Regulations and requirements may be subject to change at short notice, and you are advised to contact your doctor well in advance of your intended date of departure. Any numbers in the chart refer to the footnotes below.

	Special Precautions?	Certificate Required?
Yellow Fever	Yes	1
Cholera	Yes	2
Typhoid & Polio	Yes	-
Malaria	3	-
Food & Drink	4	-

[1]: A yellow fever vaccination certificate is required of all travellers over one year of age arriving from all countries: it is also recommended for all travellers leaving Niger.
[2]: Following WHO guidelines issued in 1973, a cholera vaccination certificate is not a condition of entry to Niger. However, cholera is a serious risk in this country and precautions are essential. Up-to-date advice should be sought before deciding whether these precautions should include vaccination as medical opinion is divided over its effectiveness. See the *Health* section at the back of the book.
[3]: Malaria risk, predominantly in the malignant *falciparum* form, exists all year throughout the country. Chloroquine-resistance has been reported.
[4]: All water should be regarded as being potentially contaminated. Water used for drinking, brushing teeth or making ice should have first been boiled or otherwise sterilised. Milk is unpasteurised and should be boiled. Powdered or tinned milk is available and is advised, but make sure that it is reconstituted with pure water. Avoid dairy products which are likely to have been made from unboiled milk. Only eat well-cooked meat and fish, preferably served hot. Pork, salad and mayonnaise may carry increased risk. Vegetables should be cooked and fruit peeled.
Rabies is present. For those at high risk, vaccination before arrival should be considered. If you are bitten abroad seek medical advice without delay. For more information consult the *Health* section at the back of the book.
Bilharzia (schistosomiasis) is present. Avoid swimming and paddling in fresh water. Swimming pools which are well-chlorinated and maintained are safe.
Health care: The two main hospitals are in Niamey and Zinder. Only the main centres have reasonable medical facilities. Personal medicines should be brought in as these can be difficult or impossible to obtain in Niger. Full health

insurance is essential, and this should include cover for emergency repatriation.

TRAVEL - International

AIR: The national airline is *Air Niger (AW)*. Most international flights are operated by *Air Afrique (RK)* and *UTA (UT)*. (There are no direct flights to Niger from the UK.)
Approximate flight time: From *London* to Niamey is six hours excluding stopover time in Paris.
International airport: *Niamey (NIM)*, 12km (7.5 miles) southeast of the city (travel time – 25 minutes). Taxi services are available to the city. Hotels have their own vehicles and provide free transport for their clients between the hotel and the airport. Airport facilities include bar, shops, post office, currency exchange and car hire. There are no duty-free facilities at Niamey airport.
ROAD: There are main roads from Kano (Nigeria) to Zinder, and from Benin, Burkina Faso and Mali. The principal trans-Sahara desert track runs from Algiers to Asamakka and Arlit, with a paved road to Agadez. Desert driving can be difficult, marker beacons may not always be visible, and petrol is not always available. **Bus** services operate from Burkina Faso, Benin and Mali.

TRAVEL - Internal

Note: It is essential that all visitors report to the police station in any town where they are making an overnight stop; see above under *Passport/Visa*.
AIR: *Air Niger* runs services from Niamey to Agadez, Tahoua, Zinder, Arlit and Maradi. Charter flights can be arranged; contact *Air Niger* or *Transniger* in Niamey.
ROAD: There are over 1500km (930 miles) of roads which are passable at all times. Principal internal roads are from Niamey to Zinder, Tahoua, Arlit and Gaya. Many tracks are impassable during heavy rain. The best season for road travel is from December to March. Petrol stations are infrequent and garages are extremely expensive. It is prohibited to travel by a different route than the one entered in the passport by the police at the previous town. **Bus:** There are reasonable services between the main centres, now that many roads have been sealed. Coach services operate from Niamey to Zinder, Agadez, N'guemi and Tera. Elsewhere, it is common practice to pay for rides in cross-country lorries; note that this can be an extremely slow and uncomfortable means of transport and that extra payment is expected of those who wish to ride in the cab. **Car hire:** Self-drive and chauffeur-driven cars are available, the latter being compulsory outside the capital. **Note:** Much of the country requires 4-wheel drive vehicles, guides and full equipment.
Documentation: An International Driving Permit and a Carnet de Passage are required. Minimum age is 23. Two photos are required.
JOURNEY TIMES: The following chart gives approximate journey times (in hours and minutes) from Niamey to other major cities and towns in Niger.

	Air	Road
Zinder	0.45	12.00
Maradi	-	9.00
Tahoua	-	7.00
Dosso	-	1.00
Tillabéri	-	4.50
Agadez	-	17.00

ACCOMMODATION

HOTELS: Hotel accommodation is difficult to obtain and reservations for major international hotels should be booked overseas. All reservations should be made well in advance. There are good hotels in Niamey, Zinder, Ayorou, La Tapoa, Maradi and Agadez. There are also 'Encampments' in Agadez, Boubon, Namaro and Tillabéri. Local hotels are available on a first-come, first-served basis. For further information contact the Société Nigérienne d'Hôtellerie (SONHOTEL), BP 11040, Niamey. Tel: 732 387 *or* 732 295. Telex: TOUROTEL 5239 NI.

RESORTS & EXCURSIONS

Niamey, spread along the northern bank of the *River Niger*, is a sprawling city with a modern centre and shanty towns on the outskirts. The two markets, the Small and Great Markets, are of interest to the visitor. Other places of interest include the *Great Mosque*, the *National Museum*, the *Franco-Nigerian Cultural Centre* and the *Hippodrome* where horse and camel races often take place on Sunday. Tours of the city are available. Outside Niamey is the famous **'W' National Park,** with its abundant wildlife including buffalo, elephants, lions, hyenas, jackals, baboons and birds.
Agadez is a beautiful old Tuareg capital which is still a caravan trading city: it also now has a thriving tourist trade. Beautiful silver and leather work can be bought in the back streets and the minaret of the mosque can be climbed at sunset for a spectacular view of the town. Expeditions can be arranged through the mountains to the springs at **Igouloulef** and **Tafadek** or the prehistoric site at **Iferouane** and beyond the *Teneré Desert* and the *Djado Mountain*.
The town of **Zinder** was the capital of Niger until 1927. The old part of the town is a maze of alleyways, typical of a Hausa town. Near the centre is the *Sultan's Palace* and the mosque, which offers a good view from the minaret. The part of the town known as *Zengou* was formerly a caravan encampment. There is an market here on Thursdays, selling leatherwork. On the route from Zinder is the town of **Dosso,** founded in the 13th century by the Zarmas after the fall of Gao. It has an exceptional palace, a lively village square and celebrates many festivals with parades and official ceremonies. Niger's economic centre is **Maradi** where the people engaged in various activities from agriculture to diverse crafts. The *Sultanate* and the *Mosque* there are well worth viewing.
The **Ayorou** region on the Mali frontier is an old trading station where a market is held every Sunday. In the region around **Tillabéri** giraffes are often encountered, often in quite large numbers. Two-day tours are available from the capital. The *Aïr Mountains*, north of Agadez, enjoy slightly more rain than the surrounding semi-desert lowlands and were, until recently, home to many species of animals not generally seen at this latitude – leopards, lions and giraffes for example. However, the drought has even taken hold here and the stranded populations are dwindling rapidly. Special permission may be required to visit the region.

SOCIAL PROFILE

FOOD & DRINK: European, Asian and African dishes are served using local fish, meat and vegetables. There is a good selection of imported beverages. Shortages of locally produced foodstuffs are, however, common due to drought. There are a few good restaurants in the main cities. Alcohol is available, but there are restrictions due to Muslim beliefs.
NIGHTLIFE: In Niamey there are nightclubs with music and dancing. There are also three open-air cinemas in the capital.
SHOPPING: Markets in the main towns, notably Niamey and Agadez, sell a range of local artefacts. The Centre des Métiers d'Art de Niger, close to the National Museum, is worth visiting, as a wide range of local goods can be bought there. Courteous bargaining is expected and items include multi-coloured blankets, leather goods, engraved calabashes, silver jewellery, swords and knives. **Shopping hours:** 0800-1200 and 1600-1900 Monday to Friday, 0800-1200 Saturday.
SPORT: Visitors can take **canoes** or **motorboats** along the Niger river to the Mali border of the 'W' game park. There are several **swimming** pools in Niamey and Agadez, but it is not advisable to swim in the lakes or rivers. There are two **riding** centres in the capital. **Fishing** is possible throughout the year, the main season being from April to September. Big-game **hunting** has been outlawed.
SPECIAL EVENTS: The following festivals are celebrated annually. The Peulh people celebrate the end of the rainy season with a lively festival. Also of interest is the *Cure salée*, when the nomads gather their cattle to lead them to the new pastures. The yearly wrestling championships are held in the traditional style. The *Agricultural Fair* draws crowds.
SOCIAL CONVENTIONS: Handshaking is customary. Casual wear is widely suitable. Women should avoid wearing revealing clothes. Traditional beliefs and Muslim customs should be respected. **Photography:** Permits are required for photography and filming, and these can be obtained from police stations. Tour operators and tourist bureaux are often able to make arrangements. Film is expensive and local facilities for processing film are not always good. Ask local people for permission before taking their photographs. Military installations, airports and administrative buildings (including the Presidential Palace) should not be photographed.
Tipping: Expected for most services, usually 10%. Most hotels add a 10-15% service charge.

BUSINESS PROFILE

ECONOMY: Niger is one of the world's poorest countries. 90% of the country's inhabitants are employed on the land, although less than 5% of the actual land area is cultivated. An already difficult situation is exacerbated by the ever-expanding desert, drought and problems with pest control. Less than one-tenth of the crops grown are cash crops – cotton and groundnuts – while the rest are grown for domestic consumption. Even so, Niger needs external aid to feed the population. The country's most valuable commodity is its deposits of uranium, of which Niger is the fifth largest non-communist producer, although world demand has been low of late following Chernobyl and the general downturn in the nuclear power industry. France buys most of Niger's uranium at a subsidised price. Otherwise Nigeria and Côte d'Ivoire are the country's main trading partners.
BUSINESS: A lightweight suit and tie are generally acceptable. A knowledge of French is essential, as interpreters are not readily available and executives seldom speak English. **Office hours:** 0730-1230 and 1530-1830 Monday to Friday; 0730-1230 Saturday.
COMMERCIAL INFORMATION: Consult the following organisation: Conseil National de Développement, c/o Ministry of Planning, Niamey. Tel: 722 233. Telex: 5214.

HISTORY & GOVERNMENT

HISTORY: Evidence of human settlement in the region now known as Niger goes back 6000 years, when the then fertile area supported a well-developed civilisation. In the thousand years up to the 19th century, power in the region was based on control of the great trans-Saharan trade routes. The Hausa kingdom dominated the central area from the 13th century. The wealth of these powers decreased from the 18th century onwards as European traders used sea-routes to make contact with West Africa. Colonised by the French in the 19th century, Niger was part of French West Africa until 1958. It achieved independence in 1960, and Hamani Diori was elected head of state. Diori was re-elected in 1965 and 1970, and his government seemed exceptionally stable until severe drought from 1968 onwards brought about widespread civil unrest. In April 1974 there was a military coup under Lt Col (later Maj Gen) Seyni Kountché, followed by a series of further coup attempts when Kountché attempted to civilianise the Government. By 1983, however, the legislative Council of Ministers was entirely composed of civilians, under Prime Minister Oumarou Maname. Kountché died in 1987, to be replaced by his staunch ally Ali Seibou who consolidated his position during the late 1980s. Seibou began his tenure by trying to diversify Niger's economy away from its current excessive dependence on uranium. Under the guidance of an IMF/World Bank Structural Adjustment Programme (SAP), Niger made good economic progress over the next few years but in 1990 the economy went into recession and the year saw a series of general strikes. Demonstrators demanded not only an end to the SAP but also the introduction of multi-party democracy. After some initial uncertainty and opposition from Seibou, the Government chose to follow the regional trend and convened a national conference to determine the country's future. After several month's deliberation, the conference decided to install an interim administration, headed by Amadou Cheiffou, to govern Niger until the end of January 1993. Multi-party elections were originally due in early 1992 but have still not been held (as of December 1992) as the interim government struggles with a chronic cash shortage and mutinous troops. Since 1990, there have been a series of clashes between security forces and guerrillas belonging to the nomadic Tuareg people, who are seeking rehabilitation in Niger, having left the country to escape the Sahel drought a few years ago. In July 1990, the governments of Algeria, Mali and Niger established a joint commission to monitor Tuareg movements across their mutual borders.
GOVERNMENT: Following a national conference which ended in November 1991, the 1989 constitution was suspended and legislative power transferred to an interim Haut Conseil de la République, which is also tasked with drafting a new constitution. The HCR and transitional government will, it is envisaged, remain in power until early 1993, at which point they will hand over to elected bodies.

CLIMATE

Summers are extremely hot. The dry season is from October to May. Heavy rains with high temperatures are common in July and August.
Required clothing: Lightweight cottons and linens are required most of the year. Warmer clothes during the cool evenings, especially in the north, are essential. Rainwear is advisable.

NIAMEY Niger (220m)

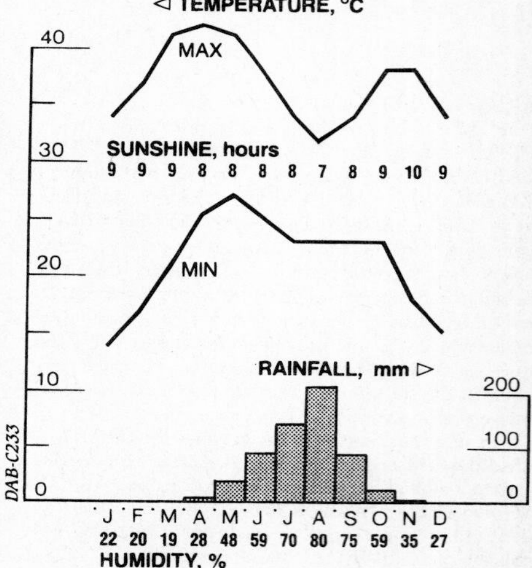

NIGERIA

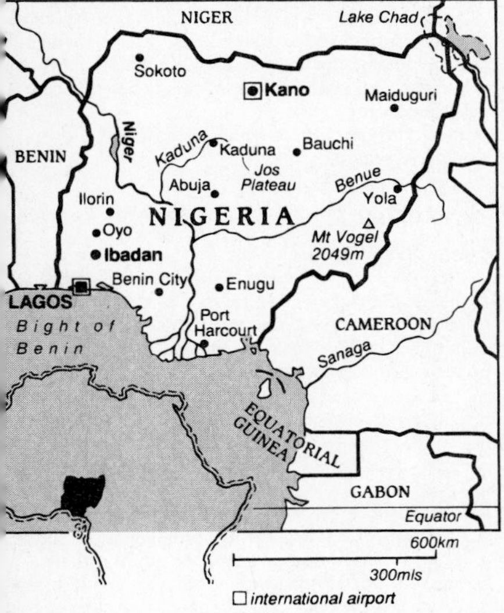

Location: West Africa.

Nigerian Tourist Board
PO Box 2944
Trade Fair Complex
Badagry Expressway
Lagos, Nigeria
Tel: (1) 883 364.

High Commission for the Federal Republic of Nigeria
Nigeria House
9 Northumberland Avenue
London
WC2N 5BX
Tel: (071) 839 1244. Fax: (071) 839 8746. Telex: 23665 or 916814.

Nigerian Consular Section
Premier House
112 Station Road
Edgware
Middlesex HA8 7AQ
Tel: (081) 905 7755. Fax: (071) 839 8746.

British High Commission
Private Mail Bag 12136
11 Eleke Crescent
Victoria Island
Lagos, Nigeria
Tel: (1) 619 531 *or* 619 537. Fax: (1) 666 909 (Visa Section). Telex: 21247 UKREP NG.

Embassy of the Federal Republic of Nigeria
2201 M Street, NW
Washington, DC
20037
Tel: (202) 822 1500.

Nigerian Consulate General
57 Lexington Avenue
New York, NY
10022
Tel: (212) 715 7200.

Embassy of the United States of America
PO Box 554
2 Eleke Crescent
Lagos, Nigeria
Tel: (1) 610 097. Fax: (1) 610 257. Telex: 23616 AMEMLA NG.

High Commission for the Federal Republic of Nigeria
295 Metcalfe Street
Ottawa
Ontario
K2P 1R9
Tel: (613) 236 0521/2/3. Fax: (613) 236 0529.

Canadian High Commission
PO Box 54506
Ikoyi Station
Committee of Vice-Chancellors Building, Plot 8a
4 Idowu-Taylor Street
Victoria Island
Lagos, Nigeria
Tel: (1) 612 382. Fax: (1) 614 691. Telex: 21275 DOMCAN NG.

AREA: 923,768 sq km (356,669 sq miles).
POPULATION: 104,957,000 (1988 estimate).
POPULATION DENSITY: 113.6 per sq km.
CAPITAL: Abuja (from Dec 12 1991). Formerly Lagos. **Population:** Lagos – 1,060,848 (1975). Foreign diplomats will continue to be accredited to Lagos for up to five years because of shortage of houses and offices.
GEOGRAPHY: Nigeria has borders with Niger to the north, Chad (across Lake Chad) to the northeast, Cameroon to the east and Benin to the west. To the south, the Gulf of Guinea is indented by the Bight of Benin and the Bight of Biafra. The country's topography and vegetation vary considerably. The coastal region is a low-lying area of lagoons, sandy beaches and mangrove swamps which merges into an area of rainforest where palm trees grow to over 30m (100ft). From here the landscape changes to savannah and open woodland, rising to the Central Jos plateau at 1800m (6000ft). The northern part of the country is desert and semi-desert, marking the southern extent of the Sahara.
LANGUAGE: The official language is English. There are over 250 local languages, the principal ones being Hausa (north), Yoruba (southwest) and Ibo (southeast).
RELIGION: Islamic majority, particularly in the north and west of the country, with a Christian minority (who make up a majority in the south). There are many local religions.
TIME: GMT + 1.
ELECTRICITY: 210/250 volts AC, 50Hz. Single phase.
COMMUNICATIONS: Telephone: Full IDD is available. Country code: 234. **Telex/telegram:** International telegraph and telex services are operated by Nigerian Telecommunications Limited (NITEL) in all large cities. **Post:** Airmail to Europe is unreliable and takes up to three weeks. Delivery may be more reliable through international couriers who are represented in major towns. **Press:** English-language newspapers include the *Daily Times*, the *Nigerian Herald*, the *Nigerian Tribune* and the *Daily Sketch*.
BBC World Service and Voice of America frequencies: From time to time these change. See the section *How to Use this Book* for more information.

BBC:				
MHz	17.79	15.40	15.07	9.410
Voice of America:				
MHz	21.49	15.60	9.525	6.035

PASSPORT/VISA

Regulations and requirements may be subject to change at short notice, and you are advised to contact the appropriate diplomatic or consular authority before finalising travel arrangements. Details of these may be found at the head of this country's entry. Any numbers in the chart refer to the footnotes below.

	Passport Required?	Visa Required?	Return Ticket Required?
Full British	Yes	Yes	Yes
BVP	Not valid	-	-
Australian	Yes	Yes	Yes
Canadian	Yes	Yes	Yes
USA	Yes	Yes	Yes
Other EC	Yes	Yes	Yes
Japanese	Yes	Yes	Yes

Restricted entry: The Government of Nigeria refuses admission to: (a) nationals of South Africa (transit permitted provided the journey is continued by the same aircraft); (b) holders of passports with a visa either valid or expired for South Africa or any other proof of contact with South Africa, eg entry or exit stamps.
PASSPORTS: Valid passport required by all.
British Visitors Passport: Not accepted.
VISAS: Required by all except nationals of Cameroon, Chad and Morocco who may stay for up to 90 days. Nationals of Benin, Burkina Faso, Cape Verde, Côte d'Ivoire, Gambia, Ghana, Guinea, Guinea-Bissau, Liberia, Mali, Mauritania, Niger, Senegal, Sierra Leone and Togo may obtain a 90-day visa on arrival.
Note: Children under 16 years of age accompanying their parents residing in Nigeria (provided the name of such a child is entered in the passport of one of the parents) do not require visas, but must, however, complete one application form accompanied by a photo. All children holding their own passport must have separate visas or re-entry permits.
Types of visa: Tourist, Transit and Business (employment/temporary work). Cost depends on nationality; UK nationals pay £30.
Transit visas: Not required by:
(a) those noted under visa exemptions above;
(b) those continuing their journey to a third country by the same aircraft and not leaving the airport;
(c) those who transit Nigeria within 48 hours, provided they hold tickets with confirmed reservations and documents valid for a third country beyond Nigeria. (They will be permitted to leave the airport, but passports will normally be retained by the immigration authorities; hotel accommodation is available near Lagos airport.)
Re-entry permits: Required by all residents who are not nationals of Nigeria. Permit must be obtained before departure.
Application to: Consulate (or Consular Section at Embassy or High Commission). For addresses, see top of entry.
Application requirements: (a) Completed application form. (b) Passport. (c) 1 photo. (d) Letter of introduction from a company or a resident of Nigeria, accepting immigration responsibility for applicant; any Nigerian inviting a visitor must attach photocopies of pages 1-5 of his own passport, while a resident must enclose a copy of his residence permit. (e) Onward or return ticket for Tourist visas.
Working days required: 2.

MONEY

Currency: Naira (N) = 100 kobo. Notes are in denominations of N20, 10, 5 and 1, and 50 kobo. Coins are in denominations of 25, 10, 5 and 1 kobo.
Credit cards: American Express is widely accepted; Diners Club, Access/Mastercard and Visa have limited use. Check with your credit card company for details of merchant acceptability and other services which may be available.
Exchange rate indicators: The following figures are included as a guide to the movements of the Nigerian Naira against Sterling and the US Dollar:

Date:	Oct '89	Oct '90	Oct '91	Oct '92
£1.00=	11.58	15.49	18.68	30.76
$1.00=	7.33	7.93	10.76	18.45

Currency restrictions: Import of foreign currency is unlimited, but it must be declared on arrival; export is limited to the amount declared. Import and export of local currency is restricted to N50 in notes. Penalties for black-market transactions are severe.
Banking hours: 0800-1500 Monday and 0800-1330 Tuesday to Friday. There are 20 commercial banks. The Government owns 60% of all foreign banks.

DUTY FREE

The following goods may be imported into Nigeria by persons over 18 years of age without incurring customs duty:
200 cigarettes or 50 cigars or 200g of tobacco;
1 litre of spirits;
A small amount of perfume.
Note: (a) If more than each of the above is imported, duty will be levied on the whole quantity. Heavy duty will be levied on luxury items such as cameras or radios unless the visitor's stay is temporary. (b) The import of champagne or sparkling wine will result in heavy fines or imprisonment. (c) It is forbidden to buy or sell antiques from or to anyone other than the Director of Antiquities or an accredited agent; visitors should obtain a clearance permit from one of the above before presenting antiques, artefacts or curios at the airport.

PUBLIC HOLIDAYS

Public holidays observed in Nigeria are as follows:
Mar 25 '93 Start of Eid al-Fitr. **Apr 9-12** Easter. **Jun 1** Eid al-Kabir. **Aug 30** Mouloud (Birth of the Prophet). **Oct 1** National Day. **Dec 25-26** Christmas. **Jan 1 '94** New Year's Day. **Mar** Start of Eid al-Fitr.
Note: Muslim festivals are timed according to local sightings of various phases of the Moon and the dates given above are approximations. During the lunar month of Ramadan that precedes Eid al-Fitr, Muslims fast during the day and feast at night and normal business patterns may be interrupted. Many restaurants are closed during the day and there may be restrictions on smoking and drinking. Some disruption may continue into Eid al-Fitr itself. Eid al-Fitr and Eid al-Kabir may last anything from two to ten days, depending on the region. For more information see the section *World of Islam* at the back of the book.

HEALTH

Regulations and requirements may be subject to change at short notice, and you are advised to contact your doctor well in advance of your intended date of departure. Any numbers in the chart refer to the footnotes below.

	Special Precautions?	Certificate Required?
Yellow Fever	Yes	1
Cholera	Yes	2
Typhoid & Polio	Yes	-
Malaria	3	-
Food & Drink	4	-

[1]: A yellow fever vaccination certificate is required of travellers over one year of age arriving from infected areas. The risk of contracting yellow fever is highest in Lagos and Kaduna States.
[2]: Following WHO guidelines issued in 1973, a cholera vaccination certificate is not a condition of entry to Nigeria. However, cholera is a serious risk in this country and precautions are essential. Up-to-date advice should be sought before deciding whether these precautions should include vaccination, as medical opinion is divided over its effectiveness. See the *Health* section at the back of the book.
[3]: Malaria risk exists all year throughout the country. The predominant *falciparum* strain has been reported to be 'resistant' to chloroquine.
[4]: All water should be regarded as being potentially contaminated. Water used for drinking, brushing teeth or making ice should have first been boiled or otherwise sterilised. Milk is unpasteurised and should be boiled. Powdered or tinned milk is available and is advised, but make sure that it is reconstituted with pure water. Avoid dairy products which are likely to have been made from unboiled milk. Only eat well-cooked meat and fish, preferably served hot. Pork, salad and mayonnaise may carry increased risk. Vegetables should be cooked and fruit peeled.
Rabies is present. For those at high risk, vaccination before arrival should be considered. If you are bitten abroad seek medical advice without delay. For more information consult the *Health* section at the back of the book.
Bilharzia (schistosomiasis) is present. Avoid swimming and paddling in fresh water. Swimming pools which are well-chlorinated and maintained are safe.
Health care: It is advisable to take a sufficient supply of drugs or medication to meet personal needs, as there are often shortages of such items in Nigeria. Medical insurance is essential.

TRAVEL - International

AIR: Nigeria's national airline is *Nigeria Airways (WT)*.
Approximate flight times: From Lagos to *London* is 7 hours 40 minutes and to *New York* is 12 hours 10 minutes.
International airports: *Lagos (LOS)* (Murtala Muhammed) is 22km (13 miles) north of Lagos (travel time – 40 minutes). Airport facilities include restaurant, bar, snack-bar, bank, post office and car hire. There is a free coach service every 10 minutes. Taxis to the city are available.
Kano (KAN) is 8km (5 miles) north of Kano (travel time – 25 minutes). Airport facilities include restaurant, bank, post office, duty-free shop and car hire. Buses leave for the city every 10 minutes 0600-2200, and taxis are available.
Abujo (ABV) is 35km (22 miles) from the city.
Departure tax: US$20 (nationals of Nigeria and alien residents with work permit N360). Transit passengers and children under two years old are exempt.
SEA: Services to Lagos, Port Harcourt and Calabar sail from London, Liverpool and other European ports.
ROAD: Links are with Benin, Niger, Chad and Cameroon. The principal trans-Saharan routes pass through Nigeria from Niger. The principal link with Benin is via the Idoroko border point along the good coast road to Lagos. All land borders, with the exception of the border with Chad which was closed in May 1984, have now been re-opened.

TRAVEL - Internal

AIR: *Nigeria Airways* operate between Lagos, Ibadan, Benin City, Port Harcourt, Enugu, Calabar, Kaduna, Kano, Jos, Sokoto, Maiduguri and Yola. Charter facilities are available in Lagos from *Aero Contractors*, *Pan-African Airlines* and *Delta Air Charter*. It is advisable to book internal flights well in advance. There is often considerable delay in internal air services.
Departure tax: N5.
SEA: Ferry services operate along the south coast and along the Niger and Benue rivers. For timetables and prices, enquire locally.
RAIL: The two main routes are from Lagos to Kano (via Ibadan–Oyo Ogbombosho–Kaduna–Zaria); and from Port Harcourt to Maiduguri (via Aba–Enugu–Makurdi–Jos). These two lines link up between Kaduna and Kafanchan. There is also a branch line from Zaria to Gusau and Kaura Namoda. A daily service runs on both main routes. Sleeping cars are available, which must be booked in advance. There are three classes and some trains have restaurant cars and air-conditioning. Trains are generally slower than buses, but cheaper.
ROAD: The national road system links all the main centres, although in some areas secondary roads become impassable during the rains. **Buses** and **taxis** (in the shape of Ford Transit vans) run between the main towns. **Car hire** is difficult to obtain even in Lagos, but it is best to go through hotels. Chaffeur-driven cars are advised.
Documentation: An International Driving Permit is required, accompanied by two photos.
URBAN: Public transport in Lagos is something of a shambles. The city suffers from chronic traffic congestion, which makes it impossible for buses and taxis to operate efficiently, especially during the rush hours. There are *Lagos State Corporation* buses, two private bus companies and several thousand private minibuses. Taxis in Lagos are yellow and fares and tip should be agreed in advance. A ferry service runs to Lagos Island.

ACCOMMODATION

HOTELS: There are first-class hotels in Lagos and in the major towns, but they are heavily booked and advance reservation is essential. Lagos is one of the most congested cities in Africa, and the majority of good hotels are on Lagos Island. Hotels are generally very expensive, but there is a variety of alternative accommodation.
OTHER ACCOMMODATION: Government-run **Catering Resthouses** are scattered throughout the country and offer accommodation in colonial-style resthouses. In many towns, **Christian missions** are able to offer good basic accommodation at a reasonable price. The universities have **guest-houses** for visiting academics, but may be able to accommodate other visitors. Most of the big towns have **sporting clubs** which offer cheap accommodation and eating facilities, and can be used by visitors who take temporary membership. Port Harcourt is the centre of the national oil industry and offers a large selection of accommodation to the industry, which is also available to tourists.

RESORTS & EXCURSIONS

Nigeria is the most populated and prosperous of the West African nations; if the Sahel countries are excluded, it is also by far the largest. For the purposes of this section (which only covers major tourist destinations), it has been divided into regions which do not necessarily reflect cultural or administrative boundaries.

The Southwest

Lagos is a busy and overcrowded city and reputed to be the most expensive city in the world. Its commercial and administrative centre is on Lagos Island at the heart of the city, linked to the mainland by two road bridges. **Ikoyi** and **Victoria** islands are also connected to **Lagos Island**, and both have wealthy residential areas and beautiful gardens. The *National Museum* at **Onikan** on Lagos Island houses numerous exhibits of Nigeria's ancient civilisations and has a craft centre which sells examples of Nigerian craft at fixed prices. In the Jankara market on Lagos Island one can bargain for locally dyed cotton and handwoven cloth, herbs and leather goods.
Ibadan is famous for its university and its market (one of the biggest in Nigeria). It is a convenient base for trips to the other, more traditional, old towns of the Western State.
The large, traditional town of **Oyo** has some old Portuguese-style houses and is the site of the capital of the old Yoruba empire.
Oshogbo is the founding centre of the internationally renowned school of Oshogbo art and home of the shrine and grove of Oshun, the Yoruba goddess of fertility. The famous *Oshun shrine* is to be found here. The *Oshun Festival* takes place towards the end of August each year.
Ile-Ife, the ancient name of the town of **Ife**, is the cradle of Yoruba culture, and includes the *Ife Museum*, which has many fine bronze and terracotta sculptures dating back to the 13th century. The university here is a centre for Batik-dying.
Akure is a good base from which to explore the seven *Olumirin Waterfalls*.

The Mouth of the Niger

Modern **Benin City** is a rapidly developing metropolis, but there are a few reminders of its long Yoruba history. The old city's moat and wall survive in places and the *National Museum* houses an interesting collection of Benin royal art. The *Oba's Palace* is worth a visit, although permission needs to be obtained in Lagos.
Many of the villages in **Cross River State** are of interest for their handicrafts and traditions of magic, but may only be accessible by foot or canoe. *Sapoba, Abaraka, Sapele, Warri* and *Auchi*, however, can be reached by road.
Calabar is a pleasant town in a beautiful setting, high on a hill above the *Calabar River*. **Ikot Ekepne** is the centre for beautiful baskets and carvings, and at **Oron** there is a museum renowned for its exhibits of Ibibio and Efik carvings. **Ikom,** on the road to Cameroon, has curious carved monoliths set in circles.
Port Harcourt has long been an important merchant port and is today the centre of Nigeria's oil industry.

The North

Kaduna is a government town laid out by the British and has fine buildings and modern amenities. The ancient walled city of **Zaria** to the north retains much of its old character and has a fine mosque and *Emir's Palace*.
Outside **Katsina,** on the border with Niger, are some old Hausa burial mounds and the city is the site of spectacular Sallah festivals (see below under *Special Events*).
Kano was the largest of the ancient Hausa cities and is today Nigeria's third largest city. The walled old town still remains and gives the city a medieval atmosphere, although the city was founded at least 1000 years ago, being of strategic importance on the trans-Saharan trade routes. *Kurmi Market* has many tourist souvenirs, including the richly embroidered Fulani horse blankets and decorations used at festivals. The famous dye pits *(Kofar Mata)*, still in use and apparently some of the oldest in Africa, are well worth a visit, as is the *Grand Mosque*. The *Emir's Palace* is an outstanding example of Hausa architecture. The city has many colonial-style sporting clubs and good restaurants and nightlife.
Jos is a favourite holiday centre on account of its situation (1200m/3900ft above sea level) and pleasant climate. The *Jos Museum* has a large collection of pottery from all over the country, and the nearby *Museum of Traditional Nigerian Architecture* holds a collection of full-size replicas representing different styles of Nigerian architecture, including *Katsina Palace, Zaria Mosque* and the *Kano Wall*. There is also a small zoo and easy access to such sights as the *Assob Falls*.
At **Maiduguri,** the Sallah festival is held three months after the festival of Eid al-Fitr, during which Borno horsemen demonstrate their equestrian prowess. The town also has a palace, park, zoo and museum.
The area around *Lake Chad* is flat and prone to flooding during and after the rains. The whole region is of special interest to the ornithologist and nature lover. In contrast, some of the most striking and fascinating mountain

NIGERIA	HEALTH REGULATIONS	VISA REGULATIONS Code-Link
GALILEO/WORLDSPAN	 TI-DFT/LOS/HE	 TI-DFT/LOS/VI
SABRE	 TIDFT/LOS/HE	TIDFT/LOS/VI

To access this information on your CRS, swipe the barcode with a light pen or type in the text under the barcode. For more information, see the introduction *How to Use This Book*.

scenery can be enjoyed around **Biu** and towards the Cameroon border.

Abuja, the new federal capital (set up in December 1991), is as yet undeveloped for tourism. It has a beautiful setting which gives magnificent views across the savannah.

SOCIAL PROFILE

FOOD & DRINK: There are restaurants of all varieties in Lagos and the major towns. European and Oriental food is readily available. Although there are self-service cafés, mainly in department stores, most restaurants have table service. Nigerian food is typical of that found throughout West Africa, and meals will often include yam, sweet potatoes, plantain and pepper soup, with regional variations. In the north, meat is more popular than in other areas; specialities are *suya* (barbecued liver and beef on sticks) and *kilishi* (spiced dried meat), in the east *egussi soup* (stew of meat, dried fish and melon seeds), and in the south goat meat and bush meat, particularly antelope, which is considered a delicacy. **Drink:** There are many brands of locally brewed and bottled beer which are very good. Spirits are expensive. Larger hotels and clubs have bars and cocktail lounges.

NIGHTLIFE: There are nightclubs in many of the hotels in Lagos and in the Surulere district. Some clubs have live entertainment, details of which are given in the local newspapers. North of Oyo in Ogbomoshe there is a lively market, particularly in the evenings. Local festivals which generally take place in the summer months provide a good opportunity to see dancing, music and traditional costumes.

SHOPPING: Markets are the most interesting places to shop. Special purchases include *adure* (patterned, indigo-dyed cloth), batiks and pottery from the southwest, leatherwork and *kaduna* cotton from the north and carvings from the east. Designs vary greatly, many towns having their own distinctive design style. Other purchases include herbs, beadwork, basketry and ceremonial masks such as those of the Ekpo. **Shopping hours:** 0800-1700 Monday to Friday; 0800-1630 Saturday.

SPORT: Swimming: The numerous beaches offer bathing, although many have strong currents and bathers should not swim far from the shore, especially in Lagos. Many of the better hotels have pools. **Tennis/squash:** Various clubs in major towns have courts where visitors are welcome to apply for temporary membership. **Golf:** Courses are attached to local sports and social clubs in many of the larger towns. **Fishing:** Good river and sea angling is available throughout the country.

SPECIAL EVENTS: In the predominantly Muslim north the most important festival is *Sallah*, celebrated three months after the feast of Eid al-Fitr, particularly in the towns of Katsina, Kano and Zaria. Every family is required to slaughter a ram and festivities last for several days, with horseback processions, musicians and dancers. Featured also in northern communities are *Durbars*, long lines of horsemen led by a band, the horses in quilted armour with the riders wearing quilted coats and wielding ceremonial swords. In the south there are masquerades and festivals marking events in local religions. At Oshogbo, the *Oshuna* festival is held at the end of the rainy season (August to September), attracting thousands of childless women who seek the help of the Yoruba goddess of fertility. Festivals in the western states include masquerades in June, the *Oro* festival in July and the *Shango* Festival in August. Other festivals are held in February, July and August in the northern town of Ogbomosho.

SOCIAL CONVENTIONS: Shaking hands with everyone is customary on meeting and departing. In Yorubaland it is a sign of respect to curtsy when introduced, and to enquire after relations, even if this is a first meeting. Unless the visitor knows someone well it is unusual to be invited to a Nigerian's home. Most entertaining, particularly in Lagos, takes place in clubs or restaurants and social customs are British oriented. A small gift of appreciation is always welcome and business souvenirs bearing the company logo are also acceptable. Casual wear is suitable and a lightweight suit and tie are only necessary for businessmen on formal meetings; on most other occasions men will not need to wear a jacket, athough a tie might be expected. Women should dress modestly, and respect local customs regarding dress, particularly in the Muslim north. It is inadvisable for women to wear trousers. There are over 250 tribes in Nigeria, the principal groups being the Hausa in the north, the Ibo in the southeast and the Yoruba in the southwest. The larger of the minor groups are the Fulani, Tiv, Kanuri, Igala, Idoma, Igbirra and Nupe in the north, the Ibibio, Efik, Ekoi and Ijaw in the east and the Edo, Urhobo, Itsekiri and Ijaw in the west. A result of this ethnic variety is the diversity of art, dance forms, language, music, customs and crafts. Nigerians have a very strong sense of ethnic allegiance. **Tipping:** Unless a service charge has been included, 10% is expected for most services. Note that for taxi drivers the fare including a tip should be agreed before the journey. Airport porters should be tipped per case.

BUSINESS PROFILE

ECONOMY: The economy is heavily dependent on oil, which accounts for over 90% of the foreign exchange revenues, and although Nigeria is a member of the OPEC cartel, its earnings are still vulnerable to fluctuations on the world market. The low world price since 1986 cut Nigeria's foreign earnings by a considerable margin. The country also has vast untapped reserves of natural gas and coal. Agriculture still occupies well over half of the population, but there is a steady drift of labour towards the towns. Government policy is concerned with reducing the reliance on oil, increasing agricultural yields, which have suffered from drought and under-investment, and increasing the standard of living of the rural population. Nevertheless, successive governments have not succeeded in restoring Nigeria's one-time self-sufficiency in food. Exports of cash crops, mostly groundnuts, cocoa and palm oil, have remained steady but are now completely overshadowed as export earners by oil. Nigeria has some minerals other than oil and gas, including tin, coal, iron ore, zinc and some uranium. The oil boom is now coming to an end, however, and Nigeria needs to diversify and boost other parts of its economy. Most major manufacturing industries have been established, but all have suffered from the world recession during the 1980s and some from a lack of spare parts caused by the shortage of foreign exchange. Nigeria now faces something of a fiscal crisis and urgently needs to reschedule its foreign debt and cut its budget deficit. A stand-by agreement with the IMF has proved elusive during 1992 because of the military government's refusal to increase prices of essential goods. Britain is the largest single exporter to the country. Germany, France, the USA and increasingly, Brazil, are other principal sources of imports. The bulk of Nigeria's exports are sold to the USA, Germany, France, Italy and Brazil.

BUSINESS: English is spoken in business circles. It is common for business meetings to take place without a prior appointment, although these should be made for government visits. Business deals will often progress at a slower pace than is common in Europe. **Office hours:** 0730-1530 Monday to Friday.

COMMERCIAL INFORMATION: The following organisation can offer advice: The Nigerian Association of Chambers of Commerce, Industry, Mines and Agriculture, Private Mail Bag 12816, 15a Ikorodu Road, Maryland, Lagos. Tel: (1) 964 737. Telex: 21368.

HISTORY & GOVERNMENT

HISTORY: The states of Kanem and Borno (which flourished from about AD10) on the shores of Lake Chad were the first imperial states in the region; their wealth was founded on control of trans-Saharan trade routes. From the 11th to 14th centuries the Islamic Hausa city states were also a dominant influence, whilst in the southwest the Yoruba cities of Ife, Oyo and Benin became major trading centres. In the 15th century the Portuguese began trading – first for spices, later for slaves. The Portuguese were later supplanted by other European trading nations. The slave trade had severe effects on the balance of power in the region and there was continuing internal instability accompanied, in the 18th century, by an expansion of the Islamic faith, which had previously been confined to the north. At the same time, Christian missionaries were coming into the area. During the 19th-20th centuries, the British conquered the territory of present-day Nigeria. In 1947, in order to reduce burgeoning tribal and religious tensions, a federal system of government was established with new administrative district divisions. With the introduction of ministerial government in 1951, a Muslim northerner, Alhaji Albubakar Tafawa Balewa, became the first Prime Minister. Independence from Britain was achieved in 1960 when, because of tribal and religious differences in Nigeria, the first government was a coalition – comprising members of the Northern People's Congress and the eastern-based National Council for Nigeria and the Cameroons. Since then the country has endured several, often violent, changes of government. The biggest single threat to the integrity of the country was during the 1967-70 civil war between Nigeria and the breakaway 'Republic' of Biafra: the secessionists were defeated. The current ruler, General Ibrahim Babangida, came to power in 1985 after the overthrow of the previous military regime of General Buhari. Elections planned for 1988 failed to materialise. In April 1990 the Government was shaken by an attempted coup by junior army officers although Babangida – an experienced coup plotter himself – was able to thwart the rebellion. Nonetheless, inter-communal tension persists and there have been several outbreaks of rioting in recent years. Babangida seems set on pursuing the course he has set for the country which will return it to democratic civilian government after the presidential elections, originally scheduled for October 1992, then December 1992, but now delayed until early 1993. The military regime has allowed the creation of just two political parties: the National Republican Convention (NRC), described by a spokesman for the Armed Forces Ruling Council as 'slightly right-of-centre', and the Social Democratic Party (SDP) which is 'a little to the left'. The NRC draws most of its support from the Muslim north while the SDP has the backing of most Ibo and Yoruba people in the southeast and west and of some dissident northerners. These two parties fought national assembly elections in July although the assembly will not start work until after the oft-postponed presidential elections. The SDP won 305 of the 593 seats in the House of Representatives and 44 seats in the Senate, just short of a majority. The real question is whether or not the new political system can inspire Nigeria's rather tired institutions and quell the restless population.

GOVERNMENT: Nigeria is currently ruled by a military government. Under the planned transition to democracy, a two-party system has been set up. Elections to the bicameral National Assembly were held in July 1992, but elections for the executive presidency have yet to be held (see above).

CLIMATE

Varies from area to area. The southern coast is hot and humid with a rainy season from March to November. During the dry season, the *Harmattan* wind blows from the Sahara. The north's rainy season is from April to September. Nights can be cold in December and January. **Required clothing:** Lightweight cottons and linens are worn, with a warm wrap advisable in the north. Rainwear is essential during the rainy season.

KANO Nigeria (470m)

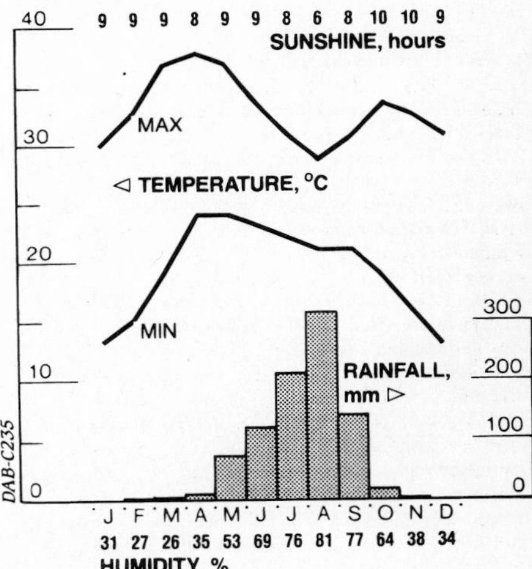

LAGOS Nigeria (3m)

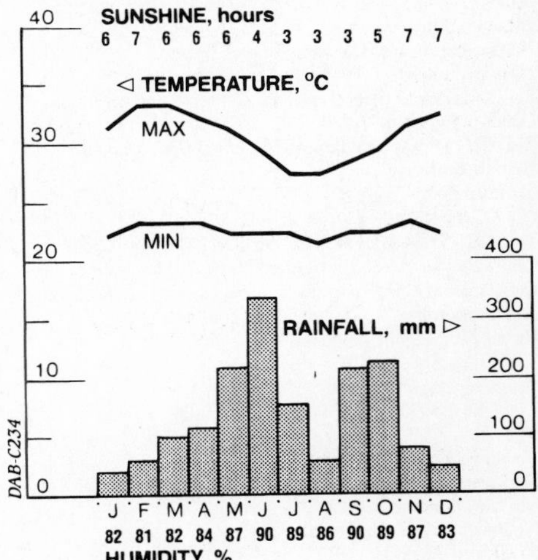

Location: Northern Europe, Scandinavia.

NORTRA (Norwegian Tourist Board)
Head Office
PO Box 499 Sentrum
0105 Oslo 1, Norway
Tel: (22) 42 70 44. Fax: (22) 33 69 98. Telex: 78582.
Royal Norwegian Embassy
25 Belgrave Square
London SW1X 8QD
Tel: (071) 235 7151. Fax: (071) 245 6993. Telex: 22321.
Opening hours: 0900-1600 Monday to Friday.
Royal Norwegian Consulate
86 George Street
Edinburgh EH2 3BU
Tel: (031) 226 5701. Fax: (031) 220 4976. Opening hours: 0900-1600 Monday to Friday.
Royal Norwegian Consulate
2 Collingwood Street
Newcastle-upon-Tyne NE1 1JH
Tel: (091) 232 6358. Fax: (091) 261 4761. Opening hours: 0930-1400 Monday to Friday.
Norwegian Tourist Board
Charles House
5 Lower Regent Street
London SW1Y 4LR
Tel: (071) 839 6255. Fax: (071) 839 6014. Opening hours: 0900-1300 and 1400-1630 Monday to Friday for general enquiries.
Norwegian State Railways Travel Bureau
Norway House
21-24 Cockspur Street
London SW1Y 5DA
Tel: (071) 930 6666. Fax: (071) 321 0624. Telex: 28380.
British Embassy
Thomas Heftyesgate 8
0244 Oslo 2, Norway
Tel: (22) 55 24 00. Fax: (22) 55 10 41. Telex: 71575.
Consulates in: Ålesund, Bergen, Harstad, Haugesund, Kristiansund (N), Kristiansund (S), Stavanger, Tromsø and Trondheim.
Royal Norwegian Embassy
2720 34th Street, NW
Washington, DC 20008
Tel: (202) 333 6000. Fax: (202) 337 0870. Telex: 892374.
Consulate Generals in: Houston, Los Angeles, Minneapolis, Miami, New York (tel: (212) 421 7333) and San Francisco.
Norwegian Tourist Board
655 Third Avenue
New York, NY
10017
Tel: (212) 949 2333. Fax: (212) 983 5260. Telex: 620681.
Embassy of the United States of America
Drammensvn 18
0255 Oslo 2, Norway
Tel: (22) 44 85 50.
Royal Norwegian Embassy
Suite 532, Royal Bank Centre
90 Sparks Street
Ottawa, Ontario
K1P 5B4
Tel: (613) 238 6571. Fax: (613) 238 2765.
Canadian Embassy
Oscar's Gate 20
0244 Oslo
Norway
Tel: (22) 46 69 55/9. Fax: (22) 69 34 67. Telex: 71880.

AREA: 323,877 sq km (125,050 sq miles).
POPULATION: 4,249,817 (1991 estimate)
POPULATION DENSITY: 13.1 per sq km.
CAPITAL: Oslo. **Population:** 461,127 (1991).
GEOGRAPHY: Norway is bordered to the north by the Arctic Ocean, to the east by the CIS, Finland and Sweden, to the south by the Skagerrak (which separates it from Denmark) and to the west by the North Sea. The coastline is 2735km (1700 miles) long, its most outstanding feature being the fjords. Most of them are between 80-160km long (50-100 miles), and are often very deep and surrounded by towering mountains. Much of northern Norway lies beyond the Arctic Circle and the landscape is stark. In the south the landscape consists of forests with many lakes and rivers.
LANGUAGE: Norwegian (Bokmål and Nynorsk). Lappish is spoken by the Sami population in the north. English is widely spoken.
RELIGION: 92% Evangelical Lutherans; other Christian denominations.
TIME: GMT + 1 (GMT + 2 in summer).
ELECTRICITY: 220 volts AC, 50Hz. Plugs are of the Continental round 2-pin type.
COMMUNICATIONS: Telephone: IDD is available. Country code: 47. **Fax:** This service is available at major hotels. **Telex/telegram:** *Televerket's* headquarters are at Teledirektor-atet, Universitetsgt 2. It is easiest to send telegrams by telephone or telex. The telephone directories give instructions in English on page 16. **Post:** Hotel receptions, shops and kiosks selling postcards will sell stamps. Airmail within Europe takes two to four days. There are *Poste Restante* facilities at post offices in all major cities. Post offices are open from 0900-1700 Monday to Friday and 0900-1300 Saturday. **Press:** The national newspapers published in Oslo are *Aftenposten, Verdens Gang, Arbeiderbladet* and *Dagbladet*. There are no English-language newspapers.
BBC World Service and Voice of America frequencies: From time to time these change. See the section *How to Use this Book* for more information.

BBC:

MHz	12.10	9.410	6.195	3.955

A service is also available on 648kHz/463m and 198kHz/1515m (0100-0500 GMT).

Voice of America:

MHz	11.97	9.670	6.040	5.995

PASSPORT/VISA

Regulations and requirements may be subject to change at short notice, and you are advised to contact the appropriate diplomatic or consular authority before finalising travel arrangements. Details of these may be found at the head of this country's entry. Any numbers in the chart refer to the footnotes below.

	Passport Required?	Visa Required?	Return Ticket Required?
Full British	1	No	No
BVP	Valid	-	-
Australian	Yes	No	No
Canadian	Yes	No	No
USA	Yes	No	No
Other EC	1	No	No
Japanese	Yes	No	No

PASSPORTS: Valid passport required by all except:
(a) [1] nationals of Belgium, Denmark, France, Germany, Italy, Luxembourg and The Netherlands if holding a national identity card, and of the UK if holding a British Visitors Passport;
(b) nationals of Austria, Finland, Iceland, Liechtenstein, Sweden and Switzerland if holding a national identity card.
Note: Passports must be valid for at least 2 months beyond the intended period of stay.
British Visitors Passport: BVPs are valid for holidays or unpaid business trips of up to 3 months. The sum duration of such visits to Denmark, Finland, Iceland, Norway and Sweden must add up to less than 3 months in any 9-month period.
VISAS: Required by all except:
(a) nationals of the countries referred to in the chart above and those exempted under *Passports*;
(b) nationals of Algeria, Andorra, Argentina, Bahamas, Barbados, Belize, Bolivia, Bosnia-Hercegovina, Botswana, Brazil, Brunei, Colombia, Costa Rica, Côte d'Ivoire, Croatia, Cuba, Cyprus, Czechoslovakia, Dominica, Dominican Republic, Ecuador, El Salvador, Fiji, Gambia, Grenada, Guatemala, Guyana, Haiti, Honduras, Hungary, Israel, Jamaica, Kenya, Kiribati, South Korea, Lesotho, Macau, Malawi, Malaysia, Malta, Mauritius, Mexico, Monaco, Namibia, New Zealand, Nicaragua, Niger, Panama, Paraguay, Peru, Poland, San Marino, Seychelles, Sierra Leone, Singapore, Slovenia, Solomon Islands, Suriname, Swaziland, Tanzania, Thailand, Togo, Trinidad & Tobago, Tuvalu, Uganda, Uruguay, Vatican City, Venezuela, Yugoslavia, Zambia and Zimbabwe.
Types of visa: Tourist/Entry visas: £14.
Validity: Up to 3 months. For renewal or extension apply to Embassy.
Application to: Consulate (or Consular Section at Embassy) from 1000-1230 Monday to Friday. For addresses, see top of entry.
Application requirements: (a) Valid passport. (b) 2 application forms. (c) 2 photos.
Working days required: 3 to 6 weeks, by post or in person.
Temporary residence: Apply to Embassy for residence and work permit if the stay exceeds 3 months.

MONEY

Currency: Norwegian Krone (NKr) = 100 øre. Notes are in denominations of NKr1000, 500, 100 and 50. Coins are in denominations of NKr10, 5 and 1, and 50 and 10 øre.
Currency exchange: *Eurocheque* cards allow encashment of personal cheques.
Credit cards: Access/Mastercard, American Express, Diners Club and Visa are accepted. Check with your credit card company for details of merchant acceptability and other services which may be available.
Travellers cheques: Accepted in banks, hotels, shops and by airlines.
Exchange rate indicators: The following figures are included as a guide to the movements of the Krone against Sterling and the US Dollar:

Date:	Oct '89	Oct '90	Oct '91	Oct '92
£1.00=	11.03	11.52	11.41	9.97
$1.00=	6.99	5.90	6.57	6.28

Currency restrictions: No restrictions on import of local currency. Free import of foreign currency, subject to declaration. The export of local currency is limited to NKr25,000. Export of foreign currency is limited to the amount declared on import.
Banking hours: 0900-1700 (or 0815-1700) Monday to Thursday in major cities and 0900-1530 Friday.

DUTY FREE

The following items can be imported into Norway without incurring customs duty by:
(a) Residents of European countries:
200 cigarettes or 250g of tobacco products and 200 leaves of cigarette paper (arrivals over 16 years of age only);
1 litre of spirits and 1 litre of wine or 2 litres of wine and 2 litres of beer (arrivals over 20 years of age only);
Small amount of perfume for personal use;
Other goods to the value of NKr1200.
(b) Residents of non-European countries:
400 cigarettes or 500g of tobacco products and 200 leaves of cigarette papers (arrivals over 16 years of age only);
1 litre of spirits and 1 litre of wine or 2 litres of wine and 2 litres of beer (arrivals over 20 years of age only);
50g of perfume and 500ml of eau de cologne;
Other goods to the value of NKr1200.
Prohibited items: Spirits over 60% volume (120° proof) and wine over 22% volume, certain foodstuffs (including eggs, potatoes, meat, meat products, dairy products and poultry), mammals, birds, exotic animals, narcotics and firearms, ammunitions and explosives.

PUBLIC HOLIDAYS

Public holidays observed in Norway are as follows:
Apr 8 '93 Maundy Thursday. **Apr 9** Good Friday. **Apr 12** Easter Monday. **May 1** May Day. **May 17** National Independence Day. **May 20** Ascension Day. **May 31** Whit Monday. **Dec 25-26** Christmas. **Jan 1 '94** New Year's Day.

HEALTH

Regulations and requirements may be subject to change at short notice, and you are advised to contact your doctor well in advance of your intended date of departure. Any numbers in the chart refer to the footnotes below.

	Special Precautions?	Certificate Required?
Yellow Fever	No	No
Cholera	No	No
Typhoid & Polio	No	-
Malaria	No	-
Food & Drink	No	-

Rabies is only present on the islands of Svalbard.
Health care: There are Reciprocal Health Agreements with most European countries. That with the UK allows free hospital in-patient treatment and ambulance travel on presentation of a UK passport. The cost of other treatment (including tooth extractions) may be partially refunded under the Norwegian social insurance scheme. Before leaving Norway, receipts should be presented at the social insurance office ('Trygdekasse') of the district where treatment was carried out. Chemists are called 'Apotek'. Standards of health care are high.

TRAVEL - International

AIR: Norwegian air travel is served by *Wideroe Norsk Air, Norway Airlines, Braathens SAFE* and *Scandinavian Airlines System (SAS)*, a Scandinavian airline. *British Airways* and *Air UK* also operate services to Norway.
Approximate flight times: From *London* to Oslo is 1 hour 45 minutes, to Bergen is 1 hour 40 minutes and to Stavanger is 1 hour 30 minutes.
From *New York* to Oslo is 10 hours 45 minutes (including stopover in London).
International airports: *Oslo (OSL)* (Fornebu) is 8km (5 miles) from the city (travel time – 25 minutes). A coach goes to the city every 20 minutes 0750-2230. Bus no 31 goes every 30 minutes 0338-0008. Taxis are available to the city. There is a surcharge after 2200. Airport facilities include banks/bureaux de change (0630-2000), duty-free shops (0600-2200), bar (1300-2200), restaurant (1230-2000), snack bar (0630-2100), chemist (open 0630-2100), various shops (0630-2200), left luggage (0600-2330), post office (0700-1730 Monday to Thursday, 0700-1830 Friday and 0830-1330 Saturday) and car rental *(Avis, Budget, Hertz* and *Tradecar)*.
Stavanger (SVG) (Sola) is 14.5km (9 miles) southwest of the city (travel time – 20 minutes). There is a coach to the Royal Atlantic Hotel, Jembaneveien 1. Bus no 40 goes every 20 minutes 0620-2400 for a fare of approximately NKr19 (travel time – 30 minutes). Taxi services are available to the city with a surcharge after 2200 (travel time – 15 minutes). Airport facilities include duty-free shops, bar (1200-2000 Monday to Friday), restaurant (1000-2000, 1000-1700 Saturday), snack bar (0615-2100 Monday to Saturday, 0800-2200 Sunday), many shops, 24-hour tourist information, post office (0830-1600 Monday to Friday, 0830-1200 Saturday), banks/bureaux de change (0745-1730 Monday to Friday, 0745-1630 Saturday and 1100-1630 Sunday), left luggage (0800-2200), 24-hour lockers and car hire *(Avis, Budget, Hertz* and *InterRent/Europcar)*.
Bergen (BGO) (Flesland) is 19km (12 miles) southwest of the city (travel time – 30 minutes). There is a coach to the city which returns from Flyterminalen Bus Station 60 minutes before flight departure. Bus (Flyplassen) service goes every 60 minutes 0645-2130. Return from Flyterminalen. Taxi services are available to the city for a fare of approximately NKr170 with a surcharge after 2200 (travel time – 25 minutes). Airport facilities include left luggage (0730-2400), lockers (0600-2400), banks (0730-1530 and until 1730 in summer), bureaux de change, post office (0830-1630 Monday to Friday, 0900-1300 Saturday), duty-free shops, bar (1200-2200 Monday to Friday), cafes, shops, tourist information

(0900-1800 Monday to Friday, 1100-1800 Saturday to Sunday), nursery (0600-2400) and car rental *(Avis, Budget, Hertz, InterRent, Europcar* and *Thrifty)*.
SEA: The main passenger ports are Oslo, Narvik, Stavanger, Kristiansund and Bergen. The main sea routes from the UK, operated by the *Color Line*, are from Newcastle to Bergen (travel time – 18 hours 30 minutes) and to Stavanger (travel time – 22 hours).
RAIL: Connections from London are via Dover/Ostend (via The Netherlands, Germany, Denmark and Sweden) or Harwich/Hook of Holland. There are two principal routes to Sweden, with daytime and overnight trains from Malmö and Stockholm.
Cheap fares: Reduced fares on rail services have vastly increased the use and range of internal services. *Nordturist* tickets, also known as *Scanrail* cards, allow 21 days' unlimited travel in Denmark, Sweden, Norway and Finland on railways and selected ferries, and a 50% reduction on other ferry services. *Inter-Rail* tickets are valid in Norway.
ROAD: The only routes are from Sweden or Finland in the far north. Camping trailers up to 2.3m (7ft 6 inches) wide, with number plates, are permitted on holiday visits.

TRAVEL - Internal

AIR: Domestic flights are run by *Scandinavian Airlines (SAS), Braathen's SAFE (BU)* and *Widerøes Air Transport Company (WF)*. Fifty airports with scheduled services exist in the fjord country of western Norway and along the remaining coast. Charter sea or land planes are available at most destinations. There is an internal service from Oslo to all towns and cities via *SAS* and *BU*. Coastal links are by *WF, SAS* and *BU*. Reduced airfare tickets are available for families, children under 12 years (who pay half price), groups and pensioners. For further information, contact Wideroe Flyveselskap A/S, Box 82, Lilleaker, N-0216 Oslo. Tel: (22) 73 66 00. Fax: (22) 73 65 90.
SEA: All coastal towns are served by ferries, catamarans and hydrofoils. The Hurtigrute (express) from Bergen to Kirkenes (near the Russian border) takes about 11 days round trip, leaving daily and stopping at 35 ports on the west coast. Various ferry trips are available (half price in spring and autumn). It is possible to embark at Trondheim, Bodø or Tromsø.
RAIL: All services are run by *NSR Travel* (Norwegian State Railways). The main internal rail routes are: Oslo–Trondheim *(Dovre Line)*; Trondheim–Bodø *(Nordland Railway)*; Oslo–Bergen *(Bergen Railway)*; Oslo–Stavanger *(Sorland Railway)*. There are also services to Charlottenburg (Stockholm) and Halden (Malmö) on routes to Sweden. Seats on express trains must be reserved. There are buffet/restaurant cars on some trains, and sleepers on long-distance overnight services. Heavy luggage may be sent in advance. The *ScanRail Pass*, valid for all of Scandinavia, offers a substantial reduction (for further information contact Norwegian State Railways, address above).

ROAD: The road system is of variable quality (especially under freezing winter conditions in the north), but supplemented by numerous car ferries across the fjords. **Bus:** Principal long-distance internal bus routes are from Bo (in Telemark) to Haugesund (8 hours); from Ålesund–Molde–Kristiansund to Trondheim (8 hours); from Fauske to Kirkenes (4 days) and links with Bo line in the north. Inter-Nordic runs from Trondheim to Stockholm. There are also extensive regional local bus services, some of which are operated by companies with interests in the ferries. The official 'Rutehefte' is a must for anyone using public transport, and gives extensive timetable information and maps of all bus, train, ferry and air routes. For further information on bus travel and bookings within Norway, contact NOR-WAY Bussekspress, Karl Johansgt. 2, N-0154 Oslo. Tel: (22) 33 08 62. Fax: (22) 42 50 33. **Taxi:** In most cases fares are metered. Taxis can be found at ranks or booked by telephone. **Car hire:** Available in airports and most towns, but costly; in general, problems of cost and parking make public transport more practical and convenient. It is also possible to hire bicycles. **Regulations:** The minimum age for driving is 18. There are severe penalties for drunken driving and illegal parking. Safety belts are compulsory. Children under 12 must travel in the back of the car. *It is obligatory for all vehicles to drive with dipped headlights at all times*, even on the brightest summer day. This includes motorcycles and mopeds. Carrying spare headlight bulbs is recommended. Speed limits are 80-90kmph (49-56mph) outside built-up areas, and 50kmph (31mph) in built-up areas. Snow chains or studded winter tyres are advised during the winter. Petrol stations are numerous, although tourists are only able to purchase petrol with credit cards in some of them. The contact for AIT (Alliance Internationale de Tourisme) is the Norwegian Automobile Association (NAF), Storgt. 2, N-1055 Oslo 2. Tel: (22) 34 14 00. **Documentation:** International Driving Permit or national driving licence and log book are required. A Green Card is strongly recommended (for those with more than Third Party cover on their domestic policy). Without it, visitors with motor insurance in their own countries are allowed the minimum legal cover in Norway; the Green Card tops this up to the level of cover provided by the visitor's own policy.
URBAN: Good public transport systems operate in the main towns. Oslo has bus, rail, metro and tramway services. Tickets are pre-purchased and self-cancelled, and there is one hour's free transfer between any of the modes. Meters on taxis are obligatory.
JOURNEY TIMES: The following chart gives approximate journey times (in hours and minutes) from Oslo to other major cities/towns in Norway.

	Air	Road	Rail
Bergen	0.35	9.00	8.00
Kristiansund	0.30	5.00	5.00
Lillehammer	0.20	3.00	2.30
Stavanger	0.35	7.00	8.00
Tromsø	1.40	20.00	-
Trondheim	0.40	10.00	9.00

ACCOMMODATION

HOTELS: First-class hotels are to be found all over the country. Facilities in all establishments are classified, as hotels must come up to official high standards; for example, there must be a reception service, dining room, and a minimum of 30 rooms, each with full bath or shower. Many hotels are still family-run establishments. Full *en pension* terms are available to guests staying at the same establishment for at least three to five days. Hotels usually allow a reduction on the same *en pension* rate for children according to age. This reduction may only apply when the child concerned occupies an extra bed in the parents' room. There are several schemes which offer visitors reduced rates in selected hotels. A **Fjord Pass** (which covers two adults with special concessions for children under 15) is accepted by 300 hotels in the period May 1 to September 30; reductions of 20% or more are

NORWAY	**HEALTH REGULATIONS**	**VISA REGULATIONS**
GALILEO/WORLDSPAN	 TI-DFT/OSL/HE	 TI-DFT/OSL/VI
SABRE	 TIDFT/OSL/HE	 TIDFT/OSL/VI

Code-Link

To access this information on your CRS, swipe the barcode with a light pen or type in the text under the barcode. For more information, see the introduction *How to Use This Book*.

possible. The **Nordic Passepartout** is a pan-Scandinavian card accepted by over 50 hotels in Norway in the main summer period and at weekends; the visitor's fifth night is free. A **Scandinavian Bonus Pass** (which covers two adults with special concessions for children under 16) is accepted by 45 hotels in Norway between May 15-September 1 and at weekends during winter; a **Scanrail** railway pass will also be accepted. **Scandinavian Hotel Express** is a travel club which enables visitors to have reductions of 50% in certain hotels. Roughly 50% of establishments belong to the Norwegian Hotel & Restaurant Association, Karl Johansgate 21, N-0159 Oslo 1. Tel: (22) 42 36 50. Fax: (22) 33 66 75. **Grading:** There is no grading system, but hotels designated *turisthotel* or *høyfjellshotell* must meet specified standards.

GUEST-HOUSES & MOUNTAIN LODGES: Guest-houses *(pensjonat)* and Mountain Lodges are generally smaller in size and offer less elaborate facilities than hotels, although many establishments can offer the same standard as those officially listed as hotels.

FARMHOUSE HOLIDAYS: Farms selected are working farms and anyone who wants to can join in the work, but guests are at liberty to plan their own day, and the hosts will generally be able to suggest tours, excursions and other activities. Contact the tourist office for further information. The tour operator Troll Park offers many farmhouse holidays and a programme printed in Norwegian, German and English is available from Troll Park A/S, Postboks 445, N-2601 Lillehammer. Tel: (61) 26 92 00. Fax: (61) 26 92 50.

SELF-CATERING: Chalets, log cabins and apartments are available for rent by groups and will generally work out less expensive per head than other kinds of holiday. Most chalets have electric lighting, heating and hot plates; some have kerosene lamps, calor gas for cooking and wood fires, while water will often have to be fetched from a nearby well or stream. Chalets are grouped near a central building which may contain such facilities as a cafeteria, lounges, TV rooms, sauna, a grocer's shop, and in some cases a swimming pool. All chalets and apartments are regularly inspected by responsible rental firms. Bookings can be made by writing to various firms. *Den Norske Hytteformidling A/S*, Box 3207 Sagene, N-Oslo 4 (tel: (22) 35 67 10; fax: (22) 71 94 13) organises chalet holidays all over Norway, with full pension or self-catering.

Rorbu holidays: A *Rorbu* is a hut or shelter used by fishermen during the winter cod-fishing season. Equipped with all the necessary facilities, these are leased to holidaymakers during the summer, providing an inexpensive form of accommodation. They will often be actually over the water. Catching your own fish will further reduce the cost of the holiday. For more information on Rorbu holidays, contact Destinasjon Lofoten, Boks 210, N-8301 Svolvaer. Tel: (88) 73000. Fax: (88) 73001.

CAMPING/CARAVANNING: Offsite camping is permitted in uninhabited areas (not lay-bys), but fires are illegal in field or woodland areas between April 15 and September 15. Farmers must be asked for permission for farmland camping. The Tourist Board publishes a list of 'Camp Sites in Norway'. Further details and a manual are available from the Norwegian Automobile Association (NAF), Storgt 2, N-0155 Oslo 2. **Grading:** There are over 1000 authorised sites in Norway, classified according to standards and amenities from **1-** to **5-stars** camps, with charges varying accordingly. Notice of available amenities is posted in each camp.

YOUTH HOSTELS: There are some 100 youth hostels spread all over Norway, some of which are open all year round. Others are in apartment houses attached to schools or universities and are open only during the summer season. Sleeping bags can be hired if necessary. Groups must always make advance bookings. All are welcome, but members of the Norwegian Youth Hostel Association (NUH), or similar associations in other countries, have priority. International membership cards can be bought at most youth hostels. Hostels vary from 1- to 3-star establishments. Breakfast is usually NKr50-60. Detailed information can be obtained from the Tourist Board's Camping/YH list, or direct from *Norske Vandrerhjem*, Dronningensgt 26, N-0154 Oslo 1. Tel: (22) 42 14 10. Fax: (22) 42 44 76.

RESORTS & EXCURSIONS

For the purposes of this section, Norway has been divided into several sections. These do not necessarily reflect cultural or administrative boundaries.

The Oslo Fjord

The region surrounding the 110km- (70-mile) long Oslo Fjord is the most popular in Norway. The coast is fringed with innumerable islands, while the interior is watered by many rivers and dotted with lakes. Here boating and bathing are the main summer attractions. There are many traces of early civilisation: rock carvings, burial mounds, ships' graves, stone churches, manor farms and fortresses.

Oslo, the capital, is Norway's most important industrial, commercial and shipping centre. Of the city's total land area, some 12% has been developed while the remainder is a network of woodland trails, islands and countless lakes offering good fishing and bathing. Oslo is also the focus of national art and culture, with major collections, maritime museums, theatres, opera, concerts and restaurants of every category.

SIGHTSEEING/EXCURSIONS: Oslo: *Akershus Castle; Munch Museum; Holmenkollen* ski jump, museum and restaurant; *Norwegian Folk Museum;* the Viking ships; *Fram Museum; Kon-Tiki Museum; Norwegian Maritime Museum* and sightseeing boat trips on the fjord.

Further afield: The *Tertitten* narrow gauge railway at **Sorumsand**, open-air zoo at **Ski**, 17th-century fortress town and *Kongsten Fortress* at **Fredrikstad**, Vansjo inland waterway system and recreational centre, the *Road of the Ancients* between **Fredrikstad** and **Skjeberg** (Bronze Age rock carvings and Viking burial mounds), the *Naval Museum* at **Horten** and the *Whaling Museum* at **Sandefjord.**

RESORTS: Holmestrand, Horten, Tonsberg, Sandefjord, Larvik, Oslo, Sarpsborg, Fredrikstad and Halden.

The Eastern Valleys

This part of Norway comprises several of the largest and loveliest valleys in the whole country. This is a typical inland region, bordered to the north, west and south by the mighty massifs of the Rondane, Dovrefjell and Jotunheimen ranges and the Hardanger plateau. Further south the country slopes down to the lakes. This area is notable for its stable climate.

Hedmark is a county of extensive forests and has Norway's longest river, the *Glomma*. There are several major tourist resorts in this area, often placed close to recreational facilities and offering varied and up-to-date accommodation. Mountain hikes, riding, glacier rambles, summer ski racing, canoeing and fishing are popular activities and larger resorts offer varied programmes of amusements.

SIGHTSEEING/EXCURSIONS: Paddle steamer trip across *Lake Mjosa; Railway Museum* at **Hamar;** 17th-century *Kongsvinger Castle; Norwegian Forestry Museum* at **Elverum;** boat excursions on *Lake Femund;* north Europe's biggest open-air museum at **Lillehammer;** *Norwegian Historical Vehicles Museum* and glassworks at **Gjovik** and **Jevnaker;** 12th-century stave churches at **Valdres;** summer skiing on *Veslejuvbreen* near **Juvasshytta;** *Blue Dye Works* at **Modum;** *Folk Museum* at **Hallingal;** and the chair lift to *Geilohøgda* at **Geilo.**

RESORTS: Winter & Summer: Geilo, Gjovik, Fagernes, Lillehammer, Otta, Dombas and Tynset. **Summer only:** Rena, Elverum, Hamar, Kongsvinger, Honefoss, Drammen and Kongsberg.

Telemark and the South Coast

This region comprises the coastal strip running from Oslo Fjord round the southern tip of Norway, a region of skerries, bathing beaches, sheltered anchorages, picturesque little harbours and villages. Further inland the country is wooded, intersected here and there by valleys running up to extensive moors and mountain ranges which have marked trails and tourist lodges for those wishing to tour on foot. This area is renowned for its cultural crafts including silverware. The *Telemark Waterway* links **Skien** on the coast with the interior by a system of locks and canals which can be negotiated by boat.

SIGHTSEEING/EXCURSIONS: The *Victoria*, sailing from Skien to **Dalen** through 18 locks and canals; canoeing on lakes and canals; *Lakeland Amusement Park* in **Skien;** *Berg-Kragero Museum* and excursions among the islands at **Kragero;** stave church from 1240 at **Heddal;** *Krosso* cable railway at **Rjukan;** old town at **Arendal;** *Ibsen Museum* at **Grimstad;** silverworks at **Setesdal;** Skerry excursions, *Christiansholm Fortress* and the zoo at **Kristiansund;** *Maritime Museum* at **Mandal;** museum at **Farsund;** and ancient monuments, rock carvings and burial mounds at **Litalandet.**

RESORTS: Winter & Summer: Bykle, Dalen, Hovden and Rjukan.
Summer only: Skien, Porsgrunn, Kragero, Risor, Arendal, Grimstad, Lillesand, Kristiansund, Mandal, Farsund, Flekkefjord and Evje.

STAVANGER

The Western Fjords

The fjord country covers the area from Stavanger in the south to Kristiansund in the north, and from the North Sea in the west to the mountain ranges in the east. Many of the fjords are only 100m (330ft) wide in places, with vertical cliffs rising over 1000m (3300ft) on either side. The longest, Sognefjord, runs for over 200km into the interior. Others include the Ryfylke Fjords, Hardanger Fjord, Sunn Fjord, Nord Fjord, Geiranger Fjord and Romsdal Fjord. In the mountain region of West Norway the glaciers often reach right down to the bottom of the adjacent valley. The whole region offers excellent river and lake fishing, as well as hiking, boat and cycling tours.

SIGHTSEEING/EXCURSIONS: There is a cathedral, an Iron Age farm and boat excursions on the fjord at **Stavanger;** daily fishing trips, an annual cultural festival (May/June), a museum and an aquarium at **Bergen;** a cable car ride to **Fløyfjell** from Bergen town centre; daily excursions to the *Hardanger Fjord* and the *Vøringfoss Falls* at **Mabodalen;** *Borgund Stâve Church* (AD1150) at **Laerdal;** the Flam railway line, dropping 900m (2952ft) in 20km (12 miles); *Sunnmøre Museum* at **Ålesund;** and the *Romsdal Museum* and jazz festival at **Molde.**

RESORTS: Winter & Summer: Voss. **Summer only:** Egersund, Stavanger, Haugesund, Bergen, Sogndal, Floro, Ålesund, Andalsnes, Molde and Kristiansund.

North Norway

In the extreme north of Norway there are majestic mountains, rolling moors, deep fertile valleys, sheltered fjords and thousands of islands. There is also continuous daylight from April to August. Due to the Gulf Stream which sweeps up the coastline, the climate is exceptionally temperate. Fishing, often combined with farming, is still the main source of livelihood. The main attraction in North Norway is the scenery, but there is also very good sea fishing, salmon rivers and thousands of lakes and rivers well stocked with trout.

SIGHTSEEING/EXCURSIONS: *Tromsø Museum, Tromsø Marine Aquarium* and *Polar Museum* in **Tromsø;** North Norway and International Deep-Sea Fishing Festivals (June/July) in **Harstad;** *Tromsø War Museum* in **Bardu;** Rock carvings (2500-4500 years old) in **Blasfjord;** primeval pine forests, cliffs and waterfalls in **Reisadalen;** *Cathedral* and sea fishing excursions in **Bodø;** the *Glom Fjord;* the *Grønnli Grotto* (stalactite cave with a subterranean waterfall); cable car to *Fagernesfjell Bird Colony* at **Røst** and **Vørøy;** Samic collections at **Karasjok;** riverboats to **Sauvtso;** church and Meridian stone at **Hammerfest;** *North Cape* (viewpoint in the extreme north of Norway); and the *King Oscar* and *St George's chapels* at **Kirkenes.**

RESORTS: Winter & Summer: Harstad, Narvik and Svolvaer.
Summer only: Rana, Mosjøen, Bodø, Narvik, Finnsnes, Tromsø, Kautokeino, Karasjok, Alta, Kirkenes, Vadsø, Hammerfest, Vardø and Nordkapp.

Trøndelag

The Trøndelag counties are bordered to the west by the Norwegian Sea and a screen of islands and skerries, past

which the Trondheim Fjord passes into rich farmland and the interior. To the east there are extensive moors dotted with well-stocked lakes, while to the south and southeast the mountain massifs of Trollheimen and Sylene dominate the scene. A number of rivers flow through rolling farm country. The region offers most outdoors activities with a special emphasis on sea and freshwater fishing, in particular salmon fishing. The climate is mild and warm enough for bathing.
SIGHTSEEING/EXCURSIONS: *Nidaros Cathedral*, 12th-century *Archbishop's Palace*, and *Ringve Musical Museum* in **Trondheim;** *Trollheimen range* with marked trails, pony trekking, salmon and trout fishing and riding camps; *Kongsvold Botanical Mountain Garden* at **Oppdal og Orkdalen;** *Rein Abbey* in **Rissa;** good fishing in the sea or rivers everywhere; prehistoric monuments including burial mounds, monoliths and stone circles at **Eggekvammen, Tingvoll;** *Helge Farm* at **Byafossen;** the Olav drama at **Stiklestad;** fortress ruins from 1525 at **Steinviksholm;** rock carvings and burial mounds at **Skogn, Hell, Leirfall** and **Lekaøya.**
RESORTS: Winter & Summer: Røros and Oppdal. **Summer only:** Orkanger, Trondheim, Stjørdal Levanger, Verdal Steinkjer, Namsos and Rorvik.

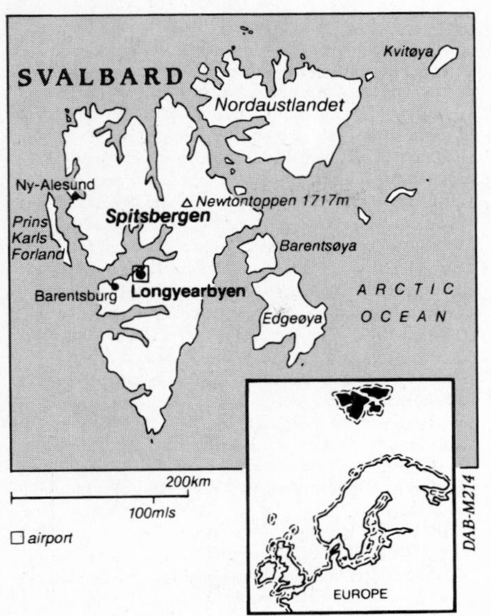

SOCIAL PROFILE

FOOD & DRINK: Breakfasts are often enormous with a variety of fish, meat, cheese and bread served from a cold buffet with coffee and boiled or fried eggs. Many hotels and restaurants serve lunch from a *koldtbord* (cold table), with smoked salmon, fresh lobster, shrimp and hot dishes. Open sandwiches are topped with meat, fish, cheese and salads. Other dishes include roast venison, *ptarmigan* in cream sauce, wild cranberries, *multer* (a berry with a unique flavour), *lutefisk* (a hot, highly flavoured cod fish) and herring prepared in various ways. **Drink:** *Aquavit* (schnapps) is a popular drink, but in general alcohol is limited and expensive, although beer and wine are generally served in restaurants. Bars have table and counter service. Licensing laws are strict and alcohol is sold only by the state through special monopoly. Licensing hours are also enforced and only wine and beer are served on Sunday.
NIGHTLIFE: Several hotels and restaurants in Oslo stage cabaret programmes and floor shows. Venues change so it is best to check in the local newspaper. Theatres, cinemas, nightclubs and discotheques are located in major centres. Resorts have dance music, and folk dancing is popular.
SHOPPING: Most towns and resorts have a shop where typical Norwegian handicrafts are on sale. Silversmiths and potteries are numerous and worth visiting. Traditional items include furs, printed textiles, woven articles, knitwear, woodcarving, silver, enamel, pewter, glass and porcelain. Tax-free cheques (which may be used to obtain tax refunds on purchases over NKr300) can be obtained from any of the 2500 shops carrying the sticker 'Tax free for tourists'. These shops save visitors 10-15% of the price paid by residents. VAT refunds are paid in cash at airports, ferries, cruise ships and border crossings. **Shopping hours:** 0900-1700 *or* 0900-1800 Monday to Friday and 0900-1500 *or* 1600 Saturday. One late night opening a week is usual, in Oslo this is on a Thursday.
SPORT: Tennis: A number of resort hotels have their own courts. **Golf:** Oslo (Bogstad links) and Stokke (between Tønsberg and Sandefjord) all have 18-hole golf courses, and there are shorter courses in Bergen, Sarpsborg, Hamar, Kristiansund and Trondheim. Most clubs are open to visitors. **Horseriding:** Riding holidays are becoming more popular. There are riding schools and clubs throughout the country with horses for hire and instruction provided, also a number of hotels keep horses. **Skiing:** Summer skiing June/July at some central resorts. Winter sports from December to April. **Fishing:** Angling is popular on Norway's many inland waters and surrounding sea. There are over 100 salmon rivers flowing into the fjords where reasonably priced sport is offered. A national fishing licence is necessary, obtainable from post offices. A permit is required for freshwater fishing. **Boating:** A number of hotels, campsites and chalets have boats for use by visitors on the coast and inland waters.
Windsurfing/water-skiing: Hotels and campsites located near stretches of water often hire out equipment for windsurfing or water-skiing and offer instruction. **Swimming:** Norway's coast and inland waters are ideal for bathing in warm months. There are several specially designated beaches for naturists. Many resort hotels have pools. **Winter Olympics:** Lillehammer will host these in 1994.
SPECIAL EVENTS: The following is a selection of major festivals and other special events celebrated in Norway. For a complete list of events in 1993/94 contact the Tourist Board. **Apr 2-12 '93** *Karasjok Easter Festival*, Karasjok. **Apr 2-4** *Voss Jazz Festival* (including both national and international artists), Voss. **May 5-12** *International Children's Culture Week* (concerts, theatre, exhibitions), Arendal. **May 2-Jun 15** *Bergen International Festival Exhibition*. **May 22-31** *Sognefjord Viking Race*. **Jun 23** *Midsummer's Eve*. **Jul 7** *Midnight Sun Marathon* Tromsø. **Jul 10-11** *Harstad International Sea Fishing Festival*. **Jul 16-25** *Coastal Culture Days*. **Jul 28-Aug 13** *Trondheim Music Festival* (chamber music festival). **Aug 1-7** *Norway Cup*, Oslo. **Aug 4-8** *Oslo Jazz Festival*. **Sep 11-Oct 10** *The Autumn Exhibition* (new paintings and sculptures), Oslo. **Oct 2-9** *Ultima-Oslo Contemporary Music Festival*. **Dec 10** *Nobel Peace Prize Presentation*, Oslo.
SOCIAL CONVENTIONS: Normal courtesies should be observed. It is customary for the guest to refrain from drinking until the host toasts their health. Casual dress is normal. The main meal of the day, lunch, may take place late in the afternoon (often as late as 1700); however, if invited out Norwegians will generally be happy to dine in the evening. If invited to the home the visitor should bring a bunch of flowers for the hostess. Punctuality is expected. Smoking is prohibited in some public buildings and on public transport. **Tipping:** It is not customary to tip taxi drivers. Waiters expect a tip of no more than 5% of the bill, porters at airports and railway stations charge per piece of luggage. Hotel porters are tipped NKr5-10 according to the number of items of luggage.

BUSINESS PROFILE

ECONOMY: There is little cultivatable land in Norway, but many farmers, the majority of whom breed livestock, combine this with tree-felling to supply Norway's numerous sawmills. Wood products and paper are consequently both strong industries. Offshore fishing has been in decline for some time, but a large number of fish-farms have been established, making Norway by far the world's largest supplier of salmon. Economic development immediately after the Second World War was concentrated in heavy engineering industries such as shipbuilding. These have also declined since the mid-1970s, but Norway has sustained its economic prosperity through development of an exceptionally strong energy sector: the country has abundant resources for hydro-electric power which have allowed much-reduced overheads for larger industries, such as aluminium production, which has established factories near power stations. In addition, from the mid-1970s Norway has, like Britain, been a major oil exporter, having discovered large deposits in the North Sea. Some advanced technological industries of world standard have developed in recent years, but the best prospects for exporters to Norway are in service industries. Britain, Germany and Sweden are the biggest importers to the country. These three countries are also Norway's largest export markets. Norway is a member of the European Free Trade Association, having decided in 1973 not to join the EC, although it enjoys wholly liberalised trade with the Community in all sectors apart from agriculture, which in Norway remains heavily protected. Moreover, EFTA established a free trade zone with the EC, known as the European Economic Area, in 1991.
BUSINESS: Business people are expected to dress smartly. Prior appointments are necessary. Norwegian business people tend to be reserved and formal. English is widely spoken. Punctuality is essential. Calling cards are common. The best months for business visits are February to May and October to December. **Office hours:** 0800-1600 Monday to Friday.
COMMERCIAL INFORMATION: The following organisation can offer advice: Norwegian Trade Council, Drammensvn 40, 0243 Oslo. Tel: (22) 92 63 00. Fax: (22) 92 64 00. Telex: 78532.
CONFERENCES/CONVENTIONS: In 1991, 127 international conventions were organised in Norway; twice as many as in 1989. Meetings for up to 9000 persons can be held in Oslo. Other towns have facilities for up to 5000 persons. Oslo, Stavanger, Bergen, Trondheim and Tromsø (each of which has its own convention bureau) are featured in a brochure produced by the Norway Convention Bureau, PO Box 499, Sentrum, N-0105 Oslo 1. Tel: (22) 42 70 44. Fax: (22) 33 69 88. Telex: 78582 NTA N.

HISTORY & GOVERNMENT

HISTORY: During the Napoleonic Wars (1813-1815), Norway entered into a union with Sweden, which lasted until the declaration of independence in 1905. The Norwegians then elected King Haakon VII, who reigned for over half a century and was succeeded by his son, Olav V. For 30 years, from 1935, the Labour Party formed the government, apart from an interruption during the war during which time the country was under the control of a Nazi puppet government headed by Vidkun Quisling, who gave his name to the English language ('quisling' is now a term for traitor). After the war, Norway dispensed with its traditional neutrality to join NATO. In 1965, a centre-right coalition unseated Einar Gerhardsen's Labour administration, but from 1973-81 minority Labour governments were in power. In 1981, another centre-right group under Prime Minister Kåre Willoch took over. Elections in 1985 kept Willoch's coalition in office, although the largest single party was the Labour Party under Mrs Gro Harlem Brundtland. Instability and severe political difficulties caused by the attempted introduction of an austerity budget brought down Willoch's government. Brundtland took office at the request of the King until the next scheduled elections (in 1989), which produced a hung parliament. A centre-right coalition under Jan Syse governed the country until it fell apart in October 1990 over the most divisive contemporary issue in Norwegian politics: the relationship between the country and the European Community. A minority Labour government then took office under Mrs Brundtland. The 1991 agreement between the EC and EFTA (the European Free Trade Association), of which Norway is a member, has brought Norway closer to the EC. In November 1992, the Norwegian parliament voted to apply for full membership, although it is not clear that this reflects the attitudes of the population at large: 1996 is a likely date for the accession of the next batch of full members, which should include Norway. Recent controversy has surrounded the Norwegian government's decision in the summer of 1992, along with several other countries (including Iceland and Japan), to resume whaling after abiding by the 6-year-long moratorium imposed by the International Whaling Commission.
GOVERNMENT: Norway is a constitutional monarchy with a parliament, the Storting, divided into two houses. Under constitutional changes agreed in 1988, the number of seats in the Storting was increased from 157 to 165. King Olav V died in January 1991 to be succeeded by his son Harald V.

CLIMATE

Coastal areas have a moderate climate due to the Gulf Stream and North Atlantic Drift. Inland temperatures are more extreme with hot summers and cold winters (November to March). In general, the lowlands of the south experience colder winters and warmer summers than the coastal areas. Rain is distributed throughout the year with frequent inland snowfalls during the winter. The northern part of the country inside the Arctic Circle has continuous daylight at midsummer, and twilight all day during winter.
Required clothing: European according to the season. Light to mediumweights are worn in summer. Warmer weights are worn during the winter. Waterproofing is advisable throughout the year.

OSLO Norway (96m)

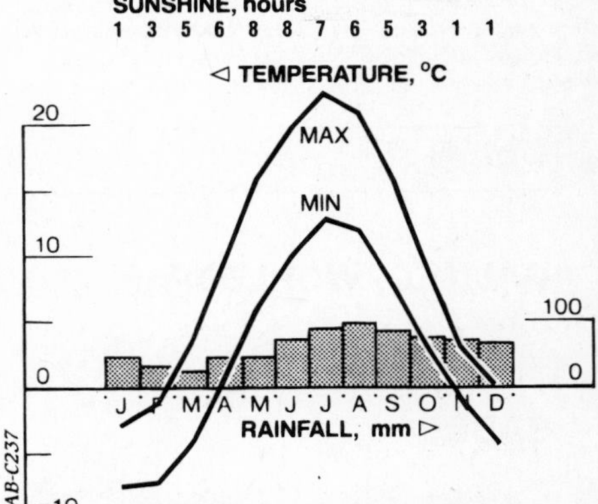

OMAN

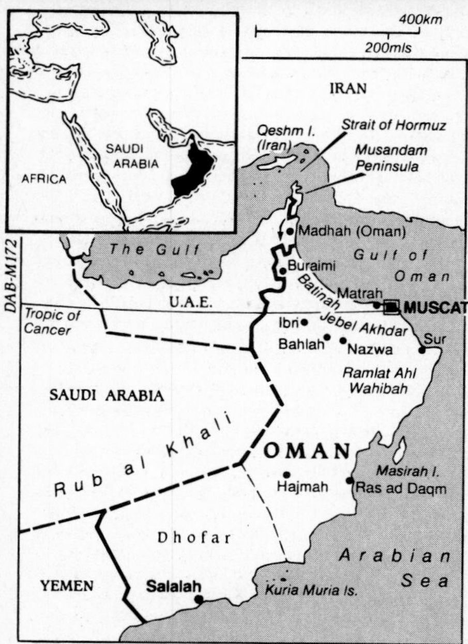

Location: Middle East, southeastern tip of Arabian Peninsula.

Embassy of the Sultanate of Oman
44a Montpelier Square
London SW7 1JJ
Tel: (071) 584 3700. Fax: (071) 225 0339. Telex: 918775. Opening hours: 0900-1530 Monday to Friday.
British Embassy
PO Box 300
Muscat, Oman
Tel: 738 501. Fax: 736 040. Telex: 5216 PRODROME ON.
Embassy of the Sultanate of Oman
2342 Massachusetts Avenue, NW
Washington, DC
20008
Tel: (202) 387 1980/1/2. Fax: (202) 387 2186. Telex: 440267.
Also deals with enquiries from Canada.
Embassy of the United States of America
PO Box 50202
Madinat Qaboos, Oman
Tel: 698 989. Fax: 699 771. Telex: 5457 USDAOMUS OM.
Canadian Consulate
PO Box 4
Moosa Abdul Rahman
Hassan Building
Al-Nboor Street
Muscat, Oman
Tel: 793 506. Fax: 709 091. Telex: 3222 MB.

AREA: 300,000 sq km (120,000 sq miles).
POPULATION: 1,502,000 (1990 estimate). In addition there were an estimated 258,260 expatriate workers in 1989.
POPULATION DENSITY: 7.1 per sq km (excluding expatriates).
CAPITAL: Muscat. **Population:** 50,000 (1981 estimate).
GEOGRAPHY: Oman is bordered to the west by the United Arab Emirates, Saudi Arabia and the Republic of Yemen. The Musandam Peninsula forms a coastal enclave on the Straits of Hormuz. The 2700km (1700 miles) of coastline are surrounded by the Arabian and Indian Seas. The Hajir Mountains divide the land stretching from the Musandam Peninsula to the southeast. To the west lies the fertile narrow plain of the Batinah coast dominated by the Jebel Akhdar. Dhofar in the south, which is divided from the north by a desert, has a coastal plain beyond which are mountains. Out to sea are the Kuria Muria Islands. The Batinah coast is inhabited by descendants of Asian merchants, Baluchi traders and other Arab nationals, who are more aware of the outside world than the tribesmen of the interior and mountains. Along the coast at Muscat and Matrah, Arab traditions remain strong despite increasing Western influence. In the southern capital of Salalah are many black Omanis descended mainly from former slaves, whereas the interior is populated by the nomadic *Bedus* (Bedouin).
LANGUAGE: Arabic and English.
RELIGION: Ibadi Muslim, with Sunni and Shia Muslim minorities.
TIME: GMT + 4.
ELECTRICITY: 220/240 volts AC, 50Hz.
COMMUNICATIONS: Telephone: IDD is available. Country code: 968. **Fax:** Services are available from Omantel. Some hotels provide facilities. **Telex/telegram:** Services are available at the counter in the Omantel office, Muscat. In case of difficulty, book calls through the international operator. **Post:** Airmail to Europe takes up to two weeks. **Press:** English-language newspapers include *The Times of Oman, Sultanate of Oman Today, Commercial Magazine* and *Oman Daily Observer*.
BBC World Service and Voice of America frequencies: From time to time these change. See the section *How to Use this Book* for more information.

BBC:

MHz	21.47	15.07	12.09	9.410

A service is also available on 1413kHz and 702kHz (0100-0500 GMT).

Voice of America:

MHz	11.97	9.670	6.040	5.995

PASSPORT/VISA

Regulations and requirements may be subject to change at short notice, and you are advised to contact the appropriate diplomatic or consular authority before finalising travel arrangements. Details of these may be found at the head of this country's entry. Any numbers in the chart refer to the footnotes below.

	Passport Required?	Visa Required?	Return Ticket Required?
Full British	Yes	Yes	Yes
BVP	Not valid	-	-
Australian	Yes	Yes	Yes
Canadian	Yes	Yes	Yes
USA	Yes	Yes	Yes
Other EC	Yes	Yes	Yes
Japanese	Yes	Yes	Yes

Restricted entry: Holders of Israeli passports or visas, or anyone showing any evidence of having visited or having links with Israel, will be refused entry.
PASSPORTS: Valid passport required by all.
British Visitors Passport: Not accepted.
VISAS: Tourist and Business visas are required by all except nationals of Bahrain, Kuwait, Qatar, Saudi Arabia and the UAE.
Note: Any visitor arriving in Oman without a visa or 'No Objection Certificate' (NOC) will be fined. Visitors are not allowed to enter Oman by road unless their visa or NOC states such validity and a designated point of entry.
Validity: Visas are valid for a visit of up to 3 weeks beginning any time during a month from the date of issue.
Application to: Consulate (or Consular Section at Embassy). For addresses, see top of entry. Applications are referred to Muscat by fax.
Application requirements: (a) 1 typed application form, completed and signed. (b) 2 recent passport-sized photos. (c) A full valid passport must be presented so that visas can be stamped into them. (d) Business letter or employer certificate. (d) Fee (for UK nationals £45; other EC nationals £21. All others should contact the Embassy for up-to-date details). Passengers who have a new passport, but whose 'No Objection Certificate' NOC is entered in a previous passport, should also carry their previous passsport.
Working days required: Approximately 7 days. Postal applications take longer.

MONEY

Currency: Omani Rial (OR) = 1000 baiza. Notes are in denominations of OR50, 20,10, 5 and 1, and 500, 250, 200 and 100 baiza. Coins are in denominations of OR500, 250, 100, 50, 25, 10 and 5, and 200 baiza.
Credit cards: American Express accepted, as are other major cards, although Access/Mastercard and Visa may have more limited acceptance. Check with your credit card company for details of merchant acceptability and other services which may be available.
Travellers cheques: Easily exchanged.
Exchange rate indicators: The following figures are included as a guide to the movements of the Omani Rial against Sterling and the US Dollar:

Date:	Oct '89	Oct '90	Oct '91	Oct '92
£1.00=	0.60	0.75	0.67	0.62
$1.00=	0.38	0.39	0.39	0.39

Currency restrictions: There are no restrictions on the import or export of local or foreign currency. Israeli currency is prohibited.
Banking hours: 0800-1200 Saturday to Wednesday and 0800-1130 Thursday.

DUTY FREE

The following items may be imported into Oman without incurring customs duty:
A reasonable quantity of tobacco products;
227ml perfume and eau de cologne.
Prohibited items: Alcohol, narcotics, fresh foods, firearms (including toys and replicas) and pornographic films/literature.

PUBLIC HOLIDAYS

Public holidays observed in Oman are as follows:
Mar 25 '93 Start of Eid al-Fitr. **Jun 21** Islamic New Year. **Jun 30** Ashoura. **Aug 30** Mouloud (Prophet's Birthday). **Nov 18** National Day. **Nov 19** Sultan's Birthday. **Feb '94** Leilat al-Meiraj (Ascension of the Prophet). **Mar** Beginning of Ramadan and Start of Eid al-Fitr.
Note: Muslim festivals are timed according to local sightings of various phases of the Moon and the dates given above are approximations. During the lunar month of Ramadan that precedes Eid al-Fitr, Muslims fast during the day and feast at night and normal business patterns may be interrupted. Many restaurants are closed during the day and there may be restrictions on smoking and drinking. Eid al-Fitr and Eid al-Adha may last anything from two to ten days, depending on the region. For more information see the section *World of Islam* at the back of the book.

HEALTH

Regulations and requirements may be subject to change at short notice, and you are advised to contact your doctor well in advance of your intended date of departure. Any numbers in the chart refer to the footnotes below.

	Special Precautions?	Certificate Required?
Yellow Fever	No	1
Cholera	Yes	2
Typhoid & Polio	Yes	-
Malaria	3	-
Food & Drink	4	-

OMAN | **HEALTH REGULATIONS** | **VISA REGULATIONS** | Code-Link

GALILEO/WORLDSPAN

TI-DFT/MCT/HE

TI-DFT/MCT/VI

SABRE

TIDFT/MCT/HE

TIDFT/MCT/VI

To access this information on your CRS, swipe the barcode with a light pen or type in the text under the barcode. For more information, see the introduction *How to Use This Book*.

[1]: A yellow fever vaccination certificate is required from travellers arriving from infected areas.
[2]: Following WHO guidelines issued in 1973, a cholera vaccination certificate is not a condition of entry to Oman. However, cholera is a risk in this country and precautions are essential. Up-to-date advice should be sought before deciding whether these precautions should include vaccination, as medical opinion is divided over its effectiveness. See the *Health* section at the back of the book.
[3]: Malaria risk, predominantly in the malignant *falciparum* form, exists throughout the year in the whole country. Chloroquine resistance has been reported.
[4]: All water should be regarded as being potentially contaminated. Water used for drinking, brushing teeth or making ice should have first been boiled or otherwise sterilised. Milk is unpasteurised and should be boiled. Powdered or tinned milk is available and is advised, but make sure that it is reconstituted with pure water. Avoid dairy products which are likely to have been made from unboiled milk. Only eat well-cooked meat and fish, preferably served hot. Salad and mayonnaise may carry increased risk. Vegetables should be cooked and fruit peeled.
Rabies is present. For those at high risk, vaccination before arrival should be considered. If you are bitten abroad seek medical advice without delay. For more information consult the *Health* section at the back of the book.
Health care: Oman has an extensive public health service (free to Omani nationals), with approximately 50 hospitals, 80 health centres and 90 preventative health centres. However, costs are high for foreigners and health insurance is essential.

TRAVEL - International

AIR: Oman's national airline is *Oman Aviation*.
Approximate flight times: From Muscat to *London* is 8 hours 10 minutes; to *Singapore* 6 hours 30 minutes and to *Sydney* 16 hours.
International airport: *Muscat (MCT)* (Seeb International) 40km (25 miles) west of the city (travel time – 30 minutes). Taxis and buses to the city are available. Airport facilities include bank/bureau de change (24 hours), duty-free shops (24 hours), 24-hour bar, restaurant (1200-1500 and 1900-0100) and car hire (*Avis*, *Budget* and *Almadar*).
Departure tax: OR3 for all departures. Transit passengers and children under 12 years old are exempt.
SEA: The main ports are Mina Qaboos and Mina Raysut. Traffic is mainly commercial.
ROAD: Travel into Oman by land is only possible with prior government permission. The best route is the north–south road from Muscat to Salalah, a journey of some ten or 12 hours. Road travel through Saudi Arabia and the United Arab Emirates is extremely limited.

TRAVEL - Internal

AIR: *Gulf Air (GFA)* runs domestic flights to Salalah from Seeb airport; the approximate flight time is two hours. Tickets for internal air travel can be obtained from *Blue Falcon Travel* in Muscat. Permission is required from the Ministry of Information.
ROAD: Principal routes run from north to south. **Bus:** *The Oman National Transport Company* has been developing a network of services in Muscat and North Oman using modern vehicles. There is competition from taxis and pick-up trucks converted for passenger service. **Taxi:** Prices are high and fares should be agreed in advance. Shared taxis are also available. **Car hire:** Available from *Zubair Travel* and *Service* in Muscat, and from *Avis*, who have offices at hotels throughout the country. **Regulations:** Visitors are not allowed to travel into the interior further up the coast than Seeb, 50km (30 miles) from Muscat, without written permission from the Ministry of the Interior. Heavy penalties are imposed for drinking and driving. **Documentation:** Holders of Tourist visas can use their national driving licence for up to seven days. For those on business, or where the stay exceeds seven days, a local licence must be obtained from the Police on presentation of their national driving licence or International Driving Permit.

ACCOMMODATION

HOTELS: There are about 12 modern hotels. Smaller hotels are cheaper but facilities are limited. There are very few hotels in provincial areas but a large hotel building programme has been initiated. Booking well in advance is strongly recommended. All rates are subject to a 15% service charge.

RESORTS & EXCURSIONS

Muscat: This old walled town is dominated by two well-preserved 16th-century Portuguese fortresses. The town consists of old houses, narrow streets and three beautifully carved original gates. The *Ali Mosque*, the *New Mosque* and the *Sultan's Palace* are well worth visiting. *Oman Museum* and the Culture area at **Qurum** encapsulate Oman's archaeology, history and culture. The coastline offers excellent fishing grounds and beaches.
Matrah-Muscat: Archaeological excavation of the tumuli at the site of *Souks Baushanos* is fascinating.
Nizwa: The holy city of the Ibadhi Imam.
Jabrin: The 17th-century fortified palace situated here is notable for its painted wooden ceilings and the splendid view across the desert to the mountains.
Bahla: This ancient town, known for its pottery, has a good *souk*, and nearby is the picturesque village of **Al Hamra.**
Jebel Akhdar: Literally 'The Green Mountain', noted for its picturesque terraced villages.
Al Hazm: On the northern slopes of the Jebel Akhdar is the fortress of Al Hazm fort, built in 1708, and the oasis town of **Rustag**.
Qurum: The *Bait Nadir Museum*, housed in a 18th-century building, has a collection of silver, jewellery, weapons and ancient stone artefacts. From here *dhows* cruise along the palm-fringed coast.

SOCIAL PROFILE

FOOD & DRINK: A number of restaurants have opened in recent years, but many people retain the habit of dining at hotels. There is a wide variety of cuisine on offer, including Arabic, Indian, Oriental, European and International dishes. Coffee houses are popular. Waiter service is usual. **Drink:** Muslim law forbids alcohol, but most hotel bars and restaurants serve alcohol. Western nationals must obtain a licence from their Embassy to buy alcohol.
NIGHTLIFE: There are a few nightclubs and bars in Muscat, mostly in the hotels. There are three air-conditioned cinemas in Ruwi and an open-air cinema at the Al Falaj Hotel showing Arab, Indian and English films.
SHOPPING: The modern shops are mostly in Ruwi. The two main *souks* (markets) are located in Matrah and Muscat. Traditional crafts include silver and gold jewellery, *khanjars* (Omani daggers), handwoven textiles, carpets and baskets. **Shopping hours:** 0800-1300 and 1600-2000 Saturday to Thursday. *Souks* open 0800-1100 and 1600-1900. Many shops close on Friday. Opening hours are one hour later during Ramadan.
SPORT: There are many beaches offering good **bathing, skindiving** and **sailing** facilities. There are also three private sports clubs with **fishing** and **water-skiing** facilities. Some hotels have pools. There are many sports clubs based in Muscat offering facilities for **tennis** and **squash**. Several **golf** clubs are open to visitors. **Hockey, football, volleyball** and **basketball** are popular spectator sports and matches are staged at the Wattayah Stadium. **Camel** and **horseraces** are held on Fridays and public holidays at the old airstrip at Seof.
SOCIAL CONVENTIONS: Shaking hands is the usual form of greeting. A small gift either promoting your company or country is well received. As far as dress is concerned it is important that women dress modestly; ie long skirts or dresses (below the knee) with long sleeves. Tight-fitting clothes must be avoided and although this is not strictly followed by Westerners, it is far better to adopt this practice and avoid offence. Shorts should never be worn in public. It is polite not to smoke in public, but generally no-smoking signs are posted where appropriate. **Tipping:** Becoming more common and 10-15% should be given.

BUSINESS PROFILE

ECONOMY: Oman was acutely underdeveloped until the discovery of oil in the early 1970s. Exports of the product now account for over 90% of GDP and almost all of the country's export earnings. Although Oman is not a member of OPEC (Organisation of Petroleum Exporting Countries), its pricing policy tends to follow that of OPEC closely. The Government has used some of its oil money to develop indigenous industries such as construction and agriculture. The latter, due to Oman's desert land, is confined to the coastal plain and a few irrigated areas in the interior. Dates, limes and alfalfa are the main products; some livestock are also bred. There are also mineral deposits of copper, chromite, marble, gypsum and limestone which are being exploited. February 1991 saw the launch of Oman's fourth 5-year economic development plan. Among the sectors which will receive particular emphasis are oil and gas, mining, agriculture and fisheries, health care, power generation, education, telecommunications, transport and construction. Industrial production (apart from oil-related industry) has increased rapidly since the early 1980s, averaging 10-15% annual growth, but still accounts for less than 10% of economic output. Japan is the country's largest trading partner, exchanging oil for manufactured goods. One deal of particular note in 1992 has been signed with the CIS member Kazakhstan. Worth perhaps US$1.5 billion, it covers the creation of an Omani-Kazakh consortium to build an oil pipeline from Kazakhstan's Tengiz field (in whose development British Gas is involved) to a suitable port. Eight possible routes have been identified but some lengthy diplomacy will be needed before a route can finally be agreed. The UK and the United Arab Emirates are the other important sources of Omani imports.
BUSINESS: Men should wear suits and ties for business and formal occasions. English is usually spoken in business circles, but a few words or phrases of Arabic will be useful and welcome. Appointments are essential and punctuality is gradually becoming more important in business circles. Visiting cards are widely used. **Office hours:** 0730-1400 Saturday to Wednesday and 0800-1300 Thursday. Many will also open 1600-1900 Saturday to Wednesday. Closed Friday. Office hours are one hour later during Ramadan.
COMMERCIAL INFORMATION: The following organisations can offer advice: Ministry of Commerce and Industry, PO Box 550, Muscat. Tel: 799 500. Fax: 794 238. Telex: 3665; *or*
Oman Chamber of Commerce and Industry, PO Box 4400, Ruwi, Muscat. Tel: 707 674. Telex: 3389.

HISTORY & GOVERNMENT

HISTORY: Archaeological excavations have recently shown that much civilisation pre-dates the Arab period. The region embraced Islam during the lifetime of the Prophet. During the 18th and 19th centuries the sultans of Muscat were often powerful figures in Arabia and East Africa, and often came into conflict with the colonial powers in the region, particularly the Portuguese, who first settled in the 16th century in an attempt to protect their eastern trade routes. Close ties have been maintained with Britain since 1798, when a treaty of friendship was concluded. The country was known as Muscat and Oman until 1970. British influence remains strong, but the number of British advisers occupying key positions in Omani government departments is diminishing. Foreign policy in the last 15 years has been dominated by the often poor relations between Oman and the neighbouring former Yemen PDR, which was alleged to have supported the unsuccessful insurgency waged by the Popular Front for the Liberation of Oman during the 1960s and 1970s. More recently, friendly relations have been established with Yemen PDR and, subsequently, with the new government of the unified Yemen republic. Oman's strategic importance has been underlined by both the Gulf War between Iran and Iraq and, in late 1990, by the Gulf crisis following the Iraqi invasion of Kuwait. Oman was used as a staging post for US and UK ships and aircraft arriving in the area as part of the multinational force confronting the Iraqis. The country was a founder member of the Gulf Co-operation Council in 1981.
GOVERNMENT: The country is ruled by Sultan Qaboos (whose family has been in power since the 18th century) with the aid of a cabinet and, until late 1991, a Consultative Assembly, although this has no direct legislative power. The Assembly has been replaced by a Consultative Council (Majlis al-Shura) with one representative from each of Oman's 59 *vilayet* (regions).

CLIMATE

The months of June and July are particularly hot. Rainfall varies according to the region. During the period June to September there is a light monsoon rain in Salalah.
Required clothing: Lightweights are worn throughout the year, with a warm wrap for cooler winter evenings. Light rainwear is advisable.

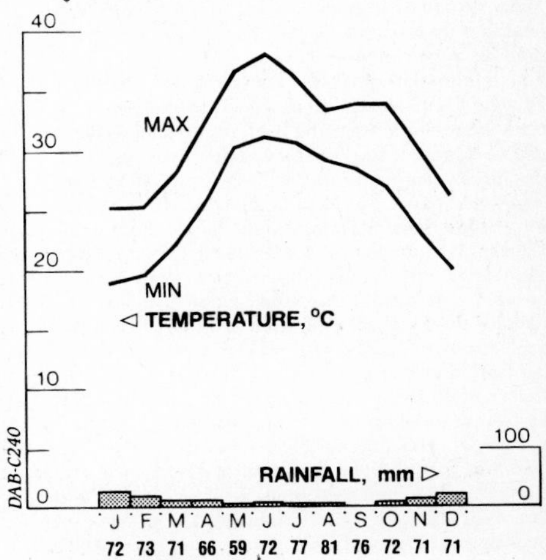

THE PACIFIC

Most of the countries in the Pacific have their own entries in the *World Travel Guide;* please consult the contents pages. Note that information on American Samoa, Guam and Hawaii is included at the end of the entry for the United States of America.

PACIFIC OVERVIEW

The vast, sparsely populated region of the Pacific Ocean, which covers a quarter of the earth's surface, has been the subject of growing interest in the last few years. It is neither easy, nor especially useful, to make generalisations about the area and the myriad of small islands peppered across it. All have unique features of geography, economy and, not least, of political history: some are newly independent; others are designated as Trust Territories; yet others are straightforward colonies. There are, nevertheless, global political and economic trends which are certain to create a substantial impact throughout the Pacific.

One significant trend of the last two decades, which will probably now be arrested, has been the growing militarisation of the Pacific. As well as the better-known nuclear testing complexes operated by France and the USA, the region saw a proliferation of intelligence-gathering, early-warning and other 'support' facilities, during the 1970s and 1980s. With the end of the Cold War, however, communist expansionism no longer provides a pretext for the strategic exploitation of the Pacific. For the Pacific islands themselves, this reduces the threat to their own autonomy from being swept up in the global superpower conflict. One by-product of this is that the major powers no longer have the same degree of incentive to underwrite the economies of those islands in which they previously took an interest. The islands must develop their own economic systems and have focused on three principal areas in which they hope to progress.

One of these is tourism. Much of the region is currently within reach of the North American traveller, but further exploitation of its tourism potential is dependent either on the development of cheaper, faster and, perhaps, less-polluting forms of long-distance transport to bring the Pacific within reach of Europe; or on a substantial increase in the disposable incomes of the populations of Asia and South America. Neither of these are likely to be realised in the short term.

Another economic asset which may produce more immediate dividends is the Pacific's awe-inspiring wealth of natural resources. Commercial fishing, notably by Japan, has long been carried out on a huge scale, but has yet to make any real impact on the ocean's deep-sea fish stocks. The region also has enormous mineral potential: much attention has been given to developing commercially viable methods of harvesting the mineral-rich manganese nodules that cover much of the ocean's abyssal plains, but there are believed to be other mineral deposits of great value. Additionally, the whole Pacific Rim has great potential as an energy source, initially from geothermal installations, later perhaps from deep-sea tidal and temperature gradient devices.

Many Pacific nations are just a few score square km of land, but their boundaries enclose hundreds of thousands of square km of ocean.

Finally, the islands stand to benefit from the rapidly growing Pacific trade axis as Japan and the fast-growing economies of other 'Pacific Rim' countries link up with the west coast of the Americas. This offers opportunities for developing transit facilities for shipping and 'offshore' financial services of the type which have long been offered by, for example, Jersey and the Cayman Islands: Nauru, Vanuatu and Tonga are likely candidates. The islands will need more than this type of business to sustain a healthy economy, and it remains to be seen whether they are able to develop their undoubted assets without becoming excessively dominated by foreign commercial interests.

On a darker note, one problem which has arisen in the last few years and is worrying several Pacific governments, concerns the possible consequences of global warming on sea levels. A number of islands face serious threats to their land mass; some, such as Nauru, could disappear altogether. The Pacific islands are consequently an increasingly vocal presence at international fora discussing global environmental questions.

THE PACIFIC ISLANDS OF MICRONESIA

(Islands formerly comprising the US-administered Pacific Trust Territory.)

Location: South Pacific, Micronesia.

Note: This region was administered by the United States on behalf of the United Nations until 1990. It includes the *Federated States of Micronesia*, the *Republic of the Marshall Islands*, the *Northern Mariana Islands* and the *Republic of Palau*. The Northern Marianas have had US Commonwealth status since 1986. Under the terms of Compacts of Free Association between the USA and the other former territories, each is a sovereign self-governing state pursuing its foreign policy along agreed guidelines, with the USA retaining responsibility for defence in exchange for economic aid. However, the position of Palau will remain effectively unaltered until it can muster a sufficiently large majority to vote for new arrangements. The *Federated States of Micronesia* and the *Republic of the Marshall Islands* became members of the United Nations in 1991.

Tourism Council of the South Pacific
Suite 433
52-54 High Holborn
London WC1V 6RB
Tel: (071) 242 3131. Fax: (071) 242 2838. Telex: 23770.
For addresses, see individual entries in this section.

AREA: 20,124,000 sq km (7,770,000 sq miles) of which 2159 sq km (833.6 sq miles) is land.
POPULATION: See individual entries.
GEOGRAPHY: Micronesia comprises four archipelagos: the Federated States of Micronesia (Caroline Islands), the Republic of the Marshall Islands, the Northern Mariana Islands and the Republic of Palau. Each archipelago is composed of hundreds of island groups, within which there are many islands varying widely in topography. A more detailed description is given under the individual entry for each country below. There are three distinct population groups: Malayans who passed through Indonesia and the Philippines; Melanesians coming from the islands of the southwest Pacific; Polynesians who inhabited the South Pacific.
LANGUAGE: English, Japanese and nine local languages.
RELIGION: Roman Catholic and Protestant with Mormon and Bahai minorities.
TIME: See individual entries.
ELECTRICITY: 110/120 volts AC, 60Hz. Plugs are the American flat 2-pin type.
COMMUNICATIONS: Telephone: IDD is available to any of the islands. See individual entries for country code. **Fax:** Available in Palau and the Northern Marianas. **Telex/telegram:** 24-hour service available in some areas. **Post:** Airmail letters to Europe take at least ten days. Post offices are located in the centre of each state. **Press:** The English-language newspapers are *Pacific Daily News* (Guam), which is the only daily newspaper in the region and is distributed throughout all the islands, *Marshall Islands Journal* (Marshall Islands), *Marianas Review* (Northern Marianas), *Marianas Variety News* (Northern Marianas) and *Palau Weekly* (Palau).
Note: Further information is provided under individual entries.
BBC World Service and Voice of America frequencies: From time to time these change. See the section *How to Use this Book* for more information.

BBC:				
MHz	15.36	9.915	7.15	5.975
Voice of America:				
MHz	18.82	15.18	9.525	1.735

PASSPORT/VISA

Note: (a) Each of the four constitutional governments is responsible for its own tourism policies, and regulations may be subject to change. (b) On many islands, especially the remoter ones, it is not the possession of documents (necessary though they are) that secures access, but the consent of the islanders.
For more details, see the individual entries in this section.

MONEY

Currency: US Dollar (US$) = 100 cents. Notes are in denominations of US$100, 50, 20, 10, 5, 2 and 1. Coins are in denominations of US$1, and 50, 25, 10, 5 and 1 cents.
Currency exchange: Foreign exchange services are limited.
Credit cards: Access/Mastercard, American Express and Visa are accepted in most urban areas. Check with your credit card company for details of merchant acceptability and other services which may be available.
Travellers cheques: US Dollar travellers cheques are advised.
Exchange rate indicators: The following figures are included as a guide to the movements of the US Dollar against Sterling:

Date:	**Oct '89**	**Oct '90**	**Oct '91**	**Oct '92**
£1.00=	**1.58**	**1.95**	**1.74**	**1.59**

Currency restrictions: No limit on the amount of foreign or local currency to be imported or exported. Any amount can be reconverted.
Banking hours: 1000-1500 Monday to Thursday, 1000-1800 Friday.

PUBLIC HOLIDAYS

US public holidays are often observed in addition to regional public holidays, though there are variations from island to island. See individual entries for main holidays in each region.

HEALTH

Regulations and requirements may be subject to change at short notice, and you are advised to contact your doctor well in advance of your intended date of departure. Any numbers in the chart refer to the footnotes below.

	Special Precautions?	Certificate Required?
Yellow Fever	Yes	1
Cholera	Yes	2
Typhoid & Polio	3	-
Malaria	No	-
Food & Drink	4	-

[1]: A yellow fever vaccination certificate is required by all visitors arriving from infected areas. Risk of yellow fever infection still exists and vaccinations are recommended for all.
[2]: Vaccination against cholera is required by all visitors arriving from an infected area. Risk of cholera infection still exists in the Marshall Islands and vaccinations are recommended for all.
[3]: Smallpox, typhoid, para-typhoid and tetanus vaccinations are strongly recommended.
[4]: Mains water is normally chlorinated, and whilst relatively safe may cause mild abdominal upsets. Drinking water outside main cities and towns may be contaminated and sterilisation is advisable. Bottled water is available and is advised for the first few weeks of the stay. Milk is pasteurised and dairy products are safe for consumption. Local meat, poultry, seafood, fruit and vegetables are generally considered safe to eat.
Health care: Health insurance is recommended. There are nine hospitals in the region, with a total of 629 beds and 55 doctors.

TRAVEL - International

AIR: The region's major airline is *Air Micronesia.*
Approximate journey times: Flight durations from London to destinations in the Pacific vary considerably depending on the route taken. The most common route would include a stopover in Los Angeles and Honolulu; eg the flight time from London to Honolulu is 19 hours 30 minutes and from Honolulu to the Marshall Islands 4 hours 30 minutes.
International airports: *Saipan (SPN)*, *Guam (GUM)* and *Palau* when entering from the north and west, *Pohnpei (PNI)* from the south and *Majuro (MAJ)* from the south and east.
Regional airlines: Scheduled inter-island travel, charters and sightseeing are offered by several local airlines. There is excellent provision for travelling from Guam and Majuro to the various islands. Flights between the islands tend to be rarer. Airlines include:
Air Marshall Islands (AMI): This government-owned airline runs charters, sightseeing tours and point-to-point flights between Majuro and other islands in the Marshalls; also international flights to Honolulu, Fiji, Kiribati and Tuvalu.
Air Micronesia (CO): Operates between islands in all four groups, and to Hawaii, Guam, the Philippines, Australia, Papua New Guinea, South Korea, Taiwan and Japan.

Several smaller airlines fly to Guam.
SEA: The major ports are Pohnpei, Majuro, Saipan, Tuik, Yap and Karor. The following cargo/passenger lines serve the islands: *Nauru Pacific, Royal Shipping Co, Daiwa Navigation Co, Oceania Line Inc, PM&O, Saipan Shipping Co* and *Tiger Line*.
There are numerous boats for touring, ranging from small speed boats to large glass-bottomed boats for fishing, sightseeing, sunset cruising, scuba diving and short-distance travel. A ferry provides service between Saipan and Tinian. Inter-island vessels provide limited and irregular service between Saipan and the smaller islands. Requests for reservations should be directed to the Office of the Government of the following: Saipan, Commonwealth of the Northern Marianas; Office of Transportation in Majuro, Marshall Islands; Konor, Palau; Kolonia, Pohnpei; Moen, Chuuk and Colonia, Yap.
Cabin space is limited, and passengers may be required to sleep on deck (bring your own mat). The field trip ships are leased by the governments to private firms, and rates are subject to change.
Cruise lines: *Princess, Royal Viking* and *Norwegian American* currently offer cruises to the islands.

TRAVEL - Internal

ROAD: Good roads are limited to the major island centres. **Bus:** There are no local bus systems other than tourist services. However, public transport is widely available in all the Micronesia district centres in the form of sedans, pickups and *jeepneys*. **Taxis:** Inexpensive taxis are available throughout Micronesia. **Car hire:** Each major centre offers rental cars, either through international or local agents. **Documentation:** A valid national driving licence is required.

ACCOMMODATION

Accommodation is extremely varied. Rooms are scarce in some districts and single guests may be required to share twin-bedded rooms with other single guests.

SOCIAL PROFILE

FOOD & DRINK: Most hotels serve Continental, Japanese, Chinese, Western-style and local cuisine. On some remote islands the arrival of a stranger calls for a feast of fish, clams, octopus, langusta, sea cucumber and eels. Breadfruit (pounded, boiled, baked or fried), taro, rice and cassava (tapioca) are popular staples. Among the regional delicacies are coconut crabs and mangrove clams. Although some dining rooms serve buffet-style fare, table service is usual and operates at a leisurely pace. See individual entries.
NIGHTLIFE: Some hotels have cocktail lounges with live entertainment. In Saipan there are nightclubs featuring music and dancing. Throughout Micronesia there are cinemas in major areas. However, tourists seek their own entertainment for the most part. See individual entries.
SPORT: There is excellent **fishing, hiking** and **watersports.** The islands are particularly appealing for skindivers, as the surrounding waters offer unsurpassed underwater scenery and marine life. See individual entries.
SPECIAL EVENTS: See individual entries.
SOCIAL CONVENTIONS: The Western understanding of private property is alien to many parts of Micronesia and personal possessions should be well looked after, though not necessarily under lock and key; outside main tourist areas, where normal precautions apply, it is usually sufficient just to keep items out of sight. All land, however, does have an owner and before using it protocol in many areas demands that permission is sought; in places this includes use of footpaths as there is not necessarily immediate right of way. A clearly expressed desire to be courteous will usually see the visitor through. See individual entries.

BUSINESS PROFILE

ECONOMY: In all four territories subsistence agriculture is a key employer. Copra, coconuts, cassava and sweet potatoes are the major crops: yields are sufficient in some cases to sustain export markets. Fishing is similarly important. The Marshalls and Palau have developed small-scale light industries engaged in food-processing, boatbuilding and the like. Tourism is growing but is generally hindered by the lack of facilities and the difficulty of access: Micronesia and the Northern Marianas have gone furthest in efforts to overcome these obstacles and develop tourist industries, relying principally on aid and foreign investment from the USA and Japan.
BUSINESS: Lightweight suits or shirt and tie are usually worn. Appointments should be made and calling cards are exchanged. Best time to visit is May to October. **Office hours:** 0800-1700 Monday to Friday. **Government office hours:** 0730-1130 and 1230-1630 Monday to Friday.

HISTORY & GOVERNMENT

The area has a turbulent history of foreign control and political change. Despite upheavals and foreign influences from Spanish, German, Japanese and American governments, many people of this vast island area have maintained much of their cultural heritage and traditions; others have lifestyles inspired mainly by the teachings of 19th-century missionaries. A slow process of local autonomy is currently taking place, but this is proceeding at different speeds in the different island groups.

CLIMATE

With 2000 islands spread over 7.8 million sq km (3 million sq miles) of the Pacific Ocean, the islands have a variety of weather. The period from autumn to winter (November to April) is the most pleasant time, while May to October is the wet season. The climate can generally be described as tropical in this part of the world, but the cooling sea-breezes prevent really extreme temperatures and humidity. For regional climate charts see under island entries below.
Required clothing: Lightweight cottons and linens and rainwear.

MARSHALL ISLANDS

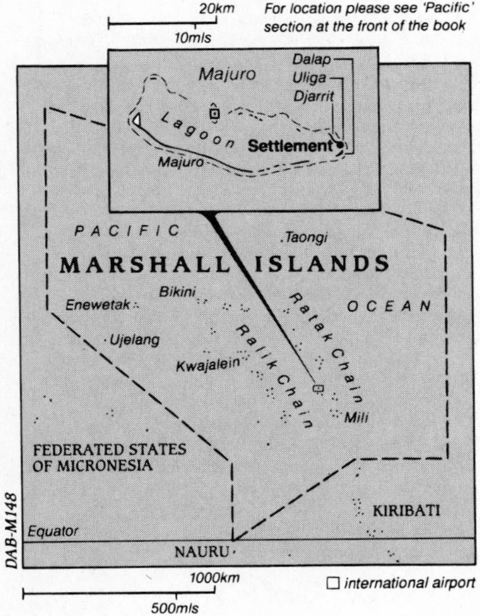

Location: Western Pacific Ocean.

Marshall Islands Visitors Authority
Ministry of Resources and Development
PO Box 1727
Majuro
Marshall Islands 96960
Tel: 625 3203 *or* 625 3206. Fax: 625 3218.
Embassy of the Republic of the Marshall Islands
2433 Massachusetts Avenue, NW
Washington, DC
20008
Tel: (202) 234 5414 *or* 232 3218. Fax: (202) 232 3236.
Consulate in: Honolulu.
Embassy of the United States of America
PO Box 680/1379
Majuro
Marshall Islands 96960
Tel: 625 4011/5. Fax: 625 4012.
Permanent Mission of the Republic of the Marshall Islands to the United Nations
7th Floor, 885 Second Avenue
New York, NY
10017
Tel: (212) 702 4850. Fax: (212) 207 9888.

AREA: 180 sq km (191 sq miles).
POPULATION: 43,355 (1988).
POPULATION DENSITY: 240.7 per sq km.
CAPITAL: Majuro. **Population:** 19,605.
GEOGRAPHY: The Marshall Islands consist of two almost parallel chains of atolls and islands and lie west of the International Date Line. Majuro atoll is 2285km west of Honolulu, 1624km east of Guam and 2625km south-east of Toyko. The eastern *Ratak* (Sunrise) Chain consists of 15 atolls and islands, and the western *Ralik* (Sunset) Chain consists of 16 atolls and islands. Together these two chains comprise 1152 islands and islets dispersed over more than 1,900,000 sq km (500,000 sq miles) of the central Pacific.
LANGUAGE: Marshallese is the offical language. English is widely understood.
RELIGION: 80% of the population belong to the independant Protestant Christian Church of the Marshall Islands.
TIME: GMT + 12.
ELECTRICITY: 110 volts AC, 60Hz. Plugs are American-style 2-pin.
COMMUNICATIONS: Telephone: IDD is available. Country code: 692. There are international satellite links. In Majuro dial 625 3399 *or* 625 3355 for the hospital; 625 3183 for the fire services; 625 3666 for police and 411 for general information. **Telex/telegram:** 24-hour telex and telegram facilities are available in Majuro, near the High School in Rita, and in Ebeye. Opening hours: 0800-1200 and 1300-1700 Monday to Friday. **Post:** A US post office is located in Majuro. Post office hours: 1000-1530 Monday to Friday; 0800-1200 Saturday. **Press:** The English-language newspaper is the *Marshall Islands Journal*.

PASSPORT/VISA

Regulations and requirements may be subject to change at short notice, and you are advised to contact the appropriate diplomatic or consular authority before finalising travel arrangements. Details of these may be found at the head of this country's entry. Any numbers in the chart refer to the footnotes below.

	Passport Required?	Visa Required?	Return Ticket Required?
Full British	Yes	Yes	Yes
BVP	Not valid	-	-
Australian	Yes	Yes	Yes
Canadian	Yes	Yes	Yes
USA	Yes	No	Yes
Other EC	Yes	Yes	Yes
Japanese	Yes	Yes	Yes

PASSPORTS: Valid passports are required by all.
British Visitors Passport: Not accepted.
VISAS: Required by all except US citizens who have a valid passport, return or onward ticket and sufficient funds for duration of stay.
Types of visa: Various.
Validity: 90 days; extensions are available.
Application to: Immigration Controller, Ministry of Foreign Affairs, Republic of the Marshall Islands, Majuro, Marshall Islands 96960. Tel: 625 3181. Fax: 625 3685. Telex: 0927 FRN AFS.
Application requirements: (a) Proof of adequate funds. (b) Return ticket.
Working days required: By post: applications are dealt with on receipt.
Temporary residence: Apply to Immigration Controller (address above).

PUBLIC HOLIDAYS

US public holidays and also the following holidays are observed in the Marshall Islands:
Mar 1 '93 Memorial and Nuclear Victim's Remembrance Day. **May 1** Constitution Day. **Jul 2** Fisherman's Day. **Sep 3** Dri Jerbal (Labour) Day. **Sep 24** Manit (Cultural) Day. **Oct 21** Independence Day. **Nov 17** President's Day. **Dec 4** Kamolol (Thanksgiving) Day. **Dec 25** Christmas Day. **Jan 1 '94** New Year's Day. **Mar 1** Memorial and Nuclear Victim's Remembrance Day.
Note: Variations occur from island to island.

HEALTH

Health care: The Marshall Islands have two main hospitals, one in Majuro and one in Ebeye. A medical facility also exists in Kwajalein.

DUTY FREE

The following items may be imported into the Marshall Islands by passengers over 18 years of age without incurring customs duty:

300 cigarettes or 75 cigars or 8oz tobacco;
2 litres of alcoholic beverage.
Prohibited items: Firearms, ammunition, drugs and pornographic materials are not permitted. Birds, animals, fruit and plants need certification from the Quarantine Division of the Ministry of Resources and Development. Coral, turtle shells and certain other natural resources cannot be exported. Any artefacts or objects of historical value cannot be taken out of the country.

TRAVEL

AIR: The *Airline of the Marshall Islands (AMI)* provides regular scheduled internal flights to ten of the atolls in the Marshall Islands and has planes available for charter. Flights are available between Honolulu and the Marshall Islands and to Fiji via Kiribati and Tuvalu. *Air Micronesia* stops in Majuro and Kwajalein on its island hopper service between Guam and Honolulu.
International airport: *Majuro International Airport (MAJ).* There are buses, taxis and hotel transport from the airport to downtown.
Departure tax: US$15 on international flights. Children under 18 years of age are exempt.
SEA: The international port is Majuro. Shipping lines servicing the Marshalls include *Matson Lines, Daiwa Lines, Tiger Lines, Nauru Pacific Line* and *Philippine, Micronesia & Orient Line.*
Four government-owned field ships connect the islands within the Marshalls on a regular schedule. Comfortable passenger cabins are available on these ships and arrangements can be made for charter trips. **Cruise:** *Royal Viking Line* sometimes calls at Majuro port, but not on a regular basis. Inter-island cruises are available. Boats can be rented from one of eight boat rental companies on the islands for sightseeing, diving tours, picnics, game fishing, snorkelling, water-skiing and other boating activities.
ROAD: All the main roads are paved. Cars are left-hand drive and driving is on the left. The minimum age is 18. **Bus:** Services run to and from Laura daily except Sundays. **Taxis:** Plentiful and cheap. Generally used on a seat-sharing basis. **Car hire:** These are usually Japanese sedans. Companies include *Martina* (tel: 625 3104), *Deluxe* (tel: 625 3665) and *Coral* (tel: 625 3724). **Documentation:** A national driving licence is valid for 30 days.

ACCOMMODATION

There are currently about 130 **hotels** in Majuro and some islands have guest-houses. Hotel space is expected to triple in the next two years to 400 rooms. **Camping** facilities are available on Majuro and various other islands. For further information contact the Visitors Authority (address at top of entry).

RESORTS & EXCURSIONS

Many of the atolls are dotted with Flame of the Forest, hibiscus and different coloured plumeria flowers. There are also at least 160 species of coral surrounding the islands. The uninhabited atolls are noted for their coconut and papaya plantations and for pandanus and breadfruit trees. The first stop in the Marshall Islands should be either **Majuro** or **Ebeye,** although visits to outer islands can be arranged. There are Sunday day-trips to **Mili** or **Maloelap** atolls where there are opportunities to snorkel over Second World War wrecks, eat local food and watch cultural dancing. There are also many historic sites and buildings. The *Alele Museum* and Visitors Authority can provide information on various sites.

SOCIAL PROFILE

FOOD & DRINK: There are several restaurants in Majuro, serving American, Western, Chinese and Marshallese specialities. Consumption of alcohol is forbidden on some of the islands.
NIGHTLIFE: There are several nightclubs on Majuro and Ebeye and some hotels offer traditional dancing.
SHOPPING: Special purchases include *kili* handbags woven by former residents of Bikini, stick charts (once used to navigate long distances between the region's scattered islands), plaited floor mats, fans, purses, shell necklaces and baskets. There is a 3% sales tax in Majuro. **Shopping hours:** 0800-2000 Monday to Thursday; 0800-2200 Friday and Saturday and 0800-1800 Sunday.
SPORT: Diving opportunities include drop-offs, coral heads, black coral and Second World War wrecks. **Fishing** expeditions can be arranged by local hotels or the Marshalls Billfish Club. **Basketball** and **volleyball, softball** and **tennis** are the favourite sports. Children play many indigenous games using local materials.
SPECIAL EVENTS: The following is a selection of the festivals and other special events celebrated annually in the Marshall Islands.
Mid-Jun *Billfish Tournament.* **Jul 4-5 (weekend)** *Marshall Islands' Fishing Tournament.* **Aug** *Folk Art Festival,* Alele Museum.
SOCIAL CONVENTIONS: Informal dress is usual for both business and social occasions. Scanty clothing (including topless bathing) is considered offensive. Use of islands, paths, beaches, etc may require permission in many areas; it is best to check locally. **Tipping** is unnecessary.

HISTORY & GOVERNMENT

HISTORY: The Marshall Islands were first sighted by European circumnavigators (including Magellan) in the early 1500s. Portuguese and Spanish influences prevailed until the middle of the 19th century, when German trading interests ensured that many of the islands were effectively German colonies. On the outbreak of hostilities in 1914, Japan occupied the Marshall Islands, its presence there being recognised, in 1920, by a 'mandate to administer' from the League of Nations. Several large military bases were built and, in 1938, Japan claimed the islands as a colony. In 1944, the islands were captured by US forces. The United Nations, post-war successor to the League of Nations, incorporated the Marshall Islands into its Trust Territory of the Pacific in 1947, under American administration. The USA, as Japan before, used the islands as a strategic military base and training area. It also established them as its main testing ground for nuclear weapons. The US Navy administered the islands from 1947-1951, when a civilian administration took over. Calls for self-determination increased from the mid-1960s onwards, with the Congress for Micronesia the main focus for debate and dissent. Finally, in 1983, a Compact of Free Association with the United States was passed by the Nitijela (the islands' assembly); it was ratified by the US Congress in 1986. Under its terms, the Marshall Islands form a sovereign self-governing state, although its foreign policy is restricted by guidelines set by the USA, which is responsible for the defence and security of the islands. The Republic of the Marshall Islands is a member of the South Pacific Forum. In 1991, the Marshall Islands were admitted as a member the United Nations.
GOVERNMENT: The locally drafted constitution came into force on May 1, 1979. It provides for a parliamentary system of government with legislative authority vested in a 33-member assembly called the Nitijela. The assembly elects a President from amongst its members.

CLIMATE

Tropical, with cooling sea-breezes and frequent rain. Tradewinds blow steadily from the northeast from December through March. Wettest months are usually October to November. The average temperature is 27°C (81°F), with a daily variation of 12 degrees.

UJELANG Marshall Is. (10m)

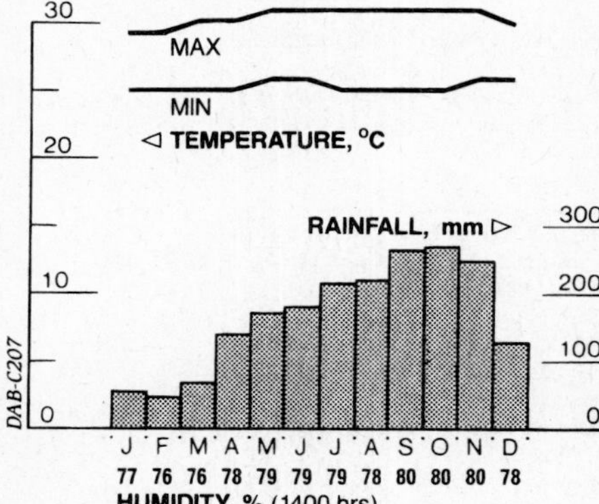

TEMPERATURE CONVERSIONS
-20 -10 0°C 10 20 30 40
0 10 20 30°F40 50 60 70 80 90 100
RAINFALL CONVERSIONS 0mm 200 400 600 800
0in 5 10 15 20 25 30

FEDERATED STATES OF MICRONESIA

Including Yap, Pohnpei, Kosrae and Chuuk (formerly Truk).

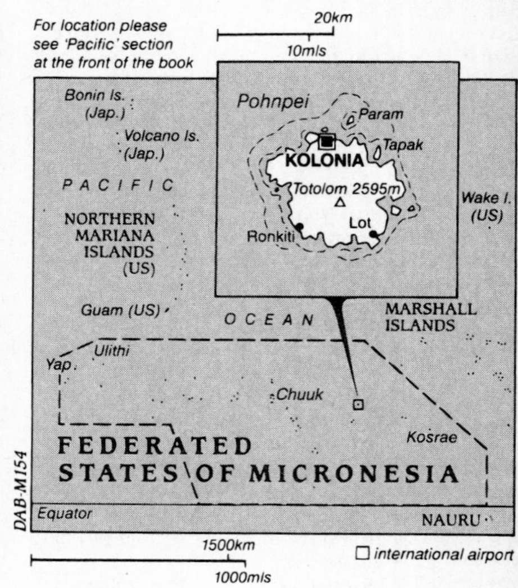

Location: Western Pacific Ocean.

Pohnpei Tourist Commission
PO Box 66
Kolonia
Pohnpei 96941
Federated States of Micronesia
Tel: 320 2421.
Chuuk Tourist Bureau
PO Box FQ
Moen
Chuuk 96942
Federated States of Micronesia
Tel: 330 4133. Fax: 330 4194.
Embassy of the Federated States of Micronesia
1725 N Street, NW
Washington, DC
20036
Tel: (202) 223 4383. Fax: (202) 223 4391.
Embassy of the United States of America
PO Box 1286
Kolonia
Pohnpei 96941
Federated States of Micronesia
Tel: 320 2187. Fax: 320 2186.

AREA: Kosrae (5 islands) 110 sq km (42 sq miles); **Pohnpei** (163 islands) 344 sq km (133 sq miles); **Chuuk (formerly Truk)** (294 islands) 127 sq km (49 sq miles); **Yap** (145 islands) 119 sq km (46 sq miles). **Total:** 700 sq km (270.3 sq miles).
POPULATION: 100,000 (1988 estimate).
POPULATION DENSITY: 143 per sq km.
CAPITAL: Pohnpei.
GEOGRAPHY: The Federated States of Micronesia lie 2300 miles north of Australia and 2500 miles west of Hawaii. They comprise 607 islands scattered over 1.6 million sq km, the most widely spread Pacific Islands groups. Yap's uplands are covered by dry meadows and scrub growth. Chuuk lagoon is circled by one of the largest barrier reefs in the world, while Pohnpei has mountains rising to over 600m (2000ft).
LANGUAGE: English; Micronesian Japanese is widely spoken (Kosrean, Ponapean, Chuukese and Yorese).
TIME: Due to the vast area covered by the islands, Micronesia spans two time zones:
Chuuk and Yap: GMT + 9.
Kosrae and Pohnpei: GMT + 10.
COMMUNICATIONS: Telephone: IDD is available. Country code: 691. **Telex/telegram:** Facilities at island capitals and main hotels. **Post:** Post offices are located in Kolonia for Pohnpei, Moen for Chuuk, Lelu for Kosrae and Colonia for Yap. Opening hours: 0830-1630 Monday to Friday and 1000-1200 Saturday. **Press:** See above under the main entry.

PASSPORT/VISA

Regulations and requirements may be subject to change at short notice, and you are advised to contact the appropriate diplomatic or consular authority before finalising travel arrangements. Details of these may be found at the head of this country's entry. Any numbers in the chart refer to the footnotes below.

	Passport Required?	Visa Required?	Return Ticket Required?
Full British	Yes	No/2	Yes
BVP	Not valid	-	-
Australian	Yes	No/2	Yes
Canadian	Yes	No/2	Yes
USA	No	No	Yes
Other EC	Yes	No/2	Yes
Japanese	1	No/2	Yes

PASSPORTS: Valid passports are required by all except:
(a) US nationals with acceptable documentation;
(b) [1] nationals of Japan with a re-entry permit issued for touristic purposes.
British Visitors Passport: Not accepted.
VISAS: [2] Not required for visits of less than 30 days; entry permits are issued on arrival. For longer stays, advance permission is required.
Types of visa: Various. Cost on application.
Validity: Various.
Application to: Division of Immigration, Office of the Attorney General, Central Office, PO Box PS 106, Palikit, Pohnpei 96941. Tel: 320 2606.
Application requirements: (a) Proof of adequate funds. (b) Return or onward ticket.
Working days required: Must apply by post; applications are dealt with on receipt.
Temporary residence: Apply to Division of Immigration (address above).
Note: Foreign-owned vessels or aircraft are required to have entry permits (visas) applied for and in their possession prior to entering Micronesia.

MONEY

Currency: Giant stone money remains in use on Yap, but not for ordinary transactions or any that are likely to involve the visitor. Coins weigh up to 4500kg (4.5 tons) with diameters of up to 3.5m (12ft). For information on convertible currency see *Money* in the introductory section above.

DUTY FREE

The following items may be imported into the Federated States of Micronesia without incurring customs duty:
200 cigarettes or 454g of cigars or tobacco;
*8 litres of beer;**
*4.5 litres of wine;**
*2.7 litres of alcoholic beverage.**
Note [*]: For passengers over 21 years of age.
Prohibited items: Firearms and ammunition. Plants and animals must be declared and will be subject to restrictions.

PUBLIC HOLIDAYS

US public holidays and also the following holidays (including local holidays in principal areas) are celebrated in the Federated States of Micronesia:
Mar 1 '93 Yap State Day. **May** Federation Day. **Sep 8** Kosrae State Day. **Sep 11** Pohnpei State Liberation Day. **Sep 23** Chuuk State Charter Day. **Nov 3** Independence Day. **Nov 8** Pohnpei Constitution Day. **Dec 24** Yap Constitution Day. **Dec 25** Christmas Day. **Jan 1 '94** New Year's Day. **Mar 1** Yap Day.
Note: Variations occur from island to island.

HEALTH

Health care: All the federated states have good government hospitals in the main cities. There are also good dental services and chemists.

TRAVEL

AIR: *Air Micronesia (CO)* flights link the major islands with Guam, Tokyo, Manila and Honolulu. *Air Nauru* provides services twice a week from Kosrae, Pohnpei, Chuuk and Guam. Flights also run daily between Pohnpei and Kosrae on *Pacific Missionary Aviation* aircraft.
Approximate flight times: See above under the main entry for the Trust Territory.
International airport: *Pohnpei* is 1.5km (1 mile) from Kolonia.
Departure tax: Chuuk US$10, Pohnpei US$5 and Kosrae US$6. There is no departure tax from Yap.
SEA: International ports are Pohnpei, Chuuk and Yap. *Nauru Pacific Shipping Lines* provide passenger sailings from Honolulu to Pohnpei and Chuuk. Inter-island trading ships based in Pohnpei, Yap and Chuuk visit the outlying islands.
ROAD: There are good roads in and around major island centres. **Bus:** No bus service. **Taxis:** Available throughout the Federated States and inexpensive. **Car hire:** Self-drive cars are available in major towns.
Documentation: National driving licence or International Driving Permit required.

ACCOMMODATION

There are hotels in the various island capitals. Parts of Chuuk, Pohnpei and Kosrae are being developed into beach resorts. There are no official **camping** grounds, but private arrangements can be made with local landowners.

RESORTS & EXCURSIONS

The most important historical sites include *The Spanish Wall* and *Catholic Bell Tower* in **Pohnpei,** the *Japanese Wartime Communication Centre* at Xavier High School in **Chuuk** and the ruins of *INSARU* in **Kosrae.** There are also small museums in Kosrae and Chuuk. The *Chuuk Lagoon* is one of the largest in the world and holds more than 60 warships. The *Enpein Marine Park* and ancient ruins of *Nan Madol* in Pohnpei are well worth visiting. All states have beautiful white sandy beaches.

SOCIAL PROFILE

FOOD & DRINK: Local specialities include breadfruit (Chuuk) and thin slices of raw fish dipped in a peppery sauce. *Sakau*, as it is known on Pohnpei, or *kava*, as it is known throughout the rest of Polynesia, is made from the root of a shrub which yields a mildly narcotic substance when squeezed through hibiscus bark. There are several *sakau* bars where visitors can sample it and watch it being made. Although some dining rooms serve buffet-style fare, table service is usual and operates at a leisurely pace. Pohnpeians have over a hundred words for yams and grow them to massive proportions (it may take several men to carry one); yams occupy a central position in local culture. Alcohol is prohibited on Chuuk (with the consequence that nearby islands are often used as picnic resorts).
NIGHTLIFE: There are good restaurants and a few cinemas in major island centres. Locals and visitors alike enjoy making their own entertainment. *Sakau* drinking is the most frequent evening activity on Pohnpei. Cultural dances can be arranged through tourist offices or hotels. Most hotels have music, dancing and discos.
SHOPPING: Favourite purchases on Chuuk include love sticks and war clubs. Yap people produce colourful grass skirts, *lava-lavas* woven from hibiscus bark, woven baby cradles, betel-nut pouches and stone money. On Pohnpei there are elaborate, carefully scaled model canoes and woven items. **Shopping hours:** 0800-1900. Some stores are open 1200-1700 Sunday.
SPORT: There are facilities available for fishing, snorkelling, scuba diving, hiking, windsurfing, tennis, canoeing, football, basketball, volleyball and baseball.
SPECIAL EVENTS: In Yap, *mitmits* are feasts, accompanied by dancing and exchanges of gifts which are given by villages reciprocally, often after a period of years has elapsed. *Liberation Day* (September 11) in Pohnpei is preceded by a week of sports and traditional events, including canoe racing. Also in Pohnpei funeral feasts are important events lasting several days. In Kosrae a notice at the airport invites visitors to participate in Sunday church services.
SOCIAL CONVENTIONS: There are considerable variations of custom and belief. 95% of Kosreans are Congregationalists with a deeply held respect for Sunday as a day of rest. Pre-European influences are stronger elsewhere and nowhere more so than in Yap where visitors are only allowed with prior permission. Use of islands, paths, beaches, etc may also require permission in many areas; it is best to check beforehand.
Photography: Permission should always be sought. Though the people are friendly, and usually accommodating, not to seek prior permission before taking pictures is considered an insult, especially on some of the remoter islands.

HISTORY & GOVERNMENT

HISTORY: The Federated States of Micronesia became a US-administered Pacific Trust Territory in 1947. This followed successive colonisations by the Portuguese, Spanish and Germans and latterly Japanese rule between the two World Wars under a mandate from the League of Nations. In November 1986, the Federated States signed a Compact of Free Association with the US administration allowing for near-independence with US defence support. Admission to and support from the South Pacific Forum, an association which groups Australasia with the smaller Pacific island nations, has been particularly valuable. Other than political matters, the governments of President John Haglelgam and his successor and former deputy, Bailey Olter, have been preoccupied with the economic situation. The Federated States suffer from their remoteness and lack of industry and infrastructure. There is some development potential, particularly in the fishing and fish-processing industry, but Micronesia has some way to go before it ceases to be dependent on aid from the United States, which will amount to US$1.3 billion between 1986 and the turn of the century. In 1991, the Federated States of Micronesia were admitted to the United Nations.
GOVERNMENT: The locally drafted constitution promulgated in May 1979 provides for a separate legislature for each of the four states of Kosrae, Yap, Pohnpei (formerly Ponape) and Chuuk (formerly Truk) and for a federal legislature (Congress) of 14 senators. Each state elects one senator for a 4-year term; these four are known as the 'senators-at-large'. The other 10 senators are elected for two years and their representation is allocated according to the population of each state. The President and Vice-President are elected by the Congress from the senators-at-large.

CLIMATE

Tropical with year-round high humidity.

POHNPEI Fed. States of Micronesia

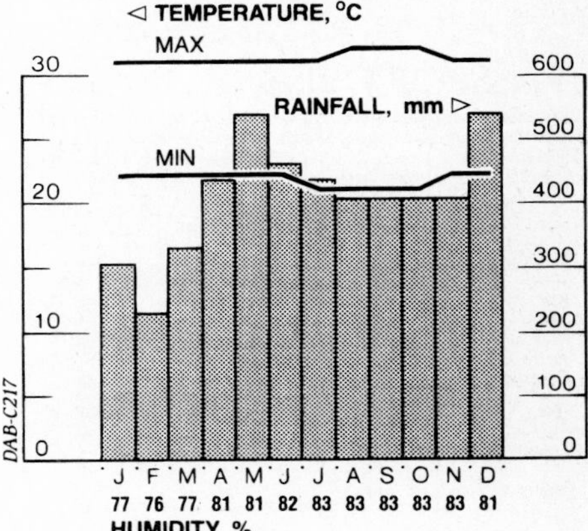

NORTHERN MARIANA ISLANDS

Saipan, Tinian and Rota (formerly the Marianas).

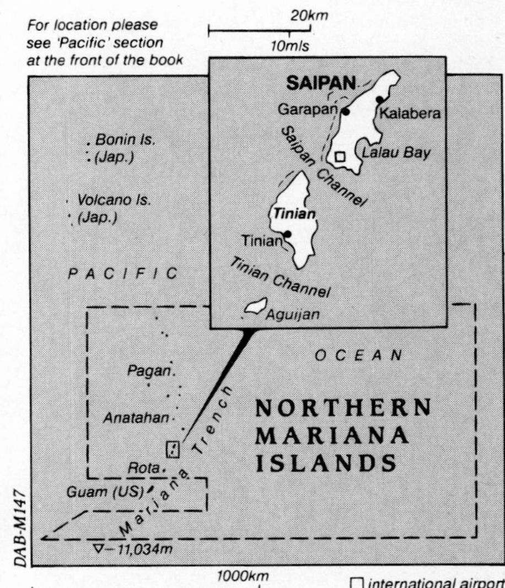

Location: Western Pacific Ocean.

Marianas Visitors' Bureau
PO Box 861
Saipan 96950
Northern Mariana Islands
Tel: 234 8327. Fax: 234 3596.
Immigration and Naturalisation Office
Commonwealth of the Northern Mariana Islands
Saipan 96950
Northern Mariana Islands
Tel: 234 7787.

AREA: 457 sq km (176.5 sq miles).
POPULATION: 31,563 (1987 estimate).
POPULATION DENSITY: 69.1 per sq km.
CAPITAL: Saipan. **Population:** 19,200 (1990).
GEOGRAPHY: Located to the south of Japan and to the north of Guam, the Northern Mariana Islands comprise 14 islands, the main ones being Saipan, Tinian and Rota. The group is compact, consisting of a single chain 650km (400 miles) long. The islands have high volcanic cones.
LANGUAGE: English. Chamorro and Carolinian are the native tongues. Japanese is widely spoken.
RELIGION: Mostly Roman Catholic.
TIME: GMT + 10.
COMMUNICATIONS: Telephone: IDD is available. Country Code: 670. There are pay-phones in Saipan and most hotels, restaurants and other public facilities have telephones which visitors can use. **Fax:** A service is available. **Telex/telegram:** Telexes and telegrams from Micronesia Telecommunications, PO Box 306, Saipan. Tel: 234 6100. Opening hours 0730-1930. **Post:** The post office in Saipan is open 0900-1600. **Press:** The English-language newspapers are the *Marianas Review* and the *Marianas Variety News*.

PASSPORT/VISA

Regulations and requirements may be subject to change at short notice, and you are advised to contact the appropriate diplomatic or consular authority before finalising travel arrangements. Details of these may be found at the head of this country's entry. Any numbers in the chart refer to the footnotes below.

	Passport Required?	Visa Required?	Return Ticket Required?
Full British	Yes	No/2	Yes
BVP	Not valid	-	-
Australian	Yes	No/2	Yes
Canadian	Yes	No/2	Yes
USA	No	No	Yes
Other EC	Yes	No/2	Yes
Japanese	1	No/2	Yes

PASSPORTS: Valid passports are required by all, except US nationals with acceptable documentation and [1] nationals of Japan with a re-entry permit issued for touristic purposes.
British Visitors Passport: Not accepted.
VISAS: [2] Not required for visits of less than 30 days; entry permits are issued on arrival. For longer stays, advance permission is required.
Types of visa: Various.
Validity: Various.
Application to: Immigration and Naturalisation Office (address above).
Application requirements: (a) Proof of adequate funds. (b) Return or onward ticket.
Working days required: By post: applications are dealt with on receipt. In person: 10-15 minutes.
Temporary residence: Apply to Immigration and Naturalisation Office (address above).

DUTY FREE

The following goods may be imported into the Northern Mariana Islands without incurring customs duty:
3 cartons of cigarettes or 454g of cigars or tobacco;
*8 litres of beer;**
*4.5 litres of wine;**
*2.7 litres of alcoholic beverage.**
Note [*]: For passengers over 21 years of age.

PUBLIC HOLIDAYS

US public holidays and also the following holidays are observed in the Northern Mariana Islands:
May 24 '93 Memorial Day. **Jul 4** US Independence Day. **Sep 6** Labour Day. **Nov 25** Thanksgiving Day. **Dec 25** Christmas Day. **Jan 1 '94** New Year's Day. **Jan 3** Commonwealth Day. **Feb 14** George Washington's Birthday celebrations. **May 23** Memorial Day.
Note: Variations occur from island to island.

TRAVEL

AIR: See the main entry for the region above.
International airport: *Saipan (SPN).*
SEA: The international port of the Northern Mariana Islands is Saipan. The following lines sail there: *Nauru Pacific Line, Royal Shipping Co* (PO Box 238, Saipan), *Daiwa Navigation Co, Oceania Line Inc, P&O, Saipan Shipping Co* and *Tiger Line.*
ROAD: There are good roads in and around major island centres. **Bus:** There is a public bus service. **Taxis:** Available in all main centres. **Car hire:** Self-drive cars are available in major towns.
Documentation: International Driving Permit or national licence accepted.

ACCOMMODATION

HOTELS: Hotels in the Northern Mariana Islands vary in standard from luxury to basic. They cater mainly for a Japanese market.

SOCIAL PROFILE

FOOD & DRINK: Local specialities include *kelaguin*, a chewy mixture of diced chicken and shredded coconut and thin slices of raw coconut dipped in a peppery sauce.
NIGHTLIFE: There are several popular bars in Garapan and a few nightclubs and discos.
SHOPPING: Special purchases here include wishing dolls, coconut masks, coconut-crab decorations and woodcarvings, plus numerous duty-free items.
Shopping hours: 0800-2100 Monday to Friday.
SPORT: Watersports are popular with many suitable **diving** and **snorkelling** locations; **windsurfing** is popular on Saipan. Local **fishing** competitions are held in several places. San Jose has a **bowling** alley and there are 9- and 18-hole **golf** courses.
SPECIAL EVENTS: Village fiestas in honour of local patron saints are among the principal annual celebrations. The *Flame Tree Festival*, which celebrates the American liberation of the islands, takes place during the two weeks preceding July 4; it consists of a variety of entertainments and coincides with the fullest flowering of the orange-red blossoms of the royal poinciana trees, hence its name. On Rota, the second weekend in October sees the largest annual event in the islands in honour of San Francisco do Borja, patron saint of Songsong village; it is a revelrous extravaganza of feasting, drinking, music, dancing and processions which attracts visitors from many neighbouring Micronesian islands. Accommodation during this period is hard to find. For further information on special events in the Northern Marianas contact the Mariana Islands Visitors' Bureau (address at top of entry), which produces an annual listing.
SOCIAL CONVENTIONS: The Chamorro culture of the original inhabitants can still be traced, although it is overlaid by strong American influences. Western conventions are well understood.

BUSINESS PROFILE

COMMERCIAL INFORMATION: For further information contact the Saipan Chamber of Commerce, PO Box 806, Chalan Kanoa, Saipan 96950. Tel: 234 6132. Fax: 234 7151.

HISTORY & GOVERNMENT

HISTORY: Formerly a Japanese colony, the Northern Marianas became part of the Pacific Trust Territory administered by the USA under a mandate granted in 1947. In 1987, following a proclamation signed by US President Reagan, the Northern Marianas assumed separate status as a US Commonwealth Territory (similar to Puerto Rico). Its constitution provides internal self-government while the inhabitants retain full civil and political rights within the United States.
GOVERNMENT: The constitution allows for an executive governor, at present Lorenzo de Leon Guerrero, and a bicameral legislature consisting of a 15-seat House of Representatives and a 9-member Senate; all are elected by universal suffrage every two years.

CLIMATE

The rainy season is July to November.

SAIPAN N.Mariana Is. (222m)

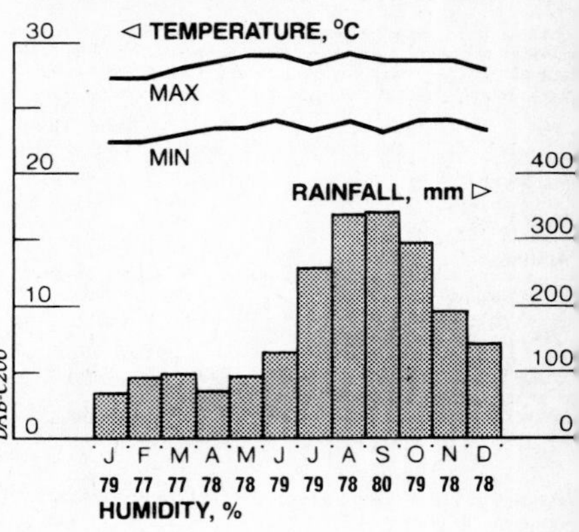

REPUBLIC OF PALAU

(Formerly part of the Caroline Islands.)

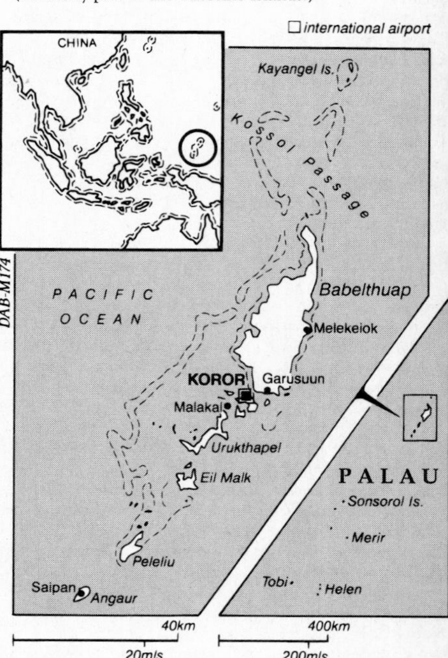

Location: Western Pacific Ocean.

Palau Visitors Authority
PO Box 256
Koror, Palau 96940
Tel: 488 2793. Fax: 488 1453. Telex: 9728-8914.
Liaison Office of the United States of America
PO Box 6028
Koror, Palau 96940
Tel: 488 2920. Fax: 488 2911.

AREA: 508 sq km (196 sq miles); Babelthuap Island: 409 sq km (160 sq miles).
POPULATION: 15,105 (1990 estimate).
POPULATION DENSITY: 29.7 per sq km.
CAPITAL: Koror. **Population:** 10,486.
GEOGRAPHY: Palau, the westernmost cluster of the six major island groups that make up the Caroline Islands, lies 1000km (600 miles) east of the Philippines. The archipelago stretches over 650km (400 miles) from the atoll of Kayangel to the islet of Tobi. The Palau Islands include more than 200 islands, of which only eight are inhabited. With three exceptions, all of the islands are located within a single barrier reef and represent two geological formations. The largest are volcanic and rugged with interior jungle and large areas of grassed terraces. The Rock Islands, now known as the Floating Garden Islands, are of limestone formation while Kayangel, at the northernmost tip, is a classic coral atoll.
LANGUAGE: English and Palauan.

ELIGION: Roman Catholic majority.
IME: GMT + 10.
OMMUNICATIONS: Telephone: IDD code: 680. **ax:** Some hotels have facilities. **Telex/telegram:** Both ervices are available in Koror. **Post:** Post office located Koror. Opening hours: 0730-1130. **Press:** The nglish-language newspaper is the *Palau Weekly*.

PASSPORT/VISA

egulations and requirements may be subject to change at short notice, and you re advised to contact the appropriate diplomatic or consular authority before nalising travel arrangements. Details of these may be found at the head of this ountry's entry. Any numbers in the chart refer to the footnotes below.

	Passport Required?	Visa Required?	Return Ticket Required?
Full British	Yes	No/2	Yes
BVP	Not valid	-	-
Australian	Yes	No/2	Yes
Canadian	Yes	No/2	Yes
USA	No	No	Yes
Other EC	Yes	No/2	Yes
Japanese	1	No/2	Yes

ASSPORTS: Valid passports are required by all except:
a) US nationals with acceptable documentation;
b) [1] nationals of Japan with a re-entry permit issued for ouristic purposes.
ritish Visitors Passport: Not accepted.
ISAS: [2] Not required for visits of less than 30 days; entry ermits are issued on arrival. For longer stays, advance per-nission is required.
ypes of visa: Various. Cost on application.
alidity: Various.
pplication to: Office of Territorial and International ffairs, OTIA Field Office, PO Box 6031, Koror, Palau 6940. Tel: 9655. Fax: 9649.
pplication requirements: (a) Proof of adequate funds. (b) eturn ticket.
Vorking days required: Postal applications are dealt with n receipt.
emporary residence: Apply to the Office of Territorial and nternational Affairs (address above).

DUTY FREE

The following goods may be imported into the Republic of Palau without incurring customs duty:
00 cigarettes or 454g of cigars or tobacco;
*litres of beer;**
*.5 litres of wine;**
*.7 litres of alcoholic beverage.**
Note [*]: For passengers over 21 years of age.

PUBLIC HOLIDAYS

JS public holidays and also the following holidays are elebrated in the Republic of Palau:
Mar 14 '93 Youth Day. **May 15** Senior Citizen's Day. **ul 9** Constitution Day. **Oct 24** UN Day. **Nov 26** Thanksgiving Day. **Dec 25** Christmas Day. **Jan 1 '94** New Year's Day. **Mar 14** Youth Day.
Note: Variations occur from island to island.

TRAVEL

AIR: *Palau Paradise Air* operates flights twice daily (except Saturday) between Babelthuap – Peleliu, Peleliu – Angaur and Babelthuap – Angaur.
nternational airport: *Palau International*, on Babelthuap sland, which is near Koror Island.
Departure tax: US$3.
SEA: International cruise lines seldom call at Palau ports. Visitors who sail privately to Palau will find Naval Oceanographic charts to be most useful. US Naval Chart HO 5500 covers the entire region of Micronesia. Unscheduled nter-island boat services to Babelthuap, Kayangel and Peleliu are available at boat docks around Koror.
ROAD: The road network is being extended but there is little central planning. **Bus:** A public bus provides an unscheduled service from Monday to Friday between Koror and Airai for a set fare each way regardless of distance. **Taxis:** There are many taxis in Koror offering comfortable travel. However, they are not metered and fares are not controlled, so it is advisable to agree on the fare in advance.

SOCIAL PROFILE

FOOD & DRINK: Several restaurants serve American and Japanese food. On request they will generally serve ocal specialities including Mangrove crab and lobster-like angusta. Fresh fish and fruits are especially delicious here.
NIGHTLIFE: Many restaurants have a bar. A few places offer evening entertainment. The Visitors Authority or agents can arrange dance shows. For address see top of entry.
SHOPPING: Palau's best-known art form is the *storyboard*. These are carvings on various lengths of wood, sometimes shaped into crocodiles, turtles or fish and painted. The story-boards depict Palauan stories taken from about 30 popular legends or recorded events. In addition to the storyboards, models of *bais* (houses), canoes and sculptured figurines called *dilukai* are also carved. Other gifts include jewellery, etchings on turtle or black oyster shells, turtleshell trays (a form of Palauan women's money) and baskets, purses, hats and mats woven from pandans and palm. **Shopping hours:** 0800-2100 Monday to Saturday.
SPORT: Palau has some of the world's most spectacular **diving** locations. For example, Jellyfish Lake offers the weird experience of **snorkelling** through a dense population of innocuous jellyfish; elsewhere the waters contain many vertical drops. Rock Island is considered to be the finest location.
SOCIAL CONVENTIONS: Traditional Palauan society was a complex matriarchal system. The people are now amongst the most enterprising in the region, though a version of traditional beliefs, *Modekngei*, exists alongside the imported Christian beliefs. The political system is modeled on that of the USA, and Western culture is being assimilated – not least because of the many Palauans who continue their education abroad. **Tipping:** Not expected.

BUSINESS PROFILE

COMMERCIAL INFORMATION: The following organisation can offer advice: The Palau Chamber of Commerce, Koror, Palau 96940.

HISTORY & GOVERNMENT

HISTORY: After liberation from Japanese occupation in World War II, Palau became part of the Trust Territory of the Pacific Islands, administered by the USA under a mandate from the UN ratified in 1947. In 1986, the Governments of Palau and the USA agreed the terms of a Compact of Free Association, similar to those reached with other Micronesian Trust members, which allows for virtual independence under an American defence umbrella. The Palau Compact has never been signed. The reason derives from the nature of Palau's constitution which was drafted locally and brought into force in 1981. The crucial clause forbids the presence of any nuclear weapons on the islands, including visits by ships equipped to carry them. This is unacceptable to the USA – in Palau as much as anywhere else – which therefore refuses to sign the Compact until the clause is rescinded. However, Palau's constitution further stipulates that any amendments can only be made with the support of a 75% majority in a national referendum. There have been no less than seven referenda on the Compact since 1983, most recently in 1990, all of which produced a majority in favour but none of sufficient size (1987 produced a near miss with 73%). Palau is thus the only remaining member of the Trust Territory of the Pacific Islands. The dispute over the Compact has produced a violent aspect into Palau's politics. President Haruu Remeliik was assassinated in 1985; his successor but one, Lazarus Salii, committed suicide in August 1988. Three months later, the present incumbent, Ngiratkel Etpison, narrowly won the election. Etpison is backed by the Ta Palau Party, which supports the Compact. The party says that the continuing uncertainty over the political situation is deterring much-needed foreign investment and leaving Palau dependent on American aid. In May 1991, the USA told the UN Trusteeship Council that if the Compact was not accepted soon, the territory should consider opening negotiations on full independence.
GOVERNMENT: Executive authority is vested in the President, who is elected for a 4-year term. Legislative authority rests with the bicameral National Congress, the Olbiil era Kelulau.

CLIMATE

Tends to be wet and hot throughout the year.

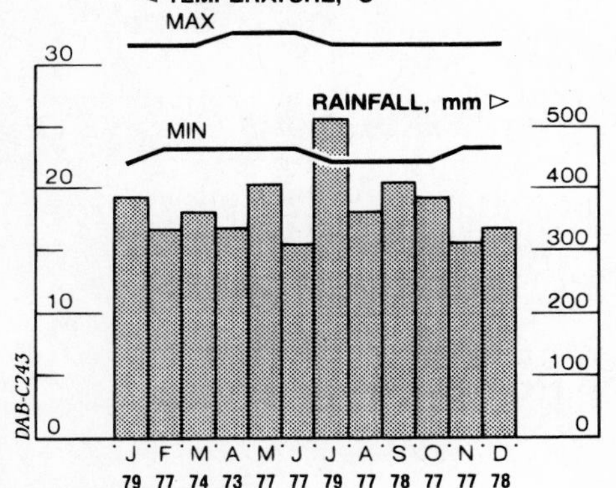

PAKISTAN

☐ *international airport*

Location: Indian subcontinent.

Pakistan Tourism Development Corporation
House No 2, Street 61
F-7/4 Islamabad, Pakistan
Tel: (51) 811 001. Fax: (51) 824 173. Telex: 54356.
High Commission of the Islamic Republic of Pakistan
35/36 Lowndes Square
London SW1X 9JN
Tel: (071) 235 2044. Fax: (071) 416 8417. Telex: 290226. General opening hours: 0930-1730 Monday to Friday. Visa Section opening hours: 1000-1300 for applications, 1630-1715 for collections.
Pakistan Tourism Development Corporation
Suite 433
High Holborn House
52-54 High Holborn
London WC1V 6RB
Tel: (071) 242 3131. Fax: (071) 242 2838. Telex: 23770.
British Embassy
PO Box 1122
Diplomatic Enclave
Ramna 5
Islamabad, Pakistan
Tel: (51) 822 131/5. Fax: (51) 823 439. Telex: 54122 UKEMBPK.
Consulates in: Karachi and Lahore.
Embassy of the Islamic Republic of Pakistan
2315 Massachusetts Avenue, NW
Washington, DC
20008
Tel: (202) 939 6200. Fax: (202) 387 0484.
Consulate General of the Islamic Republic of Pakistan
Pakistan Display Centre
747 Third Avenue
New York, NY
10017
Tel: (212) 879 5800.
Embassy of the United States of America
PO Box 1048
Unit 6220
Diplomatic Enclave
Ramna 5
Islamabad, Pakistan
Tel: (51) 826 161-79. Fax: (51) 822 004. Telex: 5864 AEISL PK.
High Commission of the Islamic Republic of Pakistan
Suite 608, Burnside Building
151 Slater Street
Ottawa, Ontario
K1P 5H3
Tel: (613) 238 7881. Fax: (613) 238 7296.
Consulates in: Montréal and Toronto.
Bestway Tours & Safaris
203-1774 West 5th Avenue
Vancouver, British Columbia
V6J 2X3
Tel: (604) 732 4686. Fax: (604) 732 9744.

Representatives for the Pakistan Tourism Development Corporation.
Canadian High Commission
PO Box 1042
Diplomatic Enclave
Sector G-5
Islamabad, Pakistan
Tel: (51) 211 101. Fax: (51) 211 540. Telex: 5700 DOCAN PK.
Consulate in: Karachi.

AREA: 796,095 sq km (307,374 sq miles).
POPULATION: 108,678,000 (1989 estimate, excluding Afghani refugees).
POPULATION DENSITY: 136.5 per sq km.
CAPITAL: Islamabad. **Population:** 204,364 (1981).
GEOGRAPHY: Pakistan has borders to the north with Afghanistan, to the east with India and to the west with Iran; the Arabian Sea lies to the south. In the far north is the disputed territory of Jammu and Kashmir, bounded by Afghanistan, China and India. Pakistan comprises distinct regions. The northern highlands – the Hindu Kush – are rugged and mountainous; the Indus Valley is a flat, alluvial plain with five major rivers dominating the upper region, eventually joining the Indus River flowing south to the Makran coast; Sind is bounded east by the Thar Desert and the Rann of Kutch, and on the west by the Kirthar Range; the Baluchistan Plateau is an arid tableland encircled by mountains.
LANGUAGE: Urdu and English with local dialects of Sindhi, Baluchi, Punjabi, Pushto, Saraiki and Hindko.
RELIGION: 97% Muslims, 2% Hindi, 1% Christian.
TIME: GMT + 5.
ELECTRICITY: 220 volts AC, 50Hz. Round 2- or 3-pin plugs.
COMMUNICATIONS: Telephone: IDD is available. Country code: 92. **Fax:** A service was introduced in 1986 by the Pakistan telephone and telegraph department. The charge is Rs40 per page and documents must be collected. **Telex/telegram:** There are services at post offices, telegraph offices and main hotels. The Central Telegraph Office at 11 Chundrigar Road, Karachi provides a 24-hour service. **Post:** Airmail takes four to five days to Europe. There are *Poste Restante* facilities in Lahore, Karachi and Rawalpindi. General Post Offices in major cities offer 24-hour services. Important letters should be registered or insured. **Press:** The English-language press enjoys a great deal of influence in business circles but most publications are in Urdu. Dailies include *The Pakistan Times*, *The Business Recorder* and *The Dawn*.
BBC World Service and Voice of America frequencies: From time to time these change. See the section *How to Use this Book* for more information.

BBC:

MHz	15.310	11.955	9.740	15.575

A service is also available on 1413kHz.

Voice of America:

MHz	21.49	15.60	9.525	6.035

PASSPORT/VISA

Regulations and requirements may be subject to change at short notice, and you are advised to contact the appropriate diplomatic or consular authority before finalising travel arrangements. Details of these may be found at the head of this country's entry. Any numbers in the chart refer to the footnotes below.

	Passport Required?	Visa Required?	Return Ticket Required?
Full British	Yes	Yes	Yes
BVP	Not valid	-	-
Australian	Yes	Yes	Yes
Canadian	Yes	Yes	Yes
USA	Yes	Yes	Yes
Other EC	Yes	Yes	Yes
Japanese	Yes	Yes	Yes

Restricted entry and transit: The Government of Pakistan refuses entry to: (a) nationals of Israel, even for transit; (b) nationals of Afghanistan (even if holding a visa for Pakistan) if their ticket or passport shows evidence of transit or boarding in India; (c) holders of passports issued by the Government of Taiwan, except for transit or to change aircraft without leaving the airport.
Nationals of South Africa must pay a deposit and a non-refundable landing fee, unless they are in direct transit.
PASSPORTS: Valid passport required by all.
British Visitors Passport: Not accepted.
VISAS: Requirements are subject to change at short notice but, at present, nationals of the following countries are exempt:
(a) South Korea, Maldives and Zambia for a period of up to 90 days;
(b) the Philippines for a period of up to 59 days;
(c) Romania, Western Samoa, Singapore and Tonga for a period of up to 30 days.
Types of visa: Single entry, generally for a maximum stay of 3 months. A multiple journey visa is also available allowing six journeys in a total period not exceeding one year, maximum 3-month stay at any one time. Visas must be used within 6 months of the date of issue. Price of visa varies according to nationality (£30 for UK nationals).
Application to: Consulate (or Consular Section at Embassy or High Commission). For addresses, see top of entry.
Application requirements: (a) Valid passport. (b) 1 application form. (c) 1 passport-size photo. (d) Confirmed return/onward ticket.

MONEY

Currency: Pakistani Rupee (Re, singular; Rs, plural) = 100 paisa. Notes are in denominations of Rs500, 100, 50, 10, 5, 2 and 1. Coins are in denominations of Rs1 and 50, 25, 10, 5, 2 and 1 paisa.
Credit cards: American Express is the most widely accepted card. Visa, Access/Mastercard and Diners Club have more limited use. Check with your credit card company for details of merchant acceptability and other services which may be available.
Travellers cheques: Generally accepted at most banks, hotels and major shops.
Exchange rate indicators: The following figures are included as a guide to the movements of the Pakistani Rupee against Sterling and the US Dollar:

Date:	Oct '89	Oct '90	Oct '91	Oct '92
£1.00=	34.50	42.00	42.54	37.00
$1.00=	21.32	22.23	24.51	23.31

Currency restrictions: The import and export of local currency is limited to Rs100 in denominations of Rs10 or less. Unlimited import of foreign currency, subject to declaration. Export of foreign currency is limited to the amount declared. All exchange transactions must be made through authorised dealers. If not declared a maximum of US$500 or US$2000 per family can be exported; larger amounts require the approval of the State Bank of Pakistan.
Banking hours: 0930-1300 and 1500-2000 Saturday to Thursday, closed Friday.

DUTY FREE

The following items may be imported into Pakistan without incurring customs duty:
200 cigarettes or 50 cigars or 500g tobacco;
250ml of perfume and toilet water (opened).
Note: (a) The import of alcohol, matches, plants, fruit and vegetables is prohibited. However, if a visitor imports alcohol by mistake or with the intention of taking it out of Pakistan, it will be held by customs and returned on departure. (b) Precious stones and jewellery can be *exported* up to a value of Rs10,000 (Rs5000 for nationals of Afghanistan, the Gulf States, Iran and Nepal) and carpets to the value of Rs25,000, if accompanied by an export permit. All items are subject to proof of having been purchased in foreign currency. The export of antiques is prohibited.

PUBLIC HOLIDAYS

Public holidays observed in Pakistan are as follows:
Mar 23 '93 Pakistan Day. **Mar 25** Eid al-Fitr (End of Ramadan). **Apr 9** Good Friday. **Apr 12** Easter Monday. **May 1** Labour Day. **Jun 1** Eid al-Adha (Feast of the Sacrifice). **Jun 21** Muharram (Islamic New Year). **Jun 30** Ashoura. **Aug 14** Independence Day. **Aug 30** Birth of the Prophet. **Sep 6** Defence Day. **Sep 11** Anniversary of the Death of Quaid-i-Azam. **Nov 9** Iqbal Day. **Dec 25** Quaid-i-Azam's Birthday and Christmas. **Dec 26** Boxing Day. **Feb '94** Beginning of Ramadan. **Mar** Eid al-Fitr (End of Ramadan). **Mar 23** Pakistan Day.
Note: (a) Muslim festivals are timed according to local sightings of various phases of the Moon and the dates given above are approximations. During the lunar month of Ramadan that precedes Eid al-Fitr, Muslims fast during the day and feast at night and normal business patterns may be interrupted. Many restaurants are closed during the day and there may be restrictions on smoking and drinking. Some disruption may continue into Eid al-Fitr itself. Eid al-Fitr and Eid al-Adha may last anything from two to ten days, depending on the region. For more information see the section *World of Islam* at the back of the book. (b) Christian holidays are taken by the Christian community only.

HEALTH

Regulations and requirements may be subject to change at short notice, and you are advised to contact your doctor well in advance of your intended date of departure. Any numbers in the chart refer to the footnotes below.

	Special Precautions?	Certificate Required?
Yellow Fever	No	1
Cholera	Yes	2
Typhoid & Polio	Yes	-
Malaria	3	-
Food & Drink	4	-

[1]: Yellow fever vaccination certificate is required of all travellers arriving from any part of a country in which yellow fever is endemic. Infants under six months of age are exempt if the mother's vaccination certificate shows her to have been vaccinated prior to the child's birth. The countries and areas that were included in the former endemic zones are considered by Pakistan to be infected areas.
[2]: Following WHO guidelines issued in 1973, a cholera vaccination certificate is no longer a condition of entry to Pakistan. However, cholera is a serious risk in this country and precautions are essential. Up-to-date advice should be sought before deciding whether these precautions should include vaccination as medical opinion is divided over its effectiveness. See the *Health* section of the end of the book.
[3]: Malaria risk exists throughout the year in all areas below 2000m. The malignant *falciparum* strain is present and has been reported to be chloroquine-resistant.
[4]: All water should be regarded as being potentially contaminated. Water used for drinking, brushing teeth or making ice should have first been boiled or otherwise sterilised. Milk is unpasteurised and should be boiled. Powdered or tinned milk is available and is advised, but make sure that it is reconstituted with pure water. Avoid dairy products which are likely to have been made from unboiled milk. Only eat well-cooked meat and fish, preferably served hot. Salad and mayonnaise may carry increased risk. Vegetables should be cooked and fruit peeled.
Rabies is present. For those at high risk, vaccination before arrival should be considered. If you are bitten abroad seek medical advice without delay. For more information consult the *Health* section at the back of the book.
Health care: Full health insurance is essential.

PAKISTAN — **HEALTH REGULATIONS** — **VISA REGULATIONS** — Code-Link

GALILEO/WORLDSPAN

TI-DFT/ISB/HE

TI-DFT/ISB/VI

SABRE

TIDFT/ISB/HE

TIDFT/ISB/VI

To access this information on your CRS, swipe the barcode with a light pen or type in the text under the barcode. For more information, see the introduction *How to Use This Book.*

TRAVEL - International

AIR: Pakistan's national airline is *Pakistan International Airlines (PK)*.

Approximate flight times: From Karachi to *London* is 11 hours 50 minutes, to *Los Angeles* is 22 hours 30 minutes, to *New York* is 21 hours 40 minutes, to *Riyadh* is 3 hours 35 minutes and to *Singapore* is 6 hours 55 minutes.

International airports: *Karachi (KHI)* (Civil), 12km (8 miles) northeast of the city (travel time – 25 minutes). Coaches to the city meet all arrivals. A bus runs from dusk to dawn every 30 minutes. Taxi services to the city are available. Good airport facilities, including duty-free shops, bar/restaurant, post office, bank and shops.

Lahore (LHE), 11km (7 miles) southeast of the city (travel time – 20 minutes). Coaches leaves every 20 minutes for the city. Buses go every 10 minutes. Taxi services to the city are also available. Airport facilities include car hire, bank, restaurant and shops.

Islamabad (ISB) (International), 8km (5 miles) east of the city (travel time – 20 minutes). Coach and taxi services to the city are available. There are full duty-free facilities.

Peshawar (PEW), 4km (2.5 miles) from the city (travel time – 20 minutes). Full bus and taxi services to the city are available.

Departure tax: Rs400 for passengers travelling first class, Rs300 for club class and Rs200 for economy class. Transit passengers and children under two years of age are exempt. Visitors exiting Pakistan by land routes are subject to a toll tax of Rs2.

SEA: The major port is Karachi (Keamari). There are a number of shipping lines serving Karachi from Europe. It is both Pakistan's and Afghanistan's port for goods, together with Port Quasim.

RAIL: The only rail link to India is a train from Lahore to Amritsar which leaves at noon daily. Passengers have to be at the station by 0900 hours for customs and immigration procedures. A rail link also extends over the Iranian border to Zahedan, but connections to and from Iran are currently provided by bus.

ROAD: Road links from Iran, India and Afghanistan. The main road link is between Karachi and Lahore. There is a road from Kabul (Afghanistan) to Rawalpindi. Another road runs from Karachi to Quetta and to the border with Iran.

TRAVEL - Internal

AIR: All domestic services are operated by *PIA*. There are many daily flights from Karachi to Lahore, Rawalpindi and other commercial centres. Air transport is the quickest and most efficient means of travel.

Departure tax: Rs20 for all passengers on internal flights.

RIVER: Traffic along the Indus River is almost exclusively commercial and many goods are carried to Punjab and the north.

RAIL: A legacy of British rule is an extensive rail network, based on the main line from Karachi to Lahore, Rawalpindi and Peshawar, which has several daytime and overnight trains. Most other routes have several daily trains. Even first-class compartments can be hot and crowded, but ice containers are provided on some trains. Travel in air-conditioned coaches is advised.

Pakistan Railways offer concessions for tourists, excluding Indian nationals travelling by rail. Discount of 25% is offered to individuals and groups, and 50% for students. Vehicles owned by foreign tourists or hired locally are also eligible to 25% discount in freight charges when transported by rail. Details from railway offices in Pakistan.

Approximate rail times: Karachi to Lahore is 16 hours; Karachi to Rawalpindi is 28 hours; Karachi to Peshawar is 32 hours.

ROAD: The highway network between cities is well made and maintained. **Bus:** Regular services run between most towns and villages. Lahore–Rawalpindi–Peshawar has an hourly service. Advance booking is recommended. **Car hire:** Available in most major cities as well as at Karachi, Lahore and Rawalpindi airports. Most hotels can book cars for guests. **Documentation:** An International Driving Permit will be issued. Take national driving licence.

URBAN: Extensive **bus** and **minibus** services operate in Lahore, Karachi and other towns, although services can be crowded. **Taxis:** Reasonably priced and widely available, they are by far the most efficient means of urban travel. Note that they may not operate after sunset during Ramadan. **Auto-rickshaws** are also available.

ACCOMMODATION

HOTELS: Pakistan offers a wide range of accommodation. Modern well-equipped hotels are to be found in most major towns and offer excellent facilities such as swimming pools and sports facilities. There are also cottages, Dak bungalows and resthouses in all principal hill stations and health resorts. A Government room tax of

5% is added to the cost of accommodation. In all cases it is advisable to book well in advance and check reservations.

YOUTH HOSTELS: The Pakistan Youth Hostel Association has nine hostels throughout the country available to members of affiliated organisations. Details can be obtained from the Pakistan Youth Hostel Association, 110 Firdous Market, Gurberg 111, Lahore. Tel: (42) 83145.

RESORTS & EXCURSIONS

KARACHI: The largest city in Pakistan, formerly the capital, is situated on the shores of the Arabian Gulf near the mouth of the Indus. The capital of Sind province, it is now a modern industrial city and Pakistan's port. Though not strictly a tourist centre there are a number of attractions, such as the fish wharf where gaily-coloured boats bring in seafood, one of the country's major foreign exchange earners. The hundreds of street restaurants, tea houses, samosa and juice stalls provide an adventurous taste of local character. Camels and horses are available for hire at Paradise Point. Boats can be hired to sail out of the harbour; to lift anchor at sunset and catch and eat crabs in the moonlight is a uniquely romantic experience. There are architectural reminders of the former British Imperialist presence, especially in the clubs. The most magnificent building, however, is the *Quaiz-i-Azam's Mazar*, the mausoleum of the founder of the Pakistani nation, made entirely of white marble with impressive North African arches and magnificent Chinese crystal chandeliers. The changing of the guards, which takes place three times a day, is the best time to visit. Other places to visit are the *National Museum*, parks, zoo and a beach at **Clifton.**

SIND: A region known for the remarkable quality of its light, with two main places of interest: *Mohenjo Daro*, a settlement dating back 5000 years, and *Tatta*, notable for its mausoleums and mosques. There are sporting facilities on *Lake Haleji*, 14km (9 miles) away.

THE PUNJAB: Lahore is a historic, bustling, dirty city with buildings of pink and white marble. There is plenty to see: bazaars, the *Badshahi Mosque*, the beautiful *Shalimar Gardens*, the *National Museum of Archaeology* and the *Gate of Chauburji*. **Other towns** in the Punjab include: Lyallpur, Taxila, Sirkap, Attock, Harappa, Multan and Bahawalpur.

Islamabad, the capital of Pakistan since 1963, and **Rawalpindi,** can both be found on the *Potowar Plain*. The decision to build a new capital city in this area transformed the sleepy town of Rawalpindi into an important twin to Islamabad. Now Rawalpindi houses a great majority of the civil servants working in the government district on the other side of the river. The old part of the town boasts fine examples of local architecture and bazaars crammed into the narrow streets with craftsmen still using the traditional methods.

As a planned capital Islamabad lacks some of the regional flair of other cities but it houses an interesting variety of modern buildings especially in the part designated for government offices. The city itself has an air of spaciousness with numerous parks, gardens and fountains below the silhouette of the *Margalla Hills*. In the midst of these lies *Daman-e-Kohj*; a terraced garden with an excellent view over the city. Well worth a visit is the *Shah Faisal Masjid* which is reputed to accommodate 100,000 worshippers. The majestic white building comprises 88m (288ft) minarets and a desert tent-like structure, the main prayer chamber. About 8km (39 miles) from the city is *Rawal Lake* with an abundance of leisure facilities including watersports and a picnic area.

KASHMIR: In this province are some of the highest mountains in the world, one of the most famous being *Nanga Parbat*. Here too is the second highest mountain in the world, *K2*, also known as Mount Godwin-Austen or Oogir Feng. The settlements of *Gilgit* and *Skardu* are well-known stop-offs on the mountaineering trail.

PESHAWAR: The capital of the former North West Frontier Province, this is the area of the Pathans. **Peshawar City** is surrounded by high walls with 20 gates leading into it. There is evidence in the lawns and parks of the former colonial days. All men carry a weapon, which is the normal equipment for a Panthan warrior. In this region is the celebrated *Khyber Pass*, a 1200m-(3960ft) high sheer rock wall separating Pakistan and Afghanistan.

SOCIAL PROFILE

FOOD & DRINK: There are three types of cuisine in Pakistan: Pakistani, Western and Chinese. Western cooking is often disappointing, although some restaurants do have European chefs. Local cuisine is based on curry or *masala* (hot and spicy) sauces accompanying chicken, mutton, shrimps and a wide choice of vegetables. Specialities include *brain masala*, *biryani* (seasoned rice with mutton, chicken and yoghurt known as *maot*), *pilao* (similar but less spicy), *sag gosht* (spinach and lamb curry) and *niramish* (fried vegetables with herbs). Lahore is the centre for Mogul-style cuisine known as *moghlai*. Specialities include *chicken tandoori*, *shish kebabs* (charcoal-grilled meat on skewers), *shami-kebabs* (patties of chopped meat fried in *ghee* or butter), *tikka-kebabs* (grilled mutton or beef seasoned and spiced) and *chicken tikka* (highly seasoned chicken quarters, charcoal-grilled). Desserts include pastries, *shahi tukray* (slices of fried bread cooked in milk or cream, sweetened with syrup and topped with nuts and saffron), *halwa* (sweetmeat made with eggs, carrots, maize cream, *sooji* and nuts) and *firni* (similar to vanilla custard). **Drink:** The national drink is tea, drunk strong with milk and often very sweet. Alcohol may be bought at major hotels by visitors who have purchased a Liquor Permit from the Excise and Taxation Office for Rs60. Wine is expensive and only available in top restaurants. Pakistani-brewed beer is widely available, as is the national drink, tea, and canned fizzy drinks. There are no bars since there are strict laws concerning alcohol, and it is illegal to drink in public. Waiter service is provided in the larger hotels and restaurants.

NIGHTLIFE: Top hotels have bars and dancing but there is little Western-style nightlife. Cinemas in the large cities show international as well as Pakistani films. Cultural programmes of traditional music and dance can be seen and the Pakistani Arts Academy performs at various times during the year. Festivals and annual celebrations are well worth seeing.

SHOPPING: Special purchases include carved wooden tables, trays, screens, silver trinkets, pottery, camel-skin lamps, bamboo decorations, brassware, cane items, conch shell ornaments, glass bangles, gold ornaments, hand-embroidered shawls, rugs and carpets, silks, cashmere shawls and *saleem shahi* shoes with upturned toes. While some of the major towns have craft centres where handicrafts from different regions are sold, bazaars often provide the most interesting shopping. It is expected that the customer should bargain for goods. **Shopping hours:** 0930-1300 1500-2000 Saturday to Thursday. Bazaars stay open longer.

SPORT: Golf: Clubs are located in the large cities and visitors are generally allowed to play a course on the introduction of a member or by acquiring temporary membership. **Tennis:** Clubs in the large cities have courts and visitors must be introduced by a member or can often obtain temporary membership through the Pakistan Tourism Development Corporation. **Watersports:** In addition to the beaches, **swimming** pools can be found in various clubs in large towns and in major hotels. Keamari sailboats or motorboats can be hired at a previously agreed price. Deep-sea night **fishing** is particularly good. There are also freshwater lakes with good fishing.

Spectator sports: Cricket, the national sport, can be watched in most major towns. **Football** and **hockey** are becoming national sports and regular matches can be seen in the stadium at Karachi and at other sportsfields all over the country. **Polo** matches can be seen in major cities and **horseracing** takes place in winter in Karachi and Lahore.

SPECIAL EVENTS: The following is a list of some of the special events taking place in Pakistan during 1993/94:

Feb-Mar '93 *Mela Chiragnan (Festival of Lamps)*, Lahore. **Mar** *National Horse and Cattle Show*, Lahore. **Mar-Apr** *Jashan-e-Khyber*, Peshawar. **Sep-Oct** *Jashan-e-Gilgit*, Gilgit. **Jan-Feb '94** *Sibi Horse and Cattle Show* (Baluchistan), Sibi.

SOCIAL CONVENTIONS: Shaking hands is the usual form of greeting. Mutual hospitality and courtesy are of great importance at all levels, whatever the social standing of the host. Visitors must remember that most Pakistanis are Muslim and should respect their customs and beliefs. Smoking is prohibited in some public places and it is polite to ask permission before lighting a cigarette. It is common for visiting business people to be entertained in hotels and restaurants. If invited to a private home a company or national souvenir is welcome. Informal dress is acceptable for most occasions. Women should avoid wearing tight clothing and should ensure that their arms and legs are covered. Pakistani society is divided into classes and within each group there is a subtle social grading. The Quran is the law for Muslims and it influences every aspect of daily life. See the section *The World of Islam* at the back of the book for more information. **Tipping:** Most hotels and restaurants add 10% service charge. Other tipping is discretionary.

BUSINESS PROFILE

ECONOMY: About half of the Pakistani labour force works in agriculture with wheat, rice, sugar cane and cotton as the main products. Poor weather and underdevelopment have hindered significant growth in this sector in recent years and the Government is attempting to stimulate other parts of the economy. Mining has considerable potential, given that deposits have been positively identified but little investment has been made in their exploitation. Oil production began during the 1980s, but remains on a small scale by world standards. Pakistan has reserves of graphite and limestone, as well as copper and some coal. Established manufacturing industries include textiles, food processing and building materials. Pakistan's lack of prosperity entitles the country to considerable foreign aid which has been more forthcoming since Pakistan managed to improve its rate of repayment – with the exception of the United States which recently cut its aid provision drastically due to Pakistan's refusal to curtail its nuclear programme. Despite that, Pakistan has made much recent economic progress: trade barriers and exchange controls have been largely removed (boosting foreign exchange accounts by US$1 billion as remittances from abroad resumed after the Gulf War); the budget deficit has been cut; and government coffers have been swelled by the proceeds of the privatisation of nearly 100 banks, industrial concerns, transport and communications organisations. Foreign investment has risen sharply, assisted by a new foreign investment law: for this reason, the Government is worried about the effect of Islamisation (see *History*) upon the economy. Japan is the country's largest trading partner, providing 16% of the country's imports and buying 10% of its exports. The USA, Saudi Arabia, Germany and the UK are the other principal trading partners.

BUSINESS: Ties should be worn for important business appointments. English is commonly used. Appointments should be made, remembering that businesses are usually closed on Fridays and Muslim holidays. Visiting cards should be used. **Government office hours:** 0830-1400 Saturday to Thursday. **Office hours:** 0900-1600 Saturday to Thursday.

COMMERCIAL INFORMATION: The following organisation can offer advice: Overseas Investors Chamber of Commerce and Industry, Talpur Road, Karachi. Tel: (21) 222 557. Telex: 2870.

HISTORY & GOVERNMENT

HISTORY: Created in response to Muslim demands for an Islamic state when India gained independence in 1947, Pakistan originally consisted of two parts, separated from each other by 1600km (1000 miles) of Indian territory. The first Governor-General of Pakistan was Muhammed Ali Jinnah, who had led the struggle for a separate Pakistan inside the Congress Party (see *India*). But in contrast to India, democracy failed to take root and Pakistan suffered prolonged periods of military rule. The first of these came in 1958 when martial law was declared and political parties abolished. The martial law co-ordinator, General (later Field Marshal) Ayub Khan, became President in 1960. He was replaced in 1969 by the Commander-in-Chief of the army, General Agha Muhammed Yahya Khan, who resisted demands for autonomy by the eastern part of the country, where civil war broke out in 1971, and the intervention of the Indian army on the side of the secessionists eventually secured an independent Bangladesh, leaving a truncated Pakistan in the west. Democratic civilian government followed the defeat, and President Zulfiqar Ali Bhutto took over as President from the discredited military regime. In 1977, however, the military again took power in a coup, and re-established martial law under General Mohammed Zia ul-Haq, who became President a year later. Bhutto was executed in 1979. However, following the death of President Zia in a plane crash in 1988, the military authorities decided to reinstitute a democratic constitution and civilian government. Despite a strong challenge from the military-backed Islamic Democratic Alliance, Bhutto's daughter, Benazir, long the focus for opposition, came to power as leader of her father's old party, the Pakistan People's Party. But the army was determined to have her removed from office and at the beginning of August 1990 they got their way when President Ghulam Ishaq Khan, exploiting obscure constitutional powers, dismissed Bhutto and her government. A caretaker President, Mustafa Jatoi, was installed until new elections could be held. At the October polls, after an exceptionally savage electoral campaign, Bhutto's Pakistan People's Party was heavily defeated by the Islamic Democratic Alliance (IDA), which almost won an overall majority. The major issues for the Sharif government have been the economy, regional security and the increasingly complex relationship between the two. The economy was badly affected by the Gulf crisis, not through the expected oil price hike (which never happened) but by the ending of remittances to their families from suddenly redundant Pakistani workers in the Gulf. The invasion of Kuwait in August 1990 was followed in October by a 90% cut in the half-billion dollar annual aid from the United States on account of Pakistan's continual refusal, after repeated warnings, to halt its nuclear weapons development programme and sign the nuclear Non-Proliferation Treaty (NPT). The programme was begun in 1971 after Pakistan's defeat by India and has progressed steadily with Chinese assistance since then: the intention has been to provide some counterweight to India's own nuclear arsenal. (Delhi, which has run a similar Soviet-backed project over several decades, has not signed the NPT either). Since the Soviet withdrawal from Afghanistan, however, Pakistan's role as a key strategic ally in South Asia has dwindled and Washington has become far less indulgent of Pakistan's nuclear aspirations. Some hard-liners in the Pakistani military have been contemplating a regional alliance with China and Iran directed against India, and are concerned about recent American overtures to Delhi (which has been historically closer to the former USSR). Their hand may be strengthened by Indian rejection of a five-party conference on nuclear issues in the region (involving the USA, CIS, China, Pakistan and India). Relations with India have long been soured by the territorial dispute over Kashmir, which is divided between the two countries and is the scene of frequent border clashes. Nawaz Sharif believes that the nuclear proliferation issue cannot be solved until Kashmir is settled. Sharif is keen to reduce tension not only for political reasons but to allow a reduction of Pakistan's considerable defence budget. An approach has been made to the IMF for financial support (the attitude of the USA here is as yet unclear), in anticipation of which the Government has introduced a programme of deregulation and privatisation. Domestic critics, principally those from the influential Muslim fundamentalist constituency, have been placated by the introduction of a version of Islamic law (*Sharia*).

GOVERNMENT: A new constitution was promulgated in 1985 which, after modifications following the death of Zia and the demise of the military government, formed the basis for Pakistan's current system of democratic government. The bicameral legislature comprises a 207-member National Assembly and an 87-member Senate, the former directly elected by universal suffrage and the latter elected by four provincial assemblies.

CLIMATE

Three seasons: winter (March to April) is warm and cooled by sea breezes on the coast, summer (April to July) has extreme temperatures, the monsoon season (July to September) has the highest rainfall on the hills. Karachi has little rain. The best time to visit the south is between November and March, when the days are cool and clear.

Required clothing: Lightweights are worn most of the year, with warmer clothes between November and April, particularly in the north. Rainwear is advisable.

KARACHI Pakistan (4m)

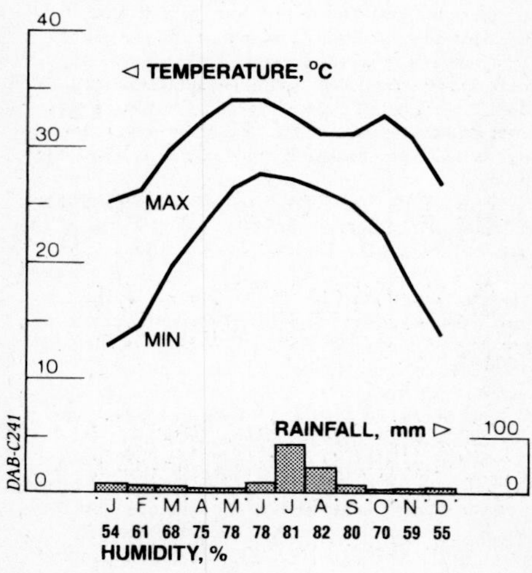

PANAMA

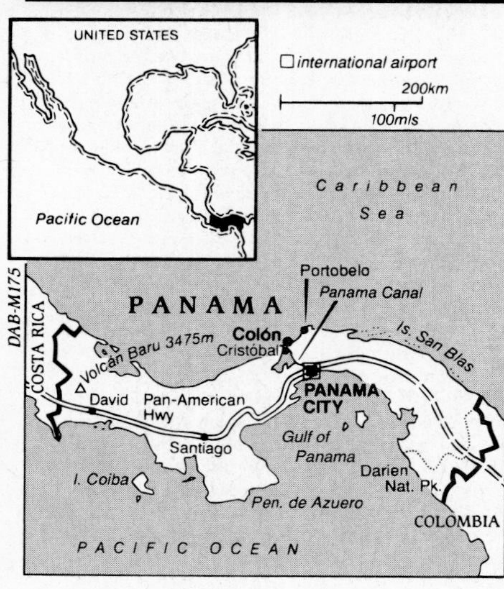

Location: Central America.

Instituto Panameño de Turismo (IPAT)
Apartado 4421
Centro de Convenciones ATLAPA
Vía Israel
Panamá 5
Republic of Panama
Tel: 267 000. Fax: 263 483. Telex: 3359.

Embassy of the Republic of Panama *and* Information & Tourist Affairs
119 Crawford Street
London W1H 1AF
Tel: (071) 487 5633. Fax: (071) 935 2764.

Panamanian Consulate
24 Tudor Street
London EC4Y OAY
Tel: (071) 353 4792. Fax: (071) 583 0008. Telex: 8812982 PANCON G. Opening hours: 1000-1200 and 1400-1600 Monday to Friday.

British Embassy
Apartado 889, Zona 1
4th & 5th Floors, Torre Banco Sur
Calle 53 Este
Urbanizacion Orbarrio
Panamá 1
Republic of Panama
Tel: 690 866 *or* 695 019 *or* 694 006. Fax: 230 730. Telex: 3620 PROPANA PG.

Embassy of the Republic of Panama
2862 McGill Terrace, NW
Washington, DC 20008
Tel: (202) 483 1407. Fax: (202) 483 8413. Telex: 64371.

Embassy of the United States of America
Apartado 6959
Avenida Balboa
Entre Calle 37 y 38
Panamá 5
Republic of Panama
Tel: 271 777. Fax: 039 470. Telex: 3583.

Panamanian Consulate
Suite 210
2788 Bathurst Street
Toronto, Ontario
L3R 3E9
Tel: (416) 787 2122 *or* 787 2724.
Consulates in: Halifax and Montréal.

Canadian Consulate
Aero Peru Piso 5B, Edificio Proconsa
Calle Manuel y Caza
Campo Alegre
Panamá City
Republic of Panama
Tel: 647 014.

AREA: 75,517 sq km (29,157 sq miles).
POPULATION: 2,466,228 (1991 estimate).
POPULATION DENSITY: 32.7 per sq km.
CAPITAL: Panama City. **Population:** 615,150 (1991).
GEOGRAPHY: Panama forms the land link between the North and South American continents. Panama borders Columbia to the east, Costa Rica to the west, and the Caribbean and the Pacific Ocean to the north and south. The country forms an S-shaped isthmus which runs east–west over a total length of 772km (480 miles) and is between 60-177km (37/110 miles) wide. The landscape is mountainous with lowlands on both coastlines cut by streams, wooded slopes and a wide area of savannah-covered plains and rolling hills called *El Interior* between the Azuero peninsula and the Central Mountains. The Caribbean and the Pacific Ocean are linked by the man-made Panama Canal, cut into a gap between the Cordillera de Talamanca and the San Blas mountain range and stretching for over 65km (40 miles); the length of the canal is often referred to as 80km (50 miles) as this is the distance between deep water points of entry. Only about a quarter of the country is inhabited. The majority of the population live either around the Canal and main cities of Panama City and Colón or the Pacific lowlands and the adjacent mountains. (Forty per cent of the population are concentrated in the two cities which control the entrance and exit of the canal.)
LANGUAGE: The official language is Spanish, but English is widely spoken.
RELIGION: 98% Roman Catholic.
TIME: GMT - 5.
ELECTRICITY: 120 volts AC, 60Hz. Plugs are the flat 2-pin American type.
COMMUNICATIONS: Telephone: IDD is available. Country code: 507. **Fax:** Some hotels have facilities. **Telex:** Facilities in Panama City and major hotels. A tax of US$1 is levied against each call. **Telegram:** Facilities in Panama City and major hotels. A tax of 50 cents is levied against each telegram. **Post:** Airmail to Europe takes from five to ten days. Main post offices have *Poste Restante* facilities. Post office hours: 0800-1700 Monday to Friday. **Press:** *El Panamá America* and *Crítica Libre* (both in Spanish) are the largest daily newspapers. *Colón News* is a weekly paper published in both English and Spanish and the US Army publish a daily newspaper in English, *Tropic Times*.
BBC World Service and Voice of America frequencies: From time to time these change. See the section *How to Use this Book* for more information.

BBC:				
MHz	17.72	11.78	9.590	5.975
Voice of America:				
MHz	15.21	11.74	9.815	6.030

PASSPORT/VISA

Regulations and requirements may be subject to change at short notice, and you are advised to contact the appropriate diplomatic or consular authority before finalising travel arrangements. Details of these may be found at the head of this country's entry. Any numbers in the chart refer to the footnotes below.

	Passport Required?	Visa Required?	Return Ticket Required?
Full British	Yes	No	Yes
BVP	Not valid	-	-
Australian	Yes	Yes	Yes
Canadian	Yes	Yes	Yes
USA	Yes	Yes	Yes
Other EC	Yes	I	Yes
Japanese	Yes	Yes	Yes

Note: (a) Panamanian immigration procedures are rigidly enforced and non-compliance with the regulations may result in fines varying from US$50-250 and transportation at carrier's expense to country of origin. Passport and visa regulations are liable to change at short notice and visitors are advised to consult the Panamanian Consul before travelling. (b) Nationals of the following countries must have authorisation from the immigration authorities in Panama before attempting to enter: Afghanistan, Albania, Algeria, Andorra, Angola, Bahrain, Bangladesh, Benin, Bhutan, Botswana, Bulgaria, Burkina Faso, Burundi, Cambodia, Cameroon, Central African Republic, China, Congo, Cuba, Czechoslovakia, Ethiopia, Fiji, Gabon, Gambia, Ghana, Hong Kong, Hungary, India, Indonesia, Iran, Iraq, Jordan, Kenya, Kiribati, Kuwait, Laos, Lesotho, Lebanon, Liberia, Libya, Madagascar, Malawi, Malaysia, Maldives, Mali, Mauritania, Mauritius, Morocco, Myanmar, Mongolia, Mozambique, Nauru, Nepal, Niger, Nigeria, North Korea, Oman, Pakistan, Papua New Guinea, Palestine, Poland, Qatar, Romania, Rwanda, Saudi Arabia, Senegal, Sierra Leone, Somalia, South Africa, Sri Lanka, Sudan, Syria, Tanzania, Togo, Tonga, Tunisia, Turkey, Tuvalu, Uganda, United Arab Emirates, CIS,

Vanuatu, Vietnam, Yemen, Yugoslavia, Zaïre, Zambia and Zimbabwe.
PASSPORTS: Valid passport required by all.
British Visitors Passport: Not accepted.
VISAS: Required by all except the following who will be issued with a Tourist Card (if travelling as tourists – all business visitors require a visa):
(a) [1] nationals of Germany, Spain and the UK;
(b) nationals of Austria, Costa Rica, Finland, Honduras and Switzerland.
Types of visa: Tourist and Business; Tourist Cards.
Validity: Validity of a Tourist or Business visa is 30 days from the date of entry, to be used within a 3-month period from date of issue. Extendable to 90 days when in Panama.
Application to: Consulate (or Consular Section at Embassy). For addresses, see top of entry.
Application requirements: (a) Valid passport. (b) 2 photos. (c) 2 completed application forms. (d) Return ticket. (e) Fee (for some nationalities). (f) For Business visa, a letter from the sponsor in the UK stating nature of business, and evidence of funds to cover expenses whilst in Panama.
Working days required: 24 hours when applying in person.

MONEY

Currency: Balboa (Ba) = 100 centésimos. There is no Panamanian paper currency; coins exist in denominations of Ba100 and 1, and 50, 25, 10, 5 and 1 centésimos. US currency circulates freely: Ba1 = US$1.
Currency exchange: Banks and *cambios* are available for changing currency.
Credit cards: Visa and American Express are the most commonly used, but Access/Mastercard and Diners Club are also accepted. Check with your credit card company for details of merchant acceptability and other services which may be available.
Exchange rate indicators: The following figures are included as a guide to the movements of the Balboa against Sterling:

Date:	**Oct '89**	**Oct '90**	**Oct '91**	**Oct '92**
£1.00=	**1.57**	**1.95**	**1.73**	**1.59**

Currency restrictions: There are no restrictions on the import and export of either foreign or local currency. Visitors must have a minimum of US$150 when entering Panama (or US$10 per day for stays exceeding 15 days).
Banking hours: 0800-1330 Monday to Friday.

DUTY FREE

The following items may be imported into Panama without incurring customs duty:
500 cigarettes or 50 cigars or 500g tobacco;
3 bottles of alcohol;
Perfume and eau de cologne in opened bottles for personal use.
Prohibited items: Fruit, vegetable and animal products.

PUBLIC HOLIDAYS

Public holidays observed in Panama are as follows:
Apr 9 '93 Good Friday. **May 1** Labour Day. **Aug 15** Foundation of Panama City (capital only). **Oct 11** Revolution Day. **Nov 1** National Anthem Day. **Nov 2** All Souls' Day. **Nov 3** Independence from Colombia (1903). **Nov 4** National Flag Day. **Nov 5** Independence Day (Colón only). **Nov 10** First Call of Independence. **Nov 28** Independence from Spain. **Dec 8** Mother's Day/Immaculate Conception. **Dec 25** Christmas Day. **Jan 1 '94** New Year's Day. **Jan 9** National Martyrs' Day. **Feb 15** Shrove Tuesday.

HEALTH

Regulations and requirements may be subject to change at short notice, and you are advised to contact your doctor well in advance of your intended date of departure. Any numbers in the chart refer to the footnotes below.

	Special Precautions?	Certificate Required?
Yellow Fever	Yes	1
Cholera	No	No
Typhoid & Polio	2	-
Malaria	3	-
Food & Drink	4	-

[1]: A yellow fever vaccination is strongly recommended for all visitors. A certificate is required for travellers over one year of age coming from an infected area.
[2]: Typhoid fevers are common, but polio is not present.
[3]: Malaria risk, predominantly in the benign *vivax* form, throughout the year in rural areas surrounding Lakes Boyana and Gatún; in Alto Chucunaque and Darién areas; and in the continental areas adjacent to the San Blas archipelago. The malignant *falciparum* form is reported to be 'resistant' to chloroquine.
[4]: Mains water is normally chlorinated, and whilst relatively safe, may cause mild abdominal upsets. Bottled water is available and is advised for the first few weeks of the stay. Drinking water outside main cities and towns is likely to be contaminated and sterilisation is considered essential. Milk is pasteurised and dairy products are safe for consumption. Local meat, poultry, seafood, fruit and vegetables are generally considered safe to eat.
Rabies is present. For those at high risk, vaccination before arrival should be considered. If you are bitten abroad seek medical advice without delay. For more information consult the *Health* section at the back of the book.
Health care: Medical facilities are of a high standard. There are approximately 7000 hospital beds and 2000 doctors in the country. Medical charges are high and health insurance is essential.

TRAVEL - International

AIR: Panama's national airline is *Air Panama International (OP)*.
Approximate flight times: From Panama City to *London* is 14 hours and to *Miami* is 2 hours 45 minutes.
International airport: *Panama City (PAC)* (Tocumen) is 27km (17 miles) northeast of the city (travel time – 25 minutes). Buses and taxis go to the city. Airport services include a bank, car hire, restaurant and full duty-free facilities.
Departure tax: US$15.
SEA: The Panama Canal is the major route from the Atlantic to the Pacific Ocean, and Panama (Balboa) is a port of call for many cruise lines and ocean vessels for both passenger and freight. Cruise lines include *Sitmar, Cunard, Royal Viking, Princess, Delta, Norwegian American* and *P&O*.
RAIL: There is an international link from Costa Rica (Puerto Cortés) to David and Bajo Baquete in the north of Panama. The *Ferrocarril de Panamá* operates a passenger and freight train service between Panama City and Colón which runs seven or eight times daily. There is also a railway operated by the *United Fruit Subsidiary* serving its plantations in Bocas del Toro and Puerto Armuelles. Trains are one class; air-conditioned accommodation is available on payment of a supplement.
ROAD: The principal route to Panama is the Pan-American Highway from Costa Rica to Panama City. The rain season causes adverse conditions on the route south to Colombia. The Trans-Isthman Highway links Panama City and Colón.

TRAVEL - Internal

AIR: Smaller airports for internal flights are: *Aeropurto Paitilla* and *Aeroperlas*. Internal air services are operated by *Cia Panameña de Aviación (COPA), Aerolineas Las Perlas* and *Alas Chiricanas* which link Panama City, Colón, David and other centres in the interior.
ROAD: Bus: There are services between most large towns, but they can be very slow. **Taxis:** Not metered, prices vary considerably. Fares should be agreed in advance. **Car hire:** Available in city centres and airport. **Documentation:** A national driving licence will be sufficient.
URBAN: Extensive bus and minibus services run in Panama City. There is a flat fare with coin-operated turnstiles at the entrances of most buses.
JOURNEY TIMES: The following chart gives approximate journey times (in hours and minutes) from Panama City to other major cities in Panama.

	Air	**Road**
Chiriquí	0.45	6.00
Santiago	0.30	3.00
Chitre	0.30	3.10

ACCOMMODATION

HOTELS: Panama is in the middle of an extensive hotel expansion programme, not only in Panama City, but also in the countryside and in mountain and seaside areas. Accommodation ranges from international standard to inexpensive country inns, very simple hotels and new resort-style hotels. There is a 10% Government tax added to hotel bills. For further information contact: Asociación Panameña de Hoteles y Restaurantes, Apartado Postal 6-100072, El Dorado, Panama City. Tel: 271 133. Fax: 270 884.
CAMPING: There are no official sites, but it is possible to camp on some beaches, and also along parts of the Pan-American Highway.

RESORTS & EXCURSIONS

Panama offers a wide variety of tourist attractions, including excellent shopping. Its position as a crossing point between the Atlantic and the Pacific has naturally made it a major commercial route. Panama City's Central Avenue, Colón's Front Street and the newer shopping sectors around the hotels, and Tucumen's duty-free stores have grown up because of this trade.
Panama City: The capital is a curious blend of old Spain, modern America and the bazaar atmosphere of the East. In the old part of the city with its narrow, cobblestoned streets and colonial buildings, most of the interesting sights are to be found. These include the *Plaza de Francia*, the *Court of Justice Building*, the *Paseo de las Bóvedas* along the massive stone wall, *San José Church* with its magnificent golden Baroque altar and the *Santo Domingo Church*, next to which is the *Museum of Colonial Religious Art*. Overlooking the bay is the President's Palace, the most impressive building in the city; further along the waterfront is the colourful public market. The most interesting museum in town is the *Museum of the Panamanian Man* north of the market and near the shopping centres. A worthwhile excursion from the city is a visit to **Panamá Viejo** and its ruins including the square tower of the old cathedral, 6km (4 miles) away. This is the original Panama City which – like Fort San Lorenzo – was, in 1671, sacked and looted by Henry Morgan. The **Panama Canal** to the west of the city itself naturally attracts many visitors; recommended is a train or bus ride alongside or a boat trip on the canal – the scenery is beautiful, and the mechanics of the canal equally fascinating. The canal was opened in 1914, and an average transit takes eight hours to complete.
Balboa: A rather Americanised suburb between the Canal quays and *Ancón Hill*. An hour's launch ride away is the island of **Taboga**, where fine beaches and quality hotels abound. The main method of transport is water taxis, known locally as *pangas*. A longer trip by launch is necessary to get to the *Pearl Islands*, which are visited mainly by sea-anglers.
Colón: The second biggest city in Panama lies on the Caribbean end of the Canal, visitors should see the cathedral and the statues on the promenade known as the *Paseo Centenario*. Front Street is famous as a shopping

PANAMA | **HEALTH REGULATIONS** | **VISA REGULATIONS** | Code-Link

GALILEO/WORLDSPAN

TI-DFT/PTY/HE

TI-DFT/PTY/VI

SABRE

TIDFT/PTY/HE

TIDFT/PTY/VI

To access this information on your CRS, swipe the barcode with a light pen or type in the text under the barcode. For more information, see the introduction *How to Use This Book*.

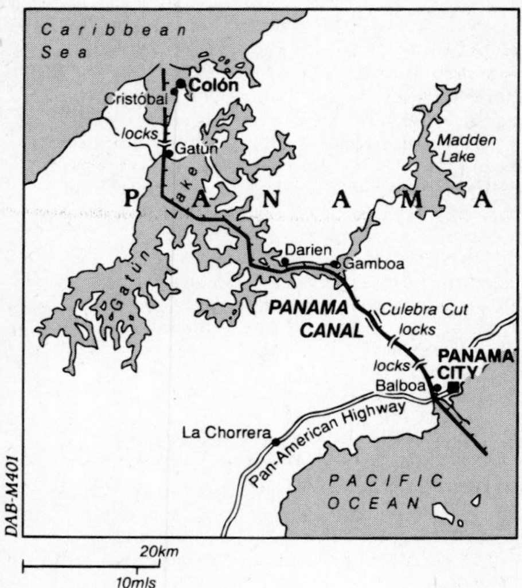

centre for duty-free luxuries, though it is now rather run down. The city is bustling and quite rough – most visitors just pass through rather than spending a lot of time here.

San Blas Islands: An interesting trip can be made from Colón to the San Blas archipelago which has 365 islands. It is the home of the Cuna Indians, the most sophisticated and politically organised of the Indians in Panama.

Portobelo: 48km east of Colón, a Spanish garrison town for two centuries with three large stone forts facing the entrance to the harbour. Also in the town are an old Spanish cannon, and the treasure house where gold and silver from Peru and Bolivia were stored before being shipped to Spain.

Azuero Peninsula: Much more relaxed and peaceful than Panama's cities is the Pacific Peninsula de Azuero, where charming small colonial towns, quiet villages and near-empty beaches await visitors who don't expect to find big hotels.

Note: The *Fiestas* in the various cities are all well worth seeing, particularly the one at Panama City during the Carnival. This is held on the four days before Ash Wednesday. Others are held to celebrate local patron saints. *Las Balserías*, a Guaymí Indian celebration held in Chiriquí Province every February, includes feasts and a contest in which the young men toss Balsa logs at one another; those who emerge undamaged may choose their mates.

SOCIAL PROFILE

FOOD & DRINK: French, Spanish and American food is available in all restaurants and hotels in Panama City and Colón. There is a huge selection of excellent restaurants in Panama City, as well as other main cities. There are also several Oriental restaurants. Native cooking is reminiscent of creole cuisine, hot and spicy. Dishes include *ceviche* (fish marinated in lime juice, onions and peppers), *palacones de plátano* (fried plantain), *sancocho* (Panamanian stew with chicken, meat and vegetables), *tamales* (seasoned pie wrapped in banana leaves), *carimañolas* and *empanadas* (turnovers filled with meat, chicken or cheese). Waiter service is the norm. The choice and availability of wines, spirits and beers in hotels, restaurants and bars is unlimited.

NIGHTLIFE: Panama City in particular has a wide range of nightlife from nightclubs and casinos to cockfights, folk ballet, belly dancing and classical theatre. There are floor shows and dancing in all the big hotels, as well as many other clubs. Other large towns and resorts have music, dancing, casinos and cinemas. Further details can be found in local papers.

SHOPPING: Panama is a duty-free haven and luxury goods from all over the world can be bought at a saving of at least one-third. Local items include leatherware, patterned, beaded necklaces made by Guaymí Indians, native costumes, handicrafts of carved wood, ceramics, *papier mâché* artefacts, macramé and mahogany bowls. **Shopping hours:** 0800-1800 Monday to Saturday.

SPORT: Fishing: Fish are abundant in the Panamanian waters of the Pacific and the Caribbean. Locations include Piñas Bay, Coiba Island, Contadora Island and Taboga on the Pacific side and the San Blas Islands and the Chiriquí Lagoon off the archipelago of Bocas Del Toro on the Caribbean.

Watersports: Surfing and **water-skiing** are popular on Pacific beaches such as Santa Clara, Nuevo Gogona and San Carlos and on the San Blas Islands. Surfing is good at Río Mar. **Golf:** There are six golf courses on the isthmus. Panama Country Club, Summit and Fort Amador's courses are all open to tourists. Guest cards are needed to play the 18-hole course at Coronado Beach Country Club.

SPECIAL EVENTS: The following is a selection of better-known festivals and events held throughout Panama. For further information contact the Tourist Office.

Feb-Mar '93 *Mardi Gras* (carnival), Panama City and Las Tablas. **Mid-Feb** *Las Balserías* (Guaymí Indian celebration – see *Resorts & Excursions* above), Chiriquí Province. **Late Apr** *Azuero Fair*. **Jul** *Boat Races*, Taboga Island. **Sep** *Agricultural Fair*, Bocas Del Toro.

SOCIAL CONVENTIONS: Handshaking is the normal form of greeting and dress should be casual. The culture is a vibrant mixture of Spanish and American lifestyles. The Mestizo majority, which is largely rural, shares many of the characteristics of Mestizo culture found throughout Central America. Only three indigenous Indian tribes have retained their individuality and traditional lifestyle as a result of withdrawing into virtually inaccessible areas.

Tipping: 10% is customary in hotels and restaurants. Taxi drivers do not expect tips and rates should be arranged before the trip.

BUSINESS PROFILE

ECONOMY: Until the political upheaval of the late 1980s, Panama enjoyed a relatively prosperous economy based on agriculture, light industry, revenues from the Panama Canal and the service sector. Over half the land area is given over to agriculture: the main cash crops are sugar cane, coffee and bananas, while the main food crops are rice, maize and beans. The country has significant reserves of timber, particularly mahogany, and good fishing stocks, amongst which shrimps are a major and valuable export earner. Local industries include food processing, clothing, paper and building materials. Panama also exports petroleum refined from imported crude oil. Further revenues are obtained from tolls levied on ships passing through the Panama Canal, which is due to come under full Panamanian control by the end of the century, and from registration fees for a plethora of 'offshore' companies exploiting Panama's strict banking and commercial secrecy laws. In mid-1990 the Endara government announced the introduction of a 'Strategy of Development and Economic Modernisation' in anticipation of a large aid injection from the USA: although receipts from this quarter have not reached Panamanian expectations, many aspects of the 'Strategy' plan have been implemented, including privatisation of state enterprises, reform of the tax and social security systems and the removal of price controls and import tariffs. About 40% of both-way trade is with the United States and Japan; Costa Rica and Germany are the country's other important trading partners. About 30% of all trade passes through the Colón freeport. Panama is attracting growing interest from Hong Kong business interests – there are historic links between Panama and China dating back to the building of the Canal – which may provide a much needed, if somewhat unexpected, source of investment in the country.

BUSINESS: Punctuality is appreciated and the exchange of business cards is normal. Suits are necessary for business meetings. **Office hours:** 0800-1200 and 1400-1700 Monday to Friday.

COMMERCIAL INFORMATION: The following organisation can offer advice: Cámara de Comercio, Industrias y Agricultura de Panamá (Chamber of Commerce), Avenida Samuel Lewis, Edificio Comosa, Planta Baja, Apdo 74, Panama 1. Tel: 271 233. Fax: 274 186. Telex: 2434.

HISTORY & GOVERNMENT

HISTORY: Under Spanish rule from the 16th century, Panama achieved independence as part of Gran Colombia in 1821. In 1903 Panama seceded from Colombia and became an American Protectorate, and construction of the Panama Canal began in the same year. In 1939, Protectorate status was abolished, and in 1946 a new constitution began a period of rapidly changing governments. A military coup led by General (later Brigadier-General) Omar Torrijos Herrera took place in 1968, and he effectively maintained power (despite surrendering the presidency) until his death in 1981. From 1984 to 1989 the country was effectively run by the armed forces chief, General Manuel Noriega. The General's policies, especially regarding future control of the Panama Canal (the governing treaty is up for renegotiation soon), and his personal activities, including alleged involvement in drug trafficking, produced very strained relations with the country's key ally, the USA. American development aid and military assistance were cut, but with little effect. USA intervention became more likely after the presidential election of May 1989. This was a straight fight between the pro-Government Coalicion de Liberacion Nacional (COLINA) and the principal opposition movement, the Alianza Democratica de Oposicion Civilista (ADOC). The ADOC candidate, Guillermo Endara Galimany, won with 62% of the vote. However, the election was almost immediately annulled without reasonable cause. After an attempted coup in October 1989, believed to have had USA backing, was quickly crushed by Noriega's forces, the only means of getting rid of the troublesome dictator was military intervention. In December 1989, US President Bush authorised an invasion of the country. After a few days of fierce fighting, mostly in the capital, the bulk of resistance to the invasion – from troops loyal to Noriega and from the paramilitary Dignity Battalions – was suppressed. Despite the relative success of the military operation, the US forces for a while failed in one key objective: the capture of Noriega himself. On Christmas Day, after delicate negotiations, Noriega was taken into the residence of the Papal Nunciate in Panama City, where he sought political asylum. Noriega's future became the subject of elaborate diplomatic manoeuvrings between the USA, the Vatican and the new Panamanian government of President Guillermo Endara. On January 4, 1990, the General finally surrendered to US forces. He was immediately flown to the United States and put on trial: in April 1992 he was convicted and sentenced to 40 years imprisonment. Back in Panama, President Endara, who was installed at the head of a new administration drawn from the ADOC coalition which had won the May 1989 election, was facing a desperate situation as the Government was virtually penniless and the war-damaged capital was almost at a standstill. Although he was installed by and firmly supports the Americans, the Bush administration proved very sluggish in offering any financial assistance and the economy has never really recovered from its near-collapse in 1989, which has led to widespread popular discontent. There have been a series of coup attempts since the beginning of 1990, mostly launched by former members of the regime who escaped capture by the Americans, but all have been easily put down. The level of discontent was made clear to US President Bush when he visited the country in June 1992. Tear gas fired at the demonstrators who greeted Bush swept over the presidential party which was forced into an ignominious retreat.

GOVERNMENT: The President has executive power. Both the unicameral legislature and the presidency are elected for five years.

CLIMATE

Temperatures are high across the whole country throughout the year, though cooler at high altitudes. The rainy season lasts from May to September. Rainfall is twice as heavy on the Pacific coast as it is on the lowlands of the Caribbean coast.

Required clothing: Lightweight cottons and linens are worn, with rainwear advisable, particularly in the rainy season. Warmer clothes are needed in the highlands.

CRISTOBAL Panama (12m)

SUNSHINE, hours

J	F	M	A	M	J	J	A	S	O	N	D
8	8	9	8	6	5	5	5	6	5	5	7

◁ TEMPERATURE, °C (0, 10, 20, 30) — MAX, MIN

RAINFALL, mm ▷ (0, 100, 200, 300, 400, 500, 600)

DAB-C244

HUMIDITY, %

J	F	M	A	M	J	J	A	S	O	N	D
82	81	80	82	87	89	89	89	89	89	89	86

PAPUA NEW GUINEA

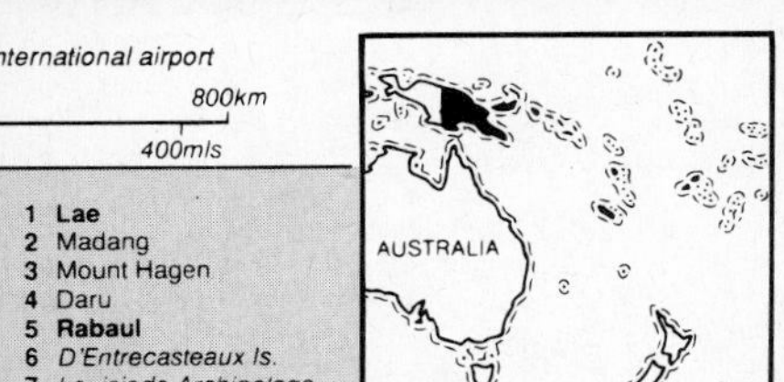

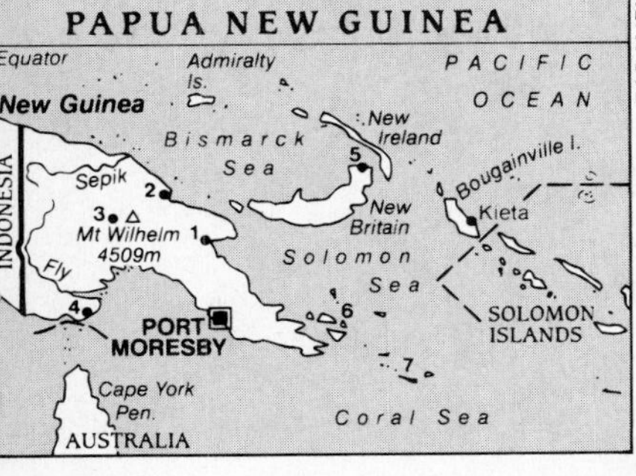

Location: South Pacific.

Tourism Development Corporation
PO Box 7144
Boroko, Papua New Guinea
Tel: 272 521. Fax: 259 447.

Papua New Guinea High Commission
14 Waterloo Place
London SW1Y 4AR
Tel: (071) 930 0922/7. Fax: (071) 930 0828. Telex: 25827 KUNDU G. Opening hours for visa applications: 0900-1300 Monday to Friday.

British High Commission
PO Box 4778, Kiroki Street
Waigani, Boroko
Papua New Guinea
Tel: 251 677. Fax: 253 547. Telex: UKREP NE 22142.

Papua New Guinea Embassy
3rd Floor, 1616 New Hampshire Avenue, NW
Washington, DC
20009
Tel: (202) 745 3680. Fax: (202) 745 3679.

Papua New Guinea Tourism Office
Suite 3000
5000 Birch Street
Newport Beach, CA
92660
Tel: (714) 752 5440. Fax: (714) 476 3741.

Embassy of the United States of America
PO Box 1492
Port Moresby, Papua New Guinea
Tel: 211 455 *or* 211 594 *or* 211 654. Fax: 213 423. Telex: 22189 USAEMB.

Papua New Guinea Consulate
Suite 501
22 St Clair Avenue East
Toronto, Ontario
M4T 2S3
Tel: (416) 926 1400.

Canadian Consulate
PO Box 851
2nd Floor, The Lodge
Brampton Street
Port Moresby, Papua New Guinea
Tel: 213 599. Fax: 213 612.

AREA: 462,840 sq km (178,704 sq miles).
POPULATION: 3,699,000 (1990 estimate).
POPULATION DENSITY: 8.0 per sq km.
CAPITAL: Port Moresby. **Population:** 145,300 (1987 estimate).
GEOGRAPHY: Papua New Guinea consists of over 600 islands and lies in the middle of the long chain of islands stretching from mainland South-East Asia. It lies in the South Pacific, 160km (100 miles) north of Australia. The country occupies the eastern half of the second largest non-continental island in the world, as well as the smaller islands of the Bismarck Archipelago (New Britain, New Ireland, Bougainville, Admiralty Island), the D'Entrecasteaux Island group and the three islands of the Louisiade Archipelago. The main island shares a land border with Irian Jaya, a province of Indonesia. The mainland and larger islands are mountainous and rugged, divided by large fertile upland valleys. Fast-flowing rivers from the highlands descend to the coastal plains. A line of active volcanoes stretches along the north coast of the mainland and continues on the island of New Britain. To the north and south of this central mountain range on the main island lie vast stretches of mangrove swamps and coastal river deltas. Volcanoes and thermal pools are also found in the southeast of other islands. Papua New Guinea also offers the greatest variety of terrestrial ecosystems in the South Pacific, including five types of lowland rainforest, 13 types of montane rainforest, five varieties of palm and swamp forest and three different mangrove forests. Two-thirds of the entire world's species of orchids come from Papua New Guinea. Birds include 38 species of the bird of paradise, and the megapode and cassowary. Marsupials and mammals include cuscus, tree kangaroos, wallabies, bandicoots, spiny ant-eaters and, in the coastal waters, the dugong. There are between 170 and 200 species of frog and 450 species of butterfly.
LANGUAGE: The official language is English, which is widely used in business and government circles. Pidgin English and Hiri Motu are more commonly used (700 other languages and dialects are also spoken).
RELIGION: 90% Christian.
TIME: GMT + 10.
ELECTRICITY: 240 volts AC, 50Hz. Australian-style 3-pin plugs are in use. Some hotels provide 110-volt outlets in guest-rooms.
COMMUNICATIONS: Telephone: IDD is available. Country code: 675. There are no area codes in Papua New Guinea. **Fax:** Services available at all major companies and government departments. **Telex/telegram:** Hotels and large businesses will have telex machines. Telegram facilities are available in main centres. **Post:** Airmail to Europe takes seven to ten days. Post office hours: 0800-1600 Monday to Friday, 0900-1200 Saturday. **Press:** The dailies include the *Niugini News* and the *Papua New Guinea Post Courier*. There are some English-language papers.
BBC World Service and Voice of America frequencies:

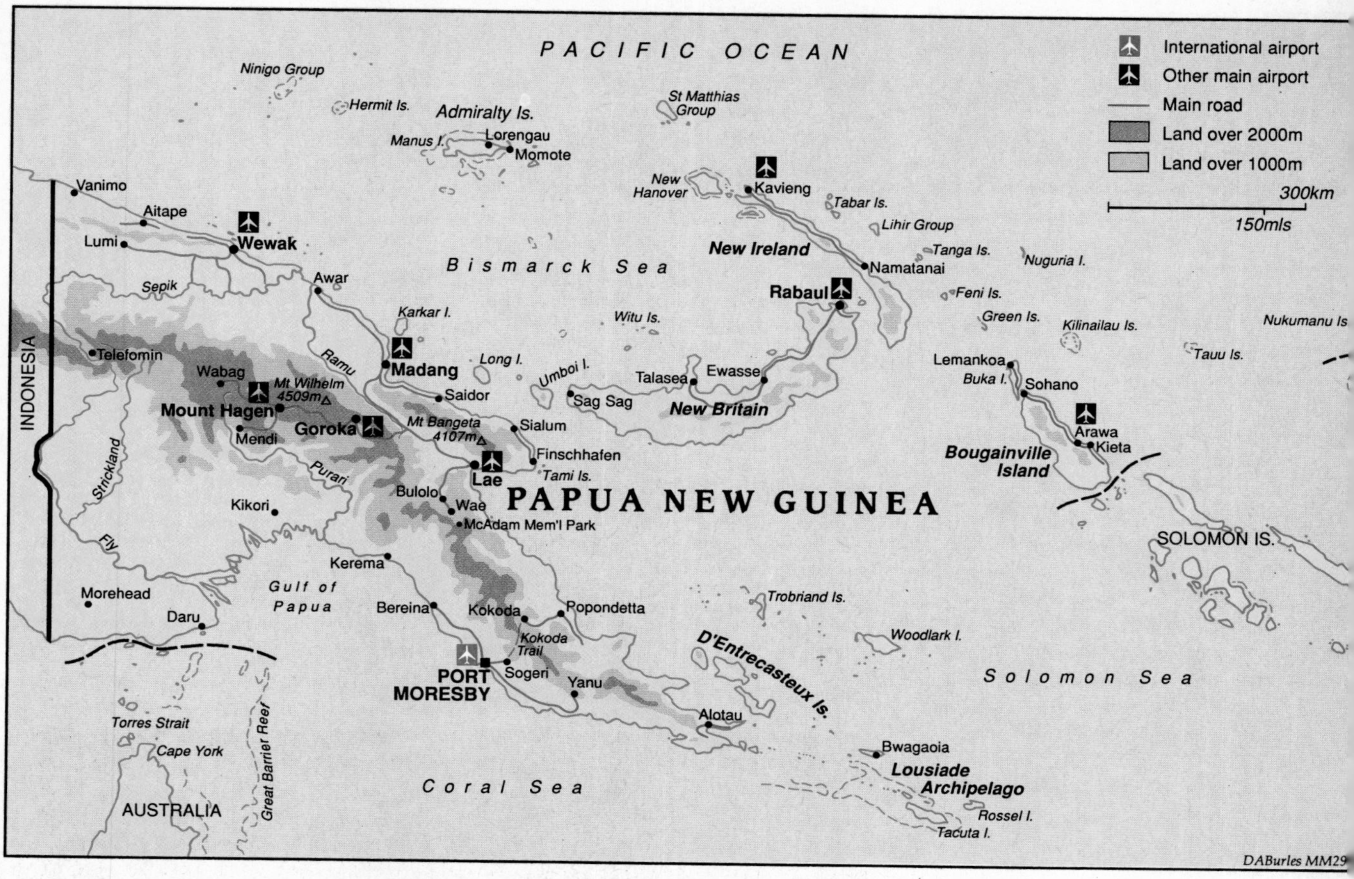

From time to time these change. See the section *How to Use this Book* for more information.

BBC:

MHz	17.83	11.95	9.740	6.195

Voice of America:

MHz	18.82	15.18	9.525	1.735

PASSPORT/VISA

Regulations and requirements may be subject to change at short notice, and you are advised to contact the appropriate diplomatic or consular authority before finalising travel arrangements. Details of these may be found at the head of this country's entry. Any numbers in the chart refer to the footnotes below.

	Passport Required?	Visa Required?	Return Ticket Required?
Full British	Yes	Yes	Yes
BVP	Not valid	-	-
Australian	Yes	Yes	Yes
Canadian	Yes	Yes	Yes
USA	Yes	Yes	Yes
Other EC	Yes	Yes	Yes
Japanese	Yes	Yes	Yes

Note: On receipt of a stamped, self-addressed envelope, the High Commission can supply information sheets on how to apply for visas for Papua New Guinea. The information below should be considered as a guide, not an exhaustive description.

Restricted entry: Nationals of South Africa and holders of dual South African nationality will be refused entry.

PASSPORTS: Valid passport required by all. Passports should be valid for one year after entry.

British Visitors Passport: Not acceptable.

VISAS: Required by all nationals.

Types of visa: *Tourist:* £7. *Business:* £7 (single entry), £105 (multiple entry). There are different charges for certain special categories of visitors (including yachtsmen and those engaged in medical, research or expedition activities). There will also be charges for extensions and costs incurred in processing documents.

Note: Visas cannot be issued at airports or seaports.

Validity: *Tourist:* 2 months. *Business:* (a) periods of not more than 3 weeks per visit within a year for single entry, *or* (b) 12 months with a maximum length of 2 months per stay for multiple entry. Details of renewals or extensions are available from the Embassy or High Commission.

Application to: Consulate (or Consular Section at Embassy or High Commission). For addresses, see top of entry.

Application requirements: (a) Completed application form (1 per passport submitted). (b) Passport with minimum 1 year remaining validity. (c) Itinerary of travel from authorised travel agent (or firm for business travellers). (d) Proof of adequate funds to cover duration of stay or a letter of invitation from friends or relations with whom you intend to reside. (e) For visa applications by mail: self-addressed, registered mail envelope and fee as postal orders or bank drafts (not personal cheques). (f) Detailed letter in support of application for Business visa covering, in particular, curriculum vitae, confirmation of ongoing project in Papua New Guinea, parent company's annual report, requirements (c) and (d) above, and confirming possession of onward/return ticket.

Working days required: 48 hours minimum for Business and Tourist visas. Temporary residence visas take up to 6 weeks or more. It is advisable for visa applications to be made a week or more before departure date.

Temporary residence: £1050 for 4 weeks to 1 year. Available for those entering for employment purposes, usually professional persons or those undertaking research, journalism, consultancy, film-making, etc. Clearance is by the Director General, Migration Division, Department of Foreign Affairs, Post Office, Wards Strip, Waigan, Port Moresby. Fax: 255 206. Telex: NE 22377.

MONEY

Currency: Kina (Ka) = 100 toea (T). Notes are in denominations of Ka50, 20, 10, 5 and 2. Coins are in denominations of Ka1, and T50, 20, 10, 5, 2 and 1.

Credit cards: Exchange facilities are available through trade banks. American Express is the most widely accepted credit card. Holders of this and other cards should check with their credit card company for details of merchant acceptability and other services which may be available.

Travellers cheques: Accepted by most shops and hotels.

Exchange rate indicators: The following figures are included as a guide to the movements of the Kina against Sterling and the US Dollar:

Date:	Oct '89	Oct '90	Oct '91	Oct '92
£1.00=	1.39	1.77	1.64	1.54
$1.00=	0.86	0.94	0.94	0.97

Currency restrictions: There are no restrictions on the import of either local or foreign currency. Export is limited to the amount imported.

Banking hours: 0900-1400 Monday to Thursday, 0900-1700 Friday.

PAPUA NEW GUINEA | **HEALTH REGULATIONS** | **VISA REGULATIONS** | Code-Link

GALILEO/WORLDSPAN

TI-DFT/POM/HE

TI-DFT/POM/VI

SABRE

TIDFT/POM/HE

TIDFT/POM/VI

To access this information on your CRS, swipe the barcode with a light pen or type in the text under the barcode. For more information, see the introduction *How to Use This Book*.

Papua-New Guinea

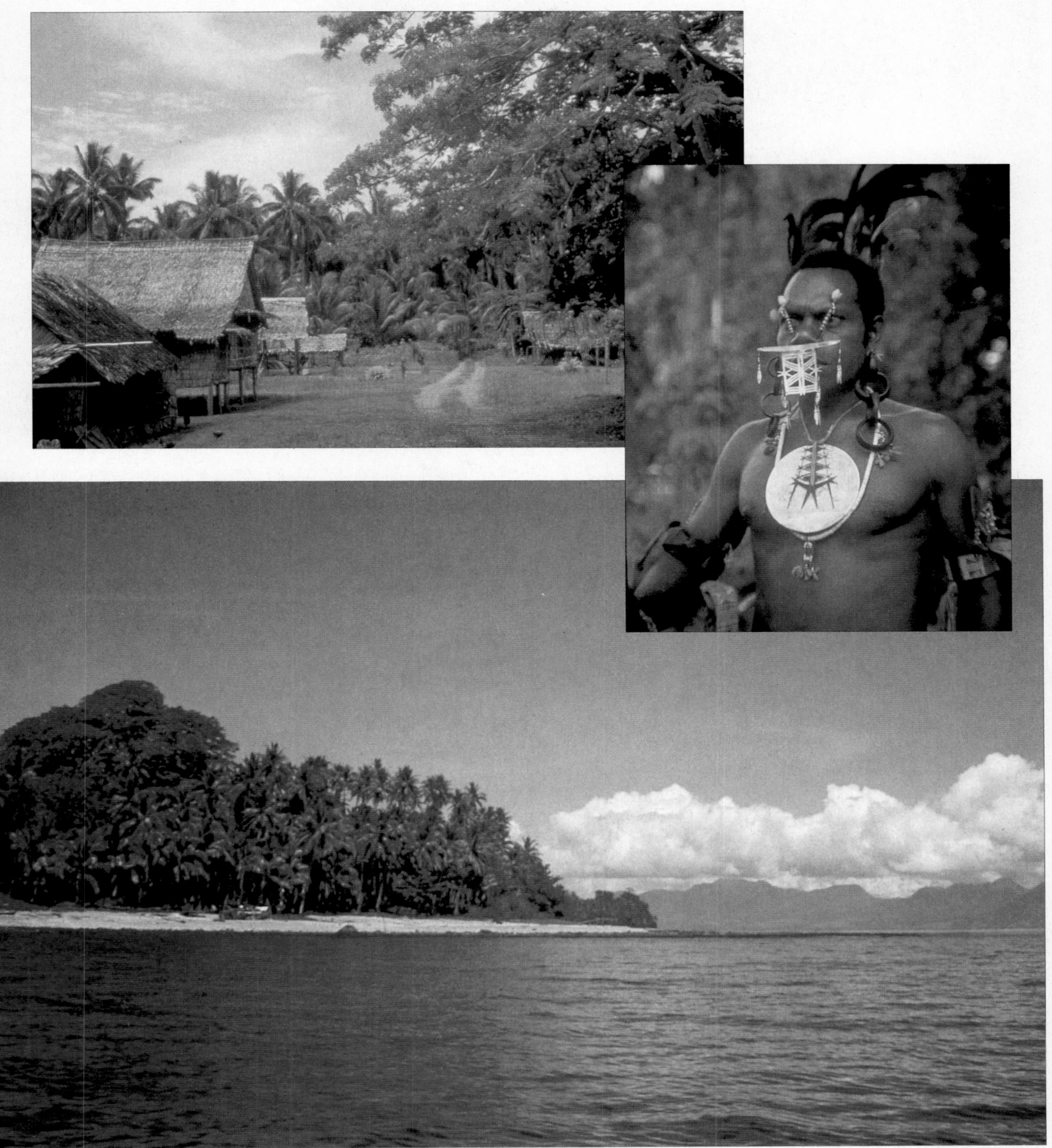

Papua New Guinea Tourist Office
PO Box 7144, Embassy Drive, Boroko, Port Moresby, Papua New Guinea
Tel: 251269. Fax: (675) 259447. Telex: NE 23472.

DUTY FREE

The following may be imported into Papua New Guinea by persons over 18 years of age without incurring customs duty:
200 cigarettes or 50 cigars or 250g tobacco;
1 litre of spirits, wine or beer;
A reasonable quantity of perfume;
Goods up to value of Ka200 (Ka100 for persons under 18 years of age) excluding radios, tape recorders, television sets, video cameras, video tapes, record players, souvenirs and gifts.

PUBLIC HOLIDAYS

Public holidays observed in Papua New Guinea are as follows:
Apr 9 '93 Good Friday. **Apr 12** Easter Monday. **Jun 7** Queen's Official Birthday. **Jul 23** Remembrance Day. **Sep 16** Independence Day and Constitution Day. **Dec 25** Christmas Day. **Dec 26** Boxing Day. **Jan 1 '94** New Year's Day.
Note: In addition, there are various regional festivals throughout the year.

HEALTH

Regulations and requirements may be subject to change at short notice, and you are advised to contact your doctor well in advance of your intended date of departure. Any numbers in the chart refer to the footnotes below.

	Special Precautions?	Certificate Required?
Yellow Fever	No	1
Cholera	Yes	2
Typhoid & Polio	Yes	-
Malaria	3	-
Food & Drink	4	-

[1]: A yellow fever vaccination certificate is required of travellers over one year of age arriving from infected areas.
[2]: Following WHO guidelines issued in 1973, a cholera vaccination certificate is not a condition of entry to Papua New Guinea. However, cholera is a serious risk in this country and precautions are essential. Up-to-date advice should be sought before deciding whether these precautions should include vaccination, as medical opinion is divided over its effectiveness. See the *Health* section at the back of the book.
[3]: Malaria risk exists all year throughout the country below 1800m. The predominant *falciparum* strain is reported to be 'highly resistant' to chloroquine and 'resistant' to sulfadoxine/pyrimethamine.
[4]: All water should be regarded as being potentially contaminated. Water used for drinking, brushing teeth or making ice should have first been boiled or otherwise sterilised. Milk is pasteurised and dairy products are safe for consumption. Only eat well-cooked meat and fish, preferably served hot. Pork, salad and mayonnaise may carry increased risk. Vegetables should be cooked and fruit peeled.
Health care: The main hospitals are Port Moresby General (Papuan region), Goroka Base (Highlands) and Angau Memorial. There are 16 others and 460 health centres throughout the country. Christian missions also provide some health services and there are private doctors in the main towns. Health insurance is essential.

TRAVEL - International

AIR: Papua New Guinea's national airline is *Air Niugini (PX)*.
Approximate flight times: The total flying time from *London* to Port Moresby is up to 30 hours (using current services and routes), but the journey takes at least two days to complete.
International airport: *Port Moresby* (Jackson Field), 8km (5 miles) from the city. Buses are available to the city (travel time – 20 minutes). There are duty-free and banking facilities at the airport.
Departure tax: Ka15 is levied on international flights. Children under two years of age and passengers not leaving the airport are exempt.
SEA: The international ports are Lae, Madang, Port Moresby, Wewak (Sepik), Rabaul (New Britain), Kieta (North Solomons) and Momote (Manus).
Passenger/cruise lines running regular services are *CTC*, *Lindblad*, *P&O* and *Sitmar*. Cargo/passenger lines are *Austasia*, *Australia/West Pacific* and *Bank Line*.

TRAVEL - Internal

AIR: Services are run by *Talair*, *Air Niugini* and *Douglas Airways* to all main centres, but are expensive. Internal services should be booked between November and February. *Air Niugini* flies to over 100 airstrips throughout the country and operates regular services to the 20 major urban centres of the country. *Air Niugini* also offers reductions for pre-booking excursions. Charter services are also in operation. The Government sometimes declares a state of emergency in Port Moresby as a result of the increase in violent crime. Travellers should make enquiries about curfew arrangements.
SEA: Cruises and excursions are available lasting three to 16 days. These go mainly to the islands and some otherwise inaccessible places on the coast. Cargo/passenger services between Madang and Lae are run by *Lutheran Shipping* with facilities including passenger cabins, accommodation and meals.
RIVER: For the local people in some regions of the country, rivers, particularly the Sepik, provide the main thoroughfares. In these areas it is possible to hire motorised canoes or obtain passage on a trading boat though, apart from cruises, there are no regular public transport operators on the rivers. See *Resorts & Excursions* section.
ROAD: Due to the rugged terrain of Papua New Guinea, road development of the interior has been slow. The network, currently 4900km, is being extended. There is a network of roads that connect the northren coast towns of Madang and Lae with the major urban centres in the Highlands region. There are few roads connecting the various provinces, however, due to the mountainous terrain. **Bus:** PMVs (public motor vehicles) operate in the main centres from bus shelters or they can be hailed. **Taxis** Available in district centres but expensive. Although operated on a metred basis, fares can be negotiated. **Car hire:** *Avis*, *Budget* and the *Travelodge Hotel Cars Service* are available in principal towns. Driving is on the left. **Documentation:** A national driving licence is sufficient.

ACCOMMODATION

Adequate and comfortable accommodation is available throughout Papua New Guinea. Generally it is more expensive than in most Australasian states.
HOTELS: There are hotels of international standard in Port Moresby, Lae, Madang and most major centres. Many motels also offer good value accommodation.
LODGES: There is a developing tourist industry and tourist accommodation is increasing in many hitherto inaccessible areas. There are lodges in the Highlands and on the Sepik River, many of which can only be reached by air or river. Generally they consist of bungalows constructed of local materials.

RESORTS & EXCURSIONS

The tribal diversity of a country with over 700 languages cannot easily be summarised, though in Papua New Guinea it is the tribal life that is most fascinating to the visitor. This section provides an introduction to what the visitor may expect.
Some of the excursions in Papua New Guinea are interestingly different to those offered elsewhere; for example the tourist can visit the coppermine in **Bougainville**, or be taken to one of the many wrecks of World War II aircrafts that lie in the jungle.
Haus Tambarans ('Spirit Houses') are a feature of many towns and villages in the country, especially in the area of the *Sepik River*, so only a few of them can be given specific mention. Only initiated men of a tribe can enter (though in places this rule is relaxed for foreigners). They are built in a variety of styles, with massive carved wooden supports being a major feature. Other carvings and masks inside represent spirits. The orator's stools in these places are not used for sitting on; bunches of leaves are slapped down on the stools as the orator makes his points.

Port Moresby

Port Moresby, the capital, is situated on the magnificent *Fairfax Harbour*. It houses the *National Parliament*, the *National Museum*, which contains exhibits of pottery from all the provinces, the *Botanical Gardens* and the *Catholic Cathedral* (which is built in the *Haus Tambaran* style). The National Museum contains a historical record stretching back over 50,000 years. There are many sporting facilities in Port Moresby, including scuba diving, windsurfing, sailing, game fishing, water-skiing, golf, tennis and squash.

There are several interesting things to see in the Port Moresby area. These include:

The Kokoda Trail and Sogeri: The Kokoda Trail is a 40km (24-mile) drive from Port Moresby. The Sogeri road offers many magnificent views and winds through rubber plantations.

Village Arts: Situated at **Six Mile,** near the airport, this is a government-owned artefacts shop with the best artefact collection in the country.

Other places of interest near Port Moresby include: the *Vairiata National Park; Moitaka Crocodile Farm; Loloata Island* and the *Sea Park Oceanarium*.

Lae and the Morobe Province

Lae is Papua New Guinea's second city and an important commercial centre and seaport. The *Botanical Gardens* are among the best in the country. *Mount Lunaman* in the centre of the town was used by the Germans and the Japanese as a lookout point. It gives a magnificent view over the *Huon Gulf* and the *Markham Valley*.

Outside Lae is **Wau,** formerly a gold-mining centre. The *Wau Ecology Institute*, a privately funded organisation, has a small museum and zoo. Visitors can see cassowaries, tree kangaroos, crocodiles, birds of paradise, native butterflies and rhododendrons. Sights near Wau are *McAdam National Park* and *Mount Kaindi*, **Finschhafen** (a very pretty coastal town) and the **Tami Islands,** whose people are renowned for their carved wooden bowls. **Sialum** is an attractive area of coastline known for its coral terraces. White-water rafting on the *Watut River* is an attraction for the adventurous.

Madang

Madang, the capital of Madang Province, is an ideal starting place for many of the tours round the islands and up the Sepik River (see below). It has a variety of shops, hotels, restaurants and markets, where storyboards depicting myths and legends can be bought. In nearby **Yabobs** and **Bilbils,** traditional pottery-making can be seen.

There are four main population groupings in the province: island, coastal, river and mountain, each with its own diet, traditions and customs. The **Manam** islanders make houses out of sago trees and toddy palms with leaves and leaf stems tied into each other. The *Ramu River* people make similar houses, but on stilts, and have a tradition of carving influenced by the cultures of the Sepik River. The mountain people are smaller in stature; they grow crops that would be familiar to an English gardener: lettuce, radishes, cabbages and potatoes. The families of the coastal population place a special value on dog's teeth necklaces, tambu shell headbands and pig tusk amulets. These items are sometimes still used as currency in tribal transactions.

The Sepik River

The Sepik River is the longest river in Papua New Guinea and has been for many centuries the trade route into the interior. It winds down from the mountains near the border with Irian Jaya, draining immense tracts of scarcely explored jungle, swamp and grassland until it meets the sea, where it is more than a mile wide. It abounds with meandering waterways, oxbow lakes, tributaries and backwaters, swamps, lagoons, lakes and channels cut by man to short-cut its looping journey. Unusually though, for a great river, it has no delta system and its waters spew directly into the sea with enormous force. From the many villages along its banks come highly prized examples of primitive art. The *Haus Tambaran* at **Angoram** possesses a display of art from almost the entire length of the river. At **Kambaramba** village, and elsewhere, houses are built on stilts as a protection against flooding and the dugout canoe is still the main local means of transport. (The visitor, however, has the option of taking a cruise.) Woodcarving is one of the main local crafts and its architectural use in gables and posts in houses is a noteworthy feature. This can be seen at the village of **Tambanum**.

In **Timbunke** village, further examples of construction techniques, including bridge-building, can be seen. Around the *Chambri Lakes* there are some of the many species of birds for which Papua New Guinea is famous. These include egrets, pied herons, brahminee kites, whistling kites, jacanas, darters, cormorants and kingfishers. Also in the Chambri area can be found a unique pottery-making village, **Aibom,** where clay fireplaces, storage and cooking pots are made by the coil method and fired in the open-air by women.

At **Kanganaman,** the slow rebuilding is taking place of a *Haus Tambaran* of national cultural importance. The rebuilding provides an excellent opportunity to see clearly the carvings on the immense Haus Posts. **Korogo** is famous for its '*Mei Masks*'.

In the upper reaches of the Sepik, insect totems dominate clan representation and artforms, using praying mantis and rhinoceros-beetle motifs and featuring distinctive insect eyes. Canoe prows are extremely elaborate, as are the tops of stepladders leading into dwellings. At **Waskusk,** the ceiling of the *Haus Tambaran* depicts the dream of a leader, but conditions on the river sometimes make this village inaccessible. At **Yigei,** Upper Sepik-style *Garamut Drums* ('Slit Gongs') can be seen (and heard); and there are dramatic designs in white and yellow along the waterway in **Swagap Village,** which also has simple, elegant pottery and fireplaces, and often very fine examples of the canoe-builders craft. In this area it is not so long since two villages concluded a peace agreement with an exchange of skulls.

The birds round Chambri Lake have already been mentioned, but the variegated wildlife of the river and its tributaries is itself a constant source of fascination. Islands of tangled vegetation and the debris of fallen trees float down the river to the Bismarck Sea. Salt and freshwater crocodiles can be seen at night, using spotlights. Along the river, great areas of swamp and grassland provide a home for waders, herons, fish-eagles and many other wildfowl. Sometimes it is possible to go on a night or early morning excursion into the jungle and experience a unique world of sound as the birds prepare for the day's hunting.

Tours along the river have a flexible itinerary in order to take advantage of river conditions and the many local customs and events which visitors may be interested in.

The Highlands

The majority of the country's population live in this least accessible part of Papua New Guinea.

The **Eastern Highlands** have the longest history of contact with the West. **Kainantu** is reached from Lae through the *Kassim Pass*. It has a large cultural centre, selling traditional artefacts; it also provides training in print-making and weaving. The largest town is **Goroka**. It is an agricultural and commercial centre for the entire Highlands region. The *J K McCarthy Museum* has a comprehensive display of regional artefacts; the Leahy wing contains photographs taken by early explorers. In the town centre the *Raun Raun Theatre* company provides contemporary performances of traditional stories and legends. **Bena Bena Village,** 10km (6 miles) from Goroka, is the largest handweaving organisation in the Highlands. Also nearby is **Asaro,** where the men coat themselves with grey mud and re-enact for visitors their historic revenge on a neighbouring village. The legend has it that, having been defeated in battle, the resourceful

villagers covered themselves in mud and paid their opponents a visit. This successfully frightened the opposition, who ran away under the impression that they were being visited by ghosts.

Kundiawa, a small town, is the capital of Simbu Province. Some of the local caves are used as burial places; others are popular with cavers. Rafting down the *Wahgi* and *Purari* rivers is also exciting. *Mount Wilhelm*, 4509m (1480ft), is in Simbu Province and is the highest mountain in Papua New Guinea.

In some ways *Mount Hagen* in the **Western Highlands** resembles a town from the Wild West. Its expansion is only recent and the local population will organise a *sing-sing* (celebration) to mark a diverse variety of events; anything from payment of a bride-price to the opening of a new road. There is also a cultural centre in the town. The *Baiyer River Wildlife Sanctuary* lies 55km (34 miles) north of Mount Hagen and is one of the best places to see the famous *birds of paradise*. Possums, tree kangaroos, parrots and cassowaries may also be seen.

The **Mendi Valley** of the **Southern Highlands** is noted for its spectacular scenery and limestone caves. It is home to the *Huli Wigmen* who wear red and yellow face-paint and elaborately decorated wigs of human hair.

Wabang in **Enga Province** has a large cultural centre with an art gallery and a museum. Young artists can be seen working on sand paintings. War shields, wigs, weapons and other artefacts from all over Papua New Guinea are on display. Enga is the most primitive of the Highland Provinces.

The Islands

The main islands are **New Britain**, **New Ireland** and the **Manus** group (together comprising the Bismarck Archipelago), the northernmost Solomon Islands of **Bougainville** and **Buka,** and an eastern group of islands including the **Trobriand** and **D'Entrecasteaux Islands**.

Rabaul on New Britain is the capital of the island and offers several hotels, clubs, restaurants, dances and other forms of entertainment. There are also sporting facilities including a golf course, though the main sporting interest is likely to centre on the various watersports on offer, which include diving, snorkelling, boating, fishing, sailing and windsurfing. A visitor who has spent the morning in these pursuits might like to spend the afternoon relaxing on a beach or on one of the smaller islands. For the sightseer Rabaul offers *Gunantabu* (the remains of Queen Emma's residence) with her private cemetery; the remains of the *German Government House* on *Namanula Hill*; a 360-mile underground tunnel system left by the Japanese; the *Admirals Bunker*, now a museum; an orchid park; and *Rabaul Market*, which is famous throughout the South Pacific. *Malmaluan* and *Namanula Lookouts* offer panoramic views, whilst really enthusiastic climbers may like to try out the extinct and active volcanoes on the island. The Baining People of the island perform a spectacular and frenzied night-time Fire Dance.

The **New Ireland** and the **Manus** group of islands are off the general tourist trail. In the Northern Western islands of the latter group there are no trees. The islanders have a tradition of making sea-going canoes out of logs that floated down the Sepik into the surrounding ocean.

Bougainville and **Buka** are separated by a narrow channel of islets. Tourists are well catered for on Bougainville, where local dancers regularly visit the hotels, retelling stories from the history of their clans. Activities include scuba diving, snorkelling, game fishing and swimming. Bushwalking and caving expeditions can also be arranged. These range from a 6-hour downhill hike from **Panguna** to **Arawa** to a 3-day jungle trek to the summit of *Mount Balbi*, a dormant volcano. Visitors should contact the Tourism Officer before undertaking a trek, as permission is required to enter villages en route. Arawa has a 9-hole golf course for those who like to do their walking in more sedate surroundings. Near Arawa there is the *Butterfly Farm* in **Kerei Village**; the Wildlife Officer can arrange a visit. Another popular, albeit unlikely, stopping place for the tourist is the Bougainville copper mine, a vast enterprise which dwarfs the visitor. Visits can be arranged through the Bougainville Copper Limited Visitors Liaison Officer.

.elics of Japanese and German occupation abound through-ut Papua New Guinea and the visitor will have no trouble nding them. However, the wreck of Admiral Yamamoto's lane in the rainforest of **Buin** may be of particular interest. 'he islands offshore to Bougainville have many white sandy eaches.

'he **Trobriands** are the most accessible of the groups of lands in Milne Bay Province. As elsewhere in the islands, wimming and snorkelling enthusiasts are well catered for. 'he harvesting of yams from May to September is accompa-ied by extended rituals and celebrations which peak in the ionths of July and August.

'he **D'Entrecasteaux Islands** rise mountainously out of the ea. In the centre of **Goodenough Island** there is a large :one decorated with mysterious paintings.

SOCIAL PROFILE

'OOD & DRINK: Hotel dining rooms cater for most visi-ors and menus in main centres are fairly extensive. The more emote the area, the more likely it is that the food will be asic and the menus simple. However, increasing use is made f fresh local meat, fish, vegetables and fruit, including ineapples, pawpaws, mangoes, passion fruit and bananas. 'raditional cuisine of Papua New Guinea is confined to root rops such as taro, kaukau and yams, sago and pig (cooked in he earth on traditional feasts). The number of European, Chinese and Indonesian restaurants is rising. Waiter service is sual. Alcohol is readily available and includes Australian nd Filipino beers.

NIGHTLIFE: Several hotels in Port Moresby have dancing n the evenings and some organise live entertainment. There re two cinemas and one drive-in cinema. The Arts Theatre tages regular performances. The local newspaper advertises rogrammes. *Sing-sings*, tribal events on a smaller scale than he biannual festival, are sometimes held.

SHOPPING: A wide range of crafts is available in shops; lternatively the visitor can buy direct from villagers. 'avourite buys include local carvings of ceremonial masks nd statuettes from Angoram and the Sepik, *Buka* basketry, rrows, bows and decorated axes, crocodile carvings from the Trobriands, pottery and local art. Supermarket facilities exist n main centres. The many butterfly farms send specimens of nusual species throughout the world. **Shopping hours:** 0900-1700 Monday to Friday, 0900-1200 Saturday (some open longer and/or Sunday).

SPORT: Fishing: Game fish are plentiful in Port Moresby, Lae, Madang, Rabaul and Wewak. Information is available from Moresby Game Fishing Club, Box 5028, Boroko. **Golf:** Port Moresby Golf Club has one of the oldest courses in Papua New Guinea, which is open to visitors. Further clubs are at Lae, Madang, Rabaul, Wau and Minj. **Riding:** Visitors are welcome to ride horses at Illimo Farm, Port Moresby, where instruction is available in the afternoons and at week-ends. **Sailing:** The Royal Papua Yacht Club makes its exten-sive facilities available to visitors; the season begins in late April. **Diving:** Skindiving facilities and qualified instructors are available. Port Moresby, Rabaul and Madang offer a wide variety of dives ranging from wrecks to reefs. Diving holidays can also be arranged at locations such as Loloaka and Wuvulu Island. There is an underwater club in Port Moresby which is open to visitors. **Squash:** Courts and equipment are available in major centres. **Hiking:** Back packing/hiking tours are on offer, ranging from simple bush walks to extended tours through the rugged interior.

SPECIAL EVENTS: National Independence Day and (in some towns) the Chinese New Year are major occasions of celebration. However the visitor to the island must not turn down any chances to go to a *sing-sing*, a colourful tribal gath-ering where there is dancing, singing and chanting. There are also some very impressive flower festivals and traditional feasts. The following is a selection:

May/Jun '93 *Kula Festival*. **Jun** *Port Moresby Show*. **Late Jul** *Mount Hagen Festival*. **Mid-Aug** *Goroka Show*. **Sep** *Hiri Maole Festival; Maborosa Festival*. **Oct** *Morobe Show*. **Oct/Nov** *Tolai Warwagira*, Rabaul. **Dec** *New Ireland Kula Festival*.

SOCIAL CONVENTIONS: Papua New Guinea's culture includes areas of society that are relatively primitive in lifestyle. There are universities at Lae (which is a University of Technology with a liberal infusion of Europeans and North Americans) and at Port Moresby. Dress should be cool and of lightweight material. Casual clothes are recommended. Informality is the order of the day and although shorts are quite acceptable, beachwear is always best confined to the beach. In the evenings some hotels expect men to wear long trousers but ties are rare. A long dress is appropriate for women on formal occasions. **Tipping:** Not customary and discouraged.

BUSINESS PROFILE

ECONOMY: Most of the population is engaged in subsis-tence agriculture. The most important commercial cash crops are copra, coffee, cocoa, timber, palm oil, rubber, tea, sugar and peanuts. In recent years the economy has been transformed by the discovery of significant mineral deposits.

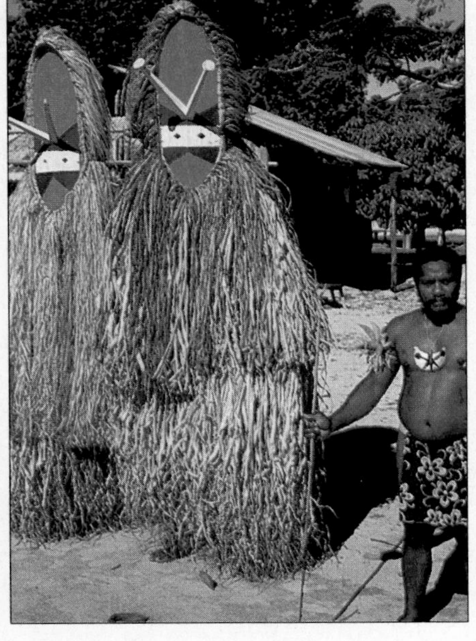

Papua New Guinea boasts the largest known supply of low-grade copper, the entire production is exported to Western Europe and Japan under long-term contract. Other identi-fied mineral deposits include gold and chromite. Traces of oil and natural gas have also been located. Earnings from gold and copper should keep the economy in a buoyant state well into the next century. The closure of the Bougainville mines (see *History* below) threw the country into recession but a recovery has been under way, fuelled by new mineral discoveries elsewhere. Light industry has grown steadily, mostly to meet consumer demands: the con-struction industry, printing, brewing, bottling and packaging are among these. At present, the economy is still heavily dependent on financial aid from Australia, although this support is due to cease in the near future. The largest importers are Australia, with 50% of the market, followed by Japan, Singapore and the USA.

BUSINESS: Business affairs tend to be conducted in a very informal fashion. A conventional suit will not be required – shirt and tie or safari suit are sufficient. **Office hours:** 0800-1700 Monday to Friday.

COMMERCIAL INFORMATION: The following organisation can offer advice: Papua New Guinea Chamber of Commerce and Industry, PO Box 1621, Port Moresby, Papua New Guinea. Tel: 213 057. Fax: 214 203.

CONFERENCES/CONVENTIONS: Some hotels pro-vide facilities.

HISTORY & GOVERNMENT

HISTORY: Papua New Guinea was formed in 1949 from two Australian territories; Papua, which had been under Australian rule since 1906, and New Guinea, a former German colony occupied in 1914 and since

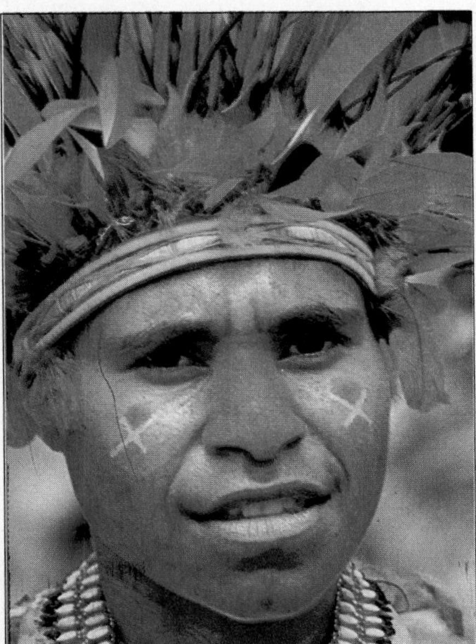

administered by the Australians under a United Nations mandate. Parts of both territories were occupied by the Japanese during the Second World War. Full indepen-dence was granted in 1975, with Michael Somare, previ-ously Chief Minister, assuming the post of Prime Minister. Somare remained in power until 1980, when Sir Julius Chan's People's Progress Party (PPP) came out of opposition to form a government. The June 1982 General Election returned Somare's Pangu Pati at the head of another coalition. Elections in June-July 1987 produced no overall majority for any party. Rabbie Namaliu, who displaced Somare as Pangu Pati leader in early 1988, took over as Prime Minister at the head of a 6-party coalition. In a photo-finish election in July 1992, Namaliu lost the premiership to Paias Wingti, leader of the People's Democratic Movement (composed of the PPP and Pangu Pati dissidents) on the casting vote of the speaker. Wingti faces, as Namaliu did, many of the classic problems which afflict developing nations. Papua New Guinea is blessed with abundant natural resources, particularly mineral deposits, but lacks the indigenous skills to exploit them. The country has therefore been obliged to rely on foreign mining interests for develop-ment and the Government has faced a balancing act in accommodating the mining companies, ensuring that the benefits of their activities accrue to the Papuan people, while protecting the rich natural environment. The Government's strategy has fallen apart spectacularly in the last two years due to the situation on the island of Bougainville, site of one of the world's largest copper mines and source of one-third of Papua's export income. In 1989 local landowners raised complaints about the pollution caused by the mine and the lack of financial benefit to the local economy. Violence broke out between the two sides and forced the closure of the mine in May 1989. The Government sent in troops who were confronted by a secessionist insurrection in the form of the Bougainville Revolutionary Army (BRA). In May 1990 Bougainville declared independence; no one recog-nised it apart from the Solomon Islands (who have close links with Bougainville). A settlement in January 1991 broke down two months later – there are apparently no prospects of a resumption of negotiations. Despite their disagreement over Bougainville, Papua and the Solomons have good official relations: together with Vanuatu, they have formed the Melanesian Spearhead Group, dedicated to preserving Melanesian cultural tra-dition and securing independence for New Caledonia. Links with ASEAN have been strengthened by the sign-ing of a friendship and co-operation treaty with Papua New Guinea.

GOVERNMENT: Papua New Guinea has a unicameral Parliamentary system, with executive power nominally held by the British Crown, represented by a Governor-General. Legislative power rests with the 109-member Parliament.

CLIMATE

Hot, tropical climate at sea level, cooling towards the highlands which also cause climatic variation from one area to another, affecting the southeast trade winds and the northwest monsoons. The majority of the rain falls between December and March due to the northwest monsoon, although Port Moresby enjoys a dry season at this time. Frost and occasional snow falls on the highest mountain peaks.

Required clothing: Tropical, lightweights and cottons are recommended. In the highlands, warmer clothing is needed. Rainwear is advised for the monsoon season (December to March).

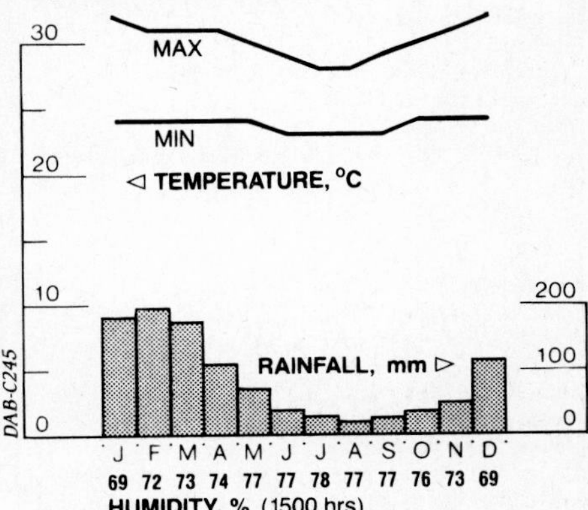

PARAGUAY

Location: Central South America.

Dirección General de Turismo
Ministerio de Obras Públicas y Communicaciones
Palma 468
Asunción, Paraguay
Tel: (21) 441 530. Telex: 162.
Embassy of the Republic of Paraguay
Braemar Lodge
Cornwall Gardens
London SW7 4AQ
Tel: (071) 937 1253. Fax: (071) 937 5687.
Visa Secton: Tel: (071) 937 6629. Opening hours: 1000-1500 Monday to Friday.
British Embassy
Casilla 404
Calle Presidente Franco 706
Asunción, Paraguay
Tel: (21) 44472 *or* 49146. Fax: (21) 446 385. Telex: PRODROME 139 PY.
Embassy of the Republic of Paraguay
2400 Massachusetts Avenue, NW
Washington, DC
20008
Tel: (202) 483 6960/1. Fax: (202) 234 4508.
Consulate Generals in: Coral Gables (Florida), Dallas, Huntington Beach (California), New Orleans, New York and San Francisco.
Embassy of the United States of America
Casilla 402
Avenida Mariscal López 1776
Asunción, Paraguay
Tel: (21) 213 715. Fax: (21) 213 728. Telex: 203.
Consulate of Paraguay
Suite 750
1130 Sherbrooke Street West
Montréal, Québec
H3A 2M8
Tel: (514) 842 8856. Fax: (514) 287 1538.
Canadian Consulate
Casilla 2577
El Paraguayo Independiente 99, Entrepiso
Oficianas 1 y 2
Asunción, Paraguay
Tel: (21) 449 505 *or* 491 730. Fax: (21) 449 506. Telex: 652.

AREA: 406,752 sq km (157,048 sq miles).
POPULATION: 4,397,306 (1991 estimate).
POPULATION DENSITY: 10.8 per sq km.
CAPITAL: Asunción. **Population:** 454,881 (1982).
GEOGRAPHY: Paraguay is a landlocked country surrounded by Argentina, Bolivia and Brazil, lying some 1440km (900 miles) up the River Paraná from the Atlantic. The River Paraguay, a tributary of the Paraná, divides the country into two sharply contrasting regions. The *Oriental* zone, which covers 159,800 sq km (61,700 sq miles), consists of undulating country intersected by chains of hills rising to about 600m (2000ft), merging into the Mato Grosso Plateau in the north; the Paraná crosses the area in the east and south. East and southeast of Asunción lie the oldest centres of settlement inhabited by the greater part of the population. This area is bordered to the west by rolling pastures, and to the south by thick primeval forests. The *Occidental* zone, or Paraguayan Chaco, covers 246,827 sq km (95,300 sq miles). It is a flat alluvial plain, composed mainly of grey clay, which is marked by large areas of permanent swamp in the southern and eastern regions. Apart from a few small settlements, it is sparsely populated.
LANGUAGE: The official language is Spanish. Guaraní is widely spoken. Most Paraguayans are bilingual, but prefer to speak Guaraní outside Asunción.
RELIGION: Roman Catholic.
TIME: GMT - 4 (GMT - 5 in summer).
ELECTRICITY: 220 volts AC, 50Hz.
COMMUNICATIONS: Telephone: IDD is available. Country code: 595. Some calls to Europe from Paraguay must be made via the international operator. Limited internal network apart from the main cities. **Fax:** Some hotels provide facilities. **Telex/telegram:** Many hotels have telex facilities. Services are also available at *Antelco* (Administracion Nacional de Telecommunicationes) from where telegrams can also be sent. **Post:** Airmail to Europe takes five days. **Press:** The main newspapers are *El Diario, ABC Color, Ultima Hora* and *Hoy*. American newspapers are available.
BBC World Service and Voice of America frequencies: From time to time these change. See the section *How to Use this Book* for more information.

BBC:				
MHz	15.26	15.18	11.75	9.915
Voice of America:				
MHz	15.21	11.58	9.775	5.995

PASSPORT/VISA

Regulations and requirements may be subject to change at short notice, and you are advised to contact the appropriate diplomatic or consular authority before finalising travel arrangements. Details of these may be found at the head of this country's entry. Any numbers in the chart refer to the footnotes below.

	Passport Required?	Visa Required?	Return Ticket Required?
Full British	Yes	No	Yes
BVP	Not valid	-	-
Australian	Yes	Yes	Yes
Canadian	Yes	No	Yes
USA	Yes	No	Yes
Other EC	Yes	1	Yes
Japanese	Yes	Yes	Yes

PASSPORTS: Valid passport required by all except nationals of Argentina, Brazil, Chile and Uruguay with valid ID cards entering as tourists from their own country.
British Visitors Passport: Not accepted.
VISAS: Required by all except nationals of the following countries entering as tourists for stays of up to 90 days:
(a) those mentioned under passsports above;
(b) **[1]** EC countries (except France, Greece, Ireland and Portugal who *do* require visas);
(c) Canada and the USA;
(d) Austria, Colombia, Ecuador, El Salvador, Israel, Norway, Sweden and Switzerland.
Types of visa: Tourist, Business and Transit.
Validity: 1-3 months.
Application to: Consulate (or Consular Section at Embassy). For addresses, see top of entry.
Application requirements: (a) Valid passport. (b) Completed application form. (c) Letter from a recognised authority, such as a tour operator. (d) 2 passport photos. (e) Sufficient funds for support during stay. (f) Onward ticket. (g) SAE for those applying by post.
Working days required: 7 maximum.
Temporary residence: Apply to immigration section of the Ministry for the Interior.

MONEY

Currency: Guaraní (G). Notes are in denominations of G50,000, 10,000, 5000, 1000, 500, 100, 50, 10, 5 and 1. Coins are in denominations of G50, 10, 5 and 1.
Currency exchange: Travellers cheques, currency and all commercial transactions must be conducted at the free market rate. Many cheap hotels will neither accept credit cards nor exchange travellers cheques. US Dollars, which are more easily negotiable than Sterling, are widely accepted throughout the country.
Credit cards: Access/Mastercard, American Express and Visa are widely accepted, while Diners Club has more limited use. Check with your credit card company for details of merchant acceptability and other services which may be available.
Travellers cheques: Banks will not cash travellers cheques in anything other than Guaranís. *Casas de cambios* will, however, give US Dollars. There are no facilities for exchanging travellers cheques at the airport.
Exchange rate indicators: The following figures are included as a guide to the movements of the Guaraní against Sterling and the US Dollar:

Date:	Oct '89	Oct '90	Oct '91	Oct '92
£1.00=	1980.05	2362.0	2284.9	2459.2
$1.00=	1253.98	1209.1	1316.5	1549.6

Currency restrictions: There are no import or export restrictions on local or foreign currency.
Banking hours: 0830-1215 Monday to Friday.

DUTY FREE

The following items may be imported into Paraguay without incurring customs duty:
A reasonable quantity of tobacco and alcoholic beverages;
A reasonable quantity of perfume for personal use.

PUBLIC HOLIDAYS

Public holidays observed in Paraguay are as follows:
Mar 1 '93 Heroes' Day. **Apr 8** Maundy Thursday. **Apr 9** Good Friday. **May 1** Labour Day. **May 15** National Independence Day. **May 20** Ascension Day. **Jun 10** Corpus Christi. **Jun 12** Peace of Chaco. **Aug 15** Founding of Asunción. **Aug 25** Constitution Day. **Sep 29** Battle of Boquerón. **Oct 12** Columbus Day. **Nov 1** All Saints' Day. **Dec 8** Immaculate Conception. **Dec 25** Christmas Day. **Jan 1 '94** New Year's Day. **Feb** San Blás (national saint). **Mar** Heroes' Day.

HEALTH

Regulations and requirements may be subject to change at short notice, and you are advised to contact your doctor well in advance of your intended date of departure. Any numbers in the chart refer to the footnotes below.

	Special Precautions?	Certificate Required?
Yellow Fever	No	1
Cholera	No	No
Typhoid & Polio	Yes	-
Malaria	2	-
Food & Drink	3	-

[1]: A yellow fever vaccination certificate is required from travellers leaving Paraguay to go to endemic areas. No certificate is required from travellers arriving in the country.
[2]: Malaria risk, predominantly in the benign *vivax* form, exists from October to May in some rural areas of Alto Paraná, Amambay, Caaguazú, Canendiyú and San Pedro Departments.
[3]: Mains water is normally chlorinated, and whilst relatively safe may cause mild abdominal upsets. Bottled water is available and is advised for the first few weeks of the stay. Drinking water outside main cities and towns is likely to be contaminated and sterilisation is considered essential. Milk is unpasteurised and should be boiled. Powdered or tinned milk is available and is advised, but make sure that it is reconstituted with pure water. Avoid dairy products which are likely to have been made from unboiled milk. Only eat well-cooked meat and fish, preferably served hot. Pork, salad and mayonnaise may carry increased risk. Vegetables should be cooked and fruit peeled.
Rabies is present. For those at high risk, vaccination before arrival should be considered. If you are bitten abroad seek medical advice without delay. For more information consult the *Health* section at the back of the book.
Health care: Health insurance is essential.

TRAVEL - International

AIR: Paraguay's national airline is *Líneas Aéreas Paraguyayas (LAP)*.
Approximate flight time: From *London* to Paraguay is 15-19 hours, depending on the route taken.
International airport: *Asunción (ASU)* (Silvio Pettirossi) is 16km (10 miles) from the city (travel time – 20 minutes). A coach and taxi service runs to the city.
Departure tax: G11,000 is levied on all international departures. Transit passengers and children under 2 years of age are exempt.
SEA: A ferry between Posadas (Argentina) and Encarnación offers an alternative to travelling to Buenos Aires, about 321km (200 miles) longer, by way of the

.rgentine provinces of Missiones and Corrientes and ɹen across the new bridge over the Paraná River to esistencia. Those who prefer to continue along the left ank of the Paraná River will have to travel to Paraná, rovincial capital of Entre Rios, crossing under the araná River in the tunnel between the cities of Paraná ıd Santa Fé.

.AIL: There is no through service to Argentina, but a eekly train from Asunción serves Posadas in Argentina y means of a train-ferry, with connections to Concordia ıd Buenos Aires. The rail services are very slow.

.OAD: The roads from Rio and São Paulo to Asunción via the Iguazú Falls) are paved and generally good, as is ıe one from Buenos Aires. **Bus:** There are daily services om São Paulo and Rio de Janeiro (Brazil), Santa Fé, .osario, Córdoba, Buenos Aires (Argentina) and Aontevideo (Uruguay).

TRAVEL - Internal

.IR: Air service is run by *LAP*, *TAM (Transportes Aero Ailitar)*, *LATN (Lineas Aéreas de Transporte Nacional)*, *Aeronorte* and *Aerosur*. The most popular visitors' flight s to the Iguazú Falls from Asunción with *Varig Airways*. Air-taxis are popular with those wishing to discover the rackless Gran Chaco (see *Geography* above). Travel gencies offer daily city tours, but services suffer from freuent upsets by weather conditions.

RAIL: A weekly service links Asunción and Encarnación – which are 431km (268 miles) apart – ısing original steam locomotives. There is also a twiceweekly service from San Salvador to Abay. Services are often unreliable, however, and whole routes may be bandoned for months at a time.

ROAD: Roads serving the main centres are in good condition. However, unsurfaced roads may be closed in bad veather. Approximately 10% of roads are surfaced. A ighway links Asunción with Iguazú Falls, a drive of up o six hours. **Bus:** Often the best and cheapest method of ransport within Paraguay. For longer distances advance ɔooking may be necessary. There are express links to najor centres. **Car hire:** Cars can be hired through local ourist agencies. **Documentation:** National driving icence or International Driving Permit are both accepted.

URBAN: Bus and minibus services are provided by private companies in Asunción, with 2-zone fares collected ɔy conductors. There also remain two routes of the government-operated tramway.

JOURNEY TIMES: The following chart gives approximate journey times (in hours and minutes) from Asunción to other major cities in Paraguay.

	Air	Road	Rail	River
PJ Caballero	1.15	11.00	-	13.00
Concepión	1.00	12.00	-	14.00
C. del Este	1.05	5.00	-	-
Valle Mí	1.30	-	-	15.00
Encarnación	1.10	5.00	14.00	9.00

ACCOMMODATION

HOTELS: Outside the capital, accommodation is limited. All accommodation must be booked in writing well in advance; details of current prices are available from the Embassy (see above). All hotels in Asunción are likely to be fully booked throughout the tourist season (July and August). Visitors are advised to consult a reputable travel agent for up-to-date information, or to ascertain the rates with hotels when making reservations.

RESORTS & EXCURSIONS

A popular tourist itinerary is the 'Central Circuit', a route of some 200km (125 miles) that takes in some of the country's most interesting sites.

Asunción: The attractive and colourful capital city is situated on the *Bay of Asunción*, an inlet off the Paraguay River. Planned on a colonial Spanish grid system, it has many fine parks and plazas. Trees such as jacaranda and orange add colour to the avenues. On the way to the waterfront the visitor enters the old part of town with a variety of architectural styles. The parks of the city should not be missed, one of the best is *Parque Calos Antonio Lopez* high above Asunción with a splendid view of the surrounding area. The *Botanical Gardens*, situated in a former estate of the Lopez family on the Paraguay River, are home to an abundance of plants as well as a golf-course and a small zoo. The *Lopez Residence* has been converted to a natural history museum and library. Package trips can be booked to see the *Iguazú Falls* and the *Salto Crystal Falls*, and river trips to **Villeta** or up the *Pilcomayo River* to the *Chaco*. **Luque**, near the capital, is the home of the famous Paraguayan harps, which can be purchased.

San Lorenzo: Founded in 1775, the town is the site of the university halls of residence and an interesting gothic-style church.

Ita: Founded in 1539 by Domingo Martinez, its main speciality is the handpainted Gallinita hens made of black clay. The highly colourful market is also an attraction.

Yaguarón: The city is set in an orange-growing district and played a part during the Spanish conquest as a base for the Franciscan missions. Their churches date back to 1775 and the tints made from local plants still add a bright sparkle to the wood carvings.

Paraguarí: Situated in the foothills of the **Cordillera des Altos,** this is a historic village with several old buildings in colonial style.

Chololo: A picturesque holiday centre where tourist facilities include bars, restaurants and bungalows for rent.

Piribebuy: The scene of bloody fighting during the war of the triple alliance. The Encaje-yú spindle lace, the 'sixty stripe' Paraní poncho and other handmade goods are produced here. It is also famous as a place of worship of the 'Virgin of Miracles'.

San Bernadino: Situated on *Lake Ypacarai*, the town is a notable holiday resort and very popular during the summer months. It has a beach, good hotels, bars and restaurants.

Ciudad Del Este is the fastest-growing town in the country and offers extensive shopping facilities. The *Monday Falls*, 10km (6 miles) from the town are also well worth a visit.

Encarnación has many colonial buildings and a sleepy waterfront area complete with *gauchos* and sandy streets.

The Paraguyan Chaco: This vast scarcely populated area consists mainly of empty plains and forests. The drive from Asunción leads through the Low Chaco, a land of palm forests and marshes, and reaches the Middle Chaco with its capital *Filadelfia*. Here mainly Mennonites of German descent have set up farms and other agricultural outlets as well as their own schools. Therefore they are considered to be the only organised community in the whole of the Chaco region.

SOCIAL PROFILE

FOOD & DRINK: Typical local dishes include *chipas* (maize bread flavoured with egg and cheese), *sopa Paraguaya* (soup of mashed corn, cheese, milk and onions), *soo-yosopy* (a soup of cornmeal and ground beef), *albondiga* (meatball soup) and *boríborí* (another soup of diced meat, vegetables and small balls of maize mixed with cheese). *Palmitos* (palm hearts), *surubí* (a fish found in the Paraná) and the local beef are excellent. There is a wide choice of restaurants in Asunción, most with table service. **Drink:** The national drink is *cana*, distilled from sugar cane and honey. Sugar cane juice, known as *mosto*, and the national red wine are well worth trying, as is *yerba maté*, a refreshing drink popular with nearly all Paraguayans. There are no strict licensing hours and alcohol is widely available.

NIGHTLIFE: Asunción has very little nightlife, but there are casinos and discotheques. The *parrilladas* or open-air restaurants offer by far the best atmosphere, especially in Asunción. There is a casino at the border towns of Ciudad Del Este and Encarnación.

SHOPPING: Special purchases include *nandutí* lace, made by the women of Itagua, and *aho poí* sports shirts, made in a variety of colours and designs. Other items include leather goods, wood handicrafts, silver *yerba maté* cups and native jewellery. **Shopping hours:** 0800-2000 Monday to Friday and 0730-1200 Saturday.

SPORT: Football is the national sport. There are **tennis** facilities at hotels and in Asunción. The Asunción Golf Club has an 18-hole **golf** course. **Water-skiing** facilities are available at one hotel on the River Paraguay. Some large hotels have **swimming** pools. **Fishing** is a special attraction. The *dorado*, found in the Paraguay, Paraná and Tebicuary rivers, can weigh up to 29kg (65 pounds). International fishing contests are held near Asunción. There are many other smaller fish that are peculiar to Paraguay such as the *surubi*, *pati*, *pacu*, *manguruyus*, *armados*, *moncholos* and *bagres*. There are also small lakes with trout and local varieties of fish.

SPECIAL EVENTS: Annual festivals of note in Paraguay are as follows (check with the Embassy for exact dates):

Mar '93 *Argentine-Paraguay Festival*. **Apr** *Semana Santa* (week-long Easter festival). **Apr 1-4** *Semana del Turismo* (week of traditional cultural and artistic attractions), Caacupe. **May** *Music Festival*, Tapiracuai. **May 15** *Dia de la Independencia* (Independence Day parades and festivities). **Jun** *Verbana de San Juan* (traditional fiesta, including walking on hot embers). **Jul** *Festival del Nanduti* (traditional music and crafts festival with parade of floats), Itaugua; *Festival Internacional de Danza* (dance festival with participants from Argentina, Brazil, Paraguay and Uruguay), Encarnación. **Aug 15** *Dia de la Virgen de la Asunción* and *Aniversario de la Fundación de Asunción* (religious and cultural celebrations). **Sep** *Festival de la Alfalfa*, Sapucai. **Oct** *Encuentro Internacional de Coros* (choir festival), Encarnación. **Nov** *Festival del Poyvi* (arts, crafts and music fair), Carpegua. **Dec** *Apertura de Temporada* (opening of the tourism season), San Bernadino.

SOCIAL CONVENTIONS: Shaking hands is the usual form of greeting. Normal codes of behaviour should be observed. Smoking is not allowed in cinemas and theatres. Dress tends to be informal and sportswear is popular. **Photography:** Avoid sensitive subjects, eg military installations. **Tipping:** 10-15% is normally included in hotel, restaurant and bar bills.

BUSINESS PROFILE

ECONOMY: Paraguay's agriculture plays an important part in its economy, supplying nearly one-third of GNP and almost all the country's export earnings. Production of Paraguay's principal cash crops, cotton and soya, has expanded rapidly during the late 1980s with the best prospects for the future in increased growth of these and other commodities. The country's agricultural potential is, in principle, immense. Recently completed hydro-electric projects, undertaken as joint projects with Brazil and including the world's largest hydro-electric dam at Itaipú, have given Paraguay self-sufficiency in energy. The economy has now recovered from the recession of the early 1980s and is one of the fastest-growing in Latin America. Unlike many other countries on the continent, it is without an excessive foreign debt. Indigenous industry has grown quickly, but there are still considerable opportunities for exports of manufactured goods. Paraguay is a member of the 11-strong Asociación Latinoamericana de Integración, which seeks to promote free trade and economic development within Latin America. Paraguay, alongside Bolivia, enjoys special tariff concessions, which may in the near future see the country develop as an export market for the rest of the continent. Brazil, the USA and Argentina are the largest trading partners. Admission to the Mercosur group of southern Latin American countries will further assist trade growth and economic development.

BUSINESS: For formal occasions or business affairs men should wear lightweight suits and ties or a dinner jacket in the evening. Most business people are able to conduct a conversation in English, but a knowledge of Spanish will be useful. Appointments and normal business courtesies apply. Best time to visit is from May to September. **Office hours:** 0800-1200 and 1500-1730/1900 Monday to Friday; 0800-1200 Saturday.

PARAGUAY	HEALTH REGULATIONS	VISA REGULATIONS
GALILEO/WORLDSPAN	 TI-DFT/ASU/HE	 TI-DFT/ASU/VI
SABRE	 TIDFT/ASU/HE	 TIDFT/ASU/VI

Code-Link

To access this information on your CRS, swipe the barcode with a light pen or type in the text under the barcode. For more information, see the introduction *How to Use This Book*.

COMMERCIAL INFORMATION: The following organisation can offer advice: Cámara y Bolsa de Comercio; Estrella 540, Asunción. Tel: (21) 47312.

HISTORY & GOVERNMENT

HISTORY: Paraguay became independent in 1811, after about 300 years of Spanish rule. Since then, the country has been ruled by a succession of dictators, and has endured costly wars against neighbouring countries, particularly in 1865 against Uruguay, Brazil and Argentina, as a result of which Paraguay lost much of its territory and roughly a half of its population. Since the 1940s Paraguay has been under military rule for most of the time, interspersed with periods of crisis and internal conflict. A spell of intense instability in the late 1940s and early 1950s was brought to an end in 1954 with a military coup by the Commander-in-Chief of the armed forces, General Alfredo Stroessner. Backed by the military, the business community and the main right-wing grouping, the Partido Colorado, Stroessner retained power for over 32 years. In February 1989, Stroessner was overthrown in a military coup led by his former deputy, General Andres Rodriguez. As Stroessner retired into Brazilian exile, a presidential election organised by the new regime, and backed by the Colorado Party, gave a large vote to Rodriguez. With firm prodding from Brazil and the USA, Rodriguez then spent the following two years attempting to drag Paraguay out of its political and economic torpor. Liberalising measures have been introduced, coupled with strict fiscal and budgetary control. The old public and private monopolies have been shaken up and are now being sold off. The Government has made attempts to crack down on smuggling, drug trafficking and tax evasion. The political system has been opened up, with the stranglehold of the Colorados gradually being weakened. Elections in November 1991 for a new 198-seat National Assembly saw the Colorado Party take two-thirds of the vote (123 seats); a vigorous opposition, led by the Partido Liberal Radical Auténtico which won 28% of the vote, has emerged after long years of repression. The army, long a dominant influence in Paraguayan politics, will necessarily see this influence curtailed: provided it is not asked to make undue sacrifices, especially in its budget, it will probably accept the reform process. The progress made by the Government so far has gained it admission as a founding member of the Mercosur group, a common market in the south of the Latin American continent including Brazil and Argentina. Indeed, the inaugural ceremony for the group was held in Asunción in March 1991.
GOVERNMENT: The newly elected National Assembly (see above) has the task of drafting a replacement for the existing 1967 Constitution.

CLIMATE

Subtropical with rapid changes in temperature throughout the year. Summer (December to March) can be very hot. Winter (June to September) is mild with few cold days. Rainfall is heaviest from December to March.
Required clothing: Lightweight cottons and linens are worn in warmer months, with some warm clothes for spring and autumn. Mediumweights are best for winter. Rainwear is advisable throughout the year

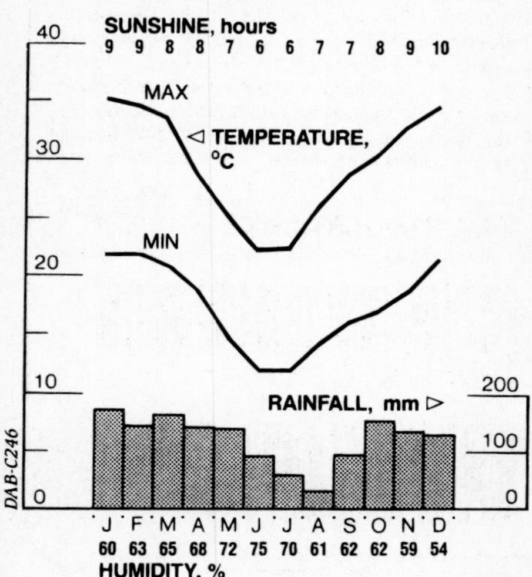

Location: Western South America.

Fondo de Promoción Turística (FOPTUR)
Jirón de la Unión 1066
Belén
Lima, Peru
Tel: (14) 323 559. Fax: (14) 429 280. Telex: 21363.
Embassy of the Republic of Peru
52 Sloane Street
London SW1X 9SP
Tel: (071) 235 1917. Fax: (071) 235 4463. Telex: 917888. Opening hours: 0930-1630 Monday to Friday.
Visa Section: Tel: (071) 235 6867. Opening hours: 1000-1300 Monday to Friday.
British Embassy
Casilla 854
Edificio El Pacífico Washington, 12°
Plaza Washington
Avenida Arequipa
Lima 100, Peru
Tel: (14) 334 738. Fax: (14) 334 735. Telex: 25230 PU PRODROME.
Consulate in: Arequipa.
Embassy of the Republic of Peru
1700 Massachusetts Avenue, NW
Washington, DC
20036
Tel: (202) 833 9860. Fax: (202) 659 8124. Telex: 197675.
Peru Tourist Office Inc
Suite 600
1000 Brickell Avenue
Miami, FL
33131
Tel: (305) 374 0023. Fax: (305) 374 4905.
Embassy of the United States of America
Apartado 1995
Avenida Garcilaso de la Vega 1400
Lima 100, Peru
Tel: (14) 338 000. Fax: (14) 316 682. Telex: 25212.
Embassy of Peru
Suite 1007
170 Laurier Avenue West
Ottawa, Ontario
K1P 5V5
Tel: (613) 238 1777. Fax: (613) 232 3062. Telex: 0533754.
Consulate in: Montréal.
Canadian Embassy
Apartado 1212
Federico Gerdes 130
Miraflores
Lima, Peru
Tel: (14) 444 015 *or* 443 841 *or* 443 893. Fax: (14) 444 347. Telex: 25323 PE DOMCAN.

AREA: 1,285,216 sq km (496,225 sq miles).
POPULATION: 22,332,000 (1990 estimate).
POPULATION DENSITY: 17.4 per sq km.
CAPITAL: Lima. **Population:** 6,233,800 (1989 estimate).
GEOGRAPHY: Peru is a large, mountainous country straddling the equator on the Pacific coast of South America. It has borders with Ecuador and Colombia to the north, Brazil and Bolivia to the east, and Chile to the south. There are four natural zones, running roughly north to south: Costa, Sierra, Montaña and Selva. The **Costa region**, which contains Lima, the capital, is a narrow coastal plain consisting of large tracts of desert broken by fertile valleys. The cotton and sugar plantations and most of the so far exploited oilfields lie in this area. The **Sierra** contains the Andes, with peaks of over 6000m (20,000ft), most of the country's mineral resources and the greater part of its livestock. The bulk of the Indian population live in this area. The **Montaña**, an area of fertile, subtropical uplands, lies between the Andes and the jungles of eastern Peru. As yet, it is largely undeveloped. Sections of a proposed international highway are at present being built through it, with some sections already in use. The **Selva**, or Amazonian jungle of eastern Peru, has vast natural resources. The absence of land communications, however, left the area largely unexplored until full-scale oil exploration began in 1973. The population is largely Indian and Mestizos with a noticeable influence from European (mainly Spanish), Chinese and African settlers.
LANGUAGE: Spanish and Quechua. English is spoken in major tourist areas.
RELIGION: 99% Roman Catholic.
TIME: GMT - 5.
ELECTRICITY: 220 volts AC, 60Hz.
COMMUNICATIONS: Telephone: IDD is available. Country code: 51. **Fax:** Some hotels have facilities. **Telex/telegram:** Facilities are available at Lima and main hotels, with services run by ENTEL PERU. These close in the evenings and during holidays. Telex services at Bolivar, Crillon and Sheraton hotels. Country code is PE. **Post:** Airmail to Europe takes up to two weeks. Postal facilities are limited outside Lima. First-class airmail from the UK addressed to PO boxes in Peru usually takes four days, but may be subject to delay. The delivery of mail to streets is erratic and subject to frequent delays. The main post office is near the Plaza de Armas and opens 0800-1800 Monday to Saturday and 0800-1200 Sunday. **Press:** Newspapers are in Spanish. Morning dailies include *La Républica, Expreso, Ojo, El Peruano* and *El Comercio*. The English-language weekly newspaper is *The Lima Times*.
BBC World Service and Voice of America frequencies: From time to time these change. See the section *How to Use this Book* for more information.

BBC:				
MHz	17.84	15.26	15.22	9.915
Voice of America:				
MHz	15.21	11.58	9.775	5.995

PASSPORT/VISA

Regulations and requirements may be subject to change at short notice, and you are advised to contact the appropriate diplomatic or consular authority before finalising travel arrangements. Details of these may be found at the head of this country's entry. Any numbers in the chart refer to the footnotes below.

	Passport Required?	Visa Required?	Return Ticket Required?
Full British	Yes	No	Yes
BVP	Not valid	-	-
Australian	Yes	Yes	Yes
Canadian	Yes	No	Yes
USA	Yes	No	Yes
Other EC	Yes	No	Yes
Japanese	Yes	No	Yes

PASSPORTS: Valid passport required by all.
British Visitors Passport: Not accepted.
VISAS: Required by all except:
(a) nationals of those countries shown in the chart above for stays of up to 3 months;
(b) nationals of Argentina, Austria, Barbados, Brazil, Finland, Honduras, Liechtenstein, Norway, South Korea, Sweden, Switzerland and Uruguay for stays of up to 3 months;
(c) nationals of Bolivia, Colombia, Ecuador and Venezuela for stays of up to 2 months (an extension to 3 months is available);
(d) nationals of Chile for stays of up to 30 days;
(e) visitors on an *approved* organised trip.
Those exempted under (a) and (b) must be in possession of a yellow *Cedula* 'C' along with documents for onward travel. The Cedula 'C' is usually issued free of charge by the carrier.

Types of visa: Visitors, approximately £12. Business, £27. Transit visas are not required by those who continue their journey to a third country within 24 hours by the same or first connecting flight, provided that they hold tickets with reserved seats and other documents for their onward journey. They may not leave the transit area of the airport.
Application to: Consulate (or Consular Section at Embassy). For addresses, see top of entry.
Application requirements: (a) Valid passport. (b) Open or through ticket to show they will be leaving Peru. (c) For *Business visas*, company letter specifying the reason for the trip. (d) Fee.
All nationals are advised to check with the Peruvian Consulate prior to departure to obtain current details of any documentation which might be required.
Working days required: Usually 24 hours.

MONEY

Currency: Nuevo Sol = 100 centimos. The Neuvo Sol replaced the Inti as the national currency in January 1991 at 1 Neuvo Sol = 1,000,000 Intis. Inti notes are still legal tender. Neuvo Sol notes are in denominations of 20 and 10. Coins are in denominations of 1 Sol, and 50, 10, 5 and 1 centimos.
Currency exchange: Changing currencies other than the US Dollar can be both difficult and, in terms of the high commission rates charged, expensive. Banco de la Nación is the only institution regularly authorised to deal in foreign exchange. The main hotels and *Casas de Cambios* are, however, allowed to exchange foreign currency as agents of the Banco de la Nación. *Casas de Cambios* are recommended for their good rates, speed and honesty.
Credit cards: American Express, Access/Mastercard, Diners Club and Visa are all accepted, but usage facilities may be limited outside Lima. Check with your credit card company for details of merchant acceptability and other services which may be available.
Travellers cheques: American Express state that they will sell travellers cheques and give out emergency money, but only in Lima. 'Exprinter' of Lima cashes travellers cheques with 1.25% commission. Outside Lima, changing travellers cheques is a slow and laborious process.
Exchange rate indicators: The following figures are included as a guide to the movements of the Inti/Nuevo Sol against Sterling and the US Dollar:

Date:	**Oct '89**	**Oct '90**	**Oct '91**	**Oct '92**
£1.00=	8723	867,786	1.47*	2.52*
$1.00=	5525	444,221	0.85*	1.59*

Note [*]: Neuvo Sol.
Currency restrictions: There are no restrictions on the import and export of local currency. Export of foreign currency is limited to the amount imported. Exchange receipts must be kept for reconversion of Neuvo Sol into foreign currency.
Banking hours: 0815-1130 Monday to Friday (January to March) and 0915-1245 Monday to Friday (April to December). Some banks may open in the afternoon.

DUTY FREE

The following items may be imported into Peru without incurring customs duty:
400 cigarettes or 50 cigars or 50g of tobacco;
2 litres of spirits or 2 litres of wine;
A reasonable amount of perfume for personal use.

PUBLIC HOLIDAYS

Public holidays observed in Peru are as follows:
Apr 8 '93 Maundy Thursday. **Apr 9** Good Friday. **May 1** Labour Day. **Jun 24** Day of the Peasant (half day). **Jun 29** St Peter and St Paul. **Jul 28-29** Independence Day. **Aug 30** St Rose of Lima. **Oct 8** Battle of Angamos. **Nov 1** All Saints' Day. **Dec 8** Immaculate Conception. **Dec 25** Christmas Day. **Jan 1 '94** New Year's Day.

HEALTH

Regulations and requirements may be subject to change at short notice, and you are advised to contact your doctor well in advance of your intended date of departure. Any numbers in the chart refer to the footnotes below.

	Special Precautions?	Certificate Required?
Yellow Fever	Yes	1
Cholera	Yes	No
Typhoid & Polio	Yes	-
Malaria	2	-
Food & Drink	3	-

[1]: A yellow fever vaccination certificate is required of travellers over six months of age arriving from infected areas. Vaccination is recommended for those intending to visit rural areas.
[2]: Malaria risk, almost exclusively in the benign *vivax* form, exists throughout the year in rural areas below 1500m of the Departments of Amazonas, Ancash, Apurimac, Ayacacho, Cajamarca, Cuzco (La Convención Province), Huánuco, Junín (Chanchamayo and Satipo Provinces), La Libertad, Lambayeque, Loreto, Madre de Dios, Piura, San Martin, Tumbes and Ucayali. *Falciparum* malaria occurs sporadically in areas bordering Bolivia (Madre de Dios River), Brazil (Yavari and Acre River), Columbia (Putumayo River), Ecuador (Napo River) and in Zarumilla Province. Resistance to chloroquine and sufadoxine/pyrimethamine of the *falciparum* strain has been reported.
[3]: Mains water is normally chlorinated, and whilst relatively safe may cause mild abdominal upsets. Bottled water is available and is advised for the first few weeks of the stay. Drinking water outside main cities and towns is likely to be contaminated and sterilisation is considered essential. Milk is unpasteurised and should be boiled. Powdered or tinned milk is available and is advised, but make sure that it is reconstituted with pure water. Avoid dairy products which are likely to have been made from unboiled milk. Only eat well-cooked meat and fish, preferably served hot. Pork, salad and mayonnaise may carry increased risk. Vegetables should be cooked and fruit peeled.
Rabies is present. For those at high risk, vaccination before arrival should be considered. If you are bitten abroad seek medical advice without delay. For more information consult the *Health* section at the back of the book.
Health care: There are approximately 450 hospitals (30,000 beds) and 12,000 doctors.

TRAVEL - International

AIR: Peru's national airlines is *Aeroperu (PL)*.
Approximate flight times: From Lima to *London* is 19 hours (including stopover in Miami), to *Los Angeles* is 8 hours 55 minutes, to *Miami* is 5 hours 55 minutes and to *New York* is 9 hours 20 minutes. Direct flights from Europe take 14 hours.
International airport: *Lima (LIM)* (Jorge Chávez International) is 16km (10 miles) northwest of the city (travel time – 35 minutes). Coaches go to the city every 5 minutes providing a 24-hour service. Return is from Le Paris Movie bus stop, La Colmena Avenue, Block 7 and pick-ups are at Hotel Crillon. Buses go to the city every 15 minutes providing a 24-hour service. Return is from Camana, Block 8. Taxis to the city are also available. Airport facilities include a duty-free and handicraft shop, bank, coffee shop, newsagent and tourist information desk.
Departure tax: US$15 is levied on all international departures. Transit passengers and children under two years are exempt.
SEA: One regular passenger line calls at Callao, the main seaport. *Delta Line Cruises* sail from San Francisco and Los Angeles every 23 days for a trip around South America via the Panama Canal, passing through the Straits of Magellan and stopping at Valparaiso and Callao. The voyage lasts 55 days.
RAIL: There are also two daily trains from Tacna to Arica (Chile) and there is a weekly rail-steamer link across Lake Titicaca from Puno to Guaqui (Bolivia); see also *Travel – Internal* below.
ROAD: The main international highway is the Pan-American Highway running north–south through the coastal desert of Peru. *TEPSA* operate Greyhound-type buses from Ecuador, through Peru to Chile.

TRAVEL - Internal

AIR: *Aeroperu* and *Faucett* handle virtually all domestic air traffic, linking Lima to Arequipa, Ayacucho, Cuzco, Iquitos, Piura, Pucallpa, Talara, Trujillo, Tumbes, Yurimagnas, Tacna, Chiclayo and other cities. *Aeroperu* offers cheap unlimited travel in Peru with a ticket lasting 15 days.
Departure tax: US$15. Passengers departing from Cuzco, Iquitos, Arequipa or Trujillo must pay a further tax of US$3.50.
RAIL: There are two main rail networks, which do not intersect. In addition, a number of short tracks have been constructed by mining interests and there is a short spur from the Chilean network reaching as far as Tacna. There are no connections between Lima and Cuzco. Fast and comfortable electric *autovagons* are operated on some routes. Visitors should be aware that railway stations and trains are the haunts of thieves at night and they are advised to travel only by day.
The *Central Railroad* links Lima, La Oroya, Huancayo and Huancavelica. The section from La Oroya to Huancayo is the highest standard-gauge railroad in the world. The narrow-gauge railway journey from Lima to La Oroya is also spectacular, and should be on every visitor's itinerary. Services are, however, liable to be disrupted by landslide damage to the track. There is a branch line from La Oroya to Cerro de Pasco, but it has been closed for several years.
The *Southern Railroad* runs from Arequipa through Juliaca to Puno on Lake Titicaca, where there is a weekly connection (Tuesday) by steamer across the lake to Bolivia (returning Friday). Always check for revised schedules as the boats are often docked for repairs and there are separate summer and winter schedules. At Juliaca, there is a branch line to Cuzco, where a short, unconnected railway has been built to Machu Picchu (it is necessary to change not just trains but stations). There is a second branch line south of Arequipa, looping through several coastal towns; it has been closed for several years. Railways have separate winter and summer schedules.
ROAD: A road connects Lima, Canta and Cerro de Pasco to Huánuco and on to Tingo María and Pucallpa on the Ucayali River. The Central Highway connects Lima with La Oroya, Huancayo, Huancavelica, Ayacucho, Cuzco, Puno and Arequipa. The grand circuit (Lima–Cuzco–Puno–Arequipa–Lima) is 2400km (1500 miles).
Few roads in Peru are paved. Landslides are frequent and road surfaces very rough, making for slow travel and frequent breakdowns. The Peruvian Touring Club helps prepare itineraries and sells excellent maps of 12 individual regions and of the country as a whole. Driving is on the right. All foreign vehicles must display a 'Customs Duty Payment Voucher' entry permit

PERU	HEALTH REGULATIONS	VISA REGULATIONS Code-Link
GALILEO/WORLDSPAN	 TI-DFT/LIM/HE	TI-DFT/LIM/VI
SABRE	TIDFT/LIM/HE	TIDFT/LIM/VI

To access this information on your CRS, swipe the barcode with a light pen or type in the text under the barcode. For more information, see the introduction *How to Use This Book.*

issued by Customs upon entering the country. Highways in some areas, particularly between the coast and the mountain region, are often blocked by landslides in the rainy season. **Bus:** Operated extensively, providing a very cheap means of travel. Greyhound-type buses are operated by *Roggero* and *TEPSA* along the Pan-American Highway. **Taxi:** Stationed at hotels and at airports. **Car hire:** *Hertz, Avis, National* and *Budget* have rental agencies in Lima and principal cities. **Documentation:** An international driving licence is required.

URBAN: About half of the public transport in Lima is provided by conventional buses, 30% by minibuses and 20% by *colectivos*, communal taxis carrying six passengers which follow set routes into the suburbs. They leave from La Colmena on both sides of the Plaza San Martín and will pick up and drop off passengers anywhere along their routes for a standard fare. Other taxis do not have meters and fares should be agreed before departure, though they are relatively inexpensive. A novel, exclusive busway with ten 'stations' is operated by articulated high-capacity buses.

JOURNEY TIMES: The following chart gives approximate journey times (generally in hours and minutes) from Lima to other major cities/towns in Peru.

	Air	Road	River
Arequipa	1.10	48.00	-
Cuzco	1.00	84.00	-
Huaraz	-	8.00	-
Iquitos	1.30	-	120.00
Nazca	0.30	6.00	-
Pucallpa	1.00	-	60.00
P. M'nado	2.15	-	84.00

Note: Times given for river journeys do not allow for road links between navigable waterways.

ACCOMMODATION

HOTELS: Lima has the largest choice of hotels in Peru, and only here can hotels of international standard be found. In many towns the only reliable hotels are the government-run *Hoteles Turistas*. Although these hotels are in many cases modern, they are frequently converted estate houses. There are many *pensiones*, some very economical, throughout Lima and in most major towns. All bills will include a 15% service charge and tourism tax. Hotel prices in the provinces are lower than in the capital. **Grading:** The standard of the state tourist hotels *(Hoteles Turistas)* in the provincial cities varies considerably, but they frequently offer the best accommodation. Hotels are classified by the star system, the highest and most luxurious being 5 stars. The level of comfort, quality of service and general infrastructure are the criteria for inclusion in each grade. All deluxe, first-class and state-tourist hotels charge 21% in taxes, but this does include service charges. Lower category hotels charge 13-19%. Under a new regulation, all places that provide accommodation must have a plaque outside bearing the letters **H** (Hotel), **HR** (Hotel Residencial) or **P** (Pension). Prices vary accordingly. For further information, contact Asosiación de Hoteles & Restaurantes, Av. Javier Pardo 620, Of, 306, Miraflores, Lima 18. Tel: (14) 468 773.

CAMPING/CARAVANNING: There are very few official camping areas anywhere in South America and no formal arrangements exist in Peru.

YOUTH HOSTELS: There are 26 youth hostels in the country with dormitory, single or twin rooms. They usually have a bar or cafeteria and a kitchen. A variety of sporting facilities is on offer: some have swimming pools, trekking, skiing and many watersports facilities. For information contact Youth Hostels – Lima, Casimiro Ulloa 328, San Antonio, Lima 18. Tel: (14) 465 488.

RESORTS & EXCURSIONS

To indicate to visitors something of the flavour of Peru, a selection of towns and notable areas is included below. These are described from south to north, and are situated in fertile plains and valleys, barren deserts, on the towering peaks of the Andes or deep in the Amazonian jungle. Visitors should be aware that Sendero Luminoso guerrillas operate in the remoter regions of Peru and it can be dangerous to stray too far from the established tourist routes.

Tacna: A frontier town on the Chilean border, containing a cathedral designed by Eiffel. The *Railway Museum* is worth visiting.

Situated 2359m (7740ft) above sea level on the slopes of Misti, **Arequipa** is known as *'White City'*. Both Spanish colonial and Andalusian influences are visible everywhere. Recommended is a visit to the *Santa Catalina Convent* – a beautiful 'city within a city'.

Puno is situated on the Collao plateau over 3800m (12,467ft) above sea level. Spaniards were lured to the region by the vast mineral wealth, and the area is dotted with colonial churches and pre-Colombian remains. Puno is the greatest centre of the Peruvian folklore tradition. Beautiful *alpaca* wool textiles, as well as *Torito de Pucara*, local pottery and silver artefacts are available. **Lake Titicaca** is described as the highest navigable lake in the world. The local Uru Indians are descendants of the original inhabitants, and continue to dwell around and make their living from the lake.

Situated 3500m (11,480ft) above sea level, **Cuzco** became the capital of the Inca Empire. Remains of granite stone walls of the Inca palaces and temples can still be seen, the most notable of which is the *Coricancha*, or Second Sun Temple. Of the several churches, the 17th-century *La Merced* and its monastery, *San Francisco Belén de los Reves*, *Santa Clara* and *San Blas* are the most interesting, and represent a blend of colonial and Indian architecture. The Cuzco market is also an attraction of the area.

Overlooking Cuzco is the immense ruined fortress of **Sacsahuaman.** Also easily accessible are the Inca sites of *Kkenkko*, *Puca Pucara*, ruined *Machay*, *Pisac*, *Ollantaytambo* – and *Machu Picchu*.

The visitor can reach **Machu Picchu** from Cuzco by train, by foot on the Inca Trail or by a combination of both. There are three types of train: local, tourist and the faster *autovagons*. The journey takes several hours. Those wishing to walk the *Inca Trail* usually catch a local train to Kilometre 88. From there it is just over 30km (20 miles) to the ruins, but due to the difficulty of the terrain, trekkers should allow at least three days to complete the journey. The stone ruins of palaces, towers, temples, staircases and other remains are currently being restored. Best viewed at dawn or dusk, Machu Picchu is claimed by many to be the Eighth Wonder of the World.

Ica and Nazca: Both cities have treasure houses containing pre-Inca primitive objects. In the arid terrain surrounding Nazca are great drawings, which depict images reminiscent of modern airport runways and have caused much speculation among archaeologists. There are inexpensive daily flights over the area of the Nazca Lines.

Ayacucho: Known as the 'town of a hundred churches'; indeed, from some aspects it seems as though there are more churches than houses. It is famous as a source of handicrafts including pottery, leatherwork, textiles and jewellery.

Lima, the capital, is an ancient Spanish city founded by Pizarro and known as the 'City of Kings'. The city's splendid museums, galleries and monuments live side by side with modern suburbs containing the new banks and businesses of an emerging third-world nation. Bullfighting is a passion for many Peruvians; in October and November the famous bullfighting festival takes place.

Trujillo is known as 'the City of the Eternal Spring'; **Chan-Chan** is the largest clay city in the world. Trujillo and the north are the centre of Animism and witchcraft.

The most northerly Peruvian town, **Tumbes** is a major sporting and deep-sea fishing centre.

The jungle: The Amazon Basin covers more than half of Peru, but it is mostly inaccessible for tourists. It is possible to take a boat from Pucallpa to Iquitos on the *Ucayali River*, but the principal means of travel to the Amazonian jungle is by plane to **Iquitos**, the most important city in the Peruvian jungle. The city has a number of parks, with a wide variety of plants and trees. Launches regularly take passengers to visit the areas inhabited by the Amazonian Indian tribes. Bathing in this region is excellent. It is also possible to fly to **Puerto Maldonado,** capital of Madre de Dios Department.

SOCIAL PROFILE

FOOD & DRINK: Despite the hot and flavoured nature of Peruvian food, created by *aji* and *ajo* (pepper and garlic), it has become celebrated at home and abroad. Peruvians enjoy a wide variety of vegetables; there are over 220 kinds of potatoes alone. Tropical fruits are abundant, as are avocados. *Ceviche* is a local speciality (uncooked fish marinated in lemon juice and hot pepper, served with corn-on-the-cob, potatoes and onions). *Escabeche* is a cooked fish appetiser eaten cold, served with peppers and onions. *Corvina* is sea bass prepared in several ways and is always an excellent choice. Scallops *(conchitas)* are excellent, as are mussels *(choros)* and shrimps *(camarones)*, which are plentiful and delicious. *Chupe de camarones* is a chowder-type soup made with shrimp, milk, eggs, potatoes and peppers. Other specialities include *sopa criolla* (spicy soup with beef and noodles), *aji de gallina* (shredded chicken in a piquant cream sauce), *anticucho* (South American shish kebab) and *lomo saltado* (morsels of beef sautéed with onions and peppers, served with fried potatoes and rice). Rice and potatoes accompany virtually every dish. Traditional desserts are *arroz con leche* (rice pudding), *mazamorra morada* (rich, fruity, purple pudding), *suspiro* and *manjar blanco*, both made from sweetened condensed milk and *picarones* (free-form doughnuts served with syrup). Table service is the norm in hotels and restaurants. **Drink:** Peruvian beers are excellent and national wines are good. The most famous drink is *pisco sour*, made from a potent grape brandy. Other pisco-based drinks are *algar-robina* (pisco and carob syrup), *chilcano* (pisco and ginger ale) or *capitán* (pisco and vermouth). *Chicha de jora* (fermented) and *chicha morada* (non-alcoholic) are popular drinks dating from Inca times.

NIGHTLIFE: Traditional Peruvian social life, for the most part, takes place at home among the family, but there are nevertheless many good bars and discotheques in the major towns and tourist resorts. *Peñas* are places of traditional Peruvian nightlife. *Peñas* always serve snacks and some serve full meals. Here one can enjoy *criolla* or folk music. Peru also has theatres and cinemas.

SHOPPING: There are many attractive Peruvian handicrafts such as *alpaca* wool sweaters, *alpaca* and *llama* rugs, Indian masks, weaving, reproduction jewellery and much more. State-run handicraft shops *(Eppaperú)* are located in most major towns. Silver, gold, leather and wooden goods are also recommended buys. **Shopping hours:** 1030-1300 and 1600-1900 Monday to Saturday.

SPORT: Golf and tennis: In Lima and suburbs. Some private clubs will make their facilities available to tourists. **Horseriding:** Central highlands and in the horse-breeding areas south as far as Ica. **Mountaineering:** There are many unconquered peaks in the Andean Range. **Exploring:** Contact South American Explorers Club. **Watersports:** Many watersports are available on the coast and **surfing** is a particular favourite as the beaches of Lima rank alongside the best in Hawaii or California. Boards may be hired. **Fishing:** Good sea fishing and trout and salmon are found in Lake Titicaca and in Conococha.

SPECIAL EVENTS: The following is a selection of the major festivals held throughout Peru. Check with the Embassy for details:

Mar-Apr '93 *Easter Week* (celebrated across the country, but particularly in Ayacucho). **Apr (third week)** *National Contest of Paso Horses*, Mamacona near Lima. **May (beginning)** *Festival of the Cross*. **Jun (whole month)** *Corpus Christi and Folklore Festival*, Cuzco. **Jun 9** *Festival of the Virgin of Perpetual Help*, Piura. **Jun 15** *Racqui Folklore Festival*, Sicuani. **Jun 24-Jul 1** *Inti Raymi* or *Festival of the Sun*, Cuzco. **Sep** *Festival of the Virgin of Cocharcas*, Huancayo. **Sep (last week)** *International Spring Festival*, Trujillo. **Oct (whole month)** *Lord of Miracles Festivities*, Lima; *Bullfighting Festival*, Lima. **Oct 1-7** *Wine Festival*, Ica. **Nov (weekends)** *Bullfighting season*, Rimac. **Nov 1-6** *Folklore Week*, Puno. **Dec 24** *Santuranticuy* (Christmas Eve), Cuzco. **Jan 6 '94** *Epiphany*. **Jan 24-Feb 14** *Virgen de la Candelaria*, Puno. **Feb-Mar** *Carnival* (the beginning of Lent is celebrated throughout the country, but particularly in Cajamarca, Puno, Trujillo (*Festival de la Marinera*), Ayacucho and Iquitos). **Mar** *La Vendimia* (wine festival), Ica.

SOCIAL CONVENTIONS: Shaking hands is the customary form of greeting. Visitors should follow normal social courtesies and the atmosphere is generally informal. A small gift from a company or home country is sufficient. Dress is usually informal, although for some social occasions men wear a jacket and tie. Many local businessmen wear an open-necked shirt called a *guayaberas* during the summer. Shorts and beach attire should only be worn in summer resorts. Life is conducted at a leisurely pace and Peruvians laughingly speak of *la hora Peruana* when referring to their tendency to arrive late for everything. **Tipping:** Service charges of 16% are added to all bills. Additional tips of 5% are expected. Taxi drivers do not generally expect tips.

BUSINESS PROFILE

ECONOMY: Peru has abundant mineral resources which produce most of the country's foreign earnings. Agriculture, which is more important for the numbers employed than for its contribution to national wealth, roduces sugar cane, potatoes, maize, rice, cereals, otton and coffee. Peru is also the world's largest proucer of coca, although the Government has an greement with the USA to try and eliminate the rop. Fishing is also important – Peru's catch was nce the world's largest – but the sector was devastatd in the early 1980s by climatic changes and has nly recovered slowly since then. Peru has some oil eserves, but these are not large and the country has uctuated between being a net exporter and net nporter during the last decade. Other mineral eposits, which are thought to be considerable, nclude copper, silver, gold, iron ore, coal and phoshates. The mining sector has been badly affected, owever, by low world prices and industrial problems. 'eru has formidable overseas debt problems, with otal external borrowings of around US$15 billion. 'he Government has recently negotiated a novel ebt-for-exports deal with the USA which should elp to lift the burden. Financial aid from the USA nd other donors has been cut in 1992 because of the uspension of democratic government (see *History*), n untimely development for the Peruvians as their conomy goes into serious recession. Growth has falln by 7-8% per annum during the last two years. 'here are signs that donors may relent in view of the eriousness of the situation. Peru is a member of the Andean Treaty and of the 11-member Asociación atinoamericana de Integración which seeks to pronote free trade and economic development in Latin America. Peru's major trading partners are the USA, apan and Germany.

BUSINESS: Some business people will speak English, but the majority speak Spanish and a business visitor to Peru who does not speak the language hould arrange for an interpreter. Appointments hould be made and confirmed and although Peruvians can be late, visitors are expected to arrive on time. Visiting cards are used. **Office hours:** 0900-1700 Monday to Friday.

COMMERCIAL INFORMATION: The following organisation can offer advice: Confederación de Cámaras de Comercio y Producción del Perú, Avda Gregorio Escobedo 398, Lima 11. Tel: (14) 633 434. Fax: (14) 632 820.

CONFERENCES/CONVENTIONS: For further information contact: Avda Andrés Reyes 320, San Isidro, Lima. Tel: (14) 700 781. Fax: (14) 429 398.

HISTORY & GOVERNMENT

HISTORY: The indigenous Inca civilisation of what is now Peru was conquered by Spain in the early 16th century. The city of Lima was founded in 1535 and became the effective capital of the viceroyalty of Peru, established seven years later. Spain ruled the country until the early 19th century, using the rich silver reserves to finance its costly imperialist struggles with France, England and The Netherlands. The wars of independence, which expelled the Spanish from virtually the entire South American continent, reached Peru in the early 1820s. After the 1821 declaration of independence in Peru was challenged by the royalists, the new government appealed for assistance to the revolutionary leader Bolívar who arrived from Colombia. The royalists were defeated at the Battle of Ayacucho in December 1824, after which Bolívar became Head of State. Relations between Peru and its neighbours were difficult in the early years of independence. There were border disputes with Brazil and Ecuador (which have not been settled to this day) but especially with Chile. The War of the Pacific, which broke out between Peru, supported by Bolivia, and Chile in 1879 ended after five years with a complete victory for Chile and the loss to Peru of some southern territories. Internal problems dominated the agenda for the next 30 years as a series of governments struggled to keep the economy, which was almost completely destroyed as a result of the Pacific War, from disintegrating. The first of Peru's many military coups was in 1914. The junta lasted five years before giving way to the civilian government of Augusto Leguia. Between 1919 and 1930, despite rampant corruption, Leguia instituted important reforms in education and social services. His tenure ended with another military takeover. While the military have always been a powerful force in Peruvian politics, their principal opponent and the country's largest political party for much of the 20th century has been the Alianza Popular Revolucinaria Americana (APRA), founded by Dr Victor Raul Haya de la Torre in 1924 as a continent-wide anti-imperialist movement, but increasingly moderate and Peruvian-centred in its appeal. APRA has nevertheless been illegal for much of its history. Civilian administrations from 1963-67 and 1980-85 were headed by the right-wing President Belaunde Terry of the Accion Popular party, although APRA was usually the largest party in the Chamber of Deputies. Under Alan Garcia, APRA took power for the first time in 1985. Garcia's administration was a failure on both the political and economic front. Garcia decided to suspend repayment on Peru's large foreign debt accumulated during the 1970s and increase state control of the economy, particularly the financial and banking sectors. Massive capital flight followed before exchange controls were introduced; investment dropped to near-zero; loans dried up and the Government's attempts to maintain living standards resulted in hyperinflation running to thousands of per cent per annum. On the political front Garcia was faced with the continuing growth of the Maoist guerrilla movement Sendero Luminoso (Shining Path), which benefited substantially from the deteriorating economic situation; the Government declared states of emergency in ten of Peru's two dozen provinces, giving the military a virtually free hand in operations against the guerrillas. By the end of the 1980s, amid rumours of a possible military coup, it was clear that Garcia's days were numbered. Local elections in November 1989 brought victory for the Democratic Front coalition, defeating a socialist grouping into second and pushing the ruling APRA into third. This pattern was expected to be repeated in the presidential elections the following year. However, these elections, held in April 1990, developed into a 2-way race between Mario Vargas Llosa, the world-renowned author who led the Democratic Front coalition, and the comparatively unknown independent centrist candidate, Alberto Fujimori, an agricultural engineer of Japanese extraction, who was the surprise landslide winner. The new government followed the trend on the Latin American continent for economic shock treatment. Most price controls and government subsidies were abolished at a stroke in August 1990, producing 400% inflation for that month. Since then the rate has dropped to a more manageable 10% monthly, heralding what the Government hopes is the start of an economic recovery. It is, however, extremely fragile: the currency is highly unstable; agricultural and manufacturing production levels are, at best, stable. The Government is relying on creating a sound fiscal environment to stimulate commercial prosperity. The strategy may be undermined by continuing capital flight (exchange controls having been lifted) and the distorting effects of the illegal cocaine economy. The Bush administration, which is concerned about cocaine production for different reasons, signed a number of agreements with the Peruvians during 1991 to increase anti-trafficking operations. As US aid to countries supposedly involved in the global narcotics industry is now conditional on the implementation of counter-measures by the recipient government, the Peruvians had little choice other than to co-operate. Peru's foreign policy under Fujimori has been devoted to economic matters – trade agreements and aid commitments – and the resolution of border disputes. The disagreement with Ecuador over access to the Amazonian river system is one of the most bitter and intractable on the continent. Several military clashes have occurred since a brief war over the issue in 1942, the most recent in 1981. A diplomatic initiative brokered by Brazil now offers the prospect of a settlement in 1992. The foreign policy priority remains, however, economic support from the international community. Unfortunately, Peruvian efforts are constantly undermined by events at home. Early in 1991, an outbreak of cholera, the inevitable result of an inadequate and neglected water treatment system, killed several thousand people and disrupted essential trade in agricultural products. Foreign investors were already reluctant to commit assets to Peru because of the escalating political violence, for which Sendero Luminoso is principally responsible. Duly convinced of their inevitable victory, Sendero absolutely refused to negotiate at any level and the response of successive governments to Sendero has been, without exception, ever increasing doses of repression. As Peru's situation grew ever more dire towards the end of 1991, Fujimori issued a series of decrees which made Peru simultaneously the most economically liberal and politically repressive country in Latin America. The security forces enjoy blanket powers of censorship and the right to expropriate any property or financial asset for reasons of national security. With the support of every political constituency outside the security forces rapidly evaporating, a prominent right-wing senator, Miguel Cruchaga, commented at the end of 1991 that "it indicates that the Government wants to transform the country into a fascist state". Prophetic words, indeed. On April 5, 1992, with the backing of the security forces, Fujimori staged a constitutional coup; congress was suspended indefinitely and the entire judiciary sent on leave pending 'reorganisation' while Fujimori now rules by decree. After four months, the coup has not been a notable success: in fact, achievements since it took place are all but impossible to list. The Government's fortunes in the war against Sendero Luminoso, which the coup was supposed to improve, have not done so (see below). And the reaction of the international community has been poor, leading to a loss of essential economic aid. Sendero, meanwhile, have made progress but are not having everything their way. The guerrillas have launched the second phase of their struggle in which, having consolidated control of the bulk of the countryside, they move to take control of the towns and cities. The basic method is to use terrorist tactics to create a political vacuum – by killing or otherwise disposing of local government officials and other manifestations of state power, into which Sendero then moves. Bomb attacks against government establishments and personnel are supplemented by attacks on the infrastructure with the aim of bringing society to a halt. A critical stage of this classic struggle between insurgency and state power has now been reached: its course during 1992 may well decide the final outcome.

GOVERNMENT: Under the 1980 constitution, executive power lies with the elected President, with a bicameral legislature consisting of a Senate and a Chamber of Deputies.

CLIMATE

Varies according to area. Winter lasts from May to September. Summer on the coast and around Lima is from October to April, which corresponds to the rainy season in the mountains and in the jungle. From May to September the mountains are clear, while coastal areas are often foggy.

Required clothing: Lightweights during summer with warmer clothes worn in upland areas. Mediumweights are advised during cooler months.

LIMA Peru (11m)

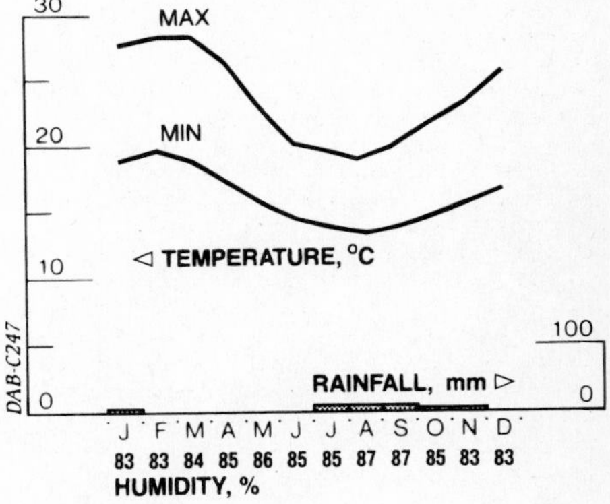

CAJAMARCA Peru (2621m)

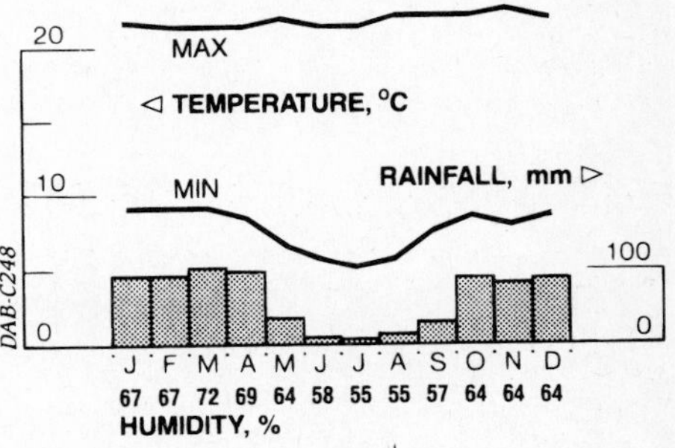

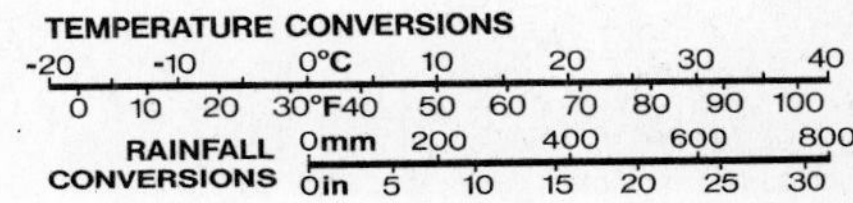

PHILIPPINES

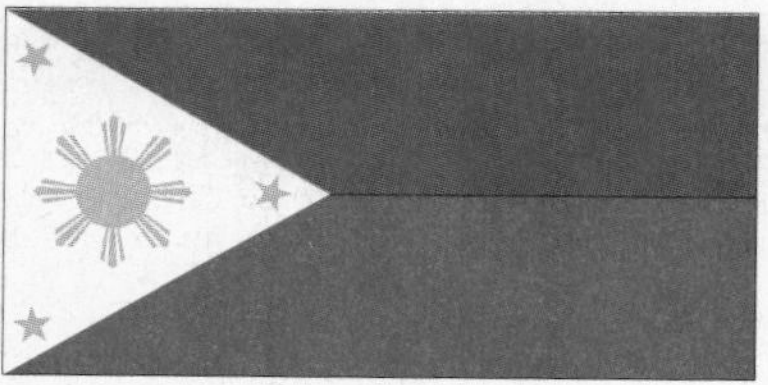

Location: South-East Asia.

Philippine Convention and Visitors Corporation
PO Box EA-459
Suite 10-17
4th Floor, Legaspi Towers
300 Roxas Boulevard
Metro Manila, Philippines
Tel: (2) 575 031. Fax: (2) 521 6165. Telex: 40604 PCVC PM.

Embassy of the Republic of the Philippines
9a Palace Green
London W8 4QE
Tel: (071) 937 1609. Fax: (071) 937 2925. Telex: 24411 AMPHIL G. Opening hours: 0900-1300 Monday to Friday.

Philippine Consulate
First Base, Enterprise House
Ocean Village
Southampton
SO1 1XB
Tel: (0703) 230 129. Fax: (0703) 332 050.

Philippine Department of Tourism
17 Albemarle Street
London W1X 7HA
Tel: (071) 499 5443 (general enquiries) *or* 499 5652 (incentive travel). Fax: (071) 499 5772. Telex: 265115 PTOE LP-G. Opening hours: 0900-1700 Monday to Friday.

British Embassy
15-17th Floors
LV Locsin Building
6752 Ayala Avenue
Makati
Metro Manila 3116, Philippines
Tel: (2) 816 7116. Fax: (2) 819 7206. Telex: 63282 PRODME PN.

Embassy of the Republic of the Philippines
Special Services Unit
(Conventions and Tourism)
1617 Massachusetts Avenue, NW
Washington, DC
20036-2274
Tel: (202) 483 1414. Fax: (202) 328 7614. Telex: 440059.
Consulate Generals in: Chicago (tel: (312) 782 1707), San Francisco (tel: (415) 433 6666) and Los Angeles (tel: (213) 387 5321).

Philippine Center
556 Fifth Avenue
New York, NY
10036
Tel: (212) 575 7915. Fax: (212) 302 6759. Telex: 6801425.
Also deals with enquiries from Canada.

Embassy of the United States of America
1201 Roxas Boulevard
Metro Manila, Philippines
Tel: (2) 521 7116. Fax: (2) 521 7116. Telex: 27366.

Embassy of the Republic of the Philippines
Suite 606
130 Albert Street
Ottawa, Ontario
K1P 5G4
Tel: (613) 233 1121. Fax: (613) 233 4165.

Canadian Embassy
9th Floor
Allied Bank Center
6754 Ayala Avenue
Makati
Metro Manila, Philippines
Tel: (2) 815 9536. Fax: (2) 815 9595. Telex: 63676.

AREA: 300,000 sq km (115,831 sq miles).
POPULATION: 60,684,887 (1990).
POPULATION DENSITY: 202.3 per sq km.
CAPITAL: Manila. **Population:** 1,598,918 (1990).
GEOGRAPHY: The Philippines lie off the southeast coast of Asia between Taiwan and Borneo in the Pacific Ocean and South China Sea. They are composed of 7107 islands and islets, 2773 of which are named. The two largest islands, Luzon in the north and Mindanao in the south, account for 65% of the total land area and contain 60% of the country's population. Between the two lie the Visayas Islands.
LANGUAGE: Filipino, based on Tagalog, is the national language. English is widely spoken, Spanish less so. The Philippines is the third largest English-speaking country in the world. There are over 100 cultural and racial groups, each with its own language or dialect.
RELIGION: 84% Roman Catholic. Other faiths are Protestant and Islam.
TIME: GMT + 8.
ELECTRICITY: 220 volts (110 volts in Baguio) AC, 60Hz. 110 volts is available in most hotels. Flat and round 2- and 3-pin plugs are in use.
COMMUNICATIONS: Telephone: IDD is available to most main towns. Country code: 63. International calls to the smaller towns must be booked through the operator. **Fax:** All 3- to 5-star hotels have facsimile services. **Telex/telegram:** Telegrams can be sent from Eastern Telecommunications Philippines Incorporated offices. Public telex booths are operated by the same company, along with Globe-Mackay Cable and Radio Corporation and RCA Communications. **Post:** Airmail to Europe takes up to ten days. Post offices are from 0900-1700. **Press:** There are about 20 daily newspapers. English-language daily newspapers include the *Philippine Star*, *Philippine Daily Inquirer*, *Manila Bulletin*, *Manila Times*, *Manila Chronicle*, *Philippine Daily Globe*, *Manila Standard* and *People Tonight*.
BBC World Service and Voice of America frequencies: From time to time these change. See the section *How to Use this Book* for more information.

BBC:				
MHz	15.36	11.95	9.74	9.57
Voice of America:				
MHz	15.43	11.72	5.985	1.143

PASSPORT/VISA

Regulations and requirements may be subject to change at short notice, and you are advised to contact the appropriate diplomatic or consular authority before finalising travel arrangements. Details of these may be found at the head of this country's entry. Any numbers in the chart refer to the footnotes below.

	Passport Required?	Visa Required?	Return Ticket Required?
Full British	Yes	1	Yes
BVP	Not valid	-	-
Australian	Yes	1	Yes
Canadian	Yes	1	Yes
USA	Yes	1	Yes
Other EC	Yes	1	Yes
Japanese	Yes	1	Yes

PASSPORTS: Valid passport required by all.
British Visitors Passport: Not acceptable.
VISAS: Required by all except:
(a) transit passengers;
(b) [1] bona fide foreign tourists (including business persons), provided stay does not exceed 21 days and they have passports valid for at least one year and onward tickets (those who wish to stay for more than 21 days require a visa); *
(c) nationals of Brazil, Gibraltar, Israel, Pakistan, Romania and Sri Lanka for entry into the Philippines for a period of not more than 59 days.
Note [*]: Nationals of Albania, Cambodia, CIS, China, Cuba, Iran, Laos, Libya, North Korea and Vietnam do require a visa to enter the Philippines for any purpose.
Types of visa: Tourist and Business. Cost: often free, but £9.70 for stays of between 21 and 59 days. Employment visa: £193.55.
Validity: Tourist and Business visas are valid for up to 59 days after entry. Refer to Commission on Immigration and Deportation for extension procedure.
Application to: Consulate (or Consular Section at Embassy). For addresses, see top of entry.
Application requirements: (a) 2 application forms. (b) 2 photos. (c) Passport valid for at least 1 year. (d) Proof of means of support during stay. (e) Fee. Application for a non-immigrant visa should be made in person.
Working days required: One.

MONEY

Currency: Philippine Peso (PP) = 100 centavos. Notes are in denominations of PP1000, 500, 100, 50, 20, 10, 5 and 2. Coins are in denominations PP1, and 50, 25, 10, 5 and 1 centavos.

Currency exchange: Travellers cheques and foreign currency may be cashed in all commercial banks and Central Bank dealers. Also accepted in most hotels, restaurants and shops. Always use authorised money-changers or banks in Manila; banks can, however, be slow. Outside the capital there is a shortage of facilities for changing foreign currency, and rates may get progressively worse further from the city.
Credit cards: American Express, Diners Club, Access/Mastercard and Visa are widely accepted. Check with your credit card company for details of merchant acceptability and other services which may be available.
Travellers cheques: See *Currency exchange* above.
Exchange rate indicators: The following figures are included as a guide to the movements of the Philippine Peso against Sterling and the US Dollar:

Date:	Oct '89	Oct '90	Oct '91	Oct '92
£1.00=	33.67	48.40	45.58	35.00
$1.00=	21.32	24.78	26.26	22.05

Currency restrictions: The import and export of local currency is limited to PP5000. Free import of foreign currency.
Banking hours: 0900-1600 Monday to Friday.

DUTY FREE

The following items may be imported into the Philippines without incurring customs duty:
400 cigarettes or 50 cigars or 250g tobacco;
2 litres of alcoholic beverage;
A reasonable amount of clothing, jewellery and perfume for personal use.
Prohibited items: Firearms, explosives, pornographic material, seditious or subversive material, narcotics and other internationally prohibited drugs (unless accompanied by a medical prescription).

PUBLIC HOLIDAYS

Public holidays observed in the Philippines are as follows:
Apr 8 '93 Maundy Thursday. **Apr 9** Good Friday. **May 1** Labour Day. **May 6** Day of Valour. **Jun 12** Independence Day. **Nov 1** All Saints' Day. **Nov 30** Bonifacio Day. **Dec 25** Christmas Day. **Dec 30** Rizal Day. **Jan 1 '94** New Year's Day.
Note: Easter is a major holiday in the Philippines and travel may be disrupted.

HEALTH

Regulations and requirements may be subject to change at short notice, and you are advised to contact your doctor well in advance of your intended date of departure. Any numbers in the chart refer to the footnotes below.

	Special Precautions?	Certificate Required?
Yellow Fever	No	1
Cholera	Yes	2
Typhoid & Polio	Yes	-
Malaria	3	-
Food & Drink	4	-

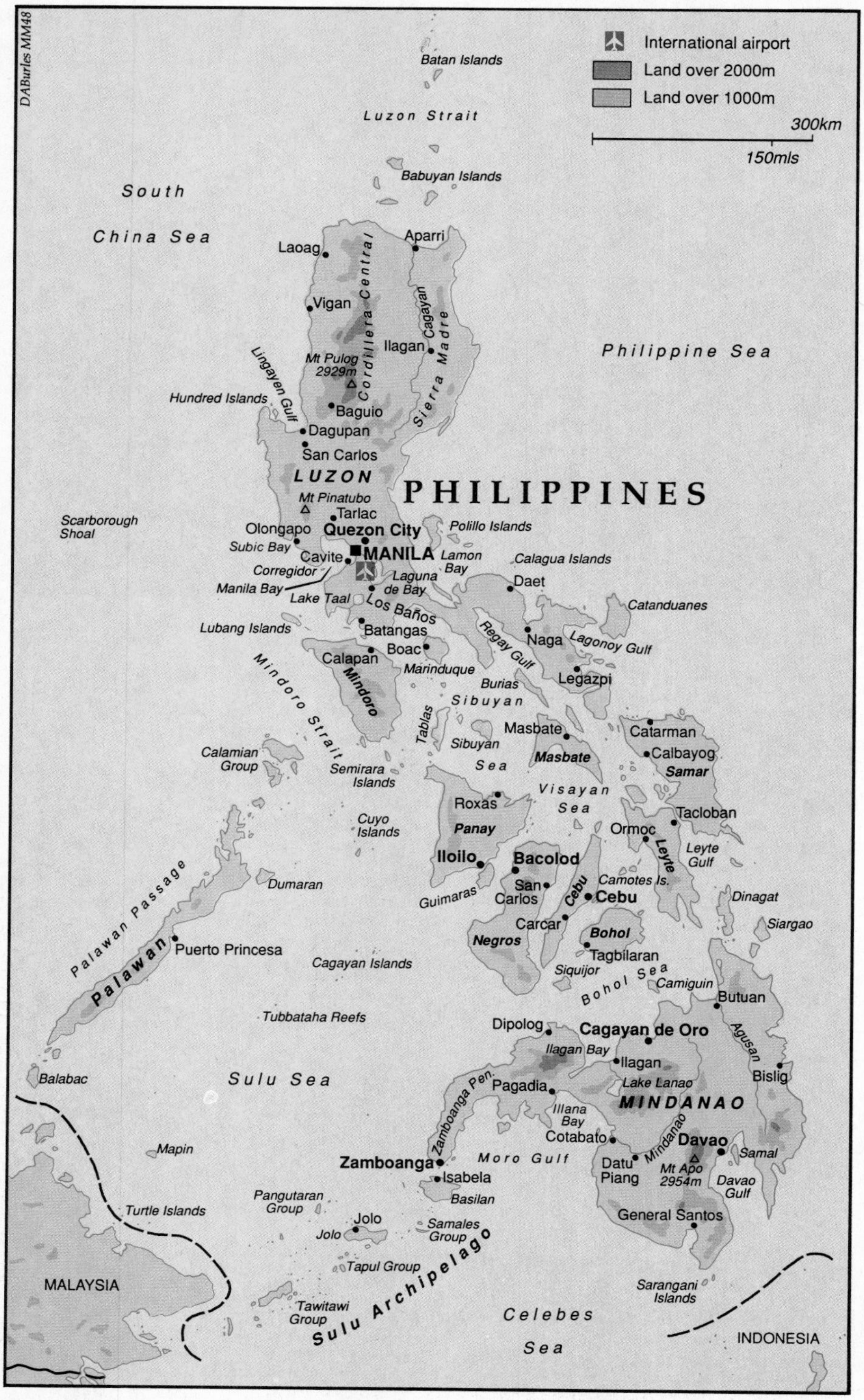

[1]: A yellow fever certificate is required from travellers arriving from infected areas, except children under one year of age, who may, however, be subject to isolation or surveillance.
[2]: Following WHO guidelines issued in 1973, a cholera vaccination certificate is not a condition of entry to the Philippines. However, cholera is a serious risk in this country and precautions are essential. Up-to-date advice should be sought before deciding whether these precautions should include vaccination, as medical opinion is divided over its effectiveness. See the *Health* section at the back of the book.
[3]: Malaria risk exists throughout the year in areas below 600m, except in the Provinces of Bohol, Catanduanes, Cebu and Leyte. No risk is considered to exist in urban areas or in the plains. The malignant *falciparum* strain is present and is reported to be 'highly resistant' to chloroquine.
[4]: All water should be regarded as being potentially contaminated. Water used for drinking, brushing teeth or making ice should have first been boiled or otherwise sterilised. Milk is unpasteurised and should be boiled. Powdered or tinned milk is available and is advised, but make sure that it is reconstituted with pure water. Avoid dairy products which are likely to have been made from unboiled milk. Only eat well-cooked meat and fish, preferably served hot. Pork, salad and mayonnaise may carry increased risk. Vegetables should be cooked and fruit peeled.
Rabies is present. For those at high risk, vaccination before arrival should be considered. If you are bitten abroad seek medical advice without delay. For more information consult the *Health* section at the back of the book.
Bilharzia (schistosomiasis) is present. Avoid swimming and paddling in fresh water. Swimming pools which are well-chlorinated and maintained are safe.
Health care: Health insurance is essential. There are approximately 1600 hospitals, three-quarters of which are private.

TRAVEL - International

AIR: The Philippines' national airline is *Philippine Airlines (PR)*.
Note: The period over Easter, from Good Friday to the following Bank holiday (and sometimes beyond), is a major holiday in the Philippines and there may be some difficulty booking a flight over this period.
Approximate flight times: From Manila to *London* is 18 hours; to *Paris* is 21 hours 15 minutes; to *Los Angeles* is 16 hours 55 minutes; to *New York* is 25 hours 20 minutes; to *Singapore* is 3 hours 10 minutes; to *Hong Kong* is 1 hour 50 minutes; to *Bangkok* is 3 hours 50 minutes; to *Tokyo* is 4 hours 15 minutes; and to *Sydney* is 8 hours 50 minutes.
International airport: *Ninoy Aquino (MNL)*, 12km (7.5 miles) southeast of Manila. Airport facilities include banks, post office, medical clinic, baggage deposit area, duty-free shops and car hire. Bus and taxi services are available to the city (travel time – 35 minutes).
Departure tax: PP250 for international departures. Children under two years of age and transit passengers are exempt.
SEA: Manila is a major seaport, a crossroads of trade in the Asia-Pacific region. Shipping lines which call at Manila include *American President Lines, Anline, Ben Line Container Ltd, Everett Lines, Hapag-Lloyd, 'K' Line, Knutsen Line, Lykes Orient Line, Orient Overseas Container Line, Scandutch, Sealand, United States Line* and the *Waterman Line*. Schedules and rates are listed in the shipping pages of daily newspapers.

TRAVEL - Internal

AIR: *Philippine Airlines* offers comprehensive internal services with a wide range of discount fares. Demand is heavy so flights should be booked in advance. Privately-owned airlines also operate.
Departure tax: PP10 on domestic flights.
SEA: Inter-island ships with first-class accommodation connect the major island ports. For details contact local shipping lines.
RAIL: The only railway is on Luzon Island, from Legaspi to San Fernando (operated by *Philippine National Railways*). This network runs three trains daily to and from Manila, one overnight with couchettes and dining car. There is also some air-conditioned accommodation.
ROAD: There are 135,300km (84,075 miles) of roads spread among the islands, with highways on the Mindanao, Visayas and Luzon island groups. Driving is on the right. **Bus:** There are bus services between the towns and also widely available 'jeepneys'. These are shared taxis using jeep-derived vehicles equipped to carry up to 14 passengers on bench seats. Fares are similar to buses. **Taxi:** Taxis are available in the cities and to smaller towns.

PHILIPPINES	HEALTH REGULATIONS	VISA REGULATIONS (Code-Link)
GALILEO/WORLDSPAN	 TI-DFT/MNL/HE	 TI-DFT/MNL/VI
SABRE	 TIDFT/MNL/HE	TIDFT/MNL/VI

To access this information on your CRS, swipe the barcode with a light pen or type in the text under the barcode. For more information, see the introduction *How to Use This Book*.

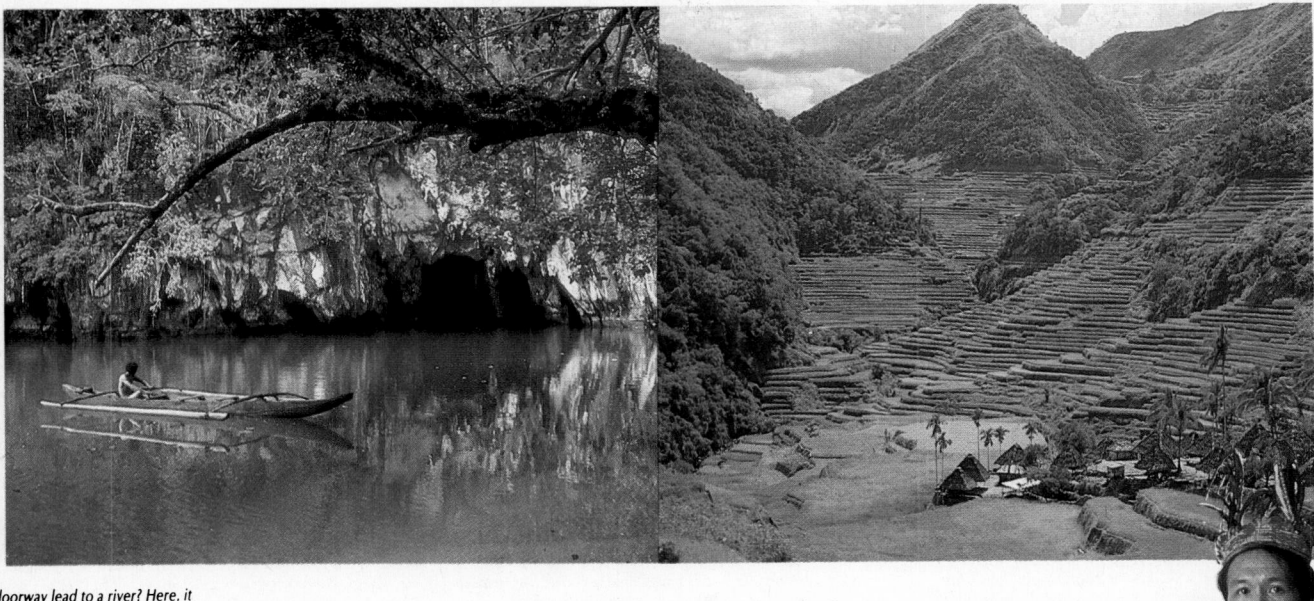

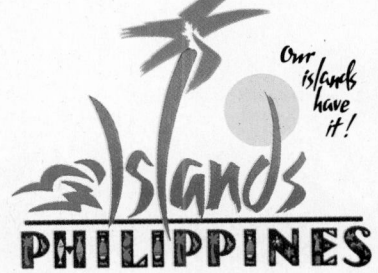

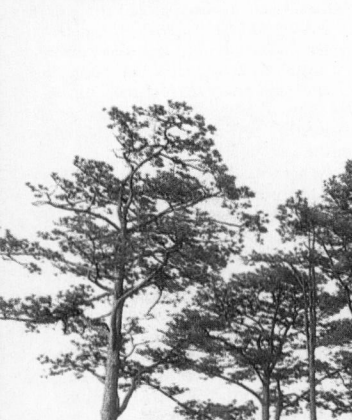

Make sure meters are used, as some taxi drivers will set an exorbitant and arbitrary rate. **Car hire:** Car rentals, with or without driver, are available in Manila and in major cities. The minimum age is 18. **Documentation:** International Driving Permit required, together with a national driving licence.
URBAN: A number of bus routes are operated by *Metro Manila Transport* using conventional vehicles, including double-deckers, and Manila's air-conditioned *Love Bus* which has become part of the city's attractions, besides providing a comfortable ride on specially designated routes. Most journeys, however, are made by *jeepneys*, of which there are an estimated 30,000 in Manila alone. The *Metro*, a light rail transit link, opened in 1984, is now fully operational. 15km (9 miles) in length, it runs from Baclaran terminal in the south to Caloocan terminal in the north.
JOURNEY TIMES: The following chart gives approximate journey times (in hours and minutes) from Manila to other major cities/towns in the Philippines.

	Air	Road	Sea
Baguio	0.50	4.00	-
Cebu	1.10	-	24.00
Cagayen de Oro	1.25	-	48.00
Laoag	1.25	7.00	-
Iloilo	1.00	-	24.00
Batangas	-	2.00	-
Banaue	*0.50	4.00	-
Davao	1.30	-	48.00
Palawan	1.10		24.00

Note [*]: As far as Baguio City and then another 4 hours by road.

ACCOMMODATION

HOTELS: In Manila there are some 10,000 first-class hotel rooms. There are numerous smaller hotels, inns, hostels and pensions. Prices are often quoted both in PP and US$. A complete directory of hotels is available from the Department of Tourism. 51% of establishments belong to the Hotel and Restaurant Association of the Philippines, Room 205, Regina Building, Trasierra, corner of Aguirre Street, Legaspi Village, Makati, Metro Manila. Tel: (2) 815 4695 *or* 815 4661/3. Fax: (2) 815 4663. In addition, most regions have their own associations. **Grading:** Hotels are graded in the following categories based on standards set by the Office of Tourism Services, Department of Tourism, Manila: economy (43% of all establishments are in this grade), standard (39%), first class (9%) and de luxe (9%).
SELF-CATERING: 'Apartels' are available for minimum stays of a week.
HOMESTAY: The National Homestay Programme provides travellers with comfortable accommodation in Filipino family homes throughout the islands. Adequate lighting, ventilation, bath and toilet are provided; home-cooked meals are usually also avaliable. There are various regional Homestay Associations. For further information contact the Department of Tourism.
CAMPING/CARAVANNING: Offered only in a very limited number of places.

RESORTS & EXCURSIONS

The Philippines are composed of 7107 islands, with a total coastline longer than that of the USA. The warm tropical waters offer for some the attractions of sunbathing and swimming, while divers can explore coral gardens and dramatic drop-offs on the sea bed. Charter planes can be hired for reaching some of the more remote islands. Inland, the rich history and culture of the Filipino people, the dramatic landscapes and thriving cities will fascinate the visitor. For the purposes of this guide, the Philippines have been divided into three, with the main tourist attractions listed under Luzon, the Visayas and Mindanao and the South.

Luzon

Luzon is the largest and most northerly of the main islands. The spectacular landscape is made up of mountainous regions in the north, the flat vistas of the central plain, lakes and volcanoes in the southern peninsula, and a coastline dotted with caves and sandy-beached islands.
Manila, capital and hub of the nation, is situated on the east coast. Manila has been a port for hundreds of years, founded in 1571 on the ruins of a Muslim settlement. The oldest part of the city, the *Intramuros* or Walled City, was protected by a massive wall, some of which still remains today despite savage fighting staged here in the Second World War. Places of interest include *San Augustin Church*, *American Cemetery*, *Coconut Palace*, *Manila Cathedral*, from which there is an excellent view of the 2072 sq km (800 sq miles) of the harbour, and the ruins of *Fort Santiago*. Outside the Intramuros is *Chinatown*, a market in the district of Binondo, crowded with shops, stalls and restaurants. The splendid *Malacanang Palace* museum, which is the former home of the Presidents of the Philippines, is open to tourists. *Luneta National Park* contains the *Rizal Monument*, a memorial to the execution of this great Filipino intellectual of the late 19th century.
Manila is a good base from which to make excursions, for instance to *Las Pinas*, situated a little way outside the city, where the famous Bamboo Organ is and the *Sarao Jeepney factory* which allows people to wander around free of charge. About an hour's drive away from Manila through coconut plantations, *Tagaytay Ridge* in **Cavite** overlooks a lake that contains *Taal Volcano*, which contains another lake. Tagaytay is a popular destination in summer when all kinds of festivities are celebrated and roadside stalls overflow with flowering plants and fruits in season.
Laguna, a short distance from Manila, is a province famous for hot sulphur springs. The 'Towns of Baths', **Pansol, Los Banos** and **Cuyab,** are situated here. The series of mineral springs of *Hidden Valley* lie secreted in a 90m (300ft) deep crater in **Aminos**, enclosed by rich forests. The pools vary in temperature from warm to cold, and the lush trails fetch up at a gorge with a waterfall.
Villa Escudero, an 800-hectare coconut plantation in **Laguna Province** less than two hours by road from Manila, is part of an actual working plantation, yielding rare glimpses into rural life. Guests are taken on a tour of a typical village on a cart drawn by a carabao, or water buffalo.
Corregidor Island, 'The Rock', a famous memorial to those who fell during the Japanese invasion, is accessible by hydrofoil. Day tours include refreshments and guide. A day trip to the town of **Pagsanjan**, 63km (39 miles) southeast of Manila, includes dug-out canoe rides down the jungle-bordered river to the *Pagsanjan Falls*. These were the location for the filming of 'Apocalypse Now', and are a popular excursion.
250km (150 miles) north of Manila is **Baguio,** 1525m (5000ft) above sea level on the *Cordillera Mountain Range*, a cool haven from the summer heat. It is accessible both by air and land, though the drive up the zigzagging *Kennon Road* is more popular as it offers spectacular views of the countryside. Baguio has a good variety of restaurants, mountain views and walking excursions. Main attractions include the various parks; *Lourdes Grotto*, a religious shrine from which there is a beautiful view of the city; *The Mansion*, summer residence of the Philippine president; *Bell Church*, a cluster of temples combining Buddhist, Taoist and Confucian influences; *Baguio Cathedral*, notable for its twin spires and one hundred steps; and the *Crystal Caves*, composed of crystalline metamorphic rocks and once an ancient burial site. There are also extensive facilities in the USAF recreation centre, *Camp John Hay*, just outside the town.
Banaue is four hours bus ride north of Baguio. A remote mountainous community lives here, and tourists can visit their settlements. The beautiful rice terraces are the main attraction of this area. A breathtaking sight, they rise majestically to an altitude of 1525m (5000ft), and encompass an area of 10,360 sq km (4000 sq miles). The terraces were hand-carved some 2000 years ago using crude tools cutting into once barren rock, each ledge completely encompassing the mountain. Banaue has a tourist hotel and many good pensions.
Hundred Islands lies off the coast of **Pangasinan,** 400 islets surrounded by white sand beaches. This area is ideal for skindiving, swimming and fishing. Hundred Islands is the second-largest marine reservation in the world, teeming with over

2000 species of aquatic life. The caves and domes of **Marcos Island** and the *Devil's Kitchen* are worth exploring.

The entire province of **Palawan** is a remarkable terrain for adventure and exploration, with its primeval rainforests, *St Paul's Underground River* and *Tubbattaha Reef*.

Mindoro island, reached by ferry from Batangas pier and south of Manila, is a place where the stunning scenery includes *Mount Halcon*, 2695m (8841ft) high, *Naujan Lake* and the *Tamarao Falls* – with a pool at their base surrounded by a thick wall of vegetation. **La Union,** situated on the northwest coast of Luzon, has some of the best beach-resort facilities on the island. There are regular buses to La Union from Manila and Baguio.

Bicol Region, situated in the east, offers beaches, hotels and sights such as the *Mayon Volcano*, a nearly perfect cone, *Tiwi Hotsprings*, *Naglambong Boiling Lake* and *Kalayukay Beach Resort*.

The Visayas

The Visayas is a group of islands between Luzon and Mindanao. The main islands are **Samar, Panay, Negros, Cebu** and **Leyte,** famous as the landing point for the American liberation forces in 1944. The two islands are linked by the *San Juanico Bridge*, the longest in the country. Leyte is also famous as the island first sighted by the Spanish explorer Ferdinand Magellan in the 16th century.

Cebu City is the main resort of the Visayas. Cebu is the most densely populated island, a commercial centre with an international harbour, and the Philippines' second city. City sights include *Magellan's Cross*, a wooden cross planted by Magellan himself over 450 years ago to commemorate the baptism into the Christian faith of Rajah Humabon and his wife Juana with 800 followers. *Fort San Pedro*, the oldest and smallest Spanish fort in the country, is a triangular bastion built on the order of conquistador Miguel Lopez de Legazpi in 1565.

Carcar town, south of Cebu City, has many preserved Castillian houses, gardens and churches. The *Chapel of the Last Supper* features hand-carved life-size statues of Christ and his apostles dating back to Spanish times. The *Magellan Monument* on **Mactan Island** was raised in 1886 to mark the spot where Magellan died, felled by the fierce chieftain, Datu Lapu-Lapu, who refused to submit to the Spanish conquerors. There is also a monument to Datu Lapu-Lapu honouring him as the first Filipino patriot. **Maribago** is the centre of the region's guitar-making industry. As well as many historical sites there are popular hotels, beach clubs and resorts such as *Tambuli Beach Resort*, *Coral Reef*, *Mar y Cielo* and others.

Iloilo on Panay is an agricultural province producing root-crops, vegetables, cacao, coffee and numerous tropical fruits.

Iloilo City is reached by air. The attractions include nearby beach resorts and the 18th-century *Miagao Church*, a unique piece of Baroque colonial architecture with a facade decorated with impressions of coconut and papaya trees. *Sicogon Island* is a haven for scuba divers, and has mountains and virgin forests to explore. *Boracay Island* is another such island paradise, accessible by air via Kalibo, followed by a bus or jeepney ride to Malay, and finally by ferry or pumpboat from Caticlan. A BMW survey considered its powdery-fine white-sand beach to be amongst the best in the world.

Bohol Island, just across the straits from Cebu in Central Visayas, is the site of some of the country's most fascinating natural wonders; hundreds of limestone hills, some 30m (100ft) high, that in summer look, for all the world, like oversized chocolate drops, earning them the name *'Chocolate Hills'*. The smooth rounded hills, covered by thin grass that dries up and turns brown under the summer sun, are a strange spectacle – mounds rising straight up from flatlands; they are situated about 55km (34 miles) northeast of **Tagbilaran City**, the island's capital. Bohol also offers handsome white-sand beaches and pretty secluded coves, accessible via good roads. The island is a coconut-growing area and its local handicrafts are mostly of woven materials: grass mats, hats and baskets. *Baclayon Church* is worth a visit, as it is probably the oldest stone church in the Philippines, dating back to 1595. The island can be reached by plane or ferry. The air journey from Cebu to Tagbilaran takes 40 minutes. Ferries go from Cebu to Tagbilaran or Tubigon, another port north of the capital.

Mindanao & the South

Mindanao is the second largest and the most southerly island, with a very different feel from the rest of the country. A variety of Muslim ethnic groups live here, now concentrated around Lake Lanao in the southernmost islands.

In the southwestern tip of Mindanao is **Zamboanga City,** considered by some as the most romantic place in the Philippines and a favourite resort amongst tourists. The city is noted for its seashells, unspoiled tropical scenery and magnificent flowers (the word *Zamboanga* is derived from the Malay word for 'land of flowers'). Zamboanga was founded by the Spanish, and the 17th-century walls of *Fort Pilar*, built to protect the Spanish and Christian Filipinos from Muslim onslaughts, are still standing. The city has excellent hotels, cars for hire, good public transport and *vintas* (small boats), often with colourful sails, available to take visitors round the city bay. The *flea market* sells Muslim pottery, clothes and brassware. About 2km (1.2 miles) from Fort Pilar are the houses of the Badjaos, which are stilted constructions on the water. Water gypsies live in boats in this area, moving to wherever the fishing is best. *Plaza Pershing* and *Pasonanca Park* are worth visiting. *Sta Cruz Island* has a sand beach which turns pink when the corals from the sea are washed ashore, and is ideal for bathing, snorkelling and scuba diving. There is also an old Muslim burial ground here.

Davao province is the industrial centre of Mindanao, renowned for its pearl and banana exports. **Davao City** is one of the most progressive industrial cities in the country. The province is the site of *Mount Apo*, the highest peak in the country, while the *Apo Range* has spectacular waterfalls, rapids, forests, springs and mountain lakes.

Cagayan de Oro, on the northern coast of Mindanao, is the gateway to some of the most beautiful islands in the Philippines. By way of contrast, in *Bukidnon* there are huge cattle ranches and the famous Del Monte pineapple fields, and *Iligan City* is the site of the hydroelectric complex driven by the *Maria Cristina Falls*.

Lanao del Sur is the province where Muslim people, known as the Maranaos, live by the shores of *Lake Lanao*. Mindanao State University overlooks the lake. Other attractions include *Signal Hill; Sacred Mountain;* the native market, *Torongan;* homes of the Maranao royalty; the various Muslim mosques on the shores of the lake; and examples of the famous brassware industry centred in *Tugaua*.

SOCIAL PROFILE

FOOD & DRINK: Unlike most Asian cooking, Filipino cuisine is distinguished by its moderate use of spices. Chinese, Malay, Spanish, Japanese and American influences have all left their mark in a subtle blending of cultures and flavours. Naturally, seafoods feature strongly, freshly harvested and often simply grilled, boiled, fried or steamed and served with *kalamansi* (the local lemon), *bagoong* (a fish paste) or vinegar with *labuyo* (the fiery native pepper). Restaurants specialising in seafoods abound, offering crabs, lobsters, prawns, oysters, tuna, freshwater fish, *bangus* (the bony but prized milkfish) and the sweet *maliputo*, found in deep-water lakes. The *lechon* (roasted whole pig, served with a bright red apple stuffed in the mouth) is prepared for fiestas and family celebrations. Other delightful specialities include *kare-kare* (an oxtail stew in peanut sauce served with bagoong), *sinigang* (meat or fish in a pleasantly sour broth) and *adobo* (braised pork and chicken, in tangy soy sauce, vinegar and garlic). Among the regional dishes, the Ilocos region's *pinakbet* (vegetables sauteed with pork and bagoong), Central Luzon's *relleno* (boned and stuffed chicken or fish) and the Visaya's *kinilaw* (raw fish marinated in a spicy vinegar dressing) top the list. Rice is a staple substance of the Filipino cuisine. Fruit is plentiful with mangoes, papayas, bananas, chicos, lanzones, guavas and rambutans. Philippine food preserves like *atsara* (a chutney-like vegetable preserve) and the numerous native desserts like the *pili nut brittle* (a crunchy sweet made with the luscious pili nuts found only in the Bicol region) can be purchased in local markets. All the regional dishes are available in Manila's excellent restaurants which, like the restaurants of all the main towns, offer a varied cuisine. For the less adventurous there are also European-style restaurants and American fast food. Restaurants are generally informal, with table service. **Drink:** Alcoholic drinks include locally brewed beer and the delicious Philippine rum. The local San Miguel beer is considered one of the best in the world. Waiter service is common in bars. There are no strict regulations regarding the sale of alcohol.

NIGHTLIFE: The choice of entertainment in Manila displays the Filipino's affinity for music. 5-star hotels offer everything from high-tech discos to lavish cultural songs and dances, as well as superb pop singers and performers, trios, show bands and classical string ensembles. On most evenings there are cultural performances by local artists or foreign groups at the many other venues for the performing arts. Free concerts are offered by several parks every week, and occasionally by banks and other corporations. The Philippines also has some unusual musical groups like the Pangwat Kawayan bamboo orchestra, which uses bamboo musical instruments, and the rondalla group which uses tiny guitars like the ukelele. Casinos are located in Manila, Cebu, Zamboanga, Iloilo and Davao.

SHOPPING: The Philippines are a haven for shoppers. Countless bargain opportunities for the handicrafts of the different regions are found in the numerous shopping complexes, which range from sleek air-conditioned department stores to open-air bazaars. The chain stores offer everything from the famous *barong tagalong* (hand-embroidered dress shirts for men in delicate jusi material) to Tiffany lamps made with capiz shells. But for local colour there's nothing like going to the flea markets where shoppers can find all kinds of cloth weaves, brassware from the south, woodcarvings and other local crafts, as well as rare seashells and other souvenirs. Some particularly good buys are the silver jewellery from Baguio, coral trinket boxes, rattan furniture, baskets in different designs, woven grass mats (*banig*), antique wooden figurines of saints, ready-to-wear clothes, garments embroidered with the traditional callado, Filipino dresses for women (usually made from banana and pineapple fibres), cigars and *abaca* placemats. Handicraft stores are found everywhere in the country, especially in cities. Large department stores sell both local and foreign manufactured goods. **Shopping hours:** These vary. Many are open 0900-1200 and 1400-1930 Monday to Saturday. Most department stores and supermarkets are open Sunday.

SPORT: Golf: Golf is popular in larger cities. There is a municipal golf course and driving range in Manila and also a miniature golf course. Most golf courses are designed by world-renowned golf architects and are equipped with amenities not just for golfers, but for non-golfers as well. Country clubs usually allow visitors to play on invitation from members; alternatively hotel staff can make arrangements. **Scuba & snorkelling:** The Philippines' crystal clear waters, tropical climate, colourful coral reefs, marine life and hospitable islands make it a rare diver's paradise, with adventures ranging from resort-based to extended trips on luxury vessels to unexplored areas. The islands of Batangas, Mindoro (particularly Apo Reef Marine Park) and Palawan offer some of the best diving sites in the country. **Boating:** *Bancas* (canoes) can be rented at all beaches. **Swimming:** Beaches and pools are ubiquitous. **Tennis:** Courts are available in most major cities and resorts. **Fishing:** The Philippines' warm waters, measuring almost 2,000,000 sq km (772,200 sq miles) of fishing grounds, rank 12th in worldwide fish production. These grounds are inhabited by some 2400 fish species, including many game fish such as giant tuna, tanguingue, king mackerel, great barracuda, swordfish and marlins. Local tour operators in Manila will help with excursions. Game fishing is best from December to August. **Spectator sports: Basketball** is popular all year round. **Horseracing, football, American baseball** and **boxing** are also popular. A unique game is ***Spa***, played with a small wicker ball, which the visitor can watch in Manila at the Rizal Court.

SPECIAL EVENTS: Dozens of colourful festivals are celebrated in the Philippines each year. A comprehensive listing, including all important Muslim festivals and Catholic feast days in honour of patron saints etc, may be obtained from the Department of Tourism. The following is a list of some of the major events in the Philippines:

Mar *Moriones* (street drama festival), Boac, Mogpop, Gasan and Marinduque. **Apr** *Turumba* (flower festival), Pakil and Laguna. **May** *Carabao Festival*, Pulilan and Bulacan. **Jun** *Parada Ng Lechon* (roast pig feast), Balayan and Batangas. **Jul** *Pagoda Sa Wawa* (water parade), Balayan and Batangas. **Aug** *Kadayawan Sa Dabaw* (street dancing and tribal shows), Davao City. **Sep** *Nuestra Senora de Penafrancia* (religious parade), Naga City. **Nov** *All Saints' Day*. **Dec** *Simbang Gabi* (Dawn masses). **Jan** *Nazareno* (religious festival), Quiapo and Metro Manila.

SOCIAL CONVENTIONS: Government officials are addressed by their titles such as Senator, Congressman or Director. Otherwise, usual modes of address and levels of politeness are expected. Casual dress is acceptable in most places, but in Muslim areas the visitor should cover up. Filipino men may wear an embroidered long-sleeved shirt or a plain white barong tagalog with black trousers for formal occasions. The Philippines are, in many respects, more Westernised than any other Asian country, but there is a rich underlay of Malaysian culture. **Tipping:** Usually 10% of the bill.

BUSINESS PROFILE

ECONOMY: The Philippines is the world's largest producer and exporter of coconuts. Other crops include copra, timber and sugar. The other main source of export earnings is mining, particularly of copper, gold and nickel. The manufacturing sector, much of which has been released from public ownership in the last few years, is concentrated in food processing, electronic equipment, textiles, chemicals and oil refining. The Government has successfully stimulated economic growth in

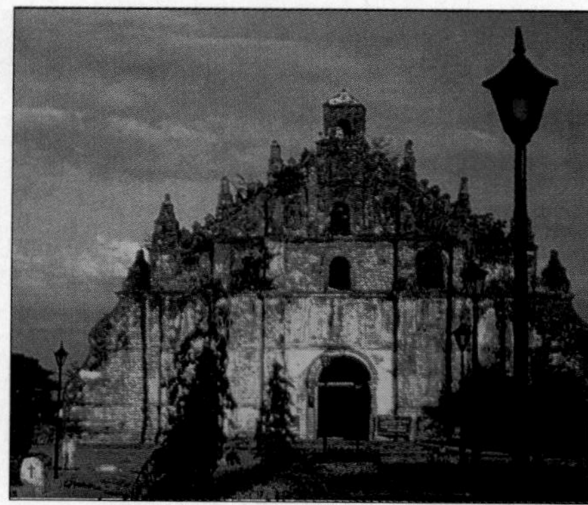

the period since the overthrow of the Marcos government and now looks to the private sector to guarantee future growth. Recent growth puts the Philippines in the same bracket as other vibrant economies in the region and the return of financial confidence among investors and donors offers reasonable economic prospects for the country. The Government's main economic concern meanwhile has been to reschedule repayments of the country's considerable foreign debt. The economy hit some problems in the early 1990s due to a spate of natural disasters: a series of typhoons and floods was followed by the eruption of Mount Pinatubo, with serious damage to agriculture. Moreover, following the Iraqi invasion of Kuwait, remittances from Filipino workers in the Gulf dried up, and the temporary rise in the oil price was a further burden on the Treasury, which subsidises petrol prices. The Philippines has a trade surplus with most of its major trading partners, including the USA, Japan, Germany and the UK.

BUSINESS: Safari suits or a long-sleeved Filipino barong tagalog can be worn for business visits. Prior appointments are necessary and it is customary to exchange business cards. Filipinos have an American business style and English is widely spoken. Best months for business visits are October to November and January to March. **Office hours:** These vary. Usually 0800/0900-1200 and 1300-1700/1800 Monday to Friday.

COMMERCIAL INFORMATION: The following organisation can offer advice: Philippine Chamber of Commerce and Industry, 7th Floor, ODC International Plaza Building, 219 Salcedo Street, Legaspi Village, Makati, Metro Manila 2801. Tel: (2) 817 6981. Telex: 62042.

CONFERENCES/CONVENTIONS: The Philippine International Convention Center has seating for up to 4000 persons. There are also several hotels with convention facilities and a broad range of back-up services; these can seat up to 1500 persons. 102 establishments belong to the Philippine Convention and Visitors Corporation (PCVC). It has US offices in Chicago, Los Angeles, New York, San Francisco, Washington DC; and also offices in Frankfurt, Hong Kong, London, Osaka, Paris, Sydney and Tokyo. For further general information contact the Philippine Convention and Visitors Corporation (address at top of entry).

HISTORY & GOVERNMENT

HISTORY: The earliest inhabitants of the Philippines were the Negritos. Other tribes later arrived from Malaysia and Indonesia. In 1521, the Portuguese navigator Ferdinand Magellan, financed by the King of Spain, landed on the islands and named them after Philip II of Spain. Friars converted the inhabitants to Christianity, and today the Philippines are the only predominantly Christian country in South-East Asia. Spanish explorer Miguel Lopez de Legaspi established the first Spanish settlement in Cebu in 1565; he moved north and defeated the Muslim Rajah Sulayman and, in 1571, established a Spanish base in Manila, extending the area under Spanish control. In 1896, a revolution against Spanish rule lead to the establishment of the first Filipino Republic in 1898 under General Emilio Aguinaldo. Later, the United States took control of the islands, and in 1935 a constitution was drawn up giving the Philippines internal self-government. The islands were occupied by the Japanese between 1942 and 1945 during the Second World War, and achieved independence in 1946. A series of American-backed presidents in the ensuing 20 years achieved little. In 1965 Ferdinand Marcos of the Nacionalista Party won the presidential elections and began a programme of rapid economic development. Before his maximum of two terms in office were over, in 1972, Marcos instituted martial law and suppressed all political opposition. He also set about large-scale looting of the country's exchequer to fill his and his family's own foreign bank accounts. Opposition to Marcos evolved in two distinct forms: the 'constitutional' opposition organised around dissenting senators such as Benigno Aquino; and the Communist Party which, linking with various tribal groups, launched an armed insurgency based in the southern islands, particularly Mindanao. By the mid-1980s, the New People's Army (NPA), the armed wing of the Communist Party, was able to sustain a major insurrection right across the country in both rural and urban areas. Large amounts of financial and military aid from the United States were poured in, especially during the Reagan administration which was very close to Marcos. The turning point for the regime came after the assassination of Benigno Aquino immediately – literally as he disembarked from the aircraft – upon his return from exile in 1983. Public opinion rallied behind his widow, Corazon Aquino, at the head of an amorphous grass-roots movement loosely organised under the rubric 'People Power'. A massive campaign of demonstrations and non-violent protest confronted Marcos. Equally important, President Reagan faced a groundswell of American public opinion in favour of Aquino, and withdrew his backing from Marcos. The Filipino military followed suit and Marcos fled into exile. Lacking any political experience whatever, Corazon Aquino took a while to settle into the Presidency. Relations between the new government and the military were the most pressing problem. The army sheltered an influential rump of support for Marcos which busied itself plotting against Aquino and had, by the end of 1989, made no less than six coup attempts. Aquino kept the bulk of the military on her side by supporting a hard line in the counter-insurgency campaign against the NPA. Military issues also dominated the Philippines key foreign relations with the USA. The Americans had maintained two large bases on Luzon Island at Subic Bay (navy) and Clark Air Base, plus a handful of smaller facilities since the end of the Second World War, but the agreement permitting their use was due to expire in 1991. Aquino again faced conflicting pressures: the economic value of the bases against nationalist demands for their removal. Amid tortuous and protracted negotiations, the problem was solved at a stroke by the volcanic eruption of Mount Pinatubo, dormant for 600 years, in the summer of 1991. Clark Air Base – 10 miles from the volcano – was damaged so badly as to render it unusable and the Americans decided to abandon it. In October 1991, the Philippines Senate accepted a deal carved out between the Government and the Americans allowing for a total pull-out by 1994. The country now turned its attention to the presidential election campaign. The constitution prevented Mrs Aquino from putting herself forward for re-election. Fidel Ramos, Aquino's erstwhile Defence Minister and a key figure in recent Filipino politics, secured her endorsement. The election was closely fought between the three principal candidates: Ramos; Aquino's younger brother, Jose 'Danding' Cojuangco; and Miriam Santiago, a fiery and popular lawyer with an impressive record as an anti-corruption campaigner. Ramos won the poll in May 1992 with 5.3 million votes. Imelda Marcos, who also stood, hoping to exploit her husband's residual popularity, came a poor fourth.

GOVERNMENT: The Constitution adopted in 1987 provides for a dual-chamber congress comprising a 24-member Senate and a House of Representatives with a maximum 250 members, of whom 200 are directly elected.

CLIMATE

Tropical climate tempered by constant sea breezes. There are three distinct seasons: the rainy season (July to October), cool and dry (November to February), and hot and mainly dry (March to June). Evenings are cooler. Typhoons occasionally occur from July to October.

Required clothing: Lightweight cottons are worn throughout most of the year. Rainwear or umbrellas are advisable for the rainy season.

MANILA Philippines (16m)

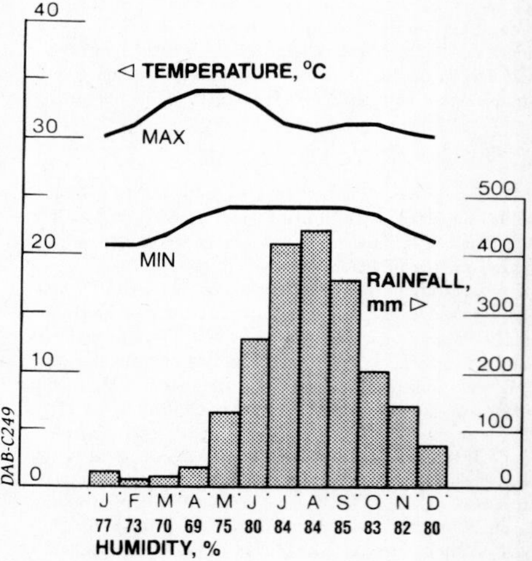

POLAND

□ *international airport*

Location: Central Europe.

Orbis SA
Ulica Bracka 16
00-028 Warsaw
Poland
Tel: (22) 260 271. Fax: (22) 271 123. Telex: 814761.

Embassy of the Republic of Poland
47 Portland Place
London W1N 3AG
Tel: (071) 580 4324. Fax: (071) 323 4018. Telex: 265691 POLAMB G. Opening hours: 0830-1630 Monday to Friday.

Consulate General of the Republic of Poland
73 New Cavendish Street
London W1M 7RB
Tel: (071) 580 0476. Fax: (071) 323 2320. Opening hours: 1000-1400 Monday to Friday, except Wednesday 1000-1200.

Polorbis Travel Limited
82 Mortimer Street
London W1N 7DE
Tel: (071) 637 4971. Fax: (071) 436 6558. Telex: 935509. Opening hours: 0900-1700 Monday to Friday, 0930-1330 Saturday.

British Embassy
Aleja Róz 1
00-556 Warsaw
Poland
Tel: (2) 628 1001. Fax: (22) 217 161. Telex: 813694 PROD PL.

Embassy of the Republic of Poland
2640 16th Street, NW
Washington, DC
20009
Tel: (202) 234 3800/1/2. Fax: (202) 328 6271.

Polish National Tourist Board
Suite 228
333 North Michigan Avenue
Chicago, IL
60601
Tel: (312) 236 9013. Fax: (312) 236 1125. Telex: 282181.
Also deals with enquiries from Canada.

Embassy of the United States of America
PO Box 5010
Aleja Ujazdowskie 29/31
00-540 Warsaw
Poland
Tel: (22) 283 041. Fax: (2) 628 8298. Telex: 813304.
Consulates in: Kraków and Poznan.

Embassy of the Republic of Poland
443 Daly Avenue
Ottawa, Ontario
K1N 6H3
Tel: (613) 236 0468. Fax: (613) 232 3463.
Consulates in: Halifax, Montréal and Toronto.

Canadian Embassy
Ulica Matejki 1/5
00-481 Warsaw
Poland
Tel: (22) 298 051. Fax: (22) 296 457. Telex: 813424 CAA PL.

AREA: 312,683 sq km (120,727 sq miles).
POPULATION: 38,183,200 (1990 estimate).
POPULATION DENSITY: 122.1 per sq km.
CAPITAL: Warsaw. **Population:** 1,655,700 (1990 estimate).
GEOGRAPHY: Poland shares borders to the north with the Baltic, to the east with the CIS and Lithuania, to the south with the Czech Republic and the Slovak Republic and to the west with Germany. The Baltic coast provides over 500km (300 miles) of sandy beaches, bays, steep cliffs and dunes. Northern Poland is dominated by lakes, islands and wooded hills joined by many rivers and canals. The Mazurian Lake District to the northeast is particularly beautiful. Lake Hancza, the deepest lake in Poland, is located in this district. The River Vistula has cut a wide valley from Gdansk on the Baltic coast to Warsaw in the heart of the country. The rest of the country rises slowly to the Sudety Mountains which run along the border with the Czech Republic. To the west, the River Oder, with Szczecin at its mouth, forms the northwest border with Germany.
LANGUAGE: Polish is the official language. There is a German-speaking minority. Some English and French are also spoken.
RELIGION: 95% Roman Catholic; the Polish Autocephalous Orthodox Church.
TIME: GMT + 1 (GMT + 2 from March 29 to September 26).
ELECTRICITY: 220 volts AC, 50Hz; Continental sockets.
COMMUNICATIONS: Telephone: Full IDD available. Country code: 48. Cheap rate on long distance calls available from 1600-0600. Tokens can be purchased from post offices for local calls. **Telex/telegram:** Telex services are available at *Foreign Trade Enterprises* and *Urzad Pocztowy* in Warsaw, 24 hours a day. *Orbis* hotels also provide services. Telegram services are provided at all main post offices and by phone. **Post:** Service to Western Europe takes up to four days. *Poste Restante* facilities are available at post offices throughout the country. Post office hours: 0800-1800 Monday to Friday. **Press:** Independent publications are flourishing following the changes in the political system; about 100 newspapers are now available. The principal dailies are *Gazeta Wyborcza, Rzeczpospolita* and *Zycie Warszawy*.
BBC World Service and Voice of America frequencies: From time to time these change. See the section *How to Use this Book* for more information.

BBC:				
MHz	15.070	12.095	9.750	6.195
Voice of America:				
MHz	9.670	6.040	5.995	1.197

PASSPORT/VISA

Regulations and requirements may be subject to change at short notice, and you are advised to contact the appropriate diplomatic or consular authority before finalising travel arrangements. Details of these may be found at the head of this country's entry. Any numbers in the chart refer to the footnotes below.

	Passport Required?	Visa Required?	Return Ticket Required?
Full British	Yes	No	No
BVP	Not valid	-	-
Australian	Yes	Yes	No
Canadian	Yes	Yes	No
USA	Yes	No	No
Other EC	Yes	1	No
Japanese	Yes	Yes	No

PASSPORTS: Valid passport required by all.
British Visitors Passport: Not accepted.
VISAS: Required by all except:
(a) **[1]** nationals of Belgium, Denmark, France, Germany, Italy*, Luxembourg, The Netherlands and the UK (other EC nationals *do* require a visa);
(b) nationals of Argentina, Austria, Bulgaria, Cuba, CIS, Czechoslovakia, Finland, Hungary, Mongolia, Norway, Romania and the USA.
Note [*]: If travelling for tourist purposes.
Types of visa: *Entry:* £20; *Transit:* £10 (both single).
Validity: Entry visa valid up to 6 months. Extensions can be arranged in Poland through the district passport office. Transit visas are valid for up to 48 hours.
Application to: Consulate (or Consular Section at Embassy). For addresses, see top of entry.
Application requirements: (a) Valid passport. (b) Completed application form. (c) 2 photos. (d) Company letter (where applicable).
Applications for visas not including these requirements will not be considered by the Consular offices and will be returned to the applicant.
Working days required: 7 (tourist); 2 (business).
Temporary residence: Apply to Consulate.

MONEY

Currency: Zloty (Zl) = 100 groszy. Notes are in denominations of Zl1,000,000, 500,000, 200,000, 100,000, 10,000, 5000, 2000, 1000, 500, 200, 100, 50, 20 and 10. Coins are in denominations of Zl10,000, 2000, 1000, 500, 200, 100, 50, 20, 10, 5, 2 and 1; and 50, 20, 10, 5, 2 and 1 groszy.
Currency exchange: Foreign currency can be exchanged at all border crossing points, all *Orbis* hotels and most others and are open 24 hours. Cash cannot be obtained from either credit cards or travellers cheques and change in foreign currency is given only when the payment exceeds 50% of a cheque value.
Credit cards: American Express, Access/Mastercard, Visa and Diners Club are widely accepted. Check with your credit card company for details of merchant acceptability and other services which may be available.
Travellers cheques: Readily exchanged *(but see above)*.
Exchange rate indicators: The following figures are included as a guide to the movements of the Zloty against Sterling and the US Dollar:

Date:	Oct '89	Oct '90	Oct '91	Oct '92
£1.00=	2893.75	18,738	19,302	23,773
$1.00=	1832.65	9592.0	11,122	14,980

Currency restrictions: The import and export of local currency is prohibited. The import of foreign currency is unlimited, provided it is declared on arrival. The export of foreign currency is limited to the balance of amounts declared on arrival.
Banking hours: 0800-1800 Monday to Friday.

DUTY FREE

The following items may be imported into Poland by persons over 17 years of age without incurring customs duty:
250 cigarettes or 50 cigars or 250g tobacco;
1 litre of wine and 1 litre other alcoholic beverages;
Gifts not exceeding US$200 in value.
Note: (a) Fur, leather and gold articles are subject to customs duty. (b) The export of antiques, works of art and certain other items from Poland is prohibited. (c) A customs declaration must be presented at the border. (d) Firearms and narcotics are prohibited. (e) Duty-free shops are located in every *Orbis* hotel and in several others, as well as at border crossing points. Payment for purchases can be made either in foreign currency, travellers cheques or credit cards.

PUBLIC HOLIDAYS

Public holidays observed in Poland are as follows:
Apr 12 '93 Easter Monday. **May 1** Labour Day. **May 3** Polish National Day. **May 9** Victory Day. **Jun 10** Corpus Christi. **Aug 15** Assumption. **Nov 1** All Saints' Day. **Nov 11** Independence Day. **Dec 25-26** Christmas. **Jan 1 '94** New Year's Day.

HEALTH

Regulations and requirements may be subject to change at short notice, and you are advised to contact your doctor well in advance of your intended date of departure. Any numbers in the chart refer to the footnotes below.

	Special Precautions?	Certificate Required?
Yellow Fever	No	No
Cholera	No	No
Typhoid & Polio	No	-
Malaria	No	-
Food & Drink	1	-

[1]: Mains water is normally chlorinated, and whilst relatively safe may cause mild abdominal upsets. Bottled water is available and is advised for the first few weeks of the stay. Milk is pasteurised and dairy products are safe for consumption. Local meat, poultry, seafood, fruit and vegetables are generally considered safe to eat.

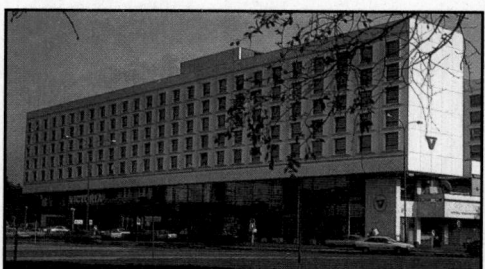

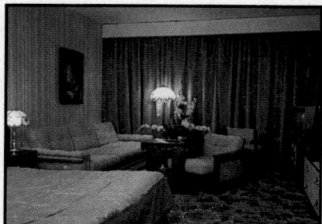

Rabies is present. For those at high risk, vaccination before arrival should be considered. If you are bitten abroad seek medical advice without delay. For more information consult the *Health* section at the back of the book.

Health care: There are Reciprocal Health Agreements with most European countries for hospital treatment and medical expenses. The Agreement with the UK allows free medical treatment (including hospital treatment) and some free dental treatment on presentation of an NHS card. UK citizens must, however, pay a call-out charge as well as 30% of the cost of prescribed medicines obtained at a public pharmacy.

TRAVEL - International

AIR: Poland's national airline is *LOT Polish Airlines (LOT)*.

Approximate flight times: From Warsaw to *Frankfurt/M* is 1 hour 50 minutes, to *London* is 2 hours 30 minutes and to *Prague* is 1 hour 10 minutes.

International airports: *Warsaw (WAW)* (Okecie) is 10km (6 miles) southwest of the city (travel time – 40 minutes by bus; 15 minutes by taxi). Full duty-free facilities are available. Airport facilites include bureaux de change (0800-2000), tourist information and car rental (*Avis* and *Orbis*). Taxis are available. A bus departs every 25 minutes from 0500-2300.

Kraków (KRK) (Balice) is 18km (10 miles) from the city centre. Buses and taxis are available. There are no duty-free facilities.

SEA: *Polish Ocean Lines* operate from Montréal in Canada to Gdynia via London and Rotterdam. Other routes operate from Poland to Australia, the Middle East, UK, Ireland, Germany, Belgium, Africa (North and West), Singapore and the Far East.

RAIL: All services from Western Europe to Poland pass through Germany, the Czech Republic or the Slovak Republic. Main routes are Berlin–Warsaw–Moscow; Paris–Warsaw; and from Vienna, Budapest and Prague to Warsaw. There is a car-sleeper service from the Hook of Holland to Poznan/Warsaw (see below). As from May 31 1993, Warsaw can be reached with EuroCity-trains from *Berlin*.

ROAD: Poland is best reached from Germany and the Czech Republic or the car-sleeper rail service from the Hook of Holland to Poznan/Warsaw. There are extensive **bus** and **coach** services.

TRAVEL - Internal

AIR: All internal airlines are operated by *LOT (Polish Airlines)* and there is a comprehensive network linking all major cities. For details of routes and fares contact *LOT* offices.

RAIL: *Polish State Railway (PKP)* services link all parts of the country in a network radiating from Warsaw. There are two classes of travel. Reservations are required on express trains. The 'Polerailpass' is available for 8, 15, 21 or 30 days. Intercity express trains are cheap and efficient.

ROAD: Unleaded petrol is available in all major cities and a full list of filling stations can be obtained from Polorbis. The Polish motoring club *Polski Zwiazek Motorowy (PZM)* can be called on 981 nationwide for assistance. For further information contact Polski Zwiazek Motorowy, Ulica Kazimierzowska 66, 02-518 Warsaw. Tel: (22) 499 361. **Bus:** There are good regional bus and coach services operated by *Polish Motor Communications (PKS)* connecting most towns. **Car hire:** Self-drive cars are available at the airport or through *Orbis* offices in town centres. The minimum age is 21. Charges are usually based on a daily rate plus a kilometre charge. **Regulations:** The speed limit is 60kmph in built-up areas, 90kmph on major roads and 110kmph on motorways. Seat belts are compulsory outside built-up areas. Trams have the right of way. **Documentation:** Tourists travelling in their own cars should have car registration cards, their national driving licence and valid Green Card motor insurance. An International Driving Permit is recommended, although not legally required.

URBAN: There are good **bus** services in all towns, with additional trams and trolleybuses operating in a dozen of the larger urban areas. Warsaw has bus, tramway and rail services. A flat fare is charged and there are pre-purchase tickets and passes. 7-day **tram** tourist tickets can be purchased. In 1983, trolleybuses were reintroduced on one route and construction was

POLAND	HEALTH REGULATIONS	VISA REGULATIONS (Code-Link)
GALILEO/WORLDSPAN	 TI-DFT/WAW/HE	 TI-DFT/WAW/VI
SABRE	 TIDFT/WAW/HE	TIDFT/WAW/VI

To access this information on your CRS, swipe the barcode with a light pen or type in the text under the barcode. For more information, see the introduction *How to Use This Book*.

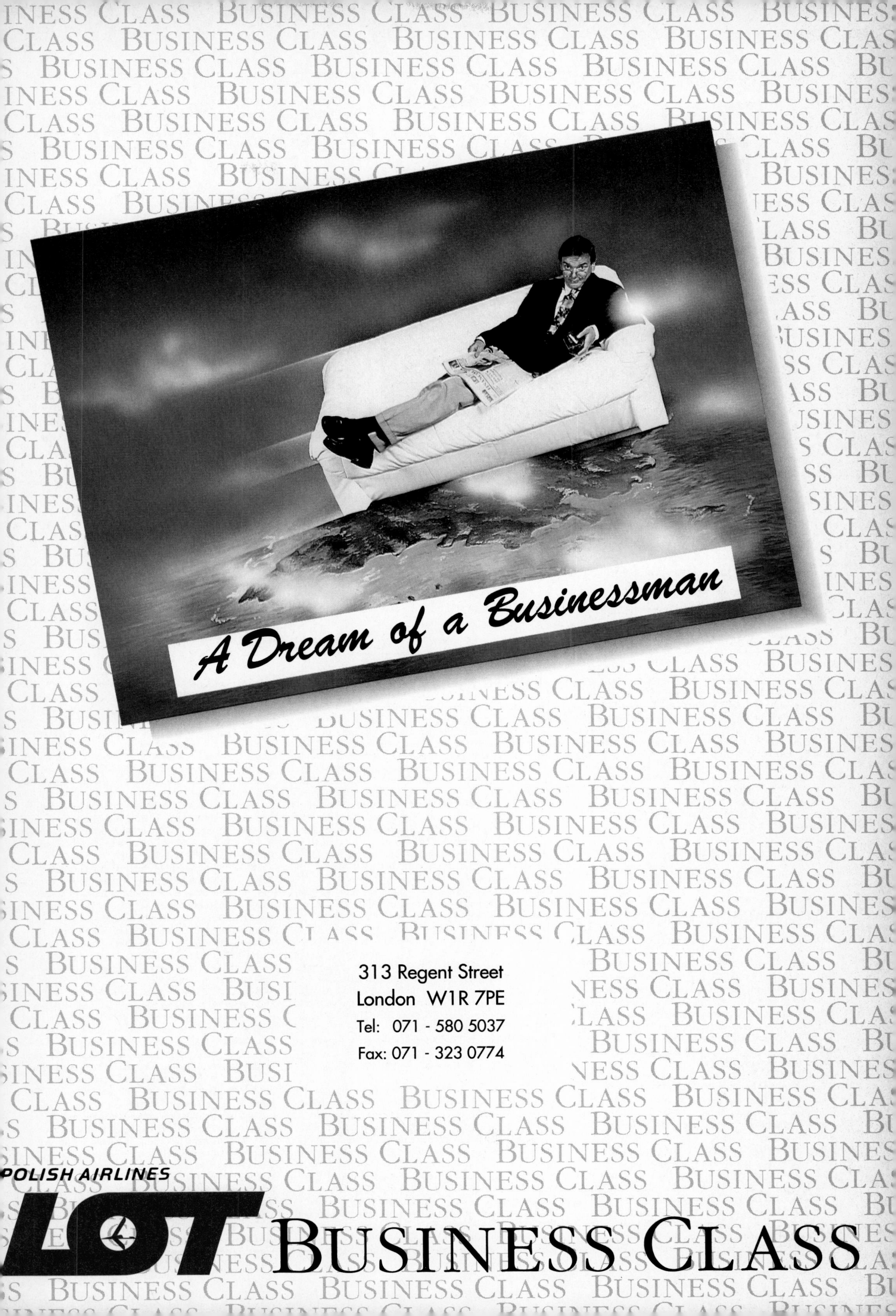
A Dream of a Businessman
313 Regent Street
London W1R 7PE
Tel: 071 - 580 5037
Fax: 071 - 323 0774
POLISH AIRLINES
LOT
BUSINESS CLASS

begun on a metro. Most public transport operates from 0530-2300. **Taxis** are available in all main towns. They are usually found at ranks or phoned. There is a surcharge from 2300-0500 and for journeys out of town as well as for weekends. Taxi drivers may insist on payment in hard currency. **Tipping** is not necessary.
JOURNEY TIMES: The following chart gives approximate journey times (in hours and minutes) from Warsaw to other major cities/towns in Poland.

	Air	Road	Rail
Kraków	1.40	4.00	4.00
Poznan	1.00	4.00	3.00
Wroclaw	1.15	6.00	6.00
Gdansk	1.00	6.00	5.00
Szczecin	2.00	8.00	6.45
Katowice	1.30	4.30	4.00
Lódz	-	2.00	2.00

ACCOMMODATION

HOTELS: National Tourist Enterprise *Orbis* (address at beginning of entry) runs over 150 hotels. International Student Hotels offer better facilities than youth hostels and are inexpensive, comfortable and pleasant. **Grading:** Hotels in Poland are graded in five categories: luxury, 4-star, 3-star, 2-star and 1-star. In addition there are tourist hotels, boarding houses and motels, each graded into three or four categories.
GUEST-HOUSES: Three categories are available in all towns and run by regional tourist boards. Reservations can be made from local offices.
CAMPING/CARAVANNING: There are over 200 campsites in Poland, nearly 75% of which are fitted with 220-volt powerpoints and several with 24-volt points for caravans. Facilities also include washrooms, canteens and nearby restaurants and food kiosks. It is advisable to have camping coupons which entitle the holders to be given priority in getting a site without reservations. The vouchers for coupons can be obtained at the exchange desks of the *Polish Motor Union* and *Orbis*, as well as at road border crossings.
YOUTH HOSTELS: There are about 1200 hostels in Poland. Addresses can be found in the *Youth Hostel Handbook* published by Youth Hostels Federation *(Almatur)*, 15 Copernika Street, 00-359 Warsaw. Tel: (22) 265 381. Fax: (22) 262 353. Telex: 813474.

RESORTS & EXCURSIONS

The following is an outline of the attractions to be encountered in a circular tour of seven of Poland's major cities. A brief description of Zakopane, Poland's premier ski resort, is also included.
WARSAW: The *River Vistula* runs through the middle of this modern capital. Warsaw was completely destroyed during the Second World War, but now the *Old Town* has been rebuilt. The *Wilanów Palace*, one of the reconstructed buildings, has a rare collection of old paintings and furniture, and in the *Orangerie* is the *Museum of Posters*. The reconstructed *Royal Castle* is well worth seeing, as is the *Palace of Culture and Science*, with its views over the whole city. The *Lazienki Palace* is set in a lovely park with an open-air Greek theatre and a monument to Chopin.
Excursions: *Zelazowa Wola*, 53km (32 miles) west of Warsaw, an attractive park in which stands the manor house where Chopin was born; *Kampinos National Park*, 340 sq km (130 sq miles) of forest, marsh and sand where it is possible to see wild boars and elks; *Bielowiezá National Park*, 1250 sq km (480 sq miles) of primeval forest straddling the border with the CIS, the last major refuge of the European bison, also inhabited by lynx, moose, wild forest ponies and other rare forest-dwellers. **Lublin**, a charming medieval city with five universities, is 164km (102 miles) southeast of Warsaw.
KRAKOW: Poland's second city also stands on the banks of the River Vistula but far to the south in the wooded foothills of the *Tatra Mountains*. It still retains its charming medieval air, having largely escaped destruction during the Second World War. In the centre is the *Cloth Hall* built in the 14th century. Opposite is *St Mary's Church* with its world-famous wooden altar carved by Wit Stwosz. The *Jagiellonian University* founded in 1364 is one of the oldest in Europe. Here Copernicus studied and visitors may see the astronomical instruments he used. Overlooking Kraków is the *Royal Castle* with its marvellous 16th-century tapestries. Next to the Castle is the *Royal Cathedral* where many of the Polish kings are buried as Kraków was Poland's capital until 1611. *Czartoryski Museum* contains ancient art, European paintings, and crafts.
Excursions: At **Wieliczka,** 13km (8 miles) from Kraków, cathedral-like salt mines are open to visitors. The route spans 4.5km leading to the oldest part of the mine through 14th- and 15th-century chapels and crystal caves. 70km (43 miles) from Kraków lies the site of **Auschwitz** (now Oswiecim) concentration camp in which 4 million people were killed. The camp area has been designated as a Monument to the Victims of Oswiecim. There is a *Museum of Martyrdom* on the site. Other excursions include the *Bledowska Desert*, perhaps the only true desert in Europe; **Wadowice,** birthplace of Pope John Paul II; and the portrait of the Madonna in the huge monastery complex at **Czestochowa**, 100km (60 miles) north of Cracow, reputed to have been painted by St Luke.
ZAKOPANE: About 112km (70 miles) south of Kraków, this charming resort and winter sports centre lies in the heart of the Tatra Mountains. There is a fairytale atmosphere here – 'gingerbread' wooden cottages and people still in national dress.
Excursions: Organised trips are available to *Dunajec Rapids; Koscieliska Valley*, through beautiful countryside; *Kasprowy Wierch*, by means of a cable car offering spectacular views; and to *Morskie Oko*, a mountain lake.
WROCLAW: The principal city of southwest Poland and capital of Lower Silesia can claim to be the cradle of the Polish state: it was here that the Polanie tribe built their first fortified settlement (on Ostrow Tumski Island). During the 14th century, it fell under the rule of the Bohemians, in the 16th century the Habsburgs, the Prussians and then the German Reich. At the end of the Second World War the town was used as the 'Festung Breslau', a Nazi stronghold. The modern city is threaded with 90km (56 miles) of canals and tributaries of the River Oder and there are more than a hundred bridges. Sights include the *Town Hall* and the *Cathedral* on **Ostrow Tumski Island** (Ostrow Tumski means 'Cathedral Island').
Excursions: The spas and health resorts of the *Klodzko Valley;* the rugged *Stolowe Mountains;* ski resorts in the *Karkonosze Mountains* on the border with the Czech Republic; and the many picturesque medieval (and earlier) towns in the region, such as **Swidnica**, **Bolslawiec** and **Paczkow**.
POZNAN: This sedate city stands beside the *River Warta* in the middle of the flatlands of western

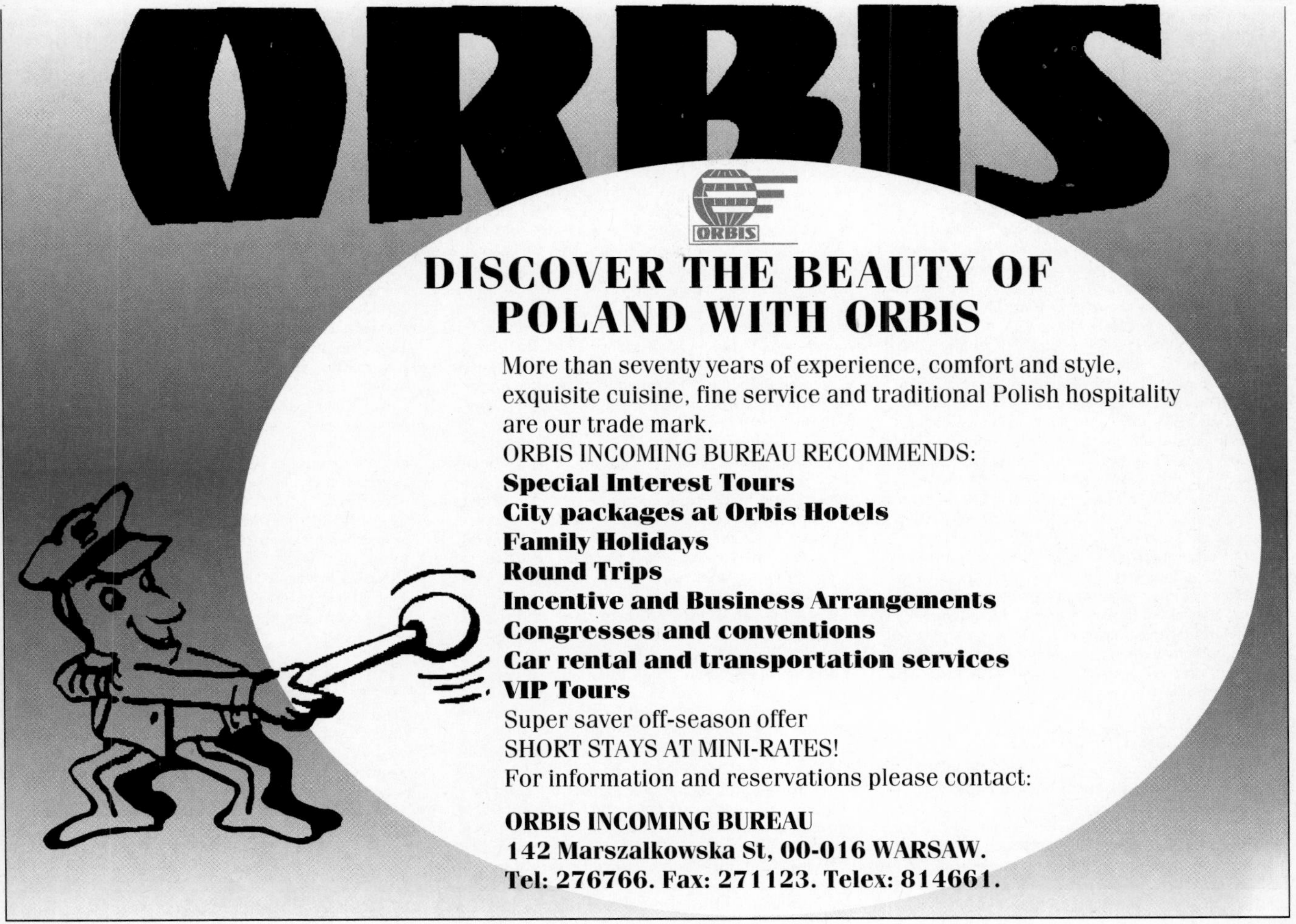

Poland. More than half of the city was destroyed during the Second World War but much has been restored. Sights include the Italianate town hall in the *Old Market Square*, the *Gorki Palace*, the *Dzyalinski Mansion* (now a hotel), the 12th-century *Church of St John* and *Przemyslaw Castle*, once seat of the Grand Dukes of Poland. Of more recent interest is the huge monument in memory of the workers killed in *Plac Mickiewicza* by the police during disturbances in 1956. Watersports can be enjoyed in and on the many lakes in the woods surrounding the city. The *Poznan International Trade Fair* is held here every year in June.
Excursions: Gniezno also claims to be the birthplace of the Polish state. Three brothers, Lech, Czech and Rus, are said to have been the founders of the Slavic nations. Lech was supposed to have settled at Gniezno on finding white eagles nesting there. The white eagle later became the symbol of Poland. At **Biskupin** nearby, there is a large and well-preserved prehistoric settlement.
SZCZECIN: Standing 60km (37 miles) upstream from the mouth of the *River Oder*, this is nonetheless the largest port on the Baltic Sea. Formerly known as Stettin, it was the capital of Pomerania and sights include the Pomeranian princes' 14th-century chateau and the 12th-century cathedral. The city was largely rebuilt in the last century, taking Paris as a model, and has a spacious feel to it, with many wide, tree-lined boulevards.
Excursions: The beach resorts of the Pomeranian coast, such as *Kolobrzeg* (large and fashionable) or *Leba* (a quiet resort with a beach of fabulous white sand); and the beech woods of the *Wolin National Park*, home of the rare European sea eagle.
GDANSK: Formerly known as Danzig, this important Baltic port has had a troubled history. The Order of Teutonic Knights took it from the Poles in the 14th century and later lost it to the Prussians. In the 20th century, it was the first city to be attacked by Nazi Germany in 1939 and its Lenin Shipyards were the birthplace of *Solidarinosc* (Solidarity) and thus of today's democratic Poland. Almost the entire city was destroyed in the Second World War, but was restored to its former beauty. The city is now a provincial capital at the mouth of the Vistula and Motlawa and a commercial, industrial and scientific centre. Sights include the *Town Hall*, restored Renaissance-style houses, the 17th-century *Golden Gate* and the largest Gothic Church in Poland, the *Church of the Virgin Mary*. The beach resort at nearby *Sopot* has Europe's longest pier (500m/1640ft).
Excursions: The forested *Hel Peninsula*; the *Kashubian Lakeland*; the narrow-gauge railway that runs along the *Vistula Spit;* the Teutonic castles at **Malbork** (Marienburg), **Gniew** and elsewhere; and the *Nicolaus Copernicus Museum* at **Torun**, his birthplace. Further east is **Mazuria**, a huge, thinly populated area of lakes, dense forests and swamps. It is rich in wildlife, including wild bison and Europe's largest herd of elks, and offers every form of outdoor pursuit – mushroom-collecting, sailing, canoeing, camping, etc. In the heart of a Mazurian forest, at **Ketrzyn** (Rastenburg), is the site of *Hitler's 'Eagle's Nest'*, the concrete bunker where members of his High Staff tried to assassinate him in August 1944.

SOCIAL PROFILE

FOOD & DRINK: Poland has a distinctive cuisine, with typical ingredients being dill, marjoram, caraway seeds, wild mushrooms and sour cream, which is frequently added to soups, sauces and braised meats. The national dish of Poland is *bigos*, made with sauerkraut, fresh cabbage, onions and any variety of leftover meat. Polish meals start with *przekaski* (starters), such as pike in aspic, marinated fish in sour cream, salted and rolled herring fillets with pickles and onions, *kulebiak* (a large mushroom and cabbage pastie) or Polish sausages such as the long, thin and highly spiced *kabanos* or the hunters' sausage *(mysliwska)* made with pork and game. Soups play an important part at mealtimes and are usually rich and very thick. Soups such as *borschtsch* (beetroot soup, excellent with sour cream) or *rosot* (beef or chicken boullion) are often served in cups with small hot pasties stuffed with meat or cabbage. For main courses, meat supplies tend to be erratic and so some of the cheaper restaurants have been forced to institute one meatless day per week. Popular dishes include *zrazy zawijane* (mushroom-stuffed beefsteak rolls in sour cream) served with boiled *kasha* (buckwheat) and pig's knuckles. Poland is also a good country for fish *(ryba)* such as carp served in sweet-and-sour jellied sauce, and poached pike with horse-radish in cream. Herring *(sledz)* is particularly popular and is served up in countless different ways. Pastries *(ciastka)* are also very good. Table service is the norm in restaurants. **Drink:** Vodka *(wódka)*, the national drink, is drunk chilled. *Wyborowa* is considered the best standard vodka, but there are many flavoured varieties such as *zubrowka* (bison grass), *tarniowka* (sloe plum), *sliwowica* (prune) and *pieprzowka* (vodka with ground white pepper). Western drinks, such as whisky, gin or brandy, can be obtained in most bars but are expensive. Wine is available but, again, is imported and expensive. The best bottled beer is *zywiec*, a fairly strong lager-type beer. Bars have table and/or counter service. Coffee shops are very popular in Poland and are the favourite places for social meetings from early morning to late at night. They do not close during the day and have the same function as do pubs in the United Kingdom. Alcoholic drinks are only served after 1300.
NIGHTLIFE: Warsaw also reflects the strong theatrical and musical traditions of Poland, with about 17 theatres, and three opera companies. Cinemas in Poland show both Polish and foreign films. There are some discos in Poland, as well as a few nightclubs and music clubs in Warsaw.
SHOPPING: Special purchases: glass and enamelware, handwoven rugs, silverware and handmade jewellery, dolls in regional costumes, woodcarvings and clay and metal sculptures. **Shopping hours:** 1000-1900 Monday to Friday.
SPORT: *Orbis* can arrange special-interest recreation stays in Poland for sports clubs, youth organisations and school children, such as **yachting** and other **watersports** on the Mazurian Lakes, **horseriding** and winter sports holidays. **Winter sports:** The most popular resorts are Zakopane in the Tatra Mountains and Krynica in the Beskidy Mountains. **Skiing** runs from November through to May. Another winter sport is **ice-boating** on Poland's frozen waterways. **Fishing:** For angling, tourists need to buy a fishing licence for about £11 which is valid for 7 days. **Sailing:** The main sailing regions are the Mazurian Lakes and the Suwalki and Augustow Lakes. **Swimming:** There are swimming pools in most cities and beaches along the Baltic coast. Swimming is also particularly good in the Mazurian Lakes. There is, however, fairly high pollu-

tion in rivers and so it is not a good idea to swim in them. **Racing:** The main horseracing tracks are Warsaw (Sluzewiec), Sopot, Raculka (near Zielona Gora), Bialy Bor (near Slupsk) and Ksiaz (near Walbrzych).

SPECIAL EVENTS: The following series of events are highlights in the Polish calendar. For further details of events in 1993/94 contact Polorbis Travel Limited (address at top of entry).

Apr '93 *Poznan Spring* (Festival of Polish Contemporary Music), Poznan. **May** *Music Festival*, Lancut. **Jun** *International Book Fair*, Warsaw. **Jul/Aug** *Dominican Market*, Gdansk. **Aug** *International Song Festival*, Sopot; *Picnic Country Festival*, Mragowa. **Sep** *Warsaw Autumn* (Festival of Contemporary Music), Warsaw. **Sep** *Festival of Highland Folklore*, Zakopane. **Oct** *Jazz Jamboree* (International Jazz Festival), Warsaw.

SOCIAL CONVENTIONS: Poles are friendly, industrious people and foreigners are usually made very welcome. There are vast contrasts between urban and rural life and the Polish peasantry is very religious and conservative, maintaining a traditional lifestyle. Roman Catholicism plays an important role in daily life and criticism or jokes about religion are not appreciated, despite the general good humour of the people. Music and art are also important aspects of Polish culture. Shaking hands is the normal form of greeting. Normal courtesies are observed when visiting private homes and it is customary to bring flowers. Fairly conservative casual wear is the most suitable attire, but dress should be formal when specified for entertaining in the evening or in a smart restaurant. Smoking is restricted in some public buildings. **Photography:** Military installations such as bridges, ports, airports, border points etc should not be photographed. **Tipping:** A service charge is usually added to restaurant bills.

BUSINESS PROFILE

ECONOMY: The working population is divided roughly in half between agriculture and industry. Although some productive land is under state control, there have long been numerous private farms which are responsible for the bulk of Polish produce. Livestock is particularly important and Polish meat is a major export earner. Rye, wheat, oats, sugarbeet and potatoes are the main crops. The main industries are shipbuilding, textiles, steel, cement, chemicals and foodstuffs. After a period of rapid growth during the 1970s, financed by relatively easy credit from the West, Polish industry has undergone severe recession, particularly in the heavier industries, and although there has been some recovery since the introduction of market reforms, the problems are still considerable. With the new non-Communist government now in place, the old facets of the Soviet-style command economy have for the most part been removed. Price controls and other financial restrictions have been dropped and Poland has embarked on a major programme of privatisation, using a voucher-based system similar to that introduced in the then Czechoslovakia. The Zloty is now partly convertible while the tax and fiscal system is undergoing a complete restructuring. Inflation has been brought down from nearly 700% to around 40% per annum (3% per month). Poland has signed an association agreement with the European Community and expects to seek membership around the turn of the century. A trade agreement with EFTA (the European Free Trade Association) is, however, being held up by disagreements over import tariff reductions. Poland's main trading partners are Germany and the CIS.

BUSINESS: Men are expected to wear a suit and tie at business meetings. In Poland a formal approach is favoured and it is therefore advisable to give plenty of notice of an intended visit. Employees in state organisations do not take a lunch break; they have their main meal after 1500. **Office hours:** 0700-1600 Monday to Friday.

COMMERCIAL INFORMATION: The following organisation can offer advice: Krajowa Izba Gospodarcza (Polish Chamber of Commerce), PO Box 361, Trebacka 4, 00-950 Warsaw. Tel: (22) 260 221. Fax: (22) 274 673. Telex: 814361.

CONFERENCES/CONVENTIONS: The most popular conference venues are in Warsaw. Events are also hosted in Cracow, whereas Wroclaw, Gdansk and other towns are used occasionally. A comprehensive range of support facilities is provided by ORBIS SA, Krakowskie Przedmiescie, 00-950 Warsaw. Tel: (22) 261 658. Fax: (22) 261 297. Telex: 814728.

HISTORY & GOVERNMENT

HISTORY: For much of the medieval and early modern period, Poland was one of the largest states in Europe, although generally cut off from the mainstream of European life. By the 18th century, however, the combination of an antiquated social structure, the emergence of powerful neighbours, an elective king with no real power and a parliament which was able to veto any legislation if so much as one member voted against it (the *Liberum Veto*) had reduced Poland to the role of little more than a confused buffer state between Austria, Prussia and Russia. One observer commented how the Polish state had 'legalised anarchy and called it a constitution'. The situation was finally resolved between 1772 and 1795 when, as a result of three partition treaties signed by Austria, Prussia and Russia, the country was carved up. A small area around Warsaw briefly enjoyed a form of independence between 1807 and 1831 (as the Grand Duchy of Warsaw and Congress Poland), but subsequently became a province of Russia. Poland did not re-acquire independence until 1918. In 1926, a military regime ousted the civilian administration and governed Poland until the country was once again dismembered by its powerful neighbours, Germany and the Soviet Union, after the 1939 Anti-Aggression Pact of the two. Prior commitments by Britain to defend Polish sovereignty led the former to declare war on Germany and initiate the Second World War. In 1941 Germany drove the USSR out of Poland, to be ejected, in turn, by the Soviets four years later. At the end of World War II, the Soviet-backed Polish Workers' Party formed a coalition government under Wladyslaw Gomulka, until the latter was dismissed for 'deviationism' in 1948. In the same year, the Polish Workers' Party merged with the Polish Socialist Party to form the Polish United Workers' Party (Polska Zjednoczona Partia Robotnicza, PZPR). In 1956, three years after Stalin's death, Gomulka returned amid growing unrest to implement a plan of gradual liberalisation of society and the economy. Following disturbances in the industrial port of Gdansk, Gomulka was replaced as First Secretary of the party by Edward Gierek. Opposition to the regime was, significantly, led by elements of the industrial workforce (in contrast to movements elsewhere in eastern Europe which were led by intellectuals, such as Charter 77) and supported by the Catholic Church, a major political force in Poland which the communists had never been able to suppress fully. This was a vital factor in the rapid growth of the Solidarnosc (Solidarity) labour movement in the late 1970s and early 1980s. The PZPR's initial response to this challenge was confused. Gierek was forced into retirement (through illness). His successor, Stanislav Kania, proved no more able to stop the growth of Solidarnosc or the declining prestige and influence of the PZPR. In December 1981, with the backing of Moscow, the former army chief-of-staff, General Wojciech Jaruzelski, who had replaced Kania two months earlier, imposed martial law and established a Military Council of National Salvation to run the country. Solidarnosc was banned and its senior figures detained, including its leader, the shipyard electrician Lech Walesa. The restrictions of martial law were gradually eased as the situation stabilised over the next few years, but it was clear that some accommodation between the Government and Solidarnosc was inevitable. The changes in the Soviet Union from 1985 onwards made this task easier. In 1988, following the near-collapse of the economy, the PZPR government resigned and was replaced by an interim Council of Ministers, which included several non-PZPR members, although it remained communist-dominated. It held serious negotiations with Solidarnosc on economic and constitutional reforms. Solidarnosc was finally legalised in 1989 to pave the way for elections to the new bicameral National Assembly (see below) in June of that year. For the first time candidates opposed to the ruling PZPR were allowed to stand for one-third of the seats; the remainder were reserved for the PZPR and its allies. Solidarnosc swept the board in those it was allowed to contest. It subsequently formed a coalition government with two smaller parties, with Tadeusz Mazowiecki becoming the first non-Communist Prime Minister of a Warsaw Pact country. General Jaruzelski was re-elected as President. The Government was almost immediately faced with a deep recession which it tackled by introducing market reforms. Ironically, this exacerbated the growing divisions within Solidarnosc. A deep split occurred in the movement in the months leading up to the first wholly free presidential election in November 1990. Walesa and Mazowiecki, respective leaders of their factions, both stood. Walesa won, with Centre Alliance backing. Mazowiecki was replaced as Prime Minister by Jan Krysztof Bielecki. October 1991 saw elections to the National Assembly. The largest proportion of the vote won by any single party was the 15% picked up by Mazowiecki's Democratic Union, which won 76 seats of 460; the former communists, now styled the Democratic Left Alliance, came second; six parties with between 5-10% of votes (25-50 seats) came next, followed by a plethora of smaller parties including the Party of the Friends of Beer with a creditable 14 seats. In all, 29 parties are represented in the Sejm. Stable government has proved elusive, however, as a succession of short-lived administrations have succumbed to the constant shifting of political alliances. The latest model, which took over in July 1992, seems to be more durable: it is a 7-party coalition led by Hanna Suchocka of the Democratic Union. One particularly important development is that Suchocka has managed to guide a law through the Sejm allowing economic decisions to be implemented by decree; this is essential to break the policy-making logjam and allow Poland to tackle its desperate economic problems. Negotiations have opened with the IMF, World Bank and the European Bank for Reconstruction and Development, and Western governments appear prepared to approve a requested US$1-billion economic aid programme. Poland's progress in introducing market economics has helped the country's standing. Eventual membership of the EC is a long-term objective.

GOVERNMENT: Legislative power in Poland is vested in a bicameral national assembly. The 460-seat lower house is the Sejm while a new 100-seat Upper Chamber has been created with the power of veto over all legislation put forward by the Sejm. Elections are by proportional representation.

CLIMATE

Temperate with warm summers, crisp, sunny autumns and cold winters. Snow covers the Sudety Mountains (mid-December to April). Rain falls throughout the year. **Required clothing:** Light to mediumweights are worn during warmer months. Medium to heavyweights are needed during winter. Rainwear is advisable all year.

WARSAW Poland (107m)

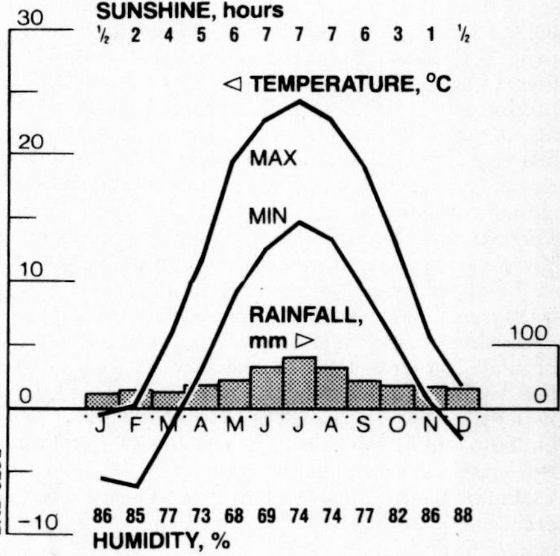

GDYNIA Poland (15m)

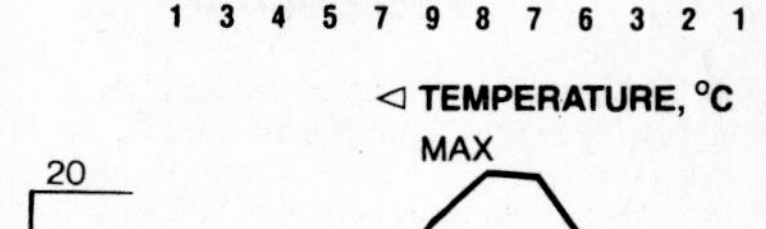

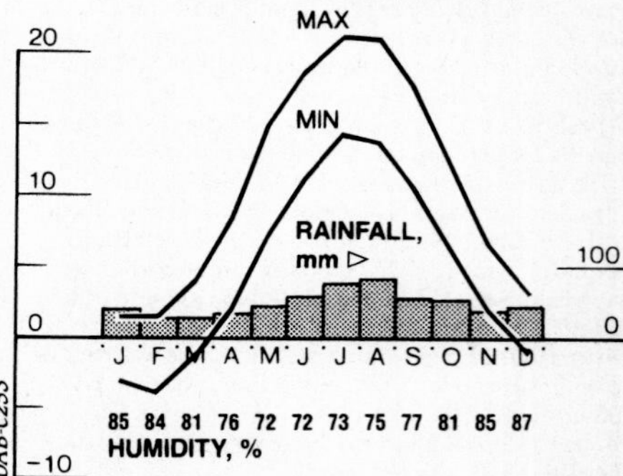

PORTUGAL

□ *international airport*

Location: Western Europe.

ICEP/Turismo
Avenida Conde Valbom 30 – 5°
1016 Lisbon
Portugal
Tel: (1) 352 5807/8.

Embassy of the Portuguese Republic
11 Belgrave Square
London SW1X 8PP
Tel: (071) 235 5331/4. Fax: (071) 245 1287. Telex: 28484. Opening hours: 1000-1300 and 1400-1700 Monday to Friday.

Portuguese Consulate
Silver City House
62 Brompton Road
London SW3 1BJ
Tel: (071) 581 8722. Fax: (071) 581 3085. Opening hours: 0900-1330 Monday to Friday.

Portuguese National Tourist Office
4th Floor
22/25a Sackville Street
London W1X 1DE
Tel: (071) 494 1441. Fax: (071) 494 1868. Telex: 265653.

British Embassy
Rua de S Domingos à Lapa 35-37
37 1200 Lisbon
Portugal
Tel: (1) 396 1191/1147/3181. Fax: (1) 397 6768. Telex: 122780.
Consulates in: Funchal (Madeira), Oporto, Ponta Delgada (Azores) and Portimão (for Macau, refer to British Trade Commission, Hong Kong).

Embassy of the Portuguese Republic
2125 Kalorama Road, NW
Washington, DC
20008
Tel: (202) 328 8610. Fax: (202) 462 3726.
Consulate Generals in: Boston, Honolulu, Houston, Los Angeles, Miami, Newark, New Bedford, New Orleans, New York (tel: (212) 246 4580), Philadelphia, Providence, San Francisco and Waterbury.

Portuguese National Tourist Office
4th Floor, 590 Fifth Avenue
New York, NY
10036-4704
Tel: (212) 354 4403. Fax: (212) 764 6137. Telex: 2341401 CTPA UR.

Embassy of the United States of America
Avenida das Forças Armadas
1600 Lisbon Codex
Portugal
Tel: (1) 726 6600 *or* 726 6659 *or* 726 8670. Fax: (1) 726 9109. Telex: 12528 AMEMB.
Consulate in: Ponta Delgada (Azores).

Embassy of the Portuguese Republic
645 Island Park Drive
Ottawa, Ontario
K1Y 0B8
Tel: (613) 729 0883 *or* 729 2922. Fax: (613) 729 4236.
Consulates in: Edmonton, Halifax, Montréal, Québec, St John's, Toronto, Vancouver and Winnipeg.

Portuguese National Tourist Office
Suite 1005
60 Bloor Street W
Toronto, Ontario
M4W 3B8
Tel: (416) 921 7376. Fax: (416) 921 1353. Telex: 06524013.

Canadian Embassy
4th Floor
Avenida da Liberdade 144/56 4°
1200 Lisbon
Portugal
Tel: (1) 347 4892. Fax: (1) 347 6466. Telex: 12377 DOMCAN P.
Consulate in: Faro.

AREA: 92,389 sq km (35,672 sq miles).
POPULATION: 10,525,000 (1990 estimate).
POPULATION DENSITY: 111.9 per sq km.
CAPITAL: Lisbon. **Population:** 807,937 (1981).
GEOGRAPHY: Portugal occupies the southwest part of the Iberian Peninsula, and shares borders in the north and the east with Spain, while to the south and west lies the Atlantic Ocean. The country is divided into various provinces, including the Atlantic islands of Madeira and the Azores; the latter lying some 1220km (760 miles) due west of Lisbon. The Douro, Tagus and Guadiana rivers flow across the border from Spain. North Portugal is mountainous, the highest part being the *Serra da Estrela*, a popular area for skiing. South of Lisbon stretch the vast plains of the *Alentejo* region. A range of mountains divides the *Alentejo* from the Algarve, which runs along the south coast, and is one of the most popular resort areas with wide sandy beaches and attractive bays.
LANGUAGE: Portuguese.
RELIGION: Roman Catholic.
TIME: GMT (GMT + 1 in summer).
ELECTRICITY: 220 volts AC, 50 Hz. 110 volts in some areas and 220 DC in parts of the south. Continental 2-pin plugs are in use.
COMMUNICATIONS: Telephone: IDD is available. Country code: 351. There are call boxes in most villages and all towns, also public phones in many cafés and bars from which international calls may be made. **Fax:** This service is available to the public at bureaux and large hotels in major cities. **Telex/telegram:** There are telegram and telex facilities at most major hotels. The public telex office at Praca D Luis 30-1, Lisbon is open 0900-1800 Monday to Friday. **Post:** Airmail to European destinations from Continental Portugal and the Azores takes three days; from Madeira up to five days. There are *Poste Restante* facilities at post offices throughout the country. **Press:** There are no English-language newspapers.
BBC World Service and Voice of America frequencies: From time to time these change. See the section *How to Use this Book* for more information.

BBC:				
MHz	**15.070**	**12.095**	**9.410**	**6.195**
Voice of America:				
MHz	**11.97**	**9.670**	**6.040**	**5.995**

PASSPORT/VISA

Regulations and requirements may be subject to change at short notice, and you are advised to contact the appropriate diplomatic or consular authority before finalising travel arrangements. Details of these may be found at the head of this country's entry. Any numbers in the chart refer to the footnotes below.

	Passport Required?	Visa Required?	Return Ticket Required?
Full British	1	No	No
BVP	Valid	No	No
Australian	Yes	No	No
Canadian	Yes	No	No
USA	Yes	No	No
Other EC	1	No	No
Japanese	Yes	No	No

PASSPORTS: [1] Valid passport required by all except nationals of Austria, Belgium, France, Germany, Greece, Italy, Liechtenstein, Luxembourg, Malta, The Netherlands, the UK, Spain and Switzerland holding national ID cards, or BVP in the case of UK citizens.
British Visitors Passport: Accepted.
VISAS: Required by all except:
(a) nationals of EC countries (including the UK) for stays of up to 3 months;
(b) nationals of Argentina, Australia, Austria, Czechoslovakia, Chile, Costa Rica, Japan, Malta, Mexico, Monaco, New Zealand, Norway, San Marino, Switzerland and Yugoslavia for stays of up to 3 months;
(c) nationals of Andorra, Canada, Ecuador, Finland, Iceland, South Korea, Liechtenstein, Malawi, Seychelles, Sweden, Uruguay and the USA for stays of up to 2 months;
(d) nationals of Brazil for stays of up to 6 months.
Nationals of other countries should consult the Portugese Consulate for further information.
Note: Usually it is sufficient for visitors to Madeira and the Azores to satisfy the entry conditions for Portugal. Exceptions are noted in the sections below on Madeira and the Azores.
Types of visa: Entry visa: £5.11 for single passport, £7.57 for family passport.
Validity: Visas are valid for 120 days after the date of issue, and up to 60 days from date of entry.
Application to: Consulate (or Consular Section at Embassy). For addresses, see top of entry.
Application requirements: (a) Valid passport. (b) Application form(s). (c) Passport-size photo(s).
Working days required: Normally 48 hours, longer if the application has to be referred to Portugal. Applications by post should be accompanied by a large SAE.
Temporary residence: Applications for residence visa must be accompanied by a declaration of interest (explanation of reasons, intentions and statement of financial capacity). Contact the Consulate for further details.

MONEY

Currency: Escudo (Esc) = 100 centavos. Notes are in denominations of Esc10,000, 5000, 1000, 500, 100 and 50. The Esc1000 note is known as a *conto*. Coins are in denominations of Esc100, 50, 20, 10, 5 , 2.5 and 1, and 50 centavos.
Currency exchange: Many UK banks offer differing exchange rates depending on the denominations of Portuguese currency being bought or sold. Check with banks for details and current rates.
Credit cards: Visa, American Express and Access/Mastercard are widely accepted. Check with your credit card company for details of merchant acceptability and other services which may be available.
Travellers cheques: Readily exchanged. *Eurocheques* may be used at many banks in conjunction with appropriate encashment cards.
Exchange rate indicators: The following figures are included as a guide to the movements of the Escudo against Sterling and the US Dollar:

Date:	**Oct '89**	**Oct '90**	**Oct '91**	**Oct '92**
£1.00=	**257.20**	**259.60**	**250.50**	**217.70**
$1.00=	**158.96**	**137.39**	**144.34**	**137.18**

Currency restrictions: There import of local or foreign currency in cash or travellers cheques is unlimited. The personal export allowance is Esc100,000 cash or (local) travellers cheques, or the equivalent of Esc1,000,000 in foreign currency. This limit may be exceeded on presentation of proof that the same or a larger amount was imported. There is no limit on the movement of credit cards, cheques, or travellers cheques issued outside Portugal in the name of the visitor. The export of gold, silver, jewellery and other valuables is limited to a value of Esc30,000 and subject to special conditions. For details contact the Embassy, see top of entry for addresses.
Banking hours: Generally, 0830-1500 Monday to Friday. Certain banks in Lisbon are open 1800-2300 Monday to Friday. In the Algarve, the bank in the Vilamoura Marina Shopping Centre is open daily from 0900-2100.

DUTY FREE

The following goods may be imported into Portugal by visitors over 17 years of age from non-EC countries without incurring customs duty or Government tax:
200 cigarettes or 100 cigarillos or 50 cigars or 250g of tobacco;
1 litre of spirits over 22% or 2 litres of spirits up to 22%;
2 litres of wine;
50g of perfume and 250ml of toilet water;
500g of coffee or 200g of coffee extract;
100g of tea or 40g of tea extract;
Further goods up to Esc7500.
Visitors over 17 years of age from EC countries may import goods in the following quantities without incurring

customs duty or Government tax:
300 cigarettes or 150 cigarillos or 75 cigars or 400g of tobacco;
1.5 litres of spirits over 22 % or 3 litres of spirits up to 22%;
5 litres of wine;
75g of perfume and 375ml of toilet water;
1kg of coffee or 400g of coffee extract;
200g of tea or 80g of tea extract;
Further goods up to Esc60,000.
Visitors over 17 years of age arriving from EC countries with duty-paid goods (as of January 1993):
800 cigarettes and 400 cigarillos and 200 cigars and 1kg of tobacco;
90 litres of wine (including up to 60 litres of sparkling wine);
10 litres of spirits;
20 litres of intermediate products (such as fortified wine);
110 litres of beer.

PUBLIC HOLIDAYS

Public holidays observed in Portugal are as follows: **Apr 9 '93** Good Friday. **Apr 25** National Day. **May 1** Labour Day. **Jun 10** Portugal Day and Corpus Christi. **Aug 15** Assumption. **Oct 5** Republic Day. **Nov 1** All Saints' Day. **Dec 1** Independence Day. **Dec 8** Immaculate Conception. **Dec 25-26** Christmas. **Jan 1 '94** New Year's Day. **Feb 15** Shrove Tuesday.
Note: The Tourist Office brochure *Portugal – Fairs, Festivals and Folk Pilgrimages* gives details of local holidays.

HEALTH

Regulations and requirements may be subject to change at short notice, and you are advised to contact your doctor well in advance of your intended date of departure. Any numbers in the chart refer to the footnotes below.

	Special Precautions?	Certificate Required?
Yellow Fever	No	1
Cholera	No	No
Typhoid & Polio	No	-
Malaria	No	-
Food & Drink	2	-

[1]: A yellow fever vaccination certificate is required from travellers over one year of age arriving in or destined for the Azores or Madeira if coming from infected areas. No certificate is, however, required from transit passengers at Funchal, Porto Santo and Santa Maria.
[2]: Mains water is normally chlorinated, and whilst relatively safe may cause mild abdominal upsets. Bottled water is available and is advised for the first few weeks of the stay. Drinking water outside main cities and towns may be contaminated and sterilisation is advisable. Milk is pasteurised and dairy products are safe for consumption. Local meat, poultry, seafood, fruit and vegetables are generally considered safe to eat.
Health care: There are Reciprocal Health Agreements with most European countries. The agreement with the UK allows free in-patient treatment in general wards of official hospitals to those presenting UK passports (other EC nationals must present form E111). Other medical treatment, all dental treatment and prescribed medicines must be paid for. This Agreement is also effective in Madeira and the Azores. Those wishing to take advantage of it should inform the doctor prior to treatment that they wish to be treated under EC social security arrangements. Medical fees paid whilst in Portugal cannot be reimbursed by the British NHS.

TRAVEL - International

AIR: Portugal's national airline is *TAP Air Portugal (TP)*.
Approximate flight times: From Lisbon to *London* is 2 hours 30 minutes and to *New York* is 8 hours.
International airports: *Lisbon (LIS)* (Portela de Sacavem), 7km (4.5 miles) north of the city (travel time – 30 minutes). Taxi and bus services are available to Lisbon. Greenline Bus, nos 44, 45 and 83, runs every 10 minutes from 0530-0100 to the city centre and main railway station. Taxi services to the city are available, with surcharge after 2200. Airport facilities include 24-hour bureau de change, tourist information (0600-0200), duty-free shops (0700-0130) and car rental (*Avis, Eurodollar, Inter-Rent* and *Hertz*).
Faro (FAO), 4km (3 miles) west of the city (travel time – 25 minutes). Bus nos 17 and 18 go to the city; taxis available.
Oporto (OPO) (Oporto Sá Carneiro), 11km (about 6.8

PORTUGAL	HEALTH REGULATIONS	VISA REGULATIONS Code-Link
GALILEO/WORLDSPAN	TI-DFT/LIS/HE	TI-DFT/LIS/VI
SABRE	TIDFT/LIS/HE	TIDFT/LIS/VI

To access this information on your CRS, swipe the barcode with a light pen or type in the text under the barcode. For more information, see the introduction *How to Use This Book*.

miles) from the city. Taxis to the city are available.
Lisbon, Faro and *Oporto* airports all have the following airport facilities: outgoing duty-free shop; bank/exchange (open normal banking hours); car hire, including *Hertz, Avis, Europcar* (in Lisbon only) and *Inter-Rent*; and a restaurant/bar.
SEA: The principal ports for international passengers are Lisbon, Leixões (Oporto), Funchal (Madeira) and Portimao (Algarve), served by *P&O, Union Castle, Olympia, Linea C, Cunard* and *Italia*. For details contact shipping lines.
RAIL: There is a daily service between London, Paris and Lisbon, taking approximately 26 hours. The 'Sud-Express' runs between Paris and Lisbon, offering first- and second-class seats, sleepers and a restaurant car.
ROAD: The only land border is shared with Spain, and there are seven frontier posts in the north and six on the western and southern border. Border posts are usually open 0700-2400, but close earlier in winter. Ferries from the UK (Plymouth) to Santander in northern Spain obviate the need to drive through France. Cars can be imported for up to six months. See below for information on **documentation** and **regulations**.

TRAVEL - Internal

AIR: *Air Portugal (TP), LAR, Portugalia* and *Airsul* run services between Lisbon, Faro, Madeira, Porto Santo, Oporto and the Azores. The airline for the Azores is *SATA (Sociedade Acoriana de Transportes Aereos) (SP)*, which operates between the various islands. Charter flights are also available.
SEA/RIVER: Internal transport is available from all coastal ports and along the major rivers. For details contact local ports.
RAIL: *Portuguese Railways (CP)* provide a rail service to every town. The tourist areas of Cascais and Sintra are connected to Lisbon by frequent express trains.
Cheap fares: On 'Blue Days', usually Monday afternoon to Thursday, special rates are available. There are also special fares (with 20-30% reductions) for groups of ten or more *(Bilhete de Grupo)*, minimum distance 75km (single journey) and 150km (return journey). Application should be made four days in advance by the group leader. Tourist Tickets (*Bilhete Turisticos*) for 7, 14 or 21 days of unlimited travel are also available. The Rail Cheque *(Cheque Trem)*, obtainable in four different values, can be in one name or a company's name and has no time limit; it gives a reduction of 15% and can be used both for purchasing tickets and many other railway services.
An International Youth Ticket *(BIJ)* entitles those aged between 12 and 26 to a discount subject to certain conditions in 24 countries including Portugal.
A Senior Citizen Card *(Cartão Dourado)* is issued free of charge on production of proof of age, to those over 65 years of age. Entitles holder to 50% reduction on all but suburban trains between 0630-0930 and 1700-2000 except Saturdays, Sundays and holidays.
Family Card, Inter-Rail Card, Rail Inclusive Tours and *Special Tourist Trips* are amongst other offers from *Portuguese Railways*, Caminhos de Ferro Portugueses, Santa Apólonia, Lisbon 1200. Tel: (1) 876 025 *or* 877 092. Telex: 15813 MARPOL P (reservations). Rail information is also available from the National Tourist Office.
ROAD: Every town and village can be reached by an adequate system of roads. Petrol stations are open between 0700 and 2400. Circulation on motorways is subject to a toll according to distance covered and type of vehicle. A small tax may be added to petrol bought with a credit card. **Taxi:** Charges are according to distance and they are all metered. **Car hire:** Available from main towns and airports, with or without driver.
Regulations: Minimum age for driving is 18. Cars may be imported for up to six months. All traffic drives on the right. Traffic signs are international. Headlights should be dipped in built-up areas and side lights used when parking in badly-lit areas. Children should not travel in the front seat. Seat belts should be worn. Warning triangles are compulsory. It is forbidden to carry cans of petrol in vehicles. Speed limits are 60kmph (37mph) in built-up areas, 90kmph (56mph) outside built-up areas and 120kmph (70mph) on motorways. Visitors who have passed their driving test for less than one year must display a yellow disc with '90' on it on the rear of their vehicle and must not go faster than 90kmph (56mph) (or lower where appropriate). Permitted speeds will vary if trailers are being used. **Documentation:** International Driving Permits or foreign driving licences are accepted. Third Party insurance is compulsory and a Green Card must be obtained. A Carnet de Passage is needed for a van.
JOURNEY TIMES: The following chart gives approximate journey times (in hours and minutes) from Lisbon to other major cities/towns in Portugal.

	Air	Road	Rail
Faro	0.35	4.00	5.00
Oporto	0.45	5.00	3.00
Funchal	1.30	-	-

ACCOMMODATION

There is a wide range of accommodation available all over the country, ranging from luxury hotels, pensions, boarding houses and inns to simple guest-houses, manor houses, campsites and youth hostels. The government-run *pousadas* offer very good value and are often situated in places of scenic beauty in converted castles, palaces or old inns (see below).
HOTELS: Most hotels have a private swimming pool and serve international cuisine as well as some typically Portuguese dishes. During the low season, hotels normally grant substantial reductions. There should be an officially authorised list of prices displayed in every bedroom, and children under eight years of age are entitled to a reduction of 50% on the price of full meals and 50% on the price of an extra bed – if sharing parents' room or apartment. Further information can be obtained from the Associação dos Hoteis de Portugal, Avenida 5 de Outubro 176 – 5 Esq, 1000 Lisbon. Tel: (1) 793 1141 Telex: 62149HP. **Grading:** Classification of hotels is according to the international **1-** to **5-star** system and their prices are officially approved. Apartment hotels are classified from 2- to 4-star, motels from 2- to 3-star and boarding houses from 1- to 4-star; there are also 4-star *albergarias*.
POUSADAS: The *pousadas* are a network of inns operated by the Government, and housed in historic buildings, castles, palaces and convents, or sometimes built especially for the purpose. They have often been geographically sited in regions not on the usual tourist itinerary to give people the opportunity to visit the whole country. The architecture and design of the pousadas has been carefully studied in order to give visitors a better knowledge of the cultural traditions of the various regions of the country, with particular attention paid to handicrafts, cuisine and wines. A guide to pousadas can be obtained from the National Tourist Office.
PRIVATE HOUSES: Rooms are available in private houses and on farms all over Portugal. Some of the old manor houses are now open to receive visitors and

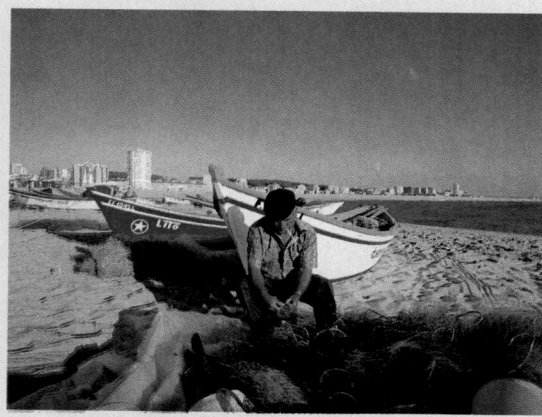

provide good opportunities for the tourist to make contact with Portuguese customs and people. For further information contact the National Tourist Office or local travel agents.

SELF-CATERING: There is self-catering tourist accommodation in deluxe, first- and second-class tourist villages and tourist apartments, particularly on the Algarve. Tour operators can arrange a wide variety of villas for self-catering parties.

YOUTH HOSTELS: Youth hostels are located to give young people the opportunity of visiting towns, countryside, mountains and coastal areas. Tourists from 14-40 years of age can obtain accommodation and meals, but must apply to the *Associação Portuguesa de Pousadas de Juventude* (Portuguese Youth Hostels Association), R Andrade Corvo 46, Lisbon. Tel: (1) 571 014. Fax: (1) 532 696.

CAMPING/CARAVANNING: Portugal provides camping and caravan parks near beaches and in thickly wooded areas. Some have model installations including swimming pools, games fields, supermarkets and restaurants. A guide published by the Directorate-General gives the names of existing parks and details of their classification, equipment and capacity. For further information contact Federacao Portuguesa de Campismo, Rua Voz do Operario, 1-r/c Esq, 1100 Lisbon. Tel: (1) 886 2350.

RESORTS & EXCURSIONS

There are six major tourist regions in Portugal. These are, from north to south: the coastal regions of the Costa Verde, the Costa de Prata, the Costa de Lisboa (including the Costa do Estoril, Costa Azul, Costa Dourada and the Algarve) and, inland, the Montanhas and the agricultural region of the Planícies.

Costa Verde

The Costa Verde is the region occupying the northwest corner of Portugal, starting at the northern border with Spain and stretching south of Oporto and as far east as Vila Real. It encompasses the rivers *Minho*, *Lima* and *Douro* together with the *Peneda-Gerês National Park*. The area has much to offer to the visitor – there are long beaches flanked by pinewoods as well as handicrafts, local cuisine and vinho verde, history and ancient monuments, amusements, casinos, rivers and fishing. The towns and villages of the region all have shrines and churches erected in thanksgiving for some special benefit or to mark a noteworthy occasion. Some places have become somewhat 'touristy', but along the coast and in the countryside such places are few and far between. The vicinity of Oporto is the home of the famous Port wine, and is developed to provide facilities for tourists. There are also natural spas in this area. Away from the main centres, the Costa Verde is an ideal place for those who want to see behind the usual holiday façade of a country and get to know the people and their way of life. The coastal area is well covered by maritime pine forests, giving it its distinctive emerald look. Wide golden beaches are to be found in many of the resorts between Espinho and the mouth of the Minho River. There are excursions away from the beaches through the Minho and Douro Valley, home of vinho verde 'green wine'. There is always something going on, whatever the time of year, including village fairs and religious processions and, in early autumn, wine harvests.

Oporto is the second-largest city in Portugal and the major town in Costa Verde. Oporto prospered under the Romans and was the birthplace of Prince Henry the Navigator, a driving force behind the great maritime discoveries of the 15th and 16th centuries. A trading agreement with England in 1703 heralded the wealth of the town and the birth of the famous Port wine trade. At the wine lodges in the area, visitors are always welcome to sample all types of Port.

Póvoa de Varzim, north of Porto, is an elegant sea resort. Here traditional industries such as fisheries and silversmiths exist next to thriving tourist institutions. In fact the city can be divided into two: the north encompasses 7km (4 miles) of sandy beaches and sporting facilities. Visitors can admires the large sloops moored at the man-made marina beside the casino.

Other towns of interest in the area include: **Espinho**, a modern beach resort; **Vila do Conde**, a quiet fishing resort famous for its traditional crafts such as 'bone lace', chocolate-making and fishing boats; **Ofir**, a vast expanse of sandy beach fringed by pinewoods; **Barcelos**, famous for its handicrafts, particularly ceramics; **Viana do Castelo**, a fortress town noted for Renaissance and Manueline architecture and local products such as ceramics, embroidery, jewellery and filigree; **Valenca**, a 13th-century border town; **Monção**, home of Alvarinho vinho verde; **Braga**, which has a 12th-century cathedral; **Peneda-Gerês National Park**, 170,000 acres of mountain countryside and wild life; and **Guimaraes**, the first medieval capital. There are *spas* at Caldelas, Gerez, Vizela and Moncao.

Resorts in the area include: Aboinha, Afife, Alem do Rio, Amarante, Arcos de Valdevez, Aver-o-Mar, Baião, Barcelos, Bom Jesus do Monte, Braga, Caldas de Canavezes, Caldas das Taipas, Caldas de Vizela, Caldelas, Canicada, Castro de Laboreiro, Entre-os-Rios, Ermesinde, Espinho, Esposende, Fafe, Felgueiras, Gerez, Granja, Guardeiras, Guimaraes, Gulpilhares, Leça do Bailio, Leça da Palmeira, Lousada, Marco de Canavezes, Matosinhos, Melgaco, Moledo do Minho, Monaco, Monte Faro, Monte de São Felix, Novelas, Ofir, Pacos de Ferreira, Paredes, Penha, Ponte da Barca, Ponte de Lima, Porto, Póvoa de Varzim, Praia de Miramar, Riba de Ave, Rio Caldo, Santa Marta, Santo Tirso, São Bento de Porta Aberta, São Martinho do Campo, São Tiago, São Vicente, Seixas, Serra do Marão, Terras do Bouro, Torre, Valenca, Valongo, Viana do Castelo, Vieira do Minho, Vila do Conde, Vila Nova de Cerveira, Vila Nova de Famalicao and Vila Praia de Âncora.

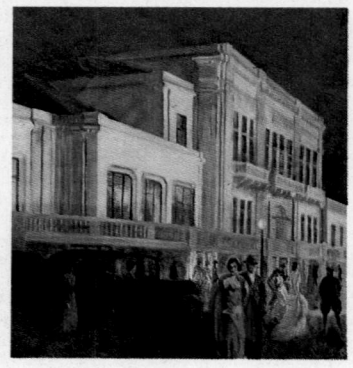

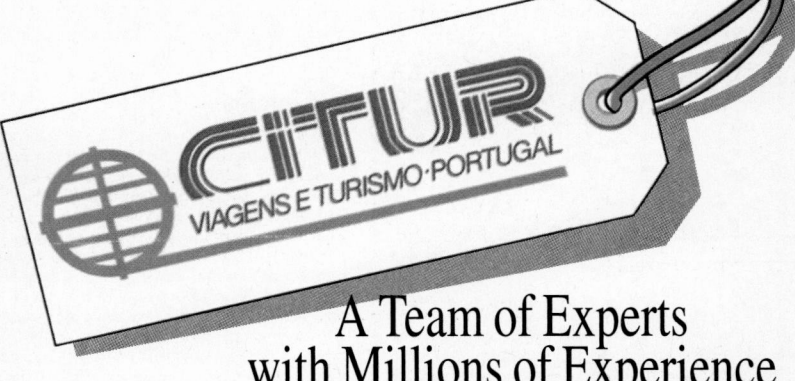

Costa de Prata

The Costa de Prata forms a long narrow strip which stretches along the coastline between the south of the Costa Verde and the north of the Costa de Lisboa regions. In the north is Espinho, and in the south, Ericeira. The region embraces Coimbra, the shrine of Fatima, and the caves of Santo Antonio and Alvados. Here there are long beaches, pinewoods, picturesque fishing boats and the Berlengas Islands, with plentiful sea fishing. There are spas at Luso and Curia and a casino at Figueira da Foz. Like the Costa Verde, this region has its fair share of monuments, temples, castles, palaces, monasteries and museums and it also boasts modern tourist resorts with good beaches. All this makes the area popular with sightseers the whole year round.

Coimbra is Portugal's third-largest city. It is an ancient university town, famous for its twisting streets, terraced houses and a particular style of *Fado*, the melancholy but moving music which is distinctive to the Portuguese. Worth visiting are the 12th-century *Sé Cathedral*, the *Art Museum* housed in a former Bishop's Palace, the *Church* and *Monastery* of the *Holy Cross*, and the *University*, one of the oldest in Europe.

Other towns of interest in the area include: **Aveiro**, the 'Venice of Portugal', surrounded by salt flats, beaches and lagoons and dominated by the central canal; **Torreira**, a typical fishing village between ocean and lagoon which can be reached by boat from Aveiro; **Anadia**, the centre of the wine-growing region of Bairrada with visits to wine cellars; **Conimbriga**, where fine Roman remains dating from AD1 can be seen; **Bussaco**, famous for its National Park founded by Carmelite friars, and for its 'enchanted forest'; **Figueira da Foz,** a modern resort with a fine beach and a casino; **Pinhal do Rei**, a beautiful pine forest; **Fatima**, centre for pilgrimages celebrating the appearance of the Virgin Mary there in 1917 (special ceremonies take place here on the 13th of each month between May and October); **Batalha**, where the *Battle Abbey* (more properly the Mosteiro de Santa Maria) commemorates the 1386 signing of the alliance between England and Portugal (the oldest alliance in Europe); the caves of **Santo António e Alvados**; the fishing village of **Nazare**; **Alcobaca**, a quiet town with narrow streets and open-air market; and **Obidos**, a medieval walled town. An annual fair takes place at the end of March at **Leiria**, a quiet country town situated between Lisbon and Oporto and dominated by a 12th-century castle built on a plateau high above the town. There are *spas* at **Caldas da Rainha**, **Curia, Luso, Vimeiro** and **Cucos**.

Resorts in the area include: Agueda, Albergaria-a-Velha, Alcobaca, Aljubarrota, Anadia, Arouca, Aveiro, Avelar, Batalha, Bombarral, Buarcos, Bussaco, Cacia, Caldas da Rainha, Caldas de São Jorge, Cantanhede, Coimbra, Cucos, Curia, Esmoriz-Barrinhas, Estarreja, Fatima, Fermentelos, Figueira de Foz, Figueiro dos Vinhos, Forte da Barra, Foz do Arelho, Ilhavo, Leiria, Luso, Marinha Grande, Mealhada, Minde, Mira de Aire, Monte Real, Murtosa, Nazare, Obidos, Oliveira de Azeméis, Oliveira do Bairro, Peniche, Piedade, Pombal, Porto de Barcas, Praia da Areia Branca, Praia da Barra, Praia do Furadouro, Praia de Mira, Praia de Pedrogao, Praia do Porto Novo, Praia de Santa Cruz, Sangalhos, Santa Luzia, São Joao da Madeira, São Martinho do Porto, São Pedro de Muel, Seixal da Lourinha, Serém, Sever do Vouga, Sobrado de Paiva, Torres Vedras, Torreira, Vale de Cambra, Vale Gracioso, Vale do Grou, Vale da Mó, Vieira de Leiria, Vila Nova de Ourem and Vimeiro.

Montanhas

The mountainous region in the northeast of Portugal is an unspoiled area of rugged countryside with castles perched on hilltops, forests, rivers and spas. There are vineyards, old mansions, mountain climbing and walks, and trout fishing.

Resorts in the area include: Alfândega da Fé, Alijo, Alpedrinha, Alto do Caçador, Arganil, Armamar, Belmonte, Braganca, Caldas de Alcafache, Caldas de Aregos, Caldas da Cavaca, Caldas da Felgueira, Caldas de São Gemil, Caramulo, Carvalhelhos, Castelo Branco, Castro de Aire, Catraia de São Romao, Celorico da Beira, Cernache do Bonjardim, Chaves, Cinfães, Coja, Covilhã, Escalhão, Figueira de Castelo Rodrigo, Fornos de Algodres, Fundão, Gândara de Espariz, Gouveia, Guarda, Lamego, Lousa, Luga do Torrao, Macedo de Cavaleiros, Mangualde, Manteigas, Miranda do Douro, Mirandela, Mogadouro, Moimenta da Beira, Monfortinho, Nelas, Oliveira de Frades, Oliveira do Hospital Orvalho, Pedras Salgadas, Penacova, Penhas da Saude, Peso da Regua, Pinhao, Pinheiro de Lafoes, Pinhel, Povoa das Quartas, Resende, Rio Torto, Sabagal, São Joao de Pesqueira, São Pedro do Sul, Seia, Serra da Estrela, Serta, Torre de Moncorvo, Urgeirica, Vidago, Vila Flor, Vila Nova de Poiares, Vila Real, Vilar Formoso, Vimioso, Vinhais, Viseu and Vouzela.

Costa de Lisboa

This area comprises Lisbon, the Estoril coast, Costa Azul, and the Costa Dourada to the south. Lisbon, the capital of Portugal, lies on seven low hills at the estuary of the River Tagus (Tejo), six miles from the Atlantic Ocean on the west coast, with the Algarve to the south and Costa de Prata and Costa Verde to the north. The Estoril coast runs along the mouth of the Tagus Estuary on to the Atlantic as far as Ericeira. Here there are long

LISBON

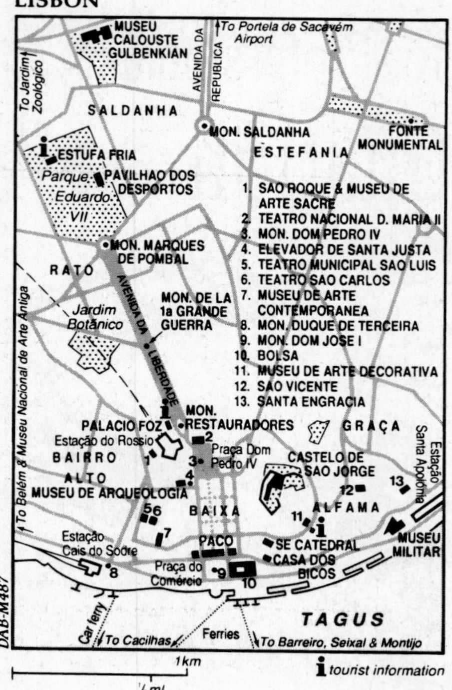

Atlantic beaches, pleasant countryside, castles, palaces and parks around Lisbon and also the international life of the Costa de Estoril, where there is a casino, varied nightlife, restaurants, watersports, golf, shopping and riding. There are water meadows, bulls and local cooking at Vila Franca and also the fishing town of Sesimbra and Troia sands. The Costa Dourada is less well-known, with wild beaches and soft sand.

Lisbon is a lively, international city possessing a distinctive character and charm and a population of one and a half million people. In the centre of the city is the medieval Castle of São Jorge, which stands with its ten towers on the hill where the original colony was situated in Phoenician times. Nearby is Alfama, the old Moorish quarter, which has narrow winding streets and white-washed houses, and the Bairro Alto, centre of *Fado* (the traditional folksongs of Lisbon).

Nearby is **Belem**, from where the ships of Vasco da Gama, Alvares Cabral and other famous explorers were launched; the town has a famous tower and the *Hieronymite Monastery*. Other points of interest include the 12th-century *Lisbon Cathedral*, the *Coach Museum*, the *Gulbenkian Museum*, the 2.5km (1.5 mile) long suspension bridge over the Tagus, and the beautiful *azulejos*, the traditional blue and white tiles which adorn so many of the city's churches.

The beach resorts of **Estoril** and **Cascais** are a few miles away from the capital. The former, once the exclusive preserve of the permanently or temporarily rich, is adjusting well to the demands of tourism and is maintaining the high standards of its hotels, which fringe the glorious *Tamariz Beach*, while making them more accessible to the 2-week holidaymaker. Cascais has changed even more quickly, from a small fishing village with good but empty beaches to a lively resort with bars, nightclubs and cheap, high-quality restaurants.

Other towns in the area include: **Sintra**, a town in the mountains 25km (15 miles) from Lisbon, with a summer palace, the Monserrate gardens and twice-monthly antique market; **Colares**, a small village famous for its red wines; **Queluz**, with the 18th-century pink rococo palace; **Mafra**, home of the Baroque monastery built in 1717; **Ericeira**, a small fishing village; **Sesimbra**, a busy fishing village with good beaches and brightly painted boats, famous for its seafood and an old Moorish castle overlooking the village; **Troia**, a modern tourist complex on a peninsula parallel to the town of Setubal with good beaches, hotels, restaurants, supermarket, swimming pools, nightclubs, golf course and nautical sports centre; **Setubal**, 39km (24 miles) south of Lisbon; and the village of **Palmela**, with its 12th-century castle and old monastery (which is now a *pousada* – see *Accommodation* above).

Resorts in the area include: Lisbon, Caparica, Palmela, Azeitao, Arrabida, Setubal, Troia, Sesimbra, Carcavelos, Estoril, Cascais, Guincho, Colares, Sintra, São Pedro de Sintra, Queluz, Ericeira, Praia das Macas, Praia Grande and Parede.

Planícies

This large inland area includes the regions of the Cova da Beira, Ribatejo and Alentejo, Monsarraz, Marvao, Moura, Monsanto. Throughout the area there are many typical Portuguese villages set in rich arable landscape. The Planícies is the country's granary, and also the source of much of its cork. Attractions include shooting and reservoir fishing, a wealth of local folklore which finds expression in the countless local festivals, and easy access to the Costa Dourada with the quiet beaches of Alentejo. The area is known for its local cuisine, particularly seafood, and its handicrafts.

Resorts in the area include: Abrantes, Alcacer do Sal, Alter do Chao, Beja, Benavente, Campo Maior, Castanheira, Castelo de Bode, Castelo de Vide, Caxarias, Charneca do Infantado, Coruche, Elvas, Entroncamento, Estremoz, Evora, Ferreira do Alentejo, Ferreira do Zezere, Grandola, Ilha do Lombo, Lagoa de Santo Andre, Marvao, Minde, Monsaraz, Monte das Flores, Montemor-o-Novo, Moura Ponte do Sor, Portalegre, Rio Maior, Rossio ao Sul do Tejo, Santa Clara-a-Velha, Santarem, Santiago do Cacem, Serpa, Sines, Tomar, Torrao, Torres Novas, Vila Nova da Barquinha, Costa Dourada from Troia to Algarve; Sines and Vila Nove de Milfontes.

The Algarve

The Algarve is located in the far south of Portugal, bordered by the Atlantic on two sides, by the mountains in the north and Spain in the east. It stretches from the Spanish border westwards to Cape St Vincent. Here there are over 250km (150 miles) of beaches, long and curving with little sandy coves hidden between varying coloured cliffs. The area has an international atmosphere with big hotels, casinos, amusements and sports facilities. There are also family-style tourist villages and camping. The hotels are up to the usual high Portuguese standards, as are the rapidly expanding villa and apartment complexes. The location of the region on the Atlantic coast makes it hardly surprising that fishing has played a major part in the region's way of life, and one of the sights worth travelling many miles to see is the lantern-lit fleet of fishing smacks leaving their berths at night. There are 14 good 18-hole golf courses. Indeed the Algarve offers excellent facilities for all types of sports, including tennis, squash, shooting, riding and every watersport under the sun.

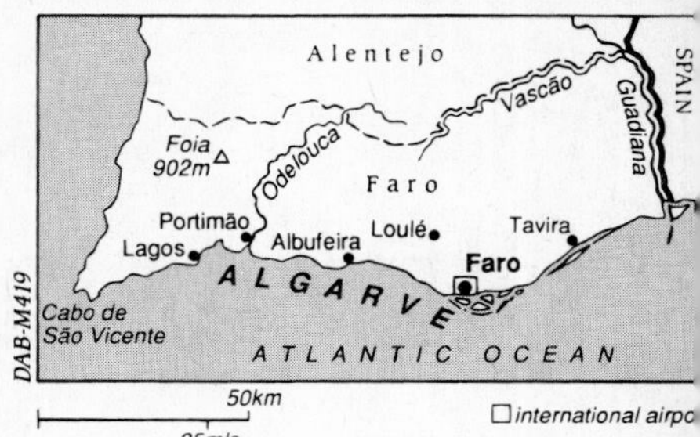

Faro, the capital of the Algarve, was destroyed by an earthquake in 1755, and only part of the old town remains. **Loulé** is a market town famous for crafts such as leather and copper. **Albufeira** is a busy market town with a Moorish atmosphere. **Armação de Pêra** is a fishing village with one of the biggest beaches on the Algarve. **Silves** is an old walled city with a 12th-century cathedral. **Carvoeiro** is an old fishing village with a picturesque harbour. **Portimao** is one of the largest towns and fishing ports in the Algarve, known for its furniture and wickerwork. **Monchique** is set high in the mountains and has a spa. **Lagos** has historical shipyards. **Sagres** is the centre of the lobster fishing industry, with a 17th-century fortress. **Cape St Vincent** is the most southwesterly point of mainland Europe.

Resorts in the area include: Albufeira, Armação de Pêra, Lagos, Portimao, Praia da Rocha, Silves, Tavira, Vila Real de Santo Antonio, Olhao, Quarteira, Carvoeiro Loule, Sagres, Vilamoura, Monte Gordo, S. Bras de Alportel, Aljezur and Monchique.

SOCIAL PROFILE

FOOD & DRINK: Seafood is popular, especially in Lisbon, but can be expensive. Soup is a main dish. Typical Portuguese dishes include *sopa de marisco* (shellfish soup cooked and served with wine), *caldo verde* (green soup), made with finely shredded green kale leaves in broth, and *bacalhau*, dried cod, cooked in over 100 different ways. *Caldeirada* is a fish stew with as many as nine kinds of fish, cooked with onions and tomatoes. Also typical is *carne de porco a Alentejana*, in which bits of fried pork are covered with a sauce of clams stewed with tomato and onions. Puddings include *arroz doce* (rice pudding), Madeira pudding and *nuvens* (egg custard). Carrot jam is worth a try – the Portuguese taste for it caused the EC to define the carrot as a fruit. Table service is normal. **Drink:** Portuguese table wines are good value. The most popular regional names are *Dao* and *Serradayres* for red wines and *Bucelas* and *Colares* for white wines. Sparkling rosé wines are mostly produced for export. *Mateus Rosé* is a famous lightweight rosé. Portuguese brandies are also good; the best are produced around Oporto where Port wines come from. There are no licensing hours.

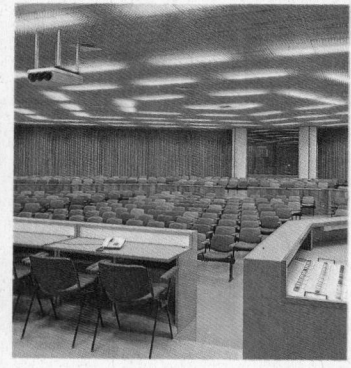

NIGHTLIFE: The large towns offer every kind of entertainment. There are many nightclubs, theatres, cinemas, stage shows, folk dancing and music performances. Besides these international amusements, Portugal offers bullfights on horseback. The traditional *Fado* can be heard in many restaurants and performances begin at about 2200. The theatre season is from October to May. Gambling is authorised and Estoril, Figueira da Foz, Espinho, Alvor, Vilamoura and Monte Gordo have casinos. The elegant Casino Monumental in Póvoa de Varzim is the most renowned.

SHOPPING: There is a wide variety of souvenirs and gifts available, whether one visits the sophisticated markets and shops of the bigger cities or the more traditional rural areas. Items include leather goods, copper, ceramics, handcrafted silver and gold, embroidery and tapestry, woodcarving, cork products, porcelain and china, crystal and glassware. **Shopping hours:** Generally 0900-1300 and 1500-1900 Monday to Friday, Saturdays 0900-1300 (December also 1500-1900). Shopping centres are usually open 1000-2400 Monday to Sunday.

SPORT: The National Tourist Office has brochures listing the hotels and centres which offer amenities for a wide range of sports. **Golf:** There are championship golf courses in most major centres where visitors can arrange to play. **Tennis:** Most resorts and cities have tennis courts available. **Horseriding:** Horses and instruction are available in many resorts. **Watersports:** Skindiving, swimming, offshore fishing, deep-sea fishing, water-skiing, sailing and windsurfing are popular. The Algarve offers watersports all year round, although the tides can be strong in the winter. **Spectator sports:** The Portugal Golf and Portugal Tennis Opens. **Other sports:** These include **clay pigeon shooting** and **squash**.

SPECIAL EVENTS: June is one of the best months for festivals in Portugal, and the festivals of St Anthony, St John and St Peter, held in Lisbon, are central events. Also of note are the *Gulbenkian Festival of Music* in winter, the *Santiago Fair* in Setubal, the *Wine Harvest Festival* at Palmela in September, the *Algarve Song* and *Dance Festival* in September and the world-famous *Our Lady of Fatima* pilgrimages during May and October. There are many other religious and *Lady Saint* festivals. There are carnivals throughout the country in the days leading up to Shrove Tuesday.

For a full list of local festivals contact the National Tourist Office.

SOCIAL CONVENTIONS: The Portuguese way of life is leisurely, and old-fashioned politeness is essential. Warm, Latin, Southern European hospitality is the norm. The country has a deeply individual national character, although each province has its own traditions and folklore. Casual wear is widely acceptable, although beachwear should not be worn in towns. The Portuguese are in general heavy smokers. In restaurants it is usual to smoke only at the end of the meal. Smoking is prohibited in cinemas, theatres and on buses. **Tipping:** Generally 10-15%. Taxi drivers are tipped 10%.

BUSINESS PROFILE

ECONOMY: Portugal has a traditionally agrarian economy that has industrialised extensively in recent years. Agriculture still employs over 25% of the workforce, producing wheat, maize, tomatoes, potatoes and grapes. Production has undergone a relative decline so that Portugal now imports a sizeable proportion of its foodstuffs after having long been self-sufficient. The manufacturing sector is dominated by the textile industry, in which there has been major investment, and both it and the footwear industry are vital export earners. Other significant products are paper, cork and other wood products, electrical appliances, chemicals and ceramics. Portugal has grown rapidly since joining the European Community in 1986. Both foreign and internal investment have been high and the country's infrastructure has been extensively modernised. There remain problems: at 12%, inflation is high by EC standards; the large agricultural sector remains very inefficient; and the disparity between the relatively prosperous north and the poorer south continues. Although Britain has historically been Portugal's main trading partner, the growth of bilateral trade has failed to keep pace with that of Portugal's other trading partners, particularly Germany, France, Spain and Italy.

BUSINESS: Business people are expected to dress smartly and formal attire is expected in some dining rooms and for important social functions. English is widely spoken in business circles, although when visiting a small family business it is best to check. Visiting cards are generally only exchanged by more senior members of a company. July and August are best avoided. **Office hours:** 0900-1300 and 1500-1900 Monday to Friday.

COMMERCIAL INFORMATION: The following organisations can offer advice: Associação Comercial de Lisboa, Rua das Portas de Santo Antão 89, 1194 Lisbon. Tel: (1) 342 7179. Fax: (1) 342 4304. Telex: 13441; *or* Confederação do Comércio Português (CCP), Rua dos Correeiros 79, 1° andar, 1100 Lisbon. Tel: (1) 347 7430. Fax: (1) 347 8638. Telex: 14829.

CONFERENCES/CONVENTIONS: Lisbon is the main centre for conventions, with venues that can seat up to 1500 persons: in 1987 the Lisbon Convention Bureau was founded and, in 1989, a major Congress Centre opened, fully integrated with the Lisbon International Fair's exhibition facilities. The Fair is a department of the Portuguese Industrial Association which promotes trade fairs, exhibitions and meetings. The Bureau is a nonprofit-making association of companies providing support services to conference organisers. Its *Services Directory* includes details of the Congress Centre and hotels with conference facilities. For information contact the: Lisbon Convention Bureau, Rua Jardim do Regedor 50, 1100 Lisbon. Tel: (1) 342 5527. Fax: (1) 346 3521. Telex: 14217 GICOL P.

HISTORY & GOVERNMENT

HISTORY: The part of Iberia which is now Portugal was occupied by the Moors until the 11th century, when Ferdinand of Leon and Castile reconquered much of the territory and established it as a province of Spain. Over the next 200 years, the remaining Moors were driven out and the boundaries of Portugal fixed. The Castilians were themselves expelled in 1385 after defeat at the hands of King João I at the Battle of Aljubarotta. From this point, the Portuguese went on to build a colonial empire in Africa, Latin America, India and the Far East. One of the most famous figures during this period was Prince Henry the Navigator, amongst whose acquisitions were the Azores (with Flemish Knights) and Madeira. One of the best-known visitors to Madeira was Christopher Columbus, who married a daughter of one of the island's governors and lived for some time on Porto Santo. The island survived a brief invasion by a French pirate in 1566, but in 1580, along with the rest of Portugal, came under Spanish domination. This arose from the recurring friction between the two kingdoms, particularly after the union of Aragon and Castile in the late 15th century. In the 16th century, with the Portuguese regime weakened by a struggle for the succession to the throne and the legacy of a disastrous 'crusade' against the Moors, Philip II of Spain (who had a claim to the Portuguese crown) invaded. Spanish rule lasted just 60 years until 1640, when the Portuguese launched a successful uprising and seceded from Spain. However, by the time they recovered their independence, the Portuguese had lost the bulk of their empire, including most of the valuable East Indies territories which had been snapped up by the Dutch. Portugal ceased to be a major player in the

European colonial scramble thereafter. The Braganza dynasty, which took power after the defeat of the Spanish, lasted until the mid-19th century, presiding over a weak economy and a largely feudal society. One of the princesses of the royal house, Catherine, married Charles II of England, confirming the friendly relations between the two countries which date back to the 14th century; this brought many advantages to English merchants in Portugal, and also on the island of Madeira where the treaty helped the rapid development of the trade in the island's wine which became popular in England. Portuguese political development lagged behind that of many European states during this period and it remained comparatively untouched by the Enlightenment until the emergence in the late 18th century of the Cardinal Richelieu-type Marquis de Pombal, who was both dictatorial yet enlightened (by the standards of the time) on matters of social reform. He did much to break the power of the landed aristocracy over the country. Occasional conflicts with the Spanish and French – sometimes in alliance – threatened the country's autonomy, but the Portuguese always managed to preserve their independence, often with the support of the British. The monarchy was finally overthrown in 1910 by republican forces, who particularly resented the strong influence of the Catholic Church on the regime. Portugal supported the Allied Powers during the First World War, but contributed little due to the presence of a strong pro-German element in the armed forces, which made several coup attempts. Finally, a right-wing dictatorship took power in 1926. Though military in composition, the key figure in the new regime was finance minister Antonio de Oliveira Salazar. Having addressed Portugal's chaotic financial situation, Salazar became President in 1932. Salazar was influenced by the populist fascism of Benito Mussolini in Italy and founded a party, the National Union, to prepare the way for an 'Estado Novo'. Despite its government's sympathies, Portugal, like Spain, stayed neutral during the Second World War. Salazar remained in power until 1968 without effecting any of the post-war reforms which had been forced upon or embraced by other European countries: the economy remained largely agricultural and under-industrialised, while the Portuguese colonies were subject to regimes more consistent with the conditions of the 19th and early 20th centuries. Salazar's eventual successor, Marcello Caetano, eased the restrictions on domestic political activity, but otherwise altered little. His downfall six years later was connected with the colonial policies inherited from his predecessor: specifically that Portugal's overseas possessions were an 'inalienable' part of the country. The strain of fighting several different nationalist movements simultaneously (see, for example, *World Travel Guide* entries on Angola, Mozambique, Guinea-Bissau and Indonesia) strained both army morale and the Government's finances. On April 25, 1974 (a date of great significance in Portugal), a group of radical army officers deposed Caetano in a bloodless coup. The African colonies were immediately abandoned: indeed, they were left with such haste that internal crises were almost inevitable. Portugal was governed for two years by a leftist military junta led by members of the Movimento das Forcas Armardas, the instigator of the revolution, while civilian politicians re-emerged and crystallised around the Socialist and Communist Parties and the right-wing Partido Popular Democratico. Under the constitution adopted in 1976, Portugal was nominally committed to a path of socialist development, but the country has since followed a standard Western European model of political pluralism. Portugal has been a member of NATO since its inception in 1949 and a member of the EC since 1986. The Government of Anibal Cavaco Silva which took office in 1987 concentrated on bridging the economic gap between Portugal and its richer fellow Community members. With average annual growth of around 5% in the last four years, the Government has been broadly successful on the economic front. This as much as anything else won Cavaco Silva's centre-right Partido Social Democrata (PSD, Social Democrats) a further endorsement from the electorate in October 1991. The PSD again won an overall majority, taking 130 of the 250 seats in the Assembly of the Republic. Cavaco Silva's second term of office is likely to prove more testing than the first. Key parts of the economy, particularly textiles and the inefficient agricultural sector, are vulnerable to competition. The Government has announced a controversial privatisation programme which aims to dispose of almost the entire state sector. Much of the proceeds will be needed, however, to hold the value of the Escudo within the the European Monetary System and keep the lid on inflation which persists in low double figures. Portugal held the European Community presidency in the first half of 1992, and is a relatively contented participant in the post-Maastricht integration process. Outside Europe, the Portuguese Foreign Ministry, co-operating closely with Italian diplomats, contributed substantially to the political settlement in Mozambique.

GOVERNMENT: Since 1982, when the Military Council of the Revolution was abolished, Portugal has been formally governed by an elected President, who is Head of State and appoints a Prime Minister and Council of Ministers. Legislation is handled by the unicameral 250-member Assembly which, like the President, is elected for a 5-year term. The Azores and Madeira (see below) are integral parts of the Portuguese republic, but since 1976 have had autonomous governments. Macau is governed by special statute (see separate entry).

CLIMATE

The northwest has mild winters with high levels of rainfall and fairly short summers. The northeast has longer winters and hot summers. In the south summers (March to October) are warm with very little rain except in early spring and autumn. High temperatures are moderated by a permanent breeze in Estoril (July to August).

Required clothing: Light to mediumweights and rainwear are advised.

LISBON Portugal (77m)

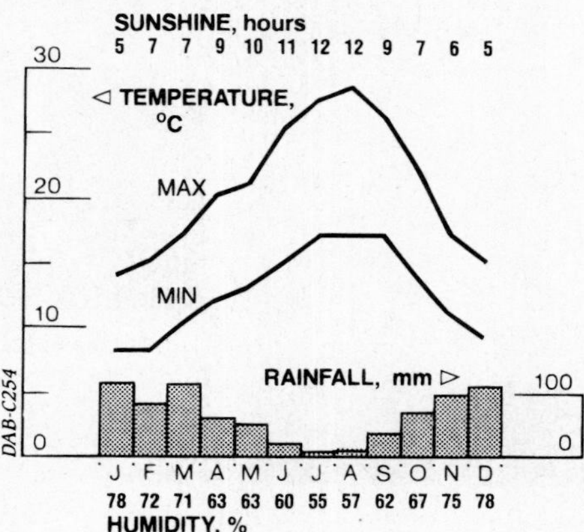

MADEIRA

Location: Atlantic Ocean, 535 nautical miles southwest of Lisbon.

AREA: 794 sq km (314 sq miles).
POPULATION: 275,000 (1989 estimate).
CAPITAL: Funchal. **Population:** 44,111 (1981).
GEOGRAPHY: The group comprises the main island of Madeira, the smaller island of Porto Santo and the three uninhabited islets of Ilheu Chao, Deserta Grande and Ilheu de Bugio. The islands are hilly and of volcanic origin and the coast of Madeira is steep and rocky with deep eroded lava gorges running down to the sea. These are particularly impressive on the north coast of Madeira island. The largest of a group of five islands formed by volcanic eruption, Madeira is in fact the summit of a mountain range rising 6.5km (4 miles) from the seabed. Its volcanic origins can be clearly seen in its mountainous interior and in the lava streams which break up the line of cliffs on its coast. At Cabo Girao, west of the capital of Funchal, is the second-highest cliff in the world. Inland, Pico Ruivo is the island's highest point (1862m/6109ft) with the slightly lower Pico de Arieiro (1810m/5940ft) nearby. Both are destinations for sightseeing tours, commanding fine views of the surrounding mountains. Madeira's volcanic origin means that it has no sandy beaches, although there is a small beach, Prainha, near the whaling village of Canical on the extreme east of the island. Madeira itself is 58km (36 miles) long and 23km (14 miles) wide. Porto Santo is much smaller, only 14km (9 miles) long and 5km (3 miles) wide, with a long, golden sandy beach, complementing Madeira.
TIME: GMT (GMT + 1 in summer).
ELECTRICITY: 220 volts AC, 50Hz. 2-pin round plugs are in use.
COMMUNICATIONS: Services are similar to those offered on the mainland.
BBC World Service and Voice of America frequencies: From time to time these change. See the section *How to Use this Book* for more information.

BBC:				
MHz	17.705	15.070	12.095	9.410
Voice of America:				
MHz	11.97	9.670	6.040	5.995

PASSPORT/VISA

The passport and visa requirements are the same as for visiting mainland Portugal, except that nationals of Malawi *do* need visas for visiting Madeira.

HEALTH

As for mainland Portugal; see above.

TRAVEL

AIR: The airline serving Madeira is *Air Portugal TAP (TP)*.
Approximate flight time: From London to *Funchal* is 3 hours 40 minutes.
International airports: *Funchal (FNC)*, 23km (14 miles) from the city, and *Porto Santo (PXO)*, which is served by flights from Funchal and Lisbon.
SEA: The main passenger port is Funchal, served by *BI, CTC, P&O, Fred Olsen, Cunard, Polish Ocean, Norwegian American, Norwegian Cruises/Union Lloyd, Costa* and *Lauro*. Ferry services from Madeira to Porto Santo take three hours.

ACCOMMODATION

HOTELS: There are many luxury hotels on the island along the coast. These tend to be fully booked during the summer and over the Christmas period, therefore early booking is advisable. Most of the hotels compensate for the lack of beaches on the island of Madeira by providing swimming pools.

RESORTS & EXCURSIONS

Much of Madeira's appeal comes from the fact that it is a spectacularly beautiful island, lush with woods, vineyards and rich farmland, pitted with valleys and with a coastline consisting mainly of sheer cliffs. It is described by the locals as a 'floating garden', which reflects the efforts of centuries of intensive cultivation. Many beautiful walks may be taken following the routes on the *levadas* (irrigation channels) which cover the island. Many people come to Madeira because of its wealth of flowers and other vegetation. As well as travelling around the island to see its abundant foliage, one should visit the *Botanical Gardens* in Funchal, beautifully laid out in the grounds of an old country house. The visitor will see extravagant terraces of tropical flowers and other more delicate varieties grown in greenhouses. Open from 1000-1700, admission to the gardens is free; there is also a superb view across the harbour.

Although a number of excursions are available on Madeira, one which should be singled out is the toboggan run down to Funchal from the villages of *Monte* or *Terreiro da Luta*. Before motor vehicles, the toboggan was commonly used in Madeira and a number of special 'runs' were constructed. Today the toboggans carry tourists with two men using ropes to control the wide 'carro', a large wicker basket mounted on wooden runners.

Madeira is an island whose success is based on providing quality service and a high standard of holidaymaking. It is nevertheless unlikely ever to be overrun by groups of conference delegates, for hoteliers are well aware of their obligations to individuals who choose to take their holiday on Madeira. It is, if nothing else, an island for the independently minded.

Funchal: There are several regular sightseeing bus tours which take in many of the town's attractions. These include the *Mercado dos Lavradores* (the lively flower and vegetable market), the *Botanical Gardens*, the *Sé* (the 15th-century cathedral), the *Quinta das Cruzes* and the *Museu de Arte Sacra* (Museum of Sacred Art), a large villa containing many European works of art. A visit to the wine lodge is recommended; there one may taste and buy various Madeira wines. The lodge is conveniently situated next door to the Madeira Tourist Office in Avenida Arriaga, which can provide information on all aspects of excursions on the island.
Baia de Zarco is the new name given by the Madeira Tourist Office to a key tourist area located 24km (15 miles) from Funchal. The principal villages are **Agua de Pera, Machico, Canical, Portela, Porto da Cruz, Santa de Serra** and **Santa Cruz**. The area offers a wide variety of watersports, golf and tennis, and has a selection of hotels and holiday villas. **Prainha**, near the island's eastern tip, has Madeira's best sand beach.
The coast: Most coastal towns offer a wide variety of watersports; these can be reached from Funchal by means of a road network which offers spectacular views. Many of the towns have fine churches and other examples of Portuguese colonial architecture. The main centres on the more accessible southern coast include the fishing village of **Camara de Lobos**, a favourite spot of Winston Churchill, 8km (5 miles) west of Funchal; **Calheta**; and **Porta do Sol**, which is situated on both sides of a deep ravine. The roads are often rough, but the sea views are magnificent. The scenery in the north is wilder and even more spectacular, and the area contains many of the island's best vineyards and colonial architecture. **Porto do Moniz, São Vincente** and **Santana** are the main towns.
Inland Madeira: The moutainous interior is served by a network of twisting roads, many of which go up to the summits of some of the highest peaks. Places particularly worth a visit include **Camacha**, centre of the wickerwork industry; *Eira do Serrado*, the crater of an extinct volcano inside which lies the hidden village of **Curral das Freiras;** and *Pico Ruivo*, the island's highest point. The return journey to Funchal from **Monte** or **Terreiro da Luta** can be made by means of the toboggan run.
Porto Santo is 15 minutes from Funchal by plane (advance booking essential). The terrain is flatter and has more sandy beaches than Madeira. Day trips from Madeira can be organised. The tiny capital, **Vila Baleira**, contains the house where Christopher Columbus once lived.

SOCIAL PROFILE

FOOD & DRINK: Regional dishes include *sopa de tomate e cebola* (tomato and onion soup), *caldeirada* (fish soup), *bife de atum e milho frito* (tuna steak and fried maize), *carne vinho e alho* (pickled pork and garlic), *espetada* (fresh black scabbard fish) and *bolo de mel* (Madeira honey cake). **Drink:** Popular wines of Madeira are *malmsey* (Malvasia), a sweet dessert wine, *bual* and the dry *xercial*. Wines, spirits and beers imported from mainland Portugal and Europe are also available. *Galao*, a glass of milky coffee and *bica*, a small cup of very black coffee, are also popular.
NIGHTLIFE: Some hotels have excellent nightclubs with music for dancing and international cabaret entertainment. Folk entertainment is also included in the weekly programme of these hotels and in most cases non-residents are welcome.
SHOPPING: In Funchal there is a wide variety of shops selling everyday goods, as well as many souvenirs. Special purchases include Madeira folk art such as embroidery, tapestry and wickerwork. Madeira wine is a popular gift.
SPORT: Golf: Santo da Serra is Madeira's only golf course. It has nine holes, and caddies and clubs are available. The course is located 29km (18 miles) from Funchal. Many hotels have their own **tennis** courts and some allow non-residents to use them. **Watersports:** As well as the sea, there are many **swimming** pools, some on hotel rooftops and others along the seafront. There is also a Lido, large enough for 2000 people, with pools, shops and restaurants. Arrangements for watersports, including **water-skiing, windsurfing, snorkelling, scuba diving** and **fishing**, can be made through some hotels.
SPECIAL EVENTS: Throughout the year numerous events take place on Madeira and it is a good idea to visit at the time of a specific festival. Around Christmas and New Year, for example, there are some really spectacular celebrations. Cruise ships often stop the night of December 31 in Funchal Harbour so that passengers can appreciate the firework displays, accompanied by church bells and ships' sirens, which herald the New Year. The *Flower Festival* in April, the *Bach Music Festival* in June, the *Wine Festival* in September, *Carnival* in February and the *Saint Silvester Festival* in December are just a few of the events that can add a memorable highlight to a holiday.

CLIMATE

Mild subtropical climate with warm summers and extremely mild winters.
Required clothing: Mid-seasonal wear (as for the Azores).

FUNCHAL Madeira (25m)

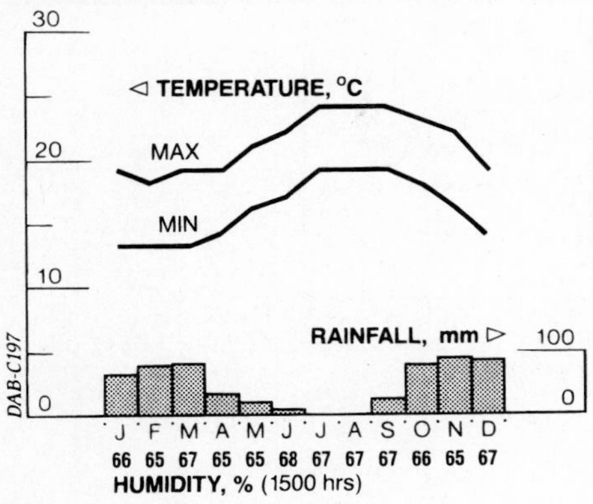

AZORES

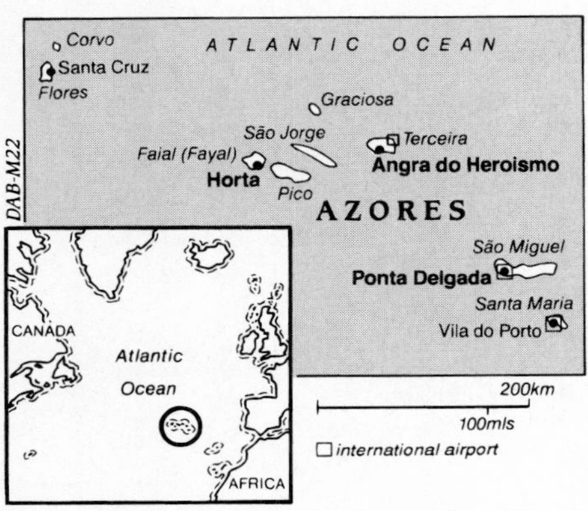

Location: Atlantic, 1220km (760 miles) due west of Portugal.

AREA: 2247 sq km (868 sq miles).
POPULATION: 253,100 (1989).
CAPITAL: Ponta Delgada *(on São Miguel)*; Horta *(on Faial)*; Angra do Heroismo *(on Terceira)*.
GEOGRAPHY: The Azores are a widely separated group of nine islands in the Atlantic, due west of mainland Portugal. Principal groups of islands are São Miguel and Santa Maria, Terceira, Graciosa, São Jorge, Pico, Faial, Flores and Corvo. The islands are mountainous in the interior and forested, leading down to long beaches and fishing harbours. There are several hot springs and spas.
TIME: GMT - 1 (GMT from Mar 29).
ELECTRICITY: 220/110 volts. 2-pin round plugs are in use.
COMMUNICATIONS: Services are similar to, but less extensive than, those offered on the mainland.
BBC World Service and Voice of America frequencies: From time to time these change. See the section *How to Use this Book* for more information.

BBC:				
MHz	6.195	15.070	12.095	9.410
Voice of America:				
MHz	11.97	9.670	6.040	5.995

PASSPORT/VISA

The passport and visa requirements are the same as for visiting mainland Portugal (see above), except that nationals of Canada, Malawi and Swaziland *do* need visas for visiting the Azores.

HEALTH

As for mainland Portugal; see above.

TRAVEL

AIR: The Azores' local airline is *SATA (SP)*, which runs inter-connecting flights between the islands.
Approximate flight time: From London to the *Azores* is 3 hours 10 minutes, plus stopover time in Lisbon of 2-12 hours.
International airports: *Ponta Delgada (PDL)* (São Miguel), *Santa Maria (SMX)* (Vila do Porto), and *Terceira (TER)* (Terceira).
SEA: *CTC* and *P&O* run cruises to the main port of Ponta Delgada.

ACCOMMODATION

The main islands have a reasonably good selection of hotel accommodation, and hotels are rarely full, so although it is a good safeguard, it is not vital to book in advance.

RESORTS & EXCURSIONS

During the last 500 years the Azores have remained almost completely unspoilt, and the tranquillity of the islands is ideal for visitors who want to get away from it all. There are no hotel blocks, not too many people, no obvious commercialism; instead, the visitor will be met with great natural beauty and clean, unpolluted sea and sky. Volcanic craters form lakes, and there are high cliffs, gentle valleys, unusual flowers amid lush vegetation, geysers, mineral water springs and secluded coves. Inland the countryside is speckled with whitewashed cottages.
Santa Maria was the first island to be discovered and contains vineyards, green fields, palm trees and windmills. There are two excellent beaches with soft sand at São Lourenco and Praia. There is also a 15th-century parish church and the town hall is located in a former 16th-century convent. The island is ideal for underwater fishing and water-skiing.
São Miguel is the largest island in the group and perhaps the most beautiful. Certainly one of the most spectacular sights on any of the islands is São Miguel's *Sete Cidades* – a 40 sq km (15 sq miles) extinct crater with two lakes, one of deep blue and the other emerald green. At *Furnas* you can bathe in the volcanic streams and therapeutic sulphurous springs. Embroideries and pineapple products are the main souvenirs of this island.
Terceira: Called the 'Lilac Isle' because of the distinctive colouring of its sunsets, this gently rural island is the home of unique rope bullfights. This island too is covered with an abundance of hydrangeas and azaleas and along the highways are gaily coloured little stands that serve as altar stations for the Whitsun Festival of the Holy Spirit – also celebrated throughout the Azores.
Graciosa contains the geological curiosity of *Furna de Enxofre*, a small, warm sulphur lake in a grotto beneath a crater, access to which is via a spiral staircase 80m (270ft) down. The island also boasts the black underground *Lake Caldeira*, and the hot springs with bathhouse of *Carapacho*. Here many of the islands' typical windmills are scattered amongst the fields. Vineyards form a major part of the island's economy. **Santa Cruz**, the capital, is a village with 18th-century houses.
São Jorge is surrounded by sheer, black rock cliffs and a profusion of vegetation that covers the steep slopes down to the sea. Cedar woods surround the island's capital of *Velas*, which has old buildings and a 17th-century church. São Jorge is the centre for the Azore's dairy produce.
Fayal: The name means 'beech tree', but the islands's main trees are now the strawberry trees or *arbutus*. Blue hydrangea hedges line the fields. The coast is indented with many sheltered bays, and vegetation consists of pines and exotic trees from Japan and elsewhere. *Horta* is the islands' main port, an ideal harbour for yachts and a meeting point for yachtsmen who cross the ocean, as well as a place where large cruise liners dock. *Caldeira* is an immense crater carpeted with greenery and has breathtaking views.
Pico gets its name from the mountain at its centre, which is Portugal's highest peak (2364m/7755ft). The snow-capped cone's hues vary constantly in the different lights during the day from the grey sunrise to the fiery colours of the sunset. The island is renowned for its vineyards that grow the famous 'verdelho' wine of Pico. This harsh and rocky island is also a centre for the Azores whaling industry.
Flores was named after its profusion of flowers. It is often regarded as the prettiest of the islands, with its rugged terrain, flowers growing in the deep canyons, and waterfalls casting hues of blue and green as they splash down into the sea. The island is ideal for watersports.

Corvo, the smallest island, has only one village and its few hundred inhabitants are related to one another. Nobody ever locks their front door and there is no jail or courthouse. Corvo has the living traditions of a pastoral and fishing community.

SOCIAL PROFILE

FOOD & DRINK: Generally the food is Portuguese; crayfish and rabbit are specialities. Locally produced wines are recommended, as are the brandies distilled on the islands.
SHOPPING: Locally made linens and woollen goods, lace and pottery make good buys.
SPORT: Watersports, including deep-sea **fishing**, are catered for at many coastal resorts, particularly on São Miguel where tourist facilities are more developed. Some hotels have **tennis** courts, and **golf** is available.

CLIMATE

Subtropical due to the Gulf Stream. Very equable and slightly humid climate. The rainy season is from November to March.
Required clothing: Mid-season clothes are best; the temperatures are mild at all times of the year.

PONTA DELGADA Azores (35m)

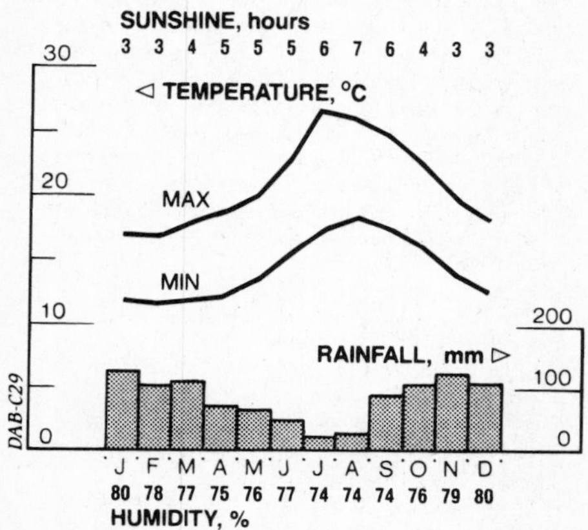

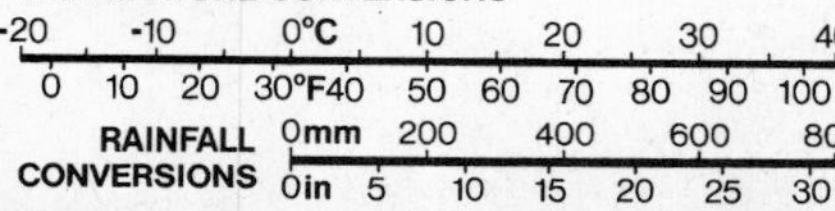

PUERTO RICO

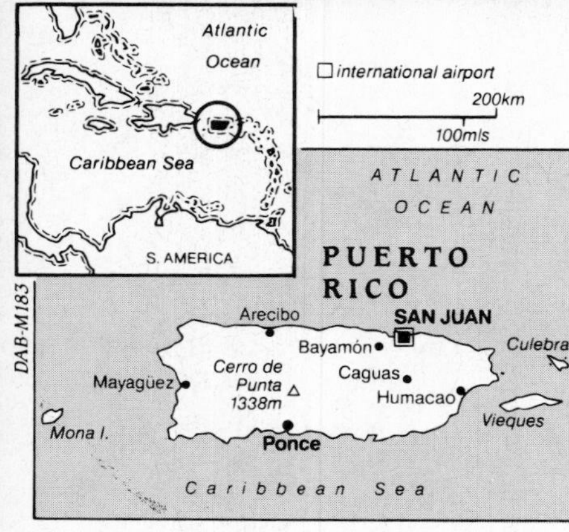

Location: Caribbean.

Diplomatic representation: As an *estado libre asociado* (a 'commonwealth state') of the USA, Puerto Rico manages its own affairs, but is represented abroad by US Embassies and Consulates. Addresses of these and of US Tourist Offices may be found in the *United States of America* entry later in the *World Travel Guide*. Tourist information may also be obtained from:

Puerto Rico Hotel and Tourism Association
Suite 702, Plaza Center
954 Ponce de León Avenue
Miramar
Santurce 00907, Puerto Rico
Tel: 725 2902.

Commonwealth of Puerto Rico Tourism Company
PO Box 4435
301 San Justo Street
Old San Juan Station
San Juan 00905, Puerto Rico
Tel: 721 2400. Fax: 725 4417. Telex: 3450158.

British Consulate
Suite 5E
1 Taft Street
Santurce 00911, Puerto Rico
Tel: 728 6715. Telex: 3454325.

Commonwealth of Puerto Rico Tourism Company
23rd Floor, 575 Fifth Avenue
New York, NY 10017
Tel: (212) 599 6262. Fax: (212) 818 1866.

Commonwealth of Puerto Rico Tourism Company
Suite 700, 2 Bloor Street West
Toronto, Ontario
M4W 3R1
Tel: (416) 969 9025. Fax: (416) 969 9478.

AREA: 8959 sq km (3459 sq miles).
POPULATION: 3,605,000 (1990 estimate).
POPULATION DENSITY: 402.4 per sq km.
CAPITAL: San Juan. **Population:** 434,849 (1980).
GEOGRAPHY: Puerto Rico is an island east of the Dominican Republic and west of the British Virgin Islands. Also included are several smaller islands, such as Culebra, Mona and Vieques. The island is comparatively small, 8959 sq km (3459 sq miles), with a central mountain range reaching an altitude of 1337m (4389ft) at Cerro La Punta, and surrounded by low coastal plains. The capital is on the northeast shore. Much of the natural forest has been cleared for agriculture, but the trees in the northeast are protected as a national park. The other main towns are Ponce, Bayamón and Caguas.
LANGUAGE: Spanish is the official language; English is widely spoken.
RELIGION: 85% Roman Catholic; the remainder are other Christian denominations and Jews.
TIME: GMT - 4. The island does not observe Daylight Saving Time.
ELECTRICITY: 120 volts AC, 60Hz.
COMMUNICATIONS: Telephone: IDD service is available. Country code: 1 809. **Telex:** Facilities are available in the capital and in main hotels. **Post:** Airmail to Europe takes up to a week. **Press:** The English-language newspaper published in Puerto Rico is *The San Juan Star*; others include *El Vocero de Puerto Rico*, *El Nuevo Dia* and *El Mundo*.
BBC World Service and Voice of America frequencies: From time to time these change. See the section *How to Use this Book* for more information.

BBC:

MHz	17.840	15.220	9.915	5.975

Voice of America:

MHz	15.21	11.70	6.130	0.930

PASSPORT/VISA

The passport and visa requirements for entering Puerto Rico are the same as for entering the USA. See the *Passport/Visa* section in the *United States of America* entry later in the *World Travel Guide*.

MONEY

Currency: US Dollar (US$) = 100 cents. For denominations, see the *Money* section of the general USA entry later in the book.
Credit cards: All international credit cards are accepted.
Travellers cheques: Cheques in various currencies are accepted, but US Dollar cheques are preferred.
Currency restrictions: As for the USA; see later in the *World Travel Guide*.
Banking hours: 0900-1430 Monday to Thursday; 0900-1430 and 1530-1700 Friday.

DUTY FREE

As for the USA; see later in the *World Travel Guide*.

PUBLIC HOLIDAYS

Public holidays observed in Puerto Rico are as follows:
Mar 22 '93 Emancipation of the Slaves. **Apr 9** Good Friday. **Apr 16*** José de Diego's Birthday. **May 31** Memorial Day. **Jun 24** Feast of St John the Baptist. **Jul 5** US Independence Day. **Jul 17** Luis Muñoz Rivera's Birthday. **Jul 26** Constitution Day. **Jul 27** José Celso Barbosa's Birthday. **Sep 6** Labour Day. **Oct 11** Columbus Day. **Nov 11** Veterans' Day. **Nov 19** Discovery of Puerto Rico Day. **Nov 25** Thanksgiving Day. **Dec 25** Christmas Day. **Jan 1 '94** New Year's Day. **Jan 6** Epiphany. **Jan 11** Birthday of Eugenio Maria de Hostos. **Jan 17** Martin Luther King Day. **Feb 21** Washington-Lincoln Day. **Mar 22** Emancipation of the Slaves.
Note: [*] Half-day holidays (shut in the afternoon), but some shops and offices may close for the whole day. If a holiday falls on a Sunday, the next day becomes a holiday.

HEALTH

Regulations and requirements may be subject to change at short notice, and you are advised to contact your doctor well in advance of your intended date of departure. Any numbers in the chart refer to the footnotes below.

	Special Precautions?	Certificate Required?
Yellow Fever	No	No
Cholera	No	No
Typhoid & Polio	Yes	-
Malaria	No	-
Food & Drink	1	-

[1]: Water is purified in main areas, although bottled water may be preferable. Tap water is considered safe to drink. Milk is pasteurised and dairy products are safe for consumption. Local meat, poultry, seafood, fruit and vegetables are generally considered safe to eat.
Rabies is present. For those at high risk, vaccination before arrival should be considered. If you are bitten abroad seek medical advice without delay. For more information consult the *Health* section at the back of the book.
Bilharzia (schistosomiasis) is present. Avoid swimming and paddling in fresh water. Swimming pools which are well-chlorinated and maintained are safe.
Health care: Health services are good but costly; health insurance is recommended.

TRAVEL - International

AIR: There is no local airline, but frequent flights connect Puerto Rico with other islands and cities in the Caribbean.
Approximate flight times: From Puerto Rico to *Chicago* is 5 hours 40 minutes, to *London* is 8 hours (direct), to *Los Angeles* is 10 hours 45 minutes, to *Miami* is 2 hours 35 minutes, to *New York* is 4 hours and to *Washington DC* is 3 hours 50 minutes.
International airport: *Luis Muñoz Marin (SJU)* is 14km (9 miles) east of San Juan. Airport facilities include a restaurant, bar, bank, post office, hotel reservations, a duty-free shop and car hire. Bus T2 runs every 30 minutes from 0600-2300. Taxis are available.

SEA: The main passenger port is San Juan. The following cruise lines run services to San Juan: *NCL, Commodore, Royal Caribbean, Costa, Cunard, Chandris, Astor United Cruises, Sitmar, Home Lines, Norwegian Viking* and *Princess Cruises*.

TRAVEL - Internal

AIR: *Prinair (PQ)* run high-frequency commuter services to Ponce and Mayagüez.

ROAD: Taxi: A special service called a *linea* will pick up and drop off passengers where they wish. They operate between San Juan and most towns, at a fixed rate. **Car hire:** Available at the airport and city agencies. Rental companies include: *AAA, Afro, Atlantic, Avis, Budget* and *Discount*. **Documentation:** International Driving Licence.

URBAN: Bus: San Juan has local bus services (*Guaguas*) and there are bus terminals in Bayamón, Catano, Country Club and Rio Piedras, as well as the capital. Buses tend not to run after 2100. There are also coach and bus companies offering sightseeing trips. These include: *American Sightseeing/Travel Service Inc, Gray Line Sightseeing Tours, Normandie Tours, Rico Sun Tours, Taino Tours Inc* and *Will Rey Tours*. **Taxi:** *Publicos* (shared taxis) have P or PD at the end of licence plate numbers and run regular routes between established points. They usually operate only during daylight hours and depart from the main *plaza* (central square) of a town. *Publicos* must be insured by law and the Public Service Commission fixes their routes and reasonable rates. Conventional taxis are hired by the hour, and charges are metered except in charter trips outside the usual taxi zones. They can be hailed in the street, or called by telephone. They are available at the airport and at stands at most hotels. Taxi drivers expect a 15% tip.

JOURNEY TIMES: The following chart gives approximate journey times (in hours and minutes) from San Juan to other major cities and resorts in Puerto Rico.

	Air	Road	Sea
Ponce	0.30	1.30	-
Mayagüez	0.30	2.30	-
Vieques	0.30	*0.45	2.00
Fajardo	-	0.45	-
Dorado	-	0.35	-
Humacao-Palmas -	0.45	-	

Note [*]: To Fajardo.

ACCOMMODATION

HOTELS: San Juan has modern Americanised hotels and there is similar lodging in Ponce. *Paradores* (government-sponsored inns) are less modern, but of a good standard. For further information contact the Puerto Rico Hotel and Tourism Association (for address, see above).

APARTMENTS & CONDOMINIUMS: Available from a number of companies specialising in renting this type of accommodation. See under *Accommodation* in the general introduction to the United States later in the *World Travel Guide*. Condominiums and flats are best around Luquillo Beach to the northeast.

RESORTS & EXCURSIONS

The capital city of **San Juan** is divided into the old and the new. The old part was founded in 1521 and is now officially declared a National Historic Zone, and many 16th- and 17th-century buildings have been restored and refurbished in the original Spanish style. The city boasts many shops, restaurants, art galleries and museums. The *Pablo Casals Museum* has manuscripts and photographs relating to the work of the famous cellist. Videotapes of performances from past Casals festivals (held every June) can be viewed on request. *Casa de los Contrafuertes* houses the *Latin American Graphic Arts Museum* and the *Pharmacy Museum*, with its recreated apothecary shop. *Casa del Callejon* is a traditional Spanish-style home, which holds the *Museum of Colonial Architecture* and the *Museum of the Puerto Rican Family*. *Casa del Libro* holds a rare collection of early manuscripts and books, some dating back to the 15th century. The *San Juan Museum of Art & History* was built in 1855 as a market and restored in 1979 as a cultural centre where the patio is often used for concerts. *Plaza de San José*, at the 'top' of old San Juan and marked by a statue of Juan Ponce de León, is a cosy area of small museums and pleasant cafés. Other places of interest in Old San Juan include *El Morro* (a 16th-century Spanish fortress) and the 18th-century fort of *San Cristobal*, built in 1771. Both buildings are perched on clifftops at the tip of a peninsula. El Morro, in particular, has many exhibits documenting Puerto Rico's role in the discovery of the New World and was instrumental in the defence of San Juan in the 16th century and its continuing survival.

Casa Blanca, dating from 1523, was built as a home for Ponce de León, and the *Dominican convent* (also started in 1523) now houses the *Instituto de Cultura Puertorriquena*. *La Fortaleza*, completed in 1540, is now the Governor's residence – the oldest of its kind in the Western hemisphere. The old *San Juan City Wall*, dating from the 1630s, was built by the Spanish and it follows the peninsula contour, providing picturesque vantage points for viewing Old San Juan and the sea. *San Juan Cathedral*, originally built in the 1520s, was completely restored in 1977. *San José Church* is the second-oldest church in the western hemisphere – Ponce de León's body was interred here until the early 20th century. The *Alcaldia*, or City Hall, was built between 1604-1789. The *Casino* (not to be confused with gambling clubs) is a beautiful building dating from 1917. Recently refurbished, the rich interior boasts marble floors, exquisite plasterwork and 12ft chandeliers.

New San Juan is connected to the old town by a narrow neck of land, and modern architecture has flourished in recent years. There are *Botanical Gardens* and a *Museum of Anthropology* for the leisurely visitor. Bay cruises are also available, which offer excellent views of the city.

El Yunque, east of the capital, is a 27,000-acre rainforest (with over 240 species of trees) and bird sanctuary, which can be visited by narrow-gauge train or road. It is the only tropical rainforest in the US National Forest System and is located in the *Luquillo Mountains*.

The beautiful town of **Ponce**, on the southern side of the island and connected to the capital by a toll road, is situated near many excellent beaches. It hosts an *Indian Ceremonial Park* and also has several buildings of interest, including a sugar mill and rum museum. The *Museum of Art* there contains more than 1000 paintings and 400 sculptures, ranging from ancient classical to contemporary art. Its collection of 19th-century Pre-Raphaelite paintings is among the best in the Americas.

The Arroyo to Ponce train stops at **Guayama,** where the station has been restored as a crafts centre.

The *Tibes Indian Ceremonial Centre*, a short drive from Ponce, is an ancient Indian burial ground. A replica of a Taino Indian village has been built near the small museum, reception area and exhibition hall. The museum is open 0900-1600 Tuesday to Sunday.

The *Phosphorescent Bay*, near **La Parguera** in the southwest of the island, is a major attraction. Here, marine life, microscopic in size, lights up when disturbed by fish, boats or any movement. The phenomenon – especially vivid on moonless nights – is rarely found elsewhere. Boat trips are available at night. There is another phosphorescent bay in **Vieques.**

The *Camuy Caves*, near **Arecibo** on the north coast, is the third largest cave system in the world. There are well-paved access roads, a reception area, and electric trains to the entrance of the caves. The *Arecibo Observatory* is the site of the largest radar/radio telescope in the world. Located in the unusual karst country of Puerto Rico, the 20-acre dish is best seen from a small airplane flight between San Juan and Mayagüez. Visitors are welcome 1400-1630 Sundays. The *Caguana Indian Ceremonial Park*, south of the Arecibo Observatory, was built by Taino Indians as a site for recreation and worship 800 years ago. There is another Ceremonial Park in Ponce.

There are old colonial towns at **San German** and **Mayagüez** and a *Tropical Agricultural Research Station* near the Mayagüez division of the University of Puerto Rico, with cuttings of hundreds of tropical plants; visitors are allowed in the gardens 0730-1200 and 1300-1630 Monday to Friday.

Many of the drives through the centre of the island take in spectacular scenery and are to be recommended. The **Espirito Santo** is a navigable river that flows from the Luquillo Mountains to the Atlantic, and has 24-passenger launches available for river tours along 8km (5 miles) of the route. Special arrangements can be made for groups and the boat ride usually takes about two hours.

SOCIAL PROFILE

FOOD & DRINK: Puerto Rico (and especially San Juan) abounds with good restaurants, catering for all tastes from Spanish to Chinese, Italian, French and Greek. The island cuisine is Spanish-based, with rice and beans as the staple diet. *Paella*, chicken dishes, black bean soup, *sacocho* (beef stew), *jueyes* (land crabs) and *pan de agua* (native bread) are all excellent, as is the delicately seasoned *langosta*. Island rums such as *barrilito* are not to be missed.

NIGHTLIFE: Abundant, ranging from spectacular shows in large hotels to jazz recitals, classical concerts and discos. There is also gambling in San Juan, with casinos at the *Carib Inn, Caribe Hilton, Concha, Condado Plaza, Sands* and *Ramada* hotels, to name a few. Some casinos do require formal wear after 2000.

SHOPPING: Special purchases are cigars, hammocks, straw weaving, sculpture, *santos* (carved religious figures), coconut devil masks and stringed musical instruments. **Shopping hours:** 0900-1700 Monday to Saturday. Some shops open on Sunday if cruise liners are in port.

SPORT: There is **horseracing** at Rio Pedras (El Comandante) all year round. **Horseriding** is available from various ranches on the island, such as Rancho Borinquen, Rancho Criollo and Rancho Guayama. There are eight **baseball** teams in the league and the San Juan-Santurce stadium seats close to 25,000 people. There are other ball parks at Arecibo, Caguas, Mayagüez and Ponce. There are many **golf** courses, including *Punto Borinquen* at Aguadillo (18 holes), and the *Dorado Del Mar Country Club* (18 holes – there are four 18-hole courses at Dorado). **Tennis** courts are available all over the island, especially at major hotels. In addition, play is available on 17 floodlit public courts in San Juan's Central Park, which is open daily. There are also six courts available at the *Dorado Del Mar Country Club* at Dorado. Deep-sea **fishing** is available, with blue and white marlin, sailfish, wahoo, Allison tuna, mackerel, dolphin, tarpon and snook to be found. Fully equipped boats with crew are available for charter all over the island. Palmas del Mar rents small-to medium-sized boats for day **sailing** and the resort is headquarters for the annual Copa del Palmas, the major 1-design regatta in Puerto Rico. Motorboats and rowing boats are also available. Puerto Rico's shoreline has many areas protected by beautiful coral reefs and keys, and **snorkelling** in shallow reef waters and mangrove areas is an excellent way of seeing the beautiful and colourful underworld of the sea. **Scuba diving** instruction and equipment rental are available at watersports offices of major hotels and resorts. Many beaches cater for **surfing** and **windsurfing,** for example Pine Grove and Condado beaches.

SPECIAL EVENTS: The following is a selection of the special events taking place in Puerto Rico 1993/94: **Apr '93** *Puerto Rico Orchid Show*, Hato Rey; *Mavi Festival* (costumes, floats, arts & crafts shows and mavi drinking – a local drink made from sassafras), Juana Diaz. **May** *Semana de la Danza* (a week-long celebration of a national dance form – *la danza*), Old San Juan; *Pineapple Festival*, Lajas. **Jun** *Bomba y Piena Festival* (Afro-Caribbean heritage celebration), Ponce; *San Juan Bautista Day* (begins a week of festivities celebrating San Juan's patron saint), San Juan. **Jul** *Barranquitas Artisans Fair*, Barranquitas. **Sep** *Inter-American Festival of the Arts*, San Juan. **Oct** *National Plantain Festival*, Corozal; *Puerto Rico Tennis Open*, Dorado. **Nov** *Arts & Crafts Fair*, Mayagüez and Cabo Rojo; *Jayuya Indian Festival*, Jayuya. **Nov-Dec** *Fiesta de la Musica Puertorriquena* (annual classical and folk music concerts), Old San Juan; *Festival of Typical Dishes*, Luquillo Beach. **Dec-Jan** *Navidades* (island-wide Christmas festivities). **Dec 24-28** *Hatillo Festival of the Masks*, Hatillo. **Jan '94** *San Sebastian Street Festival*, Old San Juan. **Feb** *San Blas Marathon*, Coamo.

PUERTO RICO | **HEALTH REGULATIONS** | **VISA REGULATIONS** | Code-Link

GALILEO/WORLDSPAN

TI-DFT/SJU/HE

TI-DFT/SJU/VI

SABRE

TIDFT/SJU/HE

TIDFT/SJU/VI

To access this information on your CRS, swipe the barcode with a light pen or type in the text under the barcode. For more information, see the introduction *How to Use This Book*.

'Fiestas Patronales' celebrations are held in each town's plaza to honour the area's patron saint. These fiestas usually last for ten days and include religious processions, games, local food and dance. For further details contact the Commonwealth of Puerto Rico Tourism Company.
SOCIAL CONVENTIONS: Handshaking is the customary form of greeting. Casual dress is acceptable, but shorts should not be worn in hotel dining rooms or casinos, where formal dress is required after 2000. Spanish and American manners and conventions exist side by side on the island. Some hotels do require formal dress. **Tipping:** Generally 15-20% if not included on the bill.

BUSINESS PROFILE

ECONOMY: Puerto Rico has few natural resources, although some nickel and copper has been located. Manufacturing has overtaken agriculture as the main source of income following an intensive programme of industrialisation by the Government. Pharmaceuticals, electrical and electronic equipment, processed food, textiles, clothing, rum, petrochemicals and refined oil are the main industries. In the agricultural sector, dairy and livestock produce is now more important than sugar cane, the island's main crop. Fresh fruit and vegetables are increasingly grown for export. Tourism is the main service industry. The USA and American corporations dominate the economy and Puerto Rican trade patterns, although the country has important trading links with Japan, the Dominican Republic and Venezuela.
BUSINESS: A knowledge of Spanish (the official language) is very useful, although English is widely spoken; most people in the tourist industry and the greater metropolitan areas are bilingual. Lightweight suits are advised for business meetings. **Office hours:** 0830-1630 Monday to Friday.
COMMERCIAL INFORMATION: The following organisation can offer advice: Chamber of Commerce of Puerto Rico, Chamber of Commerce Buildings, PO Box S-3789, Tetuán 100, San Juan 00904. Tel: 721 6060. Fax: 723 1891.

HISTORY & GOVERNMENT

HISTORY: The Taino Indians were the first Puerto Rican inhabitants. The island was 'discovered' by Columbus in 1493 on his second voyage to the New World and was governed by Ponce de León from 1508. Puerto Rico *(Rich Port)* was eventually ceded to the USA in 1898 at the end of the Spanish-American War. In 1917 Puerto Ricans were granted US citizenship and in 1952 the island became a self-governing, a Commonwealth in association with the USA. Many people regard this situation as a compromise between the two alternatives of full membership of the USA or full independence. Various political groupings support these views; the Partido Popular Democrático (PPD) is broadly in favour of Commonwealth status, while the Partido Neuvo Progresista (PNP) supports full state membership. Some left-wing groups are working towards independence, including a couple of extremist groups who advocate and use violence: independence remains a sensitive issue on the island. Puerto Rico has a representative in the US House of Representatives; the inhabitants of the island are US citizens, but they may not vote in presidential elections.
GOVERNMENT: Executive power is held by the Governor, who is elected by universal adult suffrage for a 4-year term, assisted by a 15-member Cabinet staffed by appointees. A bicameral assembly, a scaled-down version of the US Congress, is responsible for legislation.

CLIMATE

Hot tropical climate. The temperature varies little throughout the year. Cooler in the upland areas.
Required clothing: Lightweight tropical clothes.

SAN JUAN Puerto Rico (15m)

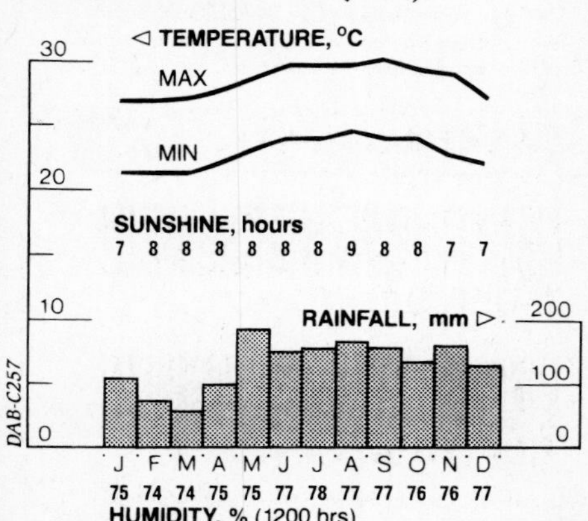

QATAR

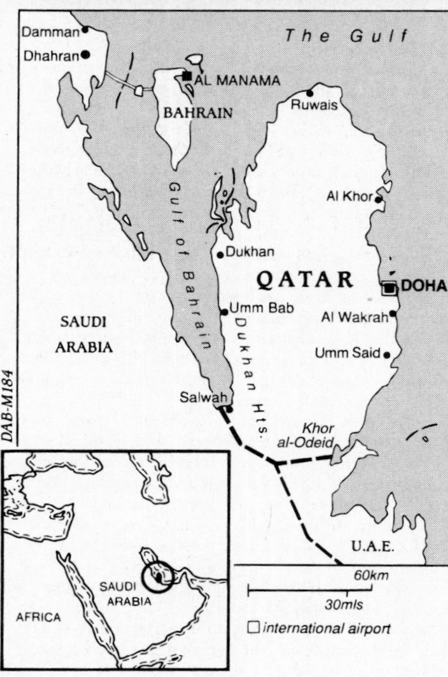

Location: Middle East, Gulf Coast.

Ministry of Information and Culture
PO Box 1836
Doha, Qatar
Tel: 831 333. Fax: 831 860. Telex: 4229.
Embassy of the State of Qatar
27 Chesham Place
London SW1X 8HG
Tel: (071) 235 0851. Fax: (071) 235 7584. Telex: 28469.
Opening hours: 0930-1600 Monday to Friday.
Qatar Consulate
115 Queen's Gate
London SW7 5LP
Tel: (071) 581 8611/9. Fax: (071) 581 4292. Telex: 893191 QATINF. Opening hours: 0930-1600 Monday to Friday.
British Embassy
PO Box 3
Doha, Qatar
Tel: 421 991. Fax: 438 692. Telex: 4205 PRODRO DH.
Embassy of the State of Qatar
Suite 1180
600 New Hampshire Avenue, NW
Washington, DC
20037
Tel: (202) 338 0111.
Embassy of the United States of America
PO Box 2399
149 Ali Bin Ahmed Street
Farig Bin Omran
Doha, Qatar
Tel: 864 701/2/3. Fax: 861 669. Telex: 4847.
The Permanent Mission of Qatar to the United Nations
22nd Floor
747 Third Avenue
New York, NY
10017
Tel: (212) 486 9367/8. Fax: (212) 458 4952.
Canadian Embassy to Qatar
c/o Canadian Embassy
PO Box 25281
13113 Safat
Kuwait City, Kuwait
Tel: (965) 256 3025. Fax: (965) 256 4167. Telex: MCAN 23549 KT.

AREA: 11,437 sq km (4416 sq miles).
POPULATION: 422,000 (1989 estimate).
POPULATION DENSITY: 36.9 per sq km.
CAPITAL: Doha. **Population:** 217,294 (1986).
GEOGRAPHY: Qatar is an oil-rich peninsula jutting out into the Gulf between Bahrain and the United Arab Emirates. There are hills in the northwest, but the rest of the country consists of sand dunes and salt flats, with scattered vegetation towards the north.
LANGUAGE: Arabic is the official language. Some English is spoken.
RELIGION: Muslim.
TIME: GMT + 3.
ELECTRICITY: 240/415 volts AC, 50Hz.
COMMUNICATIONS: Telephone: IDD is available. Country code: 974. **Fax:** Available at some major hotels. **Telex/telegram:** The Cable and Wireless Office in Doha (open 0600-2300) and major hotels provide these services. **Post:** Airmail to Europe takes up to a week. **Press:** The main dailies are *Al-Arrayah* and *Al-Arab*. English-language newspapers include *The Gulf Times*.
BBC World Service and Voice of America frequencies: From time to time these change. See the section *How to Use this Book* for more information.

BBC:

MHz	15.07	12.10	9.670	6.180

A service is also available on 1413kHz and 702kHz (0100-0500 GMT).

Voice of America:

MHz	11.97	9.670	6.040	5.995

PASSPORT/VISA

Regulations and requirements may be subject to change at short notice, and you are advised to contact the appropriate diplomatic or consular authority before finalising travel arrangements. Details of these may be found at the head of this country's entry. Any numbers in the chart refer to the footnotes below.

	Passport Required?	Visa Required?	Return Ticket Required?
Full British	Yes	No/1	Yes
BVP	Not valid	-	-
Australian	Yes	Yes	Yes
Canadian	Yes	Yes	Yes
USA	Yes	Yes	Yes
Other EC	Yes	Yes	Yes
Japanese	Yes	Yes	Yes

Restricted entry: The Government refuses entry and transit to holders of passports issued by Israel or South Africa, or to those with stamps issued by these countries in their passports.
PASSPORTS: Valid passport required by all.
British Visitors Passport: Not accepted.
VISAS: Required by all except:
(a) **[1]** nationals of the UK (applicable only to passport holders born and residing in the UK) for a stay not exceeding 30 days;
(b) nationals of Bahrain, Kuwait, Oman, Saudi Arabia and the United Arab Emirates.
Types of visa: Entry visa and 72-hour visa. Entry visas are valid for two weeks. A 72-hour visa can be granted at Doha Airport if the traveller has a valid passport, an onward ticket, proof of being a representative of a commercial company and is met at Doha Airport by a recognised commercial company representative in Qatar.
Application to: Consulate (or Consular Section at Embassy). For address, see top of entry. An Entry visa valid for two weeks can be obtained by applying to the Qatar National Company for Hotels. If there is no objection, the concerned authorities will in turn inform the appropriate hotel of their approval who will notify the applicant accordingly. The approval remains valid for one month from the date of issue. For longer-period visas apply to the Immigration Department, Ministry of Interior, PO Box 2433, Doha, Qatar.
Application requirements: (a) Completed visa application form. (b) 3 photos. (c) Fee of £24 for single entry; £44 for up to 6 months multiple entry and £84 for up to 12 months multiple entry.
Working days required: 24 hours, although applications should be made well in advance of the intended departure date.

MONEY

Currency: Qatar Riyal (QR) = 100 dirhams. Notes are in denominations of QR500, 100, 50, 10, 5 and 1. Coins are in denominations of 50, 25, 10 and 5 dirhams.
Credit cards: Visa, American Express, Access/Mastercard and Diners Club are widely accepted. Check with your credit card company for details of merchant acceptability and other services which may be available.
Travellers cheques: Widely accepted.
Exchange rate indicators: The following figures are included as a guide to the movements of the Riyal

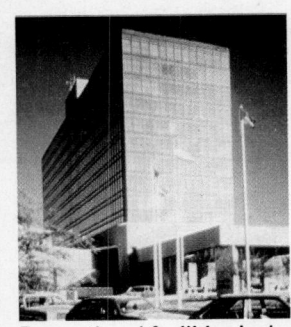

against Sterling and the US Dollar:

Date:	Oct '89	Oct '90	Oct '91	Oct '92
£1.00=	5.76	7.12	6.33	5.88
$1.00=	3.65	3.64	3.64	3.70

Currency restrictions: There are no restrictions on the import or export of either local or foreign currency, execpt that Israeli currency is prohibited.
Banking hours: 0730-1130 Saturday to Thursday.

DUTY FREE

The following goods may be imported into Qatar without incurring customs duty:
454g of tobacco;
Perfume to the value of QR1000.
Prohibited items: All alcohol is prohibited to those who do not hold a licence. Firearms can only be imported with a licence obtained in advance from the Ministry of Defence, Government of Qatar. Israeli currency is prohibited.

PUBLIC HOLIDAYS

Public holidays observed in Qatar are as follows:
Mar 25 '93 Start of Eid al-Fitr. **Jun 1** Start of Eid al-Ahda. **Jun 21** Islamic New Year. **Sep 3** National Day. **Jan 9 '94** Leilat al-Meiraj. **Feb 11** Start of Ramadan. **Feb 22** Accession of HH The Amir. **Mar 13** Start of Eid al-Fitr.
Note: Muslim festivals are timed according to local sightings of various phases of the Moon and the dates given above are approximations. During the lunar month of Ramadan that precedes Eid al-Fitr, Muslims fast during the day and feast at night and normal business patterns may be interrupted. Many restaurants are closed during the day and there may be restrictions on smoking and drinking. Some disruption may continue into Eid al-Fitr itself. Eid al-Fitr and Eid al-Adha may last anything from two to ten days, depending on the region. For more information see the section *World of Islam* at the back of the book.

HEALTH

Regulations and requirements may be subject to change at short notice, and you are advised to contact your doctor well in advance of your intended date of departure. Any numbers in the chart refer to the footnotes below.

	Special Precautions?	Certificate Required?
Yellow Fever	No	1
Cholera	Yes	No
Typhoid & Polio	Yes	-
Malaria	No	-
Food & Drink	2	-

[1]: A yellow fever vaccination certificate is required from travellers over one year of age arriving from infected areas.
[2]: All water should be regarded as being potentially contaminated. Water used for drinking, brushing teeth or making ice should have first been boiled or otherwise sterilised. Milk is unpasteurised and should be boiled. Powdered or tinned milk is available and is advised, but make sure that it is reconstituted with pure water. Avoid dairy products which are likely to have been made from unboiled milk. Only eat well-cooked meat and fish, preferably served hot. Salad and mayonnaise may carry increased risk. Vegetables should be cooked and fruit peeled.
Rabies is present. For those at high risk, vaccination before arrival should be considered. If you are bitten abroad seek medical advice without delay. For more information consult the *Health* section at the back of the book.
Note: Certificates proving the visitor to be HIV negative and free of tuberculosis, syphilis, leprosy and hepatitis B are required.
Health care: There are several hospitals in Qatar, the most recent and modern being the Hamad General Hospital. The Poly Clinic has good dentists. Charges are high and health insurance is essential. Due to the intense heat, visitors should maintain a high salt and fluid intake.

TRAVEL - International

AIR: *Gulf Air (GF)* is the major airline serving Qatar.
Approximate flight times: From Doha to *Calcutta* is 50 minutes, to *Colombo* is 4 hours 20 minutes and to *London* is 7 hours 15 minutes.
International airport: *Doha (DOH)* is 8km (5 miles) southeast of the city (travel time – 25 minutes). Facilities include car hire, bank, restaurant and a duty-free shop. Taxis are available to the city with official rates displayed.
SEA: The main international ports are Doha and Umm Said. The traffic is mostly commercial, but some passenger lines call at Doha.
ROAD: Access is possible via both the UAE and Saudi Arabia, but the main international route from Saudi Arabia is unreliable and often impassable during the rainy season.

TRAVEL - Internal

ROAD: The road system is fair, but conditions are poor during the wet season. Driving is on the right. **Bus:** No organised public bus service. **Taxi:** These have black and yellow number plates and are metered. Can be hired on an hourly basis. **Car hire:** Available from local companies at the airport and hotels. **Documentation:** A 90-day Temporary Driving Permit will be granted at The Traffic and Licence Office on presentation of a national driving licence or an International Driving Permit. Applicants will be required to pass an oral highway code test and should be accompanied by someone who knows the procedure. A renewal at the end of the 90-day period is possible. Third Party insurance is necessary.

ACCOMMODATION

HOTELS: Recent building ensures that Qatar is well served by first-class hotels. There are also a number of 3- or 4-star hotels offering reasonable accommodation. Advanced booking is strongly advised. All rates are subject to a 15% service charge.

RESORTS & EXCURSIONS

DOHA: The city is a rich mixture of traditional Arabic and modern architecture which gives it an interesting flair with its over 700 mosques. The *Grand Mosque* with its multiple domes and the *Abu Bakir al-Siddiq Mosque* are especially worth a visit. There is an excellent *National Museum* in Doha tracing the country's development. The modern town clusters around the Grand Mosque, the *New Amir's Palace* and the *Clock Tower*.
THE NORTH: This area contains most of the historic sites, including **Umm Salal Mohammed,** a relatively large village dominated by the ruins of a 19th-century fort. At **Zubara** is the *Qalit Marir fortress*. **Al Khor** is the second largest city, situated around a natural shallow harbour. A new corniche and sea wall aim to make the city a centre for weekend leisure. **Gharya** has a golden sandy beach stretching for miles. **Ruwais** boasts a picturesque harbour, from where there is an occasional *dhow* service to Bahrain. There are also good beaches at **Fuwairat**, on the northeast coast, and **Ras Abruk,** opposite Hawar Island.
THE WEST COAST: There are beaches at **Umm Bab** ('The Palm Tree Beach'), **Dukhan** and **Salwah,** near the Saudi frontier.
THE SOUTH: This is a region of sand dunes and beaches, offering opportunities to go pearl hunting, or to practise any of a number of watersports. The 'inland sea' of **Khor al-Odeid** is the centre of a region of outstanding natural beauty, surrounded by the Sandi Hills, accessible only to 4-wheel drive vehicles.

SOCIAL PROFILE

FOOD & DRINK: While the best food is generally found in hotels, Western, Chinese, Indian and American cuisine is also available. All the major hotels have good public restaurants and most offer

QATAR	HEALTH REGULATIONS	VISA REGULATIONS
GALILEO/WORLDSPAN	 TI-DFT/DOH/HE	 TI-DFT/DOH/VI
SABRE	 TIDFT/DOH/HE	TIDFT/DOH/VI

Code-Link

To access this information on your CRS, swipe the barcode with a light pen or type in the text under the barcode. For more information, see the introduction *How to Use This Book.*

outside catering of high quality; waiters, crockery and cutlery will be provided on request. There are a reasonable number of places to eat in Doha, including snack bars serving fast foods, as well as the traditional Levantine *shawarma* and Egyptian *foul* and *taamiyeh*. Restaurants are scarce outside the capital. Alcohol is prohibited.
NIGHTLIFE: Public entertainment is rather limited. Doha has a cinema showing English-language films and the National Theatre. Live entertainment is infrequent, but some international artistes do perform in Qatar.
SPORT: Football is the national sport. Doha boasts several marinas, sub-aqua clubs and **sailing** facilities as well as a number of sports clubs which are open to visitors. There are several **camel race** tracks, the main one just off the road to Dukhan, but spectators need a 4-wheel drive vehicle to follow the race. The graded track is 18km (11 miles) long through the desert and sometimes more than 250 camels take part with big money prizes and prestige at stake.
SOCIAL CONVENTIONS: The visitor should be fully aware of Muslim religious laws and customs. Women should always dress modestly. Also observe that it is acceptable to cross your legs, whereas showing the sole of the foot or unknowingly pointing it at a person is considered an insult. At business and social functions, the traditional Qatari coffee in tiny handleless cups, will invariably be served. This is a ritual of welcome with strict rules: guests are served in order of seniority – a few drops at first, then, after three or four others have been served, the server returns to fill the first cup; always hold the cup in the right hand; two cups are polite, but never take only one or more than three. It is also worth noting that catering staff are treated with the same respect as other employees. See the section *World of Islam* at the back of the book for further information. **Tipping:** Taxi drivers do not expect a tip. A service charge is often added to bills in hotels and most restaurants, otherwise 10% is appropriate.

BUSINESS PROFILE

ECONOMY: Oil transformed Qatar from an impoverished outcrop on the Arabian peninsula into one of the richest countries in the world in terms of per capita income. Crude petroleum, which is of a very high grade, provides virtually all the country's income. Revenues are dictated by world prices and the requirements of OPEC, of which Qatar is a member, and although prices and production have fallen from their peak in the 1970s, Qatar continues to enjoy a healthy trade surplus. Part of the revenues have been used to develop indigenous industry, mainly based on petrochemicals and refining but also including a steel plant and flour mill. Industrial development is likely to increase sharply during the next few years, observers believe, following the appointment of a new Industry and Works Minister. Agriculture is necessarily limited by the climate and the nature of the country's water resources, although the Government has established a number of experimental projects with artificial resources. The most important economic development in Qatar in recent years has been the discovery of the North Dome gas field, now confirmed as the world's largest. Most of Qatar's oil is sold to Japan and Italy, with whom Qatar signed a 5-year economic and technical co-operation agreement in January 1992. EC countries, Japan and the USA share most of the country's trade.
BUSINESS: Politeness and patience in business dealings are needed. **Office hours:** 0730-1200 and 1500-1800 Saturday to Thursday.
COMMERCIAL INFORMATION: The following organisation can offer advice: The Qatar Chamber of Commerce, PO Box 402, Doha. Tel: 425 131. Fax: 324 338. Telex: 4078 TIJARA DH.
CONFERENCES/CONVENTIONS: Several of Doha's largest hotels provide facilities with extensive support services, including simultaneous translation systems and full audio-visual capability. Contact individual hotels for more information.

HISTORY & GOVERNMENT

HISTORY: Like the rest of the Arabian peninsula, Qatar was occupied by the Turks and incorporated into the Ottoman Empire. After the latter's collapse during the First World War, Qatar came under British rule. The British recognised the Al-Thani family as rulers of the peninsula, providing military protection in exchange for control of Qatar's external affairs under treaties signed in 1916 and 1934. British troops were moved out of the Gulf in 1968 as part of the 'East of Suez' withdrawals. Plans to enhance Qatar's security through federations with Bahrain and the Trucial States (now the United Arab Emirates) failed and in 1971 Qatar assumed full independence under the rule of Sheikh Ahmad. Rivalries within the Al-Thani family immediately after independence culminated in a coup by the chief minister, Sheikh Khalifa Bin Hamad Al-Thani. Under Khalifa's regime, Qatar has used its substantial oil revenues to develop a modern infrastructure, health and education services. It has allied itself closely with Saudi Arabia on regional and international issues (but see below). Qatar was also one of the instigators of the Gulf Co-operation Council, inaugurated in 1981, which seeks to establish an EC-style trade structure in the Gulf area and to provide for a regional defence policy. The security aspect of the Council's work has received greater attention since the Iraqi invasion of Kuwait. In July 1991 the Council was involved in calming a dispute between Qatar and Bahrain over a group of small but potentially oil-rich islands in the Gulf; the issue is now under deliberation by the International Court of Justice. A more recent border dispute with Saudi Arabia, which has led to the tearing-up of a bilateral agreement signed in 1965, has yet to be solved. Despite formal support for its fellow Arabs in Iraq in the war against Iran, Qatar avoided the same level of involvement in the conflict as some of its Gulf neighbours, although it did play a major role during the protracted peace negotiations. Qatar was an active participant in the multinational alliance assembled to liberate Kuwait in 1990. Regional upheavals have shown little sign as yet of prompting a liberalisation of Qatar's autocratic political system. However, the presentation of a petition in January 1992 to the Amir, signed by 50 prominent Qataris and demanding the establishment of a consultative assembly (a *majlis as-shura*, similar to that existing in other Gulf states) shows that there is pressure for reform.
GOVERNMENT: The Al-Thani family rules Qatar as an absolute monarchy without independent legislature and without political parties. Executive power is partially devolved to a Council of Ministers appointed by the Amir who is both Head of State and Prime Minister. An advisory council with 30 appointees was created in 1972.

CLIMATE

Summer (June to September) is very hot with low rainfall. Winter is cooler with occasional rainfall. Spring and autumn are warm and pleasant.
Required clothing: Lightweight cottons and linens are worn during summer months, with warm clothes for cooler evenings and during the winter. Rainwear is advisable during winter.

BAHRAIN (5m)

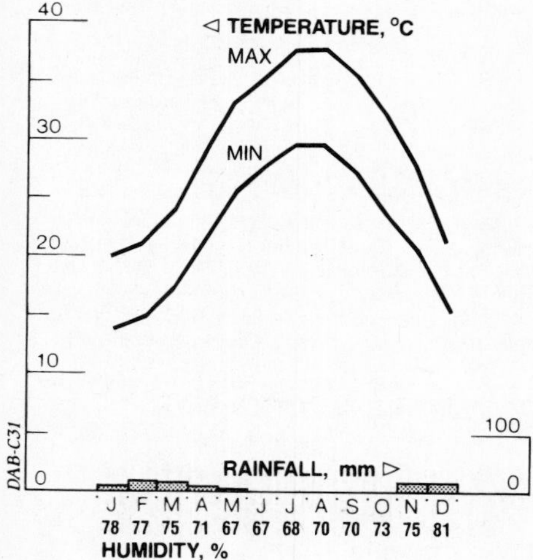

TEMPERATURE CONVERSIONS
-20 -10 0°C 10 20 30 40
0 10 20 30°F40 50 60 70 80 90 100
RAINFALL CONVERSIONS 0mm 200 400 600 800
0in 5 10 15 20 25 30

REUNION

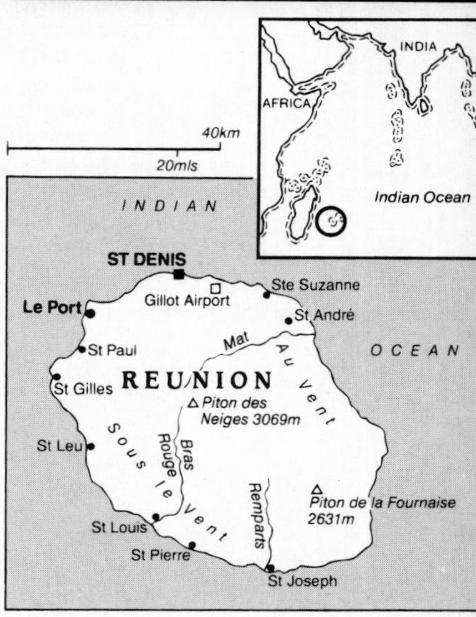

Location: Due east of Madagascar, in the Indian Ocean.

Diplomatic Representation: Réunion is an Overseas Département of the Republic of France; addresses of French Embassies, Consulates and Tourist Offices may be found in the *France* section earlier in the *World Travel Guide*. Tourist information may also be obtained from:
Comité du Tourisme de la Réunion
BP 1119
Residence Vetiver
23 Rue Tourette
97482 Saint-Denis Cedex
Réunion
Tel: 210 041 *or* 418 441. Fax: 202 593. Telex: 916068.
Comité du Tourisme de la Réunion
90 rue la Boétie
75008 Paris
France
Tel: (1) 40 75 02 79. Fax: (1) 40 75 02 73.

AREA: 2512 sq km (970 sq miles).
POPULATION: 597,828 (1990).
POPULATION DENSITY: 238 per sq km.
CAPITAL: Saint-Denis. **Population:** 122,000 (1990).
GEOGRAPHY: Réunion lies 760km (407 miles) due east of Madagascar in the Indian Ocean. Running diagonally across the island is a chain of volcanic peaks, separating a green humid eastern zone *(Le Vent)* from a dry, sheltered south and west *(Sous le Vent)*. The majority of the population lives along the coast. Sugar-cane production accounts for over half the arable land in a country where many basic foodstuffs are imported. Five smaller islands, with a total area of less than 50 sq km (20 sq miles), are all uninhabited.
LANGUAGE: French is the official language. Local Creole *patois* is also spoken.
RELIGION: The majority of the population is Roman Catholic with a Muslim minority.
TIME: GMT + 4.
ELECTRICITY: 220 volts AC, 50Hz.
COMMUNICATIONS: Telephone: IDD is available. Country code: 262. **Telex/telegram:** Facilities are available in Saint-Denis. **Post:** Airmail to Europe takes up to three weeks. *Poste Restante* facilities are available in Saint-Denis. **Press:** The two biggest dailies are the *Quotidien de la Réunion* and the *Journal de l'Ile de la Réunion*. There are no English-language dailies.
BBC World Service and Voice of America frequencies: From time to time these change. See the section *How to Use this Book* for more information.

BBC:				
MHz	21.470	17.885	15.420	9.630
Voice of America:				
MHz	21.49	15.60	9.525	6.035

PASSPORT/VISA

Regulations and requirements may be subject to change at short notice, and you are advised to contact the appropriate diplomatic or consular authority before finalising travel arrangements. Details of these may be found at the head of this country's entry. Any numbers in the chart refer to the footnotes below.

	Passport Required?	Visa Required?	Return Ticket Required?
Full British	Yes	No	Yes
BVP	Not valid	-	-
Australian	Yes	Yes	Yes
Canadian	Yes	No	Yes
USA	Yes	No	Yes
Other EC	Yes	No	Yes
Japanese	Yes	No	Yes

PASSPORTS: Valid passport required by all.
British Visitors Passport: Not accepted.
VISAS: Required by all except:
(a) nationals of countries shown in the chart above for stays of up to 3 months;
(b) nationals of Andorra, Austria, Cyprus, Czechoslovakia, Finland, Hungary, Liechtenstein, Malta, Monaco, New Zealand, Norway, Poland, San Marino, Sweden, Switzerland and the Vatican City for stays of up to 3 months;
(c) nationals of Mauritius for stays of up to 15 days, to whom visas are issued on arrival (these cannot be granted more than 6 times a year at intervals of at least 1 month).
Application to: French Consulate General. For address, see top of *France* entry.
Application requirements: (a) 3 forms. (b) 3 photos. (c) Travel documentation.
Working days required: Usually one day, although longer in the case of some nationalities.

MONEY

Currency: French Franc (FFr) = 100 centimes. Notes are in denominations of FFr500, 200, 100, 50, 20 and 10. Coins are in denominations of FFr10, 5, 2 and 1, and 50, 20, 10 and 5 centimes.
Credit cards: American Express, Visa and Diners Club are widely accepted. Access/Mastercard has more limited use. Check with your credit card company for details of merchant acceptability and other services which may be available.
Travellers cheques: Accepted in all the usual institutions.
Exchange rate indicators: The following figures are included as a guide to the movements of the French Franc against Sterling and the US Dollar:

Date:	Oct '89	Oct '90	Oct '91	Oct '92
£1.00=	10.10	9.97	9.92	8.27
$1.00=	6.40	5.10	5.72	5.21

Currency restrictions: Restrictions on the import and export of both foreign and local currency are the same as those for France. See the entry for *France* earlier in the *World Travel Guide*.
Banking hours: 0800-1600 Monday to Friday.

DUTY FREE

The following goods may be imported into Réunion without incurring customs duty:
200 cigarettes or 100 cigarillos or 50 cigars or 250g of tobacco;
1 litre of spirits over 22% proof or 2 litres of spirits;
2 litres of sparkling wine of less than 22% proof;
50g of perfume and 250ml of toilet water;
Other goods to the value of FFr300.
For passengers arriving from Mauritius:
200 cigarettes or 50 cigars or 250g tobacco.

PUBLIC HOLIDAYS

Public holidays celebrated in Réunion are the same as in France. See the entry for *France* earlier in the *World Travel Guide.*

HEALTH

Regulations and requirements may be subject to change at short notice, and you are advised to contact your doctor well in advance of your intended date of departure. Any numbers in the chart refer to the footnotes below.

	Special Precautions?	Certificate Required?
Yellow Fever	No	1
Cholera	No	-
Typhoid & Polio	2	-
Malaria	No	-
Food & Drink	3	-

[1]: A yellow fever vaccination certificate is required from travellers over one year of age arriving from infected areas.
[2]: There is a risk of typhoid, but not of polio.
[3]: All water should be regarded as being potentially contaminated. Water used for drinking, brushing teeth or making ice should have first been boiled or otherwise sterilised. Facilities are limited and full health insurance is advised. Milk is unpasteurised and should be boiled. Powdered or tinned milk is available and is advised, but make sure that it is reconstituted with pure water. Avoid dairy products which are likely to have been made from unboiled milk. Only eat well-cooked meat and fish, preferably served hot. Pork, salad and mayonnaise may carry increased risk. Vegetables should be cooked and fruit peeled.
Rabies is present. For those at high risk, vaccination before arrival should be considered. If you are bitten abroad seek medical advice without delay. For more information consult the *Health* section at the back of the book.
Health care: There are 19 hospitals and there is an outpatient clinic in each town or village. The French national health scheme is in force and there is a Reciprocal Health Agreement with the UK; see the entry for *France* earlier in the *World Travel Guide* for details.

TRAVEL - International

AIR: The main airlines to serve Réunion are *Air France (AF)* and *UTA (UT)*.
Approximate flight time: From *London* to Gillot is 14 hours 40 minutes.
International airport: *Saint-Denis (RUN)* (Gillot) is 5.5km (3.5 miles) from Saint-Denis (travel time – 20 minutes).
SEA: Both freight and passenger lines (a large number are French) put in at Pointe-des-Galets.

TRAVEL - Internal

AIR: Aero-clubs at Gillot Airport hire planes for flights over the island, which are well worth the price.
SEA: Four shipping lines run services around the island.
ROAD: Roads are fair and over 2975km (1850 miles) of highway are tarred. Speed limits are the same as in France. The main road runs on a north–south axis. The island can be easily crossed by bus, taxi or hired car. The **bus** services are excellent and luxurious, with very comfortable vehicles. Buses stop by request. **Car hire:** Available from the airport and from rental firms in Saint-Denis. **Documentation:** An International Driving Permit is recommended, though not legally required.

ACCOMMODATION

There is a good range of hotels, inns, lodges and *pensions*. Prices are high (and plumbing somewhat basic), but the food is often excellent. Tariffs usually include bed and breakfast, tax and service charges. There are *gîtes* (shelters) for hikers in the mountains, and good camping facilities. For further information contact Relais Départmental de Gîtes Ruraux, 18 rue Sainte-Anne, 97400 Saint-Denis. Tel: 203 190 *or* 218 336. Telex: 916068. **Grading:** Hotels range from **1** to **4 stars.**

RESORTS & EXCURSIONS

Saint-Denis, the capital, has several places of interest, including the *Natural History Museum* and the *Leon Dierx Art Gallery* with its collection of French Impressionists. There are various temples, a mosque and a cathedral, a sign of the cultural and religious variety of the island population. Around town a number of trips are recommended, such as the *Plaine d'Affouches* in **La Montagne** which is lined by lush tamarind trees and *calumets*, a type of wild fig tree. From **Brûlé** a footpath leads to the *Roche-Ecrite*, a 2227m-high summit which overlooks the whole of the northern part of the island and slopes down to the cirques of Malfate and Salazie. All in all, over 600km (370 miles) of marked and excellently maintained footpaths lead through the great natural beauty of the island. A special feature on Réunion are the so-called *cirques* – large volcanic valleys surrounded by mountains, creating an impressive natural amphitheatre of about 10km in diameter, washed into the rock by time and erosion. Day-long sightseeing trips to the cirques may be arranged with travel agents in Saint-Denis.
Cilaos, once infamous as a refuge for escaped slaves, is a lovely mountain area rising to about 1220m (4000ft) with impressive views from *Le Bras Sec* and *Ilet à Cordres*.
The most beautiful cirque is probably **Salazie**, with its magnificent waterfalls, especially those known as *Le Voile de la Mariée* (The Bride's Veil) near **Hell-Bourg.** The trout farm here is worth a visit and there is a lovely day trip to **Grand-Ilet** taking in spectacularly rugged scenery. *Piton des Neiges* is the highest point on the island and is an enjoyable hike from Hell-Bourg.
Mafate is the most secluded of the valleys, unconnected by any road with the outside world. Whilst there, it is worth visiting the historic town of **St Paul,** Réunion's original capital, and birthplace of Leconte de Lisle.
There are tours to the island's still-active volcano, *La Fournaise*.
Nez-de-Boeuf ('ox's nose') affords a splendid view over the *Rivière des Remparts*, 1000m (3300ft) below, the *Plaine des Sables* and the *Belle Combe* pass. The *Enclos Fouque* crater and the highest peak of the 2631m (8632ft) *Fournaise* can both be explored on foot. The still active *Bory* and *Brûlant* craters are also well worth a visit.
Réunion abounds with tropical flowers, trees and fruit and there are tours which aim to show the visitor some of the many species on the island, before returning to the *Botanical Gardens* at Saint-Denis.
Beaches: Réunion does not have particularly extensive beaches, but those on the leeward west coast are particularly beautiful with yellow, black or white sands. Some of the best beaches are to be found at *Saint-Gilles, Saint-Leu* and *Etang-Sale*. These are mostly shallow coral, running out to the reef. The *Corail Turtle Farm* near Saint Leu is worth a visit.

SOCIAL PROFILE

FOOD & DRINK: A variety of excellent restaurants, some run by hotels, offer good French cuisine and Creole specialities, notably *rougail* (seafood with sauces) and

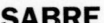

RÉUNION | **HEALTH REGULATIONS** | **VISA REGULATIONS** | Code-Link

GALILEO/WORLDSPAN

TI-DFT/RUN/HE

TI-DFT/RUN/VI

SABRE

TIDFT/RUN/HE

TIDFT/RUN/VI

To access this information on your CRS, swipe the barcode with a light pen or type in the text under the barcode. For more information, see the introduction *How to Use This Book*.

many different unique curries – these include duck, eel and octopus curry *(zourite)*. Worth trying is *bredes*, a delicious local vegetable rather like spinach. Traditional spicy Indian cuisine also appears on the menu, under the heading *massalés*. There are about ten good first-class restaurants in Saint-Denis. Seaside restaurants in particular serve authentic local cuisine – a mixture of Chinese, African and Indian cooking. **Drink:** Arab coffee *(café Bourbon)*, French wine and liqueurs, and good local rum such as *rhum arrange* (white rum with vanilla, orchids, aniseed and cinnamon). Local beer and wine are also very good. A full range of alcoholic drinks is available. Licensing hours are largely unrestricted.
SHOPPING: Local handicrafts include lace and embroidery, coral jewellery and basketwork. Tamarind wood, olive wood and ironwood provide the material for furniture in the traditional 'colonial' style, and are used by sculptors and other craftsmen. Rum, vanilla and extracts of vetiver, geranium and ylang-ylang are also recommended purchases. In Saint-Denis the main shopping streets are the rue du Maréchal-Leclerc, the rue Jean-Chatel, and the rue Juliette-Dodu. **Shopping hours:** 0830-1200 and 1430-1800 Monday to Saturday.
SPORT: Watersports: Good swimming and other activities are to be found along the *Sous le Vent* coast, especially at Saint-Gilles-des-Bains, which has a reef-protected lagoon. On the more remote beaches, sharks may be a danger, so it is best to enquire locally. **Walking/trekking:** There are excellent walking opportunities in the mountains. **Mountaineering:** Good climbing is to be had among the volcanic peaks. **Spas:** Rest cures are available in mountain resorts, such as Cilaos, which is a mountain spa. **Fishing:** Trout fishing is to be found at the Takamaka Falls.
SPECIAL EVENTS: Traditional Creole dancing *(Sega* and *Maloya)* is performed on special occasions and the Asian communities occasionally perform rituals such as *Malabar* dancing and fire-walking.
SOCIAL CONVENTIONS: The islanders have always followed French fashion and so dress should be casual – except for evening wear. Normal social courtesies should be observed. The immigrants from India, Pakistan and Europe have kept their cultural identities, and have not been assimilated into mainstream Réunion society. **Tipping:** Widely practiced and 10% is normal.

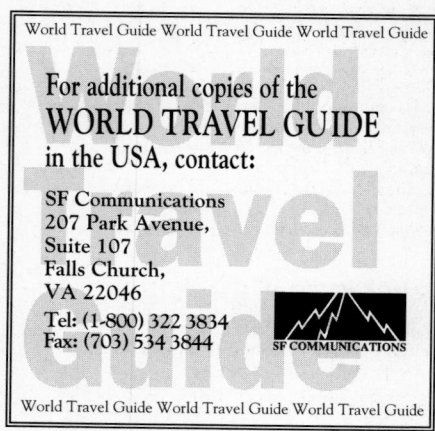

BUSINESS PROFILE

ECONOMY: Sugar cane is the principal crop and export earner in this mainly agricultural economy. Other crops which are grown, given that the soil is mostly of volcanic origin, include vanilla, tobacco, vetiver and ylang-ylang, the last two of which are used in tropical essences. The only industries are those for processing sugar and making rum. Réunion is thus far from self-sufficient in food or anything else and relies on large injections of French aid to cover its trade and budgetary deficits. Apart from France, Réunion trades with Germany, Italy, South Africa and Bahrain.
BUSINESS: The atmosphere is relaxed and friendly; suits will only be required for the smartest meetings. A sound knowledge of French language will be useful, since there are no formal interpreter services available. Prices should be quoted in French Francs, and all trade literature should be in French. **Office hours:** 0800-1200 and 1400-1800 Monday to Friday.
COMMERCIAL INFORMATION: The following organisation can offer advice: Chambre de Commerce et d'Industrie de la Réunion, BP 120, 5 bis rue de Paris, 97463 Saint-Denis Cedex. Tel: 215 366. Fax: 418 034. Telex: 916278.

HISTORY & GOVERNMENT

HISTORY: Réunion was occupied by the French in the 1640s. The island became prosperous during the 18th century, along with nearby Mauritius, when it lay on the shipping routes which carried trade between Europe and Asia. Sugar plantations, worked by slaves imported from Africa, formed the other main economic sector. Réunion was ruled as a colony until 1946 when it was granted the status of an Overseas Department of France, under which it is an integral part of the French state: the Government is represented by a Commissioner. Politics in recent years have been primarily concerned with internal autonomy: most people appear to favour an increase beyond the present level but very few support a complete severing of the link with France, particularly as the island is largely dependent economically upon aid from the French government. The current administration in Paris has guaranteed that support will continue, and broadly supports the islanders' desire for greater autonomy. The main political parties on the island are the Gaullist Rassemblement pour la République (RPR), the centre-right Union pour la Démocratie Française (UDF), the Parti Socialiste (PS) – all three adjuncts of mainland parties – the Parti Communiste Réunionnais (PCR) and a newish right-wing outfit called France-Réunion-Avenir (FRA, literally France-Réunion-Future). Of the five seats allocated to Réunion in the French National Assembly (increased from three in 1986), the Communists hold two seats and the UDF, RPR and FRA hold one each. In the concurrent elections for the Regional Council, one of the two elected ruling bodies on the island, the RPR-UDF alliance, won 18 of the 45 seats and the FRA won 8, giving the right-wing parties a working majority. Pierre Lagourgue of the FRA was elected President of the Regional Council. The Communists (13) and the Socialists (6) are the main opposition parties. The balance of forces on the 44-seat General Council, elections for which were held in 1988, is similar.
GOVERNMENT: Apart from the Governor, who represents the French government, there are two councils with local powers, both of which are elected for 6-year terms by proportional representation. Réunion sends three representatives to the French National Assembly, and two to the Senate. As a Départment of the French Republic, it is also entitled to representation at the European Parliament in Strasbourg.

CLIMATE

Hot tropical climate. The best months are from May to October on the coasts. Temperatures are cooler in the hills, occasionally dropping to freezing point in the mountains at night. The cyclone season (January to March) is hot and wet. The eastern half of the island around *Le Vent* and the mountain slopes have a fairly high rainfall throughout the year.
Required clothing: Lightweights are worn throughout most of the year on the coast. Warmer clothes are needed in the hills and mountains. Rainwear is advisable, especially during the wet season.

ST DENIS Réunion

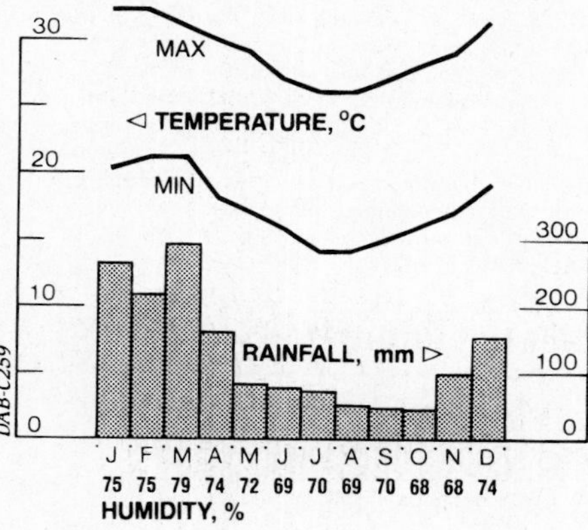

ROMANIA

Location: Eastern Europe.

National Tourist Office (Carpati)
Boulevard Magheru 7
Bucharest 1
Romania
Telex: 11270.
Embassy of Romania
4 Palace Green
London
W8 4QD
Tel: (071) 937 9666/8. Fax: (071) 937 8069. Telex: 22232 ROMANOCORN LDN. Opening hours: 0900-1700 Monday to Friday. *Visa Section:* Tel: (071) 937 9667. Opening hours: 1000-1200 Monday to Friday.
Romanian National Tourist Office (Carpati)
17 Nottingham Street
London
W1M 3RD
Tel: (071) 224 3692. Telex: 262107.
British Embassy
Strada Jules Michelet 24
70154 Bucharest, Romania
Tel: (1) 266 2888. Fax: (1) 595 090. Telex: 11295.
Embassy of Romania
1607 23rd Street, NW
Washington, DC
20008
Tel: (202) 232 4747 *or* 232 6634 *or* 232 6593. Fax: (202) 232 4748.
Romanian National Tourist Office
573 Third Avenue
New York, NY
10016
Tel: (212) 697 6971.
Embassy of the United States of America
Strada Tudor Arghezi 7-9
Bucharest, Romania
Tel: (1) 610 4040. Fax: (1) 612 0395. Telex: 11416.
Embassy of Romania
655 Rideau Street
Ottawa, Ontario
K1N 6A3
Tel: (613) 232 5345 *or* 232 3001. Fax: (613) 567 4356.
Consulates in: Montréal and Toronto.
Romanian Tourist Information Office
Suite 530
111 Peter Street
Toronto, Ontario
M5V 2G9
Tel: (416) 585 5802. Fax: (416) 585 4798.
Canadian Embassy
PO Box 2966 Post Office 22
36 Nicolae Lorga
71118 Bucharest, Romania
Tel: (1) 650 6140 *or* 659 7394. Fax: (1) 612 0366.
Telex: 10690 CANAD R.

AREA: 237,500 sq km (91,699 sq miles).
POPULATION: 23,190,000 (1990 estimate).
POPULATION DENSITY: 97.6 per sq km.
CAPITAL: Bucharest. **Population:** 2,200,000 (1989 estimate).
GEOGRAPHY: Romania is bordered to the north and east by the CIS, the southeast by the Black Sea, the south by Bulgaria, the southwest and west by Yugoslavia and in the west by Hungary. The country is divided into four geographical areas. Transylvania, a belt of Alpine massifs and forests, and Moldavia compose the northern half of the country, which is divided down the middle by the north–south strip of the Carpathian Mountains. South of the east–west line of the Carpathians lies the flat Danube plain of Walachia with the capital Bucharest, its border with Bulgaria being defined by the course of the Danube. Romania's coastline is along the Black Sea, incorporating the Black Sea port of Constanta, the Danube Delta and some fine resorts.
LANGUAGE: Romanian is the official language. Some Hungarian and German is spoken in border areas, while English and French are spoken by those in the tourist industry.
RELIGION: Romanian Orthodox with Roman Catholic, Lutheran, Muslim and Jewish minorities.
TIME: GMT + 2 (GMT + 3 in summer).
ELECTRICITY: 220 volts AC, 50Hz.
COMMUNICATIONS: Telephone: IDD is available into Romania, but outgoing calls must be made through the operator. Country code: 40. Public telephones are widely available. Hotels often impose a high service charge for long-distance calls. **Telex/telegram:** Facilities at post offices and a night telegram service (2000-0700) are available in Bucharest. Telex facilities are available at large hotels. **Post:** Airmail to western Europe takes up to two weeks. **Press:** There are daily and weekly newspapers published in Romanian, Hungarian and German.
BBC World Service and Voice of America frequencies: From time to time these change. See the section *How to Use this Book* for more information.

BBC:				
MHz	17.640	15.070	9.410	6.180
Voice of America:				
MHz	9.670	6.040	5.995	1.197

PASSPORT/VISA

Regulations and requirements may be subject to change at short notice, and you are advised to contact the appropriate diplomatic or consular authority before finalising travel arrangements. Details of these may be found at the head of this country's entry. Any numbers in the chart refer to the footnotes below.

	Passport Required?	Visa Required?	Return Ticket Required?
Full British	Yes	Yes	Yes
BVP	Not Valid	-	-
Australian	Yes	Yes	Yes
Canadian	Yes	Yes	Yes
USA	Yes	Yes	Yes
Other EC	Yes	Yes	Yes
Japanese	Yes	Yes	Yes

PASSPORTS: Valid passport with a minimum validity of 3 months after return required by all.
British Visitors Passport: Not acceptable.
VISAS: Required by all except:
(a) nationals of the former Eastern bloc countries – Bulgaria, USSR, Croatia, Czechoslovakia, Estonia, Hungary, Latvia, Lithuania, Poland and Yugoslavia (nationals of Albania *do* need a visa);
(b) nationals of the Central African Republic, Congo, Costa Rica, Cuba, Guinea Republic, Mauritania, Mexico, Mongolia, Morocco, San Marino, São Tomé e Principe, Sierra Leone, Tanzania, Tunisia, Turkey and Zambia.
Types of visa: Business, Tourist, Transit (single and double) visas are available, as well as a reduced Tourist visa for all-inclusive package tours. Standard prices for 3-month Business and Tourist visas are £20 for British Passport holders and £17 for other nationals. Tourist visas for package tourists are £10 for all nationals. Transit visas are £20 for British subjects and £10 (Single Transit) and £17 (Double Transit) for other nationals.
Note: Visa fees fluctuate according to the exchange rate of the Pound Sterling against the US Dollar. Contact the consulate in advance regarding fees.
Validity: The Business visa is valid for a stay of up to 60 days. Transit visa is valid for 72 hours within 3 months of the date of issue. Transit visas are obtainable at any frontier crossing or airport.
Application to: Consulate (or Consular Section at Embassy). For address, see top of entry. Visas are also

ROMANIA	HEALTH REGULATIONS	VISA REGULATIONS
		Code-Link
GALILEO/WORLDSPAN	 TI-DFT/BUH/HE	 TI-DFT/BUH/VI
SABRE	 TIDFT/BUH/HE	TIDFT/BUH/VI

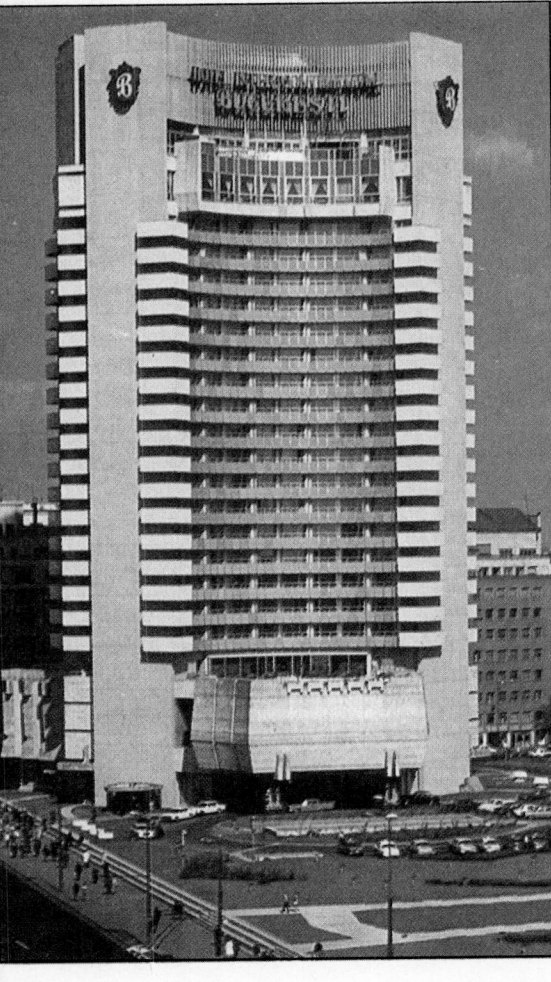

To access this information on your CRS, swipe the barcode with a light pen or type in the text under the barcode. For more information, see the introduction *How to Use This Book*.

granted by any Romanian Embassy or, for those with prepaid accommodation, on arrival in Romania, by any border point, including airports.
Application requirements: (a) Valid passport (due to expire no less than 3 months after return from Romania). (b) Letter indicating date of departure and length of stay (Business visa applications should also include the name of the sponsoring Romanian company). (c) Fee (no cheques). (d) For reduced package-tour visas a confirmation of booking by the tour operator must be included. (e) Postal applications should be accompanied by a stamped, self-addressed envelope.
Working days required: Visas can be processed within 24 hours for an extra cost of £4. Non-urgent standard 3-month visas are issued within 7 or more working days at £20 for British subjects and £17 for all other nationals.
Temporary residence: Enquire at Embassy.

MONEY

Currency: Leu (plural Lei) = 100 bani. Notes are in denominations of 1000, 500, 100, 50, 25 and 10 Lei. Coins are in denominations of 5, 3 and 1 Lei, and 25, 15 and 5 bani.
Credit cards: Access/Mastercard, American Express, Diners Club and Visa are all widely accepted. Check with your credit card company for details of merchant acceptability and other services which may be available.
Travellers cheques: Like credit cards, these will be useful in hotels, restaurants, shops and for obtaining cash at the Tourist Office.
Exchange rate indicators: The following figures are included as a guide to the movements of the Leu against Sterling and the US Dollar:

Date	Oct '89	Oct '90	Oct '91	Oct '92
£1.00=	14.22	38.58	104.07	677.79
$1.00=	9.01	19.75	59.96	427.09

Currency restrictions: The import or export of local currency is prohibited. There are no restrictions on the import of foreign currency. Foreigners may export up to the unused amount.
Banking hours: 0900-1200 and 1300-1500 Monday to Friday; 0900-1230 Saturday.

DUTY FREE

The following items may be imported into Romania without incurring customs duty:
200 cigarettes or 300g of tobacco;
2 litres of of spirits;
4 litres of wine or beer;
Gifts up to value of 2000 Lei.

PUBLIC HOLIDAYS

Public holidays observed in Romania are as follows:
Apr 9 '93 Good Friday. **Apr 12** Easter Monday. **May 1-2** International Labour Day. **Dec 1** National Day. **Dec 25** Christmas. **Jan 1-2 '94** New Year.

HEALTH

Regulations and requirements may be subject to change at short notice, and you are advised to contact your doctor well in advance of your intended date of departure. Any numbers in the chart refer to the footnotes below.

	Special Precautions?	Certificate Required?
Yellow Fever	No	No
Cholera	No	No
Typhoid & Polio	Yes	-
Malaria	No	-
Food & Drink	1	-

[1]: Mains water is normally chlorinated, and whilst relatively safe may cause mild abdominal upsets. Bottled water is available and is advised for the first few days of the stay. Milk is pasteurised and dairy products are safe for consumption. Local meat, poultry, seafood, fruit and vegetables are generally considered safe to eat.
Health care: There is a Reciprocal Health Agreement with the UK. Those presenting a UK passport and a driver's licence or NHS card are entitled to free treatment in hospitals and some free medical and dental treatment elsewhere. Charges are made for medicine supplied by a public chemist. Other nationals should contact a Romanian Embassy for details of other agreements.

TRAVEL - International

AIR: Romania's national airline is *Tarom (RO)*.
Approximate flight time: From *London* to Bucharest is 3 hours 30 minutes.
International airport: *Bucharest (BUH)* (Otopeni) is 16km (10 miles) north of the city (travel time – 35 minutes). Full duty-free facilities are available. A 24-hour coach service runs every 60 minutes. Return is from Tarom Agency, 10 Brezoianu Street. Bus no 49 runs every 20 minutes from 0530-2350. Return is from Scinteia House, Press Square. Taxis are also available.
SEA: The main international passenger ports are Constanta and Sulina on the Black Sea. There is a ferry service on the Danube, starting from Orsova, to Yugoslavia and to Bulgaria. **River cruises:** Sailing from Vienna to the Black Sea along the Danube, these stop at various places of interest, including Vienna, Bratislava, Budapest, Belgrade, Bazias, Giurgiu, Calafat and Bucharest. The cruises incorporate varied itineraries: historic towns, museums, art collections, monasteries, spas, archaeological sites, folk evenings, nature reserves (the Danube Delta alone contains more than 250 species of fauna) and of course the dramatic scenery of eastern Europe, including Transylvania. For further information, contact the National Tourist Office; address at top of entry.
RAIL: Main international trains from western Europe to Romania (Bucharest) are the *Orient Express* and the *Wiener Waltzer*.
The *Orient Express* departs from Paris Gare de l'Est at 2315, reaching Bucharest at 1220 two days later (total travel time – about 38 hours). Sleeping cars from Paris run four times a week (not in the summer). All have first- and second-class carriages. The *Wiener Waltzer* runs to Bucharest in summer only (June to September) and includes two nights' travel from Basel, arriving in Bucharest two days later at 0815. There are no through carriages from Basel, which means moving to the Bucharest coaches in Vienna. As well as day carriages, there are sleeping cars from Vienna to both Bucharest and Constanta on the Black Sea coast. There are also through trains from other east European cities.
ROAD: The most direct international routes to Romania are via Germany, Austria and Hungary. The best route from Hungary is the E64 from Budapest to Szeged through Arad, Brasov, Campina and Ploiesti. There is also a route from Szeged to Timisoara. A more frequently used route from Hungary to Germany is through Oradea (the E60).
See below for information on **documentation**.

TRAVEL - Internal

AIR: The main airport for internal flights is *Baneasa* (travel time – 20 minutes to Otopeni). *Tarom (RO)* operates regular services from there to Constanta, Arad, Bacau, Caransebes, Baia Mare, Cluj-Napoca, Iasi, Satu Mare, Timisoara, Oradea, Tirgu Mures, Sibiu, Suceava and Tulcea.
RAIL: *Romanian State Railways* run efficient and cheap services, some with sleeping and restaurant cars. Supplements are payable on rapide and express trains, for which seats must be reserved in advance. Rail Inclusive Tour tickets include transport and hotel accommodation.
ROAD: The *Romanian Automobile Club* (ACR) has its headquarters in Bucharest and offers services through all its branches to *AA* and *RAC* members. The petrol coupon system has been abandoned. Speed limits are 60kmph (37mph) in built-up areas and up to 90kmph (57mph) on main roads. Traffic drives on the right. Driving after any alcohol intake is forbidden. For further information contact the national car association, *Automobil Clubul Román (ACR)*, Strada Take Ionescu 27, 70154 Bucharest. Tel: (1) 615 5510. **Bus:** Local services operate to most towns and villages. **Taxi:** Metered taxis can be hailed in the street or called from hotels. Drivers expect a 10% tip. **Car hire:** Available at hotels and at Bucharest Airport. **Documentation:** National driving licence or International Driving Permit and Green Card insurance are required.
URBAN: Good public transport facilities are provided in the main centres. Bucharest has a good bus system and a metro. Tickets are pre-purchased from agents, and there are stamping machines on board buses and trains. There are are also daily, weekly and fortnightly passes. A separate 18-route minibus network is operated.

ACCOMMODATION

HOTELS: Visitors are advised to purchase prepaid vouchers for accommodation through a travel agency which has contract links with the National Tourist Office. Bookings will be confirmed by telex (any booking not confirmed may not be honoured).
SELF-CATERING: Addresses of private accommodation and self-catering establishments are available from local tourist offices.
CAMPING/CARAVANNING: There are around 100 campsites in Romania. Prepaid tourist coupons valid from May to September are available from specialised travel agencies.
YOUTH HOSTELS: Hostels (Strada Onesti) are open in July and August. Information is available from the Youth Tourist Bureau, Strada Onesti 4-6, Bucharest, or through a travel agent specialising in Balkan travel.

RESORTS & EXCURSIONS

Romania's main resort areas are the **Black Sea Coast,** the **Danube Delta,** the **Carpathian Mountains, Bukovina** and **Transylvania.**
BLACK SEA COAST: This coastline is the principal tourist area of Romania and ideal for family holidays. Its 70km (43 miles) of fine white sandy beaches boast many resorts, the main ones being *Mamaia, Eforie Nord, Techirghiol, Eforie Sud, Costinesti, Neptun-Olimp, Jupiter, Venus-Aurora, Saturn* and *Mangalia.* There are ten boating centres for watersports on the sea and lakes, and both daytime and evening cruises from the Dobrudja region to other resorts. The curative properties of the salt waters and the mud from *Lake Techirghiol* (whose thermal springs have a year-round temperature of 24°C), Mangalia, Eforie and Neptun, make the Romanian Riviera popular with those seeking spa treatments, especially for rheumatism. The Greek/Byzantine port of **Constanta,** founded in the 6th century BC, is worth a visit, and inland there are interesting archaeological sites including the ancient Greek city ruins of *Histria, Tomis* and *Callatis.* The area is inhabited by foxes, otters, wildcats and boars and in the migratory periods one can see over 300 species of birds.
DANUBE DELTA: A vast expanse of protected watery wilderness in the north of the Romanian Black Sea Coast, comprised by the three main arms of the Danube with numerous little waterways, wetlands, small patches of forest and a rich and varied wildlife including over 300 species of birds. The backwaters can be explored by fishing boat or floating hotel, and several hotels and campsites welcome visitors. The main town of the Delta is **Tulcea** with its excellent *Danube Delta Museum.*
CARPATHIAN MOUNTAINS: This beautiful and densely forested mountainous area lends itself to many sporting and leisure activities such as skiing, bob sleighing, horseriding and tennis. Situated in picturesque valleys and on mountain slopes are many health and winter resorts, open all year round and well equipped with ski-hire facilities etc. The major resorts are: *Sinaia* (bob-sleigh tracks); *Busteni; Predeal* and *Poiana Brasov* (illuminated ski slopes); *Semenic; Paltinis; Bilea; Borsa* and *Durau.*
All are equipped to cater for a long winter sports season running from December to April. Spectacular mountain lakes are found in the *Fagaras* and *Retezat* ranges, and caves in the *Apuseni, Mehedinti* and *Bihor* regions.
BUKOVINA: An area in the northern Carpathian foothills which has unique churches and monasteries with exceptional frescoes dating back 500 years. **Sucevita** is the home of a monastery with the largest number of frescoes in the region. 29km (18 miles) west of Sucevita is **Moldovita,** renowned for its most spectacular monastical paintings. The Moldavian region has 48 monasteries in total, nearly all of them built to celebrate a victory over the Turks in the 14th and 15th centuries.
TRANSYLVANIA: Since Roman times Romanian Spas have been known for their miraculous healing powers. Transylvania holds many well-equipped spa towns, such as **Baile Felix, Baile Herculane, Sovata** and **Covasana,** some of which have facilities offering acupuncture, acupressure and slimming cures. This is also the heart of Dracula country, the famous Bram Stoker character based on the medieval King of the region, Vlad 'the Impaler'. One of Dracula's abodes, *Bran Castle,* set in a commanding position with its thick walls and peaked tower, offers a highly dramatic view. From here one can travel to **Sibiu** where rich and authentic traditional costumes can be seen in the old market place.

SOCIAL PROFILE

FOOD & DRINK: Although there are some regional differences between the provinces, there is a definite national culinary tradition. Dishes include *ciorba de perisoare* (soup with meatballs), *ciorba tanancasca* (meat with vegetables), lamb *bors,* giblet soup and a variety of fish soups. Sour cream or eggs are often added to soups. *Mamaliga* (a staple of mashed cornmeal) is served in many ways. Other national specialities include *tocana* (pork, beef or mutton stew seasoned with onions and

served with *mamaliga*), *ghiveci* (over 20 vegetables cooked in oil and served cold), Moldavian *parjoale* (flat meat patties, highly spiced and served with garnishes), *sarmale* (pork balls in cabbage leaves), *mititei* (a variety of highly seasoned charcoal-grilled meat) and *patricieni* (charcoal-grilled sausages similar to frankfurters). Fish dishes include *nisetru la gratar* (grilled Black Sea sturgeon), *raci* (crayfish) and *scrumbii la gratar* (grilled herring). Desserts include *placinte cu poale in briu* (rolled cheese pies), Moldavian *cozonac* (brioche) and *pasca* (a sweet cheese-cake). Although there are inexpensive self-service snack bars, table service is the norm. **Drink:** A traditional drink with entrées is *tzuica* (plum brandy) which varies in strength, dryness and smell according to locality. *Tzuica de Bihor* is the strongest and generally known as *palinca*. Romanian wines have won international prizes and include *pinot noir* and *chardonnay* from the Murfatlar vineyards. *Grasa* and *feteasa* from Moldavia's Cotnari vineyards are also recommended. Many Romanian wines are taken with soda water. Romanian beers are also good. There are no licensing hours, but the legal age for drinking in a bar is 18.

NIGHTLIFE: Bucharest has a growing number of popular discotheques and nightspots with entertainment and live dancing. Restaurants at most major hotels double as nightclubs and there are also several Parisian-style cafés. Opera is performed at the Romanian Opera House and the Romanian Athenaeum has two symphony orchestras. Folk entertainment is performed at the Rapsodia Romana Artistic Ensemble Hall and there are numerous theatres.

SHOPPING: Specialist purchases include embroideries, pottery, fabrics, woodcarvings, metal and leather items. Rugs, glass paintings and silk dresses are particularly attractive. **Shopping hours:** 0600-2100 Monday to Saturday and 0600-1200 Sunday, although these vary according to season.

SPORT: Tennis: There are lawn tennis courts in seaside and mountain resorts and in many towns. **Horseriding:** Centres at Izvin (Banat), Mangalia (the sea coast), Radauti (Northern Moldavia) and Simbata de Jos (near Fagaras). The state racecourse is at Ploiesti. **Winter sports:** There are numerous facilities. Pistes of varying degrees of difficulty are found in almost all mountain resorts, the majority of which are equipped with cable cars. National and international **skiing** and **bob-sleighing** competitions are organised in the main winter sports resorts (Sinaia, Predeal and Poiana Brasov). **Sledging** tracks, **skating** and **ice hockey** are available at most mountain resorts. **Angling:** Romania has many easily accessible places for fishing. **Watersports:** Beautiful beaches and luxury resorts line the Black Sea coast. The seas are clean and tideless and a full range of facilities is available.

SPECIAL EVENTS: Folk festivals include dances, music and displays of traditional art. Contact the National Tourist Office for full details of events. The following are of special interest:

May *Simbra Oilor*, Oas; *The Lilac Feast*, Ponoare. **Jun** *The Hercules Festival*, Baile Herculane Spa. **Aug** *The Romanian Calusul* (parade of costume and dance), Slatina; *The Mountain Song*, Lainici. **Mid-Aug** *Hora de la Prislop*. **Sep** *Vintage celebrations*, Odobesti. **Dec** *Marmatia*.

SOCIAL CONVENTIONS: Handshaking is the most common form of greeting. Visitors should follow normal European courtesies on social occasions. Dress tends to be rather conservative but casual wear is suitable. Beachwear should not be worn away from the beach or poolside. Smoking is prohibited on public transport, in cinemas and theatres. **Photography:** Sensitive installations with military importance should not be photographed. **Tipping:** A 12% service charge is added in most restaurants. Porters and taxi drivers expect tips.

BUSINESS PROFILE

ECONOMY: Agriculture is a key sector of the economy employing nearly one-third of the workforce. The country is an important producer of wheat and maize, but it also grows vegetables, fruit, sugar beet and vegetable oil seeds; many farms also breed livestock. The sector as a whole has suffered from lack of investment due to economic policies which have favoured heavy industry. Forestry is being developed under a long-term programme. Romanian industry produces industrial and transport equipment, metals, furniture, chemical products and manufactured consumer goods, but the most important sector is oil, natural gas and oil-derived products (petrochemicals, paints and varnishes). The development of the sector has been unsteady and despite its oil deposits and other energy schemes, including hydro-electric and nuclear, Romanians have suffered severe power shortages. Similarly the food supply situation deteriorated during the 1980s. Part of the reason was the Ceausescu government's overriding desire to eliminate its foreign debt which meant that every conceivable product was assigned for export even to the detriment of the population. The bulk of Romania's imports during the 1980s comprised machinery, equipment and raw materials in accordance with industrial development plans; consumer goods were given a very low priority. The National Salvation Front government has concentrated upon turning Romania into a market economy. A fair amount of progress has been made: the Leu is now directly convertible; price controls have been removed; and the National Privatisation Agency has distributed over 4 million share certificates preparatory to the sale of state assets, 30% of which have been allocated to the general public. For all that, Romania's current economic health is poor: inflation is approaching 100% per annum, unemployment is rising and economic output fell by 13% during 1991. Romania has recently signed a trade agreement with the European Free Trade Association, an economic co-operation agreement with the European Community, and has access to loans from the European Bank for Reconstruction and Development. The CIS is the largest trading partner, followed by Egypt, Italy and Germany. It is unclear as yet whether there will be any significant change in Romanian trade patterns.

BUSINESS: A suit is essential at all business meetings and only on very hot days are shirt-sleeves acceptable. English, German and French are used in business circles. Appointments are necessary and punctuality expected. Business cards are widely used. **Office hours:** 0700-1530 Monday to Friday, 0700-1230 Saturday.

COMMERCIAL INFORMATION: The following organisations can offer advice: Ministrul Comertului Exterior si Cooperari Economice Internationale (Ministry of Foreign Trade and Economic Co-operation), Boulevard Republicii 14, Bucharest. Tel: (1) 616 6850. Telex: 10533; *or*

Chamber of Commerce and Industry of Romania, Boulevard Nicolae Balcescu 22, 79502 Bucharest. Tel: (1) 612 1312. Fax: (1) 613 0091. Telex: 11374.

HISTORY & GOVERNMENT

HISTORY: Ethnic Romanians are descendants of the Dacians, one of the Thracian tribes that inhabited the Balkan peninsula during the first millenium BC. After surviving numerous invasions and regional upheavals, during which provinces were annexed variously to Hungary, Austria and the Ottoman Empire, Romania became an independent country with a monarchy in 1881. Romania entered the Second World War on the side of the Axis powers but, following military defeats and internal political pressure, the regime was overthrown in 1944 and replaced by a coalition government of communists, liberals and social democrats. The communists gradually established their political hegemony within the Government. In 1947 the monarchy was deposed and the Government declared the Romanian People's Republic. Nicolae Ceausescu assumed the post of First Secretary of the Romanian Communist Party (RCP) in 1965 and held power in the country until the dramatic, bloody and largely unpredicted revolution during Christmas 1989. Despite being a member of the Warsaw Pact and the COMECON trading bloc, Romania was inclined to pursue independent policies, particularly with regard to military and foreign policy matters: Ceausescu refused to allow other Warsaw Pact military forces to maintain bases in the country, and in 1968 he vigorously denounced the Soviet-led invasion of Czechoslovakia. In the era of Gorbachev, whose policies Ceausescu considered to be irrelevant for his own country, Romania lost this unique advantage as the draconian and uncompromising nature of the President's domestic policies, including forced assimmilation of minorities, tight rationing of basic needs and severe cultural and political repression, became apparent. In mid-December 1989, protests in the city of Timisoara triggered a nationwide revolt. A large part of the army defected from the regime to join the revolutionaries – under the loose umbrella of the National Salvation Front (NSF) – and for several days the country was in a state of open civil war as the pro-Ceausescu Securitate (the security forces) mounted a desperate bid to prevent the collapse of the regime, during which thousands were killed. The President and his wife were captured, quickly tried and executed. The new government, under the then provisional leadership of Ion Iliescu (the former Communist Central Committee Secretary) was faced with a number of acute problems: the pacification of the country; the disbanding of the Securitate; the restoration of the economy; and the need to prepare Romania for peaceful multi-party elections. Iliescu was confirmed in office by a presidential election in May 1990 at which he took 85% of the vote as the NSF candidate. Simultaneous elections to the two chambers of the national assembly produced similarly large majorities for the Front (263 of 387 seats in the House of Deputies and 91 of 119 in the Senate). The new government of Prime Minister Petre Roman, composed mainly of young technocrats, started to introduce a reform programme similar to those elsewhere in Eastern Europe and worked hard to improve Romania's image abroad. Foreign aid gradually resumed and the IMF approved a much-needed economic support package. The response at home, where the measures bit hard and quickly, was less generous. Violent civil unrest broke out on several occasions during 1990 between pro- and anti-NSF elements. Petre Roman resigned in September 1990. He was replaced by Teodor Stolojan, previously Finance Minister, who continued the policies pursued by Roman. Stolojan, who leads a non-party interim government, successfully guided Romania's new constitution through the hurdles of a referendum and a vote in the national assembly. It establishes Romania as a republic with a market economy and individual rights of free speech, religious adherence and private ownership. The ruling National Salvation Front split into two factions led by Petre Roman and President Ion Iliescu, who has formed his own breakaway party, the Democratic National Salvation Front. Iliescu again prevailed at the next presidential elections held in October 1992, capturing 60% of the vote; at simultaneous parliamentary elections, his party did less well but remains the largest bloc in the new assembly. An unstable coalition government, which is essentially opposed to Iliescu, holds office. The future of Romania's economic reform programme may now be in jeopardy. The other main problem facing the Government, the upheaval in the former Soviet republic of Moldova, is also in need of urgent attention.

GOVERNMENT: Under the provisions of the constitution adopted in December 1991, Romania is a republic. Executive power is vested in a government subordinate to the President, who is elected every four years and is limited to a maximum of two terms in office. The legislature is a bicameral national assembly, elected every four years, comprising the Assembly of Deputies (387 seats) and the Senate (119 seats).

CLIMATE

Romania has four seasons. Summer temperatures are moderated on the coast by sea breezes while inland at sea level it is hot. Winters are coldest in the Carpathian Mountains where there is snow from December through to April. Snow also falls throughout most of the country. Winters are mildest on the coast.

Required clothing: Lightweights are worn in summer on the coast and in low inland areas. Warmer clothes are needed in winter and throughout the year in the uplands. Rainwear is recommended in the spring and autumn.

BUCHAREST Romania (82m)

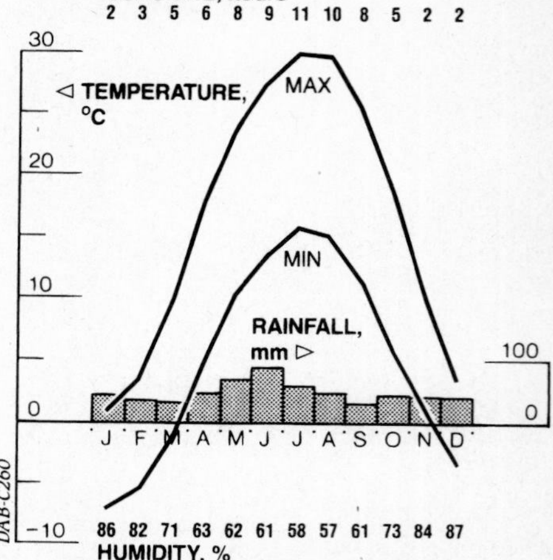

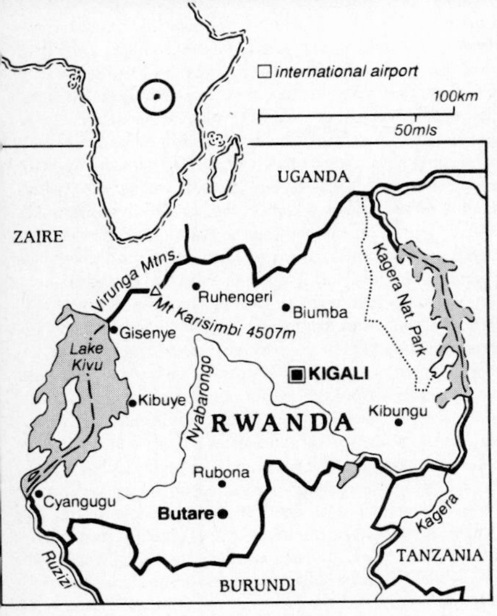

Location: Central Africa.

Office rwandais du tourisme et des parcs nationaux (ORTPN)
BP 905
Kigali, Rwanda
Tel: 76514. Fax: 76512.

Embassy of the Republic of Rwanda
1 avenue des Fleurs
Woluwe St Pierre
1150 Brussels, Belgium
Tel: (2) 763 0705. Telex: 26653.
Consulate in: Antwerp.

British Consulate
BP 356
avenue Paul VI
Kigali, Rwanda
Tel: 75219 *or* 75905. Telex: 509 RWANDEX RW.

Embassy of the Republic of Rwanda
1714 New Hampshire Avenue, NW
Washington, DC
20009
Tel: (202) 232 2882. Fax: (202) 232 4544. Telex: 248505.

Embassy of the United States of America
BP 28
boulevard de la Révolution
Kigali, Rwanda
Tel: 75601/2/3. Fax: 72128.

Embassy of the Republic of Rwanda
121 Sherwood Drive
Ottawa, Ontario
K1Y 3V1
Tel: (613) 722 5835 *or* 722 7921. Fax: (613) 729 3291.
Consulates in: Montréal and Toronto.

Canadian Embassy
PO Box 1177
rue Akagera
Kigali, Rwanda
Tel: 73210 *or* 73278 *or* 73787. Fax: 72719. Telex: 22592 DOMCAN RW.

AREA: 26,338 sq km (10,169 sq miles).
POPULATION: 7,000,000 (1990 estimate).
POPULATION DENSITY: 265.8 per sq km.
CAPITAL: Kigali. **Population:** 225,000 (1990).
GEOGRAPHY: Rwanda is a small mountainous country in central Africa, bordered to the north by Uganda, to the east by Tanzania, to the south by Burundi and to the west by Zaïre. The country is divided by great peaks of up to 3000m (9842ft) which run across the country from north to south. The Birunga volcanoes, rising steeply from Lake Kivu in the west, slope down first to a hilly central plateau and further eastwards to an area of marshy lakes around the upper reaches of the Kagera River, where the Kagera National Park is situated.
LANGUAGE: The official languages are Kinyarwanda and French. Kiswahili is used for trade and commerce.
RELIGION: Christian (mostly Roman Catholic) with Islamic and Animist minorities.
TIME: GMT + 2.
ELECTRICITY: 220 volts AC, 50Hz.
COMMUNICATIONS: Telephone: IDD is available. Country code: 250. **Telex/telegram:** Facilities are available in Kigali and main hotels. **Post:** In Kigali post offices open 0800-1200 and 1400-1700 Monday to Friday, 0800-1200 Saturday. Airmail to Europe takes approximately 14 days. **Press:** There are no English-language newspapers. Publications are in French or Kinyarwanda and are weekly or quarterly.
BBC World Service and Voice of America frequencies: From time to time these change. See the section *How to Use this Book* for more information.

BBC:				
MHz	21.470	17.885	15.420	9.630
Voice of America:				
MHz	21.49	15.60	9.525	6.035

PASSPORT/VISA

Regulations and requirements may be subject to change at short notice, and you are advised to contact the appropriate diplomatic or consular authority before finalising travel arrangements. Details of these may be found at the head of this country's entry. Any numbers in the chart refer to the footnotes below.

	Passport Required?	Visa Required?	Return Ticket Required?
Full British	Yes	Yes	Yes
BVP	Not valid	-	-
Australian	Yes	Yes	Yes
Canadian	Yes	Yes	Yes
USA	Yes	Yes	Yes
Other EC	Yes	1	Yes
Japanese	Yes	Yes	Yes

Restricted entry: The Government refuses admission and transit to nationals of Burundi without a regular visa. Visa-free transit by nationals of Burundi is only permitted by the same flight without leaving the airport.
PASSPORTS: Valid passport required by all.
British Visitors Passport: Not accepted.
VISAS: Required by all except:
(a) **[1]** nationals of Germany;
(b) nationals of Tanzania.
Validity: Generally 3 months.
Transit: Visas are not required by those who continue their journey to a third country on the same day, without leaving the airport.
Types of visa: Tourist or Business. Cost: BFr500 (payment must be in *Belgian* Francs) plus BFr300 if the passport is to be returned by registered mail.
Application to: Representatives of Rwanda in Addis Ababa, Beijing, Berne, Bonn, Brussels, Bujumbura, Cairo, Dar es Salaam, Kampala, Kinshasa, Mainz, Mombasa, Montréal, Moscow, Nairobi, New York, Ottawa, Paris, Pretoria, Tokyo, Toronto *or* Washington.
Application requirements: (a) Valid passport. (b) 2 photos. (c) Yellow fever vaccination certificate. (d) 2 completed application forms. (e) Company letters or guarantee. (f) Fee.
Temporary residence: Visas can be extended at the Immigration Office in Kigali.

MONEY

Currency: Rwandese Franc (Rw Fr) = 100 centimes. Notes are in denominations of Rw Fr5000, 1000, 500 and 100. Coins are in denominations of Rw Fr50, 20, 10, 5, 2 and 1.
Credit cards: Access/Mastercard is most widely accepted, with more limited use of Diners Club. Check with your credit card company for details of merchant acceptability and other services which may be available.
Exchange rate indicators: The following figures are included as a guide to the movements of the Rwandese Franc against Sterling and the US Dollar:

Date:	Oct '89	Oct '90	Oct '91	Oct '92
£1.00=	128.71	137.52	216.94	234.60
$1.00=	81.51	70.34	125.00	147.83

Currency restrictions: The import and export of local currency is limited to Rw Fr5000. The import of foreign currency is unlimited, subject to declaration. The export is limited to the amount declared.
Banking hours: 0800-1200 and 1400-1800 Monday to Friday, 0800-1300 Saturday.

DUTY FREE

The following items may be imported into Rwanda by persons over 16 years of age without incurring customs duty:
200 cigarettes or 50 cigars or 454g tobacco;
2 bottles of spirits or wine (opened);
A reasonable amount of perfume.

PUBLIC HOLIDAYS

Public holidays observed in Rwanda are as follows:
Apr 12 '93 Easter Monday. **May 1** Labour Day. **May 20** Ascension Day. **May 31** Whit Monday. **Jul 1** Anniversary of Independence. **Jul 5** National Peace and Unity Day. **Aug 15** Assumption. **Sep 25** Kamarampaka Day. **Oct 26** Armed Forces Day. **Nov 1** All Saints' Day. **Dec 25** Christmas. **Jan 1 '94** New Year's Day. **Jan 28** Democracy Day.

HEALTH

Regulations and requirements may be subject to change at short notice, and you are advised to contact your doctor well in advance of your intended date of departure. Any numbers in the chart refer to the footnotes below.

	Special Precautions?	Certificate Required?
Yellow Fever	Yes	1
Cholera	Yes	2
Typhoid & Polio	Yes	-
Malaria	3	-
Food & Drink	4	-

[1]: A yellow fever vaccination certificate is required from all travellers over one year of age.
[2]: Following WHO guidelines issued in 1973, a cholera vaccination certificate is not a condition of entry to Rwanda. However, cholera is a serious risk in this country and precautions are essential. Up-to-date advice should be sought before deciding whether these precautions should include vaccination, as medical opinion is divided over its effectiveness. See the *Health* section at the back of the book.
[3]: Malaria risk exists all year throughout the country. The predominant *falciparum* strain is reported to be 'highly resistant' to chloroquine and 'resistant' to sulfadoxine-pyrimethamine.
[4]: All water should be regarded as being potentially contaminated. Water used for drinking, brushing teeth or making ice should have first been boiled or otherwise sterilised. Milk is unpasteurised and should be boiled. Powdered or tinned milk is available and is advised, but make sure that it is reconstituted with pure water. Avoid dairy products which are likely to have been made from unboiled milk. Only eat well-cooked meat and fish, preferably served hot. Pork, salad and mayonnaise may carry increased risk. Vegetables should be cooked and fruit peeled.
Rabies is present. For those at high risk, vaccination before arrival should be considered. If you are bitten abroad seek medical advice without delay. For more information consult the *Health* section at the back of the book.
Bilharzia (schistosomiasis) is present. Avoid swimming and paddling in fresh water. Swimming pools which are well-chlorinated and maintained are safe.
Health care: There are approximately 250 hospitals and clinics, with a total of 8000 beds and 1200 doctors. Medical insurance, including cover for emergency repatriation, is essential.

TRAVEL - International

AIR: Rwanda's national airline *Air Rwanda (NR)* does not operate international services, except to Entebbe in Uganda and Bujumbura in Burundi. *Air France* is the general sales agent in the United Kingdom, representing *Air Burundi (PB)*, the local airline running services in the region. Normally flights operate via Paris and there are two flights a week.
Approximate flight time: From *London* to Kigali is 13 hours, including stopovers.
International airport: *Kigali (KGL)* (Kanombe), 12km (7.5 miles) east of Kigali (travel time – 25 minutes). Airport facilities include bar, duty-free shop, post office and currency exchange. Coach and taxi services are available.
Departure tax: Rw Fr1500 is levied on all international departures. Transit passengers are exempt.
ROAD: International routes are available from the surrounding countries of Zaïre, Uganda and Tanzania. **Bus:** There is a regular twice-weekly service from Kampala in Uganda to Kigali on Wednesday and Saturday.

TRAVEL - Internal

AIR: *Air Rwanda (NR)* runs internal services to the main towns. Chartered planes are also available though expensive.

Departure tax: Rw Fr300 for all domestic flights.
ROAD: The network is sparse and most roads are in bad condition, although the roads linking the capital with Butare, Bugarana and the frontier posts are of better quality. **Bus:** Services are operated by *L'Office National des Transports en Commun* and are classified into three groups: Urban (route numbers prefixed by A, B or C); Suburban (D routes); and Interurban. A timetable and tariff booklet is available in Rwanda. **Taxi:** Available in Kigali and other large towns. Fares should be agreed in advance. Tipping is not expected. **Car hire:** Limited facilities in Rwanda. There are no international car hire firms operating, but there are local companies in Kigali. **Documentation:** An International Driving Permit is required.

ACCOMMODATION

HOTELS: Found mostly in Kigali; they are expensive. Missions with dormitory accommodation are recommended, particularly in remote districts and smaller towns. Ruhengeri and Gisenye mission station hotels are excellent, the former providing good food as well as beds.
GUEST-HOUSES: Outside the main towns there are guest-houses which are generally cheaper than hotels. There is a guest-house at the edge of the Kagera National Park at Byumba in the northeast of the country.
CAMPING: This is now forbidden. Rest huts are available on the expedition route in the Virunga Volcanoes.

RESORTS & EXCURSIONS

Rwanda is a mountainous land in the heart of Africa, split by the Rift Valley, and dominated by a mountain range which traverses the country from north to south. The three areas of principal interest are the Virunga Volcanoes, the Kagera National Park and the region around Lake Kivu. The capital city of **Kigali** is mainly a commercial and administrative centre and has little in the way of tourist attractions.
Kibungu, in the east of the country, is in the centre of a region of lakes and waterfalls, including *Lake Mungesera* and the *Rusumo Falls*. It is also close to the southern tip of the **Kagera National Park**, which covers over 2500 sq km (1000 sq miles) of savannah to the west of the *Kagera River* (the frontier with Tanzania). The park has a variety of wildlife and is a habitat for over 500 species of birds. There are accommodation facilities on the edge of the park at **Gabiro**, 100km (60 miles) to the north. Reservations should be made in advance. In the rainy season (December, March and April) many of the routes become impassable.
West of Kagera is the **Parc des Volcans**, one of the last sanctuaries of the mountain gorilla. The ORTPN bureau in Kigali can organise guided tours of the park for small parties; it is advisable to book well in advance. This region is composed of volcanic mountains of which two, across the frontier in Zaïre, are still active.
Gisenye is the main centre for excursions in the Parc des Volcans. Plane trips can be made from here to view the craters. Situated on the north of *Lake Kivu*, it also offers many opportunities for water sports or for excursions on the lake. **Kibuye**, further south, is another lakeside resort. Near **Cyangugu**, on the southern shores of the lake, are the spectacular grottoes of *Kaboza* and *Nyenji*, and the thermal waters at **Nyakabuye**. Nearby, the *Rugege Forest* is the home of many rare species of wildlife.
East of Cyangugu is **Butare**, the intellectual capital of the country. It boasts an interesting museum, craft shops and a botanical garden. North of Butare is **Gitarama**, which has a good art museum; nearby is the cathedral town of **Kabgayi**; and at **Mushubati** the grottoes of *Bihongori*.
ORTPN in Kigali can give up-to-date information about tours and excursions in the country. For address, see above.

SOCIAL PROFILE

FOOD & DRINK: Hotels generally serve a reasonable choice of European dishes while restaurants serve Franco-Belgian cuisine and some African dishes. **Drink:** A fairly good selection of beers, spirits and wines is available. Beer is also brewed locally.
NIGHTLIFE: Apart from the many small bars, there is little in the way of nightlife. There are a few cinemas in Kigali. The Rwanda National Ballet is famous for its traditional dancing and singing and can be seen either at national ceremonies or sometimes on request in the villages.
SHOPPING: Special purchases include baskets with pointed lids, clay statuettes, masks, charms and knives called *pangas* or *umuhoro*, with blades shaped like a question mark. Don't buy souvenir gorilla skulls; if they are offered, report the trader to the police. **Shopping hours:** Dawn to dusk.
SPORT: Safaris: Kagera National Park at Gabiro, accessible by air or road, is devoted to game preservation and has lions, zebras, antelopes, hippos, buffalo, leopards, apes, impala, crested herons, fish eagles and cormorants. **Climbing/expeditions:** The Virunga Volcanoes between Ruhengeri and Gisenye are popular with climbers. Nyiragongo in Zaïre is the most commonly climbed from Gisenye. Rwandan guides are available for 2- or 3-day expeditions to view the craters. **Watersports:** There is a sandy beach at Gisenye and **swimming** is safe in Lake Kivu. **Water-skiing** is also possible.
SOCIAL CONVENTIONS: The traditional way of life is based on agriculture and cattle. The Rwandese settle in the fertile areas, but they do not form villages, each family being surrounded by its own fields. The majority of the population belong to the Hutu tribe. There is a significant minority (15%) Tutsi population and a smaller minority of Twa, a mixed race of pygmies and probably the country's first inhabitants, traditionally potters and hunters. After internal unrest in the past, a degree of tolerance between the various groups now exists. Normal social courtesies apply. **Tipping:** 10% is normal.

BUSINESS PROFILE

ECONOMY: Subsistence agriculture is the core of the Rwandan economy. During the last decade the Government has tried to redirect the agricultural sector towards the production of cash crops such as tea and coffee, of which the latter is a particularly important export earner. Rice and sugar plantations have also been developed. Rwanda has some mineral deposits, mainly tin but also several rare ores which are in heavy demand in the world market. However, exploitation has not always been worthwhile: tungsten mining ceased in 1987 when it proved uneconomic. One bright prospect for the future is the discovery of natural gas deposits which may be among the world's largest. Rwanda's economic indicators are good by African standards; inflation is in single figures and external debts are manageable. However, the collapse of the world coffee price during 1990, coinciding with serious internal political problems, has darkened the outlook. Rwanda will need to rely on its long-term contacts with the European Community, particularly Belgium and Germany, which have guaranteed a steady flow of development aid. Outside the EC, Kenya, Uganda and the USA are Rwanda's main trading partners. Trade with Britain is worth less than £10 million per annum, with a large surplus in Britain's favour.
BUSINESS: Lightweight suits are advised and appointments are necessary. Best time to visit is from April to October or December to January. A knowledge of French is useful as only few executives speak English. **Office hours:** 0800-1600 Monday to Friday; 0800-1200 Saturday.
COMMERCIAL INFORMATION: The following can offer advice: Chambre de Commerce et d'Industrie du Rwanda, BP 319, Kigali. Tel: 72319. Telex: 22662.

HISTORY & GOVERNMENT

HISTORY: In the late 13th century, pastoral Tutsi tribes arriving from the south conquered the agricultural Hutu and hunter-gatherer Twa inhabitants of Rwanda and established a feudal kingdom. This lasted until the end of the 19th century, when Rwanda first became a province of German East Africa then, in 1916, part of the territory of Rwanda-Urundi administered by Belgium under a League of Nations mandate. The Belgians sponsored the continued dominance of the Tutsi minority at the expense of the Hutu but were forced in the early 1960s to concede internal autonomy and then independence under majority Hutu rule. With many Tutsi unwilling to relinquish power, inter-tribal violence continued in the years after independence. Many Tutsi fled into exile in neighbouring Burundi, Uganda and Tanzania during this period and a Tutsi government-in-exile still remains in the Ugandan capital, Kampala. In 1973, after further inter-tribal conflict, Major-General Juvénal Habyarimana led a bloodless coup which established a military government. A few years later the National Revolutionary Movement for Development was founded and has remained in power ever since. Relations between Rwanda and its neighbours, particularly Uganda, have been strained by the maltreatment of Rwandan exiles. The Rwandan government has occasionally closed its borders with both Uganda and Tanzania but, needing access to ports in these countries since Rwanda is landlocked, these periods have been kept to a minimum. The internal political situation had been very stable until October 1990 when a full-scale invasion was launched from across the Ugandan border. The force, styling itself the Rwandan Patriotic Front, was composed mainly of Tutsi dissidents and led by a Rwandan refugee, Fred Rwigyema, who had served as a senior commander in the Ugandan national resistance Army under Yoweri Museveni. After some initial successes in the northeast of the country, the rebels struck for the capital but came up against large government forces backed by regular units from the Zaïrois army. After a month the rebels accepted a cease-fire and although sporadic fighting continued during 1991 the situation is calm. In mid-1990, before the invasion, Habyarimana had declared that Rwanda would have multi-party government by 1992 at the latest. This schedule has been thrown into jeopardy and the Government's intentions in this respect are uncertain. By the summer of 1992 it appeared that this schedule was somewhat optimistic. There were, however, signs that a peace settlement opening the way to democratic reforms might be possible. The government and the Patriotic Front held several rounds of talks in the Kenyan capital, Nairobi, and agreed to convene a 50-member all-African military team to monitor a cease-fire. The parties also agreed to go to the next, most delicate stage: talks about power-sharing between the two communities.
GOVERNMENT: Legislation is controlled jointly by the President, who is Head of State, and the National Development Council. The President holds executive power, assisted by an appointed council of ministers.

CLIMATE

Despite its proximity to the Equator the climate in Rwanda is cooled by the high altitude. It is warm throughout most of the country but cooler in the mountains. There are two rainy seasons: mid-January to April and mid-October to mid-December.
Required clothing: Lightweights are required for most of the year with warmer clothes for cooler upland evenings. Rainwear is advisable

RUBONA Rwanda (1706m)

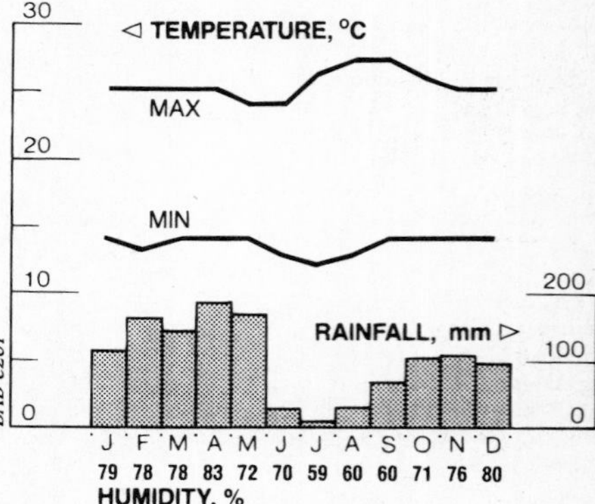

RWANDA | **HEALTH REGULATIONS** | **VISA REGULATIONS** | Code-Link

GALILEO/WORLDSPAN

TI-DFT/KGL/HE

TI-DFT/KGL/VI

SABRE

TIDFT/KGL/HE

TIDFT/KGL/VI

To access this information on your CRS, swipe the barcode with a light pen or type in the text under the barcode. For more information, see the introduction *How to Use This Book*.

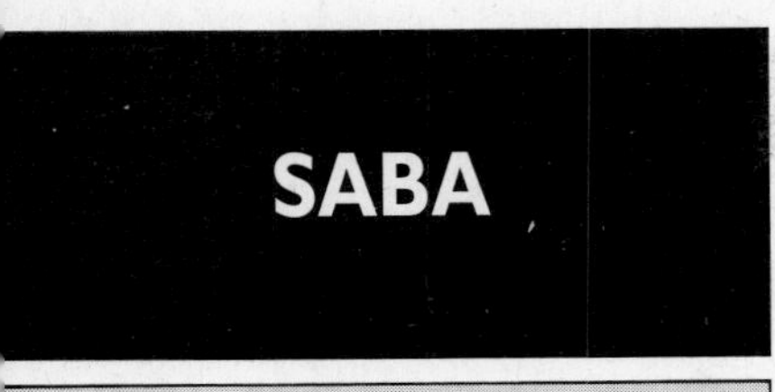

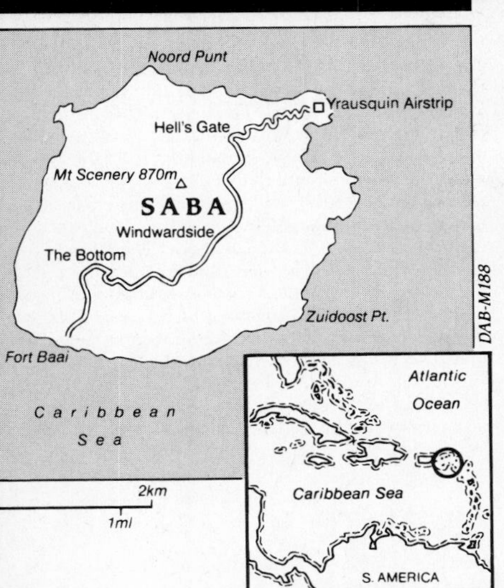

Location: Eastern Caribbean, Windward Islands.

Diplomatic representation: Although the Netherlands Antilles are part of the Kingdom of the Netherlands, they are not formally represented by Royal Netherlands Embassies. Information and advice may be obtained at the addresses below.

Saba Tourist Office
PO Box 527
Windwardside, Saba NA
Tel: (4) 2231. Fax: (4) 2350. Telex: 8006.
Office of the Minister Plenipotentiary of the Netherlands Antilles *and* **The Netherlands Antilles Organisation**
PO Box 90706
2509 LS The Hague
The Netherlands
Tel: (70) 351 2811. Fax: (70) 351 2722. Telex: 31161.
Saba Tourist Office
Suite 2305
1500 Broadway
New York, NY
10036
Tel: (212) 840 6655.
Saba Tourist Bureau
c/o New Concepts-Canada
Suite 70
2455 Cawthra Road
Mississauga, Ontario
L5A 3P1
Tel: (416) 803 0131. Fax: (416) 803 0132.

AREA: 13 sq km (5 sq miles).
POPULATION: 1119 (1990 estimate).
POPULATION DENSITY: 86.1 per sq km.
CAPITAL: The Bottom. NA capital: Willemstad, Curaçao.
GEOGRAPHY: Saba is one of three Windward Islands in the Netherlands Antilles, although geographically it is part of the Leeward Group of the Lesser Antilles, lying 265km (165 miles) east of Puerto Rico, 44km (27 miles) south of St Maarten and 21km (13 miles) west of St Eustatius. Saba is the peak of a submerged extinct volcano, Mount Scenery, thick with forest and rising to almost 900m (3000ft) in less than 2km (1.2 miles). There are four villages, until recently connected only by thousands of steps cut from the rock. A road now links the airport with The Bottom.
LANGUAGE: Popularly English, but Dutch (the official language of the Netherlands Antilles) is used for legal documents and taught in schools.
RELIGION: Roman Catholic majority; also Anglican and Wesleyan.
TIME: GMT - 4.
ELECTRICITY: 110 volts AC, 60Hz.
COMMUNICATIONS: Telephone: Fully automatic system with good IDD. Country code: 599. Calls made through the operator are more expensive and include a 15% tax. The exchange is located in The Bottom. **Telegram:** Services operated by *Lands Radio Dienst* and *All American Cables*. **Post:** The Post Office is in The Bottom. Airmail to Europe takes four to six days, surface mail four to six weeks. **Press:** The *Saba Herald* is published monthly in English.
BBC World Service and Voice of America frequencies: From time to time these change. See the section *How to Use this Book* for more information.

BBC:				
MHz	17.840	15.220	9.915	5.975
Voice of America:				
MHz	15.21	11.70	6.130	0.930

PASSPORT/VISA

Regulations and requirements may be subject to change at short notice, and you are advised to contact the appropriate diplomatic or consular authority before finalising travel arrangements. Details of these may be found at the head of this country's entry. Any numbers in the chart refer to the footnotes below.

	Passport Required?	Visa Required?	Return Ticket Required?
Full British	Yes	No	Yes
BVP	Valid/1	-	-
Australian	Yes	4	Yes
Canadian	2	4	Yes
USA	3	4	Yes
Other EC	1	4/5	Yes
Japanese	Yes	4	Yes

PASSPORTS: Valid passport required by all except:
(a) [1] nationals of Belgium, Luxembourg and The Netherlands holding a tourist card, nationals of Germany holding an identity card and UK nationals holding a British Visitors Passport;
(c) [2] nationals of Canada with birth certificate or proof of citizenship;
(b) [3] nationals of the USA holding voters registration card or birth certificate, and alien residents of the USA with acceptable documentation;
(d) nationals of San Marino holding a national ID card.
British Visitors Passport: Acceptable.
VISAS: [4] Visas are only required for nationals of the Dominican Republic resident there. All other nationals are allowed to stay in Saba for 14 days without a visa (but might need a Certificate of Admission, see below) provided they have a return or onward ticket. All visitors staying more than 90 days require a visa. Transit passengers staying no longer than 24 hours holding confirmed tickets and valid passports do not require visas or Certificates of Admission.
For stays of between 14 and 28 days a **Temporary Certificate of Admission** is required, which in the case of the following countries will be issued by the Immigration authorities on arrival in Saba:
(a) [5] Belgium, Germany, Luxembourg, The Netherlands, Spain and the UK;
(b) Bolivia, Burkina Faso, Chile, Colombia, Costa Rica, Czechoslovakia, Ecuador, Hungary, Israel, Jamaica, South Korea, Malawi, Mauritius, Niger, The Philippines, Poland, San Marino, Swaziland and Togo.
The following must apply in writing and *before* entering the country even for tourist purposes for a Certificate of Admission: nationals of Albania, Bulgaria, Cambodia, China, Cuba, North Korea, Libya, Romania, CIS, Vietnam and holders of Rhodesian passports issued on or after November 11, 1965.
All other nationals have to apply for the Certificate after 14 days of stay.
Further information about visa requirements may be obtained from the Office of the Minister Plenipotentiary of the Netherlands Antilles; and whilst Royal Netherlands Embassies do not formally represent the Netherlands Antilles in any way, they might also be able to offer limited advice and information. For addresses, see top of this entry and top of the *Netherlands* entry above.
Temporary residence: Enquire at the Office of the Minister Plenipotentiary of the Netherlands Antilles.

MONEY

Currency: Netherlands Antilles Guilder or Florin (NAG) = 100 cents. Notes are in the denominations of NAG500, 250, 100, 50, 25, 10 and 5. Coins are in the denominations of NAG2.50 and 1, and 50, 25, 10, 5 and 1 cents. There are in addition a large number of commemorative coins which are legal tender.
Credit cards: Access/Mastercard and Visa are accepted in large establishments. Check with your credit card company for details of merchant acceptability and other services which may be available.
Exchange rate indicators: The following figures are included as a guide to the movement of the Netherlands Antilles Florin against Sterling and the US Dollar:

Date:	Oct '89	Oct '90	Oct '91	Oct '92
£1.00=	2.84	3.49	3.11	2.83
$1.00=	*1.79	*1.79	*1.79	*1.79

Note: [*] The NAG is linked to the US Dollar.
Currency restrictions: The import and export of local currency is limited to NAG200. There is no limit on foreign currency.
Banking hours: 0830-1200 and 1330-1630 Monday to Friday.

DUTY FREE

The following items may be imported into Saba by tourists over 15 years of age only without incurring customs duty:
400 cigarettes or 50 cigars or 250g tobacco;
2 litres of alcoholic beverages;
250ml of perfume (entire amount will be dutiable if more is imported);
Gifts to a value of NAG100.
Prohibited items: It is forbidden to import parrots and parakeets, dogs and cats from Central and South America. The import of souvenirs and leather goods from Haiti is not advisable.

PUBLIC HOLIDAYS

Public holidays observed on Saba are as follows:
Apr 9-12 '93 Easter. **Apr 30** Queen's Birthday. **May 1** Labour Day. **May 20** Ascension Day. **May 31** Whit Monday.**Dec 6** Saba Day. **Dec 25-26** Christmas. **Jan 1 '94** New Year's Day.

HEALTH

Regulations and requirements may be subject to change at short notice, and you are advised to contact your doctor well in advance of your intended date of departure. Any numbers in the chart refer to the footnotes below.

	Special Precautions?	Certificate Required?
Yellow Fever	No	1
Cholera	No	No
Typhoid & Polio	Yes	-
Malaria	No	-
Food & Drink	2	-

[1]: A yellow fever certificate is required from travellers over six months of age arriving from infected areas.
[2]: Water on the island is considered safe to drink. Bottled mineral water is widely available. Milk is pasteurised and dairy products are safe for consumption. Local meat, poultry, seafood, fruit and vegetables are generally considered safe to eat.
Health care: There is a hospital in The Bottom. Medical insurance is essential.

TRAVEL - International

AIR: The national airline of the Netherlands Antilles is *ALM (LM)*.
Approximate flight times: From Saba to *London* is 13 hours, to *Los Angeles* is 10 hours, to *New York* is 6 hours and to *Singapore* is 34 hours (all depending on connections).
International airport: *Juancho Yrausquin (SAB)* at Cove Bay. The runway, at 400m (1300ft), is one of the shortest in the world. There are daily STOL turboprop flights to St Eustatius and St Kitts (and thus the airport may be classified as 'international') and thrice-daily to St Maarten.
Departure tax: US$2 for flights to other Windward Islands, US$5 to St Kitts.
SEA: Small boats operate from the Leo A Chance Pier at Fort Baai. There is a regular ferry service to St Maarten and a weekly cargo boat brings groceries and other supplies from St Maarten. Cruise ships call occasionally.

TRAVEL - Internal

ROAD: Saba has one road, 15km (9.5 miles) long, bisecting the island from the airport to Fort Baai. Taxis are available. Driving is on the right. Self-drive cars may be hired at Douglas Johnson's *The Square Nickel*.

ACCOMMODATION

GUEST-HOUSES: There are five guest-houses – *Captain's Quarters, Cranston's Antique Inn, Scout's Inn, Juliana's Apartments* and *Sharon's Ocean View* – with a total of 50 rooms. Each has its own restaurant and bar.

RESORTS & EXCURSIONS

Mount Scenery is an extinct volcano rising from the floor of the Caribbean; the 250m (800ft) above sea level are known as Saba. There is only one road and with a population of just over 1000, Saba is the most unspoilt of the Netherlands Antilles; the inhabitants will claim that visitors are so few that each one is something of a celebrity. The island's four villages are mere clusters of ornate timber cottages dangling on the flanks of the mountain. Vegetation becomes increasingly lush towards the summit and the crater itself holds a tropical rainforest splattered with exotic flowers – begonias, giant heliconias and orchids. Tours may be taken by taxi from the airport or pier, or on foot via the forest trails and thousands of stone-cut steps linking the villages. The *Harry L Johnson Memorial Museum* in **Windwardside** is the restored home of a Dutch sea captain; visitors are offered a plate of pork, freshly cooked in the kitchen's rock oven. Windwardside also contains the *Tourist Office*, the island's two largest guest-houses and most of its shops. The island's capital, **The Bottom,** is situated 250m (820ft) above the ocean on a plateau surrounded by volcanic domes. Here, the *Artisan Foundation* exhibits early examples of Saba Lace; intricate embroidery on linen that resembles lace. The climate is milder than neighbouring St Eustatius (21km/13 miles away), but the island is subject to sudden downpours.

SOCIAL PROFILE

FOOD & DRINK: Fine local cuisine is offered at the island's guest-houses and there are several public restaurants, including the *Saba Chinese Restaurant* and *Guido's Italian Restaurant*. Local specialities include *calaloo soup*, curried goat, breadfruit, soursop ice cream and exotic fruit grown on the island – mangoes, papayas, figs, bananas and bitter mangoes. Restaurants and bars are usually closed by midnight. **Drink:** Most well-known brands of drink are available and Saba has its own brand of rum – *Saba Spice*, a blend of rum, aniseed, cinnamon, orange peel, cloves, nutmeg, spice bush and brown sugar.
NIGHTLIFE: There are few visitors to the island and generally evenings are quiet, but on Friday and Saturday nights there is dancing at *Guido's Italian Restaurant* and at *Lime Time*. The *Captain's Quarters* and *Scout's Place* guest-houses have lively bars.
SHOPPING: By the middle of the last century, the decline in the demand for sugar throughout the world and indigo had left Saba looking at a very bleak future; the plantations, the only source of employment, reverted to forest. Undaunted, the men built boats and became fishermen, the women stayed at home and embroidered napkins and table cloths using a technique remembered by Mary Gertrude Johnson from her days in a Venezuelan convent. The fishing industry is now marginal but the embroidery has become Saba's chief claim to fame. *The Saba Artisans' Foundation* (founded in 1972 with money from the United Nations' Development Programme) in The Bottom promotes local lacework, silk-screened fabrics and garments printed and handmade by Sabans, as does the *Island Craft Shop* in Windwardside. *Saba Spice*, a 150-proof rum of local manufacture, is an acquired taste – a good gift to take home for friends and relatives. **Shopping hours:** 0800-1200 and 1400-1800 Monday to Saturday.
SPORT: There are few facilities for organised sport on the island. There is a concrete **tennis** court at the Sunny Valley Youth Centre in The Bottom and a **swimming** pool at the Captain's Quarters and at Scout's Place. There are no beaches. **Hiking** to the summit of Mount Scenery is popular with visitors – Bernard Johnson offers guided tours – but Saba's greatest sporting potential is in **scuba diving**. The waters around the island have been declared a protected marine park in recognition of the unique opportunities for wall diving they present to experienced divers. Visibility varies from 20-30m (75-100ft) with a water temperature of 30°C in summer, whilst in winter visibility is up to 40m (125ft) with a water temperature of 24°C. The fragile coral reefs clinging to the submerged mountain slopes are teeming with colourful grazing fish, preyed on by sharks and barracuda. Giant sea turtles and humpback whales are seasonal visitors. There are already two dive shops on the island, *Saba Deep* in Fort Baai and *Sea Saba* in Windwardside. Both have their own boats and diving equipment (beginners are confined to the shallow waters of Fort Baai) and qualified divemasters, such as *Sea Saba*'s Greg Johnson, can provide tuition at all levels.
SPECIAL EVENTS: *Saba Days* are celebrated on the first weekend in December with donkey racing, dancing and parties. The *Carnival* is held every July with colourful costumes, dancing and Caribbean music.
SOCIAL CONVENTIONS: Dutch customs are still important throughout the Netherlands Antilles, but tourism on neighbouring St Maarten has brought some US influence to Saba (several businesses are US-owned). Dress is casual and lightweight cottons are advised. **Tipping:** A surcharge of 15% is usually added to guest-house and restaurant bills to cover government and utility taxes. Elsewhere 10-15% is appreciated but never expected.

BUSINESS PROFILE

ECONOMY: Falling oil prices and the recent trend towards transhipment have badly affected the Netherlands Antilles, once regarded as among the most affluent islands in the Caribbean, but as oil-related industries are confined to Curaçao and, to a lesser extent, Bonaire, the Windward Islands – of which Saba is one – probably have less to lose. Saba continues to earn a modest income from fishing and handmade textiles. Tourism has, as is the case elsewhere in the island group, become of increasing importance.
BUSINESS: Business is fairly formal and visitors should wear a tropical suit. Appointments should be made and always kept as it is very discourteous to be late. **Office hours:** 0800-1200 and 1330-1630 Monday to Friday.
COMMERCIAL INFORMATION: The following organisations can offer advice:
Curaçao Chamber of Commerce and Industry, PO Box 10, Kaya Junior Salas 1, Willemstad, Curaçao. Tel: (9) 611 451. Fax: (9) 615 652; *or*
St Maarten Chamber of Commerce and Industry, PO Box 454, Voorstraat, Philipsburg, St Maarten. Tel: (6) 23590.

HISTORY & GOVERNMENT

HISTORY: Saba was sighted by Christopher Columbus in 1493, by Sir Francis Drake in 1595 and by two Dutch expeditions in the 1620s. In 1632, a party of Englishmen was shipwrecked on the tiny island and found it uninhabited, although there were traces of Carib occupation. Permanent settlement by Europeans did not occur until the second half of the 17th century, when the Dutch were consolidating their Caribbean empire, based on Curaçao. The settlers founded an agricultural economy with sugar and indigo as the key crops. The decline in these markets forced the population to maintain their modest prosperity through fishing and embroidery, which together with low-key tourism remain the major sources of income. The island changed hands 12 times between 1632 and 1816, when it was finally confirmed as a Dutch possession. As part of the Netherlands Antilles, Saba gained partial independence from The Netherlands in 1954.
GOVERNMENT: The Netherlands Antilles, Aruba and The Netherlands each have equal status within the Kingdom of the Netherlands as autonomous regions in internal affairs. The Queen is repesented locally by a Governor, while the Netherlands Antilles are represented in the Government of the Kingdom by a Minister Plenipotentiary. Foreign policy and defence matters are decided by a Council of Ministers of the Kingdom, including the Plenipotentiary, and executed under the authority of the Governor. The internal affairs of the Netherlands Antilles are administered by the central government of the Netherlands Antilles, based in Willemstad, Curaçao, which is responsible to the Staten or legislative assembly. Saba may elect by non-compulsory adult suffrage one of 22 members to the Staten. Routine local affairs on each island group (Bonaire, Curaçao and the Windward Islands) are managed by an elected Island Council, presided over by a Lieutenant-Governor.

CLIMATE

Hot, but tempered by cooling trade winds. The annual mean temperature is 27°C, varying by no more than two or three degrees throughout the year; average rainfall is 1667mm. The temperature can drop to 16°C on winter evenings. When climbing Mount Scenery, the temperature will drop by approximately 0.2°C for each 100m (330ft) gained in altitude.
Required clothing: Tropicals and cottons are worn throughout the year. Umbrellas or light waterproofs are needed for the rainy season.

PLYMOUTH Montserrat (40m)

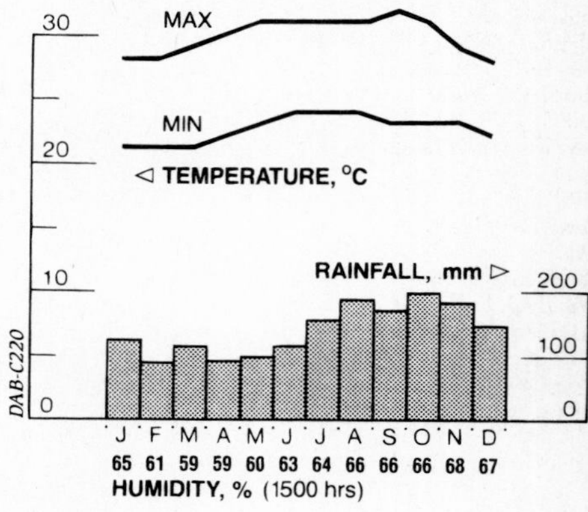

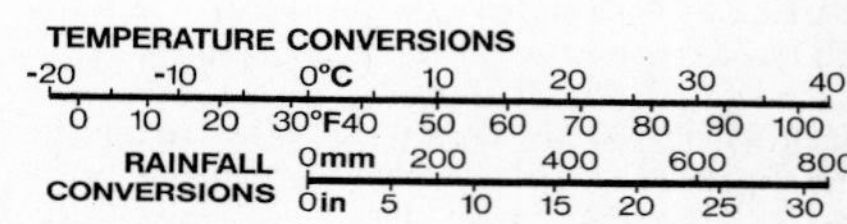

SABA	HEALTH REGULATIONS	VISA REGULATIONS
		Code-Link
GALILEO/WORLDSPAN	TI-DFT/SAB/HE	TI-DFT/SAB/VI
SABRE	TIDFT/SAB/HE	TIDFT/SAB/VI

To access this information on your CRS, swipe the barcode with a light pen or type in the text under the barcode. For more information, see the introduction *How to Use This Book*.

ST EUSTATIUS

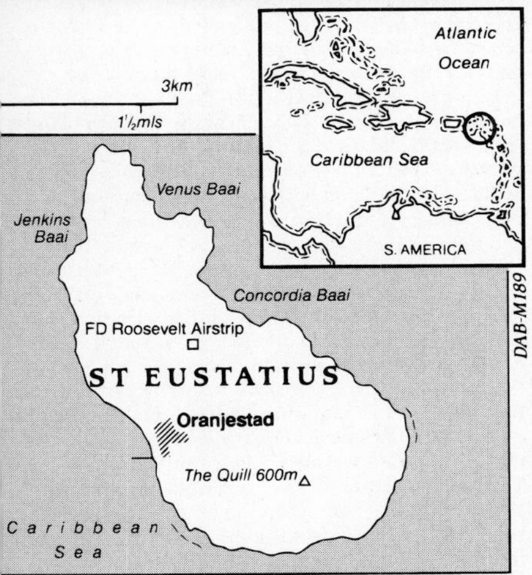

Location: Eastern Caribbean, Windward Islands.

Diplomatic representation: Although the Netherlands Antilles are part of the Kingdom of the Netherlands, they are not formally represented by Royal Netherlands Embassies. Information and advice may be obtained at the addresses below.

St Eustatius Tourist Bureau
Fort Oranjestad z/n
Oranjestad
St Eustatius, NA
Tel: (3) 82433. Fax: (3) 82433. Telex: 8080.
Office of the Minister Plenipotentiary of the Netherlands Antilles *and* **The Netherlands Antilles Organisation**
PO Box 90706
2509 LS The Hague
The Netherlands
Tel: (70) 351 2811. Fax: (70) 351 2722.
The British Embassy in Venezuela deals with enquiries relating to St Eustatius:
British Embassy
Edificio Torre Las Mercedes (Piso 3)
Avenida La Estancia
Chuao
Caracas 1060
Venezuela
Tel: (2) 926 542. Fax: (2) 923 292. Telex: 23468 PROCA VE.

AREA: 21 sq km (8 sq miles).
POPULATION: 1715 (1990 estimate).
POPULATION DENSITY: 81.7 per sq km.
CAPITAL: Oranjestad; NA capital: Willemstad, Curaçao.
GEOGRAPHY: Politically, St Eustatius is one of three Windward Islands in the Netherlands Antilles; geographically it is part of the Leeward Group of the Lesser Antilles. It lies 286km (178 miles) east of Puerto Rico, 171km (106 miles) east of St Croix, 56km (35 miles) due south of St Maarten and 14km (9 miles) northwest of St Christopher (St Kitts). On the south end of the island is an extinct volcano called *The Quill*, which has a lush rainforest in the crater. Twice a year, sea turtles clamber up onto the black volcanic sands that rim the island to lay their eggs; giant land crabs hunt on the beaches every night.
LANGUAGE: English is the official language of the Windward Islands. Papiamento (a local *patois*), French and Spanish may also be spoken.
RELIGION: The majority are Protestant with a Roman Catholic minority.
TIME: GMT - 4.
ELECTRICITY: 110/220 volts AC, 60Hz.
COMMUNICATIONS: Telephone: Fully automatic system with good IDD connections. Country code: 599. Calls made through the operator are more expensive and include a 15% tax. **Telegram:** Services operated by *Lands Radio Dienst* and *All American Cables*.
Post: Airmail to Europe takes four to six days, surface mail four to six weeks. **Press:** No newspapers are published on St Eustatius, but an English-language daily, *The News*, is published on Curaçao. All other newspapers in the Netherlands Antilles are published in Dutch or Papiamento.
BBC World Service and Voice of America frequencies: From time to time these change. See the section *How to Use this Book* for more information.

BBC:				
MHz	17.840	15.220	9.915	5.975
Voice of America:				
MHz	15.21	11.70	6.130	0.930

PASSPORT/VISA

Regulations and requirements may be subject to change at short notice, and you are advised to contact the appropriate diplomatic or consular authority before finalising travel arrangements. Details of these may be found at the head of this country's entry. Any numbers in the chart refer to the footnotes below.

	Passport Required?	Visa Required?	Return Ticket Required?
Full British	Yes	No	Yes
BVP	Valid/1	-	-
Australian	Yes	4	Yes
Canadian	3	4	Yes
USA	2	4	Yes
Other EC	1	4/5	Yes
Japanese	Yes	4	Yes

PASSPORTS: Valid passport required by all except:
(a) **[1]** nationals of Belgium, Luxembourg and The Netherlands holding a tourist card, nationals of Germany holding an identity card and UK nationals holding a British Visitors Passport;
(b) **[2]** nationals of the USA holding voters registration card or birth certificate, and alien residents of the USA with acceptable documentation;
(c) **[3]** nationals of Canada with birth certificate or proof of citizenship;
(d) nationals of San Marino holding a national ID card.
British Visitors Passport: Acceptable.
VISAS: [4] Visas are only required for nationals of the Dominican Republic resident there. All other nationals are allowed to stay in St Eustatius for 14 days without a visa (but might need a Certificate of Admission, see below) provided they have a return or onward ticket. All visitors staying more than 90 days require a visa. Transit passengers staying no longer than 24 hours holding confirmed tickets and valid passports do not require visas or Certificates of Admission.
For stays of between 14 and 28 days a **Temporary Certificate of Admission** is required, which in the case of the following countries will be issued by the Immigration authorities on arrival in St Eustatius:
(a) **[5]** Belgium, Germany, Luxembourg, The Netherlands, Spain and the UK;
(b) Bolivia, Burkina Faso, Chile, Colombia, Costa Rica, Czechoslovakia, Ecuador, Hungary, Israel, Jamaica, Malawi, Mauritius, Niger, The Philippines, Poland, San Marino, South Korea, Swaziland and Togo.
The following must apply in writing and *before* entering the country even for tourist purposes for a Certificate of Admission: nationals of Albania, Bulgaria, Cambodia, China, Cuba, Libya, North Korea, Romania, CIS, Vietnam and holders of Rhodesian passports issued on or after November 11, 1965.
All other nationals have to apply for the Certificate after 14 days of stay.
Further information about visa requirements may be obtained from the Office of the Minister Plenipotentiary of the Netherlands Antilles; and whilst Royal Netherlands Embassies do not formally represent the Netherlands Antilles in any way, they might also be able to offer limited advice and information. For addresses, see top of this entry and top of the *Netherlands* entry above.
Temporary residence: Enquire at the Office of the Minister Plenipotentiary of the Netherlands Antilles.

MONEY

Currency: Netherlands Antilles Guilder or Florin (NAG) = 100 cents. Notes are in the denominations of NAG500, 250, 100, 50, 25, 10 and 5. Coins are in the denominations of NAG2.50 and 1, and 50, 25,10, 5 and 1 cents. There are in addition a large number of commemorative coins which are legal tender.
Credit cards: Access/Mastercard and Visa are accepted in large establishments. Check with your credit card company for details of merchant acceptability and other services which may be available.
Exchange rate indicators: The following figures are included as a guide to the movement of the Netherlands Antilles Florin against Sterling and the US Dollar:

Date:	**Oct '89**	**Oct '90**	**Oct '91**	**Oct '92**
£1.00=	2.84	3.49	3.11	2.83
$1.00=	*1.79	*1.79	*1.79	*1.79

Note [*]: The NAG is linked to the US Dollar.
Currency restrictions: The import and export of local currency is limited to NAG200. The import and export of foreign currency is unlimited.
Banking hours: 0830-1200 and 1330-1630 Monday to Friday.

DUTY FREE

The following items may be imported into St Eustatius by tourists over 15 years of age only without incurring customs duty:
400 cigarettes or 50 cigars or 250g tobacco;
2 litres of alcoholic beverages;
250ml perfume (entire amount will be dutiable if more is imported);
Gifts to a value of NAG100.
Prohibited items: It is forbidden to import parrots and parakeets, dogs and cats from Central and South America. The import of souvenirs and leather goods from Haiti is not advisable.

PUBLIC HOLIDAYS

Public holidays observed in St Eustatius are as follows:
Apr 9-12 '93 Easter. **Apr 30** Queen's Day. **May 1** Labour Day. **May 20** Ascension Day. **May 31** Whit Monday. **Nov 16** St Eustatius Day. **Dec 25** Christmas Day. **Dec 26** Boxing Day. **Jan 1 '94** New Year's Day.

HEALTH

Regulations and requirements may be subject to change at short notice, and you are advised to contact your doctor well in advance of your intended date of departure. Any numbers in the chart refer to the footnotes below.

	Special Precautions?	Certificate Required?
Yellow Fever	No	1
Cholera	No	No
Typhoid & Polio	Yes	-
Malaria	No	-
Food & Drink	2	-

[1]: A yellow fever certificate is required from travellers arriving from infected areas.
[2]: Water on the island is considered safe to drink. Bottled mineral water is widely available. Milk is pasteurised and dairy products are safe for consumption. Local meat, poultry, seafood, fruit and vegetables are generally considered safe to eat.
Health care: There is one hospital on St Eustatius. Health insurance is advised.

TRAVEL - International

AIR: The national airline of the Netherlands Antilles is *ALM (LM)*.
Approximate flight times: From St Eustatius to *London* is 12 hours, to *Los Angeles* is 9 hours, to *New York* is 5 hours and to *Singapore* is 33 hours (these will vary considerably, depending on connections).
International airport: *F.D. Roosevelt (EUX)*, 1km (0.6 miles) from Oranjestad, is served by daily scheduled flights from St Kitts and Nevis, from St Maarten (four times daily, flight time – 30 minutes) and from Saba. The runway is too small for jets.
Departure tax: US$5 for international departures.
SEA: A 900m (3000ft) long deep-water pier at Oranjestad can accommodate ocean liners. Small boats operate to the other islands in the Leeward Group; the 21km (13-mile) trip to Saba takes about two hours.

TRAVEL - Internal

ROAD: St Eustatius is a very small island and consequently has very few roads; a road of sorts runs right around the coast and a track leads up to the rim of *The*

Quill, an extinct volcano in the south. The entire system can be walked in a few hours, but there are 15 **car-hire** and **taxi** companies in Oranjestad. There are an equal number of cars and donkeys on the island; the latter may also be hired. **Documentation:** A national driving licence is acceptable.

ACCOMMODATION

There are three small hotels – *Golden Era*, *La Maison Sur La Plage* and *The Old Gin House* – offering a total of 50 beds, and several guest-houses. There are also several fully equipped apartments available for weekly rental. Advance booking is advised.

RESORTS & EXCURSIONS

St Eustatius, popularly known as 'Statia', was a thriving transhipment port during the 17th and 18th centuries, becoming known throughout the Caribbean as 'The Golden Rock'. The subsequent decline of the island has only recently been halted by a moderate influx of tourists. Statia is quiet and unhurried, with reminders of its bustling commercial past surviving only in the ruins of old warehouses, the weed-choked *Jewish Cemetery* (attached to the second-oldest synagogue in the New World), colonial houses, *Fort Amsterdam* above the town, and the foundations of the Dutch sea walls, now sunk beneath the clear waters of the bay. Many of the submerged ruins can be seen by scuba divers or snorkellers; equipment can be hired and trips organised by the *Happy Hooker Watersports Centre* in the lower town, next to the small tourist complex known as 'The Inns of Gallows Bay', and at *Surfside Statia* near 'The Old Gin House'. Other attractions of the island include walking up *The Quill*, a forested dormant volcano; donkey rides along the black sand beach to *Forte de Windt;* surfing off the northeast coast; and fishing trips. Contact the Tourist Office for details.

SOCIAL PROFILE

FOOD & DRINK: Despite the island's small size, it has nine restaurants offering nine different blends of imported and local cuisine. The hotel restaurants are probably the best – indeed the *Mooshay Bay Dining Room* at 'The Old Gin House', where Continental food is served on old pewter plates, has been given a 5-star rating by Gourmet Magazine – but the local Creole-style cooking is particularly suited for seafood dishes: pickled conch shell meat, grilled spicy fish and lobster, and turtle dishes are recommended. The *Chinese Restaurant* offers authentic Cantonese cuisine; other restaurants also offer Cantonese dishes, together with American, French and local specialities. **Drink:** There are no licensing hours on the island (although most restaurants and bars are usually closed by midnight), and alcohol is virtually tax free. Most well-known brand names are available; a 'greenie' is a Heineken.
NIGHTLIFE: Centred on the main hotels and restaurants, including dancing to both taped Western music and live local bands, who may play one of the two different indigenous blends of reggae and calypso – 'Pim Pim' and 'Hippy'.
SHOPPING: The reductions on duty-free imports make the purchase of some perfume, jewellery or alcohol well worthwhile. **Shopping hours:** 0800-1200 and 1400-1800 Monday to Saturday.
SPORT: Watersports predominate, and for almost every visitor will form the central part of any holiday. **Snorkelling, windsurfing** and **water-skiing** are all available with facilities and tuition as necessary, but the island is perhaps becoming best-known as a centre for **scuba diving**. Many wrecks lie on the black sand amid coral reefs and the submerged old port just off Oranjestad and have long attracted a staggering variety of marine life; since the opening of *Surfside Statia*, a large and modern scuba centre adjacent to 'The Old Gin House', the fish have been joined by increasing numbers of expert divers, drawn by a unique combination of first-rate facilities, with warm and clear water, countless wrecks, coral, and – onshore – comfortable hotels and excellent cuisine. The centre has two air compressors, 60 tanks, and two dive boats; training is available for beginners. The *Happy Hooker Watersports Centre* in the lower town also hires out equipment.
SPECIAL EVENTS: The *Carnival* sweeps back and forth through the island every year during the month of July; this is of course a popular time to visit and advance booking is essential.
SOCIAL CONVENTIONS: Dutch customs are still important throughout the Netherlands Antilles, but American influences from the Virgin Islands nearby are dominant on St Eustatius. Dress is casual and lightweight cottons are advised. Bathing suits should be confined to beach and poolside areas only. It is common to dress up in the evening. **Tipping:** Hotels add a 5-10% Government tax and 10-15% service charge. Doormen and waiters expect a 10% tip, but taxi drivers are not usually tipped.

BUSINESS PROFILE

ECONOMY: Falling oil prices and the trend towards transhipment at sea in recent years have badly affected the Netherlands Antilles, once regarded as among the most affluent island groups in the Caribbean, but as oil-related industries are confined to Curaçao and, to a lesser extent, Bonaire (Aruba is no longer part of the Netherlands Antilles), the Windward Islands perhaps had less to lose. St Eustatius earns a modest income from agriculture and from a major petroleum transhipment installation, but it is tourism which dominates the economy. There have been some efforts to develop the fishing industry but, for the time being, government employment (in the administration for the Netherlands Antilles group) is the most important source of regular employment.
BUSINESS: Office hours: 0800-1200 and 1330-1630 Monday to Friday.
COMMERCIAL INFORMATION: The following organisation can offer advice: Windward Islands Chamber of Commerce and Industry, PO Box 454, Voorstraat, Philipsburg, St Maarten. Tel: (5) 23590.

HISTORY & GOVERNMENT

HISTORY: St Eustatius was sighted by Christopher Columbus in 1493, but not settled until the 17th century when the Dutch were consolidating their Caribbean empire, based on Curaçao. Within 100 years, the island was the most important transhipment port in the New World, visited by as many as 3000 ships a year, with as many as 200 anchored at the same time. The island has changed hands 22 times since settlement, with the French, Spanish and British ever eager to wrest it from the Dutch. It was an important supply port for the American settlers during the American War of Independence; indeed, the Dutch administration of St Eustatius was the first state to recognise the United States of America, on November 16, 1776. This act provoked the British to send a fleet (under Admiral Rodney) to exact revenge and in 1781 the island was virtually laid bare by British guns. Rebuilt by the Dutch, it continued to be an important trading centre until the advent of larger ships sent it sliding into obscurity.
GOVERNMENT: The Netherlands Antilles, Aruba, and The Netherlands each have equal status within the Kingdom of the Netherlands as regions autonomous in internal affairs. The Queen is represented locally by a Governor, while the Netherlands Antilles is represented in the Government of the Kingdom by a Minister Plenipotentiary. Foreign policy and defence matters are decided by a Council of Ministers of the Kingdom, including the Plenipotentiary, and executed under the authority of the Governor. The internal affairs of the Netherlands Antilles are administered by the central government of the Netherlands Antilles, based in Willemstad, Curaçao, which is responsible to the Staten, or legislative assembly. St Eustatius may elect by non-compulsory adult suffrage one of 22 members to the Staten. Routine local affairs on each island group (Bonaire, Curaçao and the Windward Islands) are managed by an elected Island Council, presided over by a Lieutenant-Governor.

CLIMATE

Hot, but tempered by cooling trade winds. The annual mean temperature is 27°C, varying by no more than two or three degrees throughout the year; the average rainfall is 1771mm.
Required clothing: Tropicals and lightweight cottons are worn throughout the year. Umbrellas or light waterproofs are also advisable.

PLYMOUTH Montserrat (40m)

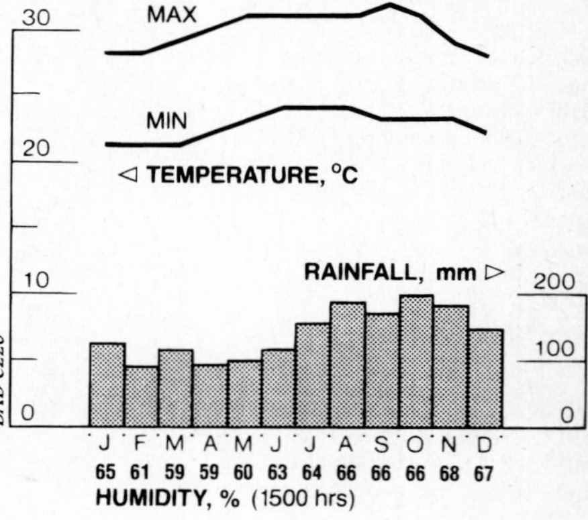

TEMPERATURE CONVERSIONS
-20 -10 0°C 10 20 30 40
0 10 20 30°F40 50 60 70 80 90 100

RAINFALL CONVERSIONS
0mm 200 400 600 800
0in 5 10 15 20 25 30

ST EUSTATIUS	HEALTH REGULATIONS	VISA REGULATIONS
GALILEO/WORLDSPAN	 TI-DFT/EUX/HE	TI-DFT/EUX/VI
SABRE	TIDFT/EUX/HE	TIDFT/EUX/VI

Code-Link

To access this information on your CRS, swipe the barcode with a light pen or type in the text under the barcode. For more information, see the introduction *How to Use This Book*.

ST KITTS & NEVIS

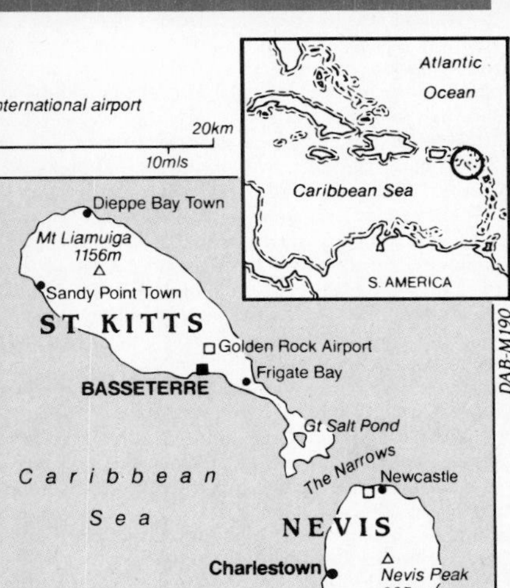

Location: Eastern Caribbean, Leeward Islands.

St Kitts & Nevis Department of Tourism
PO Box 132
Bay Road
Basseterre, St Kitts
Tel: 465 2620 *or* 465 4040. Fax: 465 8794; *or*
Main Street
Charlestown, Nevis
Tel: 469 5521. Fax: 469 1806.

High Commission for Eastern Caribbean States
10 Kensington Court
London W8 5DL
Tel: (071) 937 9522. Fax: (071) 937 5514. Telex: 913047 ECACOM G. Opening hours: 0930-1730 Monday to Friday.

St Kitts & Nevis Tourism Office
Address as for High Commission.
Tel: (071) 376 0881. Fax: (071) 937 3611. Opening hours: 0930-1730 Monday to Friday.

The British High Commission in Antigua deals with enquiries relating to St Kitts & Nevis:

British High Commission
PO Box 483
Old Parham Road
St John's, Antigua
Tel: 462 0008/9. Fax: 462 2806. Telex: 2113 UKREP ANT AK.

Consulate of the Federation of St Christopher & Nevis
Suite 608
2100 M Street, NW
Washington, DC
20037
Tel: (202) 833 3550. Fax: (202) 833 3553. Telex: 6387679.

St Kitts & Nevis Tourist Office
414 East 75th Street
New York, NY
10021
Tel: (212) 535 1234. Fax: (212) 879 4789.

Honorary Consulate of the Federation of St Christopher & Nevis
602 CLL Group Building
2695 Dutch Village Road
Halifax, Nova Scotia
B3J 4T9
Tel: (902) 455 9090.

St Kitts & Nevis Tourist Board
Suite 508
11 Yorkville Avenue
Toronto, Ontario
M4W 1L3
Tel: (416) 921 7717 *or* 921 7558. Fax: (416) 921 7997.

The Canadian High Commission in Barbados deals with enquiries relating to St Kitts & Nevis:

Canadian High Commission
PO Box 404
Bishops Court Hill
St Michaels
Bridgetown, Barbados
Tel: 429 3550. Fax: 429 3780. Telex: 2247 CANADA WB.

AREA: St Kitts: 168.4 sq km (65.1 sq miles); **Nevis:** 93.2 sq km (36.0 sq miles). **Total:** 261.6 sq km (101.1 sq miles).
POPULATION: 44,000 (1987 estimate).
POPULATION DENSITY: 168.2 per sq km.
CAPITAL: Basseterre. **Population:** 14,725 (1983).
GEOGRAPHY: St Kitts (officially known as St Christopher) lies in the northern part of the Leeward Islands in the eastern Caribbean. The high central body of the island is made up of three groups of rugged volcanic peaks split by deep ravines. The vegetation on the central mountain range is rainforest, thinning higher up to dense bushy cover. From here the island's volcanic crater, Mount Liamuiga, rises to almost 1200m (4000ft). The foothills,

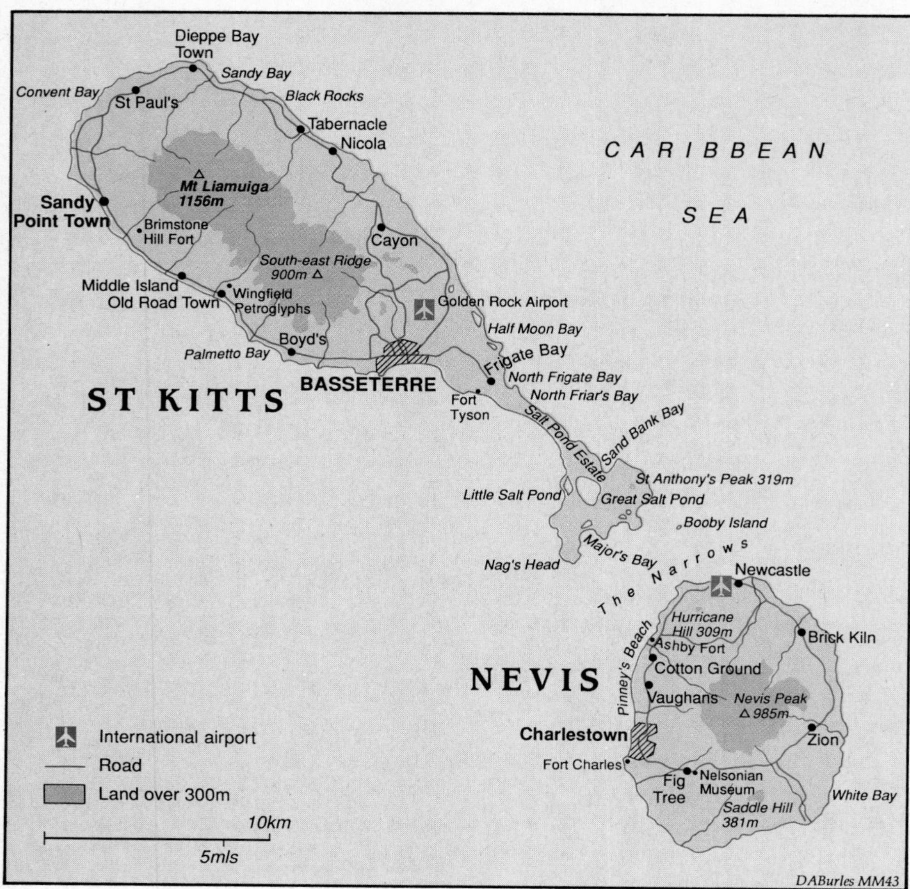

particularly to the north, form a gently rolling landscape of sugar-cane plantations and grassland, while uncultivated lowland slopes are covered with thick tropical woodland and exotic fruits such as papaya, mangoes, avocados, bananas and breadfruit. To the southeast of the island a low-lying peninsula, on which there are many excellent beaches, stretches towards Nevis.

3km (2 miles) to the south and only minutes away by air or ferry across The Narrows channel is the smaller island of **Nevis**, which is almost circular in shape. The island is skirted by miles of silver sand beaches, golden coconut groves and a calm, turquoise sea in which great brown pelicans dive for the rich harvest of fish. The central peak of the island, Mount Nevis, is 1090m (3576ft) high and its tip is usually capped with white clouds. The mountain is flanked on the north and south sides by two lesser mountains, Saddle Hill and Hurricane Hill, which once served as look-out posts for Nelson's fleet. Hurricane Hill on the north side commands a view of St Kitts and Barbuda. On the island's west side massed rows of palm trees form a coconut forest. There are pleasant coral beaches on the island's north and west coasts.

LANGUAGE: The official language is English.

RELIGION: Anglican Communion Church and other Christian denominations.

TIME: GMT - 4.

ELECTRICITY: 230 volts AC, 60Hz (110 volts available in some hotels).

COMMUNICATIONS: Telephone: IDD is available to St Kitts & Nevis (country code: St Kitts – 1 809; Nevis – 1 809), but outgoing international calls must go through the operator (dial 0). There is fully automated dialling for domestic calls. **Fax:** This service is available to the public at the offices of *SKANTEL* (see below) and at some hotels. **Telex/telegram:** Facilities available at main hotels and at the offices of *SKANTEL* at Cayon Street, Basseterre and Main Street, Charlestown. Opening hours: 0700-1900 Monday to Friday, 0700-1400 and 1900-2000 Saturday and 0800-1000 and 1900-2000 Sundays and public holidays. **Post:** Airmail to Europe takes five to seven days. Post offices are open 0800-1500 Monday to Friday and Saturday; 0800-1100 Thursday. **Press:** There are two newspapers, both published in English – the weekly *Democrat* and the twice-weekly *Labour Spokesman*.

BBC World Service and Voice of America frequencies: From time to time these change. See the section *How to Use this Book* for more information.

BBC:				
MHz	17.840	15.220	9.915	5.975
Voice of America:				
MHz	15.21	11.70	6.130	0.930

PASSPORT/VISA

Regulations and requirements may be subject to change at short notice, and you are advised to contact the appropriate diplomatic or consular authority before finalising travel arrangements. Details of these may be found at the head of this country's entry. Any numbers in the chart refer to the footnotes below.

	Passport Required?	Visa Required?	Return Ticket Required?
Full British	Yes	2	Yes
BVP	Not valid/1	-	-
Australian	Yes	No	Yes
Canadian	No	No	Yes
USA	No	No	Yes
Other EC	Yes	2	Yes
Japanese	Yes	No	Yes

PASSPORTS: Valid passport required by all except nationals of Canada and the USA with valid ID (for up to 6 months).

British Visitors Passport: [1] Not officially accepted. Although the immigration authorities of this country may in certain circumstances accept British Visitors Passports for persons arriving for holidays or unpaid business trips of up to 3 months, travellers are reminded that no formal agreement exists to this effect and the situation may, therefore, change at short notice. In addition, UK nationals using a BVP and returning to the UK from a country with which no such formal agreement exists may be subject to delays and interrogation by UK immigration.

VISAS: Required by all except:
(a) **[2]** nationals of most EC countries (nationals of Portugal *do* require visas);
(b) nationals of Commonwealth countries;
(c) nationals of Austria, Bahrain, China, Egypt, Finland, Iceland, Israel, Japan, Jordan, Kuwait, Liechtenstein, Monaco, Netherlands Antilles, Norway, Oman, Qatar, Saudi Arabia, South Africa, South Korea, Sweden, Switzerland, Turkey and United Arab Emirates;
(d) nationals of most OAS countries, namely: Bolivia, Brazil, Chile, Colombia, Costa Rica, Dominica, Ecuador, El Salvador, Grenada, Guatemala, Honduras, Jamaica, Mexico, Nicaragua, Panama, Paraguay, Peru, Puerto Rico, St Lucia, St Vincent & the Grenadines, Suriname, Trinidad & Tobago, Uruguay, US Virgin Islands, USA and Venezuela (nationals of Haiti and the Dominican Republic *do* require visas).

Types of visa: Ordinary. Cost depends on nationality of applicant.

Validity: Usually up to 6 months.

Application to: Consulate (or Consular Section at Embassy or High Commission) or Tourist Board. For addresses, see top of entry.

Working days required: 2-3 days.

Temporary residence: Apply to the Ministry of Home Affairs, Basseterre, St Kitts, West Indies.

MONEY

Currency: Eastern Caribbean Dollar (EC$) = 100 cents. Notes are in denominations of EC$100, 20, 10, 5 and 1. Coins are in denominations of EC$1, and 50, 25, 10, 5, 2 and 1 cents. The Eastern Caribbean Dollar is pegged to the US Dollar and US Dollars are also legal tender on the islands.

Credit cards: Visa is widely accepted, and Access/Mastercard and Diners Club have more limited acceptance. Check with your credit card company for details of merchant acceptability and other services which may be available.

Exchange rate indicators: The following figures are included as a guide to the movements of the Eastern Caribbean Dollar against Sterling and the US Dollar:

Date:	Oct '89	Oct '90	Oct '91	Oct '92
£1.00=	4.27	5.27	4.69	4.27
$1.00=	2.70	2.70	2.70	2.70

Currency restrictions: There are no restrictions on the import or export of local currency. There is free import of foreign currency, subject to declaration. Export of foreign currency is limited to the amount imported and declared.

Banking hours: 0800-1300 Monday to Thursday; 0800-1300 and 1500-1700 Friday; 0830-1130 Saturday.

DUTY FREE

The following goods may be imported into St Kitts & Nevis without incurring customs duty:
200 cigarettes or 50 cigars or 225g of tobacco;
1.136 litres of wine or spirits;
175ml perfume.

Note: There are several duty-free shops, selling a range of goods, including perfumes, textiles, clothing, porcelain, crystal and jewellery.

ST KITTS & NEVIS | **HEALTH REGULATIONS** | **VISA REGULATIONS** | Code-Link

GALILEO/WORLDSPAN

TI-DFT/SKB/HE

TI-DFT/SKB/VI

SABRE

TIDFT/SKB/HE

TIDFT/SKB/VI

To access this information on your CRS, swipe the barcode with a light pen or type in the text under the barcode. For more information, see the introduction *How to Use This Book*.

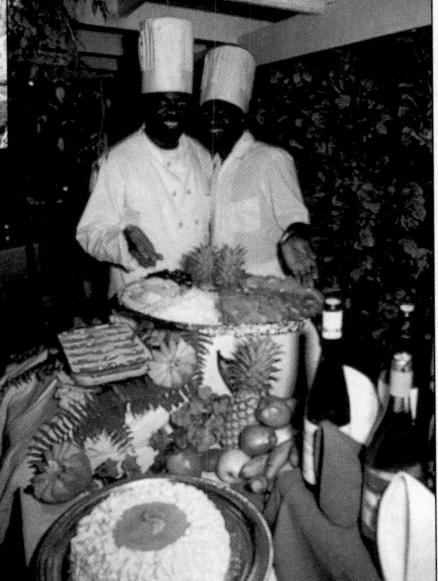

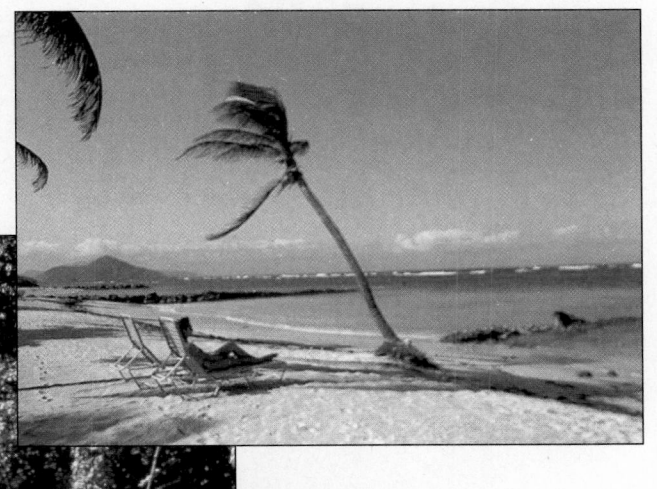

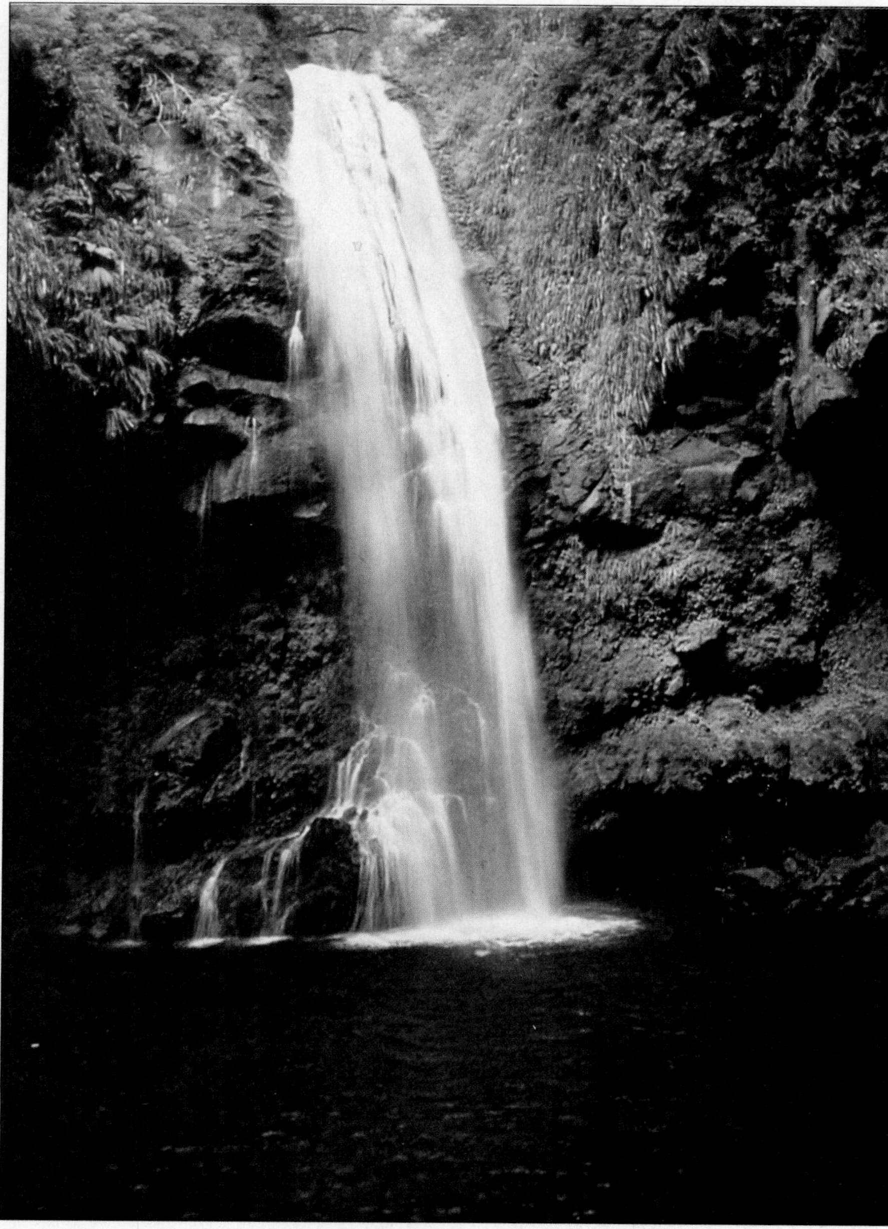

TRAVEL - Internal

AIR: The local airline, *LIAT (LI)*, runs five flights daily between St Kitts and the island of Nevis. The airport for Nevis is *Newcastle (NEV)*.
SEA: There is a regular passenger ferry service between Basseterre (St Kitts) and Charlestown (Nevis) with four sailings daily except Thursday and Sunday (travel time – 40 minutes). For information contact the General Manager, St Kitts & Nevis Port Authority, Basseterre, St Kitts, West Indies.
ROAD: A good road network on both islands makes any area accessible within minutes. Driving is on the left. **Bus:** There are privately-run bus services, which are comfortable and make regular but unscheduled runs between villages. **Taxi:** Services on both islands have set rates. A schedule of taxi rates is obtainable at the government headquarters. On St Kitts, there is a 25% surcharge between 2300-0600. On Nevis, there is a 50% surcharge between 2200-0600. Taxi drivers expect a 10% tip. **Car & moped hire:** A selection of cars and mopeds can be hired from several companies. It is best to book cars through the airline well in advance. **Documentation:** Before driving any vehicle, including motorcycles, a local Temporary Driver's Licence must be obtained from the Police Traffic Department. This is readily issued on presentation of an International Driving Permit or national driving licence and a fee of EC$30, and is valid for one year.
JOURNEY TIMES: The following chart gives journey times from Basseterre, St Kitts (in hours and minutes) to other major towns on the islands.

	Air	Road	Sea
Newcastle, Nevis	0.05	-	-
Charlestown, Nevis	-	-	0.45
Sandy Point	-	0.20	-
Brimstone Hill	-	0.35	-
Frigate Bay	-	0.10	-
Cockleshell Bay	-	0.35	-

ACCOMMODATION

Daily tariffs for hotel and other accommodation vary according to the standard of the establishment. In general, prices are considerably lower in the low season (mid-April to mid-December). Group discounts and package rates are offered by most hotels on request. A Government tax of 7% is levied on all hotel bills and the hotels themselves add 10% service charge.
HOTELS: There are over 20 hotels on the two islands, the majority being on St Kitts; most are small and owner-managed, offering a high standard of facilities and comfort. Many are converted from the great houses and sugar mills on the old estates. Further development on St Kitts will add 200 more beds. A full list of hotels can be obtained from the Embassy, High Commission or Tourist Board. The majority of hotels belong to the St Kitts & Nevis Hotel Association (SKANHA), PO Box 438, Basseterre, St Kitts. Tel/fax: 465 5304. **Grading:** Though not a grading structure, many hotels in the Caribbean offer accommodation according to one of a number of plans: **FAP** is **Full American Plan**: room with all meals (including afternoon tea, supper etc). **AP** is **American Plan**: room with three meals. **MAP** is **Modified American Plan**: breakfast and dinner included with the price of the room plus, in some places, British-style afternoon tea. **CP** is **Continental Plan**: room and breakfast only. **EP** is **European Plan**: room only.
GUEST-HOUSES: There are several guest-houses on both islands. A list is available from the Tourist Board.
SELF-CATERING: There are villas and apartments available. A list and full details are available from the Tourist Board.

PUBLIC HOLIDAYS

Public holidays observed in St Kitts & Nevis are as follows:
Apr 9 '93 Good Friday. **Apr 12** Easter Monday. **May 3** Labour Day. **May 31** Whit Monday. **Jun 12** Queen's Official Birthday. **Aug 2** August Monday. **Aug 3** Culturama (Nevis only). **Sep 19** Independence Day. **Dec 25** Christmas Day. **Dec 26** Boxing Day. **Jan 1 '94** New Year's Day/Carnival Day.

HEALTH

Regulations and requirements may be subject to change at short notice, and you are advised to contact your doctor well in advance of your intended date of departure. Any numbers in the chart refer to the footnotes below.

	Special Precautions?	Certificate Required?
Yellow Fever	No	1
Cholera	No	No
Typhoid & Polio	Yes	-
Malaria	No	-
Food & Drink	2	-

[1]: A yellow fever vaccination certificate is required from travellers over one year of age arriving from infected areas.
[2]: Mains water is normally chlorinated, and whilst relatively safe may cause mild abdominal upsets. Bottled water is available and is advised for the first few weeks of the stay. Drinking water outside main cities and towns may be contaminated and sterilisation is advisable. Milk is pasteurised and dairy products are safe for consumption. Local meat, poultry, seafood, fruit and vegetables are generally considered safe to eat.
Health care: There are large general hospitals in Basseterre and Charlestown, and a smaller public hospital at Sandy Point, St Kitts. There are no private hospitals, but several doctors and dentists are in private practice. Health insurance is advised.

TRAVEL - International

AIR: *LIAT (LI)* runs six flights a week from Antigua and offers day trip charters to Montserrat, St Maarten (for duty-free shopping), Antigua and Barbuda. Other airlines serving the islands include *Air BVI, American Eagle, BWIA International* and *Windward Islands Airways*.
Approximate flight times: From *London* to St Kitts is 10 hours, including stopover in Antigua. From *New York* to St Kitts is 5 hours.
International airports: *St Kitts (SKB)* (Golden Rock) is 3.2km (2 miles) from Basseterre on St Kitts. Airport facilities include restaurant and duty-free shop. There are at present no exchange facilities at the airport. Taxi fares are regulated; fares from the airport to Basseterre are approximately EC$13-16 (50 cents is charged on each additional piece of luggage over one).
Newcastle Airfield is 11km (7 miles) from Charlestown on Nevis.
Departure tax: EC$20 (US$8).
SEA: Basseterre is a deep-water port capable of berthing ships up to 120m (400ft) and is regularly visited by cruise liners operated by *Cunard, Ocean Cruise, Regency Cruise, Royal Caribbean Cruises, Regency Cruise, Pacquet Cruise* and *P&O*.

RESORTS & EXCURSIONS

St Kitts

Basseterre: The capital retains the flavour of both French and British occupation, and there are many Georgian buildings surrounding *Independence Square*. A deep-water harbour for cruise ships has recently been completed. Sights in or near the capital include: *The Circus, Independence Square*, the market, *St George's Church, Craft House, Brimstone Hill Fortress, Black Rocks, Caribelle Batik Factory* (considered to be the most beautiful factory in the world), the *Primate Research Centre, Frigate Bay Development*, the southeastern peninsula and *Mount Liamuiga's volcanic crater*.
Brimstone Hill: One of the most impressive New World forts, built on the peak of a sulphuric prominence, known as 'The Gibraltar of the West Indies'. It commands the southern approach to what were the sugar mill plains, and commands a view of the nearby islands of Saba and St Eustatius. Built in 1690, it was the scene of a number of Franco/British battles during the 18th century.

Frigate Bay: This is the main resort area on the island and has been designated a Tourist Area by the Government. It boasts two fine beaches, hotels, a golf course and a casino.
Day trip *charter flights* to neighbouring islands depart regularly from Golden Rock.

Nevis

Since the 18th century, Nevis has been known as the 'Queen of the Caribbean', and over the last 100 years the island has become one of the world's most exclusive resorts and spas. Most of the original plantation owners lived on the island and it became renowned as a centre of elegant and gracious living. Although Nevis has lived through an earthquake and a tidal wave which is claimed to have buried the former capital, the island is still dotted, as is St Kitts, with fascinating old buildings and historic sites.
Charlestown: The capital is a delightful town, with weathered wooden buildings decorated like delicate gingerbread and great arches of brilliantly coloured bougainvillea. The town contains several reminders of Nevisian history, such as the *Cotton Ginnery*, Alexander Hamilton's birthplace and museum, the *Court House*, the *War Memorial*, the *Alexandra Hospital* and the *Jewish Cemetery*. Some of the plantation houses have now been transformed into superb hotels, such as the famous *Nisbett*. Other sights in or near Charlestown include: *Nevis Philatelic Bureau, Public Library*, the market, *Bath House* (one of the oldest hotels in the Leeward Islands), Eva Wilkin's studio, Eden Brown's Great House, *Fig Tree Church, Nelson Museum, Bath Hot Springs* and the *Newcastle Pottery*.
Elsewhere: North of Charlestown is *Pinney's Beach*, one of the best on the island, an expanse of silver sand, backed by palm trees. Further north still, *Black Sand Beach* and *Hurricane Hill* offer an excellent view of both St Kitts and Barbuda.

SOCIAL PROFILE

FOOD & DRINK: St Kitts & Nevis has built up a widely established reputation for fine food, a reputation which the local restauranteurs guard zealously. Restaurants specialise in West Indian, Creole, Continental, Indian, Chinese and French cuisine. Most restaurants in St Kitts offer a continental menu with island variations. Local dishes include roast suckling pig, spiny lobster, crab back or curries. Restaurants that cater more for locals also offer conch (curried, soused or in salad), turtle stews, rice and peas and goat's water (mutton stew). Christophine, yams, breadfruit and papaya are also served. Nevis is less grand and Charlestown's small restaurants cater more to Nevisians than visitors. Local specialities are native vegetable soup, lobster, mutton, beef and turtle stews. Fruit, including mangoes, papayas and bananas, is sold at the waterfront market. **Drink:** The locally produced CSR (cane spirit), belonging to the Baron Rothschild family, is excellent. A wide range of imported drinks is available.
NIGHTLIFE: Very low key. A number of hotels and inns have string or steel bands to dance to on Saturday nights in the peak season, and there is a disco called *J's Place* at the foot of the Brimstone Hill Fortress in St Kitts. *Mingles Night Club*, also in St Kitts, is open until the small hours. St Kitts has a casino at the *Royal St Kitts*, complete with slot machines, roulette wheels and blackjack tables. Otherwise entertainment centres around the pleasant bars of the inns and hotels.
SHOPPING: Local crafts include carvings, batik, wall hangings, leather art and coconut work. Local textiles and designs are also available. Stamp collectors should note the excellent Philatelic Bureau in Basseterre. Duty-free shopping is relatively new to St Kitts and as yet, only a few shops feature imported merchandise at substantial savings. Nevis' hot pepper sauce, ranked among the Caribbean's best, is a good take-home item and can be bought at the Main Street grocery in Charlestown. **Shopping hours:** 0800-1600 Monday to Wednesday and Friday; 0800-1200 Thursday; and 0800-1800 Saturday.
SPORT: Swimming is excellent; most hotels have freshwater pools and some have their own beaches. **Scuba** and **snorkelling** are catered for and beach hotels generally have equipment. Several Basseterre skippers are equipped to take scuba parties. **Sailing** boats can be hired from beach hotels, although Nevis has very limited facilities. Fast boats and **water-skiing** equipment are available for hire. **Fishing** trips can be organised. Deep-sea fishing is a speciality. An 18-hole international **golf** championship course is at Frigate Bay and a 9-hole course at Golden Rock, both on St Kitts. There is also an 18-hole championship golf course on Nevis. A number of **tennis** courts are available on both islands, and clubs welcome visitors. Many of the hotels have their own (mainly hard) tennis courts. Other sports include **mountaineering, hiking, cricket, football** and **horseriding.**

SPECIAL EVENTS: Festivals in St Kitts & Nevis have a special atmosphere and visitors are encouraged to take part in the parades, pageants and parties. The following are a few special events celebrated during 1993/4:
May-Jun '93 *Windsurfing/Sunfish Race*. **End Jun-Early Jul** *Caribbean Offshore Race*. **Jul 30-Aug 3** *Culturama* (a celebration of folklore, art and culture), Nevis. **Sep-Oct** *Rotary Fun Rally*. **Dec 24-Jan 1 '94** *Carnival*, masquerades, street dancing, calypso competitions and cultural presentations, as well as the usual Christmas dances and celebrations.
SOCIAL CONVENTIONS: Commercialisation has not yet taken over and the easy-going, quiet way of life of the local people remains almost unspoiled. All visitors to the islands are cordially welcome; marriages are valid after two days residence. Islanders maintain traditions of calypso dancing and music and this can be seen particularly during the summer months. Dress is informal at most hotels. It is suggested that visitors be suitably attired when in town and in places of business. For more formal occasions and functions, a lightweight suit and tie is recommended. **Tipping:** 10% service charge is added to hotel bills. In restaurants leave 10-15% and tip taxi drivers 10% of the fare.

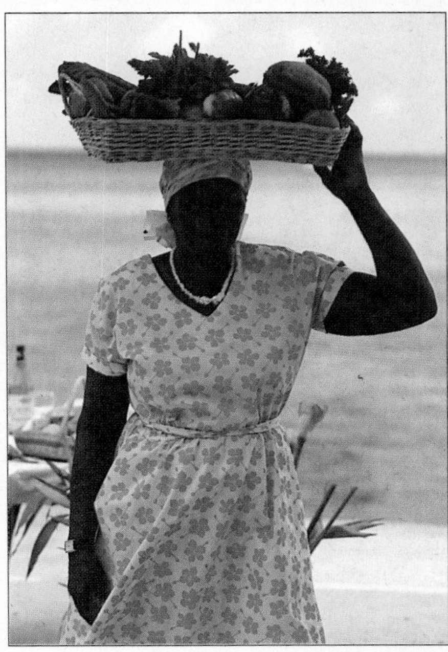

BUSINESS PROFILE

ECONOMY: St Kitts & Nevis has an agricultural economy, the mainstay of which is the sugar industry. As the world sugar price has been very low in the past few years, St Kitts & Nevis has come to rely on regular injections of

foreign aid to prevent economic collapse. The Government is trying to broaden the range of the islands' manufacturing industry, which was taken into state ownership in 1975. One notable result of this policy has been the establishment of a thriving electronics and data processing sector. Tourism is also seen as a promising growth area and is developing rapidly, especially on Nevis, though political uncertainties have hampered infrastructure development. The UK and the USA are the islands' main trading partners.

BUSINESS: Business wear for men usually consists of a short- or long-sleeved shirt and tie, or open-neck tunic-shirt, or alternatively, safari-type suits. **Office hours:** 0800-1200 and 1300-1600 Monday to Saturday; early closing on Thursday.

COMMERCIAL INFORMATION: The following organisation can offer advice: St Kitts-Nevis Chamber of Industry and Commerce, PO Box 332, South Square Street, Basseterre, St Kitts. Tel: 465 2980. Fax: 465 4490. Telex: 6822.

CONFERENCES/CONVENTIONS: For further information on conferences and convention possibilities, contact the St Kitts & Nevis Hotel Association (for address, see *Accommodation* above).

HISTORY & GOVERNMENT

HISTORY: The islands of St Kitts and Nevis were originally settled by Indians from South America. Britain, France and, to a lesser extent, Spain squabbled over possession of the islands throughout the 16th century. By 1623, Britain had prevailed and set about cultivating sugar on the islands on plantations worked by large numbers of slaves. It was not until September 1983 that the islands became an independent state within the Commonwealth. Two general elections were held since then. At the latest polls in March 1989, six of the 11 elected seats were won by the People's Action Movement (PAM) and the remainder divided between the Labour Party, the Nevis Reformation Party (NRP) and the Concerned Citizens' Movement. The present government is a coalition of the PAM and NRP led by Dr Kennedy Simmonds. Since September 1989, the Government's immediate priority has been to administer the reconstruction of the islands in the wake of the devastation caused by Hurricane Hugo. In the longer term, the main political issue is the much-debated possibility of merger with other Leeward Islands and the Virgin Islands. There is also a long-running dispute over the relative political influence of the island of Nevis, which many Kittitians feel to be excessive in proportion to Nevis' size and population. In June 1992, elections were held for the Nevis Island Assembly. The Nevis Reformation Party retained 2 seats, while the other 3 were won by the Concerned Citizens' Movement.

GOVERNMENT: The Head of State of the Federation of St Christopher and Nevis (the islands' formal title) is the British monarch, represented locally by a Governor-General. Legislative power is vested in the Governor and the National Assembly, which has 11 members elected directly by universal suffrage and three appointed members. Nevis Island also has a separate legislature which, subject to certain conditions written into the constitution, may secede from the Government of the Federation.

CLIMATE

Hot and tropical climate tempered by trade winds throughout most of the year. The driest period is from January to April and there is increased rainfall in summer and towards the end of the year. The volume of rain varies according to altitude; rain showers can occur throughout the year. The average annual rainfall is about 125cm (50 inches) to 200cm (80 inches) with a wetter season from May to October. Like the other Leeward Islands, St Kitts lies in the track of violent tropical hurricanes which are most likely to develop between August and October.

Required clothing: Lightweights are worn throughout the year, with warmer clothes for cooler evenings, especially in winter (October to February). A light raincoat is advisable.

PLYMOUTH Montserrat (40m)

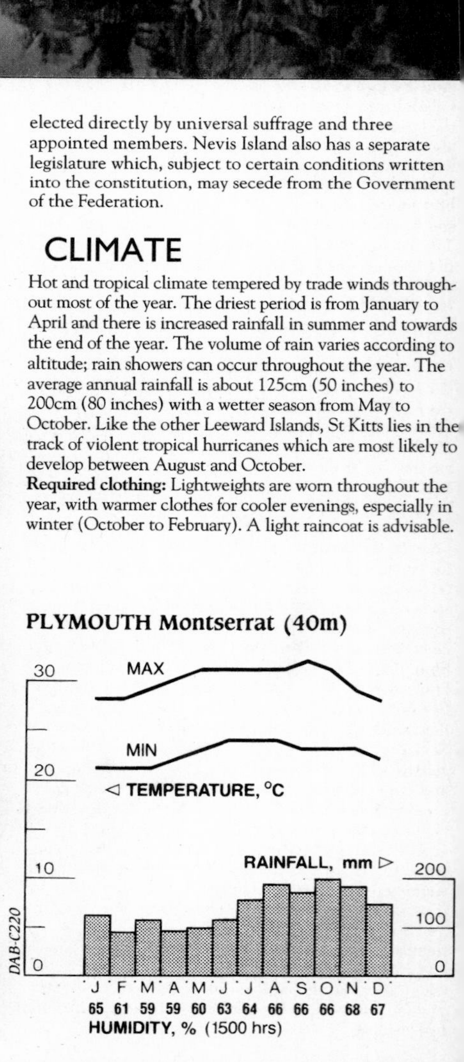

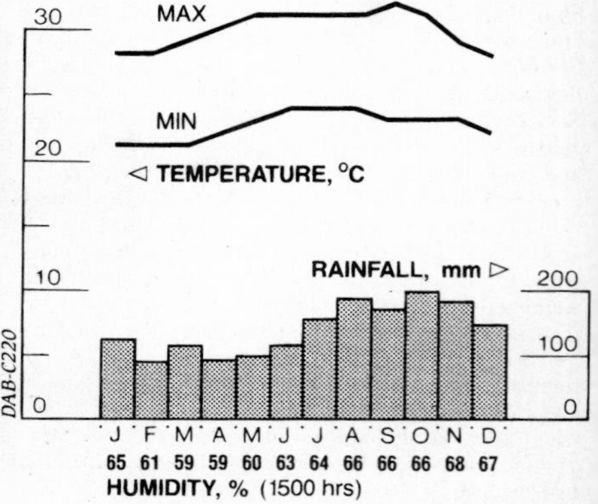

ST LUCIA

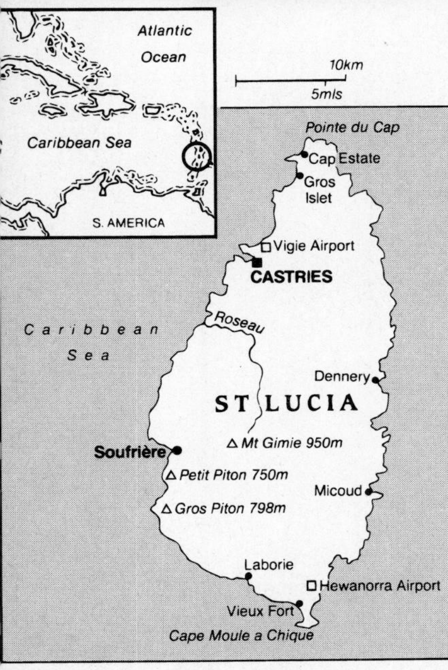

Location: Eastern Caribbean, Windward Islands.

St Lucia Tourist Board
PO Box 221
Pointe Seraphine
Castries, St Lucia
Tel: 24094. Fax: 31121. Telex: 6380.

High Commission for Eastern Caribbean States
10 Kensington Court
London W8 5DL
Tel: (071) 937 9522. Fax: (071) 937 5514. Telex: 913047 ECACOM G. Opening hours: 0930-1730 Monday to Friday.

St Lucia Tourist Board
Address as for High Commission.
Tel:(071) 937 1969. Fax: (071) 937 3611.

British High Commission
24 Micoud Street
Castries, St Lucia
Tel: 22485.

Embassy of St Lucia
Suite 309
2100 M Street, NW
Washington, DC
20037
Tel: (202) 463 7378/9. Fax: (202) 887 5746. Telex: 6711478.

St Lucia Tourist Board
9th Floor
820 Second Avenue
New York, NY
10017
Tel: (212) 867 2950/1. Fax: (212) 370 7867. Telex: 666762.

Honorary Consulate of the Federation of St Lucia
3 Dewberry Drive
Markham, Ontario
L3S 2R7
Tel: (416) 472 1423. Fax: (416) 472 6379.

St Lucia Tourist Board
Suite 425
151 Bloor Street
Toronto, Ontario
M5S 1S4
Tel: (416) 961 5606. Fax: (416) 961 4317. Telex: 06217775.

The Canadian High Commission in Barbados deals with enquiries relating to St Lucia:
Canadian High Commission
PO Box 404
Bridgetown
Barbados
Tel: 429 3550. Fax: 429 3780. Telex: 2247 CANADA WB.

AREA: 616.3 sq km (238 sq miles).
POPULATION: 151,290 (1990 estimate).
POPULATION DENSITY: 245.5 per sq km.
CAPITAL: Castries. **Population:** 57,322 (1990).
GEOGRAPHY: St Lucia is the second largest of the Windward Islands. It has some of the finest mountain scenery in the West Indies, rich with tropical vegetation. For so small an island, 43km (27 miles) by 23km (14 miles), St Lucia has a great variety of plant and animal life. Orchids and exotic plants of the genus *anthurium* grow wild in the rainforests and the roadsides are covered with many colourful and sweet-smelling tropical flowers. Flamboyant trees spread shade and blossom everywhere. Indigenous wildlife includes a species of ground lizard unique to St Lucia, and the *agouti* and the *manicou*, two rabbit-like animals, common throughout the island. The Amazon versicolor parrot is another, though more elusive, inhabitant of the deep interior rainforest. The highest peak is Mt Gimie, 960m (3145ft). Most spectacular are Gros Piton and Petit Piton, ancient, volcanic forest-covered cones which rise out of the sea on the west coast. *Soufri* (vents in a volcano which exude hydrogen sulphide, steam and other gases) and boiling water-pools can be seen here. The mountains are intersected by short rivers which in some areas form broad fertile valleys. The island has excellent beaches and is surrounded by a clear, warm sea.
LANGUAGE: English and local French *patois*.
RELIGION: 82% Roman Catholic, also Anglican, Methodist, Seventh Day Adventist and Baptist.
TIME: GMT - 4.
ELECTRICITY: 220 volts AC, 50Hz.
COMMUNICATIONS: Telephone: IDD is available. Country code: 809 45. **Fax:** Available to the public in Castries at the offices of *Cable & Wireless* (tel: 23301) and at some hotels. **Telex/telegram:** Facilities limited to main towns and hotels and at the public telex booth at Cable & Wireless. **Post:** Airmail to Europe takes up to a week. *Poste Restante* mail will only be released on presentation of suitable identification. Post office hours: 0800-1630 Monday to Friday and 0900-1330 Saturday. **Press:** The main newspapers are *The Voice of St Lucia* and *The Crusader*.
BBC World Service and Voice of America frequencies: From time to time these change. See the section *How to Use this Book* for more information.

BBC:				
MHz	17.84	15.22	9.915	5.975
Voice of America:				
MHz	15.21	11.70	6.130	0.930

PASSPORT/VISA

Regulations and requirements may be subject to change at short notice, and you are advised to contact the appropriate diplomatic or consular authority before finalising travel arrangements. Details of these may be found at the head of this country's entry. Any numbers in the chart refer to the footnotes below.

	Passport Required?	Visa Required?	Return Ticket Required?
Full British	Yes	No	Yes
BVP	Not valid/2	-	-
Australian	Yes	No	Yes
Canadian	1	No	Yes
USA	1	No	Yes
Other EC	Yes	No	Yes
Japanese	Yes	Yes	Yes

PASSPORTS: [1] Valid passports are required by all except nationals of Canada and the USA with valid proof of identity (for visits of up to 6 months).
British Visitors Passport: [2] Not officially accepted. Although the immigration authorities of this country may in certain circumstances accept British Visitors Passports for persons arriving for holidays or unpaid business trips of up to 3 months, travellers are reminded that no formal agreement exists to this effect and the situation may, therefore, change at short notice. In addition, UK nationals using a BVP and returning to the UK from a country with which no such formal agreement exists may be subject to delays and interrogation by UK immigration.
VISAS: Required by all except:
(a) nationals of countries as shown in the chart above;
(b) nationals of all Commonwealth countries;
(c) nationals of Austria, Finland, Iceland, Liechtenstein, Norway, San Marino, Sweden, Switzerland, Turkey and most European countries (nationals of Eastern European countries should contact the High Commission);
(d) nationals of the following countries belonging to the Organisation of American States: Antigua & Barbuda, Argentina, Bahamas, Barbados, Bolivia, Brazil, Costa Rica, Dominica, Dominican Republic, Ecuador, El Salvador, Grenada, Guatemala, Haiti, Honduras, Jamaica, Mexico, Nicaragua, Panama, Peru, St Kitts & Nevis, St Vincent & the Grenadines, Suriname, Trinidad & Tobago, Uruguay, the USA and Venezuela (nationals of Chile, Colombia and Paraguay *do* need visas);
(e) nationals of most African countries (nationals of Libya and South Africa *do* need visas).
Transit: Transit passengers who continue their journey within 14 days do not require a transit visa. This does not apply for nationals of Cuba and Eastern bloc countries.
Types of visa: Ordinary; cost depends on nationality of the applicant.
Validity: Up to 6 months.
Application to: Consulate (or Consular Section at Embassy or High Commission). For addresses, see top of entry.
Application requirements: (a) Completed application form(s). (b) Photo(s). (c) Sufficient funds to cover duration of stay.
Working days required: Dependent upon nationality of applicant, normally 2-4 days.
Temporary residence: Refer applications or enquiries to Consulate, Embassy or High Commission. Processed through the Ministry of Foreign Affairs, Castries.

MONEY

Currency: Eastern Caribbean Dollar (EC$) = 100 cents. Notes are in denominations of EC$100, 20, 10, 5 and 1. Coins are in denominations of EC$1, and 50, 25, 10, 5, 2 and 1 cents. US dollars are also accepted as legal tender.
Currency exchange: US dollars ensure a better exchange rate.
Credit cards: Access/Mastercard, American Express, Diners Club and Visa are all widely accepted. Check with your credit card company for details of merchant acceptability and other services which may be available.
Travellers cheques: Accepted. US Dollar cheques preferred.
Exchange rate indicators: The following figures are included as a guide to the movements of the Eastern Caribbean Dollar against Sterling and the US Dollar:

Date:	**Oct '89**	**Oct '90**	**Oct '91**	**Oct '92**
£1.00=	4.27	5.27	4.69	4.27
$1.00=	*2.70	*2.70	*2.70	*2.70

Note [*]: The Eastern Caribbean Dollar is tied to the US Dollar.
Currency restrictions: Free import of local currency, subject to declaration. Export of local currency is limited to the amount declared on import. There are no restrictions on the import or export of foreign currency.
Banking hours: Generally 0800-1500 Monday to Thursday and 0800-1700 Friday. Some banks are open 0800-1200 Saturday. These hours vary between banks.

DUTY FREE

The following items may be imported into St Lucia without incurring customs duty:
200 cigarettes or 250g tobacco products;
1 litre alcoholic beverage.

PUBLIC HOLIDAYS

Public holidays observed in St Lucia are as follows:
Apr 9 '93 Good Friday. **Apr 12** Easter Monday. **May 1** Labour Day. **May 31** Whit Monday. **Jun 5** Queen's Official Birthday. **Jun 10** Corpus Christi. **Aug 2** August Bank Holiday. **Oct 4** Thanksgiving Day. **Dec 13** St Lucia Day. **Dec 25-26** Christmas. **Jan 1-2 '94** New Year. **Feb 22** Independence Day. **Feb 22-23** Carnival.

HEALTH

Regulations and requirements may be subject to change at short notice, and you are advised to contact your doctor well in advance of your intended date of departure. Any numbers in the chart refer to the footnotes below.

	Special Precautions?	Certificate Required?
Yellow Fever	No	1
Cholera	No	No
Typhoid & Polio	Yes	-
Malaria	No	-
Food & Drink	2	-

[1]: A yellow fever vaccination certificate is required from travellers over one year of age from infected areas.
[2]: Mains water is normally chlorinated, and whilst relatively safe may cause mild abdominal upsets. Bottled water is available and is advised for the first few weeks of the stay. Milk is pasteurised and dairy products are safe for consumption. Local meat, poultry, seafood, fruit and vegetables are generally considered safe to eat.
Bilharzia (schistosomiasis) is present. Avoid swimming

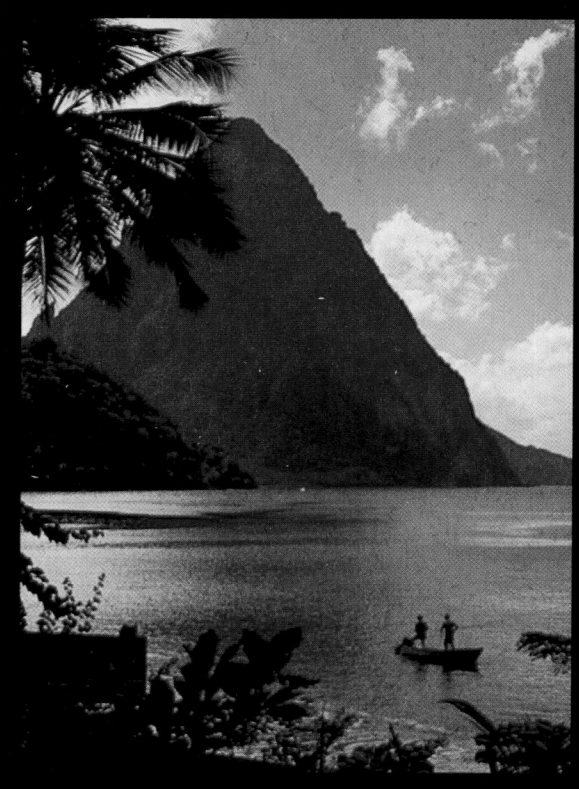

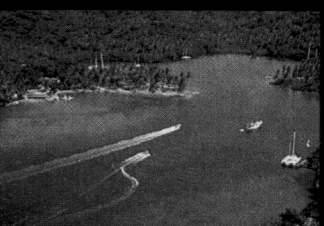

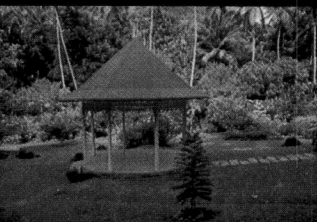

and paddling in fresh water. Swimming pools which are well-chlorinated and maintained are safe.
Health care: Costs of health care are high and full health insurance is essential.

TRAVEL - International

AIR: St Lucia is served direct by *British Airways* and by *British West Indian Airways*.
Approximate flight times: From Castries to *Barbados* is 30 minutes, to *London* is 8 hours 25 minutes (via Barbados), to *Los Angeles* is 9 hours, to *New York* is 5 hours and to *Singapore* is 33 hours.
International airports: *Vigie (SLU)* and *Hewanorra (UVF)*, 3km (2 miles) and 67km (42 miles) from Castries respectively. Taxis or buses are available from airports to Castries. Both runways are equipped for jets. Airport facilities at Vigie include a bar/restaurant and car hire; at Hewanorra there is a bar/restaurant, shops and tourist information, outgoing duty-free shop and a car hire outlet.
Departure tax: EC$27 on all international departures and EC$20 for Caribbean destinations. Transit passengers and children under two years are exempt.
SEA: St Lucia is served by a number of cruise lines as well as local passenger/freight lines. Lines include *Cunard, Costa, P&O* and *Sun Line*. The main ports are Castries, Vieux Fort and Soufrière. The duty-free port at Pointe Seraphine offers 2-berth cruise ship facilities, duty-free shopping, restaurants and bars; it may be visited by any tourist holding a current passport (further information in the *Shopping* section below). Work on the construction of a third berth for cruise ships began in 1989.

TRAVEL - Internal

AIR: It is possible to charter planes. Charter flights operate between Vigie and Hewanorra airports. The regional airline *LIAT* offers flights to neighbouring islands.
SEA: Boat charters are easily available at Castries, Marigot Bay and Rodney Bay.
ROAD: All major centres are served by a reasonable network. The main cross-island route runs from Vieux Fort in the south of the island to Castries in the north. Traffic drives on the left. **Bus:** Services connect rural areas with the capital. There is a good service from Castries to Gros Islet in the north of the island with buses departing every 30 minutes during the day. **Taxi:** Hiring a taxi is easy and cheap. Tipping is unnecessary. **Car hire:** Cars can be obtained either in Castries, Soufrière and Vieux Fort, or through hotels. Minimokes are particularly popular. Hotels and local tour operators run coach trips for groups. **Documentation:** On presentation of a national driving licence or International Driving Permit a local licence will be issued.

ACCOMMODATION

HOTELS: St Lucia has a range of accommodation to suit every taste and every budget, from deluxe hotels to self-catering apartments. All-inclusive holidays are also proving very popular and several hotels now offer this option. Most hotels provide some form of entertainment in the evening, from calypso music to the ever-popular limbo dancing. Details are available from hotels' reservation desks. A Government tax of 8% and service charge of 10-15% are added to bills. A leaflet giving hotel and guest-house rates is produced by the St Lucia Hotel and Tourism Association, PO Box 545, Vide Boutielle, Castries. Tel: 25978. Fax: 27967. **Grading:** Though not a grading structure, many hotels in the Caribbean offer accommodation according to one of a number of plans: **AP** is **American Plan**; room with three meals. **MAP** is **Modified American Plan**; breakfast and dinner included with the price of the room plus, in some places, British-style afternoon tea. **CP** is **Continental Plan**; room and breakfast only. **EP** is **European Plan**; room only. Hotels in St Lucia are also graded on a scale from **3** to **5 stars.**
GUEST-HOUSES: A range of accommodation is available, some of which offers self-catering facilities.

RESORTS & EXCURSIONS

St Lucia is a beautiful volcanic island with green jungles, undulating agricultural land and dazzling beaches. It is an island of contrasts, and the visitor can stroll for hours along unspoiled beaches, enjoy the tropical splendour of the lush rainforests in its interior, marvel at the hot springs in the world's only 'drive-in' volcano, go horseriding on rugged mountain trails, play golf or simply

ST LUCIA	HEALTH REGULATIONS	VISA REGULATIONS (Code-Link)
GALILEO/WORLDSPAN	 TI-DFT/SLU/HE	TI-DFT/SLU/VI
SABRE	 TIDFT/SLU/HE	 TIDFT/SLU/VI

To access this information on your CRS, swipe the barcode with a light pen or type in the text under the barcode. For more information, see the introduction *How to Use This Book*.

sunbathe; all among some of the most varied scenery in the Caribbean. Considerable French influence is still felt throughout the island.

Castries and the North

Castries is one of the most beautifully situated Caribbean cities. Surrounded by hills, its large, safe, land-locked harbour at the head of a wide bay is a constant hive of activity. Castries is a major port of call for cruise ships, which dock at Pointe Seraphine. The spacious *Columbus Square* boasts tropical scenery and the 19th-century *Catholic Cathedral* (where the art of gospel singing is very much alive). There is also a colourful, bustling market. **Morne Fortune,** 'the hill of good luck', affords the visitor the chance to inspect the fortification which defends Castries. It also provides a magnificent panorama of the city and the surrounding area.

Gros Islet, on the northwest coast of the island, stages an 'impromptu' street party every Friday. Nearby **Pigeon Point** has a small museum telling the history of the island. It was from here that Admiral Rodney set sail in 1782 and destroyed the French Fleet in one of the most decisive engagements in European history. This end of the island is now being developed as a centre for tourism. **Anse La Raye,** on the west coast south of Castries, is a vividly coloured fishing village where locals make boats from gum trees and sails from chicken feathers. **Marigot Bay,** also on the west coast, is a secluded and idyllic palm-fringed yachtsman's paradise. Above Marigot Bay lies **Cul de Sac,** an area of three large banana plantations. From above, they look like gently moving oceans of green leaves. It was here that 'Dr Doolittle' was filmed.

Soufrière and the South

Soufrière is the second largest settlement on the island. This deep-water port stands at the foot of two extinct volcanoes, the **Pitons**. Rising to 798m (2619ft) above sea level, these are probably St Lucia's most famous attractions. The town itself is typically West Indian, a cluster of brightly painted arcaded buildings set hard against the jungle.

The road between Soufrière and Fond St Jacques runs eastwards through lush rainforest; here are the **Diamond Waterfalls** and **Sulphur Springs.**

The picturesque little villages of **Choiseul** and **Laborie** are surrounded by splendid vegetation.

On the east of the island, the headlands project into the ocean; a visit to **Dennery** and **Micoud** is highly recommended.

Coastal Excursions

There are several boat trips which offer the visitor an exhilarating day viewing the island from the sea and possibly weighing anchor to picnic at an exciting location. Alternative means of transport include brigs, catamarans and private yachts.

SOCIAL PROFILE

FOOD & DRINK: Most hotels have restaurants, in addition to a wide range in the major towns serving many different types of food. Waiter service is the norm. Local dishes include *langouste* (local lobster)

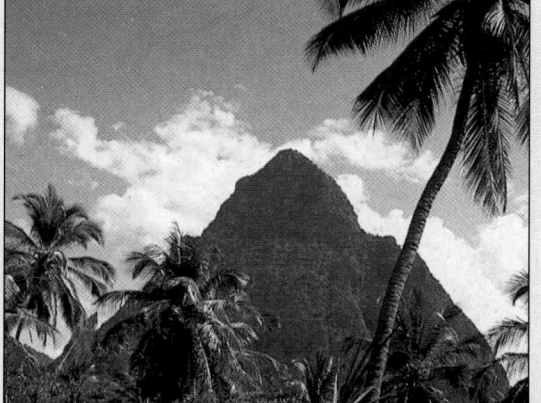

cooked in a variety of ways, *lambi* (conch) and other fresh seafood, breadfruit and other local fruit and vegetables. *Pepper pot* and fried plantain are two local specialities worth trying. In general the food is a combination of Creole with West Indian and French influences. **Drink:** Many imported spirits are available, but the local drink is rum, often served in punch and cocktails. Caribbean beer and plenty of delicious fresh fruit juices are also available.
NIGHTLIFE: Centres mainly in hotels, particularly the *St Lucian, Halcyon* and *Le Sport* hotels. During summer there is little nightlife, but during the winter the resorts are lively, with plenty of local music and dance.
SHOPPING: Special purchases include unique batik and silkscreen designs made into shifts, sports shirts, table mats, cocktail napkins and shopping bags produced at a studio on the road between Castries and La Toc. Other craft outlets sell locally made bowls, beads, straw hats, flour-sack shirts, sisal rugs, bags, sandals and woodwork. Work began in 1989 on the expansion of the recently opened duty-free port at *Pointe Seraphine*, which already has 23 duty-free shops, bars and restaurants placed around an open piazza. Duty-free shopping is available to all visitors, provided they present their passport or airline ticket when purchasing goods. **Shopping hours:** 0800-1800 Monday to Friday and 0800-1200 Saturdays.
SPORT: Watersports: St Lucia is one of the world's breeziest places, where the trade winds blow in from the sea to the southern shore. The sandy beach of Anse de Sable offers ideal windsurfing conditions for both novice and expert. The west coast, too, offers a selection of resorts and hotels geared to the special needs of the active watersports enthusiast, while elsewhere on the island guests can enjoy water-skiing or scuba diving. Enthusiasts' equipment is happily accommodated by *British Airways* (who fly direct) and *BWIA*, with windsurfers' boards carried as excess baggage and charged according to size. Hotels hire out hobbycats, dinghies and small speedboats by the hour or half-day. From Marigot Bay and Rodney Bay the more experienced sailor can hire a variety of craft from comparatively basic, small yachts to larger 12m (40ft) and 18m (60ft) vessels, with crew if required. Tour operators can also arrange for stays of a week or more on the island to be coupled with a 'free floating' holiday on board a chartered yacht visiting the neighbouring islands. All west coast beaches have good swimming. The Atlantic coast has rugged surf and is not recommended to anyone with little experience and ability, and even an extremely proficient swimmer should not go unaccompanied. Many of the sports facilities are available free of charge. **Walking:** Tours to Mount du Cap and Pigeon Point can be arranged at *Le Sport Hotel*. Tours into the rainforest, plantations and the Pitons can be arranged through *Anse Chastenet*. **Golf:** There are courses at Cap Estate, the northern tip of the island, and at La Toc. **Tennis:** All the main hotels have courts and arrangements can be made through hotels to play at *St Lucia Tennis Club*.

Fishing: Sea trips are possible, fishing for barracuda, mackerel, kingfish etc. **Climbing:** Local guides are available to help climbers tackle the Pitons. **Horseriding:** There are stables at Cap Estate.
SPECIAL EVENTS: The following are important events which take place annually on St Lucia: **Jun 6-8 '93** *Aqua Action Weekend* (watersports festival; activities include novelty events such as a 'non-mariners race', windsurfing and sunfish sailing races and a unique 'match racing' event, the only one of its kind in the Caribbean). **Jun 29** *St Peter's Day/Fisherman's Feast* (fishermen celebrate by decorating all the fishing boats). **Aug 29** *Market Vendor's Festival*. **Aug 30** *Feast of St Rose of Lima* (flower festival and street parade). **Sep 27-Oct 1** *Tourism Week*. **Oct 17** *Feast of St Margaret Mary Alacoque* (flower festival and street parade). **Nov 22** *St Cecilia's Day* ('Musician's Day'). **Dec 13** *National Day* (cultural and sporting activities throughout the island in celebration of the island's patron saint – St Lucia). **Dec 21** *Atlantic Rally for Cruisers*. **Jan 1-2 '94** *Fiesta at Vigie Playground*, Castries. **Feb 22-23** *Carnival*.
SOCIAL CONVENTIONS: Some French influence still remain alongside the West Indian style of life. The people are friendly and hospitable and encourage visitors to relax and enjoy their leisurely lifestyle. The *madras* and *foulards* are not often seen in towns, but are sometimes worn at festivals such as the *Feast of St Rose of Lima*, August. Casual wear is acceptable, although some hotels and restaurants encourage guests to dress for dinner. Beachwear should not be worn in towns. **Tipping:** 10-15% is added to bills. Taxi drivers do not expect tips.

BUSINESS PROFILE

ECONOMY: Although the economy still relies heavily on agriculture (the main exports are bananas, coconuts and cocoa), tourism is an increasingly important source of income. There is a small, light industrial sector producing plastic, textiles and industrial gases, and assembling electronic components. Foreign investment has been slow in arriving but has grown steadily since the early 1980s. The industrial development programme has gradually reduced the economy's dependency on agriculture. The late 1980s saw a construction and consumer spending boom which threatened to over-

Scenic Castries Harbour

Exciting Castries Market

Secluded Marigot Bay

heat the economy, despite the damage wrought by Hurricane Hugo in late 1989, but the Government has managed to avoid serious recession. The USA and the UK are the main trading partners; the USA for imports and the UK for exports.
BUSINESS: Short- or long-sleeved shirt and tie or a safari suit are suitable for most business visits. **Office hours:** 0800-1600 Monday to Friday.
COMMERCIAL INFORMATION: The following organisation can offer advice: St Lucia Chamber of Commerce, Industry and Agriculture, PO Box 482, 2nd Floor, Monplaisir's Building, Brazil Street, Castries. Tel: 23165.
CONFERENCES/CONVENTIONS: A few hotels offer conference and back-up facilities, with seating for up to 200 persons. The St Lucia Tourist Board can provide details (address at top of entry).

HISTORY & GOVERNMENT

HISTORY: Fierce resistance from the indigenous Carib Indians kept British and French colonists away from the island for 50 years. Then, between the signing of a peace treaty with the French in 1660 and the British takeover of the island in 1814, ownership changed no less than 14 times. The British maintained control until 1979, when St Lucia was granted independence. Recent politics have been dominated by the 3-way struggle between the ruling conservative United Workers' Party, the social democratic St Lucia Labour Party (SLP) and the left-leaning Progressive Labour Party (PLP), which split from the SLP in 1981. St Lucia joined the Organisation of American States and the Organisation of Eastern Caribbean States on independence. St Lucian forces participated in the US-led invasion of Grenada in 1983. The United Workers' Party holds power at present, having won the last election held in 1992, with a slim majority over the SLP/PLP opposition. The next election is due to be held in 1997 and promises to be a hard-fought affair since the reorganisation of the Labour Party which has been out of office for more than a decade. St Lucia has been prominent in the lobby for the creation of a unitary Eastern Caribbean state, although progress has been slow as most of the Windward Islands group favour a slower process of political and economic integration.
GOVERNMENT: Under the independence constitution, the Head of State is the British monarch, represented by a Governor-General. Legislation is the responsibility of the 17-member House of Assembly, which is directly elected by universal adult suffrage for a 5-year term, and the 11-member Senate, composed of appointees of the Prime Minister (six nominations), the leader of the main opposition party (three nominations) and the Governor-General (two nominations).

CLIMATE

Hot, tropical climate tempered by trade winds throughout most of the year. The driest period is from January to April and there is increased rainfall in summer and towards the end of the year.
Required clothing: Lightweight cottons and linens, with rainwear or an umbrella for sharp showers and a warm wrap for evenings.

SOUFRIERE St Lucia (3m)

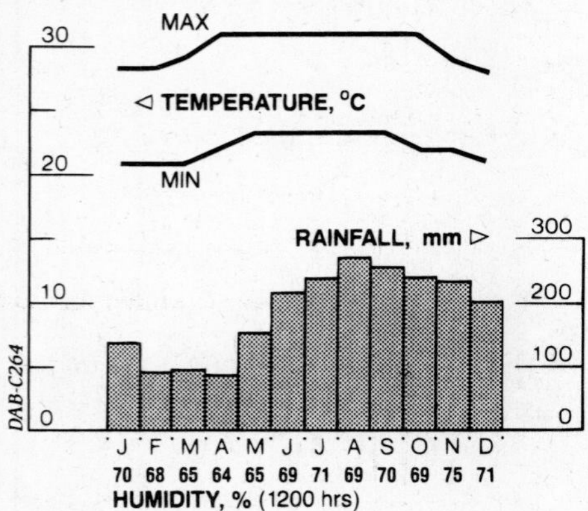

ST MAARTEN

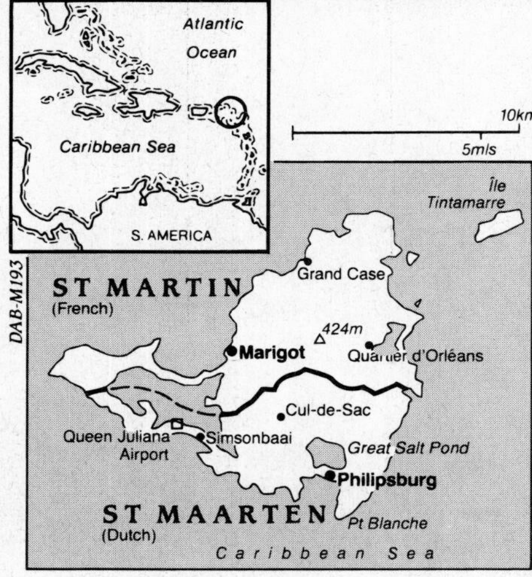

Location: Eastern Caribbean, Windward Islands.

Diplomatic representation: Although the Netherlands Antilles are part of the Kingdom of the Netherlands, they are not formally represented by Royal Netherlands Embassies. Information and advice may be obtained at the addresses below.

St Maarten Tourist Board
Cyrus Wathey Square
Philipsburg
St Maarten, NA
Tel: 22337. Fax: 24884.
Office of the Minister Plenipotentiary of the Netherlands Antilles *and* **The Netherlands Antilles Organisation**
PO Box 90706
2509 LS The Hague
The Netherlands
Tel: (70) 351 2811. Fax: (70) 351 2722.
St Maarten Tourist Information Office
275 Seventh Avenue
New York, NY
10001
Tel: (212) 989 0000.
St Maarten Government Tourist Information Office
243 Ellerslie Avenue
Willowdale, Ontario
M2N 1M8
Tel: (416) 223 3501. Fax: (416) 223 6887.

AREA: 34 sq km (13 sq miles).
POPULATION: 26,994 (1988 estimate).
POPULATION DENSITY: 793.9 per sq km.
CAPITAL: Philipsburg. NA capital: Willemstad, Curaçao.
GEOGRAPHY: Politically, St Maarten is one of three Windward Islands in the Netherlands Antilles, although geographically it is part of the Leeward Group of the Lesser Antilles, and not strictly an island – it occupies just one-third of an island otherwise under French control (the French sector is called St Martin), lying 8km (5 miles) south of Anguilla, 232km (144 miles) east of Puerto Rico and 56km (35 miles) due north of St Eustatius. St Maarten is the southern sector, an area of wooded mountains rising from white sandy beaches. To the west, the mountains give way to lagoons and salt flats.
LANGUAGE: Mainly English although Dutch (the official language of the Netherlands Antilles) is used for legal documents and taught in schools. Papiamento is the local *patois*; French may also be spoken.
RELIGION: Protestant, with Roman Catholic and Jewish minorities.
TIME: GMT - 4.
ELECTRICITY: 110/220 volts AC, 60Hz.
COMMUNICATIONS: Telephone: Fully automatic system with good IDD. Country code: 599 5. Calls made through the operator are more expensive and include a 15% tax. **Fax:** Some hotels provide facilitie **Telegram:** Services operated by *Lands Radio Dienst* and *All American Cables*. **Post:** Airmail to Europe takes four to six days, surface mail four to six weeks. **Press:** No newspapers are published on St Maarten, but an English-language daily, *The News*, is publishec on Curaçao. All other newspapers in the Netherlands Antilles are published in Dutch or Papiamento.
BBC World Service and Voice of America frequencies: From time to time these change. See the sectior *How to Use this Book* for more information.

BBC:				
MHz	17.840	15.220	9.915	5.975
Voice of America:				
MHz	15.21	11.70	6.130	0.930

PASSPORT/VISA

Regulations and requirements may be subject to change at short notice, and y are advised to contact the appropriate diplomatic or consular authority befo finalising travel arrangements. Details of these may be found at the head of th country's entry. Any numbers in the chart refer to the footnotes below.

	Passport Required?	Visa Required?	Return Ticke Required?
Full British	Yes	No	Yes
BVP	Valid/1	-	-
Australian	Yes	4	Yes
Canadian	3	4	Yes
USA	2	4	Yes
Other EC	1	4/5	Yes
Japanese	Yes	4	Yes

PASSPORTS: Valid passport required by all except:
(a) [1] nationals of Belgium, Luxembourg and The Netherlands holding a tourist card, nationals of Germany holding an identity card and UK nationals holding a British Visitors Passport;
(b) [2] nationals of the USA holding voters registration card or birth certificate, and alien residents of the USA with acceptable documentation;
(c) [3] nationals of Canada with birth certificate or proof of citizenship;
(d) nationals of San Marino holding a national ID card.
British Visitors Passport: Acceptable.
VISAS: [4] Visas are only required for nationals of the Dominican Republic resident there. All other nationals are allowed to stay in St Maarten for 14 days without a visa (but might need a Temporary Certificate of Admission, see below) provided they have a return or onward ticket. All visitors staying more than 90 days require a visa. Transit passengers staying no longer than 24 hours holding confirmed tickets and valid passports do not require visas or Certificates of Admission.
For stays of between 14 and 90 days a **Temporary Certificate of Admission** is required, which in the case of the following countries will be issued by the Immigration authorities on arrival in St Maarten:
(a) [5] Belgium, Germany, Luxembourg, The Netherlands, Spain and the UK;
(b) Bolivia, Burkina Faso, Chile, Colombia, Costa Rica, Czechoslovakia, Ecuador, Hungary, Israel, Jamaica, South Korea, Malawi, Mauritius, Niger, The Philippines, Poland, San Marino, Swaziland and Togo.
The following must apply in writing and *before* entering the country even for tourist purposes for a Temporary Certificate of Admission: nationals of Albania, Bulgaria, Cambodia, China, Cuba, North Korea, Libya, Romania, CIS, Vietnam and holders of Rhodesian passports issued on or after November 11, 1965.
All other nationals have to apply for the Certificate after 14 days of stay.
Further information about visa requirements may be obtained from the Office of the Minister Plenipotentiary of the Netherlands Antilles; and whilst Royal Netherlands Embassies do not formally represent the Netherlands Antilles in any way, they might also be able to offer limited advice and information. For addresses, see top of this entry and top of the *Netherlands* entry above.
Temporary residence: Enquire at the Office of the Minister Plenipotentiary of the Netherlands Antilles.

MONEY

Currency: Netherlands Antilles Guilder or Florin (NAG) = 100 cents. Notes are in the denominations of NAG500, 250, 100, 50, 25, 10 and 5. Coins are in the denominations of NAG2.50 and 1, and 50, 25, 10, 5 and

cents. There are also a large number of commemorative ›ins which are legal tender.
redit cards: Access/Mastercard and Visa are accepted ɑ large establishments. Check with your credit card ɔmpany for details of merchant acceptability and other ɛrvices which may be available.
xchange rate indicators: The following figures are ɑcluded as a guide to the movement of the Netherlands .ntilles Florin against Sterling and the US Dollar:

ate:	Oct '89	Oct '90	Oct '91	Oct '92
1.00=	2.84	3.49	3.11	2.83
1.00=	*1.79	*1.79	*1.79	*1.79

Iote [*]: The NAG is linked to the US Dollar.
'urrency restrictions: The import and export of local ɹrrency is limited to NAG200. There are no restrictions n the import and export of foreign currency. The import f Dutch or Suriname silver coins is prohibited.
anking hours: 0830-1200 and 1330-1630 Monday to riday.

DUTY FREE

'he following items may be imported into St Maarten by isitors over 15 years of age without incurring customs duty:
00 cigarettes or 50 cigars or 250g tobacco;
litres of alcoholic beverages;
50ml of perfume (entire amount will be dutiable if more is nported);
ïifts to a value of NAG100.
'rohibited items: It is forbidden to import parrots, paraeets, dogs and cats from Central and South America.
'he import of souvenirs and leather goods from Haiti is .ot advisable.

PUBLIC HOLIDAYS

'ublic holidays observed in St Maarten are as follows:
Apr 9-12 '93 Easter. **Apr 30** Queen Beatrix's Birthday. **Iay 1** Labour Day. **May 20** Ascension Day. **May 31** Whit Monday. **Nov 11** St Maarten Day. **Dec 25** Christmas Day. **Dec 26** Boxing Day. **Jan 1 '94** New 'ear's Day.

HEALTH

Regulations and requirements may be subject to change at short notice, and you are advised to contact your doctor well in advance of your intended date of departure. Any numbers in the chart refer to the footnotes below.

	Special Precautions?	Certificate Required?
Yellow Fever	No	1
Cholera	No	No
Typhoid & Polio	Yes	-
Malaria	No	-
Food & Drink	2	-

1]: A yellow fever certificate is required from travellers over six months of age arriving from infected areas.
2]: Water on the island is considered safe to drink. Bottled mineral water is widely available. Milk is pasteurised and dairy products are safe for consumption. Local meat, poultry, seafood, fruit and vegetables are generally considered safe to eat.
Health care: There is one general hospital, the St Rose Hospital in Philipsburg. Medical insurance is advised.

TRAVEL - International

AIR: The national airline of the Netherlands Antilles is ALM (LM). The government-owned *Windward Islands Airways International (WIA – Winair)*, based at *Juliana Airport*, has scheduled flights to the Lesser Antilles, as well as charter flights to destinations throughout the Eastern Caribbean.
Approximate flight times: From St Maarten to *London* is 12-14 hours, to *Los Angeles* is 9 hours, to *New York* is 4 hours 10 minutes, to *St Croix* is 45 minutes and to *Singapore* is 33 hours (all depending on connections).
International airports: *Juliana (SXM)*, 15km (9.5 miles) west of Philipsburg, receives regular scheduled flights from other Caribbean islands, the USA and Europe. Good bus services to Philipsburg; taxis are available. *Esperance (SFG)* in the French sector is smaller and not equipped for jets.
Departure tax: NAG9 for all international departures. Transit passengers and children under two years of age are exempt.
SEA: St Maarten is a leading port of call for cruise liners. Cruises operated by *Holland America, Cunard, Prince's Cruise* and *Royal Viking* regularly stop at Philipsburg.

TRAVEL - Internal

SEA: Small boats may be chartered for fishing trips, scuba diving, water-skiing or visits to neighbouring islands.
ROADS: Most roads are good and driving is on the right. There are good **taxi** services on the island running from the airport, main hotels and towns. **Car hire:** There are plenty of car-hire firms in the city and at the airport. Chauffeur-driven cars are also available. **Documentation:** A national driving licence is acceptable.

ACCOMMODATION

HOTELS: St Maarten has long been a popular holiday destination and is well prepared for the year-round onrush, with over 40 hotels offering a total of nearly 9000 beds – more than 500 to be found in one hotel, the *Mullet Bay Resort* by the airport. This and other luxury hotels are equipped with everything a visitor could ever need, from casinos to beauty parlours, and have extensive watersports facilities on the premises; even modest beachside establishments usually have their own swimming pool, restaurant and a few skis to lend. A Government tax of 5% is levied on all hotel bills and many hotels add a 10-15% service charge. Some even add a further 10% as an energy surcharge. Further information about hotels is available from the St Maarten Hotel Association, PO Box 486, Promenade 14, Philipsburg, St Maarten. Tel: 23133. Telex: 8014.
GUEST-HOUSES: Several guest-houses cater for the less demanding; apartments may be rented.

RESORTS & EXCURSIONS

The most prominent physical feature in St Maarten is the thickly wooded *Mt Flagstaff*, an extinct volcano, but the most important is undoubtedly the excellent beach that follows the south and west coasts. Beach activities and shopping at duty-free centres satisfy most tourists but there are several places of interest for the more enterprising visitor.
Philipsburg, the only town of any size, is situated on a sand bar that separates *Great Salt Pond*, an *étang* or salt marsh, from the ocean. The entire town consists of two streets, Voorstraat (Front Street) and Achterstraat (Back Street), running the length of the isthmus and joined by short, narrow alleys. Land has been reclaimed from the marsh for the construction of a ring road; local wits have suggested that this should be called Nieuwstraat (New Street) to preserve a Dutch feel of the place. Indeed, many buildings do date back to the early colonial era, and despite the multitude of duty-free shops, Philipsburg retains a predominantly colonial atmosphere. Worth seeing are its nine shingled churches and the *Queen Wilhelmina Golden Jubilee Monument*. Nearby is *Fort Amsterdam*, dating from the time of the earliest settlers. Inland are the picturesque ruins of several plantation mansions, set in the wooded hills around Mount Flagstaff, and the *Border Monument*, celebrating 300 years of co-operation between the French and the Dutch. Across the border (no passports are required) is the charming market town of **Marigot**.
EXCURSIONS: Small boats are available for various watersports and fishing.

SOCIAL PROFILE

FOOD & DRINK: St Maarten's cuisine is as varied as its history, combining Dutch, French, English, Creole and, more recently, international, influences. Seafood is, of course, a speciality. **Drink:** Duty on alcohol (and other goods) is low and prices in St Maarten are as cheap as duty-free havens elsewhere. Most well-known brands are available.
NIGHTLIFE: Many of the restaurants and bars have live entertainment and dancing until the early hours. All the large hotels have casinos.
SHOPPING: There is a good range of high quality duty-free shopping available in Philipsburg. **Shopping hours:** 0800-1200 and 1400-1800 Monday to Saturday.
SPORT: Most large hotels have equipment for the full range of **watersports** – snorkelling, scuba diving, water-skiing, windsurfing and sailing – and most have their own swimming pools and **tennis** courts. There is a **golf** course at the Sheraton Mullet Bay Resort.
SPECIAL EVENTS: *Carnival*, which commences in mid-April, lasts for three weeks, and finishes spectacularly with the burning of King Moui-Moui. Lighthearted races for prizes take place monthly, and each year there is a relay race in which the tussle for the island between the French and the Dutch is re-enacted. In February each year a regatta is held.
SOCIAL CONVENTIONS: Dutch customs are still important throughout the Netherlands Antilles, but tourism has brought increasing American influences and St Maarten is perhaps more easy-going than the southern islands. Dress is casual and lightweight cottons are advised, but it is common to dress up in the evening. **Tipping:** Hotel bills always include a Government tax of 5% and often a service charge of 10-15%. Elsewhere, 10-15% is acceptable for doormen, waiters and bar staff. Taxi drivers do not expect a tip.

BUSINESS PROFILE

ECONOMY: During its time as a Dutch colony, sugar cane and livestock were the major products, despite the fact that the poor soil and lack of rain made these activities somewhat unprofitable. With the end of slavery in 1863, resulting in the breakdown of the plantation system, these activities declined as many ex-slaves left the island to look for other work. The island had a brief period as a major exporter of salt to the USA and neighbouring islands from the rich deposits found in the Great Salt Pond near Philipsburg, but by 1949 this industry had also ended and a further exodus of the population took place. Since then the island has resorted to subsistence farming and fishing, making tourism its major emphasis. It now totally dominates the economy: 70% of all visitors to the Netherlands Antilles visit St Maarten, resulting in over 900,000 tourists annually. Further investment in tourist infrastructure is planned, including a new major port capable of docking eight cruise ships simultaneously. Government service provides one of the few alternative sources of employment.
BUSINESS: Formality in business is expected in most of the Netherlands Antilles and lightweight tropical suits should be worn. Appointments should be made in

ST MAARTEN	**HEALTH REGULATIONS**	**VISA REGULATIONS** Code-Link
GALILEO/WORLDSPAN	TI-DFT/SXM/HE	TI-DFT/SXM/VI
SABRE	TIDFT/SXM/HE	 TIDFT/SXM/VI

To access this information on your CRS, swipe the barcode with a light pen or type in the text under the barcode. For more information, see the introduction *How to Use This Book*.

advance and punctuality is taken very seriously. **Office hours:** 0800-1200 and 1330-1630 Monday to Friday.
COMMERCIAL INFORMATION: The following organisation can offer advice:
Windward Islands Chamber of Commerce and Industry, PO Box 454, Voorstraat, Philipsburg, St Maarten. Tel: 23590.

HISTORY & GOVERNMENT

HISTORY: Occupied since prehistory by Carib Indians, St Maarten was sighted by Christopher Columbus on St Martin's Day in 1493. However, the first European settlers were French and Dutch who, in 1648, partitioned the island. The island has remained under dual sovereignty ever since, the Dutch sector achieving partial independence from The Netherlands in 1954 with the establishment of the Netherlands Antilles.
GOVERNMENT: The Netherlands Antilles, Aruba and The Netherlands each have equal status within the Kingdom of the Netherlands as regions autonomous in internal affairs. The Queen is represented locally by a Governor, while the Netherlands Antilles are represented in the Government by a Minister Plenipotentiary. Foreign policy and defence matters are decided by a Council of Ministers of the Kingdom, including the Plenipotentiary, and executed under the authority of the Governor. The internal affairs of the Netherlands Antilles are administered by the central government of the Netherlands Antilles, based in Willemstad, Curaçao, which is responsible to the Staten (legislative assembly). St Maarten may elect by non-compulsory adult suffrage three of 22 members to the Staten. Routine local affairs on each island group (Bonaire, Curaçao and the Windward Islands) are managed by an elected Island Council, presided over by a Lieutenant-Governor.

CLIMATE

Hot but tempered by cooling trade winds. The annual mean temperature is 27°C, varying by no more than two or three degrees throughout the year; average rainfall is 1772mm.
Required clothing: Tropicals and cottons are worn throughout the year. Umbrellas or light waterproofs are advisable

KINGSTOWN St Vincent

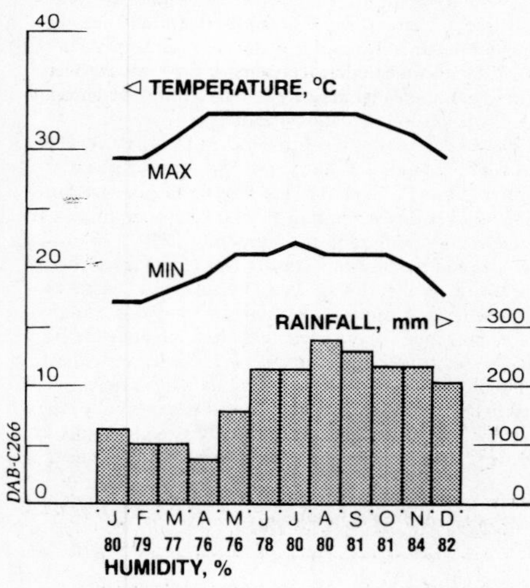

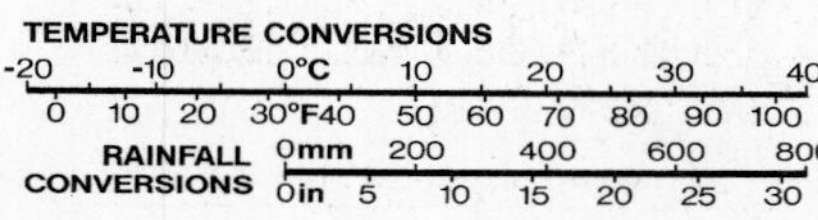

ST VINCENT & THE GRENADINES

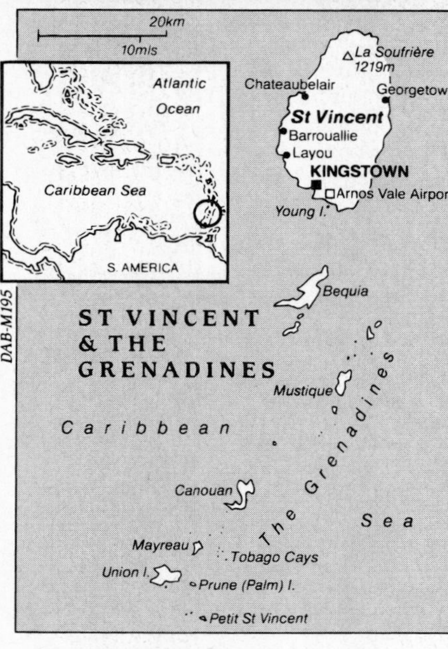

Location: Eastern Caribbean, Windward Islands.

St Vincent & the Grenadines Department of Tourism
PO Box 834
Bay Street
Kingstown, St Vincent
Tel: 71502. Fax: 72880. Telex: 7531/7484 FOREIGN VQ. Opening hours: 0800-1200 and 1300-1615 Monday to Friday.
High Commission for Eastern Caribbean States
10 Kensington Court
London W8 5DL
Tel: (071) 937 9522. Fax: (071) 937 5514. Telex: 913047 ECACOM G. Opening hours: 0930-1730 Monday to Friday.
St Vincent & the Grenadines Tourist Office
Address as for High Commision.
Tel: (071) 937 6570. Fax: (071) 937 3611. Opening hours: 1000-1530 Monday to Friday.
British High Commission
PO Box 132
Granby Street
Kingstown, St Vincent
Tel: 71701/2. Fax: 62750. Telex: 7516 UKREP SVT VQ.
Embassy of St Vincent & the Grenadines
Suite 102
1717 Massachusetts Avenue, NW
Washington, DC
20036
Tel: (212) 687 4491.
St Vincent & the Grenadines Tourist Office
21st Floor, 801 Second Avenue
New York, NY
10017
Tel: (212) 687 4981. Fax: (212) 949 5946. Telex: 427711 SVGUN.
St Vincent & the Grenadines Consulate
73 Harvest Moon Drive
Markham, Ontario
L3R 4M2
Tel: (416) 897 2060.
St Vincent & the Grenadines Tourism Office
Suite 504, 100 University Avenue
Toronto, Ontario
M5J 1V6
Tel: (416) 971 9666. Fax: (416) 971 9667.
The Canadian High Commission in Barbados deals with enquiries relating to St Vincent & the Grenadines:
The Canadian High Commission
PO Box 404
Bishops Court Hill, St Michael
Bridgetown, Barbados
Tel: 429 3550. Fax: 429 3780. Telex: 2247 CANADA WB.

AREA: St Vincent: 344 sq km (133 sq miles). **Grenadine** 45.3 sq km (16.7 sq miles). **Total:** 389.3 sq km (150.3 sq miles).
POPULATION: 107,598 (1991).
POPULATION DENSITY: 276.4 per sq km.
CAPITAL: Kingstown. **Population:** 19,345 (1989 estimate
GEOGRAPHY: St Vincent and the Grenadines make up part of the Windward Islands and lie south of St Lucia. St Vincent, like all the Windwards, is volcanic and mountainous with luxuriant vegetation and black sand beaches. The highest peak of St Vincent, *La Soufrière* (1234m, 4048ft), is volcanic, and deep down in the crater is a lake. The 'tail' of the Comet of St Vincent (the Grenadines) is a string of islands and cays that splays south from Bequia (pronounce Beck-Way), Petit Nevis, Isle à Quatre and Pigeon Island to Battowia, Baliceaux, Mustique, Petit Mustique, Savan, Canouan, Petit Canouan, Mayreau and the Tobago Cays, Union Island, Palm Island and Petit St Vincent. All of the Grenadines are famous for their white beaches, clear water and green scenery.
LANGUAGE: English.
RELIGION: Roman Catholic, Anglican, Methodist and other Christian denominations.
TIME: GMT - 4.
ELECTRICITY: 220/240 volts AC, 50 Hz.
COMMUNICATIONS: Telephone: IDD is available. Country code: 1 809 45. **Fax:** Faxes can be sent from most hotels. **Telex/telegram:** Facilities limited to main towns and hotels. **Post:** Airmail to Europe takes up to two weeks. Post office hours: 0830-1500 Monday to Friday and 0830-1130 Saturday. **Press:** All newspapers are in English and are published weekly or twice weekly.
BBC World Service and Voice of America frequencies: From time to time these change. See the section *How to Use this Book* for more information.

BBC:				
MHz	17.84	15.22	9.915	5.975
Voice of America:				
MHz	15.21	11.70	6.130	0.930

PASSPORT/VISA

Regulations and requirements may be subject to change at short notice, and you are advised to contact the appropriate diplomatic or consular authority before finalising travel arrangements. Details of these may be found at the head of this country's entry. Any numbers in the chart refer to the footnotes below.

	Passport Required?	Visa Required?	Return Ticket Required?
Full British	Yes	No	Yes
BVP	Not valid/2	-	-
Australian	Yes	No	Yes
Canadian	Yes	No	Yes
USA	1	No	Yes
Other EC	Yes	No	Yes
Japanese	Yes	No	Yes

PASSPORTS: [1] Valid passports required by all except nationals of the USA holding proof of identity if the stay does not exceed 6 months.
British Visitors Passport: [2] Although the immigration authorities of this country may in certain circumstances accept British Visitors Passports for persons arriving for holidays or unpaid business trips of up to 3 months, travellers are reminded that no formal agreement exists and the situation may, therefore, change at short notice. In addition, UK nationals using a BVP and returning to the UK from a country without such formal agreement exists may be subject to delays and interrogation by UK immigration.
VISAS: Not required. Length of stay is determined by immigration authority on arrival, if necessary.
Temporary residence: Refer applications or enquiries to the Tourist Board, Embassy or High Commission (addresses at top of entry) or to the Ministry of Foreign Affairs.

MONEY

Currency: Eastern Caribbean Dollar (EC$) = 100 cents. Notes are in denominations of EC$100, 20, 10, 5 and 1. Coins are in denominations of 50, 25, 10, 5, 2 and 1 cents.
Credit cards: All major credit cards are widely accepted. Check with your credit card company for details of merchant acceptability and other services which may be available.
Exchange rate indicators: The following figures are included as a guide to the movements of the Eastern Caribbean Dollar against Sterling and the US Dollar:

Date:	Oct '89	Oct '90	Oct '91	Oct '92
£1.00=	4.26	5.27	4.69	4.27
$1.00=	*2.70	*2.70	*2.70	*2.70

Note [*]: Eastern Caribbean Dollar is tied to the US Dollar.
Currency restrictions: There are no currency restrictions. Unlimited travellers cheques and other currencies.

Free import of local currency, subject to declaration. **Banking hours:** 0800-1300 Monday to Thursday, 0800-1300 and 1400/1500-1700 Friday. The bank at *E T Joshua Airport* opens 0700-1700 Monday to Saturday with additional extensions during the major festivals.

DUTY FREE

The following items may be imported into St Vincent & the Grenadines without incurring customs duty:
200 cigarettes or 50 cigars or 250g of tobacco;
1.136 litres of alcoholic beverage.

PUBLIC HOLIDAYS

Public holidays observed in St Vincent & the Grenadines are as follows:
Apr 9 '93 Good Friday. **Apr 12** Easter Monday. **May 3** Labour Day. **May 31** Whit Monday. **Jul 5** CARICOM Day. **Jul 6** Carnival. **Aug 2** Emancipation Day. **Oct 27** National Day. **Dec 25-6** Christmas. **Jan 1 '94** New Year's Day. **Jan 22** St Vincent & the Grenadines Day.

HEALTH

Regulations and requirements may be subject to change at short notice, and you are advised to contact your doctor well in advance of your intended date of departure. Any numbers in the chart refer to the footnotes below.

	Special Precautions?	Certificate Required?
Yellow Fever	No	1
Cholera	No	No
Typhoid & Polio	Yes	-
Malaria	No	-
Food & Drink	2	-

[1]: A yellow fever vaccination certificate is required from travellers over one year of age arriving from infected areas.
[2]: Mains water is normally chlorinated, and whilst relatively safe may cause mild abdominal upsets. Bottled water is available. Milk is pasteurised and dairy products are safe for consumption. Local meat, poultry, seafood, fruit and vegetables are generally considered safe to eat.
Health care: Health insurance is recommended. There is one large hospital, the Central General Hospital, augmented by a further 30 or so state-run clinics and dispensaries.

TRAVEL - International

AIR: The main airline to serve St Vincent & the Grenadines is *LIAT (LI)* (handled by British Airways). *Mustique Airways* and *Aero Services* run services from Barbados and *Air Martinique* from the French West Indies.
Approximate flight times: From St Vincent to *London* (via Barbados) is 9 hours, to *Los Angeles* is 9 hours, to *New York* is 5 hours and to *Singapore* is 33 hours.
International airport: *E T Joshua (SVD)* is 3.2km (2 miles) from Kingstown. Buses and taxis go from the airport to the city. There are standard fares to a number of major hotels throughout the island. There are also small airstrips on Union Island, Canouan and Mustique for small planes.
Departure tax: EC$15 on all international departures and EC$10 for Caribbean destinations.
SEA: Kingstown and some of the Grenadines are ports of call for a number of cruise lines; *CIC, Epirotiki, Paquet Cruises, Hapag Lloyd* and *Princess Cruises*, for example. Some lines also put in at one or other of the Grenadines. Smaller boats ply between the islands, especially to and from Barbados.

TRAVEL - Internal

AIR: Local and charter services are available. Small planes can be chartered for inter-island travel. *Aero Services, Mustique Air* and *Air Martinique* run regular services to Mustique, Canouan and Union Island.
SEA: Yacht chartering is easy and one of the best ways to explore the Grenadines. Yachts can be hired locally, with or without crew. There is a regular service to Bequia, Mustique, Canouan and Union Island from St Vincent. A mail boat runs twice-weekly through the Grenadines. The Tourist Office can help with all details.
ROAD: Bus: Services run regularly throughout St Vincent. The buses are open air and brightly coloured. Small minibuses run a shared *route-taxi* service with a standard fare anywhere along the route. Public transport is crowded but cheap. **Taxi:** Taxis are shared and charge standard rates (fixed by the Government). A list is available from the Tourist Board. **Car hire:** Easily arranged through a number of national and international firms. **Documentation:** A local driving licence is essential and can be obtained on presentation of a valid national or international licence either at the Airport or at the Police Station in Bay Street, Kingstown, or at the Licensing Authority in Halifax Street, Kingstown (opening hours: 0900-1500 Monday to Friday). Fee: EC$20.

ACCOMMODATION

From casual and economical to elegant and exclusive, lodgings in St Vincent & the Grenadines offer something for every taste and budget. The choice ranges from a rustic cottage on the beach or a historic country hotel in the mountains, to a luxury resort with an island to itself. Young Island, a small island off the south coast of St Vincent, with a cottage community of separate huts including all modern facilities, is widely considered to be the closest place to paradise in the whole of the Caribbean. All hotels are small and stress personal service. A list of rates is available from the St Vincent Department of Tourism and all its overseas offices. All rooms are subject to a 5% hotel tax. **Grading:** Many hotels in the Caribbean offer accommodation according to one of a number of plans: **FAP** (Full American Plan): room and all meals supplied (including afternoon tea, supper etc); **AP** (American Plan): room and three meals supplied; **MAP** (Modified American Plan): breakfast and dinner included with the price of the room plus, in some places, British-style afternoon tea; **CP** (Continental Plan): room and breakfast only; **EP** (European Plan): room only.

RESORTS & EXCURSIONS

St Vincent

St Vincent is a lush, volcanic island of steep mountain ridges, valleys and waterfalls. The rugged eastern coast is lined with cliffs and rocky shores, while the western coastline dips sharply down to black and gold beaches. To the north, *La Soufrière*, St Vincent's volcano, rises over 1220m (4000ft). St Vincent has frequent rains and volcanic soil, which produces an abundance of fruits, vegetables and spices. The interior flatlands and valleys are planted with coconuts, bananas, breadfruit, nutmeg and arrowroot.
Kingstown, capital of St Vincent, is a lively port town on the southern coast. The town contains 12 small blocks with a variety of shops and a busy dock area which is the centre of commerce for the islands. The Saturday morning market, comprising many stalls piled high with fresh fruits and vegetables, brings everyone to town. In the centre of Kingstown, *St Mary's Roman Catholic Cathedral*, built of grey stone, is a combination of several European architectural styles displaying Romanesque arches, Gothic spires and Moorish ornamentation. The ruins of *Fort Charlotte* overlook a 180m (590ft) ridge north of town and offer a magnificent southward view of the Grenadines. The oldest *Botanical Gardens* in the western hemisphere occupy 20 acres to the north of Kingstown and contain a display of tropical trees, blossoms and plants, including a breadfruit tree descended from the original one brought to the island in 1765 by Captain Bligh. Within the gardens there is also an extensive collection of ancient stone artefacts.
The *Falls of Baleine*, at the northern tip of St Vincent, are accessible only by boat. The 18m (59ft) freshwater falls stream from volcanic slopes and form a series of shallow pools at the base. A hike for the more adventurous is just over 5km (3 miles) journey up *La Soufrière*, St Vincent's northern volcano which affords a wonderful view of the crater and its islands, all of St Vincent and the Caribbean. Strung along the western coast are fishing villages

ST VINCENT	HEALTH REGULATIONS	VISA REGULATIONS
GALILEO/WORLDSPAN	 TI-DFT/SVD/HE	 TI-DFT/SVD/VI
SABRE	TIDFT/SVD/HE	TIDFT/SVD/VI

Code-Link

To access this information on your CRS, swipe the barcode with a light pen or type in the text under the barcode. For more information, see the introduction *How to Use This Book.*

Questelles, **Layou**, **Barrouallie** and **Châteaubelair**, all of which have charming pastel-coloured cottages and black sand beaches from which fishermen set out daily in small brightly painted boats.
Young Island: Only 180m (590ft) off St Vincent, Young Island rises from the sea, a 25-acre mountain blanketed with tropical foliage and blossoms. Young Island provides an excellent view of the procession of yachts sailing into the harbour of St Vincent. The entire island comprises one resort called 'Young Island Resort', which consists of 29 cottages set on the beaches and hillsides. There is a freshwater pool and tennis courts in the hilltop trees. Adjoining Young Island is the 18th-century *Fort Duvernette*, sculpted from an enormous rock, towering 60m (200ft) above the sea. A ferry, a smaller version of the *African Queen*, runs constantly between Young Island and St Vincent.

The Grenadines

Bequia: This island lies 14km (9 miles) south of St Vincent and is the largest of the Grenadines, measuring 18 sq km (7 sq miles). Little changed by time, it is an island on which life is completely oriented to the sea. It can be reached by boat, although an airstrip was opened in May 1992. Its seclusion has ensured it retains its age-old traditions of boat building and fishing. In the marine park, spear-fishing, snares and nets are prohibited. The islanders themselves are some the world's last hand harpooners and their activities do not affect marine stocks, unlike the mechanised fishing of some fleets. The centre of the island is hilly and forested, providing a dramatic backdrop to the bays and beaches.
Admiralty Bay, the island's natural harbour, is a favourite anchoring spot for yachtsmen from all over the world, and here you can watch men building their boats by hand on the shores. The attractive region around *Lower Bay* has good opportunities for swimming and other watersports.
The quaint waterfront of **Port Elizabeth** is lined with bars, restaurants and craft shops. Bequia is encircled by gold sand beaches, many of which disappear into coves, excellent for sailing, scuba diving and snorkelling. Lodgings vary from luxurious resort cottages to small, simple West Indian inns. Much of the nightlife centres on the hotels and beachside barbecues, invariably accompanied by a steel band.
Mustique: Heading south, the next port of call is Mustique, a gem in the ocean only taking up 4.5 sq km (2 sq miles). Mustique is privately owned, with a landscape as gentle as its lifestyle – green hills roll into soft white-sand beaches and turquoise waters. This island has long been a hiding place for the rich and famous, including Princess Margaret and other members of the British Royal Family. A sprawling 18th-century plantation house has been converted into the island's only resort. Elegant accommodation is available in several stone houses, separated for seclusion. The public rooms of the *Main House* are beautifully decorated with antiques and afternoon tea is served daily on the veranda. There is a hilltop swimming pool with a magnificent panorama, as well as tennis, horseriding, motorcycling and all watersports.
Canouan: The island claims some of the best beaches in the Caribbean – long stretches of powder white sands, wide shallows and coral. The island stretches over 11 sq km (7.9 sq miles) and has two hotels: *Crystal Sands Beach*, with accommodation in seafront villas, and *Canouan Beach Hotel*.
Tobago Cays: South of Canouan are the Tobago Cays, numerous islets and coves guarded by some of the most spectacular coral reefs in the world. You can sail, snorkel and beachcomb in complete seclusion. The only way to get here is by chartered yacht.
Mayreau: East of the Cays is Mayreau, one of the smaller Grenadines, which is a privately-owned island with few residents. *Salt Whistle Bay Resort*, the only hotel, welcomes guests and can be reached by boat from Union Island.
Union Island: *Mount Parnassus* on Union Island soars 275m (900ft) from the sea – guarding the entrance to the southern Grenadines. The 2100-acre mountainous island is fringed by superb beaches and is the stopping-off point for yachtsmen and visitors heading to some of the smaller Grenadines.
Clifton Harbour, the main town, is small and commercial. There are several beachfront inns with a relaxed atmosphere.
Palm Island: The 110-acre flat Palm Island acquired its name due to the graceful coconut palms that line the beaches – 8000 in all. This private island has been turned into a resort; the *Palm Island Beach Club*, made up of 20 beachfront stone cottages. Here it is possible to dine in the open air and all watersports take place off the wide, white shores.
Petit St Vincent: The southernmost Grenadine governed by St Vincent is Petit St Vincent, a 113-acre resort set on beaches. The luxuriant foliage and the 22 villas of Petit St Vincent offer guests the ultimate luxury and seclusion, including private patios and seaside vistas. Visitors gather for meals in beachfront pavilions and the ambience is carefree and festive.

SOCIAL PROFILE

FOOD & DRINK: St Vincent is one of the few islands where good West Indian cuisine can almost always be enjoyed in hotels. Specialities include *red snapper*, kingfish, *lambi* (a sea shellfish), *calaloo* soup, *souse* (a sauce made from pigs' foot) and sea-moss drink. There are plenty of fresh fruits, vegetables and seafoods. Lobster is available in season.
Drink: Vincentian beer and rum, a major ingredient in punch and cocktails, are the local drinks, as are a wide variety of local exotic fruit juices.
NIGHTLIFE: Most evening events take place in hotels and it is best to ask at individual hotels. The *Aquatic Club* is now operated as a supper club by *Basil's Bar*, of Mustique fame. *The Attic* in Kingstown features a wide variety of music during the week and live entertainment on weekends. There is one casino on the island, at Peniston.
SHOPPING: Designs on sea-island cottons can be bought and made up into clothes within two or three days. Handicrafts and all varieties of straw-made items, grass rugs and other souvenirs can be bought at a number of workshops and giftshops. **Shopping hours:** 0800-1200 and 1300-1600 Monday to Friday, 0800-1200 Saturdays.
SPORT: Sailing and all kinds of **watersports** are a major pastime. Various boats head south regularly through the Grenadines. For the novice, professionals are available to handle the sails. You can, of course, bring your own yacht, or charter one, either with or without crew. Yachts are available for charter from *Caribbean Sailing Yachts* (tel: 458 4308; fax: 458 9255) and *Frangipani Yacht Services* (tel: 458 3244; fax: 458 3824). Other watersports, particularly **scuba diving**, can be arranged through some hotels. **Fishing:** Deep-sea fishing excursions are available. **Spectator sports: Cricket** and **football** are very popular. **Tennis:** Courts are available at *Kingstown Tennis Club* and facilities may also be arranged through hotels. **Horseriding:** Can be arranged by certain hotels.
SPECIAL EVENTS: The following major events occur annually in St Vincent & the Grenadines:
Bequia Regatta (Easter Weekend) features races for all classes of vessel, sporting competitions and games.
Union Island Easter Sports and Games (Easter) – regattas, sports, games, calypso competition and cultural pageants.
Union Island Big Drum Festival (May) featuring the Big Drum Dance.
St Vincent & the Grenadines Carnival (first week in July) is one of the largest in the West Indies and lasts for 10 days, ending with the Street Parade. The Festival exposes the islands' artistic talents in music, brass bands, steel bands and calypsos, costume design, folk dances and calypso dances. The street parades, featuring costumed bands with as many as ten sections, depict scenes from mythology and folklore, as well as contemporary and futuristic themes. A Carnival King and Queen as well as a Calypso King will be chosen. The greatest experience is *playing mas* (participating in one of the costumed bands).
Canouan Annual Yacht Races (beginning of August) – activities include a fishing competition, a cricket match, 'Greasy Pig', donkey relay races, a Queen and Calypso competition, crab races and various regattas.
Tourism Week (November) – a celebration including competitions for those involved in the industry, awards ceremonies, tourism awareness programmes at schools and on radio and television and special entertainments – steelbands, fashion shows and barbecues.
Nine Mornings (December) – nine mornings before Christmas people parade through the streets of Kingstown long before dawn. The most recent addition to St Vincent's unique Christmas celebration is the organised dances held in St Vincent's dance halls on each of the nine mornings.
SOCIAL CONVENTIONS: The Vincentians are fun-loving and easy-going people, and the informal and relaxed lifestyle combines many English influences with West Indian. The Saturday market in Kingstown is bustling with life seemingly involving all islanders. All visitors are made welcome and casual wear is widely acceptable. Refrain, however, from wearing beachwear or mini shorts on the streets or while shopping. **Tipping:** 10-15% service added to the bill. Taxi drivers do not expect tips.

BUSINESS PROFILE

ECONOMY: St Vincent is poor by Eastern Caribbean standards, with agriculture being the main source of income and export earnings. Bananas are the main crop and St Vincent is also the world's leading producer of arrowroot; other exotic fruit, vegetables and root crops also make a contribution to the economy. The Single European Market, introduced in 1992, is regarded as a potentially serious threat to St Vincent's export markets. Sugar has been reintroduced to reach self-sufficiency and reduce the import bill rather than as an export commodity. Fishing has also been revitalised and a processing complex built. Tourism is little-developed by regional standards and its growth has been hampered by the lack of suitable infrastructure. Apart from the USA and the UK, St Vincent has important trade links with Trinidad & Tobago, Barbados and St Lucia.
BUSINESS: Short- or long-sleeved shirt and tie or safari suit are suitable for most business visits. **Government office hours** vary from department to department but generally 0800-1615 Monday to Friday, with some opening for a few hours on Saturday morning.
COMMERCIAL INFORMATION: The following organisation can offer advice:
St Vincent & the Grenadines Chamber of Industry and Commerce, PO Box 134, Halifax Street, Kingstown. Tel: 71464. Fax: 62944.

HISTORY & GOVERNMENT

HISTORY: According to popular belief, St Vincent was discovered by Christopher Columbus on his third voyage in 1498. The island remained in undisputed possession until 1627 when it was granted to Lord Carlisle. However, the indigenous Caribs fought furiously to keep possession of it. In 1783 the Treaty of Versailles restored St Vincent to Britain after the French had temporarily taken possession of it. Carib resistance was finally crushed in 1795, after which the settlement of St Vincent proceeded on more conventional lines. During the late 19th and 20th century, St Vincent endured a series of natural disasters: in 1812, the first recorded eruption of the La Soufrière volcano, during which many lives were lost; in 1896, floods; two years later, a hurricane; and in 1902, the second eruption of La Soufrière killed 2000 inhabitants. The next eruptions, neither of which caused loss of life, occurred in the 1970s. By this time the political development of the island had assumed a more orthodox course. Soon after the Second World War, the right to vote was at last extended to the entire adult population after decades of restriction. This was an essential preparatory move on the road to independence, the key issue of the day. For the small Caribbean islands like St Vincent & the Grenadines, a variety of proposals were studied during the 1960s, leading in 1969 to St Vincent's adoption of Associate Statehood with the UK, under which it was internally self-governing while London looked after foreign and defence matters. It also gave St Vincent the right to declare full independence at any time which it finally did in October 1979. The viability of St Vincent as a nation state has been the subject of constant debate ever since, and never more so than under the present government led by James Mitchell of the New Democratic Party. The NDP enjoys the unusual position of having been elected to every single seat in parliament, a privilege normally confined to political parties unencumbered by an opposition. The main opposition party, the St Vincent Labour Party, and two smaller socialist parties, fought the NDP in the last poll in 1989, but are now considering an electoral pact at the next election, due in 1994, in order to avoid another humiliating defeat. They may be too late to prevent St Vincent from pressing forward with the proposed economic and political union of the Windward Islands: Mitchell and the NDP are firm supporters of the integration plan which they believe is essential to restore the health of St Vincent's ailing economy.
GOVERNMENT: The British monarch, represented locally by a Governor-General, is Head of State. The Governor-General, who is appointed upon the advice of the Prime Minister, exercises executive authority. The 15 representatives in the House of Assembly, which has legislative power, are elected every 5 years by universal adult suffrage.

CLIMATE

Tropical, with trade winds tempering the hottest months, June and July.
Required clothing: Lightweights and waterproofs.

KINGSTOWN St Vincent

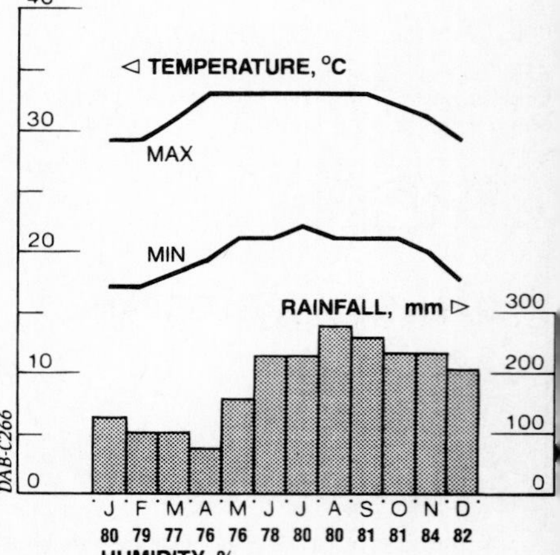

SAN MARINO

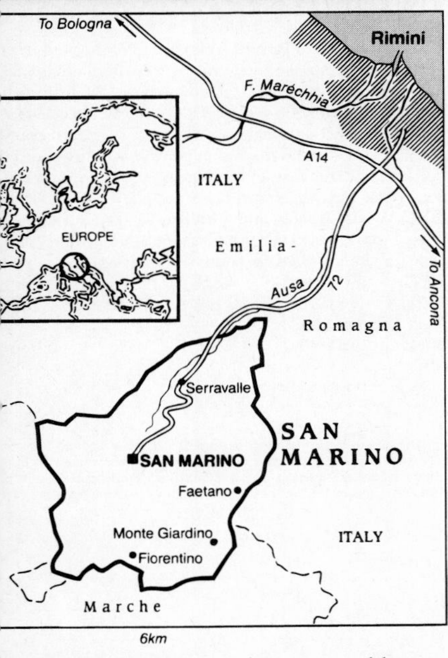

Location: Western Europe; northeastern part of the Italian peninsula.

Ufficio di Stato per il Turismo
Palazzo del Turismo
47031 Repubblica di San Marino
Tel: 882 400. Fax: 990 388. Telex: 282.

Secretariat of State for Foreign and Political Affairs
Palazzo Begni
Republicca di San Marino
Tel: 882 209. Fax: 992 018.

British Consulate
Palazzo Castelbarco
Lungarno Corsini 2
50123 Firenze, Italy
Tel: (55) 212 594. Fax: (55) 219 112.

Consulate General of San Marino
27 McNider Avenue
Montréal, Québec
H2V 3X4
Tel: (514) 871 3838. Fax: (514) 876 4217.
Consulate in: Toronto.

AREA: 60.5 sq km (23.4 sq miles).
POPULATION: 23,676 (1991).
POPULATION DENSITY: 391.3 per sq km.
CAPITAL: San Marino. **Population:** 4185 (1990 estimate).
GEOGRAPHY: San Marino is a tiny state bordered by the Italian regions of Emilia-Romagna to the north and east and Marche to the south and west. The landscape is for the most part green with rolling hills, dominated by the three peaks of Mount Titano. Within San Marino lie the capital of the same name and eight villages.
LANGUAGE: Italian.
RELIGION: Roman Catholic.
TIME: GMT + 1 (GMT + 2 in summer).
ELECTRICITY: 220 volts AC, 50Hz.
COMMUNICATIONS: Telephone: IDD is available. Country code: 39 (same as Italy), plus area code 549. There no local codes. **Telex/telegram:** Telex country code: 505 1 SO. Facilities are available in main hotels. **Post:** Good postal service. Airmail to European destinations takes approximately four days. *Poste Restante* facilities are available at all post offices. **Press:** No daily newspapers are published in San Marino; Italian newspapers are widely available.
BBC World Service and Voice of America frequencies: From time to time these change. See the section *How to Use this Book* for more information.

BBC:

MHz	17.64	15.57	12.09	6.195

A service is also available on 648kHz and 198kHz (0100-0500 GMT).

Voice of America:

MHz	11.97	9.670	6.040	5.995

PASSPORT/VISA

Travellers will necessarily enter San Marino from Italy. As there are no frontier formalities imposed, any person visiting San Marino must comply with Italian passport/visa regulations; refer to the *Passport/Visa* section in the *Italy* entry, earlier in the *World Travel Guide*.

MONEY

Currency: Italian Lira (Lit). Notes are in denominations of Lit100,000, 50,000, 20,000, 10,000, 5000, 2000, 1000. Coins are in denominations of Lit1000, 500, 200, 100, 50, 20, 10 and 5.
Currency exchange: Many UK banks offer differing exchange rates depending on the denominations of Italian currency being bought or sold. Check with banks for details and current rates.
Exchange rate indicators: The following figures are included as a guide to the movements of the Lira against Sterling and the US Dollar:

Date:	Oct '89	Oct '90	Oct '91	Oct '92
£1.00=	2182	2230	2178	2108
$1.00=	1382	1142	1254	1328

Note: For further information, see the *Money* section in the *Italy* entry earlier in this book.

DUTY FREE

Visitors must comply with Italian customs regulations; see the relevant *Italy* section in the *World Travel Guide*.

PUBLIC HOLIDAYS

Public holidays observed in San Marino are as follows:
Mar 25 '93 Anniversary of the Arengo. **Apr 1** Captains-Regent Investiture. **Apr 12** Easter Monday. **May 1** Labour Day. **Jun 10** Corpus Christi. **Jul 28** Anniversary of the Fall of Fascism. **Aug 15** Assumption. **Sep 3** San Marino Day and Republic Day. **Oct 1** Captains-Regent Investiture. **Nov 1** All Saints' Day. **Nov 2** Commemoration of the Dead. **Dec 8** Immaculate Conception. **Dec 25** Christmas. **Dec 26** St Stephen's Day. **Jan 1 '94** New Year's Day. **Jan 6** Epiphany. **Feb 5** Liberation and St Agatha's Day. **Mar 25** Anniversary of the Arengo.

HEALTH

The health regulations and recommendations are the same as for Italy. See the *Health* section in the entry for Italy, earlier in the *World Travel Guide*.

TRAVEL

AIR: The Italian national airline is *Alitalia (AZ)*.
Approximate flight time: From *London* to Bologna/Rimini is 2 hours 30 minutes.
International airports: *Bologna (BLQ)* is 125km from San Marino and *Rimini (RMI)* is 27km from San Marino. Good bus services are available to San Marino.
RAIL: The nearest railhead is at Rimini. A funicular serves the capital and Borgo Maggiore. There are no internal railways.

ACCOMMODATION

All hotels in San Marino are comfortable and of a good standard. Every hotel allows special reductions for groups, children and large families. Full-board and half-board arrangements are also available. For more information contact the national Tourist Board (address at beginning of entry). **Grading:** Hotels in San Marino are classified in four categories, with 1/A category hotels at the luxury end of the market, 1/B category hotels being slightly more modest, and 2 and 3 category hotels for budget travellers.

RESORTS & EXCURSIONS

The whole of the centre of the city of San Marino is a perfectly preserved medieval square and there are also museums, galleries and various churches. The lower cliffs of *Mount Titano* are capped with three fortified towers, linked by a system of walls and pathways that are accessible from the city below. The city itself is enclosed by three walls with numerous gateways, towers, ramparts, churches and medieval houses. Other places worth visiting are the *Government Palace;* the *Basilica;* the *State Museum* and *Art Gallery; St Francis' Church,* which also has a museum and art gallery; the *Capuccin Friars Church of St Quirino;* and the *Exhibition of San Marino Handicrafts*.
Eight villages are scattered around the countryside outside the capital. Places of interest include *Malatesta Castle* at **Serraville**; the modern church and the stamp and coin museum at **Borgo Maggiore;** the church and convent at **Valdragone**; and the fort at **Pennarossa**. Ancient ruins can be seen throughout the Republic. Attractions outside the city and villages include *Mount Titano*, pine woods, springs, streams, lakes and hunting and fishing reserves. There is easy access to Italian beaches on the Adriatic coast nearby.

SOCIAL PROFILE

FOOD & DRINK: Italian cuisine is widely available. Popular first courses include *tortellini, passatelle* (broth), *tagliatelle, lasagne, ravioli, cannelloni* and *arbalester's passaduri* (a local speciality). Main dishes include roast rabbit with fennel, devilled chicken, quails, veal escalopes, Bolognese veal cutlets, assorted 'mouthfuls' (three types of tender meat) and Roman veal escalopes. San Marino tart and *caccietello* (similar to crême caramel) may be ordered for desert. There is a wide selection of restaurants, both in the capital and in the outlying villages. Table service is customary, although a few are self-service. **Drink:** San Marino muscat, *briancele, albana* and *sangiovese* are all good quality wines produced locally. *Mistra* is the local liqueur.
NIGHTLIFE: Reviews, festivals and theatrical productions are popular. During the summer, frequent folk festivals, the most important being the crossbow competition, are held in the capital on San Marino's National Day (September 3) annually.
SHOPPING: Special purchases include locally-made ceramics; stamps and coins bought from the *State Numismatic & Philatelic Office*, local wines and liqueurs, local jewellery, playing cards and cigarettes. **Shopping hours:** 0830-1300 and 1530-1930 Monday to Saturday.
SPORT: There are facilities for **tennis, roller skating, basketball, gymnastics, hunting, fishing, swimming** and **bowls**. There is a sports club at Serraville with modern equipment and there are numerous tennis courts and **football** pitches throughout the Republic.
SOCIAL CONVENTIONS: Normal European courtesies and codes of conduct should be observed.

SAN MARINO | **HEALTH REGULATIONS** | **VISA REGULATIONS** | Code-Link

GALILEO/WORLDSPAN

TI-DFT/BLQ/HE

TI-DFT/BLQ/VI

SABRE

TIDFT/BLQ/HE

TIDFT/BLQ/VI

To access this information on your CRS, swipe the barcode with a light pen or type in the text under the barcode. For more information, see the introduction *How to Use This Book*.

Tipping: Service charges are generally included in hotel bills. An extra tip is usual.

BUSINESS PROFILE

ECONOMY: The only agricultural product exported is wine. The other principal crops are wheat, barley, maize and olive oil. Other exports include woollen goods, furniture and ceramics. Tourism provides most of the Republic's income, with approximately three million visitors each year accounting for over 60% of the national income. An unusual source of revenue is postage stamps, which are produced several times a year and sold almost entirely to collectors and bring in 10% of the national income. Details of San Marino's external trade are included with those of Italy with whom San Marino maintains a customs union.
BUSINESS: A suit is recommended and prior appointments are absolutely essential. Avoid making appointments early in the morning or straight after lunch. A knowledge of Italian is useful.

HISTORY & GOVERNMENT

HISTORY: San Marino is the only surviving Italian city-state. Like Andorra, Liechtenstein and Monaco, it is an anachronism, a reminder of the times when Europe – particularly Germany, Italy and the Pyrenees – was made up of tiny political units, often extending no further than a cannon could fire from a city's walls. Of all the small European countries, San Marino's survival is the most surprising. Apart from the Vatican City (whose development followed a different course), it is the only one which is completely surrounded by one other country. Various treaties of friendship have been signed with Italy since the latter's unification, but San Marino proudly asserts its independence where possible. Having joined the Council of Europe as a full member in 1988, San Marino held the chair of the organisation during the first half of 1990. Domestically, San Marino has evolved a pluralistic system of government similar to that in Italy. The major political parties are the Progressive Democrats (ex-Communists), Socialists, Christian Democrats, Social Democrats and the leftist Partito Socialista Unitario. Like their Italian counterparts, the Communists decided to change their title soon after the collapse of communist rule in eastern Europe. The country was governed by a coalition of the Progressive Democratic Party and the Christian Democrats from 1990 until March 1992, when the Christian Democrats decided that their alliance with the progressive democrats was 'outdated' and immediately moved into coalition with the Socialists to form the ruling bloc. The same month, San Marino became a member of the United Nations.
GOVERNMENT: Legislative power is vested in the Consiglio Grande e Generale (Great and General Council) which has 60 members elected by universal adult suffrage for five year terms. The country is divided into nine 'Castles', representing the nine original parishes. Each is governed by a 'Castle-Captain', who holds office for two years. Two 'Castles-Regents', elected by the Council for 6-month terms, act as joint Heads of State.

CLIMATE

Temperate. Moderate snow in winter, some brief showers in summer. The atmosphere is clean, typical of low mountain and hill country with sea breezes.
Required clothing: Light to mediumweights and rainwear are required.

SAN MARINO

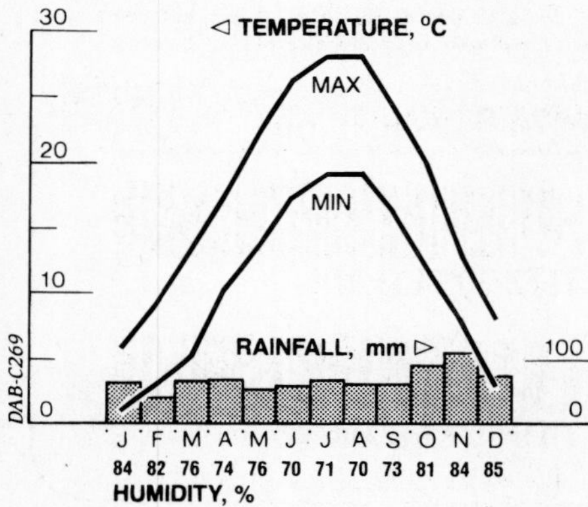

SÃO TOMÉ E PRÍNCIPE

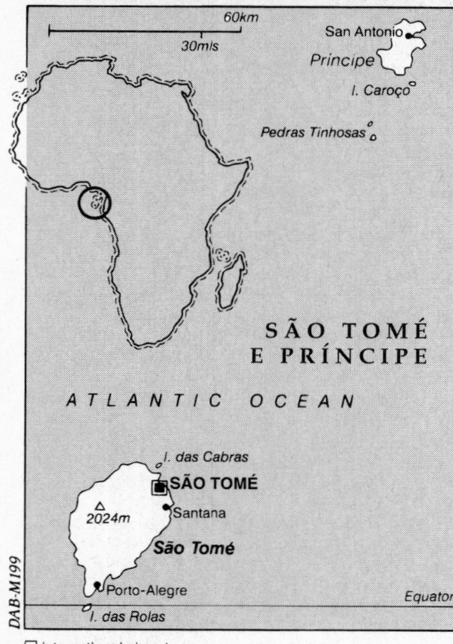

□ international airport

Location: West Africa, Gulf of Guinea.

Ministry of Foreign Affairs
São Tomé, São Tomé e Príncipe
Tel: 21446. Telex: 211.

Honorary Consulate of the Democratic Republic of São Tomé and Príncipe
42 North Audley Street
London
W1A 4PY
Tel: (071) 499 1995. Fax: (071) 629 6460. Telex: 262513. Opening hours: 0900-1730 Monday to Friday.

Embassy of the Democratic Republic of São Tomé and Príncipe
42 avenue Brugman
B-1060 Brussels
Belgium
Tel: (2) 347 6067 *or* 347 5375. Fax: (2) 347 5408. Telex: 65313.

British Consulate
c/o Hull Blythe (Angola) Ltd
BP 15
São Tomé, São Tomé e Príncipe
Telex: 220 HBALTD ST.

Equatorial Airlines of São Tomé and Príncipe
BP 45
Avenida Marginal 12 de Julho
São Tomé, São Tomé e Príncipe
Tel: 21160. Telex: 216.

Embassy of the Democratic Republic of São Tomé and Príncipe
c/o The Permanent Mission of São Tomé and Príncipe to the United Nations
Suite 1504
801 Second Avenue
New York, NY
10017
Tel: (212) 697 4211/2. Fax: (212) 687 8389.

Consulate of the Democratic Republic of São Tomé and Príncipe
4068 Beaconsfield Avenue
Montréal, Québec
H4A 2H3
Tel: (514) 484 2706.

AREA: 964 sq km (372 sq miles).
POPULATION: 116,000 (1989 estimate).
POPULATION DENSITY: 120 per sq km.
CAPITAL: São Tomé.
GEOGRAPHY: São Tomé e Príncipe comprises two main islands (Saõ Tomé and Príncipe) and the islets Cabras, Gago Coutinho, Pedras Tinhosas and Rolas. These lie approximately 200km (120 miles) off the west coast of Gabon, in the gulf of Guinea. The country is rugged and has a great deal of forest cover and few natural resources.
LANGUAGE: Portuguese and native dialects (Fôrro and Angolares). Some English spoken, but French is more common.
RELIGION: Roman Catholic majority.
TIME: GMT.
ELECTRICITY: 220 volts AC.
COMMUNICATIONS: Telephone: Very limited IDD is available. Country code: 239. There are no area codes. All international calls must be booked through the International Operator. 45% of all local calls are placed through automatic exchanges. **Telex/telegram:** Facilities in the capital and main hotels, telex code ST. **Post:** Airmail to Europe takes up to two weeks. **Press:** Newspapers are in Portuguese.
BBC World Service and Voice of America frequencies: From time to time these change. See the section *How to Use this Book* for more information.

BBC:				
MHz	25.75	17.88	15.40	7.105
Voice of America:				
MHz	21.49	15.60	9.525	6.035

PASSPORT/VISA

Regulations and requirements may be subject to change at short notice, and you are advised to contact the appropriate diplomatic or consular authority before finalising travel arrangements. Details of these may be found at the head of this country's entry. Any numbers in the chart refer to the footnotes below.

	Passport Required?	Visa Required?	Return Ticket Required?
Full British	Yes	Yes	Yes
BVP	Not valid	-	-
Australian	Yes	Yes	Yes
Canadian	Yes	Yes	Yes
USA	Yes	Yes	Yes
Other EC	Yes	Yes	Yes
Japanese	Yes	Yes	Yes

PASSPORTS: Valid passport required by all.
British Visitors Passport: Not accepted.
VISAS: Required by all. *Transit* visas not required by those holding tickets with reserved seats and other documents for onward or return travel the same day.
Validity: Enquire at Embassy.
Application requirements: (a) £25 fee. (b) Cost of postage. (c) 2 passport photos.
Applications to: Consulate (or Consular Section at Embassy). For addresses, see top of entry.
Working days required: One.
Temporary residence: Enquire at Embassy.

MONEY

Currency: Dobra (Db) = 100 centavos. Notes are in denominations of Db1000, 500, 100 and 50. Coins are in denominations of Db20, 10, 5, 2 and 1, and 50 centavos.
Exchange rate indicators: The following figures are included as a guide to the movements of the Dobra against Sterling and the US Dollar:

Date:	Oct '89	Nov '90	Oct '91	Oct '92
£1.00=	169.15	294.09	417.00	379.56
$1.00=	107.12	150.55	240.28	239.17

Currency restrictions: Free import and export of local and foreign currency, subject to declaration.
Banking hours: 0730-1130 Monday to Friday.

DUTY FREE

The following may be imported into São Tomé e Príncipe without incurring customs duty:
Reasonable quantities of tobacco products, alcohol (opened) and perfume (opened).

PUBLIC HOLIDAYS

Public holidays observed in São Tomé e Príncipe are as follows:
Mar 23 '93 Shrove Tuesday. **Apr 9** Good Friday. **Apr 12** Easter Monday. **May 1** Workers' Day. **May 28** Ascension. **Jun 18** Corpus Christi. **Jul 12** Independence Day. **Aug 15** Assumption. **Sep 30** Agricultural Nationalisation Day. **Nov 1** All Saints' Day. **Dec 21** People's Popular Power Day. **Dec 25-26** Christmas. **Jan 1 '94** New Year's Day. **Feb 3** Commemoration of the 1953 Massacre. **Feb 15** Shrove Tuesday.

HEALTH

Regulations and requirements may be subject to change at short notice, and you are advised to contact your doctor well in advance of your intended date of departure. Any numbers in the chart refer to the footnotes below.

	Special Precautions?	Certificate Required?
Yellow Fever	No	1
Cholera	Yes	2
Typhoid & Polio	Yes	-
Malaria	3	-
Food & Drink	4	-

[1]: A yellow fever vaccination certificate is required from travellers over one year of age arriving from all countries, except travellers arriving from a non-infected area and staying less than two weeks in the country.
[2]: Following WHO guidelines issued in 1973, a cholera vaccination certificate is not a condition of entry to São Tomé e Príncipe. However, cholera is a risk in this country and precautions are essential. Up-to-date advice should be sought before deciding whether these precautions should include vaccination, as medical opinion is divided over its effectiveness. See the *Health* section at the back of the book.
[3]: Malaria risk exists all year throughout the country. Chloroquine-resistance in the *falciparum* strain has been reported.
[4]: All water should be regarded as being potentially contaminated. Water used for drinking, brushing teeth or making ice should have first been boiled or otherwise sterilised. Milk is unpasteurised and should be boiled. Powdered or tinned milk is available and is advised, but make sure that it is reconstituted with pure water. Avoid dairy products which are likely to have been made from unboiled milk. Only eat well-cooked meat and fish, preferably served hot. Pork, salad and mayonnaise may carry increased risk. Vegetables should be cooked and fruit peeled.
Rabies is present. For those at high risk, vaccination before arrival should be considered. If you are bitten abroad seek medical advice without delay. For more information consult the *Health* section at the back of the book.
Bilharzia (schistosomiasis) is present. Avoid swimming and paddling in fresh water. Swimming pools which are well-chlorinated and maintained are safe.
Health care: Health insurance is essential. There are 16 hospitals and clinics and approximately 40 doctors.

TRAVEL - International

AIR: The national airline is *Equatorial International Airlines of São Tomé and Príncipe (GJ)*. It operates four flights weekly between São Tomé and Libreville (Gabon), where they connect with ingoing or outgoing longhaul flights to or from Europe.
Approximate flight time: From *London* to São Tomé is 10 hours.
International airport: *São Tomé (TMS)*, 5.5km (3.5 miles) from the town.
Departure tax: US$20 per adult, payable in cash on departure for all international flights. US$10 must be paid for children and US$2 for infants.
SEA: The main port is São Tomé, but this is not deep-water and few international cruise lines or other passenger ships call there.

TRAVEL - Internal

AIR/SEA: There are three flights a week from São Tomé to Príncipe (travel time – 50 minutes) and a limited ferry service.
ROAD: There are over 280km (175 miles) of roads, although in general these are deteriorating. Some of them are asphalted around São Tomé town, but 4-wheel drive vehicles are necessary to get further afield. There is a **bus** network, and **taxis** are also in operation. **Car hire** can be arranged through the *Miramar Hotel* (see below).
Documentation: An International Driving Permit is required.

ACCOMMODATION

There are currently about 10 hotels in the country, including the 50-room luxury establishment *Miramar Hotel* in the capital São Tomé, opened in 1986 to coincide with the initiation of a campaign to promote tourism. It has restaurants, a coffee shop, snack bar, swimming pool, duty-free shop, two bars, a swimming pool, tennis and squash courts, a snooker table, in-house video and satellite TV, a marina with facilities for watersports (including scuba diving) and fishing, and conference facilities for up to 200 delegates. The *Bom Bom Island Resort* on the northern coast of Príncipe offers 25 first-class bungalows. Apart from the hotels there is also a chain of state-run inns, operated at more modest levels of comfort.

RESORTS & EXCURSIONS

The islands lie on an alignment of once-active volcanoes, with rugged landscapes, dense forests and virgin palm-fringed beaches. Still almost totally undiscovered by the tourist trade, indeed only open to tourists since 1987, these islands provide unspoiled beauty and isolation from the world now rarely found anywhere else. The history of the islands is dominated by the slave trade and slave-worked plantations. These plantations, now mostly nationalised, still remain a major feature of the landscape. The town of **São Tomé** is picturesque, with colonial Portuguese architecture and attractive parks. Excursions by car or boat and watersports can usually be arranged at the hotel.

SOCIAL PROFILE

FOOD & DRINK: There are several restaurants in the capital, augmented by a considerable number of more informal eating establishments patronised by the inhabitants. Reservations are nearly always required, even at the higher profile restaurants, not for lack of space but to allow the proprietor to obtain sufficient food in advance. Grilled fish and chicken are popular. Most dishes are highly spiced.
SOCIAL CONVENTIONS: The Portuguese influence is very strong. The people are friendly and courteous. Every greeting is accompanied by a handshake. Normal social courtesies should be observed. Alcohol is available and smoking is acceptable. **Tipping:** Not always welcomed.

BUSINESS PROFILE

ECONOMY: The economy is based on the export of agricultural products, mainly cocoa, palm oil, bananas, coffee and coconuts. This concentration on cash crops, most of which are exported, means the country has to import the bulk of its food requirements. Efforts to develop the fishing industry have not been particularly successful, as local fishermen have had to compete against 'factory ships' from the former Soviet Union and Australia. The Government therefore decided to sell fishing rights in São Tomé's territorial waters to the countries which operate the big fleets. There is virtually no manufacturing industry apart from some food-processing plants and factories producing consumer items such as soap, textiles and beer. Portugal and Angola have a significant corner of the import market, while many exports are bought by The Netherlands.
BUSINESS: Bush jackets or safari suits are commonly worn and appointments are advised. Generally an informal atmosphere prevails. Business is conducted in Portuguese; a knowledge of French is also useful.
COMMERCIAL INFORMATION: The following organisation can offer advice: Ministry of Foreign Affairs and Co-operation, BP 111, São Tomé. Tel: 21077. Fax: 22597. Telex: 211.

HISTORY & GOVERNMENT

HISTORY: The islands were first settled by Portuguese navigators in the late 15th century, and were formally annexed to the Portuguese crown 100 years later. The islands became a major transhipment centre for the slave trade. In 1875 slavery was abolished and a system of contract labour introduced, which brought in people from other African countries to work on the plantations. There was, however, little improvement in the conditions of the native population and there were a number of rebellions against the Portuguese colonists. In 1975, following the fall of President Salazar in Portugal, the nationalist movement, the Movimento de Libertação de São Tomé e Príncipe (MLSTP), forced the new Portuguese government to grant independence. There have since been a number of attempted coups, all of which have been put down. In foreign affairs, São Tomé e Príncipe maintains close links with other former Portuguese colonies and with Gabon, Cameroon and Equatorial Guinea on the neighbouring mainland. Until 1984 it was also unquestionably a Soviet satellite. However, later that year President da Costa declared São Tomé e Príncipe to be non-aligned and in 1985 the USA agreed to allow a small number of São Toméan troops to be trained in the USA. Da Costa was subsequently involved in mediating the talks that brought the long-running civil war in Angola to a close. The MLSTP remained committed to some political liberalisation. A new constitution was introduced in March 1990 allowing for the formation of opposition parties and the conducting of multi-party elections. These were originally set for the end of 1990 but postponed until January 1991. Four main parties contested the poll: the ruling MLSTP; the main opposition party, the Patrido de Convergência Democratíca – Grupo de Reflexão (PCD); the Coligação Democratico da Oposição (CDO); and the Frente Democratica Crista. The MLSTP and PCD shared the bulk of the seats, with the PCD coming out on top with 54% of the vote and 33 of 55 seats in the National Assembly. A presidential election followed in March: an independent, Miguel dos Anjos da Cunha Lisboa Trovoada, was the victor. 1992 saw some instability in the country, manifested in a series of clashes between police and troops.
GOVERNMENT: Under the new constitution, legislative power is vested in the National Assembly, elected by popular vote for a period of four years. The Head of State is the President of the Republic, who governs with the assistance of a Council of Ministers, led by the Prime Minister. The President, whose tenure is limited to two succcessive terms, is elected for a period of five years.

CLIMATE

An equatorial climate with heavy rainfall, high temperatures and humidity. The south of the main island, being mountainous, is wetter than the north. The main dry season is from early June to late September. There is also a little dry season, the 'pequenha Gravana', from the end of December to the start of February.
Required clothing: Tropicals and lightweight cottons throughout the year. Umbrellas or light waterproofs for the rainy season are advised.

SÃO TOMÉ (5m)

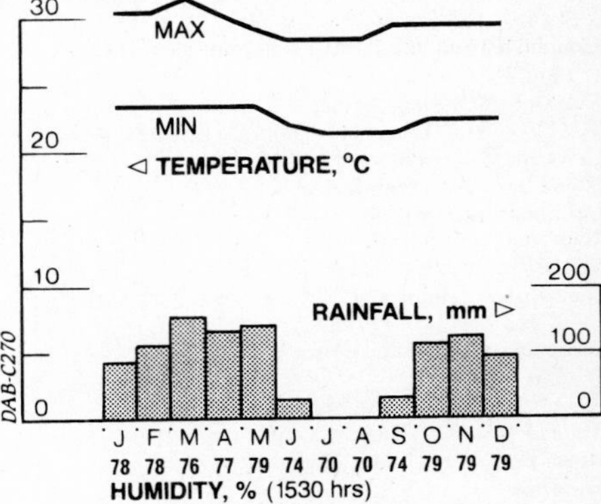

SÃO TOMÉ E PRINCIPE | **HEALTH REGULATIONS** | **VISA REGULATIONS** | Code-Link

GALILEO/WORLDSPAN

TI-DFT/TMS/HE

TI-DFT/TMS/VI

SABRE

TIDFT/TMS/HE

TIDFT/TMS/VI

To access this information on your CRS, swipe the barcode with a light pen or type in the text under the barcode. For more information, see the introduction *How to Use This Book*.

SAUDI ARABIA

Location: Middle East.

Saudi Hotels and Resort Co (SHARACO)
PO Box 5500
Riyadh 11422, Saudi Arabia
Tel: (1) 465 7177. Fax: (1) 465 7172. Telex: 400366.

Saudi Arabian Ministry of Foreign Affairs
Nasseriya Street
Riyadh 11124, Saudi Arabia
Tel: (1) 406 7777. Telex: 405000.

Royal Embassy of Saudi Arabia
32 Charles Street
London W1X 7PM
Tel: (071) 917 3000. Fax: (071) 917 3255. Opening hours: 0900-1500 Monday to Friday.

Saudi Arabian Information Centre
Cavendish House
18 Cavendish Square
London W1M 0AQ
Tel: (071) 629 8803. Fax: (071) 629 0374. Telex: 266065 SAINFC G.

British Embassy
PO Box 94351
Riyadh 11693, Saudi Arabia
Tel: (1) 488 0077. Fax: (1) 488 2373. Telex: 406488.
Consulate in: Jeddah.

Royal Embassy of Saudi Arabia
601 New Hampshire Avenue, NW
Washington, DC 20037
Tel: (202) 342 3800. Telex: 440132.
Consulates in: Houston, Los Angeles and New York (tel: (212) 752 2740).

Embassy of the United States of America
PO Box 9041
Riyadh 11413, Saudi Arabia
Tel: (1) 488 3800. Telex: 406866.

Royal Embassy of Saudi Arabia
Suite 901
99 Bank Street
Ottawa, Ontario K1P 6B9
Tel: (613) 237 4100/1/2/3/4/5. Fax: (613) 237 0567. Telex: 0534285.

Canadian Embassy
PO Box 94321
Riyadh 11693, Saudi Arabia
Tel: (1) 488 2288. Fax: (1) 488 0137. Telex: 404893 DOMCAN SJ.

AREA: 2,240,000 sq km (864,869 sq miles).
POPULATION: 14,870,000 (1990 estimate).
POPULATION DENSITY: 6.6 per sq km.
CAPITAL: Riyadh. **Population:** 2,000,000 (1989).
GEOGRAPHY: Saudi Arabia occupies four-fifths of the Arabian peninsula. It is bordered to the northwest by Jordan, to the north by Iraq and Kuwait, to the west by the Red Sea and to the east Qatar, the United Arab Emirates and Oman, and to the south by Yemen. To the west lies the Red Sea. Along the Red Sea coast is a narrow coastal strip *(Tihama)* which becomes relatively hotter and more humid towards the south and has areas of extensive tidal flats and lava fields. Behind this is a series of plateaux reaching up to 2000m (6560ft). The southern part of this range, *Asir*, has some peaks of over 3000m (9840ft). North of these mountains, is *an Nafud*, a sand sea and further south the landscape rises to *Najd*, a semi-desert area scattered with oases. Still further south the land falls away, levelling out to unremitting desert, the uninhabited 'Empty Quarter' or *Rub al Khali*. Along the Gulf coast is a low fertile plain giving way to limestone ridges inland.
LANGUAGE: Arabic. English is spoken in business circles.
RELIGION: The majority of Saudi Arabians are Sunni Muslim, but Shi'ites predominate in the Eastern Province.
TIME: GMT + 3.
ELECTRICITY: 125/215 volts AC, 50/60 Hz.
COMMUNICATIONS: Telephone: A sophisticated telecommunications network and satellite, microwave and cable systems span the country. Full IDD is available. Country code: 966. **Fax:** Major hotels provide facilities. **Telex/telegram:** Telegrams can be sent from all post offices. All major hotels have telex facilities. **Post:** Internal and international services available from the Central Post Office. Post is delivered to box numbers. Airmail to Europe takes up to a week. Surface mail takes up to five months **Press:** The main newspapers include *Al-Riyadh* and *Al-Jizirah*. English-language dailies include *Arab News*, *Saudi Gazette* and *Saudi Review*.
BBC World Service and Voice of America frequencies: From time to time these change. See the section *How to Use this Book* for more information.

BBC:

MHz	21.47	15.57	11.76	9.410

A service is also available on 1413kHz and 702kHz (0100-0500 GMT).

Voice of America:

MHz	9.670	6.040	5.995	1.260

PASSPORT/VISA

Restricted entry: The Saudi Arabian authorities will refuse entry to: (a) holders of Israeli passports; (b) holders of passports containing a valid or expired visa for Israel; (c) Jewish passengers; (d) those improperly dressed by Saudi Arabian standards or arriving in an apparently intoxicated state.
Note: (a) Unaccompanied women must be met at the airport by their sponsor or husband or have confirmed onward reservations as far as their final destination in Saudi Arabia. If met by a sponsor, it is worth noting that there are restrictions on women travelling by car with men who are not related by blood or marriage: enquire at the Information Centre or Embassy. (b) No foreign passenger who is working as a domestic servant in Saudi Arabia should be transported to Saudi Arabia unless holding a valid non-refundable return ticket.

Regulations and requirements may be subject to change at short notice, and you are advised to contact the appropriate diplomatic or consular authority before finalising travel arrangements. Details of these may be found at the head of this country's entry. Any numbers in the chart refer to the footnotes below.

	Passport Required?	Visa Required?	Return Ticket Required?
Full British	Yes	Yes	Yes
BVP	Not valid	-	-
Australian	Yes	Yes	Yes
Canadian	Yes	Yes	Yes
USA	Yes	Yes	Yes
Other EC	Yes	Yes	Yes
Japanese	Yes	Yes	Yes

PASSPORTS: A valid passport is required by all except Muslim pilgrims holding 'Pilgrim Passes', tickets and other documents for their onward or return journey and entering the country via Jeddah or Dhahran. All passports must be valid for at least 6 months beyond the estimated stay in Saudi Arabia.
British Visitors Passport: Not accepted.
VISAS: Required by all except nationals of Bahrain, Kuwait, Oman, Qatar and the United Arab Emirates (not of Jewish origin) and holders of re-entry permits and 'Landing Permits' issued by the Saudi Arabian Ministry of Foreign Affairs (address above).
Types of visa: Business, Transit and Single- or Multiple-entry (the latter are *not* Tourist visas and are meant only for those visiting relatives, etc). Transit visas are not required by passengers proceeding to a third country if in possession of confirmed tickets and other onward travel documentation. Travellers must not leave the airport confines and must continue their journey by the same or next connecting flight (maximum 12 hours stay permitted at Dhahran and Jeddah). This is not applicable to nationals of Albania, Bulgaria, Cuba, Czechoslovakia, the People's Republic of China, Hungary, Mongolia, Poland, Romania, CIS, Vietnam and Yugoslavia.
Application to: Consulate (or Consular Section at Embassy). For addresses, see top of entry.
Application requirements: For a Business visa, a letter endorsed by the Saudi Minister of Foreign Affairs is required, together with a valid passport and 2 photos. Cost: £7.15 (depending on exchange rate).

MONEY

Currency: Saudi Arabian Riyal (SA R) = 100 halalah; 5 halalah = 20 qurush. Notes are in denominations of SA R500, 100, 50, 10, 5 and 1. Coins are in denominations of 50, 25, 10, 5 and 1 halalah.
Credit cards: Access/Mastercard, American Express, Diners Club and Visa are all widely accepted. Check with your credit card company for details of merchant acceptability and other services which may be available.
Exchange rate indicators: The following figures are included as a guide to the movements of the Riyal against Sterling and the US Dollar:

Date:	Oct '89	Oct '90	Oct '91	Oct '92
£1.00=	5.93	7.33	6.51	6.06
$1.00=	3.76	3.75	3.75	3.82

Currency restrictions: Free import and export of both local and foreign currency. Israeli currency is prohibited.
Banking hours: 0830-1200 and 1700-1900 Saturday to Wednesday, 0830-1200 Thursday.

DUTY FREE

The following items may be imported into Saudi Arabia without incurring customs duty:
600 cigarettes or 100 cigars or 500g tobacco;
Perfume for personal use.
Note: Duty is levied on cameras and typewriters, but if these articles are re-exported within 90 days the customs charges may be refunded. It is advisable not to put film in the camera.
Prohibited items: Alcohol, pornography, pork, contraceptives, firearms, pearls, children's dolls, jewellery or

SAUDI ARABIA | **HEALTH REGULATIONS** | **VISA REGULATIONS** | Code-Link

GALILEO/WORLDSPAN

TI-DFT/RUH/HE

TI-DFT/RUH/VI

SABRE

TIDFT/RUH/HE

TIDFT/RUH/VI

To access this information on your CRS, swipe the barcode with a light pen or type in the text under the barcode. For more information, see the introduction *How to Use This Book.*

statues shaped in the form of an animal or human, musical instruments and items listed as prohibited by the Arab League (copy available from the Embassy).

PUBLIC HOLIDAYS

Public holidays observed in Saudi Arabia are as follows: **Mar 25 '93** Start of Eid al-Fitr. **Jun 1-5** Eid al-Adha (Feast of the Sacrifice). **Jun 21** Muharram, Islamic New Year. **Jun 30** Ashoura. **Aug 30** Mouloud (Prophet's Birthday). **Feb '94** Leilat al-Meiraj. **Mar** Start of Eid al-Fitr.

Note: Muslim festivals are timed according to local sightings of various phases of the Moon and the dates given above are approximations. During the lunar month of Ramadan that precedes Eid al-Fitr, Muslims fast during the day and feast at night and normal business patterns may be interrupted. Some disruption may continue into Eid al-Fitr itself. Eid al-Fitr and Eid al-Adha may last anything from two to ten days, depending on the region. During Hajj (when pilgrims visit Mecca) all government establishments and some businesses will be closed for five to ten days. For more information see the section *World of Islam* at the back of the book.

HEALTH

Regulations and requirements may be subject to change at short notice, and you are advised to contact your doctor well in advance of your intended date of departure. Any numbers in the chart refer to the footnotes below.

	Special Precautions?	Certificate Required?
Yellow Fever	No	1
Cholera	Yes	2
Typhoid & Polio	Yes	-
Malaria	3	-
Food & Drink	4	-

[1]: A yellow fever vaccination certificate is required from all travellers arriving from countries of which any parts are infected.

[2]: Following WHO guidelines issued in 1973, a cholera vaccination certificate is not a condition of entry to Saudi Arabia, except perhaps for certain pilgrims arriving during Hajj. However, cholera is a risk in this country and precautions are essential. Up-to-date advice should be sought before deciding whether these precautions should include vaccination, as medical opinion is divided over its effectiveness. See the *Health* section at the back of the book.

[3]: Malaria risk, predominantly in the malignant *falciparum* form, throughout the year in areas other than the Eastern, Northern and Central Provinces, the high altitude areas of Asir Province, and the urban areas of the Western Province (Jeddah, Mecca, Medina and Taif). Resistance to chloroquine has been reported.

[4]: All water should be regarded as being potentially contaminated. Water used for drinking, brushing teeth or making ice should have first been boiled or otherwise sterilised. Milk is unpasteurised and should be boiled. Powdered or tinned milk is available and is advised, but make sure that it is reconstituted with pure water. Avoid dairy products which are likely to have been made from unboiled milk. Only eat well-cooked meat and fish,

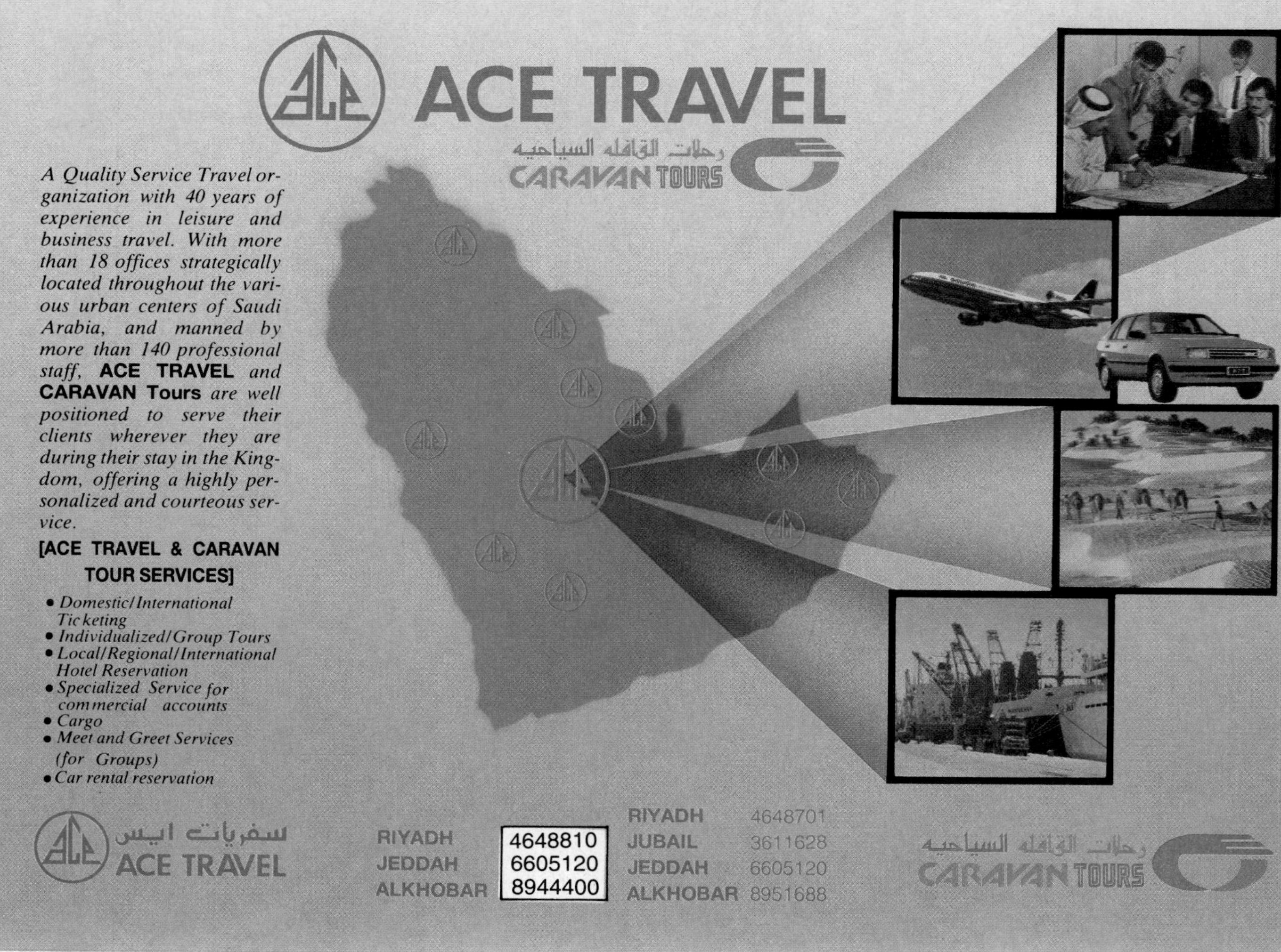

preferably served hot. Salad and mayonnaise may carry increased risk. Vegetables should be cooked and fruit peeled.

Note: During the Hajj (annual pilgrimage to Mecca) Saudi Arabia requires vaccination of pilgrims against *meningococcal meningitis*. Although this applies mainly to pilgrims, other travellers may find themselves affected, especially during the month of August.

Rabies is present. For those at high risk, vaccination before arrival should be considered. If you are bitten abroad seek medical advice without delay. For more information consult the *Health* section at the back of the book.

Bilharzia (schistosomiasis) is present. Avoid swimming and paddling in fresh water. Swimming pools which are well-chlorinated and maintained are safe.

Health care: Medical facilities are generally of a high standard, but treatment is expensive. Health insurance is essential.

TRAVEL - International

AIR: Saudi Arabia's national airline is *Saudia (SV)*.

Approximate flight times: From *London* to Dhahran is 6 hours 25 minutes, to Jeddah is 5 hours 50 minutes and to Riyadh is 6 hours 25 minutes.

From *Los Angeles* to Jeddah is 18 hours 45 minutes and to Riyadh is 21 hours 15 minutes.

From *New York* to Jeddah is 12 hours 5 minutes and to Riyadh is 15 hours 45 minutes.

From *Singapore* to Jeddah is 11 hours 55 minutes.

International airports: *Riyadh (RUH)* (King Khalid International) airport, 35km (22 miles) north of the city. Good bus and taxi services.

Dhahran (DHA) (Al Khobar) airport, 8km (5 miles) southeast of the complex (travel time – 20 minutes). Taxis are available.

Jeddah (JED) (King Abdul Aziz) airport, 18km (11 miles) north of the city (travel time – 40 minutes). Buses leave every 30 minutes (24-hour service) for Jeddah and there are also buses for Mecca, Medina and Taif. Taxis are available. This airport occupies the largest area in the world.

SEA: The main international passenger ports are Dammam (Gulf), and Jeddah and Yanbu (Red Sea).

ROAD: The principal international routes from Jordan are Amman to Dammam, Medina and Jeddah. There are also roads to Yemen (from Jeddah), Kuwait, Qatar and the United Arab Emirates. A causeway has recently been opened to link Al Khobar with Bahrain.

TRAVEL - Internal

AIR: There are 19 domestic airports and air travel is by far the most convenient form of travelling around the country. *Saudia* connects all main centres. 'Arabian Express' economy class (75 minutes) connects Jeddah with Riyadh and Riyadh with Dhahran (no advance reservations). Get a boarding pass the evening before departure. There are special flights for pilgrims arriving at or departing from Jeddah during Hajj.

SEA: Dhows may be chartered for outings on both coasts.

RAIL: The only functioning railway is the Riyadh–Dammam line, which is via Dhahran, Abqaiq, Hofuf, Harad and Yamamah. There is a daily service in air-conditioned trains with dining car. A new line from Riyadh to Dammam is currently being built. The railway on the west coast made famous by Lawrence's raid has long since been abandoned to the desert.

ROAD: There are 25,000km (15,000 miles) of roads linking the main towns and rural areas. The network is constantly being upgraded and expanded (most recently, an expressway has been built from Jeddah to Medina and the trans-peninsula road from Jeddah to Dammam has been upgraded) and on the main routes, much of it is of the highest standard. The corniche that winds down the escarpment between Taif and Mecca is as spectacular a feat of engineering as may be seen anywhere. However, standards of driving are erratic, particularly in the Eastern Province, where it is not unknown for lorry drivers to equip their vehicles with hub-knives similar to those seen in the film 'Ben Hur'. Criteria for apportioning blame after traffic accidents are also erratic and many driving offences carry an automatic prison sentence. As foreigners are tolerated rather than welcomed in Saudi Arabia, it is best to drive with extreme caution at all times. Non-Muslims may not enter Mecca or the immediate area; police are stationed to ensure that they turn off onto a specially-built ring road, known amongst expatriates as the 'Christian Bypass'. **Bus:** Services have recently been developed by SAPTCO to serve inter-urban and local needs. Modern vehicles have been acquired, including air-conditioned double deckers. All buses must have a screened-off section for the exclusive use of female passengers. **Taxis:** Available in all cities, but often very expensive. Few have meters, and fares should be negotiated in advance. **Car hire:** The major international car rental agencies have offices in Saudi Arabia. The minimum age is 25. **Documentation:** A national driving licence is valid for up to three months if accompanied by an officially-sanctioned translation into Arabic. An International Driving Permit (with translation) is recommended, but not required by law. Women are not allowed to drive or travel with men other than their husbands or a blood relative.

ACCOMMODATION

HOTELS: There is a good range of hotel accommodation throughout the country, the price of which varies according to standard and facilities. Accommodation is generally easy to find, except during the pilgrim season when advance reservations are recommended. Service charges are fixed at 15% for deluxe and first-category hotels and at 10% for all others. Hotel charges double in Mecca and Medina during the pilgrimage season, and increase by 25% during the summer months in resort areas such as Taif, Abha, Kamis Mushait and Al-Baha.

Grading: There are seven grades of hotel in Saudi Arabia: deluxe, first-class A and B, second-class A and B and third-class A and B.

RESORTS & EXCURSIONS

For the purposes of this section, the country has been divided into four sections: The Najd, The Hejaz, Hasa and The Asir. This does not necessarily represent tribal or administrative boundaries.

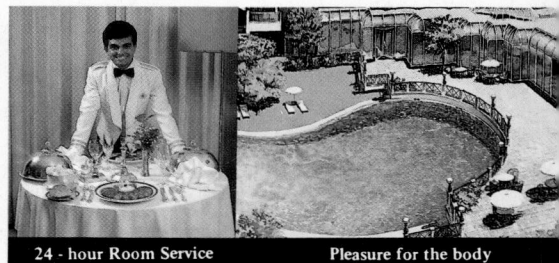

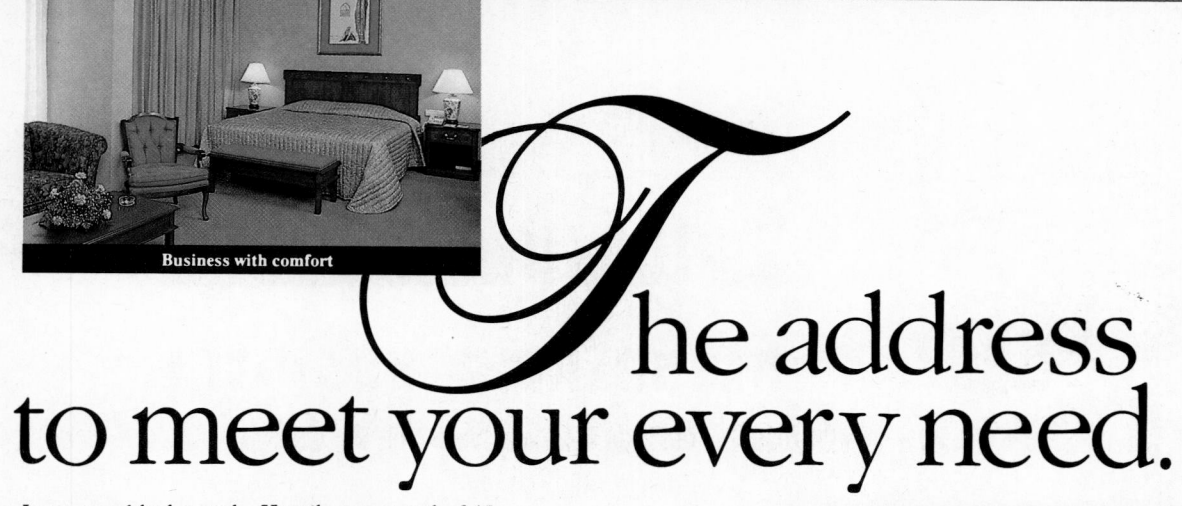

The Najd (Central Region)

The Najd is a stony desert plateau somewhat isolated from the rest of the peninsula. It was from here that Ibn Saud led his tribe of nomads out to create a new kingdom through conquest. Despite oil wealth, some Najdis still lead a semi-nomadic life, tending camels and sheep, but many have settled in the same towns they once milked for tribute with threats of violence.
Watchtowers, standing guard on all the high points in Najd, are a reminder of this age-old conflict between nomad and farmer.
Riyadh (Ryad), the royal capital, is a modern city built on the site of the first town captured by Ibn Saud, when he stormed the *Musmat Fort* in 1902 (a spearhead embedded in the main door is said to be the one with which Ibn Saud killed the Turkish governor). Apart from the fort and a few traditional Najdi palaces near Deera Square, little trace of the old town remains. The *King's Camel Races* are held near the city in April or May.
Other places of interest in Najd are **Diriya, Wadi Hanifa, Shaib Awsat, Shaib Laha, Al-Hair, Wadi-al-Jafi, Tumair, Towqr, Aneyzah, Qassim** and **Hail**.

The Hejaz (Western Region)

The west coast is a centre for trade, but of equal importance is the concentration of Islamic holy cities, including Mecca and Medina, which attract pilgrims from all over the world. The region also includes the city of Jeddah, which was until recently Saudi Arabia's diplomatic capital and remains the most important commercial and cultural gateway to the country.
Mecca: The spiritual centre of the Islamic world, forbidden to non-Muslims. Places of significance to Muslims include the *Kaabah Enclosure*, the *Mountain of Light*, the *Plain of Arafat* and the house of Abdullah Bin Abdul Muttalib, where Mohammed was born.
Medina: The second-holiest city in Islam and also forbidden to non-Muslims.
Jeddah: Although the city has grown phenomenally, priority is being given to the preservation of the ancient city. The ragged, coral-coloured Ottoman buildings are currently being renovated. Leisure facilities have increased and the corniche has a 'Brighton' feel about it. There is an amusement park and a wonderful creek allowing both sailing and snorkelling. Its hotels and restaurants are cosmopolitan and there are good fish and meat markets.
Taif: Perched on top of a 900m (3000ft) cliff at the edge of the plateau above Mecca, this resort town enjoys a milder climate than much of the country and was for a long time the official summer capital. It is noted for its pink palaces and for the astounding modern corniche road that winds down the sheer cliffs of the Taif escarpment to the hot coastal plain.
Other important towns in the Hejaz include **Usta, Wadi Fatima, Hanakiyah, Khaybar** and **Yanbu.**

Hasa (Eastern Region)

Fertile lowland coastal plains inhabited by the kingdom's Shi'ite minority, who have traditionally lived by fishing, diving for pearls, raising date palms and trading abroad and with the interior. All of Saudi Arabia's vast stocks of oil lie under Hasa or beneath the Gulf and the province's indigenous population is now out-numbered by foreign oil-workers from a multitude of nations.
Places retaining some flavour of old Hasa include **Hofuf,** a lively oasis with Turkish influence and a camel market; **Jebel-al-Qara,** where the potteries have been worked by eight generations of the same family; **Abqaiq,** which has a 5000-year-old saltmine, still in operation; the ruined customs house at **Uqair,** once an important Portuguese port and caravan terminus; and **Tarut Island,** site of the oldest town on the peninsula, now a picturesque settlement of fishermen and weavers.

The Asir (South Region)

A range of coastal mountains and the only part of the kingdom where there is significant wild vegetation, mostly palms and evergreen bushes. Millet, wheat and dates are grown using largely traditional methods. The inhabitants are darker than other Saudis, being in part descended from African slaves. Baboons, gazelles, leopards, honey badgers, mongooses and other 'African' animals inhabit remoter areas. Unique to Asir are the ancient *gasaba* towers, phallus-shaped and of unknown purpose.
Places to visit include the ancient caravan city of **Qaryat-al-Fau,** currently being excavated; the great dam and temple at **Najran**; and nearby, amidst orchards of pomegranates, limes and bananas, the ornate ruins of the ancient cities of **Timna** and **Shiban.**

SOCIAL PROFILE

FOOD & DRINK: Local food is often strongly flavoured and spicy. The staple diet is *pitta* bread (flat, unleavened bread) which accompanies every dish. Rice, lentils, chick peas *(hummus)*, and cracked wheat *(burghul)* are also enjoyed. The most common meats are lamb and chicken. Beef is rare and pork is proscribed under Islam laws. The main meat meal of the day is lunch, either *kultra* (meat on skewers) or *kebabs* served with soup and vegetables. Arabic cakes, cream desserts and rice pudding *(muhalabia)* also feature in the diet. *Mezzeh*, the equivalent of hôrs d'oeuvres, may include up to 40 dishes. Many foreign cuisines are on offer in larger towns and the whole range of international cuisine, including fast food, is available in the oil-producing Eastern Province and in Jeddah. Restaurants have table service. **Drink:** There are no bars. Alcohol is forbidden by law, and there are severe penalties for infringement; it is important to note that this applies to all nationals regardless of religion. Arabic coffee and fruit drinks are popular alternatives. Alcohol-free beers and cocktails are served in hotel bars.
NIGHTLIFE: Apart from restaurants and hotels there is no nightlife in the Western sense.
SHOPPING: *Souks* (markets) sell incense and incense burners, jewellery, bronze and brassware, richly decorated daggers and swords, and in the Eastern Provinces huge brass-bonded chests. Bargaining is often expected, even for modern goods such as cameras and electrical equipment (which can be very good value). **Shopping hours:** 0900-1300 and 1630-2000 Saturday to Thursday (Ramadan 2000-0100). These hours differ in various parts of the country.
SPORT: Obhir Creek, 50km (30 miles) north of Jeddah, has good facilities for **swimming, water-skiing, fishing** and **sailing**, and there are similar beaches on the Gulf coast south of Al Khobar. Elsewhere, hotels have swimming pools. The British and US embassies have men-only health clubs as well as swimming pools, **golf** clubs and **squash** and **tennis** facilities. Most companies employing foreign workers also have some sports facilities. The desert terrain provides great opportunities for off-road **motorcycling** but this sport is prohibited from time to time. **Football** is popular and most large towns have modern stadia.
SOCIAL CONVENTIONS: Saudi culture is based on

Islam and the perfection of the Arabic language. The Saudi form of Islam is conservative and fundamentalist, based on the 18th-century revivalist movement of Najdi leader Shaikh Mohammed Ibn Abdel-Wahhab. This still has a great effect on Saudi society, especially on the position of women, who do not generally go out without being totally covered in black robes *(abaya)* and masks, although there are regional variations of dress. The Najd and other remote areas remain true to Wahhabi tradition, but throughout the country this way of life is being threatened by modernisation and rapid development. For more information see *World of Islam* at the back of the book. Shaking hands is the customary form of greeting. Invitations to private homes are unusual. Entertaining is usually in hotels or restaurants and although the custom of eating with the right hand persists, it is more likely that knives and forks will be used. A small gift either promoting the company or representing your country will generally be well received. Women are expected to dress modestly and it is best to do so to avoid offence. Men should not wear shorts in public or go without a shirt. Customs regarding smoking are the same as in Europe and non-smoking areas are indicated. During Ramadan, Muslims are not allowed to eat, smoke or drink during the day and it is illegal for a foreign visitor to do so in public. **Tipping:** The practice of tipping is becoming much more common and waiters, hotel porters and taxi drivers should be given 10-15%.

BUSINESS PROFILE

ECONOMY: Oil and natural gas products account for all but a tiny fraction of Saudi exports (representing two-thirds of GNP and 90% of exports). Saudi Arabia is the world's third-largest producer of oil (after the CIS and the USA) and it dominates the economy; its discovery transformed a barren and impoverished desert state into a wealthy and increasingly modern economy. Revenues have fluctuated with the price of oil on the world market and the production quotas imposed by OPEC: they have therefore been relatively depressed during the 1980s. Although economic activity has slowed somewhat as a result, Saudi Arabia has vast reserves – the largest known in the world – and few long-term worries. The remainder of the economy is engaged in agriculture and newly developed industries. Agriculture supports one-sixth of the workforce, producing wheat, fruit, vegetables, barley, eggs and poultry, in most of which the kingdom is now self-sufficient. Considerable effort has been put into ensuring adequate irrigation in a country with miniscule rainfall. The industrial sector produces petrochemicals, steel, engineering products and a wide range of consumer goods. Construction is also a key industry. Service industries such as finance and business services, consultancies and property are the fastest growing sectors at present. Japan and the USA are the largest exporters to Saudi Arabia, while most of the kingdom's oil is sold to Germany, Italy, France and South Korea. Britain is also an important and long-established trading partner, and the country's principal supplier of armaments, of which the Saudis buy a very great deal. The *Al-Yamamah* contract signed in 1986 is, at £20 billion over ten years, the largest weapons contract in history.

BUSINESS: Appointments are necessary. Visiting cards printed in English with an Arab translation are usually exchanged. Men should wear suits for business meetings and formal social occasions. Thursday and Friday are official holidays. **Office hours:** 0900-1300 and 1630-2000 Saturday to Thursday (Ramadan 2000-0100), with some regional variation (eg Dhahran offices: 0700-1130 and 1300-1630 Saturday to Wednesday). **Government office hours:** 0730-1430 Saturday to Wednesday.

COMMERCIAL INFORMATION: The following organisation can offer advice: Council of Saudi Arabian Chambers of Commerce and Industry, PO Box 16683, Riyadh 11474. Tel: (1) 405 3200. Fax: (1) 402 4747. Telex: 405808.

HISTORY & GOVERNMENT

HISTORY: The Arabian Peninsula was occupied by the Abyssinians before the 6th century AD. Around AD576 they were driven out of the southern regions by the Persians, who made it a province of their empire. The year AD622, which has been adopted as the beginning of the Muslim era, was significant for the flight of the prophet Mohammed from his home town of Mecca to nearby Medina, where he organised his followers before launching a successful campaign to recapture Mecca. Many Arab tribes joined Mohammed before his death in 632 and afterwards the Muslims continued their expansion across the Arabian peninsula and into Syria, Mesopotamia (Iraq), Persia and westwards into Egypt and North Africa. The towns of Mecca and Medina, both of which were thriving cultural and commercial centres before and after Mohammed, are the holiest cities of Islam and the Saudis take the responsibility for protecting their integrity with the utmost seriousness. Arabia was absorbed into the Turkish Ottoman Empire during the 16th century, after the capture of Mecca by the Turks in 1517, but subsequent local rulers were allowed a great deal of autonomy. Under Turkish supervision, successive Sherifs of Mecca governed the territory of Hijaz, which covered the western part of the peninsula including the Red Sea coast as far south as Yemen, until the onset of the First World War. In 1914 the British armed forces chief Lord Kitchener offered the Sherif of Mecca a deal under which Hijaz would acquire independence, guaranteed by Britain, on condition that the Sherif supported the military campaign against the Turks. The Sherif accepted, and after the Turkish defeat, the Kingdom of Hijaz was recognised as independent at the 1920 Treaty of Sèvres. On the other side of the peninsula, the leading potentate was Abdul Aziz ibn Abdar-Rahman, better known as 'Ibn Saud', ruler of the province of Najd. In 1915, the Government of India, then under British rule, recognised Najd and some other territories along the Persian Gulf as possessions of Ibn Saud. Throughout the 1920s, military clashes between Ibn Saud's troops and forces loyal to the Hashemite King of Hijaz, Hussein, grew more frequent as the decisive struggle for control of the peninsula took place. The British and other Western powers switched their support between the two sides as it suited them. Eventually, Ibn Saud pushed out the Hashemites, and in 1926 was recognised as ruler of the Kingdom of Hijaz and Najd. In 1932 this became the United Kingdom of Saudi Arabia. The Hashemites were consoled with the thrones of Iraq and Transjordan (later Jordan). In 1933 the first explorations began for oil, vast deposits of which were discovered in the eastern part of the country. This set Saudi Arabia on the road to its current prosperity. Ibn Saud, who ruled as King until his death in 1953, used the accumulating revenues to develop a national infrastructure and basic state services. Political and social development in the kingdom, by Western standards at any rate, lagged somewhat behind economic developments: slavery, for example, was not abolished until 1962. Ibn Saud's descendents comprise the dynasty which has since ruled Saudi Arabia. They are, like most Saudis, adherents to the Wahhabi sect which subscribes to Sunni Muslim doctrine and Islamic laws are strictly enforced by the Religious Police. The oil search of the 1930s brought the Americans into contact with Saudi Arabia for the first time and they quickly became the country's principal Western ally. The British, who had initially vied for the privilege, concentrated on the littoral states – Yemen, Oman, and the Gulf sheikdoms thereafter. As US-Saudi relations evolved, the Americans implicitly assumed a major responsibility for the security of Saudi Arabia, a state of affairs which the Saudis, worried by their own lack of military clout, a consequence of their small population and large land area, accepted gladly. In 1957 the Saudis permitted the use of Dharhan air base in the east of the country. (This base became the principal forward base for American aircraft during the 1991 Gulf War.) During the next two decades, Saudi Arabia emerged as the most important Arab ally of the USA. It consistently opposed the radical pan-Arab policies promoted by Egypt's president Nasser: Saudi troops fought Egyptians in North Yemen during the 1960s to prevent a pro-Nasser government from taking power. In the end a moderate nationalist government was installed. Nonetheless, there was one issue on which Saudi and American policies were implacably opposed: Israel. Washington's consistent support for the Jewish state was a constant source of friction. This became spectacularly clear in 1973 when Saudi Arabia and Iran, two of America's staunchest allies in the region, led the OPEC cartel in trebling the price of oil overnight in response to the West's support for Israel during the Yom Kippur War. The period of cool relations which followed came to an end with the revolution in Iran in 1979. Fundamentalist Iran gradually assumed an important and increasingly hostile posture in Saudi eyes: firstly, because of Saudi backing for Iraq during the Iran-Iraq war; and then, in 1986, after an incident in which several hundred Iranians died during a confrontation with Saudi security forces in the course of making the annual *Hajj* pilgrimage to Mecca. 1986 also saw the dismissal by King Fahd of the veteran Saudi oil minister, Sheikh Yamani, the engineer of the 1973 oil 'shock', after a dispute over OPEC pricing policy. The Saudis are constantly concerned about their security, both external and internal, and events since the beginning of 1990 have done nothing to ease this. After the Iraqi invasion of Kuwait in August 1990, the initial disposition of the invasion forces in Kuwait was interpreted as potentially threatening to Saudi Arabia (although it is unlikely Saddam Hussein had any serious designs on the country). This became the main pretext for the arrival of the American-led multinational force and Saudi Arabia was subsequently the launch-pad for the counter-invasion of Kuwait to expel Saddam's army, a prospect which the Saudi government considered with some trepidation since, whatever the ultimate fate of Saddam's regime, the Saudis would have to live with him or his successor as neighbours. This and an obvious reluctance to play host to a war forced the Saudi government into urgent diplomatic activity. Talks with the Iraqis, brokered through Jordan, concentrated on a comprehensive regional settlement, at the core of which was the controversial issue of 'linkage' between solutions to the Kuwait problem and to the Palestinian issue. Despite the Saudis' ready agreement to allow American and allied forces into the country, the decision was not without cost for the Government. It has experienced increasing difficulties with the growing Islamic fundamentalist constituency which objected to the American military presence for a host of reasons. The regime has also come under unusual pressure from several directions – foreign governments, domestic opponents and younger members of the ruling family – to improve its presently non-existent democratic credentials. To that end, King Fahd announced in October 1990 the formation of a *majlis al-shura* (consultative council) to advise on the running of the country, although sceptical observers recall similar past initiatives which either failed to materialise or rapidly withered away. By the beginning of 1992, press censorship and political control had returned to pre-Gulf War levels. How long the increasingly educated populace is prepared to accept the current autocracy is unclear, but with an army of politically impotent expatriates available to keep the country running, Saudi Arabia is unlikely to make hasty progress towards political pluralism. Internationally, Saudi influence and prestige in the aftermath of the Gulf War has been at a peak. The main reason is oil: the Saudis promised the Bush administration that they will continually adjust their own production level to meet world demand. Current Saudi production already compensates for the absence of oil from Kuwait (under repairs) and Iraq (embargoed). Saudi motives are twofold: to keep firm control of OPEC and to build up their financial reserves after the expenses incurred as a result of the Gulf War. Among Saudi Arabia's southern neighbours, relations with Yemen have been particularly bad since Yemen decided to support Iraq rather than Kuwait in 1990. The Saudis have reactivated an ancient border dispute and counselled oil companies who were relishing the prospect of drilling in Yemen not to do so. The Saudis are also playing an important role, largely behind the scenes, in the Arab-Israeli peace process. Prince Bandar bin Sultan, Saudi Arabian ambassador to Washington and a key figure in the regime, has held talks with American Jewish leaders. He has also offered to provide funds for joint Arab-Israeli development projects – an astute and tempting move. Having decided to become involved, the Saudis are in a position to exercise very great influence.

GOVERNMENT: Saudi Arabia is an absolute monarchy with no political parties or representative assembly. King Fahd, who succeeded in 1982, appoints a Council of Ministers to run day-to-day affairs. The establishment of a consultative council, numbering about 60, is apparently under consideration.

CLIMATE

Saudi Arabia has a desert climate. In Jeddah it is warm for most of the year. Riyadh, which is inland, is hotter in summer and colder in winter, when occasional heavy rainstorms occur. The Rub al Khali seldom receives rain, making Saudi Arabia one of the driest countries in the world.

Required clothing: Tropical or lightweight clothing.

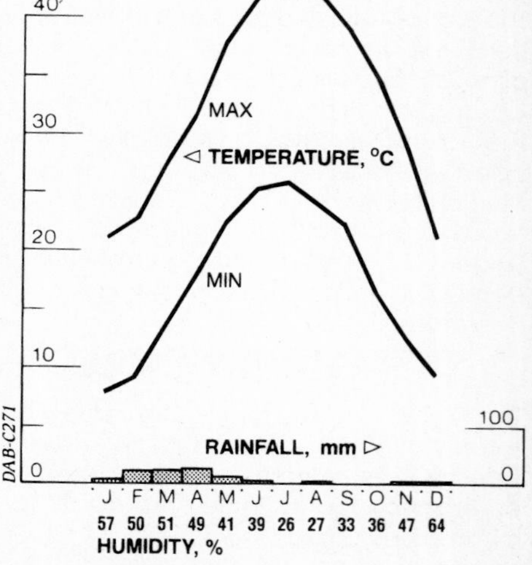

SENEGAL

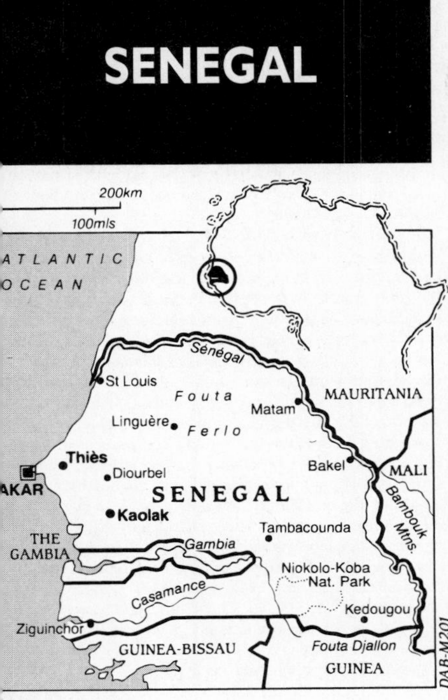

international airport

ocation: West Africa.

Note: The Senegambian Confederation, established in 981 with the aim of bringing the economy and foreign olicy of Senegal and The Gambia into line (while retaining full sovereignty) was peacefully dissolved in 1989.

Ministry of Tourism and Environmental Protection
BP 4049
avenue André Peytavin
Dakar, Senegal
Tel: 225 376.

Embassy of the Republic of Senegal
11 Phillimore Gardens
London W8 7QG
Tel: (071) 937 0925/6. Fax: (071) 937 8130. Telex: 917119. Opening hours: 0930-1700 Monday to Friday.

British Embassy
BP 6025
20 rue du Docteur Guillet
Dakar, Senegal
Tel: 237 392. Fax: 232 766. Telex: 21690.

Embassy of the Republic of Senegal
2112 Wyoming Avenue, NW
Washington, DC
20008
Tel: (202) 234 0540/1. Fax: (202) 352 6315.

Embassy of the United States of America
BP 49
avenue Jean XXIII
Dakar, Senegal
Tel: 234 296. Fax: 222 991. Telex: 21793.

Embassy of the Republic of Senegal
57 Malborough Avenue
Ottawa, Ontario
K1N 8E8
Tel: (613) 238 6392. Fax: (613) 238 2695. Telex: 0534531.

Canadian Embassy
PO Box 3373
Immeuble Daniel Sorano
45 boulevard de la République
Dakar, Senegal
Tel: 239 290. Fax: 238 749. Telex: 51632.

AREA: 196,722 sq km (75,955 sq miles).
POPULATION: 6,881,919 (1988 estimate).
POPULATION DENSITY: 35 per sq km.
CAPITAL: Dakar. **Population:** 850,000 (1979 estimate).
GEOGRAPHY: Senegal is bordered by Guinea to the south, Mali to the east and Mauritania to the north, and encloses the confederated state of The Gambia. To the west lies the Atlantic Ocean. Most land is less than 100m (330ft) above sea-level, except for the Fouta Djallon foothills in the southeast and the Bambouk Mountains on the Mali border. On the coast between Dakar and Saint-Louis is a strip of shifting dunes. South of Dakar there are shallow estuaries along the coastline, which is fringed by palm trees. In the northern part of the country, south of the Senegal Basin, lies the arid Fouto Ferlo, a hot dry Sahelian plain with little vegetation.
LANGUAGE: The official language is French. There are many local languages, the principal one being Wolof. Other groups include Senegalo-Guinean, Mandé and Peulh.
RELIGION: 90% Muslim, 5% Roman Catholic and Protestant, and a minority of traditional beliefs.
TIME: GMT.
ELECTRICITY: 220 volts AC, 50Hz.
COMMUNICATIONS: Telephone: IDD is available. Country code: 221. **Fax:** SONATEL (responsible for all telecommunications) has a fax machine. Some hotels also have facilities. **Telex/telegram:** There are facilities at main post offices and several hotels. **Post:** Airmail to Europe takes between seven and ten days, and surface mail between two and six weeks. **Press:** All newspapers are in French and nearly all are controlled directly by political parties.
BBC World Service and Voice of America frequencies: From time to time these change. See the section *How to Use this Book* for more information.

BBC:				
MHz	21.71	15.40	94.10	6.005
Voice of America:				
MHz	21.49	15.60	9.525	6.035

PASSPORT/VISA

Regulations and requirements may be subject to change at short notice, and you are advised to contact the appropriate diplomatic or consular authority before finalising travel arrangements. Details of these may be found at the head of this country's entry. Any numbers in the chart refer to the footnotes below.

	Passport Required?	Visa Required?	Return Ticket Required?
Full British	Yes	No	Yes
BVP	Not valid	-	-
Australian	Yes	Yes	Yes
Canadian	Yes	Yes	Yes
USA	Yes	Yes	Yes
Other EC	Yes	1	Yes
Japanese	Yes	Yes	Yes

PASSPORTS: Valid passport required by all.
British Visitors Passport: Not accepted.
VISAS: Required by all except:
(a) **[1]** nationals of Denmark, France (unless travelling via The Gambia), Germany, Ireland, Italy and the UK (nationals of other EC countries *do* need visas);
(b) nationals of Benin, Burkina Faso, Cape Verde, Central African Republic, Congo, Côte d'Ivoire, Gabon, The Gambia, Guinea-Bissau, Mali, Mauritania, Mauritius, Morocco, Niger, Rwanda, Sierra Leone, Togo and Tunisia.
Types of visa: *Multiple-entry visa* (tourist and business): £12.50 (for stays of up to 1 month) and £17.50 (for stays between 1 and 3 months). *Transit visa:* £2.50 (required by all except those nationals referred to above in visa exemptions, and passengers holding confirmed reservation and travel documents for onward journey by same or next connecting flight).
Validity: 3 months from the date of issue.
Application to: Consulate (or Consular Section at Embassy). For addresses, see top of entry.
Application requirements: (a) Valid passport. (b) 2 passport photos. (c) Company letter for Business visa. (d) Yellow fever vaccination certificate.
Working days required: 1 (use registered post for postal applications).

MONEY

Currency: CFA Franc (CFA Fr) = 100 centimes. Notes are in denominations of CFA Fr10,000, 5000, 1000, 500 and 100. Coins are in denominations of CFA Fr100, 50, 25, 10, 5, 2 and 1. The notes are also legal tender in the republics which formerly comprised French West Africa, ie Benin, Burkina Faso, Côte d'Ivoire, Mali, Niger and Togo. Senegal is part of the French Monetary Area.
Credit cards: American Express is the most widely accepted, although Access/Mastercard, Diners Club and Visa have limited use. Check with your credit card company for details of merchant acceptability and other services which may be available.
Exchange rate indicators: The following figures are included as a guide to the movements of the CFA Franc against Sterling and the US Dollar:

Date:	Oct '89	Nov '90	Oct '91	Oct '92
£1.00=	505.13	498.38	496.13	413.75
$1.00=	319.91	255.12	285.87	260.71

Currency restrictions: Import of both foreign and local currency is unlimited, subject to declaration. Export of local currency is restricted to CFA Fr20,000. Export of foreign currency equivalent to more than CFA Fr50,000 is limited to the amount declared on arrival and a detailed list of all exchanges must be shown.
Banking hours: 0800-1115 and 1430-1630 Monday to Friday.

DUTY FREE

The following items may be imported into Senegal by persons over 18 years of age without incurring customs duty:
200 cigarettes or 50 cigars or 250g tobacco;
A reasonable quantity of perfume for personal use.
Note: There is no free import of alcoholic beverages.

PUBLIC HOLIDAYS

Public holidays observed in Senegal are as follows:
Mar 25 '93 Korité (End of Ramadan). **Apr 4** National Day. **Apr 9** Good Friday. **Apr 12** Easter Monday. **May 1** Labour Day. **May 20** Ascension Day. **May 31** Whit Monday. **Jun 1** Tabaski (Feast of the Sacrifice). **Jul 14** Day of Association. **Aug 15** Assumption. **Aug 30** Mouloud (Prophet's Birthday). **Nov 1** All Saints' Day. **Dec 25** Christmas. **Jan 1 '94** New Year's Day. **Mar** Korité.
Note: Muslim festivals are timed according to local sightings of various phases of the Moon and the dates given above are approximations. During the lunar month of Ramadan that precedes Korité (Eid al-Fitr), Muslims fast during the day and feast at night and normal business patterns may be interrupted. Many restaurants are closed during the day and there may be restrictions on smoking and drinking. Some disruption may continue into Korité itself. Korité and Tabaski (Eid al-Adha) may last anything from two to ten days, depending on the region. For more information see the section *World of Islam* at the back of the book.

HEALTH

Regulations and requirements may be subject to change at short notice, and you are advised to contact your doctor well in advance of your intended date of departure. Any numbers in the chart refer to the footnotes below.

	Special Precautions?	Certificate Required?
Yellow Fever	Yes	1
Cholera	Yes	2
Typhoid & Polio	Yes	-
Malaria	3	-
Food & Drink	4	-

[1]: A yellow fever vaccination certificate is required from all travellers over one year of age.
[2]: Following WHO guidelines issued in 1973, a cholera vaccination certificate is not a condition of entry to Senegal. However, cholera is a risk in this country and precautions are essential. Up-to-date advice should be sought before deciding whether these precautions should include vaccination, as medical opinion is divided over its effectiveness. See the *Health* section at the back of the book.
[3]: Malaria risk, predominantly in the malignant *falciparum* form, all year throughout the country; there is a lower risk in the Cap Vert region from January to June. Resistance to chloroquine has been reported.
[4]: All water should be regarded as being potentially contaminated. Water used for drinking, brushing teeth or making ice should first be boiled or otherwise sterilised. Milk is unpasteurised and should be boiled. Powdered or tinned milk is available and is advised, but make sure that it is reconstituted with pure water. Avoid dairy products which are likely to have been made from unboiled milk. Only eat well-cooked meat and fish, preferably served hot. Pork, salad and mayonnaise may carry increased risk. Vegetables should be cooked and fruit peeled.
Rabies is present. For those at high risk, vaccination before arrival should be considered. If you are bitten abroad seek medical advice without delay. For more information consult the *Health* section at the back of the book.
Bilharzia (schistosomiasis) is present. Avoid swimming and paddling in fresh water. Swimming pools which are well-chlorinated and maintained are safe.
Health care: In Dakar, doctors are plentiful and most medicines are available. Up-country, however, facilities are minimal. Health insurance is essential.

TRAVEL - International

AIR: Senegal's national airline is *Air Sénégal/SONATRA (DS)*.
Approximate flight times: From Dakar to *London* is 8 hours 10 minutes, to *New York* is 8 hours 10 minutes and to *Paris* is 7 hours.
International airport: *Dakar (DKR)* (Dakar-Yoff) is 17km (10.5 miles) northwest of the city (travel time – 25 minutes). Regular coach and bus services go to and from Dakar.

Metered taxis are available. Airport facilities include duty-free shop, bar/restaurant, bank, post office and car hire.
Departure tax: CFA Fr5000 for international flights and CFA Fr4000 for flights within Africa.
SEA: There are regular sailings from France, the Canary Islands, Morocco, Spain and several South American and West African ports. Fares tend to be expensive. The main port is Dakar.
RAIL: There are two passenger trains (one Senegalian and one Malian) with restaurant and sleeping cars, running from Bamako, Mali, twice a week. The journey can take between 30 and 36 hours. It is advisable to travel on the Senegalese train (well up to Western standards), rather than the Malian train, as the latter is very basic indeed.
ROADS: Roads from Mauritania are tarred and in good condition; the best place to cross the border is at Rosso. Roads from Guinea-Bissau are not yet tarred; there is a border crossing at São Domingo. There is a route from Senegal to Mali via Tambacounda. There is access across the Sahara by a 5500km (2120 miles) road that runs from Algeria via Mali. The trans-Gambian highway crosses the River Gambia by ferry. There is a good network of **buses** and **taxis** running across the major borders.

TRAVEL - Internal

AIR: *Air Senegal* runs services to all the main towns in Senegal.
Gambia Air Shuttle offers flights from Dakar to Banjul (Gambia) twice a day.
Departure tax: CFA Fr2000 for all internal flights.
SEA: A boat operating on a weekly basis runs from Dakar to Ziguinchor.
RAIL: The country has a network of about 1034km (643 miles) of rail track. Trains run from Dakar to towns en route for Mali. There is also a service between Dakar and St Louis. There is an ongoing programme of upgrading and expansion.
ROAD: There are approximately 2951km (1834 miles) of asphalt roads linking the major towns and in the coastal region. The network of roads in the interior are rough (about 10,400km/6460 miles in all) and may become impassable during the rainy season. There are often police checkpoints at the entrance and exit to villages to enforce speed restrictions; fines are paid on the spot. **Bus:** Long distance services operate subject to demand only. **Taxis** are available in most towns and fares are metered. It is cheaper to hail a taxi in the street than arrange to be collected from the hotel. Bush taxis and estate cars are good for journeys into the interior. **Car hire** companies are found in Dakar and the main towns. **Documentation:** A French or International Driving Permit is required.
URBAN: Bus and minibus services operate in Dakar.

ACCOMMODATION

HOTELS: The government-controlled expansion of tourism has lead to an increasing number of hotels. There are a number which are of international standard, and more development is under way, including a number of hotels on the Petite Côte (the stretch of beaches between Dakar and Joal). In Casamance some luxury resorts like the *Club Mediterranée* have been built. It is advisable to book accommodation in advance, particularly in Dakar where there is an increased demand during the tourist season, which lasts from December to May. Hotels in Dakar generally have air-conditioning but tend to be expensive. An establishment in its own class is the *Bou el Mogdad*, the River Region floating hotel, which has comfortable cabins and a lively shipboard life.
CAMPING: Government campsites (*campements*) provide a few beds, but no bedding. There are basic facilities for the traveller who prefers to wander from the beaten track, although camping independently is strongly discouraged. Sometimes bungalows or grass huts are available; visitors must otherwise provide their own tents.
MISSIONS: Catholic missions will accommodate tourists only in cases of real need.
VILLAGE HUTS: A village will sometimes courteously offer a stranger one of the local huts as living accommodation, but it is necessary for visitors to provide their own bedding.

RESORTS & EXCURSIONS

Dakar is a bustling modern city and major port with good restaurants and shops and a lively nightlife. There is a ferry-boat ride to **Gorée Island,** an old fortified slaving station and one of the first French settlements on the continent. There is a museum on the island, along with a zoo, colonial mansions and slaves' houses. Dakar's markets include the *Sandaga* and the *Kermel*, the former being famous for its silverworking. There is a pleasant trip from Dakar to the beach at *N'Gor*, near the airport.
St Louis is another old French fortified settlement, from the days of slave-trading. There are good beaches. A cruise lasting several days up the Senegal River departs from here.
Ziguinchor is a good base for visiting the **Basse Casamance** region, with mangrove swamps and palm trees.
On the island of **Karaban** the ruins of a Breton church and a colonial settlement can be seen.
There are a number of national parks in Senegal, particularly rich in birdlife. The best time for viewing is usually winter: *Niokolo Koba, Basse Casamance, Langue de Barbarie* and *Djoudi* are especially recommended. All these parks have basic accommodation, mostly in the form of *campements*.
The *Lac de Guiers* is the home of a wide variety of birds.
The area around the source of the *River Saloum* is rich in archaeological remains – relics of an ancient civilisation about which little is known.

SOCIAL PROFILE

FOOD & DRINK: Senegalese food is considered among the best in Africa. The basis of many dishes is chicken or fish, but the distinctive taste is due to ingredients not found outside Africa. This food is served in many restaurants in Dakar. Provincial resthouses serve less sophisticated but delicious variations. Dishes include *chicken au yassa* (chicken with lemon, pimentos and onions), *tiebou dienne* (rice and fish), *dem à la St Louis* (stuffed mullet), *maffe* (chicken or mutton in peanut sauce) and *accras* (a kind of fritter). Suckling pig is popular in the Casamance region. Fruit and vegetables are plentiful. Waiter service is normal and table manners often follow the Muslim tradition of eating with the right hand, especially when with Senegalese hosts. Western-style restaurants have knives and forks.
Drink: There are bars in some hotels and clubs. Although predominantly a Muslim country, alcohol is available. The traditional drink is mint tea, the first cup drunk slightly bitter, the second with more sugar and the third very sweet. The Casamance drink is palm wine, which is drunk either fresh or fermented. *Toufam* (a kind of yoghurt thinned with sugared water) is served to guests in Toucouleur villages. A unique drink is home-roasted coffee with pimento.
NIGHTLIFE: Traditional Senegalese festivals are held throughout the year and are well worth watching. There are several nightclubs in Dakar and a casino on the route de N'Gor. There are cinemas showing the latest French films.
SHOPPING: Bargaining is customary. At Soumbedionne, on the Corniche de Fann, is a craft village where you can watch craftsmen at work and buy their handicrafts. Purchases include woodcarving in the form of African gaming boards, masks and statues; musical instruments; and metalwork, including copper pendants, bowls and statuettes. Most markets and centres sell traditional fabric, embroidery, pottery, necklaces of clay beads and costume jewellery of wood or various seeds. **Shopping hours:** Generally 0800-1200 and 1430-1800 Monday to Saturday. Some shops open Sunday mornings, others are closed on Mondays.
SPORT: Swimming: There are swimming pools in many hotels and at the Dakar Lido. There is good bathing at N'Gor Beach, Hann Bay, the Petite Côte and Casamance. The coast from Cap Vert to Saint Louis is not suitable for swimming. **Water-skiing:** Facilities are available at Dakar alongside the 'Children's Beach' on the lagoon between N'Gor and its island and at the Marinas in Hanns Bay. **Fishing:** The Centre de Pêche Sportive at Dakar port and the Hann Bay Marinas have fully equipped deep-sea fishing boats for hire. **Skindiving:** Underwater enthusiasts will find good diving waters all around the Cap Vert Peninsula. **Horseriding:** Horses are available for riding in the Cap Vert area. **Tennis:** Courts are at N'Gor, Nianing, Dakar and Cap Skirring. **Golf:** There is a 9-hole golf course at Camberene and miniature golf at Dakar-Yoff. **Spectator sports:** Senegalese are keen **footballers** and followers of African **wrestling**. There are matches every Sunday at the Fass arena and in the suburbs or at the Iba Mar Diop Stadium near the Great Mosque.
SOCIAL CONVENTIONS: It is customary to say 'good morning', 'good afternoon' etc, when coming across local people, especially in the bush, and the visitor should make the effort to learn its translation in one of the local dialects. Handshaking on meeting, regardless of how many times a day you meet the person, is normal. When visiting a village it is polite to call upon the village headman or school-teacher to explain that you want to visit the area. They will often act as interpreter and will be helpful guides to the customs of the village and also in terms of money, ensuring that a traveller does not find himself in the embarrassing position of paying for hospitality that was given in friendship. Return hospitality with a gift of medicines, food or money for the community. It is not advisable to give money indiscriminately as tourists have encouraged the practice of begging. Casual wear is widely acceptable. Scanty swimwear should be reserved for the beach. Smoking is prohibited in some public places (especially mosques). **Tipping:** A service charge of 10-15% is included in all hotel and restaurant bills. Taxi drivers are not normally given a tip.

BUSINESS PROFILE

ECONOMY: In a good year, Senegal is the world's leading producer of groundnuts, which are the country's key export commodity. The country's finances are therefore hostage to the volume of the groundnut harvest and price levels. In recent years, both have been unfavourable and Senegal has consequently had to appeal for foreign aid to purchase necessary imported foodstuffs. Other agricultural produce – rice, sugar and cotton – are being successfully cultivated and have been introduced in pursuit of diversification, which has occurred, but slowly. There are plentiful fishing grounds with a wide range of species suitable for export, although the accessible area is small. Currently exploitable mineral deposits are limited to phosphates (the chemical industry draws on sizeable deposits of lime phosphate and aluminium phosphate within Senegal); some iron ore has been identified and there is thought to be oil inland. Senegal is the most industrialised country in French West Africa after Côte d'Ivoire. The main industries are involved in the processing of agricultural products and phosphates, milling, textiles, commercial vehicle assembly, food and drink, farming materials (implements, fertilisers etc), paint, asbestos, cement, printing and boat-building. The country remains nonetheless heavily dependent on foreign aid and its finances remain weak. The IMF has had one of its longest Structural Adjustment Programmes in operation in Senegal but the results have been mediocre and the Fund appears to view some of the problems as virtually insoluble. Senegal is a member of the CFA Franc zone. France is the major trading partner, followed by Côte d'Ivoire, Mali, Spain and the USA.
BUSINESS: A lightweight suit is acceptable for business. French will generally be needed for meetings. Appointments should be made and punctuality is expected, despite the fact that a customer may be slightly late. Visiting cards are essential, preferably in French and English. The period from July to October should be avoided for business visits, as many people are on holiday. **Office hours:** 0800-1200 and 1430-1800 Monday to Friday and 0800-1200 Saturday; during Ramadan some offices open 0730-1430.
COMMERCIAL INFORMATION: The following organisations can offer advice:
Chambre de Commerce et d'Industrie de la Région de Dakar, BP 118, 1 place de l'Indépendance, Dakar. Tel: 237 189. Telex: 61112; *or*

SENEGAL | **HEALTH REGULATIONS** | **VISA REGULATIONS** | Code-Link

GALILEO/WORLDSPAN

TI-DFT/DKR/HE

TI-DFT/DKR/VI

SABRE

TIDFT/DKR/HE

TIDFT/DKR/VI

To access this information on your CRS, swipe the barcode with a light pen or type in the text under the barcode. For more information, see the introduction *How to Use This Book*.

Syndicat des Commerçants Importateurs et Exportateurs de la République du Sénégal (SCIMPEX), BP 806, angle rue Parent et ave Abdoulaye Fadiga, Dakar. Tel: 213 662.

HISTORY & GOVERNMENT

HISTORY: In medieval times, parts of Senegal belonged to the empires of Mali, Ghana and Songhai. During the colonial era, Senegal came initially under French control. It was then ceded to Britain in 1763 as part of the settlement of the Seven Years War (over North American territories) but returned to the French in 1817. From 1959-60 it was part of the Federation of Mali. Senegal achieved full independence in 1960; after a brief and unsuccessful attempt to forge administrative links with Mali, Léopold Senghor became the country's first President that year, and remained in office for 20 years. The Parti Socialiste Senegalais (PSS) has been in power since independence, although the country is not a one-party state. Foreign policy is dominated by relations with The Gambia, which Senegal surrounds. During the 1980s these have fluctuated considerably, ranging from very close to rather cool. Links were at their closest following the 1981 coup attempt against the Jawara government in The Gambia which was put down with the assistance of Senegalese troops. Soon afterwards, in February 1982, the *Senegambian Confederation* was established, the object of which was to co-ordinate policy with the long-term aim of creating a full economic and monetary union. It was peacefully dissolved in 1989 after continual and unresolved arguments over trade. An extremely cold spell of relations followed. 1989 brought a sudden and drastic deterioration of relations with Mauritania. Long-standing ethnic and economic rivalries between the two countries exploded into blood-letting, with several hundred killed in each country and thousands of refugees crossing the (disputed) border in both directions. War was narrowly averted and the quarrel has since been patched up; diplomatic relations, cut in 1990, were restored in April 1992. Relations with Guinea-Bissau are also poor owing to a territorial dispute over an area which may yield oil deposits. In 1990 President Diouf conducted a reorganisation of the Government. The regime has made a continuing commitment to multi-party politics, and opposition parties continue to operate unhindered, although the dissident press is still subject to heavy political pressure. In the last 12 months some changes have been made to Senegal's electoral law (see below) and a review of the judiciary has been announced.
GOVERNMENT: The President holds executive power and is elected, from 1993 onwards, for a maximum of two 7-year terms. The unicameral National Assembly, which has 120 elected members and a 5-year term of office, is responsible for legislation.

CLIMATE

The best time to visit Senegal is during the dry season which runs from December through to May. In coastal areas there are cool trade winds during the dry period. Throughout the rest of the year a hot monsoon wind blows from the south bringing the rainy season and hot, humid weather. Rainfall is heavy in Casamance and in the southeast and slight in the Sahelian region in the north and northeast, where temperatures tend to be higher.
Required clothing: Lightweight clothing is worn all year. Rainwear is advisable from May to November. Warmer clothes are necessary for the evenings during the period from December to April, especially in Dakar.

DAKAR Senegal (23m)

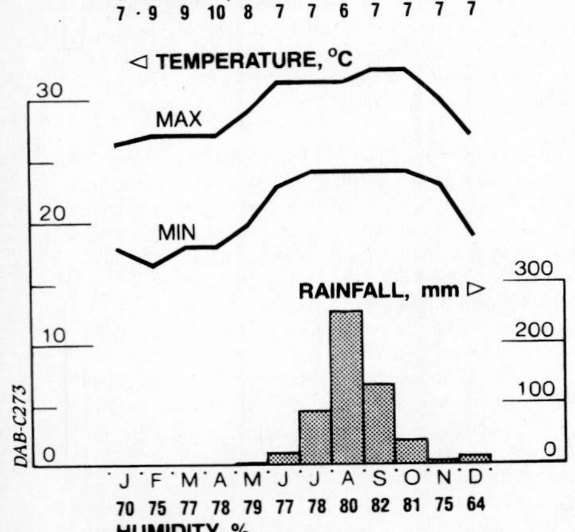

SEYCHELLES

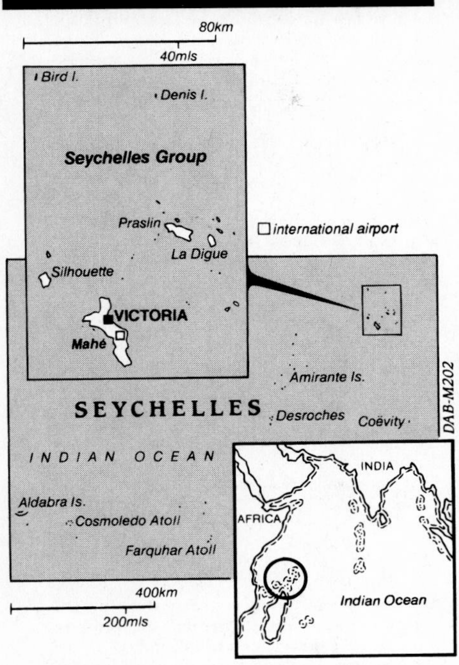

Location: Indian Ocean, 1600km (990 miles) east of Kenya.

Seychelles Tourist Board
PO Box 92
Independence House
Victoria
Mahé, Seychelles
Tel: 25333. Telex: 2275 SEYTOB SZ.
High Commission for the Republic of the Seychelles
PO Box 4PE
2nd Floor, Eros House
111 Baker Street
London W1M 1FE
Tel: (071) 224 1660. Fax: (071) 487 5756. Telex: 281446. Opening hours: 0900-1630 Monday to Thursday and 0900-1200 Friday.
Seychelles Tourist Office
Address as for High Commission.
Tel: (071) 224 1670. Fax: (071) 487 5756. Telex: 281446. Opening hours 0900-1600 Monday to Friday.
British High Commission
PO Box 161
3rd Floor, Victoria House
Victoria
Mahé, Seychelles
Tel: 25256. Fax: 25189. Telex: 2269 UKREP SZ.
Embassy of the Republic of the Seychelles
Suite 927, 820 Second Avenue
New York, NY
10017
Tel: (212) 687 9766/7. Fax: (212) 808 4975. Telex: 220032 SMUN UR.
Also deals with enquiries from Canada.
Seychelles Tourist Office
Suite 900F, 820 Second Avenue
New York, NY
10017
Tel: (212) 687 9766. Fax: (212) 922 9177. Telex: 220032 SMUN UR.
Also deals with enquiries from Canada.
Embassy of the United States of America
PO Box 251
Victoria House
Victoria
Mahé, Seychelles
Tel: 25256. Fax: 25189.

AREA: 443 sq km (171 sq miles).
POPULATION: 67,038 (1989 estimate). There is no permanent population on the Coralline Islands.
POPULATION DENSITY: 147.7 per sq km.
CAPITAL: Victoria, Mahé. **Population:** 24,325 (1987).
GEOGRAPHY: The Seychelles Archipelago occupies 400,000 sq km (150,000 sq miles) of the Indian Ocean northeast of Madagascar and contains 115 islands and islets. These fall into two groups of markedly different appearance, stemming from their distinct geologies:
Granitic: A dense cluster of 42 islands, unique in being the only mid-ocean group in the world with a granite rock formation. Their lush green vegetation is tropical in character, with a profusion of coconut palms, bananas, mangoes, yams, breadfruit and other tropical fruit. Indigenous forest exists on the higher slopes where cinnamon and tea are planted. All, including the second largest, Praslin, are less than 65km (40 miles) from Mahé.
Coralline: Isolated coral outcrops speckling a vast area of the Indian Ocean to the southwest of the granitic group. They rise only a few feet above sea level but are covered with rich and dense vegetation due to fertilisation by copious amounts of guano. There is no permanent population. Aldabra, the largest atoll in the world, contains one-third of all Seychellois land and is a UNESCO-designated World Heritage Site.
The largest island in either group is **Mahé**, lying 4°S of the equator. It is 27km (17 miles) long by 8km (5 miles) wide and contains Victoria, the capital and main port, and 90% of the population. Mahé is typical of the granitic islands, being mountainous and covered with jungle vegetation. Its highest point, indeed the highest point in the Seychelles, is Morne Seychellois (905m/2970ft). The isolated nature of the Seychelles has given rise to the evolution of many unique species of flora and fauna, including the coco-de-mer palm (producing the world's heaviest seed pods) and unique varieties of orchid, giant tortoise, gecko, chameleon and 'flying fox' (fruitbat). Several national parks and reserves have been set up to protect this heritage.
The Seychellois are born out of a mixture of French and British landowners, freed African slaves and a small number of Indian and Chinese immigrants, creating a unique culture.
LANGUAGE: The official language is Creole, but English and French are widely spoken.
RELIGION: 92% Roman Catholic with Anglican, Seventh Day Adventist, Muslim and other minorities.
TIME: GMT + 4 (GMT + 3 in summer).
ELECTRICITY: 240 volts AC, 50Hz. British 3-pin plugs are in use.
COMMUNICATIONS: Telecommunications: SEYTELS offers a 24-hour service for telexes, telegrams, telephones and telefaxes via SEYTELS/Cable & Wireless Ltd, Francis Rachel Street, Victoria, Mahé. Phonecards were introduced in 1988. IDD is available. Country code: 248. **Post:** The main post office is in Victoria. Airmail collections are at 1500 weekdays and 1200 Saturdays; airmail to Europe normally takes up to a week. Post office hours: 0800-1200 and 1300-1600 Monday to Friday, and 0800-1200 Saturday. **Press:** English-language newspapers include *The Seychelles Nation* (morning daily) and the *Seychelles Weekend Nation*, *The People* (monthly, published by the Seychelles Progressive Front) and *Seychelles Today* (monthly news review).
BBC World Service and Voice of America frequencies: From time to time these change. See the section *How to Use this Book* for more information.

BBC:				
MHz	21.470	17.885	15.575	9.630
Voice of America:				
MHz	21.49	15.60	9.525	6.035

Radio Television Seychelles broadcasts a full news bulletin in English at 1900 daily on 1368kHz; headlines are broadcast in English at 0700 and 1300.

PASSPORT/VISA

Regulations and requirements may be subject to change at short notice, and you are advised to contact the appropriate diplomatic or consular authority before finalising travel arrangements. Details of these may be found at the head of this country's entry. Any numbers in the chart refer to the footnotes below.

	Passport Required?	Visa Required?	Return Ticket Required?
Full British	Yes	No	Yes
BVP	Valid	-	-
Australian	Yes	No	Yes
Canadian	Yes	No	Yes
USA	Yes	No	Yes
Other EC	Yes	No	Yes
Japanese	Yes	No	Yes

PASSPORTS: Valid passport required by all.
British Visitors Passport: Accepted.
VISAS: Not required. A visitor's permit, valid initially

for 4 weeks, is issued on arrival, subject to possession of a return or onward ticket, booked accommodation and sufficient funds to cover the duration of stay; alternatively a deposit may be made by 'security' bond in lieu. The pass may be renewed for up to three months for a fee of S Rs200. For further information contact the nearest Seychelles Tourist Office.
Transit: Passengers in transit must have tickets with reserved seats for their onward journey.
Temporary residence: Enquire at the High Commission or Embassy.

MONEY

Currency: Seychelles Rupee (S Re: singular; S Rs: plural) = 100 cents. Notes are in denominations of S Rs100, 50, 25 and 10. Coins are in denominations of S Rs5 and 1, and 25, 10, 5 and 1 cents. A number of gold and silver coins are also minted (with face values as high as S Rs1500), but these are not in general circulation.
Currency exchange: Exchange facilities are available at the airport banks, which are open for all flight departures and arrivals. The following banks have branches in the Seychelles and will exchange travellers cheques and foreign currency: *Barclays Bank International Limited, Bank of Baroda, Banque Française Commerciale, Development Bank of Seychelles, Habib Bank Limited* and *Standard Chartered Bank Plc*.
Credit cards: American Express and Visa are widely accepted, Access/Mastercard and Diners Club have more limited use. Check with your credit card company for details of merchant acceptability and other services which may be available.
Travellers cheques: Accepted in most hotels, guest-houses, restaurants and shops.
Exchange rate indicators: The following figures are included as a guide to the movements of the Seychelles Rupee against Sterling and the US Dollar:

Date:	Oct '89	Oct '90	Oct '91	Oct '92
£1.00=	9.10	9.83	9.08	7.85
$1.00=	5.76	5.03	5.23	4.95

Currency restrictions: There are no restrictions on the import and export of foreign currency. The import of local currency is unlimited; export is restricted to S Rs100 in notes and S Rs10 in coins.
Banking hours: 0830-1300 Monday to Friday, 0830-1100 Saturday.

DUTY FREE

The following items may be imported into the Seychelles without incurring customs duty:
Cigarettes or cigars or tobacco to the value of S Rs100;
2 litres of spirits;
2 litres of wine;
200cc of perfume and 200cc toilet water;
Other dutiable goods to a total not exceeding S Rs1000 (S Rs500 for children).
Prohibited items: The importation of non-prescribed drugs and all firearms, including air pistols, air rifles and spearfishing guns, is prohibited. The importation of animals and food and other agricultural produce is strictly controlled and subject to licensing. No pets are admitted without written permission from the Chief Veterinary Officer, Seychelles. There is a 15-day quarantine period on arrival.

PUBLIC HOLIDAYS

Public holidays observed in the Seychelles are as follows:
Apr 9-10 '93 Easter. **May 1** Labour Day. **Jun 5** Liberation Day. **Jun 10** Corpus Christi. **Jun 29** Independence Day. **Aug 15** Assumption Day. **Nov 1** All Saints' Day. **Dec 8** Immaculate Conception. **Dec 25** Christmas Day. **Jan 1-2 '94** New Year's Day.

HEALTH

Regulations and requirements may be subject to change at short notice, and you are advised to contact your doctor well in advance of your intended date of departure. Any numbers in the chart refer to the footnotes below.

	Special Precautions?	Certificate Required?
Yellow Fever	No	No
Cholera	No	No
Typhoid & Polio	Yes	-
Malaria	No	-
Food & Drink	1	-

[1]: Mains water is normally chlorinated, and whilst relatively safe may cause mild abdominal upsets. Bottled water is available and is advised for the first few weeks of the stay. Milk is pasteurised and dairy products are safe for consumption. Local meat, poultry, seafood, fruit and vegetables are generally considered safe to eat.
Rabies may be present in certain areas. For those at high risk, vaccination before arrival should be considered. If you are bitten abroad seek medical advice without delay. For more information consult the *Health* section at the back of the book.
Health care: There is a large general hospital in Victoria and there are clinics elsewhere on Mahé, Praslin and La Digue. Visitors may obtain emergency treatment for a basic consultancy fee of S Rs75. Additional medical insurance is advised.

TRAVEL - International

AIR: The Seychelles' national airline is *Air Seychelles (HM)*. Other airlines flying to the Seychelles include *British Airways, Air France, Kenya Airways, Air India, Somali Airways* and *Aeroflot*.
Approximate flight times: From *London* to Mahé is 11 hours 30 minutes (15 hours via Nairobi) and from *New York* is 24 hours (via London).
International airport: *Mahé Island (SEZ)* (Seychelles International) is 10km (16 miles) southeast from Victoria (travel time – 20 minutes). Some coach services are provided by agents and taxis are available. Airport facilities include an outgoing duty-free shop, banking and exchange facilities (0830-1230 Monday to Friday; 0830-1200 Saturday), car hire and a restaurant and bar (0800-last flight).
SEA: Cruise and cargo ships call at Mahé but there are no scheduled services.

TRAVEL - Internal

AIR: *Air Seychelles* provides an efficient network of scheduled and chartered services from Mahé to Praslin, Denis, Bird, Frégate and Desroches islands.
SEA: Privately owned schooners provide regular inter-island connections between Mahé, Praslin and La Digue. Government-run ferries also operate on some routes.
ROAD: There are paved roads only on the two largest islands, Mahé and Praslin; elsewhere the roads are sandy tracks. **Bus:** *SPTC* buses run on a regular basis on Mahé between the rural areas and Victoria, the main town. A bus service also operates on Praslin from 0530-1900 and on La Digue. There are a number of 18-seater coaches for airport transfers and excursions. Prices for buses and coaches are very reasonable. **Taxi:** There are about 135 taxis on Mahé and Praslin and the rates are fixed by the Government. Rates on Praslin are 25% higher and there is a surcharge between 2000-0600 on both islands. **Car hire:** There are over 550 cars for hire on Mahé, and a limited number on Praslin. It is advisable to make advance reservations, especially in the high season. Conditions of hire and insurance should be carefully checked. Hire is on an unlimited mileage basis and the price includes Third Party insurance and tax. Minimum age is 21. Petrol is approximately 30% more expensive than in Europe. Bicycles may be hired on Praslin and La Digue. **Traffic regulations:** Driving is on the left and there is a speed limit of 65kmph (40mph) on the open road, decreasing to 40kmph (25mph) in built-up areas and throughout Praslin. **Documentation:** A national driving licence is sufficient.
JOURNEY TIMES: The following chart gives approximate journey times (in hours and minutes) from Mahé to other islands in the Seychelles.

	Air	Sea
Praslin	0.15	2.30
La Digue	-	3.15
Bird Is.	0.30	7.00
Denis Is.	0.30	6.00
Round Is.	-	0.30
Frégate Is.	0.15	2.00
Moyenne	-	0.30
Desroches	1.00	-

Note: The ferry from Praslin to La Digue takes approximately 30 minutes.

ACCOMMODATION

Although the Seychelles have been a popular tourist destination for more than ten years and now offer the full range of accommodation from self-catering apartments to luxury hotels, careful planning has ensured that the islands have retained the astonishing beauty and quiet charm that attracted the first tourists. Right from the start, the Government decreed that no new building could be higher than the surrounding palm trees, with the result that big-city levels of comfort and convenience have been achieved in thoroughly Seychellois settings. There are approximately 4500 hotel beds on the islands and it is advisable to confirm reservations with a deposit, particularly during the high season from December to January and in August.
HOTELS & GUEST-HOUSES: All recently-built hotels come well up to international standards and there are a number of large resort hotels equipped with air-conditioning, private bathrooms, swimming pools and full sporting facilities. Older hotels and guest-houses on the smaller islands may lack some sophistication, but their charming seclusion has long recommended them to those seeking complete peace and privacy: the late Somerset Maugham once sought out the quietest so that he could write a novel without interruption. Many are former plantation houses modestly modernised and run in a relaxed manner by the resident owner. Thatched-roof chalets and guest-houses, built in the local style, are to be found mainly on outlying islands. The Seychelles Hotel Association comprises ten hotels on the islands. More information is available from the association at PO Box 595, Victoria, Mahé. There are no Youth Hostels and camping is not permitted. For up-to-date prices, contact the Tourist Office.
SELF-CATERING: Self-catering units are available on the main islands. For details, contact the Tourist Office.

RESORTS & EXCURSIONS

Granitic Islands

Mahé: Surrounded by coral reefs, this is the largest of the islands, and houses the international airport, the port and capital (Victoria), the majority of the population and most of the hotels. It is an island of powdery white sands (there are almost 70 beaches on Mahé alone) and lush vegetation, rising through plantations of coconut palms and cinnamon to forested peaks that afford unparalleled views of neighbouring islands.
Excursions may be made in glass-bottomed boats from Victoria to nearby *St Anne Marine National Park*, which encloses the islands of St Anne, Cerf, Long, Round and Moyenne; or by coach, taking in such attractions as the market, the *Botanical Gardens* (with coco-de-mer, giant tortoises and orchids), and a replica of London's *Vauxhall Bridge Tower* in Victoria, before setting off around the island to visit Colonial-style mansions in graceful decline, old plantations of cinnamon and vanilla, and everywhere the greenest of vibrant green jungles. Tourists may also visit the *Morne Seychellois National Park*, occupying the highest part of the island. The *National Museum* in Victoria celebrates Seychellois history, folklore and music, and has particularly fine displays depicting the history of spice cultivation.
Praslin: The second largest island is two to three hours by boat or 15 minutes by air (20 scheduled flights per day) from Mahé. It is famous for the *Vallée de Mai*, which contains the double-nutted coco-de-mer palm. Regular excursions are available to smaller islands such as Cousin, Aride, Curieuse and La Digue.
La Digue: Three to three and a half hours by schooner from Mahé or half an hour from Praslin, this beautiful island is the breeding ground of the rare Black Paradise Flycatcher. There are very few cars and the ox-cart remains the principal means of transport (although bicycles may be hired). There are beautiful old plantation houses, including *Chateau Saint-Cloud*, as well as a vanilla plantation, copra factories and superb beaches.
Frégate: The most easterly and isolated of the granitic islands, Frégate is associated with pirates (Ian Fleming was obsessed with the notion that a pirate's hoard was buried here somewhere). It is also the home of the almost extinct Seychelles magpie robin. Frégate is 15 minutes by air from Mahé.
Thérèse: Notable for its warm rock-pools and the tortoise colony.
Cousin: Two hours by boat from Mahé, Cousin was bought (in 1968) by the International Council for Bird Protection, who operate it as a nature reserve. Amongst the rare bird species thus protected are the brush warbler, the Seychelles toc-toc and the fairy tern. The best time to visit is April or May, when a quarter of a million birds nest on the island. All visits to the island must be made as part of an organised tour. Local rangers act as guides; a full tour of the island takes between one and two hours. Local operators can arrange these trips, usually in conjunction with visits to other islands.
Aride: Two hours from Mahé, Aride is the most northerly of the granitic islands. Home to vast colonies of seabirds, in 1973 it was bought by Christopher Cadbury, President of the Royal Society

for Nature Conservation. It is open to visitors from October to the end of April.
Curieuse: Approximately 3km (2 miles) long, Curieuse is covered by lush vegetation and huge takamaka trees. It has been designated a reserve for giant tortoises (imported from Aldabra). Day trips may be arranged from Praslin.
Silhouette: Thought to have been home to one of the Indian Ocean's most notorious pirates, Hodoul, this island may be seen from Beau Vallon Beach on Mahé. It has a population of about 200. Sights include an old plantation house of traditional Seychellois timber construction.

Coralline Islands

Denis: Five to seven hours by boat or 30 minutes by air from Mahé, Denis is also on the edge of the continental shelf and attracts many deep-sea fishermen. Marlin may be caught from October to December. The island's seabird population has, over the years, left rich deposits of guano, which has encouraged the growth of lush vegetation. The minimum stay is two days.
Bird: Six to eight hours by boat or 30 minutes by plane from Mahé, this island is famous for the millions of sooty terns who migrate here to breed between May and September. Its location at the edge of the Seychelles continental shelf (the sea floor drops rapidly to 2000m) also makes it a favoured destination for fishermen. A third claim to fame is Esmeralda, said to be 150 years old and the largest tortoise in the world.
Desroches: The largest of the Amirantes archipelago, Desroches is 193km (120 miles) southwest of Mahé (one hour by air). The surrounding coral reef keeps the coastal waters calm and makes it an ideal destination for those seeking watersports. Although Desroches was only recently developed as a resort, there are facilities for water-skiing, windsurfing, sailing, fishing and scuba diving; water scooters may also be hired. The diving is particularly good: there are sea cliffs, tunnels and caves – and, of course, multitudes of fish of many different species. Lessons are available. Visibility is best from September to May. Accommodation is in 20 chalets set amongst casuarina trees and coconut palms.

Plants and Wildlife

As a result of their extraordinary, isolated history, the Seychelles are rich in rare plants which flourish nowhere else on the planet. 81 species are unique survivors from the luxuriant tropical forests which covered the islands until man's belated arrival two centuries ago. Outstanding amongst these is the coco-de-mer (sea coconut), native to Praslin, which grows in the Vallée de Mai. Its seed is the largest in nature, and gave rise to many legends when it was washed ashore on the coasts of Africa, India and Indonesia. Since the islands were unknown, the nuts were thought to have grown under the sea – hence the name. Among the many orchids is the vanilla, once widely cultivated for the essence produced from its aromatic pods. Its ornate leaves and lovely flowers make a wonderful display. It is not, however, necessary to travel the length and breadth of the islands to see interesting plants, as many of them can be viewed in Victoria's Botanical Gardens. The Seychelles are also a major attraction for birdwatchers. Millions of terns nest on some of the islands – among them that most beautiful of seabirds, the fairy tern. Up to two million sooty terns nest on Bird Island, and on Aride can be found the world's largest colonies of lesser noddies, roseate terns and other tropical birds. Some species, on the other hand, are less well represented and are rare almost to the point of extinction. The paradise flycatcher has dwindled to some 30 pairs on one island, La Digue. The Seychelles magpie robin is confined to Frégate, the black parrot to Praslin and the melodious brush warbler to Cousin.
It was only some 20 years ago that active conservation of endangered species began in the Seychelles. Since then, with the establishment of island sanctuaries and nature reserves, much has been done to make the Seychelles a paradise for birds – and for all those who love to watch them.

SOCIAL PROFILE

FOOD & DRINK: Seychellois Creole cuisine is influenced by French, African, Chinese, Indian and English traditions. The careful blending of spices is a major feature and much use is made of coconut milk and breadfruit. Local specialities include *kat-kat banane*, coconut curries, *chatini requin*, *bourgeois grillé*, *soupe de tectec*, *bouillon brède*, *chauve-souris* (fruit bat), *cari bernique*, *salade de palmiste* (made from the 'heart' of the coconut palm and sometimes known as 'millionaire's salad') and *la daube* (made from breadfruit, yams, cassavas and bananas). Breadfruit is prepared in similar ways to the potato (mashed, chipped, roasted etc) but has a slightly sweeter taste. Other locally produced fruits and vegetables include aubergines, calabashes, choux choutes, patoles, paw-paws (papaya), bananas, mangoes, avocados, jack-fruits, grapefruits, guavas, lychees, pineapples, melons, limes and golden apples. The tomato is romantically known as the *pomme d'amour*. Lobster, octopus, pork and chicken are used more frequently than beef or lamb, which must be imported. Most restaurants offer a few items of what is termed 'international' cuisine, generally with a bias towards preparations of fresh fish and shellfish, as well as the Creole delicacies mentioned above. There are Italian and Chinese restaurants on Mahé. Some of the main hotels have bakeries and home-baked bread is also a feature of some of the small guest-houses and lodges. Waiter service is the norm. All restaurants which are members of the *Seychelles Restaurateurs' Association* quote an average price per person for a 3-course meal inclusive of two glasses of wine and coffee. Prior notice should be given in restaurants for groups of four or more and advance bookings should be made for restaurants on Round and Cerf and for *La Réserve* restaurant on Praslin. **Drink:** A wide range of wines, spirits and other alcoholic beverages is available in the Seychelles. *Seybrew*, a German style lager, is made locally. The same company also produces *Guinness* under licence and soft drinks. Local tea is also popular – see below under *Shopping*. A hotel licence permits hotel residents to drink at any time. Alcohol can be sold to anyone between 1400-1800 Monday to Friday, and 0800-1200 and 1400-1800 Saturday. Other bars open 1130-1500 and 1800-2200. It is illegal to drink alcohol on any road or in public.
NIGHTLIFE: Largely undeveloped and unsophisticated. There is, however, much to be enjoyed in the evenings, and a speciality is the local *camtolet* music, often accompanied by dancers. Several hotels have evening barbecues and dinner dances. Theatre productions are often staged (in Creole, French and English) and there are cinemas in Victoria and casinos at *Beau Vallon Bay Hotel* and the *Plantation Club*.
SHOPPING: Local handicrafts include work with textiles (such as batik), fibres (such as basketwares, tablemats and hats) and wood (such as traditional furniture, ornaments and model boats). Pottery and paintings may also be bought. Special souvenirs might include a coco-de-mer or jewellery made from green snail shells. Tea growing and manufacturing in the Seychelles is done on a small scale. Local tea can be bought in the shops or when visiting the tea factory on Mahé, where many blends of tea may be sampled at the *Tea Tavern*. Vanilla is cultivated as a climbing plant around the base of trees because pollination can be done by hand. Pods can be bought in shops and used as flavouring. Cinnamon grows wild on all the islands. It can be bought as oil or in quills made from dried bark which can be freshly grated before use. **Shopping hours:** 0800-1700 Monday to Friday and 0800-1200 Saturday. Some shops close 1200-1300 weekdays.

SPORT: Golf: The *Reef Hotel* has a 9-hole golf course at Anse Aux Pins, on Mahé, and visitors can arrange temporary membership at the clubhouse, as well as hire equipment. **Fishing:** Game fishing is a comparatively new sport in the Seychelles, but the abundance of fish has already made the islands popular with enthusiasts. Fishing seasons are governed by weather conditions: from May to September, the trade winds blow from the southeast; and from November to February, from the northwest. Black, blue and striped marlin, sailfish, yellowfish and dogtooth tuna, wahoo and barracuda are just a few of the game fish found in these tropical waters. **Boat charters:** Power boats, cabin cruisers and yachts are available for charter for anglers and others wishing to explore the islands at their own pace. Vessels may be booked in advance by the day, week or month. Reservations may be made at local agents or through *The Marine Charter Association*, PO Box 469, Victoria, Mahé. Tel: 22126. Telex: 2359 MCA SZ. **Diving:** Coral reef diving is perhaps the main sporting attraction in the Seychelles. Spearfishing is forbidden and, perhaps as a consequence, the fish are not afraid of people. The clear water makes conditions perfect for underwater photography. The coastal waters are a haven for 100 species of coral and over 900 species of fish. The *Seychelles Underwater Centre* is run by professional divers and is affiliated to the *British Sub Aqua Club*. The address is PO Box 384, Victoria, Mahé. Tel: 47357. **Watersports:** Windsurfers, canoes, sailing dinghies, etc may be hired on the more popular beaches, such as Beau Vallon Bay on Mahé, and water-skiing and paragliding are available at many other resort areas. Equipment may be hired. **Other:** There are also opportunities for **squash, tennis** and **badminton.**

SPECIAL EVENTS: The following events are celebrated annually in the Seychelles:

End Sep *La Fête La Digue Annual Regatta*. **End Oct** *Creole Festival*. **Nov** *Annual Fishing Competition*.

SOCIAL CONVENTIONS: The people live a simple and unsophisticated island life and tourism is carefully controlled to protect the unspoilt charm of the islands. Before the international airport opened in 1971, the islands could be reached only by sea, and since they are miles from anywhere, visitors were few and far between and the people were little influenced by the outside world. They developed their own language and culture which – like so many things in the islands – are unique. Shaking hands is the customary form of greeting. The Seychellois are extremely hospitable and welcome guests into their homes. When visiting someone's home a gift is acceptable. A mixture of imperial and metric systems is in operation. For example, petrol is dispensed in litres, whilst bars sell bottled and draught beer in half-pint measures. Casual wear is essential and formal clothes are only worn by church-goers. Swimwear should only be worn on the beaches. **Tipping:** Tips in restaurants, hotels, taxi drivers, porters etc are usually 5-10% of the bill or fare. All hotel and restaurant tariffs include a service charge, but payment is not obligatory.

BUSINESS PROFILE

ECONOMY: During the early 1970s, tourism overtook agriculture as the largest sector in the Seychelles economy and now accounts for approximately 20% of domestic economic activity and draws 90% of Seychelles' foreign exchange earnings. The rapid overall growth the economy experienced during the 1970s as a result of the tourist boom has faltered in the 1980s, undermined by high fares, insufficient routes and internal political uncertainty. Shaken by the prospect of economic decline so soon after the advent of prosperity, the Government is seeking to diversify the economy. The fishing fleet is to be modernised and expanded and a 200-mile exclusion zone has been declared. Local industry is concentrated in brewing and tobacco, plastics, soap and detergent; there is also some small-scale manufacturing. The National Oil Corporation was set up to encourage exploration after gas was discovered offshore in 1980. Fish, copra and cinnamon are the main exports while food, fuel, manufactured goods and transport equipment are the main imports. Seychelles' geographical position allows for a thriving re-export business.

BUSINESS: Businessmen do not wear suits and ties, although a smart appearance is advised. Most executives speak English and/or French. **Office hours:** 0800-1200 and 1300-1600 Monday to Friday.

COMMERCIAL INFORMATION: The following organisation can offer advice: Seychelles Chamber of Commerce and Industry, PO Box 443, 38 Premier Building, Victoria, Mahé. Tel: 23812.

HISTORY & GOVERNMENT

HISTORY: It is thought that the Seychelles Archipelago may have been visited by early Arab, Phoenician and Indonesian traders but the first recorded sighting was by the Portuguese navigator Vasco da Gama at the beginning of the 16th century. Until as little as 200 years ago, it remained uninhabited. In 1756 French planters claimed Mahé and seven other islands for France. The archipelago, until then known as the Amirantes (Admiral da Gama had named them after himself), was re-named in honour of the French king's accountant, Vicomte Moreau de Séchelles. The Seychelles were ceded to Britain in 1814, following the Napoleonic Wars. The British placed the group under the administration of Mauritius, settled it with 'old India hands', men and women with proven tropical expertise. For the next 150 years, isolated from the rest of the world and all but ignored by the major European powers, the Seychelles developed its own traditions, language and culture. The islands became a Crown Colony in 1903. Internal self-government was granted in 1975 and independence a year later. By now, tourism had become the major contributor to the GDP; one-third of the new republic's working population were employed by the tourist industry. This isolated island paradise might have seemed an unlikely setting for the cut and thrust of Cold War politics, but in the years after independence, Seychellois politics was dominated by precisely that. The first post-independence Prime Minister, James Mancham, leader of the Seychelles Democratic Party, believed that tourism and offshore financial services offered the best economic future for the islands. The Seychelles People's United Party, under Albert René, thought otherwise. While Mancham attended the 1977 Commonwealth Conference, armed SPUP supporters staged a coup and installed René at the head of a one-party state. In foreign affairs, the René government pursued a policy of strategic non-alignment, trading with and receiving aid from both superpowers. In the last few years, the Government has felt at ease, with a healthy economic outlook, generated by recent liberalisation policies and political stability. It had no intention, apparently, of opening up the political system. However, international pressure, mainly from aid donors France and Britain, for the Seychelles to follow the African trend by introducing multi-party politics had its effect in December 1991 when René announced to a stunned People's Progressive Party (renamed from SPUP) congress that presidential elections would be held before the end of 1992. James Mancham, who said that he would return to the islands when elections were held, did so as leader of the newly-formed Democratic Party. The first poll, which was contested by the ruling People's Progressive Party, the Democratic Party, the Liberal Party and the Parti Seselwa (Creole), was for the 20-person membership of the constitutional commission. With 58% of the vote, the PPP will enjoy an absolute majority on the commission.

GOVERNMENT: Under the constitution adopted in 1979, Seychelles is a single-party state. The President holds executive power, while legislation is in the hands of the 25-member National Assembly. Both President and Assembly are subject to popular elections every five years.

CLIMATE

The islands lie outside the cyclone belt but receive monsoon rains from November to February with the northwest trade winds. This hot and humid season gives way to a period of cooler weather (but temperatures rarely fall below 24°C) and rougher seas when the trade winds blow from the southeast (May to September).

Required clothing: Informal lightweight cottons and linens.

VICTORIA Seychelles (5m)

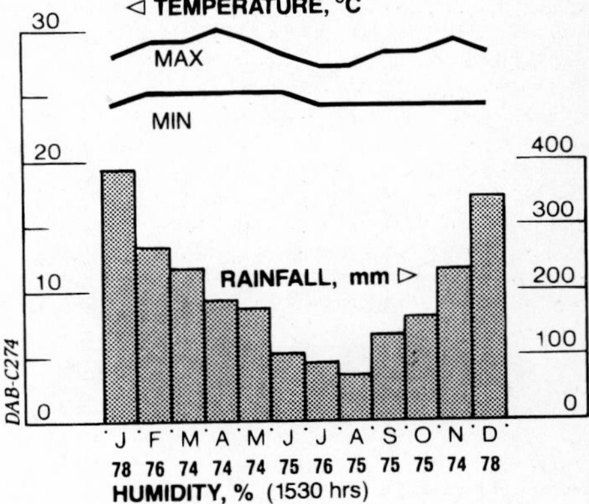

TEMPERATURE CONVERSIONS
-20 -10 0°C 10 20 30 40
0 10 20 30°F40 50 60 70 80 90 100

RAINFALL CONVERSIONS
0mm 200 400 600 800
0in 5 10 15 20 25 30

SIERRA LEONE

□ international airport

Location: West Africa.

Ministry of Tourism and Cultural Affairs
Wallace Johnson Street
Freetown, Sierra Leone
Tel: (22) 26345.

High Commission for the Republic of Sierra Leone
33 Portland Place
London W1N 3AG
Tel: (071) 636 6483. Fax: (071) 323 3159. Opening hours: 1000-1300 and 1430 to 1530 Monday to Friday.

National Tourist Board of Sierra Leone
375 Upper Richmond Road West
London SW14 7NX
Tel: (081) 392 9188. Fax: (081) 392 1318. Opening hours: 0900-1800 Monday to Friday.

British High Commission
Standard Chartered Bank Building of Sierra Leone Ltd
Lightfoot Boston Street
Freetown, Sierra Leone
Tel: (22) 3961. Telex: 3235.

Embassy of the Republic of Sierra Leone
1701 19th Street, NW
Washington, DC
20009
Tel: (202) 939 9261.
Also deals with enquiries from Canada.

Embassy of the United States of America
Corner of Walpole and Siaka Stevens Streets
Freetown, Sierra Leone
Tel: (22) 226 481 *or* 226 155. Fax: (22) 225 471. Telex: 3509 USEMBSL.

AREA: 71,740 sq km (27,699 sq miles).
POPULATION: 4,151,000 (1990 estimate).
POPULATION DENSITY: 57.9 per sq km.
CAPITAL: Freetown. **Population:** 469,776 (1985).
GEOGRAPHY: Sierra Leone is bordered to the northwest, north and northeast by Guinea Republic, and to the southeast by Liberia. To the south and southwest lies the Atlantic Ocean. A flat plain up to 110km (70 miles) wide stretches the length of the coast except for the Freetown peninsula, where the Sierra Lyoa Mountains rise to 1000m (3280ft). In some coastal areas, sand bars have formed that stretch out as far as 112km (70 miles). Behind the coastal plain is the central forested area, drained by eight principal rivers, which has been cleared for agriculture. The land rises in altitude towards the east to the Guinea Highlands, a high plateau with peaks rising to over 1830m (6000ft) in the Loma Mountains and Tingi Hills area. The population represents a wide cross-section of tribal origins with some groups predominant in certain areas, particularly Mende in the south and Temne in the west and central areas.
LANGUAGE: The official language is English. Krio is more widely spoken. Other local dialects are Mende and Temne.
RELIGION: Principally Animist with Muslim and Christian minorities.
TIME: GMT.
ELECTRICITY: 230/240 volts AC, 50Hz. Supply subject to fluctuations.
COMMUNICATIONS: Telephone: IDD is available. Country code: 232. **Telex/telegram:** Facilities at Slecom House, 7 Wallace Johnson Street, Freetown. **Post:** Airmail to Europe takes about five days. **Press:** Sierra Leone's English-language daily is *The Daily Mail.*
BBC World Service and Voice of America frequencies: From time to time these change. See the section *How to Use this Book* for more information.

BBC:				
MHz	17.79	15.07	15.40	9.410
Voice of America:				
MHz	21.49	15.60	9.525	6.035

PASSPORT/VISA

Regulations and requirements may be subject to change at short notice, and you are advised to contact the appropriate diplomatic or consular authority before finalising travel arrangements. Details of these may be found at the head of this country's entry. Any numbers in the chart refer to the footnotes below.

	Passport Required?	Visa Required?	Return Ticket Required?
Full British	Yes	Yes	Yes
BVP	Not valid	-	-
Australian	Yes	Yes	Yes
Canadian	Yes	Yes	Yes
USA	Yes	Yes	Yes
Other EC	Yes	Yes	Yes
Japanese	Yes	Yes	Yes

Restricted entry: 'White' nationals of South Africa should check with the High Commission, since visa applications are judged individually.
PASSPORTS: Valid passport required by all.
British Visitors Passport: Not accepted.
VISAS: Required by all except:
(a) nationals of Benin, Burkina Faso, Cape Verde, Côte d'Ivoire, Gambia, Ghana, Guinea Republic, Guinea-Bissau, Mali, Mauritania, Niger, Nigeria, Senegal and Togo;
(b) holders of a re-entry permit.
Types of visa: Tourist and Business. Cost: £20 (Tourist); £30 (Business).
Validity: Entry Permits and visas generally allow a stay of 1 week extendable up to 6 months in Sierra Leone.
Application to: Consulate (or Consular Section at Embassy or High Commission). For addresses, see top of entry.
Application requirements: (a) Completed application form. (b) 3 passport-size photos. (c) Passport. (d) Company letter for Business visa.
Working days required: 3 days. Several weeks where referral to authorities in Sierra Leone is necessary.

MONEY

Currency: Leone (Le) = 100 cents. Notes are in denominations of Le100, 50, 20, 10, 5, 2 and 1. Coins are in denominations of Le1, and 100, 50, 20, 10, 5 and 1 cents. In June 1986, a system of 'floating' exchange rates was introduced to correct persistent over-valuation of the Leone.
Credit cards: American Express is widely accepted and Access/Mastercard, Diners Club and Visa have limited acceptance. Check with your credit card company for details of merchant acceptability and other facilities which might be available.
Exchange rate indicators: The following figures are included as a guide to the movements of the Leone against Sterling and the US Dollar:

Date:	Oct '89	Oct '90	Oct '91	Oct '92
£1.00=	99.26	330.50	608.12	798.85
$1.00=	62.86	169.18	350.40	503.37

Currency restrictions: The import and export of local currency is limited to Le20. Foreign currency must be declared on entry and the amount exported is restricted to £25 or equivalent. An amount of at least US$100 or equivalent must be exchanged on arrival in Sierra Leone.
Banking hours: 0800-1330 Monday to Thursday; 0800-1400 Friday.

DUTY FREE

The following may be imported into Sierra Leone without incurring customs duty:
200 cigarettes or 225g tobacco;
1.136 litres of wine or spirits;
1.136 litres of perfume.

PUBLIC HOLIDAYS

Public holidays observed in Sierra Leone are as follows:
Mar 25 '93 Start of Eid al-Fitr. **Apr 9-12** Easter. **Apr 27** Independence Day. **Jun 1** Start of Eid al-Adha (Feast of the Sacrifice). **Aug 30** Mouloud (Prophet's Birthday). **Dec 25-26** Christmas. **Jan 1 '94** New Year's Day. **Mar** Eid al-Fitr.
Note: Muslim festivals are timed according to local sightings of various phases of the Moon and the dates given above are approximations. During the lunar month of Ramadan that precedes Eid al-Fitr, Muslims fast during the day and feast at night and normal business patterns may be interrupted. Many restaurants are closed during the day and there may be restrictions on smoking and drinking. Some disruption may continue into Eid al-Fitr itself. Eid al-Fitr and Eid al-Adha may last anything from two to ten days, depending on the region. For more information see the section *World of Islam* at the back of the book.

HEALTH

Regulations and requirements may be subject to change at short notice, and you are advised to contact your doctor well in advance of your intended date of departure. Any numbers in the chart refer to the footnotes below.

	Special Precautions?	Certificate Required?
Yellow Fever	Yes	1
Cholera	Yes	2
Typhoid & Polio	Yes	-
Malaria	3	-
Food & Drink	4	-

[1]: A yellow fever certificate is required of travellers arriving from infected areas.
[2]: Following WHO guidelines issued in 1973, a cholera vaccination certificate is not a condition of entry to Sierra Leone. However, cholera is a serious risk in this country and precautions are essential. Up-to-date advice should be sought before deciding whether these precautions should include vaccination, as medical opinion is divided over its effectiveness. See the *Health* section at the back of the book.
[3]: Malaria risk exists, predominantly in the malignant *falciparum* form, all year throughout the country. Resistance to chloroquine has been reported.
[4]: All water should be regarded as being potentially contaminated. Water used for drinking, brushing teeth or making ice should have first been boiled or otherwise sterilised.

SIERRA LEONE | **HEALTH REGULATIONS** | **VISA REGULATIONS** | Code-Link

GALILEO/WORLDSPAN

TI-DFT/FNA/HE

TI-DFT/FNA/VI

SABRE

TIDFT/FNA/HE

TIDFT/FNA/VI

To access this information on your CRS, swipe the barcode with a light pen or type in the text under the barcode. For more information, see the introduction *How to Use This Book.*

Milk is unpasteurised and should be boiled. Powdered or tinned milk is available and is advised, but make sure that it is reconstituted with pure water. Avoid dairy products which are likely to have been made from unboiled milk. Only eat well-cooked meat and fish, preferably served hot. Pork, salad and mayonnaise may carry increased risk. Vegetables should be cooked and fruit peeled.
Rabies is present. For those at high risk, vaccination before arrival should be considered. If you are bitten abroad seek medical advice without delay. For more information consult the *Health* section at the back of the book.
Bilharzia (schistosomiasis) is present. Avoid swimming and paddling in fresh water. Swimming pools which are well-chlorinated and maintained are safe.
Health care: Medical facilities are extremely limited and are, if anything, continuing to decline. According to UN estimates, Sierra Leone has the highest death rate, the second-highest infant mortality rate (200 out of every 1000 infants die within a year of birth) and the lowest life expectancy of any nation in the world (an average age of 34 recorded for the years 1980-1985). Christian missions and foreign aid organisations provide some medical facilities and social services. Health insurance is strongly recommended. It is advisable to take personal medical supplies.

TRAVEL - International

AIR: Sierra Leone's national airline is *Sierra National Airlines*. It currently operates flights only between Freetown and Paris. Other airlines serving Sierra Leone are *Air Gambia*, *KLM* and *UTA*.
Approximate flight time: From *London* to Freetown is 6 hours 30 minutes (direct flight).
International airport: *Freetown (FNA)* (Lungi), is 24km (18 miles) north of the city (travel time – 2 hours). There is a hovercraft/ferry link as well as taxi and bus services to the city. Airport facilities include a post office, bar, shops and currency exchange.
Departure tax: Le5000 on international departures. Transit passengers are exempt.
SEA: The principal port is Freetown which has services to Liberia and Guinea Republic.
RAIL: There are no passenger services at present.
ROAD: There are routes from Guinea Republic and Liberia, but access depends on the prevailing political situation. Contact the Embassy or High Commission for up-to-date information.

TRAVEL - Internal

AIR: *Sierra National Airlines* run daily flights to Hastings, Kenema, Bo, Gbangbatoke, Yengema and Bonthe.
SEA: Ferries connect all coastal ports. For details contact local authorities.
ROAD: Sierra Leone has over 6440km (4000 miles) of roads. Although the principal highways have a bitumen surface, the secondary roads are poorly maintained and often impassable during the rainy season. **Bus:** Local and long-distance bus services are operated by the *Sierra Leone Road Transport Corporation*. Buses are fast and cheap and connect all the major centres. **Documentation:** An International Driving Permit is required.
URBAN: Limited bus services in Freetown are operated by the *Road Transport Corporation*, though most of the city's public transport is provided by minibuses and taxis.

ACCOMMODATION

There are hotels in Freetown of international standard with air-conditioning and swimming pools. It is always advisable to make reservations in advance. Additionally, there are three luxury hotels located on the peninsular at Lakka and Tokay. The YMCA in Freetown offers clean, cheap accommodation with shared bathroom and kitchen facilities. Hotels in the interior are rare, though there is some fairly rudimentary accommodation in Bo and Kenema. There are also resthouses, for which application must be made to the Ministry of the Interior; guests must bring their own linen.

RESORTS & EXCURSIONS

The most accessible part of Sierra Leone for the tourist is the **Freetown Peninsula**, where palm trees shade sandy bays. From *Leicester Peak* superb views of the city between the sea and the mountains unfold below, and a narrow, steep road through the mountains leads to the old Creole Villages (dating from 1800) of **Leicester, Gloucester** and **Regent**. The area was chosen as a resettlement area for liberated slaves who built the villages of **Sussex, York, Kent, Waterloo, Hastings** and **Wellington.** The roads cross the picturesque *Grafton Valley* and run past *Guma Valley* to *Dam Lake*. The beaches on the peninsula, such as *Bureh Town* or *Number Two River*, are beautiful and ideal for swimming. **Freetown** itself, surrounded by thickly vegetated hills, is both a colourful and historic port. Attractions include a 500-year-old cotton tree; the museum; the *De Ruyter Stone*; *Government Wharf* and *'King's Yard'* (where freed slaves waited to be given land); *Fourah Bay College*, the oldest university in West Africa; *Marcon's Church*, built in 1820; and the *City Hotel*, immortalised in Graham Greene's novel 'The Heart of the Matter'. The *King Jimmy Market* and the bazaars offer a colourful spectacle.
There is a boat trip up the *Rokel River* to **Bunce Island**, one of the first slave trading stations of West Africa.
GAME PARKS: Permits, obtainable from the Ministry of Agriculture and Forestry in Freetown, are necessary for visits to Reserves, and a guide is provided. For hunting, a special pass is required, for which 48 hours notice is needed.
The Outamba-Kilimi National Park in northern Sierra Leone, which can be reached from Freetown by road or air, offers varied and spectacular scenery and, at this and other reserves, there are game animals such as elephants, chimpanzees and pigmy hippos. The **Sakanbiarwa** plant reserve has an extensive collection of orchids, which are at their best early in the year.

SOCIAL PROFILE

FOOD & DRINK: Various restaurants in the capital serve English, French, Armenian and Lebanese food. African food is served in many hotels; local dishes include excellent fish, lobster and prawns, exotic fruit and vegetables.
NIGHTLIFE: Freetown has nightclubs and two casinos and there is music, dancing and local entertainment arranged by the hotels along Lumley Beach in the Cape Sierra district.
SHOPPING: Opening hours: 0800-1200 and 1400-1700 Monday to Saturday.
SPORT: The tourist resorts in the Cape Sierra, Lakka and Tokay have good beaches with safe **swimming** and there are facilities for **windsurfing, yachting** and game **fishing**. The beautiful coral in the clear waters off York and Lumley beaches are an added attraction for **divers**. There is also a first-class **golf** course. In Freetown, the Siaka stadium and sports complex has facilities for **football,** swimming, diving, **basketball, gymnastics** and **athletics.** Domestic football league matches can be seen at the stadium.
SOCIAL CONVENTIONS: The majority of people in Sierra Leone still live a traditional, agricultural way of life, with ruling chiefs, religions and secret societies which preserve social stability and local music, dance and traditions. When visiting the country normal social courtesies should be observed and handshaking is the normal form of greeting. It is usual to be entertained in a hotel or restaurant, particularly for business visitors. Small tokens of appreciation, a momento from home or a company souvenir, are always welcome. Casual wear is suitable everywhere. Men are rarely expected to wear suits and ties, except for very important occasions. **Tipping:** Most hotels and restaurants include a service charge of 10-15%. Taxi drivers don't expect tips.

BUSINESS PROFILE

ECONOMY: One of Africa's poorest countries, agriculture employs over two-thirds of the workforce in Sierra Leone, growing coffee, cocoa, palm kernels, nuts, ginger and cassava. Fishing is also significant. Industry is confined to light manufacturing, mostly of consumer goods such as textiles, furniture and suitcases. The mainstay of the economy is mining, which supplies the bulk of the country's foreign exchange: diamonds are the main commodity, with gold (which is growing in importance), bauxite and titanium ore making up the balance. Titanium is the most lucrative of these products and production is likely to increase rapidly following the discovery of new deposits. Sierra Leone has had problems, however, with its oil industry: although deposits have been identified they are proving difficult to develop and Sierra Leone has had to buy most of its needs on the world market, using up much precious foreign exchange. In 1986 a barter arrangement was reached with Britain which eased the pressure. Since then Sierra Leone has entered into agreements with the IMF, all of which have been aborted because of the failure to curb expenditure and reduce its debt. The UK is the largest trading partner, followed by the USA, Germany and The Netherlands.
BUSINESS: English is the most common language in business circles. Appointments and punctuality are expected. Visiting cards are essential. September to June are the best months for business visits. **Office hours:** 0800-1200 and 1400-1645 Monday to Friday.
COMMERCIAL INFORMATION: The following organisation can offer advice: Sierra Leone Chamber of Commerce, Industry and Agriculture, PO Box 502, 5th Floor, Guma Building, Lamina, Sankoh Street, Freetown. Tel: (22) 26305.

HISTORY & GOVERNMENT

HISTORY: In the late 18th century, British philanthropists decided that freed slaves should have a homeland in Africa and after much discussion amongst themselves (but not with the indigenous people of West Africa) they chose a recently acquired territory which became known as Sierra Leone. In 1821, Sierra Leone was merged with Gambia and Gold Coast (now Ghana) to create the British West African Territories. Over the next 50 years, the British navy landed 70,000 slaves in Sierra Leone; the population of Freetown, the capital, was further boosted by the migration of indigenous tribes from the interior. Sierra Leone made a quiet transition to independence, which it achieved in 1961, under the Sierra Leone People's Party led by the Margais (Sir Milton Margai and his half-brother Sir Albert). A disputed election in 1967, won by the rival All Peoples' Congress (APC) under the leadership of Siaka Stevens, led to a brief period of military government, ended by a second coup the following year which allowed the APC to form a civilian government under Dr Siaka Stevens. A republican constitution was adopted in 1971, with Stevens as President, to be replaced in 1978 by a constitution allowing the APC to be the sole legal party. Elections in 1985 gave the presidency and leadership of the APC to Major General Joseph Momoh, the sole candidate, and he began a programme of administrative and economic reform. The IMF and World Bank offered enthusiastic support initially, but as the Momoh government proved increasingly reluctant to implement the measures recommended by the two institutions, their support faded; a much-vaunted Structural Adjustment Programme was discarded. During the late 1980s Sierra Leone's economy drifted into decline until the end of the decade when uncontrolled government expenditure and a sudden drop in export earnings brought on a major crisis. Foreign policy over the last few years has been dominated by poor relations with its principal neighbours, Liberia and Nigeria. Difficulties with Nigeria date from Sierra Leone's support for the Biafran rebels during the 1967-70 Nigerian civil war. Meanwhile, relations with Liberia are in crisis and now pose a major threat to Sierra Leone, as several armed groups launch incursions into Sierra Leone. Mediation, perhaps by Côte d'Ivoire, appeared to offer the best prospect of a settlement. That was, until disaffected junior officers, tired of fighting without pay for an increasingly corrupt regime, launched a coup of their own at the end of April 1992. At the head of the new National Provisional Ruling Council was 27-year-old Captain Valentine Strasser. The policies of the new government have not yet taken shape, but the clear priority is to bring the war with Taylor's forces to an end. After that, the restoration of the economy, devastated by corruption and mismanagement, is imperative. There is a wide expectation in the country that Strasser and his youthful colleagues, who are somewhat reminiscent of Thomas Sankara and company in Burkina Faso, can turn around Sierra Leone's fortunes following its decline into one of the world's poorest nations.
GOVERNMENT: Executive power is vested in the President, aided by two Vice-Presidents. The legislature is the single-chamber House of Representatives, which has 104 members, 85 of whom are elected by universal adult suffrage for terms of five years; the remainder are regional leaders, known as Paramount Chiefs, and presidential appointees.

CLIMATE

Tropical and humid all year. The best time to visit is between November and April. The coastal areas are cooled by sea breezes. In December and January the dry dusty *Harmattan* wind blows from the Sahara. During the rainy season between May and November rainfall can be torrential.
Required clothing: Tropical clothing recommended with an umbrella during the rainy season.

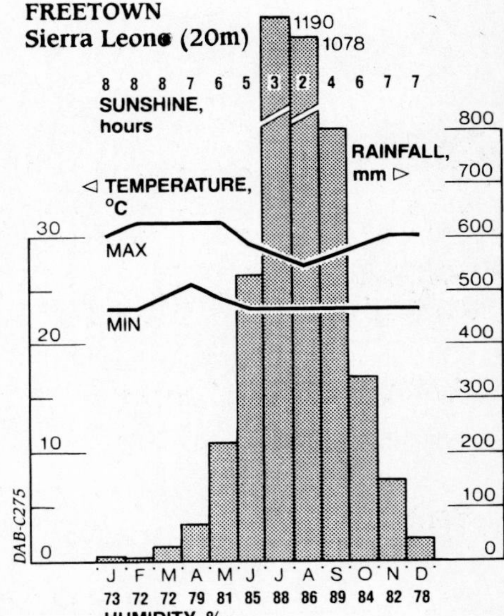

SINGAPORE

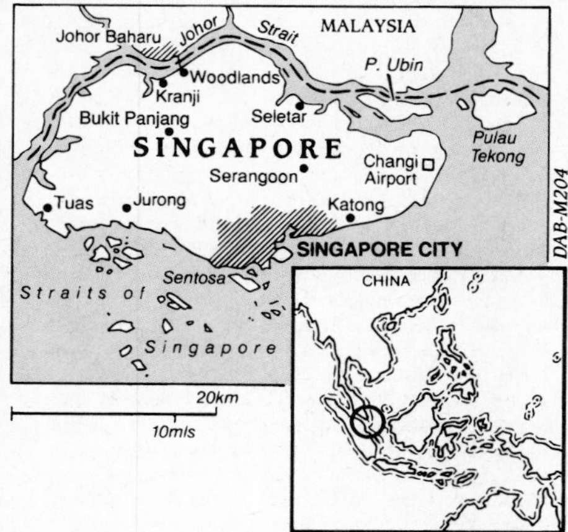

Location: South-East Asia.

Singapore Tourist Promotion Board
Raffles City Tower #36-04
250 North Bridge Road
Singapore 0617
Tel: 339 6622. Fax: 339 9423. Telex: 33375.
High Commission for the Republic of Singapore
9 Wilton Crescent
London SW1X 8SA
Tel: (071) 235 8315. Fax: (071) 245 6583. Telex: 51262564.
Visa Section: Tel: (071) 235 5441. Fax: (071) 245 6583. Telex: 262564. Opening hours: 1000-1230 and 1400-1600 Monday to Friday.
Singapore Tourist Promotion Board
1st Floor, Carrington House
126-130 Regent Street
London W1R 5FE
Tel: (071) 437 0033. Fax: (071) 734 2191. Telex: 893491 STBLON G. Opening hours: 0900-1700 Monday to Friday.
British High Commission
Tanglin Road
Singapore 1024
Tel: 473 9333. Fax: 475 2320 *or* 475 9706. Telex: 21218 UKREP SP RS.

Embassy of the Republic of Singapore
1824 R Street, NW
Washington, DC
20009
Tel: (202) 667 7555. Fax: (202) 265 7915.
High Commission of Singapore
c/o The Permanent Mission of the Republic of Singapore to the United Nations
25th Floor, Two United Nations Plaza
New York, NY
10017
Tel: (212) 826 0840/1/2/3/4. Fax: (212) 826 2964.
Also deals with enquiries from Canada.
Singapore Tourist Promotion Board
NBR, 12th Floor
590 Fifth Avenue
New York, NY
10036
Tel: (212) 302 4861. Fax: (212) 302 4801. Telex: 220843 SING UR.
Office also in: Chicago.
Embassy of the United States of America
30 Hill Street
Singapore 0617
Tel: 338 0251. Fax: 338 4550.
Consulate of Singapore
c/o Russel and Dumoulin
1700-1075 West Georgia Street
Vancouver, BC
V6E 3G2
Singapore Tourist Promotion Board
Suite 1112
175 Bloor Street East
Toronto, Ontario
M4W 3R8
Tel: (416) 323 9139. Fax: (416) 323 3514. Telex: 06 217510 SINGA POR TOR.
Canadian High Commission
PO Box 845
14th and 15th Floors, IBM Towers
80 Anson Road
Singapore 9016
Tel: 225 6363. Fax: 225 2450. Telex: 21277 DOMCAN RS.

Chettiar Temple

AREA: 626.4 sq km (241.9 sq miles).
POPULATION: 2,685,400 (1989 estimate).
POPULATION DENSITY: 4287 per sq km.
GEOGRAPHY: The island of Singapore is situated off the southern extremity of the Malay Peninsula, to which it is joined by a causeway carrying a road, railway and waterpipe. The Straits of Johor between the island and the mainland are about 1km (0.75 miles) wide. The Republic of Singapore includes some 58 islets. It is a mainly flat country with low hills, the highest being Bukit Timah at 163m (545ft). In the northeast of the island large areas have been reclaimed, and much of the original jungle and swamp covering the low-lying areas has been cleared.
LANGUAGE: Chinese (Mandarin), English, Malay and Tamil. Most Singaporeans are bilingual and speak English, which is used for business and administration.
RELIGION: Confucian, Taoist, Buddhist, Christian, Hindu and Muslim.
TIME: GMT + 8.
ELECTRICITY: 220/240 volts AC, 50Hz. Plug fittings of the 3-pin square type are in use. Many hotels have 110-volt outlets.
COMMUNICATIONS: Telephone: Full IDD is available. Country code: 65. **Fax:** There are services at many major hotels and at the Telecoms buildings in Robinson Road and Exeter Road. **Telex/telegram:** Telegrams can be sent from post offices, hotels, the Central Telegraph Office at 35 Robinson Road and Comcentre near Orchard Road. Outgoing telexes can be sent from public telex booths, Telecoms service counters and at many hotels. Incoming international telexes are accepted only when replying to an outgoing telex from Singapore and when sender is present. **Post:** Airmail to Europe takes up to a week. There are limited postal facilities at many hotels. Post office hours: 0900-1700 Monday to Friday, except Wednesday when they are open until 2100. The Airport and Orchard Point branches are open 0800-2000 daily. **Press:** The two local English-language newspapers

TB23/92 UK
Blazing satay, ice-cold coconut juice.
Laughing buddhas, dancing lions, eight year olds that are eight feet tall.
Space-age shopping centres and quaint old shops in historic back lanes.
High tea at 700 feet above sea level.
Singapore
The most surprising tropical island on Earth
For more information contact Singapore Tourist Promotion Board. Tel: 071 437 0033.

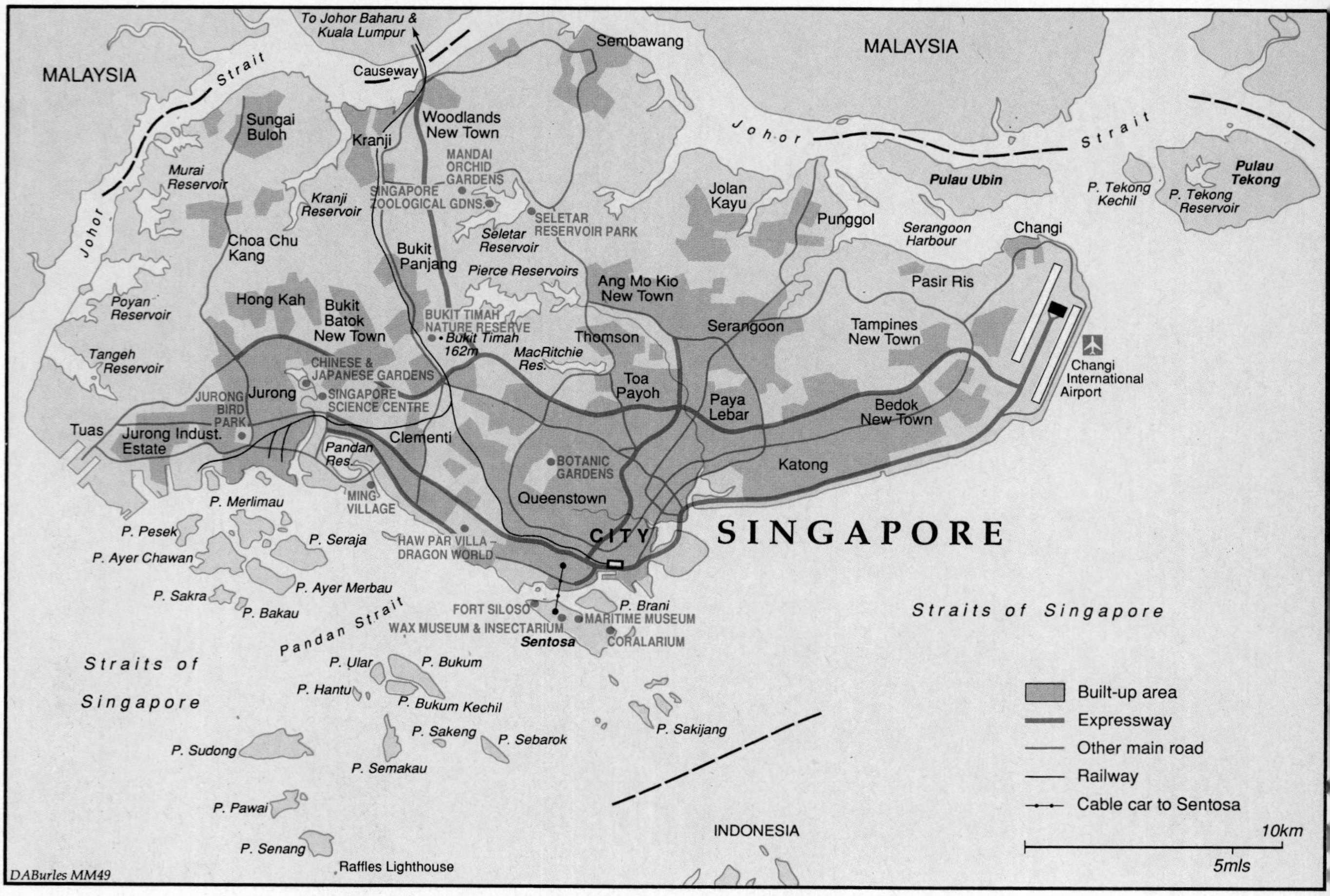

are *Business Times* and *Straits Times*.

BBC World Service and Voice of America frequencies: From time to time these change. See the section *How to Use this Book* for more information.

BBC:

MHz	88.9			
Voice of America:				
MHz	15.43	11.72	5.985	1.143

PASSPORT/VISA

Regulations and requirements may be subject to change at short notice, and you are advised to contact the appropriate diplomatic or consular authority before finalising travel arrangements. Details of these may be found at the head of this country's entry. Any numbers in the chart refer to the footnotes below.

	Passport Required?	Visa Required?	Return Ticket Required?
Full British	Yes	No	Yes
BVP	Not valid	-	-
Australian	Yes	No	Yes
Canadian	Yes	No	Yes
USA	Yes	No	Yes
Other EC	Yes	No	Yes
Japanese	Yes	No	Yes

Note: (a) Women in an advanced state of pregnancy must obtain a Social Visit Pass prior to arrival; apply at the nearest Singapore Embassy or High Commission. (b) Severe penalties are imposed on those found in possession of narcotics; the death penalty is in force for those convicted of trafficking in heroin or morphine.

PASSPORTS: Valid passport required by all.

British Visitors Passport: Not acceptable.

VISAS: Required only by the following:
(a) nationals of Afghanistan, Algeria, Cambodia, China, India, Iraq, Jordan, Laos, Lebanon, Syria, Tunisia, USSR, Vietnam and Yemen;
(b) those holding Refugee Travel Documents issued by Middle East countries to refugees from Palestine, Hong Kong ID cards or travel documents of Arab countries.
Visitors from Thailand and the Philippines need a visa if their stay exceeds 14 days. All other nationals require a 14-day Social Visit Pass, which is issued on arrival, provided the traveller holds a valid national passport, confirmed onward or return travel documentation, and sufficient funds to cover expenses for duration of stay. For a stay of up to 2 weeks, the passport has to be valid for 3 months after departure from Singapore. For stays exceeding 2 weeks, the passport has to be valid for six months after departure from Singapore. The Social Visit Pass can be extended to a maximum of 3 months on application to the Singapore Immigration Department in Singapore.

Types of visa: *Visa* (enquire at Embassy or High Commission for costs), *Social Visit/Student Pass* (cost dependent on nationality of applicant, for UK passport holders approximately £5.10, payable in cash or by postal order) and *Professional Visit Pass* (cost: S$25, to be paid on arrival in local currency). *Transit Visas* are not normally required if the visitor has confirmed onward travel documents and leaves Singapore within 14 days. This facility is not, however, available to nationals of the following countries: Afghanistan, Algeria, Cambodia, China, India, Iraq, Jordan, Laos, Lebanon, Syria, Tunisia, USSR, Vietnam and Yemen.

Note: Holders of valid USSR or Chinese passports *may* visit for a maximum of 24 hours without visas provided they hold confirmed onward/return bookings.

Validity: *Social Visit/Student Pass:* Maximum of 3 months. *Professional Visit Pass:* Up to 6 months. *Visa:* Enquire at Embassy or High Commission.

Application to: Consulate (or Consular Section at Embassy or High Commission). For addresses, see top of entry.

Application requirements: *For Social Visit Pass:* (a) Valid travel documents. (b) Sufficient funds. (c) 1 passport-size photo. (d) 2 completed application forms. *For Student Pass:* (a) Valid travel documents. (b) 2 passport-size photos. (c) 2 copies of acceptance letter from college/university in Singapore. (d) 2 completed application forms. *For Professional Visit Pass:* (a) Valid travel documents (photocopy of passport will suffice). (b) 2 passport-size photos. (c) 2 copies respectively of letters from own and sponsoring company. (d) 2 copies of letter stating the reason for visit. (e) 2 completed application forms. *For Visa:* (a) Valid passport. (b) 2 completed application forms. (c) 2 passport-size photos. (d) 2 copies of letter stating reason for visit. (e) 2 copies of a letter from your local sponsor in Singapore.

Working days required: 6-8 weeks.

Temporary residence: Apply to Consulate (or Consular Section of Embassy or High Commission), who will forward application to the authorities in Singapore.

SINGAPORE | **HEALTH REGULATIONS** | **VISA REGULATIONS** | Code-Link

GALILEO/WORLDSPAN

TI-DFT/SIN/HE

TI-DFT/SIN/VI

SABRE

TIDFT/SIN/HE

TIDFT/SIN/VI

To access this information on your CRS, swipe the barcode with a light pen or type in the text under the barcode. For more information, see the introduction *How to Use This Book*.

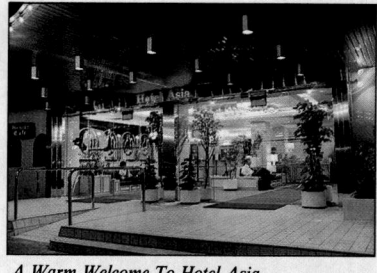

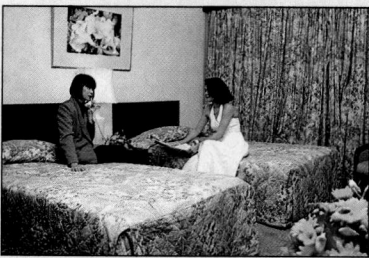

MONEY

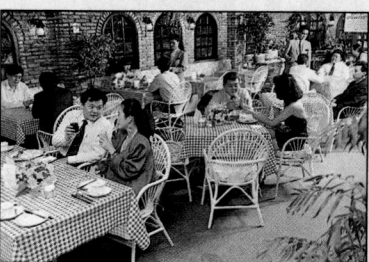

Currency: Singapore Dollar (Sing$) = 100 cents. Notes are in denominations of Sing$10,000, 1000, 500, 100, 50, 20, 10, 5, 2 and 1. Coins are in denominations of Sing$1, and 50, 20, 10, 5 and 1 cents.
The currency of Brunei is also legal tender; 1 Brunei Dollar = 1 Singapore Dollar.
Credit cards: Access/Mastercard, American Express, Diners Club and Visa are widely accepted. Check with your credit card company for details of merchant acceptance and other facilities which may be available.
Exchange rate indicators: The following figures are included as a guide to the movements of the Singapore Dollar against Sterling and the US Dollar:

Date:	**Oct '89**	**Oct '90**	**Oct '91**	**Oct '92**
£1.00=	3.10	3.35	2.93	2.57
$1.00=	1.96	1.72	1.69	1.62

Currency restrictions: There is no restriction on the import and export of local or foreign currency.
Banking hours: 1000-1500 Monday to Friday and 1100-1600 Saturday. Branches of certain major banks on Orchard Road are open 0930-1500 Sunday.

DUTY FREE

The following goods may be imported into Singapore without incurring customs duty:
1 litre of spirits;
1 litre of wine and beer.
Note: These allowances do not apply if arriving from Malaysia.
Prohibited items: Firearms, non-prescribed drugs, all pornographic films and literature. There are severe penalties for possession of narcotics. Export permits are required for arms, ammunition, explosives, animals, precious metals and stones, drugs and poisons.

PUBLIC HOLIDAYS

Public holidays observed in Singapore are as follows:
Mar 25 '93 Hari Raya Puasa (End of Ramadan). **Apr 9** Good Friday. **May 1** Labour Day. **May/Jun** Vesak Day. **Jun 1** Hari Raya Haji (Feast of the Sacrifice). **Aug 9** National Day. **Nov 13** Deepavali. **Dec 25** Christmas Day. **Jan 1 '94** New Year. **Feb 10** Chinese New Year. **Mar** Start of Hari Raya Puasa.

Note: (a) Not all Muslim festivals listed above are national holidays, but all will affect Muslim businesses. Muslim festivals are timed according to local sightings of various phases of the Moon and the dates given above are approximations. During the lunar month of Ramadan that precedes Hari Raya Puasa (Eid al-Fitr), Muslims fast during the day and feast at night and normal business patterns may be interrupted. Many restaurants are closed during the day and there may be restrictions on smoking and drinking. Some disruption may continue into Hari Raya Puasa itself. Hari Raya Puasa and Hari Raya Haji (Eid al-Adha) may last anything from two to ten days, depending on the town. For more information see the section *World of Islam* at the back of the book. (b) Hindu festivals are declared according to local astronomical observations and it is only possible to forecast the month of their occurrence.

HEALTH

Regulations and requirements may be subject to change at short notice, and you are advised to contact your doctor well in advance of your intended date of departure. Any numbers in the chart refer to the footnotes below.

	Special Precautions?	Certificate Required?
Yellow Fever	No	1
Cholera	Yes	-
Typhoid & Polio	2	-
Malaria	No	-
Food & Drink	3	-

[1]: A yellow fever certificate of vaccination is required from persons over one year of age who have been in or passed through any country classified either partly or wholly as a yellow fever endemic zone within the previous six days. The countries formerly classified as endemic zones are considered by the Singapore authorities to be still infected.
[2]: Polio has been eliminated, but there may be a risk of typhoid.
[3]: Mains water is normally chlorinated, and whilst relatively safe may cause mild abdominal upsets. Bottled water is available and is advised for the first few weeks of the stay. Milk is pasteurised and dairy products are safe for consumption. Local meat, poultry, seafood, fruit and vegetables are generally considered safe to eat.
Health care: Singapore General Hospital receives emergency cases and health care is exceptionally good. There is a large private sector. Health insurance is recommended.

TRAVEL - International

AIR: Singapore's national airline is *Singapore Airlines (SQ)*.
Approximate flight times: From *London* to Singapore is 13 hours, from *Los Angeles* is 20 hours 25 minutes, from *New York* is 21 hours 55 minutes and from *Sydney* is 9 hours 15 minutes.
International airport: *Changi (SIN)*, 20km (12 miles) east of the city (travel time – 30 minutes). Buses run to the city every 10 minutes 0700-2330 (not recommended for the elderly or those with baggage). Full taxi service to the city is available by metered cabs, with surcharge of Sing$3 for taxis from the airport and 50% surcharge for fares 2400-0600. Airport facilities include duty-free shops, shops, restaurant, banks, car hire and hotel reservation service.
Departure tax: Sing$5 levied on flights to Brunei and Malaysia, Sing$12 on all other international flights. Transit passengers and children under two years of age are exempt.
SEA: The international port is Singapore itself, the second-busiest in the world.
RAIL: Trains run to Kuala Lumpur and Butterworth (Malaysia) on a route which extends to Bangkok. There are five trains daily between Singapore and Kuala Lumpur, some of which offer air-conditioning and dining cars. There are also overnight trains with sleepers.
ROAD: Singapore is connected to Malaysia and the mainland of Asia by a causeway which crosses the Straits of Johor; bus and coach services operate to the Malaysian town of Johor Bahru and beyond.

TRAVEL - Internal

AIR: Sightseeing flights can be arranged locally through the *Republic of Singapore Flying Club*.
SEA: A ferry leaves The World Trade Centre for Sentosa every 15 minutes from 0730, everyday. There are cruises of the harbour and islands and cruises in junks.

Boat dwellings

ROAD: Bus: There is a well-developed system of local services run by two main companies. The service is cheap and efficient. There are additional peak-hours-only shuttle and minibus services. A flat fare system operates on the one-man routes. A timetable and route map are available from bookstores. **Car hire:** There are several car hire/self-drive firms with offices in the airport and at hotels. **Documentation:** International Driving Permit required.
URBAN: Taxi: These are numerous and relatively cheap. They can be picked up from outside hotels and official ranks or flagged down on the streets. Taxis are often scarce during the rush hours (0700-1015 and 1600-1800) and during heavy rain storms. Fares are metered and only this fare must be paid but there are a number of surcharges: 50 cents on the metered fare for each passenger if more than two adults (three children under 12 count as two adults); Sing$1 for all luggage placed in the boot; 50% on the metered fare for journeys 2400-0600; Sing$3 for all journeys starting at the airport; Sing$2 for all taxis booked by telephone; Sing$3 if booked more than half an hour in advance; Sing$1 for all trips starting in the Central Business District 1600-1900 Monday to Friday and 1200-1500 Saturday. It is possible to negotiate hourly rates for round-island tours. **Metro:** Singapore has one of the most advanced metro systems in the world. When complete, the network of two lines will serve 42 stations over 67km (42 miles) of track. The trains operate 0600-2400 with stations being served on average every six minutes. Fares range from 50 cents to Sing$1.10. **Central Business District:** To reduce congestion, no car or taxi may enter the CBD carrying less than four persons (including the driver) from 0730-1015 and 1630-1830 Monday to Saturday unless an area licence sticker is displayed on the windscreen. These may be purchased for Sing$3 from kiosks on the main roads into the area.

ACCOMMODATION

HOTELS: There is a wide variety of accommodation, characterised by new, high-class hotels (over 60 hotels in Singapore have more than 50 rooms). These have extensive facilities including swimming pools, health clubs, several restaurants, full business services and shopping arcades. It is advisable to make advance reservations. All rooms are subject to 4% tax and 10% service charge. For further information on accommodation in Singapore contact the Singapore Tourist Promotion Board (addresses at beginning of entry) who can supply the *Singapore Hotels* brochure. The following organisation also offers information: Singapore Hotel Association, 24 Nassim Hill, Singapore. Tel: 235 9533. **Grading:** Some hotels are designated as being 'International Standard' with all modern conveniences such as swimming pools and air-conditioning and prices ranging from Sing$100 a night.

RESORTS & EXCURSIONS

Singapore is truly fascinating and cosmopolitan, an interesting mixture of every major world culture: Chinese, Indian, Japanese, Arab, European and Malay to name but a few. The Singapore Tourist Promotion Board publishes a wide range of brochures and booklets giving information on every aspect of the country of interest to a foreign visitor. Below are listed some of the main attractions in Singapore City itself, including the several parks and gardens, and descriptions of the most popular outlying islands.

Singapore City

Singapore City was founded in 1819 by Sir Stamford Raffles of the British East India Company, who recommended that different areas of the town be set aside for the various ethnic groups. Although there has been some cultural assimilation there are still fascinating pockets where traditional cultures exist, principally in Chinatown, Arab Street, Serangoon Road (focus of the Indian community) and Padang Square with very strong colonial associations. The best way to experience the remarkable diversity of the city is on foot: the traditional architecture, customs and cuisines of the various ethnic areas are, in turn, in fascinating contrast to the lavish, space-age shopping centres of Orchard Road and Raffles City.
Arab Street is the centre of the Arabian quarter of Singapore. Other streets with excellent shopping opportunities are *Baghdad Street* and *Bussorah Street*, while *Sultan Plaza* is a centre for cloth traders. The golden dome of the *Sultan Mosque* dominates the area; nearby are two historic Muslim burial grounds.
Chinatown is a bustling and colourful area with many shops and restaurants, and also several temples such as the *Fuk Tak Ch'i in* Telok Ayer Street and the *Temple of the Calm Sea.* Ancient crafts of calligraphy, paper-making and fortune-telling are practised, and a wide range of traditional goods and foodstuffs can be bought.
Serangoon Road is the centre of the Indian quarter. Apart from the shops and restaurants, attractions in the area include the *Sri Veeramakalimman Temple*, the *Mahatma Gandhi Memorial Hall* in Race Course Lane and *Farrer Park.*
No trip to Singapore would be complete without a visit to *Raffles*, one of the most famous hotels in the world. A Singapore Sling in the Long Bar is almost *de rigeur*; alternatively, drop into the *Writer's Bar* which provided inspiration for, amongst others, Noel Coward, Somerset Maugham and Joseph Conrad. A statue of the man himself – Sir Stamford Raffles – has been erected on the banks of the Singapore River on the spot where he is believed to have first set foot in Singapore. Nearby is the *Parliament House*, the oldest government building in the country, the core of which

SINGAPORE CITY

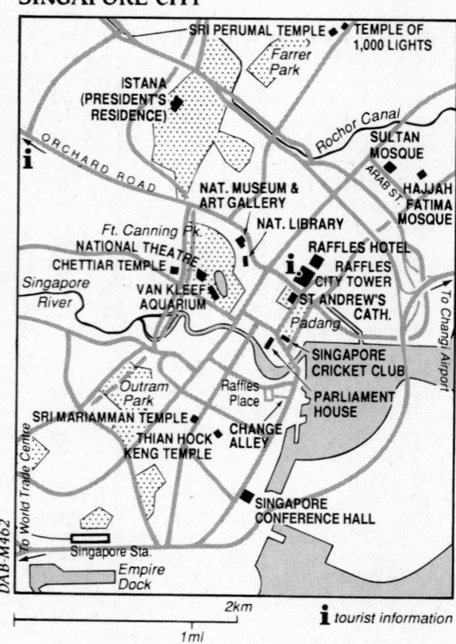

dates back to the 1820s.

Not far from Raffles Hotel is the beautiful *Armenian Church* in Hill Street, the oldest church in Singapore. This building is also a reminder of another nationality who contributed so much to the development of this cosmopolitan city.

Nowhere is a culture's personality more strongly expressed than in its religious architecture and Singapore provides fascinating examples of this. Buddhist temples, mosques, Catholic and Anglican cathedrals and Hindu temples can all be encountered during a comparatively brief walk around some of the central areas of Singapore. *St Andrew's Cathedral*, the *Cathedral of the Good Shepherd*, the *Al-Abrar Mosque*, the *Kong Meng Sang Phor Kark See Temple Complex*, the *Chettiar Hindu Temple* and the *Sri Mariamman Temple* are only a few of these. The *Singapore Official Guide* (a handy pocket-sized publication) gives further information on these and other religious buildings in Singapore.

The *Singapore Science Centre* in Jurong is a remarkable complex which includes hundreds of exhibits (many of which are 'hands-on'), the Aviation Gallery which traces the history of flight and the Omnitheatre, a cinema with a planetarium-like screen. It is open 1000-1800 Tuesday to Sunday.

The *New Ming Village* in Pandan Road is certainly the place to visit if you are interested in Chinese porcelain. Craftsman produce almost indistinguishable imitations of ancient masterpieces of Ming and Qing culture, and many of the items are available for purchase. Opening hours: 0900-1730 daily.

Other attractions of interest in Singapore City include the *National Museum & Art Gallery*, *Merlion Park*, the *Thong Chai Medical Institution*, *The Singapore Mint Coin Gallery*, *The Singapore Crocodilarium* (feeding time at 1100, crocodile wrestling at 1315 and 1615), the informal *bird singing contest* every Sunday at 0800 at the corner of Tiong Bahru and Seng Poh Roads, and the *Van Kleef Aquarium* in River Valley Road, with over 6000 species of freshwater and marine animals.

Parks & Gardens

The Botanic Gardens, over 47 hectares of landscaped parkland and primary jungle, are situated to the west of the city (Napier/Cluny Roads), and are home to a wide range of animal and plant life. The gardens are open 0500-2300 Monday to Friday and until midnight at weekends and public holidays. Admission is free.

The Bukit Timah Reserve, northwest of the Botanic Gardens on Bukit Timah Road, consists of tropical vegetation with clearly marked trails which lead up to the highest hill in Singapore, Bukit Timah. Admission is free.

Fort Canning Park, on Fort Canning Rise, was once an ancient fort of the Malay kings covering seven acres. The ruins still survive, as does a 19th-century Christian cemetery.

Haw Par Villa (The Tiger Balm Gardens) in Pasir Panjang Road are a monument to Chinese mythology, with many stone statues offering fascinating glimpses into ancient beliefs and superstitions. The Gardens are open 0800-1800 daily.

The Chinese and Japanese Gardens are to be found west of the centre. The two are linked by a 65m (200ft) ornamental bridge, and are superb examples of the master skills of oriental landscape gardeners, with thousands of varieties of flowers, shrubs and trees. The gardens are open 0900-1900 Monday to Saturday and 0830-1900 Sundays and public holidays. An admission fee is charged.

The Mandai Orchid Garden is a commercial orchid farm with a hillside of exotic orchids of many different species and a spectacular water garden. Opening hours: 0900-1730 daily. A small admission fee is charged.

The Jurong Bird Park on Jurong Hill (near the Chinese and Japanese Gardens) covers more than 20 hectares and is home to an incomparable collection of South-East Asian birds. There is also the world's largest walk-in aviary, a nocturnal house and several spectacular bird shows. The park is open 0900-1800 daily.

The Singapore Zoological Gardens, towards the north of the island of Singapore, is largely an 'open' zoo, using natural barriers rather than iron bars. Over 170 animals live here, including many which are rare or endangered, such as orang-utans, Sumatran tigers, Komodo dragons and clouded leopards. Daily attractions include breakfast or tea with an orang-utan (0900, 1500 respectively) and Animal Showtime (1030, 1130, 1430 and 1530). The zoo is open daily 0830-1800.

The Islands

Sentosa is the largest and best known of Singapore's offshore islands, and also one of the closest to the mainland. It is a multi-million dollar pleasure resort offering a wide range of activities and attractions. These include the *Butterfly Park*, with over 50 species; the *Maritime Museum*, which traces Singapore's remarkable history as a port; the *Rare Stone Museum*; the *Garden Plaza*; the *Rasa Sentosa Food Centre*, *The New Food Centre* and the *Pasar Malam Night Bazaar*.

Sentosa's beaches are among its most popular attractions and a wide range of watersports are available.

How to get there: Sentosa is linked to Singapore by regular ferry services (every 15 minutes 0730-2245) and a cable car (1000-2100 weekdays and 0900-2100 Sundays and public holidays). An admission fee for entry to the island is charged and composite tickets can also be bought which give admission to some of the attractions; enquire locally for details.

St John's Island is large, hilly and tree-shaded with several excellent beaches. There are also several walking trails.

How to get there: There is a regular ferry service from the World Trade Centre which takes about one hour.

Kusu Island is noted for two landmarks: the *'Keramat'* (a Muslim shrine) and the Chinese *Tua Pekong Temple*.

How to get there: There is a regular ferry service from the World Trade Centre which takes about 30 minutes.

Pulau Hantu, Pulau Sekeng and **Sisters islands** (the latter being part of the group of Southern Islands) are ideal for fishing, snorkelling and swimming enthusiasts.

How to get there: There are no regular ferry services but boats can be chartered; enquire locally for information.

Malaysia: The east coast of the Malaysian Peninsula is a popular resort area, particularly Desaru. For more information, see the entry on *Malaysia* above.

SOCIAL PROFILE

FOOD & DRINK: Singapore is a gourmet's paradise, ranging from humble street stalls to 5-star restaurants. There are over 30 different cooking styles, including various regional styles of Chinese cuisine, Indian, Malay, Indonesian, Japanese, Korean, Italian, Swiss, American, Russian, French and English. Malay cuisine is a favourite, famed for its use of spices and coconut milk. *Satay* (skewers of marinated chicken cooked over charcoal) served with peanut sauce, cucumber, onion and rice is popular. Hot, spicy or sweet Indonesian cuisine includes *beef rendang* (coconut milk curry), *chicken sambal* and *gado gado* (a fruit and vegetable salad in peanut sauce). One of the best ways to eat in Singapore is in the open, at one of the 8000 street foodstalls. Some are quiet and casual while others are in areas bustling with activity. All have a vast selection of cheap, mouth-watering food. Newton Circus and Rasa Singapura are food centres where all types of Asian food can be sampled cheaply. Although there are many self-service establishments, waiter service is more common in restaurants. **Drink:** Bars/cocktail lounges often have table and counter service. There are no licensing hours. 'Happy hours' with discounts on drinks are usually from 1700-1900.

NIGHTLIFE: There are cultural shows, street operas, special types of street theatre, fine theatres and international films providing inexpensive entertainment. Most hotels have bars or cocktail lounges which stay open until the early hours of the morning. Nightclubs have international entertainers and generally serve a wide range of food.

SHOPPING: The vast range of available goods and competitive prices have led to Singapore rightly being known as a shopper's paradise. Special purchases include Chinese, Indian, Malay, Balinese and Filipino antiques; batiks; cameras; Chinese, Persian and Indian carpets; imported or tailored clothing; jewellery and specialised items made of reptile and snake skins, including shoes, briefcases, handbags and wallets. Silks, perfumes, silverware and wigs are other favourite buys. The herding of shop owners from 'Chinatown' into multi-storey complexes lost some of the exciting shopping atmosphere, although these huge centres do provide an air-conditioned environment. Orchard Road is the main shopping street, although many of the large hotel complexes, such as Marina Square, have shopping centres attached. Although most outlets operate on Western-style fixed pricing, bargains can in some places still be made but generally only after good research and shrewd negotiating. There is a Pasar Malam (night bazaar) every Wednesday, Saturday and Sunday in the afternoon and early evening at the Singapore Handicraft Centre. Electrical equipment of all types can be bought at Sungei Road, but caution is advised as there are many imitation products around. For more information on shopping in Singapore, see the *Singapore Shopping* brochure published by the Singapore Tourist Promotion Board. **Shopping hours:** 0930-2100 Monday to Sunday.

SPORT: Many sports associations and clubs welcome visitors. **Badminton** is almost a national sport played all year round. **Cricket** is also played in Singapore, the *Singapore Cricket Club* being one of the oldest sporting associations in the world. It has a sports ground where cricket, soccer, tennis, hockey and rugby are played. **Bowling** is also very popular with several lanes catering for the enthusiast. The *Singapore Island Country Golf Club*, the *Keppel Club* and Sentosa Island have 18-hole **golf** courses. Night-time driving, pitching and putting are available until 2100 at the country club. *Singapore Turf Club* is responsible for all **horseracing** meetings. **Polo** matches are played regularly at the *Singapore Polo Club*. **Fishing** is a year-round sport. Boats and equipment, inexpensive to hire, are available at the Jardine Steps, Changi Park. **Canoeing** and **windsurfing** faculties are found at Sentosa Island and windsurfing at East Coast Park. Many Singaporeans drive over to Malaysia to enjoy the **watersports** off the East coast. For further information the *Malaysia* entry.

SPECIAL EVENTS: The cosmopolitan character of Singapore means that a great number of festivals and special events are regularly celebrated; indeed a visitor staying for more than a few days would be unlucky not to catch at least one. The following is a selection of the main festivals.. For more information and for exact dates, see the *Singapore Calender of Festivals* leaflet published by the Singapore Tourist Promotion Board.

Mar 25 '93 *Hari Raya Puasa* – The Muslim area of Geylang Serai is lit up from 1930 every night and hundreds of stalls offering Malay goods will be open.

Apr 16-May 1 *Singapore International Film Festival.*

May 28 *Birthday of the Third Prince.*

Jun 12-20 *17th South-East Asia Games.*

Jun 26-27 *Singapore World Invitational Dragon Boat Race; Singapore Dragon Boat Festival* – Held in honour of the poet Qu Yuan who drowned himself in protest against political injustice and corruption. Competitors from all over the world race their boats; *The Festival of Arts* – A month-long celebration of music, dance, theatre, ballet and opera.

Aug *Singapore River Regatta* – Competing teams of jet skiers, dragon boats and canoes; *Singapore Art Fair* – This 10-day festival promotes visual arts and is an opportunity for artists to exhibit their work; *National Day* – The anniversary of Singapore's independence is marked with parades, processions of decorated floats and fireworks displays.

Aug 18-Sep 15 *Festival of Hungry Ghosts*– The belief that the spirits of the dead walk the earth during the eighth lunar month marks this festival. Street festivities are staged (including *wayangs*, operas) to ensure a prosperous year.

Beach on the Southern Islands

Sep 30 *Mooncake Festival* – A traditional Chinese festival with lantern-lit processions and the consumption of sweet 'mooncakes'. Tradition has it that the Chinese concealed messages in such cakes when plotting a revolt against Mongol rule.

Oct 15 *Navarathivi* – This is an excellent opportunity to see classical performances, accompanied by Indian music.

Nov *Christmas Light-up* – The length of Orchard Road, the famous shopping area, is transformed into a fairyland with a million lights until early January.

Nov 1 *Thimithi* – The Fire-Walking Festival is an ancient celebration where Hindu ascetics walk across a pot of burning coals at the Sri Mariamman Temple in South Bridge Road.

Nov 13 *Deepavali* – The Festival of Light is celebrated with a special light-up in Serrangoon Road.

Dec *Mobil International Marathon.*

Jan '94 *Ponggal* – The Southern Indians celebrate the harvest for four days with ritual music and the offering of food in thanksgiving to the gods. The Perumal Temple in Serangoon Road is the best place to view the spectacle.

Feb *Thaipusam* – This Hindu festival is one of the most spectacular festivals in the world. Penitents carry brightly decorated steel arches, *kavadis*, fastened to the devotees' bodies by hooks and spears. The 5km- (3-mile) procession winds its way from Serangoon Road to Tank Road to the accompaniment of religious music.

Feb 10-11 *Chinese New Year* – Chinatown comes alive for the celebrations, with bright red lanterns and crowds shopping for Chinese delicacies. The vigorous and noisy *Chingay Parade* features lion and dragon dancers, decorated floats, and acrobats.

SOCIAL CONVENTIONS: Handshaking is the usual form of greeting, regardless of race. Social courtesies are often fairly formal. When invited to a private home a gift is appreciated and if on business a company souvenir is appropriate. Dress is informal. Most first-class restaurants and some hotel dining rooms expect men to wear a jacket and tie in the evenings; a smart appearance is expected for business meetings. Evening dress for local men and women is unusual. Each of the diverse racial groups in Singapore has retained its own cultural and religious identity while developing as an integral part of the Singapore community. Over 50% of the population is under 20 years of age. Laws relating to jaywalking and littering are strictly enforced in the urban areas. Smoking is widely discouraged and illegal in enclosed public places (including restaurants). Dropping a cigarette end in the street or smoking illegally can lead to an immediate fine of up to Sing$500. **Tipping:** Officially discouraged in restaurants, hotels and the airport. A 10% service charge is included in restaurant bills.

BUSINESS PROFILE

ECONOMY: Singapore's fortunes rely on entrepôt trade, shipbuilding and repairing, oil refining, electronics, banking and, to a slightly lesser extent, tourism. From the late 1970s, the Government initiated a strategy of upgrading the economy by establishing export-oriented and service industries

Parliament House

with the intention of making Singapore an economic fulcrum of the region. High-technology manufacturing, particularly computer and telecommunications equipment, and financial services, mainly banking and insurance, have performed particularly well and gone some way to fulfilling the Government's intentions. The state has also started to benefit from the political situation in Hong Kong (see the *History & Government* section of Hong Kong for more information) with the result that many companies in the region have decided to relocate their operations in Singapore: corporate telecommunications is one striking example, with Singapore now the most important hub in South-East Asia. The vibrant economic activity more than compensates for Singapore's lack of natural resources. All foodstuffs and raw materials have to be imported. The only important natural resource is the superb natural harbour which, with the exception of Rotterdam's, is the busiest in the world. The per capita income is second in the region only to that of Japan. The largest exporters to Singapore are Japan, the US and Malaysia, who between them collect nearly half of Singapore's US$70 billion annual import bill. The same three countries are also Singapore's principal overseas market.

BUSINESS: English is widely spoken in business circles. Appointments should be made and punctuality is important. Chinese people should be addressed with their surnames first, while Malays do not have surnames but use the initial of their father's name before their own. Visiting cards are essential, although it is policy for government officials not to use them.

COMMERCIAL INFORMATION: The following organisations can offer advice:
Singapore Federation of Chambers of Commerce and Industry, #03-01 Chinese Chamber of Commerce Building, 47 Hill Street, Singapore 0617. Tel: 338 9761. Fax: 339 5630. Telex: 26228; *or*
Singapore International Chamber of Commerce, 6 Raffles Quay, #05-00 Denmark House, Singapore 0104. Tel: 224 1255. Fax: 224 2785. Telex: RS 25235 INTCHAM.

CONFERENCES/CONVENTIONS: Singapore is the top convention city in Asia and ranks among the top ten meetings destinations in the world. There are many hotels with extensive conference facilities, including the latest audio-visual equipment, secretarial services, translation and simultaneous interpretation systems, whilst Raffles City, a brand new and completely self-contained convention city, can accommodate up to 6000 delegates under one roof. Full information on Singapore as a conference destination can be obtained from the Singapore Convention Bureau, Raffles City Tower #37-00, 250 North Bridge Road, Singapore 0617. Tel: 339 6622. Fax: 339 9423. Telex: STBSIN RS 33375. The Bureau, a division within the Singapore Tourist Promotion Board, is a non-profitmaking organisation with the dual objectives of marketing Singapore as an international exhibition and convention city and of assisting with the planning and staging of individual events.

HISTORY & GOVERNMENT

HISTORY: For centuries before Sir Stamford Raffles acquired it from the Sultan of Johor in 1819, Singapore had been virtually abandoned. However, within decades of the change of ownership, in an historical echo of its role today, Singapore had become the main commercial and strategic centre for the region. In 1867, it became a British Crown Colony and housed one of Britain's most important naval bases. This remained unchanged until 1942 when the Japanese army swept down through Malaya and occupied the colony. Three and a half years later the British took the Japanese surrender in Singapore and the colony resumed its previous status. With the dissolution of the British empire, Singapore was granted internal self-government in 1958 and then, in 1963, independence as part of the Federation of Malaysia. Two years later, Singapore was expelled when Lee Kuan Yew, first elected Prime Minister in 1959 and re-elected eight times since, refused to implement a federal edict granting Malays a privileged economic position. The initial outlook was unpromising: Singapore is tiny and has no natural resources apart from a good harbour. However, Lee managed to exploit the situation to galvanise the population into building a strong, export-led manufacturing and service economy. Lee Kuan Yew and the party which he led, the People's Action Party, have enjoyed a virtual monopoly of political power since 1972. In 1988, Lee Kuan Yew started his eighth term in office; on doing so, he announced that he would not complete the term nor seek subsequent office. Indeed, in October 1990, Lee formally handed over the premiership to a long-standing colleague, Goh Chok Tong, although Lee will remain an important, probably decisive influence behind the scenes. Some Singaporeans believe that Goh is merely a transitional figure between Lee Kuan Yew and his son Lee Hsien Loong, who has entered politics after a glittering academic and military career and currently serves as deputy prime minister.

GOVERNMENT: The parliament is unicameral; executive power nominally rests with the president but effectively lies with the Prime Minister and the Cabinet. The presidency is a largely ceremonial post whose incumbent is elected by Parliament to serve a 4-year term.

CLIMATE

Warm and humid through most of the year. There is no distinct wet/dry season. Most rain falls during the northeast monsoon (November to January) and showers are usually sudden and heavy.

Required clothing: Lightweight cottons and linens. An umbrella or light raincoat is recommended.

SINGAPORE (10m)

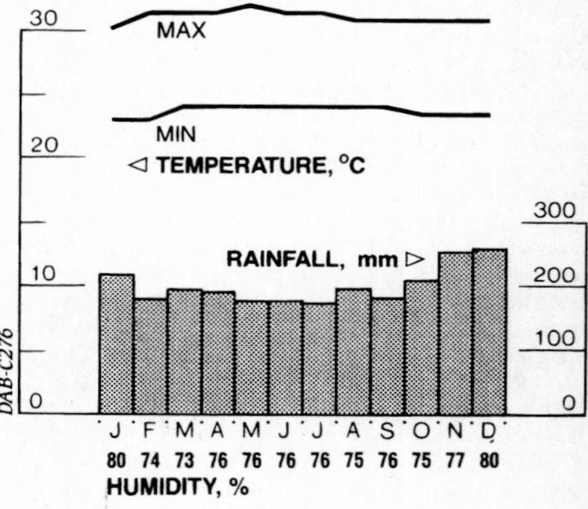

SLOVAK REPUBLIC

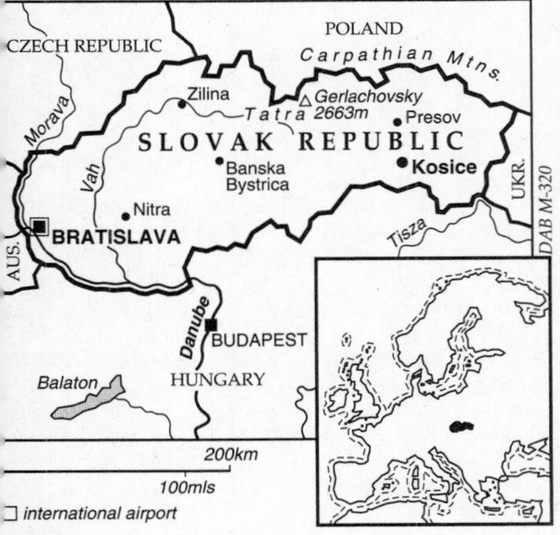

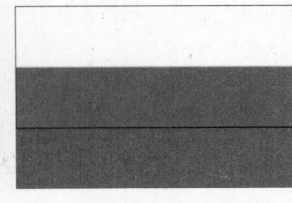

Location: Central Europe.

Ministry of Economy of the Slovak Republic
Tourism Section
Spitálska 8
81315 Bratislava
Slovak Republic
Tel: (7) 59371 *or* 51095. Fax: (7) 490 093.

Cedok (Travel Bureau)
Mileticova 1
82472 Bratislava
Slovak Republic
Tel: (7) 212 828. Fax: (7) 212 664.

Embassy of the Slovak Republic
25 Kensington Palace Gardens
London W8 4QY
Tel: (071) 229 1255. Fax: (071) 727 5824. Telex: 28276 OBZALD G. Opening hours: 0900-1700 Monday to Friday.

Cedok (London) Ltd (Travel Bureau)
49 Southwark Street
London SE1 1RU
Tel: (071) 378 6009 (general enquiries & independent travellers) *or* (071) 378 1341 (group bookings). Fax: (071) 403 2321. Telex: 21164 CEDOKL G. Opening hours: 0930-1730 Monday to Friday.

Embassy of the Czech Republic and Slovak Republic
3900 Linnean Avenue, NW
Washington, DC
20008
Tel: (202) 363 6315/6. Fax: (202) 966 8540.

Embassy of the United States of America
Hviezdoslavovo námestie 8
811 02 Bratislava
Tel: (7) 330 861 *or* 333 338. Fax: (7) 335 439.

Cedok
Suite 1902
10 East 40th Street
New York, NY
10016
Tel: (212) 689 9720. Fax: (212) 481 0597. Telex: 62467.

Embassy of the Czech Republic and Slovak Republic
50 Rideau Terrace
Ottawa, Ontario
K1M 2A1
Tel: (613) 749 4442 *or* (613) 749 4450. Fax: (613) 749 4989.

Cedok (Travel Bureau)
Cedok Canada
Suite 201

1212 Pine Street West
Montréal, Québec
H3G 1A9
Tel: (514) 849 8983. Fax: (514) 849 4117.

AREA: 49,035 sq km (sq miles).
POPULATION: 5,310,154 (1990 estimate).
POPULATION DENSITY: 108 per sq km.
CAPITAL: Bratislava. **Population:** 444,482 (1990 estimate).
GEOGRAPHY: The Slovak Republic is situated in central Europe, sharing frontiers with the Czech Republic, Austria, Poland, Hungary and the CIS. The republic is hilly and picturesque, with historic castles, dense forests, pure mountain streams, romantic valleys and lakes, as well as excellent facilities to 'take the waters' at one of the famous spas or to ski and hike in the mountains. The Tatra range and the foothills of the Carpathians descend to the huge and fertile Danube Plain, located in the southwest near Bratislava. The famous Danube River flows through the southeast of the Slovak Republic and into Hungary. The Slovak Republic was once under Hungarian rule and reflects this in its music, food and architecture, especially in the south.
LANGUAGE: The official language is Slovak. Czech, Russian, German and English are also spoken.
RELIGION: The majority are Roman Catholic. Protestant churches have the next highest following, such as the Reformed, Lutheran, Methodist, Moravian and Baptist.
TIME: GMT + 1 (GMT + 2 in summer).
ELECTRICITY: Generally 220 volts AC, 50Hz. Most major hotels have standard international 2-pin razor plugs. Lamp fittings are normally of the screw type.
COMMUNICATIONS: Telephone: IDD available. Country code: 42. There are public telephone booths, including special kiosks for international calls. Surcharges can be quite high on long-distance calls from hotels. Local calls cost Kcs1. **Telex/telegram:** Facilities are available at all main towns and hotels. Services are available 24 hours at Kollárska 12 (centre of the city) and next to the main railway station on Dimitrovovo námestie. **Post:** *Poste Restante* services are available. Post office hours: 0800-1800 Monday to Friday. **Press:** There are no English-language newspapers published.
BBC World Service and Voice of America frequencies: From time to time these change. See the section *How to Use this Book* for more information.

BBC:				
MHz	15.575	12.095	6.195	9.410
Voice of America:				
MHz	9.670	6.040	5.995	1.197

PASSPORT/VISA

Regulations and requirements may be subject to change at short notice, and you are advised to contact the appropriate diplomatic or consular authority before finalising travel arrangements. Details of these may be found at the head of this country's entry. Any numbers in the chart refer to the footnotes below.

	Passport Required?	Visa Required?	Return Ticket Required?
Full British	Yes	No	No
BVP	Not valid	-	-
Australian	Yes	Yes	No
Canadian	Yes	Yes	No
USA	Yes	No	No
Other EC	Yes	No	No
Japanese	Yes	Yes	No

PASSPORTS: Valid passport required by all. Passports must be valid for at least eight months at the time of application.
British Visitors Passport: Not accepted.
VISAS: Required by all except:
(a) nationals of EC countries;
(b) nationals of other European non-EC countries (nationals of Albania, Cyprus and Turkey *do* need visas);
(c) nationals of Cuba and Malaysia;
(d) nationals of the USA for a stay of 30 days.
Types of visa: Tourist, Transit and Double Transit. Cost depends on nationality and range from £2 to £60, but Tourist visas are generally £14-£29. Children aged 15 or under do not have to pay for a visa.
Validity: *Transit:* 48 hours. *Tourist:* 6 months from date of issue for 30-day visit.
Application to: Consulate (or Consular Section at Embassy). For addresses, see top of entry.
Application requirements: (a) Completed application form (2 for double transit). (b) 2 passport-size photos. (c) Passport valid for at least 8 months, with one blank page. (d) Fee (cash or postal orders only).
Working days required: Same day in most cases.
Temporary residence: Special application form required. Enquire at Embassy.

MONEY

Currency: Koruna (Kcs) or Crown = 100 haléru (single: heller). Notes are in denominations of Kcs1000, 500, 100, 50, 20 and 10. Coins are in denominations of Kcs10, 5, 2 and 1, and 50, 20, 10 and 5 haléru.
Currency exchange: Foreign currency (including travellers cheques) can be exchanged at exchange offices, Cedok offices, main hotels, *Tuzex* stores and road border crossings, as well as post offices and some travel agencies.
Credit cards: Major cards such as American Express, Diners Club, Visa and Access/Mastercard may be used to exchange currency and are also accepted in better hotels, restaurants and shops. Check with your credit card company for details of merchant acceptability and other services which may be available.
Travellers cheques: These are widely accepted (see *Currency exchange* above).
Exchange rate indicators: The following figures are included as a guide to the movements of the Koruna against Sterling and the US Dollar:

Date:	**Oct '89**	**Oct '90**	**Oct '91**	**Oct '92**
£1.00=	15.75	58.67	51.81	43.32
$1.00=	9.97	30.03	29.85	27.30

Currency restrictions: The import and export of local currency is not permitted. There is no restriction on foreign currency.
Banking hours: Generally 0800-1700 Monday to Friday.

DUTY FREE

The following goods may be imported into the Slovak Republic by visitors 18 years of age or older without incurring customs duty:
250 cigarettes (or corresponding quantity of tobacco products);
1 litre of spirits;
2 litres of wine;
500ml of perfume;
Gifts up to Kcs1000;
All goods bought at Tuzex shops by tourists.
Prohibited items: All forms of pornography. All items of value, such as cameras and tents, must be declared at Customs on entry to enable export clearance on departure.

PUBLIC HOLIDAYS

Public holidays observed in the Slovak Republic are as follows:
Apr 12 '93 Easter Monday. **May 1** Labour Day. **May 8** Liberation Day. **Jul 5** National Day, Day of the Apostles St Cyril and St Method. **Oct 28** National Day, Anniversary of Independence. **Dec 24-26** Christmas. **Jan 1 '94** New Year's Day.

HEALTH

Regulations and requirements may be subject to change at short notice, and you are advised to contact your doctor well in advance of your intended date of departure. Any numbers in the chart refer to the footnotes below.

	Special Precautions?	Certificate Required?
Yellow Fever	No	No
Cholera	No	No
Typhoid & Polio	No	-
Malaria	No	-
Food & Drink	1	-

[1]: Mains water is normally chlorinated, and whilst relatively safe may cause mild abdominal upsets. Bottled water is available and is advised for the first few weeks of the stay. Milk is pasteurised and dairy products are safe for consumption. Local meat, poultry, seafood, fruit and vegetables are generally considered safe to eat.
Health care: There is a Reciprocal Health Agreement with the UK. On the production of a UK

SLOVAK REPUBLIC | **HEALTH REGULATIONS** | **VISA REGULATIONS** | Code-Link

GALILEO/WORLDSPAN

TI-DFT/BTS/HE

TI-DFT/BTS/VI

SABRE

TIDFT/BTS/HE

TIDFT/BTS/VI

To access this information on your CRS, swipe the barcode with a light pen or type in the text under the barcode. For more information, see the introduction *How to Use This Book*.

passport, hospital and other medical care will be provided free of charge should visitors fall ill or have an accident while on holiday. Prescribed medicine will be charged for.

TRAVEL - International

AIR: The Slovak Republic is served by *Czechoslovak Airlines (OK)*, *Tatra Air* and *Aeroflot*.
Approximate flight time: From *London* to Bratislava is 1 hour 45 minutes.
International airport: *Bratislava (BTS)* (Ivánka), 12km (7.5 miles) from the city centre, is served from Continental Europe only. Airport express bus runs to the city centre for Kcs6 (travel time – 20 minutes). Another bus runs to the city, stopping en route, for Kcs3 (travel time – 30 minutes). Taxis are also available (travel time – 15 minutes). Airport facilities include duty-free shops (0700-1900 Monday to Friday), bank (0800-1430 Monday to Friday), post office (0700-1500 Monday to Friday), restaurant (until 1900), bar (0700-1900), snack bar (0700-1900), 24-hour flight information, 24-hour left luggage, 24-hour tourist information, 24-hour first aid, disabled facilities and car hire (*Budget, Europcar, Hertz* and *Univox*).
Poprad-Tatry is 5km (2.5 miles) from the city.
Vienna International Airport (Schwechat) is 50km (31 miles) from Bratislava and can be used as a gateway for inter-continental travellers.
Departure tax: US$5.98.
RAIL: The most convenient route to the Slovak Republic from Western Europe is via Vienna or Prague. There are also routes from Budapest and Kiev (Ukraine).
ROAD: The Slovak Republic can be entered via the Czech Republic, Poland, the CIS, Hungary or Austria. There is a motorway from Bratislava via Brno to Prague. Petrol coupons must be purchased before entering the country and are available at border crossings.

TRAVEL - Internal

AIR: *Czechoslovak Airlines* operates an extensive domestic network that includes flights from Bratislava to most major cities including Poprad, Presov, Piestany, Bystrica and Kosice. The domestic airline *Slov Air* operates scheduled and chartered flights from Ivank Airport, Bratislava. Tel: (7) 226 172.
RIVER: Navigable waterways can be found in the country and the main river ports are located at Bratislava and Komarno.
RAIL: The rail network is operated by *Czechoslovakian State Railways*. There are several daily express trains between Bratislava and main cities and resorts. Reservations should be made in advance on major routes. Fares are low, but supplements are charged for travel by express trains. Details can be obtained from Cedok.
ROAD: The major route is from Bratislava to Presov, via Trencin, Banská Bystrica, Zilina, Kralovany and Poprad. **Bus:** The extensive network covers areas not accessible by rail, and is efficient and comfortable. **Car hire:** Self-drive cars may be pre-booked through Cedok in main towns and resorts. Seat belts are compulsory and drinking is absolutely prohibited. Filling stations tend to be closed in the evenings. **Documentation:** A valid national driving licence is sufficient for car hire.
URBAN: Buses, trolleybuses and tramways exist in Bratislava and several other towns. Most services run from 0430-2400. All the cities operate flat-fare systems and pre-purchased passes are available. Tickets should be punched in the appropriate machine on entering the tram or bus. A separate ticket is usually required when changing routes. There is a fine for fare evasion. Blue badges on tram and bus stops indicate an all-night service. Taxis are available in all the main towns, and are metered and cheap; higher fares are charged at night.
JOURNEY TIMES: The following chart gives approximate journey times from Bratislava (in hours and minutes) to other major towns in the Slovak Republic.

	Air	Road	Rail
Poprad	0.45	4.00	4.30
Kosice	1.00	5.30	7.00
B. Bystrica	-	2.30	4.10
Piestany Spa	-	0.50	0.50

ACCOMMODATION

HOTELS: Prices compare very favourably with Western hotels, though services and facilities are often more limited. There is an acute shortage of accommodation in the Slovak Republic in the peak seasons (May to October, but especially during July and August), and it is wise to pre-book. At present, higher standard hotels are to be found primarily in Bratislava and other cities and spas of national and international significance. The new *Hotel Forum Bratislava* has recently been built in the city centre with 200 rooms, a number of restaurants and conference facilities. The 4-star *Hotel Danube* is also recommended, particularly for business travellers. A national hotel association is currently in the process of being established. **Grading:** The international 5-star system has recently been introduced for hotel classification, but the old **ABC** system may still be encountered in remote areas. The present system is: **5-star** (formerly **A+** or **Deluxe**), **4-star** (formerly **A**), **3-star** (formerly **B+**), **2-star** (formerly **B**), and **1-star** (formerly **C**). You can expect rooms with private bath or shower in hotels classified 3-star (or B+) and upwards.
MOTELS: Motels are split into two categories. **Grading:** In **B motels** every room is provided with central heating and a wash-basin with hot and cold water; on every floor there is a separate bathroom and WC for men and women. **A motels** are provided with the following extras: a lift, a bathroom or shower with every room, a radio receiver and in some cases a TV set. Car parking facilities are available in both types. Details can be obtained from Cedok offices.
PRIVATE HOUSES: Cedok (London) Ltd can arrange stays in private houses in the Slovak Republic throughout the year.
SELF-CATERING: Chalet Communities in many parts of the country are available in two categories. **Grading: B chalets** offer drinking water, WC, the possibility of obtaining meals, and heating in winter. **A chalets** have the following extras: electric lighting in the chalets, flushing WC, washroom with running water, washing and ironing facilities, and a sports ground. For further information, contact Cedok (London) Ltd.
CAMPING/CARAVANNING: Campsites have all the regular facilities such as showers, cooking amenities, shops and, in some cases, caravans for hire. A map, marking and listing sites throughout the country, is obtainable through Cedok. **Car camps:** In the **B** category these have a car park, fenced-in campsite, day and night service, washroom, WC, drinking water and a roofed structure with cookers and washing-up equipment. Car camps in the **A** category are provided with the following extras: sale of refreshments, showers with hot and cold water, flushing WC, washing and ironing facilities, a reception office, a social room, sale of toilet requisites and souvenirs.

Slovak Radio is the first public service broadcasting institution under licence in the former Eastern Block. It has been established by the Slovak National Council (Act No. 255/91) and designated as an organisation for cultural information. In the legal as well as popular sense it has become a successor to the Czechoslovak State Radio on the terrritory of the Slovak Republik in the CSFR, and the successor of a radio broadcasting tradition which started in 1926. Slovak Radio has four broadcasting networks:

Slovakia 1 News and current affairs programmes

Slovakia 2 A network for discerning listeners, made up of artistic and cultural programmes

Slovakia 3 A network for regional broadcasting, co-ordinated by the regional studios in Kosice and Banska Bystrica.

Slovak Radio's fourth programme is **Radio Rock FM** – unpolitical, musical and commercial broadcasting. The popular family station – broadcasting live, 24 hours a day. Slovak Radio ensures broadcasting for ethnic minorities in Hungarian, Ukrainian and Ruthenian.

PhDr. Vladimir Stefko, CSc.
General President

The Radio Bratislava Symphony Orchestra, Radio Bratislava Big Band the Radio Bratislava Folk Instrument Orchestra and the Radio Bratislava Children's Choir are also part of Slovak Radio.

The station has 1400 employees – its budget is composed as follows:

65% subscription fees (concessional)

18% state subsidies

17% commercial activities, which consist of advertising, agency activity in the production of classical, folk and pop music production, leasing of recording studios, publishing (books, records, CDs, audio tapes).

By licence Slovak Radio is entitled to develop business activities, leading to the launch of the subsidiary firm **Radio Media** (contact: **Radio Media**, Mileticova Street 40, 821 08 Bratislava, CSFR. Tel and fax: 615 19).

According to a proposal by the Radio Council, Dr. Vladimr Stefko CSc. has been appointed by the board of the Slovak National Council as the General President of Slovak Radio (contact: Slovak Radio, Mytna Street No. 1, 812 90 Bratislava, CSFR. Tel: 497 332. Fax: 493 626).

Vice Presidents of Slovak Radio are:

Ernest Weidler – responsible for programme and regional broadcasting, Tel: 498 978. Fax: 493 626.

Dr. Michael Berko – responsible for the news service, commercial activities and ethnic broadcasting. Tel: 496 600. Fax: 493 626.

Commercial Department – Tel: 493 086. Fax: 495 633.

Slovak Radio, **Bratislava**

RESORTS & EXCURSIONS

Every historical period and century has left behind monuments now admired by the world. Alongside castles, manors, chateaux and historical buildings, visitors to the Slovak Republic will also find great natural beauty: towering mountain peaks and quiet valleys, rivers, mountain lakes with crystal-clear waters and extensive cave systems.

The capital of the Slovak Republic, **Bratislava**, is the political, economic and cultural centre of the country. Its history is inextricably linked with the Celtic and Roman periods; there is also archaeological evidence dating back to the Great Moravian period. The fortified settlement grew in importance over the years and was granted town privileges in 1291. Matthias Corvinus established the first university, the *Academia Istropolitana*, in 1465. After the Battle of Mohácz in 1536, Bratislava became the capital and coronation town of Hungary and remained so for 250 years. The city contains palaces bearing the architectural style of almost every age: Rococo, Baroque, classical and Renaissance. The *Devín Castle,* recently renovated, dominates the city. Other sights include the 13th-century *Old Town Hall*, the *Primate's Palace* (1777), *Michael's Tower* (14th-15th centuries), *St Martin's Cathedral* (14th and 15th centuries), *Segner's Mansion* (1648) and *Roland's Fountain* (1573). On a walk through the Kapitulská, Klariská, Laurinská and Nálepkova streets, visitors will pass especially fine parish houses. Throughout the city are numerous examples of sacral buildings such as cloisters and churches. There are fine views of the Danube and the elegant modern bridge leading to Austria. Its theatres and concert halls are outstanding. The most important art museum is *The Slovak National Gallery*. There is also a *Pharmaceutical Museum* and a zoo.

The medieval town of **Bardejov** centres around an oblong square lined with fine examples of Gothic *burgher houses* with additions made during the Renaissance period. The 16th-century *Town Hall* also combines aspects of Gothic and Renaissance styles and should not be missed. The town can only be accessed through the four gates in the 14th-century *city walls*, circling the centre. The 15th-century *St Egydius Church* is also worth a visit.

Nitra, the centre of the principality of the same name, is an old Slavonic fortified settlement which developed between the 6th and 9th centuries. It is renowned for the *castle complex*, the *monastery*, the *Franciscan Church* (1624), the *Provost's Palace* (1779), the *Old Administration Building* (1874) and *Our Lady's Column* (1739).

The history of **Trnava** dates back as far as the Neolithic Age and the Great Moravian Period. In 1238 it became a royal town and was the centre for church administration for Hungary for 250 years from 1541 onwards. The city offers fine examples of 17th- and 18th-century architecture in the *university* buildings (founded 1635).

The mining tradition of **Banská Stiavnica** can be traced back to the 13th century. Renaissance-style *burgher houses* can be found in the city centre; other sights include the *old castle* (1548), several sacral buildings and the 11 buildings of the *Mining and Forestry Academy* dating from the 18th and 19th centuries.

Kezmarok was proclaimed a free Royal town in 1442. Well worth a visit is the 15th-century Gothic *chateau* with its 17th-century chapel. Throughout the city are the remnants of the town and castle walls dating from the 14th and 16th centuries. Also of interest are the *Lyceum* (1755) and the *Belfry* (1586).

Mining and coin-minting (granted in 1328) played an important role in the history of **Kremnica.** Historic buildings include the *Town Castle* (14th-19th centuries) with an extensive complex of Gothic and Renaissance buildings, the *St Trinity Pest Column* (1767-72) and the miners' small *gallery houses* (18th-19th centuries).

The region of **Spis** is dotted with numerous historic medieval towns, townlets and other settlements. The most important is **Levoca,** which can look back to an eventful history. In 1271 it became the capital of the Union of Spis Saxons and in 1323 it was declared a free royal town. This is reflected in the repeated alterations to *St James Church*, which originally dates from the 14th century. It houses the highest Gothic altar in the world (18.6m high and 6m wide) built by Master Pavol and complemented by 12 side altars. Also of importance is the town square flanked by the Renaissance *Town Hall*, the *Building of Town Weights* and over 50 burgher houses. **Spisská Kapitula** has been the seat of provosts and later bishops since the 13th century. Developing around a 12th-century church is a city reminiscent of a medieval townlet. It houses such ecclesiastic buildings as the *Cloister of the Brothers of Mercy* and a fine Baroque church.

Kosice is the capital of the eastern Slovak region and bears significant reminders of its rich history, with its numerous Gothic buildings. Towering over the city is the monumental *St Elisabeth Cathedral*.

WINTER SPORTS: The mountains, forests and lakes are enchanting and ideal for outdoor holidaying as well as winter sports. There are popular winter sports centres in 30 mountain regions, of which the *Tatra Mountains* are the best. Other popular mountain areas include the *Slovensky raj* range, with its deep canyons, and the *Malá Fatra* range with its neighbouring *Vratna Dolina Valley*. There are also numerous lakes and rivers amidst the glacial landscape, offering excellent fishing, canoeing, boating and freshwater swimming. The primary water-sports areas are at **Orava, Liptovská Mara** and **Zemplínska Sírava.**

NATIONAL PARKS: There are five national parks and 15 protected landscape areas in the Slovak Republic. Protected landscape areas are to a large extent untouched by human hand. The countryside is dotted with varied natural formations and numerous species of flora and fauna.

The **Low Tatras National Park** covers the second highest mountain range within the western Carpathians. Within the boundaries of the national park are several ski and recreation resorts, the most renowned lying in the foothills of the *Chopok* (2024m). Also situated in the park is the *Demänová Valley*, running over a length of 15km, with an extensive cave system. The *Demänová Cave of Liberty* and the *Demänová Ice Cave* are open to the public.

The **Tatra National Park** is the oldest national park in the country, housing large numbers of wildlife (including chamois and marmot) and plants. This is due to the great difference in elevation covering a range from 900-2655m. The park caters for all needs of recreation with a good selection of accommodation and sporting facilities (mountaineering and hiking). An ideal starting point for tours into the eastern part of the High Tatras is **Tatranská Lomnica.** Founded in 1892 as a State climatic spa, it nestles in the foothills of *Skalnaté Pleso* (1751m) which boasts the best downhill ski track in the Tatras. The town offers extensive skiing facilities such as a ski-tow, two ski-jumps and a bobsleigh track. Trips to the astronomical observatory can be arranged. A sky-tram goes up to *Lomnicky stít*, the second highest peak in the Tatras (2632m). The picturesque Goral village of **Zdiar** lies at the divide of the Belianske Tatry and the Spisská Magura mountain ranges. Several ski tows and excellent ski terrains are suitable for beginners in particular.

The **Pieniny National Park** is a bilateral national park shared with Poland, 30km northeast of the High Tatras. The **Little Fatra National Park** (200 sq km) is renowned for the scenic beauty of its valleys and gorges and its abundant wildlife. It is a favourite with hikers in both winter and summer.

Canyons, up to 200m deep, cut through the **Slovensky raj (Slovak Paradise) National Park.** The area is riddled with basins and waterfalls in a rugged landscape. *Hrabusice-Podleskok* is an ideal starting point for extensive hiking tours.

SPAS: The country offers a great wealth of curative springs, thermal spas, climatic health resorts and natural mineral waters which are renowned throughout the world.

Bardejovské kúpele was already established as a health resort in the 13th century; **Dudince's** spring is rated among the best in the area due to its mineral composition; the world-famous thermal health resort of **Piestany** specialises in rheumatic treatment; **Sliac** was first mentioned in 1244 and is the most important spa for the treatment of cardio-vascular disorders; and **Trencianske Teplice**, known since 1488, is situated near a sulphuric spring and is suitable for the treatment of nervous disorders.

SOCIAL PROFILE

FOOD & DRINK: Food is often based on Austro-Hungarian dishes; *wiener schnitzel* and sauerkraut, dumplings and pork are very popular. The national peciality is *bryndzove halusky* (potato pasta with sheep's heese and small pieces of fried bacon) and in the east isitors should sample the gruel made of mushrooms and our cream, served with black rye bread. The mountainous region of the Slovak Republic is renowned for different varieties of roasted mutton, whereas the southern art of the country serves geese, baked in charcoal ovens. Western-style fresh vegetables are often missing. There is wide selection of restaurants, beer taverns and wine cellars with counter service, but table service is often available. **Drink:** Popular beverages include fresh fruit juices, iqueurs and wines. A particular speciality is *borovicka* strong gin) and the aromatic *marhulovica* (apricot brandy). Beers, *slivovica* (plum brandy) and sparkling wine from the Bratislava region are also famous. There are no rigid licensing hours.

NIGHTLIFE: Theatre and opera are of a high standard all over Eastern Europe. Much of the nightlife takes place in hotels, although nightclubs are to be found in major cities.

SHOPPING: Souvenirs include pottery, porcelain, wooden folk carvings, hand-embroidered clothing and food items. As well as *Tuzex* outlets, of which a current list can be obtained from Cedok offices, there are a number of excellent shops specialising in glass and crystal, while various associations of regional artists and craftsmen run their own retail outlets (pay in local currency). Other special purchases folk ceramics from eastern Slovak Republic and woodcarvings from Spisska Bela. **Shopping hours:** 0900-1200 and 1400-1800 Monday to Friday, 0900-1200 Saturday (many shops close all day).

SPORT: Football, volleyball, tennis and **ice hockey** are popular. There is a very good network of marked trails in all mountain areas, and it is possible to plan a **walking** tour in advance.

Winter sports tours can be arranged by Cedok; check for details. The many and varied rivers and lakes provide excellent opportunities for **watersports – canoeing, sailing, water-skiing, fishing,** etc (see *Resorts & Excursions* above).

SPECIAL EVENTS: Most towns have their own folk festivals, with dancing, local costumes and food. These tend to be in the summer months leading up to the harvest festivals in September. The following is a selection of festivals celebrated during 1993/94 in the Slovak Republic.

Mar-Apr '93 *Danube Cup* (International Modern Dance Competition), Bratislava. **Apr** *Celebration of Choir Songs*, Bratislava. **Jun** *International Folk Festival*, Kosice. **Jul** *Folk Festival*, Vjchodná; *Celebration under Poléna*, Detra. **Sep** *Biennale of Children's Phantasy* (international competition and exhibition of children's art), Mertin. **Sep/Oct** *Bratislava Music Festival*, Bratislava.

There are also folk festivals at Vychodná, Detva and Terchova. For further details of special events, contact Cedok, who also arranges music festival tours.

SOCIAL CONVENTIONS: Dress should be casual, but conservative, except at formal dinners and at quality hotels or restaurants. **Photography:** Areas where there are military installations should not be photographed. **Tipping:** A 5-10% tip will be discreetly accepted; some alteration in customs is to be expected in the wake of political and social changes.

BUSINESS PROFILE

ECONOMY: Of all the Soviet bloc economies, the then Czechoslovakia experienced the highest degree of state control, without even the small-scale private enterprise that existed to some extent in all Eastern European economies. Under central planning, and particularly in the aftermath of the 'Prague Spring', economic development concentrated on heavy industry at the expense of traditional strengths in light and craft-based industries, such as textiles, clothing, glass and ceramics (though these remain significant). These inefficient and, in some cases, redundant industrial monoliths are now a considerable millstone around the economy, particularly in the Slovak Republic. The other problem is a dearth of natural resources – the country had hitherto relied heavily on the former Soviet Union for most of their raw materials, particularly oil, supplies of which have been cut to one-third and payment required in hard currency. The oil shortage reached crisis proportions at the end of 1990 and was resolved satisfactorily only after urgent personal discussions between Presidents Havel and Gorbachev. The following year, the Government embarked on an ambitious programme of privatisation as the cornerstone of its declared policy of introducing a market economy. This has happened at breakneck speed despite the misgivings of observers from across the political spectrum who have raised questions about the lack of financial infrastructure, possible consequences of extensive foreign ownership, and the use of an untried 'voucher' scheme which gives equity stakes in industrial enterprises to any individuals who apply (this was apparently inspired by an obscure Western academic paper). The autumn of 1991 saw 1700 enterprises denationalised in the space of just two weeks. This was the first part of a two-phase plan, beginning in May 1992 and ending in December, which placed most of the industry and agriculture in private hands. There has also been extensive fiscal and budgetary reform, with the aim of creating a fully-fledged capitalist financial system with strong safeguards against inflation. Limited currency convertibility has also been introduced as a necessary step towards promoting foreign investment. This is being keenly sought. The Slovak Republic has changed its approach towards privatisation methods, introducing direct sales, tenders and auctions. Priority areas are machinery industries, chemical industries, textiles, leather, shoes, glass, electronics, nuclear energy and car manufacturing. Agriculture is particularly important as an export sector (beer and timber are much in demand). For the time being, the majority of trade is conducted with former members of COMECON, the defunct Soviet bloc economic union, but the focus at present is on developing links with Western Europe. The then Czechoslovakia negotiated associate membership with the European Community. Since the split the negotiations will continue with either republic, acknowledging their separate status. Future trade patterns are likely to see the Slovak Republic improve its links with Poland, the Ukraine and Hungary, but also establishing new ones with countries such as Germany, France, Austria and the USA.

BUSINESS: Businessmen wear suits. A knowledge of German or Hungarian is useful as English is not widely spoken. Long business lunches are usual. Avoid visits during July and August as many businesses close for holidays. **Office hours:** 0800-1600 Monday to Friday.

COMMERCIAL INFORMATION: The following organisation can offer advice: Slovak Chamber of Commerce and Industry, Gorkeho 9, 81 603 Bratislava. Tel: (7) 59198. Fax: (7) 330 754.

HISTORY & GOVERNMENT

HISTORY: Before Czechoslovakia came into existence in 1918, two of its component republics, Moravia and Bohemia, were Austrian-controlled, while the third, Slovakia, was under Hungarian domination, with Bratislava being the capital of Hungary. The large German population in an area of the new country known as the Sudetenland prompted Hitler to annexe it in 1938. The rump of Bohemia and Moravia were occupied the following year while Slovakia was left nominally independent with a pro-German puppet government. After the war, Czechoslovakia was reconstituted and in 1948 came under communist and subsequently Soviet control. Apart from a brief period known as the 'Prague Spring' in 1968, during which a reform-minded government under Alexander Dubcek attempted to introduce a more pluralistic political and economic structure, links between the two countries remained strong. Reactions to the new spirit of *glasnost* under President Gorbachev, 20 years later, were cautious at first, as evinced by a wave of arrests of dissidents in 1988 and 1989. During November 1989, however, large demonstrations took place in all of the country's major cities, culminating in the resignation of the Communist Party leader, Milos Jakes, along with many members of the ruling Politburo. Prime Minister Ladislav Adamec led discussions in the same month with representatives from the main opposition group, Civic Forum, including the playwright Václav Havel. Here, Adamec conceded that the 'leading role' of the Communist Party should end and with it the Party's domination of the Government. These proposals were subsequently endorsed by the National Parliament. Civic Forum's influence over new appointments led to the appointment of Václav Havel as President while the country set about introducing a pluralistic political system and market economy. The country was also set free to pursue its own foreign and defence policies. Multi-party elections for a new national assembly in June 1990 were won by Civic Forum (and its Slovakian ally, Public

Hotels Slo

Hotel Junior Bratislava

▲ Located in a quiet area close to the centre of Bratislava, the capital of Slovakia. Bratislava, a town rich in history and culture, is situated on the foothills of the Small Carpathian Mountains, on the Danube. Hotel Junior offers 240 beds in double and triple rooms including toilet, bathroom, phone, satellite TV and radio. Restaurant, bars, café and exchange-office.

Attractions consist of boat-trips on the Danube, bus excursions to Vienna and Budapest, trips to the Small Carpathian Mountains and parties in a typical Slovak 'Koliba' restaurant.

Hotel Junior Bratislava, Drieňová ul. 14 821 01 Bratislava. Tel: 07 230 021/234 340. Fax: 07 238 065.

Hotel Junior Tatranská Štrba

◀ Tatranská Štrba is located in the High Tatras National Park, 946m above sea level close to the ski resort of Štrbské Pleso.

The hotel offers 96 beds in double rooms including toilets, bathroom, satellite TV and loggias with a magnificent view of the mountain peaks, restaurant, café and nightclub. Activities include skiing for skilled sportsmen as well as beginners, aeroplane and helicopter sight-seeing trips, sports equipment rental and day trips in the summer and winter.

Hotel Junior RYSY 059 41 Tatranská Štrba. Tel: 0969 926 91.
Fax: 0969 922 96.

▼ Located in th
ern part of the Low
National Park
favourable location
it utilisation dur
whole year. The ho
uated above a lak
the most famous

Hot

▼ Situated in th
Tatras National
1200m above sea le
the Demänovská D
the best ski ar
Czecho-Slovakia
hotel offers 260 b
comfortable room

H

akia

e in Czecho-Slovakia. The hotel offers 183 beds in single and e rooms with satellite TV, toilet, bathroom, ra dio, telephone alcony. Facilities include restaurant, café, day-bar, night-bar, s centre, bowling alley, billiards and swimming pool. Activities de angling, boating, surfing, riding, day-trips in the summer, g and skiing in the winter approx 200m from the hotel.
Junior Krpáčovo, 976 98 Lopej.
0867 811 43. Fax: 0867 811 43.

nior Krpácovo

rate facilities, satellite TV and radio. Two restaurants serving tional Slovak food, ski bar, nightclub and banqueting room. vities include swimming pool, massages, solarium, health , tennis court, basketball and vollyball as well as paragliding, e riding, ski school, sightseeing and full- and half-day excurs. Traditional Slovak evening at 'Koliba' restaurant.
el Junior Jasná 032 51 Demänovská Dolina.
0849 915 71-3. Fax: 0849 915 75.

Junior Jasná

HOTELY MLÁDEŽE SLOVAKIA
PRAŽSKA UL. 11
CS-816 36 BRATISLAVA
TEL: 07 498 090; 498 541-5.
FAX: 07 491 805.

Hotel Junior Banská Bystrica

▲ Banská Bystrica is in the heart of Central Slovakia, in the Zvolen Valley surrounded by the Kremnica Mountains. The hotel is in the very centre of the city, close to the ancient square of Banská Bystrica and offers 112 beds (double/triple rooms with wash basin), showers and toilets (provided on each floor), restaurant, café and day-bar. Activities include winter and summer trips, skiing, open-air and indoor swimming pools close to the hotel, tours to the historical monuments of Banská Bystrica and bus trips to the ancient cities of Zvolen, Kremnica and Banská Štiavnica.
Hotel Junior Banská Bystrica, Národná ul. 12, 974 58 Banská Bystrica.
Tel: 088 233 67; 255 93-4. Fax: 088 233 95.

Hotel Junior Björnson

◀ The Hotel preserves the typical atmosphere of a wooden mountain hotel and is situated in the neighbourhood of the Hotel Jasná (100m) close to the funicular railway station. It offers accommodation in double and triple rooms, Slovak restaurant and bar. Hotel guests are welcome to use all the facilities available at the Hotel Jasná.

Against Violence) under the leadership of Marián Calfa. Divisions within the victorious party quickly emerged. The decisive split occurred in January 1991 when the right-wing federal Finance Minister Václav Klaus, the architect and chief engineer of the privatisation programme, left the Forum with his supporters to create the Civic Democratic Party (ODS). With Marián Calfa largely discredited by his previous associations with the Communists, Klaus emerged as the most powerful figure within the federal government. Slovak pressure for secession increased among the region's parliamentary deputies and the wider public once the economic plans of finance minister Vaclav Klaus (now Prime Minister) became clear. Klaus favoured a rapid transition to a market economy and mass privatisation of state-controlled businesses. Many Slovaks felt that such prescriptions were inappropriate for their own part of the country with its heavy industrial base. Despite the firm opposition of President Havel, who considered that the country could ill afford the diversion of a national split at such a critical stage in its development, negotiations opened between representatives of the two republican governments in November 1991. The talks broke down within weeks and both sides retired to await the June 1992 national election which promised to be, in effect, a referendum on the future structure of the country. At the poll on June 5 and 6, Klaus' ODS took 34% of the national vote – over 50% in the Czech part of the country. The main Slovak party, the Movement for a Democratic Slovakia (HZDS), led by an ex-communist turned nationalist, Vladimir Meciar, polled 37% nationally and the lion's share in Slovakia, where most of the population favoured the autonomy proposals put forward by Meciar suggesting that the two parts of the country share defence and foreign policies and little else. A complete split into two independent countries was quickly accepted as the only viable solution. The process of achieving this 'velvet divorce' proved more awkward than envisaged. The date of the formal division was January 1993. President Havel, who led the velvet revolution, has since been re-elected as the President of the new Czech Republic.

GOVERNMENT: The Slovak Republic ratified its national constitution in September 1992.

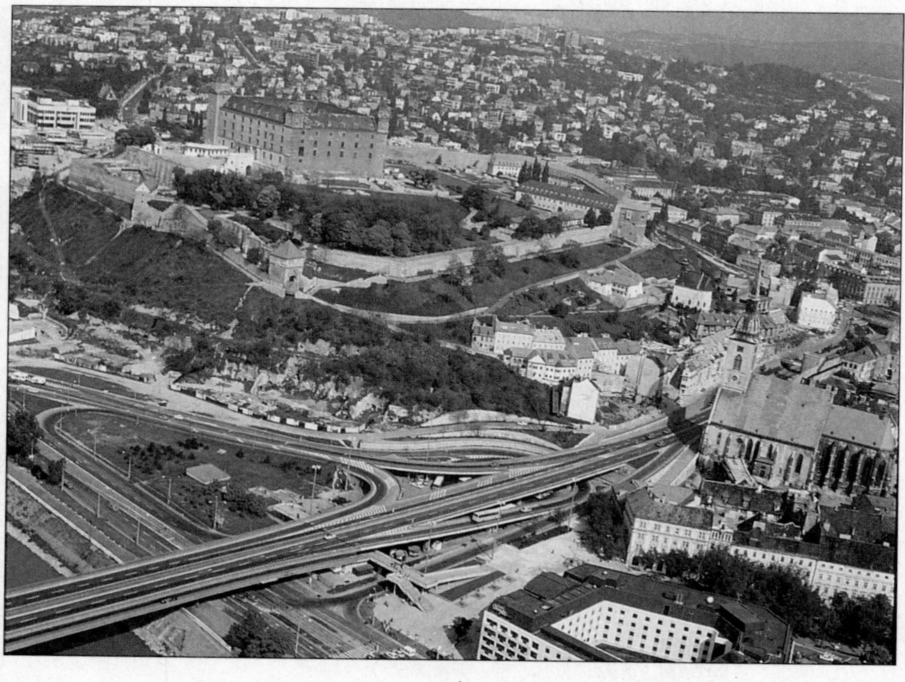

CLIMATE

Cold winters, mild summers.

Required clothing: Mediumweights, heavy topcoat and overshoes for winter; lightweights for summer. Rainwear throughout the year.

BRATISLAVA Slovak Republic (133m)

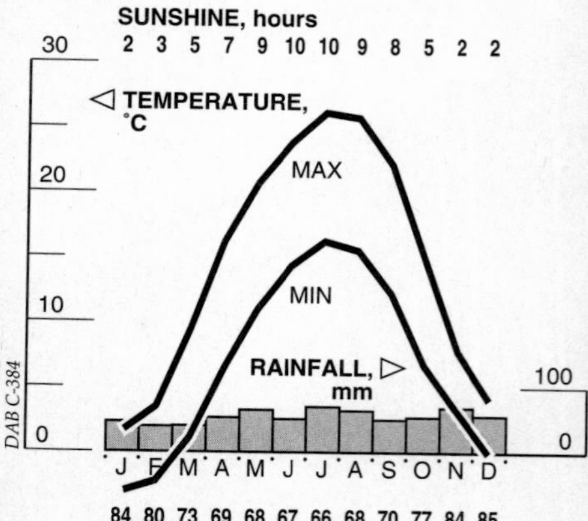

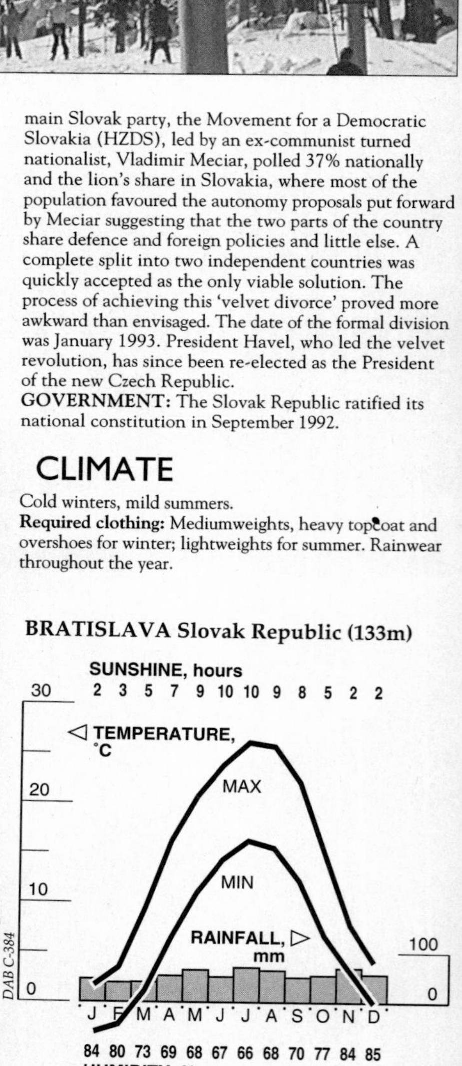

SLOVENIA

Location: Southern Central Europe.

Note: Along with the rest of the EC, the UK recognised Slovenia in January 1992.

Tourist Association of Slovenia
Milosiceva 38
61000 Ljubljana, Slovenia
Tel: (61) 120 141. Fax: (61) 301 570.
Centre for Tourist and Economic Promotion
Cesta VII, Korpusa 1
61000 Ljubljana, Slovenia
Tel: (61) 129 345. Fax: (61) 315 944.
Embassy of the Republic of Slovenia
Heather Lodge
Kingston Hill
Kingston-upon-Thames
Surrey KT2 7LX
Tel: (081) 974 8300. Fax: (081) 974 6552. Opening hours: 1000-1200 Monday to Friday.
Adria Airways
49 Conduit Street
London W1R 9FB
Tel: (071) 734 4630 *or* 437 0143. Fax: (071) 287 5476.
Telex: 264465.
Ljubljanska Banka Representative Office
7 Birchin Lane
London EC3V 9BY
Tel: (071) 626 8848/9. Fax: (071) 626 0710.
British Embassy
Holiday Inn
Miklosiceva 3
61000 Ljubljana, Slovenia
Tel: (61) 155 051. Fax: (61) 150 323.
Embassy of the Republic of Slovenia
1300 19th Street, NW
Washington, DC
20036
Tel: (202) 828 1650. Fax: (202) 828 1654.
Consulates in: Cleveland (Ohio) and New York (tel: (212) 702 4884).
Embassy of the United States of America
c/o American Center
Cankarjeva 11
61000 Ljubljana, Slovenia
Tel: (61) 210 190 *or* 158 226. Fax: (61) 210 190.
Consulate of the Republic of Slovenia
Suite 700
67 Younge Street
Toronto, Ontario
M5E 1J8
Tel: (416) 363 3442 *or* 234 8103. Fax: (416) 863 5006.

AREA: 20,251 sq km (7819 sq miles), or 7.9% of the territory of the former Yugoslav federation (its fifth largest republic).
POPULATION: 1,974,839 (1991 census), or 8% of the total population of the former Yugoslav federation.
POPULATION DENSITY: 97.5 per sq km.
CAPITAL: Ljubljana. **Population:** 323,300 (1991).
GEOGRAPHY: A compact and strategically important country dominated by mountains, rivers and major north–south and east–west transit routes, Slovenia borders Italy to the west, Austria to the north, Hungary to the northwest and Croatia to the southeast, plus a 47km Adriatic Sea coastline, where the main port is Koper.
LANGUAGE: Slovene (Latinate alphabet) which is closely related to the Serbo-Croat (or Croato-Serb) of the ex-Yugoslav republics to the southeast.
RELIGION: 90% Roman Catholic Slovenes, 3.2% Roman Catholic Croats, 2.6% Eastern Orthodox Serbs, plus smaller ethnic Italian and Hungarian minorities. As the most religiously homogeneous of the ex-Yugoslav republics, Slovenia has consequently been relatively peaceful since a brief war with the federal army in 1991, although there is still widespread concern about the ultimate consequences of the ongoing civil war to the southeast.
TIME: GMT + 1 (GMT + 2 from March to September).
ELECTRICITY: 220 volts AC, 50Hz.
COMMUNICATIONS: Telephone: IDD available as part of the former Yugoslav federation. Telephone lines between Ljubljana and Belgrade have been indefinitely cut, although services to and from Zagreb are generally available. Country code: 38. Calls can be made either with tokens or phonecards. **Fax:** Available to and from Western Europe. **Telex/telegram:** Telex facilities are limited. **Post:** Reasonable internal service. Stamps can be bought at bookstalls. Post office hours: 0800-1900 Monday to Friday; 0800-1300 Saturday. The post office at Cigaletova 5 is open 24 hours. **Press:** The main local newspaper is *Delo* (Ljubljana). The state news agency, *STA*, produces material in English for international distribution on a daily basis. Unlike the other ex-Yugoslav republics, Slovenia is also well provided with English-language monthly and other magazines specifically aimed at Western business interests and available on subscription abroad. Two of the most prominent are *Slovenian Business Report* (tel: (61) 318 389) and MM *(Marketing Magazine) Slovenija* (tel: (61) 318 593). Both are available abroad on subscription. The state TV and radio station *RTS* produces regular news and other broadcasts in English and other West European languages during the tourist season.
BBC World Service and Voice of America frequencies: From time to time these change. See the section *How to Use this Book* for more information.

BBC:				
MHz	15.07	12.10	9.410	6.195
Voice of America:				
MHz	9.670	6.040	5.995	1.260

PASSPORT/VISA

Regulations and requirements may be subject to change at short notice, and you are advised to contact the appropriate diplomatic or consular authority before finalising travel arrangements. Details of these may be found at the head of this country's entry. Any numbers in the chart refer to the footnotes below.

	Passport Required?	Visa Required?	Return Ticket Required?
Full British	1	No	Yes
BVP	Valid/2	-	-
Australian	1	Yes/4	Yes
Canadian	1	Yes/4	Yes
USA	1	Yes/4	Yes
Other EC	1	3	Yes
Japanese	1	No	Yes

PASSPORTS: Required by all. **[1]** However, most nationals (except nationals of Greece) can enter Slovenia with a national ID card (BVP for UK nationals) or other form of identification. Upon purchase of a Tourist Pass at the border they can enter for up to 30 days.
British Visitors Passport: [2] Acceptable if travelling for tourist purposes only upon purchase of a Tourist Pass.
VISAS: These can be issued at border points and are required by all except:
(a) **[3]** nationals of EC countries for stays of up to three months (nationals of Greece *do* require a visa);
(b) nationals of Argentina, Algeria, Austria, Bolivia, Bosnia-Hercegovina, Chile, Costa Rica, Croatia, Cyprus, Finland, Iceland, Iran, Iraq, Liechtenstein, Macedonia, Malta, Monaco, Morocco, Norway, San Marino, Switzerland, Sweden and Tunisia for stays of up to 90 days;
(c) nationals of Japan for stays of up to 90 days;
(d) nationals of Bulgaria, CIS, Czechoslovakia, Hungary and Poland for stays of up to 30 days.
Note: [4] Nationals of Australia, Canada and the USA can obtain visas at the border free of charge.
Types of visa: Single entry and Transit: £5; Multiple entry: £14.
Validity: *Transit:* 7 days. *Single and Multiple entry:* Negotiable from 1 week up to 1 year.
Application to: Consulate (or Consulate Section at Embassy). For addresses, see top of entry.
Application requirements: (a) Valid passport. (b) Completed application form. (c) Fee.
Note: Applications for visas *must* be applied for in person.
Working days required: 1-2 working days.

MONEY

Currency: Slovene Tolar (SIT) = 100 stotins. The Tolar replaced the Yugoslav Dinar in October 1991. Local hyperinflation (over 300% in 1991) is undermining the SIT despite the aim of its introduction being to rid Slovenia of this problem.
Currency exchange: As elsewhere in the ex-Yugoslav republics, the only true repositories of value and real mediums of exchange locally are the German DM and the US$ (the UK£ is rarely used or seen in the republic). Austrian and Italian currencies are also used to a lesser extent. Much foreign currency is reportedly in circulation in private hands in Slovenia, and the Government has used non-confiscatory means, such as real estate sales, to gain access to some of it. The banking system functions well, with auditing of local financial institutions now widely done by Western auditors, as in the case of the Bank of Slovenia.
Credit cards: All main cards are widely accepted.
Travellers cheques: Widely accepted.
Exchange rate indicators: The following figures are included as a guide to the exchange rate of the Slovene Tolar against Sterling and the US Dollar:

Date:	**Oct '92**
£1.00=	**143.31**
$1.00=	**90.30**

Currency restrictions: The import and export of local currency is limited to SIT5000. There is unrestricted import and export of foreign currency.
Banking hours: 0800-1800 Monday to Friday. Some branches are open 0730-1200 Saturdays for payments and withdrawals.

DUTY FREE

The following goods can be imported into Slovenia without incurring customs duty:
200 cigarettes or 50 cigars or 250g of tobacco;
1 litre of wine;
750ml of spirits;
50ml perfume;
250ml eau de toilette;
Gifts of up to DM100 in value.

PUBLIC HOLIDAYS

Public holidays observed in Slovenia are as follows:
Apr 12 '93 Easter Monday. **Apr 27** Resistance Day. **May 1-2** Labour Days. **May 30** Whit Sunday. **Jun 25** Statehood Day. **Aug 15** Assumption. **Oct 31** Reformation Day. **Nov 1** Remembrance Day. **Dec 25** Christmas Day. **Dec 26** Independence Day. **Jan 1-2 '94** New Year. **Feb 8** Culture Day.

HEALTH

Regulations and requirements may be subject to change at short notice, and you are advised to contact your doctor well in advance of your intended date of departure. Any numbers in the chart refer to the footnotes below.

	Special Precautions?	Certificate Required?
Yellow Fever	No	No
Cholera	No	No
Typhoid & Polio	No	-
Malaria	No	-
Food & Drink	1	-

[1]: Mains water is normally chlorinated, and whilst relatively safe may cause mild abdominal upsets. Bottled water is available and is advised for the first few weeks of the stay. Milk is pasteurised and dairy products are safe for consumption. Local meat, poultry, seafood, fruit and vegetables are generally considered safe to eat.
Rabies is present. For those at high risk, vaccination before arrival should be considered. If you are bitten abroad seek medical advice without delay. For more information consult the *Health* section at the back of the book.
Health care: There is a Reciprocal Health Agreement with the UK, allowing free hospital and other medical treatment and some free dental treatment to those

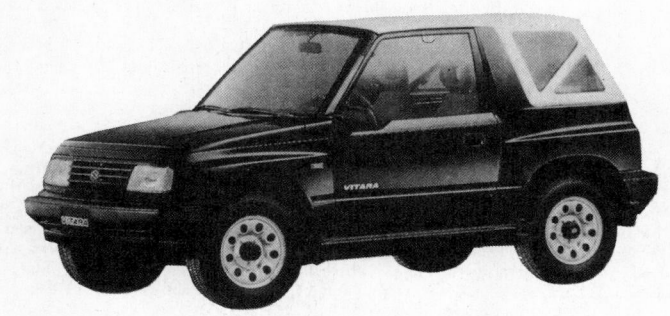

presenting a UK passport. Prescribed medicines must be paid for.

TRAVEL - International

Note: Due to the war to the southeast, Slovenia does not as yet fully control all of its airspace. Contact the FCO's travel advice unit prior to any visit. Tel: (071) 270 4129.
AIR: Slovenia's national airline is *Adria Airways* which operates direct flights from London to Ljubljana.
Approximate flight times: From *London* to Ljubljana is 2 hours.
International airports: *Ljubljana (LJU)* (Brnik) is 25km (15 miles) from the city. Buses are available to Kranj (travel time – 15 minutes) and to Ljubljana (travel time – 45 minutes). Taxis are also available. Airport facilities include bank (0900-1200 and 1430-1730), post office (0700-1800 Monday-Friday, 0700-1200 Saturday), duty-free shops (0700-2100), bars (0730-2000), restaurants (0800-1900), snack bar (0730-2000), shops (0800-1900) and car hire (*Hertz* and *Budget*).
Maribor also has some international connections.
Departure tax: DM22.
SEA: Ferries link the Adriatic Coast with Italian ports.
RAIL: Connections and through coaches are available from principal east and west European cities. There are other links, particularly via Venice and Vienna. International trains have couchette coaches as well as bar and dining cars. On some lines transport for cars is provided.
ROAD: The following frontier posts are open for road traffic:
From **Italy:** San Bartolomeo–Lazaret; Albaro Veskova–Skofije; Pesse–Kozina; Lipizza–Lipica; Fernetti–Fernetici (Sezana); Gorizia–Nova Gorica; Stupizza–Robic; Uccea–Uceja; Passo del Predil–Predel; and Fusine Laghi–Ratece.
From **Austria:** Wurzenpass (Villach)–Korensko Sedlo; Loibl–tunnel–Ljubelj; Seebergsattel–Jezersko; Grablach–Holmec; Rabenstein–Vic; Eibiswald–Radlji od Dravi; Langegg–Jurij; Spielfeld–Sentilj; Mureck–Trate; Sicheldorf–Gederovci; Radkersburg–Gornja Radgona; and Bonisdorf–Kuzma.
From **Hungary:** Bajansenye–Hodos.
Nearly all the passes mentioned above are open 24 hours a day.
See below for information regarding **documentation** and **traffic regulations**.

TRAVEL - Internal

AIR: There are domestic airports at Maribor in the east of the country and on the Adriatic Coast at Portoroz.
SEA: Slovenia has ports at Koper, Izola and Piran.
ROAD: There is a good network of high-quality roads in Slovenia. However, due to the war, they now effectively stop at Zagreb. There are extensive detours via Hungary for traffic going to and coming from Belgrade further south. For further information contact the national automobile club Auto-Moto Zveza Slovenije (AMZS), Dunajska 128, 61000 Ljubljana. Tel: (61) 181 111.
Speed limits: 120kmph (75mph) on motorways, 100kmph (62mph) on other roads. In cities it is 60kmph (38mph). School buses cannot be overtaken. The alcohol limit is 0.5%. **Documentation:** Full national driving licences are accepted. No customs documents are required, but car log books and Third Party Green Card insurance are necessary.
URBAN: Ljubljana has bus services and taxis are widely available.
JOURNEY TIMES: The following chart gives approximate journey times from Ljubljana (in hours and minutes) to other major cities in Slovenia.

	Road	Rail
Portoroz	1.30	2.30
Maribor	2.00	2.30
Lipica	1.00	-
Bled	0.45	1.15
Murska Sobota	3.00	3.30
Postojna	0.45	1.00
Novo Mesto	1.00	1.30

ACCOMMODATION

HOTELS: Slovenia has over 75,000 beds in hotels throughout the country. Standards are high and

SLOVENIA	HEALTH REGULATIONS	VISA REGULATIONS
GALILEO/WORLDSPAN	 TI-DFT/LJU/HE	TI-DFT/LJU/VI
SABRE	 TIDFT/LJU/HE	TIDFT/LJU/VI

Code-Link

To access this information on your CRS, swipe the barcode with a light pen or type in the text under the barcode. For more information, see the introduction *How to Use This Book*.

accommodation is classified from Deluxe to A, B, C and D class. Further hotel information is available from the Centre for Tourist and Economic Promotion (for address, see top of entry).

RESORTS & EXCURSIONS

The Slovene capital, **Ljubljana**, stretches along the banks of the Ljubljanca River. The old part of the town is particularly picturesque. Three bridges cross the river, one leading directly to the *Town Hall* (1718) and its Baroque fountain. The two open courtyards are not to be missed. Towering over the city are the twin towers of *Ljubljana Cathedral* (1708) which contain impressive frescoes. The *Castle*, situated on a hill, overlooks the river. Part of the Castle is currently undergoing repairs and only part of it is open to the public. The tower offers a splendid view of the city. On the eastern bank of the river is the *Town Museum* with an extensive collection of Roman artefacts. Near to the *University* is the *Ursuline Church* (1726) with an altar by Robba. The *National Museum* is well worth a visit. The *National Gallery*, the *Municipal Gallery* and the *Modern Art Gallery* with the quiet *Tivoli Gardens* should be part of every itinerary. The **Julian Alps** are a popular skiing area in the winter, particularly the resorts of **Kranjska Gora** and **Bovec**. **Podkoren** is situated in the mountains near the Austrian border. The fashionable mountain resort of **Bled** is set on the idyllic *Lake Bled*, a place of skating and curling in the winter, and swimming and rowing in the summer. The trout and carp fishing is also very good. Sights include the neo-Gothic *Parish Church* (1904) with its interesting frescoes and *Bled Castle*, the former seat of the bishops of Brixen. Perching above a 100m drop, the castle offers magnificent views over the city and lake. **Ptuj** contains Roman remains, a medieval centre and is the scene of traditional carnivals. **Portoroz** is the largest and best-known resort in Slovenia. The port of **Koper** still retains an Italian flair. The old town, entered through *Muda Gate*, is particularly worth exploring. Passing the *Bridge Fountain*, the street widens onto the city's central square. In general, the sights are clustered around the *Town Tower* (1480) which dominates the skyline. Fine examples of the Venetian Gothic style are given by the 15th-century *cathedral*, the *loggia* and the *Praetor's Palace*; also of interest is the Romanesque *Carmin Rotunda* (1317). Well worth a visit is the excellent *Provincial Museum* which houses old maps of the area.

SOCIAL PROFILE

FOOD & DRINK: Slovenia's national cuisine shows an Austro-German influence with sauerkraut, grilled sausage and apple strudel often appearing on menus.
SHOPPING: Shopping hours: 0800-1900 Monday to Friday.
NIGHTLIFE: There is a good selection of theatres, cinemas and clubs in the larger towns. Ljubljana also has a good opera house and the symphony orchestra plays regularly in the Big Hall of the Cultural and Congress Centre.
SPORT: Skiing and **spa resorts** exist in all regions, but particularly Bled, Bohinj and Vogal. **Fishing** permits are available from hotels or local authorities. Fishing on the Adriatic coast is unrestricted, but freshwater angling and fishing with equipment require a permit. 'Fish-linking' with a local small craft owner is popular. **Sailing** is popular along the coast. Berths and boats can be hired at all ports. Permits are needed for boats brought into the country. **Spectator sports:** Football is very popular.
SPECIAL EVENTS: The following event is celebrated annually in Slovenia. Many major cities hold theatre festivals in October. For a complete list, contact the Embassy.
Bohinj: *'Cattle Ball'* (third Sunday in September).
SOCIAL CONVENTIONS: Shaking hands is the normal form of greeting. The visitor will find the Slovenes a very hospitable and generous people; usual social conventions apply and informal dress is widely acceptable. Smoking is prohibited on public transport, in cinemas, theatres, public offices and in waiting rooms. **Tipping:** 10% is generally expected in hotels, restaurants and for taxis.

BUSINESS PROFILE

ECONOMY: By far the richest and most economically developed of the former Yugoslav republics, Slovenia accounted for 20% of Yugoslavia's GDP (around US$10.7 billion) and industrial output, and 30% of its exports (60% of which went to Western convertible currency markets) in 1990, with a GDP per capita of around US$5000 in the same year (double the Yugoslav average, but only a third of that then prevailing in nearby Austria). A highly industrialised economy with a foodstuffs deficit and no natural resources, Slovenia was seriously affected by the various adverse consequences of the civil war (notably the collapse of the old Yugoslav market) in 1991, when the GDP fell by 15% (with another 10% fall expected in 1992). Real living standards fell by 30% and previously non-existent unemployment rose to 10% of the working population. Consequently, the Government wants to see free trade arrangements between the various ex-Yugoslav republics, but these remain politically improbable due to Croatian government objections and the imposition of UN economic sanctions against Serbia and Montenegro in June 1992. Slovenia's main problem is its domestic market which is too small to be viable in the longer term, while exports to Western markets will have to increase by over 300% to maintain present living standards. Export performances declined in 1991, mainly due to supply problems from the southern republics, diminishing stocks of capital and a deteriorating infrastructure. Foreign economic assistance and investment is thus urgently required, with forthcoming IMF membership likely to expedite its arrival, but not on the large scale envisaged by the Government, whose previous relative success in attracting such external resources was due to its position within a larger all-Yugoslav market. Another possible impediment to increased foreign interest in Slovenia is the relatively slow pace of socio-economic reform, with key legislation (notably on privatisation) endlessly delayed since 1990 by political squabbling within the Government and elsewhere. In the longer term, all this could threaten the repayments of the republic's agreed share of the former federation's foreign debt (US$1.8 billion, plus around 20% of unallocated federal debt, or around 20% of the total Yugoslav foreign debt). As of June 1992, when the Bank of Slovenia had foreign exchange reserves of around US$500 million, Slovenia was unique among the ex-Yugoslav republics in repaying its foreign debt share more or less according to schedule. Prior to the imposition of UN economic sanctions against Serbia and Montenegro in June 1992, Slovenia accounted for around 25% of bilateral UK trade with Yugoslavia in 1991 (the Serbian share of such trade was around

65%), when British creditor interests also held around 8% of Slovenia's foreign debt.

BUSINESS: Smart dress is advised. Appointments are usual and visitors should be punctual. Visiting cards are essential. Slovenia is the most efficient and reliable of the ex-Yugoslav republics, being in many respects comparable to Austria and Germany. Executives will generally have a good knowledge of German, English and sometimes Italian. There is a well-developed network of local agents, advisers, consultants and lawyers willing to act for foreign companies. **Office hours:** 0700-1500 Monday to Friday.

COMMERCIAL INFORMATION: The following organisation can offer advice: Chamber of Economy of Slovenia, Slovenska cesta 41, 61000 Ljubljana. Tel: (61) 150 122. Fax: (61) 219 536.

CONFERENCES/CONVENTIONS: Slovenia's tradition as a meeting place goes back to 1821, when it played host to the Congress of the Holy Alliance. The main conference locations are Ljubljana, Bled, Portoroz, Radenci and Rogaska Slatina, where there are meeting facilities for up to 2000 participants. For more information contact Kulturni in Kongresni Center Cankarsev Dom, Kidricev Park 1, 61000 Ljubljana. Tel: (61) 158 121 *or* 224 133. Fax: (61) 217 431 *or* 224 279. Telex: 32111 LJ *or* 32101 LJ.

HISTORY & GOVERNMENT

HISTORY: Historically settled in four distinct areas (Styria, Carniola, Carinthia and Gorizia) since the 5th century, the Slav and later Roman Catholic Slovenes were henceforth variously dominated by the Bavarians, the Frankish Empire of the Carolingians, and the German-dominated Holy Roman Empire, whose rule lasted in one form or another from the 9th to the 19th centuries. In the 14th century, the Slovene territories became hereditary possessions of the House of Habsburg. After 1867, when the Habsburg realm became the Dual Monarchy of Austria and Hungary, the Slovenes fell under the jurisdiction of the Austrian Crown. Despite considerable socio-economic progress locally thereafter, the ancient threat posed to Slovene survival and cultural identity by Germanisation pushed local political sentiment towards supporting the growing South Slav movement of the Croats and Serbs. Thus, following the destruction of the Austro-Hungarian empire during the First World War, Slovenia became a part of the new 'Kingdom of Serbs, Croats and Slovenes' in 1918 (renamed 'Yugoslavia' in 1929). In 1941, when the Axis powers dismembered Yugoslavia, Slovenia was carved up between Germany, Italy and Hungary. Local resistance, initially non-communist nationalist, was forcibly hijacked by the Yugoslav Communist Party led by Josip Broz Tito, himself partly of Slovene origin. In 1945, after the communists emerged as victors, Slovenia became a constituent republic of the new Yugoslav federation. The ruling League of Communists of Slovenia (LCS) supported the Croats in the demand for an effectively confederal Yugoslavia during the 1960s and 1970s, although never to the point of provoking Tito into repression, as took place in Croatia in 1971. Among other things, this caution made a relatively politically liberal atmosphere in Slovenia possible, culminating in a pluralist 'Slovene Spring' after Milan Kucan became LCS leader in 1986. The nationalist Kucan steered Slovenia towards independence following multi-party national assembly elections in April 1990 which brought to power a six-party centre-right coalition, calling itself DEMOS, led by premier Lozle Peterle. After 14 months during which Slovenia and Croatia became increasingly alienated from Belgrade, Slovenia declared independence. Thus provoked, the central government sent in armoured convoys to take control of federal border posts and key installations in the capital Ljubljana. The army was clearly not expecting the resistance put up by well-prepared Slovene irregulars and after a few weeks of sporadic and largely inconclusive fighting, a ceasefire was reached. By October 1991, all federal military forces had left the republic, which proclaimed its full independence on October 8, following the expiry of a EC-agreed 3-month moratorium on disassociation from the Yugoslav federation. Full international recognition followed in January 1992, after which the DEMOS government collapsed, having achieved its sole objective of securing international recognition. Slovenia was admitted to the United Nations in June. A non-party government of technocrats led by Janez Drnovesk, replacing Lozle Peterle as Prime Minister, took over pending new elections. Slovenia is the only one of the ex-Yugoslav republics to have a substantial as opposed to a merely nominal multi-party democracy, although it is on the road to permanent coalition politics domestically.

GOVERNMENT: The constitution promulgated in December 1991 allows for the election of a new bicameral legislature to which elections will be held in late 1992. The State Presidency has five members of which the President of the presidency is Head of State.

CLIMATE

Continental climate with warm summers and cold winters (snowfalls in the Alps). Mediterranean climate on the coast.

Required clothing: Mediumweight clothing and heavy overcoats in winter; lightweight clothing and raincoats for the summer, particularly for the higher Alpine north.

LJUBLJANA Slovenia (299m)

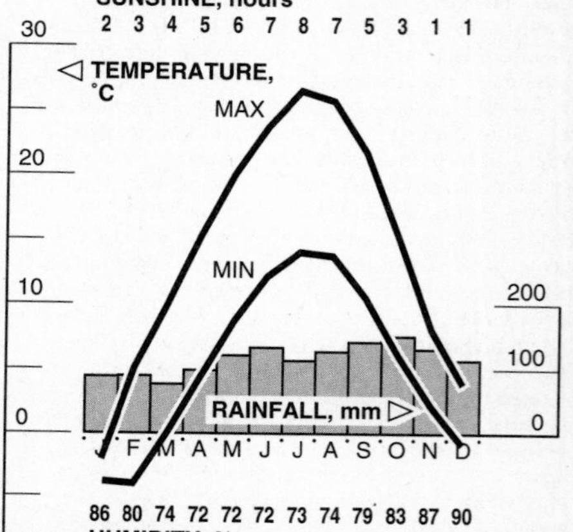

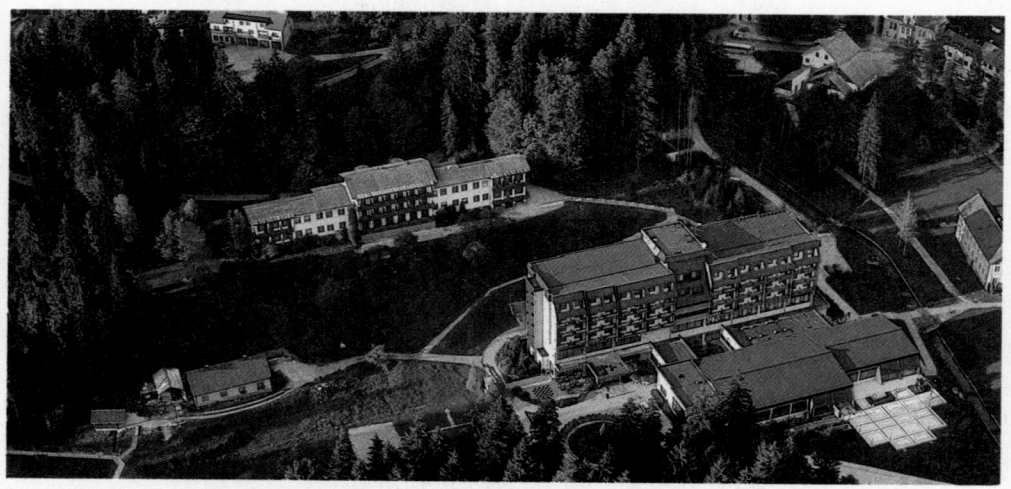

SOLOMON ISLANDS

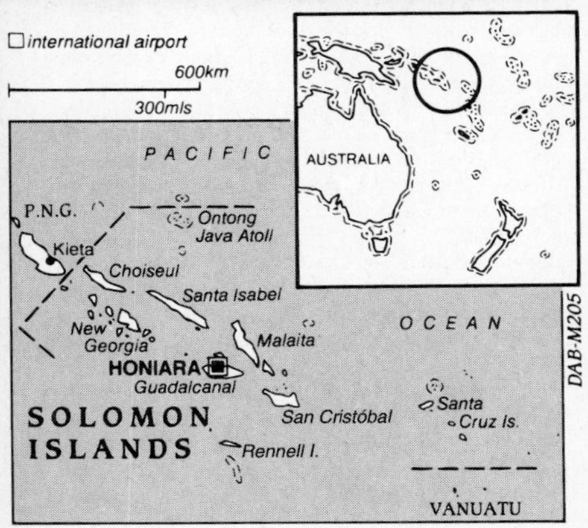

Location: Southwestern Pacific.

Solomon Islands Tourist Authority
PO Box 321
Honiara, Solomon Islands
Tel: 22442. Fax: 23986. Telex: 66436.

Ministry of Foreign Affairs and Trade Relations
PO Box G10
Honiara, Solomon Islands
Tel: 22223. Telex: 66311.

Solomon Island Airways
Sevenoaks Station
London Road
Sevenoaks, Kent TN13 1DP
Tel: (0732) 743050.

British High Commission
PO Box 676
Telekom House
Mendana Avenue
Honiara, Solomon Islands
Tel: 21705/6. Fax: 21549. Telex: 66324.

Solomon Islands Tourist Authority
c/o The Permanent Mission to the United Nations
Suite 800
820 Second Avenue
New York, NY
10017
Tel: (212) 599 6193/4. Fax: (212) 972 3970 Telex: 960945.
Also deals with enquiries from Canada.

Embassy of the United States of America
PO Box 561
Honiara, Solomon Islands
Tel: 20725. Fax: 23488. Telex: 66461.

The Canadian High Commission in Australia deals with enquiries relating to the Soloman Islands:
The Canadian High Commission
Commonwealth Avenue
Canberra ACT 2600
Tel: (6) 273 3844. Fax: (6) 273 3285.

AREA: 27,566 sq km (10,639 sq miles).
POPULATION: 318,707 (1990 estimate).
POPULATION DENSITY: 11.6 per sq km.
CAPITAL: Honiara. **Population:** 35,288 (1990 estimate).
GEOGRAPHY: The Solomon Islands Archipelago is scattered in the southwestern Pacific, east of Papua New Guinea. The group comprises most of the Solomon Islands (those in the northwest belonging to Papua New Guinea), the Ontong Java Islands, Rennell Island and the Santa Cruz Islands, which lie further to the east. The larger of the islands are 145-193km (90-120 miles) in length, while the smallest are no more than coral outcrops. The terrain is generally quite rugged, with foothills that rise gently to a peak and then fall away steeply to the sea on the other side. The capital Honiara is situated on Guadalcanal Island which also has the highest mountain, Mount Makarakombu, at 2447m (8028ft). There are a number of dormant volcanoes scattered throughout the archipelago.
LANGUAGE: English is the official language. Pidgin English and over 87 different local dialects are also spoken.
RELIGION: More than 95% of the population are Christian.
TIME: GMT + 11.
ELECTRICITY: 240 volts AC, 50Hz. Australian type flat 3-pin plugs are in use.
COMMUNICATIONS: Telephone: IDD is available. Country code: 677. **Fax:** *Solomon Telekom* provides services at its offices in Honiara, though introduction elsewhere has been gradual and only some hotels have facilities. Address: Solomon Telekom, PO Box 148, Honiara, Guadalcanal. Tel: 21576. Fax: 23110. Telex: 66301. **Telex/telegram:** Services available 24 hours a day administered by Solomon Telekom (address above). **Post:** Airmail to Europe takes approximately seven days. The main post office in Honiara opens 0900-1630 Monday to Friday and 0900-1100 Saturday. Other post office opening hours are 0800-1630 Monday to Friday and 0800-1200 Saturday. **Press:** The main newspaper is the weekly *The Solomon Star*.
BBC World Service and Voice of America frequencies: From time to time these change. See the section *How to Use this Book* for more information.

BBC:				
MHz	17.10	15.36	9.740	7.150
Voice of America:				
MHz	18.82	15.18	9.525	1.735

PASSPORT/VISA

Regulations and requirements may be subject to change at short notice, and you are advised to contact the appropriate diplomatic or consular authority before finalising travel arrangements. Details of these may be found at the head of this country's entry. Any numbers in the chart refer to the footnotes below.

	Passport Required?	Visa Required?	Return Ticket Required?
Full British	Yes	No	Yes
BVP	Not valid	-	-
Australian	Yes	No	Yes
Canadian	Yes	No	Yes
USA	Yes	No	Yes
Other EC	Yes	1	Yes
Japanese	Yes	No	Yes

PASSPORTS: Valid passport required by all.
British Visitors Passport: Not accepted.
VISAS: Required by all except:
(a) those referred to in the chart above;
(b) **[1]** nationals of Belgium, Denmark, France, Germany, Greece, Italy, Luxembourg and Spain (all other EC nationals *do* require visas);
(c) nationals of Bahamas, Bangladesh, Barbados, Botswana, Cyprus, Dominica, Fiji, Finland, Gambia, Ghana, Grenada, Guyana, Iceland, India, Jamaica, Kenya, Kiribati, Lesotho, Liechtenstein, Malawi, Malaysia, Malta, Mauritius, Nauru, New Zealand, Nigeria, Norway, Papua New Guinea, St Lucia, St Vincent & the Grenadines, San Marino, Seychelles, Sierra Leone, Singapore, Sri Lanka, Swaziland, Sweden, Switzerland, Tanzania, Tonga, Trinidad & Tobago, Tunisia, Turkey, Tuvalu, Uganda, Uruguay, Western Samoa, Zambia and Zimbabwe.
Note: Visitor's Permits for up to two months will be issued on arrival to the above nationals provided they have a passport and return ticket.
Types of visa: Tourist, Transit; price on application. Transit visas are not required by those continuing their journey to a third country within 7 days and holding tickets with reserved seats for their onward journey. However, this does not apply to nationals of Albania, Bulgaria, China, Cuba, Czechoslovakia, Hungary, North Korea, Lebanon, Mongolia, Poland, Romania, USSR, Vietnam and Yugoslavia.
Application to: Principal Immigration Officer, Ministry of Commerce and Primary Industries, PO Box G26, Honiara. Tel: 21140. Telex: 66311.
Application requirements: Enquire at Immigration Division, Ministry of Commerce and Primary Industries.
Working days required: Apply well in advance.
Temporary residence: Ministry of Commerce and Primary Industries.

MONEY

Currency: Solomon Islands Dollar (SI$) = 100 cents. Notes are in denominations of SI$50, 20, 10, 5 and 2. Coins are in denominations of SI$1, and 50, 20, 10, 5, 2 and 1 cents.
Credit cards: Diners Club is accepted on a limited basis. Check with your credit card company for details of merchant acceptability and other facilities which may be available.
Travellers cheques: Can be exchanged at banks.
Exchange rate indicators: The following figures are included as a guide to the movements of the Solomon Islands Dollar against Sterling and the US Dollar:

Date:	Oct '89	Oct '90	Oct '91	Oct '92
£1.00=	3.77	5.02	4.77	4.72
$1.00=	2.39	2.57	2.75	2.97

Currency restrictions: Free import of foreign currency, subject to declaration; export limited to amount declared on arrival. Free import of local currency, export limited to SI$250.
Banking hours: 0900-1500 Monday to Friday.

DUTY FREE

The following items may be imported into the Solomon Islands without incurring customs duty:
200 cigarettes or 250g cigars or 250g of tobacco;
2 litres of wine/spirits;
Other dutiable goods to a total value of SI$40.
Prohibited items: Unlicensed firearms or other weapons.

PUBLIC HOLIDAYS

Public holidays observed in the Solomon Islands are as follows:
Apr 9-12 '93 Easter. **May 31** Whit Monday. **Jun 4** Queen's Official Birthday. **Jul 7** Independence Day. **Dec 25-26** Christmas. **Jan 1 '94** New Year's Day.

HEALTH

Regulations and requirements may be subject to change at short notice, and you are advised to contact your doctor well in advance of your intended date of departure. Any numbers in the chart refer to the footnotes below.

	Special Precautions?	Certificate Required?
Yellow Fever	No	1
Cholera	No	No
Typhoid & Polio	Yes	-
Malaria	2	-
Food & Drink	3	-

[1]: A yellow fever vaccination certificate is required by travellers arriving from infected areas.
[2]: Malaria risk exists throughout the year except in some outlying islets in the east and south. The malignant *falciparum* strain is present and is reported to be 'resistant' to chloroquine.
[3]: All water should be regarded as being a potential health risk. Water used for drinking, brushing teeth or making ice should first be boiled or otherwise sterilised. Milk is unpasteurised and should be boiled. Powdered or tinned milk is available and is advised, but make sure that it is reconstituted with pure water. Avoid dairy products which are likely to have been made from unboiled milk. Only eat well-cooked meat and fish, preferably served hot. Pork, salad and mayonnaise may carry increased risk. Vegetables should be cooked and fruit peeled.
Health care: There are eight hospitals, the largest being the Central Hospital in Honiara, Guadalcanal. Church missions provide medical facilities on outlying islands. Health insurance is essential.

TRAVEL - International

AIR: The Solomon Islands' national airline is *Solomon Island Airways (IE)*.
Approximate flight time: From *London* to Honiara is 29 hours 45 minutes, excluding stopover time in Brisbane.
International airport: *Honiara (HIR)* (Henderson Field) on Guadalcanal Island, 20km (8 miles) from Honiara (travel time – 20 minutes). Bus and taxi services are available.
Departure tax: SI$30 for all departures. Transit passengers and children under two years are exempt.
SEA: International ports are Honiara (Guadalcanal Island) and Yandina (Russell Island). Plans are in hand to build a new deep-sea harbour at Noro on New Georgia, which will replace the port at Gizo. The two principal passenger lines with services to the Solomons are *P&O* and *Sitmar*.

TRAVEL - Internal

AIR: Domestic scheduled and charter services are run by *Solomon Island Airways (IE)* from Henderson Field to most main islands and towns in the Solomons. Flightseeing tours can be arranged.
SEA: Large and small ships provide the best means of travelling between islands. Services are run by the Government and by a host of private operators; some of the Christian missions even have their own fleets.
ROAD: There are over 1300km (800 miles) of roads throughout the islands. About 455km (280 miles) are

main roads and a further 800km (500 miles) are privately maintained roads for plantation use. Road maintenance is limited and the general condition of the roads is poor. **Taxi:** Available in Honiara and Auki. It is advisable to agree the fare beforehand. **Car hire:** This is available through hotels in Honiara. **Documentation:** A national driving licence will suffice.

ACCOMMODATION

HOTELS: There are only six hotels in Honiara. Visitors are advised to make advance reservations. The *Tavanipupu Island Resort* in the Marau Sound (Guadalcanal) is accessible by air and sea. Accommodation is also available in the Reef Islands, Western Solomons and Malaita. A number of lodges and resorts on the islands offer a variety of leisure activities. A full list of accommodation and rates is available from the Solomon Islands Tourist Authority (address at top of entry).

Camping is rare and is best confined to remoter areas. Permission should always be obtained from the landowner, usually the village chief, before pitching your tent.

RESORTS & EXCURSIONS

Guadalcanal, Malaita, Cghoiseul, New Georgia, San Cristobal and **Santa Isabella** are the main islands. They are up to 200km (120 miles) long and up to 50km (30 miles) wide. The wildlife on the islands is of great interest, consisting of a mixture of introduced and indigenous species. Most islands are populated with a range of reptiles (including turtles), as well as marsupials including 'flying foxes' (fruitbats), phalangers and opossums. Later introductions include pigs and chickens. Europeans brought cats, horses, cattle and goats. Hawks, cuckoos, waders and other often colourful birds exhibit the diversity of behaviour typical of island creatures. The buff-headed coucal is the world's largest cuckoo. The ubiquitous ants, beetles, spiders, moths, butterflies and frogs also come in a variety of forms. The ocean around the islands is crammed with exotic creatures, though a visitor would be well advised to be cautious of some of them.

Honiara, the capital on **Guadalcanal,** has a museum, botanical gardens and Chinatown. There are World War II relics in and around the town and noticeboards indicate major battles and incidents that took place during the battle for Guadalcanal. Villages and scenic drives are within easy reach.

Three travel agencies can arrange excursions around Guadalcanal and other islands. Popular tours include the battlefields of World War II, the *Betikama* carving centre, *Chapura* and *Tambea* villages on Guadalcanal, and *Laulasi* and *Alite* villages on the island of **Malaita**, where shells are broken, rounded and, after further working, strung together. They are used to denote status and as gifts and items of barter in inter-tribal deals. The strings of shells can be worn as bracelets, necklaces, belts and earrings. They may also include animal and fish teeth, and, in times past, the teeth of murderers. Collectively, these items are known as 'shell money'.

Carvings for the tourist trade are made on **Rennell** and **Bellona.** Miniature daggers, spears and clubs are very popular. Other carvings show scenes from life on the Solomon Islands, both human and animal.

Tourists can easily organise their own excursions, with timetables and information provided by the tourist authority and travel agents.

SOCIAL PROFILE

FOOD & DRINK: Local recipes include *tapioca* pudding and *taro* roots with *taro* leaves. There are a few restaurants outside the hotels in Honaria. Both Asian and European food is served and the cuisine is generally good. There are two Chinese restaurants in Honiara which are quite popular. Spirits, wine and beer are available. Table service is normal.

NIGHTLIFE: Honiara is a comparatively quiet town, although there are a few clubs with music and dancing, the occasional film show and snooker and darts. The clubs offer temporary membership to visitors.

SHOPPING: Local purchases include mother-of-pearl items, walking sticks, carved and inlaid wood, copper murals, conch shells and rare varieties of cowrie. New Georgia in the western district is known for carved fish, turtles and birds. Carvings in ebony, inlaid with shell, are unique. Duty-free shopping is available at a number of stores in Honiara. **Shopping hours:** 0800-1700 Monday to Friday and 0800-1230 Saturday.

SPORT: Surrounding waters have good **fishing** potential and enquiries may be made at the *Point Cruz Yacht Club*, which welcomes visitors. A number of resorts now offer a broad variety of sea and other sports. **Swimming** is not recommended in the sea around Honiara because of sharks. In any case, swimmers should be beware of sea urchins, bristle-worms, stinging corals, crown of thorn starfish and further exotic sealife. There are a number of swimming pools. **Tennis** courts are at the *Guadalcanal Club* and arrangements can be made through the hotels. **Dives** are arranged most weekends by the *Skin Diver Association* which can be contacted through the Solomon Islands Tourist Authority. There is a 9-hole **golf** course outside Honiara and local tourist agents will make arrangements. The *Tamba Village Resort* west of Honiara has a miniature golf course.

SPECIAL EVENTS: Each part of the Solomon Islands has its own *Province Day*. These are listed below:

Jun 8 '93 *Temotu*. **Jun 29** *Central*. **Jul 8** *Isabel*. **Jul 31** *Guadalcanal*. **Aug 3** *Makira*. **Aug 14** *Malaita*. **Dec 7** *Western*.

SOCIAL CONVENTIONS: A casual atmosphere prevails and European customs exist alongside local traditions. Informal wear is widely suitable although women often wear long dresses for evening functions. Men need never wear ties. It is customary to cover thighs. Visitors are discouraged from wearing beachwear and shorts around towns and villages. **Tipping:** There is no tipping on the Solomon Islands and visitors are requested to honour this local custom.

BUSINESS PROFILE

ECONOMY: The economy continues to depend on subsistence agriculture, employing about 90% of the population in producing coconuts, sweet potatoes, cassava, fruit and vegetables, although fish and related products have been the most important exports since 1984. A great deal of copra continues to be produced, but the world price has in recent years been steadily declining and government economic policy is concerned with increasing foreign investment and commercial development. New agricultural products included cocoa and palm oil while an indigenous timber industry was successfully developed and some rich mineral deposits have been located. The latter include phosphates, bauxite and asbestos and there is a possibility of gold, silver and copper. Tourism is relatively minor as yet but may develop significantly in the future. The Solomon Islands also enjoy substantial overseas aid. Australia and Japan are the main trading partners. The islands' total trade in 1987 was US$130 million.

BUSINESS: Shirt and smart trousers or skirt will suffice. English and French are widely spoken. Best time to visit is May to October. **Office hours:** 0800-1200 and 1300-1630 Monday to Friday and 0730-1200 Saturday.

COMMERCIAL INFORMATION: The following organisation can offer advice: Solomon Islands Chamber of Commerce, PO Box 64, Honiara. Tel: 22960. Telex: 66448.

HISTORY & GOVERNMENT

HISTORY: The modern nation of the Solomon Islands is an amalgamation of two archipelagos created by the British in the last years of the 19th century, the high point of the imperial rivalry in the Pacific between the major European powers. The northern group was first claimed by the Spanish in the 16th century, then annexed by the Germans and finally ceded to the British (in exchange for part of the Samoan island group) who administered it together with the southern group, which they already controlled, as the British Solomon Islands Protectorate. Apart from a brief spell under Japanese occupation during the Second World War, the Solomon Islands remained under British rule until the 1970s. Self-government was granted in 1976 and full independence was achieved two years later. The main political debate since then has concerned the issue of decentralisation, whose advocates seek the division of the archipelago into separate administrative regions. Opponents maintain, however, that such divisions operate excessively in favour of those islands which are most commercially developed. (These lie mainly in the west, closer to Papua New Guinea and Australia.) After initial successes by the devolution lobby, the results of recent elections have backed those who wish to reassert the power of central government. Although closer to Asia and Australasia than many other Pacific micro-states, the Solomons' development has been hampered at times by governments prone to haphazard decision-making. Following the latest elections, held in February 1989, the People's Alliance Party with 11 seats became the largest single party in the 38-seat assembly, while party leader Solomon Mamaloni assumed the office of Prime Minister. The new premier immediately announced the suspension of all overseas aid to his country, an extraordinary decision which deprived the Solomons of a sum equivalent to almost one-fifth of GDP. The economy has been in steady decline throughout the 1990s and the islands' prospects can only be described as uncertain. Abroad, foreign relations have been dominated by the dispute with Papua New Guinea over the Solomons' alleged support for the secessionists of Bougainville (see *Papua New Guinea*). Despite this, the two countries have joined together with Vanuatu to form a Melanesian Spearhead Group which seeks to protect Melanesian cultural integrity and political interests, particularly independence for the islanders of New Caledonia.

GOVERNMENT: The British monarch, represented by a Governor-General, is the Head of State, but real power is held by the Prime Minister, who presides over a cabinet of 14 other ministers. The legislature is unicameral and is made up of members of the four main political groups as well as many independents; in the 1989 general election 14 out of 38 members returned had no party affiliation.

CLIMATE

Semi-tropical, mainly hot and humid, with little annual variation in temperature. The wet season (November to April) can bring severe tropical storms.

Required clothing: Tropical, lightweights and cottons are recommended. Rainwear from November to April.

KIETA Papua New Guinea (73m)

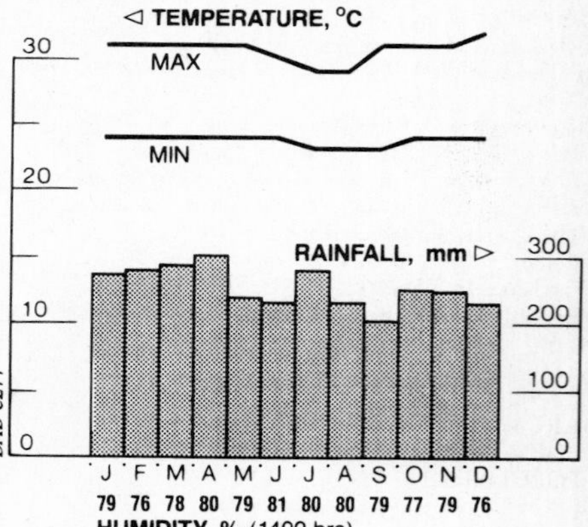

SOLOMON ISLANDS	HEALTH REGULATIONS	VISA REGULATIONS
GALILEO/WORLDSPAN	 TI-DFT/HIR/HE	TI-DFT/HIR/VI
SABRE	TIDFT/HIR/HE	TIDFT/HIR/VI

Code-Link

To access this information on your CRS, swipe the barcode with a light pen or type in the text under the barcode. For more information, see the introduction *How to Use This Book*.

SOMALIA

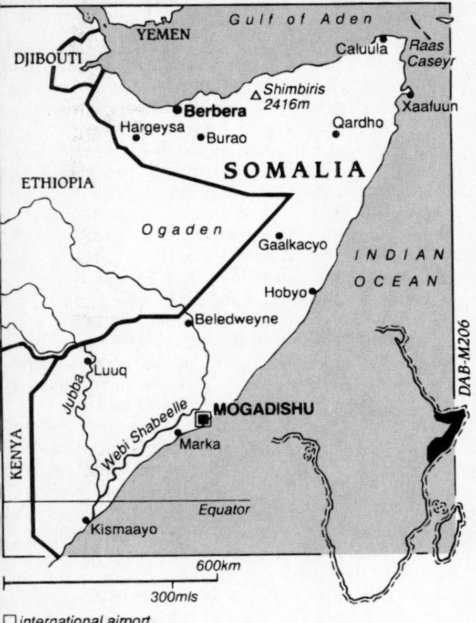

Location: East Africa.

Note: At the time of writing (January 1993), there is fierce fighting in the capital and other parts of the country, diplomatic representations are closed and prospective visitors should contact the Foreign Office (or exterior affairs department of their country) for information about the current level and geographical extent of the conflict. The embassies are currently closed and the following information largely represents the situation before the current civil war, and is presented in the hope that it will again prove useful.

Embassy of the Somali Democratic Republic
(Presently closed.)
60 Portland Place
London W1N 3DG
Tel: (071) 580 7148. Telex: 267672 SOMDIP. Opening hours: 1000-1530 Monday to Friday.
British Embassy
PO Box 1036
Hassan Geedi Abtow
Mogadishu, Somalia
Tel: (1) 20288. Telex: 3617.
Embassy of the Somali Democratic Republic
Suite 710
600 New Hampshire Avenue, NW
Washington, DC
20037
Tel: (202) 342 1575.
The Canadian Embassy in Kenya deals with enquiries relating to Somalia:
The Canadian High Commission
PO Box 30481
Comcraft House, Haile Selassie Avenue,
Nairobi, Kenya
Tel: (2) 214 804. Fax: (2) 226 987.

AREA: 637,657 sq km (246,201 sq miles).
POPULATION: 7,691,000 (1991 estimate).
POPULATION DENSITY: 11.2 per sq km.
CAPITAL: Mogadishu. **Population:** 500,000 (1981).
GEOGRAPHY: Somalia is bounded to the north by the Gulf of Aden, to the south and west by Kenya, to the west by Ethiopia and to the northwest by Djibouti. To the east lies the Indian Ocean. Somalia is an arid country and the scenery includes mountains in the north, the flat semi-desert plains in the interior and the subtropical region in the south. Separated from the sea by a narrow coastal plain, the mountains slope south and west to the central, almost waterless plateau which makes up most of the country. The beaches are protected by a coral reef that runs from Mogadishu to the Kenyan border in the south. They are among the longest in the world. There are only two rivers, the Juba and the Shebelle, and both rise in the Ogaden region of Ethiopia. Along their banks is most of the country's agricultural land. The Somali population is concentrated in the coastal towns, in the wetter, northern areas and in the south near the two rivers. A large nomadic population is scattered over the interior, although drought in recent years has led to many settling as farmers or fishermen in newly formed communities.
LANGUAGE: Somali and Arabic are the official languages. Swahili is spoken, particularly in the south. Some English and Italian are also spoken.
RELIGION: 90% Muslim, with a Christian (mostly Roman Catholic) minority.
TIME: GMT + 3.
ELECTRICITY: 220 volts AC, 50Hz.
COMMUNICATIONS: Telephone: IDD is available. Country code: 252. **Telex/telegram:** There are limited facilities in the capital, but the main Post Office in Mogadishu, opposite the Hotel Juba, offers services. **Post:** Airmail to Europe takes up to two weeks. **Press:** No English-language dailies are published.
BBC World Service and Voice of America frequencies: From time to time these change. See the section *How to Use this Book* for more information.

BBC:

MHz	21.47	17.64	15.42	6.005

A service is also available on 1413kHz (0100-0500 GMT).

Voice of America:

MHz	21.49	15.60	9.525	6.035

PASSPORT/VISA

Regulations and requirements may be subject to change at short notice, and you are advised to contact the appropriate diplomatic or consular authority before finalising travel arrangements. Details of these may be found at the head of this country's entry. Any numbers in the chart refer to the footnotes below.

	Passport Required?	Visa Required?	Return Ticket Required?
Full British	Yes	Yes	Yes
BVP	Not valid	-	-
Australian	Yes	Yes	Yes
Canadian	Yes	Yes	Yes
USA	Yes	Yes	Yes
Other EC	Yes	Yes	Yes
Japanese	Yes	Yes	Yes

Note: The Somali Embassy is currently closed due to civil war in Somalia. Contact the Foreign Office (tel: (071) 270 2894) for any information regarding entry into Somalia.
PASSPORTS: Valid passport required by all.
British Visitors Passport: Not accepted.
VISAS: Required by all. Transit visas not required by visitors with booked seats and documents for onward travel who continue their journey to a third country by the same aircraft on the day of arrival without leaving the airport.
Types of visa: Tourist and Business, cost £10; Transit.
Validity: Depends on nationality.
Application to: Immigration Department in Mogadishu or Consulate (or Consular Section at Embassy). For addresses, see top of entry.
Application requirements: (a) 2 completed application forms. (b) 2 photos. (c) Fee. (d) Confirmation telex from sponsor in Somalia (for Business visa). (e) Letter from sponsor (for Business visa).
Working days required: 1 month.
Temporary residence: Apply to Embassy.

MONEY

Currency: Somali Shilling (SoSh) = 100 cents. Notes are in denominations of SoSh100, 50, 20, 10 and 5. Coins are in denominations of SoSh1, and 50, 10 and 5 cents.
Credit cards: Diners Club has limited acceptability. Check with your credit card company for details of merchant acceptability and other facilities which may be available.
Travellers cheques: US travellers cheques are preferred. These can be cashed at banks and some hotels.
Exchange rate indicators: The following figures are included as a guide to the movements of the Somali Shilling against Sterling and the US Dollar:

Date:	Oct '89	Oct '90	Oct '91	Oct '92
£1.00=	648.21	5112.9	4552.25	3985.38
$1.00=	410.52	2617.3	2623.02	2511.27

Note: The Shilling has been devalued a number of times in recent years.
Currency restrictions: The import and export of local currency is limited to SoSh200. Free import of foreign currency, subject to declaration on arrival and exchange at the National Banks within five days. Export of foreign currency limited to the amount declared on import. All foreign exchange transactions should be recorded on the official currency form which may be required prior to departure from Somalia.
Banking hours: 0800-1130 Saturday to Thursday.

DUTY FREE

The following goods may be imported into Somalia without incurring customs duty:
400 cigarettes or 400g of tobacco;
1 bottle of wine or spirits;
A reasonable amount of perfume for personal use.

PUBLIC HOLIDAYS

Public holidays observed in Somalia are as follows:
Mar 25 '93 Start of Eid al-Fitr. **May 1** Labour Day. **Jun 1** Eid al-Adha. **Jun 26** Independence Day. **Jun 30** Ashoura. **Jul 1** Foundation of the Republic. **Aug 30** Mouloud (Birth of the Prophet). **Jan 1 '94** New Year's Day. **Mar '94** Start of Eid al-Fitr.
Note: Muslim festivals are timed according to local sightings of various phases of the Moon and the dates given above are approximations. During the lunar month of Ramadan that precedes Eid al-Fitr, Muslims fast during the day and feast at night and normal business patterns may be interrupted. Many restaurants are closed during the day and there may be restrictions on smoking and drinking. Some disruption may continue into Eid al-Fitr itself. Eid al-Fitr and Eid al-Adha may last anything from two to ten days, depending on the region. For more information see the section *World of Islam* at the back of the book.

HEALTH

Regulations and requirements may be subject to change at short notice, and you are advised to contact your doctor well in advance of your intended date of departure. Any numbers in the chart refer to the footnotes below.

	Special Precautions?	Certificate Required?
Yellow Fever	Yes	1
Cholera	Yes	2
Typhoid & Polio	Yes	-
Malaria	3	-
Food & Drink	4	-

[1]: A yellow fever vaccination certificate is required from travellers arriving from infected areas.
[2]: A cholera vaccination certificate is required from all travellers.
[3]: Malaria risk, predominantly in the malignant *falciparum* form, exists all year throughout the country. Resistance to chloroquine has been reported.
[4]: Mains water is normally chlorinated, and whilst relatively safe may cause mild abdominal upsets. Bottled water is available and is advised for the first few weeks of stay. Drinking water outside main cities and towns is likely to be contaminated and sterilisation is considered essential. Milk is unpasteurised and should be boiled. Powdered or tinned milk is available and is advised, but make sure that it is reconstituted with pure water. Avoid dairy products which are likely to have been made from unboiled milk. Only eat well-cooked meat and fish, preferably served hot. Pork, salad and mayonnaise may carry increased risk. Vegetables should be cooked and fruit peeled.
Rabies is present. For those at high risk, vaccination before arrival should be considered. If you are bitten abroad seek medical advice without delay. For more information consult the *Health* section at the back of the book.
Bilharzia (schistosomiasis) is present. Avoid swimming and paddling in fresh water. Swimming pools which are well-chlorinated and maintained are safe.
Health care: Health insurance is essential. Medical treatment at government-run hospitals and dispensaries is free for Somalians and may sometimes be free for visitors.

TRAVEL - International

AIR: Somalia's national airline is *Somali Airlines (HH)*.
Approximate flight time: From *London* to Mogadishu is 11 hours 35 minutes, excluding stopover time in Rome.
International airport: *Mogadishu (MGQ)* is 6km (4 miles) west of the city. There is a taxi service to the city centre.

Departure tax: The equivalent of US$20 is levied on all international departures. Transit passengers and children under two years are exempt.
SEA: The principal ports are Mogadishu, Kismayo, Berbera and Merca. The *Norwegian American Line* operates a passenger service to Mogadishu.
ROAD: There are routes to Somalia from Djibouti and Kenya. There is no border crossing with Ethiopia at present. Roads are underdeveloped, and travel requires suitable 4-wheel drive desert vehicles.

TRAVEL - Internal

AIR: *Somali Airlines (HH)* run regular services to all major towns.
SEA: Modern Somalia is essentially a broad strip of coastal desert. Roads are poor and consequently, coastal shipping is an important form of transport, both socially and economically.
ROAD: It is difficult to travel outside Mogadishu by car. Existing roads run from the capital to Burao and Baidoa and there are sealed roads between Mogadishu and Kisamayu and Mogadishu and Hargeisa. Passenger transport is restricted almost entirely to road haulage. There are few cars and buses although there are reasonable bus services between the major centres in the south. **Taxi:** Taxis are available in large towns. **Car hire:** Available in Mogadishu. **Documentation:** An International Driving Permit is required.
URBAN: Minibuses and shared taxi-type services run in Mogadishu, but availability may be restricted outside the normal working hours of 0700-1400 Saturday to Thursday.

ACCOMMODATION

HOTELS: In the main cities of Mogadishu and Hargeisa there are international standard hotels. There are also hotels in Afgoi, Berbera, Borama, Burao, Kismayu and Merca. The latter boasts the best hotel in Somalia, set in attractive parkland offering ethnic accommodation in chalets.
REST-HOUSES: Government-run rest-houses are located in many places with dormitory accommodation for four to ten people.
LODGES: There are tourist and hunting lodges in national parks at Lac Badana and Bush-Bush as well as in other areas.

RESORTS & EXCURSIONS

Kismayu National Park, in the southwest, contains many common and a few rare East African species. **Hargeisa** in the north contains rarer species. A third park has recently opened outside Mogadishu and there are ten game reserves.

SOCIAL PROFILE

FOOD & DRINK: In peacetime, restaurants in the major city serve European, Chinese, Italian and Somali food. Local food includes lobster, prawn, squid, crab, fresh tuna, Somali bananas, mangoes and papaya. A traditional Somali meal is roast kid and spiced rice.
NIGHTLIFE: Local bands playing European and African music perform at nightclubs. There are frequent traditional feasts with ritualistic and recreational dance, music and folk songs.
SHOPPING: Traditional crafts include gold, silver jewellery, woven cloth and baskets from the Benadir region, *meerschaum* and woodcarvings. **Shopping hours:** 0800/0900-1230 and 1630-1900 Saturday to Thursday.
SPORT: Miles of sandy beaches offer safe **bathing**, protected from sharks by the coral reef. Some hotels have swimming pools. The **golf** club and *Anglo-American Beach Club* in Mogadishu are both open to non-members. There is some good **fishing**, particularly along the northeast coast, which is believed to be among the richest fishing grounds in the world.
SOCIAL CONVENTIONS: Traditional dance, music, song and craftsmanship flourish despite gradual modern development. Informal wear is acceptable and there is no objection to bikinis on the beach. **Tipping:** 10-15% is normal in hotels and restaurants.

BUSINESS PROFILE

ECONOMY: Somalia's economy has been almost completely dislocated by years of military action and political strife which, together with the severe East African drought, have caused an acute refugee problem which has strained the country's already limited resources. The present phase of civil strife has set the country back yet further, to the point where it now ranks amongst the most deprived countries in the world. Subsistence agriculture and livestock rearing occupy most of the working population, although any improvements have been hampered by primitive techniques, poor soil and climatic conditions, and a chronic shortage of skilled labour. Exports of livestock, hide and skins provide about 80% of the country's export earnings although revenue has been seriously affected by a ban on purchases of Somali animals imposed by the main buyer, Saudi Arabia, on health grounds. Cash crops can be grown in some areas where there is adequate irrigation: bananas are grown for export; cotton, maize, sorghum and other crops are produced for domestic consumption. Plans to develop the fishing industry have been formulated but have yet to be implemented. Similarly, port facilities have potential but have not been developed to any degree, except by the superpowers for their own strategic purposes. There is no industry to speak of, but Somalia does have considerable potential as a source of minerals. However, no deposits have been found that would prove to be both commercially viable and practicable in terms of investment, labour and political stability. The main suppliers of imported goods to Somalia are Italy, the USA, Germany, Saudi Arabia and the UK. Somalia has a large foreign debt, which only large aid packages have rendered manageable. Aid provision to the country has, in recent years, been more often determined by geo-political considerations than economic requirements. The current civil war has badly damaged Somalia's future economic prospects.
BUSINESS: For business, wear lightweight suits or safari-style jackets without a tie in hot weather. The best time to visit is October to May. **Government office hours:** 0800-1400 Saturday to Thursday.
Office hours: 0800-1230 and 1630-1900 Saturday to Thursday.
COMMERCIAL INFORMATION: The following organisation can offer advice: Chamber of Commerce, Industry and Agriculture, PO Box 27, Via Asha, Mogadishu. Tel: (1) 3209.

HISTORY & GOVERNMENT

HISTORY: The British, Italians and also the French established protectorates on the Somali coast during the late 19th century. These were the subject of various treaties, forged amid frequent border clashes, between the colonial powers and the neighbouring Ethiopians and between the European powers themselves. Modern Somalia was created from British and Italian Somalilands, on July 1, 1960. Inherited tribal rivalries and territorial disputes have dominated its subsequent history. The Somali Youth League held on to power throughout the 1960s, mostly under the leadership of President Shermake. Throughout the decade, the Government aggressively pursued claims to the Ethiopian Ogaden region and parts of Kenya's Northern Frontier District, the latter resulting in a severance of diplomatic relations with the UK from 1964 to 1968. President Shermake was assassinated by a policeman in October 1969 and a military coup a few days later installed Mohamed Siad Barre as President of the renamed Somali Democratic Republic. The new government continued to pursue an aggressive foreign policy, declaring that all ethnic Somalis should have a 'right to self-determination', and relations with Ethiopia and Kenya continued to decline throughout the 1970s. In 1977, the Somali government supported an invasion of the Ethiopian Ogaden by the Western Somali Liberation Front, forcing the then USSR to withdraw its military, political and economic support for Somalia in order to maintain its stronger relations with Ethiopia. Siad Barre responded by building up links with the West, and in particular with the USA. The Americans sensed an opportunity to bolster its position in East Africa and granted Somalia military and economic aid. After 1982, however, Washington seemed to have had second thoughts, believing, probably correctly, that Siad Barre was simply playing the superpowers off against each other and that there was little to be gained. The restoration of diplomatic relations with the USSR in October 1986 appeared to confirm the Somali tendency to tilt between camps. Relations with Kenya improved during the 1980s; and in April 1988 Siad Barre met Lt-Col Mengistu of Ethiopia and each agreed to respect the other's territorial integrity. Such rapprochements were probably triggered by the worsening domestic situation in Somalia. The Siad Barre regime enjoyed comparative stability in the mid-1980s, having survived a period of sectarian unrest that arose from the distribution of political power between the main groupings. Armed opposition resurfaced in the northwest in January 1987, when the dissident Somali National Movement (SNM) briefly cut Somalia's road links with Djibouti by occupying the town Hargeisa. The SNM again took over Hargeisa from May to August 1988, and in February 1989 captured several others towns in the region after heavy fighting. During the summer of 1989, fighting broke out in the centre of the country following an army mutiny involving members of the Ogaden clan. A battalion of troops composed of members of Siad Barre's own Marehan tribe were sent to crush the revolt, which they did successfully. In January 1990, there were unconfirmed reports that units of the Somali army loyal to Siad Barre were again active against remote populations in the northwest, and that their campaign was being waged with a ferocity verging on genocide. Throughout 1990, with news of the situation inside Somalia scarce, the extent and intensity of the fighting could be gauged from the numbers of refugees flee-

SOMALIA	HEALTH REGULATIONS	VISA REGULATIONS
GALILEO/WORLDSPAN	 TI-DFT/MGQ/HE	TI-DFT/MGQ/VI
SABRE	 TIDFT/MGQ/HE	TIDFT/MGQ/VI

Code-Link

To access this information on your CRS, swipe the barcode with a light pen or type in the text under the barcode. For more information, see the introduction *How to Use This Book.*

ing across the border into camps in Ethiopia and Kenya. The portion of the country under government control inexorably shrank to the point where, by the end of 1990, its writ barely extended beyond the capital, Mogadishu. Only disagreements between the various rebel groups fighting the regime had prevented a swifter victory. The three most important of these groups are each drawn predominantly from a single clan. The Somali National Movement (SNM) is dominated by the Issaq people who inhabit the north of the country and now control virtually the entire region. The Somali Patriotic Movement (SPM), drawn mainly from the Ogadeni clan, holds the south. The third major group is the now-split United Somali Congress (USC) which is composed mostly of people from the Hawiye clan and has borne the brunt of the recent battle for the capital which began at the end of December 1990. At the end of January 1991 Siad Barre fled. It was expected that at this point the United Somali Congress would march victorious into Mogadishu and install their commander, General Mohammed Farah Aideed, as president. It didn't happen: by the time the USC armed forces arrived, they discovered that the local affiliate of the USC, known as the Manifesto group, had already taken over the remaining administrative structure and voted in their own man, Ali Mahdi Mohammed, to the presidency. The departure of Siad Barre brought an end to any semblance of central government in Somalia, and the country has effectively been divided into autonomous regions since the middle of 1991. In particular, the northern provinces, formerly British Somaliland, formally seceded in May. This precipitated the total disintegration of the country. Relations between the two main power-brokers in the capital, Ali Mahdi Mohammed and General Aideed, deteriorated into armed conflict. Even though both were supported by the Hawiye-based USC, Somali clan politics conspired to exacerbate the dispute. The two main sub-clans within the Hawiye, the Abgal and the Habr Gedir Saad, backed Ali Mahdi and General Aideed respectively. In November 1991, Ali Mahdi temporarily fled the capital after heavy fighting broke out. A cease-fire which is, at the time of writing, just holding was agreed in the early summer of 1992 with Mahdi's forces in control of north Mogadishu and Aideed's the south. By this time, all civilian authority had collapsed, both inside and outside the capital, normal services had ground to a halt and food supplies were becoming desperately short. The United Nations, whose attention was finally drawn away from Yugoslavia, imposed an arms embargo and started to organise relief shipments for the starving population. Without armed guards on the ground, the UN quickly found that the shipments were mostly looted by one armed faction or another. In December 1992, a contingent of roughly 20,000 mainly US troops entered Somalia to protect the aid shipments.
GOVERNMENT: The country is in a state of civil war without any effective central government. General Aideed, military commander of the United Somalia Congress, is in control of the capital.

CLIMATE

There are four seasons. The *Jilal* starts around January and is the harshest period, hot and very dry. *Gu* is the first rainy season lasting from March to June. *Hagaa*, during August, is a time of dry monsoon winds and dust clouds. The second rainy season is from September to December and is called *Dayr*.
Required clothing: Lightweights and rainwear.

MOGADISHU Somalia (17m)

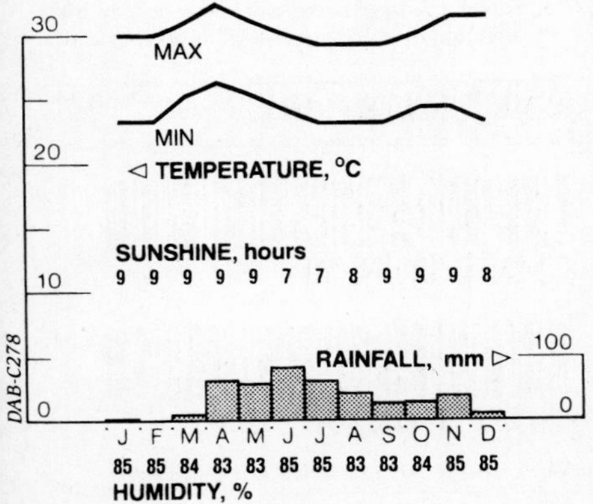

SOUTH AFRICA

Location: Southern Africa.

South African Tourism Board
Private Bag X164, 442 Rigel Avenue South
Frasmusrand
Pretoria 0001, South Africa
Tel: (12) 347 0600. Fax: (12) 454 768. Telex: 320457.
Embassy of the Republic of South Africa
South Africa House
Trafalgar Square
London WC2N 5DP
Tel: (071) 930 4488. Fax: (071) 925 0367. Telex: 267672 *or* 8952626. Opening hours: 1000-1200 and 1400-1600 Monday to Friday.
South African Consulate
8 Duncannon Street
London WC2N
Tel: (071) 839 2211.
Opening hours (personal applications only): 1000-1200 and 1400-1600 Monday to Friday.
South African Tourism Board (SATOUR)
5-6 Alt Grove
Wimbledon
London SW19 4DZ
Tel: (081) 944 8080. Fax: (081) 944 6705.
British Embassy
July-December
255 Hill Street
Arcadia
Pretoria 0002, South Africa
Tel: (12) 433 121. Fax: (12) 433 207. Telex: 321323.
January-June
91 Parliament Street
Cape Town 8001, South Africa
Tel: (21) 461 7220. Fax: (21) 461 0017. Telex: 527301.
Consulates in: Johannesburg, East London, Port Elizabeth and Durban.
Embassy of the Republic of South Africa
3051 Massachusetts Avenue, NW
Washington, DC 20008
Tel: (202) 232 4400. Fax: (202) 265 1607. Telex: 248364.
Consulates in: Chicago, Houston, Los Angeles and New York (tel: (212) 213 4880).
South African Tourism Board (SATOUR)
20th Floor
747 Third Avenue
New York, NY 10017
Tel: (212) 838 8841. Fax: (212) 826 6928. Telex: 23649535. *SATOUR also in:* Los Angeles.
Embassy of the United States of America
7th Floor, Thibault House
Pretorius Street
Pretoria, South Africa
Tel: (12) 284 266. Fax: (12) 219 278. Telex: 322143.
Embassy of the Republic of South Africa
15 Sussex Drive
Ottawa, Ontario
K1M 1M8
Tel: (613) 744 0330. Fax: (613) 711 1639. Telex: 0534185.
Consulates in: Montréal and Toronto.
South African Tourism Board
Suite 205, 4117 Lawrence Avenue East
Scarborough, Ontario
M1E 2S2
Tel: (416) 283 0563. Fax: (416) 283 5465.
Canadian Embassy
PO Box 26006
Arcadia
Pertoria 0007, South Africa
Tel: (12) 324 3970. Fax: (12) 323 1564. Telex: 5322112.

AREA: 1,125,500 sq km (434,558 sq miles), excluding Transkei, Bophuthatswana, Ciskei and Venda. Including the four 'homelands' the area of the country is 1,221,037 (471,445 sq miles).
POPULATION: 30,797,000 (1990 estimate). The population of the country including the four 'homelands' is estimated at 33,849,000 (1985).
POPULATION DENSITY: 27.4 per sq km.
CAPITAL: Pretoria (administrative). **Population:** 588,773 (1991).
Cape Town (legislative). **Population:** 776,617 (1985).
Bloemfontein (judicial). **Population:** 272,846 (1991).
GEOGRAPHY: The Republic of South Africa lies at the southern end of the African continent. It is bounded by the Indian Ocean to the east and the Atlantic Ocean to the west, and is bordered at the north by Namibia, Botswana, Zimbabwe, Mozambique and Swaziland and totally encloses Lesotho. South Africa has three major geographical regions, namely plateau, mountains and the coastal belt. The high plateau has sharp escarpments which rise above the plains, or *veld*. The vegetation is open grassland, changing to bush in the Northern Transvaal, and the Thornveld in the arid southwest. Despite two major river systems, the Limpopo and the Orange, most of the plateau lacks surface water. Along the coastline are beaches and coves, and the vegetation is shrublike. The mountainous regions which run along the coastline from the Cape of Good Hope to the Limpopo Valley in the northeast are split into the Drakensberg, Nuweveldberg and Stormberg ranges.
LANGUAGE: The official languages are Afrikaans and English. There are nine main African languages, the most widely spoken being Xhosa, Zulu and Sesotho.
RELIGION: Dutch Reform Church, Nederduitsch Hervormde, Church of England, Roman Catholic, Congregational, Methodist, Lutheran and other Christian groups. There are also Jews, independent black church movements, Hindus and Muslims.
TIME: GMT + 2.
ELECTRICITY: 250 volts AC (Pretoria) and 220/230 volts AC elsewhere, 50Hz.
COMMUNICATIONS: Telephone: IDD is available. Country code: 27. **Fax:** Most main hotels have this service. **Telex/telegram:** Telegraph services are available in all towns. Public telex facilities are available in Cape Town, Durban, Johannesburg (24-hour service) and Pretoria post offices. **Post:** Airmail to Europe takes up to seven days. Post offices are generally open 0800-1630 Monday to Friday and 0800-1200 Saturday. Some transactions may not be carried out after 1530 Monday to Friday or after 1100 Saturday. The smaller post offices close for lunch between 1300 and 1400. *Poste Restante* services are available throughout the country. **Press:** The main newspapers are in English and Afrikaans, and include *Business Day*, *Cape Times*, *The Argus*, *The Citizen*, *The Star*, *Sowetan* and *Natal Mercury*.
BBC World Service and Voice of America frequencies: From time to time these change. See the section *How to Use this Book* for more information.

BBC:				
MHz	25.75	21.66	11.94	6.190
Voice of America:				
MHz	21.49	15.60	9.525	6.035

PASSPORT/VISA

Regulations and requirements may be subject to change at short notice, and you are advised to contact the appropriate diplomatic or consular authority before finalising travel arrangements. Details of these may be found at the head of this country's entry. Any numbers in the chart refer to the footnotes below.

	Passport Required?	Visa Required?	Return Ticket Required?
Full British	Yes	1	Yes
BVP	Not valid	-	-
Australian	Yes	Yes	Yes
Canadian	Yes	Yes	Yes
USA	Yes	Yes	Yes
Other EC	Yes	1	Yes
Japanese	Yes	No	-

PASSPORTS: Valid passport required by all (must be valid for at least 6 months beyond applicants' departure from South Africa).
British Visitors Passport: Not accepted.
VISAS: Required by all except:
(a) [1] nationals of Germany, Ireland and the UK for business and holiday visits;
(b) nationals of Liechtenstein, Namibia and Switzerland for business and holiday visits;
(c) nationals of Botswana, Côte d'Ivoire, Lesotho, Swaziland and Zaïre for a visit of less than 15 days;
(d) nationals of Austria, Gabon, Hong Kong (holding passports of British Hong Kong), Japan, Kenya, Madagascar, Malawi, Mauritius, Singapore, South Korea and Thailand for business and holiday visits of less than 15 days;
(e) nationals of Turkey for business and holiday visits of less than 30 days;
(f) nationals of Bolivia, Costa Rica, Kenya, Malaysia, Mauritius and Zambia for business and holiday visits of 30 days or less.
Note: Holders of Visitors' visas are not allowed to take up employment in South Africa.
Types of visas: Transit, Visitor's (which, subject to certain conditions, may be used for business purposes) and Study and Employment visas (longer term). All visas are issued free of charge.
Application to: Consulate (or Consular Section at Embassy). For addresses, see top of entry. Applicants in countries where South Africa is not represented may send their applications direct to the Director-General for Home Affairs, Private Bag X114, Pretoria 0001, South Africa. Tel: (12) 314 8911. Fax: (12) 326 4571. Telex: 3668 *or* 3664.
Application requirements: (a) Valid passport. (b) 2 photos. (c) 1 application form correctly filled out (failure to complete the application fully and in detail may result in visa being delayed or refused). (d) Sufficient funds to cover expenses of visit. (e) Onward/return ticket (or sufficient funds to pay for one) and, if in transit, proof of sufficient documentation for admission to the country of destination. (f) No criminal record. (g) Visitors should be of sound mind and body. (h) Applications for Employment or Study must be accompanied by completed medical forms IM10 and IM13 if stay is for over one year. (i) In the case of failure to comply with any regulations, a visitor may be required to leave a deposit with the Immigration Officer.
Working days required: Applications should be made well in advance. Although the minimum time taken is two days, nationals requiring a visa applying from the UK are advised to apply up to 10 weeks beforehand.
Temporary residence: Temporary residence permits are available at the airport on arrival, valid for a period of 3 months. Extensions must be applied for to the Director-General for Home Affairs in Pretoria or its nearest regional office, or at a police station if none of the former are available.

MONEY

Currency: Rand (R) = 100 cents. Notes are in denominations of R50, 20, 10 and 5. Coins are in denominations of R2 and 1, and 50, 20, 10, 5, 2 and 1 cents.
Credit cards: Access/Mastercard, American Express, Diners Club and Visa are widely accepted. Check with your credit card company for details of merchant acceptability and other facilities which may be available.
Travellers cheques: Valid at banks, hotels, restaurants and shops.
Exchange rate indicators: The following figures are included as a guide to the movements of the Rand against Sterling and the US Dollar:

Date:	Oct '89	Oct '90	Oct '91	Oct '92
£1.00=	*4.26	*4.94	*4.89	*4.68
$1.00=	*2.70	*2.53	*2.81	*2.95

Note [*]: Commercial rate.
Currency restrictions: The import and export of SA Reserve Bank notes is limited to R500. Free import of foreign currency, subject to declaration. The export of foreign currency is limited to the amount declared on arrival.
Banking hours: 0830-1530 Monday to Friday, and 0800-1130 Saturday.

DUTY FREE

The following goods may be imported into South Africa by passengers over 16 years of age without incurring customs duty:
400 cigarettes and 50 cigars and 250g of tobacco;
1 litre of spirits and 2 litres of wine;
50ml of perfume and 250ml toilet water per person;
Gifts up to a value of R500 per person.
There is a flat-rate duty of 20% on gifts in excess of R500 and up to R10,000.

PUBLIC HOLIDAYS

Public holidays observed in South Africa are as follows:
Apr 6 '93 Founder's Day. **Apr 9** Good Friday. **Apr 12** Family Day. **May 1** Workers' Day. **May 20** Ascension Day. **May 31** Republic Day. **Oct 10** Kruger Day. **Dec 16** Day of the Vow. **Dec 25** Christmas Day. **Dec 26** Day of Goodwill. **Jan 1 '94** New Year's Day.

HEALTH

Regulations and requirements may be subject to change at short notice, and you are advised to contact your doctor well in advance of your intended date of departure. Any numbers in the chart refer to the footnotes below.

	Special Precautions?	Certificate Required?
Yellow Fever	No	1
Cholera	Yes	2
Typhoid & Polio	Yes	-
Malaria	3	-
Food & Drink	4	-

[1]: A yellow fever vaccination certificate is required from travellers over one year of age arriving from infected areas. Those African countries formerly classified as endemic zones are considered by the South African authorities to be infected areas. Travellers arriving on flights with scheduled airlines that originated outside an infected area, and passengers who transited through an infected area but remained at the scheduled airport or in the adjacent town during transit, do not require a certificate. Passengers arriving by unscheduled flights at airports other than those used by scheduled airlines must possess a certificate. Infants under one year of age without a certificate may be subject to surveillance and will not be allowed into Natal or to the Lowveld of the Transvaal within six days of leaving an infected area.
[2]: Following WHO guidelines issued in 1973, a cholera vaccination certificate is not a condition of entry to South Africa. However, cholera is a risk in parts of this country, particularly in rural areas, and precautions are recommended for those likely to be at risk. Up-to-date advice should be sought before deciding whether these precautions should include vaccination, as medical opinion is divided over its effectiveness. See the *Health* section at the back of the book.
[3]: Malaria risk, predominantly in the malignant *falciparum* form, exists throughout the year in Northern Transvaal, Eastern Lowveld and Northern Natal. 'Resistance' to chloroquine has been reported. It is strongly recommended that visitors to these areas take anti-malaria tablets before entering these zones (tablets are available from pharmacies without prescription).
[4]: Tap water is considered safe to drink in urban areas but may be contaminated elsewhere and sterilisation is advisable. Milk is pasteurised and dairy products are safe for consumption. Local meat, poultry, seafood, fruit and vegetables are generally considered safe to eat.
Rabies is present. For those at high risk, vaccination before arrival should be considered. If you are bitten abroad seek medical advice without delay. For more information consult the *Health* section at the back of the book.
Bilharzia (schistosomiasis) is common in the north and east and may be present elsewhere. Avoid swimming and paddling in fresh water. Swimming pools which are well-chlorinated and maintained are safe.
Health care: Medical facilities are excellent. Health insurance is recommended.

TRAVEL - International

AIR: South Africa's national airline is *South African Airways (SAA)*.
Approximate flight times: From *London* to Cape Town is 12 hours 50 minutes, to Durban 12 hours 45 minutes and to Johannesburg is 12 hours 50 minutes. From *Los Angeles* to Johannesburg is 23 hours 5 minutes (no direct flight available).
International airports: *D F Malan Airport (CPT)* (Cape Town), 22km (14 miles) southeast of the city (travel time – 25 minutes). Tel: (21) 934 0407. *Inter-Cape* buses meet all inward and outgoing flights. Courtesy buses are operated by some hotels. Taxis are available, with a surcharge after 2300. Airport facilities include an outgoing duty-free shop, car rental (0600-0305), bank/exchange facilities (0830-1630 Monday to Friday, 0830-1200 Saturday) and a restaurant and bar (0600-0305).
Louis Botha Airport (DUR) (Durban), 16km (10 miles) southwest of the city (travel time – 20 minutes). Tel: (31) 426 111 *or* 426 145. Coaches meets all arrivals 0800-2200. Taxis are available. Airport facilities include an outgoing duty-free shop, car rental (0600-1330), bank/exchange facilities (0830-1630 Monday to Friday, 0830-1200 Saturday) and a bar/restaurant (0600-1330).
Jan Smuts International Airport (JNB) (Johannesburg), 24km (15 miles) east of the city (travel time – 30 minutes). Bus services to Pretoria and Johannesburg are available 0500-2200. Trains link Kempton Park with Johannesburg. Taxis are available. Courtesy coaches are operated by some major hotels. Airport facilities include incoming and outgoing duty-free shops, post office, car rental, bank/exchange facilities (24 hours), restaurant (0700-2200) and bar (1000-2400).
SEA: The main ports are Cape Town, Durban, Port Elizabeth and East London. *St Helena Shipping Co Ltd* runs a regular passenger service from Avonmouth to Cape Town. *The Royal Viking Line* includes South Africa on its Southern Africa cruise. Cruises are offered by various companies between South Africa and the Indian Ocean Islands. Cruise lines include *P&O* and *Cunard*.
RAIL: The main routes are from South Africa to Zimbabwe, Botswana and Mozambique. Contact *South African Railways (TRANSNET)*.
ROAD: There are two main routes into South Africa: from Zimbabwe (via Beit Bridge) and Botswana (via Ramatlabama).

TRAVEL - Internal

AIR: Daily flights link Cape Town, Durban, Pretoria, Port Elizabeth, East London, Kimberley and Bloemfontein with other connecting flights to provincial towns. *South African Airways (SAA)* operate on the principal routes.
Discounts: An 'Africa Explorer' fare is available to foreign visitors entering South Africa with an IATA airline. It offers a significant saving for anyone planning to use *SAA's* internal network. The fare is valid for a minimum of seven days and a maximum of one month: travel may originate and terminate at any point within South Africa which is served by the airline. Travel is not permitted more than once in the same direction over any given sector. There is also a

SOUTH AFRICA	**HEALTH REGULATIONS**	**VISA REGULATIONS** Code-Link
GALILEO/WORLDSPAN	TI-DFT/DUR/HE	 TI-DFT/DUR/VI
SABRE	 TIDFT/DUR/HE	TIDFT/DUR/VI

To access this information on your CRS, swipe the barcode with a light pen or type in the text under the barcode. For more information, see the introduction *How to Use This Book*.

30% reduction on some standby fares. *SAA* can offer various other discount domestic fares including Apex, Slumber, Supersaver and Saver fares. Contact *SAA* for details.
SEA: *Starlight Cruises* offer links between major ports.
RAIL: The principal intercity services are as follows: the **Blue Train** (luxury express) between Pretoria, Johannesburg and Cape Town (every other day); the **Trans-Oranje** between Cape Town and Durban via Kimberley and Bloemfontein (weekly); the **Trans-Natal Express** between Durban and Johannesburg (daily); *Rovos Rail* offer luxury steam safaris to the eastern Transvaal. The Transnet Museum also offer various steam safaris around South Africa and Zimbabwe; and the **Trans-Karoo Express** between Cape Town and Johannesburg and Pretoria (four times a week). All long-distance trains are equipped with sleeping compartments, included in fares, and most have restaurant cars. Reservations are recommended for principal trains and all overnight journeys. There are frequent local trains in the Cape Town and Pretoria/Johannesburg urban areas. All trains have first- and second-class accommodation.
ROAD: There is a well-maintained network of roads and motorways in populous regions. 30% of roads are paved (with all major roads tarred to a high standard). Driving is on the left. Fines for speeding are very heavy. It is illegal to carry petrol other than in built-in petrol tanks. Petrol stations are usually open all week 0700-1900. Some are open 24 hours. **Bus/coach:** Various operators, such as *Greyhound* and *Translux* run intercity express links using modern air-conditioned coaches. Courier/drivers supervise the tours. On many of the intercity tours passengers may break their journey at any scheduled stop en route by prior arrangement at time of booking and continue on a subsequent coach at no extra cost other than for additional accommodation. **Taxis:** Available throughout the country, at all towns, hotels and airports, with rates for distance and time. For long-distance travel, a quotation should be sought. **Car hire:** Self-drive and chauffeur-driven cars are available at most airports and in major city centres. *Avis*, *Imperial* and *Budget* are nationwide. **Documentation:** An International Driving Permit is required. British visitors who are planning to drive in South Africa should check with the *AA* or *RAC* prior to departure that they have all the correct documentation.
URBAN: There are good bus and suburban rail networks in all the main towns, with trolleybuses in Johannesburg. Fares in Cape Town and Johannesburg are zonal, with payment in cash or with 10-ride pre-purchase 'clipcards' from kiosks. In Pretoria there are various pre-purchase ticket systems, including a cheap pass for off-peak travel only. In Durban, conventional buses face stiff competition from minibuses and combi taxis (both legal and illegal), which are also found in other South African towns. These should be used with care. For ordinary taxis, fares within the city areas are more expensive than long distances. Taxis do not cruise and must be called from a rank. Taxi drivers expect a 10% tip.
JOURNEY TIMES: The following chart gives approximate journey times (in hours and minutes) from Cape Town to other major cities/towns in South Africa.

	Air	Road	Rail
Johannesburg	2.00	15.00	25.00
Durban	2.00	18.00	38.00
Pretoria	2.00	16.00	26.00
Port Elizabeth	1.00	7.00	-
Bloemfontein	1.30	10.00	21.00

ACCOMMODATION

South Africa offers a wide range of accommodation from luxury 5-star hotels to thatched huts *(rondavels)* in game reserves. 'Time-sharing condominiums' are developing in popular resorts. Comprehensive accommodation guides giving details of facilities, including provision for the handicapped, are available at all SATOUR offices and from tourism board regional offices. Information covers hotels, motels, game park rest camps, caravan and camping sites and supplementary accommodation such as beach cottages, holiday flats and bungalows. Rates should always be confirmed at time of booking. It is forbidden by law to levy service charges (though phone calls may be charged for).
HOTELS: All hotels are registered with the South African Tourism Board, which controls standards. For further information contact: SATOUR Standards Department, Private Bag X164, Pretoria 0001. Tel: (12) 347 0600. Fax: (12) 454 768. Telex: 320457. 800 hotels are members of the Federated Hotel Association of South Africa (FEDHASA), PO Box 514, Rivonia 2128. Tel: (11) 444 8982. Fax: (11) 444 8987. FEDHASA has regional offices throughout the country. **Grading:** Hotels are graded from **1 to 5 stars.** Each hotel has a plaque which displays its grading. 1236 establishments follow this system, 747 of which are 1 star.
Plaques also state the terms of its licence to sell alcohol, as follows:
Y: Licensed to sell wine and beer with meals.
YY: Licensed to sell only wine and beer.
YYY: Licensed to sell wine, spirits and beer.
R on this plaque means that less than half the occupancy is transitory; **T** means that more than half the occupancy is transitory.
SELF-CATERING: Holiday flats, guest-farms, resorts and health spas are available along main routes.
CAMPING/CARAVANNING: Caravan parks are to be found along all the tourist routes in South Africa, particularly at places favoured for recreational activities and sightseeing. The standard is usually high. Many caravan parks also have campsites. A number of companies can arrange motor camper rentals, with a wide range of fully equipped vehicles. Full details can be obtained from SATOUR.
GAME RESERVES: Game reserve rest camps are protected enclosures within the confines of the park. Accommodation is usually in thatched huts known as *rondavels*, or in small cottages. Some camps provide air-conditioned accommodation. Most *rondavels* and

cottages are self-contained, with private baths and showers, and sometimes kitchens. Some camps have luxury air-conditioned accommodation.

RESORTS & EXCURSIONS

For the purposes of this section, South Africa has been divided up into the following regions: the Southern Transvaal; the Eastern Transvaal; the Northern Cape; the Eastern Cape; and the Western and Southern Cape.

The Southern Transvaal

Nicknamed 'Witwatersrand' (Ridge of White Waters) by 19th-century prospectors, the area contains the richest gold reef in the world. The man-made lakes scattered along the reef provide facilities for boating, fishing and birdwatching, and the area is rich in parks, nature reserves and gardens.

JOHANNESBURG: The discovery of gold near Johannesburg in 1886 turned a small shanty town into the bustling modern city which is today the centre of the world's gold-mining industry and the commercial nucleus of South Africa.

Sightseeing: *Carlton Panorama* is 202m (663ft) high, providing stunning views over Johannesburg, along with a sound and light show. *Northcliff Ridge* is the highest natural point in Johannesburg, affording a panoramic view of the city. *Gold Reef City* is a living replica of early Johannesburg, complete with hotels, bars, shops and theatres. *Johannesburg Art Gallery* has a fine collection of English, Dutch, French and South African art. *The Planetarium* is well worth a visit, as are the craft markets at *Zoo Lake* and *Hillbrow*. *The Florence Bloom Bird Sanctuary*, within Delta Park, is home for a large variety of birds, as is the *Melrose Bird Sanctuary*. *The Harvey Wild Flower Reserve* at **Linksfield** has lovely views over Johannesburg and Magaliesberg. *The Zoological Gardens* have a wide variety of animals and *The Botanic Gardens* contain exotic trees, over 4000 species of roses, and a herb garden.

Museums: Johannesburg has numerous museums. *The Adler Museum of the History of Medicine* includes an African herbarium and a witch doctor's premises; *The Afrikana Museum* contains exhibitions of early Johannesburg memorabilia in their settlement of the Cape; *The Africana Museum* contains a vast ethnological collection; *The Bensusan Museum of Photography* has early equipment and a history of photography; *The Bernberg Museum of Costume* houses 18th- and 19th-century period costumes; and *The Jewish Museum* has displays of ceremonial art and a history of South African Judaism from the 1920s to the present day.

PRETORIA: Named after the Voortrekker leader Andries Pretorius, Pretoria is the administrative capital of the country with many parks and gardens. The city is known as the 'Jacaranda City' because of the flowering trees lining its streets in late spring. Its indigenous flora include protea, aloe, cycad, acacia, wild fig and fever trees.

Sightseeing: *Church Street* is 26km (16 miles) long and one of the world's longest straight streets. There are many museums, including *The Fort Klapperkop Military Museum*, *The Museum of Geological Survey* (with its collection of fossils and precious/semi-precious stones), *The Pretoria Art Museum* and *The Transvaal Museum of Natural History*. *The State Theatre* has facilities for all the performing arts. *The Austin Roberts Bird Sanctuary* features a variety of waterbirds. Other nature sanctuaries include *Derdepoort Regional Park*, *Fountains Valley Nature Reserve*, *Wonderboom Nature Reserve*, *The National Botanic Garden* and *Meyers Park Nature Reserve*.

EXCURSIONS: The Southern Transvaal's many attractions include dozens of nature reserves. The beautiful *Magaliesberg* mountain range, named after Magali, chief of the Po tribe, has abundant flora and fauna in private game and nature reserves, providing a nesting ground for the endangered Cape vulture. The area boasts the *Hartbeespoort Dam*, a popular recreational spot, complete with watersports, fishing, hiking and camping facilities. *The Aquarium*, 3km (2 miles) from the dam, has indigenous and exotic fish, as well as crocodiles and performing seals. There is a zoo and snake park and a nature reserve.

Near **Krugersdorp,** the *Sterkfontein Caves* contain a one-million-year-old female skull.

The Eastern Transvaal

The high and virtually treeless grassland plateau of the Transvaal stretches for hundreds of kilometres until it reaches the Drakensberg range of mountains, plunging into a beautiful subtropical woodland known as the *Lowveld*. Vast numbers of animals can be found here.

EXCURSIONS: The **Kruger National Park** comprises about 2,000,000 hectares and has a variety of animal species unequalled elsewhere on the African continent. Species include zebra, giraffe, wildebeest, elephant, impala, leopard, cheetah, rhino, buffalo, cicada, ostrich, lilac-breasted roller, hornbill and fish eagle. There is excellent accommodation in the park.

Manyeleti Game Reserve, to the east of the Kruger, houses two trail camps, *Khoka Moya* and *Honey Guide*, who cater particularly for those game-viewing on foot. Open vehicle game drives take place in the evening. Khoka Moya comprises four double ensuite cabins and separate dining, lounge and bar areas. Honey Guide accommodates a maximum of 12 in six large East African tents. Two- and three-day package safaris are a speciality.

The western border of the Kruger National Park has seen the development of several private game reserves, to provide sanctuaries for the Lowveld flora and fauna. The **Sabi Sabi Private Game Reserve** offers excellent wildlife game-viewing of giraffe, antelope, warthog, lion, elephant, rhinocerous, buffalo, leopard, hyena, zebra and bountiful birdlife. Thatched bungalows and a roster of activities are also available to visitors.

Other game reserves in this region include the *Klaserie* and *Timbavati* and the *Umbabat Nature Reserve*.

There are many panoramic routes which can be taken through this area, but one of the most famous is the **Summit Route**. This takes in *Long Tom Pass*, 2150m (7050ft) above sea level; *Sabie*, situated against Mauchsberg and Mount Anderson with an abundance of waterfalls and wild flowers; *Graskop*, a forestry village perched on a spur of the Drakensberg escarpment; *Pilgrim's Rest*, a gold-rush town with many historic buildings; *Mount Sheba Nature Reserve*, embracing 1500 hectares of ravines and waterfalls; *Pinnacle Rock*, a massive, free-standing granite column; *God's Window*, a spectacular viewing point over the Lowveld 1000m (3300ft) below; *Lisbon Falls* and *Berlin Falls*; *Bourke's Luck Potholes*, formed by the swirling action of pebble-laden flood water over the course of time; *Blyde River Canyon* and the *Blyderivierspoort Nature Reserve*, an immense ravine containing a multitude of flora and fauna and with spectacular viewing points; *F H Odendaal Camp*, with good vantage points and accommodation facilities; *Sybrand Van Nierkerk*

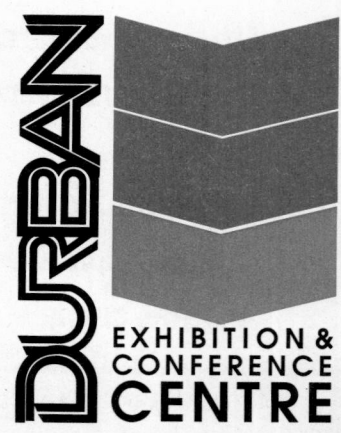

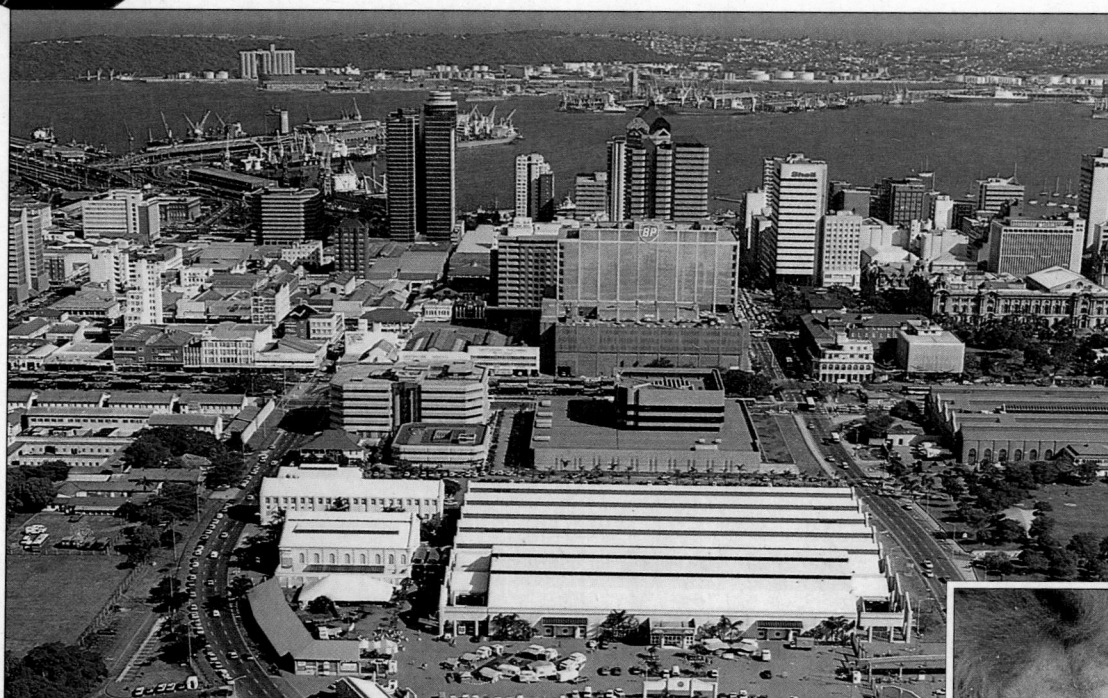

XPERIENCE AFRICA: COME TO URBAN

or over a century, Durban has been nd still is Southern Africa's favourite oliday destination for millions of sitors who flock there each year. Vith 230 sunny days a year to relax in opical splendour on the warm Indian cean shores, the hospitality frastructure developed to the extent at it is unrivalled in Africa. So, when ou announce that you will be tending a conference in Durban, the mily will want to accompany you.

isitors will find extensive commercial nd industrial development and a rich

teraction between Western and ulu traditions while the Eastern fluence through 133 years of ettlement in the region is evident verywhere: mosques, temples, astern markets, spice emporia and ari shops abound and the annual stivals such as Diwali with thousands f Hindu homes being lit up in elebration, are joyous and peaceful ccasions.

Vhen it comes to night clubs, coffee ars and restaurants, Durban excels ith a wide variety of cuisines ncluding eastern, Chinese, Italian, rench, Greek, Spanish, Portuguese nd western selections. For those vho enjoy the sport of Kings, two ace courses in the City and one in ietermaritzburg provide the pportunity of relaxation and a utter on Wednesdays and aturdays and many other sporting acilities, including numerous golf courses, are available.

The Playhouse is the home of the internationally renowned Natal Philharmonic Orchestra which, while specialising in classical, operatic and ballet works, lets its hair down on a regular basis, inside the Playhouse or outside in the many beautiful parks, to feature big band, light classical and prom concerts, West end or Broadway musicals and current favourites of interest to the resident population and visitors.

A quick look at the availability of theatres and cinemas plus Durban fun spots will reveal a combined total of over 60 to choose from.

For those who love the sea, the surfing fraternity begin "catching waves" immediately after sunrise from 05:00 in the Spring and Summer months and the mild winters plus warm Indian ocean currents ensure it remains pleasant for surfing, swimming and relaxation on the beaches from 07:00 in the Autumn and Winter months. The natural sea harbour, where arrangements can be made for deep sea, coastal or harbour fishing, yachting or motor pleasure boat cruises is the busiest in Africa.

Durban is also the ideal pivot point for your exploration of the numerous attractions of Natal including the majestic Drakensberg mountains, the Valley of a Thousand Hills, the historical battlefields in the Natal

midlands, the magnificent Northern Natal Game Parks, conservation and forest zones, abounding in birdlife, wildlife and nature trails, the northern and southern beach resorts and the Wild Coast.

Direct flights are available to Durban's Louis Botha International Airport to or from 45 Cities on all five continents.

Large cities compete for conferences and exhibitions. Durban is certainly no exception and caters for this market in numerous hotels and at the Durban Exhibition and Conference Centre. This versatile and spacious centre in the heart of the Central Business District, within 2 km of all the major hotels, is undergoing renovations to meet the up market needs of small or large conferences for from 20 to 2600 delegates and exhibitions which require up to 9600m^2 of undercover space.

And to keep up with expected demands well into the next century, the complex is being expanded to provide an International Convention Centre with world class facilities, by 1996.

So whether your conference or exhibition, or conference linked to an exhibition is being planned to take place within the next two years or ten years, make up your mind now to come to Durban, stay at least an extra week and experience what this unique part of Africa has to offer.

(Swadini Camp), dominated by Mariepskop and the cliffs of Swadini buttress, with a reptile park just outside the nature reserve; *The Museum of Man* containing rock paintings and archaeological excavations; the *Echo Caves* at the head of the *Molopong Valley*, with their Stone and Iron Age tools; and the *Abel Erasmus Pass* and *J G Strijdom Tunnel*, rising 335m (1100ft) above the *Ohrigstad River* before descending more than 700m (2300ft) to the beautiful *Olifants River*.

Nelspruit is a good base for seeing the famous *Sudwala Caves*. The caves (extending far into the Mankelekele Mountain) are of immense interest to scientists as well as tourists and comprise a linked series of chambers adorned with stalactites and stalagmites. Some of the chambers are vast, such as the *PR Owen Hall*, a subterranean amphitheatre with acoustics so good that concerts have been held there. Guided tours are available. There is a *Dinosaur Park* near the caves containing life-size replicas of the kind of prehistoric reptiles that roamed South Africa 250 million years ago.

The Northern Cape

This area, a vast (and often barren) wilderness, is watered by the *Orange River* and is home to large numbers of animals, many of them protected species. The discovery of vast diamond deposits in the northern Cape helped to create its principal town, Kimberley. In Namaqualand in the west, the discovery of copper as well as precious and semi-precious stones has continued since the 1850s. The area is also famous for its Bushmen rock-art.

KIMBERLEY: In 1866 a boy found a shiny 'pebble' at *Hopetown*, 128km (80 miles) south of Kimberley, allowing a primitive and sparsely populated settlement to become what is now the diamond capital of the world. Today, Kimberley is an attractive city with broad tree-lined streets and good shopping centres. Its attractions include *The Big Hole*, which is the largest man-made excavation in the world, and *The Kimberley Mine Museum*, with its replicas of 19th-century Kimberley at the height of the gold rush. *The De Beers Hall Museum* houses a display of cut and uncut diamonds; here can be seen the famous '616' – at 616 carats, the largest uncut diamond in the world – and the 'Eureka' diamond, the first to be discovered in South Africa. *The William Humphreys Art Gallery* has one of the finest collections of South African art, along with French, English, Dutch and Flemish contributions.

EXCURSIONS: Nooitgedacht, near Kimberley, has pavements of Ventersdorp lava, over 2500 million years old, polished by slow-moving glaciers during an ice age 250 million years ago. The area also has some very fine examples of Bushmen, or *San*, art, in the form of rock paintings. The paintings are scattered over an area stretching from the Cape to the Zambezi and from the east coast lowlands to South West Africa. The engravings are usually 'pecked' into the rock with flint and similar sharp implements, and are characterised by a boldness and simplicity of design combined with extremely accurate draughtsmanship and limited use of colour. They are believed to be about 10,000 years old.

Olifantshoek has rock engravings and is known as the *Gateway to the White and Roaring Sands* at **Witsand,** 70km (45 miles) away. Any disturbance of the 100m (330ft) high sands, particularly in hot weather, produces a strange moaning noise.

The national park at **Vaalbos** has eland, kudu, giraffe, red hartebeest and springbok.

There are ancient and extensive mines on the southern slopes of the *Gatkopies*, near **Postmasburg.** Archaeological findings indicate that Hottentots mined here for specularite from AD700.

Augrabies is a Hottentot name for 'place of great noise', which accurately describes the falls plummeting 56m (184ft) into a 20m (66ft) wide ravine, 120km (75 miles) west of **Upington.** There are spectacular rapids as the river drops a further 35m (115ft) along the ravine's 18km (11-mile) length. The area is a national park, and is home to many animal species, including baboons, vervet monkeys, rhino and antelope.

The **Kalahari Gemsbok National Park** shares a common boundary with the Botswana National Park, a staggering area of 127,135 sq km (79,000 sq miles). It is the largest nature conservation area in Southern Africa and one of the largest unspoilt ecosystems in the world, supporting fauna and flora in bewildering variety.

Namaqualand is a vast area of seemingly barren semi-desert, harbouring a treasure-house of floral beauty, appearing after the desired amount of winter rains: daisies, aloes, lilies, perennial herbs and many other flower species. The rich deposits of copper in the region had been used for centuries by the Nama tribe of Hottentots before the advent of white settlers in the 17th century; in 1685 the Governor of the Cape, Simon van der Stel, led an expedition to the 'Copper Mountain', near to the present town of **Springbok.** The copper boom finally began in earnest in the 19th century.

The Eastern Cape & The Garden Route

The Eastern Cape has an extraordinary variety of scenic beauty, ranging from the vast and arid Great Karoo to the Knysna forest, the fertile agricultural lands of the Little Karoo and the Long Kloof. Two of the country's major seaports (East London and Port Elizabeth) are located in this area.

PORT ELIZABETH: This city has a thriving cultural life. The Cape Performing Arts Board presents ballet, opera, music and drama productions in the newly restored *Opera House* and there are productions of Shakespeare in *The Mannville Open Air Theatre* in St George's Park. The city boasts excellent shops and amenities, including extensive parks and public gardens. Plans are underway to 'reclaim' the city's beaches along the sheltered warm water bay, where all sorts of watersports can be enjoyed.

Sightseeing: Tourist attractions include the *Apple Express*, one of the few remaining narrow-gauge steam trains, in operation since 1906 and running from Port Elizabeth to Loerie in Long Kloof. The *City Hall* and *Market Square* are worth a visit, with a replica of the *Dias Cross*, a memorial to the Portuguese navigator Bartholomew Dias. There is also a memorial to Prester John here.

The Oceanarium, Snake Park and *Tropical House* are on the seafront at Humewood. *The King George IV Art Gallery & Fine Arts Hall* has an excellent collection of 19th- and 20th-century art. *Settler's Park Nature Reserve* at How Avenue abounds with indigenous flora and *St George's Park* has open-air exhibitions and craft fairs, as well as theatrical productions.

EXCURSIONS: The **Addo Elephant National Park**, 72km (45 miles) north of Port Elizabeth, was created in 1931 to protect the last of the Eastern Cape elephants. There are also black rhino, buffalo and antelope and more than 170 species of birds.

The **Zuurberg National Park** is situated in the *Winterhoek Mountains* and contains a large variety of flor and fauna, including the *Alexandria Forest*, an evergreen coastal high forest, where black eagles breed.

East London is situated on the magnificent coastline of the eastern seaboard, part of the 'Romantic Coast'. There are excellent beaches at *Eastern Beach, Nahoon Beach* and *Orient Beach*. The city has very good amenities. The *Museum* contains a fine natural history collection.

The **Karoo** is a vast and beautiful upland area with spectacular sunsets. The novelist, Olive Schreiner, made the area famous and her house at *Cradock* has been restored. The *Mountain Zebra National Park* is worth a visit, on the northern slopes of the Bankberg range. The town of **Graaff-Reinet** is situated in the heart of the *Karoo Nature Reserve*, at the foot of the *Sneeuberg Mountains*. It has many attractive 18th- and 19th-century buildings, as well as parks and museums, and is an excellent centre for exploration of the area.

The Garden Route encompasses the *Outeniqua Mountains* inland, the arid plains of the *Little Karoo*, the *Tsitsikamma Coastal National Park* and the *Swartberg Mountains* with their immense subterranean *Cango Caves*. There is a spectacular variety of flora, including the protected red 'George' lily. *Jeffrey's Bay* offers spectacular surfing. *St Francis Bay* has wide, unspoilt beaches and is a shell-collector's paradise. The lagoon at *Paradise Beach* is a sanctuary for many birds, including flamingo and swans. **Knysna** is situated between lush inland forests and the Knysna lagoon and is a popular tourist resort. The lagoon is a National Park area, stretching from *Buffels Bay* to *Noetzie*, both with beautiful beaches. *The Wilderness National Lakes* area, with its ferns, lakes and tidal rivers, lies between Knysna and **George.** The latter town is known as the 'Garden City' because of its magnificent yellowwood and stinkwood trees. *Oudtshoorn* is famous for its ostrich farms.

The Western & Southern Cape

An area of outstanding natural (especially floral) beauty, stretching from the remote rocky outcrops beyond Lambert's Bay in the West to the mountains of the southern peninsula. The area is famous for its wine production.

CAPE TOWN: South Africa's administrative capital is situated at the foot of *Table Mountain* looking out onto the Atlantic Ocean. Places of interest include *The Castle of Good Hope* in Darling Street, built in 1666; *The Cultural History Museum*; the Malay quarter; *The Nico Malan Theatre Complex*; and *The Old Townhouse* on Greenmarket Square, housing a permanent collection of 17th-century Dutch and Flemish paintings. *The Victoria & Alfred Waterfront*, the old Victorian harbour which has been restored, offers free entertainment, a variety of shops, taverns and restaurants has become a major attraction. There are excellent sporting and shopping facilities.

EXCURSIONS: The **Cape of Good Hope Nature Reserve** covers the southern tip of the Cape peninsula, with a profusion of flowers, birds and animals. There are many fishing villages and holiday resorts around the bay, including *Llandudno, Hout Bay, Kommetjie* and *Fish Hoek; Chapman's Peak* has a spectacular scenic drive from *Hout Bay*, traversing *Chapman's Peak Mountain*.

Stellenbosch, centre for wine production, has many attractive buildings, including the *Village Museum* and the *Dutch Reform Church*. **Franschhoek** is also a wine production centre, which originally hosted refugee

Huguenots from France, many of them involved in wine-growing, who brought their vinicultural skills to South Africa.
The **Franschhoek Pass** is a spectacular mountain pass. The *Drakenstein Valley* has picturesque vineyards, orchards and farms and there are many 'wine routes' which can be followed. The **Bontebok National Park,** near Swellendam, has many varieties of game.
The fertility of the Southern Cape region gradually gives way to the rugged and beautiful **West Coast,** which has abundant shellfish.

SOCIAL PROFILE

FOOD & DRINK: A thriving agricultural sector yields excellent fresh produce, meat, fruit and wines. Typical South African dishes include *sosaties* (a type of kebab), *bobotie* (a curried mince dish), *bredies* (meat, tomato and vegetable casseroles), crayfish (or rock lobster) and many other seafood dishes traditional to the Western Cape Province. Curries and chutneys are excellent. *Biltong* (dried meat) is a savoury speciality. Although there is a wide choice of self-service restaurants, most have table service. **Drink:** There are excellent local red and white wines, and sherries. Beer is also very good. Bars/cocktail lounges have bartender service. 'Liquor stores' are open 0900-1700 weekdays and close at 1300 Saturdays.
NIGHTLIFE: Cinemas show a variety of international films. In the large cities there are regular plays, operas and symphony concerts. There are a number of nightclubs and discotheques open until late. The large hotels usually have a danceband or cabaret.
SHOPPING: Stores are generally modern. Special purchases include Swakara coats, gold, diamond and semi-precious stone jewellery, leather and suede goods, ceramics and African handicrafts, safari suits and feathers. **Shopping hours:** 0830-1700 Monday to Friday, 0830-1300 Saturday. Some shops are open Sunday.
SPORT: South Africans are ardent sports enthusiasts. Visitors are made welcome at many venues. **Golf:** Played on more than 400 courses. Visitors can play on weekdays. Fees are not exorbitant and equipment and caddies can be hired. **Tennis/squash:** Many hotels can arrange tennis and squash facilities. **Hunting:** Details of various game hunting tours are available from SATOUR. **Sailing:** Hotels on the coast will arrange sailing and yachting. **Swimming:** Hotels in coastal areas will give advice on the best sea bathing and surfing locations. Most hotels have swimming pools. **Fishing:** Sea fishing is particularly popular off the Indian Ocean coast.
SPECIAL EVENTS: The following is a selection of events and festivals celebrated during 1993/4 in South Africa. For further details contact SATOUR.
Mar '93 *Pearl Nouveau Wine Festival*, Pearl, Cape. **Apr 2-18** *Grand Rand Show*, Johannesburg. **May 3-Jun 5** *Music Festival*, Pretoria. **Jul 11-17** *J22 International Yacht Regatta*, Durban. **Aug 31-Sep 3** *The Africa Show*, Johannesburg. **Sep 10-15** *Flora '93*, Cape Town. **Oct 1-10** *National Motor Show*, Johannesburg. **Nov 17-22** *Cherry Festival*, Ficksburg. **Jan 10-Feb 5 '94** *International Music Competition*, Pretoria.
SOCIAL CONVENTIONS: Handshaking is the usual form of greeting. Normal courtesies should be shown when visiting someone's home. Casual wear is widely acceptable. Formal social functions often call for a dinner jacket and black tie for men and full-length dresses for women; this will be specified on the invitation. Smoking is prohibited during cinema and theatre performances. The internal situation in South Africa is tense and complex, and visitors should avoid making casual remarks or expressing dogmatic opinions on the subject. **Tipping:** Normally 10% if service is not included. It is customary to tip porters, waiters, taxi drivers, caddies and room service. Porters and room service are usually given a R2 tip. By law, hotel rates do not include a service charge.

BUSINESS PROFILE

ECONOMY: South Africa has one of the world's largest economies and completely dominates the southern part of the African continent. Agriculture is strong enough to allow South Africa virtual self-sufficiency in foodstuffs: livestock is widespread, sugar, maize and cereals are produced in large quantities. The foundation of the modern South African economy, however, is mining. The country has considerable deposits of common minerals such as coal, but also of valuable ores which are in high demand but are scarce outside the CIS: chromium, manganese, vanadium and platinum appear in the largest concentrations anywhere in the world. Its most valuable minerals, however, are gold and diamonds, and South Africa has long been the world's largest producer and exporter of both. Despite the importance of mining, manufacturing is the largest sector of the economy. Metal industries include steel and heavy engineering, producing machinery and transport equipment. Advanced technological and service industries have emerged in recent years, but have yet to compete in scale or sophistication with their counterparts in Europe, North America or Japan. The only key mineral that South Africa lacks is oil. Although this is the subject of a long-standing United Nations embargo, the South African government has gone to very great lengths to ensure an adequate supply of oil by clandestine purchases on the world market and the construction of a unique coal-to-oil conversion plant. South Africa is also the target of an embargo on the sale of armaments. Pretoria's response has been the creation of an indigenous defence manufacturing industry which has been successful enough to become an important exporter in its own right. (South African products of all descriptions are generally disguised before or during export to deceive or reassure purchasers as to the origin.) Despite managing to avoid serious damage from economic sanctions, South Africa effectively spent most of the 1980s in recession. This stemmed from excessive government spending compounded by a sharp fall in foreign investment and, in some cases, outright withdrawal. High inflation and foreign debt, plus a weak currency, forced the Government into unprecedented debt rescheduling in 1989. This had immense political consequences which have not yet been fully resolved. The future of the economy is a key item on the political agenda: both domestic and foreign business interests are hoping for a stable political transition and an operating environment relatively free of control and regulation. The short- and medium-term outlook is not good, however, as recessionary forces continue to depress the economy into the 1990s. Severe drought has badly affected the agricultural sector. The USA, the UK, Germany and Japan are South Africa's main trading partners. Israel and Taiwan are also important.
BUSINESS: Suits are generally expected to be worn for meetings, safari-style suits are often suitable for summer. Appointments are generally necessary and

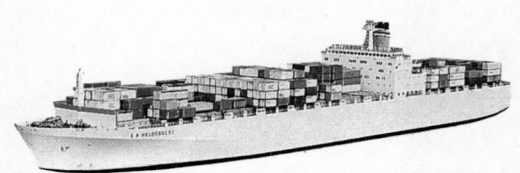

unctuality is expected. Visiting cards are widely sed. **Office hours:** 0830-1630 Monday to Friday.

COMMERCIAL INFORMATION: The following rganisations can offer advice:
South African Chamber of Business (SACOB), PO Box 91267, Auckland Park 2006. Tel: (11) 482 2524. Fax: (11) 726 1344. Telex: 422497; *or*
South African Foreign Trade Organisation (SAFTO), PO Box 782706, Sandton 2146. Tel: (11) 883 3737. Fax: (11) 883 6569. Telex: 424111.

CONFERENCES/CONVENTIONS: There are oughly 815 conference venues in South Africa of which 326 are in the Transvaal, 226 in the Cape, 55 in Natal and 39 in the Orange Free State. The main conference venues are in Pretoria and Johannesburg though facilities exist in all other major towns, provided mainly by hotels and universities. The Conference and Incentive Promotions Division of SATOUR exists to promote South African venues and to ensure high standards of service and facilities for the conference organiser. Address: SATOUR Conference Division, Private Bag X164, Pretoria 0001. Tel: (12) 347 0600. Fax: (12) 454 768 *or* 454 1419. Telex: 3204575 SA.

HISTORY & GOVERNMENT

HISTORY: Evidence for human and humanoid occupation of South Africa extends back two million years. Stone Age artefacts date from 40,000 years ago, from which time there appears to have been a continuous human culture. This culture has been identified as being related to that of the Khoisan peoples and it lasted until the arrival of the Europeans and the Bantus – who largely absorbed them. The Bantu population of the region arrived as a result of the great southernward migrations of Bantu peoples across central and southern Africa which occurred during the early and middle parts of this millenium. This largely displaced the Bushmen (whose aboriginal culture – still surviving in the Kalahari – is rivalled only in Australia) and the Khoiknoi ('Hottentots'). The European discovery of South Africa was roughly contemporaneous – the Portuguese navigator Bartholomew Dias 'discovered' the Cape of Good Hope in 1488. In 1652 Dutch settlers, under Commander Jan van Riebeeck, arrived to start a victualling station for the Dutch East India Company. Numbers were swelled by French Huguenots in 1688 and again in 1820 by British settlers, after the British occupation of the Cape. During the 18th and 19th centuries, British and Boer settlers fought a series of wars with the local tribes. Control of the Cape region was also a matter of dispute – between the Dutch and the British. The latter finally gained control in 1806 and, dissatisfied with their new rulers, the Boer pioneers, or *Voortrekkers*, moved northward to establish the independent republics of the Orange Free State and the Transvaal, bringing them into contact (and sometimes conflict) with the indigenous Africans, in particular, members of the Sotho and Nguni groups. In 1869, diamonds (and later gold) were discovered in the Transvaal, attracting huge numbers of fortune hunters, many of them British. President Paul Kruger of the Transvaal, fearing British domination, invoked strict franchise requirements. Britain's attempts at intervention resulted in the Anglo-Boer War, and the British victory in 1902 eventually resulted in the establishment of the Union of South Africa in 1910. In 1948 the National Party came to power, and has remained in office ever since. The National Party has cemented the policy of apartheid, officially the separate development of all racial groups, effectively the creation of semi-autonomous 'homelands' and the preservation of white supremacy elsewhere. There are now four 'homelands' (Transkei, Bophuthatswana, Venda and Ciskei) comprising 13% of all land in the country. Though they are officially styled 'independent', the 'homelands' are not recognised internationally and remain entirely dependent on South Africa.

The principal black opposition movement to the government has been the African National Congress (ANC). The bulk of the ANC's organisation and resources, including its military wing Umkhonto we Sizwe, worked in exile elsewhere in southern Africa until very recently, since it was made illegal. The most important black political force outside the ANC has been Chief Buthelezi's Inkatha movement, with a substantial power base in the Zulu areas in the south-east of the country. In the absence of organised, legal black political movements (trade unions were also banned until the mid-1980s). The major role in focussing opposition to the Government was played by the church, which enjoyed the advantage of being impossible to ban (on political grounds). There was also growing opposition to the Government among whites. This derived from two distinct quarters: firstly, from right-wing Afrikaners such as the Conservative Party, which made significant parliamentary gains during the late 1980s, and the quasi-paramilitary AWB (Afrikaner Resistance Movement); secondly, and more crucially for the Government, from the business community. However, the continuing presence of Botha – 'The Crocodile' to South African columnists – seemed to preclude any great shift in government attitudes. Then in February 1989, ill health suddenly provided the opportunity for Botha's Cabinet opponents to force his resignation as leader of the National Party (although he retained his role of State President). The Education Minister, F W de Klerk, was selected to lead the Party. De Klerk, despite a reputation as a hard-liner, has proved more flexible, imaginative and conciliatory than his predecessor. The decisive factor in the Government's concessions was economic. South Africa's foreign creditors – multinational banks, for the most part – refused to reschedule overdue loan repayments without a major change in the domestic policies which, the bankers felt, would surely lead to disaster. It was made quite clear to Pretoria that they had the full backing of all major western governments in taking this line. The new government, which was rapidly running out of money, was presented with little choice and promptly set about drafting further reforms. In the run-up to the September elections, de Klerk worked hard, and mostly successfully, to sell these to his own party. The new government also scored some quick foreign policy gains by ending the war in Namibia and curtailing the South African-backed guerrilla groups in Angola and Mozambique, partly by rapprochement with the newly accommodating USSR. Botha resigned his post of State President in August 1989. Elections in early September 1989 returned the National Party to power, but with inroads made on their majority from both left- and right-wing opponents. The peaceful settlement in Namibia, initially seen as something of a gamble in Pretoria, has paid off for de Klerk, as did his controversial decision to release seven leading members of the African National Congress (including several colleagues of Nelson Mandela who were jailed at the same time). On February 2, 1990, de Klerk announced: the 'unbanning' of the ANC, the South African Communist Party and 30 other anti-apartheid groups; the relaxation of the state of emergency; and the unconditional release of Nelson Mandela. This last long-awaited event finally took place on February 11. The ANC immediately appointed Mandela Vice-President, effectively leader due to the absence through illness of the movement's President Oliver Tambo. Mandela and selected ANC colleagues quickly sat down to start negotiating a final political settlement with the white government. While the white community is far from united, the ANC must also deal with internal diasagreements. The ANC is not a unitary movement, but a coalition of numerous diverse interests: Mandela describes it as 'an African parliament'. The internal dissent which is potentially damaging comes from the younger, township-based activists who are suspicious of contacts with the Government.

More important than this is the deep schism which emerged between the ANC and Inkatha, which has exploded into disturbingly frequent violence between Zulu supporters of Inkatha and the Xhosas who predominantly back the ANC. Several thousand have been killed in two years of intercommunal violence. Much of it was initiated by Inkatha, apparently as a strategic ploy to force its way to the negotiating table. It later transpired that the security forces were covertly financing Inkatha violence and in some cases instigating attacks against ANC cadres. Inkatha eventually got its way, although in December 1991 it pulled out of the multi-party talks. By this time the talks had been running for six months and, in an atmosphere of increasing suspicion between the Government and the ANC, progress was slow. However, at the end of November a Convention for a Democratic South Africa (CODESA) was signed by the Government, ANC, Inkatha and over a dozen other interested parties which set down basic parameters for political transition. CODESA now provides the principal forum for the negotiations, at which the Government and the ANC are the major participants, to define a new constitutional structure for South Africa. The allegations of security force collusion in political violence have damaged the process considerably, and there remain doubts as to whether the Government can actually control the large and powerful security apparatus. In February 1992, amid mounting white opposition, de Klerk decided to call a snap referendum on the constitutional changes. The outcome of the all-white referendum, which was held on March 17, 1992, was a larger than expected majority in favour of the reform process. With this result secured, de Klerk entered the CODESA negotiations. De Klerk's confidence was apparent from the Government's conduct of the negotiations, which have covered much ground since the spring of 1992, but have reached an impasse over the percentage of the vote in a new proposed parliament which must be achieved to effect future constitutional change: the Government have insisted on 75%; the ANC have offered 70%. The minutiae of the negotiations became increasingly irrelevant, however, as it became clear that the Government was doing nothing to reign in its security establishment which continued to sponsor Inkatha violence against the ANC. This factor and the massacres of unarmed demonstrators in the Johannesburg shanty town of Boipatong in June and on the border of the Ciskei 'homeland' in October have all but driven the ANC away from the negotiating table. However, there is little doubt in Government quarters and among foreign observers that CODESA will resume: indeed, discreet contacts between the two sides have continued behind the scenes: too much is at stake for a complete breakdown. Certainly, the alternative to violent insurrection hardly bears contemplation. The pace may be forced in the near future by the worsening economic outlook. Unemployment amongst all communities is at its highest level since the 1930s – and it was that experience of the Great Depression for South Africa's whites that laid the original foundations for the introduction of apartheid.

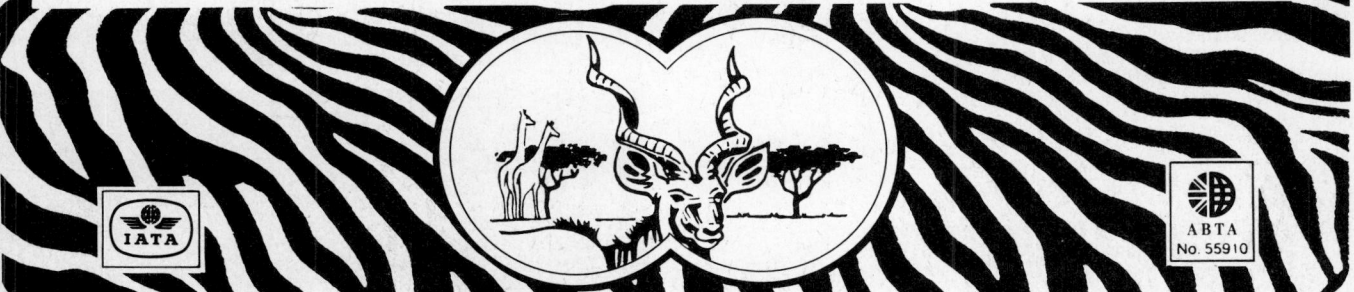

GOVERNMENT: Until 1984, all South Africans were governed by a parliament drawn from and elected by whites only. The State President, also a white, and the members of the parliament, were elected for five years. A tricameral parliament was introduced in 1984 as a result of a constitutional reform under which representation was extended to both Asians and coloureds. The white, coloured and Asian parliaments contain 178, 85 and 45 members respectively, elected exclusively by members of their own ethnic group. Each parliament is responsible for legislation governing its own community, but matters of 'national' import require the agreement of all three houses, over which the whites have a built-in majority. Negotiations for the introduction of a new constitution have been taking place under the auspices of the Convention for a Democratic South Africa, in which representatives of all communities have been involved.

CLIMATE

South Africa's climate is generally sunny and pleasant. Winters are usually mild, although snow falls on the mountain ranges of the Cape and Natal and occasionally in lower-lying areas, when a brief cold spell can be expected throughout the country. Since South Africa lies south of the Equator, the seasons are the reverse of those in the northern hemisphere.

Required clothing: Lightweight cottons and linens and rainwear. Warmer clothes are required for winter.

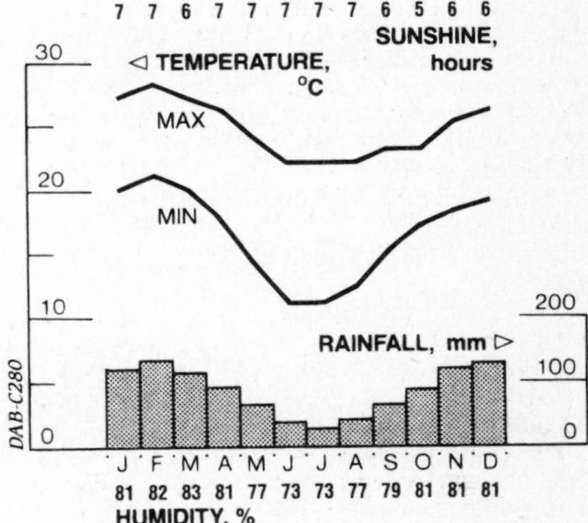

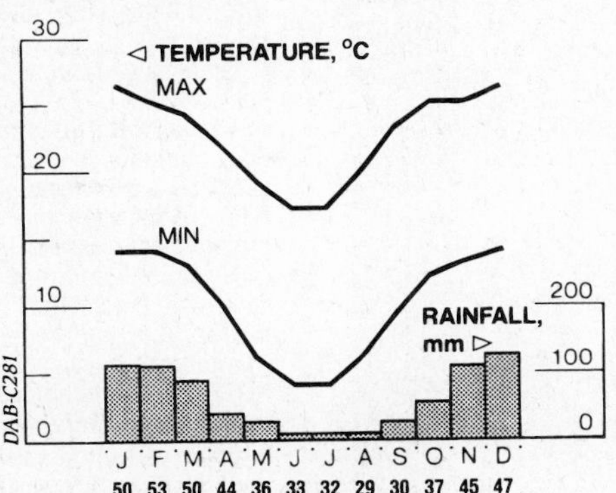

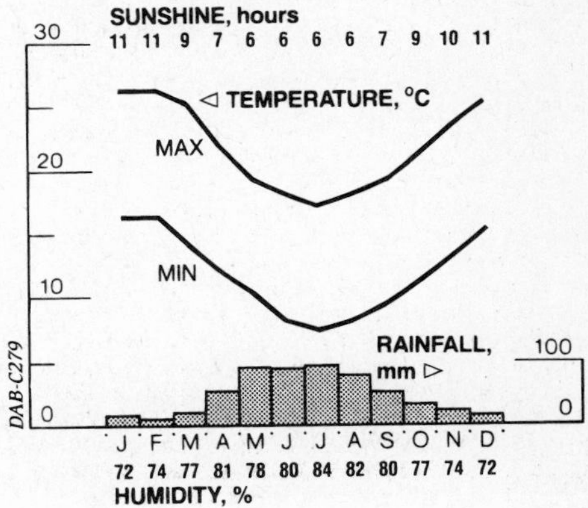

Bophuthatswana

LOCATION: Southern Africa.

TOURISM DEVELOPMENT UNIT (Bophuthatswana Tourism Council Boptour)
PO Box 4488
Suite 101, Borekelong House
8681 Mmabatho, Bophuthatswana
Tel: (140) 843 040. Fax: (140) 842 542.
BOPTOUR SUN CITY
PO Box 171
Sun City Entertainment Centre
0136 Sun City, Bophuthatswana
Tel: (1465) 21358. Fax: (1465) 21359.
BOPTOUR JOHANNESBURG
PO Box 7727
Shop No 3, Nedbank Mall
145 Commissioner Street
2000 Johannesburg
Tel: (011) 331 9330/6/8/9. Fax: (011) 331 9351.
BOPTOUR REPRESENTATIVES ABROAD:
GERMANY
Frankfurt Office
Kettenhofweg 33
W-6000 Frankfurt/M 1, Germany
Tel: (69) 720 797/8. Fax: (69) 720799.
FRANCE
Président de l'Association d'Amitié France-Bophuthatswana
18 Square de l'Avenue Foche (80)
75116 Paris, France
Tel:(1) 45 00 05 89 *or* 45 00 01 42. Fax: (1) 45 01 84 78.
ISRAEL
Bophuthatswana Trade Mission
Beit Asia
4 Weizman Street
Tel Aviv 64239, Israel
Tel: (3) 269 151/5. Fax: (3) 269 157.
ITALY
General Consultant Bophuthatswana
Via Po 44/46
00198 Rome, Italy
Tel: (6) 841 5497/8. Fax: (6) 844 3291.
UNITED KINGDOM
Bophuthatswana International Affairs
Piccadilly House
33/37 Lower Regent Street
London SW1Y 4NE
Tel: (071) 439 8611/5. Fax: (071) 734 0346.
TAIWAN
Bophuthatswana Trade and Tourism Centre
16th Floor, Room 16/3
333 International Trade Building
Keelung Road
Section 1
Taipei, Taiwan.

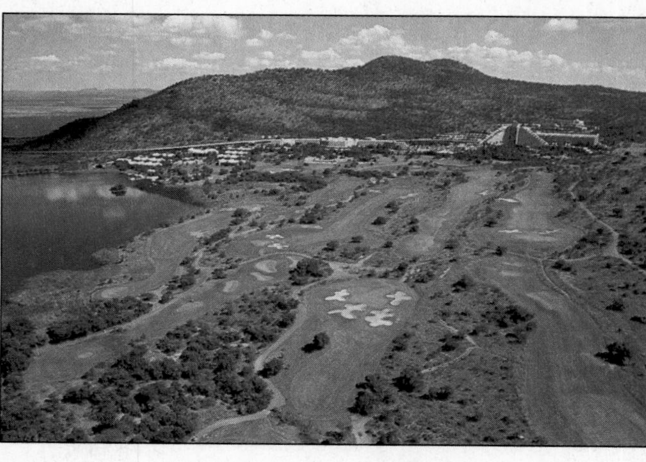

AREA: 44,000 SQ KM.
POPULATION: 3.2 million (1.8 million reside in Bophuthswana and 1.4 million outside Bophuthatswana).
DENSITY: 24.4 per sq km.
CAPITAL: Mmabatho.
GEOGRAPHY: Bophuthatswana is a flat country at an altitude of between 1000-2000m with gently rolling hills and consists of six separate geographical units in a east–west line, ranging between the populous gold mining heartland of Southern Africa and the arid areas of the Kalahari Desert. A remote region of the state is situated in the south east in the wheat growing belt of central Southern Africa. The country shares borders of 2790km with South Africa, except the Lehurutshe and Molopo regions which border Botswana. It is also roughly bounded in the south by the Orange River and in the north by the Limpopo River. On the south east border are the Vaal and Hartz rivers. The largest area measures 16,000 sq km in the Kudumane and Ganyesa Districts, comparable to the size of Switzerland. The capital, Mmabatho, including Mafikeng (Mafeking) and the Montshiwa small industries area, borders on less populated areas of the west.

LANGUAGE: Setswana, Afrikaans and English are spoken, with Setswana as the national and English as the commercial language.
RELIGION: Church of England, Roman Catholic, Lutheran, Methodist and other black church movements. There are also independent church movements.
TIME: GMT + 2.
ELECTRICITY: 220/230AC, 50Hz.
TELEPHONE: IDD is available. Country code: 27. **Fax:** Most hotels and conference establishements have facilities. **Telex/telegram:** Available at all post offices. **Post:** Airmail to overseas countries can take up to ten days. There are no deliveries and mail must be collected from post boxes or tribal offices. **Press:** The weekly newspapers are *The Mail* and *Seipone*. South African daily newspapers are widely available, including *The Star, The Citizen* and *Sowetan*, as well as periodicals such as *News Week, Time, Financial Mail* and others.
PASSPORT: Valid passport required by all.
VISAS: Required by all except:
(a) nationals of the UK and Germany;
(b) nationals of South Africa, Lesotho, Botswana, Swaziland, Transkei, Ciskei and Venda.
APPLICATION REQUIREMENTS
For Tourists and Visitors' visas (Single entry): (a) Apply formally on a prescribed TS S 94 form. (b) Submit two identical passport-size photos (c) Fee: R15. (£3 UK sterling or US$5).
Employment visas: as in above plus: (a) Company letter. (b) Copy of relevant qualifications and/or testimony of appropriate experience and skills in the case of an employment visa.
Visitors may apply for visas at the nearest Bophuthatswana representative (for addresses, see above).
NOTE: Visa requirements at airports and road posts are the same as those at the border. Visitors must comply with requirements as outlined above. Over and above the South African visas, the holder has to acquire a Bophuthatswana visa when entering through border posts.

Types of visas
(a) Single-entry visas for holidaymakers, visitors and tourists;
(b) Multiple-entry visas for employment and schooling;
(b) Shopping visas issued to nationals who require a visa but hold temporary residence in Botswana.
It takes approximately six weeks to process a postal application. Faxed applications must be legible in order to be processed.
Note: There are no border controls between Bophuthatswana and South Africa. However, visas are required when entering or leaving the country through the borders shared with Botswana.

MONEY

CURRENCY: South African Rand (R) = 100 cents. Notes are in dominations of R50, 20, 10 and 5. Coins are in denominations of R2, R1 and 50, 20, 10, 5, 2 and 1 cent.
CREDIT CARDS: Access/Mastercard, American Express, Diners Club and Visa are widely accepted. Check with your credit card company for details of merchant acceptability and other facilities which may be available.
TRAVELLERS CHEQUES: Valid at banks, hotels, some restaurants and other shops.
EXCHANGE RATE INDICATORS: The following figures are included as a guide to the movements of the Rand against Sterling and the US Dollar:

Date:	Oct '89	Oct '90	Oct '91	Oct '92
£1=	*4.26	*4.94	*4.89	*4.75
US$1=	*2.70	*2.53	*2.81	*3.02

Note [*]: Commercial rate.
BANKING HOURS: 0900-1530 Monday to Friday and 0830-1100 Saturday.

DUTY FREE

The following goods per person may be imported into Bophuthatswana by passengers over 16 years of age without incurring customs duty:
400 cigarettes and 50 cigars and 250g of tobacco;
1 litre of spirits and 9 litres of wine;
50ml of perfume and 250ml of toilet water;
Gifts up to the value of R500.

HEALTH

	Special precautions advised	*Certificate required?*
YELLOW FEVER	No	1
CHOLERA	Yes	2
TYPHOID & POLIO	Yes	-
MALARIA	3	-
FOOD & DRINK	4	-

[1]: A yellow fever vaccination certificate is required from travellers over one year of age arriving with scheduled airlines that originated from infected areas. Travellers arriving on flights with scheduled airlines that originated from infected areas but remained at the scheduled airport or in the adjacent town during transit, do not require a certificate. Passengers arriving by unscheduled flights at airports other than those used by scheduled airlines must possess a certificate.
[2]: Following WHO guidelines issued in 1973, a cholera vaccination certificate is not a condition of entry into Bophuthatswana. However, cholera is a risk in parts of the country, particularly in rural areas and precaution is recommended for those likely to be at risk. Up-to-date advice should be sought before deciding whether these precautions should include vaccination.
[3]: Malaria risk, predominantly in the malignant *falciparum* form, exists throughout the year. Resistance to chloroquine has been reported. It is strongly recommended that visitors take anti-malaria tablets before entering the country.
[4]: Tap water is considered safe to drink in urban areas but may be contaminated elsewhere and sterilisation is advisable. Milk is pasteurised and diary products are safe for consumption. Local meat, poultry, seafood, fruit and vetgetables are generally considered safe to eat.
Health care: Medical facilities are excellent and hospitals are sprinkled in all the regions. There are chemist and pharmacy supplies. Health insurance is recommended.

TRAVEL INTERNATIONAL

AIR: *Jan Smuts Airport* serves as the main gateway into Bophuthatswana for scheduled international flights. *Mmabatho International Airport* takes wide-bodied aircraft such as Boeing 747s. Connnecting flights between Mmabatho and Johannesburg and various destinations in Bophuthatswana and Southern Africa are available at Mmabatho International Airport.
RAIL: There are regular rail links between major centres in Botswana, Zimbabwe, Namibia and South Africa to Bophuthatswana.
ROAD: For those wishing to travel by car/bus, there are excellent tarred roads making Botswana, Zimbabwe, Namibia and South Africa easily accessible to and from Bophuthatswana.

TRAVEL INTERNAL

AIR: *BopAir* offers scheduled flights from Johannesburg to Mmabatho, Johannesburg to Pilanesberg and Mmabatho. *BopAir* offers charters within Bophuthatswana connecting major regions. There are airports at Mmabatho,

Thaba Nchu and Pilanesberg.
ROAD: The road system is well developed in urban areas and poor in rural areas. There is a well-maintained network of roads and motorways in populous regions. Driving is on the right. It is illegal to carry petrol other than in petrol tanks. **Taxi:** Commuter-type taxis are available throughout the country in all towns.

ACCOMMODATION

Bophuthatswana offers a wide variety of accommodation graded from luxury 5-star to budget hotels. Each hotel must display a plaque showing the relevant grading. Hotels are registered with the Bophuthatswana Tourism Council which controls standards and can be contacted at PO Box 4488, 8681 Mmabatho. Tel: (140) 843 040/6. Fax: (140) 842 524.

Where to Stay

The country boasts a wide variety of accommodation in luxurious hotels, game lodges, chalets and cabins, safari tents, caravan parks and camping sites. The rating is done by Boptour and is as follows:

Hotels

Sun City (★★★★★) Cascades (★★★★★)
Thaba Nchu Sun (★★★★★) Mmabatho Sun (★★★★)
Morula Sun (★★★★) The Cabanas (★★★)
Tlhabane Sun (★★★) Naledi Sun (★★★)
Taung Sun (★★★) Molopo Sun (★★★)
Carousel (Grading pending).

The Palace of the Lost City

The most magnificent hotel ever built. The theme is 'mythical Africa'. The vision is incredible. Here, the watchword is opulence. The rooms are luxuriously appointed, standard features include air-conditioning and 24-hour room service. The decor of each room is designed as though if it were in an emperor's residence. Eight towers provide dramatic views of the jungle, one of the restaurants is on an island, the other overlooking a rainforest and lake. Experience a prelude wave-splash in an in-land sea at the Lost City.

Lodges/Resorts

Kwa Maritane Time Share Resort (★★★);
Baskubung Time Share Resort (Grading pending);
Manyane Game Lodge.

Budget Hotels

Protea (★★) Surrey (★)
Crews (★) Thaba Nchu (★)
Thebe Patshwa (★) Oasis (★)

There is also safari accommodation in three National Parks in chalets, cabins, safari tents, caravan and camping sites.
CAMPING/CARAVAN: Caravan parks are to be found in various regions of Bophuthatswana. Camping is only allowed in specified areas.

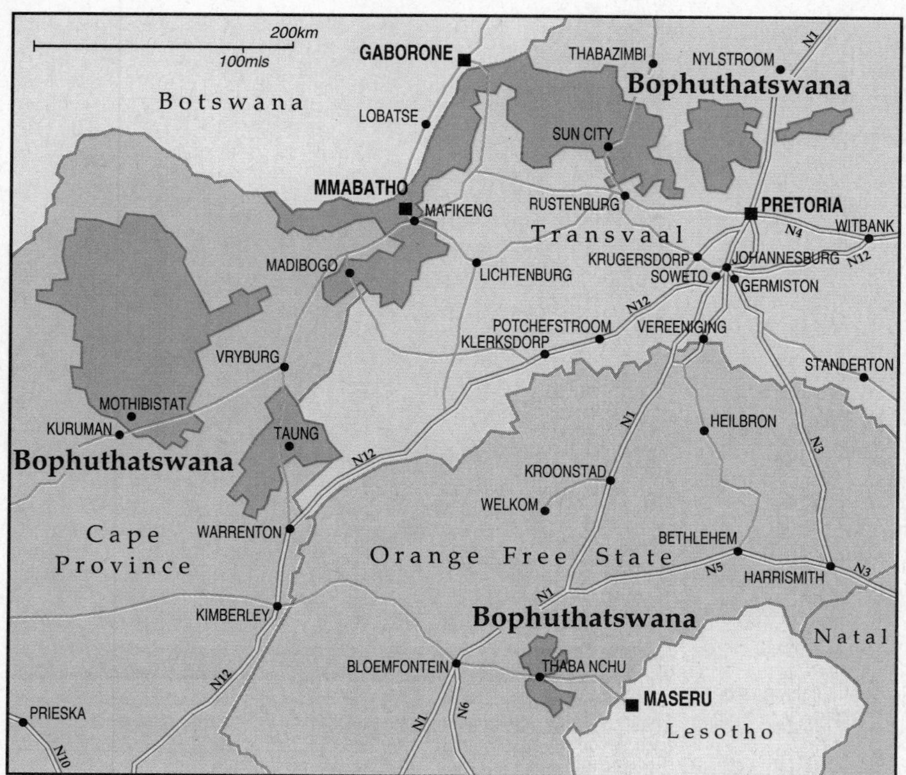

SOCIAL PROFILE

FOOD & DRINK: Ranges from traditional dishes to international cuisine. National specialities include sour porridge made from sorghum (*bogobe*) and meat (*nama*). Traditional beer is also made from sorghum (*bojalwa*).
SHOPPING: There are small rural markets or large ultra-modern centres where shopping for curios or imported gourmet delicacies and pottery, jewellery and a variety of garments can be made. **Shopping hours:** 0830-1700 Monday to Friday, 0800-1300 Saturday.
SPORT: Sporting activities include golf, tennis, fishing and water-skiing. There is a man-made lake at the Sun City Complex for various watersports including sailing and water-skiing.
SPECIAL EVENTS: Independence Day (December 6) is celebrated with traditional dancing, musical events, floats and many other spectacular performances.
SOCIAL CONVENTIONS: As in many African countries, a traditional way of life prevails. Handshaking is the usual form of greeting. Dress is informal during the day. Sports shirts and shorts or trousers for cool evenings. Women need little more than light dresses, skirts, trousers or shorts and top. When dining out, jacket and tie are recommended for men and smart dress for women.

BUSINESS PROFILE

ECONOMY: Bophuthatswana espouses the free-enterprise system with mining as the major source of foreign income. The western world's second largest producer of platinum, Bophuthatswana also has large deposits of chromium, salt, iron ore, diamonds, limestone, lead, copper, zinc, coal, uranium, asbestos, manganese and vanadium. The country produces a large variety of agricultural products: maize, sorghum, wheat, soya beans, sunflower seed, groundnuts, cotton, beef, poultry and vegetables. Industry is flourishing and manufactured products include clothing, furniture, domestic and commercial appliances, building materials and explosives for the mining industry. The region is one of the fastest foreign exchange earners with phenomenal development in the hotel industry.

HISTORY

The Tswana nation is one of the older indigenous populations in Southern Africa. Living on the central highland plateau, they can trace their early democratic principles in everyday life to at least 400 years ago – before the American and French revolutions. The Batswana form one of the main black populations of the region. They are the largest branch of the Sotho group and number over four million. In colonial times, the British divided the Bechuanaland Protectorate into two ares: to the north, the Bechuanaland Protectorate (now Botswana); and to the south, British Bechuanaland (now Bophuthatswana). At the end of the 19th century, British Bechuanaland was ceded to the Cape Colony 'for ease of administration', despite solemn undertakings from the British allies that this would not happen. This decision was, as they saw it, as honourable as it was disloyal. Yet it was the Batswana who fought alongside the garrsion at the siege of Mafikeng (anglicised to 'Mafeking') in the Anglo-Boer war – one of the most famous victories in English colonial history. Once their lands were joined to the Cape, however, their fate was sealed. In due course this was to become part of the Union of South Africa. So deprived of their cherished freedom, the Batswana found themselves becoming second-class citizens – in their own ancestral lands.
GOVERNMENT: Bophuthatswana is governed by an Executive President at the head of an Exective Council (cabinet), a National Assembly, Regional Authorities, tribal and community authorities. The chief or headman appoints councillors for five years in accordance with local laws and customs. The councillors are overseen by the 12 regional authorities. The tribal and community authorities fall under the Governor's jurisdiction and are represented by two appointed members per tribe or community plus the chief or headman. The chairman and vice-chairman of regional authorities are elected by the members of the tribal council authorities, with only chiefs eligible for election. Regional authorities advise and assist the Government, the tribal and community authorites falling within their jurisdiction, and pass regulations. The sovereign legislature of Bophuthatswana is the National Assembly, consisting of 108 members. Executive powers are vested in the President, who consults with various ministers in the Executive Council. The present Executive Council consists of the President, 15 cabinet ministers and six deputy ministers.

CLIMATE:

The climate follows that of a dry steppe with warm to hot summers and cool, though sun-drenched winters. Temperatures range from 22°C in summer to 12°C in winter. Rainfall occurs in summer from November until early April measuring from 300mm in the dry west to 700mm in the east, which suffices for dry land agriculture.

Location: Western Europe.

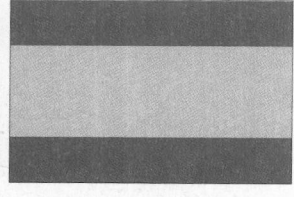

Secretaría General de Turismo
Mariá de Molina 50
28006 Madrid, Spain
Tel: (1) 411 4014. Fax: (1) 411 4232. Telex: 23100.

Embassy of the Kingdom of Spain
24 Belgrave Square
London SW1 8QA
Tel: (071) 235 5555. Fax: (071) 828 3067. Telex: 21110 *or* 261333.

Spanish Consulate
20 Draycott Place
London SW3 2RZ
Tel: (071) 581 5921/4. *Visa Information*: Tel: (071) 581 5924/5. Fax: (071) 235 2263. Opening hours: 0930-1200 Monday to Friday.
Manchester: Tel: (061) 236 1233. Fax: (061) 228 7467. Telex: 667591.
Edinburgh: Tel: (031) 220 1843.

Spanish Institute/Cultural Attaché
(for information on language courses in Spain etc)
102 Eaton Square
London SW1
Tel: (071) 235 1484/5. Fax: (071) 235 4115.

Spanish Labour Office
(for information on working and free health care in Spain)
20 Peel Street
London W8 7PD
Tel: (071) 221 0098. Fax: (071) 229 7270. Telex: 919140 SPANL OG.

Spanish National Tourist Office
Metro House
57-58 St James's Street
London SW1A 1LD
Tel: 499 0901 (general information) *or* 499 4593 (travel agents) *or* 499 9237 (promotional material) *or* 499 1243 (exhibitions) *or* 499 3257 (PR). Fax: (071) 629 4257. Telex: 888138 TURESP G.

British Embassy
Calle de Fernando el Santo 16
28010 Madrid
Spain
Tel: (1) 319 0200. Fax: (1) 319 0423. Telex: 27656.
Consulates in: Algeciras, Seville, Alicante, Barcelona, Tarragona, Bilbao, Las Palmas (Grand Canary), Santa Cruz de Tenerife (Canary Islands), Málaga, Palma, Ibiza, Santander, Menorca and Vigo.

Embassy of the Kingdom of Spain
2700 15th Street, NW
Washington, DC
20009
Tel: (202) 265 0190/1. Fax: (202) 328 3212. Telex: 440061SPA UI.
Consulates in: Boston, Chicago, Houston, Los Angeles,

Miami, New Orleans, New York (tel: (212) 265 0190), Puerto Rico and San Francisco.
Spanish National Tourist Office
665 Fifth Avenue
New York, NY
10022
Tel: (212) 759 8822. Fax: (212) 980 1053. Telex: 426782 SNTO UI.
Offices also in: Chicago, Los Angeles and Miami.
Embassy of the United States of America
Serrano 75
28006 Madrid, Spain
Tel: (1) 577 4000. Fax: (1) 575 8655. Telex: 27763.
Embassy of the Kingdom of Spain
Suite 802
350 Sparks Street
Ottawa, Ontario
K1R 7S8
Tel: (613) 237 2193/4. Fax: (613) 236 1502.
Consulates in: Calgary, Halifax, Montréal, Québec, Saskatoon, St John's and Toronto.

Spanish National Tourist Office
Suite 1400
102 Bloor Street West
Toronto, Ontario
MS5 1M8
Tel: (416) 961 3131. Fax: (461) 961 1992. Telex: 06 218206.
Canadian Embassy
Edificio Goya
Calle Nunez de Balboa 35
28080 Madrid, Spain
Tel: (1) 431 4300. Fax: (1) 431 2367. Telex: 27347 DOMCAN E.
Consulates in: Barcelona, Málaga and Seville.

AREA: 504,782 sq km (194,897 sq miles).
POPULATION: 39,321,604 (1990 estimate).
POPULATION DENSITY: 77.9 per sq km.
CAPITAL: Madrid. **Population:** 2,984,576 (1991 estimate).

GEOGRAPHY: Spain shares the Iberian peninsula with Portugal and is bounded to the north by the Pyrenees, which separate Spain from France. The Balearic Islands (Mallorca, Menorca, Ibiza and Formentera), 193km (120 miles) southeast of Barcelona, and the Canary Islands off the West Coast of Africa are part of Spain, as are the tiny enclaves of Ceuta, Chafarinas, Melilla and Jadu on the North African mainland. With the exception of Switzerland, mainland Spain is the highest and most mountainous country in Europe, with an average height of 610m (2000ft). The Pyrenees stretch roughly 400km (249 miles) from the Basque Country in the west to the Mediterranean Sea; at times the peaks rise to over 1524m (5000ft), the highest point being 3404m (11,169ft). The main physical feature of Spain is the vast central plateau, or *Meseta*, divided by several chains of sierras. The higher northern area includes Castile and León, the southern section comprises Castile/La Mancha and Extremadura. In the south the plateau drops abruptly at the Sierra Morena, beyond which lies the valley of Guadalquivir. Southeast of Granada is the Sierra Nevada, part of the

SPAIN	HEALTH REGULATIONS	VISA REGULATIONS Code-Link
GALILEO/WORLDSPAN	 TI-DFT/MAD/HE	 TI-DFT/MAD/VI
SABRE	 TIDFT/MAD/HE	TIDFT/MAD/VI

To access this information on your CRS, swipe the barcode with a light pen or type in the text under the barcode. For more information, see the introduction *How to Use This Book.*

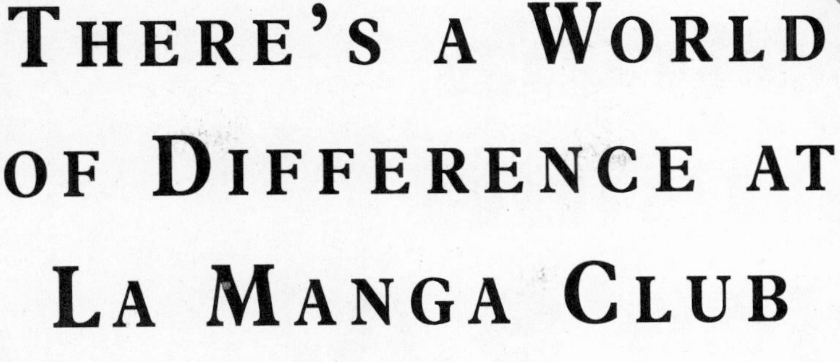

NEW FIVE STAR PRINCE FELIPE HOTEL OPENS JUNE 1993

GOLF - 3 x 18 hole Championship courses (1 x 18 hole 'Dave Thomas' course); Driving range; Pro coaching; PGA of Europe College; PGA of Europe Tournament venue; 18 hole pitch and putt.

TENNIS - 18 courts; Coaching; Practice facilities; Venue for Spanish Championships.

SQUASH

BOWLS

HORSE RIDING

HEALTH CENTRE - Jacuzzi; Gym; Beautician; Sauna.

WATERSPORTS SCHOOL - Sailing; Skiing; Jet Skiing; Snorkel; Scuba; Turbo Ride.

RESTAURANTS

PIANO BARS

CONFERENCE FACILITIES

VILLAS AND APARTMENTS- For all property enquiries at La Manga Club can contact Richard Gower, Sales Manager on (68) 56 45 11 or our UK contact on 0800 252 235

There's a world of difference at La Manga Club.

A world where time stands still and sky blue days thread lazily one to another...

A world where a new hotel, breathtaking villas and beautiful apartments are the last word in style and comfort.

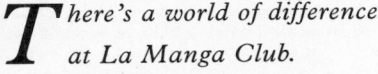

Where the challenge of the three championship golf courses, a driving range and professional coaches are a stone's throw from your door. Fun, exciting and special, it is a paradise for all sports enthusiasts.

This exclusive European resort opens its state-of-the-art five star hotel in June.

Stay for a week...

Or the rest of your life.

It's the resort of the future...

It's a world apart.

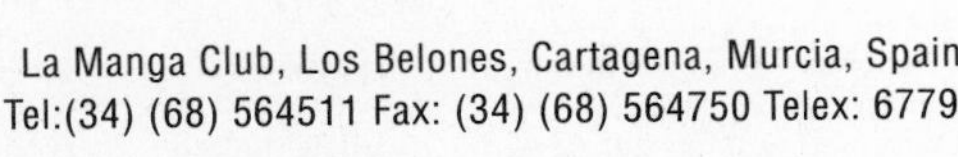

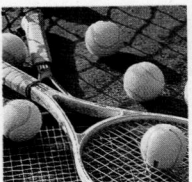

La Manga Club, Los Belones, Cartagena, Murcia, Spain
Tel:(34) (68) 564511 Fax: (34) (68) 564750 Telex: 67798

Betic Cordillera, which runs parallel to the Mediterranean, rising to 3481m (11,420ft) and the highest point on the Spanish peninsula (the Pico del Teide on Tenerife in the Canaries is the highest peak in Spain). The Mediterranean coastal area reaches from the French frontier in the northeast down to the Straits of Gibraltar, the narrow strip of water linking the Mediterranean with the Atlantic and separating Spain from North Africa.
LANGUAGE: Spanish (Castilian), Catalan, Galician and Basque.
RELIGION: Roman Catholic majority.
TIME: Mainland Spain/Balearics: GMT + 1 (GMT + 2 in summer).
The Canary Islands: GMT (GMT + 1 in summer).
ELECTRICITY: 220 volts AC (110/125 volts in some older buildings), 50Hz. Generally, round 2-pin plugs and screw-type lamp fittings are in use.
COMMUNICATIONS: Telephone: IDD is available. Country code: 34. Area codes for a selection of major centres: Madrid 1, Alicante 6, Balearic Islands 71, Barcelona 3, Benidorm 6, Bilbao 4, Granada 58, Las Palmas 28, Málaga and Torremolinos 52, Santander 42, Seville 5, Tenerife 22 and Valencia 6. Inside Spain a 9 has to be dialled before the above numbers. **Fax:** This is generally available at 4- and 5-star hotels, especially those catering for the business and conference traveller. **Telex/telegram:** Facilities are available at main post offices. A 24-hour service is available in Madrid at Plaza de la Cibeles; in Barcelona at Plaza Antonio Lopez; in Bilbao at 15 Calle Alameda Urquillo. There are also facilities in major hotels. Charges for automatically connected telex transmissions are by the minute, with a 1-minute minimum charge. Transmissions through the operator are at the same rate, with a 3-minute minimum charge. Urgent business transmissions to Britain can be made from the British Embassy in Madrid, the British Consulates General at Barcelona and Bilbao, and the British Consulates at Seville and the Canary Islands. There is a surcharge of 90% of the cost during normal working hours. **Post:** There are efficient internal and international postal services to all countries. Airmail within Europe usually takes about five days. *Poste Restante* facilities are available at main post offices. **Press:** The English-language daily is *The Iberian Daily Sun*. Other dailies with large circulations include *ABC*, *Dairio 16* and *El Pais*.

BBC World Service and Voice of America frequencies: From time to time these change. See the section *How to Use this Book* for more information.
BBC:

MHz	17.705	15.575	12.095	6.195

A service is also available on 648kHz and 198kHz (0100-0500 GMT).
Voice of America:

MHz	11.97	9.670	6.040	5.995

PASSPORT/VISA

Regulations and requirements may be subject to change at short notice, and you are advised to contact the appropriate diplomatic or consular authority before finalising travel arrangements. Details of these may be found at the head of this country's entry. Any numbers in the chart refer to the footnotes below.

	Passport Required?	Visa Required?	Return Ticket Required?
Full British	1	No	No
BVP	Valid	No	No
Australian	Yes	No	Yes
Canadian	Yes	No	No
USA	Yes	No	Yes
Other EC	1	No	No
Japanese	Yes	No	Yes

PASSPORTS: Valid passport required by all except:
(a) [1] nationals of EC countries with valid ID cards (BVPs if UK nationals); and nationals of Belgium, France, Luxembourg, The Netherlands and Portugal with passports expired less than a maximum of 5 years (nationals of Denmark and Ireland *do* require passports);
(b) nationals of Andorra, Austria, Liechtenstein, Malta, Monaco and Switzerland holding valid ID cards or expired passports (maximum of 5 years).
British Visitors Passport: A BVP is valid for holidays or unpaid business trips of up to 3 months.
VISAS: Required by all except:
(a) nationals of EC countries for visits not exceeding 90 days;
(b) nationals of Canada and the USA and for stays not exceeding 90 days;
(c) nationals of Andorra, Argentina, Austria, Bolivia, Brazil, Chile, Colombia, Costa Rica, Croatia, Cyprus, Czechoslovakia, Dominican Republic, Ecuador, El Salvador, Finland, Grenada, Guatemala, Honduras, Hungary, Iceland, Japan, Kenya, South Korea, Liechtenstein, Malta, Mexico, Monaco, New Zealand, Nicaragua, Norway, Panama, Paraguay, San Marino, Seychelles, Singapore, Slovenia, Sweden, Switzerland, Uruguay, Vatican City, Venezuela and Yugoslavia for stays not exceeding 90 days;
(d) nationals Australia (two entries), Bahrain, Hong Kong, Malaysia, Oman, Qatar, Saudi Arabia, United Arab Emirates and Yemen for one stay of up to 30 days in any 6-month period;
(e) nationals of Algeria, Morocco, Tunisia and Turkey for one entry not exceeding 30 days per year, provided they have 'leave to stay or remain in the UK or an EC country for an indefinite period' (nationals of Morocco on business *do* require visas);
(f) children of any nationality under 14 years of age holding valid passports and accompanied by an adult.
Note: (a) British subjects holding passports issued in Gibraltar *do* require visas. (b) Holders of Netherlands Antilles passports should enquire at a Spanish Consulate to establish whether visas are required. (c) Visas are required by nationals of all countries not exempted above and are generally valid for stays of up to 30 days or 7 days transit. For further information contact the Consulate (for addresses, see above).
Types of visa: Special, Tourist and Business; prices range from £14 to £40 in the UK. Transit visas are not required by: (a) those not needing Tourist visas; (b) those making only one landing in Spain and continuing their journey within 24 hours without leaving the airport.
Validity: Visas are normally valid for up to 30 days (but see above). Visitors wishing to stay longer should make an application for a Special visa.
Application to: Consulate (or Consular Section at Embassy). For addresses, see top of entry.
Application requirements: (a) 3 application forms. (b) 3 photos. (c) Valid passport. (d) Closed travel tickets. (e) Confirmed accommodation. (e) Written invitation from company or organisation in Spain, or proof of trade/professional interest in Spain (for Business visas). (f) A stamped, self-addressed envelope if applying by post. (g) Proof of means of support to cover the intended stay may be requested by the

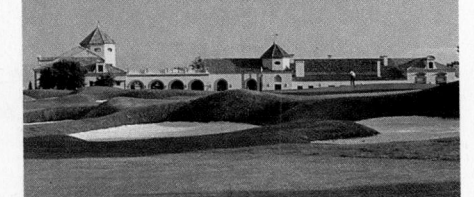

Passport Control Authorities upon arrival in Spain.
Note: Requirements for visas vary according to nationality, passport, travel document used and the purpose and duration of the trip. For further information contact the Consulate (for addresses, see above).
Working days required: Between 1 day and 6 weeks depending on nationality.
Temporary residence: Refer enquiries to Consulate.

MONEY

Currency: Peseta (Pta) = 100 centimos. Notes are in denominations of Pta10,000, 5000, 2000, 1000 and 500. Coins are in denominations of Pta500, 200, 100, 50, 25, 10, 5, 2 and 1.
Currency exchange: Money can be changed in any bank and most travel agencies. National Girobank Postcheques may be used to withdraw cash from UK accounts at main Spanish post offices. If buying Pesetas in advance, note that rates of exchange at many UK banks depend on the denominations of Spanish currency being bought or sold. Check with banks for details and current rates.
Credit cards: Access/Mastercard, American Express, Diners Club and Visa are widely accepted. Check with your credit card company for details of merchant acceptability and other facilities which may be available.
Travellers cheques: International travellers cheques and Eurocheques are widely accepted.
Exchange rate indicators: The following figures are included as a guide to the movements of the Peseta against Sterling and the US Dollar:

Date:	Oct '89	Oct '90	Oct '91	Oct '92
£1.00=	188.60	186.60	184.00	172.65
$1.00=	119.44	95.52	106.02	108.79

Currency restrictions: The import and export of local currency is subject to declaration if the amount exceeds Pta1,000,000 and the amount exported must not exceed the amount declared on arrival. The import and export of foreign currency is unlimited, but should be declared if the quantity exceeds Pta500,000 per person per journey, to avoid difficulties on leaving Spain.
Banking hours: 0830-1630 Monday to Thursday, 0830-1400 Friday and 0830-1300 Saturday (October to May); 0830-1400 Monday to Friday (June to September).

DUTY FREE

The following items may be imported into Spain without incurring customs duty:
(a) Passengers of 17 years or older from Europe and the Mediterranean countries of Asia and Africa:
200 cigarettes or 100 cigarillos or 50 cigars or 250g tobacco ;
1 litre of spirits if exceeding 22% volume or 2 litres of alcoholic beverage not exceeding 22% volume;
2 litres of wine;
250ml eau de toilet and 50g of perfume;
Gifts to the value of Pta5000 (Pta2000 for children under 15 years of age).
(b) Passengers over 17 years of age arriving from EC countries with duty-paid goods (as of January 1993):
800 cigarettes and 400 cigarillos and 200 cigars and 1kg of tobacco;
90 litres of wine (including up to 60 litres of sparkling wine);
10 litres of spirits;
20 litres of intermediate products (such as fortified wine);
110 litres of beer.
Note: [1] The allowance on tobacco products is doubled for all other nationals. There are no import restrictions for the Canary Islands (except for goods which may be imported if valued at no more than Pta8000).

PUBLIC HOLIDAYS

Public holidays observed in Spain are as follows:
Apr 8 '93 Maundy Thursday (except Barcelona). **Apr 9** Good Friday. **Apr 12** Easter Monday (Barcelona and Palma de Mallorca only). **May 1** St Joseph the Workman. **May 15** St Isidro (Madrid only). **Jun 10** Corpus Christi. **Jun 24** King Juan Carlos' Saint's Day. **Jul 25** St James of Compostela. **Aug 15** Assumption. **Oct 12** National Day. **Nov 1** All Saints' Day. **Dec 6** Constitution Day. **Dec 8** Immaculate Conception (except Barcelona). **Dec 25** Christmas Day. **Dec 26** Boxing Day (Barcelona and Palma de Mallorca only). **Jan 1 '94** New Year's Day. **Jan 6** Epiphany.
Note: Different cities, towns and villages have their own festivals in addition to the holidays mentioned above.

HEALTH

Regulations and requirements may be subject to change at short notice, and you are advised to contact your doctor well in advance of your intended date of departure. Any numbers in the chart refer to the footnotes below.

	Special Precautions?	Certificate Required?
Yellow Fever	No	No
Cholera	No	No
Typhoid & Polio	No	-
Malaria	No	-
Food & Drink	1	-

[1]: Mains water is normally chlorinated, and whilst relatively safe may cause mild abdominal upsets. Bottled water is available and is advised for the first few weeks of the stay. Milk is pasteurised and dairy products are safe for consumption. Local meat, poultry, seafood, fruit and vegetables are generally considered safe to eat.
Health care: There is a Reciprocal Health Agreement with the UK. Medical treatment provided by state scheme doctors at state scheme hospitals and health centres (*ambulatorios*) is free to UK citizens if on arrival in Spain, they exchange form E111 for a book of vouchers. This form is available at post offices. This Agreement is, however, implemented to a limited degree in most holiday resorts and health insurance is *strongly advised*. Prescribed medicines and dental treatment must be paid for by all visitors. Further information is available from the Labour Office; for address see top of entry.

TRAVEL - International

Note: For information on travel to and within the **Canary Islands** and the **Balearic Islands** see the respective entries below.
AIR: Spain's national airlines is *IBERIA (IB)*.
Approximate flight times: From *London* to Barcelona is 2 hours, to Ibiza is 2 hours 20 minutes, to Madrid is 2 hours and to Málaga is 2 hours 20 minutes.
From *Los Angeles* to Madrid is 13 hours.
From *New York* to Madrid is 7 hours 25 minutes.
From *Sydney* to Madrid is 29 hours 5 minutes.
International airports: *Alicante (ALC)* (Altet), 12km (7.4 miles) southwest of the city. Coach service runs every 80 minutes to the city from 0700-2200. A taxi service is available to the city. There is a taxi connection between Alicante and Valencia Airport. Airport facilities include a duty-free shop, bank, exchange office, car rental desk and restaurant.
Barcelona (BCN) (del Prat), 10km (6 miles) southwest of the city. Bus service to the city every 30 minutes from 0630-2300. Rail service is every 30 minutes from 0612-2212. Taxi service to the city is available. Airport facilities include a 24-hour bank, restaurant, bar, several car rental companies and a duty-free shop.
Bilbao (BIO), 9km (6 miles) north of the city. Bus service runs every 20 minutes. Taxi service to the city is available. Airport facilities include a restaurant and car rental offices.
Madrid (MAD) (Barajas), 16km (10 miles) east of the city. Coach service to the city every 15 minutes from 0545-0055. Taxi service is available. Airport facilities include restaurants and bars (0700-2400), banks (24 hours), several car rental offices and an outgoing duty-free shop.
Málaga (AGP), 8km (5 miles) southwest of the city. Bus runs every 20 minutes from 0600-2310. Train service runs every 30 minutes from 0611-2241. Taxi service to the city is available. Airport facilities include duty-free shop, bank, restaurant and car hire firms.
Santiago de Compostela (SCQ), 10km (6.5 miles) northeast of the city. Bus service and taxis are available to the city centre.
Seville (SVQ), 12km (7.5 miles) from the city. Bus service from 0700-2215 according to flights. Taxis are available to the city centre.
Valencia (VLC) (Manises), 13km (8 miles) from the city. Bus service runs every 80 minutes from 0635-2105 according to flights. Taxis are available to the city centre. Airport facilities include several car hire firms, 24-hour bank, restaurant, bar and duty-free shop.
SEA: *Brittany Ferries* operate a service to Santander (on the north coast) from Plymouth, taking 24 hours.
RAIL: There are direct trains from Lisbon, Paris and Geneva. Otherwise, a change of train is necessary.
ROAD: The main route from the UK is via France. The main autoroutes to Spain from France are via Bordeaux or Toulouse to Bilbao (north Spain) and via Marseille or Toulouse to Barcelona (east Spain). A number of coach operators offer services to Spain. For more information contact the Spanish National Tourist Office.
See the next page for information on **documentation** and **traffic regulations**.

TRAVEL - Internal

AIR: Domestic flights are run by *Iberia (IB)* and *Aviaco (AO)*.
Scheduled flights connect all main towns as well as to the Balearic and Canary Islands and enclaves in North Africa. Air taxis are available at most airports. Reservations should be made well in advance.
SEA: There are regular hydrofoil and car and passenger ferry sailings from Algeciras to Ceuta (North African enclave); Málaga and Almeria to Melilla (North African enclave); Barcelona, Valencia and Alicante to the Balearic Islands; and Cádiz to the Canary Islands. There are also inter-island services.
RAIL: In 1988, *Spanish National Railways (RENFE)*, which operates a large network throughout the country, introduced the **RENFE Tourist Card** valid for 8, 15 or 22 days which allows unrestricted travel on all first- and second-class trains, including international trains (with the exception of the Paris–Madrid Talgo train); this card is only available outside Spain – for details contact *RENFE* at the address below. Principal trains are air-conditioned, and many have restaurant or buffet service. Reservations are required on all express trains. There are also *Dias Azules* (Blue Days), as specified on the train timetable, which are cheaper than normal. These days take up about a half to a third of the year. For further details contact RENFE, 1-3 avenue Marceau, 75116 Paris, France. Tel: (1) 47 23 52 01. Fax: (1) 46 47 88 33.
ROAD: There are more than 150,000km (95,000 miles) of roads. Motorways are well-maintained; most sections are toll roads. Trunk roads between major cities are generally fast and well-maintained. Rural roads are of uneven quality. **Bus:** There are bus lines which are efficient and cheap, operating between cities and towns. Departures are generally from a central terminal at which the operators will have individual booths selling tickets. Most places have a bus link of some kind, even the more remote villages. **Car hire:** All major car-hire companies are represented in major cities. Minimum age for car hire is 21 years. **Motorcycles:** No person under 18 may hire or ride a vehicle over 75cc. Crash helmets must be worn. **Traffic regulations:** Driving is on the right. Side lights must be used at night in built-up areas. Spare bulbs and red hazard triangles must be kept in all vehicles. Traffic lights: green for go, amber, then red for stop; two red lights mean 'No Entry'. Seat belts to be worn by travellers of any age on the front seats. The speed limit for motorways is 120kmph (75mph) in general, but for buses and lorries the limit is 100kmph (60 mph); in built-up areas the limit is 50kmph (31mph); for other roads it is 90kmph (56mph). **Documentation:** An International Driving Permit is required or a translation of the national driving licence (available from the Consulate), or a new EC format driving licence (3-part pink document). Third Party insurance is also required and a Green Card is strongly recommended.
URBAN: Traffic in Spanish cities is normally heavy, and urban driving takes some time to adjust to. City public transport facilities are generally good. Barcelona and Madrid have metros as well as buses. Pre-purchase multi-journey tickets are sold. Other towns and resorts are well served by local buses. Metered taxis are available in most major cities and taxi drivers expect a 2-3% tip.
JOURNEY TIMES: The following chart gives approximate journey times (in hours and minutes) from Madrid to other major cities/towns in Spain.

	Air	Road	Rail
Barcelona	1.00	8.00	8.00
Valencia	0.50	5.00	4.00
Bilbao	0.50	5.00	6.00
Seville	0.55	6.00	7.00
Mallorca	1.00	-	-
Canary Is.	2.30	-	-
Málaga	1.00	8.30	7.00
Santander	0.50	5.00	6.00
Palma	1.10	*6.00	*5.00

Note [*]: Plus 9 hours by boat.

ACCOMMODATION

HOTELS & HOSTELS: A variety of hotel-type accommodation is available including apartment-hotels, hotel-residencias and motels. The term *residencia* denotes an establishment where dining room facilities are not provided, although there must be provisions for the serving of breakfast and a cafeteria. Detailed information is available from Federación Española de Hoteles, Orense 32, 28020 Madrid. Tel: (1) 556 7112 *or* 556 7202. Fax: (1) 556 7361; *or* from ZONTUR, Paseo de Almeria, 69-5º, 04001 Almería.
Grading: Most accommodation in Spain is provided in hotels, classified from 1 to 5 stars (the few exceptions have a Grande De Luxe category), or hostels or *pensiones*, classified from 1 to 3 stars.
The following is an outline of the facilities available in the hotel and hostel categories.
5-star hotels: Air-conditioning in all public rooms and bedrooms, central heating, two or more lifts, lounges, bar, garage (within towns), hairdressers, all bedrooms with en suite bathrooms and telephone, some suites with sitting rooms, and laundry and ironing service.
4-star hotels: Air-conditioning in every room, unless climatic conditions require central heating or refrigeration only, the minimum of two hotel lounges, 75% of the bedrooms with en suite bathroom and the rest with shower, washbasin, WC and hot and cold running water, laundry and ironing service, telephone in every room, garage parking (in towns), lift and bar.
3-star hotels: Permanently installed heating or air-conditioning according to climate, lounge, lift, bar, 50% of the bedrooms have en suite bathrooms, 50% have shower, washbasin, WC and hot and cold running water, laundry and ironing service, telephone in every room.
2-star hotels: Permanently installed heating or air-conditioning according to climate, lounge, lift in buildings of two or more storeys, bar, 15% of rooms with en suite bathrooms, 45% with shower, washbasin and WC and the rest with shower, washbasin and hot and cold running water, one common bathroom to every six rooms, laundry and ironing service, telephone in every room.
1-star hotels: Permanently installed heating, lift in buildings of more than four storeys, lounge, 25% of bedrooms with shower, washbasin and WC, 25% with shower and washbasin, the rest have washbasin and hot and cold running water, one common bathroom every seven rooms, laundry and ironing service, telephone on every floor.
3-star hostels: Permanently installed heating, lift in buildings of more than four storeys, lounge, 5% of bedrooms with en suite bathroom, 10% with shower, washbasin and WC, 85% with shower and washbasin and hot and cold running water, one common bathroom to every eight rooms, laundry and ironing service, telephone in every room.
2-star hostels: Permanently installed heating, lift in buildings of five storeys or more, lounge or comfortable lobby, one common bathroom to every ten rooms, all bedrooms with washbasin and hot and cold water, general telephone.
1-star hostels: All rooms with washbasins and cold

running water; one bathroom for every 12 rooms; general telephone.
It is always advisable to book accommodation well in advance, particularly during festivals or at popular resorts on the coast from late spring to October. Reservations may be made by writing direct to the hotels, lists of which may be obtained from the SNTO, or through travel agents or certain hotel booking services. Letters to 5-, 4- or 3-star hotels may be written in English, but it is advisable to write in Spanish to lower categories.
GOVERNMENT LODGES: A chain of lodging places has been set up by the Ministry of Tourism in places of special interest or remote locations. These include attractive modern buildings and ancient monuments of historic interest, such as monasteries, convents, old palaces and castles. Standards are uniformly high, but not at the expense of individual charm and character. Below is a brief description of each type of lodging:
Paradores (National Tourist Inns): Each Parador is a hotel with all modern amenities including rooms with private bathroom, hot and cold running water, central heating, telephone in every room, public sitting rooms, garages and complementary services. Advance booking is advised. For further information contact: Central De Reservas De Espana, Calle Velázquez 18, Madrid 28001. Tel: (1) 435 9700 *or* 435 9744 *or* 435 9768. Fax: (1) 435 9944. Telex: 44607 RRPP. Alternatively, contact the UK representative, Keytel International, 402 Edgware Road, London W2. Tel: (071) 402 8182. Fax: (071) 724 9503. Telex: 21780 KEYTEL G.
Hosterias (Traditional restaurants): These are typical restaurants, decorated in the style of the region in which they are situated and serve excellent meals.
GUEST-HOUSES: *Pensiones* are common throughout Spain and vary in quality from austere to relatively luxurious. They are usually run by the family on the premises and provide bed and board only, with showers extra.
CAMPING/CARAVANNING: There are numerous campsites throughout the country, again covering a wide quality and price range. Permission from the local police and landowner is essential for off-site camping provided there are not more than three tents/caravans or ten campers in any one place. Regulations demand that off-site camping is in isolated areas only. Spanish Federation of Camping has recently opened a new booking centre. For further information contact: ANCE, General Oraa 52, 2°, 28006 Madrid. Tel: (1) 262 9994. Fax: (1) 563 7094. Telex: 42066 FCCV E; *or*
The Interprovincial Association for Campsites, Edificio Espana, Grupo 6, puerta 11, despacho 3, Gran Via 88, 28013 Madrid. Tel: (1) 242 3168.

RESORTS & EXCURSIONS

The Kingdom of Spain occupies four-fifths of the Iberian peninsula and is a land of great geographical and cultural diversity with much to offer the tourist. Spain's beach resorts on the south and northwest Mediterranean coasts continue to attract sunseekers, but increasingly tourists are discovering the immense beauty and cultural heritage away from the beaches. Every sort of landscape may be enjoyed in Spain: dense deciduous and coniferous forests, endless arid plains, lush salt marshes, picturesque rocky bays, mist-shrouded mountain tops haunted by vultures, broad sandy beaches, uniquely Spanish medieval cities, ancient rivers meandering through orchards and streams plunging through chasms, and everywhere castles, palaces and reminders of Spain's incomparably rich history.
The wide range of influences on Spanish **architecture** through the ages makes it difficult to isolate a style and define it as typically Spanish; major influences include Roman, Visigoth, Romanesque, Moorish, Byzantine, Medieval, Renaissance, Baroque and Art Nouveau styles. Throughout Spain a sense of the historical traditions that have shaped the country is reflected in the castles, churches, monuments and houses.

Certain examples defining the pure style of these influences can be seen: Roman remains at Italica, Sagunto, Tarragona, Mérida (theatre and amphitheatre), Segovia (aqueduct) and Alcudia; Moorish architecture at Córdoba (the Great Mosque), Seville (the Alcázar, the Giralda tower) and, above all, at Granada (the Alhambra). The Mudejar style, developed from the interaction of Christian and Muslim ideas, can be seen in the finely detailed ceramic work at Teruel. Gothic churches from the early, middle and late periods can be found at Burgos, Toledo, León, Barcelona, Gerona, Pamplona, Segovia and Seville, and fine examples of the Baroque style at Salamanca and Valladolid.
The majority of castles adopted as the standard image of the country date from the 15th century. The 16th, 17th and 18th centuries saw the construction of many beautiful palaces and religious and civic buildings, adding to an already rich architectural heritage. The 19th and early 20th centuries added only moderately to this heritage, although the work of Antonio Gaudí stands out as being exceptional (see *Barcelona* below).
Spanish **wildlife** is also enormously diverse. Amongst the more exotic mammals are: bears, ibexes and chamois in the foothills of the great northern mountains; wild boars, lynxes, mongooses and even wild camels amidst the marshes and sand dunes of the Coto de Doñana (also home to chameleons, tarantulas, scorpions, tortoises and terrapins); and wolves in Murcia and perhaps elsewhere. There are resident populations of flamingoes, ibises, spoonbills, bee-eaters and golden orioles in the Coto de Doñana; hoopoes, bustards, owls and eagles may be seen throughout the country; vultures inhabit the highest peaks, including, in the Pyrenees, rare lammergeiers – large, shy birds that drop scavenged bones from a great height onto rocks to break them open and release the nutritious marrow. Several major migration routes cross Spain and, at the right time of year, the skies are filled with millions of birds of many different species heading north from Africa. The white stork is amongst those that stop to breed, and in spring and summer almost every church tower seems to be capped by a large, shaggy nest. There are excellent opportunities for sea and river fishing. Salmon abound in the inlets along the northwest coast and most rivers and streams have healthy populations of trout.
Spain's 52 provinces have, since 1983, been administered as 17 Autonomous Communities, each with a degree of self-government. For the purposes of this section, however, the country has been divided into eight regions, which do not necessarily reflect political or cultural boundaries: **Andalucia, Ceuta & Melilla,** *including the*

Costa de Almería, the Costa del Sol and the Costa de la Luz; **Castile/La Mancha & Extremadura; Madrid; Castile/León & La Rioja; The Northern Region,** *including the Basque Country, Cantabria, Asturias and Galicia;* **Navarre & Aragón; Catalonia,** *including the Costa Brava and the Costa Dorada;* and **Valencia & Murcia,** *including the Costa del Azahar, Costa Blanca and the Costa Calida.* The regional map below gives the frontiers of these regions; the dotted lines denote Autonomous Communities. There is also a separate section on Spain's **Ski Resorts.**

Information on **The Balearic Islands** and **The Canary Islands,** both integral parts of the Kingdom of Spain, may be found in the separate entries immediately following Spain's *Climate* section.

Andalucia, Ceuta & Melilla

Including the **Costa de Almería,** the **Costa del Sol** and the **Costa de la Luz.**

Andalucia is a mountainous region in the far south of Spain, rich in minerals and an important centre for the production of olives, grapes, oranges and lemons.

INLAND: The regional capital is **Seville,** one of the largest cities in Spain, and one bearing numerous traces of the 500 years of Moorish occupation. Seville is the romantic heart of the country, the city of Carmen and Don Juan; its cathedral is the largest Gothic building in the world and has a superlative collection of art and period stonework. Christopher Columbus and St Ferdinand are buried here. Of great importance also is the *Alcázar,* the palace-fortress of the Arab kings, together with *Giralda* and *Torre de Oro,* reputedly once covered in gold leaf, and the *River Guadalquivir.* Holy Week in Seville embodies the religious fervour of the Spanish, and is one of the most interesting festivals in the country. Early booking for accommodation at festival time is essential. Holy Week is followed closely by the famous April Fair, during which couples parade the fairground mounted on fine Andalucian horses, dressed in the traditional flamenco costume. Drinking, eating, song and dance are the order of the day for the whole week and the fairground with its coloured lanterns and *casetas* bordering the streets is a continuous movement of colour.

SEVILLE

Córdoba to the northeast has further relics of the Mussulman Empire, the most spectacular being the 8th-century mosque with painted columns and arches. The building is so magnificent that it has been preserved through the changes of religion.

Granada contains probably the greatest tribute to the Moorish Empire in Spain, the *Alhambra.* This fortress palace, home of the Moorish kings, defies accurate description for its sumptuous elegance and beauty. It is surrounded by the exquisite gardens of the *Generalife,* whose ponds and fountains help to cool the hot summer air. The Alhambra is possibly the single most splendid building in a country bearing relics of numerous epochs and civilisations. Granada's magnificent cathedral houses the tombs of King Ferdinand and Queen Isabella.

South of Granada, and only about 40km (25 miles) from the coast, is the upland area of the **Sierra Nevada,** a mountain range running roughly east to west. It contains the highest peaks in Iberia; one of these, the Pico de Veleta (over 3400m/11,155ft) is accessible for most of its height by road, and coach trips are available. The region offers the unique opportunity to combine a holiday of winter sports with coastal sunshine and watersports in the Mediterranean (see below). Mountain resorts include *Capileira* (south of the Pico de Veleta), *Borreguiles* and *Pradollano* (both in the Solynieve region).

Jaén, capital of the northwestern Sierra Nevada, is an ancient town rich in historic buildings and art treasures; the *Provincial Museum,* the *Cathedral* and the *Castle of Santa Catalina* are among them. **Baeza,** 48km (30 miles) from Jaén, displays architectural styles which span Romanesque to Renaissance. Baeza as a whole has an air of nobility and strength; the aristocratic design and countless nobles' mansions are enhanced in appearance by the prevailing golden hue of the stone.

Barely 10km (6 miles) from Baeza and 58km (36 miles) from Jaén lies **Ubeda,** with Renaissance palaces to be seen on all sides.

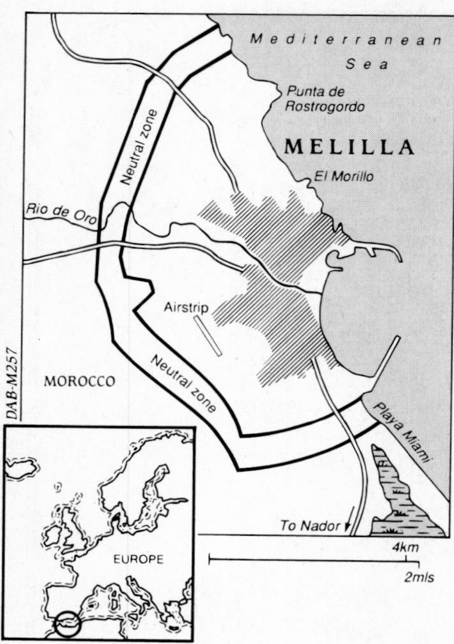

COSTA DE ALMERIA: To the east of the Costa del Sol is the province of **Almería.** The capital of the same name is a Roman port with many Moorish-style houses, dominated by two castles. It is surrounded by subtropical vegetation and hills and is situated within a wide bay. Attractions in the town include the 16th-century *Cathedral*, the *Church of Santiago el Viejo* and the Moorish *Alcazaba*.

Resorts on the Costa de Almería: Adra, Roquetas, Cabo de Gata, Aguadulce, Mojácar and San José.

COSTA DEL SOL: This extends along almost all of the Mediterranean coast of Andalucía from the Costa de Almería to Tarifa in the south. The Costa del Sol is a densely populated tourist area mainly because of the fine beaches and picturesque towns.

The main city of this area, **Málaga,** lies only a few miles from the famous tourist resorts of **Marbella** and **Torremolinos.** Over 160km (100 miles) of coastline ensure that, despite its popularity, it is still possible to find a relatively uncrowded beach. In the same province is **Nerja,** known as the 'Balcony of Europe' on account of its having a promontory look-out which is perched high above the sea with commanding views of the Mediterranean. It is also the home of well-preserved prehistoric caves. An excursion can be made from Málaga into the hinterland to the old Spanish mountain town of **Ronda**, spectacularly situated in the *Sierra de Ronda*.

Resorts on the Costa del Sol: Calahonda, Torre del Mar, El Palo, Málaga, Nerja, Torremolinos, Benalmádena Costa, Fuengirola/Mijas, Marbella, San Pedro de Alcántara and Estepona.

COSTA DE LA LUZ: This runs along the southern Atlantic coast of Spain between Tarifa and the Portuguese border, featuring long sandy beaches and unspoilt sand dunes.

From **Algeciras** ferries run to Tangier and Ceuta on the North African coast, as well as to the Canary Islands. Taking the road from Algeciras to **Cádiz** is one of the most enjoyable drives in the country, offering spectacular views of the Straits of Gibraltar, the North African coastline and the Atlas Mountains. Cádiz is characterised by palm trees, look-out towers and white-fronted houses. It is one of the oldest towns in Iberia, founded by the Phoenicians around 1000BC. Less than half an hour away is the sherry town of **Jerez,** housing the great *bodegas* whose product has linked the town with England since importation of 'sherris-sack' into this country began in the 16th century.

In the province of Huelva is the town of **El Rocío** where one of the most important Spanish festivals is held, that of the *Virgin of El Rocío*. Also of interest are the beautiful stalactite caves of *Gruta de las Maravillas* in **Aracena** in the north of Huelva province and the national park, *Coto de Doñana* (see the general introduction above).

Resorts on the Costa de la Luz: Barbate, Algeciras, Tarifa, Conil de la Frontera, Chiclana de la Frontera, Cádiz, El Puerto de Santa María, Rota, Chipiona, Sanlúcar de Barrameda, Torre la Higuera, Mazagón, Punta Umbría, El Rompido, La Antilla and Isla Cristina.

THE AFRICAN ENCLAVES: Ceuta is a free port on the north coast of Africa. The city is dominated by the *Plaza de Africa* in the town centre, and by the cathedral. The promontory has the remains of the old fortress. Bus services are available into Morocco, and there are regular car ferry sailings from Algeciras. **Melilla** is also a free port on the north coast of Africa, and is served by car ferries from Málaga and Almería. The town is mainly modern, but there are several older buildings, including a 16th-century church.

Balearic & Canary Islands

See separate entries below.

Castile/La Mancha & Extremadura

This inland region lies between Madrid and Andalucia. Bordered by mountains to the north, east and south, it is irrigated by two large rivers, the *Tajo* and the *Guadiana*, both of which flow westwards to Portugal and thence to the Atlantic. Castile/La Mancha, the higher, western part of the region, is also known as *Castilla La Nueva* (New Castile).

CASTILE/LA MANCHA: To the south of Madrid is the ancient Spanish capital of **Toledo.** Rising above the plains and a gorge of the River Tajo, the city is dominated by the magnificent cathedral and Alcazar. The town seems tortured by streets as narrow as the steel blades for which it is famous. Toledo is justly proud of its collection of paintings by El Greco, who lived and painted here. El Greco's most famous painting, 'The Burial of the Conde Orgaz', is preserved in the *Santo Tome Church*.

Guadalajara, capital of the province of the same name, is situated northeast of the capital, on the Rio Henares. Sights include the 15th-century *Palacio del Infantado* and the *Church of San Gines*.

The provincial capital of **Ciudad Real** is the chief town in the La Mancha region, the home of Don Quixote. There are many places in the surrounding area associated with Don Quixote, including *Campo de Criptana*, believed to be the setting for his fight with the windmills.

Cuenca, also a provincial capital, is famous for its hanging houses. It is one of the most attractive of Spain's medieval towns, and the Gothic cathedral is particularly richly decorated. The nearby countryside includes woods, lakes, spectacular caves, towering mountains and valleys, many with fortified towns and villages clinging to their sides.

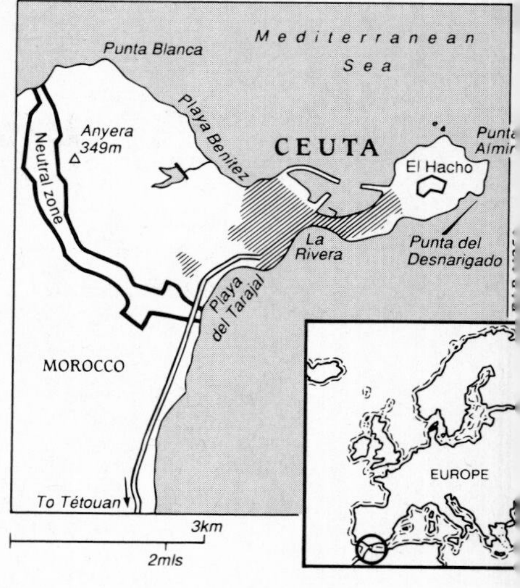

Albacete is the centre of a wine-producing region. The town witnessed two exceptionally bloody battles during the Reconquista, but the considerable rebuilding of the town has left few reminders of its history. More evidence, however, is scattered in the surrounding countryside, where such places as the Moorish castle at **Almansa** and the old fortified towns of **Chinchilla de Monte Aragón** and **Villena** reflect the area's stormy past.

EXTREMEDURA: This region consists of the provinces of Cáceres and Badajoz. **Cáceres** was founded in the 1st century BC by the Romans, and was later destroyed by the Visigoths and rebuilt by the Moors. There are traces of all the stages of the city's history, although most of the buildings date from Cáceres' Golden Age during the 16th century. Nearby is the beautiful village of **Arroyo de la Luz.** 48km (30 miles) away is the town of **Trujillo,** the birthplace of Pizarro. Also in this province is **Plasencia**, founded in the 12th century, which has a beautiful medieval aqueduct and a cathedral. The ancient fortified town of **Badajoz** (in the province of the same name), is situated very close to the Portuguese frontier, and was founded by the Romans. The Alcazaba,

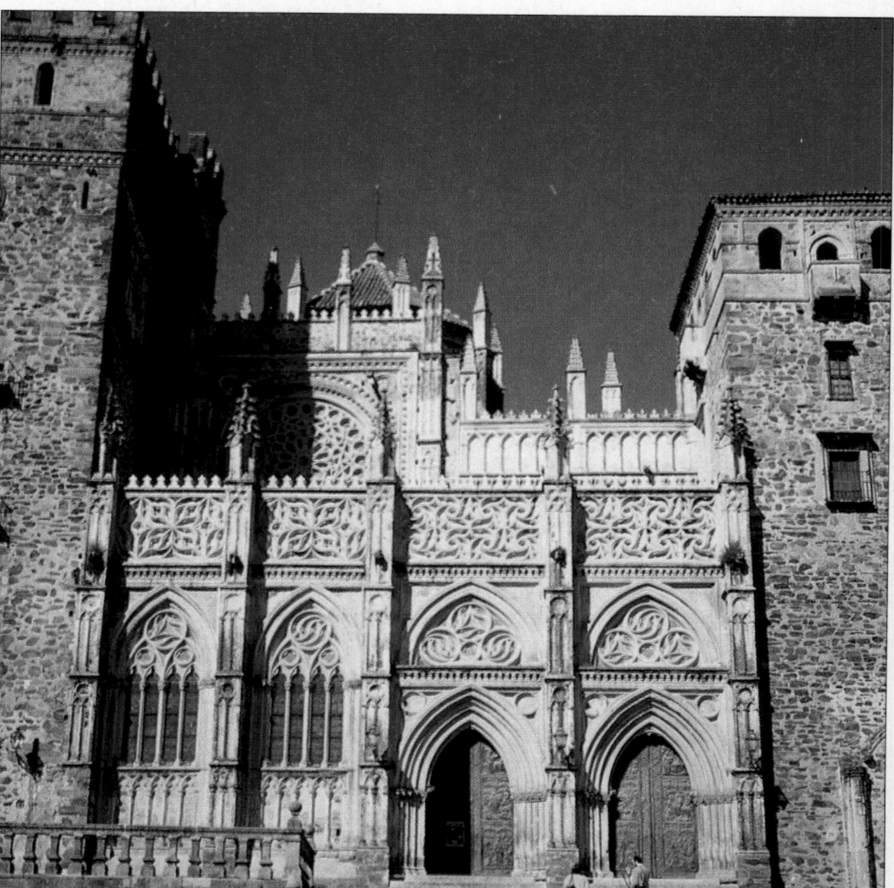

Monastery, Cáceres

MADRID

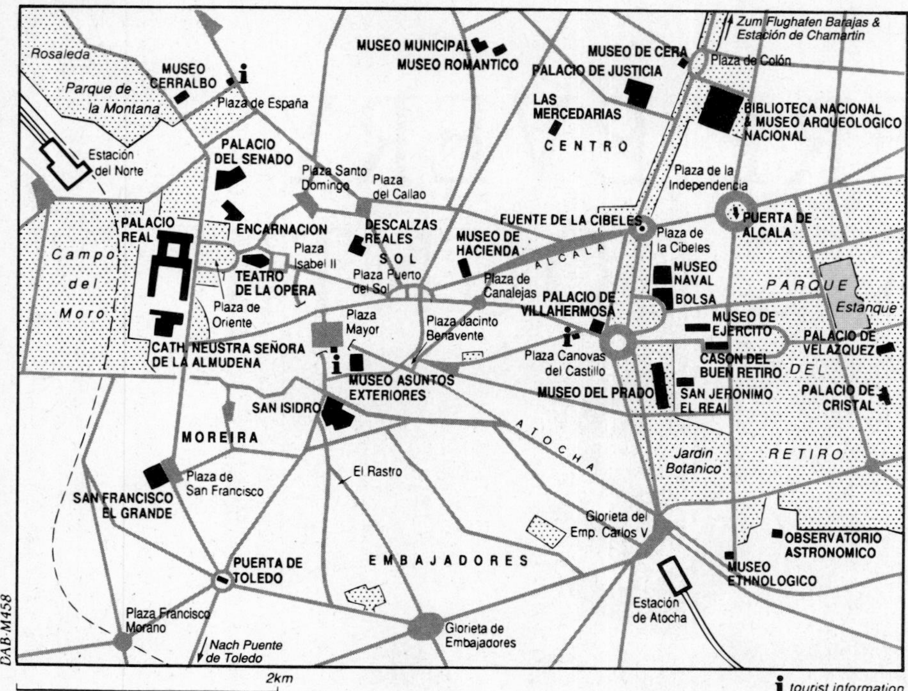

the Moorish part of the town, is on a hill in the northeast of the town. Not far away is the town of **Alburquerque**, which has the ruins of a massive castle and a large Gothic church. In the same province is the town of **Mérida**, famous for ancient Roman ruins; the remains are housed in the *Museum of Archaeology*. A few kilometres away is **Medellín**, where Cortés was born in 1485.

Madrid

The capital city **Madrid,** in the region of the same name, is a cosmopolitan metropolis with many theatres, cinemas and opera houses, and over 50 museums and art galleries. These include the *Prado*, one of the most celebrated and comprehensive art galleries in the world (see below), and the *Royal Palace*, set in a luxurious 18th-century garden, housing paintings, tapestries, carpets, armour, and an outstanding collection of clocks. The popular centre of Madrid is the *Puerta del Sol*, from which ten streets radiate. To its south is the site of 'Kilometre Zero', a stone slab from which all distances are measured in Spain. A short walk southwest of the Puerta del Sol leads to the *Plaza Mayor*, a spacious square surrounded by arcades sheltering small shops. From here one can explore an area which still has some of the flavour of Old Madrid.

The Prado Museum has one of the most remarkable art collections in the world, including many supreme works of art acquired by Spanish monarchs. Works by El Greco, Murillo, Goya, Velazquez, Titian, Raphael, Botticelli, Veronese, Tintoretto, Breughel and Bosch can be found here. Plans are being made to assemble a collection by Spain's most famous 20th-century artist, Pablo Picasso. 'Guernica', one of his greatest masterpieces – a monument to the people's suffering during the Civil War – has now been returned to Spain and hangs in the *Centro Cultural Reina Sofia*. The recently opened *Thyssen-Bornemisza Museum* housed in the *Villahermosa Palace* opposite the Prado Museum is, with its 800 works of art, one of the largest private collections in the world.

EXCURSIONS: There are many places of interest within easy reach of the city. The great *Monastery of San Lorenzo del Escorial* is situated about 40km (25 miles) north of Madrid, and includes a church, a royal palace, a monastery, a mausoleum and a famous library. The Escorial was built in 1563-84 by Philip II, and is now a burial place of Spanish kings and queens. 9km (6 miles) from the Escorial is the *Valle de los Caídos* (Valley of the Fallen), a huge crypt cut into the mountainside surmounted by a stone cross reaching 152m (500ft) into the sky. It stands as a massive tribute to those who died in the Civil War, and is the resting place of General Franco. **Alcalá de Henares** is the birthplace of Cervantes and Catherine of Aragón. **Aranjuez** is famous for its summer palace and the *Casita del Labrador*, situated near the banks of the cooling *River Tagus*, on whose fertile soil are grown the asparagus and strawberries for which the town is also renowned.

September sees the *Ferias Mayores* (Great Fairs) and the Easter processions of Semana Santa, both typically extravagant and colourful affairs. Several special tours are available, including the 'Castles in Spain Tour', run by Viajes Marsans for three days, departing from Madrid.

The *Guadarrama* region offers the possibility of winter sports. For further information see the *Ski Resorts* section below.

Castile/León & La Rioja

The inland region of Castile and León lies to the north and northwest of Madrid and occupies the northern part of the Meseta Central, the plateau that covers much of central Spain. As with the previous region, Castile and León is hemmed in by high mountains to the north, east and south and is the catchment area for a large river, the Douro, which flows westward into Portugal. Hot and dry throughout much of the year, the region's extensive plains nonetheless make it an important agricultural asset for a country as mountainous as Spain.

CASTILE LA VIEJA: Avila is the highest provincial capital in the country, its medieval quality retained and enhanced by the magnificence of its surrounding walls. The celebrated *Convent of St Therese the Mystic* is here. **Segovia** has a working Roman aqueduct, one of the best preserved structures of its kind in the world. There are many unspoilt Romanesque churches, dominated by the cathedral and by the Arab Alcazar. The turrets soaring from its rocky outcrop are said to be the inspiration for Walt Disney's fairytale castles.

The province of **Soria** has a large number of archaeological remains of the Celtiberian and Roman civilizations, and many of these may be seen in the *Museo Numantino* in the provincial capital of the same name. 9km (6 miles) north of the town is the site of *Numancia*, a fortified Celtiberian town. Attractions in the town of Soria include the 13th-century *Church of San Juan de Duero*, the *Cathedral of San Pedro* and *Renaissance Palacio de los Condes de Gómara*.

La Rioja is a province famous for its vineyards. The capital, **Logroño**, is in the centre of the province. It is a district with a great historical past; the origins of poetry in the Castilian language lie here, and it contains the channel of a European stream of culture – the *Road to Santiago*.

Burgos was the birthplace of the great knight El Cid, the embodiment of a strong, romantic tradition of chivalry and honour. His tomb can be seen at Valladolid (see below).

Palencia, the capital of the province of the same name, was the one-time residence of the Kings of Castile and seat of the Cortes of Castile. The cathedral is one of the finest late-Gothic buildings in the country. The city has several other late-medieval buildings and an archaeological museum.

The city of **Valladolid** is the capital of a province rich in castles and other ancient buildings. It is famous for its lush gardens, which provide such a refreshing contrast to the aridity of much of the surrounding landscape, and also for its *Ferias Mayores* (Great Fairs) in September, and its Easter Procession. Book early if a visit is planned at either of these times. The city is also associated with four of the most famous names in the history of the Iberian peninsula: Columbus (although not a Spaniard) died here in 1506, and his house can be visited; so too can the old home of Cervantes, which has now been turned into a museum; and Ferdinand and Isabella were married here in 1469, bringing together the crowns of Castile and Aragón. The city also has a beautiful medieval cathedral and a university.

LEON: The city of **León** was recaptured from the Moors in 850, and the architecture reflects its long history under Christian rule. The cathedral is one of the finest examples of the Gothic style in the country. There are several places of interest within easy reach of León, including the spectacular **Puerto de Pajares, Benavente** and the attractive region around **Astorga,** a town which, like other towns in the region, was a stopping point on the *Way of St James* (see the section on Santiago de Compostela in the *Northern Region* below).

South of León is the province of **Zamora;** the provincial capital of the same name was the scene of many fierce struggles between the Moors and the Christians during the *Reconquista*, in which the Spanish hero El Cid figured prominently. The town has a Romanesque cathedral and several 12th-century churches. 19km (12 miles) northwest of the town is an artificial lake, created in 1931; on the shores of the lake, in **El Campillo,** is a Visigoth church dating from the 7th century, which was moved when its original site was flooded by the new reservoir.

The southernmost province of León, **Salamanca**, has as its capital the ancient university town of the same name. It is situated on the swiftly flowing *Tormes River*, and has many superb old buildings, weathered to a golden-brown hue. The most famous of these is the *Cathedral*, built between the early 16th and the mid-18th centuries, and reflecting the styles of architecture prevalent during the various stages of its construction. The university buildings and the fine houses around the *Plaza Mayor* are also particularly striking. The fiesta in September is very popular, and bookings should be made well in advance.

The Northern Region

Including the **Basque Country, Cantabria, Asturias** and **Galicia.**

This region consists of the northwestern part of the country and the northern coastal region stretching to the French frontier. The eastern coastal area adjacent to the French border is now made up of fashionable tourist beaches and picturesque small towns.

THE BASQUE COUNTRY: The provinces of **Guipúzcoa, Vizcaya** and **Alava** form the Basque provinces, occupying a coastal position in the eastern part of the *Cantabrian Mountains*. The economy of this fertile region is strongly based on agricultural produce, although recently the area has also become one of Spain's foremost industrial areas. The Basques themselves are a very ancient pre-Indo-European race, and the origins of their language have baffled etymologists for centuries. The area managed to maintain a considerable degree of independence until the 19th century.

The main city of the region is **Bilbao,** founded in the early 14th century. The *Old Town* has a Gothic Cathedral, and an attractive town hall. The provincial capital of **San Sebastián,** situated very close to the French frontier, is one of the most fashionable and popular Spanish seaside resorts. 7km (4 miles) west of the town is *Monte Ulia*, which offers superb views across the countryside and the *Bay of Biscay*. The art treasures found in San Sebastián and Bilbao and in the 13th-century *Castle of Butron*, near Bilbao, are also worthy of note.

The third provincial capital of the Basque region, and also the regional capital, is **Vitoria,** famous as being the site of a British victory during the Peninsula War, an event commemorated in various places in the city. Vitoria is remarkable for having two cathedrals; one was completed in the 15th century, whilst the other, on which work commenced in 1907, has yet to be finished.

SANTANDER: Although the province of Santander is historically in Old Castile, owing to its position on the coast, it has been included in this section. The historical capital of **Santander** is set in a beautiful bay ringed with hills. The Gothic Cathedral was destroyed by fire in 1941, but has been carefully restored. The *Municipal Museum* contains a fine collection of paintings by many 17th and 18th-century artists. Nearby are the fine beaches of *El Sardinero* and *Magdalena*. The latter makes a convenient base for expeditions to the highest of the *Cantabrian Mountains*, the vulture-haunted *Picos de Europa* (actually in Asturias), several attractive beach resorts such as **Comillas** and **San Vincente,** and the *Caves of Altamira*, with detailed wall paintings dating back 13,000 years. Admission is now very limited and

Tielve, Asturias

must be applied for. **Solares** is a town in this region noted for the therapeutic qualities of its mineral waters. There are several pleasant resorts, including **Santillana del Mar,** a completely preserved medieval town.

ASTURIAS: This formerly independent principality contains two towns of note; Oviedo, the capital, and the port and industrial centre of Gijón. The chief interest in **Oviedo** is the small, old central area, dominated by the cathedral. The port of **Gijón** has a large and very popular beach and there are others nearby.

GALICIA: Comprising the provinces of La Coruña, Lugo, Orense and Pontevedra, Galicia is a mountainous region with large tracts of heathland broken by steep-sided gorges and fast-flowing rivers. The coastline has many sandy bays, often backed with forests of fir and eucalyptus, and deep fjord-like estuaries *(rías)* which cut into the land at the river-mouths. The dominant building material is granite.

La Coruña (Corunna) is the largest town in this region, and was possibly founded by the Phoenicians. Since then it has enjoyed a tempestuous history. Its most attractive feature is the *Ciudad Vega* on the north spur of the harbour. The famous pilgrimage town of **Santiago de Compostela** is also in the province; for further information, see below under the section on the *Way of St James*. The Roman town of **Lugo** is noted for having one of the finest surviving examples of Roman walls. **Orense** first attracted the Romans on account of its therapeutic waters. The 13th-century Cathedral was built on the site of one dating from the 6th century. **Pontevedra**, the region's fourth provincial capital, is a granite town with arcaded streets and many ancient buildings. Further south is the important port of **Vigo**, the centre of a region of attractive countryside. A good view of the town and the bay can be had from the *Castillo del Castro*.

THE WAY OF ST JAMES: During the Middle Ages, the tomb of St James at Santiago de Compostela was regarded as one of the most holy sites in Christendom, and thousands of pilgrims travelled through Spain each year to visit the shrine. This route, the *Way of St James*, was lined with monasteries, religious houses, chapels and hospices to cater for the pilgrims. Many of these buildings still survive, and any traveller following the route today will find it an uplifting introduction to the religious architecture of medieval Spain. The route began in Navarre, at Canfranc or Valcarlos; from there, travelling west, the main stopping places were Pamplona, Santo Domingo de la Calzada, Logroño, Burgos, León, Astorga and Santiago de Compostela. The Saint's feast day, July 25 (the term 'day' is a misnomer since the festival runs for a full week) is celebrated in vigorous style in Santiago de Compostela, and accommodation should be booked well in advance. There are several specialist books on the subject of this and other old pilgrim routes which may be followed, both in Spain and elsewhere in Europe.

NORTH ATLANTIC COASTAL RESORTS: The region's coastline – stretching from the French frontier along the Cantabrian coast to Cap Finisterre, and then southwards to the border with Portugal – has many fine beaches which are as yet largely undiscovered. This is at least partly due to the climate being slightly harsher than in the south of the country. The beaches are mostly of fine sand, often surrounded by cliffs and crags. Much of the hinterland is lush, earning the coast of Asturias the title of Costa Verde. In Galicia the rivers have fjord-like estuaries called *rias*.

Resorts on the North Atlantic Coast: Fuenterrabia, San Sebastián, Orio, Zaraúz, Guetaria, Zumaya, Deva, Motrico, Ondarroa, Lequeitio, Ibarranguelua, Pedernales, Mundaca, Baquio, Gorliz, Plencia, Sopelana, Algorta, Las Arenas, Abanto y Ciervana, Castro Urdiales, Laredo, Isla, Ajo, Somo, Santander, Santa Cruz de Bezana, Liencres, Miengo, Suances, Cobreces, Comillas, San Vicente de la Barquera, Pechón, Colombres, Llanes, Ribadesella, Colunga, Villaviciosa, Gijón, Luanco, Salinas, Cudillero, Luarca, Tapia de Casariego, Castropol, Ribadeo, Barreiros, Foz, Ceruo, Jove, Vivero, Vicedo, El Barquero, Ortiguerira, Cedeira, Valdovino, San Martin de Covas, El Ferrol del Caudillo, Cabanas, Mino, Sada, Mera, Santa Cruz, Santa Cristina, La Coruña, Cayon, Malpica, Lage, Camarinas, Finisterre, Curcubion, Carnota, Muros, Noya, Puerto del Son, Santa Eugenia de Ribera, Puebla del Caraminal, Rianjo, Villagarcía de Arosa, Villanueva de Arosa, Cambados, El Grove, La Toja, Sangenjo, Poyo, Pontevedra, Marín, Bueu, Cangas de Morrazo, Redondela, Vigo, Nigran, Bayona and La Guardia.

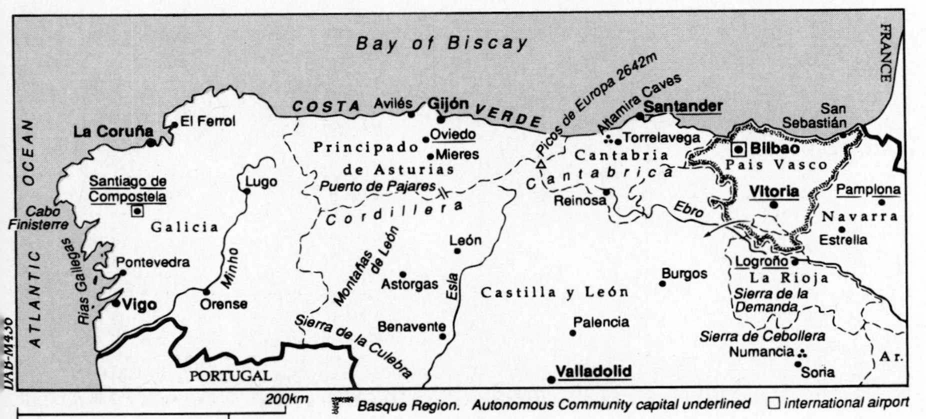

MOUNTAIN RESORTS: The *Cantabrian Range* stretches between the *Cantabrian Corniche* and the *Rías Gallegas*. The highest peaks are the Picos de Europa (2615m/8579ft), favoured by walkers, climbers and wildlife enthusiasts. Parts of the Cantabrian Range are suitable for winter sports. For more information, see the *Ski Resorts* section below.

Navarre & Aragón

These two former medieval Iberian kingdoms lie southwest of the French border, with the Pyrenees to the northeast. The landscape offers spectacular views from the mountains contrasting with the lush valleys of the lower ground.

NAVARRE: The approximate frontiers of the old strategically placed Kingdom of Navarre still survive in this region of dry, dusty uplands and rich, fertile valleys. Both Navarre and Aragón have been largely ignored by visitors, with a few notable exceptions: one such is **Pamplona**, once the capital of the Kingdom of Navarre, and now the regional capital. It is famous for the *Corrida*, the 'running of the bulls', at the festival of *San Fermín* (July). On these days the young men of the town and anyone else who feels sufficiently brave can prove themselves by running in front of a large herd of bulls that virtually stampede through the closed streets of the town. The town was the spiritual home of Ernest Hemingway and is now a very popular tourist attraction. Book early and expect relatively high prices.

ARAGON: Another old Iberian kingdom, Aragón is geographically a fairly featureless region, with many remote plains. The kingdom rose to prominence in the late 15th century. Many of the kings resided at **Zaragoza** (Saragossa), now the regional capital. Like most settlements of any size in Aragón, the town is situated in a *huerta*, a narrow oasis following the course of a river. Zaragoza is a university town, with a medieval cathedral and an excellent museum. In the surrounding countryside there are several areas noted for their wine production, such as **Borja** and **Cariñena,** and several castles. **Huesca**, situated in the foothills of the Pyrenees, is an important market town. There are several attractions within easy reach, including the *Parque Nacional de Ordesa*, excellent walking and climbing country; the popular summer holiday resort of **Arguis** in the *Puerto de Monrepós* region; the spa town of **Balneario de Panticosa;** and the high-altitude resort and frontier town of **Canfranc.**

The third and southernmost province of Aragón is **Teruel**. The provincial capital is on a hill surrounded by the gorges of the Rio Turia. It has a very strong Moorish influence (the last mosque was not closed until ten years after the end of the Reconquista in 1492), and there are several architectural survivals from its Islamic period. Nearby is the small episcopal city of **Sergobe,** spectacularly situated between two castle-crowned hills.

THE PYRENEES: There are several mountain resorts in Navarre and Aragón, some of which offer excellent skiing, sometimes for up to six months of the year. For more information, see the *Ski Resorts* section below.

Catalonia

Including the **Costa Brava** and the **Costa Dorada.** Catalonia is a hilly coastal region in Spain's northwest corner, bordering France. It has an ancient culture distinct from those of neighbouring regions and many of the inhabitants speak Catalan as a first language. The environs of Barcelona are Spain's industrial and commercial powerhouse, but inland and up the coast, the rocky, forested landscape is largely unspoilt and Catalonia attracts many tourists, mainly to seaside resorts on the Costa Brava and Costa Dorada. Despite its energetic bustle, tourists are also drawn to Barcelona itself, a city of great charm, many fine buildings and a vibrant nightlife. The region is also an important centre for the production of olive oil, wine, almonds and fruit.

BARCELONA: This, the second largest city in the country, is Spain's major commercial and industrial centre and one of the most important Mediterranean ports. The *Old Town* near the railway station has a museum with a fine collection of Picasso's early sketches. The *Ramblas*, originally the site of the ancient city walls, is now the major promenade area of the city, where one goes to see and be seen. Museums worth visiting include the *Picasso Museum*, the *Museum of Catalan Art*, the *Maritime Museum* and the *Zoological Museum*. The old cathedral, the *Episcopal Palace*, the *Palacio de la Generalidad* and the *Plaza del Rey* have architecture to rival the Baroque splendours of central Europe and, like most towns and cities in Catalonia, Barcelona is famous for its excellent Romanesque art; and of course it contains the most famous examples of the work of the visionary Catalan architect, Antonio Gaudí (see below). The funicular to Tibidabo, the highest of the peaks that enclose Barcelona, and the cable car to *Montjuic* in the southern suburbs, offer spectacular views over the city.

Gaudí was born in the 1850s, and began work at the age of 32 on what is now one of the world's most extraordinary churches, the *Sagrada Familia* in Barcelona. Statues portraying biblical scenes are sculpted into the walls of the building, surrounded by stone palm leaves, strange viney branches and fungus-like vegetation. George Orwell once described the church as 'one of the most hideous buildings in the world', and although unfinished (Gaudí died while work was still in progress) the people of Barcelona are intensely proud of it. Now a century old, construction still continues. Other examples of his work are the *Casa Batlló*, the *Casa Mila* (an apartment block taking the

BARCELONA

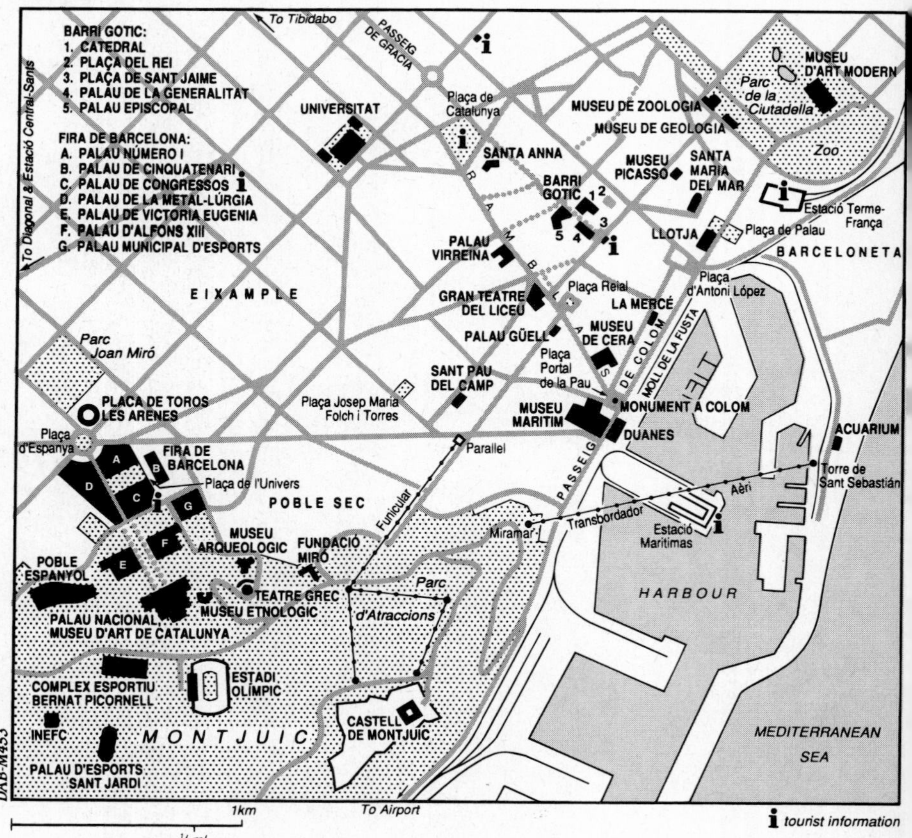

form of a dragon perched precariously on top of a melting slab of cheese) and the *Parque Güell*, all to be found in Barcelona.

THE COSTA BRAVA: This coast, which begins 65km (40 miles) northeast of Barcelona, is a stretch of spectacular pine-clad rocky coastline interspersed with fine sandy bays, and is one of the most famous resort areas in the country. Some places (such as Tossa de Mar) remain relatively unspoilt by the massive influx of holidaymakers and retain the small-town flavour of the original town; others (such as Lloret de Mar), have an intensely developed tourist industry. Summer is very crowded everywhere, but with persistence and a short walk relatively isolated beaches can be found. Coastal ferries operate between most resorts on the Costa Brava.

Although most visitors come to the Costa Brava for a relaxing holiday of sun and sea rather than serious sightseeing, there are nevertheless certain points of cultural interest in the area. These include **Girona** (Gerona), one of Catalonia's oldest cities; **Figueras,** home of the *Salvador Dali Museum;* **Cadaquès,** an enchanting fishing village nestling on the coast about 30 minutes bus drive from Figueras, where Dali lived for many years; and **Ampurias** with its impressive Greco-Roman remains.

Resorts on the Costa Brava: Rosas, San Pedro Pescador, San Martín de Ampurias, La Escala, Estartit, Bagur, Palafrugell, Palamós, Playa de Aro, S'Agaro, Sant Feliú de Guixols (the market is worth a visit), Tossa de Mar, Lloret de Mar and Blanes.

THE COSTA DORADA: This extends south from Barcelona to Tarragona, with fine sandy beaches that are often separated by the road or railway from the interior.

The lively and cosmopolitan resort town of **Sitges** on the Costa Dorada has several museums, in particular the *Cav-Ferrat* which houses two paintings by El Greco. Off the A2 motorway towards Lerida are two monasteries, the Cistercian *Monastery of Santa Cruz* dating back to 1159 and, near the ancient medieval town of **Montblanc**, the *Santa María* at **Poblet**. **Lerida** itself is the capital of a province that includes the wildest, most mountainous area of the Pyrenees. Its wealth of scenery and monuments make it one of the most interesting and attractive areas in Spain. The coastal city of **Tarragona** is one of the finest examples of a Roman city in existence, virtually built on the Roman plan. The amphitheatre overlooking the sea is well preserved and atmospheric; in addition there is an aqueduct. The town of **Manresa** has a 14th-century church noted for its stained glass. 60km (37 miles) northwest of Barcelona is **Montserrat**, the site of a world-famous monastery, the legendary home of the Holy Grail, and the actual home of the famous Black Madonna. Founded in 880, it is set in the 'serrated mountain' landscape 1135m (3725ft) above the *Llobregat River* valley. There are inspiring views from the monastery and on the mountain walk from the *Hermitage of San Jeronimo*.

Resorts on the Costa Dorada: Calella de la Costa, Arenys de Mar, Castelldefels, Sitges, Calafell, Comarruga, Torredembarra, Tarragona, Salou, Cambrils, Miami Playa, Hospital del Infante and San Carlos de la Rapita.

THE PYRENEES: There are several mountain resorts in Catalonia, some of which offer excellent skiing for up to six months of the year. For more information, see the *Ski Resorts* section below.

SP del Pinatar, Murcia

Valencia/Murcia

Including the **Costa del Azahar,** the **Costa Blanca** and the **Costa Calida.**

VALENCIA: The city of Valencia is famous for its orange groves and is a popular tourist resort with two main beaches, both a short bus ride from the town. It has a 13th-century church which also claims possession of the Holy Grail. The chief attraction is the *Fallas* (March 19), a festival culminating in the burning of papier-mâché effigies satirising famous Spanish figures. There is also a magnificent fireworks display.

THE COSTA DEL AZAHAR: This extends from Vinaroz along the coast of Castellón province and the Gulf of Valencia to beyond Denia. The region has expansive beaches, but its most outstanding feature is perhaps the ancient fortress town of **Peñiscola,** a dramatic sight when viewed from a distance. Other places of interest are the ruined castle of **Chisvert,** inland from Peñiscola; the 16th-century *Torre del Rey* at **Oropesa;** and the Carmelite monastery at the *Desierto de las Palmas*. North of Valencia is the attractive provincial capital of Castellón, **Castellón de la Plana**. It is situated on a fertile plain, and is the centre of a thriving trade in citrus fruits.

Resorts along the Costa del Azahar: Vinaroz, Benicarlo, Peñiscola, Alcosebre, Oropesa, Benicasim, Valencia, Cullera, Gandia and Oliva.

ALICANTE & THE COSTA BLANCA: Further south along the coast is **Alicante**, situated centrally on the Costa Blanca (the White Coast). The town is dominated by the vast Moorish castle of *Santa Barbara*, which offers superb views of the city. Excursions from Alicante include a run inland to **Guadalest,** a village perched like an eagle's eyrie high in the mountains and accessible in the last stages only by donkey or on foot. Also of great interest are several historical sites, including castles at **Elda** and **Villena,** and **Elche,** where there is a forest of over a million palm trees, *Botanical Gardens* and the *Basilica*, where the medieval 'Mystery' passion play takes place every August.

The region of the **Costa Blanca** has expanded rapidly in recent years and has developed most of the coastal towns between the Peñón de Ifach and Alicante as tourist resorts. Being further south, temperatures are slightly hotter than the Costa Brava and in general the beaches are larger, particularly the beautiful twin bays of Benidorm, the largest and most popular resort. All resorts are very busy during the summer.

One of the many places to visit here is the *Peñón of Ifach* (Ifach Rock), 5km (3 miles) off the main road past the walled town of **Calpe.** 1.5km (1 mile) further on is the 300m (1000ft) monolith of *Penon*, surrounded by legend and accessible through a tunnel.

Resorts on the Costa Blanca: Denia, Javea, Moraira, Calpe, Benidorm, Villajoyosa, Alicante, Los Arenales del Sol, Santa Pola, Guardamar del Segura, Torrevieja, Campoamor, Santiago de la Ribera, La Manga del Mar Menor, Puerto de Mazarrón and Aguilas.

MURCIA & COSTA CALIDA: This region lies to the south of Valencia and Alicante and is thinly populated except in the areas around the river valleys. The mountains of Andalucía reach right down to the sea.

Murcia, the town, has both a university and a cathedral. In summer the temperatures can be almost unbearably hot. The most impressive festivals are in Holy Week, and during the spring when there is a 'Battle of the Flowers'.

The coastal region of Murcia, the **Costa** (which is often regarded as being part of the Costa Blanca), has a few resorts. These include *Mar Menor*, *La Unión*,

Carboneras, *Puerto de Mazarrón*, *Aguilas* and the area's main coastal town, **Cartagena**, founded, as its name implies, by the Carthaginians in 221BC. The museum here has a good collection of Roman and pre-Roman artefacts.

Ski Resorts

Spain offers many possibilities for a winter sports holiday, and in many regions (particularly in the Penibetic Chain) there is a unique opportunity to combine winter sports with coastal sunshine. There are many natural ski-runs and many winter resorts, equipped with modern facilities, all blessed with the promise of warm sun and blue skies. There is also a wide range of hotels, inns and refuges from which to choose.

There are five main skiing regions in Spain; these are the Pyrénéan Range, the Cantabrian Range, the Iberian Chain, the Central Chain and the Penibetic Chain. These ranges have diverse characteristics, and all are attractive for mountaineering in general and in particular for winter sports. A brief description of these regions, together with a list of major resorts, is given below. More detailed information may be found by consulting the many booklets and leaflets published or distributed by the Spanish National Tourist Office, in particular the trilingual (English-Spanish-French) book entitled *Guide to Winter & Mountain Resorts* and the English-language booklet *Winter Sports – Spain*. These publications provide invaluable information on individual resorts, accommodation available, transport, etc in greater detail than is possible here.

In the following section, each resort is listed in **bold**, followed by the province in which it is situated. The nearest airport, the range of altitudes and the area of snow are given afterwards in *italics*.

Most resorts offer rental or sale of equipment; nightclub; bars; hospital; nursery; a Catholic church; and accommodation either at the resort or within 30km (19 miles). Some offer facilities such as a heated pool; tennis; mini-golf; riding; skeet shooting and bowling. All have ski lifts (apart from the Nordic skiing centres), many have baby lifts and chair lifts, and some also have cabin lifts, cable cars or funiculars. Further details may be found by consulting either of the publications referred to above.

THE PYRENEAN RANGE:

A region of high valleys allowing steep descents, with most of the resorts concentrated in the Catalonian area. The Aragónese Pyrenees contain the highest altitudes in the range; some are over 3400m (11,155ft). The Navarran Pyrenees have no mountain resorts, and are notable for their gentle slopes and superb forests.

Catalonian Pyrenees

Vallter 2000, Gerona. *Airport:* Gerona 90km (55 miles). Barcelona 150km (93 miles). *Alt:* 2000-2650m (6560-8400ft). *Snow area:* 50 sq km (20 sq miles).

Nuria, Gerona. *Airport:* Gerona 110km (68 miles). Barcelona 135km (84 miles). *Alt:* 1960-2920m (6430-9580ft). *Snow area:* 79 sq km (30 sq miles).

La Molina-Supermolina, Gerona. *Airport:* Gerona 140km (87 miles). Barcelona 160km (99 miles). *Alt:* 1436-2540m (4711-8333ft). *Snow area:* 70 sq km (27 sq miles).

Masella, Gerona. *Airport:* Gerona 160km (99 miles). Barcelona 175km (108 miles). *Alt:* 1600-2530m (5249-8300ft). *Snow area:* 43 sq km (16 sq miles).

Rasos de Peguera, Barcelona. *Airport:* Barcelona 135km (83 miles). *Alt:* 1800-2050m (5903-6725ft). *Snow area:* 15 sq km (6 sq miles).

Port de Comte, Lérida. *Airport:* Barcelona 160km (99 miles). *Alt:* 1700-2380m (5577-7808ft). *Snow area:* 80 sq km (30 sq miles).

San Juan de l'Erm, Lérida. (Nordic skiing). *Airport:* Cerdaña (light aircraft). *Alt:* 1600-2150m (5249-7053ft). *Snow area:* 40 sq km (15 sq miles).

Lles, Lérida (Nordic skiing). *Airport:* Cerdaña (light aircraft). *Alt:* 1900-2300m (6233-7545ft). *Snow area:* 30 sq km (11 sq miles).

Llessúy, Lérida. *Airport:* Barcelona 258km (160 miles). *Alt:* 1280-2900m (4199-9514ft). *Snow area:* 30 sq km (11 sq miles).

Super Espot, Lérida. *Airport:* Barcelona 270km (167 miles). *Alt:* 1480-2320m (4855-7611ft).

Baqueira Beret, Lérida (the largest resort). *Airport:* Barcelona 309km (192 miles). *Alt:* 1520-2470m (4986-8103ft). *Snow area:* 40 sq km (15 sq miles).

Tuca-Betrén, Lérida. *Airport:* Barcelona 295km (183 miles). *Alt:* 1050-2250m (3444-6381ft). *Snow area:* 15 sq km (5 sq miles).

Aragónese Pyrenees

Cerler, Huesca. *Airport:* Zaragoza 227km (141 miles). Barcelona 300km (186 miles). *Alt:* 1500-2850m (4921-1770ft). *Snow area:* 24 sq km (9 sq miles).

Panticosa, Huesca. *Airport:* Zaragoza 168km (104 miles). *Alt:* 1165-2100m (3822-6889ft).

El Formigal, Huesca. *Airport:* Zaragoza 167km (103 miles). *Alt:* 1500-2350m (4921-7709ft). *Snow area:* 38 sq km (14 sq miles).

Candanchú, Huesca. *Airport:* Zaragoza 180km (111 miles). *Alt:* 1450-2400m (4757-7874ft). *Snow area:* 18 sq km (7 sq miles).

Astún, Huesca. *Airport:* Zaragoza 180km (111 miles). *Alt:* 1420-2400m (4658-7874ft). *Snow area:* 40 sq km (15 sq miles).

In addition to the above-mentioned resorts, there are throughout the Pyrenees other places which are highly suitable for skiing in which modern facilities will soon be installed to make best use of their excellent natural advantages. Enquire at the Spanish National Tourist Office for up-to-date details of the facilities available. Of these, the main resorts/areas are:

Tossa de Das, Barcelona; *Camprodon*, Gerona; *Valle de Farreras*, Lérida; *Bosost*, Lérida; *La Maladeta*, Huesca; *Val de Broto*, Huesca; *Bielsa*, Huesca; *Isaba*, Navarra; and *Burguete*, Navarra.

THE CANTABRIAN RANGE:

Situated in the north of the country, the Cantabrian Range drops sharply towards the Atlantic, but falls away more gently to the south. It is more rugged at its eastern end than in Galicia and has a number of important ski centres. The Enol Lakes are also a major attraction of this region.

Alto Campo, Santander. *Airport:* Cantabria 99km (61 miles). *Alt:* 1515-2150m (4970-7053ft). *Snow area:* 20 sq km (7 sq miles).

Valgrande-Pajares, Asturias & León. *Airport:* Oviedo 100km (62 miles). *Alt:* 1350-1834m (4429-6017ft). *Snow area:* 75 sq km (28 sq miles).

San Isidro, León & Asturias. *Airport:* Oviedo 70km (43 miles). *Alt:* 1500-1955m (4921-6414ft). *Snow area:* 60 sq km (23 sq miles).

Cabeza de Manzaneda, Orense. *Airport:* Santiago de Compostela 190km (118 miles). *Alt:* 1450-1760m (4757-5774ft). *Snow area:* 20 sq km (7 sq miles).

Other winter sports centres in this region include *Riaño-Maraña* on the slopes of Mampodre; *San Emiliano* in the northwestern part of the region; and *Leitariegos* in the western part of the range.

IBERIAN SYSTEM:

This extends northwest from the Demanda Range in Burgos to the Alcaraz Range on the Mediterranean.

Many of the slopes are pine-forested. The highest point in the system is the Moncayo summit 2313m (7588ft).
Valdezcaray, Logroño. *Airport*: Villafía (Burgos) for light aircraft 100km (62 miles). *Alt*: 1550-1860m (5085-2821ft). *Snow area*: 8 sq km (3 sq miles).
Lunada-Espinosa, Burgos. *Airport*: Villafía (Burgos) for light aircraft.
Valle del Sol, Burgos. *Airport*: Villafría (Burgos) for light aircraft 100km (62 miles). *Alt*: 1500-1700m (4921-5577ft). *Snow area*: 15 sq km (5 sq miles).
Sierra de Gudar, Teruel. *Airport*: Valencia 135 km (83 miles). *Alt*: 1600-2025m (5249-6643ft). *Snow area*: 15 sq km (5 sq miles).
CENTRAL SYSTEM:
This is also known as the Carpetan Range and runs from northeast to southwest dividing the central Meseta into two parts, although there are several passes which allow lines of communication. The Guadarrama and Gredos ranges are found within this system. The highest peak rises to over 2500m (8202ft). The region is within easy reach of Madrid.
La Pinilla, Segovia. *Airport*: Madrid 112km (69 miles). *Alt*: 1500-2270m (4921-7447ft). *Snow area*: 15 sq km (5 sq miles).
Valcotos, Madrid. *Airport*: Madrid 82km (50 miles). *Alt*: 1785-2270m (5856-7447ft). *Snow area*: 30 sq km (11 sq miles).
Valdesqui, Madrid. *Airport*: Madrid 85km (52 miles). *Alt*: 1876-2260m (6154-7414ft). *Snow area*: 20 sq km (7 sq miles).
Puerto de Navacerrada, Madrid. *Airport*: 75km (46 miles). *Alt*: 1700-2200m (5577-7217ft). *Snow area*: 42 sq km (16 sq miles).
PENIBETIC SYSTEM:
This is in the south of the country, and the range is broken by a fault line dividing it into a northern and a southern block. The southern block contains the main skiing areas, and also the highest peaks in the Spanish mainland (Sierra Nevada), reaching to over 3440m. The effect of river erosion has opened deep gorges leading to meadows and beaches on the Mediterranean coast. Some of the ski runs are less than 35km (21 miles) from the famous city of Granada.
Solynieve, Granada. *Airport*: Granada 34km (21 miles). *Alt*: 2100-3470m (6889-11384ft). *Snow area*: 40 sq km (10 sq miles).

SOCIAL PROFILE

FOOD & DRINK: Eating out in Spain is often cheap and meals are substantial rather than gourmet. One of the best ways to sample Spanish food is to try *tapas*, or snacks, which are served at any time of day in local bars. These range from cheese and olives to squid or meat delicacies, and are priced accordingly. Many of the specialities of Spanish cuisine are based on seafood, although regional specialities are easier to find inland than along the coast. In the northern Basque provinces, there is cod *vizcaina* or cod *pil-pil; angulas*, the tasty baby eels from Aguinaga; bream and squid. Asturias has its bean soup, *fabada*, cheeses and the best cider in Spain, and in Galicia there are shellfish, especially good in casseroles, and a number of regional seafood dishes such as *hake à la gallega*.
In the eastern regions the *paella* has a well-deserved reputation. It can be prepared in many ways, based on meat or seafood. Catalonia offers, among its outstanding specialities, lobster Catalan, sausages stewed with beans, and partridge with cabbage.
The Castile area specialises in roast meats, mainly lamb, beef, veal and suckling pig, but there are also stews, sausages, country ham and partridges. Andalucía is noted for its cooking (which shows a strong Arab influence), especially *gazpacho*, a delicious cold vegetable soup, a variety of fried fish including fresh anchovies, *jabugo* ham from Huelva and many dishes based on the fish which the coast provides in such abundance. Restaurants are classified by the Government and many offer tourist menus (*menu del día*). Restaurants and cafés have table service. **Drink:** Spain is essentially a wine-drinking country, with sherry one of the principal export products. Its English name is the anglicised version of the producing town Jerez (pronounced *kherez*), from which the wine was first shipped to England. Today, Britain buys about 75% of all sherry exports. There are four main types: *fino* (very pale and very dry), *amontillado* (dry, richer in body and darker in colour), *oloroso* (medium, full-bodied, fragrant and golden) and *dulce* (sweet). Sanlúcar de Barrameda and Puerto de Santa María are other towns famous for their sherry and well worth visiting. Tourists are able to visit one of the *bodegas* (above-ground wine stores) in Jerez. In the Basque Country a favourite is *chacolí*, a 'green' wine, slightly sparkling and a little sour, rather than dry.
The principal table wines are the *riojas* and *valdepenas*, named after the regions in which they are produced. In

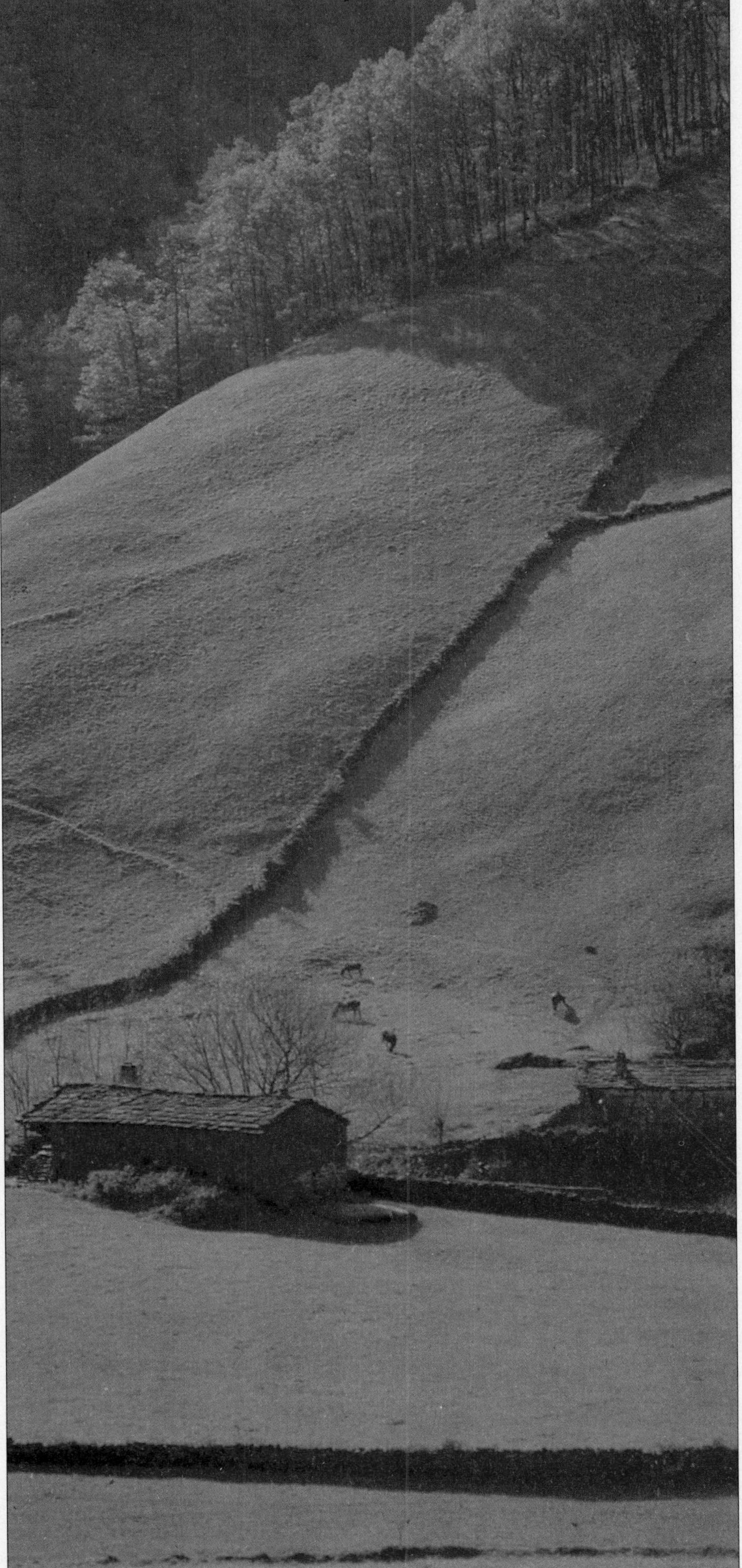

Vega del Pas, Cantabria

general, *rioja*, from the region around Logroño in the northeast, resembles the French Bordeaux, though it is less delicate. *Valdepenas* is a rougher wine, but pleasant and hearty. It will be found at its best in the region where it is grown, midway between Madrid and Cordóba. In Catalonia the *ampurdán* and *perelada* wines tend to be heavy and those that are not rather sweet are harsh, with the exception of the magnificent full-bodied Burgundy-type *penedés* wines. Alicante wine, dry and strong, is really a light aperitif. Nearby, the Murcia region produces excellent wine. Often it makes a pleasant change to try the unbottled wines of the house *(vino de la casa)*. It is much cheaper than the bottled wines and even in small places is usually good. Similarly inexpensive supermarket wine is very acceptable. Among the many brands of sparkling wines known locally as *champan* or *cava*, the most popular are *Codorniú* and *Freixenet*, dry or semi-dry. The majority of Spanish sparkling wines are sweet and fruity.

Spanish brandy is as different from French as Scotch whisky is from Irish. It is relatively cheap and pleasant, although most brandy drinkers find it a little sweet. Spain has several good mineral waters. A popular brand is *Lanjarón* which comes from the town of the same name. It can be still or fizzy. *Vichy Catalan* is almost exactly like French Vichy. *Malavella* is slightly effervescent and *Font Vella* is still. Cocktail lounges have table and/or counter service. There are no licensing hours.

NIGHTLIFE: In the cities, there are nightclubs, cafés and restaurants as in most of Europe. Each city or resort has its own type of entertainment, ranging from flamenco or other regional dancing to the discos and nightclubs. The entertainment, wherever you are, tends to start – and finish – quite late in the evening.

SHOPPING: In Spain the shopper can find items of high quality and fair price, not only in the cities, but in the small towns as well. In Madrid the Rastro Market is recommended, particularly on Sunday. Half of the market takes place in the open air and half in more permanent galleries, and has a character all its own. Catalonian textiles are world famous and there are important mills throughout the region. Spanish leather goods are prized throughout the world, offering high-fashion originals at reasonable prices. Of note are the suede coats and jackets. The furriers of Spain are also outstanding. In general all leather goods, particularly those of Andalucía, combine excellent craftsmanship with high-quality design. Fine, handcrafted wooden furniture is one of the outstanding products. Valencia is especially important in this field, and has a yearly international furniture fair. Alicante is an important centre for toy manufacturing. Shoe manufacturing is also of an especially high quality; the production centres are in Alicante and the Balearics. Fine rugs and carpets are made in Cáceres, Granada and Murcia. The numerous excellent sherries, wines and spirits produced in Spain make good souvenirs to take home.

Shopping hours: 0930/1000-1300/1330 and 1630/1730-1930/2000 Monday to Saturday. Department stores open 0930/1000-2000 Monday to Saturday.

SPORTS: There are excellent facilities for **tennis**, **sailing**, **racing** and other sports in most major cities and throughout the islands. Climatic conditions in southern Spain make outdoor sporting activities possible throughout the year. **Golf** is becoming increasingly popular; at present Spain has nearly 200 golf courses. **Watersports:** Water-skiing, swimming, sailing, sea fishing and windsurfing facilities can be found at all seaside resorts on the Costa del Sol, Costa Brava and Costa Blanca. These can be busy in the summer months. Windsurfing world championships are held in Tarifa, near Cádiz. **Winter sports:** Spain offers ideal conditions for winter sports and climbing; see the *Ski Resorts* section above for further information. **Spectator sports:** A typical and spectacular sport is *pelota vasca*, or ***jai-alai***. In the principal northern Spanish cities are courts where there are daily matches from October to June. In the towns and cities of the Basque regions the game is played in summer as well. **Football** is probably the most popular spectator sport, with clubs such as Real Madrid and Barcelona being among the most famous in the world; first-class matches are usually played on Sundays. International matches are also staged from time to time. **Horseracing:** There is a magnificent track in Madrid with meetings in the autumn and spring; there is racing in San Sebastián in the summer and in Seville in winter. Palma de Mallorca has a track for trotting races.

SPECIAL EVENTS: Folklore is very much alive and there is always some form of folk festival taking place. It is almost impossible for a visitor to be anywhere in the country for more than a fortnight without something taking place. The Ministry of Tourism produces a booklet listing and describing Spain's many national, regional and international feasts and festivals, of which there are over 3000 each year. Fiestas, Saints' Days, *Romerías* (picnics to religious shrines) and *Verbenas* (night festivals on the eve of religious holidays) are all celebrated with great spirit and energy. 'Holy Week' is probably the best time of year to visit for celebrations and it is then that the individuality of each region's style of pageantry is best revealed. For further information contact the Spanish Fair Association (AFE), C/General Pardiñas, 112 bis-1º Izq, 28006 Madrid. Tel: (1) 262 1022.

The following is a list of some of the more notable *fiestas* of interest to a visitor:

Mar 19 '93 *Fallas* (Fire Festival), Valencia. **Apr 4-11** *Holy Week*, Seville. **Apr 22-24** *Moors and Christians* (processions, displays and dancing), Alcoy, Alicante. **Apr 27- May 2** *Fair*, Seville. **May 9-16** *Horse Fair*, Jerez, Cádiz. **Jul 6-14** *Running of the Bulls*, Pamplona. **Jul 25** *Jubilee Year Festival* (culmination of year-round celebrations), La Coruña, Santiago de Compostela. **Aug** *International Festival* (month-long celebrations), Santander. **Oct 31** *The Saffron Festival*, Consuegra, Toledo.

Note: See also the list of individual town festivals for 1993/4 given in the *Public Holidays* section above.

SOCIAL CONVENTIONS: Spanish life has undergone rapid change in recent years and many of the stricter religious customs are giving way to more modern ways, particularly in the cities and among women. Nonetheless, old customs, manners and traditions have not faded and hospitality, chivalry and courtesy remain important. Handshaking is the customary form of greeting. Normal social courtesies should be observed when visiting someone's home. If invited to a private home, a small present is appreciated. Flowers are only sent for special celebrations. Conservative casual wear is widely acceptable. Some hotels and restaurants encourage men to wear jackets. Black tie is only necessary for very formal occasions and is usually specified if required. Outside resorts, scanty beachwear should be confined to beach or poolside. Smoking is widely accepted. **Tipping:** Service charges and taxes are normally included in hotel bills, however in addition, a tip should be left for the chambermaid and porters should be tipped per bag. It is also customary to leave a tip for the waiter. Restaurants include service in the bill and a tip is discretionary. In cafés and bars it is usual to leave loose change. Tip taxis 2-3% when metered.

BUSINESS PROFILE

ECONOMY: Spain is a major industrialised European economy with a large agricultural sector. Until 1975, under the Franco regime, the Spanish economy developed almost in isolation, protected from foreign competition by tight import controls and high tariffs, and evolved from an essentially agrarian economy to an industrial one. Spain joined the European Community in 1986, and the transition, which was widely expected to be very difficult, has actually gone exceptionally well. Despite the decline of many of its industries, such as shipbuilding, steel and textiles – all of which were badly hit during the world recession – Spain achieved the highest average growth rate in the Community during the 1980s. Inflation, which threatened at one point to get out of control, has been tamed especially since the Peseta was tied to the European Monetary System. Unemployment, however, has remained stubbornly high. Spain's economy ranks eighth in the world according to its GNP. The agricultural sector produces cereals, vegetables, citrus fruit, olive oil and wine: EC investment and modernisation have fostered a vast improvement in efficiency. The processed foods industry has expanded rapidly. The fishing fleet, once among the world's largest, has shrunk although it remains important. Energy requirements are met by indigenous coal and natural gas, imported oil (mostly from Algeria) and a sizeable nuclear power programme. In the manufacturing sector, the decline of older industries has been offset by rapid expansion in chemicals, electronics, information technology and industrial design. Tourism also contributes substantially to the economy. The EC countries, the USA and Japan are the country's main trading partners.

BUSINESS: Business people are generally expected to dress smartly. Although English is widely spoken, an interest in Spanish and an effort on the part of the visitor to speak even a few words will be appreciated. Business cards are exchanged frequently as a matter of courtesy and appointments should be made. **Office hours:** Tend to vary considerably. Business people are advised to check before making calls.

COMMERCIAL INFORMATION: The following organisations can offer advice:

Consejo Superior de Cámaras Oficiales de Comercio, Industria y Navegación de Espana, Calle Claudio Coello 19, 1º, 28001 Madrid. Tel: (1) 575 3400. Telex: 23227; *or* Cámara de Comercio Internacional (same address, telephone and telex number).

CONFERENCES/CONVENTIONS: In 1982 the Spanish Convention Bureau was founded as a non-profit-making organisation, by a confederation of 14 towns for the purpose of helping conference organisers select locations for their events with suitable facilities and back-up services. Most of these towns have dedicated convention centres in addition to the facilities provided by hotels. Seating capacity ranges from 540 in Jaca to 4200 in Palma de Mallorca; Madrid can seat up to 2650 persons. Full details can be obtained from the Spain Convention Bureau, Nuncio 8, 28005 Madrid. Tel: (1) 266 560. Fax: (1) 265 5482. Telex: 47716 FEMP E.

HISTORY & GOVERNMENT

HISTORY: Spain was under Roman rule for five centuries from 218BC, leaving remnants of their culture throughout the country. Spain then came under the rule of the Visigoths who rapidly integrated with the inhabitants until driven north by invading Arabs. Muslim culture soon established itself, most notably in the south, where Arabic influence and architecture are still a common sight. During the Middle Ages, Christianity gradually gained ground. Many kingdoms – Aragon, Castile, Navarre, León and Portugal being the major ones – were established, most of them on a more or less constant war footing. The spirit of *Reconquista*, the fierce flame which burned throughout so much of the medieval period, matching the Islamic concept of *Jihad* (holy war), produced heroes, folklore, legend, staggering architectural achievements and great acts of bravery and chivalrous folly; it also, after centuries of intermittent fighting, produced a final triumph for Christianity. In 1492, Ferdinand and Isabella – respectively King of Aragon and Queen of Castile, then the two most powerful kingdoms in Iberia, united by marriage – captured Granada, the last Muslim foothold in the Peninsula. The same year saw Columbus' discovery of America, financed by Castile, and the beginning of Spain's 'Golden Age' as the centre of the far-flung Habsburg Empire of Charles V (Charles, or Carlos, I of Spain). The reign of Philip II during the late 16th century was also one of the most artistically fertile in the country's history, with Cervantes, Lope de Vega, Velazquez and El Greco coming to prominence at this time. The Habsburg monarchy became progressively less able to deal with the serious political and economic problems of their empire during the 17th century, and the dynasty reached its nadir under the inept King Carlos II. There was a revival under the Bourbons, notably Carlos III, but the late 18th and early 19th centuries saw Spain suffering from the drain of the Napoleonic wars and internal political vendettas. The abdication of King Alfonso XIII in 1931 brought a left-wing republic. This was short-lived and was effectively crushed by General Franco in the Civil War of 1936-1939. His fascist regime lasted until his death in 1975 when the monarchy was restored. By March 1978 a democratic constitutional monarchy had been put in place. Domestic politics during the 1980s have been dominated by the Socialist Party under the leadership of Felipe Gonzalez, an archetype of the new generation of Spanish socialists who favoured pragmatism and technocratic development in place of ideology. In 1982 and again in 1986, the Socialists won an absolute majority in the Cortes (national assembly). In October 1989, Gonzalez again went to the country to seek his third successive term. However, disillusion on the left with 'Felipismo', and particularly the unequal distribution of the benefits of rapid economic growth, deprived Gonzalez' Socialists of many seats, eventually reducing the governing party to the leadership of a minority government. The Gonzalez government's particular achievement in foreign policy has been to establish Spain as a valuable and enthusiastic member of the European Community, which it joined in 1986. The country has benefited considerably from membership. As one enthusiast put it: "To think we Spaniards spent all those years searching for El Dorado in America when all the time it was right here in Europe – in Brussels". That impression has doubtless been reinforced after the Maastricht summit of European leaders in December 1991 at which Spain won a major readjustment of the Community's budget worth approximately £700 million to Madrid. The Spanish are sufficiently concerned to defend it to threaten a veto of future expansion of the EC, unless a new redistribution mechanism is introduced. In 1992 national pride and coffers received a boost from both Expo '92 in Seville and the Olympic Games in Barcelona. Cooler heads are, however, looking beyond El Dorado to the Single European Market and the potential threat which it poses to Spain's relatively uncompetitive industry. It is certainly preoccupying Finance Minister Carlos Solchaga, who emerged in 1991 as the key figure in the Government after the dismissal of his left-wing rival Alfonso Guerra, the Government's link-man with the trades unions and Gonzalez' former deputy. The main outstanding political issue for Spain in Europe is Gibraltar. Although co-operation with the British has improved at almost every level in the last five years, the single-mindedness of the Rock's inhabitants limits the political options available to either government (see *Gibraltar* section for details). Outside

Europe, Spain has special relations with Latin America and the Arab world as a result of historical and cultural ties. Spain has also been a member of NATO since 1982 and continued membership was confirmed in a referendum held in 1986. However, the referendum also showed a popular desire to end the 1982 agreement allowing the USA to establish naval and air bases on Spanish territory.
GOVERNMENT: The 1978 Constitution created a bicameral *Cortes* (Parliament), divided into the Congress of Deputies and the Senate, which holds legislative power. The 350-strong Congress is elected every four years by proportional representation; the 202 senators are chosen by direct election. There are also 17 autonomous regions whose governments are elected every four years.

CLIMATE

Spain's climate varies from temperate in the north to dry and hot in the south. The best months are from April to October, although mid-summer (July to August) can be excessively hot throughout the country except the coastal regions. The central plateau can be bitterly cold in winter.
Required clothing: Light to mediumweights and rainwear, according to the season

BARCELONA Spain (95m)

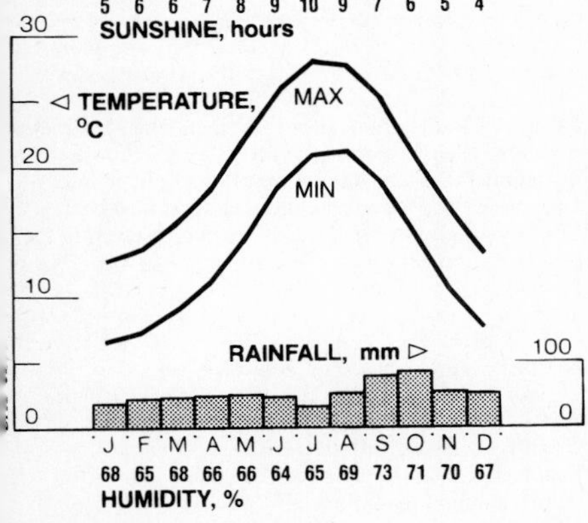

MADRID Spain (667m)

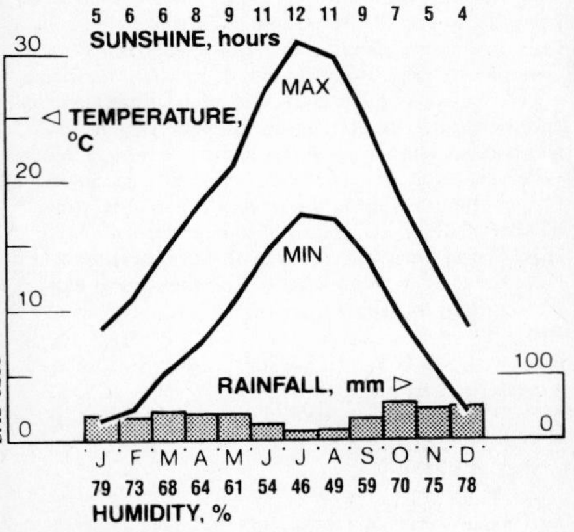

SEVILLE Spain (30m)

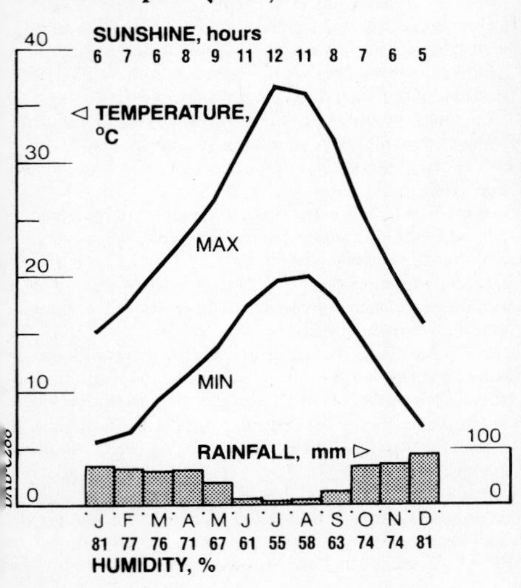

BALEARIC ISLANDS

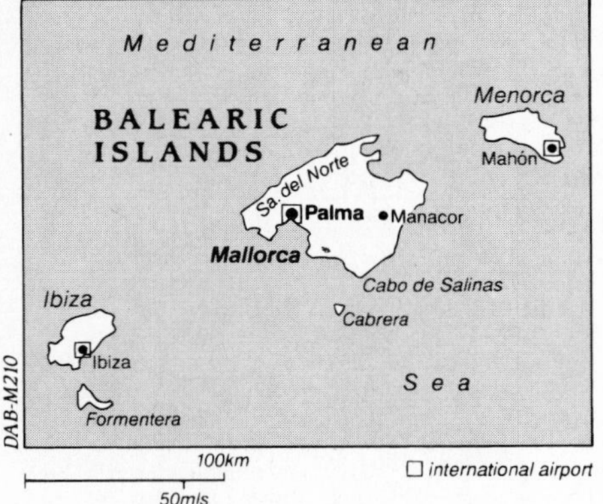

Ibiza, Mallorca, Menorca & Formentera
Location: Mediterranean, 240km (150 miles) due east of Valencia on the Spanish coast.

Note: The *Passport/Visa* and *Health* requirements for visiting the Balearic Islands are exactly the same as for visiting mainland Spain, and information may be found by consulting the respective sections above. Likewise, Spanish currency is used, and all the details given in the *Money* section apply.

AREA: Total: 5014 sq km (1935 sq miles). **Mallorca:** 3640 sq km (1405 sq miles). **Menorca:** 700 sq km (270 sq miles). **Ibiza:** 572 sq km (220 sq miles). **Formentera:** 100 sq km (38 sq miles).
POPULATION: 739,501 (1991 estimate).
POPULATION DENSITY: 147.5 per sq km.
CAPITAL: Palma de Mallorca. **Population:** 308,616 (1991 estimate).
GEOGRAPHY: Mallorca, Menorca and Ibiza are the main islands in this group, which is situated 193km (120 miles) south of Barcelona off the east coast of Spain. The landscape of these islands is characterised by woodlands, almond trees, fertile plains and magnificent coastlines with numerous sandy coves separated by craggy cliffs. The largest island, **Mallorca** (also known as the 'Isle of Dreams'), has a varied landscape, mountains and valleys, rocky coves and sandy beaches. The main geographical feature is the Sierra del Norte, a mountain range running along the northern coast. The island is covered with fresh green pines, ancient olive and almond trees, which blanket the countryside with blossoms in springtime. **Menorca** has evidence of ancient history and a strong feeling of connection with Britain, due to Admiral Nelson's stay on the island. Both the capital Mahón and the old town of Ciudadela at the north end of the island are set at the apex of deep inlets forming natural harbours. There are many bays and lovely beaches on this unspoilt and relatively quiet island.
Ibiza, the third largest island, has a rugged coastline with many fruit orchards and woods. The main town of the same name is situated above a busy harbour. A narrow channel separates Ibiza from **Formentera**, the smallest inhabited island in the group.

TRAVEL

AIR: Approximate flight times: From *London* to Palma de Mallorca is 2 hours 15 minutes, to Menorca is 3 hours 30 minutes (including stopover in Palma) and to Ibiza is 3 hours 30 minutes (including stopover in Barcelona).
International airports: *Palma de Mallorca (PMI)* (Son San Juan), 9km (5.5 miles) southeast of the city. Coaches to the city leave every 30 minutes 0630-2400. Return from Iberia Office, Archiduque, Luis Salvador 2. Taxis to the city are also available. The airport has a duty-free shop.
Mahón (MAH), 6km (4 miles) from Mahón. Taxi or coach is available to the town.
Ibiza (IBZ), 8km (5 miles) from the town of Ibiza. Bus to

Cala Conta, Ibiza

the city leaves every hour from 0730-2230. Taxis are available to the city.
SEA: The following shipping lines run services to the Balearic Islands: *Compañía Transmediterránea* (car ferry) from Alicante, Barcelona, Valencia and inter-island; *Isnasa-Islena de Navegación; CNAN – Compagnie Nationale Algerienne de Navigation* (car ferry) from Algiers; *DFDS* (car ferry) from Italy. There is also a ferry service from Sète (France) to Palma.
Local: There are regular ferries from Ibiza to Formentera.
RAIL: On Mallorca, narrow-gauge trains run from Palma to Soller five times daily, and to Inca every hour. Inter-Rail passes are not valid. There are no railways on any of the other islands.
ROAD: There are generally good bus services on the islands connecting resorts with main towns. Car and scooter hire is generally available. The steep, narrow inland roads make it difficult for coaches and cars to pass each other (although there are special passing points). It is best to check coach timetables before commencing your journey to avoid difficulties; hotels can often provide this information.

ACCOMMODATION

There are establishments of all categories: hotels catering for over 227,000 visitors, chaltes, apartments and bungalows. It is possible to rent furnished or unfurnished chalets for the season, although visitors must book in advance due to demand. Rates vary according to season and the standard of accommodation. Numerous 'packages' are available.

RESORTS & EXCURSIONS

Mallorca: Of all the Balearic Islands, Mallorca probably has the most to see and explore, lending itself to a number of half- and full-day excursions (especially to the north of the island), all of which can be made from Palma, and include Mallorca's highlights. The trip from Palma to Puerto Soller by special train is highly recommended, as is a trip to the Formentor Peninsula at the island's northeastern tip. This area is famous for its pine woods and secluded coves and for the more inquisitive visitor, there are plenty of half-hidden bays and mountain villages to be discovered.
The island's coastline is 300km (186 miles) long and although some tourist centres have suffered from overdevelopment, there are still numerous beautiful bays and the interior offers scope for many interesting excursions. Apart from the area around Palma, most of the resorts are on the eastern coast. The north is the least developed region; the mountainous terrain ensures that the road is close to the coast in only a few places, and after Puerto Soller it stays well inland until reaching Formentor. Only one side-road manages to fight its way through to La Colobra on the coast, and elsewhere, the only access to the sea is by path. The inland plain is noted for its almond trees, of which there are estimated to be over six million. **Palma,** the capital, clearly demonstrates its long association with maritime commerce and its history as a major Mediterranean port. The old city is beautifully situated in the middle of the broad sweep of *Palma Bay*, with modern developments to the east and west. Palma is overlooked by the 14th-century *Castle of Belver*, and other notable buildings include the golden sandstone Cathedral *(La Seo)*, the *Archbishop's Palace*, the *Monastery and Church of San Francisco* and the *Montesion Church*. Apart from these major buildings, there are many beautiful palaces and churches in the city, many of which were built from the profits of commerce.
Menorca: The second largest island, lies some 40km (25 miles) northeast of Mallorca. The capital of **Mahón** (on the east coast) is a compact town, with many of the buildings dating back to the period of British occupation, and is best explored on foot. The main attractions include the Town Hall *(Casa Consistorial)*, the *Church of Santa Maria* and the *Church of San Francisco*. Trips are available around the harbour. A good highway links Mahón with the older town of **Ciudadela** (the former capital) on the opposite side of the island. It has a Cathedral which dates back in part, to the 14th century, and also boasts several elegant Palacios and medieval churches. Despite the lack of coastal roads, it is nevertheless possible to make a wide variety of excursions from these two main centres, both of which also have several good beaches within easy reach. All over the island the visitor will come across prehistoric dolmans, taulas or talayouts. At **Talah** there is a construction resembling Stonehenge, believed to have been erected 4000 years ago. Menorca has preserved its stock-farming and leather-working traditions, making its economy less dependent on the revenue earned through tourism.
Ibiza: The third largest in the group and a very popular tourist destination, the island still retains some of its traditional atmosphere. The north and south in particular are still densely wooded with pine, and elsewhere there are many orchards. Large sandy beaches are found south of the capital. **Ibiza Town**, dominated by a medieval fortress, and the *Dalt Vila* (Upper Town), are well worth exploring. To the southwest of the town centre is the *Puig des Molins*, a Punic Cemetery. The two other major tourist centres are the coastal towns of *San Antonio Abad* and *Santa Eulalia del Río*.
Formentera: Separated from Ibiza by a 4km (2.4-mile) channel (hourly boat services operate during the summer), the main settlement is the large village of *San Francisco Javier*. Like the other islands in the group, Formentera has no shortage of pine woods and sandy beaches, and the pace of life is generally even more relaxed than on neighbouring Ibiza.

SOCIAL PROFILE

FOOD & DRINK: The varied local cuisine includes rabbit, a wide selection of seafood and pork dishes and numerous locally grown fruits and vegetables. Dishes include Mallorcan *ensaimada* (light pastry roll), Ibizan *flao, graixonere de peix, tumbet, escaldums* of chicken, *sobresada, frit* (chips), Mallorcan soups, and mayonnaise, the famous culinary invention from Menorca. **Drink:** The islands have plenty of good wines and aromatic liqueurs, such as *palo*, which is made from locally grown *St John's bread* (carob beans) and *frigola*. Imported alcoholic and soft drinks are also widely available.
NIGHTLIFE: There are numerous nightclubs and discotheques, some with terraces for dancing outside overlooking the sea, floorshows, live bands and orchestras. There are also many cinemas, theatres, concerts and art exhibitions. 18km (11 miles) west of Palma, in Magaluf, there is an elegant casino with a large restaurant. For the latest news on the local nightlife, and details of current events, artistic and cultural, consult the local English-language newspaper *The Bulletin*.
SHOPPING: On the Balearic Islands there is a strong tradition of craftsmanship. Purchases include: furniture, hand embroideries, handpainted ceramics, carved olive-wood panels, wrought ironwork, glassware, items made from raffia and palm leaves, handmade shoes, the famous pearls made in Mallorca and other costume jewellery from Menorca.
SPORT: Swimming: It is possible to swim in the sea virtually all year round. Innumerable heated swimming pools are also available. **Sailing:** There are facilities for different forms of sailing in the many sheltered bays. The Balearic Islands are also an arrival point on all Mediterranean yacht cruises. Mooring fees in any of the yacht clubs (Palma de Mallorca, Mahón, Ciudadela, Andraitx and Ibiza) are reasonable. **Watersports:** Facilities for most other water activities are available including water-skiing, windsurfing, parasailing and sub-aqua. Underwater fishing is especially popular and there are plentiful sea bass, sole, dentex, dorado and sea bream. **Tennis** can be played in the Real Club of Palma and in Ibiza, as well as on the private courts of the major hotels of the different towns. **Golf:** There are golf courses attached to the big hotels, and numerous mini-golf courses on all the islands. **Bowling:** American bowling rinks are available on all the islands.

CLIMATE

The islands enjoy a temperate, Mediterranean climate. The maximum temperatures are not excessive, even in high summer, due to the cooling influence of the sea. The climate during the winter is mild and dry and temperatures below zero are practically unknown.

PALMA Mallorca (28m)

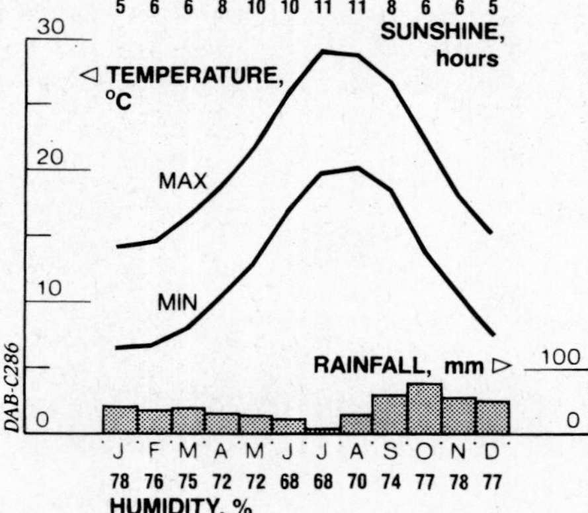

CANARY ISLANDS

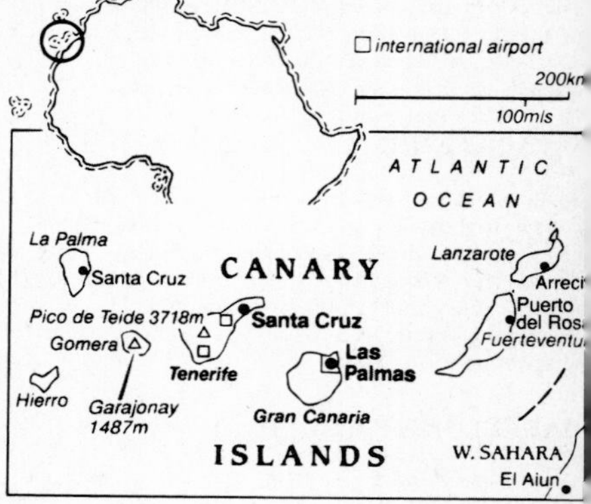

Location: North Atlantic, west of the African coast.

Note: The *Passport/Visa* and *Health* requirements for visiting the Canary Islands are exactly the same as for visiting mainland Spain, and information may be found by consulting the respective sections above. Likewise, Spanish currency is used, and all the details given in the *Money* section apply.

AREA: 7242 sq km (2796 sq miles).
POPULATION: 1,601,812 (1991).
POPULATION DENSITY: 221.2 per sq km.
CAPITAL: Santa Cruz de Tenerife (Tenerife). **Population:** 191,974 (1991 estimate). Las Palmas de Gran Canaria. **Population:** 347,688 (1991 estimate).
GEOGRAPHY: The Canary Islands are situated off the northwest coast of Africa and consist of seven islands which are divided into two provinces. **Las Palmas** comprises the islands of Gran Canaria, Fuerteventura and Lanzarote. **Santa Cruz de Tenerife** is made up of Tenerife, La Palma, Gomera and Hierro. All the islands are of volcanic origin and the climate is subtropical, dry and warm throughout the year. The landscape is varied, and includes imposing peaks and mountain ranges, hidden valleys, volcanic deserts, abrupt rocky cliffs, geometrically perfect craters and beautiful forests.
TIME: GMT (GMT + 1 April to September).
BBC World Service and Voice of America frequencies: From time to time these change. See the section *How to Use this Book* for more information.

BBC:				
MHz	17.705	15.070	12.095	9.410
Voice of America:				
MHz	11.97	9.670	6.040	5.995

TRAVEL

AIR: Approximate flight times: From *London* to Las Palmas is 5 hours 30 minutes and to Tenerife is 9 hours (including stopover in Las Palmas).
International airports: *Las Palmas (LPA)*, 22km (14 miles) south of the city on Gran Canaria. Hotel coach to city (30 minutes) operates 0610-0110. Return is from Iberia terminal (Hotel Iberia), Avenida Maritima from 0530-2330. Public bus service to the city leaves every 15 minutes, 24-hour service. Return is from the bus station, Parque de San Telmo. Taxis to the city are available, with a surcharge after 2200.
Tenerife-Norte Los Rodeos (TCI), in the north of the island, is 13km (8 miles) from Santa Cruz. Bus service runs every 30 minutes from 0600-2300.
Tenerife-Sur Reina Sofia (TFS), in the south of the island, is used for resorts such as Playa de las Americas. Bus service is according to flight arrivals.
Local flights run by *Iberia (IB)* link all the islands with the exception of Gomera.
SEA: The majority of cruises stop in the Canaries. Further details available from the Spanish National Tourist Office, or from *P&O* in Folkestone (representatives of the company *Transmediterránea*).
Local: All the islands are linked by regular car and passenger ferries. Day trips to the smaller islands are quickly and easily arranged.
ROAD: There are bus services available. Cars may be hired.

RESORTS & EXCURSIONS

Tenerife is the largest of the islands, and is dominated by a central mountain range and several spectacular valleys. It has a National Park, a gigantic natural crater some 19km (12 miles) in diameter and, to the north, the *Pico del Teide*, the highest mountain in Spain. The capital, **Santa Cruz**, is a city rich in architecture (including the *Church of San Francisco)* and museums housing art treasures and historical momentoes of the Canaries. **Puerto de la Cruz** is the most important resort, and also has several buildings which date back to the 17th century. Elsewhere on the island, places to visit include the second city of **La Laguna, La Orotava** (centre of a beautiful valley), **Güimar, Garachico** (the 'Pearl by the Sea') and **Los Cristianos.**

La Palma has the greatest altitudes in the world in relation to its perimeter, and in its centre is one of the largest craters in the world, the *Caldera de Taburiente*, best viewed from the La Cumbrecita look-out point. The island's capital of **Santa Cruz** (not to be confused with Santa Cruz de Tenerife) is also worth exploring with its examples of 16th-century architecture and the *Natural History Museum*. Other places of interest on the island include **Los Llanos de Aridane, Tazacorte, Mazo,** the *Belmaco Cave* and *Cueva Bonita*, a beautiful natural grotto.

Gomera (capital **San Sebastián)** is rich in vegetation and has several white sand beaches. The landscape is rugged, although not as mountainous as other islands in the group, and the most practical method of transportation around the island is often by sea. San Sebastián is interesting for its connections with the explorer Christopher Columbus, who is commemorated by the *Torre del Conde*, an old fortress, now an historic national monument. Gomera is also famous for its *whistling* language, which is used by the islanders to call from mountain to mountain. Other interesting places on the island include **Hermigüa, El Bosque del Cedro,** the uniquely beautiful **Vallehermoso** and the fishing ports of **Playa de Santiago** and **La Rajita.**

Hierro is the most westerly island with **Valverde** as its capital. The island has hardly any beaches, as most of the coastline consists of sheer cliffs; this explains why, of all the islands in the Canaries, Hierro is the only one with an inland capital. The highest point, *Malpaso*, is over 1300m (4265ft). It is an island of unspoilt, rugged, pine-clad countryside, dotted with small villages; **La Restinga** (the most southern point of the Canaries, and hence Spain, and hence – politically if not strictly geographically – of Europe as well), **Taibique, Frontera** and **El Barrio** (the 'suburb'), a collection of settlements close to the main town. Most of the western part of the island is wholly uninhabited.

Gran Canaria is the third largest island in the archipelago, and has as its capital the city of **Las Palmas** (not to be confused with the smaller island of La Palma). It has been called a 'miniature continent', as plants usually associated with Europe, Africa and America all flourish here. There are splendid beaches, including the *Playa del Inglés* and *Maspalomas* which is nearly four miles long. The capital is a major city with many sites of historical and architectural interest. These include the *Museo de Nestor*, the *Old Town* and the Gothic *Cathedral of Santa Ana*. Columbus lived here for a time before setting out on his voyage of discovery. Other places worth a visit include **Telde, Tejeda, Ingenio** (famous for its crafts), **San Bartolomé de Tirajana** (situated in the crater of a volcano), **Agüimes, Arinaga, San Agustín, Playa del Inglés,** the historic cities of **Galdar** and **Agaete**, the *Tara Caves* and the maritime town of **Sardina del Norte.**

Fuerteventura is the second largest of the Canary Islands, and has a large number of fine beaches. The island's capital, **Puerto del Rosario**, is home of about one-third of the island's population, and was built in the late 18th century. Attractions on the island include **Corralejo** in the far north (where straw hats are woven in the traditional manner); the many prehistoric sites and, to the west, the Norman castle of *Rico Roque*, near **Cotillo. Betancuria,** the ancient capital of the island, houses its most important monument, the *Church of Santa María*, noted for its painted ceiling and murals. One of the most attractive areas is *Jandía* in the south, particularly notable for its beaches. Camels are a common method of transport on this sandy island.

Lanzarote is the most easterly of the Canaries, a dry and fairly flat island which owes its eerie landscape to the activity of volcanoes long since dormant. The volcanic ash and craters have now been turned to the islanders' advantage in a novel method of vine cultivation. The capital, the port of **Arrecife**, is to be found on the south-east coast and in the area of flattest land on the island, so communications with nearby towns are good. The highest areas are in the north and east. Places of interest include **Teguise** (the old capital), with the *Guanapay Castle* set on a volcanic cone; the oasis-like **Haría; Malpaís de la Corona**, where an immense volcanic cave called *Los Verdes*, 6.5km (3.5 miles) long, is located; and the nearby *Jameo del Agua* lagoon. The *National Park of Timanfaya* is a spectacular stretch of lava which covers nearly one-third of the island and is awe-inspiring in its majesty and barrenness. The most popular excursion is to the volcanoes on camels.

SOCIAL PROFILE

FOOD & DRINK: The cuisine of the Canaries offers many dishes based on fish, which are usually served with wrinkled potatoes and a special sauce called *mojo picón*. The traditional dishes are watercress soup and the popular *sancocho canario*, a dish based on a fish salad, with a hot sauce. Locally grown bananas, tomatoes, avocados and papayas also play an important part in the Canaries cuisine. Corn meal, wheat flour, corn or barley, previously roasted, are eaten instead of bread with certain local dishes. In pastry are found the excellent *tirijalas, bienmesabes, frangollo, bizcochos lustrados*, meat pies, nougats of corn meal and molasses. In the main resorts restaurants offer the full range of international cuisine, as well as local delicacies. Often restaurants cater for the tastes of particular nationalities. **Drink:** Full range of wines, spirits and liqueurs from throughout the world. Spanish wines and spirits are particularly good value and spirits are slightly cheaper than in the UK. Local beers are *pilsner*-type lagers and, on the whole, rather weak. Local wines are also produced: typical of the island of Hierro are the *quesadillas* as well as the *rapaduras y marquesotes* of La Palma. Other drinks originating from the islands are rum, honey-rum and malmsey wine.

SHOPPING: Besides the excellent duty-free shopping there are numerous local items to tempt the visitor. Craftsmanship is represented mainly by skilled openwork and embroidery. Pottery, basket-work based on palm leaves, cane and reed and delicate woodcarvings are also popular. Tobacco produced here is excellent and world famous. Cigars from the Canary Islands are outstanding in quality.

SPORT: The islands provide an ideal setting for all kinds of sport. The warm, clear sea is excellent for underwater **fishing, diving, snorkelling** and **swimming**. Facilities for **water-skiing** and **windsurfing** are also available from beaches or from hotels. There are numerous **tennis** courts (often owned by the hotel or attached to one's apartment), **golf** courses and riding stables. **Spectator sports** include *jai-alai*, the stick game (a sort of fencing with long poles), the famous Canaries wrestling and the *garrocha* which is especially practised on the island of La Palma.

CLIMATE

The climate in the northern island of the Canaries is subtropical; the south of the islands tend to be hotter and drier, although rainfall is generally low throughout the islands.

Required clothing: Lightweight cottons and linens, with light to mediumweight clothes for winter.

LAS PALMAS Canary Is. (6m)

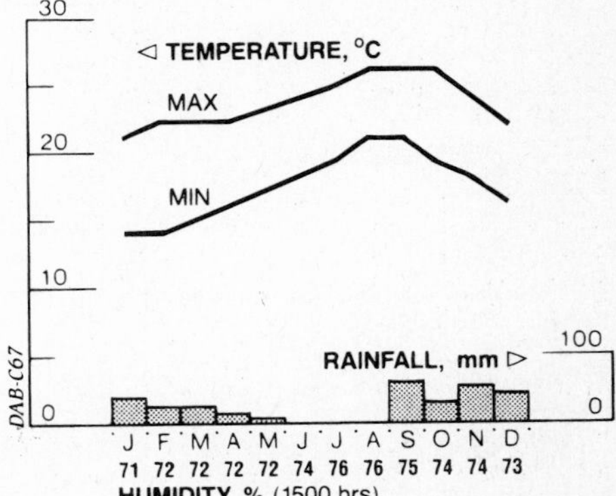

SRI LANKA

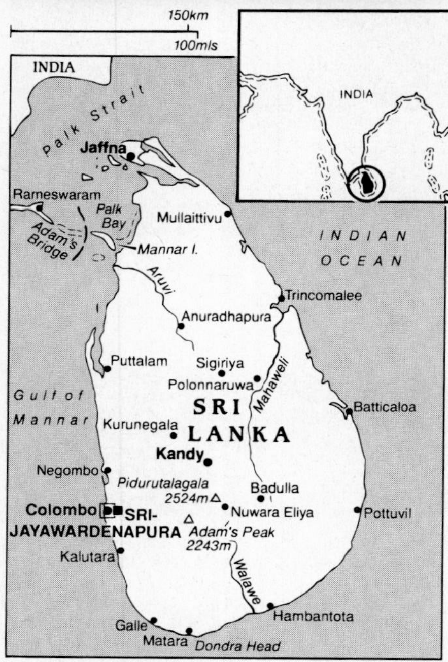

□ international airport

Location: Indian sub-continent.

Note: There has been some conflict in the northern provinces between Tamil separatists and government troops and travellers are advised to avoid the area. Anyone who must travel either to or near a trouble zone should contact the relevant diplomatic representation in Sri Lanka for an up-to-date report on the situation for travellers.

Sri Lankan Tourist Board
PO Box 1504
78 Stewart Place
Colombo 3, Sri Lanka
Tel: (1) 437 059. Fax: (1) 437 953. Telex: 21867.

High Commission for the Democratic Socialist Republic of Sri Lanka
13 Hyde Park Gardens
London W2 2LU
Tel: (071) 262 1841/7. Fax: (071) 262 7970. Telex: 25844. Opening hours: 0915-1700 Monday to Friday; *Visa Section*: 0930-1300 Monday to Friday.

Sri Lankan Tourist Board
Address as for High Commission.
Tel: (071) 262 5009 *or* 262 1841. Fax: (071) 262 7970. Telex: 25844 LETCON G.

British Embassy
PO Box 1433
190 Galle Road
Kollupitiya
Colombo 3, Sri Lanka
Tel: (1) 437 336. Fax: (1) 437 344. Telex: 21101.

Embassy of the Democratic Socialist Republic of Sri Lanka
2148 Wyoming Avenue, NW
Washington, DC
20008
Tel: (202) 483 4025. Fax: (202) 232 7181. Telex: 248312.

Embassy of the United States of America
PO Box 106
210 Galle Road
Colombo 3, Sri Lanka
Tel: (1) 548 007. Fax: (1) 549 070. Telex: 21305.

High Commission for the Democratic Socialist Republic of Sri Lanka
Suites 102-4
85 Range Road
Ottawa, Ontario
K1N 8J6
Tel: (613) 233 8449. Fax: (613) 238 8448.
Consulate in: Vancouver.

Canadian High Commission
PO Box 1006
6 Gregory's Road
Cinnamon Gardens
Colombo 7, Sri Lanka
Tel: (1) 695 841. Fax: (1) 687 049. Telex: 21106 DOMCAN CE.

AREA: 64,454 sq km (24,886 sq miles).
POPULATION: 16,993,060 (1990 estimate).
POPULATION DENSITY: 264 per sq km.
CAPITAL: Colombo. **Population:** 615,000 (1990 estimate).
GEOGRAPHY: Sri Lanka is an island off the southeast coast of the Indian state of Tamil Nadu. It is separated from India by the Indian Ocean, in which lie the chain of islands called Adam's Bridge. Sri Lanka has an irregular surface with low-lying coastal plains running inland from the northern and eastern shores. The central and southern areas slope into hills and mountains. The highest peak is Pidurutalagala (2524m), also known as Adam's Peak.
LANGUAGE: Sinhala, Tamil and English.
RELIGION: Buddhist, with Hindu, Christian and Muslim minorities.
TIME: GMT + 5.5.
ELECTRICITY: 230/240 volts AC, 50Hz. Round 3-pin plugs are usual, with bayonet lamp fittings.
COMMUNICATIONS: Telephone: IDD facilities are available to the principal cities. Country code: 94. **Fax:** The General Post Office in Colombo (address below) provides a service. Many hotels also have facilities. **Telex/telegram:** Telex facilities are available at the Overseas Telephone Service Counter, Duke Street Post Office, Colombo. Telegrams can be sent from all post offices. **Post:** Airmail to Europe takes up to a week. **Press:** Daily newspapers published in the English Language include the *Daily News*, *The Island* and the *Observer*.
BBC World Service and Voice of America frequencies: From time to time these change. See the section *How to Use this Book* for more information.

BBC:

MHz	15.31	11.96	9.740	6.180

A service is also available on 1413kHz.

Voice of America:

MHz	21.49	15.60	9.525	6.035

PASSPORT/VISA

Regulations and requirements may be subject to change at short notice, and you are advised to contact the appropriate diplomatic or consular authority before finalising travel arrangements. Details of these may be found at the head of this country's entry. Any numbers in the chart refer to the footnotes below.

	Passport Required?	Visa Required?	Return Ticket Required?
Full British	Yes	No	Yes
BVP	Not valid	-	-
Australian	Yes	No	Yes
Canadian	Yes	No	Yes
USA	Yes	No	Yes
Other EC	Yes	No	Yes
Japanese	Yes	No	Yes

PASSPORTS: Valid passport required by all.
British Visitors Passport: Not accepted.
VISAS: Required by all except:
(a) nationals of EC-countries entering as tourists for a maximum stay of 90 days;
(b) nationals of Australia, Bangladesh, Finland, Malaysia, New Zealand, Philippines, Sweden and the USA, who will be given a free 90-day Entry visa at point of entry;
(c) nationals of Albania, Austria, Bahrain, Bosnia-Hercegovina, Bulgaria, Canada, Croatia, Cyprus, Czechoslovakia, Estonia, Hungary, Indonesia, Israel, Japan, Kuwait, Latvia, Lithuania, Maldives, Norway, Nepal, Oman, Pakistan, Poland, Qatar, Romania, Saudi Arabia, Singapore, Slovenia, South Korea, Switzerland, Thailand, Turkey, United Arab Emirates, USSR and Yugoslavia entering as tourists for a maximum stay of 30 days.
Note: All business visitors require a visa.
Types of visa: Tourist and Business. Prices vary according to nationality.
Validity: 30 days. Visitors can request to extend their stay by applying to the Department of Immigration & Emigration in Colombo. This is issued at the discretion of the authorities who must be satisfied that the applicant has at least US$35 per day for the stay and holds an onward or return ticket for travel.
Application to: Consulate (or Consular Section at Embassy or High Commission). For addresses, see top of entry.
Application requirements: (a) Full valid passport. (b) Completed application form. (c) 1 passport photo signed on the back by applicant. (d) Fee with self-addressed envelope, stamped for US$2, for return of passport. (e) Proof of sufficient funds for duration of stay. (f) For Business visa, a letter from sponsor in the national's own country.
Working days required: At least 3.
Temporary residence: Enquire at Embassy or High Commission.

MONEY

Currency: Sri Lanka Rupee (SL Re) = 100 cents. Notes are in denominations of SL Rs1000, 500, 100, 50, 20, 10, 5 and 2. Coins are in denominations of SL Rs10, 5, 2 and 1, and 50, 25, 10, 5, 2 and 1 cents. There are also a large number of commemorative coins in circulation.
Currency exchange: Foreign currency must be changed only at authorised exchanges, banks and hotels, and these establishments must endorse such exchanges on the visitor's Exchange Control D form which is issued on arrival and must usually be returned at time of departure.
Credit cards: American Express, Visa and Access/Mastercard are widely accepted. Diners Club has more limited acceptance. Check with your credit card company for details of merchant acceptability and other services which may be available.
Travellers cheques: The rate of exchange for travellers cheques is better than the rate of exchange for cash.
Exchange rate indicators: The following figures are included as a guide to the movements of the Sri Lanka Rupee against Sterling and the US Dollar:

Date:	Nov '89	Oct '90	Oct '91	Oct '92
£1.00=	62.10	78.20	72.86	67.00
$1.00=	39.50	40.03	41.98	42.22

Currency restrictions: The import and export of local currency is limited to SL Rs1000. The import of notes from India and Pakistan is not allowed, otherwise the import of foreign currency is not restricted but subject to declaration. Export of foreign currency is limited to the amount declared on import.
Banking hours: 0900-1300 Monday and Saturday, 0900-1500 Tuesday to Friday. Colombo Airport's banking facilities serve all incoming and outgoing flights.

DUTY FREE

The following items may be imported into Sri Lanka without incurring customs duty:
200 cigarettes or 50 cigars or 375g of tobacco or a combination of these not exceeding 375g;
2 bottles of wine and 1.5 litres of spirits;
Small quantity of perfume or 250ml of toilet water.
Note: (a) Precious metals, including gold, platinum and silver (and including jewellery), must be declared on arrival in Sri Lanka. (b) There is no free gift allowance.

PUBLIC HOLIDAYS

Public holidays observed in Sri Lanka are as follows:
Mar 25 '93 Eid al-Fitr. **Apr 9** Good Friday. **Apr 12** Easter Monday. **May 1** May Day. **May 22** National Heroes' Day. **Jun 1** Eid al-Adha. **Jun 30** Special Bank Holiday. **Aug 30** Milad un-Nabi (Birth of the Prophet). **Dec 25** Christmas Day. **Dec 26** Boxing Day. **Dec 31** Special Bank Holiday. **Jan 1 '94** New Year's Day. **Feb 4** Independence Commemoration Day. **Mar** Eid al-Fitr.
Note: (a) In addition to the above there is a *poya* holiday on the day of each full moon. In general, Hindu and Buddhist festivals are declared according to local astronomical observations and it is often only possible to forecast the approximate time of their occurrence. (b) Muslim festivals are timed according to local sightings of various phases of the Moon and the dates given above are approximations. During the lunar month of Ramadan that precedes Eid al-Fitr, Muslims fast during the day and feast at night and normal business patterns may be interrupted – however, since Sri Lanka is not a predominantly Muslim country restrictions (which travellers may experience elsewhere) are unlikely to cause problems.

HEALTH

Regulations and requirements may be subject to change at short notice, and you are advised to contact your doctor well in advance of your intended date of departure. Any numbers in the chart refer to the footnotes below.

	Special Precautions?	Certificate Required?
Yellow Fever	No	1
Cholera	Yes	2
Typhoid & Polio	Yes	-
Malaria	3	-
Food & Drink	4	-

[1]: A yellow fever vaccination certificate is required from travellers over one year of age arriving from infected areas.
[2]: Following WHO guidelines issued in 1973, a cholera vaccination certificate is not a condition of entry to Sri Lanka. However, cholera is a serious risk in this country and precautions are essential. Up-to-date advice should be sought before deciding whether these precautions should include vaccination as medical opinion is divided over its effectiveness. See the *Health* section at the back of the book.
[3]: Malaria risk, predominantly in the benign *vivax* form, exists throughout the year in the Districts of Amparai, Anuradhapura, Batticoloa, Badulla, Hambantota, Jaffna, Kandy, Kegalle, Kuranegala, Mannar, Matale, Matara, Moneragala, Polonnaruwa, Puttalam, Ratnapura, Trincomalee and Vavuniya. The malignant *falciparum* strain is also present and is reported to be 'highly resistant' to chloroquine.
[4]: All water should be regarded as being potentially contaminated. Water used for drinking, brushing teeth or making ice should have first been boiled or otherwise sterilised. Bottled water and a variety of mineral waters are available at most hotels. Unpasteurised milk should be boiled. Powdered or tinned milk is available and is advised, but make sure that it is reconstituted with pure water. Pasteurised and sterilised milk is available in some hotels and shops. Avoid all dairy products made from unboiled milk. Only eat well-cooked meat and fish, preferably served hot. Pork, salad and mayonnaise may carry increased risk. Vegetables should be cooked and fruit peeled.
Rabies is present. For those at high risk, vaccination before arrival should be considered. If you are bitten abroad seek medical advice without delay. For more information consult the *Health* section at the back of the book.
Health care: Treatment is free at government hospitals and dispensaries; 24-hour treatment is available at Colombo General Hospital. Some hotels also have doctors.

TRAVEL - International

AIR: Sri Lanka's national airline is *Air Lanka (UL)*.
Approximate flight times: From *Hong Kong* to Colombo is 5 hours 10 minutes, from *London* is 13 hours 45 minutes, from the *Seychelles* is 3 hours 55 minutes and from *Tokyo* is 12 hours.
International airport: *Colombo (CMB)* (Katunayake) is 32km (21 miles) from the city. Bus no 240 goes to the city every 30 minutes 0600-2100. It returns from Pettah bus station, Olcott Mawatha Street. Bus no 187 goes to the city every 60 minutes 0600-2100. It returns from Fort bus station, Olcott Mawatha Street. Taxis to the city are available. There is a train to Maradana station (one mile from the city centre) at 0756, 0830, 1632 and 1720 (travel time – 1 hour 25 mins). Return is from Fort railway station, Olcott Mawatha Street at 0510, 0526, 1340 and 1520. There are full duty-free facilities at Colombo airport, as well as a restaurant, bar, snack bar, bank, post office and car hire.
Departure tax: SL Rs400 is levied on all international departures. Transit passengers and children under two years are exempt.
SEA: International ports include Colombo, Talaimannar, Trincomalee and Galle. Passenger services to Sri Lanka are operated by *Flagship Cruises, Holland America, Nauru Line, Norwegian American, P&O, Royal Viking, CIT* and *Cunard*. Cargo/passenger lines running services to Sri Lanka include *Bank, Hauraise, Lloyd, Triestine, Swedish American* and *United Yugoslav*. There is a ferry service to Rameswaram on the Indian side of Adam's Bridge, but it suffers occasional disruption due to the political disturbances in the northern parts of Sri Lanka.
RAIL: The Talaimannar line connects with the India ferry service (see above).

TRAVEL - Internal

AIR: The major domestic airport is *Ratmalana* at Columbo. There are daily flights to smaller airports at Batticoloa, Gal Oya, Palali and Trincomalee. The airport at Jaffna is currently closed.
Helicopter tours: *Helitours of Ceylon*, with pilots from the Sri Lanka Air Force, offers charter tours of major tourist areas.
RAIL: Trains connect Colombo with all tourist towns, but first-class carriages, air-conditioning and dining cars are available on only a few. New fast services operate on the principal routes, otherwise journeys are fairly leisurely. The total network covers 1500km (900 miles).
Note: Rail services to Jaffna have recently been much reduced due to the violent political disruptions in the northern area.
ROAD: Most roads are tarred, with a 56kmph (35mph) speed limit in built-up areas and 75kmph (45mph) outside towns. **Bus:** An extensive network of services of reasonable quality is provided by the *Sri Lanka Central Transport Board*. **Taxi:** These are available in most towns. **Car hire:** This is available from several international agencies. Air-conditioned minibuses are also available. Chaffeur-driven cars are less expensive and well recommended. **Documentation:** In order to avoid bureaucratic formalities in Sri Lanka, an International Driving Permit should be obtained before departure. If not, a temporary licence to drive is obtainable on presentation of a valid national driving licence. This must be endorsed at the AA office in Colombo. The minimum age for driving a car is 18.
URBAN: Bus: The Central Transport Board provides intensive urban bus operations in Colombo, where there are also private buses and minibuses. Fares are generally collected by conductors. Services are often crowded. **Taxi:** Taxis are metered with yellow tops and red and white plates. Drivers expect a 5% tip.
JOURNEY TIMES: The following chart gives approximate journey times (in hours and minutes) from Colombo to other major cities/towns in Sri Lanka.

	Air	Road	Rail
Kandy	-	2.30	3.00
Galle	-	3.00	3.00
Bentota	-	1.45	1.45
Matara	-	4.00	4.30
Badulla	-	9.30	9.00
Negombo	-	0.45	0.45
Nuwaraeliya	-	3.30	5.00
Anuradhapura	0.45	5.30	6.00
Pollonnaruwa	1.00	6.00	7.00
Trincomalee	1.00	6.00	7.00
Kataragama	-	6.30	-

ACCOMMODATION

Sri Lanka offers a wide choice of accommodation. Hotels are classified from 1 to 5 stars. There are seven international-class 5-star hotels with every modern facility. Inns, guest-houses and resthouses offer comfortable but informal accommodation. For the visitor who would like to get to know the Sri Lankans and see how they live, arrangements can be made to stay in private homes or on a tea or rubber plantation. There are also many park bungalows run by the Department of Wild Life Conservation which are furnished and equipped for comfort rather than sophistication. Information about youth hostels can be obtained from the YHA.

RESORTS & EXCURSIONS

Ancient sites include Anuradhapura, Polonnaruwa, Sigiriya, Dambulla, Panduwasnuwara and Yapahuwa. All these places contain the remains of a great civilisation which grew through the centuries under the influence of Buddhism, a gentle faith still preserved in Sri Lanka in its purest form. Vast man-made lakes, large parks, shrines, temples and monasteries speak eloquently of the grandeur of the past and bear testimony to a cultured and imaginative people. The regions in the following guide are used for convenience only and have no administrative significance.

Colombo

Sri Lanka's capital is a fascinating city, blending its older culture with modern Western influences. A palm-fringed drive of 34km (21 miles) leads from the Katunayake (Colombo) International Airport to Colombo city.
Fort: So called as it was a military garrison during the Portuguese and Dutch occupation from the 16th to the 18th century, today it is the commercial capital of Sri Lanka.
Pettah: A mile from Fort is the busy bazaar area known as the Pettah.
Buddhist temples: *Kelani Rajamaha Viharaya*, 10km (6 miles) from Fort; the *Vajiraramaya* at Bambalapitiya, 6km (4 miles) from Fort; *Dipaduttaramaya* at Kotahena, 5km (3 miles) from Fort; and *Gotami Vihare* at Borella, 7km (4.5 miles) from Fort. Also worth visiting are *Gangaramaya Bhikkhu Training Centre* and *Sima Malaka* at 61, Sri Jinaratana Road, Colombo, 3km (2 miles) from Fort; the *Purana Viharaya* at Metharamaya, Lauries Road, Colombo 4; and the *Purana Viharaya* at Hendala, half a mile on the Colombo–Negombo road, en route to the *Pegasus Reef Hotel*.
Hindu temples: At Kochikade Kotahena, Pettah and Bambalapitiya, Colombo 4; Sri Siva Subramania Swami Kovil, Gintupitiya – within walking distance of Sea Street, Colombo 11 (Pettah).
Mosques: Davatagaha mosque at Union Place, Colombo 2; Afar Jumma mosque in the Pettah.
Parliament Building is at Sri Jayawardenepura, Kotte.
Parks: The *Vihara Maha Devi Park*, named after the mother of one of Sri Lanka's greatest kings, is noteworthy for its collection of beautiful flowering trees, a lovely spectacle in March, April and early May. The park is open until 2100 daily and is well illuminated.
Other attractions: *The Planetarium, The National Zoological Gardens* and several museums and art galleries.

Kandy & the Hill Country

Kandy, a picturesque, naturally fortified town, 115km (72 miles) from Colombo, was the last stronghold of the Kandyan Kings. It withheld foreign conquest until 1815 when it was ceded to the British by treaty. It is now a cultural sanctuary where age-old customs, arts, crafts, rituals and ways of life are well-preserved.
Good sightseeing trips should include: the Temple of the Sacred Tooth Relic (Dalada Maligawa); Embekke Devale; Lankatillaka; Gadaladeniya; Degaldoruwa temples; museums; Royal Botanic Gardens; Peradeniya; Elephants' Bath at Katugastota; the Kandyan Arts Association; Kalapura (Craftsmen's Village) at Nattarampotha (6.5km/4 miles from Kandy); and Henawela Village – famous for its 'Dumbara Mats' (16km/10 miles from Kandy).

Beaches

Sri Lanka has approximately 1600km (1000 miles) of beautiful palm-shaded beaches as well as warm, pure seas and colourful coral reefs.
Southwest coast: At its best from November to April. The east coast is best from April to September.
Mt Lavinia, 11km (7 miles) from Colombo is a good beach resort close to Colombo and the domestic airport.
Beruwela, 58km (36 miles) from Colombo, has good bathing in the bay all year round.
Bentota, 61km (38 miles) from Colombo is a pleasant self-contained resort destination, between the sea and the river.
Hikkaduwa, 99km (62 miles) from Colombo is a beautiful coral reef and beach.
Galle, 115km (72 miles) from Colombo, is famous for its old Dutch fort, and is also a centre for lace-making, ebony-carving and gem-polishing.

SRI LANKA | **HEALTH REGULATIONS** | **VISA REGULATIONS** | Code-Link

GALILEO/WORLDSPAN

TI-DFT/CMB/HE

TI-DFT/CMB/VI

SABRE

TIDFT/CMB/HE

TIDFT/CMB/VI

To access this information on your CRS, swipe the barcode with a light pen or type in the text under the barcode. For more information, see the introduction *How to Use This Book*.

Tangale, 195km (122 miles) from Colombo, is a beautiful bay and there is safe swimming all year round.
Negombo, 37km (32 miles) from Colombo near Katunayake International Airport, is Sri Lanka's oldest and best-known fishing village. It stands on a strand separating the sea from a lagoon. The seafood here, particularly the shellfish, is a speciality.
East coast & Jaffna: *Visitors are advised to check with the Tourist Board regarding the situation in these areas prior to departure.*
Trincomalee, 265km (160 miles) from Colombo, is the ideal refuge for the beach addict. It boasts one of the finest natural harbours in the world and excellent beaches. All watersports, including fishing, are available here.
Batticaloa, 312km (195 miles) from Colombo: famous for the 'singing fish' and the old Dutch fort.
Kalkudah, 32km (20 miles) from Batticaloa: here the sea is clear, calm and reef-protected, and ideal for bathing.
Passekudah, close to Kaludah, has a fine bay, clear waters and safe swimming.
Nilaveli, 18km (11 miles) from Trincomalee, very much a resort centre, all beach and watersports.
Arugam Bay, 314km (196 miles) from Colombo, 3km (2 miles) from Potuvil has a beautiful bay and has good surfing.
Jaffna 396km (240 miles) from Colombo: Jaffna, the unofficial capital of the Tamil separatists, is different from the rest of Sri Lanka in its topography, history, people and way of life. The city was devastated during the prolonged siege by Indian forces in 1987, but was once noted for its Hindu temples, Dutch forts, the Keerimalai Baths, the tidal well and the Chundikulam sanctuary. Jaffna has many scenic beaches, the best known of which is Casuarina Beach. Check with the Tourist Board, Embassy or High Commission whether the area is off-limits to foreign visitors.

SOCIAL PROFILE

FOOD & DRINK: Standard foods are spicy and it is advised to approach curries with caution. There are many vegetables, fruits, meats and seafoods. Continental, Chinese, Indian and Japanese menus are available in Colombo. A speciality is basic curry, made with coconut juice, sliced onion, green chili, aromatic spices such as cloves, nutmeg, cinnamon and saffron and aromatic leaves. *Hoppers* is a cross between a muffin and a crumpet with a wafer crisp edge, served with a fresh egg soft-baked on top. *Stringhoppers* are steamed circlets of rice flour, a little more delicate than noodles or spaghetti. *Jaggery* is a fudge made from the crystallised sap of the kitul palm. The *durian* fruit is considered a high delicacy. **Drink:** Tea is the national drink and considered to be amongst the best in the world. *Toddy*, the sap of the palm tree, is a popular local drink; fermented, it becomes *arrack* which, it should be noted, comes in varying degrees of strength. Alcohol cannot be sold on *poya* holidays (which occur each lunar month on the day of the full moon).
NIGHTLIFE: Some Colombo hotels have supper clubs with music for dancing. There are theatres in Colombo, cinemas showing films from the USA, ballet, concerts and theatre productions.
SHOPPING: Special purchases include handicrafts and curios of silver, brass, bone, ceramics, wood and terracotta. Also cane baskets, straw hats, reed mats and tea. Some of the masks, which are used in dance-dramas, in processions and on festival days, can be bought by tourists. The '18-disease' mask shows a demon in possession of a victim; he is surrounded by 18 faces – each of which cures a specific ailment. Versions produced for the tourist market are often of a high standard. Sri Lanka is also rich in gems. Fabrics include batiks, cottons, rayons, silk and fine lace. **Shopping hours:** 0800/0900-1700 Monday to Friday. Many stores also open Saturday morning.
SPORT: Golf: Offered on a temporary membership basis at several courses. **Fishing:** Sport fishing is popular in Sri Lanka and several clubs offer membership to visitors. **Skindiving:** *Underwater Safaris*, 25 Barnes Place, Colombo 7, conducts skindiving expeditions and supplies equipment. **Swimming:** With over 1600km (1000 miles) of fine beaches and several swimming clubs, there is plenty of scope for swimmers. **Water-skiing:** Available with *Sun Stream Boat Services* (National Holiday Resort, Bentota). **Windsurfing** is a sport that is gaining popularity and facilities are located in Kalutara, Bentota, Beruwela and Negombo. **Other sports: Rugby, hockey, cricket, football, squash** and other indoor games are also available. Apply to a local Travel Information Centre.
SPECIAL EVENTS: The following list is a selection of the events taking place in Sri Lanka annually. For further information and exact dates, contact the Tourist Board. **Jan** *Duruthu Perahera Festival* (commemorating a visit of the Buddha to Sri Lanka), Kelaniya; *Thai Pongal* (traditional Hindu festival where thanksgiving prayers are offered to the deities, and milk rice is boiled at dawn in the direction of the rising sun). **Feb** *Navam Perahera Festival* (colourful street procession with about 100 elephants and 'low country' dancers), Colombo. **Feb 4** *Independence Commemoration Day* (commemorating the granting of political independence to the country in 1948, after 150 years of British colonial rule). **Apr 13-14** *Sinhala* and *Tamil New Year*. **May** *Vesak Festival* (commemorates the Birth, Enlightenment and Death of the Buddha). **Jul/Aug** *Kataragama Festival*, Tissamaharama; *Esala Perahera Festival*, Kandy. **Dec** *Sanghamitta Day*.
SOCIAL CONVENTIONS: Shaking hands is the normal form of greeting. It is customary to be offered tea when visiting and it is considered impolite to refuse. Punctuality is appreciated. A small token of appreciation like a souvenir from home or your company is always welcomed. Informal, Western dress is suitable. Visitors should be decently clothed when visiting any place of worship. Beachwear is not suitable for temples and shrines, and shoes and hats must be removed. Jackets and ties are not required by men in the evenings except for formal functions when lightweight suits should be worn.
Tipping: Most hotels include a service charge of 10%. Extra tipping is optional.

BUSINESS PROFILE

ECONOMY: The economy is predominantly agricultural. The main cash crops are tea, rubber and coconuts, which provide over 75% of export earnings. Rice is grown mainly for domestic consumption, and Sri Lanka is almost self-sufficient in rice. The main industrial sectors are mining and manufacturing, which are currently doing most to support the growth of the Sri Lankan economy. Graphite is the most important mineral, but recent growth is largely a result of increasing export of gemstones. Iron ore, limestone, clay and uranium are present in commercially exploitable quantities. Oil exploration has so far failed to yield significant deposits, but a number of major oil companies have signed long-term contracts to continue test drilling. Several key manufacturing industries are under government control, including cement and textiles – the latter being an important export industry – which are typical of the Government's strategy of promoting export-oriented industries within the country. Forestry and fishing are also important. Hydroelectricity is the main source of power. The biggest problem facing the economy at present is the dislocation caused by the internal security situation, although it has picked up in the early 1990s with a sharp fall in the trade and current account deficits and a recovery of the tourism industry which was hit particularly badly. Sri Lanka's principal imports are foodstuffs, oil and machinery; the market for consumer goods is comparatively underdeveloped and offers promising future opportunities for exporters. The UK is the third largest exporter to Sri Lanka after Japan and the USA and also the third largest overseas market for Sri Lankan goods. Sri Lanka has run a sizeable trade deficit for years, which is met through overseas aid and loans.
BUSINESS: Business attire is casual. English is widely spoken in business circles. Appointments are necessary and it is considered polite to arrive punctually. It is usual to exchange visiting cards on first introduction. **Office hours:** 0830/0900-1615/1700.
COMMERCIAL INFORMATION: The following organisations can offer advice: Federation of Chambers of Commerce and Industry of Sri Lanka, People's Bank Building, 220 Deans Road, Colombo 10. Tel: (1) 699 530.

HISTORY & GOVERNMENT

HISTORY: Sri Lanka was part of the empire of Asoka during the 3rd century, during which time the population became converted to Buddhism. The Sinhalese inhabitants later moved their capital to Polonnaruva in the south of the island to escape from repeated Tamil invasions during the 11th and 12th centuries. The first Europeans to arrive were the Portuguese, quickly supplanted by the Dutch in the 17th century. In 1796 Sri Lanka (as Ceylon) was acquired from the Dutch by the British. Initially, administration of the island was shared between the East India Company and the Crown, but the latter assumed full control in 1802. Sri Lanka (then Ceylon) eventually won independence in 1948. Past colonisation by the Indians, Portuguese, Dutch and British have all left their mark in architecture, customs, languages and agriculture. The country became a republic in 1972, adopting a new constitution along with the Sinhala name, Sri Lanka. The majority (70%) of the population are Buddhists of Sinhalese descent, but the north and parts of the east of Sri Lanka are dominated by the Tamil population (15%), Hindu by religion, associated with the Tamils of southern India. Serious conflict has arisen out of the minority Tamils' demands for a separate Tamil state (Eelam), and terrorist activity since the 1970s has led to states of emergencies being called by the Government, the latest in 1983. Since 1983, the Indian government has taken an increasingly active role in attempts to resolve the situation, acting as official mediator between the Tamils and the Sri Lankan government from 1985 to 1987, when a failed armistice drove the Sri Lankan government to invite India to intervene militarily. A large Indian force engaged the Tamils and, by the end of the year, the crucial Jaffna peninsula had been taken, with heavy losses on both sides. However, all the key Tamil leaders and many of the guerrillas escaped into the jungle. With more than 1000 Indian soldiers dead, Indian Prime Minister Rajiv Ghandi struggled to persuade the Sri Lankan government to guarantee certain rights for the Tamil minority, but the Government was constrained by the increasing violence of the militant Sinhalese JVP party. The Indian troops have now withdrawn and, while the security situation is less volatile compared to 1985-87, neither the main Tamil guerrilla group – the Liberation Tigers of Tamil Eelam – nor the Sinhalese JVP have been disarmed. The much-maligned Sri Lankan army, meanwhile, has clearly benefited from its crash training by foreign instructors and scored several significant victories during 1990, including the relief of the siege of Jaffna in September. At the New Year, the Tigers announced a unilateral ceasefire. This was the final move in a year-long series of secret peace talks. They were a failure and came to an abrupt end shortly afterwards. Throughout 1991 and 1992, the war of attrition continued without decisive military developments or peace manoeuvres. The Tigers are evidently willing to continue their struggle indefinitely. In the summer of 1992, the Government was awaiting the deliberations of a multi-party committee established to work out a basis for a dialogue with the Tigers. The Tamil cause suffered a political setback during the same period following the assassination of Rajiv Ghandi for which the Tigers are widely held to be responsible: there followed a distinct cooling of support for them in the south of India, upon which the Tigers rely heavily for training and logistics support, followed in 1992 by their outlawing by the Indian government.
GOVERNMENT: Executive and legislative power are vested in the President and a single chamber assembly respectively. The President is directly elected for a 6-year term. The 255-member assembly is elected by proportional representation.

CLIMATE

Tropical climate. Upland areas are cooler and more temperate and coastal areas are cooled by sea breezes. There are two monsoons, which occur May to July and December to January.
Required clothing: Lightweights and rainwear.

NUWARA ELIYA Sri Lanka (1880m)

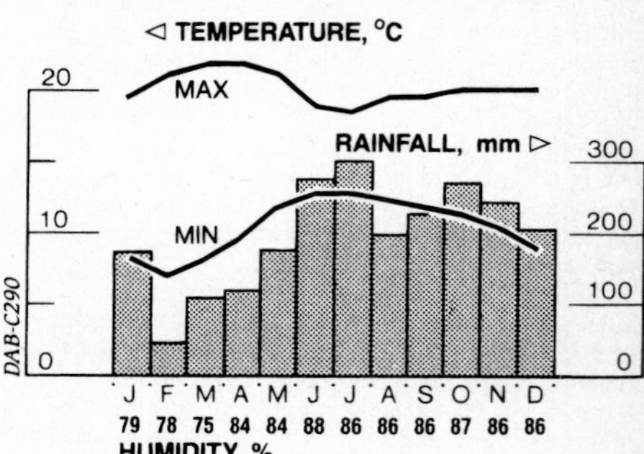

COLOMBO Sri Lanka (7m)

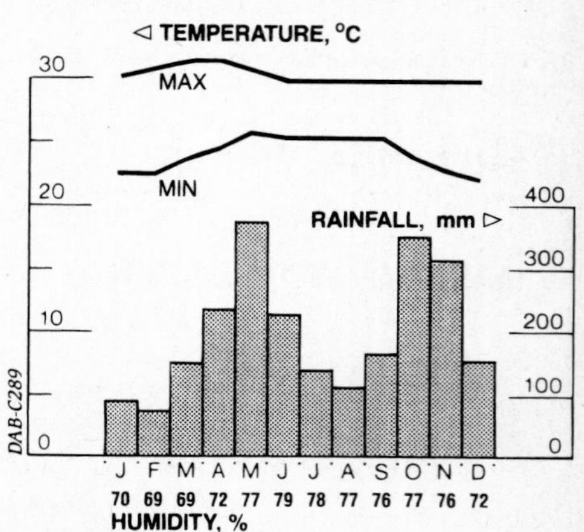

SUDAN

Location: Northeast Africa.

Public Corporation of Tourism and Hotels
PO Box 7104
Khartoum, Sudan
Tel: 74053. Telex: 22203.

Embassy of the Democratic Republic of Sudan
3 Cleveland Row
St James' Street
London SW1A 1DD
Tel: (071) 839 8080. Fax: (071) 839 7560. Opening hours: 0900-1600 Monday to Friday.

British Embassy
PO Box 801
Street 10
Off Sharia Al Baladiya
Khartoum East, Sudan
Tel: 70760/6/9. Telex: 22189 PRDM SD.

Embassy of the Democratic Republic of Sudan
2210 Massachusetts Avenue, NW
Washington, DC
20008
Tel: (202) 338 8565/6/7. Fax: (202) 667 2406.

Embassy of the United States of America
PO Box 699
Sharia Ali Abdul Latif
Khartoum, Sudan
Tel: 74700 *or* 74611. Telex: 22619 AMEM SD.

Embassy of the Democratic Republic of Sudan
Suite 407
85 Range Road
Ottawa, Ontario
K1N 8J6
Tel: (613) 235 4000. Fax: (613) 235 6880.

The Canadian Embassy in Ethiopia deals with enquiries relating to Sudan:
c/o The Canadian Embassy
PO Box 1130
6th Floor, African Solidarity Insurance Building
Churchill Avenue
Addis Ababa, Ethiopia
Tel: (1) 511 343 *or* 511 228 *or* 511 319. Fax: (1) 512 818.
Telex: 21053 DOMCAN ET.

AREA: 2,505,813 sq km (967,500 sq miles).
POPULATION: 23,797,000 (1988 estimate).
POPULATION DENSITY: 9.5 per sq km.
CAPITAL: Khartoum. **Population:** 476,218 (1983).
GEOGRAPHY: Sudan is bordered by Egypt to the north, the Red Sea to the northeast, Ethiopia to the east, Kenya, Uganda and Zaïre to the south, the Central African Republic and Chad to the west and Libya to the northwest. There is a marked difference between the climate, culture and geography of northern and southern Sudan. The far north consists of the contiguous Libyan and Nubian Deserts which extend as far south as the capital, Khartoum, and are barren except for small areas beside the Nile River and a few scattered oases. This gives way to the central steppes which cover the country between 15°N and 10°N, a region of short, coarse grass and bushes, turning to open savannah towards the south, largely flat to the east but rising to two large plateaux in the west and south, the Janub Darfur (3088m/10,131ft) and Janub Kordofan (500m/1640ft) respectively. Most of Sudan's agriculture occurs in these latitudes in a fertile pocket between the Blue and White Niles which meet at Khartoum. South of the steppes is a vast shallow basin traversed by the White Nile and its tributaries, with the Sudd, a 120,000 sq km (46,332 sq miles) marshland, in the centre. This gives way to equatorial forest towards the south, rising to jungle-clad mountains on the Ugandan border, the highest being Mount Kinyeti, at 3187m (10,465ft).
LANGUAGE: Arabic is the official language. English and many local dialects are widely spoken.
RELIGION: Muslim in the north; Christian and traditional Animist religions in the south.
TIME: GMT + 2.
ELECTRICITY: 240 volts AC, 50Hz.
COMMUNICATIONS: Telephone: IDD is available. Country code: 249. **Telex/telegram:** Central telegraph office is open at Khartoum (Gamma Avenue) 24 hours a day including holidays. Telex facilities at main post offices. All previous three digit numbers are now preceeded by 22. **Post:** Post offices are open 0830-1200 and 1730-1830 Saturday to Thursday. Airmail to Europe takes up to a week. **Press:** The main dailies are *El Sudan*, *El Watini* and *El Muslaha*. There is an English-language magazine called *Sudan Now*.
BBC World Service and Voice of America frequencies: From time to time these change. See the section *How to Use this Book* for more information.

BBC:				
MHz	21.47	17.64	15.07	9.410
Voice of America:				
MHz	21.49	15.60	9.525	6.035

PASSPORT/VISA

Regulations and requirements may be subject to change at short notice, and you are advised to contact the appropriate diplomatic or consular authority before finalising travel arrangements. Details of these may be found at the head of this country's entry. Any numbers in the chart refer to the footnotes below.

	Passport Required?	Visa Required?	Return Ticket Required?
Full British	Yes	Yes	Yes
BVP	Not valid	-	-
Australian	Yes	Yes	Yes
Canadian	Yes	Yes	Yes
USA	Yes	Yes	Yes
Other EC	Yes	Yes	Yes
Japanese	Yes	Yes	Yes

Restricted entry: The Sudanese authorities refuse entry and transit to nationals of Israel, South Africa and holders of passports that contain visas for Israel or South Africa (either valid or expired).
PASSPORTS: Valid passport required by all. Passport must have been valid for at least 6 months.
British Visitors Passport: Not accepted.
VISAS: Required by all except nationals of Sudan, Egypt and Tanzania.
Types of visa: Tourist or Business; cost: £20 (postal order, company cheque or cash).
Validity: 3 months from the date of issue. Enquire at Embassy.
Transit visa: Required by all passengers who continue their journey to a third country within 24 hours by the same or first connecting aircraft. Visitors must remain in the airport and must hold confirmed reservations and the necessary documents for their onward journey. There is no hotel accommodation at the airport.
Application to: Consulate (or Consular Section at Embassy). For addresses, see top of entry.
Application requirements: (a) 2 completed application forms. (b) 2 photographs. (c) Fee. (d) Company letter or invitation from Sudan for Business visas. (e) Return/onward ticket. (f) Travellers cheques for Tourist visas.
Working days required: 7 days to 3 weeks.
Temporary residence: Enquire at Embassy.
Note: Special permits are required for travel to all parts of Sudan, apart from the capital, they are obtainable from the Passport and Immigration office in Khartoum. Two days should be allowed for the issue of a permit.

MONEY

Currency: Sudanese Pound (Sud£) = 100 piastres. Notes are in denominations of Sud£20, 10, 5 and 1, and 50 and 25 piastres. Coins are in denominations of 10, 5, 2 and 1 piastres. There are also a number of commemorative coins in circulation.
Credit cards: American Express is widely accepted, Diners Club and Access/Mastercard have more limited use. Check with your credit card company for merchant acceptance and other services which may be available.
Travellers cheques: These have limited acceptance, and should be in a major currency.
Exchange rate indicators: The following figures are included as a guide to the movements of the Sudanese Pound against Sterling and the US Dollar:

Date:	Oct '89	Oct '90	Oct '91	Oct '92
£1.00=	7.11	8.78	7.82	15.82
$1.00=	4.51	4.49	4.51	9.97

Currency restrictions: There is no limit on the import and export of foreign currency, subject to declaration. The import and export of local currency is prohibited.
Banking hours: 0830-1200 Saturday to Thursday.

DUTY FREE

The following items may be imported into Sudan by visitors over 10 years of age without incurring customs duty:
200 cigarettes or 50 cigars or 225g of tobacco;
Perfume and toilet water for personal use.
Prohibited items: The import of goods from South Africa and Israel is prohibited. Sudan also adheres to the list of prohibited goods drawn up by the Arab League and these include alcoholic beverages.

PUBLIC HOLIDAYS

Public holidays observed in Sudan are as follows:
Mar 3 '93 Unity Day. **Mar 25** Eid al-Fitr (End of Ramadan). **Apr 6** Uprising Day. **Apr 19** Sham an-Nassim (Coptic Easter Monday). **Jun 1** Eid al-Adha (Feast of the Sacrifice). **Jun 21** Islamic New Year. **Jul 1** Decentralisation Day. **Aug 30** Mouloud (Prophet's Birthday). **Dec 25** Christmas. **Jan 1 '94** Independence Day. **Mar** Start of Eid al-Fitr. **Mar 3** Unity Day.
Note: Muslim festivals are timed according to local sightings of various phases of the Moon and the dates given above are approximations. During the lunar month of Ramadan that precedes Eid al-Fitr, Muslims fast during the day and feast at night and normal business patterns may be interrupted. Many restaurants are closed during the day and there may be restrictions on smoking and drinking. Some disruption may continue into Eid al-Fitr itself. Eid al-Fitr and Eid al-Adha may last anything from two to ten days, depending on the region. For more information see the section *World of Islam* at the back of the book.

HEALTH

Regulations and requirements may be subject to change at short notice, and you are advised to contact your doctor well in advance of your intended date of departure. Any numbers in the chart refer to the footnotes below.

	Special Precautions?	Certificate Required?
Yellow Fever	1	1
Cholera	Yes	2
Typhoid & Polio	Yes	-
Malaria	3	-
Food & Drink	4	-

[1]: The risk of yellow fever is primarily in the equatorial south. A yellow fever vaccination certificate is required from travellers over one year of age arriving from infected areas, and may be required from travellers leaving Sudan. Those countries and areas formerly classified as endemic zones are considered by the Sudanese authorities to be infected areas.
[2]: Following WHO guidelines issued in 1973, a cholera vaccination certificate is no longer a condition of entry to Sudan. However, cholera is a serious risk in the country and precautions are essential. Up-to-date advice should be sought before deciding whether these precautions should include vaccination as medical opinion is divided over its effectiveness. See the *Health* section at the back of the book.
[3]: Malaria risk, predominantly in the malignant *falciparum* form, exists throughout the year throughout the country. High resistance to chloroquine had been reported.
[4]: All water should be regarded as being a potential health risk. Water used for drinking, brushing teeth or making ice should have first been boiled or otherwise sterilised. Milk is unpasteurised and should be boiled. Powdered or tinned milk is available and is advised but make sure that it is reconstituted with pure water. Avoid dairy products which are likely to have been made from unboiled milk. Only eat well-cooked meat

and fish, preferably served hot. Pork, salad and mayonnaise may carry increased risk. Vegetables should be cooked and fruit peeled.
Rabies is present. For those at high risk vaccination before arrival should be considered. If you are bitten abroad seek medical advice without delay. For more information consult the *Health* section at the back of the book.
Bilharzia (schistosomiasis) is present. Avoid swimming and paddling in fresh water. Swimming pools which are well-chlorinated and maintained are safe.
Visceral leishmaniasis is currently highly endemic in the country. Vaccination is strongly recommended. The disease is transferred through sandflies which mainly occur on river banks and in wooded areas.
Health care: Medical treatment may be free at certain establishments but health insurance is essential and should include cover for emergency repatriation. Medical facilities are limited outside Khartoum.

TRAVEL - International

AIR: The national airline is *Sudan Airways (SD)*.
Approximate flight time: From *London* to Khartoum is 8 hours, including stopover.
International airport: *Khartoum (KRT)* (Civil), 4km (2.5 miles) southeast of the city (travel time – 20 minutes). Taxi services are available with a surcharge after 2200. There are full duty-free facilities at Khartoum airport.
Departure tax: Sud£50 is levied on international departures. Transit passengers and children under two years are exempt.
SEA: The only sea port is Port Sudan on the Red Sea, served by passenger lines from Europe *(Polish Ocean Lines)*, the USA *(Hellenic Lines)* and several African countries. *Sudan River Transport Corporation* operates regular Nile cruises from Aswan and Abu Simbel in Egypt, calling at Wadi Halfa. There are services from Saudi Arabia and Yemen *(Fayez Trading Company* and *Mohammed Sadaka Establishment Company)*.
RAIL: Rail links run from Cairo (Egypt) to Aswan High Dam and then by riverboat to Wadi Halfa.
ROAD: Sudan can be reached by road from Egypt, Libya, Chad, Uganda and the Central African Republic. Entry via Ethiopia is at present not possible. Motorists must apply for permission to drive through Sudan well in advance. Applications must be made to government representatives abroad or in Khartoum, listing vehicle and passenger details, with documents from a recognised automobile club or guarantee from a bank or business firm.

TRAVEL - Internal

Note: Travel to the southern provinces is restricted; see *Passport/Visa* section above.
AIR: *Sudan Airways (SD)* run services to 20 airports, including Dongola, Juba, Port Sudan and El Obeid. The most reliable route is Port Sudan to Khartoum. There is also an air-taxi service operating twice weekly to Nyala, available from Khartoum.
Departure tax: Sud£30 on domestic flights.
SEA: River steamers serve all towns on the Nile but conditions are mostly unsuitable for tourist travel. Services depend on fluctuating water levels. It is advisable to take food and water. Destinations include Dongola, Karima, Kosti and Juba. A 320km (200 miles) navigable canal, the *Jonglei*, is under construction in the south.
RAIL: Sudan has an extensive rail network but the service is extremely slow and uncomfortable. There are three normal classes of travel plus *mumtaza* (deluxe). Sleeping cars are available on main routes from Khartoum to Wau/Nyala, Khartoum to Kassala/Wadi Halfa and Port Sudan to Khartoum. There are a few air-conditioned carriages, for which a supplement is charged.
ROAD: Only a small proportion of roads are asphalted; road conditions are poor outside towns and roads to the north are often closed during the rainy season (July to September). Due to the bad conditions, a full set of spare parts should be carried for long journeys, and vehicles must be in good working condition. **Bus:** Services run between the main towns and depart from the market places. *Souk* (market) lorries are a cheap but uncomfortable method of transport. **Taxi:** These can be found at ranks or hailed in the street. Taxis are not metered, fares must be agreed in advance. **Car hire:** Available in the main towns and at major hotels but charges are high. **Documentation:** *Carnet de Passage*, adequate finance and roadworthiness certificate (from Sudanese Embassy) are all needed. An International Driving Permit is recommended, although not legally required. A temporary driving licence is available from local authorities on presentation of a valid British or Northern Ireland driving licence. Trailers and cars of less than 1500cc are refused entry.
URBAN: Publicly-operated bus services in Khartoum have of late become unreliable and irregular which has led to the proliferation of private *bakassi* minibuses, nicknamed *boks*. They pick up and set down with no fixed stops. These operations are on the fringes of legality and should be used with care.

ACCOMMODATION

HOTELS: Accommodation is scarce outside Khartoum and Port Sudan. Khartoum has 11 medium-sized hotels, including some of international standard, and Port Sudan has three. There are a few smaller hotels in the main towns and several hostels.
YOUTH HOSTELS: Contact the Youth Hostel Association, PO Box 1705, Khartoum. Tel: 81464 *or* 22087.

RESORTS & EXCURSIONS

Sudan has only recently been developed as a tourist destination and communications and facilities are still limited outside Khartoum. Travel restrictions are also in force in much of the country (see *Passport/Visa* section above) due to the presence of separatist insurgents.
KHARTOUM: The capital is situated at the confluence of the Blue and White Niles. With **Omdurman**, the old national capital, and **Khartoum North**, it forms one unit called the 'three towns capital'. Among the tourist attractions are the Omdurman camel market and the Arab *souk*, where the visitor may find every item of local handicraft from carved ebony to leather work and silver and gold jewellery. A good selection of Sudanese handicrafts is sold in several shops in the centre and in the reception halls of some of the bigger hotels.
Particularly noteworthy from an historic and artistic point of view is a visit to the well-organised *National Museum* which contains archaeological treasures dating back to 4000BC and earlier. A visit to the *Khalifa's House Museum* will reward those who are interested in Sudan's more recent history, especially the reign of the Mahdi (1881-1899).
Excursions: A visit to the Gezira model farm or a trip along the Nile to the dam at *Jebel Aulia*, where the Nile is especially rich in fish. Sunset on the river is spectacular.
THE NORTH & EAST: The main areas of archaeological interest in Sudan are to be found beside the Nile north of Khartoum. They include **Bajrawiya, Naga, Musawarat, El Kurru, Nuri** and **Meroe.**
The Zinder National Park, covering 6475 sq km (2500 sq miles) southeast of Khartoum on the Ethiopian border, is one of the largest in the world. There are many species of wild animals, including lions, giraffes, leopards, kudus, bushbuck and antelope, and birds such as guinea fowl, vultures, pelicans, storks, kingfishers and the beautiful crown crane. Special three-day trips from Khartoum are organised in the high season (December to April).
The Red Sea, with the transparency of its water, the variety of its fish and the charm of its marine gardens and coral reefs, is one of Sudan's main tourist attractions. The busy **Port Sudan, Suakin,** famous during the Ottoman era, and the **Arous Tourist Village,** 50km (30 miles) north of Port Sudan, are just three centres from which to explore the coast. **Erkowit,** 1200m (3930ft) above sea-level, is a beautiful resort in the coastal mountains and is renowned for its evergreen vegetation.
THE WEST: Jebel Marra, at more than 3088m (10,100ft), is the highest peak in the Darfur region of western Sudan. It is a region of outstanding scenic beauty, with waterfalls and volcanic lakes and a pleasant climate, and consequently a favoured resort.
THE SOUTH: The Southern Provinces are characterised by green forests, open parkland, waterfalls and treeless swamps abounding with birds and wild animals such as elephants, black and white rhinos, common elands, Nile lechwes, lesser kudus, bisa oryxes, zebras, crocodiles, hippos, hyenas, buffaloes and the almost extinct shoebill. The **Gemmeiza Tourist Village,** situated in the heart of East Equatoria, is considered of special interest, owing to the abundance of game in that area.
Note: The people of the south are largely Christian and this has led to friction with the ruling Muslim factions in the north. Civil war is a constant threat. Check with the Embassy before travelling if you intend to visit this region (see also the*Passport/Visa* section above).

SOCIAL PROFILE

FOOD & DRINK: The staple diet is *fool*, a type of bean, and *dura*, cooked maize or millet, which are eaten with various vegetables. The hotel restaurants in Khartoum and Port Sudan serve international cuisine and there are a few Greek and Middle Eastern restaurants. If invited to a Sudanese home more exotic food will usually be served. Alcohol is banned by the Islamic *Sharia* code.
NIGHTLIFE: The best entertainment is found in Khartoum and Omdurman, with a national theatre, music hall, cinemas, open air and hotel entertainment.
SHOPPING: The *souk* has stalls selling food, local crafts, spices, cheap jewellery and silver. Special purchases include basketwork, ebony, gold and silver and assorted handicrafts. Visitors must not buy cheetah skins: the slaughter of cheetahs is prohibited and they are a protected species under the World Wildlife Act. **Shopping hours:** 0800-1330 and 1730-2000 Saturday to Thursday.
SPORT: There is great scope for **watersports** on the Red Sea coast, including **swimming, skindiving** on coral reefs and **fishing** for barracuda, sharks and grey cod.
SOCIAL CONVENTIONS: In the north Arab culture predominates while the people in the more fertile south belong to many diverse tribes, each with their own lifestyle and beliefs. Because Sudan is largely Muslim, women should not wear revealing clothing. Official and social functions and some restaurants will expect formal clothes to be worn. The Sudanese have a great reputation for hospitality. **Tipping:** Not customary.

BUSINESS PROFILE

ECONOMY: Once described as the bread basket of the Arab world, Sudan is a country of high, though largely unrealised, economic potential which is presently crippled by repeated droughts, civil war and a massive foreign debt. Agriculture employs most of the workforce producing cotton – the major export – wheat, groundnuts, sorghum and sugar cane. Gum arabic, once important, has declined through the introduction of synthetic substitutes and increasing competition, particularly from West Africa. So has

SUDAN	HEALTH REGULATIONS	VISA REGULATIONS (Code-Link)
GALILEO/WORLDSPAN	TI-DFT/KRT/HE	TI-DFT/KRT/VI
SABRE	TIDFT/KRT/HE	 TIDFT/KRT/VI

To access this information on your CRS, swipe the barcode with a light pen or type in the text under the barcode. For more information, see the introduction *How to Use This Book.*

.vestock breeding, mainly because of drought. The mall manufacturing sector concentrates on processing he country's agricultural output – sugar refining, for xample – and the production of consumer goods such s textiles, cigarettes and batteries. There are commer-ially significant, though not vast oil deposits but arnings from these have been depressed by the low vorld oil price. Other mineral deposits have been ocated but have yet to be fully exploited. Sudan's rade has fallen sharply since the early 1980s, because f a chronic shortage of foreign exchange. What esources the Government can muster are devoted to neeting repayments of Sudan's US$15 billion foreign lebt. Saudi Arabia is the largest exporter to Sudan, ollowed by the UK, Italy, the USA and Germany. British exports to Sudan in 1989 were valued at JS$135 million (9%). Sudan finds markets for its xports in Egypt, Saudi Arabia, Italy and Japan. Foreign aid is vital to stave off total economic collapse.

BUSINESS: Businessmen should wear a lightweight uit. Muslim customs should be respected by visiting business people. English is widely spoken in business ircles although knowledge of a few words of Arabic will be well received. Punctuality is less important han patience and politeness. Personal introductions re an advantage; business cards should have an Arabic translation on the reverse. **Office hours:** 0830-1300 Saturday to Thursday.

COMMERCIAL INFORMATION: The following organisations can offer advice: Sudan Development Corporation, PO Box 710, 21 al-Amarat. Khartoum. Tel: 42425. Fax: 40473. Telex: 24078 SDC SD; *or* Sudan Chamber of Commerce, PO Box 81, Khartoum. Tel: 72346.

HISTORY & GOVERNMENT

HISTORY: The provinces of Nubia, Senaar and Kordofan which make up modern Sudan were conquered by the Egyptians in a campaign between 1820 and 1822. In the 1880s, the country fell under British and Egyptian control. Local resistance at this time was led by the legendary Mahdi Mohammed Ahmed, who defeated first a British-led force of Egyptian troops in 1883. He retained control of Sudan until the British reconquered the territory in 1898. An Anglo-Egyptian condominium was established in 1899. In 1914, Egypt itself was made a British protectorate and Sudan taken under British rule accordingly. When the protectorate was dissolved in 1922, the future of Sudan was left open subject to further negotiations, but a condominium was restored in 1929. A further Anglo-Egyptian treaty in 1936 allowed Egyptian troops and civilian immigrants to enter Sudan without restriction. After the Second World War, Sudan became the subject of serious contention between Britain and Egypt. Efforts to co-opt Sudan under Egyptian control in 1951 were firmly resisted by the Sudanese. The overthrow of King Farouk in 1952 brought to power a radical republican government, led by Colonel Gamal Abdel Nasser, which was more sympathetic to Sudanese aspirations to independence. In 1952, Britain and Egypt agreed upon a constitution for Sudan allowing free elections and a referendum on independence which was granted in 1956. The Sudanese house of representatives, elected in November 1953, chose Abdullah Khalil, leader of the Umma (People's) Party to premiership. However, Khalil's government lasted less than two years before it was overthrown by army chief Ibrahim Abboud and his supporters. The Abboud regime fell in 1964, unseated by unrest throughout the country but especially in the south. Resenting the political domination of the predominately Muslim north, the mostly Christian and animist southerners launched an insurrection against the Khartoum government. In a pattern to be repeated time and again, the new regime held talks with southern leaders and offered limited autonomy; the south rejected the terms as inadequate. Fighting resumed and continued for the next five years. During that time a general election brought to power a civilian government under Mohammed Ahmed Mahgoub. In May 1969, Mahgoub was deposed in a military coup in which Jafaar al-Nimeri became President. Nimeri negotiated a settlement in 1972 with the south. But when it collapsed 1983, it signalled the beginning of the end for Nimeri himself. The main cause was the introduction of Islamic *Sharia* law, intended to placate increasingly troublesome Muslim elements complaining about the austerity programme introduced on the instructions of the IMF earlier in the year. Not surprisingly, it was not well received in the south, and was later withdrawn. Soon afterwards, the southerners returned to fully-fledged armed struggle under the banner of the Sudanese People's Liberation Front (SPLF) and its military arm, the Sudanese People's Liberation Army (SPLA), led by John Garang. Nimeri was deposed by a coup while he visited the United States. The general election which followed returned Sudan to civilian rule under a coalition government headed by Sadiq al-Mahdi (a descendant of the 19th-century Mahdi), but the Government seemed unable to tackle the inherited problems of debt, famine and the war in the south. Severe droughts in 1986, 1987 and 1988 were followed by a flood that devastated the crucial agricultural regions. Another military coup in July 1989 toppled the civilian government and brought a group of second-ranking army officers, led by Brigadier Omar Hassan Ahmed al-Bashir, to power. Their political programme was vague beyond a general commitment to sue for peace with the SPLF. Their terms were clearly inadequate for the rebels, as in January 1990 the southern town of Juba came under siege by the SPLF. Two coup attempts in April and September 1990, both organised by dissident army elements, were crushed, but the Government was otherwise able to do little to alleviate the country's problems. Sharia was once again introduced at the beginning of 1991. An accommodation with the SPLF may still be possible, despite the Government's Islamic persuasion. Talks between the two sides opened in the Nigerian capital, Abuja, in October 1991 under the auspices of the Organisation of African Unity. The Government found itself in a stronger position than for some time; its acquisition of new friends abroad contrasted with a damaging split in the opposition: the loyalist 'Torit' faction, mostly Dinka tribespeople, which stayed with Garang; and the breakaway 'Nasir' faction led by Riek Machar who are predominantly from the Nu'er tribe. The SPLA had, moreover, lost one of its principal foreign backers in President Mengistu of Ethiopia. During 1992, repeated attempts at negotiation have quickly broken down, and the Government made important military gains in the dry season offensive. This war is, though, far from over.

GOVERNMENT: An interim constitution was agreed prior to the 1986 elections under which legislative power was vested in the National Assembly. Executive power was wielded by a Council of Ministers, headed by a Prime Minister and responsible to the National Assembly. A Supreme Council, comprising the Prime Minister and five others, acts collectively as Head of State.

CLIMATE

Extremely hot (less so November to March). Sandstorms blow across the Sahara from April to September. In the extreme north there is little rain but the central region has some rainfall from July to August. The southern region has much higher rainfall, the wet season lasting May to October. Summers are very hot throughout the country, whilst winters are cooler in the north.

Required clothing: Tropical clothes all year, warmer clothes for cool morning and evenings (especially in the desert).

KHARTOUM Sudan (380m)

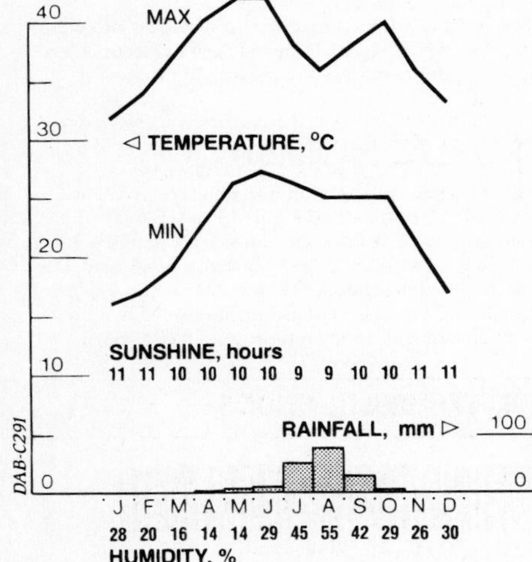

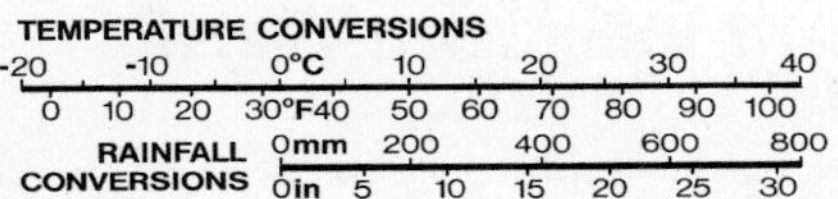

SURINAME

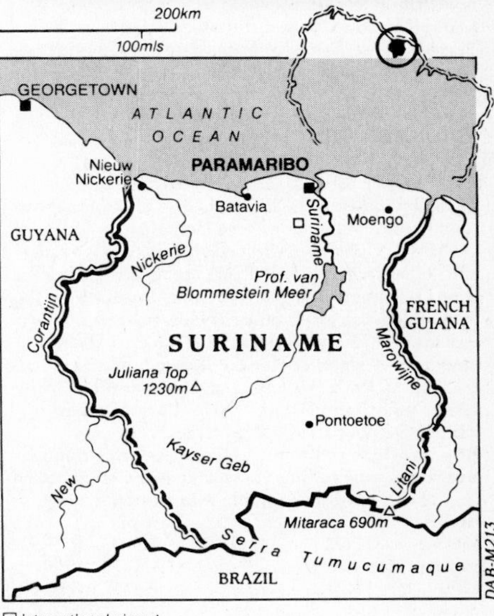

Location: North coast of South America.

Suriname Tourism and Catering Department
PO Box 656
Waterkant 8
Paramaribo
Suriname
Tel: 71163. Telex: 118.

Embassy of the Republic of Suriname
Alexander Gogelweg 2
2517 JH The Hague
The Netherlands
Tel: (70) 650 844. Fax: (70) 617 445. Telex: 32220.

Consulaat-Generaal van de Republick Suriname
De Cuserstraat 11
1081 CK Amsterdam
The Netherlands
Tel: (20) 642 6137 *or* 642 6717.

British Honorary Consulate
c/o VSH United Buildings
PO Box 1300
Van't Hogerhuysstraat
Paramaribo
Suriname
Tel: 72870. Fax: 75515. Telex: 144 UNITED SN.

Embassy of the Republic of Suriname
Suite 108, Van Ness Centre
4301 Connecticut Avenue, NW
Washington, DC
20008
Tel: (202) 244 7488 *or* 244 7490/1/2. Fax: (202) 244 5878. Telex: 892656.
Consulate General in: Miami.
Also deals with enquiries from Canada.

Embassy of the United States of America
PO Box 1821
Dr Sophie Redmondstraat 129
Paramaribo
Suriname
Tel: 72900. Fax: 10025. Telex: 373 AMEM SU SN.

The Canadian High Commission in Guyana deals with enquiries relating to Suriname:

Canadian High Commission
PO Box 10880
High and Young Streets
Georgetown, Guyana
Tel: (2) 72081/5 *or* 58337. Fax: (2) 58380. Telex: 2215 DOMCAN GY.

AREA: 163,265 sq km (63,037 sq miles).
POPULATION: 394,768 (1987 estimate).
POPULATION DENSITY: 2.4 per sq km.
CAPITAL: Paramaribo. **Population:** 150,000 (1988 estimate).
GEOGRAPHY: Suriname is bordered to the north by

the Atlantic Ocean, to the east by the Marowijne River which separates it from French Guiana, to the west by the Corantijn River dividing it from Guyana, and to the south by forests and savannas which separate it from Brazil. In the northern part of the country are coastal lowlands covered with mangrove swamps. Further inland runs a narrow strip of savannah land. To the south the land becomes hilly and then mountainous, covered with dense tropical forest, and cut by numerous rivers and streams.

LANGUAGE: Dutch is the official language. 'Negro English' *(Taki-Taki* or *Sranan Tongo)*, originating in Creole, is the popular language. The other main languages are Hindi and Javanese. English, Chinese, French and Spanish are also spoken.

RELIGION: 45% Christian, 27% Hindu, 18% Muslim.

TIME: GMT - 3.

ELECTRICITY: 127/220 volts AC, 60Hz. European round 2-pin plugs. Screw-type lamp fittings.

COMMUNICATIONS: Telephone: IDD is available. Country code: 597. There are no area codes. **Telex/telegram:** Telegrams can only be sent from the government telegraph office at Gravenstraat 33, Paramaribo. International telex services available. Only a few post offices have telegram facilities outside the capital. **Post:** Airmail to and from Europe usually takes a month or longer to arrive. **Press:** Dailies include *De West* and *De Ware Tijd*.

BBC World Service and Voice of America frequencies: From time to time these change. See the section *How to Use this Book* for more information.

BBC:				
MHz	17.72	11.78	9.590	5.975
Voice of America:				
MHz	15.21	11.74	9.815	6.030

PASSPORT/VISA

Regulations and requirements may be subject to change at short notice, and you are advised to contact the appropriate diplomatic or consular authority before finalising travel arrangements. Details of these may be found at the head of this country's entry. Any numbers in the chart refer to the footnotes below.

	Passport Required?	Visa Required?	Return Ticket Required?
Full British	Yes	No	Yes
BVP	Not Valid	-	-
Australian	Yes	Yes	Yes
Canadian	Yes	Yes	Yes
USA	Yes	Yes	Yes
Other EC	Yes	1	Yes
Japanese	Yes	No	Yes

PASSPORTS: Valid passport required by all.

British Visitors Passport: Not accepted.

VISAS: Required by all except:

(a) **[1]** nationals of Denmark and the UK (all other EC nationals *do* require visas);

(b) nationals of Antigua & Barbuda, Brazil, Chile, Dominican Republic, Ecuador, Finland, Gambia, Grenada, Guyana, Japan, Netherland Antilles, Norway, St Lucia, South Korea, Sweden, Switzerland, Trinidad & Tobago and Venezuela.

Those exempted above do, however, require 60-day Tourist Cards, which are issued on arrival for a fee of S Gld25 to those able to present a valid passport, 1 passport photograph and onward or return tickets. For stays of over 60 days, enquire at a Suriname mission (see below).

Transit visas: Not required by those continuing their journey to a third country by the same or the first connecting aircraft.

Visa applications: Those requiring visas should apply to:

(a) Suriname missions in Belgium or The Netherlands if holding a West European passport;

(b) Suriname missions in Belgium, Guyana or The Netherlands if holding an East European passport;

(c) any Suriname mission if holding an Asian or African passport;

(d) the Suriname mission in Washington DC or Miami if holding a North, Central or South American passport;

(e) the office of *Suriname Airways* in Curaçao, NA, if holding a Caribbean passport (other offices of *Suriname Airways* may in some circumstances be able to issue visas to would-be visitors from the Caribbean and elsewhere, but check well in advance of the intended departure date).

Cost: For further information enquire at the appropriate office.

Application requirements: (a) 1 completed application form. (b) 1 passport photo. (c) A passport that is valid for at least 3 months. (d) A valid ticket.

Working days required: 1-6 weeks, although applications can be processed in approximately 1 week if this is necessary.

MONEY

Currency: Suriname Guilder (S Gld) = 100 cents. Notes are in denominations of S Gld500, 250, 100, 25, 10 and 5. Coins are in denominations of S Gld2.5 and 1, and 25, 10, 5 and 1 cents.

Currency exchange: Suriname Guilders and cents are the only legal tender. Banks and some hotels are authorised to exchange money.

Credit cards: American Express is the most widely accepted credit card; Diners Club has limited acceptance. Check with your credit card company for merchant acceptability and other facilities which may be available.

Travellers cheques: Must be changed at banks.

Exchange rate indicators: The following figures are included as a guide to the movements of the Suriname Guilder against Sterling and the US Dollar:

Date:	Oct '89	Oct '90	Oct '91	Oct '92
£1.00=	2.82	3.48	3.10	2.82
$1.00=	1.79	1.78	1.79	1.78

Currency restrictions: The import and export of local currency is limited to S Gld100. Foreign currency must be declared if it exceeds the equivalent of S Gld5000. On departure, the imported currency can be exported again, providing an exchange permit is produced.

Banking hours: 0730-1400 Monday to Friday.

DUTY FREE

The following items may be imported into Suriname without incurring customs duty:

400 cigarettes or 100 cigars or 200 cigarillos or 500g of tobacco;
2 litres of spirits;
4 litres of wine;
50g of perfume;
1 litre of toilet water;
8 rolls of unexposed film;
60m of unexposed ciné film;
100m of unrecorded tape.

Prohibited items: Fruit (except that of reasonable quality from The Netherlands), meat and meat products, unless a valid health certificate is shown.

PUBLIC HOLIDAYS

Public holidays observed in Suriname are as follows: **Mar '93*** Phagwa. **Mar 25** Eid al-Fitr (End of Ramadan). **Apr 9-12** Easter. **May 1** Labour Day. **Jul 1** National Union Day. **Nov 25** Independence Day. **Dec 25-26** Christmas. **Jan 1 '94** New Year's Day. **Feb 25** Revolution Day. **Mar** Eid al-Fitr; Phagwa.

Note: (a) In addition, Chinese, Jewish and Indian businesses will be closed for their own religious holidays. (b) Muslim festivals are timed according to local sightings of various phases of the Moon and the dates given above are approximations. During the lunar month of Ramadan that precedes Eid al-Fitr, Muslims fast during the day and feast at night and normal business patterns may be interrupted. Many restaurants are closed during the day and there may be restrictions on smoking and drinking. Some disruption may continue into Eid al-Fitr itself, which may last anything from two to ten days, depending on the region. For more information see the section *World of Islam* at the back of the book. (c) [*] Hindu festivals are declared according to local astronomical observations and it is only possible to forecast the approximate time of their occurrence.

HEALTH

Regulations and requirements may be subject to change at short notice, and you are advised to contact your doctor well in advance of your intended date of departure. Any numbers in the chart refer to the footnotes below.

	Special Precautions?	Certificate Required?
Yellow Fever	Yes	1
Cholera	No	No
Typhoid & Polio	Yes	-
Malaria	2	-
Food & Drink	3	-

[1]: A yellow fever vaccination certificate is required from travellers arriving from infected areas.

[2]: Malaria risk throughout the year in the whole country excluding Paramaribo District and coastal areas north of 5°N. The predominant *falciparum* strain is reported to be 'highly resistant' to chloroquine and 'resistant' to sulfadoxine/pyrimethamine.

[3]: Mains water is normally chlorinated, and whilst relatively safe may cause mild abdominal upsets. Bottled water is available and is advised for the first few weeks of the stay. Drinking water outside main cities and towns is likely to be contaminated and sterilisation is considered essential. Milk is unpasteurised and should be boiled. Powdered or tinned milk is available and is advised, but make sure that it is reconstituted with pure water. Avoid dairy products which are likely to have been made from unboiled milk. Only eat well-cooked meat and fish, preferably served hot. Pork, salad and mayonnaise may carry increased risk. Vegetables should be cooked and fruit peeled.

Rabies is present. For those at high risk vaccination before arrival should be considered. If you are bitten abroad seek medical advice without delay. For more information consult the *Health* section at the back of the book.

Bilharzia (schistosomiasis) is present. Avoid swimming and paddling in fresh water. Swimming pools which are well-chlorinated and maintained are safe.

Health care: Health insurance is strongly recommended. There are five well-equipped hospitals in Paramaribo and a few in outlying areas.

TRAVEL - International

AIR: The national airline is *Suriname Airways (ALM)*. *KLM* and *Cruzeiro* also operate to Suriname.

Approximate flight time: From *London* to Paramaribo is 10 hours, excluding stopover time in Amsterdam or Miami, either of which may involve an overnight stay, due to a lack of connecting flights.

International airport: *Paramaribo (PBM)* (Zanderij) is 45km (28 miles) south of the city. A coach meets all arrivals. There are also buses or taxis to the city.

SEA: The main international port is Paramaribo. *Suriname Navigation Company* sails from New Orleans

SURINAME | **HEALTH REGULATIONS** | **VISA REGULATIONS** | Code-Link

GALILEO/WORLDSPAN — TI-DFT/PBM/HE — TI-DFT/PBM/VI

SABRE — TIDFT/PBM/HE — TIDFT/PBM/VI

To access this information on your CRS, swipe the barcode with a light pen or type in the text under the barcode. For more information, see the introduction *How to Use This Book.*

and Mexico monthly. There are coastal services between ports and services to The Netherlands and Germany. The *Royal Netherlands Steamship Company* provides a service from Amsterdam to Suriname with limited passenger accommodation. There are regular ferry services across the Suriname River and Marowijne River to French Guiana and across the Corantine River to Guyana.
RAIL: There is a weekly train from Ovenwacht to Bronsweg.
ROAD: The coastal road from Paramaribo serves the borders of Guyana and French Guiana.

TRAVEL - Internal

AIR: Domestic flights to towns in the interior are operated from Paramaribo and Zorg en Hoop by *Suriname Airways (ALM)*. They also provide services from Paramaribo to the Nieuw Nickerie district, and maintain a charter service.
Note: It is advisable to check the weather conditions before setting out for the interior, as heavy rains can cause delays.
ROAD: There is a reasonable, if patchy, road network. Drivers using their own cars should make sure they carry a full set of spares. **Bus:** There are services from the capital to most villages, with fixed routes at low prices. **Taxi:** Taxis are not metered, prices should be agreed before departure and tipping is unnecessary. **Car hire:** Available at airport and in Paramaribo through main hotels. **Documentation:** International Driving Permit is not required, but recommended.

ACCOMMODATION

HOTELS: Paramaribo has a number of modern hotels with air-conditioning, but advance booking is essential due to the limited number of beds. A 10% service charge is added. There are several small guest-houses and pensions in the city and elsewhere but it is advisable to check with the tourist office for further information. Hotels and restaurants are rare outside the capital, and travellers are advised to bring their own hammock and food.
CAMPING: Cola Creek and Blaka Watra are inland resorts where both picnic grounds and camping/bathing facilities are available.
YOUTH HOSTELS: There is a YWCA in Paramaribo.

RESORTS & EXCURSIONS

PARAMARIBO: The capital is graced with attractive Dutch colonial architecture. The nearby restored Fort Zeelandia houses the *Suriname Museum*. Other attractions include the 19th-century Roman Catholic cathedral (made entirely of wood), *Unity Square*, the *Presidential Palace* (with an attractive palm garden) and the lively waterfront and market districts. *Palmetuin* is a pleasant park, as is the *Cultuurtuin*, but the latter is a fair distance from the town and there are no buses.
ELSEWHERE: The countryside is sparsely populated, and the scenery and the tropical vegetation and wildlife provide the main attractions: mangrove swamps, rivers of all sizes, jungles and mountains, and jaguars, tapirs, snakes, tropical birds and giant sea turtles. There are no beaches. There are a number of nature reserves, including the *Raleighvallen/Noltzberg Nature Reserve* and *Brownsberg Nature Park*. Some offer accommodation in lodges.

SOCIAL PROFILE

FOOD & DRINK: Due to the diverse ethnic mixture of the population, Suriname offers a good variety of dishes including European, Indonesian, Creole, Chinese, Indian and American. Indonesian dishes are recommended, usually *rijsttafel* with rice (boiled or fried) and a number of spicy meat and vegetable side dishes, *nasi goreng* (Indonesian fried rice) and *bami goreng* (Indonesian fried noodles). Creole dishes include *pom* (ground tayer roots and poultry), *pastei* (chicken pie with various vegetables) and peanut soup. Indian dishes such as *roti* (dough pancake) served with curried chicken and potatoes and Chinese dishes such as *chow-mein* and *chop suey* are excellent. *Mocksie metie* (various meats served on rice) is a local favourite. Restaurants are rarely encountered outside the capital.
NIGHTLIFE: There are several nightclubs in Paramaribo, often attached to a hotel, with live music and dancing. There are also a number of discotheques and several cinemas including a drive-in. In general it is best to stick to the hotels unless accompanied by locals who know the reputations of other nightspots, in particular those out of the town centre. The *Local Events Bulletin* lists all current activities and is usually available in hotels.
SHOPPING: Popular items include Maroon tribal woodcarvings, hand-carved and hand-painted trays and gourds, bows and arrows, cotton hammocks, wicker and ceramic objects, gold and silver jewellery, Javanese bamboo and batik, as well as tobacco and liquor products. Chinese shops sell imported jade, silks, glass, dolls, needlework and wall decorations. **Shopping hours:** 0730-1600 Monday to Friday and 0730-1300 Saturday.
SPORT: Swimming: Besides the beaches (which are not of the highest standard), there are hotel pools and, in Paramaribo, there is a public pool. Visitors can also swim in the city's private clubs if introduced. **Tennis:** Some private clubs have tennis courts and games can be arranged through an introduction. Hotels provide further information. **Golf:** An 18-hole golf course is located 5km (3 miles) from Paramaribo on the airport road. **Sailing:** There are facilities at *Jachthaven Ornamibo*. **Fishing:** Tarpon and piranha offer excellent sport. **Spectator sports: Football** can be seen regularly at the Suriname Stadium and **basketball** matches are held at the Sports Hall (both in Paramaribo).
SOCIAL CONVENTIONS: Informal dress is suitable for most occasions. *Guayabera* or safari outfits are increasingly worn in place of jackets and ties. Women should wear long trousers on trips to the interior. Beachwear should be confined to the beach or poolside. **Photography:** It is inadvisable to photograph public places, particularly of a political or military nature (including police stations). There is a general sensitivity about the taking of photographs – it is advisable to seek prior permission. **Tipping:** Hotels include 10-15% service charge and restaurants may also add 10% to the bill.

BUSINESS PROFILE

ECONOMY: Until the civil war, aluminium and related industries provided over 75% of the country's foreign exchange earnings. Other raw materials include iron ore, copper, nickel, gold and platinum. The vast resources held within Suriname's extensive jungles remain largely untapped, although the timber industry is developing rapidly. There is great agricultural potential; rice, citrus fruits, sugar and bananas are the main crops. Shrimp fishing is both important and lucrative. There is a small manufacturing sector producing goods ranging from soap to telephone exchanges for the domestic market. Economic relations with The Netherlands, once crucial to the economy, suffered following the military takeover, and The Netherlands suspended its aid programme. By early 1987, the civil war had brought the aluminium industry to a standstill and destroyed crucial sectors of the country's infrastructure. The establishment of a transitional government restored some of the mother country's goodwill and aid resumed in February 1988. It was, however, suspended once again after a further military coup in December 1990 – and resumed again following the 1991 elections. The economy has since shown signs of improvement, generating a trade surplus, although there seems to be some danger of overheating as inflation has risen sharply from single-figure levels in the late 1980s. Suriname signed a loan agreement with Brazil in January 1988. The leading importers into Suriname are the USA, The Netherlands, Trinidad & Tobago and Brazil. Suriname has observer status within the Carribean trade bloc CARICOM.
BUSINESS: A suit is expected for business. **Office hours:** 0700-1500 Monday to Friday and 0700-1430 Saturday. **Government office hours:** 0700-1500 Monday to Thursday and 0700-1430 Saturday.
COMMERCIAL INFORMATION: The following organisation can offer advice: Suriname Chamber of Commerce and Industry, PO Box 149, Mr Dr J C de Mirandastraat 10, Paramaribo. Tel: 73527. Fax: 74779. Telex: 375.

HISTORY & GOVERNMENT

HISTORY: Discovered by the Spaniards in the late 15th century and later colonised by the Dutch, the country often changed hands between the French, English and Dutch before finally being confirmed as a Dutch possession by the terms of the Treaty of Vienna in 1815. In 1954 Suriname, with the Netherlands Antilles, became an autonomous region within the Kingdom of The Netherlands. Full independence was achieved in 1975. In February 1980, a National Military Council replaced the coalition government which had been in power since independence. The new regime followed a left-wing political line at the expense of those with The Netherlands and a ban on all political parties. The economic burden of the civil war which broke out between the regime and jungle-based dissident elements prompted the military regime to announce a return to civilian rule. A transitional constitution was agreed in March 1987 and elections in November gave 40 out of the 51 seats in the National Assembly to the Front for Democracy and Development. A ceasefire agreed with guerrillas for January 1988 was later withdrawn, but a settlement was finally reached with the guerrillas in 1992. Diplomatic relations with The Netherlands have see-sawed continually since the early 1980s, depending largely on the extent of Dutch aid. Following a dispute with the elected president, Ransewak Shankar, Lt-Col Bouterse launched another coup in 1990. The National Assembly rapidly approved a new government, dominated by the National Democratic Party (NDP) which, despite having won just two seats at the 1987 election, had the strong backing of the army. The elderly Johan Kraag was installed as President although in practice the Government was dominated by the vice-president and premier Jules Wijdenbosch. The next general election was held in May 1991. The New Front, successor to the Front for Democracy and Development, was again victorious, taking 30 out of 51 seats; the army-backed NDP did rather better than previously with 12 seats, while the 2-month-old Democratic Alternative '91 took a respectable nine seats. With the army managing to stay out of the main political arena, the all-important Dutch aid tap started to flow once again. Economic reform, particularly the reduction of state involvement, is now on top of the Government's agenda.
GOVERNMENT: The 51-seat National Assembly has legislative powers and is elected, along with the President, every four years. The National State Council, which includes members of the military, has an ill-defined 'advisory' role. The President is currently Ronald Venetiaan. The Vice-President and Prime Minister is Jules Adjodhia of the left-wing Progressive Reform Party, a constituent of the New Front alliance.

CLIMATE

Tropical climate cooled by the northeast tradewinds. The best time to visit is December to April. The hot season runs from May to October and has the highest rainfall.
Required clothing: Lightweights and rainwear.

PARAMARIBO Suriname (3m)

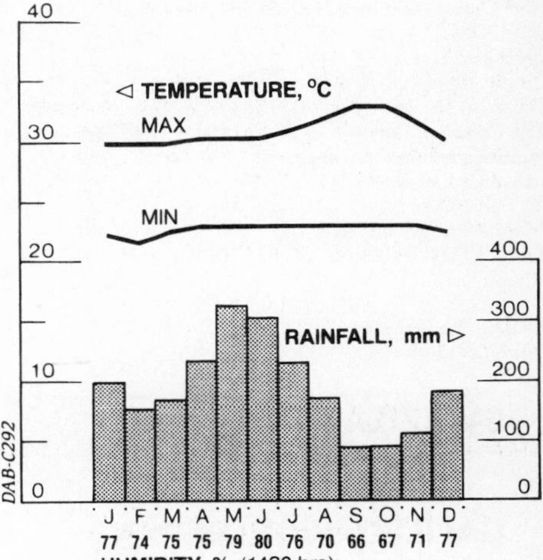

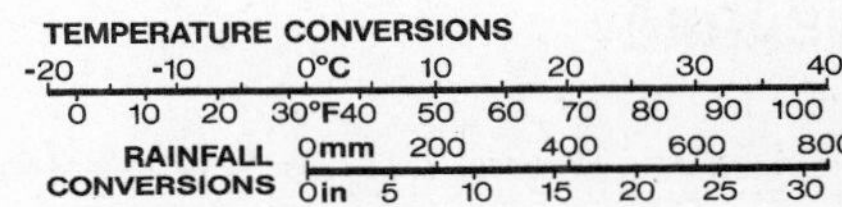

SWAZILAND

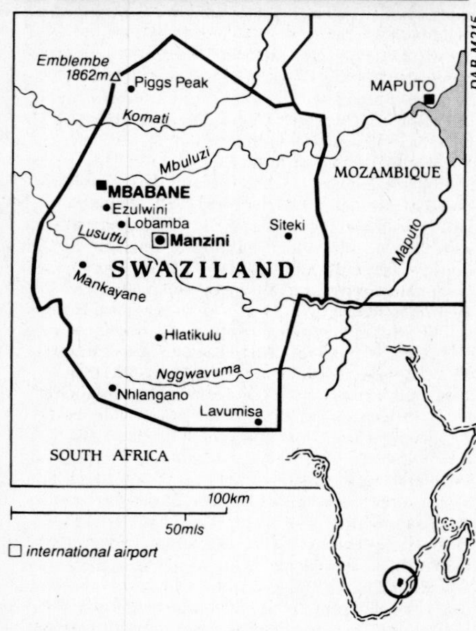

Location: Southern Africa.

Ministry of Broadcasting, Information and Tourism
PO Box 338
Mbabane, Swaziland.
Kingdom of Swaziland High Commission
58 Pont Street
London SW1X 0AE
Tel: (071) 581 4976/7/8. Fax: (071) 589 5332. Telex: 28853 SWAZI G. Opening hours: 0900-1630 Monday to Thursday and 0900-1600 Friday.
British High Commission
Allister Miller Street
Mbabane, Swaziland
Tel: 42581. Fax: 42585. Telex: 2079 WD.
Embassy of the Kingdom of Swaziland
3400 International Drive, NW
Washington, DC 20008
Tel: (202) 362 6683/5. Fax: (202) 244 8059.
Embassy of the United States of America
PO Box 199
Central Bank Building
Warner Street
Mbabane, Swaziland
Tel: 46441/5. Fax: 45959. Telex: 2016 WD.
High Commission for the Kingdom of Swaziland
Suite 1204
130 Albert Street
Ottawa, Ontario, K1P 5G4
Tel: (613) 567 1480. Fax: (613) 567 1058. Telex: 0533185.
The Canadian Embassy in South Africa deals with enquiries relating to Swaziland:
Canadian Embassy
PO Box 26006
Pretoria 0007, South Africa
Tel: (12) 324 3970. Fax: (12) 323 1564.

AREA: 17,363 sq km (6704 sq miles).
POPULATION: 750,000 (1991 estimate).
POPULATION DENSITY: 43.2 per sq km.
CAPITAL: Mbabane. **Population:** 38,636 (1982).
GEOGRAPHY: Swaziland is surrounded to the north, west and south by the Transvaal of South Africa and to the east by Mozambique. There are four main topographical regions: the Highveld Inkangala, a wide ribbon of partly reforested, rugged country including the Usutu pine forest; the Peak Timbers in the northwest; the Middleveld, which rolls down from the Highveld through hills and fertile valleys; and the Lowveld, or bush country, with hills rising from 170-360m (560-1180ft). The Lubombo plateau is an escarpment along the eastern fringe of the lowveld, comprising mainly cattle country and mixed farmland. One of the best-watered areas in southern Africa, Swaziland's four major rivers are the Komati, Usutu, Mbuluzi and Ngwavuma, flowing from west to east to the Indian Ocean.
LANGUAGE: English and Siswati.
RELIGION: Christian with an Animist minority.
TIME: GMT + 2.
ELECTRICITY: 220 volts AC, 50Hz. 15-amp round pin plugs are in use.
COMMUNICATIONS: Telephone: IDD is available. Country code: 9268. Public telephones are available. **Fax:** Some hotels have facilities. **Telex/telegram:** Facilities in the capital. **Post:** Post offices are in all main centres. Airmail to Europe takes up to two weeks. Post office opening hours: 0800-1300 and 1400-1700 Monday to Friday and 0800-1100 Saturday. **Press:** The two English-language newspapers in Swaziland are *The Times of Swaziland* (Monday to Friday) and the *Swazi Observer* (Sunday).
BBC World Service and Voice of America frequencies: From time to time these change. See the section *How to Use this Book* for more information.

BBC:				
MHz	21.660	3.255	11.940	6.190
Voice of America:				
MHz	21.49	15.60	9.525	6.035

PASSPORT/VISA

Regulations and requirements may be subject to change at short notice, and you are advised to contact the appropriate diplomatic or consular authority before finalising travel arrangements. Details of these may be found at the head of this country's entry. Any numbers in the chart refer to the footnotes below.

	Passport Required?	Visa Required?	Return Ticket Required?
Full British	Yes	No	2
BVP	Not valid	-	-
Australian	Yes	No	2
Canadian	Yes	No	2
USA	Yes	No	2
Other EC	Yes	1	2
Japanese	Yes	Yes	2

PASSPORTS: Valid passport required by all.
British Visitors Passport: Not accepted.
VISAS: Required by all except:
(a) nationals of countries as shown in the chart above;
(b) [1] nationals of EC countries (nationals of France, Germany and Spain *do* require a visa);
(c) nationals of Bahamas, Barbados, Botswana, Cyprus, Finland, Gambia, Ghana, Grenada, Guyana, Iceland, Israel, Jamaica, Kenya, Lesotho, Liechtenstein, Malawi, Malaysia, Malta, Nauru, New Zealand, Nigeria, Norway, Papua New Guinea, San Marino, Seychelles, Sierra Leone, Singapore, Solomon Islands, South Africa, Sweden, Tanzania, Tonga, Trinidad & Tobago, Uganda, Uruguay, Western Samoa, Zambia and Zimbabwe (including holders of an unexpired Rhodesian passport).
Note: [2] A return ticket is recommended but not essential.
Types of visa: Entry visa. Cost: £2. Available free of charge to those EC citizens requiring visas (see above) upon arrival at the port of entry.
Validity: Entry visa is valid for 3 months. Any visitor wishing to extend stay should apply for a temporary residence permit from the Chief Immigration Officer in Swaziland.
Application to: Consulate (or Consular Section at Embassy or High Commission). For addresses, see top of entry.
Application requirements: (a) Application form. (b) 2 photographs. (c) Fee. (d) Valid passport. (e) Proof of means of support during stay.
Working days required: Postal: 48 hours; personal: 24 hours.
Temporary residence: Apply to Chief Immigration Office.

MONEY

Currency: Lilangeni (E) = 100 cents. The plural of Lilangeni is Emalangeni. Notes are in denominations of E20, 10 and 5. Coins are in denominations of E2 and 1, and 50, 20, 10, 5, 2 and 1 cents. The South African Rand is also accepted as legal tender (E1 = 1 Rand) although coins are not accepted.
Currency exchange: Visitors are advised to exchange Emalangeni back to their own currency before leaving.
Credit cards: American Express and Access/Mastercard are widely accepted. Visa has more limited use. Check with your credit card company for details of merchant acceptability and other facilities which may be available.
Travellers cheques: Widely accepted.
Exchange rate indicators: The following figures are included as a guide to the movements of the Lilangeni against Sterling and the US Dollar:

Date:	Oct '89	Oct '90	Oct '91	Oct '92
£1.00=	4.27	4.94	4.89	4.68
$1.00=	2.70	2.53	2.82	2.95

Currency restrictions: The import and export of foreign and local currency is unrestricted.
Banking hours: 0830-1300 Monday to Friday and 0830-1100 Saturday.

DUTY FREE

The following items may be imported into Swaziland without incurring customs duty:
400 cigarettes and 50 cigars and 250g of tobacco;
1 litre of spirits and 2 litres of wine;
50ml of perfume and 250ml toilet water per person;
Gifts up to a value of E200 per person.

PUBLIC HOLIDAYS

Public holidays observed in Swaziland are as follows:
Mar 8 '93 Commonwealth Day. **Apr 9** Good Friday. **Apr 12** Easter Monday. **Apr 25** National Flag Day. **May 20** Ascension Day. **Jul 22** Birthday of the late King Sobhuza. **Aug 24** Umhlanga Day. **Sep 6** Somhlolo, Independence Day. **Oct 24** United Nations Day. **Dec 25** Christmas Day. **Dec 26** Boxing Day. **Dec/Jan** Incwala Day (see *Special Events* below). **Jan 1 '94** New Year's Day. **Mar 8** Commonwealth Day.

HEALTH

Regulations and requirements may be subject to change at short notice, and you are advised to contact your doctor well in advance of your intended date of departure. Any numbers in the chart refer to the footnotes below.

	Special Precautions?	Certificate Required?
Yellow Fever	No	1
Cholera	Yes	-
Typhoid & Polio	Yes	-
Malaria	2	-
Food & Drink	3	-

[1]: A yellow fever vaccination certificate is required of travellers arriving from infected areas.
[2]: Malaria risk exists throughout the year in all lowveld areas. The predominant *falciparum* strain is reported to be 'highly resistant' to chloroquine.
[3]: Tap water is considered safe to drink. Drinking water outside main cities and towns may be contaminated and

SWAZILAND | **HEALTH REGULATIONS** | **VISA REGULATIONS** | Code-Link

GALILEO/WORLDSPAN

TI-DFT/MTS/HE

TI-DFT/MTS/VI

SABRE

TIDFT/MTS/HE

TIDFT/MTS/VI

To access this information on your CRS, swipe the barcode with a light pen or type in the text under the barcode. For more information, see the introduction *How to Use This Book*.

terilisation is advisable. Milk is pasteurised and dairy products are safe for consumption. Local meat, poultry, seafood, fruit and vegetables are generally considered safe to eat.
Rabies is present. For those at high risk vaccination before arrival should be considered. If you are bitten abroad seek medical advice without delay. For more information consult the *Health* section at the back of the book.
Bilharzia (schistosomiasis) is present. Avoid swimming and paddling in fresh water. Swimming pools which are well-chlorinated and maintained are safe.
Health care: Health insurance is recommended.

TRAVEL - International

AIR: Swaziland's national airline is *Royal Swazi National Airways Corporation (ZC)*.
Approximate flight time: From *London* to Swaziland is 16 hours including stopover.
International airport: *Manzini (MTS)* (Matsapha), 8km (5 miles) from the city. Coach and taxi service is available at all arrivals. Airport facilities include banks/bureaux de change (0700-1730), restaurants and snack bar.
Departure tax: E10.
ROAD: There are good roads from Johannesburg, Durban and northern Zululand, as well as tourist buses running from Natal and the Transvaal. There is a weekly **bus** service from Mbabane and Manzini to Johannesburg, and a twice-weekly service from Mbabane to Maputo.

TRAVEL - Internal

ROAD: The road system is largely well developed, although some roads are often winding depending on the topography of the different areas. The maximum speed limit on all roads is 80kmph (50mph). **Bus:** There are numerous buses connecting the different parts of the country, including non-stop buses. **Car hire:** There are a number of car hire companies in Swaziland such as *Hertz, Imperial, Avis* etc. **Documentation:** National driving licences are valid for up to six months if they are printed in English or accompanied by a certified translation. International Driving Permits are also recognised.
JOURNEY TIMES: The following chart gives approximate journey times (in hours and minutes) from Mbabane to other major towns in Swaziland.

	Road
Manzini	0.45
Nhlangano	2.00
Pigg's Peak	1.00
Siteki	1.30

ACCOMMODATION

There are some good hotels in Swaziland, some of international standard, but it is necessary to book well in advance. There are also smaller motels and inns, camp sites and caravan parks outside the city. For further information contact: The Hotel and Tourism Association of Swaziland, PO Box 462, Empire Building, Allister Miller Street, Mbabane. Tel: 42218. Fax: 44516. **Grading:** The star-grading system is in use.

RESORTS & EXCURSIONS

The lush **Ezulwini Valley** is a miracle of nature and the seat of Swaziland's major tourist attractions. Though Swaziland is regarded as one of the most beautiful countries in Africa, it was not until an Italian and South African syndicate erected southern Africa's first casino hotel on a prime valley site 12 years ago that Swaziland geared itself towards tourism.
Here in the valley is the magnificent Royal Swazi golf course, the casino, the hot mineral spring – one of eight in the country – known by locals and guests as the 'Cuddle Puddle', the superb health studio and a cluster of fine hotels forming the *Holiday Valley* complex.
Swaziland's industrial centre of **Manzini** lies east across the valley, a half hour's drive. On the way are signposts to Swaziland's most famous waterfall, the *Mantenga Falls*, the thriving *Mantenga Arts & Crafts Centre*, *Mlilwane Game Sanctuary*, **Lobamba**, the spiritual and legislative capital, Matsapha Airport and the industrial area of **Matsapha**, which produces everything from beer to televisions.
Mlilwane, the oldest established game sanctuary in Swaziland, once privately owned, was offered to the nation as a sanctuary for wild animals. There has been a strong effort made to bring back wildlife to the country.
Following the establishment of Mlilwane, two other game sanctuaries have been proclaimed: **Malolotsha**, in the north near Pigg's Peak, and **Hlane** in the north east. Hlane has wide open spaces supporting big herds of game. Malolotsha, situated on top of a mountain range and surrounded by steep canyons and waterfalls, is breathtaking.
Although southern Swaziland is currently being developed for tourism, there are at present no plans for a game sanctuary in this area. The first project in the development of the southern region has been the erection of another casino hotel at **Nhlangano**, about 120km (75 miles) south of Mbabane. The sports facilities, which include a golf course and swimming pool, are excellent. The nearby **Mkondo River** twists its way through gorges and valleys, past waterfalls, pools and rapids and, in the distance, the mountain ranges gleam brown, mauve and blue. Some of Swaziland's finest Bushmen paintings are found in this area – others are located in the mountains north of Mbabane.

SOCIAL PROFILE

FOOD & DRINK: Restaurants are found mainly in the larger centres and at hotels. Most serve international cuisine; Greek, Hungarian and Indian food is available. Food stalls in the local markets sell traditional meat stew and maize meal or stamped mealies and roasted corn on the cob. **Drink:** There is a good selection of spirits, beers and wines. Traditional Swazi beer can be tasted in rural areas. There are no prescribed licensing hours.
NIGHTLIFE: In Mbabane and Ezulwini Valley are nightclubs and discotheques some with live music and cabaret. The main attraction in Ezulwini Valley is the casino at the Royal Swazi Hotel.
SHOPPING: There is a modern shopping complex in Mbabane and many local markets. Purchases from craft centres include beadwork, basketry, grass and sisal mats, copperware, local gemstone jewellery, wooden and soapstone carvings, calabashes, knobkerries, battleaxes, walking sticks, *karosses* (animal skin mats), drums, woven cloth and batik and tie-dye, which are often incorporated into traditional Swazi garments. **Shopping hours:** 0800-1700 Monday to Friday and 0800-1300 Saturday.
SPORT: Golf: There is an 18-hole golf course in the Ezulwini Valley at the Royal Swazi Sun Hotel and Spa and the Havelock Golf Course. **Tennis:** Courts are available at major hotels, notably the Royal Swazi. **Swimming:** Several hotels have pools and non-residents are generally able to use the facilities. **Hiking:** A popular hike is up Sheba's Breasts. Others include the ascent to Malolotsha Falls at Pigg's Peak and the climb up Emlembe, Swaziland's highest peak.
SPECIAL EVENTS: Every December or January at a time carefully chosen by astrologers the *Incwala* ('Fruit Ceremony') takes place. It is a 4-day ceremony encompassing the entire nation and culminates in a ritual during which the King eats the first fruit of the new season. The ceremony confers the blessing of their ancestors on the nation's consumption of these fruits. In August or September the *Umhlanga* ('Reed Dance') is an event in which young women pay homage to the Queen Mother.
SOCIAL CONVENTIONS: Traditional ways of life are still strong and Swazi culture in the form of religious music, dance, poetry and craftsmanship play an important part in daily life. Casual wear is normal although more formal wear is customary at the casino and sophisticated hotels. Visitors wishing to camp near villages should inform the headman first. He can normally help with customs. **Photography:** Permission to photograph individuals should always be sought. In some cases a gratuity may be asked for (especially if the photographee has gone to some effort to make a show – for example, by wearing traditional regalia). It is prohibited to photograph the Royal Palace, the Royal Family, uniformed police, army personnel, army vehicles or aircraft and bank buildings. Visitors wishing to photograph traditional ceremonies should first contact the Government Information Service, PO Box 338, Mbabane. **Tipping:** 10%.

BUSINESS PROFILE

ECONOMY: The economy is dominated by and closely linked with that of South Africa and the country is a member of the Southern African Customs Union and part of the Rand Monetary Area. Agriculture is by far the largest part of the economy, employing over 75% of the working population. Sugar, citrus fruits and pineapples are the main cash crops. Important industries include sugar refining, forestry, asbestos and coal. Tourism is increasing. In recent years the country has suffered from a reduction in world demand for its main exports and a shortage of foreign capital. Government policy is currently concerned with trying to encourage investment in the agricultural and mining sectors but is hampered by the frequent suspicion that much of its apparent trade comprises goods in transit to and from South Africa in order to evade international embargoes. This practice, proven by a US Congressional inquiry in 1987, declined temporarily but soon resumed its previous level. The end of international sanctions against South Africa will ease pressure on the Swazi economy, although there may be some short-term loss of revenue. Expansion of the mining sector is the most promising avenue for economic growth which has been at best sluggish in recent years. Apart from South Africa, which dominates Swazi trade, the most important trading partners are the UK and France.
BUSINESS: Lightweight suits are generally expected for business. Appointments are necessary and business cards are exchanged. English is widely spoken in business circles.
Office hours: 0800-1300 and 1400-1700 Monday to Friday and 0800-1300 Saturday.
COMMERCIAL INFORMATION: The following organisations can offer advice:
Swaziland Industrial Development Corporation Ltd, PO Box 866, Mbabane. Tel: 43391. Fax: 45619. Telex: 2052; *or*
Swaziland Chamber of Commerce and Industry, PO Box 72, Mbabane. Tel/Fax: 44408. Telex: 2032.
CONFERENCES/CONVENTIONS: The principal facilities are at the Royal Swazi Convention Centre in the Ezulwini Valley, which has seating for up to 600. Several hotels have facilities for smaller numbers, with back-up services. The Ministry of Broadcasting, Information and Tourism (address at beginning of entry) can supply information.

HISTORY & GOVERNMENT

HISTORY: Swaziland became a British Protectorate in 1907 as a result of the Boer War of 1899-1902; previously it had been ruled jointly by the UK and the South African Republic. The country became independent in September 1968, after repeated South African requests that the territory be handed over to them had been refused by the British, who administered Swaziland (like Botswana and Lesotho) as a Trust Territory. Between 1973 and 1978, the existing constitution was suspended, at the instigation of the King and with the approval of Parliament. In 1978, a new constitution concentrated political power in the hands of the monarch, who appointed a Prime Minister and Cabinet. An elected Parliament, the Libandla, in which political parties remained illegal, was established, but its functions were restricted to conveying advice to the King and his principal advisory body, the Liqoqo (Supreme Council of State). The current monarch, King Mswati III, was crowned in April 1986. Sotsha Dlamini was appointed Prime Minister in November 1987 after which a new Parliament was elected. Sotsha Dlamini was dismissed in July 1989 for 'disobedience' and replaced with Obed Dlamini (no relation). Political stability proved elusive during the late 1980s: the Mswati monarchy was repeatedly threatened by plots organised by dissident members of the royal family and disaffected politicians but all have been stifled with apparent ease. Recent political developments in South Africa have, however, given rise to pressure of a different kind on the regime. The gradual liberalisation across the border inspired demands for democracy which the Government largely ignored or resisted until the beginning of 1992. Despite frequent harassment of opposition activists, dissent continues to grow; as does industrial unrest. The focus of opposition has been the People's United Democratic Movement (PUDEMO) which operated largely clandestinely until February 1992, when it declared itself a legal opposition party. This followed the appointment by King Mswati of the Vusela committee to take soundings of popular opinion on the subject of electoral reform. On the economic front, the extensive illicit trade through Swaziland (see *Economy*) can be regulated at last. The only significant problem in Swazi-South African relations has been territorial: sporadic negotiations continue for the transfer of land, amid Zulu objections, from South Africa to Swaziland.
GOVERNMENT: The current constitution dates from 1978; the monarch is the Head of State who appoints the ministers. Parliament consists of the Senate, with 10 appointed and 10 elected members, and the House of Assembly, with 10 appointees and 40 elected representatives. Elections are not direct but made by an electoral college which itself is directly elected on a regional basis through the *Tinkhundla* (chieftaincies).

CLIMATE

Due to the variations in altitude the weather is changeable. Except in the lowland it is rarely uncomfortably hot and nowhere very cold. The Middleveld and Lubombo are drier and sub-tropical with most rain from October to March.
Required clothing: Lightweights and rainwear.

MBABANE Swaziland (1163m)

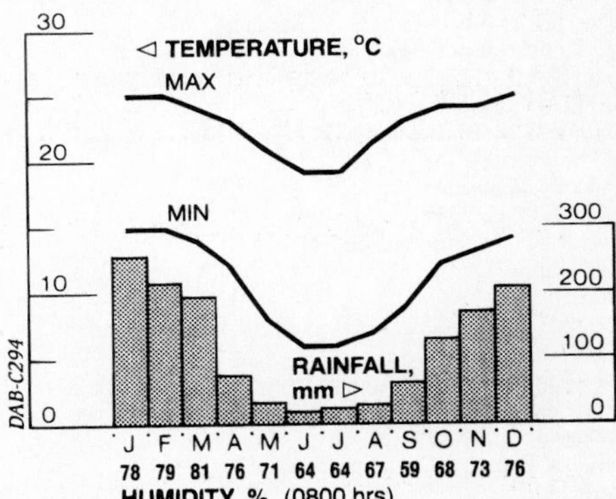

SWEDEN

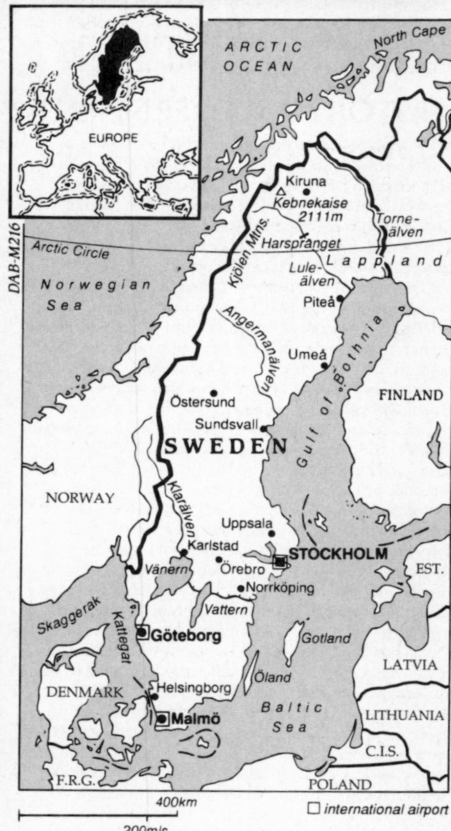

Location: Northeast Europe, Scandinavia.

Swedish Travel & Tourism Council
PO Box 10134
121 28 Stockholm, Sweden
Tel: (8) 725 5500. Fax: (8) 649 8882.
Embassy of Sweden
11 Montagu Place
London W1H 2AL
Tel: (071) 724 2101. Fax: (071) 724 4174. Telex: 28249 SVENSK G.
Visa Section: Tel: (071) 917 6413. Fax: (071) 917 6475.
Opening hours: 0900-1230 Monday to Friday.
Telephone enquiries: 0900-1230 and 1400-1600 Monday to Friday.
Swedish Travel & Tourism Council
73 Welbeck Street
London W1M 8AN
Tel: (071) 487 5007. Fax: (071) 935 5853. Opening hours: 0930-1600 Monday to Friday.
Svenska Turistföreningen (Swedish Touring Club)
PO Box 25
Drottninggatan 31-33
101 20 Stockholm, Sweden
Tel: (8) 790 3100. Fax: (8) 201 332. Telex: 17760.
British Embassy
Skarpögatan 6-8
115 27 Stockholm, Sweden
Tel: (8) 667 0140. Fax: (8) 662 9989. Telex: 19340 BRITEMB S.
Consulates in: Gothenburg (Göteborg), Malmö, Luleå and Sundsvall.
Embassy of Sweden
Suites 1200 and 715
600 New Hampshire Avenue, NW
Washington, DC
20037
Tel: (202) 944 5600. Fax: (202) 342 1319. Telex: 248347.
Consulate Generals in: Chicago, Houston, Los Angeles, Minneapolis, New York (tel: (212) 751 5900) and San Francisco.
Swedish Travel & Tourism Council
18th Floor
655 Third Avenue
New York, NY
10017
Tel: (212) 949 2333. Fax: (212) 697 0835. Telex: 620681.
Scandinavian Tourist Boards in: Chicago and Beverly Hills.
Embassy of the United States of America
Strandvägen 101
115 89 Stockholm, Sweden
Tel: (8) 783 5300. Fax: (8) 661 1964.
Embassy of Sweden
Mercury Court
377 Dalhousie Street
Ottawa, Ontario
K1P 9N8
Tel: (613) 236 8553. Fax: (613) 236 5720. Telex: 0533331 SVENSK OTT.
Consulates in: Calgary, Edmonton, Halifax, Montréal, Québec, Regina, Saint John, St John's, Saskatoon, Toronto, Vancouver and Winnipeg.
Canadian Embassy
PO Box 16129
7th Floor
Tegelbacken 4
103 23 Stockholm, Sweden
Tel: (8) 237 920. Fax: (8) 242 491. Telex: 10687 DOMCAN S.

AREA: 440,945 sq km (170,250 sq miles).
POPULATION: 8,590,630 (1990 estimate).
POPULATION DENSITY: 19.5 per sq km.
CAPITAL: Stockholm. **Population:** 674,452 (1990).
GEOGRAPHY: Sweden is bordered by Norway to the west and Finland to the northeast, with a long Baltic coast to the east and south. Approximately half the country is forested and most of the many thousands of lakes are situated in the southern central area. The largest lake is Vänern, with an area of 5540 sq km (2140 sq miles). Swedish Lappland to the north is mountainous and extends into the Arctic Circle.
LANGUAGE: Swedish. Lapp is spoken by the Sami population in the north. English is taught as the first foreign language from the age of ten.
RELIGION: Swedish State Church (Evangelical Lutheran); other Protestant minorities.
TIME: GMT + 1 (GMT + 2 in summer).
ELECTRICITY: 220 volts, 3-phase AC, 50Hz. 2-pin continental plugs are used.
COMMUNICATIONS: Telephone: Full IDD is available. Country code: 46. Unlike other European countries, telephones are not found in post offices but in special 'Telegraph Offices'. **Fax:** Widely available throughout the country. **Telex/telegram:** Facilities are available in every main town. **Post:** Post offices are open during normal shopping hours (0900-1800 Monday to Friday and 1000-1300 Saturday). Some branches may be closed on Saturdays during July. Post boxes are yellow. Stamps and aerograms are on sale at post offices and also at most bookstalls and stationers. Airmail within Europe takes three to four days. *Poste Restante* facilities are widely available in post offices.
Press: The provinces have their own newspapers which are widely read in their respective regions; the major dailies are confined largely to the capital. Many papers are financed by political parties but independence and freedom of the press is firmly maintained. All papers are published in Swedish.
BBC World Service and Voice of America frequencies: From time to time these change. See the section *How to Use this Book* for more information.

BBC:				
MHz	15.57	9.410	6.195	3.955
Voice of America:				
MHz	11.97	9.670	6.040	5.995

PASSPORT/VISA

Regulations and requirements may be subject to change at short notice, and you are advised to contact the appropriate diplomatic or consular authority before finalising travel arrangements. Details of these may be found at the head of this country's entry. Any numbers in the chart refer to the footnotes below.

	Passport Required?	Visa Required?	Return Ticket Required?
Full British	1	No	No
BVP	Valid	-	-
Australian	Yes	No	No
Canadian	Yes	No	No
USA	Yes	No	No
Other EC	2	No	No
Japanese	Yes	No	No

PASSPORTS: Valid passport required by all except:
(a) [1] nationals of the UK holding a BVP;
(b) [2] nationals of Belgium, France, Germany, Italy, Luxembourg and The Netherlands, provided they hold a valid ID card (for a stay of up to 3 months);
(c) nationals of Austria, Switzerland and Liechtenstein provided they hold valid ID cards (for a stay of up to 3 months).
British Visitors Passport: BVPs are valid for holidays or unpaid business trips of up to 3 months. Visits to Denmark, Sweden, Norway and Iceland as a group must not exceed 3 months in any 9-month period.
VISAS: Required by all except:
(a) nationals of the countries referred to in the chart above (but note that UK passport holders who are subject to British Immigration controls may need visas);
(b) nationals of Andorra, Argentina, Austria, Bahamas, Barbados, Belize, Bolivia, Botswana, Brazil, Brunei, Chile, Colombia, Costa Rica, Côte d'Ivoire, Croatia, Cuba, Cyprus, Czechoslovakia, Dominica, Dominican Republic, Ecuador, El Salvador, Fiji, Finland, Gambia, Grenada, Guatemala, Haiti, Honduras, Hong Kong (UK passport holders), Hungary, Iceland, Israel, Jamaica, Kenya, Kiribati, Lesotho, Liechtenstein, Malaysia, Malta, Malawi, Mauritius, Mexico, Monaco, Namibia, New Zealand, Nicaragua, Niger, Norway, Panama, Paraguay, Peru, Poland, St Lucia, St Vincent & the Grenadines, San Marino, Seychelles, Singapore, Slovenia, Solomon Islands, South Korea, Suriname, Swaziland, Switzerland, Tanzania, Thailand, Togo, Trinidad & Tobago, Tuvalu, Uganda, Uruguay, Venezuala, Yugoslavia, Zambia and Zimbabwe.
Types of visa: Ordinary (tourist/business) and Transit.
Cost: £15. Visa fees are waived for the following:
(a) applicants under 16 years of age;
(b) British Protected Persons travelling on UK passports;
(c) nationals of Algeria, Antigua & Barbuda, Bangladesh, Benin, Bosnia-Hercegovina, Bulgaria, Burkina Faso, China, Guyana, India, Iraq, North Korea, Kuwait, Maldives, Morocco, Pakistan, Papua New Guinea, Philippines, St Kitts & Nevis, Sri Lanka, Syria, Tunisia, Turkey and the USSR.
Validity: 90 days.
Application to: Consulate (or Consular Section at Embassy). For addresses, see top of entry.
Application requirements: (a) Valid passport. (b) 2 photographs. (c) Fee (cheque or postal order only if sent by post). (d) Completed application form. (e) SAE if sending by post for return of passport.
Working days required: 2-8 weeks.
Temporary residence: Enquire at Embassy.

MONEY

Currency: Swedish Krona (SKr) = 100 öre. Notes are in denominations of SKr10,000, 1000, 500, 100, 50 and 20. Coins are in denominations of SKr10, 5 and 1, 50 öre.
Currency exchange: Personal cheques can be cashed in Swedish banks under the Eurocheque system.
Credit cards: Diners Club, American Express, Visa and Access/Mastercard are all widely accepted. Check with your credit card company for details of merchant acceptability and other facilities which may be available.
Travellers cheques: Widely accepted.
Exchange rate indicators: The following figures are included as a guide to the movements of the Swedish Krona against Sterling and the US Dollar:

Date:	Oct '89	Oct '90	Oct '91	Oct '92
£1.00=	10.23	11.00	10.64	9.17
$1.00=	6.48	5.63	6.13	5.78

Currency restrictions: There are no restrictions on the import or export of local or foreign currencies.
Banking hours: Generally 0930-1500 Monday to Friday, but in many large cities banks close at 1800. All banks are closed on Saturday.

DUTY FREE

The following items may be imported into Sweden without incurring customs duty by:
(a) European residents:
200 cigarettes or 100 cigarillos or 50 cigars or 250g of tobacco;
1 litre wine (2 litres if no spirits are imported);
1 litre spirits (over 20 years of age);
2 litres of beer (over 20 years of age);
A reasonable quantity of perfume;
Gifts up to the value of SKr1000.
(b) Non-European residents:
400 cigarettes or 500g of tobacco or tobacco products;
The same quantity of other duty-free items as European residents.
Note: Drink regulations are strictly enforced.

PUBLIC HOLIDAYS

Public holidays observed in Sweden are as follows:
Apr 9 '93 Good Friday. **Apr 12** Easter Monday. **May 1** Labour Day. **May 20** Ascension Day. **May 31** Whit Monday. **Jun 26** Midsummer's Day. **Nov 6** All Saints' Day. **Dec 24-26** Christmas. **Dec 31** New Year's Eve. **Jan 1 '94** New Year's Day. **Jan 6** Epiphany.

HEALTH

Regulations and requirements may be subject to change at short notice, and you are advised to contact your doctor well in advance of your intended date of departure. Any numbers in the chart refer to the footnotes below.

	Special Precautions?	Certificate Required?
Yellow Fever	No	No
Cholera	No	No
Typhoid & Polio	No	-
Malaria	No	-
Food & Drink	No	-

Health care: There are full Reciprocal Health Agreements with most other European countries including the UK. The UK Agreement allows free hospital in-patient treatment (including medicines) to those presenting a UK passport; children are also allowed free dental treatment. Out-patient treatment at hospitals, all treatment at clinics and general surgeries, most prescribed medicines and ambulance travel must be paid for. Travelling expenses to and from hospital may be partially refunded.

TRAVEL - International

AIR: The national airline is *SAS Scandinavian Airlines (SK)*.
Approximate flight times: From *London* to Stockholm is 2 hours 30 minutes and to Gothenburg is 1 hour 45 minutes. From *Los Angeles* to Stockholm is 14 hours 10 minutes. From *New York* to Stockholm is 7 hours 45 minutes.
International airports: *Stockholm (STO)* (Arlanda) is 41km (25 miles) north of the city. There is a frequent coach service between the airport and the city (travel time – 40 minutes). Limousine and taxi services are available. Airport facilities: full outgoing duty-free shop; car hire (several major firms); bank/exchange (0700-2200 daily); restaurant/bar (1130-2130 daily); and coffee shop (open 0630-2130 Monday to Friday and 0630-0030 weekends).
Gothenburg (GOT) (Landvetter) is 25km (15 miles) east of the city (travel time – 25 minutes). Frequent coach services travel between the airport and the Central Station. Limousine and taxi services are available. Airport facilities: full outgoing duty-free shop; car hire; bank/exchange (0800-2000 Monday to Friday, 0800-1200 and 1300-1700 Saturday and 1230-1700 and 1800-2000 Sunday); restaurant/bar (1145-1930 Monday to Friday, 1200-1730 Saturday and 1200-1900 Sunday); and coffee shop (0600-2145).
Malmö (MMA) (Sturup) is 31km (20 miles) southeast of the city (travel time – 40 minutes). Bus and taxi services go to the city.
Malmö Harbour Hoverport (HMA), 200m (650ft) from the Central Station, is now the city's main terminal for international air passengers using the hovercraft service operated by *SAS* which connects with flights at *Copenhagen Airport*. The terminal has its own duty-free facilities. Taxi services are available.
SEA: *Scandinavian Seaways* ferries sail all year round from Harwich to Gothenburg and in summer from Newcastle to Gothenburg. There are also ferry connections with Copenhagen and Helsingör.
RAIL: The UK–Sweden route is from London (Victoria and Liverpool Street) to either the Hook of Holland or Ostend, and onwards via Copenhagen; the journey time is approximately 22-25 hours. There are connections by ferry from Denmark and through rail routes from Norway (Oslo, Narvik and Trondheim).
ROAD: From the UK you can either drive to Sweden through Europe via Denmark or Germany, or catch a car ferry from Harwich (all year) to Gothenburg on the southwest coast (sailing time – 24 hours).
Coaches: There are services from London (Victoria) to a number of Swedish cities throughout the year (restricted service in winter). Contact the Swedish Travel & Tourism Council for a list of operators.
See below for information on **documentation** and **traffic regulations.**

SWEDEN	HEALTH REGULATIONS	VISA REGULATIONS Code-Link
GALILEO/WORLDSPAN	 TI-DFT/STO/HE	 TI-DFT/STO/VI
SABRE	 TIDFT/STO/HE	TIDFT/STO/VI

To access this information on your CRS, swipe the barcode with a light pen or type in the text under the barcode. For more information, see the introduction *How to Use This Book.*

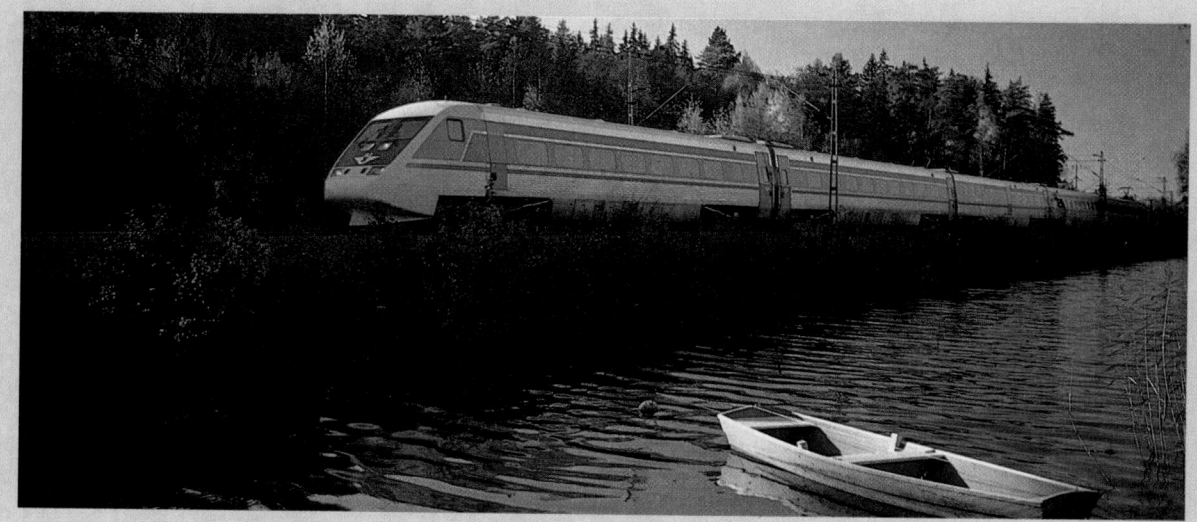

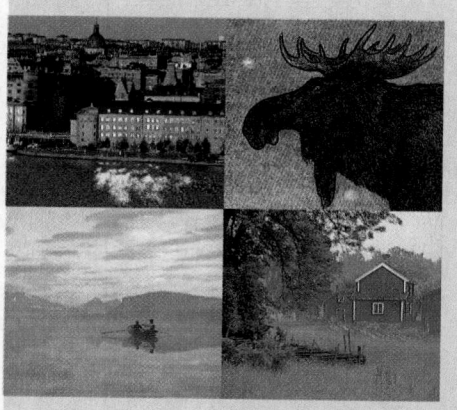

TRAVEL - Internal

AIR: SAS and *Linjeflyg (LF)* serve over 30 local airports. Travel by air is relatively cheap and there are a number of reduced fares offered by *Linjeflyg* and *SAS*. Contact airlines for further details.

SEA/LAKE: Frequent coastal sailings to all ports and on the hundreds of lakes throughout the country, especially in the north. For details contact local authorities.

RAIL: The excellent and extensive rail system is run by *Swedish State Railways (SJ)*, 105 50 Stockholm. Tel: (8) 762 2000. Fax: (8) 108 309. The network is more concentrated in the populated south where hourly services run between the main cities, but routes extend into the forested and sparsely populated lake area of the north, which is a scenic and popular holiday destination. Restaurant cars and sleepers are provided on many trains. Reservations are essential for most express services. Motorail car-sleeper services are operated during the summer on the long-distance routes from Malmö, Gothenburg and Västerås to Kiruna and Luleå.

Cheap fares: There are reductions for families and regular passengers, as well as a link-up with other Scandinavian countries via the *Nord-Turist Railpass* (also known as the *Scanrail Card*), which provides unlimited travel in Denmark, Norway, Finland and Sweden for 21 days. It also gives free travel on the ferries between Helsingör and Helsingborg. Children under 16 travel at half the fare or reduced fare, two children under 12 accompanied by an adult travel free. Half-price fares are available for second-class travel on specified offpeak trains within Sweden throughout the week. The discount applies on trains shown in the timetable as 'low price' or 'red departures'.

ROAD: Sweden's roads are well-maintained and relatively uncrowded but watch out for game crossing the road in remote areas. Credit cards are becoming more acceptable as a means of payment at filling stations. Most filling stations have 24-hour automatic petrol pumps; they accept SKr100, 50 and 10 notes. **Bus:** Express coach services and local buses are run by *GDG* and *Swebus*, and also the *Swedish Post Office* in the north. Cheap and efficient links are available to all towns. Many coach operators do special offers on tickets at the weekends (Fridays to Sundays). Information available in Sweden from local tourist offices. **Taxi:** Available in all towns and airports. Intercity taxis are also available. **Car hire:** Available in most towns and cities. All international agencies are represented. **Regulations:** Speed limits outside built-up areas are 110, 90 or 70kmph (68, 56 or 43mph) depending on road width and traffic density. In built-up areas the limit is 50kmph (31mph) or 30kmph (19mph) in school areas. Severe fines and sometimes prison sentences are imposed on drivers over the alcohol limit. There are on-the-spot fines for traffic offences. The use of dipped headlights is compulsory in the daytime for cars and motorcycles. Crash helmets are compulsory for motorcyclists. Children under seven may not travel in a car if it is not equipped with a special child restraint or a normal seat belt adapted for the child's use. Emergency warning triangles are strongly advised. Spiked tyres are only permitted from October 1 to April 30. **Documentation:** National driving licence is sufficient. The minimum age for car drivers is 18; for motorcyclists it is 17. The car's log book and written permission must be carried if driving someone else's car. A Green Card is not required by Swedish authorities, but it tops up the cover provided by a domestic policy. It is advisable to check the validity of insurance policies prior to departure.

URBAN: Public transport is efficient, comprehensive and well-integrated. Stockholm has bus, trams, metro *(T-banan)* and local rail services. Pre-purchase multi-tickets and passes are sold, though single tickets can also be obtained on the bus. There are trams in Gothenburg and Norrköping. Taxis are widely available and several of the main cities, particularly Stockholm, have boat excursions and services. See *Resorts & Excursions* below.

JOURNEY TIMES: The following chart gives approximate journey times (in hours and minutes) from Stockholm to other major cities/towns in Sweden.

	Air	Road	Rail
Gothenburg	0.50	6.00	4.30
Malmö	1.05	8.00	6.45
östersund	0.55	8.00	6.30
Karlstad	0.40	5.00	3.30
Luleå	1.15	20.00	15.00
Mora	1.00	6.00	4.30

ACCOMMODATION

Accommodation in Sweden is generally of a very good standard, ranging from first-class hotels to overnight accommodation in a *Rum* or youth hostel.

HOTELS: These are usually of a high standard. Most have a restaurant and/or cafeteria and a TV lounge. Good first- and medium-class hotels are found in every Swedish town. They are mostly private but are, in many cases, operated by hotel groups and offer special reduced rates for the summer and weekends. Special packages are available throughout the year in Stockholm, Malmö and Gothenburg. **Grading:** There is no formal grading structure but most first-class hotels display the *SHR* sign indicating that they belong to the *Swedish Hotel & Restaurant Association (SHR)*, Sveriges Hotell & Restaurang Förbund, PO Box 1158, Kammarkargatan 39, 111 81 Stockholm. Tel: (8) 231 290. Fax: (8) 215 861.

Tourist hotels: All over Sweden you can find country hotels, characterised by good food and attractive settings. Some are renovated and modernised manor houses or centuries-old farmhouses which have frequently been in the same family for generations. They are mostly independently owned and are often located in picturesque surroundings – by the sea or a lake, in the heart of the mountains or in a place of special historic or cultural interest. Others are traditional old inns. During the summer many hotels offer facilities for swimming, fishing, boating, golf and flower-spotting or bird-watching excursions.

Mountain hotels: There are also a number of mountain hotels which are ideal for those who want a get-away-from-it-all holiday. They provide a good base for expeditions in the mountains and guided walks are often arranged, as well as other activities like keep-fit classes, fishing and canoeing. Many are also popular skiing hotels in the winter.

Hotel discount schemes: Many Swedish hotels offer discounted rates throughout the summer and at weekends during the winter and some of the leading chains have special deals which can be booked in advance, including the *SARA Hotels Scandinavian Bonus Pass*, the *Scandic Hotel Cheque* scheme and the *Sweden Hotel Pass*. Details of these offers and other discount schemes are contained in the annual guide *Hotels in Sweden*, obtainable from the Swedish Travel & Tourism Council.

MOTELS: Sweden has a large number of motels, most of which are new, usually situated on the outskirts of towns or in the countryside. Parking is free. They may have swimming pools, a gymnasium and saunas, restaurants and self-service cafeterias.

FARMHOUSE ACCOMMODATION: A limited number of farms throughout Sweden offer accommodation, either in the main farmhouse or in an adjoining cottage. Accommodation is normally on a bed & breakfast basis, with self-catering facilities. Some farms offer full board. Accommodation can be booked through local tourist offices.

SELF-CATERING: Forest cabins and chalets are available throughout the country, generally set in beautiful surroundings, near lakes, in quiet forest glades or on an island in some remote archipelago. Many chalets have been built by the local authorities, maintaining rigid standards of quality and hygiene; purpose-built chalets generally consist of a living room, two or three bedrooms, a well-equipped kitchen and a toilet. They can generally accommodate up to six people, and cooking utensils, cutlery, blankets and pillows are provided. Visitors will have to supply only sheets and towels. Log cabins offer a slightly more simple type of accommodation. Renovated cottages and farm buildings are also available, usually in remote spots.

Chalet villages: Sweden's 250 chalet villages offer the advantage of amenities such as a grocery, general shops, leisure facilities, restaurants, swimming pools, saunas, a launderette, playgrounds, mini-golf, tennis, badminton or volleyball. Some have programmes of special activities such as music, dancing, barbecues, riding, fishing, walking trails and other excursions. It is often possible to rent boats or bicycles. The price of renting a cottage varies according to standard, size and location but generally they are more expensive in the high season (mid-June to mid-August) and also in February, when Swedish schools have their winter holiday. Several holiday companies offer inclusive packages combining chalet rental with your car-ferry crossing to Sweden. Information on rental of holiday cottages or flats can be obtained from specialist agencies, local tourist offices in Sweden or the Swedish Travel & Tourism Council.

CAMPING/CARAVANNING: Family camping holidays are extremely popular in Sweden and there is a tremendous variety of attractive sites. Most are located in picturesque surroundings, often on a lakeside or by the sea with free bathing facilities close at hand. There are about 750 campsites, all officially approved and classified by the Swedish Travel & Tourism Council. Many offer facilities such as boat or bicycle rental, mini-golf, tennis, riding or saunas.

There are 50 campsites in the mountain region, 12 of which are within the Arctic Circle, where there is 24 hours of daylight in summer. Many campsites have facilities for the handicapped. Most authorised sites are open with full service between June 1 and August 15. Many sites are also open in April or May but the full range of ancillary facilities, such as the post office, may not be open. About 200 sites remain open in the winter, particularly in the wintersports areas in central and northern Sweden. All sites open during the winter have electric sockets for caravans.

Camping/Caravanning holidays in Sweden are inexpensive. The price for one night for the whole family plus tent or caravan and use of services is one of the lowest rates in Europe, although at some sites there are small charges for the use of services like showers or launderette. A camping *carnet* is needed at most sites. It is issued at the first site you visit and is then valid for the whole season. The *carnet* is not required by holders of the 'Camping International' card. Standards of facilities and cleanliness at Swedish campsites are probably the highest in Europe. Approved sites are inspected annually by the Swedish Travel & Tourism Council and are awarded a 1-2- or 3-star rating according to the facilities provided, as follows:

3-star: Supervision 24 hours a day, postal service, car wash, cafeteria, cooking facilities, play and recreational activities and assembly room.

2-star: Supervision throughout the day, illuminated and fenced-in area, drains for caravans, shaving points, kiosk, grocery shop, telephone and electric sockets for caravans.

1-star: Daily inspection, a barrier at the entrance, dustbin, drinking water, toilets, washing facilities and hot water for dish-washing, laundering and showers.

Camping Cheques, valid at more than 350 sites, can be purchased before your holiday but only as part of a package including your return car-ferry journey. Each cheque is valid for one night's stay for a family with car plus tent or caravan.

Detailed information about camping in Sweden is contained in a pamphlet which is available free of charge from the Swedish Travel & Tourism Council; an abbreviated list of campsites is also available. Motor homes and caravans can be rented. Further information from the Swedish Travel & Tourism Council.

Fuel: *Camping Gaz* is not normally available in Sweden and you are recommended to take your own supplies with you. Only propane gas (eg Primus) is obtainable. This is

widely available at more than 2000 Primus dealers along with the necessary equipment at reasonable prices. It is important to ensure that equipment designed to burn butane is not refilled with propane; this is both illegal and highly dangerous.

CAMPING CABINS: A useful alternative to tent or caravan camping is to rent one of 4400 camping cabins which are available at 350 sites. The cabins have between two and six beds and are usually equipped with a cooking range and kitchen utensils (but not generally with bedclothes). You can use services on the campsite.

YOUTH HOSTELS: The 280 hostels range from mansions to a renovated sailing ship, the *Af Chapman*, in the centre of Stockholm, and there are also many purpose-built hostels. There are no restrictions on who may use Sweden's hostels. Hostels have 2-4 beds per room, or family rooms and self-catering facilities. The hostels are run by the *Swedish Touring Club (STF)* but members of the UK *Youth Hostels Association* or *Scottish Youth Hostels Association* qualify for a cheaper rate, on production of a membership card. All youth hostels are open during the summer and some for the whole year. They are closed during the day but are open to check in new guests 0800-0930 and 1700-2200. During the summer it is advisable to book in advance. A list of Swedish youth hostels can be ordered direct from *STF*; address at beginning of entry. The hostels are also listed in the 'International Youth Hostel Handbook', available through the *YHA* in the UK.

SWEDISH TOURING CLUB: The *Swedish Touring Club (STF)* runs Sweden's youth hostels and several mountain stations in the north of the country and looks after the many mountain huts along the long-distance hiking trails. *STF* also publishes a list of guest harbours and issues guidance to hikers and canoeing enthusiasts.

RESORTS & EXCURSIONS

For the purpose of clarity, information on resorts and excursions has been divided into nine main sections: Stockholm and the islands; Gothenburg; Skåne; the Glass Country; the West Coast; the Golden Coast; Gotland and Öland; Swedish Lakeland; the Midnight Sun Coast; and Lappland. The natural environment is protected by a law called Allemanrätten, allowing visitors to stay in places of natural beauty providing they don't damage the environment. For further information contact: Swedish Travel & Tourism Council, the Swedish Touring Club or a local tourist information centre.

Stockholm and the islands

Built on a string of islands, **Stockholm** was founded 700 years ago by King Birger Jarl at the strategic point where the fresh water of Lake Mälaren meets the salt water of the Baltic. A good starting point for an exploration of the city is the 'Old Town' *(Gamla Stan)*, a cluster of old buildings and narrow cobbled streets which formed the original Stockholm. The old buildings are beautifully preserved and the main streets, Österlånggatan and Västerlånggatan, are pedestrian precincts with a host of boutiques, handicrafts and antique shops. The Old Town has three churches of historic interest, *Storkyrkan* and *Riddarholm Church*, both dating from the 13th century and the German church with its magnificent Baroque interior. Overlooking the harbour is the *Royal Palace*, which contains the State Apartments, the Crown Jewels, the Hall of State and Chapel Royal, Royal Armoury and Palace Museum. Within easy reach of the Old Town, in a magnificent setting on the edge of Lake Mälaren, is Stockholm's elegant City Hall *(Stadshuset)*, inaugurated about 60 years ago. There is a spectacular view of the capital from the top of the 100m (350ft) tower. Another spot for a magnificent view is the observation platform on the *Kaknäs* communications tower which, at 155m (508ft), is the highest building in Scandinavia.

The island of **Djurgården,** can be reached either by bus from the city centre or by ferry across the busy harbour. The best-known attraction here is the purpose-built *Vasa Museum* housing the restored 360-year-old wooden warship which was recovered from the depths of Stockholm's harbour in 1961. Also in Djurgården is *Skansen*, an open-air folk museum which celebrated its centenary in 1991. It has about 150 traditional buildings from different regions of Sweden, as well as an open-air zoo and an aquarium. Across the road is *Gröna Lund*, a lively amusement park.

The city boasts over 50 museums. No less than eight can be visited in the Djurgården area, including the Nordic Museum *(Nordiska Museet)*, *Waldemarsudde House*, which was the home of the artist Prince Eugen until 1947, and *Liljevalchs Konsthall*. The Historical Museum *(Historiska Museet)* has some priceless treasures and implements from prehistoric Sweden, as well as examples of medieval art. *The National Museum* is Sweden's central museum for the national collections of painting, sculpture, applied arts, printing and drawings.

Every visitor to Stockholm should invest in a special discount card, the 'Stockholm Card' *(Stockholmskortet)* which cuts sightseeing and entertainment costs dramatically. Cards of longer validity are available at an extra charge, available in Stockholm from the Stockholm Tourist Centre.

EXCURSIONS: There is a whole armada of boat excursions on offer. 'Under the Bridges of Stockholm' takes a circular tour through part of the harbour as well as *Lake Mälaren*. A longer trip can be taken out into the archipelago to resorts like **Sandhamn, Saltsjöbaden** or **Vaxholm**. You can also take a boat from the City Hall to *Drottningholm Palace*. The Royal Theatre has been preserved in its original 18th-century form and plays are still performed there in period costume. There is also a museum depicting the development of the theatre since the Renaissance period.

Gothenburg

The history of Sweden's second city **Gothenburg** (Göteborg) is closely tied to the sea, and is still the arrival point for hundreds of thousands of visitors from abroad each year. The basic pattern of the city owes much to the Dutch architects who designed it; the spacious streets are laid out at right angles and there is a network of canals. The *Nordstaden Kronhuset* area houses the oldest building of the city, built in 1643 and now the City Museum. Nearby is *Kronhusbodarna*, an arts and craft workshop centre dating from the 18th century. A visit to the Botanical Gardens *(Botaniska Trädgården)* is a must; the rock garden there is regarded as one of the most impressive in the world, with about 3000 species of Alpine plants. In the city centre is the beautiful *Garden of Trädgårdsföreningen* with its restored *Palm House*, built in the style of what was London's Crystal Palace.

Another must during the summer is the *Liseberg Amusement Park*, an ideal spot for children. There are also many museums, such as the Maritime Museum *(Sjöfartsmuseet)* which illustrates Sweden's maritime history and the development of its shipbuilding industry. The 'Gothenburg Discount Card' can be purchased for free admission to many tourist attractions.

EXCURSIONS: One of the best ways of sightseeing in Gothenburg is on one of the famous *Paddan* boats. Departure is from the terminal at Kungsportsplatsen for an hour-long tour under 20 bridges and out into the busy harbour. Another popular boat trip is to the 17th-century *Nya Elfsborg Fortress* built on an island at the harbour mouth. There are also sightseeing tours of varying duration by bus with an English-speaking guide. A cheap way of travelling around the city is to buy a 24-hour ticket on the tram network. Gothenburg is the starting point for the classic three-day trip to Stockholm through Sweden's great lakes and the historic *Göta Canal*.

RESORTS: See *The Golden Coast* below.

Skåne

At the southernmost tip of Sweden is the province of **Skåne**, an area of fertile fields and meadows which was ruled by the Danes until 1658. To this day the Skånians have maintained their own distinctive dialect. As a reminder of the days of Danish rule there are more than 200 castles and manors scattered over the province, often forming part of a farm. This region is famous for its food, and the landscape is characterised by rolling fields and pastures and forests but only a few lakes. The best spots for swimming and fishing are along the east, south and west coasts. Inland there are countless small lanes ideal for cycling tours. For golfers, Skåne has some of the finest and most beautifully located courses in Sweden.

Especially recommended is the 'Malmö Card' which can be purchased at the Malmö Tourist Board and entitles you to free travel on local buses, free admission to museums

and discounts on a wide variety of purchases.
EXCURSIONS: The medieval town of **Lund** has a 12th-century cathedral and 14th-century astrological clock.
RESORTS: Malmö, Lund, Helsingborg, Ystad, Falsterbo, Mölle and Båstad.

The Glass Country

In the middle of the 18th century, German immigrants established the province of **Småland**, north of Skåne, as the home of the Swedish glass-making industry. Småland is a very large province and the 'glass country' forms only a small part of it. It is also good holiday country with vast forests, pleasant lakes and winding lanes along which red cottages are dotted. In the province of **Blekinge** there are large oak forests and softer landscapes. This region has many coastal towns that stretch along the Baltic. The *Mörrumsån river* is noted for salmon and sea trout and *Lake Vättern* for char fishing. Three quarters of the Swedish glassworks are found in the counties of **Kronoberg** and **Kalmar.** They are located off the beaten track surrounded by vast tracts of forest and attract many visitors each year.
EXCURSIONS: Visitors are welcome to watch the craftsmen in most of the glassworks 0800-1500 Monday to Friday. Most of the works have their own shops. Boat trips are available to the island of **Visingsö** on Lake Vättern. *High Chaparral* is a reconstructed wild west town. There is a fortress on the Baltic island of Öland (see below).
RESORTS: Sölvesborg, Karlshamn, Ronneby, Karlskrona, Ljungby, Värnamo, Gislaved, Gnosjö, Jönköping, Växjö and Kalmar.

The West Coast

Halland is a long, narrow province strung out along the picturesque west coast. Unlike its northern neighbour, Bohuslän (see below), its landscape is gentle, with mile after mile of long sandy beaches, often fringed with pinewoods. Inland, the scenery changes as it meets the tableland of Småland and the landscape is characterised by a series of ridges and valleys. There are also vast forests and heather-covered moors.
Areas of note are **Kungsbacka**, a northern market town and the nearby Onsala peninsula, ideal for bathing, sailing and fishing, and **Fjärås Bräcka,** an unusual gravel ridge formed during the Ice Age. Further south is **Varberg,** one of Halland's main coastal resorts, dominated by the 13th-century *Varberg Fortress*. Other resorts are the port of **Falkenberg** and **Tylösand,** with its long sandy beach sheltered by dunes and pine trees. Halland's capital is the important seaport and industrial town of **Halmstad**.
Warmed by the waters of the Gulf Stream, the west coast is a natural choice for seaside holidays. The long narrow province of **Bohuslän** has countless spots where the visitor can enjoy an idyllic holiday in the sun. The coastline is deeply indented and there are hundreds of rocky islands. All along the coast are picturesque villages with their typical red-painted huts where the nets are hung out to dry. The province is also one of the most important centres of ancient Swedish civilisation and there are many archaeological relics dating back to the Bronze Age and Viking times.

The Golden Coast

This area is situated in the southwest of Sweden and has vast stretches of beaches, warm sea and holiday resorts reaching for 400km (250 miles) from **Laholm** in the south to **Strömstad** in the north. Here there are flat, sandy beaches, bare rocks and fjord-like inlets with meadows stretching down to the seashore and tiny fishing villages.
RESORTS: Gothenburg (see above), Halmstad, Lysekil, Tylösand, Falkenberg, Varberg, Bovallstrand, Hunnebostrand, Kungshamn and Smögen and the islands of Orust and Tjörn.

Gotland and Öland

These are Sweden's largest islands, situated off the southeast coast in the Baltic Sea. There is more sunshine here than elsewhere, making it a favourite summer holiday spot with the Swedes, and as a the result the beaches are rather crowded. The islands are of particular interest to ornithologists and flower lovers and there is a wealth of historic sites. Several ferries serve both islands and daily coach trips are available to Öland over Europe's longest bridge, starting just outside Kalmar on the mainland. Cycles can be hired on the islands.
EXCURSIONS: There are Stone, Bronze and Iron Age sites on both islands. On **Gotland** the *Lummelunda Caves* with their spectacular stalactites and stalagmites and a preserved medieval town at *Kattlundsgård*. On **Öland** are the Royal summer residence at **Solliden**; *Borgholm Castle;* a restored medieval church at **Gärdslösa**; a recently excavated fortified village at **Eketorp**; and many Viking stones and the local windmills.
RESORTS: Visby and Borgholm.

Swedish Lakeland

This region comprises the nine provinces of **Västergötland, Dalsland** and **Värmland** in the west, **Närke, Västmanland** and **Dalarna** in the north, and **Östergötland, Södermanland** and **Uppland** to the east. These form a large part of Sweden with a mixture of open water, vast lakes, plains and meadows – an area of wild natural scenery. The provinces in the west are dominated by Vänern, Sweden's largest lake, while in the north and east are the lakes of Vättern, Mälaren, Hjälmaren and Siljan as well as the Baltic Sea. The whole region is considered the cradle of Swedish culture, and it is here that the majority of Swedes live. For visitors there is a wide variety of hotels, campsites and country inns.
EXCURSIONS: Västergötland has the castle of *Läckö*, the *Trollhättan* hydro-electric waterfalls, canoe trips and fishing. **Närke** contains the *Stjerhov Manor* and a 17th-century inn at *Grythyttan* in Västmanland. In **Dalarna** visitors can meet Father Christmas at the Santaworld theme park. On the island of **Sollerön** there are Viking graves and in **Kolmården** there is a zoo and safari park. *Gripsholm Castle* is in **Södermanland,** with the university city of **Uppsala** and the baroque *Castle of Skokloster*, with a vintage car museum in Uppland.
RESORTS: Skara, Karlstad, Lidköping, Örebro, Askersund, Grythyttan, Rättvik, Leksand, Vadstena, Linköping, Tällberg, Sunne, Mariefred, Uppsala, Sigtuna and Björkön.

The Midnight Sun Coast

The midnight sun coast is a 1500km (900 mile) stretch of Baltic coastline which runs all the way to the Finnish border. In the south are the spruce forests of the province of **Gästrikland**; immediately to the north of this region is **Hälsingland** with its spectacular views, extensive lakes and typical wood-built mansions. Forestry has traditionally been the dominant industry of **Medelpad**, today one of Sweden's most industrialised areas, although there are plenty of opportunities for visitors who want to fish in unspoilt outback country or rent a cottage in the middle of a countryside rich in prehistoric monuments and relics of ancient cultures.
In the province of **Ångermanland** is some of Sweden's most breathtaking scenery, consisting of forests, lakes, islands, fjords and mountains plunging dramatically to the sea. This magnificent district is called the High Coast. **Västerbotten** offers unspoilt wilderness and the **Norrland Riviera** coastline is ideal for a relaxed holiday. There are also countless clear lakes and rivers teeming with fish, and excellent roads lead inland to the southern part of Lappland. Further north along the coast at **Lövånger** there are hundreds of renovated timber cottages which are rented out to holidaymakers. Nearer the Arctic Circle the air and water temperatures in the summer are much the same as in the Mediterranean and this area has an excellent sunshine record. **Norrbotten** is a fisherman's paradise with plenty of mountain streams and sea fishing.
RESORTS: Furuvik, Gävle, Söderhamn, Hudiksvall, Bollnäs, Ljusdal, Arbrå, Järvsö, Sundsvall, Härnösand, Örnsköldsvik, Ramsele, Umeå, Piteå, Luleå and Boden.

Lappland

The enormous expanse of **Lappland**, one of Europe's last wildernesses, covers a quarter of the area of Sweden but has only 5% of the population. It is both inviting and inhospitable at the same time. Fell-walkers who leave the marked routes do so at their own risk. The best-known route is *Kungsleden*, which also gives experienced mountaineers the chance to climb Sweden's highest peak, *Kebnekaise*. Other favourite areas for walking are the national parks of *Sarek* and *Padjelanta*. In the west the mountains soar up towards the Norwegian border and the region experiences rapid changes in the weather. **Jämtland**, bordering southern Lappland, has plenty of good hiking and fast-flowing rivers for fishermen. It is known for its skiing. Wildlife is abundant in **Härjedalen,** with reindeer, buzzard, beaver, lynx and Sweden's only herd of musk ox.
EXCURSIONS: Lapps celebrate their annual church festivals in **Gällivare.** In **Jokkmokk** there are collections of Lapp art and culture, and a *Lapp Staden*, an old village of 70 cone-shaped Lapp huts. **Arjeplog** has an interesting Lapp museum. Iron Age burial grounds and a medieval church are on the island of **Frösö**. The cable car trip from **Åre** leads up to the summit of Åreskutan.
RESORTS: Kiruna, Gällivare, Jokkmokk, Arvidsjaur, Ammarnäs, Tärnaby, Åre, Storlien, Storuman, Sylarna, Blåhammaren and Östersund. Ski resorts include Åre and Storlien.

SOCIAL PROFILE

FOOD & DRINK: Swedes like straightforward meals, simply prepared from the freshest ingredients. As a seafaring country with many freshwater lakes, fish dishes are prominent on hotel or restaurant menus. The Scandinavian cold table, called *smörgåsbord*, is to be appreciated properly when you eat the various dishes in their traditional order. First try pickled herring with boiled potatoes, then perhaps a couple more fish courses, smoked salmon or anchovies followed by cold meat, pâté, sliced beef, stuffed veal or smoked reindeer. The hot dishes come next, for instance, another herring dish, small meatballs (*köttbullar*) or an omelette. A fruit salad and cheese with various crispbreads round off the meal. Other dishes to look out for are smoked reindeer from Lappland; *gravlax*, salmon that has been specially prepared and pickled; wild strawberries; and the cloudberries that are unique to Scandinavia. Once on the open road the traveller is well catered for with numerous picnic sites on the way, often with wooden tables and seats.
Restaurants: Top-class restaurants in Sweden are usually fairly expensive, but even the smallest towns have reasonably priced self-service restaurants and grill bars. Many restaurants all over Sweden offer a special dish of the day at a reduced price which includes main course, salad, soft drink and coffee. Waiter service is common although there are many self-service snack bars. **Drink:** *Snapps*, the collective name for *aquavit* or *brännvin*, is a Swedish liqueur which is traditionally drunk chilled with *smörgåsbord*. It is made under a variety of brand names with flavours varying from practically tasteless to sweetly spiced. Swedish beers are lager and pilsner type brews and come in four strengths. The minimum age for buying alcoholic beverages is 20. Wine, spirits and beer are sold through the state-owned monopoly, *Systembolaget*, open during normal shopping hours. Before 1300 on Sundays alcohol cannot be bought in bars, cafés or restaurants. After midnight alcohol can only be bought in nightclubs that stay open until 0200 or 0300. In a restaurant or a nightclub, the minimum age for buying alcoholic beverages is 18. Stiff penalties are enforced for drinking and driving.
NIGHTLIFE: Stockholm has pubs, cafés, discos, restaurants, cinemas and theatres. In the more rural areas evenings tend to be tranquil. From August to June the Royal Ballet performs in Stockholm. Music and theatre productions take place in many cities during the summer at open air venues. Outside Stockholm in the 18th-century Court Theatre of the Palace of Drottningholm there are performances of 18th-century opera.
SHOPPING: VAT (*Moms*) is refundable to tourists or visitors who are residents outside the Nordic countries on goods bought at shops participating in the Tax-Free Shopping scheme. The refund is payable to the customer when departing from Sweden at either airports or customs offices at ports. Special purchases include glassware and crystal, stainless steel and silver, *hemslöjd* (cottage industry artefacts) and wood carvings. Women's and children's clothes are good buys, especially handknitted Nordic sweaters. **Shopping hours:** 0900-1800 Monday to Friday and 1000-1300 Saturday. In larger towns, certain department stores open some evenings until 2000/2200 and some are also open 1200-1600 Sundays. In rural areas, shops and petrol stations close by 1700/1800.
SPORT: Hiking routes are on well laid-out paths in almost every part of the country. **Cycling** is a popular holiday recreation, particularly in the south. The *Swedish Cycling Promotion Institute*, in co-operation with regional tourist offices, has scheduled cycling tours in almost every region. **Golf:** There are excellent golf courses and facilities provided for members and visitors. Sweden has about 150 courses. One situated north of the Arctic Circle enjoys 24 hour daylight during the summer months and many midsummer championships take place at midnight. Clubs and golf carts can usually be rented. **Winter sports:** There are excellent facilities for **skiing, skating, tobogganing** and **dog-sledging.** Most skiing takes place in the north, particularly in Jämtland, Dalarna and Härjedalen. **Watersports:** Sweden has hundreds of miles of beaches, particularly on the west coast, and 96,000 lakes. There are numerous **water-skiing** and **windsurfing** centres on the coast and more accessible lakes. **Skindiving** is mostly confined to the rocky coasts and islets on the west coast both north and south of Gothenburg. Courses are held from June to August. **Boating:** There are about 50 centres where you can hire a canoe. Many campsites offer a hire service. Sailing boats and motor-cruisers can be hired in more than 25 places in Sweden or visitors can bring their own. Many

of Sweden's canals run through beautiful countryside and are well maintained to provide an ideal boating holiday. Short sightseeing trips are available on several canals but the classic journey is by steamer along the Göta Canal. All meals and accommodation are included in the prices. Many cruises, some in vintage steamers, are operated from Stockholm out into the archipelago with its 30,000 islands. In August the World Championship for Soling class sailing boats will be held at Karlshamn (Blekinge).
Fishing: Sweden has more than 96,000 lakes and visitors can enjoy fishing in most of them. There are also thousands of miles of rivers, streams and brooks and a coastline of 6760km (4200 miles). The salmon season at Mörrum near Karlshamn opens at the beginning of spring. Sea-trout can be caught throughout the year, except in high summer, which is the best time for char and grayling (typical fish from the northern part of the country). Fishing is generally free all along the coastline and in the larger lakes, including Mälaren, Vättern and Vänern, but a special permit is required to fish in other lakes and rivers. Information is available from local tourist offices. Sea-fishing tours of varying lengths are arranged on the west coast and in the south. Guest harbours are available all round the coast and on Lakes Mälaren, Vänern and Vättern. The *Swedish Touring Club (STF)* publishes a list of 330 with some information in English.
SPECIAL EVENTS: The following is a selection of major festivals and other special events celebrated in Sweden during 1993/94. For a complete list, contact the the Swedish Travel & Tourism Council.
Jun '93 *Midsummer Celebrations*. **Jul** *Tall Ships' Race*, Karlskrona. **Aug 7-15** *Stockholm Water Festival*. **Dec 10** *Nobel Prize Ceremony*. **Dec 13** *St Lucia*. **First weekend of Feb '94** *Winter Fair*, Jokkmokk (Lappland). **First weekend of Mar** *Vasaloppet cross-country ski race from Sälen to Mora*, Dalarna.
SOCIAL CONVENTIONS: Normal courtesies should be observed. It is customary for the guest to refrain from drinking until the host makes a toast. He should also thank him for the meal with 'Tack för maten'. Casual dress is acceptable for everyday occasions; smarter wear for social occasions, exclusive restaurants and clubs. Evening wear (black tie) will usually be specified when required. Smoking is prohibited on public transport and in most public buildings.
Tipping: Hotel prices include a service charge. Service in restaurants is included in the bill. Late at night the service charge is higher. Taxi drivers are always tipped at least 10% of the fare on the meter.

BUSINESS PROFILE

ECONOMY: Sweden boasts one of Europe's most advanced industrial economies and one of the highest standards of social welfare in the world. A prolonged period of peace, which included a policy of neutrality during both World Wars, has contributed much to its economic development. Over half of the country is covered by forests, supplying raw material for the wood-based industries – paper, wood pulp and finished products such as furniture – which account for 20% of Swedish exports. Other major exports are vehicles, office and telecommunications equipment and chemicals. Many industries are state-owned. The country is rich in mineral resources, which include 15% of the world's identified uranium deposits and large deposits of iron ore, although production has declined sharply since the 1970s. Parts of the south and central regions are given over to agriculture. Lacking indigenous fossil fuels, which must be imported, Sweden has a large nuclear power programme meeting around 40% of total energy requirements. Domestic political considerations mean that this proportion is unlikely to be increased. Oil and coal are the largest items on Sweden's import bill; manufactured goods make up most of the rest. Sweden is a member of the European Free Trade Association (EFTA) which links the economies of those Western European nations outside the European Community. This trade will be boosted by the creation in 1991 of the European Economic Area, a free-trade zone encompassing the EC and EFTA, and perhaps future membership of the EC itself (see the *History* section below). Sweden's major bilateral trading partners are Germany, the UK and the USA.
BUSINESS: Business people are expected to dress smartly. English is widely spoken in business circles. Punctuality is important for business and social occasions. Business cards are commonly used. **Office hours:** Flexible working hours are a widespread practice, with lunch between 1200-1300.
COMMERCIAL INFORMATION: The following organisation can offer advice:
Federation of Swedish Commerce and Trade, PO Box 5512, Grevgatan 34, 114 85 Stockholm. Tel: (8) 666 1100. Fax: (8) 662 7457. Telex: 19673.
There are also chambers of commerce for other major towns and regions in Sweden.
CONFERENCES/CONVENTIONS: The main venues are in Stockholm, Gothenburg and Malmö; the Swedish Travel & Tourism Council also lists two in Lappland. The Globe Arena in Stockholm can seat up to 5000 persons and there are other venues in the city catering for up to 3000 persons. Elsewhere in Sweden most venues have facilities for 200-500 persons (although Malmö and Gothenburg have capacity for 1500). The Swedish Travel & Tourism Council's *Meetings and Incentive Planner* gives information on over 30 venues; it also supplies addresses for the main regional organisers.

HISTORY & GOVERNMENT

HISTORY: Sweden's contact with Europe is first recorded in the Viking period, when the country traded furs and arms along the eastern passage with Russia. During the 13th century a form of feudalism began to be introduced, a hereditary nobility was established and a thriving middle class of burghers emerged in the towns. Political history in this period is complex, but some sense of order, however transitory, was engendered by the accession of Margaret, then regent of Denmark and ruler of Norway, to the throne in 1387. She made an attempt to establish a united Scandinavia (the Union of Kalmar), but this did not long survive her death, and during the 15th century the nobility were able to do much as they pleased at the expense of royal authority. The most significant event of this period was the Massacre of Stockholm in 1520, occasioned by Christian of Denmark's ill-judged attempt to reassert his authority in Sweden; this led to a national revolt, headed by Gustav Ericksson Vasa. The Danes were defeated and Gustav was crowned Gustav I in 1523, establishing the House of Vasa and heralding the beginning of Sweden's ascendancy in Europe. Protestantism became firmly established by the Convention of Uppsala in 1593. In 1611, Gustav II Adolf, one of the most famous names in Swedish history, became king. The war with Russia was brought to a successful conclusion, as a result of which Russia was cut off from the Baltic. Many internal reforms, enlightened by the standard of the day, were also introduced by the king and his Chancellor Axel Oxenstierna. Much of the foreign policy of the 17th century was dominated by the desire to turn the Baltic into a Swedish lake: this was the main motivation behind Gustav II's entry into the Thirty Years War in 1629; despite his perceived role as a champion of Protestantism, he soon came to an alliance with Catholic France to oppose their common enemy, the Emperor Ferdinand II. Sweden won the last remaining Baltic territories not under their control, Prussia and Pomerania. Another consequence was the death of Gustav, killed at the Battle of Lutzen in 1632. Although the Peace of Westphalia (1648) confirmed Sweden as a major power, this dominance proved to be short-lived. Gustav was succeeded by his infant daughter Christina. She abdicated in 1654 and the reigns of her three successors (1654-1718) were dominated by military campaigns, characterised by a slow retreat (in the face of Russia and Austria) and punctuated by spectacular but indecisive victories, such as Narva (1701). An alliance against the growth of Swedish power eventually defeated Karl (the Great Northern War) and by the mid-18th century Sweden had lost most of its possessions outside Scandinavia. Another casualty of the defeat was absolutism, established by Karl XI, but abolished on the accession of his sister Eleanora. Factions at court involved the country in further European conflicts, including another war with Russia, and in 1772 Gustav III felt strong enough to reimpose absolutist rule. Despite an aggressive and successful foreign policy his regime did not long survive his own assassination in 1792. After the Peace of Kiel in 1814, Sweden was confirmed in possession of Norway but was forced to cede several German regions to Denmark and Finland to Russia, marking the termination of Swedish interests on mainland Europe. Absolutism was not broken until the mid-19th century, as a result of Liberal opposition to Karl XV. The latter years of the century were dominated by economic expansion and the emergence of Norwegian nationalism, culminating in the latter's declaration of full independence in 1905. By this time a parliamentary form of government had emerged in Sweden, with a strong Socialist opposition; they gained power in the early 1920s and introduced many social reforms. Sweden has since been ruled by a succession of governments of varying complexions, and also several coalitions. Sweden remained neutral in both world wars. The post-war years have been characterised by economic prosperity, continued investment in the welfare state, the forging of close links with other Scandinavian countries and an important role on the international stage as well-respected 'neutrals'. Nobody exemplified this more than Olof Palme, Prime Minister and leader of the Socialdemokratiska Arbetarepartiet (SDAP, Social Democrats) from 1970 until his assassination in 1986. At the 1988 election the Green party emerged as a major electoral force, attracting 20% of the poll. By this time relations with the EC had become the major issue in Swedish politics and, while the Government pursued liberalising economic measures, it was reluctant to compromise Swedish neutrality by making a formal application for membership. At the October 1991 election, all the major parties (Social Democrats, Conservatives, Liberals and Greens) backed a broadly pro-Community platform. The contest therefore centred upon domestic issues, particularly a reform of the welfare and tax systems and economic policy. The emergence of a right-wing populist party, New Democracy, cast further uncertainty on the outcome. The result was a four-party centre-right coalition led by the Conservatives under Carl Bildt. With 170 seats, he is just short of an outright majority and has to rely on the 23-member New Democracy caucus. Liberalisation and deregulation have accelerated under Bildt; privatisation of state companies has been introduced and foreign ownership encouraged. Government spending has been drastically cut. Sweden is now, along with Austria, considered to be at the front of the queue for EC membership.
GOVERNMENT: Sweden is a constitutional monarchy with legislative power vested in the 349-member Riksdag (parliament) which is elected for a 3-year term. A prime minister and cabinet are drawn from the largest party or coalition of parties.

CLIMATE

In spite of its northern position, Sweden has a relatively mild climate which varies due to its great length. The summers can be very hot but get shorter further north. The midnight sun can be seen between mid-May and mid-June above the Arctic Circle. Winters can be bitterly cold, especially in the north.
Required clothing: Lightweight for summer, heavy-weights for winter and all year.

STOCKHOLM Sweden (44m)

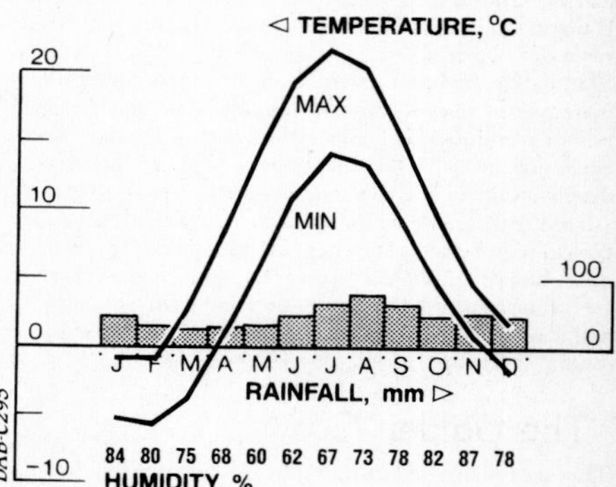

GÖTEBORG Sweden (31m)

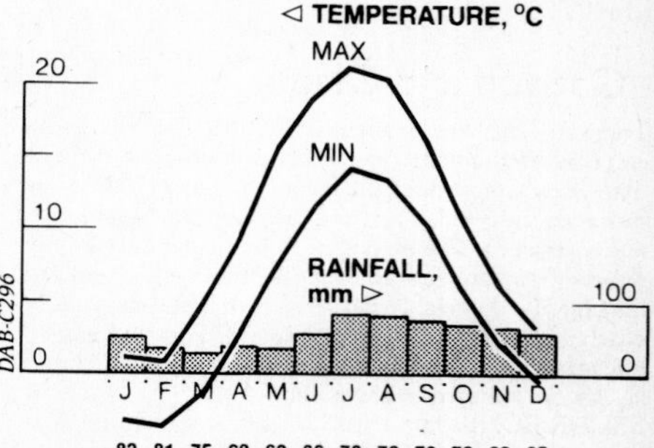

SWITZERLAND

Location: Western Europe.

Swiss National Tourist Office
Bellariastrasse 38
CH-8027 Zürich, Switzerland
Tel: (1) 288 1111. Fax: (1) 288 1205. Telex: 815391.
Embassy of the Swiss Confederation
16-18 Montagu Place
London W1H 2BQ
Tel: (071) 723 0701. Fax: (071) 724 7001. Telex: 28212 AMSWIS G. Opening hours: 0930-1230 Monday to Friday.
Swiss Consulate General
24th Floor, Sunley Tower
Piccadilly Plaza
Manchester M1 4BT
Tel: (061) 236 2933. Fax: (061) 236 4689. Telex: 665918 CONSUI G.
Swiss National Tourist Office
Swiss Centre
Swiss Court
London W1V 8EE
Tel: (071) 734 1921. Fax: (071) 437 4577. Opening hours: 0900-1700 Monday to Friday.
British Embassy
Thunstrasse 50
CH-3000 Bern 15, Switzerland
Tel: (31) 445 021. Fax: (31) 440 583. Telex: 911929 UKBE CH.
Consulates in: Geneva, Montreux, Zürich and Lugano.
Embassy of the Swiss Confederation
2900 Cathedral Avenue, NW
Washington, DC
20008
Tel: (202) 745 7900. Fax: (202) 387 2564. Telex: 440055.
Swiss National Tourist Office
608 Fifth Avenue
New York, NY
10020
Tel: (212) 757 5944. Fax: (212) 262 6116. Telex: 236058.
Also in: San Francisco, Los Angeles and Chicago.
Embassy of the United States of America
Jubiläumsstrasse 93
CH-3005 Bern, Switzerland
Tel: (31) 437 011. Fax: (31) 437 344. Telex: 912603.
Consulates in: Geneva and Zürich.
Embassy of the Swiss Confederation
5 Marlborough Avenue
Ottawa, Ontario
K1N 8E6
Tel: (613) 235 1837/8. Fax: (613) 563 1394. Telex: 0533648.
Consulates in: Calgary, Edmonton, Montréal, Québec, Toronto and Vancouver.
Swiss National Tourist Office
Suite 610
154 University Avenue
Toronto, Ontario
M5H 3Y9
Tel: (416) 971 9734. Fax: (416) 971 6425.
Canadian Embassy
PO Box 3000
Kirchenfeldstrasse 88
CH-3005 Bern, Switzerland
Tel: (31) 446 381/2/3/4/5. Fax: (31) 447 315. Telex: 911308 DMCN CH.
Consulate in: Bern.

AREA: 41,293 sq km (15,943 sq miles).
POPULATION: 6,673,850 (1989 estimate).
POPULATION DENSITY: 161.6 per sq km.
CAPITAL: Bern. **Population:** 134,393 (1989 estimate).
GEOGRAPHY: Switzerland is bordered by France to the west, Germany to the north, Austria to the east and Italy to the south. It has the highest mountains in Europe, waterfalls and lakes set amid green pastures and the spring Alpine flowers covering the valleys and lower mountain slopes. The highest peaks are Monte Rosa, 4634m (15,217ft), on the Italian border; the Dom, 4548m (14,917ft); the Matterhorn, 4477m (14,698ft); and the Jungfrau, 4166m (13,669ft). The most popular areas are: the Engadine, the Berner Oberland, the Valais and the Ticino.
LANGUAGE: 73% German in central and eastern areas, 20% French in the west and 4% Italian in the south. Raeto-Romansch is spoken in the southeast by 1%. English is spoken by many. Overlapping cultural influences characterise the country.
RELIGION: Roman Catholic and Protestant.
TIME: GMT + 1 (GMT + 2 in summer).
ELECTRICITY: 220 volts AC, 50Hz.
COMMUNICATIONS: Telephone: Full IDD is available. Country code: 41. International calls can be made from all call-boxes. **Fax:** Facilities are available in all telegraph offices and most major hotels and post offices. **Telex/telegram:** Many hotels have telex facilities, and telegrams and telex messages can be sent from post offices. **Post:** Airmail within Europe takes three days. *Poste Restante* is available at all post offices. Post offices are open 0730-1200 and 1345-1830 Monday to Friday. Saturday closing is at 1100 except in major cities. **Press:** The high level of interest in local politics throughout Switzerland has led to a large number of regional newspapers. However, the most popular dailies are *Blick* and *Tages-Anzeiger Zürich*. European newspapers are widely available. There are no local English-language newspapers printed in Switzerland.
BBC World Service and Voice of America frequencies: From time to time these change. See the section *How to Use this Book* for more information.

BBC:

MHz	15.070	9.410	6.195	3.955

A service is also available on 648kHz and 198kHz (0100-0500 GMT).

Voice of America:

MHz	11.97	9.670	6.040	5.995

PASSPORT/VISA

Regulations and requirements may be subject to change at short notice, and you are advised to contact the appropriate diplomatic or consular authority before finalising travel arrangements. Details of these may be found at the head of this country's entry. Any numbers in the chart refer to the footnotes below.

	Passport Required?	Visa Required?	Return Ticket Required?
Full British	1	No	Yes
BVP	Valid	-	-
Australian	Yes	No	Yes
Canadian	Yes	No	Yes
USA	Yes	No	Yes
Other EC	1	No	Yes
Japanese	Yes	No	Yes

PASSPORTS: Valid passport required by all except:
(a) **[1]** nationals of EC countries holding a national ID card or, in the case of UK nationals, a BVP;
(b) nationals of Austria, Cyprus, Finland, Liechtenstein, Malta, Monaco and San Marino holding national ID cards.
British Visitors Passport: Acceptable.
VISAS: Required by all except:
(a) nationals of countries referred to in the chart above;
(b) nationals of countries in South and Central America (nationals of Belize *do* need a visa);
(c) nationals of Caribbean island states (nationals of the Dominican Republic and Haiti *do* need a visa);
(d) nationals of Andorra, Austria, Brunei, Cyprus, Czechoslovakia, Fiji, Finland, Hungary, Iceland, Israel, Kiribati, Liechtenstein, Malaysia, Malta, Monaco, New Zealand, Norway, Poland, San Marino, Singapore, Solomon Islands, South Africa, South Korea, Sweden, Tuvalu and Vatican City;
(e) nationals of Bosnia-Hercegovina, Croatia and Turkey provided they are resident in an EC or EFTA country, Canada or the USA;
(f) nationals of Yugoslavia provided they are resident in an EC or EFTA country.
The exemptions listed under (a)-(f) are for stays of up to three months provided that the visitor does not engage in employment or other gainful activity. If staying longer than six months within a 12-month period, a 'Residence Permit' is required which has to be applied for within eight days of entry to Switzerland.
Types of visa: Single-, Multiple-entry and Transit visas (maximum 24 hours in country). Cost: £11 for passengers over 18 years of age; £5.50 for unmarried passengers under 18.
Validity: 3 months.
Application to: Consulate (or Consular Section at Embassy). For addresses, see top of entry. UK applicants should note that residents of Northern Ireland, Scotland, Cheshire, Cleveland, Cumbria, Derbyshire, Durham, Greater Manchester, Humberside, Isle of Man, Lancashire, Leicestershire, Lincolnshire, Merseyside, Northumberland, Nottinghamshire, Tyne & Wear and Yorkshire must obtain their visas from the Swiss Consulate General in Manchester.
Application requirements: (a) 1 completed application form. (b) 1 passport-size photo. (c) Passport or travel document valid for at least 6 months after intended visit. (d) Return/onward ticket and visa for next country of destination if required. (e) Proof of sufficient funds, ie SFr100 (£40) for each day of stay, or SFr30 (£13) per day for students presenting a valid student ID card and letter from their university. (f) For visitors staying with Swiss residents, an invitation from the host stating that the visitor's expenses would be met by the host, which must then be approved, stamped and signed by the Aliens Police of the resident's canton). (g) For a Business visa, proof of existing business connections or invitation from Swiss company or business partner.
Temporary residence: For nationals listed above an 'Assurance of a Residence Permit' must be obtained prior to entry from the employer in Switzerland by all those taking up residence or employment there. Students who wish to attend a school, college or university for more than 3 months need not apply for this assurance in advance, but must apply to the local Aliens Police for a residence permit after entry.

MONEY

Currency: Swiss Franc (SFr) = 100 rappen or centimes. Notes are in denominations of SFr1000, 500, 100, 50, 20 and 10. Coins are in denominations of SFr5, 2, 1 and 0.5, and 20, 10 and 5 centimes.
Currency exchange: Personal cheques within the 'Eurocheque' system are accepted.
Credit cards: Access/Mastercard, American Express, Diners Club and Visa are widely accepted. Check with your credit card company for details of merchant acceptability and other facilities which may be available.
Travellers cheques: Pound Sterling, US Dollar or Swiss Franc cheques are accepted at airports, railway stations and banks.
Exchange rate indicators: The following figures are included as a guide to the movements of the Swiss Franc against Sterling and the US Dollar:

Date:	Oct '89	Nov '90	Oct '91	Oct '92
£1.00=	2.60	2.51	2.55	2.17
$1.00	1.64	1.29	1.47	1.37

Currency restrictions: There are no restrictions on the import or export of local or foreign currencies.
Banking hours: 0830-1630 Monday to Friday.

DUTY FREE

The following items may be imported into Switzerland by persons over 17 years of age without incurring customs duty by:
(a) Visitors from European countries:
200 cigarettes or 50 cigars or 250g of pipe tobacco;
2 litres of alcohol (up to 15° proof);
1 litre of alcohol (over 15° proof);
Gifts up to SFr100 (SFr50 for passengers under 17 years of age).
(b) Visitors from non-European countries:
400 cigarettes or 100 cigars or 500g of pipe tobacco;
2 litres of alcohol (up to 15° proof);
1 litre of alcohol (over 15° proof);
Gifts up to SFr100 (SFr50 for passengers under 17 years of age).
Prohibited items: All meat and processed meat, absinth

and narcotics are prohibited. There are strict regulations on importing animals and firearms.

PUBLIC HOLIDAYS

Public holidays observed in Switzerland are as follows: **Apr 9 '93** Good Friday. **Apr 12** Easter Monday. **May 20** Ascension Day. **May 31** Whit Monday. **Aug 1** National Day. **Dec 25-26** Christmas. **Jan 1-2 '94** New Year.
Note: There are in addition some local and regional holidays which are only observed in certain areas.

HEALTH

Regulations and requirements may be subject to change at short notice, and you are advised to contact your doctor well in advance of your intended date of departure. Any numbers in the chart refer to the footnotes below.

	Special Precautions?	Certificate Required?
Yellow Fever	No	No
Cholera	No	No
Typhoid & Polio	No	-
Malaria	No	-
Food & Drink	No	-

Health care: Health insurance is essential. Medical facilities in Switzerland are among the best in Europe but treatment is expensive. Various leaflets giving information on health spas and clinics are available from the SNTO.

TRAVEL - International

AIR: Switzerland's national airline is *Swissair (SR)*.
Approximate flight times: From *London* to Basel, Bern, Geneva or Zürich is 1 hour 30 minutes.
From *Los Angeles* to Geneva is 17 hours and to Zürich is 14 hours 35 minutes.
From *New York* to Geneva is 9 hours 45 minutes and to Zürich is 7 hours 20 minutes.
International airports: *Zürich (ZRH)* (Kloten), 13km (8 miles) from the city (travel time – 10 minutes). Trains run every 20 minutes from 0600-2400, from under Terminal B. Passengers arriving in Switzerland by air via Zürich, Geneva or Basel Airports can check in their baggage from the airport abroad through to their Swiss destination. Home-going air travellers whose flights are booked from Basel, Zürich or Geneva airports can check their luggage through to their final destination from many Swiss towns and resorts. Return is from Hauptbahnhof (main railway station). Taxis to the city are available.
Geneva (GVA) (Gen), 5km (3 miles) northwest of the city. Taxis to the city are available. There is a regular train service to Geneva Cornavin Station (travel time – 7 minutes).
Bern (BRN) (Belp), 9km (5.5 miles) from the city (travel time – 20 minutes). Bus services are available to Bern Bahnhof. A rail service runs from Bern to Zürich Airport (0455-2147). Taxis are also available.
Basel (BSL) (Basel-Mulhouse), 12km (7 miles) from the city. Bus runs to Basel SBB Luftreisebüro. Taxis are also available.
Note: Portable computers may not be carried as hand luggage on international flights departing from Swiss airports. This ban was introduced as a security measure and may be lifted at any time; check with your airline before travelling.
RAIL: Connections from London via the main channel crossings are available (minimum journey time of about 14-15 hours to Basel and Lausanne, the main points of entry). There are also through trains from many other European cities.
ROAD: Switzerland can be reached by road from Italy, Germany, France and Austria. Some approximate driving times to Geneva and Zürich by the most direct routes are: Calais–Geneva: 12/13 hours (747km/464 miles); Dunkirk–Geneva: 12/13 hours (732km/454 miles); Calais–Zürich: 13-14 hours (790km/490 miles); and Dunkirk–Zürich: 14-15 hours (880km/546 miles).
Coach: There are coach services to Switzerland, such as 'Europabus', as well as scheduled coach tour operators. See below for information on **documentation** and **traffic regulations**.

TRAVEL - Internal

AIR: All services are operated by *Swissair* and *Crossair*. Domestic air travel is fast but expensive, and with the exception of the Geneva to Zürich flight (travel time – 45 minutes), many business people prefer to travel by rail or road.
RAIL: Rail transport is particularly well-developed in Switzerland, with excellent services provided by the *Schweizerischen Bundesbahnen (SBB)* and many other operators. Use of the 'Swiss Pass' (see below) is a superb way to view the scenery, although mainline services are geared to the needs of the hurried business traveller. Trains run at least hourly from the major centres and there is a country-wide timetable of regular services. There are dining cars on many trains, and snacks and refreshments are widely available. Independent railways, such as the *Rhätische Bahn* in the Grisons and the *Berner Oberlandbahn*, provide services in certain parts of the country. There are also a large number of mountain railways which are sometimes the only means of access to winter resorts. The SBB has introduced specialised cars for disabled people using wheelchairs. Facilities include a lift for wheelchairs, a specially adapted WC and radios adapted for people with hearing difficulties.
Cheap fares are available from SNTO. The 'Swiss Pass' gives unlimited travel on rail services, those of other main regional operators, lake steamers and the extensive network of postal buses, as well as reduced price travel on other mountain railways not included in the full scheme. If travelling with parents on a family ticket, children up to 15 travel free and from 16-25 pay half price. Senior citizen cards are available and provide a significant discount. There are also regional tickets for unlimited travel in different parts of Switzerland at various rates. There is a leaflet describing all the schemes which is available from the SNTO. A comprehensive timetable for all Swiss public transport can also be purchased. Inter-Rail cards are valid.
ROAD: Road quality is generally good. Many mountain roads are winding and narrow, and often closed in heavy winter conditions; otherwise chains and snow tyres may be necessary. Rail is often more efficient than driving.
Coach: Postal motor coaches provide a service to even the remotest villages, but under the integrated national transport policy few long-distance coaches are allowed to operate. **Taxi:** All taxis have meters for short and long trips, although it is advisable to agree the fare for longer distances out of town. **Car hire:** Available in all towns from hotels and airports and at all manned rail stations. All major European companies are represented.
Regulations: Seat-belts are obligatory and children under 12 years must travel in the back of the car. Dipped headlights are compulsory in bad light. Drink-driving fines are heavy. **Speed limits:** 80kmph (50mph); 120kmph (75mph) on motorways; 50kmph (31mph) in towns. **Organisations:** The AA and RAC in the UK are linked with *TCS (Touring Club Suisse)* and *ACS (Automobil Club der Schweiz)*. Contact the *Automobil Club der Schweiz (ACS)*, Wasserwerkgasse 39, CH-3000 Bern 13. Tel: (31) 224 722. Fax: (31) 220 310.
Motorway tax (Vignette): Since January 1, 1985 an annual road tax of SFr30 has been levied on all cars using Swiss motorways. An additional fee of SFr30 applies to trailers and caravans. The vignette (sticker) is valid between December 1 of the year preceding and January 31 of the one following the year printed on the vignette. These permits, which are available at the border crossings, are valid for multiple re-entry into Switzerland within the duration of the licensed period. To avoid hold-ups at the frontier, however, it is advisable to purchase the vignette in advance from the nearest SNTO.
Documentation: A national driving licence is sufficient. Green Card insurance is advised – ordinary domestic policies insurance are valid but do not provide full cover. The Green Card tops the cover up to the level provided by the visitor's domestic policy.
URBAN: Highly efficient and integrated urban public transport systems serve as a model for other countries. There are tramways and light rail services in Basel, Bern, Geneva, Neuchâtel and Zürich and these and a further dozen cities also have trolleybuses. Fares systems are generally automated with machines issuing single or multiple tickets at the roadside. Tickets are also available at enquiry offices. Fares are generally zonal. There is a day ticket for travel in one or more Swiss cities on any given day at a standard fare. Taxis are widely available and drivers expect a 15% tip.
JOURNEY TIMES: The following chart gives approximate journey times (in hours and minutes) from Zürich to other major cities/towns in Switzerland.

	Air	Road	Rail
Basel	0.30	1.10	1.05
Bern	-	1.15	1.10
Geneva	0.40	2.45	2.55
Lugano	0.45	3.00	3.00

ACCOMMODATION

HOTELS: Hotels are of high quality and in high demand. Advance booking is advised. Bookings cannot be made through the SNTO. All standards from luxury to family hotels and pensions are available. 40% of hotels in Switzerland are affiliated to the *Schweizer Hotelier Verein* (Swiss Hotels Association) (SHV), PO Box 2657, Monbijoustrasse 130, CH-3001 Bern. Tel: (31) 507 111. Fax: (31) 507 444. 75% of all overnight stays in the country are at SHV member hotels.
Grading: The SHV classifies all its hotels according to a 5-star rating system, which stipulates a range of facilities as follows:
5-star (luxury): Very high standard of comfort and facilities including all rooms with private bath, colour television and 16/24-hour room service. Minimum size of hotel: 35 rooms. There are 87 SHV-classified 5-star hotels.

SWITZERLAND	HEALTH REGULATIONS	VISA REGULATIONS (Code-Link)
GALILEO/WORLDSPAN	 TI-DFT/ZRH/HE	 TI-DFT/ZRH/VI
SABRE	 TIDFT/ZRH/HE	TIDFT/ZRH/VI

To access this information on your CRS, swipe the barcode with a light pen or type in the text under the barcode. For more information, see the introduction *How to Use This Book*.

4-star (First class): High standard of comfort and facilities including all rooms with private bath and 16/24-hour room service. 60% of rooms with colour television. Minimum size of hotel: 25 rooms. There are 438 SHV-classified 4-star hotels.
3-star (Good middle-class): Very good standard of comfort and facilities including 75% of rooms with private bath. Minimum size of hotel: 10 rooms. There are 1037 SHV-classified 3-star hotels.
2-star (comfortable): Good standard of comfort and facilities including 30% of rooms with private bath. There are 565 SHV-classified 2-star hotels.
1-star (simple): Simple, clean accommodation offering basic amenities. There are 295 SHV-classified 1-star hotels.
Note: Membership of the SHV is, however, voluntary, and there may be some first-class hotels which do not have the star rating.
Prices will vary slightly according to the popularity of the resort.
The SHV (see above for address) issues a yearly guide of 2700 member hotels and pensions. This shows the rates, addresses, telephone/telex numbers, opening dates and amenities of the various hotels. Also included are lists of spas, resorts, sports facilities and climate. A list of hotels and restaurants catering for Jewish visitors is available from the SHV, as well as a hotel guide for the disabled and a list of hotels especially suitable for families. All lists are available from the SNTO.
CHALETS & APARTMENTS: Information regarding the rental of chalets, houses, flats and furnished apartments is available from local tourist offices and estate agents in Switzerland. A list of contacts is available from the SNTO.
SPAS: Switzerland has about 22 different mineral springs for the treatment of various health conditions. A guide to Swiss spas, including hotels, is available from the SNTO. Information can also be obtained from the Swiss Spa Association (SSA), PO Box 1456, CH-5400 Baden. Tel: (56) 225 318.
PRIVATE CLINICS: Details of accommodation in private sanatoria and clinics is included in the publication *Private Clinics in Switzerland*, available from the SNTO.
CAMPING: There are approximately 450 campsites in Switzerland. Camping on farmland is not advisable. Local area laws and fees vary. Camping guides published by the *Swiss Camping Federation* and the *Swiss Camping Association* can be purchased from the SNTO. The *Swiss Camping Association (SCA)* can be contacted at Seestrasse 119, CH-3800 Interlaken. Tel: (36) 233 523.
YOUTH HOSTELS: Youth hostel accommodation is available for tourists up to the age of 25 years. Hostellers over 25 are admitted if there is room. Visitors from abroad must hold a membership card of a national organisation affiliated to the *International Youth Hostels Federation*. To avoid disappointment, wardens of youth hostels should be given prior notice (at least five days) of arrival. An *International Reply Paid Postcard (Youth Hostel Edition)* should be used if confirmation is required.
A list of Swiss youth hostels is obtainable from the SNTO or from the *Schweizerischer Bund für Jugendherbergen (SBJ)* (Swiss Youth Hostel Federation), Neufeldstrasse 9, CH-3012 Bern. Tel: (31) 245 503.

RESORTS & EXCURSIONS

For purposes of this guide Switzerland has been divided into six resort sections: Western, Northern, Central, Eastern and Southern Switzerland; and Ski Resorts.

Western Switzerland

Jura, Neuchâtel & Fribourg: The Lakes of Biel, Murten and Neuchâtel are strung along the foot of the Jura. Although not one of the most popular regions for tourists, the rolling hills, the *Franches Montagnes* in the Neuchâtel region and the foothills of the Alps of the canton of Fribourg on the other side of the lakes are excellent for hiking, camping and fishing. The waterfalls of the *Doubs* and the gorges of the *Areuse* are very impressive. Well worth a visit is the *Lac Talliers*, the medieval town of **Romont**, south of **Morat** and the *Folk Art Museum* at **Tafers. Fribourg** where a romanesque-germanic atmosphere prevails, is one of the most interesting historical cities in Switzerland. In the south of the canton Fribourg is the Gruyère region, in the foothills of the Alps. It is famous for its dairy farming which produces one of the best Swiss cheeses: Gruyère. The town of **Gruyères** is still completely surrounded by its old city walls. Swiss precision watches are produced in Western Switzerland; do not miss the *Horological Museum* at **La-Chaux-de-Fonds.** Visitors can try to solve the mystery of the precision watch at the watch-making factories at **La-Chaux-de-Fonds** and **Le Locle**. The area is also famous for its food wines.
Resorts: Saint Blaise, La Chaux-de-Fonds, Le Locle, Le Font, Neuchâtel, Auvernier, Colombier, La Neuveville, Boudry, Fribourg, Gruyères, Les Bioux, Murten, Le Brassus and St Ursanne.
Geneva & Lake Geneva (Lac Léman in French; **Genfer See** in German): Geneva is a university town set at the Rhône-outlet of the lake at the foot of the Jura. It owes its cosmopolitan nature to the presence of the United Nations, the International Red Cross and many other international organisations. The *Palais des Nations* should be part of every itinerary. Its popularity is, however, not only due to its excellent surroundings. Elegant shops, nightclubs, restaurants, fine museums and art galleries and an extensive calendar of cultural activities make it a favourite with many visitors. The old city centre should be explored on foot. One of the finest examples of Romanesque architecture is the *Cathedral St Pierre Genève*. There is also an original flower clock in the *Jardin Anglais*. Do not miss a boat-trip on the lake. The lake, which is dominated by the *Jet d'Eau*, a 145m-high water fountain, is generally covered with sailing boats. A crisp breeze known as the *bise* blows across the lake and there are facilities for all kinds of watersports, as well as golf and riding. Mountaineering is popular at *Mont Salève*, south of the city, where there is an excellent school. In winter there is skiing, skating, curling and covered swimming. Vineyards cover the slopes of Monts de Lavaux; the villages of Riez and Epesse produce delicious wines. *Chateau d'Oex*, in the canton of Vaud, is the gateway to the *Pays d'Enhaut* ('upper land').
Lausanne, the capital of the canton, is situated on the northern shore of Lac Léman. The symbol of the city is the *Cathedral Notre Dame* in the *Cité*, the old centre, and the *Château St Maire* (1397-1431). A walk along the promenade of the old *Port d'Ouchy* reverts to a slower pace of life; or a funicular can be taken from Ouchy to the inner city of Lausanne. Several rivulets and rolling hills dominate the canton Vaud, a famous wine-producing region. In the midst of vineyards is the *Château d'Aigle*, the former residence of the Bernse Landvogts. Also in this area is one of the most important historical buildings of Switzerland: the Benedictine monastery church of *St Pierre* (11th century) in the small town of **Romainmotier**. There is summer skiing on the glacier at **Les Diablerets** (noteworthy for its panoramic views of *Mont Blanc* and the icy peaks and green valleys of the Alps), and rafting or hydrospeeding precariously down the *Sarine*, from *Chateau d'Oex*, is the area's newest sport. Each summer there is a rock festival at **Leysin. Montreux** is renowned for its mild climate and the International Jazz Festival. At **Villars** there is an 18-hole golf course. The region's more traditional activities include wood sculpture, cheese-making and paper cut-out artistry.
Summer resorts: Lausanne, Montreux, Yverdon, Nyon-Coppet, Morges, Lausanne Chexbres, Vevey, Villeneuve, Château d'Oex, Les Diablerets, Leysin, Villars, Gryon, Payerne, Sainte Croix, Orbe and Vallée de Joux.
Winter resorts: Rochers-de-Naye, Les Avants, Château d'Oex, Rougemont, Les Diablerets, Leysin, Villars, Gryon, Saint Cergue, Sainte Croix, Vallée de Joux.

Northern Switzerland

Zürich: Switzerland's largest city is set on its own lake on the banks of the *Limmat River*, and is a German-speaking business and banking centre. The old part of the town is picturesque, and the town has a full cultural season. Plays are performed in the *Zürcher Schauspielhaus*, which is counted among the most prestigious German-speaking theatres. On a walk through the old centre do not miss the *Basilica Fraumünster* (11th-13th century) with its three naves and the stained glass windows by Marc Chagall. The skyline is dominated by the *Grossmünster* with its twin towers. Other sights include the impressive *Town Hall*, a fine example for the later Renaissance (17th century), the *Swiss Country Museum* and the porcelain collection at the Baroque *Zunfthaus zur Meisen*. Local trains and buses leave for the hills, woods and parks that surround Zürich; during the summer, steamer cruises on the lake are also popular. Zürich is set in the Mittelland ('middle country'), a very lush and picturesque region dotted with small historic towns, spotless villages and vineyards. **Regensberg** is one of the most appealing medieval cities in the country; the medieval castle at **Rapperswil** is well worth a visit. A day-trip to the *Uetliberg* is recommended. On clear days the panorama from the platform includes the Valais and Berner Alps to the west and in the east the Black Forest. **Schaffhausen** is set above the *Rhine Falls* on the norther bank.
Northwest Switzerland: Not one of the more important tourist areas, but there are a few well-known holiday resorts. **Basel,** the ancient university and trading city, straddles the Rhine between the Jura and the Alsace, and is a centre of art and research. During the three days of the *Basler Fasnacht* (carnival), no serious sightseeing should and can be done, as visitors are required to take part. The towns people even built a *Fasnacht Fountain* in front of the City Theatre. The collection in the *Art Museum* ranges from Cranach and Holbein via Rembrandt to Monet, Picasso and Max Ernst. The old city centre houses the *Münster* (parts date from the 9th-13th century) with its two towers. Other sights include the *Spulentor* (1370) and the *Church of St Peter* (15th century). Away from the town, mountain paths zigzag up to the heights of the Jura. The prevalent architectural styles of **Solothurn** are Renaissance and Baroque. Day trips to **Aarau** and **Baden** are also recommended. Do not miss the 13th-century moated castle at **Binningen,** the *Waldenburg* and the spa resort of *Rheinfelden*.

Central Switzerland

The **Berner Oberland** with Interlaken and Jungfraujoch is one of the main tourist areas of Switzerland with a spectacular scenery of famous peaks, mountain lakes, alpine streams and wild flowers. **Adelboden, Grindelwald** and **Lenk** were already famous with the European noblesse and artists of the 19th century.
Interlaken, situated between the lakes of Thun and Brienz, is a renowned climatic health resort and the gateway to the Berner Oberland. From here a network of roads and mountain railways serves the resorts in the Jungfrau region. Jungfrau (4158m), Mönch (4099m) and Eiger (3970m), whose dangerous, nearly perpendicular northern ascend was climbed 1938 for the first time, are the Finsteraarhorn Group. Finsteraarhorn (4275m), the highest peak of the Berner Alps, is dominated by glaciers

which reach from the upper Aare and the Rhône valley to Lac Léman. Excursions to the Schilthorn and the Allmendhubel with funiculars, the waterfalls at **Giessbach** and the open-air museum at **Ballenberg** are recommended. **Adelboden** and **Zweisimmen** are reached from Spiez on *Lake Thun*. *Thun's Castle* should not be missed.

Bern, the ancient capital, provides opportunities for sightseeing and shopping in the 11th-century arcaded streets. The backdrop is provided by the Jura in the west and the south is dominated by the Alps and their foothills. On the *Aare Peninsula* is the medieval city centre between the *Zeitglockenturm* and the *Nydeggchurch*. Vegetable and flowerstalls are scattered over the pretty *Bear Market* on Tuesday and Saturday mornings.

Summer resorts: Interlaken, Mürren, Wengen, Lenk, Grindelwald, Brienz, Meiringen, Thun and Spiez.

Winter resorts: Interlaken, Mürren, Wengen, Grindelwald, Gstaad, Lauterbrunnen, Scheidegg, Zweisimmen and Meiringen.

Lucerne area: This region of mountains, lakes, pine forests and meadows is traditionally a very popular tourist area. The lakes of *Zug*, *Ageri* and *Lauerz* surround the Rigi massif. **Lucerne** is on the *Vierwaldstätter See*. Its medieval old town remains intact; important buildings include the *Hofkirche*, the old *Town Hall* (1602-1606) and the famous *Lion Memorial*. Spanning the Reuss is the 170m-long, covered wooden *Chapel Bridge*, the oldest in Switzerland (1333). Lucerne also houses the *Richard Wagner Museum* and the transport museum. An international music festival is held here every year. Cablecars, passenger lifts, and cogwheel railways provide transport to the *Sonnenberg*, the *Gütsch*, the *Pilatus* and other mountains.

Summer resorts: Lucerne, Engelberg, Weggis, Vitznau, Schwyz, Sarnen, Küssnacht, Hergiswil, Gersau, Einsiedel and Brunnen.

Winter resorts: Engelberg, Andermatt, Melchsee-Frutt, Rigi Kaltbad and Sorenberg.

Eastern Switzerland

Graubünden: There are 150 valleys in the rugged mountainous country of the Grisons. The climatic health resorts of St Moritz, Davos, Klosters and Arosa are renowned the world over, not only for their winter sports facilities. Typical Engadine stone-houses characterise the cities of **St Moritz, Pontresina** and **Zuos.** The highest peak in the canton is the Bernina (4049m) on the border to Italy and Austria. **Chur**, the oldest Swiss city, is the hub for *St Moritz, Davos, Klosters, Arosa* and countless other ski resorts. Sights of the city include the *St Lucius Church*, the *Cathedral* (12th-13th century) and the *Rhaetic Museum*. A bus ride from Chur to **Bellinzona** goes over the *San Bernardino Pass*. In the Engadine valley, small villages beyond **Zernez** and the *Swiss National Park* have cross-country skiing or summer walking areas. This mountain republic has probably the longest history of any region of Switzerland and has castles, fortresses and countless churches and chapels. The 168-sq-km Swiss National Park is covered to a third with dense forest and home to several wildlife species, among them roe and deer, eagles, marmot and lizards.

All-year resorts: Flims, St Moritz, Arosa, Davos, Bad Scuol, Bad Tarasp-Vulpera, Bad Vals, Bergun, Chur, Disentis, Grusch, Klosters, Laax, Lenzerheide, Mustair, Obersaxen, Pontresina, Poschiavo, San Bernardino, Samedan, Savognin, Sedrun, Sils, Silvaplana and Zernez.

East & North of Lake Constance: This area of Eastern Switzerland rises slowly over the rugged range of the Churfirsten near St Gallen to the Glarner Alps. **Appenzell,** in the northeastern part of Switzerland, with its highest peak Säntis (2504m), is ideal for hiking tours. The Rhine, which springs from Lake Toma in the *St Gotthard*, runs through Lake Constance and cascades into the fall at Schaffhausen. **Stein am Rhein** is a picturesque small town with a medieval atmosphere. **St Gallen's** old city centre is dominated by burgher houses from the 17th and 18th century. Not to be missed is the Baroque *Cathedral*, the famous *Abbey Library* in the courtyard of the old Benedictine monastery (incunabula and illuminated manuscripts) and the city library, *Vadiana* (1551). Old traditions remain very much alive in Appenzell, and national costumes are still worn for village and folk festivals. The wild valley of the Linth, lakeboat trips on Lake Constance to **Friedrichshafen** in Germany, excursions to the Berner Oberland and to the Valais and the Duchy of Liechtenstein can easily be arranged.

Summer resorts: Schaffhausen, Toggenburg, Stein am Rhein, Lake Constance, Wildhaus and Unterwasser.

Winter resorts: The Toggenburg Valley, Wildhaus and Unterwasser.

Southern Switzerland

Valais: The valley stretches all the way from the Rhône glacier past **Brig**, **Sion** and **Martigny** down to **Lake Geneva.** Nestling between the northern and the southern side of the Alps is a diverse landscape which will entice every visitor. Glaciers can be found on all peaks of the Valais Alps which are also the highest in Switzerland: Monte Rosa (4635m), Dom (4551m), Weisshorn (4509m) and the Matterhorn (4479m). Small villages of weathered wooden-beamed houses, with flowers pouring out of the windowboxes in summer, perch in clearings high on the slopes. High transverse valleys give access to their resorts at the foot of the alpine giants such as **Saas Fee** in the Saas Valley and **Zermatt** in the Nikolai Valley; the Matterhorn provides a magnificent backdrop for the latter. In the internationally well-known resort of Zermatt, cars are not allowed and transport is either on foot or horse and cart. There are well-posted walks and cable-cars, with lifts and tows to the tops of the slopes for more ambitious climbing. The historic town of **Brig** boasts the most important Baroque castle in Switzerland, the *Stockalperschloss*. **Sion**, an episcopal town, and **Martigny**, with a castle ruin, are worth a visit and are also ideal starting points for excursions to the surrounding area. Castle enthusiasts should visit **Leuk**, **Sierre** and **Monthey**. Europe's highest aerial cable goes up to the *Little Matterhorn* at **Zermatt**. Any visit to the area should include the *Rhône Glacier* and grotto at **Gletsch** and the subterranean lake at **Saint Leonard**.

All-year resorts: Zermatt, Saas Fee, Crans Montana, Leukerbad, Champex, Champery, Riederalp, Bettmeralp and Verbier.

Winter resorts: Bellwald, Fiesch, Grachen, Les Marecottes, Champery-Planachaux, Morgins, Salvan and Finhaut.

Ticino: The Italian-speaking, southernmost tip of Switzerland is the Ticino. The climate is subtropical and the atmosphere Mediterranean. From the Alpine valleys the road runs down to the narrow streets, pavement cafés and lakeside lido of **Locarno,** on the shores of Lago di Maggiore. The largest tessinian city **Lugano** is a health and holiday resort and lies on the Lago di Lugano between the peaks of *San Salvatore* and *Monte Bré*. It is a favourite holiday destination for the Swiss. Piazzas, palazzos, palms, the *Cathedral San Lorenzo* and the promenade along the lake shore give the city a special flair. During spring the area is in full bloom with fig and olive trees, pommegranates and myrtle. Local buses visit the picturesque villages of the area and funiculars run to the top of *Mount San Salvatore*. Coach excursions to the great passes of *Furka, Oberalp* and *Lukmanier,* and to Milan and Venice, can be arranged locally. The islands of **Brissago** are worth a visit; on the larger is an interesting botanical garden with Mediterranean flora. The unspoiled wilderness of **Bolle di Magadino** is a must for nature enthusiasts and the *Paleological Museum* at **Meride** is also interesting.

Resorts: Locarno, Ascona, Brissago, Lugano, Morcote and Gandria.

Ski Resorts

ADELBODEN AREA: Adelboden: Christmas to beginning of April. Quiet town and nightlife, mainly for serious skiers. **Lenk:** Season is mid-December to end March. Superb skiing, but very quiet. Excellent for families. Little nightlife. **Kandersteg:** All types of skiing but not extensive. Does not share lift pass.

CRANS/MONTANA AREA: Crans sur Sierre: Mid-December to mid-April. Very chic, with plenty of choice of nightlife. **Montana:** More rustic and down to earth. Nightlife varied, but restrained. **Anzere:** Mid-December to mid-March. A young people's place. Close-knit English community. **Grimentz:** Small attractive village. Limited nightlife, but all standards of skiing. **Zinal:** Beginners and intermediates. Good nightlife.

DAVOS/KLOSTERS AREA: Davos: Beginning of December to mid-April. Fewer facilities for younger people. Lots of varied après-ski. **Klosters:** December to mid-April. Quiet and expensive après-ski. More a resort for the middle-aged. **Arosa:** Beginning of December to end of April. Good for skiers and non-skiers. Horse-drawn sleighs.

ENGADINE AREA: St Moritz: Early December to end of April. Large expensive resort. All types and ages. Varied nightlife. **Pontresina:** Near St Moritz. Early December to mid-April. **Celerina:** Attractive, traditional village. For nightlife, St Moritz is up the road. **Samnaun (Grisons):** Many Germans. Good cross-country skiing. Duty-free area. **Zuoz:** Limited downhill skiing. Charming village.

FLIMS AREA: Laax: Ancient farming village. Excellent skiing sites of all types. **Flims:** Mid-December to mid-April. Quiet. Ski school. Excellent standard. Good facilities for non-skiers.

GSTAAD (WEISSES HOCHLAND) AREA: Gstaad: Christmas to beginning of April. Very glamorous resort. Trendy and expensive. Much après-ski. **Château d'Oex:** Mostly beginners. Traditional town. Most accommodation in chalets. **Rougemont:** Unspoiled village. Good cross-country. Quiet nightlife. **Saanenmoser, Schonried and Saanen:** Also has summer skiing on glacier. Attractive chalets. Runs to suit all standards. **Zweisimmen:** Small town. Ski school. All standards. Quiet nightlife. **Les Diablerets:** Mid-December to mid-April. Quiet. Ideal for families. Good nursery slopes. Non-skiing activities. Summer skiing on glacier. **Leysin:** Mid-December to mid-March. Nightlife gentle. Lots of school children. **Villars sur Ollon:** Mid-December to end of March. Quiet. Typically Swiss. Restricted nightlife. **Les Mosses:** Intermediates and beginners. Nightlife quiet.

JUNGFRAU AREA: Grindelwald: Mid-December to end March. Rather old-fashioned. Quiet in the evening. **Wengen:** December to April. A lot of English spoken. Plenty of non-skiing activity. **Mürren:** Early December to mid-April. Rustic village with chalet accommodation.

LENZERHEIDE AREA: Valbella: Varied skiing. One difficult run. Suitable for families. Very beautiful area. **Lenzerheide:** Mid-December to mid-April. Good food. Nightlife moderate.

OBERTOGGENBURG AREA: Alt St Johann: Picturesque. Popular but not too crowded. Intermediate with some advanced runs. **Wildhaus:** Not too crowded. Runs for all standards. Good for non-skiers. Nightlife mostly in hotels.

PORTES DU SOLEIL AREA: Champery: Mid-December to beginning of April. Quiet. Family resort. **Champoussin:** Lots of English-speaking instructors. Excellent skiing for all standards. **Morgins:** Pretty resort. Skiing relatively easy. Good resort for families.

RIEDERALP AREA: Bettmeralp: Two beginner runs, two advanced, the rest intermediate. Good restaurants. Prices reasonable. **Riederalp:** Early December to end of March. Minimal nightlife. Beautiful surroundings. Peaceful.

SARGANS AREA: Wangs-Pizol: Some exhilarating skiing. Good ski school for children and beginners. Nightlife minimal. **Braunwald:** Does not share lift pass. Beginners and intermediate. **Flumserberge:** Suitable for cross-country skiing. Good for families. Few non-skiing activities. **Malbun:** Intermediates and beginners. One advanced run. Nightlife is noisy and lively.

VERBIER/LES QUATRE VALLÉES AREA: Verbier: Mid-December to end of April. Serious skiers and lots of facilities for young people. **Bruson:** Quieter. Main slopes suitable for beginners and intermediates. **Super St Bernard:** More a ski station. No accommodation. Good day's outing. All standards. **Thyon 2000:** Modern resort. One long run, the rest suitable for beginners and intermediate. Not lively but suitable for groups and families.

ANDERMATT AREA: Andermatt: Mid-December to mid-April. Nightlife quite lively. Plenty of non-skiing activities. **Engelberg:** Mid-December to mid-April. Historic town. Some runs very difficult. Some nightlife. Casino. Some intermediate. **Hoch-Ybrig** (Central Switzerland): Good place for families. Nightlife moderate. Beautiful area.

ZERMATT AREA: Zermatt: Early December to mid-April. Much variety of skiing and nightlife. Plenty of non-skiing activities. **Saas Fee:** Early December to mid-April. Après-ski quiet, but fun. No cars. **Grachen:** Beginners and intermediates. Good non-ski facilities.

SOCIAL PROFILE

FOOD & DRINK: Swiss cuisine is varied. The great speciality is *fondue*, the delicious concoction of *Gruyère* and *Emmental* cheese, melted and mixed with white wine, flour, *Kirsch* and a little garlic. Other cheese specialities are *Emmental* and *Tête de Moine*. Regional specialities include *viande sechée* (dried beef or pork) from Valais and the Grisons where it is called *bündnerfleisch*. The meat is cut wafer thin, with pickled spring onions and gherkins. *Papet vaudoir* is a delicious dish made from leeks and potatoes. Geneva's great speciality is *pieds de porc au mad* (pigs feet). Pork sausages or salami come in a variety of local recipes including *landjäger, beinwurst, engadinerwurst, leberwurst* (pâté), *kalbsleberwurst* (calf's liver pâté) and *knackerli*. Try *rösti* (shredded fried potatoes) and *Fondue Bourguignonne* (cubes of steak with various sauces). Cakes and pastries are also varied: *leckerli* are Basel specialities (spiced honey cakes topped with icing sugar); in Bern they are decorated with a white sugar bear; *gugelhopf* (a type of sponge cake with a hollow centre), *fastnachtküchli* (sugar-dusted pastries eaten during Carnival) and *schaffhausen* (cream-filled cakes) are also popular. Although there are many self-service snack bars, table service is normal.

Drink: A great variety of Swiss wines are available

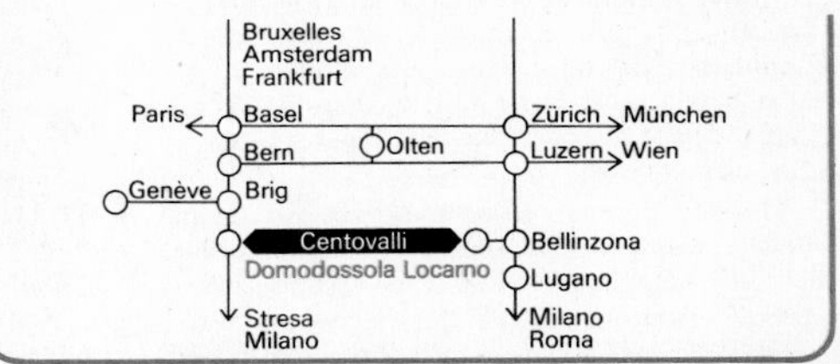

The fastest railway connection between Ticino and Geneva-Bern

LOCARNO

Locarno, with its exceptionally mild climate, is the Swiss town where spring blossoms earlier, where the summer is longer and autumn lasts until December.
Nestling along the Verbano shore at 198 meters above sea level Locarno has a population of 15 500. The surrounding valleys are a favorite haunt of mountain and nature lovers who appreciate the infinite possibilities for hikes and excursions.
The lake, offers enchanting places to visit such as the Brissago Islands, and, further south, the Borromeo Islands. There are numerous place of interest for the visitor to discover. The Sanctuary of Madonna del Sasso, is the symbol of Locarno and one of its main attractions, remarkable not only for the beauty of the building itself, but for the splendid view from its balconies.
Also worhty of a visit is the Visconti Castle, ancient fortress and the largest edifice of its kind in Ticino, as well as the eight churches of the town with their various architectural styles.
Piazza Grande marks the centre of the town and it is here that a fort-nightly open market takes place. It is in this piazza, with its cobbled paving and characteristic arcades, that the International Film Festival takes place each year in August.
The Old Town is justly proud of its patrician houses and threads its way through typical alleyways.
Easily reached by rail, road and air, Locarno rewards the visitor with a wide range of interesting activities, whether cultural, recreational, sporting or sight-seeing.

throughout the country. There are also spirits made from fruit, the most popular being *Kirsch*, *Marc*, *Pflümli* and *Williams*. Swiss beer of a lager type is also available. Bottled mineral water is an accepted beverage, local brands including *Henniez* and *Passuger*. Bars/cocktail lounges have table and/or counter service.
NIGHTLIFE: Most major towns and resorts have nightclubs or discotheques with music and dancing, sometimes serving food. There are also cinemas and theatres, and some bars and restaurants have local folk entertainment.
SHOPPING: Special purchases include embroidery and linen, Bernse woodcarving, chocolate, cheese from the mountains, Swiss army knives, and luxury handmade timepieces. **Shopping hours:** 0830-1200 and 1330-1830 Monday to Friday, 0800-1200 and 1330-1600 Saturday.
SPORT: Mountaineering/hiking: Switzerland's topography is ideal for climbers of every class from the highly experienced to the casual hill walker. However, whatever their standard, all participants must be aware of basic safety, well informed on the weather forecasts and suitably equipped. **Golf:** A list of courses is available at the SNTO. **Tennis:** Many hotels have courts. **Cycling:** Bicycle hire is available. **Watersports:** Lakes such as Lake Geneva, Lugano and Neuchâtel offer sailing, water-skiing and canoeing. **Winter sports:** Switzerland's winter resorts are a principal international tourist attraction and Swiss teams participate in all international skiing events. Skiing and winter sport facilities are innumerable. For more details, contact the SNTO.
SPECIAL EVENTS: Special events for 1993 include: **Mar 1-3 '93** *Fasnacht* (carnival), Basel. **Mar 28-Apr 4** *Curling World Championships*, Geneva. **Apr 9-12** *Osterfestspiele* (Easter concerts), Lucerne. **Apr 18-19** *Sechseläuten* (spring festival), Zürich. **May 2-8** *Golden Rose of Montreux TV Festival*. **May 11-15** *EIBTM, Incentive, Business Travel and Meetings Exhibition*, Geneva. **Jun 1-30** *International Festival Weeks*, Zürich. **Aug 14-Sep 8** *International Music Festival*, Lucerne. **Aug 24-29** *International Folklore Rally*, Fribourg. **Sep** *Wine Harvest Festival*, Neuchâtel.
For further details, contact the SNTO.
SOCIAL CONVENTIONS: It is customary to give unwrapped flowers to the hostess when invited for a meal. Avoid red roses; never give chrysanthemums or white asters as they are considered funeral flowers. Informal wear is widely acceptable. First-class restaurants, hotel dining rooms and important social occasions may warrant jackets and ties. Black tie is usually specified when needed.
Tipping: A service charge of 15% is included in all hotel, restaurant, café, bar, taxi and hairdressing services by law.

BUSINESS PROFILE

ECONOMY: Switzerland has a typical West European mixed economy with a bias towards light and craft-based industries: precision manufacturing such as watch-making is renowned throughout the world. The country is highly industrialised and heavily dependent on exports of finished goods. In manufacturing, the machinery and equipment industry specialises in precision and advanced technology products: machine tools, printing and photographic equipment, electronic control and medical equipment. There is also a substantial chemical industry, employing 10% of the workforce, which continues to experience steady growth. Although half the country's food is imported, the agricultural sector is strong and a major employer. The processed foods industry has a high international profile, particularly in chocolate, cheese and baby foods. The service sector is dominated by banking. Uninterrupted peace since 1815 initially made Switzerland an attractive location for depositors concerned about political stability. More recently, the particular reputation of the Swiss banking community for discretion has attracted large deposits. Inevitably, some of this money has been illegally procured and the Swiss authorities have come under heavy pressure, especially from Washington, to relax the country's strict banking secrecy laws to assist international criminal investigation. For the time being, Switzerland remains one of Europe's major financial centres. Among other service industries, tourism is of growing importance. Switzerland is not a member of the EC, although nearly two-thirds of its exports are sold to Community countries. It may apply to join before the end of the 1990s depending on the political situation (see *History* below). As a member of the European Free Trade Association (EFTA), however, Switzerland does belong to the European Economic Area, the combined EC/EFTA trading bloc established in 1991. In May 1992, Switzerland gained admission to the IMF and World Bank. Switzerland's main export markets are: Germany (22%), France (10%), Italy (9%) and the UK (6%).
BUSINESS: Business people are expected to wear suits. Although English is widely spoken, it is always appreciated if a visitor attempts to say a few words in the language of the host. When visiting a firm a visiting card is essential.
Office hours: 0800-1200 and 1400-1700 Monday to Friday.
COMMERCIAL INFORMATION: The following organisation can offer advice: Schweizerische Zentrale für Handelsförderung – Office Suisse d'Expansion Commerciale (OSEC), Stampfenbachstrasse 85, CH-8035 Zürich. Tel: (1) 365 5151. Fax: (1) 365 5221. Telex: 817272.
Information can also be obtained from the regional chambers of commerce in each canton.
CONFERENCES/CONVENTIONS: The neutrality, stability and conveniently central location of Switzerland make the country a favourite meeting place for conventions and international organisations. It has an extensive and highly developed network of conference destinations with all the major cities and many of the smaller alpine and lake resorts offering hotels and convention centres which are fully equipped with a complete range of facilities including interpretation and audio-visual services. Each of Switzerland's main cities has its own Convention Bureau, whilst the Association of Swiss Convention Centres, *Swiss Congress*, oversees meetings activity throughout the country. The organisation is made up of the 19 leading congress locations in Switzerland and can help with the organisation of a meeting in any region of the country. Contact the Swiss Congress and Incentives (SCI), avenue de Belmont 23, CH-1820 Montreux. Tel: (21) 963 1759. Fax: (21) 963 1837.

HISTORY & GOVERNMENT

HISTORY: The history of Switzerland has followed a broadly different course from that of its European neighbours, mainly because no ruler since the 14th century was able to claim more than a theoretical suzerainty over the small, well-organised and prosperous group of cantons that was to become Switzerland. In the period between 1315 and 1388, they inflicted a series of crushing defeats on the armies of the Dukes of Austria, resulting in several other cantons joining the original three in the Swiss Confederation. Their location left them well placed to interfere in the interminable power-struggles of the period, and their influence was backed up by the formidable reputation of their army, probably the most powerful in Europe at the end of the 15th century. Swiss mercenaries were to be found taking part in most of the major battles of the period. The Reformation led to a division in Swiss society between the followers of the reformer Zwingli and, later, Calvin, and the Catholics. The bitter controversy considerably reduced Swiss influence in Europe, and the Confederation was lucky to survive a series of defeats. Swiss independence from the Holy Roman Empire was one of the results of the Peace of Westphalia (1648) which concluded the Thirty Years' War, in which Switzerland had suffered badly. In the following 100 years little progress was made towards a formal union of the cantons, and the religious controversy rumbled on; the dominance of the Protestants was not decided until after the Second Villmergen War in 1712. In the late 18th century Switzerland, and in particular Geneva and Zürich, became a centre of European intellectual life, and this period is particularly associated with the great names of Rousseau and Voltaire. The dramatic events of the French Revolution and the Napoleonic Empire resulted in a confusing period, with much of the country being annexed by France. Independence was restored by the Congress of Vienna in 1815 (which also laid down the principle of the perpetual neutrality of Switzerland), but the repressive policies of the cantons and the lack of any central power continued to work against political unity or economic growth. It was not until the end of the 19th century that the Federal Government began to be truly effective, although the cantons continue to enjoy wide powers. Swiss neutrality was tested to the limit by two World Wars but survived unscathed. Domestic politics since 1945 have been dominated by four political parties: the Social Democrats, Radical Democrats, the Swiss People's Party and the Christian Democratic People's Party. These four have governed the country in various coalition combinations; at present, all four are allied. The principal question in Swiss politics is the European Community, which is responsible for 50% of Switzerland's trade. Referenda are a common feature of Swiss public life, and the question will doubtless be raised in this way eventually. Campaigning for the latest general election in October 1991 focused extensively upon it. The erosion of cantonal power, immigration levels and the threat of absorption into its larger neighbours are the most-voiced concerns. The results of the October 1991 poll returned the coalition to office. Both pro- and anti-EC parties gained seats at the expense of fence-sitters, showing that on this issue, as on others confronting Switzerland today, the end of relative isolation threatens to bring a divided nation. That division was apparent from the result of the referendum held in December 1992 on Swiss membership of the European Economic Area, a free-trade agreement between the EC and EFTA (of which Switzerland is a member): opponents of the pact won with 50.3% of the vote. Switzerland's participation in future European integration initiatives is now in serious doubt.
GOVERNMENT: The present constitution dates back to 1874. There are 26 cantons (three of which are subdivided) and over 3000 communes. The federal assembly is bicameral, comprising a Council of State (upper house) with 46 members and a 200-strong National Council (lower house) whose members are elected every four years. Executive power is vested in the 7-member Federal Council, elected by the Assembly, headed by an annually elected President.

CLIMATE

The Alps cause many climatic variations throughout Switzerland. In the higher Alpine regions temperatures tend to be low, while the lower land of the northern area has higher temperatures and warm summers.
Required clothing: Warm clothes and rainwear; lighter clothes for summer.

ZURICH Switzerland (569m)

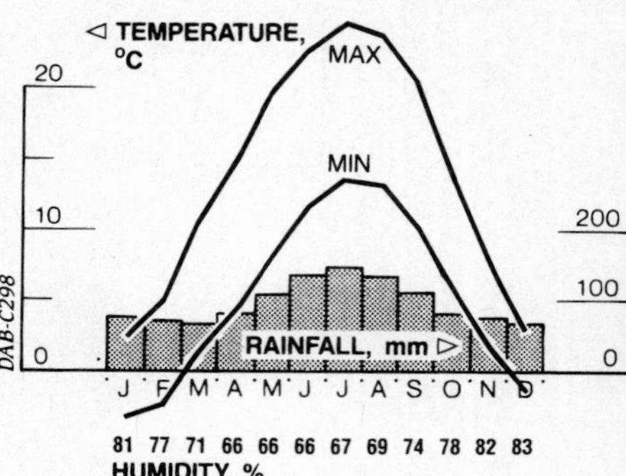

SANTIS Switzerland (2500m)

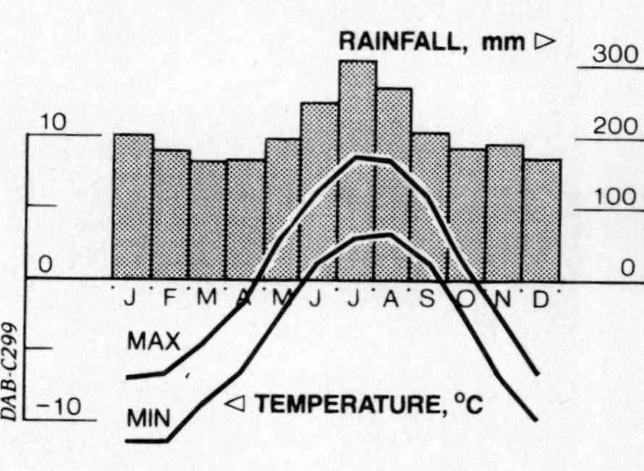

LOCARNO Switzerland

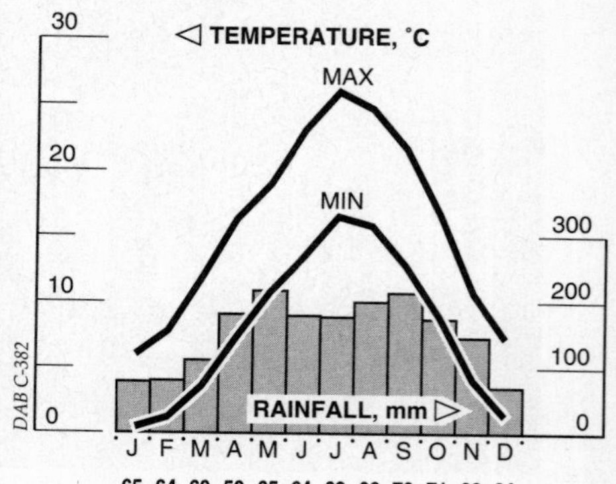

SYRIAN ARAB REPUBLIC

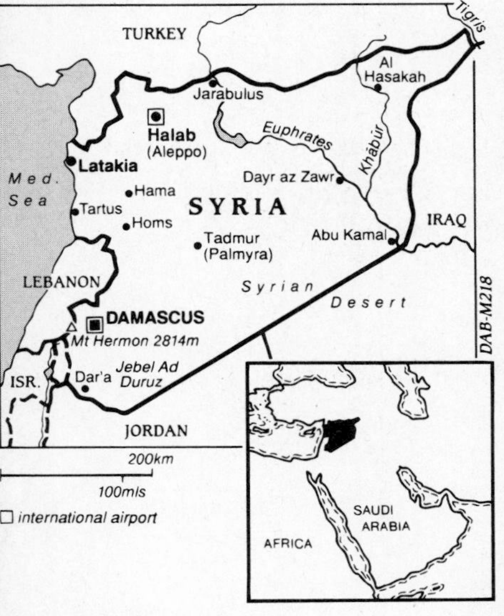

AREA: 185,180 sq km (71,498 sq miles).
POPULATION: 11,719,000 (1989 estimate).
POPULATION DENSITY: 63.7 per sq km.
CAPITAL: Damascus. **Population:** 2,800,000 (1988 estimate).
GEOGRAPHY: Syria shares borders with the Mediterranean and Lebanon in the west, Israel and Jordan in the south, Iraq in the east and Turkey in the north. The country can be divided geographically into four main areas: the fertile coastal plain in the north-east, the plateau and mountain areas in the west, the central plains and the desert and steppe region in the central and southeastern areas. The Euphrates flows from Turkey in the north, through Syria, down to Iraq in the southeast. It is the longest river in Syria, the total length being 2330km (1450 miles), of which 600km (370 miles) pass through Syria. The Khabur River supports the al-Khabur Basin in the northeast.
LANGUAGE: Arabic, French and English.
RELIGION: 70% Sunni Muslim, 12% Christians (mostly Orthodox and Greek Catholic) and 18% other minority groups including Jews and Druzes.
TIME: GMT + 2 (GMT + 3 from April 1 until September 29).
ELECTRICITY: 220 volts AC, 50Hz.
COMMUNICATIONS: Telephone: IDD is available. Country code: 963. **Telex/telegram:** A public telex service is available from main hotels and the main telegraph office in Damascus. **Post:** Airmail to Europe takes up to two weeks. Parcels sent from Syria should be packed at the post office and a good deal of time and bureaucracy may be involved. There are post offices in virtually all towns. Post office hours are 0900-1500; larger branches will be open all day. **Press:** Most newspapers will have political or governmental affiliations. The English-language daily newspaper is the government-controlled *Syria Times*, whilst the most important Arab publications are *al-Baath*, *Tishrin* and *al-Thawrah*.
BBC World Service and Voice of America frequencies: From time to time these change. See the section *How to Use this Book* for more information.

BBC:				
MHz	15.57	1.323	12.09	21.47
Voice of America:				
MHz	9.670	6.040	5.995	1.260

Location: Middle East.

Ministry of Tourism
rue Victoria
Damascus
Syria
Tel: (11) 215 916. Telex: 411672.
Embassy of the Syrian Arab Republic
8 Belgrave Square
London
SW1X 8PH
Tel: (071) 245 9012. Fax: (071) 235 4621. Opening hours (for visa applications): 1000-1200 Monday to Friday.
British Embassy
PO Box 37
Quarter Malki
11 rue Muhammed Kurd Ali
Immeuble Kotob
Damascus
Syria
Tel: (11) 712 561/2/3. Fax: (11) 713 592. Telex: 411049 BRITEM SY.
British Consulate
PO Box 199
Aleppo
Syria
Tel: (21) 332 133. Telex: 331 627 ACCO SY.
Embassy of the Syrian Arab Republic
2215 Wyoming Avenue, NW
Washington, DC
20008
Tel: (202) 232 6313. Fax: (202) 234 9548.
Honorary Consulate in: Houston.
Embassy of the United States of America
BP 29
Abu Roumaneh
rue al-Mansur 2
Damascus
Syria
Tel: (11) 333 052
or 332 557
or 330 416. Fax: (11) 718 687. Telex: 411919 USDAMA SY.
Consulate General of the Syrian Arab Republic
324 Arlington Crescent
Beaconsfield
Québec
H9W 2K3
Tel: (514) 630 4339. Fax: (514) 697 0081.
Consulate in: Toronto.
Canadian Embassy
PO Box 3394
Block 12
Mezzeh Autostrade
Damascus
Syria
Tel: (11) 236 851 *or* 236 892. Fax: (11) 228 034. Telex: 412422 CANADA SY.

Amphitheatre, Bosra

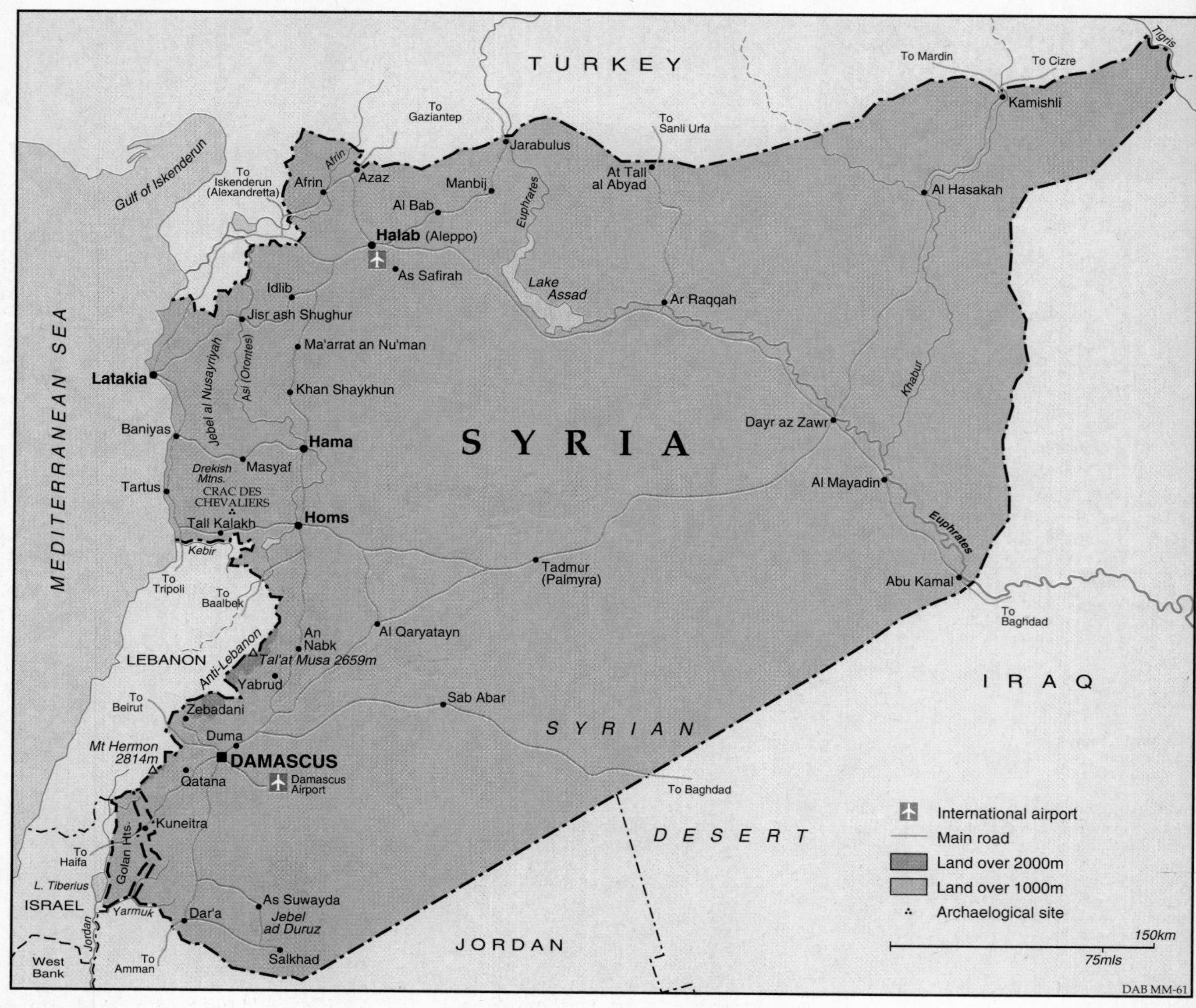

PASSPORT/VISA

Regulations and requirements may be subject to change at short notice, and you are advised to contact the appropriate diplomatic or consular authority before finalising travel arrangements. Details of these may be found at the head of this country's entry. Any numbers in the chart refer to the footnotes below.

	Passport Required?	Visa Required?	Return Ticket Required?
Full British	Yes	Yes	Yes
BVP	Not valid	-	-
Australian	Yes	Yes	Yes
Canadian	Yes	Yes	Yes
USA	Yes	Yes	Yes
Other EC	Yes	Yes	Yes
Japanese	Yes	Yes	Yes

Restricted entry and transit: Holders of Israeli and South African passports will be refused admission; so will any passenger holding a passport containing a visa (valid or expired) for Israel or South Africa and those holding a stamp indicating an Israel-Jordan border crossing. Nationals of South Korea and Chinese residents of Taiwan, even if holding an entry visa, will be refused entry.

PASSPORTS: Valid passport required by all except holders of national ID cards of Lebanon.

British Visitors Passport: Not accepted.

VISAS: Required by all except nationals of Algeria, Bahrain, Iraq, Jordan, Kuwait, Lebanon, Libya, Mauritania, Morocco, Oman, Qatar, Saudi Arabia, Somalia, Sudan, Tunisia, United Arab Emirates and Yemen.

Note: Travel regulations are liable to change at short notice and prospective visitors are advised to consult the Embassy for up-to-date information.

Types of visa: Tourist and business (single, double, multiple entry); transit. Transit visas not required by those who continue their journey to a third country within 24 hours by the same or first connecting aircraft without leaving the transit area. Documents for the next destination, including visas (where applicable) and tickets with confirmed onward reservations, must be held. Fees vary according to nationality.

Validity: *Tourist:* 3 months; *Transit:* 3 months; *Business:* 6 months.

Application to: Consulate (or Consular Section at Embassy). For addresses, see top of entry.

Application requirements: (a) 1 completed application form. (b) Passport. (c) 1 photograph. (d) Business visa: company letter stating nature of business. (e) Tourist visa: letter indicating the itinerary in the Middle East and stating the number of journeys into Syria. (f) Fee. (g) A stamped, self-addressed envelope.

Working days required: 3-4.

Temporary residence: Applications to the Syrian Immigration Department, Damascus.

MONEY

Currency: Syrian Pound (S£) = 100 piastres. Notes are in denominations of S£500, 100, 50, 25, 10, 5 and 1. Coins are in denominations of S£1, and 50, 25, 10, 5 and 2.5 piastres.

SYRIA	HEALTH REGULATIONS	VISA REGULATIONS (Code-Link)
GALILEO/WORLDSPAN	TI-DFT/DAM/HE	TI-DFT/DAM/VI
SABRE	TIDFT/DAM/HE	TIDFT/DAM/VI

To access this information on your CRS, swipe the barcode with a light pen or type in the text under the barcode. For more information, see the introduction *How to Use This Book*.

Hama, a traditional village

Currency exchange: Since 1986 stringent restrictions on illegal currency transactions have forced the black market to all but disappear. Syrian currency cannot generally be reconverted to hard currency. The country's banking system is state-owned, and there will be at least one branch of the Commercial Bank of Syria in every main town.
Credit cards: American Express and Diners Club are most readily accepted; some hotels will accept Access/Mastercard. Tickets may be bought with credit cards. Check with your credit card company for merchant acceptability and for other services which may be available.
Travellers cheques: Not always exchangeable at Damascus airport.
Exchange rate indicators: The following figures are included as a guide to the movements of the Syrian Pound against Sterling and the US Dollar:

Date:	Oct '89	Oct '90	Oct '91	Oct '92
£1.00=	33.20	40.98	36.49	35.55
$1.00=	21.02	21.00	21.03	22.40

Currency restrictions: The import of local currency is unlimited; its export is prohibited. Import of foreign currency is unlimited, although amounts over US$500 must be declared upon arrival. The export of foreign currency is limited to US$5000, or up to the amount declared on arrival.
Banking hours: 0800-1400 Saturday to Thursday (tend to close early on Thursday).

DUTY FREE

The following items may be imported into Syria without incurring customs duty:
200 cigarettes or 50 cigars or 250g of tobacco;
1 litre of spirits and 1 bottle of wine;
A reasonable quantity of perfume and toilet water.
Note: All gold jewellery must be declared on arrival.

PUBLIC HOLIDAYS

Public holidays observed in Syria are as follows:
Mar 8 '93 Revolution Day. **Mar 25** Start of Eid al-Fitr. **Apr 16-19** Easter (Greek Orthodox). **Jun 1** Eid al-Adha. **Jun 21** Islamic New Year. **Jul 23** Egypt's Revolution Day. **Aug 30** Mouloud (Birth of the Prophet). **Sep 1** Union of Syria, Egypt and Libya. **Oct 6** Beginning of October War. **Nov 16** National Day. **Dec 25** Christmas Day. **Jan 1 '94** New Year's Day. **Feb** Leilat al-Meiraj. **Mar 8** Revolution Day. **Mar** Start of Eid al-Fitr.
Note: Muslim festivals are timed according to local sightings of various phases of the Moon and the dates given above are approximations. During the lunar month of Ramadan that precedes Eid al-Fitr, Muslims fast during the day and feast at night and normal business patterns may be interrupted. Many restaurants are closed during the day and there may be restrictions on smoking and drinking. Some disruption may continue into Eid al-Fitr itself. Eid al-Fitr and Eid al-Adha may last anything from two to ten days, depending on the region. For more information see the section *World of Islam* at the back of the book.

HEALTH

Regulations and requirements may be subject to change at short notice, and you are advised to contact your doctor well in advance of your intended date of departure. Any numbers in the chart refer to the footnotes below.

	Special Precautions?	Certificate Required?
Yellow Fever	No	1
Cholera	Yes	2
Typhoid & Polio	Yes	-
Malaria	3	-
Food & Drink	4	-

[1]: A yellow fever vaccination certificate is required from travellers coming from infected areas.
[2]: Following WHO guidelines issued in 1973, a cholera vaccination certificate is not a condition of entry to Syria. However, cholera is a risk in this country and precautions are essential. Up-to-date advice should be sought before deciding whether these precautions should include vaccination, as medical opinion is divided over its effectiveness. See the *Health* section at the back of the book.
[3]: Malaria risk, exclusively in the benign *vivax* form, exists from May to October in the whole country, excluding urban areas and the Districts of Dayr as Zawr and Sweida.
[4]: Mains water is normally chlorinated, and whilst relatively safe may cause mild abdominal upsets. Bottled water is available and is advised for the first few weeks of the stay. Drinking water outside main cities and towns is likely to be contaminated and sterilisation is considered essential. Milk is unpasteurised and should be boiled. Powdered or tinned milk is available and is advised but make sure that it is reconstituted with pure water. Avoid dairy products which are likely to have been made from unboiled milk. Only eat well-cooked meat and fish, preferably served hot. Pork, salad and mayonnaise may carry increased risk. Vegetables should be cooked and fruit peeled.
Rabies is present. For those at high risk, vaccination before arrival should be considered. If you are bitten abroad seek medical advice without delay. For more information consult the *Health* section at the back of the book.
Bilharzia (schistosomiasis) is present. Avoid swimming and paddling in fresh water. Swimming pools which are well-chlorinated and maintained are safe.

Hama, Mhardeh Church

Bas relief, Palmyra

Health care: Health insurance is recommended. There is no Reciprocal Health Agreement with the UK. There are about 200 hospitals (12,000 beds) and 6000 doctors. Medical care is provided free of charge to those who cannot afford to pay.

TRAVEL - International

AIR: Syria's national airline is *Syrian Arab Airlines (RB)*.
Approximate flight times: From *London* to Damascus is 7 hours 30 minutes (including stopover time of 3 hours in Amman) and to Aleppo is 4 hours 20 minutes.

International airports: *Damascus (DAM)*, 30km (18 miles) southeast of the city (travel time – 30 minutes). A bus service runs every 60 minutes. Return is from the Central Post Office. Taxis are available, but it is advisable to negotiate fares beforehand. Facilities include banking, restaurants/snack bars, duty-free shop and tourist information.
Aleppo (ALP) (Nejrab), 10km (6.5 miles) from the city (travel time –20 minutes). Bus and taxi services go to the city. Facilities include banking, restaurants/snack bars and tourist information.
Departure tax: S£100. Transit passengers are exempt.

Statue of the Star

SEA: The principal ports are Latakia, Tartous and Banias. The nearest car ferry sails to Badrum in western Turkey. There are no passenger lines.
RAIL: Links go via Istanbul and Ankara (Turkey). Change at Ankara for the *Taurus Express* to Aleppo. There are twice-weekly trains from Damascus to Amman (Jordan). There is also a connection from Haleb to Beirut (Lebanon).
ROAD: The principal international routes are from Istanbul, the E5 road to Ankara, Adana and Iskeuderun in Turkey. Enter at Bab-al-Hawa for Aleppo, or at Kassab for Latakia. From the south the best routes are from Akaba on the Red Sea in Jordan. **Bus:** Services across the desert on routes from Baghdad via Damascus and Amman to Damascus. See below for information on **documentation** and **traffic regulations**.

TRAVEL - Internal

AIR: *Syrian Arab Airlines (RB)* fly to Aleppo, Palmyra, Dayr as Zawr, Qamishlye and Latakia. Fares in general are exceedingly cheap.
RAIL: The railway extends 3735km (2321 miles), of which 1785km (1054 miles) are of standard gauge, the rest narrow gauge. Services are provided to the north of the country from Damascus but these are irregular and there are no sleeping or restaurant cars except in the through train to Turkey. Some air-conditioned accommodation is available.
ROAD: The road network comprises 30,208km, of which about 22,500km are surfaced. Second-class roads are unreliable during the wet season. The principal route is Aleppo to Damascus and Dera'a (north–south axis). **Bus:** Services run from Damascus and Aleppo to most towns and are cheap and efficient. There are orange and white air-conditioned *Karnak* (government-operated) buses. Reservations should be made well in advance. Karnak bus routes serve their own terminals, which are usually in or near the city centres. There are also privately run bus and microbus services which are cheaper but less comfortable and with no fixed timetables. **Taxi:** Shared taxis are available to all parts of the country. Service taxis (old limousines) run on major routes and cost 50-70% more than Karnak buses. **Regulations:** Speed limits: 20kmph (12mph) in the city; 80kmph (50mph) on highways. **Documentation:** International Driving Permit required. Green Cards are not yet accepted in Syria. Insurance is required by law and a customs certificate is needed. These are available from touring and automobile clubs.
URBAN: Publicly owned bus services operate in all major towns and cities, while Damascus and Aleppo also have two public elevators and a funicular. Most buses outside the capital, however, have no signs in a European script to indicate destination or stops, which can make travelling rather difficult. Taxis are widely available. Fares should be agreed in advance.
JOURNEY TIMES: The following chart gives approximate journey times (in hours and minutes) from Damascus to other major cities/towns in the Syrian Arab Republic.

	Air	Road
Aleppo	1.00	5.30
Latakia	1.00	5.00
Dayr as Zawr	1.00	8.00
Qameshliye	1.00	8.00
Palmyra	1.25	3.00
Dera'a	-	5.00
Hasake	-	8.00
Homs	-	1.30
Hama	-	2.00
Tartous	-	3.00

ACCOMMODATION

HOTELS: Accommodation can be difficult to obtain and care should be taken to confirm bookings. Tariffs are the same throughout the year. All rates are subject to a 15% service charge. **Grading:** Hotels range from fairly low grade to luxurious 5-star accommodation. The best-quality hotels are found in Damascus, where there are three 5-star hotels, and several other hotels with the lowest grade being 3-star. Aleppo has several hotels, ranging from 2- to 3-star. In addition there are hotels in Homs (with a range of 2- to 3-star), Hama (1-star hotels only), Latakia (with a good range, from 2- to 5-star), the Latakia suburbs in the mountains (1-star hotels only) and Tartous (1- to 3-star). There is one hotel in Edleb (2-star), a 5-star hotel in Palmyra and there are 3-star hotels in Swaida and lower-quality hotels in Hasake, Qameshliye, Dayr as Zawr, Ra and Dera'a.
GUEST-HOUSES: At Damascus, Zabedani, Aleppo, Idlib, Dera'a and Bosra. *Cités Universitaires* offer summer accommodation.

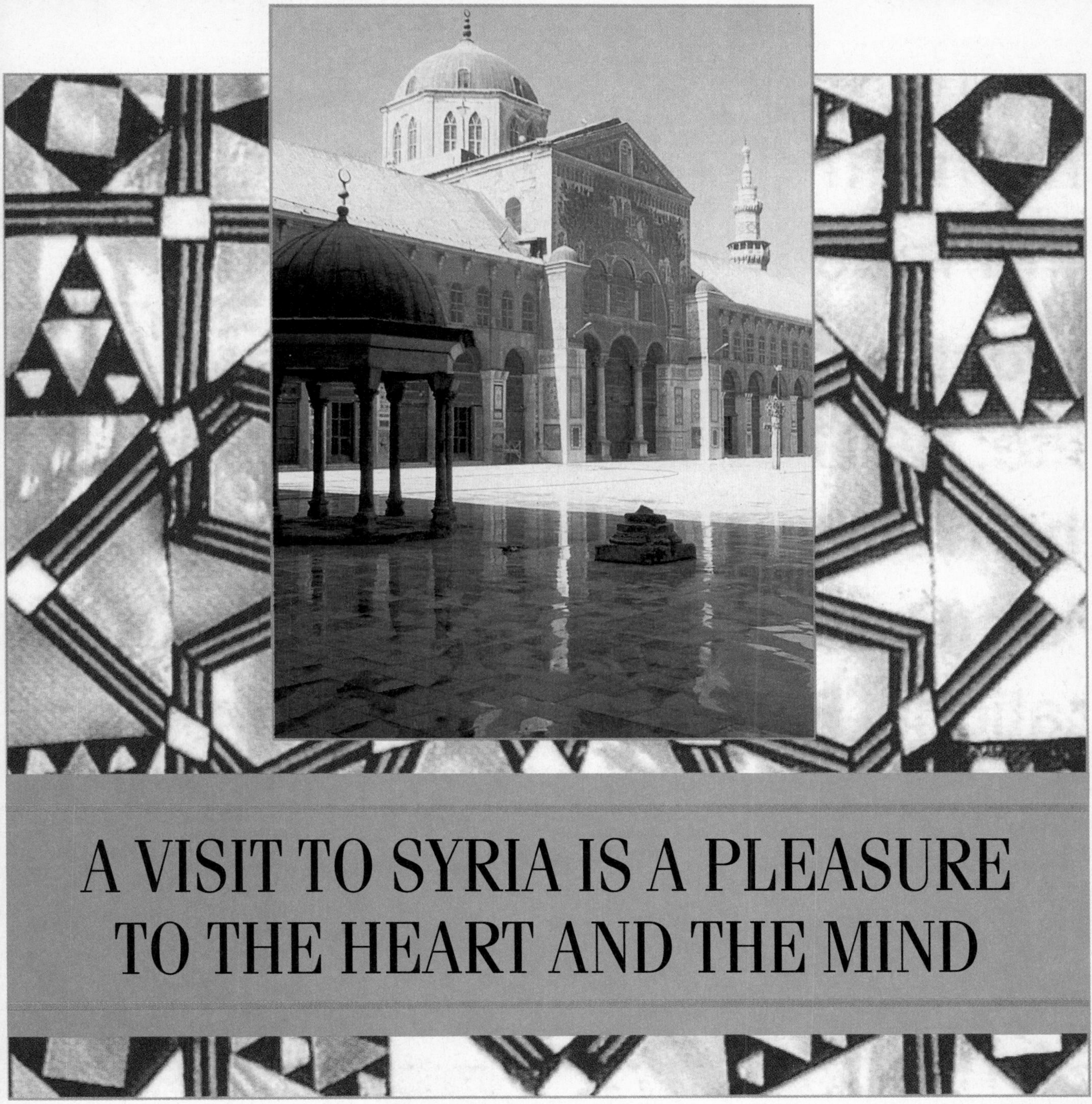

CAMPING/CARAVANNING: There are two official sites near Damascus. Otherwise, camping is permitted near resorts.

RESORTS & EXCURSIONS

For the purposes of covering the main areas of interest to the visitor Syria is divided laterally into three regions; South, Central and North.

The South

Damascus: The capital of Syria is the world's oldest inhabited city. A central feature of this cluttered and clamorous city is the *Ummayyad Mosque*, entered by passing through the the *Al-Hamidiyah Bazaar*. The history of the mosque in many ways traces the history of Damascus; built on the site of a temple to the ancient Aramean god Haddad, the original temple was adapted and enlarged by the Romans and used as a temple to Jupiter. It was later knocked down by the Byzantines, who replaced the pagan temple with the Cathedral of John the Baptist, and subsequently converted into a mosque to accommodate the Islamic teachings brought by the Arabs in 636. The mosque houses the *Tomb of St John the Baptist*. The *Tikiyeh* mosque, built in the mid-16th century, stands out by its two elegant minarets and great dome. The 18th-century *Al-Azem* palace is now a national museum, where there are, amongst other examples of Islamic art, beautifully illuminated copies of the Koran. Situated in old Damascus, a little way off the famous *Via Vector*, or 'Straight Street', is the *House of Hanania*, where St Paul hid, using the underground chapel for worship. The prison cell in the Damascus Wall from where St Paul escaped in a basket is also still preserved. Other attractions include: the *Sayyida Zainab Shrine* (the granddaughter of the Prophet), the *Tomb of Saladin* at the backyard of *Ummayyad Mosque*, and the outskirts of Damascus, especially Dummar, with seasonal entertainment, restaurants, and Ghota, the fruit orchards surrounding Damascus – at its best during the blooming of apricot, plums, cherries and other trees in early spring.
Busra: A Roman city with a well-preserved amphitheatre in which the musical festival is held every year. Also worth seeing is The *Long Souk*.

Central Region

Palmyra: Thought to have been founded by King Solomon. Set in a desert oasis, the city was ruled by the legendary Queen Zenobia, who stood against the two great empires of the Romans and the Persians. Zenobia was taken captive to Rome when the Emperor Aurelian captured and destroyed the city in 272. The ruins of the *Valley of Tombs*, the *Hypogeum of the Three Brothers*, the *Temple of Baal* and the *Monumental Arch* are some of the fine remains found over a wide radius of the city, prized as some of the most famous monuments to classical times in the Middle East.
Homs: The third-largest city in Syria, Homs is known for its industry, and is the site of Syria's first oil refinery. Of historical interest is the mausoleum of *Khalid Ibn al-Walid*.
Crac des Chevaliers: 65km (40 miles) outside Homs, Crac des Chevaliers is the most famous crusader castle in the world. A stronghold of the Hospitallers during the days of the Latin Kingdom of Jerusalem (1100-1290), it maintained a garrison of a couple of thousand soldiers in peacetime, and is a good example of French military architecture. The castle, rising from an altitude of 670m (2200ft), was protected by watch-towers and supplied with food from the surrounding fertile countryside. The crusader castles of *Sahyn* and *Markab* are also worth a visit.
Hama: 45km (28 miles) from Homs. Situated on the *River Orontes*, Hama dates back to beyond 5000BC. The *Norias*, gigantic Roman wooden water-wheels, are a unique feature, still used to provide water for the city and to irrigate the many public gardens. The orchards, the *Great Mosque* and the *Al Azem Palace's Museum* are also of interest.

The North

Aleppo: Older possibly even than Damascus, Aleppo's massive *Citadel* stands on the site of a Hittite acropolis. This is one of the most magnificent examples of Islamic Arab military architecture in Syria. There is an impressive number of mosques in the city. For the tourist, the *souk*, made up of 16km (10 miles) of meandering low corridors lined with shops and bustling with activity, is probably the greatest attraction. The well preserved *hammams*, or public baths, are worth a visit, as are the ancient *khans* (resthouses). Some fine artefacts and historic reminders of Syria's rich cultural past are housed in the archaeological museum. Aleppo is also the commercial and industrial centre of Syria.
Latakia: Syria's principal port and the metropolitan city of the country. Set on the Mediterranean coast, Latakia is a major holiday resort. The city stands at the foot of the forested chain of mountains overlooking the coastal strip on one side and the edge of the *Fertile Crescent* (the 'Cradle of Civilisation') on the other. There are a number of antiquities, including the ruined *Temple of Bacchus* and a triumphal arch.
Resorts/excursions: Tartous, beaches and mountains, Latakia mountain resorts of *Kassab* and *Slounfeh*. 10km (6 miles) inland, near Tartous, are the *Drekish Mountains*, famous for the purity of its waters.

SOCIAL PROFILE

FOOD & DRINK: There are numerous restaurants in Damascus and Aleppo serving a variety of Oriental and European dishes. National dishes are *kubbeh* (minced semolina and meat formed in balls and stuffed with minced meat, onion and nuts), *yabrak* (vine leaves stuffed with rice and minced meat), *ouzi* (pastry stuffed with rice and minced meat) and a variety of vegetables cooked with meat and tomato sauce, usually presented on separate plates and eaten by mixing it with cooked rice. Among these vegetables are *okra*, French beans and *malukhiyya*. Table service is the norm and a meal is paid for afterwards.
Drink: There are bars serving a wide range of alcoholic drinks. Alcohol is permitted but restrictions are imposed during Ramadan when it is illegal to drink in public from dawn to dusk, even for non-Muslims.
SHOPPING: *Souks* (markets) are the best places, notably those in Aleppo. Local handicrafts in Syria are numerous and precious, including mother-of-pearl items (such as backgammon boards), olive-wood carvings, weaving and embroidery, leather goods and gold and silver jewellery. **Shopping hours:** 0930-1400 and 1630-2100 Saturday to Thursday (summer); 0930-1400 and 1600-2000 Saturday to Thursday (winter).
SPORT: The Mediterranean resorts offer **canoeing**, **scuba diving** and other **watersports**. Inland, there are numerous hotel **swimming** pools and public baths, particularly in Aleppo.
SPECIAL EVENTS: The following is a selection of the major festivals and other special events celebrated annually in Syria.
Apr *Flower Show*, Latakia. **May** *International Flower Exhibition*, Damascus. **Jul** *Vine Festival*, Suwayda; *Cotton Festival*, Aleppo. **Aug-Sep** *International Fair*, Damascus. **Oct** *Festival of Folklore and Music*, Bosra. **Nov** *Film and Theatre Festival*, Damascus.
SOCIAL CONVENTIONS: The Syrians appear to take more pride in their modern amenities than in their unique heritage or in the tradition of exquisite craftsmanship but both should be appreciated. Visitors will enjoy the hospitality that is a deep-rooted Arab tradition and sharing the pleasures of an attractive Oriental way of life. It is customary to shake hands on meeting and on departure. A visitor will be treated with great courtesy and will frequently be offered refreshment, usually coffee. As a guest in someone's home or, more usually, in a restaurant, visitors should respect Arab customs and traditions. A souvenir from the visitors home or company is well received. Conservative casual wear is suitable. Beachwear or shorts should not be worn away from the beach or poolside. Smoking follows Western habits and in most cases it is obvious where not to smoke. Smoking is prohibited in public from dawn to dusk during Ramadan. **Photography:** No attempt should be made to photograph anything remotely connected with the armed forces or in the vicinity of defence installations, which even includes radio transmission aerials. It is wise to take a good look at what will be appearing in the background of holiday snaps before pointing the camera. **Tipping:** Not necessary but 10% is acceptable for most services.

BUSINESS PROFILE

ECONOMY: The main components of the Syrian economy are agriculture and oil. In the agricultural sector, which employs one-third of the working population, cotton is the main commodity as well as a key export. Wheat, barley, fruit and vegetables are the other main products, the bulk of which are grown for domestic consumption. With little manufacturing industry beyond that established to meet local demand, the Syrian economy has survived only by virtue of its oil reserves. However, problems with certain aspects of the industry, the low world price and the closure of the main pipeline (which runs through Iraq), plus the high cost of maintaining a large military presence in Lebanon, caused a severe financial crisis in 1987, which was alleviated by Soviet and Iranian aid of various sorts. By 1989 the economy had recovered sufficiently to the extent that Syria enjoyed its first trade surplus for 30 years. The oil sector has been especially buoyant. The Gulf War was a mixed blessing. Like all Iraq's neighbours, Syria's trade suffered but, by joining the US-led coalition, Damascus benefited from aid packages from the West and the Gulf states. Upheaval in the Soviet Union has caused some difficulties, since Syria was historically a major trading partner and a recipient of much Soviet heavy machinery, particularly armaments, but increased oil production and greater international support produced a healthy 6% growth in 1990. Further economic progress depends significantly on reform of the top-heavy state sector. The economic issue most worrying the Syrian government at the turn of the 1990s was the restriction on water supplies which followed the

pening of the Ataturk dam in Turkey, but this was ettled by an inter-government treaty in 1992. Iran nd Italy are the country's main trading partners. 'rade with Britain declined to near zero after the iplomatic breach in 1986 but has since picked up.
USINESS: Formal suits are necessary for business. usiness people generally speak English and French. ppointments are necessary and visiting cards are idely used. Arabs often discuss business with more han one person at a time. Good Arabic translators re difficult to find; a list of notarised translators is vailable at the British Embassy. **Office hours:** 0800-430 Saturday to Thursday. All government offices, anks and Muslim firms close on Friday and remain pen Sunday; Christian firms are generally open riday and closed Sunday. During the month of amadan, Government offices start work one hour ater than usual and the pace generally slows down.
OMMERCIAL INFORMATION: The following rganisations can offer advice:
ederation of Syrian Chambers of Commerce and the Damascus Chamber of Commerce, BP 1040, rue Aou'awiah, Damascus. Tel: (11) 211 339. Telex: 11326.

HISTORY & GOVERNMENT

HISTORY: Syria has been inhabited for tens of housands of years and, as a result, has a rich cultural istory. Jericho on the River Jordan was a settlement n about 10,000BC. The area which is now Syria was art of the Empire of Mesopotamia around 2300BC, uring which time the cities of Jericho, Ugarit (where he oldest written alphabet in the world is believed to ave been developed) and Byblos grew to become owerful commercial centres. By about 1500BC, outhern Syria had fallen under the control of Egypt, while the northern principalities had been welded nto the Mitanni Empire. Within a few centuries, owever, the Hittites from the north had overrun all of Syria, an empire which in turn collapsed in the ace of invasions by the Philistines. The history of the ollowing centuries, until the eventual destruction of he kingdom of Judah in 539BC, is one of a struggle y Israel, the Philistines, the Assyrians and many other tribes and empires for control of the Syrian rade. Alexander the Great absorbed Syria into his empire in 333BC, but for the next two centuries control of the region was disputed, on this occasion between the various people trying to gain control of his inheritance. For several centuries, the Province of Syria enjoyed the mixed blessings of the *Pax Romana* and later a province of the Eastern (Byzantine) Empire after the division of the Roman Empire, but even then Syria was always regarded as a frontier region, bordered to the east by the Arabs and Persians. The Persian invasions were repulsed but Syria eventually fell to the Muslims in the mid-7th century. From then on, Syria was to be firmly part of the Muslim world, although retaining Christian and Jewish populations. Muslim control of Syria was vital to the defeat of the Christians and their expulsion from Jerusalem. During the 13th century a far greater threat was, however, the terrifying force of the Mongols. In the space of 50 years they swept through Asia, creating an empire which stretched from Korea to Moscow. By 1260, having overrun Syria and deposed the Abbasaid Khalif, the Muslim world – and, indeed, the Christian one as well – seemed doomed, but the Mamluk General Baybars in that year defeated the massive army of Hulagu at the Battle of Goliath's Well, a victory which, in retrospect, must be seen as one of the world's most decisive military engagements. By 1520, the region had fallen under the sway of the Ottoman Turks, and for the most part Syria prospered once again as a result. The 19th century was a period of increasing restiveness in the area: Napoleon's campaign in 1799-1800, the Egyptian invasion in the 1830s and the insurrection in 1860-61 are three instances of this. The Turks were defeated in World War I and Syria was occupied for a short time by the French. Syria was granted full independence in 1946. Three years later the country came under the first of a series of military dictatorships which have governed the country for most of the subsequent period. As in the rest of the Middle East, Arab nationalism became a major political force during the 1950s: indeed, the influence of Nasser's revolution in Egypt on the Syrians was so strong that, in 1958, Syria joined Egypt in forming the United Arab Republic. The alliance was short-lived, Syria seceding in 1961 to form the Syrian Arab Republic. The most powerful political force in Syria since then has been the Ba'ath Party (Arab Socialist Renaissance – see *Iraq*), led since 1971 by Hafiz al-Assad. The Syrians have suffered two major military defeats, in 1967 and 1973, at the hands of the Israelis and have now apparently concluded that they are unlikely to fare any better in the forseeable future. Assad can, however, point to a significant strategic victory over the Israelis in asserting political hegemony over Lebanon after a bloody struggle of attrition throughout the 1980s. The installation of the pro-Syrian government of Elias Hrawi was followed by the election in 1992 of a majority of pro-Syrian candidates to a new national assembly. This was prinicpally a result of Syria's decision to join the US-led coalition force which defated the Iraqis after the occupation of Kuwait in August 1990. Subsequently, the Syrians were necessarily key participants in the Middle East peace talks organised by then US Secretary of State James Baker; these began in December 1991. The Syrians have taken a hard line in each of the negotiating sessions, insisting that Israel must declare its intention to withdraw from the occupied Golan Heights before Syria would consider peace. Ever watchful of his domestic position, Assad stood for re-election at a national poll in December 1991. As the only candidate, he was comfortably returned to office. The Syrians have responded positively to the change of government in Israel. In 1992, they signalled a desire to improve relations by granting exit permits to the 4000 strong Syrian Jewish community.
GOVERNMENT: Syria is a Republican Democracy with an Executive led by a President. It has a Cabinet, one House of Parliament and an independent judiciary. Members of Parliament and local government counsellors are all directly elected by the people.

Palymra

CLIMATE

Syria's climate is characterised by hot, dry summers and fairly cold winters. Nights are often cool.
Required clothing: Lightweights are essential in summer with protective headwear. Heavy winter clothing is advisable from November to March.

DAMASCUS Syria (720m)

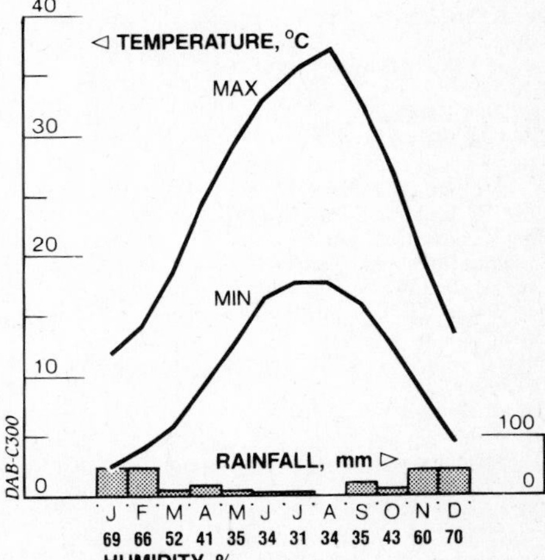

TAIWAN (CHINA)

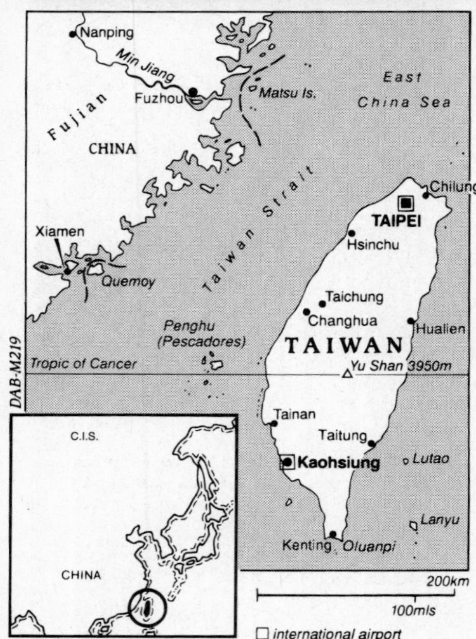

Location: Between the South and East China Seas, off the southeast coast of the People's Republic of China.

Taiwan Visitors Association
5th Floor
9 Minchuan East Road, Section 2
Taipei, Taiwan
Tel: (2) 594 3261. Fax: (2) 594 3265. Telex: 20335.
Tourism Bureau, Ministry of Communications
PO Box 1490
9th Floor
290 Chunghsiao East Road, Section 4
Taipei, Taiwan
Tel: (2) 721 8541. Fax: (2) 773 5487. Telex: 26408.
Taipei Representative Office in the UK
4th Floor, Dorland House
14-16 Regent Street
London
SW1Y 4PH
Tel: (071) 930 9553/4. Fax: (071) 321 0043. Telex: 24324 FCCLDN G. Opening hours: 1000-1300 Monday to Friday.
Visa Section: tel: (071) 930 5767. Opening hours: 0930-1730 Monday to Friday.
Republic of China Co-ordination Council – Information Division (CCNAA Office)
4201 Wisconsin Avenue, NW
Washington, DC
20016
Tel: (202) 895 1850. Fax: (202) 362 6144.
Also in: Atlanta, Boston, Chicago, Honolulu, Houston, Kansas City, Los Angeles, New York, San Francisco and Seattle.
Taiwan Visitors Bureau
Suite 7953
1 World Trade Center
New York, NY
10048
Tel: (212) 466 0691. Fax: (212) 432 6436. Telex: 226000 ETLX UR ATTN: BXT 1472 ROCNY.
Also in: Chicago and San Francisco.
American Institute in Taiwan
Suite 7, Lane 134
Hsin Yi Road, Section 3
Taipei, Taiwan
Tel: (2) 709 2000. Fax: (2) 702 7675. Telex: 23890 USTRADE.
Taiwan Visitors Association
Suite 820
222 Spadina Avenue
Toronto, Ontario
M5T 3A2
Tel: (416) 971 6912. Fax: (416) 490 0083. *Visa Information:* Tel: (416) 369 9030. Fax: (416) 369 1473.

AREA: 36,000 sq km (13,900 sq miles).
POPULATION: 20,550,000 (1991).
POPULATION DENSITY: 570.8 per sq km.
CAPITAL: Taipei. **Population:** 2,718,757 (1991).
GEOGRAPHY: Taiwan is the main island of a group of 78 islands. It is dominated by the Central Mountain Range covering 75% of its land area and running its full length north to south on the eastern seaboard. Over 60 peaks exceed 3000m (9850ft), the highest being *Yu Shan* (Jade Mountain) at 3950m (1290ft), and most are heavily forested. About 25% of the country is alluvial plain, most of it on the coastal strip. The Pescadores (Fisherman's Isles), which the Chinese call Penghu, comprise 64 islands west of Taiwan with a total area of 127 sq km (49 sq miles). The offshore island fortress of Quemoy (Kinmen) and Matsu, that form part of the mainland province of Fukien, are occupied by armed forces from Taiwan.
LANGUAGE: The official language is Northern Chinese (Mandarin). English and Japanese are widely spoken.
RELIGION: Buddhism; also Taoism, Christianity (Roman Catholic and Protestant) and Muslim.
TIME: GMT + 8.
ELECTRICITY: 110 volts AC, 60Hz.
COMMUNICATIONS: Telephone: Full IDD is available. Country code: 886. There is an extensive internal telephone system. **Fax:** Facilities are available at the ITA main office, 28 Hangchow South Road, Section 1, Taipei. Good hotels also have facilities. **Telex/telegram:** Telegrams may be sent from the ITA office (address above), or one of four branch offices. Telex equipment is available at major hotels or at the ITA main office. **Post:** Airmail to Europe takes up to ten days. *Poste Restante* facilities are available in main cities. **Press:** English-language dailies include *China News, China Post* and *Free China Journal.*
BBC World Service and Voice of America frequencies: From time to time these change. See the section *How to Use this Book* for more information.

BBC:				
MHz	11.955	15.360	11.955	9.740
Voice of America:				
MHz	17.74	11.76	7.275	1.575

PASSPORT/VISA

Regulations and requirements may be subject to change at short notice, and you are advised to contact the appropriate diplomatic or consular authority before finalising travel arrangements. Details of these may be found at the head of this country's entry. Any numbers in the chart refer to the footnotes below.

	Passport Required?	Visa Required?	Return Ticket Required?
Full British	Yes	Yes	1
BVP	Not valid	-	-
Australian	Yes	Yes	1
Canadian	Yes	Yes	1
USA	Yes	Yes	1
Other EC	Yes	Yes	1
Japanese	Yes	Yes	1

Restricted entry and transit: Passengers holding passports issued by the People's Republic of China will be refused entry to Taiwan.
Return tickets: [1] Open-ended tickets *may* be accepted in the case of business visitors or in other special circumstances.
PASSPORTS: Passport valid for at least 6 months required by all.
British Visitors Passport: Not acceptable.
VISAS: Required by all.
Note: No visa is required if continuing journey by the same or connecting aircraft on the same day of arrival, provided the visitor has confirmed onward tickets, the necessary travel documentation and does not depart from the transit lounge.
Types of visa: Single Visitor and Multiple Entry; cost: approximately £10 for Single Visitor visa; £20 for Multiple Entry.
Validity: Visitor: 60 days (valid for 3 months from date of issue). Business Multiple Entry: valid over a period of 6 months.
Application to: Taipei Representative Office in the UK or Taiwan Visitors' Bureau (addresses at beginning of entry) who will issue a letter of introduction for a visa to be issued on arrival in Taiwan.
Application requirements: (a) Application forms. (b) 2 photos. (c) Passport. (d) Tickets and letter from company for business visit. (e) Certificates declaring immunity against cholera and yellow fever if having arrived or passed through an infected area.
Working days required: 24 hours.
Temporary residence: Those wishing to stay more than 6 months must apply for a resident visa. Contact the Taipei Representative Office in the UK for further information (see address above).

MONEY

Currency: New Taiwan Dollar (NT$) = 100 cents. Notes are in denominations of NT$1000, 500, 100 and 50. Coins are in denominations of NT$50, 10, 5 and 1, and 50 cents.
Credit cards: Accepted in most hotels, restaurants and shops.
Travellers cheques: Accepted in most hotels, restaurants and shops.
Exchange rate indicators: The following figures are included as a guide to the movements of the New Taiwan Dollar against Sterling and the US Dollar:

Date:	Oct '89	Oct '90	Oct '91	Oct '92
£1.00=	40.45	53.90	45.97	40.23
$1.00=	25.62	27.59	26.49	25.35

Currency restrictions: The import of local currency is limited to NT$40,000 and only NT$8000 is allowed to be taken out. Government permission is required for larger amounts. Free import of foreign currency is allowed, subject to declaration. The export of foreign currency is limited to the equivalent of US$5000 for passengers leaving within six months of arrival, or up to the amount imported and declared. All exchange receipts must be retained.
Banking hours: 0900-1530 Monday to Friday and 0900-1200 Saturday.

DUTY FREE

The following items may be imported into Taiwan by travellers over 20 years of age without incurring customs duty:
200 cigarettes or 25 cigars or 454g of tobacco;
1 bottle of alcoholic beverage;
1 camera.
Note: Prohibited items include narcotics, gambling articles, non-canned meat products and toy pistols. All baggage must be itemised and declared in writing.

PUBLIC HOLIDAYS

Public holidays observed in Taiwan are as follows:
Mar 29 '93 Youth Day. **Apr 5** Women and Children's Day; Tomb Sweeping Day and Death of President Chiang Kai-shek. **May 1** Labour Day. **Jun 24** Dragon Boat Festival. **Sep 28** Birthday of Confucius (Teachers Day). **Sep 30** Mid-Autumn Moon Festival. **Oct 10** Double Tenth National Day. **Oct 25** Retrocession Day. **Oct 31** Birthday of Chiang Kai-shek (Veteran's Day). **Nov 12** Dr Sun Yat Sen's Birthday. **Dec 25** Constitution Day. **Jan 1 '94** National Holiday and Founding Day. **Feb 10** Chinese New Year. **Mar 29** Youth Day.

HEALTH

Regulations and requirements may be subject to change at short notice, and you are advised to contact your doctor well in advance of your intended date of departure. Any numbers in the chart refer to the footnotes below.

	Special Precautions?	Certificate Required?
Yellow Fever	No	1
Cholera	Yes	2
Typhoid & Polio	Yes	-
Malaria	No	-
Food & Drink	3	-

[1]: A yellow fever vaccination certificate is required of travellers arriving from infected areas.
[2]: Following WHO guidelines issued in 1973, a cholera vaccination certificate is not a condition of entry to Taiwan. However, cholera is a risk in this country and precautions are essential. Up-to-date advice should be sought before deciding whether these precautions should include vaccination, as medical opinion is divided over its effectiveness. See the *Health* section at the back of the book.
[3]: All water should be regarded as being potentially contaminated. Water used for drinking, brushing teeth or making ice should have first been boiled or otherwise sterilised. Milk is unpasteurised and should be boiled. Powdered or tinned milk is available and is advised, but make sure that it is reconstituted with pure water. Avoid dairy products which are likely to

have been made from unboiled milk. Only eat well-cooked meat and fish, preferably served hot. Pork, salad and mayonnaise may carry increased risk. Vegetables should be cooked and fruit peeled.
Rabies is present. For those at high risk, vaccination before arrival should be considered. If you are bitten abroad seek medical advice without delay. For more information consult the *Health* section at the back of the book.
Health care: Emergency health care is available at the Mackey Memorial Hospital in Taipei. Imported medicines are expensive, but locally produced and manufactured medicines are plentiful. Health insurance is recommended.

TRAVEL - International

AIR: Taiwan's national airline is *China Airlines (CI)*.
Approximate flight time: From *London* to Taipei is 20 hours, including connection in Amsterdam and subsequent stopovers.
International airports: *Taipei (TPE)* (Chiang Kai-shek) is 40km (25 miles) southwest of the city (travel time – 40 minutes). Airport facilities include an outgoing duty-free shop (0800-1900), post office, car hire (0900-1900), bank/exchange (0900-1900), bar/restaurant (0900-1900) and a tourism bureau. The coach to the city returns from the railway station (Chung Hsiao East Road). Bus no 1 goes every 15 minutes from 0640-2300. Return is from *Sung Shan* (domestic) airport bus terminal at Tun-Hwa North Road. Taxi service is available to the city. A bus service goes every 15 minutes from 0630-2230 (travel time – 45 minutes) to *Sung Shan*, which is located in the city itself; the journey takes approximately 40 minutes.
Kaohsiung International (KHH) is 9km (4 miles) from the town centre. A free hotel bus service is available (travel time – 30 minutes). There is a taxi service to the town. Airport facilities include an outgoing duty-free shop (0800-1900), car hire (0900-1900), bank/exchange services (0900-1900) and bar/restaurant (0900-1900).
Departure tax: NT$300 is levied on international departures. Transit passengers and children under two years are exempt.
SEA: Taiwan has sea links with Macau, Hong Kong and Japan.

TRAVEL - Internal

AIR: *China Airlines (CI)* and *Far Eastern Air Transport* run services to major cities from *Sung Shan* airport, Taipei. See above for information on shuttle bus to *Chiang Kai-shek* international airport.
SEA: There are reasonable connections from local ports. For details contact port authorities.
RAIL: Services are provided by the *Taiwan Railway Administration* along west and east coast routes. Air-conditioned electric trains run at least hourly from Taipei to Kaohsiung; some trains have restaurant and sleeping cars.
ROAD: There is an adequate road system joining all major cities. Some main streets have English signs.
Bus: There are both local and long-distance bus and coach services. **Taxi:** These are plentiful and inexpensive (metered). The destination must be written in Chinese for the driver. **Car hire:** This is available in major towns. **Documentation:** An International Driving Permit is required.
URBAN: A number of private bus companies provide extensive services in Taipei. Metered taxis are available in Taipei and tipping is not expected, but is starting to come into practice.
JOURNEY TIMES: The following chart gives approximate journey times (in hours and minutes) from Taipei to other major cities/towns in Taiwan.

	Air	Road	Rail
Kaohsiung	0.40	5.30	6.00
Tainan	0.40	4.30	5.00
Taichung	-	2.30	3.00
Hualien	0.30	7.00	3.00
Taitung	0.50	10.00	5.30
Sun Moon L.	-	4.30	-
Alishan	-	6.00	-
Kenting	-	6.30	-
Makung	0.40	-	-

ACCOMMODATION

HOTELS: There are over 100 tourist hotels in Taiwan offering a broad range of accommodation and services. Prices range from US$30-50 a day for smaller hotels with US$90-150 a day being average. For details contact the Press Division of the Taipei Representative Office in the UK or the Taiwan Visitors Bureau. Many hotels belong to the Taipei Tourism Hotel Association, 8F-1, 369 Fu-Hsing N Road, Taipei. Tel: (2) 717 2155. Fax: (2) 717 2453. **Grading:** Hotels are rated on a scale of **1** to **5 'Plum Blossoms'** using a system equivalent to the more familiar 5-star system, with Three Plum Blossoms being about average:
4 to 5 Plum Blossoms: 50 hotels (half of which are in Taipei) are in these categories. The hotels are luxury class with a range of services and facilities, eg tennis courts, swimming pools and beauty salons.
2 and 3 Plum Blossoms: The 80 hotels in these categories are clean, comfortable and functional.
CAMPING/CARAVANNING: Campsites are available.
YOUTH HOSTELS: Dormitory and non-dormitory rooms are available in major cities and in scenic areas.

RESORTS & EXCURSIONS

For the purposes of this section, the country has been divided into four regions: Taipei; North Taiwan; Central Taiwan; and South Taiwan.

Taipei

The principal city in northern Taiwan, Taipei was designated a 'special municipality' in July 1967, thus acquiring the same status as a province and its mayor the same rank as a provincial governor. The area of the city has expanded to four times its original size, making it the fastest growing city in Asia.
Sightseeing: The city centre contains the *National Museum of History*, the *Taipei Fine Arts Museum*, the *Taiwan Provincial Museum* and *Chung Cheng (Chiang Kai-shek) Memorial Hall*, which is a fine example of classical Chinese architecture. The magnificent main entrance is more than 30m (100ft) high.
The *Lungshan (Dragon Mountain) Temple* is dedicated to Kuan Yin, the Goddess of Mercy, and was built in 1740. The temple, one of more than 5000 temples and shrines in Taiwan, is regarded as the island's finest example of temple architecture.
Among other outstanding buildings of classical Chinese architecture in Taipei are the *Martyrs' Shrine*, the *Sun Yat-sen Memorial Hall* and the *Chungsham Building* in the Yangmingshan district of the metropolis, 40 minutes drive from the centre of Taipei, where the *National Palace Museum* can also be found; it houses the world's largest and most priceless collection of Chinese art treasures. *Yangmingshan Park* is famous throughout Taiwan for its cherry and azalea trees and attracts thousands of visitors at blossom time.

North Taiwan

Keelung has an imposing hilltop statue of *Kuan Yin*, the Goddess of Mercy. The northeast coastal road offers a spectacular drive, passing the foothills of the Central Mountain Range and overlooking the East China Sea and the Pacific Ocean. The traveller will pass through many small villages whose lifestyles have changed little with the advent of high technology.
Other outstanding attractions of the area include **Yehliu**, noted for its fantastic rock formations (Queen's Head); *Green Bay* and *Chinshan* beaches, with full beach resort facilities; *Shihmen Dam;* and **Wulai**, a mountain resort south of Taipei. Wulai is the site of a hilltop park and of a village inhabited by aboriginals who, besides making and selling artefacts, give lively song and dance performances for tourists. The **Northeast Coast National Scenic Area**, also with unusual rock formations, is not only good for swimming, diving, surfing, water-skiing and camping, but also the best place for seashore fishing and rock climbing. *Window on China* at **Lungtan**, 53km (33 miles) southwest of Taipei, contains reproductions on a scale of 1:25 of historical and other notable Chinese sites.

Central Taiwan

The centre of the island has the most varied landscape. The east–west cross-island highway passes through spectacular mountain passes, most notably the *Taroko Gorge*, a ravine with towering cliffs shot through with extensive marble deposits. **Lishan**, located 1945m (6381ft) up on *Pear Mountain*, is a popular mountain resort. Other popular sights in the mountains include the *Sun Moon Lake*, the *Chitou Forest* recreation area, *Yu Shan* (Jade Mountain), and the alpine railway to **Alishan**.
Throughout the central area there are numerous temples. The region's main towns are **Taichung**, one of the largest ports on the island, and **Hualien** located in the east.

South Taiwan

Kenting National Park is a popular forest recreation area boasting fine beaches, coral lakes, a bird sanctuary and, more recently, facilities for watersports and golf, all set amidst tropical coastal forest. **Kaohsiung** is the main industrial centre and has the island's only other main airport, besides Taipei's Chiang Kai-shek. **Tainan**, the oldest city on the island, is known as the 'City of 100 Temples'; there are in fact 220, amongst them some of the best examples of Confucian temple architecture on the island. **Lanyu** (Orchid Island), one of the smaller islands off the east coast, is the home of the aboriginal Yami, one of the world's last surviving hunter-gatherer tribes. *Lotus Lake* is the site of the Spring and Autumn Pavilions and of the Dragon and Tiger Pagodas.

SOCIAL PROFILE

FOOD & DRINK: The Chinese, never at a loss for vivid description, describe their cuisine as an 'ancient art of ultimate harmony: pleasing to the eye; mouth-watering; and a delight to the palate'. Taiwan's restauranteurs see themselves as the guardians of this tradition. Culinary styles include Canton, Peking, Szechuan, Shanghai, Hunan, Mongolia and Taiwan. Cantonese food is more colourful and sweeter than that of other regions. Dishes include fried shrimp with cashews, onion-marinated chicken, beef with oyster sauce and sweet-and-sour pork. Pastries include steamed dumplings stuffed with meat, sweet paste or preserves, buns, deep-fried spring rolls and tarts. Pekinese cooking is mild, combining roast or barbecued meat (often cooked at the table), vegetables and flat pancake wrappers. Dishes include *Peking duck*, carp cooked three ways, steamed prawns, chicken-in-paper, diced chicken in heavy sauce, eels with pepper sauce and ham marrow sauce. Szechuan cooking is hot and spicy, based on red chilli pepper and garlic. Dishes include *Mother Ma's bean curd*, aubergine with garlic sauce, *Gungbao chicken*, fried prawns with pepper

TAIWAN	HEALTH REGULATIONS	VISA REGULATIONS
GALILEO/WORLDSPAN	 TI-DFT/TPE/HE	 TI-DFT/TPE/VI
SABRE	 TIDFT/TPE/HE	TIDFT/TPE/VI

Code-Link

To access this information on your CRS, swipe the barcode with a light pen or type in the text under the barcode. For more information, see the introduction *How to Use This Book.*

sauce, minced chicken with *Gingko* nuts. Fried breads make a pleasant change from rice.

Shanghai cooking is mostly seafood with rich salty sauces. Dishes include shark's fin in chicken, mushroom with crab meat, *ningpo* (fried eel), shark's fin soup and West Lake fish. Hunan has both spicy and steamed dishes including steamed ham and honey sauce, diced chicken with peanuts, steamed silver thread rolls and smoked duck. Mongolian comprises two basic dishes of *huoguo* ('firepot' – meat dipped in a sauce based on sesame paste, shrimp oil, ginger juice and bean paste) and barbecue (various slices of meat and vegetables cooked on an iron grill and eaten in a sesame bun). Taiwanese cooking is mostly seafood with thick sauces. It relies on garlic in the north and soy sauce in the south. Dishes include spring rolls with peanut butter, sweet-and-sour spare ribs, bean curd in red sauce, oyster omelette and numerous excellent seafoods. More information on Chinese cuisine can be found by consulting the corresponding sections in the entries for China (People's Republic of) and Hong Kong; see the *Contents* pages for details.

Restaurants/bars: Restaurants almost always have table service although some hotels have buffet/barbecue lunches. Most hotels have restaurants offering both Western and Chinese cuisine and some of the larger hotels offer several styles of Chinese cooking (the Chinese word for hotel, *fan-dien*, means 'eating place'). Most bars have counter service. **Drink:** There are no set licensing hours and alcohol is widely available.

NIGHTLIFE: Most top hotels have nightclubs with dinner, dancing and a show. Smaller bars often present 'entertainments'. Taiwanese opera is performed on the streets, in open spaces, outside temples and anywhere a stage can be erected. Ballet, opera and drama can be seen at the National Theatre and the City Hall in Taipei. Performances with puppets are offered in villages and temples during festivals. There are also cinemas which show both Chinese and foreign-language films.

SHOPPING: One of the best ways to shop in Taiwan is to visit the night-markets. Purchases include Formosan sea-grass mats, hats, handbags and slippers, bamboo items, Chinese musical instruments, various dolls in costume, handpainted palace lanterns made from silk, lacquerware, ceramics, teak furniture, coral, veinstone and Taiwan jade items, *ramie* fibre rugs, brassware, handmade shoes, fabrics and chop sticks (decorated, personalised sticks of wood or marble). Cashback on duty free can be claimed at the following address: Ministry of Finance (MOF), 85 Hsinsheng S Road, Section 1, Taipei. Tel: (2) 741 3181.

SPORT: Fishing: There are lakes, rivers and fish farms and the sea with mainly unrestricted fishing. Near Taipei there is good fishing at the Tamsui and Hsintien rivers, Green Lake and Shihmen Reservoir. **Golf:** There are several year-round golf courses. Sponsorship, if needed, can be arranged through travel agencies. For further information contact the *Chinese Taipei Golf Association*, 75 Lane 187, Tunhua South Road, Taipei. **Mountaineering:** Slopes range from beginner to bare rock faces. **Skating:** There are several roller-skating rinks in major cities and two ice rinks in Taipei. **Skindiving:** The coral reefs of southern Taiwan and the Pescadores Islands are considered good skindiving areas. Contact *Chinese Diving Federation*, 123 Chui Chuan Street, Taipei. **Swimming:** Rivers, lakes and the sea are ideal for swimming. Best time for swimming on the north coast is May to September while on the south coast the water is warm all year. **Tennis:** There are tennis courts at most universities, colleges and many hotels. Every major city has bowling alleys. **Hot springs** abound throughout Taiwan. Some of the sites are easily accessible and provide baths, hot tubs and hotel facilities.

SPECIAL EVENTS: There are numerous festivals throughout the year, all with variable dates. For an up-to-date list, contact the Taipei Representative Office in the UK or the Taiwan Visitors Bureau (for addresses see top of entry), but a selection is included here: **Mar 11 '93** *Birthday of Kuan Yin* (Goddess of Mercy). **Apr 10-14** *Taipei International Flower Show*, Taipei World Trade Centre. **Apr 14** *Festival of the Birth of Matsu, Goddess of the Sea;* Matsu temples around the island with major celebration at Peikang's Chaotien Temple. **Apr** *Flying Fish Festival of the Yami people*, Lanyu. **May 23-26** *Taipei International Design Exhibition (TIDEX)*, Taipei World Trade Centre. **Jun 2-5** *Lukang Folk Arts Festival*, Lukang. **Jun 1-5** *Computex Taipei International Computer Show*, Taipei World Trade Centre. **Jun 24** *Dragon Boat Festival.* **Jul 2** *Birthday of Cheng Huang.* **Aug** *Harvest Festival of the Ami people*, Hualien and Taitung counties; *Harvest Festival of the Rukai people*, Kaohsiung, Pingtung and Taitung counties. **Aug 19-22** *Taipei Aerospace Technology Exhibition*, Taipei World Trade Centre. **Aug 31** *Ghost Month* begins. **Sep 26-29** *Taipei International Toy Show*, Taipei World Trade Centre. **Sep 30** *Mid Autumn Moon Festival.* **Feb 10-11 '94** *Chinese Lunar New Year* (Lantern Festival). **Mar** *Festival of the Birth of Kuan Yin* (Goddess of Mercy).

SOCIAL CONVENTIONS: Handshaking is common. Casual wear is widely acceptable. Ancient festivals and customs are celebrated enthusiastically and traditional holidays are important. Entertainment is usually offered in restaurants, not at home. Visitors are not expected to entertain. Conversation about mainland China is common. Chinese culture in the form of drama, opera and art is also very strong in Taiwan. Despite rapid industrialisation and development the way of life in Taiwan is very much Chinese, steeped in tradition and old values. **Tipping:** Tipping is not an established custom, although it is on the increase. Taipei hotels and restaurants add 10% service charge and extra tipping is not expected. It is not customary to tip taxi-drivers.

BUSINESS PROFILE

ECONOMY: After phenomenal economic growth from the 1950s onwards, Taiwan had by 1980, emerged among the top 20 trading nations in the world. The island's success has been on a policy of rapid industrialisation, coupled with low overheads and labour costs which have allowed Taiwanese products to compete successfully in world markets. Textiles, shipbuilding, metals, plywood, furniture and petrochemicals are the principal industries; the Government is now seeking to promote financial services, electronics and information technology to sustain Taiwan's economic growth. Agriculture and fisheries, despite declining in relative terms, are large enough to afford Taiwan a considerable measure of self-sufficiency in food. The island leads the 'Tiger economies' of the Pacific basin, boasting the highest standard of living in East Asia outside Japan and the largest reserves of foreign currency (US$87 billion in 1991) – valued at around US$70,000 million – of any country in the world. Exports in 1988 totalled US$53.5 billion. Apart from the USA, Taiwan's major trading partners are Japan, Germany, Australia, Saudi Arabia (which supplies much of Taiwan's oil requirements) and mainland China, with whom both-way trade now exceeds US$5 billion. Taiwanese investors, both private and government-sponsored, have also been active in Europe in recent years. The domestic boom is showing definite signs of deflating: growth is sluggish and investment tailing off. However, reduced trade barriers and the relaxation of foreign exchange controls have made exporting easier. The Gulf crisis and the consequent oil price hike has sharply increased the island's import bill.

BUSINESS: Although many business people speak English, interpreters may be needed. Appointments should be made and punctuality is expected. Visiting cards are widely used. **Office hours:** 0830-1730 Monday to Friday, 0830-1230 Saturday.

COMMERCIAL INFORMATION: The following organisations can offer advice: General Chamber of Commerce, 6th Floor, 390 Fu Hsing South Road, Section 1, Taipei. Tel: (2) 701 2671. Fax: (2) 754 2107. Telex: 11396; *or*

China External Trade Development Council, 4th-7th Floors, 333 Keelung Road, Section 1, Taipei 10548. Tel: (2) 725 5200. Fax: (2) 757 6653. Telex: 21676.

CONFERENCES/CONVENTIONS: The Tourism Bureau's brochure *Convention Facilities in Taiwan* lists 27 venues of which the largest is Sun Yat-Sen Memorial Hall, with seating for up to 2653 persons; several other venues can seat over 2000. Hotels offer a comprehensive range of facilities and there are some with seating for 1000 and over. For further information contact: Taipei International Convention Center (TICC), 1 Hsin Yi Road, Section 5, Taipei. Tel: (2) 723 2535. Fax: (2) 723 2590.

HISTORY & GOVERNMENT

HISTORY: Taiwan is an island off the south-east coast of China, a country of which it is also a part, and is claimed to be the custodian and preserver of the world's oldest culture. Taiwan has a varied history, originally inhabited by mainland Chinese until the 17th century when the Dutch occupied the islands along with the Spanish for about 40 years. In 1684 it was occupied mainly by supporters of the deposed Ming Dynasty and was a *tao* (a province and a county) of the province of Fukien across the Taiwan Straits. In 1885 it was completely controlled by the Qing Dynasty and made into an official province. In 1895 it was put into the control of the Japanese by a treaty which dated from the first Sino-Japanese War. This rule was fiercely opposed by the local people until the handing back of power in 1945. The KMT (Kuomintang) Party has dominated Taiwanese politics since the fleeing of Chiang Kai-shek to the island and has concentrated on ensuring its own political survival and developing the economy. The latter, it has done successfully, and Taiwan is now recognised as one of the fast-developing 'Tiger economies' of the Pacific Rim. Politically, Taiwan relied for a long time upon the support of the United States until the 1970s when the rapprochement between Washington and Peking took place. Despite the distance between mainland China and Taiwan, co-operation has grown during the last decade. In 1991 two-way trade was US$5.8 billion and one million Taiwanese visited China. In July 1992, Taiwan's legislature passed a law allowing most forms of direct contact with China. The KMT stranglehold has recently been challenged by students who have adopted a strategy of protest with growing representation for KMT opponents in the national assembly. The Government has been occasionally preoccupied by territorial disputes such as the 6-way squabble over the ownership of the potentially oil-rich Spratly Islands.

GOVERNMENT: The Assembly is nominally elected by adult suffrage every six years, but many of the 1020 seats have been allocated to life members. Much political power is held by the five *Yuans* (governing bodies) whose responsibilities are: presentation of legislation to the National Assembly; government administration; oversight of the executive; interpretation of the law; and control of the recruitment of government officials. The majority of *Yuan* members are appointed for life.

CLIMATE

A subtropical climate with moderate temperatures in the north, where there is a winter season. The southern areas enjoy sunshine every day and temperatures are slightly higher and has no winter season.The typhoon season is from June to October.

Required clothing: Light to mediumweights, with rainwear advised.

TAIPEI Taiwan (8m)

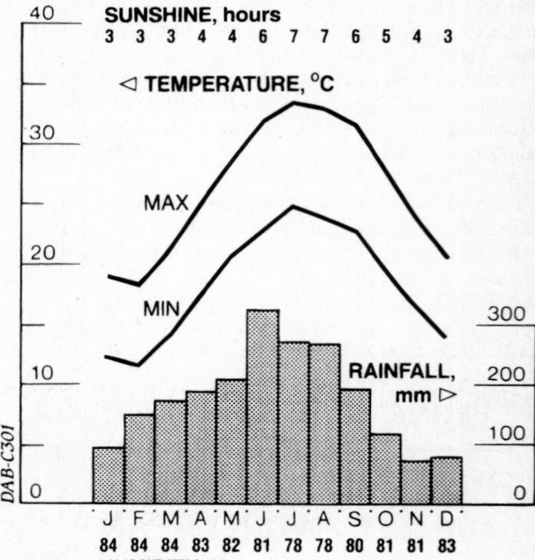

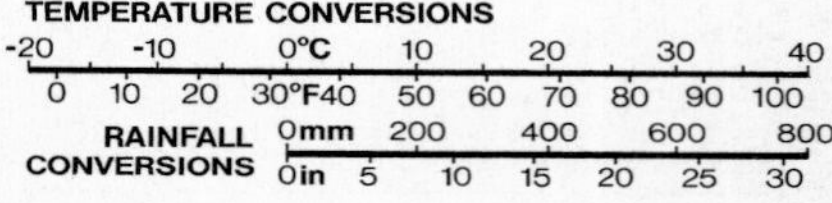

TANZANIA

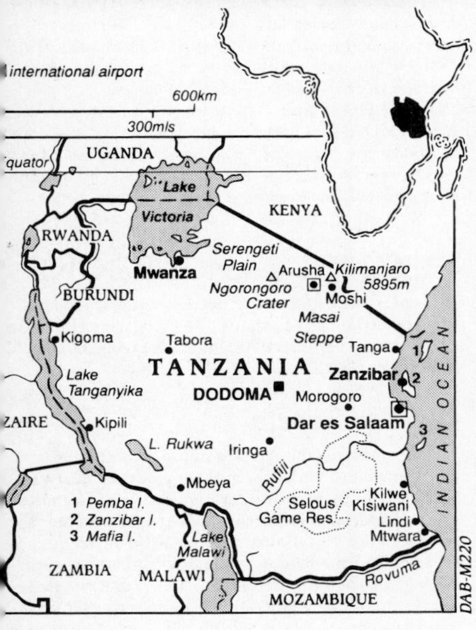

ocation: East Africa.

Tanzania Tourist Corporation
O Box 2485
Dar es Salaam, Tanzania
Tel: (51) 27671. Fax: (51) 46780. Telex: 41061.
Tanzania Wildlife Corporation
O Box 1144
Arusha, Tanzania
Tel: (57) 8830. Fax: (57) 8239. Telex: 42080.
High Commission for the United Republic of Tanzania
3 Hertford Street
London
W1Y 8DB
Tel: (071) 499 8951-4. Fax: (071) 491 9321. Telex: 262504. Opening hours: 0900-1230 (for visa enquiries) and 1400-1700 Monday to Friday.
Tanzanian Trade Centre
78-80 Borough High Street
London SE1 1LL
Tel: (071) 407 0566. Fax: (071) 403 2003. Opening hours: 0900-1700 Monday to Friday.
British High Commission
PO Box 9200
Hifadhi House
Samora Avenue
Dar es Salaam, Tanzania
Tel: (51) 29601. Fax: (51) 46301. Telex: 41004.
Embassy of the United Republic of Tanzania
2139 R Street, NW
Washington, DC
20008
Tel: (202) 939 6125. Fax: (202) 797 7408. Telex: 64213.
Tanzania Tourist Office
8th Floor
205 East 42nd Street
New York, NY
10017
Tel: (212) 972 9160. Telex: 220782 TTCNY UR.
Also deals with enquiries from Canada.
Embassy of the United States of America
PO Box 9123
36 Laibon Road
Dar es Salaam, Tanzania
Tel: (51) 66010/3. Fax: (51) 66701. Telex: 41250.
High Commission for the United Republic of Tanzania
50 Range Road
Ottawa, Ontario
K1N 8J4
Tel: (613) 232 1500/9. Fax: (613) 232 5184.
Canadian High Commission
PO Box 1022
38 Mirambo Street
Dar es Salaam, Tanzania
Tel: (51) 46000/11. Fax: (51) 46005. Telex: 41015 DOMCAN TZ.

AREA: 945,087 sq km (364,900 sq miles).
POPULATION: 23,997,000 (1988 estimate).
POPULATION DENSITY: 25.4 per sq km.
CAPITAL: Dodoma (administrative capital).
Population: 85,000 (1985 estimate). Dar es Salaam remains the commercial capital for the time being.
Population: 1,096,000.
GEOGRAPHY: The United Republic of Tanzania lies on the Indian Ocean and is bordered by Kenya and Uganda to the north, by Burundi, Rwanda and Zaïre to the west, and by Zambia, Malawi and Mozambique to the south. The Tanzanian mainland is divided into several clearly defined regions: the coastal plains, which vary in width from 16-64km (10-39 miles) and have lush, tropical vegetation; the Masai Steppe in the north, 213-1067m (698-3500ft) above sea level; and a high plateau in the southern area towards Zambia and Lake Nyasa. Savannah and bush cover over half the country, and semi-desert accounts for the remaining land area, with the exception of the coastal plains. Over 53,000 sq km (20,463 sq miles) is inland water, mostly lakes formed in the Rift Valley. The United Republic of Tanzania includes the islands of Zanzibar and Pemba, about 45km (28 miles) off the coast to the northeast of the country.
LANGUAGE: Swahili and English are the official languages. Other African languages such as Bantu and those of Nilo-Hamitic and Khoisan origin are also spoken.
RELIGION: Muslim, Christian, Hindu and various traditional beliefs.
TIME: GMT + 3.
ELECTRICITY: 230 volts AC, 50Hz. Plugs may be round or square 3-pin, fused or unfused.
COMMUNICATIONS: Telephone: IDD is available. Country code: 255. There are many public call boxes in post offices and main towns. **Telex/Telegram:** Telex facilities are available at the *Kilimanjaro Hotel*, Dar es Salaam, *Mount Meru Hotel* in Arusha and at the post office in Dar es Salaam. Telegrams can be sent from the post office. **Post:** Airmail to Europe takes five days. **Press:** The English-language newspaper is *Daily News*, a government publication, printed in Dar es Salaam.
BBC World Service and Voice of America frequencies: From time to time these change. See the section *How to Use this Book* for more information.

BBC:				
MHz	21.470	17.885	15.420	9.630
Voice of America:				
MHz	21.49	15.60	9.525	6.035

PASSPORT/VISA

Regulations and requirements may be subject to change at short notice, and you are advised to contact the appropriate diplomatic or consular authority before finalising travel arrangements. Details of these may be found at the head of this country's entry. Any numbers in the chart refer to the footnotes below.

	Passport Required?	Visa Required?	Return Ticket Required?
Full British	Yes	No	Yes
BVP	Not valid	-	-
Australian	Yes	Yes	Yes
Canadian	Yes	Yes	Yes
USA	Yes	Yes	Yes
Other EC	Yes	1	Yes
Japanese	Yes	Yes	Yes

PASSPORTS: Valid passport required by all.
British Visitors Passport: Not accepted.
VISAS: Required by all except:
(a) **[1]** nationals of Denmark, Ireland and the UK . All other EC nationals *do* require a visa;
(b) nationals of Antigua & Barbuda, Bahamas, Bangladesh, Barbados, Belize, Botswana, Brunei, Cyprus, Dominica, Fiji, Finland, Gambia, Ghana, Grenada, Guyana, Iceland, Jamaica, Kenya, Kiribati, Lesotho, Malawi, Malaysia, Maldives, Malta, Mauritius, Nauru, Norway, Papua New Guinea, Rwanda, St Kitts & Nevis, St Lucia, St Vincent & the Grenadines, Seychelles, Sierra Leone, Singapore, Solomon Islands, Sri Lanka, Swaziland, Sweden, Tonga, Trinidad & Tobago, Tuvalu, Uganda, Vanuatu, Western Samoa, Zambia and Zimbabwe;
(c) holders of a Tanzanian re-entry pass.
However, *all* temporary visitors must hold a *Visitor's Pass*. Visitors are advised to obtain such a Pass from Tanzanian representations before the commencement of their journey.
Type of visa: Cost of visa depends on nationality. Visitor's Pass is issued free of charge.
Application requirements (for Visas and Passes): (a) 1 completed application form (different form for Visa and Visitor's Pass). (b) Letter of invitation (for business visitors). (c) 2 passport-size photos. (d) Passport. (e) Fee (visas only).
Application to: Consulate (or Consular Section at Embassy or High Commission). For addresses, see top of entry.
Working days required: 5 days.
Temporary residence: Enquire at Embassy or High Commission.

MONEY

Currency: Tanzanian Shilling (TSh) = 100 cents. Notes are in denominations of TSh1000, 500, 200, 100 and 50. Coins are in denominations of TSh20, 10, 5 and 1, and 50, 20, 10 and 5 cents.
Currency exchange: Money may be changed at authorised dealers or bureaux de change.
Credit cards: Access/Mastercard and Diners Club both have limited acceptance. Check with your credit card company for details of merchant acceptability and other facilities which may be available.
Travellers cheques: May be cashed with authorised dealers or bureaux de change.
Exchange rate indicators: The following figures are included as a guide to the movements of the Tanzanian Shilling against Sterling and the US Dollar:

Date:	Oct '89	Oct '90	Oct '91	Oct '92
£1.00=	230.00	380.65	397.54	506.08
$1.00=	145.66	194.85	229.06	318.90

Currency restrictions: The import and export of local currency is prohibited. The import of foreign currency is unlimited, subject to declaration. The export of foreign currency is limited to TSh4000 or the amount declared on arrival.
Banking hours: 0830-1230 Monday to Friday, 0830-1130 Saturday and 0900-1130 Sunday.

DUTY FREE

The following items may be imported into Tanzania without incurring customs duty:
200 cigarettes or 50 cigars or 250g of tobacco;
1 litre of wine or 1 litre of spirits;
250ml of perfume.

PUBLIC HOLIDAYS

Public holidays observed in Tanzania are as follows:
Mar 25 '93 Start of Eid al-Fitr. **Apr 9-12** Easter. **Apr 26** Union Day. **May 1** Labour Day. **Jun 1** Start of Eid al-Haji. **Jul 7** Peasants' Day. **Aug 30** Prophet's Birthday. **Dec 9** Independence Day. **Dec 25** Christmas Day. **Jan 12 '94** Zanzibar Revolution Day. **Feb 5** Chama Cha Mapinduzi Day. **Mar** Eid al-Fitr.
Note: Muslim festivals are timed according to local sightings of various phases of the Moon and the dates given above are approximations. During the lunar month of Ramadan that precedes Eid al-Fitr, Muslims fast during the day and feast at night and normal business patterns may be interrupted. Many restaurants are closed during the day and there may be restrictions on smoking and drinking. Some disruption may continue into Eid al-Fitr itself. Eid al-Fitr and Eid al-Haji (Eid al-Adha) may last anything from two to ten days, depending on the region. For more information see the section *World of Islam* at the back of the book.

HEALTH

Regulations and requirements may be subject to change at short notice, and you are advised to contact your doctor well in advance of your intended date of departure. Any numbers in the chart refer to the footnotes below.

	Special Precautions?	Certificate Required?
Yellow Fever	Yes	1
Cholera	Yes	2
Typhoid & Polio	Yes	-
Malaria	3	-
Food & Drink	4	-

[1]: A yellow fever vaccination certificate is required of all travellers over one year of age.
[2]: A vaccination certificate is an essential requirement for entry into Zanzibar. Following WHO guidelines issued in 1973, a cholera vaccination certificate is no longer a condition of entry to Tanzania. However, cholera is a risk in this country and precautions are essential. Up-to-date advice should be sought before deciding whether these precautions should include

vaccination as medical opinion is divided over its effectivenss. See the *Health* section at the back of the book.
[3]: Malaria risk, predominantly in the malignant *falciparum* form, exists all year throughout the country below 1800m. The strain is reported to be 'highly resistant' to chloroquine and 'resistant' to sulfadoxine/pyrimethamine.
[4]: All water should be regarded as being potentially contaminated. Water used for drinking, brushing teeth or making ice should have first been boiled or otherwise sterilised. Milk is unpasteurised and should be boiled. Powdered or tinned milk is available and is advised, but make sure that it is reconstituted with pure water. Avoid dairy products which are likely to have been made from unboiled milk. Only eat well-cooked meat and fish, preferably served hot. Pork, salad and mayonnaise may carry increased risk. Vegetables should be cooked and fruit peeled.
Rabies is present. For those at high risk, vaccination before arrival should be considered. If you are bitten abroad seek medical advice without delay. For more information consult the *Health* section at the back of the book.
Bilharzia (schistosomiasis) is present. Avoid swimming and paddling in fresh water. Swimming pools which are well-chlorinated and maintained are safe.
Health care: Private health insurance is recommended. There are 2000-3000 hospitals and clinics; some Christian missions also provide medical treatment.

TRAVEL - International

AIR: Tanzania's national airline is *Air Tanzania Corporation*.
Approximate flight times: From London to *Dar es Salaam* is 12 hours 45 minutes and to *Kilimanjaro* is 14 hours.
International airports: *Dar es Salaam International (DAR)*, 15km (9 miles) southwest of the city (travel time – 25 minutes). A shuttle bus service and taxi services to the city are available. Airport facilities include outgoing duty-free shop, car hire, post office, banking and exchange facilities, a bar and restaurant.
Kilimanjaro International Airport (JRO). Shuttle bus services and taxis are available to the nearest town of Arusha. Airport facilities include shops, post office, bar and restaurant.
Departure tax: *Residents:* TSh1000; *non-residents:* US$20. The latter has to be paid in US Dollars. Transit passengers and children under two years are exempt.
SEA: Dar es Salaam is served by ocean freighters and passenger liners. Contact the *National Shipping Agencies Co Ltd (NASACO)*, PO Box 9082, Dar es Salaam (telex: 41235); *or the Tanzanian Harbours Authority (THA)*, PO Box 9184, Dar es Salaam. Tel: (51) 21212. Fax: (51) 32066. Telex: 41346.
RAIL: There is a twice-weekly restaurant car service by *Tanzania – Zambia Railway Authority (Tazara)* from Dar es Salaam to Kapiri Mposhi (Zambia), with a change of train at the border. Lake steamer connections operate from railheads at Kigoma and Mwanza to Burundi, Rwanda and Uganda. Trains may get very crowded but officials can be readily persuaded to find seats for tourists. Travellers should take special care of their baggage. It is unwise to forward luggage. Rail connections between Tanzania and Kenya have been suspended for many years, following a dispute over ownership of locomotives and rolling stock.
ROAD: The tarmac road connecting Tanzania with Zambia is in good condition, as is the road north to Kenya. From Lusaka in Zambia the Great North Road is paved all the way to Dar es Salaam. Road links from Rwanda and Mozambique are poor.

TRAVEL - Internal

AIR: *Air Tanzania* runs regular services to all main towns. These are reliable and efficiently run, but check with the town airline office before leaving for the airport. All national parks have airstrips and there are two charter companies operating single- and twin-engined aircraft to any town or bush strip in the country. In addition there are numerous bush airfields and airstrips in many towns which can be used by the charter companies.
SEA/LAKE: There is a daily speed-boat service between Dar es Salaam and Zanzibar which takes 2-3 hours in each direction. There is also a sailing from Zanzibar to Pemba Island. Both Lake Tanganyika and Lake Victoria have a steamer service. First-, second- and third-class seating is available on both services, though first class has more comfortable seats and is likely to be less crowded. The service on Lake Victoria calls at the ports of Bukoba, Mwanza and Musoma, but the timetable for the service is unlikely to be reliable. For further details contact the *Tanzania Railways Corporation* or *NASACO*.
RAIL: *Tanzania Railways Corporation (TRC)* provides the principal services, while those on the route to Zambia are run by *Tazara*. *TRC* runs a daily service from Dar es Salaam to Mwanza on Lake Victoria and Kigoma on Lake Tanganyika with a restaurant car. There are also daily trains from Dar es Salaam to Moshi and Arusha. *Tazara* runs daily trains to the Zambian border.
ROAD: Tanzania has a good network of tarmac and all-weather roads connecting all major towns. Most minor roads are in bad condition becoming impassable to all except 4-wheel drive vehicles during the long rains in April and May. It is not advisable to drive at night because of wild animals, cattle and goats on the road. There are often petrol shortages and spare parts for vehicles are hard to find. **Bus:** Inexpensive buses connecting most places are operated by the *State Travel Service*, but services are often unreliable or break down. The worst times to travel by bus are at the end of the month and during the April/May rains. **Car hire:** Self-drive car hire is extremely expensive and is discouraged by most companies. Vehicles with drivers are offered, and this is often more reliable. **Documentation:** An International Driving Licence is recommended, although it is not legally required; it must be endorsed by the police on arrival. A temporary licence to drive is available from the police on presentation of a valid national driving licence.
URBAN: Buses and minibuses operate in Dar es Salaam on a flat fare basis. Services are usually crowded and inefficient. In Dar es Salaam, taxis at hotels have fixed rates for journeys within the city. In other towns, taxi fares should be negotiated in advance. Drivers expect a tip of 10%.

ACCOMMODATION

HOTELS: Tanzania has a range of accommodation from very good, expensive hotels to cheaper hotels which, although adequate, lack comfort. Although accommodation is on the expensive side, it is often possible for two people to share a single room except in top hotels. The less expensive hotels are often fully booked.
WILDLIFE LODGES: There are wildlife lodges in all national parks. Reservations can be booked through the *Tanzania Tourist Corporation (TTC)* in Dar es Salaam or the Tanzania Wildlife Corporation in Arusha (see top of entry for addresses and telephone numbers).
GUEST-HOUSES: These are often offshoots of local bars and provide cheap accommodation, but there may be problems with drunken behaviour and theft. Sharing a room is advisable and special attention to possessions should be paid while staying there. These are not bookable in advance. Prices of guest-houses are higher in the larger towns, but in general the quality can be assessed from the tariffs.
CAMPING/CARAVANNING: There are campsites in Arusha, Arusha National Park (four), Tarangire National Park (two), Lake Manyara National Park (two), Ngorongoro Conservation Area Authority (two), Serengeti National Park (seven), Kilimanjaro National Park (one), Mikumi National Park (two) and Ruaha National Park (two). Some have standard facilities, including taps, toilets, bivouac huts and firewood; others are more basic. Permits for entry to each park and also for photography and filming must be obtained before arrival. It is advisable to check on the prices and site procedure before arrival. All bookings can be made through the office of the Director, Tanzania National Parks, PO Box 3134, Arusha. Tel: (57) 3471. Alternatively, write directly to the Park Warden in charge of the individual parks.
YOUTH HOSTELS: There are youth hostels in Lake Manyara National Park (primarily educational groups) and Serengeti National Park, YMCA hostels in Moshi and Dar es Salaam, and a YWCA hostel, which takes couples as well as women, in Dar es Salaam.

RESORTS & EXCURSIONS

For convenience and ease of reference, this section has been divided into five regions: Dar es Salaam; The Coast; Zanzibar & Mafia Island; Mount Kilimanjaro; and The National Parks.

Dar es Salaam

The capital city (though this function is gradually being moved to Dodoma) and a major port, **Dar es Salaam** is an ideal centre for holidaying in Tanzania. The international airport is the stepping-off point for wild-life viewing holidays, Mount Kilimanjaro, Dodoma and the nearby island of Zanzibar, big-game fishing, a wide variety of marine sports and the more simple and relaxing pleasures of swimming and sunbathing. Parts of Dar es Salaam have a restful air that belie the industrial and commercial activity which is visibly expanding the city in size and influence. The bustling metropolis is full of interest and colour, with its mosques, churches and temples, markets, bazaar, shops, hotels, restaurants, cinemas and gardens.
Places to visit: The *National Museum*, housing the skull of Nutcracker Man, *Observation Hill* with the campus and facilities of the University of Dar es Salaam, and the *Village Museum* with exhibits of traditional housing and crafts.

The Coast

The fishing village of **Msasani**, 8km (5 miles) from the capital, contains tombs dating back to the 17th century. Further south, at **Kilwa Klsiwani,** there are ruins of Portuguese and Arab architecture.
Many beautiful beaches are within easy reach of Dar es Salaam, such as those at **Kunduchi, Mjimwena** and **Mbwa Maji. Kunduchi,** 24km (15 miles) north of the city, is a quaint fishing village with adjacent ruins of Persian tombs and mosques and is highly recommended. The *Bahari* and *Kunduchi Beach Hotels* are within 3km (2 miles) of offshore **Mbudya Island**. This uninhabited island forms part of the protective coral reef which is ideal for diving, snorkelling and fishing. The *African Vacation Village* on a peninsula near Kunduchi is another independent hotel complex. **Sinda Island**, some 14km (9 miles) off Dar es Salaam, also offers facilities for snorkelling and shell fishing.
A 72km (45-mile) drive north of Dar es Salaam is **Bagamoyo**, a one-time slave port and terminus for the caravans. This tiny township is the nearest mainland point to Zanzibar and possesses sandy beaches set in a beautiful bay. Livingstone's body rested in the tiny chapel of the convent here on its way back to London. The town mosque and Arab tombs date from the 18th and 19th centuries. 5km (3 miles) to the south is the village of **Kaole,** near which are the ruins of a mosque and pillars believed to be 800 years old.

TANZANIA	HEALTH REGULATIONS	VISA REGULATIONS (Code-Link)
GALILEO/WORLDSPAN	 TI-DFT/DAR/HE	 TI-DFT/DAR/VI
SABRE	 TIDFT/DAR/HE	TIDFT/DAR/VI

To access this information on your CRS, swipe the barcode with a light pen or type in the text under the barcode. For more information, see the introduction *How to Use This Book.*

To the north of Bagamoyo is the country's second port, **Tanga.** From here the visitor can drive to the beautiful *Usambara Mountains* and **Moshi** on the slopes of Mount Kilimanjaro.

Zanzibar & Mafia Island

The beautiful island of **Zanzibar** is only 20 minutes flight from Dar es Salaam. The visitor can still see the house where Dr Livingstone lived, as well as that used by Burton and Speke. The *Anglican Cathedral Church of Christ* stands on the site of the old slave market, while on the seafront are the palace of the former sultan and the towering *Beit-el-Ajaib* ('The House of Wonders'). Zanzibar is the 'Island of Spices' where cloves, nutmeg and cinnamon are grown. To enjoy the old town the visitor should walk, thus being able to see at close hand the handsome carved buildings. The surrounding countryside with its palaces, forts, stone aqueducts and baths scattered in the tropical setting adds to the spell of the island. **Note:** Visitors to Zanzibar should observe the strict Muslim rules regarding dress. For more information, see the section *World of Islam* at the back of the book.

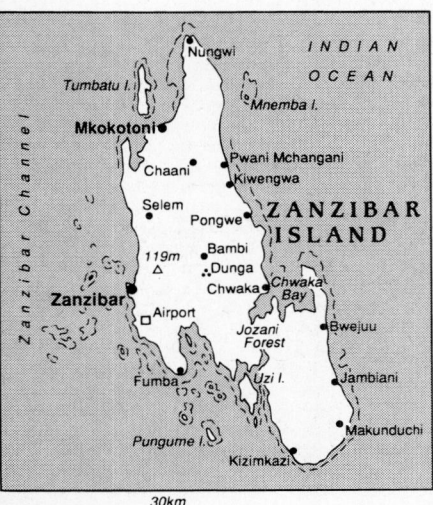

Only 40 minutes flight south of Dar es Salaam, **Mafia Island** is one of the most exciting big-game fishing locations in the world and also a unique marine park. *Mafia Island Lodge* caters for enthusiasts who come from all parts of the world. Powered boats and tackle are available for hire.

Mount Kilimanjaro

At 5895m (19,341ft), Africa's highest mountain is a major attraction for mountaineers. Expeditions must be accompanied by a guide, and very warm clothes are required for the last section of the climb. The ascent takes about three days, allowing for rests at the three huts and a day or so at the final hut to acclimatise before tackling the final stage to the summit. See also the *Sport* section below.

The National Parks

Tanzania has 11 national parks, extending over some 33,660 sq km (13,000 sq miles). In addition there is the unique *Ngorongoro Conservation Unit*, in which wildlife is protected and where the Masai tribesmen also live and herd their cattle. There are also some ten game reserves where government-approved hunting safaris operate under licence and about 40 controlled areas where the hunting of game is controlled by a quota system.

Serengeti National Park: This is a plain-dwellers' stronghold of 13,000 sq km (5000 sq miles), claimed to be the finest in Africa. Here are 35 species of plain-dwelling animals, including wildebeest and zebra, which feature in the spectacular Serengeti migration, and also an extensive selection of birdlife. Probably the best time to see them is from December to May.

Ngorongo Crater: Rising high above the plains of the Serengeti is the rim of the Ngorongo Crater, the location of another animal world. The 260 sq km (100 sq miles) of a collapsed volcano is the home of zebra, wildebeest, gazelles, elephant, rhino, leopard and buffalo.

Lake Manyara National Park: Famous for its tree-climbing lions. The wall of the *Great Rift Valley* forms a backdrop to the park, before which lies forest, open grassland, swamp and the soda lake. Wildlife includes lions, herds of buffalo, baboons, elephant, rhino, impala, giraffe, leopard, zebra, bushbuck, reedbuck, waterbuck and blue and vervet monkeys. Manyara is also noted for its birdlife, particularly the flamingoes which form a line of shimmering pink which stretches miles along the still waters.

Arusha National Park: This park lies within the *Ngurdoto Crater*, a volcano that has probably been extinct for a quarter of a million years. Visitors are able to view wildlife from special vantage points, from where it is possible to see herds of buffalo, rhino, elephant, giraffe and warthog.

Mikumi National Park: This park, 1300 sq km (500 sq miles) in area, offers a chance to see lion, zebra, hippopotamus, leopard, cheetah, giraffe, impala, wildebeest and warthog. A popular spot for visitors is the *Kikaboga Hippo Pool*. Although December to March is the ideal time for viewing at Mikumi, animals are to be seen throughout the year.

Ruaha National Park: The largest elephant sanctuary in the country, lying 118km (73 miles) from Iringa in the Southern Highlands along an all-weather road. The park affords views of unparalleled scenery along the *Ruaha Gorge*, with many sightings of antelope. **Iringa** is also connected with Dar es Salaam and other centres by air and bus service. The best time to visit is from July to November.

Tarangire National Park: Only 130km (80 miles) from **Arusha** and 8km (5 miles) off the Great Cape to Cairo road, it is nonetheless an area which compares favourably with the Serengeti in terms of wildlife density.

Gombe National Park: This park is near **Kigoma** on the shores of *Lake Tanganyika* and is the home of about 200 chimpanzees, more easily seen here in their natural habitat than anywhere else in the world. This is the place where Jane Goodall has devoted her entire life to recording chimpanzee ethology, in the deepest study ever undertaken (over 30 years); this has yielded many surprises and will almost certainly in the future yield more about man's closest cousin, providing human interference doesn't force the chimp into extinction.

Selous Game Reserve in southern Tanzania is one of

the largest in the world and one of the world's largest elephant populations. There is also a high concentration of stalking lions and other game. The possibilities of undertaking walking safaris (accompanied by an armed ranger) and boat trips past countless hippos and crocodiles make the game reserve even more attractive.

SOCIAL PROFILE

FOOD & DRINK: Most hotels serve local Tanzanian food of maize and beans or maizemeal with fish or meat, while the major hotels offer Western food. There is a variety of good seafood such as tuna and shark and an abundance of tropical fruit such as coconuts, pawpaws, mangoes, pineapples and bananas. Table service is normal in restaurants. **Drink:** Coffee and tea are of high quality. Tanzania is a non-secular state and alcohol is not prohibited. A good lager beer is produced locally, as is a popular gin called *Konyagi*, a chocolate and coconut liqueur called *Afrikoko* and wine called *Dodoma*, which comes in red or rosé. Bars generally have counter service.
NIGHTLIFE: In Dar es Salaam there are four nightclubs and cabaret. There are seven cinemas, all air-conditioned, and one drive-in cinema. There is also a *Little Theatre* at Oyster Bay. Generally the nightlife centres are in the top tourist hotels.
SHOPPING: The city and town centres usually have markets which sell curios such as African drums, old brass and copper, carved chess sets, jewellery, zebra skins and one speciality, large wooden salad bowls carved from one piece of teak, *mninga* or ebony.
Shopping hours: 0800-1200 and 1400-1800 Monday to Saturday.
SPORT: Temporary membership can be obtained for hotels and private clubs' sports facilities. Sports facilities offered in resorts include **tennis** and **basketball**.
Mountaineering: It is possible to climb mountains such as Mount Kilimanjaro, but it is essential to have the right equipment (such as warm clothing, boots, gloves and a hat) and some experience. All climbers should be aware that guides and porters are essential even to the lower peaks. Organised climbs with food and staff can be arranged at some cost through selected hotels. It is advisable to book well in advance. Slightly cheaper and more rough-and-ready safaris can be organised through the *Kibo Hotel*, PO Box 102, Marangu; *Marangu Hotel*, PO Box 40, Moshi; *or* the YMCA, PO Box 558, Moshi. Tel: (55) 2362. Alternatively, climbers can bring their own supplies and hire staff and equipment (Arctic sleeping bags and extra trousers) at the park gate. **Watersports: Sailing, swimming** and **fishing** in the coastal resorts. The main fishing season is from September to March.
SPECIAL EVENTS: The *Sukuma* (or *Bujora) Museum*, 15km (9 miles) east of Mwanza, gives approximately weekly performances of traditional dances of the Wasukuma tribe, including the *Bugobobobo* (Sukuma Snake Dance). During the Muslim festival of *Eid al-Fitr*, there is an event at Makunduchi in Zanzibar in which men from the north and south flail each other with banana branches, followed by the townswomen singing traditional songs and a night of feasting and dancing.
SOCIAL CONVENTIONS: When meeting and parting, hands are always shaken; this applies throughout the country in both rural and urban areas. The standard greeting when addressing an individual is *Jambo* to which the reply is also *Jambo*. The greeting for a group is *Hamjambo* to which the reply is *Hatujambo*. People are delighted if visitors can greet them in Kiswahili. There is no fixed protocol to do with hospitality, but when invited for a meal the food is traditionally eaten with hands. A token of appreciation is welcome when invited for a meal. Dress is smart and a good appearance is highly regarded. Suits and ties or safari suits are worn by men and suits or dresses by women. Ashtrays are usually an indication of permission for a visitor to smoke. Smoking is prohibited in cinemas and on public transport.
Photography: In some places a charge wil be levied on visitors wishing to take photographs; elsewhere a permit may be required. **Tipping:** Discouraged except in 'Western situations', when waiters, porters and others may be tipped.

BUSINESS PROFILE

ECONOMY: Agriculture employs 90% of the working population, much of it subsistence but cash crops, including cotton, coffee, tea, sisal, tobacco and cashew nuts, are the country's main export earners. Depressed prices have kept Tanzanian revenues at a static level despite increases in production. There is a small minerals sector: diamonds are mined commercially along with, on a smaller scale, gold and other gemstones. The Government has granted exploration licences in the hope of locating offshore deposits of oil and gas. The industrial sector is small: sugar processing, brewing, textiles and cigarette manufacture are the most important industries. Many of Tanzania's imported goods come through Kenya. This is due in part to the superior port facilities of Mombasa compared to those of Dar es Salaam, along with the more acceptable trading conditions in Kenya. Nevertheless, there are many port agents available at Dar es Salaam. The UK is Tanzania's largest supplier; currently there exists a 6-year backlog of commercial debt (value of £70m) with UK commercial suppliers. Aid organisations (principally World Bank and EC aid) are an important source of finance for Tanzanian imports. The Government has also been forced to adopt austerity measures, including currency devaluation and strict budgetary controls, by the IMF in exchange for financial support.
BUSINESS: Normal courtesies should be shown when

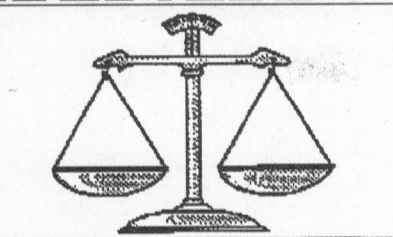

visiting local business people. Almost all executives speak English. **Office hours:** 0730-1430 Monday to Friday and 0730-1200 Saturday.

COMMERCIAL INFORMATION: The following organisation can offer advice: Dar es Salaam Chamber of Commerce, PO Box 41, Dar es Salaam. Tel: (51) 21893.

HISTORY & GOVERNMENT

HISTORY: The present country came into being in 1964 with the union of Tanganyika and Zanzibar. There are over 120 tribes on the mainland, most of whom migrated from other parts of Africa. Zanzibar, also known as the Spice Island, on the other hand has a history of contact with virtually every Old World civilization except the Roman and Greek – and they certainly knew of it. Tanganyika was a component (along with Rwanda and Burundi) of the colony of German East Africa between 1884 and 1918. After the First World War it was administered by the UK under successive League of Nations and United Nations mandates. Tanganyika became independent within the Commonwealth in 1961 after a period of self-government during which the principal nationalist party, the Tanganyika African National Union (TANU), emerged as the dominant political force. Its charismatic leader, Julius Nyerere, held the post of President from Independence to 1985; he occupied the position of Chairman until 1990. In 1964, Tanganyika joined with Zanzibar and became Tanzania. Prior to that, Zanzibar had been a British protectorate (established in 1890) and, in 1963, an independent sultanate. The sultan lasted less than 12 months before being deposed in a coup by radicals from the Afro-Shirazi Party, which quickly amalgamated with TANU on the mainland to form the country's sole political party, Chama Cha Mapinduzi (CCM), the Revolutionary Party of Tanzania. Nyerere's main objective was the successful application of socialist principles to an African agricultural society and economy. Nyerere's ideas, particularly the introduction of *ujamaa*, were articulated in the famous Arusha Declaration. Unfortunately, mismanagement and external events conspired to wreck Nyerere's plans, with dire consequences for the economy. In foreign policy, Tanzania has leant towards China rather than the USSR but has always maintained fair relations with the West. Moreover, Tanzania has proved itself an active player in regional politics, having given consistent support to anti-colonial guerrilla movements in Southern Africa (and now the African National Congress in South Africa) and intervened militarily in Uganda in 1979 to overthrow the Amin regime. Tanzania was a founder-member of the Southern African Development Co-ordination Conference and has been a prominent participant in the Organisation of African Unity. Nyerere retired from the Presidency in 1985 and was replaced by Ali Hassan Mwinyi, former Vice-President and President of Zanzibar. Mwinyi favoured re-orienting the economy towards private enterprise and market forces but faces formidable obstacles, especially a large and fairly corrupt state bureaucracy. He is also taking on the challenge – common to the rest of the continent – of introducing multi-party politics to Tanzania. In March 1991, Mwinyi established a presidential commission to examine this latter issue. Early in 1992 draft amendments to the constitution were presented to the National Assembly. No definite timetable has yet been set out for the process to be completed.

GOVERNMENT: The country is a one-party state with a unicameral National Assembly which is elected every five years. In 1985, Ali Hassan Mwinyi succeeded Julius Nyerere as Head of State, ending an impressive rule of 24 years. Zanzibar has its own internal administration, headed by a president who is elected for a 5-year term, under the terms of the 1979 Constitution, amended in 1985. Constitutional amendments allowing for the introduction of a multi-party system are making their their way through the National Assembly.

CLIMATE

The climate is tropical, and coastal areas are hot and humid. The rainy season lasts from March to May. The central plateau is dry and arid. The northwestern highlands are cool and temperate and the rainy season here lasts from November to December and February to May.

Required clothing: Tropical clothing is worn throughout the year, but in the cooler season from June to September jackets and sweaters may be needed, especially in the evenings.

DAR-ES-SALAAM Tanzania (14m)

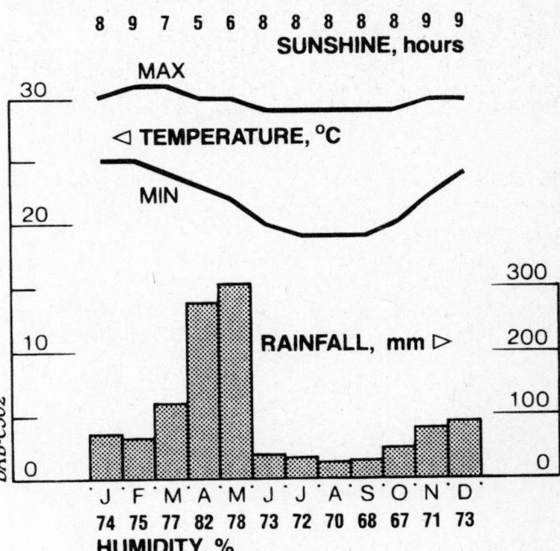

TABORA Tanzania (1265m)

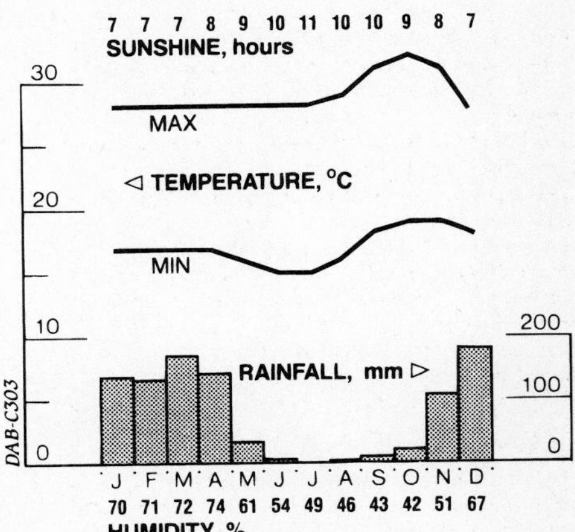

THAILAND

Location: South-East Asia.

Tourism Authority of Thailand
4 Ratchadamnoen Nok Avenue
Bangkok 10100, Thailand
Tel: (2) 28 21 14 37. Fax: (2) 280 1744. Telex: 72059 TAT BKK TH.

Royal Thai Embassy
29-30 Queen's Gate
London SW7 5JB
Tel: (071) 589 2944 (main switchboard) *or* 589 0173 (Consular section) *or* 589 2857 (recorded visa information) *or* 584 5421 (information bureau). Fax: (071) 823 9695. Consular section opening hours: 0930-1300 Monday to Friday.

Royal Thai Consulates
Birmingham: Tel: (021) 643 9977. Fax: (021) 632 1256. Telex: 336730.
Glasgow: Tel: (041) 248 6677. Fax: (041) 204 1351.
Liverpool: Tel: (051) 255 0504. Fax: (051) 255 1070.
Cardiff: Tel: (0222) 766 993. Fax: (0222) 766 993.
Hull: Tel: (0482) 29925. Fax: (0482) 224 225. Telex: 592 112 HSSG.
Dublin: Tel: (353) 1 781 599. Fax: (353) 1 752 426. Telex: 93277.

Tourism Authority of Thailand
49 Albemarle Street
London W1X 3FE
Tel: (071) 499 7679. Fax: (071) 629 5519. Opening hours: 0900-1700 Monday to Friday.

British Embassy
Wireless Road
Bangkok 10330, Thailand
Tel: (2) 253 0191. Fax: (2) 255 8619. Telex: 82263 PRODROM TH.

Royal Thai Embassy
2300 Kalorama Road, NW
Washington, DC 20008
Tel: (202) 483 7200. Fax: (202) 234 4498. Telex: 64232.
Consulates in: Chicago, El Paso, Honolulu, Los Angeles, Montgomery, New Orleans and New York (tel: (212) 732 8166).

Embassy of the United States of America
95 Wireless Road
Bangkok 10330, Thailand
Tel: (2) 252 5040. Fax: (2) 254 2990.

Royal Thai Embassy
180 Island Park Drive
Ottawa, Ontario
K1Y 0A2
Tel: (613) 722 4444. Fax: (613) 722 6624.
Consulates in: Edmonton, Montréal, Toronto and Vancouver.

Tourism Authority of Thailand (Western Canada)
Suite 104
1530 West 8th Avenue
Vancouver, British Columbia
V6H 3V9
Tel: (604) 737 8170. Fax: (604) 736 7761.

Tourism Authority of Thailand (Eastern Canada)
Suite 306
250 St Clair Avenue West
Toronto, Ontario
M4V 1R6
Tel: (416) 925 9329. Fax: (416) 925 2868.

Canadian Embassy
PO Box 2090
11th Floor, Boonmitr Building
138 Silom Road
Bangkok 10500, Thailand
Tel: (2) 237 4126. Fax: (2) 236 6463. Telex: 82671 DOMCAN TH.

AREA: 513,115 sq km (198,115 sq miles).
POPULATION: 56,340,000 (1990 estimate).
POPULATION DENSITY: 109.8 per sq km.
CAPITAL: Bangkok. **Population:** 5,845,152, including Thon Buri (1989).
GEOGRAPHY: Thailand is bounded to the west by Myanmar and the Indian Ocean, to the south and east by Malaysia and the Gulf of Thailand, to the east by Cambodia, and to the north and east by Laos. Central Thailand is dominated by the Chao Phraya River. In the northeast the Korat Plateau rises about 305m (1000ft) above the central plain. This largely arid region covers approximately one-third of the country. In the north, another one-third consists of forested hills.
LANGUAGE: Thai is the official language. English, Malay and a dialect of Chinese (Tachew) are also spoken.
RELIGION: The vast majority adhere to Buddhism (Theravada), with Muslim and Christian minorities.
TIME: GMT + 7.
ELECTRICITY: 220 volts AC, 50Hz. A variety of plugs and light fittings is in use.
COMMUNICATIONS: Telephone: IDD is available. Country code: 66. Public international telephone facilities are available at the Central General Post Office, New Road, Bangkok. **Fax:** The *Communications Authority of Thailand* provides a service. Many hotels have facilities. **Telex/telegram:** Telegrams can be sent from the GPO Building or from any telegraph office. Public telex facilities are available at the GPO Building and hotels (at extra cost). **Post:** Airmail to Europe takes up to one week. The Central Post Office in Bangkok is open 0800-1800 Monday to Friday and 0900-1300 weekends and holidays. Post offices up-country are open 0800-1630. **Press:** English-language dailies include *Bangkok Post* and *The Nation*.
BBC World Service and Voice of America frequencies: From time to time these change. See the section *How to Use this Book* for more information.

BBC:				
MHz	17.790	11.750	9.740	6.195
Voice of America:				
MHz	9.670	6.040	5.995	1.260

PASSPORT/VISA

Regulations and requirements may be subject to change at short notice, and you are advised to contact the appropriate diplomatic or consular authority before finalising travel arrangements. Details of these may be found at the head of this country's entry. Any numbers in the chart refer to the footnotes below.

	Passport Required?	Visa Required?	Return Ticket Required?
Full British	Yes	No	Yes
BVP	Not valid	-	-
Australian	Yes	No	Yes
Canadian	Yes	No	Yes
USA	Yes	No	Yes
Other EC	Yes	No	Yes
Japanese	Yes	No	Yes

Restricted entry: The Government of Thailand may refuse entry to persons whose general appearance and clothing does not comply with government requirements. The Government of Thailand does not recognise identity cards issued for children by Germany (*Kinderausweis*).
PASSPORTS: A valid passport is required by all except holders of Hong Kong certificate of identity bearing a Thai visa issued in Hong Kong.
British Visitors Passport: Not accepted.
VISAS: The following are permitted to stay in Thailand *for a maximum of 15 days* without a visa provided they are bona fide tourists with valid passports and hold a confirmed date return ticket:
(a) nationals of countries exempted in the chart above (but see note above concerning German identity cards);
(b) nationals of Argentina, Austria, Brazil, Brunei, Fiji, Finland, Hong Kong (holders of British passports), Iceland, Indonesia, Kenya, Malaysia, Mexico, Myanmar, New Zealand (for a maximum of 3 months), Norway, Papua New Guinea, Philippines, Senegal, Singapore, South Korea (for a maximum of 3 months), Sweden, Switzerland, Turkey, Vanuatu, Western Samoa and Yugoslavia.
The following are permitted to enter Thailand for tourist purposes without a visa provided a valid passport and a confirmed return or onward ticket is held and a visa is obtained (for a period of 15 days maximum) on arrival at the immigration checkpoints at Don Muang airport near Bangkok: nationals of Andorra, Antigua & Barbuda, Bahamas, Bangladesh, Barbados, Belize, Bhutan, Bolivia, Botswana, Burkina Faso, Burundi, Cameroon, Cape Verde, Central African Republic, Chad, Chile, Colombia, Comoro Islands, Costa Rica, Côte d'Ivoire, Cyprus, Djibouti, Dominica, Dominican Republic, Ecuador, Equatorial Guinea, Gabon, Gambia, Grenada, Guatemala, Guinea-Bissau, Guinea Republic, Haiti, Honduras, India, Jamaica, Kiribati, Lesotho, Liberia, Liechtenstein, Malawi, Maldives, Mali, Malta, Mauritania, Mauritius, Monaco, Morocco, Nauru, Nepal, Niger, Pakistan, Panama, Paraguay, Peru, Rwanda, St Kitts & Nevis, St Lucia, St Vincent & the Grenadines, San Marino, São Tomé e Príncipe, Seychelles, Sierra Leone, Solomon Islands, Somalia, South Africa, Suriname, Swaziland, Tanzania, Togo, Tonga, Trinidad & Tobago, Tuvalu, Uganda, Uruguay, Vatican City, Venezuela, Zaïre, Zambia and Zimbabwe.
Types of visa: Transit, for visits of up to 30 days. Cost: £5. Tourist, for visits of up to 60 days. Cost: £8. Non-immigrant (including business visits), for visits of up to 90

THAILAND	**HEALTH REGULATIONS**	**VISA REGULATIONS** Code-Link
GALILEO/WORLDSPAN	 TI-DFT/BKK/HE	 TI-DFT/BKK/VI
SABRE	TIDFT/BKK/HE	 TIDFT/BKK/VI

To access this information on your CRS, swipe the barcode with a light pen or type in the text under the barcode. For more information, see the introduction *How to Use This Book*.

Phuket

days. Cost: £15. All visas are valid for 90 days from date of issue, strictly not extendable and single entry only.
Application to: Consulate (or Consular Section at Embassy). For addresses, see top of entry.
Application requirements: (a) Passport (valid for at least 6 months previously). (b) 1 completed application form. (c) 2 recent photographs. (d) Fee (cash or postal order). (e) If requesting non-immigrant visa for business visit, letter from sponsor in country of origin guaranteeing financial status and repatriation costs. (f) Stamped self-addressed envelope for postal enquiries.
Working days required: At least 48 hours.

MONEY

Currency: Baht (Bt) = 100 satang. Notes are in denominations of Bt500, 100, 50, 20, 10, 5 and 1. The three smallest of these denominations are no longer issued, but are still legal tender. Coins are in denominations of Bt10, 5, 2 and 1, and 50 and 25 satangs. In addition, there are a vast number of commemorative coins which are also legal tender.
Credit cards: Access/Mastercard and Visa are widely accepted, while Diners Club has more limited use. Check with your credit card company for details of merchant acceptability and other facilities which may be available.
Travellers cheques: Accepted by all banks and large hotels and shops.
Exchange rate indicators: The following figures are included as a guide to the movements of the Baht against Sterling and the US Dollar:

Date:	Oct '89	Oct '90	Oct '91	Oct '92
£1.00=	40.82	48.70	44.16	40.13
$1.00=	25.85	24.93	25.44	25.28

Currency restrictions: The import of local currency is limited to Bt50,000. There are no restrictions on the import of foreign currency but it should be declared. Export of local and foreign currency is unrestricted, except for travel to Cambodia, Myanmar or Vietnam, when it is limited to Bt100,000 per person.
Banking hours: 0830-1530 Monday to Friday.

DUTY FREE

The following goods may be imported into Thailand without incurring customs duty:
200 cigarettes or 250g of tobacco;
1 litre of wine or spirits;
Goods to the value of Bt100,000.
Note: There are restrictions on the export of items of archaeological interest or historical value without a certificate of authorisation from the Department of Fine Arts in Thailand, and also a total prohibition on the export of images of Buddha.

PUBLIC HOLIDAYS

Public holidays observed in Thailand are as follows:
Mar 7 '93 Magha Puja. **Apr 6** Chakri Day. **Apr 12-14** Songkran Festival. **May 5** Coronation Day. **May 17** Royal Ploughing Ceremony. **Jun 4** Visakha Puja. **Jul*** Buddhist Lent. **Aug 2** Asalha Puja. **Aug 3** Khao Phansa. **Aug 12** Queen's Birthday. **Oct 23** Chulalongkorn Day. **Dec 5** King's Birthday. **Dec 10** Constitution Day. **Dec 31** New Year's Eve. **Jan 1 '94** New Year's Day. **Feb/Mar** * Magha Puja. **Feb 10-11** Chinese New Year.
Note [*]: Date to be confirmed.

HEALTH

Regulations and requirements may be subject to change at short notice, and you are advised to contact your doctor well in advance of your intended date of departure. Any numbers in the chart refer to the footnotes below.

	Special Precautions?	Certificate Required?
Yellow Fever	No	1
Cholera	Yes	2
Typhoid & Polio	Yes	-
Malaria	3	-
Food & Drink	4	-

[1]: A yellow fever vaccination certificate is required from travellers over one year of age arriving from infected areas. Countries and areas included in endemic zones are considered to be infected areas.

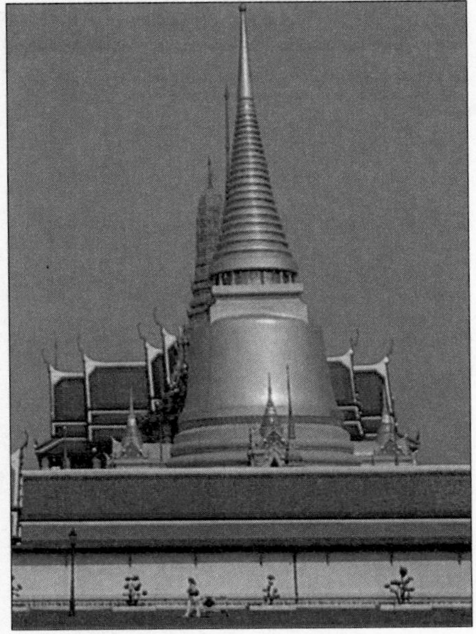

Grand Palace

[2]: Following WHO guidelines issued in 1973, a cholera vaccination certificate is not a condition of entry to Thailand. However, cholera is a serious risk in this country and precautions are essential. Up-to-date advice should be sought before deciding whether these precautions should include vaccination, as medical opinion is divided over its effectiveness. See the *Health* section at the back of the book.
[3]: Malaria risk throughout the year in rural areas throughout the country, and especially in forested and hilly areas. There is no risk in cities and the main tourist resorts, eg Bangkok, Chiang Mai, Pattaya and Phuket. The malignant *falciparum* form is present and is reported to be 'highly resistant' to chloroquine and 'resistant' to sulfadoxine/pyrimethamine and mefloquine.
[4]: All water should be regarded as being potentially contaminated. Water used for drinking, brushing teeth or making ice should have first been boiled or otherwise sterilised. Unpasteurised milk should be boiled, although there are a number of good dairies in Thailand (as a result of joint ventures with various Western governments), where pasteurised or homogenised milk may be bought. Powdered or tinned milk is available and is advised, but make sure that it is reconstituted with pure water. Avoid dairy products which are likely to have been made from unboiled milk. Only eat well-cooked meat and fish, preferably served hot. Pork, salad and mayonnaise may carry increased risk. Vegetables should be cooked and fruit peeled.
Rabies is present. For those at high risk, vaccination before arrival should be considered. If you are bitten abroad seek medical advice without delay. For more information consult the *Health* section at the back of the book.
Health care: Health insurance is recommended. Medical facilities are good in main centres. All major hotels have doctors on call.
Precautions should be taken to guard against mosquito bites due to the risk of *Japanese encephalitis* which exists particularly in rural areas between June and October. A vaccine is available, and travellers are advised to consult their doctor prior to departure.

TRAVEL - International

AIR: Thailand's national airline is *Thai Airways International (TG)*.
Approximate flight times: From *London* to Bangkok is 13 hours 40 minutes; from *Manila* is 3 hours 10 minutes; from *Singapore* is 2 hours 15 minutes and from *Sydney* is 11 hours.
International airports: *Bangkok International (BKK)* (Don Muang) is 30km (19 miles) north of the city (travel time – 30/45 minutes). There is a regular airport bus service to the City Terminal (Asia Hotel) every 30 minutes 0600-2100 daily. Children under five travel free of charge. There is also a direct coach service to Pattaya at 0900, 1200 and 1900, returning at 0600 and 1600. Limousines are available at all hours: service is every 20 minutes depending on flights. Airport facilities include a

Royal Garden Resorts, 257/1-3 Charoen Nakorn Road, Thonburi, Bangkok 10600

Tel: (662) 476 0021/2. Fax: (662) 476 1120 or 460 1805.

Six **'Uniquely Thai'** resorts, surrounded by beautiful tropical gardens, lily ponds, swimming pools, pristine beaches and exot riverfront. All offer luxurious accommodation, impeccable service, sumptuous restaurants and a wide variety of sports activiti

The Royal Garden Riverside

Bangkok's newest city-resort, on the 'River of Kings', has 420 rooms with private balconies and magnificent river views. Restaurants include world-famous Benihana's and Trader Vic's, plus excellent Chinese and Thai venues. In addition, there are tennis courts, a spa and health club, deluxe shopping plaza and cruises on the hotel's own river rice barge. Easy access by car or the hotel's river taxis to the airport, golf courses and nearby tourist attractions.

The Royal Garden Resort Pattaya

Opened in 1991, this 'family-friendly' hotel in the heart of Pattaya is surrounded by peaceful gardens and lily ponds, and boasts the largest hotel swimming pool in the city. The 300 rooms command fine balcony views of Pattaya Bay and the pool. Restaurants and the poolside barbecue serve excellent Thai and international cuisine. Golf, tennis, watersports, shops and the exciting nightlife scene are only a few minutes walk away.

A summer retreat for Thailand's Royal Family since 1920, this resort treats all its guests like royalty. Located on a magnificent private beach, all 220 rooms have uninterrupted views of the Gulf of Siam. Restaurants serve international, Italian and Thai cuisine. Entertainment and recreation includes a disco, a gym, "live" traditional Thai and popular music and sports galore.

The Royal Garden Resort Hua Hin

This 'Uniquely Thai' village resort is set amid 14 acres of gardens and ponds. Luxurious villas, decorated with Thai art and antiques, are accompanied by sumptuous seafood and barbecue specialities. The pristine private beach offers many watersports, plus tennis courts. Golf and tourist attractions are within easy reach. Theme parties are a speciality in this exclusive, exotic setting.

The Royal Garden Village Hua Hin

The Royal Garden Village Chieng Mai

Overlooking rice terraces and the stunning Mae Rim Valley, this resort offers 68 rooms in deluxe Thai villas. Superb dining and extensive recreational facilities are available, and culture-rich Chieng Mai city, orchid and butterfly farms, elephant shows and authentic village life are within easy reach.

The Royal Garden Village Phuket

158 rooms set in 26 acres of lush gardens on Phuket's longest beachfront. Fine dining and a wide selection of sports and recreation amid pools, lagoons and the pristine private beach guarantee an idyllic holiday. Golf courses and the airport are just a few minutes away, and next door is Phuket's beautiful national park.

duty-free shop, car hire (*Avis, Hertz, Sintat* and *Rent-a-Car*), banking and exchange facilities (24 hours), restaurant (24 hours) and bar inside the departure lounge (0630-2315), post office (24 hours) situated inside the departure lounge, accommodation and insurance bureaux (0700-2200 hours).
Chiang Mai International Airport (CNX). Nearest city – Chiang Mai. Taxi service is available to the city centre. Airport facilities include car hire (*Avis, Hertz, Sintat* and *Rent-a-Car*), banking and exchange facilities (0830-1530), restaurant (0800-2200) and bar (2100-0200).
Phuket International Airport (HKT) is 35 km (21.8 miles) from Phuket. Airport facilities include car hire (*Avis, Hertz, Sintat* and *Rent-a-Car*), restaurant (0800-2200) and bar (2100-0200).
Hat Yai International has recently been opened; so far it is only used for flights to Asian destinations and domestic flights. Nearest town – Songkhla (approximatley 20km/12.5 miles). Taxis, bus and train services are available.
Departure tax: Bt200 for all international departures. Transit passengers and children under two years of age are exempt.
SEA: The main international port is Bangkok. Limited passenger services are available. Cargo/passenger lines: *Ben Shipping, Glen, Hansa, Polish Ocean, Royal Inter-Ocean* and *States Steamship*.
RAIL: Through trains operate to Kuala Lumpur, with connections to Singapore (three times a week), and to the borders with Cambodia (at Aranyaprathet) and Laos. The journey to Singapore takes approximately 48 hours.
ROAD: There are international roads from Malaysia but those leading into Myanmar, Laos and Cambodia are not officially open.

TRAVEL - Internal

AIR: *Thai Airways International (TG)* and *Bangkok Airways* run services to all major towns. Discounts are available in off-peak seasons and during special promotional periods.
Departure tax:. Bt20 on all domestic flights.
RIVER: Thailand has, depending on the season, up to 1600km of navigable inland waterway. Services operate between Thanon Tok and Nonthaburi, and luxury cruises are available on the *Oriental Queen*. Long-tailed motorboats and taxi-boat ferries also operate.
RAIL: The railway network extends over 4450km linking all major towns with the exception of Phuket. It has recently been extended to serve centres on the east coast. There are four main trunk routes to the northern, eastern, southern and northeastern regions, and also a line serving Thon Buri, River Kwai Bridge and Nam Tok. There are several daily services on each route, with air-conditioned, sleeping and restaurant cars on the principal trains. The journeys are leisurely but comfortable, and travelling by train is certainly one of the best ways to get around the country. The *Southern Line Express* stops at Surat Thani for those who wish then to take the bus and ferry to the offshore island of Koh Samui. Some railway timetables are published in English.
ROAD: There is a reasonable road network comprising many highways and 44,400km of national and provincial roads. All major roads are metalled. **Bus:** There are inter-urban routes to all provinces. Fares are very cheap, and the buses very crowded. Privately owned air-conditioned buses (seats bookable) are comfortable and moderately priced. **Taxi:** There are plenty of taxis, which operate day and night. Rates should be agreed before departure; drivers rarely understand English. Tipping is not expected. **Car hire:** Available in all main cities. **Documentation:** International Driving Permit required.
URBAN: Conventional bus services in Bangkok are operated by the *Government Mass Transit Authority*, but there are also extensive private minibus operations and passenger-carrying trucks. Premium fares are charged for air-conditioned and express buses. Fares are generally low and are collected by conductors. When taking buses around the city, leave the back seat free for the saffron-robed monks. There are also boat services and taxi-boat ferries. On arrival in Bangkok, visitors are advised to buy a copy of the detailed bus map available, as the city can be very confusing to the newcomer.
JOURNEY TIMES: The following chart gives approximate journey times (in hours and minutes) from Bangkok to other major cities/towns in Thailand.

	Air	Road	Rail
Chiang Rai	1.15	12.00	-
Chiang Mai	1.00	10.00	14.00
Hat-Yai	1.15	15.00	17.00
Hua Hin	0.40	2.45	4.00
Pattaya	-	1.45	-
Phitsanulok	0.45	5.30	6.00
Phuket	1.10	10.45	-
Samui	1.10	10.45	12.00
Surat-Thani	1.00	9.00	13.00
U-R*	1.45	8.00	8.30
Udonthani	1.35	8.00	10.15

Note [*]: Ubon-Ratchathani.

Samui

ACCOMMODATION

HOTELS: Bangkok has some of Asia's finest hotels, with over 12,000 rooms meeting international standard. All luxury hotels have swimming pools, 24-hour room service, air-conditioning and a high staff-to-guest ratio. Accommodation styles cover every range, however, and the budget traveller is also well catered for. Hotels outside the capital and developed tourist areas are less lavish but extremely economical and promise a high standard of personal attention and hospitality. Member hotels of the Thai Hotels Association can be booked on arrival at the counter of Bangkok's Don Muang Airport, and at similar counters in some provincial airports. Thai Hotel Association, 1 Soi Phra Chen, Wireless Road, Lumpini, Bangkok 10330. Tel: (2) 251 3017. Fax: (2) 252 5582. Telex: 21422 THAOFF TH. **Grading:** There is no official system of grading hotels but prices generally give a good indication of standards. The Tourism Authority of Thailand publishes regional accommodation guides which give comprehensive details on pricing and facilities.
SELF-CATERING: Holiday villas and flats can be rented. For details, look in the English newspapers' advertisements columns.
CAMPING/CARAVANNING: Most of Thailand's campsites are in the area of the National Parks which are under the management of the Department of Forestry; there are also some private tourist resorts which provide camping facilities. In general, camping in Thailand is not popular, as other accommodation is available at such reasonable prices.
YOUTH HOSTELS: YMCA, YWCA and small, cheap hotels are available all over the country.

RESORTS & EXCURSIONS

Bangkok, the capital, although highly westernised in appearance, still has a strong undercurrent of traditional ways not yet eroded by the effects of modernisation. *Excursions:* The Grand Palace; Wat Phra Kaeo, the Chapel of the Emerald Buddha; Wat Pho, Bangkok's largest temple complex; Lak Muang (the city stone) and the Erewan shrine, where local offerings are made daily; the National Museum; the many splendid Buddhist temples including Wat Suthat, Wat Ratchabophit and Wat Arun. Water tours on the Chao Phraya River are popular, with visits to the floating market and the Royal Barges. Up-river is the old capital of **Ayodhaya** and the old summer palace at **Bang Pa-In**; tropical gardens, old Thai houses and precious antiques at the Suan Pakkard Palace; Jim Thompson's House; the Bangkok zoo; the snake farm at the Red Cross centre and the markets.
East of Bangkok lies the *Ancient City*, a vast private parkland with models, some full-sized, some reduced, of most of Thailand's historic monuments, and the temple ruins of the Khmer Empire, situated near the Cambodian border; also just outside the city is the Rose Garden Country Resort with daily performances of Thai music, dance, games and ceremonies.

The Central Plains north of Bangkok form the prosperous heart of the country, a rich environment that has seen the rise and fall of great cities and kingdoms. Phitsanulok makes a convenient base for excursions into the area. From Phitsanulok one can visit the ancient city kingdoms of *Sukothai* and *Kamphaeng Phet*.

The western province of **Kanchanaburi** now has modern hotels from which trips around this most beautiful part of Thailand, west of Bangkok, can be made. Kanchanaburi is the site of the famous *Bridge Over The River Kwai*; several beautiful waterfalls and limestone caves are other attractions.

In the **northeast**, about three hours by road from Bangkok, is the *Khao Yai National Park & Wildlife Reserve*. The most popular of the country's national parks, it has been developed into a modest resort. As well as the wildlife and jungle attractions, the park can be used as a base to visit the many ancient and historical sites in the northeast of Thailand. Also in the northeast there are several centres with the remains of richly cultured ancient Khmer Empire. Among these are **Pimai, Lop Buri** and **Phanom Rung**. While Cambodia remains closed such remains cannot be seen anywhere else. The northeast also provides its own special festival celebrations, the most exciting being the elephant round-up at **Surin** each November.

Chiang Mai in the far north is Thailand's second-largest city and a centre for excursions to the region's ancient and beautiful temples, the teak forests and their working elephants, caves and waterfalls, and journeys to visit the northern tribes with their unique culture. There are many small villages in the area surrounding the city where local handicrafts are produced, and excursions to these can be arranged locally. In the *Mae Sa Valley* there is an elephant training school and nearby, an orchid farm; longer trips can be made to the *Doi Inthanon National Park* and to Chiang Rai, from which the *Mekong River* and the *Golden Triangle* can be reached.

Beach resorts: In the Eastern Gulf is *Pattaya*, South-East Asia's most renowned beach resort, and the much quieter resort of *Bang Saen*. Two hours south of Bangkok are *Cha'am* and *Hua Hin*. The latter was a royal watering place and is currently enjoying a renaissance.

The island of **Phuket** (attached by a causeway to the mainland) in the southwest corner of the country is one of several resorts on the Indian Ocean. In the last couple of years many new hotels have opened in Phuket, which now challenges Pattaya as the number one beach resort in South-East Asia. *Phang Nga Bay*, which is readily reached from Phuket, boasts one of the world's most stunning seascapes; the area was featured in a James Bond film.

Songkhla, on the eastern side of the Gulf, is 1300km (800 miles) from Bangkok. It is a pleasant, relaxed resort with a Chinese ambience. Closer to Bangkok is the resort island of **Koh Samui,** three hours from the mainland, and renowned for its coconuts.

BANGKOK

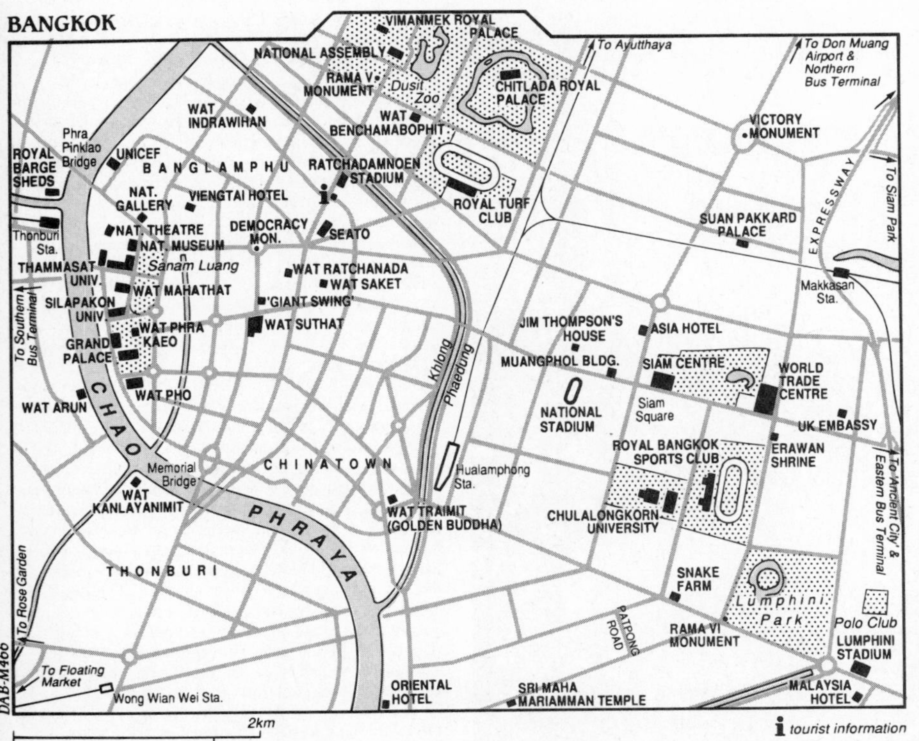

SOCIAL PROFILE

FOOD & DRINK: There are many European and Asian restaurants. Thai food is hot and spicy, but most tourist restaurants tone down the food. *Pri-kee-noo*, a tiny red or green pepper is one of the hot ingredients that might best be left at the side of the plate. Thai dishes include *tom yam* (a soup prepared with *makroot* leaves, lemon grass

herbs, prawns, chicken or fish); *gang pet* (hot curry with coconut juice, herbs, garlic, chillies, shrimp paste, coriander and seasoning) served with rice and *gai yang* (barbecued chicken); and *kao pat* (fried rice with pieces of crab meat, chicken, pork, onion, egg and saffron) served with onions, cucumber, soy sauce and chillies. Desserts include *salim* (sweet noodles in coconut milk) and *songkaya* (pudding of coconut milk, eggs and sugar often served in a coconut shell). Well worth trying is sticky rice and mangoes (rice cooked in coconut milk served with slices of mango) served in the mango season (March to May). Other popular fruits are *mangosteens*, *rambutans*, *pomelos* (similar to grapefruits) and, above all, *durians* which *farangs* (foreigners) either love or hate. In a Thai restaurant food is eaten with a spoon and fork while chopsticks are used in Chinese restaurants (a knife and fork can be provided). Also in a Chinese restaurant guests will be handed hot or cold towels to wipe their faces, necks and hands. Bars have counter or table service. There are no licensing laws. *Mekhong* whisky is worth sampling.
NIGHTLIFE: Bangkok's nightlife is famous the world over; there are nightclubs, open-air restaurants, classical dancing and films. Nightclubs are air-conditioned and many of the sleazier variety provide hostesses.
SHOPPING: Good buys include Thai silks and cottons, silver, pottery with *celadon* green glaze, dolls, masks, lacquerware, bamboo artefacts and bronzeware. The weekend market at *Chatuchak Park* in Bangkok is a regular cornucopia with items ranging from genuine antiques to fighting fish. **Shopping hours:** 1000-1900 (department stores), 0800-2100 (others) Monday to Sunday.
SPORT: Golf courses are available in most major tourist areas. **Skindiving** is popular at Pattaya and Phuket seaside resorts, and **water-skiing** at the coastal resort of Pattaya, inland on the Chao Phraya at Nonthaburi and at Pakred outside Bangkok. **Spectator sports: Thai kick boxing** can be seen at the Lumpini Stadium three evenings a week and on Saturday afternoons. Rajdamnem Stadium has bouts four times a week. **Horseraces** are held at the Royal Bangkok Sports Club on Saturdays and at the Royal Turf Club on Sundays.
SPECIAL EVENTS: The following is a list of major events and festivals celebrated in various parts of Thailand during 1993. For further details contact the Tourism Authority of Thailand.
Mar 4-7 '93 *Asean Barred Ground Dove Festival*, Yala. **Mar 5-7** *Lam Duan Flower Festival*, Si Sa Ket. **Mar 23-Apr 3** *Thao Suranari Fair*, Nakhon Ratchasima. **Apr 3-7** *Phanom Rung Fair*, Buri Ram. **Apr 12-14** *Songkran Festival*. **Apr 13** *Turtle Releasing Fair*, Phuket. **Apr 19-25** *Pattaya Festival*, Pattaya. **May 8-9** *Rocket Festival*, Yasothon. **May 17** *Royal Ploughing Ceremony*, Bangkok. **Jun 26-27** *Phi Ta Khon Festival*, Loei. **Jul 18** *Phuket International Marathon*, Phuket. **Aug** *Candle Festival*, Ubon Ratchathani. **Aug 6-14** *Trang Vegetarian Festival*, Trang. **Sep 3-5** *Phichit Boat Races*, Phichit. **Sep 11-12** *Thailand International Swan-Boat Races '93*, Bangkok. **Sep 29-Oct 1** *Chinese Lunar Festival*, Songkhla. **Oct 1-10** *World Stamp Exhibition-Bangkok 1993*, Bangkok. **Oct 27-30** *Wax Castle & Boat Racing Festival*, Sakon Nakhon. **Oct 27-31** *Illuminated Boat Procession*, Nakhon Phanom. **Oct 31** *Tak Bat Devo*, Uthai Thani. **Nov** *Festival of Lights*, Ayutthaya. **Nov-Dec** *Mexican Sunflower Blooming Season*, Mae Hong Son. **Nov 20-21** *Surin Elephant Round-up*, Surin. **Nov 26-28** *Loi Krathong and Candle Festival*, Sukhotani. **Nov 28** *Chinese Banquet for Monkeys*, Lop Buri. **Dec 5-11** *Phuket King's Cup Regatta '93*, Phuket. **Dec 11-12** *I-San Kite Festival*, Buri Ram.
SOCIAL CONVENTIONS: Present-day Thai society is the result of centuries of cultural interchange, particularly with China and India but more latterly with Western influences. Western visitors will generally receive a handshake on meeting someone. A Thai will be greeted with the traditional closed hands and a slight bow of the head. Shoes should be removed before entering someone's home. A meal will generally be eaten with a fork and spoon, but mainly Western etiquette prevails. Informal dress is widely acceptable and men are seldom, if ever, expected to wear suits. A traditional Thai shirt is the most suitable attire for men at any official function. Beachwear should be confined to the beach. Smoking is widely acceptable. **Tipping:** Most hotels will add a 10% service charge and an 11% Government tax to the bill. Taxi drivers are not tipped.

BUSINESS PROFILE

ECONOMY: Thailand is relatively prosperous by Asian standards. Nevertheless, certain aspects of the economic performance have in recent years given cause for concern, notably the foreign debt and the shortcomings of the taxation system. Agriculture is the main economic activity, but continues to decline in relative importance as the industrial base expands and develops. The main crops are rice – of which Thailand is the world's leading exporter – sugar, cassava, maize, rubber, cotton and tobacco. Fishing is substantial. Timber has suffered from excessive logging, although the Government has plans to replant the now treeless areas. In the meantime, there is an extensive military-run timber trade with Myanmar, which is desperately short of foreign exchange. Thailand's other important natural resource is tin, although earnings from this too have suffered following the collapse in the mid-1980s of the London-based International Tin Council which controlled most of the world trade in the metal. The most promising discovery of late has been offshore deposits of natural gas. Industrialisation got under way in the early 1960s and Thailand now has a strong base in cement manufacturing, electronics, jewellery, sugar and oil refining. In the service sector, tourism has grown steadily during the last two decades, although it has recently been hit by political upheaval: a quick recovery is hoped for provided political stability can be maintained. Trade has been boosted by a sharp increase in industrial investment and consequent demand for machinery and equipment. Thailand's rapid and consistent growth suggests that these conditions will prevail for some time, notwithstanding the recent military coup and subsequent unrest which has raised concern over future relations between Thailand and a number of its major trading partners. Recent social unrest has also had a bad effect on Thailand's economic performance although foreign investors will have been reassured by the reappointment of Anand Parachayun as Premier. However, GDP growth slipped from 9% in 1991 to 5% in 1992.
BUSINESS: Most people in senior management speak English but in very small companies, or those situated outside the industrial belt of Bangkok, English is less well-known. Most businesses of substantial size prefer visitors to make appointments. Visiting cards are essential. **Office hours:** 0830-1630 Monday to Friday. Some have a half-day on Saturday.
COMMERCIAL INFORMATION: The following organisation can offer advice: Thai Chamber of Commerce, 150 Rajbopit Road, Bangkok 10200. Tel: (2) 225 0086. Fax: (2) 225 3372. Telex: 72093.
CONFERENCES/CONVENTIONS: The Thailand Incentive and Convention Association has 191 members representing all sectors of business interested in conventions and incentives. Members include hotels, airlines, publishing houses, advertising agencies, cruise companies, travel agents, lawyers, equipment suppliers and banks. The aim of the association is to provide help with every possible query that an organiser may have as well as providing practical assistance. It publishes a quarterly newsletter, an annual guide, a gift-ideas catalogue and a social programme. The Bangkok Convention Center is the largest venue in the country but there are many other venues (including hotels) in Bangkok and elsewhere. The largest markets for delegates in 1988 were Malaysia, Japan, the USA, Taiwan and Australia, though interest from Canada and Germany showed a considerable increase. In October 1991, Thailand hosted the annual meeting of the World Bank and International Monetary Fund attend-

Kok River, Chang Mai

ed by 15,000 delegates. Further information can be obtained from the Thailand Incentive and Convention Association, Room 1509/2, 15th Floor, Bangkok Bank Buildings, 333 Silom Road, Bangkok 10500. Tel: (2) 235 0731/2. Fax: (2) 235 0730. Telex: 22228 TCPA TH.

HISTORY & GOVERNMENT

HISTORY: The Kingdom of Thailand, known as Siam until 1939, was ruled by the Khmers, based in what is now neighbouring Cambodia, during the 11th and 12th centuries. In 1238 two Thai chieftains rebelled against Khmer domination and established the first independent Thai kingdom. Ayudhya, to the north of Bangkok, was the capital of the kingdom from the early 1300s until its destruction by Burmese invaders in 1767. The Burmese were quickly forced out and the monarchy re-established. The absolute rule of the monarchy lasted until 1932 when it was replaced by a system of constitutional monarchy. In the period since then, Thai politics have been dominated by the military. Since the end of absolute monarchy, Thailand has made slow progress towards a democratic, pluralistic system of government. Democratic governments were a rarity in the region and Thailand's chief strategic ally, the United States, was more concerned with Thailand's role as a bulwark against encroaching communism from elsewhere in South-East Asia. In this respect, Thailand has been an influential member of the anti-communist Association of South-East Asian Nations (ASEAN) but with the Cold War at an end, Thailand has taken the lead in proposing the reformation of ASEAN into a regional trading bloc (see *Economy*). Thailand's uniformly hostile attitude towards its communist neighbours was dropped after a reappraisal of Thai foreign policy in 1988/89, since then, relations with Cambodia, Laos and Vietnam have improved dramatically. This switch was one of the successes of the Government led by Chatichai Choonhaven, who governed the country from his election in 1988 until his overthrow in a military coup in February 1991. This uprising, the 17th since 1932, was led by army chief General Suchinda Kraprayoon, who emerged at the head of a new ruling body entitled the National Peacekeeping Council (NPKC). The NPKC appointed a former diplomat and businessman, Anand Panyarachun, as Premier. Anand led a group of technocratic ministers – there was no government as such – which gained many international plaudits for its competent management and comparative honesty in a country where corrutpion and graft are commonplace. Elections were held in March 1992. Eleven parties won seats in the new national assembly, led by Samakkhi Tham and Chart Thai which allied with four other parties to form a government in which General Suchinda took the premiership. The public reaction to Suchinda's assumption of the post, given that no-one had elected him to anything, was immediate and furious. Massive demonstrations demanding his resignation were met by fierce measures from the military. The decisive intervention in the crisis was then made by King Bhumibol, who normally refrains strictly from involvement in politics. The King is revered as a semi-deity by Thais and his pronouncements treated as gospel. In an extraordinary televised encounter, Bhumibol castigated the prostrate Suchinda whose resignation followed almost immediately on May 24. On June 10, Anand Parachayun was recalled as Prime Minister to restore stability prior to the holding of new elections. These were held in September; Chart Thai again did well but the real winner was the Democrat Party which doubled its representation to become the largest single party. Allied with four others, the Democrat Party leder Chuan Leekpai managed to put togther a coalition government which took office at the end of September.

GOVERNMENT: The present constitution, promulgated in December 1991, allows for an elected House of Representatives with 360 members and a 270-strong Senate composed of military appointees.

CLIMATE

Generally hot, particularly between mid-February and June. The monsoon season runs from May to October, when the climate is still hot with torrential rains. The best time for travelling is November to February, which is the cool season.

Required clothing: Lightweights and rainwear are advised for all seasons.

BANGKOK Thailand (2m)

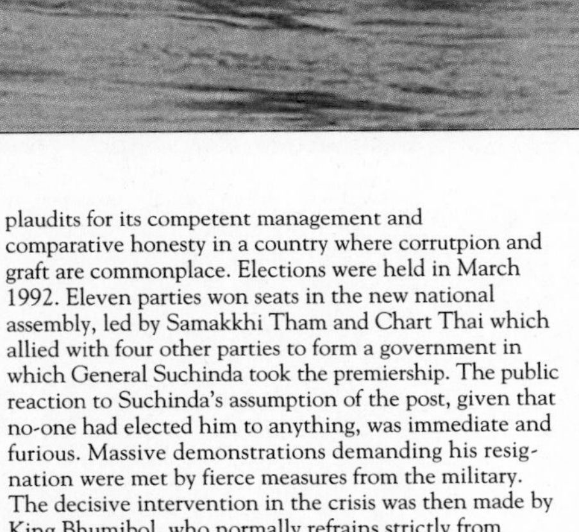

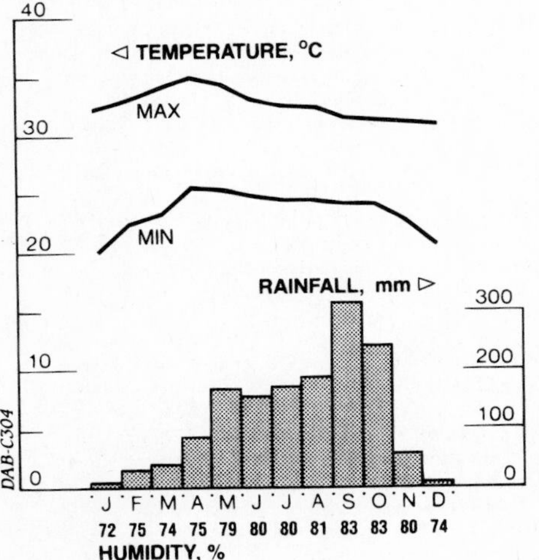

CHIANG MAI Thailand (314m)

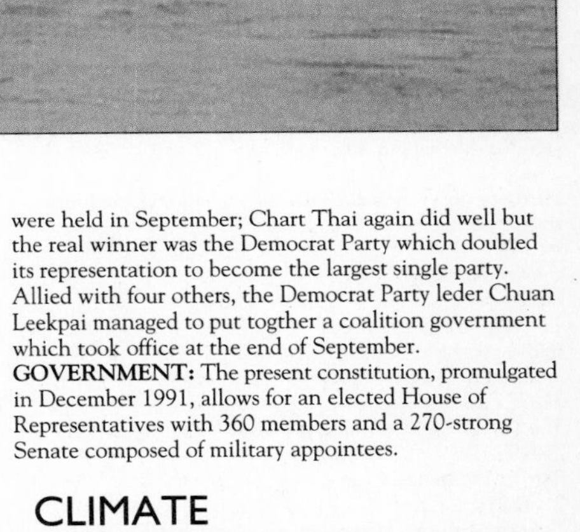

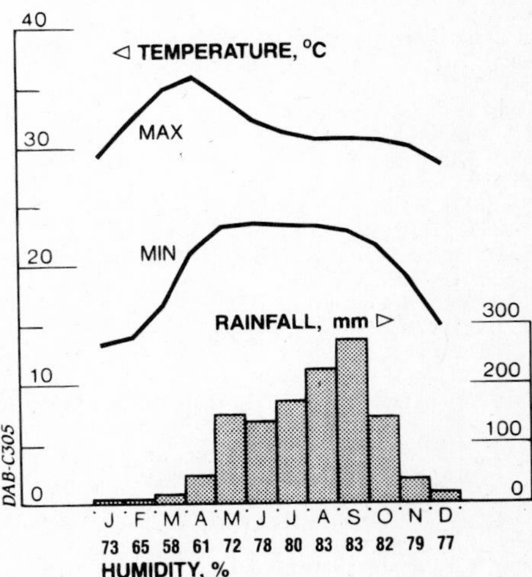

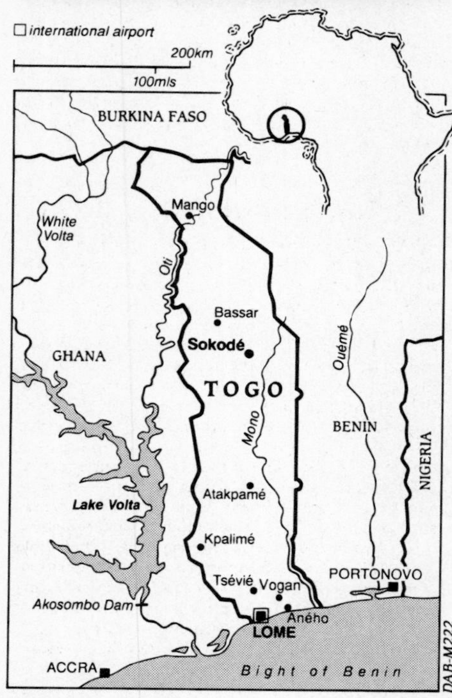

Location: West Africa.

Ministry of Tourism, Crafts and Small and Medium-sized Enterprises
BP 3114
avenue Sarakawa
Lomé, Togo
Tel: 215 352. Telex: 5007.

Embassy of the Republic of Togo
8 rue Alfred Roll
75017 Paris, France
Tel: (1) 45 25 99 40. Fax: (1) 43 80 90 71. Telex: 290497.

British Honorary Consulate
BP 60958
Agence Maritime Atlantique du Togo SARL
1 rue l'Hotel Miramar
Ablogame 2
Lomé, Togo
Tel: 214 082. Telex: 5153 AMATO TG.

Embassy of the Republic of Togo *and* **Togo Tourist Information Office**
2208 Massachusetts Avenue, NW
Washington, DC
20008
Tel: (202) 234 4212/3.

Embassy of the United States of America
BP 852
angle rue Pelletier Caventou et rue Vauban
Lomé, Togo
Tel: 217 717 *or* 212 991/2/3/4. Fax: 217 952.

Embassy of the Republic of Togo
12 Range Road
Ottawa, Ontario
K1N 8J3
Tel: (613) 238 5916/7. Fax: (613) 235 6425.
Consulates in: Calgary, Montréal and Toronto.

The Canadian High Commission in Ghana deals with enquiries relating to Togo:
Canadian High Commission
PO Box 1639
42 Independence Avenue
Accra, Ghana
Tel: (21) 773 791. Fax: (21) 773 792. Telex: 2024 DOMCAN GH.

AREA: 56,785 sq km (21,925 sq miles).
POPULATION: 3,349,000 (1989 estimate).
POPULATION DENSITY: 59 per sq km.
CAPITAL: Lomé. **Population:** 500,000 (1987).
GEOGRAPHY: Togo shares borders with Burkina Faso to the north, Benin to the east and Ghana to the west with a short coast on the Atlantic in the south. The country is a narrow strip, rising behind coastal lagoons and swampy plains to an undulating plateau. Northwards, the plateau descends to a wide plain irrigated by the River Oti. The central area is covered by deciduous forest while savannah stretches to the north and south. In the east, the River Mono runs to the sea; long sandy beaches shaded by palms characterise the coastline between Lomé and Cotonou.
LANGUAGE: French is the official language, while Ewe, Watchi and Kabiyé are the most widely spoken African languages. Very little English is spoken.
RELIGION: 50% traditional or animist, 35% Christian and 15% Muslim.
TIME: GMT.
ELECTRICITY: 220 volts AC, 50Hz single phase. Plugs are square or round 2-pin.
COMMUNICATIONS: Telephone: IDD is available to main cities. Country code: 228. There are no area codes. **Telex/telegram:** Slow, limited and expensive services are available only in the capital (the facilities at the main post office are the least expensive). The telegram service is dependable; calls to France and West Africa are less expensive. **Post:** Postal facilities are limited to main towns. *Post Restante* facilities are available and are very reliable. Airmail to Europe takes up to two weeks. **Press:** Newspapers are exclusively in the French language. The main newspaper is the government-owned *La Nouvelle Marche*.
BBC World Service and Voice of America frequencies: From time to time these change. See the section *How to Use this Book* for more information.

BBC:				
MHz	17.79	15.40	15.07	9.600
Voice of America:				
MHz	21.49	15.60	9.525	6.035

PASSPORT/VISA

Regulations and requirements may be subject to change at short notice, and you are advised to contact the appropriate diplomatic or consular authority before finalising travel arrangements. Details of these may be found at the head of this country's entry. Any numbers in the chart refer to the footnotes below.

	Passport Required?	Visa Required?	Return Ticket Required?
Full British	Yes	No	Yes
BVP	Not valid	-	-
Australian	Yes	Yes	Yes
Canadian	Yes	No	Yes
USA	Yes	No	Yes
Other EC	Yes	1	Yes
Japanese	Yes	Yes	Yes

Restricted entry: The Government of Togo refuses admission to nationals of South Africa, and holders of communist country passports must acquire special permission on arrival.
PASSPORTS: Valid passport required by all except nationals of Benin, Burkina Faso, Central African Republic, Chad, Côte d'Ivoire, Ghana, Guinea Republic, Mali, Mauritania, Niger, Nigeria and Senegal bearing a 'Carnet de Voyage' national ID card.
Note: Joint passports are not accepted.
British Visitors Passport: Not accepted.
VISAS: Required by all except:
(a) **[1]** nationals of France for any length of stay;
(b) **[1]** nationals of Belgium, Denmark, Germany, Greece, Ireland, Italy, Luxembourg, The Netherlands and the UK for visits not exceeding 90 days;
(c) nationals of Canada, Cape Verde, Gabon, Gambia, Guinea-Bissau, Liberia, Nigeria, Norway, Sierra Leone and Sweden for visits not exceeding 90 days and nationals of Cameroon for visits not exceeding 10 days;
(d) nationals of Andorra, Benin, Burkina Faso, Central African Republic, Chad, Côte d'Ivoire, Ghana, Guinea Republic, Madagascar, Mali, Mauritania, Monaco, Niger, Senegal and the USA for any length of stay.
Types of visa: Tourist and Business. Group visas can also be obtained. Check with embassy for visa fees.
Validity: 30 days. Business and Tourist visas can be extended on arrival in Lomé at the Sûreté Nationale for visits not exceeding 6 months.
Application to: Consulate (or Consular Section at Embassy). For addresses, see top of entry.
Application requirements: (a) 2 completed application forms. (b) 3 passport photos. (c) Company letter for Business visa.
Working days required: 2 days.
Temporary residence: Apply in Togo.

MONEY

Currency: CFA Franc (CFA Fr) = 100 centimes. Notes are in denominations of CFA Fr10,000, 5000, 1000 and 500. Coins are in denominations of CFA Fr100, 50, 10, 5 and 1.
Currency exchange: Togo currency is legal tender in the countries which formerly comprised French West Africa (Benin, Côte d'Ivoire, Niger, Senegal, Togo and Burkina Faso). Togo belongs to the French Franc Zone and is a member of the West African Monetary Union. The CFA Fr is pegged to the French Franc at a fixed rate.
Credit cards: American Express is widely accepted, with more limited use of Diners Club, Visa and Access/Mastercard. Check with your credit card company for details of merchant acceptability and other facilities which may be available.
Travellers cheques: International travellers cheques are accepted in Lomé.
Exchange rate indicators: The following figures are included as a guide to the movements of the CFA Franc against Sterling and the US Dollar:

Date:	**Oct '89**	**Oct '90**	**Oct '91**	**Oct '92**
£1.00=	505.1	498.38	496.13	431.75
$1.00=	319.9	255.12	285.87	260.71

Currency restrictions: The import of local currency is limited to CFA Fr1 million, the export to CFA Fr25,000. There are no restrictions on the import of foreign currency, subject to declaration. The export of foreign currency is limited to the amount declared on entry.
Banking hours: 0800-1600 Monday to Friday.

DUTY FREE

The following goods may be imported into Togo without incurring customs duty:
100 cigarettes or 50 cigars or 1kg of tobacco;
1 bottle of spirits and 1 bottle of wine;
A reasonable quantity of perfume for personal use.
Note: Visitors may also import for the duration of their stay clothes (not new) and personal effects, two cameras with film, one pair of binoculars, one musical instrument, one typewriter and small items of camping and sporting equipment.

PUBLIC HOLIDAYS

Public holidays observed in Togo are as follows:
Mar 25 '93 Eid al-Fitr (End of Ramadan). **Apr 12** Easter Monday. **Apr 24** Victory Day. **Apr 27** Independence Day. **May 1** Labour Day. **May 20** Ascension Day. **May 31** Whit Monday. **Jun 1** Tabaski (Feast of the Sacrifice). **Aug 15** Assumption. **Sep 24** Anniversary of failed attack on Lomé. **Nov 1** All Saints' Day. **Dec 25** Christmas Day. **Jan 1 '94** New Year's Day. **Jan 13** Liberation Day. **Jan 24** Day of Victory (anniversary of the failed attack at Sarakawa). **Mar** Start of Eid al-Fitr.
Note: Muslim festivals are timed according to local sightings of various phases of the Moon and the dates given above are approximations. During the lunar month of Ramadan that precedes Eid al-Fitr, Muslims fast during the day and feast at night and normal business patterns may be interrupted. Many restaurants are closed during the day and there may be restrictions on smoking and drinking. Some disruption may continue into Eid al-Fitr itself. Eid al-Fitr and Tabaski (Eid al-Adha) may last anything from two to ten days, depending on the region. For more information see the section *World of Islam* at the back of the book.

HEALTH

Regulations and requirements may be subject to change at short notice, and you are advised to contact your doctor well in advance of your intended date of departure. Any numbers in the chart refer to the footnotes below.

	Special Precautions?	Certificate Required?
Yellow Fever	Yes	1
Cholera	Yes	2
Typhoid & Polio	Yes	-
Malaria	3	-
Food & Drink	4	-

[1]: A yellow fever vaccination certificate is required from travellers over one year of age from all countries.
[2]: Following WHO guidelines issued in 1973, a cholera vaccination certificate is not a condition of

entry to Togo. However, cholera is a serious risk in this country and precautions are essential. Up-to-date advice should be sought before deciding whether these precautions should include vaccination, as medical opinion is divided over its effectiveness. See the *Health* section at the back of the book.

[3]: Malaria risk exists throughout the year in the whole country. The predominant malignant *falciparum* form is reported to be resistant to chloroquine.

[4]: All water should be regarded as being a potential health risk. Water used for drinking, brushing teeth or making ice should have first been boiled or otherwise sterilised. Milk is unpasteurised and should be boiled. Powdered or tinned milk is available and is advised but make sure that it is reconstituted with pure water. Avoid dairy products which are likely to have been made from unboiled milk. Only eat well-cooked meat and fish, preferably served hot. Pork, salad and mayonnaise may carry increased risk. Vegetables should be cooked and fruit peeled.

Rabies is present. For those at high risk, vaccination before arrival should be considered. If you are bitten abroad seek medical advice without delay. For more information consult the *Health* section at the back of the book.

Bilharzia (schistosomiasis) is present. Avoid swimming and paddling in fresh water. Swimming pools which are well-chlorinated and maintained are safe.

Health care: Health insurance and a good supply of personal medical provisions are advised. There is one doctor for every 20,000 inhabitants.

TRAVEL - International

AIR: The main airline running services to Togo is *Air Afrique (RK)*, in which Togo is a shareholder. Togo has become an important transit point for air travel in Africa. There are frequent flights to most major African destinations.

Approximate flight time: From *London* to Lomé is 7 hours.

International airport: *Lomé (LFW)* is 4km (2.5 miles) northeast of the city. Airport facilities include bar, restaurant, snack bar, shops, bank, post office, duty-free shop and car hire. Taxi and bus services are available to the city centre.

SEA: Ferries from Benin and Ghana call at Lomé and coastal ports. For details contact port authorities.

ROAD: There are routes from Benin, Ghana and Burkina Faso but conditions are unreliable.

TRAVEL - Internal

AIR: *Air Togo* runs services to Sokodé, Mango, Dapango, Lama-Kara, Niamtougou and Lomé.

SEA: Ferries run along the coast. For details contact port authorities.

RAIL: There are services between Lomé, Atakpamé and Blitta; Lomé and Kpalimé; and Lomé and Aného. Trains run at least daily on each route.

ROAD: Surfaced roads run to the border countries and the major northern route is called 'The Highway of Unity'. There are roads linking most settlements but these are largely impassable during the rainy season. Driving is on the right. **Bus/taxi:** National bus and taxi systems are reasonably efficient and cheap. Taxis are widely available in Lomé and shared taxis are available between towns. Drivers do not expect a tip. **Car hire:** This is available in Lomé. **Documentation:** An International Driving Permit is required.

ACCOMMODATION

HOTELS: Only Lomé and Lama-Kara have international-class accommodation but there are hotels in all the main towns. There is a severe shortage of accommodation, so it is advisable to book in advance.

CAMPING: This is available free of charge though not recommended.

RESORTS & EXCURSIONS

Lomé: Togo boasts the only capital in the world which is placed directly at a border. The city itself is a mixture of traditional parts, especially around the *Grand Marché*, and modern buildings like Lomé 2000. Tourists and nationals, however, tend to stay near the market and old part of town, which is still the heart of commercial dealings in Lomé. Traders from neighbouring countries sell their products here and the fetish market, with its interesting and intriguing voodoo charms and various lotions and potions, is well worth a visit. The seaside is rather disappointing and visitors have to leave the city well behind to find a nice spot.

Other towns of interest include **Togoville,** where the colonial treaty between the Germans and the ruler Mlapa III was signed. The chief still shows copies of the treaty to visitors. In the village itself, there are numerous voodoo shrines and the Roman Catholic Cathedral, built by the Germans. **Aného** has the most colonial atmosphere of any town in Togo, which is reflected in such attractions as the 19th-century *Peter and Paul Church*, the *Protestant Church* and the *German Cemetery*. The short coastline is home to several small fishing villages, sometimes with examples of colonial architecture, though unfortunately in bad repair.

Togo's wildlife parks include the *Fazao National Park* outside **Sokodé,** with many monkeys and one of Togo's last remaining elephant herds; the *Kéran National Park* near **Kara,** with many baboons and antelopes; and the *Fosse aux Lions* (Lions' Den) southwest of **Dapaong,** which has a few more of Togo's small population of elephants.

SOCIAL PROFILE

FOOD & DRINK: Most restaurants catering for visitors tend to be French orientated, although some do serve African dishes. In Lomé in particular, there are many small cafés serving local food. Dishes include soups based on palm nut, groundnut and maize. Meat, poultry and seafoods are plentiful and well prepared, as are the local fruit and vegetables. **Drink:** A good selection of alcoholic drinks is available and a number are produced locally.

NIGHTLIFE: There are numerous nightclubs, particularly in Lomé. Most serve food and are open until the early hours of the morning for dancing to a mixture of West African and Western popular music. There are also cinemas showing French and English-language films.

SHOPPING: Markets are interesting places to shop and bargain purchases include wax prints, indigo cloth, Kente and dye-stamped Adinkira cloth from Ghana, embroideries, batik and lace from The Netherlands, locally-made heavy marble ashtrays, gold and silver jewellery, traditional masks, wood sculpture and religious statuettes. Voodoo stalls display an extraordinary range of items used in magic, like cowrie shells (once used as currency). **Shopping hours:** 0800-1730 Monday to Friday, 0730-1230 Saturday.

SPORT: Beaches are unsafe for all but the best swimmers, but there are several pools along the beach at Lomé. Hotel pools and the lakeside resort of Porto Seguro (a short drive from Lomé) offer safe **swimming.** There are also **water-skiing** and **sailing** facilities at Porto Seguro. Some hotels have **tennis** courts and non-residents can generally arrange to play on them.

SPECIAL EVENTS: Mid-Jul *Evala* (initiation ceremonies, a custom which involves traditional wrestling), Kabyé region; *Akpema* (girls' initiation ceremonies), Kabyé region. **Aug** *Kpessosso* (a harvest festival of the Guens); *Ayize* (Bean Harvest Festival celebrated by the Ewe). **First Thursday in Sep** *Agbogbozan* (Ewe Diaspora Festival). **First Week of Sep** *Dipontre* (Yam Festival), Bassar region. **Dec** *Kamou* (Harvest Festival), Kabyé region.

SOCIAL CONVENTIONS: Music and dance are the most popular forms of culture. The Togolese have had a varied colonial heritage which has resulted in the variety of Christian denominations and European languages; the voodoo religion is a strong influence in the country and many young girls, after fulfilling an initiation period, will devote their lives to serving the religion and the voodoo village priest. Practical, casual clothes are suitable. Beachwear should not be worn away from the beach or poolside. **Tipping:** When not included, a tip of about 10% is customary. Taxi drivers do not usually expect a tip.

BUSINESS PROFILE

ECONOMY: Although most of the population is employed in agriculture, Togo's principal export earners are the ores from the country's phosphate mines. A wide range of tropical crops is produced: cocoa, coffee, palm kernels, cotton, copra, groundnuts and maize. New projects include the growing of tomatoes, herbs and sugar. Most of the country's industry is based on the processing of these products, apart from a handful of factories engaged in textiles, marble and consumer goods for domestic consumption. There is little other industrial output apart from the very high-quality phosphate which is one of the country's main sources of foreign exchange. The mining industry is under government control. France is Togo's leading trading partner followed by The Netherlands. In the region, Côte d'Ivoire and Senegal have significant trade links, much of it based on re-export from Togo of imported consumer goods. IMF-imposed austerity measures, in force throughout the 1980s, have continued into the next decade. The economy remains weak, suffering from low commodity prices and a lack of investment arising from continuing political unrest.

BUSINESS: It is generally acceptable for visiting business people to wear a safari suit except on very formal business and social occasions. Business is conducted in French, only a few executives speak English. Appointments should be made and business cards should be carried. **Office hours:** 0700-1730 Monday to Friday.

COMMERCIAL INFORMATION: The following organisation can offer advice: Chambre de Commerce, d'Agriculture et d'Industrie du Togo (CCAIT), BP 360, angle avenue de la Présidence, Lomé. Tel: 217 065. Telex: 5023.

HISTORY & GOVERNMENT

HISTORY: Togoland, of which modern Togo was formerly a part, was colonised by the Germans in 1894. Their administration was overthrown by a joint Anglo-French force early in World War I after which the country was divided into a French-controlled eastern part and a British-occupied Western sector, each of which was governed under a League of Nations mandate. After a UN-sponsored referendum in 1956, the British sector merged with the neighbouring colony of Gold Coast to form Ghana, while the French part chose later in the year to become the autonomous Republic of Togo. It was granted full independence in 1960. The civilian government which took power at this point lasted just seven years before a military coup in January 1967 brought Lieutenant-Colonel Etienne Gnassingbe Eyadéma to power. Eyadéma has remained in office ever since, with the support of the country's sole political party, the Rassemblement du Peuple Togolais (RPT). Eyadéma's authoritarian style of government spawned

TOGO	HEALTH REGULATIONS	VISA REGULATIONS Code-Link
GALILEO/WORLDSPAN	 TI-DFT/LFW/HE	TI-DFT/LFW/VI
SABRE	TIDFT/LFW/HE	TIDFT/LFW/VI

To access this information on your CRS, swipe the barcode with a light pen or type in the text under the barcode. For more information, see the introduction *How to Use This Book.*

numerous opponents and several coup attempts were directed against him. Surprisingly, Togo was initially in the vanguard of the democratic revolution which swept Africa during 1991. In common with other Francophone countries on the continent, the Togolese government was told that continuing economic and political support from Paris would henceforth be conditional upon the institution of democratic government. In August 1991, a national conference of the country's major political forces was convened to chart the path to democratic government. By a large majority, the conference stripped Eyadéma of his executive powers (although he retained his position) and installed a transitional administration, the High Council of the Republic led by Kokou Koffigoh. However, in late November 1991, the Government made a serious tactical error by banning the RPT, Eyadéma's political power base. Threatened with a complete loss of political power, the army mutinied, determined this time to bring Koffigoh down. The arrival of French paratroops in neighbouring Benin brought the violence to a halt. After negotiations between Eyadéma and Koffigoh, a compromise solution was reached under which Koffigoh would remain in office at the head of a 'government of national unity' to oversee the transitional process. During 1992, political turbulence continued in Togo. A provisional schedule for multi-party elections has been postponed several times, and it now appears that Eyadéma is determined to hold on to power, come what may.

GOVERNMENT: A government of national unity led by Kokou Koffigoh runs Togo while plans are made for a new system of democratic government. The Head of State in the interim period is the long-serving Gnassingbe Eyadéma.

CLIMATE

Togo's climate is not as hot as some parts of the West African coast. From December to January the *Harmattan* wind blows from the north. The rainy season lasts from April to July. Short rains occur from October to November. The driest and hottest months are February and March.

Required clothing: Lightweights, a few warm clothes and rainwear is advised.

LOME Togo

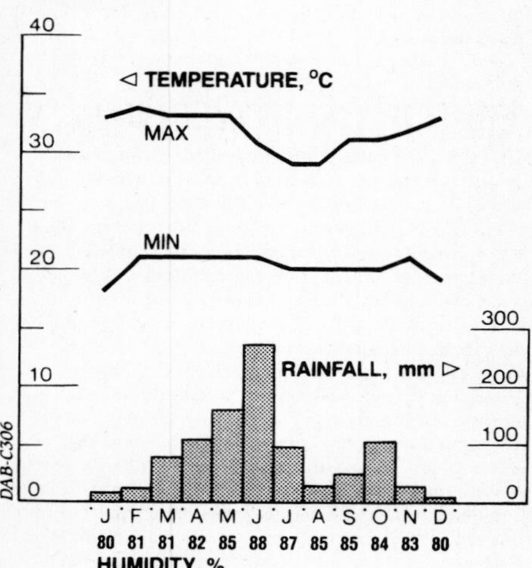

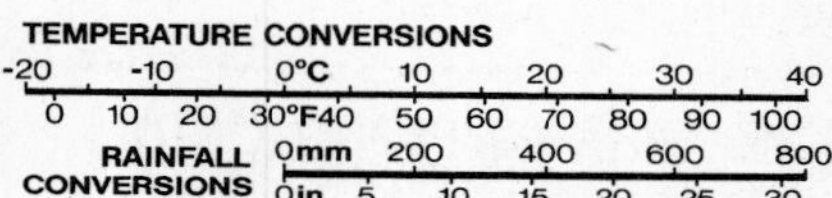

For information on the way in which each country's entry is presented, refer to the introductory section *How to Use this Book.*

TONGA

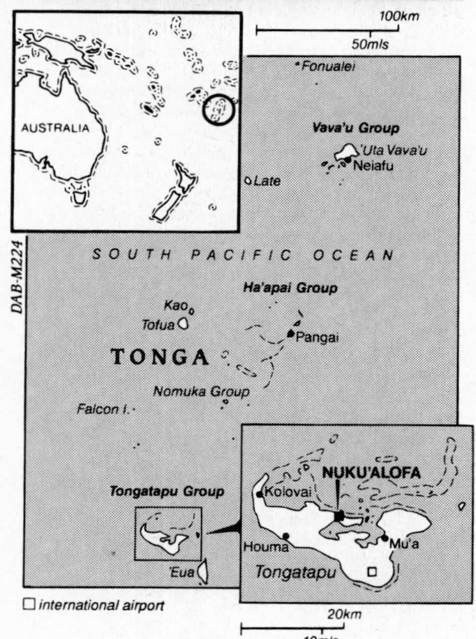

Location: South Pacific.

Tonga Visitors Bureau
PO Box 37
Vuna Road
Nuku'alofa, Tonga
Tel: 21733 *or* 23507. Fax: 22129. Telex: 66269 PRIMO TS.

High Commission for the Kingdom of Tonga
36 Molyneux Street
London W1H 6AB
Tel: (071) 724 5828. Fax: (071) 723 9074. Telex: 8954094. Opening hours: 0900-1300 and 1400-1700 Monday to Friday.

British High Commission
PO Box 56
Vuna Road
Nuku'alofa, Tonga
Tel: 21020/1. Fax: 24109. Telex: 66226 UKREP TS.

Tonga General Consulate
Suite 604
360 Post Street
San Francisco, CA
94108
Tel: (415) 781 0365. Fax: (415) 781 3964.

The Canadian High Commission in New Zealand deals with enquiries relating to Tonga:

Canadian High Commission
PO Box 12-049
61 Molesworth Street
Thorndon
Wellington, New Zealand
Tel: (4) 473 9577. Fax: (4) 471 2082. Telex: CANAD NZ3577.

AREA: 748 sq km (289 sq miles).
POPULATION: 94,649 (1986).
POPULATION DENSITY: 126.5 per sq km.
CAPITAL: Nuku'alofa (Tongatapu Island). **Population:** 21,383 (1986).

GEOGRAPHY: Tonga is an archipelago of 172 islands in the South Pacific, most of which are uninhabited, covering an area of 7700 sq km (3000 sq miles). The major island groups are Tongatapu and 'Eua, Ha'apai and Vava'u. Tonga's high volcanic and low coral forms give the islands a unique character. Some volcanoes are still active and Falcon Island in the Vava'u group is a submerged volcano that erupts periodically, its lava and ash rising above sea level forming a visible island which disappears when the eruption is over. Nuku'alofa, on Tongatapu Island, has a reef-protected harbour lined with palms. The island is flat with a large lagoon, but no running streams, and many surrounding smaller islands. 'Eua Island is hilly and forested with high cliffs and beautiful beaches. The Ha'apai Islands, a curving archipelago 160km (100 miles) north of Tongatapu, have excellent beaches. Tofua, the largest island in the group, is an active volcano with a hot steaming lake in its crater. The Vava'u Islands, 90km (50 miles) north of Ha'apai, are hilly, densely wooded and interspersed with a maze of narrow channels. They are known for their stalagmite-filled caves.

LANGUAGE: Tongan and English are the official languages.
RELIGION: Wesleyan Church, Roman Catholic, Anglicans.
TIME: GMT + 13.
ELECTRICITY: 240 volts AC, 50 Hz.

COMMUNICATIONS: Telephone: IDD is available. Country code: 676. There are no area codes. **Fax:** *Cable & Wireless* provide fax services. **Telex/telegram:** Telegrams and cables can be booked through *Cable & Wireless Limited,* Tonga. **Post:** The main post office is located in the centre of Nuku'alofa. Open 0830-1600 Monday to Friday. All mail must be collected from the post office. Airmail to Europe takes approximately ten days. There are branch offices on Ha'apai and Vava'u. **Press:** The *Tonga Chronicle* and *The Times of Tonga* are the weekly newspapers.

BBC World Service and Voice of America frequencies: From time to time these change. See the section *How to Use this Book* for more information.

BBC:

MHz	17.83	15.34	9.640	11.95

Voice of America:

MHz	18.82	15.18	9.525	1.735

PASSPORT/VISA

Regulations and requirements may be subject to change at short notice, and you are advised to contact the appropriate diplomatic or consular authority before finalising travel arrangements. Details of these may be found at the head of this country's entry. Any numbers in the chart refer to the footnotes below.

	Passport Required?	Visa Required?	Return Ticket Required?
Full British	Yes	No	Yes
BVP	Not valid	-	-
Australian	Yes	No	Yes
Canadian	Yes	No	Yes
USA	Yes	No	Yes
Other EC	Yes	No	Yes
Japanese	Yes	No	Yes

Note: All passengers must be in possession of valid onward or return tickets and have proof of adequate funds for their stay. If visitors wish to extend their stay beyond 30 days, they must request permission from the Principal Immigration Officer, who may grant permission for up to 6 months.

PASSPORTS: Valid passport required by all.
British Visitors Passport: Not accepted.
VISAS: Required by all except:
(a) nationals of Commonwealth countries;
(b) nationals of EC countries;
(c) nationals of Japan and the USA.
Types of visa: Tourist and Business. Cost: free
Validity: 30 days.
Application to: Consulate (or Consular Section at Embassy or High Commission). For addresses, see top of entry.
Working days: 2 to 7.

MONEY

Currency: Pa'anga (T$) = 100 seniti. Notes are in denominations of T$50, 20, 10, 5, 2 and 1, and 50 seniti. Coins are in denominations of T$2 and 1, and 50, 20, 10, 5, 2 and 1 seniti.

Credit cards: Limited use of both Visa and Diners Club. Check with your credit card company for details of merchant acceptability and other facilities which may be available.

Travellers cheques: Accepted at banks and at some hotels and tourist shops.

Exchange rate indicators: The following figures are included as a guide to the movements of the Pa'anga against Sterling and the US Dollar:

Date:	Oct '89	Oct '90	Oct '91	Oct '92
£1.00	2.01	2.46	2.18	2.22
$1.00	1.27	1.26	1.26	1.40

Currency restrictions: There are no restrictions on the import or export of foreign currency. Free import and export of local currency.

Banking hours: 0930-1530 Monday to Friday, 0800-1200 Saturday.

DUTY FREE

The following goods may be imported into Tonga by persons over 18 years of age without incurring customs duty:
200 cigarettes;
1 litre of spirits or wine.
Note: (a) The import of arms, ammunition and pornography is prohibited. (b) Birds, animals, fruit and plants are subject to quarantine regulations. (c) There are several duty-free shops in Tonga. (d) The export of valuable artefacts and certain flora and fauna is restricted.

PUBLIC HOLIDAYS

Public holidays observed in Tonga are as follows:
Apr 9-12 '93 Easter. **Apr 25** Anzac Day. **May 4** Crown Prince's Birthday. **June 4** Independence Day. **Jul 4** King's Birthday. **Nov 4** Constitution Day. **Dec 4** King George Tupou I Day. **Dec 25** Christmas. **Dec 26** Boxing Day. **Jan 1 '94** New Year's Day.

HEALTH

Regulations and requirements may be subject to change at short notice, and you are advised to contact your doctor well in advance of your intended date of departure. Any numbers in the chart refer to the footnotes below.

	Special Precautions?	Certificate Required?
Yellow Fever	No	1
Cholera	No	No
Typhoid & Polio	Yes	-
Malaria	No	-
Food & Drink	2	-

[1]: A yellow fever vaccination certificate is required from travellers over one year of age arriving from infected areas.
[2]: Mains water in Nuku'alofa is normally chlorinated, and whilst relatively safe may cause mild abdominal upsets. Drinking water outside the capital should be considered a potential health risk and sterilisation is advisable. Bottled water is available and is advised for the first few weeks of the stay. Milk is pasteurised and dairy products are safe for consumption. Local meat, poultry, seafood, fruit and vegetables are generally considered safe to eat.
Health care: Health insurance is recommended. There are medical facilities in all major centres. For emergency services, dial 911.

TRAVEL - International

AIR: The main airline serving Tonga is *Air Pacific (FJ)*. *Air New Zealand* and *Polynesian Airways* also serve the country. *Polynesian Airways* offer a 'Polypass' which allows the holder to fly anywhere on the airline's network: Sydney (Australia), Auckland (New Zealand), Western Samoa, American Samoa, the Cook Islands, Vanuatu, New Caledonia, Fiji and, on payment of a supplement, Tahiti. The pass is valid for 30 days.
Approximate flight time: From *London* to Nuku'alofa is 20 hours.
International airport: *Tongatapu (TBU)* is 21km (13 miles) from Nuku'alofa. Transport by taxi and bus is available. There are car-hire services and a duty-free shop.
Departure tax: T$20 is levied on all international departures and is payable at the airport. There are no exemptions.
SEA: Ports of entry are Nuku'alofa, Pangai, Neiafu, Niuatoputapu. There are no regular passenger services, but berths may be available on cruise ships.

TRAVEL - Internal

AIR: *Royal Tongan Airlines* provide regular service between Vava'u, Ha'apai, 'Eua, Niuatoputapu and Tongatapu. Bookings and information from Royal Tongan Airlines, Nuku'alofa.
SEA: Local ferries sail between all the island groups. There are regular sailings from Faua Wharf in Nuku'alofa to Ha'apai and Vava'u. Ferry schedules are subject to change according to demand or the weather.
ROAD: There is a good network of sealed roads. Driving is on the left. Horses are extensively used. **Bus:** Minibus services are available throughout Tongatapu. **Taxi:** Saloon car taxis, mini-mokes, minibuses and *ve'etolus*, 3-wheeler open-air taxis. There are no fixed rates, therefore it is advisable to negotiate the cost beforehand. **Car hire:** May be arranged through various agencies. Self-drive or chauffeur-driven cars are available. **Documentation:** A current local driving licence is required, available from the Police Traffic Department in Nuku'alofa on production of a valid national or international licence, T$8 and a passport. The minimum driving age is 18.
JOURNEY TIMES: The following chart gives approximate journey times (in hours and minutes) from Nuku'alofa to other major centres on Tonga.

	Air	Sea
Neiafu (Vava'u)	1.00	24.00
Pangai (Ha'apai)	0.30	18.00
'Eua	0.10	3.00

ACCOMMODATION

HOTELS: There are excellent hotels, motels and resort villages of Tongan-style houses. Traditional boarding houses are also very popular with tourists. There is a growing selection of accommodation and capacity is expected to increase to 900 rooms. Contact the Tonga Visitors Bureau for a complete list of available accommodation.
CAMPING: Niu-akalo Hotel offers camping grounds.

RESORTS & EXCURSIONS

Tongatapu Group

Sightseeing on Tongatapu should include the *Royal Palace* on the waterfront in **Nuku'alofa,** just beyond Vuna Wharf where Vuna Road turns into Taufa'ahau Road. The Palace was completed in 1867 displaying Victorian-style spires and turrets. The grounds are decorated with tropical shrubs and flowers. While visitors are not allowed to enter the palace or gardens, there are good views from the low surrounding walls. The *Royal Chapel* was completed in 1882 in a similar style to that of the Palace. The interior, however, is in a style known as 'Pacific Gothic', rich with dark-polished woods and carvings. Visitors are invited to attend Sunday evening services here.
The *Mala'ekula* (Royal Tombs) are situated in the southern part of the business district along Taufa'ahau Road. The tombs have been a burial place for Tongan royalty since 1893.
A short stroll on Vuna Road from the *International Dateline Hotel* are the *Fa'onelua Tropical Gardens*, which contain a variety of flowers and plants indigenous to the South Pacific, including several different types of hibiscus. Within the gardens is a model Tongan village.
One of the most impressive sights in Tonga are the *Blow Holes*, found along the coastline at **Houma**, 14.5km (9 miles) from Nuku'alofa. Waves send sea water spurting some 18m (60 feet) into the air through holes in the coral reef. This stretch of coastline is known as the **Mapu 'a Vaea** (the Chief's Whistle) by Tongans because of the whistling sound made by the geyser-like spouts.
At **Kolovai**, 18km (11 miles) west of Nuku'alofa, one can find the rare *flying foxes*, dark brown fruit-bats, some with wingspans of up to 1m (3ft). The *Ha'atafu* and *Monotapu* beaches are also situated at the western end of the island; they are easily accessible and well protected.
On the eastern end of the island are the *Langi* (Terraced Tombs), 9.5km (6 miles) from the Ha'amonga Trilithon (see below) towards Nuku'alofa. The tombs form quadrilateral mounds faced with huge blocks of stone rising in terraces to heights of 4m (13 feet), built for the old *Tu'i tonga* (Spiritual Kings). The stones are of coral, built around AD1200, possibly carried from Wallis Island on large canoes known as *lomipeau*.
Ha'amonga Trilithon is a massive stone arch possibly used as a seasonal calendar, erected at the same time as the Terraced Tombs and again made from coral. Each stone is thought to weigh in the region of 40,000kg (about 40 tons).
Other sights include: the *Anahulu Cave*, an underground cavern of stalactites and stalagmites near the beach of the same name, about 24km (15 miles) from the capital; and *Oholei Beach*, with good bathing and excellent barbecues organised by the *International Dateline Hotel*.
The island of **'Eua,** a 10-minute flight away from Tongatapu, has recently been promoted as a tourist destination. It offers a blend of modern comfort (the island has one hotel and one motel) and the traditional South Sea island lifestyle. Many species of exotic birds live on the island.

Vava'u Group

Lying 240km (150 miles) north of Tongatapu, this cluster of 50 or so thickly wooded islands has two hotels, two motels and two guest-houses. There is a daily 1-hour flight from the capital and a weekly ferry service; private cruisers and ferries also operate from the harbour at **Neiafu,** the main town. There is excellent diving, with visibility often as much as 30m (100 ft). Other attractions include the *Fangatongo Royal Residence*, the view from *Mount Talau* and *Sailoame Market* in Neiafu.

SOCIAL PROFILE

FOOD & DRINK: Restaurants have table service, and are found mainly in hotels. Apart from hotel and boarding-house dining rooms, there are restaurants featuring Tongan food, French, Taiwanese and Japanese cuisine. Local staples are *'ufi* (a large white yam) and *taro*. Other dishes include *lu pullu* (meat and onions, marinaded in coconut milk, baked in *taro* leaves in an underground oven), *feke* (grilled octopus or squid in coconut sauce), devilled clams, *'ota* (raw fish marinaded in lemon juice) and lobster. Tropical fruits and salads are excellent. Feasts play a major role in the Tongan lifestyle. Up to 30 different dishes may be served on a *pola* (a long tray of plaited coconut fronds), and will typically include suckling pig, crayfish, chicken, octopus, pork and vegetables steamed in an *umu* (underground oven), served with a variety of tropical fruits.
NIGHTLIFE: Nightlife is sedate, limited to music and dancing in the hotels, clubs and occasionally at the *Yacht Club* and the *Banana Shed*. Floorshows are held on some nights in the main hotels and Tongan feasts and entertainment are also organised.
SHOPPING: Special purchases are hand-decorated and woven *tapa* cloth, woven floor coverings, *To'avala pandanus* mats, woven *pandanus* baskets, 'Ali Baba' laundry baskets, polished coconut-shell goblets and ashtrays, model outrigger canoes, tortoiseshell ornaments, brooches, earrings, rings and silver inlaid knives. Tongan stamps and coins are collectors' items; complete sets are on sale at the philatelic section of the Tongan Treasury. There are duty-free shops on Tongatapu and Vava'u. A Government tax of 5% is added to all bills for goods and services. **Shopping hours:** 0800-1700 Monday to Friday and 0800-1200 Saturday.
SPORT: There are sandy beaches and excellent **swimming** throughout the islands, with pools at some hotels. **Surfing:** There is a world-standard surfing beach on the island of 'Eua, 11km (7 miles) from Tongatapu. Niutoua Beach, on the main island, and Ha'apai and Vava'u islands are also good for surfing. **Riding:** Horses are available on 'Eua, Vava'u and Tongatapu Islands. **Fishing:** There are plentiful game fish including barracuda, tuna, marlin and sailfish. Charter boats are available. **Water-skiing:** Available in Tongatapu. **Diving:** Tongan coral

TONGA	HEALTH REGULATIONS	VISA REGULATIONS
GALILEO/WORLDSPAN	 TI-DFT/TBU/HE	 TI-DFT/TBU/VI
SABRE	 TIDFT/TBU/HE	 TIDFT/TBU/VI

Code-Link

To access this information on your CRS, swipe the barcode with a light pen or type in the text under the barcode. For more information, see the introduction *How to Use This Book.*

reefs provide great beauty and variety for **scuba diving** and **snorkelling;** fully equipped boats, scuba diving and snorkelling equipment can be hired. Contact the Tonga Visitors Bureau for information.
SPECIAL EVENTS: May '93 *Vava'u Festival.* **Jul** *Heilala Festival.*
SOCIAL CONVENTIONS: Shaking hands is a suitable form of greeting. Although by Western standards Tongan people are by no means rich, meals served to visitors will always be memorable. A token of appreciation, while not expected, is always welcome, especially gifts from your homeland. Casual wear is acceptable, but beachwear should be confined to the beach. *It is illegal not to wear a shirt in public.* Sunday is regarded as a sacred day, an aspect of Tongan life thrown into sharp relief by the controversy surrounding the so-called 'Tongan loop'. The international date line forms a loop around the islands, thereby making them a day ahead of Samoa, even though Samoa is almost due north of Tonga. Members of the Seventh Day Adventist Church therefore maintain that a Tongan Sunday is really a Saturday, and are unwilling to attend church on a day which is only a Sunday because of an apparently arbitrary manifestation of international law. This complex and almost insoluable problem may cause visitors a certain amount of confusion, but travellers to Tonga are advised to respect the religious beliefs of the islanders, even though enforcement of the Sabbath law affecting tourists can, at times, be irksome and inconvenient. **Tipping:** Not encouraged, but no offence is caused if services are rewarded in this way.

BUSINESS PROFILE

ECONOMY: Tonga's economy produces little more than agricultural items – mostly copra, bananas and dessicated coconut meal. Manufacturing activities are scarce other than handicrafts to supply the slowly growing tourist trade, although small manufacturing enterprises and food processing are potential growth areas. The search for oil continues offshore despite repeated failures to find deposits. The island's main imports are flour, meat, oil products, machinery and transport equipment, as well as manufactured goods. Australia and New Zealand are the main suppliers and the largest markets for Tongan goods. Some UK exports appear in Tonga as re-exported products from Australia and New Zealand. In a recent development, Tonga has exploited its geographical position to lay claim to six geostationary satellite positions to be used for trans-Pacific communications. With the approval of the relevant international governing body (Intelsat), the Tongasat company earns valuable revenue for the country by leasing these facilities to foreign telecommunications operators.
BUSINESS: Shirts and ties will suffice for most business visits. English and French are widely spoken. **Office hours:** 0830-1630 Monday to Friday and 0800-1200 Saturday.
COMMERCIAL INFORMATION: The following organisation can offer advice: Office of the Minister of Labour, Commerce and Industries, PO Box 110, Nuku'alofa. Tel: 23688. Fax: 23887. Telex: 66235.

HISTORY & GOVERNMENT

HISTORY: Tonga is the last remaining Polynesian kingdom; its ruling family can be traced back more than 1000 years. The island group was first visited by Europeans in the early 17th century, although it was not colonised due to the ruling family's adoption of Christianity and policy of accommodation with the British, then the principal imperial power in the area. King Taufa'ahau, the great-great-great grandfather of the present ruler and the first chief to rule over all of Tonga, also introduced representative government to the islands during the mid-19th century. A Treaty of Friendship was signed with the British in 1879 which afforded it the unique status of a 'Protected State' (as distinct from a Protectorate, which allowed for less autonomy in government). Under revisions to the treaty effected in 1968, the islands assumed complete responsibility for internal affairs, before being granted full independence in 1970. King Taufa'ahau Tupou IV, who has held power since then, has pursued a uniformly pro-Western foreign policy, including (unusually for the region) expression of support for French nuclear testing in the Pacific. Domestic politics are totally dominated by the Crown; there are no organised political parties.
GOVERNMENT: Tonga is a hereditary monarchy. The monarch is head of both state and government, and appoints a Privy Council which acts as a Cabinet of Ministers. The single-chamber Legislative Assembly has 29 members, including the King, the Cabinet and 9 representatives elected by universal suffrage every three years. The Assembly meets once a year.

CLIMATE

Tonga's climate is marginally cooler than most tropical areas. The best time is from May to November. Heavy rains occur from December to March.
Required clothing: Lightweights with warm clothes for cool evenings are advised.

NUKU'ALOFA Tonga

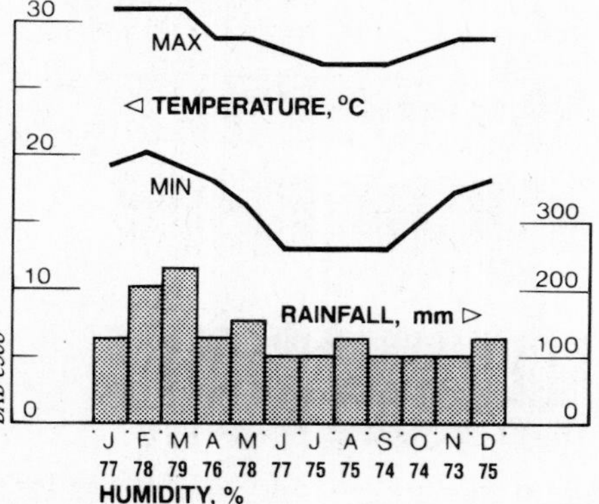

TRINIDAD & TOBAGO

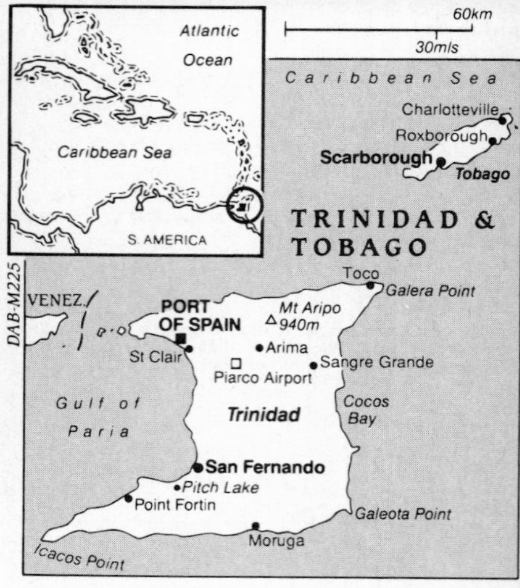

Location: Southern Caribbean, off Venezuelan coast.

Trinidad & Tobago Tourism Development Authority
134-138 Frederick Street
Port of Spain, Trinidad
Tel: 623 1932. Fax: 623 3848.
Trinidad & Tobago Hotel and Tourism Association
Room 202
Queen's Park Hotel
5-5a Queen's Park West
Port of Spain, Trinidad
Tel: 625 1061 *or* 625 1066.
High Commission for the Republic of Trinidad & Tobago
42 Belgrave Square
London SW1X 8NT
Tel: (071) 245 9351. Fax: (071) 823 1065. Opening hours: 0900-1700 Monday to Friday; 1000-1400 Monday to Friday (for visa applications).
Trinidad & Tobago Tourism Office
8a Hammersmith Broadway
London W6 7AL
Tel: (081) 741 4466. Fax: (081) 741 1013. Opening hours: 0900-1700 Monday to Friday.
British High Commission
PO Box 778
3rd & 4th Floors, Furness House
90 Independence Square
Port of Spain, Trinidad
Tel: 625 2861. Fax: 623 0621. Telex: 22224 UKREP WG.
Embassy of the Republic of Trinidad & Tobago
1708 Massachusetts Avenue, NW
Washington, DC
20036
Tel: (202) 467 6490. Fax: (202) 785 3130.
Consulate in: New York (tel: (212) 682 7272).
Trinidad & Tobago Tourism Development Authority
Suite 1508
25 West 43rd Street
New York, NY
10036
Tel: (212) 719 0540. Fax: (212) 719 0988.
Also deals with enquiries from Canada.
Embassy of the United States of America
PO Box 752
15 Queen's Park West
Port of Spain, Trinidad
Tel: 622 6372/6 *or* 622 6176. Fax: 628 5462.
High Commission for the Republic of Trinidad & Tobago
Suite 508
75 Albert Street
Ottawa, Ontario
K1P 5E7
Tel: (613) 232 2418/9. Fax: (613) 232 4349.
Consulates in: Willowdale and Winnipeg.
Canadian High Commission
PO Box 1246
Huggins Building

72 South Quay
Port of Spain, Trinidad
Tel: 623 7254. Fax: 624 4016. Telex: 22429 DOMCAN WG.

AREA: 5128 sq km (1980 sq miles).
POPULATION: 1,235,400 (1988 estimate).
POPULATION DENSITY: 240.9 per sq km.
CAPITAL: Port of Spain. **Population:** 59,200 (1988 estimate).
GEOGRAPHY: Trinidad and her tiny sister island of Tobago lie off the Venezuelan coast. Along the north of Trinidad runs the Northern Range of mountains, looming over the country's capital, Port of Spain. South of Port of Spain on the west coast the terrain is low, and the Caroni Swamps contain a magnificent bird sanctuary largely inhabited by the Scarlet Ibis. On the north and east coast lie beautiful beaches. Central Trinidad is flat and largely given over to agriculture.
LANGUAGE: The official language is English. French, Spanish, Hindi and Chinese are also spoken.
RELIGION: 36% Roman Catholic, 23% Hindu, 21% Anglican, 14% other Christian denominations and 6% Muslim.
TIME: GMT - 4.
ELECTRICITY: 115 volts AC, 60Hz. Continental 2-pin plugs are standard, though variations may be found.
COMMUNICATIONS: Telephone: IDD is available. Country code: 1 809. There are no area codes. **Fax:** Some hotels have facilities. **Telex/telegram:** Port of Spain has good facilities in Independence Square and Edward Street; *Textel* is open 24 hours a day. Cables can also be sent from hotels and airport. Telex facilities are also available in Scarborough, Tobago, run by *Cable & Wireless (WI) Ltd.* **Post:** The main post office is on Wrightson Road, Port of Spain. Airmail to Europe takes up to two weeks. **Press:** English-language dailies include *The Sun, Trinidad Guardian* and *The Trinidad & Tobago Express*.
BBC World Service and Voice of America frequencies: From time to time these change. See the section *How to Use this Book* for more information.

BBC:				
MHz	17.840	15.220	9.915	5.975
Voice of America:				
MHz	15.21	11.70	6.130	0.930

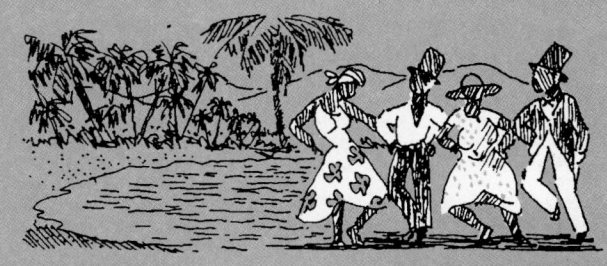

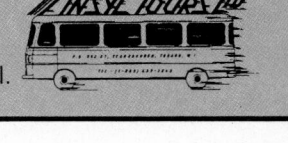

PASSPORT/VISA

Regulations and requirements may be subject to change at short notice, and you are advised to contact the appropriate diplomatic or consular authority before finalising travel arrangements. Details of these may be found at the head of this country's entry. Any numbers in the chart refer to the footnotes below.

	Passport Required?	Visa Required?	Return Ticket Required?
Full British	Yes	No	Yes
BVP	Not valid	-	-
Australian	Yes	Yes	Yes
Canadian	Yes	No	Yes
USA	Yes	No	Yes
Other EC	Yes	No	Yes
Japanese	Yes	Yes	Yes

Restricted entry: Passports issued by the Republic of South Africa are not valid for entry into Trinidad & Tobago. Alternative documentation may be accepted, and a visa issued, in some circumstances. Advice should be sought from the Embassy, Consulate or High Commission.
PASSPORTS: Valid passport required by all persons 16 years and over. Passports must be valid at least for the duration of stay and visitors must be in possession of a valid return ticket to their country of residence or citizenship and sufficient funds to maintain themselves whilst in Trinidad & Tobago.
British Visitors Passport: Not accepted.
VISAS: Required by all except:
(a) nationals of EC countries;
(b) nationals of the USA arriving as tourists for a stay not exceeding 2 months;
(c) nationals of Antigua & Barbuda, Austria, Bahamas, Bangladesh, Barbados, Belize, Botswana, Brazil, Canada, Colombia, Cyprus, Dominica, Finland, Gambia, Ghana, Grenada, Guyana, Iceland, Israel, Jamaica, Kenya, Kiribati, Lesotho, Liechtenstein, Malawi, Malaysia, Malta, Mauritius, Nauru, Norway, St Kitts & Nevis, St Lucia, St Vincent & the Grenadines, Seychelles, Sierra Leone, Singapore, Solomon Islands, Sweden, Swaziland, Switzerland, Tonga, Turkey, Tuvalu, Vanuatu, Western Samoa, Zambia and Zimbabwe for a stay not exceeding 3 months;
(d) nationals of Venezuela arriving from Venezuela for a stay not exceeding 14 days.
Types of visa: Tourist. Cost: £8.
Validity: 3 months.
Application to: Consulate (or Consular Section at Embassy or High Commission). For addresses, see top of entry.
Working days required: Tourist visas will normally be issued within 48 hours. Applications from the following nationals must be made at least 3-4 weeks prior to the proposed date of departure: Albania, Bulgaria, China, Cuba, Czechoslovakia, Hungary, North Korea, Poland, Romania, Taiwan, USSR, Vietnam and Yugoslavia.
Temporary residence: Enquire at Embassy or High Commission.

MONEY

Currency: Trinidad & Tobago Dollar (TT$) = 100 cents. Notes are in denominations of TT$100, 20, 10, 5 and 1. Coins are in denominations of TT$1, and 50, 25, 10, 5 and 1 cents.
Currency exchange: Foreign currency can only be exchanged at authorised banks and some hotels. Delay may be experienced in obtaining foreign exchange, though banks are authorised to sell up to £50 in sterling notes for legitimate travelling requirements.
Credit cards: Access/Mastercard, Diners Club, American Express and Visa are accepted by selected banks, shops and tourist facilities. Check with your credit card company for details of merchant acceptability and other services which may be available.
Travellers cheques: These are very widely accepted and will often prove the most convenient means of transaction. Banks charge a fee for exchanging travellers

TRINIDAD & TOBAGO | **HEALTH REGULATIONS** | **VISA REGULATIONS** | Code-Link

GALILEO/WORLDSPAN

TI-DFT/POS/HE

TI-DFT/POS/VI

SABRE

TIDFT/POS/HE

TIDFT/POS/VI

To access this information on your CRS, swipe the barcode with a light pen or type in the text under the barcode. For more information, see the introduction *How to Use This Book*.

cheques. Check for the best rates.
Exchange rate indicators: The following figures are included as a guide to the movements of the Trinidad & Tobago Dollar against Sterling and the US Dollar:

Date:	Oct '89	Oct '90	Oct '91	Oct '92
£1.00=	6.72	8.86	7.38	7.20
$1.00=	4.26	4.25	4.25	4.53

Currency restrictions: The import of local currency is limited to TT$200. The export of local currency is limited to TT$2500. There is free import of foreign currency, subject to declaration. The export of foreign currency is limited to the amount declared on entry.
Banking hours: 0900-1400 Monday to Thursday, 0900-1200 and 1500-1700 Friday.

DUTY FREE

The following goods may be imported into Trinidad & Tobago by persons over 17 years of age without incurring customs duty:
200 cigarettes or 50 cigars or 250g of tobacco;
1 litre of wine or spirits;
Gifts up to the value of TT$50.

PUBLIC HOLIDAYS

Public holidays observed in Trinidad & Tobago are as follows:
Mar 25 '93 Start of Eid al-Fitr. **Apr 9** Good Friday. **Apr 12** Easter Monday. **May 31** Whit Monday. **Jun 10** Corpus Christi. **Jun 19** Labour Day. **Aug 1** Emancipation Day. **Aug 31** Independence Day. **Sep 24** Republic Day. **Oct** Divali. **Dec 25-26** Christmas. **Jan 1 '94** New Year's Day. **Feb/Mar** Carnival. **Mar** Start of Eid al-Fitr.
Note: (a) See *Special Events* in the *Profile* section for details of Carnival. (b) Muslim festivals are timed according to local sightings of various phases of the Moon and the dates given above are approximations. During the lunar month of Ramadan that precedes Eid al-Fitr, Muslims fast during the day and feast at night and normal business patterns may be interrupted. Many restaurants are closed during the day and there may be restrictions on smoking and drinking. Some disruption may continue into Eid al-Fitr itself. Eid al-Fitr and Eid al-Adha may last anything from two to ten days, depending on the region. For more information see the section *World of Islam* at the back of the book. (c) Hindu festivals are declared according to local astronomical observations and it is only possible to forecast the month of their occurrence.

HEALTH

Regulations and requirements may be subject to change at short notice, and you are advised to contact your doctor well in advance of your intended date of departure. Any numbers in the chart refer to the footnotes below.

	Special Precautions?	Certificate Required?
Yellow Fever	No	1
Cholera	No	No
Typhoid & Polio	Yes	-
Malaria	No	-
Food & Drink	2	-

[1]: A yellow fever vaccination certificate is required of travellers over one year of age arriving from infected areas.
[2]: Mains water is normally chlorinated, and whilst relatively safe may cause mild abdominal upsets. Bottled water is available and is advised for the first few weeks of the stay. Drinking water outside main cities and towns may be contaminated and sterilisation is advisable. Milk is pasteurised and dairy products are safe for consumption. Local meat, poultry, seafood, fruit and vegetables are generally considered safe to eat.
Rabies is present. For those at high risk, vaccination before arrival should be considered. If you are bitten abroad seek medical advice without delay. Bats are a problem as far as the transmission of rabies is concerned. For more information consult the *Health* section at the back of the book.
Health care: Health insurance is recommended. There is one doctor for every 1500 inhabitants.

TRAVEL - International

AIR: Trinidad & Tobago's national airline is *BWIA (BW)*. *BWIA* fly to other Caribbean islands and to several towns on the South American coast. *LIAT (LI)* also offer inter-Caribbean flights.
Approximate flight times: From *Barbados* to Port of Spain is 45 minutes.
From *London* is 10 hours 30 minutes (with a further 30-minute flight to Scarborough, Tobago).
From *New York* is 10 hours 20 minutes and from *St Lucia* is 50 minutes.
International airport: *Port of Spain (POS)* is 25.5km (16 miles) southeast of the city. There are taxis to the city for hotels throughout the island with set fares posted in taxis. Fares increase after midnight. Sharing taxis is an accepted practice. Buses operate to Port of Spain. Airport facilities include a duty-free shop.
Departure tax: TT$50 is levied on international departures. Transit passengers and children under five years of age are exempt.
SEA: The main ports are Port of Spain, Point-à-Pierre and Point Lisas.

TRAVEL - Internal

AIR: There are regular flights run by *BWIA* to Scarborough *(Crown Point Airport)* on Tobago, 13km (8 miles) south of the town. Flights are usually every hour, with some night services. During peak seasons these are often heavily booked.
SEA: There is a regular car ferry/passenger service from Port of Spain to Tobago (Scarborough) (travel time – 5 hours). The day journey gives a good view of the two islands but the night journey can be uncomfortable. Return by plane is recommended; fares are quite low.
ROAD: The road network in Trinidad between major towns is good. Two major highways run north–south and east–west. Off major routes roads are very unpredictable, and all are susceptible to poor weather conditions. **Bus:** Services are operated by the state *Public Service Corporation (PTSC)*. In the absence of a railway, the main towns are served by bus but although cheap, they are crowded and unreliable. The use of shared taxis has increased due to the shortcomings of the bus network; these are available both outside and within Port of Spain. **Taxi:** All taxis have registration 'H'. *Route* taxis serve standard routes within Trinidad & Tobago. These have fixed rates. **Car hire:** Cars and motorcycles are available in Port of Spain or Scarborough, and can be arranged via hotels. **Documentation:** Visitors in possession of a valid driving permit issued in any of the countries listed below may drive in Trinidad & Tobago for a period of up to three months. They are, however, entitled to drive only a motor vehicle of the class specified on their permit. Drivers must at all times have in their possession (a) their National Driver's Permit and (b) any travel document on which is certified their date of arrival in Trinidad & Tobago. Visitors whose stay exceeds the 3-month period are requested to apply to the Licensing Department, Wrightson Road, Port of Spain, for a local Driving Permit. The above information applies to all signatories to the Convention on International Driver's Permits including: USA, Canada, France, UK, Germany and the Bahamas. *Excluded:* China, South Africa and Vietnam.
URBAN: Due to the deterioration of bus services, most public transport journeys in Port of Spain are now made by shared taxis, which may take the form of either cars or minibuses. They serve specific zones, and are coloured accordingly. Zone fares are standardised. Basic operations are on fixed routes, with pick-ups at central points, but they can also be hailed anywhere along the route; drivers will often sound their horns to indicate that there is room in the vehicles. The taxis will generally not start the journey until full. Most route taxis terminate at points around Independence Square, Port of Spain. Other roaming taxis are much more expensive, and rates should be agreed in advance. The Tourism Development Authority publishes a list of fares for standard routes.

ACCOMMODATION

HOTELS: There are major international chain hotels in Port of Spain, and a number of smaller hotels in the surrounding areas. Resort hotels are recommended, especially in Tobago. There is a wide range of prices. For further information contact The Trinidad & Tobago Hotel and Tourism Association (for address, see top of entry). There is a 10% Government room tax and VAT levied.
GUEST-HOUSES: The Tourism Development Authority publishes a list of guest-houses found throughout Trinidad & Tobago.
Note: All types of accommodation must be booked well in advance for the Carnival (see below under *Social Profile*).

RESORTS & EXCURSIONS

The home of carnival, steel bands, calypso and limbo dancing, Trinidad & Tobago's blend of different cultures give them an air of cosmopolitan excitement.

Trinidad

Port of Spain, surrounded by lush green hills, is the capital and business hub of oil-rich Trinidad. The city captures the variety of Trinidadian life, with bazaars thronging beneath modern skyscrapers and mosques rubbing shoulders with cathedrals. The architecture of the city incorporates a mixture of styles: these include Victorian houses with gingerbread fretwork; the *German Renaissance Queen's Royal College; Stollmeyer's Castle*, an imitation of a Rhine fortress; the President of the Republic's residence and the Prime Minister's office at **Whitehall** (both built in Moorish style); and the 19th-century Gothic *Holy Trinity Cathedral*. Places of interest include the shopping district centred on Frederick Street; the *Royal Botanic Gardens;* the *Red House* (a stately colonial building now the seat of government); and the *National Museum* and *Art Gallery*.
Queen's Park Savannah, a magnificent park just to the north of the capital and well within walking distance, is spread out at the foot of the Northern Range. A mixture of natural and manmade beauty, with attractive trees and shrubs (including the African Tulip, or 'Flame of the Forest'), it forms a backdrop to a racecourse and playing fields and the elaborate mansions, now mostly government offices.
On the outskirts of the city is *Fort George*. Built in 1804, it offers an excellent view of Port of Spain and the mountains of northern Venezuela.
Maracas Bay, Las Cuevas and *Chaguaramas* are the nearest beaches to the Port of Spain.
13km (8 miles) to the south of the capital by road and boat is the *Caroni Bird Sanctuary*, home of the Scarlet Ibis (see also below under 'Wildlife'). The *Diego Mountain Valley*, 16km (10 miles) from Port of Spain, contains one of the island's most beautiful water wheels. In the village of **Chaguanas** it is possible to sample the most exotic of West Indian culinary specialities. **Ariman** the third largest town on the island has an *Amerindian Museum* at the *Cleaver Woods Recreation Centre* on the west side of town. About 8 miles north is the *Asa Wright Nature Centre* at **Blanchisseuse**, containing a collection of rare bird specimens such as the Oilbird or *Guacharo*. The *Aripo Caves* are noted for their stalactites and stalagmites.
On the east coast is *Valencia*, a lush tropical forest near the Hollis Reservoir. **Cocal** and **Mayaro** are also worth visiting.
San Fernando is the island's second town. Close by is the fascinating natural phenomenon of the *Pitch Lake*, a 90-acre lake of asphalt which constantly replenishes itself.

Tobago

Tobago is very different from its larger neighbour 32km (20 miles) away. It is a tranquil island with calm waters and vast stretches of white sand beaches. The capital, **Scarborough**, has many quaint houses which spill down from the hilltop to the waterside, as well as interesting *Botanic Gardens*. It is overshadowed by the *King George Fort*, built in 1779 during the many struggles between the French and the English, an excellent point from which to view the sunset. Nearby is the small town of **Plymouth** with its tombstone inscriptions dating from 1700.
There are a number of fine beaches. They include *Pigeon Point* on the southwest coast (admission is charged); *Store Bay*, where brown pelicans can be seen diving into the waters to catch fish; *Man O'War Bay*, at the opposite end of the island, and *Mount Irvine* and *Bacolet Bays*. *Buccoo Reef* is an extensive coral reef lying a mile offshore from Pigeon Point. Excursions can be made in glass-bottomed boats and it is an excellent place for snorkelling.
At *Fort James* there is a well-maintained red brick building, and at *Whim*, a large plantation house. *Arnos Vale Hotel* is a former sugar plantation, now an hotel; a disused sugar mill fitted out with formidable crushing wheels, made in 1857, is still in the grounds. Birdwatching is a favourite pastime here.
Charlotteville is a fishing town commanding precipitous views of the headlands. Looming above the town is *Pigeon Peak*, the highest point on the island. There are good swimming beaches in the region. *Tobago Forest Reserve* has many trails which provide excellent long hikes for the more active visitor.
On the Atlantic side of the island are the tiny villages of **Mesopotamia**, **Goldsborough** and **Roxborough** and several beautiful bays. **Speyside** is a colourful beach settlement, from which can be seen tiny **Goat Island** and **Little Tobago,** a 450-acre bird sanctuary.

Wildlife

These islands have a unique wealth of wild birds and flowers, butterflies and fish, mostly undisturbed, yet accessible. The island boasts no less than 622 species of **butterfly** and over 700 species of **orchid**. The latter are perhaps best seen in Trinidad's *Botanic Gardens* in Port of Spain (along with a wide selection of indigenous trees, shrubs, ferns and cacti). The *Emperor Valley Zoo* has a similarly representative selection of local wildlife – reptile as well as mammal. Birdwatchers on Trinidad should head for the *Nariva Swamp*, the *Aripo Savannah* and the *Asa Wright Nature Centre* and look out in particular for the national bird, the **Scarlet Ibis**, conserved in the *Caroni Bird Sanctuary*. The sight of these scarlet birds flying in formation to roost before sundown is a stunning and colourful spectacle. While on Tobago a visit to *Little Tobago Island* is recommended. **Hummingbirds** are ubiquitous on Tobago; there are 19 recorded species, seven of which are unique to the island. Beneath the waters of the Caribbean is a spectacular treasure trove of tropical fish and coral gardens lying easily visible just below the waters' surface, the *Buccoo Reef*.

SOCIAL PROFILE

FOOD & DRINK: Bars and restaurants open until late, with a very wide choice of local and Western food and drink. Chinese, Indian and West Indian cooking is available in Trinidad. British, American and Creole cooking is available in Tobago, as well as some notable seafood specialities such as lobster, conch and jackfish. Local dishes include pilau rice and Creole soups, the best being *sans coche*, *calaloo* and peppery pigeon pea soup. *Tatoo, manicou*, pork souse, green salad, *tum-tum* (mashed green plantains), roast venison, *lappe* (island rabbit), *quenk* (wild pig), wild duck and *pastelles* (meat folded into cornmeal and wrapped in a banana leaf) are also available. Seafood including bean-sized oysters, *chip-chip* (tiny shellfish similar in taste to clams) and crab *malete* is excellent, as is the freshwater fish *cascadou*. Indian dishes include *roti* (dough stuffed with chicken, fish or meat) and hot curries. **Drink:** Excellent rums and Angostura bitters are used to make rum punch. The local beers are *Carib* and *Stag*, which are best drunk very cold.
NIGHTLIFE: Trinidad has a wide and varied nightlife including hotel entertainment and nightclubs with *calypso*, limbo dancers and steel bands.
SHOPPING: Goods from all over the world can be found in Port of Spain, but local goods are always available. Special purchases include Calypso records, steel drums, leather bags and sandals, ceramics and woodcarvings. Gold and silver jewellery can be good value, as can Indian silks and fabrics. Rum should also be considered. Bright, printed fabrics and other summer garments are available in Trinidad & Tobago. **Shopping hours:** 0800-1600 Monday to Friday, 0800-1200 Saturday. Some shops stay open later in Port of Spain. Shops close on public holidays, especially during Carnival.
SPORT: Tennis: There are facilities at most large hotels for tennis. **Golf:** May be enjoyed just outside Port of Spain or in Tobago at the marvellous Mount Irvine Golf Course. **Fishing:** Fishing of all kinds from deep-sea to inland is widely available and usually rewarding on and off both islands. Kingfish, Spanish mackerel, wahoo, bonito, dolphin and yellow tuna are the usual catches, with grouper, salmon and snapper also to be found off the west and north coasts of Trinidad. **Cricket:** This is the major spectator sport and the season runs from February to June. The best national and international matches can be seen at the Queen's Park Oval, in Port of Spain. **Racing:** Trinidadians are great sportsmen and the Queen's Park Savannah hosts a number of major meetings, particularly around New Year and Easter. The meetings are well organised. **Watersports:** There are good facilities for all types of watersports, especially at the beaches along the north and east coasts of Trinidad, and all around Tobago. Buccoo Reef, just off the southwest coast of Tobago, offers exciting **scuba diving** with its magnificent coral formations and abundant marine life. Trips in glass-bottomed boats are very popular.
SPECIAL EVENTS: A vast mixture of races has led to a varied cultural life, the diversity of which is reflected in costume, religion, architecture, music, dance and place names.
The major event in Trinidad is the *Carnival*, renowned throughout the Caribbean and the rest of the world. The festivities climax at the beginning of Lent, on the two days immediately preceding Ash Wednesday, although the run-up to Carnival starts immediately after Christmas when the Calypso tents open and the Calypsonians perform their latest compositions and arrangements. During Carnival normal life grinds to a halt and the whole of Trinidad & Tobago is absorbed in the festivities.
A week before the Carnival proper, *Panorama* is staged. This is the Grand Steel Drum (pan) tournament; all the big steel bands parade their skills around the Savannah, the large park in the north of Port of Spain. *Hosay*, coinciding with the Muslim New Year, sees the Muslim population of Port of Spain, San Fernando and Tunapuna take to the streets in a festival of their own. Contact the Tourism Development Authority for dates of all of the above. The following is a selection of festivals and other special events celebrated in Trinidad & Tobago:
Mar 5-6 '93 *Tobago Jazz Festival*, Palm Tree Village, Tobago. **Mar 13-14** *National Flower Show*, Port of Spain. **Apr 17** *Fun Run*, Port of Spain. **May-Jun** *National Best Village Programme*. **May 2** *La Divina Pastora Festival*, Siparia. **May 9** *Trinidad & Tobago Song Festival*, St Ann's. **Jun** *Tobago Harvest Festival*, Tobago. **Jun 6** *Trinidad & Tobago Marathon*, Port of Spain. **Jun 6-13** *Week of Hockey*. **Jun-Jul** *Fishermans' Festival; St Peter's Day*, Carenage. **Jul 16-Aug 1** *Tobago Heritage Festival*, Tobago. **Jul-Aug** *Hosay; Sand Sculpture Competition*. **Aug 15** *Santa Rosa Festival*, Arima. **Sep 9-18** *Caribbean Cup Volleyball Championships*, Port of Spain. **Oct** *Ramleela Hindu Festival; National Flower Show; Orchid Show; School Steelband Music Festival*. **Oct 2-23** *National Indoor Hockey Championships*, Port of Spain. **Oct 24-30** *Amerindian Heritage Festival*, Arima. **Nov 11-13** *Trinidad & Tobago Pan Jazz Festival*. **Dec 12** *International Drag Racing*, Wallerfield.
Note: It is no exaggeration to say that the Trinidadians, like most of the people living in the Caribbean, are warm and friendly with an exuberant love of life. Nevertheless, visitors are well-advised to exercise care with their personal belongings during Carnival.
SOCIAL CONVENTIONS: *Liming*, or talking for talking's sake, is a popular pastime, as is talking about, watching and playing cricket. Many local attitudes are often reflected in the lyrics of the *calypso*, the accepted medium for political and social satire. Hospitality is important and entertaining is commonly done at home. Casual wear is usual with shirt sleeves generally accepted for business and social gatherings. Beachwear is not worn in towns. **Tipping:** Most hotels and guest-houses add 10% service charge to the bill, otherwise a 10-15% tip is usual in hotels and restaurants.

BUSINESS PROFILE

ECONOMY: The economy has steadily contracted since the early 1980s when the country's oil production, begun ten years earlier, started to decline. By way of compensation, however, large reserves of natural gas have been located and these have provided the raw material for the islands' burgeoning petrochemical industry in which the Government has rested many of its hopes for future economic development. The revenues have also been used to establish indigenous plastics and electronics industries. A major expansion of this sector was launched in 1991. Apart from oil and gas, Trinidad has the world's largest deposits of asphalt. The other important foreign exchange earner is tourism although this has not reached its full potential as the Government has been reluctant to make extensive investments. The agricultural sector is small with sugar as the main commodity. Once a net exporter of foodstuffs, Trinidad now imports the bulk of its requirements. Trinidad & Tobago is a member of the Caribbean economic union, CARICOM. The three largest exporters to Trinidad and Tobago are the USA, Japan and the UK. Machinery and transport equipment are the islands' main imports other than foodstuffs. In 1992, the Government announced a limited programme of privatisation.
BUSINESS: Lightweight suits or 'shirt jacks' should be worn. The best time to visit is from December to April, avoiding the Christmas festivities. **Office hours:** 0800-1600 Monday to Friday.
COMMERCIAL INFORMATION: The following organisation can offer advice: Trinidad and Tobago Chamber of Industry and Commerce, PO Box 499, 31 Frederick Street, Port of Spain. Tel: 623 1561. Fax: 623 5363. Telex: 22462.

HISTORY & GOVERNMENT

HISTORY: The history of Trinidad & Tobago is one of invasion and conquest from its first discovery in 1498 by Christopher Columbus, who claimed it for Spain. A Spanish colony was founded on Trinidad in 1532 but was destroyed by Sir Walter Raleigh in 1595. Subsequently it was raided by the Dutch, the French (with the Spanish as their allies on this occasion) and finally the British, which resulted in the island's being ceded to the British Crown in 1802. Tobago's history was equally stormy after the Spaniards first defeated the native Caribs. After many attempts to settle there by the English, French, Dutch and various pirates of indeterminate nationality, the island was finally ceded to the British in 1877. In 1888 Tobago was politically amalgamated with Trinidad, and after the break-up of the West Indian Federation the islands were granted full independence in 1962. The islands' leading political figure since then has been Eric Williams, who served as Prime Minister from independence until his death in 1981. His party, the People's National Movement (PNM), won every general election from independence until the mid-1980s. At the general election in 1986, the 3-year-old National Alliance for Reconstruction, a coalition of four opposition parties under the leadership of Arthur Robinson, formed a government for the first time. Since then, the parlous condition of the economy has preoccupied the Robinson administration. The low level of the world oil price has done considerable damage to Trinidad's finances, although Trinidad has benefited from the introduction of a single market by the Caribbean Common Market (CARICOM) in 1988. The domestic political arena was relatively quiet until July 1990 when an attempted coup was staged by a 100-strong fanatical Muslim group led by a Trinidadian, one Yasim Abu Bakr. For five days, the group held the Government building and the nearby television centre from where they broadcast their various demands and threats to kill the hostages which they had taken, including Prime Minister Robinson. Although the coup was successfully beaten, at the cost of a handful of fatalities and the destruction of a few parts of the city, Trinidad's political innocence was swept away. In December 1991, a year and a half after surviving the coup attempt, Arthur Robinson and the NAR were heavily defeated at the polls by the People's National Movement whose leader Patrick Manning has taken over as Prime Minister.
GOVERNMENT: The President is the Constitutional Head of State, with executive power vested in a Prime Minister and a Cabinet. Parliament is bicameral, comprising the Senate, with 31 appointed members, and the House of Representatives, with 36 members elected by universal adult suffrage. Since 1980, Tobago has had its own 15-seat House of Assembly, with 12 members elected and 3 selected by the ruling party. The island was granted full internal self-government in January 1987.

CLIMATE

The tropical climate is tempered by northeast trade winds. The dry season is from November to May, but it is hottest between June and October.
Required clothing: Tropical lightweights are required. Rainwear is advisable, especially for the wet season.

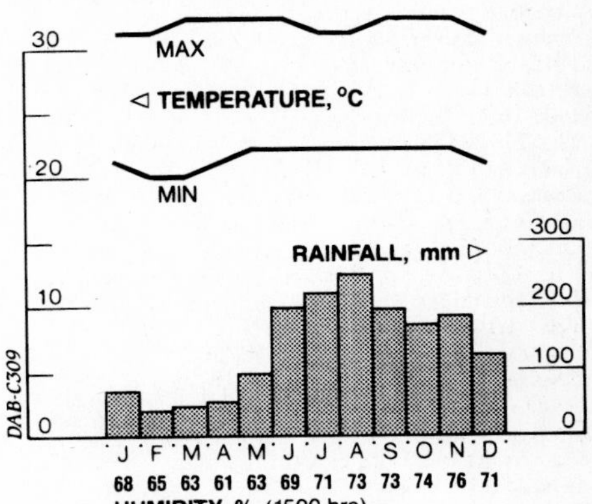

TUNISIA

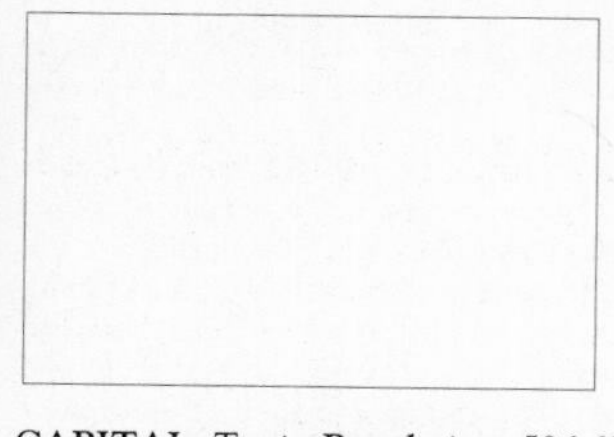

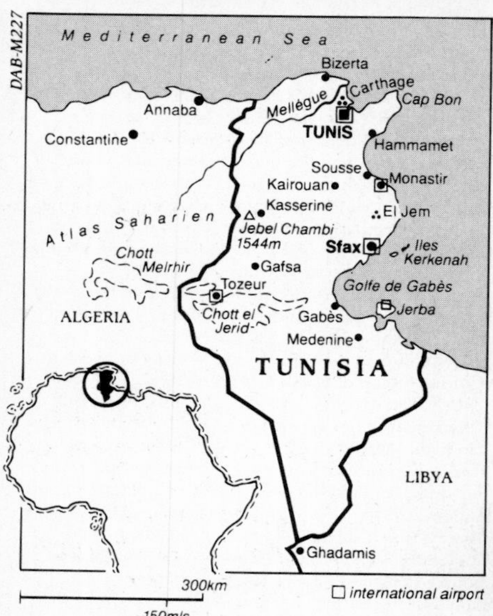

Location: North Africa.

Office National du Tourisme Tunisien
1 avenue Mohamed V
Tunis, Tunisia
Tel: (1) 341 077. Fax: (1) 350 997. Telex: 14381.

Embassy of the Republic of Tunisia
29 Prince's Gate
London SW7 1QG
Tel: (071) 584 8117. Fax: (071) 225 2884. Telex: 23736.
General opening hours: 0900-1630 Monday to Friday.
Opening hours for visa enquiries: 0930-1300 Monday to Friday.

Tunisian National Tourist Office
77a Wigmore Street
London W1H 9LJ
Tel: (071) 224 5561 (enquiries) *or* 224 5598 (administration). Fax: (071) 224 4053. Telex: 261368 TTOLDN.
Opening hours: 0930-1730 Monday to Friday.

British Embassy
5 place de la Victoire
Tunis, Tunisia
Tel: (1) 245 100 *or* 245 649 *or* 245 324. Fax: 354 877.
Telex: 14007 PRDROM TN.

Embassy of the Republic of Tunisia
1515 Massachusetts Avenue, NW
Washington, DC
20005
Tel: (202) 862 1850. Fax: (202) 862 1858.
Consulate in: San Francisco.

Embassy of the United States of America
144 avenue de la Liberté
Belvédère
1002 Tunis, Tunisia
Tel: (1) 782 566. Fax: (1) 789 719. Telex: 13379 AMTUN TN.

Embassy of the Republic of Tunisia
515 O' Connor Street
Ottawa, Ontario
K1S 3P8
Tel: (613) 237 0330 *or* 237 0332. Fax: (613) 237 7939.
Telex: 053 4161.
Consulate in: Montréal.

Canadian Embassy
PO Box 31
3 rue du Sénégal
Place d'Afrique
Belvédère
Tunis, Tunisia
Tel: (1) 286 577 *or* 286 337 *or* 286 619. Fax: (1) 792 371.
Telex: 15324 DOMCAN TN.

AREA: 154,000 sq km (59,460 sq miles).
POPULATION: 8,200,000 (1991 estimate).
POPULATION DENSITY: 53.3 per sq km.

CAPITAL: Tunis. **Population:** 596,654 (1984).
GEOGRAPHY: The Republic of Tunisia lies on the Mediterranean coast of Africa, 130km (80 miles) southwest of Sicily and 160km (100 miles) due south of Sardinia. The landscape varies from the cliffs of the north coast to the woodlands of the interior, from deep valleys of rich arable land to desert, and from towering mountains to salt pans lower than sea level. South of Gafsa and Gabès is the Sahara desert. The 1100km (700 miles) of coastline is dotted with small islands, notably Jerbain the south and Kerkenah in the east, and from the northwest to the southeast the coastline is backed successively by pine-clad hills, lush pasture, orchards, vineyards and olive groves.
LANGUAGE: The official language is Arabic. A knowledge of French is essential for business travellers and useful for tourists – it is taught as a second language in schools. English is spoken in major cities and resorts.
RELIGION: The principal religion is Islam; there are Roman Catholic and Protestant minorities.
TIME: GMT + 1.
ELECTRICITY: 220 volts AC, 50Hz. A 2-pin continental plug/adaptor is needed.
COMMUNICATIONS: Telephone: Full IDD is available. Country code: 216. Automatic dialling extends to almost every part of the country and covers direct international calls. Area codes for major cities and towns: Tunis 1, Bizerte and Menzel Bourguiba 2, Sousse 3, Gabès 5, Kairouan 7. **Fax:** Facilities are available in main towns. **Telex/telegram:** The Telecommunications Centre in Tunis (29 Jamal Abdelnasser) is equipped with a public telex system. Telegraph facilities are available at the Central Post Office at rue Charles de Gaulle, Tunis. **Post:** Airmail to Europe takes three to five days. *Post Restante* facilities are available in main cities. Post office hours: *Summer* (approximately June 15-September 15): 0800-1300 Monday to Saturday. *Winter* (approximately September 16-June 15): 0800-1200 and 1400-1800 Monday to Friday, 0800-1200

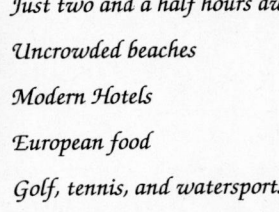

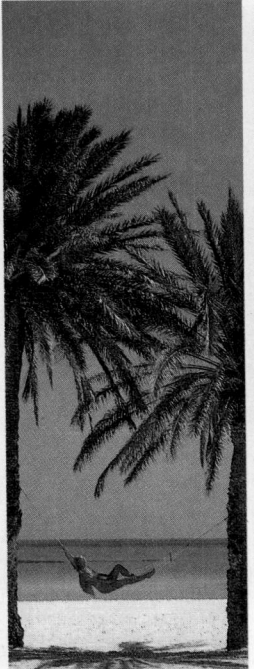

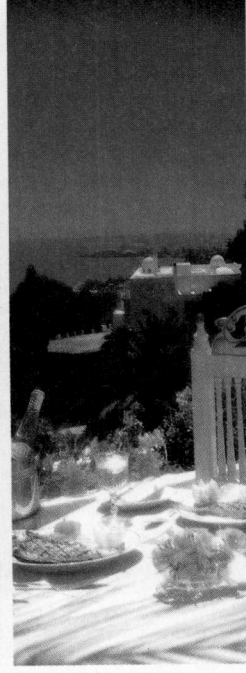

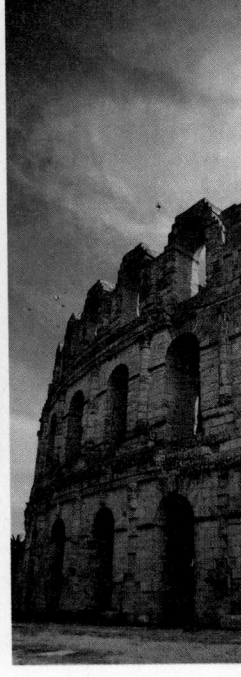

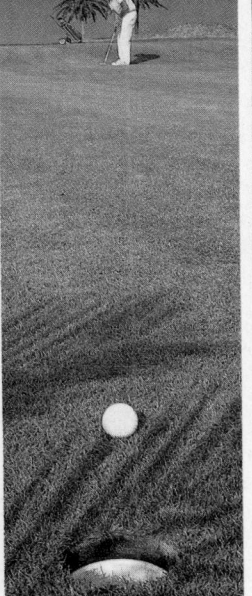

Saturday. *During Ramadan:* 0800-1500 Monday to Saturday. **Press:** Daily newspapers are printed in Arabic or French, the most popular being *As-Sabah*, *L'Action*, *Al-Amal* and *La Presse*.
BBC World Service and Voice of America frequencies: From time to time these change. See the section *How to Use this Book* for more information.

BBC:				
MHz	21.71	15.07	12.10	9.410
Voice of America:				
MHz	21.49	15.60	9.525	6.035

PASSPORT/VISA

Regulations and requirements may be subject to change at short notice, and you are advised to contact the appropriate diplomatic or consular authority before finalising travel arrangements. Details of these may be found at the head of this country's entry. Any numbers in the chart refer to the footnotes below.

	Passport Required?	Visa Required?	Return Ticket Required?
Full British	1	No	Yes
BVP	Valid	-	-
Australian	Yes	Yes	Yes
Canadian	Yes	No	Yes
USA	Yes	No	Yes
Other EC	Yes	No	Yes
Japanese	Yes	No	Yes

Restricted entry: Holders of Israeli and South African passports are refused entry.
PASSPORTS: [1] Valid passport required by all except UK nationals in possession of a British Visitors Passport.
British Visitors Passport: Acceptable. BVPs may be used for holidays or unpaid business trips of up to three months.
VISAS: Required by all except:
(a) nationals of countries referred to in the chart above;
(b) nationals of Algeria, Antigua & Barbuda, Austria, Bahrain, Barbados, Belize, Bermuda, Brunei, Bulgaria, Chile, Côte d'Ivoire, Dominica, Fiji, Finland, Gambia, Ghana, Guinea Republic, Hong Kong, Iceland, Kiribati, Kuwait, Libya, Liechtenstein, Malaysia, Mali, Malta, Mauritania, Mauritius, Monaco, Montserrat, Morocco, Niger, Norway, Oman, Qatar, Romania, St Kitts & Nevis, St Lucia, St Vincent & Grenadines, San Marino, Saudi Arabia, Senegal, Seychelles, Solomon Islands, South Korea, Sweden, Switzerland, Turkey, United Arab Emirates, Vatican City and Yugoslavia.
Check with the Embassy for details of length of stay.
Types of visa: Tourist and Transit. Cost: £3.71.
Note: Transit visas are not required for passengers holding confirmed onward tickets and travel documents valid for departure within 48 hours (24 hours for nationals of People's Republic of China, Lebanon and Syria) by the same or first connecting flight provided they do not leave the airport.
Validity: *Tourist:* up to 4 months; *Transit:* 7 days.
Application to: Consulate (or Consular Section at Embassy). For addresses, see top of entry.
Application requirements: (a) Valid passport. (b) 2 completed application forms. (c) 2 photos.
Working days required: 2-3 weeks, for both postal and personal applications.
Temporary residence: Apply to Ministry of Interior, avenue Habib Bourquiba, Tunis, Tunisia.

MONEY

Currency: Tunisian Dinar (TD) = 1000 millimes. Notes are in denominations of TD20, 10 and 5. Coins are in denominations of TD1, and 500, 100, 50, 20, 10 and 5 millimes.
Currency exchange: All banks change money, as do most hotels of three stars and above.
Credit cards: Access/Mastercard, American Express, Diners Club and Visa are widely accepted. Check with your credit card company for details of merchant acceptability and other services which may be available.
Travellers cheques: Readily cashed in banks and the usual authorised establishments.
Exchange rate indicators: The following figures are included as a guide to the movements of the Tunisian Dinar against Sterling and the US Dollar:

Date:	Oct '89	Oct '90	Oct '91	Oct '92
£1.00=	1.52	1.66	1.64	1.41
$1.00=	0.96	0.85	0.94	0.89

Currency restrictions: The import and export of local currency is strictly prohibited. The import of foreign

TUNISIA	HEALTH REGULATIONS	VISA REGULATIONS Code-Link
GALILEO/WORLDSPAN	 TI-DFT/TUN/HE	 TI-DFT/TUN/VI
SABRE	 TIDFT/TUN/HE	TIDFT/TUN/VI

To access this information on your CRS, swipe the barcode with a light pen or type in the text under the barcode. For more information, see the introduction *How to Use This Book*.

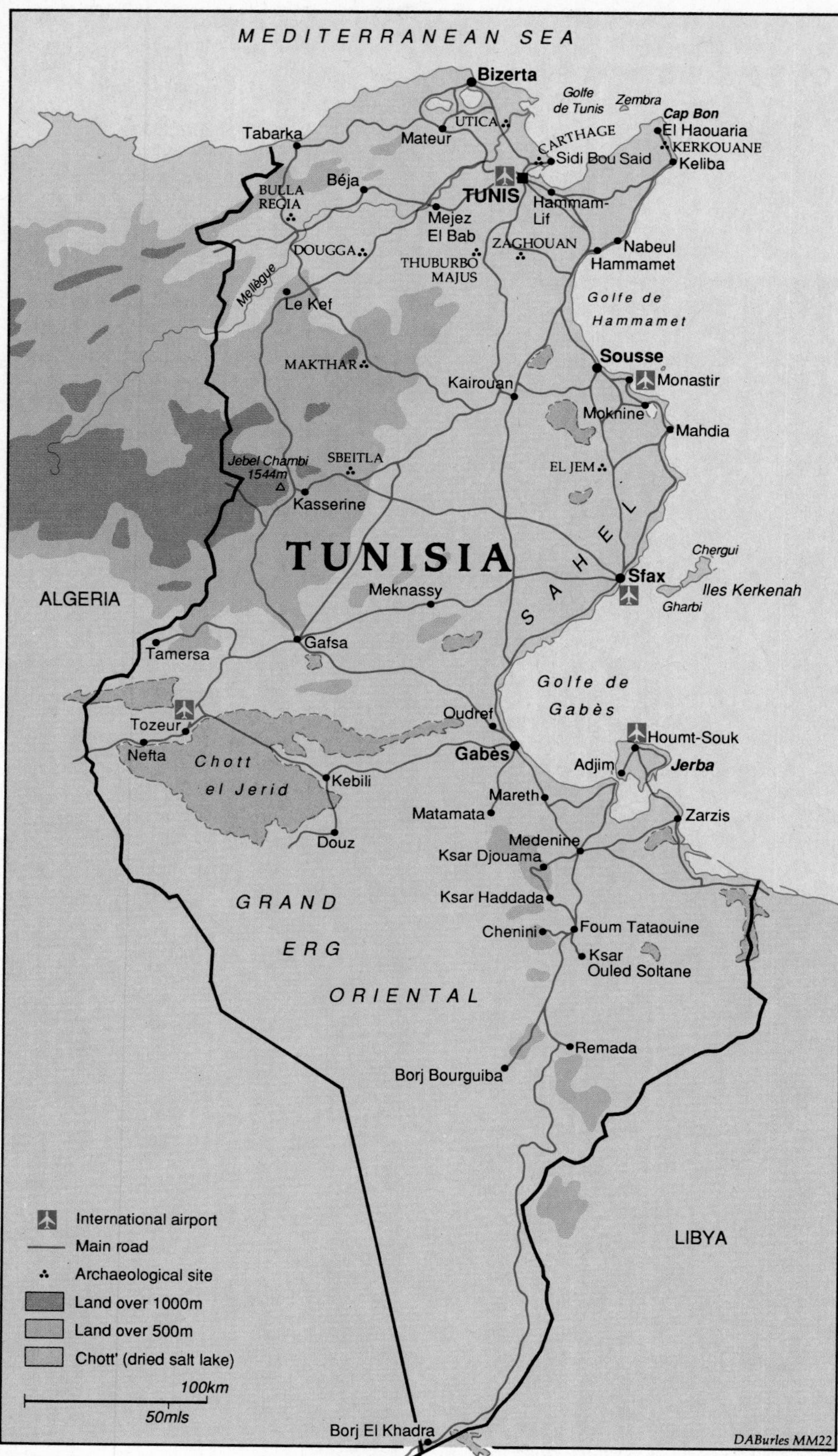

currency is unlimited, although amounts over the value of TD500 must be declared. The export of foreign currency is limited to the amount imported. All currency documentation must be retained. Reconversion of local into foreign currency is possible for up to 30% of total foreign currency imported or TD100 per person, whichever is the larger.
Note: Tunisian currency is not valid in duty-free shops.
Banking hours: 0730-1100 Monday to Friday (summer); 0800-1100 and 1400-1600 Monday to Thursday, 0800-1130 and 1300-1515 Friday (winter).

DUTY FREE

The following goods may be imported into Tunisia without incurring customs duty:
400 cigarettes or 100 cigars or 500g of tobacco;
1 litre of spirits of more than 25% alcohol;
2 litres of alcoholic beverages of up to 25% alcohol;
0.25 litres of toilet water;
Gifts up to value of TD10.

PUBLIC HOLIDAYS

Public holidays observed in Tunisia are as follows:
Mar 20 '93 Independence Day. **Mar 21** Youth Day. **Mar 24** Aid el-Seghir (End of Ramadan). **Apr 9** Martyr's Day. **May 1** Labour Day. **May 31** Aid el-Kebir. **Jun 21** Ras El Am Hejri (Muslim New Year's Day). **Jul 25** Republic Day. **Aug 13** Women's Day. **Aug 29** Mouloud (Prophet's Birthday). **Nov 7** New Era Day. **Jan 1 '94** New Year's Day. **Mar 20** Independence Day. **Mar 21** Youth Day. **Mar** Aid el-Seghir (End of Ramadan).
Note: Muslim festivals are timed according to local sightings of various phases of the Moon and the dates given above are approximations. During the lunar month of Ramadan that precedes Aid el-Seghir (Eid al-Fitr), Muslims fast during the day and feast at night and normal business patterns may be interrupted. Many restaurants are closed during the day and there may be restrictions on smoking and drinking. Some disruption may continue into Aid el-Seghir itself. Aid el-Seghir and Aid el-Kebir (Eid al-Adha) may last anything from two to ten days, depending on the region. For more information see the section *World of Islam* at the back of the book.

HEALTH

Regulations and requirements may be subject to change at short notice, and you are advised to contact your doctor well in advance of your intended date of departure. Any numbers in the chart refer to the footnotes below.

	Special Precautions?	Certificate Required?
Yellow Fever	No	1
Cholera	Yes	2
Typhoid & Polio	Yes	-
Malaria	No	-
Food & Drink	3	-

[1]: A yellow fever certificate is required from travellers over one year of age arriving from infected areas.
[2]: Following WHO guidelines issued in 1973, a cholera vaccination certificate is not a condition of entry to Tunisia. However, cholera is a risk in this country and precautions are essential. Up-to-date advice should be sought before deciding whether these precautions should include vaccination, as medical opinion is divided over its effectiveness. See the *Health* section at the back of the book.
[3]: Mains water is normally chlorinated, and whilst safe may cause mild abdominal upsets. Bottled water is available and is advised for the first few weeks of the stay. Drinking water outside main cities and towns is likely to be contaminated and sterilisation is considered essential. Milk is unpasteurised and should be boiled. Powdered or tinned milk is available and is advised but make sure that it is reconstituted with pure water. Avoid dairy products which are likely to have been made from unboiled milk. Only eat well-cooked meat and fish, preferably served hot. Pork, salad and mayonnaise may carry increased risk. Vegetables should be cooked and fruit peeled.
Rabies is present. For those at high risk, vaccination before arrival should be considered. If you are bitten abroad seek medical advice without delay. For more information consult the *Health* section at the back of the book.
Health care: Health insurance is recommended. Tunisia has a comparatively well-developed public health service and 70% of the population qualify for free medical treatment. There is one doctor for every 7000 inhabitants.

TRAVEL - International

AIR: The national airline is *Tunis Air (TU)*.
Approximate flight times: From London to *Tunis* is 2 hours 30 minutes, to *Jerba*is 3 hours, to *Monastir* is 2 hours 45 minutes and to *Sfax* is 3 hours.
International airports: *Tunis (TUN)* (Carthage International) is 8km (5 miles) northeast of the city (travel time – 10 minutes). There is a duty-free shop open both to incoming and outgoing passengers. Five banks are open all day for currency exchange, and at least one remains open for night flights. An airport–city coach service operates every 15 minutes, and buses depart every 30 minutes. Return is from Hotel Africa Meridien (city air terminal). Taxis are available; a surcharge is levied at night.
Jerba (DJE) (Melita) is 8km (5 miles) from the city.
Monastir (MIR) (Skanes) is 8km (5 miles) from the city.
Sfax (SFA) is 15km (8 miles) from the city.
Tozeur (TOE) (Nefta) is 10km (6 miles) from the city.
All the above airports have bars, restaurants and both incoming and outgoing duty-free shops. Taxis are available at all the airports.
Departure tax: TD4.50.
Note: Tunisian currency is *not* valid in duty-free shops.
SEA: There are regular shipping services from France and Italy to Tunisia. All the shipping lines have representatives in European cities. For details contact the National Tourist Office. The following are major routes and journey times:
Marseilles–Tunis: 21-24 hours.
Genoa–Tunis: 21-24 hours.
Naples–Tunis: 21-24 hours.
Palermo–Tunis: 10 hours.
Sicily (Trepani)–Kelibia: 3 hours [1]
Note [1]: hydrofoil July-September.
RAIL: There is a rail link from Tunis to Algiers (subject to closures due to the political situation in Algeria; check before departure).
ROAD: There are several points of entry by road from Algeria, normally served by buses and long-distance

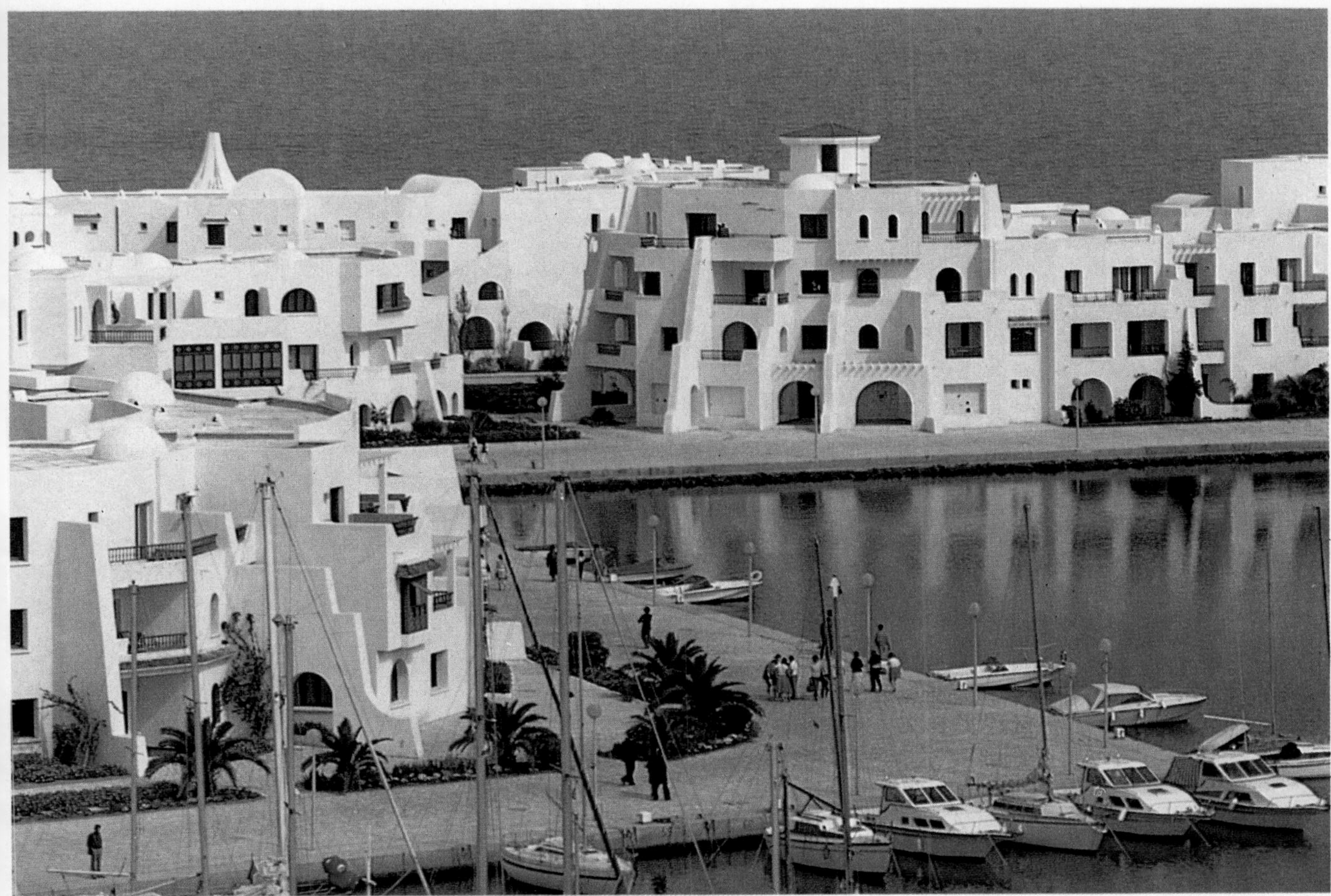

taxis: Annaba (in Algeria) to Tabaka (following the coast road); Souk Ahras (in Algeria) to Ghardimaou; and El Oued (Algeria) to Gafsa. Entry by road from Libya is via the coast road at Gabès, via Ben Gardane and Ras Agedir.
See below for information on **documentation**.

TRAVEL - Internal

AIR: Regular daily services run six times daily between Tunis and Jerba airports (flight time – 1 hour 5 minutes). There is a daily flight to Sfax from Tunis and two on Wednesday and Thursday, and a weekly flight to Monastir. Tozeur is served from Tunis by two flights on Monday and one on Thursday, Friday, Saturday and Sunday. A new set of flights will run from Tunis to the newly-opened airport at Tabarka. All the above services are operated by the domestic airline *Tuninter*, represented internationally by *Tunis Air*. Prices are reasonable and services are normally heavily subscribed, so it is advisable to book ahead. Air taxis are operated by *Tunis Avia*. For details contact *Tunis Avia*, 19 ave Habib Bourguiba, Tunis. Tel: 254 239.
SEA: Ferries operate between Sfax and the Kerkenah Islands twice daily, and between Jorf and Jerba Island regularly during the day.
RAIL: Regular trains (run by the SNCFT) connect Tunis, Hammamet, Nabeul, Sousse, Sfax, Sbeitla, Kasserine, Mateur, Bizerte, Tabarka, Beja, Ghardimaou, Zarzis, Gabès and Medenine. It is essential to purchase a ticket before boarding the train, or the traveller will have to pay double the fare. Several daily trains run on each route, many with air-conditioned accommodation and a buffet. It is highly advisable to book in advance, if possible, especially for the more popular air-conditioned routes.
Tunis–Gabès: A special business-class service runs between Tunis and Gabès, offering very comfortable accommodation and music.
Cheap fares: A reduction is made on round-trip tickets and children (4-10 years) travel at half price.
ROAD: Tunisia has a widespread road network. In case of breakdown, the *Garde Nationale* (National Guard) will assist free of charge (they usually contact the nearest garage). **Bus:** *Societé Nationale des Transports* and other buses connect all the main cities and towns. Inter-city bus services are cheap and reasonably comfortable. Passengers are allowed 10kg of luggage without additional charge. Each piece of luggage must, however, be registered. The major (but far from insurmountable) difficulty for most tourists will be finding out which bus is going where. **Taxi:** Long-distance taxis (usually large Mercedes or similar), called *louages*, are authorised to carry five passengers. They have no fixed schedule and leave their respective departure points when full. They serve the whole of Tunisia. This is the quickest form of public road transport. There are many *louage* stations and prices are similar to those of buses and trains. **Car hire:** This can be very expensive. To rent a self-drive car the driver must be over 21 years of age. A full driving licence, which has been valid for at least one year, is acceptable. **Speed limits:** 50kmph (31mph) in towns; 100kmph (62mph) on major highways.
Documentation: Log books, valid national driving licences and Green Card insurance are essential. Both the *RAC* and *AA* are affiliated to the *National Automobile Club (NACT)* based in Tunis. Insurance valid for up to 21 days can be purchased at the border.
Note: For safety reasons, it is forbidden to drive a car in the Sahara without first contacting the National Guard Post at the nearest town, giving the planned itinerary and the expected point of exit from the area. Full provisions, a suitable vehicle and an experienced guide are necessary for any travel in the Sahara.
URBAN: Publicly owned transport services *(SNT)* operate in all major towns, and are extensive but crowded. There is a rail link from Tunis to the suburbs of Goulette and La Marsa. **Taxi:** Within Tunis and other cities, city taxis are numbered and have meters. The price on the meter is what you should pay. There is a 50% surcharge on night fares.
JOURNEY TIMES: The following chart gives approximate journey times (in hours and minutes) from Tunis to other major cities/towns in Tunisia.

	Air	Road	Rail
Hammamet	-	0.45	1.00
Nabeul	-	0.45	1.00
Sousse	-	2.00	2.30
Port el Kantaoui	-	2.00	2.30
Monastir	0.35	3.00	3.00
Sfax	0.30	4.00	4.00
Gabès	-	5.00	6.00
Jerba	0.45	7.00	-
Tozeur	0.40	6.00	-

Note: Travellers to Port el Kantaoui are advised to take the train to Sousse, and travel the remaining 7km (4 miles) by taxi. For Monastir they should change in Sousse for the Metro Leger. For Jerbathey should take the train to Gabès and then the shuttle bus.

ACCOMMODATION

HOTELS: Tunisia has approximately 124,000 hotel beds. There are also several Vacation Villages within each area. A full list of hotel and other types of accommodation is available from the Fédération Tunisienne de l'Hôtellerie, 62 rue d'Iran, Tunis. Tel: (1) 256 766 *or* 349 374. **Grading:** Hotel accommodation is classified by a star system ranging from deluxe **(5-star)** to clean but simple **(1-star)**.
Marhalas are converted caravanserais and often consist of several connected underground houses *(matmata* and *ksars* – ancient granaries), where sleeping quarters and communal bathing and toilet facilities have been installed. They also have their own simple, but clean and adequate, restaurants. There are *Marhalas* at Houmt Souk, Nefta and Kairouan.
CAMPING/CARAVANNING: You can pitch a tent or park a trailer on beaches and in parks with permission from the property owner or from the nearest Police or National Guard station. The major campsites are *Le Moulin Bleu* (Blue Mill) at Hammam-Plage, 20km (12 miles) from Tunis; *L'Auberge des Jasmins* (Jasmin Inn) at Nabeul, 65km (40 miles) from Tunis, equipped with showers, wash-basins, toilets, hot and cold running water, shop, restaurant and outdoor theatre in an extensive orange grove; *L'Idéal Camping* at Hammamet, 60km (35 miles) from Tunis, with restaurant facilities; *Sonia Camping & Caravan Site* at Zarzis, 505km (313 miles) from Tunis; and *The Youth Centre of Gabès*, 404km (251 miles) from Tunis (summer only).
YOUTH HOSTELS: Youth Hostels are open to all young people who are members of the *International Youth Hostel Association*. It is recommended to make reservations well in advance, especially for groups. For details contact the National Tourist Office.

RESORTS & EXCURSIONS

For the purposes of this section, Tunisia has been divided into six main regions. There is also information on the major historic sites in the country.

Tunis & the suburbs

Tunis is a modern international metropolis with sophisticated hotels, shops, entertainment and flower-lined avenues but within it is **The Medina,** one of the best-preserved medieval cities in the Islamic world. The main entrance to this area – by the Porte de France and the

British Embassy – leads straight into the rue Djamaa Ez-Zitouna. This is the main street of the *souk* markets. From here many other individual *souks* branch off, often specialising in particular types of product. If you get lost, your landmark is the Grand Mosque, *Djamaa Ez-Zitouna*, in the street of the same name.

The *Bardo Museum*, housed in what was once the Bey's palace, contains important Carthaginian, Roman, Byzantine and Arab treasures. The *National Museum* holds prehistoric, Punic, Roman and Byzantine exhibits and stands over the remains of the *Baths of Antoninus*, which are open to the public.

The city is overlooked by the cool, wooded **Belvedere Park** which has a delightful Muslim pavilion, and a zoo. There is a golf course and a riding stable in the suburbs of **La Soukra.**

RESORTS: To the northeast of Tunis is the beach resort and port of **La Goulette**, where on hot summer nights the outdoor restaurants and cafés offer fresh fish specialities, as well as typical Tunisian cuisine. Further along the coast are the remains of **Carthage**, once the equal of Ancient Rome (described more fully in *Historic Sites* below), then **Sidi-bou Said**, **La Marsa** and **Gammarth**. All these towns are linked by rail with Tunis. Sidi-bou Said is on a headland bedecked with bougainvillaea, carnations, geraniums and the bright blue doors and shutters of white Andalusian-style villas. The town is a centre for the production of domed wire-filigree birdcages which may become the envy of neighbour's canaries, and is also famous for its cafés. Amid greenery sweeping down to superb sandy beaches, La Marsa, Gammarth and Raouad have fine hotels, cosmopolitan restaurants and nightlife.

In the southern suburbs lies **Hammam-Lif**, a small resort village on the beach, dominated by *Jebel Bou Kornine* ('two-horned mountain').

The Coral Coast

Often known as 'Green Tunisia', this is a delightful part of the country, a region of hills, mountains and fertile plains. Temperature variations can be great, and occasional snow covers the peaks of Khroumiria. The weather is cooler in the summer season than in the south. First-rate hotels are situated on this coast.

Bizerte, formerly the Roman city of Hippo Diarrytus, was a key port in the last war. It retains its old fishing harbour, a kasbah and medina, the Andalusian quarter, wide avenues and a palm-fringed promenade. Modern hotels in landscaped gardens and a splendid *Congress Hall* are spread along the Corniche above sand dunes.

Scenic drives can be enjoyed around *Cap Bizerte* and *Cap Blanc* or around *Lake Bizerte* and *Lake Ichkeul*. The latter provides the habitat for numerous varieties of wildfowl, and the wooded mountain of *Jebel Ichkeul* is the home of buffalo sent as a royal gift to the Bey of Tunis.

Utica, 32km (20 miles) from both Bizerte and Tunis, is an old Phoenician settlement; see the *Historic Sites* section below. Nearby **Raf Raf** is a charming hilltop town.

Tabarka, a picturesque port and resort about 140km (90 miles) west of Bizerte, can be reached by an undulating country route through **Teskraia** and **Djebel Abiod,** a horse-breeding centre. Tabarka is now a more peaceful place than its formidable Genoese fortress would suggest; today, it is given over largely to coral fishing, with spectacular scope for skindivers on the coral reefs, and for the netting of red mullet and hake. It is enlivened by an arts and music festival in July and August, when many visitors stay in a hut village on the beach.

Tabarka's importance in the expanding tourist trade is exemplified by the construction of a 10,000-bed complex based around a marina, as well as the building of a new international airport.

The wooded and flower-decked foothills of Khroumiria, behind The Coral Coast, have more than a hint of unspoiled Provence, although the forests are of cork trees rather than olive. Deer, lynx, civets and jackals may be glimpsed by naturalists throughout the year. Southwards, past **Bulla Regia** (see *Historic Sites*) stands lofty **Le Kef** which has thermal springs. The region also has historical associations stretching from Roman, Punic and early Christian days up to the time of the Second World War.

Cap Bon

Hammamet, where no hotel may be built higher than the tallest of the adjacent trees, is situated on the southern corner of fertile Cap Bon, about 65km (40 miles) from Tunis. It is Tunisia's major and most mature seaside playground. The numerous hotels are built in various modern Moorish styles, which sometimes mirror the white domes of the picturesque *medina* (old town) nearby. The sea-girt *medina* is walled, and guarded by a tawny-coloured *kasbah* whose towers offer a hawk's-eye view of the neat warren of narrow streets below, with their workshops, souvenir arcades and boutiques selling leather and woollen goods, sponges and embroidery. Like the *kasbah* and mosque, the Turkish baths *(hammam)* date from the 15th century. Foreigners are welcome to use them.

A wide sandy beach leads from the old town to the resort area; just behind this, quite near the medina, is a complex of shops, restaurants, nightclubs, bars and cafés. The holiday hotels themselves tend to have plenty of in-house entertainment, including discos and folklore evenings, while beach activities can include horse or camel rides.

One of the most beautiful gardens in Tunisia is that of the *International Cultural Centre*, originally a villa created by Georges Sebastien, friend and host to many French artists and writers. Churchill stayed here and, during the Tunisian campaign, Rommel requisitioned the villa for his personal use. Now the centre is the setting for open-air concerts and plays of international interest, as well as for Tunisian folklore performances.

Nabeul is a relatively modern town, about 10km (6 miles) north of Hammamet. It stands on an ancient Punic and Roman site and maintains a centuries-old tradition in its manufacture of pottery and fine ceramics, perfumes (from local orange and jasmine blossom), lace and leatherwork. There is a camel market here every Friday. The holiday hotels, sometimes containing traditional-style bungalows for self-caterers, look onto a sand beach as fine as that in Hammamet, and have facilities and entertainments similar to those of the bigger resorts. The line of hotels eventually merges into the orchards and fields of Cap Bon, with their hedges of prickly pear and cactus. For further information, see the *Accommodation* section above.

Cap Bon has a maritime climate (mild throughout the year), varied landscapes and an easily accessible coast, a combination of features which made this a popular holiday region amongst the Punic and Roman aristocrats. Jutting out between the Gulf of Tunis and the Gulf of Hammamet, Cap Bon encompasses important wine-growing areas and produces fine figs, olives, oranges, lemons and cereals. At **Korbous,** a former palace of the Bey of Tunis has been converted into a centre for the treatment of arthritis and skin ailments with therapeutic spa waters. Nearby **Sidi Daoud** is a fishing centre, and from here the islets of **Zembra** and **Zembretta** can be reached.

El Haouraria, a village in a wooded region near the end of the cape, is the site of a falconry festival every spring – it is on the migratory path of several bird species. Nearby cliffs soar to 400m (1300ft). **Kerkouane** has an important Punic archaeological site. **Kelibia** has a romantic

Jerba

castle ruin and a thriving fishing port. The local inhabitants, many of whom have blue eyes and red hair, are known as 'Lengleez', and are believed to be descended from British sailors shipwrecked years ago.
Inland from Cap Bon are **Zaghouan** and **Thuburbo Majus** – for further information see *Historic Sites* below.

The Sahel

This central coastal area is a region of hills and plains, with gardens and groves of olive, pomegranate and almond trees. The hills slope down towards a coastline of white sandy beaches or occasional rocky cliffs and underwater reefs.
The Sahel today is the most densely populated region of Tunisia. A common feature of the sun-bleached villages which dot the stony landscape is the cultivation of olive and fruit trees. In the small country museums there are collections of gold jewellery dating back many centuries and this is still a speciality of town artisans today. The region is traditionally known for its weaving. The visitor will especially appreciate the cottons of Ksar Hellal and the wool embroidery of Mahdia and El Jem (see *Historic Sites* below). Some of the smallest villages offer the most original handicrafts; the inhabitants of **Hergla**, for example, make the alfalfa filters that are used all over the country in olive presses.
Many of the towns and villages in the Sahel stand on the remains of Roman or Punic urban centres. The museums of Sousse and El Jem have collections of unusually rich mosaics which show the extraordinary wealth of the area during the Roman era. It was for this reason that the Arabs founded their most important capitals, Kairouan, an important spiritual centre, and Mahdia, today an important holiday centre, in this region.
Sousse, a major port and Tunisia's third largest city, is set in a convenient central position on the eastern coast. The sand beaches, with horse and camel riding, reach beyond Port el Kantaoui, 7km (4 miles) to the north (see below). Most of Sousse's beach hotels are outside the modern town, whose cafés, bars, discos and excellent restaurants are alternative attractions to the hotels' in-house activities and folklore evenings. Impressive ancient ramparts surround the old town. The 8th-century Ribat is one of a chain of fortified monasteries built to defend North Africa from Christian attacks. The men and women who inhabited its spartan quarters had vowed to die if necessary to preserve the Muslim faith. Its watchtower gives a splendid view over the *medina*, as does the garden terrace of Sousse's museum – whose intriguing 'cartoon strip' mosaics should be seen, especially by those who have not visited the Bardo Museum in Tunis.
Port el Kantaoui is a garden village which has an 18-hole championship golf course and a marina. Several of the hotels have spacious lawns facing the soft sand beach. There are good opportunities for sea fishing from here.
Monastir is 24km (15 miles) further south, an intimate and fashionable small resort which is famous for its 10th-century *Mosque*. The town is served by Skanes – Monastir airport. Monastir is a mixture of ancient and modern. The 20th century has given Monastir other attractions, such as the elegant yacht marina which nestles between small sandy coves.
There are many festivals throughout the high season, horseracing to watch and a museum of Islamic arts to visit. A new rail link to Sousse has recently opened; this helps to attract business people to its well-equipped International Convention Centre. There will soon be a second golf course near the town.
21km (13 miles) to the south is the market town of **Moknine**. Part of its population is Jewish and the traditional jewellery items they make are among the exhibits in the town's fascinating little folk museum.
Mahdia, 25km (17 miles) further along the coast, is a fishing port and beach resort, a town with an important place in Arab Muslim history. The all-powerful Obaid Allah, known as the Mahdi, developed it in the 10th century as a stronghold and capital of the Fatimite dynasty.

The Isles of Jerba & Kerkenah

The island of **Jerba**, 614 sq km (240 sq miles), is joined to the mainland by a 6km-long causeway. There is also a ferry-boat service and an air link. The main centre, **Houmt Souk,** is a small market town serving outlying farms and villages, most of which have fine examples of the distinctive local architecture. The island has several beach hotels.
The inhabitants of two Jerban villages are Jews, descendants of refugees who fled from Jerusalem after the Roman conquest of the city in AD70. Their influence is seen in the design of the jewellery sold locally. Jerban villages often specialise in one product. At **Guellala**, for instance, it is pottery; whilst at **Adjim,** it is sponges.
Kerkenah's two inhabited islands, **Gharbi** and **Chergui**, can be reached by car ferry from the pleasant city of **Sfax**. A holiday village and a few hotels and bars indicate that tourism has (however unobtrusively) arrived to supplement the islands' staple industry of fishing. Kerkenah is also notable for its traditional and colourful wedding ceremonies, which visitors are welcome to watch.

Central Tunisia

The oases and the *chotts* (vast dried salt lakes) provide a strange, unearthly atmosphere. The *chotts,* white-crusted in summer (when roads across them are most negotiable), give an impression of infinite open space; even more so than the sand-duned desert further south. A ground haze shimmers in the sun, and a far-distant camel train seems to be floating on air. Mirages of palm trees can sometimes be seen in the afternoon, as in the Sahara. The main oases, which must have seemed visions of paradise to early travellers, nourish countless date palms. Pomegranates, bananas and other fruits are cultivated by their limpid streams. Palm sap is made into a wine called *lagmi*, for whose potency there are prodigious claims.
The easily accessible **Gabès**, site of a southerly seaside oasis which can be toured in a horse-drawn *caleche*, is also a port and a good base for excursions through the *chotts* to the inland oases of **Gafsa, Tozeur, Nefta** and **Douz**, or southwards to the Sahara and the *Matmata Mountains* (see *The Deep South* section).
Gafsa, about 160km (100 miles) inland, is a city of rose-pink walls, whose 86°F thermal water spring bubbles up into three large Roman cisterns. Just out of town is a zoo displaying indigenous animals and birds, as well as the oasis, which can be toured by horse-drawn carriage.
Tozeur has perhaps the most luxuriant oasis of all. Its 200 springs feed thousands of the best date-palms – each towering tree is said to need 100 cubic metres (3500 cubic ft) of water a day. It can be toured by donkey or camel, and contains a 'Paradise Garden' profuse with exotic flowers and fruits. Tozeur's town buildings are built with unfired yellow bricks picked out in geometric patterns similar to those found on Arab rugs. There is an international airport and Tozeur and Nefta are sometimes featured as destinations in package deals, 'twin-centering' them with a coastal resort.
Nefta's oasis resembles a bowl, and is known locally as a basket or 'horn of plenty'. The town, made up of sand-coloured houses, is on a plateau above it. Guides are available for the trek on donkey back to the oasis. Nefta has the feeling of being a rather remote frontier post (but

Excursion in the south of the country

less so than Douz), although it has a 4-star deluxe hotel. North of Tozeur and Nefta are the mainly mud-walled villages of **Chebika**, **Tamerza** and **Mides**.
To the southeast, via Kebili, lies **Douz**, on the *Grand Erg Oriental*, the great sand-sea of the eastern Sahara. Its Thursday camel market is a camera-worthy event, as is the *marhoul* ceremony celebrating the start of the seasonal desert migration. Such rituals – as well as camel-wrestling, poetry 'jousts' and folk dance and music – are incorporated into a Sahara Festival which takes place near Douz every January.
Around this region live veiled people of pure Berber stock. You may also find a 'desert rose' of crystalline minerals baked by the sun into petal-like formations.
Note: Any trip into the desert region must be planned carefully, using suitable transport, adequate provisions and a guide (see *Travel* section above). Overnight lodging and restaurants can be found throughout southern Tunisia. Hard-topped roads and dirt tracks make it possible to drive to all points of interest, even across the crusted beds of the *chotts*.

The Deep South

A hole-in-the-ground hotel in a lunar landscape; civilised cave dwellings tunnelled into a mountainside; homes like giant honeycomb cells in ancient stone granaries; these are just some of the intriguing sights to be investigated on trips southwards from Gabès, Jerba or Zarzis.
Matmata (a location used during the filming of 'Star Wars') consists (as do other Berber villages) largely of sizeable holes burrowed into the ground, a useful defence against the fierce summer heat and cold winter winds. Their homes are built on two levels, the upper one containing storage rooms. In some cases, several of these underground dwellings have been connected together to make hotels and restaurants. 'Mod cons' are generally available, although the furnishings are normally traditional. The mosque there is underground, as is communal bakery. There are even subterranean oil factories where olives are pressed by a camel-driven mill with a huge olive trunk. Domes that rise above ground level usually mark *marabouts*, the shrines of holy men.
The Matmata landscape is typified by deeply-eroded, conical hillocks separated by narrow ravines, where olive and fig trees sometimes grow. The region is speckled with flat plots of land where goats are pastured among the gardens and clumps of olive trees.
The road southeast from Gabès leads through **Mareth**, scene of a battle in 1943, to **Medenine**. This market town has a *ksar*, a fortified citadel surrounded by former grain stores *(ghorfas)*, some two or three storeys high, sometimes used as homes. Some *ghorfas* have been converted into tourist accommodation and others are now little shops selling Bedouin silver jewellery.
On a circular route from Medenine to Foum Tataouine are several more *ksars*, including **Ksar Djouama,** probably 14th century in origin; **Beni Kheddache,** on a mountain-top; **Ksar Haddada,** with a small hotel; and **Ghoumrassen,** in a valley. All have cave dwellings. The road is rough and is best negotiated by jeep.
Two of the most beautiful mountain *ksars* are **Ouled Soltane,** south of Tataouine, and **Chenini,** to the west. The road to Chenini is a memorable one, zigzagging through a cinnamon-coloured mountainscape.
The fringes of the Sahara lie to the south of **Tataouine, Remada** and **Borj Bourguiba.** Some internal tour operators arrange Land Rover treks into the desert. Independent travellers wishing to visit it should note that, as a precaution against their becoming stranded or lost, it is a strict requirement that they should first contact the National Guard Post in Medenine or nearest town. Vehicles should be suitable for this kind of travel, and be equipped with ample water, provisions, repair kits and a tent. An experienced accompanying guide is advisable, as is a preliminary check of the meteorological conditions – particularly before a trip of any length. Drivers (preferably in convoy) should stop at every guard post on the way and tell the officer in charge where they are going.
Zarzis, on the coast facing Jerba, is a beach resort in a coastal oasis of about 500,000 palm trees and 100,000 olive trees.

Historic Sites

Tunisia has a wide variety of historical settlements, Punic, Roman, Byzantine and Islamic, many of which are in excellent condition.
Tunisia's most famous historic site is probably **Carthage,** in the suburbs of Tunis. It was the city of the legendary Queen Dido, and once the great rival of Rome in the struggle for domination of the Meditterranean. When the Romans, furious at humiliations inflicted by Hannibal and the Carthaginians, conquered it in 146BC, they razed and ploughed it into the ground, which they symbolically sterilised with salt. Later they rebuilt the city, making it their provincial capital of North Africa. Then the city suffered at the hands of the Vandals who conquered the region at the end of the 5th century. They lived up to their name, vandalising many of the Roman statues by chipping off their proud noses. Then again, in AD698, it was razed to the ground – this time by Arab invaders.
The small whitewashed town of **El Jem** (about 40km/25 miles inland from Mahdia) is dominated by the well-preserved Colosseum. Its lion-coloured outer walls are 35m (120ft) high and there was seating for 30,000.
Kairouan (50km/30 miles inland from Sousse) is the fourth most holy city in the Islamic world – after Mecca, Medina and Jerusalem. It was founded in AD670 by a disciple of the Prophet Mohammed and is situated on the spot where a new spring of water and other miraculous revelations were manifested to him during a journey. According to legend, seven visits to Kairouan equal one to Mecca. The courtyard in front of its great Mosque (which can be visited by non-Muslims) is said to be able to hold 200,000 pilgrims on holy days. There are many other mosques and shrines, but the Great Mosque is the most sanctified place. Its prayer room is supported by a variegated 'forest of pillars' of Roman, Byzantine and Arab periods, made of stone, marble or porphyry. The 5m (18ft) high, gloriously carved wooden pulpit dates from the 9th century – as does its minaret with 128 steps.
Utica, reached from Tunis or Bizerte, was a Phoenician colony founded around 1100BC – earlier than Carthage, its rival in later centuries. After entering by a great arched gateway, one can see marble flooring of a mansion set in a garden fragrant with rosemary. Mosaics depicting sea fish decorate a water-basin and the pool of a former fountain. The remains of several other houses reveal decorated flooring of the Punic, Roman and Byzantine periods, and the Punic tombs contain interesting remains.
Dougga is a major Roman site in a lofty setting 100km (60 miles) southwest of Tunis. The theatre, built in AD168 to seat 3500, resounds again when Greek-based classical plays and other performances are staged, sometimes by the *Comédie Française*. Visitors with a more down-to-earth humour may be amused by the neighbourly arrangement of 12 seats over latrines in the Bath of Cyclops. However, decorum is restored with a view of the city's capitol, claimed by some to be the grandest in North Africa.
Bulla Regia, south of Tabarka, is a site with at least 23 special features from the Roman, early Christian and Byzantine periods. Some of its best mosaics have been removed to the Bardo Museum in Tunis, but its 'Hunting Palace' has vivid mosaics of wild animals and the chase, and recognisable remnants of a dining room, kitchen and bedrooms.
Sbeitla, 160km (100 miles) inland from Sousse and Sfax, is one of the country's largest archaeological sites. Its numerous attractions include Roman temples and baths, early Christian churches and Byzantine fortresses.
It is possible in most resorts to arrange excursions to important historical sites.

Carthage

SOCIAL PROFILE

FOOD & DRINK: Tunisian food is well prepared and delicious, particularly the authentic lamb or *dorado* (bream) *cous-cous*, the fish dishes, *tajine* and *brik* or *brik à l'oeuf* (egg and a tasty filling fried in an envelope of pastry). Tunisian dishes are cooked with olive oil, spiced with aniseed, coriander, cumin, caraway, cinnamon or saffron and flavoured with mint, orange blossom or rose water. Restaurants catering for tourists tend to serve rather bland dishes and 'international' cuisine, and visitors are advised to try the smaller restaurants. Prices vary enormously, and higher prices do not necessarily mean better meals. Tunis and the main cities also have French, Italian and other international restaurants. Self-service may sometimes be found but table service is more common. **Drink:** Moorish cafés, with their traditional decor, serve excellent Turkish coffee or mint tea with pine nuts. Although Tunisia is an Islamic country, alcohol is not prohibited. Tunisia produces a range of excellent table wines, sparkling wines, beers, aperitifs and local liqueurs, notably *Bouka* (distilled from figs) and *Thibarine* (from dates).

NIGHTLIFE: In Tunisia the theatre season lasts from October to June when local and foreign (especially French) companies put on productions and concerts. International groups appear at Tunis Theatre and in the towns of Hammet and Sousse. There are numerous cinemas in the larger cities. There are nightclubs in most of the beach hotels as well as in the big city hotels. Belly dancing is a common cabaret feature and lively local bands often play traditional music.

SHOPPING: Special purchases include copperware (engraved trays, ashtrays and other utensils); articles sculpted in olive wood; leather goods (wallets, purses, handbags); clothing (kaftans, jelabas, burnuses); pottery and ceramics; dolls in traditional dress; beautiful embroidery; fine silverware and enamelled jewellery. Among the most valuable of Tunisia's products are carpets. The two major types are woven (or non-pile) and knotted (or pile). The quality of all carpets is strictly controlled by the National Handicrafts Office, so be sure to check the ONA seal before buying. **Shopping hours:** 0800-1200 and 1600-1900 (summer), 0830-1200 and 1500-1800 (winter). **Weekly markets:** A source of good purchases are the markets which are set up on certain days in many Tunisian towns and villages. All the products of the region are displayed, including handicrafts, farm produce and second-hand goods. There are ONA workshops and stores throughout the country where visitors can buy items at fixed prices (payment can be made by cheque with a bankers card). ONA stores make a reduction of 10% on the price of goods purchased in foreign currency. No duty is payable on articles up to £900 in value which are shipped to EC countries, accompanied by an EUR1 form. Visitors who make a purchase of more than five dinars anywhere in Tunisia should ask for a sales slip and keep it safe, along with bank receipts for any currency exchanged, for Customs inspection.

SPORT: Gliding: The best-known venue for gliding enthusiasts is the Federal Gliding Centre at Jebel Rassas, 25km (15 miles) from Tunis, where gliders and qualified instruction in the sport are available to visitors. **Golf:** The Tunisian Open Golf Tournament 1982-85 became one of the major tournaments on the PGA European tour. There are excellent courses at Port El Kantaoui near Sousse, Monastir and Hammamet; others are being developed at Jerba, Tabarka and Tunis. Players of all abilities will find very high-quality facilities. The Open Golf Championships there have already attracted many leading competitors from all over the world. Created by eminent golf-course architects, the courses are dotted with palm, olive and pomegranate trees, and are next to the sea. Each of the 18 holes is on a different kind of terrain, and treated turf has been imported from California. The courses are well-suited to all players. There are luxurious clubhouses, equipment to rent, and training/practice grounds with putting green. In Tunis, the golf course at the Country Club at La Soukra is presently undergoing extension and re-landscaping. More courses are planned for every major resort. **Fishing:** The abundance and great variety of fish makes fishing a popular sport. Underwater fishing is also good. The range includes mullet, ray, dogfish, groupers, red rock mullet, crayfish and shrimp. A wetsuit is necessary only between November and April. You can watch coral fishing at Tabarka, octopus fishing off the Kerkenah Islands, sponge fishing at Sfax, on the island of Jerba and in the Gulf of Gabès, and tuna fishing by the experts at Sidi Daoud. These 'fishing spectacles' take place in May and June. **Scuba diving:** A fully equipped scuba diving centre was opened in 1980 in Tabarka and Port El Kantaoui. For underwater fishing, it is necessary to bring your own equipment, and obtain details of conservationist underwater fishing restrictions from the National Tourist Office. Visitors who have brought their own equipment can refill their air bottles at the offices of the *Société d'Air Liquide* at Mégrine, 7km (4 miles) from Tunis, and at Sfax. In case of accident, there are decompression chambers at the Naval Station at Bizerte. **Swimming:** Tunis has three public swimming pools open to visitors. Most hotels on the coast have a heated pool as well as a private beach. **Birdwatching:** Tunisia has many species of birds, many of which are protected in national parks. The cork oak forests of Ain Draham, the lake and marshes of Ichkeul near Bizerte, the coastal lagoons round Tunis and Sousse, the rocky hills and steps from Kef to Kasserine, and the oases and deserts of the south all have their characteristic birds. Birdlife also varies with the seasons; in winter, spoonbills, geese, ducks, robins and wagtails seek refuge from the cold further north, while in spring and autumn migrant swallows and warblers and birds of prey at Cap Bon pass through on their journeys between Africa and Europe. In summer, Mediterranean species like storks, bee-eaters and rollers stay to nest. **Health spas:** There are about 100 hot-spring stations throughout Tunisia – mostly in the north of the country. Many of the spas have been used for this purpose since Roman and Punic times. The most important stations are run by personnel specialised in the medical and paramedical fields and treatments are available for rheumatism, arthritis, a variety of lung and skin complaints, circulatory troubles, gynaecology and paediatrics. More information is available at the National Tourist Office. **Sailing:** Port el Kantaoui is a port of international standard offering mooring for 340 boats, harbour-master's office, deep-sea navigation school, sailing school, ship-chandler, boat-rental, and a dry docking area with maintenance shops. Prices are competitive, especially for winter careening services. There is a newly opened marina at Cap Monastir with similar facilities. Among other sailing (and water-skiing) centres is *Le Club Nautique de Sidi-bou-Said,* which has a marina complex. A new marina is nearing completion at Tabarka.

SPECIAL EVENTS: The following information gives some idea of Tunisian festivals in 1993. A complete list is available from the National Tourist Office. **Jun '93** *Festival of the Sparrow Hawk*, El Haouaria, near Nabeul. **Jun** *Festival of Malouf* (Andalusian folklore), Testour. **Jun** *Ulysses Festival* (traditional songs and dances of the island of Jerba), Houmt Souk. **Jun** *Festival of Dougga* (classical plays in Roman theatre), Beja. **Jul** *El Jem Festival*, Roman colosseum. **Jul-Aug** *Festival of Carthage* (music, theatre, dance and folklore), Roman theatre. **Jul-Aug** *Monastir Festival* (international music, dance and theatre). **Aug** *Festival of Hammamet* (music, theatre, dance, folklore), International Cultural Centre. **Sep** *Festival of Cavalry* (traditional Arab horse festival with racing and dancing), Kairouan. **Nov** *Festival of the Tozeur Oasis* (parades of decorated floats, folklore, camel fights). **Dec** *Douz Festival* (folklore, camel racing, cavalry and music), Sahara.

SOCIAL CONVENTIONS: Arabic in culture and tradition, Tunisia is nevertheless one of the more liberal and tolerant Muslim countries. The nomadic Bedouin still follow their traditional way of life in the southern desert. The Tunisians' varied origins are shown in the architecture, crafts, music and regional folk dances. Tunisia has also developed an international reputation as an intellectual and cultural centre. Shaking hands is the usual form of greeting. Hospitality is very important and a small gift in appreciation of hospitality or as a token of friendship is always appropriate. Dress can be informal but should respect the conventions of Islam when visiting religious monuments, ie shoulders and knees must be covered. Outside tourist resorts scanty beachwear should not be worn. **Tipping:** 10-15% for all services.

BUSINESS PROFILE

ECONOMY: Tunisia lacks the vast natural resources of its immediate neighbours, but careful and successful economic management has brought the country reasonable prosperity. Agriculture and mining are the foundations of the economy. The main agricultural products are wheat, barley, olive oil, wine and fruit, but large quantities of other foodstuffs have to be imported. Large quantities of phosphate ores are mined, along with iron, lead and zinc. Tunisia is also a modest oil exporter, although this sector has recently been in decline. There is a small manufacturing sector which is involved in processing organic chemicals derived from petroleum and purifying the phosphate ore. The economy has suffered from recent falls in oil and phosphate prices, which has forced the Government to relax price controls on basic commodities. France and Italy are Tunisia's principal trading partners. The Government is trying to broaden the base of the economy by introducing more liberal economic policies, backed by the IMF which has offered soft loans

Sidi Bou Said

in exchange for a brake on public expenditure and an export drive.

BUSINESS: Arabic and French are the most widely used languages in business circles and a knowledge of either is useful. Interpreter services are available. Appointments are required. **Office hours:** 0800-1230 and 1430-1800 Monday to Friday, 0800-1200 Saturday (winter); 0700-1300 Monday to Saturday (summer).

COMMERCIAL INFORMATION: The following organisations can offer advice: Agence de Promotion de l'Industrie (API), 63 rue de Syrie, 1002 Tunis. Tel: (1) 792 144. Fax: (1) 782 482. Telex: 14166; *or*

Chambre de Commerce de Tunis, 1 rue des Entrepreneurs, 1000 Tunis. Tel: (1) 242 872. Fax: (1) 354 744. Telex: 14718.

CONFERENCES/CONVENTIONS: The following organisation can supply details: Office National du Tourisme Tunisien, 1 avenue Mohamed V, 1002 Tunis. Tel: (1) 341 077. Fax: (1) 350 997. Telex: 14381.

HISTORY & GOVERNMENT

HISTORY: Tunisia was ruled by an hereditary monarchy until the French made the country a protectorate in 1883. Nationalist pressure for independence began in 1934 with the formation of the Néo-Destour (New Constitution) Party (NDP) under the leadership of Habib Bourguiba. Internal self-government was granted in 1955; independence as a constitutional monarchy under the Bey of Tunis came a year later. In 1957, the Bey was overthrown and a republic proclaimed, with Bourguiba as President. Despite independence, the French insisted on holding onto a naval base at Bizerte on the northern coast but lost it in 1963 after a naval blockade by the Tunisians and several months of heavy fighting. The ruling Parti Socialiste Destourien (renamed Rassemblement Constitutionel Démocratique in 1988), successor to the NDP, has maintained a strong grip. Bourguiba pursued unsuccessful socialist policies in the early part of his regime, but in the 1970s opened the economy up to foreign investment and allowed the development of a private sector. By the crude measure of per capita domestic income, the lot of the Tunisians greatly improved during this second phase. At the time of his fall from power in November 1987, Bourguiba had been in control for 30 years, at first through elections to the single party, and after 1975 as President-for-Life. Following a pronouncement by his own team of doctors that Bourguiba was no longer of sound mind, Prime Minister Zein al-Abideen Ben Ali assumed the Presidency unopposed. Tunisia has played host to the leadership and many of the fighters of the Palestine Liberation Organisation since their enforced departure from the Lebanon following the Israeli invasion in 1982. Elections were held in 1989 at which opposition parties, including Islamic fundamentalists, were allowed to stand for the first time. The poll was, however, conducted on a constituency 'first past the post' system; no opponents of the Government were elected. An important foreign policy development occurred in February 1989 with the formation of the Union Of The Arab Maghreb, conceived as a political and economic bloc in North Africa and comprising Algeria, Libya, Morocco, Mauritania and Tunisia. This was part of a more general realignment of Tunisian foreign policy away from the West towards a pro-Arab stance. One consequence of this was Tunisian support for Saddam Hussein during the 1990-91 Gulf crisis, leading to a sharp deterioration in relations with pro-coalition Arab states, particularly Egypt, Saudi Arabia and Kuwait itself. As President Ben Ali consolidated his position, the Government introduced economic reforms to complement the political liberalisation process: state control of certain industries was relaxed, trade controls were abolished, and the Government intends to make the Tunisian Dinar fully convertible within the next few years. The objective is to broaden the base of the economy which remains principally agricultural and thus vulnerable to drought. These occurred frequently during the late 1980s and threatened to undermine the economic system. Negotiations were held with the International Monetary Fund and a 'Structural Adjustment Programme' agreed but the Tunisian government has been slow to effect the necessary changes. During 1991, Tunis has watched developments in neighbouring Algeria with increasing concern. Tunisia has its own influential Islamic movement, Nahda, but the Government has not yet allowed it to operate legally as a political party. Nahda has grown quickly in the last few years and may have benefited from Saudi funding.

GOVERNMENT: Legislation is carried out by the unicameral Chamber of Deputies, whose 125 members are elected by universal adult suffrage for five years. Since 1981, candidates for election can be put forward by more than one political party: prior to that, only the Parti Socialiste Destourien (PSD) could nominate candidates. In February 1988 the PSD renamed itself Rassemblement Constitutionel Démocratique (RCD). The Communist Party, the Democratic Socialist Party and the Party of Popular Unity are also legally recognised. The main Islamic Party, Nahda, is not (see above). The President, as Head of State, appoints a Prime Minister and a Council of Ministers who exercise executive power under his leadership. There are also various advisory bodies: the State Council, the Social and Economic Council, the Constitutional Council and the Higher Islamic Council.

CLIMATE

Tunisia has a warm climate all year. Best periods are spring and autumn. Temperatures can be extremely high inland. Winter is mild and has the highest rainfall.

Required clothing: Lightweights in summer, mediumweights and rainwear in winter. Sunglasses are advised.

GABES Tunisia (2m)

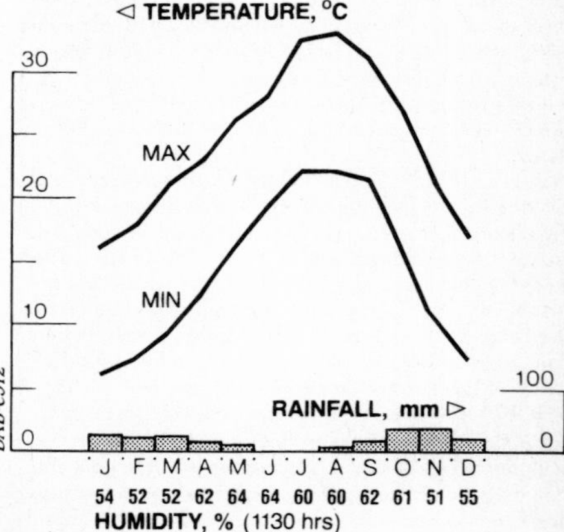

TUNIS Tunisia (3m)

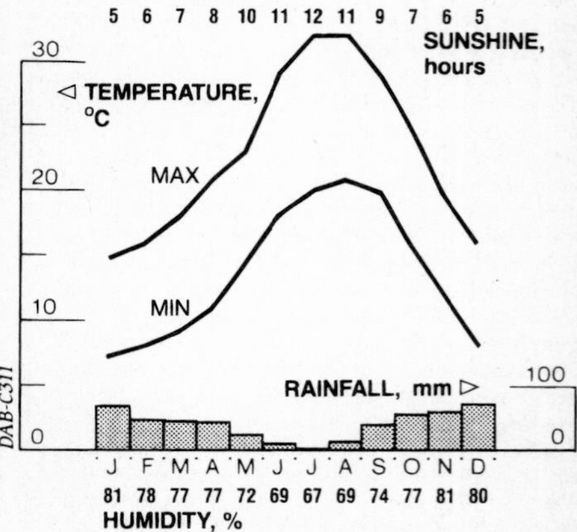

The Colosseum, El Jem

TURKEY

□ international airport

Location: Southeastern Europe/Asia Minor.

Ministry of Tourism
Bahçelievler
Ankara, Turkey
Tel: (4) 212 8300. Fax: (4) 213 6887.
Embassy of the Republic of Turkey
43 Belgrave Square
London SW1X 8PA
Tel: (071) 235 5252/3/4. Fax: (071) 235 8093. Telex: 884236.
Turkish Consulate General
Rutland Lodge
Rutland Gardens
London SW7 1BW
Tel: (071) 589 0360 *or* 589 0949. Fax: (071) 584 6235.
Opening hours: 0930-1200 (for visas) and 1430-1600 (other enquiries) Monday to Friday.
Turkish Embassy Information Counsellor's Office
170 Piccadilly
London W1V 9DD
Tel: (071) 734 8681. Fax: (071) 491 0773. Opening hours: 0930-1730 Monday to Friday.
British Embassy
Sehit Ersan Caddesi 46A
Cankaya
Ankara, Turkey
Tel: (4) 427 4310/1/2/3/4/5. Fax: (4) 468 3214. Telex: 42320 PROD TR.
Consulates in: Antalya, Bodrum, Istanbul, Iskenderun, Izmir, Marmaris and Mersin.
Embassy of the Republic of Turkey
1714 Massachusetts Avenue, NW
Washington, DC
20036
Tel: (202) 659 8200. Fax: (202) 659 0744.
Consulate Generals in: Chicago, Los Angeles and New York.
Turkish Culture & Information Office
821 UN Plaza
New York, NY
10017
Tel: (212) 687 2194. Fax: (212) 599 7568. Telex: 42428.
Also in: Washington DC.
Embassy of the United States of America
PO Box 5000
Atatürk Bulvar 110
Ankara, Turkey
Tel: (4) 426 5470. Fax: (4) 467 0057.
Consulates in: Istanbul, Izmir and Adana.
Embassy of the Republic of Turkey
197 Wurtemburg Street
Ottawa, Ontario
K1N 8L9
Tel: (613) 232 1577/8. Fax: (613) 232 5498.
Consulates in: Montréal and Winnipeg.
Canadian Embassy
Nenehatun Caddesi 75
Gaziosmanpasa 06700
Ankara, Turkey
Tel: (4) 136 1275/6/7/8/9. Fax: (4) 146 4437. Telex: 42369 DCAN TR.
Consulate in: Istanbul.

AREA: 779,452 sq km (300,948 sq miles).
POPULATION: 57,000,000 (1991 estimate).
POPULATION DENSITY: 73.1 per sq km.
CAPITAL: Ankara. **Population:** 3,200,000 (1991).
GEOGRAPHY: Turkey borders the Black Sea and the CIS to the northeast, Iran to the east, Iraq to the southeast, Syria and the Mediterranean to the south, the Aegean Sea to the west and Greece and Bulgaria to the northwest. Asia Minor (or Anatolia) accounts for 97% of the country and forms a long, wide peninsula 1650km (1025 miles) from east to west, 650km (400 miles) from north to south. Two east–west mountain ranges, the Pontic in the north and the Taurus in the south, enclose the central Anatolian plateau, but join up in a vast mountainous region in the far east of the country. Here the ancient Tigris and Euphrates rivers rise.
LANGUAGE: Turkish and Kurdish (9%). French, German and English are widely spoken in cities.
RELIGION: Muslim with small Christian minority. Turkey is a secular state which guarantees freedom of worship to non-Muslims.
TIME: GMT + 2 (GMT + 3 in summer).
ELECTRICITY: 220 volts AC, 50Hz.
COMMUNICATIONS: Telephone: IDD is available. Country code: 90. There is an extensive internal telephone network, but often an interpreter will be needed for more remote areas. **Fax:** Some hotels have facilities. **Telex/telegram:** There is a public telex office in the main post office at Ulus, Ankara, open 0900-1900. Telegrams may be sent from the office of *Telegraf Gisesi* at Sirkeci, Istanbul, open 24 hours. **Post:** Airmail to Europe takes three days. Turkish post offices are recognisable by their yellow *PTT* signs. Major post offices are open 0800-2400 Monday to Saturday and 0900-1900 Sunday. Small post offices have the same opening hours as government offices. **Press:** The main newspapers are *Hurriyet, Sabah* and *Milliyet*. English-language daily newspapers include *The Turkish Daily News*.
BBC World Service and Voice of America frequencies: From time to time these change. See the section *How to Use this Book* for more information.

BBC:				
MHz	12.095	15.070	9.410	6.180
Voice of America:				
MHz	9.670	6.040	5.995	1.260

PASSPORT/VISA

Regulations and requirements may be subject to change at short notice, and you are advised to contact the appropriate diplomatic or consular authority before finalising travel arrangements. Details of these may be found at the head of this country's entry. Any numbers in the chart refer to the footnotes below.

	Passport Required?	Visa Required?	Return Ticket Required?
Full British	Yes	Yes	Yes
BVP	Valid	-	-
Australian	Yes	No	Yes
Canadian	Yes	No	Yes
USA	Yes	No	Yes
Other EC	1	2	Yes
Japanese	Yes	No	Yes

PASSPORTS: Required by all except the following if travelling as tourists and able to present a valid national ID card:
(a) **[1]** nationals of Belgium, France, Germany, Greece, Luxembourg and The Netherlands (all other EC nationals require passports);
(b) nationals of Malta and Switzerland.
British Visitors Passport: Accepted for touristic visits of up to 3 months.
VISAS: Required by all except the following for stays of up to 3 months (unless otherwise indicated):
(a) nationals of the countries referred to in the chart above;
(b) **[2]** nationals of EC countries (nationals of the UK, Ireland and Italy *do* need visas); nationals of Portugal need a visa if stay exceeds two months;
(c) nationals of Liechtenstein and Switzerland;
(d) nationals of Argentina, The Bahamas, Bahrain, Barbados, Belize, Bolivia, Chile, Djibouti, Ecuador, Fiji, Finland, Grenada, Iceland, Iran, Jamaica, Kenya, South Korea, Kuwait, Liechtenstein, Malaysia, Malta, Mauritius, Monaco, Morocco, New Zealand, Norway, Oman, Qatar, St Lucia, San Marino, Saudi Arabia, Seychelles, Singapore, Sweden, Switzerland, Trinidad & Tobago, Tunisia, Turkish Cyprus, United Arab Emirates and Vatican City;
(e) nationals of Romania and Yugoslavia for stays of up to 2 months;
(f) nationals of South Africa for 21 days.
Note: (a) Tourists and business visitors from Austria, Czechoslovakia, Hungary, Ireland, Italy, Poland, the UK and Spain travelling to Turkey for less that 3 months *must* obtain their visas at the point of entry at the time of arrival; visitors from the UK, Ireland and Hong Kong pay £5; Austria As150; Italy US$5; Spain US$10; CIS US$10 (only at the borders of Sarp, Istanbul-Atatürk and Ankara-Esenboga); Czechoslovakia, Hungary and Poland US$10. Those staying longer or travelling for the purposes of employment, education, research or residence *must* obtain their visas in advance from the nearest Turkish consular mission; cost for UK applicants – Single entry, £40; Multiple entry/Business, £40; for Employment, Education or Research, £60; Residence visa, £80. (b) Visas issued to nationals of the following countries will be stamped on a removable insert in the passport: Greek Cyprus, North Korea and Taiwan.
Types of visa: Tourist/Business single-entry visa; Tourist/Business multiple-entry visa; Employment, Education, Residence or Research visa; and Transit visa. Prices vary according to nationality; see above for prices for UK applicants.
Transit visas are *not* required by:
(a) those exempted from Tourist/Business visas;
(b) those continuing their journey by the same or the first connecting aircraft, if in possession of confirmed onward tickets (and visas when appropriate).
Transit visas are required by all others continuing their journey within 72 hours; full visas are required for longer transit periods. Transit visas are only issued to those with valid passports and confirmed onward documentation. The cost varies according to the nationality of the applicant. All other nationals should contact the nearest Turkish consulate. All holders of travel documents must obtain visas before travelling to Turkey. Others may obtain Transit visas on arrival if travelling from a country where there is no Turkish consular mission, but nationals of Hungary, India, Peru and South Africa must have travelled directly from their home country.
Validity: Dependent on nationality of applicant.
Application to: Consulate General. For addresses, see top of entry.
Working days required: Up to 5.

MONEY

Currency: Turkish Lira (TL). Notes are in denominations of TL20,000, 10,000, 5000, 1000, 500 and 100. Coins are in denominations of TL100, 50, 25 and 10.
Currency exchange: All exchange certificates and purchase receipts must be retained to prove that legally exchanged currency was used. Many UK banks offer differing rates of exchange depending on what denominations of Turkish currency are being bought or sold. Check with banks for details and current rates.
Credit cards: American Express, Access/Mastercard, Visa and Diners Club are accepted. Check with your credit card company for details of merchant acceptability and other services which may be available.
Travellers cheques & Eurocheques: Can be cashed immediately upon proof of identity. However, it may take several days to cash cheques from private accounts.
Exchange rate indicators: The following figures are included as a guide to the movements of the Turkish Lira against Sterling and the US Dollar:

Date:	Oct '89	Oct '90	Oct '91	Oct '92
£1.00=	3643	5377	8277	12,567
$1.00=	2307	2753	4769	7919

Currency restrictions: There are no restrictions on the import of foreign currency, though visitors bringing in a large amount of foreign currency should obtain a written declaration from the Turkish authorities. No more than the equivalent of US$5000 in local currency may be exported. Foreign currency may be exported up to US$5000, but no more than the amount imported and declared.
Banking hours: 0830-1200 and 1300-1700 Monday to Friday.

DUTY FREE

The following goods may be imported into Turkey without incurring customs duty:
5 litre bottles or 7 bottles of spirits (70cc), of which no more than 3 can be of the same brand;
200 cigarettes and 50 cigars and 200g of tobacco **[1]**;
1.5kg of coffee;
1.5kg of instant coffee;
500g of tea;
1kg of chocolate;
1kg of sweets;
5 bottles of eau de cologne (120ml), eau de toilette, perfume

or lavender water or lotion;
Gifts up to a value of £170.
Note: (a) **[1]** A further 400 cigarettes or 100 cigars and 500g of tobacco may be imported if purchased on arrival at a duty-free shop. (b) Very specific amounts and categories of personal belongings may be imported duty free, according to a list available from the Consulate General. Most tourists are unlikely to find themselves exceeding these allowances, but should note that the limits imposed on personal belongings include: one camera and five rolls of film; one pocket calculator; one table clock; one manual typewriter (duty must be paid on electric and electronic models); one video camera and five blank cassettes; one 8mm cine-camera and ten blank cassettes; one portable radio or radio/cassette (speakers should not be detachable); five LPs or compact discs (no two the same); and one portable computer with no more than 4K bytes of memory. (c) Sharp implements and weapons may not be imported without permission. (d) Marijuana and other narcotics are strictly prohibited in Turkey.
Export restrictions: (a) The export of souvenirs such as carpets is subject to customs regulations regarding age and value. (b) The export of antiques is forbidden. (c) Minerals may only be exported under licence from the General Directorate of Mining Exploration & Research.

PUBLIC HOLIDAYS

Public holidays observed in Turkey are as follows:
Mar 25 '93 Seker Bayram (End of Ramadan). **Apr 23** National Independence and Children's Day. **May 1** Spring Day. **May 19** Atatürk's Commemoration Day, Youth and Sports Day. **Jun 1** Kurban Bayrami (Feast of Sacrifice). **Aug 30** Victory Day. **Oct 29** Republic Day. **Jan 1 '94** New Year's Day. **Mar** Seker Bayram (End of Ramadan).
Note: Muslim festivals are timed according to local sightings of various phases of the Moon and the dates given above are approximations. During the lunar month of Ramadan that precedes Seker Bayram (Eid al-Fitr), Muslims fast during the day and feast at night and normal business patterns may be interrupted. Some restaurants are closed during the day and there may be restrictions on smoking and drinking. Some disruption may continue into Seker Bayram itself. Seker Bayram and Kurban Bayrami (Eid al-Adha) may last anything from two to ten days, depending on the region. For more information see the section *World of Islam* at the back of the book.

HEALTH

Regulations and requirements may be subject to change at short notice, and you are advised to contact your doctor well in advance of your intended date of departure. Any numbers in the chart refer to the footnotes below.

	Special Precautions?	Certificate Required?
Yellow Fever	No	No
Cholera	1	No
Typhoid & Polio	Yes	-
Malaria	2	-
Food & Drink	3	-

[1]: The Turkish Health Authorities have reported no cases of cholera in recent years. A vaccination is recommended to give improved protection against the disease. It is, however, wise to follow simple precautions when eating and drinking – see **[3]** below.
[2]: Potential malaria risk (exclusively in the benign *vivax* form) from March to the end of November in the Çukorova/Amikova area and from mid-May to mid-October in southeast Anatolia.
[3]: Tap water is usually chlorinated in larger towns and cities, but should not be assumed to have been so treated: if used for drinking, brushing teeth or making ice it should have first been boiled or otherwise sterilised. If a water source bears the words *içilmez*, it means that it is not for drinking; sources labelled *içilir*, *içme suyu* or *içilebilir* are safe to drink. Bottled spring water is widely available. Milk is unpasteurised and should be boiled. Powdered or tinned milk is available and is advised, but make sure that it is reconstituted with safe water. Avoid dairy products which are likely to have been made from unboiled milk. Only eat well-cooked meat and fish, preferably served hot. Salad and mayonnaise may carry increased risk. Vegetables should be cooked and fruit peeled.
Rabies is present. For those at high risk, vaccination before arrival should be considered. If you are bitten abroad seek medical advice without delay. For more information consult the *Health* section at the back of the book.
Health care: Turkey has a large health sector: one doctor and one hospital bed for, respectively, every 1700 and 470 inhabitants. A great number of Turkish doctors and dentists speak a foreign language, particularly at major hospitals. Private health insurance is recommended.

TRAVEL - International

AIR: Turkey's national airline is *THY Turkish Airlines (TK)*.
Approximate flight times: From *Frankfurt* to Istanbul is 2 hours 45 minutes, from *London* is 3 hours 45 minutes and from *New York* is 11 hours.
International airports: *Ankara (ANK)* (Esenboga) is 28km (17.5 miles) northeast of the city. THY buses go from the city 90 minutes before domestic flights and 135 minutes before international flights. There is a taxi service to the city available. Airport facilities include incoming and outgoing duty-free shops; bank/exchange services; restaurant and bar.
Istanbul (IST) (Atatürk, formerly Yesikoy) is 24km (15 miles) west of the city (travel time – 30 minutes). A coach (THY bus) goes every 15 minutes to the THY terminal. There are taxi services to the city. Airport facilities include incoming and outgoing duty-free shop (open 24 hours); bank/exchange services; restaurant; bar and car hire *(Avis* and *Europcar)*.
Izmir (IZM) (Adnan Menderes). A THY bus leaves from the city 75 minutes before departure. Airport facilities include bank/exchange services; restaurant and bar.
SEA: Major ports are Istanbul, Izmir, Mersin, Antalya and Bodrum. Cruise lines: *TUI Cruises*, *Epirotiki*, *BI*, *Lauro*, *Costa*, *CTC*, *Norwegian American*, *Turkish Maritime*, *'K' Lines* and *Sun Line*. *Turkish Maritime Lines* operate car-ferry services from Izmir to Venice.
RAIL: There are connections from London (Liverpool Street) via Hook of Holland, Cologne and Belgrade to Istanbul on the *Istanbul Express*, which also carries cars from several other European cities. There is a weekly sleeper from Moscow. *Interrail* tickets are available in the European part of Turkey as far as Istanbul.
ROAD: There are roads from the CIS, Greece, Bulgaria and Iran. **Coaches:** There are regular services between Turkey and Austria, France, Germany and Switzerland, also Jordan, Iran, Saudi Arabia and Syria.

TRAVEL - Internal

AIR: *Turkish Airlines* provides an important network of internal flights from Istanbul, Ankara and Izmir to all of the major Turkish cities. *Turkish Airlines* offers reductions of 60% on international flights (with the exception of Middle Eastern destinations) and 10% on domestic flights to holders of International Student Travel Conference (ISTC) cards.
SEA: *Turkish Maritime Lines* offer several coastal services with their *Adriatic Line* subsidiary, providing excellent opportunities for sightseeing; they also operate a car ferry between Mersin and Magosa (via Latakia). The *Mersin Tourist Line* operates from Mersin to Izmir and Istanbul via Antalya, Bodrum and Kusadasi. There are also services between Istanbul and Izmir, with overnight accommodation and ferry routes along Turkey's northern Black Sea coast. A frequent car ferry crosses the Dardenelles at Gallipoli, from Canakkale to Eceabat and Gelibolu to Lapseki.
Turkish Maritime Lines offer discounts of 15% on single and 25% on return passages for international routes and 50% for domestic routes to holders of ISTC cards.
RAIL: Many trains of the *Turkish State Railways (TCDD)* have sleeping cars, couchettes and restaurant cars, but there is no air-conditioned accommodation. Fares are more expensive for express and mail trains, even though express trains are relatively slow, and some routes are indirect. Steam engines, such as the *Anatolia Express* which traverses eastern Turkey, are retained for tourist trains on some routes. Tickets can be purchased at *TCDD* offices at the stations and *TCDD*-appointed agents. *TCDD* offer discounts of 20% to holders of ISTC cards.
ROAD: There is an extensive road maintenance and building programme; 1400km (900 miles) of motorway are under construction. In case of an accident, contact the Turkish Touring & Automobile Association *(Turkiye Turing ve Otomobil Kurumu)*. **Coach:** Many private companies provide frequent day and night services between all Turkish cities. Services are often faster than the trains and there is much competition between operators which leads to lower fares. Tickets are sold at the bus or coach companies' branch offices either at stations or in town centres. One should shop around the ticket offices for the best prices. Coaches depart from the bus stations *(otogar)* in large towns and from the town centre in small towns. **Car hire:** Both chauffeur and self-drive cars are available in all large towns. All international companies are represented.
Documentation: For stays longer than three months it is necessary to apply to the Turkish Touring & Automobile Club for a customs *triptique*. An International Driving Permit is required for vehicles hired in Turkey, but a valid national driving licence is sufficient for those bringing in their own car. Insurance requirements are a Green Card (or similar international cover) endorsed for Turkish territory.
URBAN: Extensive conventional bus (and some trolley-bus) services operate in Istanbul, Ankara and Izmir. There are buses in all other towns of size. They are generally reliable, modern and easy to use, although publicity is non-existent. Tickets are bought in advance from kiosks and dropped into a box by the driver. There are many types of taxi, shared taxi and minibus in operation. Taxis are numerous in all Turkish cities and are recognisable by their chequered black and yellow bands. Metered taxis are now available in Ankara and Istanbul. Where no metered taxis are available, the fare should be agreed beforehand.
A *dolmus* is a collective taxi which follows specific routes and is recognisable by its yellow band. Each passenger pays according to the distance travelled to specific stops. The fares are fixed by the municipality. The *dolmus* provides services within large cities to suburbs, airports and often to neighbouring towns. This is a very practical means of transport and much cheaper than a taxi, but one should beware of fares which may be demanded for unusual journeys, or journeys at night or in bad weather; in such cases, a 'special' (ie higher) rate will be demanded. Taxis may turn into a *dolmus* and vice versa according to demand. There are extensive cross-Bosphorus and short-hop ferries between the parts of Istanbul. In 1988 a second bridge over the river was opened. There are plans to construct a metro system in Ankara.
JOURNEY TIMES: The following chart gives approximate journey times (in hours and minutes) from Ankara to other major cities/towns in Turkey.

	Air	Road	Rail
Istanbul	0.45	8.00	8.00
Izmir	0.50	10.00	14.00
Antalya	1.00	9.00	-
Adana	0.55	8.00	13.00
Erzurum	1.15	11.00	18.00
Van	1.15	15.00	23.00
Trabzon	1.40	13.00	-
Mugla	1.25	10.00	-

TURKEY | **HEALTH REGULATIONS** | **VISA REGULATIONS** | Code-Link

GALILEO/WORLDSPAN

TI-DFT/ANK/HE

TI-DFT/ANK/VI

SABRE

TIDFT/ANK/HE

TIDFT/ANK/VI

To access this information on your CRS, swipe the barcode with a light pen or type in the text under the barcode. For more information, see the introduction *How to Use This Book.*

ACCOMMODATION

HOTELS: In recent years Turkey has made a considerable effort to develop its hotel facilities. As is usually the case, the major hotels are concentrated in the larger cities, especially in Istanbul, Ankara and Izmir.
At the coastal resorts and tourist centres there are a number of hotels, motels and camping facilities.
However, in the more remote areas of Turkey the number of hotels corresponding to Western standards is limited, most offering only basic comforts.
It is compulsory for establishments to have a book in which guests can register remarks, suggestions and complaints. Complaints can also be made direct to the Ministry of Tourism (address above), or to the Ministry of Tourism Directorate of the city concerned. **Grading:** Hotels are graded from **1 star** (tek yildizi) to **5 stars** (5 yildizi). Motels and holiday villas are first class (1 sinif) or second class (2 sinif).
GUEST-HOUSES: Guest-houses (pensions) can be found in holiday resorts and major towns.
SELF-CATERING: Villas and apartments can be rented. Contact the Information Counsellor's Office.
CAMPING/CARAVANNING: There are numerous sites but facilities are generally limited.
YOUTH HOSTELS: Holders of ISTC cards, International Youth Hostel Federation cards and those registered as 'student' or 'teacher' on their passports can benefit from the youth holiday opportunities available in Turkey. There are youth hostels in Istanbul, Kumla and Canakkale.
Some Turkish organisations, such as *Turkish Airlines*, recognise the ISTC card and accordingly grant reductions to holders.

RESORTS & EXCURSIONS

For the purpose of this section the country has been divided into several regions; in addition, there is also a section on ski resorts. Please see also the map of Turkey for the location of the main towns, resorts and communication routes.

Istanbul

Spanning the continents of Europe and Asia, Istanbul is spectacularly situated on the Golden Horn peninsula. Istanbul is a bustling, cosmopolitan city, and its eventful past as a former capital of the Roman, Byzantine and Ottoman Empires has left a rich legacy. Innumerable mosques, museums and magnificent palaces, the colourful waterside life and the covered bazaars all combine to create a compelling atmosphere.
Istanbul is made up of three distinct cities. The old city of **Istanbul** is decorated with parks and gardens. The main attractions include *Topkapi*, the residential palace of the Ottoman sultans overlooking the *Sea of Marmara* and the *Bosphorus*; the *Blue Mosque*, the only mosque in the world with six minarets; *St Sophia*, once a Byzantine cathedral, later a mosque and now a museum; and, underground, the Byzantine cistern supported by 336 Corinthian columns. (*St Sophia* is the largest free-standing building in the world and has survived several earthquakes which have destroyed the foundations of smaller structures.)
Across the Golden Horn, in stark contrast, is modern Istanbul, **Pera**, with large hotels, spacious squares and an international nightlife.
On the third shore lies **Uskudar** (Scutari), the Asian part of Istanbul, where Florence Nightingale nursed the sick during the Crimean War. Two suspension bridges (the longest in Europe) now span the Bosphorus and afford the most unforgettable panoramic view of Istanbul. One of the delights of Istanbul is that many seaside resorts on the Bosphorus, including *Tarabya* and *Machka*, are only a short drive away. Other attractions are the ancient fortifications at *Rumeli Hisarti*, the *National Park* of *Mount Olympus*, the ruins of *Troy* and the boat trips on the Bosphorus to the Princes Islands.

Thrace & Marmara

The Dardanelles, the Sea of Marmara and the Bosphorus separate the rolling hills and sunflower fields of European Thrace from Turkey's heartland in Asia. **Edirne,** the provincial capital, is a city rich in history. Three of the finest Turkish mosques, the *Eski Cami*, *Uc Serefeli Cami* and the famed *Selimiye* are among the various attractions. The landscape is made up of forests, mountains and sandy beaches, and Marmara is a particularly beautiful region. It is an important leisure area; there are coastal resorts at *Yalova*, *Erdek* and *Gemlik*. *Mount Uludag*, the ancient Mount Olympus of Mysia, is now Turkey's most popular ski resort. Lying at the foot of *Mount Uludag*, the thermal resort and historic city of **Bursa** is noted for the many elegant Ottoman buildings, including the *Green Mausoleum* and *Great Mosque*. **Iznik** has many Roman, Byzantine, Seljuk and Ottoman remains throughout the city. It is also famous for the tiles used to decorate mosques and palaces throughout Turkey. The city of **Izmit**, now sadly polluted, has ancient walls and a Roman aqueduct.

Aegean Coast

The magnificent coast of ancient Ionia, one of the earliest cradles of western civilization, boasts many important sites and picturesque resorts. It is thought that the remains of Troy lie along this coast. Of the nine levels of the excavated settlement mound, the sixth is supposed to be the Troy depicted in Homer's Iliad. The ruins of the great city of *Pergamum* (modern *Bergama*) lie to the south of Troy. The city was once famous in antiquity for its splendid library. Visit the *Sanctuary of Asclepieion* and the two fine temples, the Acropolis and the red-brick Basilica.
Izmir, the birthplace of Homer, is Turkey's third city and an important port. A modern metropolis with many large hotels, Izmir lies in a beautiful curving bay and is surrounded by terraced hillsides. As a result of earthquakes and a great fire, there are only a few reminders of old *Smyrna – Kadifekale*, the 4th-century fortress situated on top of *Mount Pagos*. The fortress affords a superb view of the city and the *Gulf of Izmir*, the Roman agora with some well-preserved porticos and the *Statues of Poseidon and Artemis*. **Cesme** is one of the many popular resorts in the Izmir region, and is noted for its excellent beaches, thermal springs and 15th-century fortress. The picturesque port of *Sigacik*, the ruins of the ancient Ionian city of **Teos** and the sandy beach at a *Akkum* are all situated between Izmir and Cesme. The remains of the Hellenistic and Roman city of Ephesus (modern **Seljuk**) founded in the 13th century BC, lie at the foot of Mount Pion. The *Grand Theatre* has been restored and there is a 2nd-century *Temple to Serapis* and an elegant facade to the temple of Hadrian. The site of *Meryemana*, the reputed house of the Virgin Mary, lies very close to **Ephesus** in a small vale of *Mount Bulbul Dagi* (Nightingale Mountain). It has become a world famous shrine, attracting thousands of pilgrims each year. The ruins of *Priene*, *Miletus* and *Didyma* are also of great interest and, like Ephesus, are within easy reach of **Kusadasi**, an attractive resort, surrounded by sandy bays, and an ideal excursion centre.
The attractions of the southwest Aegean include the popular seaside town of **Bodrum**, dominated by the magnificent 15th-century castle of St Peter; *Marmaris*, set in a deep fjord-like inlet and surrounded by pine woods; the fishing village of **Datca**; and the Lycian rock tombs in **Fethiye**. Not far from Fethiye is the newly discovered holiday beauty spot of *Ölü Deniz*, a stunning crystal clear lagoon surrounded by pine covered mountains and protected from rampant commercial development by its status as a national park.
Pamukkale, near Denizli, is famous for its spectacular calcified waterfall and thermal waters, used since Roman times for their therapeutic powers. Pamukkale also contains the ruins of the Roman city of *Hierapolis* and the often photographed swimming pool littered with ancient columns.

Western Mediterranean Coast

With sunshine for most of the year and a magnificent coastline of secluded, sandy bays, the Mediterranean (or Turquoise) Coast is a popular holiday area. It is also a region steeped in history and legend, lavishly endowed with important sites and great Crusader castles.
Situated on a cliff promontory, **Antalya** is a delightful resort and, with its modern hotels, is the ideal starting point for tours to the outlying Roman cities of *Perge*, *Aspendos* and *Side*. Antalya itself has the attraction of the monumental *Hadrian's Gate*, *Kesik Minare* and *Yivli Minare* mosques and *Hidirlik Kulesi*, the round Roman tower. One of the largest and best-preserved Roman stadiums lies outside the Hellenistic wall which surrounds the ruins of Perge. In addition to the magnificent *Victory Portal*, thermal bath and agora, the marks of chariot wheels can still be detected. The remarkable 2nd-century theatre at **Aspendos** is the finest surviving example of the ancient world and is still used for performances of classical plays. Turkey's finest Roman aqueduct lies to the north of the city. In **Side**, now a thriving seaside resort, the Greek enclosure walls are still virtually undamaged. The town also boasts an exquisite fountain, a theatre, two agoras and Roman baths. Nestling at the foot of a rocky promontory and crowned by a Seljuk fortress, **Alanya** is one of the finest sights in the Mediterranean. Take a boat trip round its magnificent cliffs, bristling with coves and inlets, and climb to the triple-walled citadel for a breathtaking view.

Eastern Mediterranean Coast

A spectacularly scenic road connects **Anamur**, striking for the Byzantine castle standing on a towering cliff, and **Silifke.** The museum in ancient Silifke contains finds from the numerous archaeological sites in the vicinity. **Mersin,** built on a site dating back to Paleolithic times, is a major port with some good hotels. The prosperous city of **Adana,** in the middle of the flat Cukurova plain, is the centre of Turkey's cotton industry. The massive *Taskopru bridge*, built by Hadrian in the 2nd century, the ancient covered bazaar and nearby Crusader castles and Hittite settlements are all worth a visit. The road from **Iskenderun** leads through the Belen Pass to **Antakya,** the Biblical Antioch, where St Peter founded the first Christian community. The grotto where he preached can be seen just outside the town.

The Black Sea Coast

This rugged, mountainous region of Turkey has a wild beauty, but lacks the historical and climatic attractions of the rest of the country. Despite the variable weather, there are several coastal resorts with good, sandy beaches. These include, from east to west, *Kilyos*, *Sile*, *Akcakoca*, *Unye*, *Ordu* and *Giresun*. Accommodation is, however, often very basic. A good and scenic coastal road connects **Samsun** and **Trabzon**, the two regional centres.
Although little remains to testify to its ancient origins, Samsun's important place in modern history is reflected by one of the finest monuments in Turkey; the War of Independence began here in 1919. The ruins of a Byzantine fortress can still be seen in Trabzon, together with many fine buildings including the *Church of St Sophia* which was built during the Comnene's 200-year rule. 54km (34 miles) from Trabzon is the 14th-century convent dedicated to the Virgin Mary. Set into the face of a sheer cliff, 300m (1000ft) above the valley floor, it contains some magnificent frescoes.

Central Anatolia

The hub of this vast, central plateau – the cradle of the ancient Hittite and Phrygian civilizations – is the modern metropolis of **Ankara**. Kemal Atatürk supervised the construction of Ankara, a capital to replace Istanbul, in this hitherto underpopulated region during the 1920s and 1930s. Memorials to this national hero abound and the mausoleum of Atatürk dominates the new city.
Ankara was, however, built on the site of more ancient settlements and it is fitting that the *Museum of Anatolian Civilizations*, built under the ramparts of the Citadel, should house such a unique and magnificent collection of Neolithic and Hittite works. There are also reminders of the area's more recent past – as part of the Roman and Seljuk Empires – and many fine mosques, some dating back to the 12th century. The Hittite state archives were found in **Bogazkale** (Hattusas) in 1906, and contained within the Bogazkale–Alacahoyuk–Yazilikaya triangle are the most important sites of the Hittite Empire.
Sungurlu is a good base for visitors to this fascinating but underdeveloped region. **Amasya,** one of the most attractive towns in Anatolia, was the capital of the Pontic kingdom. The rock tombs of the Pontic kings and the ruins of a citadel, perched on a rock face and containing the remains of an Ottoman palace, can still be seen. The nearby towns of **Tokat** and **Sivas** are noted for their Seljuk architecture.
Cappadocia is a spectacular, almost surreal landscape of rock and cones, capped pinnacles and fretted ravines, just beginning to feature on tourist itineraries. Dwellings have been hewn from the soft, volcanic rock since 400BC, and the elaborate cave systems have sheltered generations of persecuted settlers. Some villages, notably **Soganli**, are still inhabited but most have been evacuated due to the persistent threat of rock falls. At **Goreme** there are magnificent rock churches with Byzantine frescoes and at **Zelve** a somewhat eerie monastic complex. The villages of *Ortahisar* and **Uchisar**, clustered around rock pinnacles and crowned by citadels, offer panoramic views. The canyon of *Ihlara* and the underground cities of **Kaymakli** and **Derinkuyu** should not be missed. Small, friendly hostels and campsites are dotted around Cappadocia, but the best hotels are to be found in the main towns of **Nevsehir** and **Urgup**. The ancient settlements of *Kanes*, *Karum* and *Fraktin* (now a ski resort), near the old city of **Kayseri**, are worth a visit.
Konya, the old Seljuk capital and Turkey's fourth largest city, is one of the world's oldest settlements, dating back to the 7th millenium BC. Konya was also the home of Mevlana, Islam's most celebrated mystic and founder of the Order of Whirling Dervishes. The mausoleum of Mevlana became a museum in 1927 under Atatürk's secularisation policy, but to many a place of worship. Other places of interest include Alaeddin's 13th-century mosque, the *Ince Minare Medrese* and the *Iplikci Mosque*,

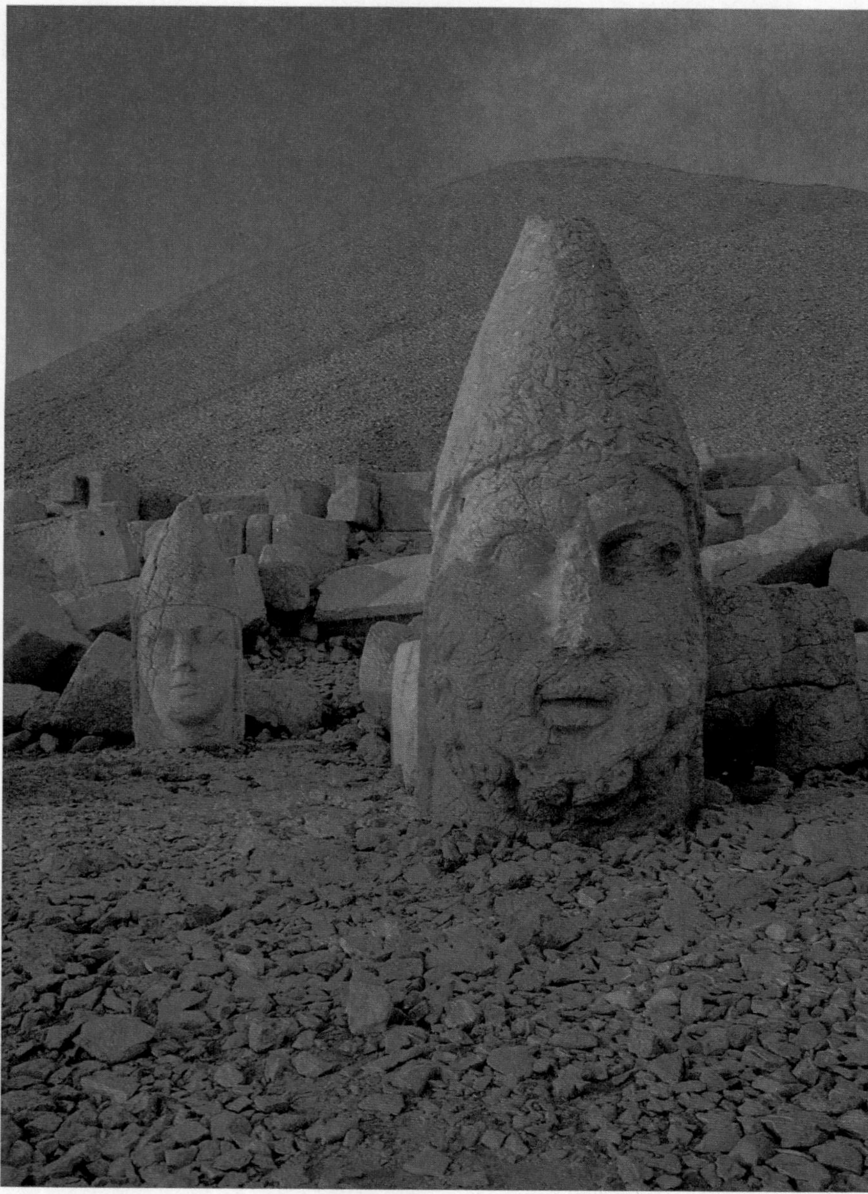
Statues at Nemrut Dagi

Konya's oldest structure. The ancient sites of *Beysehir*, *Catalhoyuk* and *Binbir Kilise* are all close to Konya.

The Eastern Provinces

The vast, empty expanse of eastern Anatolia differs profoundly from the rest of the country. It is a miraculously untamed area, and a land of extreme temperatures. The landscape has a desolate beauty, with ochre red plains and fertile valleys, lakes, waterfalls and snow-capped peaks. There are fine mosques, palaces and monuments. **Erzurum,** the largest town in the region, was one of the eastern bastions of Byzantium for many centuries, and has mosques and mausolea from the Seljuk and Mongol eras, Byzantine walls and two Koranic colleges characterised by minarets and finely carved portals. The frontier town of **Kars**, to the north of Erzurum, is dominated by a formidable 12th-century Georgian fortress. The ruins of the 10th-century *Ani* lie east of Kars. Overshadowed by *Agri Dagri*, the Biblical Mount Ararat where Noah's Ark came to rest, is the fairytale palace and mosque of *Ishak Pasha* at **Dogubayazit.** The view from the palace is spectacular. The walled town of **Van,** on the eastern shore of the immense *Lake Van*, was an important Urartu fortress from 800-600BC. The citadel dominates the ruins of Seljuk and Ottoman mosques and many rock tombs. On the island of **Akdamar**, in Lake Van, is the enchanting 10th-century *Church of the Holy Cross.* Other places of interest include **Diyarbakir**, built in the 4th century and surrounded by forbidding triple walls of black basalt; the white coloured medieval architecture and Roman citadel of **Mardin; Urfa**; and **Nemrut Dagi**, the home of the colossal stone statues erected by King Antiochus I in the 1st century BC.
Accommodation in this area is very basic and often hard to find.

Ski Resorts

Winter sports resorts in Turkey are generally located in forested mountains of average height. The following ski centres are easily accessible by road or *Turkish Airlines* domestic flights.
Bursa – Uludag: 36km (22 miles) south of Bursa, this resort is accessible by a good asphalt road or by cable car. The season runs from January to April. There are beginners' slopes, slalom and giant slalom courses, three ski lifts, three chair lifts and après-ski facilities. A wide range of accommodation is available – hotels and chalets with a capacity for 3100 – and the resort also has a small hospital.
Antalya – Saklikent: 48km (30 miles) north of Antalya, in the Bakirli Dagi mountain range, reaches 2546m (8353ft) high. Accommodation consists of pensions and chalets, with a capacity of 2500. The special attraction of this centre is that in March and April one can ski in the morning, then drive down to the coast and swim in the warm waters of the Mediterranean in the afternoon.
Bolu – Koroglu: This resort is situated on the Istanbul–Ankara highway, 50km (30 miles) from Bolu and surrounded by pine forests; the ski area is between 1900m and 2350m (6235ft to 7710ft) high. The second-class Kartal hotel with 400-bed capacity has a swimming pool, ski lift, equipment for hire, and ski instructors.
Erzurum – Palandoken: This centre, 6km (4 miles) from Erzurum, lies at an altitude of 2200m to 3100m (7200ft to 10,000ft) with some of the longest and most difficult courses in Turkey. Skiers must have prior permission from the General Director of Physical Training (Beden Terbiyesi GM Kayak Federasyonu, Ulus Ishani, A-Blok, Ulus, Ankara). Accommodation is available at a 100-bed, centrally heated ski lodge, with a chair lift, ski instructors and equipment for hire. There is also a number of hotels in Erzurum. December to April is the most popular season.
Kars – Sarikamis: Situated near Kars at 2250m (7400ft), this centre has good runs and ideal snow conditions. The best season is January to March. There is accommodation in Kars and at the 60-bed, centrally heated ski lodge with a chair lift and ski instructors.
Kayseri – Erciyes: 25km (15 miles) from Kayseri, this centre lies at 2150m (7050ft) on the eastern face of Erciyes Dagi. The season runs from November to May and there is a 120-bed ski lodge, equipment hire facilities and instructors. To ski at this resort, permission from the General Directorate of Physical Training is required (see above).

SOCIAL PROFILE

FOOD & DRINK: Most hotels have their own restaurants; there is also a large number of other eating places. Turkish food is world famous, combining culinary traditions of a pastoral people originating from central Asia and the influences of the Mediterranean regions. Turkish cuisine is noted for its pure quality stemming from the freshness of the fruit, vegetables, meat and fish in a country which produces all its own food. Lamb is a basic meat featured on all menus, often as *sis kebab* (pieces of meat threaded on a skewer and grilled), *doner kebab* (pieces of lamb packed tightly round a revolving spit). Fish and shellfish are very fresh and *barbunya* (red mullet) and *kilic baligi* (swordfish) are delicious. *Dolma* (vine leaves stuffed with nuts and currants) and *karniyarik* (aubergine stuffed with minced meat) are other popular dishes. Guests are always able to go into a kitchen and choose from the pots if they cannot understand the names of the dishes. Table service is common. **Drink:** *Ayran* (a refreshing yoghurt drink) and strong black Turkish coffee are widely available. Turkey is a secular state and alcohol is not prohibited, although during Ramadan it is considered polite for the visitor to avoid drinking alcohol. Turkish beer, red and white wines are excellent. The national drink is *raki* (anisette) which clouds when water is added, known as 'lion's milk'. Drinking *raki* is a ritual and is traditionally accompanied by a variety of *meze* (hors d'oeuvres).
NIGHTLIFE: There are nightclubs in most main centres, either Western or Oriental, with music and dancing. There are theatres with concerts in Izmir, Istanbul and Ankara and most towns have cinemas. Restaurants and hotels sometimes offer floorshows. Turkish baths are popular.
SHOPPING: Istanbul's *Kapali Carsi Bazaar* has jewellery, carpets and antiques for sale. Turkish handicrafts include a rich variety of textiles and embroideries, articles of copper, onyx and tile, mother of pearl, inlaid articles, leather and suede products, jewellery and, above all, carpets and *kilims*. **Shopping hours:** 0900-1300 and 1400-1900 Monday to Saturday (closed Sunday). Summer: In the Aegean and Mediterranean regions of Turkey, government offices and many other establishments are closed during the afternoon in the summer months. The summer hours are fixed each year by the provincial governors.
SPORT: Mountaineering: Turkey has a number of mountain ranges with peaks ranging from heights of 3250m (10,660ft) to the 5165m (16,945ft) of Mount Agri (Ararat), the highest mountain in Anatolia, which provide excellent climbing possibilities for both the amateur and more expert climber. Permission is required from the *Turkish Mountaineering Club*. **Skiing:** Winter sports resorts in Turkey are generally located in forested mountains. Ski centres are often easily accessible by road or by *Turkish Airlines* domestic flights. Most resorts are in the north (near Ankara) and the western interior. **Watersports:** The Mediterranean coast, particularly Izmir, has very warm waters and watersports are widely available.
SPECIAL EVENTS: The following is a selection of some of the festivals to be held in Turkey during 1993/4: **Mar 18 '93** *Anniversary of the 1915 Sea Victory*, Çanakkale. **Apr 3** *International Film Festival*, Istanbul. **Apr 23** *International Children's Festival*, Ankara. **May 6-10** *International Yunus Emre Culture and Art Week*, Eskisehir. **May-Jun** *The Biennial International Asian-European Art Festival*, Ankara. **Jun 4-9** *International Folk Music and Dance Festival*, Antalya. **Jun** *Kafkasor Culture and Art Festival*, Artvin. **Jun 7-13** *International Bergama Fair*, Izmir. **Jul 14-24** *International Hitite Festival*, Çorum. **Aug 4-12** *Insuyu Festival*, Burder. **Aug 10-18** *Festival of Troy*, Izmir. **Sep 6-7** *Seyh Edebal Tribute and Culture Festival*, Bilecik. **Oct 26-28** *International Bozburun Gulet Festival*, Mugla. **Nov 1-6** *Marmaris International Yacht Races Week*, Mugla. **Dec 10-17** *Tribute to Melvana Ceremonies*, Konya. **Mar '94** *Anniversary of the 1915 Sea Victory*.
SOCIAL CONVENTIONS: Shaking hands is the normal form of greeting. Hospitality is very important and

isitors should respect Islamic customs. Informal wear is cceptable, but beachwear should be confined to the each or poolside. Smoking is widely acceptable but pro-ibited in cinemas, theatres, city buses and *dolmuses*. **ipping:** A service charge is included in hotel and estaurant bills.

BUSINESS PROFILE

CONOMY: Agriculture is still the most important sec-or, particularly the production of export crops such as obacco and cotton. Other products include wheat, sugar eet, grapes, olives and citrus fruit. The sector has shown isappointing growth in recent years, especially by com-arison with Turkish industry. In mining, Turkey is an mportant producer of copper, chromium, borax, and to a esser extent, bauxite and coal. There is a small manufac-uring sector, concentrated in textiles, iron and steel. Tourism is in a phase of rapid expansion and is now a key ource of foreign exchange. The economy is generally weak, but stable. Turkish trade patterns have shifted rom the Middle East in favour of Europe and the EC in articular. The Turkish government has repeatedly xpressed a desire to join the EC, although the majority f the Community have reacted coolly to the proposal Britain under Margaret Thatcher was the major excep-ion to this attitude). Germany (which employs many Turkish immigrant workers), the USA, Iran and Iraq are Turkey's main trading partners. In 1992, a regional eco-omic co-operation agreement was signed in Istanbul by leven countries (Turkey, Greece, the Russian ederation, Ukraine, Moldova, Bulgaria, Romania, Albania, Armenia, Azerbaijan and Georgia).
BUSINESS: A formal suit or jacket and tie should always be worn for business. English is widely spoken in business circles, although an effort by the visitor to speak a little Turkish is appreciated. The majority of people in business value punctuality and visiting cards are widely used. **Office hours:** 0830-1200 and 1300-1730 Monday to Friday.
COMMERCIAL INFORMATION: The following organisation can offer advice: Union of Chambers of Commerce, Industry, Maritime Commerce and Commodity Exchanges of Turkey (UCCET), Atatürk Bul 149, Bakanliklar, Ankara. Tel: (4) 417 7700. Telex: 42343.

HISTORY & GOVERNMENT

HISTORY: Turkey, or Asia Minor as it was called during much of the pre-modern period, was for over a thousand years the heartland of the Eastern Roman (Byzantine) Empire, with Constantinople as its glori-ous capital. Founded by Constantine the Great in AD330, it survived the collapse of the Western Empire in the 5th century. It was the capital from which the brilliant and enigmatic Emperor Justinian (527-565) launched his ambitious projects to reunite the old Roman Empire, the western provinces of which had been occupied by Germanic people from northern Europe. The Byzantine Empire, from the death of Justinian until its eventual fall in 1453, was engaged in a long retreat in the face of numerous enemies, mainly the forces of Islam. However, the Byzantines took advantage of the success of the First Crusade (1096-1100) whose armies re-took many Byzantine posses-sions in Asia Minor, Syria and Palestine although, as later events were to prove, the interests of the Byzantines and of the Christian Crusader states in Palestine were not always identical. But the Byzantine state never fully recovered, and on many occasions dur-ing the next three centuries a final defeat was only pre-vented by the disunity of their enemies and, particular-ly, by the massive fortifications of the city of Constantinople. The conquest of Constantinople in 1204 – the only time the fortifications were breached – was followed by one of the most savage and rapacious sacks of any city in the history of the world: the trea-sures of Byzantium were beyond count or value, and many priceless works of art were removed to Europe (mainly to Venice) during this time. The Byzantines set up a rival capital at Nicea until the reconquest of Constantinople in 1261, but by this time the Empire had effectively lost control of most of its territories, and by the 14th century, Byzantine control of Asia Minor was little more than an empty theory. The real power in the region were fast becoming the Ottomans, inhabitants of a state based in Bithynia. They steadily expanded their territorial control from Turkey itself and constructed the Ottoman empire, which at its zenith in the mid-16th century (a period associated with the reign of Suleman the Magnificent) covered southeast Europe, including the Balkans and Hungary; North Africa as far as Morocco; Crimea and Georgia; the Levant; Syria; Iraq; and most of the Arabian penin-sula. The most famous conquest, from a symbolic and strategic point of view, was that of Constantinople itself in 1453; with its fall, the Roman Empire, in a strictly legalistic sense, finally came to an end. The ter-ritorial ambitions of the Ottomans regarding control of the Mediterranean and central Europe brought the empire into conflict with the major European powers of the day, particularly the Habsburgs. The Venetians and, later, the Russians were almost constant enemies of the Ottomans during the late-17th and 18th cen-turies, during which time the empire sank into decline. Attempts were made by some rulers in the late 18th century to reform the empire, but with little effect. The diplomatic history of central Europe in the early modern period is highly complex, and the Ottoman Empire became increasingly a pawn and victim of the various power struggles. The term 'the sick man of Europe' was applied to Turkey during this period. Turkish history can thereafter be characterised by a constant struggle between the forces of absolutism and reform. In 1914, the country became embroiled in the First World War on the side of Germany. After the war, most of the Ottoman possessions came under British or French control with the support of the newly-formed League of Nations. In Turkey itself, the Ottoman dynasty was overthrown in 1923 by a revolu-tionary movement led by Mustafa Kemal – better known as Atatürk ('the father of the Turks') – who established a single-party republic with himself at the head. The period after the War of Independence saw sweeping social reforms and economic modernisation, including the abolition of the Islamic social infrastruc-ture and the development of manufacturing industry. Atatürk's successor, Ismet Inönü, kept Turkey out of World War II (bar the last four months) and intro-duced multi-party politics. The first elections were held in 1950. There have since been two prolonged periods of military rule, the second ending with elec-tions in 1983, won by Turgut Özal and the Motherland Party. Martial law, however, remained in force in many provinces until further elections in 1987, in which the Motherland Party took 99% of the vote. Turkey joined NATO in 1952 and, following the lifting of suspen-sions with the end of military rule, is once more a member of the OECD and the Council of Europe and an associate member of the EC; full EC membership is actively being sought. At the beginning of 1990, the Armenian/Azeri conflict created tension in Turkey's eastern provinces. Turkey was the first country to recognise the independence of Azerbaijan and has pro-vided consistent diplomatic support for the Azeris against Armenia. Turkey is also seeking to develop closer political and economic links with the Turkic republics of the former Soviet Union: several of these Central Asian states view Turkey, with its largely secu-lar polity and mixed economy, as a suitable model to pursue in the course of their own development. Later in 1990, Turkey became deeply involved in the Gulf crisis sparked off by the Iraqi invasion of Kuwait. As Iraq's only neighbour belonging to NATO, Turkey's position has been a valuable one for the West. Turkey's prompt action in backing UN sanctions and imple-menting measures to make them reasonably effective garnered both financial benefits and a free hand to deal with the Kurdish Workers' Party insurgency operating in southeast Turkey. However, President Özal could not send troops to join the multinational force in Saudi Arabia because of the weakness of his domestic position, reflected in massive unpopularity and con-stant ministerial resignations. Six months after the end of the war, in October 1991, national elections were held in Turkey. Four main parties fought the election: the True Path Party (DYP) led by Suleyman Demirel which won 27% of the vote; the Motherland Party (ANAP) led by Prime Minister Mesut Yilmaz (24%); the Socialist Democratic Populist Party (Erdal Inonu, 21%); and the Islamic fundamentalist Welfare Party (Necmettin Erbakan, 16%). True Path and the Socialist Democratic Populists formed a coalition which gave them a majority of 40 seats in the National Assembly. Suleyman Demirel, six times premier and twice deposed by the military, once again became Prime Minister.
GOVERNMENT: Under the constitution of 1987, legislative power is vested in a single chamber, the 400-member National Assembly, elected through uni-versal adult suffrage. This, in turn, elects the President for a 7-year term. The President holds executive power and is advised by a Council of Ministers.

CLIMATE

Marmara and the Aegean and Mediterranean coasts have a typical Mediterranean climate with hot summers and mild winters.
Required clothing: Light to mediumweights and rain-wear for all seasons.

ISTANBUL Turkey (114m)

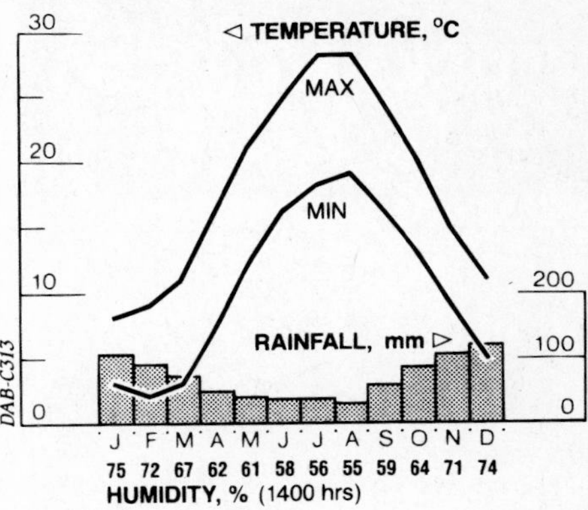

IZMIR Turkey (28m)

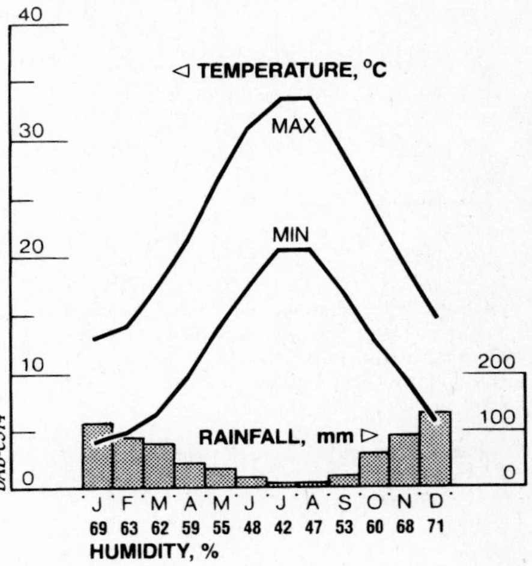

ANTALYA Turkey (40m)

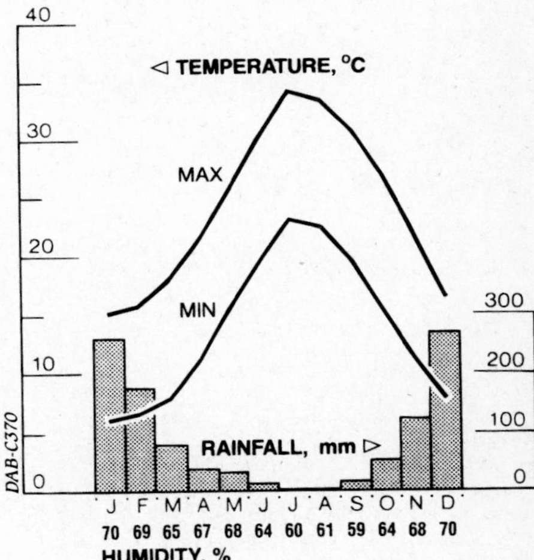

SAMSUN Turkey (40m)

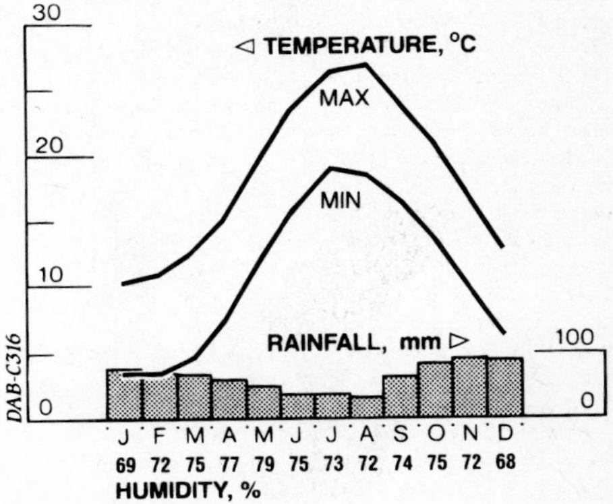

TURKS & CAICOS

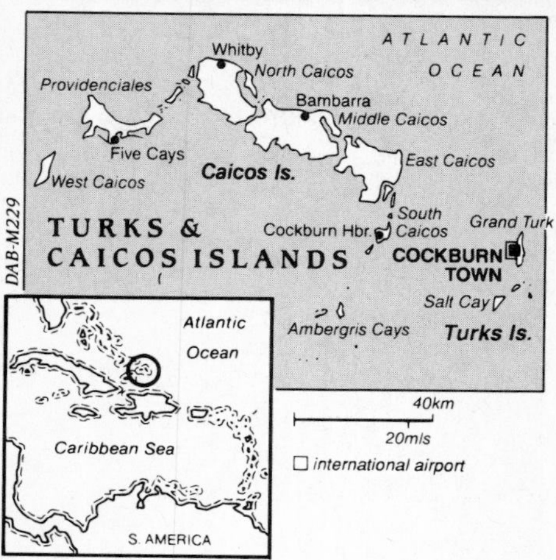

Location: Caribbean, southeast of the Bahamas.

Diplomatic representation: The Turks & Caicos Islands are a British Dependent Territory and are formally represented abroad by British diplomatic missions. However, information and advice may be obtained at the addresses below.

Turks & Caicos Islands Tourist Board
PO Box 128
Pond Street
Grand Turk
Turks & Caicos Islands
Tel: 946 2321. Fax: 946 2733. Telex: 8227.

Turks & Caicos Tourist Information Office
International House
47 Chase Side
Enfield EN2 6NB
Tel: (081) 364 5188. Fax: (081) 367 9949. Telex: 24457.
Opening hours: 0900-1730 Monday to Friday.

Commonwealth Information Centre
Commonwealth Institute
Kensington High Street
London W8 6NQ
Tel: (071) 603 4535, ext 210 (information). Fax: (071) 602 7374. Telex: 8955822.

Turks and Caicos Travel Bureau
PO Box 594023
Miami, FL
33159
Tel: (305) 667 0966.

Turks and Caicos IslandsTourist Board
Taurus House
512 Duplex Avenue
Toronto, Ontario
M4R 2E3
Tel: (416) 485 7827. Fax: (416) 485 8256.

AREA: 5000 sq km (193 sq miles).
POPULATION: 12,350 (1990).
POPULATION DENSITY: 24.7 per sq km.
CAPITAL: Cockburn Town (Grand Turk). **Population:** 3761 (1990).
GEOGRAPHY: The Turks & Caicos are an archipelago of more than 40 islands forming the southeastern end of the Bahamas chain. There are two principal groups, each surrounded by a continuous coral reef. Caicos is the larger group and includes Providenciales, Middle (or Grand) Caicos, and the islands of North, South, East and West Caicos, plus numerous small cays, some of which are inhabited. The Turks group, separated by a 35km- (22-mile) wide channel of water, consists of Grand Turk, Sal Cay and a number of small uninhabited cays.
LANGUAGE: English.
RELIGION: Roman Catholic, Anglican, Methodist, Baptist, Seventh Day Adventist and Pentecostal.
TIME: GMT - 5 (GMT - 4 from Apr 7 to Oct 26).
ELECTRICITY: 110 volts AC.
COMMUNICATIONS: Telephone: IDD is available Country code: 809 946. There are no area codes. Good communications network run by *Cable & Wireless (WI) Ltd*, with automatic exchange on all the islands. USA 800 calls are charged at the normal rate. The local telephone directory lists charges for international calls. There is a 10% tax on all calls. Public card-phones are in operation on all the islands; phonecards are available from *Cable & Wireless* and outlets near phone booths, in US$20, 10 and 5 denominations, plus 10% tax. Cheap rates are in operation 1900-0600 weekdays and all day Saturday and Sunday. **Fax:** All the islands have facsimile services. **Telex/telegram:** International services are available from the capital and main hotels; 0800-1800 Monday to Saturday. **Post:** The General Post Office is on Grand Turk, with sub-offices in South Caicos, Salt Cay and Providenciales. Airmail to Europe takes five days. Post office hours: 0800-1600 Monday to Thursday, 0800-1530 Friday. **Press:** *The Turks & Caicos Free Press* is published weekly, *The Turks and Caicos News* bi-weekly, *The Times of the Islands Magazine* quarterly, with *The Turks and Caicos Pocket Guide* appearing seasonally.
BBC World Service and Voice of America frequencies: From time to time these change. See the section *How to Use this Book* for more information.

BBC:				
MHz	17.790	11.750	9.740	6.195
Voice of America:				
MHz	15.21	11.70	6.130	0.930

Providenciales

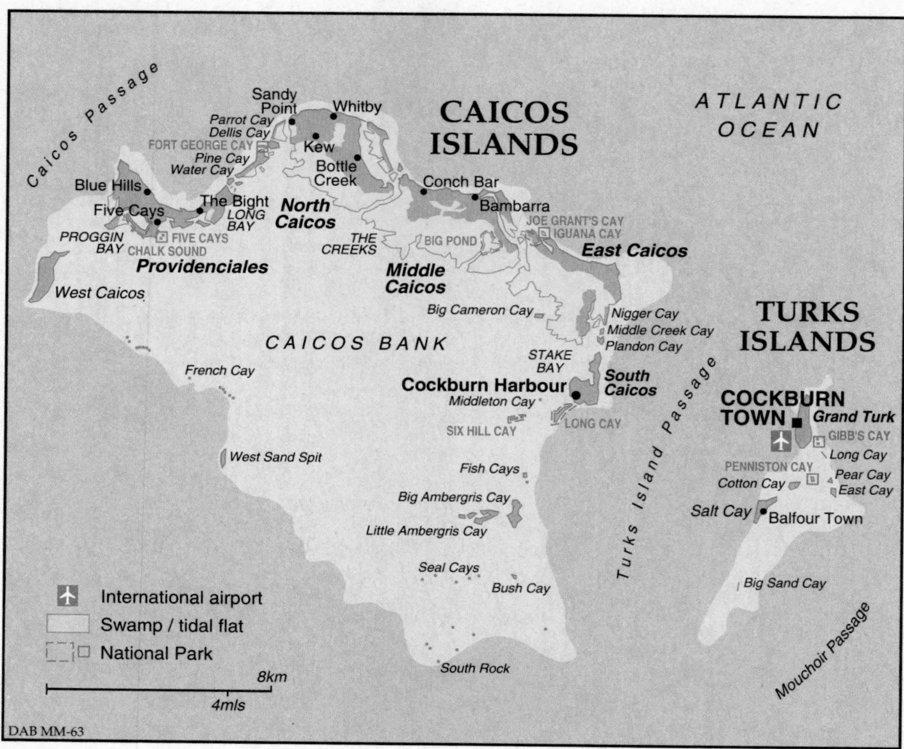

PASSPORT/VISA

Regulations and requirements may be subject to change at short notice, and you are advised to contact the appropriate diplomatic or consular authority before finalising travel arrangements. Details of these may be found at the head of this country's entry. Any numbers in the chart refer to the footnotes below.

	Passport Required?	Visa Required?	Return Ticket Required?
Full British	Yes	No	Yes
BVP	Not valid	-	-
Australian	Yes	No	Yes
Canadian	1	No	Yes
USA	1	No	Yes
Other EC	Yes	No	Yes
Japanese	Yes	Yes	Yes

PASSPORTS: Valid passport required by all except [1] nationals of Canada and the USA if holding proof of identity (ie a voter's card).
British Visitors Passport: Not acceptable.
VISAS: Required by Eastern bloc countries and some non-Commonwealth countries. Since visa regulations are subject to frequent change, it is, however, strongly advised to check with the visa department of the British Passport Office prior to departure (see below).
Types of visa: Entry visa. Cost: £20 (£33 if the application has to be referred to Grand Turk).
Validity: Variable; each application is judged on individual merit.
Application to: British Passport Office, Clive House, Petty France, London SW7. Tel: (071) 279 4000 *or* 271 8552 (visa department). Opening hours: 0900-1600 Monday to Friday.
Application requirements: (a) Passport. (b) Photo. (c) Return or onward ticket.
Temporary residence: Work and residence permits are required; apply to the Chief Immigration Officer, Government Buildings, Grand Turk.

MONEY

Currency: US Dollar (US$) = 100 cents. Notes are in denominations of US$100, 50, 20, 10, 5, 2 and 1. Coins are in denominations of US$1, and 50, 25, 10, 5 and 1 cents.
Credit cards: Access/Mastercard and Visa are widely accepted. Check with your credit card company for details of merchant acceptability and other services which may be available.
Travellers cheques: Accepted in most hotels, shops and banks.
Exchange rate indicators: The following figures are included as a guide to the movements of the US Dollar against Sterling:

Date:	Oct '89	Oct '90	Oct '91	Oct '92
£1.00=	1.58	1.95	1.74	1.58

Banking hours: 0830-1430 Monday to Thursday, 0830-1230 and 1430-1630 Friday (Barclays Bank); 0830-1430 Monday to Thursday and 0830-1630 Friday (Scotia Bank).

DUTY FREE

The following items may be imported into the Turks & Caicos Islands without incurring customs duty:
200 cigarettes or 50 cigars or 225g of tobacco;
1.136 litres of spirits or wine.
Note: (a) The above applies to UK residents over 17 years of age. Allowances for other nationals vary, and it is advisable to consult the Tourist Board for details. (b) There are no restrictions on the import of cameras, films or sports equipment except spear guns. Firearms are prohibited without a permit.

PUBLIC HOLIDAYS

Public holidays observed in the Turks & Caicos Islands are as follows:
Mar 8 '93 Commonwealth Day. **Apr 9** Good Friday. **Apr 12** Easter Monday. **May 17** National Heroes' Day. **Jun 6** Memorial Day. **Jun 12** Queen's Official Birthday. **Aug 1** Emancipation Day. **Sep 24** National Youth Day. **Oct 12** Columbus Day. **Oct 24** International Human Rights Day. **Dec 25** Christmas Day. **Dec 26** Boxing Day. **Jan 1 '94** New Years Day. **Mar 8** Commonwealth Day.

HEALTH

Regulations and requirements may be subject to change at short notice, and you are advised to contact your doctor well in advance of your intended date of departure. Any numbers in the chart refer to the footnotes below.

	Special Precautions?	Certificate Required?
Yellow Fever	No	No
Cholera	No	No
Typhoid & Polio	Yes	-
Malaria	No	-
Food & Drink	1	-

[1]: All water should be regarded as being potentially contaminated. Water used for drinking, brushing teeth or making ice should have first been boiled or otherwise sterilised. Powdered or tinned milk is available and is advised, but make sure that it is reconstituted with pure water. Only eat well-cooked meat and fish, preferably served hot. Pork, salad and mayonnaise may carry increased risk. Vegetables should be cooked and fruit peeled.
Health care: There is a Reciprocal Health Agreement with the UK. On presentation of proof of residence in

TURKS & CAICOS ISLANDS | **HEALTH REGULATIONS** | **VISA REGULATIONS** | Code-Link

GALILEO/WORLDSPAN

TI-DFT/GDT/HE

TI-DFT/GDT/VI

SABRE

TIDFT/GDT/HE

TIDFT/GDT/VI

To access this information on your CRS, swipe the barcode with a light pen or type in the text under the barcode. For more information, see the introduction *How to Use This Book.*

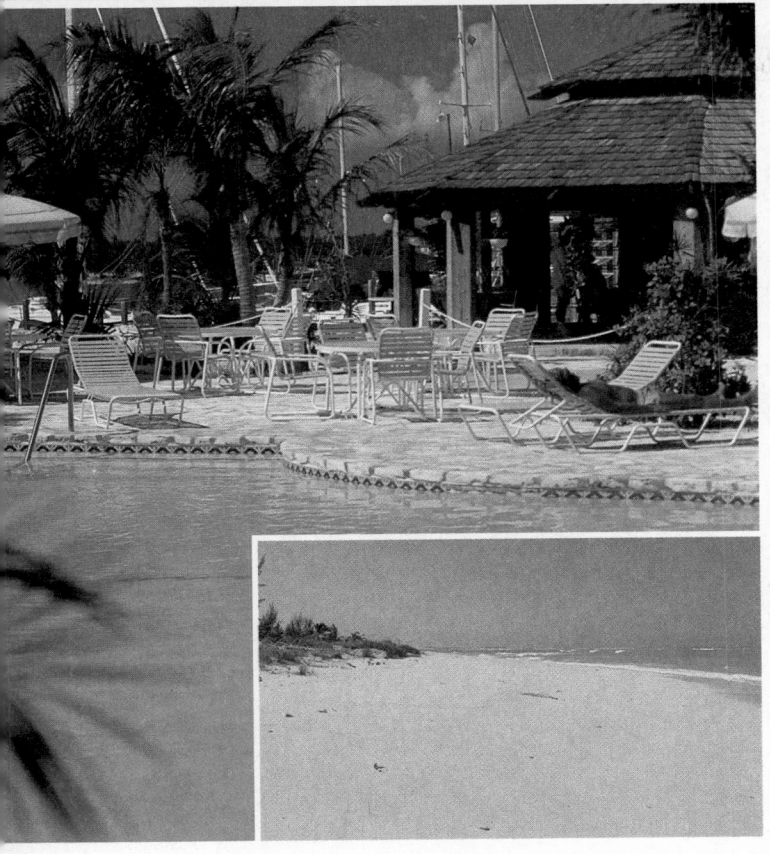

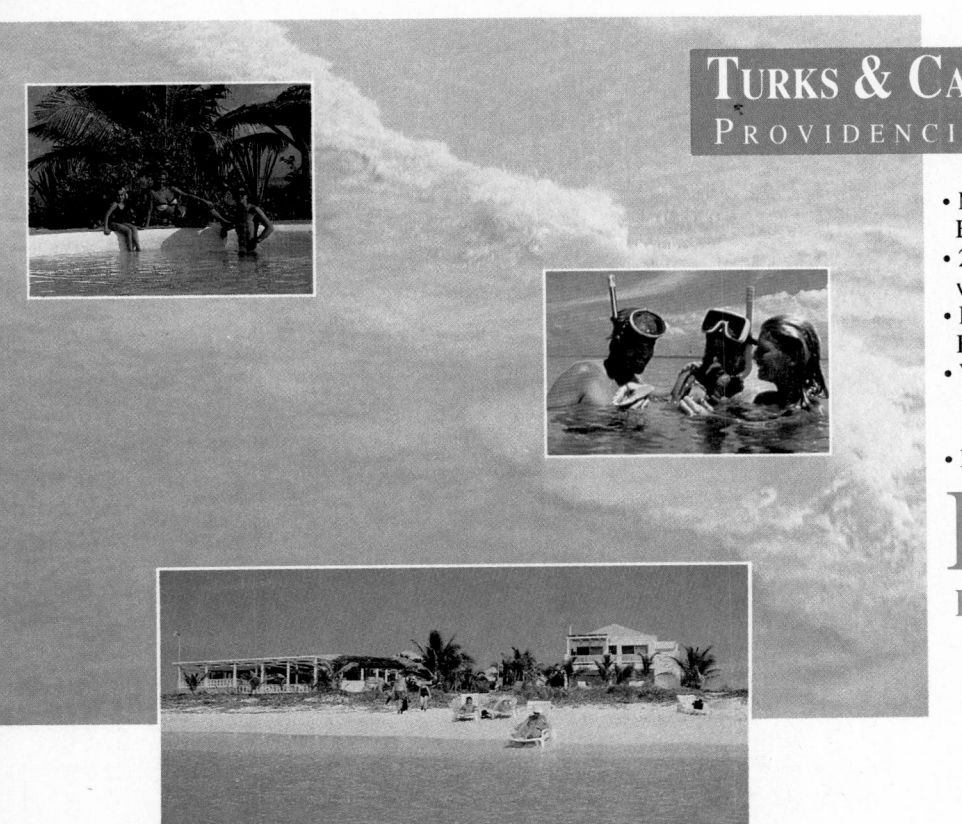

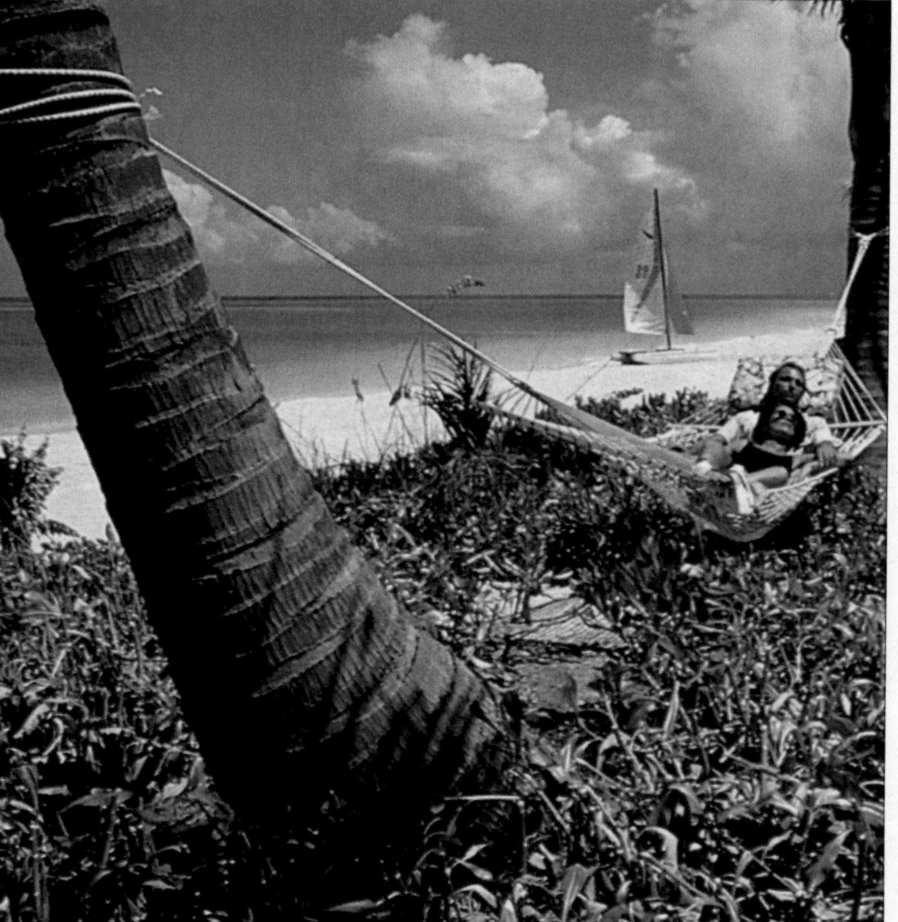

the UK (NHS card, driving licence, etc), those under 16 or over 65 receive all medical and dental treatment free of charge. Other UK residents are entitled to free treatment as follows: on *Grand Turk*, dental treatment, prescribed medicines and ambulance travel; on the *outer islands*, medical treatment at government clinics and prescribed medicines. There is a hospital on Grand Turk, and clinics on South Caicos, Middle Caicos, North Caicos, Providenciales and Salt Cay.

TRAVEL - International

AIR: The main airline is *Turks & Caicos Airways (QW)*. Other airlines are *American Airlines (AAL)* and *Cayman Airways (KAY)*.

Approximate flight times: From *London* to Grand Turk is 13 hours 30 minutes, including a stopover of 1 hour in Nassau; the route via Miami usually involves an overnight stop.

From *Miami* to Grand Turk is 1 hour 45 minutes and to Providenciales is 1 hour 35 minutes.

From *New York* to Grand Turk is 6 hours and to Providenciales is 5 hours 50 minutes.

International airports: *Grand Turk (GDT)*. There is a taxi service from Grand Turk to hotels; prices vary. Airport facilities include incoming duty-free shop; car hire; bank/exchange services (0800-1300 and 1400-1630 Monday to Friday, 0800-1200 Saturday).

There are international airstrips on *South Caicos* and *Providenciales*.

Departure tax: US$10.

SEA: The archipelago is off the beaten track for most major cruise lines. Boats can be chartered to sail to the islands in Bahamas or Haiti. The main ports are Cockburn Harbour and Salt Cay (South Caicos), Grand Turk and Providenciales. Harbour facilities on South Caicos are currently being improved. There are plans to build a new port on North Caicos.

TRAVEL - Internal

AIR: In addition to the international airports on Grand Turk, South Caicos and Providenciales (see above), there are landing strips on Middle Caicos, Pine Cay, Parrot Cay, North Caicos and Salt Cay. *Turks & Caicos Airways* run a twice-daily air-taxi service to all the inhabited islands as well as flights to the Puerto Plata,

Cape Haïtien and Nassau. Charter flights at competitive rates are also available.

SEA: Limited coast-hopping and inter-island services. Boats may be chartered at most of the inhabited islands.

ROAD: There are over 120km (75 miles) of roads in the islands, of which about one-fifth are sealed. **Taxi:** Available at most airports, but the supply may be limited and sharing is often necessary. **Car hire:** Limited selection available from some local firms on Grand Turk, Providenciales and South Caicos. **Documentation:** Local licence available for a fee if holding national driving licence or International Driving Permit.

JOURNEY TIMES: The following chart gives approximate journey times (in hours and minutes) from Grand Turk to other major cities/towns on the islands.

	Air
Salt Cay	0.05
South Caicos	0.15
Middle Caicos	0.20
North Caicos	0.25
Pine Cay	0.30
Providenciales	0.30

ACCOMMODATION

There is accommodation on Grand Turk, North and South Caicos, Salt Cay, Providenciales and Pine Cay, including hotels, inns, a guest-house and self-catering apartment complexes. The standard is high, and many have beach frontage, private gardens, swimming pool and extensive watersports facilities. On Providenciales there is a *Club Med Village* and a *Ramada Resort Hotel*. All rooms are subject to 7% tax and 10% service charge. Advance reservation is necessary. The Tourist Board can supply further details and make reservations. Information is also available from the Turks & Caicos Islands Resort Association, c/o the Ramada Hotel. Tel: 946 5555. Fax: 946 5522. **Grading:** There are a number of standard hotels as well as two luxury and two deluxe hotels.

RESORTS & EXCURSIONS

The Turks & Caicos Islands are a perfect destination for those who wish to get away from it all. Numerous national parks, nature preserves, sanctuaries and historical sites are recommended excursions. The islands remain uncommercialised and unspoilt with small, personal places to stay.

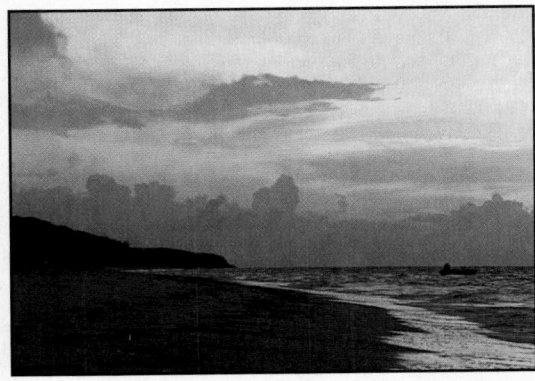

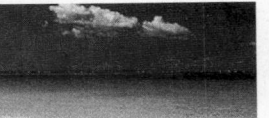

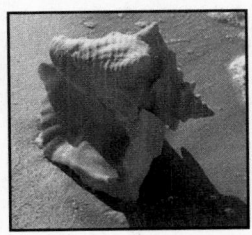

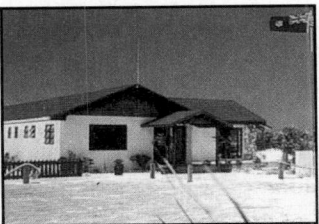

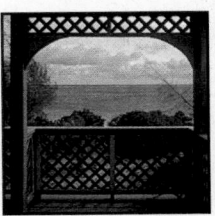

The Caicos Group

There are six principal islands and numerous small cays, some of which are uninhabited.

Providenciales is the centre of the islands' major tourist development, with a *Club Mediterranée* centre. Its beautiful beaches, shoreline and hills provide impressive land- and seascapes with every conceivable shade of green and blue. The main tourist centre lies around Turtle Cove with its peaceful yacht basin.

The abrupt coastline and deep water make **West Caicos** a fine fishing ground and provide opportunities for some dramatic scuba diving. Uninhabited, it is presently only visited by the occasional adventurous yachtsman and fishermen, and by many thousands of sea birds.

North Caicos is known as the 'Garden Island' of the Caicos, its better-quality soils and water providing good farmland. Along its miles of deserted white sand beaches lies a hotel development, the *Prospect of Whitby*. Here you can walk or relax in absolute peace and seclusion.

Pine Cay has one of the most beautiful beaches in the Caicos Islands, if not the Caribbean. It is also the home of *The Meridian Club*, one of the islands' select tourist developments, and is part of the *Caicos Cays National Underwater Park*. Be sure not to miss the reefs of the Caicos bank, with their rich variety of corals and vividly coloured fish.

Parrot Cay lies between Providenciales and North Caicos. Although hardly inhabited at present, it is earmarked for a sophisticated holiday development.

Middle Caicos, or Grand Caicos, is without any development and is noted for the hospitality and the imperturbability of its people. Blessed with a highly romantic coastline, to the west of Conch Bar the shore line swirls in and out with bluffs and enticing small coves. Visitors should be sure not to miss the island's most spectacular caves.

East Caicos is uninhabited but when flying it to South Caicos, look down at the salmon in the translucent green water. Some of the most beautiful beaches in the Caribbean are to be found here.

The town of Cockburn Harbour is situated on a small ridge at the extreme southwest of the island of **South Caicos**. It was once the chief port for the shipment of salt from the islands. The town is a quiet and pleasant place to potter around in the evening. During the day there are numerous beaches to explore, and, as everywhere in the Turks & Caicos group, there is superb diving, yachting and big-game fishing.

The Turks Group

These are smaller, separated from the Caicos' by the 35km (22-mile) deep-water channel 'Turks Island Passage', and consist of two main islands and a number of small, uninhabited cays.

Grand Turk, a few minutes from South Caicos by air, with the small metropolis Cockburn Town, is the islands' seat of government and commerce, as well as its historic and cultural centre. The *Turks and Caicos National Museum* situated on the water front, tells the story of the oldest shipwreck discovered in the Americas and exhibits rare prints and manuscripts from all of the islands. Front Street has a number of colonial-style buildings, dating from the early 19th century. They have imposing entrances in the high, whitewashed walls which surround their gardens. There are many delightful bays on the eastern shores of Grand Turk. The island is also a fine base for diving and fishing.

Salt Cay, set in an opalescent sea, is the most charming and atmospheric of all the Salt Islands. There are fine beaches, and also considerable interest in the still productive salt ponds. The island is dominated by a great white house, built in the 1830s in solid Bermudian style.

SOCIAL PROFILE

FOOD & DRINK: With rare exceptions, dining takes place in hotels. Island specialities include whelk soup, conch chowder, lobster and special types of fresh fish. Continental dishes are also available as are American/ European snacks such as hot dogs and hamburgers. Although some establishments have buffet-style serveries, table service is common. **Drink:** Alcohol is freely available. Rum-based punch and cocktails are delicious and a wide selection of imported beer, wines and spirits can be found in most bars.

NIGHTLIFE: There are small local nightclubs and discotheques and hotels often arrange beach parties and other entertainments. Events are broadcast in advance on local radio.

SHOPPING: The islands' small shops sell locally made baskets, shells, sponges, hand-screened cloth, souvenir T-shirts and rare conch pearls.

SPORT: Swimming: With more than 370km (230 miles) of beaches, there is plenty of opportunity for safe bathing supplemented by hotel pools. **Scuba diving:** The spectacular reefs and underwater life surrounding the islands attract divers from all over the world. Most clubs and centres have qualified instructors, equipment can be hired and diving trips arranged. **Fishing:** There is good fishing off all the islands; boats can be hired from most hotels and individual island fishermen can be hired as guides. **Golf:** A new 18-hole championship course has recently been opened in Providenciales. **Tennis:** Courts are available on Pine Cay at *The Meridian Club* (rackets and balls for hire) Grand Turk and Providenciales also have courts available. **Birdwatching:** There are many bird and butterfly sanctuaries.

SPECIAL EVENTS: The following is a list of special events taking place in 1993/4 on the islands:

Apr '93 *Kite Flying Festival*, Grand Turk; *Ripsaw Festival*, Grand Turk. **May** *Regatta*, South Caicos. **Jun/Aug** *Salt Cay Day Celebrations*, Salt Cay. **Jun 27-Jul 2** *Annual Turks and Caicos Billfish Tournament*, Providenciales. **Jul** *Festarama*, North Caicos. **Aug** *M C Expo*, Middle Caicos; *Cactus Fest*, Grand Turk. **Oct** *Columbus Celebrations*, Grand Turk. **Nov** *Eco-Tourism Conference*. **Dec 31** *Dandamist*, (New Year's Eve Cultural Festival), Grand Turk.

SOCIAL CONVENTIONS: Shaking hands is the normal form of greeting. Hospitality is important and, when visiting someone's home, normal social courtesies should be observed – if possible a return invitation should be made. A souvenir from home is well received. Informal dress is accepted for most events, but beachwear should be confined to the beach. **Tipping:** There is no tipping in hotels on any of the islands, 10% is added to every bill. In restaurants, tip 10-15%.

BUSINESS PROFILE

ECONOMY: Since salt mining ceased in the mid-1960s, the Turks & Caicos Islands have relied on tourism and offshore financial services for most of their income. The expansion of tourism, recommended in a recent official report, is now seen as essential to the islands' future economic health. Fishing is the other main industry and the sole contributor to the islands' food requirements, the remainder of which must be imported; it is also a valuable export earner, particularly from the USA which buys much of the catch. Aid from Britain is needed to balance the budget and fund capital projects. The UK is the largest single trading partner.

BUSINESS: The informal relaxed atmosphere prevails even in business circles. A lightweight tropical suit will be the most needed. Best months to visit are from April to October. **Office hours:** 0800-1300 and 1400-1630 Monday to Friday, 0800-1200 Saturday.

COMMERCIAL INFORMATION: The following organisation can offer advice: Chamber of Commerce, c/o Turks and Caicos Banking Co Ltd, PO Box 123, Harbour House, Grand Turk. Tel: 946 2364/8. Fax: 946 2365.

HISTORY & GOVERNMENT

HISTORY: None of the Arawak Indians, who occupied the islands when Columbus first discovered them, survived the 16th century. Until the 19th century the islands were a source of salt for the American mainland, slaves being used as labour. During the 19th century control of the islands changed hands several times. In 1962 the Turks & Caicos Islands became a separate British Colony, having been a Jamaican dependency for some 75 years. The islands held their first general election in 1976, the winning party, the People's Democratic Movement (PDM), pursuing a policy of full independence for the islands. The next election, in 1980, was effectively a referendum on the independence issue and was won by the the pro-dependency Progressive National Party (PNP), which won again four years later. A major political scandal erupted in 1985 (and continued the following year) in which the Chief Minister, the Minister of Development & Commerce and a leading PNP member were implicated in illegal drug trafficking. A new party was formed, the National Democratic Alliance (NDA), and a general election was held in 1988 with the PDM winning 11 of the 13 seats. By 1990, the islands had managed to put the corruption scandals behind them (although the drug-trafficking problem has not wholly vanished) and concentrate on the development of tourism, financial services and overseas investment. At the latest election, held in 1991, the revitalised PNP fought a winning campaign against initial public scepticism under a new leader, Washington Missick, who is now Chief Minister.

GOVERNMENT: The British monarch is Head of State, represented locally by a Governor. The Government comprises Legislative and Executive Councils. The former consists of a Speaker, three ex-officio members of the Executive Council, three appointees, and 11 members elected by universal adult suffrage. The Executive Council consists of a Chief Minister and four other Ministers drawn from the Legislative Council, plus three appointees to the posts of Chief Secretary, Financial Secretary and Attorney-General. In 1986 the ministerial form of government was suspended and not reintroduced until March 1988.

CLIMATE

Tropical; tempered by trade winds, generally pleasant. Cool nights. Rain in winter.

Required clothing: Tropical lightweights. Light sweaters are advised for evenings.

GRAND TURK Turks & Caicos Is. (3m)

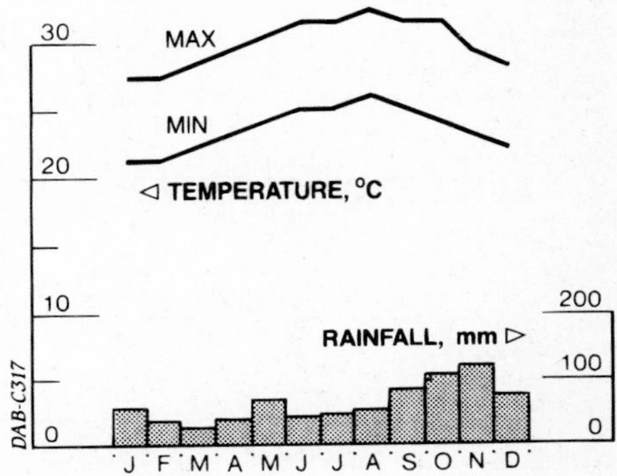

TUVALU

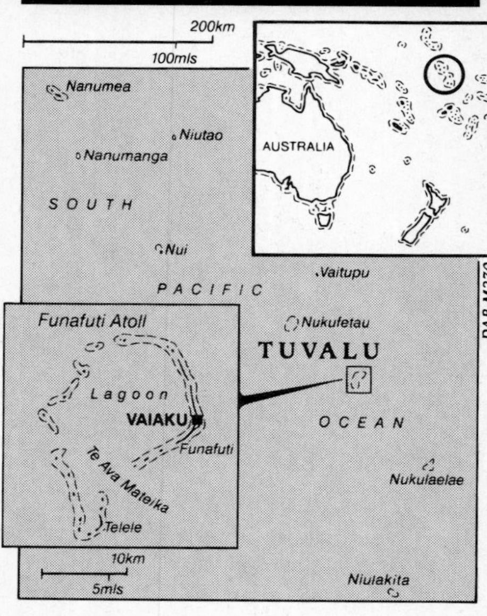

Location: West Pacific.

Ministry of Commerce (Tourist Information)
Vaiaku
Funafuti, Tuvalu
Fax: 829. Telex: 4803.

Honorary Consulate General of Tuvalu
Klövensteenweg 115A
W-2000 Hamburg 56, Germany
Tel: (40) 810 580. Fax: (40) 811 016.

The British Embassy in Fiji is accredited to Tuvalu on a non-resident basis:

British Embassy
PO Box 1355
Victoria House
47 Gladstone Road
Suva, Fiji
Tel: 311 033. Fax: 301 406. Telex: 2129.

The Canadian High Commission in New Zealand deals with enquiries relating to Tuvalu:

Canadian High Commission
PO Box 12-049
61 Molesworth Street
Thorndon
Wellington, New Zealand
Tel: (4) 473 9577. Fax: (4) 471 2082. Telex: 3577 CANAD NZ.

AREA: 26 sq km (10 sq miles).
POPULATION: 9500 (1991).
POPULATION DENSITY: 365.4 per sq km.
CAPITAL: Funafuti. **Population:** 2810.
GEOGRAPHY: Tuvalu (formerly the Ellice Islands) is a scattered group of nine small atolls in the western Pacific Ocean extending about 560km (350 miles) from north to south. Nearest neighbours are Fiji (to the south), Kiribati (north) and the Solomon Islands (west). The main island, Funafuti, is also the capital and lies 1200 miles north of Suva, Fiji.
LANGUAGE: Tuvaluan and English are the main languages.
RELIGION: Approximately 98% Protestant.
TIME: GMT + 12.
ELECTRICITY: 240 volts AC, 50Hz (Funafuti only).
COMMUNICATIONS: Telephone: IDD service is available. Country code: 688. There are no area codes. However, demand is high and the capacity as yet limited. Operator-controlled calls are available at the following times: 1930-0830 Monday to Thursday; 1930-0300 Friday; 0400-0800 and 2200-2400 weekends and public holidays. **Fax:** Available at the Telecommunication Centre in Funafuti. **Telex/telegrams:** Public telex facility available at the Telecommunication Centre in Funafuti (Telex: TV Comm 4800). Overseas telegrams may be sent via the Post Office in Funafuti. **Post:** Airmail services to Europe take between five and ten days to arrive, but can be erratic. **Press:** The Government Broadcasting and Information Division publishes *Sikuleo o Tuvalu* (in Tuvaluan) and *Tuvalu Echoes* (in English, on a fortnightly basis).
BBC World Service and Voice of America frequencies: From time to time these change. See the section *How to Use this Book* for more information.

BBC:

MHz	17.830	15.340	9.640	11.955

Voice of America:

MHz	18.82	15.18	9.525	1.735

PASSPORT/VISA

Regulations and requirements may be subject to change at short notice, and you are advised to contact the appropriate diplomatic or consular authority before finalising travel arrangements. Details of these may be found at the head of this country's entry. Any numbers in the chart refer to the footnotes below.

	Passport Required?	Visa Required?	Return Ticket Required?
Full British	Yes	No	Yes
BVP	Not valid	-	-
Australian	Yes	No	Yes
Canadian	Yes	No	Yes
USA	Yes	Yes	Yes
Other EC	Yes	1	Yes
Japanese	Yes	Yes	Yes

PASSPORTS: Valid passports required by all.
British Visitors Passport: Not accepted.
VISAS: Not required for:
(a) nationals referrred to in the chart above;
(b) [1] nationals of Belgium, Denmark, Germany, Greece, Italy, Luxembourg, The Netherlands, Spain and the UK, provided that they have proof of onward travel and sufficient funds for stays of up to 1 month (other EC nationals *do* need a visa);
(c) nationals of Antigua & Barbuda, Bahamas, Bangladesh, Barbados, Belize, Botswana, Cyprus, Dominica, Fiji, Finland, Gambia, Ghana, Grenada, Guyana, Iceland, India, Jamaica, Kenya, Kiribati, Lesotho, Liechtenstein, Malawi, Malaysia, Maldives, Malta, Mauritius, Nauru, New Zealand, Nigeria, Norway, Papua New Guinea, St Lucia, St Vincent & the Grenadines, San Marino, Seychelles, Sierra Leone, Singapore, Solomon Islands, Sri Lanka, Swaziland, Sweden, Switzerland, Tanzania, Tonga, Trinidad & Tobago, Tunisia, Turkey, Uganda, Uruguay, Vanuatu, Western Samoa, Zambia and Zimbabwe.
Types of visa: Entry and Transit.
Validity: Visitors are normally permitted to remain in Tuvalu for up to 1 month, after meeting the visa requirements; their visit may then be extended for a maximum of 3 months.
Application requirements: Visas may be obtained on arrival by passengers with onward tickets and valid passports.

MONEY

Currency: Australian and Tuvaluan currency are both in use, but transactions over one Dollar are always conducted in Australian Dollars.
Australian Dollar (A$) = 100 cents. Notes are in denominations of A$100, 50, 20, 10 and 5. Coins are in denominations of A$2 and 1, and 50, 20, 10 and 5 cents.
Tuvaluan Dollar = 100 cents. Coins are in denominations of 1 dollar, and 50, 20, 10, 5, 2 and 1 cents.
Credit cards: Credit cards are not accepted, but Visa may be used at the National Bank of Tuvalu.
Exchange rate indicators: The following figures are included as a guide to movements of the Australian Dollar against Sterling and the US Dollar:

Date:	Oct '89	Oct '90	Oct '91	Oct '92
£1.00=	2.01	2.46	2.18	2.22
$1.00=	1.27	1.26	1.26	1.40

Currency restrictions: There are no restrictions on the import and export of foreign or local currency.

DUTY FREE

The following items may be imported into Tuvalu without incurring customs duty:
200 cigarettes or 225g tobacco or cigars;
1 litre of spirits and 1 litre of wine (if over 18);
Goods up to A$25.
Prohibited items: Pornography, pure alcohol, narcotics, arms and ammunition. All plant and animal material must be declared and quarantined.

PUBLIC HOLIDAYS

Public holidays observed in Tuvalu are as follows:
Mar 8 '93 Commonwealth Day. **Apr 9-12** Easter. **Jun 14** Queen's Official Birthday. **Aug 2** National Children's Day. **Oct 1-2** Tuvalu Day. **Nov 14** Prince of Wales's Birthday. **Dec 25** Christmas Day. **Jan 1 '94** New Year's Day. **Mar** Commonwealth Day.

HEALTH

Regulations and requirements may be subject to change at short notice, and you are advised to contact your doctor well in advance of your intended date of departure. Any numbers in the chart refer to the footnotes below.

	Special Precautions?	Certificate Required?
Yellow Fever	No	1
Cholera	No	2
Typhoid & Polio	Yes	-
Malaria	No	-
Food & Drink	3	-

[1]: A yellow fever vaccination certificate is required of travellers over one year of age arriving from an infected or endemic area.
[2]: A cholera vaccination certificate is required of travellers over one year of age who have been in an infected area prior to arrival.
[3]: All water is stored in tanks so waste should be avoided. Take local advice.
Health care: Visitors are advised to bring antiseptic cream as cuts are inclined to turn septic, but apart from this precaution there are no serious health risks. The mosquitos are non-malarial, but the visitor may nevertheless wish to take defensive measures. There is a well-equipped 31-bed hospital on Funafuti's main island.

TRAVEL -International

AIR: There are plans to implement a national airline in the near future. Presently *Air Marshall*, the airline of the Marshall Islands, offers return flights twice a week from *Majuro* (Marshall Islands) to *Tarawa* (Kiribati), *Funafuti* and *Nadi* (Fiji's main international airport). It is advisable to book in advance.

TUVALU	HEALTH REGULATIONS	VISA REGULATIONS (Code-Link)
GALILEO/WORLDSPAN	 TI-DFT/FUN/HE	TI-DFT/FUN/VI
SABRE	 TIDFT/FUN/HE	 TIDFT/FUN/VI

To access this information on your CRS, swipe the barcode with a light pen or type in the text under the barcode. For more information, see the introduction *How to Use This Book.*

International airport: *Funafuti International (FUN)*. There is a pick-up service to the only hotel.
Departure tax: A$10 is levied on international departures.
SEA: Shipping services operate from Fiji, Australia and New Zealand, calling at the main port of Funafuti. Adventure cruises organised by *Society Expeditions of Seattle* (USA) also call from time to time.

TRAVEL - Internal

AIR: The only airstrip is at Funafuti. There is no internal air service in Tuvalu.
SEA: The islands are served by a passenger and cargo vessel, the *Nivaga II*, based at Funafuti, which occasionally calls at Suva (Fiji).
ROAD: There are a few roads, constructed from impacted coral, and several dirt tracks that span the islands. There are no **taxis,** but limited transport service is provided by privately operated **minibuses.** The usual form of transport on the islands are small **motorcycles** and **pushbikes,** which can be hired at the hotel. For more information contact The Travel Office, Funafuti. Tel: 737.

ACCOMMODATION

The only hotel in Tuvalu is the Vaiaku Lagi Hotel in Funafuti. As there are only seven rooms at present, visitors are advised to book early and may be asked to share rooms. There are plans to upgrade existing facilities to a 16-room hotel with amenities for meetings. In addition there are a few private guest-houses available. The Travel Office can supply details (for address see above).

RESORTS & EXCURSIONS

Tuvalu is said to fulfill the classic image of a South Sea paradise and visitors come to the islands to enjoy the unspoilt peaceful atmosphere. Pandanus, papaya, banana, breadfruit and most commonly coconut palms are typical. The greatest attraction is the beautiful (and enormous) *Funafuti Lagoon*, which is 14km wide and about 18km long. In the Funafuti area, tourists will find many palm-fringed islands of scenic beauty. Boats for sightseeing and excursions can be hired from the Government or from private operators. Adjacent to the Government offices in Vaiaku is the open-sided national Parliament *(maneapa)*. The handicraft centre near the airport is well worth visiting. Traditional buildings with thatched roofs can be seen virtually everywhere on the islands.

SOCIAL PROFILE

FOOD & DRINK: The emphasis is on fish and local tropical foods. The Vaiaku Lagi Hotel serves meals daily and has a barbecue in the courtyard once a fortnight. There are also a number of privately owned snackfood shops and a restaurant on Funafuti's main island. **Drink:** Beer is imported.
NIGHTLIFE: There is a fortnightly disco at the Vaiaku Lagi Hotel.
SHOPPING: Near the hotel there is a handicraft centre selling handmade articles from all the islands ranging from hats, mats and shell necklaces to traditional lidded wooden boxes *(tulumas)* used by fishermen. Visitors should be aware that general shopping facilities are limited and many things that visitors take for granted elsewhere may be unobtainable, eg developing of photographs. **Shopping hours:** 0630-1730 Monday to Saturday.
SPORT: Visitors interested in **watersports** should bring their own equipment as there is none for hire. **Swimmers** should wear sandshoes as stonefish are an occasional hazard. Due to the strong tide, swimming in the ocean is very dangerous. Swimming in the lagoon is considered fairly safe. Visitors who wish to use the hotel's **tennis** court should bring their own rackets and balls. **Football** is very popular, as is *kilikiti*, a local version of cricket. *Te ano* is a much-loved traditional ballgame reminiscent of volleyball.
SOCIAL CONVENTIONS: Traditional values continue to dominate Tuvaluan culture. Footwear should be removed when entering a church, a village meeting house *(manepa)*, or private house. The consumption of alcohol outside licensed premises is not permitted. Whilst dress is usually casual, it is customary for women to keep their thighs covered and beachwear should be confined to the beach or poolside. There are procedures which should be followed by those invited to a feast and visitors should take local advice about this and other matters. It is customary not to speak a foreign language in the presence of a person who does not know it, so apparent indications of a desire to hold a private or confidential conversation should be interpreted as simple courtesy to fellow-islanders. Visitors are welcome to join in the numerous local festivals and celebrations with feasting and traditional entertainment. **Tipping:** Not customary.

BUSINESS PROFILE

ECONOMY: The main source of income for the islands is remittances from abroad. Stamp sales are the principal foreign currency earner. The indigenous economy is dominated by fishing, and Tuvalu also receives valuable revenue from licences granted to American and Japanese fleets to fish in Tuvalu waters. On land, copra is the only significant export since the soil is of unsuitable quality for agriculture. Australia, New Zealand and Fiji are the main trading partners, while the UK provides an aid package mainly to assist the development of the island's infrastructure. A Trust Fund has been established to generate income for development projects from foreign investment.
BUSINESS: A high standard of business ethics is to be expected, given that the overwhelming majority of the population are congregationalists. **Government office hours:** 0730-1615 Monday to Thursday and 0730-1245 Friday.
COMMERCIAL INFORMATION: The following organisations can offer advice: Tuvalu Co-operative Society Ltd, PO Box 17, Funafuti. Tel: 724. Fax: 800. Telex: 4800; *or*
Business Development Advisory Bureau, PO Box 9, Funafuti. Tel: 850. Telex: 4800.

HISTORY & GOVERNMENT

HISTORY: Formerly known as the Ellice or Lagoon Islands, Tuvalu was a slaving post, a situation which, along with imported European diseases, cut the population from 20,000 in 1850 to 3000 in 1875. Two years later the islands were taken under British jurisdiction and ruled from Fiji. In 1916, they were taken into the Gilbert and Ellice Islands and ruled as a colony until internal self-government was granted in 1974. The islands were split from the Gilberts (which became Kiribati) in 1976 and became independent as Tuvalu in 1978. Now the world's smallest sovereign state (apart from Nauru), Tuvalu's post-independence governments have been much concerned with the problems of sustaining a subsistence economy. Other major political issues include French nuclear testing in the region – which Tuvalu strongly opposes – and Tuvalu's constitutional position: a referendum in 1986 favoured the islands retaining its existing status of a constitutional monarchy, rejecting the alternative option of becoming a republic. A treaty of friendship was signed with the USA in 1983. Despite the difficulties of running a country and an economy spread over three-quarters of a billion square kilometres with a land area of 0.003% of that figure (26 sq km), Tuvalu has nonetheless made substantial progress in education, health care and economy under the premierships of Tomasi Puapua and the current Prime Minister Bikenibeu Paeniu. Paeniu gained the premiership after the most recent general election in Tuvalu held in September 1989, displacing his predecessor and principal rival, Tomasi Puapua.
GOVERNMENT: Tuvalu is a constitutional monarchy. The British monarch is the Head of State, exercising executive authority through an appointed Governor-General. The post is allocated on the recommendation of the Prime Minister and Cabinet. A Parliament is elected every four years by universal adult suffrage; the Prime Minister and Cabinet are elected from its ranks by the members.

CLIMATE

The climate is humid and hot with a mean annual temperature of 28°C and comparatively little seasonal variation. March to October tends to be cooler and more pleasant, whilst some discomfort may be experienced during the wet season from November to February. The average rainfall is about 3000mm annually.
Required clothing: Lightweight for summer, rainwear for the wet season.

SUVA Fiji (6m)

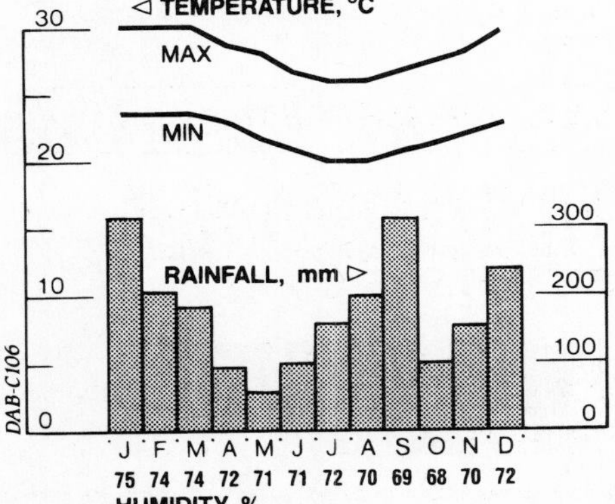

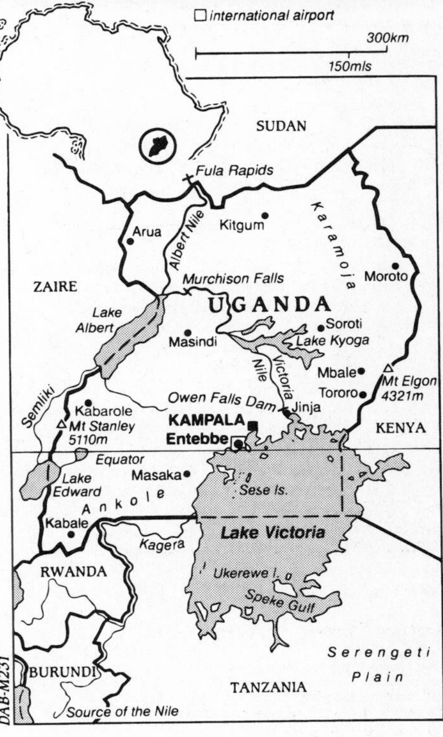

Location: Central/East Africa.

Uganda Tourism Development Corporation
PO Box 7211
Plot 6, 2nd Street
Kampala, Uganda
Tel: (41) 245 261. Telex: 61150.
Ministry of Tourism, Wildlife and Antiquities
PO Box 4241
Parliament Avenue
Kampala, Uganda
Tel: (41) 232 971. Telex: 62218.
High Commission for the Republic of Uganda
Uganda House
58-59 Trafalgar Square
London
WC2N 5DX
Tel: (071) 839 5783. Fax: (071) 839 8925. Telex: 915141. Opening hours: 0930-1300 and 1400-1730 Monday to Friday.
British High Commission
PO Box 7070
10-12 Parliament Avenue
Kampala, Uganda
Tel: (41) 257 301/4 *or* 257 054/9. Fax: (41) 257 304. Telex: 61202 UKREP KLA.
Embassy of the Republic of Uganda
5909 16th Street, NW
Washington, DC
20011
Tel: (202) 726 7100. Fax: (202) 726 1727.
Consulate in: New York (tel: (212) 949 0110).
Embassy of the United States of America
PO Box 7007
Kampala, Uganda
Tel: (41) 259 792/3/5.
High Commission for the Republic of Uganda
231 Cobourg Street
Ottawa, Ontario
K1N 8J2
Tel: (613) 233 7797/8. Fax: (613) 232 6689.
Canadian Consulate
c/o Uganda Bata
PO Box 422
Fifth Street
Industrial Area
Kampala, Uganda
Tel: (41) 258 141. Fax: (41) 241 380 . Telex: 61049 BATA UGA.

AREA: 241,139 sq km (93,104 sq miles).
POPULATION: 16,582,674 (1991 estimate).
POPULATION DENSITY: 68.8 per sq km.
CAPITAL: Kampala. **Population:** 773,550 (1991).
GEOGRAPHY: Uganda shares borders with Sudan to the north, Kenya to the east, Lake Victoria to the south-east, Tanzania and Rwanda to the south and Zaïre to the west. Kampala is on the shores of Lake Victoria, and the White Nile flowing out of the lake traverses much of the country. The varied scenery includes tropical forest and tea plantations on the slopes of the snow-capped Ruwenzori Mountains, the arid plains of the Karamoja, the lush, heavily populated Buganda, the rolling savannah of Acholi, Bunyoro, Tororo and Ankde, and the fertile cotton area of Teso.
LANGUAGE: English is the official language, with Luganda and Kiswahili also widely spoken.
RELIGION: 60% Christian, 32% Animist and 8% Muslim.
TIME: GMT + 3 (GMT + 2 in summer).
ELECTRICITY: 240 volts AC, 50Hz.
COMMUNICATIONS: Telephone: IDD is available to and from principal towns in Uganda. Country code: 256. Service for local calls can be unreliable. **Fax/Telex:** Telex and fax service available at the *Postal & Telecommunications Office*, 35 Kampala Road, Kampala, central post offices in Jinja and Mbale between 0800-1600, and some hotels. **Post:** Airmail to Europe can take from three days to several weeks. Post office hours: 0830-1230 and 1400-1630 Monday to Friday. **Press:** The English-language papers are *The Monitor, The People, New Vision, The Star* (dailies) and the weekly *Topic*.
BBC World Service and Voice of America frequencies: From time to time these change. See the section *How to Use this Book* for more information.

BBC:				
MHz	21.470	17.885	15.420	9.630
Voice of America:				
MHz	21.49	15.60	9.525	6.035

PASSPORT/VISA

Regulations and requirements may be subject to change at short notice, and you are advised to contact the appropriate diplomatic or consular authority before finalising travel arrangements. Details of these may be found at the head of this country's entry. Any numbers in the chart refer to the footnotes below.

	Passport Required?	Visa Required?	Return Ticket Required?
Full British	Yes	Yes	Yes
BVP	Not valid	-	-
Australian	Yes	No	Yes
Canadian	Yes	Yes	Yes
USA	Yes	Yes	Yes
Other EC	Yes	1	Yes
Japanese	Yes	Yes	Yes

PASSPORTS: Valid passport required by all.
British Visitors Passport: Not valid.
VISAS: Required by all except:
(a) [1] nationals of Denmark, Ireland and Spain (all other EC nationals *do* require visas);
(b) nationals of Angola, Antigua & Barbuda, Australia, Bahamas, Bangladesh, Barbados, Belize, Botswana, Burundi, Comoros, Cyprus, Djibouti, Dominica, Ethiopia, Fiji, Finland, Gambia, Ghana, Grenada, Guyana, Kenya, Lesotho, Malawi, Maldives, Malta, Mauritius, Mozambique, New Zealand, Nigeria, Norway, Papua New Guinea, Rwanda, San Marino, Seychelles, Sierra Leone, Singapore,Solomon Islands, Somalia, Sri Lanka, St Lucia, St Vincent & the Grenadines, Sudan, Swaziland, Sweden, Tanzania, Togo, Trinidad & Tobago, Turkey, Tuvalu, Uruguay, Vanuatu, Western Samoa, Yugoslavia, Zambia and Zimbabwe.
Restricted entry: Entry may be refused to passengers not holding sufficient funds, return or onward tickets and other necessary travel documents.
Types of visa: Tourist and Business; Single and Multiple entry. **Cost:** *Single entry:* £20 (UK nationals) and £10 (other nationals and students under 25); *multiple entry*: £40 (UK nationals) and £20 (other nationals and students under 25).
Validity: Single entry: 3 months from date of issue; multiple entry: 6 months from date of issue.
Application to: Consulate (or Consular Section at Embassy or High Commission). For addresses, see top of entry.
Application requirements: (a) Valid passport. (b) 2 completed application forms. (c) 2 passport size photos. (d) Fee (cash or postal orders only). (e) Letter from sponsor in UK if travelling on business.
Working days required: 5 days.
Temporary residence: Enquire at Embassy or High Commission.

MONEY

Currency: Uganda Shilling (USh) = 100 cents. Notes are in denominations of USh1000, 500, 100, 50, 20, 10 and 5. Some coins for smaller denominations exist but are not generally used. The Shilling is not a stable currency and has been substantially devalued several times in recent years.
Currency exchange: Money should be changed at the tourist exchange rate (known as 'Window 2') which is more advantageous than the official bank rate. Tourists should not be tempted to use unofficial alternatives, which are numerous and widespread, as heavy fines and even prison sentences are imposed on offenders.
Credit cards: Visa is widely accepted with less widespread use of Access/Mastercard. Check with your credit card company for details of merchant acceptability and other services which may be available.
Exchange rate indicators: The following figures are included as a guide to the movements of the Uganda Shilling against Sterling and the US Dollar:

Date:	**Oct '89**	**Oct '90**	**Oct '91**	**Oct '92**
£1.00=	316.02	938.14	1473.90	1856.25
$1.00=	200.14	480.24	849.27	1169.66

Currency restrictions: The import and export of local currency is prohibited (although Kenyan, Tanzanian and Ugandan currencies may be carried between the three countries up to the equivalent of US$5). Free import of foreign currency if declared on arrival. It is imperative to obtain a currency declaration form on arrival in Uganda. The export of foreign currency is limited to the amount imported and declared.
Banking hours: 0830-1400 Monday to Friday and 0830-1300 Saturday.

DUTY FREE

The following items may be imported into Uganda without incurring customs duty:
200 cigarettes or 225g of tobacco;
1 bottle of spirits or wine;
568ml of perfume.

PUBLIC HOLIDAYS

Public holidays observed in Uganda are as follows:
Mar 8 '93 International Women's Day. **Mar 25** Eid al-Fitr (End of Ramadan). **Apr 9** Good Friday. **Apr 12** Easter Monday. **May 1** Labour Day. **Jun 1** Eid al-Adha (Feast of the Sacrifice). **Jun 3** Martyrs' Day. **Jun 9** Heroes' Day. **Oct 9** Independence Day. **Dec 25** Christmas Day. **Dec 26** Boxing Day. **Jan 1 '94** New Year's Day. **Mar** Eid al-Fitr.
Note: Muslim festivals are timed according to local sightings of various phases of the Moon and the dates given above are approximations. During the lunar month of Ramadan that precedes Eid al-Fitr, Muslims fast during the day and feast at night and normal business patterns may be interrupted. Many restaurants are closed during the day and there may be restrictions on smoking and drinking. Some disruption may continue into Eid al-Fitr itself. Eid al-Fitr and Eid al-Adha may last anything from two to ten days, depending on the region. For more information see the section *World of Islam* at the back of the book.

HEALTH

Regulations and requirements may be subject to change at short notice, and you are advised to contact your doctor well in advance of your intended date of departure. Any numbers in the chart refer to the footnotes below.

	Special Precautions?	Certificate Required?
Yellow Fever	Yes	1
Cholera	Yes	2
Typhoid & Polio	Yes	-
Malaria	3	-
Food & Drink	4	-

[1]: A yellow fever vaccination certificate is required from travellers over one year of age arriving from infected areas.
[2]: Following WHO guidelines issued in 1973, a cholera vaccination certificate is not an official condition of entry to Uganda. However, cholera is a serious risk in this country and precautions are essential. Up-to-date advice should be sought before deciding whether these precautions should include vaccination, as medical opinion is divided over its effectiveness. See the *Health* section at the back of the book.
[3]: Malaria risk, predominantly in the malignant *falciparum* form, all year throughout the country, including urban areas. Resistance to chloroquine has been reported.
[4]: All water should be regarded as being a potential health risk. Water used for drinking, brushing teeth or making ice should have first been boiled or otherwise sterilised. Milk is unpasteurised and should be boiled. Powdered or tinned milk is available and is advised, but make sure that it is reconstituted with pure water. Avoid dairy products which are likely to have been made from unboiled milk. Only eat well-cooked meat and fish, preferably served hot. Pork, salad and mayonnaise may carry increased risk. Vegetables should be cooked and fruit peeled.
Rabies is present. For those at high risk, vaccination before arrival should be considered. If you are bitten abroad seek medical advice without delay. For more information consult the *Health* section at the back of the book.
Bilharzia (schistosomiasis) is present. Avoid swimming and paddling in fresh water. Swimming pools which are well-chlorinated and maintained are safe.
Health care: Bring personal supplies of medicines that are likely to be needed, but enquire first at Embassy or High Commission whether such supplies may be freely imported. Comprehensive health insurance is essential and should include cover for emergency air repatriation in case of serious accident or illness. The Ugandan health service has still not recovered from the mass departure of foreign personnel in 1972 and there are medical facilities of a reasonable standard only in large towns and cities.

TRAVEL - International

AIR: Uganda's main airline is *Uganda Airlines Corporation (QU)*.
Approximate flight time: From *London* to Kampala is 8 hours.
International airport: *Entebbe (EBB)* is 35.5km (22 miles) south of Kampala (travel time – 30 minutes). Coach services to Kampala go every three hours 0800-1800. Bus services go every 2 hours 0800-1600. Taxis are also available. Airport facilities include a duty-free shop, restaurant, bank, post office, car hire and hotel reservations.

UGANDA | **HEALTH REGULATIONS** | **VISA REGULATIONS** | Code-Link

GALILEO/WORLDSPAN

TI-DFT/EBB/HE

TI-DFT/EBB/VI

SABRE

TIDFT/EBB/HE

TIDFT/EBB/VI

To access this information on your CRS, swipe the barcode with a light pen or type in the text under the barcode. For more information, see the introduction *How to Use This Book*.

Departure tax: US$23 is levied on international departures. Transit passengers and children under two years old are exempt.
Note: All airline tickets purchased in Uganda must be paid for in hard currency.
RAIL: The line from Nairobi (Kenya) crosses the border at Tororo. It may be necessary to change trains to travel further into Uganda. Rail travel can be slow and uncomfortable.
ROAD: There are connections with all neighbouring countries. Road access from Kenya is good, roads to Rwanda are currently being improved. The Uganda/Rwanda border is closed at weekends. **Bus:** The road from Kenya is used by buses and tour company coaches from Nairobi. There is a twice-weekly service from Kampala to Kigali (Rwanda).

TRAVEL - Internal

AIR: *Uganda Airlines* offer flights from Entebbe to all main towns including Arua and Kasese. Charter flights are also available.
RAIL: There are more than 1000km (625 miles) of track, running in a single arc from Pakwach on Lake Albert (Lake Mobutu) near the border with Zaïre, through several northern towns to Tororo on the Kenyan border, then on to Lake Victoria and Kampala and finally to Kasese, near Lake George. Trains run twice daily from Tororo to Kampala, and once daily elsewhere. Passenger facilities are limited, but the rolling stock is new and reasonably comfortable. Timetables are somewhat erratic.
ROAD: The road network extends over 27,540km (17,113 miles). The roads are of variable quality and radiate from Kampala, although the network is sparse in the north. There are still some army and police check points on roads and railways. **Buses** run between most parts of Uganda but are unreliable and often very crowded. Scheduled services operate between Entebbe and Kampala (travel time – 1 hour) and to and from the airport (see above).
Documentation: A national driving licence or International Driving Permit is required.

ACCOMMODATION

HOTELS: Several hotels, both private and government owned, are available in all large towns, but they are of limited quality. Some of the major National Parks offer accommodation (see below).

RESORTS & EXCURSIONS

Kampala: The capital is set among hills with fine modern architecture, tree-lined avenues, cathedrals, mosques and palaces of the old Kingdom of Buganda and the Uganda Museum. The *Kabaka Tombs* are on *Kasubi Hill*, where shoes must be removed before entering the buildings.
Jinja: The second largest town in Uganda lies on the shores of Lake Victoria. Though somewhat under-populated there is a very lively Saturday market. The nearby *Owen Falls Dam* is the source of the Nile.
Entebbe: The major gateway to Uganda for air travellers, it has fine botanical gardens and a lakeside beach, although bathing is not recommended because of bilharzia.
Fort Portal: A good base for exploring the *Ruwenzori Mountains*, the hot springs at **Bundibugyo** and the *Toro Game Reserve*.
Kisoro: The starting point for climbing expeditions to *Mounts Muhavura* and *Mgahinga*. There are seven lakes in the vicinity which offer fishing and possible duck fowl shooting.
Mbale: Set in fertile and lush country near *Mount Elgon*, which is popular with hikers and inexperienced mountaineers.
National Parks: There are a number of good national parks and game reserves, some acclaimed as being among Africa's best. The major parks are *Kabalega*, *Ruwenzori* and *Kidepo*. *Kabalega* and *Ruwenzori* have good accommodation facilities; *Ruwenzori National Park* (also known as Queen Elizabeth National Park) is regarded as one of the most spectacular in Africa. The *East National Park* near Kampala has good lodges, *banda* (cabins) and campsites.

SOCIAL PROFILE

FOOD & DRINK: There are restaurants in and around Kampala. All state-owned hotels serve local food. Popular dishes include *matoke* (a staple made from bananas), millet bread, *cassava*, sweet potatoes, chicken and beef stews and freshwater fish. **Drink:** The national drink is *waragi*, a banana gin, popular among visitors as a cocktail base.
SHOPPING: Purchases include bangles, necklaces and bracelets, wood carvings, basketry, tea, coffee and ceramics. **Shopping hours:** 0830-1700 Monday to Friday and 0830-1900 Saturday.
SPORT: Climbing expeditions to Mount Muhavura and Mount Mgahinga, starting from Kisoro, are popular with climbers, while the ascent of Mount Elgon from Mbale is popular with hikers. There is excellent **fishing** in numerous inland waters, notably the seven lakes in the vicinity of Kisoro. It is unwise to **swim** in most of the lakes, with the exception of Lake Nagubo in the Kigezi hills, due to bilharzia.
SPECIAL EVENTS: The following is a selection of events taking place in 1993/94. For full details contact the Uganda Tourism Development Corporation.
Mar 8 '93 *Women's Day*. **Jun 9** *Heroes' Day*. **Jan 26 '94** *National Resistance Movement Victory Celebrations*.
SOCIAL CONVENTIONS: Shaking hands is the normal form of greeting. Casual dress is usual for most occasions in the daytime or evening. **Photography:** Since June 1992, photography has been allowed in all areas with the exception of military installations. However, some areas are still sensitive and it is advisable to take local advice. **Tipping:** It is customary to give waiters and taxi drivers a 10% tip.

BUSINESS PROFILE

ECONOMY: Uganda's thriving agricultural economy has been damaged by the oil crisis, local mismanagement and the military campaigns of 1979 which saw the overthrow of General Amin and the civil war that followed. Coffee is the main export commodity, while tea is developing well from a low base. Copper mining, once important, is being re-established. Manufacturing is also recovering: tobacco, brewing and sugar refining have been successfully rehabilitated. The Government has also sponsored a large amount of barter trade. Despite these successes, excessive military expenditure and the uncertain security situation ensured that at the end of the 1980s the economy's long-term prospects looked bleak. But during the last three years there has been a remarkable improvement. The Government has made full use of a better security situation to support economic development and (under pressure from foreign aid donors) cut military spending. GDP growth of 6% in 1990 exceeded all expectations and it now seems that Uganda may at last be on the road to fulfilling at least some of its immense potential. The UK is the largest exporter to Uganda with, according to 1986 figures, about 8% of the US$330-million market.
BUSINESS: A suit and tie are best worn by men for business meetings. English is used for all business discussions. Appointments should always be made. **Office hours:** 0800-1230 and 1400-1630 Monday to Friday.
COMMERCIAL INFORMATION: The following organisations can offer advice: Uganda National Chamber of Commerce and Industry, PO Box 3809, Plot 17/19 Jinja Road, Kampala. Tel: (41) 58791. Telex: 61272; *or*
Uganda Investment Authority, PO Box 7418, Kampala. Tel: (41) 234 105. Fax: (41) 242 903.
CONFERENCES/CONVENTIONS: The Uganda International Conference Centre with its main auditorium and its three committee rooms has seating for up to 2000 persons. It is adjacent to the 4-star Nile Hotel and is 3km (2 miles) from the centre of Kampala. For further information contact the Uganda International Conference Centre, PO Box 3496, Kampala. Tel: (41) 258 619 *or* 258 081/9. Fax: (41) 259 130 *or* 257 824. Telex: 61092 INTLCONF.

HISTORY & GOVERNMENT

HISTORY: For most of the period since independence in 1962, politically inspired violence has been endemic in Uganda. President Obote (who had banned opposition parties in 1969) was overthrown by the notorious Idi Amin, who remained in power until he was deposed by Tanzanian forces and Ugandan exiles in 1979. Obote subsequently returned to office, but he too found himself fighting guerrilla groups (remnants of Amin's army), notably Yoweri Museveni's National Resistance Army (NLA). The actions of the ill-disciplined Uganda National Liberation Army (UNLA), fighting both Museveni and tribesmen loyal to Amin in the former West Nile district, led to the displacement of large numbers of the population. In July 1985, Obote was replaced by a military council under General Tito Okello. The whole period of Okello's government was dominated by the struggle against the NRA. The latter, enjoying much more popular support than Okello's UNLA, continued their struggle against the Government and took control of the capital in January 1986. A National Resistance Council was established to take over legislative responsibilities. Many of Uganda's problems in recent years have had their origins in relations with its various neighbours. Relations with Kenya are for the moment good, but, Sudan alleges Ugandan support for the Sudanese People's Liberation Army, which is fighting a secessionist war in the south of Sudan, and relations remain very bad. A joint force of Ugandan rebels and Sudanese army units crossed the northern border in late 1989; it was defeated. Then, in early 1990, an insurgency by guerrilla forces that had been defeated by the NRA was launched from Zaïre; it too was successfully countered, but at some cost in displaced civilians. The Rwandan problem, however, is much more serious. Uganda is home to at least 100,000 Tutsi refugees from ethnic conflict in their own country. Many Tutsi signed up with the NRA at the beginning of Museveni's insurgency. Thus trained and armed, in October 1990 they returned to the south to lead an invasion force into Rwanda (see *Rwanda*). Despite these difficulties Uganda is now more peaceful than at any time in the last 20 years. Economic reconstruction continues apace with some notable successes registered, particularly in re-establishing the important coffee industry as a major currency earner. The economy has recorded growth estimated at around 7% per annum. Corruption, which threatened to engulf the Museveni regime, as it had many before it, is commonly accepted to have been brought under reasonable control, although elections in February 1989 to an expanded National Resistance Council (generally accepted as free and fair) returned some politicians renowned for their propensity for graft. The NRA-dominated Council's mandate is due to expire in 1995, and in January 1992 the Council announced that a new constitution will be drafted and elections held before January 1995. Local elections were held in February and March 1992.
GOVERNMENT: Legislative power is in the hands of the 278-strong National Resistance Council, 210 of whose members are elected and the remainder appointed by the President who is Head of State and holds executive authority. Political activity has been suspended for the time being, although political parties have not been outlawed. A new constitution is due to be introduced and national elections held before January 1995.

CLIMATE

Temperatures in some parts of the country can be quite cool owing to the country's high altitude, despite its position on the Equator. The mountain areas become much cooler and the top of Mount Elgon is often snow-covered. Other parts of the country are much warmer. There is heavy rain between March and May and October and November.
Required clothing: Lightweights and rainwear, with warm wraps for the evenings are advised

ENTEBBE Uganda (1146m)

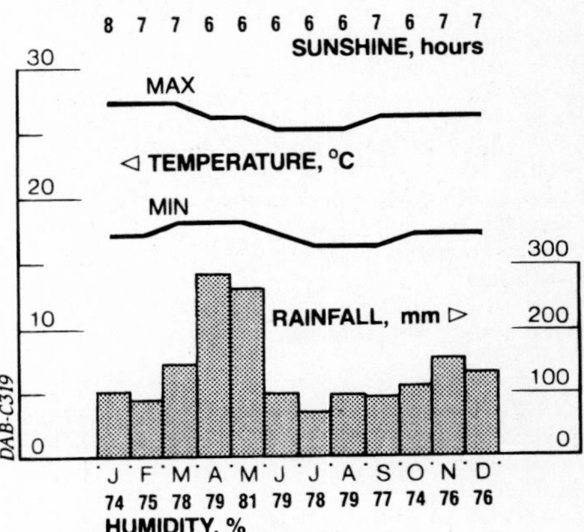

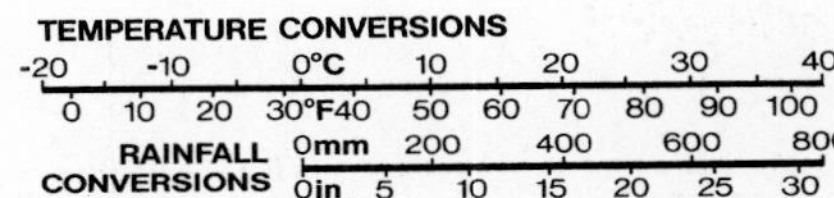

UNITED ARAB EMIRATES

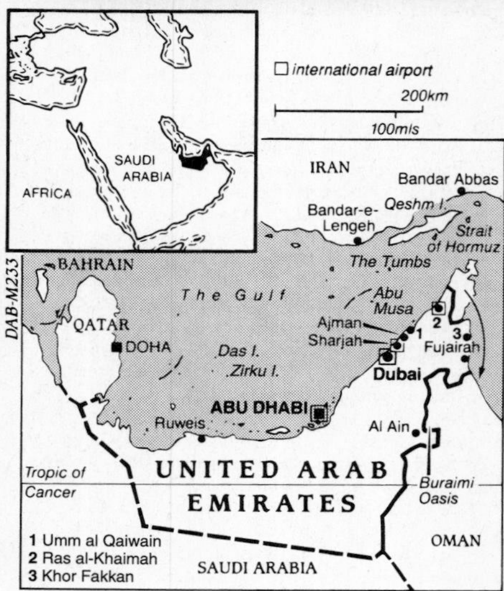

Location: Middle East.

Dubai Commerce and Tourism Promotion Board
PO Box 594
Dubai, UAE
Tel: (4) 511 600. Fax: (4) 511 711. Telex: 46182 DCTPB EM.

Federal Ministry of Information & Culture
PO Box 17
Abu Dhabi, UAE
Tel: (2) 463 100. Telex: 22283.

Embassy of the United Arab Emirates
30 Prince's Gate
London SW7 1PT
Tel: (071) 581 1281. Fax: (071) 581 9616. Telex: 918459 EMARAT. Opening hours: 0930-1500 Monday to Friday.

Consulate of the United Arab Emirates
48 Prince's Gate
London SW7 1PT
Tel: (071) 589 3434. Fax: (071) 581 9616. Opening hours: 0930-1500 Monday to Friday.

Dubai Commerce and Tourism Promotion Board
34 Buckingham Palace Road
London SW1 0RE
Tel: (071) 828 5961. Fax: (071) 630 9750.

British Embassy
PO Box 248
Abu Dhabi, UAE
Tel: (2) 326 600 (7 lines). Fax: (2) 341 744 *or* 318 138. Telex: 22234 PRODRO EM;
and
PO Box 65
Dubai, UAE
Tel: (4) 521 070. Fax: (4) 525 750. Telex: 45426 PRODR EM.

Embassy of the United Arab Emirates
Suite 740
600 New Hampshire Avenue, NW
Washington, DC 20037
Tel: (202) 338 6500.

Embassy of the United States of America
PO Box 4009
Abu Dhabi, UAE
Tel: (2) 336 691. Fax: (2) 213 771. Telex: 23513 AMEMBY EM.

Embassy of the United Arab Emirates
747 Third Avenue
New York, NY
10017
Tel: (212) 371 0480. Fax: (212) 319 5433.
Also deals with enquiries from Canada.

The Canadian Embassy in Kuwait deals with enquiries relating to the United Arab Emirates:

Canadian Embassy
PO Box 25281
13113 Safat
Kuwait City, Kuwait
Tel: 256 3025. Fax: 256 4167. Telex: 23549 MCAN KT.

AREA: 77,700 sq km (30,000 sq miles).
POPULATION: 1,909,000 (1991).
POPULATION DENSITY: 24.6 per sq km.
CAPITAL: Abu Dhabi. **Population:** 798,000 (1991).
GEOGRAPHY: The Emirates are bordered to the north by the Gulf and the Musandam Peninsula, to the east by Oman, to the south and west by Saudi Arabia and to the northwest by Qatar. They comprise a federation of seven small former sheikhdoms. Abu Dhabi is the largest Emirate, and the remainder (Dubai, Sharjah, Ajman, Fujairah, Umm al Qaiwain and Ras al Khaimah) are known collectively as the Northern States. The land is mountainous and mostly desert. **Abu Dhabi** is flat and sandy, and within its boundaries is the Buraimi oasis. **Dubai** has a 16km (10-mile) deep-water creek, giving it the popular name of 'Pearl of the Gulf'. **Sharjah** has a deep-water port on the Batinah coast at Khor Fakkan, facing the Indian Ocean. **Ras al-Khaimah** is the fourth emirate in size. **Fujairah,** one of the three smaller sheikhdoms located on the Batinah coast, has agricultural potential, while **Ajman** and **Umm al Qaiwain** were once small coastal fishing villages.
LANGUAGE: Arabic is the official language. English is widely spoken.
RELIGION: 96% Sunni Muslim.
TIME: GMT + 4.
ELECTRICITY: Abu Dhabi: 220/240 volts AC, 50Hz. **Northern States:** 220 volts AC, 50Hz. Square 3-pin plugs are widespread.
COMMUNICATIONS: Telephone: IDD is available both to and from all states. Country code: 971. Main area codes: Abu Dhabi 2, Ajman, Sharjah and Umm al Qaiwain 6, Al Ain 3, Dubai 4, Fujairah 9, Jebel Ali 084 and Ras al-Khaimah 7. There is a good local telephone network. Telephone calls *within* each state are free. **Fax:** *ETISALAT* offices at main centres provide a service. All hotels have facilities. **Telex/telegram:** Services are run by *ETISALAT*, which has offices throughout the Emirates and are also available through main post offices. **Post:** Airmail letters and parcels take about five days to reach Europe. **Press:** English-language daily newspapers include *Gulf News, Khaleej Times,* and *Emirates News.*
BBC World Service and Voice of America frequencies: From time to time these change. See the section *How to Use this Book* for more information.

BBC:

MHz	15.07	12.10	9.670	6.180

A service is also available on 1413kHz and 702kHz (0100-0500 GMT).

Voice of America:

MHz	11.97	9.670	6.040	5.995

PASSPORT/VISA

Regulations and requirements may be subject to change at short notice, and you are advised to contact the appropriate diplomatic or consular authority before finalising travel arrangements. Details of these may be found at the head of this country's entry. Any numbers in the chart refer to the footnotes below.

	Passport Required?	Visa Required?	Return Ticket Required?
Full British	Yes	1	Yes
BVP	Not valid	-	-
Australian	Yes	Yes	Yes
Canadian	Yes	Yes	Yes
USA	Yes	Yes	Yes
Other EC	Yes	Yes	Yes
Japanese	Yes	Yes	Yes

Restricted entry: The United Arab Emirates refuse admission and transit to nationals of Israel and to holders of passports containing a visa (valid or expired) for Israel. Travel documents and certificates of identity issued under the Convention of 1951 are not accepted.
PASSPORTS: Valid passport required by all. Often a sponsor will hold a visitor's passport. In these cases a receipt will be issued. This will generally be accepted in place of a passport where a transaction may require one.
British Visitors Passport: Not accepted.
VISAS: Required by all except:
(a) nationals of Bahrain, Kuwait, Oman, Qatar and Saudi Arabia;
(b) [1] UK nationals for a maximum of 30 days.
Note: As a general rule, visas for tourists and travellers (intending to visit family) must be arranged via the hotel/package tour operator or UAE resident concerned. To obtain approval the sponsor will require the visitor's proposed flight and passport details in advance. Business visits are made by invitation only.
Flights between airports in the UAE are regarded as international and visitors intending to visit more than one state should have a multiple-entry visa.
Types of visa: 30-day Visitors' visa and 14-day Transit visa available by prior arrangement through a UAE sponsor. Transit visas are not required by travellers continuing their journey by the same or first connecting flight, provided they do not leave the confines of the airport.
Application to: Consulate (or Consular Section at Embassy). For addresses, see top of entry.
Application requirements: (a) Valid passport. (b) 2 completed application forms. (c) 2 photos. (d) Fee. (e) For business visits, letter in duplicate from sponsor in country of origin. (f) Fax of invitation from sponsor in UAE, which must be sent direct to Embassy (fax: (071) 581 9616).
Note: Applications *must* be made in person.

MONEY

Currency: UEA Dirham (UEA Dh) = 100 fils. Notes are in denominations of UEA Dh1000, 500, 100, 50, 10, 5 and 1. Coins are in denominations of UEA Dh1, and 50, 25, 10, 5 and 1 fils.
Currency exchange: Most hotels will handle the exchange of foreign currency.
Credit cards: American Express, Diners Club, Visa and Access/Mastercard are widely accepted. Check with your credit card company for details of merchant acceptability and other services which may be available.
Travellers cheques: These are widely accepted.
Exchange rate indicators: The following figures are included as a guide to the movements of the UEA Dirham against Sterling and the US Dollar:

Date:	Oct '89	Oct '90	Oct '91	Oct '92
£1.00=	5.81	7.18	6.38	5.92
$1.00=	3.68	3.67	3.68	3.73

Currency restrictions: The import and export of both local and foreign currency are unrestricted. South African Rand and Israeli Sheklim are prohibited.
Banking hours: 0800-1200 Saturday to Wednesday; and 0800-1100 Thursday in Abu Dhabi and 0800-1200 Thursday in the Northern States. Some are also open 1600-1730.

DUTY FREE

The following items may be imported into the United Arab Emirates without customs duty:
250 cigarettes or 400 cigars or 2kg of tobacco;
2 litres of spirits and 2 litres of wine (non-Muslims only);
A reasonable amount of perfume for personal use (opened).
Prohibited items: Drugs, firearms and ammunition.

PUBLIC HOLIDAYS

Public holidays observed in the United Arab Emirates are as follows:
Mar 25 '93 Eid al-Fitr (End of Ramadan). **Jun 1** Eid al-Adha (Feast of the Sacrifice). **Jun 21** Islamic New Year. **Aug 6** Accession of the Ruler of Abu Dhabi. **Aug 30** Mouloud (Prophet's Birthday). **Dec 2** National Day. **Dec 25** Christmas Day. **Jan 1 '94** New Year's Day. **Jan 9** Leilat al-Meiraj (Ascension of Mohammed). **Feb 11** Beginning of Ramadan. **Mar** Eid al-Fitr.
Note: Muslim festivals are timed according to local sightings of various phases of the Moon and the dates given above are approximations. During the lunar month of Ramadan that precedes Eid al-Fitr, Muslims fast during the day and feast at night and normal business patterns may be interrupted. Many restaurants are closed during the day and there may be restrictions on smoking and drinking. Some disruption may continue into Eid al-Fitr itself. Eid al-Fitr and Eid al-Adha may last anything from two to ten days, depending on the region. For more information see the section *World of Islam* at the back of the book.

HEALTH

Regulations and requirements may be subject to change at short notice, and you are advised to contact your doctor well in advance of your intended date of departure. Any numbers in the chart refer to the footnotes below.

	Special Precautions?	Certificate Required?
Yellow Fever	No	No
Cholera	Yes	1
Typhoid & Polio	Yes	-
Malaria	2	-
Food & Drink	3	-

[1]: Following WHO guidelines issued in 1973, a cholera vaccination certificate is not a condition of entry to the United Arab Emirates. However, cholera is a risk in this country and precautions are essential.

Up-to-date advice should be sought before deciding whether these precautions should include vaccination, as medical opinion is divided over its effectiveness. See the *Health* section at the back of the book.

[2]: Malaria is not present in the Emirate of Abu Dhabi nor in the cities of Dubai, Sharjah, Ajman or Umm al Qaiwain. There is, however, a risk of contracting the disease (predominantly the benign *vivax* form) in the valleys and on the lower slopes of mountainous areas of the Northern States.

[3]: Tap water in major cities is safe to drink, but in small villages it should be filtered, or bottled water should be used. Water used for drinking, brushing teeth or making ice should have first been boiled or otherwise sterilised. Milk is unpasteurised and should be boiled. Powdered or tinned milk is available and is advised, but make sure that it is reconstituted with pure water. Avoid dairy products which are likely to have been made from unboiled milk. Only eat well-cooked meat and fish, preferably served hot. Salad and mayonnaise may carry increased risk. Vegetables should be cooked and fruit peeled.

Rabies is present. For those at high risk, vaccination before arrival should be considered. If you are bitten abroad seek medical advice without delay. For more information consult the *Health* section at the back of the book.

Health care: Medical facilities are of a very high quality, but are extremely expensive. Private health insurance is essential.

TRAVEL - International

AIR: The national airlines are *Emirates (EK)* and *Gulf Air (GF)*. *Emirates* operates international flights to and from Dubai; *Gulf Air* serves all UAE airports. *Emirates* is expanding services to the Far East.

Approximate flight time: From *London* to Abu Dhabi is 6 hours 35 minutes and to Dubai is 7 hours; from *Frankfurt* to Dubai is 6 hours; from *Hong Kong* to Dubai is 8 hours; and from *Nairobi* to Dubai is 4 hours.

International airports: *Abu Dhabi (AUH)* (Nadia) is 37km (23 miles) southwest of the city (travel time – 25 minutes). Airport facilities include duty-free shop, 24-hour bank, bar, snack bar and car hire. Bus and taxis are available at the airport.

Dubai (DBX) is 4km (2.5 miles) from the city (travel time – 10 minutes). Airport facilities include duty-free shop, bank, post office, shops, car hire, restaurant, snack bar and bar. Taxis are available at the airport.

Ras al-Khaimah (RKT) is 15km (9 miles) from the city. Airport facilities include a duty-free shop and restaurant/snack bar. Taxis are available at the airport.

Sharjah (SHJ) is 10km (6 miles) from the city. Airport facilities include duty-free shop, car hire, bar, restaurant, snackbar and bank (only open restricted hours). Taxis are available at the airport.

There is also an airport at *Fujairah* with duty-free facilities, and one is being constructed at *Al Ain*.

SEA: The main international ports are Jebel Ali, Rashid and Zayed (Abu Dhabi), Khalid (Sharjah), Saqr (Ras al-Khaimah) and Fujairah. Cruise ships call at Abu Dhabi, and there are passenger/cargo services to the USA, Far East, Australia and Europe.

ROAD: There is a good road into Oman and a fair one into Qatar which connects with the Trans-Arabian Highway on the overland route to Europe. See below for information on **documentation**.

TRAVEL - Internal

AIR: A daily flight now links Abu Dhabi and Dubai. Flights can also be chartered and there are small landing fields throughout the United Arab Emirates.

SEA: Commercial and passenger services serve all coastal ports. A water taxi travels between Dubai and Deira across the Creek.

ROAD: There are good tarmac roads running along the west coast between Abu Dhabi and Dubai, Sharjah and Ras al-Khaimah; between Sharjah and Dhaid; and linking Dubai with other northern states and the interior. Driving is on the right and the speed limit in built-up areas is 60kmph and 80-100kmph elsewhere. **Bus:** Limited services link most towns. However, most hotels run their own scheduled bus services to the airport, city centre and beach resorts. **Taxis:** Available in all towns. In Abu Dhabi, urban journey fares are metered, whilst fares for longer journeys should be agreed in advance. There is a surcharge for

UNITED ARAB EMIRATES	HEALTH REGULATIONS	VISA REGULATIONS
GALILEO/WORLDSPAN	 TI-DFT/AUH/HE	 TI-DFT/AUH/VI
SABRE	 TIDFT/AUH/HE	 TIDFT/AUH/VI

Code-Link

To access this information on your CRS, swipe the barcode with a light pen or type in the text under the barcode. For more information, see the introduction *How to Use This Book*.

air-conditioned taxis. Many travellers find taxis to be the quickest and most convenient method of travel from Abu Dhabi to Dubai. **Car hire:** Most international car hire companies have offices at airports or hotels. **Documentation:** An International Driving Permit is recommended, although it is not legally required. A local driving licence can be issued on presentation of a valid national driving licence. A letter from the visitor's sponsor is also required.

ACCOMMODATION

Accommodation is plentiful and some very reasonable prices can be found, with rates remaining constant all year round. Most of the major international hotel chains are represented, ie Hyatt, Forte, Sheraton, Hilton, Inter-Continental, Marriott and Ramada. There are also top-class beach resort hotels at Jebel Ali and Chicago Beach and a mountain resort hotel at Hatta Fort. Confirmation of reservation by fax or telex is necessary.

RESORTS & EXCURSIONS

For the purposes of this survey, the United Arab Emirates have been divided into the following areas: Abu Dhabi Emirate, The Desert, Dubai, The East Coast and The Northern Emirates.

Abu Dhabi

A predominantly modern city, Abu Dhabi nevertheless retains some of its ancient past. The *Diwan Amiri* (White Fort) was built in 1793 and still survives. There are many mosques, from the massive blue mosque on the corner of the *Corniche* to the tiny one in the centre of Khalifa Street Roundabout, surrounded by trees. There is also a museum. The oldest part of the town is the *Batin* area, served daily by the fishing dhows bringing their catch of Gulf prawns and other fish to the small harbours. The old building yards demonstrate craftsmen's skills which have remained unchanged for centuries. The city has ancient burial mounds at *Um al Nar*.
Excursions: Al Ain, 100km (60 miles) from Abu Dhabi, is an oasis and former caravan stop, built on a huge fertile plain. There is spectacular scenery along the journey from Abu Dhabi. The resort includes a camel market, zoo and museum containing old and new artefacts and Mesopotamian pottery. There is also a water spring at **Ain Faidha,** 14km (9 miles) from Al Ain. There are important archaeological digs at **Hili,** 10km (6 miles) from Al Ain. The stone tombs, including the famous 'Great Sepulchre', date back 5000 years. South of Al Ain is the *Hafit Mountain*, containing ancient tombs, pottery and swords. There are more ancient sites worth visiting at **Um Al Nar,** and **Badi'i Bent Saud.** A fun park is situated at **Al-Hir** and majestic sand seas are to be seen at **Liwa.** Other areas of great scenic beauty include **Qarn Island, Belghilam Island** (famous for its gazelle breeding), near to **Sadiyat Island,** and **Abul-Abyadh Island.**

Dubai

The 'Pearl of the Arabian Gulf' is concentrated mainly on its exquisite creek, the finest natural shelter in 1600km (1000 miles) of coastline. Bur Dubai, the original town, has substantial areas of old buildings, atmospheric alleyways and *souks* (markets). There is also the *Sikket-El-Kheil souk* and a museum. The modern city is on the Deira-side of the creek and is cosmopolitan and lively, with many attractive gardens and first-class shopping facilities, ranging from Western-style shops to the ancient *souks* where spices, perfume, clothing, antiques, handicrafts and jewels are available. One-fifth of the world's gold passes through Dubai by air or sea. There are outstanding sporting facilities in Dubai, including powerboat racing, water-skiing, snorkelling and ice skating. The recreation and sporting complex en route to **Jebel Ali** includes a golf course, with an all-grass cricket pitch under construction. Freshwater lakes can also be seen here, full of Japanese carp. There is an all-grass 18-hole golf course at the *Emirates Golf Club*, 20km west of Dubai City, which also offers a swimming pool, tennis courts, squash courts and a snooker room. Another all-grass 18-hole golf course was recently landscaped in Dubai at the new *Dubai Creek Golf Club* on the Creek. The project should be completed in 1993 and will also feature a miniature golf course, tennis courts, picnic and barbecue sites, children's play areas, cycling and jogging tracks and acres of beautiful gardens. The three main parks in Dubai are the *Mushrif Park*, *Jumeira Beach Park* and the *Safa Park* (currently under renovation).
Excursions: The ancient fortressed village of **Hatta** and *Wadi Hatta*, a lush and attractive valley in the foothills of the Hajar Mountains with superb desert scenery on the journey from Dubai.

The Desert

A spectacular and varied wilderness of magnificent red dunes and stark mountains with pockets of green oases. It is possible to meet the nomadic *Bedu* folk, whose hospitality is famous, and to watch camel races at dawn.
Excursions: Include visits to Bedu villages and to the beautiful white sand dunes at *Awir*, where there is a national park. There are now quite a few 'safari' holidays available.

The East Coast

This impressive stretch of lush coastline makes a dramatic change after the desert, with steep mountains, unspoilt sandy bays and beaches, ancient fortress, and date palm groves sloping down to the edge of the Indian Ocean with its host of marine life. Scuba diving and snorkelling are very popular here and many forms of watersports are available at the hotels.
Excursions: Include visits to the resorts of *Dibba* and *Fujairah*, where there is a museum, a Necropolis, an old fort and, nearby, many small mountain villages.

The Northern Emirates

This region has undergone a dramatic transformation since the discovery of natural gas in 1980 and there has been a considerable amount of expansion in the commercial sector. **Sharjah** is an excellent shopping centre, with its new *souk* containing hundreds of shops. There is also an ancient fort.
Excursions: Include visits to **Ras al-Khaimah,** where there is an old seaport with spectacular views over the coast and the *Hajar Mountains;* and also visits to the *Dhaid* and *Khatt* oases, the latter with mineral water springs. There are also trips available to the natural harbour at *Dibba* and the beautiful *Khor Kalba*, one of the most famous shell beaches in the world. The archaeological site at *Mileiha* (in **Sharjah** itself) dates back to the 4th century BC; 80-million-year-old fossils are to be seen here. Other archaeological sites include the *Dur* site at **Umm al Qaiwain** where Hellenistic ruins can be seen (210-100BC), the *Drabhaniya* ruins in **Ras al-Khaimah** and the *Zaura* ruins in **Ajman.** Important resort areas are *Khor Fakkan*, which has excellent beaches and watersports facilities and *Khalid Lagoon* (an aquatic park with several islands and a miniature Disneyland).

SOCIAL PROFILE

FOOD & DRINK: Specialities of Arab cuisine include *hoummus* (chickpea and sesame paste), *tabbouleh* (bulghur wheat with mint and parsley), *ghuzi* (roast lamb with rice and nuts), *warak enab* (stuffed vine leaves) and *koussa mashi* (stuffed courgettes). In the Emirates *makbous* (spicy lamb with rice) and seafood with spicy rice are also popular. Local fruit and vegetables are increasingly available and there is excellent local fish. Hotels serve both European and Arab food and there are also a number of Chinese, Indian and other restaurants. Frozen foods from all over the world are available in supermarkets. **Drink:** All the Emirates, with the exception of Sharjah, permit the consumption of alcohol by non-Muslims. It is illegal to drink alcohol in the street or to buy it for a UAE citizen. *Ayran* (a refreshing yoghurt drink) or strong black coffee are served on many occasions.
NIGHTLIFE: There are several nightclubs located in major centres and entertainment ranges from Arabic singers and dancers to international pop stars. Bars are found in all top hotels and range from sophisticated cocktail lounges to English-style pubs. Some hotels also have discos. Traditional dances are performed on public holidays. Most large towns have cinemas showing English-language films.
SHOPPING: Customs duties are low and therefore luxury goods are cheaper than in most countries. The Dubai duty-free shop is one of the cheapest in the world. *Souks* sell traditional Emirate leather goods, gold, brass and silverware.
SPORT: Golf: The *Emirates Golf Club*, Dubai, which opened in 1988, was the first grass golf course in the Gulf. In addition, there is also the recently completed *Dubai Creek Golf Club*. **Fishing:** There is an abundance of game fish in the Gulf. Fully equipped boats with crew can be hired from the Jebel Ali Hotel

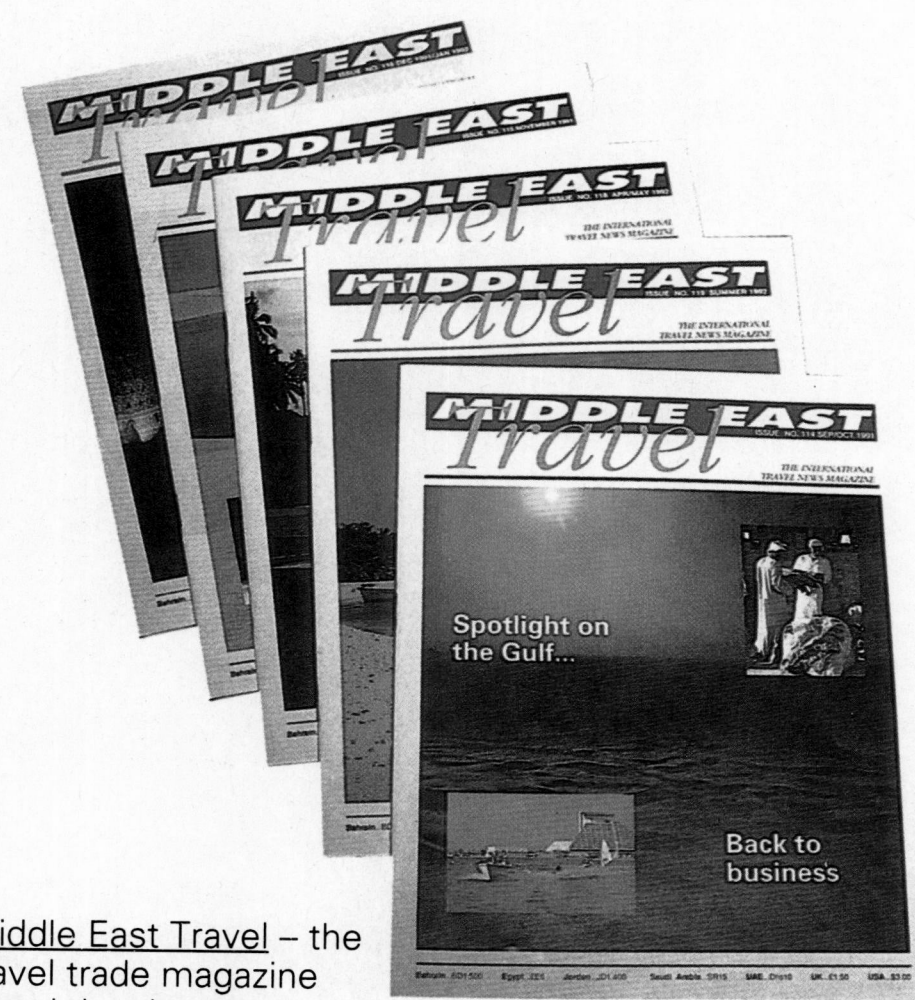

marina for deep-sea fishing trips. **Water-skiing:** Boats and water-skiing equipment are available for hire. **Sailing** and **windsurfing** are popular around Dubai and boats are available for hire from the Dubai Offshore Sailing Club. **Swimming:** Bathing is possible in the many hotel pools or beaches. **Ice skating:** Dubai has two year-round ice rinks and skates and instruction are available. **Horseriding:** Available at several riding centres, and rides through the desert are organised regularly. **Tennis/squash:** Many hotels and clubs have tennis courts and there are squash courts in main centres. **Bowling** alleys can be found in hotels and clubs. **Scuba diving:** The waters off Dubai are considered among the best areas in the world for diving. There are sub-aqua clubs in main centres and an extensive range of equipment is available for hire. **Spectator sports:** A boat race for about 30 rowers is a traditional sport that is becoming increasingly popular. Camel and horse races are also held at various race tracks. **Football** has become more popular and can be seen in most large towns and there are three thriving **rugby** clubs in Dubai. **Falconry** is very popular among Arabs.

SPECIAL EVENTS: The following is a selection of major festivals and other special events celebrated in the United Arab Emirates during 1993.

Apr 2 '93 *Powerboat Race*, Mina Seyaha. **Apr 14-20** *International Spring Trade Fair*, Dubai. **Apr 28-May 1** *UK in the Gulf* (exhibition of products from the UK), Dubai. **May 22-31** *Haj Pilgrimage* (religious event attracting Muslims from around the World). **Oct 1** *Dubai Duty-Free Snooker Classic*, Al Nasr Club. **Oct 1-Nov 1** *Dubai Aviation Cup* (open tennis tournament), Dubai. **Oct 20-23** *Motexha* (trade fair for fashion and textiles), Dubai. **Oct 31-Nov 1** *Computer Technology for the Middle East Conference*, Dubai. **Nov 1** *Dubai Duty-Free Powerboat Race and Beach Carnival*. **Nov 24-28** *Middle East International Motor Show*, Dubai.

SOCIAL CONVENTIONS: Muslim religious laws should be observed. Women are expected to dress modestly and men should dress formally for most occasions. Smoking is the same as in Europe and in most cases it is obvious where not to smoke, except during Ramadan when it is illegal to eat, drink or smoke in public. **Tipping:** Most hotels, restaurants and clubs add fairly high service charges to the bill, therefore tipping is not necessary. Taxi drivers are not tipped.

BUSINESS PROFILE

ECONOMY: Oil and gas are the Emirates' main industry and underpin the country's considerable prosperity. Although revenues declined in real terms during the 1980s, due to low world oil prices and OPEC-imposed production ceilings, the Emirates have had sufficient money to invest in major industrial and infrastructural projects: a large foreign workforce (estimated at two-thirds of the total population) has been recruited for these. Outside the oil and gas sector, most economic activity is government-sponsored and designed to diversify the economy and reduce dependence on oil. There are major construction projects, including a new international airport, and several industrial zones have been established to produce materials for domestic consumption. Imports into the UAE are dominated by the Japanese, who hold about two-thirds of the US$7-billion market, followed by the USA and Turkey.

BUSINESS: Business entertaining will often be lavish. Suits should be worn and prior appointments are essential. English is widely spoken in business circles, but translation services are likely to be available. **Office hours:** 0800-1300 and 1600-1900 Saturday to Wednesday and 0700-1200 Thursday. **Government office hours:** 0730-1330 Saturday to Wednesday and 0730-1200 Thursday (winter); 0700-1300 Saturday to Thursday (summer). All offices are closed every afternoon during the month of Ramadan.

COMMERCIAL INFORMATION: The following organisations can offer advice: Federation of Chambers of Commerce and Industry, PO Box 3014, Abu Dhabi. Tel: (2) 214 144. Fax: (2) 339 210. Telex: 23883 GHURAFEM; *or*

Federation of Chambers of Commerce and Industry, PO Box 8886, Dubai. Tel: (4) 212 977. Fax: (4) 235 498. Telex: 48752.

In addition, each of the Emirates has its own Chamber of Commerce.

CONFERENCES/CONVENTIONS: Though the Emirates are not primary convention locations, there are many first-class hotels with meeting facilities. The Dubai World Trade Centre hosts a multitude of events (including car rallies and tennis exhibitions). For further information on conference and convention facilities, contact the Dubai World Trade Centre, PO Box 9292, Dubai. Tel: (4) 314 200. Fax: (4) 306 4089. Telex: 47474.

HISTORY & GOVERNMENT

HISTORY: Formerly the Trucial States, this group of small sheikhdoms was brought under British suzerainty in the 1820s after attacks on British-owned shipping by pirates operating in the Gulf region. A treaty was signed between the local Arab rulers and the British in 1853, under which the local rulers accepted British military protection and promised to refrain from piracy. In the 1950s, the British sought to weld the seven distinct regimes of the Trucial States into a single administrative bloc. Two factors set the future course of the territory: the 1968 decision by the British to withdraw military forces from the Gulf area; and the discovery of oil which gave a sudden and rapid boost to the economy of the region. The United Arab Emirates came into being as an independent state on December 2, 1971. Internal politics remain somewhat unstable because of the uncertain nature of the federation and boundary disputes. Sharjah, in particular, has been the subject of a couple of coup attempts. After a quiet start on the international stage, the UAE have taken an active role in Middle Eastern politics both as a member of the Gulf Co-operation Council (of which it was a founder) and in offering itself, successfully on several occasions, as a mediation party in disputes between Israel and the Palestinians, Morocco and Algeria, Iran and Iraq, and between Oman and Yemen. It also developed links further afield, by establishing diplomatic relations with China and the CIS, in anticipation of the East–West thaw and before other countries in the region. The prospects of peace offered by the end of the Iran-Iraq war in 1988 were briefly threatened; the Iraqi invasion of Kuwait in August 1990, once again put the Emirates close to the centre of a major regional dispute. In common with other members of the Gulf Co-operation Council, the UAE gave their firm backing to the US-led anti-Iraqi coalition. In October 1990, one of the veteran leaders of the UAE, Sheikh Rashid bin Said al-Maktoum of Dubai, died aged 80 after nearly 20 years at the top. He was succeeded by his son, Sheikh Maktoum bin Rashid al-Maktoum. In the other main emirate, Abu Dhabi, Sheikh Zayed has been linked with the collapse of the Bank of Credit and Commerce International in July 1991, in which the ruling family was the major shareholder with 77%.

GOVERNMENT: The highest federal authority is the Supreme Council of Rulers comprising the absolute rulers of the seven emirates. Decisions reached by the Council must have the agreement of at least five members including Abu Dhabi and Dubai, the two largest members. The Council appoints a President to act as Head of State. There are no political parties.

CLIMATE

The best time to visit is between October and May. The hottest time is from June to September with little rainfall. **Required clothing:** Lightweights with mediumweights from November to March, warmer clothes for evening.

SHARJAH, UAE (5m)

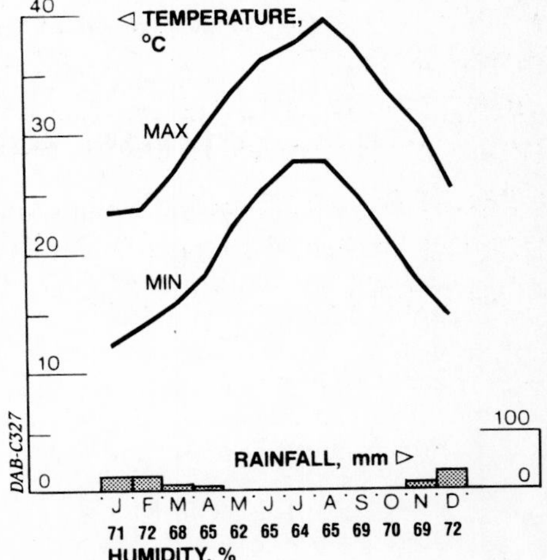

UNITED KINGDOM

□ major international airport

Location: Northwest Europe.

British Tourist Authority & English Tourist Board
Thames Tower
Black's Road
London W6 9EL
Tel: (081) 846 9000 *or* (071) 730 3488. Fax: (081) 563 0302. Telex: 21231 BTA ADM G *or* 266975. Opening hours: 0900-1800 Monday to Friday, 0900-1700 Saturday.

Scottish Tourist Board
23 Ravelston Terrace
Edinburgh EH4 3EU
Tel: (031) 332 2433. Fax: (031) 343 1513. Telex: 72272.

Wales Tourist Board
Brunel House
2 Fitzalan Road
Cardiff CF2 1UY
Tel: (0222) 499 909. Fax: (0222) 485 031.

Northern Ireland Tourist Board
St Anne's Court
59 North Street
Belfast BT1 1NB
Tel: (0232) 231 221. Fax: (0232) 240 960. Telex: 748087.

Embassy of the United Kingdom of Great Britain and Northern Ireland
3100 Massachusetts Avenue, NW
Washington, DC
20008
Tel: (202) 462 1340. Fax: (202) 898 4255. Telex: 892384PRODROM B WSH.
Consulate Generals in: Atlanta, Boston, Chicago, Cleveland, Dallas, Houston, Los Angeles, New York (tel: (212) 745 0200) and San Francisco.

British Tourist Authority
7th Floor
551 Fifth Avenue
New York, NY
10176
Tel: (212) 986 2200 *or* 986 2266. Fax: (212) 986 1188.
Also in: Atlanta, Chicago and Los Angeles.

United States Embassy
24-31 Grosvenor Square
London W1A 1AE
Tel: (071) 499 9000. Fax: (071) 409 1637.

British High Commission
80 Elgin Street
Ottawa, Ontario
K1P 5K7
Tel: (613) 237 1530. Fax: (613) 237 7980.
Consulates in: Halifax, Montréal, St John's, Toronto, Vancouver and Winnipeg.

British Tourist Authority
Suite 450
111 Avenue Road
Toronto, Ontario
M5R 3J8
Tel: (416) 925 6326. Fax: (416) 961 2175.

Canadian High Commission
Macdonald House
1 Grosvenor Square
London W1X 0AB
Tel: (071) 629 9492. Fax: (071) 258 6506. Telex: 261592 CDALDN G.

INTRODUCTION

The United Kingdom of Great Britain and Northern Ireland consists of *England, Scotland, Wales* and *Northern Ireland*. Although they form one administrative unit (with regional exceptions) they have had separate cultures, languages and political histories. Within this entry are also the *Channel Islands* and the *Isle of Man* which, although only dependencies of the British Crown, are included for convenience of reference. The *United Kingdom* entry has been arranged as follows. First, a general introduction, covering the aspects which the four countries have in common. Then follow sections devoted to the four constituent countries and finally sections dealing respectively with the Channel Islands and the Isle of Man. *Jersey* and *Guernsey* have separate entries earlier in the *World Travel Guide*.

AREA: 242,521 sq km (93,638 sq miles).
POPULATION: 57,236,200 (1989 estimate).
POPULATION DENSITY: 236 per sq km.
CAPITAL: London. **Population:** 6,756,400 (Greater London, 1989).
GEOGRAPHY: The British landscape can be divided roughly into two kinds of terrain – highland and lowland. The highlands area comprise the mountainous

regions of Scotland, Northern Ireland, northern England and north Wales. The English Lake District in the northwest contains lakes and fells. The lowland area is broken up by sandstone and limestone hills, long valleys and basins such as the Wash on the east coast. In the southeast, the North and South Downs culminate in the White Cliffs of Dover. The coastline includes fjord-like inlets in the northwest of Scotland, spectacular cliffs and wild sandy beaches on the east coast and, further south, beaches of rocks, shale and sand sometimes backed by dunes, and large areas of fenland in East Anglia.
Note: More detailed geographical descriptions of the various countries may be found under the respective entries.
LANGUAGE: English. Some Welsh is spoken in parts of Wales, Gaelic in parts of Scotland and Northern Ireland, and French and Norman French in the Channel Islands. The many ethnic minorities within the UK also speak their own dialects and languages (eg Hindi, Urdu, Turkish, Greek, Cantonese, Mandarin, etc).
RELIGION: Predominantly Protestant (Church of England), but many other Christian denominations also: Roman Catholic, Church of Scotland, Evangelical, Nonconformist and Baptist. There are sizeable Jewish, Muslim and Hindu minorities.
TIME: GMT (GMT + 1 from March 29 to October 29).
ELECTRICITY: 240 volts AC, 50Hz. Square 3-pin plugs are standard and the visitor is unlikely to come across the older round 3-pin type.

COMMUNICATIONS: Telephone: IDD is available. Country code: 44. There are numerous public call boxes. Some boxes take coins, others phone cards only. There are two suppliers of telecommunication networks, British Telecom and Mercury. **Fax:** There are many high street bureaux in major cities. Most hotels have facilities.
Telex/telemessage: There are telex bureaux in all the main cities. Telemessages may be sent from a post office or from a private telephone. **Post:** Stamps are available from post offices and many shops and stores. There are stamp machines outside some post offices. Post boxes are red. First-class internal mail normally reaches its destination the day after posting (except in remote areas of Scotland), and most second-class mail the day after that. International postal connections are good. Post office opening hours are 0900-1730 Monday to Friday and 0900-1230 Saturday. **Press:** Dominated by about ten major newspapers, UK circulation figures are amongst the highest in the world. The most influential newspapers are *The Times*, *The Guardian*, *The Daily Telegraph*, *The Financial Times* and *The Independent*. The more popular 'tabloid' newspapers are *The Sun*, *The Daily Mirror*, *The Daily Express*, *The Daily Mail* and *Today*. Most papers have an associated Sunday newspaper, though there are some independents, most notably *The Observer*. There are also daily regional newspapers, particularly in Scotland and the North. The London *Evening Standard* is produced in several editions daily, the first being in the early afternoon.

PASSPORT/VISA

Regulations and requirements may be subject to change at short notice, and you are advised to contact the appropriate diplomatic or consular authority before finalising travel arrangements. Details of these may be found at the head of this country's entry. Any numbers in the chart refer to the footnotes below.

	Passport Required?	Visa Required?	Return Ticket Required?
Full British	1	No	No
BVP	Valid	No	No
Australian	Yes	No	No
Canadian	Yes	No	No
USA	Yes	No	No
Other EC	2	No	No
Japanese	Yes	No	No

PASSPORTS: Valid passport required by all except:
(a) [1] nationals of the United Kingdom and colonies holding a BVP;
(b) [2] nationals of EC countries with a national ID card for tourist visits not exceeding 3 months;
(c) nationals of Austria, Liechtenstein, Monaco and Switzerland holding national ID card for touristic/social visits of less than 6 months and in possession of a Visitor's Card available from travel agencies.
Note: (a) A passport is not required for travel between

UNITED KINGDOM	HEALTH REGULATIONS	VISA REGULATIONS (Code-Link)
GALILEO/WORLDSPAN	 TI-DFT/LHR/HE	 TI-DFT/LHR/VI
SABRE	 TIDFT/LHR/HE	TIDFT/LHR/VI

To access this information on your CRS, swipe the barcode with a light pen or type in the text under the barcode. For more information, see the introduction *How to Use This Book*.

Great Britain and Ireland, Northern Ireland, the Channel Islands or the Isle of Man. (b) Passports should be valid for at least 6 months beyond the period of intended stay. (c) Passengers transiting the UK to the Republic of Ireland are advised to hold return tickets to avoid delay and interrogation.
British Visitors Passport: Accepted.
VISAS: Required by the following:
(a) *Commonwealth:* nationals of Bangladesh, Ghana, India, Nigeria, Pakistan, Sri Lanka and Uganda. Citizens of these countries must generally have their passport or identity document endorsed with a valid United Kingdom visa, issued for the purpose for which they seek entry. Those who have settled in the UK may be exempt: enquire at the UK Passport Office if in the UK, otherwise at a British Embassy or High Commission;
(b) *Europe:* nationals of Albania, Bulgaria, Georgia, Poland, Romania, Turkey and CIS (Armenia, Azerbaijan, Belarus, Kazakhstan, Kirghizia, Moldova, Russian Federation, Tajikstan, Turkmenistan, Ukraine and Uzbekistan);
(c) *Asia:* All *except* nationals of Bahrain, Israel, Japan, South Korea, Kuwait, Qatar and United Arab Emirates;
(d) *Africa:* All *except* nationals of Côte d'Ivoire, Niger and South Africa;
(e) *The Americas:* nationals of Haiti and Cuba.
Types of visa: Temporary visitor's and Business. Cost: £20 (£10 for travellers under 25). A 6-month Multiple-entry visa costs £30. Visa prices are standard. *Transit visas* are not required if continuing the journey to a third country by the first connecting aircraft within 24 hours, and possessing confirmed onward travel documentation. Travellers who do not qualify for this exemption must possess a Transit visa, which is valid for 7 days.
Application to: The nearest visa issuing post in the country in question, ie British Consulate (or Consular Section at Embassy or High Commission). For addresses, see top of entry.
Application requirements: Depends on nationality of applicant.
Working days required: Depends on nationality of applicant. Applications that are referred to the Home Office may take 6 weeks or more.
Temporary residence: Enquire at nearest British Consulate, Embassy or High Commission.

MONEY

Note: For information on currency specific to Jersey and Guernsey, see their separate entries earlier in the book; for the Isle of Man and Northern Ireland, see the sub-sections that follow this general UK entry.
Currency: Pound (£) = 100 pence. Notes are in denominations of £50, 20, 10 and 5. There are in addition bank notes issued by Scottish banks which are legal tender in all parts of the UK. Coins are in denominations of £1, and 50, 20, 10, 5, 2 and 1 pence. In 1990 a new smaller 5-pence piece came into circulation; the old 5-pence piece is no longer legal tender. On September 30, 1992, a new smaller 10-pence piece was introduced; the old 10-pence piece remains legal tender.
Currency exchange: Money can be exchanged in banks, exchange bureaux and many hotels. The exchange bureaux are often open outside banking hours but charge higher commission rates.
Credit cards: Access/Mastercard, American Express, Diners Club and Visa are all widely accepted. Check with your credit card company for details of merchant acceptability and other services which may be available.
Travellers cheques: Widely accepted.
Exchange rate indicators: The following figures are included as a guide to the movements of Sterling against the US Dollar:

Date:	Oct '89	Oct '90	Oct '91	Oct '92
$1.00=	0.62	0.52	0.58	0.63

Currency restrictions: There are no restrictions on the import or export of either local or foreign currency.
Banking hours: 0930-1530/1630 Monday to Friday (there may be some further variation in closing times). Some branches of certain banks are open on Saturday morning. Some branches of the Co-operative Bank stay open until 1730.

DUTY FREE

Note: The Channel Islands are treated as being outside of the EC for the *Duty Free* section.
The following items may be imported into the UK without incurring customs duty by:
(a) European residents arriving from the EC countries (duty and tax paid within the EC):
300 cigarettes or 150 cigarillos or 75 cigars or 400g of tobacco;
5 litres non-sparkling table wine and one of the following:
(a) 1.5 litres of spirits over 22°,
(b) 3 litres of fortirfied/sparkling wine (under 22°),
(c) 3 litres of non-sparkling table wine;
90cc of perfume and 375cc of toilet water;
Goods to the value of £420; this may include an allowance of 50 litres of beer and 25 mechanical lighters.
(b) Passengers arriving from non-EC countries or if goods were obtained duty free within the EC:
200 cigarettes or 100 cigarillos or 50 cigars or 250g of tobacco;
2 litres non-sparkling table wine and one of the following:
(a) 1 litre of spirits over 22°,
(b) 2 litres of fortified/sparkling wine (under 22°),
(c) 2 litres of non-sparkling table wine;
60cc of perfume and 250cc of toilet water;
Goods to the value of £32 this may include an allowance of 50 litres of beer and 25 mechanical lighters.
(c) Visitors over 17 years of age arriving from EC countries with duty-paid goods (as of January 1993):
800 cigarettes and 400 cigarillos and 200 cigars and 1kg of tobacco;
90 litres of wine (including up to 60 litres of sparkling wine);
10 litres of spirits;
20 litres of intermediate products (such as fortified wine);
110 litres of beer.
Note: The UK is one of the few regions of the world completely free of rabies, and all cats and dogs imported into the country must spend six months in quarantine. To bring animals and birds into the UK, an import licence must be obtained, at least six months in advance. *Severe penalties are imposed on persons attempting to smuggle domestic animals into the country. An illegally imported animal is liable to be destroyed.* For further information contact The Ministry of Agriculture, Fisheries & Food, Government Buildings, Hook Rise South, Kingston Bypass, Tolworth, Surbiton, Surrey KT6 7NF. Tel: (081) 330 4411 *or* the nearest British mission abroad.

PUBLIC HOLIDAYS

Public holidays observed in the UK are as follows:
Apr 9 '93 Good Friday. **Apr 12** Easter Monday. **May 3** May Day Bank Holiday. **May 31** Spring Bank Holiday. **Aug 2** Summer Bank Holiday (Scotland only). **Aug 30** Late Summer Bank Holiday. **Dec 25** Christmas Day. **Dec 26** Boxing Day. **Jan 1 '94** New Year's Day.

Note: Public holidays are often referred to as 'bank holidays' in the UK.

HEALTH

Regulations and requirements may be subject to change at short notice, and you are advised to contact your doctor well in advance of your intended date of departure. Any numbers in the chart refer to the footnotes below.

	Special Precautions?	Certificate Required?
Yellow Fever	No	No
Cholera	No	No
Typhoid & Polio	No	-
Malaria	No	-
Food & Drink	No	-

Health care: The National Health Service provides free medical treatment (at hospitals and general surgeries) to all who are ordinarily resident in the UK but requires payment for dental treatment, prescriptions and spectacles. Immediate first aid/emergency treatment is free for all visitors, after which charges are made unless the visitor's country has a Reciprocal Health Agreement with the UK. The following have signed such Agreements: all EC countries (but Danish residents of the Faroe Islands are not covered), Anguilla, Australia, Austria, British Virgin Islands, Bulgaria, Channel Islands (applies only if visitor is staying less than three months), Falkland Islands, Finland, Hong Kong, Hungary, Iceland, Isle of Man, Malta (for visits up to 30 days), Montserrat, New Zealand, Norway, Poland, Romania, St Helena, Sweden and the Turks & Caicos Islands. The Agreements provide differing degrees of exemption for different nationalities; full details of individual Agreements are available from the Department of Health. See also the *Health* section at the back of this book.

TRAVEL - International

AIR: The principle national airline is *British Airways* (*BA*).

Approximate flight times: From *Birmingham* to Amsterdam is 1 hour; to Dublin is 50 minutes; to Düsseldorf is 1 hour 15 minutes; to Frankfurt/M is 1 hour 30 minutes; and to Paris is 1 hour 5 minutes.

From *Glasgow* to Paris is 1 hour 35 minutes.

From *Manchester* to Amsterdam is 1 hour 5 minutes; to Brussels is 30 minutes; to Copenhagen is 1 hour 45 minutes; to Dublin is 45 minutes; to Düsseldorf is 1 hour 20 minutes; to Frankfurt/M is 1 hour 45 minutes; to Milan is 2 hours 5 minutes; to Nice is 2 hours 5 minutes; to Paris is 1 hour 15 minutes; to Rome is 2 hours 40 minutes; and to Zurich is 2 hours 50 minutes.

For approximate durations of international flights from London, see *Travel* sections in entries of destination country.

International airports: See relevant country sections below for information on UK airports.

SEA: There are many ports offering ferry connections between the UK and mainland Europe, Ireland, the Channel Islands, the Isle of Wight, the Scilly Isles and the Isle of Man.

RAIL: *British Rail* trains meet connecting ferries at Dover, Newhaven, Portsmouth, Weymouth and Folkestone sailing for France, Germany and Belgium (board at Victoria Station in London); and at Harwich sailing for The Netherlands and Scandinavia (board at Liverpool Street).

ROAD: Few formalities are encountered when driving between Northern Ireland and the Republic of Ireland.

TRAVEL - Internal

Note: This section is a general introduction to transport within the UK. Further information is given in the Travel sections for England, Scotland, Wales, Northern

Ireland, the Channel Islands and the Isle of Man below.
AIR: *British Airways* operates a shuttle service to Belfast, Edinburgh, Glasgow and Manchester. Other internal operators include: *Aer Lingus, Air UK, British Midland Airways, Dan-Air, Inter City Airlines, Jersey European Airways, Logan Air, London City Airlines* and *Ryanair*.
Approximate flight times: From *London* to Aberdeen is 1 hour 25 minutes; to Belfast is 1 hour 10 minutes; to Edinburgh is 1 hour 10 minutes; to Glasgow is 1 hour 10 minutes; to Jersey is 50 minutes; to Manchester is 50 minutes; and to Newcastle is 1 hour.
From *Aberdeen* to Birmingham is 1 hour 40 minutes; to Glasgow is 50 minutes; to London is 1 hour 25 minutes; to Manchester is 1 hour 35 minutes; to Orkney is 45 minutes; and to Shetland is 1 hour 5 minutes.
From *Belfast* to Birmingham is 50 minutes; to Glasgow is 45 minutes; to London is 1 hour 5 minutes; and to Manchester is 45 minutes.
From *Birmingham* to Aberdeen is 1 hour 40 minutes; to Belfast is 55 minutes; to Edinburgh is 55 minutes; to Glasgow is 1 hour; and to Manchester is 30 minutes.
From *Edinburgh* to Birmingham is 55 minutes and to London is 50 minutes.
From *Glasgow* to Aberdeen is 50 minutes; to Belfast is 50 minutes; to Birmingham is 55 minutes; to Inverness is 50 minutes; to London is 1 hour 10 minutes; to Manchester is 50 minutes; and to Stornoway is 1 hour 5 minutes.
From *Jersey* to London is 50 minutes and to Manchester is 1 hour 5 minutes.
From *Manchester* to Aberdeen is 1 hour; to Belfast is 45 minutes; to Birmingham is 30 minutes; to Glasgow is 50 minutes; to Jersey is 1 hour 5 minutes; and to London is 50 minutes.
SEA: Information on travel to the Scottish islands is given below under Scotland.
RAIL: The UK is served by an excellent network of railways (16,000km/10,000 miles – in total). *Intercity* lines provide fast services between London and major cities, and there are services to the southeast and to major cities in the Midlands and the north, South Wales and between Edinburgh and Glasgow. Some rural areas are less well served (eg, the north coast of the west country, parts of East Anglia, North Yorkshire and Northumberland, parts of inland Wales, Northern Ireland and southern and northern Scotland), although local rail services are generally fairly comprehensive. There is a Motor Rail service across the country; this enables travellers to travel quickly by train while still having the facility of their car at the other end.
There are many **discretionary fares** and visitors using trains may like to consider an all-line *British Rail* pass giving unlimited travel. Contact *British Rail* for details. Disabled travellers are also entitled to discounted train fares; see the relevant section at the back of the book. *Inter-Rail* cards are valid; holders may be entitled to discounts on ferry fares.
ROAD: There are trunk roads ('A' roads) linking all major towns and cities in the UK. Roads in rural areas ('B' roads) can be slow and winding, and in upland areas may become impassable in winter. Motorways radiate from London and there is also a good east–west and north–south network in the north and the Midlands. The M25 motorway circles London and connects at various junctions with the M1, M4, M3, M40, M10 and M11. The only motorway that leaves England is the M4 from London to South Wales. Access to Scotland is by the A1/A1(M) or the A68 to Edinburgh, or the M6 to Carlisle followed by the A74 to Glasgow. Within Scotland, motorways link Edinburgh, Glasgow and Perth. In Northern Ireland, motorways run from Belfast to Dungannon and from Belfast to Antrim. For further information on roads within each country, see the respective sections below. **Coaches:** Every major city has a coach terminus, in London it is Victoria Coach station, about 1km from the train station. There are rapid coach services to all parts of the country. Many coaches have on-board toilets, refreshments and video. Private coaches may be hired by groups wishing to tour the UK; these can be booked in advance and will visit most major tourist attractions. Many of these destinations now have coach parks nearby. The main carrier is *National Express*.
Traffic regulations: Driving is on the left. Speed limits are 30mph (48kmph) in urban areas, 70mph (113kmph) on motorways and dual carriageways, elsewhere 50mph (80kmph) or 60mph (97kmph) as marked. Petrol is graded in a star system: 2-star (90 octane), 3-star (94 octane) and 4-star (97 octane). Unleaded petrol is now available at many petrol stations and is sold at a lower price than leaded petrol. **Documentation:** National driving licences are valid for one year. Drivers must have Third Party insurance and vehicle registration documents.
Automobile associations: Able to provide a full range of services to UK members touring the UK, they can also assist people who are travelling from abroad with maps, tourist information and specially marked routes to major events or places of interest.
URBAN: All cities and towns have bus services of varying efficiency and cost. London, Newcastle and Glasgow have metros, London and Glasgow's being very old and Newcastle's very new. The urban areas of Glasgow, Cardiff, Manchester, Liverpool and Birmingham are also well served by local railway trains. Licensed taxi operators are generally metered; small supplements may be charged for weekends, 'bank holidays', excess baggage and late night travel. In the larger cities, unlicensed operators offer a cheaper (but less efficient and knowledgeable) unmetered service with fares based loosely on elapsed clock mileage; these taxis are known as mini-cabs and must be summoned by telephone.

ACCOMMODATION

Accommodation in all parts of the UK is plentiful.
HOTELS: These tend to be much more expensive in large cities, especially London. Different classification schemes are used by the various countries. See the relevant country sections below. More information is also available from: British Hospitality Association, 40 Duke Street, London W1M 6HR. Tel: (071) 499 6641. Fax: (071) 355 4596.
GUEST-HOUSES: There are guest-houses and bed & breakfast facilities throughout the country.
SELF-CATERING: Cottages can be rented in many areas. For information contact the RTB or consult the relevant section in local and national papers.
CAMPING/CARAVANNING: There are camping and caravan sites throughout the UK, for short and long stays. Some sites hire out tents or a caravan to those

without their own equipment. Most sites offer basic facilities, while some have playgrounds, clubs, shops, phones and sports areas.
HOLIDAY CAMPS: These offer accommadation, food and a full range of leisure activities generally at an all-inclusive price. Good holidays for families, some run baby sitting and children's clubs.
YOUTH HOSTELS: Standards vary greatly, from very basic night-time accommodation for hikers and cyclists, to modern hostels and motels which are often used by families and groups. Prices are very reasonable. For infomation contact the Youth Hostel Association, 8 St Stephen's Hill, St Albans AL1 2DY. Tel: (0727) 855 215. Fax: (0727) 844 126.

RESORTS & EXCURSIONS

Details of resorts and places of interest throughout the four countries of the UK may be found by consulting the respective entries below.

SOCIAL PROFILE

Each of the countries of the United Kingdom has its own particular national dishes and drinks, festivals and other events of interest, its own attractions for shoppers and its own nightlife and other entertainments. Details may be found by consulting the respective entries below.
SOCIAL CONVENTIONS: The monarchy, though now only symbolic, is a powerful and often subconscious unifying force, and members of the Royal family are the subject of unceasing fascination, with their every move avidly followed and reported by the popular press, both in Britain and abroad. Handshaking is the customary form of greeting. Normal social courtesies should be observed when visiting someone's home and a small present such as flowers or chocolates is appreciated. It is not customary to start eating until everyone is served. **Clothing:** A tie, trousers and shoes (as opposed to jeans and trainers) are necessary for entry to some nightclubs and restaurants, otherwise casual wear is widely acceptable. **Use of Public Places:** Topless sunbathing is allowed on some beaches and tolerated in some parks. Smoking or non-smoking areas will usually be clearly marked. Cigarettes should not legally be sold to children under 16. **Tipping:** In hotels, a service charge of 10-15% is usual, which may be added to the bill. 10% is usual for restaurants and it too is often added to the bill, in which case a further tip is not required. 10% is also usual for taxi drivers and hairdressers but this is *not* included in the bill. There is no legal requirement to pay service charges that have been added to bills and if the service has been unsatisfactory, it may be deducted by the customer. Remember, however, that in the UK wage levels for catering staff are set at a deliberately low level in the expectation that tips will make up the difference.

BUSINESS PROFILE

ECONOMY: The UK is one of the world's leading industrial nations. North Sea oil is one of the mainstays of the economy, together with heavy engineering, chemicals, electronics, textiles and service industries including tourism, financial services and media. Agriculture and fishing are also important but employ only 3% of the population. Recent government policy under the Conservative governments has been dominated by principles of non-intervention, privatisation and tight controls on public spending. Many former state-owned industries, including oil, telecommunications, gas and electricity, have been sold to private shareholders. The 1980s saw a significant shift from manufacturing – which suffered badly from the recession of the early 1980s – to service industries. The beginning of the 1990s, however, has brought further recession which hit those sectors, principally building and retail, which had largely escaped the slump of the previous decade. The bulk of the UK's trade is conducted with the European Community and the United States. EC trade is set to grow substantially following the introduction of the Single European Market at the end of 1992.

Note: The economies of mainland UK countries are closely linked and are therefore dealt with together in this section. For information about Jersey and Guernsey, see their separate entries earlier in the book; for the Isle of Man and Northern Ireland, see the subsections that follow this general UK entry.
BUSINESS: Business people are generally expected to dress smartly (suits are the norm). Appointments should be made and the exchange of business cards is customary. A knowledge of English is essential. **Office hours:** 0900-1700 *or* 0930-1730 Monday to Friday.
COMMERCIAL INFORMATION: The following organisation can offer advice: Association of British Chambers of Commerce, 9 Tufton Street, London SW1P 3QB. Tel: (071) 222 1555. Fax: (071) 799 2202.
CONFERENCES/CONVENTIONS: The UK conference scene is well-organised with several publications comprehensively listing every possible kind of venue (including dedicated centres, hotels, universities, football grounds, race courses, manor houses, castles and theatres). In addition regional and local tourist boards promote their own areas vigorously. London and Birmingham have an international reputation; there are several excellent conference venues. There are other towns with facilities of near comparable size, and comprehensive back-up services are available everywhere. Glasgow, Manchester, Newcastle and Bristol are among the great cities offering a variety of venues, whilst smaller towns such as Chester, Salisbury, York, Llandudno and Inverness offer uniquely attractive environments without sacrificing efficiency. The large political parties of the UK traditionally hold their conferences in seaside towns during the winter; locations include Blackpool (the famous *Winter Gardens*), Bournemouth and Brighton. Those looking for conventional venues will find the maximum seating capacity (19,000 persons) in London; however, if an organiser wished to book the Wembley Stadium he could probably do it, so, effectively, there is no upper limit. All parts of the UK are easily accessible by rail and air from London. *The British Conference Destinations Directory* gives brief regional details and is published by the British Association of Conference Towns (BACT), First Floor, Elizabeth House, 22 Suffolk Street, Queensway, Birmingham B1 1LS. Tel: (021) 616 1400. Fax: (021) 616 1364. Enquiries can also be made to the *International Congress and Convention Association* (ICCA), UK-1 Secretariat, 137 Sheen Road, Richmond, Surrey TW9 1YJ. Tel: (081) 940 3431. Fax: (081) 332 1920.

HISTORY & GOVERNMENT

HISTORY: The Romans conquered and settled the major part of the British mainland between the 1st and 5th centuries AD, although their influence was limited in the northern and western regions. After their withdrawal (410-442) the island was invaded by Jutes, Saxons and Angles, who soon established seven kingdoms in the area south of Hadrian's Wall. Scotland and Wales remained Pictish/Celtic. By the early 9th century Wessex had emerged as the dominant kingdom and was the spearhead of resistance to the Danish invasions, particularly during the reign of Alfred the Great. By the time of Edward the Confessor (1042-1066), England was the most highly organised state in Europe and this position was consolidated when Norman military feudal organisation was imposed by William I and his successors (notably Henry I and Henry II) after 1066. Inheritance and dynastic marriage had given England control of most of France by the 12th century and the territorial disputes were not settled until the end of the Hundred Years' War in 1453. The 12th century also saw the conquest of Ireland, although it was never fully integrated into the political life of the mainland (see *History & Government* for Ireland). The constitutional history of England between the 11th and 15th centuries can be viewed in terms of the gradual expansion of the powers of the crown and the increasing efficiency and sophistication of the monarch's administration. This was a policy which often ran contrary to the interests of the aristocracy and on many occasions, notably during the reigns of Stephen, John, Henry III, Edward II and Richard II, constitutional conflicts developed which checked or reversed the trend; indeed the last two of these were deposed to make way for a ruler whom the barons felt would be more amenable to their wishes. The deposition of Richard II and the accession of his cousin Henry IV of Lancaster ushered in 60 years of largely weak central government and low royal prestige (Henry V's dazzling victory at Agincourt in 1415 and his subsequent conquest of most of France notwithstanding) which culminated in the dynastic conflict known as the Wars of the Roses. The throne changed hands on six occasions between 1461 and 1485, when Henry VII (Tudor) defeated the Yorkist Richard III at the Battle of Bosworth. Probably the most able English monarch, Henry VII managed considerably to revive the power and prestige of the crown. In 1509 his son Henry VIII succeeded to a state in many ways stronger and wealthier than it had ever been before. Scotland's political development during this period was dominated by largely unsuccessful royal attempts at centralisation; nevertheless the kingdom did manage to protect its independence in the face of constant English aggression, largely as a result of the talents of the members of the house of Stuart who managed to preserve some semblance of royal authority, despite that every ruler between 1437 and 1625 came to the throne whilst a minor. Their reward came in 1603 when James VI succeeded Elizabeth I of England (see below). Wales remained as a Principality during this time, occasionally united and usually very much at the mercy of English political ambitions. The Tudor period in England (1485-1603) witnessed several important developments: the re-establishment of central power, the break with Rome under Henry VIII, the beginnings of overseas expansion, the union of England and Wales and the flowering of Elizabethan and Jacobean drama. In retrospect, possibly the most important development was the remarkable growth of the power of parliament. Accustomed since its slightly hazy beginnings in the baronial revolts of the 1260s to have a say in representing grievances and – particularly as a consequence of Edward III's urgent need for money to fight the French – to granting taxation, the institution acquired a new purpose in the 1530s. Henry VIII used it as a vehicle for passing the Act of Supremacy and other legislation pertaining to the break with Rome, thus giving parliament a prestige and self-confidence to interfere in and influence the affairs of state which it never lost. Elizabeth I was succeeded by her cousin James VI of Scotland, although the formal union of the countries was not effected until 1707. The increasing power of Parliament (see above) was to prove a more effective force in curtailing the power of the crown than the medieval barons had been, and the English Civil War in the 1640s proved how real and effective this power had become: the conflict finally ended with the dramatic and, to most contemporaries, horrific spectacle of the execution of Charles I in 1649 and the establishment of a confused series of republics and Protectorates during the English Revolution (1649-1660). Despite the prodigious wealth of political ideas which surfaced in this period – which ranged from the re-establishment of the monarchy under Oliver Cromwell to the creation of an Evangelical Republic to prepare for the imminently expected Second Coming – by

1660 the Revolution had run out of viable ideas and Charles II was invited back almost on his own terms. Amazingly, within 20 years he almost managed to assert absolutism, although this opportunity finally disappeared with the abdication and flight of the unpopular (and Catholic) successor, his brother James II. On this occasion, Parliament made no mistake, inviting – this time on *their* terms – the Protestant William III of Orange to take the crown in 1689. From this date on the powers of the crown became severely curtailed: his successor, Queen Anne, was the last monarch to refuse the royal assent to an Act of Parliament. The 18th century saw Great Britain's (so-called after 1707) emergence as a major colonial and industrial power, mainly at the expense of France in such conflicts as the Seven Year's War. The American colonies were lost in 1776, but victory in the Napoleonic Wars confirmed British naval supremacy. By this time, Great Britain was one of the world's leading military and industrial powers, having spear-headed in the Industrial Revolution techniques in almost every field of production. While the growth of the colonies provided markets and sources of raw materials, the demographic increase gave the new industries a ready supply of cheap labour, and the explosion of urban wealth and population was probably the most dramatic social change since the introduction of feudalism. Great Britain and Ireland were formally united in 1801 under the name of the United Kingdom. The long reign of Victoria (1837-1901) is associated with the period of greatest British involvement, conquest, conversion and settlement, as well as further domestic economic and demographic growth. The First World War, in which Britain suffered heavy losses, marked in retrospect the end of the old system of European and colonial empires and was followed in Britain by a depression, the first signs of an economic decline which is still evident to this day. Relations between Britain and Ireland, never good, flared into civil war in 1916, and all but the six largely Protestant northeastern counties became independent in 1921. The colonial possessions were given up after the defeat of Nazi Germany in the Second World War and since then the outlook of the United Kingdom has been dominated by European concerns, although British influence (often covert) in the ex-colonies remains strong. Certain vestiges of the empire, such as the Falkland Islands, Hong Kong and Gibraltar, have caused varying degrees of friction with other states. After the Second World War, the empire was effectively finished: the opposition of the Americans, who had now assumed the mantle of the world's principal power, saw to that. At home, the Liberal Party was challenged, and quickly overtaken, as the main opposition to the Conservative Party by the Labour Party, which had its roots in the organised labour movement which grew up around the turn of the century. Labour formed its first government under Ramsay MacDonald in 1924. After a wartime coalition government of national unity – with both Labour and Conservative represented under Winston Churchill – between 1940 and 1945, Labour and Conservative have exerted a two-party stranglehold on the Government of the UK. The Labour government of 1945-51 was significant for major reforms of the health, education, housing and social service systems. The consensus started to break down in the 1970s as economic stagnation, endemic inflation and a growing trade deficit made it clear to many that the post-war prescriptions were no longer valid or relevant. It was against this background, and the decline of traditional industries on which the fortune of the nation had been built, that Thatcher came to power at the head of a radical Conservative government in 1979. The 1980s was a decade characterised internally by radical domestic policies of privatisation, local government reform and a revision of the tax-structure – leading to the introduction of the controversial 'Community

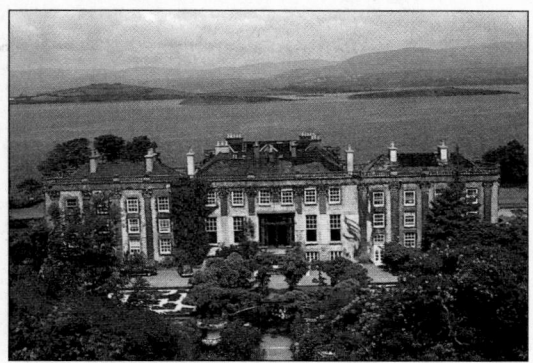

Charge' ('Poll Tax'). In spite of Government enthusiasm for the Single European Market, UK attitudes to issues as diverse as European monetary union, South African sanctions and German unification have caused strains in relationships with other EC countries; though many of these differences bear the interpretation of being about degrees of sovereignty and the timing of events rather than about fundamentals. British politics during the 1980s were dominated by Margaret Thatcher, who having taken office in May 1979, went on to win general elections in 1983 and 1987.
Her eventual political demise in November 1990 came not from a decision of the electorate, but from a lack of confidence within her own Conservative Party over the electoral consequences of her policies and her single-minded approach to their implementation. The deeply unpopular poll tax and the Government's uncertainty over European issues, along with the presence of a large contingent of disaffected and influential Tory MPs (many of them ex-ministers) combined in the autumn of 1990 to produce a concerted challenge to Thatcher's leadership. Her anointed successor, who won the second ballot comfortably with her blessing, was the Chancellor of the Exchequer, John Major. Since taking office, Major has enjoyed fairly good fortune in establishing his credentials domestically and on the international stage. His immediate inheritance was a series of potential problems, not least Gulf crisis to which Britain sent 30,000 troops, sailors and airmen. Another, rather different international crisis central to British foreign policy has been South Africa where Margaret Thatcher had attracted much opprobrium from her apparent support for the apartheid state. Recent developments in that country have made the Major government's continuation of existing policy towards South Africa that much less risky. The dominant foreign policy issue remains that of the EC. At the European Summit held at Maastricht in The Netherlands in November 1991, Britain's attitude was notable for its refusal, alone among the twelve, to be committed to any of the major policies which the EC is developing: the British negotiating team secured 'opt-outs' on both the introduction of a single European currency and on the European Social Charter. The British refusal was widely suspected to be motivated by the need to placate the Eurosceptics on the right of his party as much as by principle. On the domestic front, Major dealt effectively with the poll tax by abolishing it. The economy has proved more intractable, however, and repeated assurances by Major and Chancellor of the Exchequer Norman Lamont that the recession that began in 1990 has ended, is ending or will end soon have yet to be fulfilled. All of these issues, the economy in particular, were high on the agends during the April 1992 election: much to the surprise of most observers, the Conservatives were yet again victorious, although with a much reduced and vunerable majority of 21. Within months, during the ratification of the controversial Maastricht Treaty, they came within three votes of defeat. The management of the economy and the EC are likely to remain the dominant political concerns for the forseeable future.
GOVERNMENT: Hereditary monarchy, with real power being held by the Prime Minister, who is the leader of the largest parliamentary party and the head of the Cabinet. The two main political parties are the Conservatives (Tories) and Labour, although a centre party (the Liberal-SDP Alliance, later merged as the Liberal Democrats) threatened to disturb this old balance in the mid-1980s. None of the major British parties hold seats in Northern Ireland, where the political map is largely divided between the Unionists and the SDLP. Scotland and Wales return a handful of Nationalist MPs. The lack of any system of proportional representation in parliamentary elections does not, however, encourage the prosperity of smaller parties in Britain. Elections must be held every five years, though the timing is at the discretion of the Prime Minister. The legislature is bicameral; the House of Commons is elected, while the House of Lords is a peculiar mixture of appointed members, judges, bishops and hereditary peers. Britain is almost unique in the world in having no written constitution, and the political and administrative machine is powered by a mixture of common and statute law, judicial decisions and long-standing conventions; the royal assent to an Act of Parliament, for instance, is still proclaimed in Norman French.

CLIMATE

Owing to its being an island, the UK is subject to very changeable weather. Extremes of temperature are rare but snow, hail, torrential rain and heatwaves can occur almost without warning. Detailed descriptions follow in the respective sections below.
Required clothing: Waterproofing throughout the year. Warm clothing is advisable at all times, and is essential for any visits to upland areas.

ENGLAND

Location: Great Britain.

English Tourist Board
Thames Tower
Black's Road
London W6 9EL
Tel: (071) 846 9000 *or* (071) 730 3488. Fax: (081) 563 0302. Telex: 21231 BTA ADM G *or* 266975.

AREA: 130,439 sq km (50,362 sq miles).
POPULATION: 47,689,400 (1989 estimate).
POPULATION DENSITY: 365.6 per sq km.
CAPITAL: London. **Population:** 6,756,000 (Greater London, 1989).
GEOGRAPHY: Much of the countryside is relatively flat, consisting of fertile plains and gentle hills. Mountains, moors and steeper hills are found mainly in the north and the west; the Lake District (Cumbria) and the northwest are divided from the Dales of Yorkshire, and the northeast, by the (relatively) high-rising Pennines, 'the backbone of England'. The eastern part of the country, particularly East Anglia, is the most low-lying. The coastline is varied, and ranges from long stretches of sandy beaches to steep cliffs and isolated rocky coves.
LANGUAGE: English. The multiplicity of local dialects throughout the country, overlaid with class, and town and country accents make English a language of astonishing diversity – words and forms of syntax which are obsolete in the southeast may often be found elsewhere. Cornish is still spoken by a few people in Cornwall. In the larger cities, particularly London, there are many communities who do not speak English as a first language (or who have a *patois* – originating outside of this country – which adds yet more variety to the English language).
NOTE: *For information on time, electricity, communications, passport/visa, money, duty free, health, public holidays and business see the general UK section above.*

TRAVEL

AIR: England's principle international airports are:
Heathrow (LHR): Located: 24km (15 miles) west of central London. Airport information: (081) 745 7702. The airport has three passenger terminals grouped together in the airport's central area. The fourth terminal, a short distance from the main complex, handled 7,787,900 passengers in 1989. **Facilities:** Banks (7 days a week) and currency exchange in all terminals (T1/T2: 0700-2300; T3: 24 hours for arrivals, 0630-2130 for departures; T4: 24 hours for arrivals with a mobile bureau de change in departure lounge 0700-2100 daily); left luggage in all terminals; post office in T2 (0830-1800 Monday to Saturday, 0900-1800 Friday, 0900-1300 Sunday and public holidays); T1, T3 and T4 have pillar boxes and coin-operated stamp machines; T4 also has a sub-post office in the bureau de change in the departures area; buffet in all terminals (24-hour); quick grill and restaurant facilities in all terminals (24-hour); airside bars (0700-2230); full restaurant service at the 'Petit Four' (T4) and 'Runway Restaurant' (T2); babycare rooms in all terminals (0700-2200); St George's Chapel, opposite entrance to T2 car park (tel: (081) 745 4261); duty free in all terminals; gift/general shops in all terminals; Travel Care Unit in Queen's Building (tel: (081) 745 7495, open 0900-1800 Monday to Friday, and 0930-1630 Saturday and Sunday); Heathrow Business Centre, next to T2 (tel: (081) 745 5757); 24-hour emergency medical service; hotel reservation service in all terminals; facilities for the disabled: wheelchairs, telephones, toilets, special parking bays in short-term car park and coach link to long-term car park. There is also an induction loop link system for the hard of hearing.
Underground: The airport is linked to the entire Greater London area by the underground railway network. Stations for Heathrow Terminals 1, 2, 3 and 4 are on the Piccadilly Line, with direct trains to Hammersmith (change for Victoria), Earl's Court, South Kensington (change for Paddington, Blackfriars, Cannon Street and Tower Hill), Knightsbridge, Green Park (change for Charing Cross and Baker Street), Piccadilly Circus (change for Waterloo and Marylebone), Leicester Square (change for Euston), Holborn (change for Bank and Liverpool Street), Kings Cross (change for Moorgate and London Bridge) and Finsbury Park. The travel time to the West End takes 47 minutes, and to the British Rail stations Kings Cross and St Pancras 55 minutes. All other main-line stations can be reached with only one change of train in central London (see above for suggested connections). Services run 0508-0018 Monday to Saturday, and 0601-2352 Sunday. More information on the *London Regional Transport* network may be obtained by dialling (071) 222 1234 day or night.
Train: *British Rail* operates a Rail Air Link, with frequent express coaches connecting Heathrow with trains at Reading and Woking stations. The Reading Link takes 55 minutes and runs 0700-2300. The Woking Link operates 0820-2120 and takes 45 minutes. Details are available from British Rail desks in each terminal. Tel: (081) 745 7582. **Coach:** *London Transport* operates *Airbuses* with three express services operating between Heathrow and London. Airbuses call at all terminals and have ample space for passengers and baggage. There are also wheelchair facilities for the disabled. The A1 service to Victoria Station runs every 20 minutes, from Heathrow 0620-2210, and from Victoria 0640-2110. The A2 service to Woburn Place, W1, and other central and west London stops runs every 30 minutes from Heathrow 0610-2130 and from Woburn Place 0630-2030 (travel time – 1 hour 10 minutes). *London Country/Green Line's Jetlink 777* operates every 30 minutes (0630-2300) to Gatwick. The journey takes 1 hour 10 minutes. The service has now been extended to Luton airport, running approximately every 1.5 hours from 0700-2330. Further *London Country/Green Line* services include: *701/724:* Maidenhead, Windsor, Hammersmith and Victoria; *724:* Windsor, Egham, Staines, Watford, Hatfield, Welwyn Garden City, Hertford and Harlow; *726:* Windsor, Slough, Ashford, Kingston, Sutton, Croydon, Bromley and Dartford; and *727:* Crawley, Gatwick, Reigate, Epsom, Kingston, Uxbridge, Watford and Luton. Tel: (071) 730 0202 for information on all services.
National Express runs direct Rapide coach services from Heathrow to most parts of the UK including Manchester six times a day (travel time – 6 hours); Bristol 14 times a day (travel time –1 hour 55 minutes); Birmingham eight times a day (travel time –3 hours 15 minutes); and Liverpool five times a day (travel time – 6 hours 20 minutes). Tel: (071) 730 0202 (information and bookings). Speedlink coaches connect Heathrow with Gatwick and Stansted (travel time – 1 hour 20 minutes). Many private companies have long-distance coach services linking Heathrow with the rest of the country. Oxford and West Midlands area: *Flights Coaches*, tel: (021) 554 5232. East Anglia: *Cambridge Coaches*, tel: (0223) 236 333. Southend and Basildon: *Southend Transport*, tel: (0702) 355 711. Birmingham: *Aziz Coach Services*, tel: (021) 440 2015.
Local Bus: *London Transport's* services A1, A2, 105, 111, 140, 223, 285 and its night bus N97 operate from Heathrow Central bus station to various parts of London (tel: (071) 222 1234). Oxford/South Midland's 390 operates to Henley, Wallingford, Abingdon and Oxford; and 790 to Uxbridge, High Wycombe, Wheatley and Oxford. The X70 service runs directly between Heathrow and Oxford at hourly and half-hourly intervals, depending on the time of day. Tel: (0865) 774 611. *London Country/Green Line* also operate local services (see above for coach operations). **Note:** London Travelcheck (tel: (071) 222 1200) gives up-to-the-minute information on how London services are running.
Taxi: Available for hire outside each airport terminal. Each terminal has its own taxi rank and the information desk can give an indication of fares.
Car hire: *Avis, Budget, Hertz* and *Europcar* self-drive and chauffeur driven cars can be hired from desks in each airport

terminal. To central London takes 30 minutes to 1 hour. **Private car:** Heathrow, 24 miles from central London, is reached either through the tunnel of the M4 motorway spur or from the A4 (Bath) road. It is also close to the M25 orbital motorway, making journeys to virtually all parts of the country relatively simple. It is advisable to avoid the area driving during peak times (0700-1300 Friday to Sunday), especially in summer. Unloading but no waiting is allowed outside terminals. Short- and long-term car parking is available; coach connection from long-term car park to all terminals.

Gatwick (LGW): Located: 45km (27 miles) south of central London. Airport information: (0293) 535 353. **Facilities:** Banks/exchange, shops, restaurants, left luggage, duty-free shops, chapel, babycare rooms, medical room and facilities for the disabled. All facilities are available 24 hours. **Train:** *British Rail's* London to Brighton line runs underneath the Gatwick terminal and there are non-stop trains from Victoria Station (travel time – 1 hour) at 15-minute intervals during the day and hourly throughout the night for 24 hours all week (0520-2200). Tel: (081) 668 7261. Passengers travelling with *British Airways* or scheduled airlines handled by them can check in their luggage at the air terminal at Victoria Station. There are also services to Gatwick from London Bridge Station every half hour (travel time – 35 minutes). There are fast and frequent trains from Gatwick which connect with mainline stations throughout south-east England. There are three direct trains daily between Gatwick and Manchester, Birmingham, Coventry, Edinburgh, Glasgow, Luton, Oxford, Stoke-on-Trent and Wolverhampton, with stops en route. Tel: (071) 928 5100 for services in the south of England; tel: (071) 278 2477 for services to the northeast of England. Gatwick Travel Centre, tel: (0294) 543 445. **Coach:** *Speedlink* luxury non-stop service links Gatwick with all four terminals at Heathrow. Services depart every 15 minutes to 1300, every 30 minutes in the afternoon and the evening until 2200 (travel time – 60 minutes). Tel: (0293) 502 001. *Flightline 777* to Victoria Coach Station runs every hour 0515-2200 (travel time – 70 minutes). *Jetlink 747* to Heathrow runs every 30 minutes 0705-1605 and hourly thereafter (travel time – 60 minutes), with an extension to Luton airport every hour. The service to Heathrow continues every hour until 0005 with additional journeys at 0600 and 2200. There is a surcharge for services operating 0000-0659. Tel: (081) 668 7261 *or* (0293) 502 116. *National Express* have direct coach services to most parts of the UK including Birmingham, eight times a day (travel time – 5 hours 5 minutes); Leicester, seven times a day (travel time – 3 hours 25 minutes); Manchester, six times a day (travel time – 6 hours 45 minutes). Tel: (071) 730 0202 (information and bookings). Flightlink goes from Manchester and Birmingham. *Other services* calling at the terminal include Oxford Citylink, National Express 015 (from Bournemouth and Poole), 825 (from Manchester and Birmingham) and Caledonian Express (from Glasgow). Certain charter tour operators also provide coaches from Gatwick for arriving passengers. Check with relevant tour operator. **Local bus:** There are local buses to Crawley and Horley on routes C1, C2, 405, 455 and 773. Tel: (0293) 502 116. **Taxi:** Available outside the terminal. Travel time to central London – 1 hour. Tel: (0293) 502 808. **Car hire:** *Avis*, *Europcar*, *Budget* and *Hertz* self-drive and chauffeur driven cars can be hired from desks in the arrivals hall. **Private car:** Gatwick can be reached from London on the A23 or M23 motorway. It is also close to the M25 orbital motorway, linking all main routes from London. There are ample parking facilities for short and long stays. Fee enquiries: tel: (0293) 502 737 (North Terminal) *or* 502 896 (South Terminal).

London City Airport (LCY): Located: 10km (6 miles) east of the City of London. This new airport, situated in the Royal Docks in the London Borough of Newham, opened in autumn 1987 and provides frequent scheduled air services linking the City of London with Paris, Amsterdam, Rotterdam, Lille, Strasbourg and Brussels. The airport works on the STOL-port concept, for aircraft capable of Short Take Off and Landing. Scheduled Airlines include *Air France*, *Brymon Airways*, *Flexair*, *London City Airways* and *Sabena*. All scheduled services are business class. Check-in time is usually about ten minutes. **Facilities:** Duty-free shops (0600-2200), car hire, bank and bureau de change, restaurant and bars, newsagent and bookstore, and business centre with meeting rooms for up to 40 persons. **Train/Underground:** Silvertown Station on the North London Link is 300 yards from the airport terminal, connecting with the Underground at West Ham (District and Hammersmith and City Lines), Stratford (Central and Docklands Light Railway), Highbury and Islington (Victoria Line), West Hampstead (Jubilee Line) and Willesden Junction (Bakerloo Line). Plaistow (District Line) is approximately two miles from the airport; it has its own taxi rank. **Coach/bus:** No 69 from Stratford and Plaistow and no 276 from Stratford and West Ham underground stations. **Riverbus:** Hourly service from Charing Cross Pier (Embankment Station) at ten minutes past the hour and Swan Lane Pier (Monument Station) at 15 minutes past the hour (except at 1315). Travel time – 35 minutes. Leaves the airport at 30 minutes past the hour. **Taxi:** Widely available; may be booked in-flight. **Car hire:** *Europcar* and *Hertz* both offer hire cars. Tel: (071) 474 5555 (City Airport), ext 2531 and 2525 respectively. **Private car:** The airport is reached from the City via Commercial Road/East India Dock Road (A13) over the Canning Town Flyover, turning right into Prince Regent Lane; from the M25 via the M11 and North Circular (A406) or the A13. Access from the City of London will usually present no problems provided the morning and evening rush hours are avoided. London City Airport has ample car parking space located just two minutes walk from the terminal building.

Stansted (STN): Located: 55km (34 miles) northeast of central London. Airport information: (0279) 662 379. **Facilities:** Information desk, executive lounge, lost property, bureau de change, landside buffet and bar plus self-service restaurant, airside buffet and 24-hour bar, nursing mothers' room, 24-hour emergency medical service, duty-free shop, wheelchairs and toilets for the disabled as well as induction loop system in the international departures lounge. **Train:** Services run throughout the day (every 30 minutes) from London Liverpool Street to Bishop's Stortford station and then taxi or bus (see below) to the airport, approximately four miles away (travel time – 41 minutes) 0600-2300 Monday to Friday, 0700-2300 Saturday, 0730-2300 Sunday. Further information is available from *British Rail* (tel: (071) 928 5100). There are also services from Stansted to Cambridge and the North. Tel: (0223) 311 999. **Coach:** *National Express* and *Cambridge Coach Services* operate a range of services to and from Stansted, including London Victoria, Norwich (four times daily, travel time – 2 hours 20 minutes), Norfolk and the Midlands. Tel: (0223) 460 711 (National Express) and (0223) 236 333 (Cambridge Coach Services). *Eastern National* run services to Braintree, Chelmsford, Colchester, and Harlow. Rail Air Link services 33, 333 and X70 operate between Bishop's Stortford station and the airport to connect with all scheduled services (travel time – 15 minutes). Service is

hourly on Sundays. Tel: (0245) 353 104. There are services daily (bus 38) to London Victoria from the airport. Tel: (0223) 460 711 (National Express) *or* (071) 730 0202 (London Victoria Coach Station). **Taxi:** To Central London takes 1.5 hours. **Car hire:** Cars can be hired from desks in the terminal building. For details contact: *Budget Rent-a-Car* (0279) 681 194; *Hertz* (0279) 680 154/5. For air taxis/business aviation services contact: *Artac (Titan)* (0279) 680 680. **Private car:** Situated 34 miles northeast of London, the airport is easily accessible by road on M25/M11 from London. The Midlands and the North are reached via the A1, A604 and M11. Long- and short-term car parking space is available.

Birmingham (BHX): Located: 14km (9 miles) southeast of the city centre. Airport information: (021) 767 7145. **Facilities** include bank and foreign exchange services, buffet, bar, duty-free shop, facilities for the disabled, nursing mothers' room, shops, spectators' viewing gallery and left-luggage office. **Train:** The terminal is linked to Birmingham International Station by the Maglev shuttle which takes 90 seconds and is free of charge. Birmingham International is connected to the Intercity network and regional lines and has a fast service to London Euston (80 minutes). Train information: (021) 643 2711. Birmingham New Street Station, in the city centre, is 10 minutes away by Intercity or local services and provides interchange for services throughout the rest of the country. Tel: (021) 643 2711. **Coach/bus:** *West Midlands Travel* operates local services into the suburbs. *National Express* service 825 offers a daily service, every two hours, to central Birmingham, Coventry, Lancashire and the London airports. Service 305 runs to Birmingham, Coventry, Northampton, Cambridge and Clacton/Lowestoft. Service 307 runs to Birmingham, Coventry, Northampton, Corby, Peterborough and King's Lynn. Tel: (021) 622 4373. *United Counties Coachlink* service X64 runs to Birmingham, Coventry, Daventry, Northampton, Wellingborough, Kettering and Corby. Tel: (0604) 36681. Frequent coaches run to and from Birmingham from London Victoria and most major cities and towns throughout the country. **Local bus:** Service 900 runs to the city centre Monday to Friday. Travel time – 40 minutes. **Taxi:** Travel time to city centre – 25 minutes. Taxis are available outside the airport. **Car hire:** *Avis*, *Hertz* and *Europcar* have offices at the airport. **Private car:** M1, M5, M6, M42 and M40 are the main routes to Birmingham. The airport is well signposted from the city. There is multi-storey and open-air parking (over 8000 spaces) at the airport.

Note: A new terminal (the 'Eurohub' terminal) opened in July 1991. The aim is to facilitate flight-transfer in anticipation of a change in intra- and extra-European air travel organisation towards a more American system, in which major airports serve as hubs from which flights radiate out to other airports in an integrated fashion, making more use of connecting flights.

Luton (LTN): Located: 48km (30 miles) northwest of London. Airport information: (0582) 405 100. Scheduled flights: *Britannia Airways, British Airways, British Midland, Manx Airlines, Netherlines* and *Ryanair*. **Facilities:** Landside bank (with extended opening hours), general shops, grill restaurant (0700-2300), bar, 24-hour buffet/ bar, nursing mothers' room, free-play area (2-8 years) in departure lounge, duty-free shop, medical services and facilities for the disabled – wheelchairs, toilets and ambulift. **Train:** There is a service from London St Pancras to Luton railway station from 0518 to late in the evening, except Sundays. Frequent buses connect with the airport. The present hourly service from 2400 to 0600 continues. There are also frequent trains from Luton to Bedford, Leicester, Nottingham, Derby and Sheffield. Tel: (0582) 27612. **Coach:** *National Express* service 825 runs every two hours to Birmingham, Manchester, Heathrow and Gatwick. Services also run to most other parts of the UK (tel: (0733) 237 141 or, for information, (071) 730 0202). *Speedline* 750/751 operates at two hourly intervals from the airport to Hemel Hempstead, Hertford, Hitchin, Rickmansworth, Stevenage, Uxbridge and Ware (tel: (0923) 257 405). *Green Line's Jetlink 747* is a direct (limited stop) service from Stevenage, calling at Luton and continuing to Heathrow and Gatwick, which operates hourly from Luton and twice-hourly from Stevenage. It runs via Hemel Hempstead and Watford. *Flightline* 757 Express travels to London Victoria via Marble Arch, Hyde Park Corner (every 30 minutes Monday to Saturday during the day, and hourly at night and Sundays; travel time – 70 minutes). *United Counties* operate directly to Bedford (with connection to Cambridge), Huntingdon, Northampton, Peterborough and St Neots. Services are twice-hourly. Tel: (0234) 262 151 for details. *Flightlink Ltd* operates direct between the airport and Birmingham, Coventry and Wolverhampton (all 7 times daily), and Stafford, Stoke (Newcastle) and Manchester (all 5 times daily). **Local bus:** Buses no 12 and 38 run from the airport to Luton bus and rail stations, with frequent services

1 Durham
2 West Yorkshire
3 South Yorkshire
4 Nottinghamshire
5 Gtr. Manchester
6 Merseyside
7 Cheshire
8 Derbyshire
9 Staffordshire
10 Shropshire
11 West Midlands
12 Warwickshire
13 Leicestershire
14 Northamptonshire
15 Bedfordshire
16 Cambridgeshire
17 Hereford & Worcester
18 Gloucestershire
19 Oxfordshire
20 Buckinghamshire
21 Hertfordshire
22 Greater London
23 Surrey
24 Berkshire
25 Hampshire
26 Wiltshire

during the day, and hourly evening and Sunday services. Summer-only services run to Bournemouth and Southampton. Tel: (0582) 404 074. **Taxi:** Can be hired from the rank immediately outside the terminal building. **Car hire:** *Avis*, *Swan National* and local operators *Intercity Cars* and *Woodside Private Hire* have desks at the airport. **Private car:** The airport can be reached on the M1 exiting at Junction 10. Access to the airport from the east is via the A505 dual carriageway from Hitchin. The M25 connects all motorways and the airport can therefore be accessed from the East, South and West via M25, M4, M11 and M23. Travelling from the west also provides several routes from the Dunstable area through Luton. Airport signs should be followed throughout. Long- and short-term car-parking is available within the airport boundary.

Manchester (MAN): Located: 16km (10 miles) south of the city centre. Airport information: (061) 489 3000. **Facilities:** Restaurant (0700-2230), buffet, bar, ice-cream parlour, duty-free shop, nursery, chemist, gift shop, newsagent, banking service and three service tills, bureau de change, post office, full facilities for the disabled and range of other shops. **Train:** The nearest railway station is Heald Green, 3km (2 miles) from the airport. Frequent train services to Manchester (Piccadilly) and Crewe via Wilmslow are available for connections with main Intercity services. Services to the north of England are from Manchester Piccadilly station. Tel: (061) 228 2141. **Coach/bus:** *National Express* runs daily services to most parts of the UK including Scotland, tel: (061) 228 3881. Express coach service 100 runs throughout the week to Victoria and Piccadilly rail stations and the city centre. Service 44 runs every 20 minutes throughout the week to Manchester Piccadilly via Gatley, Northenden and Withington. Service 500 runs to Bolton via Stockport and various other stops. The 757 Airport shuttle (Monday to Saturday) provides a regular service to the city centre every 45 minutes 0600-2300. For more detailed information on times and frequency of these services contact *Greater Manchester Buses*, tel: (061) 228 7811. **Taxi:** Travel time to the city centre – 25 minutes. A taxi-rank is situated at ground level adjacent to the arrival hall in Terminals A and B. **Car hire:** *Hertz* (tel: (061) 437 8208), *Avis* (tel: (061) 436 2020), *Europcar* (tel: (061) 834 5845) and *Swan National* (tel: (061) 499 3320) have booking offices in both the arrivals halls. **Private car:** The airport is at the heart of the country's motorway network and a specially constructed spur from the M56 runs directly into the terminal building. Road connections serve Greater Manchester, Merseyside, Lancashire, Cheshire, the Midlands and West and South Yorkshire. There is car parking space within the airport boundary.

Newcastle (NCL): Located: 10km (6 miles) northwest of the city centre. Airport information: (091) 286 0966. **Facilities:** Bureau de change (0600-2145 Sunday to Friday, 0600-1830 Saturday), restaurant/bars (1200-2000), shops (0600-2030), duty-free shop, emergency medical services and facilities for the disabled. **Metro:** The Tyneside Metro Rapid Transport system extends to Kenton Bank Foot, 3km (2 miles) south of the airport and bus services 76 and 77 link the airport with the city. *Busways* provide a linkup with the Metro at Kenton Bank Foot every ten minutes and takes 15-20 minutes. The Metro runs to Newcastle city centre, across the River Tyne to Gateshead and South Shields and to Tynemouth and the coast. Traveline (Public Transport Information): (091) 232 5325. **Train:** Nearest railway station is Newcastle Central, 11km (7 miles) from the airport, linked by express buses operated by *Busways*, which run every 30 minutes Monday to Saturday, and every hour on Sunday. Tel: (091) 232 6262. **Buses:** The X77 ('Airport Express') provides a direct link to Newcastle city centre, operating 16 hours a day (half-hourly 1035-1735); the travel time is 25 minutes. Services 75, 76, 76E, 77, 77E, 78, 78E and 79 run from Eldon Square bus concourse, in the centre of Newcastle. These stop on the main road at the airport entrance (travel time – 20 minutes). *Blue Bus Services*, tel: (091) 276 5657. **Coach:** *National Express* and *Scottish Citylink* operate services to the airport from most major cities in Scotland and the North and Midlands of England. **Car hire:** *Hertz* (tel: (091) 286 0966), *Avis* (tel: (091) 286 0815) and *Europcar* (tel: (091) 286 0966) self-drive agents are located at the airport. **Taxi:** Travel time to city centre – 15-20 minutes. A taxi rank is situated outside the railway station, and at the Haymarket near the Eldon Square bus concourse in Newcastle city centre. Only licensed taxi cabs are allowed to pick up at the airport. **Private car:** The airport can be reached from the south by the A1 (M) north, then the A696 Jedburgh trunk road, and from the north by the A1 south, then the A696 Jedburgh trunk road. Open-air long- and short-term parking facilities are available (no advanced booking required).

SEA: See list of ferry operators.

RAIL: The *Intercity* network serves all main cities in the UK mainland. All routes radiate from London. For general travel enquiries, weekdays only, tel: (071) 928 5100. Alternatively, and at weekends, ring the number of the appropriate terminus station for information. Terminus stations in London serve the following regions: Southern England and South London: *Charing Cross, Victoria* and *Waterloo*. Tel: (071) 928 5100. East Anglia, Essex, North East and East London: *Liverpool Street*. Tel: (071) 928 5100. South Midlands, West of England, South Wales and West London: *Paddington*. Tel: (071) 262 6767. East and West Midlands, North Wales, North East England, West Coast of Scotland and West London: *Euston, St Pancras* and *Marylebone*. Tel: (071) 387 7070. East and North East England, East Coast of Scotland and North London: *Kings Cross*. Tel: (071) 278 2477.

There are also many smaller lines which operate less frequently. There are services to the Republic of Ireland via Holyhead, and to Northern Ireland. Tel: (071) 387 7070. Services to the Republic of Ireland via Fishguard are also available. Tel: (071) 262 6767.

ROAD: England is served by a good network of motorways and trunk roads which connect all the main cities and towns.

The main motorways are: **M1:** London, Luton, Leicester, Sheffield, Leeds. **M2/A2:** London to Dover. **M3:** London to Winchester. **M4:** London, Reading, Bristol, Newport, Cardiff, Swansea. **M5:** Birmingham, Gloucester, Bristol, Exeter. **M6:** Coventry, Birmingham, Stoke, Warrington (connecting with the M62 for Liverpool and Manchester), Preston (connecting with the M55 for Blackpool), Morecambe, Carlisle. **M11:** London to Cambridge. **M20/A20:** London to Folkestone. **M40:** London to Oxford. **M62:** Liverpool, Warrington, Manchester, Huddersfield, Leeds, Hull. **M25:** London orbital.

The main trunk roads are: **A1/A1(M):** (Motorway in parts.) London, Peterborough, Doncaster, Darlington, Newcastle, Edinburgh. **A2:** London to Dover. **A3:** London, Guildford, Portsmouth. **A5:** London, St Albans, Nuneaton, Birmingham area, Shrewsbury, across inland North Wales to Holyhead. **A6:** London, Bedford, Leicester, Manchester. **A11:** London to Norwich. **A12:** London, Ipswich, Great Yarmouth. **A23:** London to Brighton. **A30:** London, Basingstoke, Yeovil, Exeter, Penzance. **A40:** London, Oxford (M40), Gloucester, Cheltenham, across inland South Wales to Fishguard.

Distances from London (by road): To Birmingham 169km (105 miles), Manchester 299km (186 miles), Liverpool 325km (202 miles), Exeter 278km (173 miles), Penzance 452km (281 miles), Bristol 185km (115 miles), Carlisle 484km (301 miles), Newcastle 441km (274 miles), Sheffield 257km (160 miles), York 311km (193 miles), Cambridge 89km (55 miles), Southampton 124km (77 miles), Dover 114km (71 miles), Oxford 92km (57 miles), Norwich 182km (113 miles), Portsmouth 113km (70 miles) and to Harwich 122km (76 miles).

Coach: Many coach companies offer express and stopping services throughout England and the rest of the UK. The *National Express* enquiry office provides nationwide coach information. Tel: (071) 730 0202. The head office is at 4 Vicarage Road, Edgbaston, Birmingham B15. Tel: (021) 456 1122.
URBAN: All towns and cities have bus services. In addition, the areas of Birmingham, Liverpool, Manchester and the cities of South Yorkshire and Newcastle have suburban rail services. Newcastle also has a metro, which consists of a circular line with three branches. It connects with Newcastle Central, Manors and Heworth *British Rail* stations and terminates at South Shields (ferry connection to North Shields, also on the Metro), St James and Bank Foot. All cities have taxi services, many using London-type black cabs. Taxi ranks are usually placed near bus stations, railway stations and town centres. Local telephone directories give the numbers of minicabs and hire cars.
LONDON: Travel enquiries: For bus and underground enquiries, tel: (071) 222 1234 (24-hour service). For *British Rail* enquiries, phone the number of the *British Rail* terminus for your region. Maps and leaflets are widely available.
The Underground: The 'tube' is the oldest and one of the most extensive underground railway networks in the world. There are eleven lines, including the recently opened *Docklands Light Railway*, and some such as the *Central* and the *Metropolitan* extend well into the surrounding suburbs. Each line has its own colour on the network map, copies of which are widely available. Some lines operate certain sections during peak hours and some stations close altogether in the evenings or at weekends. There is also an extensive network of *British Rail* services in the London area, particularly in the southeast, many of which connect with *Underground* services. All the *British Rail* terminus stations connect with at least one *Underground* line, with the exception of Fenchurch Street (which is however virtually adjacent to Tower Hill). Various travel discounts are available. The one-day *Travelcard* offers unlimited travel on bus, underground and *British Rail* in one or more zones; it is is one of the best methods for visitors to travel throughout London. Weekly and monthly Travelcards require a passport-size photograph. **Note:** The maps of the *Underground* and *British Rail* networks are diagrammatic, and do not indicate the relative distances between stations.
Bus: London is served by an excellent network of buses (about 300 routes), although recent policy has been to cut some of the lesser-used services. Some operate only partial routes at specific times or may discontinue service in the evenings or at weekends. During rush hours, bus travel in central London can become agonisingly slow, although the introduction of bus lanes and 'red routes' on some roads has partly improved this situation. There is a good timetabled network of night bus services, and all routes passing through central London call at Trafalgar Square.
Taxi/car hire: Black cabs can be hailed in the street or ordered by phone. Fares are metered but surcharges are levied for extra passengers, large amounts of luggage, for travel at night, and Sundays or public holidays. Over 3000 new black cabs have facilities for wheelchair-bound passengers. Minicabs and hire cars are also available; numbers are listed in the telephone directory yellow pages.

ACCOMMODATION

Accommodation is available at hotels, motels and posthouses, guest-houses, farmhouses, inns and self-catering establishments and on campsites.
HOTELS: It is rare to find a town in England, how-ever small, which does not have at least one hotel, in villages very often doubling as the local pub. Some London hotels, for example the Savoy, are famous the world over but there are many newer first-class hotels. In addition, there are many smaller hotels throughout the larger cities; in London, Earls Court and the area around Kings Cross are famous for their many streets of small hotels bearing such names as the *Apollo*, *Victoria* or *Albany*. For further information, contact the British Hospitality Association, 40 Duke Street, London W1M 6HR. Tel: (071) 499 6641. Fax: (071) 355 4596, *or* the British Federation of Hotel, Guest-Houses & Self-Catering Associations, 5 Sandicroft Road, Blackpool FY1 2RY. Tel: (0253) 52683. **Grading:** The English Tourist Board has a 'crown' classification system which is used throughout their publications; RTB brochures also use this system. There are 11,000 places to stay that have a national crown rating; 13,000 holiday homes have a key rating and 900 holiday Q rating. (The AA and RAC use a star system which is similar to the ETB crowns.) The main hotel classifications are as follows:
'Listed': Clean and comfortable accommodation, although the facilities and services may be limited.
1-crown: Better equipped accommodation with a wider range of facilities including washbasins in all rooms and a lounge area.
2-crown: Accommodation offering more extensive facilities and services (the latter in particular) including early morning tea/coffee and calls.
3-crown: The range of facilities increases, with at least one third of bedrooms having bath or shower and WC en suite, plus easy chair and full length mirror in all bedrooms.
4-crown: An even wider range of facilities and services. Colour TV, radio and telephone in all bedrooms. At least three-quarters of bedrooms have bath or shower and WC en suite.
5-crown: The highest classification, with an extensive range of facilities and services, including room service, night porter and laundry service. All rooms have bath, shower and WC en suite.
Brochures, booklets and leaflets giving full information on accommodation are available from the English Tourist Board, or from any of the 12 regional Tourist Boards; for addresses, see the relevant section below.
GUEST-HOUSES: There are guest-houses and bed & breakfast facilities throughout the country. For listings contact the RTB for regional information.
SELF-CATERING: Cottages and bungalows can be rented in many areas. For information contact the RTB or look in the relevant section in local and national papers. Standards may vary.
CAMPING/CARAVANNING: There are camping and caravan sites throughout the UK, for short and long stays. Some sites hire out tents or caravans. Most sites offer basic facilities, while some have playgrounds, clubs, shops, phones and sporting areas.
HOLIDAY CAMPS: Offer accommodation, food and a full range of leisure activities generally at an all inclusive price.
YOUTH HOSTELS: Standards vary greatly, from very basic night-time accommodation for hikers and cyclists, to modern hostels and motels which are often used by families and groups. Prices are very reasonable. For infomation contact the *Youth Hostel Association*, 8 St Stephen's Hill, St Albans AL1 2DY. Tel: (0727) 855 215. Fax: (0727) 844 126.

RESORTS & EXCURSIONS

This section has been divided into 12 regions, following the divisions employed by the English Tourist Board. Except in the case of Dorset (which is split between the South West and Southern England) and the Peak District of Derbyshire (which comes under the North West), all these divisions follow county boundaries. At the head of each sub-section is the address and telephone number of the local tourist board which can supply further information.

For further information on *National Trust* properties in England, Wales and Northern Ireland, 36 Queen's Anne's Gate, London SW1H 9AS. Tel: (071) 222 9251. Fax: (071) 222 5097.

London

The London Tourist Board & Convention Bureau, 26 Grosvenor Gardens, London SW1 W 0DU. Tel: (071) 730 3450 (group bookings) *or* (071) 730 3488 (individuals). Fax: (071) 730 9367.

London is a city without an easily recognisable centre, a result of the fact that it grew out of two distinct cities: the *City of London*, the site of the original Roman settlement and, further west, the *City of Westminster*. Before long, these two settlements had grown together and were engulfing surrounding villages and hamlets. It was not until the Green Belt legislation of the 1950s that this expansion was halted. Today, the 32 London boroughs and the City of London cover an area of nearly 385 sq km (1000 sq miles), but the way in which the city has grown has left it with a comparatively low population density as well as a great deal of open parkland, commons and even woods.

The **Central Area** of London, roughly bounded by the Circle Line of the Underground, includes the West End, Westminster and the City of London. The West End contains many of the principal theatres, cinemas, restaurants, hotels and nightclubs, as well as some of the best-known shopping areas, such as Oxford Street, Covent Garden, Regent Street, Knightsbridge and Bond Street. The main places of interest in this area are *Westminster Abbey, Big Ben* and the *Houses of Parliament, The National Gallery* in *Trafalgar Square*, the *British Museum, Buckingham Palace*, the buildings of the *Horse Guards* in **Whitehall** and the *Tate Gallery* in Pimlico. At the *Rock Circus*, created by the Tussaud's Group, the story of rock and pop music is brought to life. The Courtauld Institute paintings are on display at *Somerset House* (which formerly housed records of births, marriages and deaths). Further west, in **Kensington** and **Chelsea**, are several other famous shopping streets (King's Road, Knightsbridge and Portobello Road), as well as three of London's largest museums *(The Victoria & Albert, Science* and *Natural History)*, and the *Albert Hall*, home of the Promenade Concerts during the summer. The central area of London also contains four parks: Hyde Park (by far the largest), St James's Park, Green Park and, slightly further north, Regent's Park.

The **City of London**, with a population of less than 5000, is, during the day, the workplace of over half a million people. Its best-known building is *St Paul's Cathedral*, completed in 1711. Clearly visible from the City, although in fact just beyond its boundaries and in the neighbouring borough of Tower Hamlets, is *The Tower of London*, built by William the Conqueror in the 11th century. The Tower Hill Pageant, a history of the River Thames, has recently opened. *The Bank of England, The Stock Exchange, Lloyd's of London* (the world's leading insurance market), *Mansion House* (the official residence of the Lord Mayor), *The Central Criminal Court* ('The Old Bailey'), *Dr Johnson's House* behind Fleet Street, *The Monument* and *The Royal Exchange* are other famous landmarks; a more recent addition to the City skyline is the *Barbican* centre which contains an arts complex which is home to both the Royal Shakespeare Company and the London Symphony Orchestra. *Tower Bridge* is one of the most famous bridges in the world, and it is now possible to visit the control room containing the machinery for raising and lowering the central section and to walk along the overhead walkway. *HMS Belfast*, which can be viewed from the bridge, is moored at Symons Wharf near Tooley Street and is open to visitors. Nearby is *Hay's Galleria*, an exciting mix of shops, restaurants, bars and entertainment. The City is best explored during evenings, weekends or public holidays, and its narrow alleyways and passages, which contain impressive but often half-hidden 17th- and 18th-century buildings, make travel on foot or by bicycle recommended. Contact the London Tourist Board for details of organised walks.

South London is in general less often visited by tourists. *The South Bank Arts Centre*, near Waterloo Station, is among the most famous and accessible attractions south of the river; it contains the *Royal National Theatre* and the *Royal Festival Hall*. In this complex, too, can be found *MOMI* (The Museum of the Moving Image) which traces the story of moving images from the earliest cinematic experiments to the latest TV technology. Nearby is *The Old Vic*, recently refurbished and one of London's best-known theatres. *Southwark Cathedral*, near London Bridge, is one of the finest Gothic churches in the city. Also in Southwark, reconstruction of Shakespeare's famous *Globe Theatre* is underway, due for completion in 1993 (coincidentally work started just as the site of the nearby, and similar, *Swan Theatre* was discovered). Other attractions near the river include *The Imperial War Museum* in **Lambeth**, *Lambeth Palace*, the *Florence Nightingale Museum*, based at St Thomas' Hospital, *Battersea Park* and, further west, *The Botanical Gardens* (and palace) at **Kew**, and *Richmond Park*, where thousands of deer are free to graze. 15 minutes' journey by train from Charing Cross is **Greenwich**, home of *The National Maritime Museum*, the clipper *Cutty Sark* (one of the fastest ships before, and at times even after, the Age of Steam), *The Royal Naval College* and *The Royal Observatory*, through which runs the Greenwich Meridian, zero degrees longitude. In Greenwich you can also find the *Queen's House* which has recently been restored to its 17th-century glory. From April 1991 visitors will be able to see over 2000 fans displayed at the new *Fan Museum* in Greenwich. Other attractions in south London include *The National Sports Centre* at **Crystal Palace**, *The All England Tennis Club* at **Wimbledon,** the attractive 'village' of **Dulwich,** which has the oldest art gallery in England, and *Brunel's Engine House* in **Rotherhithe**, the site of the world's first underwater tunnel.

West London: London's two major exhibition centres, **Earl's Court** and **Olympia,** are situated slightly to the west of the central London area. The Boat Show and the Ideal Home Exhibition are among their principal events. Not far away, Whiteleys of **Bayswater** is a luxury Edwardian shopping centre comprising over 80 shops, also restaurants and a multi-screen cinema. *Chiswick House* in **Chiswick** is a superb Italian-style villa. Further west is *Syon Park* in **Brentford** (which includes a beautiful 16th-century house), the *British Motor Industry Museum* and the *London Butterfly House*; nearby is the *Musical Museum*, the *Living Steam Museum* and the *Waterman's Arts Centre*. South of Brentford and Chiswick are several elegant riverside houses which are open to the public, the greatest of these being *Hampton Court Palace*, built by Cardinal Wolsey in the early 16th century and added to by Henry VIII, Charles I,

LONDON

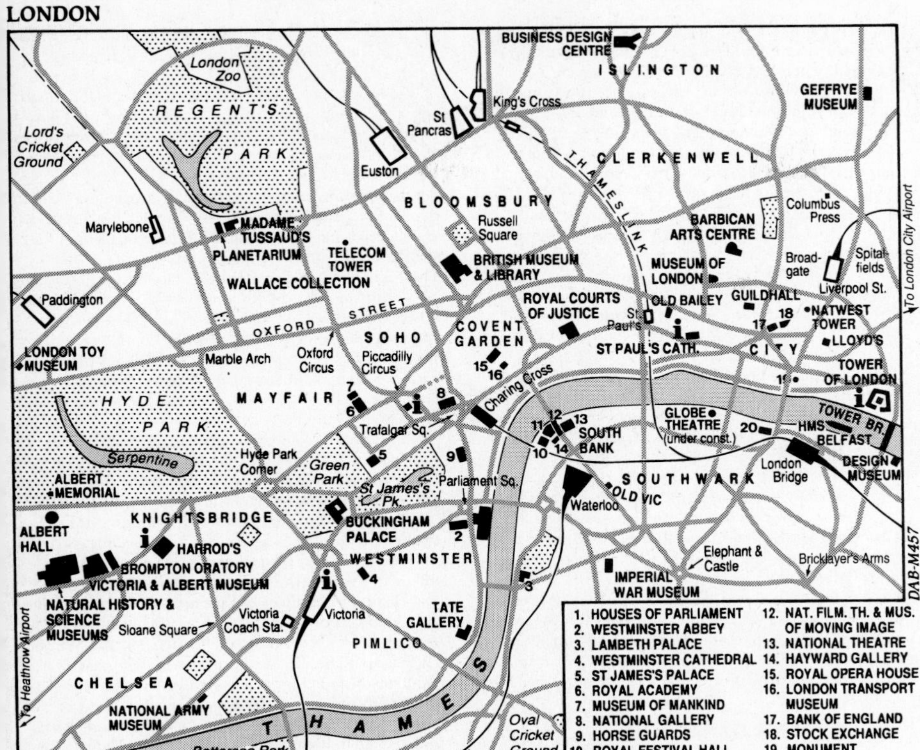

Charles II and William III; others include the *Orleans House Gallery*, *Ham House* and *Marble Hill House*. In northwest London is *Wembley Stadium* (England's premier football ground) and *Wembley Arena and Conference Centre*. The August Bank Holiday weekend is celebrated in the **Notting Hill** area with the famous West Indian Carnival.

North London contains the fashionable residential area of **Hampstead,** set on a steep hill to the north of Central London. *Hampstead Heath* is one of the largest expanses of parkland to be found in any big city anywhere in the world. Hampstead itself has many narrow twisting streets and alleyways and numerous cafés, restaurants, wine bars and shops. Places to visit include *Burgh House*, *The Kenwood Bequest* (a Georgian country house, which contains a fine collection of paintings, and set in beautiful parkland) and *Keats' House* in Wentworth Place. Slightly to the east, and also on a hill, is **Highgate**, another attractive former village, best known for its cemetery which includes the graves of Karl Marx and George Eliot. In St John's Wood visitors can find the Gestetner Tours of *Lords' Cricket Ground.*

East London and in particular the East End (Whitechapel, Bethnal Green, Mile End and Bow) is in many ways the 'real London', although the architecture of this part of the capital suffered badly both during the Second World War and at the hands of the urban planners in the 1960s. Today the City is encroaching on the traditional East End areas of **Whitechapel** and **Aldgate**. The *Whitechapel Art Gallery* is, however, a source of local pride. One major area of recreational redevelopment is the *Lea Valley Park*, which stretches from Hertfordshire to Bromley-by-Bow in the East End and has extensive leisure and recreational facilities. Attractions include the 16th-century *Queen Elizabeth's Hunting Lodge* in **Chingford** and the 11th-century *Waltham Abbey*. Of more recent construction is the remarkable *Thames Flood Barrier*, situated down-river from Greenwich. The renovated *St Katharine's Dock* is now a yacht harbour and at **Wapping** there are many old warehouses, the majority of which have been converted into homes and amenities – a process which is under way throughout East London. Here can be found *Tobacco Dock*, a leisure complex with restaurants and entertainment. Two replica 18th-century pirate ships are moored at the quayside. The whole docklands area, on both banks of the river, is undergoing much redevelopment and a new light railway opened in July 1987, giving greater access to the area of the **Isle of Dogs**. A separate development, *Canary Wharf*, with its 245m- (800ft) high tower was completed in 1992. Walks along the river and in the dockland areas are often very rewarding, offering unexpected glimpses of 18th- and 19th-century London.

London in literature: The Tower of London and the royal palaces have probably had more written about them in works of historical romance than anywhere else. But, these aside, it is the works of Charles Dickens, in particular, that have coloured visitor's (and even Londoner's) perceptions of the city, though it is probably true to say that, apart from the Inns of Court, very little remains of the London he depicted – not even the famous *pea-souper* (London fog) famously depicted in *Bleak House*. The site of the debtors' prison in Marshalsea Road (into which Mr Pickwick was cast) retains squalid associations even now. It is perhaps worth bearing in mind that many of the changes (though certainly not all) would have been welcomed by Dickens; the London we have now is, to some extent, his handiwork. The most famous fictional citizen of London is undoubtedly Sherlock Holmes of Baker Street (who, as a fictional recipient of fan mail, probably comes second only to Santa Claus). Of the diarists who have strong associations with London, Pepys occupies the first place; his account of the plague in 1665 and of the Fire of London in 1666 resonates through places that have long since changed their character. There are many tours based on London's literary associations. From 1993 the reconstructed *Globe Theatre* in **Southwark** will stage the plays of Shakepeares.

Tours: Addresses of companies which offer guided tours of London and the surrounding area (either by car or on foot) may be obtained from the London Tourist Board or Tourist Information Centres. The London Tourist Board and the individual borough councils also produce a range of booklets and pamphlets giving information on events and attractions in the capital; these range from street markets, sports centres, guided walks, fringe theatre to festivals and flower shows. There is a great variety of entertainment in the capital, not all restricted to the centre.

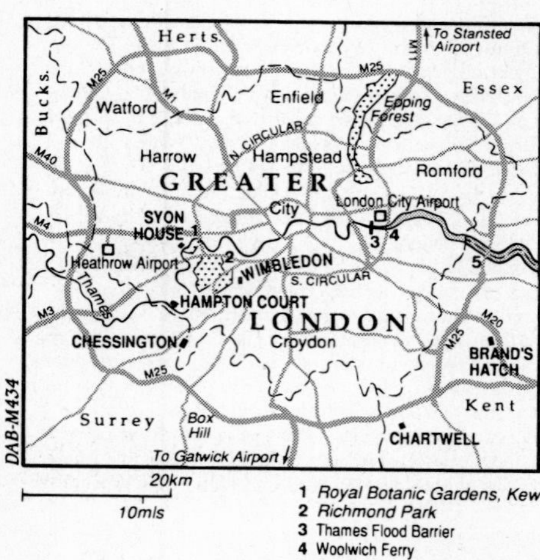

South East

East Sussex, Kent, Surrey, West Sussex.

South East England Tourist Board, The Old Brew House, Warwick Park, Tunbridge Wells, Kent TN2 5TU. Tel: (0892) 540 766. Fax: (0892) 511 008.

The sparkling array of seaside resorts, such as Brighton, Eastbourne, Margate and Worthing, are as popular now as they were with 18th-century patrons. With safe beaches, seafront gardens, piers (except Margate) and promenades, they all are strongly associated with the great British seaside holiday.

Brighton is perhaps the most popular and lively of the southeast resorts, made famous by the Prince of Wales (later George IV) who had the remarkable *Pavilion* constructed here. There are splendid 19th-century terraces and crescents, two piers, the 'Lanes' area of antique shops, a museum and an art gallery.

Other resorts include **Dover**, famous for the *White Cliffs*, the remains of the Pharos, a Phoenician lighthouse, and the Norman *Dover Castle* with the new *White Cliffs Experience*. The one-time Cinque Port of **Hythe** still contains three *Martello Towers*. There are Roman remains at *Saltwood Castle* and *Lympne Castle*. The former port of **Rye** has a medieval atmosphere and retains its 14th-century walls, albeit crumbling.

Behind the resorts spread the *South Downs*: an expanse of farmland, hills and woods, with the South Downs Way (a long-distance footpath) stretching some 130km (80 miles) from Eastbourne to the Hampshire border.

Nestling at the foot of the Downs is the historic county town of **Lewes**, with its famous castle and picturesque High Street, while nearby the world-renowned opera house of *Glyndebourne* sits in its own grounds and welcomes the greatest singers from all over the world each year for its summer season. There are many villages of interest in the area including half-timbered **Biddenden** and **Chiddingstone** and the old smuggling centres of **Rye, Dymchurch, Hawkhurst** and **Alfriston**, all of which are on the boundaries of the Romney marshes. There remain, to this day, smuggling tunnels under the town of Rye and there are ancient escape routes across the marshes that only the smugglers would dare to use.

Other places of interest include **Runnymede**, the riverside fields where the Magna Carta was signed; the historic town of **Guildford** in Surrey; and *Hever Castle* in Kent, the childhood home of Anne Boleyn.

The *North Downs* swing from Surrey into Kent and curving across the hills from Farnham to Dover is another long-distance footpath, the North Downs Way, which merges in places with the traditional Pilgrims' Way leading to the archiepiscopal city of **Canterbury**, which retains its medieval charms and is famous for *Canterbury Cathedral* where Thomas a' Becket was murdered in 1170. It is also the centre of the Anglican Church. *St Martin's Church* is one of the oldest churches in use in the country and services were held as far back as AD500.

The Kent countryside has been dubbed the 'Garden of England' for its copious quantities of fruit, hops and garden produce. The best time to visit is in April or May when the orchards and woodlands are clouded with blossom. **Rochester** in Kent is a charming old town and has strong connections with Dickens, including *Restoration House*, which is thought to be the prototype for Miss Haversham's house in *Great Expectations*.

The South East offers an excellent choice of bases for longer stays or weekends away: the elegant spa of **Tunbridge Wells; Maidstone**, in the centre of the hop-growing country; **Chichester**, in West Sussex, with its lively harbour and 12th-century cathedral.

The South East has many historic houses and gardens, such as *Penshurst Place*, *Leeds Castle*, the *Martello Towers* at Dymchurch, Seaford and Eastbourne and numerous castles and battlefields which bear witness to the area's position as the invader's gateway to England.

Southern England

Hampshire, Eastern Dorset, the Isle of Wight.

Southern Tourist Board, 40 Chamberlayne Road, Eastleigh, Hants SO5 5JH. Tel: (0703) 620 006. Fax: (0703) 620 010.

Southern England, comprising Hampshire, Dorset, the Isle of Wight and South Wiltshire, embraces some of the best-known beauty spots, spectacular coastline and historic towns and cities in the country.

The **New Forest** was decreed as a Royal Hunting Preserve in 1079, its 145 sq miles of undulating heaths and woodlands are dotted with picturesque cottages and grazing animals. To the west of the Forest lie the seaside resorts of **Bournemouth**, **Poole** and **Swanage**. In the east, Southern England can lay claim to two of the greatest maritime centres, **Southampton** and **Portsmouth**, each with a host of naval heritage and attractions to see.

Also in the area are the picturesque *Hamble* and *Test* valleys with their famous chalk streams. To the north lies 'Hampshire Borders' with its wealth of pretty villages and rolling countryside.

Isle of Wight: Less than two hours by train from London (and a short car ferry or passenger ride from Southampton, Portsmouth or Lymington), the Isle of Wight, with its beautiful countryside, rugged downland, unspoilt coastline and mile after mile of sandy beaches, is blessed with one of the best sunshine records in the country. Quiet and relaxing or sporting and energetic, it has all the ingredients to make the visitor's stay unforgettable. Craft centres, country parks, historic buildings, sporting and leisure facilities, the island with its stunning contrasts in scenery and entertainment is often described as 'England in Miniature'.

Cowes, world famous for yachting, also plays host to many national and international events, from sailing to power boating. Traditional English and foreign restaurants, cafés, pubs and wine bars provide a wide ranging choice of cuisine which can be complemented with a local wine from one of the island's five vineyards.

Dorset is a delightful county that has plenty for everyone. Historic towns, pretty villages nestling in idyllic English countryside, scenic coastline and lively resorts.

Called the 'Garden City by the sea', the Dorset resort of **Bournemouth,** just two hours from London, is foremost among British holiday locations for its sense of style. It has fine sandy beaches, excellent shopping, top-class entertainment and comfortable hotels and flats making the town an ever-popular holiday resort.

Nearby **Poole** has the second-largest natural harbour in the world and the lovely island nature reserve of *Brownsea* lies in its midst. Pleasure boats wait at the quayside and regularly make the short trip over. The new *Tower Park* leisure complex offers a host of up-to-the-minute entertainments. The town's old Quay retains its 18th-century atmosphere and has become an ideal location for displaying maritime influences on the area. The new waterfront museum can be visited here.

Just to the west of Poole is an area known as the **Isle of Purbeck**. The coastline is full of variety and is known for its dramatic coastal scenery and the popular holiday resort of **Swanage.**

Hampshire: Lovers of the sea and open spaces will delight in this county. The region is one of great natural beauty but also enjoys the benefits of up-to-the-minute shopping, leisure facilities and nightlife. The county is justly famous for the **New Forest**, 145 sq miles of open heathland, where ponies, deer and cattle roam freely. The New Forest is a paradise for riders and walkers there are lots of lovely places to stay and campsites are plentiful. *Beaulieu Motor Museum* and *Bucklers Hard* are well worth a visit.

Southampton is one of the most rapidly expanding cities on the South Coast with exciting new marinas, leisure facilities and shopping malls including the *Waterfront*, *Ocean Village* and the new *Bargate* shopping centre.

There is a wealth of maritime history in the neighbouring city of **Portsmouth** – *HMS Victory*, *HMS Warrior*, the *Mary Rose* and the *Royal Naval Museum*. *The D-Day Museum* at **Southsea** tells the story of the 1944 allied Normandy landings.

Winchester, in central Hampshire, and Romsey to the south are worth including in any itinerary. Winchester has a magnificent 11th-century *Cathedral* and is surrounded by the most lovely rolling countryside. Romsey is an attractive old market town proud to be associated with *Broadlands*, the 18th-century home of Lord Mountbatten.

Yachtsmen are well catered for in Hampshire. **Lymington** is a very attractive small town lying on the edge of the New Forest, with it's own pretty harbour. **Hamble** to the east is a mecca for yachtsmen, the *Hamble River* providing good sheltered moorings, making it an ideal place to start a cruise around its waters or over to the Isle of Wight.

The **Hampshire Borders**, in the north of the county, have some lovely countryside and the area is home to a past winner of the Best Kept Village competition, **Hartley Wintney**. There are a number of historic houses in the region and lots of military museums. A wide variety of accommodation can be found in and around **Basingstoke**, making it a good base from which to explore and the area is well connected by road and rail to London.

The West Country

Cornwall, Devon, Somerset, Wiltshire, Avon, Western Dorset, Isles of Scilly.

The West Country Tourist Board, 60 St David's Hill, Exeter EX4 4SY. Tel: (0392) 76351. Fax: (0392) 420 891.

The superb West Country resorts, together with 1000km (650 miles) of varied and spectacular coastline, have always been a great attraction for holidaymakers.

The coastline of **Cornwall**, which has both the southernmost and westernmost points on the English mainland, is characterised by tiny harbours, rocky headlands and magnificent cliffs. The north coast, washed by Atlantic breakers, has particularly good stretches of fine golden sandy beaches. **Bude**, the picturesque harbour at **Boscastle** and the clifftop castle at **Tintagel** are worth visiting. **Newquay** is the region's main resort, and has excellent beaches, modern hotels and good shops. **St Ives** is an old fishing port and a delightful holiday centre.

The south coast is in complete contrast, generally less dramatic, with many wooded estuaries, sheltered coves, picturesque fishing ports and several popular resorts. There are excellent facilities for sailing and deep-sea fishing at **Penzance** and **Fowey**. **Falmouth**, a town of many beaches and several beautiful gardens, is the main resort.

Mevagissey and **Looe** are fine examples of traditional Cornish fishing ports. The coastline is also notable for its old smuggling villages, such as **Coverack**.

Inland Cornwall consists mainly of flower-bordered lanes, gentle valleys and granite-capped moors. The three main towns inland are **Bodmin, Launceston** (the county town of Cornwall) and the cathedral city of **Truro**. *Bodmin Moor* is an area of stark natural beauty, and the setting for Daphne du Maurier's famous novel *Jamaica Inn*.

Devon: The area known as the *English Riviera* comprises **Torquay**, **Brixham** and **Paignton**. The major city in this region is **Plymouth**, a principal English seaport for over 500 years and the place where the Westcountryman Sir Francis Drake finished his leisurely game of bowls before setting sail to defeat the Spanish Armada. In 1620 the Pilgrim Fathers set out for the New World from Plymouth on the *Mayflower*, and parts of the town dating from this period still survive. Seaside trips in this region can also be combined with holidays inland into the peaceful wilderness of the *Dartmoor National Park* where native wild ponies roam freely across a beautiful landscape dotted with prehistoric remains. The county town, **Exeter**, has a long history and there are remains of Roman walls, underground passages, a beautiful cathedral and the oldest Guildhall in the kingdom.

Western Dorset: Virtually all of the coast and much of the inland regions of the county has been designated an 'Area of Outstanding Natural Beauty'. Along the coast from **Christchurch to Lyme Regis** there is a fascinating variety of sandy beaches, towering cliffs and shingle banks, whilst inland is a rich mixture of lonely heaths, fertile valleys, historic houses and beautiful villages of thatch and mellow sandstone buildings. **Weymouth** is the main resort in this part of the country. Weymouth, with its top, clean 'Blue

Flag' award beach, has panoramic Georgian Bay and picturesque harbour. There is entertainment and activities for all the family plus many top attractions and events including the new *Brewer's Quay* leisure and shopping development. Inland, the hills of Dorset abound with ancient trackways and early British hill forts; the county town of Dorchester was itself founded by the Romans.

The north of the county is a region of farms, woods and river valleys. The three other main towns are **Sherborne, Sturminster Newton** and **Shaftesbury**. A little further westwards is the holiday town of **Portland**, joined to Weymouth by the *Chesil Beach* and causeway, is a fascinating island. Famous for its stone, the Island also has several castles, a lighthouse and small, sheltered coves.

Lying inland, northeast of Weymouth, is **Shaftesbury**, Dorset's most ancient hilltop town, characterised by steep cobbled streets. Slightly to the south is the handsome 18th-century town of **Blandford Forum**. A little further south east is **Wimborne Minster**, a small market town, with the distinction of having one of the most unusual churches in Dorset.

Somerset, another attractive rural county, has three fine coastal resorts, **Weston-super-Mare, Burnham-on-Sea** and **Minehead**. Much of west Somerset lies within the *Exmoor National Park*. Attractions in this region include the tiny *Culbone Church*, the clapper bridge at *Tarr Steps*, the idyllic villages of *Selworthy*, *Dunster* or a climb to the top of *Dunkery Beacon*. The county town of **Taunton** is to the west of the county, near the southern end of the wooded *Quantock Hills*. The county's northern boundary is emphasised by the limestone range of the *Mendip Hills*. Along the southern edge are the attractions of the *Cheddar Gorge*, *Wookey Hole* and the great cathedral at **Wells**, where Stoppa Collins was a choir-boy. The southeastern corner of the county around **Yeovil** has many historic houses open to the public.

Even in prehistoric times the inland county of **Wiltshire** proved attractive to early settlers, and the evidence of long occupation – at places such as **Stonehenge, Avebury, Old Sarum** and others – make Wiltshire the best county for exploring prehistoric remains. In addition, some of England's greatest stately homes are in Wiltshire, including *Longleat*, *Wilton*, *Lacock Abbey*, *Corsham* and *Stourhead*. Longleat is a very grand Elizabethan mansion, famous for its safari pak, and Stourhead, built in 1722, has particularly fine gardens leading down to its own lake and *Wilton House*.

The city of **Salisbury** is dominated by the 123m (404ft) cathedral spire, the tallest in England. The area contains many notable houses that are open to the public *The Barchester Chronicles* of Anthony Trollope, which provide an entertaining account of life in a 19th-century cathedral town, are a fictional counterpart to Salisbury. *Mompesson House* is a perfectly preserved 18th-century home and *Malmesbury House* was once sanctuary for King Charles II, who was fleeing after the Battle of Worcester in the 17th century. The city has a harmonious blend of gabled houses, historic inns and 18th-century architecture and offers a great choice of hotels, restaurants and shopping. Guided tours can be taken around the city by open-top bus or horse-drawn omnibus. The remains of *Old Sarum*, an ancient city and Norman fortress, can be seen but the most important site is *Stonehenge*, 3km (2 miles) away on Salisbury Plain. The enormous stones are arranged in an inner and an outer circle, and the site is believed to have been first used as long ago as 1500BC.

The new county of **Avon** has two cities of note: **Bristol**, which is one of the largest ports in the country (the Cathedral and *St Mary Redcliffe Church* are worth seeing, as is Brunel's impressive *Clifton Suspension Bridge*, which spans the Avon Gorge) and **Bath**, which is usually regarded as the most elegant Georgian city in the country, and has been immortalised in countless photographs, paintings and novels. The city also has Roman remains and an abbey.

Historical and literary associations can be found in many places throughout the West Country; King Alfred reputedly burnt his cakes at Athelney, while Cadbury may have been *Camelot*. RD Blackmore's novel *Lorna Doone* was set in Exmoor (now a national park), while many of Daphne du Maurier's were set in Cornwall. Lyme Regis, in Dorset, was one of Jane Austen's favourite towns, and, along with Bath, was one of the settings for her novel *Persuasion*.

Dorchester is the birthplace of Thomas Hardy, the West Country's most famous literary figure, who immortalised both this town and much of the surrounding countryside – referred to in his books as 'Wessex', the name of the old Saxon kingdom in that area. Hardy's cottage lies 5km (3 miles) out of town. The museum in Dorchester contains many pre-Roman exhibits and a Thomas Hardy memorial room. *Maiden Castle*, 3km (2 miles) from Dorchester is one of the most impressive prehistoric sites in the country.

The **Isles of Scilly** lie 50km (30 miles) off Land's End. Though there are about a hundred of them, only five are inhabited. They are a popular holiday destination, as the climate is warmer and more temperate than on the mainland. The tourism industry was undoubtedly boosted when, during his prime ministership, it became known that Harold Wilson had a holiday home there. Horticulture is now the islands' second-largest industry. Boat trips to visit the smaller islands are popular, particularly from *St Mary's*, the largest of the islands. The Isles of Scilly can be reached by ferry or helicopter.

Heart of England

Gloucestershire, Herefordshire, Shropshire, Staffordshire, Warwickshire, Worcestershire, The West Midlands Boroughs.

Heart of England Tourist Board, Larkhill Road, Worcester, Worcestershire WR5 2EF. Tel: (0905) 763 436. Fax: (0905) 763 450.

Some of the country's most famous landscapes lie in the Heart of England. Little has changed over the centuries in the **Cotswolds**, where gentle uplands are studded with beautiful old villages and towns, many of which are frequently built from the locality's yellow limestone and graced by magnificent churches erected chiefly from the wealth of the medieval wool trade.

Two important rivers cross this heartland. The Severn winds through the ancient city of **Worcester**, skirting the *Malvern Hills* to meet the Avon at Tewkesbury. The Avon flows past the fertile *Vale of Evesham* and passes **Stratford**, home of William Shakespeare.

The dark mountains of Wales give way to the border area called *The Marches* and the English hills of *Long Mynd*, *Wenlock Edge* and *Clun Forest*. This area was once less tranquil than it is today and its turbulent past is indicated by ancient barrows, pre-Roman camps and the entrenchment of *Offa's Dyke* (now a long-distance footpath). In turn, the Normans and Plantagenets left remains of splendid castles at **Shrewsbury, Goodrich** and **Ludlow**, built to protect England from invasion.

The first sparks of the Industrial Revolution ignited at **Ironbridge**, now a showplace of industrial archaeology, while in neighbouring Staffordshire, where the scenery rises to peaks and moorland, that same era bequeathed a legacy of canals (now popular for pleasure-craft) and the Potteries with their famous china factories.

Gloucestershire & The Cotswolds: This region comprises a range of low limestone hills stretching in a curve from Bath to the vicinity of Stratford-upon-Avon. The charming and well-preserved towns and villages of the Cotswolds are built in a honey-coloured stone, and are set in one of the finest areas of unspoilt countryside in England. Historically, the area's wealth was based on sheep farming and the wool industry, and sheep are still very much in evidence today. The area is accessible by road from London, and many of the towns by rail from Paddington. Gloucester is an ancient cathedral city on the River Severn. Many of the streets and parts of the old city wall date back to the Middle Ages. The revitalised docks now have massive warehouses which are gradually being filled. The *National Waterways Museum* opened in 1988, while the *Marina and Tall Ships*, plus the fascinating *Opic Collection of Packaging*, are already open to the public. **Cheltenham**, an elegant Regency spa town, is famous for its *National Hunt Racecourse* and annual music and literature festival. The flowers and gardens of the suburbs are also worth seeing. **Malmesbury** contains a fine example of Norman building in its abbey, the ruins of a 12th-century castle, a market square and several attractive 17th- and 18th-century houses. **Cirencester** contains extensive Roman remains, and is a good centre for exploring the Cotswolds. To the east of the Wye Valley is the *Forest of Dean*, 130 sq km (50 sq miles) of ancient hunting forest, once the property of the medieval kings but now given over to trails and picnic sites.

Herefordshire & Worcestershire: The stretch of country between Worcester and the Welsh border is one of the richest farming areas in Great Britain, with fields and meadows full of cider apples, hops and white-faced red cattle. Characteristic black and white half-timbered buildings decorate the villages and market towns such as **Ledbury**. The Wye Valley, the Malvern Hills and the *Teme Valley* all add to the area's beauty.

The **Wye Valley** is an exceedingly beautiful region, with the river flowing at first through water meadows and gentle countryside but later winding its way through spectacular gorges in the region of Symonds Yat. The town of **Ross-on-Wye** provides a good base for exploring this area. Northwest of Ross is **Hereford**, also on the *River Wye*, an attractive cathedral city and a thriving market centre. There is a city museum and art gallery as well as a cider museum. Nell Gwynne was said to be have been born here. To the west of Hereford is the *Golden Valley*, a remote region containing many attractive villages. At the northern tip of the valley on the Welsh border is the town of **Hay-on-Wye**, famous for having one of the largest second-hand bookshops in the world. The ancient city of **Worcester** on the bank of the *River Severn* has a cathedral, the museum and factory of the famous Royal Worcester Porcelain Company, a magnificent Guildhall with a Queen Anne facade and a number of streets with overhanging half-timbered houses from the Tudor period. Worcester is also the ancient Commandey, once the battle headquarters of Charles II, and now housing a Civil War audio-visual display. South of Worcester are the *Malvern Hills*, a very steep range topped with open moorland which offer superb views across the rich agricultural landscape. The spa town of **Great Malvern** was built as a fashionable spa resort in the 19th century; Malvern spring water can still be tasted at *St Anne's Well*. 32km (20 miles) north of Worcester is the *Wyre Forest*, ideal for walking and riding. The main towns in this region are **Stourport**, **Bewdley** and **Kidderminster**, terminus for the Severn Valley Railway, the longest full-gauge steam railway in England.

Warwickshire & The West Midlands: The industrial heart of Britain on the edge of some lovely countryside, particularly in Warwickshire. **Birmingham**, Britain's second-largest city, is a centre both of industry and culture. It has a magnificent library, and the *Central Museum & Art Gallery* is one of the finest in the country. **Birmingham** is the home of the *National Exhibition Centre*, site of many of the major exhibitions and fairs for which Britain is renowned. Birmingham also lies at the centre of a vast network of canals – there are more kilometres of canals in the West Midlands than there are in Venice – most of which are still navigable. Canal holidays represent one of the best ways of seeing not only the countryside of the area but also some unusual views of the gaunt architecture of the industrial revolution in the cities. There are also many museums which trace the region's industrial past. **Coventry** is famous for its new cathedral, designed by Sir Basil Spence after the original one was destroyed in the Second World War. **Warwick** contains many 17th- and 18th-century houses and the castle, one of the most imposing medieval strongholds in the country, is open to visitors even though it is still inhabited. The *Church of St Mary*, the *Lord Leycester Hospital* and the *Doll Museum* are all worth visiting.

Stratford-upon-Avon, in the county of Warwickshire, is one of the most famous towns in the country. It was the birth and burial place of *William Shakespeare*, and the life and works of the great playwright are commemorated throughout the year in almost every aspect of the town's public life, chiefly through the productions of his works at the Royal Shakespeare Theatre. Other buildings in the town associated with Shakespeare include his birthplace in Henley Street, the 15th-century grammar school which he attended, the early home of his wife Anne Hathaway, the *Shakespeare Centre*, *Holy Trinity Church*, where Shakespeare and his family are buried and *Halls Croft*, once the home of Shakespeare's daughter. Other buildings of note include the *Motor Museum*; the RSC's other venues, the 'Other Place' and the 'Swan Theatre'; and *Harvard House*, built in the late 16th century and owned by the family who founded the American University of the same name. The whole of Stratford is a beautifully preserved town, with many excellent examples of Elizabethan, Jacobean, Restoration and Georgian buildings. It makes an ideal centre for exploring the surrounding towns and countryside. Places of interest close to Stratford include *Ragley Hall* and *Coughton Court* near Alcester, *Charlecote Park* and *Upton House*, Edge Hill.

Staffordshire is both an industrial and an agricultural county. Part of it lies within the *Peak District National Park* and contains some of the most spectacular countryside in England, such as *Thor's Cave* and the limestone gorge at **Dovedale**. East of the industrial region of the Potteries lie the scenic *Churnet Valley* and the *Vale of Trent*, the latter containing *Cannock Chase*, an attractive area of heath and woodland. One of the most famous sights in the county is *Lichfield Cathedral*, which has three spires. Nearby **Tamworth** has a fine castle.

Shropshire is a county with a varied landscape, including moorlands, forests, gentle hills and open pastures. Despite this appearance of rural tranquillity, Shropshire is also the county where the industrial revolution began, evidence of which may be seen in the area of *Ironbridge Gorge*, which includes the towns of **Coalbrookdale**, **Coalport** and **Ironbridge**. The *Ironbridge Gorge Museum* is spread out over a large number of sites but the area's most famous landmark is probably the Ironbridge itself, built in 1779. On the eastern boundary of this district is the magnificent Restoration house and parkland known as *Weston Park*. Nearby is **Boscobel** where the future Charles II hid in the now famous Royal Oak after the Battle of Worcester. To the west is the area of *The Wrekin*, a conical-shaped hill that figures in many local tales and legends. The county's capital of **Shrewsbury** is one of the finest Tudor towns in England, celebrated for the flower market held every summer. South and southwest of Shrewsbury are the *Shropshire Hills*, designated as an area of outstanding natural beauty. **Ludlow** (dominated by the ruins of its castle), *Church Stretton*, *Bishop's Castle*, *Much Wenlock* and *Bridgenorth* are also worth visiting. The *Severn Valley Railway* is the longest full-gauge steam railway in England. The north of the county is dominated by a large plain with many quiet roads, making it ideally suited to a cycling or walking holiday. **Market Drayton, Wem** (famous for its beer), **Whitchurch** and **Oswestry** are the major market towns in this region.

Thames & Chilterns

Oxfordshire, Berkshire, Buckinghamshire, Bedfordshire, Hertfordshire.

BritishTourist Authority & English Tourist Board, Thames Tower, Black's Road, London W6 9EL. Tel: (081) 846 9000 *or* (071) 730 3488. Fax: (081) 563 0302.

There are several good ways to discover the Thames and Chilterns region: perhaps on a narrow boat on the Kennet and Avon Canal; on a footpath ramble through the Chiltern Hills; at a picnic on the banks of the River Great Ouse; exploring Blenheim Palace or Luton Hoo or taking an open-top bus tour of Oxford or Windsor.

The Thames, with its many riverside pubs and hotels, winds its way through the region, passing through attractive and colourful towns and villages such as **Abingdon** and **Wallingford** and the regatta towns of **Marlow** and **Henley**. The ancient university city of **Oxford** also lies on the Thames. The college buildings, gardens, squares, cathedral and gracious streets that make up this historic city are probably best appreciated on foot or on an open-top bus tour. Northwest of Oxford, on the fringes of the Cotswolds, is impressive *Blenheim Palace*, birthplace of Sir Winston Churchill.

Almost on the outskirts of London but still on the Thames, is **Windsor**, dominated by its famous castle. For the 900 years since William the Conqueror, Windsor has been the home of the monarch and is today the home of Her Majesty the Queen. The fire of 1992 destroyed the *St George's Chapel* and larger parts of the *State Apartments*. Renovation and repair works are currently underway and access to the castle during this time is restricted. Guided tours of the town are available, as well as bus tours and river cruises. At Windsor's Central Station a recreation of Queen Victoria's Jubilee in 1897 brings famous Victorian figures to life using the latest computerised techniques. Across a footbridge lies **Eton**, home of the famous college founded by Henry VI. Nearby are the 4800 acres of *Windsor Great Park*, containing glorious gardens and the famous *Safari Park* (currently threatened by closure) comprising seven drive-through reserves.

The Berkshire Downs are criss-crossed with ancient by-ways and dotted with interesting towns and villages. There is **Wantage**, birthplace of King Alfred the Great, and **Newbury**, home of the famous race course and annual Spring Festival. In the beautiful Kennet Valley lies **Hungerford**, known for the unusual antiques arcade. Astride the *River Lambourn* at **Bagnor**, near Newbury, stands the jewel-box *Watermill Theatre*, renowned for its varied and entertaining plays.

The *Great Ouse* winds gently through the county of **Bedfordshire**, a region of great natural beauty, with a number of country parks and riverside walks. It has many historic connections, including the 4000-year-old *Icknield Way* and the *Roman Watling Street*, both crossing the county, and historic houses such as *Woburn Abbey* and *Luton Hoo*. John Bunyan is a famous son of Bedfordshire and many associations with him can be found in and around Bedford.

Buckinghamshire has been called the Queen of the Home Counties. It boasts many picturesque villages and fine old towns such as **Olney** and **Buckingham**, as well as the new city of **Milton Keynes** in the north, with its extensive covered shopping centre. The Ouse and the *Grand Union Canal* flow through the north of the county, and the Thames through the south, with the magnificent beechwoods of the Chilterns running along its eastern edge.

Hertfordshire is a region of gently undulating countryside. The historic town of **St Albans** contains many reminders of the town's great past when, as Verulamium, it was one of the great cities of the Roman Empire. The *Verulamium Museum* reveals these Roman connections through a nationally important collection of Iron Age and Roman artefacts. Other museums of note in the county include the *Tring Zoological Museum*, a branch of the British Museum; *St Albans Organ Museum* with its magnificent collection of fairground and dance-hall organs and the innovative *Stevenage Museum* which tells the town's history from prehistory to the present through displays of everyday objects.

The region has many **historic houses**, including Woburn Abbey, Luton Hoo (Beds); Windsor Castle, Highclere Castle (Berks); Cliveden, Hughendon Manor (Bucks); Hatfield House, Knebworth House (Herts); Blenheim Palace and Broughton Castle (Oxon).

Wildlife parks and zoos: Windsor Safari Park & Marine World (Berks); Woburn Wild Animal Kingdom and Whipsnade Wild Animal Park (Beds); and the Cotswold Wildlife Park (Oxon).

East Anglia

Norfolk, Suffolk, Essex, Cambridgeshire.

East Anglia Tourist Board, Toppesfield Hall, Hadleigh, Ipswich, Suffolk IP7 5DN. Tel: (0473) 822 922. Fax: (0473) 823 063.

The county of **Essex** has some lovely remote and unspoilt villages including **Epping** (and Epping forest), **Thaxted** (with its medieval church and windmill), **Saffron Walden** and **Dunmow**. Also in Essex are the well-known seaside resorts of **Southend, Clacton-on-Sea** and **Maldon,** a maritime town on the estuary of the *River Blackwater*. **Colchester** the oldest continuously occupied town in the country with the Roman Walls still remaining. The town is a good base for exploring the neighbouring Constable Country.

A relatively under-exploited part of East Anglia is the marshland called the **Fens**, drained in the 17th and 18th centuries by Dutch engineers to create a system of canals. The main centres in the Fens are the cathedral cities of **Ely** and **Peterborough**. Not as famous is the heath area known as **Breckland**, now overgrown with pine forests. Many archaeological discoveries have been made here. **Thetford** is a good base from which to visit this area.

The towns in East Anglia show many examples of the wealthy past of the region. The late 14th, 15th and 16th centuries were a period of great prosperity, largely as a result of the wool trade; the architecture of towns such as **Lavenham** being superb testimony to the wealth of the Tudor wool merchants. Many of Cambridge's colleges were founded at this time and elsewhere in the region solid stone guildhalls, manor houses and thatched inns were built, as well as a wealth of churches. Because the towns largely escaped the influence of the Industrial Revolution, Norman

castles, medieval churches, Tudor half-timbered houses and 18th-century mansions are still numerous.
Cambridge is famous for its university (the second-oldest in the country) and gracious buildings, including *Henry VI's Chapel* at King's College, the *Great Court* at Trinity College, the *Bridge of Sighs* at St John's College and the *Cloister Court* at Queens' College. A river trip along the *Cam* affords the best view of the colleges whose lawns sweep down to the river, a view known as 'the Backs'. Bear in mind that most of the colleges are closed to visitors during the exam periods in the early summer.
Cromwell House, home of Oliver Cromwell, is open to the public. **Ipswich**, county town of Suffolk, retains much of its medieval street pattern and several of the buildings from this period remain. **Kings Lynn** is a medieval town, once one of the country's major ports. **Norwich** is an attractive city with a Norman cathedral, a castle with a museum and art gallery, and medieval houses set in narrow streets. The *Maddermarket Theatre* is an Elizabethan theatre with an apron stage. Over 160km (100 miles) of navigable waterways make up *The Broads*, an area of reed-fringed lagoons and rivers, teeming with wildlife and waterfowl, and ideal for a boating holiday. In between many of the coastal resorts are secluded marshes and estuaries, popular among birdwatchers and yachtsmen.
The region has many **historic houses**, including *Audley End*, *Sandringham*, *Ickworth* and *Wimpole Hall*.
Seaside resorts: *Essex:* Southend, Clacton, Walton, Frinton and Harwich. *Norfolk:* Cromer, Wells-next-the-Sea, Sheringham, where a steam railway operates daily in the summer, and Great Yarmouth, one of Britain's largest and most popular resorts. *Suffolk:* Lowestoft, as well as being a major resort, is also the home of England's main fishing fleet. To the south is Oulton Broad and the resort of Southwold. Beyond Southwold is Aldeburgh, home of a summer music festival. Hunstanton gives a magnificent view of the Wash, and is also notable for its red- and-white striped cliffs.

East Midlands

Derbyshire, Leicestershire, Lincolnshire, Northamptonshire, Nottinghamshire.
East Midlands Tourist Board, Exchequergate, Lincoln, Lincolnshire LN2 1PZ. Tel: (0522) 531 521. Fax: (0522) 532 501.
Solid, historic houses make their presence felt throughout the area: *Chatsworth*; medieval *Haddon Hall*; *Althorp*, family home of the Princess of Wales; *Sudbury Hall* with its Museum of Childhood; the gardens at *Melbourne Hall*; and Elizabethan *Doddington Hall*. A strong sense of history can be felt throughout the region – in the cathedrals of Lincoln and Southwell, in Leicester's Guildhall, Nottingham's Castle and at Derby's Industrial Museum, and also in the wealth of churches, particularly in Lincolnshire and Northamptonshire.
The traditional dining-table of this area reflects the presence of the English landed gentry over the centuries. Sporting specialities include game soup, flavoured with port wine; Melton Mowbray pork pies; and Melton Hunt Cake, made to a 120-year-old recipe. Red Leicester and Stilton cheeses and Bakewell Pudding are other local favourites.
The spa town of **Buxton** in **Derbyshire**, makes a good base from which to explore the Peak District, now a 1300 sq km (500-sq-mile) National Park with limestone dales and open moors. Other places of interest in Derbyshire include **Matlock Bath**, with its cable car ride across the *Derwent Gorge* and show-caves to visit; **Bolsover**, a small market town with a 17th-century castle set in rich farmland; **Creswell Crags**, with the Visitor Centre at the site of archaeological finds such as Creswellian Man; **Chesterfield**, another convenient base for exploring the Peak District and famous for its crooked spire church; Chatsworth House, Baslow; Kedleston Hall, near Derby; and Sudbury Hall, Sudbury.
The county town of **Derby** is the home of Royal Crown Derby porcelain and the city's cathedral, museums and Assembly Rooms – all worth visiting.
Nottinghamshire was the home of Robin Hood, and parts of his Sherwood Forest still survive the Country Park. The city of Nottingham has a beautiful neo-classical Council House, a castle which overlooks the city, and Wollaton Hall, an Elizabethan mansion now housing a natural history museum. North Nottinghamshire is a rural area with many old villages, and the home of several of the Pilgrim Fathers. Newark-on-Trent in the heart of the county has a 12th-century castle. Rufford County Park at Ollerton is also worth visiting.
Lincolnshire, the largest county in the East Midlands and the only one with a coastline, has several seaside resorts, notably **Skegness** and **Mablethorpe**, both of which are towns with good sunshine records. Inland are the gently rolling hills of the Lincolnshire Wolds, where Tennyson spent much of his early life. The area around **Spalding** is the richest farmland in the country, and is famous for growing bulbs. During the 12th century, **Boston** was one of the three most important ports in England, and from here many of the Pilgrim Fathers planned to set sail for The Netherlands to find religious freedom, but were betrayed and imprisoned in cells still in Boston Guildhall. The county town of **Lincoln** is a well-preserved medieval city and the cathedral, set on a limestone hill, has three towers, a fine Norman West Front and a particularly beautiful 13th-century presbytery. The aptly named *Steep Hill* has some interesting shops and the 'Jew's House', halfway up its incline, is worth a visit.
Stamford, situated at the border of four counties, is another medieval town, with several fine churches and buildings of mellow stone. Nearby is *Burghley House*, built by one of Elizabeth I's most powerful ministers. The medieval Old Hall at **Gainsborough** in north Lincolnshire is also worth a visit.
The county of **Leicestershire** has many castles, manor houses and market towns. **Leicester** has Roman remains and a great deal of medieval architecture, but is nowadays more important as a major shopping centre. Other towns of interest in the county include **Market Harborough, Oakham, Lutterworth** (the home of John Wycliffe) and **Melton Mowbray**, the home of Stilton cheese and pork pies. Near Leicester is Market Bosworth, the site of one of the most famous battles in English history, when Henry Tudor defeated Richard III, the last Plantagenet king. Also worth visiting are *Belvoir Castle* near *Melton Mowbray* and *Oakham Castle*, with its collection of decorative horseshoes.
Northamptonshire is traversed by major road and rail links but most of the countryside remains unspoilt. One of the most attractive regions is the *Rockingham Forest* area, which contains several historic houses. Of *Fotheringhay Castle* (where Mary Queen of Scots was executed in 1587) only the mound remains but most of the other houses are in much better condition, and many are still occupied. Of these, *Althorp* and *Rockingham Castle*, north of **Corby**, are particularly worth visiting. Other places of interest include the *Nene Valley Steam Railway* and the Central museum in Northampton with its fine shoe collection.

The North West

Cheshire, Greater Manchester, Lancashire, Merseyside, the High Peak District of Derbyshire.
North West Tourist Board, Swan House, Swan Meadow Road, Wigan Pier, Wigan WN3 5BB. Tel: (0942) 821 222. Fax: (0942) 820 002.
The North West's 250km (150-mile) coastline is characterised by dune-backed sandy beaches. The seven large resorts, the most popular of which is **Blackpool**, attract millions of holiday-makers each year. Other resorts include **Lytham St Annes, Ainsdale, Fleetwood, Morecambe** and **Southport**. All have extensive facilities and a wide choice of accommodation and entertainment.
Further north, **Blackburn, Bolton, Nelson** and **Burnley** offer varied accommodation as bases for trips round the western slopes of the *Pennines*, while long stretches of footpaths and bridleways wind through the landscape of heather and wild bilberries. Throughout the area there are fine examples of the stately homes of England: 16th-century *Speke Hall* near Liverpool; *Gawsworth Hall* near Macclesfield; timbered *Bramall Hall* near Stockport; and *Tatton Park* near Knutsford, whose interior is familiar to viewers of the BBC television adaptation of Evelyn Waugh's *Brideshead Revisited*.
The countryside includes the gentle *Cheshire Plain* dotted with small natural lakes, old water-wheels and distinctive villages with black and white houses. In the *Peak District National Park*, the limestone valleys and vast caverns of the White Peak give way to the dramatic moorlands of the Dark Peak.
In the south is the *Mersey Estuary* and the port of **Liverpool**, home of the Beatles. It also contains the *Walker Art Gallery* with Dutch, French, Italian and English paintings, and two cathedrals, one Anglican and one Roman Catholic. Attractions in and around the city include the *Merseyside County Museum*, *St George's Hall* and the 16th-century *Speke Hall*. From Liverpool there are regular ferry sailings to the Isle of Man.
Across the river is the *Wirral Peninsula* with the resort of **New Brighton** and a large country park. From here there are views across the Dee estuary to the Welsh Hills. On the *River Dee* near the Welsh border is the historic walled city of **Chester**, well-known for its concentration of Cheshire's black and white 'magpie' houses. To the east of the city is the 4000-acre *Delamere Forest* and the rich pastures of the Cheshire Plain, a region which has a network of canals several hundred kilometres long.Northeast of Cheshire is the city of **Manchester**, in many ways the 'capital' of the north of England. Attractions here include the *Opera House*, the *Palace Theatre*, the *Royal Exchange Theatre* (in the building that, 100 years ago, was at the very centre of the world's cotton industry), the *Free Trade Hall* and the mock-Gothic *John Rylands Library*. The city's cathedral was built in the 15th century, although most of the more immediately noticeable buildings date from the city's period of greatest prosperity in the 19th century.
Further north is the *Forest of Bowland*, a vast and lonely area of high moor-backed hills which also contains the beautiful wooded valley of the River *Ribble*. The historic county town of **Lancaster** is to the northwest, a short distance inland from the resorts of **Morecambe** and **Heysham**.

Cumbria

Cumbria Tourist Board, Ashleigh, Holly Road, Windermere, Cumbria LA23 2AQ. Tel: (05394) 44444. Fax: (05394) 44041.
Cumbria is proud to boast England's largest national park, containing the highest English peak (Scafell Pike) and Windermere, the largest lake. Cumbria is climbing country, with easy fell walks, and sailing, fishing, canoeing and pony-trekking facilities in a stunningly beautiful setting of mountains and lakes. This dramatic landscape is enhanced by the highest level of rainfall in England rendering the grass greener and the flowers brighter than elsewhere. The ancient sport of Cumberland and Westmorland wrestling takes place at the annual sports meetings in Grasmere, Ambleside and Coniston. Traditional fell-racing (to the top of the nearest hill and back) can also be seen at some of the Cumbrian sports meetings.
Many of the towns and villages, hidden among moorland, perched on mountainsides or tucked away along the coast, hold fairs, shows and sheepdog trials throughout the year. Local crafts are practised and workshops, smithies and potteries welcome visitors. It is possible to watch weaving in Grasmere, pencils made at Keswick and clogs fashioned in **Whitehaven**. Sweaters sold in Ambleside are made from the wool of local Herdwick sheep.
Grasmere is a small, circular lake with a small island in the middle. The village of **Grasmere** is where Wordsworth lived for several years and his home, *Dove Cottage*, is open to the public. He also lived at the nearby *Rydal Mount*. **Keswick**, on the shores of *Derwent Water*, is an attractive market town with a museum, the *Fitz Park*, which contains many manuscripts and letters of Shelley, Southey, Wordsworth and Coleridge. The region also has several coastal resorts such as Maryport, Silloth, St Bees and Grange-over-Sands.

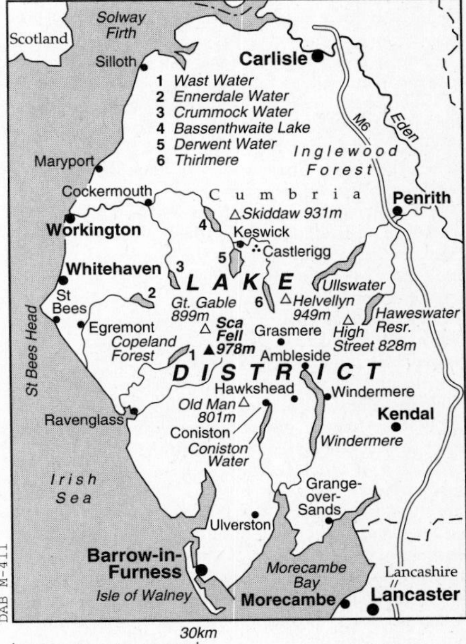

To the north of the county is the 2000-year-old cathedral city of **Carlisle**, close to Hadrian's wall and once a Roman camp. Likewise, the once important 18th-century trading port of Whitehaven today preserves an echo of former glories in its Georgian buildings. Another historic town, **Penrith**, makes a good base for touring the rich and peaceful *Eden Valley* and the wide-open spaces of the *Cumbrian Pennines*.

Yorkshire & Humberside

Humberside, North Yorkshire, South Yorkshire, West Yorkshire.

Yorkshire and Humberside Tourist Board, 312 Tadcaster Road, York YO2 2HF. Tel: (0904) 707 961. Fax: (0904) 701 414.

Yorkshire and Humberside is a region of scenic softness, rugged castles, stately homes and ancient churches all packed tightly into a compact area with good transport communications.

For many people, the scenic grandeur of the *Yorkshire Dales National Park* – 680 sq miles of unspoilt countryside, rivers, caves and unforgettable views – is a major attraction all year round. This is the landscape made famous by JMW Turner and, most recently, by the worldwide success of the books and TV series featuring Dales vet, James Herriot. The surgery and locations used in the filming can be seen in **Askrigg**, in Wensleydale. Walking is a very popular pastime in the area, with everything from gentle strolls to hearty climbs such as the ascent of the *Three Peaks* of Ingleborough, Whernside and Pen-y-ghent. An even bigger challenge is the *Pennine Way*, the toughest of many long-distance footpaths to be found in Yorkshire and Humberside. Historic castles abound in the region, such as the great fortresses of Richmond and Middleham, the latter associated with Richard III. *Bolton Castle* in **Wensleydale** once served as a prison for the ill-fated Mary Queen of Scots, whilst an even more tragic scenario was played out at *Pontefract Castle* in **West Yorkshire**, where Richard II was murdered.

A more stable period for the aristocracy is reflected in the great houses to be found dotted throughout the region, notably *Castle Howard*, near **Malton**, world famous as the setting for Evelyn Waugh's *Brideshead Revisited*. Other fine houses open to the public include *Harewood House*, *Duncombe Park*, *Nostell Priory*, *Sledmere House* and *Burton Constable Hall*.

The great city of **York**, with its unparalleled wealth of historic sites, continues to be a strong magnet for visitors; more than two million people visit the Minster – Northern Europe's largest Gothic cathedral – every year. Other top attractions are the *National Railway Museum*, the *Castle Museum* and the *Jorvik Viking Centre*, whilst many people come to see the medieval ring of walls or to shop in the Shambles, York's most quaint street.

Humberside is a maritime county with powerful links with Britain's proud seafaring tradition. The city of **Hull** is an important working port, and has recently been transformed by the new waterfront marina development, whilst the majestic *Humber Bridge* is an attraction in its own right. Beyond Hull is the gentle lowland area of **Holderness**, which ends in the bird sanctuary at lonely *Spurn Point*. To the north lies the ancient market town of **Beverley**, with its Georgian houses in the shadow of the minster. Close by is the racecourse and the fascinating *Museum of Army Transport*.

The **North York Moors** National Park has miles of open moorland with picturesque villages nestling in hollows. The North Yorkshire Moors Railway, starting at **Pickering**, is one of the most scenic in Britain, and is one of the many steam railways in the region – others include the *Embsay Steam Railway* at **Skipton** and the *Keighley and Worth Valley Railway*.

On the coast, traditional family resorts like **Scarborough**, **Bridlington** and **Cleethorpes** have added many new attractions in recent times, such as Bridlington's popular *Leisure World Complex*. There are also many smaller resorts, each with their own special character, such as **Whitby** with its busy harbour and clifftop abbey, linked to Bram Stoker's *Dracula*.

Between the coast and the Vale of York lie *The Wolds*, a gentle range of rolling hills with timeless villages and quiet lanes, ideal for walking or cycling. On the edge of *The Wolds* is **Malton**, one of the many interesting towns to be found dotted throughout the region – others worth a visit include *Thirsk*, *Skipton*, *Selby*, *Ilkley* and *Harrogate*.

The cities of South and West Yorkshire make interesting destinations, their potent industrial heritage combined with a new spirit of renovation and renewal. **Bradford** has led the way, with the award-winning *National Museum of Photography, Film and Television*. **Wakefield** boasts *Caphouse Colliery*, home of the *Yorkshire Mining Museum*. Close by are the Wild Moors of the Pennines including the Brontë Village of **Haworth**.

Northumbria

Cleveland, Durham, Tyne & Wear, Northumberland.

Northumbria Tourist Board, Aykley Heads, Durham, Co Durham DH1 5UX. Tel: (091) 384 6905. Fax: (091) 386 0899.

A region of contrasts, Northumbria offers miles of coastline, city lights, quiet countryside, castles and cathedrals, industrial tourism, Hadrian's Wall and much more.

Northumberland, lying between the Scottish Border and Tyne and Wear, is a rural county with numerous attractive villages and market towns. On its northern boundary it has **Hadrian's Wall** as its most famous landmark. The wall was built to protect Roman Britain from the incursions of the Picts and Scots from north of the border; much of the surviving architecture tells of centuries of border warfare, such as the chain of castles built to defend the countryside and the long Northumberland coastline. These include dramatic **Bamburgh**, gaunt craggy **Dunstanburgh** and impressive **Alnwick**. In contrast, the simple cross at **Chollerford, Lindisfarne** (Holy Island) and *St Wilfred's* at **Hexham** reflect the important role Northumberland played in the spread of Christianity. Hexham makes a good base from which to explore the whole Northumbrian region. Much of the county is a National Park, with rolling moorlands stretching from the North Sea to the *Cheviot Hills* on the Scottish border. England's most northerly town, **Berwick-upon-Tweed**, was a regular casualty in the border battles, and changed hands between Scotland and England at least 13 times. Its medieval town walls, reconstructed in Elizabethan times, are among the best-preserved in Europe. Today the town makes a convenient base for touring northern Northumberland and the Borderlands.

Tyne and Wear spans the mouths of the two major rivers in its name. **Newcastle-upon-Tyne** (originally no more than a fort on Hadrian's Wall) has city centre shopping, museums, theatres, hotels, restaurants and all the services expected in a major city. There is also a cathedral and a castle. Across the river are **Gateshead** with the *Metro Centre* indoor shopping and **South Shields**, home of popular author Catherine Cookson. **Sunderland** stands at the mouth of the *River Wear* and nearby is **Washington**, famous as the original home of US President George Washington's family. Christian Heritage comes to the fore at *Tynemouth Priory* and **Jarrow**, home of The Venerable Bede.

Transport in the Newcastle area is particularly good owing to its excellent Metro.

County Durham, where Prince Bishops ruled for 600 years, surrounds **Durham City** with its spectacular castle and Norman Cathedral built overlooking a gorge on the River Wear. Surrounding countryside is pleasant and studded with small market towns such as **Bishop Auckland** and *Barnard Castle*. *The Bowes Museum*, *Raby Castle*, *High Force Waterfall* and *Beamish Open Air Museum* attract thousands of visitors to the county each year. There are several castles, in varying stages of dilapidation. **Bishop Auckland** is an ancient market town; nearby is an 800-acre deer park. Also within this county is the wild region of the North Pennines, Weardale and Teesdale. **Darlington**, which made its name in the 19th century with the world's first passenger railway to nearby Stockton, has a famous railway museum. There are many other attractive towns and villages throughout County Durham, and many opportunities for walks in the hills and moors.

Cleveland, in the south of the region close to the Yorkshire border, is an industrial county dominated by **Middlesbrough**. It boasts Australia's discoverer Captain Cook as its most famous son. The *Captain Cook Birthplace Museum* in Middlesbrough tells his story. Coastal towns include **Redcar**, **Saltburn** and **Hartlepool**, with its maritime museum, restored ships and marina (under construction). Cleveland's long industrial history dates from the early 19th century (the world's first passenger train steamed into Stockton-on-Tees in 1825). Towns of interest include **Marske**, **Guisborough** and **Upleatham**, with reputedly the smallest church in England.

SOCIAL PROFILE

FOOD & DRINK: Good English cooking is superb and there are restaurants specialising in old English dishes. In general, the north of the country tends to offer more substantial and traditional food, at more reasonable prices than the south. Every region, however, will have its own speciality; these will include roast beef and Yorkshire pudding, game or venison pies, rack of lamb and many fish dishes. Britain is still the home of puddings: *spotted dick* (suet pudding with currants and raisins); *plum duff* (suet roll stuffed with plums); and *syllabub* (a medieval dish consisting of double cream, white wine and lemon juice). Delicious baking is to be found in Britain and visitors may sample a four o'clock tea of scones, jam, little quarter sandwiches and cakes of all descriptions. The West Country cream tea consists of clotted or double cream and jam instead of butter and jam. There are many regional varieties in baking: the flat pancake-type scones of the North of England and Scotland; Scottish black bun, a fruit cake on a pastry base; Bakewell tart, a pastry base covered with jam, almond filling and topped with icing; and breads of all description. For those who want variety, London offers every type of ethnic food imaginable, Indian and Chinese being particularly popular and good value for money. There are many celebrated British cheeses, of which *Cheddar* and *Stilton* are the most famous. Tipping is not compulsory and it is up to the individual to pay the 10% service charge often added automatically to bills. Table service is usual but there are self-service snack bars. Set price lunches, especially on Sundays, with a choice of about three dishes, are particularly good value, as is pub food. **Drink:** The British pub is nothing short of a national institution and even the smallest village in the remotest corner of the country will usually have at least one. There are about as many beers in England as there are cheeses in France and the recent revival of real ale has greatly improved the range and qualities of brews available. Look out for the sign 'Free House' outside a pub, meaning that beer from more than one brewery will be sold there. Bitter and lager are the most popular beers, but Guinness, pale ale, brown ale and cider are also widely drunk. Wine bars and cocktail bars are now common in the larger cities and towns, and the latter will often have a 'happy hour' (when prices are reduced) in the early evening. Under 18's may not be served with alcohol and children under 16 are not generally allowed into pubs, although they may sit in the garden. Licensing hours vary from Monday to Saturday but many pubs, especially in main centres, are open typically 1100-2300; the visitor should not be surprised however if he finds a pub closing for a period in the afternoon. On Sundays, hours are 1200-1500 and 1900-2230. Private clubs often have an extension to these hours.

NIGHTLIFE: The main cities, London in particular, have a vast range to choose from: theatre (including open air in the summer), opera, ballet, concerts, films, restaurants, nightclubs and discotheques, as well as, of course, pubs. In the provinces the choice is not as great. The weekly magazines *Time Out* and *City Limits* publish a comprehensive guide to the events in the capital.

SHOPPING: Woollen and woven goods such as *Harris Tweeds* are famous. Printed cottons and silks are to be found, as well as fashionable ready-made clothes. China and porcelain *Wedgewood*, *Crown Derby*, *Royal Worcester* and *Royal Doulton* are good buys, as are luxury food and chocolates. Antiques are to be found all over the country. In London, Charing Cross Road is famous for bookshops, and there are the street markets: Petticoat Lane for clothes and Bermondsey for antiques, to name just two. **Tax Free Shopping:** Many shops throughout the country now operate a tax-free shopping scheme for overseas visitors. The store will provide a form which should be completed at the time of purchase. Upon arrival at Customs, present the goods and the forms (within three months) to the Customs Officer, who will stamp the vouchers certifying that the goods are being exported, and that you will be entitled to a refund of Value Added Tax. For further information contact the British Tourist Office which will be able to supply details. **Shopping hours:** In major cities 0900-1730 Monday to Saturday; in London's West End and other large shopping centres, shops stay open to 2000. Many local shops stay open to 1900 or 2000 and some even later; many of these are open on Sunday mornings or all day. Some towns and areas of cities may have early closing one day a week, usually Wednesday or Thursday.

SPORTS: Golf, tennis, squash, riding, sailing and **swimming** are all possible. Swimmers should be warned that the sea is invigorating rather than warm. In Cornwall there are some opportunities for **surfing**. Spectator sports include **horseracing** (both flat and steeplechasing, according to the season); **rugby; football** from mid-August to April (there are 92 first-class clubs in England and Wales); **tennis** (particularly at Wimbledon); and **cricket**; 17 counties have first class-cricket teams playing from April to September. The most famous ground is Lords' in north London, the home of cricket.

SPECIAL EVENTS: The following is a selection of the major festivals and other special events celebrated annually in England. For a complete list contact the English Tourist Board.

Mar 9-20 '93 *Chelsea Antiques Fair*, London. **Mar 18-Apr 12** *Daily Mail Ideal Home Exhibition*, London. **Mar 20-Nov 3** *Durham Cathedral 900th Anniversary Celebrations*. **Apr-Jan** *Shakespeare Festival Season*, Stratford-upon-Avon. **May 1-3** *Classic and Sports Car Exhibition*, Birmingham. **May 7-30** *Brighton International Festival*. **May 15** *FA Challenge Cup Final*, Wembley, London. **May 29-Jun 12** *English Riviera Dance Festival*, Torquay, Devon. **May 25-28** *Chelsea Flower Show*,

London. **May 29-30** *Air Fete '93*, Bury St Edmunds, Suffolk. **Jun 9** *Appleby Horse Fair*, Cumbria. **Jun 12** *Trooping the Colour*, The Queen's Official Birthday Parade, London. **Jun 21-Jul 4** *Lawn Tennis Championships*, Wimbledon, London. **Jul 2-11** *Cambridge Festival*. **Jul 4-21** *City of London Festival*. **Jul 16-Sep 11** *Henry Wood Promenade Concerts*, Royal Albert Hall, London. **Aug 29-30** *Notting Hill Carnival*, London. **Sep 9-11** *International Sheepdog Trials*, Armathwaite, Cumbria. **Sep 10-18** *Southampton International Boat Show*. **Oct 21-31** *Motorfair – The London Motor Show*, Earls Court, London. **Nov 7** *London to Brighton Veteran Car Run*. **Nov 13** *Lord Mayor's Procession and Show*, London. **Feb 13 '94** *Chinese New Year Celebrations*, London. **Mar 10-13** *Crufts Dog Show*, London.

CLIMATE

The climate is temperate with warm wet summers and cool wet winters. It is variable from day to day and throughout the country as a whole. The west coast and mountainous areas receive the most rain; the east coast, particularly in the north, is colder and windier. The southeast is sunnier than the north with less rain and a climate approaching the continental. The southwest has overall the mildest climate.
Required clothing: European according to season, plus rainwear.

LONDON England (5m)

SUNSHINE, hours
1 2 4 5 6 7 6 6 5 3 2 1

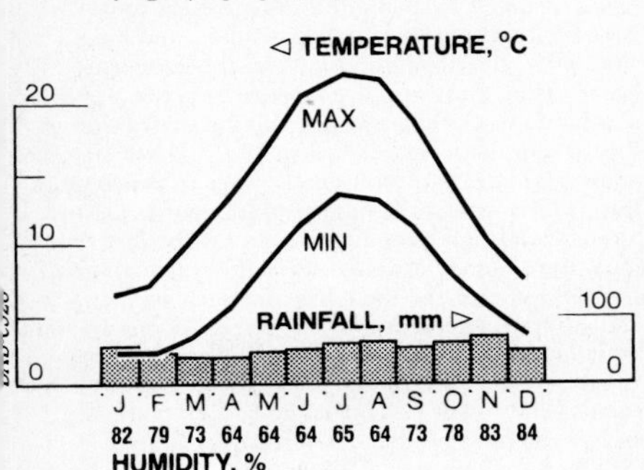

MORECAMBE England (7m)

SUNSHINE, hours
2 2 4 6 7 7 6 6 4 3 2 1

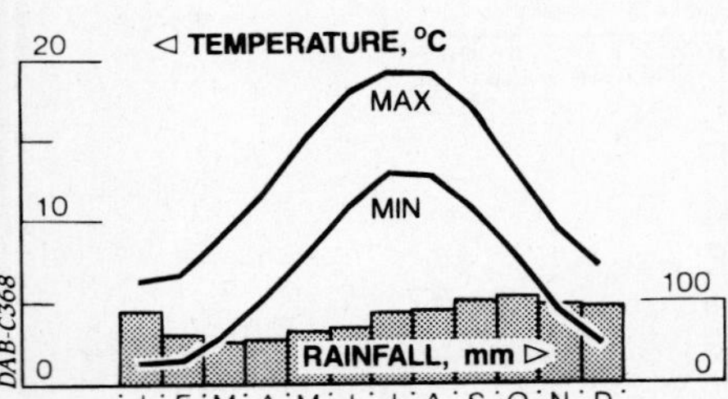

SCARBOROUGH England (36m)

SUNSHINE, hours
1 2 3 5 6 6 6 5 5 3 2 1

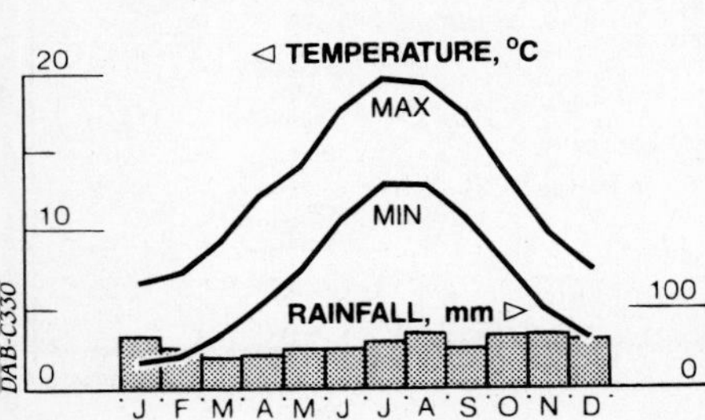

SCOTLAND

Location: Northern part of Great Britain.

Scottish Tourist Board
23 Ravelston Terrace
Edinburgh EH4 3EU
Tel: (031) 332 2433. Fax: (031) 343 1513. Telex: 72272.

AREA: 77,167 sq km (27,478 sq miles).
POPULATION: 5,090,700 (1989 estimate).
POPULATION DENSITY: 66 per sq km.
CAPITAL: Edinburgh. **Population:** 433,200 (1989 estimate).
GEOGRAPHY: The country consists of the southern Lowland area, a region of moorland and pastoral scenery – where most of the population lives – and the Northern Highlands, dominated by the Grampian Mountains and Ben Nevis, the highest peak in the British Isles. The whole of the exceedingly beautiful coastline is indented with lochs (particularly in the north and west). Off the west coast there are many islands, the largest of which are Skye and Lewis, the latter being part of the Outer Hebrides. The Orkney and Shetland Islands lie to the northeast of the Scottish mainland, across the Pentland Firth from John O'Groats.
LANGUAGE: English. Gaelic is still spoken by some, mostly in the West and Highlands.
NOTE: *For information on time, electricity, communications, passport/visa, duty free, money and health, see general UK entry above.*

PUBLIC HOLIDAYS

Public holidays observed in Scotland are similar to those observed in the rest of the UK (*see the general entry above*), with the addition of:
May 1 '93 May Day. **Aug 2** Bank Holiday. **Nov 30** St Andrew's Day. **Dec 31** *Hogmanay* (New Year's Eve, celebrated with particular fervour in Scotland). **Jan '94** Bank Holiday.

TRAVEL

AIR: Scotland's main international airports are *Edinburgh* and *Glasgow*:
Edinburgh (EDI): Located: 11km (7 miles) west of the city centre. Airport information: (031) 344 3136. **Facilities** include duty free; general shop; 24-hour coffee shop; banks (0800-1900 Monday to Friday, 0900-1430 Saturday, 1100-1700 Sunday with extensions to all these times in summer); emergency medical services; nursing mothers' room; restaurant, bar and buffet; hotel reservation service; conference facilities for 30; facilities for the disabled – wheelchairs, telephones and toilets; Salmon Pool (Scottish and English delicacies). **Train/bus:** Airlink bus 100 links the airport with Waverley Bridge station Monday to Friday (0715-2235) every 15 minutes and every hour Saturday and Sunday (0910-1730) and less frequently outside these times. Travel time – 25 minutes. Details: (031) 220 4111. Edinburgh Airbus to city centre (Waverley Bridge) Monday to Friday every 30 minutes (0630-2030); Saturday and Sunday (0800-1920). Tel: (031) 556 2244. From Waverley Bridge Station there are trains to the rest of Scotland and to England. **Taxi:** Travel time to city centre – 25 minutes. Available from the rank outside the airport. **Car hire:** *Alamo, Avis, Hertz, Europcar* and *Swan National* self-drive and chauffeur-driven cars can be hired from desks within the terminal. **Private car:** The A8 runs direct to the airport from the city centre. If coming from the west or north follow the signs on the M9, M8 and A90.
Glasgow (GLA): Located: 14km (9 miles) west of the city centre. Airport information: (041) 887 1111. **Facilities** include 24-hour emergency medical services, left luggage (0700-2230), general shops, pharmacy (24-hour), post office (0900-1300 and 1400-1730 Monday to Friday, 0900-1300 Saturday), buffet (24-hour), 'Paisley' bar/diner (1000-2300 Monday to Saturday, 1230-1430 and 1830-2300 on Sunday), 'Gallery' (1200-2200, last orders at 2000), duty-free shop, hotel reservation service, conference facilities for 40 (tel: (041) 887 1111) and facilities for the disabled – wheelchairs, toilets and telephones. **Train:** Paisley Gilmour Street station is 1.6km (1 mile) from the airport. Services run every 15 minutes from 0630-2346 Monday to Saturday; every 30 minutes on Sunday (0925-2348). Travel time – 10 minutes. Main line connections are available to most parts of the country. *British Rail*: (041) 2042844. **Coach:** *Airlink* services 160 and 180 (Clydeside) coach link from airport to Paisley Gilmore Street every 10 minutes in the day and every 30 minutes in the evening (0605-2315). Travel time – 10 minutes. A limited stop service runs to Erskine, calling at Glasgow airport. *Scottish Citylink* service 500 runs from the airport to Glasgow and Edinburgh via the M8. Travel time to Edinburgh is 1 hour 50 minutes (20 minutes to Glasgow city centre). **Bus:** Services 500 and 502 Scottish City Link to city centre Monday to Saturday every 30 minutes every hour in the evening (0625-2355) and every hour on Sunday (0755-2255). Bus information: (041) 332 9644. **Local bus:** Regular service to Renfrew and Paisley. **Taxi:** To the city centre is 20 minutes; to Paisley BR station is 5 minutes. Taxis are available from the rank at the western end of the terminal building. **Car hire:** *Avis, Euro Dollar, Hertz* and *Europcar* have desks in the Domestic Arrivals Hall. **Private car:** The M8 runs direct to the airport from the city centre. Car parking space is available for 2000 cars.
Other airports: *Inverness (INV)* is the major airport serving the Highlands, with transfer connections available to airports in the north of Scotland.
There are several smaller airports in the north of Scotland which are served by flights from Glasgow and, in some cases, from Aberdeen, Inverness and Edinburgh as well. These include *Kirkall* (Orkney), *Lerwick* (Shetland), *Skye, Tiree, Stornoway, Benbecula* and *Barra*. For further information, contact Glasgow Airport. Tel: (041) 887 1111.
SEA: Ferry services operate between the mainland and all the Scottish islands but many of these will be infrequent. *Caledonian MacBrayne* operate the largest network of ferries, serving 23 islands including the Inner and Outer Hebrides. During the summer, services often operate hourly or half-hourly but in the winter they are less frequent. For details of fares,

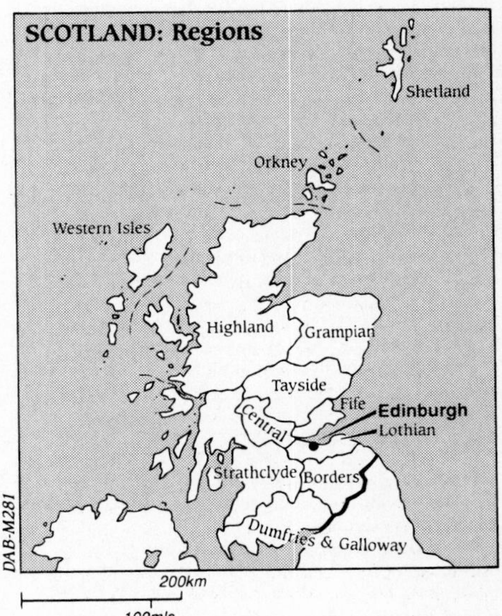

routes and timetables contact *Gourock*. Tel: (0475) 33755. Fax: (0475) 37607. *P&O Ferries* operate services to the Orkneys and Shetlands; from Aberdeen to Lerwick up to three times a week (travel time–14 hours); and from Scrabster to Stromness up to 11 times a week (travel time – 2 hours). Tel: (0224) 572 615. Fax: (0224) 574 411.
Other routes include *P&O's* service between Cairnryan and Larne up to five times a day (travel time – 2 hours 20 minutes); and *Sealink's* service between Stranraer and Larne eight times a day (travel time – 2 hours 15 minutes). *Seacat* have opened a new route between Stranraer and Belfast Harbour five times a day and four crossings daily during the low season (travel time – 1 hour 30 minutes). Tel: (041) 204 2266. Fax: (0304) 240 088.
RAIL: There are two main line routes into Scotland from England: from Euston up the west coast to Glasgow and beyond to Perth and Inverness; and from King's Cross up the east coast to Edinburgh and beyond to Dundee and Aberdeen. Tel: (071) 387 7070 (Euston) *or* (071) 278 2477 (King's Cross). Particularly in the Edinburgh-Glasgow area, there are good services connecting all the main towns. Many of the routes which pass through the highlands (such as the Perth to Inverness, Inverness to Kyle of Lochalsh and the Glasgow to Mallaig via Fort William) are very spectacular. The network extends right up to Thurso and Wick in the extreme north of the country. Sleeper services are available on Intercity routes from England.
ROAD: Scotland is connected to the main UK road network by good trunk roads, and has several internal motorways. Main access from England is via the A74 (Carlisle to Glasgow), the A696/A68 (Newcastle to Edinburgh via the Cheviots) and the A1 (Newcastle to Edinburgh via the coast). The main motorways within Scotland connect Edinburgh with Glasgow (M8), Edinburgh with Stirling (M9), and the Forth Bridge, near Edinburgh, with Perth (M90). In general, the internal trunk road network is better and more direct on the east coast, and roads north of Inverness tend to be slower and often single track. Driving in winter in the highland areas can be dangerous and motorists are advised to follow local advice concerning weather conditions. The main cross-country road, the A9, connects Perth with Inverness and Thurso.
Car hire: Self-drive cars are widely available in the major centres. The Scottish Tourist Board will be able to supply a list of companies in each area.
Distances: *From London:* Edinburgh 610km (378 miles), Glasgow 640km (397 miles), Aberdeen 810km (503 miles), Inverness 860km (536 miles), Fort William 640km (398 miles), Perth 670km (415 miles) and Thurso 1945km (651 miles).
From Edinburgh: Glasgow 65km (42 miles), Aberdeen 200km (125 miles), Inverness 255km (158 miles), Fort William 235km (146 miles), Perth 70km (44 miles) and Thurso 450km (278 miles).
URBAN: All the major towns and cities have bus services. Glasgow also has an underground and a suburban train network.

ACCOMMODATION

The Scottish Tourist Board publishes a series of *Where to Stay* brochures, covering *Hotels and Guest-houses; Bed and Breakfast; Camping and Caravan* and *Self-catering*. Tel: (031) 332 2433. Fax: (031) 343 1543.
HOTELS: There is a wide range of hotel accommodation available in Scotland, with many hotels having been built, modernised or refurbished during the last few years. See above for details of guides available. **Grading:** As well as the UK-wide crown grading system, hotels are classified as *Highly Commended* (122), *Commended* (679), *Approved* (188), *Classification Only* (15); the latter meet minimum requirements. There are more than 4500 establishments as well as the above hotels that follow this system.
CAMPING: There are many campsites throughout the country with good facilities. Campsites come under the new 'Thistle Commendation Scheme', in which sites are inspected each year.
SELF-CATERING: Self-catering holidays are very popular in Scotland and accommodation is available throughout the country. See above for details of guides available.

RESORTS & EXCURSIONS

Scotland is a beautiful and sparsely populated country with rolling lowland, dramatic mountains, lochs and many offshore islands.
For further information on historical properties belonging to The National Trust for Scotland, contact 5 Charlotte Square, Edinburgh EH2 4DU. Tel: (031) 226 5922. Fax: (031) 220 6266.

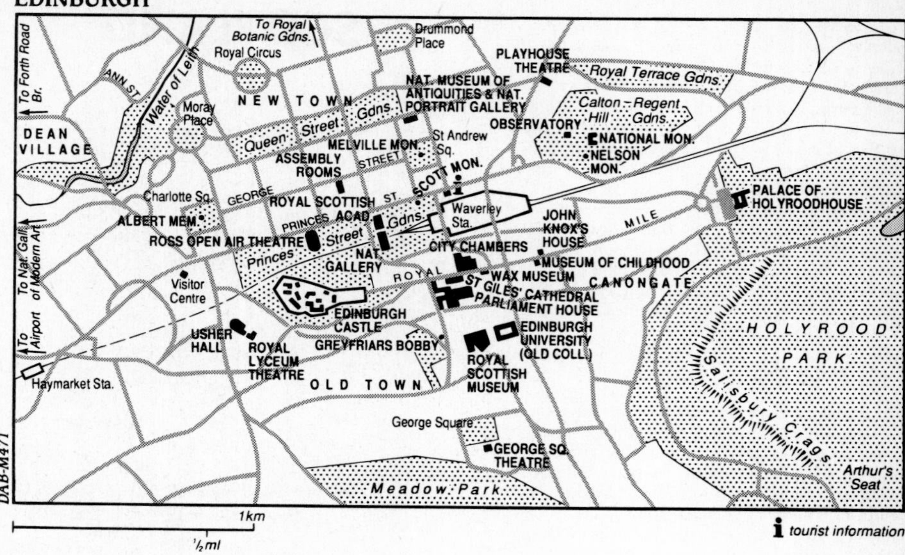

Edinburgh

One of the most beautiful cities in Great Britain, Edinburgh is the social and cultural centre of Scotland. *The Royal Mile* in the oldest part of the city runs from *Edinburgh Castle* past *St Giles Cathedral* to *John Knox's House* and on to *The Palace of Holyroodhouse*. The Castle was originally built by the Saxon King Edwin of Northumbria, but most of the present-day buildings date from after Bruce's storming of the city in 1313. The 'Honours of Scotland' – crown, sceptre, sword and other treasures dating back to the 16th century – are kept there. The Castle gives a superb view across the city, as does *The Scott Monument* in Prince's Street and *Arthur's Seat* in Holyrood Park. Holyroodhouse was built by David I as part of the Abbey of Holyrood, but its most famous owner was Mary Queen of Scots, and it was here that many of the dramatic events of that period took place. Most of the present buildings date from the late 17th century.
The central part of the city between the Castle, Waverley Station, Princes Street and the Royal Mile is occupied by the attractive *Princes Street Gardens*. Princes Street itself has many fine shops and buildings. To the north is the *New Town*, an area of Georgian crescents, streets and squares, all preserved in their original elegant condition. Edinburgh's museums include the *National Gallery of Scotland*, the *Scottish National Portrait Gallery*, the *National Museum of Antiquities*, the *Scottish National Gallery of Modern Art*, the *Royal Scottish Museum* (natural history, science and technology exhibits), the *People's Story* and the *Museum of Childhood*. The *Edinburgh Festival* is held from late August to early September each year. Attractions close to Edinburgh include the resort of **Aberdour**; **Dunfermline**, whose abbey is the burial place of several Scottish kings; *Blackness*, *Dunbar* and *Tantallon* castles; and the old village of **Dalmeny**.

The East Coast

St Andrews, north of Edinburgh in Fife, is the home of golf. In addition the town has a university, castle and a cathedral. The *Lammas Fair* takes place in August. Across the Firth of Tay is the city of **Dundee**. Some 25km (15 miles) to the north is **Glamis**, whose castle was the home of Shakespeare's Macbeth and the birthplace of Princess Margaret. West of Dundee is **Perth**, an attractive market town whose most famous literary association is Scott's *The Fair Maid of Perth*. King James I, one of Scotland's most able rulers, was murdered here, and John Knox preached one of his earliest sermons in the town. **Scone**, where many of Scotland's kings were crowned, is a few kilometres away and was the centre of the Pictish kingdom during the period of Roman occupation south of *Hadrian's Wall*. Further up the coast from Dundee is **Arbroath** which has a famous ruined abbey. To the north, the town of **Montrose** is noted for its golf course. 56km (35 miles) north of Montrose is **Aberdeen**, Scotland's third city, built largely of granite. Aberdeen is now the centre of Britain's North Sea oil industry, which has had the effect of inflating prices in the region. The city itself has a 16th-century cathedral, a 15th-century university and a 14th-century bridge, the 'Brig O'Balgownie'. Nearby **Braemar** is the site of the most famous of the highland gatherings. There are several National Trust properties within easy reach of Aberdeen, including *Craigievar* and *Castle Fraser*. The A92 continues north to **Peterhead** and **Fraserburgh**, passing through some spectacular countryside dotted with ruined fortresses, but the A96 and railway both turn inland towards Inverness. On the way is **Elgin** which has a ruined cathedral and a well-restored abbey church. **Inverness** is the northernmost large town in the country; many of the buildings date back to the 17th century. Inverness is also famous for being situated at the head of *Loch Ness*, the deep-water home of the elusive monster. Nearby is the site of the Battle of Culloden where the forces of Bonnie Prince Charlie were crushed in 1746. There are many highland gatherings and games in this region. Beyond Inverness, the countryside consists mainly of moorlands, glens and forests and is the last remaining home of some of Britain's once common indigenous animals, including red deer, wild cats and golden eagles. Most of the towns in this area are little more than villages, and include *Golspie*, *Ullapool* and *Lybster*, near which are several neolithic tombs. The towns of **Thurso** and **Wick** mark the end of the railway line. The village of **John O'Groats**, due north of Wick, is the northernmost point on the British mainland.

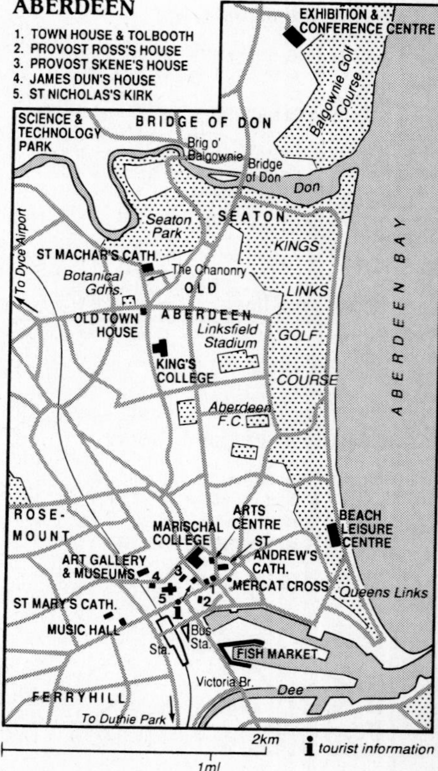

GLASGOW

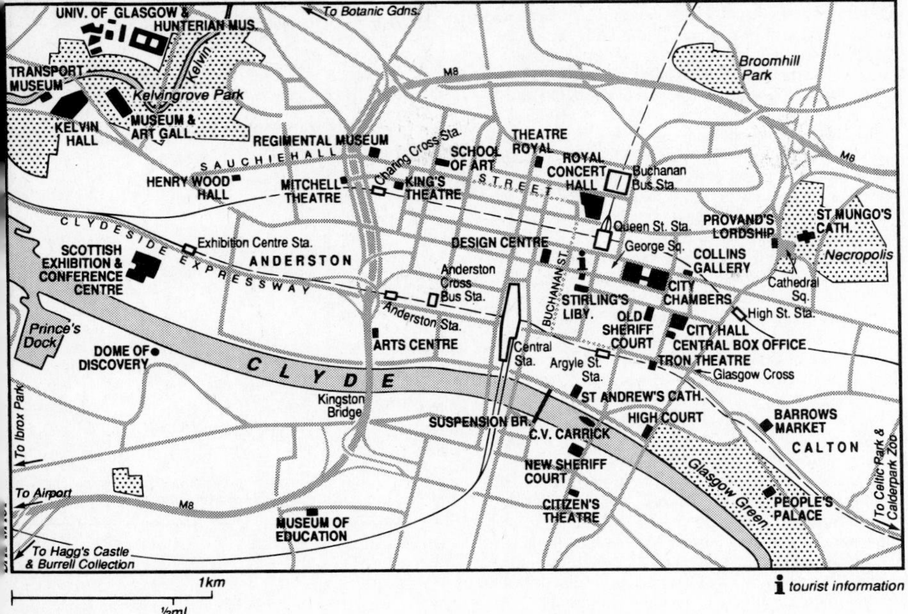

Glasgow

This former industrial city is the largest and possibly most lively city in Scotland; it is also becoming a major cultural centre with a variety of exciting events taking place – and of course the recent opening of the *Burrell Collection* and the *Royal Concert Hall*. Indeed, Glasgow was the 1990 Cultural Capital of Europe. It has some fine parks and the only complete medieval cathedral in Scotland (containing the tomb of St Mungo). A short ride away from George Square is *Kelvingrove Park*; the art gallery has paintings by some of the most famous Renaissance and modern painters. Glasgow's *Theatre Royal* is the home of the Scottish Opera, and the city is also the headquarters of the Scottish National Orchestra. Attractions near Glasgow include **Ayr**, on the coast and **Alloway**, the birthplace of Robert Burns and, on a cliff overlooking the Firth of Clyde, *Culzean Castle*, once the home of the American Kennedy family. Another lowland place of interest is *Loch Lomond*.

Dumfries, Galloway & the Borders

These regions are the southernmost in Scotland. Much of their area is lowland, rising in the north towards the Southern Uplands. The **Borders** area was the setting for many of the battles which were regularly fought between Scotland and England through the centuries. It is a region of lush green hills and moorlands, occasionally pitted with valleys, gorges and roaring waterfalls. The area's wealth, despite such disadvantages, allowed the construction of several outstanding ecclesiastical buildings, notably the abbeys at *Jedburgh*, *Dryburgh* and *Melrose*. The ancient border towns of **Selkirk**, **Galashiels**, **Peebles** and **Hawick** are still the centre of a thriving wool, tweed and knitwear industry. **Abbotsford** in this area was the home of Sir Walter Scott. The region of **Dumfries** and **Galloway** consists of open, undulating countryside, lakes and pine forests. The main town is Dumfries, an important market town and the place where Burns died. Galloway has many great country houses, such as *Ardwell* and *Logan*, as well as *Dundrennan* where Mary Queen of Scots passed her last night in her home country before her long years of imprisonment in England.

The Highlands & the West Coast

The **Scottish Highlands** contains probably the most breathtaking scenery in the British Isles. Railway and road traverse the countryside between the capital and Inverness, passing through the *Grampian Mountains* and the *Forest of Atholl*. The lochs of the central highlands feed the River Tay, one of the best fishing rivers in the British Isles. Also in the Highlands are the *Pass of Killiecrankie*, *Blair Atholl*, *Kingussie* and *Aviemore*, the winter skiing resort.
The West Coast has some pretty coastal resorts and also some exceedingly beautiful scenery, particularly the mainland opposite Skye.
Fort William is one of the best-known towns on this coast, as well as one of the largest. Nearby is **Glencoe** where the Campbells massacred the Macdonald clan; when shrouded in mist, Glencoe still has an ominous air about it. At the mouth of Loch Linnhe is **Oban**, the gateway to many of the islands and the beautiful region of *Kintyre*. Between Kintyre and the coast of Strathclyde is the island of **Arran**, while to the west of Kintyre are **Islay** and **Jura**. **Iona**, the burial place of many Scottish kings, **Mull** and the *Outer Hebrides* can be visited from Oban. Further north is the town of **Mallaig** which is, like Oban, situated at the end of a railway line from Glasgow. Separated from the mainland by the Sound of Sleat and the Inner Sound is the island of **Skye**, which can be reached from Mallaig or *Kyle of Lochalsh* (also on the railway). The town of **Ullapool** is still an important fishing port, and is also the departure point for car ferries to the Isle of Lewis in the Outer Hebrides. Further up the coast is **Unapool**, close to which is the beautiful *Inverpolly Nature Reserve*. Other towns worth visiting in this part of the coast include **Lochinvar**, **Aultbea** and **Gairloch**. Inland, in the bleak area of Sutherland, is *Loch Shin*, on the southern edge of which is the town of **Lairg**. To the northwest and north the coastline is rocky, deep-hewn with lochs, while the countryside is often wholly deserted. Travelling along the north coast, the road skirts around several lochs, passing towns such as Durness and Melvich, before reaching **Thurso**, embarkation point for ferries to the Orkney Islands, and to *John O' Groats*.

The Orkney & Shetland Islands

These two island groups lie northeast of the Scottish mainland, and can be reached by air or sea. See the *Travel* section above.
The Orkneys: 67 islands, 29 of which are inhabited, the Orkneys are separated from the mainland by the Pentland Firth. The islands are fertile although with very few trees, and enjoy a predominantly mild, although variable climate. The main town situated on the island known as Mainland, is **Kirkwall**, built in Norwegian style, and boasting an impressive 12th-century cathedral. The islands are rich in archaeological remains, including the Stone Age village of **Skara Brae**, the Maes Howe burial mound, and the standing stones at the *Ring of Brogar*. On the other side of Scapa Flow is the island of **Hoy**, whose sheer cliffs and windswept sandstone landscape make it one of the most dramatic islands of the Orkney group. Other islands of interest include **Westray** and **South Ronaldsay.** The islands are of particular interest to birdwatchers and sea anglers.
Birds are also the main attraction on **Fair Isle,** between the Orkneys and the Shetlands. It is owned by the National Trust for Scotland, who should be contacted by anyone planning a visit (tel: (031) 226 5922). It is served by air and sea from both the Orkneys and Shetlands.
The Shetlands: This group of 100 rugged, hilly and heather-rich islands is located at the most northerly point of Britain. Their climate is surprisingly mild considering their northerly latitude (the same as Leningrad, Hudson Bay and Southern Alaska). The largest island (also called Mainland) is riddled with fjords and inlets. The chief town of **Lerwick** relied in former days almost solely on fishing but now, like most parts of the Shetlands and Orkneys, has benefited from the North Sea oil boom. Other places of interest include the Bronze Age tomb at **Jarlshof**, the island of **Bressay**, the nature reserve on the island of **Noss**, **Mousa Broch** on the uninhabited island of **Mousa**, and, reputedly, the most northern castle in the world on the island of **Unst**. All the islands in the group can be reached from Lerwick and, like the Orkneys, their main attraction is their remoteness, their birdlife and, in good weather, opportunities for sea fishing. Weather conditions can change suddenly and local advice should be sought and heeded.

SOCIAL PROFILE

FOOD & DRINK: In the main cities and towns, a wide variety of British and continental food is available. Local dishes include *haggis* (chopped oatmeal and offal cooked in the stomach of a sheep), *cullen skink* (fish soup), smoked haddock and salmon and *partan bree* (crab with rice and cream). Baked food such as cakes and biscuits are exceedingly popular and some of the more famous are flat pancake-type scones, oatcakes and *black bun*, a fruit cake on a pastry base. **Drink:** Scotch whisky is the national drink, and is famous the world over. There are also many local beers, known as *light* and *heavy*, as well as lager. Licensing hours are subject to greater variation than in England; some pubs may be open from 1030-2400, others only 1130-1430 and 1830-2300.
NIGHTLIFE: In major cities there are many bars, restaurants, nightclubs, theatres and cinemas. Nightlife may be more limited in the smaller villages and islands.
SPORT: Golf is one of the most popular national sports and St Andrew's has arguably the finest course in the world. Gleneagles and Troon are also excellent. **Fishing** is popular throughout the country and the salmon fishing in particular is widely regarded as being among the best in the world. **Spectator sports** include **rugby** and **football**. The Scottish countryside is also ideal for **birdwatching, walking** and **pony trekking**. There are also several **winter sports** centres, notably at Glencoe, the Nevis Range, Glenshee and Aviemore, in the Cairngorms.
SPECIAL EVENTS: The highlight of the cultural year in Scotland is the *Edinburgh Festival*, which runs during the last two weeks of August and the first week of September. Almost every room in the city large enough to hold an audience is in use during this time, and it is possible to see as many as ten shows in one day; these might range from a short open-air concert to a full-scale production by the RSC or the LSO. Accommodation in Edinburgh is booked up months in advance at this time. There are also many Highland Games during the summer, which include caber tossing and hammer-throwing competitions. The following is a selection of other events in Scotland (for a complete list contact the Scottish Tourist Board):
Apr 2-11 '93 *Edinburgh International Folk Festival*. **Apr 10-24** *International Science and Technology Festival*, Edinburgh. **Apr 30-May 22** *Mayfest*, Glasgow. **Jun 21-27** *Glasgow International Folk Festival*. **Jun 24-27** *Royal Highland Show*, Edinburgh. **Jul 6-10** *Bell's Scottish Open Golf*, Auchterarder. **Aug 6-28** *Military Tattoo*, Edinburgh. **Aug 14** *World Pipe Band Championships*, Glasgow. **Aug 27-28** *Cowal Highland Gathering* (Centenary Year), Dunoon. **Sep 4** *Braemar Royal Highland Gathering*, Braemar.
Note: Some of the above dates are provisional.

BUSINESS PROFILE

CONFERENCES/CONVENTIONS: In 1988 the Greater Glasgow Tourist Board and Convention Bureau was voted the UK's Best Convention Bureau by organisers. The Scottish Tourist Board has a number of publications for conference organisers. For information contact the Scottish Convention Bureau, c/o the Scottish Tourist Board, 23 Ravelston Terrace, Edinburgh EH4 3EU. Tel: (031) 343 1608. Fax: (031) 343 1844. Telex: 72272.
Note: See the general UK section for other business information.

CLIMATE

Scotland is rarely much colder than England, despite its more northerly latitude. The west tends to be wetter and warmer than the cool dry east. On upland areas snow is common in winter, and fog and mist may occur at any time of year.
Required clothing: Similar to the rest of the UK, according to season. Waterproofing advised throughout the year and warm clothing for the Highlands.

EDINBURGH Scotland (134m)

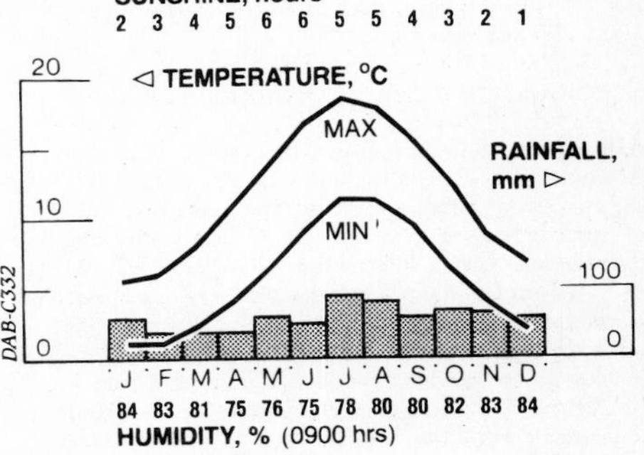

WALES

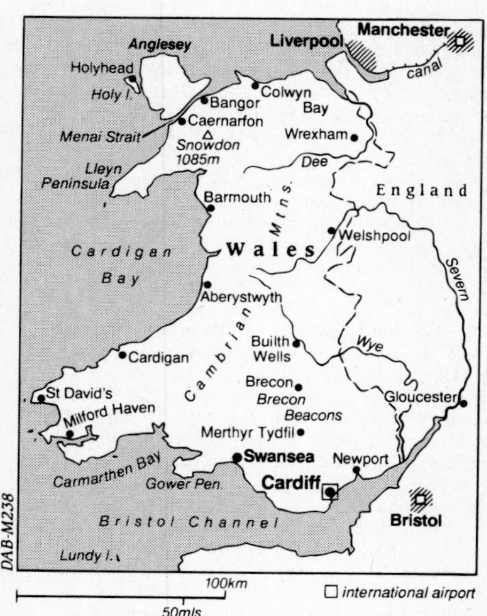

Location: Western Great Britain.

Wales Tourist Board
Brunel House
2 Fitzalan Road
Cardiff CF2 1UY
Tel: (0222) 499 909. Fax: (0222) 485 031.
Wales Tourist Board
c/o British Tourist Authority
7th Floor
551 Fifth Avenue
New York, NY
10176
Tel: (212) 986 2200 *or* 986 2266. Fax: (212) 986 1188.

AREA: 20,768 sq km (8018 sq miles).
POPULATION: 2,873,100 (1989 estimate).
POPULATION DENSITY: 138.3 per sq km.
CAPITAL: Cardiff. **Population:** 284,900 (1989).
GEOGRAPHY: Wales is a country of great geographical variation with many long stretches of attractive and often rugged coastline. South Wales is mainly known for its coal and steel but the western part of the coast between Camarthen Bay and St Davids is similar to that of the more pastoral west country of England, and backed by some equally beautiful countryside. The scenery of mid-Wales includes rich farming valleys, the broad sandy sweep of Cardigan Bay and rolling hill country. North Wales is one of the most popular tourist areas in the British Isles, with many lively coastal resorts. Inland, the region of Snowdonia has long been popular with walkers and climbers. Much of the central inland area of the country is mountainous, with some breathtaking scenery.
LANGUAGE: English, but at least a fifth of the population also speaks Welsh.
NOTE: *For information on time, electricity, communications, passport/visa, duty free, health, money and business see the general UK section above.*

PUBLIC HOLIDAYS

Public holidays observed in Wales are the same as for the rest of the UK (*see the general entry above*), with the addition of:
Mar 1 '93 St David's Day.

TRAVEL

AIR: Wales' international airport is ***Cardiff Wales Airport* (CWL).** Facilities include free flow-buffet and bar, bureau de change, duty-free, news and gift shop, restaurant, medical room and first aid, and facilities for the disabled. Airport Information: (0446) 711 111, ext 2201. **Train:** Local buses link the airport with Cardiff Central station, which is 12 miles away. The station is served by the Intercity network and regional lines, including a fast service to London Paddington. Tel: (0222) 228 000. **Coach:** Regular coach services operate to Cardiff Central Bus Station from London Victoria and other major destinations with connections to the rest of the country. **Local bus:** A local bus no X51 runs from Cardiff bus station to the airport on an hourly basis.
Taxi: Available through local operator *Panda Cars*. Tel: (0446) 710 693. **Car hire:** *Europcar* has an office at the airport. Tel: (0222) 497 111. **Private car:** Cardiff is reached on the M4 from London, exiting at Junction 33 and following the signs. Car-parking facilities are available at the airport for short- and long-term stays.
SEA: The main ports are Pembroke Dock and Fishguard (Dyfed) and Holyhead (Anglesey), all of which receive ferries from the Republic of Ireland.
RAIL: There are two main-line routes into Wales. One runs from London Paddington to Fishguard along the South Wales coast (branching at Whitland to serve Haverfordwest and Milford Haven), while the other links Holyhead with Chester and northeast England. In addition, the line from Cardiff to Chester (via Newport, Hereford and Shrewsbury) links the South Wales cities with Abergavenny in Gwent to Wrexham in Clwyd. There are also two smaller cross-country lines: these run from Shrewsbury to Welshpool, Aberystwyth, Barmouth, Harlech, Porthmadog and Pwllheli; and from Craven Arms (on the Shrewsbury to Ludlow line) through Llandrindod Wells and Llandovery down to the south coast to Swansea.
There are also a large number of local steam railways, rescued by railway enthusiasts during the Beeching era, known collectively as **The Great Little Trains of Wales.** The most famous of these is the one at Ffestiniog at Porthmadog in Snowdonia, which has lovingly restored locomotives and carriages from the last century. Others include the Welshpool and Llanfair Railway (in north Powys), the Fairbourne and Talyllyn Railways (both near Barmouth in Cardigan Bay) and the Bala Lake Railway. Wanderers' Tickets are available, giving access to all the railways for a specific period. For further information, contact The Great Little Trains of Wales, c/o Talyllyn Railway, Wharf Station, Tywyn, Gwynedd. Tel: (0654) 710 472. Fax: (0654) 711 755.
ROAD: The best road approach to Wales from southern England is via the M4 motorway, which runs from west London to Newport, Cardiff and Swansea, almost to Carmarthen. The A5 links London and the Midlands with the ferry port of Holyhead, and the A55 links Holyhead with Chester. The best cross-country road is probably the A44/A470 from Oxford to Aberystwyth. Many of the smaller roads are slow, and in upland areas may become impassable during bad weather.
Distances: From *London* to Cardiff is 250km (157 miles), to Fishguard is 420km (260 miles), to Holyhead is 430km (268 miles) and to Aberystwyth is 340km (210 miles).
URBAN: All the main cities have local bus services. There is a good network of local train services radiating from Cardiff.

ACCOMMODATION

HOTELS: All hotels are inspected by the Wales Tourist Board. **Grading:** Hotels in Wales are subject to the Wales Tourist Board's 'crown' classification scheme – which is part of the UK-wide classification scheme. The higher the crown rating, the greater the range of equipment, facilities and services on offer. The system is not intended as a guide to quality but only to show the level of facilities provided at each hotel. All hotels participating in this scheme are inspected annually. Further information may be obtained from the brochures produced by the Wales Tourist Board. Tel: (0222) 499 909. In addition, the Board's North, Mid- and South Wales regional offices have lists of accommodation available in their areas. For North Wales, tel: (0492) 531 731; Mid-Wales, tel: (0654) 702 653; and South Wales, tel: (0792) 781 212.
SELF-CATERING: There is a very wide range of self-catering accommodation, ranging from holiday villages in or near popular coastal resorts to remote cottages in the mountains of Snowdonia. Contact the regional offices referred to above for an up-to-date list. **Grading:** Accommodation is graded on a scale of 1 to 5 as follows: **1** – Standard. **2** – Approved. **3** – Good. **4** – Very good. **5** – Excellent.
CAMPING/CARAVANNING: There are over 300 caravan parks in the country, both permanent and touring parks and all sites referred to in accommodation lists or brochures supplied by tourist offices will meet certain minimum requirements. There are many campsites throughout the country. **Grading:** Sites are graded with from 1 to 5 'Q's reflecting quality, neatness and cleanliness but not necessarily facilities.

RESORTS & EXCURSIONS

Wales may be divided into three areas: South Wales, containing the capital Cardiff, the cities of Swansea and Newport, Camarthen Bay and the Brecon Beacons; Mid Wales, with the Cambrian Mountains and the attractive coastal resorts of Cardigan Bay; and North Wales, with the popular resorts of Llandudno and Rhyl, the island of Anglesey and the Snowdonia National Park, containing *Mount Snowdon*, the highest mountain in Wales. Cardiff is connected to London by road, rail and air and is a convenient starting point for a journey through Wales from south to north.

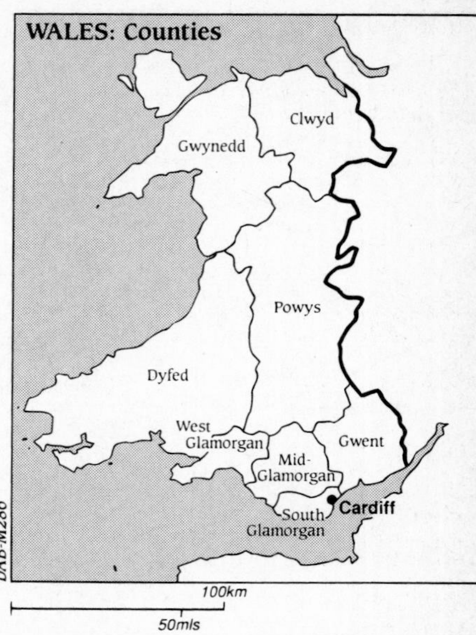

South Wales

Cardiff is the principality's capital and principal seaport. The castle, much of which dates back to the Middle Ages, was extensively added to during the 19th century, thus creating a strongly Victorian Gothic result. Cardiff also houses the *National Museum of Wales*, with Welsh archaeology, arts and crafts as well as European paintings. 8km (5 miles) west of Cardiff is **St Fagans** with its open-air *Welsh Folk Museum*.
Travelling towards England, the town of **Chepstow** straddles the border. The castle dates from the reign of King Edward I and the narrow streets are still in part enclosed by the medieval town walls. Nearby **Caerwent** is rich in Roman remains. Between Cardiff and the English border is *Newport*, the country's third largest town which has a 15th-century cathedral.
There are several resorts on the coast between Cardiff and Swansea with sandy beaches; these include *Barry*, *Porthcawl* and *Aberavon*, near Port Talbot.
Swansea is Wales' second city and a major cultural, industrial and shipping centre. Swansea has over 45 parks, a fact which only partly compensates for the grim industrial aspect of much of the city and the surrounding towns, but it is also a popular seaside resort, as well as being conveniently situated close to the *Gower Peninsula*. *The Mumbles*, almost a suburb of Swansea, is the main resort in this region. In the Penclawdd region, cockle-gathering is still carried on in the traditional way, on donkey-back. Other resorts on the Gower peninsula include *Oxwich* and *Port Eynon*.
The most popular inland destination in South Wales is the area of the *Brecon Beacons*, a national park stretching from the Vale of Towey to the Usk Valley. Brecon and Abergavenny are the major centres for touring the Brecon Beacons. There is a narrow gauge railway, the *Brecon Mountain Railway*, which runs for a few kilometres through the hills, giving superb views across the countryside. For more information, see under 'The Great Little Trains of Wales' in the *Travel* section above. West of Brecon, across the other side of the Black Mountains, is **Carmarthen**, a quiet country town set in gentle undulating countryside which comes alive on market days.
Across Carmarthen Bay is the resort town of **Tenby**, beyond which lies the old region of Pembroke. This part of the country was colonised by Normans, and from the 11th century onwards by weavers from Flanders. Henry Tudor, later to become Henry VII after the Battle of Bosworth, was born in *Pembroke Castle*, the remains of which still survive. The whole region has many castles, as well as several monasteries, abbeys and priories. The most famous religious building in the area, however, is undoubtedly the cathedral at **St David's,** founded in the late 12th century. St David's was for for many centuries a place of pilgrimage. Nearby are the larger towns of **Haverfordwest** and the deep-water port of **Milford Haven,** near which there are several island bird sanctuaries. To the north is the ferry port of **Fishguard**.

Mid-Wales

The town of **Cardigan** on Cardigan Bay is a pleasant market town which makes a good starting point for exploring Mid-Wales. Between Cardigan and Aberystwyth there are many small towns and villages, most of which are unpronounceable to non Welsh-speakers, with small rocky coves and sandy beaches. The university town of **Aberystwyth**, about midway round the bay, is a popular resort and base for visits to *Devil's Bridge*, one of the most notable beauty spots in the British Isles which is linked to the town by a narrow-gauge steam railway. There are two other narrow-gauge steam railways close by; the *Talyllyn Railway*, which runs for about 10km (16 miles) through beautiful countryside in the hills behind the town of Tywyn where it terminates. **Barmouth** was once one of the most popular resorts in the British Isles and was frequented by, amongst others, Charles Darwin and Lord Tennyson. There are good beaches, both in the town and also near *Dyffryn Ardudwy*, a few kilometres to the north. Inland from Barmouth is **Dolgellau**, at the foot of Cader Idris, a small and attractive market town. Other towns of interest inland from Aberystwyth or Barmouth include **Builth Wells**, an important cattle trading town; **Strata Florida Abbey**; the towns of **Lampeter** and **Tregaron** on the *River Teifi* and **Llandrindod Wells**, one of many towns with therapeutic waters, and Wales' leading spa in the late 18th and early 19th centuries, leaving a legacy of elegant architecture to be enjoyed by its latter-day inhabitants and visitors. Beyond Barmouth, on the northern tip of Cardigan Bay, is **Harlech**, famous both for its castle which overlooks the peaks of Snowdonia and for the song 'Men of Harlech', referring to the defence of the castle in the 15th century. South of Harlech is **Llanbedr**, a popular yachting centre.

North Wales

This region is one of the oldest-established tourist areas in the British Isles, and resorts such as **Llandudno** and **Rhyl** are still exceedingly popular.

North of the *Mawddoch Estuary* is the town of **Porthmadog**, a holiday resort with excellent facilities. It has the oldest independent narrow-gauge railway in the world, now known as the *Ffestiniog Railway*, which carries thousands of visitors each year. West from Porthmadog is the *Lign peninsula*, where there are many good beaches, particularly on the south coast, at towns such as **Criccieth** (Lloyd George's birthplace), **Pwllheli** (the end of the railway line), **Abersoch, Aberdaron,** and, on the northern coast, **Nefyn** and **Clynnog-Fawr.** Further north, facing the Isle of Anglesey across the Menai Strait, is **Caernarfon**, a town still surrounded by 13th-century walls and dominated by the 13th-century castle. It was here that Prince Charles was invested as Prince of Wales in 1969. The **Isle of Anglesey,** once known as Mona, is notable for a remarkable bridge, the ferry port of **Holyhead** and the town of **Llanfair PG**, the abbreviation for its real name, whose 58 letters make it the longest place name in the world (the sign on the platform of the the local railway station is worth photographing). The main town on the island, **Beaumaris**, has excellent leisure facilities and a castle built by Edward I. Back on the mainland on the other side of the Strait is the university and cathedral city of **Bangor;** its attractions include a huge doll collection housed in *Penrhyn Castle*.

The **Snowdonia National Park,** 2200 sq km (840 sq miles) of some of the most beautiful countryside in the British Isles, with 14 peaks over 915m (3000ft), the highest of which is *Mount Snowdon*. The Snowdon Mountain Railway, running from Llanberis, is certainly the least exacting way of reaching the summit of the mountain. Other attractions in the region include *Betws-y-Coed*, in the Gwydyr Forest; *Bethesda*, southeast of Bangor; *Bala Lake*, which also has a narrow-gauge railway; and *Beddgelert* in the Nant Gwynant valley.

On the north coast, continuing east from Bangor, is the historic town of **Conwy**, with a mighty medieval castle and complete medieval town walls. Nearby is the superb *Bodnant Gardens*. At the other side of Great Ormes Head is **Llandudno,** one of the country's most popular tourist resorts. It has almost every possible facility and amenity as well as being within striking distance of the beautiful hinterland which includes the Snowdonia National Park. The chain of resorts continues almost unbroken for several miles; *Rhos-on-Sea, Colwyn Bay, Abergele* and *Prestatyn* all have good beaches, and in particular **Rhyl**, a town with a 5km- (3-mile) long promenade and extensive leisure and recreation facilities. It is also a good base for excursions to *St Asaph*, a city with the smallest medieval cathedral in Britain. Further east lies *Bagillt* and *Flint*, once the capital of the tiny county of the same name.

To the southeast of Flint is **Wrexham**, a kilometre south of which is *Erdigg*, a 17th-century squire's house containing much of the traditional furniture and with many of the outbuildings still in their original condition and in working order. Further south is *Chirk Castle*, a 14th-century Marcher fortress built to guard the frontier between England and Wales which it straddles. To the west and the south is an area of great natural beauty, including the forests of *Dyfnant*, *Ceiriog* and *Penllyn*. Southwest of Wrexham is **Llangollen**, set in forested landscape overlooking the salmon-rich River Dee and containing a bridge that is a masterpiece of medieval engineering. It is also the setting for the International Musical Eisteddfod – for further information, see the *Social Profile* section below. Nearby is the 13th-century *Vale Crucis Abbey* and the beautiful *Horseshoe Pass*. Due south of Llangollen is **Welshpool**, an attractive town with many Georgian buildings and a narrow-gauge railway. South of the town is *Powys Castle*, built in the 13th century and modernised during the 16th.

SOCIAL PROFILE

FOOD & DRINK: In most major centres, British and continental food is available. Welsh cooking is, in general simple, with abundant fresh local produce, particularly meat and fish. Near the coast, seafood is also widely available. Local dishes include *Welsh rarebit*, *leek soup* and *laver bread*, which is made with seaweed. **Drink:** In some Welsh counties, drinking laws differ from the rest of the UK and it may not be possible to buy alcohol on Sundays except in a hotel in which you are a guest.
NIGHTLIFE: In general similar to that in an English town of comparable size, with bars, restaurants and cinemas being common in the cities and large towns.
SPORT: Rugby is the national sport, and is played to the very highest level of skill. There are a huge number of local clubs and the international team plays matches at the national stadium *Cardiff Arms Park*. **Cricket** (Glamorgan CCC) and, to a lesser extent, **football** are also popular spectator sports. There are many **golf** courses, **tennis** courts and sports centres throughout the country. **Sea fishing** is good off all coasts and there are also many opportunities for **coarse** and **game fishing** inland; the areas of Snowdonia, Brecon and the River Teifi (Cardigan) are among the most popular.
SPECIAL EVENTS: Many Welsh villages hold an *Eisteddfod* once a year – a contest for local poets, singers and musicians. All but the largest ones are generally only advertised inside the town itself but visitors are welcome to attend. The largest of these are:
Apr 20-May 16 '93 *Holyhead Arts Festival*. **Jun 13-19** *Cardiff Singer of the World Competition*. **Jul 6-11** *International Musical Eisteddfod*, Llangollen. **Jul 19-22** *Royal Welsh Agricultural Show*, Buith Wells. **Jul 19-31** *Gower Festival*, Gower, West Glamorgan. **Jul 31-Aug 7** *Royal National Eisteddfod*, Builth Wells. **Aug 13-15** *Brecon Jazz Festival*, Powys. **Aug 21-29** *Llandrindod Wells Victorian Festival*. **Aug 27-30** *Brecon Cathedral Flower Festival* (900th Anniversary of the Cathedral), Powys. **Sep 9-11** *24th Annual Welsh Antiques Fair*, Brecon. **Sep 19-25** *North Wales Music Festival*, St Asaph, Clwyd. **Sep 27-Nov 6** *Swansea Music Festival*. **May '94** *May Day*.
Note: For further details on events contact the relevant tourist board. Accommodation at festival times should be booked well in advance.

CLIMATE

Wales tends to be wetter than England, and has slightly less sunshine. The coastal areas, however, can be very warm in summer. Conditions in upland areas can be dangerous and changeable at all times of the year.
Required clothing: Similar to the rest of the UK, according to season. Waterproofing advised throughout the year, and warm clothes are required for upland areas.

CARDIFF Wales (62m)

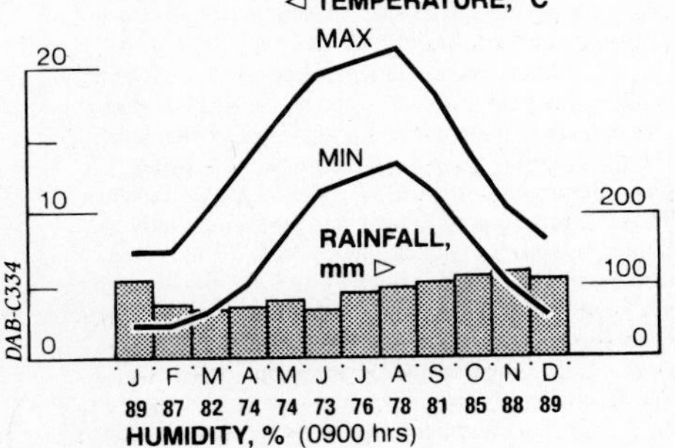

NORTHERN IRELAND

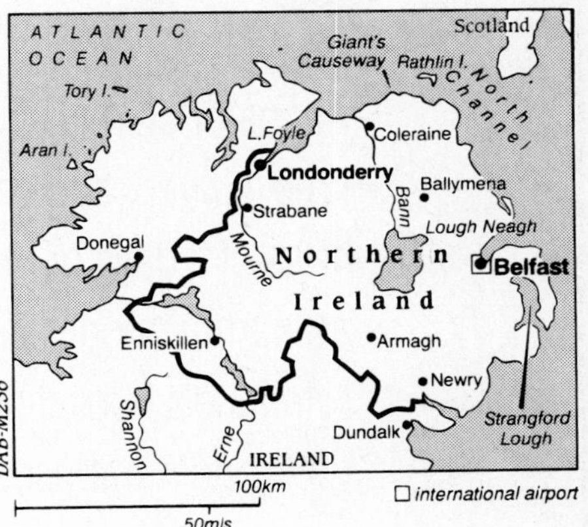

Location: Northern Ireland.

Note: Due to the political situation in Northern Ireland, visitors should take care when visiting certain parts of the main cities and the border area. No problems should arise providing the visitor follows local advice and avoids expressing dogmatic opinions on political or religious topics.

Northern Ireland Tourist Board/Business Centre
11 Berkeley Street
London W1X 6BU
Tel: (071) 493 0601. Fax: (071) 499 3731. Opening hours 0800-1700 Monday to Friday;
or
St Anne's Court
59 North Street
Belfast BT1 1NB
Tel: (0232) 231 221. Fax: (0232) 240 960. Telex: 748087.
Tourist Information Centre
Ireland Desk British Travel Centre
4-12 Lower Regent Street
London SW1Y 4PQ
Tel: (071) 839 8416/7. Fax: (071) 839 6179. Opening hours: 0900-1830 Monday to Friday, 1000-1600 Saturday and Sunday.
Northern Ireland Tourist Board
Suite 500, 5th Floor
276 Fifth Avenue
New York, NY
10001
Tel: (212) 686 6250. Fax: (212) 686 8061.

AREA: 14,147 sq km (5462 sq miles).
POPULATION: 1,583,000 (1988 estimate).
POPULATION DENSITY: 111.9 per sq km.
CAPITAL: Belfast. **Population:** 299,600 (1987).
GEOGRAPHY: Northern Ireland contains some beautiful scenery, from the rugged coastline in the north and northeast to the gentle fruit-growing regions of Armagh. To the west are the Sperrin Mountains and the lake of Fermanagh, where the winding River Erne provides excellent fishing. The high moorland plateau of Antrim in the northeast gives way to the Glens further south and to the Drumlin country of County Down; further south still the Mountains of Mourne stretch down to the sea.
LANGUAGE: English.
NOTE: *For information on time, electricity, communications, duty free, health, public holidays and passport/visa see the general UK entry above. No passports are needed for travel between Northern Ireland and the mainland.*

MONEY

NOTE: For travelling around and staying at small hotels or farmhouses, cash is needed. Elsewhere, as in England, cheques backed by a banker's card are widely accepted. For **currency, credit cards** etc, see the general UK entry above.
Banking hours: In very small villages, the bank may open two or three days a week only, so aim to get cash in the bigger centres.

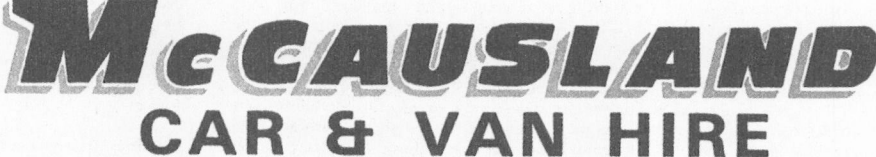

Changing money outside banking hours: *Thomas Cook*, 11 Donegall Place, Belfast 1, is open 0900-1730 Monday to Saturday. Some hotels will also change money, but *Thomas Cook* and the banks give the best rate of exchange.

PUBLIC HOLIDAYS

Public holidays observed in Northern Ireland are the same as those observed in the rest of the UK *(see the general entry above)* with the addition of:
Mar 17 '93 St Patrick's Day. **Jul 12** Orangemen's Day.
Mar 17 '94 St Patrick's Day.

TRAVEL

AIR: Northern Ireland's international airport is ***Belfast International Airport (BFS),*** 29km (18 miles) northwest of the city centre. Airport information: (08494) 22888.
Facilities include bureau de change, duty-free shop, restaurant/buffet, bar, general shops, emergency medical services, nursing mothers' room, wheelchairs for the disabled, freeport facilities and business centre. *Belfast International Airport* has been designated a freeport for Northern Ireland. The 70-acre freeport site is located in the northwestern corner of the airport complex and has first-class access by road as well as internal access from the aircraft movements area and freight village. Freeport Northern Ireland operates on a 24-hour, 7-days-a-week basis. A modern, well-appointed business and conference centre operates five days per week and on request at weekends. Full state-of-the-art office equipment, secretarial services and restaurant facilities are available – for parties/groups of up to 100. **Train:** There is at present no direct rail link to Belfast International Airport, but trains run from Londonderry, Coleraine, Portrush, Ballymoney, Ballymena and Belfast to Antrim (8km/5 miles away) from where a taxi may be hired to the airport. There are also train connections from Lurgan, Portadown, Dundalk, Drogheda and Dublin. **Bus:** *Airbus* (Ulsterbus) runs to city centre Monday to Saturday half-hourly (0645-2215) and Sunday hourly (0715-2215). **Taxi:** Travel time to city centre – 35 minutes. Taxis are available for hire outside the main airport building. **Car hire:** *Godfrey Davis/Europcar, Avis, Hertz* and *McCausland Car Hire* are represented at the airport. **Private car:** The M1 provides the main link with Fermanagh and the west of the Province whilst forming part of the journey to and from Dublin and the east coast of Ireland. The M2 is the airport's main link with the centre of Belfast and to Londonderry, 72 miles (116km) to the northwest. There is nearby car parking for short and long stays. Access is from the M1 and M2 (parking is available) or train to Antrim and then taxi. Regular bus services run to the city centre. Car hire and taxi services are available.
The small airport at *Belfast Harbour* is handy for flights to some provincial British cities, such as Liverpool and Manchester and also the Isle of Man. Regular train and bus services run to the city centre. Tel: (0232) 457 745.
Note: For approximate durations of a selection of domestic flights from Belfast, see the *Travel* section in the general UK entry above.
SEA: Two ferry companies operate direct services between mainland Europe and Ireland. *Irish Ferries* operate between Le Havre and Rosslare with three departures per week in each direction (approximate travel time – 22 hours). Their ships also ply between Cherbourg and Rosslare and a peak summer-only Cork-Lettaire service. *Brittany Ferries* operate the Roscoff–Cork route with one departure per week in each direction during the summer season only (travel time – 16 hours).
When travelling via Great Britain to Northern Ireland there is a choice of three services across the Irish Sea: Stranraer (southern Scotland) to Larne, frequent daily services by *Sealink Scotland* (2 hours 15 minutes); and Cairnryan (southern Scotland) to Larne, frequent daily services (2 hours) by *P&O European Ferries*.
In addition there are daily crossings between Stranraer and Belfast Harbour (1 hour 30 minutes) by *Seacat*. Northern Ireland's only inhabited island is Rathlin, a few kilometres off the north coast. There are frequent passenger boats between Ballycastle and the island.
At peak holiday times a sailing/regulation ticket is required as well as a travel ticket. Check when booking. It is always advisable to book your journey both ways before leaving home.
RAIL: There are three main rail routes from Belfast Central Station north to Londonderry City via Ballymena and Coleraine, east to Bangor along the shores of Belfast Lough, and south to Dublin, in the Irish Republic, via Lisburn and Newry. The Belfast – Dublin non-stop express takes two hours. There are six trains daily in both directions (only three on Sundays). The busiest times are holiday weekends and the first and last trains on Fridays and Sundays, when it is best to reserve seats. Rail runabout tickets (seven days unlimited travel on scheduled rail services from April to October) are available from main Northern Ireland railway stations.
A special rail-link bus runs between York Road and the Central Station regularly from 0730-2030 Monday to Saturday. Outside those hours other buses will take you to Oxford Street bus station or City Hall.
For information on timetables for *all* rail services, contact Northern Ireland Railways Information Centre, Central Station, East Bridge Street, Belfast BT1 3PB. Tel: (0232) 230 310. Open until 1800.
ROAD: Bus: Northern Ireland has an excellent bus network and there are particularly good bus links between those towns which are not served by rail. Belfast has two main bus stations: Great Victoria Street, near Europa Hotel and Oxford Street, near the main rail station. Express buses run from Belfast to Antrim, Armagh, Ballymena, Banbridge, Coleraine, Cookstown, Dungannon, Enniskillin, Hillsborough, Larne (port), Londonderry, Lurgan, Magherafelt, Newry, Omagh, Portadown, Portrush (near Giant's Causeway) and Strabane. In July and August *Ulsterbus* run day and half-day tours to the glens of Antrim, Antrim Coast and Giant's Causeway, Fermanagh Lakeland, the Mountains of Mourne, Ards Peninsula and Armagh. Tours leave Belfast (Great Victoria Street Bus Station) seven days a week. Excursions include Lammas Fair and Ulster Grand Prix. Cheap day-returns include Causeway, Newcastle and Cushendun (from Oxford Street Bus Station) and unlimited travel bus tickets. Contact *Ulsterbus:* (0232) 320 011. *Citybus* enquiries (Belfast area only): (0232) 246 485.
Traffic regulations: Driving is on the left. The speed limit is 30mph (48kmph) in towns and cities unless you see a sign showing 40mph (64kmph) or 50mph (80kmph). On country roads the limit is 60mph (96kmph); on dual carriageways, trunk roads and motorways 70 mph (112kmph) is the speed limit unless signs show otherwise.
Breakdowns: If the car is rented, contact the rental company. If you are a member of the Continental equivalent of the *Automobile Association (AA)* you can contact their 24-hour breakdown service. Tel: (0800) 887 766. The *Royal Automobile Club (RAC)* provides a similar service. Tel: (0232) 240 261. They can be contacted from their roadside phones or from any call box. If you are not a member of the motoring organisation you should consult the Yellow Pages for breakdown services.
Parking: Permitted where there is a blue 'P' sign, which indicates a car park in towns or a lay-by at the roadside

outside towns. You can park elsewhere on the street except when there is a single yellow line, when parking is permitted only at the times shown on the yellow signs nearby; or when there is a double yellow line which prohibits all parking. Control Zones, which are usually in town centres, are indicated by yellow signs 'Control Zone. No Unattended Parking'. An unattended car in a Control Zone is treated as a security risk. Never park on zigzag markings near pedestrian crossings. In some towns you may find the centre sealed off at certain times, particularly overnight. Alternative routes will be signposted.
Car hire: The main firms – *Avis*, *Hertz* and *Europcar* – all operate in Northern Ireland and have desks at Aldergrove Airport with cars available on the spot. There is also a host of smaller firms.
Taxis: Available at main stations, ports and Belfast Airport and are also bookable by telephone in larger towns and cities.

ACCOMMODATION

A wide range of accommodation is available in Northern Ireland. Contact the Northern Ireland Tourist Board for brochures and booklets giving full lists of available accommodation.
HOTELS: Brochures from the Northern Ireland Tourist Board give full details of services. All establishments belong to the Northern Ireland Hotel and Catering Association.
Grading: The Northern Irish Tourist Board operates a 'star' classification system which is used throughout their publications. The main hotel classifications are as follows:
4-star: High standard of comfort and service, including room service and well-equipped premises. Food and beverages are obliged to meet the most exacting standards.
3-star: Good facilities and a wide range of services in comfortable surroundings, including en suite bathroom. Refreshments are available during the day.
2-star: Good facilities, offering satisfactory standards of accommodation and food, with en suite bathroom.
1-star: Acceptable standards of accommodation and food. Some bedrooms offer en suite bathroom.
For further information, contact the Northern Ireland Hotel and Caterers Association, 108-110 Midland Buildings, Whitla Street, Belfast BT15 1JP. Tel: (0232) 351 110. Fax: (0232) 351 509.
FARM & COUNTRY HOUSE HOLIDAYS: This is currently one of the most popular forms of holidaying in Northern Ireland. The *Northern Ireland Farm & Country Holidays Association* produces an accommodation voucher, valid for bed and breakfast for one night. The brochure *Farm & Country Holidays* can be obtained from the Northern Ireland Tourist Board. *The Northern Ireland Town & Seaside House Association* has houses in some of Northern Ireland's most beautiful areas, from the Mourne Mountains to the Causeway Coast, from the Fermanagh Lakes to the Ards Peninsula, each house offering good home-cooking and a traditional Ulster welcome. The Association offers a Tour Operator rate and is happy to arrange 'go as you please' itineraries. A brochure, *Town and Seaside House Holidays*, is obtainable from the Northern Ireland Tourist Board. For further information contact: The Northern Ireland Farm and Country Holidays Association, Greenmount Lodge, 58 Greenmount Road, Gortaclare, Omagh BT79 0YE. Tel: (0662) 841 325.
SELF-CATERING: There are self-catering establishments in all of Northern Ireland's six counties. For further information contact Mrs Reid at the Northern Ireland Self-Catering Association. Tel: (0365) 658 181.
CAMPING/CARAVANNING: There are over 100 caravan and camp sites throughout the six counties of Northern Ireland. Details of the prices and facilities are contained in an information bulletin *Camping & Caravan Parks*, available from the Northern Ireland Tourist Board. The Northern Ireland Forest Service issues permits for camping in forest areas. Contact Forest Services, Department of Agriculture, Dundonald House, Newtowners Road, Belfast BT4 3SB. Tel: (0232) 650 111, ext 456.
YOUTH HOSTELS: For further information contact: The Youth Hostel Association of Northern Ireland, 56 Bradbury Place, Belfast BT7 1RU. Tel: (0232) 324 733. Fax: (0232) 439 699.

RESORTS & EXCURSIONS

Northern Ireland, often referred to as the 'six counties', is described county by county in this guide, with an additional section on *Farm Study Tours*.

Antrim

To the southeast of the county, **Belfast** provides 6-day shopping and city entertainment in the shape of theatres, cinema, a wide range of restaurants, the *Grand Opera House* and all the other attractions of any capital city. To the northwest lies the *Causeway Coast*, with its holiday resorts and the *Giant's Causeway* as the dominant

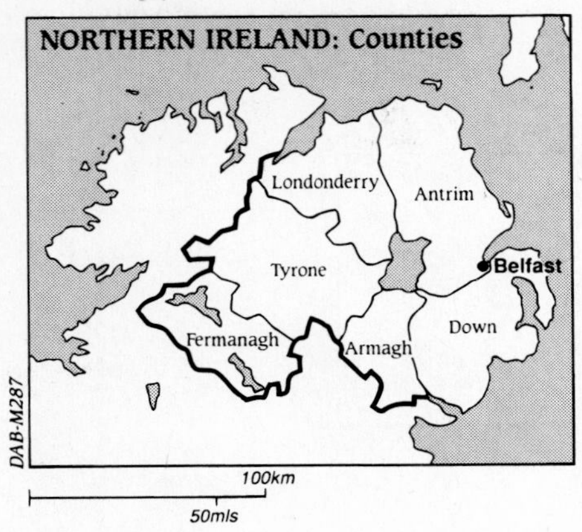

feature. There are many sleepy villages between the nine glens of Antrim and the spectacular coast road, and inland are towns like Antrim with its ancient round tower and splendid park. There is a lakeside steam railway at *Shane's Castle*, golf at **Portrush** and elsewhere throughout the county, as well as bathing, boating and fishing along its 160km (100 miles) of coast.

Down

Attractions include the *Folk and Transport Museum* at **Cultra** and the ancient shrines of St Patrick's country around the cathedral hill of *Downpatrick*; the flat sandy beaches of the *Ards Peninsula* and the beautiful *Mountains of Mourne;* lively **Newcastle** with its seaside festival; and stately homes like *Mount Stewart* and *Castle Ward* open to visitors. At **Rostrevor,** a small sheltered resort on *Carlingford Lough*, orchids and palm trees flourish in the balmy climate. Horseriding, sailing, angling and golf are within easy reach, also motor racing at **Kirkistown** and sea angling in Strangford Lough.

Armagh

Northern Ireland's smallest county rises gently from *Lough Neagh's* banks, southwards through apple orchards, farmland and hill forest to the rocky summit of *Slieve Gullion*, mountain of Cuchulain. The crown of **Armagh** is the city itself, a religious capital older than Canterbury, with two cathedrals, the *Georgian Mall* and the *Planetarium/Space Centre*. **Craigavon** has a leisure centre and ski-slope, with lakes for watersports; and there is sailing on *Lough Neagh* and angling and canoeing on the *Blackwater River*.

Fermanagh

Ulster's lakeland spreads its web of waterways, islands, forest and glen, castles and abbey ruins right across the county. **Enniskillen**, county town and shopping centre, strides the narrows between Upper and Lower Lough Erne. From there pleasure boats run daily cruises in summer. Golf, sailing, water-skiing and even pleasure flying are available nearby. Fishermen need no reminder that these are the waters where record catches are made. Two of Ireland's finest houses, *Florence Court* and *Castle Coole*, are open to the public. The nearby *Marble Arch Caves* were opened to the public for the first time in May 1985 and the tour begins with an underground boat trip through the caves (opening times: 0900-1800 September to May, 0900-2200 June to August). Visitors to the old pottery at **Belleek** can watch craftsmen at work on fine porcelain.

Londonderry

This is a fertile agricultural county, with small farms scattered across the broad sweeping land, and long Atlantic beaches. The city of **Derry** is best known for its massive ring of fortified walls and 'singing pubs'. In the county's northeast corner is **Coleraine** (with one of the main campuses of the University of Ulster), conveniently close to the seaside resorts of **Portstewart** and **Castlerock** for sea angling, golf and children's amusements. For rewarding scenic drives the *Sperrin Mountains* are best approached from Limavady and the beautiful Roe Valley Country Park. The *Bann River* is noted for trout and salmon.

Tyrone

Between the Sperrins in the north and the green Clogher Valley with its village cathedral in the south lies a region of great historical interest. The county's associations with the USA are recalled in the *Ulster-American Folk Park* near **Omagh**. Gray's old printing shop at **Strabane** still contains its 19th-century presses. A mysterious ceremonial site of stone circles and cairns near *Davagh Forest* has recently been uncovered and there are other Stone Age and Bronze Age remains in the area. There are forest parks, *Gortin Glen* and *Drum Manor*, for driving or rambling, excellent trout and salmon waters near Newtonstewart, market towns for shopping and recreation. **Dungannon** is notable for its fine glassware, Tyrone Crystal.

Farm Study Tours

Northern Ireland is primarily an agricultural country and is world-famous for its farming techniques. Study tours can be arranged for specialised or general visits with guides and experts on hand. Options for Study Tours: Greenmount, Loughry and Enniskillen Colleges of Agriculture offer research facilities on residential courses or visit the research establishment at Loughgall, County Armagh, Hillsborough, County Down, Cross-na-Creevy, Castlereagh, the Northern Ireland Pig Testing Station, Antrim and the Veterinary Research Laboratories at Stormont, Belfast. Major horticulture centres include Greenmount, Grovelands, Balmoral or Loughgall. Fane Valley, Fair Country Fruit Growers and Killyman Cooperatives are also well worth a visit, as is the Ulster Folk and Transport Museum.

SOCIAL PROFILE

FOOD & DRINK: The best value for money meals in Ulster are to be had at lunchtime (midday), when many restaurants and pubs offer special menus. Most Ulster families have high tea at about 1800 and many hotels and restaurants offer the same. High tea usually consists of a lightly cooked meal (an Ulster fry – perhaps eggs, sausages, ham or fish with chips) and a wide variety of bread, scones and cakes. Dinner is served from about 1900. Typical Northern Ireland foods include shellfish, home-made vegetable soups, potato dishes, dried seaweed, locally grown fruit and home-baked cakes and pastries. A useful booklet is *Where to Eat in Northern Ireland*, available from newsagents and Tourist Information centres, which lists all the places where food is served, a price indication and brief description of the sort of food. It is advisable to book ahead for the more popular restaurants, especially towards the weekend. **Drink:** The pubs are open all day 1130-2300 Monday to Saturday and 1230-1430/1900-2200 Sunday with half an hour 'drinking up' time. Popular drinks are, of course, *Guinness* – a dark heavy stout with a creamy head – and *whiskey* (Northern Ireland also boasts the world's oldest whiskey distillery at Bushmills). Irish whiskey is often drunk along with a bottle of stout. Real ale fans can try *Hilden* produced at Lisburn and obtainable locally.
NIGHTLIFE: There are summer theatres in Newcastle and Portrush, plus the Riverside Theatre at Coleraine. The Belfast Festival at Queen's (three weeks in November each year) is Europe's biggest arts festival after Edinburgh. There is an Autumn festival in Armagh and Londonderry and towns like Newry, Omagh and Enniskillen have first-rate theatre and music. Traditional Irish music in 'singing pubs' provides a good evening's entertainment in many places, particularly Belfast and Londonderry.
SHOPPING: Shops in Belfast city centre are open 0900-1730 six days a week (late-night shopping on Thursday). Other cities and towns close half day one day a week (it differs from town to town) and some small shops close at lunchtime. Modern shopping centres on the outskirts of towns have late night shopping to 2100 Thursday and Friday. Shopping bags and contents may be examined at the door of big stores. Ulster is well known for its pure Irish linen; cut-glass goblets, decanters, bowls; creamy Belleek pottery; handwoven tweed; pure wool jumpers and cardigans hand-knitted in traditional patterns; hand-embroidered wall hangings; Carrickmacross lace and silver jewellery.
SPORT: Fishing: Sea fishing is popular all along the coast and skippered boats of all sizes can be hired at most resorts. Strangford Lough is famous for its skate and tope. Carlingford Lough is nearly as good and the coast of Belfast Lough is dotted with sea angling clubs. There are superb waters for river and lake fishing, particularly in the Mournes area of Down, the Glens of Antrim and the River Bann. In most areas a rod licence and a coarse fishing permit are necessary. Day permits are available. Check at the nearest tackle shop. **Golf:** Some of the best golf courses are situated on the coast – at Whitehead, Bangor, Royal Portrush, Ballycastle, Royal County Down at Newcastle and the Chairndhu Club near to Larne. Weekly and daily rates for playing on the courses are available from the club itself or the nearest tourist information centre. **Walking:** There is a multitude of walks around Northern Ireland – from the Mourne Mountains and forest parks in County Down to the nine Glens in County Antrim. The Ulster Way is an 800km (500-mile) walking route around Northern Ireland and various walking holidays are arranged throughout the summer. **Sub-aqua:** Northern Ireland can offer the

experienced diving enthusiast several areas to explore; these include Strangford Lough, some 29km (18 miles) long and averaging 6km (3.5 miles) wide, a fascinating underwater world with many contrasting dive sites. The long history of sea traffic has left a legacy of wrecks in and around the Lough such as the 'Lees' wreck, an old liberty ship now lying at 12m (39ft), or the remains of the largest vessel wrecked on the Co Down coast, the American troopship 'Georgetown Victory'. Also of interest to experienced divers is the rugged, towering coast of Rathlin Island and Northern Ireland's famous north coast. **Cruising:** Loch Erne has in recent years become very popular for cruising holidays and several tour operators and local companies can arrange holidays. Contact the Tourist Board for further details. **Other sports:** Leisure centres have been springing up in most Ulster towns over the past few years. They have facilities for squash, badminton, tennis, gymnastics and other sports. There is also hang-gliding, gliding and rock climbing in the Mournes, Co Down; gliding, hang-gliding and parascending at Magilligan, Bellarena and Aghadowey, Co Londonderry; water-skiing on the River Bann at Coleraine; archery at Groomsport; canoeing at Bangor and Newcastle; pony trekking in the mountains and forests around Newcastle and Castlewellan, North Down coast and the Causeway Coast.

SPECIAL EVENTS: The following is a selection of the major festivals and other special events celebrated annually in Northern Ireland. For a complete list, contact the Northern Ireland Tourist Board.

Mar 17 '93 *St Patrick's Day Celebrations.* **Apr 10-13** *Circuit of Ireland International Motor Rally*, Newcastle. **May 3** *Belfast Marathon.* **May 9-15** *P&O European Ferries Classic Fishing Festival*, Fermanagh. **May 12-14** *Royal Ulster Show* (agricultural show), King's Hall, Belfast. **May 25-30** *British Amateur Open Golf Championships*, Royal Portrush, Causeway Coast. **Jun 7-11** *Black Bush Amateur Golf Tournament*, Causeway Coast. **Jul 5** *Pearl International, Athletics Meeting*, Mary Peter's Track, Belfast. **Jul 23-25** *Irish Powerboat Grand Prix*, Belfast. **Aug 26-29** *Northern Ireland Game Fair* (European Horse Trials Championships), Templepatrick. **Aug 30-31** *Oul 'Lammas Fair* (ancient crafts and livestock fair), Ballycastle. **Sep 7-18** *Ideal Home Exhibition*, Belfast. **Sep 10-12** *Belfast Folk Festival.* **Oct 2** *Mounthill Fair*, Larne. **Nov 2-4** *Belfast Festival at Queen's.* **Mar 17 '94** *St Patrick's Day.*

BUSINESS PROFILE

ECONOMY: The Northern Ireland economy has traditionally been divided between manufacturing, concentrated in shipbuilding and aerospace in the east of the province, and agriculture, which is prevalent throughout. The province is one of the poorest regions of the UK and suffered disproportionately under the recession of the early 1980s. Central government and European support have produced some improvement in Northern Ireland's economic fortunes, but the hoped-for boom in advanced technological industries (parallel to that in the Irish Republic) has not happened and the security situation continues to deter many would-be investors.

COMMERCIAL INFORMATION: The following organisation can offer advice: Northern Ireland Chamber of Commerce and Industry, Chamber of Commerce House, 22 Great Victoria Street, Belfast BT2 7BJ. Tel: (0232) 244 113. Fax: (0232) 247 024.

CLIMATE

In general, the weather is similar to the rest of the United Kingdom, but Northern Ireland tends to have less sunshine and more rain. Extremes of temperature are rare but conditions can be changeable.

Required clothing: Similar to the rest of the UK, according to season. Waterproofs are advisable throughout the year.

BELFAST N.Ireland (67m)

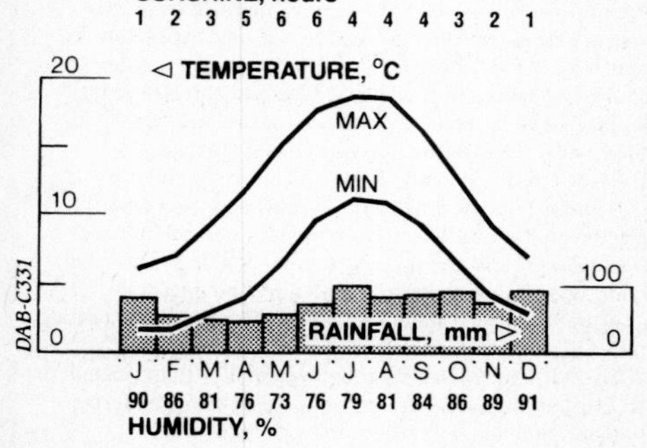

ISLE OF MAN

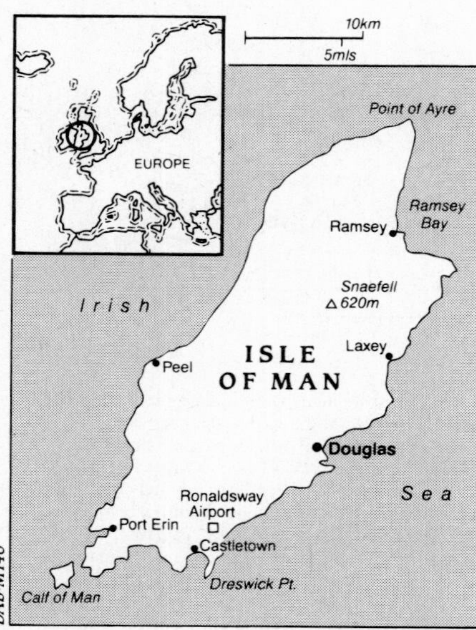

Location: Irish Sea.

Isle of Man Tourist Board
Sea Terminal Buildings
Douglas
Isle of Man
Tel: (0624) 674 323. Fax: (0624) 672 872. Telex: 637793 FG.

AREA: 572 sq km (221 sq miles).
POPULATION: 64,282 (1986).
POPULATION DENSITY: 112.4 per sq km.
CAPITAL: Douglas. **Population:** 20,368 (1986).
GEOGRAPHY: The Isle of Man is situated in the Irish Sea, 114km (71 miles) from Liverpool and 133km (83 miles) from Dublin. The island has a mountain range down the middle, the highest peak being Snaefell at 620m (2036ft) and a flat northern plain to the Point of Ayre, the most northerly point. The Calf of Man, an islet off the southwest coast, is administered as a nature reserve and bird sanctuary by the Manx Museum and National Trust.
LANGUAGE: Manx Gaelic, the indigenous language, is an offshoot of Scots and Irish Gaelic. At one time spoken by all the Manx, the tongue was replaced by English during the last century, and now only 50 or so people speak it. On Tynwald Day, summaries of the new laws are read out in Manx and English. Manx Gaelic evening classes are regularly held, and a weekly radio programme and newspaper column appear in the language.
TIME: GMT (GMT + 1 from March 29 to October 31).
ELECTRICITY: 220 volts AC, 50Hz.
COMMUNICATIONS: Telephone: To telephone the Isle of Man from the UK, the STD (area) code is 0624. **Fax:** Services are available. **Post:** Services are administered by the Isle of Man Post Office Authority which issues its own postage stamps, recognised internationally under the auspices of the Universal Postal Union. Only Isle of Man Post Office Authority stamps are valid for postal purposes in the Island. **Press:** There are several local papers published on the island and English papers are widely available.

PASSPORT/VISA

No passports are required for travel between the UK and the Isle of Man. See the *Passport/Visa* section of the general UK entry above.

MONEY

Currency: The Isle of Man Government issues its own decimal coinage, and currency notes of £50, £20, £10 and £1, all of which are on a par with the UK's equivalents. The coins and notes of England, Scotland and Northern Ireland circulate freely in the Island. The coins and notes of Eire are not equivalent to Manx or UK currency, although they may be accepted at the appropriate exchange rate at some establishments.
Banking hours: 1000-1530 Monday to Friday. Some are open 1000-1300 Saturdays.

DUTY FREE

There are no duty- free allowances between the UK and the Isle of Man. Duty-free allowances are available between the Isle of Man and the Republic of Ireland.

PUBLIC HOLIDAYS

Public holidays observed in the Isle of Man are as follows:
Apr 9 '93 Good Friday. **Apr 12** Easter Monday. **May 3** May Day. **May 31** Spring Holiday. **Jul 5** Tynwald Fair Day. **Aug 30** Late Summer Bank Holiday. **Dec 25** Christmas Day. **Dec 26** Boxing Day. **Dec 27** Bank Holiday. **Jan 1 '94** New Year's Day.
Note: The Friday of the *Isle of Man TT* (motorcycle race) week is also a holiday.

HEALTH

No vaccination certificates are required to enter the Isle of Man. There is a Reciprocal Health Agreement with the UK, allowing all visitors from the mainland free medical treatment; dental treatment and prescribed medicines must be paid for. No proof of UK residence is required to benefit from the Agreement. The island has two first-class hospitals and many dental practices.

TRAVEL

AIR: *Manx Airlines (JE)* operate year-round services between the Isle of Man and London Heathrow, Manchester, Liverpool, Birmingham, Luton, Glasgow, Blackpool, Belfast and Dublin.
The island's airport is **Ronaldsway (IOM),** 11km (7 miles) from Douglas. Airport information: (0624) 823 311. **Facilities** include restaurant, buffet, bar (normal licensing hours), general shop and newsagents, fruit and flower shop, duty-free shop, and facilities for the disabled. **Airport opening times:** 0615-2045 Monday to Friday, 0615-2045 Saturday, and 0700-2045 Sunday. Airport opening times may change in summer. There are regular coach services to and from the airport in summer. A **local bus** operates approximately half hourly in summer, and hourly in winter. **Taxis** and **car hire** are also available. *Athol Garage Car Hire*, tel: (0624) 823 311, ext 234. *Mylchreests Car Hire*, tel: (0624) 823 533. It is ten miles to Douglas by private car. There is one contract and one public car park.
SEA: Daily sailings by *The Isle of Man Steam Packet Company* from Heysham. In addition the *Company* operates summer sailings from Belfast, Dublin and Liverpool.
RAIL: Horse trams run along the 3km (2 miles) of the Douglas Promenade during the summer. *The Steam Railway* operates from Douglas to Port Erin and *The Manx Electric Railway* runs from Douglas to Ramsey and the top of Snaefell in the summer months.
ROAD: The island is served by *Isle of Man National Transport* buses throughout the year. There are also a number of coach operators who operate full-day and half-day excursions. Private **taxis** operate all year round and there are a number of **car hire** firms. **Bicycles** are available for hire in the summer months. **Regulations:** Driving is on the left. There is no maximum speed limit except in built-up areas. **Documentation:** Full UK driving licence is acceptable.

ACCOMMODATION

Hotel, guest-house and self-catering accommodation is available, but pre-booking is necessary in the summer months. Camping is only permitted on the official campsite. The importation of caravans is prohibited.

RESORTS & EXCURSIONS

For information on National Trust properties in the Isle of Man, contact the Manx Museum and National Trust, tel: (0624) 675 522.
Douglas is set in a bay at the confluence of the *Dhoo* and *Glass* rivers, and has a promenade 3km (2 miles) long. *The Manx Museum* in Finch Road has exhibits illustrating the island's history, works by local artists and items dating to Celtic and Viking periods. At *Ballasalla* are the ruins of *Rushen Abbey*, which was founded in 1134, and dissolved at a later date than those of the British Isles. *Creigneish* is the most southerly point of the island and includes such sights as the *Mull* or *Meayll Circles*, a group of six chamber tombs, and *The Manx Open Air Folk Museum* which has a group of thatched cottages restored to their original furnishing. The scenery in this part of the island is fairly wild and rugged and cliffs fall away steeply to the sea. Across the Calf Sound lies the *Calf of Man*, a bird reserve with a large population of rare sea-birds, as well as seals. The sanctuary can be visited outside the nesting season by boat from Port Erin. **Peel** is a picturesque fishing port on the west coast of the island at the mouth of the *River Neb*, and it is claimed produces some of the best kippers. Linked to the town by a causeway is *St*

Patrick's Isle which houses a tiny cathedral, and *Peel Castle*, a red sandstone structure enclosed by walls. From Laxey it is possible to take an electric mountain train up **Snaefell**, the island's highest point, from which the four countries of England, Wales, Scotland and Northern Ireland can be seen on a clear day.
Museums: The Manx Museum, off Crellin's Hill, Douglas. Open weekdays, entrance free. The Folk Museum, Manx Cottages, Creigneish. The Nautical Museum, Bridge Street, Castletown. The Grove Rural Life Museum, Andreas Road, Ramsey. The Railway Museum, Port Erin. Motorcycle Museum, Snaefell. The Motor Museum, Church Road, Port Erin. Fenton's Photographic Museum, Strand Road, Port Erin. 'Odin's Raven', Viking Longboat House, Mill Road East, Peel.

SOCIAL PROFILE

FOOD & DRINK: Cuisine is English and Manx. Local specialities include *queenies* (small scallops) and world-famous Manx kippers. A wide variety of alcoholic beverages are available, including Real Manx Ale from the wood and Manx whiskey, gin and vodka. All drinks are relatively cheaper than the UK. **Licensing hours:** From Maundy Thursday to September 30 (inclusive) public houses are open 1030-2245 Monday to Saturday. On Sundays public houses are open 1200-1330 and 2000-2000. Special opening hours apply to the Christmas/New Year period.
SHOPPING: VAT is at the same rate as the UK and prices are in general similar to those in the UK. Special purchases include Manx tartan, crafts and pottery. **Shopping hours:** 0900-1800 Monday to Saturday. Early closing on Thursdays during the winter months.
SPORT: There are seven **golf** courses on the island and green fees are much cheaper than in the UK. The resorts have facilities for squash, badminton, tennis, bowls, putting and miniature golf. There are boating lakes in Onchan and Ramsey. There is a sailboard and water-skiing centre in the south of the island. The waters around the island are ideal for yachting.
Note: For information on people, religion, social conventions, business, tipping and eating and drinking, see the general UK entry above.
SPECIAL EVENTS: The following is a selection of the major motoring events held throughout the year. For a complete list, contact the Isle of Man Tourist Board.
May 31-Jun 11 '93 *Isle of Man TT* (motorcycle race). **Jul 12-15** *Southern 100* (motorcycle race). **Aug 21-Sep 3** *Manx Grand Prix* (motorcar racing). **Sep 14-17** *Manx International Rally* (motorcar racing). **Sep 22-25** *Classic Car Racing*.

BUSINESS PROFILE

ECONOMY: The Island's economy has taken off in the financial and business sector and is now a leading financial services base. Exports include Manx tweeds, foodstuffs, herring and shellfish; the principal imports are fish, fertilisers and timber.
COMMERCIAL INFORMATION: The following organisation can offer advice: Isle of Man Chamber of Commerce, 17 Drinkwater Street, Douglas. Tel: (0624) 674 941. Fax: (0624) 663 367.
CONFERENCES/CONVENTIONS: Seating is available for up to 1000 persons, though facilities on the island lend themselves very well to meetings of 100 persons or less. Conferences hosted include those of the National Federation of Young Farmers' Clubs and the Union of Communication Workers. All conference hotels have superb back-up services. For further information contact the Department of Tourism.

HISTORY & GOVERNMENT

HISTORY: The original inhabitants were the Neolithic and Mesolithic tribes, followed by the people of the Bronze Age and the Celts whose civilisation is the basis of Manx culture. Christianity was introduced during the 5th and 6th centuries. The Scandinavian Vikings arrived over 1000 years ago and from 979 to 1266 Norse rule prevailed in the establishment of the Kingdom of Man and the Isles. The Vikings founded the Tynwald Parliament which has a continuous unbroken tradition and celebrated its millenium in 1979. After a brief period of Scottish rule, the Kingdom of Man passed to the English Crown, eventually being given in 1403 to Sir John Stanley, whose descendants were Lords of Man for 362 years before the Lordship reverted to the Crown by purchase. During this period the island became a haven for smuggling operations.
GOVERNMENT: The Isle of Man is not constitutionally part of the UK; it is a self-governed dependency of the Crown within the British Commonwealth. The parliamentary institution of Tynwald (stemming from the Scandinavian 'Thing', assembly and 'vollr', field) comprising the Legislative Council and the 24 elected members of the House of Keys legislates for the island, levies taxation and has control of the island's finances. A contribution is paid annually to the UK Treasury. The Acts of Tynwald require the Royal Assent, and are proclaimed to the people in July each year at the open-air assembly on Tynwald Hill at St John's, thus maintaining the Norse tradition. The Government of the Isle of Man maintains its own education, health, national insurance, social security, police, postal and other public services. The Lieutenant-Governor is appointed by the Crown.

CLIMATE

The climate of the Isle of Man is temperate. There is a considerable variation in rainfall over the island, the driest parts being in the extreme south and over the northern plain; the wettest being the hilly interior. Frost and snow occur much less frequently than in other parts of the British Isles.

DOUGLAS Isle of Man (87m)

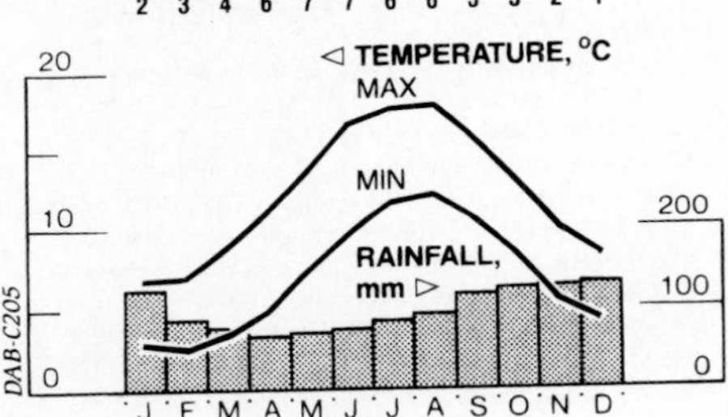

TEMPERATURE CONVERSIONS
-20 -10 0°C 10 20 30 40
0 10 20 30°F40 50 60 70 80 90 100
RAINFALL CONVERSIONS 0mm 200 400 600 800
0in 5 10 15 20 25 30

CHANNEL ISLANDS

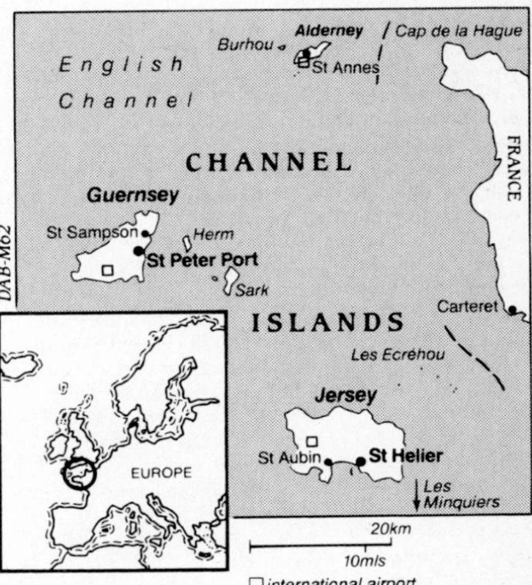

Alderney, Guernsey, Jersey, Sark & Herm.
There are other, very small islands in the group, but these are not normally open to visitors. Guernsey and Jersey have their own sections elsewhere in this book.

ALDERNEY

Location: English Channel, the northernmost Channel Island; off the north coast of France.

States of Alderney Tourism Office
Alderney
Channel Isles
Tel: (0481 82) 2994.

AREA: 7.9 sq km (3.1 sq miles).
POPULATION: 2000 (1985).
POPULATION DENSITY: 253.1 per sq km.
CAPITAL: St Anne's.
GEOGRAPHY: The most northerly of the Channel Islands, Alderney lies 12km (8 miles) off the coast of Normandy in France and some 32km (20 miles) from Guernsey. The central part of the island is a plateau varying in height from 76-90m (250-296ft). The land is flat to the edge of the southern and southwestern cliffs where it falls abruptly to the sea. On the northern, eastern and southeastern sides it slopes gradually towards rocky and sandy bays and quiet beaches.
LANGUAGE: English.
TIME: GMT.
ELECTRICITY: 240 volts AC, 50Hz.
COMMUNICATIONS: Telephone: Alderney is linked to the English STD service; the area code is 0481 82 (4-figure numbers) or 0481 (6-figure numbers). **Post:** Only Guernsey and Alderney stamps will be accepted on outgoing mail. **Press:** Jersey, Guernsey and British papers are available on the island.

PASSPORT/VISA

No passports are required for travel between the UK, the other Channel Islands and Alderney. See the *Passport/Visa* section of the general UK entry above.

MONEY

The currency is Sterling. UK notes and coins are legal tender and circulate together with Channel Islands issue, which are in the same denominations. Channel Islands notes can be reconverted at parity in UK banks, although they are not accepted as legal tender in the UK.
Banking hours: 0930-1300 and 1430-1530 Monday to Friday.

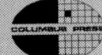

DUTY FREE

The following items can be imported into Alderney without incurring customs duty on arrival in the UK:
200 cigarettes or 50 cigars or 100 cigarillos or 250g of tobacco (double the above quantities for those living outside the UK);
1 litre of alcoholic beverages if over 38.8% proof or 2 litres if under 38.8% proof or 4 litres of wine (2 sparkling and 2 still);
50g perfume and 250ml of toilet water.

PUBLIC HOLIDAYS

Public holidays observed in Alderney are as follows:
Apr 9 '93 Good Friday. **Apr 12** Easter Monday. **May 3** Labour Day. **May 8** Liberation Day. **May 31** Spring Bank Holiday. **Aug 30** Late Summer Holiday. **Dec 25-26** Christmas. **Jan 1 '94** New Year's Day.

HEALTH

No vaccination certificates are required to enter Alderney. There is a Reciprocal Health Agreement with the UK, allowing all short-stay visitors (three months maximum) from the mainland free medical treatment and free emergency dental treatment; prescribed medicines must be paid for. Proof of UK residence (driving licence, NHS card, etc) is required to benefit from the Agreement. The island has a small hospital and two medical and dental practices.

TRAVEL

AIR: The island's airport is ***The Blaye (ACI)*** with flights to Southampton, Bournemouth, Guernsey, Jersey and Cherbourg. **Facilities:** Buffet and shop (0800-1830 winter, 0800-1930 summer); taxis (rank adjacent to Terminal Building).
SEA: During the summer months *Torbay Seaways* have direct sailings from Torquay to Alderney. *Condor of Guernsey* have twice-weekly hydrofoil services during the summer between Guernsey and Alderney.
ROAD: Caravans may not be imported to Alderney. **Bus:** During the summer months an internal bus service operates on the island running from St Anne's to the five main beaches. **Taxi:** Private taxi companies operate on the island. **Car hire:** There is a car hire company on the island and a number of garages have rental cars. **Bicycle hire:** There are several bike hire firms that rent out bicycles at daily or weekly rates. **Regulations:** Driving is on the left. Maximum speed limit is 30mph (48kmph). **Documentation:** Full UK driving licence is accepted.

ACCOMMODATION

Hotel, guest-house and self-catering accommodation is available, but pre-booking is necessary in the summer months. Camping is only permitted on the one official campsite. The import of caravans is prohibited.

RESORTS & EXCURSIONS

The island is almost treeless and has a heavily indented shoreline which has created many sandy bays and rugged crags. The principal town, **St Anne's**, dates back to the 15th century and has many shops and inns lining its cobbled streets.

SOCIAL PROFILE

FOOD & DRINK: Cuisine is largely French influenced. The local speciality is shellfish. A wide variety of alcoholic beverages is available. Spirits, beers and wines are relatively cheaper than on the mainland.
SHOPPING: There is no VAT but a Guernsey Bailiwick tax is imposed on certain goods such as spirits, wines, beers and tobacco. Prices on luxury goods are relatively cheaper than in the UK, although the overall cost of foodstuffs is higher. Special purchases include Alderney pullovers, local pottery and crafts. **Shopping hours:** These vary, but the majority of shops are open 0930-1230 and 1430-1730. Shops generally close earlier on Wednesdays.
SPORT: Golf: There is a well-maintained 9-hole golf course with a bowling green. **Windsurfing/surfing:** Surf/sail boards are available for hire on the island; ask at the tourist office for further information. **Sailing:** The sailing club facilities are open to visiting yachtsmen from established clubs. Various open events are held during the summer. **Tennis/squash:** Facilities are available on the island for both squash and tennis.
SPECIAL EVENTS: *Alderney Week* takes place in late July/early August and the first Saturday in August sees a cavalcade and torchlight procession.
NOTE: For information relating to Alderney on people, religion, social conventions, business, tipping, as well as information on the government, economy and history, see the separate entry on *Guernsey*.

CLIMATE

The island enjoys a temperate climate with warm summers and milder winter temperatures than those experienced in the UK.

GUERNSEY

For information on Guernsey, see the separate entry earlier in the *World Travel Guide*.

JERSEY

For information on Jersey, see the separate entry earlier in the *World Travel Guide*.

SARK & HERM

Location: English Channel.

Sark Tourism Information Centre
Tel: (0481 83) 2345. Fax: (0481 83) 2483.
Herm Island Administration Office
Tel: (0481) 622 377. Fax: (0481) 671 0066.

AREA: Sark: 5.5 sq km (2.1 sq miles). **Herm:** 2 sq km (0.8 sq miles).
POPULATION: Sark: 420 (1984). **Herm:** 107, including Jethou (1971).
POPULATION DENSITY: Sark: 76.4 per sq km. **Herm:** 53.5 per sq km.
GEOGRAPHY: Sark is an hour's boat journey east of Guernsey. It is almost two islands, the two parts being joined by a narrow isthmus known as *La Coupée*. Most of the people live on La Collinette on a steep hill overlooking the harbour of La Maseline. The coastline is rugged, with many cliffs and caves. **Herm** lies between Guernsey and Sark. It has lush and varied scenery, with meadows, unusual wild flowers and steep cliffs overlooking secluded coves and pounding surf. Herm attracts up to 3000 visitors a day during the summer.
LANGUAGE: Local *patois*, a mixture of Norman French and Old English. English widely spoken.
COMMUNICATIONS: Sark and Herm are connected to the UK STD telephone network. Area codes: **Sark** 0481 83; **Herm** 0481 (same as Guernsey).
NOTE: *For information on time, electricity, communications, money, passport/visa, climate and health, see the separate entry on Guernsey earlier in this book.*

TRAVEL

SEA: Sark and Herm can be reached by sea from either Jersey or Guernsey.
ROAD: No cars are allowed on either island but there are 58 tractors on Sark – indeed, even the ambulance on Sark is drawn by a tractor. The Sark 'Taxi' is a horse-drawn carriage which takes visitors around the island.

ACCOMMODATION

There are a few hotels on Sark. Herm has one country inn, surrounded by flower gardens. For further information, contact the Guernsey Tourist Office. Tel: (0481) 624 411. Fax: (0481) 672 1246.

RESORTS & EXCURSIONS

Sark: A feudal state ruled over by a single man – the grandson of the famous Dame of Sark. There is a medieval parliament called the Chief Pleas. The *Island Hall* is a wooden building used for dances, film shows, card games and many other forms of entertainment. There are several excellent beaches, including the *Venus Pool*, *Adonis Pool* and *Creux Derrible*; most of these beaches can only be reached at low tide. Most of the island's accommodation is to be found at *Dixcart Bay*.
Herm: Privately leased, and run as a resort island. Attractions include a 'Tom Thumb' village restored from derelict houses, a restored chapel, woods, caves, the shell beach, covered by countless shells deposited by the Gulf Stream, some from as far away as Mexico, swimming in rock pools. There are quite a few pubs on the island which devise their own opening hours on a rota system; one will almost always be open.

ST HELIER Jersey (9m)

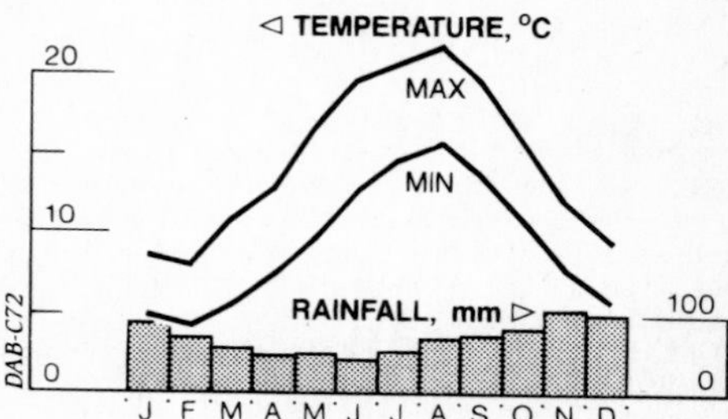

UNITED STATES OF AMERICA

Location: North America.

United States Travel and Tourism Administration
14 Constitution Avenue, NW
Washington, DC
20230
Tel: (202) 482 4904. Fax: (202) 482 2887.
Embassy of the United States of America
24 Grosvenor Square
London
W1A 1AE
Tel: (071) 499 9000.
United States Consulate General
(Visa Branch)
5 Upper Grosvenor Street
London W1A 2JB
Tel: (071) 499 6846 (visa information) *or* (0891) 200 290 (recorded information). Fax: (071) 495 5012. Opening hours: 0830-1130 Monday to Friday.
United States Consulate General
3 Regent Terrace
Edinburgh EH7 5BW
Tel: (031) 556 8315. Fax: (031) 557 6023. Opening hours: 1000-1200 and 1300-1600 Monday, Wednesday and Friday; 1000-1200 Tuesday and Thursday.
United States Immigration Department
5 Upper Grosvenor Street
London W1A 2JB
Tel: (071) 499 9000 *or* (0891) 200 290 (recorded information). Fax: (071) 495 4330. Opening hours: 0900-1200 Monday to Friday.
United States Travel & Tourism Administration (USTTA)
PO Box 1EN
London W1A 1EN
Tel: (071) 495 4466. Fax: (071) 495 4377. Information can be obtained by phone, fax or post only. Opening hours: 0900-1600 Monday to Friday.
British Embassy
3100 Massachusetts Avenue, NW
Washington, DC
20008
Tel: (202) 462 1340. Fax: (202) 898 4255. Telex: 892384 PRODROME B WSH.
Consulates in: Anchorage, Atlanta, Boston, Chicago, Cleveland, Dallas, Houston, Kansas City, Los Angeles (tel: (310) 477 3322), New Orleans, New York (tel: (212) 745 0200), Miami, Norfolk, Philadelphia, Portland (Oregon), Puerto Rico, San Francisco and Seattle.
British Consulate-General
845 Third Avenue
New York, NY
10022
Tel: (212) 745 0200. Fax: (212) 735 3062. Telex: 216756.
Also in: Atlanta, Boston, Chicago, Houston and Los Angeles.
Embassy of the United States of America
PO Box 866
100 Wellington Street
Station B
Ottawa, Ontario
K1P 5T1
Tel: (613) 238 5335 *or* 238 4470. Fax: (613) 238 5720.
Consulates in: Ottawa, Calgary, Halifax, Montréal, Québec, Toronto and Vancouver.
United States Travel & Tourism Administration (USTTA)
Suite 602
480 University Avenue
Toronto
Ontario
M5G 1V2
Tel: (416) 595 5082 (trade enquiries) *or* 595 0335 (consumer enquiries). Fax: (416) 595 5211.
Also in: Montréal and Vancouver.
Canadian Embassy
501 Pennsylvania Avenue, NW
Washington, DC
20001
Tel: (202) 682 1740. Fax: (202) 682 7726. Telex: 89664 DOMCAN A WSH.
Consulates in: Atlanta, Boston, Buffalo, Chicago, Cleveland, Dallas, Detroit, Los Angeles (tel: (213) 687 7412), Minneapolis, New York (tel: (212) 768 2400), San Francisco and Seattle.

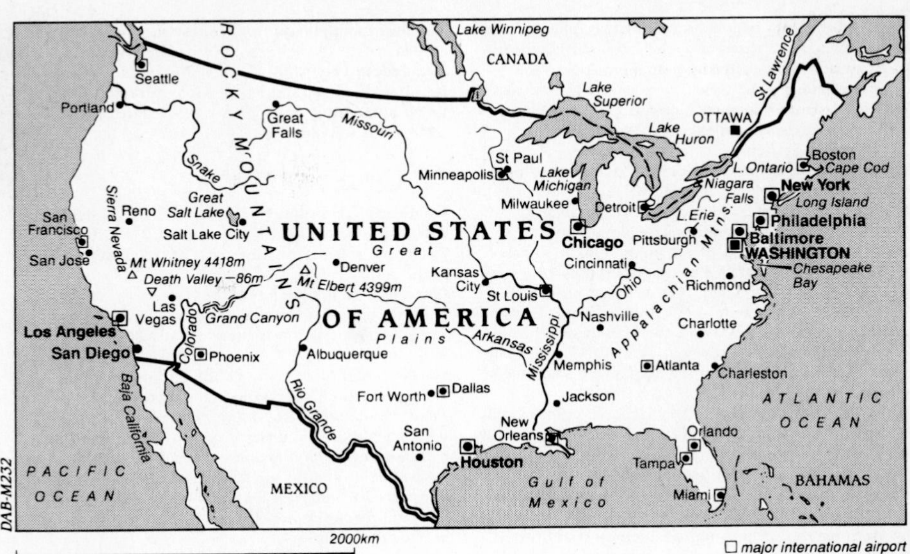

INTRODUCTION

Information on the United States of America is provided in three sections: the general factfinder (immediately below); the *States A-Z* section, which briefly covers all states not included under *US Gateways* and gives sources of further information; and the *US Gateways* section, providing detailed information on the major tourist destinations – details of travel, excursions, leisure activities and special events in the states of Arizona, California, Florida, Georgia, Illinois, Louisiana, Maryland, Massachusetts, Michigan, Minnesota, Missouri, New Jersey, New York, Pennsylvania, Texas, Washington and Washington DC (all of these states have gateway airports). A section on the state of Hawaii, American Samoa, Guam and the US Virgin Islands follows the *Gateways* section.

AREA: 9,372,614 sq km (3,618,770 sq miles).
POPULATION: 250,885,000 (1990 estimate).
POPULATION DENSITY: 26.8 per sq km.
CAPITAL: Washington DC. **Population:** 617,000 (1988 estimate). Sixteen other cities have a population larger than that of Washington DC. New York is the largest city, with a population of over seven million. Los Angeles, Chicago, Houston, Philadelphia, San Diego and Detroit had populations of over one million in 1988.
GEOGRAPHY: Covering a large part of the North American continent, the United States of America shares borders with Canada to the north and Mexico to the south and has coasts on the Atlantic, Pacific and Arctic Oceans, the Caribbean and the Gulf of Mexico. The state of Alaska, in the northwest corner of the continent, is separated from the rest of the country by Canada, and Hawaii lies in the central Pacific Ocean. One of the largest countries in the world, the USA has an enormous diversity of geographical features. The climate ranges from subtropical to Arctic, with a corresponding breadth of flora and fauna. For a more detailed description of each region's geographical characteristics, see below under the *States A-Z*.
LANGUAGE: English. Many other languages are widely spoken in certain areas of the cities, in communities and in states bordering Mexico where Spanish has, in some areas, completely supplanted English.
RELIGION: Protestant with Roman Catholic, Jewish and many ethnic minorities. In large cities people of the same ethnic background often live within defined communities.
TIME: The USA is divided into six time zones:
Eastern Standard Time: GMT - 5.
Central Standard Time: GMT - 6.
Mountain Standard Time: GMT - 7.
Pacific Standard Time: GMT - 8.
Alaska: GMT - 9.
Hawaii: GMT - 10.
Note: When calculating travel times, bear in mind the adoption of *Daylight Saving Time (DST)* by most states in summer. From the first Sunday in April to the last Sunday in October clocks are put forward one hour, changing at 0200 hours local time. Regions not observing *DST* include most of Indiana, all of Arizona, Hawaii, the US Virgin Islands and American Samoa. The USA adopts *DST* one week later than the UK, so for a week the time difference changes.
ELECTRICITY: 110/120 volts AC, 60Hz. Plugs are of the flat 2-pin type. European electrical appliances not fitted with dual-voltage capabilities will require a plug adaptor, which is best purchased *before* arrival in the USA.
COMMUNICATIONS: Telephone: Full IDD is available. Country code: 1. For emergency police, fire or medical services in major cities, dial 911. **Fax:** There are bureaux in all main centres, and major hotels also have facilities. Fax services are very widely available. **Telex/telegram:** *Western Union* telex facilities are available throughout the USA. Telegrams can be sent through all telegraph and post offices. **Post:** There are only a limited number of post offices, so it is advisable to buy stamps in bulk. There are, however, stamp machines in hotels and shops, but these have a 25% price mark-up. Airmail to Europe takes up to a week. Post office hours: 0900-1700 (24 hours at main offices in larger cities). If sending gifts valued at less than US$50 to the USA, the recipient will not have to pay tax if the package is marked 'Unsolicited Gift'. **Press:** The most influential papers are *The New York Times*, *Washington Post*, *Los Angeles Times* and the *Wall Street Journal*. Owing to the high degree of self-government of each state, newspapers tend to be regionalised, although recent economic pressures have resulted in large-scale mergers. Even so, the USA publishes more newspapers than any other country, and has perhaps the heaviest Sunday newspapers in the world, particularly the Sunday edition of *The New York Times*.
BBC World Service frequencies: From time to time these change. See the section *How to Use this Book* for more information.

BBC:				
MHz	17.84	15.22	9.590	5.975

PASSPORT/VISA

Regulations and requirements may be subject to change at short notice, and you are advised to contact the appropriate diplomatic or consular authority before finalising travel arrangements. Details of these may be found at the head of this country's entry. Any numbers in the chart refer to the footnotes below.

	Passport Required?	Visa Required?	Return Ticket Required?
Full British	1	2	Yes
BVP	Not valid	-	-
Australian	Yes	Yes	Yes
Canadian	1	No	No
USA	-	-	-
Other EC	Yes	2	Yes
Japanese	Yes	3	Yes

Entry restrictions: The following will be refused entry to the United States of America unless a 'waiver of ineligibility' has first been obtained:
(a) anyone afflicted with communicable diseases;
(b) anyone with a criminal record;
(c) narcotics addicts or abusers and drug traffickers;
(d) anyone who has been deported from or denied admission to the USA within the previous 5 years.
PASSPORTS: [1] A valid passport is required on entry by all except: (a) Canadian nationals arriving from anywhere in the Western Hemisphere; (b) residents of Canada or Bermuda who have a common nationality

with nationals of Canada or with British subjects in Bermuda (ie are citizens of a Commonwealth country or Ireland) who are arriving from anywhere in the Western hemisphere.
British Visitors Passport: Not valid.
VISAS: Required by all except:
(a) Canadian citizens;
(b) residents of Canada or Bermuda as described in *Passports* above;
(c) [2] nationals of Belgium, Denmark, France, Germany, Italy, Luxembourg, The Netherlands, Spain and the UK who are travelling on an unexpired passport for holiday, transit or business purposes for a stay not exceeding 90 days and, if entering by air or sea, hold a non-refundable return or onward ticket and completed form I-94-W and enter aboard an air or sea carrier participating in the Visa Waiver Pilot Program (lists of participating air or sea carriers are available from most travel agents);
(d) [2] British subjects resident in the Cayman Islands or the Turks & Caicos Islands who arrive directly from those islands for non-immigration purposes;
(e) [3] nationals of Japan who are travelling on an unexpired passport for holiday, transit or business purposes for a stay not exceeding 90 days and, if entering by air or sea, hold a non-refundable return or onward ticket and completed form I-94-W and enter aboard an air or sea carrier participating in the Visa Waiver Pilot Program (lists of participating air or sea carriers are available from most travel agents);
(f) nationals of Andorra, Austria, Finland, Iceland, Liechtenstein, Monaco, New Zealand, Norway, San Marino, Sweden and Switzerland who are travelling on an unexpired passport for holiday, transit or business purposes for a stay not exceeding 90 days and, if entering by air or sea, hold a non-refundable return or onward ticket and completed form I-94-W and enter aboard an air or sea carrier participating in the Visa Waiver Pilot Progam (lists of participating air or sea carriers are available from most travel agents).
Note: (a) UK citizens may also enter the USA overland from Canada or Mexico without a visa provided they are in possession of a completed form I-94-W issued by the immigration authorities at the port of entry. (b) UK passports that indicate the bearer is a British subject rather than a British citizen do not qualify. Persons unsure about visa requirements (including those defined in 'Entry restrictions' above) should write to the US Consulate General or the Visa Department of the American Embassy (addresses and phone numbers above).
Types of visa: *Non-immigrant* (business and pleasure), *Student* (participating in academic or exchange programmes), *Journalist*, *Temporary worker* and *Transit*. For nationals of most European countries, visitor visas are often valid indefinitely for Multiple entries. There are further classifications of non-immigrant visas; enquire at the Embassy for more information. Cost varies according to nationality; the policy is to charge the same as that charged by the applicant's country of origin. Visas (if required) are issued free to UK nationals. *Transit:* Certain airlines are authorised to carry foreign nationals in transit without a visa, provided they continue their journey from the same airport within 8 hours and hold confirmed documentation for onward travel and valid entry requirements for the onward destination. In other cases, a Transit visa will be required; contact the nearest visa branch (see below) for further information.
Validity: Varies from 3 months to indefinite; some visas are valid for Multiple entry (see above). The length of stay in the USA is determined by US immigration officials at the time of entry, but is generally 6 months. For extensions, apply to the US Immigration & Naturalisation Service.
Note: A visa no longer expires with the expiry of the holder's passport. An unexpired visa may be presented in an expired passport for entry into the USA as long as the visa itself has not been cancelled and is presented with a valid non-expired passport, provided that both passports are for the same nationality.
Application to: Visa Branches at Consulate Generals. Those residing in England, Scotland, Northern Ireland or Wales should apply to the Consulate General in London. The Consulate General in Scotland no longer deals with visa applications. For addresses, see top of entry.
Application requirements: (a) Valid passport. (b) Sufficient funds for duration of stay. (c) 1 passport-size photo. (d) Completed application form.
Further documentation may be required to substantiate details and the purpose of visit plus proof of intention to return to country of residence.
Working days required: Applications will normally be dealt with within 10 working days for applications by post (although it is advisable to allow 28 days), and 48 hours for applications via a travel agency or courier service.
Residence: The law in the USA is complex for those wishing to take up residence. More information may be obtained from the Immigration Department (for address see top of entry).

MONEY

Currency: US Dollar (US$) = 100 cents. Notes are in denominations of US$500, 100, 50, 20, 10, 5, 2 and 1. Coins are in denominations of US$1, and 50, 25, 10, 5 and 1 cents.
Currency exchange: Hotels do not as a rule exchange currency and only a few major banks will exchange foreign currency, so it is therefore advisable to arrive with dollars.
Credit cards: Most major credit cards are accepted throughout the USA, including Diners Club, American Express, Access/Mastercard and Visa. Check with your credit card company for details of merchant acceptability and other services which may be available. Visitors are advised to carry at least one major credit card, as it is common to request prepayment for hotel rooms and car hire when payment is *not* by credit card.
Travellers cheques: Widely accepted in hotels, stores and restaurants, providing they are US Dollar cheques; Sterling travellers cheques are not acceptable. American Express travellers cheques are often accepted as cash, preferably in denominations of US$10 or US$20. It should be noted that many banks do not have the facility to encash travellers cheques (the US banking system differs greatly from that of the UK) and those that do are likely to charge a high commission. One or in some cases two pieces of identification (passport, credit card, driving licence) may also be required.
Exchange rate indicators: The following figures are included as a guide to the movements of the US Dollar against Sterling:

Date:	Oct '89	Oct '90	Oct '91	Oct '92
£1.00=	1.57	1.95	1.74	1.59

Currency restrictions: There are no limits on the import or export of either foreign or local currency. However, movements of more than US$10,000 or the equivalent (including 'bearer bonds') must be registered with US Customs on Form 4790. All gold coins and any quantity of gold must be declared before export.
Banking hours: Variable, but generally 0900-1500 Monday to Friday.

DUTY FREE

The following goods may be imported by visitors into the USA without incurring customs duty:
200 cigarettes or 50 cigars or 2kg of tobacco or proportionate amounts of each;
1 litre of alcoholic beverage (if aged 21 or over);
Gifts or articles up to a value of US$100 (including 100 cigars in addition to the tobacco allowance above).
Note: (a) Items should not be gift-wrapped as they must be available for customs inspection. (b) The alcoholic beverage allowance above is the national maximum; certain states allow less and if arriving in those states, the excess will be taxed or withheld. (c) The gift allowance may only be claimed once in every six months and is only available to non-residents who intend to stay in the USA for more than 72 hours. (d) For information about the importation of pets, refer to the brochure *Pets, Wildlife – US Customs*, available at US Embassies and Consulates.
Prohibited items: The following are either banned or may only be imported under licence: (a) Narcotics and dangerous drugs, unless for medical purposes (doctor's certificate required). (b) Absinthe, biological materials, some seeds, fruits and plants (including endangered species of plants and vegetables and their products). (c) Firearms and ammunition (with some exceptions – consult Customs). (d) Hazardous articles (fireworks, toxic materials). (e) Meat and poultry products. (f) Pornographic material. (g) Switchblade knives.

PUBLIC HOLIDAYS

Public holidays observed throughout the USA are as follows:
Apr 11 '93 Easter. **May 31** Memorial Day. **Jul 4** Independence Day. **Sep 6** Labor Day. **Oct 11** Columbus Day. **Nov 11** Veterans' Day. **Nov 25** Thanksgiving. **Dec 25** Christmas. **Jan 1 '94** New Year's Day. **Jan 17** Martin Luther King Day. **Feb 15** Presidents' Day.
Note: Other holidays may be observed on different dates from state to state.

HEALTH

Regulations and requirements may be subject to change at short notice, and you are advised to contact your doctor well in advance of your intended date of departure. Any numbers in the chart refer to the footnotes below.

	Special Precautions?	Certificate Required?
Yellow Fever	No	No
Cholera	No	No
Typhoid & Polio	No	-
Malaria	No	-
Food & Drink	1	-

[1]: Tap water is considered safe to drink. Milk is pasteurised and dairy products are safe for consumption. Local meat, poultry, seafood, fruit and vegetables are generally considered safe to eat.
Rabies is present. For those at high risk, vaccination before arrival should be considered. If you are bitten abroad seek medical advice without delay.
Health care: Medical insurance providing cover up to at least US$250,000 is strongly advised. Only emergency cases are treated without prior payment and treatment will often be refused without evidence of insurance or a deposit. Medical facilities are generally of an extremely high standard. Those visiting the USA for long periods with school-age children should be aware that school entry requirements include proof of immunisation against diphtheria, measles, poliomyelitis and rubella throughout the USA, and schools in many states also require immunisation against tetanus, pertussis and mumps.

TRAVEL - International

Note: The vast majority of arrivals are by air and consequently a special *US Gateways* section is included after the *States A-Z* below. The information to be found immediately below is of a more general nature.
AIR: The principal US airlines operating international services are: *American Airlines, Continental Airlines, Delta Air, Northwest Airlines, Trans World Airlines (TWA)* and *United Airlines*. Many other airlines operate services from all over the world to the USA.
Approximate flight times: From *London* to Anchorage is 8 hours 55 minutes, to Detroit is 8 hours 30 minutes, to Los Angeles is 11 hours, to Miami is 9 hours 35 minutes, to New York is 7 hours 30 minutes (3 hours 50 minutes by Concorde), to San Francisco is 10 hours 45 minutes, to Seattle is 9 hours 40 minutes and to Washington DC is 8 hours 5 minutes (all times are direct).
From *Singapore* to Los Angeles is 18 hours 45 minutes and to New York is 21 hours 25 minutes.
From *Sydney* to Los Angeles is 17 hours 55 minutes and to New York is 21 hours 5 minutes.
More international flight times may be found in the *US Gateways* section below.
International airports: See below under *US Gateways*.
Note: Flights from Europe to the USA take longer than those coming back; ie flying east to west takes longer than west to east. Flights from the east coast of the USA take approximately 30-40 minutes less and from the west coast of the USA approximately one hour less.
SEA: Numerous cruise lines sail from ports worldwide to both the east and west coasts. Contact a travel agent or the USTTA for fares and schedules.
RAIL: The US and Mexican rail networks connect at Tecate (Tijuana), Yuma, Nogales, Douglas, El Paso, Del Rio and Laredo, but there are few scheduled passenger services. There are several connections with the Canadian network. The major routes are: New York to Montréal and New York to Toronto. Milwaukee, Chicago, Detroit and Buffalo are all connected via terminals in Toronto, Hamilton and Ottawa.
ROAD: There are many crossing points from Canada to the USA. The major road routes are: New York to Montréal/Ottawa, Detroit to Toronto/Hamilton, Minneapolis to Winnipeg and Seattle to Vancouver/Edmonton/Calgary.

TRAVEL - Internal

Note: More detailed information may be found in the *States A-Z* section below.
AIR: The USA may be crossed within 5 hours from east to west and within 2 hours from north to south. Strong competition between airlines has resulted in a wide difference between fares. There is a good choice of fares: first-class, economy, excursion and discount. Night flights are generally cheaper. **Cheap fares:** Money-saving schemes for the visitor include discounts on all internal flights offered by *TWA*, *Delta* and other principal airlines. The traveller should buy tickets 21 days in advance. *Delta, British Airways* and *Virgin Atlantic* offer a *Discover America Pass* which includes a minimum of

three and a maximum of 12 coupons entitling the passenger to that number of flights within the USA at a discounted fare. The cost of the pass is according to the number of coupons requested. *Delta Air Lines* also offers a 30- or 60-day *Standby Air Travel USA Pass* available to all persons who permanently reside outside the USA, Canada, Mexico or the Caribbean, entitling them to unlimited standby air travel throughout the stated period. The cost of the 30-day pass is US$499 and for the 60-day pass is US$799. These passes must be purchased outside the USA.

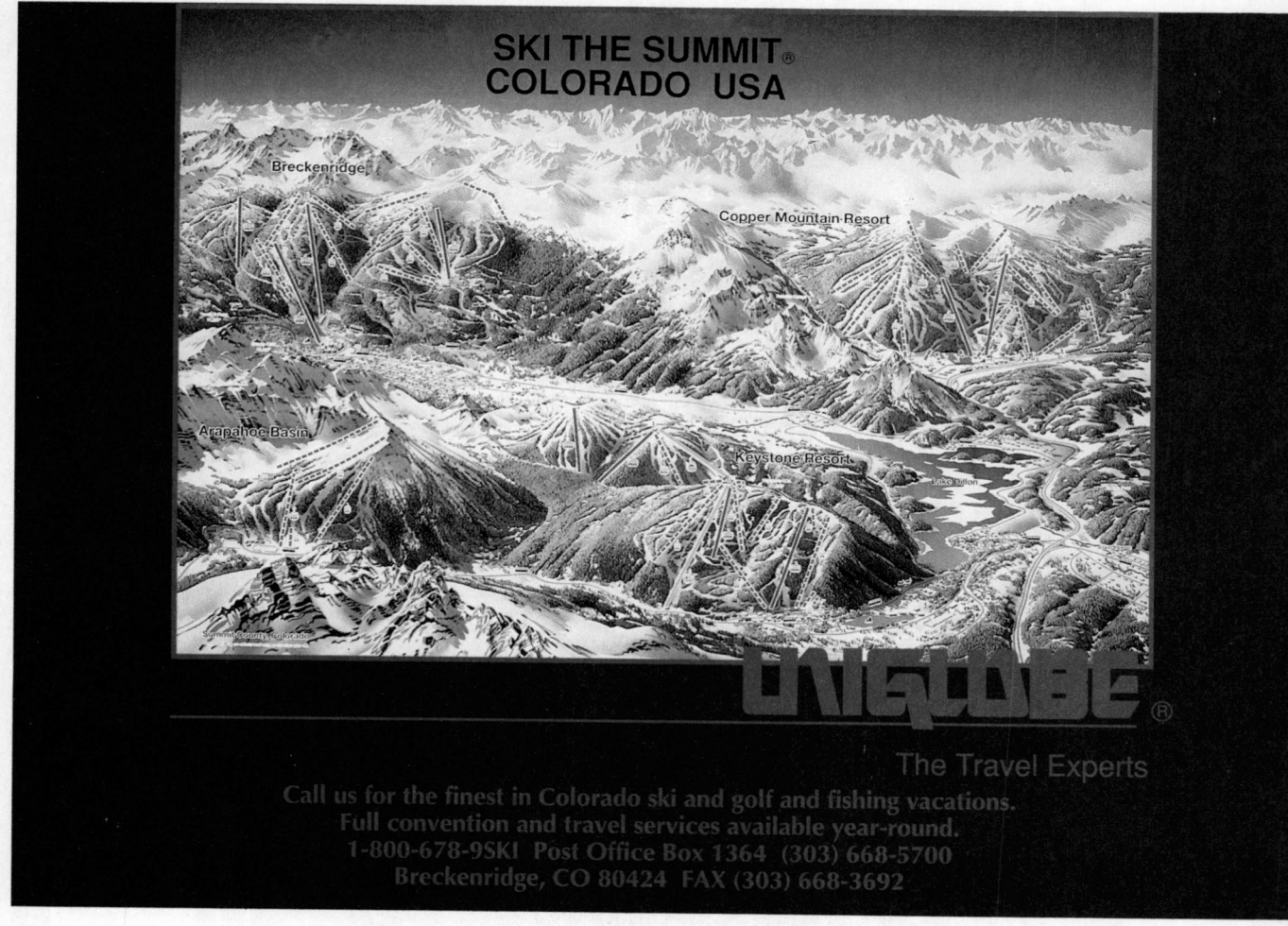

Agents are advised to contact the offices of individual airlines once a basic itinerary has been organised.

Note: Baggage allowance is often determined by number and size rather than weight.

Approximate flight times: Consult the *US Gateways* section below.

SEA & RIVER: There are extensive water communications both along the coastline and along the great rivers and lakes.

Great Lakes: The Ohio River carries more water traffic than any other inland waterway in the world. Tour ships and passenger and freight lines crisscross all the Great Lakes from Duluth, Sault Sainte Marie, Milwaukee, Chicago, Detroit, Toronto, Rochester, Cleveland and Buffalo.

RAIL: Although the US rail network has more than 300,000km (186,410 miles) of track, passenger trains run over only a small part of the system. Outside the densely populated northeast, trains run once-daily over a handful of long-distance routes. Nearly all the long-distance trains are operated by the *National Railroad Passenger Corporation (Amtrak)*, but suburban and some medium-distance services are run by local agencies. *Amtrak's* main route is the Boston–New York–Washington northeast corridor; other routes run south to Florida and New Orleans, and between Boston, New York and Washington to Chicago. From Chicago, daily services radiate to Seattle, Portland, Oakland (San Francisco), Los Angeles, San Antonio and New Orleans. There is also a thrice-weekly train from Los Angeles to New Orleans.

***Amtrak* tour packages:** There are over 74 different tours in 34 states throughout the USA. Full details are provided in the *Amtrak* brochure, which is widely available. Nearly all trains have one-class seating and air-conditioning, with a variety of sleeping accommodation available on payment of a supplementary fare. All long-distance trains have dining facilities. The railroads often pass through fine scenery, particularly on east–west routes. While most Americans drive or take the bus, the passenger trains continue to attract a discerning and ever-increasing clientele. Indeed, rail travel in the USA – as in many other countries – has undergone a considerable revival in recent years, and the signs are that this trend will continue. For further Amtrak information, tel: 1-(800) USA RAIL *or* 1-(800) 872 7245 (toll-free).

Cheap fares: There are regional and nationwide *USA Rail Passes;* nationwide passes give 15 or 30 days unlimited travel on the whole *Amtrak* network up to Montréal. Overnight sleepers, auto trains and the 'Metroliner' between New York and Washington are not included in the pass. The *National Rail Pass* is valid for rail travel anywhere in the USA for 15 or 30 days. The 15-day pass costs US$308 per person in the peak season (from May 28-Aug 29) and US$208 per person (off-peak); the 30-day pass costs US$389 per person (US$309 off-peak). Regional passes are broken down into the following: *East Region Pass* is valid for unlimited travel in the region east of Chicago and New Orleans up to Montréal for 15 or 30 days – the 15-day pass costs US$178 per person (US$158 off-peak) and the 30-day pass costs US$229 per person (US$209 off-peak); *West Region Pass* is valid for unlimited travel in the region west of Chicago to New Orleans for 15 or 30 days – the 15-day pass costs US$228 per person (US$188 off-peak) and the 30-day pass costs US$289 per person (US$259 off-peak); *Far West Pass* is valid for unlimited travel in the region from Seattle to San Diego and to Salt Lake City and Flagstaff for 15 or 30 days – the 15-day pass costs US$178 per person (US$158 off-peak) and the 30-day pass costs US$229 per person (US$209 off-peak); and *Coastal Region Pass* is valid for unlimited travel from Montréal to Miami on the east coast and from Seattle to San Diego on the west coast for 30 days only and costs US$199 per person (US$179 off-peak). These passes *cannot* be purchased in the USA. Passports must be presented at the time of purchase and passes must be used within 90 days of purchase. The passes cover coach-class travel tickets and seat reservations on *Amtrak* passenger services. *However, rail passes act as a form of payment for seats only – to guarantee a seat on any specific Amtrak train, a reservation must be made.* Travellers should contact the nearest Amtrak station to find out whether reservations are required on specific journeys they wish to make. For journeys where reservations are required, train times should be reconfirmed 24 hours prior to departure. Travellers aiming to travel during peak times should make reservations well in advance. Higher class and other accommodation is available on payment of the usual supplements. Children aged 2-15 pay half the adult fare and children under two years of age travel free. Group, family, weekend and tour packages are all available, although fares may still exceed combined bus and air fares.

In many cases, point-to-point tickets bought outside the USA will be considerably cheaper. UK nationals can check with *Destination Marketing* (tel: (071) 978 5222; fax: (071) 924 3171) for further details.

Approximate journey times: See below under *US Gateways* for approximate times for train connections between a selection of major US cities.

ROAD: Driving is a marvellous way to see the USA, although the distances between cities can be enormous. A realistic evaluation of travel times should be made to avoid over-strenuous itineraries. Driving conditions are excellent and the road system reaches every town. Petrol is cheaper than in Europe. The *American Automobile Association (AAA)* offers touring services, maps, advice and insurance policies, which are compulsory in most states, even for hiring. Tel: (407) 444 7000. Membership of a visitor's own national automobile association (eg *AA* or *RAC* membership for the UK) entitles the traveller to *AAA* benefits.

Coach: There is one major coach carrier covering the whole of the USA: *Greyhound World Travel.* This main national service is supplemented by over 11,000 other tour lines, covering the country with reasonably priced and regular services. Air-conditioning, toilets and reclining seats are available on intercity routes. *Greyhound* covers the Southern States, the Southern-Central States, the South Rockies area and also extends into Mexico and Canada. Facilities for left luggage and food are available, usually 24 hours a day. Once disembarked at a bus terminal, passengers are not permitted to wait there overnight for an onward bus (ie no sleeping in the terminal). **Cheap fares:** *Greyhound Lines* offers the *Ameripass*, which gives 7, 15 or 30 days unlimited travel throughout the USA. Extensions are available, payable by the day. The pass must be bought outside the USA through *Greyhound World Travel. Ameripass* offers half-price fares for children 5-11 years old. Unlimited stopovers are allowed on ordinary tickets. *Greyhound Lines* also offer excursion fares for point-to-point travel. *Intra* and *Intercity Tours (Greyhire)* are run throughout the USA. Contact *Greyhound Lines* at their international offices in New York (tel: (212) 917 6363) *or* Los Angeles (tel: (213) 620 1200).

Car hire: Major international companies have offices at all gateway airports and in most cities. There are excellent discounts available for foreign visitors. Credit card deposits and inclusive rates are generally required. As a guide to car sizes an 'Economy' or 'Compack' refers to a car the size of a standard European car, while a 'Standard' refers to a car the size of a limousine. Minimum ages for hirers vary according to the rental company, pick-up point and method of payment. Agents are advised to contact the individual companies for information on drivers under 25 years of age. *Columbus Press* publishes a handy booklet, *Driving In the USA*, dealing with most aspects of car hire in the USA.

Drive away: The AAA and *Auto Driveaway* provide a service enabling the traveller to drive cars to and from a given point, only paying the price of petrol. A deposit is often required and time and mileage limits are set for delivery, which leaves very little time for sightseeing (there are heavy financial penalties for those who exceed the limits). Details are published under *Automobile & Truck Transporting* in the US Yellow Pages. Some companies allow the driver to finish the journey in Canada. For further information, phone *Auto Driveaway*. Tel: (312) 341 1900.

Campers/motorhomes: The hire of self-drive campers or motorhomes, which are called 'recreational vehicles' in the USA, are a good means of getting around. Contact the USTTA Travel Information Centre for more information.

Documentation: An International Driving Permit is recommended, although it is not legally required (it is often very useful as an additional proof of identity). A full national driving licence is accepted for up to one year. *Insurance:* All travellers intending to rent or drive cars or motorhomes in the USA are strongly advised to ensure that the insurance policy covers their total requirements, covering all drivers and passengers against injury or accidental death. A yellow 'non-resident, interstate liability insurance card' which acts as evidence of financial responsibility is available through motor insurance agents.

Traffic regulations: Speed limit: usually 55mph (89kmph) on motorways, but varies from state to state. Speed limits are clearly indicated along highways and are strictly enforced, with heavy fines imposed. Note that it is illegal to pass a school bus that has stopped to unload its passengers (using indicators and warning lights), all vehicles must stop until the bus has moved back into the traffic stream. It is illegal for drivers not to have their licences immediately to hand. If stopped, do not attempt to pay a driving fine on the spot as it may be interpreted as an attempt to bribe. **Note:** There are extremely tough laws against drinking and driving throughout the USA. These laws are strictly enforced.

Approximate journey times: Approximate self-drive and *Greyhound* journey times between a selection of US cities may be found below under *US Gateways*.

URBAN: Some US cities now have good public transport services following a 'transit renaissance' after the energy crises of the 1970s. There are a number of underground train systems in operation in major cities including New York (subway), Washington (metro), Boston ('T'), Chicago (train) and San Francisco (BART – Bay Area Rapid Transit); others are being planned or built, for instance a long-overdue network in Los Angeles. There are also several tramway and trolleybus systems, including the much-loved antique trams found in San Francisco.

Note: Many of the underground train systems are dangerous during off-peak hours (the New York subway, in particular, has acquired an almost gothic reputation for violence, although this has been much exaggerated), but they offer cheap, quick and efficient travel during the working day, particularly in New York, Boston and Chicago. Travel by any other means during the day is likely to be tortuous.

ACCOMMODATION

HOTELS: There are many good traditional hotels. However, the majority are modern and part of national and international chains, often with standard prices. In general the quality of accommodation is high, with facilities such as television and telephone in each room. For further information, contact the American Hotel & Motel Association, Suite 600, 1201 New York Avenue, Washington, DC 20005-3931. Tel: (202) 289 3100. Fax: (202) 289 3199.

Grading: Basic categories fall into 'Super', 'Deluxe', 'Standard', 'Moderate' and 'Inexpensive'. Prices vary according to standards.

Pre-paid voucher schemes: Several companies offer a pre-paid voucher scheme for use at various hotel and motel chains throughout the USA. Further details are available from the USTTA Travel Information Centre.

GUEST-HOUSES: There is a network of guest-houses (boarding houses) throughout the USA. For details contact: The Director, Tourist House Association of America, PO Box 355-AA, Greentown, PA 18426. Tel: (717) 676 3222.

BED & BREAKFAST: This long-established tradition in the UK is now spreading across the USA. B&B signs are not generally displayed by individual homes, but most homes offering this service are listed in directories, which may be purchased by interested travellers.

RANCH HOLIDAYS: There are ranches all over the southern and western states offering riding, participation in cattle drives, and activity holidays in mountain and lakeland settings.

CAMPING/CARAVANNING: This is extremely popular, especially in the Rocky Mountains and New England. The camping season in the north lasts from mid-May to mid-September. Camping along the side of highways and in undesignated areas is prohibited. For information on campsites, contact: KOA (Kampgrounds of America). Tel: (406) 248 7444. The 24,000-plus campsites fall into two general categories:

Public sites: Usually linked with National or State Parks and Forests, offering modest but comfortable facilities. Most of them will have toilet blocks, electricity hook-ups and picnic areas. Campsites are usually operated on a first-come, first-served basis and will often restrict the length of stay. Advance reservations are possible at some national parks.

Privately-run sites: These range from basic to resort luxury. Most have clothes washing and drying facilities, entertainment and information services. Reservations can be made through a central reservation office in the USA.

YMCA/YOUTH HOSTELS: There are 74 YMCA centres in 68 cities throughout the USA. Membership is not neces-

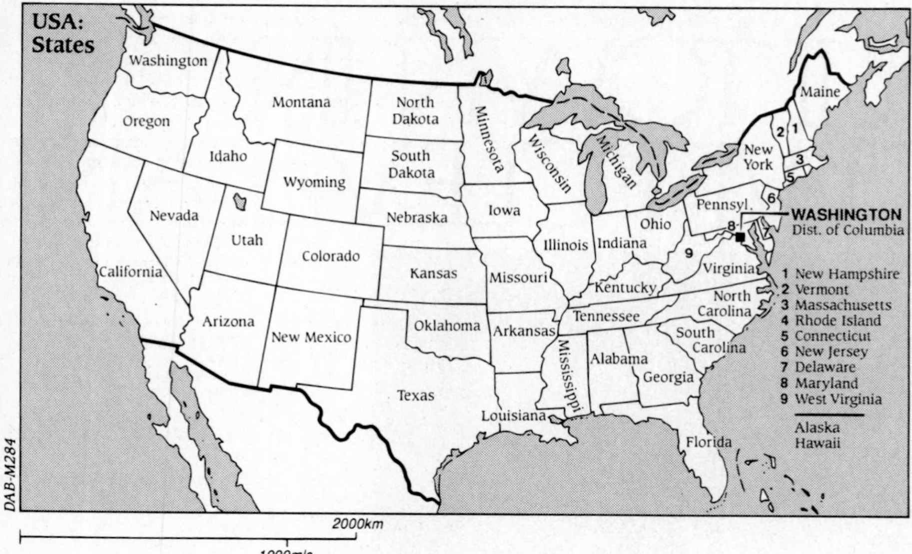

sary, but reservations should be made two days prior to arrival via the Head Offices. The *YMCA* offers centrally located accommodation at attractive rates coast to coast throughout the USA. Most centres offer single and double accommodation for both men and women and many also have sports facilities. Youth hostels offer their members simple, inexpensive overnight accommodation usually located in scenic, historical or cultural places. *Youth Hostel Association* membership is open to everyone with no age limit and there are individual, family and organisation memberships. British visitors should take out membership in the UK before travelling.

SELF-CATERING: Self-catering facilities, known in the USA as 'apartments', 'condominiums' (or 'condos'), 'efficiencies' or 'villas', are also available. Further details are available from the USTTA Travel Information Centre.

HOME EXCHANGE: There are several agents who offer home exchange programmes between the USA and the UK. Further information is available from the USTTA Travel Information Centre.

RESORTS & EXCURSIONS

Major tourist attractions are given in the section *States A-Z* and in the *Resorts & Excursions* sub-sections of *US Gateways* below.

SOCIAL PROFILE

FOOD & DRINK: In large cities restaurants are mostly of modern design and very clean, offering a vast range of cuisines, prices and facilities. American breakfasts are especially worth experiencing for such specialities as pancakes or waffles with maple syrup, home fries and grits (a Southern dish). Foreigners are often perplexed by the common question of how they would like their eggs fried, ie 'over easy' (flipped over briefly) or 'sunny side up' (fried on one side only). Fast food chains serving hot dogs ('weenies'), hamburgers and pizzas are ubiquitous. Regional specialities range from Spanish flavours in the southwest to Creole or French in the deep south. Restaurants come in all shapes and sizes, ranging from fast-food, self-service and counter service to drive-in and table service. The 'diner' is an integral part of the American way of life; consisting of a driveway, neon lights, and simple food served from the counter, it is generally located in or just outside smaller towns. Discounts on eating out include *Early Bird Dinners*, where discounts are offered for meals served prior to 1800; *Children's Platters*, selections from a low-cost children's menu; and *Restaurant Specials*, when a different specific meal is offered each day at a discount price or there is an all-you-can-eat menu. **Drink:** There are also many types of bars, ranging from the smart cocktail lounge, café-style, high 'saloon' style bars and imitations of English pubs to the 'regular' bar. In cities many have 'happy hours' with cheaper drinks and free snacks on the counter. Generally speaking, waiter/waitress service costs more. Drinking laws are set by states, counties, municipalities and towns, although traditionally closing time in bars is between 2400 and 0300. The legal age for drinking also varies from 18 to 21 from state to state and the laws on the availability of alcohol run from Nevada's policy of anytime, anywhere and to anyone, to localities where drinking is strictly prohibited. Where the laws are severe, there are often private clubs or a town only a few kilometres away from the 'dry town' where alcohol sales are legal. It is important to be aware of these laws when visiting an area and it is worth remembering that where alcohol is available, visitors may be asked to produce some form of identity that will prove their age. It should also be noted that it is illegal to have an open container of alcohol in a vehicle or on the street. Beer is the most popular and widespread drink and is served ice cold. Californian wines are gaining popularity. See also the *Food & Drink* section under *US Gateways* below.

SHOPPING: Variety, late opening hours, competitive prices and an abundance of modern goods typify American shopping. Many small stores, specialist food shops and hypermarkets are open 24 hours a day. Clothes and electronic goods can be bought direct from factories. Retail outlets range from flea markets and bargain stores to large chain department stores. Shopping in Malls is popular in the USA. Malls house a cluster of different shops in one building, often a few storeys high, connected by an indoor plaza. Note that a sales tax is levied on all items in most states and the addition is not included on the price label; 3-15% is normal. A guide to the customs and laws of American shopping is available from PO Box 95-M, Oradell, NJ 07649. **Shopping hours:** 0900/0930-1730/1800 Monday to Saturday. There may be late-night shopping one or two evenings a week. Some states permit Sunday trading.

NIGHTLIFE: Clubs generally stay open until the early hours in cities, where one can find a variety of music and theatre of all descriptions. Unlike in Europe, bars are usually for drinkers and not for social meetings. Theatre tickets for Broadway, New York's equivalent of London's West End 'Theatreland', can be booked *for groups of over 20* through *Group Sales Box Office*, 226 West 47th Street, New York, NY 10036. Tel: (212) 398 8383. Fax: (212) 398 8389. Tickets must be paid for in advance and will be kept at the theatre box office for collection on the night of the performance. Gambling is only allowed in licensed casinos and the legal age for gamblers is 21 years of age or over.

SPORT: American football, baseball and **basketball** are the national sports. The baseball season lasts from April to September, the football season from September to January, the bastketball season from November to April and the hockey season from October to March. **Ice-hockey** is also very popular, as is **tennis.** The visitor can buy temporary membership at over 200 clubs. **Golf:** A few clubs and courses are open to visitors. For information, contact the *Taconic Golf Club*, PO Box 183, Williams Town, MA 01267. Tel: (413) 458 9669. **Outward Bound:** America's vast expanses of wild country and mountains lend themselves to outdoor pursuits. The national office is *Outward Bound*, 384 Field Point Road, Greenwich, CT 06830. Tel: (203) 661 0797. **Horseracing:** The heart of racing in the USA is the 'bluegrass country', focused around the state of Kentucky. The most important races of the year, the *Bluegrass Stakes* and the *Kentucky Derby*, are run at the Churchill Downs racecourse in Louisville, Kentucky. There are also major tracks in New England. **Rodeos:** Held in Colorado, Oklahoma, Texas and throughout the western states, rodeos are a legacy of the historical development that resulted from the spread of cattle ranching. **Downhill skiing:** The principal areas are: *Eastern states* – Maine, New Hampshire, Vermont; *California* – Lake Tahoe, Squaw Valley, Mammoth Mountain; and *Colorado* – Aspen, Summit County. Skiing is also possible in Idaho, Montana, New Mexico and Utah. **Cross-country skiing:** New England, California, Minnesota, Wisconsin, Colorado and Wyoming. A *Ski Touring Guide* is published by the *Ski Touring Council*, based in New York.

SPECIAL EVENTS: The holidays which are closest to the people's hearts are Thanksgiving and Christmas. **Christmas:** The Americans celebrate Christmas in a big way, both religiously and as consumers, and much warmth and excitement is shared over the Christmas season. Northern regions have the added bonus of wintery weather and snowfall, and a 'White Christmas' (a fairly common event in the New England area and other northern states) always adds to the Christmas cheer. Chestnut-roasting over the family fireplace and cups of steaming hot chocolate or hot toddies are favourite Christmas snacks. The tree is decorated on Christmas Eve with plentiful ornaments and tinsel, and houses are also adorned with many wreaths and electric light decorations for the Christmas season.

Thanksgiving: On the last Thursday in November a holiday takes place entirely in the home amongst immediate family, sometimes with other good friends and loved ones. Blessings are shared and prayers of thanks are said over a feast of roast turkey, bread stuffing, roast potatoes and yams. This holiday originated the first year after the English arrived in the New World to thank the American Indians for their generous aid and advice in helping them come to grips with a new land.

The 4th of July: In honour of America's victory against the British in the Revolutionary War, this holiday is celebrated throughout the country with spectacular fireworks displays. American fireworks are among the best in the world and some of the most dazzling shows take place over lakes, rivers or on the coast over the ocean, where the sky can be lit up without any architectural obstacles and the light reflected from the water creates an even more brilliant effect.

Halloween: Another holiday uniquely celebrated in the USA is Halloween (Oct 31). Children dress up in costumes of their choice (often of a ghoulish nature, such as witches, devils and ghosts) and tour the neighbourhood, usually in groups, knocking on the doors of nearby houses and saying 'trick or treat' when the door is opened. The owner of the house is then obliged to give the children some sort of 'treat', usually consisting of a chocolate bar or apple. The night before Halloween is known as *Mischief Night*, when children roam their neighbourhoods doing naughty pranks such as ringing doorbells and running away or spreading toilet paper along fences and telephone poles. Both of these nights are somewhat unpopular with adults, but children have a great time and the tradition seems too engrained in American society to be discontinued. American influence throughout the world is such that other countries are beginning to celebrate Halloween, though not with such panache.

Mardi Gras: Every year New Orleans celebrates Mardi Gras, attracting visitors from all over the USA and abroad. Parades, dancing in the streets, masks and costumes abound and there is a general spirit of wild abandon during this period. This year's celebrations will take place February 1-15, 1994.

World Cup 1994: From June 17 to July 17, 1994, the USA will host World Cup Soccer 1994. Matches will take place in nine venues throughout the country, including Foxboro Stadium in Massachusetts, the Giants Stadium in the Meadowlands complex in New Jersey, RFK Stadium in Washington DC, the Citrus Bowl in Orlando, Soldier Field in Chicago, the Pontiac Silverdome in Detroit, the Cotton Bowl in Dallas, Stanford Stadium near San Francisco and the Rose Bowl in Pasadena. For further information, see the *World Cup '94* sections within the *US Gateways* entry. In addition to the above, details of special events are listed for many states under their individual headings in the *US Gateways* section.

SOCIAL CONVENTIONS: The wide variety of national origins and America's relatively short history has resulted in numerous cultural and traditional customs living alongside each other. In large cities people of the same ethnic background often live within defined communities. Shaking hands is the usual form of greeting. A relaxed and informal atmosphere is prevalent throughout most strata of society. As long as the fundamental rules of courtesy are observed there need be no fear of offending anyone of any background. Americans are renowned for their openness and friendliness to visitors. Gifts are appreciated if invited to a private home. As a rule dress is casual. Smart restaurants, hotels and clubs insist on suits and ties or long dresses. Smoking is often restricted in public buildings and on city transport. There will usually be a notice where no smoking is requested and many restaurants have smoking and non-smoking sections. **Tipping:** Widely practised, and service charges are not usually included in the bill.

Waiters generally expect 15%, as do taxi drivers and hairdressers. It should be noted that a cover charge is for admission to an establishment, not a tip for service. Porters generally expect US$1 per bag.

BUSINESS PROFILE

ECONOMY: The US economy is the world's most powerful and diverse. The physical expansion and development of the country during the 19th century (see *History* below), mass immigration, technological and marketing innovations, exploitation of natural resources and the expansion of international trade – all developments which have taken place within a political and economic system well able to exploit them – has made the USA a country of unprecedented wealth. With her large foreign investments, US interests dominate world markets in almost every sector, thus giving the dollar a crucial role. The USA has large areas under cultivation producing a wide range of commodities: the most important of these are cotton, cereals and tobacco, all of which are exported on a large scale. Mining operations produce oil and gas, coal, copper, iron, uranium and silver. The manufacturing industry is a world leader in many fields, including steel, vehicles, aerospace, telecommunications, chemicals, electronics and consumer goods. Since the late 1970s, however, the biggest employer has been the service sector, particularly finance (including banking, insurance and equities), leisure and tourism. Despite the wealth and range of its economy, there is a growing feeling in many quarters that the American economy now faces inevitable decline. Imports of many products have risen sharply during the last ten years (crucially, more quickly than exports) and previously dominant industries have found themselves under fierce competition from Japan, the European Community and the NICs – the newly-industrialised countries of the Pacific Rim. Oil, chemicals, vehicles and even advanced technology industries such as computing are threatened. There is a worrying trade deficit and a vast overspend on the Federal budget, which escalated to an astonishing US$4 trillion following the Reagan presidency. The protectionist lobby in the USA has grown quickly in the last few years and has now started to exert a significant influence on the Government. There have been a series of bilateral disputes between the USA and, successively, Japan and the European Community over a variety of products and services (semiconductors, transport and financial services). The crunch is likely to come over agriculture where both EC and Japanese farmers enjoy well-protected internal markets. The creation of the EC Single European Market in 1992 has triggered several potentially explosive arguments. Agriculture and services have been the main problem areas in the GATT talks, which have still to be resolved. On the American continent, however, free trade has scored a major success with the 3-way agreement between the USA, Canada and Mexico to establish the North American Free Trade Area (NAFTA). Subject to ratification by the US Congress, this establishes a trading bloc of remarkably similar proportions to the EC. The total population and economic output for the EC is 345 million and US$6.1 trillion respectively, and 365 million and US$6.2 trillion for NAFTA.

BUSINESS: Business people are generally expected to dress smartly, although a man may wear a short-sleeved shirt under his suit in hot weather. Normal business courtesies should be observed, although Americans often tend to be less formal than Europeans. Appointments and punctuality are normal procedure and business cards are widely used. **Office hours:** 0900-1730 Monday to Friday.

COMMERCIAL INFORMATION: The following organisations can offer advice:

New York Chamber of Commerce and Industry, 1 Battery Park Plaza, New York, NY 10004. Tel: (212) 493 7400. Fax: (212) 344 3344; *or*

Chamber of Commerce of the USA, 1615 H Street, NW, Washington, DC 20062-0001. Tel: (202) 659 6000. Fax: (202) 463 5836. Telex: 248302 CUS-UR; *or*

United States Department of Commerce, District Office, Federal Office Building, Room 3718, 26 Federal Plaza, Foley Square, New York, NY 10278. Tel: (212) 264 0600; *or*

National Foreign Trade Council Inc, 1270 Avenue of the Americas, New York, NY 10020. Tel: (212) 399 7128.

CONFERENCES/CONVENTIONS: In the last 20 years ABTA (the British Association of Travel Agents) has held its annual convention in US cities four times; its 1991 convention was in Orlando, Florida. The previously honoured places were Miami, Los Angeles and Phoenix. That no other country has been revisited so often clearly indicates the importance of the USA as a conference destination; there are state, city and regional travel and convention organisations in every part of the country, each actively promoting its own assets. With so much information available the real problem for the organiser is to find some way of getting through it all and there are several magazines devoted to this end; they include *Meeting & Conventions Magazine*, *Successful Meetings Magazine* and *Corporate Meetings and Incentive Magazine*. Of statistical interest is Chicago's status as host to more trade shows than any other city in the world. Organisers interested in US venues should contact the USTTA or the travel organisations listed in the state sections of the *USA* entry. In addition to the state organisations, this entry now includes addresses of travel and convention organisations for cities and counties.

HISTORY & GOVERNMENT

HISTORY: Before the arrival of Christopher Columbus in North America in 1492, the continent was inhabited by Indians thought to have been descended from nomadic Mongolian tribes who had travelled across the Barents Sea. The first wave of European settlers, mainly English, French and Dutch, crossed the Atlantic in the 17th century and colonised the Eastern Seaboard. The restrictions on political rights and punitive taxation which the British government imposed on the American colonists led to the American War of Independence (1775-1783), with the Declaration of Independence being signed in 1776. The outcome was a humiliating defeat for the English King, George III. The American Constitution which was born of this victory has been imitated by many other countries. By 1853, the boundaries of the United States were, with the exception of Alaska and Hawaii, as they are today, following a period of settlement, purchases from the French and Spanish and annexation of Indian and Mexican lands. Economic activity in the southern states centred on plantation agriculture. Attempts by liberally-inclined Republicans, led by Abraham Lincoln, to put an end to slavery on which it depended were fiercely opposed. The election of Lincoln to the Presidency in 1861 precipitated a political crisis in which seven southern states (joined later by three others) broke away from the Union, resulting in the American Civil War. The more powerful and better-equipped Union forces prevailed after four years of fighting. After the war, the country entered a period of consolidation, building up an industrial economy and settling the vast interior region of America commonly known as the Midwest. The mid- and late 19th century also saw the formulation of an American foreign policy with two principal elements: formal diplomatic and trading links were established with the old colonial powers; while on the American continent, the USA sought to establish itself as the regional power – a policy espoused by the Monroe Doctrine (1822) which laid the basis for intervention in support of the USA's 'national interest'. The latter has been a constant feature of US policy ever since. Successful diplomatic and commercial overtures were also made to Japan; this in turn paved the way for the growth of US power in the Pacific. In Europe, US intervention in 1917 proved decisive for the allies, and signalled the emergence of the USA as a global power. Driven by free market economic policies and innovative developments in technology and production methods – notably the growth of the motor industry – the USA had by this time undeniably become the world's leading economy. The USA entered the Second World War following the Japanese attack on the American fleet at Pearl Harbour, although its earlier neutrality had been decidedly favourable to the Allied Powers, especially Britain. Domestic post-war politics have revolved around the struggle between the Republicans and Democrats, the only two parties of any significance. The Republican Party, often referred to as the GOP or Grand Old Party, picks up most corporate support and substantial backing from wealthy individuals; the Democrats are perceived as the party supported by particular interest groups, thus the 'labor vote', 'black vote', 'Jewish vote' and so on, and as having more liberal views on social and welfare policy. The Democratic Party is, however, by no means left-wing and equally keen as its GOP counterpart to attract the votes of 'middle America' – the mostly white, middle income, middle-class folk who form the backbone of the American electorate (ie the quarter of the population who actually vote). Both Republican and Democratic candidates have been elected to the Presidency with roughly equal frequency over the history of the nation, but Republicans have been more frequent in the White House since 1945 while the Democrats have dominated Congress. The Second World War also saw the birth of nuclear weapons and the superpower conflict which has until recently dominated modern international relations. The essence of post-war American foreign policy has been the struggle against the spread of communist influence, not only for ideological reasons but also for economic motives. Despite the dangers of nuclear escalation, direct military intervention has not been eschewed, however, as in the Korean War of the 1950s (under UN auspices), the ill-fated Vietnam mission and, recently, the Middle East. The Reagan administration, which came to office in 1980, re-invigorated the ideological struggle, although relations between the USA and the then USSR improved greatly after 1985 due, almost entirely, to the 'new thinking' adopted in Soviet foreign policy under the Gorbachev regime. In November 1988, Reagan's Vice-President George Bush was elected to the White House. As far as America was concerned, the collapse of the Soviet bloc meant the Cold War was won and the foreign policy effort needed to be realigned. Thus we have the 'New World Order', a loosely defined notion coined by Bush before the war against Iraq in early 1991. The enemy, so to speak, was best defined by one White House staffer as 'that swirling pot of poison made up of zealots, crazies, drug traffickers and terrorists'. Under the aegis of the New World Order, Bush launched two major military campaigns, against Panama and Iraq. While both were successful in their immediate objectives, the long-term benefits have been less clear. A by-product of the intervention in the Gulf was the new impetus which the crisis gave to a solution of the Palestinian question in which the USA, as Israel's essential ally, has long been involved. Bush's Secretary of State James Baker managed, in the months after the war, to persuade the major participants (Israel, Lebanon, Jordan, Syria and the Palestinians) to start talking at a series of sessions at the end of 1991 and beginning of 1992. The USA continues to be a major player in the peace process, and although success is far from guaranteed there seems to be a feeling among the participants that an opportunity has arisen which must be taken. For all Bush's engagements on the international stage, his apparent neglect of the domestic situation – the state of the economy, the crises in education and health-care – told against him with the electorate. This came to haunt him in the run-up to the 1992 election as his opponent, the Democratic Governor of Arkansas, Bill Clinton, managed to capitalise on Bush's perceived policy failings, despite the Republican campaign's attempts to portray Clinton as a womanising, draft-dodging dissembler. Bush failed to repeat his achievement in 1988 of overhauling a large Democratic poll lead and Clinton won the election by a comfortable majority. The bizarre on-off candidacy of the independent candidate, billionaire H Ross Perot, had some effect on the poll, though exactly what is not clear. From Clinton's administration, the USA can expect a more interventionist government in social and perhaps industrial policy. The rest of the world may not see much change, other than in aspects of trade policy, on which Clinton has promised to take a somewhat tougher line. (The GATT settlement and the NAFTA accord can expect detailed scrutiny before ratification.)

GOVERNMENT: The USA is a Federal Republic with 50 states and the District of Columbia (as in 'Washington, DC'), which lies between Maryland and Virginia. In addition, the USA has close associations with the Commonwealth of Puerto Rico, Guam and the US Virgin Islands and exercises trusteeship on behalf of the UN over several Pacific Island groups. The Constitution (the final arbiters of which are the members of the Supreme Court) ensures the powers of the executive, legislature, judiciary, the presidency and the individual states are balanced by constitutional procedures. The President is elected by an electoral college system based on universal adult suffrage every four years. No President may be elected to serve more than two full terms of office. The current President is Bill Clinton, with Al Gore as Vice-President. The legislature is bicameral; the Senate has two members from each state while the larger House of Representatives allocates seats on the basis of population. Collectively these two bodies are known as Congress. Each state enjoys a fairly high degree of self-government.

CLIMATE

See *Climate* sections in *US Gateways* below.

STATES A-Z

The following section gives information on all the states in the USA, arranged alphabetically. More detailed information on states which have a gateway city may be found in *US Gateways* below. See also the *Introduction* above.

ALABAMA

POPULATION: 4,118,000.
CAPITAL: Montgomery.
TIME: GMT - 6. *Daylight Saving Time* is observed from the first Sunday in April to the last Sunday in October. Clocks are put forward one hour, changing at 0200 hours local time.
THE STATE: Alabama offers mountains, lakes, caverns, woodland and beaches. Birmingham is its largest city and cultural centre. Attractions include the new civic sports and arts centre and the Birmingham Museum of Art. Other tourist destinations include the Huntsville Space & Rocket Center; the Russell Cave National Monument; historic Montgomery; and Mobile, a major seaport and resort area on the Gulf Coast.
Further information from: Alabama Bureau of Tourism and Travel, PO Box 4309, 401 Adams Avenue, Montgomery, AL 36103-4309. Tel: (205) 242 4169. Fax: (205) 242 4554.
City and council information: Greater Birmingham Convention & Visitors Bureau, 2200 Ninth Avenue North, Birmingham, AL 35203-4167. Tel: (205) 252 9825. Fax: (205) 254 1649; *or*
Huntsville and Madison County Convention & Visitors Bureau, 700 Monroe Street, Huntsville, AL 35801-5570. Tel: (205) 551 2230. Fax: (205) 551 2324; *or*
Mobile Convention & Visitors Corporation, 150 South Royal Street, Mobile, AL 36602. Tel: (205) 434 7304. Fax: (205) 434 7659.

ALASKA

POPULATION: 527,000.
CAPITAL: Juneau.
TIME: GMT - 9, east of W169° 30'; GMT - 10, west of W169° 30' (the Aleutian Islands). *Daylight Saving Time* is observed from the first Sunday in April to the last Sunday in October. Clocks are put forward one hour, changing at 0200 hours local time.
THE STATE: The largest state in the USA, Alaska is a land of glaciers, rivers, waterfalls, fjords, forests, tundra and meadows. Anchorage is the largest city. Alaskan attractions include Denali National Park, Kenai Peninsula, Alyeska ski area, Chugach National Forest, Portage Glacier, Pribilof Islands and Juneau, state capital and historic gold-mining city. Mount McKinley, at 6194m (20,320ft), is the highest mountain in North America.
Further information from: Alaska Division of Tourism, PO Box 110801, Juneau, AK 99811-0801. Tel: (907) 465 2010. Fax: (907) 586 8399.
City and council information: Anchorage Convention & Visitors Bureau, Suite 200, 1600 A Street, Anchorage, AK 99501-5162. Tel: (907) 276 4118. Fax: (907) 278 5559; *or*
Fairbanks Convention & Visitors Bureau, 550 First Avenue, Fairbanks, AK 99701-4790. Tel: (907) 456 5774. Fax: (907) 452 2867.

ARIZONA

POPULATION: 3,556,000.
CAPITAL: Phoenix.
GATEWAY: Phoenix. For further information, see under *US Gateways* below.

ARKANSAS

POPULATION: 2,406,000.
CAPITAL: Little Rock.
TIME: GMT - 6. *Daylight Saving Time* is observed from the first Sunday in April to the last Sunday in October. Clocks are put forward one hour, changing at 0200 hours local time.
THE STATE: A varied landscape of plains, mountains, forests, rivers, cattle farms, industrial centres and oil wells. Its many lakes are among the chief tourist attractions. Others include the Hot Springs National Park; Blanchard Spring Caverns; Buffalo River; Crater of Diamonds State Park; Eureka Springs, a town built into the mountainside; and Mountain View, the Ozark Mountain folk centre. Little Rock, one of the state's earliest settlements, contains parks, museums and arts centers. Bill Clinton was the Governor of Arkansas with seat in Little Rock before becoming President.
Further information from: Arkansas Division of Tourism, Capitol Mall, Little Rock, AR 72201. Tel: (501) 682 7777. Fax: (501) 682 1364.
City and council information: Little Rock Convention & Visitors Bureau, PO Box 3232, Markham & Broadway, Robinson Center, Little Rock, AR 72203. Tel: (501) 376 4781. Fax: (501) 374 2255; *or*
Hot Springs Convention & Visitors Bureau, PO Box K, 134 Convention Boulevard, Hot Springs, AR 71902. Tel: (501) 321 2277. Fax: (501) 321 2136.

CALIFORNIA

POPULATION: 29,063,000.
CAPITAL: Sacramento.
GATEWAYS: Los Angeles and San Francisco. For further information, see under *US Gateways* below.

COLORADO

POPULATION: 3,317,000.
CAPITAL: Denver.
TIME: GMT - 7. *Daylight Saving Time* is observed from the first Sunday in April to the last Sunday in October. Clocks are put forward one hour, changing at 0200 hours local time.
THE STATE: Colorado stands high up in the famous Rocky Mountains and offers national parks, forests, gold-rush ghost towns, ancient Indian temples and fine ski resorts. Denver contains many museums, parks, gardens and a restored Victorian square. State attractions include Colorado Springs; Pike's Peak; the Rocky Mountain and Mesa Verde National Parks; Black Canyon and the sandstone formations of the Garden of the Gods.
Further information from: Colorado Tourism Board, Suite 1700, 1625 Broadway, Denver, CO 80202. Tel: (303) 592 5510. Fax: (303) 592 5406.
City and council information: Colorado Springs Convention & Visitors Bureau, Suite 104, 104 South Cascade Avenue, Colorado Springs, CO 80903. Tel: (719) 635 7506. Fax: (719) 635 4968; *or*
Denver Metro Convention & Visitors Bureau, 225 West Colfax Avenue, Denver, CO 80202-5399. Tel: (303) 892 1112. Fax: (303) 892 1636.

CONNECTICUT

POPULATION: 3,239,000.
CAPITAL: Hartford.
TIME: GMT - 5. *Daylight Saving Time* is observed from the first Sunday in April to the last Sunday in October. Clocks are put forward one hour, changing at 0200 hours local time.
THE STATE: Connecticut offers quiet colonial villages, upmarket 'commuter towns' for New York executives, lakes, mountains, forests and broad sandy beaches. Hartford is the insurance capital of the USA. State attractions include Mark Twain House, Hartford; New Haven, home of Yale University and the well-known Peabody Museum of Natural History; Mystic Seaport, a living museum of whaling; Long Island Sound, with its chain of resort towns and fishing ports; and the Gillette Castle Park in Hadlyme.
Further information from: Connecticut Office of Tourism, 865 Brook Street, Rocky Hill, CT 06067-3405. Tel: (203) 258 4300. Fax: (203) 529 0535.
City and council information: New Haven Visitors Bureau, 195 Church Street, New Haven, CT 06510. Tel: (203) 777 8550. Fax: (203) 782 2841; *or*
Greater Stamford Visitors Bureau, One Landmark Square, Stamford, CT 06901. Tel: (203) 359 3305. Fax: (203) 363 5069; *or*
Greater Hartford Visitors Bureau, One Civic Center Plaza, Hartford, CT 06103-1592. Tel: (203) 728 6789. Fax: (203) 293 2365; *or*
Mystic & Shoreline Visitor Center, Building 1D, Olde Mystic Village, Mystic, CT 06355. Tel: (203) 536 1641.

DELAWARE

POPULATION: 673,000.
CAPITAL: Dover.
TIME: GMT - 5. *Daylight Saving Time* is observed from the first Sunday in April to the last Sunday in October. Clocks are put forward one hour, changing at 0200 hours local time.
THE STATE: Wilmington is this small state's administrative and commercial centre. Founded in 1638, the city includes museums, galleries and a port. Its Fort Christina Historic Park is the site of Delaware's first permanent settlement. The rest of the state is mostly rural. Attractions include the small capital city of Dover; historic New Castle; the fishing town of Lewes; Rehoboth Beach and Delaware Seashore State Park.
Further information from: Delaware Tourism Office, PO Box 1401, 99 Kings Highway, Dover, DE 19903. Tel: (302) 739 4271. Fax: (302) 739 5749.
City and council information: Greater Wilmington Convention and Visitors Bureau, Suite 504, 1300 Market Street, Wilmington, DE 19801. Tel: (302) 652 4088. Fax: (302) 652 4726.

FLORIDA

POPULATION: 12,671,000.
CAPITAL: Tallahassee.
GATEWAYS: Miami, Orlando and Tampa. For further information, see under *US Gateways* below.

GEORGIA

POPULATION: 6,436,000.
CAPITAL: Atlanta.
GATEWAY: Atlanta. For further information, see under *US Gateways* below.

HAWAII

See separate entry below.

IDAHO

POPULATION: 1,014,000.
CAPITAL: Boise.
TIME: GMT - 7. *Daylight Saving Time* is observed in the greater part of the state from the first Sunday in April to the last Sunday in October. Clocks are put forward one hour, changing at 0200 hours local time.
THE STATE: Idaho includes Hell's Canyon, the deepest in North America; the largest stand of white pine in the world at Clearwater National Forest; and two of the finest big-game hunting areas in the USA – Chamberlain Basin and Selway. Boise hosts a summer festival and the August Idaho State Fair. The well-known Sun Valley resort area offers skiing and winter sports and a range of summer activities. Other attractions include the massive Shoshone Falls; the Shoshone Indian Ice Caves; historic Fort Hall; the Craters of the Moon National Monument area; the Coeur d'Alene mining district; and the Nez Perce National Historical Park.
Further information from: Idaho Department of Commerce, 700 West State Street, Boise, ID 83720-2700. Tel: (208) 334 2470. Fax: (208) 334 2631.
City and council information: Boise Convention & Visitors Bureau, PO Box 2106, Suite 200, 168 North 9th Street, Boise, ID 83701. Tel: (208) 344 7777. Fax: (208) 344 6236.

ILLINOIS

POPULATION: 11,658,000.
CAPITAL: Springfield.
GATEWAY: Chicago. For further information, see under *US Gateways* below.

INDIANA

POPULATION: 5,593,000.
CAPITAL: Indianapolis.
TIME: GMT - 5 (in the greater part of the state).
THE STATE: Indiana, bordered by Lake Michigan to the north, features lakes, deep valleys, plains, foothills, industrial areas and vast farmlands. Indianapolis is a national centre for industry, commerce and culture. Its international airport is 8km (5 miles) from the city centre. State attractions include the Indiana Dunes National Lakeshore and park; Amish Acres, a restored 19th-century Amish community at Nappanee; the Conner Prairie Pioneer Settlement; the Squire Boone Caves; and Fort Wayne, scene of many bloody battles.
Further information from: Indiana Tourism Division, Suite 700, Indiana Commerce Center, One North Capitol, Indianapolis, IN 46204-2288. Tel: (317) 232 8860.
City and council information: Greater Lafayette Convention & Visitors Bureau, PO Box 5547, 301 Frontage Road, Lafayette, IN 47905. Tel: (317) 447 9999. Fax: (317) 447 5062; *or*
Bloomington/Monroe County Convention & Visitors Bureau, 2855 North Walnut, Bloomington, IN 47404. Tel: (812) 334 8900. Fax: (812) 334 2344; *or*
Grant County Convention & Visitors Bureau, 215 South Adams Street, Marion, IN 46952. Tel: (317) 668 5435. Fax: (317) 668 5443.

IOWA

POPULATION: 2,840,000.
CAPITAL: Des Moines.
TIME: GMT - 6. *Daylight Saving Time* is observed from the first Sunday in April to the last Sunday in October. Clocks are put forward one hour, changing at 0200 hours local time.
THE STATE: Almost 95% of Iowa's gently undulating land is given over to agriculture, but it also offers cities, scenic parks and many lakes and recreation areas, such as East and West Okoboji, Spirit Lake and Clear Lake. Its rich cultural heritage is shown in the German, Swiss and Alsatian Amana colonies, with their many historic sites and museums. Pella reflects its Dutch past in its tulip fields, customs and architecture. Other attractions include the Boone and Scenic Valley Railroad; Effigy Mounds Park, with its relics of ancient Indian culture; and Fort Dodge, now restored as a museum.
Further information from: Iowa Division of Tourism, 200 East Grand Avenue, Des Moines, IA 50309. Tel: (515) 242 4705. Fax: (515) 242 4749.
City and council information: Greater Des Moines Visitors Bureau, Suite 222, 601 Ruan Two Building, Locust, Des Moines, IA 50309-2285. Tel: (515) 286 4960. Fax: (515) 244 9757; *or*
Iowa City Convention & Visitors Bureau, Suite 200, 325 East Washington Street, Iowa City, IA 52240-3959. Tel: (319) 337 6592. Fax: (319) 338 9958.

KANSAS

POPULATION: 2,513,000.
CAPITAL: Topeka.
TIME: GMT - 6. *Daylight Saving Time* is observed from the first Sunday in April to the last Sunday in October. Clocks are put forward one hour, changing at 0200 hours local time.
THE STATE: At the geographic centre of North America, Kansas is largely agricultural, with vast fields of wheat. It boasts many monuments to its Old West past, as well as numerous recreation centres, reservoirs and rivers offering all kinds of outdoor pursuits. Attractions include the restored cattle town of Dodge City; the Kansas Cosmosphere and Discovery Center in Hutchinson; and the Swedish settlers' town of Lindsborg. Wichita, its largest city, includes museums, parks, and centres for art, music, theatre and sport.
Further information from: Kansas Travel & Tourism Development, Suite 1200, 700 SW Harrison Street, Topeka, KS 66603. Tel: (913) 296 2009. Fax: (913) 296 6988. Telex: 4931494 KS.
City and council information: Wichita Convention & Visitors Bureau, Suite 100, 100 South Main, Wichita, KS 67202. Tel: (316) 265 2800. Fax: (316) 265 0162.

KENTUCKY

POPULATION: 3,727,000.
CAPITAL: Frankfort.
TIME: GMT - 5 (eastern part); GMT - 6 (western part). *Daylight Saving Time* is observed from the first Sunday in April to the last Sunday in October. Clocks are put forward one hour, changing at 0200 hours local time.
THE STATE: Kentucky is best known for horses, caves, bourbon and bluegrass. Lexington is the horse breeding centre and many of its surrounding farms welcome visitors on free tours. Louisville boasts the famous Kentucky Derby, along with historic buildings, top arts venues, a space museum and steamboat trips. Other attractions include the Fort Knox gold bullion store; the pioneer town at Kentucky Lake, one of the largest man-made lakes in the world; the Daniel Boone National Forest; and Bardstown, the 'bourbon capital of the world'.
Further information from: Kentucky Department of Travel Development, 22nd Floor, Capital Plaza Tower, 500 Mero Street, Frankfort, KY 40601. Tel: (502) 564 4930. Fax: (502) 564 5695.
City and council information: Greater Lexington Convention & Visitors Bureau, Suite 363, 430 West Vine Street, Lexington, KY 40507. Tel: (606) 233 1221. Fax: (606) 254 4555; *or*
Louisville Bureau of Tourism, 400 South First Street, Louisville, KY 40202. Tel: (502) 584 2121. Fax: (502) 584 6697; *or*
Northern Kentucky Convention & Visitors Bureau, 605 Philadelphia Street, Covington, KY 41011. Tel: (606) 261 4677. Fax: (606) 261 5135.

LOUISIANA

POPULATION: 4,382,000.
CAPITAL: Baton Rouge.
GATEWAY: New Orleans. For further information, see under *US Gateways* below.

MAINE

POPULATION: 1,222,000.
CAPITAL: Augusta.
TIME: GMT - 5. *Daylight Saving Time* is observed from the first Sunday in April to the last Sunday in October. Clocks are put forward one hour, changing at 0200 hours local time.
THE STATE: Maine offers some of the most beautiful scenery in the north. About four-fifths of its area is forested, but it also includes more than 2200 lakes, together with mountains, valleys and seashore. Bangor is a major commercial, financial and cultural centre. Portland, Maine's largest city, features a renovated old port section. Other state attractions include the Acadia National Park on the Atlantic Ocean, one of the most beautiful in the USA; Kittery, the state's oldest town; and Kennebunkport, one of the prime beauty spots on the north coast.
Further information from: Maine Office of Tourism, 189 State Street, Augusta, ME 04333. Tel: (207) 289 5710. Fax: (207) 287 5701; *or*
Maine Campground Owners, 655 Main Street, Lewiston, ME 04240. Tel: (207) 782 5874.
City and council information: Kennebunk-Kennebunkport Tourism Board, PO Box 740, Kennebunk, ME 04043. Tel: (207) 967 0858.

MARYLAND

POPULATION: 4,694,000.
CAPITAL: Annapolis.
GATEWAY: Baltimore. For further information, see under *US Gateways* below.

MASSACHUSETTS

POPULATION: 5,913,000.
CAPITAL: Boston.
GATEWAY: Boston. For further information, see under *US Gateways* below.

MICHIGAN

POPULATION: 9,273,000.
CAPITAL: Lansing.
GATEWAY: Detroit. For further information, see under *US Gateways* below.

MINNESOTA

POPULATION: 4,353,000.
CAPITAL: St Paul.
GATEWAY: Minneapolis/St Paul. For further information, see under *US Gateways* below.

MISSISSIPPI

POPULATION: 2,621,000.
CAPITAL: Jackson.
TIME: GMT - 6. *Daylight Saving Time* is observed from the first Sunday in April to the last Sunday in October. Clocks are put forward one hour, changing at 0200 hours local time.
THE STATE: Mississippi is noted for its pre-Civil War mansions, fine beaches and scenery. More than 16,000 acres have been set aside for camping and recreation, including the Clarbco and Percy Quinn state parks. National forests include Bienville, DeSoto, Delta and Holly Springs, famed for its restored country houses. Natchez, with its fine 18th- and 19th-century architecture, is near the start of the restored Natchez Trace Trail to Nashville. The route passes the ancient Indian Emerald Mound and the ghost town of Rocky Springs. Other attractions include Vicksburg, with its national military park; and Biloxi, on the state's beach-lined border with the Gulf of Mexico.
Further information from: Mississippi Division of Tourism, PO Box 849, Jackson, MS 39205. Tel: (601) 359 3297. Fax: (601) 359 2832.
City and council information: Meridian-Lauderdale County Partnership, PO Box 790, Suite 800, 721 Front Street, Meridian, MS 39301. Tel: (800) 748 9970. Fax: (601) 693 5638; *or*
Natchez-Adams County Convention & Visitors Bureau, PO Box 1485, 422 Main, Natchez, MS 39120. Tel: (601) 446 6345. Fax: (601) 442 0814.

MISSOURI

POPULATION: 5,159,000.
CAPITAL: Jefferson City.
GATEWAY: St Louis. For further information, see under *US Gateways* below.

MONTANA

POPULATION: 806,000.
CAPITAL: Helena.
TIME: GMT - 7. *Daylight Saving Time* is observed from the first Sunday in April to the last Sunday in October. Clocks are put forward one hour, changing at 0200 hours local time.
THE STATE: Montana boasts vast areas of national forest and wilderness, together with glaciers, mountain lakes, rivers, trails, waterfalls and ski resorts. Its major tourist destinations include the spectacular Yellowstone (shared with Wyoming, see below) and Glacier National Parks. Its numerous recreation areas include the Bob Marshall Wilderness Area and the huge Charlie Russell Wildlife Refuge. Helena offers fine 19th-century architecture, museums and the Gothic-style St Helena Cathedral. Other attractions include the Custer Battlefield, site of Custer's Last Stand; the restored Old West towns of Virginia City and Nevada City; and the National Bison Range.
Further information from: Montana Travel Promotion Office, 1424 9th Avenue, Helena, MT 59620. Tel: (406) 444 2654. Fax: (406) 444 2903.
City and council information: Missoula Convention and Visitors Bureau, PO Box 7577, 825 East Front, Missoula, MT 59807-7577. Tel: (406) 543 6623. Fax: (406) 543 6625.

NEBRASKA

POPULATION: 1,611,000.
CAPITAL: Lincoln.
TIME: GMT - 6. *Daylight Saving Time* is observed in the greater part of the state from the first Sunday in April to the last Sunday in October. Clocks are put forward one hour, changing at 0200 hours local time.
THE STATE: Nebraska rises from the Missouri prairie lands to the Great Plains and foothills of the Rocky Mountains. Omaha, its largest city, is one of the state's major tourist destinations. Boys Town, the famous homeless boys' community, is nearby. Lincoln boasts the State Capitol, the University of Nebraska Museum and the well-known Sheldon Art Gallery. Other state attractions include the Homestead National Monument; the pioneer landmarks of Scotts Bluff and Chimney Rock; Fort Robinson, where Chief Crazy Horse surrendered; and the Buffalo Bill Historical Park.
Further information from: Nebraska Division of Travel & Tourism, PO Box 94666, Lincoln, NE 68509. Tel: (402) 471 3796. Fax: (402) 471 3026.
City and council information: Greater Omaha Convention & Visitors Bureau, Suite 1200, 1819 Farnam Street, Omaha, NE 68183. Tel: (402) 444 4660. Fax: (402) 444 4511.

NEVADA

POPULATION: 1,111,000.
CAPITAL: Carson City.
GATEWAY: Las Vegas.
TIME: GMT - 8. *Daylight Saving Time* is observed from the first Sunday in April to the last Sunday in October. Clocks are put forward one hour, changing at 0200 hours local time.
THE STATE: Nevada includes everything from pine forests, desert, mountains and ghost towns to neon-lit cities. Las Vegas is its largest city and one of the major gambling and entertainment centres of the world. Luxury hotels, casinos and show venues line 'The Strip', a section of Las Vegas Boulevard South. A lower-priced, smaller version is found at the Downtown Casino Center. Outdoor sports, top restaurants and nightclubs are also on offer. Reno, another entertainment and casino city, is also known for its quiet residential areas and surrounding historic and natural attractions. Lake Tahoe nearby spans the California-Nevada border. It is the largest mountain lake in the USA and one of America's most famous mountain resort areas, offering year-round sports and activities. Other state attractions include the Lake Mead National Recreation Area; the Valley of Fire State Park; Pyramid Lake; Mount Charles; and the spectacular Lehman Caves and Death Valley.
Further information from: Nevada Commission on Tourism, 5151 South Carson Street, Capitol Complex, Carson City, NV 89710. Tel: (702) 687 4322. Fax: (702) 687 6779.
City and council information: Las Vegas Convention & Visitors Bureau, 3150 Paradise Road, Las Vegas, NV 89109-9096. Tel: (702) 892 0711. Fax: (702) 892 2824; *or*
Reno-Sparks Convention & Visitors Authority, PO Box 837, 4590 South Virginia Street, Reno, NV 89502. Tel: (702) 827 7600. Fax: (702) 827 7646.

NEW HAMPSHIRE

POPULATION: 1,107,000.
CAPITAL: Concord.
TIME: GMT - 5. *Daylight Saving Time* is observed from the first Sunday in April to the last Sunday in October. Clocks are put forward one hour, changing at 0200 hours local time.
THE STATE: New Hampshire is noted for its scenic beauty, from Mount Washington in the northern White Mountains and the centre-state lakes to the ocean beaches near Hampton. The Cog Railway ride to the top of Mount Washington affords panoramic views of Canada and the surrounding states. Franconia Notch, a dramatic 13km (8-mile) gorge nearby, is one of New England's most acclaimed beauty spots. Major ski resorts include Cannon Mountain, Loon Mountain and Waterville Valley. The town of Laconia, between lakes Winnipesaukee and Winnisquam, is another popular tourist destination.
Further information from: New Hampshire Office of Tourism, PO Box 856, 172 Pembroke Road, Concord, NH 03302. Tel: (603) 271 2666. Fax: (603) 271 2629; *or*
New Hampshire Lodging and Restaurant Association, PO Box 1175, 36 Pleasant Street, Concord, NH 03302-1175. Tel: (603) 228 9585.
City and council information: Mount Washington Valley Tourism Office, PO Box 2300, North Conway, NH 03860. Tel: (603) 356 5701. Fax: (603) 356 7069.

NEW JERSEY

POPULATION: 7,736,000.
CAPITAL: Trenton.
GATEWAY: Newark. For further information, see under *US Gateways* below.

NEW MEXICO

POPULATION: 1,528,000.
CAPITAL: Santa Fe.
TIME: GMT - 7. *Daylight Saving Time* is observed from the first Sunday in April to the last Sunday in October. Clocks are put forward one hour, changing at 0200 hours local time.
THE STATE: New Mexico has deserts, forests, cities, lakes and mountains. Its Pueblo Indian and Spanish cultures are still very much alive. Albuquerque, the largest city, has an international airport and its Old Town, museums and cultural centres help make it an important tourist destination and a good base for travelling through the state. Santa Fe, with its adobe architecture, is the USA's oldest state capital. Other attractions include the Sandia Peak area and ski runs; the Carlsbad Caverns; the mountain resort of Ruidoso; the Spanish colonial village of La Mesilla; prehistoric Indian sites; and the Navajo Indian Reservation near Farmington.
Further information from: New Mexico Tourism & Travel Division, Lamy Building, 491 Old Santa Fe Trail, Santa Fe, NM 87501. Tel: (505) 827 7400. Fax: (505) 827 7402.
City and council information: Albuquerque Convention & Visitors Bureau, 121 Tijeras Avenue North East, Albuquerque, NM 87102. Tel: (505) 842 9918. Fax: (505) 247 9101; *or*
Santa Fe Convention & Visitors Bureau, PO Box 909, 201 West Marcy Street, Santa Fe, NM 87504-0909. Tel: (505) 984 6760. Fax: (505) 984 6679.

NEW YORK

POPULATION: 17,950,000.
CAPITAL: Albany.
GATEWAY: New York City. For further information, see under *US Gateways* below.

NORTH CAROLINA

POPULATION: 6,571,000.
CAPITAL: Raleigh.
TIME: GMT - 5. *Daylight Saving Time* is observed from the first Sunday in April to the last Sunday in October. Clocks are put forward one hour, changing at 0200 hours local time.
THE STATE: Natural attractions in North Carolina range from sandy beaches in the east to high mountain ranges in the west. Charlotte, the largest city, is a thriving convention and entertainment centre. The Outer Banks barrier islands along the coast include resorts, fishing villages and stretches of national seashore. Cape Hatteras National Seashore also boasts areas of undeveloped beach. Other attractions include Raleigh, with its fine architecture and cultural centres, Great Smoky Mountains National Park and the Qualla Boundary Cherokee Indian Reservation.
Further information from: North Carolina Tourism Office, 430 North Salisbury Street, Raleigh, NC 27611. Tel: (919) 733 4171. Fax: (919) 733 8582.
City and council information: Asheville Area Convention & Visitors Bureau, PO Box 1010, 151 Haywood Street, Asheville, NC 28802. Tel: (704) 258 6111. Fax: (704) 251 0926; *or*
Charlotte Convention & Visitors Bureau, 122 East Stonewall Street, Charlotte, NC 28202. Tel: (704) 334 2282. Fax: (704) 342 3972.

NORTH DAKOTA

POPULATION: 660,000.
CAPITAL: Bismarck.
TIME: GMT - 6. *Daylight Saving Time* is observed in the greater part of the state from the first Sunday in April to the last Sunday in October. Clocks are put forward one hour, changing at 0200 hours local time.
THE STATE: North Dakota, one of the most rural states in the USA, is famous for its scenery and Old West heritage. The 70,000-acre Theodore Roosevelt National Park in the Badlands offers spectacular views and includes the restored cow-town of Medora. Fort Lincoln, south of Mandan, was HQ for Colonel Custer and the 7th Cavalry. The Slant Indian Village nearby traces the area's history from the first Indian settlements. Fargo is the state's largest city. Other attractions include the beaches of Lake Metigoshe; Sully's Hill Game Preserve; and the recreation areas around Lake Sakakawea and the Little Missouri River.
Further information from: North Dakota Office of Tourism, Liberty Memorial Building, 604 East Boulevard, Bismarck, ND 58505. Tel: (701) 224 2525. Fax: (701) 224 4878.
City and council information: Greater Grand Forks Tourism Office, Suite 200, 202 North 3rd Street, Grand Forks, ND 58203. Tel: (701) 746 0444. Fax: (701) 780 9025.

OHIO

POPULATION: 10,907,000.
CAPITAL: Columbus.
TIME: GMT - 5. *Daylight Saving Time* is observed from the first Sunday in April to the last Sunday in October. Clocks are put forward one hour, changing at 0200 hours local time.
THE STATE: Ohio, birthplace of seven US presidents, is an expanse of fertile farmland dotted with industrial centres. Cleveland, on the shores of Lake Erie, is a major industrial city with many tourist attractions, including museums, a planetarium, and the University Circle of performing arts venues and galleries. Cincinnati, on the Ohio River, also boasts sightseeing and cultural attractions. The Greater Cincinnati and Cleveland Hopkins international airports are nearby. Other places of interest include Cedar Point beach resort on Lake Erie; Seaworld in Aurora; the peaceful Lake Erie Islands; and the scenic Hocking Hills area around Logan.
Further information from: Ohio Division of Travel & Tourism, PO Box 1001, 77 South High Street, Columbus, OH 43266. Tel: (614) 466 8844. Fax: (614) 466 6744.
City and council information: Greater Cincinnati Convention & Visitors Bureau, 300 West Sixth Street, Cincinnati, OH 45202. Tel: (513) 621 7862. Fax: (513) 621 2156; *or*
Greater Cleveland Visitors Bureau, 3100 Terminal Tower, Tower City Center, Cleveland, OH 44113. Tel: (216) 621 4110. Fax: (216) 621 5967.

OKLAHOMA

POPULATION: 3,224,000.
CAPITAL: Oklahoma City.
TIME: GMT - 6. *Daylight Saving Time* is observed from the first Sunday in April to the last Sunday in October. Clocks are put forward one hour, changing at 0200 hours local time.
THE STATE: Oklahoma comprises mountains, forests and lakes to the east, plains and farmland in the centre, and wide-open ranching country to the west. It is the home of more Indian tribes than any other state in the USA. Oklahoma City offers many tourist attractions, including the Western Heritage Center and operating oil wells. Tulsa also has an international airport and boasts some of the West's major art centres and galleries. State park resorts and recreation areas include Eufaula Lake; Lake Texom; Arrowhead; Quartz Mountain and Western Hill. Indian City USA and the Cherokee Heritage Center recreate the Indian life of centuries ago.
Further information from: Oklahoma Tourism & Recreation, PO Box 60789, 500 Will Rogers Building, Oklahoma City, OK 73146-0789. Tel: (405) 521 2409.
City and council information: Oklahoma City Convention & Visitors Bureau, Four Santa Fe Plaza, Oklahoma City, OK 73102. Tel: (405) 278 8912. Fax: (405) 278 8916.

OREGON

POPULATION: 2,820,000.
CAPITAL: Salem.
TIME: GMT - 8. *Daylight Saving Time* is observed from the first Sunday in April to the last Sunday in October. Clocks are put forward one hour, changing at 0200 hours local time.
THE STATE: Oregon has many areas of great natural beauty and boasts more than 230 state parks and hundreds of camping areas in 13 national forests. Portland, the 'City of Roses', boasts fine gardens, restaurants, shops, concerts, jazz festivals and theatres. Its international airport is 14km (9 miles) east of downtown. State tourist destinations include the spectacular coast north of the California border; historic Astoria on the Columbia River; the Sea Lion Caves; Mount Hood Forest; Crater Lake Park; 19th-century Jacksonville; the Oregon Cave; and Hells Canyon.
Further information from: Oregon Tourism Division, 775 Summer Street NE, Salem, OR 97310. Tel: (503) 373 1270. Fax: (503) 581 5115.
City and council information: Eugenne/Springfield Visitors Bureau, PO Box 10286, 305 West Seventh Street, Eugene, OR 97440. Tel: (503) 484 5307. Fax: (503) 343 6335.

PENNSYLVANIA

POPULATION: 12,040,000.
CAPITAL: Harrisburg.
GATEWAY: Philadelphia. For further information, see under *US Gateways* below.

RHODE ISLAND

POPULATION: 998,000.
CAPITAL: Providence.
TIME: GMT - 5. *Daylight Saving Time* is observed from the first Sunday in April to the last Sunday in October. Clocks are put forward one hour, changing at 0200 hours local time.
THE STATE: Rhode Island, the smallest of the 50 states, offers broad sandy beaches, parks, cities and a wealth of historic buildings. Providence is the second-largest city in New England. Its East Side contains many fine restored homes. Newport, one of the chief resorts, has beautiful 17th- and 18th-century wooden buildings, good beaches, famous yachting events, and music and art festivals. Many of its magnificent mansions (including those built by the Vanderbilts and the Astors) are open to the public. Block Island, a summer island resort, is reached by ferry from Newport and Galilee. The state's scenic centrepiece, Narragansett Bay, is home to yachting regattas and a thriving fishing industry.
Further information from: Rhode Island Tourism Division, 7 Jackson Walkway, Providence, RI 02903. Tel: (401) 277 2601. Fax: (401) 277 2102.
City and council information: Greater Providence Convention & Visitors Bureau, Room 610, 30 Exchange Terrace, Providence, RI 02903. Tel: (401) 274 1636. Fax: (401) 751 2434.

SOUTH CAROLINA

POPULATION: 3,512,000.
CAPITAL: Columbia.
TIME: GMT - 5. *Daylight Saving Time* is observed from the first Sunday in April to the last Sunday in October. Clocks are put forward one hour, changing at 0200 hours local time.
THE STATE: South Carolina boasts a rich history and scenery ranging from lakes and mountains to some of the best beaches in the USA, as well as beautiful 'Gone With The Wind' plantations and the northwestern foothills where fierce battles were fought during the Civil War. Charleston, situated on the coast, is one of its chief tourist destinations, being the site of the first permanent English settlement. The historic downtown district of this port city has cobbled streets and hundreds of pastel-painted pre-Civil War buildings with lovely wrought-iron work and lush gardens. Carriages are available. Attractions in and around the city include the many museums, antique shops and restaurants as well as the marina, Charles Towne Landing State Park and Middleton Place Gardens, among the oldest in the USA. The nearby Magnolia Gardens, Cypress Gardens and Middelton Place Plantation have attractive landscaping and seasonal blooms and shrubs. Columbia's Riverbanks Zoo is one of the top ten in the USA. Other state attractions include Myrtle Beach, a popular resort city famous among other things for its golf, centred on the sun-drenched 95km (60 miles) stretch of coastline on the northern border; peaceful island resorts such as Kiawah, Seabrook and Hilton Head which has 20km (12 miles) of

beautiful beaches, unspoilt forest and golf courses; and the Oconee State Park in the lush northern Upcountry.
Further information from: South Carolina Division of Tourism, 121 Gloucester Place, London W1H 3PJ. Tel: (071) 224 1780. Fax: (071) 224 5164; *or*
South Carolina Division of Tourism, Suite 106, 1205 Pendleton Street, Columbia, SC 29201. Tel: (803) 734 0122. Fax: (803) 734 1017.
City and council information: Charleston Trident Visitors Bureau, PO Box 975, 81 Mary Street, Charleston, SC 29402. Tel: (803) 853 8000. Fax: (803) 723 4853.

SOUTH DAKOTA

POPULATION: 715,000.
CAPITAL: Pierre.
TIME: GMT - 6 (eastern part); GMT - 7 (western part). *Daylight Saving Time* is observed from the first Sunday in April to the last Sunday in October. Clocks are put forward one hour, changing at 0200 hours local time.
THE STATE: South Dakota includes the dramatic Badlands, fertile prairies, early pioneer towns and the Black Hills, with forests, lakes and caves. By far its biggest tourist attraction is the Mount Rushmore Memorial, where the faces of four American presidents have been blasted and carved out of the mountain. Sioux Falls and Rapid City are gateways to the area and have good air connections. State attractions include the Black Hills National Forest; Badlands National Park; and the Wind Cave National Park. All offer a host of outdoor pursuits.
Further information from: South Dakota Division of Tourism, 711 East Wells Avenue, Pierre, SD 57501. Tel: (605) 773 3301. Fax: (605) 773 3256.
City and council information: Sioux Falls Convention & Visitors Bureau, PO Box 1425, Suite 102, 200 North Philips Avenue, SD 57101-1425. Tel: (605) 336 1620. Fax: (605) 336 6499.

TENNESSEE

POPULATION: 4,940,000.
CAPITAL: Nashville.
TIME: GMT - 6. *Daylight Saving Time* is observed in the greater part of the state from the first Sunday in April to the last Sunday in October. Clocks are put forward one hour, changing at 0200 hours local time.
THE STATE: More than half of Tennessee is forested and great tracts have been set aside as state and national parks, forests, wilderness areas and game preserves. Nashville is a major music performance and recording centre. It also boasts a host of fine colleges and churches, a full-size replica of the Parthenon, the Country Music Hall of Fame and the Opryland USA music entertainment complex. Memphis, the state's largest city, is a major trading centre. Its main tourist attraction is Graceland, the home of Elvis Presley, and Beale Street is featured in many blues songs. At Chattanooga, take a ride up Lookout Mountain, with its Rock City Gardens and Ruby Falls. Gatlinburg is the starting point for trips into the Great Smoky Mountain National Park.
Further information from: Tennessee Tourism Office, PO Box 23170, Nashville, TN 37202-3170. Tel: (615) 741 2159. Fax: (615) 741 7225.
City and council information: Memphis Convention & Visitors Bureau, 47 Union Avenue, Memphis, TN 38103. Tel: (901) 543 5300. Fax: (901) 543 5350; *or*
Knoxville Convention & Visitors Bureau, PO Box 15012, 810 Clinch Avenue, Knoxville, TN 37901. Tel: (615) 523 7263. Fax: (615) 673 4400.

TEXAS

POPULATION: 16,991,000.
CAPITAL: Austin.
GATEWAYS: Dallas/Fort Worth and Houston. For further information, see under *US Gateways* below.

UTAH

POPULATION: 1,707,000.
CAPITAL: Salt Lake City.
TIME: GMT - 7. *Daylight Saving Time* is observed from the first Sunday in April to the last Sunday in October. Clocks are put forward one hour, changing at 0200 hours local time.
THE STATE: Utah's attractions include canyons, colourful towns and breathtaking national parks. Salt Lake City, with its international airport 11km (7 miles) west of downtown, is the world centre of the Mormon Church. Surrounded by the Wasatch Mountains, it boasts historic buildings, churches, museums, science exhibitions and arts festivals. Other state attractions include Zion National Park around the Virgin River Canyon, with its temple-like rock formations; Canyonlands, Arches and Capitol Reef national parks; and Timpanogos Cave and the Dinosaur National Monument near Vernal.
Further information from: Utah Travel Council, Council Hall, Capitol Hill, Salt Lake City, UT 84114-1102. Tel: (801) 538 1030. Fax: (801) 538 1399.
City and council information: Salt Lake City Convention & Visitors Bureau, 180 South West Temple, Salt Lake City, UT 84101-1493. Tel: (801) 521 2822. Fax: (801) 355 9323.

VERMONT

POPULATION: 567,000.
CAPITAL: Montpelier.
TIME: GMT - 5. *Daylight Saving Time* is observed from the first Sunday in April to the last Sunday in October. Clocks are put forward one hour, changing at 0200 hours local time.
THE STATE: Vermont is the only New England state without a seashore, but its border with Lake Champlain more than compensates. Its largest city, Burlington, affords magnificent views of the water, with its many sporting and recreation areas. The state's attractions include Stowe, the famous ski resort on the slopes of Mount Mansfield; Heritage Park, with its early New England buildings; and Green Mountain National Forest, with its historical trails and drives. Other major ski areas include Killington, Sugarbush, Mount Snow, Jay Peak, Smuggler's Notch and Haystack.
Further information from: Vermont Travel Division, 134 State Street, Montpelier, VT 05602. Tel: (802) 828 3236. Fax: (802) 828 3233.
City and council information: Burlington Visitors Bureau, PO Box 453, 209 Battery Street, Burlington, VT 05402. Tel: (802) 863 3489. Fax: (802) 863 1538.

VIRGINIA

POPULATION: 6,098,000.
CAPITAL: Richmond.
TIME: GMT - 5. *Daylight Saving Time* is observed from the first Sunday in April to the last Sunday in October. Clocks are put forward one hour, changing at 0200 hours local time.
THE STATE: Virginia is one of the country's most historic and scenic states. Some of its leading attractions are located along the Potomac River – Arlington National Cemetery, with the grave of John F Kennedy; Old Town Alexandria; and Mount Vernon, George Washington's country estate. Richmond, the capital of the Confederacy in the Civil War, has many fine old buildings. Williamsburg, Yorktown and Jamestown, the birthplace of the USA and three of its most historic sites, are situated further east. Shenandoah Valley, with its caverns, waterfalls and popular resorts, is to the west. Other attractions include Virginia Beach resort; Cumberland Gap; and the Great Falls Park. Norfolk is an important Atlantic seaport.
Further information from: Virginia Division of Tourism, 1021 East Cary Street, Richmond, VA 23219. Tel: (804) 786 2051. Fax: (804) 786 1919.
City and council information: Norfolk Convention & Visitors Bureau, 236 East Plume Street, Norfolk, VA 23510. Tel: (804) 441 5266. Fax: (804) 622 3663; *or*
Alexandria Convention & Visitors Bureau, 221 King Street, Alexandria, VA 22314. Tel: (703) 838 4200. Fax: (703) 838 4683; *or*
Virginia Beach Convention & Visitors Development, Suite 500, 2101 Parks Avenue, Virginia Beach, VA 23451. Tel: (804) 437 4700. Fax: (804) 437 4747.

WASHINGTON

POPULATION: 4,761,000.
CAPITAL: Olympia.
GATEWAY: Seattle. For further information, see under *US Gateways* below.

WEST VIRGINIA

POPULATION: 1,857,000.
CAPITAL: Charleston.
TIME: GMT - 5. *Daylight Saving Time* is observed from the first Sunday in April to the last Sunday in October. Clocks are put forward one hour, changing at 0200 hours local time.
THE STATE: Monongahela National Forest occupies a vast area in the eastern part of this mountain state and includes the Spruce Knob-Seneca Rocks National Recreation Area. West Virginia also boasts some of the nation's best state parks, with good sports and recreation facilities. These include Bluestone and Pipestem. Other attractions include the Greenbrier luxury resort; Smoke Hole Scenic Gorge; Mammoth Mound, one of the world's tallest prehistoric Indian burial grounds; and the State Capitol in Charleston, one of the best Italian Renaissance buildings in the USA.
Further information from: West Virginia Division of Commerce, 2101 Washington Street East, Charleston, WV 25305. Tel: (304) 558 2286. Fax: (304) 558 0108.
City and council information: Charleston Convention & Visitors Bureau, Room 002, 200 Civic Center Drive, Charleston, WV 25301. Tel: (304) 344 5075. Fax: (304) 344 1241; *or*
Northern West Virginia Convention & Visitors Bureau, 709 Beechurst Avenue, Morgantown, WV 26505. Tel: (304) 292 5081. Fax: (304) 291 1354.

WISCONSIN

POPULATION: 4,867,000.
CAPITAL: Madison.
TIME: GMT - 6. *Daylight Saving Time* is observed from the first Sunday in April to the last Sunday in October. Clocks are put forward one hour, changing at 0200 hours local time.
THE STATE: Wisconsin has more than 15,000 lakes and thousands of kilometres of rivers and streams. Its varied countryside also includes sandstone cliffs, sandy beaches, northern forests and rich, southern farmland. Milwaukee is the state's largest city, on the shores of Lake Michigan. It is well known for its German heritage, top performing arts companies and fine restaurants. Its parks and museums are among the best in the USA. Other state attractions include the sculptured cliffs of the Wisconsin Dells; Lake Geneva, a favourite recreation spot; and Green Bay, the state's oldest settlement.
Further information from: Wisconsin Division of Tourism, PO Box 7970, 123 West Washington Avenue, Madison, WI 53707. Tel: (608) 266 7621. Fax: (608) 267 2829.
City and council information: Greater Madison Convention & Visitors Bureau, 615 East Washington Avenue, Madison, WI 53703. Tel: (800) 255 2537. Fax: (608) 258 4950; *or*
Fond Du Lac Tourism & Visitors Bureau, 19 West Scott Street, Fond Du Lac, WI 54935. Tel: (414) 923 3010. Fax: (414) 929 6846.

WYOMING

POPULATION: 475,000.
CAPITAL: Cheyenne.
TIME: GMT - 7. *Daylight Saving Time* is observed from the first Sunday in April to the last Sunday in October. Clocks are put forward one hour, changing at 0200 hours local time.
THE STATE: Wyoming, the 'Cowboy State', boasts 11 major mountain ranges, prairies, grasslands, parks, forests, lakes and rivers. The huge Yellowstone National Park includes geysers, hot springs, canyons, mountain lakes, waterfalls and a huge variety of wildlife. Old Faithful Geyser, the park's most famous attraction, erupts almost hourly. Other state attractions include Grand Teton National Park; Devil's Tower, the core of a now extinct volcano; the Buffalo Bill Historical Center in Cody; Fort Laramie pioneer post; Bighorn Canyon; and Prior Mountain Wild Horse Range, with more than 200 free-roaming wild horses.
Further information from: Wyoming Travel Commission, I-25 & College Drive, Cheyenne, WY 82002. Tel: (307) 777 7777. Fax: (307) 777 6904.
City and council information: Green River Convention & Visitors Bureau, 1450 Uinta Drive, Green River, WY 82935. Tel: (307) 875 5711. Fax: (307) 875 1646; *or*
Cheyenne Area Convention & Visitors Bureau, PO Box 765, 309 West Lincolnway, Cheyenne, WY 82001. Tel: (307) 778 3190; *or*
Jackson Hole Visitors Council, PO Box 982, Jackson, WY 83001. Tel: (307) 733 7606. Fax: (307) 733 5585.

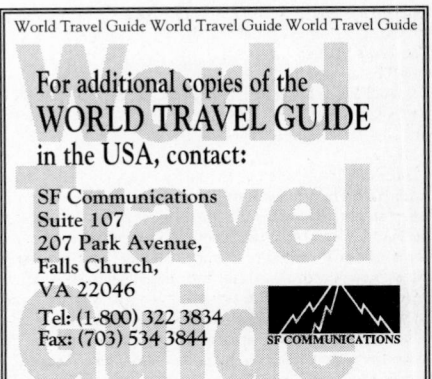

US GATEWAYS

ARIZONA

Including **Phoenix**, gateway to the southwestern States of Arizona, New Mexico, Colorado, Utah and Nevada and the western Pacific State of California.

Arizona Office of Tourism
1100 West Washington Avenue
Phoenix, AZ
85007
Tel: (602) 542 8687. Fax: (602) 542 4068.

Phoenix and Valley of the Sun Convention & Visitors Bureau
Suite 600
1 Arizona Center
400 East Van Buren
Phoenix, AZ
85004
Tel: (602) 254 6500. Fax: (602) 253 4415.

Scottsdale Chamber of Commerce
7333 Scottsdale Mall
Scottsdale, AZ
85251-4498
Tel: (602) 945 8481.

Tucson Convention & Visitors Bureau
130 South Scott Avenue
Tucson, AZ
85701
Tel: (602) 624 1817. Fax: (602) 884 7804.

TIME: GMT - 7.

THE STATE: Arizona has spectacular scenery, including arid plateaux, mountains and broad desert plains. It contains the famous Grand Canyon, Painted Desert and Petrified Forest National Parks. Phoenix, the largest city in the state, shares borders with Scottsdale, the primary resort destination in Arizona. Both cities have a variety of accommodation and attractions, unique shopping, fine art galleries and many cultural events. Other state attractions include Tucson, the second largest city; Saguaro National Monument; Arizona-Sonora Desert Museum; Kaibab Forest; Monument Valley Navajo Tribal Park; Hoover Dam; Montezuma Castle; and Tombstone, site of the infamous shoot-out at the OK Corral.

TRAVEL

AIR: Approximate flight times: From Phoenix to *Atlanta* is 3 hours 30 minutes, to *Chicago* is 3 hours 30 minutes, to *Los Angeles* is 2 hours, to *Miami* is 4 hours and to *New York* is 4 hours.

International airport: *Phoenix Sky Harbor International Airport (PHX)* is 6km (4 miles) from the city centre (tel: (602) 273 3300). Bus service to the city centre runs every 25 minutes 0600-1830; travel time – 22 minutes. (Tel: (602) 253 5000 for more detailed bus information.) 24-hour limousine service provides door-to-door service. Taxis are also available 24 hours a day. A 24-hour super-shuttle service leaves every 15 minutes 0900-2100 and less frequently 2100-0900. The newly built Terminal Four opened in 1991 to accommodate more international flights.

RAIL: *Amtrak* offers services from Phoenix to many major cities. International trains run direct to El Paso and Los Angeles. Domestic services run frequently on two *Amtrak* lines, the Sunset Limited line (Benson–Tucson–Phoenix–Yuma) and the Southwest Limited line (Winslow–Flagstaff–Seligman–Kingman). The *West Region Rail Pass* is available for 15 or 30 days unlimited travel from the midwest as far east as Chicago, from as far southeast as New Orleans and as far west as the Pacific coast. The *Far West RegionRail Pass* is also available for 15 or 30 days of travel in the west, from the Pacific coast to as far east as Denver. First-class sleeping cars can be reserved for an additional fee.

ROAD: Most major routes run east–west. **Bus:** *Greyhound* and *Continental Trailways* buses are available to many northern, central and southern city destinations. Tel: (602) 271 7249 for further information on *Greyhound* services from Phoenix. *Gray Line*, with offices in Phoenix, Tucson and Flagstaff, offers 2-hour to 2-day local sightseeing tours.

Approximate driving times: From Phoenix to *Tucson* is 2 hours, to *Las Vegas* is 7 hours, to *San Diego* is 6 hours, to *Los Angeles* is 6 hours 30 minutes, to *El Paso* is 8 hours 30 minutes and to *Albuquerque* is 9 hours.

Approximate *Greyhound* journey times: From Phoenix to *Tucson* is 2 hours, to *Las Vegas* is 7 hours 30 minutes, to *San Diego* is 8 hours, to *Los Angeles* is 8 hours 30 minutes, to *El Paso* is 9 hours and to *Albuquerque* is 10 hours.

URBAN: Bus: Phoenix buses run every 30 minutes from every bus stop throughout the day and every 10-20 minutes during peak traffic hours. Tickets are sold in books of ten and and there is a local and an express fare. An all-day local pass is available, as well as a local monthly pass. Tickets for express services are more expensive. Discount fares are available for children under 18, pensioners (over 65) and disabled persons. Special

Holy Trinity Monastery chapel, Tuscon

dial-a-ride services are available in Phoenix and Scottsdale 0630-1000 Monday to Friday. An excellent bus service is available between Phoenix and Scottsdale.
Car hire: Easily available in Phoenix with many car hire firms offering special weekend or weekly rates.

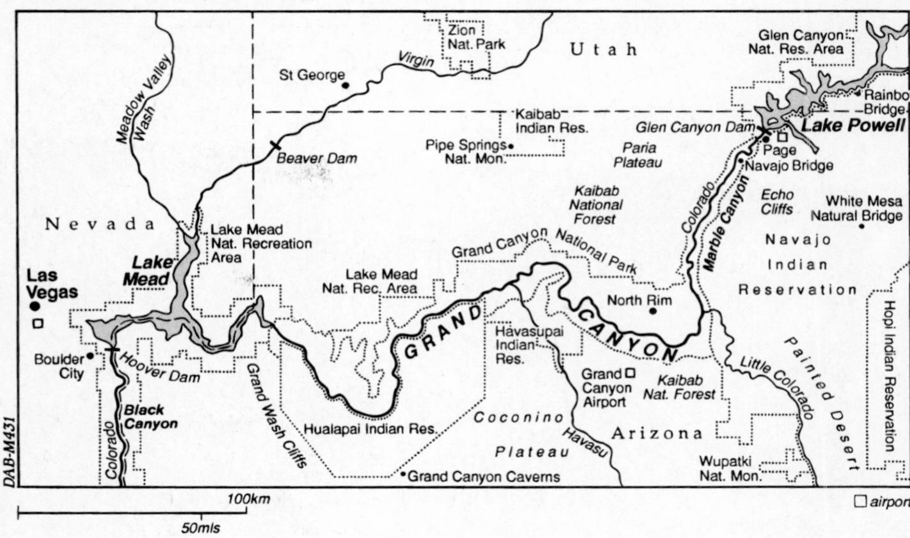

RESORTS & EXCURSIONS

PHOENIX: The eighth largest city in the USA and capital of Arizona, Phoenix has recently grown in importance, due to its improved airport facilities and recent large investment in extensive urban redevelopment. It claims to have more 5-star hotels than any other US city. Just some of the new development projects in the downtown area include: *Renaissance Square*, a 26-storey office tower with a newly completed 28-storey twin tower; the new US$20-million, 225-suite *Hilton Hotel*, located in the downtown business district; the *Arizona Center* (an 8-block complex with a 600-room hotel, offices, restaurants, shops and entertainment); and *Patriots Square Park*, in the centre of Phoenix, with a sophisticated and spectacular laser light system that is visible for miles around.
Sightseeing: *Encanto Park; Pueblo Grande; Papago Park*, including the Phoenix Zoo and Desert Botanical Garden; *South Mountain Park*; and the *Heard Museum*, devoted to the art, anthropology, history and Indian culture of Arizona.
Excursions: The Grand Canyon is accessible by airplane from the centre of Phoenix on *Arizona Air*, by helicopter on *Grand Canyon Helicopters* or by the *Grand Canyon Railroad* (tel: (602) 635 4000).
LAKE HAVASU CITY: This desert city has recently become known as the new home of *London Bridge*, where it now spans the Colorado River and is the focal point for an array of English-style shops, pubs and lodgings. Further information is available from Lake Havasu Convention & Visitors Bureau on (602) 855 4115.
SCOTTSDALE: 'The Valley of the Sun'. Founded in 1888 and known as 'The West's most Western town', Scottsdale has matured into a mecca for lovers of relaxed lifestyles. Year-round sunshine makes the outdoors a way of life in Scottsdale, with its 125 golf courses, scores of tennis courts, and pools and spas at almost every resort.
Sightseeing: *Taliesin West*, the home and workshop of the famous designer, Frank Lloyd Wright, is open for viewing daily. A new 2-storey aquarium has been built in the *Scottsdale Galleria* with over 100 species of fish and marine life.
Excursions: Many river rafting expeditions on the Salt and Verde rivers are organised by *Desert Voyagers* (tel: (602) 998 7238), as well as combination river rafting and desert jeep tours which take in the *Sonoran Desert* and its rivers. There are also special Barnstormer Bi-planes (replicas of the post-World War I open cockpit 2-winged Waco). Rides, complete with 1930s goggles and helmets, are available, with aerobatics displays for the brave. Other outdoor activities include gliders, hot-air balloons and horseriding.
SEDONA/OAK CREEK CANYON: An attractive town nestled in the extraordinary red-rock formations and cliffs at the foot of Oak Creek.
Sightseeing: The beautiful *Verde River Canyon* provides lush scenery and there are prehistoric Indian ruins to be seen.
Excursions: Trips into the canyon are available, sometimes including Western-style barbecues by the river and live entertainment.
TUCSON: This popular winter resort is one of the fastest-growing areas in the USA. Surrounded by a ring of mountain ranges in the Sonoran Desert, it is known for its constant sunshine, and its location only 100 miles from the Mexican border is apparent in its architecture, cuisine and lively fiestas and cultural festivals.
Sightseeing: *Tucson Children's Museum*, with many hands-on exhibitions, is a favourite with children and adults; *Tubac*, an artist's colony with shops and galleries, is also the site of a walled fort and archaeological dig; and *Tohono Chul Park*, a desert sanctuary where visitors can learn about and experience the desert with the added benefit of cool refreshments available at the park's Tea Room.
APACHE TRAIL: An extraordinary scenic drive passing through arid deserts, winding canyons, looming buttes, glistening lakes and the ominous volcanic dome known as Superstition Mountain.
Sightseeing: *Goldfield Ghost Town and Mine Tours; Superstition Mountain Museum; Tortilla Flat*, an old stagecoach stop offering 'killer' chilli and prickly-pear cactus ice cream; *Roosevelt Bridge*, the world's largest single-span bridge; and *Tonto National Monument*, well-preserved cliff dwellings occupied 500 years ago by the Salado Indians and featuring examples of their weavings, jewellery, weapons and tools.
GRAND CANYON: This is perhaps the most famous natural tourist site in America and its impact is awe-inspiring to most visitors. This massive rend in the earth can be reached in a variety of different ways: by airplane, helicopter, railroad, 1901 period steam train from Williams to the South Rim or by a Lake Powell tour boat from Wahweap Lodge to Rainbow Bridge (the world's biggest natural stone arch). There are some hotels in the Canyon but advanced booking is usually essential. As the Canyon is far from any city, those wanting to save time and see it all can take a 'flightseeing' trip over the Grand Canyon, the Havasupai Canyon (a remote side canyon of the Grand), Canyon de Chelly and the spectacular Monument Valley.
INDIAN RESERVATIONS: There are 64,750 sq km (25,000 sq miles) of Navajo Indian Reservation – home to 200,000 Navajos. Once a semi-nomadic and warlike people, they are known for their adaptability and have incorporated many skills into their culture from the Spanish and early settlers. They live in hogans (dome-shaped houses of log and adobe) in small, scattered settlements. In the middle of the Navajo Reservation sits the Hopi Indian Reservation, comprising 6475 sq km (2500 sq miles) and 7000 Hopis. They have lived in the region for 1500 years and are known for their amazing agricultural talents in farming dry and difficult land. The Hopis live in snug pueblo-style villages on top of mesas. This area is treasured for its outstanding natural beauty. Further information is available from Native American Travel Center, Suite 114, 4130 N Goldwater Boulevard, Scottsdale, AZ 85251 (tel: (602) 945 0771) *or* Hopi Tribal Office of Public Relations, PO Box 123, Kykotsmovi, AZ 86039 (tel: (602) 734 6648).
LAKE POWELL: A scenic wonderland of red rocks and blue waters.
Excursions: Many tour boats ply the waters of this large and beautiful lake. Information on lake cruises is available from Wahweap Lodge and Marina. Tel: (602) 645 2433.
Note: For information on attractions in neighbouring states, see above under *States A-Z*.

SOCIAL PROFILE

FOOD & DRINK: Most restaurants serve American or American/Continental food but Mexican, Chinese and Italian cuisine are also available. **Drink:** Drinking is legal in any licensed bar, restaurant, hotel or inn 0600-0100 weekdays and 1200-0100 Sunday. Minimum legal drinking age is 19. Many supermarkets and drug stores sell alcoholic beverages. Most liquor stores close at 2300.
THEATRE & CONCERTS: *Herberger Theater Center* in Phoenix is a new US$19-million development and is now home to the Arizona Theater Company, Arizona Opera, Ballet Arizona and Actors Theater of Phoenix.
NIGHTLIFE: Phoenix, Scottsdale and Tucson have various nightclubs and there is evening entertainment at many resorts in the area.
SHOPPING: Phoenix has excellent shopping facilities. The new Arizona Center in downtown Phoenix has good shopping opportunities and Mercado, also in the downtown area, is a new US$14-million shops and restaurant complex with a Mexican atmosphere. Civic Plaza, in the centre of Phoenix, is also a big and comprehensive shopping area. Special buys in Arizona include Navajo silver and turquoise jewellery, sand paintings, rug weaving and paintings; and Hopi silver jewellery, kachina carvings, pottery, basketry and paintings.
SPORT: American football games are held weekly during the football season at Sun Devil Stadium between the Phoenix Cardinals and other visiting teams. Arizona is the training ground for some excellent major-league **baseball** teams, including the Cleveland Indians (Tucson), the San Francisco Giants (Phoenix), Chicago Cubs (Mesa), Milwaukee Brewers (Sun City), Seattle Mariners (Tempe) and San Diego Padres (Yuma).
Basketball games take place between the Phoenix Suns and other visiting teams in Phoenix where construction is now underway on the new US$89-million America West Arena. **Boxing** matches take place in Phoenix and Tucson. **Horseracing** can be seen at Turf Paradise in Phoenix and Rillito Downs in Tucson. **Car racing** can be viewed in Tucson at Corona Speedway and Tucson Dragway and in Phoenix at Beeline Dragway, Manzanita Park, Phoenix Dragway and Phoenix International Raceway. **Rodeos** are popular in Arizona and there are over 25 major rodeo sites throughout the state. **Skiing** is available in the winter at The Arizona Snow Bowl near Flagstaff, Mount Lemmon (an hour outside of Tucson) and Sunrise Ski Area outside Springerville. Other sports available include **archery, horseriding, bowling, fishing, golf, hiking, hunting, swimming, river tubing, hang-gliding, ballooning** and **tennis.**
SPECIAL EVENTS: The annual *Navajo Nation Fair* is the largest Indian fair in the world. It takes place in Window Rock, capital of the Navajo Nation, for five days in September. It includes lasso competitions, rodeos, horseracing, arts and crafts exhibitions, country and western dances, song and dance competitions, livestock and agricultural exhibits, food and a big parade.
The Festival in the Sun takes place in Tucson in February/ March and is a large celebration of visual and performing arts.

CLIMATE

Warm and comfortable all year round, ranging from refreshing breezes in the mountains to hot temperatures in the desert.
Required clothing: Lightweight cotton clothing for all seasons, with a wrap for cool nights. Warmer clothing is needed in the mountains, especially in the ski areas.

SALT LAKE CITY Utah (1286m)

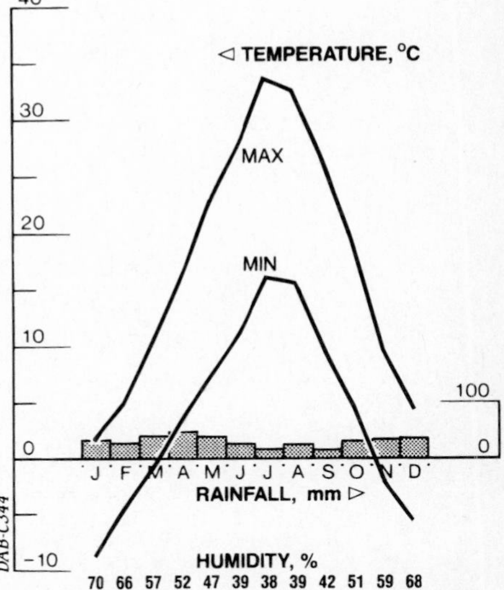

CALIFORNIA

Including **Los Angeles** and **San Francisco,** gateways to the West (Pacific) Coast, Nevada, Oregon and Arizona.

California Office of Tourism
Suite 1600
801 K Street
Sacramento, CA
95814
Tel: (916) 322 2881 *or* 322 1396. Fax: (916) 322 3402.

Fresno Convention & Visitors Bureau
808 M Street
Fresno, CA
93721
Tel: (209) 233 0836. Fax: (209) 445 0122.

Los Angeles Convention & Visitors Bureau
Suite 6000
633 West 5th Street
Los Angeles, CA
90071
Tel: (213) 624 7300. Fax: (213) 624 9746.

Palm Springs Desert Resorts Convention & Visitors Bureau
Suite 201
69-930 Highway 111
Rancho Mirage, CA
92270
Tel: (619) 770 9000. Fax: (619) 770 9001.

Sacramento Convention & Visitors Bureau
1421 K Street
Sacramento, CA
95814
Tel: (916) 264 7777. Fax: (916) 264 7788.

San Diego Convention & Visitors Bureau
Suite 824
1200 Third Avenue
San Diego, CA
92101-4190
Tel: (619) 232 3101. Fax: (619) 696 9371.

San Francisco Convention & Visitors Bureau
Suite 900
201 Third Street
San Francisco, CA
94103-3185
Tel: (415) 974 6900. Fax: (415) 227 2602.

Santa Cruz County Conference & Visitors Bureau
701 Front Street
Santa Cruz, CA
95060
Tel: (408) 425 1234. Fax: (408) 425 1260.

TIME: GMT - 8. *Daylight Saving Time* is observed from the first Sunday in April to the last Sunday in October. Clocks are put forward one hour, changing at 0200 hours local time.

THE STATE: Known as 'the Golden State' because of its sunny climate and the discovery of gold in pioneering days, California is a mixture of beaches, mountains, rugged coastline, Hollywood glamour, desert, woodland and orchards. The most populous state in the USA, its major tourist destinations include Los Angeles, San Francisco and San Diego, the lush resorts of Santa Barbara and Palm Springs and the artists' communities of Laguna Beach and Mendocino.

TRAVEL

AIR: Approximate flight times: From **Los Angeles** to *Anchorage* is 6 hours 40 minutes, to *Chicago* is 4 hours 15 minutes, to *Guatemala City* is 4 hours 35 minutes, to *Honolulu* is 5 hours 30 minutes, to *London* is 10 hours 15 minutes, to *Mexico City* is 4 hours 55 minutes, to *Miami* is 4 hours 55 minutes, to *New York* is 5 hours 20 minutes, to *Orange County* is 30 minutes, to *Papeete* (Tahiti) is 8 hours 10 minutes, to *San Diego* is 45 minutes, to *San Francisco* is 1 hour 20 minutes, to *Singapore* is 20 hours 25 minutes, to *Sydney* is 19 hours 30 minutes and to *Washington DC* is 4 hours 30 minutes.
From **San Francisco** to *Anchorage* is 5 hours 35 minutes, to *Chicago* is 4 hours 15 minutes, to *Honolulu* is 5 hours 40 minutes, to *London* is 12 hours 10 minutes, to *Los Angeles* is 1 hour 20 minutes, to *Mexico City* is 5 hours 10 minutes, to *Miami* is 6 hours 20 minutes, to *New York* is 5 hours 40 minutes, to *Papeete* (Tahiti) is 10 hours 40 minutes, to *Seattle* is 1 hour 50 minutes, to *Singapore* is 21 hours 25 minutes, to *Sydney* is 16 hours 40 minutes, to *Vancouver* is 2 hours 35 minutes and to *Washington DC* is 6 hours.
International airports: *Los Angeles International (LAX)* is located on Santa Monica Bay, 24km (15 miles) from the city centre. A train service is available and coaches provide reasonably priced services to all major downtown locations as well as many surrounding areas such as Hollywood.
San Francisco (SFO) is 25km (15 miles) southeast of the city; travel time – 30 minutes. *Airporter* buses leave every 20 minutes 0500-2300. Limousine, taxi and public bus services are also available.
Oakland (OAK), located across the Bay 32km (20 miles) from downtown San Francisco, receives international charter flights and US domestic flights. *Airporter* buses link Oakland with downtown Oakland and *San Francisco International Airport*. *Air-BART* buses connect with the BART rapid transit (underground) system, which gives access to downtown San Francisco.
Domestic airports: *Burbank (BUR)* airport is 34km (21 miles) from downtown Los Angeles, and receives US domestic services only.
San Diego International (SAN), 4.8km (3 miles) west of San Diego city centre, is primarily a gateway to southern California for domestic traffic.
SEA: A ferry service links San Francisco with the Bay communities of Sausalito, Larkspur in scenic Marin County, Tiburon, Vellejo, Oakland and Alameda. San Francisco departure is from Pier 1, adjoining the Ferry Building at the foot of Market Street.
RAIL: The *Amtrak* terminal in **Los Angeles** is Union Station at 800 North Alameda Street on the edge of the business district. It is at the western end of several major routes across the southern Rockies and is also the southern terminus of the West Coast line to Seattle (although there are frequent shuttle services heading further south to San Diego).
In **San Francisco,** the *Transbay Terminal* at 425 Mission Street is used only for limited suburban services; the *Amtrak Terminal* at Oakland, across the Bay, is far larger, being the central node on the West Coast line and also the western terminus of a line running across the high Rockies to Salt Lake City and beyond.
Amtrak provide coach shuttles between their Oakland and San Francisco terminals.
Approximate *Amtrak* journey times: From *Los Angeles* on the 'Texas Eagle' to Phoenix is 8 hours, to El Paso is 18 hours, to San Antonio is 29 hours, to Austin is 32 hours, to Fort Worth is 37 hours, to Dallas is 39 hours, to St Louis is 54 hours and to Chicago is 61 hours; on the 'Southwest Chief' to Flagstaff is 9 hours, to Albuquerque is 16 hours, to Kansas City is 32 hours and to Chicago is 38 hours; on the 'Sunset Limited' to Houston is 34 hours and to New Orleans is 43 hours; on the 'Coast Starflight' to San Jose is 9 hours, to Oakland is 11 hours, to Sacramento is 13 hours, to Portland (Oregon) is 29 hours and to Seattle is 33 hours.
From *Oakland* on the 'California Zephyr' to Reno is 6 hours, to Salt Lake City is 16 hours, to Denver is 31 hours and to Chicago is 50 hours.
ROAD: Approximate driving times: From *Los Angeles* to San Diego is 2 hours, to Las Vegas is 6 hours, to San Francisco is 8 hours, to Phoenix is 8 hours, to Reno is 10 hours, to Albuquerque is 16 hours, to Seattle is 24 hours, to Dallas is 29 hours, to Chicago is 44 hours, to Miami is 58 hours and to New York is 58 hours.
From *San Francisco* to Reno is 4 hours, to Portland is 13 hours, to Albuquerque is 12 hours, to Seattle is 16 hours, to Dallas is 36 hours, to Chicago is 45 hours, to New York is 61 hours and to Miami is 65 hours.
All times are based on non-stop driving at or below the applicable speed limits.
Approximate *Greyhound* journey times: From *Los Angeles* (tel: (213) 620 1200) to San Diego is 2 hours 30 minutes, to Las Vegas is 5 hours 30 minutes, to San Francisco is 7 hours 30 minutes, to Phoenix is 8 hours 30 minutes, to Yosemite is 10 hours 15 minutes, to Sacramento is 12 hours 30 minutes, to Albuquerque is 17 hours 30 minutes and to Portland (Oregon) is 22 hours.
From *San Francisco* (tel: (415) 495 1571) to Sacramento is 2 hours, to Lake Tahoe is 5 hours, to Reno is 5 hours 30 minutes, to Los Angeles is 7 hours 30 minutes, to Yosemite is 7 hours 30 minutes and to Portland is 16 hours.
URBAN: Los Angeles: The distances between Los Angeles' various attractions can be intimidating at first but it is a relatively easy city to get around quickly provided the visitor has a car. The freeways are well-marked, though congested during rush hours. Leading car hire and motor camper rental agencies have offices at the airport and downtown LA. Within Los Angeles County, the *Southern California Rapid Transit District (RTD)* provides a good bus service. For trips beyond Los Angeles, the *Orange County Transit District* accepts transfers from *RTD* for services throughout suburban Orange County. Buses are reasonably priced but you may have to wait some time to catch one. Though taxis are readily available, the geographic size of Los Angeles makes them expensive and impractical.
San Diego: Buses give good service at moderate prices. Taxis are expensive. Car rentals are readily available, with *Avis*, *Budget*, *Dollar-A-Day*, *Hertz* and *National* all providing services.
San Francisco: Public transport is excellent. The network of buses, streetcars and cable cars (see below under *Resorts & Excursions)* is the most economical way to get to attractions beyond walking distance. The basic fare includes transfers between the different forms of transport. Passengers must have exact change when they board, drivers carry no change. Taxis are readily available in most of the downtown area and other major streets. Because San Francisco is comparatively small in area, taxi fares tend to be less than in most other major cities. All major national car hire agencies are represented in San Francisco; motor campers may also be rented. For information on local companies, look in the San Francisco *Classified Telephone Directory*. Buses and streetcars also provide services from downtown to more distant points in the city, including Golden Gate Park, Twin Peaks, Seal Rocks, Mission Dolores, the Presidio and Golden Gate Bridge. The futuristic *Bay Area Rapid Transit (BART)* subway and surface rail system links San Francisco with communities on the east side of sprawling San Francisco Bay, including Oakland, Alameda, Fremont, Richmond and Berkeley, site of the huge University of California campus.

RESORTS & EXCURSIONS

LOS ANGELES: The 'City of Angels' is the primary gateway to Southern California and the Far West. Founded in 1781, it now has the second highest population of any US city and covers 1930 sq km (746 sq miles) between mountains and sea. Greater LA is actually a collection of many communities, each with their own distinct character.

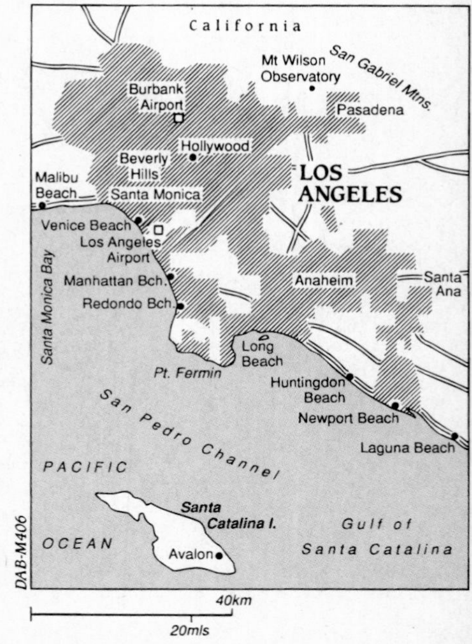

Fisherman's Village, Marina del Rey, Los Angeles

Snowcapped mountains, vast deserts, sandy beaches and canyons are all within driving distance of the city.

Sightseeing: *Beverly Hills* is one of the most elegant communities in Southern California; many of the luxurious homes are owned by film and TV stars. *Chinatown*, in the heart of LA, has the aromas, sounds and architecture of mainland China. Footprints of the stars are cast in cement outside *Mann's Chinese Theater* on *Hollywood Boulevard*. Many of the celebrities are featured in *Movieland Wax Museum* in *Buena Park*. *Griffith Park*, one of the world's largest city parks, features the *Los Angeles Zoo*, an observatory, a miniature railroad, golf courses and tennis courts. *El Pueblo de Los Angeles State Historical Park* is the original site of the city, dating back 200 years, where much of LA's Spanish heritage has been restored and preserved. Museums and galleries include *Los Angeles County Museum of Art, The Armand Hammer Museum of Art & Cultural Center, California Afro-American Museum, Japanese-American National Museum* and the *Museum of Contemporary Art*. Historical museums in Los Angeles include *Gene Autry Western Heritage Museum, George C. Page Museum, Grier-Musser Museum, Hollywood Bowl Museum, Hollywood Entertainment Museum, Wells Fargo History Museum, Los Angeles Maritime Museum, Southwest Museum, Martyrs Memorial and Museum of the Holocaust* and the *Natural History Museum of Los Angeles County*.

Excursions: Picturesque **Santa Barbara** overlooks the Pacific from the Santa Ynez foothills; *Mission Santa Barbara* is perhaps the most beautiful of all old Spanish churches in California. Other popular local tourist attractions include **Pasadena, Burbank** and **Anaheim,** home of *Knott's Berry Farm* Old West theme park.

Disneyland: The original theme park created by Walt Disney is 43km (27 miles) southeast of the Los Angeles Civic Center. Over 80 acres of land have been used to create seven theme lands. *Adventureland* explores the exotic regions of Asia, Africa and the South Pacific. *Critter Country* is a down-home backwoods setting for the 'Country Bear Playhouse' and 'Splash Mountain', which is based on the adventures of Brer Rabbit, Brer Bear and Brer Fox from the Walt Disney film 'Song of the South'. Visitors travel in hollowed-out logs through twisting backwoods waterways before descending the world's longest flume drop, which reaches a top speed of 64kmph (40mph). *Fantasyland* is a kingdom of storybook enchantment. *Frontierland* is an exciting realm of pioneers and a return to the heritage of the Old West; *Main Street USA* is a composite of small-town America around 1900. *New Orleans Square* is the home of ghosts, pirates and quaint shops. Finally, *Tomorrowland* shows the world of the future, a panorama on the move.

SAN DIEGO: This, the second largest and oldest city in California, has a distinctly Spanish flavour. A major gateway city for southern California, it is 215km (134 miles) south of Los Angeles.

Sightseeing: The easiest and cheapest way to get around San Diego is on *The Bus That Goes in Circles*, a private service connecting the major hotels and tourist attractions. *Balboa Park* is a huge leisure area containing *San Diego Zoo* (home to 3400 creatures), San Diego *Wild Animal Park, Anza Borrego Desert State Park* and *Sea World*, as well as museums, art galleries, theatres and sports facilities. *Old Town* was the first European settlement in California. There are old missions at *San Diego* and *Seaport Village*. There is a resort area at *La Jolla* and there are miles of sandy beaches to the north and south of the city.

Excursions: Tourist destinations within easy reach of San Diego include *Marineland of the Pacific* in **Rancho Palos Verdes;** the *Queen Mary* ocean liner, docked in **Long Beach** harbour; **Palm Springs,** 160km (100 miles) from Los Angeles – a wintertime destination favoured by the jet set, famed for its health resorts, spas, golf and tennis clubs, and an aerial tramway; *Six Flags Magic Mountain* entertainment complex in **Valencia;** the *John Paul Getty Museum* near **Malibu,** the wealthiest museum in the world; **Pasadena,** home of the New Year's Day *Tournament of Roses Parade* and *Rose Bowl* football game, and of the *Norton Simon Museum of Art;* and **Death Valley National Monument,** 5790 sq km (2235 sq miles) of rugged desert, sand dunes, salt flats and canyons, with extreme heat in summer (best visiting times: early November to late April).

SAN FRANCISCO: Gateway to the scenic region of the Far West, northern California, northern Nevada and Oregon. This cosmopolitan port by the Golden Gate Bridge was first settled by Spanish missionaries but its real development began with the California Gold Rush. Cable cars, a San Franciscan trademark, travel up and down its steep hills and are an exciting way to explore this beautiful city's well-known restaurants, shopping areas and many tourist attractions.

Sightseeing: *Chinatown* is the largest Chinese community outside Asia; enjoy Chinese theatres, museums, restaurants and cultural centres. *The Japan Center* is a 2-hectare complex of Japanese restaurants, shops, fountains, tea rooms and baths. *Golden Gate Bridge*, the city's most famous landmark, affords spectacular views of the city. *Alcatraz Island* in San Francisco Bay has been transformed from the USA's most infamous prison to one of the city's leading tourist attractions. *Lombard Street*, known as the 'Crookedest Street in the World', is lined with handsome homes and flower gardens. *Golden Gate Park*, one of the great city parks of the USA, has museums, beautiful lakes, botanical gardens and many miles of scenic drives, bridle paths and foot trails. The *Twin Peaks* afford one of the finest panoramic views of the city. Among San Francisco's main museums and galleries are the *San Francisco Museum of Modern Art*, the *M H de Young Memorial Museum* in Golden Gate Park, the *Asian Art Museum*, the *Cartoon Art Museum*, the *California Academy of Sciences* with its planetarium and new anthropology hall, the *Museum of the City of San Francisco*, the *California Palace of the Legion of Honour*, the *Old Mint* and *Octagon House*. Cable cars, a famous San Francisco attraction, are also a fun way to get around parts of the downtown area. The *Cable Car Museum, Powerhouse & Car Barn* shows how the system works. *North Beach* is home to many of the city's Italian-Americans, boasting art galleries, sidewalk cafés, bookshops and coffee houses.

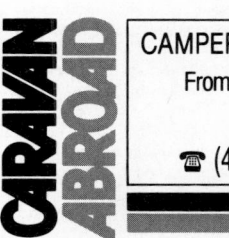

Excursions: The artists' colony of **Sausalito,** with its colourful yachts and houseboats, restaurants, galleries and antique shops, lies just across the bay. **Mendocino** is another attractive artist colony on the coast further north. **St Helena** is a small town at the centre of many well-known wineries. *Muir Woods National Monument* features centuries-old coastal redwoods, about 24km (15 miles) from San Francisco. *Great America* theme park is to be found in **Vallejo.** *Marine World/Africa USA* is on San Francisco Bay. **Redwood National Park** between Eureka and Crescent City has 23,472 hectares of redwood forest and dramatic coastline. *Lassen Volcanic National Park*, dominated by a massive plug volcano, is to be found at **Mount Lassen.** The

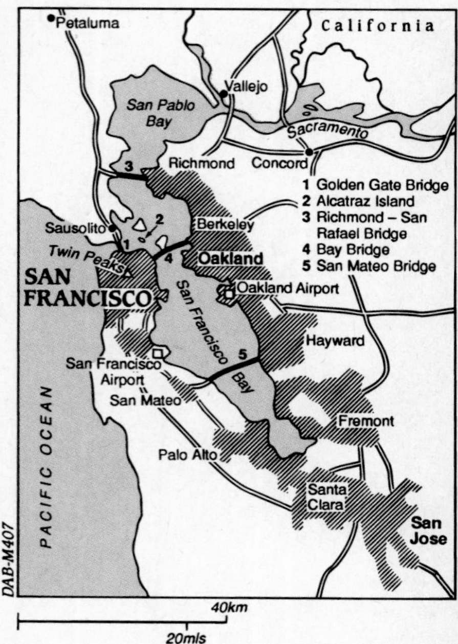

Golden Gate, San Francisco

Monterey Peninsula, where sea otters and sea lions feed in the kelp just offshore, is famous for historic **Monterey** city and its September jazz festival. The city is also known for its association with Nobel Prize-winning author, John Steinbeck; it provides the setting for several of his novels including 'Cannery Row', 'Sweet Thursday' and 'Tortilla Flat'. There is yet another artist's colony at **Carmel. Sequoia** and **Kings Canyon National Parks** have magnificent and ancient forests bordering *Mount Whitney*, the highest point in California.
Yosemite National Park, centred around a spectacular glacial valley, is famous for its mountains, meadows, pine forests, sequoia groves, waterfalls, sports and activities.
Sacramento, state capital and former gold-rush town, has California's first pioneer outpost, *Sutter's Fort. Lake Tahoe*, beneath the peaks of the Sierra Nevada and spanning the California-Nevada border, has ski areas, beaches, watersports and other activities.
Note: For information on attractions in neighbouring states, see above under *States A-Z*.

SOCIAL PROFILE

FOOD & DRINK: Los Angeles: Cosmopolitan cuisine; seafood and grilled meats are specialities of the region. **San Francisco:** A limitless variety of ethnic, American, health food and international cuisine. Sample fresh crab and shrimp at the seafood houses that line the famous Fisherman's Wharf. There are numerous 'fast food' places. **Drink:** Excellent California wines rival many of the renowned vintages of Europe.
THEATRES & CONCERTS: Los Angeles: Broadway hits can be seen at theatres in the US$34.5-million *Music Center* complex, 135 N Grand Avenue. The *Dorothy Chandler Pavilion* is home of the film industry's annual *Academy Awards* and of the *Los Angeles Philharmonic* and the *Civic Light Opera*. The world-famous *Hollywood Bowl*, 2301 N Highland Avenue, stages summer concerts. The *Universal Amphitheater* in the grounds of *Universal Studios* presents major pop and rock concerts. Other top venues include the *Mark Taper Forum*, the *Ahmanson Theater*, the *Shubert Theater* and the outdoor *Greek Theater* in Griffith Park.
San Francisco: The *Orpheum Theater* offers light opera. *Geary Theater* is the home of the *American Conservatory Theater*, which also stages special performances at *Marines Memorial Theater*. *Curran* and *Golden Gate Theaters* show major Broadway productions. The *San Francisco Symphony* performs in the magnificent new *Louise M Davies Symphony Hall*; while popular music concerts are given in the *Civic Auditorium* in July. The *San Francisco Ballet* also performs in the *Opera House* during the December holiday season. The San Francisco opera season, one of the most outstanding in the country, runs from mid-September to November.
NIGHTLIFE: Los Angeles: Nightclubs offer top-rate acts and a chance to rub shoulders with the stars. Most clubs are concentrated around Sunset Boulevard, Hollywood and the San Fernando Valley. Many hotels present star entertainment.**San Francisco:** Everything from strip joints through *chic* piano bars to elegant supper clubs.
SHOPPING: Los Angeles: Smart shops, boutiques and department stores are found in downtown Los Angeles and Beverly Hills. Good value gifts, jewellery and handicrafts are sold in Little Tokyo and Olvera Street.
San Francisco: Art, jewellery and handcrafted items are especially notable. The principal shopping district surrounds Union Square in the city centre. Others include Ghirardelli Square and the Cannery (trendy clothes, foods, art and kitchen imports); Union Street (boutiques, antiques, arts and handcrafts in restored Victorian settings); Pier 39, a shopping/restaurant complex on a long pier; Chinatown and Japantown.
SPORT: Los Angeles: Horseracing is held at Santa Anita Park, Arcadia (October and December to April); and thoroughbred racing (mid-April to late July) and night harness-racing (August to early December) at Hollywood Park, Inglewood. The area also has professional baseball (August to December), professional basketball and hockey. **San Francisco:** San Francisco offers major-league baseball (April to September) and professional football US-style (September to December). There is thoroughbred, quarterhorse and harness-racing at Bay Meadows Race Track and San Mateo (September to June) and thoroughbred racing at Golden Fields, Albany (winter and spring).
SPECIAL EVENTS: Los Angeles: The *Los Angeles County Fair* is held each September in Pomona and the *National Orange Show* is held for 11 days each spring in San Bernadino. Both of these towns are just outside of Los Angeles. The *Annual Gourmet Food and Wine Festival* takes place every February at Thousand Oaks. It is also the month of the *Golden Dragon Parade* in Chinatown, ushering in the new year with floats, dancers and other traditional activities. *Cinco de Mayo* is a traditional Mexican festival, held in El Pueblo de Los Angeles Historic Park. April sees the *Conejo Valley Days Chili Cook-Off* at the Oaks Rotary Club, attended by over 15,000 visitors. November's *Doo Dah Parade* in Pasadena has no theme, no judging, no prizes and no order of marching, and seems well worth a visit. *The Seventh International Contemporary Art Fair* at the LA Convention Center is in December. *The City of Los Angeles Marathon*, with over 20,000 competitors, is in March. *Long Beach Indy Grand Prix* takes place in May, with the famous *Rose Bowl* in Pasadena a site for the *1994 World Cup*.
San Francisco: The *Midsummer Music Festival* offers ten free Sunday afternoon programmes in the Sigmund Stern Grove, 19th Avenue and Sloat Boulevard. Performances include ballet, symphony, opera, jazz, ethnic dance programmes and musicals. From September to the end of May there is a wide range of productions from which to choose. *Fleet Week Celebration* is in October, an annual celebration of seamanship as the US Navy sails into Fisherman's Wharf. The *Great Holloween & Pumpkin Festival* at the end of October is paradise for children, featuring costume parades and festivities in the Richmond District. The *International Accordian Festival* at Fisherman's Wharf, and the *San Francisco Fall Antiques Show* are also at the end of October. The *Film Arts Festival* is a showcase of Bay Area independent film and video, and takes place at the Roxie Cinema (Mission District) at the beginning of November. In 1994, the Stanford Stadium outside of San Francisco will host *World Cup '94* games.

CLIMATE

Summers are hot, while the winter months are mild with wetter weather.
Required clothing: Lightweight during the summer with warmer wear for the cooler winter period.

LOS ANGELES California (103m)

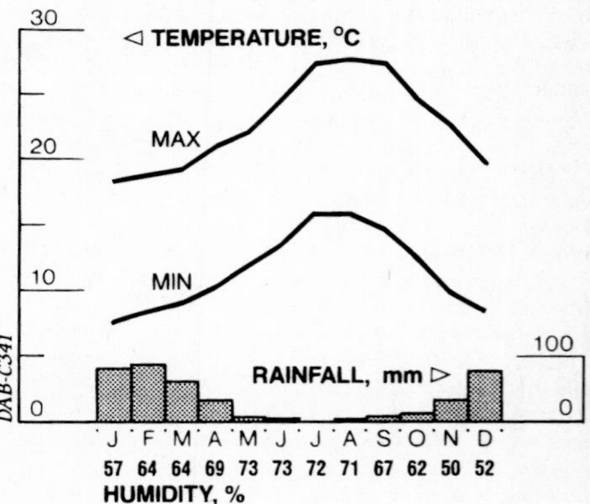

SAN FRANCISCO California (16m)

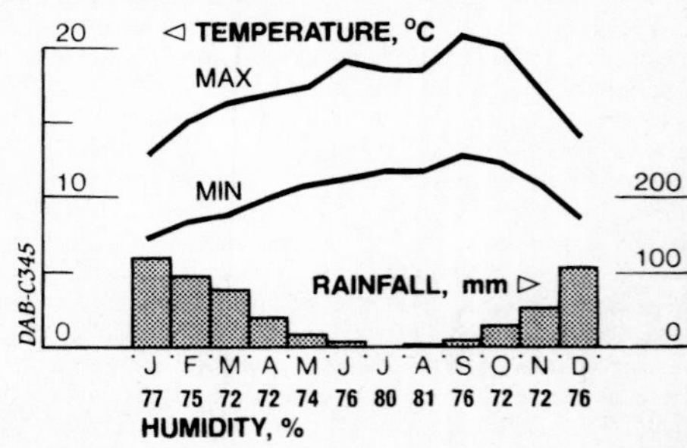

Welcome to LOS ANGELES

94

City of Dreams and Imaginations

Los Angeles, California – probably no other city in the world during the 20th century has been the centre of people's hopes, dreams and imaginations more than Los Angeles.

Even before Hollywood developed its glamorous reputation as the film capital, visitors have been drawn to this southern California mecca on the chance that its magical aura will rub off on them.

Maybe it is the city's intoxicating mix of beaches, sun, palm trees, mountains and consistently mild climate. Others have said that it is the feeling of endless opportunities and discoveries that are possible in no other major metropolitan area.

Los Angeles is a city that is constantly recreating and redefining itself, stretching the limits of innovation and providing a refuge for those who seek a new perspective on life.

Visitors coming to Los Angeles should be prepared for a multitude of experiences, sights and sounds. Los Angeles is a city that refuses to accept a simple characterisation. Instead, it is a blending of elements that are uniquely associated with this bustling metropolis.

From Gary C. Sherwin, Director of Media Relations, Los Angeles Convention & Visitors Bureau.

FISHERMAN'S VILLAGE

WORLD CUP '94

WORLD CUP LOS ANGELES

Los Angeles

Recent Major Sporting Events

Millions of visitors are attracted to the Southern California area each year, not only because of the obvious natural and commercial attractions, but to view a growing number of major national and regional sporting events. Some of the most popular have included the following:

Games of the XXIII Olympiad – Summer, 1984
Attendance: 6.2 million
National Basketball Association Finals, 1984, 85, 87, 88, 89
Attendance: 262,500 (15 games at 17,500 per game)
NFL Super Bowl, 1987
Attendance: 101,063
Major League Baseball World Series, 1988
Attendance: 112,000 (2 games at 56,000 each)
Major League Baseball All-Star Game, 1989
Attendance: 64,000 (Anaheim)
NEC World Cycling Invitational (Six nations), 1990
Attendance: 20,000
North America Nation's Cup Soccer Matches, 1991

In addition to these and other sporting events, two major sports meetings were held in the Los Angeles/ Pasadena area within the last three years, as follows:
Major League Baseball Winter Meetings, 1990
Thirteenth International Sport Summit, 1991

A number of events, held every year, regularly attract thousands of spectators. Principal among these are:
The Toyota Grand Prix of Long Beach
Attendance: 200,000
The Los Angeles Marathon
Attendance: 1.5 million spectators (+ 20,000 participants)
Los Angeles Open Golf Tournament (PGA)
Attendance: 130,000+
The Rose Bowl (NCAA Football)
Attendance: 100,000+
Virginia Slims of Los Angeles Tennis Tournament (Women)
Volvo International Tennis Tournament (Men and Women)
Western Hemisphere Marathon
(Oldest marathon in the US west of the Mississippi).

THE USA WORLD CUP '94 MARKS THE FIFTEENTH COMPETITION TO DATE. THIS QUADRENNIAL CHAMPIONSHIP REMAINS THE WORLD'S BEST IN PROFESSIONAL COMPETITIVE FOOTBALL.

THE LOCATION Los Angeles is located on the west coast of southern California, 14km (9 miles) from Pasadena, 42km (26 miles) from Disneyland, 193km (120 miles) north of San Diego, 428km (266 miles) southwest of Las Vegas and 648km (403 miles) south of San Francisco. The metropolitan area is 1209 sq km (467 sq miles) and the County of Los Angeles is 10,660 sq km (4083 sq miles). The Los Angeles 5-county area (including Los Angeles, Riverside, Ventura, Orange and San Bernardino counties) is 88,445 sq km (34,149 sq miles), which is larger than any US state excluding California, New York and Texas.

THE LANDSCAPE Los Angeles is a city with a diverse landscape – from the magnificent Pacific coastline on its west side through the cosmopolitan district to the tranquil deserts and snowcapped mountains to the east. The Los Angeles area consists of five distinct regions: the Downtown area, Hollywood, Westside, the Coast and the Valleys. The Los Angeles County coastline itself is 116km (72 miles) long, stretching from Malibu to Long Beach. The climate is sunny and warm with gentle ocean breezes in summer. Humidity is low and there is very little rain. Temperatures average 28°C (82°F) from June to October and 18°C (64°F) from November to May.

THE HISTORY AND CULTURE The city's official birthdate is September 4, 1781, when 44 *vecinos pobladores* or village settlers from the Mexican providences of Sonora and Sinaloa made their home in what is now downtown Los Angeles. Two of the 44 settlers were Spaniards, the others were Indians, blacks and mestizos (of mixed ancestry). The *pobladores* were greeted by a tribe of Indians called Yangna. The Spanish named the settlement 'El Pueblo de Nuestra Senora la Reina de Los Angeles' or 'The Town of the Queen of the Angels'. California became a territory of Mexico in March 1825 and the town of Los Angeles was officially declared a city in 1835. In August 1846, American soldiers entered Los Angeles and declared it part of the United States of America as of January 1847. However, the city has always had a strong Hispanic population (the USA's largest at 3.6 million) and has become a strong brew of many nationalities. Today, within the Los Angeles 5-county area, the population is approximately 50% white, 33% Hispanic, 8% black, 8% Asian/Pacific Islanders and 1% American Indian or other.

WHAT MAKES LOS ANGELES SPECIAL As recently as the last 20 years, Los Angeles has emerged as a city that effectively intermingles diverse cultures. It provides a visitor the chance to travel the globe without leaving the city. Communities such as Chinatown, Olvera Street, Koreatown and the Fairfax districts offer proof of the city's reputation as an international melting pot. The best way to grasp Los Angeles is to break it into five regions: Downtown, Hollywood, Westside, Coastal and the Valleys. Like a great Sunday morning buffet, it's best to sample a little bit of it all.

DOWNTOWN

Here's where it all started. Los Angeles was founded by the Spaniards in 1781 near what is now Olvera Street. Downtown has been buoyed by the recent development of high-rise offices, cultural institutions, unique public sculptures and sophisticated shopping centres. Stop in at *City Hall*, once the location of the *Daily Planet* during the Superman TV series. Inside the lobby is a holographic photo of Mayor Tom Bradley, as well as gifts presented to him by dignitaries throughout the world. One of the world's

WORLD CUP '94

Los Angeles

THE ROSEBOWL STADIUM

The Rose Bowl was built in 1922 in Pasadena, California, seven miles from downtown Los Angeles. It is the home of the UCLA Bruins football team. The Rose Bowl holds 103,985 people, making it the largest stadium participating in the 1994 World Cup. The Rose Bowl played host to several capacity crowds during the soccer competition of the 1984 Olympics, in which 101,799 fans watched France defeat Brazil, 2-0, for the Gold Medal.

largest newspapers, the *Los Angeles Times*, is across the street and offers behind-the-scenes tours of this media empire.

Downtown is a cornucopia of cultures. Chinatown, Little Tokyo, Broadway and Olvera Street stand as examples of the native lifestyles of LA residents.

Los Angeles has also been quickly establishing itself as a major cultural centre and nowhere is it more strongly evidenced than in Downtown. Near Little Tokyo is the *Museum of Contemporary Art* and the *Temporary Contemporary Museum*. Also close by are the *Museum of Neon Art* and the *Wells Fargo Museum*.

Serious shoppers can explore the Garment District and the Jewellery District, where quality merchandise is sold at discount prices. This is where major retailers often purchase their own goods.

The *Music Center*, frequent home to the Academy Awards extravaganza, offers excellent cultural performances. Tours of the complex are available.

Just south of downtown is Exposition Park, site of the *Los Angeles Memorial Coliseum* and the *Sports Arena*. At the park, the visitor can also explore the *Los Angeles County Museum of Natural History*, the *Museum of Afro-American History and Culture* and the *California State Museum of Science and Industry*, and stroll the campus of the *University of Southern California*.

HOLLYWOOD

Nearly 80 years after the first motion picture was made, Hollywood is still drawing those seeking stardom, or at least a chance to be close to it. The famous Hollywood sign, nestled in the hills above the city, stands as a constant reminder of the presence of the film industry. On *Hollywood Boulevard*, celebrity names are etched onto the 'Walk of Fame' sidewalk as a tribute to famous people.

Visitors wishing to get a behind-the-scenes peek at the film industry can do so at *Universal Studios Hollywood*. There, the secrets of film magic, as well as thrilling surprises including the shark from the film 'Jaws', are presented daily.

In the Griffith Park area, the largest urban park in the country, sights include the outstanding *Los Angeles Zoo, Griffith Park Observatory, Travel Town* and the *Gene Autry Western Heritage Museum*. Not far away is the magnificent *Hollywood Bowl*, a world-famous outdoor amphitheatre for the performing arts.

For a bit of the unusual, visit Melrose Avenue with its eclectic shops and restaurants. Nearby are *Farmers Market*, the *Los Angeles County Museum of Art, La Brea Tar Pits* and *The George C Page Museum*. And of course, a trip to Hollywood must include *Mann's Chinese Theatre* where the hand and footprints of celebrities are cast in concrete.

WESTSIDE

Once a visitor has explored where celebrities work, it's even more interesting to see where they live and play. The Westside includes some of the city's most prestigious addresses, including Beverly Hills, Century City, Westwood, Brentwood and Bel Air.

Beverly Hills is home to the most famous shopping district in the world, Rodeo Drive, where stars, Rolls Royces and the chicest shops and elegant bistros abound.

Maps to the homes of celebrities are available on streetcorners for individual exploration, but scheduled tours are plentiful. For more information, contact Los Angeles Convention & Visitors Bureau at (213) 689 8822 or (213) 461 4213.

Westwood Village is a hip place to stroll, especially for the younger set. It is one of the best spots to catch the latest movie or see collegiate sports action at the nearby *University of California*, Los Angeles.

The *Shubert Theatre* and *ABC Entertainment Center* are in Century City. Once the backlot of 20th Century Fox, it now is the site of the *Century City Marketplace*, a sophisticated outdoor shopping centre.

THE COAST

Palm trees and endless sunshine grace Los Angeles' leading beaches and the magnificent Pacific Ocean. Beaches, numerous resorts and 35km (22 miles) of bicycle paths stretch along 116km (72 miles) of coastline.

The Santa Monica Pier, built in 1909, houses a boardwalk of shops and restaurants, as well as a popular turn-of-the-century carousel. Nearby is the *Museum of Flying*, featuring 24 authentic aircraft displays.

For a classic Los Angeles experience, visit Venice Beach, named after the Italian city, where zanies skate along and street performers hang out. Also a part of Venice is Muscle Beach where strongmen flex their pectorals for bystanders.

Marina del Rey is the home of the world's largest manmade harbor for small boats and includes Fisherman's Village, a reproduction of a New England whaling community.

In the South Bay area, San Pedro is the site of Ports O'Call Village, a unique seaside shopping district, and the *Cabrillo Marine Museum*.

At the southernmost end of Los Angeles County is Long Beach, home to the liner-turned-hotel, the *Queen Mary*, and billionaire Howard Hughes' mammoth wooden flying machine, the *Spruce Goose*.

THE VALLEYS

Once known as the notorious hang-out of Valley Girls, the Valleys are three distinct areas with plentiful shopping and several major annual events.

Mulholland Drive, situated in the hills above the San Fernando Valley, offers panoramic views of the area below. Down below is Ventura Boulevard, a major shopping thoroughfare that attracts celebrities with its speciality shops and excellent restaurants.

Just north, in the Santa Clarita Valley, is *Six Flags Magic Mountain*, a major amusement park featuring thrill rides and six rollercoasters.

Burbank is the home of *NBC Studios*, where visitors can see the taping of their favourite TV programmes. Or tour the famous *Warner Bros Studios*.

Just east of the San Fernando Valley is the San Gabriel Valley. Pasadena is the site of the world's most famous New Year's Day event, the *Tournament of Roses Parade*. After the parade floats are parked, the nearby Rose Bowl hosts the nation's most prestigious collegiate championship football game.

An abundance of cultural offerings in Pasadena include the *Norton Simon Museum of Art*, the *Huntingdon Library and Gardens* and the *Los Angeles County Arboretum*. Nearby, Santa Anita offers one of the most beautiful racetracks in the world and high above, in the Angeles National Forest, is Mount Wilson, a small observatory and museum.

Los Angeles is a city so rich in attractions that it could literally take a lifetime to explore. But for those visitors with a little less time to see the city, obtaining a *Destination Los Angeles Visitor Guide* is a good start. To receive a copy, send $2 for postage and handling to the Los Angeles Convention & Visitors Bureau, Suite 6000, 633 W Fifth Street, Los Angeles, CA 90071.

THE WAY TO THE WORLD CUP

THE AIRPORTS

Los Angeles International Airport (LAX) is 27km (17 miles) from the city centre and is the third largest in the world in terms of passenger traffic, serving 85 major airlines. Arriving passengers may obtain information on airline terminals, airport services and transportation at the Information Booth located on the departure level of the Tom Bradley International Terminal. Travelers Aid of Los Angeles also operates booths in each terminal to assist visitors. Non-English speaking travellers may use the 24-hour language translation link at the Travelers Aid booth in the Tom Bradley International Terminal. There are a number of car rental companies located at the airport, including *Budget*, *Avis* and *Hertz*. A frequent, free shuttle-bus service is provided between terminals to assist travellers in making connections. Visitors should board the 'A' shuttle under the LAX Shuttle sign. LAX shuttle-buses are white with blue-and-green stripes. For further information, telephone (310) 646 5252.

Burbank-Glendale-Pasadena Airport is 21km (13 miles) from downtown Los Angeles, serving 3 million passengers a year and six major airlines: *Alaska*, *American*, *America*

★THERE WILL BE SPECIAL BUSES FROM THE AIRPORT TO THE STADIUM DURING WORLD CUP '94

Rose Bowl History

The location of the Pasadena Rose Bowl began as the Pasadena Valley Hunt Club in 1888. The First Tournament of Roses Parade and games were held there in 1890. The first football game was held in 1902 between University of Michigan and Stanford University, but by 1920 city officials declared the football facilities at Tournament Park unsafe for the growing New Year's Day crowds. By 1922, the construction of the horseshoe shaped stadium designed by Myron Hunt was completed with a seating capacity of 57,000. In 1923 the stadium was officially named 'The Rose Bowl'. In 1931 wooden sections of the Rose Bowl were removed and replaced with reinforced concrete and an additional 10,000 seats increased capacity to 83,000. In 1947, the Rose Parade was televised for the first time and the Rose Bowl football game was televised the following year. In 1949, the stadium was again enlarged to seat 100,807 and 1950 marks the first year that the Rose Bowl Game had over 100,000 spectators in attendance. In 1968, the Rose Parade and Rose Bowl Game were beamed live by satellite to other parts of the world and the following year marked the Rose Bowl celebration of the 100th Anniversary of Intercollegiate Football. In 1977, Super Bowl XI was the first to be played in Pasadena. Since then, three other Super Bowls have been played here, in 1980, 1983 and 1987. In 1993, the year of the 79th Rose Bowl Game, the Rose Bowl was designated as an engineering landmark by the American Society of Civil Engineers.

Wilshire Plaza Hotel and Garden

Presents

Elegantly Renovated Property Centrally Located Luxury Value for the Business Traveller

The Wilshire Plaza Hotel and Garden launched 1993 with a dramatic $4 million renovation. The largest and only luxury hotel property in the mid-Wilshire district, the Wilshire Plaza Hotel and Garden offers business and leisure travellers an affordable, elegant alternative to downtown Los Angeles hotels. The 393-room hotel is owned by Seoul-based Koreana Hotels Company Limited, and is the company's first US property.

Dramatic changes have swept through the Wilshire Plaza Hotel and Garden resulting in a property more conducive to domestic and international business travellers. To achieve an intimite and luxurious European style and bring the hotel to a level of world-class sophistication, improvements from structural alterations to interior design enhancements have taken place.

The hotel has an elegant entrance and foyer accented with marble floors, *trompe d'oeil* marble columns, and honey maple wood panelling

The 10th, 11th and 12th floors now comprise a private Plaza Level including guest rooms, suites and a lounge. The 11th-floor Plaza lounge has its own concierge, serves complimentary breakfast and offers snacks, television and newspapers. Plaza Level guest rooms offer amenities such Wilshire Plaza terry cloth robes, slippers, gold razors and gold toothbrushes.

All guest rooms and suites are now equipped with fax and modem capabilities, while Plaza Level rooms are upgraded with speaker phone and conference calling options. Remote control TVs enable express checkout and retrieval of phone messages. Guests also have access to a full array of television entertainment such as HBO, ESPN, CNN, pay-per-view and Guest Choice which offers more than 100 movie titles for guests to view at their leisure.

A new, authentic Japanese restaurant, *Saka-E*, flanks the lobby. Imported from the acclaimed restaurants of the same name in Seoul and Ulsan, Korea that cater to the country's high society and government officials, the Wilshire Plaza's *Saka-E* presents menus originated by the esteemed chef Do Yong Kank of Seoul. The restaurant features a Sushi bar, teppan-yaki, shabu-shabu and Korean barbecue.

Tulips Garden, the pool- and garden-level restaurant, serves breakfast, lunch and dinner. Tastefully reappointed to include poolside *al fresco* dining, *Tulips Gardens* also has new menus which feature international 'urban cuisine' – a blend of fresh California produce with epicurean style from many of the world's culinary capitals.

Featuring over 12,500 square feet of conference space, the Wilshire Plaza Hotel and Garden can accommodate up to 400 people for meetings and banquets. Catering services are also available to hotel guests or the public for either on- or off-site functions.

Sitauated in the heart of the mid-Wilshire district at the northwest corner of Wilshire and Normandie, the Wilshire Plaza Hotel and Garden is conveniently located 9.6 kilometres from the Los Angeles Convention Centre, 24 kilometres from both the Los Angeles International Airport and Burbank Glendale Airport, and is conveniently situated for all Southern California attractions.

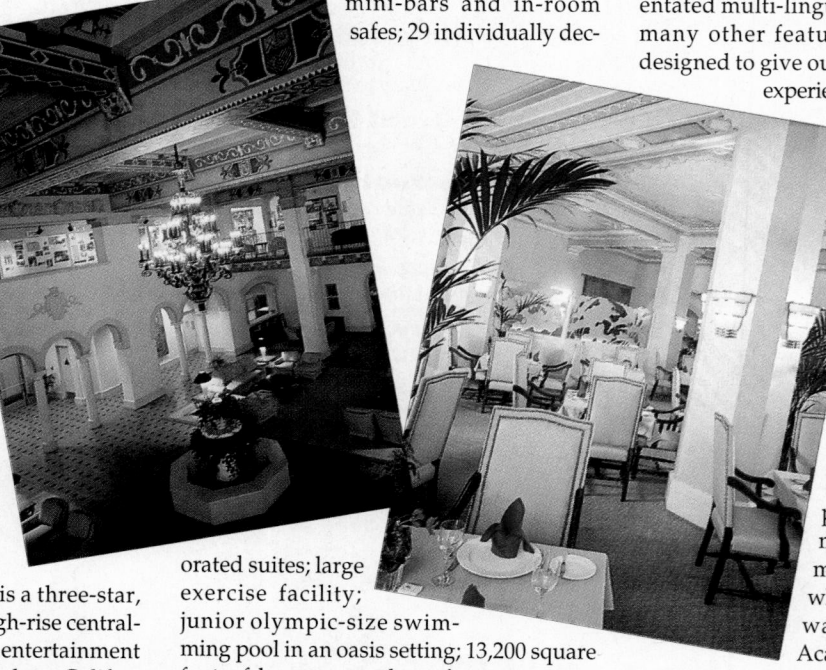

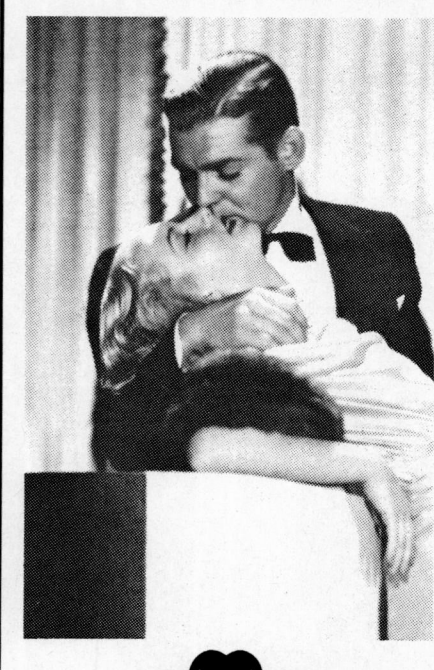

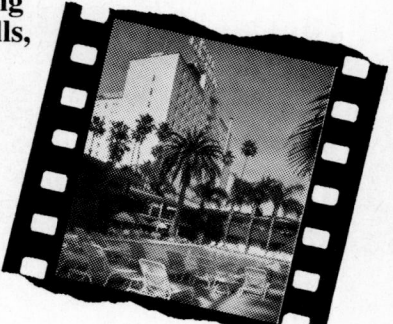

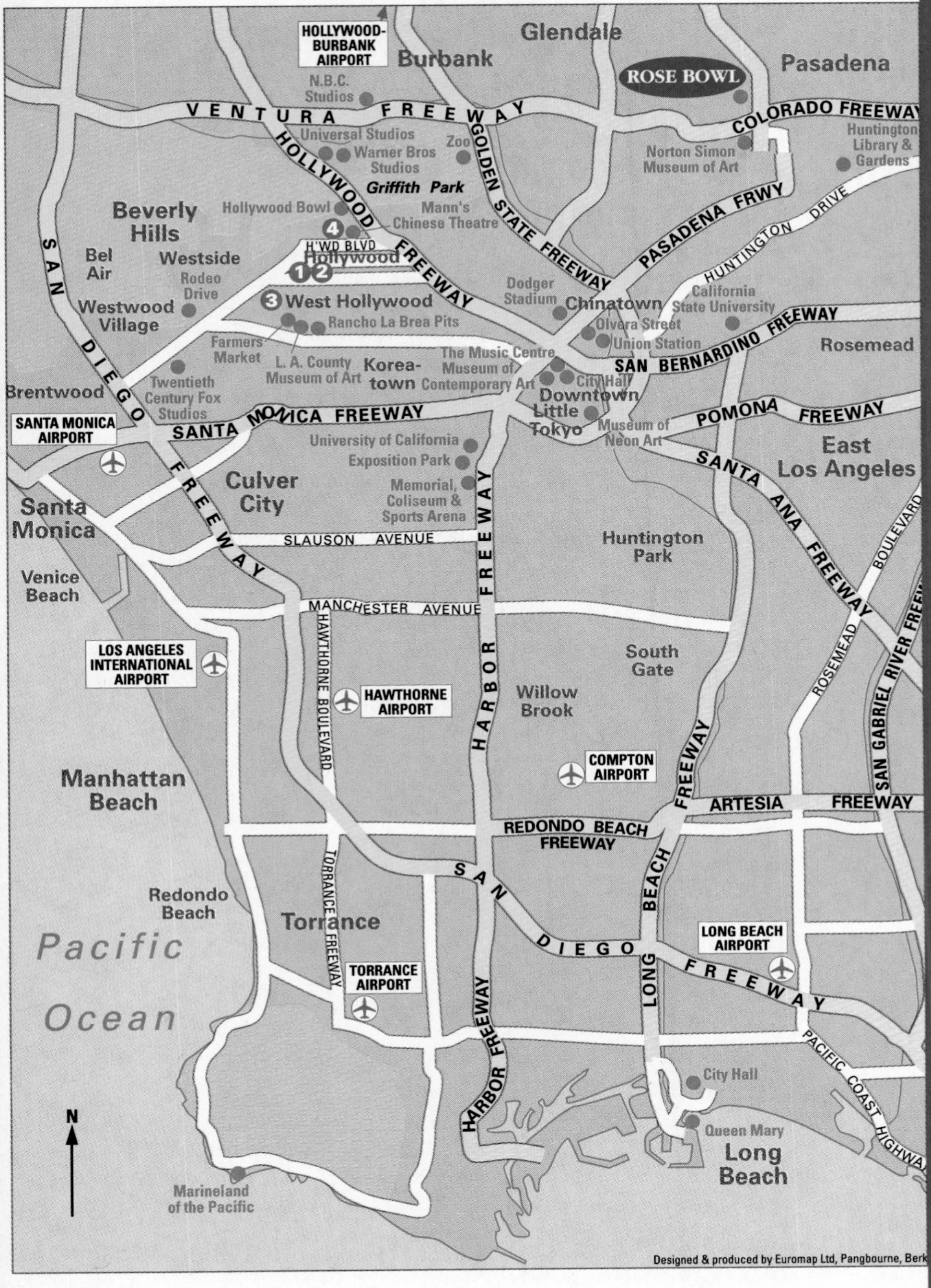

HOLLYWOOD-BURBANK AIRPORT
Burbank
Glendale
ROSE BOWL
Pasadena
N.B.C. Studios
VENTURA FREEWAY
COLORADO FREEWAY
Universal Studios
Warner Bros Studios
Zoo
Huntington Library & Gardens
Norton Simon Museum of Art
HOLLYWOOD FREEWAY
GOLDEN STATE FREEWAY
Griffith Park
Beverly Hills
Hollywood Bowl
Mann's Chinese Theatre
PASADENA FRWY
HUNTINGTON DRIVE
SAN DIEGO FREEWAY
Bel Air
Westside
H'WD BLVD
Hollywood
Rodeo Drive
Dodger Stadium
California State University
Westwood Village
West Hollywood
Chinatown
Rancho La Brea Pits
Olvera Street
Union Station
Farmers Market
L. A. County Museum of Art
Korea-town
The Music Centre
Museum of Contemporary Art
SAN BERNARDINO FREEWAY
Rosemead
Twentieth Century Fox Studios
Brentwood
City Hall
Downtown
Little Tokyo
Museum of Neon Art
SANTA MONICA AIRPORT
SANTA MONICA FREEWAY
POMONA FREEWAY
East Los Angeles
University of California
Exposition Park
Memorial, Coliseum & Sports Arena
SANTA ANA FREEWAY
Santa Monica
Culver City
SLAUSON AVENUE
Huntington Park
ROSEMEAD BOULEVARD
Venice Beach
MANCHESTER AVENUE
LOS ANGELES INTERNATIONAL AIRPORT
HAWTHORNE BOULEVARD
HAWTHORNE AIRPORT
HARBOR FREEWAY
South Gate
Willow Brook
SAN GABRIEL RIVER FREEWAY
COMPTON AIRPORT
Manhattan Beach
ARTESIA FREEWAY
REDONDO BEACH FREEWAY
LONG BEACH FREEWAY
Redondo Beach
TORRANCE FREEWAY
Torrance
LONG BEACH AIRPORT
Pacific Ocean
TORRANCE AIRPORT
PACIFIC COAST HIGHWAY
City Hall
Queen Mary
Long Beach
Marineland of the Pacific
N
Designed & produced by Euromap Ltd, Pangbourne, Berk

❶ *La Montrose Suite Hotel*

❷ *Le Reve Hotel*

❸ *Ramada West Hollywood*

❹ *The Roosevelt Hotel*

❺ *Wilshire Plaza Hotel*

E
D
F
C
G
B
A
ROSE BOWL
ROSE-MONT AVENUE
BOULEVARD
ARROYO
WEST DRIVE
SECCO STREET
N
Brookside Park

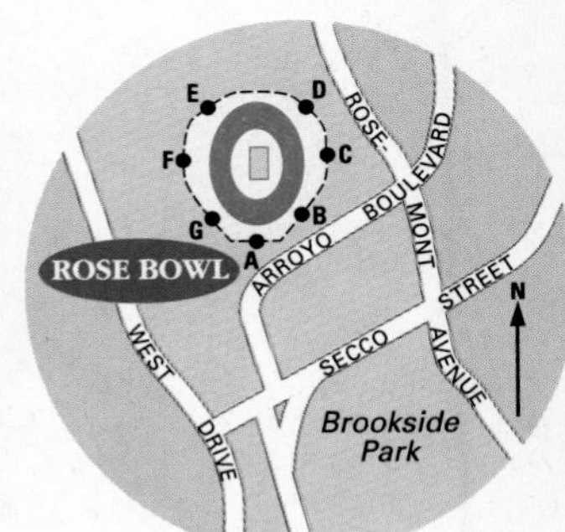

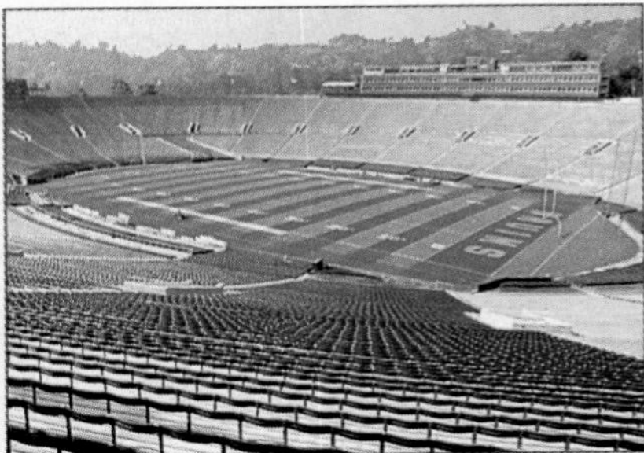

ROSEBOWL STADIUM

PROFESSIONAL SPORTS AND WHERE TO FIND THEM

Baseball
California Angels
Where: Anaheim Stadium
When: April-October
Tel: (714) 634 2000.

Los Angeles Dodgers
Where: Dodger Stadium
When: April-October
Tel: (213) 224 1491.

Basketball
Los Angeles Clippers
Where: LA Sports Arena
When: October-April
Tel: (213) 748 8000

Los Angeles Lakers
Where: The Forum
When: October-April
Tel: (310) 419 3100

American Football
Los Angeles Raiders
Where: LA Memorial Coliseum
When: August-December
Tel: (310) 322 5901

Los Angeles Rams
Where: Anaheim Stadium
When: August-December
Tel: (714) 937 6767

Hockey
Los Angeles Kings
Where: The Forum
When: November-March
Tel: (310) 673 6003

Los Angeles

West, *Delta* and *Southwest* airlines are located in Terminal A and *United* is located in Terminal B. Valet parking is available immediately across from Terminal A and rates are $5 per hour with a daily maximum of $15. For further information, telephone (818) 840 8840.

TRANSPORTATION FROM THE AIRPORTS TO LOS ANGELES

Airport Shuttles

Prime Time Shuttle: 24-hour, door-to-door luxury service from airports to residences and hotels in the Los Angeles area. For further information, telephone (310) 558 1606.
Shuttle Trak: 24-hour transportation to and from the airports, piers, bus stations and harbours. For further information, telephone (310) 216 9186.
SuperShuttle Inc.: Reliable, 24-hour, door-to-door service from the airports to hotels, offices and residences in the Los Angeles area. Also offers hourly charters to restaurants, events and special destinations. For further information, telephone (310) 338 1111.

Buses

Public bus transportation is available at the City Bus Center, located just outside the *Los Angeles (LAX) Airport* in 'Lot C' at 96th Street and Vicksburg Avenue. RTD bus fare is $1.10 (except on express buses) and exact change is required (dollar bills are accepted). However, rates are subject to change and passengers should confirm the amount before boarding. Transfers to connecting bus lines cost an additional 25 cents. Express bus services indicate travel on freeways. Arriving passengers may board a free LAX Shuttle bus at their terminal directly to 'Lot C' where the following public buses are available:
RTD Bus 42: To downtown Los Angeles;
RTD Bus 111-112: To Whittwood Center;
RTD Bus 117: To Downey;
RTD Bus 120: To Brea Mall, Orange County;
RTD Bus 220: To West Hollywood and Beverly Hills;
RTD Bus 225-226: To Palos Verdes Peninsula;
RTD Bus 232: To Long Beach;
RTD Bus 439: Express to downtown Los Angeles – fare $1.50;
RTD Bus 560: To Westwood and the San Fernando Valley – fare $1.90;
Santa Monica Bus 3: To Marina del Rey, Santa Monica;
Culver City Bus 6: To Westwood.
For further information on bus schedules and routes, telephone (213) 626 4455.

Coaches

Great American Stageline: Daily scheduled transportation from Los Angeles International Airport to Woodland Hills, the Conejo Valley and Ventura. Also offers a nationwide charter service. Coaches have WC's and radios. For further information, telephone (805) 499 4316 *or* (800) 287 8659.

Courtesy Trams

Many car rental agencies and airport area hotels provide complimentary transportation. Arriving passengers should consult the information board in the baggage claim area of each terminal where a direct information telephone is provided.

Limousines

A Gemstar Limousine Service: Full-service ground transport company specialising in airport transfers, sightseeing, tours and evenings on the town, 24 hours a day, 7 days a week. Choice of 6-, 8- or 10-passenger limousines, sedan town cars and passenger or cargo vans. Chauffeurs are multilingual. For further information, telephone (310) 457 7307 *or* (800) 835 8321.
Diva Limousine: Fleet of radio-dispatched luxury stretch limousines with full amenities and open bar available 24 hours a day. Specialises in airport transfers. Sedans and vans are also available and corporate accounts are welcome. For further information, telephone (310) 278 3482.

THE IDEA FOR A WORLD FOOTBALL CHAMPIONSHIP BEGAN IN 1904 WITH THE FORMATION OF FIFA (FÉDÉRATION INTERNATIONALE DE FOOTBALL ASSOCIATION) AND TOOK 26 YEARS TO DEVELOP. PREVIOUSLY THE OLYMPIC GAMES HAD BEEN FOOTBALL'S MOST PRESTIGIOUS CHAMPIONSHIP.

★ **FOR INFORMATION ON TICKETS TO WORLD CUP '94, SEE PAGE 1066.**

Aapex Limousine: Full-service company specialising in airport transfers, sightseeing and nights on the town. Passenger and cargo vans and sedans are also available. For further information, telephone (310) 670 3456 *or* (800) 426 4007.
Ace Limousine Service: One of LA's oldest limousine companies featuring luxury limousines for airport transportation, sightseeing or special occasions. For further information, telephone (310) 452 7083.
Dav El Chaffeured Transportation Network: Offers sedans, limousines, vans and corporate coaches, with a concierge service provided at Los Angeles International Airport. For further information, telephone (310) 642 6666 *or* (800) 328 3526.
Empire Limousine: Fully-equipped limousines and sedans offer airport and sightseeing services. For further information, telephone (818) 348 1061.
Fox Limousine Service: 24-hour service located within five minutes of Los Angeles International Airport for fast airport pick-ups. Special out-of-town airport rates are available and limousines feature first-class amenities. For further information, telephone (310) 641 9626.

Taxis

Cab stands are located at the airports and average fares from *Los Angeles (LAX) Airport* are $24.50 to downtown Los Angeles, $24 to Hollywood, $22 to Beverly Hills, $20 to Santa Monica and $44 to Pasadena. A $2.50 service charge is added to fares originating at the airport. Only taxis that display an official emblem (a picture of LA City Hall with taxi number) are authorised to offer service.

LOS ANGELES GROUND TRANSPORTATION

Rail

In a major new development, Los Angeles is constructing a light railway transportation system that will connect downtown LA with outlying districts.
Metro Blue Line: Connects downtown LA and Long Beach. For further route information, telephone (213) 626 4455 from 0530-2330.
Amtrak: Connects destinations throughout the USA. The terminal is located in downtown Los Angeles at historic Union Station on N Alameda Avenue. For information, telephone (800) 872 7245.

Buses

Los Angeles has the largest bus transit system in the nation with a passenger volume exceeding most of the country's rail systems. Bus transportation is provided primarily by the *Southern California Rapid Transit District* and several small municipal organisations. For information on RTD bus services and routes, telephone (213) 626 4455.
Greyhound: Provides transportation to various cities throughout the USA. The terminal is located at 1716 E Seventh Street in downtown LA. For additional area terminal locations, fares and schedule information, telephone (213) 620 1200.

Shuttles

DASH shuttle system, operated by the *City of Los Angeles Department of Transportation*, offers low-cost transportation in several communities. Four DASH lines in the city centre link major business, government, retail and entertainment centres. ***DASH bus service*** also operates in Hollywood, Van Nuys/Studio City, Westwood, Watts, Crenshaw/Midtown and the Fairfax districts. The fare is 25 cents and exact change is required.

Taxis

Cab stands are located at train and bus terminals and major hotels. Otherwise, taxis are radio-dispatched and must be ordered by telephone. Passing cabs will generally not stop when hailed. Fares are $1.90 on entering, plus $1.60 per mile. The following taxi companies can be phoned for services in the LA area: Checker Cab Co. Inc. – (213) 654 8400, LA Taxi – (213) 627 7000, Pedicabs – (310) 208 8898, Shuttle Trak – (310) 216 9186, Thousand Oaks Cab Co. – (805) 495 3500, United Independent Taxi Drivers – (213) 483 7604.

FREE FUN

If you are travelling on a tight budget, these free activities will help you make the most of your visit to Los Angeles:
Walk of Fame – Stroll through the terrazzo and brass stars dedicated to 1850 of Hollywood's biggest and brightest radio, movie, recording and television personalities.
Mann's Chinese Theatre – Compare your foot- and hand-prints with the stars on Hollywood Boulevard.
Griffith Park Observatory – Where stars can also be gazed at night or view the sparkling city below.
Marina Del Rey – Attend an outdoor art show or jazz concert.
Santa Monica Pier – Take in the spectacular view.
Farmers Market – Browse the boutiques, produce stands and galleries.
Forest Lawn Memorial Parks – Visit the final resting places of such Hollywood legends as Clark Gable, Nat King Cole, W C Fields, Errol Flynn and Jean Harlow.
California Museum of Science & Industry – See exhibits on the agriculture, natural resources and economy of Los Angeles.
Cabrillo Marine Museum – Experience the various marine life found in LA's coastal waters.
La Brea Tar Pits – View fossils dating back to the Ice Age.

Welcome to **PASADENA**

Pasadena is pleased to be a host for The Federation Internationale de Football Association (FIFA) World Cup, soccer's championship in the summer of 1994.

Pasadena's Rose Bowl is the venue for games on June 18, 19, 22, 26; July 3, 13, 16; and the championship game on July 17, 1994.

We are an international city, and welcome visitors from around the world for major events, conventions and leisure travel. You'll soon discover that Pasadena is a city of unparalled beauty full of tradition, and a community with an extraordinary array of culture, world-class museums and theatres. A world apart, yet just a short 30-minute drive to downtown Los Angeles and within an hour's drive of all major attractions, Pasadena is an ideal base for exploring other areas. Accommodation ranges from luxury hotels and resorts to small, intimate motels and inns.

The Rose Bowl has a seating capacity of 103,985 and will be the showcase stadium for World Cup soccer. Located in Pasadena's Arroyo Seco, a valley of parkland and natural vegetation, the stadium completed a $11.5-million renovation in August 1992. The 3-storey press box includes 23 luxury executive suites and four club suites. Perhaps the nation's most famous stadium, it was built in 1922 and boasts outstanding views. The Rose Bowl has been the site of five Super Bowls (1977, 1980, 1983, 1987 and 1993). The stadium was also used for parts of the 1932 Olympics, and again in 1984 for Olympic soccer.

Pasadena plays host to many championship events and has retained its charm and identity as a venue for world-class events for over a century. The Rose Bowl celebrates its 80-year anniversary in 1994 and the 105th Tournament of Roses Parade is cheered by one billion people watching it on television in 95 countries. Super Bowl XXVII was the most-watched show in television history with an audience of more than 30 billion people.

We hope your stay in the United States will be a memorable one and, while in our area, please stop by the Pasadena Convention and Visitors Bureau for assistance.

Pasadena Convention and Visitors Bureau, 171 S Los Robles Avenue, Pasadena, CA 91101. Tel: (818) 795 9311. Fax: (818) 795 9656.

Private, Exclusive,
Convenient!

Warm & Friendly Service with the Special Grace of a European Style Hotel.

Location: In a quiet residential neighborhood in West Hollywood, a block from Beverly Hills, steps from world famous Sunset Strip shopping & dining, just minutes from Century City, Hollywood, Pacific Design Center and Universal Studios Hollywood.

Accommodations: 115 charming suites, some with kitchenettes, each featuring color TV's and VCRs, individual air conditioning, multi-line telephones with voice mail, fireplace, private balcony, twice daily maid service.

Features: Delightful restaurant, rooftop pool & jacuzzi, lighted tennis court, full service state of the art health club, bicycles, jogging, non-smoking and handicapped rooms, meeting facilities, suite service. Bilingual staff, currency exchange, video library.

Tariff: Junior suite $145, Executive Suite $175, One bedroom suite $195.

Ask about our Weekend, Bed & Breakfast and Value Packages.

Commissions paid within 72 hours of guest departure.

le montrose

SUITE HOTEL DE GRAN LUXE

900 Hammond Street, West Hollywood, CA 90069
(310) 855-1115 Fax (310) 657-9192

URI
UNITED STATES & CANADA
APOLLO/GEMINI/GALILEO: 07683
SABRE: 05594, SYSTEM ONE: LAXVAL,
DATAS II: 01566, PARS: LAXVA

Member of THE GRANDE COLLECTION OF HOTELS

Managed by Outrigger Lodging Services
Formerly the Valadon Suite Hotel

175 Luxury Rooms to include 22 elegant loft suites.

Cable TV with remote control

Complimentary Newspaper

RAMADA
WEST HOLLYWOOD

Group/FIT Rates

Corporate Club Rates

Heated Outdoor Pool

Health Club Facilites
massage, sauna, steam & jacuzzi available

Minutes from Hollywood and Beverly Hills

Walk to Los Angeles Nightlife

Modern Artdeco Architecture

8585 Santa Monica
Hollywood, CA
90069

(310)
652-6400

FOR DETAILS AND INFORMATION CALL TOLL FREE 800-845-8585

Welcome to WEST HOLLYWOOD

Welcome to West Hollywood, home of the Sunset Strip and one of southern California's friendliest and most vibrant cities.

Centrally located, West Hollywood lies between Beverly Hills and Hollywood on Los Angeles' Westside and is just minutes away from the beaches of Santa Monica, the film and television studios of Burbank and Universal City, the museums and historic attractions of downtown Los Angeles and Pasadena, and the Rose Bowl, site of the 1994 World Cup finals.

West Hollywood's Sunset Strip has been a star-studded nightlife mecca since the 1920s. Once the site of such Hollywood legends as Ciro's, The Mocambo, Trocadero and Players, the Strip today is alive with the sounds of jazz and R&B, rock, cabaret and comedy, and is home to popular nightspots including The Roxy, Club Brasserie, Roxbury, Whisky a Go Go and The Comedy Store.

From American diners and delis to the most elegant of menus and decors, restaurants in West Hollywood afford visitors the opportunity to sample an amazing variety of cuisines. Breakfast at celebrity favourites like Hugo's and Duke's on Sunset, lunch outdoors in the California sunshine at the landmark hot-dog stand Tail o' the Pup or select from the carte de jour at the ever chic Le Dome and Chasen's and enjoy an evening meal featuring the most innovative of California cuisine at Spago or Mortons, gourmet Thai at Talesai, Spanish at La Masia, Chinese at Joss, northern Italian at Tutto Bene, French at Diaghilev, American eclectic at The Palm or Red Car Grill. Or savour the atmosphere at such legends as Formosa Café, Butterfield's and Barney's Beanery.

HOLLYWOOD AND VINE

The world-famous Melrose Avenue, the Cesar Pelli-designed Pacific Design Center and the more than 200 speciality and antique shops and interior design showrooms along the Avenues of Design attract savvy visitors from across the country and throughout the world. Sunset Plaza, an oasis of tree-lined sidewalks punctuated by outdoor cafés and boutiques – many found in no other city in the world – showcases the latest in jewellery and fashion. West Hollywood is also home to a lively art community. More than 20 galleries are located here, exhibiting the best of contemporary art from avant-garde sculpture and paintings to cutting-edge video, animation and computer art. Even the buildings here come to life with colourful murals.

Many of the area's finest hotels are in West Hollywood. Visitors can select accommodations ranging from a lavishly-appointed room in an Art Deco landmark, to an entire collection of villas – once the homes of movie stars – surrounded by lush tropical gardens. And whether the choice is on the Sunset Strip or nestled along a quiet, well-landscaped residential street, the view from the rooftop gardens, swimming pools and tennis courts of West Hollywood's hotels is always of magnificent sweeping vistas from the mountains to the Pacific Ocean.

Accept our invitation and visit West Hollywood soon. And when you do, we look forward to meeting you.

Mary Frost, Executive Director, West Hollywood Marketing Corporation.

Welcome to SAN FRANCISCO

On behalf of the San Francisco Convention & Visitors Bureau, I'd like to welcome visitors to our city. We are delighted to have been selected as one of the venues for the World Cup in 1994, and are certain that San Francisco will be as thrilling as the football competition they come to see.

San Francisco is truly a unique destination, with something for everyone. We offer you a cosmopolitan, multicultural city with spectacular scenery, mild climate, outstanding restaurants and world-renowned attractions. We hope that visitors will allow time during their visit to truly experience all that San Francisco has to offer. Whether this is their first visit, or the latest of several, we know they'll agree there is more than enough to do and see here to make them wish they had just one more day, regardless of how long their trip will be.

To help plan visits, write to our Tourism Development Department staff. They are available to assist you with brochure requests, itinerary planning and information about San Francisco's facilities, services and events (see the address in the *California* entry of the *US Gateways* section).

Once in the city, visit our Visitor Information Center, on the lower level of Hallidie Plaza at Powell and Market streets, near the cable car turnaround and BART (subway) station. The multilingual staff there can provide maps of the city (available in German, Italian, Spanish, French and Japanese, as well as English), which include scenic highlights of San Francisco. They are also happy to give advice on dining, touring and lodging, and information on transportation and city events.

International visitors may also purchase AT&T TeleTickets at the Visitor Information Center. These are phonecards that allow callers to prepay for telephone calls anywhere in the USA or abroad. Sold in 10-, 25- and 50-unit denominations for $6, $15 and $30, the cards work with any touchtone telephone and are available in English, French, German, Italian, Japanese and Spanish.

Remember, distances are short in geographically small San Francisco, which means visitors spend less time in transit and more time having fun. Many of the city's major attractions will be within walking distance from hotels. For example, Union Square, exotic Chinatown, the cafés of North Beach (the Italian quarter) and the Financial District are all just minutes from one another on foot. Fisherman's Wharf is just a short cable ride away.

San Francisco also enjoys convenient proximity to the best of Northern California. Within a short drive of the city, visitors can explore ancient redwood groves, bicycle through the Napa and Sonoma wine country, visit an array of family attractions and theme parks, hike in the Oakland hills or tour the romantic Monterey/Carmel coast.

We know visitors will enjoy their stay in our city. Please call upon us if there is anything we can do to assist you in planning travel to San Francisco.

From John A. Marks, President of the San Francisco Convention & Visitors Bureau.

SAN FRANSISCO, CITY HALL

San Francisco

SAN FRANCISCO SPORTS TRIVIA

- ★ *In the 1980s, the 49ers were led by Joe Montana, the NFL's highest-rated passer and considered by many coaches and players as one of the greatest players ever.*
- ★ *The San Francisco Giants baseball team moved from New York in 1958. Superstar players during the 1960s and early 1970s include Hall-Of-Famers Willie Mays and Willie McCovey. Present-day players include all-stars Will Clark and Barry Bonds.*
- ★ *The San Francisco Cow Palace is the temporary home to the Bay Area's new hockey team, the San Jose Sharks.*
- ★ *Former San Franciscoan 49er football player, Dwight Clark, will always be remembered for 'TheCatch' he made in a 1982 playoff game to beat the Dallas Cowboys at Candlestick Park. Today he works in the 49er front office and owns a restaurant in suburban Redwood City.*
- ★ *Herbert Hoover delivered his acceptance speech in Stanford Stadium on August 12, 1928, following his nomination to run for President on the Republican Party ticket. Formerly the manager of Stanford's first football team, Hoover was later elected the 31st President of the United States.*
- ★ *The largest crowd ever at Stanford Stadium was the audience at the 1935 Big Game. The attendance that day was an over-capacity of 94,000, all of whom were there to see Stanford's 13-0 win over California. The Indians (later to become the Cardinals) went on to capture the 1935 Rose Bowl.*

THE LOCATION San Francisco is located in northern California, not far from central California, on the west coast. It is 629km (389 miles) north of Los Angeles and 818km (508 miles) north of San Diego. Its position on the Bay creates unique weather conditions. When it's hot in New York, it's not in San Francisco. Daytime temperatures average 12-18°C (54-64°F) in summer and 9-15°C (48-59°F) in winter, far cooler than Los Angeles or San Diego. San Francisco's automatic air-conditioning is created by a unique combination of waters, winds and topography. During much of the summer a fog bank hugs the northern California coast, while in the Central Valley the temperatures soar to 38°C or more. And because air always travels from cooler to warmer surfaces, the mist moves towards the mountainous shore, where it is denied access along the 966km (600-mile) front and thrusts through the continental wall at the mouth of San Francisco Bay. The climate is invariably spring-like in this city for all seasons.

THE LANDSCAPE San Francisco Bay is a giant, irregular hourglass encompassing almost 1295 sq km (500 sq miles) of water. A few islands lie just off the coast, including Treasure Island, connected to the mainland by the 14km- (8.5-mile) long San Francisco-Oakland Bay Bridge; Angel Island, the bay's biggest island with 19km (12 miles) of roads and hiking trails; and Alcatraz, the famous high-security prison located a mile and a half from the shore which closed down in 1963. From the coastline the landscape sweeps up to a total of 42 hills overlooking the Bay. Twin Peaks (or Los Pechos de la Chola, 'The Breasts of the Indian Girl' as they were once known) are in the center of the city. Forming a 65-acre park, they are noted for their 360° view of the entire Bay area. Other magnificent vantage points include Nob Hill (overlooking Chinatown and the Bay), Russian Hill (overlooking the Bay and Golden Gate Bridge) and Telegraph Hill (overlooking the entire north and east Bay).

THE CULTURE AND HISTORY The fog that drapes the northern Californian coast hid San Francisco Bay from two centuries of European seafarers. A Spanish army expedition from Mexico finally discovered San Francisco Bay while searching for Monterey in 1769. The first colonists arrived in 1776 to found the Presidio of San Francisco and Mission Dolores. Mission Dolores was the sixth of 21 missions established by the Franciscans. Moorish, Mission and Corinthian styles are combined in the church, believed to be the oldest structure in the city. For decades a handful of missionaries laboured here to educate and convert the local Indians, members of the Costanoan tribe. It was not until July 9, 1846, that Captain John Montgomery claimed California for the United States and, 22 days later, Sam Brannan, a New York Mormon, arrived with a colonising force of 238. Less than two years later Brannan discovered gold. In one year, San Francisco's population went from 900 people to over 40,000 and the city was finally off to a roaring start and hasn't stopped since.

WHAT MAKES SAN FRANCISCO SPECIAL

THE CABLE CARS

It's hard to think of San Francisco without thinking of its beloved cable cars. They were awarded the honour of national historic landmarks in January 1964 by the US Interior Department's National Park Service. The cars are the only vehicles of their

WORLD CUP 1986: ONE OF THE MOST CONTROVERSIAL GAMES IN WORLD CUP HISTORY WAS PLAYED BETWEEN ENGLAND AND ARGENTINA WHEN MARADONA'S FIRST GOAL BECAME KNOWN AS 'THE HAND OF GOD' GOAL WHEN HE PUNCHED THE BALL INTO THE NET UNBEKNOWN TO THE REFEREE.

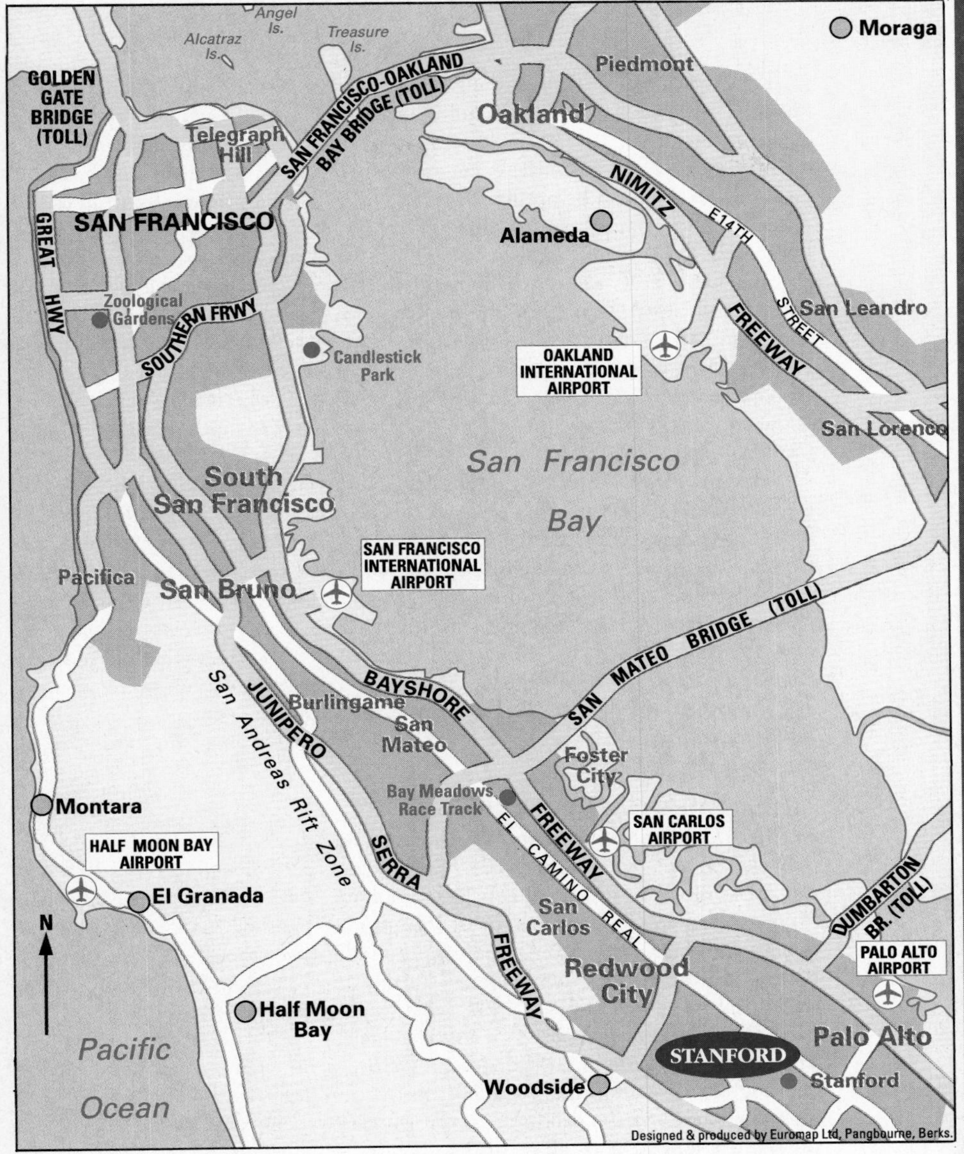

Angel Is.
Alcatraz Is.
Treasure Is.
Moraga
GOLDEN GATE BRIDGE (TOLL)
SAN FRANCISCO-OAKLAND BAY BRIDGE (TOLL)
Piedmont
Oakland
Telegraph Hill
SAN FRANCISCO
NIMITZ
E14TH STREET
Alameda
GREAT HWY
Zoological Gardens
SOUTHERN FRWY
Candlestick Park
OAKLAND INTERNATIONAL AIRPORT
FREEWAY
San Leandro
San Lorenzo
San Francisco Bay
South San Francisco
Pacifica
San Bruno
SAN FRANCISCO INTERNATIONAL AIRPORT
SAN MATEO BRIDGE (TOLL)
BAYSHORE
JUNIPERO
San Andreas Rift Zone
Burlingame
San Mateo
Foster City
Bay Meadows Race Track
Montara
HALF MOON BAY AIRPORT
EL CAMINO REAL
SAN CARLOS AIRPORT
SERRA
El Granada
San Carlos
DUMBARTON BR. (TOLL)
PALO ALTO AIRPORT
N
Redwood City
Half Moon Bay
Pacific Ocean
STANFORD
Palo Alto
Stanford
Woodside
Designed & produced by Euromap Ltd, Pangbourne, Berks.

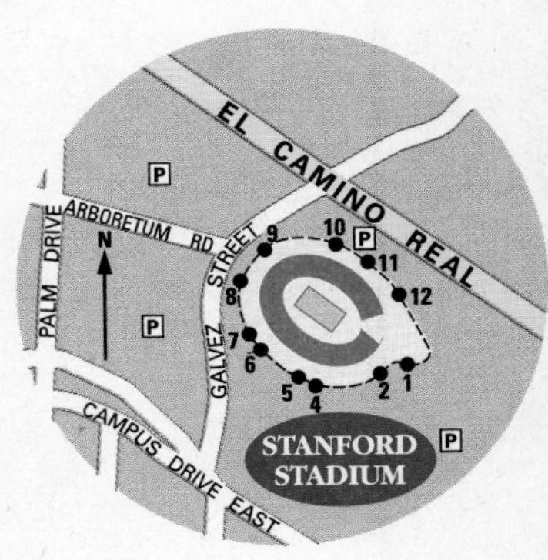

EL CAMINO REAL
P
ARBORETUM RD
PALM DRIVE
N
GALVEZ STREET
9
10
11
12
8
7
6
5
4
2
1
CAMPUS DRIVE EAST
STANFORD STADIUM

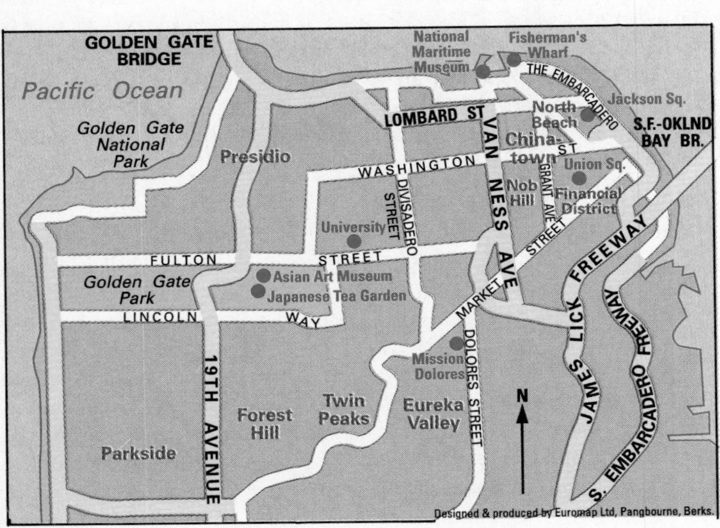

GOLDEN GATE BRIDGE
National Maritime Museum
Fisherman's Wharf
THE EMBARCADERO
Pacific Ocean
Jackson Sq.
LOMBARD ST
North Beach
S.F.-OKLND BAY BR.
Golden Gate National Park
Presidio
WASHINGTON ST
China-town
Union Sq.
VAN NESS AVE
Nob Hill
GRANT AVE
Financial District
DIVISADERO STREET
University
FULTON STREET
MARKET STREET
JAMES LICK FREEWAY
Asian Art Museum
Golden Gate Park
Japanese Tea Garden
LINCOLN WAY
EMBARCADERO FREEWAY
Mission Dolores
DOLORES STREET
19TH AVENUE
Forest Hill
Twin Peaks
Eureka Valley
N
Parkside
S. EMBARCADERO
Designed & produced by Euromap Ltd, Pangbourne, Berks.

STANFORD STADIUM

San Francisco

STANFORD STADIUM

Stanford Stadium is the largest privately owned college football facility in the United States and has been the home of the Cardinals football team for more than 70 years. It is also home of the 4-time Super Bowl Champions the San Francisco 49ers football team. In 1984 and 1985, the stadium received worldwide exposure as millions of television viewers watched both Super Bowl XIX and the Olympic Soccer competition. The eyes of the world will again focus on Stanford Stadium in 1994 as the largest event in the world comes here. At least four World Cup matches will be held at Stanford Stadium.

STANFORD STADIUM DETAILS

Stanford Stadium has a capacity of 85,500 people and there are 12 gates into the stadium. The natural turf field, considered to be one of the finest playing surfaces in the country, is composed of a mixture of rye and bermuda grass. During the football season the grass height is maintained at an even 3/4 of an inch. Sand is added every other year to absorb rainwater and provide natural drainage more effectively than any other surface in the country. This ability of the field to absorb wetness allows for play under conditions which would force many other stadiums to reschedule their events.

★ THERE WILL BE SPECIAL BUSES FROM THE AIRPORT TO THE STADIUM DURING WORLD CUP '94

kind left today, and celebrated their 100th birthday with a 10-day jubilee in 1973. Now the cable-car fleet carries 12 million passengers a year. Over 60% are tourists. The cars have a capacity of 70-80 passengers. Although the cars only travel about 15km (9.5 miles) an hour, the experience of a 90° turn or plunging down a near-perpendicular hill can be nothing short of harrowing. But there is no need to fear, as the cable cars have three separate braking devices.

Ultimately, there is no better way to sample San Francisco's sweeping vistas than by cable car. The Powell-Hyde line (the most spectacular from the standpoint of vertical and lateral 'zigzags') runs from downtown up over Nob and Russian Hills to Victorian Park on the northern waterfront. The Powell-Mason line leads from the corner of Powell and Market streets in the heart of the shopping district up over Nob Hill and down again into the colourful hubbub of Fisherman's Wharf. And the midtown route goes from the foot of California Street in the financial district to Chinatown and Nob Hill.

The cable car has had its ups and downs, figuratively as well as literally, over the years. There have been repeated moves to abolish them and replace them with more economical motor coaches, but each attempt has been met with an indignant populace. A proviso guaranteeing perpetuation of the three existing cable-car lines was written into the City Charter in 1971. This mandate can be neither revoked nor amended without the approval of the majority of San Francisco's voters. So now, after the system's $60-million renovation in 1982-84, and the fondness that San Franciscoans have developed for them over the years, their future seems secure. *The Cable Car Museum* on Washington and Mason streets is open daily from 1000-1800 free of charge for visitors wanting to find out more about the history of the cable car. Tel: (415) 474 1887.

THE GOLDEN GATE BRIDGE

Northern California's continental wall stretches for nearly 966km (600 miles). The only cleft in its mountainous coast is the Golden Gate. For well into the 20th century this mile-wide strait was considered unbridgeable: on one side lies the wild Pacific Ocean and on the other a vast (500 sq miles) natural basin nourished by 16 rivers – San Francisco Bay. At its peak, the tidal surge through the Gate is three times the flow of the Amazon and 14 times the Mississippi's. Currents sweep through at speeds up to 60mph and fierce winds whip the headlands. This is why the *Golden Gate Bridge* appeared as a near miracle.

The bridge was masterminded by Joseph B Strauss, an engineering titan barely 5ft tall, and his assistant Clifford Paine. Construction began on January 5, 1933, and took four years and the deaths of eleven workers to complete. At the time, it was the world's longest and tallest suspension structure and its 227m (746ft) towers were the highest rises west of the Empire State Building. Over 2.7km (1.7 miles) long and suspended over water 97m (318ft) deep, it allows a minimum ship clearance of 220ft and accommodates six car lanes. The great red-orange span opened to pedestrians on May 27, 1937, and to vehicles the next day, and on May 24, 1987, San Francisco marked the 50th Anniversary of its famous landmark. Nowadays, more than 40 million vehicles pass over this panoramic span and it is recognised the world over as a symbol of San Francisco.

UNION SQUARE – THE SHOPPER'S MECCA

The hub of San Francisco's shopping district, *Union Square* is a well-manicured, 2.6-acre plot planted with palms, Irish yews and bright flowers. Like Paris' Place Vendôme, Union Square has a towering, statue-topped shaft at its centre and is surrounded by smart stores and fine hotels. It also has a similar aura of elegance, but with a bit more hustle and bustle thrown in.

The Square is framed by many famous fashion houses – Saks Fifth Avenue, Burberry's of London, Macy's and Bally of Switzerland. Lining the neighbouring blocks are Gucci, Tiffany & Co., Jaeger, Brooks Brothers, Wedgwood, Gianni Versace, Scotch House and Cartier. There are 40 hotels within three blocks of the Square and flower stands grace almost every corner. Architecturally, its chief attraction is the distinctive yellow brick structure housing *Circle Gallery* at 140 Maiden Lane. Designed by Frank Lloyd Wright in 1949, the building, with its spiral interior ramp, was the prototype for his Guggenheim Museum in New York.

A haven for shoppers, sunbathers, orators, chess players and street entertainers, Union Square is an eventful place year round. It celebrates spring with *Rhododendron Days* in late April, summer with the *Cable Car Ringing Competition* and winter with the *Chinese New Year* pageant from mid-January to late February. During the Christmas season it is ablaze with many coloured lights, and throughout the year there is always something going on, including fashion shows, fundraisers, political demonstrations, sports rallies and band concerts.

THE JAPANESE TEA GARDEN

Nestled in San Francisco's *Golden Gate Park* near the *Asian Art Museum*, the *Japanese Tea Garden* could have been transplanted from a tranquil corner of Kyoto or Nikko. But its origin in San Francisco has its own story. In 1894, in the midst of a nationwide depression, the California Mid-Winter Exposition was held in Golden Gate Park in an effort to stimulate a business revival. One of the Exposition's backers was an oriental art importer, George Turner Marsh, who had spent many years in Japan where he'd become a connoisseur of the art of Japanese landscaping. For authenticity's sake, Marsh imported workmen and materials directly from Japan. The result was so unique and captivating that the Park Commission decided to retain it as a permanent feature.

A place of subtle enchantment in summer, winter and fall, the garden is spellbinding in spring. During the last weeks of March and early April, the 350 Japanese cherry trees spread their delicate blossoms in a spectacular display, along with peach, plum and quince trees. To celebrate the Tea Garden's seasonal glory, the local Japanese community stages a colourful *matsuri* festival each spring. Huge troupes of costumed performers come from all over northern and central California and Japan itself to participate in this elaborate folk rite which enlivens the city centre and *Nihonmachi* (Japantown) for two weekends in April.

The Tea Garden complements the Asian Art Museum, which spans 60 centuries of oriental civilisation – its floor-to-ceiling windows draw the garden into the galleries. Golden Gate Park's Japanese Tea Garden is the oldest in the country and there is an air of venerability about this gentle sanctuary that inspires propriety. Its gift shop and tea pavilion, where kimono-clad Japanese girls serve specially blended tea and wafers, cater to millions of visitors annually. Yet, even when the paths are crowded, voices are fittingly subdued and the garden's unruffled calm prevails.

SITTING ON THE DOCK OF THE BAY

Fisherman's Wharf remains one of the city's singular tourist attractions. Dozens of seafood restaurants sit overlooking rows of colourfully painted (and named) fishing boats. During the crab season, from mid-November to June, devotees line up for the best of the catch holding a loaf of sourdough French bread from a nearby bakery. This waterfront area was set aside in 1900 by local authorities as the province of commercial fishermen who had been catching in the bay since 1848. Now it stretches further west to Hyde Street and further east to Pier 39.

Not only does Fisherman's Wharf have some of the oldest and best seafood restaurants in the US, but there are other attractions as well. Historic ships such as *S/V Balclutha* at Hyde Street Pier (built in Scotland in 1886 and one of the last of the Cape Horn fleet), and the schooner *C A Thayer* and the engine river tug *Eppleton Hall* at the San Francisco Maritime National Historical Park make interesting viewing. There are also two newer arrivals, the *USS Pampanito* at Pier 45 (a World War II fleet submarine) and the *SS Jeremiah O'Brien* (the last unaltered World War II 'Liberty' ship) at Pier 3 East, Fort Mason. Other treats on the wharf include the *National Maritime Museum*, *The Cannery* complex off Leavenworth Street, Ghirardelli Square off Beach Street between Larkin and Polk and the Golden Gate National Recreation Area.

But for shoppers, one of the Wharf's most exciting features is *Pier 39*. Among the

Stanford Stadium History

Initially sparked by a feud with the University of California to see which school could complete a new football facility sooner, the construction of Stanford Stadium was completed in just over four months. However, having lost the stadium race, the University of California got their own back when the first game was held on November 19, 1921, between the two universities, and University of California won 42-7. The stadium has undergone renovations in 1925, 1927, 1960, 1973 and 1978. It has also been the sight of a host of national and international track and field competitions, including the United States Olympic Trials in 1960 and a 2-day meeting between the USA and the then Soviet Union teams in 1962.

THE PALACE OF FINE ARTS

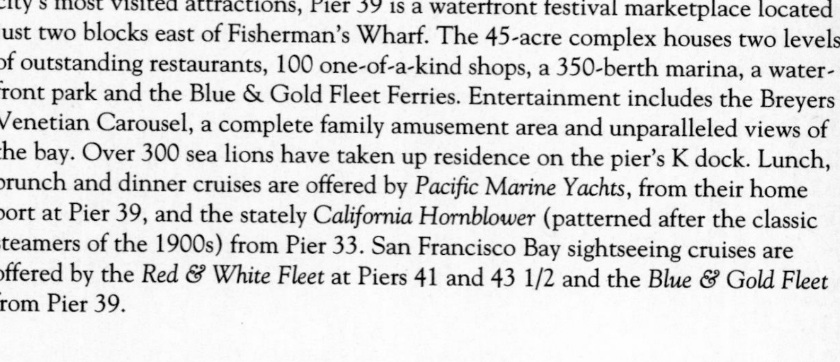
city's most visited attractions, Pier 39 is a waterfront festival marketplace located just two blocks east of Fisherman's Wharf. The 45-acre complex houses two levels of outstanding restaurants, 100 one-of-a-kind shops, a 350-berth marina, a waterfront park and the Blue & Gold Fleet Ferries. Entertainment includes the Breyers Venetian Carousel, a complete family amusement area and unparalleled views of the bay. Over 300 sea lions have taken up residence on the pier's K dock. Lunch, brunch and dinner cruises are offered by *Pacific Marine Yachts*, from their home port at Pier 39, and the stately *California Hornblower* (patterned after the classic steamers of the 1900s) from Pier 33. San Francisco Bay sightseeing cruises are offered by the *Red & White Fleet* at Piers 41 and 43 1/2 and the *Blue & Gold Fleet* from Pier 39.

San Francisco

THE WAY TO THE WORLD CUP

THE AIRPORT

San Francisco International Airport is 22km (14 miles) south of the city. It is the fifth busiest in the USA and the seventh busiest in the world. Forty-two major scheduled carriers serve the airport and there are 36,600 flights a month, 1260 a day. A $1.7-billion expansion project began in 1992 and is due to be completed in 1995.

TRANSPORTATION TO SAN FRANCISCO

Airport Shuttles

Airport Express: 30-minute service between the airport and the city costing $9. For further information, telephone (415) 775 5121.

American Airporter Shuttle: Reliable door-to-door service between the airport and San Francisco residences and hotels, as well as to Oakland airports. Advance reservations are preferred. For futher information, telephone (415) 282 8700.

Bayporter Express, Inc: Hourly door-to-door service available 24 hours a day from San Francisco and Oakland airports to any location in San Francisco and suburbs. Also offers a scheduled shuttle between San Francisco Airport and Oakland Airport. For further information, telephone (415) 467 1800.

Ez Way Out Shuttle Service: Door-to-door service available from 0600-2300 (24-hour service sometimes available) between San Francisco, Oakland and San Jose airports to residences and hotels in the area. Reservations are required. Tel: (510) 887 6226.

Francisco's Adventure: 24-hour service from San Francisco and San Jose airports to the city. Also offers tours of the city, Muir Woods/Sausalito, wine country, Monterey/Carmel and special Spanish-speaking tours. For further information, telephone (415) 821 0903.

Marin Airporter: Scheduled service available from San Francisco Airport every 30 minutes from 0430-2300, stopping at Novato, Ignacio, Terra Linda, Mill Valley and Sausalito. For further information, telephone (415) 461 4222.

OakAirporter: 24-hour daily airport shuttle service between Oakland Airport and San Francisco. Wheelchair vehicles are available on request. For further information, telephone (510) 568 RIDE.

Quake City Airport Shuttle: Service available from 0500-2400. For further information, telephone (415) 255 4899.

SFO Airporter: Motorcoach service runs every 20 minutes from 0500-2300 between San Francisco Airport, Union Square and the Financial District. Fare is $8 one-way, $12 round-trip for adults, $3 for children 2-12 and free for children under two. Reservations are unnecessary. For further information, telephone (415) 495 8404.

Supershuttle: Reliable demand-responsive door-to-door vans available 24 hours from the airport to anywhere in San Francisco. Fares will be quoted by telephone and credit cards are accepted. For further information, telephone (415) 558 8500 or (415) 871 7800.

Yellow Airport Shuttle: 24-hour, door-to-door service from San Francisco or

Oakland airports to residences and hotels in San Francisco. Fare is $9 and advance reservations are requested. Charters and tours are also available. For further information, telephone (415) 282 7433.

Taxis

Taxis are easily available from San Francisco Airport. The approximate fare to the downtown area is $24. Voluntary ride sharing for two or more persons to a maximum of three destinations is permitted. A flat fare of $24 should be divided among the passengers.

SAN FRANCISCO GROUND TRANSPORTATION

Subway

Bay Area Rapid Transit (BART): Eight San Francisco stations are linked to Daly City stations in the south and 25 East Bay stations. Trains operate 0400-2400 Monday to Friday, 0600-2400 Saturday and 0800-2400 Sunday. All tickets are dispensed from machines at the stations. Change machines for coins and 1-dollar bills are nearby. Colour-keyed wall maps are posted at each station. A special $2.60 excursion fare takes visitors around the entire system, touring the architecturally interesting stations and viewing the countryside (visitors should be careful not to go through the computerised exits at any of the stops, as this will nullify the ticket).

Rail

San Francisco Municipal Railway & Cable Cars: An extremely popular form of transportation. Fares are only $1, except on cable cars which are $3, and senior citizens only pay 25 cents. Exact change is required, as drivers do not carry change. Free transfers are valid for two changes of vehicles in any direction within two hours. Muni Passes are available for one-day ($6), three days ($10) or seven days ($15) and are valid on all Muni regularly scheduled services, including cable cars, and for a reduced fare to ballgames at Candlestick Park. Route information is published in the yellow pages or can be obtained by telephoning (415) 673 MUNI. Complete timetables are available on buses, Metro station agent booths and AC Transit booths. A comprehensive map for all Muni routes is available for $1.50. For further information, telephone (413) 673 6864.

CalTrain: The CalTrain Peninsula Commute Service operates trains daily from San Francisco to San Jose. It also operates a weekday shuttle bus from the terminal to the Financial District during peak commuter periods. For further information, telephone (800) 660 4287.

Amtrak: A daily service is provided north to Portland and Seattle and south to Los Angeles and San Diego via the 'Coast Starlight'. There are also daily services to Stockton, Merced/Yosemite, Fresno, Bakersfield and San Joaquin Valley. A service from San Francisco to Sacramento departs three times a day. The 'California Zephyr', a superliner train, runs from San Francisco to Chicago via Denver. Amtrak also provides a shuttle bus from Oakland at 16th and Wood Streets and the Transbay Terminal and CalTrain station in San Francisco. For further information, telephone (800) 872 7245.

Muni Metro Streetcars: These operate underground in the downtown area and on the streets in the outer neighbourhoods. There are five lines: 'J' (Church), 'K' (Ingleside), 'L' (Taraval), 'M' (Ocean View) and 'N' (Judah).

Buses

City buses are numbered with destinations marked on the front. Stops are usually marked by signs, curb markings and yellow bands on adjacent utility poles. ***Owl Service*** buses serve major transit corridors from 0100-0500.

AC Transit: Operates bus service to Treasure Island and communities in the East Bay (Berkeley and Oakland), as well as other cities in Alameda and Contra Costa counties, via the San Francisco-Oakland Bay Bridge. For further information, telephone (415) 839 2882.

GETTING AROUND THE GOLDEN STATE

California Coastline Limited: *Sweeping vistas of the rugged California coast captivate passengers on scenic round-trip rail excursions from Los Angeles to San Francisco. The train departs Union Station in Los Angeles for San Francisco on the first Friday of each month, returning the following Sunday. Fare includes three meals each way and hosted bar. 'Cable Car Holiday' tour packages are available in San Francisco. Reservations are accepted up to 24 hours prior to departure. For further information, telephone (800) 336 2844.*

California Parlour Car Tours: *Quality motor-coach tours offer 25 different itineraries including round-trip tours from San Francisco to Yosemite, Monterey, Lake Tahoe, as well as one-way excursions to Los Angeles with 3-, 5- or 7-day 'see California' itineraries. For reservations and departure dates, telephone 474 7500 or (800) 227 4250.*

Western Personalised Tours: *Tour packages range from two to eight days and incorporate San Francisco sites, Muir Woods/Sausalito, wine country, Yosemite and Sacramento Gold Country. Packages can be customised and include lodging, meals and transfers. For further information, telephone (510) 937 1648 or (800) 847 4822.*

San Francisco

GOLDEN GATE BRIDGE

★ FOR INFORMATION ON TICKETS TO WORLD CUP '94, SEE PAGE 1066.

Golden Gate Transit: Bus service linking San Francisco to Marin and Sonoma counties via the Golden Gate Bridge. Within San Francisco buses follow a Financial District route, a Civic Center route and a Park Presidio Boulevard route. For information on routes, schedules and fares, telephone (415) 332 6600.

Samtrans: The San Mateo County Transit District's 'Mainline Service' offers a bus service from San Francisco to San Francisco International Airport and communities on the peninsula as far as Palo Alto. For further information, telephone (800) 660 4BUS.

Greyhound: Buses are available to many destinations in the USA. For further information, telephone (415) 558 6789.

Ferries

Blue & Gold Fleet: Daily round-trip service from Oakland's Jack London Waterfront and Alameda's Gateway Center to the Ferry Building and PIER 39 at Fisherman's Wharf. There are four morning and four evening departures daily. Fares are $3.50 one-way and a $25 discount coupon book of ten round trips is available including AC Transit and Muni transfers. For further information, telephone (510) 522 3300.

Golden Gate Ferries: Ferry service departing from the south end of the Ferry Building to Sausalito and Larkspur. The MV Golden Gate makes a 30-minute crossing to Sausalito for $3.50 for adults and $2.60 for children aged 6-12. Three 725-passenger ferries provide daily service on the 21km (13-mile) route to Larkspur costing $2.20 for adults and $1.65 for children aged 6-12 on weekdays (children under five are free, but limited to two children for every one adult). Fares on weekends and holidays on this line are $3 for adults and $2.25 for children aged 12 and under. Family fares are available on the Larkspur and Sausalito ferries with children aged 12 and under travelling free if accompanied by an adult (limited to two children per adult). Handicapped persons and senior citizens receive a 50% discount. For further information, telephone (415) 332 6600.

Harbor Bay Maritime: Daily ferry service between the Ferry Building in San Francisco and Harbor Bay Island in Alameda. There are five departures a day Tuesday-Thursday and eight a day on Mondays and Fridays between 0700-1830. There are six departures a day on weekends from 1200-1800. One-way fares are $4 per person, $3 with book of ten tickets, and children of five years and under are free. For further information, telephone (510) 769 5500.

Red & White Fleet: Ferries depart daily from Pier 41 and 43½, Fisherman's Wharf, to Sausalito and Tiburon. Fares are $4.50 for adults and $2.25 for children aged 5-11. Ferries depart to Angel Island from San Francisco and Vallejo daily in the summer and on weekends only in the winter. From San Francisco the fare is $8 round trip for adults and $4 for children aged 5-11, and from Vallejo is $10.45 round trip for adults and $5.45 for children aged 4-12. A weekday commuter ferry service runs from the Ferry Building at the foot of Market Street to Tiburon and Vallejo. Ferries bound for Vallejo depart from Pier 41 and the fare is $15 round trip for adults, $12 for senior citizens and persons aged 13-18 and $6.50 for children aged 4-12. A bus shuttle service is also available to Marine World Africa USA. The package fare, including round-trip boat, bus and admission to the park, is $36 for adults, $30 for senior citizens and persons aged 13-18, and $20.50 for children aged 4-12. For further information, telephone (415) 546 BOAT.

Taxis

Taxis are easily available in San Francisco and fares are approximately $1.90 for the first mile and $1.50 for each additional mile.

NORTHERN WATERFRONT AERIEL

SCOTLAND (WHO FACE ESTONIA) AND NORTHERN IRELAND (GROUPED WITH LATVIA AND LITHUANIA) REALLY WILL BE STEPPING INTO THE UNKNOWN. ALL THREE ARE NEWLY DECLARED REPUBLICS, FOLLOWING THE BREAK-UP OF THE SOVIET UNION.

FLORIDA

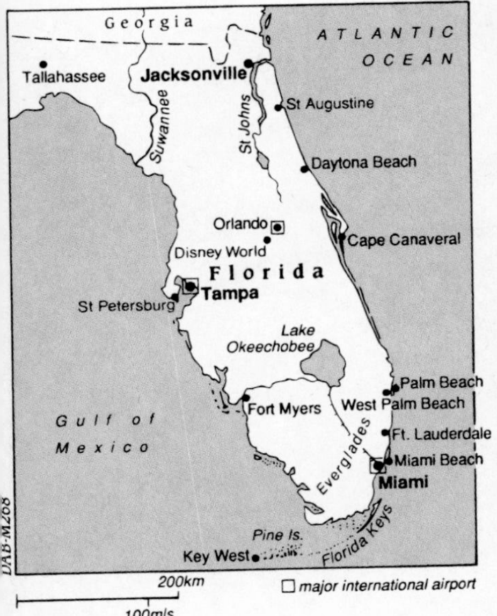

Including **Miami, Tampa** and **Orlando,** gateways to the southern States of Georgia and Alabama, as well as Central and South America and the Caribbean.

Florida Division of Tourism
18-24 Westbourne Grove
London
W2 5RH
Tel: (071) 727 1661 (recorded message). Fax: (071) 792 8633. Opening hours: 1000-1800 Monday to Friday.
Florida Division of Tourism
Suite 566
Collins Building
107 W Gaines Street
Tallahassee, FL
32399-2000
Tel: (904) 488 7598. Fax: (904) 487 0134.
Greater Fort Lauderdale Tourism Center
Suite 1500
200 East Las Olas Boulevard
Fort Lauderdale, FL
33301
Tel: (305) 765 4466. Fax: (305) 765 4467.
Greater Miami Convention & Visitors Bureau
Suite 2700
701 Brickell Avenue
Miami, FL
33131
Tel: (305) 539 3092. Fax: (305) 539 3113.
Orlando/Orange County Convention & Visitors Bureau
Suite 300
7208 Sand Lake Road
Orlando, FL
32819
Tel: (407) 363 5849. Fax: (407) 363 5899.
Tallahassee Area Convention & Visitors Bureau
PO Box 1369
200 West College Avenue
Tallahassee, FL
32302
Tel: (904) 681 9200. Fax: (904) 561 0685.

TIME: GMT - 5. *Daylight Saving Time* is observed – in the greater part of the state – from the first Sunday in April to the last Sunday in October. Clocks are put forward one hour, changing at 0200 hours local time.
THE STATE: Once an ancient Indian homeland, the Florida peninsula now offers everything from serene and simple seclusion in the sun to luxurious high-life. The state is one of the country's leading tourist regions, with winding waterways, freshwater lakes, hills, forests, swamps, cities, 13,560km (8426 miles) of coast, countless bays, inlets and islands and a legendary climate. On its southeastern tip are Miami and Miami Beach, famous and glamorous resorts where the sun shines all year long. Florida's greatest expanse of beach, the 'Miracle Strip', stretching from Apalachicola to Ensacola on the northeast coast, offers more than 160km (100 miles) of pure white and often deserted sand. Then there are the 45km (28 miles) of soft, sandy beaches along the Pinellas Suncoast near Tampa, fantasy fun at Walt Disney World, the Kennedy Space Center and much, much more.

TRAVEL

AIR: Approximate flight times: From **Miami** to *Atlanta* is 1 hour 50 minutes, to *Barbados* is 3 hours 25 minutes, to *Caracas* is 3 hours 10 minutes, to *Charlotte* is 2 hours, to *Chicago* is 3 hours 10 minutes, to *Dallas/Fort Worth* is 3 hours 20 minutes, to *Freeport* is 40 minutes, to *Grand Turk* is 1 hour 45 minutes, to *Guatemala City* is 2 hours 40 minutes, to *Honolulu* is 12 hours 15 minutes, to *Houston* is 3 hours, to *London* is 8 hours 10 minutes, to *Los Angeles* is 7 hours, to *Mexico City* is 3 hours 15 minutes, to *New York* is 2 hours 40 minutes, to *Orlando* is 55 minutes, to *Panama City* is 3 hours, to *Port-au-Prince* is 45 minutes, to *Providenciales* is 1 hour 35 minutes, to *St Croix* is 2 hours 40 minutes, to *San Francisco* is 7 hours 25 minutes, to *San Juan* is 2 hours 25 minutes, to *Santo Domingo* is 2 hours 10 minutes, to *Tampa* is 55 minutes and to *Washington DC* is 2 hours 20 minutes.
From **Tampa** to *London* is 11 hours 35 minutes (including stopover), to *Miami* is 50 minutes and to *New York* is 2 hours 40 minutes.
From **Orlando** to *London* is 12 hours (including stopover), to *Miami* is 55 minutes, to *New York* is 2 hours 30 minutes and to *Washington DC* is 2 hours 5 minutes.
International airports: *Miami (MIA)* is 8km (5 miles) northwest of the city (travel time – 25 minutes). Tel: (305) 876 7000. There is a 24-hour coach service to the downtown bus station and hotels on request. Bus no 20 departs every 30 minutes 0600-0100. Taxi and limousine services are also available. *Greyhound* run services to Homestead, Islamorada, Key Largo, Key West and Marathon.
Tampa (TPA) is 8km (5 miles) west of the city (travel time – 15 minutes). Tel: (813) 870 8700. A bus service is available to the city; limousine and taxi services are also available.
Orlando (ORL) is 12km (7 miles) south of the city (travel time – 15 minutes). Tel: (407) 825 2001. Rental cars, coach, bus, taxi and limousine services are available.
SEA: The port of Miami has been called 'the Cruise Capital of the World' and offers ocean liners for everything from business meetings and weekend getaways to luxurious extended cruises. The port of Fort Lauderdale, Port Everglades, is the second most important cruise port in Florida. Other cruise ports on the east coast include Port Canaveral and Port of Palm Beach. The main west coast cruise ports include St Petersburg and Tampa. Major cruise lines in Florida include *Admiral, Carnival, Chandris Fantasy-Celebrity Cruises, Commodore, Costa, Crown, Cunard, Dolphin, Holland America, Norwegian, Premier, Princess, Regency, Royal Caribbean, Royal Viking, Seabourn, SeaEscape, Sitmar* and *Sun Line*.
RAIL: *Amtrak's* Miami Station is 11km (7 miles) north of the downtown area. It is the southernmost point on the network, marking the southern end of the main East Coast line from New York (and ultimately Boston; see the *New York* section below for approximate journey times on this line). A branch line terminates at Sarasota, a few miles south of Tampa on the Gulf of Mexico. There are no direct services between the two.
ROAD: The best major routes through Florida are: Daytona Beach to St Petersburg (I-4), Jacksonville to the Alabama border (I-10), St Petersburg to Tampa (I-275), the lower west coast to Fort Lauderdale (State 84) and the east–west cross-state highway from Clearwater to Vero Beach (State 60). Most roads are excellent throughout the state.
Approximate driving times: From *Miami* to Orlando is 4 hours, to Tampa is 5 hours, to Daytona Beach is 5 hours, to New York is 27 hours, to Chicago is 27 hours, to Dallas is 28 hours, to Los Angeles is 57 hours and to Seattle is 69 hours.
From *Tampa* to Orlando is 1 hour 30 minutes.
All times are based on non-stop driving at or below the applicable speed limits.
Approximate *Greyhound* journey times: From Miami (tel: (305) 374 6160) to *Fort Lauderdale* is 1 hour 55 minutes, to *Palm Beach* is 3 hours, to *Orlando* is 7 hours 15 minutes, to *St Petersburg* is 8 hours 30 minutes, to *Jacksonville* is 9 hours 30 minutes, to *Tampa* is 10 hours, to *Tallahassee* is 13 hours and to *Atlanta* is 18 hours.
URBAN: Miami/Miami Beach: A new, improved public transport system has been launched for the downtown Miami area, with plans to expand it still further. It includes an elevated *Metrorail* system and an expanded bus system. The *Downtowner People Mover* combines the fun of a theme park with the convenience of above street-level travel. Buses operate frequently through most areas of Greater Miami. Fares are moderate and transfers are available. Taxis can be expensive in the Miami area; one can usually hail them but delays may be encountered at rush hours. Taxis can also be booked by telephone. Most major car hire and motor camper rental firms have offices at the airport or downtown Miami. Many provide a drop-off service in other parts of the state. Major hotels can often arrange immediate car rentals.

RESORTS & EXCURSIONS

MIAMI/MIAMI BEACH: Twin gateways to the Florida peninsula, Miami and Miami Beach also serve as the southernmost gateway to Central and South America and the Caribbean and constitute the world's largest cruise port, able to dock 14 cruise ships at one time. Once strictly a winter resort, the area is now a year-round haven for tourists. Temperatures range from about 20°C in December to around 27°C in August. Hotel and apartment rates drop in April and remain low until mid-December. Miami Beach is an island connected to the mainland by causeways and bridges. Consisting of 80 blocks and 800 buildings surrounding Flamingo Park, the area boasts the world's largest concentration of 1930s Art Deco architecture.
Sightseeing: Miami has experienced a major renovation renaissance in recent years, including the US$93-million *Bayside Marketplace*, an impressive complex of shops, restaurants and pavilions surrounding *Miami Marina*, which opened in 1988. The 28-acre *Bayfront Park* winds along the Bayfront connecting Riverwalk to Bayside. Greater Miami, or Metropolitan Dade County, is made up of many municipalities, including the city of Miami itself, Miami Beach, Coral Gables, South Miami, Haileah, Key Biscayne, Coconut Grove, Little Havana (with its Cuban restaurants and cafés) and others. The northeast area contains the popular *Sunny Isles Motel Row*. The southwest section embraces the 'Miracle Mile' shopping section in Coral Gables (with its *Venetian Municipal Pool*) and the modern university campus. To the north, *Greynolds Park* has picnic facilities, boat rentals and a 9-hole golf course, as well as the 12th-century *Cloisters of the Monastery of St Bernard de Clairvaux*, bought by newspaper magnate William Randolf Hearst and moved stone by stone from Spain. Greater Miami's 'palaces of culture' include the *Miami Wax Museum*, the *Metropolitan Museum Art Center*, the *Lowe Art Museum* (which has large collections of primitive art and of Oriental and European painting) and the *Bass Museum of Art*. *American Sightseeing Tours* offer daily tours by bus, ranging from half- to full-day trips through the Greater Miami area. Several tour companies offer boat trips. Helicopters take off regularly from **Watson Island** to give tourists a bird's-eye view of the Miami and Miami Beach area; the round trip lasts 14 minutes.
Excursions: The *Fairchild Tropical Garden*, on Old Cutler Road in South Miami, is the largest botanical garden in the USA, with 83 acres of palms, cycads and colourful tropical plants from around the world, as well as a rainforest, a sunken garden, a palm glade and a rare plant house. *HMS Bounty*, docked at Bayside, Miami, is a replica of the full-rigged 18th-century ship made famous

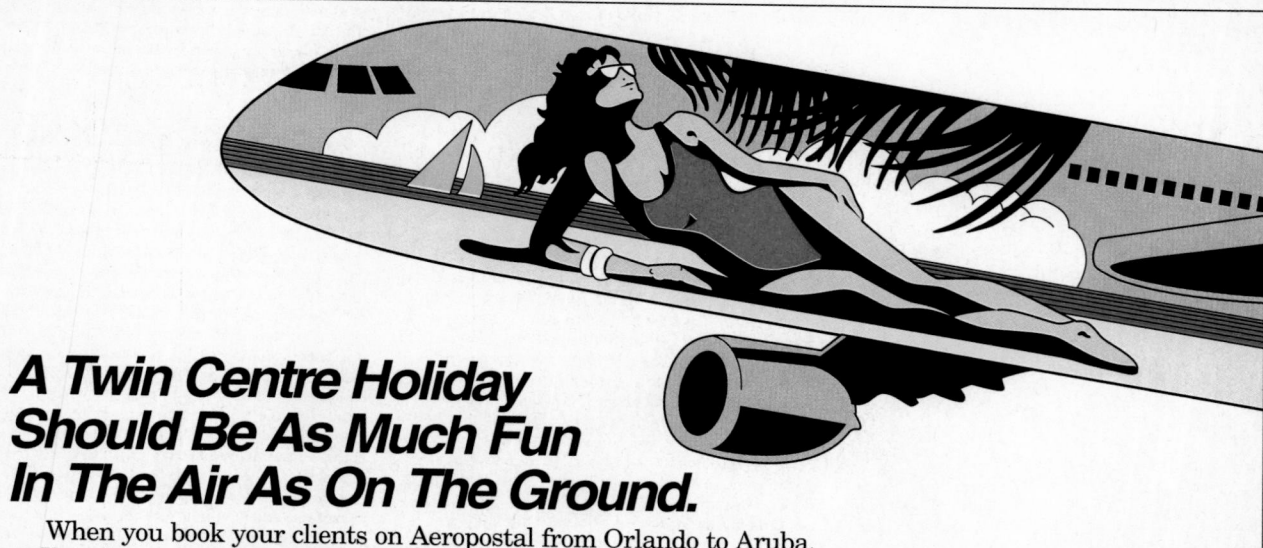

Aruba: A Tropical Getaway

With a total size of just 70 square miles, Aruba is slightly more than half the size of the U.S. island of Manhattan. But, as more and more vacationers are happy to learn each year, that's about the only similarity this wonderful tropical getaway has to hectic urban life.

The heaviest traffic Aruba's visitors will experience is a colorful school of fish swimming off the island's fabulous beaches. And though the swift and steady tradewinds that blow across this jewel of an island make sailing and windsurfing a treat, everything else in Aruba moves more leisurely.

No wonder it's regarded as one of the most hospitable of the many equatorial islands that dot the region. Aruba's 67,000 residents happily have shared their paradise with visitors for more than 20 years —even to the point of incorporating that hospitality into their national anthem: "The greatness of our people is their great cordiality. . . ," is part of one verse.

But don't, they would caution, confuse all this leisure with lack of comfort or boredom. Bordering those world-class beaches, for example, are 27 luxury hotels —with rooms that will total more than 7,100 by 1993. Resort activities include fabulous casinos, shows and exciting restaurants—all served up with the kind of friendliness and professional excellence that makes an Aruba visit extraordinary.

Duty-free shopping, dancing, sailing, diving and snorkeling, horseback riding, deep-sea fishing, tennis and sightseeing make up just a few of the other diversions.

AEROPOSTAL Airlines, which flies non-stop regularly from the U.S. cities of Atlanta, Georgia, and Orlando, Florida, to Aruba's Queen Beatrix International Airport, is one of the most convenient and comfortable ways a traveler can choose to set the mood for this special destination.

Anytime is a good time to visit Aruba. The average year-round temperature is 82 degrees. Located just 18 miles from the coast of Venezuela, the island lies outside the hurricane zone—in fact, it receives only about 20 inches of rain each year. Low humidity is a daily event.

Those weather conditions make island-exploring especially interesting because Aruba's interior is made up of colorful cactus and aloe plants, caves and picturesque rock formations.

Though it left the Netherland Antilles in 1986 and now is a separate entity in the Kingdom of the Netherlands, Aruba's 300-plus years of Dutch influence are still evident. Its principal city and capital is Oranjestad (named after the Royal House of Orange), and its official language is Dutch — though English and Spanish are widely spoken by island residents. Architecture in Oranjestad and in the second city, San Nicolas, also reflects the island's ties to the Netherlands.

by Fletcher Christian and Captain Bligh and portrayed in 'Mutiny on the Bounty'. The *Lion Country Safari*, west on Southern Boulevard, comprises a 800km (500-mile) drive through a wildlife preserve and amusement park, with about 1000 wild African, Asian and American animals roaming free in a veldt-like park. *Miami Metrozoo*, off the Florida Turnpike exit, 152nd Street West, represents state-of-the-art zoo design, with exotic animals in habitats very similar to their original homes in the wild. *Miccosukee Indian Village*, west of Miami, shows how this Indian tribe existed (and still exists) in the heart of the Florida Everglades. The *Monkey Jungle*, south on Florida Turnpike exit 216 Street West, 'where humans are caged and monkeys run wild', gives visitors the chance to see North America's first colony of wild monkeys in lush tropical jungle surroundings; other attractions there include the *Wild Monkey Swimming Pool*, the *Amazonian Rainforest* and the *Ape Encounter*. *Vizcaya*, south of downtown Miami on Biscayne Bay, is a beautiful 70-room Italian Renaissance-style palace set in ten acres of picturesque formal gardens and housing an outstanding collection of furnishings and art objects. The *Miami Museum of Science & Space Transit Planetarium*, near Vizcaya on South Miami Avenue, has many attractions, including laser shows. The *Parrot Jungle*, 18km (11 miles) south of Miami, has 1100 birds on display, including colourful macaws. The enormous *Everglades National Park*, west of Miami, is the largest subtropical wilderness in North America and at 1.4 million hectares runs into three counties and covers most of Florida's southern tip; it is the home of 600 varieties of fish, 300 species of birds, countless mammals, and plant species not found anywhere else in the world. There are hiking trails, swimming areas, campsites, guided tours, horseriding trails, as well as canoeing and boating. North of the Everglades is a stretch of road linking Miami and Tampa, known as the *Tamiami Trail*. From here the only access to the 5439 sq km (2100 sq miles) of subtropical wilderness is by water.

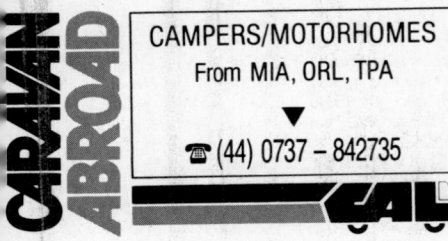

THE KEYS: The world-famous Florida Keys stretch for 290km (180 miles) over 42 bridges from Miami's Biscayne Bay to a mere 145km (90 miles) from Havana at the Dry Tortugas, known to many as the 'end of the world'. The Keys are divided into the Upper, Middle and Lower Keys (the latter including Key West). **Key Largo** is known as a diver's dream and features the only living coral reef within the continental USA. **Islamorada Key,** in the Upper Keys, is known for its sport-fishing opportunities and hosts many fishing tournaments throughout the year. Sailing, scuba diving, jet skiing and windsurfing are also popular here. Also in the Upper Keys is **Key Vaca** (or **Marathon**), with a large manatee population. The largest of the Lower Keys is **Big Pine Key,** a wildlife haven. But the most famous and popular key is **Key West,** a 13 sq km(5-sq-mile) island of charming gingerbread houses, Bahamian architecture and fascinating history (Ernest Hemingway wrote many of his major works here in the 1930s).

Sightseeing: The *Miami Seaquarium*, on **Virginia Key** and fronting on Biscayne Bay, is a tropical island paradise where visitors can see killer whales, dolphins (including the TV star 'Flipper') and sea lions. *Planet Ocean*, also on Virginia Key, via Rickenbacker Causeway, explores and explains the mysteries of the world's oceans. Visitors can see and feel a hurricane, walk through an indoor cloud and rainstorm, climb inside a submarine, listen to ships at sea, and watch the birth of the oceans. Starting at **Key Largo,** visitors can see North America's only living coral reef at the *John Pennekamp Coral Reef State Park*, with 21,000 hectares of undersea coral reef which can be viewed in glass-bottom boats and the adjacent *Key Largo National Marine Sanctuary*. **Key Biscayne,** 10.4km (6.5 miles) from

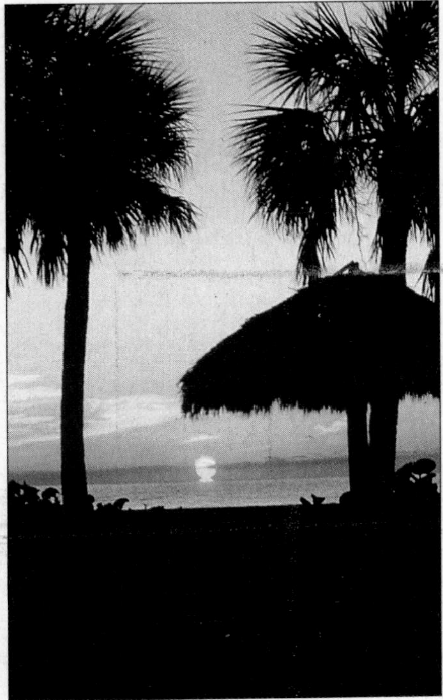

downtown Miami across Rickenbacker Causeway, has fine beaches, a zoo, picnic grove, cabanas, bath-houses, a miniature train ride and *Bill Baggs Cape Florida State Park*, with picnicking, fishing, boating and swimming. The *Theater of the Sea*, on **Islamorada Key,** is one of the oldest marine parks in the country and a favourite tourist attraction. **Big Pine Key** has the *National Key Deer Refuge* and drivers are advised to pay extra attention when driving through to avoid disturbing the deer. *Crane Point Hammock*, a 63.5-acre wilderness sanctuary, and the *Dolphin Research Center* are special attractions on **Key Vaco (Marathon). Key West** has a variety of attractions, including *Audubon House and Gardens*, the 19th-century home of the famous ornithologist; *East Martello Museum and Art Gallery; Ernest Hemingway Home and Museum; Key West Aquarium, Key West Lighthouse Museum;* and *Turtle Kraals*, home to loggerhead turtles weighing as much as 400lbs, with a touch tank and bird aviary.

FORT LAUDERDALE: North of Miami, Fort Lauderdale has been compared to Venice, because of its elegant stretches of lagoons, rivers and over 300km of canals. Watersports activities are therefore popular and include deep-sea fishing and boating. Airboat rides and day cruises are also widely available. There are 23 miles of wide sandy beach; more than 50 golf courses; 288 parks offering horseback riding, nature trails, picnicking and camping; and excellent shopping along the renowned Las Olas Boulevard. Extensive accommodation is available in elegant resorts or small properties along the beach.

Sightseeing: Boats can be hired from Bahia Mar Marina, or visitors can try the *Jungle Queen* (an Everglades cruiser). The town is home port for some 30,000 boats. *Ocean World*, in downtown Fort Lauderdale, includes dolphin and sea lion shows and demonstrations featuring sharks, alligators, sea and land turtles and tropical birds. *Bonnet House*, the winter residence of artist Fredric Bartlett, is a 35-acre subtropical estate just south of Sunrise Boulevard offering tours of the grounds. The *Discovery Center*, a hands-on science, art and history museum, is a perfect family outing and includes a planetarium and insect zoo. Interesting museums include the *International Swimming Hall of Fame Aquatic Complex, Museum and Pool*, the *Museum of Art*, with an excellent ethnic art collection, and the *Museum of Archaeology*. *Trolley Tours Inc.* offers guided historical tours of the entire city area. Day passes are available for US$8 per person and children under 10 are free. The *Voyager Sightseeing Train* also offers city tours from an open-air tram; for information, telephone (305) 463 0401.

Excursions: *Atlantis, the Water Kingdom*, located just outside of Fort Lauderdale in **Hollywood,** is south Florida's largest water theme park with 65 acres of slides, rides and attractions. The beautiful beach resort of **Palm Beach** hosts the *Henry Morrison Flagler Museum*, a tribute to the railroad mogul who established the area as a famous resort by laying out glamorous, palm-lined boulevards. Other attractions in the Palm Beach area include the *Dreher Park Zoo, Morikami Museum and Japanese Gardens, Norton Gallery of Art, South Florida Science Museum* and *Lion Country Safari Park*, with more than 1000 wild animals, free boat cruises, miniature golf and a dinosaur and reptile park. Northwest of Palm Beach is *Lake Okeechobee*, the second-largest lake in the USA, popular for large-mouth bass fishing.

TAMPA: Situated on Florida's west coast, Tampa is the state's third largest city. Long considered the preserve of the 'seriously rich', it has managed to retain the Latin colour and flavour of its Spanish origins and now has a thriving tourist industry.

Sightseeing: *Ybor City*, within the metropolitan boundary, is a thoroughly Spanish community named after Vincent Martinez Ybor who was the first Cuban cigar-maker to set up business in Tampa in 1866. Ybor City has wrought-iron balconies, plazas, arcades and sidewalk coffee shops.

Excursions: The world-famous *Pinellas Suncoast*, half an hour from Tampa on the interstate highway, is a year-round resort area with an average of 361 days of sunshine a year. Its 45km (28 miles) of sandy beaches and 205km (128 miles) of shoreline string together the Gulf Coast resorts of Clearwater Beach, Dinedin, Holiday Isles, Madeira Beach, St Peter's Beach (with its *London Wax Museum*), Tarpon Springs (with its *Sponge Docks*), Treasure Island and **St Petersburg,** one of the most popular retirement and resort cities in the USA. The *Salvador Dali Museum* in St Petersburg has the largest collection of the artist's work anywhere in the world. Further down the coastline is **Fort Myers,** with its famous palm-lined boulevards and beautifully restored turn-of-the-century downtown area. The lovely islands of **Sanibel, Captiva, Estero** and **Pine** can be visited from here. At the *Edison Winter Home*, on Fort Myers' MacGregor Boulevard, visitors can see the estate of the great inventor, with his botanical gardens, laboratory and home just as he left them. Spectacular water, light and music shows, both indoors and outdoors, can be seen at *Waltzing Waters*, south of Fort Myers. The *Homosassa Springs Nature World*, near the Gulf of Mexico, allows visitors to walk underwater with 10,000 fish and friendly manatees (aquatic mammals). *Busch Gardens* ('The Dark Continent') is a 300-acre turn-of-the-century African theme park with wild animals, and is one of Tampa's most famous attractions. There are rides of every description (including monorail, skyride, steam train and water rides to *Adventure Island*), shows, zoos and the *Moroccan Palace Theater*. The *Ringling Museum of Art*, set in the 68-acre estate of the late John Ringling in downtown **Sarasota,** is the official State Museum of Florida. Also in downtown Sarasota can be found *Bellm's Cars & Music of Yesteryear*, which has over 170 antique cars (the earliest built in 1897), over 1200 music machines, a country store, a livery stable, a blacksmith's shop and a 250-piece antique arcade. The *Everglades Wonder Gardens* in **Bonita Springs** give a glimpse of Florida's past and of the Everglades' wildlife, including bears, otters, panthers, deer, birds of prey, alligators, snakes and the endangered Everglades crocodile. *The African Safari* at the Caribbean Gardens in **Naples,** on the edge of Big Cypress Swamp, comprises 52 acres of tropical beauty with wild animals. *Fort de Soto Park* is an historic fort providing an ideal point from which to watch the ocean-going ships leaving Tampa Bay. Other parks include *Adventure Island Theme Park, Hillsborough River Park, Lowry Park* and the *Waterfront Park*.

ORLANDO: In the heart of Florida, Orlando is the centre of the state's fun attractions. It has 47 parks and 54 lakes within the city limits.

Sightseeing: *Eola Park*, the 50-acre *Le Gardens*,

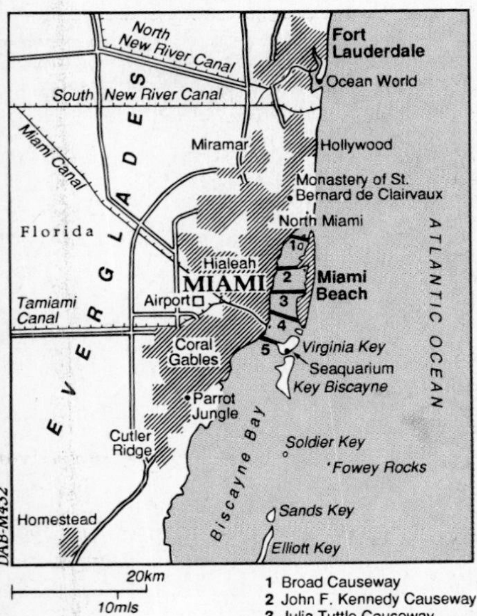

1 Broad Causeway
2 John F. Kennedy Causeway
3 Julia Tuttle Causeway
4 MacArthur Causeway
5 Rickenbacker Causeway

Orange Country Historical Museum, *Orlando International Toy Train Museum* and the *Cartoon Museum*. *Celebrity*, central Florida's only dinner theatre, has a 5-play season.
Excursions: Orlando is the closest city to **Walt Disney World,** one of the top USA tourist attractions (see section below). *Citrus Tower* on Highway 27 at **Clermont** offers visitors a wonderful view over the citrus-producing regions of central Florida. *Sea World* is the world's largest marine theme park and includes killer whales, dolphins, penguins, sharks, seals and sea lions. *Boardwalk & Baseball* is a 135-acre amusement park, with 30 thrill rides (including Florida's fastest roller coaster), shows and a midway, all connected by an authentic boardwalk. *Medieval Times*, west of **Kissimmee,** offers an 11th-century castle, banquetting, jousting and sword-fighting. The NASA Kennedy Space Center's *Spaceport USA*, on the east coast, has photographic and art exhibitions and audio-visual demonstrations with an 'IMAX Theatre' showing space shuttle launches and space activity on a huge screen. *Gatorland Zoo*, north of Kissimmee, is the world's largest alligator farm, with Florida wildlife, birds, a 'primeval swampwalk' and thousands of alligators and crocodiles. The lovely 16-acre *Florida Cypress Gardens*, started in the 1930s in **Winter Haven,** is an expanse of immaculately landscaped grounds, moss-draped cyprus, flowers, pools and grottos; it includes a zoological park and hosts the 'Southern Ice' skating review, the 'Aquacade' high-diving and synchronised swimming show and a famous water-ski show. At *Silver Springs*, visitors can cruise in glass-bottom boats through the jungle atmosphere. Nearby, the *Wild Waters* theme park has flume rides, a wave pool and a miniature golf course. Finally, for energetic walkers only, is the *Florida Hiking Trail*, which winds for 2100km (1300 miles) through the centre of the state. Orlando's latest attraction is *Universal Studios*, a 444-acre motion picture studio and entertainment attraction featuring shows and models from many hit movies, such as 'ET', 'Jaws' and 'Back to the Future'. A tour around the studio offers a behind-the-scenes look at how films and TV shows are made.
Walt Disney World: This immensely popular theme park is located 32km (20 miles) southwest of Orlando at *Lake Buena Vista*. Opened in 1971, it now attracts 20 million visitors a year. The park covers 28,000 acres, including 7200 designated as a wilderness preserve and transportation between the various attractions is by monorail train, ferry and launch. Walt Disney World is open throughout the year.
The EPCOT Center (standing for 'Experimental Prototype Community of Tomorrow') opened in 1982 and covers 260 acres. Themed areas focus on discovery and scientific achievements. Major attractions include *Spaceship Earth, The Universe of Energy, The World of Motion, Journey into Imagination, The Land, Computer Central, Horizons, The Living Seas* and *The Wonders of Life*. The *World Showcase* (also in the EPCOT Center) features exhibits celebrating eleven nations around a *World Showcase Lagoon* – Canada, the United Kingdom, France, Japan, the 'American Adventure', Italy, Germany, China, Morocco, Mexico and Norway.
Vacation Kingdom is a collection of themed resort hotels set in 2500 acres. Visitors can choose between the *Polynesian Village*, the *Disney Inn, Fort Wilderness Campground*, the *Grand Floridian Beach Resort* and the *Caribbean Beach Resort*. There are convention rooms, restaurants, shops, nightclubs, entertainment lounges, championship golf courses, tennis courts, horseriding, pools and lakes for swimming, boating and water-skiing, as well as *River Country* water thrills, *Discovery Islands* tropical gardens and wildlife sanctuary and *Typhoon Lagoon Water Park*.
Within Vacation Kingdom, the *Magic Kingdom* includes 45 major adventures on a 100-acre site. There are seven 'lands', each with entertainments, restaurants and shops based on favourite Disney themes of yesterday and tomorrow: *Adventureland, Liberty Square, Frontierland, Main Street, Fantasyland, Tomorrowland* and *Mickey's Birthday Land*.
Disney MGM Studios are a working TV and film studio, and there are production, tour and entertainment facilities.
The *Walt Disney World Village* contains the *Disney Village Market Place* (which has 30 shops, 10 restaurants, the 'Empress Lilly' riverboat and a *Village Lounge*), the *Disney Village Clubhouse & Village Resort, Hotel Plaza*, the *Village Office Plaza*, the *Conference Center* and *Pleasure Island* – a 6-acre night-time dining and entertainment complex.
JACKSONVILLE: Situated a few miles upstream from the Atlantic on the banks of the St Johns River in northern Florida, Jacksonville is a large and picturesque port. It was named after President Andrew Jackson. Jacksonville Beach has excellent shopping, dining and fishing facilities on its beach pier and boardwalk.
Sightseeing: *Fort Caroline National Memorial*, the *Cummer Gallery of Art*, the *Art Museum* and the zoo.
Excursions: St Augustine, the USA's oldest town, has winding streets and costume displays. *Zorayda Castle*, in downtown St Augustine, is a reproduction of the Alhambra, with fabulous treasures from all over the world and exhibitions on how the Moorish kings lived, entertained and ruled Spain. *Ripley's Believe-it-or-not Museum*, also in downtown St Augustine, houses a large collection of oddities, curiosities and art objects collected by Robert Ripley from around the world. *Daytona Beach* is famous for its wide beach and its speedway racing, especially the *Daytona 500*.
PENSACOLA: One of the chief resorts along the lovely northwest Florida coast, Pensacola has been under Spanish, British and French rule since the first Spanish settlers arrived in 1559.
Sightseeing: *Seville Square* (with its restaurants and speciality shops), *Plaza Ferdinand*, the *Spanish Aviation Museum*, the Spanish forts and the historic downtown area in general are all worthwhile attractions; the *Pensacola Historic District* has been designated a National Historic Landmark.
Excursions: Cedar Keys is a string of about 100 islands off the coast of northwest Florida. Three of the islands have been designated as the *Cedar Keys National Wildlife Refuge*. **Panama City** has beautiful beaches and well-known fishing areas.
Note: For information on attractions in neighbouring states, see above under *States A-Z*.

SOCIAL PROFILE

FOOD & DRINK: Miami/Miami Beach: There are more than 300 fine restaurants and most hotels maintain excellent dining rooms. Some gourmet places are rather expensive but many popular restaurants have economy prices. Cuban and Mexican food is very popular in Miami. Because Florida is surrounded almost entirely by water, seafood is a state speciality. Fresh stone crabs are available nowhere else in the USA. **Tampa:** There is a clear emphasis on Latin cuisine in Tampa but all tastes are catered for, with everything from international restaurants to fast-food shops.
THEATRE & CONCERTS: Miami/Miami Beach: There are many theatres and auditoria in the metropolis. Best known are the *Theaters of Performing Arts* at *Miami Beach Convention Center Complex*, and *Coconut Grove Playhouse*, 3500 Main Highway, which plays major Broadway hits. The *Opera Guild of Greater Miami* books major stars; their shows are usually staged at *Dade Country* or *Miami Beach Auditoria*. **Fort Lauderdale:** *Parker Playhouse* was created by Zev Buffman, owner of the Coconut Grove Playhouse, and shows usually move on from there to the Parker. *Sunrise Music Theater* features big-name performers such as Frank Sinatra and Pat Boone.
NIGHTLIFE: Miami/Miami Beach: Nightclubs exist in most hotels and resorts, and the *Coconut Grove* area, with its trendy nightclubs and lively cocktail bars, offers a swinging nightlife both inside the clubs and out on the streets, where many come just for a stroll and to be where the action is. The most lavish and lively clubs are Cuban supper clubs and *Les Violins* and *Les Folies*, both situated on Biscayne Boulevard, are highly recommended, featuring spectacular shows and excellent food.
SHOPPING: Miami: The city's main shopping streets are Flagler Street, between Biscayne Bay and Miami Avenue; and Biscayne Boulevard, between Flagler Street and north to 16th Street – site of the ultra-modern *Omni Shopping Complex*. A flea market operates every Saturday and Sunday on the grounds of *Tropicaire Drive-In Theater*, 7751 Bird Road, Miami.
Miami Beach: The principal shopping street is Lincoln Road Mall. Just north of Miami Beach is the Bal Harbour shopping district.
Tampa: The main shopping area is around Franklin Street Mall.
SPORT: Florida's sports opportunities are endless. **Greyhound racing** is held in Pensacola, Jacksonville, Daytona Beach, Orange Lake, St Petersburg, Sarasota, Tampa, Bonita Springs, Palm Beach, Miami, Fort Lauderdale and the Keys; **Jai Alai** in Chattahoochee, Daytona Beach, Tampa, Palm Beach, Fort Lauderdale and Miami; **Harness-racing** in Pompano; and **thoroughbred horseracing** in Tampa, Miami and Fort Lauderdale. Other spectator sports include **professional basketball**, played in Miami at the Miami Arena; **professional football**, with the Miami Dolphins team playing at the Joe Robbie Stadium in Miami, the Orlando Thunder team in Orlando and the Tampa Bay Buccaneers team in Tampa; and **polo**, played in Palm Beach at the Palm Beach Polo and Country Club. Other sports on offer include **golf, fishing, boat racing, motorcar racing, rodeo, baseball, tennis, hunting, sailing, diving and cycling**. Hunting and Fishing Licenses are sometimes required by persons over 16 years of age – check with the Florida Game and Freshwater Fish Commission. Tel: (904) 488 2975. For further information and brochures on any of the above-named sports, contact the Florida Sports Foundation, Room 455, 107 W Gaines Street, Collins Building, Tallahassee, FL 32399-2000. Tel: (904) 488 8347.
SPECIAL EVENTS: Qualifying matches will be held at the Citrus Bowl Stadium during the 1994 World Cup. **Mar '93** *Honda Golf Classic* (Weston); *Carnaval Miami and Calle Ocho Festival* (Little Havana); *Seafood Festival* (Port Canaveral); *Bike Week* (Daytona Beach); *Spring Break* (Daytona Beach); *Valiant Air Command Warbird Airshow* (Titusville); *St Cloud Spring Fling; Annual Spring Sidewalk Art Festival* (Winter Park); *Springtime Tallahassee; Ben Hogan Panama City Beach Golf Classic* (Panama City Beach); *FSU Flying High Circus* (Tallahassee); *Sanibel Shell Fair* (Sanibel Island); *Kissimmee Bluegrass Festival; Nestlé Invitational Golf Tournament* (Orlando); *The Players Championship* (Ponte Vedra Beach); *Gatornationals* (Gainesville); *Festival of States* (St Petersburg); *Medieval Fair* (Sarasota). **Apr** *Pompano Beach Seafood Festival; Delray Affair* (Delray Beach); *Seven-mile Bridge Run* (Marathon); *Melbourne Art Festival; Space Coast Beach Ball* (Brevard Country); *St Augustine Easter Festival; A Walk Through Time* (Micanopy); *Florida Sports Hall of Fame Induction* (Lake City); *Waldo Railroad Days; Bausch and Lomb Tennis Championship* (Amelia Island); *Ben Hogan Lake City Golf Classic* (Lake City); *Spring Arts Festival* (Gainesville); *Clay County Fair* (Green Cove Springs); *Sarasota Jazz Festival; Sailor Circus* (Sarasota); *Annual Sandestin Wine Festival* (South Walton); *Gulf Coast Offshore Powerboat Classic* (Panama City Beach); *Florida International Airshow* (Punta Gorda); *Derby Day* (Sorrento); *Sun 'n Fun EAA Fly-In* (Lakeland). **May** *Isle of Eight Flags Shrimp Festival* (Amelia Island); *Stephen Foster Folk Festival* (White Springs); *Beach Spring Festival* (St Augustine Beach); *Pioneer Days* (High Springs); *Centel Classic* (Tallahassee); *Mayfest* (Destin); *SunFest '93* (West Palm Beach); *Artworks* (Sarasota); *Gulf Coast Triathlon* (Panama City Beach); *Grayton Beach Fine Arts Festival*. **Jun** *Billy Bowlegs Festival* (Fort Walton Beach); *Annual Miami/Bahamas Goombay Festival* (Coconut Grove); *Sarasota Music Festival; Cross and Sword* (St Augustine). **Jul** *Sandblast* (Fort Lauderdale); *Lower Keys Underwater Music Festival* (Big Pine Key); *Hemingway Days Festival* (Key West); *Superstars Water Ski Tournament* (Groveland); *Fourth of July Celebrations* (Tallahassee); *Our Country Day Festival* (Keystone Heights); *Greater Jacksonville Kingfish Tournament* (Jacksonville); *Suncoast Offshore Grand Prix* (Sarasota); *Pepsi 400* (Daytona Beach). **Aug** *Panama City Beach Fishing Classic; US American Waterski Association Nationals & US Open* (South Walton).

CLIMATE

The climate is influenced by the adjacent Atlantic Ocean, which has the effect of slightly lowering temperatures in summer. It has more thunderstorms than any other state in the USA. The region is also affected by hurricanes or less severe tropical storms, which account for the heavy rainfall during the months of July to October. Winters are mild.
Required clothing: Lightweight cotton clothes and rainwear. Protective clothing against the midday sun (such as sunglasses, sun hats and long-sleeved shirts) advisable in the summer. Beachwear is popular.

MIAMI Florida (2m)

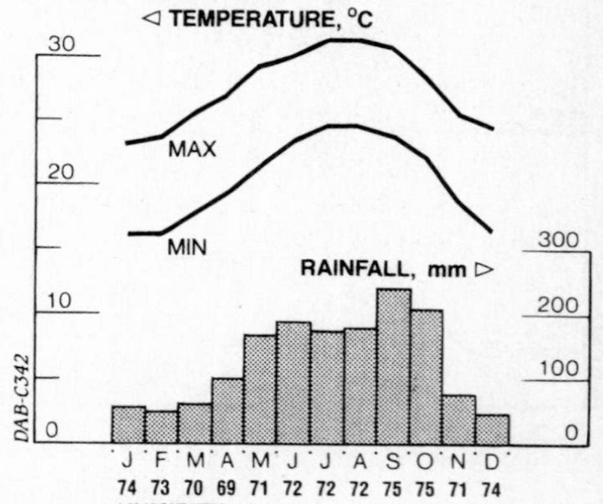

Welcome to **ORLANDO**

Orlando Welcomes International Sports Fans

Welcome to Orlando, where the magic begins the moment you arrive! Like no other city in the world, Orlando makes any visit magical. Thrills, adventure, beauty and wonder awaits visitors to this exciting one-of-a-kind destination.

ORLANDO'S MAGIC began when nature blessed the area with resplendent beauty, abundant sunshine and year-round warm weather. The opening of Walt Disney World's Magic Kingdom in 1971 paved the way for the transformation of this quiet, agricultural community into one of the world's most popular holiday destinations. Today, Central Florida is home not only to the Magic Kingdom and the Epcot Center but also to Universal Studios Florida, Sea World, Cypress Gardens, Busch Gardens, Wet 'N Wild, Spaceport USA and 50 other theme attractions.

LODGING IN ORLANDO With more than 70,000 hotel rooms, suites and villas, Orlando offers something for every taste and budget. Accommodation ranges from campsites and moderately priced lodging to suite hotels and high-class resorts.

DINING IN ORLANDO Grab a sandwich on-the-run between matches or dine in elegance on epicurean delights prepared by some of the world's most talented chefs. Sample international cuisine or chow down on barbecued gator ribs. Orlando has enough variety to satisfy any taste buds.

SAFETY TIPS Unfortunately, crime never takes a holiday. Secure valuables such as jewellery and excess cash in the hotel safe. Take only necessary valuables with you when travelling. Travellers cheques are generally regarded as the best way to meet cash needs on holiday. Determine who's there before opening hotel doors. Use peepholes, windows or phone the hotel desk. Place your room key in a safe place in a purse or on your person when at the pool, bar or dining room. Always lock your car. Lock valuables in the boot, glove box or luggage compartment. **Note:** Heat sensitive items such as film or electronic equipment may be damaged by the extreme temperatures of a parked vehicle.

CURRENCY EXCHANGE Currency exchange facilities can be found in major national and state banks, at many Central Florida hotels and at major attractions.

INTERPRETERS Orlando's Language Bank provides volunteer multilingual interpreter services. The bank provides information by phone. Arrangements for a paid interpreter or guide may also be obtained.

Welcome! You're a treasured guest in our hometown of Orlando, where dreams still come true.

From Wit Tuttle, Public Relations Representative of Orlando/Orange County Convention & Visitors Bureau.

ORLANDO WATERFRONT

ORLANDO MAGIC

ANDO WORLD CUP IS PLAYED AT THE CITRUS BOWL STADIUM

WORLD CUP ORLANDO

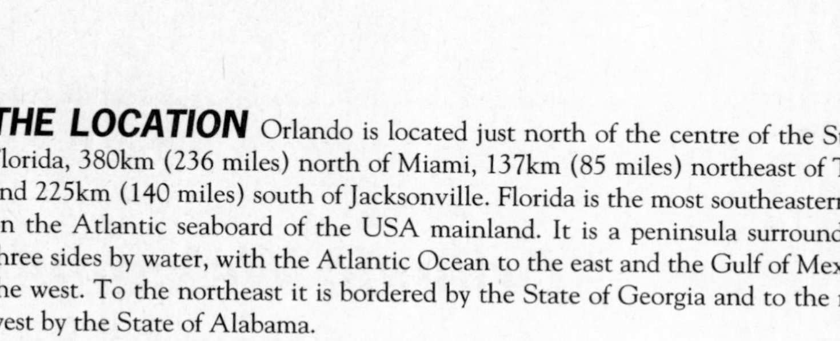

ORLANDO SPORTS TRIVIA

What NCAA college football team won the 1991 UPI Division I national championship by beating the Nebraska Cornhuskers 45-21 in the Florida Citrus Bowl in front of 72,328 fans?
The Georgia Tech Yellowjackets.

What 7ft 1 in. 300lb player was selected by the National Basketball Association's Orlando Magic with the first pick of the 1992 draft, and was consequently selected to start in the NBA all-star game in his rookie season?
Center Sharquille O'Neal.

What woman shattered the world record in three consecutive years in Orlando's Red Lobster 10km Classic?
Liz McColgan in 1987, 1988 and 1989.

What Orlando professional football team made it to the 1992 World Bowl, the championships of the World League of American Football?
The Orlando Lightning.

Who was the Most Valuable Player in the 1992 National Basketball Association's All-Star game played at the Orlando Arena?
Magic Johnson of the LA Lakers.

What golf legend designed several area golf courses and makes his home in Orlando?
Arnold Palmer.

What Orlando indoor football team played in the 1992 Arena Football League championship?
The Orlando Predators.

THE LOCATION Orlando is located just north of the centre of the State of Florida, 380km (236 miles) north of Miami, 137km (85 miles) northeast of Tampa and 225km (140 miles) south of Jacksonville. Florida is the most southeastern state on the Atlantic seaboard of the USA mainland. It is a peninsula surrounded on three sides by water, with the Atlantic Ocean to the east and the Gulf of Mexico to the west. To the northeast it is bordered by the State of Georgia and to the northwest by the State of Alabama.

THE LANDSCAPE Florida has a rich landscape, which makes it irresistable to both national and international visitors alike. From the soft, white-sand beaches that line its coasts to the palm-tree lined streets of its many attractive towns to the wild tropical flora and fauna of The Everglades, its natural beauty can be overwhelming. This idyllic environment lends itself to a variety of leisure activities with its plethora of golf courses, tennis courts and nature trails, to rowing and canoeing on Florida's massive Lake Okeechobee and inland lake chain, to an endless array of watersports available in an abundance of coastal resorts.

THE CULTURE AND HISTORY The city of Orlando is thought to have been named after a US soldier called Orlando Reeves. The story goes that he was on sentinel duty for a scouting party and, while his companions slept, an Indian approached disguised as a rolling log. Orlando saw him for what he was and fired his gun, waking the other campers and saving their lives, but was killed by the Indian's swift arrow. Before then, the community had been known as Jernigan after Aaron Jernigan who had come from Georgia and settled in the Orlando area in 1842. The first post office opened in 1850 and the city's name was changed to Orlando in 1857. It then developed a reputation as a centre for citrus production until 1971 when it became even better known as the location of Walt Disney World. Orlando is the county seat of Orange County which, until 1845, was known as Mosquito County.

WHAT MAKES ORLANDO SPECIAL

ORLANDO HAS ALL THE SPORTS

Professional and spectator sports bring big names and big leagues to Central Florida all year round. The NBA's Orlando Magic, for example, sold out its first three seasons of professional basketball at the 15,000-seat Orlando Arena. Ice hockey, concerts and other events also take place at this stadium. Orlando is also host to the Florida Citrus Bowl, a New Year's Day college football classic. Major League baseball teams from Houston and Kansas City hold spring training in and around Orlando. Two PGA-sanctioned golf tournaments are played here – the Nestlé Invitational and the Walt Disney World Classic.

There's a wealth of less structured recreation too. The Central Florida area has 44 golf courses, elaborate mini-golf, 21 tennis centres with more than 800 courts, plus hot-air ballooning, parachuting, horseriding, houseboating, canoeing, powerboating, sailing, water-skiing, fishing and swimming, all offering a relaxing change of pace.

WONDERFUL WEATHER

Florida has rightly earned its nickname of 'The Sunshine State'. Abundant sunshine and warm, pleasant temperatures are the norm in Central Florida. Summer weather (temperatures from 18-33°C; 65-92°F) arrives in Orlando in late May and

WORLD CUP 1950: ENGLAND AND THE FAR EAST DID NOT PARTICIPATE IN THE WORLD'S MOST PRESTIGIOUS FOOTBALL TOURNAMENT UNTIL 1950.

HIS VACATION, CHECK INTO A HOME...

INCREDIBLE VACATION VALUE FROM CONCORD RESORTS

As low as
;9 $139
llas Homes
per night
ommissionable

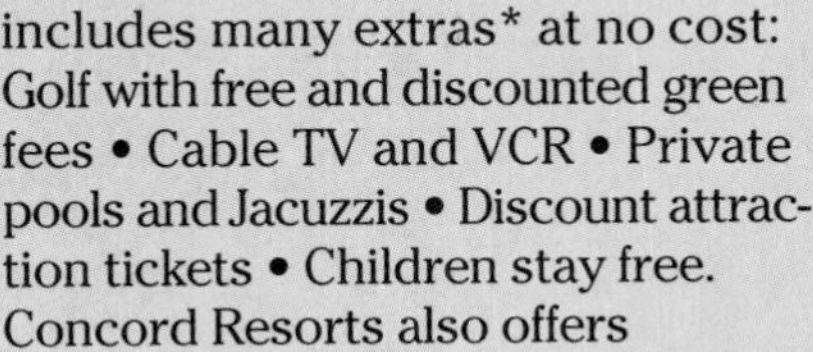

Concord Resorts offers vacationers an alternative to expensive hotels. Our beautiful homes and condo-
iniums are fully furnished
ıd include complete
tchens, washers and dry-
's, spacious rooms and
all the

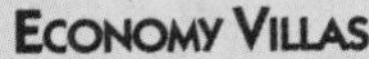

:ious
gns and
eatable
e make
cord Resorts
perfect choice
vacationing
lies.

omforts of home. That means vaca-
oners save on expensive hotel rates
nd dining costs. Plus all Concord
esorts accommodations are conve-
iently located just minutes from the
/ALT DISNEY WORLD® Resort, Sea
/orld,® Universal Studios® and other
entral Florida attractions.

A Concord Resorts vacation also includes many extras* at no cost: Golf with free and discounted green fees • Cable TV and VCR • Private pools and Jacuzzis • Discount attraction tickets • Children stay free. Concord Resorts also offers choices — select from several types of accommodations to fit your clients' lifestyles and budgets.

ECONOMY VILLAS

Budget-minded vacationers needn't sacrifice comfort or convenience when they choose our least expensive condominium rentals. These units include the listed amenities as well as tennis courts.

MODERATE VILLAS

These newer accommodations offer the same great location and amenities plus upgraded design features. Many include use of a Jacuzzi.

Located in a golf course community just a short drive from WALT DISNEY WORLD® Resort, our vacation homes even have private swimming pools.

PREMIUM VILLAS

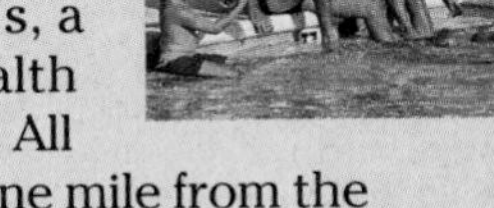

These deluxe units offer upscale furnishings and amenities including two color TVs, a VCR, and health club facilities. All located just one mile from the WALT DISNEY WORLD® Resort.

PRIVATE VACATION HOMES

Our vacation homes offer the ultimate in comfort and convenience. These new homes range in size from 1,400 to over 2,000 sq. ft. and include many extras such as private pools and free green fees.

For information and reservations call in the U.S./Canada, Puerto Rico/ V.I. toll free **1-800-999-6896**. In the U.K., call **0800-89-6650** or (407) 363-7670. Fax 1-800-866-9128 or (407) 363-9128.

WE FEATURE:
- Chelsea Square
- Villas at Shadow Bay
- Villas of Somerset
- Villas of Laguna Bay
- Villas of Sweetwater
- Parkway Village

WE MAKE ORLANDO FEEL LIKE HOME

Agent Commissions Paid Promptly

CONDOMINIUMS & VACATION HOMES

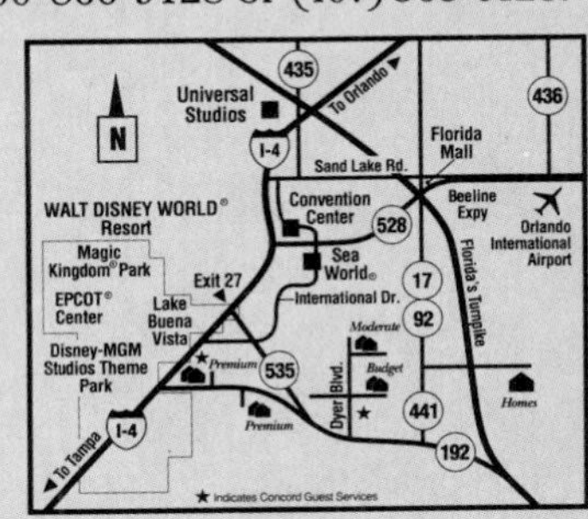

Reservation Center: 5728 Major Blvd., Suite 601, Orlando, FL 32819

*Listed amenities and features are offered at most accommodations. For specific information, contact Concord Resorts.

THE FLORIDA MALL

Great Shopping Is The Main Attraction

ORLANDO, FL.,...Situated in the heart of one of America's fastest growing cities and favorite vacation destinations, **THE FLORIDA MALL** is the premier and largest retail location within Central Florida. **THE FLORIDA MALL** blends an exceptional retail tenant mix, multi-variety food court, innovated architecture, convenient location and hotel accommodations into a total shopping experience. The 1.6 million square foot regional shopping center features · 6 fine department stores · over 200 specialty shops · a 19 unit internationally flavored Food Court · a cafeteria and family dining · the elegant 500 room Sheraton Plaza Hotel · a full Foreign Financial Service Center · and a movie theater. Situated on 225 acres in southern Orlando, these complementary components contribute to each others success.

The merchandising mix features an exceptional blend of international, national and local retailers to complement the market place, including six major department stores, Belk Lindsey, Gayfers, Dillard's East & South, JCPenney and Sears. The broad spectrum of retailers fulfills every consumer need from high fashion apparel to the basic necessities. Special shopping amenities for guests include foreign currency exchange, stroller rentals, courtesy wheelchairs, over 7500 parking spaces, mall gift certificates, foreign information services, tickets to attractions, and multi-lingual sales associates. **THE FLORIDA MALL** also features a "Frequent Shopper" Program with a chance to win valuable prizes, and the "Privilege" Program including mall-wide discount savings for world-wide visiting guests.

The 19 unit Food Court entitled "Treats" provides an exciting variety of mini eateries featuring American, Chinese, Greek, Indian, Mexican and Italian. In addition to Treats, **THE FLORIDA MALL** has a variety of eating establishments throughout its concourses including Ruby Tuesday, Morrison's Cafeteria, and Friendly's Restaurant. From traditional favorites to authentic cuisine, eating at **THE FLORIDA MALL** is a delicious experience which offers fare for all tastes.

Three distinctive architectural themes—Art Deco, Mediterranean, and Victorian—create a shopping atmosphere at **THE FLORIDA MALL** which is unequaled in Central Florida. Blending favorably with the selected merchandising mix, each of the motifs features design elements characteristic of a particular locale. Individual storefronts complement the selected decor of each area while maintaining their distinctive appeal.

THE FLORIDA MALL is conveniently located at the intersection of Sand Lake Road (S.R. 482) and South Orange Blossom Trail (Hwy. 441) in South Orlando. Accessible by two major highways including the Florida Turnpike and the Bee Line Expressway (528). **THE FLORIDA MALL** is just 4 miles east of Interstate 4 and International Drive. Area attractions such as Walt Disney World, Epcot Center, Sea World, Universal Studios Florida, Downtown Orlando and even the International Airport are all within 15 minutes of **THE FLORIDA MALL.** See map for specific directions. This retail showcase is open Monday—Saturday from 10 a.m. to 9:30 p.m., and Sunday from 11 a.m. to 6 p.m. for shopping enjoyment.

COLONIAL DRIVE S.R. 50
KIRKMAN ROAD 435
UNIVERSAL STUDIOS
WET 'N WILD
I-4
SAND LAKE ROAD S.R. 482
INTERNATIONAL DRIVE
ORLANDO CONVENTION CENTER
528
The Florida Mall
ORLANDO INTERNATIONAL AIRPORT
BEELINE EXPRESSWAY
DISNEY WORLD
LAKE BUENA VISTA
SEA WORLD
DISNEY WORLD VILLAGE
17-92
FLORIDA TURNPIKE
WALT DISNEY WORLD · RESORT
EPCOT CENTER
I-4
441
MAIN ENTRANCE
192

THE FLORIDA MALL is dedicated to our community and effectively serving our domestic and International visitors to make their visit comfortable and enjoyable. A visit to Orlando isn't complete without a stop at **THE FLORIDA MALL. . .Where Great Shopping Is The Main Attraction!**

THE FLORIDA MALL

Great Shopping Is The Main Attraction

CONTACT:
CHERYL PADILLA
Marketing Director
407-851-6255
8001 S. Orange Blossom Trail #420
Orlando, Florida 32809

International Shoppers Flock to

ALTAMONTE MALL
OF COURSE

ORLANDO, FL.,...When many international visitors arrive in Central Florida for their vacations, they bring an empty suitcase. Surprising?

Not according to ALTAMONTE MALL's assistant manager Karen E. Hipp.

"With the valuation of the dollar making traveling in the U.S. affordable and enticing, many visitors flock to Central Florida and its many attractions. While here, they find a wealth of bargains at retail stores and the empty suitcases help them take advantage," she explained.

ALTAMONTE MALL, Central Florida's only two-level high fashion regional mall, is conveniently located in Orlando's suburb of Altamonte Springs. The mall features over 175 stores, including four department stores as well as specialty shops and eateries.

It also caters to the international visitor with several exciting programs. First, all clothing retailers are able to help shoppers convert sizing into international terms with a simple to read chart posted at all dressing rooms. Also, the mall has initiated a "language bank" so non-English speaking visitors can find assistance either a store or a phone call away.

Most important, the ALTAMONTE MALL offers a special "Passport to Savings" card to all international visitors who request one or receive one from their travel agent. The credit card sized passport offers twenty percent (20%) discounts on all merchandise at nearly half of the mall's retailers. Individual, groups, or travel agents can request the cards by mail in advance of a trip to Central Florida.

The 1.3 million square foot mall houses some of the top retail names in the United States. Department stores include Gayfers, Burdines, JCPenney and Sears.

Among the high fashions retailers for women are Victoria's Secret, The Limited, Express, Ann Taylor, Lillie Rubin and Cache. Men can find a wide range of looks from Baron's Structure, J.Riggins, The Gap and Oak Tree. A host of jewelers are proving popular with tourists, among them Baily Banks & Biddle and Mayor's.

A wealth of specialty stores abound throughout the spacious mall including The Body Shop, Bentley's Luggage, Topkapi and Eckerds Drug Store where visitors can pick up anything from medical needs to fun T shirts for friends back home.

If all that shopping makes someone hungry, TREATS food court is a perfect solution. The area offers seating for over 600 and a quick meal or delectable dessert can be found at any of the fifteen (15) food retailers.

The ALTAMONTE MALL was recently renovated—it's been Central Floridians' favorite shopping mall for nearly 20 years. The wide, airy concourses make a perfect area for strolling when the summer heat proves too trying. The mall is awash with bright, light Florida colors of teal, aquamarine and peach. Dozens of skylights let in the natural sun while the professionally designed environmental control system keeps the temperature at a comfortable year-round 78 degrees.

ALTAMONTE MALL is conveniently located just 1/2 mile east of Interstate 4, the area's major thoroughfare, on State Road 436. It is just ten (10) minutes from downtown Orlando, less than thirty (30) minutes from the Disney area and International Drive.

The mall easily accommodates bus tours, is served by the area's bus service, Lynx, and has parking for over 6,000 cars.

FOR MORE INFORMATION:
Karen E. Hipp, Assistant Mall Manager

ALTAMONTE MALL
OF COURSE

451 Altamonte Avenue
Altamonte Springs, Florida 32701

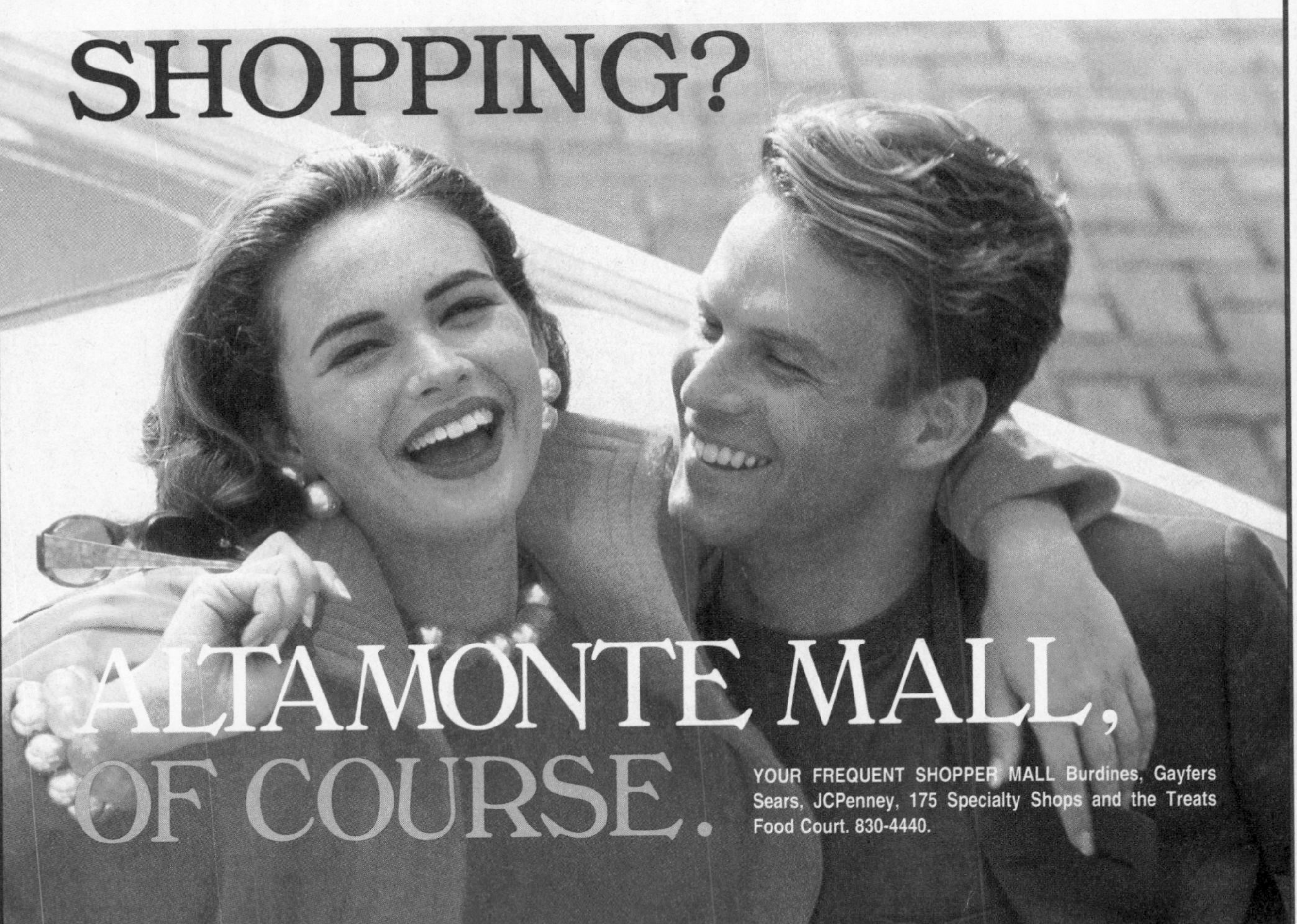

SHOPPING?
ALTAMONTE MALL,
OF COURSE.
YOUR FREQUENT SHOPPER MALL Burdines, Gayfers Sears, JCPenney, 175 Specialty Shops and the Treats Food Court. 830-4440.

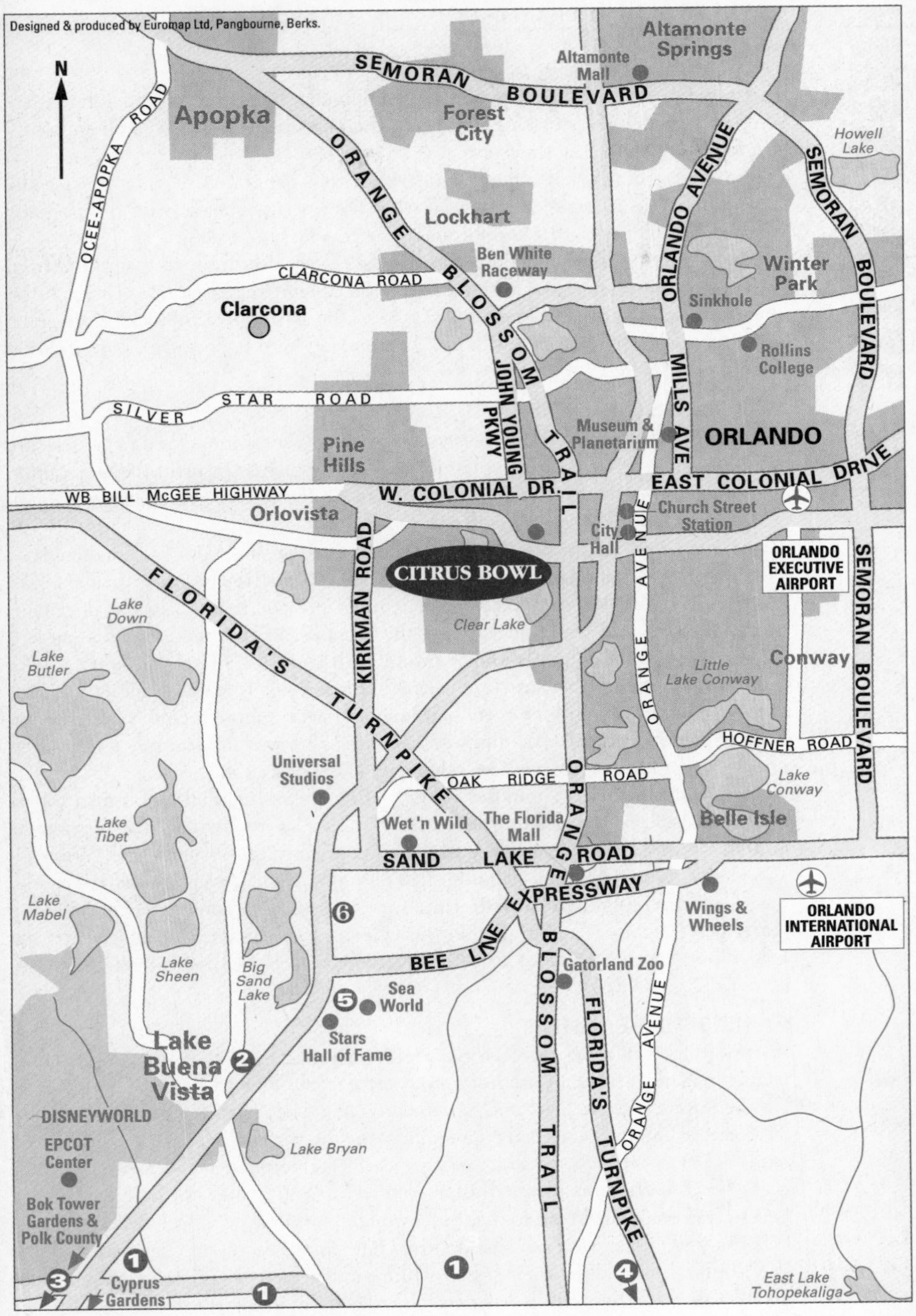

Designed & produced by Euromap Ltd, Pangbourne, Berks.

N
Altamonte Springs
Altamonte Mall
SEMORAN BOULEVARD
Apopka
Forest City
OCEE-APOPKA ROAD
ORANGE BLOSSOM TRAIL
Howell Lake
ORLANDO AVENUE
SEMORAN BOULEVARD
Lockhart
Ben White Raceway
CLARCONA ROAD
Clarcona
Winter Park
Sinkhole
Rollins College
SILVER STAR ROAD
JOHN YOUNG PKWY
MILLS AVE
Museum & Planetarium
ORLANDO
Pine Hills
WB BILL McGEE HIGHWAY
W. COLONIAL DR.
EAST COLONIAL DRIVE
Orlovista
Church Street Station
City Hall
KIRKMAN ROAD
CITRUS BOWL
ORLANDO EXECUTIVE AIRPORT
FLORIDA'S TURNPIKE
Lake Down
Clear Lake
ORANGE AVENUE
Lake Butler
Little Lake Conway
Conway
HOFFNER ROAD
Universal Studios
OAK RIDGE ROAD
Lake Conway
Lake Tibet
Wet 'n Wild
The Florida Mall
Belle Isle
SAND LAKE ROAD
ORANGE BLOSSOM TRAIL
EXPRESSWAY
Lake Mabel
Wings & Wheels
ORLANDO INTERNATIONAL AIRPORT
BEE LINE
Gatorland Zoo
Lake Sheen
Big Sand Lake
Sea World
FLORIDA'S TURNPIKE
ORANGE AVENUE
Stars Hall of Fame
Lake Buena Vista
DISNEYWORLD
EPCOT Center
Lake Bryan
Bok Tower Gardens & Polk County
Cypress Gardens
East Lake Tohopekaliga

1. *Concord Resorts*
2. *Embassy Suites Hotel*
3. *Grenelefe Resorts and Conference Centre*
4. *Jupiter Beach*
5. *Sheraton World Resort*
6. *Mercado Mediterranean Village*

★ **FOR INFORMATION ON TICKETS TO WORLD CUP '94, SEE PAGE 1066.**

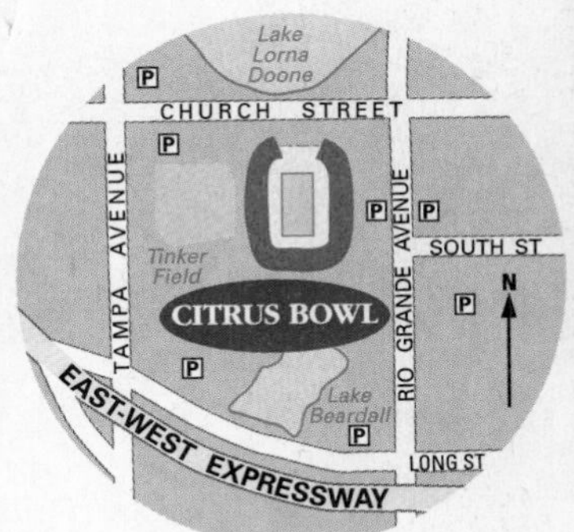

TICKETS

For ticket information, telephone John Fulgoni at Strategic Operations World Cup '94 on (310) 552 1994. Tickets might also be available through Ticketmaster on (407) 839 3900.

THE FLORIDA CITRUS BOWL

The Florida Citrus Bowl is located in Central Florida, one mile west of downtown Orlando. The stadium will host first-round World Cup 1994 matches on June 19, 24, 25 and 29, and one round of the 16-match games on July 4. Home field for the University of Central Florida football team and the WLAF Orlando Thunder American football team, it also hosts the New Year's Day football classic, The Florida Citrus Bowl, televised nationally on ABC. Other events that take place at the stadium are the Coors Lite Challenge Camel Supercross Series, the Camel Mud & Monster Truck Racing Championship and 'Rock Superbowls' – featuring such performers as The Rolling Stones, Pink Floyd and George Michael.

WORLD CUP '94

Orlando

FLORIDA CITRUS BOWL DETAILS

Seating Capacity: 70,188.
Field Dimensions:
Length – 126.5m (138.3 yds);
Width – 74.7m (81.6 yds).
Playing surface: *Natural grass.*
Press box capacity: 420.
Luxury Sky Boxes: 30.
Record Attendance: 72,328 – *Florida Citrus Bowl in January 1991.*

CITRUS BOWL STADIUM

★ THERE WILL BE SPECIAL BUSES FROM THE AIRPORT TO THE STADIM DURING WORLD CUP '94.

lasts through to the end of September. The humidity is often interrupted in the late afternoon by thunder storms. Fortunately, the rain usually lasts only half an hour – just long enough to cool things off.

The region's subtropical climate lends itself to a generally informal dress code. Lightweight, casual attire is suggested when visiting the theme parks or attending matches. Sneakers or other comfortable walking shoes are a must.

Florida's summer heat and humidity can feel especially intense to visitors from cooler, northern climates. Clothing should be of lightweight fabric such as cotton that lets skin breathe. Avoid over-exposure to the sun; apply sunblock before going outdoors and reapply every few hours. The sun can burn unprotected skin, even on overcast days.

GORGEOUS GARDENS

Oranges aren't the only thing that grow in Florida's sunshine. Florida's gardens are in bloom all year round with colourful and exotic plants. In nearby Polk County, less than an hour's drive from Orlando, can be found two grand gardens – Bok Tower Gardens and Cypress Gardens.

Bok Tower Gardens is a beautiful and serene sanctuary in the scenic highlands of Polk County that has been visited by over 20 million visitors since 1928. Thousands of azaleas, camellias and magnolias provide seasonal vistas of colour. Squirrels, quail and wood ducks roam the grounds. In the middle of the garden, amidst the reflecting pools and winding paths, is the 'Singing Tower', a 69m (225ft) stone and marble structure with 57 bronze bells. It features music from one of the world's great carillons every half hour and a 45-minute recital is presented at 1500 daily. Open 0800-1700 daily, admission is $3 for adults and free for children under 12. For further information, telephone (813) 676 1408.

Cypress Gardens, just 15 minutes north of Bok Tower Gardens, is known for its botanical displays, water-skiing shows, high diving shows, synchronised swimmers and ice skating shows. It has recently opened 'Plantation Gardens' and 'Wings of Wonder', a butterfly aviary featuring free-flying butterflies from around the world, fountains with sculptured butterflies and two chrysalis – cocoons that contain future butterflies. 'Kodak's Island in the Sky' provides a panoramic view of the gardens and Lake Eloise. Cypress Gardens is open 0900-1800 daily. For further information, telephone (800) 282 2123.

BEAUTIFUL BEACHES

With hundreds of miles of coastline, Florida is home to some of the world's most famous beaches, and many are just a short drive from Orlando.

On the Atlantic coast, Daytona, New Smyrna and Cocoa beaches are just an hour's drive east of Orlando. Cars can cruise right along the water's edge on the hard-packed sands of Daytona Beach, noted for its carnival-like atmosphere and oceanfront boardwalk. Beach enthusiasts in search of a more serene setting may opt for New Smyrna Beach, Daytona's neighbour to the south, while surfers flock to Cocoa Beach.

Less than two hours west of Orlando, the Gulf Coast beaches of Clearwater and St Petersburg are noted for their sugary-white sands which border the tranquil blue-green waters of the Gulf of Mexico. Visitors should make sure they pack their bathing suits, sunglasses and sunscreen for a few hours of blissful sunbathing and swimming and, as the sun goes down, visitors should experience Florida's exquisite beach sunsets, as they rarely fail to give an extraordinary performance.

DISNEY WORLD'S NEW ATTRACTIONS

No mention of Orlando would be complete without *Walt Disney World*. Attracting visitors from all over the world, its appeal is endless and, despite being around for 20 years, new things are still happening at Disney World.

Disney's MGM Studios Theme Park pays tribute to Walt Disney's hit movie 'Aladdin' with a daily parade called 'Aladdin's Royal Caravan'. The caravan depicts Aladdin's entrance into the city of Agrabah after discovering the magic lamp and becoming Prince Ali. A brass band leads the procession down Hollywood Boulevard followed by Aladdin's 10m (32ft) genie. Music, dance and humour com-

1958: BRAZIL STOLE MOST OF THE LIMELIGHT IN THE SIXTH WORLD CUP WITH ONE PLAYER CAUGHT IN THE HEADLINES. PÉLÉ WAS THE YOUNGEST PLAYER TO APPEAR IN A CUP FINAL AT THE AGE OF 17 AND BECAME THE FIRST OF FOOTBALL'S WORLDWIDE SUPERSTARS.

Central Florida Gives a World Class Welcome to World Cup Fans.

The world's eyes will focus on Central Florida in 1994 during World Cup soccer competition. And while preliminary competition is scheduled for Orlando, the best place for sports enthusiasts and their families to stay is Central Florida's Polk County, naturally.

Less than a sixty-minute drive from either Orlando International Airport or Tampa International Airport, Central Florida's Polk County is a sporting paradise. Enjoy the world's most famous Water Ski Show, spectacular gardens and Souther charm at Cypress Gardens. Bok Tower Gardens is known for its serene natural beauty and soothing carillon recitals. And with over 600 fresh water lakes and phosphate pits, Polk County offers plenty of opportunity for boating, water sports and exceptional angling.

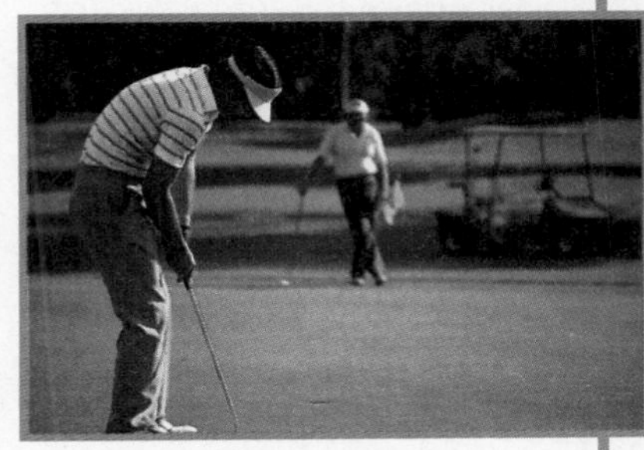

Experience the drama and excitement of one of the world's largest air shows when the annual Sun 'n Fun Experimental Aircraft Association Fly-in launches in Lakeland in April.

See professional hockey as the Tampa Bay Lightning takes to the ice at the Lakeland Civic Center for its annual training schedule. Catch a Major League Baseball game during spring training when the Detroit Tigers are in town. See the world's largest collection of Frank Lloyd Wright architecture on the campus of Florida Southern College. Enjoy a concert, play or exhibition at the Lakeland Civic Center.

If you are looking for a more relaxed pace, spend some time at Grenelefe Golf and Tennis Resort. Here you will find championship golf courses, meticulously groomed clay and grass tennis courts, croquet, swimming fishing, hiking and much more. The dining ranges from casual to gourmet at this popular meeting and convention resort. There is even a night club for good times after sundown.

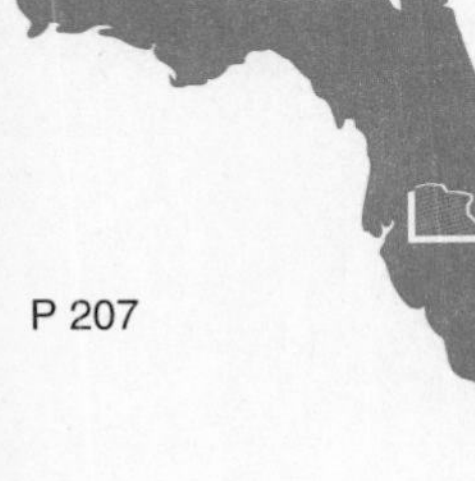

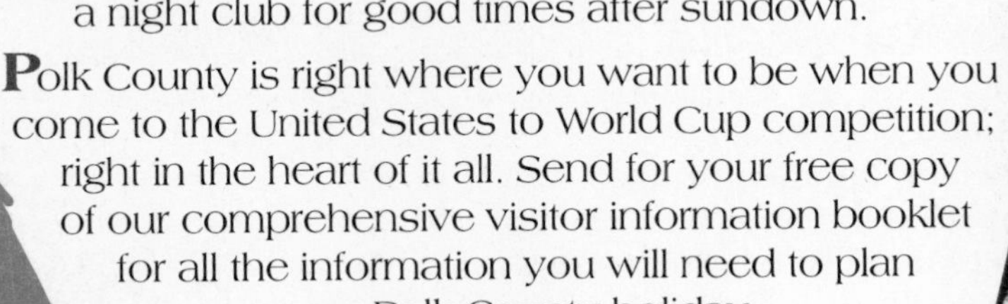

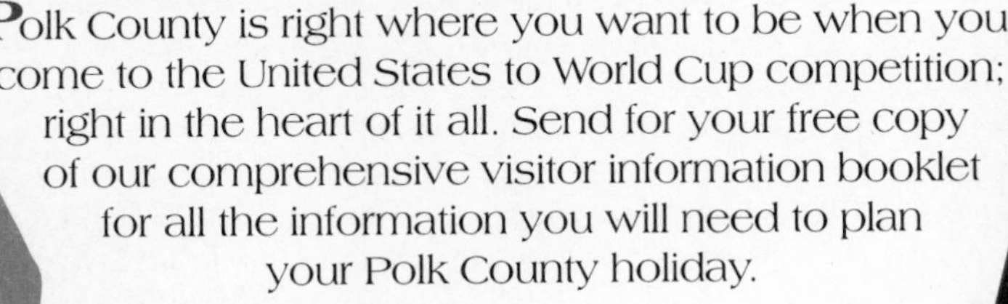

Polk County is right where you want to be when you come to the United States to World Cup competition; right in the heart of it all. Send for your free copy of our comprehensive visitor information booklet for all the information you will need to plan your Polk County holiday.

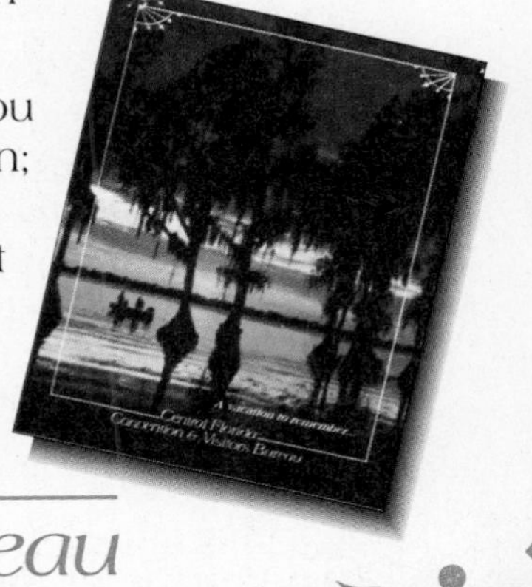

P 207

Central Florida Convention & Visitors Bureau

813/534-4375 or **FAX 813/533-1247**

P.O. Box 1839 • Bartow, FL - USA 33830

WORLD CUP '94

★ **FOR INFORMATION ON TICKETS TO WORLD CUP '94, SEE PAGE 1066.**

bine with acrobats, camels, rope climbers and snake charmers. The studios also feature the 'Voyage of the Little Mermaid'. Through the creative use of puppetry, audio-animatronics figures and film clips, this musical production takes the audience deep into the ocean with Ariel, the little mermaid. The highly acclaimed movie 'Beauty and the Beast' is the basis for a 30-minute song-and-dance stage production. One-day tickets to the theme park and tour are $34.85 for adults and $27.45 for children aged three to nine.

Disney's Epcot Center has a new night-time fireworks spectacular, 'IllumiNations', with lights, lasers, fireworks and fountains set to a classical music score. The display celebrates each of the countries represented in the World Showcase.

The Magic Kingdom's newest attraction, 'Splash Mountain', promises guests a 64kmph (40mph) descent. Disney's fastest ride is based on animated sequences in Walt Disney's 1946 film 'Song of the South' and boasts the world's longest flume drop. Four- and 5-day passes are available which include admission to all three Disney parks. Four-day passes are $117.20 for adults and $92.90 for children. Five-day passes are $153.15 for adults and $122.10 for children.

Construction begins this year on 'Celebration', Disney's $2.5-billion residential, shopping and cultural centre. Completion of the project could span two decades and will eventually include a city of 20,000 residents and 25,000 workers sitting on 4400 acres off Interstate 4 and US 192. Besides four residential communities, a shopping mall, office space and the cultural centre, Disney plans an environmental centre, three championship golf courses, schools, parks, a transportation hub and a 150-bed hospital and medical centre. Disney officials are aiming for 1995 for the opening of the residential portion of the city and the hospital.

For more information on Walt Disney World, telephone (407) 824 4531.

WATER WORLDS

As Florida is almost entirely surrounded by water, it should come as no surprise that many of its most fascinating sites should be water-orientated. From the amazing creatures that live underneath the surface to the outrageous fun that can be had on the surface, Florida has it all.

Gatorland is home to one of Florida's most famous residents – the alligator. Visitors may view 5000 alligators doing what they do naturally. Recent additions to the park include an 800-seat gator-wrestling stadium and a 10-acre breeding marsh and observation platform. The park has also added an educational and entertainment show called 'Snakes of Florida'. Future plans include a 'Crocodiles of the World' exhibit and a 'Cracker' village modelled after early 20th-century Florida settlements. For further information, telephone (407) 855 5496.

If alligators are not to one's taste, visit *Sea World of Florida*, where various species of underwater mammals, such as dolphins, sea lions, killer whales and otters, make their mark. Orlando's world-renowned marine-life park launched its largest expansion ever in 1992 with the park's first ride – 'Mission: Bermuda Triangle'. It takes guests on a scientific expedition to the mysterious depths of the Bermuda Triangle. 'Shamu's Happy Harbour', another 1992 innovation, thrills children in a 3-acre, tropically themed playground with a get-wet water maze, a 4-storey net climb and a schooner funship. Other new presentations opening in 1993/94 include 'Manatees: the Last Generation?' (opening May 1993) featuring a manatee theatre, nursing pool, habitat and rescue centre; and a Shamu (the famous killer whale) breeding and research pool, pinniped habitat and hotel-like stage. There is also a water-ski and speedboat show, botanical gardens, a Hawaiian village, Penguin and Shark Encounters, Cap'n Kids World, World of the Sea Aquarium and Sky Tower ride. For further information, telephone (407) 363 2280 *or* 351 3600.

Silver Springs is famous for its glass-bottom boat jungle cruises and was the filming site for six original Tarzan films. 'Lost River Voyage' is a 30-minute boat excursion along the river on a newly designed open-air, glass-bottom boat. The boat enables visitors to observe the beauty of the river above and below the surface, while stopping at the wildlife outpost for an informative presentation. For further information, telephone (904) 236 2121.

RECOMMENDED TIPPING

Babysitter: 10-15%
Barber/Beautician: 15%
Bartender/Waiter/Waitress: 10-15%
Bellboy/Skycap: 50 *cents to* $1 *per bag*
Chambermaid: 50-75 *cents per night*
Cloakroom: 50 *cents for coat*
Delivery Boy: 25 *cents to* $1
Masseur/Masseuse: 20%
Parking Attendant: 50 *cents to* $1
Shoe Shine: 50 *cents*
Taxi: 15% *(25 cents minimum)*
Golf Cart Attendant: $1 *per cart.*

As most establishments do not include a service charge in the bill, so it is acceptable to ask if it is or is not included. It is also suggested that you review your bill to confirm whether the gratuity is included. No tipping is required for busboys, hospital staff, maitre d's, buffet waitresses, host/hostesses, locker room attendants, lunch counter attendants, store clerks and wine stewards.

TIPS FOR VISITING THE ATTRACTIONS

Travellers can save time by following these tips on visiting major attractions:

- ★ *Guests may leave parks in the after noon after having their hands stamped, then return in the evening when crowds are smaller.*
- ★ *Shopping at the end of the day keeps guests from toting parcels through the parks.*
- ★ *Walt Disney World suggests that guests arrive early and also make dining reservations early in the day.*
- ★ *Sea World's simultaneous seating for shows and continuous viewing of exhibits make for a relaxing day, but it's still wise to pick up a show schedule when entering any park, then use it to plan the day.*
- ★ *Universal suggests that guests plan to see the major rides (Back to the Future, Kongfrontation, ET, Earthquake and The Funtastic World of Hanna Barbera) early in the morning or in late afternoon.*
- ★ *Just a few minutes of planning ensures a smoother, more memorable visit.*

But for visitors who want to really get their feet wet, Water Mania and Wet 'n Wild are the places to go. *Water Mania* has a new slide called the 'Abyss', an enclosed tube that sends guests through 91m (300ft) of blue darkness dropping into a splashing pool. A 12m (40ft) pirate ship with water cannons, tunnels and slides has recently been added to the Rain Forest children's water playground; and the 'Aqua Express', a giant train with tunnels and slides, has been added to the Squirt Pond playground. And if that's not enough, Water Mania also has the 1992 International Association of Amusement Parks and Attractions Ride of the Year – 'Wipe Out', which is a simulated surfing ride. *Wet 'n Wild* has some of the same kind of fun. Their newest slide is the Bomb Bay, which plunges thrill-seekers into a nearly vertical free-fall down a 24m (76ft) slide. In 1992, Wet 'n Wild opened the $1-million Bubba Tub, a giant inner-tube ride which sends up to five riders splashing, turning and dipping down a river of water the length of a football field. Both parks are open year-round and feature heated pools. For information on Water Mania, telephone (407) 396 2626 and for Wet 'n Wild, telephone (407) 351 1800.

NIGHTS ON THE TOWN

A night in Orlando can mean dancing until dawn, strolling in the moonlight along a quiet lakefront or laughing it up at a local comedy club. Orlando Centroplex features events at the Orlando Arena and Florida Citrus Bowl, as well as theatrical productions at *Bob Carr Performing Arts Centre*. This 2534-seat performing arts facility hosts the Southern Ballet, the Florida Symphony and visiting operas and theatrical performances. Serious music enthusiasts will also find an impressive selection of rock, jazz, country & western, blues, cajun or disco. Entertainment complexes like *Disney's Pleasure Island* or downtown Orlando's *Church Street Station* offer some of each, with a variety of nightclubs and restaurants in a themed setting. Or visitors can join the locals at popular neighbourhood spots such as a jazz & blues club in downtown Orlando or a country & western lounge with live music and dancing. Visitors should remember that wherever they go to be sure to carry identification – driver's licence or passport – as most clubs that serve alcoholic beverages require patrons to be at least 21 years of age. Casual dress is appropriate for most nightclubs, although some do not allow shorts or tank tops.

Points of interest and photo opportunities at Mercado.

Home of the Official Orlando Orange Country Visitor Information Center and named after the Spanish word meaning 'marketplace', Mercado features countless photo opportunities. Spanish architecture, arched balconies, streetscapes paved with brick and cobblestone, fountains, gardens and quaint village shop fronts combine to create an inviting 'old world' ambiance.

When you stroll through Mercado you can't help but savour the enchantment of an authentic Mediterranean village. And in the evening, Mercado takes on a magical look, as trees glitter with twinkling lights, street lamps create a warm glow and music fills the air.

For Art Lovers

As you tour Mercado, you can't help but notice the many murals, watercolours and sculpture handcrafted and designed by artist Don Reynolds, a native of Great Britain who now resides in central Florida. Don's work can be found throughout Orlando and is featured at Mercado.

OPEN 10 A.M. TO 10 P.M. DAILY. RESTAURANTS AND BARS FEATURE EXTENDED HOURS. FREE NIGHTLY ENTERTAINMENT.

Welcome to Mercado Mediterranean Village

MERCADO
MEDITERRANEAN VILLAGE
8445 International Drive,
Orlando, Florida 32819.
TEL: (407) 345-9337.

Mugsy's Merry Medley

The kids won't want to miss Mercado's very own animated variety bird show! Join Mercado's flock of feathered friends for Mugsy's Merry Medley. This songfest is performed every 20 minutes in the Marketplace, where merchants display their wares from small shops and colourful pushcart vendors offer seasonal and speciality items.

Festive Shops . . .

With a unique collection of over 60 festive shops nestled along cobblestone streetscapes, Mercado offers a truly special shopping experience! Stroll through our Village and discover treasures from the Orient and Mexico, Irish imports, precious gems plus many American favourites too! Find officially licensed Disney, Universal Studios and MGM clothing and memorabilia as well as resort wear, up-to-the-minute fashions, collectibles plus much more!

Entertainment

Mercado features free nightly entertainment for all ages in Mercado's Center Courtyard . . . Perhaps a mariachi duo or a band of merry musicians playing songs from the 60's through the 90's! Relax with a snack or a cool drink, enjoy the open air and. . . *Let us entertain you!*

THE WAY TO THE WORLD CUP

THE AIRPORT

Orlando International Airport is located 8km (5 miles) northwest of the city. *United*, *Delta* and *USAir* are Orlando's major airlines. Passengers and baggage arriving in Orlando on direct international flights must pass through US Customs and Immigration & Naturalization Services. Visitors' baggage will be transported to the main terminal baggage claim. When getting off the shuttle, visitors should check the baggage claim locations posted above the shuttle. The baggage claim areas are down the escalator on Level 2 of the main terminal. Foreign currency may be exchanged at the Main Terminal from 0700-2100 on the B-side second-level Bag Claim; on the second-level Bag Claim A or at international gates based on international arrival and departure times. Car rental agencies are available at the airport and include *Dollar* and *Hertz*. Airport Information Centers, offering a multilingual service, are located in front of the security checkpoint for Gates 1-59 in the Great Hall and in front of security checkpoint for Gates 60-99 in the Hotel Atrium. These are open every day 0700-2300. For more information, telephone (407) 825 2352 *or* 825 2118 for TDD (Tele-type Deaf Unit).

Airport Renovations

Orlando International Airport has just embarked on a 5-year $600-million expansion this year which includes upgrades and rehabilitation of the international arrivals concourse and passenger facilities to accommodate the anticipated 150% increase in international travel. There are also plans for a taxiway linking the east and west airfields and a roadway connecting the airport to the southern leg of the Central Florida Greeneway. The airport has recently completed an $800-million expansion that included a $61-million third runway, two 6-storey parking garages with 3500 parking spaces each and an expanded, automated transit system. A 450-room Hyatt Hotel opened in the airport terminal last summer boasting 32,516 sq m (35,000 sq ft) of meeting space.

TRANSPORTATION TO THE STADIUM

Shuttles will be available to the stadium from many downtown parking garages. For further information, telephone *Tri County Transit* ('The Lynx') on (407) 841 8240. For information on parking and game information, telephone (407) 849 2576.

TRANSPORTATION TO ORLANDO

Buses/Shuttle Vans/Limousines

Bus or van passage is available from the airport to International Drive or downtown Orlando. The fare is $10 one-way and $17 round-trip for adults; $7 one-way, $11 round-trip for children. Transportation to Lake Buena Vista is $12 one-way and $21 round-trip for adults; $7 one-way, $11 round-trip for children. Limousines are available from the airport to International Drive, Lake Buena Vista or downtown Orlando. Costs range from $10-$25 for adults and $5-$15 for children.

Mears Transportation Group: A full-service, 24-hour ground transportation service. Taxis and shuttles are available to all area hotels and attractions from the baggage claim level of Orlando Airport. For further information, telephone (407) 839 1670.

Alpha Shuttle Inc: Offers minibuses and luxury sedans for airport transfers and tours anywhere in Florida. For further information , telephone (407) 856 7139.

Bethany Transportation Inc: Complete transportation service offers luxury sedans, limousines, vans and buses for airport transfers and tours. Meet-and-greet service available. For further information , telephone (407) 439 3777.

Transtar Limousine Service: Transportation to and from Orlando Airport and all Orlando area hotels 24 hours a day. Sedans and limousines available. For further information, telephone (407) 856 7777.

Taxi

Visitors should use a metered cab and confirm the cost of the trip with the driver at the beginning. Rates for taxi service average $2.50 for the first mile and $1.50 for each additional mile travelled.

THE WAY TO THE WORLD CUP

CAR RENTAL

The ideal weather, the multitude of sites and the distances between them make travelling by car the best way to get around Orlando. Car hire is highly recommended for international visitors and prices in the Orlando region are reasonable. Here are some of Orlando's major car rental firms and how to contact them:

Alamo Rent-A-Car USA
(407) 857 8200
American International Rent-A-Car USA
(407) 851 6910
Avis Rent-A-Car USA
(407) 851 7600
Budget Rent-A-Car
(407) 850 6700
Dollar Rent-A-Car USA & Canada
(813) 877 5507
General Rent-A-Car
(407) 859 1340
Hertz Rent-A-Car USA
(407) 859 8400
Interamerican Car Rental
(407) 859 0414
National Car Rental
(407) 855 4170
Thrifty Rent-A-Car USA & Canada
(407) 381 2393
Value Rent-A-Car
(407) 438 7106.

When Your Clients Visit Orlando, They Expect The World... And We Give It To Them!

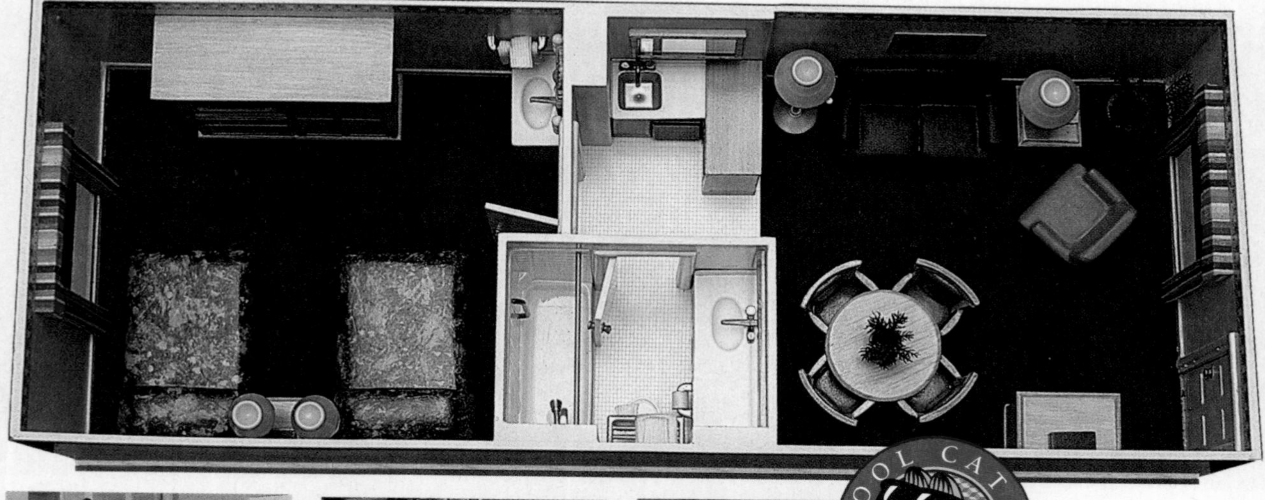

Just one mile from the WALT DISNEY WORLD® Resort Area.

Discover Lake Buena Vista's only all-suite hotel that offers so much for your clients' vacation dollar! A host of amenities, children's activities and a luxurious two-room suite, with a spacious living room and separate bedroom complement a location second to none. Embassy Suites® Resort Lake Buena Vista is only three miles from Sea World® and just seven miles from Universal Studios Florida®. We're a Free scheduled shuttle ride and just a mile from the entrance to the MAGIC KINGDOM® Park, EPCOT® Center and Disney-MGM Studios Theme Park. Plus, we're close to golf, night life and just a short drive to either coast. From recreation to relaxation, Embassy Suites Resort Lake Buena Vista has something for everyone!

TWICE THE VALUE

A typical family of 4 will **save $89 per day** by staying at Embassy Suites Resort Lake Buena Vista:

	Other Orlando Resorts	Embassy Suites Resort
Breakfast	$33.64	FREE!
Cocktails*/Soft Drinks	21.36	FREE!
Transportation to and from Disney	34.00	FREE!
Total Savings Per Day	**$89.00**	**FREE!**

EMBASSY SUITES℠

RESORT LAKE BUENA VISTA

8100 LAKE AVE., ORLANDO, FL 32836

For information and reservations, call: 44-992-441517 FAX 44-992-467731 Request Suite **MCOWD**.

Discover America Marketing, Priest House, 90 High Road, Broxbourne, Herts, EN107DZ England

Near WALT DISNEY WOLD® Resort Area. Subject to state and local laws. Represented World Wide by UTELL International.

ORLANDO GROUND TRANSPORTATION

Rail

Amtrak serves Orlando with four daily trains originating in New York, Tampa and Miami, with stops in Winter Park and Sanford.

Chaffeured Transportation

Shuttles, taxis and even stretch limousines are available for travel from airport to hotels, attractions and throughout the city. Tour operators offer group and individual services ranging from airport meet-and-greet and translation to handicapped transportation.

Self-Drive

Car rental firms in Orlando include *Alamo, Avis, Budget, Dollar, General, Major, National, Payless, Phoenix, Superior* and *Thrifty*. Vehicles range from minibuses to sleek convertibles. Recreational vehicles are available at *Holiday RV* and *Cruise America RV*. To hire a car visitors must have a valid driver's license from their own country, a major credit card and be at least 25 years of age. Some car rental companies require an international drive's license.

Orlando may be reached from the Midwest by major highway networks including Interstate 75 connecting with the Florida Turnpike, whose southern terminal is Miami; from the Atlantic coastal states via Interstate 95; and from Daytona and Tampa on Interstate 4 running east–west. Visitors should be aware that unmanned toll booths require exact change, so they should have plenty of US coins (especially quaters) to hand when driving. Also fuel tends to be 3-6 cents cheaper at self-service petrol stations.

THE ORLANDO MAGICARD

Value-conscious travellers can save hundreds with the Orlando Magicard, an areawide discount card that looks like a credit card and works like a coupon book. The free card provides savings of 10-50% at 102 area attractions, hotels, restaurants, auto and RV rental firms and retail outlets. Travellers may order the card by calling (800) 551 0181 or stopping at the Official Visitors Center at Mercado Village, 8445 International Drive, open 0800-2000 year-round. The center offers maps, directions, restaurant information, brochures, posters, hotel referrals, etc.

STATION
ORLANDO FLORIDA

GEORGIA

Including **Atlanta,** gateway to the southern Atlantic States of Georgia, North Carolina and South Carolina, and the southern states of Alabama, Tennessee and Kentucky.

Georgia Tourist Office
Suite 1000
285 Peachtree Center Avenue, NE
Atlanta, GA
30303-1232
Tel: (404) 656 3553. Fax: (404) 651 9063.
Georgia Hospitality & Travel Bureau
Suite 1500
600 West Peachtree Street
Atlanta, GA
30308
Tel: (404) 873 4482. Fax: (404) 874 5742.
Atlanta Convention & Visitors Bureau
233 Peachtree Street, NE
Atlanta, GA
30303
Tel: (404) 521 6608.
Athens Convention & Visitors Bureau
Suite 2000
7th Floor, Harris Tower
220 College Avenue
Athens, GA
30601
Tel: (706) 546 1805. Fax: (706) 549 5636.
Savannah Area Convention & Visitors Bureau
PO Box 1628
222 West Oglethorpe Avenue
Savannah, GA
31401
Tel: (912) 944 0456. Fax: (912) 944 0468

TIME: GMT - 5. *Daylight Saving Time* is observed from the first Sunday in April to the last Sunday in October. Clocks are put forward one hour, changing at 0200 hours local time.
THE STATE: Georgia, founded in 1732, is the youngest of the 13 original colonies. It is a mixture of the Old and New South, and is geographically diverse, with landscapes ranging from mountains in the northeast to the mysterious, low-lying Okefenokee Swamp in the south, called the land of the 'trembling earth' by the region's Indian tribes. Its varied climate ranges from the low humidity of the Blue Ridge Mountains to the subtropical southern coastal region.

TRAVEL

AIR: Approximate flight times: From Atlanta to *London* is 9 hours 15 minutes, to *Miami* is 1 hour 40 minutes, to *New York* is 2 hours 20 minutes and to *Washington DC* is 1 hour 30 minutes.
International airport: *Hartsfield Atlanta International Airport (ATL)* is 14.5km (9 miles) south of the city (travel time – 20 minutes). A 24-hour coach service runs every 15 minutes. Bus no 72 runs every 30 minutes 0500-2300. Taxi and limousine services are available.
RAIL: The *Amtrak* service linking New York with New Orleans stops at Brookwood Station, Peachtree Street: see the *New York* section below for approximate journey times on this line.
ROAD: *Greyhound* (tel: (404) 584 1728) and *Southern Stage* both use the Greyhound terminal at International Boulevard.
Approximate driving times: From Atlanta to *Birmingham* is 3 hours, to *Charlotte* is 5 hours, to *Nashville* is 5 hours, to *Tallahassee* is 5 hours, to *Salt Lake City* is 6 hours, to *Jacksonville* is 7 hours, to *Charleston* (South Carolina) is 7 hours, to *Memphis* is 8 hours, to *New Orleans* is 10 hours, to *Cincinnati* is 10 hours, to *Charleston* (West Virginia) is 11 hours, to *Miami* is 13 hours, to *Chicago* is 14 hours, to *New York* is 17 hours, to *Dallas* is 17 hours, to *Los Angeles* is 45 hours and to *Seattle* is 59 hours.
All times are based on non-stop driving at or below the applicable speed limits.
Approximate *Greyhound* journey times: From Atlanta to *Chattanooga* is 2 hours 30 minutes, to *Birmingham* is 3 hours, to *Charlotte* is 5 hours 30 minutes, to *Mobile* is 8 hours 30 minutes, to *Jacksonville* is 8 hours, to *St Petersburg* is 14 hours and to *Miami* is 18 hours.
URBAN: The public transport system is excellent. The most economical transport is the *Metropolitan Atlanta Rapid Transport Authority (MARTA)*, which consists of 89km (60 miles) of rapid rail or bus lines.
Car hire: Cars and motorcampers can be hired for touring the Atlanta area. Contact local companies through the Atlanta classified telephone directory.

RESORTS & EXCURSIONS

ATLANTA: Now a booming manufacturing centre with a population of more than two million, Atlanta is the city that most dramatically expresses the transition from Old South to New. Along its residential streets, magnolia and dogwood trees surround handsome Georgian-style homes, yet only blocks away, some of the country's most dazzling contemporary buildings are rising at record speed to add new beauty to Atlanta's ever-growing skyline.
Sightseeing: The *Georgia State Capitol* in Washington Street on Capitol Square, which also houses the *Georgia Hall of Fame* and the *Hall of Flags*. The *Zero Mile Post* under Central Avenue Bridge marks the city's birthplace. The *Tomb of Martin Luther King* is located at the Ebenezer Baptist Church. The 14-storey *Omni Megastructure* houses offices, a hotel, international boutiques, six cinemas, an ice-skating rink and sports area. *Underground Atlanta*, a restored 4-square block area, is located near the business centre of downtown Atlanta. *Grant Park* contains the *Atlanta Zoo*, the restored Confederate *Fort Walker*, and the *Cyclorama*, a world-famous 123m (406ft) circumference painting of the Battle of Atlanta. *Piedmont Park* has facilities for swimming, tennis and golf.
Excursions: 24km (16 miles) east of downtown Atlanta is *Stone Mountain*, where gigantic representations of three Confederate heroes – Robert E Lee, Jefferson Davis and Stonewall Jackson – have been carved into a cliff-face. Within easy travelling distance of Atlanta are: *Augusta*, home of the *Masters Golf Tournament* every April; **Dahlonega**, an old mining town where visitors can still pan for gold; and *Madison*, an antique town that was spared from ruin during Sherman's March. The nearby *Pine Mountains* area is noted for its *Callaway Gardens* and for President Franklin D Roosevelt's *Little White House* at **Warm Springs.**
SAVANNAH: On the Atlantic coast, 400km (240 miles) southeast of Atlanta, Savannah was the USA's first planned city. It has become the greatest urban historic preservation site in the USA.
Sightseeing: Much of Savannah's original beauty remains, and more than a thousand of its buildings are historically important, including the Regency-style *Owens-Thomas House* designed by William Jay, and *Davenport House*, one of the best examples of Georgian architecture in the New World. *Fort Pulaski*, one of Savannah's five forts open to the public, is named after the Polish hero of the American Revolution. *Savannah Beach* features sands, a boardwalk, fishing piers and an amusement park.
Excursions: The **Golden Isles,** south of the city, are known for their leisurely resorts, with sandy white beaches, fine golfing, tennis and fishing. **St Simons** is the largest of the islands, with vast woodlands and stretches of unspoilt marshes and coastline. **Waycross** is one of three gateways to the *Okefenokee Swamp*, one of the country's most beautiful wilderness areas. The swamp is a refuge of exotic plant and animal life including alligators.
Note: For information on attractions in neighbouring states, see above under *States A-Z*.

SOCIAL PROFILE

FOOD & DRINK: Atlanta offers a wide variety of food. Its boarding houses may offer as many as 14 or 15 main course dishes. Creole and Cajun food is well represented throughout Georgia.

THEATRES & CONCERTS: *Academy Theater* features new and experimental plays. *Alliance Theater Company*, housed in the *Memorial Arts Center*, presents an 18-week main stage season from January to May; the *Atlanta Children's Theater* performs at various locations throughout the city. *Atlanta University Center Summer Theater* presents drama for and by black people, as does *New Cosmos Cultural Theater*, a black professional resident company. The *Atlanta Ballet* performs during autumn, winter and spring.
NIGHTLIFE: Nightlife varies from intimate piano bars and dinner theatres to the underground music clubs of trendy Atlanta.
SHOPPING: Both *Peachtree Center* and *Omni Center* shelter a collection of chic boutiques. *Lenox Square Mall* and *Phipps Plaza*, both suburban shopping centres, can be reached by MARTA bus.
SPECIAL EVENTS: Mar 13 '93 *Annual Youth Arts Festival*, Georgia Southern University. **Mar 19-28** *Georgia Cherry Blossom Festival*, Macon. **Mar 26-Apr 4** *20th Annual Harness Horse Festival*, Hawkinsville. **Apr 2-4** *Taste of Columbus*, Columbus Trade Center. **Apr 15-16** *3rd Annual Arts & Crafts Show*, Rome. **May 1** *Mayfest '93*, Carrollton. **May 28-30** *Decatur Arts Festival*. **May 28-31** *Atlanta Peach Caribbean Carnival*. **Jun 11-13** *River Race Augusta*, Riverfront Marina. **Jun 12 & 26** *Kingfest '93*, Atlanta. **Jun 17-19** *Atlanta Fest at Six Flags over Georgia*. **Jul 4** Celebrations throughout the state, including the *WSB-TV Salute 2 America Parade*, Atlanta. **Early Aug** *National Black Arts Festival*, Atlanta. **Mid-Aug** *Georgia Mountain Fair*, Hiawrassee; *2nd Annual Mountain Golf Tournament*, Hiawrassee. **Sep (whole month)** *Fall Brown Bag Concert Series*, Marietta. **Mid-Sep** *18th Annual West End Festival*, Atlanta. **Mid-Oct** *Octoberfest*, various locations; *4th Annual Indian Cultural Festival*, Columbus; *Georgia National Fair*, Perry; *Atlanta International Wine Festival*. **Nov** *Veterans' Day Parade*, Atlanta. **Dec (whole month)** *Jekyll's Christmas Activities*, Jekyll Island. **Mid-Dec** *Festival of Trees*, Atlanta.

CLIMATE

Humid/hot in summer. Frequent rain. Mild winter. Cooler in the northern mountains.
Required clothing: Lightweight cotton clothes and rainwear. Warmer clothing for evenings, the winter season and mountain areas.

ATLANTA Georgia (308m)

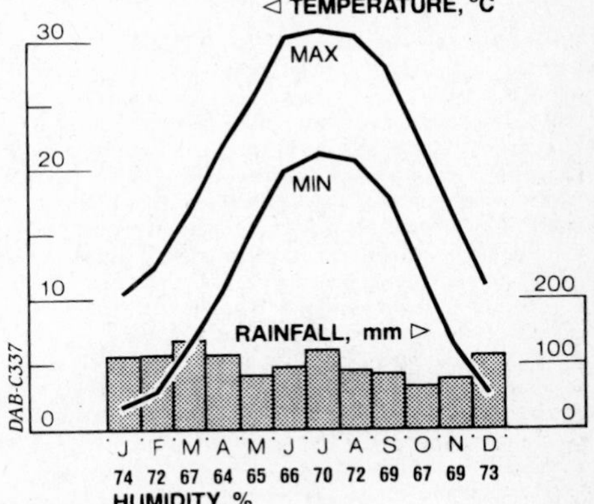

ILLINOIS

Including **Chicago,** gateway to the Great Lakes, the great plains and the northern Midwest States of Wisconsin, Iowa, Missouri, Kentucky and Indiana.

Illinois Bureau of Tourism
Suite 3-400
100 West Randolph Street
Chicago, IL
60601
Tel: (312) 814 4732. Fax: (312) 814 6581.
Chicago Southland Convention & Visitors Bureau
Suite 202
20200 Governor's Drive
Olympic Fields, IL
60461
Tel: (708) 503 1800. Fax: (708) 503 1298.
Springfield Convention & Visitors Bureau
109 North Seventh Street
Springfield, IL
62701
Tel: (217) 789 2360. Fax: (217) 544 8711.

TIME: GMT - 6. *Daylight Saving Time* is observed from the first Sunday in April to the last Sunday in October. Clocks are put forward one hour, changing at 0200 hours local time.
THE STATE: Illinois, stretching from Lake Michigan to the Mississippi River, embraces vast, rich farmlands, the giant city of Chicago, rolling glacial plains and, to the south, the hills and valleys of the Illinois Ozarks. Abraham Lincoln, the 16th US President, spent most of his professional (he was a lawyer) and political life here.

TRAVEL

AIR: Approximate flight times: From Chicago to *Anchorage* is 7 hours 30 minutes, to *Honolulu* is 10 hours 20 minutes, to *London* is 7 hours 35 minutes, to *Los Angeles* is 4 hours 45 minutes, to *Miami* is 3 hours 20 minutes, to *Montréal* is 2 hours 15 minutes, to *New York* is 2 hours 5 minutes, to *Toronto* is 1 hour 40 minutes, to *Vancouver* is 6 hours 10 minutes and to *Washington DC* is 2 hours.
International airport: *Chicago (CHI)* (O'Hare International), 35km (21 miles) northwest of the city, is the world's busiest airport. Buses, taxis and commuter trains ply to and from the city almost 24 hours a day. Most major car hire firms have offices at the airport.
Domestic airport: *Midway Airport (MDW)*, on Chicago's southwest side, handles some regional and local flights.
RAIL: Downtown Chicago's Union Station is the focal point of the rail passenger network: three of the four trans-continental lines converge here and it is also the northern terminus of north–south lines to San Antonio and New Orleans. A sixth line runs northeast to Toronto and Montréal. Services to neighbouring cities are limited.
Approximate *Amtrak* journey times: From Chicago on the 'Broadway Limited' to *Pittsburgh* is 9 hours, to *Philadelphia* is 17 hours and to *New York* is 19 hours; on the 'Lake Shore Limited' to *Toledo* is 4 hours, to *Cleveland* is 7 hours, to *Buffalo* is 10 hours and to *New York* is 18 hours; on the 'Cardinal' to *Indianapolis* is 3 hours, to *Washington DC* is 23 hours, to *Baltimore* is 24 hours and to *New York* is 27 hours; on the 'City of New Orleans' to *Memphis* is 10 hours and to *New Orleans* is 18 hours; on the 'International' to *Kalamazoo* is 2 hours, to *Port Huron* is 6 hours and to *Toronto* is 10 hours; on the 'Ann Rutledge' to *St Louis* is 6 hours and to *Kansas City* is 12 hours; on the 'Empire Builder' to *Minneapolis/St Paul* is 9 hours and to *Spokane* (connections to Portland and Seattle) is 25 hours; and on the 'Pioneer' to *Omaha* is 8 hours, to *Denver* is 18 hours, to *Salt Lake City* is 33 hours, to *Portland* is 52 hours and to *Seattle* is 56 hours. Approximate times for Chicago–Los Angeles and Chicago–Oakland services may be found in the *California* section above.
ROAD: Approximate driving times: From Chicago to *Milwaukee* is 2 hours, to *Madison* is 3 hours, to *Indianapolis* is 4 hours, to *Detroit* is 5 hours, to *St Louis* is 6 hours, to *Des Moines* is 7 hours, to *Cleveland* is 7 hours, to *Nashville* is 9 hours, to *Kansas City* is 10 hours, to *New York* is 16 hours, to *Dallas* is 19 hours, to *Miami* is 27 hours, to *Seattle* is 44 hours and to *Los Angeles* is 44 hours.
All times are based on non-stop driving at or below the applicable speed limits.
Approximate *Greyhound* journey times: From Chicago (tel: (312) 781 2900) to *Milwaukee* is 2 hours, to *Indianapolis* is 4 hours, to *Detroit* is 6 hours, to *St Louis* is 7 hours, to *Cleveland* is 7 hours 30 minutes, to *Omaha* is 10 hours 30 minutes and to *Memphis* is 11 hours 30 minutes.
URBAN: Bus: A wide network of bus routes run by the *Chicago Transit Authority (CTA)* covers the city on the major north–south and east–west streets. **Car hire:** Cars and motor campers are available.

RESORTS & EXCURSIONS

CHICAGO: Nicknamed 'Windy City', Chicago is one of the world's giant trade, industry and transportation centres and the birthplace of the skyscraper; whilst, in contrast, its Lake Michigan shoreline is dotted with sandy beaches, hundreds of parks, harbours, zoos and vast expanses of forest preserve. It is one of the USA's largest cities and the hub of the Midwest, with a population of about three million and more than 43,000 hotel rooms in the downtown and airport districts alone. For visitors to the USA, it is the gateway to the farmlands and cities of Illinois and Indiana and the recreation areas of Wisconsin.
Sightseeing: The *Museum of Science* has more than 2000 exhibits. The *Field Museum of Natural History* spans the development of the universe from 4.5 billion years ago to the present day. Other attractions include the *Art Institute of Chicago, Brookfield Zoo, Tropic World, Seven Seas Panorama* and *Six Flags Great America Amusement Park.* Many of Chicago's soaring skyscrapers have observation towers, such as *Sears Tower* and the *John Hancock Center*. The *Old Water Tower*, a landmark that survived the Great Chicago Fire of 1871, houses a tourist information centre, open daily.

The Historic Water Tower and John Hancock Center

Excursions: Springfield is the capital of Illinois. It was here that Abraham Lincoln married and began his legal career. Attractions include *Lincoln's Tomb* (a State Historical Site) and the *Illinois State Museum*. *New Salem State Park* nearby is a re-creation of the pioneer community as it was in Lincoln's day. Southern Illinois was one of the first regions of North America to be settled by the French. This colourful heritage is reflected in towns such as **Prairie du Rocher** and **Kaskaskia**. The *Shawnee National Forest*, with its huge areas of wilderness and many tourist sites, stretches across the lower part of Illinois. To the west, *Fort Crevecoeur* is a replica of a French outpost. The *Dickson Mounds* were raised by Mississippian Indians many centuries ago. To the north is **Galena,** a Victorian city, with many historic sites and tourist activities. The *Starved Rock State Park & Lodge* has hiking trails, picnic areas and excursion boats from May to September.
Note: For information on attractions in neighbouring states, see above under *States A-Z*.

SOCIAL PROFILE

FOOD & DRINK: Chicago is known for its prime rib steaks and thick-crusted Chicago pizza. It is packed with restaurants of all types, serving food from around the world.
THEATRES & CONCERTS: Major theatres include the *Goodman, Shubert, Blackstone* and *Arie Crown*. The *Auditorium Theater* stages ballet and musical events. The *Civic Center for the Performing Arts* stages performances by the *Lyric Opera Company*. The *Chicago Symphony Orchestra* performs at *Orchestra Hall*.
NIGHTLIFE: Chicago boasts everything from night-clubs, jazz spots, cinemas and discotheques to belly dancing, rock bands and folk music. It is the home of 'urban blues', a form developed by such greats as Buddy Guy and Junior Wells, continued today in Chicago and around the world by Robert Cray.
SHOPPING: The main shopping areas in Chicago include State Street Mall, North Michigan Avenue's Magnificent Mile, Woodfield Mall and the quaint speciality stores in Old Town, Lincoln Avenue and New Town.
SPECIAL EVENTS: During the summer of 1994, Illinois' Soldier Field Stadium will host qualifying matches for *World Cup '94*. The *Chicago Blues Festival* will be held in Grant Park from **May 28-30**. Sample foods from 100 restaurants at the *Taste of Chicago* event in Grant Park during **July 4** weekend. The *Chicago Jazz Festival* takes place at the same venue, from **September 10-12**. The *Illinois State Fair* takes place from **August 13-22**. The *Chicago Auto Show* is at McCormick Place in February. There is horseracing at Arlington Park from **May to September**. The *Chicago International Film Festival* takes place in **November.**

CLIMATE

Wide variation between hot summers and freezing winters, especially in the north of the state. The highest humidity is in the summer near the Great Lakes.
Required clothing: Warm winter clothes are needed in the coldest months. Light to mediumweights are advised for the summer. Rainwear may be useful.

CHICAGO Illinois (185m)

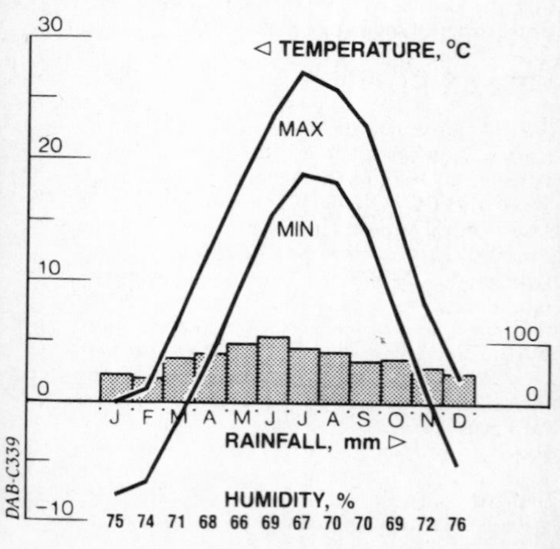

Welcome to CHICAGO

The City of Chicago and the State of Illinois welcome you to Chicago, the gateway to the heartland of the United States

Chicago is proud to be chosen to host the opening ceremony and opening game of the World Cup USA '94.

Chicago is one of the most accessible cities in the world. Soldier Field, the stadium where the World Cup will be played, is within walking distance of downtown Chicago and most of the city's hotels.

Chicago is a great sports town. The Chicago Power soccer team is Chicago's very own. The Chicago Cubs and the White Sox baseball teams play all summer long from April to October. The Bulls basketball, Blackhawks hockey and Bears football teams are crowd-pleasers during the fall and winter months.

Chicago outdoor activities include sailing, swimming and cycling along Chicago's 47km (29-mile) lakefront. During the summer, there are festivals, fairs and concerts in the park. Lincoln Park Zoo is free to everyone and is situated in a park on the lakefront. Ethnic neighbourhood festivals are a great treat.

Chicago is the entertainment capital of the Midwest. There are over 1400 professional theatres. Music is everywhere – blues, jazz, gospel, opera, rock, country & western, symphonies, new age, reggae, classical and Cajun.

Shopping is a favourite sport in Chicago. The Magnificent Mile has three indoor malls, streets lined with high-fashion boutiques and many top-name department stores. The great State Street has two architectural gems in Marshall Fields and Carson Pierre Scott.

Chicago's architecture is world-renowned. There are many tours available by boat, foot and bus. The tallest building in the world, Sears Tower, is a must for visitors.

Chicago's cultural activities cover a broad range. The Chicago Symphony Orchestra, the Lyric Opera of Chicago, the Art Institute of Chicago, the Museum of Science and Industry, Ravinia and Grant Park Outdoor Concerts, art galleries, Museum of Broadcast Communications, the Shedd Aquarium/Oceanarium, the Field Museum of Natural History and many more.

Chicago has one of the largest freshwater lakes in the USA, Lake Michigan. Other states that border the Great Lakes are Minnesota, Wisconsin, Michigan, Indiana and Ohio. The Great Lakes are an area of holiday opportunities.

Chicago's restaurants have something to tempt any taste buds. Chicago is famous for hot dogs, pizza, steaks and all types of wonderful ethnic food.

The Chicago Office of Tourism, Chicago Convention and Visitors Bureau and the Illinois Bureau of Tourism are available for any assistance they can offer to you. DON'T MISS IT!

From Mary Burns, Illinois Bureau of Tourism

CHICAGO SKYLINE

BUCKINGHAM FOUNTAIN, GRANT PARK

Chicago

A RICH SOCCER & SPORTING HERITAGE

Chicago has played a key part in the recent growth of soccer in the United States. Participation levels and interest in the sport have mushroomed in recent years. Today, soccer surpasses all other sports in levels of participation among school youth in Illinois. The following include some highlights of Chicago soccer history:

- ★ *In 1981, the Chicago Sting won the national professional championship and made front-page news. A jubilant City hailed its champions in a major downtown parade – an event unparalleled in soccer history.*
- ★ *In 1993, Illinois celebrates its 175th anniversary. Chicago's documented soccer history dates back to 1883.*
- ★ *Chicago has a host of adult and youth-club soccer leagues. Some are still divided along ethnic lines and date back decades.*
- ★ *In the summer, Chicago's parks are filled with informal soccer games, drawing soccer fans young and old from every Chicago neighbourhood.*
- ★ *The annals of the United States Soccer Federation are filled with the names of Chicagoans who have taken leadership roles. Today, their sons, daughters and grandchildren are carrying on the tradition.*
- ★ *Chicago also has two major-league baseball teams. During the summer months there is usually one of the teams at home in Chicago on any given day. Tickets can be obtained on arrival in Chicago.*

THE LOCATION Chicago is located on the southwestern shore of Lake Michigan in the northeast corner of the state of Illinois. Chicago is only 440km (275 miles) from Detroit, Michigan, another venue for World Cup '94. The state of Illinois is bordered by Wisconsin to the north, Lake Michigan to the northeast, Indiania to the east, Kentucky to the southeast, Missouri to the southwest, and Iowa to the west.

THE LANDSCAPE Chicago was the home of the very first skyscraper, the Home Insurance Company (which no longer exists), but Chicago still has the world's tallest building, Sears Tower, at 443m (1454ft). Plans are being made for an even taller building, the Miglin-Beitler Tower, to rise 594m (1950ft) and 125 storeys, which will be built just two blocks north and one block east of the Sears Tower. The city skyscape is therefore one of the most uplifting in the world and can be viewed from the top of Sears Tower from the high vantage point of the Sears Skydeck, or from the John Hancock Observatory. There are also boat tours of the skyline available on Lake Michigan. Outside the soaring city, there is much beautiful countryside dotted with farms. The Ozarks, in the south of the state are full of rolling hills and valleys, and the north around Lake Michigan has glacial moraines.

THE CULTURE AND HISTORY Chicago's worldwide reputation for commerce, culture and civic pride dates back to the earliest days. The city's central location and easy accessiblity were key factors in its growth and development. In 1673, Father Jacques Marquette, a French-born missionary, and Louis Joliet, a French explorer, were searching for a connecting link between the Atlantic Ocean and the Gulf of Mexico via the St Lawrence River, the Great Lakes and the Mississippi and instead found Chicago. Traders and explorers then began to arrive in the area, but the first known resident of Chicago was Jean Baptiste Point DuSable, a black from Santo Domingo, who built the first settlement in 1779 at the mouth of the Chicago River. In 1795 a treaty with the area's Indians ceded what is now downtown Chicago to the federal government. In 1830, lots were sold to finance construction of what would become the Illinois and Michigan Canal, connecting Chicago with the Mississippi River. Three years later, with a population of 340, the town of Chicago was incorporated, drawing its name from an Indian word meaning 'skunk', 'wild onion' or 'strong and great', depending on the interpretation. The Indians moved to reservations as the town's population grew, but in 1871 the Great Chicago Fire claimed 300 lives, left 90,000 Chicagoans without homes and destroyed $200-million worth of property. Architects from all over the world came and planned the entire city, which was quickly rebuilt. The prime planner of the city was Daniel Burnham who conceived Chicago's unobstructed lakefront, its city-wide system of parks and the development of a superhighway along Congress Street, now the Eisenhower Expressway. Chicago became a prime transportation hub with the completion of the 62km (100-mile) Illinois and Michigan Canal and the Galena & Chicago Union Railroad. It later became a centre for air traffic when the Chicago Municipal Airport was completed in 1927 – it was the world's busiest from 1945-58. O'Hare International Airport now holds the title as the world's busiest.

BRAZIL IS THE ONLY COUNTRY TO HAVE WON THE WORLD CUP OUTSIDE ITS OWN CONTINENT, A TEST THEY ACHIEVED BY BEATING SWEDEN 5-2 IN STOCKHOLM IN THE 1958 FINAL.

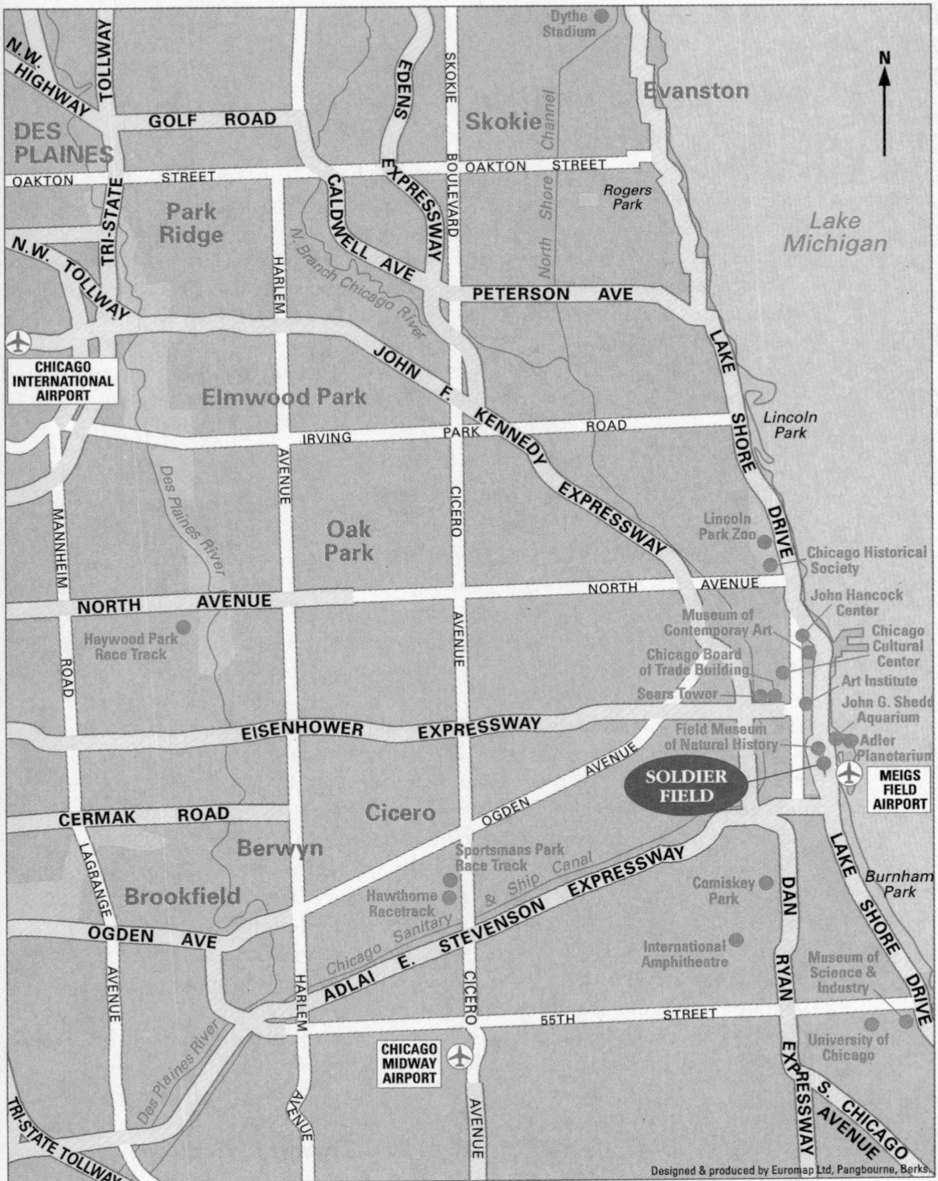

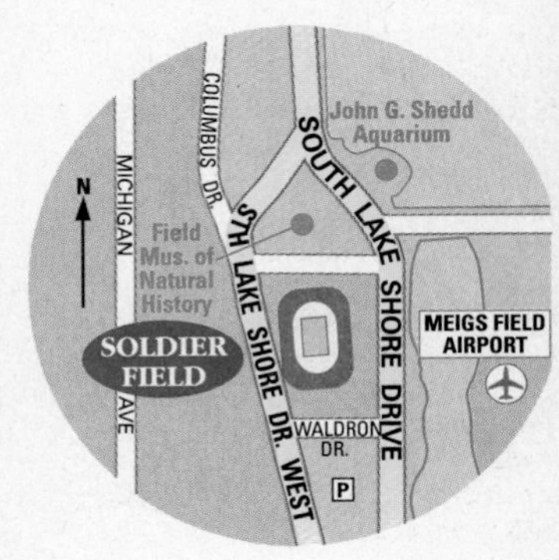

SOLDIER FIELD STADIUM

WORLD CUP '94

Chicago

SOLDIER FIELD STADIUM

Chicago's Soldier Field is an ideal setting for the World Cup Games. A traditional, historical structure, the stadium is equipped with the modern technology and conveniences required for a contemporary, world-class event. Soldier Field is located on the shores of Lake Michigan, less than 2km (1.5 miles) from the central business district and some of the city's finest museums, shops, restaurants and hotels. It is also just steps from public transportation. Spectators who prefer not to take the lovely 2km walk through Grant Park can reach the stadium on city buses or commuter trains that come directly to Soldier Field. Special city buses are also provided for major games.
From each of its 66,000 plus seats, spectators get a perfect, unobstructed view of the action on the field. Also, due to the open-air seating in Soldier Field, fans can command a view of the city's magnificent skyline and glorious lakefront. Soldier Field is also home to the Chicago Bears American football team.

WORLD CUP CHICAGO

WHAT MAKES CHICAGO SPECIAL

A MELTING POT

Chicago's long history of ethnic diversity promises to heighten the international flavour and fervour of the 1994 World Cup Games. Even today, one in ten Chicagoans is foreign-born. In terms of foreign ancestry, German-Americans are the largest group, representing 28% of the population in Chicago and other regional metropolitan areas. According to the US Census Bureau's 1980 figures, the six largest ancestry groups in this region are: German (28%), English (15%), Polish (14%), Hispanic (13%), Irish (11%) and Italian (8%).
With the Midwest being home to the nation's largest concentration of German-Americans, Chicago has a particular advantage in hosting the Opening Game, where Germany will be defending its title. Chicagoans will, no doubt, turn out in large numbers for the game.

A CITY OF NEIGHBOURHOODS

The story of the USA is told in Chicago's neighbourhoods, where wave after wave of immigrants brought their own customs, rituals, foods, crafts and philosphy of life. The true founder of Chicago, Jean Baptiste Point DuSable, was a fur trader of African and French-Canadian ancestry. Chicago's African-American population has settled primarily in areas on the city's south and west sides, such as Garfield Park, Woodlawn, South Shore, Englewood and Washington Heights. Chicago's *DuSable Museum of African-American History*, founded in 1961, tells their history.
At the city's northern border, Rogers Park and West Rogers Park (often called West Ridge) are home to a large number of Chicago's Jewish residents. Along California and Devon, visitors will find numerous synagogues, kosher butchers and bakeries and delis. In recent years, West Rogers Park has seen a tremendous influx of Asians, and Indian restaurants are also common.
A few blocks south on California is Lincoln Square, the centre of Chicago's German community, with a plethora of German restaurants, delis and cafés. Travelling east on Lawrence past Western is 'New Greektown'. Still further east is Albany Park, a former Jewish area now almost entirely Asian, with Koreans forming the largest group. Just east of here is the Edgewater/Uptown area sometimes called 'New Chinatown' but more traditionally known as 'Andersonville'. It is also the headquarters of Chicago's Swedish-American community and home to the *Swedish American Museum* and the *Swedish Historical Society*.
Along Chicago Avenue, west of the Kennedy Expressway, is the 'Ukrainian Village' and what was the centre of Chicago's Polish community. *St Nicholas Ukrainian Church, Olha Church* and the *Polish St Stanislaus Kostka Church* form the majestic backdrop against which visitors may find ethnic food, bookstores and shops. The *Ukrainian National Museum* and the *Polish Museum of America* are both located here.
A few blocks south on Halsted, between Jackson and Van Buren, is the traditional 'Greektown', where boisterous restaurants attract thousands of fun-seekers. Taking Halsted further south to 22nd Street and turning left, one comes to the Pilsen neighbourhood, the centre of Chicago's burgeoning Hispanic community, and possibly home to more outdoor murals than any other spot in the city. The new *Mexican-American Fine Arts Center Museum*, the *East Pilsen Artists Colony* and lots of Mexican restaurants can be found here. Visitors taking 22nd Street further east to Wentworth emerge in the middle of Chinatown. Dozens of Chinese and Cantonese restaurants, bakeries, bookstores and gift shops lend a unique Far-Eastern charm to the 4-block area.
Chicago is a great walking town (not a hill in the city) and there are over 77 defined neighbourhoods to explore. In summer, the neighbourhoods hold their own festivals and visitors should sample the food, music and culture that make Chicago so diverse.

BIG CITY EXPERTISE

No city in the USA can match Chicago's expertise in organising and staging large-scale festivals and events. Starting as far back as 1892 when the World's Columbian Exposition drew 26 million people to the city, Chicago has played host to hundreds of millions of tourists. Today, more than 8 million visitors come to the city every year. They can choose to stay in any of Chicagoland's 60,000 plus hotel rooms. Visitors come to attend the summer festivals, to explore the city's outstanding cultural institutions and to do business. In 1990, Chicago hosted 1100 conventions, 28,000 corporate meetings and 150 trade shows. The ease with which Chicago handles large-scale events gives the city a distinct advantage in hosting the Opening Ceremony.

CULTURAL CHICAGO

A world-renowned symphony orchestra, a highly acclaimed opera, a thriving professional theatre community and innovative dance companies can all be found in Chicago. And, as national honours, awards and recognition are heaped on these institutions, increasing numbers of tourists are including the performing arts in their trips to Chicago.

Founded in 1891, the Chicago Symphony Orchestra, based at *Orchestra Hall*, celebrates its 102nd season this year. The Orchestra is so popular that tickets are often sold out in advance, so visitors should enquire about tickets as soon as their travel plans are confirmed. Outdoor classical orchestra performances are performed by the Grant Park Symphony four times a week during the summer. Admission is free and

Chicago is only a short distance away from:

- ★ *Mississippi River – 3 hours – for a cruise and gaming.*
- ★ *Arlington Race Track – 45 minutes – for a day of family fun.*
- ★ *Frank Lloyd Wright Home and Studio in Oak Park, Illinois – 30 minutes.*
- ★ *Gurnee Mills – 45 minutes – a shopping mall with 230 discount stores.*
- ★ *Baseball – 15 minutes – at Wrigley Field or Comiskey Park.*
- ★ *Six Flags of Great America – 45 minutes – family entertainment (100 rides).*
- ★ *Galena – 3 hours – a Victorian town known for its antiques and Mississippi cruises.*

★ FOR INFORMATION ON TICKETS TO WORLD CUP '94, SEE PAGE 1066.

visitors can picnic under the stars.

Some of the hottest tickets in town are for the Lyric Opera of Chicago. New and classic productions featuring some of the world's best singers play to packed houses at the Civic Opera House, and a new company, the Chicago Opera Theatre, has been getting excellent reviews (and performances are in English).

Chicago's theatres are home to some of the most exciting, innovative and unusual performances in the nation and have been the training ground for talents such as playwright David Mamet and actors John Malkovich, John Mahoney, Joan Allen, William Peterson and others. The Steppenwolf Theatre Company, which began in a suburban garage in the 1970s, is now a major force in theatre and has recently moved into a spectacular 500-seat facility. *The Goodman Theatre*, a Chicago tradition since 1925, presents large-scale contemporary productions of classics and new plays to 200,000 theatre-lovers each year. Also, touring productions of major plays and musicals from Broadway and London are hosted by big downtown theatres such as the *Shubert*, the *Auditorium* and the newly renovated historic *Chicago Theatre*.

And last but not least, Chicago is home to a number of dance companies, including the newly formed Ballet Chicago (classical ballet), the Hubbard Street Dance Company (jazz dance), the Joseph Holmes Dance Company (modern dance), the Joel Hall Dance Company (jazz dance), the Chicago Repertory Dance Ensemble (classical modern dance) and the MoMing Dance and Arts Center (avant-garde dance). In addition, Chicago regularly hosts such visiting troupes as the Dance Theatre of Harlem, the Joffrey Ballet, the New York City Ballet and others.

The most up-to-date listing of all performances can be found in the Friday or Sunday edition of the *Chicago Tribune* or *Chicago Sun-Times* and the *Reader*, a free weekly publication available at numerous downtown locations. A copy of *Chicago's Got It!* Calendar of Events is available from the Chicago Office of Tourism. Tel: (312) 280 5740 *or* (800) 487 2446.

THE WAY TO THE WORLD CUP

THE AIRPORTS

O'Hare International Airport is 35km (21 miles) northwest of downtown Chicago. It has three permanent terminal buildings, with an interim international facility located on the ground level of the enclosed parking structure. For visitors needing information or directions, airport information booths are located on the upper level of the terminals and outside the meeters-greeters area of the international terminal. A foreign currency exchange is located in Terminal 4. For flights leaving from domestic gates, there are mobile carts nearby. For further information, telephone (312) 686 2200.

Midway Airport is located 20 minutes from downtown Chicago. The one-building airport is divided into three terminals: A and C for the arrival and departure of each airline's passengers; and B, or the Main (middle) terminal, where the information booth and all vehicle pick-up services are available. For further airport information, telephone (312) 767 0500.

Merrill C Meigs Field is a small general aviation facility just steps from Soldier Field Stadium and 10 minutes from Chicago's 'Loop'. Meigs has two commercial airlines serving various midwestern states and cities. For further information, telephone (312) 744 4787.

TRANSPORTATION FROM O'HARE AIRPORT TO CHICAGO

Subway

Chicago Transit Authority (CTA): A rapid transit train between O'Hare and downtown Chicago is easy, quick and convenient (travel time – 35 minutes). Trains run every 5-10 minutes during the day and evening, and every 30 minutes 0100-0500. The terminal is located under Terminal 4, and only one block from the other terminals via a moving sidewalk within the airport. Fare is $1.25 one-way. For further information, telephone (312) 836 7000.

Soldier Field Stadium Renovations

The stadium underwent major reconstruction in 1979, which included new lighting, playing surface, locker rooms, rebuilding of the seating area (new chairbacks, arm rests and seats) and improvement of sight lines. Additional rebuilding of the seating area occurred in 1982, along with new concourses with more restrooms and concession areas. A new press box, 60 deluxe skyboxes and a new scoreboard were also built, increasing capacity to 66,030. In 1988, the surface was changed from artificial turf to natural grass and 56 skyboxes were added along the south rim (increasing the total to 116). Overall capacity increased to 66,946. In 1992, four more seats were added to increase capacity to the current figure of 66,950.

Soldier Field History

Soldier Field was opened in November 1924 as the 45,000-seat Municipal Grant Park Stadium. Plans for the stadium began in 1919 as a memorial to the soldiers of the First World War. The field stands on 10,000 pile foundations driving an average depth of 19m (62.5ft) through fill that replaced the lake waters. The first football game was played on November 22, 1924, as a capacity crowd watched Notre Dame win over Northwestern 13-6. It went on to host the first boxing event which drew a gate of over $2.5 million (Dempsey vs Turner in 1927), the first ski meet held in a stadium and the all-time largest football crowd of over 123,000 when Notre Dame defeated Southern California, 7-6 in 1927.

WORLD CUP '94

Chicago

WORLD CUP CHICAGO

Buses

Continental Air Transport: Provides bus service to and from downtown Chicago, the Near North Side and the Northwest Suburbs from the baggage claim areas. Fare is $12.50 one-way from the airport to the 'Loop' (the centre of downtown Chicago) and $22 round-trip. For further information, telephone (312) 454 7799.

Taxis

Located on the lower level of each terminal, taxis are available 0600-0100. From O'Hare to downtown Chicago takes approximately 50 minutes and costs $25-$30. A Shared-Ride programme allows visitors to be charged a flat rate of $12.

TRANSPORTATION FROM MIDWAY AIRPORT TO CHICAGO

Buses

CTA Midway Express Bus #99M: Weekday rush-hour bus service is available from Midway to downtown Chicago. For further information, telephone (312) 836 7000.
Continental Air Transport: Buses depart from Midway to downtown Chicago every 10-15 minutes. The information and reservation booth is located at Concourse A and buses should be boarded in front of the baggage claim area. Fare is $9.50 one-way and $16.75 round-trip. For further information, telephone (312) 454 7799.

Taxis

Taxis are located in front of the Main Terminal. The fare from the airport to downtown costs $18-$22.

CHICAGO GROUND TRANSPORTATION

GETTING AROUNG THE CITY

Chicago's central location and outstanding transportation services make it easy for visiting dignitaries and guests to get to Chicago and settle in quickly and comfortably.

Rail/Bus

Chicago Transit Authority (CTA): Within Chicago's metropolitan area, the city of Chicago's Regional Transportation Authority provides public transport that is safe, clean and highly efficient. The Authority operates services to the City and 38 nearby municipalities, relying on its fleet of 1217 subway cars, 3000 buses and 950 commuter trains. In total, Chicago's public transport system offers more than 281.6 million kilometres (175 million miles) of service to approximately 680 million passengers every year.
PACE: Runs Suburban buses throughout the region.
For information on route, schedule and fare information for these two transport companies, telephone (312) 836 7000.
Metropolitan Rail (METRA): Runs commuter trains and buses between the city and suburbs. For further information, telephone (312) 322 6777.
Amtrak: For information on destinations by rail throughout the country from Chicago, telephone (312) 558 1075 *or* (800) USA RAIL.
Greyhound: For information on destinations by coach throughout the country, telephone (312) 781 2900.

Taxi

Taxis can be summoned by phoning *Checker & Yellow Cab* on (312) 829 4222 *or American United Cab* on (312) 248 7600.

Self-Drive

The city sits at the centre of an elaborate web of superhighways and expressways, making road travel direct and easy.

A CITY OF SUMMER FESTIVALS

With daytime temperatures ranging from 20-25°C (69-74°F), Chicago's June climate is ideal for outdoor activity, touring and watching sports. During the months of May, June and July, Chicago hosts some of the country's most popular music and arts festivals. The following are a few 1994 highlights:

May
International Art Expo – *hundreds of dealers and thousands of art buyers comes to Navy Pier.*

May & June
The International Theatre Festival.

June
The Chicago Blues Festival – *The world-famous festival is held at Grant Park and offers three days of brilliant music from the finest blues artists. Hundreds of thousands of people come to enjoy free outdoor concerts.*
Chicago Gospel Festival – *Two glorious days of uplifting music from national and local favourites.*

July
Taste of Chicago – *This is the city's most popular summer celebration. Lasting a whole week, it draws millions into the city to sample its ethnic cuisine. The Festival culminates in the fabulous Fourth of July fireworks.*
Chicago Country Music Festival – *Top country & western artists from across the nation perform new hits and classic favourites for two days of down-home pleasure.*

August
The Chicago Jazz Festival – *One of the world's most popular jazz events takes place in Chicago's lakefront park where fans flock to hear some of the finest musicians alive today.*

September
Viva! Chicago – *The hottest music from the greatest Latin performers in the cool breeze off Lake Michigan lasts for two exciting days.*

THE ONLY MAN TO SCAORE A HAT-TRICK IN A WORLD CUP FINAL IS ENGLAND's GEOFF HURST IN 1966.

LOUISIANA

Including **New Orleans,** gateway to the Southern States of Mississippi and Arkansas.

Louisiana Office of Tourism
PO Box 94291
Capitol Station
Baton Rouge, LA
70804-9291
Tel: (504) 342 8142. Fax: (504) 342 8390.
Greater New Orleans Tourist & Convention Commission
1520 Sugar Bowl Drive
New Orleans, LA
70112
Tel: (504) 566 5032. Fax: (504) 566 5046.
Southwest Louisiana Convention & Visitors Bureau
PO Box 1912
1211 North Lakeshore Drive
Lake Charles, LA
70601
Tel: (318) 436 9588. Fax: (318) 436 9863.
Shreveport-Bossier Convention & Visitors Bureau
PO Box 1761
629 Spring Street
Shreveport, LA
71166
Tel: (318) 222 9391. Fax: (318) 222 0056.

TIME: GMT - 6. *Daylight Saving Time* is observed from the first Sunday in April to the last Sunday in October. Clocks are put forward one hour, changing at 0200 hours local time.
THE STATE: Louisiana's marshy Mississippi valley is one of the most attractive areas of the USA. New Orleans, its largest city, is one of the country's major tourist destinations. It is famed for Dixieland jazz, its architecture, superb cuisine and its unique French Quarter. The city also boasts a wide choice of museums and galleries. Other places to see in the state include Lafayette, a city of magnificent gardens and the start of the 40km (25-mile) Azalea Trail; the Atchafalaya Basin, the largest and most remote swamp in the USA; the huge salt domes of Avery and Jefferson Islands; Alexandria, surrounded by forests and parks; and the Hot Wells resort and spa. The 138m- (452ft) high marble Capitol Building is situated in Baton Rouge.

TRAVEL

AIR: Approximate flight times: From New Orleans to *Atlanta* is 30 minutes, to *Chicago* is 1 hour, to *Los Angeles* is 4 hours, to *Miami* is 1 hour and to *New York* is 2 hours.
International airports: *New Orleans International Airport* (MSY), 23km (14 miles) from the city centre, is America's ninth largest airport (travel time – 20/30 minutes). A US$200-million airport expansion programme is presently underway. *Jefferson Transit* provides a bus service to the city centre every 15-20 minutes (weekdays) and every 30 minutes (weekends). *Greyhound* (tel: (504) 525 6075) also has buses from the airport to many destinations. *Rhodes Transportation* (tel: (504) 943 6621) offers a 24-hour limousine service to the city centre. *Mississippi Coast Limousine Service (Coastliner)* provides a shuttle service to the Gulf coast and many other places along the route, making nine trips 0800-2330 daily. Taxis are available 24 hours to the city centre. Airport facilities include two banks, shops, snack bars, restaurant/bar, post office and car hire (*Avis, Hertz, Budget, Dollar* and *National)*.
RAIL: *Amtrak* and *Southern Railways* both serve New Orleans. Amtrak offers a special *Eastern Region Rail Pass* which allows 45 days of unlimited travel to as far north as Burlington and as far west as Chicago. Passengers leave from Union Station, located at 1001 Loyola Avenue.
ROAD: Bus: Bus and coach services are provided to nearby major cities on *Greyhound* and *Trailways*.
Approximate driving times: From New Orleans to *Mobile* is 3 hours, to *Houston* is 6 hours, to *Birmingham* is 7 hours and to *Memphis* is 8 hours.
All times are based on non-stop driving at or below the applicable speed limits.
Approximate *Greyhound* journey times: From New Orleans to *Mobile* is 4 hours, to *Houston* is 8 hours, to *Birmingham* is 9 hours and to *Memphis* is 10 hours.
URBAN: Bus: The famous 'Streetcar named Desire' in New Orleans has been replaced by a bus. Extensive bus services are available throughout the city. **Car hire:** *Avis, Hertz, Budget, Dollar, Econocar, Thrifty, National* and *American International* all have offices in or near the airport. A national driving licence and a major credit card are needed to hire a car. **Streetcar:** These still run on St Charles Avenue and Carrollton in New Orleans, starting from Canal Street. **Horsecab:** Horse-drawn carriages offer a scenic means of transport through the French Quarter.

RESORTS & EXCURSIONS

NEW ORLEANS: Famous the world over for its unique charms, New Orleans offers a melting pot of influences, including French, Spanish, African, Caribbean, German and Cajun, which is apparent in its blend of architecture, cuisine and culture. It is the birthplace of jazz and the cocktail, and these perfectly describe the sort of lifestyle that New Orleans represents. The *French Quarter* is a favourite tourist haunt, full of colonial architecture, intimate courtyards, exquisite iron grillwork and the uplifting sounds of New Orleans jazz wafting through the lively streets. *Jackson Square*, the heart of the French Quarter, is a street entertainment nexus for mimes, musicians, tap dancers and sidewalk artists. There are many excellent restaurants, bars and nightclubs. Its location at the crux of the Mississippi River and the Atlantic Ocean makes it a perfect place for a walk by the river or a stroll down the esplanade overlooking the Atlantic.
Sightseeing: *Cabildo*, former seat of Spanish rulers and the setting for the Louisiana State Purchase; *Casa Hove*, a perfect example of Creole architecture; the *International Trade Mart*; *Duelling Oaks*, where affairs of honour were settled in the 18th century; *Conti Wax Museum*; *Audobon's House*, where the famous wildlife draftsman lived and worked; *Audobon Zoo and Zoological Garden* (0930-1630 Monday to Friday, 0930-1730 weekends), ranked among the top three zoos in the USA; *Aquarium of the Americas*, where four different environment simulations depict the wildlife and marine life within; *Vieux Carré; Orleans Ballroom; St Louis Cathedral*; the *French Market*, located on the waterfront, with excellent coffee bars serving french pastries; *Pontalba House*, a state museum with period furnishings and decor; *Preservation Hall*, where authentic New Orleans jazz is played nightly and *The Garden District*, featuring white-columned mansions, draping oak trees and beautiful gardens surrounded by elegant wrought-iron fences.
Excursions: There are many ferries that provide transport across or up and down the *Mississippi River*, departing from the levee at the foot of Canal Street. One- to 11-day cruises are also available: *Steamboat NATCHEZ* has harbour and dinner cruises, *Bayou Jean Lafitte* offers a 45-mile Louisiana Bayou adventure, *Cotton Blossom* has a zoo cruise between the Aquarium and Riverfront Park to the Audobon Zoo and *Bayou Segnette Swamp Boat Tours* offer special cruises through the Louisiana swamps. For further information on boat cruises, contact New Orleans Steamboat Company, 1300 World Trade Center, New Orleans, LA 70130. Tel: (504) 586 8777.
BATON ROUGE: The capital of Louisiana and heart of the Southern plantation region. The 'blues' are a large part of the Baton Rouge heritage, sung by slaves as they picked plantation cotton, and it was the original home of many of America's most well-known blues musicians. Many clubs, concerts and festivals in the area pay homage to this seminal music.
Sightseeing: *Capitol Building*, a 34-storey building with a viewing platform overlooking 27 acres of formal gardens in the Capitol grounds; the *Old Capitol*, with its Norman, Gothic and Moorish blend of architecture; the Louisiana *Governor's Mansion*, with exhibits of art, natural history and anthropology; *Baton Rouge Zoo*, 140 acres of walk-through areas and forest settings for over 400 animals; the *Louisiana Arts and Science Center Riverside*, located in a remodelled railroad station; and *The Rural Life Museum*, an outdoor museum located on the grounds of a former plantation, showing the type of work done in a 19th-century plantation community.
Excursions: Many magnificent old plantation mansions are available for viewing in this area, some offering bed & breakfast facilities as well as tours. The most spectacular plantation home in the region is called *'Le Petit Versailles'* and was owned by a 19th-century planter called Valcourt Aimé who was also known as 'Louis XIV of Louisiana'.
LAFAYETTE: The industrial and cultural hub of 'Cajun' country and home to 100,000 people, many of whom are French-speaking Canadians from Nova Scotia who settled in the region after 1764 when they were deported by the British for refusing to give up the Catholic faith or pledge allegiance to the British crown. These people were originally known as 'Acadians' but the name was eventually shortened to 'Cajuns'. The land is full of swamps and bayous.
Sightseeing: *Acadian Village* and *Vermilionville* have faithful replicas of early Cajun communities.
Excursions: Houma, a bayou town known for its many swamp tours, where alligators, wading birds and myriad other swamplife thrive; **New Iberia,** home of world-famous *Tabasco* sauce, offering tours of subtropical gardens, stately antebellum homes, rice mills and the hot sauce and pepper plant farms; **St Martinville** is a quiet and elegant town once known as 'Le Petit Paris' for its luxurious balls, operas and highlife, and its Cajun museum and church are well worth visiting; and the *Creole Nature Trail* near **Lake George,** where ducks, geese, alligators, nutria and muskrats run rampant.
NATCHITOCHES: The oldest town in Louisiana, perched on the Cane River, it was first established as a fort and trading post in 1714 to prevent the Spanish from encroaching on French territory and is now a charming river town and farm centre. It has numerous historic homes, many offering bed & breakfast, and is surrounded by pecan orchards, cotton farms and 18th-century plantation homes. The region around Natchitoches is known as the 'Crossroads' region because it is where the French and Spanish heritage of the south meets the pioneer spirit of the north. It is also a haven for country music, spawning such luminaries as Jerry Lee Lewis and Mickey Gilley, and the annual Fiddle Championship takes place in this region in Marthaville.
Excursions: Nearby **Monroe,** another river town, also has many historical homes and a museum; *The Louisiana Purchase Gardens and Zoo* in Monroe is a 100-acre park with moss-laden oaks, formal gardens and winding waterways. *Dogwood Trail Drive* is a 29km (18-mile) journey over the state's highest hills, among blossoming dogwood trees, revealing the region's particular beauty.
SHREVEPORT: A leading oil and gas centre located close to the Texas border with a distinctly American West flavour. It is also renowned as a trade and entertainment area and hosts three major annual events, attracting visitors from far and wide (see *Special Events* below). Shreve Square has an attractive cluster of nightclubs, restaurants and shops.
Sightseeing: *Louisiana State Exhibit Museum* with dioramas, an art gallery, historical murals and archaeological relics; *RW Norton Museum*, featuring Old West artists; *Pioneer Heritage Center;* and the *American Rose Center*, a famous showplace.
Excursions: This region is known as 'Sportman's Paradise' for its many forests and lakes offering opportunities for fishing, hunting, canoeing and hiking, and excursions can be arranged for these activities. An annual *Fishing Tournament* takes place at Toledo Bend. *Louisiana Downs Thoroughbred Racetrack*, across the Red River in **Bossier City,** is open for racing from late Spring until the Autumn. *Poverty Point State Commemorative Area* is an ancient Indian civilization dating from 1700BC and one of the most important archaeological finds in the USA.
Note: For information on attractions in neighbouring states, see above under *States A-Z*.

SOCIAL PROFILE

FOOD & DRINK: Creole cuisine is a speciality in Louisiana and should be experienced. The Louisiana mix of cultures has resulted in an innovative cuisine using the best elements of each nationality. The state's location makes it a prime spot for seafood, and fresh fish, shrimp, crabs, oysters and crayfish abound. Game meat is also popular in Louisiana cuisine, including rabbit and wild turkey. Exotic fruits, such as bananas and pineapples, are used often in Creole cuisine, along with spices such as hot peppers and *filé* (the ground powder for making

gumbo). The Crescent City district in New Orleans is known for its superb restaurants offering such Creole specialities as oysters Rockefeller, bananas Foster and *pompano en papillote*. Oyster bars are prevalent, especially along the seaside or riverfront. Creole cafés serve traditional favourites such as gumbo and red beans and rice. Other Cajun specialities include *étouffée, sauce piquante* and *jambalaya*. A meat pie, shaped like a half-moon and filled with a spicy mixture of ground beef and pork, is a speciality of Natchitoches. The town of Henderson, on the edge of Atchafalaya Swamp, is famous for its Cajun cuisine and its many restaurants, specialising in seafood, attract visitors from miles away. 'Southern Cookin'', found in the Crossroads region in northern Louisiana, is savoured for its delicious fried chicken, barbecued meat, cornbread and peach pie.
Drink: Given its southern climate, cold drinks are much relished in this state. Iced tea is a favourite. Alcohol can only be purchased by those over 18 years of age and is available at supermarkets and liquor stores. Some parts of northern Louisiana do not sell alcohol.
THEATRES & CONCERTS: *Le Petit Théâtre du Vieux Carré* in New Orleans is one of the oldest theatre groups in the country and is highly recommended. Shreveport also houses one of the best-known US community theatre groups in its *Little Theater*. Louisiana has engendered a rich black music scene derived from the rythmic chants of riverboat men and the soulful gospel tunes of field hands through to such jazz greats as Jelly Roll Morton and Louis Armstrong, both natives of New Orleans. Therefore, jazz, blues, gospel, rythmn 'n blues, *zydeco* (played by the French-speaking blacks of the region), Cajun and country music can all be heard in concerts throughout Louisiana. Many music concerts are held on riverboats on the Mississippi.
NIGHTLIFE: Nightlife is especially lively in New Orleans. The burlesque shows and cabarets of Bourbon Street are notorious – every third door on this famous street is a nightclub. Also, just minutes from downtown New Orleans there is a district known as *Fat City* which houses many nightclubs and 24-hour cafés.
SHOPPING: The French Quarter of New Orleans has many excellent shopping opportunities. Souvenirs are plentiful, and other good buys include Creole pecan pralines, Mardi Gras masks, beautifully bottled and handmixed perfumes, and various antiques on sale in shops on Royal Street. Other excellent shopping areas in New Orleans include Canal Place, The Esplanade, the French Market, Riverwalk and Uptown Square Shopping Center. Northgate Mall in Lafayette and Lakeside Shopping Center in Metairie are also excellent. Louisiana offers tax-free shopping to international visitors for items sold by a participating merchant. Request a tax refund voucher from any *Louisiana Tax Free Shopping (LTFS)* participator and it can be refunded at the airport on presentation of voucher, receipt and travel ticket. Refunds can also be obtained by mail if sent with voucher, receipts, travel ticket and a notarised statement stating why vouchers were not redeemed at the airport and the present whereabouts of the merchandise.
SPORT: Fishing, both freshwater and saltwater, is popular all year round. King mackerel, jewfish, marlin, bluefish, cobia, channel bass, *pompano*, red snapper and jack are found in coastal areas and the Gulf of Mexico, whereas crayfish is an inland speciality. It is one of the best states for bass fishing. Tarpon fishing is available near Houma. A freshwater fishing licence is necessary for non-residents but no licence is necessary for saltwater fishing. **Hunting** is available during the winter months with a licence and popular game includes duck, squirrel, deer, turkey and wildfowl. Bear, deer and turkey require a special licence (further information available from the *Wildlife and Fish Commission* in New Orleans). **Swimming** is available in recreation areas throughout Louisiana. 18-hole **golf** courses are available in Lafayette (City Park Golf Course), Shreveport (Andrew Querbes Park), Lakeside and New Orleans (Lakewood Country Club, which also sponsors the Greater New Orleans Open every Spring).
SPECIAL EVENTS: The New Orleans Carnival, or *Mardi Gras*, comes to a climax on Shrove Tuesday (47 days before Easter). Costumes, dazzling floats, street dancing and general wild abandon are the order of the day. Mardi Gras country-style celebrations also take place in the Cajun towns of Church Point and Mamou with music, dancing and enough gumbo to feed the whole town. The *Spring Fiesta* begins on the first Friday after Easter with jazz parades, street dancing, riverboat concerts and outdoor art shows. The *New Orleans Jazz and Heritage Festival* is held for two weeks each spring in late April and early May and is a celebration of food, music and crafts, with jazz, ragtime, gospel, blues and country music concerts, as well as parades and river cruises. The *Festival International de Louisiane*, held each April in Lafayette, is a tribute to southern Louisiana's music and food, with live bands playing Carribean music. *Festival of Lights* in Natchitoches is a Christmas celebration when elaborate scenes of multicoloured electric lights depicting camels, the Magi and other yuletide themes are turned on all at once, their reflection in the Cane River increasing their radiance; a firework display is then launched over the river. Shreveport celebrates three major annual events: the 10-day *Holiday in Dixie* in April, with flower shows, sports competitions, an air show, pet show, treasure hunt, carnival, two fancy-dress balls and a grand finale parade; the *State Fair* in the autumn, also lasting ten days, attracting half a million visitors for auto races, rodeo exhibitions, carnival rides, arts and crafts displays, band concerts and fireworks; and the *Red River Revel*, a celebration of the arts which takes place on the riverfront.

CLIMATE

Humid and subtropical. Hot temperatures in summer, mild temperatures in spring and autumn and colder temperatures in winter.
Required clothing: Lightweight cotton clothing for summer, with sweaters and jackets for winter. Rainwear or umbrella is advised for all seasons.

MARYLAND

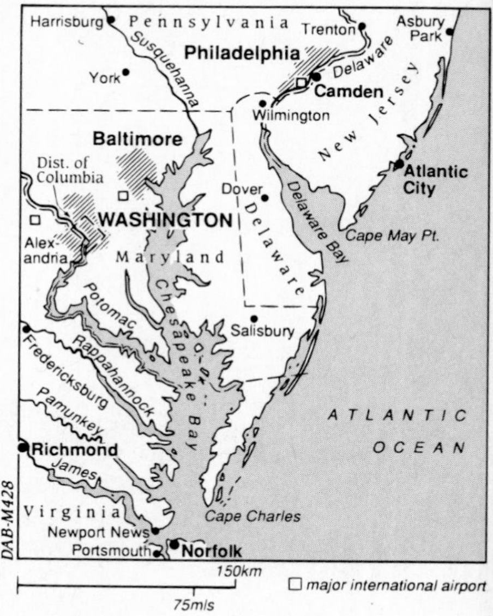

Including **Baltimore,** gateway to the northeast Atlantic coast States of Delaware and Virginia and the inland States of West Virginia and Pennsylvania.

Maryland Tourism Office
9th Floor
217 East Redwood Street
Baltimore, MD
21202
Tel: (410) 333 6611. Fax: (410) 333 6643.
Annapolis Information & Tourism Office
City Hall
160 Duke of Gloucester Street
Annapolis, MD
21401
Tel: (410) 263 7940. Fax: (410) 263 3322.
Baltimore County Office of Tourism
23 Chesapeake Avenue
Towson, MD
21204
Tel: (410) 887 8040. Fax: (410) 887 8041.
Tri-County Council for Western Maryland
111 South George Street
Cumberland, MD
21502
Tel: (301) 777 2158. Fax: (301) 777 2495.

TIME: GMT - 5. *Daylight Saving Time* is observed from the first Sunday in April to the last Sunday in October. Clocks are put forward one hour, changing at 0200 hours local time.
THE STATE: Maryland was one of the original 13 states of the USA, founded by Lord Baltimore in 1634. Its Atlantic Plain, divided by Chesapeake Bay, rises through the rolling hills and scenic farmland of the state's heartland to the Allegheny Mountains of the northwest. Its tourist destinations range from the 16km (10 miles) of white, sandy beaches at Ocean City to Baltimore's bustling Inner Harbor, located on Chesapeake Bay; its 6437km (4000 miles) of shoreline, including its tributaries, separate the eastern shore area of Maryland from the rest of the state. The twin-spanned Chesapeake Bay Bridge, 11.6km (7.25 miles) across, is the major link between the two sections. Maryland is also the 'bridge' linking Baltimore and Washington DC. The distance between the two is only about 64km (40 miles).

TRAVEL

AIR: Approximate flight times: From Baltimore to *London* is 7 hours 40 minutes (direct) and to *New York* is 1 hour 15 minutes.
International airport: *Baltimore/Washington International (BWI)* is 16km (10 miles) south of Baltimore and 55km (34 miles) northeast of Washington DC. This airport has been expanding its international services rapidly over the past year, resulting in immense profits and a greatly increased number of carriers, passengers and cargo.

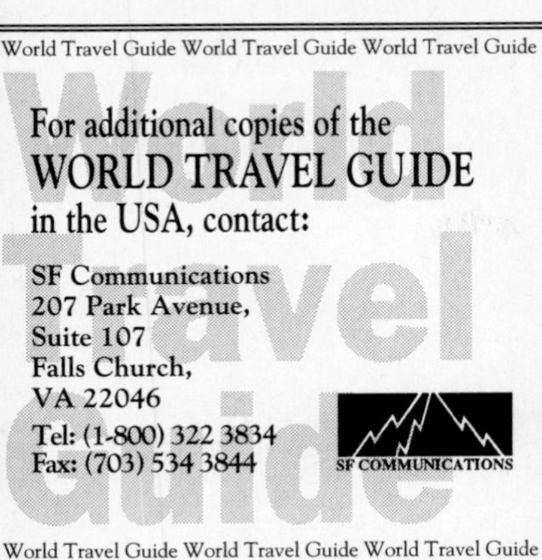

Airport buses are available to downtown Washington DC and there are frequent rail and shuttle bus connections to Baltimore. Taxis ply to and from Baltimore, but distance makes fares to Washington DC prohibitive.
RAIL: Baltimore is on the main East Coast *Amtrak* line and consequently receives direct services from as far afield as New Orleans and Miami. There are also frequent shuttles to Washington DC and New York. For approximate journey times on this line, see the *New York* section below.
ROAD: Approximate driving times: From Baltimore to *Washington DC* is 50 minutes, to *Philadelphia* is 2 hours, to *New York* is 4 hours, to *Chicago* is 15 hours, to *Miami* is 23 hours, to *Dallas* is 29 hours, to *Los Angeles* is 56 hours and to *Seattle* is 59 hours.
All times are based on non-stop driving at or below the applicable speed limits.
Approximate *Greyhound* journey times: From Baltimore (tel: (410) 744 9311) to *Washington DC* is 1 hour, to *Philadelphia* is 2 hours 15 minutes and to *New York* is 3 hours 40 minutes.
URBAN: Redevelopment in Baltimore during the last decade has provided a subway system and new expressways. The entire metropolitan area is covered by the *Mass Transit Administration*. Taxis can be hailed easily on the street or ordered by phone. Cars and motorcampers can be rented.

RESORTS & EXCURSIONS

BALTIMORE: Maryland's major city is one of the USA's busiest ports. Restoration of the city's Inner Harbor area has created one of the major tourist destinations in the mid-Atlantic region. Baltimore has a cosmopolitan population of more than two million and an attractive village-like atmosphere.
Sightseeing: Docked in the Inner Harbor at Pier 1 is the frigate *Constellation*, first ship of the US Navy (1797) and oldest ship in the world still afloat. The 3-acre Inner Harbor also contains the *World Trade Center*, the *National Aquarium*, the *Maryland Science Center* and two pavilions on the water's edge filled with shops and restaurants. An open-air amphitheatre is the site of the annual summer-long street performer's festival. Nearby is the *Charles' Center* with 22 acres of offices, tower blocks, overhead walkways, fountains and plazas; it includes the *Morris Mechanic Theater*. Also nearby is the *Baltimore Arena and Festival Hall*, site for ice hockey, music concerts and other special attractions. City museums include the *Baltimore Museum of Art*, which houses many post-impressionist works; *Walters Art Gallery*; and the *City Life Museum*, a city-block of buildings demonstrating life in Baltimore during the 19th century. *Mount Vernon Place* contains 19th-century houses and squares and various cultural institutions, such as the *Maryland Historical Society* and the *Peabody Conservatory of Music*. It also includes the *Washington Monument*, which can be climbed for a panoramic view.
Excursions: A short water-taxi ride away from the Inner Harbor is the star-shaped brick-built *Fort McHenry National Monument*, whose bombardment in 1814 inspired the writing of the 'Star Spangled Banner' and where special drills and military ceremonies are performed in the summer.
ANNAPOLIS: The state capital has an attractive harbour, the impressive campus of the US Naval Academy and beautiful period architecture.
Excursions: The *Chesapeake & Ohio Canal National Historic Park*, stretching 295km (184.5 miles) from Washington DC to Cumberland in western Maryland, is where the young Lieutenant-Colonel George Washington began his military career. His headquarters can still be seen. The canal was once a major avenue of commerce. The towpath for mule-drawn barges now serves as a popular hiking and biking trail. **Ocean City,** one of the state's main resort areas, boasts an expansive white sand beach, a 5km (3-mile) boardwalk, amusements, tram rides, boating and deep-sea fishing. *Muddy Creek Falls* is located near Deep Creek Lake, Garrett County. *Carroll Country Farm Museum* is a working 19th-century farm near **Westminster.** *Old Trinity Church*, at **Church Creek,** is the oldest Protestant church actively used in the USA.
FREDERICK: A town of quaint brick buildings and picturesque parks.
Excursions: In and around Frederick, there are a number of sights to be seen. *Gambrill State Park*, just west of town, offers outstanding panoramic views from the Catoctin peaks. *Camp David Presidential Retreat* near **Thurmont** is the traditional holiday resort for US Presidents. The public is not allowed inside but visitors can experience the same lovely landscape in *Catoctin Mountain Park*, which surrounds it. *Cunningham Falls State Park* is also nearby.
Other attractions in Maryland include **Smith Island** and *Tangier Sound*, the home of Chesapeake Bay fishermen who earn their living from oysters, crabs and clams.
Note: For information on attractions in neighbouring states, see above under *States A-Z*.

SOCIAL PROFILE

FOOD & DRINK: Baltimore is well known for its many outstanding restaurants offering fresh seafood caught in Chesapeake Bay. Establishments range from the very expensive to the cheap fast-food counters.
THEATRES & CONCERTS: The *Baltimore Symphony Orchestra* gives concerts in the *Myerhoff Symphony Hall* and the *Lyric Theater* in Baltimore. Dinner theatres are popular in Baltimore and good performances can be experienced in the lounges of hotels and supper clubs. *The Left Bank Jazz Society* gives concerts on Sunday afternoons at the *Famous Ballroom*. *Hopkins Plaza* has many music concerts and *Center Plaza* hosts various rock concerts.
NIGHTLIFE: Baltimore has many late-night clubs. Baltimore Street is a famous area for burlesque shows and there are some raunchy nightclubs in an area of Baltimore known as The Block.
SHOPPING: The main department stores are in the Howard Street area and in Harbor Place and Antique Row. Charles Street has elegant fashion and furniture. Mount Vernon Place is an attractive area with many shops and boutiques among grand 19th-century architecture.
SPECIAL EVENTS: Mar 14 '93 *St Patrick's Parade*, Baltimore. **Apr 2-4** *Maryland on Display*, Festival Hall, Baltimore. **May 15-16** 1993 *Howard County Wine and Food Festival*, Symphony Wood, Columbia. **Jun 19** *Summer Carnival Train for Children*, Westminster. **Jul 4** *July Fourth Concerts and Fireworks Display*, Harborplace Amphitheater, Baltimore. **Aug 1-31** *Party on the Bay*, Chesapeake Bay. **Sep 4-6, 11-12, 18-19 and 25-26** *17th Annual Maryland Renaissance Festival*. **Oct 2** *Paddle for People* (a charity event consisting of paddleboat races), Constellation Dock, Baltimore. **Nov 20** *Thanksgiving Parade*, Baltimore. **Dec 10-12** *Sugarloaf's 16th Annual Winter Crafts Festival*, Gaithersburg.

CLIMATE

Hot, damp summers and mild, damp winters.

WASHINGTON DC (4m)

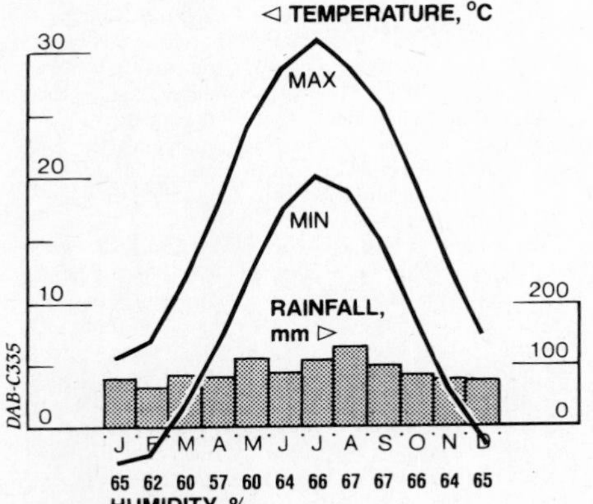

MASSACHUSETTS

Including **Boston,** gateway to New England (which comprises the States of Massachusetts, Maine, Vermont, New Hampshire, Connecticut and Rhode Island).

Massachusetts Office of Travel & Tourism
13th Floor
100 Cambridge Street
Boston, MA
02202
Tel: (617) 727 3201. Fax: (617) 727 6525.
Greater Boston Convention & Visitors Bureau
PO Box 490
Suite 400, Prudential Tower
Boston, MA
02199
Tel: (617) 536 4100. Fax: (617) 424 7664.
Greater Springfield Convention & Visitors Bureau
34 Boland Way
Springfield, MA
01103
Tel: (413) 787 1548. Fax: (413) 781 4607.
Cape Cod Chamber of Commerce
Junction Routes 6 & 132
Hyannis, MA
02601
Tel: (508) 362 3225.

TIME: GMT - 5. *Daylight Saving Time* is observed from the first Sunday in April to the last Sunday in October. Clocks are put forward one hour, changing at 0200 hours local time.
THE STATE: Massachusetts was the destination of the *Mayflower* in 1620 and is one of the original 13 states. It is now a major manufacturing state, offering everything from cobblestoned streets and village greens to space-age technology centres. The Berkshire Hills cut across its western corner. To the east the land rolls down to the sea, embracing the state capital, Boston, and the beaches of the Cape Cod National Seashore. The two regions are divided by the Connecticut River Valley.

TRAVEL

AIR: Approximate flight times: From Boston to *London* is 7 hours 15 minutes, to *New York* is 1 hour and to *Providence* is 25 minutes.
International airport: *Boston Logan International (BOS)*, 6km (4 miles) from the city centre, is the largest airport in New England. Airport services include a free shuttle-bus (marked *MASSPORT*) stopping at each airline terminal and the *MBTA* subway station which has a service every 8-12 minutes (travel time to downtown Boston – 15 minutes). Taxis and limousine service, car rentals, and buses are also available. *MASSPORT Water Shuttle*, serviced by a separate bus, offers a 7-minute boat ride from the airport to Rowes Wharf in downtown Boston.
RAIL: *Amtrak* links Boston with Washington DC, New York City, Chicago and Montréal in Canada, and offers summer service from New York City to Cape Cod.
Approximate journey time: From Boston to *New York* is 4 hours 30 minutes.

Sailboat on the Charles River

ROAD: Approximate driving times: From Boston to *Hartford* is 2 hours, to *Portland* (Maine) is 2 hours, to *Albany* is 3 hours, to *New York* is 4 hours, to *Montréal* is 6 hours, to *Chicago* is 20 hours, to *Miami* is 31 hours, to *Dallas* is 37 hours, to *Los Angeles* is 63 hours and to *Seattle* is 63 hours.
All times are based on non-stop driving at or below the applicable speed limits.
Approximate *Greyhound* journey times: From Boston (tel: (617) 423 5810) to *Albany* is 3 hours 30 minutes, to *New York* is 4 hours 30 minutes, to *Montréal* is 8 hours 30 minutes and to *St John* is 10 hours 30 minutes.
URBAN: *Massachusetts Bay Transport Authority* (MBTA or the 'T') operates Boston's subway system, as well as bus and train services throughout the city and surrounding towns. Fares are moderate and passengers can transfer easily between surface and underground transportation. Suburban buses extend travel beyond the immediate city. Taxis can be hailed throughout the city, but delays can be experienced during rush hours; they can also be called by telephone. Car hire is available. Commuter trains operate to points north, northwest, south and west of Boston.

RESORTS & EXCURSIONS

BOSTON: Boston is a city of contrasts, a gentle blend of the old and the new. The city has a very 'English' feel about it, with hilly, crooked cobblestoned streets, a thickly lawned common and cosy Victorian townhouses with polished brass door-knockers. It also played a vital role in the opposition to colonial rule that led to the American War of Independence.
Sightseeing: The *Freedom Trail* is a walk that passes 16 points of historical interest. Some of these are in the *Boston National Historical Park;* which is marked by signs and a red pavement line. The highest observation point in New England, the 60-floor *John Hancock Observatory*, offers a bird's-eye view of the city. Other attractions include harbour cruises, some of which enable the visitor to see the Boston skyline, the airport and the 1822 *USS Constitution* at Charlestown Navy Shipyard; the *Museum of Fine Arts*; the famous *Museum of Science*; the *John F Kennedy Library and Museum*; the *New England Aquarium*; the *Old North Church*; the *Boston Tea Party Ship & Museum*; *Faneuil Hall*; the *Prudential Building* viewing platform on the 52nd floor, open office hours; and the *Cheers Bar*, where the popular TV series is made.
Excursions: Cambridge lies across the Charles River from Boston. Here stands *Harvard University*, the USA's oldest university (1636). South of Boston is **Quincy,** the birthplace of Presidents John Adams and John Quincy Adams. **Salem,** north of Boston, is famous for its 1692 witch trials. Just west of Boston, **Concord** is one of the most historic and beautiful towns in the USA. *Plimoth Plantation*, in **Plymouth** is an open-air museum recreating a 1627 Pilgrim village. Nearby, the *Edaville Railroad* offers rides on an antique steam train. *Battleship Cove*, in **Fall River,** harbours 20th-century US Navy vessels and is the largest complex of its kind in the country. **New Bedford,** a restored whaling community, has the *Seamen's Bethel*, which inspired Herman Melville's description in 'Moby Dick'. **Cape Cod** has some 400km (250 miles) of beautiful beaches, and 21 seaside towns and fishing villages, making it one of the USA's prime resort areas. **Provincetown,** at the tip of the Cape, is where the pilgrims first landed. **Martha's Vineyard,** a picture-postcard island, lies off the coast of Cape Cod. Its airport in **Edgartown** receives flights from Boston and New York. **Nantucket Island,** once a great whaling port, is now a popular sun resort. *Old Sturbridge Village*, in central Massachusetts, is a living history museum recreating an 1830s New England town. Just two hours from Boston are the *Berkshire Hills* and the *Mohawk Trail*. The legendary Indian trail winds through 500,000 acres of state parks, forests and reservations. It is very popular for foliage viewing in the autumn. The *New England Science Center* in **Worcester** has a zoo, various exhibits and a range of lectures which provide an ideal learning opportunity for all members of the family.
Note: For information on attractions in neighbouring states, see above under *States A-Z*.

SOCIAL PROFILE

FOOD & DRINK: There is a wide variety of very good restaurants. Boston has many ethnic communities, and culinary opportunities range from Greek and Portuguese to Chinese and Syrian. Seafood is a speciality throughout Massachusetts, including local lobster, scallops, scrod and delicious clam chowder.
THEATRES & CONCERTS: Boston is the traditional review town for Broadway shows. The theatrical season is mainly in the autumn and winter. The *Boston Symphony Orchestra*, one of the greatest of all international ensembles, has a full schedule of autumn and winter concerts and makes its summer home at *Tanglewood* in the Berkshires. 'Boston Pops' concerts are staged in the spring and summer.
NIGHTLIFE: Boston offers a variety of jazz clubs, dance clubs and intimate piano bar lounges.
SHOPPING: The high-fashion district in Boston is Newbury Street in Back Bay. Department stores and *Filene's Bargain Basement* are in the downtown area. *Faneuil Hall Marketplace*, rather along the lines of London's Covent Garden, contains shops and restaurants.
SPECIAL EVENTS: During the summer of 1994, Boston's Foxboro Stadium will host six qualifying games for the *1994 World Cup*. The following events are celebrated annually in Boston:
Apr-Oct *Boston Red Sox Baseball*, Fenway Park. **Apr (third Monday)** *The Boston Marathon* (the USA's oldest marathon). **All summer** *Metro Parks Esplanade Concerts*, Hatch Shell, Charles River Esplanade. **Mid-Jun** *Cambridge International Fair* (ethnic performers, foods and crafts). **Late Jun** *Copley Square Book Festival*. **Jul (first week)** *Boston Harborfest*. **Jul 4** *Boston Pops Fourth of July Concert*, Charles River Esplanade. **Mid-Jul** *US Pro Tennis Championships*, Longwood; *Bay State Games*. **Jul-Aug** *Italian Feasts* (food, festivals, decorations and bands), The North End. **Dec 31** *First Night* (Boston's arts celebration of the New Year).

CLIMATE

Warm and sunny from May to October; cold winters

BOSTON Massachusetts (192m)

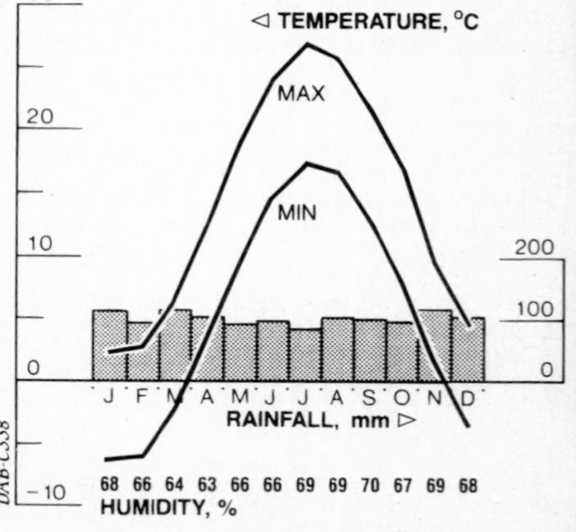

Welcome to **BOSTON**

As the 1994 World Cup Soccer venue closest to Europe, Boston is looking forward to welcoming visitors to see the games and discover the history, arts, entertainment and recreation of this world-class city.

BOSTON IS CONVENIENT, COMFORTABLE AND WALKABLE. Logan International Airport is just across the harbour from the city and accessible by water shuttle, public transportation or taxi. Downtown is compact and convenient to all of the major hotels. The attractions, shopping and restaurants are all within walking distance of each other.

BOSTON IS CHARMING. The Old World atmosphere is mixed with the excitement of today. Founded over 350 years ago, many of the old historic points of interest are situated between the newly renovated architectural gems built earlier in the century and the magnificent new towers recently added to the skyline.

BOSTON IS INTELLECTUAL. It is the centre of education and medical science in America. It has museums, concerts, performances, opera, ballet, theatre – all available to visitors to the city.

BOSTON IS EXCITEMENT. There is so much to do. Shoppers will love exploring outlets and one-of-a-kind boutiques. Diners can choose from hundreds of coffee houses, cafés, bistros, hotel fine-dining rooms and waterfront seafood restaurants. Evening entertainment ranges from local pubs like the famous Cheers, to jazz, blues and comedy clubs, rock or swing dancing.

BOSTON IS SPORTS-MINDED. When World Cup Soccer is played in Boston it will become part of a legend of international sports events. The Boston Marathon, the Head of the Charles Regatta, the US Open (golf) and the grand Regatta Columbus '92 of Tall Ships are just a few sports greats held here. Boston is also home to four professional sports teams, the Celtics (basketball), the Bruins (hockey), the Red Sox (baseball) and the New England Patriots (football). For sports history fans, there is the New England Sports Museum and the Boston Garden history tour.

BOSTON IS THE GATEWAY TO NEW ENGLAND with all the opportunities that this wonderful part of the world affords: the coast of Maine, the lakes of New Hampshire, the mountains of Vermont, the seashore of the Cape and the Islands, the rolling hills of the Berkshires. World Cup ticket holders can plan an extended vacation with their families before or after the games and they will feel welcome everywhere.

BOSTON TOURS DURING WORLD CUP SOCCER

Boston World Cup Soccer 1994 means soccer and so much more. We have a summer filled with exciting opportunities for group travel.

City Tour Options: *Historic, downtown, fashionable Back Bay, an exciting redeveloped waterfront district including shops, restaurants and hotels; world-famous Harvard University; shopping (no sales tax on clothing); world-class museums; observatories offering a panoramic city view; Boston Harbor cruises.*

1/2 Day Tour Options: *North of Boston to Salem (witch capital), oceanfront Marblehead and Rockport (artistic colony). West of Boston to scenic and historic Lexington and Concord. South of Boston to Plymouth and Plimoth Plantation (Pilgrim living-history museum). Whale watching available from Boston Harbor, Plymouth, Gloucester, Hyannis and Provincetown.*

Full-Day Tour Options: *Shopping, seafood meals, attractions. Or combine two of the 1/2-day tour options and/or include:*

North of Boston – *New England sea coast (Newburyport/York in Maine and Kennebunkport, Maine); New England Fall Foliage (White Mountains of New Hampshire/Green Mountains of Vermont); Factory Outlet Shopping in Maine and New Hampshire.*

South of Boston – *Boston & Plymouth; Factory Outlet Shopping in New Bedford and Fall River, Cape Cod; Cape Cod (Hyannisport, Sandwich and Provincetown); Newport mansions in Rhode Island; the islands of Martha's Vineyard or Nantucket; Connecticut coast including Foxwood's Gambling Casino.*

West of Boston – *Old Sturbridge Village, Pioneer Valley & Springfield, The Berkshires, the Boston Symphony in Tanglewood in the summer.*

Multi-Day Tour Options: *New England sea coast and mountains; New England/Nova Scotia with cruise; Boston–Montréal–Old Québec; New England/Eastern Canadian Maritimes; Cape Cod and islands in Massachusetts; New England and Niagara Falls; New England and New York City.*

The Greater Boston Convention & Visitors Bureau and New England-based receptive tour operators will be working with the World Cup 1994 organising committee to facilitate tour operator requests. For further information fax your request to Sue Papetti on (617) 424 7664.

BOSTON WORLD CUP PLAYED AT THE FOXBORO STADIUM

WORLD CUP '94

WORLD CUP BOSTON

Boston

BOSTON SPORTS TRIVIA

- ★ *The first Boston Marathon, the oldest in the United States, was held in 1897. It is still held annually on Patriot's Day.*
- ★ *Basketball was invented in Springfield, Massachusetts, in 1891 by Dr James Naismith.*
- ★ *The Basketball Hall of Fame is located in Springfield, Massachusetts, 1½ hours from Boston.*
- ★ *A soccer ball was used in the first basketball game played in Springfield, Massachusetts.*
- ★ *Boston was the first American city to join the National Hockey League in 1924 with the Boston Bruins hockey team.*
- ★ *Tennis was introduced in the United States in 1874 and the first tournament was played in Nahant, north of Boston.*
- ★ *The first Davis Cup tennis match was played in Boston at the Longwood Cricket Club.*
- ★ *The New England Sports Museum is located at the Cambridgeside Galleria, minutes from Boston.*
- ★ *Tours of the Boston Garden, where the Celtics basketball team and the Bruins hockey team play, are a favourite of sports fans around the world.*
- ★ *Boxing Great John L Sullivan was born in Boston and won the national championship in 1882.*
- ★ *Fenway Park, where the Boston Red Sox still play, is the oldest and smallest baseball park in the major leagues.*
- ★ *The Boston Celtics basketball team has won the world championship 16 times since 1960.*
- ★ *Ted Williams Highway (Route 9) was named to honour this Boston Red Sox legend.*
- ★ *Volleyball was founded in 1895 in Holyoke, Massachusetts, 1½ hours from Boston.*
- ★ *Baseball Hall of Fame legends who spent their entire careers with the Boston Red Sox include: Bobby Dorr, Ted Williams and Carl Yastrzemski.*
- ★ *Boston Red Sox Greats include Cy Young, Babe Ruth, Ted Williams, Carl Yastrzemski, Larry Bird and Bill Russell.*
- ★ *Boston Bruins Greats include Bobby Orr, Phil Esposito and John Bucyk.*
- ★ *Bill Rogers of Boston won the Boston Marathon four times.*
- ★ *The Head of the Charles Regatta in Boston, Cambridge, is the world's largest regatta held on a single day.*
- ★ *The Francis Quimet Museum of Golf is in Weston, Massachusetts, 30 minutes from Boston.*

THE LOCATION Boston, located in the centre of the east coast of Massachusetts, is the largest city in New England. Surrounded on three sides by water, Boston is an important harbour town with strong links to the sea. The city of Boston is 124 sq km (48 sq miles) and is the centre of a larger metropolitan area of 2849sq km (1100 sq miles). The State of Massachusetts is conveniently located in the heart of New England and borders the other New England States of New Hampshire, Maine and Vermont to the north, Connecticut and Rhode Island to the south, and New York to the west.

THE LANDSCAPE Massachusetts is a state that has landcapes to suit every eye. As Massachusetts is one of the oldest states in America, it is full of fascinating historical towns. But for the pure nature lover, there can be no disappointment. The southern shoreline of Cape Cod, with its scrub pine and sweeping sand dunes, is one of America's most popular regions, especially for those who love their sun and sand placed within an atmosphere of New England charm and culture. Inland, the Massachusetts countryside is full of quiet ponds, old farms, weathered roadside taverns and sturdy colonial churches overlooking quaint village greens, all scattered among the gently rolling landscape. In the west of the state can be found The Berkshires, a range of rolling hills and mountains. Famous for its fall foliage, its many trees and woods burst into colourful splendour from the middle of September until the end of October.

THE CULTURE AND HISTORY The state of Massachusetts is one of the oldest and most significant states involved in shaping the history of America. From the moment the Pilgrims arrived on the *Mayflower* at Plymouth Rock, the story of America unfolds. The events leading up to the American Revolution originated mainly in Boston, from the Boston Tea Party in Boston Harbor; to Paul Revere's midnight ride out of the city to warn the countryside that the British were coming; to Bunker Hill, the site of the first battle between the British and the Americans on June 17, 1775. Many important statesmen and politicians have been residents of Massachusetts, from Samuel Adams who signalled the Boston Tea Party, to John F Kennedy, whose family home, the 'Kennedy Compound', can be seen in Hyannisport. Some of America's most important writers also came from Massachusetts, including Henry Wadsworth Longfellow, Harriet Beecher Stowe, Nathaniel Hawthorne and Ralph Waldo Emerson. All in all, visitors will find the state a nexus of history and culture.

WHAT MAKES MASSACHUSETTS SPECIAL With a mix of colonial charm, urban sophistication and world-class hotel and meeting facilities, Boston is a dynamic destination for World Cup '94. The metropolitan area boasts some 20,000 hotel rooms, 14,000 of which are in Boston and Cambridge. Boston is the nation's most walkable city, as well as having an excellent public transportation system, and taxis are readily available throughout the city.

HISTORIC WALKING TOURS

Boston's popularity as a destination goes far beyond its physical attributes. Boston's role in shaping American history is unique among all other cities. People are eager to see the places where the American Revolution was conceived and began. From Paul Revere's House to the Boston Tea Party Ship to the Old North Church, history is on every corner in Boston.

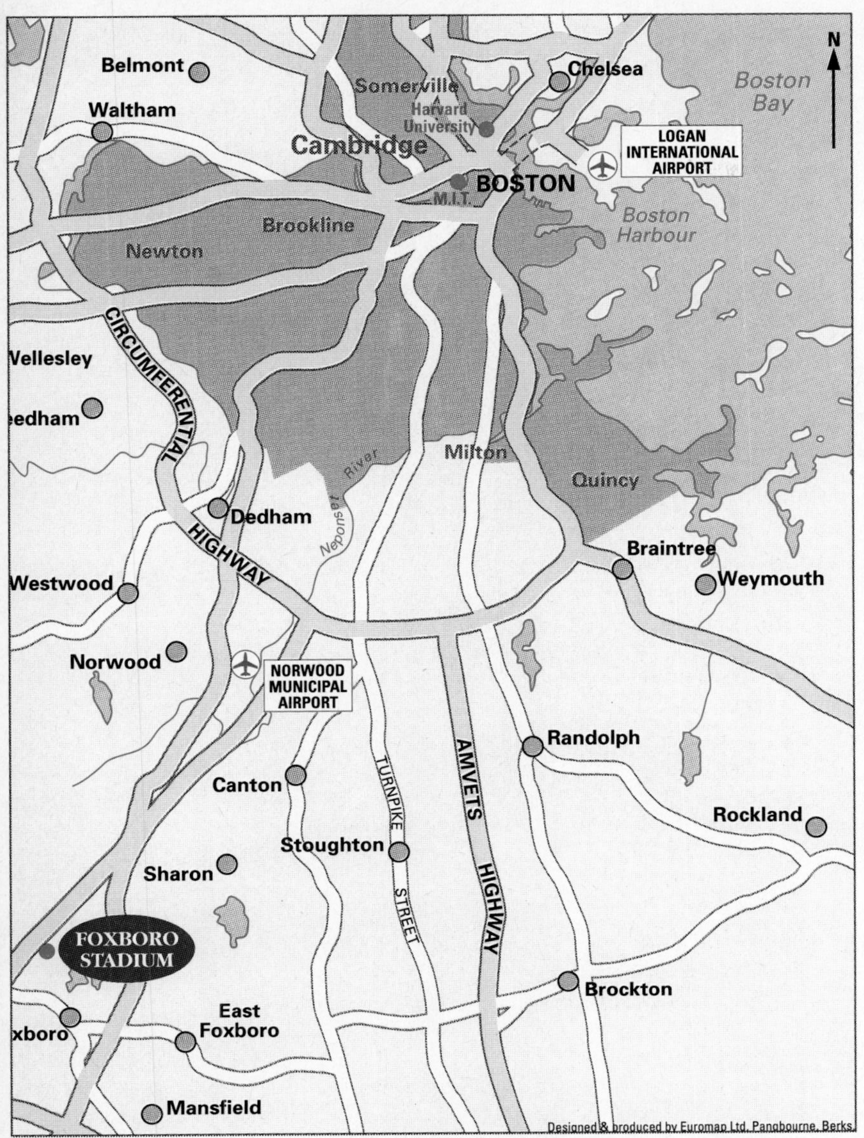

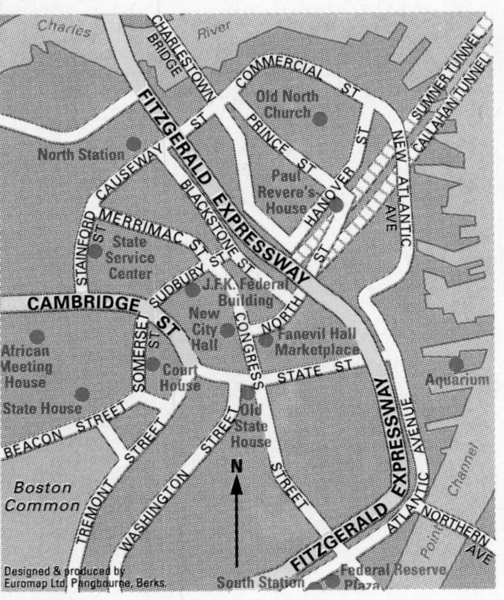

★ THERE WILL BE SPECIAL BUSES FROM THE AIRPORT TO THE STADIM DURING WORLD CUP '94.

WORLD CUP '94

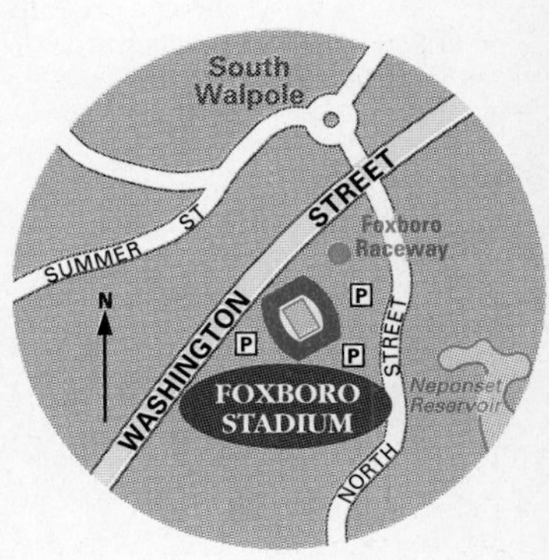

FOXBORO STADIUM DETAILS

Telephone: (508) 543 0350.
Fax: (508) 543 1409.
Playing Field Surface: *Natural grass.*
Seating Capacity: 60,290.
Luxury Suites: 666 *attendees in* 42 *suites.*
Superboxes: 104 *attendees in* 2 *boxes.*
Press Box Capacity: 175 (122 *in main press area,* 20 *seats in lounge area).*
Concession Stands: 23.
Restrooms: 10 *men,* 10 *women.*
First Aid Locations: 2. *One in the East concourse, one in the West concourse.*

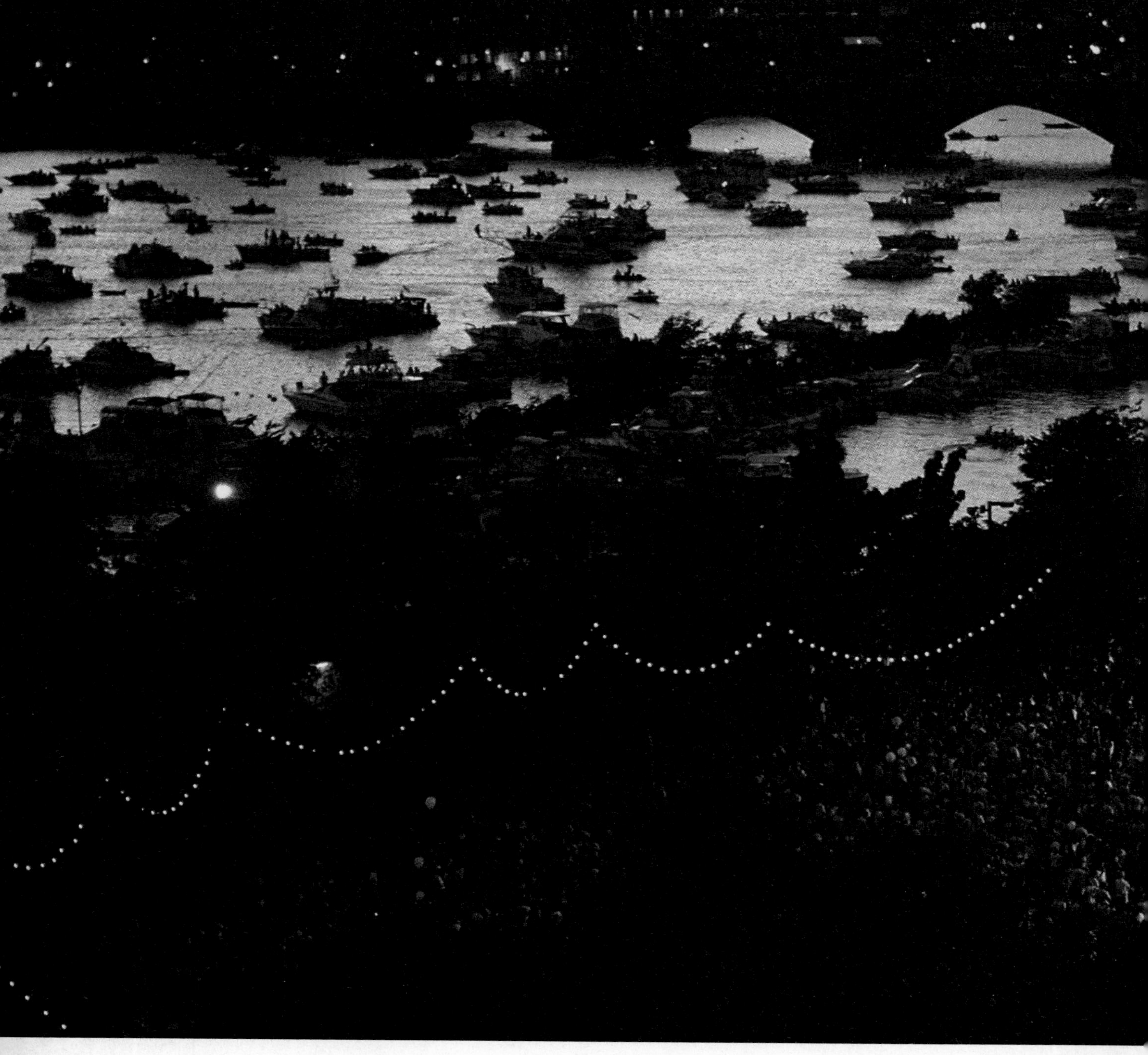

The Roar Of The Crowd, The Nor
And You Haven't Ever

This summer, as you begin to make travel plans for people heading to the United States to see 1994 World Cup Soccer, send them to one of the most historical, cultural, accessible cities in the world–Boston, the walking city. The city where every-thing is so close, all you need to bring are your trainers. From the Boston Pops playing the 1812 Overture under a dazzling sky of fireworks on

The Freedom Trail

Boston's premiere attraction, *The Freedom Trail*, is a walking tour through historic Boston, encompassing 16 of the most treasured sites in American history. The Freedom Trail is an actual red line painted on the sidewalks and streets of Boston. Besides guiding a visitor to the historic sites, the Freedom Trail is an excellent way to tour the city as it winds through many of the city's diverse neighbourhoods. Some of the historic sites on the route include *Boston Common*, the oldest public park in the country; the *Old State House*, where the Declaration of Independence was first read to Boston's citizens; the *Granary Burying Ground*, where many of America's signers of the Declaration of Independence are buried; *Paul Revere's House*, built around 1680 and considered the very oldest building in Boston; *King's Chapel*, built in 1754 and where the British troops worshipped; and *Old North Church*, where Sexton Robert Newman hung two lanterns in the steeple to signal that the British were heading towards Concord. The National Park Service offers free guided tours of the Freedom Trail for individuals and groups (telephone (617) 242 5642 for additional information and tour reservations).

Black Heritage Trail

Another walking tour, *The Black Heritage Trail*, explores the history of Boston's 19th-century black community as it guides the visitor past ten historic sites along the north slope of Beacon Hill. The heart of Heritage Trail is the *African Meeting House*, the oldest standing black church in the USA. The Meeting House became known as the 'Black Faneuil Hall' because of its status as the centre of political activity. The African Meeting House has been recently restored and is open to the public for tours, special exhibits and group functions. Other sites of interest along

FOXBORO STADIUM

the trail include *George Middleton House*, built by a black colonel during the American Revolution; *John J Smith House*, home of the distinguished black statesman who migrated from Virginia; and the *Charles Street Meeting House*, where such famous abolitionists as Frederick Douglas, Soujourner Truth and Wendall Phillips spoke from its pulpit. For additional information on the Black Heritage Trail and the African Meeting House, contact the *Museum of African American History* at (617) 742 1854.

FANEUIL HALL MARKETPLACE

Every day of the year, Faneuil Hall Marketplace is one of America's first and foremost urban attractions. From the break of dawn till the wee hours, its bubbling brew of 150 shops and restaurants, street performers and special events serves up food, fun and great people-watching for some 14 million guests annually. Retail pushcarts originated at the Marketplace and there are as many as 55 manned year-round by artisans and entrepreneurs offering hundreds of unique handcrafted and specialty items. Shops are open Monday to Saturday from 1000-2100 and on Sunday from 1200-1800. Restaurants and pubs are open until late in the evening. The Marketplace is easy to get to and comfortable to amble around in. Nestled in downtown Boston, between the Financial District and Government Center, it is convenient to the Freedom Trail, the 'T' Train and the Central Artery.

ENDLESS ENTERTAINMENT

With a wide array of diverse and interesting attractions, visitors to Boston are never at a loss for something to do. Boston's many museums, concert halls, theatres and nightclubs are always buzzing with activity and excitement. From the internationally acclaimed *Museum of Fine Arts* and *Museum of Science* to the famous *Boston Symphony Orchestra* and *Boston Pops* to an abundant local and pre-Broadway theatre scene, Boston's cultural and entertainment options are bountiful. Finally, Boston is one of the nation's top sports towns. When the Celtics, Bruins, Patriots and Red Sox play on home turf, the whole city buzzes with energy. Visitors cannot help but get caught up in all the enthusiasm.

CAMBRIDGE

Cambridge may sit just across the river from Boston, but it offers groups a flavour all of its own. It is a vibrant, colourful destination, best-known for its ties to Harvard University and the Massachusetts Institute of Technology and rich in history, culture, the arts and sciences. Cultural Cambridge combines hustle and bustle with leisurely sightseeing and museum touring. For shopping, the first place to hit is Harvard Square. 'The Square' is filled with bookstores, boutiques, unusual stores and non-stop activity. In terms of hotels, Cambridge offers groups many options. Seven major hotels are located in Cambridge, offering more than 2000 hotel rooms. Eclectic, eccentric and exciting, Cambridge is alive with youthful energy anytime of the year.

WEST OF BOSTON

Lexington and Concord

The picturesque towns of Lexington and Concord compliment any visit to the Boston area. It was on Lexington Green in the earling morning hours of April 19, 1775, that Captain John Parker of the Colonial Militia announced "Don't fire unless fired upon. But if they mean to have a war, let it begin here." Those words and the battle that followed changed the course of history. Popular sites in Lexington include the *Minute Man Statue*, *Buckman Tavern*, *Munroe Tavern* and *Hancock-Clarke House*. In Concord, the *Old North Bridge*, *Minute Man National Park*, the *Homes of Louisa May Alcott*, *Nathaniel Hawthorne* and *Ralph Waldo Emerson* and *Walden Pond*, made famous by Thoreau, are recommended. In addition to the historical attractions in this area, there are several hotel properties that can accommodate groups of all kinds. When creating day trips from Boston, Lexington and Concord are perennial favourites. The towns are only a 45-minute drive from Boston.

FOXBORO STADIUM

★ **FOR INFORMATION ON TICKETS TO WORLD CUP '94, SEE PAGE 1066.**

FOXBORO STADIUM

Foxboro Stadium has been the home of the New England Patriots for 20 years. However, to the people of New England, Foxboro Stadium has meaning far beyond the Patriots Football Club. As one of the busiest stadia in the country, Foxboro Stadium also presents popular entertainment extravaganzas on a regular basis during the spring, summer and autumn months. Over the past few years, such names as U2, Guns 'n Roses, The Rolling Stones, David Bowie and Madonna have taken centre stage. For the past two years, the stadium has hosted a day-long National Earth Day Concert featuring such talent as Indigo Girls, Steve Miller Band, 10,000 Maniacs, Jackson Browne, Midnight Oil and The Kinks, plus a host of others.

Foxboro Stadium offers a rich and diverse variety of entertainment to promoters and patrons. A full-time, professional staff from management to ticket-takers orchestrates the smooth operation of football games, concerts and special events. The stadium's choice location between Boston and Providence gives it an incredible population base from which to draw. New and innovative programmes are constantly being sought and the top-level management at the facility is one of the most approachable in the business.

FOXBORO STADIUM LOCATION

Foxboro Stadium is located on Route 1 in Foxboro, 26 miles south of Boston and 30 miles north of Providence, Rhode Island. An added benefit is Foxboro's proximity to other upper East Coast cities – 85 miles from Hartford, Connecticut and 192 miles from New York City.

TRANSPORTATION TO FOXBORO STADIUM

Air: *Boston's* Logan International Airport *provides a shuttle service to New York every half hour and direct flights to major US cities and international locations.* Mansfield Municipal Airport *accommodates corporate and private planes, and* TF Green Airport *in Warwick, Rhode Island has connecting flights to major cities.*
Rail: *MBTA commuter rail service is available for many large events directly to the stadium. Check with Boston Soccer at (617) 523 9494 for availability of service and fares during the World Cup.*
Car: *The route from Logan Airport to Foxboro by car is Route 1A South to Boston through the Sumner Tunnel to Route 93 South, then to Route 128 North, then to Route 95 South. Take Exit 9 onto Route 1 South. The stadium is 3 miles up on the left.*

Sturbridge
Old Sturbridge Village has been re-created as a rural New England town of 150 years ago, featuring demonstrations of the daily tasks of blacksmithing, weaving, buttermaking and sheepshearing. Costumed villagers wander about the homes, shops, businesses and meeting houses of a bygone era. Visitors can relax by the waterfalls and have a picnic lunch, watching the beautiful sunset over Cedar Lake, or spend the day shopping at all the antique, craft and reproduction furniture shops.

The Berkshires
In the far west of the state lie the beautiful Berkshire Hills and the Mohawk Trail, an Indian footpath that is now a 101km (63-mile) highway passing through some of the finest scenery in New England. The area attracts many trekkers and sightseers for its natural beauty, as well as hordes of music-lovers in the summer who swarm out to Tanglewood where open-air classical music concerts are performed by some of the finest orchestras and conductors in the world.

SOUTH OF BOSTON

Plymouth
Plymouth offers a resort-oriented, seaside setting that's within driving distance of Boston. Historic Plymouth, the oldest town in the country, is where the Pilgrims settled in 1620 after arriving on the *Mayflower*. Here you can view the *Mayflower II* (a reproduction); *Cranberry World,* a free museum maintained by the Ocean Spray Cranberry Company in the heart of 'cranberry country' or *Plimoth Plantation*, a re-creation of a 1627 Pilgrim village, where visitors can talk to 'Pilgrim' settlers who dress, act and speak like members of the original community.

Quincy
Known as 'the City of Presidents', it is the birthplace of John Adams and John Quincy Adams and home of the *Adams National Historic Site* mansion. The site offers an excellent historical interpretation of the Adams' contribution to our country.

Cape Cod and the Islands
The location of the region's most famous ocean resorts, this is an ideal spot for a wonderful retreat from the everyday routine. Elaborate beachfront resorts, along with small inns and cottages, allow groups of all kinds to enjoy the privacy, relaxation and resort atmosphere of Cape Cod and the Islands. 'The Cape', as it is affectionately called, boasts 483km (300 miles) of beaches, great seafood restaurants, sports activity, summer theatre, historical attractions, gift stores and museums. The best sites include the *Sandwich Glass Museum* and *Heritage Plantation* in Sandwich, the *Cape Cod National Seashore* from Eastham to Provincetown and the *Kennedy Memorial* in Hyannisport. Surfing, fishing, boating, swimming and sun-bathing are favourite activities in Cape Cod.

The two islands of Martha's Vineyard and Nantucket are located off the coast of Cape Cod. They can be reached by ferry from Hyannis, Woods Hole and New Bedford and air transportation is available from Boston, New York City and several 'Cape' towns. Martha's Vineyard is the larger and closer of the two islands, located 11km (seven miles) offshore. There are four key points of interest: Edgartown, Vineyard Haven, Oak Bluff and Gay Head. Nantucket, 48km (30 miles) off the coast, boasts cobblestone street charm and houses from the whaling days of yore. Both islands feature sailing, biking, golf courses, fishing and swimming, as well as other recreational activities.

NORTH OF BOSTON

Salem
North of Boston, Salem has the charm and lure of the sea. It is one of the country's oldest cities and its history is rooted in shipping and trade. The streets retain much of their 18th-century charm. Famous for its witchcraft hysteria in 1690 and subsequent witch trials, Salem has a *Witch Museum*. Other sites worth seeing include

WORLD CUP 1962 : THE MOST PICTURESQUE STADIUM THE WORLD CUP HAS EVER SEEN IS THE SALLS ALITE STADIUM IN VINA DEL MAR SURROUNDED BY FORESTS ON TWO SIDES AND THE PACIFIC OCEAN ON THE REMAINDER.

Pickering Wharf, the *House of Seven Gables*, the *Witch House*, the *Essex Institute*, the *Salem Maritime Historic Site* and the *Peabody Museum*.

Marblehead and Newburyport

A seafaring village whose narrow streets feature 18th-century homes and curio shops, Marblehead has many fine restaurants and makes for a wonderful stop on group tours and pre- and post-convention trips. Further north, Newburyport, the smallest city in the State, and birthplace of the United States Coast Guard, offers waterfront restaurants, quaint boutiques and miles of captivating coastline, including the sandy beaches of Plum Island.

Gloucester and Rockport

The Cape Ann towns of Gloucester and Rockport are also situated on Massachusetts' north shore. A 1- or 2-day trip to Gloucester should include visits to the *Rocky Neck Art Colony*, the *Hammond Castle*, *Paper House* and the *Beauport Museum*.

Located just a few miles from Gloucester, Rockport is one of the nation's oldest established art colonies. Visitors can explore Rockport's *Bearskin Neck*, a narrow peninsula filled with galleries, antique shops, boutiques and novelty stores. Whale-watching expeditions and harbour cruises are also popular group activities in Gloucester and Rockport. Both towns feature fine seafood restaurants and small inns.

Lowell

In the heart of the Merrimack River Valley, Lowell is the home of the American Industrial Revolution and the American labor movement. The *Lowell Heritage State Park* and the *Lowell National Historic Park* should not be missed. Here, visitors can travel by barge on a 9km (5.5-mile) canal voyage through old textile mills and power plants.

THE WAY TO THE WORLD CUP

THE AIRPORT

Logan International Airport is the gateway to Boston and the New England region. With 22 million passengers and 400,000 tons of cargo annually, Logan is the 10th busiest airport in the country and the 14th busiest in the world. As America's fourth-ranked gateway to Europe, Logan is served by more than 17 international airlines and serves 3 million international travellers each year. International passenger arrivals have been growing steadily at Logan, as more international travellers have chosen Boston and New England as a holiday destination. Logan is widely recognised as a safe airport and a user-friendly one, and for international travellers the service is world class.

Customs & Immigration

Unlike other international gateways, Boston Logan International Airport is noted for a fast and easy customs and immigration clearance process. During busy summer travel periods, additional customs agents are on staff, and an extra claims area is put in place to speed up international travellers.

Airport Facilities

International travellers are welcomed by multi-lingual interpreters, public information agents and roving ambassadors who can answer questions in nine different languages. Assistance and information is also available at Massport's information booths (in all terminals except 'B') which are open daily until the last scheduled international arrival. The *Boston Business Center*, located in Terminal C, offers a multitude of services including travel insurance, photocopying, conference room rental, workspace rental, Federal Express drop-off, fax transmissions, telephone and suite rental, foreign currency exchange, American Express moneygrams and cash advances for Visa, Mastercard and Discover cardholders. Foreign currency exchange and cash-points/service tills are available to all passengers at Logan. International travellers (who often have extra time on their hands) can enjoy a

BOSTON WORLD CUP GAMES

Boston is all geared-up for World Cup Soccer 1994! Boston games will take place at Foxboro Stadium on the following dates:

FIRST ROUND GAMES: June 21, 23, 25 & 30.

QUALIFYING GAME: July 5.

QUARTERFINAL GAME: July 9.

At present, more than 500 qualifying matches involving nearly 140 nations are being played to determine which 22 teams will join defending champion Germany and the host USA team in 1994. In December 1993, the final draw will be held to determine how the teams will be grouped and in which cities they will play the first round game.

Soccer is looming larger not only on Foxboro Stadium's landscape, but throughout New England and the USA. Summer 1994 will see the first-ever US-hosted World Cup, with six games to be played at Foxboro Stadium. Over the past two years the stadium has hosted three US Cup games, bringing the excitement of national soccer to the area's many avid soccer fans.

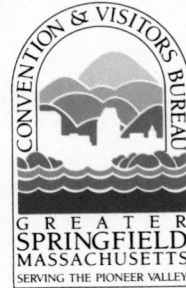

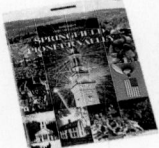

FESTIVALS AND EVENTS IN BOSTON DURING THE WORLD CUP

April to October
Boston Red Sox Baseball
Professional baseball at historic Fenway Park in the centre of Boston.

All Summer
Metro Parks Esplanade Concerts
Every summer on the Esplanade alongside the Charles River, a variety of outdoor free concerts and films take place at the Hatch Shell on the Esplanade.

Mid-June
Cambridge International Fair
Ethnic performers, food and crafts.

Late June
Copley Square Book Festival
This fair includes 100 bookstalls, children's storytellers and performers.

July 4
Boston Pops 4th of July Concert
Outdoor concert and fireworks at Charles River Esplanade.

Beginning of July
Boston Harborfest
Harborfest is a celebration of America's Independence and the Boston Harbor. More than 100 events over a 5-day period, including concerts, cruises and fireworks.
13th Annual Chowder Festival
Boston's best restaurants compete for the 'best chowder'. Visitors choose.

Mid-July
US Pro Tennis Championships
The oldest American tournament held at Longwood draws top tennis pros.
Bay State Games
Amateur competition of 13 sports to include baseball, soccer and wrestling.

July to August
Italian Feasts
The North End honours different patron saints with festivals of ethnic foods, decorations and brass bands.

food court with restaurants and concessions that offer everything from sushi to burgers. For travellers with children, Kidport in Terminal C is a great place to wait and relax at the same time.

Renovations & Modernisation
To better serve the growing number of international passengers, the Massachusetts Port Authority (Massport) plans to upgrade terminal facilities and passenger areas at Logan as part of the $1-billion Logan Airport Modernization Program. At Terminal E, the international arrivals terminal, an additional floor of passenger space will be created in the existing building, and a new and expanded federal customs and immigration centre will be built adjacent to the existing building. Plans also call for the eventual construction of a new west concourse with four new gates.

TRANSPORTATION FROM LOGAN AIRPORT TO BOSTON

Boston's Logan International Airport enjoys the extraordinary convenience of being located less than two miles from Boston's financial, medical, cultural and educational centres. Logan is well served by a full array of ground transportation services providing rapid transit to downtown and the suburbs, including car rental, taxis and airport limousines; an airport water-shuttle to downtown Boston; and a well-developed network of scheduled bus services to all regions of Massachusetts and New England.

Airport Buses

Massport Shuttle Buses: Provide free service between all Logan terminals and the MBTA Blue Line Airport subway station every 8-12 minutes from 0530-0100. Shuttle Bus 22 serves Terminals A and B. Shuttle Bus 33 serves Terminals C, D, E, the State Police and Massport's Administration Building. Shuttle Bus 11 is for transport between all airline terminals, but does not stop at the MBTA Blue Line Airport Station. For further information, telephone (617) 722 5503.
Airways Transportation: Service operates to major hotels every 30 minutes Sunday to Friday and every 60 minutes Saturday from 0800-2200. The hotels included in the destinations are *Colonnade Hotel, Copley Plaza, Copley Square, Hilton Hotel, Howard Johnson's, Lenox Hotel, Marriott Hotel, Midtown Hotel, Park Plaza Hotel, Sheraton Hotel, Tremont House* and *Westin Hotel*. The fare is $7.50. For further information, telephone (617) 442 2700.
City Transportation: Operates to downtown Boston hotels every 30 minutes 0715-2115, seven days a week. Fare is $7.50. For further information, telephone (617) 321 2282.
Peter Pan: Operates buses from Logan Airport to Peter Pan Terminal in downtown Boston. Buses depart from the airport at 0840, 1015, 1115, 1215, 1315, 1415, 1515, 1600, 1910 and 2035 Monday to Friday. On Saturday and Sunday, buses depart at 1015, 1115, 1215, 1315, 1415, 1515, 1600, 1910 and 2035 (Sundays only). Handicapped-accessible buses are available on 24-hour notice. Fare is $7. For further information, telephone (800) 237 8747.

MBTA Blue Line Subway

'T' Trains run every 8-12 minutes 0530-0100 daily. Fare is 85 cents. Visitor Passports, offering unlimited transportation on all 'T' Trains and bus lines, are available at the Airport 'T' station daily between 1200-1900 and cost $9 for a 3-day pass and $18 for a 7-day pass. For further information, telephone (617) 722 5503.

Airport Water Shuttle

Operates between Logan Airport and downtown Boston's financial district at Rowes Wharf. Free 'Airport Water Shuttle' buses provide frequent service between the Logan boat dock and all airline terminals. Connections are available to South Shore and Charlestown commuter boats at Rowes Wharf. Water shuttles run every 15 minutes 0600-2000 and every 30 minutes Sunday from 1200-2000 (there is no service on Saturday). Fares are $8 one-way for adults, $4 one-way for senior citizens and children under 12 are free.

Shuttle Vans

Logan Link at South Station: Nonstop deluxe shuttle-van service runs between Logan Airport and South Station in downtown Boston's financial district. Weekday schedules are coordinated with commuter rail services at South Station. Shuttle vans run every 30 minutes 0700-0900 and 1530-1830 Monday to Friday (there is no service on weekends). Fares are $5 one-way (or $2 one-way for MBTA Visitor Pass holders). Children under 12 and Logan Airport employees travel free.

Airport Handicap Van: There is a free handicap van service between Logan terminals. To request service, use the toll-free 'Van Phone' in the baggage claim areas, or telephone (617) 561 1769. The service is available 0530-2300 daily.

Taxis

Taxis are available at all hours at all terminals. Flat-rate fares are in effect to points beyond a 12-mile radius of downtown Boston; ask the driver or Logan dispatcher for the exact fare in advance. Fares to downtown Boston and Cambridge average about $10-$18, depending on traffic.

TRANSPORTATION TO DESTINATIONS OUTSIDE BOSTON

Logan Express Buses

Logan Express-Woburn: Operates from Logan Airport to Woburn every 30 minutes 0630-2000 weekdays and every 60 minutes 2000-2300 (the last bus leaves at 2345). On Saturday, buses operate every 60 minutes 0700-2300. Sunday service departs every 60 minutes 0700-1300, every 30 minutes 1300-2000 and every 60 minutes 2000-2300 (the last bus leaves at 2345). The fare is $5 and children under 12 are free. For further information, telephone (800) 23 LOGAN.

Logan Express-Framingham: Operates from Logan Airport to Framingham every 30 minutes 0630-2300 Monday to Friday (last bus leaves at 2345). Saturday service is 0700-2300 and Sunday service is every 60 minutes 0700-1300 and every 30 minutes 1300-2300 (last bus leaves at 2345). Handicapped-accessible buses are available with 24-hour notice. Fares are $8 Monday to Friday, and $5 Saturday and Sunday. Children under 12 are free.

Coaches

C & J Trailways: Coaches depart to Newburyport every 1-2 hours from 0730-2120, seven days a week. The fare is $14. For further information on the service, telephone (800) 258 7111.

M and L Transportation: Coaches depart to Bedford, Burlington, Chelmsford, Lowell and Woburn every 30 minutes from 0730-2300 Monday to Friday. Saturday service runs every 60 minutes 0630-2200 and Sunday service runs every 30 minutes 0830-2300. Fares are $15-$18. For further information, telephone (617) 665 7791.

Flight Line, Inc: Operates to Andover, Chelmsford, Haverhill, Lawrence, Lowell, Methuen and Tewksbury every 30 minutes 0900-2300 and by reservation 2330-0830, 24 hours a day and seven days a week. Fares are $22-$24. For reservations and information, telephone (800) 245 2525.

Peter Pan: Operates to Amherst, Northampton, Springfield and Worcester every 1-2 hours 0840-2035 Monday to Friday, and from 1015-1910 Saturday and Sunday. Handicapped-accessible buses are available with 24-hours notice. Fares are $14-$19.80. For further information, telephone (800) 237 8747.

Shuttle Vans

Marlborough-Westborough Shuttle: Departs to Marlborough and Westborough every 90 minutes from 0615-2245, everyday. For more information, telephone (800) 245 2525.

Limousines

McCarty Limousine Service: Scheduled services are at 0800 and 1745 Monday to Friday from Logan to Acton, Concord, Fort Devens and Leominster. Fares are $12-$13. For non-scheduled services, telephone (800) 675 4122.

Littleton Limo & Transportation Inc: Operates from Logan to Littleton. Fare is $34. For further information, telephone (508) 486 4600.

Destination Information:

Boston & Massachusetts
Greater Boston Convention & Visitors Bureau
PO Box 490
Prudential Tower
Boston, MA 02199
Tel: (617) 536 4100.
Fax: (617) 424 7664.
Massachusetts Office of Travel & Tourism
13th Floor
100 Cambridge Street
Boston, MA 02202
Tel: (617) 727 3201.
Fax: (617) 727 6525.
Berkshire Visitors Bureau
Berkshire Common, Plaza Level
Pittsfield, MA 01201
Tel: (413) 443 9186.
Bristol County Convention & Visitors Bureau
PO Box 976
70 Second Street
New Bedford, MA 02741
Tel: (58) 997 1250.
Fax: (508) 997 9090.
Cape Cod Chamber of Commerce
Hyannis, MA 02601
Tel: (508) 362 3225.
Fax: (508) 362 3698.
Franklin County Chamber of Commerce
PO Box 790
395 Main Street
Greenfield, MA 01302
Tel: (413) 773 5463.
Fax: (413) 773 7008.
Martha's Vineyard Chamber of Commerce
PO Box 1698
Vineyard Haven, MA 02568
Tel: (58) 693 0085.
Fax: (508) 693 7589.

Mohawk Trail Association
PO Box 722
Charlemont, MA 01339
Tel: (413) 664 6256.
Fax: (413) 458 2767.
Nantucket Island Chamber of Commerce
Nantucket, MA 02554
Tel: (508) 228 1700.
Fax: (508) 325 4925.
North of Boston Convention & Visitors Bureau
PO Box 642
Beverly, MA 01915
Tel: (508) 921 4990.
Fax: (508) 927 8108.
Plymouth County Development Council
PO Box 1620
Pembroke, MA 02359
Tel: (617) 826 3136.
Fax: (617) 826 0444.
Revolutions & Textiles of the Merrimack Valley Convention & Visitors Bureau
Howe Building
11 Kearney Square
Lowell, MA 01852
Tel: (508) 459 6150.
Fax: (508) 454 7637.
Greater Springfield Convention & Visitors Bureau
34 Boland Way
Springfield, MA 01103
Tel: (413) 787 1548.
Fax: (413) 781 4607.
Worcester County Convention & Visitors Bureau
33 Waldo Street
Worcester, MA 01608
Tel: (508) 753 2920.
Fax: (508) 754 8560.

FASCINATING FACTS

BRAZIL AND GERMANY HAVE BOTH WON THE CUP THREE TIMES, MAKING THEM POSSIBLY THE MOST FORMIDABLE TEAMS IN WORLD SOCCER HISTORY (GERMANY HOLDS THE RECORD FOR APPEARANCES IN THE FINAL (6) AND THE SEMI-FINAL (9).

TWC Limousine & Taxi: Operates from Logan to Westford and the Greater Lowell area. A mobility-impaired service is available. Fares are $18-$28. For further information, telephone (508) 692 8880.
Robert's Limousine Service: Operates from Logan to Massachusetts' North Shore. A mobility-impaired service is available. Fare is $16. For further information, telephone (800) 343 0194.

BOSTON GROUND TRANSPORTATION

Subway

The 'T' is your ticket to getting around Boston. Serving tourists, commuters and shoppers, it carries 680,000 people every day to 96 cities and towns. The 'T' is clean, safe and reliable. The 'T's Visitors Passport gives unlimited travel in Boston for 1 day ($5), 3 days ($9) or 7 days ($18), as well as discounts on popular attractions. For Visitors Passport sales locations, system route maps and timetable information, visit the Park Street Information Booth at the State Transportation Building, Room 5610, 10 Park Plaza, Boston, or call the Boston Customer Service Center on (617) 722 3200. Group discounts are also available – for information call the Pass Program at (617) 722 5548.

Rail

MBTA Commuter Rail: Sometimes called the 'Purple Line', it extends from downtown Boston to as far as 60 miles away. One can find the commuter rail at three subway stops: North Station, off the Green Line; South Station, off the Red Line; and Back Bay Station off the Orange line. For further information, telephone (617) 722 3200.
Amtrak: Trains for nationwide service arrive and depart from South Station (on the Red 'T' line) and Back Bay Station (on the Orange 'T' line).

Boston Trolley

Boston Trolley tours are one of the most convenient ways for visitors to experience Boston's extraordinary heritage. And Boston has three of them. Trolleys depart from one of 16 boarding stops frequently from 0900 every day of the year. Boarding stops include Quincy Market, North End-Boston Garden, USS Constitution ('Old Ironsides'), Boston Common, Beacon Hill-State House, West End, Cheers-'Antique Row', Newbury Street, Hynes Convention Center-South End, Copley Place Shopping, Copley Square, the Theatre District, South Station and Rowes Wharf-Tea Party Ship. The complete tour lasts 60-90 minutes and is entirely narrated by experienced driver/guides. Tickets are available on board the trolley at any of the 16 boarding stops.

Masspike

The Massachusetts Turnpike has earned a reputation as an 'economic lifeline', providing a means of safe, fast and efficient travel for thousands of motorists each day. The 135-mile toll highway runs from the western border of Massachusetts to the City of Boston, and the Sumner and Callaham Tunnels, the 1-mile harbour crossings connecting Boston with Logan Airport and the North Shore, are major links in a vital transport system that keeps the state's economy moving. All funds for maintenance, capital improvements, operation and policing of these facilities are derived solely from tolls and other revenues generated by users. The Authority receives no state or federal funds, and no petrol tax dollars. It is entirely self-supporting, primarily through the collection of tolls.

MICHIGAN

Including **Detroit,** gateway to the Great Lakes and Midwest.

Michigan Travel Bureau
PO Box 30226
Lansing, MI
48909
Tel: (517) 373 0670. Fax: (517) 373 0059.
Detroit Convention & Visitors Bureau
Suite 1950, 100 Renaissance Center
Detroit, MI
48243-1056
Tel: (313) 259 4333. Fax: (313) 259 7583.
Jackson Convention & Tourist Bureau
6007 Ann Arbor Road
Jackson, MI
49201
Tel: (517) 764 4440. Fax: (517) 764 4440.

TIME: GMT - 5. *Daylight Saving Time* is observed – in the greater part of the state – from the first Sunday in April to the last Sunday in October. Clocks are put forward one hour, changing at 0200 hours local time.
THE STATE: Michigan comprises two peninsulas. These are divided by Lake Michigan, and linked by one of the world's longest suspension bridges across the Straits of Mackinac. Lakes Superior, Huron and Erie also form the state's shorelines. The Lower Peninsula, mainly agricultural and industrial, contains inland lakes, meadows and sandy beaches as well as the 'Motor City' of Detroit. The Upper Peninsula is more rugged, and boasts forests, white beaches, trout streams and winter ski resorts.

TRAVEL

AIR: Approximate flight time: From Detroit to *London* is 7 hours 10 minutes and to *New York* is 1 hour 40 minutes.
International airport: *Detroit Metropolitan Airport* is 32km (20 miles) west of the city centre. Buses and taxis are available to downtown areas; car hire is also available.
RAIL: Detroit is on *Amtrak's* Chicago–Toronto line: see the *Illinois* section above for approximate journey times.
ROAD: Approximate driving times: From Detroit to *Cleveland* is 3 hours, to *Indianapolis* is 5 hours, to *Cincinnati* is 5 hours, to *Toronto* is 5 hours, to *Chicago* is 5 hours, to *Buffalo* is 6 hours, to *New York* is 13 hours, to *Dallas* is 24 hours, to *Miami* is 27 hours, to *Los Angeles* is 49 hours and to *Seattle* is 49 hours.
All times are based on non-stop driving at or below the applicable speed limits.
Approximate *Greyhound* journey times: From Detroit (tel: (313) 963 9840) to *Cleveland* is 4 hours, to *Cincinnati* is 6 hours, to *Chicago* is 6 hours, to *Toronto* is 6 hours, to *Indianapolis* is 7 hours and to *Duluth* is 19 hours.
URBAN: Most larger communities have bus and taxi services. Detroit also has a downtown rapid rail system, the *People Mover*.

RESORTS & EXCURSIONS

DETROIT: Industrial Detroit is the nation's car manufacturing centre. The oldest city in the Midwest, founded in 1701, it is now the ninth largest city in the USA, with a population of around one million. Its link with the St Lawrence Seaway, giving access to the Atlantic Ocean, means Detroit is also a major port.
Sightseeing: There are many museums, art galleries, zoos and amusement parks, and cultural events and major league sports are frequent crowd-pullers. The *Renaissance Center* houses dozens of restaurants, a 1400-room hotel and a variety of shops. *Belle Isle*, the nation's largest urban island park, offers biking, canoeing, an aquarium and a Great Lakes museum. The *Cultural Center* features the *Detroit Historical Museum*, the *Detroit Science Center* and the *Detroit Institute of Arts*, one of the largest art museums in the USA. The *Detroit Zoological Park* contains more than 5000 animals in natural settings (the grounds can be toured by tractor-train). *Greektown*, along Monroe Avenue, offers Greek food, entertainment and speciality shops. *Fort Wayne Military Museum* is one of the nation's best-preserved Civil War forts.
Excursions: Special tour books guide visitors around *Lake Michigan*, *Lake Superior* and *Lake Huron*. *Greenfield Village* and the *Henry Ford Museum* can be found at **Dearborn,** a Detroit suburb: the 12-acre indoor museum focuses on America's industrial development and the 240-acre village comprises more than 80 buildings, a train and a riverboat. *Cranbrook Educational Community* and *Cranbrook House and Gardens* are located in **Bloomfield Hills,** just north of Birmingham and 25 miles north of downtown Detroit. The grounds contain a beautiful country estate and landscaped gardens with an art museum, nature centre, planetarium, observatory and various educational institutions. **Ann Arbor** is the home of the *University of Michigan*. Michigan's *Great Lakes*, 60,000km (36,000 miles) of rivers and 11,000 inland lakes, offer boating, canoeing, fishing and watersports. **Traverse City,** on the west side of the state, is the heart of a recreational haven featuring sand dunes, resorts, golf and skiing. **Mackinac Island** is a well-known summer resort; cars are not allowed and visitors must walk, cycle or use horse-drawn carriages. Attractions include the impressive *Grand Hotel* and *Fort Mackinac*, a restored 18th-century military outpost. *Isle Royale National Park* is a beautiful wilderness island in Lake Superior.
Note: For information on attractions in neighbouring states, see above under *States A-Z*.

SOCIAL PROFILE

FOOD & DRINK: The state has a wide variety of American and ethnic restaurants. Steak and seafood are especially popular.
SHOPPING: Detroit's main shopping areas include the Renaissance Center, Greektown and suburban malls. Resorts have specialty shops and gallery districts.
THEATRES & CONCERTS: In Detroit, the *Fisher Theater* presents Broadway shows, and the *Detroit Symphony Orchestra* performs in *Orchestra Hall* (September to April) and at the *Meadow Bank Music Festival*, Oakland University (June to mid-August). The *Michigan Opera Theater* presents its spring season at the *Masonic Temple* and its autumn season at the *Fisher Theater*. Opera, ballet and drama are also performed at the *Music Hall Center* (October to December). Summer theatre is found throughout the state. *Cobo Arena* stages rock and soul concerts.
NIGHTLIFE: Includes supper clubs with star entertainment. Clubs offer a variety of music, ranging from 'Motown' soul music (which originated in Detroit) to classical music.
SPORT: Detroit offers professional **basketball, hockey, football** and **horseracing.** The state has more public-access **golf** courses than any other.
SPECIAL EVENTS: The *Ann Arbor Flower and Garden Show* in Saline and the biennial *Arts and Flowers Festival* at the Detroit Institute of Arts both take place in **April.** Detroit's *Riverfront Festivals* take place from **May to September,** including ethnic festivals and other special events featuring music, dancing and cuisine from various cultures held on weekends at Hart Plaza. In **June,** indy cars zoom around the Belle Isle Circuit during the 11th annual *Valvoline Detroit Grand Prix*. Belle Isle's various institutions host special events throughout the year, including six flower shows held in The Conservatory, and the *Wolverine 200 Bike-a-thon*. Each **June** sees over 500,000 fans line the island's shores for the *Spirit of Detroit Thunderfest*, hydroplane races and an airshow downtown on the Detroit River. The *International Freedom Festival* celebrates the friendship between Canada and the USA in **July.** Traverse City hosts the *National Cherry Festival* **(July)** and the *North American Vasa Cross-country Ski Race* **(February),** the second largest in the USA. The *Montreux-Detroit Jazz Festival* features some of the world's top musicians **(September).**

CLIMATE

Summers are warm with cool nights. Winters are cold, especially around the Great Lakes where conditions can be severe (however, there are good conditions for winter sports).

FIFA WORLD CUP GAME SCHEDULE – FINAL COMPETITION

17 June-17 July 1994

Stage	Round	Day	Date	LOS ANGELES Stadium Rose Bowl	SAN FRANCISCO Stadium Stanford	DETROIT Stadium Pontiac Silverdome	CHICAGO Stadium Soldier Field	BOSTON Stadium Foxboro	DALLAS Stadium Cotton Bowl	NEW YORK/ NEW JERSEY Stadium Giants	ORLANDO Stadium Citrus Bowl	WASHINGTON Stadium RFK Memorial	MATCHES/DAY
			matches/stadium	8	6	4	5	6	6	7	5	5	52
Third Stage	FINAL	31	Sunday 17 July	WA-D v WB-C									1
Third Stage	3rd/4th PLACE	30	Saturday 16 July	LA-D v LB-C									1
Third Stage	REST DAYS	29	Friday 15 July	REST DAY									
Third Stage	REST DAYS	28	Thursday 14 July	REST DAY									
Third Stage	SEMI-FINALS	27	Wednesday 13 July	WA v WD						WB v WC			2
	REST DAYS	26	Tuesday 12 July	REST DAY									
	REST DAYS	25	Monday 11 July	REST DAY									
Second Stage	QUARTER FINALS	24	Sunday 10 July		W1 v W2					W3 v W4			2
Second Stage	QUARTER FINALS	23	Saturday 9 July					W5 v W6	W7 v W8				2
Second Stage	REST DAYS	22	Friday 8 July	REST DAY									
Second Stage	REST DAYS	21	Thursday 7 July	REST DAY									
Second Stage	REST DAYS	20	Wednesday 6 July	REST DAY									
Second Stage	ROUND OF 16	19	Tuesday 5 July					1D v 3B/3E/3F		1E v 2D			2
Second Stage	ROUND OF 16	18	Monday 4 July		1B v 3A/3C/3D						1F v 2E		2
Second Stage	ROUND OF 16	17	Sunday 3 July	1A v 3C/3D/3E					2F v 2B				2
Second Stage	ROUND OF 16	16	Saturday 2 July				1C v 3A/3B/3F					2C v 2A	2
	REST DAY	15	Friday 1 July	REST DAY									
First Stage	GROUP MATCHES	14	Thursday 30 June					D2 v D3	D1 v D4				2
First Stage	GROUP MATCHES	13	Wednesday 29 June								F2 v F3	F1 v F4	2
First Stage	GROUP MATCHES	12	Tuesday 28 June		B2 v B3	B1 v B4				E2 v E3		E1 v E4	4
First Stage	GROUP MATCHES	11	Monday 27 June				C2 v C3		C1 v C4				2
First Stage	GROUP MATCHES	10	Sunday 26 June	A1 v A4	A2 v A3		D4 v D2						3
First Stage	GROUP MATCHES	9	Saturday 25 June					D1 v D3		F4 v F2	F1 v F3		3
First Stage	GROUP MATCHES	8	Friday 24 June		B1 v B3	B4 v B2					E4 v E2		3
First Stage	GROUP MATCHES	7	Thursday 23 June					C4 v C2		E1 v E3			2
First Stage	GROUP MATCHES	6	Wednesday 22 June	A1 vA3		A4 v A2							2
First Stage	GROUP MATCHES	5	Tuesday 21 June				C1 v C3	D1 v D2	D3 v D4				3
First Stage	GROUP MATCHES	4	Monday 20 June		B1 v B2							F3 v F4	2
First Stage	GROUP MATCHES	3	Sunday 19 June	B3 v B4							F1 v F2	E3 v E4	3
First Stage	GROUP MATCHES	2	Saturday 18 June	A3 v A4		A1 v A2				E1 v E2			3
First Stage	GROUP MATCHES	1	Friday 17June				C1 v C2		C3 v C4				2
				AB			CD			EF			

★ For information on how this schedule works see the Washington DC section on pages 1128 & 1129.

Welcome to DETROIT

Welcome to Detroit and the Pontiac Silverdome, home of the historic first indoor World Cup matches to be played on natural grass, on June 18, 22, 24 and 28.

The summer of '94 promises a host of activities in the Detroit area for World Cup ticket holders and visitors. In addition to the soccer matches, in early June the Motor City will offer an Indy Car Grand Prix Race on beautiful Belle Isle, a 1000-acre island park located on the Detroit River, just north of downtown Detroit. The Belle Isle Indy car event is the most unique and colourful race of the Championship Auto Racing Team (CART) series.

During the International Freedom Festival, Detroit and Windsor, Canada, celebrate jointly their independence and friendship during a 2-week gala in late June and early July that features more than 100 events in both countries. The Festival culminates with the largest firework display in North America each year.

For those who prefer watersports, each June the Detroit River is home to the annual Gold Cup 'Thunderfest' when the world's most powerful unlimited hydroplanes race at speeds in excess of 320kmph (200mph) as 400,000 sun-drenched fans line the shores.

Visitors to the Detroit area won't want to miss the Henry Ford Museum and Greenfield Village, the most visited indoor-outdoor historical museum in the country. Featuring a 12-acre indoor museum and an 81-acre outdoor museum, the complex hosts over one million visitors each year and is conveniently located in Dearborn.

Detroit's Cultural Center offers 17 institutions within one square mile, including the world-class Detroit Institute of Arts, Detroit Historical Museum, Detroit Science Center and the Museum of African American History. Near the Cultural Center is the city's emerging Theater District, which includes the fabulous Fox Theater, a 5000-seat former film palace that hosts a variety of performances and is the top-grossing theatre in its category in the nation.

In addition to the distinction of the 'Motor City', Detroit is the home of the Motown sound. On West Grand Boulevard near downtown Detroit sits 'Hitsville USA', the original 2-storey frame house where Motown founder Berry Gordy and legions of Detroit musicians recorded all those great hits. The building is now the Motown Museum and visitors can tour the historic Studio A where original sheet music with notes written by the Supremes are untouched since 1972. Tours are conducted seven days a week.

Metropolitan Detroit has over 28,000 hotel rooms and a freeway system that is the envy of most major US cities. Fine restaurants abound, featuring a variety of cuisine that reflects the area's diverse ethnic population.

Detroit Metropolitan Airport is undergoing a major renovation and offers non-stop flights from Amsterdam, Frankfurt/M, London, Montréal, Paris and Seoul.

Detroit, the Pontiac Silverdome and the local World Cup office welcome the opportunity to work with travel agents around the globe to ensure that soccer fans worldwide experience the most unique World Cup matches in the history of the world's largest single sporting event.

From Kurt Kosmowski, Media Relations Manager, Metropolitan Detroit Convention & Visitors Bureau

DETROIT CITY LIGHTS

HENRY FORD MUSEUM

WORLD CUP DETROIT

Detroit

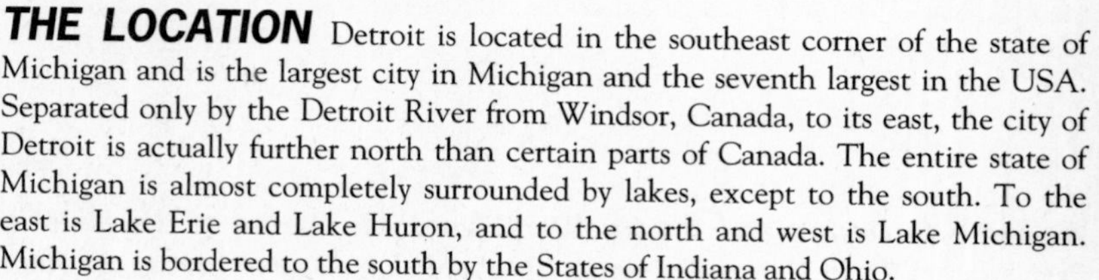

THE LOCATION Detroit is located in the southeast corner of the state of Michigan and is the largest city in Michigan and the seventh largest in the USA. Separated only by the Detroit River from Windsor, Canada, to its east, the city of Detroit is actually further north than certain parts of Canada. The entire state of Michigan is almost completely surrounded by lakes, except to the south. To the east is Lake Erie and Lake Huron, and to the north and west is Lake Michigan. Michigan is bordered to the south by the States of Indiana and Ohio.

THE LANDSCAPE The Metropolitan Detroit area encompasses 5250 sq km (2026 sq miles) and three counties – Wayne, Oakland and Macomb. Outside of Detroit, Michigan's greatest attraction has got to be the Great Lakes, which attract more than 25 million travellers a year. Michigan was carved out of the heart of the continent by glaciers, whose signature – the Great Lakes – define the state and give it its unique character. Four of the five Great Lakes surround Michigan's two peninsulas with 5152km (3200 miles) of shoreline (more than the entire Atlantic seaboard of the USA) and along with Michigan's inland lakes, there are more than 375 beaches accessible to the public. The glacial moraines have been pressed into service as ski hills, 11,000 inland lakes dot the state and 58,000km (36,000 miles) of rivers and streams and 150 waterfalls run through its 18 million acres of forest. Scores of islands punctuate the blue waters of the Great Lakes and are everything from havens of history, wildlife sanctuaries and one of America's largest urban island park, to one of America's most famous upscale resorts and America's largest island national park.

THE CULTURE AND HISTORY The oldest city in the Midwest, Detroit was discovered on July 24, 1701, when a French explorer by the name of Antoine de la Mothe Cadillac and 100 soldiers and fur traders canoed from Montréal into what is now the downtown Civic Center. They settled on this strait between two huge lakes, built a fort and started a fur trading centre named Fort-Pont-Chartrain-du-Detroit or 'Ville d'Etroit' ('City of the Strait'). It was later turned over to England as a spoil of the French and Indian War in 1760 and remained under British control until 1796. In 1805, the town became the territorial and county administrative centre with the establishment of Michigan Territory, but later that same year there was a great fire and all but one of the town's 200 structures were destroyed. The rebuilt settlement was incorporated as a city in 1815 and, with the admission of Michigan to the Union in 1837, Detroit became the state capital until 1847 when it was transferred to the present capital of Lansing.
Between 1900-1930, the population increased from 285,704 to 1,568,662, largely because of Henry Ford's car industy's moving assembly line and the $5 offered for 8 hours work a day. This was the beginning of Detroit's worldwide reputation as America's 'Motor City' and, to this day, General Motors, Ford and Chrysler (the Big Three), as well as Volkswagen of America, list Detroit as their headquarters. Also, its 51km (32 miles) of deep-water frontage on the Detroit River, connecting Lake Erie and Lake St Clair, makes it the fifth largest port. All this big business has drawn people from all over America, and the Detroit region boasts more than 100 nationalities, including large populations of African-Americans, Armenians, Asians, Bulgarians, Germans, Greeks, Hispanics, Hungarians, Irish, Italians, Native Americans, Poles and the largest Arab population outside the Middle East.

MICHIGAN SPORTS TRIVIA

- ★ *Joe Louis, the 'Brown Bomber' and former heavyweight champion, was from Detroit. His given name was Joe Louis Barrow. The present home of the Detroit Red Wings ice hockey team is the Joe Louis Arena.*
- ★ *Gordie Howe, arguably the greatest ice hockey player in the sport's history, spent most of his career with the Detroit Red Wings.*
- ★ *Ty Cobb, who registered the highest lifetime career batting in major league baseball history, played for and managed the Detroit Tigers professional baseball team.*
- ★ *In the 1930s, Detroit was often referred to as the City of Champions. The Red Wings, Tigers and American football Detroit Lions all won titles during that decade.*
- ★ *Earvin 'Magic' Johnson, arguably the greatest basketball player of all time, grew up in Lansing, Michigan, 145km (90 miles) west of Detroit, and also attended Michigan State University.*
- ★ *Former Detroit Lion players Lem Barney (member of the National Football League Hall of Fame) and Mel Farr can be heard providing background vocals on Motown Great Marvin Gaye's hit single 'What's Going On?'.*
- ★ *Boxing Great Thomas Hearns grew up in Detroit and trained at the world-famous Kronk Gym.*
- ★ *British 'soccer' star Trevor Francis came to the USA in the 1970s and starred for the Detroit Express pro soccer team. Francis' skill helped launch the sport in the Detroit area.*
- ★ *Detroit's Tiger Stadium is one of only three turn-of-the-century baseball stadiums left (Boston's Fenway Park and Chicago's Wrigley Field are the others).*
- ★ *Former US President Gerald Ford captained the University of Michigan football team in the 1940s.*
- ★ *The Pontiac Silverdome is the world's largest domed stadium and will host the first indoor World Cup games on natural grass.*

THE FIRST WORLD CUP TROPHY WAS DESIGNED BY THE FRENCH SCULPTOR ALBERT LAFLEUR. IT WAS CALLED THE JULES RIMET CUP IN HONOUR OF ITS INSTIGATOR. LEGEND HAS IT THAT DURING THE WAR, RIMET KEPT THE TROPHY UNDER HIS BED.

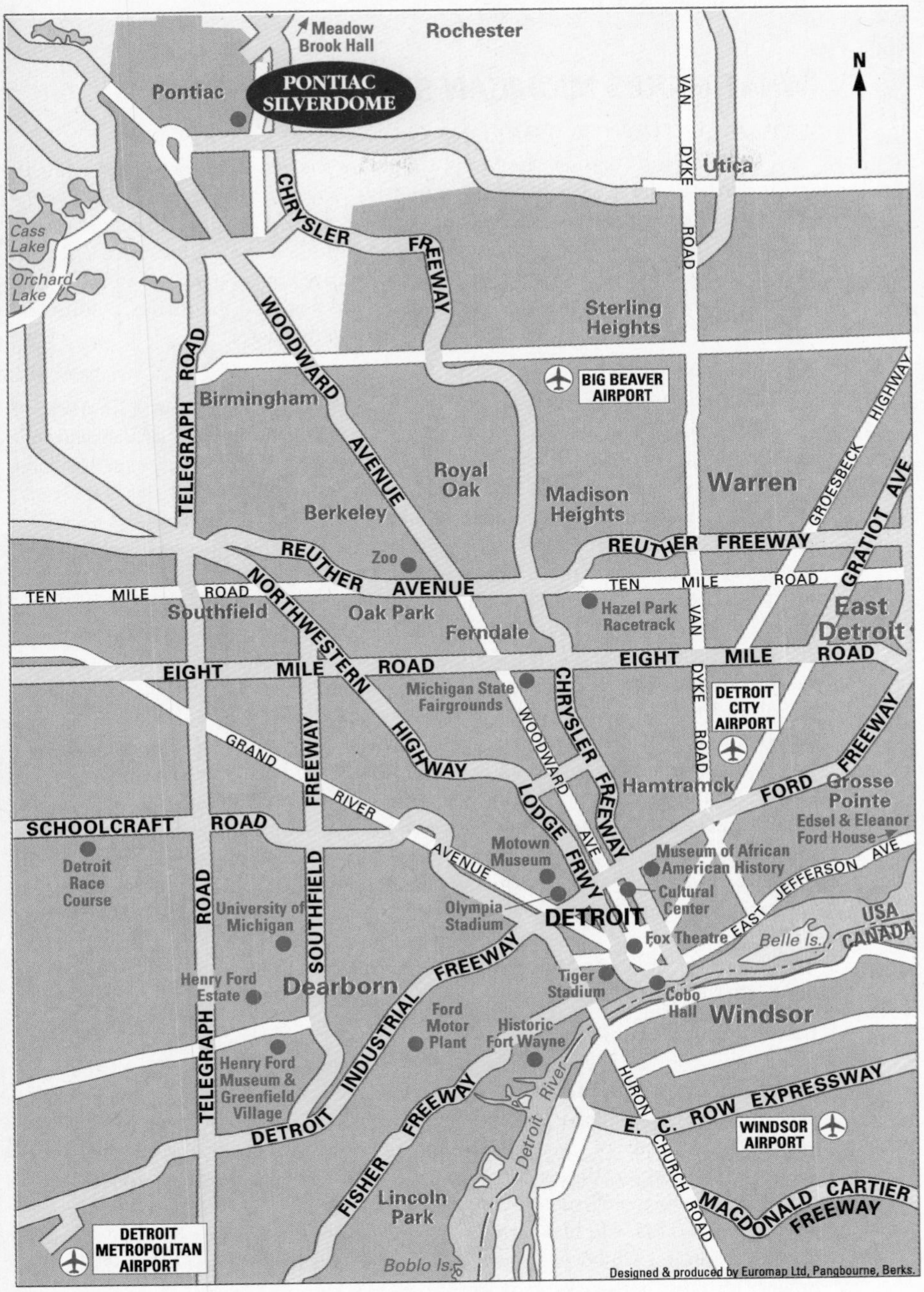

Designed & produced by Euromap Ltd, Pangbourne, Berks.

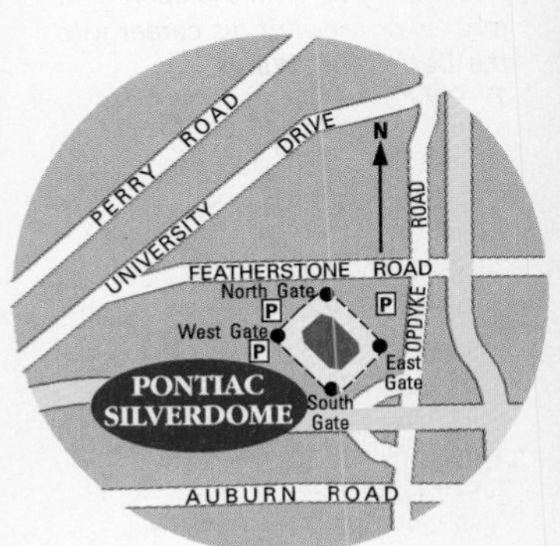

SILVERDOME STADIUM

FAMOUS PEOPLE FROM DETROIT

Detroit's list of legends is long. Here's a smattering of hometown heroes from around the metropolitan area:

Anita Baker
Sonny Bono
Aretha Franklin
Charles Lindbergh
Joe Louis
Madonna
Ted Nugent
George Peppard
Tom Selleck
George C. Scott
Lily Tomlin
Robert Wagner
Robin Williams
Stevie Wonder

Detroit

THE PONTIAC SILVERDOME

Built in 1974, the Pontiac Silverdome offers state-of-the-art comfort and theatre-style seating for 80,000 spectators. It is the world's largest air-supported, domed stadium and has enjoyed unequalled success as a major league sports/entertainment/exhibition complex.

Located within a day's drive or a 1 hour flight for 60% of the nation's population, the Silverdome boasts a solid gold record for attracting crowds to a variety of events, ranging from professional and college sports to concerts, religious crusades, political conventions, motorcross, boat shows, rodeos and truck and tractor pulls. The Silverdome is the home base for the Detroit Lions and Detroit Pistons, each of which set attendance records, respectively, for the NFL and NBA. It was the host site for the NBA All Star Game in 1979 and Super Bowl XVI in 1982 (the first NFL classic played outside the Sunbelt). The Pontiac Silverdome has even hosted a papal visit by Pope John Paul II in 1987 when 87,000 crowded inside for a glimpse of the Pope. Rock concerts ranging from 'The Who' to 'The Rolling Stones' pack tens-of-thousands inside the 'Dome'.

Strategically placed approximately 30 miles north of downtown Detroit, the Silverdome is located near several major shopping centres including the Somerset Collection which includes Neiman Marcus, Barney's, Tiffany's and other fine shops. Nearby hotels offer accommodation ranging from all-suite to budget. The stadium can also accommodate small groups, including banquets and conferences, in the spacious and elegant Stadium Club that overlooks the Silverdome floor.

★ **THERE WILL BE SPECIAL BUSES FROM THE AIRPORT TO THE STADIM DURING WORLD CUP '94.**

THE MOST VIOLENT MATCH OF THE 1934 CHAMPIONSHIPS BECAME KNOWN AS 'THE BATTLE OF BORDEAUX' WHEN NEJEDLY, THE CZECH'S STAR FORWARD, BROKE HIS LEG WHILST PLANICKA PLAYED WITH A BROKEN ARM!

WORLD CUP DETROIT

WHAT MAKES MICHIGAN SPECIAL

HOMES OF THE AUTO BARONS

As Detroit grew to become the Motor Capital of the world, opportunities to amass great fortunes grew with it. The automotive 'royalty' that emerged took on a lifestyle befitting their status. Vast estates were formed, mansions became reality and collections of art and intricate workmanship filled the impressive rooms and ornate hallways. Four of these majestic homes created by automotive wealth in the Detroit area are now open to visitors who can see firsthand the luxury, culture and hobbies that were a part of the lives of these motor magnates.

The Fisher Mansion

Lawrence Fisher, one of the founders of the Fisher Body Company and President of Cadillac Motors, spent millions of dollars of his huge fortune constructing his magnificent riverfront estate in Detroit. Completed in 1927, the Fisher Mansion was remarkable for its ornate stone and marble work, rare black walnut, rosewood parquet floors, European handcrafted stained-glass windows, Art Deco tile work and exquisite chandeliers. More than 2.8g (100 ounces) of pure gold and silver leaf highlight the decorative ceiling and moldings. Another unique feature of the estate are the boatwells, decorated with 1000 sq m (11,000 sq ft) of intricate tilework, designed to allow Fisher and his wealthy guests to dock their yachts, up to 33m (100ft) long, in the mansion's lower level. The Fishers' magnificent dining room is now Detroit's most exciting vegetarian restaurant, offering delicious cuisine amidst the opulence of polished marble floors, antique Italian serpentine rosewood pillars, Venetian silk curtains and French walnut panelling. Also on the premises is the *Bhaktivedanta Cultural Center* featuring an extraordinary multimedia presentation combining elaborate Indian sculpture with state-of-the-art audiovisual technology. The art gallery and grand ballroom display classical and contemporary paintings, as well as art objects illustrating the enlightened teachings of Indian philosophy. Situated on four acres of formal gardens with pools, fountains and roving peacocks, it is one of Detroit's most impressive attractions. The Mansion is open to the public 1230-1800 Friday to Sunday during the winter; and from 1200-1500 and 1800-2100 Tuesday to Friday, 1200-2100 Saturday and 1200-1900 Sunday during the summer. For further information, telephone (313) 331 6740.

Edsel & Eleanor Ford House

Edsel Ford, born in 1893, was the only child of Henry Ford, founder of the Ford Motor Company. Edsel served first as Secretary of the Ford Motor Company and later as its President from 1921-43. Located on 90 acres off Lake Shore Road on the Grosse Pointe shores of Lake St Clair, just northeast of Detroit, the mansion offers a world of elegance, lifestyle and quality of craftmanship rarely experienced. Construction on the 60-room house began in 1926 and was completed three years later. Edsel and his wife Eleanor brought up four children in this stately Cotswold-style mansion, for which stones were imported from the UK and split and laid by English artisans. Although many of the original paintings were left to the *Detroit Institute of Arts* by Mrs Ford in 1976, works by Van Gogh, Matisse and Diego Rivera may still be viewed in the house. Tours are available Wednesday to Sunday 1300-1600 and 1200-1600 May 1-December 31. Admission is $4 for adults, $3 for senior citizens and $2 for children. For further information, telephone (313) 884 3400.

Henry Ford Estate

Located in Dearborn, just southwest of Detroit, this 56-room Scottish baronial mansion has its own 4-storey powerhouse and a 12-car garage. Here is where the Fords lived their prosperous life, entertaining some of the world's most influential people such as Charles Lindbergh, the Duke of Windsor and President Herbert Hoover. The combined genius of Ford and Thomas Edison created the powerhouse which made the estate self-sufficient in power, heat, light and even ice. Visitors should take a walk down Jensen's Meadow to the hidden pond surrounded by a peaceful forest where Henry used to do much of his thinking. For further information, telephone (313) 593 5590.

★ FOR INFORMATION ON TICKETS TO WORLD CUP '94, SEE PAGE 1066.

Meadow Brook Hall

A bit further afield than the other estates, but worth the visit, is auto baron John Dodge's Tudor-style Meadow Brook Hall. Located north and slightly west of Detroit at Oakland University in Rochester, this 100-room mansion was never lived in by Dodge himself, who died before it was built, but became the home of his wife Matilda and her second husband, Alfred Wilson. It was begun in 1926, took three years to build and cost $4 million. Most of the construction is of native materials and there are 39 brick chimneys feeding 24 fireplaces. One of its most unique features is Knole Cottage, a home built on 2:3 scale for 12-year-old Frances Dodge. It was also the first all-electric home in the Detroit area. Donated to the state in 1957, its accompanying 1400 acres also play host every August to the Concours d'Elegance, a classic automobile show, and 'Art of Meadow Brook', an art show and sale. It is open 1000-1700 Monday to Saturday and 1300-1700 Sunday. Admission is $5 for adults, $4 for senior citizens and $3 for children (children under four years of age are admitted free). For further information, telephone (313) 370 3140.

BOBLO ISLAND

Celebrating nearly 100 years of US history, Boblo Island is situated in the Detroit River near the entrance to Lake Erie. The island is a major entertainment centre, with more than 75 amusement park rides, shows and attractions. Highlighting its history, visitors can ride a historic carousel, walk through an 1800s blockhouse and lighthouse and visit a monument erected to all sailors who died in shipwrecks on the Great Lakes. Departures to Boblo Island are made from Detroit daily by ferry, which also runs to Gibraltar, Michigan and Amherstberg, Canada. The park is open 1100-2030 Monday to Friday and 1100-2230 Saturday and Sunday, May 19-September 24. Admission is $17.50 for adults, $13.95 for senior citizens and $9.95 for children aged three to six.

THE WAY TO THE WORLD CUP

THE AIRPORT

Detroit Metropolitan Wayne County Airport is located 32km (20 miles) from the centre of Detroit. Airport facilities include seven restaurants, a cafeteria, one cocktail lounge, seven gift shops, six news-stands (and 36 newspaper machines), a bank, three cash-points/service tills, an arcade room, three duty-free shops, two barber shops, a nursery, five car-rental agencies (*Avis*, *Budget*, *Dollar*, *Hertz* and *National*) and 663 pay phones.

Approximately 13,000 on-airport parking spaces are available, plus nearby off-airport parking with a free shuttle service.The airport is also well-equipped with restroom and parking facilities for the handicapped. There are also wheelchair lift vans available (tel: (313) 941 6850) and wheelchairs are available throughout the terminals. Also, special TDD phones are available at the Marriott Hotel lobby and the Traveller's Aid Desk in the baggage claim area at the L C Smith Terminal for the deaf. Volume-control phones are available at every phone station throughout the airport. For further information, telephone (313) 942 3550.

TRANSPORTATION FROM THE AIRPORT TO DETROIT

Ground transportation to the city centre is available in the baggage claim area at all three terminals.

Airport Shuttles

Commuter Trans Vans: Services run every 30 minutes from 0645-1815 and every 60 minutes from 1900-2200. Fare is $11. For further information, telephone (800) 351 LIMO.

Commuter Transportation Company: Provides scheduled shuttles to and from the airport to all major hotels. Also offers a professional charter service with choice of tour coaches, minibuses, vans or limousines. For further information, telephone (313) 946 1000 *or* (800) 351 5466.

SILVERDOME STADIUM DETAILS

Seating Capacity: *Stadium – 80,638. Mini-dome – 35,000.*
Parking: *10,500 cars*
400 buses (on-site).
12,000 cars (off-site).
Total: 22,900.
Overall size: *770ft x 600ft.*
Main floor: *96,480 sq ft.*
Lower concourse: *25,000 sq ft.*
Roof height: *202ft.*
Constant interior temperature: *21°C (170°F)*
Main Scoreboard: *24ft x 28ft with clear instant replay, pre-programmed animation and video message capability.*
External message board: *Located on Route I-75, 2-side UNEX message board 23ft 3 ins. wide by 6ft 4 ins. deep. Accommodates up to six messages per hour, visible to 40,000 motorists daily.*
Private Suites: *102.*
Concession Stands: *38.*
Restaurant: *1.*
Banquet Rooms: *2.*
Restrooms: *44.*
Press Area: *300.*

Limousines

A Gem Limousine: Fully equipped luxury limousine service from Detroit Airport to Detroit destinations. For further information, telephone (313) 963 2120.

Taylor Winfield Ground Services Transportation: Full-service ground transportation featuring stretch limos, luxury sedans and vans to and from the airport. Fully stocked with hors d'oeuvres, beverages and continental breakfast in the morning. For further information, telephone (313) 833 2266, *or* (313) 945 5976 after business hours.

1st Class Limousine & Airport Shuttle: 24-hour airport service via limousine or luxury van. Also offers tours of city highlights. For further information, telephone (313) 569 8868.

Taxis

Taxis are available from the airport to downtown Detroit and the fare is approximately $28. For further information, telephone (313) 942 4690.

DETROIT GROUND TRANSPORTATION

Rail

Amtrak: Train services are available to destinations throughout Michigan and the USA. For further information, telephone (313) 964 5335.

Detroit People Mover: This elevated, automated transit system circles downtown Detroit's Central Business District. The system's 13 artfully decorated stations provide links with major hotels, restaurants and businesses in the area. The fare is 50 cents and children under five travel free. For further information, telephone (313) 962 RAIL *or* (800) 541 RAIL.

Buses

Detroit Department of Transportation: Provides transportation within the city. The fare is $1 and exact change is required. For schedule information, telephone (313) 933 1300.

SMART: The Suburban Mobility Authority for Regional Transportation provides buses between the city and suburbs. For information on schedules and fares, telephone (313) 962 5515.

Windsor Charter: Provides transportation from downtown Detroit to downtown Windsor, Canada. Fare is $1.50 each way. For schedule information, telephone (519) 944 4111.

Trolleys

Detroit Trolley runs four old-fashioned trolleys in the Central Business District from 0730-1800 May to November. Fare is 45 cents and exact change is required (senior citizens travel free). For further information, telephone (313) 933 1300 *or* (313) 933 8020.

Taxis

Taxis can be arranged by telephone from the following companies: Checker Cab Company (tel: (313) 963 7000), Lorraine Cab Company (tel: (313) 582 6900) *or* Southfield Cab Company (tel: (313) 356 1090).

DETROIT TROLLEY

MICHIGAN FACTS

- ★ *You are never more than 85 miles from one of the Great Lakes while in Michigan.*
- ★ *Because of the Great Lakes, the 11,000 inland lakes that dot the state and the 36,000 miles of rivers and streams that flow through it, you are never more than six miles from a body of water in Michigan.*
- ★ *Michigan has the largest flotilla of pleasure boats in the nation.*
- ★ *Michigan grows more varieties of major commercial crops (50) than any other state except California.*
- ★ *Nearly half of Michigan, more than 18 million acres, is still forested.*
- ★ *Michigan has more public golf courses than any other state in the nation (approximately 600) and more golfers per capita than any other state.*
- ★ *Michigan has more species of trees (90-100) than all of Europe.*
- ★ *Michigan is the fourth-largest exporting state in the nation, send ing $12.96 million in goods to for eign nations in 1987, and if it were an independent nation, it would rank among the top 25 producers in the world.*
- ★ *Detroit has the tallest hotel in North America – The Westin Hotel-Renaissance at 747ft.*
- ★ *The ice cream soda was invented here in 1875.*
- ★ *Detroit's Henry Ford was the first to invent airmail.*
- ★ *Detroit had the world's first under water vehicular tunnel, the Detroit/Windsor tunnel, in 1930.*
- ★ *Detroit leads the nation in potato chip ('crisp') consumption.*

FIFA WORLD CUP GAME SCHEDULE – FINAL COMPETITION

17 June-17 July 1994

Stage	Round	Day	Date	LOS ANGELES Stadium Rose Bowl	SAN FRANCISCO Stadium Stanford	DETROIT Stadium Pontiac Silverdome	CHICAGO Stadium Soldier Field	BOSTON Stadium Foxboro	DALLAS Stadium Cotton Bowl	NEW YORK/ NEW JERSEY Stadium Giants	ORLANDO Stadium Citrus Bowl	WASHINGTON Stadium RFK Memorial	MATCHES/DAY
			matches/ stadium	8	6	4	5	6	6	7	5	5	52
Third Stage	FINAL	31	Sunday 17 July	WA-D v WB-C									1
Third Stage	3rd/4th PLACE	30	Saturday 16 July	LA-D v LB-C									1
Third Stage	REST DAYS	29	Friday 15 July	REST DAY									
Third Stage	REST DAYS	28	Thursday 14 July	REST DAY									
Third Stage	SEMI-FINALS	27	Wednesday 13 July	WA v WD						WB v WC			2
	REST DAYS	26	Tuesday 12 July	REST DAY									
	REST DAYS	25	Monday 11 July	REST DAY									
Second Stage	QUARTER FINALS	24	Sunday 10 July		W1 v W2					W3 v W4			2
Second Stage	QUARTER FINALS	23	Saturday 9 July					W5 v W6	W7 v W8				2
Second Stage	REST DAYS	22	Friday 8 July	REST DAY									
Second Stage	REST DAYS	21	Thursday 7 July	REST DAY									
Second Stage	REST DAYS	20	Wednesday 6 July	REST DAY									
Second Stage	ROUND OF 16	19	Tuesday 5 July					1D v 3B/3E/3F		1E v 2D			2
Second Stage	ROUND OF 16	18	Monday 4 July		1B v 3A/3C/3D						1F v 2E		2
Second Stage	ROUND OF 16	17	Sunday 3 July	1A v 3C/3D/3E					2F v 2B				2
Second Stage	ROUND OF 16	16	Saturday 2 July				1C v 3A/3B/3F					2C v 2A	2
	REST DAY	15	Friday 1 July	REST DAY									
First Stage	GROUP MATCHES	14	Thursday 30 June					D2 v D3	D1 v D4				2
First Stage	GROUP MATCHES	13	Wednesday 29 June								F2 v F3	F1 v F4	2
First Stage	GROUP MATCHES	12	Tuesday 28 June		B2 v B3	B1 v B4				E2 v E3		E1 v E4	4
First Stage	GROUP MATCHES	11	Monday 27 June				C2 v C3		C1 v C4				2
First Stage	GROUP MATCHES	10	Sunday 26 June	A1 v A4	A2 v A3		D4 v D2						3
First Stage	GROUP MATCHES	9	Saturday 25 June					D1 v D3		F4 v F2	F1 v F3		3
First Stage	GROUP MATCHES	8	Friday 24 June		B1 v B3	B4 v B2					E4 v E2		3
First Stage	GROUP MATCHES	7	Thursday 23 June					C4 v C2		E1 v E3			2
First Stage	GROUP MATCHES	6	Wednesday 22 June	A1 vA3		A4 v A2							2
First Stage	GROUP MATCHES	5	Tuesday 21 June				C1 v C3	D1 v D2	D3 v D4				3
First Stage	GROUP MATCHES	4	Monday 20 June		B1 v B2							F3 v F4	2
First Stage	GROUP MATCHES	3	Sunday 19 June	B3 v B4							F1 v F2	E3 v E4	3
First Stage	GROUP MATCHES	2	Saturday 18 June	A3 v A4		A1 v A2				E1 v E2			3
First Stage	GROUP MATCHES	1	Friday 17June				C1 v C2		C3 v C4				2
				A B			C D			E F			

★ For information on how this schedule works see the Washington DC section on pages 1128 & 1129.

MISSOURI

Including **St Louis** and **Kansas City**, gateways to south/central USA – Missouri, Kansas, Oklahoma and Arkansas.

Missouri Division of Tourism
PO Box 1055
Jefferson City, MO
65102
Tel: (314) 751 1910. Fax: (314) 751 5160.
Greater Kansas City Convention and Visitors Bureau
Suite 2550
1100 Main Street
Kansas City, MO
64105
Tel: (816) 691 3828. Fax: (816) 691 3805.
Cape Girardeau Convention & Visitors Bureau
PO Box 98
601 North Kings Highway (63701)
Cape Girardeau, MO
63702
Tel: (314) 335 1631. Fax: (314) 335 4686.
Springfield Convention & Visitors Bureau
3315 East Battlefield Road
Springfield, MO
65804-4048
Tel: (417) 881 5300. Fax: (417) 881 7201.

TIME: GMT - 6. *Daylight Saving Time* is observed from the first Sunday in April to the last Sunday in October. Clocks are put forward one hour, changing at 0200 hours local time.
THE STATE: Missouri, in the heart of the USA, is a blend of frontier West, gracious South, the sophisticated East and industrial North. The Missouri Valley was a major pioneer route, with St Louis known as the 'Gateway to the West'. It is bounded by the Mississippi River in the east. Prairies lie north of the Missouri, the longest river in the USA, with great plains to the west, rolling hills in the south and the Mississippi cotton lands to the southeast. Its riverboat culture was immortalised by Mark Twain in 'Life on the Mississippi' and his tales of Tom Sawyer and Huckleberry Finn.

TRAVEL

AIR: Approximate flight times: From London to *St Louis* is 9 hours 10 minutes (including stopover) and to *Kansas City* is 13 hours 20 minutes (including stopover). *TWA* operate direct flights from London to St Louis.
International airports: *Lambert International Airport* is 21km (13 miles) northwest of downtown St Louis (travel time – 30 minutes). Buses, taxis, airport limousines and hire cars are available.
Kansas City International Airport (KCI) is 15km (9 miles) from the city centre (travel time – 30 minutes). Airport buses, limousines, taxis, hotel shuttle buses and hire cars are available.
RAIL: St Louis is a stopping point on *Amtrak's* Chicago–San Antonio line. Kansas City is on the Chicago–Los Angeles line. For approximate journey times on the former line, see the *Illinois* section above; for the latter see *California*. There is also a daily direct service from Kansas City (departing 1545) via St Louis (2105) and Memphis (0505 the following day) to New Orleans (arriving 1250).
ROAD: Long-distance coach companies operating in the state include *Greyhound, Gulf Transport, Great Southern* and *Vandalia.*
Approximate driving times: From *St Louis* to Kansas City is 5 hours, to Indianapolis is 5 hours, to Louisville is 5 hours, to Chicago is 6 hours, to Nashville is 6 hours, to Memphis is 6 hours, to Cincinnati is 7 hours, to Little Rock is 7 hours, to Des Moines is 7 hours, to Oklahoma City is 10 hours, to Minneapolis/St Paul is 11 hours, to Dallas is 13 hours, to New York is 19 hours, to Miami is 25 hours, to Los Angeles is 39 hours and to Seattle is 45 hours.
From *Kansas City* to Topeka is 2 hours, to Omaha is 4 hours, to Des Moines is 4 hours, to Oklahoma City is 7 hours, to Little Rock is 7 hours, to Memphis is 9 hours, to Chicago is 10 hours, to Dallas is 12 hours, to New York is 25 hours, to Miami is 30 hours, to Los Angeles is 34 hours and to Seattle is 40 hours.
All times are based on non-stop driving at or below the applicable speed limits.
Approximate *Greyhound* journey times: From *St Louis* (tel: (314) 231 4485) to Indianapolis is 5 hours, to Kansas City is 5 hours, to Louisville is 6 hours, to Chicago is 7 hours, to Memphis is 7 hours, to Tulsa is 9 hours and to Nashville is 9 hours.
From *Kansas City* (tel: (816) 698 0080) to Omaha is 5 hours, to St Louis is 5 hours, to Oklahoma City is 9 hours and to Denver is 13 hours.
URBAN: St Louis: Tour bus companies operating in the city and surrounding areas include *Gray Line, Saint Louis Sightseers* and *St Louis Tram Tours*. Hire cars and taxis are available.
Kansas City: There are public bus services around the city and surrounding suburbs. Several tour bus companies provide sightseeing trips in and around Kansas City. Hire cars and taxis are available.

RESORTS & EXCURSIONS

ST LOUIS: The largest city in Missouri and the country's largest inland port, St Louis was once a booming centre for fur traders and explorers opening up 'The West'. It is now a modern communications, commercial, industrial and cultural centre. It still retains its 'love affair' with the Mississippi River, on whose banks can be heard ragtime and Dixieland jazz. The influence of the many ethnic groups that created the city can still be seen in the German burgher houses and elegant French mansions (on its southside), and in the Italian and Serb neighbourhoods.
Sightseeing: The *Gateway Arch* on the riverfront is, at 192m (630ft), the nation's tallest memorial. It marks the starting point for settlers beginning their trek west and contains an observation deck and exhibits on the American West. Other attractions include the *Six Flags Over Mid-America* theme park; the *National Museum of Transport*; the *Missouri Botanical Garden National Historical Landmark;* and the *St Louis Zoological Park.*
Excursions: Hannibal in northeast Missouri was Mark Twain's hometown. Many museums and shows celebrate the author's life and works.
KANSAS CITY: Once the eastern terminus for some of the West's most famous trails, such as the Oregon, California and Santa Fe, Kansas City is now a major commercial and agricultural centre for the Midwest. Kansas City is situated on the state line between Missouri to the east and Kansas to the west.
Sightseeing: The *Worlds of Fun* entertainment complex has more than 120 rides, roller coasters and riverboat cruises. The *Country Club Plaza*, the nation's oldest shopping centre, was established in 1922. Other attractions include *Oceans of Fun*, a water theme park, and the *Nelson-Atkins Museum of Art.*
Excursions: Independence, 16km (10 miles) east of Kansas City, celebrates its association with Harry S Truman (he once lived there) at the *Truman Library & Museum*. Sightseeing and dinner-dance riverboat cruises are available. **St Joseph,** north of Kansas City, boasts the *Pony Express Stables Museum* and the *Patee House Museum*. The *Lake of the Ozarks* in central Missouri has more than 1600km (1000 miles) of forested shoreline and offers watersports, canoeing, golfing, tennis, caves, shows and museums. It is home to three outstanding state parks – *Bennett Springs*, the *Lake of the Ozarks* and *Ha Ha Tonka.*
Note: For information on attractions in neighbouring states, see above under *States A-Z.*

SOCIAL PROFILE

FOOD & DRINK: St Louis: Everything from elegant downtown restaurants to more casual eateries serving traditional ethnic fare. **Kansas City:** Famous for its steaks.
THEATRES & CONCERTS: St Louis: There are performances at the *Powell Symphony Hall*, the *Fox Theater* and the *Muny Theater.* **Kansas City:** The *Kansas City Philharmonic* plays at the *Music Hall. The Missouri Repertory Theater* performs on the University of Missouri's campus. Other venues include the *Lyric Theater* and *Starlight Theater.*
NIGHTLIFE: There are many clubs and restaurants on the riverfront in St Louis, some actually on the river in permanently berthed riverboats, where jazz and ragtime music is performed nightly. Discotheques exist in most modern hotels in St Louis.
SHOPPING: The most elegant shopping area in St Louis is *Plaza Frontenac* in west county, with fashionable boutiques, speciality shops, gourmet delicatessens and antique stores. The *Soulard Market* in south St Louis is a colourful and amusing place to shop on the weekends. Begun as a farmer's market in 1847, outside stalls around the main building offer fresh country goods, such as meat and home-baked items, as soon as they arrive in the city.
SPECIAL EVENTS: The following is a selection of major events celebrated in Missouri in 1993. For the complete list contact the Missouri Division of Tourism. **Mar 14 '93** *St Patrick's Day Parade* (20th Anniversary), Kansas City. **Mar 16-22** *Servies National Men's Division I Basketball Championship*, Kansas City. **Apr 16-18** *Lake of the Ozarks Dogwood Festival*, Camdenton. **Apr 29-May 2** *Storytelling Festival*, St Louis. **Apr 30-May 1** *Mushroom Festival*, Richmond. **May 7-9** *Valley of Flowers Festival*, Florissant. **May 14-16** *Harry's Hay Days*, Grandview. **May 15-16** *Maifest*, Hermann. **May 27-30** *Bluegrass Pickin' Time*, Dixon. **Jun 3-6** *Scott Joplin Ragtime Festival*, Sedalia. **Jun 5-Jul 25** *Watercolour USA*, Springfield. **Jun 11-12** *Riverfest*, Cape Girardeau. **Jun 18-20** *Hillbilly Days*, Bennett Spring State Park, Lebanon. **Jun 30-Jul 4** *National Tom Sawyer Days*, Hannibal. **Jul 3-5** *VP Fair*, St Louis. **Jul 18** *Blessing of the Fleet*, St Louis. **Jul 22-24** *Sam A Baker State Park Family Bluegrass Music Weekend*, Patterson. **Jul 23-25** *Show-Me State Games*, Columbia. **Jul 30-Aug 8** *Ozark Empire Fair*, Springfield. **Aug 14-15** *Jour de Fête*, Ste Genevieve. **Aug 19-29** *Missouri State Fair*, Sedalia. **Aug 20-22** *Fête Des Petites Cotes*, St Charles. **Aug 20-28** *Missouri River Festival of the Arts*, Boonville. **Aug 28-Sep 12** *National Quilt Festival*, Branson. **Sep 3-6** *Santa-Cali-Gon*, Independence. **Sep 9-12** *Ozark Extravaganza*, Rolla. **Sep 18** *The Great Forest Park Balloon Race*, St Louis. **Sep 20-25** *Cotton Carnival*, Sikeston. **Oct 2-3** *Harvest Fest*, Bethel. **Oct 16-17** *Maple Leaf Festival*, Carthage. **Oct 16-17** *Autumn Historic Folklife Festival*, Hannibal. **Nov 3-21** *American Royal Livestock, Horse Show and Rodeo*, Kansas City. **Nov 12-Jan 2 '94** *Ozark Mountain Christmas*, Ozark Mountain country.

CLIMATE

The region has the most continental climate of any area in the USA. Winters are cold and summers warm, with frequent heat waves.

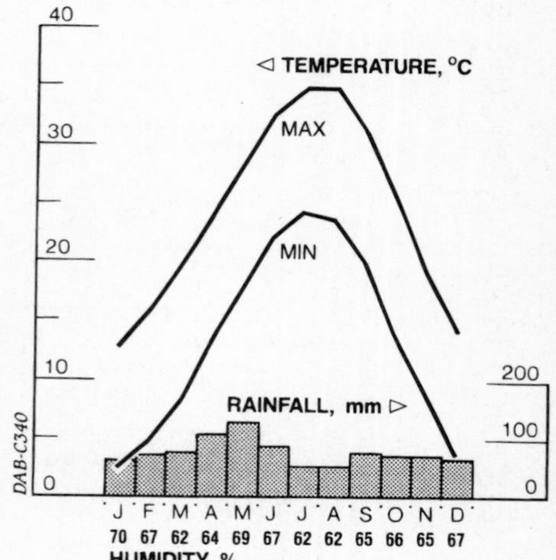

NEW JERSEY

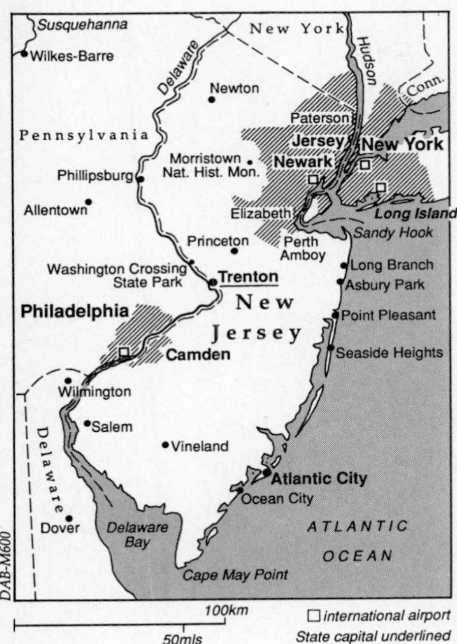

Including **Newark,** gateway to the North Atlantic States of New Jersey, New York and Maryland and the north-eastern State of Pennsylvania.

New Jersey Division of Travel and Tourism
CN 826
20 West State Street
Trenton, NJ
08625-0826
Tel: (609) 292 2470. Fax: (609) 633 7418.
Greater Atlantic City Convention & Visitors Bureau
2314 Pacific Avenue
Atlantic City, NJ
08401
Tel: (609) 348 7100. Fax: (609) 345 3685.
Newark/Meadowlands Convention & Visitors Bureau
1 Newark Center
Newark, NJ
07102
Tel: (201) 242 6237. Fax: (201) 824 6587.
Greater Wildwood Division of Tourist Information
Scheloenger Avenue
On the Boardwalk
Wildwood, NJ
08260
Tel: (609) 522 1408. Fax: (609) 729 2234.

TIME: GMT - 5. *Daylight Saving Time* is observed from the first Sunday in April to the last Sunday in October. Clocks are put forward one hour, changing at 0200 hours local time.
THE STATE: New Jersey, one of the Mid-Atlantic states, is bordered by the Atlantic Ocean to the east and the Delaware River to the west. Small in size, the state features hundreds of miles of beautiful beaches, rolling countryside and natural parkland set amidst mountains, lakes and forests. Atlantic City, one of the nation's oldest resorts, boasts luxury casino hotels and world-class entertainment by the sea. The famous Meadowlands Sports Complex is home to professional sports teams and championship horseracing. Historic towns, amusement parks and bargain shopping outlets are also scattered throughout New Jersey.

TRAVEL

AIR: Approximate flight times: See flight times from New York, as these are almost exactly the same.
International airports: *Newark International Airport (EWR)* is 27km (16 miles) southwest of midtown Manhattan. The airport has extensive facilities, including banks, a barber, shops and duty-free shops, restaurants, bars and coffee shops, a nursery and car hire (*Avis, Budget, Hertz* and *National*). There is free 24-hour bus service to other terminals and a parking lot. Bus service is available to Newark city centre and nearby New Jersey destinations.
Transportation to New York City: *New Jersey Transit* air-link bus no 302 departs every 20-30 minutes, 0605-0140 weekdays and Sundays, and every 30 minutes 0625-0155 Saturdays, and connects at Newark's Penn Station to the PATH Rapid Transit system, stopping at the World Trade Center, Christopher Street, 9th Street, 14th Street, 23rd Street and 33rd Street in Manhattan (travel time to World Trade Center – 45 minutes; to 33rd Street – 1 hour). The cost is US$4 for the bus, and US$1 for the PATH fare per person. *New Jersey Transit* express bus no 300 runs from the airport to the Port Authority Bus terminal at 42nd Street and 8th Avenue every 15-30 minutes 24 hours a day (travel time – 30 minutes). The cost is US$7 per person. For further information, contact *New Jersey Transit Center* on (201) 762 5100. *Olympia Trails* airport express bus service runs from Newark Airport to One World Trade Center in downtown Manhattan (NYC) every 30 minutes 0645-2045 weekdays and 0715-2045 weekends (travel time – 20/40 minutes). It also runs another airport express bus stopping at Grand Central Station (41st Street and Park Avenue) and Penn Station (34th Street and 8th Avenue) every 20-30 minutes between 0615 and 2400 daily (travel time – 30/60 minutes). Fares on both *Olympia Trails* buses are US$7 per person. For further information, contact *Olympia Trails* on (212) 964 6233. *Gray Line Air Shuttle* (tel: (212) 315 3006) offers a shared minibus from the airport to anywhere from 23rd-63rd Street according to passenger demand 0800-2300 at US$17 per person (travel time – 55 minutes). A 24-hour taxi service is available to downtown and mid-Manhattan (the west side between Battery Park and 72nd Street) and fares range from US$30-$31, plus tolls. For destinations on the east side of Manhattan above 14th Street, taxi drivers charge an additional US$2. There is a charge of US$1 for each piece of luggage over 24 inches in length. Limousine service is on a per person flat rate.
Transportation to New Jersey Destinations: Ground Transportation Centers are located on the lower levels of Terminals A, B and C. Information on buses, minibuses, sedans, limousines and private cars is available here, including schedules and fares. *New Jersey Transit* airlink bus no 302 departs regularly to Newark's Penn Station, the downtown business district and Broad Street Station. The fare is US$4. *New Jersey Transit* also provides a scheduled service to other New Jersey destinations stopping at Fort Dix, McGuire Air Force Base and destinations in Elizabeth, Essex, Union, Somerset and Hunterdon counties. Fares range from US$1.15-$5.30. *Princeton Airporter* run a scheduled bus service to Middlesex and Mercer counties. Fares are from US$14-$18. For further information, contact *Princeton Airporter* on (609) 587 6600. *Trans-Bridge Lines* operate a scheduled coach service to Hunterdon County. Fares range from US$9.20-$11.30. For further information, contact *Trans-Bridge Lines* on (215) 868 6001. Scheduled limousines are available to Fort Monmouth, Middlesex, Morris, Monmouth and Union counties. Fares range from US$13-$20. For further information, contact *Airport Limousine Express* on (201) 621 7300. A 24-hour taxi service is available at taxi stands which are located on the lower (arrivals) level at Terminals A, B and C. Flat rates apply to all destinations and typical fares are posted at the taxi stands. During peak hours, stands are attended by taxi dispatchers to assist passengers. Fares to the city of Newark are determined by zone. From Terminals A, B and C to points in Newark, the taxi fare will range from US$10-$14. Special 'share and save' group rates are available 0800-2400. Travelling to the airport from the city of Newark, the fare is the amount shown on the meter.
Airport transfers: *Princeton Airporter* runs a scheduled bus service from Newark Airport to JFK Airport. Fare is US$19. There is also an inter-airport helicopter service to JFK. From Port Authority Bus Terminal, connections are available to LaGuardia and JFK airports every 30 minutes from 0715-2215 via *Carey Transportation Coaches*. Fares are US$8.50 to LaGuardia and US$11 to JFK. For further information, contact *Carey Transportation Coaches* on (718) 632 0500. Limousine services are also available from Newark to JFK and LaGuardia. A flat taxi fare from Newark to JFK is US$53.50 plus tolls and to LaGuardia, the fare is US$44.50 plus tolls.
Transportation to other destinations: Limousine, bus and rail services (via *Airlink* connection) are also available to Pennsylvania, Connecticut and upstate New York.
RAIL: Penn Station in Newark serves both *Amtrak* (nationwide) and *New Jersey Transit.*
SEA: *Circle Line Tours* operates a year-round ferry service to the Statue of Liberty and Ellis Island from Liberty State Park in Jersey City. *Hoboken Ferry Service, TNT Hydrolines* and *Port Imperial Ferry* operate services to and from New York City. *Cape May-Lewes Ferry* operates a service to and from Cape May to the State of Delaware.
ROAD: Travel from New Jersey to New York City is across the George Washington Bridge or through the Lincoln and Holland Tunnels. Bridges connecting to Philadelphia, Pennsylvania are the Walt Whitman Bridge and the Benjamin Franklin Bridge. The Delaware Memorial Bridge connects New Jersey with Delaware. The New Jersey Turnpike runs north and south through the state, while the Garden State Parkway takes travellers to the shore points. **Bus:** Penn Station (McCarter Highway/Market Street, Newark) handles long-distance and regional buses.
Approximate driving times: From Newark to *Philadelphia* is 1 hour 30 minutes, to *Hartford* is 2 hours 30 minutes, to *Albany* is 3 hours 30 minutes, to *Boston* is 4 hours 30 minutes, to *Baltimore* is 3 hours 30 minutes, to *Washington DC* is 4 hours 30 minutes, to *Portland* (Maine) is 6 hours 30 minutes, to *Montréal* is 7 hours 30 minutes, to *Buffalo* is 7 hours, to *Pittsburgh* is 6 hours, to *Toronto* is 8 hours, to *Cleveland* is 9 hours, to *Indianapolis* is 14 hours, to *Chicago* is 15 hours, to *Miami* is 26 hours 30 minutes, to *Dallas* is 32 hours 30 minutes, to *Los Angeles* is 57 hours, to *San Francisco* is 60 hours and to *Seattle* is 60 hours.
All times are based on non-stop driving at or below the applicable speed limits.
Approximate *Greyhound* journey times: From New Jersey (tel: (201) 642 8205) to *Philadelphia* is 1 hour 40 minutes, to *Albany* is 3 hours, to *Washington DC* is 4 hours 40 minutes, to *Boston* is 4 hours 45 minutes, to *Montréal* is 8 hours 30 minutes, to *Buffalo* is 9 hours, to *Pittsburgh* is 9 hours and to *Cleveland* is 9 hours 30 minutes.

RESORTS & EXCURSIONS

NEWARK: Newark is the third oldest of the major US cities and the largest in New Jersey. It is a hubbub of transportation connections, arts and culture, and fast city life.
Sightseeing: The *'New' Newark Museum* is considered one of the nation's most comprehensive fine arts museums, with 66 galleries of ancient and modern art, a planetarium and a mini-zoo. *Branch Brook Park* is famous for having more cherry blossoms than Washington DC in the springtime, and plays host to an annual cherry blossom festival.
Excursions: Just east of Newark lies the *Statue of Liberty* and *Ellis Island*. The *Circle Line* ferry operates services to these important historic sites from *Liberty State Park* in **Jersey City.** North of Newark is *Palisades Interstate Park*, comprising 2500 acres of scenic roads, stunning views, picnic areas, an historic museum and nature sanctuary, and hiking and skiing trails, plus an enormous funpark that is a terrific treat for kids. For sports enthusiasts, the *Meadowlands Sports Complex*, in **East Rutherford,** northwest of Newark, is home to professional football, basketball and ice hockey teams, as well as a world-class racetrack.
ATLANTIC CITY: Known as the 'Queen of Resorts', it features 12 casino hotels, world-class entertainment, championship sporting events, gourmet restaurants, shops, beautiful beaches and the world's first boardwalk – it is one of the top tourist destinations in the USA.
Sightseeing: The *Atlantic City Boardwalk* is an attraction in itself, lined with dazzling casinos, amusement rides, games and shops on one side and by 10km (6 miles) of sand beach and surf on the other. The notorious *Trump Plaza Hotel and Trump Taj Mahal Casino* (one of the largest in the world) is to be found here (the luxurious folly of millionaire Donald Trump) and *Convention Hall*, an Art Deco architectural extravaganza which houses the world's largest pipe organ. The *Atlantic City Art Center and Historic Museum* traces the city's history as a 150-year-old seaside resort and entertainment centre, including photos and memorabilia from the Miss America Pageant which takes place here every year. *The Shoppes* on Ocean One is a modern shopping mall situated on a boardwalk pier shaped like an ocean liner.
Excursions: The Greater Atlantic City region also has a quieter side. The *Towne of Historic Smithville* is an authentic 18th-century shopping village well worth a visit, while nearby, coastal wildlife is preserved at the *Edwin B Forsythe National Wildlife Refuge*, due north of Atlantic City in **Brigantine** where the *Sea Life Museum* can also be found, open 1200-1600 Saturday and Sunday, free of charge. The region is also home to the *Renault Winery and Glass Museum* in **Egg Harbor,** one of the oldest vineyards in the USA.
TRENTON: Capital of New Jersey (and once the capital of the USA in 1794), it is also the heart of the Delaware River region. Located in the eastern heart of New Jersey, the region is steeped in history and natural beauty. Visitors to Trenton, Princeton (the home of Princeton University) and Washington Crossing State Park will learn about New Jersey's important role in the birth of the USA. Arts and culture can be experienced at the many museums and theatres in the region.
Sightseeing: *Old Barracks Museum* on Barracks Street is the site of the famous day-after-Christmas battle during the Revolutionary War and has restored soldiers' quarters, 18th-century period rooms and antiques. *William Trent House;*

Ocean City

State House, the second-oldest state hall in the USA; and *New Jersey State Planetarium and Museum*, which examines New Jersey history back to 500BC, are also well worth visiting.
Excursions: Princeton, 18km (11 miles) north of Trenton, is the home of the world-renowned Princeton University, an old and prestigious American university which sits proudly in this charming educational and historic town. The town offers excellent art exhibitions and music, as well as dance and theatre performances. Also, *Einstein's House* (when he was a Princeton University lecturer), *Princeton University Art Museum, Bainbridge House, Clarke House* on the *Princeton Battlefield*, and *Drumthwacket*, a stately Greek Revival Southern-style mansion which is now the Governor's official residence. **Camden,** a town 27 miles south of Trenton in the Delaware River region, has *Walt Whitman's House*, the *Campbell Soup Museum* and the *New Jersey Aquarium*. Historic **Salem,** 33 miles south of Camden on Route 45, has 60 18th-century buildings along *Market Street*, museums, exhibits and 500-year-old *Salem Oak* near the court house. Camping, canoeing, swimming, fishing, horseriding and hiking can be enjoyed in a venture out to the *Pine Barrens*, a national preserve that ranks as the largest wilderness area east of the Mississippi River.
SHORE REGION: Encompassing a portion of New Jersey's 127 miles of coastline, the Shore Region is ideal for vacations and excursions, boasting white sandy beaches, rolling farmland and historic sites.
Sightseeing: Dotting the shore are exciting towns like **Seaside Heights** and **Point Pleasant,** which are home to boardwalk amusement rides and games. Quieter towns like **Spring Lake** and **Ocean Grove** offer quaint bed & breakfast inns. **Asbury Park,** home of rock star Bruce Springsteen, is a somewhat dilapidated seaside circus town, but with a vibrant nightlife that will appeal to certain thrill-seeking nightowls. Exciting amusement rides and the world's largest safari park are located at *Six Flags Great Adventure* in **Jackson Township,** where a full day should be set aside for fun and games. *Allaire State Park* in **Farmingdale** is an 18th-century restored bog-iron mining village offering period shops, bakeries, churches, a blacksmith, a ride on the *Pinecreek Railroad train*, a nature centre, museum and picnic area, along with craft/antique shows and square-dancing on weekends.
Excursions: Cruises can be taken aboard the *River Belle* or *River Queen*, large stern-wheelers that ply the waters off **Point Pleasant Beach**, where deep-sea fishing boats are also available. Party cruises can be taken aboard the *Sandy Rock Lady*, an authentic paddle-wheel steamer which runs from the Atlantic highlands harbour and offers a scenic ride along the historic Shrewsbury River. Fishing is also good in the *Manasquan Inlet*.
SKYLANDS REGION: Some of the most beautiful and unspoiled land in the northeastern USA is found in the Skylands Region of northwestern New Jersey. It is a perfect vacation area for all seasons: during the winter, ski resorts such as Vernon Valley/Great Gorge provide challenging skiing for all skill levels; and during the summer, camping, hiking and watersports can be enjoyed at *Action Park*, one of the largest self-participating theme parks in the world. Numerous state and national parks offer camping and hiking opportunities; these include the Delaware Water Gap National Recreation Area. Revolutionary War historic sites, wineries, museums, antique stores and bed & breakfast inns, scattered throughout the region, are available in all seasons.
Sightseeing: The *Clinton Historical Museum* and *Spruce Run Reservoir* in **Clinton** has quaint shops and charming restaurants in an idyllic setting. *Waterloo Village* in **Stanhope** is a restored 18th-century village of colonial craftshops and homes, and hosts a summer concert series of jazz and bluegrass festivals. *Morristown National Historic Park* in **Morristown** was the site of George Washington's army winter encampments and the *Ford Mansion*, now a museum. Battle re-enactments take place throughout the year. Special treats for the children include *Land of Make Believe* in **Hope,** 30 acres of childhood fantasies – the largest childrens' amusement park in New Jersey, and *Fairy Tale Forest* in **Oak Ridge,** an enchanted forest with life-size animated characters depicting famous fairytales.
Excursions: Hiking, canoeing, fishing and river rafting on the *Delaware River* can be organised during the summer and ice-skating, tobogganing, snowmobiling, skiing and ice fishing are available during the winter. State parks ideal for winter sports include *Jenny Jump, Swartswood, Wawayanda, Worthington, Allmuchy, Spruce Run* and *Voorhees*.
SOUTHERN SHORE REGION: Located along the southeastern tip of New Jersey on the Atlantic Ocean, is a region for those who enjoy seaside culture and heritage, boardwalk amusements, fishing and birdwatching.
Sightseeing: The **Wildwoods** and **Ocean City** boardwalks buzz with excitement while **Stone Harbor** and **Avalon** are quieter retreats. **Cape May,** a National Historic Landmark, is a popular Victorian seaside town which is famous for its many bed & breakfast inns, trolley tours and the superb *Cape May County Zoo*, one of the top zoos in the world. *Wheaton Village* in **Millville** is the world's largest museum of American glass with a 7000-item collection ranging from paperweights to Tiffany masterpieces. *Cold Spring Village* in **Cold Spring** is a recreation of an old farm village, with period shops and restaurants, that displays the life and crafts of yore. Stroll through 25 different gardens, teeming with greenery and fishponds, at *Leaming's Run Gardens and Colonial Farm* in **Swainton.**
Note: For information on attractions in neighbouring states, see above under *States A-Z*.

SOCIAL PROFILE

FOOD & DRINK: New Jersey offers everything from gourmet cuisine to 'home-cooking' country food, from restaurants to diners. In addition to the staple US fare of steaks, seafood and hamburgers, cuisines from around the world can be found throughout New Jersey.
THEATRES & CONCERTS: There are numerous theatres scattered throughout New Jersey that offer productions ranging from Shakespeare to contemporary works. Concerts and special performances by the renowned *New Jersey Symphony Orchestra* and famous entertainers are held throughout the year at a variety of venues including the *Brendan Byrne Arena* at the *Meadowlands Sports Complex, Atlantic City Casino Showrooms* and the *Garden State Arts Center* in Holmdel. The *Paper Mill Playhouse*, the official state theatre of New Jersey, shows musicals and plays year round, as does the *George Street Playhouse* in New Brunswick.
NIGHTLIFE: The nightclubs and casinos of Atlantic City are open until the small hours and afford a perfect haven for gamblers. Ocean City and some of the other oceanfront towns have many clubs and entertainment centres that are open late hours and the general atmosphere along the boardwalks is lively far into the evenings.
SHOPPING: Shopping in New Jersey appeals to all tastes and budgets. Upscale malls feature the famous department stores of Macy's, Bloomingdales and Saks Fifth Avenue. Terrific bargains on brand-name merchandise can be found at the Secaucus Outlet Center in Secaucus. Similarly Liberty Village and Turntable Junction outlet centres in Flemington offer equally attractive deals. Antique stores fill New Jersey's small towns while outdoor flea markets offer an eclectic array of jewellery, clothing, housewares, furniture and more. There is no sales tax on clothing in New Jersey.
SPECIAL EVENTS: There are literally dozens of festivals and events that are celebrated throughout the state each year. The following is a list of some of the major events in New Jersey in 1993/94.
Mar 1-Jun 30 '93 *The Etruscans: Legacy of a lost civilization*, Morris Museum, Morristown. **May 31** *Tour of Somerville Bike Race*, Somerville. **Jun 12-13** *New Jersey Seafood Festival*, Belmar. **Jun 14-20** *93rd US Open*, Baltusrol Country Club, Springfield. **Jul 30** *New Jersey Festival of Ballooning*, Readington. **Aug 7** *The Hambletonian* (harness racing's most prestigious race for 3-year-old trotters), Meadowlands Racetrack, East Rutherford. **Sep 18** *Miss America Pageant*, Atlantic City. **Sep 18-19** *New Jersey State Ethnic Festival*, Liberty State Park, Jersey City. **Oct 8-17** *Victorian Week*, Cape May. **Nov 26-Jan 2** *Grand Christmas Exhibition*, Wheaton Village, Millville. **Dec 25** *Re-enactment of Washington crossing the Delaware*, Washington Crossing State Park, Titusville. **Jan '94** *New Year Celebrations*.
Details of other events are available from the New Jersey Division of Travel and Tourism.

CLIMATE

See New York gateway section immediately following for information on the climate in the New Jersey area.

Welcome to NEW JERSEY

Mr Eugene Dilbeck, Director of the New Jersey Office of Tourism, has his own special message for both travel agents and visitors to New Jersey:

The New Jersey Division of Travel & Tourism has as its primary goal to differentiate New Jersey from New York and other mid-Atlantic states as a travel destination for international visitors attending the World Cup '94 competition at Giants Stadium in East Rutherford, New Jersey.

Our goal is to increase the awareness of hospitality and travel services that are available in the state – the easy access through Newark International Airport and the outstanding dining options featuring cuisines from around the world.

We are directing the state's tourism marketing efforts to national and international audiences, creating and generating a greater awareness of the many travel experiences available in New Jersey. For agents, we are producing a variety of promotional aids, including suggested tour itineraries, and variety and easy access are key considerations for packaging New Jersey. We have the state divided into six tourism regions, each remarkably different from the other, and we also have the advantage of being a 4-seasons destination. We have spectacular winter sports, some of the country's best ocean beaches, great fall foliage, casinos, museums, professional sports and major league events all year round. No matter when the client or visitor gets here, he or she will leave satisfied.

Since the World Cup will be held during the summer season, we want to make our tour operators, travel agents and consumers aware of our beautiful ocean beaches, seaside resorts and the Queen of Resort Cities – Atlantic City, the east coast's entertainment capital. New Jersey offers a variety of first-class leisure products all at good value.

The Division will strive to get this message across to all individuals affiliated with the World Cup games around the world. Our long-range goal is to establish New Jersey as an international vacation destination with access to other renowned destination points such as New York City, Philadelphia and Washington DC. Specifically, World Cup attendees should plan to stay in New Jersey and be close to Giants Stadium and enjoy a memorable vacation in New Jersey during their visit to the USA.

ATLANTIC CITY

CAPE MAY, NEW JERSEY

WORLD CUP '94

New Jersey ☆ New York

WORLD CUP NEW JERSEY/NEW YORK

TICKETS

The service agency that will handle the distribution of World Cup tickets will also handle hotel rooms, air travel and other elements necessary for the creation of a World Cup package. The particular agency will be determined in the first quarter of 1993. The World Cup Organising Committee will supervise the activities of the service agency and will retain final authority on any and all decisions including the selection of tour operators involved, the allocation and pricing of tickets and the resale of WCOC hotel inventory. Interested tour operators should write to the World Cup office in Los Angeles at World Cup Tour Operators, Suite 4400, 2049 Century Park East, Los Angeles, CA 90067, and ask for their company to be put on the tour operators database for direct follow-up by the service agency in the second quarter of 1993.

THE LOCATION Situated on the east coast of America, along the Atlantic coast, New Jersey is bordered by Pennsylvania to the west, Delaware to the south and New York to the north. Many overseas flights now arrive at New Jersey's Newark International Airport, making New Jersey a convenient stopover for many holiday destinations and slotting easily into the visitor's itinerary.

THE LANDSCAPE New Jersey is famous for its 204km (127-mile) coastline of beautiful beaches and shore towns, but what is a delightful surprise to many visitors is the variety of New Jersey's landscape. Forests and farmland form 63% of the state, and there are also 816 sq km (315 sq miles) of scenic mountain areas with sparkling lakes, ponds and streams. The variety of natural beauty in New Jersey and its favourable climate make New Jersey an attractive vacation spot for many domestic and international visitors.

THE HISTORY AND CULTURE New Jersey's first residents were the Lenni Lenape Indian tribes who inhabited the territory for over 10,000 years before Giovanni da Verrazano arrived in 1524. Throughout the 1600s, more Europeans arrived and built colonies along the continent's North Atlantic coast. New Jersey and twelve other original British colonies in the area united in the late 1700s to break away from the authority of King George III. During the Revolutionary War, nearly 100 battles were fought on New Jersey soil. Triumphant, the 13 colonies established a national government and, in 1787, New Jersey became a state in the new union.

New Jersey's historic wealth has left behind a number of jewels for visitors to see. Key battle sites and restored colonial villages can be toured, and visitors may also witness genuine blacksmith demonstrations and Revolutionary War re-enactments. Thousands of historic homes, from a 400-year-old log cabin to a Victorian mansion, welcome visitors inside to view period furniture and exhibits depicting the daily routines followed by the people of the era.

WHAT MAKES NEW JERSEY SPECIAL Of the 50 states in the USA, New Jersey is one of the few that offers such a great variety of things to see and do, all at a short distance from one another. From the joys of swimming and boating on its excellent beaches and the endless boardwalk entertainment and casinos of its famous coastal resorts, to camping, fishing, canoeing and hiking amidst its lush forests and stunning mountain regions, New Jersey offers a never-ending multitude of outdoor activities. And as if that wasn't enough, there are also sophisticated towns and cities full of museums, music halls, performance centres, sports complexes, aquariums and restaurants serving cuisines from around the world. It is no wonder that New Jersey is the seventh most visited state in the USA – and growing all the time.

Visitors arriving in 1994 for the *World Cup 1994* games will have a number of new major attractions to see.

NEW ATTRACTIONS

GIANTS

The Liberty Science Centre

The Liberty Science Center (LSC) opens in January 1993 on a 17-acre site in New Jersey's *Liberty State Park*. The park itself offers striking views of lower Manhattan,

THE PRELIMINARY ROUND STARTS ON MARCH 1 1992 AND BY THE TIME THE QUALIFICATION PROCESS IS COMPLETED IN NOVEMBER 1993, 582 MATCHES WILL HAVE BEEN PLAYED.

★ FOR INFORMATION ON TICKETS TO WORLD CUP '94, SEE PAGE 1066.

the *Statue of Liberty* and *Ellis Island* (in fact, New Jersey is a more direct and convenient base for visits to these famous attractions), whereas the Center itself, with its exhibits, activities and interactive demonstrations, gives visitors a chance to see, feel, explore and understand the natural world.

The main exhibit space is designed around three themes: the Environment, Health and Invention. The Environment Floor will feature a Living Salt Marsh, a Bug Zoo and a solar telescope mounted in a 5m (17ft -high lighthouse. The Health Floor focuses on the senses and the human body and includes a Touch Tunnel and an Illusion Labyrinth, both experiences designed to challenge the senses. The Invention Floor features exhibits explaining modern technology.

Visitors can experience many natural phenomenas in the controlled setting of the Center. Highlights include a giant 24m (80-ft) tornado of swirling mist, a 33m (100ft) Touch Tunnel that allows visitors to explore in total darkness and a spectacular laser light show that will fill the atrium with dramatic and constantly changing imagery.

In addition, the state-of-the-art facility will feature a 50m (170ft)-high observation deck and the Kodak Omni Theater, which uses the world's largest projection dome to present films that simulate real-life challenges.

Liberty Science Center will be a full-service, handicapped-accessible facility, featuring a comfortable restaurant with a spectacular view of Manhattan and a 4m (14-ft) stained-glass window, outdoor decks, museum store, convenient parking and other amenities.

Containing over 250 continually changing exhibits, the *LSC* will be a magical experience for the tourist, as well as offering the business traveller a dynamic and unusual site for corporate parties.

Ellis Island Immigration Museum

International visitors can experience three of the United States' most important historical sites in one day – the Statue of Liberty, the Central Railroad of New Jersey Terminal and Ellis Island Immigration Museum at Liberty State Park in Jersey City.

The 1-year-old *Ellis Island Immigration Museum* has welcomed millions of visitors in its very first year of operation. The Great Hall, the focal point of the island, stands as it was in 1918 where immigrants were lined up for questionining by government inspectors. The West Wing's three floors provide a group tour area on the first floor, featuring exhibits on processing and restored hearing rooms where immigrant appeals were heard; the second and third floors offer recorded tapes of immigrants' experiences. Ellis Island celebrates its 102nd Anniversary in 1994.

The Central Railroad of New Jersey Terminal was the starting point for millions of immigrants beginning a new life in the United States. Visitors are able to tour the restored terminal as well as enjoy breathtaking views of the Manhattan skyline from this waterfront park. The nation's foremost symbol of freedom, the *Statue of Liberty*, stands proudly in New York Harbor. Millions of visitors have climbed the statue's steps to witness spectacular views of New Jersey and New York.

Ferries run every half-hour from 0930-1500. Tickets cost $6 for adults and $3 for children aged 3-12. There is no admission charge to Ellis Island or the Statue of Liberty. For more information on transportation, contact *Circle Line* on (201) 435 9499.

New Jersey State Aquarium

The New Jersey State Aquarium, located at Camden in the western part of the state, opened on February 29, 1992, and is already one of the most successful aquariums in the country. It features a 750,000-gallon open ocean tank with large sharks, an outdoor seal pool and a variety of hands-on exhibits.

THE BEACHES

Holidaymakers will find that New Jersey's shoreline, which includes parts of the Southern Shore, Greater Atlantic City and Shore Regions, offers a wealth of beautiful beaches as well as a diversity of attractions that amuse, educate and entertain.

The Southern Shore region encompasses Cape May and Cumberland counties. The

THE MEADOWLANDS COMPLEX

The state-of-the-art Meadowlands Sports Complex in East Rutherford, New Jersey has been chosen as one of nine sites to host the World Cup soccer competition in 1994.

Only 20 minutes from both Newark Airport and New York City, the Meadowlands Sports Complex is America's most extensive sports facility and the home of four professional sports teams. Every year, nearly 10 million visitors attend events at Giants Stadium, the Meadowlands Arena and the Meadowlands Racetrack.

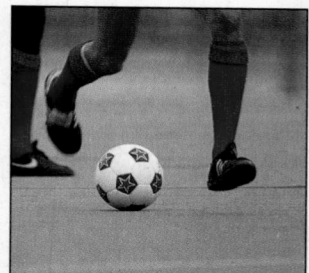

Passaic
East Rutherford
Rutherford
Meadowlands Sports Complex
GIANTS STADIUM
TETERBORO AIRPORT
Palisades Park
Bronx Zoo
Bronx
CROSS BRONX EXPRESSWAY
East-Chester bay
Yankee Stadium
BRUCKNER EXPRESSWAY
HENRY HUDSON PARKWAY
North Bergen
Nutley
Lyndhurst
HIGHWAY
McCARTER
Belle-ville
Secaucus Outlet Centre
TURNPIKE
NEW JERSEY
West New York
Hudson River
Central Park
FIFTH AVENUE
Guggenheim Museum
East River
LA GUARDIA AIRPORT
FLUSHING AIRPORT
GRAND CENTRAL
Queens
Kearny
Union City
Mus. of Modern Art
Manhattan
Empire State Building
Shea Stadium
Flushing Meadows
QUEENS BOULEVARD
EXPRESSWAY
PULASKI SKYWAY
Greenwich Village
Soho
LONG ISLAND
VAN WYCK
Newark
Jersey City
Liberty Science Center
World Trade Center
QUEENS EXPRESSWAY
NEW YORK
INTERBOROUGH PARKWAY
NEWARK INTERNATIONAL AIRPORT
Liberty State Park
Ellis Island
Statue of Liberty
FLATBUSH
ATLANTIC AVENUE
Port Elizabeth
Upper New York Bay
Brooklyn Museum
Prospect Park
CROSS BAY BOULEVARD
BELT PKWY
Bayonne
LINDEN BOULEVARD
Kill Van Kull
SHORE PARKWAY
J.F. KENNEDY INTERNATIONAL AIRPORT
N
Staten Island
VICTORY BOULEVARD
Jamaica Bay
Brooklyn
Designed & produced by Euromap Ltd, Pangbourne, Berks.

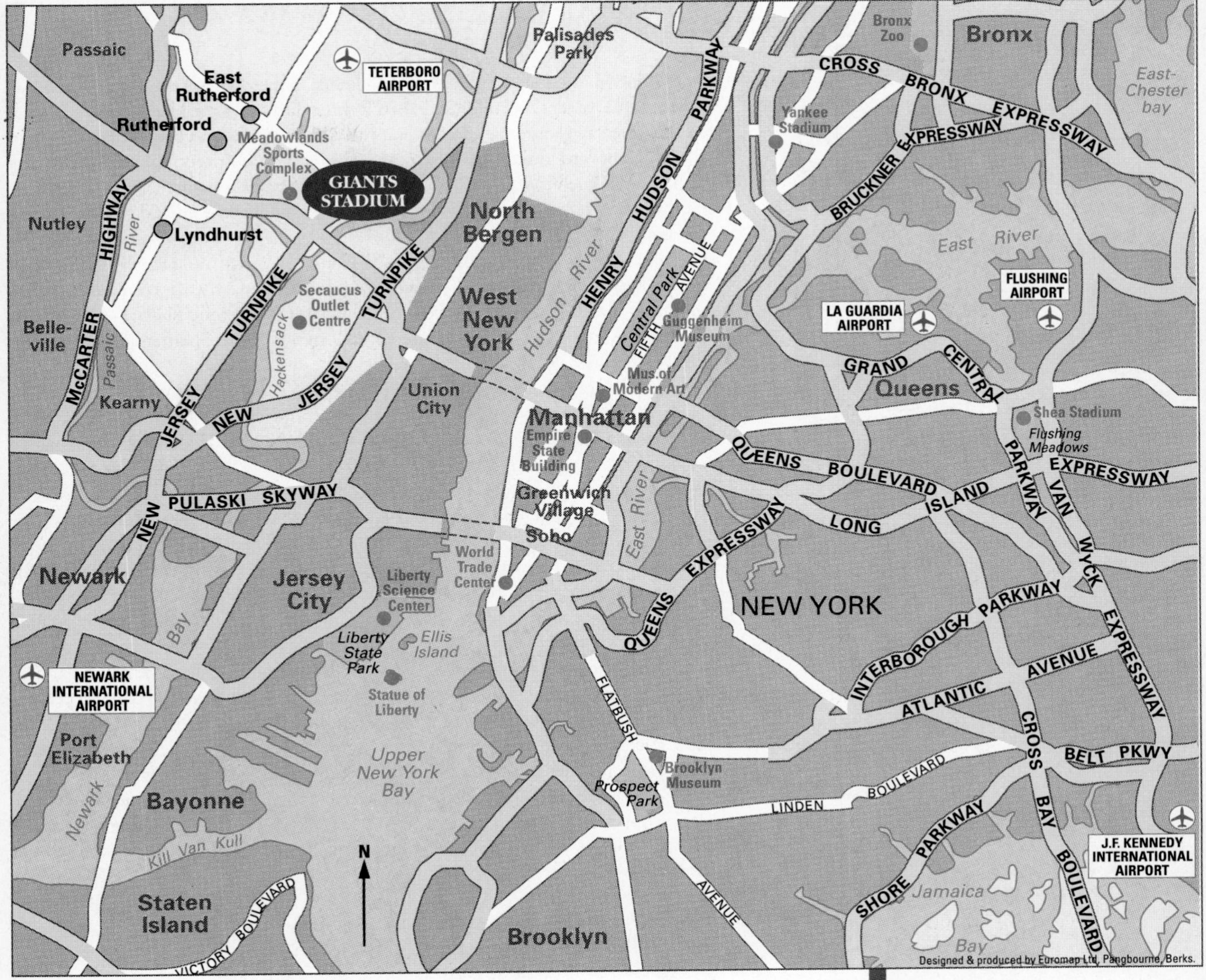

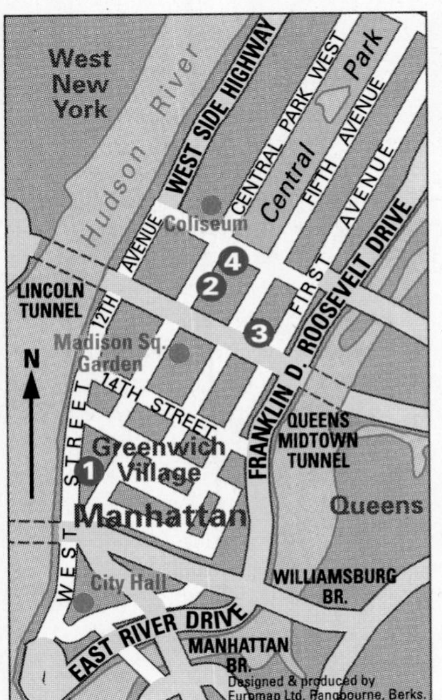
West New York
Hudson River
WEST SIDE HIGHWAY
CENTRAL PARK WEST
Central Park
FIFTH AVENUE
AVENUE
Coliseum
LINCOLN TUNNEL
12TH
FIRST AVENUE
FRANKLIN D. ROOSEVELT DRIVE
Madison Sq. Garden
N
14TH STREET
QUEENS MIDTOWN TUNNEL
Greenwich Village
Manhattan
Queens
WEST STREET
City Hall
WILLIAMSBURG BR.
EAST RIVER DRIVE
MANHATTAN BR.
Designed & produced by Euromap Ltd, Pangbourne, Berks.

1. Hotel Millenium
2. Milford Plaza
3. The Grand Hyatt (2nd Avenue)
4. St Moritz on the Park

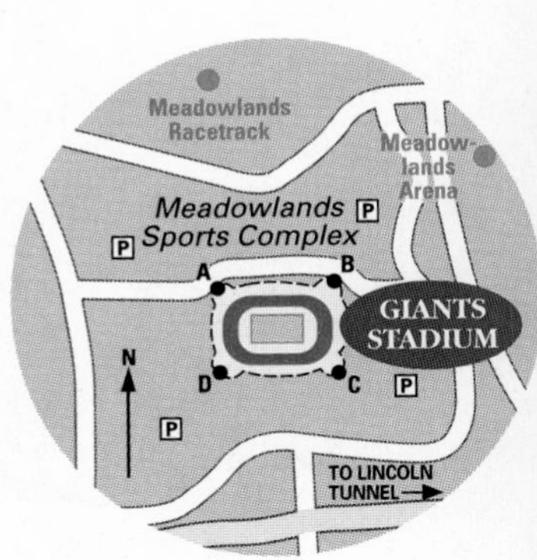
Meadowlands Racetrack
Meadow-lands Arena
Meadowlands Sports Complex
GIANTS STADIUM
N
TO LINCOLN TUNNEL

New Jersey ★ New York

GIANTS STADIUM DETAILS

The World Cup '94 games will take place in the Giants Stadium of the Meadowlands Sports Complex.

Building dimensions: 756ft by 592ft by 144ft.
Seating capacity: 76,891.
Ramps: 8.
Turnstiles: 80.
Escalators: 24.
Elevators: 4.
Ticket windows: 56.
Scoreboards: *Two Sony Jumbotron colour video scoreboards 24ft high and 32ft wide are located above the east and west seating areas. Each board contains 23,040 miniature cells (called pixels) which give the boards their colour capabilities. Next to the Jumbotrons are two Daktronics Matrix black and white scoreboards. On the north and south sides, two auxiliary boards supplement the video score-boards.*
Playing surface: *Natural grass*
Exhibition space: 19,450 sq ft.
Handicapped area: 225 *wheelchairs.*
Suites: 72.
Press Box capacity: 300.
Restaurant capacity: *The Stadium Club – 2000*
Concession stands: 40.
Restrooms: 70.

★ **THERE WILL BE SPECIAL BUSES FROM THE AIRPORT TO THE STADIM DURING WORLD CUP '94.**

GIANTS STADIUM,MEADOWLANDS SPORTS COMPLEX

town of Cape May, a National Historic Landmark, is the cornerstone of the region and features 600 Victorian-era buildings. A stroll through the town is like a journey back in time. The streets are lit by gas lamps and lined with homes and bed & breakfast inns featuring elaborate gingerbread trim and the varied architectural features of the Victorian era. Beachfront hotels, an excellent selection of restaurants, the picturesque Cape May Lighthouse, historic-home tours and special events all add to the timeless attraction of Cape May.

Other seaside towns dot the coast north of Cape May. The Wildwoods – Wildwood Crest, Wildwood and North Wildwood – are widely renowned for incredibly wide, white sandy beaches and exciting boardwalk amusements. Stone Harbor, Avalon, Sea Isle City and Ocean City complete the coastal stretch of the Southern Shore region's beach communities.

No vacationer would want to miss the excitement of Atlantic City, part of the Greater Atlantic City region and one of the nation's most popular vacation destinations. Miles of boardwalk, white-sand beaches, casino resorts and the annual Miss America Pageant provide diversions almost 24 hours a day.

Further north, New Jersey's Shore region encompasses Monmouth and Ocean counties and has garnered a fame all its own as the playground which attracts visitors year after year.

In addition to towns known for their surf, sun and sand are those towns known for their gracious atmosphere, like Ocean Grove, founded by Methodists in the late 19th century as a camp-meeting place. Its quaint houses and Great Auditorium can be toured through the Ocean Grove Historical Society. Bay Head and Spring Lake, two genteel towns along the coast, offer charming inns ideal for tranquil weekend getaways. Visitors searching for excitement will find wild amusement rides in Seaside Heights or Point Pleasant and 29km (18 miles) of shoreline fun on Long Beach Island. Lavallette, Bradley Beach, Belmar and a host of other shore towns round out the Shore region's beach communities where swimming, fishing and boating are a way of life.

Like all of New Jersey, the Shore region offers many historical and recreational opportunities. Visitors may choose to spend a day touring Monmouth Battlefield near Freehold, where General George Washington led the famous battle against the British, a day at Monmouth or Freehold racetracks or a day enjoying the amusements at Six Flags Great Adventure in Jackson.

Three historic lighthouses mark the coast of the Shore region and are also open for tours: 'Old Barney', the oft-photographed 50m (172ft) lighthouse tower at Barnegat Light; Sandy Hook Light at Fort Hancock, the oldest operating lighthouse in the United States; and Twin Lights of Navesink, a unique 2-beacon lighthouse, the first electrically operated lighthouse in the country and the site of Marconi's first ship-to-shore radio broadcast.

Whatever shore vacation visitors are looking for, the 205km (127 miles) of New Jersey coastline guarantee no shortage of either variety or quality of experience.

SPOTLIGHT ON ATLANTIC CITY

Atlantic City's 7km (4.5 miles) of broad, sandy beaches are bordered by the beautiful blue Atlantic Ocean and the picturesque Intercoastal Waterway. Ideally located at the hub of the New York City/Philadelphia/Washington DC metropolitan areas, Atlantic City is the perfect destination resort.

With such entertainers as Frank Sinatra, Diana Ross, the Rolling Stones, Kenny Rogers, Elton John, Cher, Dolly Parton and Willy Nelson, the city sparkles with excitement. Add the action of 12 world-class casinos, tempting cuisine, opulent stores and the charm of the famous Boardwalk to the mix and the city becomes the perfect place for its 32 million annual visitors.

But Atlantic City also means business. Conventions, trade shows, expositions, meetings and conferences are setting new attendance records. A $4-billion investment in new casino/convention hotels and non-casino hotels have created extraordinary meeting facilities, making Atlantic City the perfect place to mix business with pleasure.

The spacious Atlantic City Convention Center on the Boardwalk is 'new' again, thanks to a $23-million restoration programme. By 1995, a new convention centre,

New Jersey USA

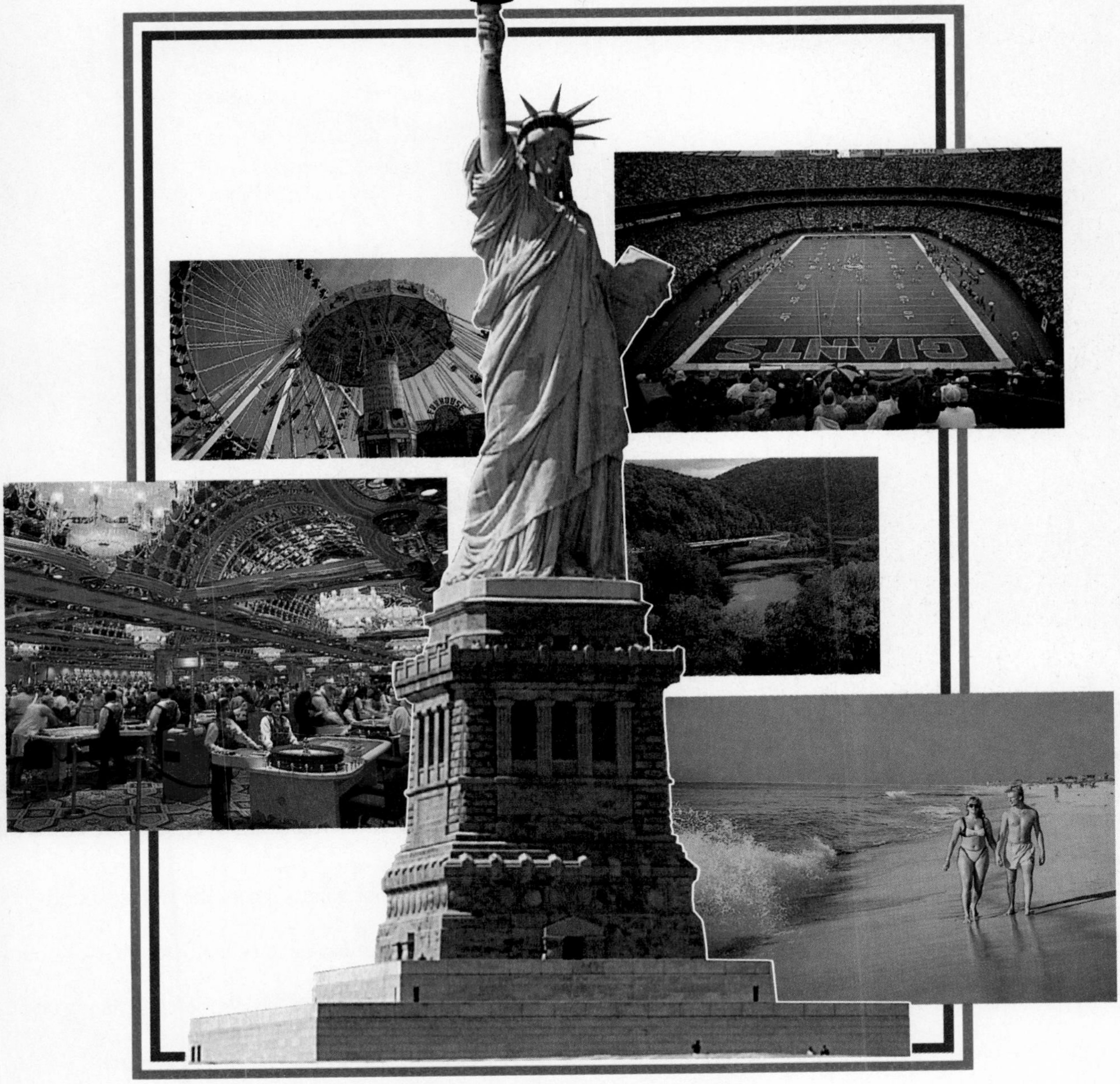

For excitement and adventure at a real value, New Jersey makes the perfect holiday. We offer miles of white sandy beaches and blue ocean, boardwalk amusements, casino games, and a variety of deluxe accommodations and dining. Sports enthusiasts will enjoy our world-class golf courses and professional sporting events. Plus, everything is easily accessible from Newark International Airport. All of which makes it possible to create a holiday with the perfect fit for every budget.

Find out more. And ask about World Cup Soccer coming our way in '94. Contact the International Travel Trade Coordinator at the NJ Division of Travel & Tourism, CN 826, Trenton, NJ 08625-0826 USA. FAX (609) 633-7418.

APPROXIMATE DISTANCE FROM NEWARK AIRPORT			
Atlantic City	174 km	Philadelphia	126 km
JFK Int. Airport	31 km	Princeton	68 km
La Guardia Airport	26 km	Trenton	80 km
Giants Stadium	18 km	Washington, DC	364 km
New York City (Times Square)	19 km		

New Jersey
YOU SHOULD SEE US NOW!

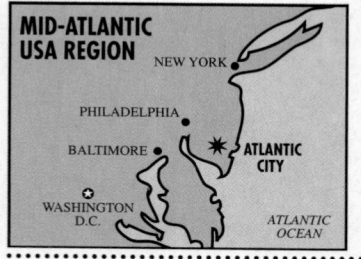

with 500,000 sq ft of exhibition space, will be completed.

This new convention centre, located at the foot of the Atlantic City Expressway, will be adjacent to the Rail Terminal, which services the *AMTRAK* Northeast Corridor. Following the recent modernisation of its terminal facilities, Atlantic City International Airport is gearing for 'take off' with an additional $35-million expansion project to double the size of the terminal and make major improvements to the parking and ground transportation facilities.

Hotel room development continues at a rapid pace led by the recently completed 295-room Ramada Renaissance Suites. Three 4-star hotels, the Trump Taj Mahal, Trump Plaza and Trump's Castle, have more than 2500 rooms. Tropworld recently added a 523-room expansion along with combined additional meeting space and Bally's Park Place boasts a magnificent 800-room tower. Other adornments of the resort skyline are the 200-room Holiday Inn on the Boardwalk and the towering 440-room Flagship Resort with its beautiful views of the ocean, bays and salt meadows.

And when the casino visitor wants to take 'time out' from the excitement of the tables and slot machines, there's plenty of golf, tennis, fishing, boating, sightseeing and shopping to satisfy anyone's desire for leisure activity.

SHOPPER'S PARADISE

Visitors are attracted to New Jersey's tremendous shopping opportunities. The state is home to two world-renowned discount outlet centres, historic towns filled with antique stores, modern shopping malls and exciting outdoor flea markets. An added incentive for shopping in New Jersey – there is no sales tax on clothing or shoes!

The vast Secaucus Outlet Center, located within 20 minutes of New York City, features over 100 outlet stores. Designer fashions, jewellery, fine china and furniture can be purchased from 20-80% off manufacturer's list prices.

Calvin Klein, Liz Claiborne, Gucci and more famous name brand merchandise can be found at the Castle Road section of the Secaucus Outlet Center, as well as at the Harmon Cove Outlet Center, the largest enclosed outlet mall in Secaucus. All stores are within easy walking distance. Harmon Cove's 'Checkerboard Food Court' offers seven eateries for hungry shoppers!

The historic town of Flemington, located an hour and a half from Manhattan, features an upscale discount shopping centre. Liberty Village Factory Outlet Complex features factory outlets, boutiques, antique shops and restaurants housed in Colonial-style buildings. Famous-name clothing, pottery, cookware, glassware and more can be purchased at bargain prices.

The Flemington Cut Glass Company has a retail outlet for china, cut crystal and glassware. Pfaltzgraff operates a discount outlet for its famous stoneware. Luxurious furs can be purchased at a tremendous discount at the Flemington Fur Company.

Historic towns like Lambertville, Lafayette, Chester, Cape May and Smithville, near Atlantic City, offer the antique lover a variety of shopping opportunities at tremendous value. Shoppers can spend an entire afternoon browsing through large indoor and outdoor flea markets that offer everything from antique tea sets to handmade items. Two famous markets are the USA's #1 Flea Market in New Brunswick and Englishtown Auction Sales in Englishtown.

For more information on outlet shopping opportunities, call Liberty Village at (908) 782 8550 or Harmon Cove Outlet Center at (201) 348 1200.

THE WAY TO THE WORLD CUP

THE AIRPORT

Newark International Airport (EWR) is 27km (16 miles) southwest of midtown Manhattan. The airport has extensive facilities, including banks, bureaux de change, barber, bookshop, chapel, dentist, information desk, lost & found office (tel: (201) 961 6230), mailbox, medical services (tel: (201) 961 2525), nursery, news-stand, telegram office, travel insurance office, baggage claim and duty-free shops, restaurant, cocktail bar, snack bar and car hire (*Avis, Budget, Hertz, Dollar* and *National*).

Giants Stadium

Home of American football's 1990 Superbowl Champion Giants and the American Football Conference Jets. The Giants have been sold out for every game they have played since October 1976. The Jets joined the Giants as residents of the stadium in 1984 and have also had mostly sold-out shows. Each fall the college American football season is launched in Giants Stadium with the Kickoff Classic, a pre-season bowl game showcasing two of the best teams from the previous year. The stadium is designed in such a way as to provide unobstructed sight lines for every fan, in addition to a close-in view of all the action that takes place on the artificial turf playing surface. High overhead, the video-matrix boards flash the latest scores and news or give spectators a second look at game action via instant replay. The Stadium has received high marks from both professional athletes and the media for its spacious team and press rooms and interview areas, and for its convenient and well-equipped training facilities. As a site for a football game, a concert presentation or any other type of entertainment event, Giants Stadium is sure to provide an enjoyable experience for spectators.

The Meadowlands (Brendan Byrne) Arena

Home of the New Jersey Nets of the National Basketball Association, this 21,000-seat arena is where you can see some of the best professional basketball stars in the world. It is also the home of the New Jersey Devils of the National Hockey League. Track and field, lacrosse, wrestling and boxing take place here, too. The arena also features lively entertainment shows, with top talent in the music, comedy and singing fields. In fact, New Jersey's own Bruce Springsteen opened the Arena in 1981 with six consecutive sold-out performances. Family shows, such as The Ringling Bros, Barnum & Bailey Circus and Ice Capades are also a major draw.

New Jersey ☆ New York

TRANSPORTATION TO NEW JERSEY DESTINATIONS

Ground Transportation Centers are located on the lower levels of Terminals A, B and C. Information on buses, mini-vans, sedans, limos and private cars is available here, including schedules and fares, and all transportation reservations can be made here.

Buses

Airlink/NJ Transit #302: A scheduled bus service is available to Newark's Penn Station, the downtown business district and Broad Street Station. The fare is $4. For further information, telephone (201) 762 5100.

NJ Transit: A scheduled bus service is available to other New Jersey destinations stopping at Fort Dix, McGuire Air Force Base, Downtown Newark, and destinations in Elizabeth, Essex, Union, Somerset and Hunterdon counties. Fares range from $1.15 to $5.30. For further information, telephone (201) 762 5100.

Princeton Airporter: Scheduled bus service to Middlesex and Mercer counties. Fares range from $14 to $18. For further information, telephone (609) 587 6600.

Coach

Trans-Bridge Lines: Scheduled coach service to Hunterdon County. Fares range from $9.20 to $11.30. For further information, telephone (215) 868 6001.

Rail

NJ Transit is the main rail service for New Jersey. For information on Northern New Jersey, telephone (201) 762 5100. For information on Southern New Jersey, telephone (215) 569 3752. For information on Atlantic City, telephone (800) 582 5946.

Limousine

Limousine service can be arranged at the Ground Transportation Centers located on the arrivals level of Terminals A, B and C at Newark Airport. ***Airport Limousine Express:*** Scheduled limousine service to Fort Monmouth, Middlesex, Morris, Monmouth and Union counties. Fares range from $13 to $20. For further information, telephone (201) 621 7300.

Taxis

24-hour taxi service is available at taxi stands which are located on the lower (arrivals) level at Terminals A, B and C. Flat rates apply to all destinations and typical fares are posted at the taxi stands. During peak hours, stands are attended by taxi dispatchers to assist passengers. Fares to the city of Newark are determined by zone. From Terminals A, B and C to points in Newark, the taxi fare will range from $10-14. Special 'share and save' group rates are available from 0800-2400. Travelling to the airport from the city of Newark, the fare is the amount shown on the meter.

TRANSPORTATION TO NEW YORK CITY

Express Buses

New Jersey Transit Express #300: Runs from the airport to the Port Authority Bus Terminal at 42nd Street and 8th Avenue every 15-30 minutes, 24 hours a day (travel time – 30 minutes). The cost is $7 per person. For further information, telephone (201) 762 5100.

Olympia Trails Express Bus: Runs from Newark Airport to One World Trade Center in downtown New York every 30 minutes from 0645-2045 weekdays and from 0715-2015 Saturday and 0715-2245 Sunday (travel time – 20/40 minutes). It also runs another airport express bus stopping at Grand Central Station (41st Street and Park Avenue) and Penn Station (34th Street and 8th Avenue) every 20-30 minutes between 0615 and 2400 daily (travel time – 30/60 minutes). Fares on both *Olympia Trails* buses are US$7 per person. For further information, telephone (212) 964 6233.

Minibus

Gray Line Air Shuttle: Offers a shared minibus from the airport to anywhere from 23rd-63rd Streets, according to passenger demand, from 0800-2300 at $17 per person (travel time – 55 minutes). For further information, telephone (212) 315 3006.

Rail

Airlink/New Jersey Transit #302: Departs every 15-30 minutes from 0605-0140 weekdays and Sundays, and every 30 minutes from 0625-0155 Saturdays, to Newark's Penn Station to the PATH Rapid Transit system, stopping at the World Trade Center, Christopher Street, 9th Street, 14th Street, 23rd Street and 33rd Street in Manhattan (travel time to World Trade Center – 45 minutes; to 33rd Street – 1 hour). The cost is $4 for the bus, $1 for the PATH fare per person. For further information, telephone (201) 460 8444.

Limousine

Limousine service is on a per person flat rate. For further information, telephone (212) 315 3006.

Taxi

Fares to downtown and mid-Manhattan (the west side between Battery Park and 72nd Street) range from $30-$31, plus tolls. For destinations on the east side of Manhattan above 14th Street, taxi drivers charge an additional $2. There is a charge of $1 for each piece of luggage over 24 inches in length.

INTER-AIRPORT CONNECTIONS

Buses

Princeton Airporter: Runs a scheduled bus service from Newark Airport to JFK Airport. Fare is $19. For further information, telephone (609) 587 6600.

Olympia Trails: Scheduled bus service runs from Newark Airport to Grand Central Terminal in midtown Manhattan every 20-30 minutes from 0615-2400, with an intermediate stop at Penn Station (34th Street and 8th Avenue). At the Grand Central stop (41st Street and Park Avenue), connections are available to either Kennedy or LaGuardia airports via *Carey Express Coaches*: to *JFK Airport* every 30 minutes 0500-0100 (fare: $11) and to *LaGuardia Airport* every 20 minutes 0600-0100 (fare: $8.50). For further information, telephone (212) 964 6233 *or* (201) 589 1188.

NJ Transit Express #300: Scheduled bus service departs from Newark Airport to the Port Authority Bus Terminal (42nd Street and 8th Avenue) every 15-30 minutes, 24 hours a day. At the Bus Terminal, connections are available to JFK and LaGuardia airports every 30 minutes from 0715-2315 via *Carey Express Coaches*. Fare is $11 to Kennedy and $8.50 to LaGuardia. For further information, telephone (201) 460 8444.

Limousines/Helicopters

Limousine services are also available from *Newark* to *JFK* and *LGA*. There is also an inter-airport helicopter service to JFK.

Taxi

The flat fare from Newark Airport to Kennedy International Airport is $53.50 plus tolls, and to LaGuardia Airport is $44.50, plus tolls.

TRANSPORTATION TO OTHER DESTINATIONS

Limousine, bus and rail services (via *Airlink* connection) are also available to Pennsylvania, Connecticut and upstate New York.

WORLD CUP USA 1994 UNVEILS FIRST TICKET SALES PLANS

The first ticket prices and sales plans for the 1994 FIFA World Cup were unveiled on February 3, 1993, at a televised New York City news conference. Making the announcement was Alan I. Rothenbeg, Chairman and Chief Executive Officer of World Cup USA, Guillermo Cañedo, chairman of FIFA's World Cup Organising Committee, Joseph S. Blatter, FIFA general secretary and chief executive officer, and Scott Parks LeTellier, managing director and chief operating officer of World

Meadowlands Racetrack

New Jersey is horse country. In fact, the horse is the official state animal, so it's not surprising to find excellent horseracing across the state. The Meadowlands Racetrack offers thrilling thoroughbred and harness racing year round and is considered to be the Number 1 harness track in America, both in terms of total wagering handle and nightly attendance. There are approximately 190 dates of harness racing from January to August and 100 dates of thoroughbred racing from September to December every year. A special feature of the track is simulcast wagering, which is betting on live races televised to and from other tracks in the state and around the country.

New Jersey★New York

WORLD CUP USA 1994 TICKET SALES USA TIMETABLE

1994 FIFA WORLD CUP

STAGES	Dates
Private Sale to members of the US Soccer Community *Stadium Series Packages only* *Mail and telephone order only*	Feb-Mar 31 '93
Public Sale *Stadium Series Packages only* *Mail and telephone order only*	June 1993
Later Round Games Public Sale *Computerised 'equal access' distribution system*	Fall 1993
Individual Game Sale (if available) *Mail, telephone order, ticket outlets*	Feb '94-Jun '94

PER GAME TICKET PRICES Competition Phase	1	2	3
Opening Game	$120	$70	$40
1st Game (Other Venues)	$75	$50	$30
1st Round $65	$45	$25	
Round of Sixteen	$85	$60	$35
Quarterfinals	$140	$80	$55
Semifinals $300	$200	$90	
Final/3rd Place Game	$475/$125	$300/$100	$180/$60

WORLD CUP NEW JERSEY/NEW YORK

Cup USA.

In his announcement, Mr Rothenberg said "Today is the beginning of yet another critical phase of our buildup to the 1994 FIFA World Cup. We have devised a ticket pricing and sales plan which we think serves the millions of soccer fans as well as World Cup USA 1994's revenue requirements. Our 'Team Ticketing' group has worked for months to ensure that everyone has an affordable way to see the world's greatest single-sport event. Of the approximately 3.6-million tickets, some 2 million are earmarked for sale within the United States and approximately 1 million of the tickets will be the lower-priced Category III tickets. Soccer is a sport played by millions of young and working-class Americans and our price structure gives them a chance to see the event live at very reasonable prices."

Single-game ticket prices range from $25 in the first round to $475 for a ticket to the World Cup Final. There will be three categories of tickets available for each game, with Category I tickets being the most expensive and Category III tickets the least expensive. FIFA General Secretary and Chief Executive Officer Mr Blatter said "FIFA is convinced that every ticket will be sold, and this will cast a very special light on the 1994 World Cup."

Members of the United States soccer family will have the first opportunity to purchase tickets to the tournament under the multi-stage sales and distribution procedure announced by World Cup USA 1994. Special ticket order forms have been distributed to members and affiliates of the United States Soccer Federation, as well as others who have been supportive of soccer and the World Cup effort. Recipients will be able to purchase Stadium Series Packages, which include a ticket to all four First Round games and the Round of Sixteen games at a particular stadium.

No more than ten such Stadium Series Packages may be purchased by any one individual. This 'private sale' opportunity extends only until March 31, 1993, after which other phases of the sales plan will begin.

Domestically, the second phase – sales to the general public – will begin this June via mail order and telephone order procedures, which will be administered by World Cup Ticketing, an operation serviced by Ticketmaster and dedicated exclusively to the sale of tickets to the general public in the United States.

World Cup USA 1994 will make available to the general public a limited number of tickets to the later round games – quarterfinals, semifinals, third place game and World Cup Final. These tickets will be sold later this year through a computerised 'equal access' system.

Managing Director and Chief Operating Officer Scott Parks LeTellier noted that the majority of tickets will be sold in Stadium Series Packages. "When we move into the general public sale in June, we will also be selling the Stadium Series Packages. We will have some innovative ticket concepts for our international visitors, such as Team Series Packages, which will allow fans to follow 'their' team and we will shortly be announcing and establishing a World Cup Travel Services company to administer travel and tour programmes throughout the world."

WORLD CUP USA 1994 TICKET ALLOCATION PLAN

Approximately 65% of all tickets to the 1994 FIFA World Cup will be distributed in the United States.

The remaining 35% will be distributed internationally to FIFA and its affiliated Football Associations, to sponsors and other commercial affiliates and World Cup Travel Services which will coordinate the sales of tickets and other travel and tour ingredients to authorised tour operators on a non-exclusive basis.

Nearly 55% of all tickets will be sold to the general public by World Cup USA 1994 through mail order, phone order and ticket outlet channels, primarily in Stadium Series Packages.

THE FINAL OF THE 1950 WORLD CUP BETWEEN URUGUAY AND BRAZIL IN RIO DE JANEIRO WAS WATCHED BY A WORLD RECORD 199,000 SPECTATORS.

Welcome to ATLANTIC CITY

This world-class resort and convention city (known as the 'Home of the Miss America Pageant') is ideal for tour packaging with such major US cities as New York, Philadelphia, Baltimore and Washington DC nearby.

ATLANTIC CITY

In 1992 Atlantic City again became the most visited resort destination in the United States (possibly the world!) by hosting nearly 32 million tourists and convention delegates.

Twelve luxurious casino/convention hotels are located along the Boardwalk and in the picturesque Marina area: Caesars, Bally's Grand, Showboat, Harrah's, Merv Griffin's Resorts, The Sands, Tropworld, Bally's Park Place, Claridge and the spectacular Trump Taj Mahal Hotel/Casino. They feature such powerhouse entertainers as Frank Sinatra, Diana Ross, Kenny Rogers, Cher – and many more fabulous show business stars who perform all year round.

Whether you like your good times wet 'n' wild with lots of excitement or dry, relaxing and easy-going you'll find a host of welcome surprises in Greater Atlantic City and Atlantic County all year round.

Enjoy fishing and boating in sheltered bay areas or the deep sea . . . sun yourself on broad, sandy beaches . . . ride the waves in the refreshing surf (Yes! Bring your surfboard) . . . stroll, jog, ride a bike or rolling chair for miles along our famous Boardwalk lined with world-class hotels and casinos offering the very best in headline entertainment.

Play one (or all!) of our fourteen challenging golf courses. Go canoeing . . . explore museums, historic attractions and a major wildlife refuge . . . shop! shop! . . . try your luck on the horses . . . visit wineries . . . or stop at a variety of excellent Atlantic County parks. Mix business with pleasure, too. Our concentration of convention, trade shows, meeting and conference facilities rank with the best in the nation.

By Anne Zernhelt, Greater Atlantic City Convention & Visitors Bureau

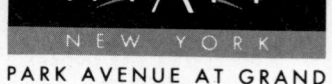

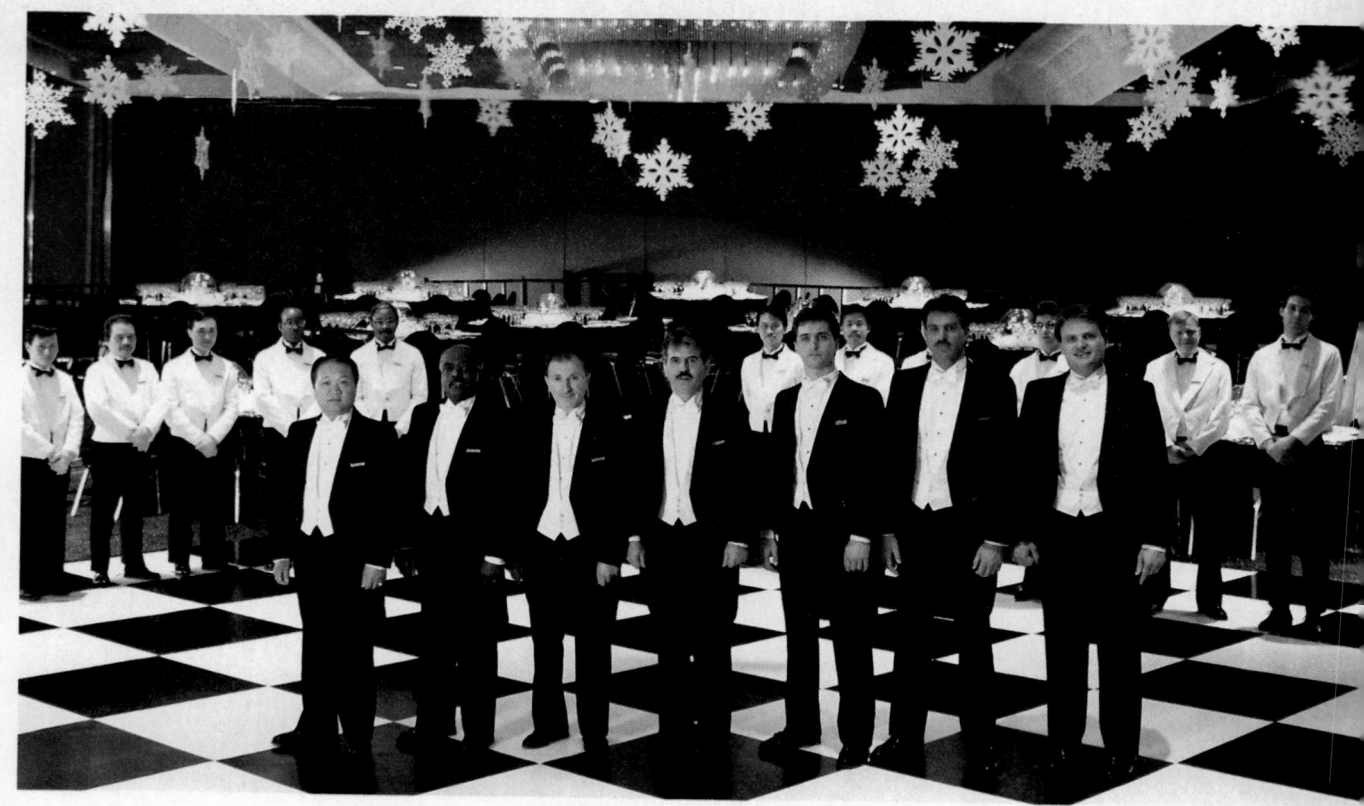

Welcome to NEW YORK

On behalf of the New York Convention & Visitors Bureau, welcome to New York City!

WORLD FINANCIAL CENTRE

GUGGENHEIM MUSEUM

We are honoured that the New York area has been chosen as a site for the FIFA 1994 World Cup semi-finals. The 'Big Apple' is a world capital of major sporting events, including the United States largest annual marathon and two premiere tennis events – the United States Open and the Virginia Slims Tournament.

New York has always been a sporting town, with the Mets and Yankees baseball teams, the Knicks basketball team, the Giants and Jets football teams and the Rangers hockey squad. Many world-class sporting events take place at Madison Square Garden, which recently underwent a $200-million renovation.

The city was also recently chosen to host the prestigious Good Will Games in 1998. This event will attract thousands of athletes and spectators from around the world.

While you are here, we hope you will take advantage of the city's exciting attractions – from the theatres of Broadway to the jazz clubs of Greenwich Village, the spacious galleries of our great art museums to the glittering stores lining the fabled Fifth Avenue. This unparalleled diversity makes New York the preferred destination for nearly 25 million visitors each year.

We look forward to welcoming you again and again to the 'Big Apple'.

From Marshall E. Murdaugh, President of the New York Convention & Visitors Bureau Inc.

New Jersey ☆ New York

THE WAY TO THE WORLD CUP AIRPORTS

New York is probably the most accessible city in the world. You can fly into any of three airports operated by the Port Authority from almost anywhere in the world – Newark Airport, LaGuardia Airport or JFK International Airport. Bus or rail links these busy airports to the 'Big Apple'.

John F Kennedy International (JFK): *24km (15 miles) southeast of central Manhattan (travel time – 1 hour). Many transatlantic flights arrive and depart here, as well as many medium-range and longhaul domestic flights. The airport is a complex of individual and shared terminals of almost 80 airlines and its Air Cargo Center is the world's largest.*

La Guardia Airport (LGA) *is 13km (8 miles) east of Manhattan, in the borough of Queens (travel time – 30 minutes). Most flights arrive and depart from the 2-level main terminal, but The Delta Shuttle to Washington DC and Boston has its own terminal (shared with Northwest Airlines).*

TRANSPORTATION TO NEW YORK CITY FROM JFK

By bus, you'll arrive in the heart of Manhattan at the Port Authority Bus Terminal at 8th Avenue and 42nd Street. By car, interconnecting parkways and highways take you across bridges or through tunnels that lead directly into the city. By train, Grand Central Station and Pennsylvania Station, both in Manhattan, serve thousands daily.

Bus/Subways

JFK Express: *An efficient 24-hour bus/underground route that runs buses every 10 minutes from 0500-2400 and every 30 minutes at other times; the bus connects with the NYC subway at Howard Beach Station on the 'A' train from where there are links to all areas of the city; return is from mid- or downtown Manhattan (travel time – 60/75 minutes). The cost of the bus is free and the subway fare is $1.25.*

THE LOCATION New York State lies in the Northeast of the United States, bordered to the south by Pennsylvania and New Jersey, to the north and west by Canada, to the northeast by Vermont and to the east by Massachusetts and Connecticut. New York City is situated at the southeastern point of the state around the mouth of the Hudson River which flows into the Atlantic Ocean. New York City is the largest city in the United States and one of the largest in the world, with a population of over seven million.

THE LANDSCAPE New York State is a vast expanse of land that stretches from the Atlantic coast to Canada and the Great Lakes. Around its capital, Albany, are scenic villages, underground waterfalls and national parkland as well as mountains. Long Island, a 241km (150-mile) glacial moraine, extends into the Atlantic, a mixture of suburbia and woods. The Hudson Valley makes a deep north–south trench on the east. To the west the Finger Lakes, rolling hills and parklands lead towards Niagara Falls. The Catskill Mountains to the northeast and, upstate, the Adirondack Mountains offer large areas of rivers, lakes and wooded slopes. The 1000 Islands, a myriad of outcrops in Lake Ontario, are also within easy reach.

THE CULTURE AND HISTORY The Lenape tribe of Native American Indians settled on the island about 3000 years ago, calling it 'Manhattes' or 'Island of the Hills'. The first European to explore the area was Hendrik Hudson, who first came there from Holland in 1609. Hudson formally bought Manhattan from the Lenape in 1626 for 60 guilders' worth of trinkets and cloth – about $24.

A busy trading port from its inception, the Dutch-named 'New Amsterdam' numbered 1500 citizens by 1664, when it was captured by the British without a battle. It was then renamed New York in honour of King Charles II's brother.

In the city's early days, most inhabitants lived south of Wall Street, where a wooden wall was built in the 1650s. Very little is left of the New York of the 1660s. Fires in the 18th and early 19th centuries swept away the Dutch and British colonial structures, while generations of building as the city progressed northward have tamped down Manhattan's hills and heights.

The city experienced enormous growth during the 19th century. In 1800, the population numbered about 60,000, and by 1880 it topped one million. In 1898, the five boroughs of Manhattan, Brooklyn, Queens, the Bronx and Staten Island united to form a single city with a combined population of nearly 3.5 million. That figure had doubled by 1950 due to several major waves of European immigration, and today it stands at 7.3 million.

WHAT MAKES NEW YORK SPECIAL What's your pleasure? From food to fashion, architecture to zoos, you'll find it in America's most exciting city.

ART AT ITS FINEST

New York leads the world as a centre for fine art. The city has 150 museums including the *Museum of Modern Art*, the *Metropolitan*, the *Whitney Museum of Modern Art*, *The Frick Collection* and the newly re-opened *Guggenheim Museum*.

New York has several art districts, including Fifth Avenue's Museum Mile, the ele-

FASCINATING FACTS

WORLD CUP 1954: FIFA REFUSED THE ENTRIES OF INDIA, PERU, VIETNAM, CUBA, ICELAND, BOLIVIA AND COSTA RICA BECAUSE OF APPLICATION FAULTS OR ENTRIES RECIEVED TOO LATE.

gant galleries lining 57th Street and upper Madison Avenue; and the avant-garde painting and sculpture galleries of SoHo.

For buyers too, New York has enough commercial galleries to satisfy every taste.

GREAT PERFORMANCES

There is more theatre in New York than in the whole of the rest of America and no trip to New York is complete without a visit to the Great White Way – Broadway. As well as the usual line-up of hit shows here, off-Broadway the theatre scene is just as thriving, particularly in the Greenwich Village and SoHo areas. It has also been enhanced by several new cabarets offering dinner and a show at moderate prices.

Visitors can enjoy opera and classical music at venues like Lincoln Center and the newly renovated Carnegie Hall. The Richmond Town Restoration on Staten Island offers opera, philarmonic concerts, chamber music and dance. Ballet aficionados can also thrill to performances by the New York City Ballet, the Joffrey Ballet and the Alvin Ailey American Dance Theatre. And for rock enthusiasts, some of rock's most contemporary sounds come of New York's music clubs and venues.

SOMETHING TO PLEASE EVERY PALATE

There are more than 17,000 restaurants, cafés, bistros, diners and food stands where visitors can take a bite of the 'Big Apple'.

Some of New York's best and most inexpensive tastes can be found on street corners, where vendors sell the city's famous hot dogs, shish kebabs and ice cream. At the other end of the spectrum, world-renowned restaurants such as Lutece, the Rainbow Room and Windows on the World dish up classic cuisine in spectacular settings. And New York City is the perfect place to experiment with a full range of national cuisines. Visitors need only visit the neighbourhoods of their favourite ethnic cuisines, where they can sample pastas and pizzas in Little Italy, dim-sum and Peking duck in Chinatown, Indian and Polish food in the East Village – the range is endless.

A WORLD OF SHOPPING CHOICES

'Born to Shop' reads a popular T-shirt – and there's no better place for shoppers than the 'Big Apple'. New York is famous for its department stores: Macy's (the biggest department store in the world), the enormous men's fashion store Barneys, Bloomingdales, the new Galleries Lafayette and the elegant 7-storey Saks Fifth Avenue.

Fine art, antique furniture, avant-garde clothing and objets d'art can be found in Greenwich Village, SoHo and the landmark Flatiron district (Fifth Avenue from 14th-23rd Streets). Antique-lovers can also visit the Manhattan Art & Antiques Center on Second Avenue between 55th and 56th Streets, and shop for bargains at the stores lining Atlantic Avenue in Brooklyn.

THE SPORTING LIFE

For a slice of the real New York, how about attending a major sports event? The Big Apple is a sporting town, with hometown loyalties running high for the Mets and Yankees baseball teams, the Knicks basketball team, the Giants and Jets football teams and the Rangers hockey squad. Many of New York's sporting events take place at Madison Square Garden, which has recently undergone a $200-million renovation. Visitors can also enjoy ball games at Shea and Yankee Stadiums, and thoroughbred racing at Aqueduct or Belmont Racetracks.

NEW YORK'S NEIGHBOURHOODS

Recently, the city has been undergoing capital improvements totalling more than $60 billion – about £35 billion. Of this amount, more than US$6 billion is being spent to enhance New York's distinctive ethnic neighbourhoods.

The city's reputation as a 'melting pot' stems from its role as a haven for immigrants in the early part of the century. It is estimated that four out of five Americans have at least one ancestor who passed through the portals of Ellis Island, now a major attraction in New York Harbour.

Take a trip around the world to New York City's neighbourhoods. Start at Arthur

Q3: *Bus/underground route that runs buses every 12-15 minutes from 0525-2125 and every 30 minutes from 2145-0145 weekdays (every 20-30 minutes weekends); the bus connects to the NYC subway 'F' or 'R' trains with links to Manhattan and Brooklyn. The cost of the bus is $1.25 (exact fare) and then another $1.25 for the subway. For further information on either the JFK Express or Q3 bus/subway route, telephone (718) 330 1234.*

Q10: *Bus/underground route that runs buses every 10 minutes from 0630-1900 and every 20-30 minutes from 1900-0630; the bus connects to subway stations at Lefferts Boulevard (for 'A' subway to Brooklyn, Lower and West Side Manhattan) and at Kew Gardens-Union Turnpike (for 'E' and 'F' subways to Queens and mid-Manhattan). Bus fare is $1.25 (exact fare) and then $1.25 for subway. For further information, telephone Green Bus Lines on (718) 995 4700.*

Buses

Carey Airport Express Coach Bus: *Departs every 30 minutes from 0600-2400, to six midtown Manhattan stops: 125 Park Avenue (opposite Grand Central Station at 41st-42nd Streets), Port Authority Bus Terminal (42nd Street between 8th-9th Avenues), New York Hilton Hotel (53rd Street and Avenue of the Americas), Sheraton Manhattan Hotel (Seventh Avenue between 51st-52nd Streets), Marriott Marquis Hotel (Broadway between 45th-46th Streets) and Holiday Inn Crowne Plaza (48th Street at Broadway). There are also buses from Grand Central Station to JFK from 0500-0100 and from Port Authority Bus Terminal to JFK from 0715-2310 and from the hotels from 0545-2200. The cost is $11-12.50 per person one way (travel time – 45/65 minutes).*

Gray Line Air Shuttle: *Available on demand from 0700-2300 for a shared minibus to anywhere from 23rd-63rd Streets in Manhattan at $15 per person (travel time – 40/60 minutes). For further information, telephone (212) 315 3006.*

Helicopters

New York Helicopters: *Offer a service throughout the day from Gate 32 Terminal to East 34th Street in midtown Manhattan for $65 per person (travel time – 10 minutes). Telephone 1 (800) 645 3494 for complete schedule information and reservations.*

Taxis

Taxis are yellow and cost an average of $28 into Manhattan, plus tolls. Taxis operate from designated taxi stands. Travellers are advised not to travel with a taxi driver who approaches them first. Always find out the standard rate since unscrupulous drivers may overcharge. A 50-cent surcharge is in effect from 2000-0600 in all yellow taxis.

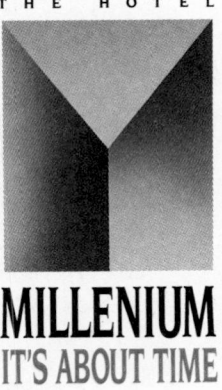

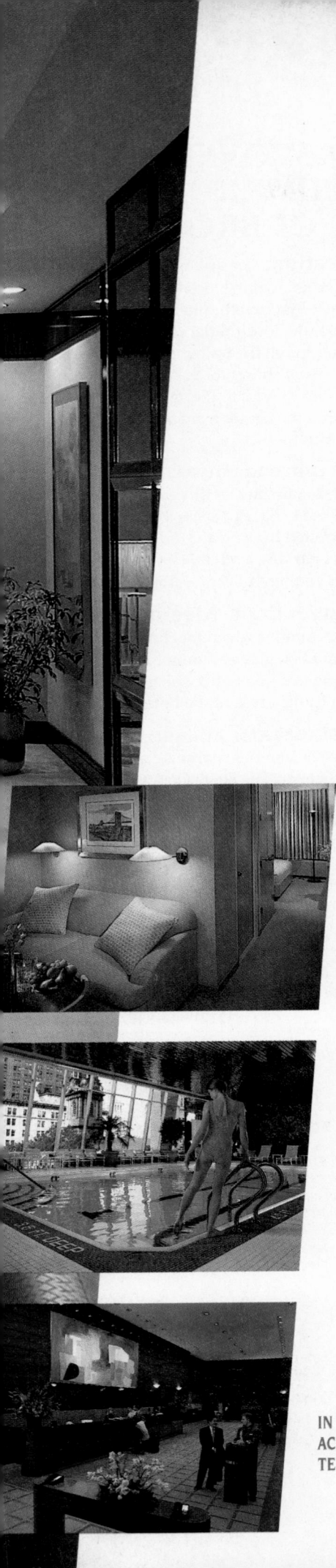

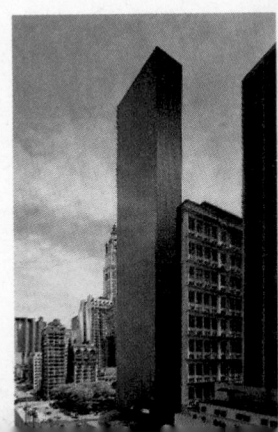

Avenue in the Bronx, where the Italian food is as authentic as any you'll find in Rome, then head south to Harlem for soul food or east to Brighton Beach, Brooklyn, for Russian blini and vodka in the district known as 'Little Odessa'.

FIVE BOROUGHS OF TOURISM ATTRACTIONS

Although most first-time visitors spend the majority of their time in Manhattan, New York City has four other boroughs: the Bronx, Brooklyn, Queens and Staten Island. If you miss them, you're missing four-fifths of the 'Big Apple'!
Below is a starter's list of top attractions in 'the other New York'.

Brooklyn

Brooklyn Museum: World-famous for its Egyptian collection, the Brooklyn Museum also has a unique outdoor sculpture garden of New York building ornaments. Visitors can also stroll through the adjoining Brooklyn Botanic Garden's 50 acres of flora or wander through the 526-acre Prospect Park. The Brooklyn Children's Museum, at 145 Brooklyn Avenue, is the oldest children's museum in the country. It's a treasure house that adults are sure to enjoy too.
New York Aquarium at Coney Island: The Brooklyn Aquarium's beloved belugas (white whales) are featured at the Aquarium's frequent outdoor shows, which also include seals, dolphins, sea lions, penguins and other aqua-stars. Down the boardwalk is Coney Island's famous amusement area featuring the Cyclone roller coaster.
Brooklyn Academy of Music: A temple for the performing arts – theatre, dance, music and film – BAM features three theatres in an impressive landmark building. The facility's latest addition is the beautifully restored Majestic Theatre, located just a few blocks from the main building.

Queens

Shea Stadium: The Mets, those 1986 world champions, continue to thrill fans in their home stadium in Flushing Meadows. The Boys of Summer play 'baseball like it oughtta be' for crowds of up to 55,000.
American Museum of the Moving Image: Located in a landmark 1920 studio building in Astoria, this new museum is part of the Kaufman-Astoria Studios, where silent films and early talkies were made and where modern movies are shot (such as 'Arthur', 'Big', 'Coming to America', 'Fatal Attraction', 'Moonstruck', 'Wall Street', 'Working Girl' and TV's 'Cosby Show'). The museum celebrates film history with permanent and changing exhibits, two film theatres and an actual set from 'The Glass Menagerie' – plus 60,000 artefacts.
Flushing Meadows-Corona Park: The former site of the 1939 and 1964 World's Fairs is now home to the Queens Museum which boasts an excellent collection of contemporary art; the New York Hall of Science where kids of all ages can learn through hands-on exhibits; and the National Tennis Center, site of the US Open Tennis Championships.
Belmont and Aqueduct Racetracks: Few thrills are more palpable than standing by the rail, cheering one's horse to victory! Both Aqueduct and Belmont feature world class racing – the latter is the world's largest thoroughbred track and home of the third jewel in horseracing's triple crown, the Belmont Stakes.

Bronx

Bronx Zoo: Thousands of creatures of all shapes and sizes inhabit this 21st-century zoo. Among the award-winning exhibits are the spooky 'World of Darkness' (nocturnal animals), 'Himalayan Highlands', 'Jungle World', 'World of Birds', the spectacular 'Wild Asia' with its Bengali Express monorail and the Children's Zoo. For an exciting overview of the entire park, visitors can ride the 'Skyfari' tramway.
Yankee Stadium: The Yankees baseball team still plays ball in here where legends were born. You can still feel the excitement created by legendary baseball greats Babe Ruth, Lou Gehrig, Joe Di Maggio, Mickey Mantle and Roger Maris.
Bronx Conservatory: The New York Botanical Garden's 1901 glass conservatory, restored to its former glory, features changing exhibits of horticultural and botanical interest, as well as lasting displays including jungles, deserts, swamps and tropical forests.

TRANSPORT TO OTHER DESTINATIONS:
Limousine services are available from JFK airport to some cities in Connecticut, Long Island and upstate New York. Coach services are available to New Jersey and Pennsylvania.

TRANSPORTION TO NEW YORK CITY FROM LAGUARDIA

Subway/Buses
Q33: *24-hour bus/underground route from the main terminal to 74th Street/Roosevelt Avenue runs every 12 minutes day and evening and every 40 minutes after 2400; the bus connects to the subway station at Jackson Heights, Queens, for the 'E', 'F', 'G', 'R' and no 7 trains.*

Buses
Carey Airport Express Coach Bus: *Departs every 30 minutes from 0645-2400, to six midtown Manhattan stops: 125 Park Avenue (opposite Grand Central Station at 41st-42nd Streets), Port Authority Bus Terminal (42nd Street between 8th-9th Avenues), New York Hilton Hotel (53rd Street and Avenue of the Americas), Sheraton Manhattan Hotel (Seventh Avenue between 51st-52nd Streets), Marriott Marquis Hotel (Broadway between 45th-46th Streets) and Holiday Inn Crowne Plaza (48th Street at Broadway). There are also buses from Grand Central Station to LaGuardia from 0600-2400 and from Port Authority Bus Terminal to LaGuardia from 0715-2315 and from the hotels from 0545-2200. The cost is $8.50-$10 per person one way (travel time – 30 minutes). For further information, telephone (718) 632 0500.*
Gray Line Air Shuttle: *Offers a service on demand from 0700-2300 from the airport to anywhere between 23rd-63rd Streets for US$12 per person (travel time – 30/45 minutes). For further information, telephone (212) 315 3006.*

Ferry
The Delta Water Shuttle: *Ferry service which departs from the Marine Air Terminal to 34th Street on the East River or to Pier 11 on Wall Street in downtown Manhattan for $25 per person one way or $45 return (travel time – 30/45 minutes). For ferry schedules ring 1-(800) 221 1212.*

Taxis
Yellow taxis are readily available from designated taxi stands. Fares to midtown Manhattan average $23 from LaGuardia.

INTER-AIRPORT TRANSFERS
Regular helicopter transfers are available on New York Helicopter (HD) between New York airports and to Newark Airport Terminal C. Salem Transportation coaches offer links between JFK and LaGuardia, as well as to Newark. A limousine service is also available from New York airports to Newark Airport. Taxis are also available.

TRANSPORTATION TO OTHER DESTINATIONS: *Limousine, bus and rail services (via Airlink connection) are also available to Pennsylvania, Connecticut and upstate New York.*

New Jersey☆New York

NYC GROUND TRANSPORTATION

Getting around the 'Big Apple' is as easy as getting there. The five boroughs of New York are all interconnected by the largest rapid transit system in the world – the city-owned subways. Daily, on more than 700 miles of track, over three million passengers ride the subways to and from work and play. The Transit Authority also provides surface transportation on over 225 bus routes amounting to more than 4828 km (3000 road miles) a day. Over 11,000 yellow cabs regulated by New York's Taxi and Limousine Commission, and metered, can take you anywhere within the five boroughs.

Subway

Despite its notorious reputation, the New York subway is fast, air-conditioned, cheap and open 24 hours a day, 7 days a week. Express trains run between major stops, local trains stop at every station. Subway maps are posted in each subway car and pocket maps are available from token booths. Tokens cost $1.25, regardless of the distance travelled, and are bought from subway booths or newsagents and can also be used on buses. There are half-fares for senior citizens (tel: (212) 577 0819 for information) and the disabled (tel: (212) 240 4131).

Buses

These are plentiful but considerably slower than the subway due to traffic congestion. Fare is $1.25, regardless of destination, and tokens or coins can be used but notes and pennies are not accepted as drivers do not give change. Night service is available on most routes. Smoking is not permitted. Three quarters of the city's buses are equipped with wheelchair lifts at the rear door.

Gray Line Bus Tours: *Located at 900 Eighth Avenue between West 53rd and West 54th Streets, Gray Line offers bus tours around the city 0800-2000 daily. There are four bus tours available: Lower Manhattan; Harlem and Upper Manhattan; the Grand Tour (most of the city); and Number 5 (including the Statue of Liberty and Upper and Lower Manhattan). For further information, telephone (212) 397 2620.*

Taxis

These are reasonably cheap and highly visible with their distinctive yellow colour. An average fare costs between $5 and $7 for a 4.5km (3-mile) ride. There is no charge for extra passengers, but there is a 50-cent surcharge after 2000.

Staten Island

Historic Richmond Town: Staten Island's architectural and historic past is preserved in this ongoing restoration of a 17th to 19th-century village. The 1695 Voorlezer's House, the oldest elementary schoolhouse remaining in the United States, is just one of the refurbished buildings at this 96-acre, early American oasis.

Snug Harbor: Formerly a home for retired seamen, this cultural centre in 80 acres of lush grounds houses the Staten Island Children's Museum, Newhouse Gallery and Veteran Memorial Hall. Concerts, art exhibits, tours and special events are scheduled year-round. Other must-see Staten Island museums include the Staten Island Institute of Arts and Sciences and the Jacques Marchais Center of Tibetan Art.

Staten Island Ferry: The world's most famous, most reasonable (50 cents round-trip) and most romantic 5-mile cruise transports you to New York City's most rustic borough.

EMPIRE STATE BUILDING

UNITED NATIONS

JULY
IV

NEW YORK

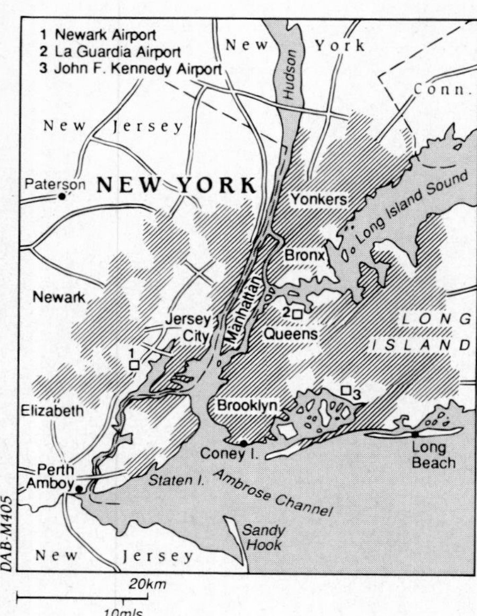

Including **New York City,** gateway to the States of the Eastern (Atlantic) Seaboard, George Washington Country and the Great Lakes.

New York State Division of Tourism
51st Floor
1515 Broadway
New York, NY
10036
Tel: (212) 827 6251. Fax: (212) 827 6279. Telex: 960981.
New York Convention & Visitors Bureau
Two Columbus Circle
New York, NY
10019
Tel: (212) 397 8222. Fax: (212) 245 5943.
Hotel Association of New York City
36th Floor
437 Madison Avenue
New York, NY
10022-7398
Tel: (212) 754 6700. Fax: (212) 754 0243.
Travellers Aid Society
2 Lafayette Street
New York, NY
10007
Tel: (212) 577 7700. Fax: (212) 385 0331.
(Multilingual staff offer help to travellers and foreign visitors, including help with legal, medical or other problems; facilities also at JFK airport.)
New York State Division of Tourism
2 Cinnamon Row
Plantation Wharf
London SW11 3TW
Tel: (071) 978 5275. Fax: (071) 924 3171. Telex: 27231 COSTRA.
Albany County Convention and Visitors Bureau
52 South Pearl Street
Albany, NY
12207
Tel: (518) 434 1217. Fax: (518) 434 0887.
Niagara Falls Convention and Visitors Bureau
Suite 101, Carborundum Center
345 Third Street
Niagara Falls, NY
14303
Tel: (716) 285 2400. Fax: (716) 285 0809.

TIME: GMT - 5. *Daylight Saving Time* is observed from the first Sunday in April to the last Sunday in October. Clocks are put forward one hour, changing at 0200 hours local time.
THE STATE: New York State is a vast expanse of land that stretches from the Atlantic coast to Canada and the Great Lakes. Its capital, Albany, offers everything from stately homes to the US$2-billion Rockefeller Empire State Plaza, as well as access to scenic villages, underground waterfalls and national parkland in the surrounding mountains. Long Island, a 241km (150 miles) glacial moraine, extends into the Atlantic, a mixture of suburbia and woodland. The Hudson Valley makes a deep north–south trench on the east. To the west, the Finger Lakes, rolling hills and parklands, lead towards Niagara Falls. The Catskill Mountains to the northeast and, upstate, the Adirondack Mountains offer large areas of rivers, lakes and wooded slopes. The 1000 Islands, a myriad of outcrops in Lake Ontario, are also within easy reach.

TRAVEL

AIR: Approximate flight times: From New York to *Anchorage* is 8 hours 30 minutes, to *Atlanta* is 2 hours 40 minutes, to *Baltimore* is 1 hour 20 minutes, to *Barbados* is 4 hours 40 minutes, to *Bermuda* is 2 hours, to *Boston* is 1 hour 10 minutes, to *Buenos Aires* is 10 hours 15 minutes, to *Buffalo* is 1 hour 50 minutes, to *Caracas* is 4 hours 55 minutes, to *Chicago* is 2 hours 50 minutes, to *Cincinnati* is 2 hours 10 minutes, to *Cleveland* is 1 hour 45 minutes, to *Dallas/Fort Worth* is 4 hours, to *Detroit* is 2 hours, to *Frankfurt/M* is 7 hours 30 minutes, to *Hartford* is 1 hour, to *Honolulu* is 12 hours, to *Houston* is 4 hours, to *London* is 6 hours 50 minutes (3 hours 50 minutes by Concorde), to *Los Angeles* is 6 hours, to *Mexico City* is 5 hours 10 minutes, to *Miami* is 3 hours 10 minutes, to *Minneapolis/St Paul* is 3 hours 10 minutes, to *Montréal* is 1 hour 25 minutes, to *Moscow* is 8 hours 50 minutes, to *Nassau* is 3 hours, to *New Orleans* is 3 hours 25 minutes, to *Norfolk* is 1 hour 30

World Trade Centre

minutes, to *Orlando* is 2 hours 50 minutes, to *Philadelphia* is 50 minutes, to *Pittsburgh* is 1 hour 30 minutes, to *Providence* is 1 hour, to *Rio de Janeiro* is 9 hours 15 minutes, to *Rome* is 8 hours 10 minutes, to *St Croix* is 4 hours, to *St Maarten* is 3 hours 50 minutes, to *St Thomas* is 3 hours 50 minutes, to *Santo Domingo* is 3 hours 50 minutes, to *San Francisco* is 6 hours 10 minutes, to *San Juan* is 3 hours 50 minutes, to *Shannon* is 6 hours 5 minutes, to *Singapore* is 21 hours 55 minutes, to *Sydney* is 26 hours, to *Tampa* is 3 hours, to *Tel Aviv* is 12 hours 30 minutes, to *Toronto* is 1 hour 30 minutes and to *Washington DC* is 1 hour 10 minutes.

International airports: *John F Kennedy (JFK)* and *LaGuardia (LGA)*. Both airports handle domestic and international flights, but most international flights into New York arrive at *JFK*. Flights from or via London *Heathrow (LHR)* to New York land at *JKF*, and flights from London *Gatwick (LGW)* land at *JFK* and *EWR* in Newark. Some transfer connections via continental Europe land at *LGA*, but the airport's primary function is to handle internal USA flights.

Travellers from Europe arriving at *JFK* will generally make their onward connection from there.

Connections to smaller locations, and connections for travellers arriving at *EWR*, may have to be made by transferring to *LGA*. For transfer details, see below under *Airport transfers*.

John F Kennedy International (JFK): 24km (15 miles) southeast of central Manhattan. For transportation into the city, *JFK Express*, an efficient 24 hour bus/underground route runs every 10 minutes 0500-2400 and every 30 minutes at other times; the bus connects to the NYC subway at Howard Beach Station on the 'A' train from where there are links to all areas of the city; return is from mid- or downtown Manhattan (travel time – 60/75 minutes). The cost of the bus is free and the subway fare is US$1.25. The *Q3* bus/underground route connects to the NYC subway 'F' or 'R' trains with links to Manhattan and Brooklyn. The cost of the bus is US$1.25 (exact fare) and then another US$1.25 for the subway. For further information on either *JFK Express* or *Q3* bus/subway routes, telephone (718) 330 1234. The *Q10* bus/underground route connects to subway stations at Lefferts Boulevard (for 'A' subway to Brooklyn, Lower and West Side Manhattan) and at Kew Gardens-Union Turnpike (for 'E' and 'F' subways to Queens and mid-Manhattan). Bus fare is US$1.25 (exact fare) and then US$1.25 for the subway. For further information, contact *Green Bus Lines* on (718) 995 4700. Bus services are provided by *Carey Transportation Coaches:* departures are every 30 minutes 0600-2400, to six midtown Manhattan stops: 125 Park Avenue (opposite Grand Central Station at 41st-42nd Streets), Port Authority Bus Terminal (42nd Street between 8th-9th Avenues), New York Hilton Hotel (53rd Street and 6th Avenue), Sheraton Manhattan Hotel (7th Avenue between 51st-52nd Streets), Marriott Marquis Hotel (Broadway between 45th-46th Streets) and the Holiday Inn Crowne Plaza (48th Street at Broadway). There are also buses from Grand Central Station to *JFK* 0500-0100 as well as from Port Authority Bus Terminal to *JFK* 0715-2215 and from the hotels 0545-2200. The cost is US$11-$12.50 per person one-way (travel time – 40/60 minutes). For further information, contact *Carey Transportation Coaches* on (718) 632 0500. *Gray Line Air Shuttle* (tel: (212) 315 3006) has a service available on demand 0700-2300 for a shared minibus to anywhere from 23rd-63rd Street in Manhattan at US$15 per person (travel time – 40/60 minutes). *New York Helicopters* offers a service throughout the day from Gate 32 Terminal to East 34th Street in midtown Manhattan for US$65 per person (travel time – 10 minutes). Call *New York Helicopters* on (800) 645 3494 for complete schedule information and reservations. Taxis are expensive (approximately US$28 into Manhattan, plus tolls) and travellers are advised not to travel with a taxi driver who approaches them first. Always find out the standard rate since unscrupulous drivers may overcharge. A 50-cent surcharge is in effect 2000-0600 in all yellow taxis.

Transport to other destinations: Limousine services are available to some cities in Connecticut, Long Island and upstate New York. Coach services are available to New Jersey and Pennsylvania.

Inter-Airport transfers: Regular helicopter transfers are available on *New York Helicopter (HD)* to Newark Airport Terminal C. *Carey Transportation Coaches* to LGA airport depart every 30 minutes 0730-2130. A limousine service is available to Newark Airport. Taxis are also available.

LaGuardia (LGA): 13km (8 miles) east of Manhattan, in the borough of Queens. For transportation into the city, bus services are provided by *Carey Transportation Coaches:* departs every 30 minutes 0645-2400, to six midtown Manhattan stops: Grand Central Station, Port Authority Bus Terminal, New York Hilton Hotel, Sheraton Manhattan Hotel, Marriott Marquis Hotel and the Holiday Inn Crowne Plaza. There are also buses from Grand Central Station to LaGuardia 0600-2400 as well as from Port Authority Bus Terminal to LaGuardia 0715-2315 and from the hotels 0545-2200. The cost is US$8.50-$10 per person one-way (travel time – 30 minutes). *Gray Line Air Shuttle* offers a service on demand 0700-2300 from the airport to anywhere between 23rd-63rd Streets for US$12 per person (travel time – 30/45 minutes). There is also a ferry service, the *Delta Water Shuttle*, which departs from the Marine Air Terminal to 34th Street on the East River or to Pier 11 on Wall Street in downtown Manhattan for US$25 per person one-way or US$45 return (travel time – 30/45 minutes). For ferry schedules, telephone (800) 221 1212. Yellow taxis are readily available from designated taxi stands. Fares to midtown Manhattan average US$23 from LaGuardia.

Airport transfers: Regular helicopter transfers are available on *New York Helicopter (HD)* between New York airports and to Newark Airport Terminal C. *Carey Transportation Coaches* offers links between *JFK* and *LaGuardia*, as well as Newark. Limousines and taxis are also available.

Transportation to other destinations: Limousine, bus and rail services (via *Airlink* connection) are also available to Pennsylvania, Connecticut and upstate New York.

SEA: The *Staten Island Ferry* operates from Battery Park (downtown) past the Statue of Liberty and Ellis Island to Staten Island. *Circle Line Tours* operate a 3-hour guided tour around Manhattan Island (departing from Pier 83, West 43rd Street), plus tours to the Statue of Liberty. Longer river tours run from New York City to Poughkeepsie. New York is a major international port.

RAIL: Pennsylvania Station (34th Street/6th Avenue) serves both the *Long Island Railroad* (Long Island and New Jersey) and *Amtrak* (nationwide). Grand Central Station (42nd Street/Park Avenue) is the terminus for services to upstate New York *(Metro North)*. There are two daily trains to Montréal and one to Toronto.

Approximate *Amtrak* journey times: From New York on the 'Adirondack' to *Montréal* is 14 hours 30 minutes; on the 'Pennsylvanian' to *Philadelphia* is 1 hour 30 minutes and to *Harrisburg* is 16 hours; on the 'Maple Leaf' to *Buffalo* is 8 hours, to *Niagara Falls* is 9 hours and to *Toronto* is 12 hours; on the 'Silver Meteor' to *Baltimore* is 3 hours, to *Washington DC* is 4 hours, to *Jacksonville* is 18 hours, to *Orlando* (Disney World) is 21 hours and to *Miami* is 26 hours; on the 'Silver Meteor' to *Tampa* is 23 hours; and on the 'Crescent' to *Charlotte* is 10 hours, to *Atlanta* is 16 hours, to *Birmingham* is 19 hours and to *New Orleans* is 27 hours. There are frequent shuttles to *Washington DC* and *Boston*, taking 3 hours 15 minutes and 4 hours 30 minutes respectively.

For journey times on lines connecting New York with Chicago, see the *Illinois* section above.

ROAD: Travel from Manhattan to New Jersey is across George Washington Bridge or through the Lincoln or Holland Tunnels. The Verrazano-Narrows Bridge connects Brooklyn with Staten Island. Queensborough Bridge links Manhattan and Queens. Take Triborough Bridge for upstate New York and the New England Thruway and Bruckner Expressway to New England.

Bus: The Port Authority Bus Terminal (40th Street/8th Avenue) handles long-distance and regional buses.

Approximate driving times: From New York to *Philadelphia* is 2 hours, to *Hartford* is 2 hours, to *Albany* is 3 hours, to *Boston* is 4 hours, to *Baltimore* is 4 hours, to *Washington DC* is 5 hours, to *Portland* (Maine) is 6 hours, to *Montréal* is 7 hours, to *Buffalo* is 8 hours, to *Pittsburgh* is 8 hours, to *Toronto* is 9 hours, to *Cleveland* is 10 hours, to *Indianapolis* is 15 hours, to *Chicago* is 16 hours, to *Miami* is 27 hours, to *Dallas* is 33 hours, to *Los Angeles* is 58 hours, to *San Francisco* is 61 hours and to *Seattle* is 61 hours.

All times are based on non-stop driving at or below the applicable speed limits.

Approximate *Greyhound* journey times: From New York (tel: (212) 971 6363) to *Philadelphia* is 2 hours 20 minutes, to *Albany* is 3 hours, to *Washington DC* is 4 hours 40 minutes, to *Boston* is 4 hours 45 minutes, to *Montréal* is 8 hours 30 minutes, to *Buffalo* is 9 hours, to *Pittsburgh* is 9 hours and to *Cleveland* is 9 hours 30 minutes.

URBAN: Streets are laid out in a grid pattern and are frequently congested. The streets and avenues mostly follow a pattern of alternate one-way flow. Broadway is an old Indian trail; it cuts right through New York State from downtown Manhattan to Albany. **Bus:** Services are extensive and are run mostly by the *New York City Transit Authority*. Tokens are available, or one may pay the driver, in which case the exact fare (cost – US$1.25, regardless of destination) is needed. Three quarters of the city's buses are equipped with wheelchair lifts at the rear door. It is advisable to get hold of a map. **Taxi:** The standard yellow cab is metered and reasonably cheap. An average fare costs between US$5 and US$7 for a 4.5km (3-mile) ride. There is no charge for extra passengers, but there is a 50-cent surcharge 2000-0600. *Gray Line Bus Tours:* Located at 900, 8th Avenue between West 53rd and West 54th Streets, *Gray Line* offers bus tours around the city. Open 0800-2000 daily. There are four bus tours available: Lower Manhattan; Harlem and Upper Manhattan; the Grand Tour (most of the city); and 'Number 5' (including the Statue of Liberty and Upper and Lower Manhattan). **Hansom cabs:** Horse-drawn carriages line up at 59th Street and Fifth Avenue, just outside the *Plaza Hotel*. **Car hire:** All the major national car rental companies are represented in New York City and many have offices at the city's airports. **Subway:** Despite its notorious reputation, the New York subway is fast, air-conditioned, cheap and runs 24 hours a day, 7 days a week. Express trains run between major stops and local trains stop at every station. Subway maps are posted in each subway car and pocket maps are available from token booths. Tokens cost US$1.25, regardless of destination. These can be purchased from subway booths or newsagents and can be used on buses. There are half-fares for senior citizens and the disabled. For further information contact the *Department of Transit* on (212) 788 4636.

NEW YORK: Lower Manhattan

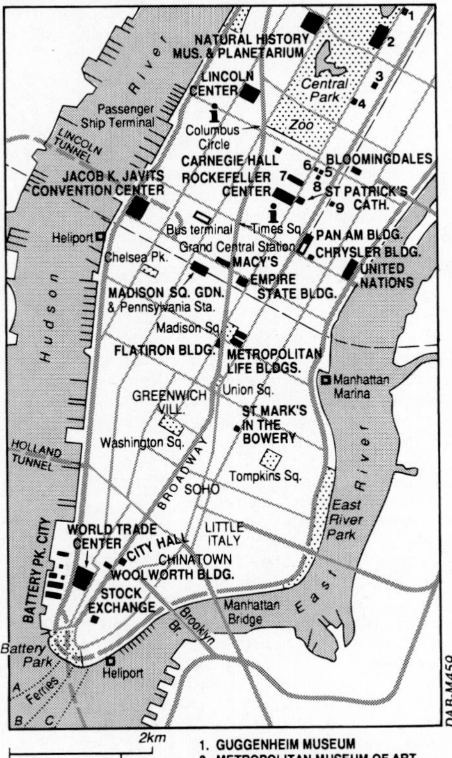

i tourist information

A. To Ellis Island
B. To Statue of Liberty
C. To Staten Island

1. GUGGENHEIM MUSEUM
2. METROPOLITAN MUSEUM OF ART
3. WHITNEY MUSEUM OF AMERICAN ART
4. FRICK COLLECTION
5. IBM TOWER
6. TRUMP TOWER
7. MUSEUM OF MODERN ART
8. AT&T BUILDING
9. SEAGRAMS BUILDING

RESORTS & EXCURSIONS

NEW YORK CITY: The 'Big Apple' has no equal. It was first settled by Dutch colonists more than 350 years ago, when the scent of flowers from Manhattan Island reached sailors on ships approaching the harbour. Nowadays, a dramatic skyline of soaring skyscrapers signals the approach to the city. New York is the third largest city in the world and the largest and most cosmopolitan in the USA. Its population of more than seven million includes Germans, Poles, Puerto Ricans, West Indians, Greeks, Scots, Hungarians, Chinese, Koreans, Irish, Italians, Africans and Romanians.

New York City is made up of five boroughs and is laid out on a grid pattern of avenues and streets. Most tourist sites and facilities are found on Manhattan Island, the business and entertainment centre of the metropolis. Its streets, running east–west, are numbered

1st-240th. Avenues, stretching north–south, run from 1-12 and A-D. South of Canal Street, the grid scatters and street names are used. The remaining four boroughs are primarily residential – the Bronx to the north, Queens to the east, Brooklyn to the southeast and Staten Island to the southwest. Each has wealthy and salubrious districts alongside slum zones – demonstrating as ever New York's uniquely varied social mix.
Sightseeing: The Manhattan skyline is one of the world's few instantly recognisable sights. Many of the skyscrapers are architecturally memorable and offer superb views of the city. The *World Trade Center* is one of several with facilities for tourists; visitors may go onto the roof of one of its two tower blocks during the day or sit in one of its restaurants or bars to see the city at night (smart dress is required in the bars and restaurants). The *Empire State Building*, one of the world's most famous skyscrapers, is on 34th Street at 5th Avenue; take a lift to the top floor for a spectacular view of the city by day or night. The *Statue of Liberty* may be reached by boat from *Battery Park* on the tip of Manhattan Island. An elevator and stairway inside the Statue takes visitors up to an observation platform. The *Staten Island Ferry* is one of the best transportation and touring bargains in the USA. The voyage is very cheap, lasts approximately 25 minutes and affords a magnificent view of Manhattan and New York harbour. *Brooklyn Bridge*, the remarkable suspension bridge across the East River, provides spectacular views of the city. The *Rockefeller Center*, between 5th and 6th Avenues, houses *Radio City Music Hall* and the *Lower Plaza*, where the café area is converted into a popular skating rink in winter. Nearby is *Broadway* and the heart of the theatre district. Other attractions include the *Lincoln Center for the Performing Arts*, the *United Nations Building* (the organisation's world headquarters), *Coney Island*, the *Bronx Zoo* and *Roosevelt Island Tramway*. The city is famous for its ethnic quarters, such as *Chinatown* and *Little Italy* in Lower Manhattan and *Germantown* along 86th Street. *Greenwich Village*, once the 'Bohemian' quarter, now has coffee and craft shops, theatres and nightclubs.
Museums & galleries: There are many dozens scattered throughout the city. The most famous is probably the *Metropolitan Museum of Art* on 5th Avenue at 82nd Street. It is the largest art museum in the western hemisphere and its outstanding collections cover all periods. A donation is requested in lieu of admission. The *Museum of Modern Art* on 11 West 53rd Street has the most important modern art collection in the USA. There is also an outdoor sculpture garden. The *Guggenheim Museum* on 5th Avenue at 88th Street is a 7-storey conical building worth visiting for its design alone (by Frank Lloyd Wright). It features 19th- and 20th-century paintings. Visitors ride an elevator to the top, then walk down a gently spiralling ramp. The *Whitney Museum of American Art* on Madison Avenue at 75th Street is a futuristic structure with exhibits of all types of American art. The *Frick Collection* on 5th Avenue at 70th Street is a neo-classical palazzo containing its original furnishings and paintings by many European masters.
Parks & gardens: The best-known parks include *Central Park* (extending from Fifth Avenue to Central Park West and 59th Street to 110th Street) with its skating rink, boating lake and zoo; *Riverside Park*, running along the Hudson; *Fort Tryon Park* at the northern tip of Manhattan; *Battery* and *Washington Square* parks in lower Manhattan; *Prospect* and *Marine* parks in Brooklyn; and *Flushing Meadows/Corona*, *Cunningham*, *Kissina* and *Jacob Riis* parks in Queens. *Clove Lake Park* and *Fort Wadsworth* on Staten Island, a quiet area beneath the Verrezano-Narrows Bridge, have impressive views of New York harbour. The Bronx has a famous *Botanical Garden* and *Pelham Bay* and *Van Cortlandt* parks. Visitors should be aware that it is dangerous to walk alone after dark in many or all of the parks.
Beaches: There are several fine beaches to the east of New York City. Nearest to Manhattan are *Coney Island*, *Brighton Beach* and *Manhattan Beach*. Beaches also run along the north and south shore of Long Island. *Jacob Riis Park* and *Rockaway Beach* are accessible from Queens and Brooklyn. Other beaches include *Orchard Beach* in Pelham Bay Park, *South Beach* and *Wolfe's Pond Park* on Staten Island. The most popular beach with New Yorkers is *Jones Beach State Park*. This 20km (12-mile) strand has all the amenities of a thriving resort. An hour's drive from the city, there are road/rail excursions available from Pennsylvania Station, and daily coach trips from the Port Authority Bus Terminal.
ALBANY: The capital of New York State, Albany stands beside the Hudson River north of New York City. It is a good base from which to explore 'upstate New York'. Cars and campers may be rented. The city is dominated by the US$2-billion *Rockefeller Empire State Plaza*.
Excursions: The quickest access to gigantic *Adirondack Park* is by plane; the *Adirondack Railway* is also fairly fast (*Amtrak* can provide more information). The park's mountainous region, which includes *Lake Placid*, site of the 1932 and 1980 Winter Olympics, offers the widest variety of winter sports in the USA. Hiking, fishing, camping and boating are also on offer. Canoeists will enjoy the *Fulton Chain of Lakes*. *Lake George* is the most popular resort region in the southeastern corner of the park. The *Saratoga Spa State Park* in the Hudson Valley just south of Lake George has mineral baths and a *Performing Arts Center*, summer home of the *Philadelphia Orchestra* and the *New York City Ballet*. *Saratoga Race Track* and *Saratoga Harness Park* are major venues for racing enthusiasts. The *Thousand Island* region along the border with Canada has in fact almost 2000 islands, ranging from the tiny to the substantial, dotted around the St Lawrence River's entrance to Lake Ontario. Boat tours are available. *Alexandria Bay* is the central resort. The *Catskill Mountains*, southwest of Albany, are another popular wilderness area.

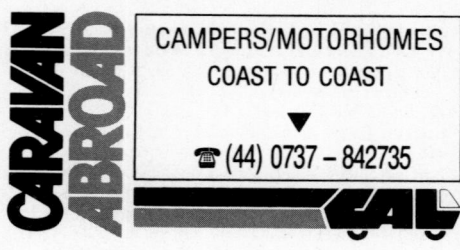

BUFFALO: Standing at the eastern extremity of Lake Erie on the border with Canada, Buffalo is a large industrial city. It is the gateway to Niagara Falls, one of the most outstanding spectacles on the North American continent and to the Finger Lakes region. It is also within easy reach of Lake Ontario and Toronto. Watkins Glen at the head of Lake Seneca has a famous motor-racing circuit.
NIAGARA FALLS: There are limousine services from *Greater Buffalo Airport (BUF)* to the city, 14.5km (9 miles) away, or direct to Niagara Falls. Taxis are also available. *Amtrak* offer rail links from Buffalo to Niagara and there are frequent local buses. *Greyhound* provide a direct service from New York to Niagara. There are in fact three main waterfalls, American, Canadian (Horseshoe) and Bridal Veil Falls, each in a different stream of the Niagara River. The drop is about 55m (180ft). Boat trips are available above and below Niagara Falls. Observation platforms set in the cliffs beside (and even behind) the Falls are reached via tunnels. Niagara is a popular honeymoon destination.
Note: For information on attractions in neighbouring states, see above under *States A-Z*.

SOCIAL PROFILE

FOOD & DRINK: New York runs the whole gamut, from *haute cuisine* to *pretzel* stalls. The staple US fare of steaks, seafood and hamburgers is sold all over the city. Excellent French food is available in the East 50s and 60s, in particular between 5th and 3rd Avenues. Authentic Spanish, Indian, Thai, Turkish, Jewish and Cuban restaurants can be found in Broadway along the Upper West Side. German, Czech and Hungarian restaurants are found in Yorkville, Italian and Chinese restaurants in Little Italy and Chinatown, and Greek and Armenian food near 5th Avenue. Greenwich Village offers predominantly Mexican, Italian and Spanish food. Uptown and midtown Manhattan offer everything from cheap, unexciting diners to coffee shops, milk bars and luxury restaurants. Late-night eateries are everywhere. Portions are large and many establishments offer good value meals.
Information on dining out: The Convention & Visitors Bureau publishes a free guide, while *New Yorker Magazine* provides weekly listings of city and suburban restaurants.
Drink: 'Singles bars' are mainly located on the Upper East Side between 59th and 86th Streets, on 3rd, 2nd and 1st Avenues. Moderate prices are charged for food and drink. Bars and lounges often stay open until 0400. They range from smart pre-theatre cocktail bars to seedy establishments for seasoned drinkers. The choice of drinks is extremely wide in most medium- to better-class establishments. 'Happy hour' is generally between 1730 and 1900 and many bars offer free hot and cold food to entice further custom.
THEATRES & CONCERTS: There are numerous theatres both 'on-' and 'off-' Broadway and many smaller, less expensive establishments are located all over the city. Concerts, revues and special performances are held at *Radio City Music Hall* throughout the year. The *Lincoln Center* complex includes the *Metropolitan Opera House*, the *New York City Opera & Ballet* and the *American Ballet Theater*. There are symphony concerts and recitals in *Carnegie Hall* during the autumn, winter and spring seasons. Greenwich Village and SoHo offer the best selection of jazz and rock clubs, cinemas and off-Broadway fringe shows in the world. (Midtown offers more commercial cinema and Broadway plays or musicals.) Cheap tickets for same-day performances can be obtained at the *TKTS* booth at 47th Street and Broadway. Free tickets for recordings of television shows are also available.
NIGHTLIFE: Few would argue that New York's nightlife is the most vibrant and diverse in the world. Entertainment magazines such as *Where*, *Promenade*, the *Village Voice* and the *New Yorker* can keep you in touch with what's going on in and around the 'Big Apple'.
Nightclubs: 'Supper clubs' are plush places for dinner or late supper, with two shows nightly by a famous entertainer. Generally the cover charge per person is quite high; 'cover charges' do not cover either food or drink. Other nightclubs have a minimum amount customers are obliged to spend. There are numerous underground clubs and discos throughout the city.
SHOPPING: There is an incomparable variety of goods and services in New York City – both in the elegant stores along 5th Avenue and in Herald Square, and in the smart uptown boutiques. The most famous department stores are Bloomingdales, Macy's (the largest), Gimbels, Alexander's and Saks Fifth Avenue. Ethnic goods may be purchased in Chinatown, Little Italy and Yorkville; bargains on Orchard Street; and an array of antiques, jewellery, leather and 'trendy' fashions catering to every imaginable taste in Greenwich Village. There are many popular galleries, bookstores, art shows and flea markets.
Bargains: These can be found on the Lower East Side, generally away from midtown. Each street has a speciality – fashion, jewellery, music, flowers or gourmet foods. Discount shops often offer better value than 'special sales' at the big-name stores.
SPECIAL EVENTS: The following are a selection of the events taking place in New York City in 1993. For full details contact the New York State Visitors Bureau. **Mar 7 '93** *Making Brooklyn Bloom Flower Show*, Brooklyn Botanic Garden. **Apr** *Easter Show*, Radio City Music Hall. **May 9** *Salute to Israel Parade*, Fifth Avenue. **Jun** *23rd Annual Lesbian/Gay Pride March*, Fifth Avenue. **Jun/Jul** *Free Metropolitan Opera concerts*, in the parks of all five boroughs. **Jul 4** *Macy's Fireworks Celebrations*, Lower Hudson River. **Jul 16-Oct 3** *Hand-Painted Pop Exhibition*, Whitney Museum of Art. **Sep 6** *West Indian American Day Carnival*, Crown Heights, Brooklyn; *Labor Day Parade*, Fifth Avenue. **Oct 11** *Columbus Day Parade*, Fifth Avenue, 44th to 86th Streets. **Nov** *The Fall Flower Show*, New York Botanical Garden, Bronx. **Nov 25** *67th Annual Macy's Thanksgiving Day*, Broadway. **Dec 31** *Runners World Midnight Run*, Central Park; *New Year's Eve Fireworks*, Prospect Park, Brooklyn and over East River; *3rd Annual First Night*, Grand Central Terminal. **Feb '94** *Chinese New Year Celebrations*.

CLIMATE

The climate is changeable with moderate rainfall throughout the year. During the summer heatwaves are common, with temperatures staying at over 37°C for several days.

NEW YORK New York (96m)

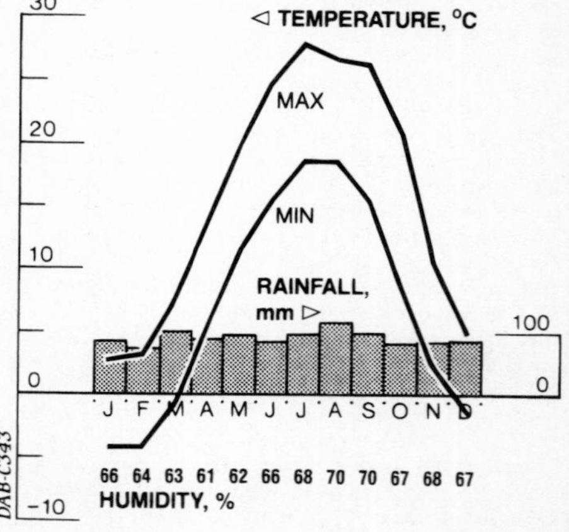

PENNSYLVANIA

Including **Philadelphia,** gateway to George Washington Country – the States of Pennsylvania, Delaware, Maryland, West Virginia and Virginia.

Pennsylvania Bureau of Travel Development
Department of Commerce
453 Forum Building
Harrisburg, PA
17120
Tel: (717) 787 5453. Fax: (717) 234 4560. Telex: 902362.

Philadelphia Convention & Visitors Bureau
Suite 2020
1515 Market Street
Philadelphia, PA
19102
Tel: (215) 636 3300. Fax: (215) 636 3327. Telex: 244442.

Gettysburg Travel Council
35 Carlisle Street
Gettysburg, PA
17325-1899
Tel: (717) 334 6274. Fax: (717) 334 1166.

TIME: GMT - 5. *Daylight Saving Time* is observed from the first Sunday in April to the last Sunday in October. Clocks are put forward one hour, changing at 0200 hours local time.

THE STATE: Pennsylvania is the state in which the USA was born. The country's Founding Fathers signed the Declaration of Independence and the Constitution at Independence Hall in Philadelphia – now one of the largest cities in the USA. Pennsylvanians represent a rich mix of cultural and ethnic backgrounds, while its boundaries embrace farmland, mountain ranges, forests, scenic rivers and waterways. Its northwestern edge borders on one of North America's Great Lakes, Lake Erie.

TRAVEL

AIR: Approximate flight times: From Philadelphia to *London* is 9 hours 25 minutes (including stopover) and to *New York* is 50 minutes.

International airports: *Philadelphia International (PHL)* is 13km (8 miles) southwest of the city (travel time – 25 minutes). The cheapest way to reach the city centre is *Southeastern Pennsylvania Transit Authority's (SEPTA) Airport Express Train*, running every 30 minutes to all three city centre stations, 0600-2400 daily. Taxis, hire cars and limousine services are also available.

Greater Pittsburgh Airport receives international, USA long-distance and regional flights. It is 22.5km (14 miles) west of Pittsburgh city centre. Limousine services, taxis, *Greyhound* buses and *Amtrak* rail services are available.

SEPTA has interconnecting buses, streetcars and elevated railways. The *Cultural Bus Loop* tours the city's major attractions.

RAIL: Philadelphia is served by *Amtrak's* shuttle service between Washington DC and New York (travel time – 1 hour 30 minutes to both cities) and also receives trains from New Orleans, Miami and Chicago. See *Illinois* and *New York* sections above for examples of journey times on several services passing through the city.

ROAD: Road travel in Pennsylvania is excellent, with good roads to Philadelphia, Scranton, Harrisburg, Pittsburgh and to outside destinations such as Binghamton in New York and Morgantown in West Virginia. The Pennsylvania Turnpike is a toll road providing swift and efficient travel across the state from New Jersey to Ohio.

Approximate driving times: From Philadelphia to *New York* is 2 hours, to *Baltimore* is 2 hours, to *Washington DC* is 3 hours, to *Pittsburgh* is 6 hours, to *Chicago* is 15 hours, to *Miami* is 25 hours, to *Dallas* is 31 hours, to *Los Angeles* is 56 hours and to *Seattle* is 59 hours.

All times are based on non-stop driving at or below the applicable speed limits.

Approximate *Greyhound* journey times: From Philadelphia (tel: (215) 931 4000) to *New York* is 2 hours, to *Washington DC* is 3 hours, to *Pittsburgh* is 7 hours, to *Chicago* is 18 hours, to *Miami* is 30 hours, to *Dallas* is 37 hours, to *Los Angeles* is 65 hours and to *Seattle* is 74 hours.

RESORTS & EXCURSIONS

PHILADELPHIA: Situated on the Delaware River, Philadelphia is the gateway for those travelling west into Pennsylvania Dutch Country, north into the ski resorts of the Pocono Mountains and southeast to the Delaware Peninsula and Atlantic Seaboard beaches. Now the fifth largest city in the USA, it is a vibrant national centre of commerce, industry, medical education, research and the arts, while preserving quiet pockets of some of the nation's most historic territory.

Sightseeing: In 1776, the Declaration of Independence and the Constitution were signed in *Independence Hall*, which stands in the centre of *Independence National Historical Park*. The glass *Liberty Bell Pavilion* houses the bell that was sounded at the first public reading of the Independence Declaration. *Franklin Court*, where Franklin's home once stood, houses an underground museum. Other places of interest include the *Old City Hall*, early home of the US Supreme Court; *Christ Church*, where Franklin and George Washington once worshipped; *Fairmount Park* by the Schuylkill River, one of the USA's

largest city parks; the *Philadelphia Museum of Art & Rodin Museum; Penn's Landing*, where state founder William Penn first arrived in 1682; and *Valley Forge National Historical Park*, just west of the city, one of the most revered shrines of the American Revolution.
PITTSBURGH: The second largest city in the state, Pittsburgh is an energetic metropolis of towering skyscrapers and landscaped parks. It was once known primarily as the USA's pre-eminent centre of steel production, but the steel mills are today in decline.
Sightseeing: The *Point State Park Fountain* symbolises the meeting of the Monongahela, Allegheny and Ohio rivers; it may be found in the breathtaking downtown area known as the *Golden Triangle*. Other attractions include the *Buhl Science Center;* the *University of Pittsburgh*, a 42-storey cathedral of learning; the *Museum of Natural History* at the *Carnegie Institute;* and the *Fort Pitt Museum*, which celebrates west Pennsylvanian history.
Excursions: *Pennsylvania Dutch Country* (actually settled by Germans in the 18th century) is in the southeast of the state. Many of the people belong to the Amish sect and retain the beliefs and customs of their forefathers. Amish men wear beards, black hats and coats. The women wear bonnets and simple, full-length dresses. Towns to visit include **Lancaster, Lititz, Strasburg, Bird-in-Hand** and **Ephrata. Harrisburg** has a magnificent 650-room State Capitol building. **Gettysburg,** the famous American Civil War battle site, features the *Gettysburg National Military Park* and the *Eisenhower National Historic Site*. The *Pocono Mountains* offer fishing, hunting, hiking, riding and camping, with skiing in the winter. Their resorts rival Niagara Falls as popular honeymoon destinations.
Note: For information on attractions in neighbouring states, see above under *States A-Z*.

SOCIAL PROFILE

FOOD & DRINK: Various regions in Pennsylvania have their own specialities. In the Pocono Mountains area, superb local mountain trout is featured in many restaurants. Pennsylvania Dutch food is a unique variation of German cuisine, including pickles, relishes, apple butter, dumplings, pretzels, molasses and shoo-fly pie. Seven sweet and seven sour dishes are served in a type of smorgasbord. There are some sausages and cold cuts that originate from this region, such as the delicious Lebanon baloney and dried beef. The best restaurants for this unique cuisine can be found around Lancaster. **Drink:** The legal age for drinking is 21 in Pennsylvania and bottled liquor is only sold in state stores.
THEATRES & CONCERTS: Summer performances in the round are staged at the *John B Kelly Playhouse*. The city's opera house and concert hall is at the *Academy of Music*, the home of the *Philadelphia Orchestra*. The huge *Mann Music Center* in Fairmount Park stages summer concerts.
NIGHTLIFE: There are numerous supper clubs, nightclubs, jazz clubs and other entertainments.
SHOPPING: Philadelphia has always been famous for antiques and handicrafts. The main shopping areas include New Market, Head House Square and the Bourse. John Wanamaker is an elegant department store in Philadelphia well worth a visit.
SPECIAL EVENTS: There are numerous and varied festivals throughout the state. The following is a list of some of the major events taking place during 1993/4. For full details contact the Philadelphia Convention and Visitors Bureau.
May 27-31 '93 *Mayfair*, Allentown. **May 28-30** *The 8th Annual Jambalaya Jam* (3-day food and music festival), Great Plaza, Penn's Landing. **Jun 4-20** *Three Rivers Arts Festival*, Pittsburgh. **Jun 13-Sep 5** *Longwood Gardens Festival of Fountains* (annual and perennial flowers in bloom), Kennett Square, Chester County. **Jun 26-Jul 4** *Gettysburg Civil War Heritage Days* (commorating the Battle of Gettysburg), Gettysburg. **Jun 26-Jul 5** *44th Annual Kutztown Folk Festival*, Kutztown. **Jul 3-Oct 17** *Pennsylvania Renaissance Faire* (16th century re-creation of Elizabethan Britain), Cornwall, Lancaster County. **Jul** *Riverblues*, Philadelphia. **Aug 5-8** *Three Rivers Regatta*, Pittsburgh. **Aug 14-22** *Musikfest* (music from Bach to Bluegrass and ethnic food), Bethlehem. **Aug 25-28** *Little League World Series*, Williamsport, Lycoming County. **Aug 27-29** *Philadelphia Folk Festival*, Schwenksville, Montgomery County. **Sep 25-Oct 2** *The Bloomsburg Fair*, Bloomsburg, Columbia County. **Oct 15-17** *Shawnee Autumn Hot Air Balloon Festival*, Shawnee-on-Delaware, Monroe County. **Nov 26-Jan 2 '94** *A Brandywine Christmas*, Chadds Ford, Delaware County.

CLIMATE

The weather can be changeable, with moderate amounts of rain throughout the year. Summers are warm with occasional heat waves.
Required clothing: Lighter weights during the summer, heavyweights for the winter months.

TEXAS

Including **Dallas/Fort Worth** and **Houston,** gateways to the southwest States of New Mexico, Oklahoma, Arkansas and Louisiana.

Texas Department of Tourism and Commerce
PO Box 12728
Suite 1190
816 Congress
Austin, TX
78711
Tel: (512) 320 9449. Fax: (512) 320 9456.
Austin Convention and Visitors Bureau
201 East 2nd Street
Austin, TX
78704
Tel: (512) 474 5171. Fax: (512) 474 5183.
Arlington Convention and Visitors Bureau
PO Box A
Suite 650
1250 East Copeland Road
Arlington, TX
76011
Tel: (817) 265 7721. Fax: (817) 265 5640.
Dallas Convention and Visitors Bureau
Suite 2000
1201 Elm Street
Dallas, TX
75270
Tel: (214) 746 6646. Fax: (214) 746 6688.
Fort Worth Convention and Visitors Bureau
415 Throckmorton Street
Fort Worth, TX
76102
Tel: (817) 336 8791. Fax: (817) 336 3282.
Greater Houston Convention and Visitors Bureau
3rd Floor
801 Congress Avenue
Houston, TX
77002
Tel: (713) 227 3100. Fax: (713) 227 6339. Telex: 203274 GHCVCUR.
San Antonio Convention and Visitors Bureau
PO Box 2277
121 Alamo Plaza
San Antonio, TX
78298
Tel: (512) 270 8700. Fax: (512) 270 8782.

TIME: GMT - 6. *Daylight Saving Time* is observed – in the greater part of the state – from the first Sunday in April to the last Sunday in October. Clocks are put forward one hour, changing at 0200 hours local time.
THE STATE: Big, bold and colourful, the 'Lone Star State' is the second largest in the USA, covering more than 431,000 sq km (262,017 sq miles). Spain was the first European power to lay claim to Texas; it also flew the flags of France and Mexico before gaining its independence in 1836. It was granted US statehood in 1846. Texas borders Mexico along the Rio Grande and embraces vast mountain ranges and canyons to the west; lakes, plantations and pine forests to the east; broad plains to the north; citrus groves, Gulf of Mexico beaches and low-lying alluvial plains to the south; and emerald hill country and clear natural springs at its heart. Its great wealth stems from its vast oil reserves. It has several booming cities: Houston, Dallas, Fort Worth, San Antonio, El Paso and its capital city, Austin.

TRAVEL

AIR: Approximate flight times: From *Dallas/Fort Worth* to Austin is 50 minutes, to London is 11 hours (including stopover), to Miami is 2 hours 40 minutes and to New York is 3 hours 30 minutes.
From *Houston* to London is 10 hours 15 minutes, to Miami is 2 hours 25 minutes and to New York is 3 hours 30 minutes.
International airports: *Dallas/Fort Worth International (DFW)* is 27km (17 miles) from both cities; travel time – 35 minutes. Complimentary coach is available to most major hotels. There are bus services to downtown areas of both cities three times daily. Taxis are also available.
Houston (IAH) (Intercontinental) is 32km (20 miles) north of the city; travel time – 30 minutes. Complimentary coaches depart for most major hotels every 30 minutes, 24 hours a day. There are buses to downtown and surrounding areas at reasonable prices. Taxis are also available, but expensive.
San Antonio International Airport is 14km (8.5 miles) from downtown, with flights from Latin America and major US cities. Express bus to the city centre costs 40 cents and there is a shuttle to the city centre for US$6. Taxis are available to the city centre for an approximate cost of US$12. Some hotels provide complimentary coaches from the airport to the hotel.
El Paso International Airport is 13km (8 miles) east of downtown; it serves as a gateway to the mountain and canyon country.
Domestic airport: *Love Field* is 9.5km (6 miles) from Dallas city centre.
RAIL: *Amtrak* journeys between main cities are difficult and can only be made on the daily long-distance trains. Dallas/Fort Worth is on the Los Angeles–San Antonio –Chicago line and Houston on the Los Angeles–New Orleans line. See *California* section above for approximate journey times. There are no local rail services.
ROAD: *Greyhound* runs frequent services connecting Dallas, Fort Worth, Houston, San Antonio and other major towns and cities in Texas and further afield. Local bus services off the main routes are not highly developed.
Approximate driving times: From *Dallas/Fort Worth* to Oklahoma City is 4 hours 30 minutes, to Houston is 4 hours 30 minutes, to San Antonio is 6 hours, to Little Rock is 7 hours, to Amarillo is 7 hours, to Kansas City is 7 hours, to Jackson is 8 hours, to New Orleans is 10 hours, to El Paso is 12 hours, to St Louis is 13 hours, to Denver is 16 hours, to Chicago is 19 hours, to Mexico City is 24 hours, to Miami is 28 hours, to Los Angeles is 29 hours, to New York is 33 hours and to Seattle is 44 hours.
From *Houston* to San Antonio is 4 hours, to Brownsville is 7 hours, to New Orleans is 7 hours, to El Paso is 15 hours, to Chicago is 24 hours, to Miami is 25 hours, to Los Angeles is 31 hours, to New York is 36 hours and to Seattle is 49 hours.
All times are based on non-stop driving at or below the applicable speed limits.
Approximate *Greyhound* journey times: From *Dallas/Fort Worth* (tel: (214) 655 7000) to Oklahoma City is 4 hours 30 minutes, to Houston is 4 hours 30 minutes, to San Antonio is 6 hours, to Tulsa is 7 hours, to Amarillo is 8 hours, to Memphis is 13 hours 30 minutes, to New Orleans is 13 hours and to El Paso is 13 hours.
From *Houston* (tel: (713) 759 6581) to San Antonio is 4 hours, to Dallas is 4 hours 30 minutes and to New Orleans is 8 hours 30 minutes.
URBAN: Dallas/Fort Worth: The various bus networks are well-run and reasonably priced. Buses between Dallas and Fort Worth are operated by *Greyhound*. Most major car-hire companies have offices in both cities. Local firms with cars and motor campers for rent are listed in the Dallas/Fort Worth classified telephone directory.
Houston: The *Metropolitan Transport Authority (METRO)* provides reasonably priced bus services. Taxis are readily available, but this type of travel can be impractical and expensive for short distances. Rental cars are the best way to get around, but visitors are advised to make advance reservations as the demand is high. For local firms see the Houston classified telephone directory under 'Car Rentals'.

RESORTS & EXCURSIONS

DALLAS: Originally a trading post, Dallas has grown into a centre for commerce and fashion of worldwide importance. It has a glittering high-rise skyline, elegant stores, fine restaurants and a rich cultural life. Located in the heart of the north Texas prairie, Dallas is a modern sophisticated city, yet still possessing the much renowned Texan hospitality and southwestern charm. It is increasingly recognised for its cosmopolitan spirit and entrepeneurial flair.

Dallas skyline

Sightseeing: Dallas is a city rich in historical sites and futuristic sights. The downtown area features shimmering glass towers and angled spires, whereas down below in the *West End Historic District* there are 100-year-old buildings now occupied by lively shops, restaurants and museums. The *McKinney Avenue Trolley* rolls down red-brick streets. *Old City Park* is a pioneer community featuring homes, a church, a schoolhouse and Main Street as it was in the days of the original settlers. The 50-storey *Reunion Tower* has a glass elevator ride to observation terraces and a revolving restaurant with night-time dancing. *Dealey Plaza* is the site where President John F Kennedy was assassinated and there is a dramatic exhibit on the event located on the sixth floor. The *John F Kennedy Memorial* at Main and Market Streets is open all year round. Popular attractions are the *DeGolyer Estate*, built by a rich oil baron and *Southfork Ranch*, the home of famous TV series' Ewing clan. Amongst its many other attractions are the *Age of Steam Museum*, *Dallas Health & Science Museum*, with many hands-on exhibitions, the *Planetarium*, *Dallas Museum of Art*, *Dallas Museum of Natural History*, with a superb dinosaur exhibition, and the *Texas Hall of State*. Favourite family activities include *Penny Whistle Park*, the *Dallas Aquarium*, the *Farmer's Market* and the *Dallas Zoo*, featuring 'the Wilds of Africa'. Outdoors activities include the *Dallas Arboretum* and the Dallas *Civic Garden Center*. The major recreational centre is *State Fair Park*. Recreational facilities available in Dallas include paddleboating among the ducks on *Bachman Lake* and horseriding through the backwoods of a real Texan ranch.

FORT WORTH: Much more 'Western' in spirit, Fort Worth started as a military outpost and then became a cow town where cattlemen brought their herds to be shipped. Much of the Old West is preserved in Fort Worth today and it continues to be a centre for the cattle industry.

Sightseeing: The historic stockyards on Northside retain the flavour of the Old West. There is also a log cabin village, a zoological park and a Japanese garden. Museums include the *Amon Carter Museum of Western Art*, the *Sid Richardson Collection of Western Art*, the *Fort Worth Art Museum* and the *Kimbell Art Museum*.

Excursions: The *Six Flags Over Texas* theme park, between Dallas and Fort Worth, offers more than 200 rides and attractions. **Abilene,** 242km (151 miles) west of Fort Worth, has a reconstructed frontier settlement. *Palo Duro Canyon State Park* near **Amarillo** in the far north of the state has startling scenery and facilities for hiking, picnicking, camping and horseriding. The *Panhandle-Plains Museum* in the nearby city of **Canyon** charts the region's development from early Indian life to modern farming and ranching.

HOUSTON: The fourth largest city in the USA and the largest in Texas, with a population of more than 2.7 million, Houston has been the centre of the US oil industry ever since 'black gold' was discovered at nearby Beaumont in 1901. The city is named after Texas hero General Sam Houston, the first President of the Republic of Texas. It is also the space headquarters of the USA (NASA's Lyndon B Johnson Space Center is nearby) and a thriving international port, being connected to the Gulf of Mexico by the 80km (50-mile) Houston Ship Canal. Houston's towering skyscrapers reflect its booming economy.

Sightseeing: Downtown attractions include the modern *Civic Center*, *Sam Houston Historical Park*, *Tranquility Park* and the *Old Market Square*. The *Houston Zoological Gardens' Discovery Hall* exhibit is popular with children for its collection of friendly and pettable animals. Admission is free. The veteran pre-World War One battleship 'Texas' is moored on the San Jacinto River near the *Battleground Monument*, which marks the 1836 battle for Texan independence. The *Lyndon B Johnson Space Center* has exhibitions of space technology and stages regular film shows explaining the US space programme.

Excursions: The spectacular *Astrodome* sports stadium is 10km (6 miles) from Houston city centre. Nearby *Astroworld* is a family entertainment park with live shows, restaurants and rides; whilst next door to that is *Waterworld*, a water recreation park. **Galveston Island,** southeast of Houston on the *Gulf of Mexico*, is rich in history and pirate lore and noted for its sandy beaches, fishing and watersports.

SAN ANTONIO: This modern, prosperous city retains much of its Spanish heritage with its fiestas, buildings and lifestyle and is the number 1 visitor city in Texas. The city's Paseo del Rio shopping and entertainments area is unique.

Sightseeing: In 1836, the *Alamo* was the site of a furious battle between a handful of independence-seeking Texans (led by Davy Crockett) and a large Mexican army. Today it is a shrine to Texan courage and patriotism. The 6-storey-high *IMAX Theater* tells the whole story of the Alamo in a gripping film. *Brackenridge Park*, nearby, embraces the headwaters of the San Antonio River and groves of ancient oaks. San Antonio is also home to two major theme parks – the world's largest marine life park, *Sea World of Texas;* and *Fiesta Texas*, which features continuous live stage shows and the world's highest and fastest wooden roller-coaster.

Excursions: Pack-trips and working ranch holidays are widely available in the hill country to the west of San Antonio. **New Braunfels,** between Austin and San Antonio, was founded by German immigrants in the 1840s. Today their descendants celebrate their heritage with traditional German festivals. **Corpus Christi** on the Gulf of Mexico, an ideal pirates' hideaway in the 1800s, is now a major seaport and resort, famous for its fishing and surfboarding competitions. Just off the coast is **Padre Island,** a narrow 170km (95-mile) barrier island with watersports and fishing centres and an impressive expanse of protected National Seashore, wildlife refuges and birdlife sites; it is connected to Corpus Christi by a causeway.

AUSTIN: The state capital, 128km (80 miles) northeast of San Antonio, is the gateway to the Texas Hill Country and the chain of Highland lakes. It is one of the most beautiful cities in the USA and the golf paradise of Texas.

Sightseeing: The *Capitol Building*, nine historical districts, the *Austin Steam Train* and *Celis Brewery*. The 300-acre *University of Texas* campus offers the *Lyndon B Johnson Presidential Library*, the *Texas Confederate Museum* and the 1856 *Governor's Mansion*.

Excursions: The 240km (150-mile) chain of *Highland Lakes*, to the northwest of the city, are excellent for fishing, boating and swimming. A day trip into the scenic hill country where several award-winning wineries are located is well worthwhile.

EL PASO: The state's westernmost city stands beside the Rio Grande in the dramatic Franklin Mountains. The largest US city on the Mexican border, it is actually closer to metropolitan areas of New Mexico, Arizona and southern California than it is to any major Texan cities. The city's

Historical Texas Landmark

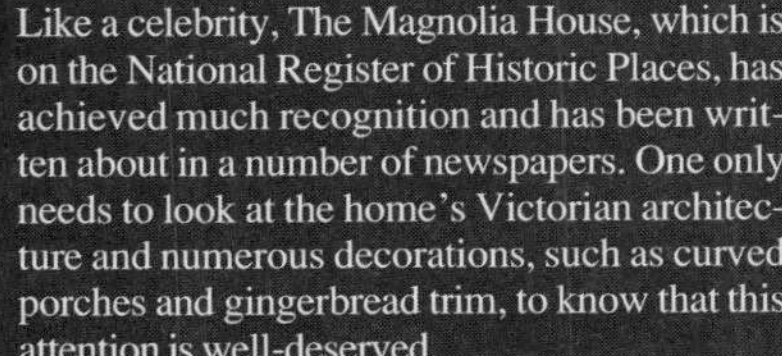

Like a celebrity, The Magnolia House, which is on the National Register of Historic Places, has achieved much recognition and has been written about in a number of newspapers. One only needs to look at the home's Victorian architecture and numerous decorations, such as curved porches and gingerbread trim, to know that this attention is well-deserved.

Built in 1895 by Dr Nathan Cass and situated on a full city block with grounds enclosed by a picket fence, the two-and-half-story wood frame residence is a lavish showplace both inside and out. The overall design is that of a Mississippi steamboat, Details are extensive, especially the intricate carvings throughout, cypress exterior siding and floor-to-ceiling windows on the porches.

the regal facade beckons one to open the front doors. First to greet you is the entry hall paneled with tight-grain curly pine, which leads to a parlor with Mozart square grand piano, circa 1850. Stair balusters are turned spindles with wheel motifs at the landing and above. A pine beaded-board wainscot lines the stair well and upstairs hall.

Perfect for private dinner parties, luncheons and receptions is the dining room with antique chandelier and built-in china cabinet. Meals can easily be prepared in the kitchen. Nearby is the pantry. Years ago, the kitchen was in a separate building, which today serves as a garage and place for storage.

Dr. Cass' office is now a library. In this room, there is an array of antique furniture, much of it dating back to the 1800s. The library mantel is of special interest since it has a secret compartment in which the doctor was said to have hidden money and drugs.

Upstairs are the bedrooms, which boast rosewood bedroom furniture that had travelled from New Orleans to Europe and then to Corsica. Also on this level is a lovely sitting room adorned with antique white wicker.

A tour of the grounds will make one feel as though they are in another time and place. A big tree, well over 100 years old, is the focal point. The Gazebo displays many of the fine qualities of the house, such as railings and brackets.

Since May of 1988, The Magnolia House has been open to the public. Now it is time to add a new chapter to this historically rich home, . . and a new owner. Rarely will one find a home so well preserved with antique fixtures but modernised with today's amenities.

Offered at US$1,200,000 including an extensive art and antique collection.

Canada's Finest Country Estate

Rarely does an estate of this importance become available. Designed, conceived and constructed by one of the world's foremost entrepreneurs for his own private country estate, with the utmost in privacy and seclusion, yet only 40 miles northwest of Toronto and only minutes form Highway 401. this private retreat is nestled on 113 picturesque acres of gently rolling hills and ponds. A magnificent stone and wrought-iron security gate with video cameras announces the arrival of your guests. A long, paved driveway winds its way thorough the professionally landscaped , manicured grounds to an exquisite custom built mansion, measuring approximately 14,000 sq ft, with a spectacular indoor swimming pool, five bedrooms, eight baths, and nine fireplaces. This prime property offers every amenity one would imagine.

Designed for grand scale entertaining and family living, the main floor features an elegant marble floored foyer, with stained and leaded glass mahogany doors. A 24ft marble floored sitting room adjoins the main dining room, 20ft by 13ft, with custom plaster hand painted ceiling and cornices. The family room features a stone fireplace and sliding glass doors open to the Banquet Hall, 35ft by 20ft, which seats 50. Designed for the most lavish dinner parties. the Banquet Hall features stripped purple heart flooring, four corinthian columns and an antique marble hand-carved French fireplace mantle. The main floor also has a marble floored library and a parquet floored den. Other entertaining rooms include the solarium, 26ft by 20ft, and the entertainment centre, 21ft by 16ft, with high cedar beamed ceiling and a floating staircase leading to the pool and recreation room.

The second floor features the master suite with a 27ft by 15ft bedroom with a two-sided quartz fireplace, private patio and lavish his and hers bath-dressing complexes. There are four additional guest suites on the second floor.

Offered at US$6,800,000.

DALLAS, TX 214-698-1736
LAKE TAHOE, RENO, NV 800-338-4664
WASHINGTON, DC 202-638-2033
TORONTO, ONTARIO 416-760-4238
NEWPORT BEACH, CA 714-675-1931
SAVANNAH, GA 912-356-3322
BEVERLY HILLS, CA 213-855-0384
SANTA BARBARA, CA 805-966-0219

PHILADELPHIA, PA 215-592-8109
PALM SPRINGS, CA 619-341-9727
SAN CLEMENTE, CA 714-492-3512

MARLYN HOFFMAN – HOFFMAN REALTY
6835 WESTLAKE,
DALLAS,
TEXAS 75214.

aerial tramway gives breathtaking views across Texas and Mexico. El Paso offers a wide variety of cultural and sports activities, including symphony concerts, theatre, museums, libraries, horse and hound racing and many other sports. The *University of Texas*, known for its Bhutanese-style architecture, and *Sun Bowl* stadium are located here.
Excursions: *Big Bend National Park*, south of El Paso, boasts spectacular views of stark desert, forests, mountains and canyons carved by the *Rio Grande*.
Note: For information on attractions in neighbouring states, see above under *States A-Z*.

SOCIAL PROFILE

FOOD & DRINK: Dallas/Fort Worth: Beef features widely, this being cattle country, but there is also a great variety of international cuisine including French, Italian, Chinese, Spanish and Mexican. Dallas has three AAA Five Diamond-rated restaurants – more than any other US city; they include The French Room at the Adolphus Hotel, The Mansion on Turtle Creek and Routh Street Café. In all, Dallas boasts more than 5000 restaurants. Country cooking is popular and includes such local specialities as chicken-fried steak and catfish fried in cornmeal batter. There are several dinner theatres where you can eat and see a show. There are also many cafeterias and coffee shops. **Houston:** A great variety of restaurants serving many different types of food. Specialities include Mexican and Spanish cuisine and Gulf seafood. The Convention & Visitors Council publishes a restaurant directory. **Austin:** Approximately 1500 restaurants offer a variety of cuisine including Texan-style steaks and barbecues, Mexican, Mediterranean, Italian, typical American and many more. **San Antonio:** Tex-Mex was practically invented here and this native cuisine can be found throughout the city, along with everything from down-home barbeque specialities to 4-star French cuisine.
THEATRES & CONCERTS: Dallas: The *Dallas Music Hall* in State Fair Park stages concerts, musicals and operas. The *Dallas Theater* presents a wide range of drama. The downtown arts district houses the *Morton H Meyerson Symphony Center, Dallas Museum of Art* and the *Arts District Theater*. Avant-garde theatres can be found in Deep Ellum. **Fort Worth:** The *William Edrington Scott Theater* presents plays, musicals and films. *Casa Manana* stages Broadway musicals during the summer. **Houston:** The *Jesse H Jones Hall for the Performing Arts* is the home of the *Houston Symphony Orchestra*, the *Houston Ballet* and the *Grand Opera*. Other venues include the renowned *Alley Theater*, the open-air *Miller Theater* in Herman Park and the *Music Hall*. **Austin:** The *Paramount Theater* presents top name entertainers in musicals, comedies, concerts and dramas. The *Zachary Scott Theater* presents musicals and plays and the *Zilker Hillside Theater* has outdoor musicals and plays. The *Frank Erwin Center* is known for its major recording artist concerts. **San Antonio:** The *Majestic Theater* hosts the *San Antonio Symphony*, as well as travelling broadway shows and concerts. The unique *Arneson Theater* is an outdoor theatre on the banks of the Paseo del Rio.
NIGHTLIFE: Dallas has clubs, cabarets, discos, singles bars and corner pubs, with music ranging from classical to jazz and from country to contemporary rock. Some clubs are listed as 'private' – ie they are located in a 'dry' area and require membership if you are to be served alcohol. Membership is usually available for a nominal fee. There are also some comedy clubs sprinkled throughout the city and others offer comedy and drama while you dine. **Fort Worth** also has a number of nightclubs, but the musical emphasis here is on country & western music. **Houston's** many night spots range from big name entertainment to supper club revues, pavement cafés, discos and singles bars. **Austin** is noted worldwide for its nightly live music venues. Historic 6th Street takes on a lively atmosphere in the evenings as people go pub-crawling between venues catering for country & western, soul, rhythm and blues, rock and roll and jazz music. **San Antonio** offers all sorts of musical entertainment, including traditional 'Tejano' sounds, Dixieland jazz, symphony concerts, country & western and college music. The Paseo del Rio is the centre for much of the city's nightlife.
SPORT: The *Dallas Cowboys* **(American football)** and the *Dallas Sidekicks* **(soccer)** play at Texas Stadium (State Highway 183 at Loop 12). The Houston football team is the *Houston Oilers*. The *Texas Rangers* play **baseball** at Arlington Stadium on the Dallas-Fort Worth Turnpike and the *Houston Astros* play baseball at the famous Astrodome. The *Dallas Blackhawks* play **hockey** in Fair Park. Professional **basketball** is played by the *Dallas Mavericks* at Reunion Arena in Dallas, by the *Houston Rockets* in Houston and by the *San Antonio Spurs* at HemisFair Arena (the *Spurs* will be moving to the new 65,000-seat Alamodome in 1993). **Golf** courses are available in and around Austin and Dallas, and San Antonio has 11 courses. Dallas also has many facilities for tennis, softball, running, bicycling and polo.
SHOPPING: Dallas/Fort Worth: The elegant and original Neiman Marcus department store should be on any tourist's itinerary. Dallas Market Center is the largest wholesale trade shopping centre in the world and also offers fine restaurants. Dallas has more shopping centres per capita than any other US city and some of the largest shopping malls in the southwest. Both cities have fine speciality shops. **Houston:** World-class shopping is available in more than 300 stores at the famous Galleria shopping centre. The best buys are Western-style clothes, hats, boots, saddles and riding equipment. A printed guide to stores is available from the Convention & Visitors Council. **San Antonio:** Authentic Mexican folk art can be found throughout the city and there are nine major shopping malls.
SPECIAL EVENTS: The following is a list of some of the events taking place in 1993/4: **Mar 6-31 '93** *Dallas Blooms*, The Dallas Arboretum. **Mar 14** *St Patrick's Day Celebrations*. **Mar 31-Apr 4** *Dallas New Car Auto Show*, Dallas Convention Center. **Apr 24-25** *9th Annual Art Walk* (street festival showcasing Texas' visual and performing artists), Deep Ellum. **May 1** *Scarborough Faire* (medieval festival with jousters and damsels in distress), Waxahachie. **May 22-24** *Artfest, Memorial Day Weekend*, Dallas. **Jun** *Junteenth Festival*, Dallas. **Jul 16-18** *The West End's 7th Annual 'Taste of Dallas'*, West End Historic District, Dallas. **Aug** *Mesquite Balloon Festival*, Mesquite. **Sep** *Dallas Morning News Dance Festival*, Artist Square. **Oct 1-24** *Texas State Fair* (the largest State Fair in the USA), Fair Park '94 Dallas. **Dec/Jan**, *Cotton Bowl Pep Rally* (a week-long festival culminating in a gala and concert at Reunion Arena on New Year's Eve and a colourful parade and football game on New Year's Day), Dallas. **Feb/Mar** *Houston Livestock Show and Rodeo* (the largest livestock show in the USA); *Mardi Gras*, Galveston Island. For full details contact the Texas Department of Commerce, Tourism Division.

CLIMATE

Dry and warm to very hot throughout the year. Occasional freak rainstorms.
Required clothing: Lightweights throughout most of the year and warmer during winter.

DALLAS Texas (146m)

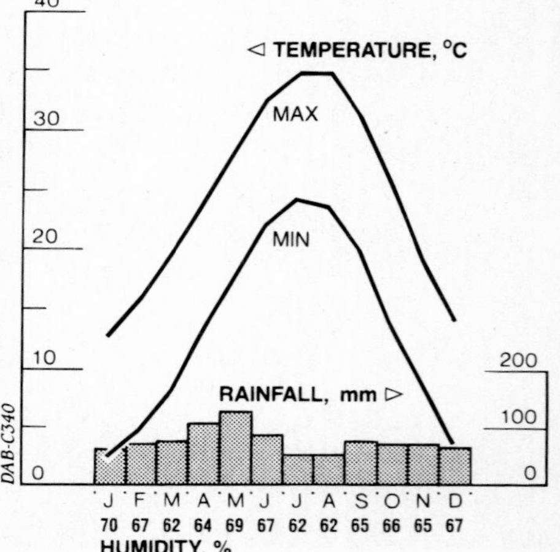

Welcome to DALLAS

Let us be the first to welcome you and your clients to Texas for the 1994 World Cup. The World Cup is destined to be the biggest sporting event to ever hit north Texas and we welcome you to take part.
World Cup fever is spreading like wildfire throughout the city of Dallas and the surrounding area, with soccer fans and volunteers gearing up for an international spectacle that surpasses even the Olympic Games. In fact, while 227 million viewers watched the last Super Bowl, over 1.3 billion people tuned into the last Championship Final of the World Cup. The 1994 World Cup means an economic bonanza for north Texas.

DALLAS WORLD CUP. Dallas scored a first in World Cup history in October when the city was awarded one of two opening-day games. Chicago and Dallas will be the only cities to host games on opening day – June 17, 1994. Between June 17 and July 10, the Cotton Bowl will host four first-round games, one round-of-sixteen game and one quarter-final. In all, as many as ten different national teams will play in Dallas, including four of the six top-ranking teams. The highlight will be the defending World Champions, Germany, who will play in the Cotton Bowl on Monday, June 17.
In addition to its advantageous game schedule, Dallas won out over Phoenix and Atlanta for the real economic blockbuster: host city for the International Broadcast Center (IBC). For approximately three months, Dallas will play host to an estimated 3000-4000 broadcasters and related technicians from around the world.
As an added bonus, FIFA, the worldwide governing body of soccer, chose Dallas for its World Cup 1994 operations headquarters. Although FIFA was expected to select a 'high profile' city such as Los Angeles or New York, Dallas was in fact their ultimate choice. During their technical inspection tour in 1992, FIFA officials Guido Tognoni and Walter Gagg stated that the combination of high-quality organisational efforts in Dallas, traditional Texas hospitality and the historic Fair Park location made Dallas the winner. Not only will Dallas be the broadcast centre, it will also be the nerve centre of the entire month-long tournament.
From their base in Fair Park, journalists will pick up the satellite signals from the nine host cities and instantly broadcast them to the world. For six weeks the entire world will hear, "Live via satellite from Dallas, Texas, USA . . ."
We think that's a wonderful sound and we hope you and your clients will join us as we kick off what is sure to be the most spectacular international event north Texas has ever seen.
Although the World Cup is not the only reason to come to Texas in 1994, it is certainly a great reason. Hospitality is our middle name and we hope you and your customers will give us the chance to show off our state.
For soccer enthusiasts and new fans alike, there is something in Texas for guests of all ages. Visitors to the north Texas area will experience a celebration that is truly international in flavour.
Experience Texas in 1994 and you will experience the world. Come see us.

FAIR PARK AND WORLD CUP VILLAGE

Fair Park, located in a 277-acre setting just 5km (three miles) from downtown Dallas, is an ideal location to house the World Cup facilities and events. Eight museums, ranging from the Age of the Steam Railroad Museum to the Museum of Natural History, are within the park grounds. The architectural style of the park is 1930s Art Deco, with fountains, outdoor courtyards, and endless gardens surrounding authentic buildings of the era.
Within Fair Park, the World Cup Village will be conveniently located 25 minutes from Dallas/Fort Worth International Airport and 15 minutes from Dallas Love Field Airport, allowing not only convenient access to international travel, but all major US cities as well. Due to its central location, Dallas is literally the 'gateway to the games'. All facilities in the Village, along with the Cotton Bowl, are located within a 5-minute walk of each other. Many of Dallas' finest restaurants and entertainment spots are located within a 5-mile radius of the Village.
The World Cup Village concept is based on the fact that all technical facilities for the World Cup will be contained within Fair Park, within easy walking distance of the stadium. The Village, situated within the beautiful and historic park, will be home to FIFA (the international football association) operations headquarters and the International Broadcast Center.

WORLD CUP '94

WORLD CUP DALLAS/FORT WORTH

Dallas☆Fort Worth

THINGS YOU ALWAYS WANTED TO KNOW ABOUT DALLAS

★ *The chicken fajita was first created in Dallas.*

★ *In July 1958, the computer chip was invented in Dallas, ushering in the computer age. Dallas has the highest concentration of high-tech companies and employees and is known as 'the Silicon Prairie'.*

★ *Dallas has more shopping space per shopper than any other city in the country.*

THE LOCATION Texas, the second largest state in the USA, is situated on the central south coast of America. Texas borders Mexico along the Rio Grande to the left, Oklahoma to the north, and Arkansas and Louisiana to the right. Dallas lies high in north central Texas, midway between both coasts.

THE LANDSCAPE Texas, big, bold and colourful, embraces a rich variety of landscape. It embraces vast mountain ranges and canyons to the west; lakes, plantations and pine forests to the east; broad plains to the north; citrus groves, Gulf-of-Mexico beaches and low-lying alluvial plains to the south; and emerald hill country and clear natural springs at its heart.

THE CULTURE AND HISTORY Dallas celebrated its 150th anniversary in 1991. In 1841, John Neely Bryan, a bachelor and lawyer from Tennessee with a taste for adventure, staked a claim on 640 acres, deciding the area would make a good trading post. He sketched out a town plan of a courthouse square with 20 streets around it and attracted farmers, traders and artisans to the area. Dallas residents have always been full of enterprise and ushered in the railroad in the 1870s, the Federal Reserve Bank in 1914, Love Field Airport in 1927 and DFW Airport in 1973. But perhaps even more significant was the discovery of oil in 1930, 161km (100 miles) east of Dallas. The East Oil Texas Field became the largest petroleum deposit in the world at the time and Dallas became a centre of oil-related activity. But Dallas' history has not always had a smooth ride. A couple of the USA's most notorious bank robbers lived in Dallas. In the early 1930s, Bonnie and Clyde called West Dallas home. In 1934, the law finally caught up with the outlaws. Clyde Barrow got 27 bullets, Bonnie Parker got 50. And their Ford got 107 bullets. And then there was November 22, 1963, when President John F Kennedy was assassinated on a downtown Dallas street – an event that devastated the nation. But Dallas has given a lot to the country as well – the Dallas Cowboys, for instance, or entrepreneurs such as Ross Perot and Mary Kay Ash. And as the 1980s came to a close, *Fortune Magazine* named Dallas/Fort Worth as the No 1 business centre in the land.

WHAT MAKES DALLAS SPECIAL For many of you, the name Dallas may conjure up a number of images, like cowboys riding the open range, or wildcat oilmen hitting a gusher, maybe even gunfighters in a high-noon shootout. For others, images of the TV show 'Dallas' may spring to mind. Legends and myths aside, no matter where you go in Dallas you're sure to encounter the ever-prevalent western spirit mixed with the sophistication of the 21st century.

BIG BUSINESS

While oil has played a prominent role in our growth, it is by no means the only business in town. In fact, some of the world's largest enterprises call Dallas home. Among these are American Airlines, J C Penney, Exxon, American Petrofina, EDS and Texas Instruments. Commercially, Dallas has enormous advantage over other cities.

ACCESSIBILITY

It is ironic that the first attempts at turning Dallas into a trading centre failed miserably. But that was 1846. Today, Dallas is heralded as one of the most easily accessible destinations in the world. This is due in great part to the Dallas/Fort Worth International Airport. Home of *American Airlines*, DFW services 172 destinations – 145 domestic and 27 international.

1966: FOUR MONTHS BEFORE THE FINAL TOURNAMENT STARTED THE JULES REMET TROPHEY WAS STOLEN WHILST ON DISPLAY IN WESTMINSTER. FINALLY A WEEK LATER A DOG CALLED PICKLES GAINED INSTANT MEDIA FAME WHEN HE DISCOVERED IT HIDDEN UNDER A BUSH IN A LONDON SUBURB. THE THIEF WAS NEVER CAUGHT.

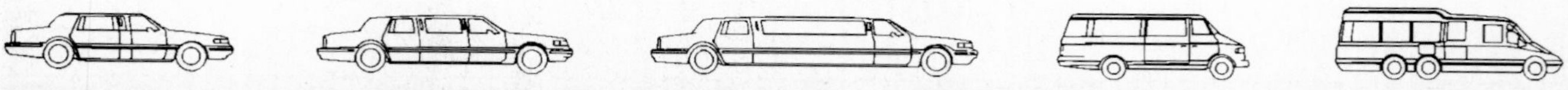

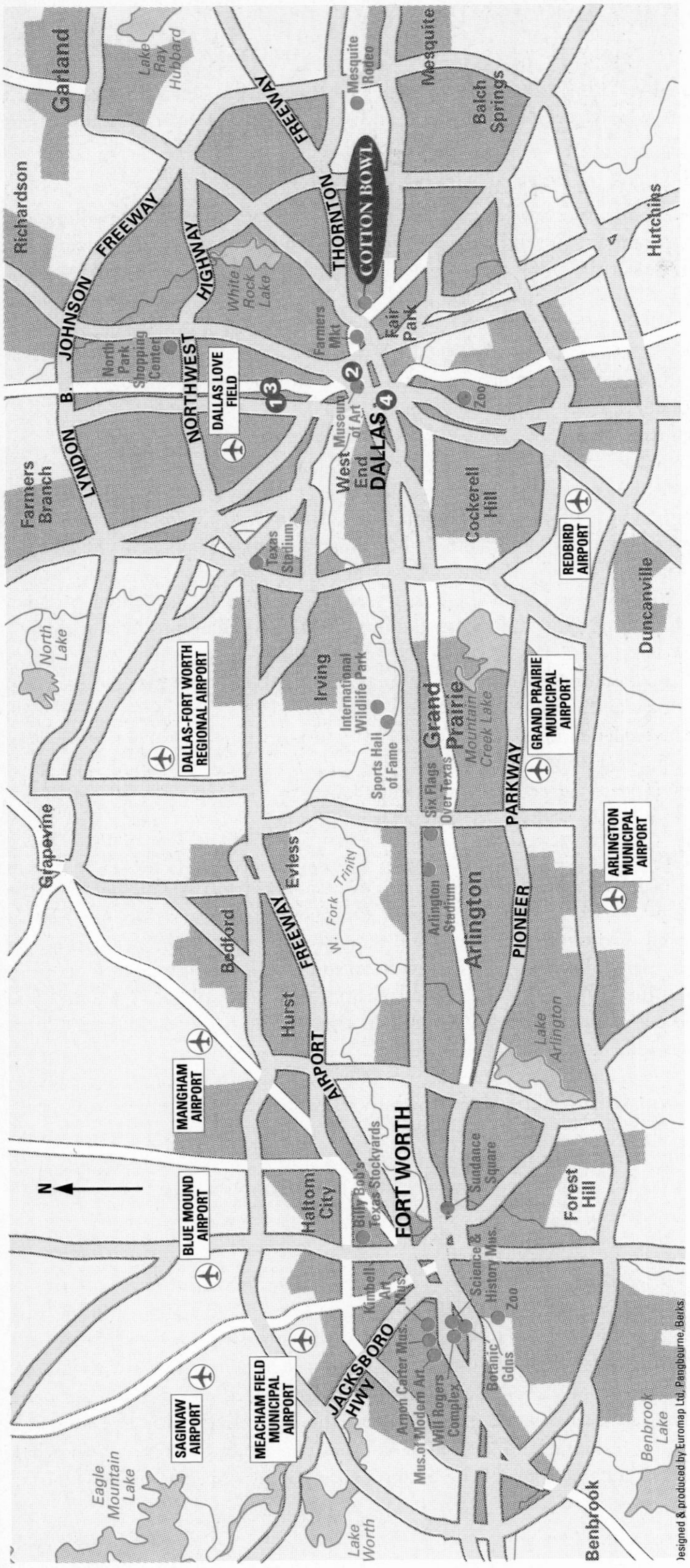

❶ *Stoneleigh Hotel*
❷ *The Plaza of the Americas*
❸ *The Mansion*
❹ *Hyatt Regency*

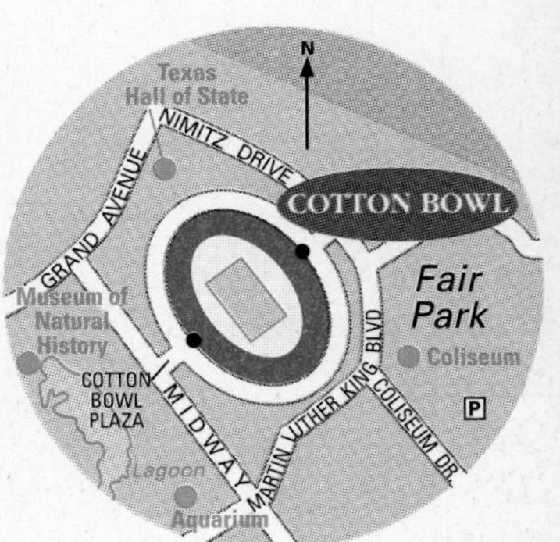

THINGS YOU ALWAYS WANTED TO KNOW ABOUT DALLAS

The idea for the Super Bowl was created in 1966 by Dallasites Lamar Hunt and Tex Schramm. Hunt was a key player in forming the American Football League. The two men discussed merger of the AFL and the NFL, and developed the idea for a championship game. Interestingly, the name 'Super Bowl' is attributed to Sharron Hunt, Lamar's daughter, who was playing with a 'super ball' the day her father was thinking of a name for the championship game.
The invention of the frozen margarita took place in Dallas.

Dallas☆Fort Worth

THERE WILL BE SPECIAL BUSES FROM THE AIRPORT TO THE STADIM DURING WORLD CUP '94.

THE COTTONBOWL STADIUM

History

The historic Cotton Bowl at Fair Park is the only stadium in the world that's been home field for three NFL teams that have won Super Bowls. The first was the original Dallas Texans who became the Kansas City Chiefs. Then there was the 1952 Dallas Texans team that became the Baltimore Colts. And, of course, there's the team that still battles Redskins, the Dallas Cowboys, who play in Texas Stadium. However, the annual Cotton Bowl game is still played in the Cotton Bowl (where else?) on New Year's Day. During the State Fair of Texas in October, the stadium hosts the annual grudgematch between the University of Texas and Oklahoma University, and the Al Lipscomb Classic, which features Grambling University as one of the teams. The Cotton Bowl also hosts state high-school football play-offs, marching band events, concerts and the annual July Fourth Freedom Fest. For further information on other Cotton Bowl games, write to the Cotton Bowl, Fair Park, Dallas, TX 75246, or telephone (214) 638 BOWL.

World Cup Renovations

Four first-round games of World Cup '94 will be played in the Cotton Bowl. Fair Park will also be the site of one game of the round of 16 games. Adding to the excitement, the Cotton Bowl will be the locale for one quarter-final game which is expected to attract 72,000 people. To prepare for the World Cup Soccer games, field wall modifications were completed on August 30, 1992, as a prerequisite to the removal of the artificial turf and its replacement with natural turf for the soccer games. The reconstruction of the wall also made way for a wider field to accommodate soccer games.

THE PRELIMINARY ROUND STARTS ON MARCH AND BY THE TIME THE QUALIFICATION PROCESS IS COMPLETED IN NOVEMBER 1993, 582 MATCHES WILL HAVE BEEN PLAYED.

WORLD CUP DALLAS/FORT WORTH

Geographically, Dallas is one of America's big hub cities. According to the US Department of Transportation, nearly 30 million people live within 10 hours driving time of Dallas.

AMERIFEST '94: A CELEBRATION OF CULTURE

During the months of May, June and July 1994, the north Texas area will experience an international cultural festival the likes of which no one has ever seen. The festival will reflect the cultural heritage and arts of our community, making it a true cross-section of our 1994 civilisation.
AmeriFest will feature:

★ Traditional Cinco de Mayo festivals (May);
★ Juneteenth Festivals (an ethnic event celebrating the historic date on which news of emancipation reached Texas);
★ ArtFest in Fair Park and ARTWALK in the Deep Ellum area;
★ Fourth of July celebrations;
★ Taste of the West End Food Festival in the Historic West End (July);
★ Fort Worth's May Fest, a celebration on the banks of the Trinity River;
★ A number of musical programmes, including the Dallas Symphony Orchestra, the Latin Jazz Festival, the Dallas Opera Series and others;
★ Dallas Summer Musicals at the Music Hall in Fair Park, Casa Manana Summer Musicals in Fort Worth, Shakespeare in the Park and numerous local theatre productions;
★ Dance programmes featuring groups such as the Anits N Martinez Ballet Folklorico and the Fort Worth Ballet;
★ Mesquite Rodeo (June-August);
★ Chisholm Trail Round-up (Fort Worth);
★ Numerous other cultural and historical events.

THE ARTS

The centre of much of this activity is the downtown Arts District, home of the *Dallas Museum of Art*, *Morton H Meyerson Symphony Center* and the *Arts District Theater* as well as other outstanding facilities. Also within the district is the *Arts Magnet High School* where young artists develop and practice their talents.
But art flourishes throughout the area, from innovative, avant-garde galleries and theatres in Deep Ellum to giant arts and crafts fairs such as the annual *Senior Citizen Craft Fair* at the Dallas Convention Center.
As Dallas has become a cultural melting pot of individuals of all backgrounds imaginable, so have its artistic endeavours grown to reflect a variety of cultures and backgrounds.
And in Dallas, children enjoy a special relationship with the arts through such activities as young people's concerts by the Dallas Symphony and the children's wing of the *Dallas Museum of Art*.

EATING & ENTERTAINMENT

Once in Dallas, there is plenty to see and do. Everything from shopping at renowned Neiman-Marcus to shuffling across a Texas-sized hall to honky-tonk piano. The centrally located Historic West End offers musical and family-orientated entertainment with the hospitality and style that is synonymous with Dallas. This 20-block area has games, music, 85 shops and more than 35 restaurants and clubs. Epicurean delights are not confined to the West End. In fact, Dallas has more than 5400 restaurants. That's more eateries per capita than New York City. These selections include some of the nation's most highly respected award-winning restaurants.

SPORTS & RECREATION

Dallas loves sports, whether it be watching or playing. After several seasons of slow but steady progress, the Texas Rangers appear ready to make a serious run at the pennant race. With a true baseball legend like Nolan Ryan on the mound and the

DALLAS

THE PLAZA OF THE AMERICAS HOTEL

You can be confident that your stay at the Plaza Of The Americas Hotel will always be handled with professionalism and care. Located in the heart of the U.S., in Dallas' arts and business districts, our $15,000,000 newly renovated hotel and complex offers world class accommodations and service for any occasion.

★ 403 elegant Texas size rooms and suites each with a dramatic view
★ 16-story atrium featuring ice skating arena, health club, two tennis courts and multi-level shopping and restaurants
★ Complete conference and meeting facilities
★ 650 North, our own award-winning restaurant, selected as one of Dallas' Top Ten and Best Hotel restaurants for 1991-92

Let us show you the difference personal care and service can make.

650 North Pearl Street in Dallas

For reservations or information on meeting arrangements call us at 800-225-5843 or 214-979-9000

More than 6,000,000 people visit Fair Park every year

Fair Park is the **site for six 1994 World Cup Soccer Games . . . and the site for the World Cup '94 International Broadcast Centre**

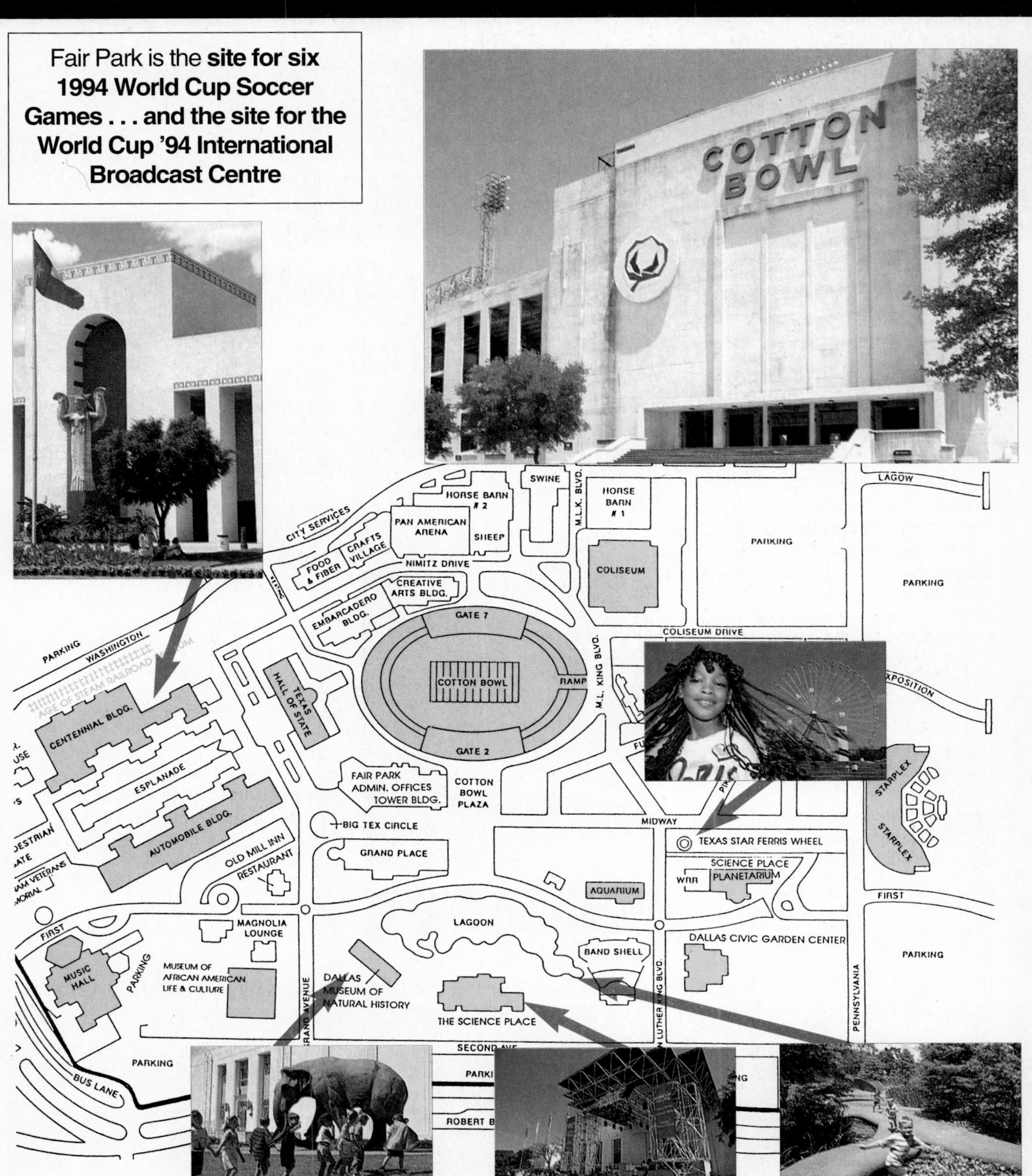

Fair Park is located 2 miles from Downtown Dallas, Texas.

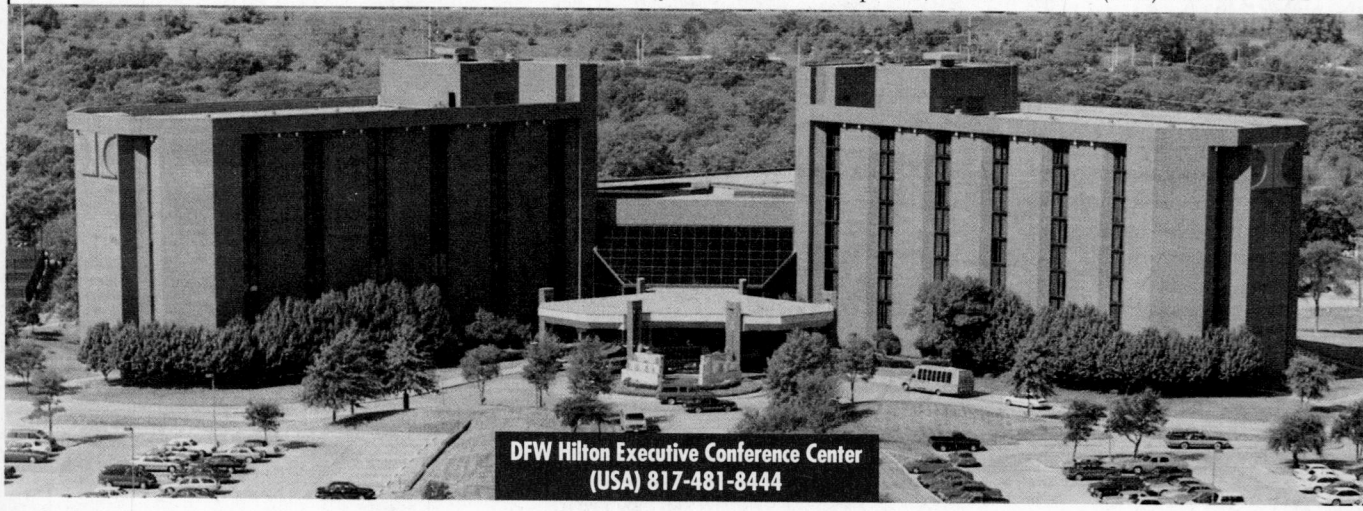

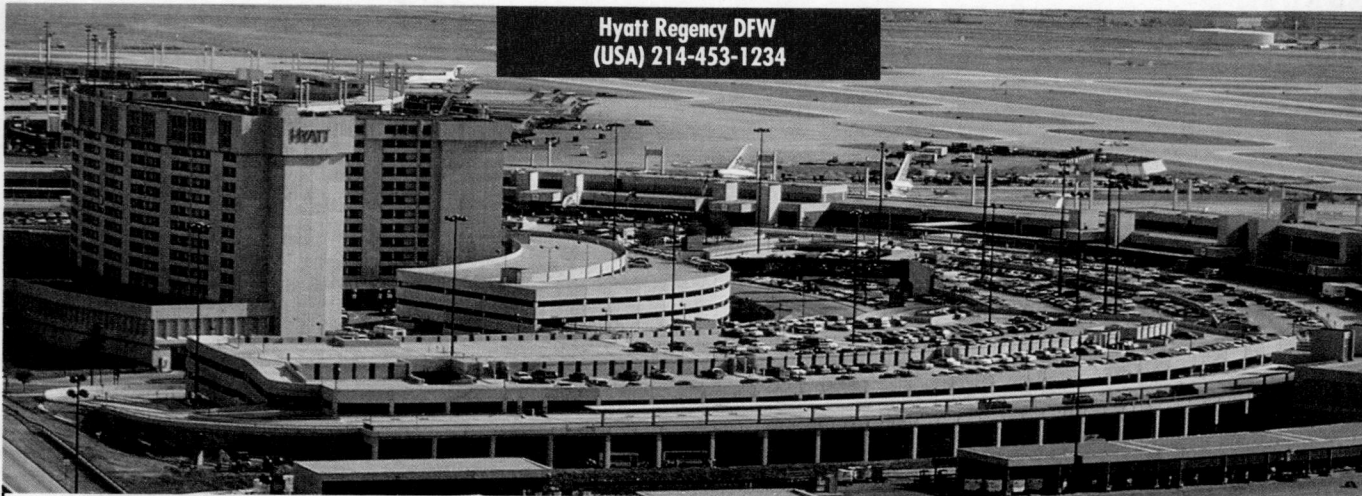

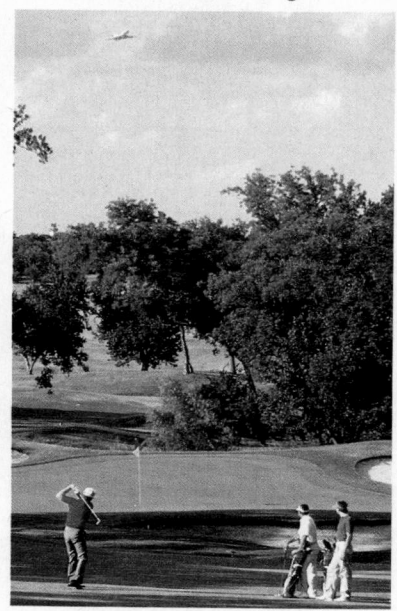

infield and outfield covered by legends-in-the-making such as Ruben Sierra, Raphael Palmeiro and Julio Franco, it will be a race well worth watching.

The hottest ticket in town is still the Dallas Cowboys under the leadership of Coach Jimmy Johnson and quarterback Troy Aikman, the Cowboys have brought winning football back to Dallas.

When it comes to participation, Dallas has something for everyone: tennis, golf, softball, running, cycling, soccer, bowling, polo, to name but a few. Even as summer turns to fall and winter, Dallas' mild climate makes it a great location to get out on the court or field and show what you've got.

That same mild weather makes Dallas a natural location for gardens and parks that bloom with flowers and activities 12 months a year. Dallas has enough parks and greenbelts to cover New York's Central Park six times over. Dallas parks are ideal for strolling and enjoying nature, but there are also plenty of hike and bike trails, tennis and basketball courts and other facilities to satisfy that urge for a little outdoor exertion. And from any point in Dallas, wide open spaces and rural backroads are never too far away.

FAIR PARK (ESPLANADE), DALLAS

DALLAS SKYLINE (TRINITY RIVER REFLECTION)

DAY TRIPS

Although there is much to see and do in the immediate Dallas area, other adventures await throughout the north central Texas area. A trip of 97-241km (60-150 miles) from Dallas in any direction will introduce you to a whole new landscape – different in topography, vegetation, flora and fauna. Also to be found on one of these trips are interesting towns and communities rich with attractions, history and recreational possibilities.

Fort Worth, Dallas' neighbour to the west, is famous for its historic Stockyards area, its Cultural District with its many museums and the Fort Worth Zoo.

To the south is Waxahachie, with plenty to see and do, from visiting shops and museums on the historic town square to seeing the homes and other structures that played starring roles in films such as 'Places in the Heart'.

Deep in the east Texas Piney Woods is Tyler, known for its acres and acres of rose gardens and scenic lakes. Nearby is Jefferson, a historic riverboat town and one of the state's major antique markets.

Also in east Texas, near Rusk, you can chug through 24 miles of scenic countryside on the Texas State Railroad.

North of Dallas on the Texas-Oklahoma border, Lake Texoma offers more than 100,000 acres of water playground. While there, you'll want to visit the birthplace of President Dwight D Eisenhower in Denison. Other attractions – all within 150 miles of Dallas – include the 2900-acre *Fossil Rim Wildlife Ranch*, *Pate Museum of Transportation* in Fort Worth and *Fort Worth Nature Center and Refuge*.

Dallas is a haven for large-scale, high-calibre events. Recent events have included the Ramses the Great exhibit of Egyptian artefacts, the Republican National convention, the final four NBA All-Star games, the State Fair of Texas, the Mobil Cotton Bowl Classic and the American Airlines Dallas Cup.

NORTH TEXAS ATTRACTIONS

The north Texas area has something to offer virtually every taste. The following attractions demonstrate the broad spectrum of entertainment available:

- ★ *Six Flags Over Texas;*
- ★ *Billy Bob's Texas;*
- ★ *Fair Park;*
- ★ *The Fort Worth Stockyards;*
- ★ *International Wildlife Park;*
- ★ *International Museum of Cultures;*
- ★ *Museum of African-American Life Studies;*
- ★ *The Sixth Floor Historical Exhibit;*
- ★ *The Wax Museum;*
- ★ *Mesquite Championship Rodeo;*
- ★ *Farmers Market;*
- ★ *West End Historical District;*
- ★ *Deep Ellum Entertainment District.*

GOING TO GRAPEVINE

Grapevine's historic Main Street offers some of the best shopping and dining in north Texas, with its antique shops, boutiques and craft shops featuring local artists. Dining in Grapevine is also a treat – the setting is as exciting as the meal itself. From feasting on native cooking in a vintage, turn-of-the-century building on Main Street to eating fresh catfish while enjoying the view at a lakefront restaurant, there's plenty of authentic home-town atmosphere.

And there is plenty to do after dinner. Main Street has one of the best live Country Western revues this side of Nashville at the Grapevine Opry. Housed in a beautifully renovated theatre, the Opry has been providing first-rate country and western entertainment since 1975 and there's a new show every weekend.

Grapevine's *Historical Museum and Calaboose*, the *Torian Log Cabin* and the old newspaper building, where the *Grapevine Sun* is still published, make enjoyable

Dallas☆Fort Worth

EVENTS IN DALLAS DURING THE WORLD CUP

Events scheduled for June and July of 1994 include:

- ★ *The Scarborough Faire Renaissance Festival;*
- ★ *Shakespeare Festival of Dallas;*
- ★ *Annual 'Hoop It Up' Basketball Tournament;*
- ★ *Freedom Fest;*
- ★ *Mesquite Balloon Festival;*
- ★ *Taste of the West End;*
- ★ *Ringling Brothers, Barnum & Bailey Circus;*
- ★ *Dallas Summer Boat Show;*
- ★ *Dallas Grand Prix in Addison.*

The area is a year-round hot spot for the best in professional and amateur sports: the NFL's Cowboys, the NBA's Mavericks, the MSL's Sidekicks, Major League Baseball's Texas Rangers, the GTE Byron Nelson Classic and the Colonial Golf Classic, the Mesquite Championship Rodeo, the Mobil Cotton Bowl Classic and much more.

outings for all the family. Or, for the more physically adventurous visitor, a day of water sports on Lake Grapevine – one of the premiere sailing and windsurfing lakes in North Texas – is great fun.

Golfers will be spoiled for choice, as there are three excellent courses in the Grapevine area. Grapevine Municipal Golf Course is an 18-hole championship course designed by Byron Nelson and rated among the top 50 municipal courses in the country. The Hyatt Bear Creek Golf and Raquet Club offers 335 acres of beautiful rolling hills with racquetball courts, indoor and outdoor tennis courts and two of the highest-rated 18-hole public golf courses in the USA.

THE WAY TO THE WORLD CUP

THE AIRPORTS

Dallas/Fort Worth International Airport DFW is one of the world's great airports. Ideally located in the centre of North America, *DFW* is within 3 1/2 hours of most major cities on the continent. Modern terminal facilities and efficient passenger services provide speedy connections.

Dallas Love Field Airport was the city's first commercial air facility and continues to serve a major role in the transportation of both business and pleasure travellers. Prior to the opening of *DFW Airport* in 1974, *Love Field* was served by all the major commercial carriers. Today, the airport is served commercially by *Southwest Airlines*, a major carrier connecting Dallas with destinations throughout Texas and its contiguous states, with connections to destinations on the West Coast and in the Midwest. *Love Field* is located within the city limits at Cedar Springs, Mockingbird Lane, Dallas, TX 75235, and is just minutes from downtown Dallas and the Dallas Convention Center, the Dallas Market Center area and North Dallas. For further information, telephone (214) 670-6080.

TRANSPORTATION TO DALLAS

Dallas' two major airports are well served by ground transportation companies that will help you get from the airport to your hotel or other locations within the area. Some of these may be operated by the hotels themselves. For airport information, telephone (214) 670 6080.

All ground transportation at *DFW International Airport* is accessed by taking the escalator or elevator from the main terminal and baggage claim level down to the lower level.

Ground transportation at *Love Field Airport* is accessed from the main terminal lobby and the baggage claim area.

Airport Shuttle Services

USA Shuttle: Direct door-to-door service between hotel, office or home and the airport, 24 hours a day, 7 days a week. A wide range of modern, radio-dispatched vehicles handle individuals or groups of any size with transportation in and around the city also available. Group and convention services are available. For further information, telephone (214) 630 6888.

Super Shuttle: Door-to-door service from hotels or office to either *DFW* or *Love Field* airports, operating 24 hours a day, 7 days a week and located in Grapevine. Also provides transportation within and around the city. A wide range of vehicles are available to handle all transportation needs. Major credit cards are accepted on board. Group and convention services are also available by telephoning (817) 329 2001. Advanced reservations are required: telephone (817) 329 2000 from *DFW Airport* or (817) 329 2025 from *Love Field Airport*.

Discount Shuttle & Tours: Located at 1911 Peters Road in Irving, TX 75061. For information, telephone (214) 445 1441.

Shuttlejack: For information, telephone (214) 484 7577.

Limousines

Allure Limousine: Located at in Dallas, Allure is a professional luxury ground transportation company serving Dallas and its surrounding areas. It offers competitive

WORLD CUP 1958: THE WORLD CUP WAS TELEVISED FOR THE FIRST TIME.

★ FOR INFORMATION ON TICKETS TO WORLD CUP '94, SEE PAGE 1066.

rates, professional chauffeurs and personalised service for corporate and personal needs. The fleet includes luxury sedans, passenger vans and buses, as well as stretch limousines loaded with all amenities. Fully licensed and insured. All major credit cards are accepted and direct billing is available. For information, telephone (214) 225 5873.

Blue Chip Limousine Inc: Located in Grapevine, Blue Chip provides professional, flexible service to the specialised needs of the corporate and market visitor. Provides luxury sedans, limousines, passenger vans and minibuses to co-ordinate the unique needs of both large and small groups. Direct billing is available. For further information, telelphone (214) 748 9117 *or* (817) 540 0032.

Valet Limousines Inc: Located in Dallas, Valet Limousines serves corporate and personal needs with new '91 stretch limos, sedans, minibus and buses. Featuring 6-, 8- and 10-passenger vehicles with cellular phones, TV/VCR, stereos and privacy windows and provides VIP treatment and transportation to the airport, sightseeing tours, sporting events, conventions, restaurants and nightclubs. Corporate accounts are welcome. For further information, telephone (214) 250 3131.

Taxis

Taxis can be found on the upper terminal/baggage claim level at *DFW Airport* and from the main terminal lobby and the baggage claim area at *Love Field Airport*. There is a $10 minimum charge for trips that exit the toll booth at *DFW Airport* and conclude on *DFW Airport* property, and a $12 minimum charge for trips that exit the toll both at *DFW Airport* and conclude off *DFW Airport* property. There is also $5 minimum charge for *DFW Airport* terminal transfers and a 50-cent loading fee at *Love Field Airport*. The basic rates are $1.50 base rate, then $1.20 for each additional mile.

Car

Dallas is accessible by car from *DFW Airport's* south exit via the Airport Freeway and from the north exit via the John W Carpenter Freeway. There are many car rental companies at the airport.

DALLAS GROUND TRANSPORTATION

Buses

DART – Dallas Area Rapid Transit: Located at 1701 Market Street, Dallas, TX 75202. Tel: (214) 828 6841. DART serves 14 cities in the Dallas area with 863 yellow and white buses. Each weekday, nearly 180,000 people ride DART's 120 bus routes. Visitors find DART an easy, inexpensive way to sample all that Dallas has to offer. Virtually all transfers are free. Ask your driver when boarding the first bus. DART's simplified fare structure consists of two basic one-way fare levels: 75 cents for Local Service and $1.75 for Premium Express and DARTAbout Van Service. Most routes within the area are the less expensive Local Service. Drivers cannot give change, so exact fare must be to hand. Downtown, DART's retail sales centres at Elm and Akard Streets or at Main and Ervay Streets can be visited for route and schedule information. Or visitors may call DART at (214) 979 1111 with their origin, destination and desired time of travel and DART will recommend the most convenient times and give advise on any necessary transfers along the way.

Downtown Hop-A-Bus: Getting around the downtown area is easy via DART's three colour-coded and distinctively decorated Hop-A-Bus routes. The Blue Bunny, Green Frog and Red Kangaroo buses run circulating routes continually each weekday, with a fare of only 25 cents and free transfers. Timetables are available at most public libraries, downtown hotels and DART retail centres.

Mobility Impaired Services: DART provides buses equipped with wheelchair lifts on many routes. DART's Handiride service also offers van and taxi service for riders with transportation needs not met by regularly scheduled bus routes. For further information, telephone (214) 828 6800.

Street Cars

McKinney Avenue Transit Authority: Located at 2098 McKinney Avenue, Dallas, TX 75204, the McKinney Avenue trolley is a fun yet practical way to get from downtown Dallas to the McKinney Avenue entertainment district north of the central city. The system features four authentic early 20th-century trolley cars that have been restored to their original splendour and ride on tracks that were abandoned over 30 years ago. The trolley can be caught on St Paul Street adjacent to the Dallas Museum of Art. From there, the trolley rumbles across Woodall Rodgers Freeway and up McKinney Avenue past a village full of restaurants, shops and nightspots. For further information, telephone (214) 855 5267.

Surreys

Dallas Surrey Services: Old-fashioned horse-drawn surreys tour the West End Historic District, Old City Park, McKinney Avenue and Turtle Creek in Dallas. The surreys can accommodate six to eight passengers and operate nightly from Market Street in the West End. For further information, telephone (214) 946 9911.

Taxis

Dallas has 24-hour taxi service provided by numerous private companies. In Dallas, the standard fare schedule is $1.50 base rate; $1.20 for each additional mile (or 30 cents for each quarter mile) and $12 per hour charge for traffic delays and waiting time. There is also a $1 charge for each additional passenger up to the rated seating capacity of the vehicle. For more information about taxi fare regulations, telephone the city of Dallas Department of Transportation on (214) 670 3161.

TRANSPORTATION TO OTHER DESTINATIONS

Rail

Amtrak passenger train service is available at Dallas' Union Station in the West End of Dallas. Trains connect Dallas with Chicago and Houston, and from Houston, connections are available to New Orleans and Los Angeles.

If you arrive by train, connections are easily made with taxis, car rental companies and city buses (DART). The station also houses restaurants on the upper level and

COTTONBOWL STADIUM

TICKETS

The organising committee for the 1994 FIFA World Cup soccer championship is now accepting ticket information requests by telephone and by mail. Tickets to the world's largest single-sport event, to be held for the first time in the United States in 1994, may be obtained by sending your name, address, daytime telephone number and self-addressed, stamped envelope to:

World Cup USA 1994
PO Box 1994
Los Angeles, CA 90051-1994
Information is also available on:
(213) 365 6300.

In addition to this number, customers can call the local Ticketmaster telephone in Dallas to receive information. Initially, two types of venues series tickets will be available. The first type will include tickets to all the first round games (a total of four) to be played at each of the nine venues. The second type will include all first round games and certain second stage games at each venue (excluding the semifinals and the final). The number of games in this series will vary, depending upon the allocation of games to each site.

"We are very pleased to give fans the chance to purchase what in essence is a season ticket to the 1994 World Cup," said World Cup 1994 Chairman Alan I. Rothenberg. "We have several innovative ticketing plans to accommodate the overwhelming worldwide demand for tickets, and for the American fans, we think the venue series will provide an efficient means of participating in what will be the greatest World Cup ever."

Ticket demand is expected to far exceed availability, according to Rothenberg. "We have already been inundated with ticket requests, and inquiries from overseas. I think there is no doubt that 1994 World Cup tickets will very rapidly become scarce," he said.

Dallas☆Fort Worth

Scott Parks LeTellier, managing director and chief operating officer of World Cup USA, also noted that members of the United States soccer family (registered players, referees and officials of the United States Soccer Federation, for example) will have priority purchase first. Once these priority rights lapse, venue series tickets will be sold by mail order on a first-come, first-served basis.

"We have a commitment to the soccer family, which has contributed mightily to the growth of the game in America," said LeTellier. "We want to ensure that they receive our complete priority ticket details and have a chance to be part of this historic occasion."

Rothenberg also outlined preliminary plans for a unique team series, in which fans will be able to buy tickets to see a specific team regardless of where they are ultimately drawn.

a Visitor Information Center operated by the Dallas Convention and Visitors Bureau.

Union Station is located within close proximity to downtown hotels, the Dallas Convention Center and the West End Historic District. The station is connected by a pedestrian tunnel to the Hyatt Regency Hotel, Reunion Tower and Reunion Arena. For more information about Amtrak Service and schedules, telephone (214) 653 1101 or (800) 872 7245.

Buses

Greyhound: There is a central Dallas terminal at the corner of Lamar and Commerce Streets in downtown Dallas. The terminal is convenient to downtown hotels, the Dallas Convention Center and the West End Historic District. For further information, telephone (214) 655 7000.

BILLY BOB'S TEXAS

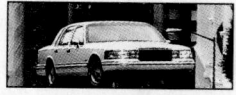

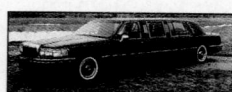

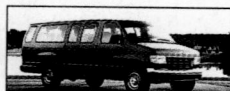

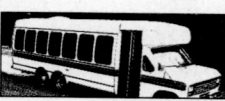

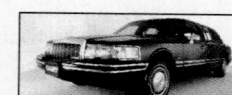

BIG TEX DAY

DOWNTOWN DALLAS

Rothenberg also outlined preliminary plans for a unique team series, in which fans will be able to buy tickets to see a specific team regardless of where they are ultimately drawn. Designed especially for fans from overseas but also available to US supporters of a particular team, the team series details will be announced later this year.

The organizing committee is also developing tour packages on a non-exclusive basis the will be targeted to what the World Cup enthusiast actually wants to see, allowing customers to make their own plans rather than be locked into rigid pre-set schedules. "Our entire ticketing philosophy is based upon satisfying the needs of the user," said Rothenberg. "We have worked very hard to devise systems which will allow us to meet our goal of selling every ticket while at the same time giving the fans the flexibility he or she wants."

Le Tellier pointed out that there will be no need for international tour packagers to buy the venue series tickets. "Our tour package plans will provide tour operators with the necessary flexibility, allowing them to obtain exactly what tickets they need to serve their clients,". Tickets for semi-finals and the final will be sold separately.

Dallas
WorldCupUSA94™
© 1991 WC '94 TM

Welcome to DALLAS ☆ Fort Worth International Airport

Your Gateway to World Cup '94

Dallas/Fort Worth International Airport (DFW), the largest airport in the United States and the second busiest in the world and, for the 140 participating nations, DFW is clearly the right connection to the World Cup!

With more than 2100 flights daily to nearly 200 destinations worldwide, DFW Airport offers 616 flights, including 137 daily nonstops to seven other World Cup cities: Los Angeles (including Orange County, Long Beach, Burbank and Ontario airports), San Francisco, Detroit, Chicago, Boston, New York City (including Newark, NJ, and New York's Kennedy and LaGuardia airports), Orlando and Washington DC (both Dulles and National airports). Dallas/Fort Worth International Airport has more than 100 boarding gates and a sophisticated ground operations system that expediates travellers to their final destination.

As an example of the airport's convenience: from DFW, travellers to Chicago can choose from 22 direct flights and 71 possible connections; travellers going through DFW on the way to Los Angeles have the option of 46 direct flights, including 38 nonstops and 152 connections. And, unlike destinations on the East or West Coast, Dallas/Fort Worth International Airport is only three and a half hours away from every major city in the United States, and just four hours away from all major cities in Canada and Mexico.

What may be most important to international travellers is quick and efficient customs clearance. With customs facilities provided in three separate terminals, clearance is measured in minutes, not hours. Currency exchange booths also are available upon arrival and departure.

The Dallas/Fort Worth area has almost 60,000 hotel rooms, beginning with the Hyatt Regency DFW, located in the centre of the airport itself. The Hyatt Regency DFW, one of the world's largest airport hotels with 1400 rooms, is just 30 minutes away from the Cotton Bowl.

Between Dallas and Fort Worth, just 10 minutes from DFW Airport, is a major entertainment corridor that includes Six Flags Over Texas amusement park, Arlington Stadium, The Palace of Wax, Ripley's Believe It or Not and numerous shopping malls.

By using DFW Airport as their gateway to the '94 World Cup, travellers can experience both the Wild West culture of Fort Worth or the urban, East Coast culture of Dallas. The airport is just 18 miles from the central business districts of both Dallas and Fort Worth.

DFW AIRPORT FACILITIES

On the ground, World Cup travellers can expect a Texas-size welcome. Whatever your appetite, you will appreciate the variety, quality and convenience of dining at any of DFW's 64 food and beverage locations. DFW travellers receive courteous attention from the Airport Assistance Center's 40 volunteers who staff the central information centre and seven information booths in the baggage claim areas at the airport. The information booths are located in Sections A and B of Terminal 2W, Sections A and C of Terminal 2E, Sections A and B of Terminal 3E and Sections B and C of Terminal 4E. The Airport Assistance Center operates 24 hours a day.

DFW Airport's passenger service agents meet every international flight, providing courteous and friendly welcome in one's own language. Passenger service agents speak 21 different languages and dialects.

Car-rental telephone counters are located near baggage claim areas, providing direct telephone service to the four rental car companies serving DFW. Rental car facilities are located on airport property and are available to visitors by a short ride on the Airport Train or rental car courtesy buses, which depart every 10 minutes from the lower level of each terminal.

Welcome to FORT WORTH

Fort Worth, Texas – where the American West begins & next door to the Dallas World Cup

The 1994 World Cup Games will bring thousands of visitors to the United States and to the games held in Dallas, Texas. Fort Worth is just 30 miles to the west of downtown Dallas and is a unique American city of 'Cowboys and Culture'. While it is the western portion of the Dallas/Fort Worth Metroplex of four million people, Fort Worth has a unique character that makes it the only large city to represent the American cowboy heritage. Fort Worth presents great opportunities for individuals and companies that wish to introduce international visitors to the American cowboy west.

FORT WORTH SKYLINE

STOCKYARDS HISTORIC DISTRICT

Fort Worth has a total of 6000 rooms to accommodate every level of budget and hotel quality desired, from luxury to economy. The Fort Worth Convention & Visitors' Bureau at (817) 336 8791 (fax: (817) 336 3282) can put you into contact with the great hotels of Fort Worth. The hotels are found throughout the entire city, but with heavy concentrations in the convenient downtown/Sundance Square area, in the Cultural District, as well as in the Stockyards. The Fort Worth Convention & Visitors Bureau can provide Visitors Guides to the city, as well as a tour package available to travel companies wishing to organise tours into the area. The Bureau also provides free step-on guides for groups staying in Fort Worth. The Convention & Visitors Bureau is pleased to work with travel organisations as well as individual travellers to advise on the appropriate and desired accommodations, as well as to identify area attractions and other tours convenient from Fort Worth.

There are a number of ranches in the surrounding area that provide various types of activities which could be of interest to travel groups. There are also many scenic day trips that could be made from Fort Worth. Fort Worth is a desirable location for weekend or weekday getaways which would be an exciting way to experience the old west and cultural attractions of Fort Worth during the interim periods between World Cup Games.

Fort Worth is a city not to be missed. It will give visitors to America a true feeling about the western cowboy experience in America. Fort Worth had great success in working the Davis Cup Tennis Final held in Fort Worth in late 1992. Many international visitors to Fort Worth from around the world have had a great experience in the city 'where the west begins'.

By Douglas Harman, President and CEO, Fort Worth Convention & Visitors Bureau

WORLD CUP DALLAS/FORT WORTH

Dallas ☆ Fort Worth

FESTIVALS, EVENTS & EXHIBITIONS IN FORT WORTH DURING WORLD CUP YEAR

JANUARY
Jan 21-Feb 6 '94
Southwestern Exposition and Livestock Show
Hundreds of thousands of people from around the world flock to Will Rogers Memorial Center for the nation's oldest livestock show and 28 performances of the world's original indoor rodeo. Fort Worth's most attended annual event. For information, telephone (817) 877 2400.

FEBRUARY
Feb 7 '92-Indefinite
Ring of Fire Exhibition
Takes viewers on a whirlwind ride around the Pacific Ocean and to the crater's edge of some of the world's most active volcanoes. Spectacular volcanic eruptions, extensive aerial photography and computer animation tell the story of these immense geologic forces and the people and cultures who coexist with them. For information, telephone (817) 732 1631.

THE LOCATION Fort Worth is located in the central northeastern sector of Texas, only 48km (30 miles) from Dallas and within walking distance of 3000 hotel rooms in historic downtown Fort Worth. The entire Dallas/Fort Worth Metroplex spans 161km (100 miles) and encompasses a population of close to four million. Within the Metroplex are many other cities, including Addison, Arlington, Duncanville, Farmers Branch, Grand Prairie, Grapevine, Glen Rose, Irving, Granbury, Lancaster, Lewisville, McKinney, Mesquite, Plano, Richardson, Waxahachie and Weatherford – each with a personality of its own.

THE LANDSCAPE Fort Worth offers a diverse landscape – from sleek modern skyscrapers to a taste of the historic Wild West. Offering both a cosmopolitan and rugged atmosphere, visitors enjoy the mild, yet varied climate. Texas blue skies, bright sunshine and clean fresh air greet the visitor, with temperatures ranging from 2-13°C in the coldest month of January to 23-35°C in the hottest months of July and August. However, even during the hottest spells, visitors will find everything air-conditioned for their convenience and comfort.

THE CULTURE AND HISTORY In its youth, Fort Worth was a rough-and-tumble frontier town, dusty and lawless, home to the brave and the brawling, the soldier, the frontiersman and the outlaw. But the grit of those early settlers, combined with the fortunes made from cattle, railroad and agricultural industries, helped Fort Worth age gracefully into the modern, bustling city it is today.

WORLD CUP '94

Dallas☆Fort Worth

'Speed' and 'Sacred Site' Exhibitions
'Speed' explores the human quest to travel ever faster, and examines the technological journey that has propelled us into the space age. 'Sacred Site' is a unique film that looks at Halley's Comet as it passes over Ayer's Rock in Australia, a sacred site to the Aborigines. For information, contact Fort Worth Museum of Science & History, Omni Theatre, Cultural District. Tel: (817) 732 1631.

Feb 8 '92-96
The Last Great Gunfight
Gambler Luke Short was the only man to ever outdraw Fort Worth's popular Marshal 'LongHair' Jim Courtright. Once was enough. Each year, mock gunfighters re-enact the last great gunfight of the West on Exchange Avenue in front of the modern-day White Elephant Saloon in the Historic Fort Worth Stockyards. Admission is free. For information, telephone (817) 624 9712.

Feb 12 '92-Indefinite
Tropical Rainforest
Tells the story of the 400-million-year evolution of tropical rainforests, their recent and rapid destruction, and scientists' efforts to understand them as they disappear. For information, contact the Fort Worth Museum of Science & History, Omni Theatre, Cultural District. Tel: (817) 732 1631.

Feb 26 '94
Fort Worth Cowtown Marathon & 10km Run
Thousands of runners from throughout the world gather in the Historic Fort Worth Stockyards for this footrace through Fort Worth neighbourhoods. For information, telephone (817) 735 2033.

MARCH
Mar 12 '94
Cowtown Goes Green
Celebration of St Paddy's Day. The festival includes a night-time parade, an Irish ballad contest, an Irish Village Fair, treasure hunt and an indoor street dance. For information, contact the Fort Worth Stockyards. Tel: (817) 926 0226.

APRIL
Apr 15-17 '94
Main Street Fort Worth Arts Festival
Fort Worth's restored Main Street becomes a marketplace of food, arts, crafts and live entertainment during this major annual festival sponsored by Downtown Fort Worth, Inc. Tel: (817) 870 1881 or 870 1692.

WORLD CUP DALLAS/FORTWORTH

Originally settled as an army outpost at a fork of the Trinity River, Camp Worth was one of eight forts assigned to protect settlers from Indian attacks. But progress helped the growing settlement survive long after other such towns had blown away with the dust of departing pioneers. After decades of progress in the cattle industry, Fort Worth prospered further with the arrival of the railroads. Later, during World War II, publisher and businessman Amon Carter used his friendship with President Franklin D Roosevelt to attract defence contractors to Fort Worth.

Today, the Historic Stockyards District looks much the same as it did 100 years ago when Exchange Avenue was filled with cattle bound for the Kansas packing houses and railroad yards and Sundance Square has been restored to its original Victorian beauty. The Fort Worth Water Garden, a spectacular complex of sculpture and fountains, now occupies what was once 'Hell's Half Acre', a brothel- and saloon-packed district where cowhands had their last bit of fun before heading to Kansas on the Chisholm Trail. It was also their first stop on the way home, and their first chance to spend their wages. Many notorious outlaws lay low in Hell's Half Acre while the law was looking for them.

Yet this 'Cowtown' has culture as well, boasting the country's third-largest cultural district. The 900-plus acres of Fort Worth's arts district are home to the Kimbell Art Museum – recognised as one of the world's finest small collections – and to the Amon Carter Museum – renowned for its collection of oils and bronze sculptures of 'Western' artists. Within walking distance of Fort Worth's celebrated museums are the Casa Manana Theatre and the Will Rogers Memorial Center. Downtown, the Sid Richardson Collection of Western Art offers a collection of Charles Russell and Frederic Remington paintings and bronze sculptures.

Yet, evidence of Fort Worth's heritage is everywhere – from the carvings of long-horn skulls on bridge pillars and public buildings to the wall-sized portraits of grand championship steers on display at Cattleman's Steak House. Just bring your pioneer spirit and you're set for the ultimate Fort Worth experience.

WHAT MAKES FORT WORTH SPECIAL

SUNDANCE SQUARE IN DOWNTOWN FORT WORTH

Fort Worth has not lost its close association with the American West. It is a unique community that places special priority on its Texas heritage and cowboy traditions. Downtown Fort Worth is known principally for 'Sundance Square', which was named after Butch Cassidy & the Sundance Kid, who were two of the most famous Western outlaws who lived in downtown Fort Worth. Many of the old buildings of that era have been restored and can be seen and visited today. The site of the last great shoot-out between a city marshal and a famous gambler was on downtown Main Street in Fort Worth. In Sundance Square, there are two museums which exhibit cowboy and western history. Also in the downtown area is the unique *Cattleman's Museum* which shows the history of ranching in the United States. No person interested in the American west should miss the great museum exhibits. The Caravan of Dreams entertainment complex in Sundance Square has become one of the nation's premier live-music clubs, attracting top-name entertainers such as Herbie Hancock, th late Dizzy Gillespie and Lyle Lovett. It also sports a rooftop grotto bar and cactus garden amidst a neon-jewelled geodesic dome.

THE FORT WORTH STOCKYARDS – A LIVING HISTORICAL DISTRICT

The Fort Worth Stockyards are one of the most popular areas to visit. Located two miles north of downtown, they have many large buildings that were critical to the operation of the Stockyards, including the *Livestock Exchange Building*, the *White Elephant Saloon*, the *Stockyards Hotel* and even the original hog and sheep pens. These pens are now a large festival market and train station location for the Tarantula excursion train, an 1896 iron-horse steam engine which operates to and from the Stockyards. To see and ride the vintage train's Victorian-styled passenger coaches through Fort Worth is to experience a moment from another era. The Tarantula departs every two hours each afternoon out of its Eighth Avenue terminal at 2318 South Eighth Avenue. For full information on the train, telephone (817) 625 RAIL.

The area was once a hangout for outlaws, cattlemen, cowboys, gamblers and other 'legends' of the west. Many of the buildings have been historically restored and the streets and courtyards are paved with red brick and cobblestone. Shops line the brick-paved Exchange Avenue where craftsmen use time-worn tools to handcraft saddles, chaps and boots.

The Stockyards are also the location of Billy Bob's, which is world famous as the largest honky-tonk in America. Every Friday and Saturday night, there is live bull riding, and Billy Bob's hosts many of the great country and western singers. It can accommodate up to 6000 people. In addition, the *Cowtown Coliseum*, which was built in 1907 and was the location of the first indoor rodeo, has regular Saturday night rodeos. 2300 people can attend these Saturday night rodeos in air-conditioned comfort.

THE CULTURAL DISTRICT – WITH COWBOYS & GREAT MUSEUMS

Fort Worth is called the city of 'Cowboys and Culture', and nowhere is this better exemplified than the city's world-famous Cultural District, only two miles to the west of downtown. The heart of this district is the 1936 *Will Rogers Complex*, including a major coliseum, art deco auditorium and an Equestrian Center acknowledged to be the best in the United States. This complex of buildings is surrounded by outstanding museums, full of enough excitement and interest to suit every taste.

The world-famous *Kimbell Art Museum* is acknowledged to be one of the great art museums in the United States and was the last building designed by Louis Kahn and thought to be one of his best. The collection includes paintings by Fra Angelico, Caravaggio, Rembrandt, Picasso and Mondrian, as well as pre-Columbian and African works. The *Amon Carter Museum* highlights American cowboy art, as well as great American art, and other artists on display include Georgia O'Keeffe and Winslow Homer. It also has one of the nation's finest photography collections with photographs by Ansel Adams, Laura Gilpin and Eliot Porter.

The *Fort Worth Museum of Modern Art* is the oldest museum in the city, with a standing collection of 20th-century paintings by Pablo Picasso, Robert Motherwell, Mark Rothko and Jackson Pollock. It is immediately adjacent to the *Fort Worth Science & History Museum*, which includes major scientific exhibits and is the most visited family attraction in Fort Worth, with over one million visitors each year. Exhibits encompass centuries-old relics, turn-of-the-century Texas dioramas, the mystery of extinct dinosaurs and fascinating computer technology. The museum is also home to the *Noble Planetarium* and the *Omni Theater*, one of the largest theatres in the world using 70mm film, which regularly shows exciting films onto a screen inside an 80ft dome.

FORT WORTH ZOO RENOVATION

Immediately south of the Botanic Gardens, which is approximately 200 acres of trees and gardens situated along the Trinity River, is the great Fort Worth Zoo. The Fort Worth Zoo Association has initiated an unprecedented renovation and redevelopment programme during the past two years, moving animals to realistic habitats which recreate their homes in the wild. It is believed the increased space and more natural settings better accommodate the behavioural requirements of the animals, and in turn increases the likelihood of successful breeding of threatened and endangered species. Two new exhibits have recently opened: 'Asian Falls' and 'World of Primates'.

The 'Asian Falls' exhibit is carved out of an existing hillside, creating a natural setting of grassy hills, waterfalls and trees. Visitors travel along elevated walkways to look down on three lush yards and view Siberian and Sumatran tigers, plus sun bears. A 40ft waterfall, 'Tiger Falls', flows into a ravine which acts as a natural bar-

Apr 21-30 '94
National Cutting Horse Association Super Stakes
Held at the Will Rogers Equestrian Center. Tel: (817) 244 6188.

Apr 22-24 '94
Cinco De Mayo Celebration
This family-oriented celebration featuring carnival rides, great food and nationally known entertainment celebrates Mexico's independence from France. Proceeds benefit the Boys & Girls Club of Great Fort Worth at Marine Park. Tel: (817) 921 9129.

MAY

May 5-8 '94
Mayfest
A family festival on the banks of the Trinity River in the Cultural District which combines all the elements of fun into a weekend that has become a Fort Worth tradition. For information, telephone (817) 332 1055.

May 28 '94
A Little Night Run
Fort Worth's only night-time run – a 5km race through the downtown area begins and ends at The Worthington Hotel with a concert by the Youth Orchestra of Greater Fort Worth. Tel: (817) 923 312.

JUNE

Jun 10-12 '94
Chisholm Trail Round Up & Chief Quanah Parker Commanche Pow Wow
The city celebrates its heritage as the last major stop on the legendary Chisholm Trail with a 3-day festival in the Fort Worth Stockyards. Tel: (817) 625 7005.

July

Jul 4 '94
Arts In The Park
Celebrate Independence Day with a patriotic festival and concert in downtown's Burnett Park, followed by fireworks at Trinity Park. Sponsored by Downtown Fort Worth, Inc. Tel: (817) 870 1692.

Dallas☆Fort Worth

Jul 6-9 '94
Miss Texas Scholarship Pageant
The Fort Worth/Tarrant County Convention Center is the setting as Texas beauties vie for the title of Miss Texas and the opportunity to compete for the dreamed-of crown of Miss America. For information, telephone (817) 334 0195.

Jul 9-17 '94
American Paint Horse Association World Championship Horse Shows
Located at Will Rogers Equestrian Center. Tel: (817) 439 3400.

AUGUST
Aug 6-13 '94
American Junior Quarter Horse Association World Championship Show
Located at Will Rogers Equestrian Center. Tel: (817) 871 8150.

SEPTEMBER
Sep 23-25 '94
Pioneer Days
A 3-day family celebration in the Fort Worth Stockyards commemorating the early days of the cattle industry and the pioneers who settled on the banks of the Trinity River. For information, telephone (817) 626 7921.

OCTOBER
Oct 1-2 '94
Oktoberfest
Five stages of continuous entertainment, German and international foods and the Buschgardens' Festhaus band and dancers are among the highlights of the festival; held at the Fort Worth/Tarrant County Convention Center. Tel: (817) 924 5881.

NOVEMBER
Nov 1-12 '94
Appaloosa World Show
At the Will Rogers Equestrian Center. Tel: (817) 871 8150.
Nov 26 '94
Parade of Lights
Horses and carriages, clowns and cars draped with twinkling lights parade down Main Street marking the official beginning of Christmas in Fort Worth. Sponsored by Downtown Fort Worth, Inc. Tel: (817) 870 1692.

rier to separate two families of endangered tigers. Streams from the waterfall empty into pools in each cat yard, where the tigers swim to escape the Texas sun. And a viewing window within the rocks lets visitors get face-to-face with a tiger.

The 'World of Primates' exhibition is of greater size and scope than any previously built at the Fort Worth Zoo. This 2.5-acre exhibit includes an indoor, climate-controlled tropical rainforest for housing critically endangered lowland gorillas in natural family groups. Visitors walk beneath a canopy of trees to see primates in a lush tropical forest under a glass roof. Indoor homes for chimpanzees, colobus monkeys and orang-utans are also located in the indoor rainforest. The chimpanzees and orangutans can be seen through huge viewing windows in the man-made rock. A connecting outdoor exhibit featuring islands surrounded by moats and wooded areas is home to various primates, including chimpanzees, colobus monkeys, gibbons, orang-utans, bonobos (pygmy chimpanzees) and baboons. In addition to other world-quality exhibits, the Zoo has the 'Texas Exhibit' which has on display all the major Texas animals, including buffalo, longhorns, horses, cattle and other animals commonly found throughout Texas. For further information, contact Fort Worth Zoo. Tel: (817) 871 7003.

THE WAY TO THE WORLD CUP

THE AIRPORT

Dallas/Fort Worth International Airport (DFW) is located in the centre of the Metroplex, midway between the cities of Dallas and Fort Worth. *DFW* offers 2000 daily flights to 1478 domestic and 35 international destinations. Last year, 48 million passengers moved through *DFW*, making it the second busiest passenger airport in the world. Airline passenger service at *DFW* is provided by 21 carriers operating in four different terminals, connected by a people mover. All baggage claim areas are located on the arrival level. Ground transportation services other than taxi cabs depart from the lower level and arrive on the upper level. Ground transportation services, other than taxi cabs, depart from the lower level and arrive on the upper roadway. International Parkway, the airport's main street, runs through the centre of the airport; all terminal buildings, parking facilities, rental car lots and the airport hotels are accessible from this roadway. For further information, telephone Dallas/Fort Worth Airport Public Affairs Department on (817) 574 8083.

TRANSPORTATION TO FORT WORTH FROM DFW AIRPORT

Bus

Airporter Bus Service: Convenient transportation between *DFW Airport* to downtown Fort Worth hotels and the park. Service is every 30 minutes from 0507-2205 (travel time – 35-56 minutes, depending on the terminal). Buses may be boarded at the lower level of each terminal – look for the signs marked 'Scheduled Transport'. The bus stops at the Airporter Park & Ride terminal, 1000 Weatherford Street, between Weatherford and 1st streets, on the northeastern edge of downtown Fort Worth, as well as Radisson Plaza, the Downtown Ramada and The Remington hotels. If boarding in Fort Worth and going to the airport, be sure to check which terminal your flight is leaving from (either Terminal 4E, 3E, 2W or 2E) and alight at the correct terminal. Fares for adults are $7 one-way; senior citizens – $3, and children 16 years or under accompanied by a paying adult are free. Tickets may be purchased at the Airporter Terminal, from downtown hotels or ask your travel agent. If you have not pre-purchased your ticket, please pay the driver. Major credit cards, travellers checks and cash are all accepted (but if paying in cash, try to have exact change, and bills over $20 cannot be changed). For further information, telephone (817) 334 0092.

Shuttle Vans

SuperShuttle: A door-to-door shared-ride system featuring clean, late model, 7-passenger vans. Services the entire Metroplex area from *DFW* and *Love Field* airports. Pick-up is at the Shared Ride Zone on the lower level. Fares begin at $7 per passenger. Major credit cards are accepted on board. For bookings and further information at the airports, telephone (817) 329 2020 (from *DFW Airport*) and (817) 329 2025 (from *Love Field*). For information from the Metroplex area, telephone (817) 329 2000 (advanced reservations necessary).

Taxis

Taxi service is available along all upper-level kerbside exits. Fares to downtown Fort Worth are about $32.

FORTWORTH GROUND TRANSPORTION

Rail

Amtrak: Serves both Dallas and Fort Worth daily. Trains depart from downtown Fort Worth from the Passenger Station. For more information, telephone (817) 332 2931.

Bus

The 'T': The Fort Worth Area Rapid Transit Authority runs a public transportation service in the Fort Worth area. Buses run from 0500-2300 weekdays, 0600-2300 Saturdays and 0700-1900 Sundays. A VisiTour bus pass is available for $3 providing two days of unlimited travel on the 'T's regular city bus service. For information on schedule and fare information, telephone (817) 871 6200.

Taxi

Taxi service is available 24 hours a day by numerous private companies. For information on taxi fare and regulations, contact the American Cab Company, Fort Worth. Tel: (817) 534 5555; *or* Yellow Checker Cab, Fort Worth. Tel: (817) 332 1919.

Nov 26-28 '94
Christkindl Markt
Traditional Christkindl Markt features German Christmas items including toys, decorations, Advent calendars, candles and ornaments. Experience the authentic German atmosphere of the Christmas market complete with a variety of entertainment, displays and refreshments. For information, telephone (817) 332 5437.

WORLD CUP '94

VANCE
HOTEL

WASHINGTON STATE

Including **Seattle,** gateway to the Pacific northwest – Washington, Oregon, Idaho and Alaska.

Washington State Tourism
PO Box 42500
101 General Administration Building
Olympia, WA
98504-0613
Tel: (206) 753 7297. Fax: (206) 753 4470.
Seattle/King County Convention and Visitors Bureau
Suite 1300
520 Pike Street
Seattle, WA
98101
Tel: (206) 461 5800. Fax: (206) 461 5855.
Washington State Convention & Trade Center
Visitor Information
Galleria Level, 800 Convention Place
Seattle, WA
98101
Tel: (206) 461 5840. Fax: (206) 461 5855. Opening hours: 0830-1700 Monday to Friday.
Port of Seattle Information Office
2 Cinnamon Row
Plantation Wharf
York Place
London
SW11 3TW
Tel: (071) 978 5233. Fax: (071) 924 3134.

TIME: GMT - 8. *Daylight Saving Time* is observed from the first Sunday in April to the last Sunday in October. Clocks are put forward one hour, changing at 0200 hours local time.
THE STATE: Washington, bordering Canada and the Pacific Ocean, offers some of the nation's finest scenery for outdoor recreation. It has the second-highest population of any western state, yet visitors can travel from any city centre to peaceful countryside within minutes. The Snake and Columbia rivers flow through eastern Washington before joining to cut a passage through the Cascades, the north–south mountain range that dominates the centre of the state, rising to 4392m (14,408ft) at Mount Rainer. There are many fine beaches and small resorts on the Pacific coast. Much of the state is covered by coniferous forest. Holiday highlights include yachting on Puget Sound, hiking along the Pacific Crest National Scenic Trail and mountain climbing in the Cascades and Olympics. Excellent accommodation is available, ranging from bed & breakfast establishments to 5-star luxury hotels.

TRAVEL

AIR: Approximate flight times: From Seattle to *London* is 9 hours 5 minutes (direct) and to *San Francisco* is 1 hour 50 minutes.
International airport: *Seattle-Tacoma International (SEA)* is 22km (14 miles) south of the city; travel time – 20 minutes. Buses link the airport to points throughout the city. Taxis are available.
SEA: *Washington State Ferries* link Seattle with the Olympic Peninsula, Bainbridge Island and other points in the region. The Victoria Clipper links Victoria and British Colombia in Canada to Seattle via high-speed catamarans.
RAIL: Seattle is on the main *Amtrak* network, which provides rail links eastwards to Chicago via Salt Lake City or Spokane and southwards to Oakland and Los Angeles (see *Illinois* and *California* sections above for approximate journey times).
ROAD: Approximate driving times: From Seattle to *Vancouver* is 2 hours, to *Portland* is 3 hours, to *Spokane* is 6 hours, to *Boise* is 10 hours, to *Calgary* is 15 hours, to *Los Angeles* is 24 hours, to *Chicago* is 44 hours, to *Dallas* is 45 hours, to *New York* is 61 hours and to *Miami* is 69 hours.
All times are based on non-stop driving at or below the applicable speed limits.
Approximate *Greyhound* journey times: From Seattle (tel: (206) 628 5526) to *Vancouver* is 4 hours, to *Portland* is 4 hours and to *Spokane* is 7 hours.
URBAN: Seattle has an excellent bus system. An underground bus tunnel operates through downtown Seattle from the International District to the Convention Center, with stops at Pioneer Square, the financial district and Westlake Center. A high-speed monorail links the downtown area with the *Seattle Center*. Public transport is free in the downtown area. Taxis and hire cars are also available.

RESORTS & EXCURSIONS

SEATTLE: The 'Emerald City' is the primary international and domestic gateway to Washington State and the Pacific northwest. The state's largest city, Seattle is surrounded by the waters of Lake Washington and Puget Sound and enjoys spectacular views of the Cascades and Olympic Mountains. The waterfront area is known for its seafood restaurants, shops and water excursions.
Sightseeing: The *Seattle Center*, built for the 1962 World Fair, is the city's cultural heart, the home of opera, symphony, ballet and repertory theatre companies. It also contains the *Space Needle*, 185m (610ft) tall with an observation deck, restaurant and cocktail bar. *Pioneer Square* is a 17-sq-block national historic district showcasing Seattle's early history with shops, art galleries, restaurants and the one-of-a-kind underground tour. *Chinatown*, location of the Oriental community, offers arts, crafts and cuisine from China and Japan. *Pike Place Public Market*, situated just above the waterfront, is the oldest continually operating farmer's market in the USA featuring abundant seafood and produce, as well as handcrafted items from the Pacific Northwest. Harbour tours and fishing excursions are easily available and the excursion to *Tillicum Village* is highly recommended. Other major attractions include *Woodland Park Zoo*, *Seattle Aquarium* and the *Japanese Garden*.
Excursions: Tacoma, south of Seattle, is the state's third largest city. Its *Point Defiance Park* is one of the finest urban parks in the Pacific northwest. *Olympic National Park*, west of Seattle, has glacier-studded mountains, rainforests, lakes, streams and miles of unspoiled coastline. **Spokane,** near the border with Idaho in eastern Washington, is the state's second largest city; it boasts the outstanding *Riverfront Park*. The famous *Ellensburg Rodeo* is held every Labour Day weekend at Ellensburg. **Kennewick, Pasco** and **Richland** are at the heart of the region's wine country. *Mount Rainier National Park*, southwest of Tacoma, offers breathtaking views and skiing and other winter sports. *Mount St Helens* in the *Gifford Pinchot National Park* in southwest Washington is the site of the infamous volcanic eruption of 1980, which left a gigantic crater in the mountain's north flank. It is possible to take short trips by light airplane over the summit.
Note: For information on attractions in neighbouring states, see above under *States A-Z*.

SOCIAL PROFILE

FOOD & DRINK: Seattle is noted for its seafood and has more than 2000 restaurants serving many different types of cuisine. Restaurant/bars can stay open until 0200 all week. Beer and wine are available in grocery stores and hard liquor in state stores, usually open 1000-2000 every day, closed Sunday. Stores in big cities have later closing hours. Minimum drinking age is 21.
THEATRES & CONCERTS: The *Seattle Opera's* season runs from September to May. The *Seattle Symphony Orchestra* plays from November to April. The *Pacific Northwest Ballet* is also recommended and both the *Pacific Northwest Ballet* and the *Seattle Repertory* seasons are from October to May.
NIGHTLIFE: Jazz spots, nightclubs and discotheques are scattered throughout the city.
SHOPPING: Westlake Center, Nordstrom, The Bon Marche and Frederick & Nelson are the major mall and department stores, located in the heart of the retail district and connected by the underground bus tunnel. Other interesting shopping areas include Pioneer Square, the Waterfront Gold Rush Strip and Pike Place Market.
SPECIAL EVENTS: The following is a list of some of the mafor events taking place in 1993/4. **Apr '93** *Skagit Valley Tulip Festival*, Mount Vernon. **May 2** *Opening Day of Yachting Season*. **May 14-Jun 7** *Seattle International Film Festival*. **May 22-25** *The Northwest Folklife Festival*.**May 24-25** *The Pike Place Market Fistival*. **Jul 10-Aug 2** *Seafair Rainier*. **Jul 17-19** *Bite of Seattle*. **Sep 4-7** *Bumbershoot Festival*. **Jan '94** *New Year Celebrations*.

CLIMATE

Washington has two distinct climate zones. Summer days west of the Cascades rarely rise above 26°C, and winter days seldom drop below 8°C, while the east of the state has warm summers and cool winters.

SEATTLE Washington (4m)

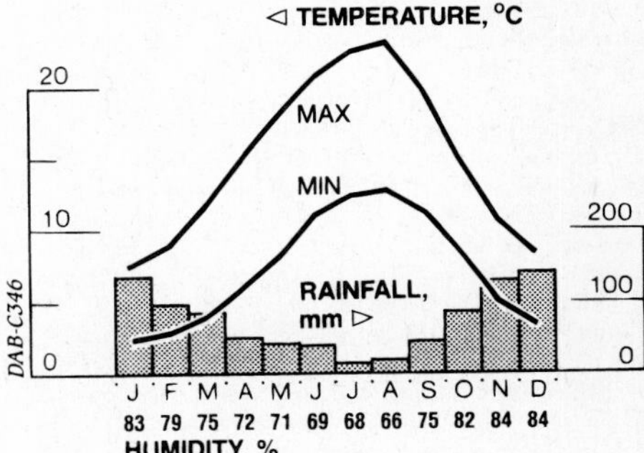

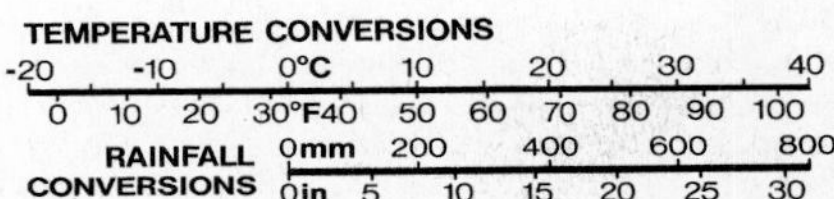

WASHINGTON DC

Gateway to George Washington Country, including Pennsylvania, Maryland, Delaware, Virginia and West Virginia.

Washington DC Convention & Visitors Association
6th Floor
1212 New York Avenue, NW
Washington, DC
20005
Tel: (202) 789 7000. Fax: (202) 789 7037.
Destination Washington DC
375 Upper Richmond Road West
London SW14 7NX
Tel: (081) 392 9187. Fax: (081) 392 1318. Opening hours: 0900-1800 Monday to Friday.

TIME: GMT - 5. *Daylight Saving Time* is observed from the first Sunday in April to the last Sunday in October. Clocks are put forward one hour, changing at 0200 hours local time.

TRAVEL

AIR: Approximate flight times: From Washington DC to *Anchorage* is 10 hours 25 minutes, to *Atlanta* is 1 hour 40 minutes, to *Chicago* is 2 hours 10 minutes, to *Frankfurt/M* is 7 hours 40 minutes, to *Honolulu* is 13 hours 40 minutes, to *London* is 6 hours 50 minutes, to *Los Angeles* is 5 hours 40 minutes, to *Miami* is 2 hours 30 minutes, to *Montréal* is 2 hours 5 minutes, to *New York* is 1 hour, to *Orlando* is 2 hours 10 minutes, to *Paris* is 8 hours 20 minutes, to *San Francisco* is 7 hours 10 minutes, to *Singapore* is 25 hours 45 minutes and to *Toronto* is 2 hours 20 minutes.
International airports: *Washington-Dulles International (WAS)* is 43km (27 miles) from the city (in Virginia); travel time – 50 minutes. Coach runs every hour from 0630-2400. Taxis are also available.
The capital is also served by *Baltimore-Washington International Airport (BWI)*, west of Baltimore; see above in entry for *Maryland*.
Domestic airport: *Washington National (DCA)* receives transfer connections from other USA gateways. It is 5km (3 miles) southwest of the city. Coach runs every 30 minutes 0700-2200. Metro rail service runs every 5 minutes 0600-2400 to Metro Center. Taxi service is also available. There is a frequent airport bus service between *Washington National* and *Dulles International* airports.
RAIL: The principal corridor is the New York–Philadelphia–Baltimore–Washington route, with frequent fast trains. There are also routes from Philadelphia and Washington to Pittsburgh. Florida-bound trains run from Washington to Richmond. There are also local trains to the Philadelphia area. The journey time to New York is 3 hours 15 minutes. See *New York* section above for further East Coast journey times.
ROAD: Approximate driving times: From Washington DC to *Baltimore* is 1 hour, to *Richmond* is 2 hours, to *Norfolk* is 4 hours, to *New York* is 5 hours, to *Pittsburgh* is 5 hours, to *Charleston* (West Virginia) is 7 hours, to *Charlotte* is 8 hours, to *Cincinnati* is 10 hours, to *Chicago* is 14 hours, to *Miami* is 22 hours, to *Dallas* is 28 hours, to *Los Angeles* is 55 hours and to *Seattle* is 58 hours.
All times are based on non-stop driving at or below the applicable speed limits.
Approximate *Greyhound* journey times: From Washington DC (tel: (202) 289 5155) to *Richmond* is 2 hours, to *Philadelphia* is 3 hours 30 minutes, to *New York* is 4 hours 30 minutes, to *Pittsburgh* is 5 hours 30 minutes and to *Knoxville* is 12 hours 30 minutes.
URBAN: The *Metro* (subway) system offers quick and comfortable transport within the downtown area; fares are zonal. Lines are being extended into the suburban areas of Maryland and northern Virginia. There are also suburban and downtown bus services. It is possible to transfer from Metro to bus without additional charge (except during rush hour), but not from bus to Metro. Taxis are available within the city area; fares are again zonal (and comparatively cheap by big city standards). Most major car hire and motor camper rental agencies have offices in Washington DC.

Jefferson Memorial

RESORTS & EXCURSIONS

WASHINGTON DC: 'DC' stands for 'District of Columbia', not a state but an administrative district created specifically to avoid having the capital city in any one state. Washington DC is a city of green parks, wide tree-lined streets, white marble buildings and, surprisingly for a US city, very few skyscrapers, which gives it a European air. It is the centre for visiting diplomats and has the fourth-largest concentration of hotel and motel rooms. Tourism is the leading private industry and business interests are increasingly attracted by the many light industrial and research companies that are now moving into the vicinity.
Sightseeing: The streets are a rectangular grid cut by long diagonals radiating from important sites such as the *Capitol* and the *White House;* the diagonals are named after states. Aligned with this grid is a grand formal vista, the *Green Mall*, which extends from *Capitol Hill* to *Potomac Park* on the river of the same name. A second rectangular garden runs northwards at right angles as far as the *White House*, which has been the home of every US President since 1800 and is visited by more than one million people every year. The *Tidal Basin*, a beautiful lake famous for its Japanese cherry trees, lies just to the southwest. The *Green Mall* contains many of Washington DC's most important monuments and institutions, including the *Lincoln* and *Jefferson Memorials;* the *Washington Monument* (at 169m/555ft, the tallest masonry structure in the world); the *Smithsonian Institute;* the old *Museum of Natural History;* the modern *National Gallery of Art*, with its stunning East Building designed by the world-famous architect I M Pei; and, of course, the *Capitol*, where Senators and Representatives meet under a magnificent 55m (180ft) dome to shape US legislative policy. It also offers many recreational activities, including boat trips on the *Potomac* (the jetty is to the south of the *Lincoln Memorial*). *Arlington National Cemetery*, on the other side of the river, contains the graves of 175,000 American soldiers who fought in wars from the Revolution onwards. Other sights include *Chinatown*, where many of the city's oriental shops and restaurants are centred; *Constitution Gardens*, with more than 50 acres of trees and lawns; the *J Edgar Hoover Building* (the FBI's headquarters) at 9th Street and Pennsylvania Avenue; the *Pentagon;* and the *US Supreme Court*, the highest court in the country.
Note: For information on attractions in neighbouring states, see above under *States A-Z*.

SOCIAL PROFILE

FOOD & DRINK: Washington has a renowned selection of good restaurants, and almost any national cuisine.
THEATRES & CONCERTS: Pennsylvania Avenue houses the *National* and *Ford Theaters*. The *John F Kennedy Center for the Performing Arts* stands at the foot of New Hampshire Avenue overlooking the Potomac River. Here there are four theatres for live performances of opera, concerts, musical plays, drama and festival occasions. A fifth theatre houses the *American Film Institute*. Open-air concerts are held at the *Jefferson Memorial* in the summer and the *National Gallery of Art* has Sunday evening concerts in the East Court Garden, September to June.
NIGHTLIFE: Washington has few bona fide nightclubs with live entertainment. However, there are numerous bars and discotheques in downtown Washington, Georgetown and the suburbs.
SHOPPING: There are several shopping areas in Washington DC. The F Street Mall (between 15th and 11th Streets) is the most traditional; Connecticut Avenue between K Street and Dupont Circle has many speciality shops; and Georgetown, in the area of Wisconsin and M Streets, offers a wide range of boutiques, antique dealers, arts and crafts shops, and pavement stalls selling jewellery and leather goods. Visit some of the government buildings for unique souvenirs and gifts.
SPECIAL EVENTS: Special events in and around Washington DC include the world-famous *Cherry Blossom Festival* and gigantic *Fourth of July* celebrations and open-air entertainments.

CLIMATE

Summers are very warm while winter temperatures can be extremely low.

WASHINGTON DC (4m)

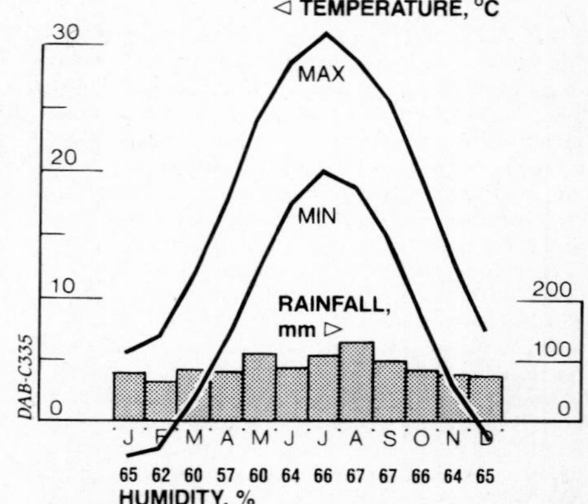

Welcome to WASHINGTON DC

Washington DC is extending a hand of hospitality to the international community as part of the 1994 World Cup. We are excited about this opportunity to play a role in the largest sporting activity in the world. The city is prepared to produce a memorable event.

Alan Rothenberg, President of the US Soccer Federation and World Cup USA 1994, promises a first-class event with sell-outs every game. He also stresses that security will be a major concern in and around stadiums. US soccer organisers and law enforcement agencies will work with European security specialists to identify potential problems. Other security proposals under consideration include: banning the sale of alcohol, separating visiting fans by rooting interests and reserving sections for American families.

Significant rule changes are also under consideration by the Federation Internationale de Football Association (FIFA). The objective of the changes are to increase scoring and reduce the number of ties. Three points would be awarded for a victory, rather than the current two, during the first round of round-robin play and sudden-death overtime would be added during elimination rounds replacing the 30-minute mandatory overtime period.

Rothenberg said plans are underway to start a pro league after the World Cup. He believes the long-term prospects for soccer in the United States are good because the public is starting to realise that soccer is a great form of entertainment. Plus, with the amount of exposure soccer will receive here during the 1994 World Cup, people in the USA should gain a new appreciation for the world's most popular sport.

THE WHITE HOUSE

As proof of the sport's popularity, a cumulative television audience of 32 billion people in over 168 countries is expected to watch the 1994 World Cup. This is an opportunity for Washington DC and those associated with the World Cup to present themselves to the world marketplace. Sponsors and supporters will not only have access to the games, but will also receive visual recognition that can be translated into increasing business development. An expected $55 million will be pumped into the local Washington DC economy alone.

THE JEFFERSON MEMORIAL

The true soul of America is in Washington DC. No other major city in the USA offers the delightful combination of history, charm, service and politics. In addition to the over 60,000 residents who call the city home, Washington DC is hometown to all the people of the United States. We are the nation's capital, headquarters for district and federal offices that serve all of its citizens, regardless of political affiliation. Washington DC's 20-million annual visitors are confirmation that the warm reception from the city invites them back again and again.

For visitor information in the United Kingdom, contact: Alison Cryer, REPRESENTATION PLUS, LTD, 375 Upper Richmond Road West, London SW14 7NX; in Germany contact Christa Dietrich, WIECHMAN TOURISM SERVICES, Scheidswaldstrasse 73, W-6000 Frankfurt/M 60; in the United States, DC Committee to Promote Washington, 1212 New York Avenue, NW, Washington, DC 20005.

WASHINGTON DC WORLD CUP IS PLAYED AT THE RFK STADIUM

Washington DC

WASHINGTON REDSKIN HEROES

Joe Gibbs – *Coach*
Mark Rypien – *Quarterback*
Art Monk – *Wide Receiver*
Doug Williams – *Quarterback*
John Riggins – *Running Back*
Joe Theismann – *Quarterback*

THE LOCATION Washington DC is the capital of the United States and the headquarters of the US government. It is a federal district, called the District of Columbia, but it is not a state nor is it part of one. It is one of the few capital cities in the world to be planned and built specifically as the seat of government. Located in a 179-sq-km (69-sq-mile) area between Virginia and Maryland, it is only 50km (31 miles) from Baltimore and 66km (41 miles) from Annapolis, the capital of Maryland.

THE LANDSCAPE Washington DC is a picture-postcard setting of massive marble buildings, gleaming white monuments and parks adorned by flowers and splashing fountains. Broad, tree-lined avenues radiate from the US Capitol and the White House, serving as a backdrop to the world-famous monuments that have been raised in honour of great men who have led the nation. The view of the capital from the *Lincoln Memorial* nearly 3km (2 miles) away is truly awe-inspiring. But outside of the centre, Washington DC becomes a city of diverse neighbourhoods, like a microcosm of America itself. The *National Arboretum*, a 440-acre stretch of gardens and woodland overlooking the Anacostia River, is a site of natural beauty, and throughout DC there are hundreds of grassy squares and riverside parkland.
Not far away, Maryland and Virginia contain some spectacular and diverse scenery, from their broad Atlantic beaches to the peaks of the Appalachians. The heavily forested *Blue Ridge Mountains* that cross Virginia are part of the Appalachian chain, and separate the Piedmont region and its rich farming country from Virginia's Shenandoah Valley. Continuing northwards, the mountains cross western Maryland, with several peaks over 1500m (3000ft). To the east, the Chesapeake Bay is like a vast inland sea, surrounded by low rolling farmland, and pine forests interspersed with marshes. The unspoilt countryside, with tobacco plantations and dairy farming, makes a fine contrast to the urbanised areas. Apart from the indented shoreline of Chesapeake Bay, Maryland and Virginia share nearly 240km (150 miles) of Atlantic coastline, from Ocean City to Virginia Beach, with peaceful barrier islands and miles of soft sandy beaches.

THE CULTURE AND HISTORY Walking the narrow cobblestoned streets of Georgetown, Washington DC's oldest neighbourhood, visitors follow in the footsteps of men who have shaped history. In 1775, George Washington and his supporters planned the Revolution here, and in 1944 a conference of world leaders at Dumbarton Oaks established a formula for peace which became the basis of the United Nations Charter. As you would expect in the nation's capital, Washington DC has an amazing array of historic buildings and points of interest. Two of the most fascinating are Ford's Theater and the Smithsonian Institute. *Ford's Theater* looks almost exactly as it did on the evening of April 14, 1865, when John Wilkes Booth crept into the presidential box and shot Abraham Lincoln. The *Smithsonian Institute* was established in 1846 with money bequeathed by an Englishman, James Smithson, the illegitimate son of the Duke of Northumberland, who desired that his fortune be used for the "increase and diffusion of knowledge among men". Today the Smithsonian has grown so large that it is said that daily visits for at least ten years would be needed to see all the displays.
Just outside Washington DC, the area is rich in history. The first English settlement in the New World was at Jamestown, Viriginia, in 1607. During the Revolutionary War, several skirmishes and battles took place along the coast between the rebellious colonists and troops loyal to the Crown, culminating in

THE FIRST TIME PENALTIES WERE USED TO DECIDE A WORLD CUP MATCH WAS IN THE 1982 SEMI-FINAL BETWEEN GERMANY AND FRANCE AFTER A 3-3 DRAW. THE GERMANS WON THE SHOOT-OUT 5-4.

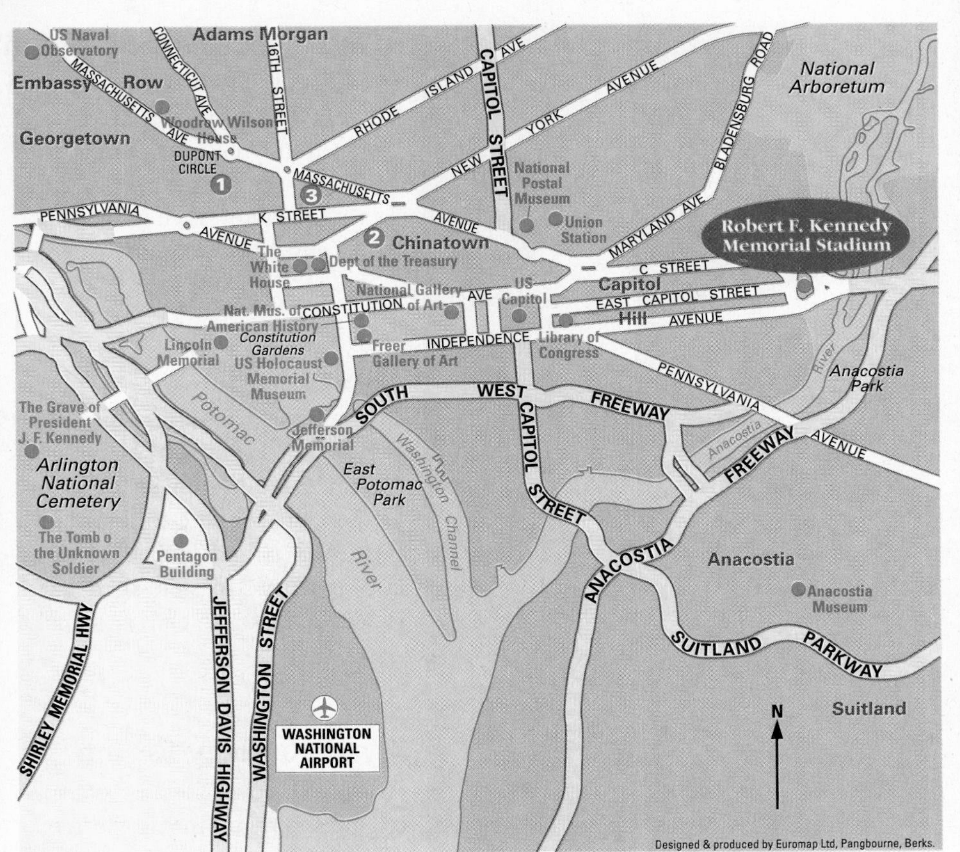

❶ *Embassy Suites*

❷ *Grand Hyatt Washington*

❸ *The Mansion*

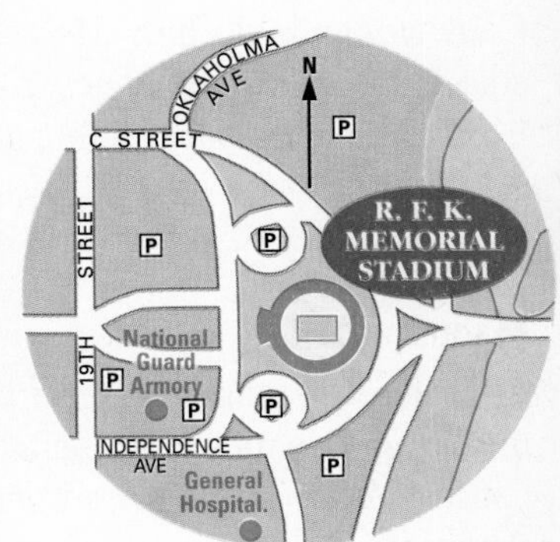

RFK STADIUM

Grand Hyatt Washington
In the heart of downtown. Walk to White House, museums and monuments on the Mall, shopping, theater. Direct access to Metro through lobby. 891 guest rooms, 60 suites. Indoor pool and health club.

Hyatt Arlington
At Washington's Key Bridge across from Georgetown; within walking distance of Arlington National Cemetery and Iwo Jima Memorial; adjacent to Metro. 302 guest rooms, 8 suites. Free indoor health club.

Hyatt Dulles
At Dulles International Airport, 30 min. from downtown Washington. Close to Wolf Trap Park and fine shopping. Free parking; free shuttle to airport. 317 suite-sized guest rooms. Free health club, pool, and whirlpool.

Park Hyatt Washington
European-style luxury hotel between historic Georgetown and downtown; convenient to Kennedy Center, Metro, art galleries, shop-ping. 224 guest rooms, 130 suites. Free indoor health spa with pool.

Hyatt Regency Bethesda
In suburban Bethesda, right at Metro; 6 miles north of The White House; 10 min. from National Zoo; 5 min. to fine shopping. 381 guest rooms, 11 suites. Free indoor rooftop health club with pool.

Hyatt Regency Crystal City
At Washington's National Airport; 5 min. to Old Town Alexandria, shopping, downtown Washington; free shuttle to Metro and airport. 685 guest rooms, 20 suites. Free outdoor pool, indoor health club.

Hyatt Regency Washington
On Capitol Hill. 2 blocks from US Capitol, Metro, Union Station; 3 blocks from Mall, Air & Space Museum, Smithsonian. 834 guest rooms, 31 suites. Free indoor pool and health club. Rooftop restaurant.

Hyatt Fair Lakes
In beautiful Fair Lakes complex, 25 min. from downtown Washington. Near George Mason U. Patriot Center. Free shuttle to fine shop-ping, Metro, and Dulles Airport; free parking. 316 suite-sized guest rooms. Free health club and pool.

Hyatt Regency Reston
At Reston Town Center. Walk to fine shopping, movie theaters. 18 miles west of downtown Washington; free parking; free Dulles Airport shuttle. 514 guest rooms, 21 suites. Free indoor health club with pool.

Everywhere in Washington you want to be...Hyatt.
The nine Hyatt Hotels of Wash-ington, DC, offer luxurious accom-modations, superb locations, and special value rates especially for weekends, summer, and holidays.

Inquire, too, about accommodations during the World Cup Soccer games in Washington June and July 1994. There's easy access from Hyatt to RFK Stadium.

For more information on special rates and packages available throughout the year, call Hyatt's sales offices at: United Kingdom—(0345) 581666; London—(071) 5808197; Frankfurt—(0130) 2929; Paris—(331) 40547819; Fukuoka—(81)(92) 4831234. For phone numbers of Hyatt sales offices in countries not listed here, call (402) 593-8800 in the U.S.

victory for the rebels when Lord Cornwallis was forced to surrender at Yorktown, Virginia in October 1781. In Fort McHenry in Baltimore the unsuccessful British bombardment in 1814 inspired Francis Scott Key to write the words of *The Star Spangled Banner*. Over 60% of the Civil War was fought in Maryland and Virginia, in a thousand battles and engagements. In Maryland, you can tour the battlefield site at Antietam, where on September 17, 1862, 25,000 men fell dead or wounded. At Moncacy Battlefield near Frederick, where Union troops delayed a Confederate march on Washington DC in 1864, there's a new visitors' centre which explains the battle and its importance to the outcome of the War.

WHAT MAKES WASHINGTON DC SPECIAL First-time visitors to America should consider a stopover in Washington DC a priority. The neighbouring states of Maryland and Virginia also offer a wealth of sightseeing options. Although the 3-tier region is intertwined socially, economically and geographically, each area maintains its own individual character. The proximity of Washington DC, Maryland and Virginia presents an excellent opportunity for travellers to sample the many historic, cultural, commercial, recreational and scenic attractions that make this part of the USA so special.

WASHINGTON'S NEIGHBOURHOODS

The compact size of the city allows easy access to many of the major attractions on foot. The visitor with limited time who comes into contact with little else is likely to return home with a true sense of awe that is conveyed by the capital city. However, those who stay longer, or who are on their second or third visit, may discover numerous attractions that lie beyond the monuments.

Capitol Hill/Northeast

This area includes the blocks surrounding the *US Capitol Building, Supreme Court, Library of Congress* and and the *Senate* and *House Office Buildings*. The shady residential streets include rows of charming townhouses, art galleries, boutiques, intimate restaurants and cafés. *Eastern Market*, an old-style farmer's market, attracts hundreds of residents every Saturday morning. A few blocks from the Capitol is *Union Station* – this historic train station has been magnificently renovated to its original 1907 Beaux-Arts style and now houses 120 shops, nine movie theatres, a host of restaurants and eateries. This neighbourhood also includes antique shops, as well as the beautifully restored Union Station, the *Capital Children's Museum* and the *National Gallery*.

Downtown

Located between Fourth Street and 17th Street, NW, and from Constitution Avenue north to M Street, the downtown area has undergone massive renovation in recent years. Several new hotels, parks, plazas, shopping complexes, office buildings, restaurants and nightclubs have emerged. Major sites in the area include the *Pavilion at the Old Post Office, Ford's Theater*, the *FBI*, the *Treasury*, the *National Archives*, the *National Theatre*, the *Navy Memorial* and the *White House*.

Dupont Circle

In the late 1800s, this was Washington DC's most fashionable residential area. *Dupont Circle*, with its impressive fountain and shaded benches, is a great place to relax and watch the street musicians, chess players and bike messengers who regularly gather here. The surrounding blocks along Connecticut Avenue from N Street through T Street, NW, are alive with museums, galleries, bookstores, record stores, restaurants and elegant Victorian row-houses.

Embassy Row

Home to diplomats and their families from all over the world, most of the city's 150 foreign embassies are found in this neighbourhood, located west of Dupont Circle and extending along Massachusetts Avenue, NW, between Sheridan and Observatory Circle. Many of the embassies are housed in fabulous mansions that were once owned by Washington DC's social elite who lost their fortunes during

RFK STADIUM

Washington DC, along with Dallas and Detroit, is one of only three venues that will host games featuring two different top seeds. Washington DC will host the First Round games on June 19 (Sunday), June 20 (Monday), June 28 (Tuesday) and June 29 (Wednesday). The June 28 and 29 matches will feature the top seed from Group E and F, respectively. In the second stage action, RFK Stadium will host a round of 16 matches on Saturday, July 2. Washington DC will host teams from Groups E and F along with New Jersey/New York and Orlando. The World Cup Final Draw, to be held in December 1993, will place each of the 24 finalists into six groups of four, enabling each venue to host two games featuring a top seed.

RFK STADIUM DETAILS

RFK Stadium is the home stadium of the Washington Redskins American football team, Superbowl Champions in 1992, 1988, 1983 and 1982. It is also home to the Washington Diplomats and Maryland Bays semi-professional soccer teams. The stadium has a seating capacity of 56,500 and has also hosted pop concerts by big names such as Michael Jackson, Pink Floyd, U2 and The Who.

the Great Depression and sold their homes to foreign legations. The *Vice President's Mansion* is located at Observatory Circle.

Chinatown

The colourful *Friendship Arch* marks the beginning of Chinatown, located between Sixth and Eighth Streets at G and H Streets, NW. The whole neighbourhood comes alive with the spectacular Chinese New Year's celebration in February.

Adams-Morgan

Located along Columbia Road between 18th Street and Kalorama Park, NW, Adams-Morgan (the name comes from two schools in the area) is all of Washington DC's multicultural neighbourhoods rolled into one. Caribbean restaurants situated alongside Latin markets, next to Middle Eastern boutiques, adjacent to antique dealers, and hip speciality stores form an eclectic mix of culture.

Foggy Bottom/West End

Once a marshy, lowland area where trader clippers docked, Foggy Bottom encompasses the area between Pennsylvania Avenue and Virginia Avenue from 18th Street to 25th Street, NW. The colourful row-houses and riverside recreational areas mix with the glamourous *Kennedy Center* and the fashionable shops at *The Watergate* to create a charming atmosphere for residents and visitors alike. Foggy Bottom is also the home of *George Washington University*.

Georgetown

Predating the city of Washington, Georgetown is in the western-most part of the city, bounded by the Potomac River on the south and by *Rock Creek Park* on the east. Once a thriving colonial port where goods from western Maryland farmlands were shipped to Europe, today Georgetown is an historic area of speciality stores, nightclubs and intriguing restaurants serving everything from Chesapeake Bay seafood to Indian, Thai and Vietnamese delicacies. It's also the starting point of the *C&O Canal* which extends north along the Potomac River for 296km (185 miles).

Southwest

Home to the Tony Award-winning *Arena Stage*, *Bannecker Circle and Fountain* and *L'Enfant Plaza*, this area is perfect for jogging, bicycling and walking. For several blocks along Maine Avenue, the *Waterfront* has developed into a shimmering array of piers, sailboats, yachts, old-time steamboats, fishing boats and seafood markets. Locals gather to purchase fresh Chesapeake Bay crabs, oysters, clams and other seafood treats brought upriver to dozens of fish markets. A string of fine restaurants provide panoramic views of the *Washington Channel*, which runs between the Waterfront and *Hains Point* to the east.

Upper Northwest

This neighbourhood stretches from above Georgetown as far as the District line at Chevy Chase, Maryland. On the north end of Wisconsin Avenue is Friendship Heights, where you'll find many delightful restaurants, shopping malls and a host of new boutiques and galleries. The predominantly residential area stretching north along Connecticut Avenue from Calvert Street, NW, is known as Woodley Park. The beautifully shaded streets and rolling hills provide a peaceful setting for the *Smithsonian's Zoological Park*, *Washington National Cathedral* and block after block of sidewalk cafés.

MUSEUM CAPITAL

Washington ranks as one of the great museum cities of the world. The Smithsonian Institute alone is a collection of 14 museums. The *Smithsonian's Freer Gallery of Art* re-opens in May 1993 for its 70th anniversary, following a 4-1/2-year construction and renovation project. Its collection of Asian Art (including Japanese, Chinese, Korean, South and Southeast Asian and Near Eastern art) is generally considered one of the world's finest. In addition, the gallery houses a collection of 19th- and early 20th-century art, including important works by James McNeill Whistler. The *Smithsonian's Anacostia Museum* is devoted to the documentation, protection and

THE MOST GOALS (146) WERE SCORED DURING A WORLD CUP TOURNAMENT IN 1982 IN SPAIN. THE MOST GOALS SCORED BY AN INDIVIDUAL WERE WHEN THE FRENCHMAN, JUSTE FONTAINE, SCORED IN EVERY GAME FRANCE PLAYED IN 1958.

Washington DC

interpretation of the American Indian experience in the Upper South. A new, free shuttle bus makes round trips between the Anacostia Museum in southeast Washington DC and other Smithsonian museums located on the *National Mall*. *Smithsonian's National Museum of American History* has a new permanent exhibition called 'American Encounters', focusing on the American southwest and the encounter between the Native American, Hispanic and Anglo-American cultures for the past 450 years. The exhibition includes objects and graphics, as well as video and audio recordings of narrative stories, music and dance of New Mexico's Rio Grande Valley. *Smithsonian's National Postal Museum* is opening in the summer of 1993. Created in cooperation with the US Postal Service, it brings 200 years of moving and sorting mail in America to life with hands-on history displays, interactive videos, video games, treasure hunts and simulations.

Another new addition to the Washington DC museum spectrum is the *US Holocaust Memorial Museum*, opening in April 1993. The exhibition tells the story of the Jews targetted for annihilation in Europe by the Nazis, and describes the fate of the other victims – gypsies, Poles, homosexuals, the handicapped, Jehovah's Witnesses, social misfits, political and religious dissidents and Soviet POWs. It will also highlight stories of resistance, rescue, heroism and survival. *The National Gallery of Art* is one of the world's great art museums which houses extensive collections of Western European and American works in its West and East buildings. Exhibits include a giant Calder mobile and Old Masters dating from the 13th century. The city is also home to a vast array of private art galleries which enjoy worldwide renown.

MAKE IT TO MARYLAND

Bordering Washington on the north and east is the state of Maryland. Located about 50km (31 miles) directly northeast of Washington, Maryland's major metropolis of **Baltimore** is widely recognised as a pace-setter in urban redevelopment. Its flagship creation is the *Inner Harbor*, a 95-acre development at the water's edge that combines sightseeing, shopping and a cultural centre.

Just 66km (41 miles) east of downtown Washington DC lies **Annapolis**. With its cobblestone streets, brick sidewalks and more 18th-century buildings than anywhere else in the country, the city resembles more a colonial waterfront town than the bustling state capital it is. Lawmakers still meet in the original *Maryland State House*, the oldest, continuously operating state house in the USA. Sitting on the shores of the *Chesapeake Bay*, Annapolis houses the largest fleet of sailing ships on the east coast during the summer and is the home of the *US Naval Academy*.

Beyond the major Maryland cities, different attractions emerge depending on the direction taken. Head west to find everything for the outdoor enthusiast. Hike the mountains, canoe the lakes and raft the rivers in summer; ski the slopes in winter. Visit Civil War battlefields and riverfront plantations. Or head east to the Maryland Atlantic Ocean resort town of **Ocean City,** or to the picturesque peninsula known as *Eastern Shore*, shared predominantly by Maryland and Virginia – a slender finger of land between the Chesapeake Bay and Atlantic Ocean.

VENTURE OUT TO VIRGINIA

Heading east, visitors won't want to miss northern Virginia, just across the Potomac River from Washington DC. This region is one of stunning contrasts – from the Kennedy grave sites at *Arlington National Cemetery* to *George Washington's Mount Vernon* plantation, to horse country and state-of-the-art shopping. (**Fairfax** has the highest concentration of shops on the east coast outside of New York City.) From the eastern shore of Virginia, it's just a short hop across the 28km (17.5-mile) Chesapeake Bay Bridge Tunnel to *Tidewater/Hampton Roads*, headquarters of NATO and site of the oldest permanent English settlement in North America. Enjoy the 45km (28 miles) Atlantic Ocean shoreline at *Virginia Beach* and the most extensive, restored 18th-century town in North America – **Colonial Williamsburg.** Tours of Colonial Willamsburg are available from Washington DC's Gray Line Terminal at Union Station. Beginning at 0800, the tour lasts approximately 15 hours and includes visits to the *Capitol of Williamsburg*, the *Palace*, the *Gaol*, *Raleigh*

HOW THE WORLD CUP SCHEDULE WORKS

The 1994 World Cup tournament features 24 teams playing a total of 52 games over the course of 31 days. The competition consists of a First Round, a Round of 16, Quarterfinals, Semifinals, a Match for 3rd Place, and the World Cup Final itself.

In the First Round, teams are divided into six groups of four teams each by means of a public draw ceremony. Six 'seeds' will be pre-determined and will be placed as the top team in each of the groups. The remainder of the teams are drawn at random to fill out the six groups, which are indicated by letters A, B, C, D, E and F.

The teams then play against each other within their group, earning two points for a win, one for a tie and no points for a defeat. When the First Round is over, 36 games will have been played (6 groups x 6 games each).

The top two teams from each group (a total of 12 teams) will qualify for the Round of 16 phase, along with the four best third-place teams as determined by a system of standings and tiebreakers.

Beginning with the Round of 16, the tournament becomes a single-elimination event – one loss and a team is eliminated. If games are tied after 90 minutes, 30 minutes of overtime is then played. If no winner is determined in the overtime (not a sudden death overtime), then penalty kicks are taken to produce a winner.

Pairings for the Round of 16 are set by FIFA Regulations and are as follows:

Game 1 Winner of Group A vs Third from Group C, D or E*
Game 2 Second of Group F vs Second of Group B
Game 3 Winner of Group E vs Second of Group D
Game 4 Winner of Group C vs Third from Group A, B or F*
Game 5 Winner of Group D vs Third from Group B, E or F*
Game 6 Winner of Group C vs Second of Group A
Game 7 Winner of Group F vs Second of Group E
Game 8 Winner of Group B vs Third from Group A, C or D*

* The specific third-place team is designated by a pre-determined chart which is applied to the four third-place qualifiers.

Tavern, *George Wythe's Home*, the *Bruton Parish Church*, the *Courthouse*, *Powder Magazine*, *Brush-Everard House* and the *College of William and Mary*. A film 'The Story of a Patriot' will be shown en route on the coach. The all-day tour is available Wednesday, Friday, Saturday or Sunday March 30-October 31 and costs $60 for adults and $50 for children (reservations required). Overnight tour packages to Williamsburg are also available. For further information, telephone (202) 289 1995.

Central Virginia mixes the genteel plantation life of some of America's greatest patriots – like Thomas Jefferson – with first-class shopping, theme parks, the historic capital of **Richmond,** and a diversity of museums enhancing the living history of Civil War battlefields and related sites.

Visitors find more natural splendour heading west to Virginia's *Shenandoah Valley* and the southwest *Blue Ridge Highlands*. Here the *Blue Ridge Parkway* joins the 168km (104 miles) of *Shenandoah National Park*, a haven for outdoor enthusiasts. In Virginia's Shenandoah Valley, there is beauty even below ground. Nature has created beautiful rock formations in deep limestone caves – *Luray*, *Dixie*, *Shenandoah* and *Endless Caverns* are among the most spectacular.

THE SPORTS SCENE

Washington DC offers a diverse range of sporting activities within minutes of the downtown area, including bicycling, golf, tennis, paddle-boating, fishing, horse-riding, even windsurfing within the city limits. In winter, ice-skating is popular on the frozen C&O Canal.

Maryland and Virginia offer visitors almost every conceivable type of sport, from powerboat racing in summer to cross-country and downhill skiing in winter. In Maryland, the Wisp ski area in the western part of the state has 23 slopes and 23km

In the Quarterfinals, the eight winners of the Round of 16 play as follows:
Match A Winner of Game 1 vs Winner of Game 2
Match B Winner of Game 3 vs Winner of Game 4
Match C Winner of Game 5 vs Winner of Game 6
Match D Winner of Game 7 vs Winner of Game 8

The Semifinal match-ups are determined as follows from the Quarterfinal winners:
Winner of Match A vs Winner of Match D
Winner of Match B vs Winner of Match C

Semifinal winners meet for the World Cup. Semifinal losers meet in the Match for 3rd Place.

Major Annual Events

Washington DC has special activities to appeal to every visitor in every season. Here's a sample of annual events in the city.

Spring: National Cherry Blossom Festival – *The capital's historic monuments are framed by thousands of delicate blossoms in late March/early April. Activities include the Cherry Blossom Festival Parade, open-air concerts, the Matsuri Festival of Japan and the Japanese Lantern Lighting Ceremony.*
St Patrick's Day Parade – *Parades down Constitution Avenue to celebrate the Irish National Day.*
White House Garden Tours – *Tours include the Jacqueline Kennedy Rose Gardens and the West Lawn Gardens; the public rooms can also be visited.*
Goodwill Embassy Tour – *Various Embassies open their doors to the public to benefit Davis Memorial Goodwill Industries.*

Summer: Smithsonian Festival of American *Folklife – American music, crafts, ethnic foods, folk heritage and occupational folklife fills the National Mall for one of the most popular events in the capital.*
National Independence Day Celebration – *This is the biggest July 4 celebration in the nation. Events begin at 1000 and continue until well into the evening, including concerts, parades and lots of free entertainment. The day culminates with a superb fireworks display over the Washinton Monument.*

Autumn: Taste of DC – *Taste the best of a vast array of international cuisine. Additional activities include arts and crafts and a special children's area.*

Winter: *National Christmas Tree Lighting/Pageant of Peace – The National Christmas Tree near the White House is lighted by the President. The tree is joined by a spectacular display of lighted Christmas trees representing each state and territory.*
White House Christmas Candlelight Tours – *Evening tours of the White House Christmas decorations, all a glow with festive candlelight.*
Chinese New Year – *Traditional firecrackers, drums and dragon dancers make their way through Chinatown's streets. The celebrations for the Lunar New Year are watched by thousands of spectators lining the colourful streets of Chinatown.*

(14 miles) of groomed trails from novice to expert.

Fishing is popular everywhere, whether in streams and rivers, or in the deeper waters of Chesapeake Bay and the Atlantic Ocean. Ocean City is famous for it charterboats and sport fishing industry.

Other outdoor activities that can be enjoyed by visitors include birdwatching, boating, kayaking and canoeing, white-water rafting, horseriding, tennis and of course, swimming, windsurfing and other watersports.

Probably the biggest sporting draw for visitors is golf. Maryland and Virginia have nearly 200 golf courses, so whether you're in the mountains or by the sea, you're never far from a challenging and enjoyable round. There are numerous golf courses and golf resorts throughout the region.

Fine resorts for skiing enthusiasts include *Massanutten*, near Harrisonburg, and *Bryce Resort* in the heart of the Shenandoah Valley at Basye.

SUPERB SHOPPING

Washington DC, together with Maryland and Virginia, has one of America's heaviest concentrations of shopping malls, department stores, speciality shops and boutiques. And as most of them are open long hours, seven days a week, shopping couldn't be easier.

Some malls have become a tourist attraction in their own right, with restaurants, cinemas and live entertainment tempting shoppers to stay all day. Some of the more famous malls are *Georgetown Park* in Georgetown, where more than 100 shops and stores are housed around a 3-storey atrium and *Mazza Gallerie*, a high-fashion indoor mall with over 50 stores in northwest Washington DC, close to the Maryland state line. Downtown Washington boasts *The Shops* at National Place, *The Pavilion* at the Old Post Office and the new shopping gallery at the restored Union Station.

In the suburbs, the selection of shopping malls increases tremendously. *Pentagon City Fashion Center*, in Virginia, and *White Flint Mall*, in Maryland, are easily reached from downtown Washington DC by Metro.

Baltimore, too, offers excellent shopping opportunities, with suburban malls and city-centre complexes like *The Gallery*, *Harborplace* and *Owings Mill Mall*, which is accessible by subway from downtown Baltimore, and *Towson Town Center Shopping Mall*, located 13km (8 miles) from downtown Baltimore, accessible by car.

Maryland has several outlet centres. Near the Chesapeake Bay bridges, factory outlets on both sides of the Bay have over 100 stores selling everything from designer clothing to craft-making materials at discount prices. In Northern Maryland, the outlet centre at Perryville is a good stop for visitors travelling the Interstate between Baltimore and Philadelphia.

In Virginia, the *Williamsburg Outlet Mall* has over 65 stores offering top-quality, name-brand products at factory prices, while *Potomac Mills Mall* near Woodbridge, with over 180 stores selling quality merchandise at discount prices, is one of the world's largest factory outlet centres.

At Waynesboro, not far from the Blue Ridge Parkway and the Skyline Drive, *Waynesboro Village Factory Outlets Mall* offers 35 designer and top-brand outlets with goods up to 50% below normal prices.

THE WAY TO THE WORLD CUP

THE AIRPORTS

Washington Dulles International Airport, where many transcontinental and international flights arrive, is 45 minutes from downtown Washington DC. For airport information, telephone (703) 471 7838 Monday to Friday 0900-1700 *or* 471 4242 (the Consumer Hotline airport information line).

Baltimore/Washington International Airport (BWI) is located approximately 1 hour from downtown Washington and serves both the nation's capital and Baltimore. For airport information, telephone (301) 859 7100.

EMBASSY SUITES HOTEL
WASHINGTON, DC
1250 22ND STREET, NW
20037
TEL: (202) 857 3388.
FAX: (202) 293 3173.

Ideally located in the heart of the business district. Six blocks from Georgetown. Most offices of National Associations, Fortune 500 companies and Embassy Row nearby. All major attractions, Capitol Hill, Smithsonian, are accessible by Metro system within four blocks of hotel. Boardrooms, Executive Meeting Suites. Limited underground parking (daily charge). nine floors and 318 suites.

EMBASSY SUITES
WASHINGTON, DC –
CHEVY CHASE PAVILLION
4300 MILITARY ROAD, NW
20015
TEL: (202) 362 9300.
FAX: (202) 686 3405.

An award-winning mixed-use facility combining a hotel, shopping mall, food court and office park all under one roof. Located along the tree lined avenues of prestigious uptown Washington, DC. Metro subway system tunnels directly under the hotel. Breath-taking atrium, glass elevators, penthouse, health and swim club. Eight floors and 198 suites.

EMBASSY SUITES HOTEL
ALEXANDRIA-OLD TOWN
1900 DIAGONAL ROAD
ALEXANDRIA, VA
22314
TEL: (703) 684 5900.
FAX: (703) 684 1403.

Located directly across the street from King Street Metro and Amtrak stations, Embassy Suites offer the advantage of being within sight of Washington, DC, but in the tranquil environment of historic Old Town Alexandria. Within walking distance of the hotel, there is a collection of speciality shops, art galleries, antique stores, 14 pubs and 37 restaurants, museums and Potomac River waterfront activities. Eight floors and 268 suites.

EMBASSY SUITES
CRYSTAL CITY –
NATIONAL AIRPORT
1300 JEFFERSON DAVIS HIGHWAY
ARLINGTON, VA
22202
TEL: (703) 979 9799.
FAX: (703) 920 5947.

Ideally situated for business and pleasure in the heart of Arlington, Virginia. Minutes away from all of Washington, DC's spectacular attractions and downtown business district; two miles from National Airport and five miles from Old Town Alexandria, Virginia. Within walking distance of the Pentagon, the Pentagon City Fashion Center and Crystal City Underground shopping. Complimentary shuttle service is available. Ten floors and 267 suites.

EMBASSY SUITES HOTEL
TYSONS CORNER
8517 LEESBURG PIKE
VIENNA, VA
22182
TEL: (703) 883 0707.
FAX: (703) 883 0694.

Located in the heart of Tysons Corner corporate park as well as central to the Tysons Corner shopping centre, the largest retail shopping area on the East Coast. Shops include Gucci, Tiffany's, Hermes, Fendi, Nordstrom's, Bloomingdales, Macy's, Neiman Marcus and Saks Fifth Avenue. Twelve miles from Dulles International Airport. 18 miles from National Airport. Complimentary shuttle service available. Eight floors and 232 suites.

Washington DC Opens Its Doors To World Cup 94

Washington Monument

Union Station

The Capitol

J. F. K Centre for the Performing Arts

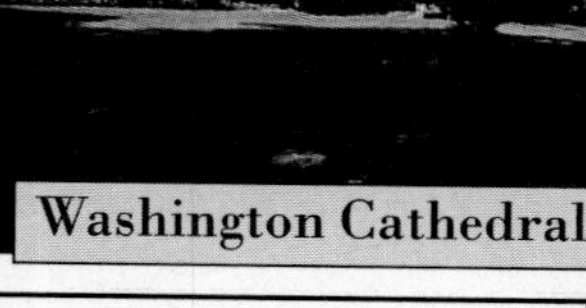

Washington Cathedral

• District of Columbia Chamber of Commerce •
• Washington Convention & Visitors Association • DC Committee to Promote Washington •
• Washington Convention Center •
In the UK: Washington Convention & Visitors Association
To request literature: Tel: 081 392 9187. Fax: 081 392 1318

Washington National Airport is located just across the Potomac River in Virginia, a 9km (5.5-mile) or 15-minute drive from downtown Washington. It is an airport for domestic flights only. For airport information, telephone (703) 685 8000 Monday to Friday 0900-1700.

TRANSPORTATION FROM DULLES AIRPORT TO NATIONAL AIRPORT

The *Washington Flyer Inter-Airport Express Buses* provide services between *Washington Dulles International Airport* and *Washington National Airport.* Buses depart from Dulles Airport every hour on the hour 0500-2300 Monday to Friday, and every two hours 0500-1300 and every hour 1300-2300 Saturday and Sunday. Buses depart from *National Airport* every hour on the hour from 0600-2300 Monday to Friday, and every two hours 0600-1400 and every hour 1400-2300 Saturday and Sunday. Fares are $16 one-way and $26 round-trip (children under six travel free). For further information, telephone (703) 685 1400.

TRANSPORTATION FROM DULLES AIRPORT TO WASHINGTON DC

Express Buses/Metrorail

Washington Flyer Express Buses provides service between *Dulles Airport* and Metrorail's West Falls Church Stations. Buses depart every 30 minutes 0600-1000, every 20 minutes 1020-1800 and every 30 minutes 1830-2230 Monday to Friday; and every 30 minutes 0730-2230 Saurday and Sunday. Buses from the Metro West Falls Church Stations to *Dulles Airport* depart every 30 minutes *from* 0630-1030, every 20 minutes 1050-1810 and every 30 minutes 1830-2300 Monday to Friday; and every 30 minutes 0800-2300 Saturday and Sunday. The fare is $8 one-way

WORLD CUP '94

(children under six travel free). For further information, telephone (703) 685 1400.

Express Buses

Washington Flyer Express Buses provide services from *Dulles Airport* to the Downtown Terminal at 1517 K Street, NW. Buses depart every 30 minutes 0520-2220 at 20 and 50 minutes past the hour Monday to Friday; and every hour from 0520-1120 at 20 and 30 minutes past the hour, and 1220-2220 at 20 and 50 minutes past the hour Saturday and Sunday. Fares are $16 one-way and $26 round-trip (children under six travel free).

Washington Flyer Courtesy Shuttles provide prompt connections from the Downtown Terminal to the following hotel locations: Mayflower (1127 Connecticut Avenue, NW), Washington Hilton (1919 Connecticut Avenue, NW), Omni Shoreham (2500 Calvert Street, NW), Sheraton Washington (2660 Woodley Road, NW), Ramada Tech World (999 9th Street, NW), Grand Hyatt (1000 H Street, NW), J W Marriott (1331 Pennsylvania Avenue, NW) and, by reservation only, to Harrington Hotel (11th & E Streets, NW).

For further information on these *Washington Flyer* services, telephone (703) 685 1400.

Taxis

At *Washington Dulles Airport*, uniformed curbside *Washington Flyer Taxi* dispatchers are on duty 24 hours a day to assist customers outside the Arrivals Level. All *Washington Flyer taxis* are equipped with electronic meters to compute fare and most are equipped with Visa, Mastercard and American Express services and cellular phones for passenger convenience. Advance reservations are accepted and handicapped-accessible vehicles are available on request. Fares are approximately $35 to the city centre. Tel: (703) 661 8230 *or* 528 4440.

TRANSPORTATION FROM BWI AIRPORT TO WASHINGTON DC

Rail

Maryland Rural Commuter Service (MARC): Operates a rail service from *BWI Airport* and downtown Baltimore to Washington DC's Union Station. For further information, telephone (800) 325 RAIL.

Amtrak: Provides services from *BWI Airport* to Washington DC. For train schedules and further information, telephone (800) 872 7245.

Express Buses

An airport express bus operates from *BWI Airport* to Washington DC. Fares are approximately $14 one-way and $25 round-trip.

Taxis

Taxis are available from *BWI Airport* to Washington DC. Fare is approximately $40 and it is best to agree the fare with the driver beforehand.

TRANSPORTATION FROM NATIONAL AIRPORT TO WASHINGTON DC

Express Buses

Washington Flyer Express Buses provide transportation from *National Airport* to Washington DC every 30 minutes 0625-2125, every 25 and 55 minutes past the hour Monday to Friday; and every 30 minutes 0625-1225 at 25 minutes past the hour, and every 30 minutes 1255-2125 at 25 and 55 minutes past the hour Saturday and Sunday. Fares are $8 one-way and $14 round-trip (children under six travel free).

Washington Flyer Courtesy Shuttles provide prompt connections from the Downtown Terminal to the following hotel locations: Mayflower (1127 Connecticut Avenue, NW), Washington Hilton (1919 Connecticut Avenue, NW), Omni Shoreham (2500 Calvert Street, NW), Sheraton Washington (2660 Woodley Road, NW), Ramada Tech World (999 9th Street, NW), Grand Hyatt (1000 H Street, NW), J W Marriott (1331 Pennsylvania Avenue, NW) and, by reservation only, to

Tours To The Surrounding Area

Chesapeake Bay, Annapolis and Baltimore

June 30-October 31

Maryland houses two former Capitols of the USA. The tour starts with a drive across the Chesapeake Bay Bridge, overlooking the city of Annapolis. Sights of Annapolis include the State Capitol, St John's Church, the US Naval Academy, the tomb of John Paul Jones and the 'Old Annapolis' dock area. In Baltimore, visit the Inner Harbor and Fort McHenry. The tour takes approximately 10 hours and departs at 0800 Wednesdays only. Reservations are required. Fares are $45 for adults and $30 for children. For more details, telephone Gray Line Inc on (202) 289 1995.

Harper's Ferry and Gettysburg Battlefield
June 28-October 25
The Blue Ridge Mountains form the magnificent backdrop for Harper's Ferry which overlooks some of the loveliest scenery in the USA. The town itself is probably best known for John Brown's raid in 1859. The tour continues to Gettysburg, a town rich in historic events. It was here that the Union forces defeated the Confederate army in the largest battle to be fought on US soil. Visit the Cemetery Ridge, site of Lincoln's Gettysburg Address, and the farm of President Eisenhower. Duration of the tour is approximately 10 hours, departure is at 0800 Mondays. Reservation required; adults pay $40 and children $20. For further information, telephone (202) 289 1995.

Monticello/Thomas Jefferson Country
July 1-October 28
Covering two centuries of US history, the tour starts with a visit to Manassas Battlefield Park. Next stop is Charlottesville and the University of Virginia (designed by Thomas Jefferson). Finally you will reach Monticello, former home of Thomas Jefferson. The tour includes a visit to one of the famous Virginia Wineries. Reservations are required; departure is at 0800 Thursdays only. Duration of the tour is 11 hours. Details can be obtained on (202) 289 1995.

Harrington Hotel (11th & E Streets, NW).
For further information on these *Washington Flyer* services, telephone (703) 685 1400.

Subway

There is a *Metrorail* subway service from *National Airport* to the city centre, starting on the Blue Line. Fare is $1 during non-rush hours and just over $1 during rush hours. Trains operate approximately every ten minutes 0530-2400 Monday to Friday, 0800-2400 Saturday and 1000-2400 Sunday.

Taxis

Washington Flyer taxis are available from *National Airport* to Washington DC destinations. Fare to the city centre is approximately $10. Tel: (703) 661 8230 *or* 528 4440.

WASHINGTON DC GROUND TRANSPORTATION

Metrorail

Most major attractions can be reached by Metro, Washington DC's clean and efficient modern subway system. The system also provides rail links to the Maryland and Virginia suburbs. Stations are readily identified by black pylons with the large white 'M' visible from the sidewalks.
To travel on the Metro, passengers must purchase a farecard from a vending machine at any of the stations. The base fare is $1 or more, depending on the destination and time of travel. Trains operate every 10 minutes on average, 0530-2400 Monday to Friday and 0800-2400 Saturday and 1000-2400 Sunday. For *Metrorail* information, telephone (202) 637 7000 (*or* 637 3780 for TDD).

Buses

Metrobus: Routes are timed with *Metrorail* routes and schedules to provide a coordinated public transportation system through Washington DC and linking it to Maryland and Virginia. For *Metrobus* information, telephone (202) 637 7000 or 637 3780 (for TDD).
Greyhound/Trailways: Provides a scheduled service to destinations throughout the USA. The Washington DC Bus Terminal is at 1st & L Streets, NE. For further information, telephone (301) 565 2662.

Rail

Amtrak: The national passenger rail system services Washington DC through the historic Union Station terminal. More than 50 trains daily link Washington to Baltimore, Philadelphia, New York and other east coast cities. For *Amtrak* reservations, telephone (800) 872 7245.
Maryland Rural Commuter System (MARC): Operates rail service from Washington DC's Union Station to Baltimore. For further informaton, telephone (800) 325 RAIL.
Virginia Railway Express: Trains connect communities such as Manassas and Fredericksburg with Washington DC.

Taxis

There are more than 9000 taxis in Washington DC and most can be hailed on the street. Cabs operate on a zone system; zones begin in the central city and spread outward. By law, basic rates must be posted in the cab. The present rates are $1.50 to begin with, then 20 cents for each additional 252 yards. There is a $1 surcharge for each additional passenger in a party and a surcharge during evening rush hours (1600-1830). Each additional suitcase, after one per passenger, is 15 cents. For trunks or similarly large articles, there is a surcharge of $1.25. For further information, telephone the DC Taxicab Commission on (202) 767 8380.

WORLD CUP 1958: ENGLAND SUFFERED A CRUEL BLOW WHEN THEY LOST MANY VITAL PLAYERS IN THE MUNICH AIR DISASTER 4 MONTHS BEFORE THE FINAL TOURNAMENT.

Self-Drive Cars

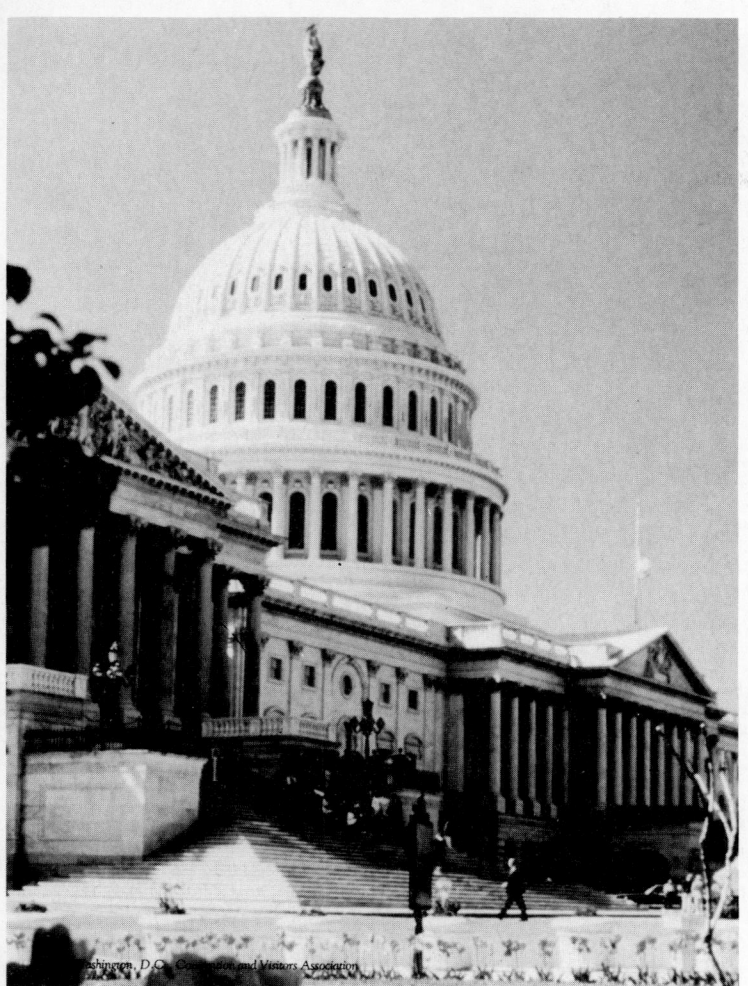

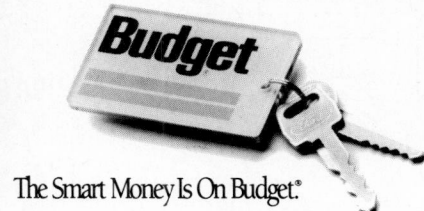

When in Washington DC, consider using public transport or other alternatives to driving. Most hotels have guest parking with bus or subway stops nearby. If you decide to drive in the city, read the parking signs carefully. If a car is causing a serious safety hazard or impeding traffic, it will be ticketed and may be towed to one of the city's impoundment lots, where the owner or renter will have to pay a $75 fine to get it back. For details on parking enforcement, call (202) 727 5000.

WASHINGTON MONUMENT

LINCOLN MEMORIAL

US ISLANDS

HAWAII

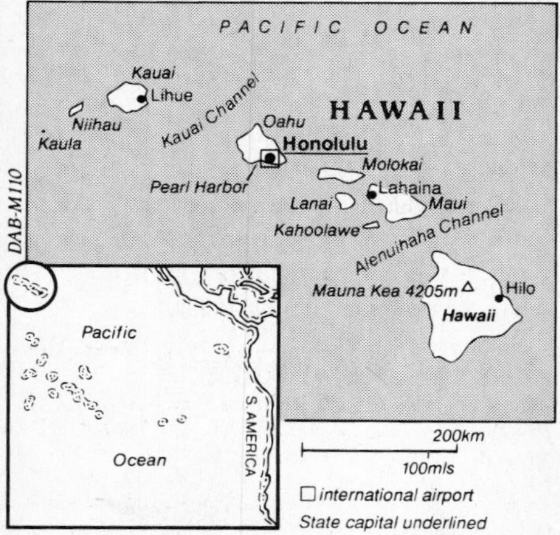

Location: Pacific Ocean.

Note: Although Hawaii is a state of the USA, information has been presented in this separate section, as the islands are in many ways a different holiday destination. Information on other states of the USA may be found in the *States A-Z* and *US Gateways* sections above.

Hawaii Visitors Bureau
Suite 801
2270 Kalakaua Avenue
Honolulu, HI
96815
Tel: 923 1811. Fax: 922 8991.

Embassy of the United States of America
For address in UK, see top of USA entry above.

Hawaii Visitors Bureau
14 The Green
Richmond
Surrey
TW9 1PX
Tel: (081) 332 6969. Fax: (081) 332 7001. Opening hours: 0930-1700 Monday to Friday.
The bureau is closed to the public.

Embassy of the United States of America
For address in Canada, see top of USA entry above.

Hawaii Visitors Bureau
Suite 205
1624 56th Street
Delta, British Columbia
V4L 2B1
Tel: (604) 943 8555.

AREA: 16,759 sq km (6471 sq miles).
POPULATION: 1,108,000 (1990). About 80% of the population lives on the island of Oahu.
POPULATION DENSITY: 66.4 per sq km.
CAPITAL: Honolulu. **Population:** 365,272 (1990 estimate).
GEOGRAPHY: The island group of Hawaii comprises over 200 islands and atolls of which seven are inhabited and make up the state itself. Oahu contains the capital, Honolulu, and is the most commercialised, while Hawaii is the biggest island. 3862km (2400 miles) from the American Pacific coast, the islands are a less wild version of Polynesia. Oahu has two diagonal mountain ranges (the Waianae and Koolau), with many beautiful waterfalls. Hawaii is cloaked in orchards and bordered by sheer cliffs. The many volcanoes on Hawaii are almost without vegetation. Maui is formed of two volcanic masses. The islands support rainforest and green flatlands.
LANGUAGE: English is the official language; Hawaiian is hardly spoken nowadays.
TIME: GMT - 10. *Daylight Saving Time* is not observed in the Hawaiian Islands.
ELECTRICITY: 120 volts AC, 60Hz.
COMMUNICATIONS: Telephone: IDD is available. Country code: 1 808. All telephone services are provided by the *Hawaiian Telephone Company*. **Fax:** Most hotels have facilities. **Telex/telegram:** *Western Union* and *ITT* provide public telex facilities. Telegrams can be sent from post and telegraph offices. **Post:** Airmail to Europe takes up to a week. Post office hours: 0900-1700 Monday to Saturday. **Press:** The two main publications are *The Honolulu Advertiser* and *Honolulu Star-Bulletin*.
BBC World Service and Voice of America frequencies: From time to time these change. See the section *How to Use this Book* for more information.

BBC:				
MHz	17.10	15.36	9.740	7.150
Voice of America:				
MHz	18.82	15.18	9.525	1.735

PASSPORT/VISA

Immigration requirements for Hawaii are the same as for mainland US states. See *USA* above.

MONEY

Currency: US Dollar (US$) = 100 cents. See the *USA* section above for information on exchange rates, credit cards, etc.
Currency exchange: There are many foreign exchange facilities at Honolulu International Airport.
Banking hours: 0900-1500 Monday to Thursday and 0830-1800 Fridays.

DUTY FREE

Duty-free allowances are as for the USA, except that goods up to the value of US$300 may be imported without incurring customs duty; see the duty-free section in the general USA entry above.

PUBLIC HOLIDAYS

The Hawaiian Islands observe all the public holidays observed in mainland US states (see *USA* above), plus the following:
Mar 26 '93 Kuhio Day. **Jun 11** Kamehamahe Day. **Mar 26 '94** Kuhio Day.

HEALTH

Regulations and requirements may be subject to change at short notice, and you are advised to contact your doctor well in advance of your intended date of departure. Any numbers in the chart refer to the footnotes below.

	Special Precautions?	Certificate Required?
Yellow Fever	No	No
Cholera	No	No
Typhoid & Polio	No	-
Malaria	No	-
Food & Drink	1	-

[1]: Tap water is considered safe to drink. Milk is pasteurised and dairy products are safe for consumption. Local meat, poultry, seafood, fruit and vegetables are considered safe to eat.
Health care: See *USA*.

TRAVEL

AIR: *Hawaiian Airlines*, *Royal Hawaiian Commuter Air* and *Aloha Airlines* offer frequent inter-island services.
Approximate flight times: From Honolulu to *Anchorage* is 5 hours 40 minutes, to *Chicago* is 9 hours 55 minutes, to *London* is 17-19 hours (including stopover, and depending on route taken), to *Los Angeles* is 5 hours 20 minutes, to *Miami* is 10 hours 35 minutes, to *New York* is 11 hours 40 minutes, to *San Francisco* is 5 hours 5 minutes, to *Singapore* is 18 hours 15 minutes, to *Sydney* is 12 hours 30 minutes and to *Washington DC* is 11 hours.
International airport: *Honolulu International Airport (HNL)* is about 6km (4 miles) west of the city and 10km (6 miles) west of Waikiki. Coaches to Waikiki hotels meet all flight arrivals during the day (travel time – 25 minutes). Bus no 8 runs every 30 minutes from 0618-0118 (travel time – 30 minutes). Taxis are available.
Local airports: *Kauai:* Hanalei, Lihue. *Molokai:* Kaunakakai, Hana. *Maui:* West Maui, Kahului, Kaanapali. *Lanai:* Lanai City. *Hawaii:* Upolu Point, Kamuela, Kona, Aloha.
SEA: Hawaii's main ports are Honolulu and Lahaina. The following cruise lines run services to Hawaii: *P & O (Honolulu)*, *Nauru Pacific*, *American Hawaii*, *Royal Viking*, *Cunard*, *Union Lloyd* and *Princess*. There is no scheduled ferry service.
ROAD: Driving is on the right. Right-hand turns are permitted in the right lane at a stop light unless signposted otherwise. Pedestrians are given the right of way most of the time. **Bus:** Deluxe modern buses operate on all islands. **Taxi:** Metered and available throughout the main islands. **Car hire:** Available through local and international agencies. Drivers must be over 21 years of age for car rentals. **Documentation:** Foreign driving licence is required.
URBAN: Good local bus services are provided on Oahu. An exact flat-fare system operates. On other islands only taxi or car hire is possible.
JOURNEY TIMES: The following chart gives approximate average journey times (in hours and minutes) from Honolulu to other major islands.

	Air
Kauai Island	0.20
Maui Island	0.20
Hawaii Island	0.25

ACCOMMODATION

HOTELS: There are modern hotels from deluxe to modest on the six largest islands. Accommodation is provided by many of the leading hotel groups. 157 establishments are registered with the Hawaii Hotel Association, 11th Floor, 2270 Kalakaua Avenue, Honolulu, HI 96815. Tel: 923 0407. Fax: 924 3843.
APARTMENTS & CONDOMINIUMS: Available from a number of companies. See the *Accommodation* section in *USA* above.

RESORTS & EXCURSIONS

OAHU: Honolulu, the capital, is the starting point for most holidays in Hawaii. *Waikiki Beach* is a particularly popular resort region of the city. Other attractions include *Kalakaua Avenue*, *Kilohana Square*, the *Ala Moana Center* and the *Kahala Mall* (all noted for their shopping); the zoo in *Kapiolani Park* (where the Honolulu Marathon is held annually); the *Punchbowl*, a grassy crater with graves of American war casualties; downtown Honolulu, including *Chinatown*; the *Academy of Arts*; *Bishop Museum*; *Castle Park*, an amusement park; *Iolani Palace* and the spectacular *Nuuanu Pali*. There are also many other parks, plus aquaria, museums and theatres in the city and its environs.
A variety of excursions are available. At least a day should be allowed for the *Grand Island Tour*, which takes in the whole of Oahu. Attractions en route include the *Sacred Falls*; *Waimea Valley* and *Waimea Falls Park*; *Pearl Harbour*; the *Polynesian Cultural Centre*; *Sea Life Park*; the *Waialua Plantation*; the *Sacred Birthstones*; *Kaena Point*; and *Sunset Beach*.
HAWAII: This is the largest island in the group. Attractions include the city of **Hilo;** beach resorts such as *Kailau-Kona* and the 'Gold Coast' of *Kawaihae*; the *National Historic Park of Honaunau*; the tropical highlands; and the two famous mountains – *Mauna Kea* and *Mauna Loa* – *Waipio Valley*, *Akaka Falls* and *Parker Ranch*.
MAUI: Attractions include the town of **Wailuku;** the more bustling town of **Kahului;** the *Iao Valley*; the historic whaling town of **Lahaina;** *Mount Haleakala*, which translates as the House of the Sun, a massive volcanic crater; the tranquil beauty of the *Eastern Shore*; the beautiful *Hana Valley*; and the waterfalls at *Wailua Cove*.
LANAI: Attractions include **Kaunolo Village;** the *Munro Trail*, leading to the spectacular *Hauola Gulch*; and the petroglyph rock carving on *Shipwreck Beach*.
MOLOKAI: Attractions include the harbour town of **Kaunakakai;** *Mount Kamakou*; the *Moaulu Falls*; the beautiful *Halowa Valley*; *Molokai Ranch Wildlife Park*; and *Father Damien's Community* at **Kalaupapa.**
KAUAI: Attractions include *Mount Waialeale*; the capital town of **Lihue;** *Waimea Canyon*; the tropical rainforest in the centre of the island; the *Wallua River*; the *Fern Grotto*; the *Na Pali Coast* and the nearby temple of *Heiau-Holo-Holo-Ku*.

SOCIAL PROFILE

FOOD & DRINK: The food is basically American with oriental influences brought in by the assortment

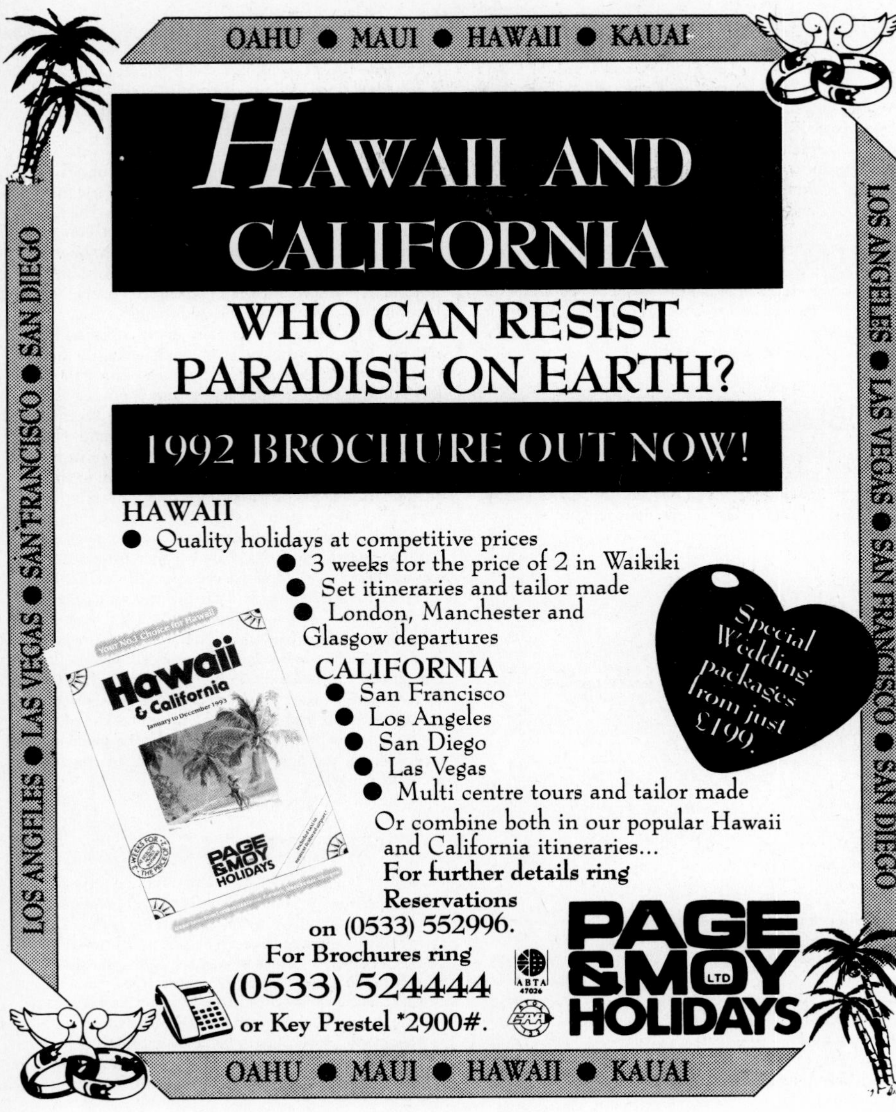

of nationals that make up the population. The classic Hawaiian feast is the *luau* based around a *puaa kalua* (whole pig) that has been skinned and rubbed with rock salt and buried in the ground. It is then placed on chicken wire, filled with hot stones from the *imu* fire, and cooked in the *imu* along with sweet potatoes, plantains and occasionally *laulaus* (pork, butterfish and spinach-like *taro* shoots wrapped in leaves and steamed). The steam is prevented from escaping by encircling the pig with corn husks and taro leaves. The *kalua* pig is eaten with the fingers and is accompanied by the traditional Hawaiian *poi* (thick paste made from ground *taro*), *opihi* (a salty, black, clam-like mollusk) and *lomi lomi* salmon (salmon rubbed with an onion and tomato marinade). *Chicken luau* comprises tender chicken pieces cooked with *taro* tops and coconut cream. Amongst the many garnishes are *limu* (dried seaweed), *paakai* rock salt and chopped roasted *kukui* nuts. Local seafoods are excellent, and include *moi* mullet *ulua*, *mahimahi* (dolphin), *opakapaka* (pink snapper), turtle, lobster and yellowfin tuna. Hawaiian breakfast specialities include macadamia nuts, banana and coconut pancakes with coconut syrup. Fresh fruit and nut ice-creams or sorbets make excellent desserts. **Drink:** The minimum legal drinking age is 21 years. It is illegal to consume alcohol in parks and on beaches.
NIGHTLIFE: There are many bars and nightclubs. Top international stars are booked whilst *luau* shows are, in themselves, a great attraction. Jazz, big band music, tea dances, hula groups, disco and Elvis (and other) impersonations are all available.
SHOPPING: The International Marketplace, Royal Hawaiian Shopping Center and the Ala Moana Shopping Center in Waikiki Beach, Honolulu, are popular shopping areas. **Opening hours:** 0900-2200 Monday to Saturday. Some shops may open 0830-1800 Sunday.
SPORT: Golf: Courses are numerous and scenic. **Hunting:** Facilities are available. **Fishing:** Deep-sea fishing is very popular off the island of Hawaii. **Watersports:** The Hawaiian islands are particularly good for watersports. **Yachting:** One-week charters are available, with or without crews. All boats are equipped with Coast Guard-approved safety equipment and are under Coast Guard supervision. **Surfing** is, of course, a very popular sport – for both participants and spectators. **Snorkelling** is best near the Molokini Crater off Maui. In addition, there are some exciting international events such as the *Canoe Race*, in which outrigger canoes race against each other across Waikiki Harbour.
SPECIAL EVENTS: *The Captain Cook Celebration* takes place in Waimea Town annually in late February. It starts on Friday afternoon and continues until late Saturday, featuring many events, in particular the foot races known as *Captain Cook's Caper*. The following is a list of events celebrated in Hawaii during 1993/94:
Mar '93 *23rd Annual Maui Marathon.* **Mar 5** *10th Anniversary Hawaii Kite Festival*, Oahu. **Mar 6** *Cherry Blossom Festival.* **Mar 14** *Marathon*, Maui. **Mar 17** *St Patrick's Day Parade.* **Mar 26** *Prince Kuhio Festival.* **Apr** *Merrie Monarch Festival*, Hilo. **May 1** *Lei Day Celebration.* **Jun** *Fiesta Filipina.* **Jun 11** *King Kamehameha Celebrations.* **Jul-Aug** *Bon Odori* (Buddhist festival). **Sep** *Aloha Week.* **Oct 30** *Ironman World Triathlon Championships*, Kailuah Kona. **Dec 12th** *21st Honolulu Marathon.* **Mar '94** *St Patrick's Day Parade.*
SOCIAL CONVENTIONS: The ancient Hawaiians were characterised as warm, friendly, hospitable people and this tradition is kept alive by the spirit of *aloha*. A garland of flowers or shells (a *lei*) symbolises this spirit and is often presented to a guest at a *luau* (feast). Several kinds of food have symbolic meanings. *Aloha* exists side by side with a very modern Westernised Hawaii and there are many commercialised versions of the customs associated with it. Topless sunbathing is not encouraged. **Tipping:** Usually 15% for restaurant and other bills. Taxi drivers expect a tip.

BUSINESS PROFILE

ECONOMY: The economy depends on federal expenditure (much of which is military), agriculture and tourism.
BUSINESS: Honolulu, especially, is a city on a par with any other modern city, and business behaviour and practice follow mainland US custom. **Office hours:** 0800-1700 Monday to Friday.
COMMERCIAL INFORMATION: The following organisation can offer advice: Chamber of Commerce of Hawaii, 735 Bishop Street, Honolulu, HI 96813. Tel: 522 8800. Fax: 522 8836.
CONFERENCES/CONVENTIONS: Oahu (where Honolulu is located) means 'the gathering place' and on this island in centuries past the kings of the Hawaiian islands used to meet. Today the East-West Centre, adjacent to the University of Hawaii, is a place of cultural interchange between the peoples of Asia, the Pacific and the USA. Many hotels have meeting rooms, and advice is available on meetings and back-up facilities. The Hawaii Visitors Bureau has 2600 members offering a variety of services. For further information contact the Department of Conventions and Meetings, c/o Hawaii Visitors Bureau. Tel: 923 1811. Fax: 922 8991.

HISTORY & GOVERNMENT

HISTORY: Captain Cook was the first European to visit the Hawaiian islands (in 1778). Having dubbed Kaua, Niihau and Oahu the 'Sandwich Islands', Cook was subsequently killed by the native inhabitants. After an agreement between the British and French not to colonise the islands, Hawaii was ruled by an indigenous monarchy until this was displaced by a US-backed republican government in 1893. Five years later Hawaii was formally annexed as part of the USA. Between the World Wars, Hawaii became the key to the USA's strategic presence in the Pacific, a fact recognised by the Japanese, whose attack on the US naval base at Pearl Harbour brought the USA into the Second World War. In 1959, Hawaii was formally admitted as the 50th state of the USA. Since then, native Hawaiians have assumed increasingly important posts within the Hawaiian state government and public service.
GOVERNMENT: Hawaii is a constituent state of the USA, and as such has a state government with the same powers as its counterparts on the mainland. For more information, see the main *History & Government* section for the USA above.

CLIMATE

Warm throughout the year with heavy rainfall from December to March.
Required clothing: Lightweights are advised throughout the year, with warmer clothes for winter. Beachwear is popular and protection from the midday sun, such as sunglasses and sun hats, is advisable.

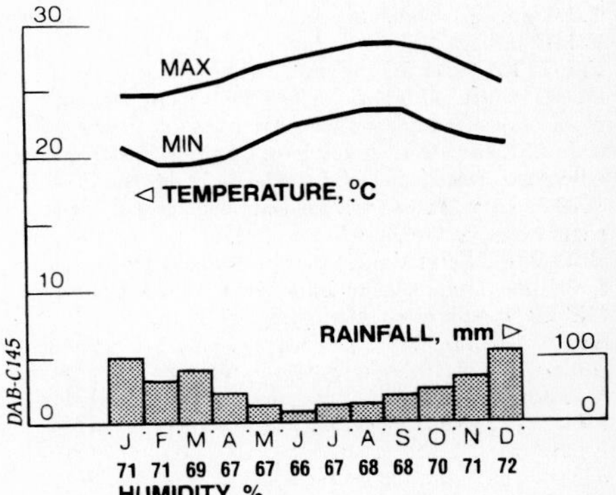

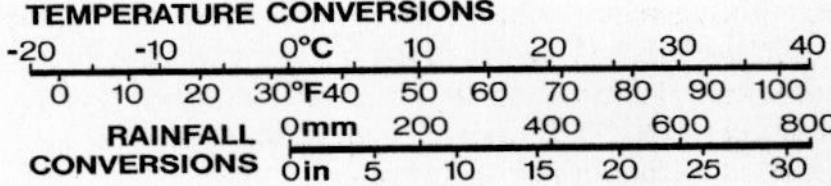

GUAM

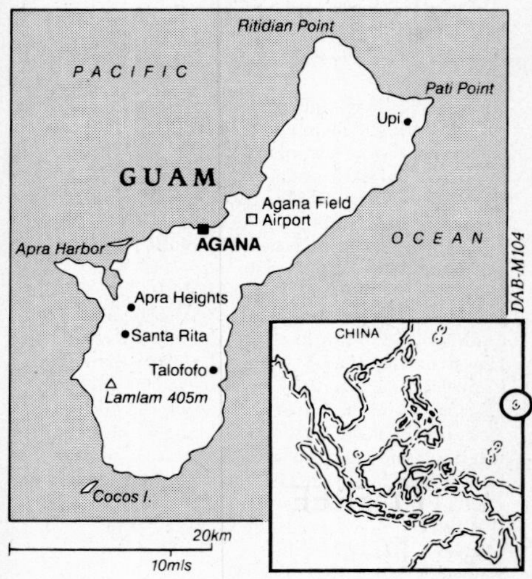

Location: Western Pacific, Micronesia.

Guam Visitors Bureau
PO Box 3520
Suite 201-205, Boon's Building
1270 North Marine Drive
Agaña, GU
96910
Tel: 646 5278/9. Fax: 646 8861. Telex: 6432.
Embassy of the United States of America
For address in UK, see top of USA entry above.
Guam Visitors Bureau
c/o The Keating Group Inc
14th Floor
425 Madison Avenue
New York, NY
10017
Tel: (212) 888 4110. Fax: (212) 888 5816.
Also deals with enquiries from Canada.
Embassy of the United States of America
For address in Canada, see top of USA entry above.

AREA: 549 sq km (212 sq miles).
POPULATION: 133,152 (1990 estimate).
POPULATION DENSITY: 242.5 per sq km.
CAPITAL: Agaña. **Population:** 5000 (1983). Tamuning is the commercial centre.
GEOGRAPHY: Guam is the largest and most southerly island of the Marianas Archipelago. It is a predominantly hilly island and its northern end is a plateau of rolling hills and cliffs rising 152m (500ft) above sea level. The cliffs are tunnelled with caves. The island narrows in the middle, with the southern half widening into a land of mountains and valleys cut by streams and waterfalls. The most sheltered beaches are on the western coast.
LANGUAGE: English and Chamorro. Japanese and Tagalog are also widely spoken.
TIME: GMT + 10.
ELECTRICITY: 120 volts AC, 60Hz.
COMMUNICATIONS: Telephone: Overseas telecommunications facilities are available in Agaña. Country code: 671. **Fax:** Many hotels have facilities. **Post:** Post offices are open 0830-1700 Monday to Friday and 0900-1200 Saturday. **Press:** The English-language daily newspaper is *The Pacific Daily News*.
BBC World Service and Voice of America frequencies: From time to time these change. See the section *How to Use this Book* for more information.

BBC:				
MHz	17.10	15.36	9.740	7.150
Voice of America:				
MHz	18.82	15.18	9.525	1.735

PASSPORT/VISA

Passports are required by all except those entering directly from the USA. Those arriving from any other country must comply with the passport and visa requirements for the USA (see *USA* above). All enquiries should be addressed to the relevant US Embassy.

MONEY

Currency: US Dollar (US$) = 100 cents. See the *USA* section above for information on currency exchange, exchange rates, etc.
Credit cards: Most major credit and charge cards are widely accepted on Guam.
Banking hours: 1000-1500 Monday to Thursday and 1000-1800 Fridays.

DUTY FREE

The list of goods exempted from payment of customs duty is the same as for the USA, as is the list of prohibited and restricted goods. See the *Duty Free* section in the general *USA* entry above.

PUBLIC HOLIDAYS

Public holidays are the same as those observed in mainland US states (see *USA* above), plus the following:
Mar 1 '93 Guam Discovery Day. **May 24** Memorial Day. **Jul 21** Independence Day. **Dec 8** Immaculate Conception. **Mar 1 '94** Guam Discovery Day.

HEALTH

Regulations and requirements may be subject to change at short notice, and you are advised to contact your doctor well in advance of your intended date of departure. Any numbers in the chart refer to the footnotes below.

	Special Precautions?	Certificate Required?
Yellow Fever	No	1
Cholera	No	No
Typhoid & Polio	Yes	-
Malaria	No	-
Food & Drink	2	-

[1]: Yellow fever certificates are required from all visitors arriving from infected areas.
[2]: Mains water is normally chlorinated, and whilst relatively safe may cause mild abdominal upsets. Bottled water is available and is advised for the first few weeks of the stay. Milk is pasteurised and dairy products are safe for consumption. Local meat, poultry, seafood, fruit and vegetables are generally considered safe to eat.
Health care: Health insurance is strongly advised. There are four hospitals.

TRAVEL

AIR: Several air taxi companies operate scheduled air commuter services daily between Saipan, Rota and Guam.
Approximate flight time: From *Guam* to London is 14 hours 30 minutes.
International airport: *Agaña Field Naval Station* is 5km (3 miles) from the city. Taxis are available.
SEA: Guam is a port of call for the following shipping lines: *Dominion Far East, Flagship Cruises, Kyowa, Daiwa, Micronesia Transport, American President, Sea-Land Services, Austfreight* and *Sitmar*.
ROAD: Bus: A reasonable service is available on a limited number of routes. **Taxi:** Fares are metered. **Car hire:** Available through most major companies. Charges are based on time and mileage plus insurance. **Documentation:** An International Driving Permit is required.

ACCOMMODATION

HOTELS: Over the past decade tourism has been growing rapidly and, to cater for this, numerous hotels have been built offering a good range of facilities to suit most tastes and pockets. Many hotels cater almost exclusively for Japanese tourists. For more details contact the US Embassy.
CAMPING: Camping is permitted on beaches and in some parks; some places are better avoided and the camper is advised to take advice. Information can be obtained from the Guam Visitors Bureau.

RESORTS & EXCURSIONS

Guam is the largest island in Micronesia and due to the large US Naval presence, the most cosmopolitan and energetic. Spain ruled the islands for nearly 250 years and **Agaña**, the capital, has many historic buildings dating from this era. Also of interest are buildings from the Spanish colonial period and the relics of the Chamorro period (a culture which remains alive today, albeit much modified, in about 55,000 persons). Many attractions are geared towards American GIs at the local US military base.
Tumon Bay, just up the coast from Agaña, is the main tourist centre. There are fine coral reefs around the coast. The interior is mountainous, particularly in the south. There are several spectacular cliffs on the north coast. There are three botanical gardens in Guam: the *Inarajan Shore Botanical Garden* by the sea in the southern part of the island; the *Nano Fall Botanical Gardens* in **Agat,** where swimming can be enjoyed in the Nano River under rushing cascades; and the *Pineapple Plantation* in **Yigo.** There are also many parks in Guam, some dedicated to the war years, such as the *South Pacific Memorial Park* in Yigo, commemorating those killed in the 1941-1945 War, and the *War in the Pacific National Historical Park,* the location of five World War II battle sites with a museum of war photos and relics. Guam has another small museum with sections dedicated to Chamorro culture, natural history and the Japanese soldier who hid in the interior until 1972, unaware that World War II was over. As most tourists to Guam are Japanese, many sites commemorate the war years. Other parks include *Latte Park,* located at the bottom of Kasamata Hill; and *Merico Pier Park,* with recreational facilities for watersports and the location of the *Merico Water Festival* held every August. It is also the gateway to **Cocos Island,** a beautiful 100-acre resort surrounded by a clear lagoon and accessible by speed boat or glass-bottomed boat. Beach parks include *Talofofo Bay Beach Park,* located at the mouth of the Talofofo River and a surfers' paradise; and *Ipao Beach Park,* once the location of an ancient Chamorro settlement, later a penal and leper colony, and now one of Guam's most popular recreational areas.

SOCIAL PROFILE

FOOD & DRINK: Guamanian cooking is very similar to Spanish cuisine. The wide selection of restaurants feature American, European, Chinese, Filipino, Indonesian, Japanese, Korean and Mexican food.
NIGHTLIFE: A choice of nightclubs feature music and dancing. Major hotels frequently stage shows with singers and musicians from the US mainland and, during the autumn, winter and spring, the *Guam Symphony & Choral Society* performs monthly. There are a number of cinemas in Agaña, most showing recent US films. Dance shows and dinner cruises are also available.
SHOPPING: The Agaña Shopping Center sells local goods but Mark's Shopping Center on the west side of Agaña and Gibson's Shopping Center at Tamuning have a wider selection of merchandise. Good buys in Guam include watches, perfume, jewellery, liquor, china, stereo equipment and cameras (Kimura Camera in the ITC Building in Agaña is excellent for both new cameras and repairs to old ones). **Shopping hours:** 1000-2100 Monday to Saturday, 1200-1800 Sundays.
SPORT: Fishing: Reef fishing with net and rod is popular, as is spearfishing for groupers and skipjacks and deep-sea fishing for marlin, tuna, wahoo, barracuda, bonito and sailfish. **Surfing:** Facilities are available at coastal resorts. **Golf:** There are several 18-hole courses. The *Windward Hills Course* has a club house and pool, as does the *Country Club of the Pacific*. Visitors are welcome at both. **Skindiving/snorkelling:** Fully equipped boats may be chartered. **Swimming:** Many hotels have swimming pools; the west coast

offers safe bathing. **Spectator sports:** Greyhound races are held three times a week. Cockfights are staged (legally) every Saturday and Sunday and on public holidays at the *Sport-O-Dome* in Tamuning, 1000-2400 (betting allowed).
SPECIAL EVENTS: Each village has its own fiesta to celebrate its patron saint. They are celebrated on the weekend closest to the *Saint's Day* and show strongly the Spanish influence on local culture. *Liberation Day* (July 21) is celebrated with fireworks, feasts and one of the year's most impressive parades (the other is on December 8 in honour of the Immaculate Conception). The *Merico Water Festival* is held every August with various watersports events. The Guam Visitors Bureau has a complete list of events.
SOCIAL CONVENTIONS: Western customs are well understood – for the visiting Westerner it is quite likely that it will not be the customs of the locals that have to be observed, but those of the visiting Japanese who make up 80% of the island's tourists. The most evident Chamorro legacy is the Chamorro language and a range of facial expressions, called 'Eyebrow', which virtually constitute a language of its own.

BUSINESS PROFILE

ECONOMY: Guam exports copra, fish and handmade goods. A petroleum refinery and a handful of light industries have been in operation since the early 1970s. The island is also an important re-export centre for distribution of goods throughout the Pacific, particularly to Micronesia. Tourism, mostly from Japan, is expanding rapidly. Government policy presently concentrates on attracting foreign investment, especially from Asian manufacturers, in order to develop an industrial base for the economy.
COMMERCIAL INFORMATION: The following organisation can offer advice: Guam Chamber of Commerce, PO Box 283, 102 Ada Plaza Center, Agaña, GU 96910. Tel: 472 8001. Fax: 472 6202.

HISTORY & GOVERNMENT

HISTORY: Guam is geographically the northernmost of the Marianas Islands, which were occupied by the Chamorro Indians from 1500BC, and who had a complex and sophisticated matrilineal society. It was claimed by the Spanish in 1565 and ruled by Madrid until the Spanish-American War of 1898. The Spanish governor was unaware of the war and, when a US frigate entered Agaña harbour with guns blazing, he apologised to the captain for not having a reciprocal salute ready. He surrendered the island the next day. US rule was interrupted by the Japanese invasion of 1941, to be re-instated after fierce fighting three years later.
GOVERNMENT: Under the terms of the 1950 Organic Act of Guam, Guam has internal self-government and its citizens are also citizens of the USA, but they are not allowed to vote in US elections. The island, which comes under the jurisdiction of the Department of the Interior, sends one delegate to the House of Representatives.

CLIMATE

Tropical, with dry and rainy seasons. The hottest months precede the rainy season, which is July to November.
Required clothing: Casual lightweight clothing, with waterproof wear needed for the rainy season.

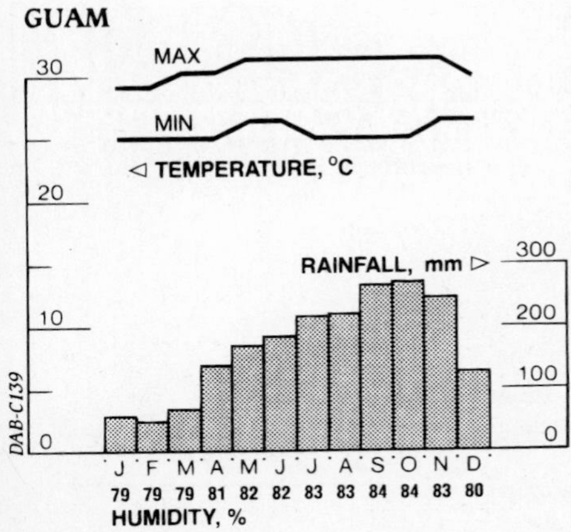

US VIRGIN ISLANDS

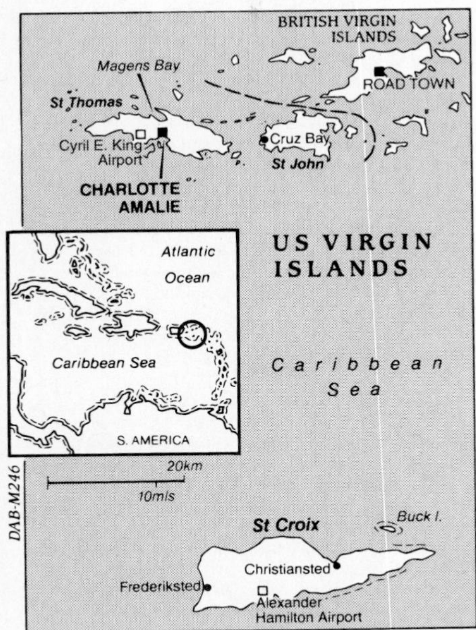

Location: Caribbean.

Virgin Islands Division of Tourism
PO Box 6400
Charlotte Amalie
St Thomas, VI
00801
Tel: 774 8784. Fax: 774 4390.

Embassy of the United States of America
For address in UK, see top of USA entry above.

US Virgin Islands Division of Tourism
2 Cinnamon Row
Plantation Wharf
York Place
London SW11 3TW
Tel: (071) 978 5262. Fax: (071) 924 3171. Telex: 27231.
Opening hours: 0930-1700 Monday to Friday.
The office is closed to the public.

US Virgin Islands Division of Tourism
1270 Avenue of the Americas
New York, NY
10020
Tel: (212) 582 4520. Fax: (212) 581 3405.

Embassy of the United States of America
For address in Canada, see top of USA entry above.

US Virgin Islands Division of Tourism
33 Niagara Street
Toronto, Ontario
M5V 1C2
Tel: (416) 362 8784. Fax: (416) 362 9841.

AREA: 354.8 sq km (137 sq miles).
POPULATION: 101,809 (1990 estimate).
POPULATION DENSITY: 287.2 per sq km.
CAPITAL: Charlotte Amalie (St Thomas). **Population:** 11,842 (1980).
GEOGRAPHY: The islands are situated 50km (30 miles) east of Puerto Rico and comprise some 50 islands covered with lush tropical vegetation and fringed by iridescent shores. St Thomas is long and thin, rising abruptly to a ridge with an excellent deep-water harbour. St John is covered partly in bay forests. St Croix consists of 218 sq km (84 sq miles) of rolling ex-plantation land.
LANGUAGE: English is the official language. Spanish and Creole are also widely spoken.
TIME: GMT - 4.
ELECTRICITY: 120 volts AC, 60Hz.
COMMUNICATIONS: Telephone: IDD is available. Country code: 1 809. There are no area codes. **Fax:** Services are available. **Telex:** Facilities are available. **Post:** Airmail to Europe takes up to a week. Post office hours: 0900-1700 Monday to Friday and 0900-1200 Saturday. **Press:** The daily newspapers are *Virgin Islands Daily News* and *St Croix Avis*.

BBC World Service and Voice of America frequencies: From time to time these change. See the section *How to Use this Book* for more information.

BBC:				
MHz	17.840	15.220	9.915	5.975
Voice of America:				
MHz	15.21	11.70	6.130	0.930

PASSPORT/VISA

Immigration requirements for the US Virgin Islands are the same as for the USA. See the general *USA* entry above.

MONEY

Currency: US Dollar (US$) = 100 cents. Import and export of amounts in excess of US$5000 must be declared. See the *USA* section above for information on currency exchange, exchange rates, credit cards, etc.
Banking hours: 0900-1430 Monday to Thursday; 0900-1400 and 1530-1700 Friday.

DUTY FREE

Duty must be paid on all gifts and alcohol brought in from abroad. Other customs regulations, duty-free exemptions and prohibitions are as for the USA. See the *Duty Free* section in *USA* above.

PUBLIC HOLIDAYS

The US Virgin Islands observes all the public holidays observed in mainland US states (see *USA* above), plus the following:
Mar 31 '93 Transfer Day. **Apr 8** Maundy Thursday. **Apr 30** Carnival. **Jun 21** Organic Act Day. **Jul 26*** Supplication Day. **Oct 18** Virgin Islands Thanksgiving Day. **Nov 1** Liberty Day. **Dec 27** Bank Holiday. **Jan 6 '94** Three Kings' Day. **Mar 31** Transfer Day.
Note [*]: Not celebrated as a full public holiday but some offices and shops may be closed.

HEALTH

Regulations and requirements may be subject to change at short notice, and you are advised to contact your doctor well in advance of your intended date of departure. Any numbers in the chart refer to the footnotes below.

	Special Precautions?	Certificate Required?
Yellow Fever	No	No
Cholera	No	No
Typhoid & Polio	Yes	-
Malaria	No	-
Food & Drink	1	-

[1]: Water precautions are advised outside the main centres. Tap water is considered safe to drink. Milk is pasteurised and dairy products are safe for consumption. Local meat, poultry, seafood, fruit and vegetables are generally considered safe to eat.
Bilharzia (schistosomiasis) may be present. Avoid swimming and paddling in fresh water. Swimming pools which are well-chlorinated and maintained are safe.
Health care: Medical costs are very high and health insurance is essential. Medical facilities are of a similar standard to those in the USA.

TRAVEL

AIR: *Continental Airlines* flies daily from New York (Newark) to St Thomas and St Croix. *American Airlines* offers daily services from New York (JFK) and Miami to St Thomas and St Croix. *Delta* flies daily from Atlanta and Orlando to St Thomas. *British Airways* has Saturday and Sunday services from London to San Juan, connecting with local commuter airlines to St Thomas and St Croix. Commuter service from San Juan is available through *Sunaire Express* and *American Eagle*. For schedules of these and other operator's routes to the US Virgin Islands, contact the airlines direct.
Approximate flight times: From St Croix to *London* is 14 hours (including stopover), to *New York* is 3 hours 45 minutes, to *Miami* is 2 hours 30 minutes, to *St Maarten* is 45 minutes and to *St Thomas* and *San Juan* is 30 minutes.
International airports: *St Thomas (STT)* (Cyril E King) is 3km (2 miles) from Charlotte Amalie, and St

Croix (STX) (Alexander Hamilton) is about 14.5km (9 miles) from Christiansted.
SEA: The main passenger ports are Charlotte Amalie (St Thomas) and Frederiksted on St Croix. A number of cruise lines operating out of Miami and San Juan include the US Virgin Islands in their itineraries around the Caribbean. Regular ferries sail between St Thomas and St John and the British Virgin Islands. Ferries leave from downtown Charlotte Amalie and Red Hook Dock on St Thomas, and Cruz Bay on St John. For more information on cruise ships to the US Virgin Islands, contact the Cruise Ship Activities Office on the West Indian Company Dock in St Thomas. Tel: 774 8784. Fax: 774 4390.
ROAD: Well-maintained roads connect all main towns, but not much else. Driving is on the left. **Bus:** Public services operate on St Thomas from Charlotte Amalie to Red Hook and Bordeaux, and St Croix has a taxi-van service between Christiansted and Frederiksted. St John has no bus services. **Taxi:** Available on all the islands. These follow standard routes between various points, and the fares for these are published. Sharing taxis is a common practise. **Car hire:** There are international car hire agencies at the airports and in the main towns on St Thomas and St Croix. St John has four rental agencies. Jeeps or mini-mokes are popular modes of travel and these too can be hired. **Documentation:** National licences are accepted; an International Driving Permit is not required.
JOURNEY TIMES: The following chart gives approximate average journey times (in hours and minutes) from Charlotte Amalie to other major cities/towns in the US Virgin Islands.

	Air	Road	Sea
Chris'sted, SC*	0.25	-	-
Cruz Bay, SJ*	-	-	0.45
Magens Bay	-	0.20	-
Coral World	-	0.40	-

Note [*]: SC = St Croix; SJ = St John.

ACCOMMODATION

HOTELS & GUEST-HOUSES: The islands have more hotels per sq mile than anywhere else in the Caribbean. Costs vary according to standard, but are generally quite high compared to other Caribbean islands. Guest-houses and 'Personality Inns' are widely available. The islands' Hotel Association has a counter at the airport to assist with reservations. The following organisations can give further information:
St John/St Thomas Hotel Association, PO Box 2300, 4D Contant, St Thomas, VI 00803. Tel: 774 6835 *or* 774 7305. Fax: 774 4993; *or*
St Croix Hotel Association, PO Box 24238, Gallows Bay, St Croix, VI 00824. Tel: 773 7117. Fax: 773 5883.
CAMPING: There are two main campsites, both on the more rural island of St John. The first is Cinnamon Bay Camp, located inside the 7028-acre St John National Park. Inexpensive bare plots and 1-room beach units are both available for a maximum stay of two weeks. The site is very popular, so reservations should be booked well in advance by contacting Cinnamon Bay Camp, Box 720, St John, VI 00830. Tel: 776 6330. The other campsite is at Maho Bay near a beautiful beach and offers 99 units. Contact Maho Bay Camp, Cruz Bay, St John, VI 00830. Tel: 776 6226. Fax: 776 6504.

RESORTS & EXCURSIONS

St Croix is the largest of the US Virgin Islands. **Christiansted** is one of the two major towns showing early Danish influence. *Fort Christiansvaern* (dating from 1774), *Government House*, the *Old Custom House and Art Gallery* and the wharf area are among its historic sites. Outside of Christiansted on West Airport Road is the *Cruz Rum Distillery* where visitors can taste the islands' rum and and watch it being made. On the way to **Frederiksted** is *Whim Greathouse*, portraying plantation life in the 1700s. Frederiksted is also of Danish origin and has a 15-acre tropical rainforest nearby.
Buck Island can easily be reached by sailing the 10km- (6-mile) channel which separates it from Christiansted. Offshore is one of the world's most impressive marine gardens, maintained by the National Park Service as an underwater protected reef.
St Thomas is the second-largest and the most interesting of this chain of islands. Like St Croix, it has many associations with the Danes and retains much Danish influence. The main town, **Charlotte Amalie,** is the group's capital. Imported goods from all over the world make it a marvellous shopping centre and stores tucked into remodelled Danish warehouses line each side of the picturesque Main Street. Cobblestone alleys with numerous boutiques lead down to the waterfront. *Blackbeard's Castle* is the earliest fortification in the US Virgin Islands. Other attractions include *Fort Christian*, built in 1672; the *Coral World Observatory;* the *Frederick Lutheran Church* of 1850; *Government House* on Government Hill, 1866; *Venus Pillar* on Magnolia Hill; *Bluebeard's Tower*, the 19th-century pirate's one-time abode; and the Synagogue on Crystal Gade, one of the oldest in the USA. On the northern coast is *Magens Bay*, claimed to be one of the world's top ten beaches.
St John is the most 'unspoilt' of the islands. It has no airport, and two-thirds of the island's deep valleys and most of its shoreline have been set aside as a National Park. *Cruz Bay* is a small town offering excellent gift shops and dive centres. *Trunk Bay* is a beautiful beach, and the diving is very good. Accommodation on the island is limited. *Caneel Bay Plantation* is a luxurious cottage colony. *Cinnamon Bay* and *Maho Bay* have campsites. Cottages can also be rented.

SOCIAL PROFILE

FOOD & DRINK: High-quality restaurants serve everything from French and Italian to Chinese cuisine. Island specialities include fresh fish and lobster. Dining out is casual and there are an increasing number of eateries on the main islands offering seafoods, burgers, steaks and native fare. **Drink:** *St John's Bay* rum is strong and distinctive.
NIGHTLIFE: Steel bands, folk singing, calypso and limbo dancing are popular. Discos are also available. St Thomas has several nightclubs; many hotels also offer entertainment. Cinemas on St Croix and St Thomas show English-language films.
SHOPPING: All luxury items up to US$200 are cheap as they are duty free. Charlotte Amalie on St Thomas is the best shopping centre. Best buys include watches, cameras, fine jewellery, china, leather goods, perfume, liquor and designer clothing. **Shopping hours:** 0900-1700/1730 Monday to Saturday.
SPORT: Golf: There are two 18-hole courses on St Croix, at Carambola Resort and at Buccaneer Hotel. A 9-hole course is located at the Reef. St Thomas has an excellent 18-hole course at Mahogany Run. **Tennis:** There are many tennis courts available on St Croix and St Thomas and a few on St John. **Horseriding** is available in Frederiksted and Christiansted on St Croix, and at Bordeaux Mountain on St John. **Watersports:** Deep-sea **fishing, scuba diving, surfing** and other watersports facilities are available on all three islands. **Parasailing** is available on St Croix and St Thomas. **Spectator sports:** Horse-racing is popular.
SPECIAL EVENTS: The following is a list of special events celebrated during 1993 in the US Virgin Islands: **Mar 3-4 '93** *Classics in the Garden*, St Thomas. **Mar 6** *USVI Calypso Competition*, St Thomas. **Mar 10-11** *USVI Fair Day*, St Thomas. **Mar 16** *2nd Annual Charter Day*, St Thomas. **Apr 9-11** *Rolex Cup Regatta – 20th Anniversary*, St Thomas. **Apr 18** *St Croix International Triathlon*, St Croix. **Apr 26** *St Thomas Carnival*, St Thomas. **May 1** *Adult Parade*, St Thomas. **May 14-16** *Jazz 'n' Paradise*, St Thomas. **May 29-31** *Memorial Day Regatta*, St Thomas/St Croix. **Jun 4-5** *Children of the Caribbean Dance*, St Croix. **Jun 13-20** *French Heritage Week*, Frenchtown. **Jun 27-Jul 5** *St John Festival and Cultural Celebration*, St John. **Jul 30-Aug 1** *6th Annual American Yacht Harbour Billfish Tournament*, St Thomas. **Aug 15** *10th Annual Texas Chili Cook-Off*. **Sep 4-9** *USVI Open Atlantic Blue Marlin Tournament*, St Thomas. **Oct 3** *Sir Francis Drake Race*, St Thomas. **Oct 14-17** *St Croix Jazz & Caribbean Music & Arts Festival*. **Nov 14** *500th Anniversary of Columbus' Arrival at Salt River*, St Croix. **Nov 20-21** *St Thomas Yacht Club Grand Prix*, St Thomas. **Nov 26-28** *Arts & Craft Fair*, St Thomas. **Dec 5** *Hibiscus Show*, St Thomas. **Dec 19** *Rising Stars Steel Band Christmas Performance*, St Thomas.

BUSINESS PROFILE

ECONOMY: When Denmark sold the islands to the United States government in 1917, they insisted that the existing privileges of the inhabitants be respected; a result of this is that the Virgin Islands are not part of the Federal Customs Area, a right which the islanders are reluctant to relinquish. This fact has helped the growth of tourism as a mainstay of the economy, but the islands also have the world's largest oil refinery and a thriving trade in rum. The current rapid population growth is causing some concern, as is the high level of immigration caused by the high quality of life and the low prices.
COMMERCIAL INFORMATION: The following organisations can offer advice: St Croix Chamber of Commerce, PO Box 4369, Kingshill, St Croix, VI 00851. Tel: 773 1435; *or*
St Thomas-St John Chamber of Commerce, PO Box 324, 6-7 Main Street, St Thomas, VI 00804. Tel: 776 0010.
CONFERENCES/CONVENTIONS: The US Virgin Islands are an idyllic place to hold a conference or convention. In St Croix, facilities are available in four major hotels for up to 200 people and in two beach resorts for up to 125. In St John, facilities are available at the Hyatt Regency for up to 350 persons and in the National Park for 50 persons. St Thomas has meeting facilities in two hotels for up to 300 persons and in seven beach resorts for up to 850 persons. For further information on conference/convention facilities in the US Virgin Islands, contact the US Virgin Islands Division of Tourism in London or New York (for addresses, see above).

HISTORY & GOVERNMENT

HISTORY: The islands were first inhabited by Carib and Arawak Indians but, in common with the rest of the Caribbean, they endured various waves of European invasion and settlement from the 1490s onwards, eventually becoming part of the Danish West Indies. The US government purchased the islands in 1917.
GOVERNMENT: Constitutionally, the islands have less autonomy than neighbouring Puerto Rico. Executive authority is vested in an elected Governor.

CLIMATE

Hot throughout the year, cooled by the eastern trade winds. Lowland areas have fairly evenly distributed rainfall, with August to October being the wettest time. Further details on the climate of the region may be found by consulting the climate charts for Dominica and Montserrat; both of these islands enjoy a similar climate to that of the US Virgin Islands.
Required clothing: Lightweight clothes throughout the year. Umbrella or light waterproof clothing is useful.

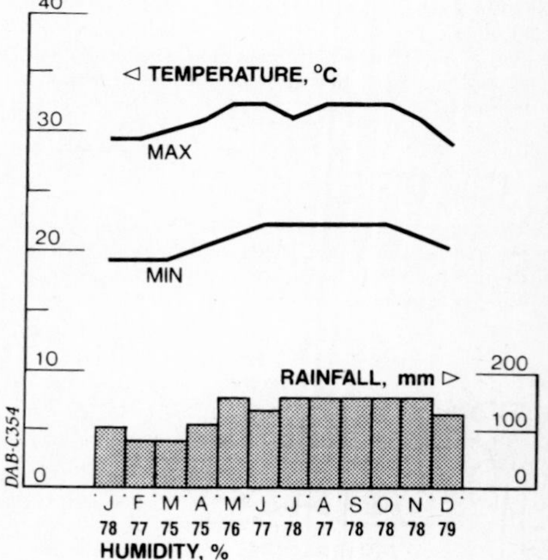

TEMPERATURE CONVERSIONS
-20 -10 0°C 10 20 30 40
0 10 20 30°F40 50 60 70 80 90 100
RAINFALL CONVERSIONS 0mm 200 400 600 800
0in 5 10 15 20 25 30

AMERICAN SAMOA

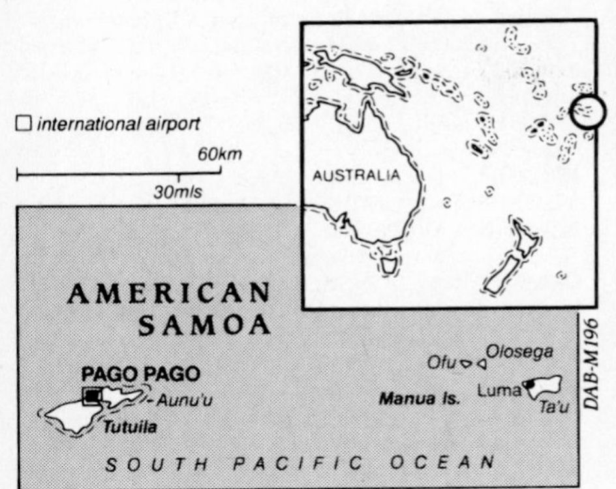

Location: South Pacific.

Office of Tourism
Convention Center
Pago Pago, AS
96799
Tel: 633 1091. Fax: 633 1094.
Embassy of the United States of America
For address in UK, see top of USA entry above.
Embassy of the United States of America
For address in Canada, see top of USA entry above.

AREA: 194.8 sq km (76.1 sq miles).
POPULATION: 46,800 (1990 estimate).
POPULATION DENSITY: 240.2 per sq km.
CAPITAL: Pago Pago. **Population:** 3075 (1980).
GEOGRAPHY: American Samoa comprises seven islands: Tutuila, the largest with an area of 53 sq miles; Ta'u, Olosega and Ofu, known as the Manu'a group; and Aunu'u, Rose and Swain's. The Manu'a group are volcanic in origin and dominated by high peaks. Rose and Swain's islands are uninhabited coral atolls located to the east and north respectively of the other two island groups.
LANGUAGE: Samoan, but a large majority of islanders speak English.
RELIGION: Half of the population are Christian Congregational; also Roman Catholics, Latter Day Saints and Protestants.
TIME: GMT - 11.
COMMUNICATIONS: Telephone: IDD is available. Country code: 684. **Fax:** Several hotels have facilities. **Telex/telegram:** Facilities are available at main towns and hotels. **Post:** The Main Post Office in the Lumana'i Building in Fagatogo is open 24 hours. There are also branches in Leone and Faguita villages, open 0800-1600 Monday to Friday and 0830-1200 Saturday. **Press:** The main English-language newspaper is the *News Bulletin*, published from Monday to Friday.
BBC World Service and Voice of America frequencies: From time to time these change. See the section *How to Use this Book* for more information.

BBC:				
MHz	17.83	15.34	9.640	11.95
Voice of America:				
MHz	18.82	15.18	9.525	1.735

PASSPORT/VISA

Regulations and requirements may be subject to change at short notice, and you are advised to contact the appropriate diplomatic or consular authority before finalising travel arrangements. Details of these may be found at the head of this country's entry. Any numbers in the chart refer to the footnotes below.

	Passport Required?	Visa Required?	Return Ticket Required?
Full British	Yes	No	Yes
BVP	Not valid	-	-
Australian	Yes	No	Yes
Canadian	Yes	No	Yes
USA	No	No	Yes
Other EC	Yes	No	Yes
Japanese	Yes	No	Yes

PASSPORTS: Passport required by all except nationals of the USA with other proof of identity. Passports have to be valid for at least 60 days beyond period of stay.
British Visitors Passport: Not accepted.

VISAS: Not required for either tourist or business visits up to 30 days, provided a confirmed reservation and documentation for onward travel is held. Travellers wishing to stay for more than 30 days should obtain special permission from the Immigration Department in Pago Pago. Approval to remain on the islands is given in 30-day periods only.
Application to: Visa Section at any US Embassy. For addresses, see top of *USA* entry.
Working days required: At least 2 weeks before departure.
Temporary residence: Apply to Immigration Department in Pago Pago.

MONEY

Currency: US Dollar (US$) = 100 cents. See the *USA* section above for information on denominations, exchange rates, etc.
Currency exchange: Exchange facilities are available at the airport and through trade banks.
Credit cards: American Express is widely accepted, whereas Access/Mastercard has more limited use. Check with your credit card company for details of merchant acceptability and other services which may be available.
Currency restrictions: Free import and export of both local and foreign currency.
Banking hours: 0900-1600 Monday to Friday.

DUTY FREE

The following items may be imported into American Samoa without incurring customs duty:
200 cigarettes or 50 cigars;
2 bottles of liquor;
A reasonable amount of perfume.

PUBLIC HOLIDAYS

American Samoa observes all the public holidays observed in mainland US states (see *USA* above),plus the following:
Apr 17 '93 Flag Day. **Jul 16** Manu'a Cession Day. **Oct 10** White Sunday. **Apr 17 '94** Flag Day.

HEALTH

Regulations and requirements may be subject to change at short notice, and you are advised to contact your doctor well in advance of your intended date of departure. Any numbers in the chart refer to the footnotes below.

	Special Precautions?	Certificate Required?
Yellow Fever	No	1
Cholera	No	No
Typhoid & Polio	Yes	-
Malaria	No	-
Food & Drink	2	-

[1]: A yellow fever vaccination certificate is required from travellers over one year of age arriving from infected areas.
[2]: Mains water is normally chlorinated, and whilst relatively safe, may cause mild abdominal upsets. Bottled water is available and is advised for the first few weeks of the stay. Drinking water outside main cities and towns may be contaminated and sterilisation is advisable. Milk is pasteurised and dairy products are safe for consumption. Local meat, poultry, seafood, fruit and vegetables are generally considered safe to eat.
Health care: There are good medical facilities at the *LBJ Tropical Medical Centre*. The *Fag'alu Institution* offers 24-hour medical and dental treatment. Health insurance is recommended.

TRAVEL

AIR: Approximate flight time: From Pago Pago to *London* is 25 hours, depending on route taken and stopover times. A typical journey would probably involve stopovers in Los Angeles and Honolulu.
International airport: *Pago Pago (PPG)* is 11.5km (7 miles) from the city. Buses and limousines are available. There are duty-free facilities at the airport. Regular scheduled trips are available to the Manu'a islands plus charters and sightseeing.
SEA: The international port is Pago Pago (Tutuila), which is served by the following passenger/cruise lines: *Chandris, Pacific Far East Line, P&O Cruises, Princess Cruises* and *Sitmar*. The port is also served by the following cargo/passenger lines: *China Navigation, Daiwa Line, Farrell Line, Polynesian Shipping* and *Union Steamship*. There is a weekly ferry service from Pago Pago to the Manu'a islands. A government-run excursion boat sails regularly around Tutuila, calling at the north coast villages of Afono, Vatia and Fagasa. Contact local authorities for details.
ROAD: There are 80km (50 miles) of asphalt road on Tutuila Island and many more miles of paved or unpaved roads throughout the islands. Driving is on the right. **Bus:** A local service operates between the airport and the centre of Pago Pago. The *aiga bus* operates an inexpensive but unscheduled service between Fagatogo and outlying villages. **Taxi:** Plentiful; the government-fixed fares are displayed in all taxis. **Car hire:** Both *Hertz* and *Avis* have agents on the islands; drivers must be at least 25 years old. There are also local companies; they impose a minimum age of 21. **Documentation:** An International Driving Permit or valid national driving licence will be accepted.

ACCOMMODATION

There is a wide range of accommodation available in American Samoa, from international standard hotels to simple guest-houses.
Fale, ma Ti (Samoan home): The Tourism Office will help to make arrangements for visitors who wish to stay in a Samoan household. This will be of particular interest to those who wish to learn more of Samoan customs.

RESORTS & EXCURSIONS

The harbour of **Pago Pago**, made famous by Somerset Maugham's short story *Rain*, is actually the crater of an extinct volcano. A spectacular cable-car ride above the harbour offers breathtaking views; Upolu in neighbouring Western Samoa is sometimes visible.
Tula Village is a traditional Samoan settlement. Situated at the far end of the eastern district of Tutuila, it overlooks a coastline of beaches and reefs that are exposed at low tide.
Amanave Village is in an area renowned for the rugged beauty of its volcanic coastline.
On the north coast of the island, a mountain-pass ride from **Fagasa**, is the *Forbidden Bay*, claimed to be one of the most beautiful in the South Pacific.
The traditional *'turtle and shark'* legend is performed **Vaitogi**. Mountain excursions are available at nearby Aoloau.
Cruises: A 2-day cruise around the islands (or one day to Western Samoa) includes an overnight stay in a local *Fale* (Samoan home) on the unspoiled island of **Savaii.**

SOCIAL PROFILE

FOOD & DRINK: Restaurants offer a variety of cuisines, including American, Chinese, Japanese, Italian and Polynesian. There are also various drive-in restaurants. The Samoan feast, *fia fia*, consists of suckling pig, chicken, fish, *palusami* (coconut cream wrapped in *taro* leaves and cooked in the *umu*, a pit oven), breadfruit, coconut, bananas, lime and mango. **Drink:** The national drink is *kava*, which is drunk in solemn and sacred ceremonies. If you become intimate with Samoans, you may be invited to a *kava* ceremony – a genuine one, as distinct from those laid on for tourists. If you attend a genuine *kava* ceremony, do not sip until you tip a little *kava* from its coconut shell cup onto the ground immediately in front of you while saying *manuia* (mah-noo-ee-ah), meaning good luck. Do not drain your cup. Leave a little and tip it out before handing the cup back to the server. Remember that drinking *kava* is a solemn, sacred ceremony and should never be confused with a casual round of drinks in Western society.
NIGHTLIFE: There are many nightspots with music and dancing. Samoan *fia fias* – feasting and traditional dancing – are organised regularly by several establishments. Samoan village *fia fias* can be arranged through local tour operators. Visitors are usually welcome at any event in the villages and churches.
SHOPPING: Special purchases include handmade *tapa* cloth, the *puletasi* (women's dress) or *lavalava* (men's costume) made by local dressmakers, shell beads and purses, woodcarvings, woven *laufala* table and floor mats, carved *kava* bowls, Samoan records and duty-free goods. **Shopping hours:** 0800-1700 Monday to Friday, 0800-1300 Saturday.
SPORT: Fishing: The surrounding waters offer spear-fishing and game-fishing for marlin, yellowfin tuna, wahoo and skipjack. Fully equipped fishing boats are available for hire through hotels or tour agents. **Watersports:** Skindiving, snorkelling and surfing facilities are excellent. Surfing is good at Carter Beach, Alofay Bay and Leone Bay. There are many safe beaches and many hotels have swimming pools. **Tennis:** Several hotels have tennis courts that are open to non-residents. **Golf:** There is a 9-hole course on Tutuila. **Hiking:** Trails lead into the interior of the islands.
SPECIAL EVENTS: During the celebrations around *Flag Day*, April 17, there are many sporting and singing competitions with events taking place for up to a week. The *Inter-island Tennis Championship* takes place around Good Friday. *Tourism Week* is at the beginning of May and hosts tourism awareness programmes and related activities. *Manu'a Cession Day* includes many singing and dancing festivities.
SOCIAL CONVENTIONS: Traditional Samoan society is still bound by very strict customs; and despite the younger generation's dissatisfaction with the old values, they are very much adhered to. The Government issues an official list of behaviour codes for both Western and

American Samoa. Revealing clothes should be avoided except when swimming or climbing coconut palms, although disapproval of shorts, if they are not *too* short, is on the wane. Samoan social behaviour conforms to strict and rather complicated rituals, to which the visitor will probably be introduced on arrival, and which should be respectfully observed. In the early evening hours, be sure to avoid making any noise that could interrupt the Samoans' prayer period. Usually three gongs are sounded. The first is the signal to return to the house, the second is for prayer and the third sounds the all-clear. In some villages, swimming and fishing are forbidden on Sunday. A visitor who happens to be invited to stay in a Samoan household should be mindful of these customs. On leaving, making a gift, a *mea alofa* (literally a 'thing of love') of shirts, belts or dress-length fabrics is most appreciated. Samoans are extremely hospitable. However, it is inappropriate to leave your first hosts before a pre-arranged date. **Tipping:** It is not customary to tip.

BUSINESS PROFILE

ECONOMY: The economy is based mainly on agriculture and fishing, with two tuna canneries providing employment for almost a quarter of the population. Recently industrial estates have been built in an effort to encourage light industrial development. Tourism is a growing industry.
BUSINESS: Shirt and smart trousers will suffice for business visits. Ties need only be worn for formal occasions. The best time to visit is May to October.
COMMERCIAL INFORMATION: The following organisation can offer advice: American Samoa Development Corporation, Pago Pago, AS 96799. Tel: 633 4241. Telex: 782511.

HISTORY & GOVERNMENT

HISTORY: For the history of American Samoa before the mid-19th century, see the entry for *Western Samoa.* US interest in Samoa emerged in the late 19th century with the search for a deep-water port in the south Pacific. When control of the islands was eventually split between the USA and Germany, the USA took Tutuila to use Pago Pago Bay as a coaling station. As Washington had no established apparatus for colonial government, the US Navy was put in charge. Despite the US presence, island life remained largely unaffected until the 1940s, when American Samoa acquired great strategic importance in the course of the Pacific war, being subject to a huge influx of US Marines. After the war, the USA started to encourage the island towards self-government. In 1956 the first indigenous Samoan Governor was appointed, followed a decade later by a new constitution that sought to guarantee the rights of the local inhabitants in matters of land ownership and civil rights. The first full election for the post of Governor was held in 1977; the post is currently held by Peter Tali Coleman.
GOVERNMENT: The Governor holds executive power, and also the right to veto laws proposed by the bicameral Legislature, called the *Fono*. The *Fono* has an 18-member Senate, elected by the tribal chiefs, and a 20-member House of Representatives, elected by popular vote for a term of two years.

CLIMATE

Very warm, tropical climate. The heaviest rainfalls are usually between December and April. The climate is best during the winter months, May to September, when there are moderate southeast trade winds.
Required clothing: Lightweight cottons and linens throughout the year with warm wrap for cooler winter evenings. Rainwear is advised for the wet season.

APIA Western Samoa (2m)

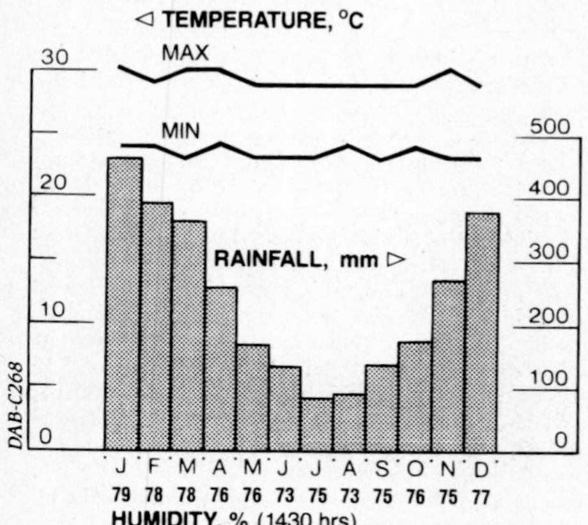

URUGUAY

Location: South America.

Dirección Nacional de Turismo
Agraciada 1409, 4°, 5° y 6°
Montevideo, Uruguay
Tel: (2) 904 148.
Embassy of the Oriental Republic of Uruguay
2nd Floor
140 Brompton Road
London SW3 1HY
Tel: (071) 584 8192 *or* 589 8735. Fax: (071) 581 9585. Telex: 264180 URUBRI G. Opening hours: 0900-1700 Monday to Friday.
Visa section: Tel: (071) 589 8735. Opening hours: 1000-1600 Monday to Friday.
British Embassy
Calle Marco Bruto 1073
11300 Montevideo, Uruguay
Tel: (2) 623 630 *or* 623 650. Fax: (2) 627 815. Telex: 22249.
Embassy of the Oriental Republic of Uruguay
1918 F Street, NW
Washington, DC
20006
Tel: (202) 331 1313. Fax: (202) 321 8142.
Consulates in: Chicago, Miami, New Orleans, New York and San Juan (Puerto Rico).
Embassy of the United States of America
Lauro Muller 1776
Montevideo, Uruguay
Tel: (2) 236 061. Fax: (2) 488 611.
Embassy of Uruguay
Suite 1905
130 Albert Street
Ottawa, Ontario
K1P 5G4
Tel: (613) 234 2727.
The Canadian Embassy in Argentina deals with enquiries relaing to Uruguay:
Canadian Embassy
Casilla de Correo 1598
Edificio Brunetta 25°
Calle Suipacha 1111
1368 Buenos Aires, Argentina
Tel: (1) 312 9081. Fax: (1) 806 1209. Telex: 21383 CANAD AR.

AREA: 176,215 sq km (68,037 sq miles).
POPULATION: 3,094,000 (1990 estimate).
POPULATION DENSITY: 17.6 per sq km.
CAPITAL: Montevideo. **Population:** 1,251,647 (1985).
GEOGRAPHY: Uruguay is one of the smallest of the South American republics. It is bounded to the north by Brazil, to the southeast by the Atlantic, and is separated from Argentina in the west and south by the River Uruguay, which widens out into the Rio de la Plata estuary. The landscape is made up of hilly meadows broken by streams and rivers. There is a string of beaches along the coast. Most of the country is grazing land for sheep and cattle. Montevideo, the most southern point of the nation, accommodates more than half of the population. About 90% of the land is suitable for agriculture, although only 12% is used in this way. Uruguay is known as the 'Oriental Republic' because it stands on the eastern bank of the Rio de la Plata.
LANGUAGE: Spanish. Some English is spoken in tourist resorts.
RELIGION: Roman Catholic.
TIME: GMT - 3 (GMT - 2 from December to February).
ELECTRICITY: 220 volts AC, 50Hz. Plugs are continental 3-pin flat or 2-pin round.
COMMUNICATIONS: Telephone: IDD is available *to* Uruguay, but callers *from* Uruguay may experience difficulty, though direct dialling is possible. Country code: 598. The local telephone service, which is operated by the government, is generally adequate but long-distance calls may take a considerable time to be put through. **Fax:** Some hotels have facilities. **Telex/telegram:** Telex services are available from Antel and at major hotels. Telegrams can be sent worldwide through *ITT Comunicaciones, Mundiales SA, Italcable* and *Western Telegraph Co Ltd.* **Post:** Post offices are open 0800-1800 (main post office in the old city, Montevideo: 0800-2200). Airmail to Europe takes three to five days. **Press:** All newspapers are in Spanish.
BBC World Service and Voice of America frequencies: From time to time these change. See the section *How to Use this Book* for more information.

BBC:

MHz	15.26	15.19	11.75	9.915

Voice of America:

MHz	15.21	11.58	9.775	5.995

PASSPORT/VISA

Regulations and requirements may be subject to change at short notice, and you are advised to contact the appropriate diplomatic or consular authority before finalising travel arrangements. Details of these may be found at the head of this country's entry. Any numbers in the chart refer to the footnotes below.

	Passport Required?	Visa Required?	Return Ticket Required?
Full British	Yes	No	Yes
BVP	Not valid	-	-
Australian	Yes	Yes	Yes
Canadian	Yes	Yes	Yes
USA	Yes	No	Yes
Other EC	Yes	1	Yes
Japanese	Yes	No	Yes

PASSPORTS: Valid passport required by all except:
(a) nationals of Uruguay who arrive from Argentina, Brazil, Chile or Paraguay who have an identity card, and foreign residents of Uruguay arriving from Argentina holding an identity card or residence permit (valid for 3 years);
(b) nationals of the independent states of the Americas (except Jamaica and Trinidad & Tobago) with appropriate identification, for stays of up to 90 days.
British Visitors Passport: Not accepted.
VISAS: Required by all except the following, for stays not exceeding 3 months:
(a) **[1]** nationals of EC countries (except nationals of France who *do* need a visa);
(b) nationals of the USA and Japan;
(c) nationals of Argentina, Austria, Belize, Bolivia, Brazil, Colombia, Costa Rica, Dominican Republic, Ecuador, Finland, Guatemala, Honduras, Hungary, Iceland, Israel, Liechtenstein, Malta, Norway, Paraguay, Peru, Poland, Seychelles, Sweden and Switzerland.
Types of visa: Transit, Business and Tourist; cost – £22. Transit visas are not required by those who continue their journey to a third country from the same airport within 8 hours after arrival. The traveller must hold tickets with confirmed seats.
Application to: Consulate (or Consular Section at Embassy). For addresses, see top of entry.
Application requirements: (a) Valid passport. (b) 1 photo. (c) Travel documentation. (d) Letter from sponsor in country of origin if requesting Business visa. (e) Postal applications should be accompanied by a stamped self-addressed envelope.
Working days required: Normally 4.
Temporary residence: Enquire at Embassy.

MONEY

Currency: New Uruguayan Peso (UN$) = 100 centésimos. Notes are in the denominations of UN$10,000, 5000, 1000, 500, 200, 100 and 50. Coins are in denominations of UN$10, 5, and 1, and 50, 20 and 10 centésimos.

Currency exchange: Visitors are advised to buy local currency at banks and exchange shops, as hotels tend to give unfavourable rates. Inflation in Uruguay, though less severe than in other Latin American countries, leads to frequent changes in the exchange rate.
Credit cards: Visa, Mastercard, Diners Club and American Express are the most commonly used. Check with your credit card company for details of merchant acceptability and other services which may be available.
Travellers cheques: Sterling travellers cheques can only be changed at *The Bank of London & South America;* visitors are therefore advised to carry US Dollar travellers cheques.
Exchange rate indicators: The following figures are included as a guide to the movements of the New Uruguayan Peso against Sterling and the US Dollar:

Date:	Oct '89	Oct '90	Oct '91	Oct '92
£1.00=	1088.72	2634.29	3868.67	5263.23
$1.00=	689.50	1348.50	2229.14	3316.47

Currency restrictions: There are no restrictions on the import or export of either local or foreign currency. It is advisable not to change more than needed in order to avoid delays and losses when changing local currency back into foreign currency.
Banking hours: 1330-1730 Monday to Friday (summer); 1300-1700 Monday to Friday (winter).

DUTY FREE

The following items may be imported into Venezuela without incurring customs duty:
(a) Residents of Uruguay arriving from Argentina, Bolivia, Brazil, Chile or Paraguay (maximum *four* times a year) [1]:
200 cigarettes or 25 cigars;
1 litre of alcohol;
2kg of foodstuffs.
(b) All other nationals [2]:
400 cigarettes or 50 cigars;
2 litres of alcohol;
5kg of foodstuffs.
[1]: Total value of exempted imports not to exceed US$30.
[2]: Total value of exempted imports not to exceed US$150.

PUBLIC HOLIDAYS

Public holidays observed in Uruguay are as follows:
Apr 19 '93 Landing of the 33 Patriots. **May 1** Labour Day. **May 18** Anniversary of Battle of Las Piedras. **Jun 19** Birth of General Artigas. **Jul 18** Constitution Day. **Aug 25** National Independence Day. **Oct 12** Discovery of America. **Nov 2** All Souls' Day. **Dec 8** Blessing of the Waters. **Dec 25** Christmas Day. **Jan 1 '94** New Year's Day. **Jan 6** Epiphany.
Note: During Carnival Week which covers Ash Wednesday week (Feb 16, 1994), many businesses are closed.

HEALTH

Regulations and requirements may be subject to change at short notice, and you are advised to contact your doctor well in advance of your intended date of departure. Any numbers in the chart refer to the footnotes below.

	Special Precautions?	Certificate Required?
Yellow Fever	No	No
Cholera	No	No
Typhoid & Polio	1	-
Malaria	No	-
Food & Drink	2	-

[1]: There is a risk of typhoid fever but no cases of polio have been reported in Uruguay in recent years.
[2]: Tap water is considered safe to drink. Drinking water outside main cities and towns may be contaminated and sterilisation is advisable. Milk is pasteurised and dairy products are safe for consumption. Local meat, poultry, seafood, fruit and vegetables are generally considered safe to eat.
Rabies is present. For those at high risk, vaccination before arrival should be considered. If you are bitten abroad seek medical advice without delay. For more information consult the *Health* section at the back of the book.
Health care: Uruguay has an excellent medical service. Private health insurance is recommended.

TRAVEL - International

AIR: Uruguay's national airline is *Primeras Líneas Uruguayas de Navegación Aérea (PLUNA) (PU).*
Approximate flight times: From *London* to Montevideo is 15 hours 15 minutes (including 1 hour 30 minutes stopover in Madrid) and from *New York* is 14 hours.
International airport: *Montevideo (MVD)* (Carrasco) is 21km (13 miles) from the city (travel time – 35 minutes). A coach leaves every two hours 0700-2100. It returns from the *IBAT* terminus, Yaguarón 1318, 0730-1930. A bus leaves every 15 minutes 0500-2400, and returns from the bus terminal, Arenal Grande, 0500-2300. Taxis are available. There is a duty-free shop.
Departure tax: US$4.50 is levied on international departures (US$2.50 to Buenos Aires). Children under two years of age are exempt.
SEA: Montevideo, the main international port, is served by cargo lines from the USA and Europe. There is a night ferry service from Buenos Aires to Montevideo (the crossing takes ten hours). There are also services from Colonia (160km/100 miles west of Montevideo) to Buenos Aires by steamer and a thrice-daily hydrofoil service.
RAIL: There are services from Brazil and Argentina.
ROAD: Coaches and *ONDA* and *TTL* buses travel regularly between Brazil and Uruguay – these are modern coaches with bar, TV, WC and radio. The travel time between Montevideo and Porto Alegre (Brazil) is 14 hours; to Rio de Janeiro (Brazil) is 59 hours. Buses run by *COIT* depart weekly for Asunción and Iguazú Falls in Paraguay, while another service, also weekly, links Montevideo and Santiago in Brazil.

TRAVEL - Internal

AIR: *PLUNA (PU)* runs daily flights to all major points within the country but flying is very costly in comparison with other means of internal travel. *TAMU*, a branch of the Uruguayan Air Force, also operates services to the main towns of Paysandú, Salto, Rivera, Artigas and Melo.
Note: There is a 3.5% surcharge on all air tickets issued and paid for in Uruguay.
SEA/RIVER: There are no scheduled boat services along the principal rivers but the Uruguayan River is navigable from Colonia to Salto, and the Rio Negro (flowing across the country from northeast to northwest) is navigable as far as the port of Mercedes.
RAIL: Four main trunk lines and branches connect Montevideo with all major cities. There are no air-conditioned coaches but a buffet service is available on some trains.
ROAD: There are 45,000km (28,000 miles) of roads in Uruguay, 80% of which are paved or otherwise improved for all-weather use. **Bus:** Three main bus lines *(CITA, COT* and *ONDA)* provide services throughout the country, connecting all towns and the Brazilian border points. **Car hire:** Available in Montevideo.
Documentation: An International Driving Permit is not legally required but recommended. A temporary licence to drive in Uruguay, valid for 90 days, must be obtained from the Town Hall *(Municipo).*
URBAN: Extensive bus and some trolleybus services operate in Montevideo and the suburbs. There are flat fares for the central area and suburban services. Metered taxis are available in all cities and from the airport. Drivers carry a list of fares. A surcharge is made for each item of baggage and for service 2400-0600. Within city limits taxis may be hired by the hour at an agreed rate.

ACCOMMODATION

HOTELS: There are numerous first-class hotels in Montevideo and along Uruguay's coastal resorts, where rates are usually a little more expensive. It is essential to book during the summer and during carnival week in Montevideo. There are several lower-priced hotels in the city for more basic accommodation. **Grading:** Hotels in Uruguay can be graded into three categories according to price and standard. Prices tend to be higher during the tourist season. There is an 18% value added tax in Montevideo. At the beaches, many hotels offer only American-plan terms (full board). After April 1 prices are greatly reduced.
CAMPING: Allowed at numerous designated sites throughout the country; elsewhere it is necessary to get police permission.
YOUTH HOSTELS: There are several youth hostels throughout Uruguay offering cheap accommodation.

RESORTS & EXCURSIONS

Uruguay draws more visitors than any other South American state. The country enjoys an ideal climate, 500km (300 miles) of fine sandy beaches on the Atlantic and the Rio de la Plata, as well as woods, mountains, hot springs, hotels, casinos, art festivals and numerous other opportunities for sport and entertainment.
Montevideo: The capital contains more than half of Uruguay's population and is the country's natural trading centre. There are nine major bathing beaches, the best of which are *Playas, Ramírez, Malvin, Pocitos, Carrasco* and *Miramar.* The suburbs have restaurants, nightclubs and hotels.
Punta del Este: The Atlantic coast resorts are popular from December to April, and have fine beaches. Most fashionable of these is Punta del Este, 145km (90 miles) from Montevideo. It has two main beaches and offers water-skiing, fishing, surfing and yachting; there is also a golf course. Villas and chalets can be rented in the wooded area on the edge of town. Two nearby islands, *Gorriti* and *Lobos*, are worth a visit.
Other attractions: To the west of Montevideo is *Colonia Suiza* ('The Swiss colony'), reached by hydrofoil from the capital. It has an excellent old quarter. Other beach resorts along the Uruguayan coast include *Atlántida, Piriápolis* and the fishing port of *Paloma. Carmelo* on the River Uruguay and *Mercedes* on the Rio Negro (a tributary) are amongst the many picturesque river ports; further up the Uruguay is *Salto*, one of the country's largest cities. *Fray Bentos*, near Mercedes, gave its name to the famous processed meat company. The journey north through *Florida* and *Duranzo* to *Tacuarembó* on the Brazilian border takes one through the heart of the country's agricultural lands. The beautiful mountains surrounding the town of *Minas* are well worth a visit, as is *Colonia del Sacramento*, which has been rebuilt in its original 18th-century style.

SOCIAL PROFILE

FOOD & DRINK: The majority of restaurants are *parrilladas* (grillrooms) and beef is a part of most meals. Dishes include *asado* (barbecued beef), *asado de tira* (ribs), *pulpa* (boneless beef), *lomo* (fillet steak) and *bife de chorrizo* (rump steak). *Costillas* (chops) and *milanesa* (a veal cutlet) are also popular, usually eaten with mixed salad or chips. *Chivito* is a sandwich filled with slices of meat, lettuce and egg. Other local dishes are *puchero* (beef with vegetables, bacon, beans and sausages), pizza, pies, barbecued pork, grilled chicken in wine, *cazuela* (stew), usually served with *mondongo* (tripe), seafood, *morcilla dulce* (sweet black sausage made from blood, orange peel and walnuts) and *morcilla salada* (salty sausage). Desserts include *chaja* (ball-shaped sponge cake filled with cream and jam), *mossini* (cream sponge), lemon pie and *yemas* (crystallized egg yolk). Table service is usual in restaurants. Cafés or bars have either table and/or counter service.
Drink: Local wines are mixed *(medio-medio,* red and white) in Montevideo and range from acceptable to undrinkable.

URUGUAY	HEALTH REGULATIONS	VISA REGULATIONS Code-Link
GALILEO/WORLDSPAN	 TI-DFT/MVD/HE	 TI-DFT/MVD/VI
SABRE	 TIDFT/MVD/HE	TIDFT/MVD/VI

To access this information on your CRS, swipe the barcode with a light pen or type in the text under the barcode. For more information, see the introduction *How to Use This Book.*

Beers are very good. Imported beverages are widely available. Local spirits are *caña*, *grappa* and locally distilled whisky and gin. There are no set licensing hours.
NIGHTLIFE: Theatre, ballet and symphonic concerts are staged in Montevideo from March to January. Nightlife, however, is minimal. There are discotheques in the Carrasco area, some with good floor shows. There are several dinner-dance places in Montevideo. Large Montevideo hotels have good bars. When there is music for dancing the prices of drinks increase quite considerably. There are also several casinos.
SHOPPING: Special purchases include suede jackets, amethyst jewellery, antiques and paintings. **Shopping hours:** 0900-1200 and 1400-1900 Monday to Friday and 0900-1230 Saturday.
SPORT: Golf: There is a municipal course in Montevideo, plus clubs at the *Victoria Plaza Hotel* and *Punta del Este Country Club*. **Fishing:** There are three fishing areas: along the Rio de la Plata from Colonia to *Piriápolis* for surf-casting; from *Piriápolis* to Punta del Este (considered one of the best fishing areas in the world); and along the Atlantic Coast towards the Brazilian border. Boats and tackle can be rented in fishing clubs in Salto, Paysandú, Fray Bentos, Punta del Este, Montevideo and Mercedes. **Swimming:** There are plenty of places to swim when the weather permits. The 'metropolitan' beaches (from Ramírez and including Pocitos) tend to be dirty and unsuitable for bathing. Those along the Atlantic coast are, however, clean and suitable for swimming. Many of the resort areas in the interior have swimming pools. The mineral baths at Minas are worth a visit. **Windsurfing** and **water-skiing** are popular along the coast. **Boating:** A favourite Uruguayan pastime. Santiago Vazquez on the St Lucia River is one of several popular centres. Arrangements can be made for rental of motor or sailing boats in Montevideo and elsewhere. **Horseracing:** There are two main tracks: *Hipodromo de Maronas* (Saturday and Sunday afternoon); and *Las Piedras* (Thursday, Saturday and Sunday). **Football:** The most popular spectator sport; matches are played regularly throughout the country.
SPECIAL EVENTS: The principal festival is the national *Carnival Week*. Although this 'fiesta' is officially only for the Monday and Tuesday preceding Ash Wednesday (ie Feburary 14 and 15, 1994), Uruguay closes down most of its shops and businesses for the entire week. Houses and streets are appropriately decorated and humorous shows are staged at open-air theatres.
SOCIAL CONVENTIONS: Shaking hands is the normal form of greeting. Uruguayans are very hospitable and like to entertain both at home and in restaurants. Normal courtesies should be observed. Smoking is not allowed in cinemas or theatres or on public transport. **Tipping:** 10% when no service charge is added. Taxi drivers expect a tip.

BUSINESS PROFILE

ECONOMY: Uruguay is one of the more prosperous Latin American countries. The economy is predominantly agricultural, with beef and wool being the most important products (cows and sheep outnumber people by about 9:1). There are also substantial dairy exports to other Latin American countries. Crop farming is widespread, producing mostly cereals, rice, fruit and vegetables, but production levels fluctuate. Uruguay relies on imported oil – exploration has proved repeatedly unsuccessful – although two recently-constructed hydro-electric power plants are sufficient to meet almost all the country's energy requirements. Development of light industry, the most productive sector of the economy, is a prime government objective: existing manufacturing capacity is concentrated in food processing, textiles, metal industries and rubber. There is no heavy industry and there are no plans to establish any. Of all the Latin American republics, Uruguay has the smallest area, one of the smallest rates of population growth, the highest literacy rate and one of the most even distributions of wealth. An efficient system of social welfare is in operation, although the Government has come under recent pressure to reduce its scope to relieve budgetary pressure. Like the rest of South America, Uruguay suffers from the continent's perennial bane, overseas debt: however, at US$6 billion, this problem is less severe (both per capita and in absolute terms) than in most other states. Uruguay is a member of the Asociación Latinoamericana de Integración (ALADI), the South American trade organisation, but also a founder member of a more influential economic body known as the Southern Common Market, Mercosur. Argentina, Brazil and Paraguay are the three other founding members of Mercosur, which was set up in March 1991. Mercosur aims to remove all tariff barriers by 1995, but a large number of exceptions have been allowed – in Uruguay's case no less than 960 separate items. Nonetheless, Uruguay should be the major beneficiary from Mercosur which will allow the country to develop its potential which has, despite a well-educated population and modern infrastructure, been hampered by the small size of its internal market. Economic fashion has also persuaded the Lacalle government to privatise some state-owned industries starting with the PTT, airline and electricity utility. The country's main trading partners are Brazil, Argentina, the USA and Germany. Lacalle sees Uruguay's economic future as the region's principal provider of financial and other services.
BUSINESS: Businessmen should wear suits and ties. As far as communication is concerned, some knowledge of Spanish will prove invaluable, although English may be spoken by many in business and tourist circles. Appointments are necessary and punctuality is expected. Visiting cards are essential and it would be an advantage to have the reverse printed in Spanish. Avoid visits during 'Carnival & Tourist Week'. **Office hours:** 0830-1200 and 1430-1830/1900 Monday to Friday. **Government office hours:** *Mid-March to mid-November:* 1200-1900 Monday to Friday; *mid-November to mid-March:* 0730-1330 Monday to Friday.
COMMERCIAL INFORMATION: The following organisation can offer advice: Cámera Nacional de Comercio, Edificio de la Bolsa de Comercio, Misiones 1400, Casilla 1000, 11000 Montevideo. Tel: (2) 961 277. Telex: 26996.

HISTORY & GOVERNMENT

HISTORY: Since independence from Spain in 1825, Uruguay has suffered frequent outbreaks of political unrest, a consequence of a body politic deeply divided between the liberally inclined Colorado Party, under the quasi-dynastic leadership of the Batlle family (commonly known as 'Reds' but by no means communist) and the right-wing Blancos ('Whites'). Under the progressive regime of José Batlle y Ordóñez between 1911 and 1915, Uruguay established Latin America's first welfare state, and the country continues to lead in this respect. Uruguay experienced relative peace until the 1960s, when economic difficulties led to an increase in labour unrest and the emergence of the Tupamaros guerrilla movement. In 1973 a military government was established and remained in power until 1985, by which time the Tupamaros had been defeated and all left-wing political activity outlawed. Dr Julio Sanguinetti of the Colorados held the Presidency from 1985 until the Presidential and Congressional elections in November 1989, when the Blancos achieved a majority in the national assembly and their candidate, Luis Alberto Lacalle Herrera, was victorious in the presidential race over the Colorado candidate, Jorge Batlle Ibáñez. The new government has adopted the South American trend in economic policy by selling off state-owned businesses, reducing government spending and attracting foreign investment and joined the Mercosur trading bloc with its neighbours (see *Economy)*. Despite the generally unfavourable climate, the Uruguayan left has undergone something of a resurgence in recent years and seems set to become the major political opposition in the country in the near future. Their leading light is the massively popular mayor of Montevideo, Tabare Vazquez, whose combination of radical politics and pragmatic problem-solving has greatly improved the quality of life in the capital. Tabare Vazquez is associated with the leftist coalition Frente Amplio (Broad Front) and may stand for the presidency in 1994.
GOVERNMENT: Legislative power is held by a bicameral Congress, which comprises a 30-member Senate and a 99-member Chamber of Representatives, and is elected by universal adult suffrage every five years. The same terms apply to the election of the President, who is Head of State and holds executive power, assisted by a Vice-President and an appointed Council of Ministers.

CLIMATE

Uruguay has an exceptionally fine temperate climate, with mild summers and winters. Summer is from December to March and is the most pleasant time; the climate during other seasons offers bright, sunny days and cool nights.
Required clothing: Lightweights for summer (December to March) with warmer clothes for cool evenings.

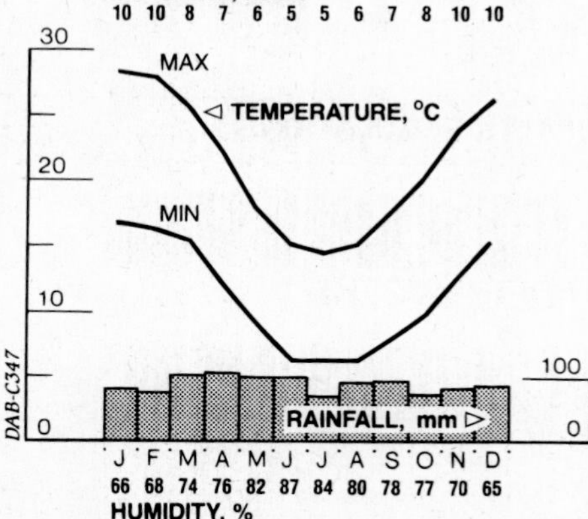

VANUATU

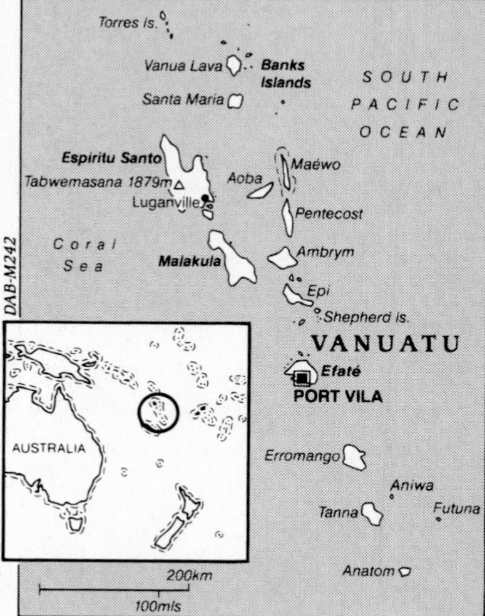

□ international airport

Location: Southwest Pacific.

National Tourism Office of Vanuatu
PO Box 209
Kumul Highway
Port Vila, Vanuatu
Tel: 22685. Fax: 23889. Telex: 1102 NATOF.
British High Commission
PO Box 567
KPMG House
rue Pasteur
Port Vila, Vanuatu
Tel: 23100. Fax: 23651. Telex: 1027 UKREP NH.
The Canadian High Commission in Canberra deals with enquiries relating to Vanuatu:
Canadian High Commission
Commonwealth Avenue
Canberra ACT 2600, Australia
Tel: (6) 273 3844. Fax: (6) 273 3285. Telex: 62017 DOMCAN AA.

AREA: 12,190 sq km (4707 sq miles).
POPULATION: 142,944 (1989).
POPULATION DENSITY: 11.7 per sq km.
CAPITAL: Port Vila (Island of Efaté). **Population:** 19,311 (1989).
GEOGRAPHY: Vanuatu, formerly called the New Hebrides, forms an incomplete double chain of islands stretching north to southeast for some 900km (560 miles). Together with the Banks and Torres islands, the chains comprise about 40 mountainous islands and 40 islets and rocks. The islands are volcanic in origin and there are five active volcanoes. Most of the islands are densely forested and mountainous with narrow bands of cultivated land along the coasts.
LANGUAGE: Bislama (Pidgin English). This most widely used day-to-day language is a Melanesian mixture of French and English. French and English are widely spoken and both English and French names exist for all towns. There are many other local dialects (totalling over 100).
RELIGION: Presbyterian, Anglican, Roman Catholic, Seventh Day Adventist, Apostolic Church and Church of Christ.
TIME: GMT + 12 (GMT + 11 in summer).
ELECTRICITY: 220-240 volts AC, 50Hz. Australian 3-pin plugs are in use.
COMMUNICATIONS: Telephone: IDD is available. Country code: 678. There are no area codes. There are public telephones at airports and post offices. **Fax:** Some hotels have facilities. **Telex/telegram:** Available at the Central Post Office in Port Vila and at main hotels. **Post:** Post offices open 0715-1130 and 1330-1600. Post offices are located on the main streets in Port Vila and

Luganville, on Santo. Airmail to Europe takes about seven days. **Press:** *Vanuatu Weekly* is published in three languages. English-language monthly: *Pacific Island Profile*. For tourist information see the publication *What's doing in Vanuatu?*
BBC World Service and Voice of America frequencies: From time to time these change. See the section *How to Use this Book* for more information.
BBC:

MHz	17.83	15.34	9.740	7.150

Voice of America:

MHz	18.82	15.18	9.525	1.735

PASSPORT/VISA

Regulations and requirements may be subject to change at short notice, and you are advised to contact the appropriate diplomatic or consular authority before finalising travel arrangements. Details of these may be found at the head of this country's entry. Any numbers in the chart refer to the footnotes below.

	Passport Required?	Visa Required?	Return Ticket Required?
Full British	Yes	No	Yes
BVP	Not valid	-	-
Australian	Yes	No	Yes
Canadian	Yes	No	Yes
USA	Yes	No	Yes
Other EC	Yes	No	Yes
Japanese	Yes	No	Yes

Restricted entry: The Government authorities of Vanuatu refuse admission to persons of dubious morality and persons who may become a public charge.
PASSPORTS: Valid passport (valid for at least 4 months beyond period of stay) required by all.
British Visitors Passport: Not accepted.
VISAS: Required by all except the following, for visits of up to 30 days, provided they are bona fide tourists in possession of confirmed onward travel documents:
(a) nationals of EC countries;
(b) nationals of all Commonwealth countries;
(c) nationals of French Overseas Departements and Territories;
(d) nationals of Austria, China, Cuba, Fiji, Finland, Japan, Federated States of Micronesia, Philippines, South Korea, Sweden, Switzerland, Taiwan, Thailand and the USA.
Types of visa: Transit and Visitors (for tourist and business purposes). Cost: V2500. Transit visas are not required for those continuing their journey to a third country by the same aircraft and not leaving the airport.
Validity: Valid for 1 month, for use within 3 months of issue. Visas may be extended once in Vanuatu.
Application to: Principal Immigration Officer, Private Mail Bag 014, Port Vila, Vanuatu. British Consulates in EC countries also issue visas for Vanuatu.
Application requirements: (a) 1 photo. (b) Valid passport. (c) Proof of sufficient funds and/or accompanying business letter.

MONEY

Currency: Vatu (V) = 100 centimes. Notes are in denominations of V1000, 500 and 100. Coins are in denominations of V100, 50, 20, 10, 5, 2 and 1. Australian Dollars are also accepted.
Currency exchange: Exchange facilities are available at the airport and trade banks.
Credit cards: Diners Club, Access/Mastercard, Visa, American Express and other major credit cards are accepted. Visitors should check with their credit card company for details of merchant acceptability and other services which may be available.
Travellers cheques: These are widely accepted.
Exchange rate indicators: The following figures are included as a guide to the movements of the Vatu against Sterling and the US Dollar:

Date:	Oct '89	Oct '90	Oct '91	Oct '92
£1.00=	187.55	209.00	192.86	181.50
$1.00=	118.77	106.99	111.12	114.37

Currency restrictions: There are no restrictions on the import or export of either local or foreign currency.
Banking hours: Generally 0830-1500 Monday to Friday, with some closing for lunch at midday.

DUTY FREE

The following items may be imported into Vanuatu without incurring customs duty:
200 cigarettes or 100 cigarillos or 50 cigars or 250g of tobacco;
1.5 litres of spirits;
2 litres of wine;
250ml of toilet water and 100ml of perfume;
Other articles up to a value of V20,000.

PUBLIC HOLIDAYS

Public holidays observed in Vanuatu are as follows:
Apr 9-12 '93 Easter. **May 3** Labour Day. **May 20** Ascension Day. **Jul 30** Independence Day. **Aug 15** Assumption. **Oct 5** Constitution Day. **Nov 29** Unity Day. **Dec 25** Christmas Day. **Jan 1 '94** New Year's Day.

HEALTH

Regulations and requirements may be subject to change at short notice, and you are advised to contact your doctor well in advance of your intended date of departure. Any numbers in the chart refer to the footnotes below.

	Special Precautions?	Certificate Required?
Yellow Fever	No	No
Cholera	No	No
Typhoid & Polio	Yes	-
Malaria	1	-
Food & Drink	2	-

[1]: Malaria risk, predominantly in the malignant *falciparum* form, exists throughout the year everywhere except Futuna Island. The strain is reported to be 'highly resistant' to chloroquine and 'resitant' to sulfadoxine-pyrimethamine.
[2]: Mains water is normally chlorinated, and whilst relatively safe may cause mild abdominal upsets. Bottled water is available and is advised for the first few weeks of the stay. Milk is pasteurised and dairy products are safe for consumption. Local meat, poultry, seafood, fruit and vegetables are generally considered safe to eat.
Health care: There are hospitals in Port Vila, Santo, Tanna, Malekula, Epi and Aoba and smaller clinics and medical dispensaries on the smaller islands. Health insurance is advised.

TRAVEL - International

AIR: The national airline is *Air Vanuatu*, which offers weekly services between Port Vila and Sydney, Brisbane and Melbourne in Australia, and Auckland (New Zealand). The airline has one Boeing 727-200. Another international airline serving the islands is *Polynesian Airways*, which offers a 'Polypass' allowing the holder to fly anywhere on the airline's network: Sydney (Australia), Auckland (New Zealand), Western Samoa, American Samoa, Cook Islands, Vanuatu, New Caledonia, Fiji and, on payment of a supplement, Tahiti. The pass is valid for 30 days.
Approximate flight time: From *London* to Vanuatu is 30 hours.
International airport: *Port Vila (VLI)* (Baver Field) is 10.3km (6 miles) from Port Vila (travel time – 15 minutes). Coaches and taxis are available. Facilities are being upgraded.
Departure tax: V1500 is levied on all departures.
SEA: The principal international ports are Port Vila and Santo. Lines operating services to Vanuatu include *P&O*, *Banks*, *Karloader* and *Messageries*.

TRAVEL - Internal

AIR: Domestic services are provided by the government-owned *Vanair*. It offers scheduled services to destinations throughout the archipelago. The airline has three Britten Norman Islanders and one Trislander.
SEA: Inter-island ferries operate from Port Vila and Santo to the northern and southern islands. *Coral* and *Hibiscus Tours* operate boats to various islands.
ROAD: Of the 1000km (600 miles) of road, 35km (22 miles) are paved. **Bus:** There are limited buses serving the town centre and the airport in Port Vila. **Taxi:** Available near *The Cultural Centre* in Port Vila. **Car hire:** Major car hire operators have offices in Port Vila. **Documentation:** A national driving licence is acceptable.

ACCOMMODATION

Accommodation is available throughout Vanuatu; it is advisable to make prior reservations. Port Vila offers a variety of accommodation, most reasonably priced. Outside Port Vila there is bungalow-style accommodation at Mele Island and Takara, and on the south coast. Accommodation is also to be found on the islands of Santo and Tanna. There is no hotel tax or service charge. Full details are available from the National Tourism Office of Vanuatu (for address, see top of entry).

RESORTS & EXCURSIONS

There are a number of tours available in Vanuatu, including trips to see volcanoes (by air), harbour cruises, sailing trips, cultural tours and visits to World War II relics. The capital, **Port Vila,** is on **Efate Island;** its *Cultural Centre* has one of the most extensive Pacific artefact collections in the world. There are also plenty of opportunities for active holidaymakers, especially those interested in watersports. On **Tanna Island** the village of the *John Frum* cargo cult can be visited; it began with the arrival of an American soldier in World War II and believers wait for him to return with great riches.
Espiritu Santo Island inspired James A Michener to write 'South Pacific'. Here, scuba divers can see where the liner *President Coolidge* and the destroyer *USS Tucker* rest on the sea-bed. On **Pentecost Island** during April and May visitors can, for a fee, see men performing the ritual leap (*Naghol*) to ensure a bountiful yam harvest; they tie vines to their ankles and leap from a 30m (100ft) tower, falling head first. Only the vine saves them from death. This ceremony was only recently opened to the public and the fee goes towards local projects. Visitors who are interested should contact the National Tourism Office of Vanuatu well in advance; the Tourism Office can also supply further information on other places of interest.

SOCIAL PROFILE

FOOD & DRINK: There are many restaurants in the main tourist areas. Seafood features strongly on hotel and restaurant menus in Port Vila and the main towns. The numerous ethnic backgrounds of the inhabitants of Vanuatu are reflected in the numerous styles of cooking. Chinese and French influences are the strongest. Food is generally excellent everywhere. French cheese, pâtés, bread, cognac and wine are available in Port Vila's two major shops. Local fruit is excellent.
NIGHTLIFE: Port Vila has several nightclubs with music and dancing. There are two cinemas and a drive-in in Port Vila. Evening cruises are also organised with wine, snacks and island music. Traditional music and dancing takes place at various island festivities to which visitors are welcome, and some hotels put on evening entertainment and dancing. Details are available from the National Tourism Office of Vanuatu.
SHOPPING: Special purchases include grass skirts from

VANUATU | **HEALTH REGULATIONS** | **VISA REGULATIONS** | Code-Link

GALILEO/WORLDSPAN

TI-DFT/VLI/HE

TI-DFT/VLI/VI

SABRE

TIDFT/VLI/HE

TIDFT/VLI/VI

To access this information on your CRS, swipe the barcode with a light pen or type in the text under the barcode. For more information, see the introduction *How to Use This Book*.

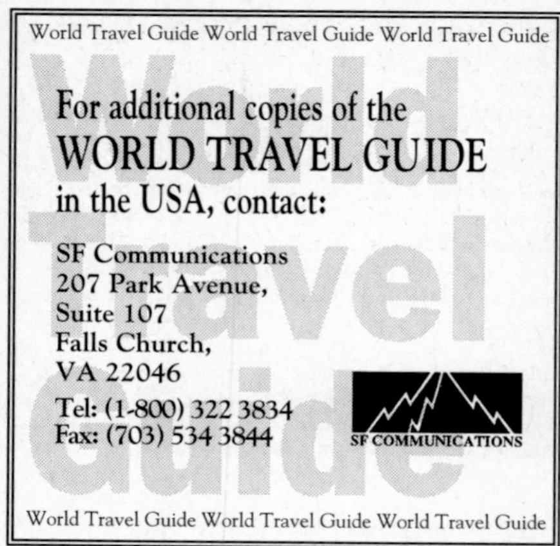

Futuna and Tanna, baskets and mats from Futuna and Pentecost, carved forms and masks from Ambrym and Malekula, woodwork from Tongoa and Santo, and pig tusks and necklaces made of shells or colourful seeds from villages near Port Vila. Duty-free shops sell a selection of luxury items. **Shopping hours:** 0730-1130 and 1330-1700 Monday to Friday. Chinese stores are open Sunday mornings from 0800 and in the evenings.

SPORT: Ornithology: Birdlife is prolific and varied, particularly in the southern islands during the breeding season (September to January). **Tennis:** There is a tennis club at Port Vila and at the hotel at Erakor Lagoon. **Golf:** There are several 9-hole golf courses; visitors can arrange games through hotels or the Vanuatu National Tourism Office. **Watersports:** There are many excellent beaches and several hotels have swimming pools. Some hotels can provide scuba equipment – the coastal waters offer excellent diving. There are several independent divers in Port Vila who provide instruction and boat charters, listed at the National Tourism Office of Vanuatu. **Game- and spearfishing** trips can be organised with local charter operators. Ask at hotels or the Vanuatu National Tourism Office for their locations.

SPECIAL EVENTS: The ritual of *Naghol* on Pentecost Island, which takes place during April and May, is described in *Resorts and Excursions* above. Visitors are also welcome at the traditional ceremonies on Tanna Island, where the foot-pounding *Toka* dance is performed.

SOCIAL CONVENTIONS: Informal wear is suitable for most occasions and men need never wear a tie. Some of the more up-market establishments appreciate men wearing long trousers in the evenings. Life goes at its own pace and, while modern influences can be seen in the main centres, in the hill villages and outlying islands age-old customs continue. **Tipping:** Contrary to Melanesian customs.

BUSINESS PROFILE

ECONOMY: Agriculture and fishing are the mainstays of the Vanuatu economy and occupy most of the working population. Fruit and vegetables are grown for domestic consumption, while copra, beef and fish are the main export commodities. Copra is particularly valuable, and responsible for around three-quarters of export earnings. There is considerable room for development, both of agriculture and associated industries such as food processing; manufacturing, which is almost entirely based on agriculture, accounts for around 5% of GDP. Tourism is growing steadily, assisted by the establishment of a national airline, *Air Vanuatu*. Vanuatu has also sought to promote offshore financial services and has created a shipping register which offers a flag of convenience. These have served to boost 'invisible' trade earnings and offset recent declines in the visible trade surplus. France, Australia and Japan are the main trading partners.

BUSINESS: A casual approach to business prevails. Shirts and smart trousers will suffice – ties are only necessary for the very smartest occasions. Business is conducted in Pidgin English or French.

COMMERCIAL INFORMATION: The following organisations can offer advice: Vanuatu Chamber of Commerce, PO Box 189, Port Vila. Tel: 23255. Telex: 1107; *or*

Ministry of Trade, Commerce, Co-operatives and Industry, PO Box 31, Port Vila. Telex: 1040.

HISTORY & GOVERNMENT

HISTORY: The island group of which Vanuatu is a part has been settled since 500BC. Up to and beyond the 13th century AD it was at the heart of the empire of Tonga. During the 19th century the islands making up Vanuatu (then called the New Hebrides) were settled by British and French missionaries, planters and traders. The UK and France eventually agreed on a condominium over the two islands. After the Second World War, a complex power struggle began between the indigenous islanders and the dual colonial interests over the future political and economic course of the islands. The constitutional position was settled in 1977 at a conference in Paris between British, French and New Hebridean representatives at which it was agreed that the islands should become fully independent within three years. At elections held in November 1979, just a few months before scheduled independence, the Vanuaaku Party (VP) under Walter Lini, an Anglican priest, took a majority in the 46-member Parliament. The VP has since held on to power, surviving further elections in November 1983 and December 1987, although the Government has been accused of abusing rights of citizenship and of political organisation. Lini has adopted radical, sometimes adventurous policies, both at home and abroad: Vanuatu is the only Pacific island to join the Non-Aligned Movement. It is also, together with Papua New Guinea and the Solomon Islands, a member of the Melanesian Spearhead Group, whose principal aims are to preserve Melanesian cultural traditions and lobby for independence for New Caledonia. Shortly before the next scheduled election in December 1991, the VP unseated Lini with a vote of no confidence, ostensibly because of his poor health but principally due to his erratic and increasingly dictatorial behaviour: half a dozen ministers had been sacked earlier in the year and all their duties assumed by Lini. Initially, Lini refused to give way to his appointed successor, education minister Donald Kalpokas, and departed with his followers to form his own party, the National United Party. The split in the VP proved a bonus to the Moderate alliance. After the election, an alliance between the Union of Moderate Parties (UMP) and Lini's new outfit overwhelmed the rump of the VP by 31 votes to 15 in Parliament. UMP leader Maxime Carlot, who stands on the right of the party, became Prime Minister.

GOVERNMENT: There is a unicameral Parliament with 46 members, elected for four years by popular vote and responsible for legislation. Executive power is the responsibility of the Council of Ministers, appointed by the Prime Minister, who is elected by the Parliament. The President, who is Head of State, is elected by an electoral college.

CLIMATE

Subtropical. Vanuatu's seasons are the reverse of those of the Northern Hemisphere. Trade winds occur from May to October. Warm, humid and wet between November and April. Rain is moderate. Cyclones are possible between December and April.

Required clothing: Lightweight for summer. Strong shoes are recommended for volcano climbing.

TANNA Vanuatu (38m)

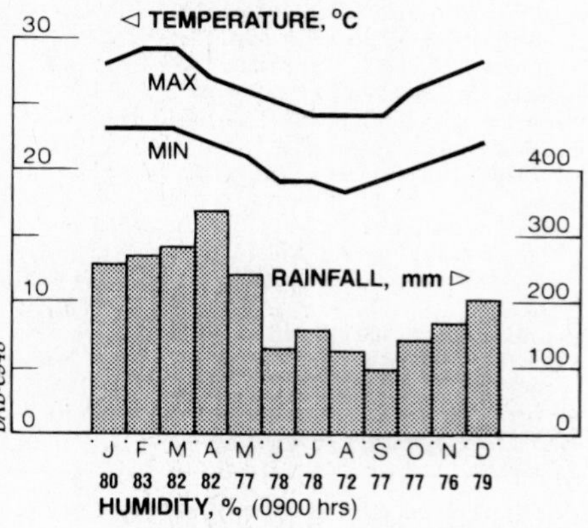

VATICAN CITY

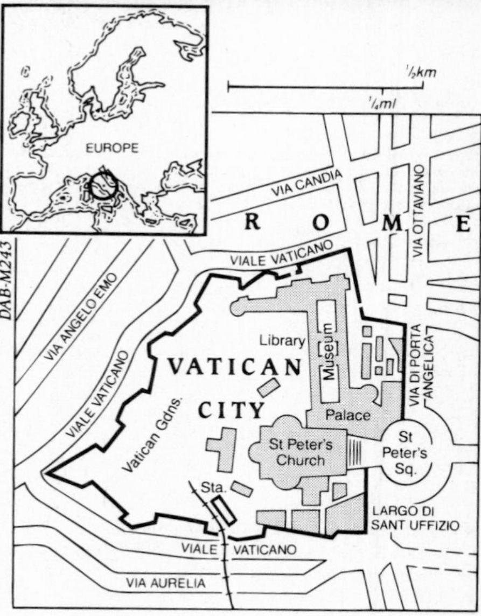

Location: Europe, Italy (Rome).

Note: Italian State Tourist Offices can provide information and advice on visiting the Vatican City. For addresses, see the top of the *Italy* section earlier in the *World Travel Guide*.

Apostolic Nunciature
54 Parkside
London SW19 5NE
Tel: (081) 946 1410. Fax: (081) 947 2494. Opening hours: 0900-1700 Monday to Friday.

British Embassy
Via Condotti 91
00187 Roma, Italy
Tel: (6) 678 9462 *or* 979 7479. Fax: (6) 684 0684. Telex: 626119 BREMB I.

Apostolic Nunciature
3339 Massachusetts Avenue, NW
Washington, DC
20008
Tel: (202) 333 7121. Fax: (202) 337 4036. Telex: 440117.

Embassy of the United States of America
Villino Pacelli
Via Aurelia 294
00165 Roma, Italy
Tel: (6) 639 0558. Fax: (6) 638 0159. Telex: 622322 AMBRMC.

Apostolic Nunciature
724 Manor Avenue
Rockliffe Park
Ottawa, Ontario
K1P 5H3
Tel: (613) 233 8900. Fax: (613) 746 4786.

Canadian Embassy
Via della Conciliazione 4/D
00193 Roma, Italy
Tel: (6) 654 7316. Fax: (6) 654 0283.

AREA: 0.44 sq km (0.17 sq mile).
POPULATION: 752 (1988 estimate).
POPULATION DENSITY: 1709 per sq km.
GEOGRAPHY: The Vatican City is situated entirely within the city of Rome, sprawling over a hill west of the River Tiber, and separated from the rest of the city by a wall. The Vatican City comprises St Peter's Church, St Peter's Square, the Vatican and the Vatican Gardens.
LANGUAGE: Italian.
TIME: GMT + 1 (GMT + 2 in summer).
ELECTRICITY: 220 volts, 50Hz.
COMMUNICATIONS: Telephone: IDD is available. The international dialling code to the Vatican switchboard is 39 6698. The Vatican has its own tele-

phone network. **Telex/telegram:** The Vatican City has its own telex and telegraph services. The telex country code is 504 VA. **Post:** Stamps issued in the Vatican City are valid throughout Rome. **Press:** The daily newspaper published in the Vatican City is *L'Osservatore Romano*, with weekly editions in English.

PASSPORT/VISA

There are no formalities required to enter the Vatican City, but entry will always be via Rome and Italian regulations must therefore be complied with. See the *Passport/Visa* section under *Italy* earlier in the *World Travel Guide*.

There is free access only to certain areas of the Vatican City; these include St Peter's Church, St Peter's Square, the Vatican Museum and the Vatican Gardens. Special permission is required to visit areas other than those mentioned.

MONEY

Currency: Vatican coins are similar in value, size and denomination to those of Italy, although the monetary system is separate from that of Italy; Italian notes and coins are, however, legal tender in the Vatican City. Refer to the *Money* section under the entry for *Italy*. Vatican coins are the Gold Lire 100 (nominal); Silver Lire 500; 'Acmonital' Lire 100 and 50; 'Italma' Lire 10, 5 and 1; and 'Bronzital' Lire 20.

DUTY FREE

There are no taxes and no customs/excise in the Vatican City. For Italian duty-free allowances refer to the *Duty Free* section under the entry for *Italy*.

PUBLIC HOLIDAYS

See the *Public Holidays* section under the entry for *Italy*.

HEALTH

See the *Health* section under the entry for *Italy*.

TRAVEL

The Vatican City has its own railway station and a helicopter pad. For travel in Rome, see the entry for *Italy*. There is a speed limit of 30kmph (19mph) in the Vatican City.

ACCOMMODATION

Board and lodging is not available to members of the general public in the Vatican City itself; for information on accommodation in Rome, see the entry for *Italy* above.

RESORTS & EXCURSIONS

The Vatican City is best known to tourists and students of architecture for the magnificent **St Peter's Basilica.** Visitors are normally admitted to the dome 1615-1800. The *Museum & Treasure House* is open 0900-1200 and 1500-1700. Leading up to it is the 17th-century **St Peter's Square,** a superb creation by Bernini. On either side are semi-circular colonnades, and in the centre of the square is an Egyptian obelisk hewn in the reign of Caligula. It is also possible to visit the *Necropoli Precostantiniana*, the excavations under St Peter's, although permission has to be obtained in advance and is usually granted only to students and teachers with a professional interest in the work being carried out. Contact the Tourist Information Office in St Peter's Square. The **Vatican Gardens** can be visited only by those on guided tours or bus tours. Tickets are available from the Tourist Information Office in St Peter's Square; it is advisable to apply two days in advance. To the right of St Peter's stands the **Vatican Palace**, the Pope's residence. Among the principal features of the Palace are the *Stanze*, the **Sistine chapel,** the *Garden House* or *Belvedere*, the *Vatican Library* and the *Vatican Collections*, containing major works of art and valuable pictures. The *Museum & Treasure House* includes the *Collection of Antiquities*, *Museo Pio-Clementino*, the *Egyptian Museum*, the *Etruscan Museum* and the *Museum of Modern Religious Art*. There is a restaurant in the museum and a bar and cafeteria on the roof of St Peter's.

BUSINESS PROFILE

ECONOMY: The Vatican has three main sources of income: the *Instituto per le Opere di Religione* (IOR, Institute of Religious Works); voluntary contributions known as 'Peter's Pence', and the interest on the Vatican's investments. The IOR – the Vatican Bank – has attracted some controversy in recent years through its association with the Banco Ambrosiano, which collapsed with debts running into hundreds of millions of pounds. Despite these heavy losses and poor recent returns on its investments which have left it running a current account deficit, the Vatican continues to wield immense financial influence. The Vatican does not produce goods for export and virtually all of its material requirements are met by the Italians.

COMMERCIAL INFORMATION: The following organisations can offer advice: Prefecture of the Economic Affairs of the Holy See, Palazzo delle Congregazioni, Largo del Colonnato 3, 00193 Rome. Tel: (6) 698 4263. Fax: (6) 698 5011; *or*

Istituto per le Opere di Religione (IOR), 00120 Città del Vaticano. Tel: (6) 698 3354. Fax: (6) 698 3809. Telex: 610030.

HISTORY & GOVERNMENT

HISTORY: For over 1000 years – from the era of Charlemagne's Frankish empire until 1870 – much of the central Italian peninsula was under the direct or indirect rule of the Pope, who at the same time wielded immense power throughout the whole of Europe. The Papacy was often deeply involved in the political issues of the times and the office itself was often in the gift of powerful lay rulers. The Popes were responsible for the launch of the Crusading movement from the late 11th century onwards and played a crucial role in almost all the major European events of the medieval period; despite such influence (often exercised very much at variance with the ideals of the Christian faith), the Papacy was also often riven by schisms, notably the Great Schism (1305-1378) when a succession of rival Popes established themselves at Avignon with the blessing of the King of France. The Reformation of the 16th century broke the spiritual dominance of the Papacy in Europe, despite the counter-reformatory work of the Council of Trent (1545-63) and from this time on the Popes, with some notable exceptions, were forced into a less dominant position in European affairs. After the unification of Italy in the late 19th century, the Pope retreated into the Vatican enclave until the Lateran treaty of 1929, between the Vatican and the Italian state, recognised Papal jurisdiction within the City. In 1978, Cardinal Karol Wojtyla became the first non-Italian encumbent of the Papacy since the 16th century, taking the title John Paul II. During his pontificate, the Vatican has experienced a major administrative upheaval and embroilment in a massive financial scandal. This applied further pressure on the already parlous Vatican finances, which are presently running a large deficit. Unlike any of his 270-odd predecessors, Pope John Paul II has made frequent overseas trips, usually to countries with a large Catholic population, and has pursued an active 'foreign policy', even where the Catholic Church has little or no direct religious influence (eg South-East Asia). Meanwhile, the world Catholic movement, particularly in the Third World where priests have been taking on political and social burdens, has become increasingly restive with what they perceive as reactionary attitudes on the part of the Vatican. At the end of 1989 the Vatican became embroiled in a major diplomatic incident when the deposed ruler of Panama, Manuel Noriega, sought asylum in the Papal Nunciature in Panama City: the crisis was settled after some adroit diplomatic footwork by the Vatican. Since then the Pope has naturally been deeply concerned with events in Eastern Europe, and particularly his native Poland, where the fall of the Communist regime has resulted in a resurgence of the Catholic Church. In the former Soviet Union, the Vatican played a mediating role during the Lithuanian crisis of 1990 and there has been an improvement in relations with Israel, which the Holy See has consistently refused to recognise since 1948. Diplomacy aside, the Vatican has displayed its customary robust attitude on social matters: a recent Italian proposal to introduce a new contraceptive pill was denounced as 'chemical warfare'.

GOVERNMENT: The Vatican City State is ruled by the Pope, who is elected for life by a 'conclave' composed of members of the College of Cardinals. The Pope appoints a Pontifical Commission to conduct the Vatican's administrative affairs, and he has legislative, executive and judicial powers within the Vatican City and in Papal possessions elsewhere.

CLIMATE

See the *Climate* section under the entry for *Italy*.

Location: South America.

Corpoturismo
Corporación de Turismo de Venezuela
Apartado 50200
Centro Capriles, 7°
Plaza Venezuela
Caracas, Venezuela
Tel: (2) 781 8370. Telex: 2396.

Embassy of the Republic of Venezuela
1 Cromwell Road
London SW7 2HW
Tel: (071) 584 4206/7. Fax: (071) 589 8887. Telex: 264186 EMVEN G. Opening hours: 0900-1600 Monday to Friday.

Venezuelan Consulate
56 Grafton Way
London W1P 5LB
Tel: (071) 387 6727. Fax: (071) 383 3253. Opening hours: 0930-1500 Monday to Friday.

VIASA Airways
19-20 Grosvenor Street
London W1X 9FD
Tel: (071) 629 1223 *or* 493 5573. Fax: (071) 493 2915. Telex: 28621.

British Embassy
Apartado 1246
Edificio Torre Las Mercedes, 3°
Avenida la Estancia, Chuao
Caracas 1060, Venezuela
Tel: (2) 751 1022 *or* 751 1166 *or* 751 1966. Fax: (2) 923 292. Telex: 23468 PROCA VE.
Consulates in: Maracaibo and Mérida.

Embassy of the Republic of Venezuela
1099 30th Street, NW
Washington, DC
20007
Tel: (202) 342 2214. Fax: (202) 387 2489.

Venezuelan Consulate General
7 East 51st Street
New York, NY
10022
Tel: (212) 826 1660.
Also in: Baltimore, Boston, Chicago, Houston, Coral Gables, New Orleans, Philadelphia, San Francisco and Santurce (Puerto Rico).

Embassy of the United States of America
PO Box 62291
Avenida Francisco de Miranda and Avenida Principal de la Floresta
Caracas 1060A, Venezuela
Tel: (2) 285 2222. Fax: (2) 285 0336. Telex: 25501 AMEMB VE.
Consulate in: Maracaibo.

Embassy of the Republic of Venezuela
32 Range Road
Ottawa, Ontario

K1N 8J4
Tel: (613) 235 5151 *or* 235 5154. Fax: (613) 235 3205.
Consulates in: Calgary, Montréal and Toronto.
Canadian Embassy
Apartado 62302
7th Floor, Edificio Torre Europe
Avenida Francisco de Miranda
Campo Alegre
Caracas 1060A, Venezuela
Tel: (2) 951 6166/7/8. Fax: (2) 951 4950. Telex: 23377 DOMCA VE.

AREA: 912,050 sq km (352,144 sq miles).
POPULATION: 19,734,968 (1990 estimate).
POPULATION DENSITY: 21.6 per sq km.
CAPITAL: Caracas. **Population:** 3,373,059 (metropolitan area, 1989 estimate).
GEOGRAPHY: Venezuela is bounded to the north by the Caribbean, to the east by Guyana and the Atlantic Ocean, to the south by Brazil, and to the west and southwest by Colombia. The country consists of four distinctive regions: the Venezuelan Highlands in the west; the Maracaibo Lowlands in the north; the vast central plain of the Llanos around the Orinoco; and the Guyana Highlands, which take up about half of the country.
LANGUAGE: Spanish is the official language. English, French, German and Portuguese are also spoken by some sections of the community.
RELIGION: Roman Catholic.
TIME: GMT - 4.
ELECTRICITY: 110 volts AC, 60Hz. American-type 2-pin plugs are the most commonly used fittings.
COMMUNICATIONS: Telephone: IDD is available. Country code: 58. **Fax:** Available at the larger hotels. **Telex/telegram:** Public telex facilities are available. Telegram services are available from public telegraph offices. **Post:** There is an efficient mail service from Venezuela to the USA and Europe. Airmail to Europe takes three to seven days. Internal mail can sometimes take longer. Surface mail to Europe takes at least a month. **Press:** The English-language daily newspaper is *The Daily Journal*, published in Caracas.
BBC World Service and Voice of America frequencies: From time to time these change. See the section *How to Use this Book* for more information.

BBC:				
MHz	17.840	15.220	9.915	5.975
Voice of America:				
MHz	15.21	11.58	9.775	5.995

PASSPORT/VISA

Regulations and requirements may be subject to change at short notice, and you are advised to contact the appropriate diplomatic or consular authority before finalising travel arrangements. Details of these may be found at the head of this country's entry. Any numbers in the chart refer to the footnotes below.

	Passport Required?	Visa Required?	Return Ticket Required?
Full British	Yes	No/1	Yes
BVP	Not valid	-	-
Australian	Yes	No/1	Yes
Canadian	Yes	No/1	Yes
USA	Yes	No/1	Yes
Other EC	Yes	1/2	Yes
Japanese	Yes	Yes	Yes

PASSPORTS: Valid passport required by all. Passports must be valid for at least 6 months.
British Visitors Passport: Not accepted.
VISAS: Required by all except [1] nationals of the following countries, who do, however, require a 60-day Tourist Card issued from an authorised air or sea carrier:
(a) [2] EC countries (except nationals of Greece and Portugal who *do* require visas);
(b) Australia, Canada and the USA;
(c) Andorra, Antigua & Barbuda, Austria, Barbados, Belize, Brazil, Costa Rica, Dominica, Finland, Iceland, Liechtenstein, Mexico, Monaco, The Netherlands Antilles, New Zealand, Norway, San Marino, St Kitts & Nevis, St Lucia, St Vincent & the Grenadines, Sweden, Switzerland, Taiwan and Trinidad & Tobago.
Note: Special authorisation is required from the Ministry of Internal Affairs to grant entry to certain nationalities; enquire at the Embassy for details.
Types of visa: Tourist, Business and Transit. Cost depends on nationality and purpose of travel.
Validity: *Tourist* and *Business:* up to 1 year; *Transit:* 3 days.
Application to: Consulate (or Consular Section at Embassy). For addresses, see top of entry.
Application requirements: (a) Completed application forms. (b) Return or onward ticket. (c) Letter of introduction from company or bank for Business visa. (d) Stamped self-addressed envelope.
Working days required: 2.
Temporary residence: Special authorisation is required from the Ministry of Internal Affairs in Caracas.

MONEY

Currency: Bolívar (B) = 100 centimos. Notes are in denominations of B500, 100, 50, 20, 10, 5 and 1. Coins are in denominations of B5, 2 and 1, and 50, 25 and 5 centimos.
Currency exchange: Banks and *cambios* will change money in Venezuela; so too will hotels, although often at a less favourable rate.
Credit cards: Visa, American Express and Access/Mastercard are widely accepted; Diners Club has more limited acceptance. Check with your credit card company for details of merchant acceptability and for other facilities which may be available.
Travellers cheques: Widely accepted, although one may be asked to produce a receipt of purchase when changing them in Venezuela. Exchange is more difficult in some places than others. Some kinds of travellers cheques are not accepted; seek advice before travelling.
Exchange rate indicators: The following figures are included as a guide to the movements of the Bolívar against Sterling and the US Dollar:

Date:	Oct '89	Oct '90	Oct '91	Oct '92
£1.00=	60.79	95.65	95.13	120.75
$1.00=	38.50	48.96	54.81	76.09

Note: The above rates are for non-commercial transactions. 'Essential Import' and 'Preferential' rates are also used.
Currency restrictions: The import and export of either foreign or local currency is unlimited.
Banking hours: 0830-1130 and 1400-1630 Monday to Friday.

DUTY FREE

The following items may be imported into Venezuela without incurring customs duty:
200 cigarettes and 25 cigars;
2 litres of alcoholic beverages;
4 small bottles of perfume.

PUBLIC HOLIDAYS

Public holidays observed in Venezuela are as follows:
Mar 10 '93 Holiday (La Guaira only). **Apr 9-12** Easter. **Apr 19** Declaration of Independence. **May 1** Labour Day. **Jun 24** Battle of Carabobo. **Jul 5** Independence Day. **Jul 24** Birth of Simón Bolívar and Battle of Lago de Maracaibo. **Sep 4** Civil Servants Day. **Oct 12** Columbus Day. **Oct 24** Holiday (Maracaibo only). **Dec 24-25** Christmas. **Dec 31** New Year's Eve. **Jan 1 '94** New Year's Day. **Feb*** Carnival. **Mar 10** Holiday (La Guaira only).
Note [*]: Check with Embassy for exact dates.

HEALTH

Regulations and requirements may be subject to change at short notice, and you are advised to contact your doctor well in advance of your intended date of departure. Any numbers in the chart refer to the footnotes below.

	Special Precautions?	Certificate Required?
Yellow Fever	Yes	1
Cholera	No	No
Typhoid & Polio	Yes	-
Malaria	2	-
Food & Drink	3	-

[1]: A yellow fever vaccination certificate is not required as a condition of entry but vaccination is advised for all travellers over one year of age who intend to venture outside urban areas.
[2]: Malaria risk exists throughout the year in rural areas in parts of Anzoátegui, Apure, Barinas, Bolívar, Mérida, Monagas, Portuguesa, Sucre, Táchira and Zulia States and the Federal Territory of Amazonas and Delta Amacuro. The malignant *falciparum* form is present and is reported to be 'highly resistant' to chloroquine.
[3]: Mains water is normally chlorinated, and whilst relatively safe may cause mild abdominal upsets. Bottled water is available and is advised for the first few weeks of the stay. Drinking water outside main cities and towns may be contaminated and sterilisation is advisable. Milk is pasteurised and dairy products are safe for consumption. Local meat, poultry, seafood, fruit and vegetables are generally considered safe to eat.
Rabies is present. For those at high risk, vaccination before arrival should be considered. If you are bitten abroad seek medical advice without delay. For more information consult the *Health* section at the back of the book.
Bilharzia (schistosomiasis) is present in north-central Venezuela. Avoid swimming and paddling in fresh water. Swimming pools which are well-chlorinated and maintained are safe.
Health care: The cost of medical and dental treatment in Venezuela is high. Facilities are good in major centres. There is one doctor for every 1270 inhabitants. Health insurance is recommended.

TRAVEL - International

AIR: Venezuela's national airline is *Viasa (VA)*.
Approximate flight time: From *London* to Caracas is 12 hours (including stopovers in Europe), from *Los Angeles* is 9 hours and from *New York* is 5 hours.
International airport: *Caracas (CCS)* (Simon Bolívar) is 22km (14 miles) from the city (travel time – 30 minutes). There is a coach to the city every 10 minutes, 24-hour service. Return is from the Parque Central terminus, Avenida Lecuna, and pick-ups are at the Hilton, Macuto, Sheraton and Inter-Continental hotels. Buses (*littoral*) are available to the city every 45 minutes from 0600-2200. Return from Nuevo Circo bus station. Taxis to the city are available on ranks. Airport facilities: duty-free shop, bank/bureau de change (0800-1830), bar/restaurant, 24-hour tourist information and car hire (*Avis, Budget* and *National*).
Departure tax: B505 is levied on all international departures (air or sea) regardless of nationality; tourists pay an extra charge of B530 for an exit form and tax stamp. Transit passengers and children under two years are exempt.
SEA: The principal Venezuelan ports are La Guaira, Puerto Cabello, Maracaibo, Guanta, Porlamar and Ciudad Bolívar (on the Orinoco River). The principal shipping lines operating to Venezuela are, from the USA: *Venezuelan Line, Delta Line Cruises* and *Royal Netherlands SS Company;* from Amsterdam, Le Havre or Bilbao: *Royal Netherlands SS Company;* from Mediterranean ports: *French Line* and the Spanish ships 'Cabo San Juan' and 'Cabo San Roque'; and from other European ports: *Polish Ocean Lines* and *Lauro*. The *Cunard* 'Countess' and

VENEZUELA | **HEALTH REGULATIONS** | **VISA REGULATIONS** | Code-Link

GALILEO/WORLDSPAN

TI-DFT/CCS/HE

TI-DFT/CCS/VI

SABRE

TIDFT/CCS/HE

TIDFT/CCS/VI

To access this information on your CRS, swipe the barcode with a light pen or type in the text under the barcode. For more information, see the introduction *How to Use This Book*.

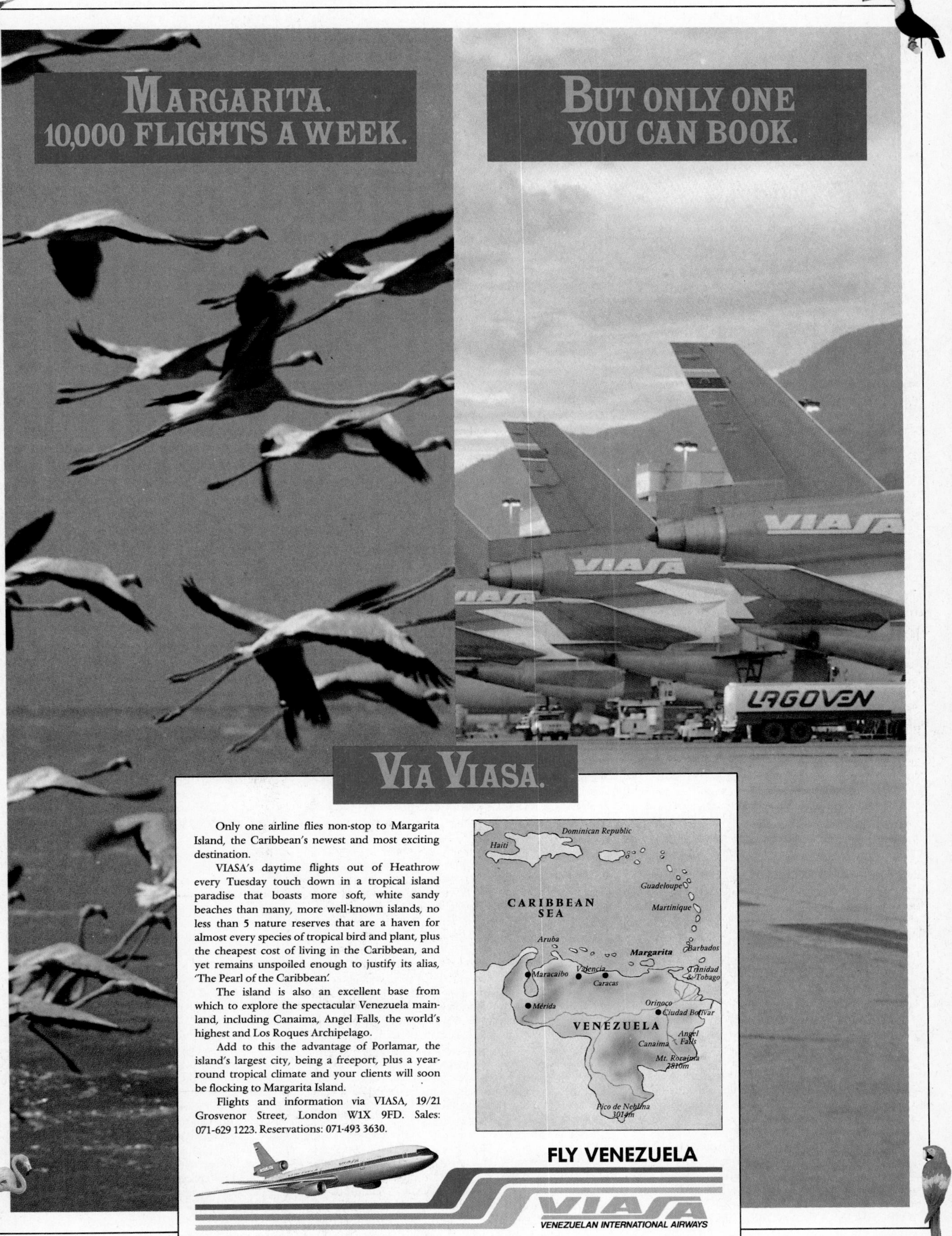
MARGARITA.
10,000 FLIGHTS A WEEK.
BUT ONLY ONE
YOU CAN BOOK.
VIASA
LAGOVEN
VIA VIASA.
Only one airline flies non-stop to Margarita Island, the Caribbean's newest and most exciting destination.
VIASA's daytime flights out of Heathrow every Tuesday touch down in a tropical island paradise that boasts more soft, white sandy beaches than many, more well-known islands, no less than 5 nature reserves that are a haven for almost every species of tropical bird and plant, plus the cheapest cost of living in the Caribbean, and yet remains unspoiled enough to justify its alias, 'The Pearl of the Caribbean'.
The island is also an excellent base from which to explore the spectacular Venezuela mainland, including Canaima, Angel Falls, the world's highest and Los Roques Archipelago.
Add to this the advantage of Porlamar, the island's largest city, being a freeport, plus a year-round tropical climate and your clients will soon be flocking to Margarita Island.
Flights and information via VIASA, 19/21 Grosvenor Street, London W1X 9FD. Sales: 071-629 1223. Reservations: 071-493 3630.
Dominican Republic
Haiti
Guadeloupe
CARIBBEAN SEA
Martinique
Aruba
Margarita
Barbados
Maracaibo
Valencia
Caracas
Trinidad & Tobago
Orinoco
Mérida
Ciudad Bolivar
VENEZUELA
Angel Falls
Canaima
Mt. Roraima 2810m
Pico de Neblina 3014m
FLY VENEZUELA
VIASA
VENEZUELAN INTERNATIONAL AIRWAYS

'Princess' offer Caribbean cruises from San Juan that include a stop in Caracas. Other cruise lines are *Costa, Princess Cruises* and *Delta Cruises*. There are ferry connections between Falcon State, Curaçao and Aruba on the Swedish *Almirante Luis Brion*, which carries 1200 passengers and 40 cars. The distance of 160km (100 miles) is covered in 3 hours 30 minutes. The ferry leaves the Muaco dock near Falcon's capital.
Departure tax: There is a tax on all sea departures regardless of nationality; enquire locally for current rate.
RAIL: There are no international rail links with Venezuela.
ROAD: Road access is from Colombia (Barranquilla and Medellin) to Maracaibo and the Amazon territory of Brazie (Manaus) to Caracas.

TRAVEL - Internal

AIR: Almost all large towns are connected with scheduled services operated by two domestic airlines: *Aeropostal (LV)* and *Avensa (VE)*. The *Avensa Air Pass* gives tourists 4, 7 or 21 days unlimited air travel within the country. Air travel is the best means of internal transport but services are often over-booked and even confirmation does not always ensure a seat. Travellers are advised to arrive at the airport well before the minimum check-in time in order to obtain confirmed seats. Schedule changes and flight cancellations with no advance warning are also likely hazards.
Departure tax: B40 for domestic departures.
SEA: Ferries link Puerto La Cruz with Margarita Island (2 hours 45 minutes).
RAIL: The only railway link runs between Barquisimeto and Puerto Cabello, with four trains daily but no air-conditioning. There are plans for a considerable extension to the rail network. There are ambitious plans for a 2000km (1200-mile) national network by the year 2000.
ROAD: Internal roads between principal cities are of a high standard, with 17,050km (10,595 miles) of paved motorways, 13,500km (8400 miles) of macadam highways and 5850km (3635 miles) of other roads. **Bus:** There are a few inter-urban bus services. **Car hire:** Self-drive cars are available at the airport and in major city centres but are expensive. **Documentation:** International Driving Permit is required.
URBAN: Caracas has a 35-station metro, which is comfortable and inexpensive. Conventional **bus** services have badly deteriorated in recent years and there has been a rapid growth in the use of *por puestos* (shared taxis). These are operated by minibus companies and tend to serve as the main form of public transport in Caracas and major cities. Fares charged are in general similar to those on the buses, although they are higher during the evenings and at weekends. **Taxis** in Caracas are metered but the fare can nonetheless be negotiated with the driver. It is customary not to use meters after midnight; the fare should be agreed before setting out. Taxi fares double after 2000. Taxi rates are posted at the airport. Motorcycles may not be used in Caracas after 2200.
JOURNEY TIMES: The following chart gives approximate journey times (in hours and minutes) from Caracas to other major cities/towns in Venezuela.

	Air
Porlamar	0.45
Los Roques	0.50
Mérida	1.00
Canaima	1.15
Cumana	0.45
Maracaibo	1.00
Ciudad Bolívar	0.50

ACCOMMODATION

HOTELS: There are many excellent hotels in Caracas. Numerous smaller hotels are open throughout the country but it is essential to make reservations at both these and the larger international hotels well in advance.
Grading: Hotels in Venezuela have been graded into three categories; 3-star (65 hotels), 4-star (22) and 5-star (15). It normally follows that the more expensive the hotel, the better the facilities. Hotels do not add a service charge, and generally there is no variation in seasonal rates.
Hotels outside the capital tend to be cheaper and the standard may not be as high. A useful guide is the *Guía Turistica de Caracas Littoral y Venezuela*, published by the Corporación de Turismo de Venezuela, available at local tourist offices. The Venezuelan Consulate holds a reference copy (address at top of entry).
CAMPING/CARAVANNING: Camping in Venezuela can involve spending a weekend at the beach, on the islands, in the Llanos or in the mountains. Camping can also be arranged with companies who run jungle expeditions. As in much of South America, however, good facilities are not widespread and camping is not used by travellers as a substitute for hotels on the main highways. No special campsites are yet provided for this purpose.

RESORTS & EXCURSIONS

Venezuela offers the tourist a great variety of landscape – tropical beaches, immense plains, enormous rivers, forests, jungle, waterfalls and great mountains. The country has, for the purposes of this survey, been divided into four major areas: Caracas, The North Coast, The Llanos and Eastern Venezuela.

Caracas

Nestling in a long narrow valley in the coastal mountain range 16km (10 miles) from the north coast, Caracas is typical of the 'new Venezuela', despite being one of the oldest established cities in the country (founded 1567). The city is constantly growing and changing but, among the new developments, there are still areas of the old towns intact – **San José** and **Las Pastora**, for example. Other periods of the country's history have left substantial monuments; these include the *Plaza Bolívar*, flanked by the old cathedral and the Archbishop's residence, the *Casa Amarilla* and the *Capitol* (the National Congress) building, erected in 1873 in only 114 days, which has a fine mural depicting Venezuelan military exploits. Other places worth visiting include the *Panteon Nacional* (which contains the body of Simon Bolívar), the *Jardín Botánicó*, the *Parque Nacional del Este*, and, for recreation, the Country Club. **Museums** in the capital include the *Museo de Bellas Artes*, the *Museo del Arte Colonial*, the *Museo del Arte Contemporáneo*, the *Museo de Transporte* and the *Casa Natal del Liberator* (a reconstruction of the house where Bolívar was born; the first was destroyed in an earthquake). Next door is a museum containing the Liberator's war relics. There are also a large number of art galleries, as well as daily concerts, theatrical productions, films and lectures. The city also has a wide range of nightclubs, bars and coffee shops, especially along the *Boulevarde Sabana Grande*.
Excursions: *Mount Avila* gives a superb view across the city and along the coast. There are several beaches within 30km (20 miles) of the capital, with excellent 'taverns' and restaurants. For further information on these and other coastal resorts, see the following section.

The North Coast

The 4000km (2800 miles) of Caribbean coastline represents the major tourist destination in the country. The area has numerous excellent beaches and resorts ranging from the comparatively luxurious to the unashamedly opulent which stretch along the coastline. **Maiquetia** is one of the best and most popular, offering wide beaches, an extensive range of watersports and some of the best fishing (including an international competition for the giant blue sailfish). There are daily air shuttles from Maiquetia to Porlamar, on **Margarita Island**, a popular tourist resort with beautiful beaches, good hotels and extensive shopping centres. Also to the west of Caracas are **Macuto, Marbella, Naiguta, Carabelleda, Leguna** and **Oriaco** which all have excellent beaches. To the north of Maiquetia is the idyllic island of **Los Roques**. **La Guaira** is the main port for Caracas. Although now heavily industrialised, the winding hilltop route from the city and the old town are worth visiting. Further west along the Inter-American highway is **Maracay** with its Opera House, bullring and *Gomez Mausoleum*. Excursions run to **Lake Valencia** and Gomez's country house, the *Rancho Grande*.
The coastal resorts of **Ocumare de la Costa** and **Cata** can be reached by way of the 1130m (3710ft) *Portachuelo Pass* through the central highlands. The coastline is dotted with fine beaches and islands, many inhabited only by flamingoes and scarlet ibis. Most can be reached by hired boat. **Morrocoy**, off the coast from Tucacas, is the most spectacular of these – hundreds of coral reefs with palm beaches ideal for scuba diving and fishing. **Palma Sola** and **Chichiriviche** are also popular. Ferries run from La Vela de Coro and Punto Fijo to the islands of Aruba and Curaçao. Journeys take about four hours and delays are to be expected.
Puerto la Cruz is a popular coastal resort with bars and restaurants and good beaches. It is also a good centre for travelling to remoter beaches. There is the Morro marina development in the Lecherías area adjacent to Puerto la Cruz, and the attractive town of **Pueblo Viejo** with 'old' Caribbean architecture and a Venetian lagoon layout – boats are the only means of transport. The attractiveness of the Puerto la Cruz area means that there has been an increase of foreign investment here in recent years.
South of Coro is **Barquisimeto**, one of the oldest settlements in Venezuela, now the country's fourth-largest city and capital of the *Llanos*, the great Venezuelan plateau and cattle range (see below for further information on this region). Its cathedral is one of the most famous modern buildings in the country.
Along the Colombian border is the **Cordillera de Mérida** and, to the east of this range, the **Cordillera Oriental**. Set in the area between these two ranges are the city of **Maracaibo** and *Lake Maracaibo*. Windless and excessively humid, the city and its environs are dominated by the machinery of oil production from the largest oilfields in the world, discovered in 1917. Sightseeing tours are available from here to the peninsula of **Guajira,** where the Motilone and Guajiro Indians live.
To the north of Maracaibo live the Goaro Indians whose lifestyle has changed little since the days of the first Spanish settlers. Their houses are raised above the lake on stilts and are in fact the original inspiration for naming the country Venezuela, or 'Little Venice'.
The **Cordillera de Mérida** are the only peaks in the country with a permanent snowline. Frosty plateaux and lofty summits characterise the landscape and many cities have grown up at the foot of the mountains, combining tradition with modern ways of life as well as diversified rural and urban scenery. The scenery in this area is extremely varied – lagoons, mountains, rivers, beaches, ancient villages, historical cities, oil camps, sand dunes and Indian lake dwellings on stilts. The **Sierra Nevada National Park** offers opportunities to ski between November and June but, at an altitude of 4270m (14,000ft), this is recommended only for the hardiest and most dedicated.
Mérida, to the south, is today a city of wide modern avenues linking mainly large-scale 20th-century developments, although, wherever possible, relics of the colonial past have been allowed to stand. A university town and tourist centre, it nestles in the *Sierra Nevada*, overshadowed by *Bolívar Peak* (5007m/15,260ft) and *Mirror Peak* (where the world's highest cable car climbs to an altitude of 4675m/14,250ft). Mérida has modern and colonial art museums and much more worth seeing, including the *Valle Grande*, the *Flower Clock*, *Los Chorros de Milla*, the lagoons of *Mucubaji*, *Los Anteojos*, *Tabay*, *Pogal*, *Los Patos*, *San-say* and the famous *Black Lagoon*. A mountain railway runs from the town to **Pico Espejo**. The view from the summit looks over the highest peaks of the Cordillera and the Llanos. *The Andean Club* in Mérida arranges trips to Los Nervados, the highest village in the mountains. Again, this is only recommended for the hardy. Other excursions from Mérida include **San Javier del Valle**, a relaxing mountain retreat, and **Jaji**, which has some fine examples of colonial architecture.

The Llanos

This is an expansive, sparsely populated area of grassland east of the Cordillera de Mérida and north of the Orinoco, reaching up to the north coast. The area is the heart of the Venezuelan cattle country and the landscape is flat and only varied here and there by slight upthrusts of land. It is veined by numerous slowly running rivers, forested along their banks. The swamps are the home of egrets, parrots, alligators and monkeys. The equestrian skills of the plainsmen can be seen at many rodeos throughout the Llanos, as well as exhibitions of cattle roping and the *Joropo*, Venezuela's national dance.

Eastern Venezuela

The coastal regions to the north of the Guyana Highlands have some fine tourist beaches and resorts. These include *Higuerote*, *La Sabana* and also *Lecheria* where the San Juan Drum Festival is held during late June.
The **Guyana Highlands** lie to the south of the Orinoco River and constitute half the land area of the country. Their main value is as a source of gold and diamonds. The Orinoco and its delta have been developed as major trade centres. **Ciudad Bolívar**, formerly known as Angostura, and the home of Angostura bitters, is an old city on the south bank of the Orinoco and still bears traces of its colonial past, although it is currently the centre of modern developments. The **Gran Sabana National Reserve** is the largest of the Venezuelan plateaux and has an extraordinary array of wildlife. **Santa Elena,** *Guri Dam* and *Danto Falls* are all worth a visit. **Santa Elena de Uairén** is a rugged frontier town which holds a Fiesta in August.
Mount Roraima, suggested as the site of Conan Doyle's 'Lost World', can be climbed on foot. A fortnight's supplies and full camping equipment should be taken as the trip can take up to two weeks. The nearest village to the mountain is **Peraitepin**. *Tepuy Peak* is also worth a visit. Trips can be arranged to the diamond mines at **Los Caribes**. In **Icaban** after a heavy rainfall it is common to see children searching the slopes for gold nuggets washed down from the slopes.
It is possible to arrange trips by boat up the Orinoco River delta to **La Tucupita**. **Canaima** (one of the world's largest national parks, comprising three million hectares) is the setting for the spectacular *Angel Falls*, which carry the waters of the *Churum River* into an abyss. At 979m

(3212ft) they are the highest in the world, a sight no visitor should miss. Trips can be arranged which take in the waterfalls and other nearby attractions, including many rare plants – Canaima has over 500 species of orchid alone. Overnight accommodation is available on the shores of the lagoon.

Other national parks in Venezuela are to be found in Bolívar State and the Amazonas Federal Territory, for example, **El Cocuy** and **Autana.**

SOCIAL PROFILE

FOOD & DRINK: Cumin and saffron are used in many dishes but the distinctive and delicate flavour of most of the popular dishes comes from the use of local roots and vegetables. Some local specialities are *tequenos*, a popular hors d'oeuvres (thin dough wrapped around a finger of local white cheese and fried crisp); *arepas* (the native bread), made from primitive ground corn, water and salt; and *tostadas*, which are used for sandwiches (the mealy centre is removed and the crisp shell filled with anything from ham and cheese to spiced meat, chicken salad or cream cheese). *Guasacaca* is a semi-hot relish used mostly with grilled meats. *Pabellón criollo* is a hash made with shredded meat and served with fried plantains and black beans on rice. *Hallaca* is a local delicacy, eaten at Christmas and New Year; cornmeal is combined with beef, pork, ham and green peppers, wrapped in individual pieces of banana leaves and cooked in boiling water. *Parrilla criolla* is beef marinated and cooked over a charcoal grill. *Hervido* is soup made with chunks of beef, chicken or fish and native vegetables or roots. *Purée de apio* is one of the more exotic local roots (boiled and puréed, with salt and butter added, it tastes like chestnuts). *Empanadas* (meat turnovers), *roast lapa* (a succulent, large rodent) and *chipi chipi* soup (made from tiny clams) are excellent. Table service is the norm and opening hours are 2100-2300. **Drink:** There is no good local wine, although foreign wines are bottled locally. There are several good local beers, mineral waters, gin and excellent rum. Coffee is very good and a *merengada* (fruit pulp, ice, milk and sugar) is recommended. *Batido* is similar but with water and no milk. *Pousse-café* is an after-dinner liqueur. Bars have either table or counter service. A *lisa* is a glass of draught beer and a *tercio* a bottled beer. Most bars are open very late and there are no licensing laws.

NIGHTLIFE: There are many nightclubs and discotheques in the major cities of Venezuela. The Nacional and Municipal Theatres offer a variety of concerts, ballet, plays, operas and operettas. There are other theatres, some of which are open-air, in Caracas, as well as several cinemas.

SHOPPING: There are many handicrafts unique to Venezuela which are made by local Indian tribes. Good purchases are gems and jewellery, *cacique* coins, gold, pearls, pompom slippers, seed necklaces, shoes and handbags, Indian bows, arrows, mats, pipes and baskets, *alpargatas* (traditional local footwear of the Campesinos), *chinchorros* (local hammocks) and many other Indian goods. **Shopping hours:** 0900-1300 and 1500-1900 Monday to Saturday.

SPORT: Jungle trips: Various companies offer 'off the beaten track' expeditions. **Golf:** There are various clubs at which temporary membership can be arranged. **Hunting:** All hunting in Venezuela has been prohibited for the past five years. **Watersports:** Available less than an hour from Caracas on the Caribbean, where there are several excellent beaches with full facilities. Sailing and yachting regattas are held every year at Macuto. There are skindiving and water-skiing facilities at Chichiriviche, Cata Bay and Macuto. The snorkeling off Margarita Island is very enjoyable. **Winter sports:** The season is from May to October. **Horseracing:** Caracas has South America's largest and most modern race track – La Rinconada – open on Saturdays and Sundays. **Boxing, baseball & football:** These are the most popular spectator sports in Venezuela and can be seen all year round. The winter baseball leagues feature many young US baseball stars. **Wrestling:** The indigenous *lucha libre* wrestling is a weekly event.

SPECIAL EVENTS: Every village and town in Venezuela celebrates the feast of its patron saint. It is during these provincial festivals that the tourist can enjoy the colourful folklore that is a mixture of the cultures of pre-Columbian Indians, African slaves and Spanish colonialists.

SOCIAL CONVENTIONS: Shaking hands or using the local *abrazo*, a cross between a hug and a handshake, are the normal forms of greeting. In Caracas conservative casual wear is the norm. Men are expected to wear suits for business, and jackets and ties are usual for dining out and social functions. Dress on the coast is less formal but beachwear and shorts should not be worn away from the beach or pool. Smoking follows European habits and in most cases it is obvious where not to smoke. Some public buildings are also non-smoking areas. **Tipping:** Tips are discretionary but in the majority of bars and restaurants 10% is added to the bill and it is customary to leave another 10% on the table. Bellboys and chambermaids should be tipped, and in Caracas tips are higher than elsewhere. Taxi drivers are not tipped unless they carry suitcases. Petrol pump attendants expect a tip.

BUSINESS PROFILE

ECONOMY: Venezuela was a primarily agricultural country until the discovery and extraction of oil began in the 1920s. Oil now dominates the economy and has made Venezuela the wealthiest country in South America. With the second-largest known reserves in the world (after Saudi Arabia) little change in the structure of the economy may be expected for the foreseeable future. Agriculture's share of the workforce has now fallen below 25%, but the sector remains important with dairy and beef farming being major export earners. Most of the rest of farming activity is devoted to staple crops for domestic consumption, although some crops – mostly rice, sugar and coffee – are grown as cash crops. The Venezuelan economy stabilised in the late 1980s after a difficult period following the collapse of the oil price which slashed revenues and brought numerous industrial and social programmes to a halt. Firm fiscal management was responsible on that occasion, despite persistent problems with debt servicing and low currency reserves, and laid the foundations for a strong economic performance in the late 1980s and early 1990s when annual growth reached 9%. However, the political uncertainty following the February 1992 coup attempt has had a knock-on effect on the economy: growth has slowed to around 5% while inflation has climbed to 30%. The Government is hoping to develop other sectors of the economy, particularly minerals including aluminium and gold, but this depends on substantial investment. Meanwhile oil revenues continue to be depressed due to low world prices. A labour shortage in key sectors of the economy has induced the Government to launch an immigration drive aimed at Eastern Europe. It is planned that 50,000 people will join the existing population of 19 million by 1997. Venezuela is a member of both OPEC and the Asociación Latinoamericana de Integración, which seeks to promote a common market for Latin America. Most kinds of industrial and consumer goods are in demand in Venezuela from foreign exporters. The USA is the dominant trade partner, followed by Germany, Japan and Brazil.

BUSINESS: English is becoming more widely spoken in business circles, particularly at executive level. Nevertheless, Spanish is essential for most business discussions. Appointments are necessary and a business visitor should be punctual. It is common to exchange visiting cards. **Office hours:** 0800-1800 Monday to Friday with a long mid-day break.

COMMERCIAL INFORMATION: The following organisation can offer advice: Federación Venezolana de Cámaras y Asociaciones de Comercio y Producción (FEDECAMARAS) (Federation of Chambers of Commerce and Industry), Apartado 2568, Edificio Fedecámaras, 5°, Avenida El Empalme, Urb. El Bosque, Caracas. Tel: (2) 731 1967. Fax: (2) 742 097. Telex: 29890.

CONFERENCES/CONVENTIONS: Larger hotels have facilities.

HISTORY & GOVERNMENT

HISTORY: Originally inhabited by Carib and Arawak Indians, Venezuela was claimed as a Spanish territory by Christopher Columbus in 1498. Spanish rule was administered from a distance, leaving the various regions to develop separately from the capital, Caracas, which was founded by Diego de Losada in 1567. An attempt to inject a measure of unification by the Spanish in the 18th century was met with widespread resistance and uprisings led by Simon Bolívar (after whom the currency is named). In 1830, Venezuela became a sovereign state led by José Paéz. The precise territorial limits were not, however, well defined and Venezuela's borders have since been the subject of periodic disputes with its neighbours. The dictatorship of Juan Vincente Goméz between 1909 and 1935 was a period of rapid economic development in Venezuela, and was marked by the opening of the country's oil fields in 1918. In 1936 and 1937, Venezuela held democratic elections for the Presidency and national assembly for the first time but the experiment in pluralism lasted only until 1945 and the first of a rapid succession of military dictatorships which lasted until 1961. That year, the current Venezuelan constitution was established. Recent politics have been dominated by the struggle between the Partido Social Cristiano, known as COPEI, and the Acción Democrática (AD).

The principal concern of the present AD government (led by Carlos Andrés Pérez) has been the domestic economy, which has been in trouble for much of the 1980s. Throughout the 1970s, Venezuela enjoyed the benefits of large oil revenues and ran up a substantial overseas debt, which has been repeatedly rescheduled although it is not on the scale of those burdening Mexico, Brazil, Argentina and others. The economic challenge for the Government in the early 1990s is to create a stable climate for export-led development, in which they have achieved a degree of success. The Government introduced austerity measures (again, in common with much of the rest of the continent) which prompted social protests during 1989 and 1990. Discontent grew through the early 1990s as living standards fell as the Government became enmired in corruption. The Government's opponents found support from sections of the army, themselves ill-equipped and badly paid, who in early February 1992, wholly unexpectedly, launched a military coup. It was put down by the majority of the armed forces who remained loyal to the Government, but Pérez was severely shocked and must consider a reappraisal of his entire policy framework. In the wake of the coup attempt, a sense of crisis and paralysis still seems to pervade the Government: promised judicial and constitutional reforms have unaccountably stalled. Loyalists in the military were still sufficiently numerous at the end of 1992 to put down a second attempted coup but their patience is wearing thin. Calls for Pérez to step down before the expiry of his term in February 1994 have been growing.

GOVERNMENT: Legislative power is vested in the dual-chamber National Congress, composed of a Senate and a Chamber of Deputies. The Senate is of variable size, with 44 elected members supplemented by all living former Presidents of the Republic. The Chamber of Deputies has 199 elected members. Executive authority rests with the elected President, who is also Head of State. All elections are conducted by universal adult suffrage every five years.

CLIMATE

The climate varies according to altitude. Lowland areas have a tropical climate. The dry season is from December to April and the rainy season from May to December. The best time to visit is between January and April.

Required clothing: Lightweights are suitable all year round in low and coastal areas, although a few warm clothes may be needed for the evenings. A light raincoat for the rainy season and warmer clothes for upland areas will be needed.

CARACAS Venezuela (1035m)

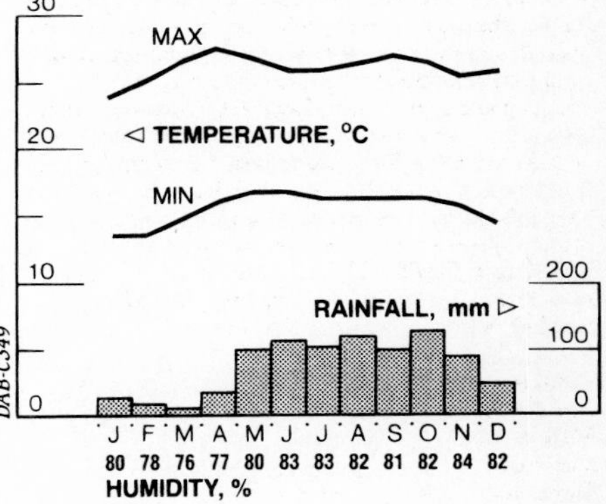

MARACAIBO Venezuela (40m)

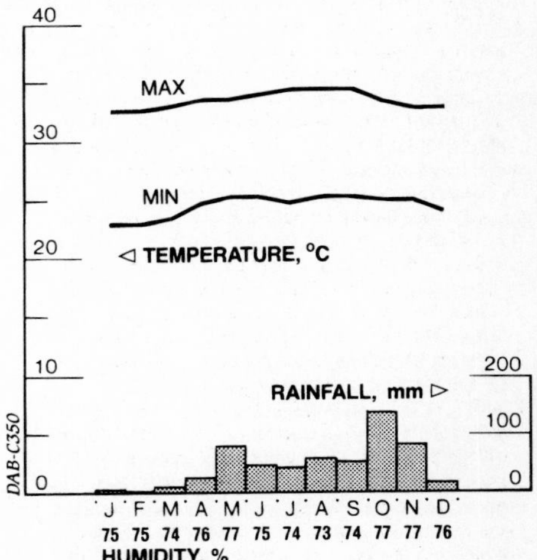

VIETNAM

Location: South-East Asia.

Vietnam Tourism
30a Ly Thuong Kiet
Hanoi, Vietnam
Tel: (4) 61151 *or* 64148. Fax: (4) 57532 *or* 57583.
Telex: 411269.

Embassy of the Socialist Republic of Vietnam
12-14 Victoria Road
London W8 5RD
Tel: (071) 937 1912. Fax: (071) 937 6108. Telex: 887361 VIETEMG. Opening hours: 0900-1200 and 1400-1800 Monday to Friday.

Regent Holidays (UK representatives of Vietnam Tourism)
15 John Street
Bristol BS1 2HR
Tel: (0272) 211 711. Fax: (0272) 254 866. Telex: 444606.

Orbittours
GPO Box 3309
428 George Street
Sydney NSW 2001, Australia
Tel: (612) 221 7322. Fax: (612) 221 7425. Telex: AA127081.

British Embassy
16 Pho Ly Thuong Kiet
Hanoi, Vietnam
Tel: (4) 52349. Fax: (4) 65762. Telex: 411405.

Embassy of the Socialist Republic of Vietnam
Suite 802
85 Range Road
Ottawa, Ontario
K1N 8J6
Tel: (613) 565 0300 *or* 565 2292. Fax: (613) 565 2595.
Telex: 053-3205.

Canadian Embassy
39 Nguyen Dinh Chieu Street
Hanoi, Vietnam
Tel: (4) 65840 *or* 65845. Fax: (4) 65837.

AREA: 330,341 sq km (127,545 sq miles).
POPULATION: 64,375 762 (1989 estimate).
POPULATION DENSITY: 194.9 per sq km.
CAPITAL: Hanoi. **Population:** 3,056,146 (1989).
GEOGRAPHY: Vietnam shares borders to the north with the People's Republic of China and to the west with Laos and Cambodia. The South China Sea lies to the east and south. The land is principally agricultural with a central tropical rainforest.
LANGUAGE: Vietnamese is the official language. French, Russian, English and Chinese are also spoken by some government officials and professionals.
RELIGION: Buddhist majority. There are Taoist, Confucian, Hoa Hao, Caodaist and Christian (predominantly Roman Catholic) minorities.
TIME: GMT + 7.
ELECTRICITY: 110/220 volts AC, 50Hz.
COMMUNICATIONS: Telephone: IDD is available. Country code: 84. **Fax:** Available in most major offices. **Telex/telegram:** Telex facilities limited to main cities only. Telegram facilities are available in most towns. **Post:** Postal services are extremely limited. Airmail to Europe takes up to a month. **Press:** Daily newspapers in Vietnam include *Hanoi Moi* and *Nhan Dan* ('The People'). No daily English-language newspapers are published.
BBC World Service and Voice of America frequencies: From time to time these change. See the section *How to Use this Book* for more information.

BBC:

MHz	11.955	11.750	9.740	6.195

Voice of America:

MHz	15.43	11.72	5.985	1.143

PASSPORT/VISA

Regulations and requirements may be subject to change at short notice, and you are advised to contact the appropriate diplomatic or consular authority before finalising travel arrangements. Details of these may be found at the head of this country's entry. Any numbers in the chart refer to the footnotes below.

	Passport Required?	Visa Required?	Return Ticket Required?
Full British	Yes	Yes	Yes
BVP	Not valid	-	-
Australian	Yes	Yes	Yes
Canadian	Yes	Yes	Yes
USA	Yes	Yes	Yes
Other EC	Yes	Yes	Yes
Japanese	Yes	Yes	Yes

PASSPORTS: Valid passport required by all.
British Visitors Passport: Not acceptable.
VISAS: Required by all. At the present time visas can be issued for either groups or individuals.
Types of visa: Tourist, Entry, Transit and Multiple entry. Cost: *Tourist*: £15; *Entry*: £20; *Multiple entry*: £45; and *Transit*: £10.
Validity: 1 month. Visas can usually be extended for another month at an extra cost of £10, but this must be done within Vietnam and is most easily achieved in Ho Chi Minh City, Nha Trang or Hué.
Application to: Consulate (or Consular Section at Embassy). Applications can also be made through *Regent Holidays* (address at beginning of entry).
Application requirements: (a) 3 completed application forms. (b) 3 photos. (c) Valid passport. (d) Fee (once application has been approved). (e) For postal applications, a registered, stamped self-addressed envelope.
Working days required: 4 days.

MONEY

Currency: New Dong (D) = 10 hao = 100 xu. Notes are in denominations of D10,000, 5000, 2000, 1000, 500, 100 and 50. Coins are in denominations of D5 and 1.
Currency exchange: The US Dollar is the most favoured foreign currency; indeed certain payments may only be made in this form. It is therefore advisable to carry US Dollars in small denominations. British, Australian, Japanese, French and German currency can usually be changed in Ho Chi Minh City and Hanoi; great difficulty may be encountered in trying to exchange any other currencies.
Credit cards: Some hotels and restaurants in Ho Chi Minh City and Hanoi accept Visa and Mastercard. Check with your credit card company for details for merchant acceptability and other services which may be available.
Travellers cheques: US currency cheques may be accepted.
Exchange rate indicators: The following figures are included as a guide to the movements of the New Dong against Sterling and the US Dollar:

Date:	Oct '89	Oct '90	Oct '91	Oct '92
£1.00=	7114	12,099	18,730	17,198
$1.00=	4505	6193	10,792	10,837

Currency restrictions: Import and export of local currency is prohibited. Import of foreign currency is unlimited subject to declaration. Export of foreign currency is limited to amount declared on arrival.

DUTY FREE

Duty-free regulations are subject to frequent amendment; check with the Embassy prior to departure. At the time of going to press, the following could be freely imported to Vietnam by foreign visitors:
200 cigarettes and 50 cigars or 250g of loose tobacco;
1 bottle of spirits;
A reasonable quantity of perfume.
Prohibited items: The importation of non-prescribed drugs, firearms and pornography (including 'Playboy' etc) is prohibited.

PUBLIC HOLIDAYS

Public holidays observed in Vietnam, are as follows:
Apr 7 '93 Emperor-Founder Hung Vuong. **Apr 30** Liberation of Saigon. **May 1** May Day. **Sep 2-3** National Day. **Jan 1 '94** New Year's Day. **Jan/Feb [1]** Têt, Lunar New Year (three days) [1].
Note [1]: Check with Embassy for the exact date. Visitors may experience difficulties during this period as shops, restaurants and public services close and prices tend to go up in the few shops that remain open.

HEALTH

Regulations and requirements may be subject to change at short notice, and you are advised to contact your doctor well in advance of your intended date of departure. Any numbers in the chart refer to the footnotes below.

	Special Precautions?	Certificate Required?
Yellow Fever	No	1
Cholera	Yes	2
Typhoid & Polio	Yes	-
Malaria	3	-
Food & Drink	4	-

[1]: A yellow fever vaccination certificate is required from travellers over one year of age arriving from infected areas.
[2]: Following WHO guidelines issued in 1973, a cholera vaccination certificate is not an official condition of entry to Vietnam. However, cholera is a serious risk in this country and precautions are essential. Up-to-date advice should be sought before deciding whether these precautions should include vaccination, as medical opinion is divided over its effectiveness. See the *Health* section at the back of the book.
[3]: Malaria risk exists throughout the year everywhere except urban areas and the river deltas. The benign *vivax* form is predominant in the northern provinces. The malignant *falciparum* form is reported to be 'highly resistant' to chloroquine and 'resistant' to sulfadoxine-pyrimethamine.
[4]: All water should be regarded as being potentially contaminated. Water used for drinking, brushing teeth or making ice should have first been boiled or otherwise sterilised. Milk is unpasteurised and should be boiled. Powdered or tinned milk is available and is advised, but make sure that it is reconstituted with pure water. Avoid dairy products which are likely to have been made from unboiled milk. Only eat well-cooked meat and fish, preferably served hot. Pork, salad and mayonnaise may carry increased risk. Vegetables should be cooked and fruit peeled.
Rabies is present. For those at high risk, vaccination before arrival should be considered. If you are bitten abroad seek medical advice without delay. For more information consult the *Health* section at the back of the book.
Bilharzia (schistosomiasis) is present in the delta of the Mekong River. Avoid swimming and paddling in fresh water. Swimming pools which are chlorinated and well-maintained are safe.
Japanese encephalitis is a risk between June and October, particularly in rural areas. A vaccine is available and travellers are advised to consult their doctors prior to departure.
Plague is present in natural foci. Further information should be sought from the Department of Health or from any of the hospitals specialising in tropical diseases listed in the *Health* section at the back of this book.
Health care: There are hospitals in major towns and cities and health care centres in all provinces but everywhere facilities are limited. Health insurance is essential and should include cover for emergency repatriation by air.

TRAVEL - International

AIR: Vietnam's national airline is *Hang Khong Vietnam (VN)*. However, its flights can only be booked in person from within Vietnam. Foreign visitors can book flights on *Thai Airways, Air France, Garuda Indonesia,*

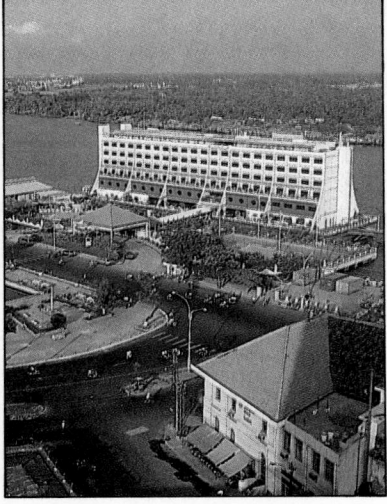

Lufthansa, Malaysian Airlines System and, to some extent, *Aeroflot*. The most usual routes to Vietnam are via Bangkok, Jakarta, Manila and Singapore.
Approximate flight time: From *London* to Hanoi via Bangkok is 17 hours, including 2 hours stopover.
International airports: *Thu Do International Airport (HAN)* at Noi Bai is 45km (28 miles) from Hanoi. Buses and a few taxis are available.
Tan Son Nhat International Airport airport is 7km (4.5 miles) from Ho Chi Minh City. Buses and a few taxis are available.
Departure tax: US$6.
SEA: The major ports are Ho Chi Minh City, Haiphong, Da Nang and Ben Thuy. There are no passenger ships available.
RAIL: There are two rail crossings to the People's Republic of China but they are unlikely to be open for regular traffic; check with Embassy for up-to-date information.
ROAD: There are routes from China and Laos but access is likely to be restricted. Contact the Embassy for details.

TRAVEL - Internal

Note: It is necessary to have a permit to travel outside Hanoi or Ho Chi Minh City for more than a day. These are issued to groups through travel agents; the permit must state all the towns on the itinerary. There are heavy fines for those caught without a permit or in a town not included in the itinerary.
AIR: *Hang Khong Vietnam* operates regular services between Hanoi, Ho Chi Minh City and seven other cities, including Da Nang, Hué and Haiphong.
SEA: A local network operates between ports. Contact the Embassy before departure.
RAIL: Visitors may use the rail transport system independently or as part of a rail tour. This can be arranged by *Regent Holidays* (address at beginning of entry). Long-distance trains are more expensive but are faster, more reliable and more comfortable.
ROAD: There is a reasonable road network. **Bus:** Services are poor and overcrowded. **Car hire:** It is possible to hire chauffeur-driven cars through *Regent Holidays* and this is probably the best way to travel and see the country. Payment must be in US Dollars and bargaining is advised. **Documentation:** An International Driving Permit is required.
URBAN: There are local bus services in Ho Chi Minh City and in Hanoi, which also has a tramway.
TOURS: Regular trips to Vietnam are organised by *Orbittours* and *Regent Holidays* (see top of entry for addresses).

ACCOMMODATION

Tourist facilities are limited but most towns have small hotels and guest-houses. The Rex Hotel in Ho Chi Minh City has conference and convention facilities. All hotels are government-owned. Although it is now possible for individual tourists to visit Vietnam, group travel remains the norm and groups often enjoy substantial discounts at hotels and elsewhere.

RESORTS & EXCURSIONS

The capital **Hanoi,** with its port **Haiphong,** sprawls on the banks of the Red River. Historic buildings, with their colonial yellow stucco facades, line the wide boulevards leading to the many lakes in the confines of the city. In the centre of the city lies the peaceful *Hoan Kiem Lake* (Lake of the Restored Sword) with the 18th-century *Ngoc Son (Jade Mountain) Temple* sitting on an island in the middle of the lake. The temple is accessible by *The Huc (Rising Sun) Bridge*, built in the 19th century and painted red. *Dong Xuan Market*, just north of the central lake, is well worth visiting for its unique collection of goods, from traditional medicines to myna birds. South of the market is the *Old Quarter* and the *Citadel* (now a military area), and west of the Citadel is Hanoi's most popular attraction, the *Ho Chi Minh Mausoleum*. Strict regulations and conduct are enforced on viewing, from the prohibition of cameras, shorts, T-shirts and hats to demands that a respectful countenance be held at all times. Putting one's hands in one's pockets is severely forbidden. His house, built in 1958, can also be seen. Museums in Hanoi include the *History Museum (Bao Tang Lich Su)*, the *Army Museum (Bao Tang Quan Doi)*, *Ho Chi Minh Museum*, *Fine Arts Museum (Bao Tang My Thuat)*, *Revolutionary Museum (Bao Tang Cach Manh)* and *Independence Museum*. Just outside of Hanoi, *Co Loa Citadel*, the first fortified citadel built in Vietnam in the 3rd century BC, is worth visiting.
To the south lies the city of **Hué**. The former capital of the emperors of Vietnam, it is known for its beautiful and picturesque architecture. The *River of Perfumes* forms the border between the city itself and the former 'Forbidden City', the mighty *Citadel*. Today, the visitor can admire this 'city within a city' with its tombs, pagodas and lakes covered in lotus flowers. Within easy reach of the city are the tombs of several of Vietnam's emperors. Well worth a visit is the *Tomb of Minh Mang* and the *Tomb of Tu Duc*. The city also houses fine examples of Buddhist pagodas and other temples, such as the *Thien Mu Pagoda*.
Set back from the delta formed by the Mekong River, **Ho Chi Minh City** (formerly Saigon) is the main commercial centre of the southern part of Vietnam, receiving its name in honour of the revolutionary Ho Chi Minh. Predominantly more modern than other Vietnamese cities, Ho Chi Minh City has retained its French colonial influences. Cafés and shops are part of the ever-changing image of the city. The colourful *Emperor of Jade Pagoda* is an excellent example of a Chinese temple. Inside, there are elaborate woodcarvings decorated with gilded characters and sculptures depicting local deities. The hustle and bustle of trading is best observed on *Ben Thanh Market* where everything that might be useful can be bought. Vegetables, fruit, clothes, household items and food are piled on the numerous stalls. 17km from Ho Chi Minh City is the *Artex Orchid Farm*. January and February form the height of the blooming season.

SOCIAL PROFILE

FOOD: Normal fare is a rather bland mixture of rice, vegetables and fruit. Seafood is the traditional weekly feast-day meal. For a traditional breakfast try *pho* (noodle soup). Local specialities include *nem* (pork mixed with noodles, eggs and mushrooms wrapped in rice paper, fried and served hot) and *banh chung* (glutinous rice, pork and onions wrapped in large leaves and cooked for up to 48 hours, to be eaten cold at any time). Vietnamese dishes are not complete without *nuoc mam* (a fish sauce) or *mam tom* (a shrimp sauce).
SHOPPING: Local specialities include lacquer painting, reed mats, embroidery, tailor-made *ao dais* (female national costume) and mother-of-pearl inlay on ornaments and furniture. **Shopping hours:** 0800-1900 Monday to Sunday.
SPECIAL EVENTS: Most regions, particularly where the minority groups live, have their own traditional festivals incorporating music, opera and dance. *Têt* (Lunar New Year) and important Buddhist festivals are celebrated during February and March each year. (Although celebrated, Buddhist and Christian festivals are not considered national holidays.)
SOCIAL CONVENTIONS: Handshaking and a vocal greeting is normal. Clothing should be kept simple, informal and discreet. Avoid shorts if possible as they are usually only worn by children. Footwear should be removed when entering Buddhist pagodas. Vietnamese people should not be touched on the head. **Photography:** There are restrictions at ports, airports and harbours, and in similar areas elsewhere. It is courteous to ask permission first before taking photographs of people. **Tipping:** Officially prohibited but widely practised, especially in the south. Discretion is advised.

BUSINESS PROFILE

ECONOMY: The economy of Vietnam was devastated by 30 years of war up to 1975, since when mismanagement and the US boycott have combined to stifle development, although there are now signs of a slow recovery. After the Communist victory in 1975, Vietnam has operated a Soviet-style command economy. However, in the wake of the political and economic upheaval in the Soviet Union and Vietnam's other former allies in COMECON, Vietnam has acted quickly to implement its own form of *perestroika*, known as *doi moi*, with market reforms and privatisation. The Government expects to sell about 500 of the country's main industrial enterprises in the next few years. War damage and the costs of maintaining the world's fourth largest standing army (which has recently disengaged from Cambodia) have also hindered economic development. The two halves of the country have distinct economies. In the south 60% of the labour force is involved in agriculture: the staple crop is rice, although significant amounts of sorghum, maize, cassava, sweet potatoes and fruit are also grown. Recent improvements in harvests have ended Vietnam's occasional reliance on UN food aid earlier in the 1980s, and the country is now virtually self-sufficient in food. The north holds most of the country's natural resources, particularly coal, and is the country's industrial centre. The exception to this pattern is oil, which is believed to be present in some quantity off Vietnam's southern coast and for which exploration licences have recently been granted. Fishing has also grown quickly in recent years with the signing of several co-operative deals with Japanese and other fishing operators. Much of Vietnam's industry was destroyed during the war but the principal industries – food processing, cement, metallurgy, chemicals, textiles and paper – have all recovered to a greater or lesser extent. Inward investment has grown quickly since 1989, however, as Japanese firms move to take advantage of cheap labour in South-East Asia's most populous country. Vietnam-Japan trade has now broken the US$1-billion barrier, making Japan the country's second largest trading partner behind the CIS (which still holds that position despite recent drastic reductions). The continuation of the US embargo still impedes Vietnam's economic development, not so much because of low bilateral economic links but because of US influence in international fora which blocks Vietnamese access to funds from international institutions such as the World Bank and IMF. Among other countries looking at commercial opportunities in Vietnam are Taiwan, China, Hong Kong and Singapore.
BUSINESS: Smart lightweight casuals would usually be worn for meetings as suits are needed for only the most formal occasions. English is not spoken by all officials and a knowledge of French will be useful. Business cards should have a Vietnamese translation on the back.
Office hours: 0730-1200 and 1300-1630 Monday to Saturday.
COMMERCIAL INFORMATION: The following organisation can offer advice: Vietcochamber (Chamber of Industry and Commerce of Vietnam), 33 Ba Trieu, Hanoi. Tel: (4) 52961. Fax: (4) 56446. Telex: 411257.

HISTORY & GOVERNMENT

HISTORY: For many years Vietnam formed part of the French colony of Indochina, along with Cambodia and Laos. With French agreement, the Japanese occupied Vietnam during their Second World War sweep through South-East Asia. Nationalist and revolutionary forces had been actively pursuing complete independence for many years and after the Japanese defeat in 1945 the Communist forces of Ho Chi Minh proclaimed the Democratic Republic of Vietnam. In 1946, France sent a large expeditionary force to re-establish their control; after eight years of fierce fighting, it was finally defeated at the humiliating siege of Dien Bien Phu (1954). The Geneva Agreement of the same year provided for the temporary partition of North and

VIETNAM	HEALTH REGULATIONS	VISA REGULATIONS (Code-Link)
GALILEO/WORLDSPAN	 TI-DFT/HAN/HE	 TI-DFT/HAN/VI
SABRE	 TIDFT/HAN/HE	TIDFT/HAN/VI

To access this information on your CRS, swipe the barcode with a light pen or type in the text under the barcode. For more information, see the introduction *How to Use This Book*.

South, to be re-unified in 1956 following general elections. The elections were not held and hostilities developed into full-scale war in which US troops intervened to back the anti-Communists. The USA withdrew in 1973 and Vietnam was reunified three years later with the victory of the Communist forces and the establishment of the Socialist Republic of Vietnam. The army, the strongest in South-East Asia, has since clashed with Chinese troops and undertaken a full-scale invasion and occupation of Cambodia to drive out the genocidal Khmer Rouge regime. Vietnamese troops finally withdrew from Cambodia in September 1989. Freed of this burden, Vietnam may now (and must) concentrate on rebuilding its own economy, having introduced a home-grown version of perestroika known as 'doi moi'. The withdrawal does not, after all, appear to have brought forward the prospect of Western aid for Vietnam: successive US governments have refused to lift the aid and trade embargo against Vietnam, and pressurised their allies to do the same, although there is hope that the Clinton administration may alter US policy. The other foreign policy issue that has been occupying Nguyen Co Thach and his government has been the negotiations with the British colonial authorities in Hong Kong concerning the future of the illegal immigrants from Vietnam: a provisional agreement involving the return of the migrants to Vietnam was reached in September 1989. The Vietnamese economy has suffered from the withdrawal of aid and subsidised goods from the former USSR and from Eastern Europe. At the 7th Congress of the ruling Communist Party held in June 1991, important changes among the leadership took place (Do Muoi was appointed party General Secretary; Vo Van Kiet Prime Minister). These indicate that the party is determined to pursue a reformist economic programme while keeping many senior military men in key positions (Defence Minister Le Duc Anh is Do Muoi's recognised deputy and army chief of staff; Do An Kue holds the party number five spot). Relations between Vietnam and China have improved following the political settlement in Cambodia in 1991, which was the main foreign issue separating the two sides. Hanoi has had some success with its attempts to improve relations with the Association of South-East Asian Nations and may even join in due course. The Vietnamese have taken the first steps by signing a friendship and co-operation treaty in July 1992. A closer relationship with ASEAN may assist a resolution of the 6-way territorial dispute (involving China, Malaysia, Taiwan, the Philippines and Brunei, as well as Vietnam) over the potentially oil-rich sandbanks known as the Spratly Islands.
GOVERNMENT: The 496-member National Assembly is responsible for legislation. The Assembly is elected every five years by universal adult suffrage from candidates proposed by the Communist Party of Vietnam. Executive power is exercised by the Council of Ministers.

CLIMATE

Tropical monsoons occur from May to October. It is almost totally dry throughout the rest of the year.
Required clothing: Tropicals and washable cottons are worn all year. Rainwear is essential during the rainy season.

HANOI Vietnam (16m)

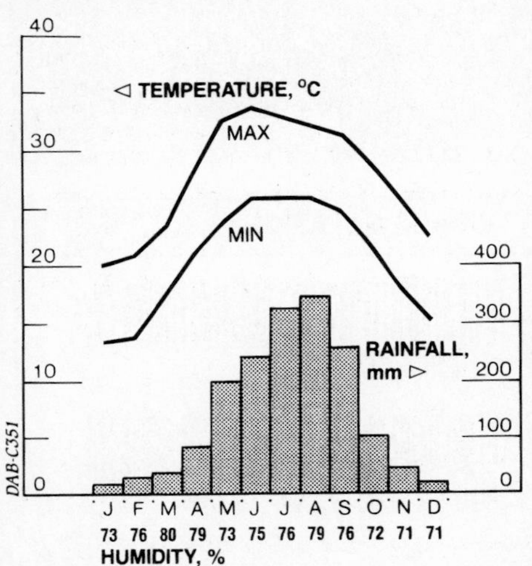

VIRGIN ISLANDS, BRITISH

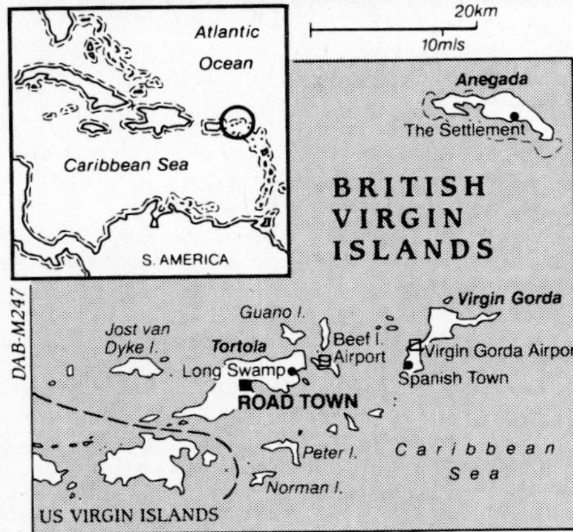

Location: Eastern Caribbean.

Diplomatic representation: The British Virgin Islands are a British Dependent Territory and are represented abroad by British Embassies. Information and advice may be obtained from the addresses below.

British Virgin Islands Tourist Board
PO Box 134
Waterfront Drive
Road Town
Tortola, British Virgin Islands
Tel: 43134. Fax: 43866. Telex: 7968.

Home Office
Clive House
Petty France
London SW1H 9HD
Tel: (071) 279 3434. Opening hours: 0900-1600 Monday to Friday.

British Virgin Islands Tourist Board
110 St Martin's Lane
London WC2N 4DY
Tel: (071) 240 4259. Fax: (071) 240 4270. Opening hours: 0930-1730 Monday to Friday.

British Virgin Islands Tourist Board
Suite 511
370 Lexington Avenue
New York, NY
10017
Tel: (212) 696 0400.
Also in: San Francisco.

AREA: 153 sq km (59 sq miles).
POPULATION: 13,000 (1989 estimate).
POPULATION DENSITY: 85 per sq km.
CAPITAL: Road Town, Tortola. **Population:** 2,500 (1987).
GEOGRAPHY: The British Virgin Islands are an archipelago of more than 40 islands, only 15 of which are inhabited, forming the northern extremity of the Leeward Islands in the eastern Caribbean. The islands are volcanic in origin, with the exception of Anegada, which is formed of coral and limestone and is the lowest lying. The topography is otherwise mountainous, the highest point being Tortola's Sage Mountain, which rises to 550m (1800ft). There are remnants of a primeval rainforest on Tortola.
LANGUAGE: English.
RELIGION: Mainly Methodist and Church of God but also Anglican, Adventist, Baptist and Roman Catholic congregations.
TIME: GMT - 4.
ELECTRICITY: 110/60 volts AC, 60Hz. American 2-pin plugs are used.
COMMUNICATIONS: Telephone: IDD is available. Country code: 1 809 49. There are no area codes. **Fax:** Cable & Wireless provides a service. **Telex/telegram:** Operated by Cable & Wireless. There are limited facilities outside main towns. **Post:** Airmail to Europe takes up to a week. **Press:** *The BVI Beacon* is published weekly.
BBC World Service and Voice of America frequencies: From time to time these change. See the section *How to Use this Book* for more information.

BBC:				
MHz	17.840	15.220	9.915	5.975
Voice of America:				
MHz	15.21	11.70	6.130	0.930

PASSPORT/VISA

Regulations and requirements may be subject to change at short notice, and you are advised to contact the appropriate diplomatic or consular authority before finalising travel arrangements. Details of these may be found at the head of this country's entry. Any numbers in the chart refer to the footnotes below.

	Passport Required?	Visa Required?	Return Ticket Required?
Full British	Yes	No	Yes
BVP	Not valid	-	-
Australian	Yes	No	Yes
Canadian	No	No	Yes
USA	No	No	Yes
Other EC	Yes	1	Yes
Japanese	Yes	Yes	Yes

PASSPORTS: Valid passport required by all except nationals of the USA and Canada in possession of recognised form of identity.
British Visitors Passport: Not acceptable.
VISAS: Required by all except:
(a) nationals of countries referred to in the chart above;
(b) **[1]** nationals of EC countries (except nationals of Ireland and Portugal who *do* require visas). Nationals of Germany for up to 1 month;
(c) nationals of Venezuela for stays of up to 1 month;
(d) nationals of Commonwealth countries;
(e) nationals of Finland, Iceland, Liechtenstein, Norway, San Marino, Sweden, Switzerland, Tunisia, Turkey and Uruguay, providing they are in possession of a confirmed return or onward travel document, have sufficient funds for support and pre-arranged accommodation.
Types of visa: Tourist, Business and Transit; fees vary according to nationality. Transit visas are not required by those with confirmed tickets for onward travel within 14 days of arrival; this facility is not available to nationals of Eastern bloc countries, who *do* require Transit visas for stays of less than 14 days (and Business/Tourist visas for longer stays).
Application to: The Home Office (address at top of entry) or the nearest British Consulate or Embassy.
Application requirements: (a) Application form. (b) Photo. (c) Valid passport. (d) Proof of sufficient funds to cover stay.
Working days required: Varies according to nationality of applicant.
Temporary residence: Work permit and residence permit required.

MONEY

Currency: US Dollar (US$) = 100 cents. Notes are in denominations of US$100, 50, 20, 10, 5, 2 and 1. Coins are in denominations of US$1, and 50, 25, 10, 5 and 1 cents.
Credit cards: American Express, Diners Club and Visa have limited acceptance. Check with your credit card company for details of merchant acceptability and other services which may be available.
Travellers cheques: Widely accepted, particularly US Dollar cheques. All cheques are liable to a 10% stamp duty. Personal cheques are not accepted.
Exchange rate indicators: The following figures are included as a guide to the movements of the US Dollar against Sterling:

Date:	**Oct '89**	**Oct '90**	**Oct '91**	**Oct '92**
£1.00=	1.57	1.95	1.73	1.59

Currency restrictions: The import of local and foreign currency is unlimited, subject to declaration. The export of foreign and local currency is restricted to the amount declared on import.
Banking hours: 0900-1400 Monday to Thursday, 0900-1400 and 1600-1800 Friday.

DUTY FREE

There is no limit on the quantity of consumable items which can be imported for personal use, though these are subject to duty, applied at varying rates. Some non-consumable items may be imported on a non-permanent basis free from duty, while certain items will require a 'good faith bond'. For details about specific items, contact the Tourist Board.

PUBLIC HOLIDAYS

Public holidays observed in the British Virgin Islands are as follows:

Mar 8 '93 Commonwealth Day. **Apr 9-12** Easter. **May 31** Whit Monday. **Jun 7** Queen's Official Birthday. **Jul 1** Territory Day. **Aug 2-4** August Monday, Tuesday and Wednesday. **Oct 21** St Ursula's Day. **Nov 14** Prince of Wales' Birthday. **Dec 25-26** Christmas. **Jan 1 '94** New Year's Day. **Mar** Commonwealth Day.

HEALTH

Regulations and requirements may be subject to change at short notice, and you are advised to contact your doctor well in advance of your intended date of departure. Any numbers in the chart refer to the footnotes below.

	Special Precautions?	Certificate Required?
Yellow Fever	No	No
Cholera	No	No
Typhoid & Polio	Yes	-
Malaria	No	-
Food & Drink	1	-

[1]: Mains water is normally chlorinated, and whilst relatively safe may cause mild abdominal upsets. Bottled water is available and is advised for the first few weeks of the stay. Milk is pasteurised and dairy products are safe for consumption. Local meat, poultry, seafood, fruit and vegetables are generally considered safe to eat.
Health care: Health insurance is recommended. There are good medical facilities on Tortola and six clinics on the other islands.

TRAVEL - International

AIR: The British Virgin Islands' national airline is *Air BVI (BL)*. Correspondence should be addressed to the Tourist Board (see top of entry for address).
Approximate flight time: From *London* to Beef Island or Virgin Gorda is 10 hours, including stopover time in Antigua or San Juan.
International airports: *Beef Island (EIS)* is 14.5km (9 miles) from Road Town on Tortola (travel time – 30 minutes). Taxis are available and there is a bar/restaurant.
Virgin Gorda (VIJ) is 5km (3 miles) from Spanish Town on Virgin Gorda. Taxis are available.
There is also an airport on the island of *Anegada.*
Departure tax: US$5 for all international departures.
SEA: The British Virgin Islands' four main ports of entry are Bellamy Cay, Beef Island and Spanish Town on Tortola as well as the Yacht Harbour on Virgin Gorda. *Commodore Cruises* and *Charger Inc* sail regularly from both Tortola and Virgin Gorda to all the US Virgin Islands.
Departure tax: US$4 for all international departures.

TRAVEL - Internal

AIR: *Air BVI (BL)* offers regular shuttle services to Virgin Gorda, Tortola and Anegada. It is also possible to charter planes for island hopping.
SEA: Yacht charter is one of the major industries and *Bareboats* can be hired for all cruises. A permit is required for all charter boat passengers. Local boats can be hired for special tours and ferry services can be arranged, given adequate notice. The high season is from December to April. For current prices and a full list of boats for charter and hire, contact the Tourist Board.
ROAD: There is a good network. Driving is on the left and there is a maximum speed limit of 30mph (48kmph) throughout all the islands. **Taxi:** The BVI Taxi Association operates a wide range of vehicles on a range of standard journeys at fixed rates. All drivers are capable tour guides. Taxis can also be hired on an hourly or daily basis. **Car hire:** There are nine car hire companies in the British Virgin Islands. **Documentation:** A temporary British Virgin Islands licence is required; this will be issued on production of a current foreign licence for US$10. Insurance and British Virgin Islands licences are available from rental companies.
JOURNEY TIMES: The following chart gives approximate journey times (in hours and minutes) from Beef Island, Tortola to other major destinations in the British Virgin Islands and the surrounding area.

	Air	Road	Sea
Virgin Gorda	0.05	0.30	-
Peter Is.	-	-	0.35
Guano Is.		-	0.20
Jost van Dyke	0.55	-	-
St Thomas	0.15	0.55	-
San Juan (PR)	0.45	-	-

Note: PR = Puerto Rico; USVI = US Virgin Islands.

ACCOMMODATION

HOTELS: A wide range of hotel accommodation is available; a full list can be obtained from the Tourist Board (addresses at beginning of entry). There is a 7% hotel accommodation tax added to all hotel bills. For further information contact the British Virgin Islands Hotel and Commerce Association, PO Box 376, Wickham's Cay, Road Town, Tortola. Tel: 46179. **Grading:** Though there is no grading structure, many hotels in the Caribbean offer accommodation according to one of a number of plans: **FAP** is **Full American Plan**; room with all meals (including afternoon tea, supper etc). **AP** is **American Plan**; room with three meals. **MAP** is **Modified American Plan**; breakfast and dinner included with the price of the room plus, in some places, British-style afternoon tea. **CP** is **Continental Plan**; room and breakfast only. **EP** is **European Plan**; room only.
SELF-CATERING: Villas, houses and cottages can be hired on a weekly or longer basis. Information on properties is available from the Tourist Board.
CAMPING: Only permitted on authorised sites. Details of sites and facilities are available from the Tourist Board. Backpacking is actively discouraged.

RESORTS & EXCURSIONS

There are more than 40 islands in the archipelago but only 15 are inhabited. All of them, apart from Anegada, are volcanic in origin. In general the atmosphere is quiet and uncommercialised, with miles of beautiful unspoilt beaches and concealed bays offering privacy and peace. The islands are situated in one of the finest sailing areas in the world. The scenery ranges from jagged mountain peaks covered with frangipani to banana and mango groves and palm trees.
Tortola, with a population of about 9000, is the largest island of the group. It is linked by a bridge to **Beef Island**, site of the international airport. **Road Town,** on the south coast of Tortola, is the capital of the British Virgin Islands. It has a colourful market and delightful West Indian-style houses.
The 'Bomba Charger', hydrofoil runs between Tortola and Virgin Gorda or St Thomas (US Virgin Islands). A submarine, the Aqua Sub, gives tourists a unique opportunity to view marine life without getting wet. Tortola is a major yachting centre.
Many of the best beaches are on the northern part of the island, with names such as *Smugglers' Cove, Long Bay, Cane Garden Bay* and *Brewer's Bay*. There is an excellent view of the island and its coast from **Mount Sage,** 550m (1800ft) above sea level.
Other islands worth visiting are the coral island of **Anegada; Salt Island,** where salt is harvested each year and a bag sent to HRH Queen Elizabeth II; **Norman Island,** with caves and a wealth of local sea-shanties and tales of treasure; and **Virgin Gorda**. Here may be found the famous *Baths*, a unique rock formation of dimly-lit grottoes and caves. Most of its attractions can be reached only by foot or boat. The smaller islands have strange names that are often the result of a historical connection with smuggling and piracy – for example, *Fallen Jerusalem, Necker Island* (owned by Richard Branson), *Great Camanoe, Great Dogs* and *Ginger Island.*

SOCIAL PROFILE

FOOD & DRINK: There is no shortage of excellent restaurants and inns serving local and international dishes. Food is imported but local island specialities are often available. These include lobster and fish *chowder*, mussel pie, conch stew, shark and other fish delicacies. In addition to the hotels, eating places can be found on Tortola, Virgin Gorda and Jost van Dyke. All kinds of rum punch and cocktails are served, plus a wide selection of imported beers, wines and spirits.
NIGHTLIFE: Many hotels have special nights with live music or dancing. There is one cinema (on Tortola) and several low-key nightclubs and discotheques. The Tourist Board publishes details of all forthcoming events.
SHOPPING: Special purchases include carved wooden items, straw-work, jewellery made from conch (pronounced 'konk') shell, seeds and very attractive *batik* material, designed and made locally.
SPORT: Sailing: Amongst the best in the Caribbean. There are numerous modern marinas and the Yacht Club in Road Town, Tortola organises races and regattas and offers instruction in sailing and navigation. **Fishing:**

VIRGIN ISLANDS, BRITISH | **HEALTH REGULATIONS** | **VISA REGULATIONS** | Code-Link

GALILEO/WORLDSPAN

TI-DFT/TOV/HE

TI-DFT/TOV/VI

SABRE

TIDFT/TOV/HE

TIDFT/TOV/VI

To access this information on your CRS, swipe the barcode with a light pen or type in the text under the barcode. For more information, see the introduction *How to Use This Book.*

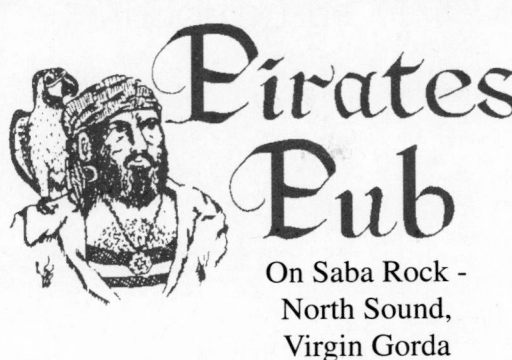

Charters can be arranged for offshore fishing trips.
Diving: The clear waters provide ideal diving conditions and qualified instructors are available. The wreck of HMS Rhone off Salt Island is a favourite diving location.
Tennis: There are numerous courts on Tortola; those on Virgin Gorda are for hotel guests only.
SPECIAL EVENTS: Events likely to be of interest to the visitor include the *Spring Regatta* in Sir Francis Drake's Channel and the *Carnival* at the beginning of August. For further details contact the Tourist Board.
SOCIAL CONVENTIONS: The British Virgin Islands remain linked to the British Commonwealth and the islanders reflect many British traditions and customs. The development of tourism proceeds with great caution; hence the unspoilt charm of these islands and cays remains the chief attraction. The pace of life is very easy-going and the visitor can expect good manners and old fashioned British courtesies everywhere. Shaking hands is the customary form of greeting. Dress is informal for most occasions apart from the formal requirements of Little Dix Bay. Beachwear should be confined to the beach. **Tipping:** All hotels add a 10-12% service charge.

BUSINESS PROFILE

ECONOMY: Tourism is the islands' main economic activity. The number of visitors has steadily risen throughout the mid- and late 1980s, mostly coming from the USA. Agricultural production is limited by poor soils, but some fruit and vegetables are produced for export, along with fish, livestock, gravel and sand. The largest export, however, is rum. The largest market for all these products is the USA. The British Virgin Islands import most of their foodstuffs and consumer goods from the US Virgin Islands, the USA itself, Puerto Rico, the UK and Europe. The whole economy suffered a dip at the end of 1989 following widespread damage caused by Hurricane Hugo but the islands recovered with remarkable speed; production, exports and growth have all now returned to their earlier levels. A burgeoning offshore financial sector has been operating since the mid-1980s and has proved to be a spectacular success by virtue of the British connection and a benign piece of customised legislation (the 1984 International Business Companies Ordinance) designed to assist offshore activities. Many companies formerly registered in Panama have moved to the islands since the US invasion of that country in 1990. Annual GDP growth reached 15% during the late 1980s.
BUSINESS: A shirt and tie are required for the summer months, with lightweight suits being acceptable at all other times. Best time to visit is April to October. **Office hours:** 0830-1700 Monday to Friday. **Government office hours:** 0830-1630 Monday to Friday.
COMMERCIAL INFORMATION: The following organisation can offer advice: Development Bank of the British Virgin Islands, PO Box 275, Wickhams Cay 1, Road Town, Tortola. Tel: 43737.

HISTORY & GOVERNMENT

HISTORY: The islands were annexed by the British in 1672. Two hundred years later, they were incorporated into the British colony of the Leeward Islands. The Governor of the Leewards continued to run the Virgin Islands until 1960, when direct responsibility was assumed by an appointed Administrator (retitled Governor in 1971). Party politics are dominated by two main parties, the Virgin Islands' Party (VIP) and the United Party (UP), but because there are only nine elected members (out of 11) on the ruling Legislative Council, the balance of power has often been held by independents. In August 1986, the Legislative Council was dissolved by the Governor shortly before a scheduled debate on a motion of 'no confidence' in the then Chief Minister. Elections the following month produced a majority for the VIP and led to VIP leader Lavity Stoutt being appointed Chief Minister for his third term since 1967. The principal political concern in recent years has been the growing traffic in, and local use of, illegal drugs. This has led to at least one high-level investigation conducted jointly by British police and the US Drug Enforcement Administration. The islands' government has since, with British assistance, established air and maritime surveillance systems to combat the traffickers and introduced legislation to curtail their use of the Virgin Islands. Stoutt was returned for yet another term at the November 1990 general election; the VIP gained one seat and now holds six out of the Legislative Council's nine elected seats.
GOVERNMENT: The present constitution, introduced in 1967 and amended ten years later, allows for a large measure of internal self-government. Nine of the 11 members of the Legislative Council are elected. The Executive Council is composed of the Chief Minister and three other ministers, all of whom are chosen from the Legislative Council, plus the Governor and the Attorney-General. The Governor is appointed from London and is responsible for defence, foreign affairs and internal security.

CLIMATE

The climate is tropical, tempered by trade winds. There is little variation between summer and winter. Rainfall is low, varying slightly from island to island. Night-time temperatures drop to a comfortable level.
Required clothing: Tropical lightweights. Dress is generally informal but beachwear is confined to beaches.

ROAD TOWN Virgin Is.,UK

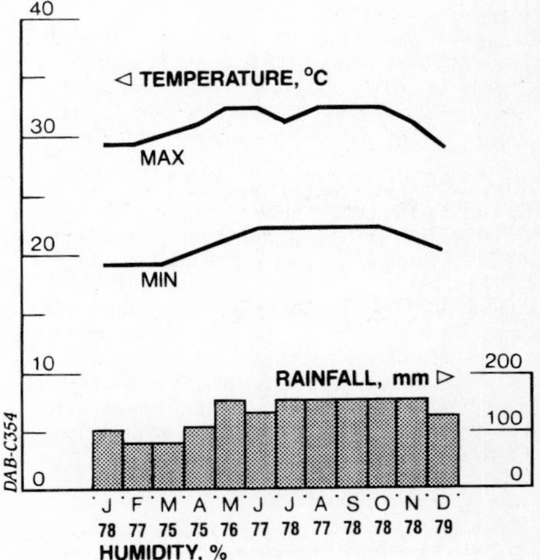

WESTERN SAMOA

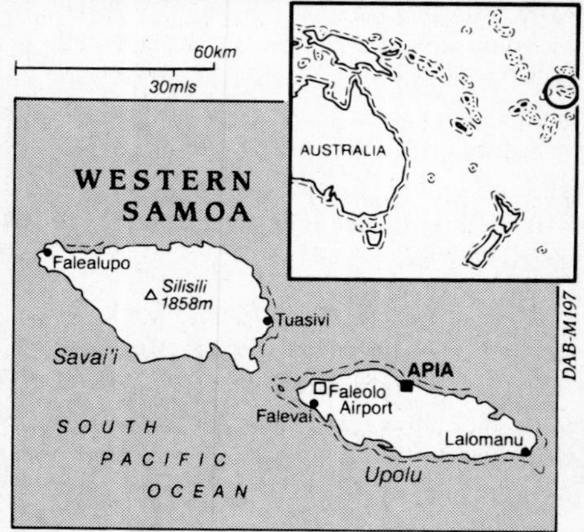

Location: South Pacific.

Western Samoan Visitors' Bureau
PO Box 2272
Apia, Western Samoa
Tel: 20878. Fax: 20886.
Embassy of Western Samoa
avenue Franklin D Roosevelt 123
B-1050 Brussels, Belgium
Tel: (2) 660 8454. Fax: (2) 675 0336. Telex: 2567.
Tourism Council of the South Pacific
52-4 High Holborn
London WC1V 6RB
Tel: (071) 242 3131. Fax: (071) 242 2838. Telex: 23770.
Office of the Honorary British Representative
PO Box 2029
c/o Apia Kruse Va'ai and Barlow
Apia, Western Samoa
Tel: 21895. Fax: 21407.
Embassy of Western Samoa
Suite 510
1155 15th Street, NW
Washington, DC
20005
Tel: (202) 833 1743. Fax: (202) 833 1746.
Embassy of the United States of America
PO Box 3430
Apia, Western Samoa
Tel: 21613. Fax: 22030. Telex: 779275 AMEMBSX.
Western Samoan Mission to the United Nations
Suite 800D
820 Second Avenue
New York, NY
10017
Tel: (212) 599 6196. Fax: (212) 972 3970.
Also deals with enquiries from Canada.
The Canadian High Commission in New Zealand deals with enquiries relating to Western Samoa:
Canadian High Commission
PO Box 12049
61 Molesworth Street
Thorndon
Wellington, New Zealand
Tel: (4) 473 9577. Fax: (4) 471 2082. Telex: 3577 CANAD NZ.

AREA: 2831 sq km (1093 sq miles).
POPULATION: 160,000 (1991).
POPULATION DENSITY: 56.2 per sq km.
CAPITAL: Apia (Upolu Island). **Population:** 36,000 (1984).
GEOGRAPHY: Western Samoa consists of nine islands. The largest of these is Savai'i, which covers 1610 sq km (622 sq miles); fertile Upolu, the second-largest (1120 sq km/433 sq miles), lies 13km (8 miles) to the southeast across the Apolima Strait. The islands are quiescent volcanoes and reach heights of up to 1857m (6094ft) on Savai'i and 1100m (3608ft) on Upolu. Volcanic activity has not occurred since 1911. The main city, Apia, is located in the north of Upolu.
LANGUAGE: Samoan is the national language. In business and commerce English is customary.
RELIGION: Congregational Church, Roman Catholic, Methodist and Latter Day Saints.
TIME: GMT - 11.
ELECTRICITY: 110 volts AC, 60Hz.
COMMUNICATIONS: Telephone: Ingoing IDD is available, but all calls out of Western Samoa must be made through the international operator. Country code: 685. There are no area codes. **Fax:** Services are available from the telegraph office above the post office. There are hotels with facilities. **Telex/telegram:** Available from the telegraph office above the post office. Also in main towns and at major hotels. **Post:** The main post office is open from 0900-1200 and 1300-1630 Monday to Friday. Airmail to Europe takes about three weeks. **Press:** The main newspapers are *The Observer* and *The Samoa Times*.
BBC World Service and Voice of America frequencies: From time to time these change. See the section *How to Use this Book* for more information.

BBC:				
MHz	17.10	15.36	9.740	7.150
Voice of America:				
MHz	18.82	15.18	9.525	1.735

PASSPORT/VISA

Regulations and requirements may be subject to change at short notice, and you are advised to contact the appropriate diplomatic or consular authority before finalising travel arrangements. Details of these may be found at the head of this country's entry. Any numbers in the chart refer to the footnotes below.

	Passport Required?	Visa Required?	Return Ticket Required?
Full British	Yes	No	Yes
BVP	Not Valid	-	-
Australian	Yes	No	Yes
Canadian	Yes	No	Yes
USA	Yes	No	Yes
Other EC	Yes	No	Yes
Japanese	Yes	No	Yes

PASSPORTS: Required by all. Passports must be valid 6 months beyond the intended stay in Western Samoa.
British Visitors Passport: Not accepted.
VISAS: Not required for visits up to a maximum of 30 days provided the visitor holds confirmed onward travel documentation and a valid passport. For longer stays, visas should be obtained before arrival.
Types of visa: Tourist or Business; cost – £3.
Application to: The Immigration Division of the Ministry of Foreign Affairs in Apia (PO Box L1861), or any Western Samoan, New Zealand or British Consulate, Embassy or High Commission.
Working days required: Apply at least 2 months in advance.
Temporary residence: Not considered.

MONEY

Currency: Western Samoa Dollar or Tala (S$) = 100 sene. Notes are in denominations of S$100, 50, 20, 10, 5 and 2. Coins are in denominations of S$1, and 50, 20, 10, 5, 2 and 1 sene.
Currency exchange: Available at the airport or through trade banks.
Credit cards: Access/Mastercard is accepted on a limited basis. Check with your credit card company for details of merchant acceptability and other services which may be available.
Travellers cheques: Accepted in major hotels, banks and tourist shops.
Exchange rate indicators: The following figures are included as a guide to the movements of the Western Samoa Dollar against Sterling and the US Dollar:

Date:	Oct '89	Oct '90	Oct '91	Oct '92
£1.00=	3.60	4.54	4.15	3.88
$1.00=	2.28	2.33	2.39	2.45

Currency restrictions: There are no restrictions on the import and export of either local or foreign currency.
Banking hours: 0900-1500 Monday to Friday; some banks open 0830-1230 Saturday.

DUTY FREE

The following items may be imported into Western Samoa without incurring customs duty:
200 cigarettes or 50 cigars or 680g of tobacco;
750ml of spirits.
Prohibited items: Firearms, ammunition, explosives, non-prescribed drugs and indecent publications. Live animals and plants (including seeds, fruit, soil, etc) may not be imported without prior permission from the Director of Agriculture, Apia (PO Box 206).

PUBLIC HOLIDAYS

Public holidays observed in Western Samoa are as follows:
Apr 9-12 '93 Easter. **Apr 25** Anzac Day. **May 31** Whit Monday. **Jun 1-3** Independence Holiday. **Nov 25** National Women's Day. **Dec 25** Christmas Day. **Dec 26** Boxing Day. **Jan 1-2 '94** New Year's Day.

HEALTH

Regulations and requirements may be subject to change at short notice, and you are advised to contact your doctor well in advance of your intended date of departure. Any numbers in the chart refer to the footnotes below.

	Special Precautions?	Certificate Required?
Yellow Fever	No	1
Cholera	No	No
Typhoid & Polio	Yes	-
Malaria	No	-
Food & Drink	2	-

[1]: A yellow fever vaccination certificate is required from travellers over one year of age if arriving six days after leaving or transiting an infected area.
[2]: Mains water is normally chlorinated, and whilst relatively safe may cause mild abdominal upsets. Bottled water is available and is advised for the first few weeks of the stay. Drinking water outside main cities and towns may be contaminated and sterilisation is advisable. Milk is pasteurised and dairy products are safe for consumption. Local meat, poultry, seafood, fruit and vegetables are generally considered safe to eat.
Health care: Health insurance is recommended. Emergency medical facilities are available at Apia General Hospital. Private medical and dental treatment are also available. There are over 30 district hospitals and medical centres.

TRAVEL - International

AIR: Western Samoa's national airline is *Polynesian Airways (PH)*. Others operating to the islands are *Air Pacific, Air New Zealand, Air Nauru* and *Hawaiian Airlines*. *Polynesian Airways* offer a 'Polypass' which allows the holder to fly anywhere on the airline's network: Sydney (Australia), Auckland (New Zealand), Western Samoa, American Samoa, Cook Islands, Vanuatu, New Caledonia, Fiji and, on payment of a supplement, Tahiti. The pass is valid for 30 days.
Approximate flight time: From *London* to Apia is 26 hours 30 minutes, excluding stopover time in Honolulu but including stopover in Pago Pago (American Samoa). There are two direct flights a week from Honolulu, four from Auckland, one from Sydney, two from Tonga, two from Suva and six from Pago Pago.
International airport: *Apia (APW)* (Faleolo) is 34km (21 miles) from the capital (travel time – 40 minutes). Airport facilities include banks/bureaux de change, post office (0800-1630 Monday to Friday), duty-free shop and car rental (*Budget* and national firms). Buses and taxis operate to the city.
Departure tax: S$20. Transit passengers and children under two years are exempt.
SEA: The international port is Apia, on Upolu. It is served by both cargo and passenger ships from New Zealand, Australia, Japan, Europe and the USA. There is also a thrice-weekly ferry service from Pago Pago on American Samoa.

TRAVEL - Internal

AIR: *Polynesian Airways (PH)* operates daily flights from Apia or Faleolo on Upolu to Asau and Maota on Savai'i. Charter and sightseeing flights are available.
SEA: There are passenger/vehicle ferries between Upolu (Apia) and Savai'i (travel time – 90 minutes).
ROAD: Traffic drives on the right. **Buses:** Public transport covers most of the islands. There are no timetables; policemen at the New Market Bus Stand in Apia have information on bus departures. **Taxis:** Cheap and readily available in Apia. They are not metered and prices should be negotiated in advance. **Car hire:** Available from several agencies. Deposit and insurance are usually required. The Transport Ministry issues a local licence for a small fee. **Bicycles** and **motor scooters** are also available.
Documentation: An international driving licence for drivers over 21 years; or a valid national licence.

ACCOMMODATION

There is a government-backed programme to improve and extend facilities for visitors. In recent years new

hotels and resorts have opened. Bookings for aerial sightseeing tours and charter flights can be arranged through *Polynesian Airlines* (tel: 21261).
HOTELS: There are a number of distinctive hotels in Western Samoa; they are of a high standard and reasonably priced. At some, prices are inclusive of meals. There are also hotels located in rural areas, including Upolu's south coast and Savai'i.
SELF-CATERING: A village resort offers the opportunity for self-catering though, if visitors prefer, a restaurant is also provided. There are many sporting and other facilities for guests. Beach cottages are less expensive and offer fewer facilities, though many of them can be found nearby.

RESORTS & EXCURSIONS

UPOLU: The most populous island. **Apia,** the capital and main commercial centre, lies on the beautiful north coast. At **Vailima** nearby is the house built by the Scottish poet and novelist Robert Louis Stevenson, who lived there from 1888 until his death (the local name for him was *Tusitala,* meaning 'teller of tales'). From the lawn, one can see his tomb on top of *Mount Vaea.* The house is now the official home of Western Samoa's Head of State.
Aleipata district: A 65km (40-mile) drive along the east coast from Apia are the *Falefa Falls, Mafa Pass* and *Fuipisia Falls.* This area is the most beautiful part of Samoa and has a 55m (180ft) waterfall, white sand beaches, an old village and four offshore islets.
Lefaga Village: On the southwest coast, an attractive village can be reached by a cross-island road. 'Return to Paradise' was filmed here in 1952.
Manono Island: Just off the coast of Upolu, this island was the inspiration for the legendary 'Bali Hai' in Rodgers and Hammerstein's musical, 'South Pacific'.
SAVAI'I: The largest island in the Samoan archipelago, this has been described as 'Polynesia at its truest'. There are scheduled flights and a regular car ferry from Apia on Upolu.
EXCURSIONS: A drive anywhere on the two larger islands will inevitably pass through regions of remarkable beauty. Ferries sail regularly between Upolu and Savai'i. The smaller islands are more difficult to reach.

SOCIAL PROFILE

FOOD & DRINK: There are hotel dining rooms but no elaborate restaurants. A variety of Chinese food is available in a few places and there are several snack and light meal restaurants in Apia serving fast food and other Western food. At Samoan feasts the traditional fare includes fresh seafood, roast suckling pig, chicken, breadfruit and fruit. **Drink:** *Kava* is the national drink (see also entry on *American Samoa* under *US Islands*). Liquor may not be purchased on Sundays except by hotel residents and their guests.
NIGHTLIFE: Several nightclubs offer dancing and other entertainment. Several cinemas show English-language films and Chinese films with subtitles.
SHOPPING: Local items include *siapo* (tapa) cloth, made from mulberry bark and painted with native dyes; mats and baskets; *kava* drinking bowls, made of hardwood and polished to a high gloss; shell jewellery; and Samoan stamps, available from the Philatelic Bureau. **Shopping hours:** 0800-1200 and 1330-1630 Monday to Friday, 0800-1230 Saturday. Some shops remain open during the lunch hour.
SPORT: Boating: Boats can be hired for net-, spear-, snorkel- and deep-sea fishing. **Golf:** The 18-hole course belonging to the Royal Samoa Golf Club at Fagali'i is open to non-members. **Bowling:** The bowling club at Apia is open to visitors. **Diving:** Western Samoa is a diver's paradise but diving equipment is difficult to obtain. Contact: *Marine Ltd,* PO Box 4700, Apia. Tel: 24550. **Swimming:** There are many beautiful beaches and there is excellent freshwater swimming at Falefa Falls, Puila Cave Pool, Fogaafu Falls and Papase'ea Sliding Rock. **Tennis:** Played all year on grass, concrete and asphalt courts. Games can be arranged through hotels. **Spectator sports: Boxing** matches are held weekly from July to October. A type of **cricket** is played locally and is very popular. British-rules cricket matches are played from November to March. The Apia Rugby Union **rugby** season is from March to June and schools also play at this time. Popular matches can be seen on Saturday afternoons at Apia Park.
SPECIAL EVENTS: The following festivals are celebrated annually in Western Samoa. For a complete list contact the Tourist Board.
Jun '93 *Independence Day with the Fautasi* (long boat races). **Oct** *White Sunday.* **Dec** *Christmas and New Year.*
SOCIAL CONVENTIONS: Even more than their American Samoan neighbours, Western Samoans adhere to traditional moral and religious codes of behaviour. According to the Government, the Samoan is the purest surviving Polynesian type, with a reputation for being upright and dignified in character. Life in each village is still regulated by a council of chiefs with considerable financial and territorial power; this 'extended family' social system is intricately and unusually linked with the overall political system. Within certain limits, dress is relatively informal; men do not need to wear ties, though in outside resorts and hotels it is preferable for women to wear dresses. Beachwear should not be worn in the street or when shopping but shorts are acceptable for men.
Tipping: Not customary.

BUSINESS PROFILE

ECONOMY: The majority of Samoans are involved in subsistence agriculture but some cash crops are also grown for export, the most important of which are coconut, cocoa and bananas. A newly built coconut-oil mill has recently come into operation to allow the islands to move into the world copra market, and there are also plans to develop a large-scale timber industry. Timber is currently exported in small quantities but volumes are declining due to the poor quality of the wood. This setback has been typical of Western Samoa's recent economic fortunes: coconut production has fallen sharply and banana exports are scarcely more than zero. There is some small-scale manufacturing industry, mostly concerned with food processing, textiles, woodworking and light engineering. There are also a number of small factories producing consumer goods for the domestic market. The Government is trying to promote tourism and export-oriented manufacturing to develop the economy. Overseas aid and remittances from Western Samoans working overseas (mostly New Zealand and, to a lesser extent, Australia) keep the economy afloat while it recovers from the damage wrought by Cyclone Ofa (which struck during 1990 and resulted in a fall in GDP of around 3% for that year) and Cyclone Val in December 1991 which repeated the damage. Food, oil, machinery and transport equipment are the main imports. New Zealand, Australia, Singapore, Fiji, Japan and the USA are the major trading partners. Western Samoa is a member of the South Pacific Forum.
BUSINESS: Shirt and smart trousers will suffice for business visits. Ties need only be worn for formal occasions. Best time to visit is from May to October. **Office hours:** 0800-1200 and 1300-1630 Monday to Friday.
COMMERCIAL INFORMATION: The following organisation can offer advice: Department of Economic Affairs, PO Box 862, Apia. Tel: 20471.

HISTORY & GOVERNMENT

HISTORY: The Polynesian inhabitants of the Samoan islands had been in residence for some 2000 years before the first European colonialists became interested. After missionaries had converted many of the islanders to Christianity in the 1830s, it was the Germans and Americans who vied to take control. Ultimately, the island group was divided between the two. Contemporary Western Samoa comprises those islands colonised by the Germans, who formally declared a protectorate over them in 1899. During World War I, the Germans were driven out by New Zealand, which later acquired a United Nations mandate to administer the territory. Measures towards local autonomy were introduced in the 1950s, and the Independent State of Western Samoa was created in 1962. Political parties in the normal sense did not feature in Western Samoan politics until the late 1970s when a group of Fono (national assembly) members in opposition to the Government created the Human Rights Protection Party (HRPP). Three years after its creation, the party won the 1982 general election. Its sole rival, the Christian Democratic Party, was formed in 1985 but the Human Rights Protection Party formed the next government both then and in 1988. Despite the best efforts of the traditionalists – among them the head of the influential Catholic Church, Cardinal Pio Taofinuu – party politics appear to have taken a firm hold. At the most recent election in April 1991, universal suffrage was introduced for the first time, and the electorate responded with a 90% turn-out. The Human Rights Protection Party was again returned to office under the leadership of Tofilau Eti Alesana. With 28 seats out of 47, Alesana now enjoys a comfortable majority in parliament. Two new Fono seats created in early 1992 were both won by the HRPP.
GOVERNMENT: Western Samoa has a 49-member Legislative Assembly (the *Fono*) which is elected by universal suffrage for a 5-year term. 47 members are elected from the ranks of the 16,000 *Matai* (titleholders); the other two seats are reserved for non-Samoan candidates. The Fono appoints the Head of State for a 5-year term. Executive power rests with the cabinet, comprising the Prime Minister and eight other ministers, appointed by the Head of State with the approval of the Fono.

CLIMATE

A warm tropical climate tempered by trade winds between May and September. Temperatures remain relatively constant throughout the year, becoming cooler at night. There are more than 2500 hours of sunshine annually. Rainfall is heaviest between December and April. Sea temperatures rarely fall below 24°C.
Required clothing: Lightweight cottons and linens with warmer clothes for evenings. Rainwear is advisable.

APIA Western Samoa (2m)

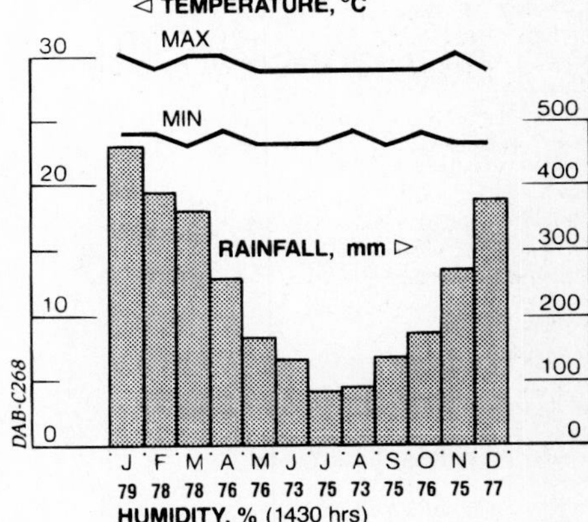

WESTERN SAMOA | **HEALTH REGULATIONS** | **VISA REGULATIONS** | Code-Link

GALILEO/WORLDSPAN

TI-DFT/APW/HE

TI-DFT/APW/VI

SABRE

TIDFT/APW/HE

TIDFT/APW/VI

To access this information on your CRS, swipe the barcode with a light pen or type in the text under the barcode. For more information, see the introduction *How to Use This Book.*

YEMEN, REPUBLIC OF

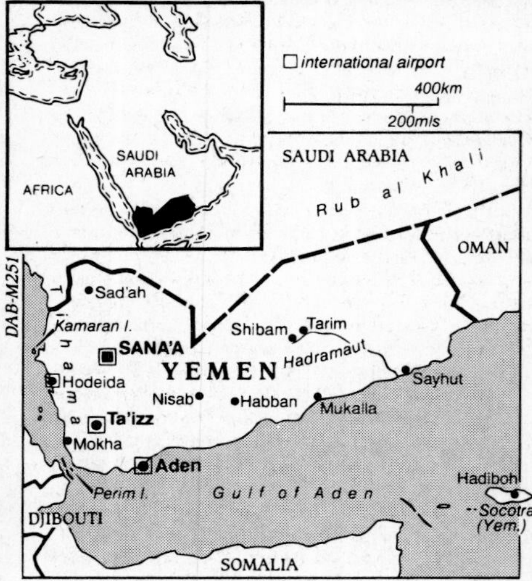

Location: Middle East, Arabian Peninsula.

Note: On May 22, 1990, the merger of the Yemen Arab Republic and the Yemen People's Democratic Republic took place. Complete integration of currency and other regulations has not yet been achieved, so where necessary there are different entries for the differing parts of the newly-unified country. During the coming period the present situation is expected to change.

Yemen Tourist Company
PO Box 1526
Sana'a
Republic of Yemen
Tel: (1) 271 970.

Embassy of the Republic of Yemen
41 South Street
London W1Y 5PD
Tel: (071) 629 9905 *or* 499 1521. Fax: (071) 491 9915. Telex: 262733. Opening hours: 0930-1230 and 1300-1630 Monday to Friday (restricted during Ramadan).

Yemen Airways
52 Stratton Street
London W1X 5FF
Tel: (071) 409 2171 *or* 491 7186. Fax: (071) 355 3062. Telex: 269292 LONZQIY.

British Embassy
PO Box 1287
129 Haddah Road
Sana'a
Republic of Yemen
Tel: (1) 215 630. Fax: (1) 263 059. Telex: 2251.

British Consulate General
PO Box 6304
28 Shara Hi Chi Minh
Khormaksar
Aden
Republic of Yemen
Tel: (2) 32712/6.

Embassy of the Republic of Yemen
Suite 840
600 New Hampshire Avenue, NW
Washington, DC
20037
Tel: (202) 965 4760/1. Fax: (202) 337 2017. Telex: 897027.

Embassy of the United States of America
PO Box 22347
Dhahr Himyar Zone
Sheraton Hotel District
Sana'a
Republic of Yemen
Tel: (2) 238 842 or 238 852. Fax: (2) 251 563. Telex: 2697.

Embassy of the Republic of Yemen
Suite 1100
350 Sparks Street
Ottawa, Ontario
K1R 7S8
Tel: (613) 232 8525 *or* 232 8582. Fax: (613) 232 8276.
Consulate in: Ottawa.

Canadian Consulate
c/o Yemen Computer Co Ltd
PO Box 340
Building 4
Street 11, off Haddah Street
Sana'a
Republic of Yemen
Tel: (2) 709 480.

AREA: 536,869 sq km (207,285 sq miles).
POPULATION: 12,500,000 (1990 estimate).
POPULATION DENSITY: 23.3 per sq km.
CAPITAL: Sana'a. **Population:** 427,150 (1986).
Economic & Commercial Capital: Aden.
Population: 407,000 (1986).
GEOGRAPHY: The Republic of Yemen is bordered in the northwest, north and northeast by Saudi Arabia, in the east by Oman and in the south by the Gulf of Aden. To the west lies the Red Sea. The islands of Perim and Karam in the southern Red Sea are also part of the Republic. Yemen is predominantly mountainous, supporting terraced agriculture. The Hadramaut is a range of high mountains in the centre of the country. Highlands rise steeply in the Central Yemen, ranging in height from approximately 200m (656ft) to the 4000m (13,123ft) peak of Jabal Nabi Shoveb. In contrast is *Tihama*, a flat semi-desert coastal plain to the west, 50-100km (30-60 miles) wide. Surface water flows down from the mountains through the valleys during the rainy season and the area is cultivated for cotton and grain. In the east the mountains drop away to the *Rub al-Khali* or 'Empty Quarter' of the Arabian Peninsula, a vast sea of sand. The arid coastal plains are fringed with sandy beaches.
LANGUAGE: Arabic. English is spoken in some urban areas.
RELIGION: Sunni Muslim (especially in the north) and Shia Muslim, small Christian and Hindu communities.
TIME: GMT + 3.
ELECTRICITY: 220/230 volts AC, 50Hz.
COMMUNICATIONS: Telephone: IDD is available in parts of the country. Country code: 967 and 969. **Fax:** Some hotels have facilities. **Telex/telegram:** Telex messages may be sent through *Cable & Wireless Ltd* in Sana'a (Gamal Abdul Nasser Street), Hodeida (Alamnie Building, 26 September Street) and Ta'izz (Hayel Saeed Building, Agaba Street). The better hotels, business houses, banks etc have telex facilities. Telegram facilities are available. *Yemen Telecommunications Co.* have offices at Steamer Point (24 hours) and at Crater. Telexes can be sent from the *Aden Frantel Hotel* and from public offices at Steamer Point and Khormaksar. **Post:** Airmail to Europe from Sana'a takes about four days; mail to and from other towns may take longer. Post office hours: 0800-1400 and 1600-2000 Saturday to Thursday. **Press:** No English-language newspapers papers are published in the Republic of Yemen. Dailies include *Al-Jumhuriya* and *Al-Thaura*.
BBC World Service and Voice of America frequencies: From time to time these change. See the section *How to Use this Book* for more information.

BBC:

MHz	21.47	15.57	12.09	9.410

A service is also available on 1413kHz (0100-0500 GMT).

Voice of America:

MHz	11.97	9.670	6.040	5.995

PASSPORT/VISA

Regulations and requirements may be subject to change at short notice, and you are advised to contact the appropriate diplomatic or consular authority before finalising travel arrangements. Details of these may be found at the head of this country's entry. Any numbers in the chart refer to the footnotes below.

	Passport Required?	Visa Required?	Return Ticket Required?
Full British	Yes	Yes	Yes
BVP	Not valid	-	-
Australian	Yes	Yes	Yes
Canadian	Yes	Yes	Yes
USA	Yes	Yes	Yes
Other EC	Yes	Yes	Yes
Japanese	Yes	Yes	Yes

Entry restrictions: The Government of the Republic of Yemen refuse entry and transit facilities to: (a) holders of Israeli and South African passports; (b) holders of passports containing visas valid or expired for Israel or South Africa or any indication, such as entry or exit stamps, that the holder has visited these countries.
PASSPORTS: Required by all.
British Visitors Passport: Not accepted.
VISAS: Required by all except nationals of Egypt, Iraq, Jordan, Syria and holders of re-entry permits.
Types of visa: Tourist and Business. Cost: £20 for British passport holders; £25 for other nationalities. Transit visas may also be required.
Validity: 1 month during a 3- month period.
Application to: Consulate (or Consular Section at Embassy). For addresses, see top of entry.
Application requirements: (a) Completed application form. (b) 2 passport photos. (c) Return ticket. (d) Valid passport.

MONEY

Note: The currency of the former Yemen Arab Republic and the currency of the Yemen People's Democratic Republic are both in circulation (1 Dinar = 26 Riyals). No date has yet been fixed for the adoption of a single currency. Some details of the two currencies are therefore listed separately below.
Currency exchange: It is inadvisable to change too much money as local currency is not easily reconverted.
Credit cards: Diners Club and American Express are the most widely accepted cards. Check with your credit card company for details of merchant acceptability and other services which may be available.
Travellers cheques: Can be exchanged at some banks and hotels.
Banking hours: 0800-1200 Saturday to Wednesday, and 0800-1130 Thursday.

YEMENI RIYAL (FORMER YAR CURRENCY)
Currency: Yemen Riyal (YR) = 100 fils. Notes are in denominations of YR100, 50, 20, 10, 5 and 1. Coins are in denominations of 50, 25, 10, 5 and 1 fils.
Exchange rate indicators: The following figures are included as a guide to the movements of the Yemen Riyal against Sterling and the US Dollar:

Date:	Oct '89	Oct '90	Oct '91	Oct '92
£1.00=	15.41	23.52	21.02	26.09
$1.00=	9.76	12.04	12.11	16.44

YEMENI DINAR (FORMER YPDR CURRENCY)
Currency: Yemeni Dinar (YD) = 1000 fils. Notes are in denominations of YD500, 250, 10, 5 and 1. Coins are in denominations of 250, 100, 50, 25, 5, 2 and 1 fils.
Exchange rate indicators: The following figures are included as a guide to the movements of the Yemeni Dinar against Sterling and the US Dollar:

Date:	Oct '89	Oct '90	Oct '91	Oct '92
£1.00=	0.54	0.90	0.80	0.74
$1.00=	0.34	0.46	0.46	0.46

Currency restrictions: There are no restrictions on the import of foreign currency, subject to declaration; export is limited to the amount declared (not exceeding US$2000). The limit on the import and export of local currency is YR5000 (or equivalent).

DUTY FREE

The following items may be imported into the Republic of Yemen without incurring customs duty:
200 cigarettes or 50 cigars or 250g of tobacco;
2 quarts of alcoholic beverages (non-Muslims only);
568ml of perfume or toilet water.

PUBLIC HOLIDAYS

Public holidays observed in the Republic of Yemen are as follows:
Mar 8 '93 International Women's Day. **Apr 4** Eid al-Fitr (End of Ramadan). **May 1** Labour Day. **May 22** Reunification Day. **Jun 11** Eid al-Adha (Feast of the Sacrifice). **Jun 13** Corrective Movement Anniversary. **Jun 30** Ashoura. **Jul 2** Muharram (Islamic New Year). **Sep 10** Mouloud (Prophet's Birthday). **Sep 26** Anniversary of the Revolution. **Oct 14** National Day. **Jan 1 '94** New Year's Day. **Jan 20** Leilat al-Meiraj. **Mar** Eid al-Fitr. **Mar 8** International Women's Day.
Note: Muslim festivals are timed according to local sightings of various phases of the Moon and the dates given above are approximations. During the lunar month of Ramadan that precedes Eid al-Fitr, Muslims fast during the day and feast at night and normal business patterns may be interrupted. Many restaurants are closed during the day and there may be restrictions on smoking and drinking. Some disruption may continue into Eid al-Fitr itself. Eid al-Fitr and Eid al-Adha may last anything from two to ten days, depending on the region. For more information see the section *World of Islam* at the back of the book.

HEALTH

Regulations and requirements may be subject to change at short notice, and you are advised to contact your doctor well in advance of your intended date of departure. Any numbers in the chart refer to the footnotes below.

	Special Precautions?	Certificate Required?
Yellow Fever	No	1
Cholera	Yes	2
Typhoid & Polio	Yes	-
Malaria	3	-
Food & Drink	4	-

[1]: A yellow fever vaccination certificate is required from travellers over one year of age arriving from infected areas.
[2]: Following WHO guidelines issued in 1973, a cholera vaccination certificate is not an official condition of entry to the Republic of Yemen. However, cholera is a risk in this country and precautions are essential. Up-to-date advice should be sought before deciding whether these precautions should include vaccination, as medical opinion is divided over its effectiveness. See the *Health* section at the back of the book.
[3]: Malaria risk, almost exclusively in the malignant *falciparum* form, exists throughout the year, but mainly from September through February, in the whole country excluding Aden and the immediate surrounding areas. Resistance to chloroquine has been reported.
[4]: Whilst relatively safe, where mains water is chlorinated it may cause mild abdominal upsets; supplies in Sana'a are said to be safe. Bottled water is available and is advised for the first few weeks of the stay. Drinking water outside main cities and towns is likely to be contaminated and sterilisation is considered essential. Water used for drinking, brushing teeth or making ice should have first been boiled or otherwise sterilised. Milk is unpasteurised and should be boiled. Powdered or tinned milk is available and is advised but make sure that it is reconstituted with pure water. Avoid dairy products which are likely to have been made from unboiled milk. Only eat well-cooked meat and fish, preferably served hot. Salad and mayonnaise may carry increased risk. Vegetables should be cooked and fruit peeled.
Rabies is present. For those at high risk, vaccination before arrival should be considered. If you are bitten abroad seek medical advice without delay. For more information consult the *Health* section at the back of the book.
Bilharzia (schistosomiasis) is present. Avoid swimming and paddling in fresh water. Swimming pools which are well-chlorinated and maintained are safe.
Health care: Medical facilities are limited. Acclimatisation may be necessary for high altitude. Medical insurance is essential.

TRAVEL - International

AIR: The Republic of Yemen's national airline is *Yemen Airways (Yemenia) (IY)*.
Approximate flight time: From *London* to Sana'a is 10 hours (direct) and to Aden is 9 hours, excluding stopover time.
International airports: *Sana'a (SAH)* (El-Rahaba) is 3km (2 miles) north of the city (travel time – 20 minutes). Taxis and buses are available. Airport facilities include a bank (0600-2200) and car hire.
Ta'izz (TAI) (al-Janad) is 4km (2.5 miles) from the city (travel time – 10 minutes). Taxis, buses and hire cars are available.
Hodeida (HOD) is 8km (5 miles) from the city. Taxis, buses and hire cars are available.
Aden (ADE) (Khormaksar) is 9.5km (6 miles) from the city (travel time – 20 minutes). Limited bus and taxi services available.
Departure tax: YR100 on international flights.
SEA: The main international ports are Aden, Hodeida, Mokha, Sulif and Lohenja. Cargo vessels with passenger berths call at Hodeida. *Norwegian American* operate a shipping service to Aden.
ROAD: Driving to Yemen is not recommended but there are routes from Riyadh, Mecca and Jeddah (in Saudi Arabia) to Sana'a.

TRAVEL - Internal

AIR: *Yemen Airways (IY)* operate services between Sana'a, Ta'izz and Hodeida. There are also flights from Aden. Flight reservations and times should be double-checked.
Departure tax: YR30 on domestic flights.
SEA: Local ferries connect local ports. For details contact port authorities.
ROAD: Within Sana'a and from Ta'izz to Mokha, the roads are reliable. From Aden to Ta'izz is three to five hours driving time. A road links Aden and Sana'a, otherwise the road network is mainly limited to desert tracks. Use of 4-wheel drive vehicles and a guide is recommended. There is a road from Aden to Mukalla of 500km (310 miles). **Bus:** Regular intercity bus services. The *Yemen Tourism Company* runs landcruisers and tourist coaches to all towns. **Taxi:** Recognisable by yellow licence plates. Taxi sharing is the cheapest transport between cities. There are minimum charges within main cities but fares should be negotiated beforehand for inter-city journeys. **Car hire:** Available in main towns. **Documentation:** An International Driving Permit is required.
JOURNEY TIMES: The following chart gives approximate journey times (in hours and minutes) from Sana'a to other major cities/towns in the Yemen Republic.

	Air	Road
Ta'izz	0.45	3.30
Hodeida	0.40	3.00
Aden	0.45	4.30

ACCOMMODATION

HOTELS: In Sana'a, there are two 5-star hotels, one 4-star hotel and five 3-star hotels; there are also a number of 3-star hotels in Ta'izz and Hodeida, and a 3-star hotel in Mareb. In Aden, the hotels for foreign visitors (including two of 'international' standard) are located in Tawahi. There are also hotels at Mukalla (al-Shaab), Seiyyum (al-Salaam), Shihr (al-Sharq), Mukheiras and Jaar. Outside the main centres, facilities are limited. Accommodation varies from ancient palace hotels and modern luxury hotels to *funduks* and tribal huts. It is necessary to book in advance and to receive a written confirmation. Winter and summer rates are the same. All bills are subject to a 15% service charge.
CAMPING: Khokha and Mokha have campsites; details may be obtained from local travel agents in Sana'a.

RESORTS & EXCURSIONS

The Republic of Yemen is the least known and in many ways the most spectacular region of all Arabia. As much of the Central Highlands rise over 3000m (10,000ft), travellers should be prepared for the high altitudes. The attraction of the Republic of Yemen for the visitor is largely its striking scenery, spectacular Islamic and pre-Islamic architecture and the deep sense of the past. Tours are available within and around the major cities; enquire at local travel agents for details.

The Central Region

This area has been intensely cultivated for centuries and is the site of many of the major towns.
Sana'a, the modern capital and long an important citadel along the trade route between Aden and Mecca, dates back to the first century and, according to popular legend, to early biblical days. The citadel, *Qasr al-Silah*, was rebuilt after the arrival of Islam in the 7th century and is still intact. The old centre is surrounded by the remains of the city walls, which can be seen in the south along Zuberi Street before Bab al-Yemen, in the east along *Mount Nugum* starting from the walls of the citadel, and in the north on the road from Bab Sha'oob to Taherir Square. The 1000-year-old *Bab al-Yemen Market* is divided into 40 different crafts and trades. The spice market is one of the best to visit, standing out from the rest by the rich aroma of incense and famed Arabian spices. Other markets include the *Souk al-Nahaas*, once the copper market, now selling embroidered head-dresses, belts and *jambias* (curved daggers). The *Great Mosque of Sana'a* is the oldest and largest of the mosques in Sana'a and one of the oldest in the Muslim world, constructed in the lifetime of the prophet and enlarged in AD705. The layout is typical of early Islamic architecture, with an open square courtyard, surrounded by roofed galleries. The *National Museum* is located in Taherir Square in **Dar al-Shukr** (or the 'Palace of Gratefulness'); it contains engravings of pre-Islamic times, bronze statues, a beautiful *mashrabia* (cooling place for water) and several examples of folk art. It offers a good view of Taherir Square and the *Muttawakelite Estate* from the roof.
Rawdha, 8km (5 miles) north of Sana'a, is a garden city, famous for its sweet grapes, the mosque built by Ahmed ibn al-Qasim and the *Rawdha Palace*, now used as a hotel.
Amran, north of Rawdha, lies on the edge of the fertile basin of *al-Bawn*. The city is surrounded by the old clay city walls of pre-Islamic, Sabean origin.
Hajja is a day's journey to the northwest of Sana'a. The countryside is made up of high mountains and large valleys, including the *Wadi Sherez*, 1000m (3280 ft), and *Kohlan*, 2400m (7875ft). Hajja itself is a citadel, situated on the central hill of Hajja, famous for underground prison cells used by the Imams.
Hadda Mountain, south of Sana'a, is dotted with villages and orchards growing apricots, peaches, walnuts and almonds. The village of Hadda has two old Turkish mills.
Wadi Dhar, 10km (6 miles) from Sana'a, is an idyllic valley filled with grapes, pomegranates and citrus fruits, surrounded by a barren plateau.
Shibam, 36km (22 miles) from Sana'a, is a pre-Islamic settlement, protected by the great fortification of *Koukaban*.

The West & Southwest

The **Tihama** in the west has a negligible rainfall and is predominantly hot, humid and sparsely populated. The road south from Sana'a runs through extremely mountainous countryside and passes the towns of **Dhofar**, the ancient capital of the Himyarites (115BC-AD525), and **Ibb**, a once important stopping point on the Sana'a to Ta'izz road. Remains of the city walls and an aqueduct can still be seen. The **Sumara Pass,** at an altitude of 2700m (8860ft), gives a spectacular panoramic view over the Yarim and Dhamar basins.
Ta'izz lies in the south at an altitude of 1400m (4590ft). The old city has been all but swallowed up by the fast-growing modern city around it but beautiful old houses and mosques remain within the line of the 13th-century city wall, which is still intact along the southern side. To the north only the gates of *Bab Musa* and *al-Bab al-Kabir* remain. The southern wall offers a splendid view of Ta'izz. *Al-Qahera*, within the city walls, is the fortress and the oldest part of the city. *Al-Ashrafiya* and *al-Mudhaffar* are two of the most beautiful mosques in Yemen. The museum in the *Palace of Imam Ahmed* contains the personal effects of the last Imam, and has preserved the spirit of Yemen from before the beginning of the Republic. The *Salah Palace*, to the east just outside the city, is another museum of the royal family. The *Souk Ta'izz* sells a variety of goods, including silverware and carpets.
Mount Saber is 18km (11 miles) from Ta'izz and offers a breathtaking view of the city and the Ta'izz basin. A heavy-duty vehicle is needed to drive to the top. The mountain rises to an altitude of 3000m (9840ft) and the weather can be very cold. **Mokha** is an old Himyarite port on the Red Sea. In the 17th and 18th centuries Mokha underwent a boom period exporting coffee, which was becoming fashionable in Europe (particularly Venice and Amsterdam, where the first coffee houses were opened). Coffee was later cultivated elsewhere and Mokha fell into decline. In recent years the Government has improved the harbour and communications within Mokha in an attempt to resurrect this once

YEMEN, REPUBLIC OF	HEALTH REGULATIONS	VISA REGULATIONS Code-Link
GALILEO/WORLDSPAN	 TI-DFT/SAH/HE	 TI-DFT/SAH/VI
SABRE	 TIDFT/SAH/HE	TIDFT/SAH/VI

To access this information on your CRS, swipe the barcode with a light pen or type in the text under the barcode. For more information, see the introduction *How to Use This Book*.

prosperous city. **Hodeida** is reached via the mountains of *Manakha*. A modern city port on the Red Sea, the harbour itself was completed in 1961. There is little here of historical interest apart from the fish market, where fishing boats are built from wood in the same way they have been for hundreds of years. **Beit al-Faqih**, 60km (37 miles) from Hodeida, has a good craft market. **Manakha**, once a road station for the Ottoman Turks, is situated on a saddle of the *Haraz Mountains*. Traditional Ismaeli villages lie to the east. This area is exceptionally good for hiking.

The Northern Region

Between Sana'a and Sada in the north lies the **Wadi Wa'aar.** The climate here is subtropical and mangoes, papayas and bananas grow freely. Out of this rises the **Shahara,** a huge mountain massif, the highest point being nearly 3000m (9840ft) above sea level. This can be climbed by foot or by 4-wheel drive car; *Shahara City* offers overnight accommodation. *Shahara Bridge*, built in the 17th century, connects two mountains and can still be crossed by foot. **Sada,** a walled city, was once an iron mining and tanning centre and an important station along the Himyarite Sana'a–Mecca trade route. Later Sada was chosen as the capital of the Zaydi state and became the centre of Zaydi learning. The *al-Hadi Mosque* is still an important institution for education in Zaydism. It is possible to walk along the top of the city walls, which afford good views of the city. The *Najran Gate* in the north is the most interesting of the gates, protected by an alleyway leading to the doors. The *Great Mosque* is the central building in the city. The market sells traditional stone necklaces and some fine silverware. The *Sada Fortress* is the seat of the provincial government, thickly walled, and once the Imam's residence. Outside the city is the *Zaydi Graveyard*, filled with some of the most beautiful gravestones in Yemen. The *Sada Basin* is strikingly fertile, providing Yemen's early crops of grapes, and is excellent for walking and hiking.

The Eastern Region

The **Eastern Mountains** (al-Mashrik) slope down from an altitude of 3000-1100m (9840-3610ft). The landscape gradually turns to sand dunes where the population decreases; agriculture is concentrated around wadies. **Mareb** was once the capital of the kingdom of Sheba but the city is now largely in a state of disrepair. Blocks of stone with Sabean writing bear testament to the history of the city. Southwest of Mareb is the ancient *Mareb Dam*, used thousands of years ago to irrigate the surrounding land. The dam fell into disuse around AD570, after which large numbers of people emigrated northwards. The stonework is impressive, measuring 600m (1968ft) wide and 18m (60ft) deep.

Aden

The history of **Aden** as a port goes back a long way; it is mentioned in the Biblical *Book of Ezekiel* (circa 6th century BC). There is a collection of pre-Islamic artefacts in the *National Museum of Antiquities* near Tawahi Harbour. *Crater*, the oldest part of the city, lies in the crater of an extinct volcano and is where the most ancient constructions in Aden may be seen. These are the *Aden Tanks*, manmade reservoirs, partly cut out of the rock, with a storage capacity of 50,000,000 litres. When it rains the upper basins fill up first and then overflow into the lower basins. Also in Crater may be found the *Ethnographical Museum* and *Military Museum*. The 14th-century *Mosque of Sayyid Abdullah al-Aidrus* commemorates the patron saint of Aden. In *Ma'allah* the visitor can see traditional Arab boats. To the south of Aden is *Little Aden*, also in the crater of an extinct volcano; this is an area of small fishing villages in sheltered bays, with several superb beaches fringing the Indian Ocean.

SOCIAL PROFILE

FOOD & DRINK: Hotel restaurants serve both Western and oriental dishes, particularly Indian and Chinese. There are a few independent restaurants serving international and Arab cuisine. Seafood is particularly recommended, as is *haradha* (a mincemeat and pepper dish). **Drink:** Alcohol is not generally available but may be served in hotels. It is illegal to buy alcohol for a Yemeni citizen.
SHOPPING: *Souks* (markets) are interesting places to shop and buy handicrafts. Purchases include *foutah* (national costume), leather goods, *jambia* (daggers), candlesticks, scarves (woven with gold thread), amber beads, brightly coloured cushions and ceramics. Other items include gold and silver work, spice, perfume, *bukhur* incense with charcoal and pottery containers in which to burn it, coloured mats and sharks' teeth. **Shopping hours:** 0800-1200/1300 and 1600-2100 Sunday to Thursday.
NIGHTLIFE: This is generally centred on the major hotels; see above under *Accommodation*.
SPORTS: Most major hotels have squash and tennis courts, swimming pools and saunas. Many beaches along the coast offer safe swimming. There are swimming clubs offering temporary membership for visitors.
SOCIAL CONVENTIONS: Traditional values are still very much part of everyday life and visitors will be treated with traditional courtesies and hospitality. Many of the population work in agriculture, with several thousand dependent on fishing. The rest live and work in towns and there is a small nomadic minority living along the northern edges of the desert. Guns become more noticeable further north, slung over the shoulder and carried in addition to the traditional *jambia*. In towns, women are veiled with black or coloured cloth, while in the villages such customs are not observed. Yemenis commonly chew *qat*, a locally-grown shrub bearing shoots that have a narcotic effect, chewed in markets and cafés but more stylishly sitting on cushions in a guestroom or *mafrai* at the top of a multi-storeyed Yemeni house. For the visitor, conservative casual clothes are suitable; visiting businessmen are expected to wear suits. Men need to wear a jacket and tie for formal occasions and in smart dining rooms. Women are expected to dress modestly and beachwear and shorts should be confined to the beach or poolside. Smoking is forbidden during Ramadan.
Tipping: The practice of tipping is becoming more common. Waiters and taxi drivers should be tipped 10-15%.

BUSINESS PROFILE

ECONOMY: The northwestern part of the country, formerly the Yemen Arab Republic, is the most fertile region on the Arabian peninsula and thus agriculture employs most of the population. The principal crops are cereals, cotton, coffee, fruit, vegetables and qat (a narcotic leaf). Livestock is also important. Fishing is underdeveloped and has prospects for growth. Industry is a small but growing sector. Goods are produced mostly for domestic consumption. Salt mining has been in progress for some years and continues to expand steadily. By contrast, the southern part of the the country (formerly the People's Democratic Republic) is almost entirely arid; agriculture is mostly subsistence and although the country can, for the most part, meet its own requirements for vegetables, most of its grain has to be imported. Only 1% of the Aden hinterland is cultivable. Fishing is a more promising industry, particularly given the rich waters of the Arabian Sea, and much recent investment in the economy has been directed to this sector. At the moment it is hampered by poor equipment and an inadequate marketing and distribution system.The main Yemeni export earners are oil and gas which, although not large by regional standards, have done much to improve the state of the economy. In Aden, formerly the capital of the south, oil refining is now the major economic activity: the city never recovered from the decline of its port after independence, before which its earnings as a freeport and the key staging post on the sea route via Suez to India and the Far East was a great national asset. There was much foreign interest in oil exploration in Yemen after several onshore discoveries during 1983, but exploitation has been stalled by oil companies' reluctance to offend the Saudis (see *History*). Yemen continues to suffer considerable economic problems as a result of the Gulf War, both from the collapse of regional trade and the Government's policy of supporting Iraq. Total losses are estimated at around $2 billion a year for 1991 and 1992. Almost one million workers were expelled from Saudi Arabia and their arrival back in Yemen has put severe strains upon the economic and social fabric. Western aid provisions have also been drastically reduced, mainly due to Saudi diplomatic pressure on donors. The United Arab Emirates, the UK and Japan are the largest importers into Yemen.
BUSINESS: Business people are expected to dress smartly for meetings and formal social occasions. English is commonly used in business circles. Appointments are needed and visitors should be punctual. Visiting cards are often exchanged. Do not be surprised during a meeting if Yemeni businessmen chew *qat*. **Office hours:** 0800-1230 and 1600-1900 Monday to Wednesday, and 0800-1100 Thursday.
Government office hours: 0800-1400 Sunday to Thursday.
COMMERCIAL INFORMATION: The following organisations can offer advice: General Corporation for Foreign Trade, PO Box 77, 163 Al-Matar Street, Sana'a. Tel: (1) 223 858. Telex: 2348; *or*
Federation of Chambers of Commerce, PO Box 16992, Sana'a. Tel: (1) 224 262. Telex: 2229.

HISTORY & GOVERNMENT

HISTORY: To the Romans, Yemen was *Arabia Felix*, as through its ports, Aden and Qana, the forest and animal wealth of Africa flowed along the Silk and Incense Roads. Subsequently, the region came within the Islamic sphere of influence. From the 16th and 17th centuries, European powers and the Ottoman Empire were involved in the region. From 1839, the port of Aden was developed by the British as a commercial, naval and military base, and a vital staging post on the Suez route to India and the Far East. The Yemeni hinterland was, for the most part, under the loose control of the Ottoman Empire throughout the 19th century until 1918 when the Imam Yahya took power in what became the Yemen Arab Republic. Aden and its surroundings, meanwhile, were firmly established as a British colony. Yahya was assassinated in 1948 and his son Ahmed took over. From 1958-1961, the YAR was federated with Egypt and Syria in the United Arab States. Ahmed died in 1962 and an army coup led to civil war between Egypt-backed Republicans and Saudi-backed Royalists. By this time, in the south, the British colonial forces faced armed opposition from both the leftist National Liberation Front and the Front for the Liberation of Occupied South Yemen (FLOSY). In November 1967, just before the formation of the Yemen Democratic People's Republic in the south by the victorious NLF forces, a Republican government took control in the north. There was intermittent warfare between the two Yemens throughout the late 1960s and early 1970s and political instability in the north throughout the 1970s. In 1978, Lt Col Ali Abdullah Saleh became Head of State. In 1983 he was unanimously re-elected by the People's Assembly. In the south, meanwhile, Ali Nasser Muhammad became Head of State in 1978. In January 1986, civil war between rival elements within the armed forces broke out after an attempted Politburo purge. A new government was formed under the former Construction Minister, Haydar Abu Bakr al-Attas. The long-promised merger of the two Yemens took place in 1990 with unexpected ease. Ali Abdullah Saleh became leader of the unified Republic of Yemen. The newly-created republic gave firm diplomatic support to Iraq during the 1990/91 Gulf crisis. This made little practical difference but subsequently caused considerable problems for the Yemenis in their relations with Saudi Arabia: one million Yemeni workers were expelled from the kingdom and remittances back home (a mainstay of the economy) dried up. Aid from the USA and other Western donors was also drastically cut under Saudi pressure. This has put substantial strain upon the Yemeni economy, which has in turn created social tension. Nonetheless, the Government went ahead with planned multi-party elections which were won by the principal northern party, the General People's Congress, with the moderate Islamic party Al-Islah coming second and the southern-based Socialists in third place.
GOVERNMENT: Executive power is held by the President who is elected for a 5-year term by the Consultative Council and rules with the assistance of an appointed Council of Ministers. The final constitutional structure of the new Yemeni state has not yet been finalised. Parliament was given 30 months to agree the format of the new constitution and to prepare for elections.

CLIMATE

The climate varies according to altitude. The coastal plain is hot and dusty throughout most of the year. The highlands are warm in summer and during winter, from October to March, nights can be very cold in the mountains. Annual rainfall is extremely low and temperatures, particularly in summer, are very high. The most pleasant time is from October to April.
Required clothing: Lightweight clothes are worn in the coastal plain all year. Warmer clothes are needed from November to April in the Highlands.

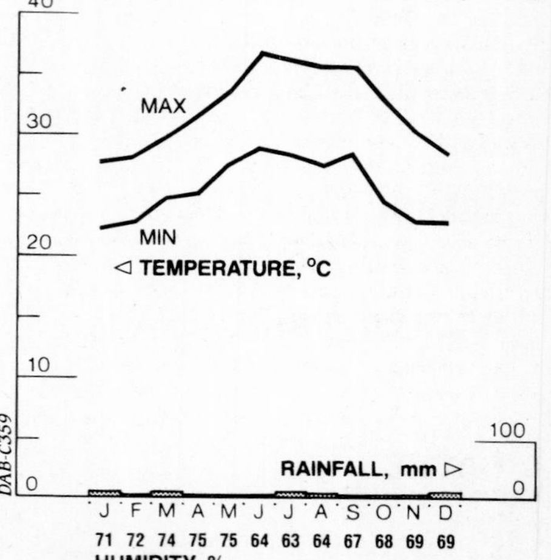

YUGOSLAVIA

Location: Southern Central Europe.

Note: In 1992 the republics of Serbia and Montenegro agreed to uphold the Yugoslav state, thereby limiting the borders to the boundaries of these two republics. Due to the extreme political instability in the region at the time of writing, travel is not advised. Prospective travellers are advised to contact the Foreign Office (or exterior affairs department of the respective country) before considering travel. At the time of writing, UN sanctions were applied against the newly styled Federal Republic of Yugoslavia, including a ban on all commercial transactions and the suspension of air links. The following information reflects the situation before the present conflict and is included in the hope that it will be useful again in the future.

Turisticki savez Jugoslavije (Tourist Association of Yugoslavia)
Postanski fah 595
Mose Pijade 8/IV
11001 Belgrade, Yugoslavia
Tel: (11) 339 041. Fax: (11) 634 677. Telex: 11863.

ECGD (Country Policy Desk)
Tel: (071) 512 7000.
Note: ECGD policy is that all the ex-Yugoslav republics are off cover for all medium- and long-term insurance. Short-term cover is now only available from private sector insurers, who will not and cannot involve themselves in so risky an area as Yugoslavia in accordance with UN sanctions since June 1992.

Foreign Office Travel Advice Unit
Tel: (071) 270 4129.

Embassy of the Federal Republic of Yugoslavia
5-7 Lexham Gardens
London W8 5JJ
Tel: (071) 370 6105. Fax: (071) 370 3838. Telex: 928542. Opening hours: 1000-1300 Monday to Friday.
Note: The Embassy does not have an ambassador. The Second Secretary is the *de facto* ambassador.

British Embassy
Ulica Generala Zdanova 46
11000 Belgrade, Yugoslavia
Tel: (11) 645 055 *or* 645 034 *or* 645 043 *or* 645 087. Fax: (11) 659 651. Telex: 11468 PROBEL YU.
Note: Although the UK still maintains an Embassy in Belgrade, it does not formally recognise the Federal Republic of Yugoslavia (Serbia and Montenegro). However, *de facto* recognition does exist. The Embassy deals with Serbia and Montenegro only.

Embassy of Yugoslavia
2410 California Avenue, NW
Washingto DC, 20008
Tel: (202) 462 6566. Fax: (202) 797 9663.
Consulates in: Chicago, Cleveland, New York (tel: (212) 535 2154œ), Pittsburgh and San Francisco.

Yugoslavia National Tourist Office
630 Fifth Avenue
New York, NY 10111
Tel: (212) 879 8700. Telex: 66558.
Also deals with enquiries from Canada.

Embassy of the United States of America
PO Box 5070
Unit 25402
Belgrade, Yugoslavia
Tel: (11) 645 655. Fax: (11) 645 221. Telex: 11529 AMEMBA YU.

Embassy of the Federal Republic of Yugoslavia
17 Blackburn Avenue
Ottawa, Ontario K1N 8A2
Tel: (613) 233 6289. Fax: (613) 233 7850.
Consulates in: Montréal, Toronto and Vancouver.

Canadian Embassy
Kneza Milosa 75
11000 Belgrade, Yugoslavia
Tel: (11) 644 666. Fax: (11) 641 480. Telex: 11137 YU DOMCA.

AREA: Now comprising only Serbia with 88,361 sq km (34,116 sq miles) and Montenegro with 13,812 sq km (5331 sq miles), respectively the largest and smallest of the former republics, Yugoslavia officially covers 102,173 sq km (39,449 sq miles), or 40% of the territory of the former federation (255,804 sq km; 98,766 sq miles). Unofficially it is around 50% larger, given that various Serbian politico-military entities loyal to Belgrade control 65% of the disputed territory of Bosnia-Hercegovina and 30% of the disputed territory of Croatia, thereby giving the Federal Republic of Yugoslavia or 'Greater Serbia' around 60% of the former territory of the former Yugoslav federation.
POPULATION: Together, Serbia (9,791,475; 1991) and Montenegro (615,267; 1991), respectively the most and least populous of the ex-Yugoslav republics, have a total population of 10,406,742 or around 45% of the population of the former Yugoslav federation. However, if the Serbs of Bosnia-Hercegovina (33% of a total 1991 population of 4.5 million) and Croatia (11-20% of the 1991 population of 4.69 million) are included, then the total population reaches around 12.5 million, amounting to 55% of the population of the former Yugoslav federation.
POPULATION DENSITY: 100.9 per sq km (Serbia and Montenegro only; 83.3 per sq km if including Serb-controlled territories in Croatia and Bosnia-Hercegovina).
CAPITAL: Belgrade (Beograd). **Population:** 1,554,826 (1991).
GEOGRAPHY: Roughly rectangular in shape and on a major European communications axis north–west and south–east, the Federal Republic of Yugoslavia borders Hungary to the north, Romania to the northeast, Bulgaria to the southeast, Macedonia to the south, Bosnia-Hercegovina to the west and Croatia to the northwest. The southern half of Serbia is mountainous and thickly forested, whilst the north is dominated by the flat, fertile farmland of the Danube and Tisza valleys. The scenery varies from rich Alpine valleys, vast fertile plains and rolling green hills to bare, rocky gorges as much as 1140m (3800ft) deep, thick forests and gaunt limestone mountain regions. Belgrade, the capital of the new Federal Republic, lies on the Danube. Montenegro is a small mountainous region on the Adriatic coast north of Albania, bordering on Bosnia-Hercegovina to the west. Its small Adriatic coastline comprises the main ports of Bar and those in the Bay of Kotor.
LANGUAGE: Serbo-Croat, using the Cyrillic alphabet. Albanian and Hungarian are also spoken in Kosovo and Vojvodina respectively.
RELIGION: 70% Eastern Orthodox Serbs, with a large Muslim ethnic Albanian minority (especially in the province of Kosovo) and a small Roman Catholic ethnic Hungarian minority (mainly located in Vojvodina).
TIME: GMT + 1 (GMT + 2 from March to September).
ELECTRICITY: 220 volts AC, 50Hz.
COMMUNICATIONS: Telephone: IDD is still available as part of the former Yugoslav federation. Country code: 38. Telephone links with Zagreb, Ljubljana and Sarajevo have been completely cut, whereas Skopje can still be reached intermittently. **Fax** and **telex** transmissions are available to and from western Europe. **Post:** All postal services between the former Yugoslav republics have been suspended indefinitely. Postal services within Serbia are reasonable. Due to the UN sanctions, international postal services take twice as long as before, ie one week to ten days for airmail via third parties to the UK. **Press:** The main local newspapers and magazines, in decreasing order of circulation, are *Vecernje Novosti* (Belgrade), *Politika Ekspres* (Belgrade), *Politika* (Belgrade), *NIN* (Belgrade) and *Pobjeda* (Podgorica). The state news agency, *TANJUG* (PO Box 439, Obilicév Venac 2, 11000 Belgrade; tel: (11) 332 230; telex: 11220), produces material in English for international distribution, plus *Newsday*, a daily newspaper in English, and *Yugoslav Life*, a quarterly magazine in the same language. *TANJUG* also provides a CITI service for business subscribers worldwide. The state TV/radio station, *RTV Serbia* (formerly *RTV Belgrade*), also produces a daily (1700-2300) unscrambled programme, including news in English, for a worldwide audience via *Eutelsat 1F4*.
BBC World Service and Voice of America frequencies: From time to time these change. See the section *How to Use this Book* for more information.

BBC:				
MHz	**15.575**	**12.095**	**9.410**	**6.195**
Voice of America:				
MHz	**9.670**	**6.040**	**5.995**	**1.260**

Note: *CNN* is also available via satellite (*Astra*) in a number of Belgrade and Montenegrin hotels.

PASSPORT/VISA

Regulations and requirements may be subject to change at short notice, and you are advised to contact the appropriate diplomatic or consular authority before finalising travel arrangements. Details of these may be found at the head of this country's entry. Any numbers in the chart refer to the footnotes below.

	Passport Required?	Visa Required?	Return Ticket Required?
Full British	1	No	No
BVP	Valid	-	-
Australian	Yes	Yes	No
Canadian	Yes	Yes	No
USA	Yes	Yes	No
Other EC	Yes	2	No
Japanese	Yes	No	No

Note: Entry requirements are liable to change at short notice. The suspension of air links and commercial transactions in accordance with UN sanctions have made legal border crossings difficult for foreign nationals. It is advisable to contact the Embassy or the Foreign & Commonwealth Office for up-to-date information (see addresses at top of entry).
PASSPORTS: [1] Valid passport required by all with the exception of nationals of the UK entering as tourists and in possession of a valid British Visitors Passport (see below). Entry is allowed for up to 90 days.
British Visitors Passport: Acceptable for holidays or unpaid business trips to Yugoslavia. A stay beyond 90 days will require permission from the local authorities.
VISAS: Nationals of Afghanistan, Albania, Australia, Bangladesh, Canada, Ghana, [2] Greece, Iran, Lebanon, Nigeria, Pakistan, the Philippines, Sri Lanka, Turkey and the USA require visas to enter Yugoslavia.
Types of visas: Single entry/single exit: £6.80; double entry/double exit: £14; and multiple entry: £20. Transit visas, valid for 7 days (to be used within 6 months of issue), cost £6.80 for single transit, £14 for double transit and £20 for multiple transit. Transit visas are not

required, however, by those holding tickets with confirmed onward reservations who depart within 24 hours and who do not leave the airport.
Validity: Where they are required, visas are valid for 6 months from date of issue and cannot be postdated.
Application to: Consulate (or Consular Section at Embassy). For addresses, see top of entry. Visas may be issued at frontier posts only in special circumstances.
Application requirements: (a) Completed application form. (b) Valid passport. (c) Self-addressed, stamped, registered envelope for return of documents. (d) Fee payable to Embassy in cash or by postal order (cheques only accepted from travel agencies and companies).
Note: Nationals who require visas may on entry be expected to state that they have at least US$150 per person per day for their intended stay in Yugoslavia, and may be asked to produce a return ticket.
Working days required: Immediate issue to personal callers. Postal applications: 7 days.
Temporary residence: Enquire at Embassy. Visas can be extended if local authorities are contacted within 7 days of arrival.

MONEY

Currency: New Yugoslav Dinar (Yu D) = 100 paras. Notes are in denominations of Yu D50,000, 20,000, 500, 200, 100 and 50. Coins are in denominations of Yu D50, 20, 10, 5, 2 and 1. The second New Yugoslav Dinar, issued in December 1991, is still the official currency, although a new Serbian Dinar is reportedly planned. The currency was initially pegged to the Mark at an official parity of DM1 = Yu D13; in September 1992 it stood at DM1 = Yu D136, following repeated devaluations earlier in the year. In August 1992, inflation waaround 75% per month in Serbia and 95% in Montenegro.
Currency exchange: As elsewhere in the ex-Yugoslav republics, the only true repositories of value and real mediums of exchange are the German DM and the US Dollar (the Pound Sterling is rarely used in the republic). The New Yugoslav Dinar is completely unconvertible and worthless. Local hyper-inflation is the basic cause of the collapse of the Yu D. Certain Serbian commercial banks even offer rates of 300-450% above the entirely nominal exchange rates against the DM and the US Dollar. The thriving black market only started trading after the economic sanctions came into force, and is fuelled by high war-related government expenditure.
Credit cards/Travellers cheques: Eurocheques, travellers cheques and credit card payments are prohibited under the terms of the UN trade embargo. The only means to pay in Yugoslavia is by direct cash settlement.
Exchange rate indicators: The following figures are included as a guide to the movement of the New Yugoslav Dinar against Sterling and the US Dollar:

Date:	Nov '89	Oct '90	Mar '91	Oct '92
£1.00=	113,001	20.98	26.42	325.00
$1.00=	72,413	10.74	15.19	204.79

Note: On January 1, 1990, Yugoslavia launched the New Yugoslav Dinar and on December 31, 1991, the second New Yugoslav Dinar.
Banking hours: 0700-1500 Monday to Friday, some branches are open on Saturdays for payments and withdrawals.

DUTY FREE

The following items may be imported into Yugoslavia by persons over 16 years of age without incurring duty:
200 cigarettes or 50 cigars or 250g of tobacco;
750ml of spirits or 1 litre of wine;
250ml of toilet water;
A reasonable quantity of perfume.

PUBLIC HOLIDAYS

Public holidays observed in the Federal Republic of Yugoslavia are as follows:
Mar 28 '93 Public Holiday (Serbia only). **Apr 24** Eastern Orthodox Good Friday. **May 1-2** Labour Days. **Jul 4** Fighters' Day. **Jul 7** Serbian National Day. **Jul 13** Montenegrin National Day. **Nov 29-30** Republic Days. **Jan 1-2 '94** New Year. **Jan 7** Eastern Orthodox Christmas. **Mar 28** Public Holiday (Serbia only).
Note: Orthodox Christian holidays may also be celebrated throughout much of the region.

HEALTH

Regulations and requirements may be subject to change at short notice, and you are advised to contact your doctor well in advance of your intended date of departure. Any numbers in the chart refer to the footnotes below.

	Special Precautions?	Certificate Required?
Yellow Fever	No	No
Cholera	No	No
Typhoid & Polio	No	-
Malaria	No	-
Food & Drink	1	-

[1]: Mains water is normally chlorinated, and whilst relatively safe may cause mild abdominal upsets. Bottled water is available and is advised for the first few weeks of the stay. Milk is pasteurised and dairy products are safe for consumption. Local meat, poultry, seafood, fruit and vegetables are generally considered safe to eat.
Rabies is present. For those at high risk, vaccination before arrival should be considered. If you are bitten abroad seek medical advice without delay. For more information consult the *Health* section.
Health care: Prescribed medicines must be paid for. Insurance with emergency repatriation recommended.

TRAVEL - International

Note: Present Foreign Office advice is to avoid the Federal Republic of Yugoslavia until further notice. It is unclear if this is a direct result of the UN sanctions or stems from the local security situation. However, serious intra-ethnic conflict is expected in Kosovo and possibly Vojvodina, while war in Serbia and Montenegro cannot be ruled out.
AIR: The national airline is *JAT Yugoslav Airlines*. It is itself grounded at Belgrade and no foreign carrier is allowed to offer regular services to Belgrade in accordance with UN sanctions as of June 1992.
International airport: *Belgrade (BEG)* (Surcin) is 20km (12 miles) west of the city. Minor airports exist elsewhere, such as *Podgorica* (formerly Titograd) in Montenegro.
SEA: Note: Services provided by *Jadrolinija* (Rijeka) and other foreign sea carriers along the Adriatic coast are forbidden from calling at any Montenegrin port as a result of UN sanctions. The entire area, and particularly points south of Dubrovnik/Split, is now an actual or potential war zone.
The principal passenger ports are Bar and Kotor. *BI* serves Kotor. Ferries link the Yugoslav Adriatic coast with Italian and Greek ports. The principal ferry routes are:
Bari–Bar–Bari (ferry 'Sveti Stefan' of the *Prekooceanska Plovidba Company*, from Bar);
Rijeka–Rab–Zadar–Split–Hvar–Korcula–Dubrovnik–Bar–Corfu–Igoumenitsa (*Jadrolinija* ferry-boat).
RAIL: Connections and through coaches are available from principal east and west European cities. From London, the main connection is the *Simplon Express:* (London)–Paris–Milan–Belgrade.
International trains have couchette coaches as well as bar and dining cars. On some lines transport for cars is provided.
ROAD: The following frontier posts are open for road traffic, usually 24 hours a day:
From **Hungary:** Redics–Dolga Vas; Letenye–Gorican; Barcs–Terezino Polje; Dravaszabolcs–Donji Miholjac; Udvar–Knezevo; Hercegszanto–Backi Breg (Bezdan); Tompa–Kelebija; and Roszke–Horgos.
From **Romania:** Jimbolia–Srpska Crnja; Stamora Moravita–Vatin; Naidas–Kaludaerova (Bela Crkva); and Portile de Fier–(Turnu Severin)–Daerdap (Kladovo).
From **Bulgaria:** Bregovo–Mokranje (Negotin); Kula–Vrska Cuka (Zajecar); Kalotina–Gradina; Otomanci–Ribarci; Kjustendil–Deve Bair (Kriva Palanka); Blagoevgrad –Delcevo; and Petric–Novo Selo.
From **Albania:** Podgradec–Cafa San (Struga); Kukes–Vrbnica; and Han i Hotit–Bozaj.

TRAVEL - Internal

AIR: *JAT* offers connections between Belgrade and Podgorica.
RAIL/ROAD: On account of the ongoing conflict with Croatia, the main road/rail route to and from Western Europe is now closed, with extensive detours via Hungary for international traffic going south–north to and from Greece. Due to the Greco-Serbian economic blockade of Macedonia (which is itself attempting to comply with UN economic sanctions against its northern neighbour), rail services between Serbia and Greece are uncertain and intermittent. The same is true in relation to connections between Bulgaria and Serbia. Internal rail services are in general poor. Delays should be expected when crossing the border from Hungary, Macedonia (Greece) and Bulgaria by car. Drivers should not rely on local petrol stations for fuel, due to continually worsening shortages of oil caused by the UN trade embargo, although hard currency might make otherwise rationed and scarce petrol available. **Coach:** Efficient and cheap coaches connect all towns. The fuel shortages have restricted the services severely. **Taxi:** Main cities have metered taxis. **Car hire:** Available from airports and main towns. **Speed limits:** 120kmph (75mph) on motorways and 100kmph (62mph) on other roads.
Documentation: Full national driving licence is accepted. No customs documents are required but car log books and third party Green Card insurance are necessary.
URBAN: There are good bus services in the main towns, with tramways and trolleybuses in Belgrade. Multi-journey tickets are sold in advance through tobacconists for self-cancellation on board. Fares paid to the driver are at double the pre-purchase prices.

ACCOMMODATION

HOTELS: Deluxe/A-class hotels are confined to Belgrade and a number of Montenegrin Adriatic resorts, most notably the exclusive island of Sveti Stefan. Further down the scale, and particularly in the smaller towns, services are poor. The best hotels are always heavily booked, so advanced booking is essential. Prices are very high, and payable in hard currency for visiting foreign nationals. Also, the Montenegrin resorts are now impossibly overcrowded, following the closure of the Croatian coastline to all Yugoslav nationals. **Grading:** Classification is from deluxe to A, B, C and D class. **Pensions:** 1st, 2nd and 3rd class pensions are available throughout the country.
Inns: Motels are found on most main roads. Prices are set independently according to region, tourist season and the quality of service.
GUEST-HOUSES: Many people offer rooms, often with meals, to tourists in villages without hotels. Discounts are available off-season. Contact tourist offices or travel agencies for details.
SELF-CATERING: Holiday villages are available in many resorts as well as a selection of apartments and villas. Travel agencies and tourist offices have further information.
CAMPING/CARAVANNING: Only available on official sites. A permit from the local tourist office is required for off-site camping. A list is available from the National Tourist Office. *Alpine Club* mountain huts are available in all mountain areas. Camping and caravan holidays are offered by a number of tour operators (*Yugotours* etc).
Note: Caravans are allowed in duty free for up to one year.
YOUTH HOSTELS: *The Youth Hostel Authority* is at Farijalni Savez Jugoslavije, Mose Pijade 12/1, 11000 Belgrade. Tel: (11) 339 666 *or* 339 802. Student and youth travel is arranged by *Naromtravel,* Mose Pijade 12, 11000 Belgrade. Tel: (11) 331 610.

YUGOSLAVIA | **HEALTH REGULATIONS** | **VISA REGULATIONS** | Code-Link

GALILEO/WORLDSPAN

TI-DFT/BEG/HE

TI-DFT/BEG/VI

SABRE

TIDFT/BEG/HE

TIDFT/BEG/VI

To access this information on your CRS, swipe the barcode with a light pen or type in the text under the barcode. For more information, see the introduction *How to Use This Book.*

RESORTS & EXCURSIONS

Serbia

The largest of the republics, Serbia was under Turkish rule and traces of Muslim influence remain, particularly in the Kosovo-Metohija region. **Belgrade** is the capital of Serbia and the national capital. Its strategic location on the edge of the Carpathian Basin near the joining of the Sava River and the Danube and also its position on the Stambul Road from Turkey into Central Europe made it a centre of commerce and communications. Many of the buildings were built after the Second World War. The *Kalemegdan Citadel* straddles a hilltop overlooking the junction of the Sava and Danube. The *National Museum* is interesting, and there is also the *Museum of Modern Art* and the *Ethnographical Museum*. Well worth a visit is the *Palace of Princess Ljubica* (1831) with a good collection of period funiture. **Skadarlija** is the 19th-century Bohemian quarter with cafés, street dancers, singers and open-air theatres. **Pristina**, the capital of Kosovo, contains the *Imperial Mosque* built in the 15th century and also several 19th-century Turkish buildings. Near **Kraljevo** is the restored *Monastery of Zica*, now painted bright red as it was in medieval times. It was there that the Kings of Serbia were crowned. The *Kalenic Monastery* is a fine example of the Serbian style.

Montenegro

Montenegro (given as the birthplace of Rex Stout's fictional American detective, Nero Wolfe) is at the southern end of Yugoslavia's coast, an area of spectacular mountain ranges with villages perched like eagles' nests on high peaks. This stands in direct contrast to the republic's coastal region, which extends from the *Bay of Kotor* to the Albanian border. **Kotor** itself is a bustling port with a picturesque old city quarter. The general architecture is mainly of Venetian origin, as this power dominated the region until 1797. Entering the city through the town gate brings the visitor to the square with the 17th-century *Clock Tower*, overshadowed by the twin towers of the *Cathedral of St Tryphon* (12th century). A visit to the *Naval Museum* and the *Church of St Lucas* (1195) should not be missed.

SOCIAL PROFILE

FOOD & DRINK: Cuisine varies greatly from one region to another. On the whole the meat specialities are better than the fish dishes. National favourites include *pihtije* (jellied pork or duck), *prsut* (smoked ham), *cevapcici* (charcoal-grilled minced meat), *raznjici* (skewered meat), *sarma* or *japrak* (vine or cabbage leaves stuffed with meat and rice). Desserts are heavy and sweet including *strukli* (nuts and plums stuffed into cheese balls and then boiled), *lokum* (Turkish delight) and *alva* (nuts crushed in honey). Table service is usual in hotel restaurants. **Drink:** Wine is widely available and cheap. Ljutomer, Traminer and Riesling wines from Montenegro are the best known. Varieties include *Dingac*, *Postup*, *Krstac* and *Vranac*. The white *Vugava* produced in Vis is excellent. Popular national spirits are *slivovica* (a potent plum brandy), *loza* and *maraskino* (made of morello cherries). Bars and cafés have counter and table service. Most places serving alcohol close by 2200.
NIGHTLIFE: There is a wide range of nightlife in all the main cities and resorts, including bars, nightclubs, cinemas and theatres. Cinemas stay open until 2300, nightclubs to 0300 and restaurants to 2400.
SHOPPING: Special purchases include embroidery, lace, leatherwork, *Pec* filigree work, metalwork and Turkish coffee sets. **Shopping hours:** 0800-1200 and 1700-2000 Monday to Friday, 0800-1500 Saturday.
SPORT: Skiing and **spa resorts** exist in all regions, but particularly Kopaonik and Brezovica (Serbia). **Fishing** permits are available from hotels or local authorities. Local information is necessary. Fishing on the Adriatic coast is unrestricted, but freshwater angling and fishing with equipment needs a permit. 'Fish-linking' with a local small-craft owner is popular. **Sailing** is popular along the coast. Berths and boats can be hired at all ports. Permits are needed for boats brought into the country. **Spectator sports: Football** is one of the more popular.
SPECIAL EVENTS: The following is a selection of the major festivals and other special events celebrated annually in Yugoslavia. For a complete list, contact the Yugoslav National Tourist Office.
Belgrade: *Summer Festival* (mid-July to mid-September).
Kotor: *Boka Night* (July).
Nationwide: Many major cities hold theatre festivals in October.
SOCIAL CONVENTIONS: Hitherto a relatively open, informal and secure society, Yugoslavia is now changing for the worse under the impact of war and its various consequences. Once virtually non-existent, violent crime is now common in the big cities, while xenophobic sentiments are growing. A superficial veneer of normality belies underlying social tensions, often exploding into violence. Foreign nationality is no longer a guarantee of safety.

BUSINESS PROFILE

Note: All business and commercial transactions are indefinitely suspended in accordance with UN sanctions effective from June 1992.
ECONOMY: The new Yugoslav federation of Serbia and Montenegro is estimated to possess about 50% of the natural resources of the former Yugoslavia, 40% of its GDP, 50% of its agricultural and electrical output, 35% of its industrial output and 30% of industrial employment. GDP per capita, previously close to the former average of US$2600 (1990), declined to US$1500 in 1991-92 because of the collapse of the internal Yugoslav market and the violent conflicts that followed. Unemployment levels reached 20% even before the UN imposed sanctions and displaced about 500,000 persons. Despite widespread sanction-busting, the socio-economic consequences in 1993 are going to be catastrophic, as industrial output and GDP fell to approximately 20-30% in the period 1991-92, while unemployment has risen to 30-40%. Only the relatively high degree of self-sufficiency in foodstuffs and electricity generation (coal) will prevent a complete collapse, as the present population ratio will probably change in favour of the relatively unpopulated countryside.
The historically poor export performance, especially to Western markets, further declined with a fall of 18% in the first quarter of 1992 over the same period in 1991; previously large trade deficits were cut over the same period by reducing imports. The loss of these important markets means that the Government cannot hope to service its share of the foreign debt of the former federation. Including unallocated federal debts, Serbia is liable for US$8 billion and Montenegro for a further US$1 billion. Under the present conditions a formal debt rescheduling is unlikely to be granted by creditors, as the majority of the National Bank of Yugoslavia's hard currency reserves (US$2 billion in 1992) were frozen by various governments. Thereby, the ultimate default and following international bankruptcy are inevitable.
Prior to June 1992, and based upon DTI data for 1990-91, Serbia's share of bilateral UK trade with the former federation was 65%, with a surplus on the UK side. At that time the UK was the fourth most important EC trading partner of the former Yugoslavia.
BUSINESS: As with Croatia, but unlike Slovenia, things go very slowly or not at all on account of the cumbersome bureaucracy and general socio-economic collapse. Communication, however, is not a major problem, as English is popular as a second language. **Office hours:** 0700-1430 Monday to Friday. **Government office hours:** 0700-1500 Monday to Friday.
COMMERCIAL INFORMATION: The following organisations can offer advice: Privredna Komora Jugoslavije (Yugoslav Chamber of Economy), PO Box 1003, Terazije 23, 11000 Belgrade. Tel: (11) 339 461. Fax: (11) 631 928. Telex: 11638; *or*
Chamber of Economy of Serbia, Ulica Generala Zdanova 13-15, 11000 Belgrade. Tel: (11) 340 611. Fax: (11) 330 949; *or*
Chamber of Economy of Montenegro, Novaka Miloseva 29/II, 81000 Podgorica. Tel: (81) 31071. Fax: (81) 34926.

HISTORY & GOVERNMENT

HISTORY: The history of Yugoslavia (and indeed of the Balkan area) is exceedingly complex, as it is a region which has long been prey to the ambitions of its neighbours on every side, from the Ancient Greeks to the Austro-Hungarian empire of the Habsburgs. The occupation of the Balkans by itinerant Slavic peoples was completed by around AD650. One of these, the Serbs, came under the hegemony of the Byzantine empire. Unity among the fractious Serbian clans was not achieved until the end of the 11th century with the Serbian expansion into Montenegro where the independent state of Zeta was established in 1081. Montenegro has since been a close ally of Serbia, a relationship which was noticeable during the 1991 civil war. By the 11th century, Christianity had come to the Balkans, laying the foundations of future enmity between Serbs, who subscribed to Eastern (Orthodox) Christianity, and Croats, who embraced Roman Catholicism. Croatia was further separated from the other Balkan states by being absorbed into neighbouring Hungary in 1102, and the rest of the century was characterised by fighting between successive Serbian kings and the Hungarians. The Magyars dominated the region, taking control of Northern Serbia, then Bosnia and Hercegovina. In 1276, Dragutin forcibly took over the crown by deposing his father with Hungary's support; however, he was almost immediately attacked and defeated by the Greeks and abdicated. Dragutin's illegitimate grandson, Stephen Dechanski, who became King Stephen Urosh III, had more success in the military sphere: his forces overran territory in Macedonia and on the Adriatic coast and vanquished a combined force of Greeks and Bulgarians at Küstendil in 1330. His successor, Stjepan Dusan (Stephen Urosh IV) built on this success and by 1344 the Serbs had subjugated all of Macedonia, Albania, Thessaly and Epirus and pacified Bulgaria. Bosnia was then conquered in 1349 and Hungary itself in 1353. This period also marked the zenith of the Serbian Orthodox Church, which had become firmly established after the destruction of the medieval Serbian empire, and which was instrumental in forming national culture and identity. In June 1389, a decisive confrontation took place which would settle the fate of the region for centuries to come and serve as the key symbol in Serbian national consciousness. This was the Battle of Kosovo in southern Serbia in which an allied force of Serbs and Bosnians (backed by some Albanians and Wallachians) under Prince Lazar was defeated by the advancing Turks. Serbia thereafter became an Ottoman vassal state, resulting in an exodus of Serbian settlers into what is now Vojvodina, Croatia and Bosnia-Hercegovina. Soon afterwards, Hungary recovered Croatia and the Dalmatian coast from Bosnian control. In 1459, Serbia was definitively conquered by the Turks and incorporated into the Ottoman empire. Montenegro was the only region not absorbed by the Ottoman Empire by this time. In the 18th century, Ottoman power began its long decline in Europe, but Serbia remained relatively quiet under Turkish rule until the early 19th century when, with Russian support, anti-Turkish uprisings began in Inner Serbia. The Turks ceded some control to the local ruler Milos, Prince of Serbia. Michael, his son, assumed the throne in 1860, determined to expel the Turks. After five years of sporadic fighting, Turkish troops left the territory. Serbia then signed a series of secret alliances with Montenegro, Romania and Greece with the aim of bolstering its own security. The Serbia-Greece pact was particularly important as it settled the ownership of disputed territories: Bosnia and Hercegovina went to Serbia; Thessaly and Epirus were taken by the Greeks. Another insurrection in 1876, followed by a declaration of war on Turkey, led to another Serbian defeat. However, a new player in the region, the Austrians, offered protection to the Serbs and prevented them from falling under Turkish suzerainty again. The Balkan republics now started to assume their modern form. Bosnia and Hercegovina merged in 1876; two years later the new republic was occupied by the Austro-Hungarian Empire. Serbian independence was settled at the Treaty of Berlin in 1878, where Montenegro was also recognised as an independent state and was doubled in size.
In the first years of the 1900s, however, the Serbian-Habsburg relationship began to sour and by 1905 Serbian policy had become avowedly nationalist and anti-Austrian. The stability of the region deteriorated further when Austria annexed Bosnia-Hercegovina in 1908. Serbia objected vehemently to the Austrian action and the two sides almost went to war over the annexation. Ultimately, Serbia was forced to back down, and the crisis left relations between the two very tense. In 1910, Nicholas I (1860-1918) proclaimed himself King of Montenegro and became Serbia's closest ally, which soon became vital in the Balkan War. In 1912 Serbia and Bulgaria signed an alliance treaty which was principally directed against Turkey and the First Balkan War in 1912-13 pitted Serbia and Bulgaria, backed by Greece, against Turkey. The fighting was ended by the Treaty of London in May 1913 which settled the status of Albania and of the Aegean islands, most of which remained under Greek control. The position of Macedonia, variously claimed by Serbia, Bulgaria and Greece, was unresolved and the particular dispute between Bulgaria and Serbia was the principal cause of the Second Balkan War which was waged for two months in the summer of 1913. Bulgaria was rapidly defeated once Turkey and Romania had entered the war against it, and the Treaty of Bucharest put an end to Bulgarian aspirations in Macedonia, which was divided between Serbia and Greece. Serbia briefly invaded Albania but quickly pulled out when threatened by Austria-Hungary. Although doubled in size as a result of the conflict, Serbia nevertheless had only limited access to the Adriatic Sea via Montenegro on account of Austrian insistence upon an independent Albanian state. This issue, plus the Austrian presence in Bosnia-Hercegovina, brought the simmering friction between Serbia and the Habsburgs suddenly to a head in June 1914 with the assassination of the Austrian Archduke Francis Ferdinand by a Serb revolutionary, Gavrilo Princip, in the Bosnian capital Sarajevo. Austria-Hungary treated the issue as a matter of national honour, as well as seeing an opportunity to deal with the Serbs once and for all. On July 28, war was declared. This brought to collapse the elaborate system of treaties and alliances which was holding together a fragile European peace. Russia, a would-be guarantor of Balkan stability, came in on the Serbian side despite German threats that they too would enter the war. Germany was challenged by

Britain and France, rejecting offers to agree the neutrality of smaller Western European states (Luxembourg and Belgium). Convinced that France would come to Russia's aid, Germany declared war on August 3. Britain, allied to France, entered the war within days. Serbia, exhausted by the Balkan wars, initially stayed out of the wider European conflict. In 1915, however, Austria-Hungary carried out their long-threatened invasion and the dispute over Macedonia again brought Serbia into conflict with Bulgaria. Serbia was occupied by enemy forces for much of the next three years, but after the end of the war and the political settlement which followed the Balkan republics concluded that some form of unity would be conducive to their future security. The 'Kingdom of Serbs, Croats and Slovenes' was formed in 1918 from the Kingdom of Serbia and the southern Slav states of the former Austro-Hungarian Empire (Croatia, Slovenia and Bosnia-Hercegovina). The Kingdom was renamed Yugoslavia in 1929. During the inter-war period, when a highly unitary system of government was imposed on the triune kingdom from Belgrade by Prince Alexander of Serbia, 'Greater Serbia' and 'Yugoslavia' became one and the same thing for the separatist Croats. Alexander was assassinated by Croatian nationalists in 1934: his brother, Prince Paul, took over. The new ruler made no secret of his pro-Nazi sympathies. During the Second World War, 1.1 million people (mostly Serb) died, largely in a genocide of Serbs by the Croatian clerico-fascist Ustasa in what later became Bosnia-Hercegovina. In 1941, a military coup led by air force officers deposed Paul, whereupon the Germans and Italians invaded the country. During the ensuing struggle, which lasted until almost the end of World War II in 1945, the Communist Party of Yugoslavia under Josip Broz (known as Tito) gained wide support for its partisan activities and in 1945 Tito took power. Later, after the war, more Serbs were killed in the power struggle carried on between royalist *Chetniks*, loyal to the ex-King Peter II exiled in London, and *Partisans* under the control of Tito's Communist Party of Yugoslavia. In 1946, a Soviet-style constitution was adopted, but two years later Yugoslavia was expelled from the Soviet alliance (the Cominform). New constitutions adopted in 1953, 1963 and 1974 extended this autonomy throughout the social and economic sphere, despite evidence that its results left much to be desired. The amended constitutions also gave considerable autonomy to the country's constituent republics. During this period Yugoslavia's foreign policy was rigorously non-aligned, which attracted much interest, particularly from countries which sought to escape the influence of one or other superpower. Yugoslavia was a founder and subsequently a prominent member of the Non-Aligned Movement.
Following Tito's death in 1980, however, foreign policy became irrelevant as the rotating collective presidency Tito had designed to replace him became increasingly concerned with holding the country together and preventing chronic economic decline. The disparity between the comparatively richer northern republics of Slovenia and Croatia and the rest became a major source of friction as the two wealthier republics increasingly questioned the use and distribution of central funds – to which they were the sole net contributors. Friction between the country's republics and different ethnic groups, suppression of which had been the key to Tito's longevity, also came to the fore. Serious difficulties began in late 1989, but the disintegration of Yugoslavia began in earnest in the spring of 1990 when Slovenia and Croatia both held multi-party elections which returned governments committed to the pursuit of outright independence in both republics. After fourteen months during which Slovenia and Croatia became increasingly alienated from Belgrade, Slovenia declared independence. The federal government immediately despatched a column of troops into Slovenia to secure federal border posts and key installations in the Slovene capital, Ljubljana. After a few weeks of inconclusive skirmishing, a ceasefire was reached. By October 1991, all federal military forces had left Slovenia which rapidly moved to full independence and international recognition. The Belgrade government, under its nationalist demagogue Slobodan Milosevic, was evidently prepared to let Slovenia, ethnically homogenous and geographically isolated, go its own way. Croatia, with its sizeable Serb population and dominance of the Yugoslav coastline, was a different matter. Tension had been rising in Croatia since the election of the Croat nationalist government led by Franjo Tudjman in May 1990. In October, the Serb minority in the Croatian region of Krajina declared autonomy: disturbances increased when Croat security forces tried to disarm Serb paramilitary groups and full-scale fighting broke out when the federal army intervened. The army's officer corps was overwhelmingly Serbian and those ranks who were not Serbs or Montenegrans defected to their own republics. The army henceforth operates as essentially a Serb army: this has given the Serbs the military edge. The seceding republics, under pressure from the EC, agreed to put their declarations of independence 'on ice' for three months while negotiators sought a settlement. In the autumn of 1991, the federal side started to develop its strategy. If Croatia was going to secede, then Belgrade would try and separate off by force those parts of it with a Serbian majority. The other Yugoslav republics staked out their positions in the conflict: Montenegro backed Serbia; Macedonia wanted autonomy as part of Greece; the 3-way ethnic split in Bosnia-Hercegovina (Muslim, Croat and Serb) gave rise to different aspirations for the ethnic groups. Bosnian Serbs voted in November 1991 to become part of 'Greater Serbia' while the Muslims and some Croats favoured independence: in December, they declared it. By this time the fighting between the Croat forces and Serbs had reached a peak, particularly around the Croat towns of Osijek and Vukovar in the north and Dubrovnik in the south. Federal and Serb shelling of Dubrovnik in particular, including the ancient and architecturally outstanding old town, raised international concerns to an unprecedented level. By the time a UN-brokered ceasefire took effect in January 1992, 30% of Croatian territory had been lost to Serb control. An uneasy peace under the supervision of the 14,000-strong UN Protection Forces for Yugoslavia (UNPROFOR) held briefly in Croatia, while the focus of the fighting moved to Bosnia. A similar pattern emerged here as Serb paramilitaries attempted to bring particular areas under their control. This entailed the practice of 'ethnic cleansing' in which non-Serbs have been driven out of targetted areas and their property and possessions handed over to Serbs. The focus of attention during 1992 has been the Bosnian capital of Sarajevo, which has been besieged for several months, relying on aid shipments by the UN. The UN and the European Community have worked in tandem throughout the crisis in the search of a settlement. Both have appointed special representatives to try and arrange a ceasefire and negotiated settlement: Cyrus Vance acts for the UN, while first Lord Carrington and now Lord Owen, represent the EC. The international community has cast rump Yugoslavia – Serbia and its ally Montenegro – as the aggressors and imposed economic sanctions against both. Although a steady supply of goods from the Danube has undermined the effectiveness of this, it has put strain on the Serb/Montenegrin economy. In the negotiations during the summer of 1992, an apparent difference has emerged between Serb leader Milosevic and the federal Yugoslav leadership. The split may have a bearing on the future of the crisis, particularly as Milosevic is increasingly unpopular at home. Renewed fighting has broken out in Croatia with Serbian bombing of a hydroelectric dam threatening massive flooding. At the time of writing, the future role and scope of UN peace-keeping forces remains uncertain.
GOVERNMENT: The Federal Republic of Yugoslavia, comprising Serbia and Montenegro, was established in April 1992. Still ruled by Milosevic's Serbian Socialist Party and Bulatovic's League of Communists of Montenegro, Yugoslavia is now confronted by immense internal and external problems, not least of which is something as basic as survival. Legislative power rests with the Federal Assembly, which has two chambers, the Chamber of Republics and the Chamber of Citizens, both comprising representatives from Serbia and Montenegro. The Assembly elects the President of the Republic. Both Serbia and Montenegro also have distinct republican assemblies.

CLIMATE

Serbia has a continental climate with cold winters and warm summers. Montenegro is largely the same, but with alpine conditions in the mountains and Mediterranean ones on the Adriatic coast.
Required clothing: *Winter:* medium-weight clothing and overcoat. *Summer:* lightweight clothing and raincoat.

BELGRADE Serbia (132m)

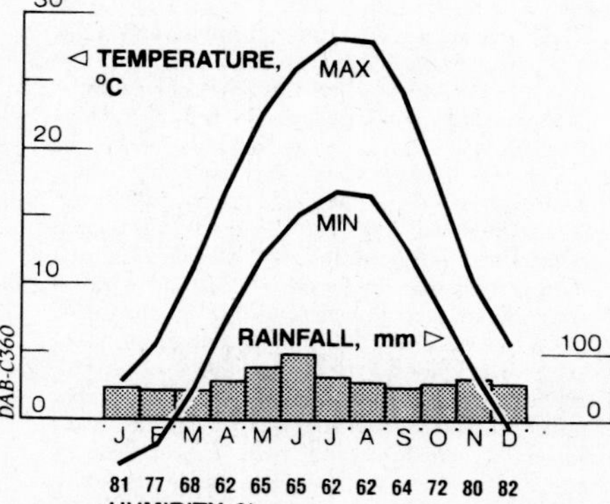

ZAIRE

Location: Central Africa.

Office National du Tourisme
BP 9502
2a/2b avenue des Orangers
Kinshasa-Gombe, Zaïre
Tel: (12) 30070.
Embassy of the Republic of Zaïre
26 Chesham Place
London SW1X 8HH
Tel: (071) 235 6137. Fax: (071) 235 9048. Telex: 25651 ZAIRE G. Opening hours (for visa enquiries): 0900-1230 Monday to Friday.
British Embassy
BP 8049
5ème étage
191 avenue de l'Equateur
Kinshasa, Zaïre
Tel: (12) 21327. Telex: 21689.
Consulates in: Lubumbashi, Goma and Kishangani.
Embassy of the Republic of Zaïre
1800 New Hampshire Avenue, NW
Washington, DC
20009
Tel: (202) 234 7690/1.
Embassy of the United States of America
310 avenue des Aviateurs
Kinshasa, Zaïre
Tel: (12) 21532 *or* 21628. Fax: (12) 21232. Telex: 21405 US EMB ZR.
Consulate in: Lubumbashi.
Embassy of the Republic of Zaïre
18 Range Road
Ottawa, Ontario
K1N 8J3
Tel: (613) 236 7103/4 *or* 236 4815. Fax: (613) 567 1404. Telex: 0534314.
Consulate in: Montréal.
Canadian Embassy
PO Box 8341
17 Pumbu Avenue
Kinshasa, Zaïre
Tel: (12) 60213. Telex: 21303 DOMCAN ZR.

AREA: 2,344,885 sq km (905,365 sq miles).
POPULATION: 33,458,000 (1988 estimate).
POPULATION DENSITY: 14.3 per sq km.
CAPITAL: Kinshasa. **Population:** 2,778,281 (including Maluku) (1985).
GEOGRAPHY: Zaïre is the third largest country in Africa and is bordered to the north by the Central African Republic and Sudan, to the east by Uganda, Rwanda, Burundi and Tanzania, to the south by Zambia and Angola and to the west by the Congo. Zaïre has a coastline of only 27km (17 miles), at the outlet of the Zaïre river, which flows into the Atlantic. The country straddles the Equator and has widely differing geographi-

cal features, including mountain ranges in the north and west, a vast central plain through which the Zaïre River flows, and the volcanoes and lakes of the Kivu region. The Zaïre River has given rise to extensive tropical rain forests on the western border with the Congo.
LANGUAGE: The official language is French. There are many local dialects, the most widely spoken being Lingala, Swahili, Tshiluba and Kikongo.
RELIGION: Predominantly Roman Catholic, with a minority of Protestant and traditional beliefs.
TIME: GMT + 1 (Kinshasa and Mbandaka) and GMT + 2 (Haut-Zaïre, Kasai, Kivu and Shaba).
ELECTRICITY: 220 volts AC, 50Hz.
COMMUNICATIONS: Telephone: IDD is available. Country code: 243. Internal telephone service is often unreliable. **Fax:** A few hotels have facilities. **Telex/telegram:** Telex facilities are only available at Kinshasa and Lubumbashi post offices and at the *Intercontinental Hotel*. Telegrams can be sent from chief telegraph offices, but are unreliable and sometimes subject to delays – particularly internal. **Post:** Post office opening hours: 0800-1800 Monday to Saturday. Zaïre is included in the Universal Postal Union and the African Postal Union. Airmail to Europe takes 4-18 days. **Press:** The daily newspapers are in various African languages. The two main newspapers are *Elima* and *Salongo*, both government-owned.
BBC World Service and Voice of America frequencies: From time to time these change. See the section *How to Use this Book* for more information.

BBC:				
MHz	21.660	21.470	17.790	15.400
Voice of America:				
MHz	21.49	15.60	9.525	6.035

PASSPORT/VISA

Regulations and requirements may be subject to change at short notice, and you are advised to contact the appropriate diplomatic or consular authority before finalising travel arrangements. Details of these may be found at the head of this country's entry. Any numbers in the chart refer to the footnotes below.

	Passport Required?	Visa Required?	Return Ticket Required?
Full British	Yes	Yes	Yes
BVP	Not valid	-	-
Australian	Yes	Yes	Yes
Canadian	Yes	Yes	Yes
USA	Yes	Yes	Yes
Other EC	Yes	Yes	Yes
Japanese	Yes	Yes	Yes

PASSPORTS: Required by all.
British Visitors Passport: Not acceptable.
VISAS: Required by all except nationals of Chad, Central African Republic, Congo, Sudan, Tanzania, Uganda and Zambia.
Types of visa: Tourist, Transit and Business; valid for single or multiple entry for 1, 2, 3 or 6 months. Transit visas are required by all except those noted above and persons continuing their journey within 48 hours provided they hold confirmed onward tickets.
Application to: Consulate (or Consular Section at Embassy). For addresses, see top of entry.
Application requirements: (a) Valid passport. (b) 1 application form. (c) 1 photo. (d) Yellow fever vaccination certificate. (e) Return or onward travel documentation. (f) Stamped, addressed envelope (or cost of return postage) with postal application.
Further documentation may be required depending on the purpose of travel eg, for visits to relatives or family, a letter of invitation from them approved by the Zaïrean authorities; for tourist visits, letters from employer/university and from bank to prove sufficient funds are held to cover duration of stay; for business visits, letters from sponsors in both country of origin and Zaïre. Fees are payable on collection of visa, in cash or certified banker's drafts/cheques only.
Cost: Transit – £25 (one way) and £50 (return); single entry (1 month) – £42; multiple entry (1 month) – £67; single entry (2 months) – £75; multiple entry (2 months) – £100; single entry (3 months) – £109; multiple entry (3 months) – £125; single entry (6 months) – £150; multiple entry (6 months) – £200.
Working days required: 48 hours minimum, in person or by post.
Temporary residence: Apply to Embassy.

MONEY

Currency: Zaïre (Z) = 100 makuta. Notes are in denominations of Z10,000, 5000, 1000, 500, 100, 50, 10 and 5. Coins are in denominations of Z10, 5 and 1.
Currency exchange: There is a thriving black market for foreign currency, but it is illegal to exchange money through any but official exchange bureaux. Note that purchase of airline tickets within Zaïre can be made only with officially exchanged money.
Credit cards: The use of Access/Mastercard and Visa are limited to main towns only. Check with your credit card company for details of merchant acceptability and other services which may be available.
Exchange rate indicators: The following figures are included as a guide to the movements of the Zaïre against Sterling and the US Dollar:

Date:	Oct '89	Oct '90	Oct '91	Oct '92
£1.00=	652	1407	31,592	2,391,600
$1.00=	413	720	18,203	1,506,994

Currency restrictions: Import and export of local currency is prohibited. Import of foreign currency is unlimited subject to declaration. Export of foreign currency is limited to the amount declared on import.
Banking hours: 0800-1130 Monday to Friday.

DUTY FREE

The following items may be imported into Zaïre without incurring customs duty:
100 cigarettes or 50 cigars or equivalent in tobacco;
1 bottle of alcoholic beverage (opened);
A reasonable amount of perfume for personal use.
Note: An import licence is required for arms and ammunition.

PUBLIC HOLIDAYS

Public holidays observed in Zaïre are as follows:
May 1 '93 Labour Day. **May 20** Anniversary of the Mouvement Populaire de la Révolution. **Jun 24** Anniversary of Zaïre currency, Promulgation of the 1967 Constitution and Day of the Fishermen. **Jun 30** Independence Day. **Aug 1** Parents' Day. **Oct 14** Youth Day and Birthday of President Mobutu. **Oct 27** Anniversary of country's change of name to Zaïre. **Nov 17** Army Day. **Nov 24** Anniversary of the Second Republic. **Dec 25** Christmas Day. **Jan 1 '94** New Year's Day. **Jan 4** Day of the Martyrs of Independence.

HEALTH

Regulations and requirements may be subject to change at short notice, and you are advised to contact your doctor well in advance of your intended date of departure. Any numbers in the chart refer to the footnotes below.

	Special Precautions?	Certificate Required?
Yellow Fever	Yes	1
Cholera	Yes	2
Typhoid & Polio	Yes	3
Malaria	4	-
Food & Drink	5	-

[1]: A yellow fever vaccination certificate is required of travellers over one year of age.
[2]: Following WHO guidelines issued in 1973, a cholera vaccination certificate is not an official condition of entry to Zaïre. However, cholera is a serious risk in this country and precautions are essential. Up-to-date advice should be sought before deciding whether these precautions should include vaccination as medical opinion is divided over its effectiveness. See the *Health* section at the back of the book.
[3]: The WHO recommends a vaccination against typhoid.
[4]: Malaria risk, predominantly in the malignant *falciparum* form, throughout the year in the whole country. The strain is reported to be 'highly resistant' to chloroquine.
[5]: All water should be regarded as being a potential health risk. Water used for drinking, brushing teeth or making ice should have first been boiled or otherwise sterilised. Milk is unpasteurised and should be boiled. Powdered or tinned milk is available and is advised, but make sure that it is reconstituted with pure water. Avoid dairy products which are likely to have been made from unboiled milk. Only eat well-cooked meat and fish, preferably served hot. Pork, salad and mayonnaise may carry increased risk. Vegetables should be cooked and fruit peeled.
Rabies is present. For those at high risk vaccination before arrival should be considered. If you are bitten abroad seek medical advice without delay. For more information consult the *Health* section at the back of the book.
Bilharzia (schistosomiasis) is present. Avoid swimming and paddling in fresh water. Swimming pools which are well-chlorinated and maintained are safe.
Plague is present in natural foci. Further information should be sought from the Department of Health or from any of the hospitals specialising in tropical diseases listed in the *Health* section at the back of this book.
Health care: Government expenditure on health is low, even by African standards. It is advisable to take specific personal medicines as medical facilities are available only in larger centres. Health insurance is *essential* and it is advisable to include cover for emergency air evacuation.

TRAVEL - International

Note: There are indefinite restrictions for entry into the Republic of Zaïre. Travellers wishing to either enter or cross the country should note that (a) entry by air is only permitted at the capital, Kinshasa, and (b) entry from Rwanda is only permitted at Goma and only for visits to the Kahuzi-Biega National Park in Bukavu (return must be by the same route).
AIR: Zaïre's national airline is *Air Zaïre (QC)*.
Approximate flight time: From *London* to Kinshasa is 7-9 hours.
International airport: *Kinshasa (FIH)* (N'djili) is 25km (15 miles) east of the city (travel time – 45 minutes). Coach to and from city with return from Hotel Memling, 50 avenue du Tchad. Taxis available. Airport facilities include 24-hour bank/bureau de change, post office, restaurant and car hire (*Avis, Budget, Europcar, InterRent* and *Hertz*).
Departure tax: US$20 for all international departures.
SEA: The international port is Matadi on the Zaïre River. There are services to Antwerp, run by *Compagnie Maritime Belge* and the *Compagnie Maritime du Zaïre*, and to the UK by *Elder Dempster Lines* and *Palm Line*.
RAIL: There are rail connections to Dar es Salaam in Tanzania and to Zambia, Zimbabwe, Mozambique and South Africa. The rail link to Lobito in Angola is unreliable due to the unstable political situation.
ROAD: The majority of Zaïre has connecting roads to surrounding countries, the major routes being through the Sudan, Uganda and Zambia. At the time of going to press, it is not advisable to travel from Zaïre to Kenya via Uganda because of the uncertain political situation in the latter country. Ferries from the western border with the Congo and the northern border with the Central African Republic run across the Zaïre and Oubangui rivers.

ZAIRE — **HEALTH REGULATIONS** — **VISA REGULATIONS** — Code-Link

GALILEO/WORLDSPAN

TI-DFT/FIH/HE

TI-DFT/FIH/VI

SABRE

TIDFT/FIH/HE

TIDFT/FIH/VI

To access this information on your CRS, swipe the barcode with a light pen or type in the text under the barcode. For more information, see the introduction *How to Use This Book*.

TRAVEL - Internal

Note: There are indefinite restrictions for tourist travel within or across Zaïre. Overland journeys by local public transport, hitch-hiking, or by foreign vehicle or motorcycle (with a foreign registration number) are forbidden.
AIR: *Air Zaïre* (QC) connects *N'djili Airport* (Kinshasa) to over 40 internal airports and 150 landing strips. Small planes are available for charter.
Departure tax: US$8 for adults and US$6 for children on all domestic departures.
RIVER: Over 1600km (1000 miles) of the Zaïre River is navigable and there are services from Kinshasa to the upriver ports of Kisangani and Ilebo. This is one of the best ways to travel, but services can be unreliable due to fuel shortages.
RAIL: The main internal railway runs from Lubumbashi to Ilebo, with a branch to Kalemie and Kindu, and from Kinshasa to the port of Matadi. Rail services are generally basic, although deluxe and first-class cars are comparable to those in Europe. There is no air-conditioning, but there are couchettes and dining cars on the principal trains.
ROAD: Due to poor maintenance, the roads are among the worst in Africa and only achieve a fair standard around the main towns. It is wise to check that bridges are safe before crossing. **Bus:** Services run between the main towns but are crowded and unreliable. **Taxi:** Available in Kinshasa but unreliable. **Car hire:** Available on a limited basis at the airport.
Documentation: International Driving Permit required.
URBAN: Conventional bus services in Kinshasa can be severely overcrowded. Minibuses and converted truck-buses also offer public transport, and are known as *fula fulas*. Pick-up trucks are known as 'taxibuses'. A better standard of transport is provided by shared taxis, which are widely available. There is little or no public transport in most other large centres.

ACCOMMODATION

Zaïre is not the easiest country for the tourist as it is crippled by transport problems while the difficult terrain has resulted in relatively few settlements except along river banks. Accommodation is therefore largely restricted to the main cities, and is scarce in the interior. For further details contact the Embassy.
HOTELS: The few hotels that cater for European visitors are expensive and generally booked-up well in advance. The majority of hotels are in Kinshasa, with others in Muanda, Boma, Matadi, Mbanzangunu, Mbandaka, Lubumbashi, Bukavu, Kolwezi, Kanga and Kisangani. Information can be obtained from the Société Zaïroise de l'Hotellerie, Immeuble Memling, BP 1076, Kinshasa. Tel: (12) 23260.

RESORTS & EXCURSIONS

Zaïre is a vast country, made even larger by inadequate transport infrastructure. It has not been developed for tourism, but the visitor armed with patience and a relaxed attitude to difficulties encountered will find its diversity fascinating.

Kinshasa

The capital does not have many sights of historic interest, but the visitor interested in the past should not miss the prehistoric and ethnological museums at the *Kinshasa University*, an ensemble of light, rectangular and well laid out buildings standing on a hillside. A brightly coloured chapel crowns the top of the hill. Nearby is a corner of the equatorial forest surrounding a beautiful lake called 'Ma Valée' with a charming tavern on its banks.
Other attractions include the fishing port of **Kinkole**, the *Gardens of the Presidential Farm of Nsele* made of pagodas, and the extensive pools where angling and swimming may be enjoyed. In both the markets and the suburbs of Kinshasa, there are craftsmen who produce wood and metal items. Visit the *National Museum* which includes some unique pieces of genuine Zaïrean art.

Southwest Zaïre & Bandundu

The *Insiki Falls* (60m/197ft) at **Zongo** and the caves in the region of Mbanza-Ngungu may be visited in one day, but it is preferable to stay for two or three days, for **Mbanza-Ngungu** is a pleasant resort with a good climate. While in the Mbanza-Ngungu area the visitor should not fail to stop at Kisantu to visit the *'Frère Gillet' Botanic Gardens* with their world-famous rare orchids.
Further west are the wild slopes and gorges of the *River Kwilu*, 120km (75 miles) from Mataoi; on the right bank of the river is a spot of rugged beauty called *Inga*. The woods, caves and waterfalls of *Boma* and equatorial **Mayumbe** and the *Tombs of Tshela*, can be visited on the way to the ocean beach of *Moanda*.
Less easily accessible is the upper valley of the *Kwango* in the southwest. A long journey through a region of unspoiled natural beauty leads to the *Tembo* (formerly *Guillaume) Falls*.

Kasai & Shaba

In the south, the *Upemba National Park* straddles the *Lualaba River*, northeast of Bugama, and includes several lakes inhabited by hippos, crocodiles and numerous aquatic birds. Here too are numerous fishermen, cattle farmers and peasants, as well as a number of mining communities. **Kananga** and **M'Buji-Mayi** are typical tropical towns; **Kalemie** and the banks of *Lake Tanganyika* are reminiscent of the French Riviera.
The whole of the south of Zaïre is punctuated with freshwater lakes such as *Munkamba, Fwa* and *Kasai;* there are also numerous impressive waterfalls, such as *Kiobo*, on the Lufira, and *Lofol* 384m (1259ft) high, north of Lubumbashi.

Upper Zaïre & the Kivu

The high plateaux of Zaïre extend across the eastern part of the country, around lakes Tanganyika, Kivu, Idi Amin, Mobutu Sese Seko and Bukavu. **Goma** and **Bunia** are small, pretty towns featuring villas, restaurants and hotels.
In the north is the **Garamba National Park**, covering 400,000 hectares and featuring lions, leopards, elephants, rhinos and giraffes.
Lake Mobutu Sese Seko, which contains more fish than any other lake in Africa, lies at an altitude of over 618m (2027ft). It can be reached from Bunia, which is also the point of departure for numerous excursions into the forests and mountains, the Pygmy villages, the *Caves of Mount Hoyo* and the *'Escaliers de Venus' Falls. Lake Idi Amin Dada* is the home of birds of all sizes and colours. The highest peak in the Ruwenzori range is the *Pic Marguerite*, at an altitude of 5119m (15,795ft). The snowline is at 450m (1776ft). This region is also inhabited by gorillas and by the extremely rare okapi.
The mountain scenery between Goma and Beni is regarded as some of the most spectacular in Africa, although the road is not always in good condition.

Virunga National Park

Covering an area of 12,000 sq km (4633 sq miles), this comprises an immense plain bounded by two jagged mountain ranges that serve as a natural enclosure for the animals which roam at liberty in this huge natural reserve. Game includes numerous lions, elephants, buffaloes, warthogs, antelopes, hippos and colourful aquatic birds. In this park, near Goma, you can also climb the still-active volcanoes of *Nyamuragira*, 3055m (10,022ft), and *Nyiragongo*, 3470m (11,385ft).

SOCIAL PROFILE

FOOD & DRINK: There are about 20 good restaurants in Kinshasa and Lubumbashi, but prices are high. Hotels and restaurants which cater for Europeans are generally expensive and serve international and Zaïrean dishes. A typical speciality is *moambe* chicken, cooked in fresh palm oil with rice and spinach. The capital Kinshasa offers French, Belgian and Zaïrean cuisine, but again restaurants are expensive and cater largely for businessmen. Small restaurants and snack bars offer Chinese, Tunisian and Greek food.
NIGHTLIFE: Kinshasa is the best place for nightlife, especially in the sprawling township of the 'Cité', where most of the population live. There are four main casinos and several large nightclubs. Local bands offer an exciting evening and have a keen local following.
SHOPPING: Local craftware includes bracelets, ebony carvings and local paintings. The large towns all have markets and shopping centres, selling everything from fresh ginger to baskets and African carvings.
Shopping hours: 0800-1800 Monday to Saturday.
SPORT: Mountaineering is a growing sport, especially in the Ruwenzori mountain range. There are eight **safari** reserves, and touring is popular. Most of the rivers and lakes yield excellent **fishing**. Facilities for **sailing** available at the country's only seaport of Matadi. **Tennis** and **golf** are also popular.
SPECIAL EVENTS: The *Kinshasa Fair* takes place in 1994, it is a biennial event running from mid-June to mid-July.
SOCIAL CONVENTIONS: Casual clothes are widely suitable although scanty beachwear should be confined to the beach or poolside. **Photography:** A permit is required. Even then, local authorities are likely to be sensitive. Avoid official areas. **Tipping:** 10% service charge is added to hotel and restaurant bills. Extra tipping is unnecessary.

BUSINESS PROFILE

ECONOMY: With rich agricultural land and extensive mineral and energy deposits, Zaïre is potentially one of Africa's richest countries. The country has rich natural resources and, by regional standards, a highly industrialised base manufacturing for the domestic market. However, two thirds of the population are still involved in subsistence farming and industry runs well below capacity due to a lack of spare parts and foreign exchange with which to acquire them. The mining sector, which enjoys investment priority and is equipped with some of the latest available technology, also produces cobalt, manganese, zinc, uranium and tin. There are also large offshore oil deposits. Compared to mining, the rest of Zaïre's industry is comparatively underdeveloped. Most enterprises turn out consumer goods – textiles, cement, food and beverages, wood products and plastics – for domestic consumption. Agriculture remains the largest employer, however, and an important source of foreign exchange. Zaïrean farmers produce palm oil, coffee, tea, cocoa, rubber, cotton, tropical woods, fruit, vegetables and rice. Any economic improvement depends – in the short-term at any rate – on increases in commodity prices on world markets. Long-term development will need considerable improvement to the country's poor infrastructure and external financial assistance which may not be forthcoming since the IMF, with which Zaïre has had a difficult relationship, declared it a 'non-cooperative' nation in April 1992. Bilateral assistance has been cut as a result of the poltical upheaval, which has also deterred foreign investors. China, the USA, Belgium and other EC countries are Zaïre's main trading partners.
BUSINESS: Business people should wear lightweight suits. Interpreter and translation services are available as business is mainly conducted in French. The best time to visit is in the cool season (which varies from one part of the country to another). *Citoyen* is the term used to address men and *Citoyenne* is used to address women.
Office hours: 0730-1700 Monday to Friday and 0730-1200 Saturday.
COMMERCIAL INFORMATION: The following organisation can offer advice: Chambre de Commerce, d'Industrie et d'Agriculture du Zaïre, BP 7247, 10 avenue des Aviateurs, Kinshasa. Tel: (12) 24623. Telex: 21071.

HISTORY & GOVERNMENT

HISTORY: The Belgian Congo was established in what is now Zaïre in 1895. Apart from extracting minerals, and creating the necessary support infrastructure (railways etc), the Belgians did very little to develop the country. In 1925, the territories of Rwanda and Urundi (now Burundi) were united administratively to the Belgian Congo under a League of Nations mandate. Independence came to the country after a very brief struggle in June 1960. The first post-independence government, headed by Joseph Kasavupu and Patrice Lumumba, immediately faced army mutiny, which led to the departure of the country's entire (Belgian) civil service, and to a series of attempted tribal secessions. By December 1960, military rule had been established by Colonel Joseph-Désiré Mobutu (who later changed his name to Mobutu Sese Seko). With his support, a civil government was formed under Cyrille Adoula in 1961, after Kasavupu and Lumumba had died in suspicious circumstances. In 1965 Mobutu, now the general and Chief-of-Staff, again seized power and formed a military-based regime which has lasted to the present day. In 1966, General Mobutu formed the sole legal party, the MPR (Mouvement Populaire de la Révolution), but Zaïre is not so much a one-party state as a one-man state. Although there is a National Legislative Council, Mobutu ('The Supreme Guide') has until recently operated as effective sole ruler through the political bureau of the MPR. From early 1990 onwards, Mobutu made various announcements concerning the impending introduction of multi-party democracy, but as the months went by and nothing changed, sentiment mounted that Mobutu was merely trying to ward off pressure from his Western political backers and aid donors. As 1991 progressed, discontent among the population at large grew sharply and Mobutu's position seemed increasingly threatened. Some 200 opposition parties were created after Mobutu's limitations on the number of such parties was quietly dropped. By September the situation was becoming desperate: food shortages and hyper-inflation running to several thousand per cent annually (estimates vary) had brought angry, unpaid and hungry demonstrators and soldiers onto the streets. On September 30, as

French and Belgian troops escorted foreign nationals out of riot-torn Kinshasa, which was quite literally stripped bare by the mobs, Mobutu sat down in the capital with Zaïre's two principal opposition figures, Etienne Tshisekedi and Nguza Karl-i-Bond, both veteran politicians predominant in the coalition of opposition parties known as the Sacred Union. Mobutu reluctantly accepted Tshisekedi as head of an interim government but insisted that he retain the presidency. After threats by army supporters of Mobutu, Tshisekedi stood down in favour of a former ally of Moboutu's, Nguza Karl-i-Bond. The following month the new government took steps to decide its future by adopting a model recently seen elsewhere in Africa: a constitutional conference. In August, delegates elected Tshisekedi once again as Prime Minister. Mobutu, whose supporters have now boycotted the conference, shows no sign of relinquishing the presidency. The delegates also passed motions granting political power to an elected parliament and reverting the country to its previous name (in use until October 1971), Congo. National elections are now expected between February and August 1994. Still, the internal situation is far from peaceful. Renewed fighting broke out and Kinshasa airport is under siege while French and Belgian troups are on standby to evacuate foreign nationals to Brazzaville (Congo).
GOVERNMENT: A national conference was convened, initially in August 1991, to determine the future of the the country, including the drafting of a new constitution. The conference declared itself sovereign in April 1992 and has elected a Prime Minister while accepting President Mobutu's remaining in office as Head of State.

CLIMATE

Varies according to distance from the Equator, which lies across the north of the country. The dry season in the north is from December to March, and in the south May to October. The annual temperatures are warm and humidity is high.
Required clothing: Lightweight clothes are recommended all year, with rainwear during rainy season.

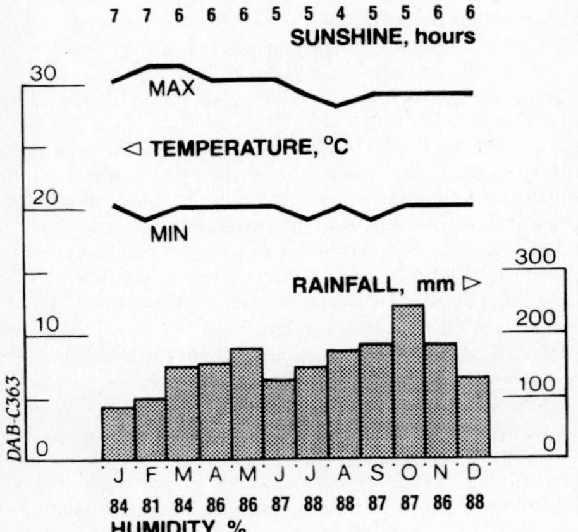

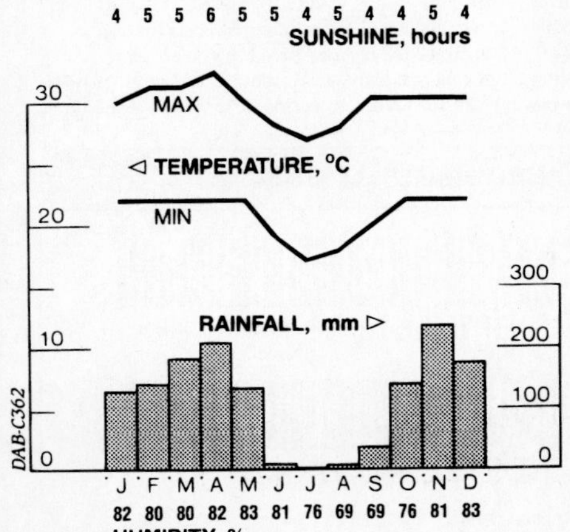

ZAMBIA

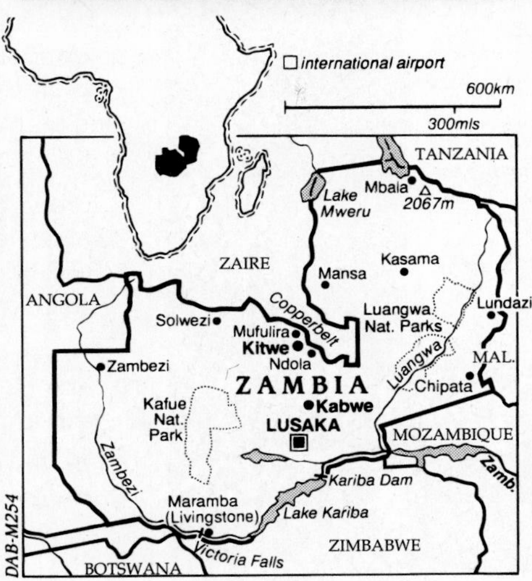

Location: Central Southern Africa.

Zambia National Tourist Board
PO Box 30017
Century House
Cairo Road
Lusaka, Zambia
Tel: (1) 229 087. Telex: 41780.
High Commission for the Republic of Zambia
2 Palace Gate
London W8 5NG
Tel: (071) 589 6655. Fax: (071) 581 1353. Telex: 263544. Opening hours: 1000-1700 Monday to Friday.
Zambia National Tourist Board
Address as High Commission.
Tel: (071) 589 6343/4. Fax: (071) 581 1353. Telex: 28956. Opening hours: 0930-1700 Monday to Friday.
British High Commission
PO Box 50050
Plot 5201, Independence Avenue
Lusaka, Zambia
Tel: (1) 228 955. Fax: (1) 253 421. Telex: 41150.
Embassy of the Republic of Zambia
2419 Massachusetts Avenue, NW
Washington, DC
20008
Tel: (202) 265 9717. Fax: (202) 332 0826.
Zambia National Tourist Board
237 East 52nd Street
New York, NY
10022
Tel: (212) 308 2155.
Embassy of the United States of America
PO Box 31617
corner of Independence and United Nations Avenues
Lusaka, Zambia
Tel: (1) 228 595 *or* 228 601/2/3. Fax: (1) 251 578.
Telex: 41970 AMEMB ZA.
High Commission of the Republic of Zambia
Suite 1610
130 Albert Street
Ottawa, Ontario
K1P 5G4
Tel: (613) 563 0712. Fax: (613) 235 0430.
Canadian High Commission
PO Box 31312
North End Branch
Barclays Bank Building
Cairo Road
Lusaka, Zambia
Tel: (1) 228 811. Fax: (1) 225 160. Telex: 42480 DOMCAN ZA.

AREA: 752,614 sq km (290,586 sq miles).
POPULATION: 7,804,000 (1989 estimate).
POPULATION DENSITY: 10.4 per sq km.
CAPITAL: Lusaka. **Population:** 870,030 (1988 estimate).
GEOGRAPHY: Zambia is a vast plateau bordered by Angola to the west, Zaïre to the north, Tanzania to the northeast, Malawi to the east, Mozambique to the southeast, Zimbabwe and Botswana to the south and the Caprivi Strip of Namibia to the southwest. The broad flood plain of the Zambezi River marks the western border. In the south, the Zambezi River, together with Lake Kariba, forms the frontier with Zimbabwe. Victoria Falls, at the southern end of the man-made Lake Kariba, is one of the most spectacular sights in Africa (if not the world). In the east and northeast the country rises to a plateau 1200m (3937ft) high, covered by deciduous savannah, small trees, grassy plains or marshland. The magnificent Luangwa and Kafue National Parks have one of the most prolific animal populations in Africa.
LANGUAGE: English is the official language, but over 73 tribal dialects, including Nyanja, Tonga, Bemba, Lozi and Luvale, are also spoken.
RELIGION: Predominantly Christian, with a minority of traditional beliefs and some Muslims and Hindus.
TIME: GMT + 2.
ELECTRICITY: 220 volts AC, 50Hz.
COMMUNICATIONS: Telephone: IDD is available. Country code: 260. There are no public telephones and most calls are made through a post office. **Telex/telegram:** There are public telex facilities at the Central Post Office in Lusaka (24 hours) and at principal hotels. Telegrams may be sent from telegraph offices in main centres, open 0800-1630 Monday to Friday, 0800-1230 Saturday, and 0900-1200 Sunday and public holidays. The central telegraph office in Lusaka accepts telegrams up to 1600 Monday to Saturday. **Post:** Airmail to Europe takes five to seven days. **Press:** The two daily newspapers, both published in English, are *The Times of Zambia* and *The Zambia Daily Mail.*
BBC World Service and Voice of America frequencies: From time to time these change. See the section *How to Use this Book* for more information.

BBC:				
MHz	21.66	3.255	11.94	6.005
Voice of America:				
MHz	21.49	15.60	9.525	6.035

PASSPORT/VISA

Regulations and requirements may be subject to change at short notice, and you are advised to contact the appropriate diplomatic or consular authority before finalising travel arrangements. Details of these may be found at the head of this country's entry. Any numbers in the chart refer to the footnotes below.

	Passport Required?	Visa Required?	Return Ticket Required?
Full British	Yes	No	Yes
BVP	Not valid	-	-
Australian	Yes	No	Yes
Canadian	Yes	No	Yes
USA	Yes	Yes	Yes
Other EC	Yes	1	Yes
Japanese	Yes	Yes	Yes

PASSPORTS: Valid passport required by all.
British Visitors Passport: Not accepted.
VISAS: Required by all except:
(a) **[1]** nationals of the UK and Ireland (nationals of other EC countries *do* require visas);
(b) nationals of Commonwealth, Dependent and Associated states;
(c) nationals of Fiji, Finland, Norway, Romania, Sweden and Yugoslavia.
Note: All visitors entering from South Africa require a visa.
Types of visa: Tourist, Business and Transit; cost – £6. Transit visas are not required by those exempted from full visas or by those continuing their journeys by the same or next connecting flight within 24 hours and not leaving the airport.
Validity: Visas may be used 3 months from date of issue, for a maximum stay of 90 days.
Application to: Consulate (or Consular Section at Embassy or High Commission). For addresses, see top of entry.
Application requirements: (a) 2 completed application forms. (b) 2 passport photos. (c) Valid passport. (d) Sufficient funds to cover stay. (e) Business applications must be covered by an explanatory letter.
Working days required: At least 3 days.
Temporary residence: Apply to Chief Immigration Officer (CIO), PO Box 50300, Lusaka (for visits in excess of 90 days).

MONEY

Currency: Kwacha (K) = 100 ngwee. Notes are in denominations of K500, 100, 50, 20, 10, 5 and 2. Coins are in denominations of K1, and 20, 10, 4, 2 and 1 ngwee.

Credit cards: American Express is widely accepted, with more limited use of Access/Mastercard, Diners Club and Visa. Check with your credit card company for details of merchant acceptability and other services which may be available.
Exchange rate indicators: The following figures are included as a guide to the movements of the Kwacha against Sterling and the US Dollar:

Date:	Oct '89	Oct '90	Oct '91	Oct '92
£1.00=	25.40	76.60	128.05	317.88
$1.00=	16.08	39.21	73.78	200.30

Currency restrictions: The import and export of local currency is limited to K2000. Free import of foreign currency subject to declaration on arrival. The export of foreign currency is limited to the amount declared on import. Exchange of foreign currency is strictly limited to authorised banks.
Note: Currency declaration forms and exchange receipts must be shown if purchasing airline tickets in Zambia.
Banking hours: 0815-1430 Monday to Friday.

DUTY FREE

The following items may be imported into Zambia without incurring customs duty:
400 cigarettes or 500g of pipe tobacco or cigars;
1 bottle of spirits and wine and 1 litre of beer (opened);
2.5 litres of beer;
1oz bottle of perfume.
Note: Souvenirs may be exported without restriction but game trophies such as tooth, bone, horn, shell, claw, skin, hair, feather or other durable items are subject to export permits.

PUBLIC HOLIDAYS

Public holidays observed in Zambia are as follows:
Mar 11 '93 Youth Day. **Apr 9-12** Easter. **May 1** Labour Day. **May 24** African Freedom Day. **Jul 5** Heroes' Day. **Jul 8** Unity Day. **Aug 5** Farmers' Day. **Oct 24** Independence Day. **Dec 25** Christmas Day. **Jan 1 '94** New Year's Day. **Mar 11** Youth Day.
Note: Dates of public holidays tend to vary and are sometimes changed at short notice. It is advisable to check dates in advance.

HEALTH

Regulations and requirements may be subject to change at short notice, and you are advised to contact your doctor well in advance of your intended date of departure. Any numbers in the chart refer to the footnotes below.

	Special Precautions?	Certificate Required?
Yellow Fever	Yes	1
Cholera	Yes	2
Typhoid & Polio	Yes	-
Malaria	3	-
Food & Drink	4	-

[1]: A yellow fever vaccination certificate is required from travellers over one year of age arriving from infected areas. All passengers must hold an 'International Certificate of Vaccination' booklet even if no vaccination is required.
[2]: Following WHO guidelines issued in 1973, a cholera vaccination certificate is not a condition of entry to Zambia. However, cholera is a risk in this country and precautions are essential. Up-to-date advice should be sought before deciding whether these precautions should include vaccination, as medical opinion is divided over its effectiveness. See the *Health* section at the back of the book.
[3]: Malaria risk exists, predominantly in the malignant *falciparum* form, throughout the country from November to May and throughout the year in the Zambezi valley. The strain is reported to be 'highly resistant' to chloroquine.
[4]: All water should be regarded as being a potential health risk. Water for drinking, brushing teeth or making ice should have first been boiled or otherwise sterilised. Milk is pasteurised and dairy products are generally safe for consumption. Only eat well-cooked meat and fish, preferably served hot. Pork, salad and mayonnaise may carry increased risk. Vegetables should be cooked and fruit peeled.
Rabies is present. For those at high risk, vaccination before arrival should be considered. If you are bitten abroad seek medical advice without delay. For more information consult the *Health* section at the back of the book.

ZAMBIA	HEALTH REGULATIONS	VISA REGULATIONS
GALILEO/WORLDSPAN	 TI-DFT/LUN/HE	TI-DFT/LUN/VI
SABRE	 TIDFT/LUN/HE	 TIDFT/LUN/VI

Code-Link

To access this information on your CRS, swipe the barcode with a light pen or type in the text under the barcode. For more information, see the introduction *How to Use This Book.*

Bilharzia (schistosomiasis) is present. Avoid swimming and paddling in fresh water. Swimming pools which are well-chlorinated and maintained are safe.
Health care: Health service is free, an exception are private clinics; however, health insurance is advisable. Adequate health care cannot be assured outside main towns. It is advisable to carry basic medical supplies.

TRAVEL - International

AIR: Zambia's national airline is *Zambia Airways (QZ)*.
Approximate flight time: From *London* to Lusaka is 10 hours.
International airport: *Lusaka (LUN)* is 26km (16 miles) east of the city (travel time – 30 minutes). Airport and city bus services are available. Taxi service is also available to the city. Return by prior arrangement with taxis from *Pamodzi*, *Ridgeway*, *Intercontinental* and *Lusaka* hotels (taxi fares are negotiable). Airport facilities include outgoing duty-free shop (0600 until last flight); car hire, bank/exchange (0600 until last flight), restaurant (0400 until last flight) and post office (0600-1430 Monday to Friday, 0600-110 Saturday).
Departure tax: K2600 for residents and Zambian nationals or US$20 for foreign nationals. Transit passengers are exempt.
RIVER/LAKE: Zambia has no coastline but there are crossings from Mpulungu across Lake Tanganyika to Kigoma in Tanzania, and a service across the Zambezi from Kazungula to Botswana.
RAIL: There are two major rail routes linking Zambia with Zimbabwe and Tanzania. *Zambia Railways* serves Livingstone and has a connection across the Victoria Falls to Bulawayo in Zimbabwe. There are two trains daily in either direction, the journey taking 9-12 hours depending on whether the ordinary or express service is used. *Tanzania–Zambia Railways Authority (TAZARA)* operates trains Mondays, Tuesdays and Fridays from Kapiri Mposhi to Dar es Salaam in Tanzania. Services are often suspended and it is advisable to check at the tourist office in Lusaka for details.
ROAD: The main routes are from Zimbabwe via Chirunda, Kariba and Livingstone; from Botswana via Kansane and Kazungula; from Mozambique via Villa Gambito and Zumbo; from Tanzania via Nakonde and Mbala; from Malawi via Chipata and Lundazi; and from Zaïre via Kashiba, Mwenda, Sakania, Mokamba, Kasumbalesa and Kapushi.
Note: All visitors entering from South Africa require a visa.

TRAVEL - Internal

AIR: *Zambia Airways (QZ)* operates domestic services, often to small landing strips rather than airports. There are over 127 airports, aerodromes and airstrips throughout the country.
Departure tax: K300 for domestic services.
RIVER/LAKE: Local ferries operate on all waterways. Contact local authorities for details.
RAIL: The routes described above in *Travel - International* also serve Lusaka, Ndola, Kitwe and Mulobezi. Local services, centred on Lusaka, are very limited.
ROAD: There is a fairly good network of roads but much of it is often hazardous during the rainy season.
Bus: The network of inter-urban bus services is run by *Zambia Motorways, Post & Telecommunications (PTC)*. The service can be unreliable and the buses often crowded. *PTC's* comfortable coach service, linking Lusaka with the Copperbelt and Livingstone on alternate days, should be booked well in advance. *Eagle Travel Tours Division Ltd* also operates a luxury coach service linking Lusaka with Livingstone (Victoria Falls) twice a week there and back, and this also requires advance booking. They also offer services to the Kariba Dam and Kafue National Park, and sightseeing tours of Lusaka. **Car hire:** A number of firms operate in main centres. Information is available from the National Tourist Board (address at top of entry) or the *Automobile Association of Zambia Limited*, PO Box 300, Dedan Kumatni Road, Lusaka. *Eagle Travel Tours Division Ltd* and *Big Five Travel & Tours Ltd* can provide chauffeur-driven cars.
Documentation: An International Driving Permit is legally required and is valid for six months. Thereafter, a Zambian driving licence is required, granted after passing a local driving test.
URBAN: Bus services in Lusaka are provided by *UBZ*; there are also private minibuses and shared taxis. The buses are somewhat basic, and can become very crowded. Taxis are not metered and fares should be agreed in advance.
JOURNEY TIMES: The following chart gives approximate journey times (in hours and minutes) from Lusaka to other major cities/towns in Zambia:

	Air	Road	Rail
Livingstone	1.20	6.30	11.00
Ndola	1.00	4.00	6.30
Kitwe	1.00	4.30	7.00
Mfuwe	1.30	-	-

ACCOMMODATION

Accommodation in Zambia may be divided into four main categories: hotels, motels, lodges and camps; and two minor categories: GRZ-resthouses and camping/caravan sites. Zambia is a fairly large, wild and, as yet, largely undeveloped country. Only the major tourist sites are fully prepared to cater for the needs of the visitor.
HOTELS & MOTELS: Hotels are concentrated around Lusaka, Livingstone and the Copperbelt region. Others are widely dispersed around the country along principal roads or near towns. It is advisable to book in advance and to obtain confirmation in writing. All bills are subject to a 10% service charge in lieu of tips and 10% sales tax. Tipping in hotels has been abolished by law.
Grading: These are graded according to a 5-star system ranging from an ungraded class to a few first-class hotels.
NATIONAL PARKS: All lodges and many camps in the parks are offered on a fully catered basis. As the quality of accommodation and associated facilities varies enormously from one place to another, visitors intending to stay should contact the relevant tour operator/tourist board for detailed information.
Lodges: These are generally stone buildings with thatched roofs designed to complement the natural environment, housing a maximum of 40 beds.
Camps: The most common and most widely used accommodation for safaris. In general, standard facilities cover hot and cold running water, electricity and water-borne sanitation plus the basic accoutrements for comfortable living. For instance, Luangwa's camps have beds, clean linen, refrigerator, crockery, cutlery, mosquito nets, lamps, toilets and showers. At non-catering camps visitors must bring their own food and drink. Some are open all year round while others open from June to October or November.
GRZ-RESTHOUSES: These are available throughout the provinces. They have a small capacity, averaging five rooms, rising in exceptional cases to 24 rooms.
CAMPING/CARAVANNING: Sites are available at most of the tourist centres, including several national parks. It is best to make reservations well in advance. If booking is more than four weeks in advance some operators will charge a 50% deposit. The peak seasons are June 1 to October 13, December 15 to January 4, and Easter. Prices may increase by 20-30% during these periods. For information contact the National Tourist Board, who can also supply a list of Zambian tour operators.

RESORTS & EXCURSIONS

Note: Most tourist organisations are controlled by the government and prices of tours need to be fixed well in advance.
NATIONAL PARKS: The Zambian government has long recognised the economic importance of its wildernesses and gives a high priority to conservation matters: almost 9% of the country is given over to national parks and game reserves. Most tourism is concentrated in five of the 19 parks – Sumbu, Kafue, Lochinvar, Luangwa and Mosi-oa-Tunya – the remainder as yet having meagre facilities. In general, safaris are limited to six to eight persons per vehicle (always accompanied by experienced guides), permitting the animal/bird lover to appreciate, in uninterrupted peace, the African wildlife roaming through an unspoilt natural environment. Herds of buffalo, elephant and antelope are readily seen and there are numerous lions and zebra. Other animals include rhinoceroses, monkeys, baboons, wild pigs, hippopotami and crocodiles. Birdlife is also prolific; 400 different species have been recorded in Lochinvar alone. The flood plains and river banks teem with water birds, especially in the Lochinvar and Luangwa National Parks. Fishing is also highly popular and international fishing competitions are often held on Zambian lakes.
The usual method of game viewing is from an open-topped Land Rover but walking tours are available for the more adventurous. As a precaution, no more than six may make up a walking party and the guide will be armed. Nocturnal safaris are also available in Land Rovers specially equipped with searchlights.
All the main national parks are accessible by car and plane. National parks require an entry permit bought from the main gate during opening hours (0600-1800 seven days a week).
For further and more detailed information about safaris, contact the National Tourist Board.
Kafue National Park: Situated in the centre of the southern half of the country, Kafue encompasses a huge area (22,500 sq km/8687 sq miles) and is one of the biggest game sanctuaries in Africa. Noted for its beauty, the park is bisected by the Kafue River, which attracts hundreds of species of birds and offers good game fishing. Eight-day walking and driving tours are available. The principal attraction is the prolific wildlife. Accommodation is provided throughout the year at *Chunga Safari Village* (no guided safaris during the rainy season, November to April), *Ngoma* and *Musungwa Lodges*, and at *New Kalala Camp* (non-catered). There are also several seasonal non-catered camps.
Luangwa Valley National Park: Regarded as one of the most exciting game reserves in the world, the Luangwa Valley is home for a huge variety of animals: among many others, elephants, hippopotami, lions, zebras, giraffes, antelopes, buffaloes, monkeys and wild dogs. Blossoming trees and exotic flowers are also to be found. Game viewing drives and walking tours are available. The main rainy season runs from November/December to May. There are lodges at *Chichele* (all year), *Luamfwa* (dry season), *Mfuwe* (all year) and *Tundwe* (dry season) and catered camps at *Chibembe* (dry season), and *Chinzombo* (all year). There are also several seasonal non-catered camps. Facilities in the park include luxury double rooms in chalets, private baths and toilets, full 3-course meals, bar facilities and swimming pools.
Lochinvar National Park: Exceptional diversity of birdlife. One lodge, open throughout the year.
Sumbu National Park: The sandy shorelines of *Lake Tanganyika* provide the setting for three all-year beach resorts: at *Kasaba*, *Ndole* and *Nkamba* bays. There is also a small non-catered camp. Activities include swimming, sunbathing and freshwater big-game fishing for the goliath tigerfish (up to 35kg), giant catfish and the Nile perch (both up to 50kg and more). It is possible to arrange visits into the surrounding bush for game viewing. *Kasaba Lodge* boasts an afternoon tea service, a bar and beach barbecues. *Nkamba Bay Lodge* offers exactly the same facilities as Kasaba but facilities are housed in rondavels. The park's spectacular sunsets are not to be missed.
Victoria Falls/Mosi-oa-Tunya National Park: Located on the southernmost edge of Zambia bordering Zimbabwe, the astonishing Victoria Falls are the mightiest cataracts in the world – the 2.5km (1.5 miles) wide Zambezi River drops 100m (330ft) into a narrow chasm at the rate of 550 million litres every minute. The spray can be seen 30km (20 miles) away. The Mosi-oa-Tunya National Park nearby is small by Zambian standards but is home to most of Zambia's more common wild animals. Also nearby is **Livingstone,** 'Tourist Capital of Zambia', with several luxury hotels, a casino, and the *National Museum*, housing Livingstone memorabilia and anthropological exhibits.
Adventure holidays: Rafting adventure holidays are becoming very popular and 7-day navigations of the Zambezi from the base of the Victoria Falls to Lake Kariba and shorter white-water raft safaris are available.
LUSAKA: Attractions in the capital include nightclubs, restaurants, cinemas, the *Kabwata Cultural Village* (devoted to the preservation of indigenous arts and crafts and displays of native dancing), the *Cathedral of the Holy Cross* and the *Munda Wanga Botanical Gardens and Zoo*.

SOCIAL PROFILE

FOOD & DRINK: Since the devaluation of the Kwacha in 1985, tourists have found restaurants to be good value. Food shortages are also reported to have become rarer. Local specialities include bream from the Zambezi, Kafue and Luapula rivers, and Nile perch, lake salmon and other freshwater fish. **Drink:** *Mosi* and *Muchinga* beers and all soft drinks are available (but there may occasionally be shortages of the latter). Spirits are expensive.
NIGHTLIFE: Lusaka has dancing and floorshows in the main hotels, cinemas (including a drive-in), theatre and casinos at the *Intercontinental* and *Pamdozi* hotels. The Copperbelt and Livingstone offer a variety of entertainments including casinos and dancing.
SHOPPING: Lusaka has modern shops, supermarkets and an open-air market. Special purchases include African carvings, pottery and copperware, beadwork and local gemstones. **Shopping hours:** 0800-1700 Monday to Friday and 0800-1300 Saturday.
SPORT: Tennis, bowls and **golf** (good course at Chingola in the Copperbelt) are all available. Sports facilities are available through private clubs, many of which offer temporary membership to visitors if introduced by a member. There is a major **horseracing** centre at Kitwe. **Swimming**, **speedboating** and other **watersports** are available at Mindola Dam in the Copperbelt. Many private clubs have **swimming** pools and clubs in Lusaka offer facilities for **sailing**.
SPECIAL EVENTS: Events likely to be of interest to the visitor include *N'Cwala* on February 24 when the chief of the Ngoni people tastes the first fresh fruit of the year, the *Ku-omboka* (February/March), when the Lozi chief (*Litunga*) together with his entire household is paddled up canals

from Leaului to Limulunga, his residence in the rainy season. In July, the *Kufulehela* is the occasion of his move back to Leaului. On July 29, *Mutumboka* is celebrated by the Lunda people of Luapala Province, and in September/October *Shimunenga* is a ceremony of the Ba-Ila people at Maala on the Kafue Flats.
SOCIAL CONVENTIONS: African culture and traditions remain prominent and there are various customs, folklore and traditional crafts in the different regions. Traditional dancing is popular and there are many colourful annual ceremonies that take place throughout the country. Visitors to the outlying areas should expect to be met with curiosity. Shaking hands is the normal form of greeting. A small inexpensive item from one's company or homeland would make an appropriate gift. Informal, practical clothes are suitable. Smoking is widely accepted. **Photography:** Do not take photographs in sensitive areas. **Tipping:** A 10% sales tax is added to all bills. Tipping in hotels has been abolished by law but 10% may be expected or included in bills elsewhere.

BUSINESS PROFILE

ECONOMY: The geographical isolation imposed by Southern Rhodesia's UDI in 1965, together with its landlocked position, crippled Zambia's economy during the first decade after independence (forcing it into heavy expenditure on transport to maintain its trade links) and the country has since had to struggle to achieve economic self-sufficiency, gradually nationalising the copper mines and (with Chinese help) building a long rail link to Tanzania. Copper has been the mainstay of the economy. The world depression of the 1970s hit copper prices badly, and the mining industry has suffered from low world prices throughout the 1980s; real income per head halved between 1974 and 1980. Meanwhile, agriculture (in which 65% of the population is engaged) has been afflicted by a series of droughts, of which the present one is the most serious, causing further damage to an already inefficient and poorly equipped industry. Maize and cattle are the main cash producers in this sector, while the bulk of other products are earmarked for domestic consumption but have to be supplemented by large-scale food imports. Despite a slight recovery in both agriculture and world copper prices in the late 1980s, the economy has remained weak, with aid and debt rescheduling essential to sustain it. Aid is in the hands of the 'Paris Club' of Western donors who are, at least for the time being, better disposed towards the new Government of Frederick Chiluba than its predecessor, to whom aid was cut off because of Kaunda's failure to adhere to previous terms agreed with the IMF. Chiluba's administration has adopted the standard set of market-orientated reforms (subsidy cuts, trade liberalisation, privatisation) and resumed debt repayments, as a result of which financial and development aid have been resumed. The Government has now agreed a three-year Structural Adjustment Programme with the IMF and World Bank as a main plank of its economic programme. Zambia is a member of the Southern African Development and Co-operation Council. Leading trading partners are Japan, the UK and China (for exports), and Japan, South Africa, the UK and the USA (for imports).
BUSINESS: A lightweight jacket and tie or a safari suit will be acceptable for men at business meetings. English is widely used in business circles and visiting cards are becoming common. **Office hours:** 0800-1300 and 1400-1700 Monday to Friday.
COMMERCIAL INFORMATION: The following organisations can offer advice:
Ministry of Commerce, Trade and Industry, PO Box 31968, Kwacha Annex, Cairo Road, Lusaka. Tel: (1) 213 767. Telex: 45630; *or*
Lusaka Chamber of Commerce and Industry, PO Box 30844, Lusaka. Tel: (1) 252 369. Fax: (1) 252 483. Telex: 40124.

HISTORY & GOVERNMENT

HISTORY: Zambia was first colonised by the British South African Company in 1889 but it was not until 1924, when the company ceded administrative control to the British Crown (whereupon it became the colony of Northern Rhodesia), that serious exploitation of the country's main natural resource, copper, began. From 1953-63 the country found itself forming the northern part of the Central African Federation, essentially a pale form of apartheid, which enjoyed no support whatsoever among the blacks. The colonial authorities ceded independence in 1964. The pre-independence elections were won by Kaunda's United National Independence Party. The country soon became involved in the war in southern Rhodesia. Kaunda closed Zambia's southern border and gave safe haven to cadres from Joshua Nkomo's ZAPU party and its associated guerrilla army ZIPRA. Relations with the Zimbabweans have naturally improved since that country became independent in 1980, and Kaunda's foreign policy subsequently focussed elsewhere. Kaunda played a major part in peace initiatives in Namibia and was elected chairman of the OAU in 1987. Zambia was a one-party state from 1973 until 1991. During 1990, a wave of demonstrations and riots, initially sparked by food price rises, then developed into demands for a more democratic system of government. Kaunda promised a national referendum on the issue but postponed it after further disturbances in July 1990. The principal opposition to the disintegrating UNIP was the Movement for Multi-party Democracy (MMD) led by Frederick Chiluba, chair of the Zambian Council of Trades Unions, the focus of much opposition activity under the one-party state. The election took place on October 1, 1991 and gave a substantial majority to the MMD candidate, Chiluba. The new president has promised to relax restrictions on foreign enterprises, normalise trade relations with South Africa and recognise Israel. While Chiluba is unlikely to be threatened politically while the opposition parties, including the formerly long-ruling UNIP, persist in their current disarray, he cannot afford to be complacent about popular feeling. The drought afflicting southern Africa as a whole is a particular cause of concern. Nonetheless, Zambia has successfully made a political transition which has so far eluded many other countries in Africa.
GOVERNMENT: The present constitution dates from 1973. Legislative power is held by the unicameral National Assembly with 135 members, 125 of whom are elected every five years by universal adult suffrage (the remaining ten are presidential appointees). Executive power is held by the President who appoints a Cabinet, headed by a Prime Minister, to conduct the administration of the Government.

CLIMATE

Although Zambia lies in the tropics, the height of the plateau ensures that the climate is seldom unpleasantly hot, except in valleys. There are three seasons: the cool, dry winter season from May to September; the hot, dry season in October and November; and the rainy season, which is even hotter, from December to April.
Required clothing: Lightweights or tropical with rainwear.

LUSAKA Zambia (1274m)

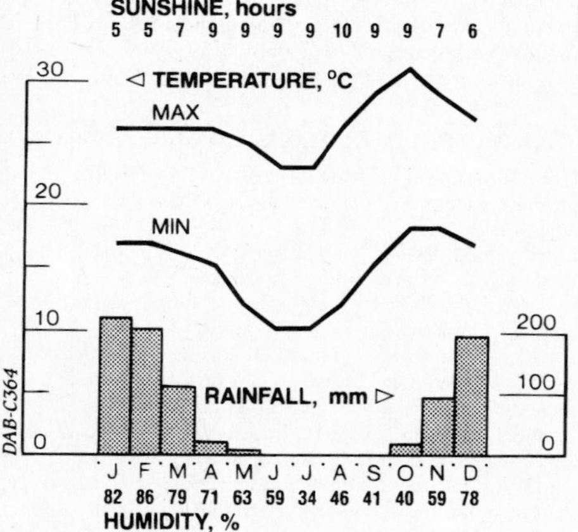

KASAMA Zambia (1382m)

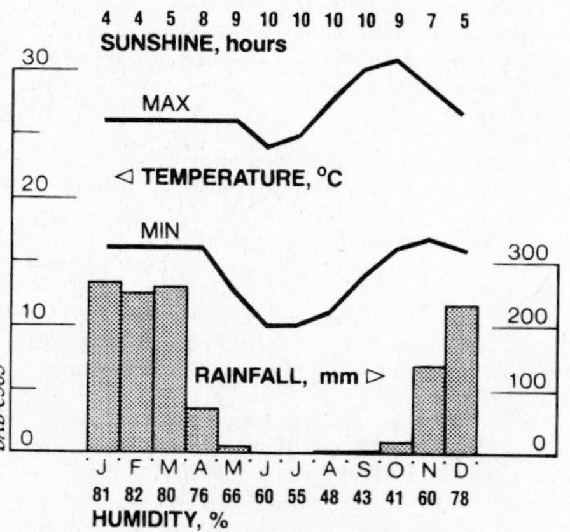

ZIMBABWE

Location: Southern Africa.

Zimbabwe Tourist Development Corporation (ZTDC)
PO Box 8052
corner of Jason Moyo Avenue and Fourth Street
Causeway
Harare, Zimbabwe
Tel: (4) 793 666. Fax: (4) 793 669. Telex: 26082 ZIMTOR ZW.
High Commission for the Republic of Zimbabwe
Zimbabwe House
429 Strand
London WC2R 0QE
Tel: (071) 836 7755. Fax: (071) 379 1167. Telex: 262014. Opening hours: 0900-1700 Monday to Friday. *Visa Section:* 0900-1300 Monday to Friday.
Zimbabwe Tourist Board
Zimbabwe House
429 Strand
London WC2R 0QE
Tel: (071) 836 7755. Fax: (071) 379 1167. Telex: 262014. Opening hours: 0930-1230 and 1530-1630 Monday to Friday.
British High Commission
PO Box 4490
Stanley House
Jason Moyo Avenue
Harare, Zimbabwe
Tel: (4) 793 781 *or* 728 716. Fax: (4) 728 380. Telex: 24607 UKREP ZW.
Embassy of the Republic of Zimbabwe
1608 New Hampshire Avenue, NW
Washington, DC
20009
Tel: (202) 332 7100. Fax: (202) 483 9326. Telex: 248402.
Zimbabwe Tourist Office
Suite 412
1270 Avenue of the Americas
New York, NY
10020
Tel: (212) 332 1090. Telex: 261038 ZTDC UR.
Also deals with enquiries from Canada.
Embassy of the United States of America
PO Box 3340
172 Herbert Chitapo Avenue
Harare, Zimbabwe
Tel: (4) 794 521. Fax: (4) 796 488. Telex: 24591 USFCS ZW.
High Commission for the Republic of Zimbabwe
332 Somerset Street West
Ottawa, Ontario
K2P 0J9
Tel: (613) 237 4388/9 *or* 237 4484. Fax: (613) 563 8269.
Canadian High Commission
PO Box 1430
45 Baines Avenue
Harare, Zimbabwe
Tel: (4) 733 881/2/3/4/5. Fax: (4) 732 917. Telex: 24465 CANADA ZW.

ACACIA HOTELS

Further Information
And Reservations
Acacia Hotels
Kariba Office
PO Box 292, Kariba, Zimbabwe.
Tel: Kariba 2525. Telex: 41296 ZW.
Accounts
PO Box 5615, Harare, Zimbabwe.
Tel: Hahare 707438.

ZATSO

Fothergill Island, Kariba

THE Island is named after Rupert Fothergill who during the late fifties, masterminded Operation Noah when thousands of wild animals were rescued from the advancing waters of the newly-built Lake Kariba. Cradled at the foot of the rugged Matusadona National Park, Fothergill is now home for a myriad of species, making it a mecca for those people who have a soul-felt love and respect for the beauty of Africa and her wildlife.

The comfortable, open-style thatched lodges have en suite showers and flush toilets, and boast memorable views over the lake and its game-rich flood plain. The double storey, thatched dining lodge with its swimming pool and bar acts as a base for the day's activities and becomes the hub of camp-life once night falls. It's an experience which is enhanced immeasurably by the infectious enthusiasm that the professional guides display for their job. A variety of game and bird viewing safaris and fishing excursions are conducted on foot, in vehicles or boats.

RACK RATES - 1993
Fothergill

All Inclusive	USD 180-00
Single Supplement	USD 42-00
Trsf p.p. 1 way	USD 35-00 Breezes Marina
	USD 40-00 Kariba Airport

The Hide

All Inclusive	USD 250-00
Single Supplement	USD 66-00

Transfers included in above tariff

Chikwenya

All Inclusive	USD 250-00
Single Supplement	USD 66-00
Trsf p.p. 1way	USD 87-50

Chikwenya Safari Camp, Zambesi

Situated on the confluence of the Zambezi and Sapi Rivers, Chikwenya is in the heart of what is widely considered one of the loveliest wilderness areas, with varying riverine and inland vegetation, including park-like woodlands, and abundant and varied wildlife and birds.

Chikwenya offers game and bird viewing by vehicle or on foot with a professional guide in the parklands, or in a unique rivercraft on the Zambezi, in addition to a viewing platform and hides for those who prefer to be more leisurely.

Al fresco meals are served in the "natural" dining area under a dense canopy of Natal Mahogany trees. Evenings around the camp fire in the dining area with the surrounding sound of the bush and adjacent river are in themselves a special experience.

The camp is open during Zimbabwe's dry season, from March to November, and caters for a maximum of 16 people at a time. Transfers are made by light aircraft from Kariba Airport daily.

The Hide

The Hide offers visitors the idealised "Out of Africa" notion of the African safari experience, situated adjacent to Hwange National Park on its eastern boundary. Unlike most other commercial Safari Camps in the area, it is located within the park itself. Hwange is Zimbabwe's largest National Park covering 14,650 square kilometres containing 107 species of animals and 405 species of birds. It is one of few remaining sanctuaries in Africa where herds of up to 100 elephant may be seen.

The Hide does not cater to a mass market, instead you will be one of no more than fourteen people drawn together by a genuine desire to gain a deeper appreciation of the land and its wildlife.

Guests are accommodated in East African canvas tents, each with en suite running water, toilet and shower facilities. Each tent has a large front porch area where visitors can relax and view game from their tents.

Meals consist of a full course breakfast, lunch and dinner served and eaten round an open dining table, in elegance and style.

The Hide recognises that visitors to Hwange want to see game, and is ideally situated to afford guests the opportunity to view an abundance of wildlife. Game viewing excursions by vehicle or on foot are organised twice daily accompanied by licensed professional guides. There are also specially adapted game viewing hides. Each one overlooks a watering hole which makes The Hide a photographer's paradise.

The Hide can be reached daily by flight to Hwange Airport from harare, kariba, Victoria Falls and Bulawayol From there transfer by minibus.

AREA: 390,759 sq km (150,873 sq miles).
POPULATION: 9,120,000 (1989 estimate).
POPULATION DENSITY: 23.3 per sq km.
CAPITAL: Harare. **Population:** 681,000 (1983 estimate).
GEOGRAPHY: Zimbabwe is bordered by Zambia to the northwest, Mozambique to the northeast, South Africa to the south and Botswana to the southwest. The central zone of hills gives rise to many rivers, which drain into the man-made Lake Kariba to the north, the marshes of Botswana to the west or into the Zambezi River to the northeast. The *highveld* landscape is dotted with *kopjes* (massive granite outcrops). Along the eastern border for some 350km (220 miles) is a high mountainous region of great scenic beauty, rising to 2592m (8504ft) at Mount Inyangani, the country's highest point. Zimbabwe offers some of the best wildlife parks in southern Africa, notably Hwange (southwest), Matapos (south) and Nyanga (northeast) National Parks. These, together with the Victoria Falls and Great Zimbabwe, are the principal attractions for visitors.
LANGUAGE: The official languages are English and the Shona and Ndebele dialects.
RELIGION: Christianity with traditional beliefs in rural areas, and some Hindu and Moslim minorities.
TIME: GMT + 2.
ELECTRICITY: 220/240 volts AC, 50Hz.
COMMUNICATIONS: Telephone: Full IDD is available. Country code: 263. **Fax:** A few hotels have facilities. **Telex/telegram:** Available at post offices and major hotels. **Post:** Airmail to Europe takes up to a week. **Press:** The two dailies, both in the English Language, are *The Herald* and *The Chronicle*.
BBC World Service and Voice of America frequencies: From time to time these change. See the section *How to Use this Book* for more information.

BBC:				
MHz	21.660	11.940	6.190	3.255
Voice of America:				
MHz	11.97	9.670	6.040	5.995

PASSPORT/VISA

Regulations and requirements may be subject to change at short notice, and you are advised to contact the appropriate diplomatic or consular authority before finalising travel arrangements. Details of these may be found at the head of this country's entry. Any numbers in the chart refer to the footnotes below.

	Passport Required?	Visa Required?	Return Ticket Required?
Full British	Yes	Yes	Yes
BVP	1	-	-
Australian	Yes	No	Yes
Canadian	Yes	No	Yes
USA	Yes	No	Yes
Other EC	Yes	2/3	Yes
Japanese	Yes	No	Yes

Restricted entry: Nationals of South Korea and Taiwan are refused entry. This situation is subject to change, and those concerned are advised to contact a Consulate or Embassy (see addresses at top of entry) for up-to-date information.
PASSPORTS: Valid passport required by all.
British Visitors Passport: [1] Although the immigration authorities may in certain circumstances accept BVPs for persons arriving for holidays or unpaid business trips of up to 3 months, travellers are reminded that no formal agreement exists and the situation may, therefore, change at short notice. In addition, UK nationals using a BVP and returning to the UK from a country with which no such formal agreement exists may be subject to delays and interrogation by UK immigration officials.
VISAS: Required by all except:
(a) nationals of countries referred to in the chart above;
(b) **[2]** nationals of EC countries (nationals of Portugal *do* need a visa);
(c) **[3]** nationals of all French overseas territories;
(d) nationals of Andorra, Antigua & Barbuda, Austria, Bahamas, Bangladesh, Barbados, Belize, Botswana, Brunei, Cyprus, Dominica, Dominican Republic, Fiji, Gambia, Ghana, Grenada, Guyana, Iceland, India, Jamaica, Kenya, Kiribati, Lesotho, Liechtenstein, Malawi, Malaysia, Maldives, Malta, Mauritius, Monaco, Nauru, Nepal, New Zealand, Norway, Pakistan, Papua New Guinea, San Marino, Seychelles, Sierra Leone, Singapore, Solomon Islands, Sri Lanka, St Lucia, Swaziland, Sweden, Switzerland, Tanzania, Tonga, Trinidad & Tobago, Tuvalu, Uganda, Vanuatu, Western Samoa, Yugoslavia and Zambia.
Nationals of other countries, *apart from those specified in the list below*, may obtain visas on arrival in Zimbabwe: Afghanistan, Albania, Algeria, Angola, Bhutan, Bulgaria, Cambodia, Cape Verde, China, CIS, Cuba, Czechoslovakia, Ethiopia, Guinea-Bissau, Hungary, Iran, Iraq, Israel, Laos, Lebanon, Libya, Mali, Mongolia, Mozambique, Myanmar, North Korea, Philippines, Portugal, Poland, Romania, Senegal, Somalia, Sudan, Syria, Vietnam, Yemen and Zaïre.
Types of visa: Single, Double and Multiple entry.
Cost: Single: US$25; Double: US$40; Multiple: US$50.
Validity: 3 months from date of issue.
Application to: If not available at the border (see above), apply to a Consulate (or Consular Section at an Embassy or High Commission). For addresses, see top of entry.
Application requirements: (a) Completed application form(s). (b) Return or onward ticket. (c) Evidence of sufficient funds to cover the stay in Zimbabwe.
Working days required: Up to 1 week on receipt of fee payment.
Temporary residence: Application to The Chief Immigration Officer, Private Bag 7717, Causeway, Harare, Zimbabwe.

MONEY

Currency: Zimbabwe Dollar (Z$) = 100 cents. Notes are in denominations of Z$20, 10, 5 and 2. Coins are in denominations of Z$1, and 50, 20, 10, 5 and 1 cents.
Currency exchange: Major foreign currencies can be exchanged at banks and major hotels at the official exchange rate.
Credit cards: American Express, Diners Club and Visa are widely accepted, whilst Access/Mastercard has more limited use. Check with your credit card company for details of merchant acceptability and other services which may be available.
Travellers cheques: Banks and major hotels will exchange these.
Exchange rate indicators: The following figures are included as a guide to the movements of the Zimbabwe Dollar against Sterling and the US Dollar:

Date:	**Oct '89**	**Oct '90**	**Oct '91**	**Oct '92**
£1.00=	3.52	4.90	8.70	8.25
$1.00=	2.23	2.51	5.01	5.20

Currency restrictions: The import of local currency is limited to Z$100. Export is limited to Z$100 in bank notes. Unrestricted import of foreign currency, subject to declaration. The export of foreign currency is limited to the amount declared on import, supported by the visitor's currency declaration form.
Banking hours: 0800-1500 Monday, Tuesday, Thursday and Friday; 0800-1300 Wednesday and 0800-1130 Saturday.

DUTY FREE

The following items may be imported into Zimbabwe without incurring customs duty:
Goods up to a value of Z$500 inclusive of tobacco, perfume and gifts;
5 litres of alcoholic beverages (up to 2 litres of which may be spirits);
New articles for personal use up to a value of Z$30,000.
Prohibited items: (a) The import of agricultural products including bulbs, cuttings, cycads, eggs, fresh meat, fruit, honey, plants, seeds and vegetables; animals, birds and used bee keeping equipment are prohibited. (b) Permission for the import of non-prescribed drugs, firearms and replicas, flick knives, lockable knives, ammunition and explosives, indecent films and publications, and telecommunications equipment has to be obtained on arrival.

PUBLIC HOLIDAYS

Public holidays observed in Zimbabwe are as follows:
Apr 9-12 '93 Easter. **Apr 18** Independence Day. **May 1** Workers' Day. **May 25** Africa Day. **Aug 11-12** Heroes' Day. **Dec 25-26** Christmas. **Jan 1 '94** New Year's Day.

HEALTH

Regulations and requirements may be subject to change at short notice, and you are advised to contact your doctor well in advance of your intended date of departure. Any numbers in the chart refer to the footnotes below.

	Special Precautions?	Certificate Required?
Yellow Fever	No	1
Cholera	Yes	2
Typhoid & Polio	Yes	-
Malaria	3	-
Food & Drink	4	-

[1]: A yellow fever vaccination certificate is required from travellers arriving from infected areas.
[2]: Following WHO guidelines issued in 1973, a cholera vaccination certificate is not a condition of entry to Zimbabwe. However, cholera is a risk in this country and precautions are essential. Up-to-date advice should be sought before deciding whether these precautions should include vaccination, as medical opinion is divided over its effectiveness. See the *Health* section at the back of the book.
[3]: Malaria risk, predominantly in the malignant *falciparum* form, exists from November to June in all areas below 1200m and throughout the year in the Zambezi Valley. Resistance to chloroquine has been reported.
[4]: All water should be regarded as being a potential health risk. Water used for drinking, brushing teeth or making ice should have first been boiled or otherwise sterilised. Milk is unpasteurised and should be boiled. Powdered or tinned milk is available and is advised but make sure that it is reconstituted with pure water. Avoid dairy products which are likely to have been made from unboiled milk. Only eat well-cooked meat and fish, preferably served hot. Pork, salad and mayonnaise may carry increased risk. Vegetables should be cooked and fruit peeled.
Rabies is present. For those at high risk, vaccination before arrival should be considered. If you are bitten abroad seek medical advice without delay. For more information consult the *Health* section at the back of the book.
Bilharzia (schistosomiasis) is present. Avoid swimming and paddling in fresh water. Swimming pools which are well-chlorinated and maintained are safe.
Health care: Medical facilities are good in the major towns and there are well-equipped clinics in most outlying areas. Health insurance is essential.

TRAVEL - International

AIR: Zimbabwe's national airline is *Air Zimbabwe (RH)*.
Approximate flight time: From *London* to Harare is 9 hours 50 minutes (there are no direct flights connecting London with Bulawayo or Victoria Falls; connections from the capital to either take approximately 1 hour).
International airports: *Harare (HRE)* is 12km (7.5 miles) southeast of the city. Coach (travel time – 30 minutes) every hour 0600-2000. Taxis and full duty-free facilities are available. Airport facilities include post office (0830-1600 Monday to Friday; 0830-1130

ZIMBABWE | **HEALTH REGULATIONS** | **VISA REGULATIONS** | Code-Link

GALILEO/WORLDSPAN

TI-DFT/HRE/HE

TI-DFT/HRE/VI

SABRE

TIDFT/HRE/HE

TIDFT/HRE/VI

To access this information on your CRS, swipe the barcode with a light pen or type in the text under the barcode. For more information, see the introduction *How to Use This Book*.

Saturday), restaurant (1200-1430 and 1800-2230) and bank/bureau de change.

Bulawayo (BUQ) is 24km (15 miles) from the city. Limited bus and taxi services are available.

Victoria Falls (VFA) is 22km (13 miles) from the town. Limited bus and taxi services are available.

Departure tax: US$10 (non-residents) or Z$10 (residents) for all international departures. Children under 12 years are exempt.

RAIL: There are train connections from South Africa through Botswana to Bulawayo. There is a link to Zambia via Victoria Falls. Trains to Mozambique are currently suspended because of the civil war there.

ROAD: There are roads from Tanzania, Malawi, South Africa, Mozambique, Botswana and Zambia. Off the main routes (Beitbridge and Victoria Falls) travel conditions are often primitive and difficult during heavy rains. For details contact the Embassy or High Commission; addresses at top of entry.

TRAVEL - Internal

AIR: Connections to Kariba, Hwange, Victoria Falls, Bulawayo, Gweru, Masvingo and Buffalo Range are run by *Air Zimbabwe (RH)*.

RAIL: There are daily trains between Plumtree, Bulawayo, Victoria Falls, Harare, Mutare and Triangle, run by *National Railways of Zimbabwe*.

ROAD: There is an excellent road network, with paved roads connecting all major towns and many rural areas. **Bus/coach:** The *Zimbabwe Omnibus Company* – a British-owned operation – provides services in most parts of the country. Routes via Great Zimbabwe, Masvingo, Nyanga, Rusape and Harare are run by *Express Motorways Africa (Central) Limited*. For more details contact the Tourist Board. **Car hire:** Available at airports and main hotels. **Documentation:** International Driving Permit required.

URBAN: A reasonable bus service is provided in Harare by a subsidiary of the *Zimbabwe Omnibus Company*. Tickets are bought in advance from booths. There is also a local bus network in Bulawayo.

ACCOMMODATION

HOTELS: There are hotels and lodges (which are similar to guest-houses and provide bed and breakfast). A list of registered hotels is available from the Tourist Board. **Grading:** All hotels are graded on a 5-star system, with those classified 1-star or above being registered with the Tourist Board. Over 70 hotels are registered.

CAMPING/CARAVANNING: Most centres and tourist areas have caravan parks and campsites, except in national parks where lodges and chalets are available.

RESORTS & EXCURSIONS

Now almost recovered from the effects of the savage civil war (and the economic boycott) that followed Rhodesia's Unilateral Declaration of Independence in 1965, Zimbabwe has emerged once more as a beautiful and unique part of Africa. Nowhere else on the continent is there such a balance between wilderness and civilisation. The best months to visit are from July to October. For details contact the Tourist Board.

The Highveld

Running from northeast to southwest down the centre of the country, and connecting its two largest cities, this chain of low mountains constitutes Zimbabwe's most populous area.

Harare: Formerly Salisbury, the capital is Zimbabwe's commercial and industrial centre and also the usual starting point for any visit. It is a clean and sophisticated city, characterised by blossoming trees, colourful parks and contemporary architecture. Local sightseeing includes the modern museum and art gallery, the *Robert McIlwaine Recreational Park*, which has a lake and game reserve, the *Lion & Cheetah Park*, the *Larvon Bird Gardens* and the landscaped gardens of aloes and cycads at *Ewanrigg Botanical Gardens*. Because of its sunny climate, Harare is known as the 'Sunshine City'.

Bulawayo: Zimbabwe's second city is a major commercial, industrial and tourist centre. The city is rich in historical associations and is the home of the National Museum and headquarters of the National Railways of Zimbabwe. Nearby are the ancient *Khami ruins*, while to the south is the *Rhodes Matopos National Park*, notable for its exotic formations of huge granite boulders. Dams with excellent fishing, caves with rock paintings, Cecil Rhodes' grave and a well-stocked game park make this area popular with visitors.

Parks & Wildlife

From the forested mountains of the Eastern highlands to the sun-washed grasslands of Hwange National Park, from the hot Mopani Forest to the shores of Lake Kariba, more than 11% of Zimbabwe's area – 44,688 sq km (17,254 sq miles) – has been set aside as parks and wildlife estates. There are ten national parks and ten recreational parks around the country, plus several botanical gardens, sanctuaries and 14 national safari areas for hunting (which helps to finance the conservation programme and is strictly controlled).

Hwange (formerly Wankie) **National Park** is the largest national park, both in size, 14,620 sq km (5,644 sq miles), and in the variety of animals and birds that may be seen. From the three camps, networks of game viewing roads guide visitors to areas with good animal concentrations and to waterholes where, in the evenings, great numbers of wild animals congregate. At some waterholes platforms are erected where one can observe game closely and in safety. Hwange is one of the last of the great elephant sanctuaries in Africa and herds of up to 100 elephants may be seen drinking and bathing at the waterholes, particularly at the end of the dry season in September. In recent years, Hwange's elephants have prospered too well and the resident population is limited through culling despite outrage from conservationists in far-off Europe.

120km (75 miles) from the Hwange National Park are the **Victoria Falls**, the largest waterfalls in the world – 2.5km (1.5 miles) wide, 550 million litres of water plunge every minute 100m (330ft) into a narrow chasm; the spray can be seen 30km (20 miles) away. To gain an overall impression of the Falls, the 'Flight of the Angels' light plane trip is a must, as is a cruise up the mighty Zambezi River. It is possible to walk across to Zambia (with the minimum of formalities) to view from the other side; this is also highly recommended, for the Falls are without a doubt one of the world's grandest natural spectacles and every viewpoint reveals something new. Nearby is the **Zambezi National Park,** where sable antelopes and other exotic animals graze in a parkland setting.

Mana Pools National Park is one of Zimbabwe's most beautiful national parks, occupying 2196 sq km (848 sq miles) of forest along the shores of the Zambezi River. The animal population includes hippos, elephants,

rhinos, buffaloes and many types of antelope. Game viewing on foot is allowed. The birdlife along the river and in the bush is particularly prolific. It is possible to fish for tigerfish, bream and the giant vundu.
Lake Kariba, in the northwest of the country on the Zambian border, covers 7770 sq km (3000 sq miles) and holds a million gallons of water. Game can be viewed from the luxury of the *Bumi Hills Safari Lodge*, the comfort of various safari camps, or from well-appointed cruise vessels and self-contained safari-crafts.
A holiday in Zimbabwe would be incomplete without a visit to the **Great Zimbabwe National Monument**. This forms the largest complex of ruins in Africa south of the pyramids in Egypt. *The Main Enclosure*, or *Temple*, has walls over 9m (30ft) tall, 4m (14ft) thick and over 228m (250 yards) in circumference, giving approximately 485,521 cubic metres (635,000 cubic ft) of hand-trimmed mortarless stonework. The remains are what is left of a city-state that flourished between the 13th and 15th centuries, trading in gold. **Lake Kyle National Park** is not far away; there is a well-organised campsite close to the lake.
Note: For safety reasons, visitors may not enter any national park by motorcycle.

The Eastern Highlands

The *Inyanga*, *Vumba* and *Chimanimani* mountain ranges are one of the country's principal holiday areas for both Zimbabweans and tourists and are ideal for those who want to relax and enjoy crisp mountain air. The country's highest mountain, *Inyangani* (2592m/8504ft), is in this area. The scenery is striking in its variety, with deep valleys, gorges, bare granite peaks, pine-forested slopes and bubbling trout streams rolling down to steep cliffs. There are challenging hilly golf courses and pony rides through the heather, as well as the opportunity for mountain climbing, squash, tennis, bowls, fishing, snooker and gambling in the casino. Because of the mountainous and forested terrain, game viewing in this region is more a matter of chance but for the lucky there are leopards and rare forest antelopes.

SOCIAL PROFILE

FOOD & DRINK: Zimbabwe is a cosmopolitan society and enjoys both local and international cuisine. Eating out is popular and comparatively cheap. Meat dishes are usually excellent. A traditional dish is *sadza* (a stiff maize meal) eaten with meat and/or gravy and a relish. Table service is the norm in restaurants. **Drink:** Beer is the most widely drunk alcoholic beverage, both lager and ale. Imported wines, spirits and liqueurs are available in hotels. Traditional maize beer, *whawha*, is made in large quantities on special occasions. Public bars are almost always part of a hotel. Licensing hours in Zimbabwe are 1030-1500 and 1630-2300. Major hotels have 24-hour bars and room service.
NIGHTLIFE: Rather limited outside the cities with the emphasis on eating and discos, but larger cities have nightclubs, cinemas and repertory theatres. The three main tourist areas have casinos.
SHOPPING: A sales tax of 15-18% is added to all purchases except those which are to be exported. Special purchases are copper, wooden and soapstone carvings, game skin and leather products, pottery and basketwork. **Shopping hours:** 0800-1700 Monday to Friday and 0800-1300 Saturday.
SPORT: Football and **cricket** are the national sports, while **tennis, squash, riding, rugby** and **hockey** are also popular. For the adventurous there are clubs for **hang-gliding, water-skiing, windsurfing** and **parachuting.**
SPECIAL EVENTS: Early Apr *Zimbabwe Trade Fair*, Bulawayo.
SOCIAL CONVENTIONS: Urban culture in Zimbabwe is greatly influenced by Western culture and education but in rural areas traditional values and crafts continue. Shaking hands is the customary form of greeting. European courtesies and codes of practice should be observed when visiting someone's home. Return invitations are appreciated. Giving a token of appreciation is optional. Casual wear is suitable for daytime and men are only expected to wear suits and ties for business meetings. Smart restaurants or hotel bars require male guests to wear a jacket and tie. Smoking is common, although it is prohibited on public transport and in some public buildings. **Tipping:** A 10-15% tip is usual.

BUSINESS PROFILE

ECONOMY: Zimbabwe is fortunate in its strong agricultural base, which did not suffer so badly from the drought problems which afflicted much of the rest of the continent. Tobacco and other cash crops, including sugar, coffee, cotton, tea and groundnuts, are key export earners. In addition, Zimbabwe exports high-quality beef to the EC under the terms of the Lomé Convention (which governs trade between the EC and the ACP – African, Caribbean and Pacific – countries). The mining industry is also important with chromium, copper, tungsten and asbestos produced for export. Large coal deposits supply the country's power stations. Other minerals are processed before being exported: ferro-chrome and refined gold are examples. The manufacturing industry is well-developed by regional standards, significantly as the result of import substitution projects set up while international trade sanctions were applied against Rhodesia during UDI. The Government has identified the manufacturing sector as the key for guaranteeing sustained economic growth in the future: this offers one of the best opportunities for British exporters, since much of Zimbabwean industry relies on very old equipment which needs replacing. Zimbabwe remains somewhat dependent on South Africa economically, both for imports of manufactured goods and for seaports (Zimbabwe is landlocked) to transport exports, and the Government has taken Zimbabwe into the Southern African Development Co-ordination Conference which aims to reduce South African economic domination of the region.
Nonetheless, the economy is fairly strong – GDP growth is around 4% per annum – and its prospects are reasonably bright if the country can survive the present crisis caused by drought and a chronic shortage of foreign exchange (which hinders the importation of goods needed for expansion and development). A five-year programme agreed with the IMF commits Zimbabwe to reducing government controls throughout the economy in exchange for financial assistance. Economic issues currently dominate the domestic political arena: trade liberalisation, which is being introduced after three years of debate, and land reform are the most important of these. Import quotas are being replaced by a general license system. Main export markets: Germany, Japan, the UK and the USA. Main import sources: South Africa, the UK, the USA and Germany.
BUSINESS: Normal courtesies should be observed and men should wear a suit and tie. The atmosphere will generally be less formal than in many European countries. **Office hours:** 0800-1630 Monday to Friday.
COMMERCIAL INFORMATION: The following organisations can offer advice:
Ministry of Industry & Commerce, Private Bag 7708, 12-14th Floor, Mukwati Building, Fourth Street, Causeway, Harare. Tel: (4) 702 731. Telex: 24472; *or*
Zimbabwe National Chambers of Commerce, PO Box 1934, Equity House, Rezende Street, Harare. Tel: (4) 708 611. Telex: 22531.

HISTORY & GOVERNMENT

HISTORY: Present-day Zimbabwe was the site of a large and complex African civilisation in the 13th and 14th centuries. The people of the area resisted European colonisation until the late 1890s, when British mining interests under Cecil Rhodes' British South Africa Company seized control. The BSAC ran the country, called 'Southern Rhodesia', until 1923, when it became, nominally, a British colony. This followed a referendum (for whites only) on joining the Union of South Africa. Despite attractive terms by South African leader Smuts, there was a heavy vote against the merger. From 1953-1963 Southern Rhodesia formed part of the Central African Federation with neighbouring Northern Rhodesia (now Zambia) and Nayasaland (now Malawi). In 1965, to resist decolonisation, the settlers, with South African support, issued a Unilateral Declaration of Independence (UDI). This triggered a bitter civil war between the white minority government and fighters for African independence, ending only in 1980 with the granting of independence and the holding of a general election under British auspices, which was won decisively by Robert Mugabe's ZANU Party. The main focus of dissent in the early years was Joshua Nkomo's ZAPU opposition party. From 1985, however, the two parties moved towards merger, which was achieved peacefully in January 1988. Still named ZANU-PF, the party again swept the board in the 1990 national elections, taking 147 of 150 seats. Mugabe's original intention was apparently to institute a one-party state once he had achieved a sufficiently large parliamentary majority. Having acquired it, however, he suddenly became curiously reluctant to continue down that path. The reason was political developments elsewhere in Africa, which are, almost without exception, moving away from one-party rule and towards pluralism; furthermore, Zimbabwe's Western backers no doubt made clear their displeasure at Mugabe's proposal. There the matter rested. With Nkomo's party neutralised as an opposition force, the charismatic ex-guerilla commander Edgar Tekere has emerged as the principal opposition to Mugabe and his party's continued domination of Zimbabwean politics. Tekere's Zimbabwe Unity Movement (ZUM) made a strong showing in the 1990 elections, campaigning on an anti-corruption platform, but was still overwhelmed by ZANU-PF and has since faded. Since then, Mugabe has definitely dropped plans to introduce a one-party state. On the economic front, Mugabe has committed his government to pursuing liberal economic policies in which market forces will play a dominant role: trade liberalisation and land reform are the main economic policies at present. With two million unemployed and inflation approaching 50%, in the middle of the worst drought for a century, quick results are needed. The Mugabe government's strong anti-apartheid stance dominates foreign affairs, and the country watches developments across the southern border with some trepidation. Foreign policy is otherwise characterised by attempts to maintain friendly relations both with the West (particularly the UK) and other EC countries, as well as China, North Korea and Eastern Europe. A large detachment of Zimbabwean troops remains in Mozambique to protect the Beira railway, which is vital to landlocked Zimbabwe for much of its export traffic. The recent political settlement in Mozambique has been a cause of considerable relief in Harare.
GOVERNMENT: Under the terms of the 1980 Constitution, executive power is formally vested in the President, consulted by a Prime Minister, who in reality wields most power. He, in turn, is advised by the Cabinet, which is responsible to the bi-cameral Parliament, which wields all legislative authority. This consists of a House of Assembly, with 150 members of whom 120 are elected by universal adult suffrage, 12 are nominated by the President, ten are traditional Chiefs and eight are Provincial Governors.

CLIMATE

Although located in the tropics, temperate conditions prevail all year, moderated by altitude and the inland position of the country. The hot and dry season is from September to October, and the rainy season from November to March. The best months to visit are April to May and August to September.
Required clothing: Tropical lightweights and rainwear for the wet season.

HARARE Zimbabwe (1470m)

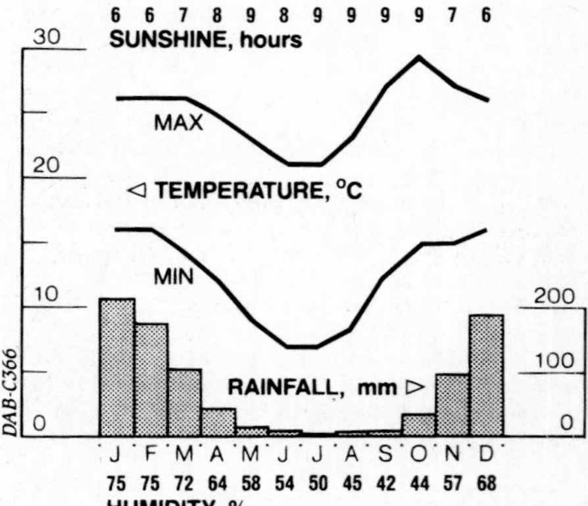

BULAWAYO Zimbabwe (1344m)

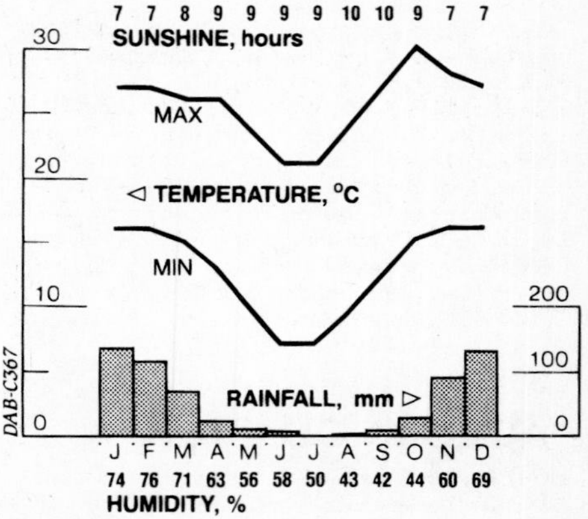

INTERNATIONAL MEDIA

This section has been designed to provide an overview of the main travel trade publications worldwide, and will be of interest both to travel trade professionals and to persons in other sectors who need to know more about the trends and developments in the travel industry. We have tried to provide as much information as will be useful for determining the suitability of the publication for the intended purpose, as well as main addresses and contact numbers. Entries are arranged alphabetically by title. This list should not be regarded as fully comprehensive and any suggestions for titles to be included in future Columbus Press publications will be gratefully received. Please address suggestions to: The Editor, World Travel Guide, Columbus Press Ltd, 5-7 Luke Street. London EC2A 4PX, UK. Tel: +44 (71) 729 4535. Fax: +44 (71) 729 1156.

Please note that all the information, including the publication summary, was provided by the publications themselves and has been reproduced in good faith. Much of the information, while correct at time of going to press, may be subject to change at short notice; for this reason, advertising rates have not been included.

Any enquiries concerning the information given in this section should be addressed to the magazine(s) concerned, not to Columbus Press.

INTERNATIONAL TRAVEL PUBLICATIONS

Agent Canada

#300, 1534 West Second Avenue
Vancouver
British Columbia V6J 1H2
Canada

Tel: (604) 731 0481.
Fax: (604) 731 2589.

Media Information

Circulation:	11,201.
Frequency:	Weekly.
Distribution:	Courier and postal system.
Trim Size (depth x width):	274mm x 209mm. 10⅞ ins. x 8¼ ins.
Language:	English.
Published in:	Canada.
Publisher:	Douglas W Keough.
Year Established:	1978.

Additional Information

Agent Canada is published weekly with a circulation of over 11,000 magazines reaching all travel agencies in Canada. Three regional distributions – *Agent West*, *Agent America* and *Agent Ontario* – are published twice a month, as well as the ACTA *Annual Directory* distributed every August for the Canadian Travel Industry. *Agent Canada* now also publish *Skal World News* six times a year. It is a 25,000-member global club with 500 branches in 100 countries and technically a supplement of *Agent Canada*.

AL DIA/Travel Agent

Editorial: *Pepperdine Enterprises Inc.*
1212 Brampton Place
Heathrow, FL
32746, USA
Advertising: *Travel Media International*
2nd Floor, Nat West Building
23 East Street
Chesham, Bucks, HP5 1DG, UK

Tel (Editorial): (407) 333 3393.
Tel (Advertising): (4094) 791 179.
Fax: (407) 333 3533.
Fax (Advertising): (4094) 775 220.

Media Information

Circulation:	5000.
Frequency:	Monthly from Mar-Nov.
Distribution:	ABC audited circulation.
Trim Size (depth x width):	273mm x 204mm. 10¾ ins. x 8⅛ ins.
Language:	Spanish and English.
Published in:	USA.
Publisher:	Noemi Pepperdine.
Year Established:	1991.

Additional Information

AL DIA/Travel Agent is an excellent trade publication for all major advertisers, enabling them to cost-effectively target Latin American travel agents, exporters, wholesalers and tour operators. The remainder is read by travel professionals such as national tourist offices, airlines, cruise lines etc. The magazine contains technical, specialised articles and useful information for the travel agent (such as special discounts on familiarisation tours, interviews with key travel executives and a travel trade Calendar of Events) as well as being a quick, entertaining and exciting read.

Al-Hayat Al-Siyahiya

1a Kings Avenue
London SW4 8DK
UK

Tel: (071) 274 9381.
Fax: (071) 326 1783.

Media Information

Circulation:	38,000.
Frequency:	Monthly.
Distribution:	Newsagent or subscription.
Trim Size (depth x width):	280mm x 210mm. 11 ins. x 8¼ ins.
Language:	Arabic.
Published in:	UK.
Publisher:	Dahabi Idrissi.
Year Established:	1983.

Additional Information

Al-Hayat Al-Siyahiya is a leading international tourist and travel magazine distributed throughout the Arab world and in Europe. It provides the latest travel news and information and is meant for everyone who takes an interest in tourism, especially the top executive professionals working in the travel and tourist field. It has also opened travel horizons by providing advice to millions of Arab tourists on the best way to spend their holidays.

Ambassador (Safeer)

Ambassador
66 Clifton Court
Northwick Terrace
London NW8 8HU
UK

Tel: (071) 289 5903.
Fax: (071) 289 2664.

Media Information

Circulation:	40,000.
Frequency:	Quarterly.
Distribution:	Airmail.
Trim Size (depth x width):	197mm x 210mm. 7⅞ ins x 8¼ ins.
Language:	English and Urdu.
Published in:	Pakistan.
Year Established:	1992.

Additional Information

This is Pakistan's first ever travel, leisure and business quarterly. *Ambassador* is set to be the highest circulated and widest read publication of Pakistan. The magazine will be distributed in the new Jinnah Terminal in Karachi and it is estimated that 7 million national and international passengers will be embarking, disembarking and passing through its gateways in transit.

Asia Travel Trade

190 Middle Road
#11-01 Fortune Centre
Singapore 0718

Tel: 339 7622.
Fax: 339 8521.

Media Information

Circulation:	14,056.
Frequency:	Monthly.
Distribution:	Surface Mail.
Trim Size (depth x width):	279mm x 205mm. 10⅞ ins. x 8⅛ ins.
Language:	English.
Published in:	Singapore.
Publisher:	John Tan.
Year Established:	1969.

Additional Information

Asia Travel Trade is targeted to middle and senior management staff of all sectors of Asia Pacific's travel and tourist industry. It is dedicated to providing principled and responsible news reporting and analysis which all industry professionals require in order to make informed decisions about the business of tourism and its development in the Asia Pacific region.

ASTA Agency Management

Pace Communications
1301 Carolina Street
Greensboro, NC
27401
USA

Tel: (919) 378 6065.
Fax: (919) 378 6828.

Media Information

Circulation:	25,000.
Frequency:	Monthly.
Distribution:	ASTA members worldwide.
Trim Size (depth x width):	276mm x 207mm. 10¾ ins. x 8⅛ ins.
Language:	English.
Published in:	USA.
Publisher:	William A Lawrence.
Year Established:	1987 ('75 as ASTA Travel News).

Additional Information

ASTA Agency Management is an upscale business publication targeted to the owner/manager of America's travel agencies. It delivers the information needed to make well-informed and profitable business decisions and provides in-depth coverage in two main areas: industry trends (with reports that ask and answer the tough business questions that have an effect on agencies) and travel agency management (including articles that provide readers with ideas, suggestions, facts, figures and instructions on how to be a more profitable and professional agency).

Benelux Travel World

Aspress BV Publications
Eilandstraat 16
B-1981 Hofstade
Belgium

Fax (Advertising): (15) 612 994.

Media Information

Circulation:	9800.
Frequency:	9 per year (not Jul, Aug, Dec).
Distribution:	Controlled circulation.
Trim Size (depth x width):	297mm x 210mm. 11¾ ins. x 8¼ ins.
Language:	Dutch, French and English.
Published in:	Benelux countries.
Publisher:	Herman Stenuit.
Year Established:	1989.

Additional Information

Benelux Travel World is a magazine for tour operators, travel agents and their employees, aviation companies, tourist offices and the best hotels and travel managers in multinational companies.

Business Class

Aspress BV Publications
Eilandstraat 16
B-1981 Hofstade
Belgium

Tel: (15) 613 596.
Fax: (15) 612 994.

Media Information

Circulation:	28,000.
Frequency:	9 per year (not Jul, Aug and Jan).
Distribution:	Post.
Trim Size (depth x width):	297mm x 210mm. 11¾ ins. x 8¼ ins.
Language:	Dutch, French and English.
Published in:	Belgium.
Publisher:	Herman Stenuit.
Year Established:	1986.

Additional Information

Business Class is a glossy, full-colour magazine published on the 20th of each month, excluding July, August and January. It provides important and up-to-date information to Belgian travel agencies, frequent business travellers and travel managers of international companies. Written in three languages (Dutch, French and English). It serves as a vital tool for any international business traveller.

Business Travel News

600 Community Drive
Manhasset, NY
11030
USA

Tel (Editorial): (212) 562 5511.
Tel (Advertising): (212) 562 5772.
Fax: (516) 562 5465.

Media Information

Circulation:	63,000.
Frequency:	27 per year.
Distribution:	Controlled circulation (post).
Trim Size (depth x width):	365mm x 273mm. 14⅜ ins. x 10¾ins.
Language:	English.
Published in:	USA.
Publisher:	Bill Besch.
Year Established:	1984.

Additional Information

Edited for corporate executives and travel agents who plan, purchase and manage business travel and small meetings. Every issue includes news and analysis of travel management trends, supplier activities (airline, hotel, car rental etc), international business travel and major business travel and meetings destinations worldwide. Pull-out supplements include *Business Travel Decisions*, emphasising how to implement travel management strategies, and *Meetings Under 100*, which covers the information needs of subscribers booking short-term corporate meetings.

Canadian Travel Press

310 Dupont Street
Toronto
Ontario M5R 1V9
Canada

Tel: (416) 968 7252.
Fax: (416) 968 2377.

Media Information

Circulation:	12,8000.
Frequency:	Weekly.
Distribution:	First-class mail/private delivery.
Trim Size (depth x width):	337mm x 251mm. 13¼ ins. x 9⅞ ins.
Language:	English.
Published in:	Canada.
Publisher:	David McClung.
Year Established:	1968.

Additional Information

Canadian Travel Press is a high-quality, glossy, tabloid-size magazine published 46 times a year. It deals with timely coverage of events of concern to the travel industry and carries in-depth reports on such destinations as Canada, the United States, the Caribbean, the Pacific and Africa, to name but a few. Periodically, issues such as automation, business travel, tax and legal matters affecting the industry and forecasting will be dealt with. The magazine is distributed to subscribers in every province within Canada, as well as in key border cities in the United States.

Delegates

Premier House
10 Greycoat Place
London SW1P 1SB
UK

Tel (Editorial): (071) 222 8866.
Tel (Advertising): (071) 222 9843.
Fax: (071) 222 5689.

Media Information

Circulation:	19,731.
Frequency:	Bi-monthly.
Distribution:	Controlled circulation.
Trim Size (depth x width):	297mm x 210mm. 11¾ ins. x 8¼ ins.
Language:	English.
Published in:	UK.
Publisher:	Audrey Brindley.
Year Established:	1985.

Additional Information

Delegates magazine is a publication for the buyers of incentive and conference facilities worldwide with regard to how the buyers view the marketplace. It is the magazine for the buyers about the buyers in the industry and is totally international in its editorial coverage, its circulation and its advertising.

Duty & Tax Free Markets

B.I.A Enterprises, S.A.
66 Clifton Court
London NW8 HU
UK

Tel: (071) 289 5903.
Fax: (071) 289 2664.

Media Information

Circulation:	12,000.
Frequency:	Bi-monthly (6 issues annually).
Distribution:	Controlled circulation.
Trim Size (depth x width):	297mm x 210mm. 11¾ ins. x 8¼ ins.
Language:	Arabic and English.
Published in:	UK.
Publisher:	Headley Brothers.
Year Established:	1990.

Additional Information

Duty & Tax Free Markets is a bi-monthly trade publication which reflects the purchasing attitudes and economic trends as they affect the duty- and tax-free trade in the Middle East and Africa. The magazine's aim is to encourage and stimulate the developing countries' operators, markets and products to seek international opportunities offered by the trade. While providing a regular update of new developments in these regions, it serves as a contact forum for both purchasers and suppliers.

Editur

Grand Via Carlos III, 86 7°
08028 Barcelona
Spain

Tel: (3) 330 7052.
Fax: (3) 330 7496 *or* 330 2401.

Media Information

Circulation:	12,750.
Frequency:	Weekly.
Distribution:	Subscription.
Trim Size (depth x width):	340mm x 240mm. 13⅜ ins. x 9½ ins.
Language:	Spanish.
Published in:	Spain.
Publisher:	Jorge Vila Fradera.
Year Established:	1960.

Additional Information

Editur is Spain's only weekly publication devoted to the professional world of tourism in its many facets. It is circulated entirely by subscription among travel agencies, tour operators, hotels, apartments, airlines, railway and overland carriers, property developers, holiday industry suppliers etc. Eight other travel magazines are published regularly by the company, and all represent an important aid for the professional in Spain and for those in other countries who work with ours.

FVW International

PO Box 323462
Redaktion
Junfrauenthal 47
W-2000 Hamburg 13
Federal Republic of Germany

Tel (Editorial): (40) 441 87383.
Tel (Advertising): (40) 441 87382.
Tel (Subscription): (40) 441 87381.
Fax: (40) 441 87329.

Media Information

Circulation:	22,103.
Frequency:	Bi-weekly.
Distribution:	Mail subscription.
Trim Size (depth x width):	315mm x 227mm. 12⅜ ins. x 8⅞ ins.
Language:	German; some in English.
Published in:	Federal Republic of Germany.
Publisher:	Dieter Niedecken.
Year Established:	1967.

Additional Information

FVW International is the leading German travel market magazine in terms of editorial pages, paid and distributed circulation and total advertisement volume. It is an informative and critical working tool for travel agencies, company travel departments and tour operators and has a very loyal readership.

GIT (Guia Internacional de Trafico)

3rd Floor, Suipacha 207
Officina 316
1088 Buenos Aires
Argentina

Tel (Editorial): (1) 35 4893/35 6945.
Tel (Advertising): (1) 35 6934/35 6400.
Fax: (1) 35 5146.
Telex: 25955 ARVIL AR.

Media Information

Circulation:	10,000.
Frequency:	Monthly.
Distribution:	Mail.
Trim Size (depth x width):	260mm x 180mm. 10¼ ins. x 7⅛ ins.
Language:	Spanish.
Published in:	Argentina.
Publisher:	A Rodrígues/J C Villa Larlaudet.
Year Established:	1963.

Additional Information

GIT is a leading airline guide and travel trade magazine reaching Argentina, Paraguay, Uruguay and Miami in the USA. There are more than 450 pages of travel industry news, features and information offering public relations and marketing services, as well as promotional activities (such as organising workshops). The magazine serves as an invaluable source of reference for anyone whose job involves planning in the travel business.

Greek Travel Pages

International Publications Ltd
6 Psylla and Filellinon Streets
10557 Athens
Greece

Tel: (1) 324 7511.
Fax: (1) 325 4775 *or* 324 9996.

Media Information

Circulation:	6000.
Frequency:	Monthly.
Distribution:	Airmail.
Trim Size (depth x width):	220mm x 150mm. 8⅝ ins. x 5⅞ ins.
Language:	English.
Published in:	Greece.
Publisher:	Eleftherios Theofanopoulos.
Year Established:	1975.

Additional Information

Greek Travel Pages is a publication used by tourist professsionals worldwide and gives comprehensive travel information.

Group Travel Organiser

4th Floor, Quadrant House
250 Kennington Lane
London SE11 5RD
UK

Tel (Editorial): (071) 735 5240.
Tel (Advertising): (071) 735 5058.
Fax: (071) 587 0497.

Media Information

Circulation:	8500.
Frequency:	10 per year.
Distribution:	Controlled mailing.
Trim Size (depth x width):	297mm x 210mm. 11¾ ins. x 8¼ ins.
Language:	English.
Published in:	UK.
Publisher:	Peter Stonham.
Year Established:	1988.

Additional Information

Group Travel Organiser is the only magazine specifically dedicated to the arena of group travel. It reaches more than 8000 named individuals known to be active group travel organisers for sports and social clubs affiliated to companies, women's institutes, retirement associations and various other special interest groups. It also has a trade readership exceeding 1000 and covers news and features on group travel opportunities throughout the UK and abroad.

GSA Travel Marketing

PO Box 3239
407 Tulbagh Centre
Hans Strijdom Avenue
Cape Town 8000
South Africa

Tel: (21) 419 1671.
Fax: (21) 419 4851.

Media Information

Circulation:	3500.
Frequency:	Monthly.
Distribution:	Subscription.
Trim Size (depth x width):	297mm x 210mm. 11¾ ins. x 8¼ ins.
Language:	English.
Published in:	South Africa.
Publisher:	Jeff Hawthorne.
Year Established:	1980.

Additional Information

Since its inception in February 1980, *GSA Travel Marketing* has grown to become the most comprehensive reference source available to the Southern African Travel Industry. Published monthly, it contains updated information on tour operators, hotels, general sales agents, airlines, car rental companies, cruise operators, other travel-related services and visa requirements.
More than 700 agencies from Southern Africa and beyond subscribe to over 3500 copies a month and it is used constantly every day by travel personnel actively selling to their clients.

Guida Viaggi

Via Larga 2
20122 Milano
Italy

Tel: (2) 876 936 *or* 866 562.
Fax: (2) 866 561.

Media Information

Circulation:	7500.
Frequency:	Weekly.
Distribution:	Free.
Trim Size (depth x width):	420mm x 305mm. 16½ ins. x 12 ins.
Language:	Italian.
Published in:	Italy.
Publisher:	Givi Srl.
Year Established:	1971.

Additional Information

Guida Viaggi is a publication providing articles, news and information concerning the travel market. It is addressed to travel agents, airlines, shipping lines, touristic agents, local tourist organisations for workers' free-time activities and magazines and newspapers with tourist columns.

Guida Viaggi

the weekly magazine for italian travel agents

SETTIMANALE D'OPINIONE

GUIDA VIAGGI

Maldiviana Sea Club di Athuruga

MALDIVE

quota «companion» sconto del 50%

ogni giovedì da Roma fino al 9 aprile

Numero 452
Anno XXI
24/31 gennaio 1992

SPEDIZIONE IN ABBONAMENTO POSTALE GRUPPO I. IN CASO DI MANCATO RECAPITO RESTITUIRE AL MITTENTE: 20122 MILANO, VIA LARGA 2

Chi si rivede: i premi!

Un fenomeno che lede la professionalità, crea malcontento e limita scelte imprenditoriali

Mario Nacci - a pag. 8

In nome della Dea Vacanza

Gloria Vanni - a pag. 4

L'inverno ci salverà?

Foderaro invoca un organismo centrale permanente di coordinamento del settore

Ettore Carminati - a pag. 6

«90 Tour» dichiarata fallita

È la società di Alitalia e FS che gestì i mondiali di calcio

Marco Ricci - a pag. 10

Si consolida la Btl

Servizio a pag. 14

Il censimento dei liner in servizio

Il più vecchio è il DC3, ma altri gli sono vicini — Franco Goy - a pag. 12

In Kenya, nella quiete del Kivulini Village

Maria Cristina Cuttica - a pag. 15

Continua la missione nel Pacifico

Sulle orme dei Marines

Gian Paolo Bonomi - a pag. 3

Questo giornale è stampato su carta ecologica.

20122 Milano - Via Larga, 2 - Ph. 39-2-876936 - Fax 39-2-866561

Holiday Marketing

Prestige Publications (UK) Ltd.
Lindsay House
19 Lindsay Road
New Haw
Addlestone
Surrey KT15 3BD
UK

Tel/Fax (Editorial): (0932) 353 687.
Tel/Fax (Advertising): (0932) 347 658.

Media Information

Circulation:	14,030.
Frequency:	11 per year.
Distribution:	Post.
Trim Size (depth x width):	297mm x 210mm. 11¾ ins. x 8¼ ins.
Language:	English.
Published in:	UK.
Publisher:	Nick Barbasiewicz.
Year Established:	1986.

Additional Information

Holiday Marketing is the only travel trade magazine to concentrate on marketing and selling. Like its predecessor, *Holiday Shop Magazine* (which it now incorporates) it is dedicated to covering tour operators's programmes. Plus features, legal advice, reader feedback and brochure reviews.

IATA Review

PO Box 672
33 route de l'Aéroport
1215 Geneva 15
Switzerland

Tel (Editorial): (22) 799 2967 (Geneva).
Tel (Advertising): (514) 844 6311 (Montréal).
Fax: (22) 799 2685 (Geneva).

Media Information

Circulation:	12,000.
Frequency:	6 per year.
Distribution:	Direct mail.
Trim Size (depth x width):	280mm x 210mm. 11 ins. x 8¼ ins.
Language:	English.
Published in:	Switzerland.
Publisher:	IATA Public Relations.
Year Established:	1966.

Additional Information

IATA Review is the news magazine of the International Air Transport Association. It contains news, commentary and background information relating both to IATA activities and to the civil aviation industry in general. Its editorial content, written by IATA specialists and external industry experts, covers a wide range of technical, regulatory, commercial and financial issues affecting air transport. Readership includes airline chief executives, directors of civil aviation, ministers of transport, airport authorities, aircraft manufacturers, financiers, tourist boards, travel agents, consumer organisations, academic institutions and the media.

Interline & Travel News

Via Bissolati 54
00187 Roma
Italy

Tel: (6) 474 1095.
Fax: (6) 482 7632.

Media Information

Circulation:	10,000.
Frequency:	Bi-monthly/monthly (Jul & Aug).
Distribution:	Post.
Trim Size (depth x width):	300mm x 211mm. 11⅞ ins. x 8¼ ins.
Language:	Italian; some in English.
Published in:	Italy.
Publisher:	Alberto Marani.
Year Established:	1970.

Additional Information

Interline & Travel News has been the official mouthpiece for airline and tourism personnel for over 20 years. Each issue, of which 8000 copies are distributed in Italy and 2000 worldwide, is the official publication of the Interline Italia Club, which promotes the many special offers available to the staff of international airlines, travel agencies, airports and civil aviation boards who are club members. It lists countless travel opportunities at amazing prices and is an ideal vehicle for operators, airlines and other tourism-related organisations to present, promote and sell their products through both advertising and editorial support.

Jax Fax Marketing

PO Box 403
397 Post Road
Darien, CT
06820-1413
USA

Tel (Editorial): (203) 655 8746.
Tel (Advertising): (203) 655 5257.
Fax: (203) 655 6257.

Media Information

Circulation:	28,000.
Frequency:	Monthly.
Distribution:	Mail.
Trim Size (depth x width):	277mm x 206mm. 10⅞ ins. x 8⅛ ins.
Language:	English.
Published in:	USA.
Publisher:	Clifton N Cooke.
Year Established:	1973.

Additional Information

Jax Fax Marketing is for reservations, sales and management personnel of retail travel agencies, tour wholesalers, group and incentive organisers and all those engaged in the sale and marketing of air transportation and inclusive tours on both scheduled and charter flights. It has over 3000 listings of low-cost high-value flights and/or tours for international and domestic destinations (including departure date, return date, number of days, price range, type of flight or tour and name of the airline), and 100 pages on new travel products, destinations and companies.

L'Agenzia di Viaggi

Via Rasella 155
00187 Rome
Italy

Tel: (6) 482 1539.
Fax: (6) 482 6721.

Media Information

Circulation:	12,450.
Frequency:	Daily.
Distribution:	72.5% to paying subscribers.
Trim Size (depth x width):	280mm x 400mm. 10⅜ ins. x 15¾ ins.
Language:	Italian.
Published in:	Italy.
Publisher:	Marco Valerio Ambrosini.
Year Established:	1965.

Additional Information

L'Agenzia di Viaggi is a daily travel magazine offering impartial travel news and in-depth reporting on tourism in Italy and throughout the world. Articles include reports on trends and styles in where to go, how to get there and where to stay. The Saturday edition is 4-colour and features special destinations and resorts. It is practically the only Italian travel trade market magazine in Italy.

L'Echo Touristique

6 rue Marius Aufan
92300 Levallois-Perret
France

Tel: (1) 47 58 20 00.
Fax: (1) 47 58 72 00.

Media Information

Circulation:	9000.
Frequency:	Weekly.
Distribution:	Subscription.
Trim Size (depth x width):	280mm x 395mm. 11 ins. x 15½ ins.
Language:	French.
Published in:	France.
Publisher:	Claude Barou.
Year Established:	1930.

Additional Information

L'Echo Touristique is a trade-only magazine devoted to the travel industry. It provides information on tour operators, travel agencies, hotels, transportation and international markets, as well as features every week on tourism destinations or on tourism companies and leaders. Several times during the year there are special features, such as articles on wages in tourism, results of the French tourism companies, training in tourism etc. It has a reputation for reliability, accuracy and objectivity.

Middle East Travel

CMC Media
127 Butlers Wharf
Shad Thames
London SE1 2YE
UK

Tel (Editorial): (4) 206 5709 (Dubai).
Tel (Advertising): (4) 294 804 (Dubai) *or* (071) 357 6624 (London).
Fax: (071) 357 6623 (London).

Media Information

Circulation:	7240.
Frequency:	9 per year.
Distribution:	Controlled circ./subscription.
Trim Size (depth x width):	270mm x 210mm. 10⅝ ins. x 8¼ ins.
Language:	English.
Published in:	UK.
Publisher:	Colin Miller.
Year Established:	1977.

Additional Information

Middle East Travel is the leading travel news magazine for this region, providing up-to-date and authoritative comment on developments affecting the airline, hotel and travel industries. Circulated to the major tour operators, travel agents, hotels and airlines, as well as the Ministries of Tourism throughout the Arab world, it is recognised as the main source of information in this growing market.

MLD Canadian Traveller

Suite #210, 1015 Burrard Street
Vancouver
British Columbia V6Z 1Y5
Canada

Tel (Editorial): (604) 669 7737.
Fax: (604) 684 2562.

Media Information

Circulation:	15,000.
Frequency:	Monthly.
Distribution:	Marketing Support Services /post.
Trim Size (depth x width):	210mm x 276mm. 8¼ ins. x 10⅞ ins.
Language:	English.
Published in:	Canada.
Publisher:	Marilynne Prupas.
Year Established:	1985 (as *Travel Trade Canada*).

Additional Information

MLD Canadian Traveller provides in-depth information about the travel destinations of the world, and is written for and distributed to Canadian travel agents. The editorial style is colourful and concise, and is designed to aid agents in selling destinations to their clients. It also supplies practical, reliable destination information of benefit to both leisure and corporate travellers, as well as frequent special issues, such as their Railways of the World issues. Their readership includes tour operators, government tourism bureaux, carriers, hotels and resorts.

OPAS The Travel Magazine

Mariankatu 14
SF-00170 Helsinki
Finland

Tel: (0) 171 737.
Fax: (0) 665 491.

Media Information

Circulation:	22,000 per quarter.
Frequency:	Quarterly.
Distribution:	Subscription/news-stands.
Trim Size (depth x width):	290mm x 212mm. 11⅓ ins. x 8⅓ ins.
Language:	Finnish and English.
Published in:	Finland.
Publisher:	Tony Ilmoni.
Year Established:	1988.

Additional Information

OPAS is one of the leading travel magazines in Scandinavia, and the only independent travel publication in Finland. There are regular extensive features covering various parts of the world – focusing on business travel, leisure, culture, gourmet travel and also practical information. There are four separate sections for different target groups – business and incentive travel, independent and group travel, tourism within Finland and the travel trade (through the Travel News supplement). The magazine carries advertising which reaches the most affluent and active group of Finns.

Panrotas Guide

Av. Jabaquara 1761
04045-901 São Paulo
Brazil

Tel: (11) 584 0211.
Fax: (11) 276 1602.

Media Information

Circulation:	11,214.
Frequency:	Monthly.
Distribution:	Annual subscriptions.
Trim Size (depth x width):	280mm x 210mm. 11 ins. x 8¼ ins.
Language:	Portuguese.
Published in:	Brazil.
Publisher:	M V M Condomi Alcorta.
Year Established:	1974.

Additional Information

Panrotas Guide is ordered by qualified travel retailers, wholesalers, transportation and promotion departments, and others who sell or influence the sale of travel to the public. Besides the domestic and international schedules and tariffs, airline ticket offices and embassies' addresses, and a wide range of technical and useful information for those who work in the travel industry, each issue also contains destination features, specialised articles to support the marketing of the travel industry, details of new packages, tours, airlines, hotels, tour operators and interviews with key industry personnel.

PTN Asia/Pacific

100 Beach Road
#2600 Shaw Towers
Singapore 0718
Tel (Editorial): 833 5022 (Hong Kong); 294 3366 (Singapore); (3) 255 7314/12 (Malaysia); 255 1480 (Thailand); (21) 337 379 (Indonesia).
Tel (Advertising): 833 5022 (Hong Kong); 294 3366 (Singapore); (3) 255 7314/24 (Malaysia); (212) 382 3960 (USA).
Tel (Production): 294 3366 (Singapore).
Tel (Circulation): 294 3366 (Singapore).
Fax: 834 5132 (Hong Kong).

Media Information

Circulation:	13,291.
Frequency:	Monthly.
Distribution:	Free if within terms of control.
Trim Size (depth x width):	285mm x 210mm. 11¼ ins. x 8¼ ins.
Language:	English.
Published in:	Singapore.
Publisher:	Chris Sweeting.
Year Established:	1987.

Additional Information

PTN Asia/Pacific is the official monthly magazine for the *Pacific Asia Travel Association* (PATA) in the Asia/Pacific region. The publication's editorial is pertinent, authoritative and well-recognised by key professionals and decision-makers in the travel industry. Its carefully controlled circulation to travel management and PATA members provides an efficient and cost-effective way to reach the people who buy travel.

PTN Europe

Morgan Grampian House
London SE18 6QH
UK

Tel (Editorial): (081) 855 7777.
Tel (Advertising): (081) 316 3460.
Fax: (081) 316 3119.

Media Information

Circulation:	14,520.
Frequency:	6 times per year.
Distribution:	Controlled postal circulation.
Trim Size (depth x width):	285mm x 210mm. 11¼ ins. x 8¼ ins.
Language:	English.
Published in:	UK.
Publisher:	Kevin Rolfe.
Year Established:	1988.

Additional Information

PTN Europe is the official PATA publication for Europe, bringing the Asia/Pacific travel market closer to the people of Europe who buy travel, including every ABTA travel agent in the UK, every IATA travel agent in continental Europe and Scandinavia and every full member of PATA. It offers cost-effective rates to advertisers, everything needed to plan a promotional campaign anywhere in Europe and covers all the important news, events and people in the far-reaching business of travel.

Publituris Travel Trade

Rua Marechal Saldanha 4-1
1200 Lisbon
Portugal

Tel (Editorial): (1) 346 0045.
Tel (Advertising): (1) 347 5201.
Fax: (1) 342 7718.

Media Information

Circulation:	7500.
Frequency:	Fortnightly; 1st and 15th.
Distribution:	Subscription.
Trim Size (depth x width):	280mm x 190mm. 11 ins. x 7½ ins.
Language:	Portuguese.
Published in:	Portugal.
Publisher:	Publiotel Ltd.
Year Established:	1968.

Additional Information

Publituris is a travel publication for travel agencies, airlines, hotels, car hire companies, real estate companies, meetings and congress organisers, tourist offices, hotel and restaurant schools and other travel trade organisations.

Reiseliv

Editorial address:
Fred. Olsensgt 1
0152 Oslo 1
Norway

Publisher's address:
Northra Produksjon AS
PO Box 591 Sentrum
0106 Oslo, Norway

Tel (Editorial): (2) 414 660.
Tel (Advertising): (2) 419 305.
Fax (Editorial): (2) 337 277.
Fax (Publishers): (2) 336 672.

Media Information

Circulation:	5000.
Frequency:	10 issues annually.
Distribution:	Post.
Trim Size (depth x width):	297mm x 210mm. 11¾ ins. x 8¼ ins.
Language:	Norwegian.
Published in:	Norway.
Publisher:	Annar Lille-Maehlum.
Year Established:	1921.

Additional Information

Reiseliv (which means 'travel business/trade') is aimed especially at key persons within the travel business and among public servants and politicians dealing with the travel industry. The articles are concerned with travel politics and the development of incoming trade and traffic, describing market conditions, activities, what other countries have to offer, as well as surveys and reports of product developments within the travel trade.

Reisrevue

Postbus 1110
3600 B0 Maarssen
The Netherlands

Tel: (3465) 50611.
Fax: (3465) 50282.

Media Information

Circulation:	15,000.
Frequency:	Weekly.
Distribution:	Subscription & free copies basis.
Trim Size (depth x width):	260mm x 194mm. 10¼ ins. x 7⅝ ins.
Language:	Dutch.
Published in:	The Netherlands.
Publisher:	Uitgeversmÿ Misset BV.
Year Established:	1982.

Additional Information

Reisrevue provides a news summary of the Dutch travel market for travel agencies, airline/cruise/ferry companies and hotels. It includes compact information about the travel products of tour operators, airlines and others in the travel business, as well as developments in the Dutch and European market, with background information and comments when necessary. The style is short, powerful and to the point.

Reisvakmagazine DIT

Postbus 122
3100 AC Schiedam
The Netherlands

Tel: (10) 427 4100.
Fax: (10) 473 9911.

Media Information

Circulation:	3000.
Frequency:	Fortnightly.
Distribution:	Subscription by mail.
Trim Size (depth x width):	272mm x 185mm. 10¾ ins. x 7¼ ins.
Language:	Dutch.
Published in:	The Netherlands.
Publisher:	Bert van Loon.
Year Established:	1958.

Additional Information

Reisvakmagazine DIT is a travel trade magazine and professional trade journal for the entire travel market in The Netherlands and includes an independent editorial content of key issues of concern, such as information on market and industry developments and practical information for the day-to-day running of business operations. Its fortnightly circulation guarantees up-to-date information and makes it a good medium for flexible and intensive advertising strategies. The magazine was restyled and relaunched in 1989.

resFLEX

PinfoR ab
Box 14045
720 14 Västerås
Sweden

Tel: (21) 35 48 00.
Fax: (21) 35 43 20.

Media Information

Circulation:	10,000.
Frequency:	Monthly (except July).
Distribution:	Subscription by mail.
Trim Size (depth x width):	370mm x 245mm. 14⅜ ins. x 9⅝ ins.
Language:	Swedish.
Published in:	Sweden.
Publisher:	PinfoR ab.
Year Established:	1986.

Additional Information

resFLEX is a Swedish travel trade monthly magazine which specialises in keeping the companies in the travel trade in Scandinavia informed about news concerning travel, hotels, transport companies, actual problems etc of interest for the travel market.
resFLEX is read by people employed in all areas of the travel trade such as travel agents, airline companies, tour operators and transport companies and will also be found at the biggest companies in Sweden.

Scottish Travel Agents

31 Henderson Street
Bridge of Allan
Scotland FK9 4HN
UK

Tel: (0786) 834 238.
Fax: (0786) 834 238.

Media Information

Circulation:	750 (trade only).
Frequency:	Weekly.
Distribution:	Mail.
Trim Size (depth x width):	300mm x 210mm. 11⁹⁄₁₀ ins. x 8³⁄₁₀ ins.
Language:	English.
Published in:	Scotland.
Publisher:	S&G Publishing (Scotland) Ltd.
Year Established:	1990.

Additional Information

Scottish Travel Agents News contains news, editorial and advertising of interest to all Scottish Travel Agents.

Selling Long-Haul

BMI Publications Ltd
Enterprise House
17/21 George Street
Croydon
Surrey CR0 1LA
UK

Tel: (081) 649 7233.
Fax: (081) 649 7234.

Media Information

Circulation:	16,000.
Frequency:	10 issues annually.
Distribution:	UK agents/long-haul principals.
Trim Size (depth x width):	297mm x 210mm. 11¾ ins. x 8¼ ins.
Language:	English.
Published in:	UK.
Publisher:	Alan Orbell.
Year Established:	1990.

Additional Information

Selling Long-Haul tells travel agents and incentive travel organisers how to sell long-haul products and services. Every editorial item and advertisement carries a unique Fast Facts number to request further information about the products and services that interest them. All of these sale leads (more than 170,000 to date) are processed and mailed directly to the companies concerned to be converted into firm business. During 1992 *Selling Long-Haul* was nominated the UK's number one travel trade publication for long-haul travel.

Stand By Travel Trade

1 Vester Farimagsgade
DK-1606 Copenhagen V
Denmark

Tel: 33 93 87 00.
Fax: 33 93 87 01.

Media Information

Circulation:	15,000.
Frequency:	Monthly, except Jan, Jul, Aug.
Distribution:	First-class mail.
Trim Size (depth x width):	360mm x 266mm. 14¼ ins. x 10½ ins.
Language:	Danish, Swedish and English.
Published in:	Denmark.
Publisher:	Preben Jack Petersen.
Year Established:	1982.

Additional Information

Stand By Travel Trade Journal is distributed as paid subscription in Denmark, Norway, Sweden and Finland, as well as the Faroe Islands, Iceland and Greenland. Its readership includes on-line and off-line tour operators, travel agents, hotels, tourist bus companies, tourist offices, foreign tourist representatives, top companies in Scandinavia and all members of Dansk Rejse-Klub (the Scandinavian equivalent of IAPA).

NEWS IN ENGLISH PAGES 53-55

Udenlandske investorer i Service Partner og Aero-Chef

KØBENHAVN: Udenlandske cateringfirmaer forventes meget snart at få indflydelse på henholdsvis *SAS Service Partner* og *Aero-Chef*.

SAS Service Partner, der har en årsomsætning på 5000 MSEK, har planer om en omfattende ekspansion på verdensbasis, men SAS' bestyrelse har meddelt, at SSP må hente den nødvendige kapital eksternt.

Det menes, at det ...nerikanske cate...ngfirma *Dobbs* vil ...lle den fornødne ...pital til rådighed ...d at få halvdelen ...ktierne i SSP. I ...vejen samarbej... Dobbs og SSP i ...ago.

...ngående Aero-... ...agter ejeren, ...ing *Airways*, at ... omkring halv-... af firmaet for ...enge i kassen. ...tale med det ...ir-ejede *Gate-... et* er klar til ...krivelse.

KØBENHAVN: *Airbus*-skandalen i *Spies*koncernen udvikler sig dramatisk.

To af de tre *Airbus-300*-fly, som det egyptiske luftfartsselskab *ZAS* har på lease fra *Conair*, har i mere end to måneder stået parkeret i en afkrog af Cairos internationale lufthavn. Efter sigende har de haft startforbud.

Samtidig afsløres det, at Conair's flyflåde er pantsat for 2420 MDKK – lang mere end, hvad flyene er værd!

Den engelske flyhandler *Arnold Martin* forbereder ved *Den Internationale Voldgiftsdomstol* i London en ny retssag mod Conair. Han er pånysat ud på et sidespor af Spieskoncernen, og nu vil han have sin totale avance udbetalt – i alt 66 MUSD.

I kølvandet på disse dramatiske oplysninger lufter Spieskoncernens ejer, *Janni Spies*, salgsplaner. Bl.a. er *LTU* i Tyskland interesseret i at overtage såvel *Tjæreborg Rejser* som *Spies Rejser*.

Pages 8-9

OY-CNA er det ene af de to Conair-fly, der i mere end to måneder har stået parkeret i Cairos lufthavn forsynet med et rødt cover over air in-take. (Foto: Per Helmer)

CONAIR'S FLY ER PANTSATTE FOR 2400 MDKK

SPIRITUS PÅ FÆRØERNE

AKUREYRI: For syvende år i træk har den nordatlantiske rejsemesse *Vest-Norden Travel Mart* fundet sted – denne gang i Akureyri på nordsiden af Island 23.-26. september.

Udbydere fra transportselskaber, hoteller etc. præsenterede deres produkter overfor købere fra et stort antal lande.

Samtidig kunne *Grønlandsfly* glæde udenlandske touroperatører med oplysningen om, at en ny trafikstruktur snart vil gøre det billigere at flyve domestic i Grønland, og færingerne kunne fortælle, at det nu er muligt at få et glas vin til maden på ø-gruppens hoteller.

Pages 34-37

Den færøske rejsebureauejer Sámal Bláhamer på ... (Foto: Preben Jack Petersen)

Take Off

Frederiksberg Allé 3
DK-1621 Copenhagen V
Denmark

Tel: 31 23 80 99.
Fax: 31 23 70 42.

Media Information

Circulation:	5800.
Frequency:	15th of every month.
Distribution:	Subscription.
Trim Size (depth x width):	270mm x 187mm. 10⅝ ins. x 7⅜ ins.
Language:	Dan/Swed/Norweg/Eng.
Published in:	Scandinavia.
Publisher:	Skandinavisk Bladforlag A/S.
Year Established:	1955.

Additional Information

Take Off is a major high-quality Scandinavian travel trade magazine. It is an active and serious publication written by experts for experts with a modern layout. Written by journalists with an excellent knowledge of the travel and tourist trade in Scandinavia and other parts of the world, it keeps abreast of new developments in travel wherever the news breaks – in air travel, ferry travel, hotels, travel agencies, tour operators, or any other area of the travel trade.

The Meeting Manager

Meeting Planners International
1950 Stemmons Freeway
Dallas, TX
75207-3109
USA

Tel (Editorial): (214) 712 7733.
Tel (Advertising): (214) 712 7738.
Fax: (214) 712 7770.

Media Information

Circulation:	11,000.
Frequency:	Monthly.
Distribution:	2nd Class Mail.
Trim Size (depth x width):	280mm x 210mm. 11 ins. x 8¼ ins.
Language:	English.
Published in:	USA.
Publisher:	Edwin L Griffin Jr., CAE.
Year Established:	1980.

Additional Information

The Meeting Manager is designed exclusively for the meetings professional and contains information and instruction on a range of meeting management topics, plus news on industry people and trends, and the issues that are making an impact on the travel trade. It is packed with vital information on sales and marketing, international meetings, computers, personal management, taxes and legal topics, as well as other relevant in-depth features. A classified advertising section, listing positions wanted and available, also provides a useful resource for travel professionals.

The UK Travel Agent

83 Glebe Street
London W4 2BE
UK

Tel: (081) 742 3456.
Fax: (081) 742 3016.

Media Information

Circulation:	22,000
Frequency:	Quarterly.
Distribution:	Travel Agents Requested ATD.
Trim Size (depth x width):	297mm x 210mm. 11¾ ins. x 8¼ ins.
Language:	English.
Published in:	UK.
Publisher:	John Warren.
Year Established:	1991.

Additional Information

The UK Travel Agent is a glossy magazine aiming to develop its own membership and promote travel products to the people who sell them to the public, thus providing a communications vehicle between agents and supplier companie;, publishes letters, comments and reports by members on trips, seminars and exhibitions they have attended; provides photo coverage of promotional events and people in the industry; and offers special travel opportunities, destination and resort offers, competitions and consumer discounts to its members.

Tour & Travel News

600 Community Drive
Manhasset, NY
11030
USA

Tel: (Editorial): (516) 562 5649.
Tel: (Advertising): (516) 562 5708.
Fax: (516) 562 5465.

Media Information

Circulation:	53,452.
Frequency:	Weekly.
Distribution:	ABC and BFA audited circ.
Trim Size (depth x width):	347.5mm x 266.7mm. 13¹¹⁄₁₆ ins. 10½ ins.
Language:	English.
Published in:	USA.
Publisher:	Bob Sullivan.
Year Established:	1985.

Additional Information

Tour & Travel News, the weekly paper for the retail travel industry, is written for retail travel agencies, travel consortium headquarters and travel consulting/management companies, tour operators, incentive travel companies, meeting planning and trade show producers and other travel businesses. It covers the news in a timely manner and includes special departments and destinations sections. *Tour & Travel* publishes *Travel Counselor*, the magazine for CTCs and career travel agents, four times per year; *Tour & Travel Marketplace* and special magazines and supplements.

Tourist Guide of Greece

137 Patission Street
112 51 Athens
Greece

Tel: (1) 864 1688/9 *or* (1) 864 9000.
Fax: (1) 864 1693.
Telex: 215182 TGOGR.

Media Information

Circulation:	26,000.
Frequency:	Annual.
Distribution:	Subscription and free copies.
Trim Size (depth x width):	280mm x 210mm. 11 ins. x 8¼ ins.
Language:	English.
Published in:	Greece.
Publisher:	Sophocles Papaioannou.
Year Established:	1972.

Additional Information

The *Tourist Guide of Greece* is an annual publication containing all tourist enterprises in Greece as follows: airlines, shipping companies, cruise lines, yacht brokers, hotel groups and representatives, travel agencies, car rental companies, camping sites, convention centres and organisers, licensed air taxi operators, special interest holidays, museums and archaeological sites, international travel agencies co-operating with Greece, and the GNTO offices abroad. The purpose is to promote tourist enterprises and to attract tourists to Greece. The *Tourist Guide* organises Greek stands at international Tourism exhibitions such as WTM and ITB.

check-in

YOUR GUIDE TO THE CMP TRAVELGROUP OF PUBLICATIONS

Presenting *Check-in*, the newsletter of the CMP Travel Group, to the readers of The World Travel Guide.

We invite you use *Check-in* as your guide to our media network of travel publications: *Business Travel News, Tour & Travel News, Travel Counselor, Tour & Travel Marketplace* and the *Special Supplements Division*—designed to deliver the highest quality editorial products and read by the most qualified professionals in the industry.

TOUR & TRAVEL NEWS: A NEW LOOK FOR '93

Tour & Travel News, the weekly newspaper for the retail travel industry, is the only trade publication to focus all of its attention on the role of retailers and the many travel products they sell and recommend. To help our over 207,000* readers find the information they need quickly and with regularity, each issue is separated into easy to locate departments and destination sections . In addition, *Tour & Travel News' Travel USA* special pullout sections will continue to be a strong focus in our editorial line-up, publishing six times in 1993.

TOUR&TRAVEL NEWS

All-Inclusives: How Many Are Too Many?

Club Vacations Cuts Charters, Gets Marsans

AmEx Promotes Use Of Agents

Can Egypt Save Its Ancient Ruins?

And now, *Tour & Travel News* has a new look: headlines that are easier to read and provide more detail; better information graphics; improved paperstock; and new features that highlight the news in each issue, including a Late News Report and News Summary.

BUSINESS TRAVEL NEWS COVERS CORPORATE TRAVEL

Business Travel News is a bi-weekly newspaper written for corporate executives responsible for business travel and meetings purchasing, policy-making and negotiating; and for travel agency personnel who specialize in the business travel and meetings field. Established in 1984, *Business Travel News,* the only newspaper in the business travel and meetings market, reaches over 266,000** readers and offers advertisers unmatched timeliness and immediacy.

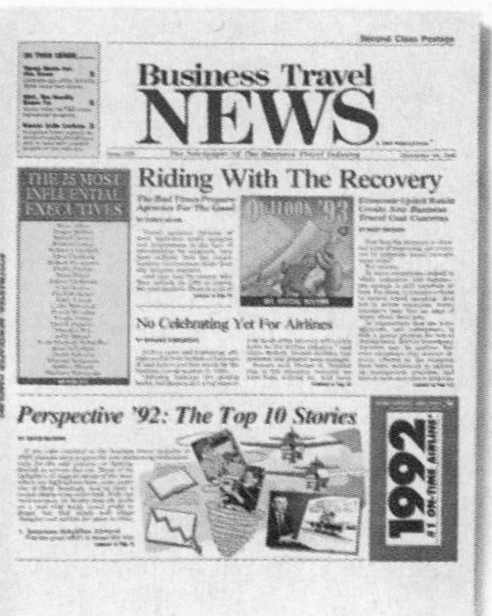

Business Travel NEWS

Riding With The Recovery

No Celebrating Yet For Airlines

Perspective '92: The Top 10 Stories

1992

The editorial focus of *Business Travel News* is on news, news analysis, and instructional features. Regular departments cover suppliers, business travel technology, travel management, U.S. destinations and international business travel. Special supplements include *Meetings Today* and the *Official Business Travel Handbook.*

Business Travel News
Tour & Travel News

Travel Counselor
Tour & Travel Marketplace
Special Supplements

World Travel Guide Special Edition 1993

Travel Counselor: Value-Added For CTCs & Career Travel Agents

The CMP Travel Group will continue to publish four editions of *Travel Counselor* under the direction of ICTA, the Institute of Certified Travel Agents, in 1993. *Travel Counselor* addresses the needs of those travel agents who have chosen to build their careers in the industry—the key decision makers at the very core of retail and commercial travel.

H. Wayne Berens, CTC, ICTA chairman, says,"We intend to make *Travel Counselor* one of the most valuable tools in professional travel counselors' libraries."

Direct Response With Tour & Travel Marketplace

Tour & Travel Marketplace is the most active direct-response publication in the industry. Delivered bi-monthly with *Tour & Travel News,* TTM offers an exciting vehicle that guarantees prompt delivery and response, with a special editorial platform–Marketplace Spotlights.

Special Supplements: The Creative Approach

In addition to its many features, departments, sections and special reports, *Business Travel News* and *Tour & Travel News* publish dozens of market driven special sections, sales guides, private-label publications, newsletters and in-flight magazines and supplements.

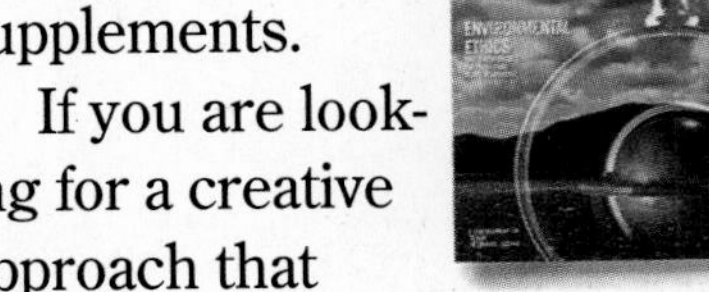

If you are looking for a creative approach that goes beyond the scope of our editorial calendars, please give us a call.

For More Information About The CMP Travel Group, Check-In With:

Jerry R. Landress
Vice President/Group Publisher
(516) 562-5704

- **Business Travel News:**
  Bill Besch, Divisional Director of Marketing Product Development
  (516) 562-5772
- **Tour & Travel News:**
  Bob Sullivan, Publisher
  (516) 562-5708
- **Travel Counselor:**
  Joanne N. Nelson, Director of Advertising
  (516) 562-5701
- **Tour & Travel Marketplace/ Special Supplements Division:**
  Doug Corper, Director
  (516) 562-5961

*November 1991 BPA projected research study of pass-along receivership
**BPA Supplementary Audit Publication Research Study November 1989

Touristik Aktuell

Jaeger Verlag Gmbh
Postfach 110452
W-6100 Darmstadt
Federal Republic of Germany

Tel (Editorial): (6154) 6995-311.
Tel (Advertising): (6154) 6995-320.
Fax: (6154) 6995-325.

Media Information

Circulation:	14,485.
Frequency:	Weekly.
Distribution:	Subscription and free copies.
Trim Size (depth x width):	310mm x 220mm. 12½ ins. x 8⅝ ins.
Language:	German.
Published in:	Federal Republic of Germany.
Publisher:	Günter M Hulwa.
Year Established:	1969.

Additional Information

Touristik Aktuell's reports centre on the product seen from two angles: 'Product Philosophy' from the point of view of travel organisers, carriers and hotels, supplemented by reports on actual experiences behind the counter, enhanced by brief information about trends within the branch and economic developments of significance to daily work. Monthly reports give information on the German and the Asian Pacific market. Case studies provide first-hand information on problem solving, helping readers to keep track of things in this increasingly complicated day-to-day business.

Touristik Management

Reichenhaller Strasse 46
W-8000 München 90
Federal Republic of Germany

Tel: (89) 692 2522.
Fax: (89) 695 771.

Media Information

Circulation:	17,200.
Frequency:	10 a year.
Distribution:	Subscription controlled circ.
Trim Size (depth x width):	252mm x 184mm. 10 ins. x 7¼ ins.
Language:	German.
Published in:	Federal Republic of Germany.
Publisher:	Axel Thunig.
Year Established:	1983.

Additional Information

Touristik Management is a professional trade magazine for travel agencies, counter staff, tour operators and company travel departments. It is the only German-speaking trade publication with a 'Counter trainer' for counter staff. The magazine deals with both tourism and business travel and informs its readers of all the specific problems and developments in this field and gives them practical help in their daily work.

Touristik R.E.P.O.R.T.

WDV Wirtschaftsdienst
Gesellschaft für Medien & Kommunikation mbH & Co. OHG
Lange Straße 13
PO Box No 112041
W-6000 Frankfurt/M 1
Federal Republic of Germany

Tel: (69) 29907-0.
Fax: (69) 29907-144.

Media Information

Circulation:	14,853.
Frequency:	Fortnightly.
Distribution:	Mail.
Trim Size (depth x width):	297mm x 210mm. 11¾ ins. x 8¼ ins.
Language:	German.
Published in:	Federal Republic of Germany.
Publisher:	Heiner Berninger.
Year Established:	1980.

Additional Information

Touristik R.E.P.O.R.T. is the authoritative trade magazine for the travel and tourist industry. Articles in *Touristik R.E.P.O.R.T.* are researched in-house and statements and information are carefully checked while analysis is supported by facts and data. It cultivates specialist, critical journalism, takes on burning issues and is free and independent in its reporting. *Touristik R.E.P.O.R.T.* reports on and for all areas of the travel trade including travel agents, tour operators, hotels, airlines, tourist offices and health resorts.

Travel Agency

Maclean Hunter House
Chalk Lane
Cockfosters Road
Barnet
Herts EN4 0BU
UK

Tel: (081) 975 9759.
Fax: (081) 975 9753.

Media Information

Circulation:	10,284.
Frequency:	Monthly.
Distribution:	Free circulation control.
Trim Size (depth x width):	260mm x 184mm. 10¼ ins. x 7¼ ins.
Language:	English.
Published in:	UK.
Publisher:	Ann Hughes.
Year Established:	1963 (From 1925 as *Travel Topics*).

Additional Information

Travel Agency is a publication that offers all the information required by ABTA travel agents to help them buy and sell business and leisure travel.

Travel Australia

The Australian Tourism Magazine Pty Ltd
GPO Box 7039
Sydney NSW 2001
Australia

Tel: (2) 233 6789.
Fax: (2) 231 5559.

Media Information

Circulation:	6703.
Frequency:	Monthly.
Distribution:	Subscription.
Trim Size (depth x width):	295mm x 210mm. 11⅝ ins. x 8¼ ins.
Language:	English.
Published in:	Australia.
Publisher:	Shamoli Dutt.
Year Established	1987.

Additional Information

Travel Australia is the only Australian trade paper dedicated entirely to the domestic and inbound markets. Its policy is to provide accurate, balanced and concise news and features coverage on developments in Australian tourism. It provides a vital communication link between the principals of the travel trade – airlines, hotels, tour operators, retail and wholesale travel agents – in Australia and worldwide.

Travel Britain

3rd Floor, Foundation House
Perseverance Works
38 Kingsland Road
London E2 8DD
UK

Tel (Editorial): (071) 729 5171.
Tel (Advertising): (071) 729 4337.
Fax: (071) 729 1716.

Media Information

Circulation:	25,000 (US travel trade only).
Frequency:	Quarterly.
Distribution:	Express Surface Post/airmail.
Trim Size (depth x width):	400mm x 290mm. 15¾ ins. x 11¾ ins.
Language:	English.
Published in:	UK.
Publisher:	Bob MacBeth-Seath.
Year Established:	1989.

Additional Information

Travel Britain is the only travel trade paper promoting tour packages, car hire, air travel, hotels, conference centres/venues, coach and rail travel etc to and throughout the UK, to the US travel trade. The USA is the UK's biggest tourism revenue earner and *Travel Britain* has established itself – being published as it is in the UK – as the mouthpiece of all tourism in Britain.

Travel Business Analyst

Asia Pacific Edition
GPO Box 12761
Hong Kong

Tel: 507 4620.

Media Information

Circulation:	N/A.
Frequency:	Monthly.
Distribution:	Paid.
Trim Size (depth x width):	280mm x 205mm. 11 ins. x 8⅛ ins.
Language:	English.
Published in:	Hong Kong.
Publisher:	Travel Business Analyst Ltd.
Year Established:	1988.

Additional Information

Travel Business Analyst specialises in travel business information, statistics and analysis for senior management in the travel industry and investors in the travel business.

Travel Business Analyst

Europe Edition
10 rue Auguste Vitu
75015 Paris
France

Tel: 45 79 50 19.

Media Information

Circulation:	N/A
Frequency:	10 yearly.
Distribution:	Paid.
Trim Size (depth x width):	280mm x 205mm. 11 ins. x 8⅛ ins.
Language:	English.
Published in:	France.
Publisher:	Travel Business Analyst Ltd.
Year Established:	1981.

Additional Information

Travel Business Analyst specialises in travel business information, statistics and analysis for senior management in the travel industry and investors in the travel business.

Travel Days

Judd House
65 Judd Street
London WC1
UK

Tel: (071) 833 0820.
Fax: (071) 833 3386.

Media Information

Circulation:	20,530.
Frequency:	Fortnightly
Distribution:	Direct mailing.
Trim Size (depth x width):	430mm x 305mm. 17 ins. x 12 ins.
Language:	English.
Published in:	UK.
Publisher:	Tommaso Bruccoleri.
Year Established:	1991.

Additional Information

Travel Days was established in 1991 as the European independent voice of the travel trade covering segments of the travel and tourism market often overlooked by existing publications. For this reason, it is the product of an independent mind and is privately funded. It has been warmly accepted since its first issue by the world of tourism, and its independent voice is becoming stronger and stronger whilst following a new concept in strategy and growth.

Travel GBI

3rd Floor, Foundation House
Perseverance Works
38 Kingsland Road
London E2 8DD
UK

Tel (Editorial): (071) 729 5171.
Tel (Advertising): (071) 729 4337.
Tel (Administration): (071) 729 4337.
Tel (Ad Production): (071) 729 4337.
Fax: (071) 729 1716.

Media Information

Circulation:	18,385 (ABC).
Frequency:	Monthly.
Distribution:	Mailed controlled circulation.
Trim Size (depth x width):	402mm x 290mm. 15¾ ins. x 11⅜ ins.
Language:	English.
Published in:	UK.
Publisher:	Robert MacBeth-Seath.
Year Established:	1978.

Additional Information

Travel GBI is the UK's only domestic travel trade newspaper for any marketing plans involving the UK business or leisure travel industry. It plays a cost-effective advertising role in the domestic marketplace and reflects modern developments and thinking within the travel trade. Insight features offer a complete update on various subjects, companies and destinations in an easy-to-read format. The new look – created in November 1990 – afforded more colour, a cleaner page layout, a strong new logo and improved comprehensive editorial coverage of all sectors of the market.

TRAVEL DAYS

The independent voice of the Travel Trade

TRAVEL DAYS

Greetings from the World Travel Market

View from W.T.M.

Khalid A. bin Sulayen, Director of Dubai Commerce & Tourism Promotion Board, Ghaith Al Ghaith and Patpong Abhijatapong.

Virgin Atlantic Airways: Ian E. Dockreay, Chris Moss, Jane Breeden, Richard Worrall and Lynn Summos.

Bahrain Stand with Dr. Kadhim E. Rajab, Directorate of Tourism & Archeology.

Representative team of North Cyprus with Mehmet Bayram Minister of Communications Public Works and Tourism.

Air Seychelles: Kate Carolus, Mr. Hodoul, Tadashi Washimi, Harrie Morshuis and Liz Lower.

TRAVEL DAYS

...mmission

...A Probe

...zdala, Classified Sales Manager, Peter Clifton-Gould, Advertisement Director and Katherine ... Membership Secretary, NAITA.

... EVENING STANDARD AND NAITA STAND TOGETHER AT WTM

...iation of Independent Travel Agents (NAITA) make their first ever ...orld Travel Market, sharing a stand with the London Evening Standard. ...d Business Class Lounge, otherwise known as "The Bar", stand number ...o-hosted by the Chartered Institute of Marketing Travel Industry ...stitute of Travel and Tourism (ITT) and Sigma 4, a US represent-

...ning Standard travel display advertising sales executive, said: ...nts us with the opportunity to demonstrate the high level of ...that the Evening Standard has with travel industry professionals ...and suppliers are invited to join us at the World Travel Market ...ar of growth and development for NAITA, and to discuss ...ortunities for 1992", commented Katherine Murray, NAITA

TRAVEL DAYS

For complimentary copies write or fax to:

TRAVEL DAYS

Cityjet House 65, Judd Street London WC1H 9QY

Tel: 071-833 0820 Fax: 071-833 3386

Travel News Asia

2/F Kai Tak Commercial Building
317 Des Voeux Road Central
Hong Kong

Tel (Editorial): 545 3028 (Hong Kong); (071) 706 1513 (London).
Tel (Advertising): 545 3028 (Hong Kong); (071) 636 3961 (London).
Fax: 544 6979 (Hong Kong).

Media Information

Circulation:	17,843.
Frequency:	Fortnightly.
Distribution:	Controlled to Asia travel trade.
Trim Size (depth x width):	414mm x 287mm. 16 1/4 ins. x 11 1/4 ins.
Language:	English.
Published in:	Hong Kong.
Publisher:	Jack Maisano.
Year Established:	1974.

Additional Information

Travel News Asia is the most widely read travel trade publication in Asia. 65% of its readers are travel agents and tour operators, giving it the widest agents/operators reach of any travel trade publication in the region. The magazine reports on issues that affect the day-to-day travel business in Asia, as well as new projects, services and trends. It provides distinct sections on airlines, hotels, agents/operators, tourism, technology and a comprehensive section which helps the industry come to grips with the latest technological changes going on in the business. Its reputation as an educational resource for travel agents makes it Asia's first choice.

Travelscope

3rd Floor, Foundation House
Perseverance Works
38 Kingsland Road
London E2 8DD
UK

Tel: (071) 729 4337.
Fax: (071) 729 1716.

Media Information

Circulation:	400,000-500,000 per quarter.
Frequency:	Dec, Mar, Jun and Sep.
Distribution:	Personalised, paid for and circulated by travel agents.
Trim Size (depth x width):	421mm x 315mm. 16½ ins. x 12⅜ ins.
Language:	English.
Published in:	UK.
Publisher:	Robert MacBeth-Seath.
Year Established:	1974.

Additional Information

Travelscope publishes the world's largest grouping of consumer travel newspapers, with personalised newspapers for leading ABTA/IATA travel agency outlets to be distributed by them to their established clients and relevant households in their areas. They are designed specifically for retail companies. Advertisers appear in all the newspapers, affording a complete approach to consumer travel marketing and generating sales and consumer demand for those advertisers appearing within, thus creating closer ties and increased sales for the participating advertisers.

Traveltrade

Business Press International Pty Ltd
9th Floor, 162 Goulburn Street
Darlinghurst, Sydney
Box 204, Strawberry Hills
NSW 2012
Australia

Tel (Editorial): (2) 379 5500.
Tel (Advertising): (2) 379 5000.
Fax: (2) 267 1223.

Media Information

Circulation:	8048 (ABC audited paid).
Frequency:	Fortnightly.
Distribution:	Mail.
Trim Size (depth x width):	420mm x 300mm. 16½ ins. x 11¾ ins.
Language:	English.
Published in:	Australia.
Publisher:	Reed Business Publishing.
Year Established:	1964.

Additional Information

Traveltrade is an independent fortnightly tabloid, primarily news orientated, with in-depth analysis of major news stories written specifically for travel agents and retail sellers of travel. First published in 1964, it is the longest established and most authoritative Australian travel industry publication and, backed by the worldwide news resources of Reed Business Publishing, it is an unquestionable market leader in Australia. The publication is audited by the *Audit Bureau of Circulations (ABC)*.

Traveltrade Magazine

13 Cheshire Street
Parnell, Auckland
New Zealand

Tel: (9) 3795 5500.
Fax: (9) 3309 4825.

Media Information

Circulation:	1700.
Frequency:	2nd & 4th Fri. of each month.
Distribution:	Paid subscription.
Trim Size (depth x width):	420mm x 290mm. 16 1/2 ins. x 11 3/8 ins.
Language:	English.
Published in:	New Zealand.
Publisher:	Chauncy Stark.
Year Established:	1972.

Additional Information

Traveltrade Magazine is a fortnightly tabloid publication produced for the travel trade in New Zealand. It is directed towards the frontline consultant and the person whose job it is to sell travel. The magazine is very informative and has regular destination and educational features. Produced on high-quality glossy paper, it contains the latest up-to-date news and events and is by far the leading trade publication in New Zealand.

Travel Trader's News

Case Postale 2244
13 rue Chantepoulet
1211 Genève 1
Switzerland

Tel: (22) 738 5858.
Fax: (22) 738 5888.

Media Information

Circulation:	6000.
Frequency:	Weekly.
Distribution:	Subscription.
Trim Size (depth x width):	290mm x 210mm. 11 3/8 ins. x 8 1/4 ins.
Language:	French.
Published in:	Switzerland.
Publisher:	Trinidad Nanzer.
Year Established:	1988.

Additional Information

Travel Trader's News (TTN) is the leading Swiss magazine for the professional world of tourism. It is distributed all over Switzerland and neighbouring France (Lyon, Grenoble, Besançon and Colmar) as well as some other countries. The editorial staff is composed of journalists and photographers who are specialists in tourism and the magazine's main goals are to inform professionals in the travel field and to help them communicate with each other.

Travel Week

Peter Isaacson Publications Pty Ltd.
46 Porter Street
Prahran
VIC 3181
Australia

Tel (Editorial): (3) 520 5555.
Tel (Advertising): (3) 520 5555.
Fax: (3) 510 3491.

Media Information

Circulation:	8650.
Frequency:	Fortnightly.
Distribution:	Post and hand delivery.
Trim Size (depth x width):	408mm x 285mm. 16 ins. x 11¹/₄ ins.
Language:	English.
Published in:	Australia.
Publisher:	Peter Isaacson Publications P/L.
Year Established:	1961.

Additional Information

Travel Week is Australia's leading travel industry newspaper with the most experienced editorial and advertising team, the highest ABC and CAB audited circulation and the greater market share of any Australian travel industry publication (MMS Research). It has a strong commitment to editorial excellence, production quality, readership relevance and advertising cost-effectiveness. As part of an international family of top travel industry publications (*TTG Asia, TTG Europa* and *TTG UK & Ireland*), it offers unbeatable advertising opportunities for the travel industry.

Travelweek Bulletin

553 Church Street
Toronto
Ontario M4Y 2E2
Canada

Tel: (416) 924 0963.
Fax: (416) 924 5721.

Media Information

Circulation:	7200.
Frequency:	Mon & Thur (Sep-Apr), then Thur only.
Distribution:	Distribution by Alltours/post.
Trim Size (depth x width):	210mm x 273mm. 8¹/₄ ins. x 10³/₄ ins.
Language:	English.
Published in:	Canada.
Publisher:	Wayne Lahtinen.
Year Established:	1974.

Additional Information

Travelweek Bulletin is a travel trade publication serving the Canadian market. It is circulated to every travel agency in Canada, twice per week in the peak winter season and once a week in summer. The magazine is a 'hard news' vehicle specialising in keeping the travel agent informed of fast-breaking events in an industry known for its rapid changes. It publishes over 30 'Spotlight Reports' every year, featuring major destinations, trade shows and other areas of interest to the trade.

Travel Weekly

11 Francis Street
London SW1P 1BZ
UK

Tel: (071) 828 8989.
Fax: (071) 798 9710.

Media Information

Circulation:	48,729.
Frequency:	Weekly.
Distribution:	Controlled circulation (ABC).
Trim Size (depth x width):	403mm x 298mm. 15⁷/₈ ins. x 11³/₄ ins.
Language:	English.
Published in:	UK and Ireland.
Publisher:	Mike Orlov.
Year Established:	1969.

Additional Information

Travel Weekly is a travel trade publication that delivers 'the news that matters to the people that matter.' Its content includes comparison news stories and features drawing from the world market for outbound business and leisure travel. The magazine caters to key decision-makers from the top downwards in airlines, tour operators' offices, hotels, travel agencies, transport companies and other associated industries. It is part of the *Reed Travel Group*.

Travel Weekly

500 Plaza Drive
Secaucus, NJ
07096
USA

Tel: (201) 902 2000.
Fax: (201) 319 1755.

Media Information

Circulation:	48,729 (ABC audited).
Frequency:	Bi-weekly/Focus Issues monthly.
Distribution:	Drop ship, polybag with label.
Trim Size (depth x width):	347mm x 267mm. 13 ³/₄ ins. x 10¹/₂ ins.
Language:	English.
Published in:	USA.
Publisher:	William D Scott II.
Year Established:	1958.

Additional Information

The *Travel Weekly* group of publications – newspapers, focus issues, special sections and reference guides – provide the latest news, industry feature articles and destination stories for US travel agents, tour operators, corporate travel executives and travel industry suppliers. It also publishes the biennial *US Travel Agency Survey* and a number of travel agent polls on pertinent topics as a special service to the industry. Reaching over 203,000 US travel agents per issue, it is the only 100% paid publication in the field.

Travel World News

1 Morgan Avenue
Norwalk, CT
06851
USA

Tel (Editorial): (203) 853 4955.
Tel (Advertising): (203) 838 4594.
Fax: (203) 866 1153.

Media Information

Circulation:	40,000.
Frequency:	Monthly.
Distribution:	Mailed controlled circulation.
Trim Size (depth x width):	276mm x 206mm. 10⁷/₈ ins. x 8¹/₈ ins.
Language:	English.
Published in:	USA.
Publisher:	Charlie Gatt.
Year Established:	1988.

Additional Information

Travel World News is a monthly review trade magazine for travel agents, supplying them with all the important industry news and product information of the month in a concise, easy-to-read format. Regular sections include industry news, an events calendar, cruises, flights, agents' familiarisation trips, special interest articles and destination features on North America, the Caribbean, Latin America, Africa, the Middle East, Eastern Europe and Europe.

TTG Asia

100 Beach Road
#26-00 Shaw Tours
Singapore 0718

Tel (Editorial): 833 5022 (HK); 294 3366 (Singapore); (3) 255 7314/24 (Malaysia); 255 1480 (Thailand); (21) 337 379 (Indonesia).
Tel (Advertising): 833 5022 (HK); 294 3366 (Singapore); (3) 255 7314/24 (Malaysia); (201) 850 8339 (USA).
Tel (Production): 294 3366 (Singapore).
Tel (Circulation): 294 3366 (Singapore).
Fax: 298 5534 (Singapore).

Media Information

Circulation:	16,130.
Frequency:	Weekly.
Distribution:	Free if within terms of control.
Trim Size (depth x width):	420mm x 282mm. $16^1/_2$ ins. x $11^1/_8$ ins.
Language:	English.
Published in:	Singapore.
Publisher:	Darren Ng.
Year Established:	1974.

Additional Information

TTG Asia is the region's only weekly travel newspaper and is widely read and held in high esteem by the area's travel professionals. With its comprehensive network of correspondents, it provides readers with the latest news and information required to keep abreast of the fast-paced and constantly changing travel industry. It has a wide network of news correspondents with three full-time bureaux, a high level of advertising support and reciprocal news agreements with its associate travel trade publications. With the impact of its high-quality reproduction and glossy paper, it keeps readers in touch with events both regionwide and throughout the world.

TTG Chinese

Asian Business Press Ltd
100 Beach Road
#26-00 Shaw Towers
Singapore 0718
Tel (Editorial): 833 5022 (HK); 294 3366 (Singapore); (3) 255 7314/24 (Malaysia); 255 1480 (Thailand); (21) 337 379 (Indonesia).
Tel (Advertising): 833 5022 (HK); 294 3366 (Singapore); (3) 255 7314/24 (Malaysia); (212) 382 3960 (USA).
Tel (Production): 294 3366 (Singapore).
Tel (Circulation): 294 3366 (Singapore).
Fax: 298 5534 (Singapore).

Media Information

Circulation:	7720.
Frequency:	Monthly.
Distribution:	Free controlled circulation.
Trim Size (depth x width):	210mm x 285mm. $8^1/_4$ ins. x $11^1/_4$ ins.
Language:	Chinese.
Published in:	Singapore.
Publisher:	Darren Ng.
Year Established:	1992.

Additional Information

TTG Chinese is a Chinese-language travel trade publication for travel agents and corporate travel planners in Taiwan, Hong Kong, China and other Chinese-speaking communities in Asia. It is the only monthly travel trade publication with a region-wide appeal to Chinese-speaking professionals in the travel trade.

TTG Europa

Travel Trade Gazette Ltd.
Morgan Grampian House
London SE18 6PH
UK

Tel (Editorial): (081) 855 7777.
Tel (Advertising): (081) 316 3481.
Fax: (081) 316 3119.

Media Information

Circulation:	16,251.
Frequency:	26 times a year.
Distribution:	Controlled circulation by post.
Trim Size (depth x width):	400mm x 292mm. $15^5/_8$ ins. x $11^1/_2$ ins.
Language:	English.
Published in:	UK.
Publisher:	Kevin Rolfe.
Year Established:	1974.

Additional Information

TTG Europa is the only pan-European travel trade publication. It reaches all IATA agents in 18 countries across Europe and Scandinavia. The comprehensive circulation encompasses over 100,000 decision-makers responsible for 63 million travel bookings a year plus and covers the whole of the European travel industry. For advertisers it is the ideal cost-effective opportunity to nestle between up-to-the-minute editorial, gathered by TTG's network of reporters, that spans the globe.

TTG Italia

Via Nota 6
10122 Torino
Italy

Tel: (11) 436 6300.
Fax: (11) 436 6500.

Media Information

Circulation:	8000.
Frequency:	Weekly.
Distribution:	Controlled circulation by mail.
Trim Size (depth x width):	264mm x 396mm. $11^3/_8$ ins. x $16^7/_8$ ins.
Language:	Italian.
Published in:	Italy.
Publisher:	Renzo Druetto.
Year Established:	1973.

Additional Information

TTG Italia is an authoritative Italian travel newspaper seeking to keep travel professionals reliably informed. A member of the international TTG Group, the magazine is sent to the entire tourism market and fully covers all travel news in Italian territory.

TTG Japan

100 Beach Road
#26-00 Shaw Towers
Singapore 0718
Tel (Editorial): 833 5022 (HK); 294 3366 (Singapore); (3) 255 7314/24 (Malaysia); 255 1480 (Thailand); (21) 337 379 (Indonesia).
Tel (Advertising): 833 5022 (HK); 294 3366 (Singapore); (3) 255 7314/24 (Malaysia); (212) 382 3960 (USA).
Tel (Production): 294 3366 (Singapore).
Tel (Circulation): 294 3366 (Singapore).
Fax: 298 5534 (Singapore).
Fax: 834 5132 (Hong Kong).

Media Information

Circulation:	5120.
Frequency:	Monthly.
Distribution:	Free if within terms of control.
Trim Size (depth x width):	210mm x 285mm. $8^1/_4$ ins. x $11^1/_4$ ins.
Language:	Japanese.
Published in:	Singapore.
Publisher:	Darren Ng.
Year Established:	1990.

Additional Information

Launched in October 1990, *TTG Japan* provides Japanese producers and buyers with an update on the latest products and developments in the Asian market in an easy-to-read format and in their own language, and is the only Japanese-language publication that supplies Japanese outbound travel agents with travel product information about the Asia-Pacific.

PLEAS
DO NO
TOUC
THIS ARE

TTG UK & Ireland

Travel Trade Gazette Ltd
Morgan Grampian House
London SE18 6QH
UK

Tel (Editorial): (081) 316 3536.
Tel (Advertising): (081) 316 3460.
Fax: (081) 316 3119.

Media Information

Circulation:	24,435.
Frequency:	Weekly.
Distribution:	Controlled circulation.
Trim Size (depth x width):	402mm x 292mm. 15¾ ins. x 11½ ins.
Language:	English.
Published in:	UK.
Publisher:	Kevin Rolfe.
Year Established:	1953.

Additional Information

TTG UK & Ireland has led the way in reporting travel industry news for 40 years. It gives the reader a full picture of the travel business, offers a wide range of comment and informative writing and seeks to be the first to break big news stories. Added to this are quality features on business travel and leisure destinations, such as the Far East, Australia and the USA, and is an invaluable tool in the day-to-day work within the travel industry. Its award-winning journalists have made it a newspaper enjoyed by advertisers and readers alike.

Turizmus

Muzeum u. 11
H-1088 Budapest
Hungary

Tel: (1) 138 4638.
(1) 138 4098.
Fax: (1) 138 4293.

Media Information

Circulation:	10,000.
Frequency:	Bi-weekly.
Distribution:	Subscription.
Trim Size (depth x width):	420mm x 296mm. 16½ ins. x 11¾ ins.
Language:	Hungarian.
Published in:	Hungary.
Publisher:	Kurir Rt.
Year Established:	1962.

Additional Information

Turizmus is the leading travel trade paper in Hungary and is subscribed to by all the country's travel agencies, tour operators, hotels, guest-houses, catering companies, major restaurants, airlines and coach operators. *Turizmus* also reaches the travel consultants of the most prominent industrial and trade companies of Hungary. The paper is published by a private publishing company, but was founded by the Hungarian Tourist Board which still considers *Turizmus* to be the official paper of this governmental body.

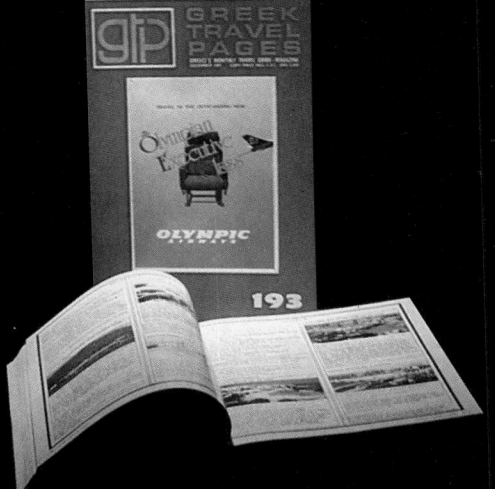

GOLF

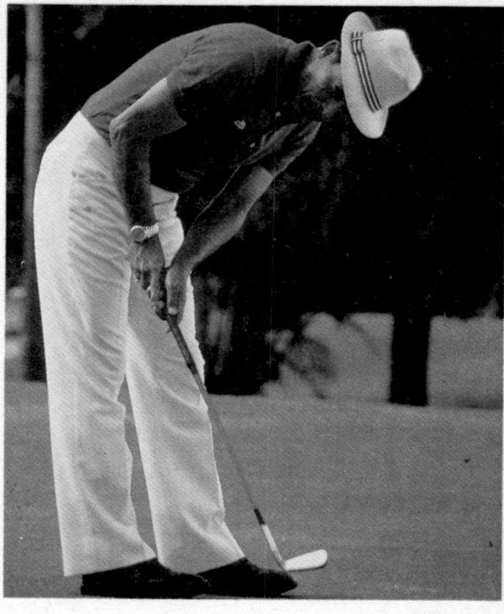

OVERVIEW

by Graham Lowing

Gathering recession throughout the world has knocked the game of golf to a little below par.

Late 1991 and last year saw a change in the order of golf holidays which have traditionally been regarded as a second vacation and usually taken in a winter sun destination.

However, the gloom of the UK's economic indicators has hit the winter golf holiday market. Fears in the United Kingdom about job security, plus money worries, meant golfers stayed on their home courses, forsaking the sun element for a while.

Despite this, all has not been lost for golf holiday operators. The effect of a winter golf downturn has been to increase summer activity by around five per cent. Recession or no recession, summer holidays are still taken and many are becoming golf breaks.

The golfing groups market has been among the worst hit, with party numbers falling in the last two years by up to 20 per cent.

Thankfully other opportunities have come forward for specialist golf operators. Particular targets are older families, those with teenage children who are beginning to take up the sport of swings seriously, and older couples.

Couples aged 40 years plus – categorised as 'empty nesters' because their children have left home – have low or no mortgage commitments, leaving disposable income in their hands, often for more than one holiday per year.

Adrian Murray, product boss of the *Sovereign* golf programme in the UK, said: "There is some evidence that these particular categories are including golf in their main summer holidays and are taking more golf-dedicated packages."

Operators are keen to capture more of the novices' market in the form of tuition weeks. Working with patient teachers on a sun-soaked course can do wonders for students' concentration and be a more enlightening experience than learning on a cold and windswept English or Scottish course.

The cost of green fees is always a major debate, with Spain, Portugal and the USA – of the sunshine destinations – getting their share of criticism.

The Far East countries have spotted the huge potential in golf as part of its tourism product and are furiously spending billions of dollars on new courses. Seeing the mistakes of other destinations, they are selling their golf on a value-for-money ticket.

In Thailand, a round can be as little as the equivalent of £4 on weekdays and £7 at weekends, and in Malaysia midweek prices are around £2.25 per round.

Malaysia is planning to increase its 91 courses by 25 per cent in the next two years, while in Thailand there are massive plans to build a golf future. The country has 60 courses but up to 500 more are under some form of development or scheduled for opening over the next four years.

Indonesia has also set aside a huge budget for improving existing courses and building new ones.

The Philippines is so convinced of its role as a golf destination that it has produced a guide dedicated to its many courses. More courses are also planned for the future.

Elsewhere, golf development goes on apace. Ireland, a top venue for travelling North American, British and Japanese players, has targeted golf as a top tourism priority.

With European Community and Irish Government cash in addition to private investment, an extra 306 holes of top-standard golf with hotels will have been added by later this year.

Golf has yet to make in-roads into Africa, but there again neither has tourism. Golf has followed the tourism pattern through Morocco and, to a greater extent, Tunisia in the north of Africa, Kenya and South Africa, who, because of strong tourism trade, carry the torch for the rest of the continent.

While golfers now have a global choice, the countries that first catered for their fanaticism for the game are still the leaders. No matter how hard the Far East, Africa and northern European countries work at it, Spain and Portugal, in the short-haul market, and the USA, in the long haul, will dominate as preferred destinations for some years to come.

AUSTRIA

The high life of Alpine golfing is being increasingly promoted by the *Austrian National Tourist Office*.

Austria is the surprise package in European golf geography with an astonishing number of top-quality courses, many in spectacular mountain locations; an additional bonus for golfers is that the higher the altitude, the further those tee shots fly through the thinner air.

The courses are of international quality, as is the *Altentann* venue designed by Jack Nicklaus near Salzburg.

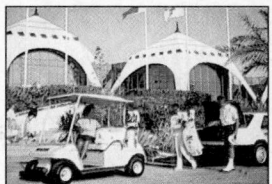

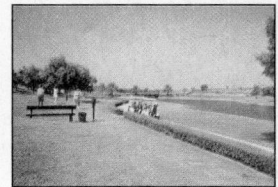

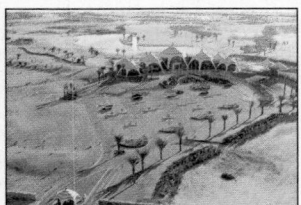

Lower Austria boasts the *Donnerskirchen* in the Tyrol, where resorts better known for their winter sports facilities are bidding for summer golf traffic too. The Alpine ski resorts of *Seefeld* and *Kitzbühl* have excellent courses in the middle of lofty mountain settings. The Seefeld venue is also the home of a golf academy.
The Tyrol has ten 18-hole and 9-hole courses in towns better known to skiers.
The southernmost province of Carinthia, with its mixture of mountains and lakes, is home to the country's oldest course at *Dellach* which was built in 1927.
Hoteliers and golf course administrators have liaised to form the Golf Green Austria organisation aimed at promoting playing packages and solidifying Austria's claims as a strong golf destination. Various areas of Austria have published special golf guides including hotels which offer thermal baths and a range of other sporting activities.

DUBAI

Golf has quite literally changed the face of Dubai. The game has brought oases of verdant green to the arid, sub-tropical landscape of the second largest of the United Arab Emirates.
The first major development to take the emirate away from sand golf where players carried their own piece of turf from which to tee off, was the 7100-yard, par 72 *Emirates Golf Club*.
It took just 18 months to carve the course out of the sand to the design of American architect Karl Litten. Players who have competed among the four lakes and amid the thousands of trees transplanted from North and South America, report the course as being quite formidable.
Last October a second big golf course opened at the *Dubai Creek* complex which includes a 5-star, 300-room hotel plus marina. Golf facilities are a further Litten-designed championship course, 9-hole floodlit course and driving range. Technical details include the creation of six lakes, grass imported from Georgia, USA, and one million gallons of desalinated water used on the course each day at the height of summer.
No expense has been spared on the Dubai courses to unite some of the best golf facilities in the world with year-round sunshine.

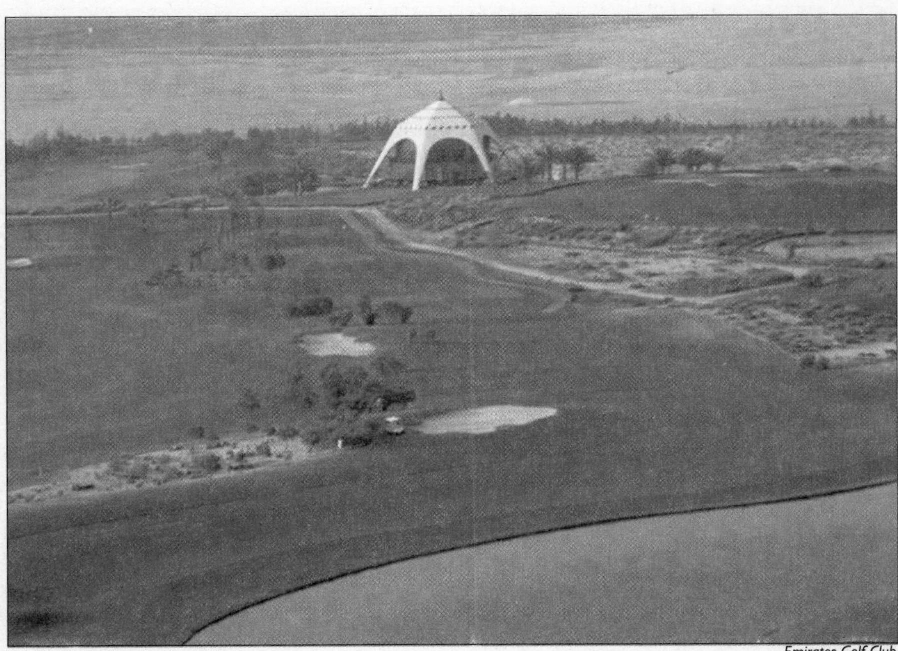

Emirates Golf Club

FLORIDA

Florida, as the Number One golf destination in the USA, has not had it easy over the last two years. The Sunshine State's golf industry hauled itself out of the surprise 1991 slump by reducing prices for 1992.
As a result by shopping around the Florida courses – of which there are more than 1000 and rising – some excellent deals can be had. The price of a game varies from £24 at the *Metrowest* course, through to £40 at some of the Walt Disney resort courses in Orlando to around £50 at the new *Disney Osprey* and *Eagle Pines* courses.
The state has suffered its share of criticism over pricing, but it counters that with almost guaranteed year-round sun and some of the best-kept courses in the world.

Slump or no slump, golf earns Florida about US$5 billion a year – that is about 55 million rounds a year – as a return on the many billions that have gone into developing the industry throughout the state. Six Florida courses are rated among the top 100 in North America.
Florida courses are generally long and flat and riddled with bunkers and the much-loved water hazards of American course builders.
Hotels are more golf-orientated in Florida than anywhere else in the world and consequently few are built without a course or alternatively, few courses are built without adjacent resort accommodation.
These hotels have catered for family demands – golf for the golfers and other pursuits for non-playing husbands, wives and children.

Grenelefe Golf & Tennis Resort

3200 State Road 546, Haines City, FL (Orlando) 33844-9732.
Tel: (813) 422 7511. Fax: (813) 421 5000.
Grenelefe is listed under Sterling Reservations Systems, Code UR (Ultimate Resorts).

Description

- 1,000-acre nationally-recognised sports resort and conference center in Central Florida.
- 950 elegant one- and two-bedroom villas/suites and deluxe club rooms nestled in secluded oak tree clusters.
- 70,000-plus square feet of state-of-the-art flexible meeting and function space.
- Three 18-hole championship golf course.
- 20 world-class tennis courts.
- Full-service marina on 6,400-acre Lake Marion with wildlife cruises and fishing charters.
- Four swimming pools; two jacuzzis; dry saunas.
- 1.7-mile fitness/nature trail with 32 exercise stations.
- Three restaurants; two snack bars.

Location

Situated between Tampa and Orlando, Grenelefe Golf and Tennis Resort is only 45 minutes from Orlando International Airport and 75 minutes from Tampa International Airport near Haines City, Florida. December through March temperatures average low 60s at night and mid 70s during the day: summer daytime temperatures average mid 80s, dropping to the high 70s at night.

Accommodation

One-and two-bedroom fariway villa/suites include two double beds and separate entrances for each guest room, full baths, fully-equipped kitchen and spacious living/dining room area with queen-sized sleeper sofa. All units have porch or patio overlooking golf courses, color television with cable and movie channels and video message/checkout service. Seasonal rentals (30 days or more) are available through real estate office.

Meeting Facilities

More than 70,000 square feet of meeting and function space accommodate groups of 10 to 2,000. A 5,000 square foot poolside pavillion seats up to 500 guests. Scenic outdoor settings include various decks, poolside courts and marina beach. Extensive in-house audio-visual and teleconferencing facilities are also available. The business center services include fax, copier, computer, secretarial, translation, message service and shipping services.

Transportation

Complimentary shuttles provide transportation around the resort quickly and efficiently. Group and individual transportation rates to and from Orlando International Airport are available. Discounts for car rental at both Tampa and Orlando airports and transportation to area attractions can be arranged.

Golf

Grenelefe West – The 7,325-yard par 72 West Course features both elevated and small trap greens. *The East Course* features shorter, straighter fairways and level greens with traps to the sides. *The South Course* offers challenging greens and is interspersed with water hazards and sand traps. Two driving ranges and putting greens are available. Two Pro Shops provide complete service. Golf carts and instruction packages are available year-round.

Tennis

The complex includes a 1,700-seat center stadium court, and three playing surfaces (grass, clay and hard). It is ranked among the top 50 in the country.

Marina/Fishing

Daytime and evening charters available on covered pontoon boats on beautiful Lake Marion showcasing its abundant wildlife, including eagles, blue herons, alligators and snowy egrets.

Nearby Attractions

Walt Disney World's Magic Kingdom, EPCOT, MGM Studios	*35 minutes.*
Sea World	*40 minutes.*
Universal Studios	*45 minutes.*
Cypress Gardens	*10 minutes.*
Busch Gardens	*90 minutes.*
Kennedy Space Centre	*90 minutes.*

Awards

Silver Medal – *Golf Magazine.*
Gold Tee Award – *Meetings and Conventions.*
Top Golf/Tennis Resorts – *Successful Meetings.*

Florida's northeast coast is growing in tourism popularity – and with it its golf facilities are increasing. Daytona Beach's *Indigo Lakes* course has the largest greens in the state and rates in the top 20. Daytona boasts enough courses within a 40-mile radius to play a different venue each day in a week's stay in the area.

Other top venues in the area are *Baymeadows* and the PGA Tour course at Jacksonville, as well as Palm Beach's *Cypress Knoll*.

Rival state South Carolina is progressing well with its golf ambitions and new courses, as with Florida, continue to be developed. A spoiled game here can even mean cash refunds thanks to weather insurance. The *Sands Oceanfront Resorts* group offers a policy with a US$5 premium per US$100 insured. More than one tenth of an inch of rain per hour can mean a payout for lost golfing time.

FRANCE

France is a latecomer to the European golf scene and has become something of a star destination with some specialist tour operators. And this despite the fact that much of France is meteorologically similar to Britain with golfers forced to travel to the Côte d'Azur to claim some winter sunshine.

French courses, being more accessible, have given a new meaning to driving holidays. Fewer restrictions, other than a courtesy call ahead to check availability, apply in France.

With golf not specifically associated with France and the country yet to produce a world star of the greens, development has nevertheless been ongoing.

For British leisure golfers, France is a short-break hop across the Channel, and with the imminent opening of the Channel Tunnel, France can expect an even bigger influx.

Among the most popular destination courses are those in the Pas de Calais, Normandy, the Loire Valley, Brittany, Bordeaux and upmarket Biarritz. Southern sun areas include the Languedoc, Provence and the Riviera.

It is generally accepted that the French have not taken the sport to their hearts as obsessively as the British and Americans.

This in turn, however, ensures a very peaceful experience on uncrowded French courses, particularly during midweek. Green fees, as a result, represent better value than European neighbours at an average of £20.

A further attempt to encourage the wandering golfer, regions like the Vendée have instigated golfpass schemes over the last couple of years and have reported successful uptakes.

More French hotels are offering packages, while the Brittany-Western Loire region has persuaded its 47 golf courses to sign a tourism charter and issued a brochure dedicated to golf.

PORTUGAL

Recently it has been Portugal's turn as the main target for the annual round robin of criticism of over-priced green fees on some of its 29 mainland and offshore courses. The attacks were on rates to the public at

Algarve courses which have given the impression that Portugal had forgotten its much-vaunted value-for-money claims.

Average fees are £25 but are less expensive in package holidays due to the negotiating power of the specialist golf operators.

It remains to be seen if the Portuguese golf authorities will opt to reduce the bad press by cutting fees or varying rates for different times of the year.

The criticism is ironic because Spain once enjoyed a clear lead as the sunshine golf destination of Europe. It too, bore the brunt of criticism over high green fees and found that Portugal, determined to keep the cost of the sport to reasonable proportions, had emerged as the more economically attractive proposition in the battle for golf supremacy on the Iberian peninsular.

The recession has pushed the number of Portugal's golf visitors down in the last year. That is not an indictment of the country's facilities, merely that fewer golfers are travelling.

The Algarve region, in Portugal's south, is its top golfing area, but the *Portuguese National Tourist Office* is keen to diversify its golf centres around the country where the climate varies only slightly from the Algarve hot spots.

Alternative golf areas have been established around the capital, Lisbon, and the nearby Estoril Coast holiday area.

Portugal founded its golf academy, the *Academia Internacional de Golfe*, in this area at the *Estoril-Sol* club. Further course development is going on apace as Portugal seeks to stay ahead of its rival Spain.

On the Costa Verde, the birthplace of golf in Portugal, there are three courses near Porto, following the traditions of the English in the port wine trade at the turn of the century who built the first course.

Even the country's Atlantic satellite of Madeira is not being left out; a fifth course is being built on the island that does so well in the winter sun holiday market.

Two courses are under construction near Lisbon and two more in the Algarve. Among the latest to open late last year was the Vila Sol on the Algarve coast – a short distance from Vilamoura, Quinta do Lago and Vale do Lobo which figure among the area's favourites.

SPAIN

Last year Spain acted to halt criticism over spiralling golf fees. More temporary memberships were made available at privately owned clubs to visiting players from overseas via tour operators and hotels offering packages.

As an example, the average cost of £33 per round throughout the Balearic Islands was reduced to around £25.

Spanish hotels have increased the number of packages on offer, and conference organisers are also pushing the sport's facilities in the country. They are mindful of the value of having a golf element to enhance convention venues.

NINE KILOMETRES OF VIRGIN BEACH AND A 27-HOLE GOLF COURSE AT YOUR DOORSTEP

The spectacular new **Royal Andalus Golf,** weds a golfer's Paradise to a beach-lover's dream by setting its exceptional facilities right in the middle.

The challenging golf course, designed by champion **Seve Ballesteros**, is of international standards and host to leading tournaments. Our guests enjoy special green fees.

The beach, a natural marvel of golden sands and green-topped dunes, stretches its virgin beauty along nine kilomtres of unspoiled coastline.

The new, four-star **Royal Andalus Golf** lives up to its surroundings. Its exterior architecture is strikingly modern, while its interior is pure Andalusian charm, filled with light and interior gardens.There are two outdoor swimming pools and a heated indoor pool, a variety of restaurants and bars, and a Sports Complex with tennis, squash, a gymnasium and sauna, and a Health Farm. Located in the exclusive, new Novo Sancti Petri urbanization in Chiclana de la Frontera, Cádiz, Spain, the hotel is within easy reach of four airports: Jerez, Gibraltar, Seville and Málaga. Add to all this the natural beauty of Andalusia, with its warm and dry year-round climate, its majestic mountains and sleepy white villages, its centuries-old customs and hospitable people.

The **Hotel Royal Andalus Golf.** somthing new and unforgettable under the sun.

Hotel Royal Andalus Golf
* * * *

Urbanización Novo Sancti Petri.
Chiclana de la Frontera. Cádiz.

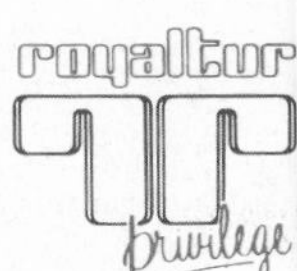

JOSÉ Mª CEREZUELA
ROYALTUR ESPAÑA S.A.
Gremio Horneros 23
07009 Palma de Mallorca
Tel: 71-20 72 12 ♠ Fax: 71-20 12 67

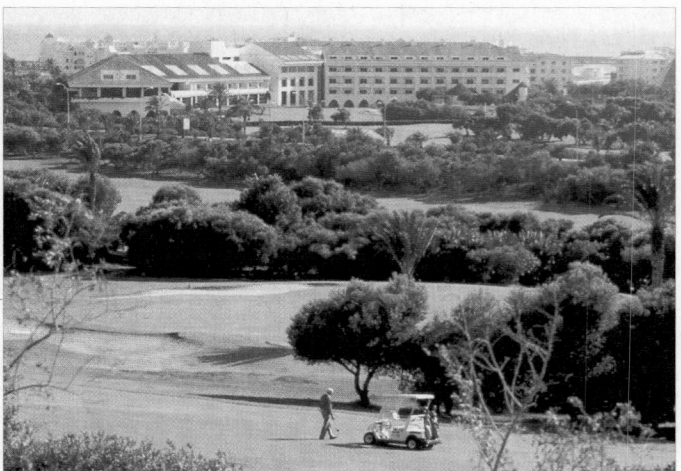

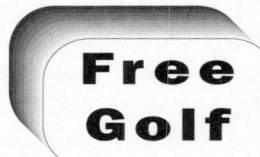

The Spanish tourism authorities have had their promotion budgets pegged for 1993, but are keen to keep up the golf impetus. Spain has 90 courses, mostly concentrated in the southern sun belt of the Costa del Sol and the Balearics.

The capital Madrid has 11 courses and there are 12 more scattered among the woods and hills of the in the northern Cantabrian area of 'green' Spain between La Coruna and San Sebastian in the Basque Country. The Costa Brava's newcomer is the championship-standard course at Mas Nou.

La Manga, probably the best-known sports holiday venue in the world, is spending more than £20 million on a new hotel and a third 18-hole golf course.

New Spanish courses are planned or under way at Estepona, Val D'Or and Santa Ponsa.

On the Balearic Islands of Mallorca, Menorca and Ibiza, golf will have a greater presence in the future. The islands' government has declared golf developments as 'environmentally friendly tourism'. Mallorca, the largest of the islands has at least 20 more golf courses being planned for the future. The 11th addition to Mallorca's golf courses was the £65-million Jack Nicklaus-designed venture near Valldemosa.

The split-level course, developed by a British company, includes a golf school and training course.

Ibiza's single 9-hole course, the *Roca Llisa* in Santa Eulalia, was combined with the new *Golf Ibiza* complex to form a 27-hole complex last year.

Menorca's single 9-hole course, the Son Parc, will be bolstered by two new courses in the next four years.

UK & SCOTLAND

The British Isles, the birthplace of golf, relies on hotels to bring the game into the tourism domain. While it is perfectly possible to put together a self-drive itinerary of some of the big names in Scotland and England, it is not necessarily a trouble-free experience.

With a recent report claiming that the UK needs dozens more courses to keep pace with demand and the number of newcomers taking up the game, prior arrangements are necessary to avoid disappointment; even so, this will not always get the roving player on some of the top names in the sport.

The Scottish Tourist Board especially continues to promote the country's golf heriatge, particularly in Germany, Scandinavia, Finland, France and the Benelux countries.

The *Gleneagles Hotel* and golf complex in Scotland has been expanded and provides some of the best upmarket golfing holidays in the UK as well as offering access to Scotland's many other top courses.

Following the Florida influence but unfortunately without the sunshine, British hotels offering special breaks provide the best opportunities, with the number of properties offering golf, either on its own course or at a nearby club, growing rapidly.

Luxury accommodation is the order of the day, as provided by the many Best Western hotels dedicated to golf in the consortium's brochure. Breaks like this offer the chance to stroll from the breakfast table right on to the first tee.

In keeping with US thinking, British hotels offer a range of sporting facilities for non-golfing companions.

HEALTH

The health of any traveller abroad may not be protected by services and legislation well-established at home. Changes in food and water may bring unexpected problems, as may insects and insect-borne diseases, especially in hot countries. Few have at their fingertips the current detailed knowledge needed to advise the traveller going to a particular country and personal reminiscences may not always reflect current or common problems. A danger of generalising is that it may be forgotten, for example, that malaria is a risk in Turkey, poliomyelitis occurs in Europe, and the *Hepatitis A* virus occurs worldwide and is not destroyed by many methods of purifying drinking water. Specific advice on which diseases are present in countries to be visited is likely to be complicated. A practical starting point for the traveller seeking advice is to consider which diseases can be prevented by immunisation, prophylactic tablets, or other measures, and decide whether it is appropriate to do so for each individual.

An unpredictable environment is especially a problem for the overland traveller who plans his own journey, and he needs greater knowledge of disease prevention and management than the traveller in an airplane or on a sea cruise, whose environment, food and drink are largely in the hands of the operator. Unforeseen changes in timetables may lead to stays in accommodation not of the expected standard. Delays at airports can take place in overcrowded and unhygienic conditions where the facilities have not kept pace with increased demand, and also insect-borne diseases may be contracted. Jetlag and exhaustion may prompt a traveller to take risks with food and drink. More experienced travellers tend to have fewer health problems. Better planning, immunisations and experience in prevention may all play a part, as well as salutary lessons learnt on previous occasions.

A questionnaire survey of returning travellers (most of whom had been to Europe, especially the Mediterranean countries) showed that half had had diarrhoea or respiratory symptoms while abroad. Excessive alcohol, sun and late nights can add to the problems. About one in 100 package holidaymakers who take out a health insurance policy make a claim. Diarrhoea and sunburn are principal reasons, but accidents are also common. Injuries occur especially in and around swimming pools, to pedestrians forgetting that traffic drives on the right, and from unfamiliar equipment such as gates on lifts. Sexually transmitted diseases may be contracted and may require urgent treatment.

Long-stay travellers may adapt to these initial problems, but then find themselves suffering from diseases endemic in their chosen country, such as malaria, hepatitis, diarrhoea and skin problems. Two per cent of British Voluntary Service Overseas personnel contract *Hepatitis A* within eight months if they are not protected. Poliomyelitis would be common if most travellers were not effectively immunised. Car accidents occur while driving on unmetalled roads, and some emotional problems may be resolved only by an early return home.

The traveller should be insured against medical expenses and most policies include the cost of emergency repatriation when appropriate. Such insurance, however, rarely covers a service overseas similar to that available at home. Language and administrative differences are likely to present problems. Leaflet *T4* issued yearly by the Department of Health describes the free or reduced-cost medical treatments available in other countries and the documents (passport, NHS medical card, form *E111*) which the traveller has to have with him or her. Reciprocal arrangements between countries differ and money may have to be paid and then reclaimed in the visited country itself, which can be time consuming. Extra provision should be made for such emergencies. Any reciprocal arrangement between the UK and a country is mentioned in each country's entry.

Form *E111*, obtainable from post offices, is needed in some countries of the European Community. Only a 'small' supply of medicines for personal use may be taken out of Britain, unless Home Office permission is obtained. Medicines and immunisations which are used to prevent diseases contracted abroad should not be prescribed on form *FP10*.

ADVICE CENTRES

Note: Members of the public should be aware that personal medical advice cannot necessarily be obtained from organisations listed in this section. In many cases their own medical practitioner will be in the best position to take account of relevant personal factors. Where specialist advice is supplied to members of the public (very often for a fee) this has been noted. Some addresses, however, are provided particularly to assist professionals in the travel trade who wish to keep abreast of developments in the rapidly changing medical world.

UK

MASTA (Medical Advisory Service for Travellers Abroad) of the London School of Hygiene and Tropical Medicine offers a print-out of the necessary immunisation and definitive malaria advice for any journey for a fee of £5 (fax service, £7). Tel: (071) 631 4408.

BA TRAVEL CLINICS Tel: (071) 831 5333 for nearest location.
25 clinics nationwide.

HOSPITAL FOR TROPICAL DISEASES TRAVEL CLINIC 180-182 Tottenham Court Road, London NW1 0PE.Tel: (071) 388 9600.

HEALTHLINE Tel: (0898) 345 081.
This is a regularly updated advice line (with inter-active technology) for travellers seeking information about vaccinations etc in most countries and regions.

COMMUNICABLE DISEASES (Scotland) Unit) Ruchill Hospital, Glasgow G20 9NB. Tel: (041) 946 7120. Fax: (041) 946 4359.

DEPARTMENT OF COMMUNICABLE AND TROPICAL DISEASES Immunisation Section, East Birmingham Hospital, Yardley Green Road, Birmingham B9 5PX, Tel: (021) 772 3679.

DEPARTMENT OF HEALTH ISD 1B, Room 324, Hannibal House, Elephant & Castle, London SE1 6TE. Tel: (071) 972 2654. Fax: (071) 972 2326.

LIVERPOOL SCHOOL OF TROPICAL MEDICINE Pembroke Place, Liverpool L3 5QA, Tel: (051) 708 9393. Fax: (051) 708 8733.

DEPARTMENT OF INFECTIOUS DISEASES & TROPICAL MEDICINE Monsall Hospital, Monsall Road, Newton Heath, Manchester M10 8WR, Tel: (061) 205 2393. Fax: (061) 203 5513.

ROSS INSTITUTE MALARIA ADVISORY SERVICE London School of Hygiene and Tropical Medicine, Keppel Street, London WC1E 7HT, Tel: (071) 636 7921 (24-hour tape).

BRITISH DIABETIC ASSOCIATION 10 Queen Anne Street, London W1M 0BD.Tel: (071) 323 1531. Fax: (071) 637 3644.
Issues leaflets and travel guides to the more popular countries with advice pertinent to the diabetic.

RADAR 25 Mortimer Street, London W1N 8AB Tel: (071) 637 5400. Fax: (071) 637 1827.
A wide range of leaflets and services are available to help the handicapped arrange, insure and enjoy their travels. (See separate section on *The Disabled Traveller.*)

SWITZERLAND

INTERNATIONAL ASSOCIATION FOR MEDICAL ASSISTANCE TO TRAVELLERS Gotthardstrasse 17, CH-6300 Zug, Switzerland.
Membership is free, but voluntary contributions are welcome. The association issues a directory of English-speaking doctors and leaflets on climate, acclimatisation, immunisation etc.

USA

CENTERS FOR DISEASE CONTROL TRAVELERS' HEALTH SECTION Tel: (404) 332 4559.
In Atlanta. Run a 24-hour automated telephone system giving advice by region and on special problems such as malaria, food and water precautions and for pregnant travellers.

CONVENIENCE CARE CENTERS Suite 100, 10301 East Darvey, Armani, CA 91733.
Undertakes all the necessary vaccinations for overseas travel.

INTERNATIONAL ASSOCIATION FOR MEDICAL ASSISTANCE TO TRAVELERS 417 Center Street, Lewiston, NY 14092.
A non-profit organisation dedicated to the gathering and dissemination of health and sanitary information worldwide.

US DEPARTMENT OF HEALTH AND HUMAN SERVICES Public Health Service, Centers for Disease Control, Center for Prevention Services, Division of Quarantine, Atlanta, GA 30333. Tel: (404) 331 2316. Intermedic, 777 Third Avenue, New York, NY 10017.
A list of recommended English-speaking doctors in many countries is available to members (subscription US$6).

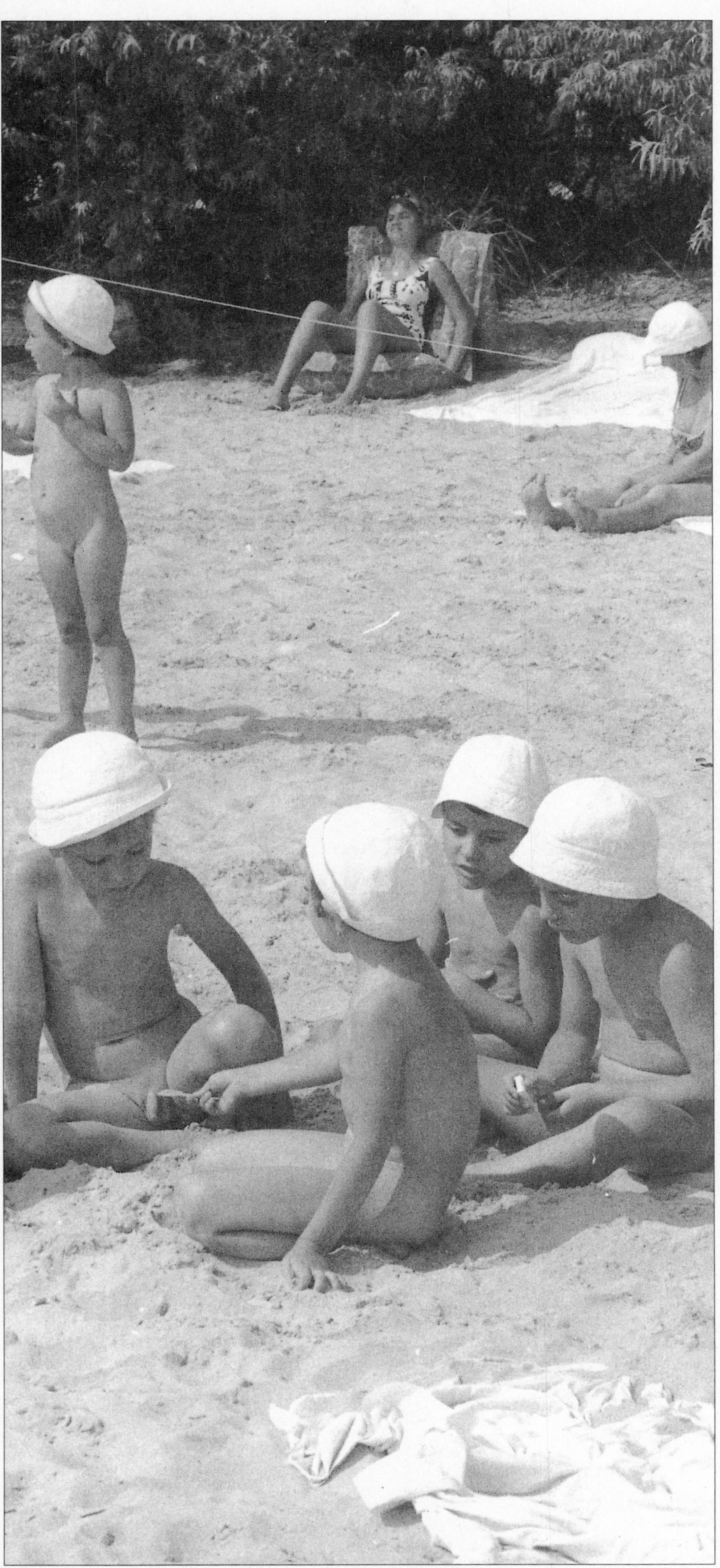

IMMUNISATION

YELLOW FEVER: This disease is caused by a virus that circulates in animals indigenous to certain tropical forested areas. It mainly infects monkeys, but if man enters these areas the virus may be transmitted to him by mosquitoes whose normal hosts are monkeys. This is *jungle yellow fever*. It occurs haphazardly and is clearly related to man's habits. If, from an animal source, the virus begins to circulate between man and his own mosquitoes, primarily *Aedes aegypti*, epidemics of *urban yellow fever* result. Immunisation protects the individual and is effective in preventing the spread of the virus to countries where *Aedes aegypti* is prevalent. It is therefore reasonable for such countries to request a certificate of vaccination of all travellers from areas where human cases are occurring. Many national administrations, however, require immunisation of all travellers over one year of age from all countries, or else all travellers over one year from countries where enzootic *foci* occur. A map of zones where yellow fever is endemic (enzootic) can be found on page 1225. Immunisation is clearly not indicated when travelling outside the enzootic zones. Within the zones, if it is not compulsory, it is not always necessary. For instance, in the absence of an epidemic of yellow fever, a business trip within the confines of Nairobi would be perfectly safe. Nevertheless, local and current knowledge of cases is required for such decisions to be made, so in practice immunisation is recommended to all travellers within enzootic zones. Immunisation in the United Kingdom is undertaken only at recognised yellow fever vaccination centres (see below).

Once immunised (a single vaccination is used), the vaccination certificate is valid after ten days for ten years. It is not recommended for pregnant women and children under nine months.

CHOLERA: In 1973 the WHO, recognising that immunisation cannot stop the spread of cholera among countries, deleted from the International Health Regulations the requirement of cholera immunisation as a condition of admission to any country. In 1990 the WHO stated that immunisation against cholera was not effective and they do not recommend it. In 1991 the WHO confirmed that certification was no longer required by any country or territory. Nevertheless, some countries do still require certificatin form travellers entering from an infected area. When immunisation is for certification one dose will suffice and the certificate is valid after six days for six months. It is not to be given to children under six months of age.

TYPHOID FEVER: Typhoid fever is endemic worldwide and is usually spread faecal-orally. The risk of infection is increased in areas of high carriage rates and poor hygiene. The risk is not significantly increased for the traveller to areas with public health standards similar to those of the UK – namely, northern Europe, USA, Canada, Australia, New Zealand and Japan – and immunisation for these areas is not necessary. Outside these areas the risks reflect not only local hygiene and carriage rates but also lifestyle. Travelling or living rough, living in rural areas, or 'eating out' make transmission more likely. The risks are therefore small for the air traveller with full board at a reputable hotel, and immunisation is unnecessary. On the other hand, overland travel to Australia would be a clear indication for immunisation. Between these extremes there are many circumstances for which risks cannot be precisely defined. Typhoid vaccine is now no longer routinely recommended for the millions of tourists to southern Europe each year, although it may still be advisable not only for those whose lifestyle or occupation increase the risk of such exposure, but also during local outbreaks such as occurred on the island of Kos in 1984.

HEPATITIS A: The *Hepatitis* A virus is endemic worldwide and spread by the faecal-oral route; protection from symptomatic infection can be provided by active immunisation or passively acquired immuno-globulin. The virus circulates freely in our own population however, and many travellers will be immune already. Protection should be offered to the same groups as are offered typhoid immunisation, as exposure to one infection would imply the risk of exposure to the other. The recurrent tropical traveller may now have his antibodies against *Hepatitis A* checked as this test has become widely available. If antibodies are present, that person is immune. If antibodies are absent, immunoglobulin or inactivated *Hepatitis* A vaccine should be given. Immunoglobulin requires to be given at least every six months while the risk continues. *Hepatitis* A in children is usually mild and more often asymptomatic, so immunoglobulin is not essential. It can, however, be given in reduced doses.

Worldwide H
Quality H

Imagine being thousands of miles away from home, ill, and frustrated because the doctor doesn't speak your language and can't understand what's wrong. When traveling, for business or pleasure, locally or internationally, quality healthcare in a time of need can make a world of difference. Through the work of the International Medical Institute with a mission to ease access to quality healthcare for people of all nations.

The Atlanta International Clinic

The Atlanta International Clinic is designed to serve the healthcare needs of both international and local area residents. Special attention is given to patient's unique cultural, language and

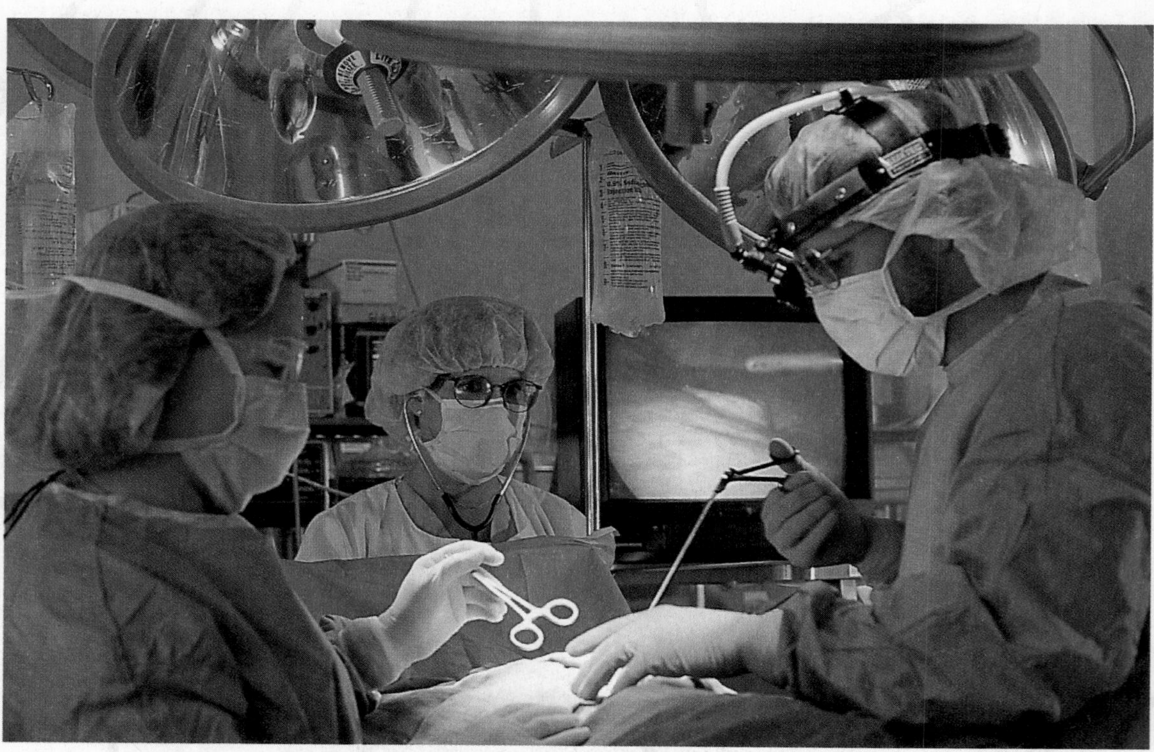

and communication technology advancements it is possible to obtain quality medical attention virtually anywhere in the world. IMI incorporates a worldwide network of physicians and hospitals dedicated to mutual empowerment through information transfer, education and international cooperation

travel needs. The Atlanta International Clinic provides quality healthcare to world travelers accessing them to expert medical treatment. Similar clinics will soon be launched in over twenty five international cities worldwide.

THE ATLANTA INTERNATIONAL CLINIC

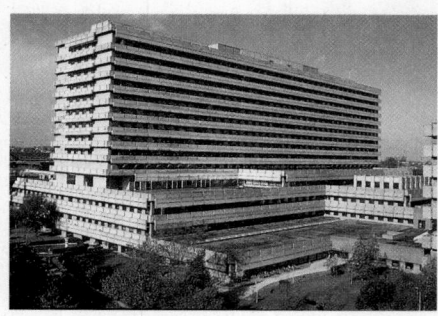

POLIOMYELITIS: A survey undertaken in England in 1978 showed that 40 per cent of the tested population did not have antibodies to all three serotypes of poliovirus. Hence a consultation about travel abroad is a vital opportunity to complete primary courses or boost immunisations which are nationally recommended. Oral poliomyelitis vaccine is given, but supplies of inactivated polio vaccine are available if oral vaccine is contra-indicated.
TETANUS: As with poliomyelitis, all individuals should gain or maintain immunity to tetanus. It is as firmly recommended for life in the UK as for travel abroad.

SPECIAL/RARE DISEASES

Rabies: Most doctors do not think it is necessary to immunise the ordinary traveller going to areas where rabies is endemic, although it may be advisable for those in remote areas who would be many days' travel away from a source of vaccine and rabies immunoglobulin. However, all travellers should avoid contact with animals, especially cats and dogs. If they do get bitten, wounds should be promptly washed with copious soap and water followed by the application of alcohol (spirits like gin and whisky can be used). If the animal's owner is available, it should be checked whether the animal has been vaccinated against rabies (check certification). A forwarding address or telephone number should be left to enable contact to be made should the animal become unwell over the next two weeks. Seek local medical advice promptly and give details of the incident to the local police. On return, the traveller's medical practitioner should be informed.
Diphtheria: Diphtheria is endemic worldwide. From 1983 to 1987, only seven cases were notified in the United Kingdom, mostly from an imported source. Most morbidity and mortality are in children and they should be immunised as nationally recommended (initial primary course and booster on school entry). Adult travellers with a high risk of infection are those in contact with children in poorer areas – for example, health workers and teachers. Such travellers may have their immunity boosted, without Schick testing, by a low dose preparation of diphtheria toxoid. Contact: Regent Laboratories. Tel: (081) 965 3637. Fax: (081) 961 9311.
Meningococcal meningitis: Although the bacteria responsible for this illness circulate widely throughout the world, certain areas, like the dry areas bordering the southern Sahara, are renowned for recurrent epidemics and many areas suffer occasional epidemics, as in India, Nepal and Brazil, and during the Mecca pilgrimages in recent years. Immunisation is available for the types of meningococci usually responsible for these outbreaks, and should be considered for travellers to such areas with current outbreaks, particularly those staying long-term.
Tick-borne encephalitis: Tick-borne encephalitis is caused by an arbovirus, transmitted by the bite of an infected tick. Its distribution is confined to warm and low-forested areas in parts of central Europe and Scandinavia, particularly Austria, the Czech Republic, the Slovak Republic, Germany and Yugoslavia. The forests are usually deciduous with heavy undergrowth. Those normally at risk are foresters and those clearing such areas, but increasing contact will occur with increased recreational use, such as camping and walking. Most human illness occurs in late spring and early summer. Tick bites are best avoided by limiting contact with such areas, wearing clothing to cover most of the skin surface and using insect repellents on outer clothes and socks. Where prolonged contact is necessary, a killed vaccine is available from Immuno Ltd on a named patient basis. Tel: (0732) 458 101. Fax: (0732) 455 175.
Japanese B encephalitis: This virus infection is transmitted by mosquitoes in certain rural areas of eastern Asia, the Indian subcontinent and a few Pacific islands. Occasional larger outbreaks develop and this infection tends to have a higher mortality than the many other similar viruses that can cause encephalitis. If planning to sleep in rural areas with a high risk or an active outbreak, immunisation should be considered; this is available from Cambridge Self Care Diagnostics. Tel: (091) 261 5950. Fax: (091) 261 5915. Considerable protection is offered by avoiding mosquito bites (see below in the *Malaria Prophylaxis* section) and staying indoors at night in rural areas where known cases are occurring.
Plague: Plague is an infection of wild rodents transmitted by fleas. It exists in many rural areas of Africa, Asia and the Americas. The risk to the traveller from the bite of an infected flea is *low*. Routine immunisation is not recommended. In enzootic areas, usually rural and hilly, contact with rodents should be discouraged by preventing their access to food and waste, avoiding dead rodents and rodent burrows. Fleas can be discouraged by insect repellents. When prolonged stay in a rural enzootic area is expected and avoidance of rodents is impracticable – for example, during wars or after disasters – an inactivated vaccine is available from Bayer UK Ltd. Tel: (0284) 763 200. Fax: (0284) 702 810. Two doses are necessary four to 12 weeks apart with boosters necessary every six months.
Hepatitis B: Vaccination should be considered for groups such as medical, nursing and laboratory staff planning to work among populations with high HBsAg carriage rates. The recommended regimen consists of three doses, the boosters being given one month and six months after the initial dose. Immunity is predicted to last about five years but those who remain at risk should have antibodies checked three months after completion of course.
AIDS: This disease develops in people who have been infected with the human immunodeficiency virus (HIV). People infected with HIV, and who may appear perfectly well, pass on the infection by sexual intercourse or if their blood is inoculated into other people, as in the sharing of needles by drug users, the transfusion of untested blood, or the re-use of injection needles without sterilisation between patients. Although prevalent worldwide, certain areas of the world, such as parts of tropical Africa, South America and Asia have a higher number of carriers of HIV. There is therefore a greater risk of infection in such areas during casual sexual intercourse and, if not avoided, the use of condoms and spermicidal cream should reduce the level of risk. Thought must also be given to the need for blood transfusions, where blood is not tested for HIV antibodies, and the need for injections where there is doubt about the sterility of the needles (these may be sterilised by placing in boiling water for 20 minutes). Kits containing appropriate needles and syringes are available. Travellers should know their blood group. The World Health Organisation is vigorously opposed to any country requiring travellers to present a certificate stating that they are free from HIV infection. Besides being against International Health Regulations, it is both clinically unsound and epidemiologically unjustifiable as a

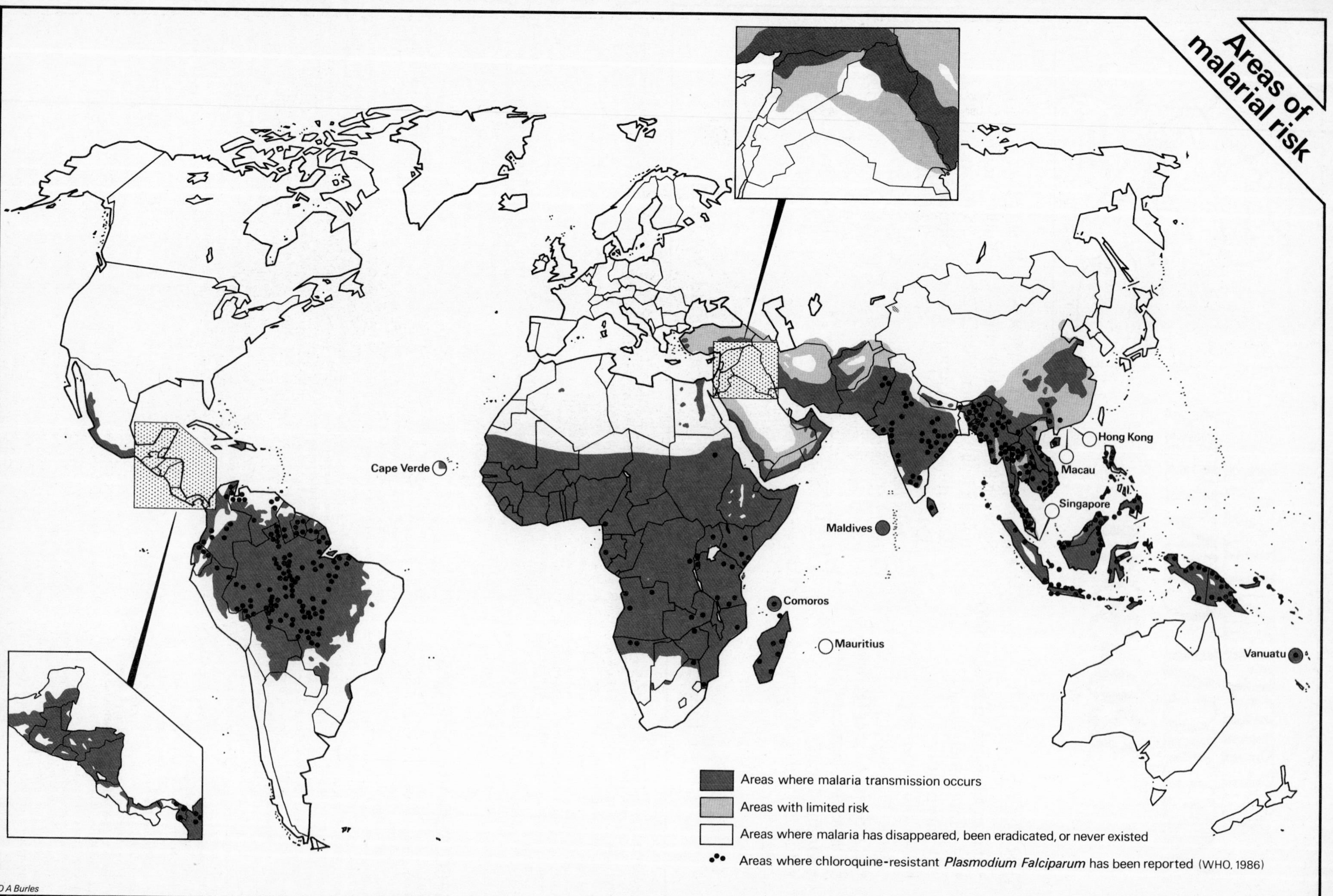

Areas of malarial risk
Cape Verde
Hong Kong
Macau
Singapore
Maldives
Comoros
Mauritius
Vanuatu
Areas where malaria transmission occurs
Areas with limited risk
Areas where malaria has disappeared, been eradicated, or never existed
Areas where chloroquine-resistant Plasmodium Falciparum has been reported (WHO, 1986)
D A Burles

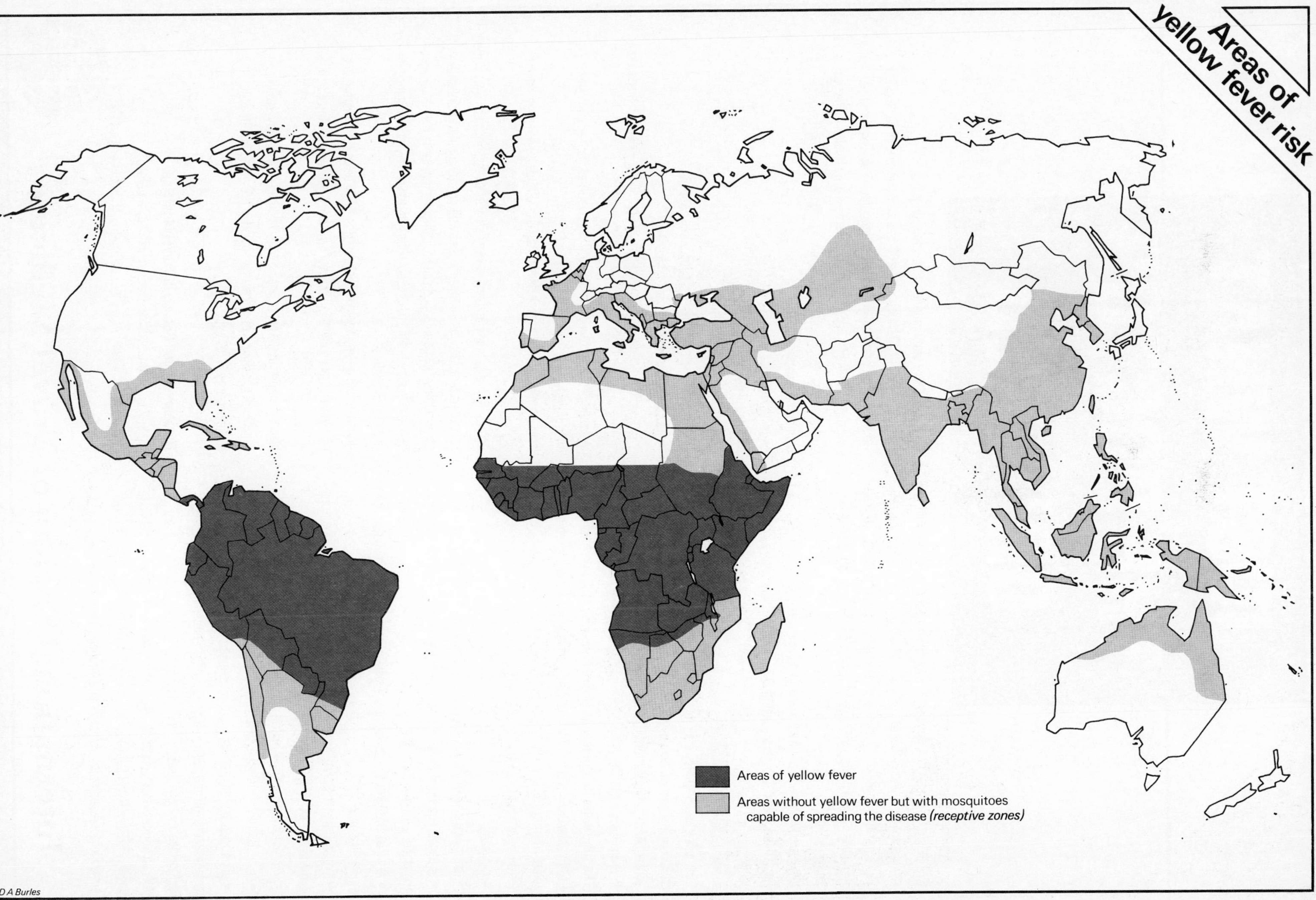
Areas of yellow fever risk
Areas of yellow fever
Areas without yellow fever but with mosquitoes capable of spreading the disease *(receptive zones)*
D A Burles

means of limiting infection. However, at least 40 countries have introduced restrictions, such as compulsory HIV testing or refusal of entry of 'suspicious' visitors, though mostly those planning to stay, work or study long-term.

MALARIA PROPHYLAXIS

Malaria is widespread in tropical and subtropical areas of the world and is spread by the bite of a female anopheline mosquito that has been infected by the malaria parasite. During the 1960s, control measures in many areas appeared to be bringing malaria under control. A resurgence has occurred, however, particularly in the Indian subcontinent, parts of South America and Turkey.

The increasing mobility of the population, especially through air travel, brings a further hazard since travellers may be bitten by mosquitoes at airports en route as well as in the countries where they stay. The speed of travel means that first symptoms may occur in a country and in a context where the disease will not be immediately considered. Mosquitoes may even be brought in airplanes to non-endemic areas and infect, for example, airport staff or travellers' relatives. Infection also occurs through blood transfusion (cold storage does not destroy the parasites) and the sharing of needles by drug users.

The most immediately life-threatening form of malaria is caused by *Plasmodium falciparum*. Because of the travelling habits of those living in the UK, this form of malaria is usually imported from Africa but also from Asia. Prevention is primarily aimed at this parasite. Nevertheless, the same advice is given to those likely to be exposed to the less dangerous *P vivax*, *P malariae*, and *P ovale*, partly to prevent an unpleasant illness but also because *P falciparum* infection can never be presumed to be absent in any malarious area. There is no immediate prospect of an effective vaccine, so regular ingestion of prophylactic tablets is necessary. This requires habits which some find difficult or even distasteful, and because of increasing resistance to these tablets, they can no longer guarantee protection from illness. Bites must be avoided or reduced (see below) and any flu-like illness with fever and shivers lasting more than two days should be promptly diagnosed. If such symptoms develop after return, even months afterwards, the attending doctor should be reminded of the date and place of travel.

Note: A map showing areas of malarial risk and areas where chloroquine resistance has been reported is printed on page 1224. Sorce: WHO, Geneva.

Personal precautions:

(1) Avoid mosquito bites, especially after sunset, when the anopheline mosquitoes responsible for transmitting malaria are most active. Long trousers, sleeves and dresses, netting on windows, and mosquito nets over beds help to prevent mosquito bites.

(2) Insect repellents may be used on exposed skin and insecticides inside buildings or on breeding sites. Repellent-impregnated wrist and ankle bands, and electrical insecticide vaporisers may also be used.

(3) Mosquitoes should not be encouraged to breed by leaving stagnant water – for example, in blocked drains or around plant pots.

(4) Prophylactic tablets are necessary because the above measures, although valuable, are unlikely to be fully effective.

Precautions before travel:

(a) Start tablets one week before departure to confirm tolerance and obtain adequate blood concentrations before exposure.

(b) Take the tablets *with absolute regularity*. Prophylactic doses of drugs are not normally curative once the infection is established.

(c) Continue prophylaxis for at least four weeks after leaving an endemic area: all forms of the parasite develop first in the liver and only later re-enter the blood, where most prophylactic drugs take effect.

(d) Seek advice on which type of tablet to take from an advice centre (see beginning of entry).

ACCIDENTS AND BITES

As children begin to crawl and walk they become more vulnerable to faecal-oral infections and hazards such as bites, accidents and burns. Open wounds should be kept clean and covered with dressings until healed. Deaths from scorpion bites are unusual but mostly occur in children aged under two years. Allowing toddlers to play outside unattended can be particularly hazardous.

Taking adequate malarial prophylaxis should not encourage the traveller to ignore the risks from other mosquito-borne diseases such as dengue, which can be more severe in children. Protection from mosquito bites is also important in those children who are strongly allergic to them. Appropriate clothes and bed or window netting at night are usually more valuable in the long term than insect repellents.

PREGNANCY

Live vaccinations are best not given during pregnancy, although if someone unprotected against yellow fever is going to live in a high risk area, the theoretical risk of vaccination is outweighed by the serious nature of the illness. If the vaccine is not given, a doctor's letter endorsed with a health board or authority stamp to say the inoculation is contra-indicated is usually accepted. Inactivated poliomyelitis vaccine may be used instead of oral live vaccine.

A mother immunised against tetanus passes on protection to her baby over the neonatal period and a booster can be given during pregnancy if necessary.

Hepatitis A in pregnancy may be more severe and also result in premature labour. Prevention with normal immunoglobulin is generally encouraged for those at risk. Malarial prophylaxis should be maintained throughout pregnancy but the risks of some drugs have to be balanced against the type of malaria and likelihood of its transmission in different areas and specialist advice should be sought.

CONTRACEPTION

Those using oral contraceptives should be aware that absorption may be affected during gastrointestinal illnesses, that some brands may not be available locally, and that they may be continued over the usual break in the cycle if menstruation is going to occur at an inconvenient time such as during a long journey. They may contribute to the fluid retention that some people experience in hot climates.

STAY HEALTHY WHILE YOU TRAVEL

The information of the following pages has been extractred from the Columbus Press publication Stay Healthy While Your Travel adn is designed to answer the most frequently posed questions by those planning a trip abroa, Copies of the booklet, which is packed with useful advi e and vital infomatink are available form Columbus Press Subscriptions Department, 5-7 Luke Street, London EC2A 4PX. Tel: +44 (0) 71 729 4535, Fax: +44 (0) 71 729 1156.

JABS

Do I Really Have to Have Jabs?
Having the right jabs is like carrying an umbrella to protect you against the rain. Jabs or oral vaccines against diseases like polio, tetanus, hepatitis, tuberculosis, typhoid, diphtheria and yellow fever are for your protection.

Many countries may not let you in without an up-to-date yellow fever certificate, in case you are carrying the disease. Remember, the yellow fever jab, being a live virus, is not recommended if you are pregnant (see the section on *pregnancy* below) or if you are taking immuno-suppressive drugs like steroids. Check with your GP. Other vaccines can be live too: the usual type of polio vaccine for instance. In general, yellow fever is the only disease where you will be asked for a certificate of inoculation.

Where Can I Get the Right Travel Health Advice Before I Go?
Contact one of the reputable travel health specialist centres listed under *Advice Centres* above. It is crucial to get accurate, up-to-date advice on the protection you need. Help them to give you the best advice by telling them where you are going, including any transit stops, how you are getting there and what you plan to do when you get there.

Remember that embassies, travel agents and even GPs are often *not* the best sources of information – after all, travel health is not their speciality. Nevertheless, if you are already taking medicine or have allergies or other medical conditions – or are pregnant – always check with your GP about your trip. For a start, you may need an extra supply of your medicine.

How Long Before I Travel Should I Get my Jabs?
Ideally 6 to 8 weeks before you depart. Finish them several days before you set off. Some jabs – a first course against typhoid for example – require 2 injections at least 4 weeks apart. Yellow fever only requires 1 injection which should not be within 3 weeks of other live vaccines such as polio.

TEETH

Should I get my Teeth Checked Before I Go?
Yes! Dental problems can ruin your holiday. Worse, in some countries you may put yourself at risk from contracting AIDS or hepatitis B from dental treatment because of inadequately sterilised instruments, or you might imbibe contaminated water in the surgery.

Always get a proper check-up before going abroad. If you wear false teeth, it is a good idea to carry a spare set with you.

THE JOURNEY

What Can I do to Make a Long Plane Journey More Bearable?
(1) Wear comfortable shoes for flying. Your feet may swell so be careful. If you take your shoes off for comfort you should wear something like canvas espadrilles to squeeze swollen feet back into after the flight. It pays to get up and walk about every 1-2 hours to restore the circulation.
(2) Recently had a cold? Prone to blocked sinuses? Before flying, take something to dry out your sinuses, available over the counter in chemists. Otherwise you could experience a searing and startling pain in your head when the plane comes down to land.
(3) If you wear contact lenses keep a supply of lens solution with you, as lenses can dry out in the very low humidity in pressurised cabins.

How do I Deal with Motion/Travel Sickness?
Some people think motion sickness is psychological – if you are determined not to be sick you will be just fine. Whether there is any truth in the 'Mind-over-Matter' theory or not, feeling nauseous is very unpleasant.
Travel/motion sickness affects 5-15 year olds the most. If young children are prone to motion sickness, do not encourage them to read on the journey – read *to* them, if necessary.
There are many effective remedies for motion sickness. Choose the one that works best for you and stick to it.

Sea Bands are two knitted elasticated wrist bands. A plastic button on the band presses against the wrist at a spot known in the ancient Chinese science of acupressure as the 'Nei Kuan-point'. No drugs are involved so there are no apparent side effects. They also seem to work well for children. They are available in most chemists.

Always inform the pharmacist if you are pregnant or suffer from eye conditions like glaucoma, and about any other drugs you or your children are taking before buying a motion-sickness drug. Make sure you give children the correct, smaller dose (ask your GP or pharmacist). Never combine travel sickness preparations with alcohol or tranquillisers.

If you do not like modern drugs, there are traditional remedies like ripe bananas, green apples, ginger or glucose. You can ask your GP to refer you to a homeopathist for a homeopathic seasickness remedy.

SUN, SEA AND SAND

But Isn't That What I'm Going on Holiday For?
Bear in mind the incredible power of the sun as you get closer to the Equator, especially with all the powerful reflections from white sands and blue seas, catching you even under a swaying palm. Nor does cloud cover filter out all the harmful rays.

Our 'indoor skin' is never adapted to the tremendous burning power of the sun. Only now, with millions and millions of European tourists fleeing to the hotter climes for their holidays, is it becoming apparent just how dangerous the great golden orb can be.

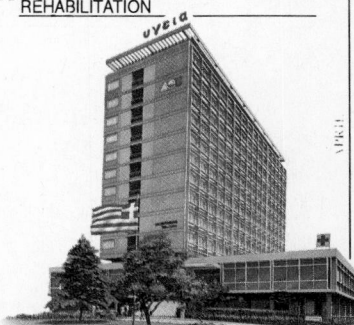

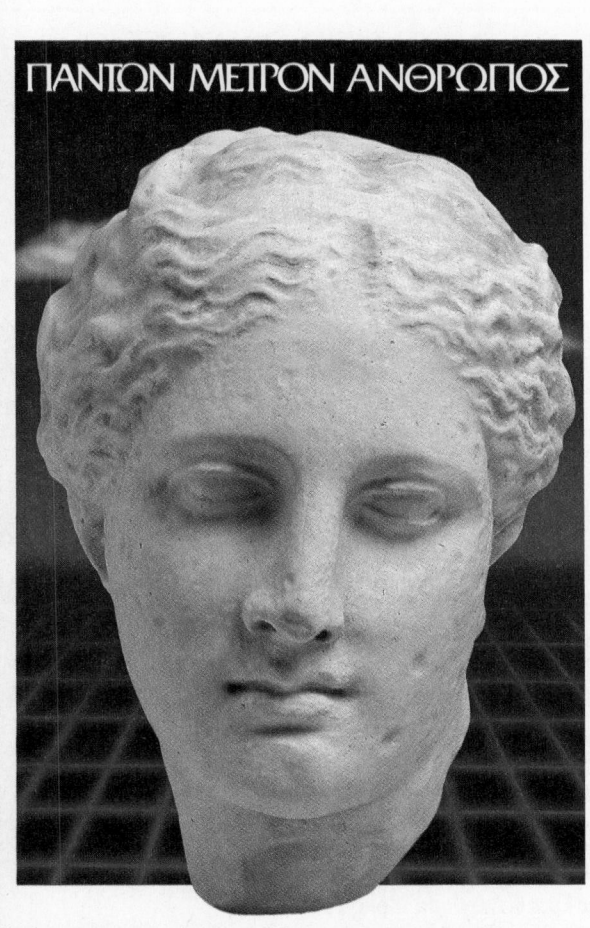

But I Really Want to Sunbathe!
In that case, go for gold. If you must sunbathe, a golden tan is safer than a dark brown one. Medical advice these days is 'Do not bake in the sun'. You can age and damage the skin severely and even get skin cancer, particularly if you are fair-haired, red-haired, fair-skinned, blue-eyed, or a child.
Make sure you allow your skin to acclimatise gently, particularly during the first few days. Subsequently, avoid the searing heat in the middle of the day. Some people try to prepare by taking a course on sun-beds. No one knows if this causes long-term damage, but the probability is high. Remember, you should use a sunscreen even with artificial sun. The sunscreen number should be just as high as you expect to use at the resort. The higher the sunscreen number, the higher the protection. Use plenty – and keep the sunscreen simple. The fewer extra ingredients like perfume, colourants or exotic fruity oils, the less chance there is of combining with sunshine to give you a nasty rash. Look for water-resistant sunscreen preparations with a high factor. Apply double the amount you might back home. Continue to slap on sun protection cream even after you have got a tan. Do not use last year's sun protection creams and lotions if you have opened them, as the chemicals may have degraded.

Bear in mind also that sunshine can sometimes interact violently with drugs you are taking – such as tetracyclines – or with perfumes.

Treat a bad sunburn as a bad burn or scald – severe infection can result. Apply cold compresses – wet, non-fluffy material will do – and see a doctor. If you do get sunburn, natural yogurt spread over the affected area will help to soothe it. Children's young skin is extremely vulnerable to strong sun. High-protection products for children are available.

What About Heatstroke?
Heatstroke is a life-endangering emergency often caused as a result of sheer foolishness in ignoring the tremendous heat and exposure you are receiving. Sweating can actually stop – in fact, that is one of the warning signs. The skin becomes dry and hot. Your temperature can climb to 40°C (105°F). This can be accompanied by vomiting, dizziness and headache. The pulse rate increases. In severe stages there is delirium and loss of consciousness. You must get the temperature down fast but do not try diving into cold water.

Move the person to a cool, shady place and then remove all clothing and if possible immerse them in a bath of cool water. Keep the person wet by throwing water over their body constantly. Fan the body continuously. As recuperation takes place, make the victim drink plenty of water or fruit juice, adding about a teaspoonful of salt to the pint (about half a litre), to replace loss. Stop cooling when the body temperature falls below 39°C (103°F). Get a doctor as soon as you can.

What Effect will a Hot Climate Have on Skin Conditions like Eczema, Herpes and Psoriasis?
These and other skin conditions can be made worse in hot or humid climates; consult your doctor before you leave.

What is Prickly Heat?
It is known in medical circles as *miliaria rubra* – red millet seeds – because you get huge numbers of tiny blisters on a red, quite inflamed skin, mostly around your waist, upper body, front of elbows and armpits. Women may find rashes where the bra rubs just under the breast. The rash is accompanied by terrible prickly sensations. Prickly heat is probably caused by continuous wetting of the skin by unevaporated sweat, especially in hot and humid climates. To prevent it, keep cool, wash carefully each day, use cotton or silk bras and underwear, and put on plenty of talcum powder. Once you are suffering from prickly heat, take cool showers, dab-dry (do not rub skin) and touch on calamine lotion and zinc oxide dusting powder.

EARS AND EYES

If you have any eye or ear conditions be sure to get medication for them before you go.

Ears: Swimming and diving can lead to ear infections because of moisture left in the canal. Use cotton wool buds to gently dry. An antibiotic ear-drop like *Otosporin* may be required if infection sets in.

If you have any ear conditions then scuba diving may not be a suitable activity for you on holiday. People who have recently had even a moderate cold are certainly not advised to dive as the ear passages may be blocked.

Eyes: If you wear glasses, pack a spare pair. If you wear contact lenses, then take a pair of glasses as well. Dust and sand can become trapped behind contact lenses; if you experience any discomfort then switch to your specs for a day or so. Cleaning and rinsing fluids may not be available on your holiday, so be sure to take a good supply with you.

Wear sunglasses! The best kind filter out most of the ultra-violet light and, while more expensive, are worth it. Always wear sunglasses in bright light; you may end up with a peculiar 'panda' effect round your eyes for the first few days, but that is a lot better than the pain of overexposure to sunlight.

Infections can be caused from tiny pieces of coral getting in your eye while swimming in the sea: dirt and sand are other hazards. In such cases remember the golden rule – do *not* rub your eyes. Bathe them in clean water, or a proprietary eye lotion. If you can see the foreign body, use the edge of a clean handkerchief to wipe it away. If the object is sharp, go to a doctor. Many minor eye problems are cured by resting, preferably with a clean pad over the eyes. Thin slices of cucumber are also useful in relieving irritation caused by dust or coral. If the discomfort or discharge persists for more than a day or so then you should seek medical advice.

STOMACH PROBLEMS

How do I Avoid Stomach Problems on Holiday?
Let's be perfectly clear – it is likely to be very, very difficult. Holiday *WHICH?* (May 1988) reported a remarkably high incidence of stomach afflictions among tourists staying in even 3-star hotels in the Mediterranean regions, Africa, Asia and Latin America. A nasty stomach bug can really ruin your holiday, even if it provides cruel humour for the other guests (until they get it too). Remember, an awful lot of tummy upsets at the very start of the holiday come because you have gone barmy on food and drink. This can give you frequent loose watery stools, sometimes accompanied by temperature, nausea and a colicky left-sided abdominal pain. This should clear up by itself.

If you get food poisoning on holiday, it is likely to be because you have eaten food contaminated with human or animal excreta. In other words, the salad you ate had sewage on it. Or you ate partly-cooked contaminated meat. Or those ice-cubes in your cold drink were made from unclean water. Local water in poor countries can be little more than diluted sewage and hotel or restaurant staff may not have washed their hands properly before preparing your food.

How Can I Avoid Getting an Upset Stomach?
Try following these rules:

1. Never eat food which has been standing around, even in a top hotel or in restaurants (that includes those delicious-looking buffets). Flies may have infected it. Remember, local flies carry local diseases. Also be wary of foods like meat-balls or delicacies which require a lot of handling in their preparation.

2. Always order hot food. You are usually safe with freshly grilled or fried foods. Thorough cooking helps to kill off the bugs. So make sure meat, especially chicken, has been cooked right through. The meat should have no trace of red left in it. Chicken especially is a classic home for dangerous salmonella food-poisoning.

3. Be particularly careful if you are pregnant – many upsets may cause only mild illness in adults but can have a very serious effect on the unborn baby.

4. Do without shellfish unless you are certain it comes from unpolluted water and has been kept properly chilled or iced, and has then been cooked for at least 10 minutes. Otherwise, it can be very dangerous indeed. Never eat raw or even pickled oysters, clams, lobster or crab. They can carry typhoid, bacillary dysentery or hepatitis.

5. Avoid leaf salads, as they may have been washed in contaminated water and touched with unclean kitchen hands. If you have to eat salad, dose it well with lemon or a strong vinegar dressing. This will slightly reduce the risk. Try to eat fruit you yourself can peel, such as bananas, oranges and peaches.

6. Avoid milk and local milk products made from unboiled milk, including milk-shakes and ice-creams (however tempting) in case the milk is not pasteurised. Remember that in poorer countries, milk is often sold diluted with contaminated water.

What do I do if I Get an Upset Stomach?
Most doctors believe you should give your own immune system a chance to cure mild upset stomachs. Avoid anti-diarrhoeal agents like Codeïne, Diphenoxylate (Lomotil) and Kaolin, unless you temporarily need to block yourself up (if you are travelling, for example).

If you do get an upset stomach, try not to eat for 24 hours, stay off anti-diarrhoea treatments initially unless the symptoms are intolerable, rest and constantly replace salt and fluids fast. You should drink plenty of fluids such as weak lemon tea, fizzy drinks, clean water, mild herb teas or a light, clear salty soup. Sip little and often to lessen the risk of vomiting. It is very important to take in as much fluid as possible to avoid dehydration. Do not drink strong tea, coffee, alcoholic drinks or milk. Do not take antibiotics unless prescribed by a competent medical authority. In some cases of diarrhoea, antibiotics would be completely wrong.

If someone is vomiting or has diarrhoea, give them a rehydration cocktail. Either make up a solution of the internationally famous 'après diarrhoea cocktail' – half a teaspoon of salt and two teaspoons of sugar in a pint (half litre) of clean or sterilised water. Keep sipping little and often. A 'Cognac Quickie' (a measure of cognac with a little grated nutmeg) will calm the spasms. As the diarrhoea lessens, eat dry toast, biscuits, ripe bananas, boiled rice with a squeeze of lemon juice, soups, but avoid any dairy products. The pectin in ripe bananas acts as a binding agent. Return to normal eating habits on the third day.

When Should I Call a Doctor?
An upset tummy may be the mild uncomfortable inconvenience of loose stools or a life-threatening attack of cholera or dysentery. Attacks of diarrhoea vary so much it is difficult to give precise guidelines as to when to call the doctor.

You should always call a doctor when: there is blood in the stools; the diarrhoea lasts longer than three days (one day in a baby); the temperature lies above 38.6°C (101°F) and stays above for more than two days or when the diarrhoea is particularly severe or frequent.

WATER

How much Liquid Will I Need?
This is a very difficult one. Even if you do not exert yourself in hot countries, you may be sweating ten to fifteen pints of liquid a day. You will need a large amount of water in hot countries: but make sure it is safe. As a rough guide, drink enough fluid to pass at least 1.5 pints (800ml) of water a day.

How do I Know if the Water is Clean?
Water is an ideal way for various unpleasant things, through faecal contamination, to find a new and unwilling host – you. Among the risks are worm infections, typhoid, cholera, amoebic dysentery, polio, Hepatitis A and viral diarrhoea. Tap water in most countries in the tropics and parts of the Mediterranean should be regarded as potentially contaminated, although you are likely to experience fewer problems in high-quality resorts and hotels. You have to take charge of your water intake in many hot countries, exercising extreme caution as you do so.

If in doubt, do not drink tap water or even rinse your toothbrush in it. Even chlorine does not kill off all the bugs. Nor does alcohol – unless it is above 100% proof, which can obviously cause other problems. Always carry a few water-purification tablets with you and follow the instructions. These are available from most chemists; otherwise two drops of iodine per pint (500ml) of water in a glass is a good idea. If the water is cloudy, add four drops and leave for 15 minutes. If you have purchased a light-weight water purifier, use the purified water extensively, even to the extent of washing your own fruit from the local markets with it, or for drinking with a safe snack at the hotel or beach.

Buy bottled drinks with metal tops and reliable labels. Fizzy drinks are acidic and more likely to be safe than still drinks. Alcohol dehydrates you and is unwise in hot climates: so does caffeine. Buy bottles of mineral water where possible, and check that the seal is unbroken –

QUICK GUIDE TO VACCINATION/PROPHYLAXIS REQUIREMENTS & PROGRAMMES

When time permits, immunisation should be started well in advance so that adequate intervals between doses can be maintained. If notice to travel is short, a rapid course may be given, but the immunity provided will not be as good.
Children should be up-to-date with routine UK vaccination schedule. Extra consideration should be given to the need for vaccinating pregnant women. If it is known that a full initial (primary) course of any of these vaccines has been given, then only single booster doses are necessary.

Against	No. of injections in primary programme (inc. period of protection)	Validity of certificate	Revaccination	Other details
Yellow Fever	One injection gives protection for 10 years.	10 days after inoculation for 10 years.	Every 10 years validity taking immediate effect.*	Reactions to vaccination are rare, though some discomfort might be experienced. Not for infants under 9 months or pregnant women.
Cholera **	2 injections given 4-6 weeks apart give some protection for 6 months. See note below.	6 days after inoculation for 6 months	A single booster must be acquired before expiry of every six month period, and lasts 6 months. Takes immediate effect	Local tenderness, swelling and redness with slight general upset may occur. Not for infants under 1 year
Typhoid Fever				
(a) Inactivated	Two injections separated by 4-6 weeks give reasonable protection for 3 years.	Not applicable.	Single booster every 3 years.	Local tenderness, swelling and redness with slight general upset may occur. Not for infants under 1 year
(b) Vi vaccine	One injection.	Not applicable.	Single booster.	Local and systematic reactions less than above. More expensive. Not for children under 18 months of age.
(c) Oral	One capsule on alternate days for 3 doses.	Not applicable.	3 dose booster annually for recurrent travellers.	Only mild reactions expected. To be kept refrigerated. Do not use with antibiotics, within 12 hours of mefloquine, in pregnant or immunocompromised or concurrent oral polio vaccine. Not for children under 6 years of age.
Tetanus	Three injections given 6-12 weeks between first and second and 6 months between second and third.	Not applicable.	Single booster every 10 years.	Local tenderness, swelling and redness may occur.
Poliomyelitis	Three oral vaccinations with with 4-8 weeks between doses.	Not applicable.	Single booster every 10 years.	Different (inactivated) vaccine available for pregnant women.
Hepatitis A				
(c) Immunoglobulin	One injection of Gamma globulin taken just prior to departure gives reasonable protection for up to 6 months	Not applicable.	Further Gamma globulin should be given within every 6-month period if risk persists.	Immediately protective for travel at short notice.
(b) Vaccine	Three injections given 2-4 weeks between first and second and 6 months between second and third. Expected to last 10 years.	Not applicable.	Single booster may be required after 10 years.	Equally protective as immunogloulin. Useful for young recurrent travellers.
Malaria	Tablets should be taken a few days prior to departure and continued regularly while in malarial zone. It is essential to continue taking tablets for 4 weeks after leaving zone (see *Malaria Prophylaxis*).	Not applicable.	Not applicable.	Pregnant women and newborn infants require special consideration.

* If vaccination is recorded on a new certificate, travellers are advised to retain thier old certificate until their new certificate is valid.
** The World Health Organisation state that vaccination against cholera cannot prevent the introduction of the infection into a country. The WHO therefore amended the International Health Regulations in 1973 so that *cholera vaccination should no longer be required of any traveller,* although some countries still request a certificate as a condition of entry or the granting of a visa.

P U B L I C A T I O N S

The following list is selective, but includes sources that are readily available and frequently updated.

HEALTH ADVICE FOR TRAVELLERS (T4) – DEPARTMENT OF HEALTH

These are available free by dialling (0800) 555 777. If more than ten copies are required, thay can be ordered form Health Publications Unit, NO 2 Site, Heywood Stores, Manchester Road, Heywood, Lancs OL10 2PZ. This is a yearly publication containing advice on how to reduce health risks, with a list, by country, of compulsory and recommended immunisations. It advises about travel insurance and entitlement to reduced cost medical treatment in other countries.

INTERNATIONAL TRAVEL AND HEALTH World Health Organisaiton, Geneva, yearly

This lists, by country, compulsory immunisations and the risk of malaria and gives the distributuion by geo graphical area of other health risks and appropriate advice. It is aimed particularly at national health adminis trations and is not recommended for the individual traveller without medical knowledge.

TRAVELLERS'S HEALTH (3RD EDITION) ed. R. Dawood, Oxford University Press, 1992.

A multi-author book by mostly tropical disease specialists. some medical knowledge is necessary to under stan the extensive coverage of many conditions met by the traveller. Most suitable for those residing long-term in tropical climates and highly motivatded to understatnd their health needs.

ABC OF HEALTHY TRAVEL E. Walker, G. Williams, British Medical Journal , 1989

An easy-to-read guide to the health problems of travel intended for the general practioner and informed lay person.

PRESERVATION OF PERSONAL HEALTH IN WARM CLIMATES

Ross Institute of Tropical Hygien, 1992, Aimed at the traveller, particularly those becoming resident abroad, A concise and detailed account of health problems, how they arise and how they may be modified.

BRITISH MEDICAL JOURNAL 1988 – WELL AWAY E. Walker, G. Williams.

Less detailed than the above, but more understandable for the average traveller without medical knowledge.

THE TRAVELLER'S HEALTH GUIDE A.C. Turner, Lascelles, 1985.

Aimed at the average traveller but with much more background and historical detail, which tends to dilute the main messages. Useful summaries at the end about immunisations for each country and about malaria prophylaxis.

STAY HEALTHY WHILE YOU TRAVEL Tim Symonds and Lesley Abdela, Columbus Press, 1988

An invaluable travel-size guide which gives the traveller basic information needed for safe travel in hot countries.

CARE IN THE AIR Air Transport Users Committee, 2nd Floor, Kinsway House, 103 Kingsway, London WC2B 6QX. Tel: (071) 242 3882.

Advice for handicappped travellers.

YOUR PATIENT AND AIR TRAVEL British Airways Health Centre, Passenger Clearance Department, Queens Building, Ground Floor (N121) Heathrow Airport, Hounslow, Middlesex TQW6 2JA. Tel: (081) 562 7070.

Useful booklet for medical practitioners with advice on fitness to travel and specific contra-indications.

THE CARE OF BABIES AND YOUNG CHILDREN IN THE TROPICS D. Morley, National Association for Maternal and Child Welfare, 1st Floor, 40-42 Osnaburgh Street, London NW1 3ND. Tel: (071) 383 4115.

HEALTH INFORMATION FOR INTERNATIONAL TRAVEL, available from Superintendent of Documents, US Govt Printing Office, Washington, DC 20402.

bottles refilled from the tap are a welcome extra income to hotel staff in many poorer countries. Order carbonated water instead.

Remember, ice-cubes may have been prepared from contaminated water, so avoid them. You can cool drinks by placing the bottle on ice or wrapping it in a damp cloth (it will cool by evaporation). Ask the tour operator on the spot, or other resident foreigners, whether the tap water is safe.

Tea (without milk) and other hot drinks are a good bet simply because the water has been boiled, although some unpleasant bugs can survive nearly half an hour of boiling.

So What Should I do About all of This?

1. A plastic thermos-type flask with a shoulder strap is a very useful item for travellers 'on trek' or taking a day excursion. Fill it up each day with water you know is clean (or purified) and take it with you to the beach, bush or in the car. Combined with a personal water-purifier, it is a great combination. Try squeezing a little fresh lime into the flask to freshen the taste.

2. If you are setting off up-country it is a good idea to take your own mug and cutlery.

3. Make sure your hands are clean when you eat food.

3. That 'under-the-weather-feeling' in the heat could be from dehydration. Women who are menstruating may also feel like that for a day or two, so drink a bottle of fizzy, non-alcoholic drink. It can provide swift therapy and will probably be hygienic.

MOSQUITOES

What About Mosquitoes?

When in the tropics, these insects spread diseases. Even in Mediterranean areas, you should take measures to restrict bites to a minimum as far as possible; mosquitoes can carry all sorts of nasty bugs. Take no prisoners – remember, it is them or you.

You must keep down the number of mosquito bites you receive on your trip. We cannot emphasise this too much. These insects can carry more than 80 different diseases (though not AIDS or Hepatitis B). Some may be extremely severe and amongst the most unpleasant ones are malaria, dengue fever and yellow fever. Reducing the risk will also keep down other flying insect bites which transmit viruses, bacteria, worms and protozoa which can harm your health.

The simplest way to ward off mosquitoes during romantic evenings on the verandah is to wear long sleeves, long trousers or skirts, and use a repellent at strategic parts of the body, particularly around the ankles.

Where am I Most Likely to be Plagued by Mosquitoes?

You will be at your most vulnerable to attack by the pool-side bar in the early evening, sitting on the terrace watching the sunset or in a restaurant for dinner and in bed. In addition, mosquitoes are most prevalent in monsoon seasons.

There are certain geographic hot-spots you need to be especially aware of, such as some tropical beaches at sun-up and in the evening. Beaches to be avoided are those with foliage nearby, very little breeze or stagnant water. In many hotels in tropical paradises, at dawn and in the evenings, the pool-side and dining area are virtually no-go zones without lashings of mosquito repellent. Watch out for hotel lobbies with indoor pools or pot plants. Mosquitoes do not like draughts and breezes. If you stay in a hotel on a coastline with a cooling breeze, or on a cruise ship, or sit under one of those great old ceiling fans, you are more or less OK. Air-conditioning in your bedroom will also help keep them out.

How do I Keep Mosquitoes Away?

Most chemists supply a variety of insect repellent – ask your chemist to recommend the right one for your needs.

Remember, measures to keep mosquitoes off will also help avoid the bites of other dangerous insects, including the tsetse fly which spreads sleeping sickness. Mosquito nets will give good protection (particularly if treated with an insecticide) but their effectiveness is vastly reduced if they are holed or if they touch any part of the body.

Do I Have to Keep Taking Anti-Malaria Tablets After I Get Home?

Yes. Remember, the malaria parasite goes through several life stages in your liver and red blood cells; you must continue to take the pills for at least four weeks after your return home. This suppresses the development of the red blood cell forms of the parasite. If you feel ill or have flu-like symptoms on your return, even a year later, you must tell your doctor that you have been in the tropics. Present-day anti-malaria drugs are not 100% effective. You could get malaria up to 12 months or more after your return.

What About Dengue Fever?

This unpleasant fever, like malaria, is carried by mosquitoes. It is prevalent in South-East Asia, the Pacific, Africa, the Caribbean and the Americas, including Puerto Rico. The first you know about it is a sudden onset of headache, severe muscle and joint pain (dengue fever is sometimes called 'breakbone fever') and recurring fever. A rash usually appears between the third and fifth day, starting on the body and spreading to limbs and face. A few days later it goes, with no serious complications. No vaccine is available, so you should be very careful to minimise contact with mosquitoes.

RABIES

Rabies is an ever-present danger in almost every country in the world, particularly in the tropics and sub-tropics. Never touch or even go near an animal abroad. Specifically forbid any children to go near dogs or cats, or wild animals that appear tame. Appearing tame can be an early-warning sign that the animal has rabies. British children in particular are not aware of rabid animals.

If you do get bitten, wash the bitten area well with soap and water. Apply tincture of iodine, if available. Get to a doctor fast. Cover the wound with a clean bandage or sterile gauze. It will help if the animal's owner can be traced and the animal observed for 10 to 14 days, to see if it dies, foaming at the mouth. If it does not, you might be able to discontinue the treatment. On the plus side, the modern vaccine HDCV is safe and not that painful; it is normally no longer necessary to have the jabs in your stomach.

If you are exposed to extra risks abroad you should have the pre-exposure rabies vaccine, known as the human diploid cell strain vaccine (HDCV), before you go. This is strongly recommended.

COUNTRY CURRENCY CODES

COUNTRY	CURRENCY	CODE
Afghanistan	Afghani	AFA
Albania	Lek	ALL
Algeria	Algerian Dinar	DZD
Andorra	Spanish Peseta	ESP
	French Franc	FRF
Angola	Kwanza	AOK
Anguilla	East Caribbean Dollar	XCD
Antarctica	No universal currency	-
Antigua & Barbuda	East Caribbean Dollar	XCD
Argentina	Argentine Peso	ARS
Aruba	Aruban Guilder	AWG
Australia	Australian Dollar	AUD
Austria	Schilling	ATS
Bahamas	Bahamian Dollar	BSD
Bahrain	Bahraini Dinar	BHD
Bangladesh	Taka	BDT
Barbados	Barbados Dollar	BBD
Belgium	Belgian Franc	BEF
Belize	Belize Dollar	BZD
Benin	CFA Franc	XOF
Bermuda	Bermudian Dollar	BMD
Bhutan	Indian Rupee	INR
	Ngultrum	BTN
Bolivia	Bolivian Peso	BOB
Bonaire	Netherland Antillian Guilder	ANG
Bosnia-Hercegovina	New Yugoslav Dinar	YUN
Botswana	Pula	BWP
Brazil	Brazil Cruzeiro	BRC
British Dep. Territories	Ocean Territory US Dollar	USD
Brunei	Brunei Dollar	BND
Bulgaria	Lev	BGL
Burkina Faso	CFA Franc	XOF
Burundi	Burundi Franc	BIF
Cambodia	Riel	KHR
Cameroon	CFA Franc	XAF
Canada	Canadian Dollar	CAD
Cape Verde Islands	Cape Verde Escudo	CVE
Cayman Islands	Cayman Island Dollar	KYD
Central African Republic	CFA Franc	XAF
Chad	CFA Franc	XAF
Chile	Chilean Peso	CLP
China, People's Republic of	Yuan Renminbi	CNY
Colombia	Colombian Peso	COP
CIS	Rouble	SUR
Comoro Islands	Comoro Franc	KMF
Congo	CFA Franc	XAF
Cook Islands	New Zealand Dollar	NZD
Costa Rica	Costa Rican Colon	CRC
Côte d'Ivoire	CFA Franc	XOF
Croatia	Croatian Dinar	HRD
Cuba	Cuban Peso	CUP
Curaçao	Netherland Antillian Guilder	ANG
Cyprus	Cyprus Pound	CYP
Czech Republic	Koruna	CSK
Denmark	Danish Krone	DKK
Djibouti	Djibouti Franc	DJF
Dominica	East Caribbean Dollar	XCD
Dominican Republic	Dominican Peso	DOP
Ecuador	Sucre	ESC
Egypt	Egyptian Pound	EGP
El Salvador	El Salvador Colón	SVC
Equatorial Guinea	CFA Franc	XAF
Estonia	Kroon	EEK
Ethiopia	Ethiopian Birr	ETB
Falkland Islands	Falkland Island Pound	FKP
Fiji	Fiji Dollar	FJD
Finland	Markka	FIM
France	French Franc	FRF
French Guiana	French Franc	FRF
French Overseas Possessions	French Franc	FRF
French Polynesia	CFP Franc	XPF
Gabon	CFA Franc	XAF
Gambia, The	Dalasi	GMD
Germany	Deutsche Mark	DEM
Ghana	Cedi	GHC
Gibraltar	Gibraltar Pound	GIP
Greece	Drachma	GRD
Greenland	Danish Krone	DKK
Grenada	East Caribbean Dollar	XCD
Guadeloupe	French Franc	FRF
Guatemala	Quetzal	GTQ
Guinea Republic	Guinea Franc	GNF
Guinea-Bissau	Guinea-Bissau Peso	GWP
Guyana	Guyana Dollar	GYD
Haiti	Gourde	HTG
	US Dollar	USD
Honduras	Lempira	HNL
Hong Kong	Hong Kong Dollar	HKD
Hungary	Forint	HUF
Iceland	Iceland Krona	ISK
India	Indian Rupee	INR
Indonesia	Rupiah	IDR
Iran	Iranian Rial	IRR
Iraq	Iraqi Dinar	IQD
Ireland, Republic of	Irish Punt	IEP
Israel	Shekel	ILS
Italy	Italian Lira	ITL
Jamaica	Jamaican Dollar	JMD
Japan	Yen	JPY
Jordan	Jordanian Dollar	JOD
Kenya	Kenyan Shilling	KES
Kiribati	Australian Dollar	AUD
Korea (North)	North Korean Won	KPW
Korea (South)	Won	KRW
Kuwait	Kuwaiti Dinar	KWD
Laos	Kip	LAK
Latvia	Rouble	SUR
Lebanon	Lebanese Pound	LBP

Three-letter codes assigned to each of the world's currencies by the International Standards Organisation.

COUNTRY	CURRENCY	CODE
Lesotho	Rand	ZAR
	Loti	LSL
Liberia	Liberian Dollar	LRD
Libya	Libyan Dinar	LYD
Liechtenstein	Swiss Franc	CHF
Lithuania	Lithuanian Rouble	LAR
Luxembourg	Luxembourg Franc	LUF
Macau	Pataca	MOP
Macedonia	New Yugoslav Dinar	YUX
Madagascar	Malagasy Franc	MGF
Malawi	Kwacha	MWK
Malaysia	Malaysian Ringgit	MYR
Maldives Republic	Rufiyaa	MVR
Mali	CFA Franc	XOF
Malta	Maltese Lira	MTL
Martinique	French Franc	FRF
Mauritania	Ouguiya	MRO
Mauritius	Mauritius Rupee	MUR
Mexico	Mexican Peso	MXN
Monaco	French Franc	FRF
Mongolia	Tugrik	MNT
Montserrat	East Caribbean Dollar	XCD
Morocco	Moroccan Dirham	MAD
Mozambique	Metical	MZM
Myanmar	Kyat	BUK
Namibia	Rand	ZAR
Nauru	Australian Dollar	AUD
Nepal	Nepalese Rupee	NPR
Netherlands, The	Netherland Guilder	NLG
New Caledonia	CFP Franc	XPF
New Zealand	New Zealand Dollar	NZD
Nicaragua	Córdoba	NIC
Niger	CFA Franc	XOF
Nigeria	Naira	NGN
Norway	Norwegian Krone	NOK
Oman	Rial Omani	OMR
Pacific Islands of Micronesia	US Dollar	USD
Pakistan	Pakistani Rupee	PKR
Panama	Balboa	PAB
	US Dollar	USD
Papua New Guinea	Kina	PGK
Paraguay	Guaraní	PYG
Peru	Nuevo Sol	PES
Philippines	Philippine Peso	PHP
Poland	Zloty	PLZ
Portugal	Portuguese Escudo	PTE
Puerto Rico	US Dollar	USD
Qatar	Qatari Rial	QAR
Réunion	French Franc	FRF
Romania	Leu	ROL
Rwanda	Rwanda Franc	RWF
Saba	Netherland Antillian Guilder	ANG
St Eustatius	Netherland Antillian Guilder	ANG
St Kitts & Nevis	East Caribbean Dollar	XCD
St Lucia	East Caribbean Dollar	XCD
St Maarten	Netherland Antillian Guilder	ANG
St Vincent & the Grenadines	East Caribbean Dollar	XCD
San Marino	Italian Lira	ITL
São Tomé e Príncipe	Dobra	STD
Saudi Arabia	Saudi Riyal	SAR
Senegal	CFA Franc	XOF
Seychelles	Seychelles Rupee	SCR
Sierra Leone	Leone	SLL
Singapore	Singapore Dollar	SGD
Slovak Republic	Koruna	CSK
Slovenia	Slovene Tolar	SIT
Solomon Islands	Solomon Islands Dollar	SBD
Somalia	Somali Shilling	SOS
South Africa	Rand	ZAR
Spain	Spanish Peseta	ESP
Sri Lanka	Sri Lanka Rupee	LKR
Sudan	Sudanese Pound	XSD
Suriname	Suriname Guilder	SRG
Swaziland	Lilangeni	SZL
Sweden	Swedish Krona	SEK
Switzerland	Swiss Franc	CHF
Syria	Syrian Pound	SYP
Taiwan (China)	New Taiwan Dollar	TWD
Tanzania	Tanzanian Shilling	TZS
Thailand	Baht	THB
Togo	CFA Franc	XOF
Tonga	Pa'anga	TOP
Trinidad & Tobago	Trinidad & Tobago Dollar	TTD
Tunisia	Tunisian Dinar	TND
Turkey	Turkish Lira	TRL
Turks & Caicos Islands	US Dollar	USD
Tuvalu	Australian Dollar	AUD
Uganda	Uganda Shilling	UGX
United Arab Emirates	UAE Dirham	AED
United Kingdom	Pound Sterling	GBP
United States of America	US Dollar	USD
US Islands		
American Samoa	US Dollar	USD
Guam	US Dollar	USD
US Virgin Islands	US Dollar	USD
Uruguay	Uruguayan Peso	UYP
Vanuatu	Vatu	VUV
Vatican City	Italian Lira	ITL
Venezuela	Bolívar	VEB
Vietnam	Dong	VND
Virgin Islands, British	US Dollar	USD
Western Samoa	Tala	WST
Yemen, Republic of	Yemeni Rial	YER
	Yemeni Dinar	YDD
Yugoslavia	New Yugoslav Dinar	YUN
Zaïre	Zaïre	ZRZ
Zambia	Kwacha	ZMK
Zimbabwe	Zimbabwe Dollar	ZWD

THE DISABLED TRAVELLER

INTRODUCTION

Disability – whether short term or permanent – does not stop people *wanting* to travel for pleasure, or *needing* to travel for business. Arranging travel for someone who has impaired vision or hearing, or who may be confined to a wheelchair, can be an alarming prospect, but does not have to be an impossible problem.

Careful and sometimes painstaking planning is needed, but provided you and your client are frank with one another over what you can and cannot do, there is no reason why both of you should not be happy with the outcome.

What disablement means: Disability can take many forms: to be disabled means having an impairment which takes away abilities which someone would otherwise be able to enjoy.

When a person is confined to a wheelchair, or can only move about on sticks and crutches, their disability is only too evident. Although they are likely to have the greatest difficulties in travelling, there are many more people who may not be obviously disabled, but have some problem which can make it difficult to move about easily and to enjoy a holiday without problems or worries. People who have had strokes or are arthritic, blind or epileptic are likely to be among these.

There are also many people whose mobility is impaired temporarily, such as those who may have broken limbs, or women who are in the late stages of pregnancy.

Travel opportunities and choice for disabled people have grown dramatically over the past few years, and travel agents can play an important role in ensuring the success of what may, in many cases, be a first trip away from home.

HELPING THE TRAVELLER

In order to help a disabled traveller to plan a holiday or business trip, the most important thing is to obtain as much information as possible. Find out when, where and for how long the person has travelled on previous occasions, and what problems, if any, were encountered.

It is also necessary to know whether he or she will be travelling alone and, if so, whether he or she is able to be completely independent – in a different environment, possibly in an unfamiliar climate that could cause discomfort, and where language may be a problem. Help will usually be at hand at terminals and in hotels, but should not be expected nor relied upon unless confirmed in writing beforehand. If complete independence is impossible, he or she *must* be accompanied by someone who can give the extra help needed. If this is out of the question, there are some organisations specialising in holidays for severely disabled unaccompanied people, both in this country and abroad. For details, contact the *Holiday Care Service* at the address below.

The name of the person's disability and its effects are also vital information. There are many kinds of disability, both temporary and permanent. Not all confine someone to a wheelchair or limit their mobility; a broken leg creates different problems from a heart condition or respiratory complaint. The following checklist covers the kind of information that needs to be communicated to tour operators, carriers and hoteliers:

- The name of the disability;
- The limitations to mobility – for example, ability to walk unaided, the use of a stick or crutches, the need to hold someone's arm to help over long distances;
- Whether the use of a wheelchair is permanent, most of the time, or for distance only;
- Whether transfer from a wheelchair into a coach, air or train seat is easy or difficult;
- Whether one or both legs need to be fully extended whilst travelling;
- The overall dimensions of the wheelchair, whether it is collapsable and if it is battery operated;
- Any other effects of the disability;
- Whether the person is being accompanied by someone who can provide all the personal assistance needed whilst on holiday and, if not, whether help will be required with feeding, washing, bathing, toileting, dressing or simply pushing the wheelchair. If this kind of help is needed, and the traveller will not be accompanied by a friend or relative, it will probably be necessary to join a special holiday for disabled people where such assistance is available: *Holiday Care Service* has details;

Any special requirements for the holiday or the journey, such as a special diet, oxygen or other aids;

Any other information which may be helpful to the travel agent or tour operator in ensuring the most comfortable trip;

If travelling as a group, apart from the usual questions about budget, it is useful to know the proportion of able-bodied to disabled people; the nature of the disabilities; the number of wheelchairs; how many of those in wheelchairs are totally confined to them; whether or not there is a doctor or nurse in the party; and the age groups involved.

ARRANGING THE TOUR

Booking an inclusive tour: The *Holiday Care Service* provides a list of operators whose programmes can be considered by a disabled traveller (some mention this in their brochures and give a contact name and telephone number). If a particular country or resort has been asked for, the service can tell you which operators serve that destination, and in some cases will be able to give detailed information about facilities for disabled people in hotels there.

Communication is essential when booking a disabled client on a package tour. It is the travel agent's task to provide all the information a tour operator might need to ensure the success of the trip for the client.

Misunderstandings will be minimised if the enquiry and booking are backed up with a letter clearly stating the client's needs, and requesting written confirmation that these can be met. The points to be covered will include transport to, from and at the destination; accommodation; and facilities at the resort and during excursions. The paragraphs which follow on transport and accommodation will also help to ask the tour operator the right questions.

Arrangements for the independent traveller: As long as the necessary information is available, it should not be difficult to meet the requirements for a business trip or holiday – but every detail must be double-checked, particularly on a complicated journey where the risk of a problem is greater.

By air: Where there is a choice of airlines, check on their policy and attitude towards carrying disabled people; the facilities they have for them (both on the ground and in the air); the type of aircraft (some are more comfortable than others); the availability of special diets; the method of boarding and disembarking people; and so on.

The time of day for travelling can be important to someone with a disability, as can the difference between a non-stop flight or one which involves stopovers.

The most comprehensive advice on air travel for disabled people is found in 'Care in the Air', available free from the Air Transport Users Committee, 2nd Floor, Kingsway House, 103 Kingsway, London WC2B 6QX. Tel: (071) 242 3882. Fax: (071) 831 4132.

Each UK airport gives details of the services that they can offer to disabled travellers. For information contact the relevant airport. The 'Welcome to Gatwick' publication covers provision for disabled people at Gatwick Airport. This is available from Gatwick Airport Ltd, Gatwick, West Sussex RH6 0HZ.

The Heathrow Airport 'A Commitment for People with Special Needs' booklet provides information for disabled travellers who wish to fly to and from the airport. This is available from Heathrow Airport Ltd, Hounslow, Middlesex, TW6 1JH. Tel: (081) 745 6156.

British Airways publishes a leaflet intended as a general guide to doctors entitled 'Your Patient and Air Travel'.

Details of facilities and services for disabled people at over 280 airports in 40 countries are contained in 'Access Travel; Airports', published by the US Department of Transportation, and available from Access America, Washington, DC 20202, USA.

Publications such as these should only provide preliminary guidance; checking is still important.

Check to make certain the arrangements for checking in and boarding and remember that equal care is needed at the end of the journey; ensure any airport transfer arrangements are appropriate, and provide the traveller with the telephone numbers needed to confirm arrangements for the homeward journey; if there is a change in the time, airline or airport, the new arrangements will have to be checked for their suitability.

Sea: An increasing number of ferries have incorporated special facilities for disabled people and, where there is a choice of routes and/or companies, you can check which offers the best facilities. Not all the vessels in a fleet will have the same facilities.

The *Holiday Care Service* keeps details of what is currently available; whether or not a ferry or hovercraft offers special facilities, it is still vitally important that the company is informed in advance that someone is disabled.

When booking a crossing for a disabled passenger, ensure the company knows the nature of the disability and the sort of help needed during the journey.

Cruises can be especially attractive to elderly and disabled people, and most shipping lines offering cruises or fly/cruises are used to carrying disabled passengers. However, the following problems should be borne in mind:

- A cruise is almost certainly out of the question for someone who cannot walk at all and is unaccompanied;
- Shore excursions may not be possible, especially if tendering is involved and passengers have to board launches;
- Coaches on shore excursions are unlikely to have any special facility for a disabled person;
- Bad weather can be distressing for everyone, but especially so for someone not too steady on their feet or confined to a wheelchair.

When booking a disabled client on a cruise, and they are confined to a wheelchair, obtain the following information before making definite reservations:

- Width of lift floors, and whether they offer access to all parts of the ship;
- Width of cabin and toilet/bathroom doors; whether the doors open outwards, and if not, whether they block the plumbing; whether any existing steps at the doorways can be ramped temporarily;
- Whether any cabins have an extra basin in the room to save some trips to the bathroom; where they are located; how much they cost, and their location in relation to lifts, etc;
- Whether a wheelchair user is excluded from any part of the ship because of stairs, narrow doorways or other obstacles;
- Which excursions ashore require a launch to be used, and whether help would be available if the stairs down to the launch cannot be used; whether the gangplank used by passengers is too steep for a wheelchair user, and whether the one used by the crew is any lower and could be used instead;
- What special arrangements might be needed at the start and finish of the cruise;
- What special diets are available;
- Any restrictions on the type of wheelchair used;
- Availability of laundry and/or launderette facilities.

Road and **Rail:** The provision of facilities for disabled travellers in coaches, taxis, hire cars and trains varies considerably from country to country. Even where there are specially adapted vehicles, as in the United Kingdom, these may not be available on all routes or at more than a few locations. Check with the relevant carrier for further information.

British Rail in the UK has done much recently to improve the service offered to disabled passengers. This includes *Motor Rail* services; all terminals now have wheelchairs available to assist disabled people. For full details ask for the 'Motor Rail' brochure, available from stations, travel centres and BR-appointed travel agents. 'Disabled Person's Railcard' gives discounts to holders and is available to people with a variety of disabilities. For information ask for the leaflet 'Disabled Person's Railcard' at stations, travel centres and post offices, which gives details and includes an application form. Blind or partially sighted travellers who do not have a 'Disabled Person's Railcard' are entitled to discounts on standard and season tickets. Guide dogs accompanying blind people are always conveyed free of charge. British Rail can give assistance to disabled travellers from the moment they leave the door, through to the time they reach their destination. For full details ask for the 'British Rail and Disabled Travellers' leaflet available free from all stations and travel centres. The leaflet also gives the name and addresses of the Area Manager who should be contacted in advance of travel. This gives the opportunity for all the relevant information to be compiled so that a comprehensive service can be offered at the time of travel.

Note: Since November 1989 all new *licensed London cabs* have been equipped to carry wheelchairs. There are now approximately 3900 cabs that are capable of this, and it is hoped that by 1999 all cabs in service will be able to take wheelchairs on board. These cabs

are available from cab ranks at stations, airports, hotels across London and can be hailed in the normal way. Where there are no special facilities, it may still be possible for a disabled person to travel by road or rail, always ensuring that prior notification is given to the operator, giving precise details of route and timing. Where appropriate, help may then be provided.
The *Holiday Care Service* can advise on what services are available in the UK and abroad, but details and availability will need to be checked carefully.
Car rental: Some international car rental firms have cars equipped with hand controls for drivers with lower limb disability. For further details, contact car hire companies.

ACCOMMODATION

The nature and degree of the disability will dictate the type of accommodation required. The points below will be important, and are particularly relevant to wheelchair users; however, when booking, ask what facilities will be needed for minimum and maximum comfort, request these facilities, back up your request with a letter, and ask for confirmation in writing that they are available.

Access: For wheelchair access, entrance or side doors need to be ramped or level, with a minimum width of 75cm. Interior doors also need to be at least this width, with no steps leading into public rooms (restaurant, lounge, bar, toilets, etc).
There are many disabled people who do not use wheelchairs, but are unable to use steps or stairs. A number of accommodation guides, details of which can be obtained from the *Holiday Care Service*, show where there are ground-floor bedrooms. Most of these also show where there is a lift available, so even if there are no ground-floor bedrooms, access may be just as feasible because there is a lift. If making enquiries about a hotel or guest-house with a lift, do make sure that the bedroom is as near to the lift as possible, and do ask whether there are any steps in the corridor between the lift doors and the bedroom.

General facilities: If ground-floor bedrooms are not available, there should be a lift large enough to take a wheelchair, ie at least 120cm deep by 80cm wide.

Bedroom: The door should be at least 75cm wide; there should be sufficient turning space for a wheelchair, ie 120cm by 120cm, and free width of at least 80cm to one side of the bed.
Bathroom: The door should be at least 75cm wide; enough room is needed to enter in a wheelchair and close the door, with space beside the WC for a wheelchair to enable sideways transfer; support rails near the bath and WC are also needed.

Outside: There should be a route without steps and with a firm smooth surface which wheelchairs can use; this would ideally facilitate access to the swimming pool or beach without needing to negotiate steps; the accommodation should be in a central position with shopping and entertainment facilities within easy reach, otherwise specially arranged transport would be needed to enable the disabled holidaymaker to go on trips or excursions.

The Accessible Symbol: The *Hotel and Holiday Consortium*, made up of 21 organisations including ABTA, the BTA and the British Hotels, Restaurants & Caterers Association, has drawn up a range of minimum standards which must be met by an establishment before the Accessible Symbol can be awarded. Requirements for the new symbol are as follows:

A public entrance to the building must be accessible to disabled people from a setting-down or car-parking point;

Where an establishment has a car park, a parking space must be reserved for a disabled guest on request;

Disabled people must have access to the following areas (if provided): reception, restaurant or dining room, lounge, TV lounge (unless TV is provided in the bedroom) and bar;

A minimum of one guest room with bath or shower and WC facilities en suite, which is suitable for a wheelchair user, should be provided. Where these facilities are not en suite, a unisex WC compartment and a bath or shower room suitable for a wheelchair user must be provided on the same floor level.

ORGANISATIONS

HOLIDAY CARE SERVICE

2 Old Bank Chambers, Station Road, Horley, Surrey RH6 9HW. Tel: (0293) 774 535. Fax: (0293) 784 647. Minicom: (0293) 776 943.
The *Holiday Care Service*, which was established as a registered charity in 1981, is the UK's central source of holiday information for people whose age, disability, or other personal or family circumstances make it difficult for them to find a holiday. An entirely non-commercial organisation, it provides details of accommodation, transport, facilities or publications which are most appropriate to the person's needs, although it does not make reservations direct. A Holiday Helper scheme is also run by the *Holiday Care Service*, which matches a volunteer to act as a helper on a holiday.
At present the following areas of information are covered by the service; new topics are being added continuously.
Overseas holidays for disabled people: Planning and booking the holiday; insurance; specialised group holidays; commercial packages; cruises; handling agents; self-catering; camping and caravanning; car hire; pilgrimages; serviced accommodation; transport advice; resort information and hotel descriptions for the major European tourist destinations.
UK holidays for disabled people: Specialist commercial and voluntary operators; access, accommodation and catering guides; self-catering accommodation; hotels and guest-houses; special interest and activity holidays; farm holidays; specially adapted accommodation; group facilities; university and college accommodation; holiday camps and centres; accommodation where personal or nursing care is provided; boating holidays; coach, rail, taxi and ambulance information; car hire; non-smoking accommodation; holidays suitable for those with epilepsy; holidays for people with learning difficulties; opportunities for the mentally ill; escorts; financial assistance; information for deaf and/or blind people; various holidays for physically, mentally and/or sensorily handicapped children; use of oxygen on holiday; holiday facilities for kidney dialysis.
It is vital that adequate insurance cover is arranged. One of the most difficult problems disabled people have faced in the past has been the inclusion in policies of a 'pre-existing medical condition' exclusion clause. These still appear in the policies offered by quite a number of tour operators. Do check very carefully that the policy offered does not have this clause. Even those who exclude nothing often require that a 'fitness to travel' certificate is obtained from a doctor beforehand. The *Holiday Care Service* offers an insurance policy specifically designed for disabled travellers. Details are contained in the organisation's 'Holiday Insurance' leaflet.
As a travel agent, it would be useful to find out how your client got on, if anything went wrong or if the client has any handy hints to pass on. Any feedback, whether good or bad, is helpful to you and to disabled people.

RADAR

(Royal Association for Disability and Rehabilitation), 25 Mortimer Street, London W1N 8AB. Tel: (071) 637 5400. Fax: (071) 637 1827. Minicom: (071) 637 5315. RADAR is a national organisation working with and for physically disabled people. It acts as a pressure group to improve the environment for disabled people, campaigning for their rights and needs, and challenging negative attitudes and stereotypes. *RADAR* is particularly involved with education, health, social services, employment, housing, mobility and holidays. The organisation publishes several books, including 'Holidays and Travel Abroad. A Guide for the Disabled' and 'Holidays in the British Isles. A Guide For Disabled People', as well as a number of fact sheets covering all aspects of travel.

ACROSS TRUST

Bridge House, 70/72 Bridge Road, East Molesey, Surrey KT8 9HF. Tel: (081) 783 1355. Fax: (081) 941 2730. *Across Trust* arranges holidays for the severely disabled through *Jumbulance Holidays Across Europe*.

BREAK

20 Hooks Hill Road, Sherringham, Norfolk NR26 8NL. Tel: (0263) 823 170. Fax: (0263) 825 560. *Break* caters mainly for physically and mentally handicapped children and adults. *Break* can supply an information pack which also includes an application form. Write to the address above.

BRITISH RED CROSS SOCIETY

9 Grosvenor Crescent, London SW1X 7EJ. Tel: (071) 235 5454. Fax: (071) 245 6315. An information pack can be supplied on request. The *Red Cross* will provide regional contact addresses and telephone numbers, so that local help can be found.
Much of the information contained above is based on material supplied by *Holiday Care* Service; the publishers wish to thank them for their help in preparing this section of the 'World Travel Guide'.

THE WORLD OF ISLAM

INTRODUCTION

Mohammed, the Prophet of Islam, was born in AD570, the posthumous son of a Hashemite from Mecca. His mother died when he was about six and he was brought up by his grandfather, who had him set up as a merchant by the time he was 25. His teachings began around 612, but despite gaining some followers he was rejected by the townsmen and was forced to leave for Medina in 622. For the next decade he organised the Commonwealth of Islam, creating a community based on the will of God. A considerable amount of conflict was caused by his activities, mainly with the Meccans, but by his death in 632 many of the Arab tribes had been subdued.

Within a year of the Prophet's death, the Muslims had advanced into Iraq, and by the early years of the following century had reached the River Indus and the Pyrénées. In the context of this remarkable expansion, the victory of Charles Martel at Tours (732) must rank as one of the most decisive in history. Most of the countries which were conquered during this period still remain Islamic or else have large Muslim populations.

The history of Islam and its influence on Christian Europe, with which it coexisted uneasily for centuries, repays careful study. Certain European countries, notably Spain, Portugal and Sicily, have fascinating reminders of both cultures; it is also worth remembering that during the Middle Ages the Islamic world was far advanced compared with those of the west in the fields of philosophy, medicine, science, geography, poetry and music. Many classical works only survived because they were translated into Arabic during the so-called 'Dark Ages' before being brought to Western Europe in the 12th century; the rediscovery of the works of Aristotle in this way was of fundamental importance to the development of Western philosophy. During the Crusades (1100-1290), armies of Christian Europe and Islam came into violent conflict, and there is little doubt that it was the Muslims who in general displayed greater tolerance and humanity. In recent years an understanding of Islam has often been obscured by political complexities, and the following section is an attempt to explain some of the important tenets of the faith. Anyone planning to visit a Muslim country should familiarise themselves with at least a little of the history, culture and beliefs of this increasingly influential religion. Many books cover the subject in considerably more depth than is possible here.

ISLAM

The Islamic religion is based on the 'submission to the will of God (Allah)'. Islam has teachings for the mind, body and spirit; also laws on education, economy, politics, science, crimes and punishment, human behaviour and all aspects of morality in daily life for individuals (men and women of any race), families, governments and whole societies anywhere in the world.

The **Quran/Koran** and **Sunnah** are the two basic sources of Islamic teachings, law and order. The *Koran* is the main religious book for Muslims; it is the spoken word of **Allah** (God) and has 30 volumes which contain 114 chapters (or *Sura*) in Arabic. The *Sunnah* is complementary to the *Quran* and contains the sayings of the **Prophet Mohammed** and his way of life.

The Prophet received the spoken word of Allah containing the foundation of the faith (the *Quran/Koran*) while in **Mecca** in the 7th century AD. The city is now Islam's principal holy city. **Medina**, also in Saudi Arabia, a little over 300km (200 miles) due north of Mecca, is second only to Mecca in importance. It was to Medina that Mohammed and his followers moved after his monotheistic beliefs were given a hostile reception by some Meccans. The journey from Mecca to Medina *(Hijra)* is celebrated each year, the event being taken as the starting point of the Islamic calendar (Ah 1). Prior to their return to Mecca the Prophet and his followers made a pilgrimage *(Hajj)* to the Holy City during the month of *Ramadan*. After Mohammed's death in AD632 temporal authority was assumed by a series of khalifahs, with various sects developing. Today the strongest sects within Islam (that is those with the most followers) are the *Sunni* (in Indonesia, India, Malaysia, Pakistan, Bangladesh, Syria, parts of Lebanon, Egypt, north Africa, Saudi Arabia, the Gulf States and large parts of Turkey) and the *Shi'ite* (in Iraq, southern Lebanon and the greater part of Iran).

THE FIVE PILLARS OF ISLAM

There are five basic religious tenets, generally called the *Five Pillars of Islam:*

Shahada – The profession of faith: 'I testify there is no God but Allah and Mohammed is the Messenger of Allah.'

Salah – The faithful must turn towards Mecca and recite a prescribed prayer five times daily at dawn, noon, *asr* (between noon and sunset), sunset and before sleeping. In some Muslim countries the activities of the day stop at the time of prayer. The *muezzin* calls to prayer, chanting from the minaret of each mosque. For obvious practical reasons, not all Muslims go to a mosque for prayer. Shopkeepers and businessmen will offer prayers on their premises, usually on a mat set to one side. Non-Muslims should not be embarrassed if they happen to witness this.

The most important prayer is the Friday prayer, delivered from a pulpit of the mosque by a prayer leader. In many Muslim countries, Friday is a holiday, with banks and shops closed all day.

Zakat – A form of almsgiving which was originally an obligatory act of charity, and is now a property tax for the benefit of widows, the poor and children within the community. It is a religious duty to give alms to the needy, especially during Ramadan.

Ramadan – All Muslims are required to fast during the Holy Month of Ramadan (a lunar month of four weeks, which falls 11 days earlier each year, depending on sightings of the moon). All Muslims abstain totally from food, drink, sex and tobacco from dawn to dusk. Non-Muslims should respect this practice and wherever possible avoid infringing these laws in front of Muslims, since this would be considered an insult. Practically speaking, when Ramadan falls during the summer months, the abstentions become a test of endurance. Often shops and restaurants will open much earlier and close during the afternoons and in smaller towns some will close altogether, but some businesses do open at night. At sunset most, if not all, Muslims will break their fast, and little business or travel will be practical for the visitor at this time.

Originally the festival celebrated the month during which the *Koran* was first revealed and later when Mohammed's followers won a great victory over opponents to his faith in Mecca. *Eid al-Fitr*, an official holiday in some Muslim countries of three or more days, takes place at the end of Ramadan. It is a celebratory feast when those luxuries which have been denied are enjoyed with relish.

Hajj – The pilgrimage to Mecca. Every Muslim who can afford it and is fit enough must make the journey. Some Muslims, especially those in Saudi Arabia, make the pilgrimage more than once. At the time of the pilgrimage, the pilgrim *(hajji/hajja)* enters the holy precincts of Mecca wearing a white, seamless garment *(ihram)* and performs the sevenfold circumambulation of the *Kaabah* (the black stone housed in the centre of the Holy mosque) and the sevenfold course between the little hills of Safa and Marwah near Mecca. Muslims perform this in memory of Haggar who is mentioned in the Old Testament, who ran seven times between Safa and Marwah seeking a spring for her thirsty son. The *Hajj* lasts from the seventh to the eighth of *Dhu-al-Hijja*. On the ninth day pilgrims stand praying on the mountain **Arafat** – an essential part of the ritual of the *Hajj*. The pilgrimage formally ends with *Eid al-Adha* (Feast of the Sacrifice), which is an official holiday of four or more days, in which a camel, sheep or horned domestic animal is sacrificed on the tenth of *Dhu-al-Hijja*. After shaving the head the *ihram* is discarded and normal dress *(ihlal)* resumed. As long as the *hajji/hajja* is in a *muhrim* (sanctified place) he/she must refrain from sexual intercourse, the shedding of blood, hunting and the uprooting of plants. All of the different activities of the *Hajj* are symbolic and have stories associated with them.

SOCIAL CUSTOMS

Muslims regard Islam as an integral part of daily life, resulting in an ordered society in which a man's social, spiritual and economic status is clearly defined. This way of life is for the most part drawn from the *Koran*. Greetings and replies in particular are formal and stylised. Manners and courtesy reflect a deeply held convention of hospitality and mutual respect. It is customary for Muslim households to extend hospitality to people whom Western society would disregard socially. For instance, tradition dictates that anyone who appears at meal times must be invited to share the meal, and this would apply as much to strangers or tradesmen, whatever the reason for their call, as it would to friends or relatives. Hospitality was a part of Arab culture before Islam and the laws and teaching of Islam reinforced it. Subjects such as illness or death are not surrounded by taboo as they are in many Western societies, and are discussed with frankness by all. Muslims are encouraged to have close relationships and keep an open heart, an understanding of others and to try and help with their problems.

The label of a family can cover any number of individuals rather than just those related by blood ties. Arab families are close-knit, and the importance of family unity cannot be stressed too strongly. Inter-family disputes are a cause for public shame and require immediate attention.

WOMEN AND ISLAM

Probably the aspect of Islam which non-Muslims find most difficult to accept is the treatment of women, and it is the aspect most deeply criticised. The demand that women should dress and behave modestly is seen by Muslims as symbolic of the importance and value placed on women as mothers and guardians of the family. The Prophet encouraged monogamy although polygamy was allowed, provided that the husband was in a position to provide for all wives and treated them equally. Polygamy may also occur in special circumstances, such as when the number of women in society is larger than the number of men, or when the wife is chronically ill or sterile. Today monogamy is more common, polygamy being allowed but not encouraged. Many, but not all, royal families have employed polygamy to ensure succession, and for practical reasons such as providing ministers and administrators, but otherwise it is not the norm.

The theory behind modest dress and veil for women is to preserve respect, dignity and virginity and safeguard them from interference or abuse by men, although for some time this tradition has been slowly relaxed in many countries through contact with non-Islamic cultures. Other traditions, however, such as arranged marriages or the seating of females upstairs or at a separate table in a restaurant, are still rigidly observed. Many of the public traditions serve to distinguish male dominance in society. Women are allowed to work in some cases, especially when the need arises, but the Islamic code of dress and modesty must always be observed. In some jobs it is obligatory to have female teachers or doctors, for example when dealing with Muslim girls or women. Today in the Arab and Muslim world, many Muslim women are working because of financial need and because of the liberalising of religious practice or observance.

Women invariably rule the household and the family. Given the importance of the family, this affords the older women considerable influence. Younger women, however, hold no such position and although many Islamic countries have relaxed restrictions and women have begun to play an active part in many spheres of activity (particularly in medicine, education, public services and the media), a number of countries still follow traditional practices.

The difference between the measure of adherence to Koranic practices of one country and another is most easily judged by the degree of freedom afforded to women. Fundamentalism, enjoying a resurgence in many Islamic countries, is as much as anything else an articulation of the resentment felt at the interference of stronger foreign economies in their internal affairs. However, this can often manifest itself in a retreat back to almost medieval traditions as a positive form of disapproval of the decadence of the West. Thus, in many countries the position of women can be protected and their role in society appreciated, whilst at the same time their ability to control their own lives is largely denied.

Note: The above account of women and Islam, which describes widely-held beliefs and customs, should not be taken as authoritative. *Women in Islam*, published by the Islamic Foundation, gives an account of one of the sessions of the International Islamic Conference held in London in 1976. The session was addressed by two Islamic women with a Western background and followed by a discussion. *Women in Islam* looks at issues more deeply and is a useful starting point for those who wish to learn about issues in Islam today.

SOCIAL CONVENTIONS

Forms of address: The Arabic equivalent of 'Mr' is *Sayyid* (for Muslims) and *Khawaja* (for Christians), while married women should be addressed as *Sayyida* or *Sitt*, and girls as *Anissa*. In Islam it is also encouraged to call a Muslim man 'my brother' and a Muslim woman 'my sister'. Islam regards men as equal, but social conventions, hospitality and politeness of Islamic societies prevent overfamiliarity.

Greeting: There follows a short list of Arabic greetings and phrases. The transliterations are phonetic and intended to assist pronunciation.

Marharba - Hello;
Markhabtain - Hello (reply);
Ma'a Salama - Goodbye;
Ahlan wa sahlan - Welcome;
Ahlan feekum - Welcome (reply);
Sabah al-khir - Good morning;
Sabah innoor - Good morning (reply).

These were all originally purely Arabic greetings. In Islam the common greeting still widely used is *Assalmu Alaykum* ('Peace be with you').

Note: Throughout the Arab world English is widely spoken in business, and it is not essential for English-speakers to learn Arabic. However, attempts to say even a few words and phrases in Arabic are generally very much appreciated.

Business: This must *always* be conducted on a personal introduction or invitation basis only. Without invitations or introductions a business visit, while being courteously received, will ultimately amount to nothing. Honesty is the basis of all business dealings in Islamic countries and a word is a bond. Arguing and haggling over prices is the norm and an Arabic tradition of buying and selling. Once a bargain has been struck the deal cannot be renegotiated or cancelled unless either party cannot raise the money.
Clothing conventions: These are derived in part from religious beliefs and in part from climatic necessity. Western business suits are only practical during the summer if they are lightweight. Businessmen will be accepted if they wear open-necked shirts, as long as they are well turned out. Women are advised not to wear revealing clothes as this will attract unwelcome attention or ridicule at best, and resentment and hostility at worst. Women should also cover their heads when entering a Mosque. Muslim women are generally advised to show face and hands only.
Do not sit in a position which places the soles of the feet towards anyone, as this is considered a deliberate insult. Shoes should be removed upon entering a Mosque or a house.
Sexual politics: Remember the position that women hold in Islam (see above), and that some gestures considered normal by westerners can be interpreted as serious insults. Divorce and marriage are considered civil matters and while divorce is not a common practice it is relatively easy. Adultery is considered an insult to Allah and society and severely punished, often by flogging, but sometimes by stoning to death.
Giving and receiving: Always use the right hand. To offer gifts with the left hand is considered an insult.
Drug use: Although many countries cultivate hashish or marijuana, it is not culturally acceptable and in the majority of countries the possession, use or trading of drugs is severely punished. Drug abuse is not permitted in Islam, particularly hard drugs such as heroin, morphine or cocaine, but also any drug which interferes with the consciousness, reasoning or judgement, affecting work, study or family life.
Alcohol: The consumption of alcohol is forbidden by law. Many non-practising Muslims will, however, drink alcohol and will offer them to guests when outside their own country. Most Islamic countries (with the exception of Libya, Saudi Arabia and Kuwait) permit the sale and consumption of alcohol by non-Muslims. Generally the sale of alcohol will be confined to international hotels, but visitors may in some cases buy alcohol from wholesalers with a permit from their company or local Embassy. Bars are usually closed during Ramadan. Never drink alcohol while eating. Drunkenness is considered disgraceful, and the visitor is advised to *never* consume more than he or she can gracefully manage.
Gambling: This is considered by most Islamic countries to be an evil, and is strictly outlawed.
Smoking: This is also discouraged in Islam because of the health hazards associated with it. However, do not refuse a cigarette unless you are an ardent non-smoker, as an offer of a cigarette is often a compliment, especially from one's host. If invited to smoke a *narghileh* (hookah) do not refuse and follow the ritual behaviour exhibited. This essentially social activity is popular in some, but by no means all, Arab countries.
Food: Pork is forbidden by Islamic law and all meat is killed by cutting the animal's throat and draining the blood. This is called *halal* meat. It is customary for the host/hostess to cut up whole items of food (especially with *mezzeh*, the Arabic equivalent of hors d'oeuvres) and distribute them. It is also customary to offer guests the most succulent parts of the meal, often the entrails or eyes. To refuse these is considered an insult. In restaurants the person who makes the invitation pays the bill and it is considered an insult to contravene.
Note: Etiquette in all Islamic countries is complicated and highly evolved, and all those wishing to learn more are advised to read books on the subject.

THE ISLAMIC CALENDAR

Based on lunar months, the first of each month coincides with the date of the actual new moon. In 'Common' years of 354 days, the months are alternately 30 and 29 days long; in the 'Kabishah' year of 355 days the last month has 30 days. During a 30-year period there are 19 Common and 11 Kabishah years. The ninth month is Ramadan. The Islamic months are as follows:
Muharram, Safar, Rarabia (1), Rarabia (2), Jumada (1), Jumada (2), Rajab, Shaaban, Ramadan, Shawwal, Dhul-al-Qa'da, Dhu-al-Hijja.
These months are used especially in Saudi Arabia.

For further information contact:
Muslim Information Services
233 Seven Sisters Road
London N4 2DA
Tel: (071) 272 5170.

THE WORLD OF CHRISTIANITY

BELIEF AND PRACTICE

The Bible consists of the Old Testament inherited from Judaism and the New Testament which tells the story of Jesus and his apostles, and also contains letters written to Christian communities, especially those by St Paul. Discussion of the Old Testament and St Paul's letters is omitted in the following for reasons of space.

The New Testament Story

The Christian belief is based on the life and teachings of Jesus who, as recorded in the gospels of Matthew, Mark, Luke and John, travelled through Palestine for three years declaring his message and performing miracles until he was arrested, accused of being a rebel against the occupying Roman authorities and crucified. The Jewish authorities were particularly upset by his claim to be the son of God, and therefore the long-awaited Messiah. Three days after his crucifixion Jesus rose from the dead and for the next few weeks appeared several times, until he 'ascended' to heaven.
Subsequent to his death, resurrection and Ascension his apostles (see below) and other disciples travelled through the Roman Empire preaching and gaining converts. Of these converts St Paul, who was in the first place fanatically anti-Christian, is perhaps the most important; many Christian doctrines are based on his letters to the various Christian communities.

The Miracles

In the gospels, Jesus is often portrayed as reluctant to perform miracles, performing them only out of compassion, with a reminder that people should not believe in him for his miracles. The miracles most often mentioned involve making the lame walk and the blind see, from others he 'casts out devils' (a phrase now given a psychological slant by many). A few seem to have a mystical or symbolic significance: turning the water to wine at the wedding in Cana, the feeding of the five thousand (with two loaves and three fishes) and calming the storm on Lake Galilee seem to fall into this category.

The Parables

The miracles are often a prelude to a discussion in which a parable, or maybe several, are told. Jesus is not primarily someone who lays down moral laws; it is the attitude and approach to life of his listeners that he targets. Taken collectively the parables form a set of yardsticks against which the Christian can measure himself. As they are stories, rather than codes of behaviour, their origin many years ago in a largely pastoral and Roman-occupied Middle East does not confine and date them. Phrases from the parables occur naturally in conversations of those who live in societies moulded by Christianity (no matter how secular they have become). A 'Good Samaritan' is a person who helps a stranger in need; a 'Prodigal Son' is one who is wayward; 'to sort out the sheep from the goats' is to separate the good from the bad; 'to turn the other cheek' is to withhold retaliation. There are many other examples. The parables emphasise ethical percepts central to Christianity: returning good for evil, forgiveness, welcoming the sinner and valuing a person for *what* he is, not for *who* he is. The most direct statements of Christian ethics in the Bible are perhaps to be found in the Beatitudes, the most famous being 'Blessed are the meek for they shall inherit the Earth'.

The Apostles

The 12 apostles were disciples who were particularly close to Jesus; several were fishermen. Notable among the apostles was Peter (meaning 'stone'), who through force of character, or perhaps conviction, was able to overcome his weaknesses. Another apostle, Matthew, symbolises the universal nature of the Christian appeal; he had been a tax-collector (a universally corrupt and despised profession in the Roman Empire). Most notorious was Judas Iscariot, who betrayed Jesus to the authorities; down the centuries his actions, and those of the priests he assisted, have been used as a justification for persecution of the Jewish people throughout the centuries.

Gospels & the Acts of the Apostles

John's gospel is accepted as being the closest eye-witness account. The visionary nature of his work, however, inclines many interpreters against being over-literal. The other gospels are called collectively the 'synoptic' gospels; though there are differences between them, they draw on the same source material. Mark's, the earliest, is a bald 'no frills' narrative; the aim is clearly to bring the material together and put it in writing. Matthew's is written from a Jewish perspective and has a clear emphasis on putting the story into the context of Jewish tradition. Luke, on the other hand, as a gentile convert, emphasises the universal elements of the story. From Luke also comes the Acts of the Apostles, an account of the early days of Christianity, which significantly gives us a picture of the second major progenitor of Christianity: St Paul.

Practices

Whilst Christian denominations vary radically in their practices, virtually all perform the Act of Holy Communion (see below) and hold services on Sunday (the day of the Resurrection, traditionally the Christian day of rest), though such activities are not necessarily confined to Sunday. A prayer ('grace') is often said at table before meals, especially the evening meal. It may be read or memorised and may also give mention to preoccupations or current events. It is customary for persons in attendance to lower their eyes, bow their head and clasp their hands in front of them or hold the hand of the persons sitting next to them. The prayer always finishes with the word 'Amen' (meaning 'So be it'), at which time those attending can resume their normal posture and begin their meal. It is a breach of manners to begin eating before the prayer is completed.
In general, practising Christians are definably members of a community centred on their church; originally the act of baptism symbolised the acceptance of a Christian as a full member, but it is now performed at so young an age (in most denominations) that there is usually some other recognised form of acceptance, which occurs when a person is old enough to take responsibility for his actions. The nature of this form of acceptance varies greatly, but what is centrally important, and sets Christianity apart, is that individuals are offered the choice of whether or not to accept it.

Communion

At the Last Supper, when Jesus celebrated the Jewish Passover immediately before being taken prisoner and crucified, he broke bread and drank wine with his apostles, saying: "Do this in remembrance of me". This has become the Christian sacrament of Communion when by re-enacting this event Christians renew their ties with God. There is no particular time or place for this sacrament, though over the centuries many rites and practices have grown around it, mostly perhaps in the Roman Catholic Mass.

The Christian Calendar

The most important event in the Christian calendar is Easter, which celebrates the death and resurrection of Jesus: Good Friday, the day when hope was lost; Easter Sunday, the day it was restored. Very much second in importance is Christmas, which celebrates the Birth of Jesus. The Christmas tradition of exchanging gifts and family celebration is very much a secular affair and not rooted in any Christian doctrine. The older European tradition is to celebrate on St Nicholas' Day (December 6) whilst other churches prefer to commemorate the arrival of the Magi with their gifts. Many other events in the life of Jesus are celebrated in the Christian calendar.
The most important dates are as follows:
Christmas (generally: December 25; Orthodox: variable) – Celebrates the Birth of Jesus; see above.
Epiphany (January 6, 12 days after Christmas) – The coming of the wise men with their gifts.
Ash Wednesday (40 days before Easter) – Commencement of Lent, traditionally a period of fasting and self-denial leading up to Easter.
Palm Sunday (a week before Easter) – Celebrates the arrival into Jerusalem of Jesus riding on a mule.
Good Friday (two days before Easter) – Traditionally referred to as three days before Easter Sunday, this commemorates the crucifixion.
Easter Sunday (*) – The day of the Resurrection.

See above for more detailed information.
Note [*]: This is a moveable Feast which usually occurs in March or April. Western and Orthodox churches determine its date according to different calendars.
Ascension Day (40 days after Easter) – The day Jesus ascended to heaven on a cloud following his resurrection and last appearances on Earth.
Whit Sunday (6 weeks after Easter) – Marking the day the Holy Spirit entered the disciples left behind and the beginning of their ministry.
The above dates are marked by virtually all Christian churches; Orthodox and Catholic churches, in particular, mark other occasions such as Noah's Flood (Orthodox) and the Immaculate Conception (Roman Catholic).

Doctrines

Only the foolhardy could set out a list of Christian doctrines; the following beliefs are held, with differing degrees of literalness, by most Christians:
(1) There is only one God.
(2) Jesus is his son.
(3) He was born of the Virgin Mary.
(4) He lived, was crucified, resurrected from the dead and ascended to heaven (the meaning of this is explained separately, see below).
(5) Through the working of the Holy Spirit his apostles were moved to preach in the name of Jesus, and establish the church as we know it.
(6) God, Jesus and the Holy Spirit are not three entities but one and the same (the complex doctrine of the Trinity).
(7) The Bible, including the Jewish Old Testament seen in the light of the New Testament, represents the word of God to his people.
(8) God remains today in commune with his church and its members.
There is a broad range of attitudes to these beliefs, from the Roman Catholics' insistence on orthodoxy to the Quakers' belief in the 'still, small voice'.

Significance of the Resurrection

'The death and resurrection of one man saved the entire world – you included – if only you would believe it'. That, in summary, has been the message of the Christian church down the ages. The story of Jesus is the story of a man who was angered by hypocrisy, who relished debate, who spoke of forgiveness and returning love for hate and who, having spoken of these things, was betrayed and abandoned by those closest to him; who was so desolate that he himself gave up hope, and compassionate enough, even on the cross, to give reassurance to the thief dying beside him. In this giving up hope and in his death he fully joins humanity. And then in the resurrection Jesus joins humanity again, but this time with his divinity in the ascendant, and with the assurance that if he can defeat death so can all who believe in him.

Denominations

The following is a list of some of the main Christian denominations worldwide, together with a brief description of their particular customs.
Roman Catholic (worldwide, especially in Latin countries and Europe): Roman Catholics believe that the Pope inherits supreme authority within the church directly from St Peter. Elaborate rituals are performed and the role of the priest is central; it is his responsibility to listen to *Confession*, assign penances and give absolution (forgiveness). Many saints are venerated and countries with the Roman Catholic denomination are often noted for their fiestas on Saints' Days; spectacular carnivals before or after Easter also occur. Modesty in dress when visiting churches is required (eg covering the head for women).
Orthodox (Russia, Middle East & Central Europe): Orthodox churches are similar to Catholic ones in the elaborate style of their liturgies and rituals (called 'Greek Rite'). Services are long with the congregation standing throughout; stress is laid on the importance of the Ascension and saints are highly regarded. In some places, icons (usually miniature religious paintings on small pieces of wood) are used as an aid to contemplation. Each *province* has its own Patriarch and, whilst there is no overriding central control, the Patriarch of Istanbul is recognised as the most senior. Modesty in dress when visiting churches is required (eg covering the head for women).
Anglican & Episcopalian (English-speaking countries): The Church of England parted from the Roman Catholic church in the 16th century. Many of its rites are similar to those of the Catholic church, although over the centuries the influences of Puritanism and non-conformity have, for the most part, tended to concentrate worship on the main doctrines and away from the veneration of saints etc. The priest is also less of an intermediary between his congregation and God. Anglican and Episcopalian churches throughout the world have forms of service derived from that of the Church of England. The church is broad and 'high' churches tend to be similar in character to Roman Catholicism, whilst 'low' churches look more to non-conformist influences. Requirements on dress are not as strict as those of Catholic and Orthodox churches, but respect is always appreciated.
Methodist, Presbyterian & Congregationalist (English-speaking countries & the Pacific): Industriousness, temperance (meaning more than just sobriety), straightforwardness and honesty are the values of these churches; qualities which the New Testament sums up in the concept of 'stewardship'. In form of service, some are similar to the 'low' church of the Church of England whilst others are more austere and Calvinistic (putting emphasis on the relationship man–God, strongly opposing the role of priest as mediator). In some more isolated parts of the world the influence of Victorian morality is strong, eg where there is a requirement to keep certain parts of the body covered.
Baptist (CIS, USA & parts of the Far East): Most churches practise baptism within a few weeks of birth. For Baptists the consent of the baptised is essential if the rite is to be significant and adult, or 'believer's baptism', is practised. Congregations are autonomous and independent of each other though each belongs to a national union. Other beliefs are similar to those described above under *Methodist etc.*
Pentecostal (Caribbean & USA): These are the most exuberant churches of all, with much community singing and uninhibited celebration; 'speaking in tongues' and dancing often enter into church services. Beliefs are usually fundamentalist.
Seventh Day Adventist (USA & Pacific): This Fundamentalist church celebrates the Sabbath on Saturday (the 'seventh day'). Church members look forward to the 'Second Coming' when Jesus will return to Earth and there is a heavy emphasis on the Old Testament.
Evangelical: Many churches have evangelical congregations and this is an area in which the Pentecostal church has been influential. The importance of proclaiming God's word is emphasised.

GROWTH OF CHRISTIANITY

The history of Christianity is central to the history of the world and pervades every aspect of philosophy, politics and culture, certainly in Europe. Space here does not permit more than a brief survey and it should be remembered that although originally a Near Eastern religion, it was in Europe that Christianity most firmly took root and survived. The following survey has been written largely from a western European viewpoint; this is not to belittle the achievements of the many founding fathers of the Church, many of whom lived in Syria and North Africa.
The early church, initially small groups converted by the remaining Apostles and St Paul, grew rapidly in the Roman Empire but suffered considerable persecution and also many heresies and schisms. The remarkable spread of the religion culminated in the reign of the Emperor Constantine (306-337), who became a Christian himself and summoned the first Ecumenical council of the Church (325) in an attempt to settle the matter of the Arian heresy, the first sign of a split between the eastern and western churches which was never subsequently healed. The church was at this time organised under the leadership of several patriachs (at Alexandra, Antioch, Jerusalem, Constantinople and Rome), with the latter accorded a somewhat vague primacy. Christianity spread rapidly throughout Europe during the so-called Dark Ages (although parts of eastern and northeastern Europe were not converted until the 11th/12th centuries), a growth mirroring the breakdown of secular power.
The propensity of Christianity to produce heretical and schismatic groups in no way abated during this period and led to the establishment of many diverse Christian groups, such as the Coptics and Maronites, which still survive to this day. The rapid and dramatic spread of Islam in the 7th century resulted in many Christian lands (such as Spain and almost all of the near East) being over-run; the conquest of Jerusalem was particularly keenly felt, the city being revered by Christians, as well as by Muslims and Jews. The career of Charlemagne (771-814) produced a revival both of Christianity and of secular power, and his coronation as Holy Roman Emperor in Rome on Christmas Day 800 – thus recreating the Roman Empire in the west and formalising the concept of Christendom – was an event of enormous significance, not least because it brought into sharp focus the conflicting aspirations of church and state. It was widely believed that Constantine had granted the church ultimate supremacy in earthly affairs (the so-called 'Donation of Constantine', later proved to be a forgery), and this dispute rumbled on throughout the Middle Ages, often flaring into armed conflict. The launching of the Crusades in 1096 was motivated not only by a desire to reinforce ecclesiastical supremacy in the West, but also as a response from the Orthodox Byzantine Empire to assist in the defence of their empire; there existed also the fainter hope of producing a reconciliation between Rome and Constantinople. The astounding success of the First Crusade, which led to the establishment of Christian states in the Near East for almost 200 years, brought Christianity, Judaism and Islam into sharp and violent conflict. The triumph of Islam in the East was assured after the conquest of Constantinople in 1453; the Eastern (Orthodox) church retained its hold in Greece and Russia, and also in many isolated (and often heretical) communities in the Near East.
Shortly afterwards the 'seamless robe of Christ' was split still further by the Reformation and the teachings of Luther, Calvin and Zwingli. By the end of the 16th century, despite the work of the Counter-Reformation and the Council of Trent, much of Northern Europe had turned to Protestantism. Increasingly, the religious split in Europe manifested itself in many of the wars of the period – the French Wars of Religion, the Dutch War of Independence and the English Civil War and Revolution, for instance – culminating in the gruesome politico-religious violence of the Thirty Years War (1618-1648). By this time most of the major European powers had started to establish overseas empires, exporting religion at the same time, and by the 18th century Christianity had established itself as the most widely spread faith in the world. Methodism was the last of the major Christian denominations to take root, and by that time most of the established churches in Europe had achieved a more tranquil *modus vivendi* with their secular counterparts by the rationalism of the Enlightenment. From this time on the most zealous Christians, from the Jesuits to Evangelicals, were finding that the most fertile ground for their teaching lay in the colonies: during the 19th century the work of conversion in all parts of the world proceeded apace. The 20th century has seen the Christian Church in Europe holding an increasingly small constituency and relying more on moral and ethical, rather than theological, influence on the life of its adherents. Certainly the increasing power and sophistication of the state has, in our century, resolved the ancient church – state dispute very firmly in favour of the secular arm. The foundation of the ecumenical World Council of Churches in 1948 can be seen partly as an attempt to bury old differences between the denominations. Despite the increasing drift away from religion in the west, revivals, often of a dramatic nature, have taken place throughout the century, and one should in particular cite the recent rise of fundamentalist preachers in the USA. Two other events are worthy of particular mention. Firstly, the work of the Second Vatican Council in the 1960s, an attempt to bring the Catholic Church in line with the needs of the modern world: it has been said that, convened 500 years earlier, it would certainly have prevented the Reformation. Secondly, the spread of the so-called 'Liberation theology' in the Third World and Eastern Europe, born of an attempt to use the moral authority and teachings of the Church to aid the struggle against political and social oppression. Although in many ways a return to the fundamental teaching of Christ, the development is viewed with alarm by the Vatican and, to a lesser extent, by other church leaders. The legacy of Christianity to the world is incalculable: almost every work of literature, art and music before about 1600 – and many after this date – were inspired by the faith, while the soaring cathedrals of both western and eastern Europe rank among the greatest achievements of mankind. Certainly the religion will continue to guide, comfort and inspire countless millions across the globe, although it seems unlikely to spawn any further major global changes.

INFORMATION

Contact a local church or the Council of Churches for Britain & Ireland, Inter-Church House, 35-41 Lower Marsh, London SE1 7RL. Tel: (071) 620 4444. Fax: (071) 928 0010.

THE WORLD OF BUDDHISM

INTRODUCTION

Buddhism was born as a result of the works and teachings of Siddhartha, a member of the Shakyan clan who lived in and around the Ganges Plain during the 5th and 6th centuries BC. He is believed to have been born in 563BC, and was for many years a follower of the Vedic religion, a very diffuse set of spiritual and philosophical beliefs, one aspect of which was Brahmanism.

Siddhartha's religion, achieved as a result of an 'Enlightenment', was in many ways a critique of Vedic doctrines. In particular, he was highly critical of its caste system and the use of sacrifices. In its place he developed a spiritualism which would enable man to escape from the pain and suffering of the world and achieve *Nirvana*.

The word 'Buddha' means 'enlightened', and the achieving of this is the ultimate goal. Siddhartha was very keen to stress that he was neither God, nor the son of God, nor even a prophet but merely an ordinary man who had, through his own spiritualism, achieved enlightenment.

The religion was non-theistic, having at its centre not a God but man in a fully enlightened state. Full enlightenment is striven for through meditation and personal religious experience, combined with a strict morality and altruism. It is not regarded as being a static state but one which constantly changes; Siddhartha himself modified his teachings throughout his life in the light of circumstances and his own personal experiences.

Having established itself in northern India during the 5th century BC, Buddhism was contained within the subcontinent for about a hundred years. The teaching spread to Nepal by the 4th century BC, and reached Kashmir, Sri Lanka and Central Asia by the 2nd century BC. The later spread of the religion occurred partly through trade and partly through the work of missionaries. By the time of the Birth of Christ, Buddhism was established in China, reaching Korea by the end of the 3rd century. The increased trade in the Far East at this time gave greater impetus to the spread of the religion, and by the 7th century Buddhists were to be found in Java, Sumatra, Japan, Tibet, Thailand and Myanmar. Further westward expansion was halted by Islamic conquests but conversion still persisted; Bhutan, for instance, was not reached until the 9th century but today is one of the most strongly Buddhist countries in the world.

The spread of Buddhism over a period of over 1500 years led to the development of three different strands:

Theravada Buddhism, found in Thailand, Sri Lanka, Myanmar, Laos and Cambodia. The monks are distinguished by orange or yellow robes.

Mahayana Buddhism, found in China, Japan and Korea. The priests wear brown, grey or black robes.

Vajrayana Buddhism, found in Tibet, Nepal, Sikkim, Bhutan and Mongolia. The monks wear maroon robes.

Buddhism is not a centralised religion with centralised institutions, although it does have a hierarchical form of organisation within each of the three main groups (see above). In countries such as Thailand, Sri Lanka, Myanmar and Bhutan, where the Government and a large part of the population are Buddhist, the State is very closely associated with the religion and its organisation and institutions tend to be more formalised. In other countries, such as Japan, the religion exists within a looser framework.

FESTIVALS

Visitors are welcome to attend the many festivals which are an integral part of Buddhist life. The major obstacle is finding out the date, as these are scheduled by the lunar calendar and often take place on the full moon, and therefore change annually. Each country also has its own special festivals, so it is advisable to check well in advance. This can be done either by consulting the relevant country entries in this book under *Public Holidays*, or by contacting the embassies or tourist boards (addresses are at the beginning of each entry). The main festivals are as follows:

Wesak (Buddha Day) – Commemorating the Buddha's enlightenment (as well as his birthday and death). It is celebrated in the Theravada countries around the full moon in May. Houses and streets are decorated and roads are packed with processions. Long lines of monks and worshippers throng the temples either meditating or listening to religious discourses.

Tooth Ceremony – Takes place annually in Kandy, Sri Lanka, lasting for about a week in July or August. Up to 100 elephants take part.

Songkran – Celebrated in Thailand during April, this 3-day festival involves water-splashing, the freeing of fish, fighting kites, dancing etc.

Hana Matsuri (the flower festival in April), **Jodo-e** (December) and **Nehan-e** (February) are celebrated in Japan to commemorate respectively the Birth, Enlightenment and Death of Buddha.

Chinese New Year – The main festival celebrated in China, the Vajrayana countries and by the Chinese populations in Malaysia, Taiwan, Hong Kong and Hawaii. This is actually a pre-Buddhist festival to mark the beginning of spring. It usually falls in February or late January and lasts for up to a week. The third day is the *Feast of Lanterns* when the long painted dragons dance in the streets.

Vajrayana countries also have very colourful festivals and ceremonies, with demon-dancing and the blowing of enormous long horns by brightly hatted monks. The dates for these festivals are variable, so it is best to enquire nearer the time when more information will be available.

FURTHER INFORMATION

The information contained in this section was based on material kindly supplied by Dharmadhara of the Buddhist Information Service, who may be contacted for further information.

Friends of the Western Buddhist Order (FWBO)
'Padmaloka'
Lesingham House
Surlingham
Norwich NR14 7AL
Tel: (05088) 310.

Alternatively, contact the London Buddhist Centre on (081) 981 1225.

WEATHER

The following gives an indication of the way in which weather conditions affect people. The comfort or discomfort felt in different conditions depends on temperature, humidity and wind. For information on weather conditions in each country, see the relevant country entry.

HUMIDITY

Humidity is the amount of moisture in the air. Expressed as a percentage, a relative humidity of 100% is the maximum possible moisture content held at any given temperature. As air can hold more moisture at greater heat, so 100% humidity at 26°C (79°F) holds more moisture than 100% humidity at 10°C (50°F). Low humidity results in rapid evaporation; perspiration evaporates easily and wet clothes dry quickly. Such conditions prevail in hot and dry climates, where one experiences far less discomfort and can endure relatively high temperatures. In a hot climate with high humidity conditions, perspiration cannot evaporate easily and clothes dry slowly. One feels hot and uncomfortable as heat loss through perspiration is minimised. A breeze can sometimes relieve the discomfort associated with high humidity. Below the freezing point the air can hold very little moisture and humidity has little effect. Although damp (raw) cold is less pleasant than dry cold in temperatures above freezing point, wind is a more important factor.

WIND

One feels cooler in wind because air movement around the body has the effect of carrying body heat away. In hot weather the body temperature is regulated chiefly by the evaporation of perspiration. When the air temperature exceeds normal skin temperature (about 34°C; 93°F), in a dry climate the cooling power of wind becomes critical. In low temperatures the wind speed is equally critical. A temperature of 0°C (32°F) with a wind speed of 50kmph (30mph) feels colder than the lower temperature of -20°C (4°F) in calm conditions. High wind speeds can increase the risk of frostbite.

Many regions have particular winds which occur at certain times of the day or seasons of the year, and there are general rules – for instance, winds generally drop at night and increase by day (especially on the coast). Wind speed almost always increases with altitude. However, average wind statistics are almost impossible to supply although forecasts are given in some countries, such as the USA, on television and radio or in newspapers.

WIND CHILL FACTOR

The wind chill factor indicates outdoor conditions and how a suitably dressed person would feel, and can be deduced from wind speeds and average temperatures. In less extreme conditions a sunny day will produce extra warmth. The rate of heat loss from the body can be measured in kilogram calories per square metre of body surface per hour. The wind chill factor is often given in weather bulletins.

TEMPERATURE RANGE

This can be estimated by measuring the difference between the maximum and minimum temperatures, which usually occur just after midday and just before dawn. In cloudy, rainy areas the range may be quite small but in very sunny, dry climates such as deserts or mountainous regions there may be a large range with surprisingly cold nights. As a general rule the greatest range is inland and the lowest on the coast.

PRECIPITATION

Precipitation includes all forms of moisture falling on the ground as rain, snow, sleet, hail or fog drip. Generally this is rain but on high mountains, or in countries with very cold winters such as Canada, the CIS, parts of the USA, China or Scandinavia, it may well fall as snow. All forms are measured as the melted equivalent of rain, one foot of snow being roughly equivalent to one inch of rain. Generally, below 2°C (36°F) snow or sleet are as likely as rain. At freezing point or below, snow is most likely. Rain falling below freezing point, although rare, is very dangerous especially on roads.

PRECAUTIONS

Height above sea level: The general fall in temperature is at the rate of 0.6°C for every 100m (1°F for every 300ft), especially in cloud. Higher altitudes can also mean a wide range of day and night-time temperatures. Atmosphere becomes thinner over 1800m (6000ft), the sun's rays are more powerful and breathing and exertion become more difficult. Adequate clothing should always be taken when walking or climbing.

Heat: In high temperatures the body keeps cool by sweating. However, if the humidity is too low or evaporation is increased by wind, the body may not sweat fast enough to match the rate of evaporation. In such conditions the risk of heat exhaustion or heatstroke increases.

Heat Exhaustion: Symptoms are loss of appetite, lassitude and general discomfort, with possible hallucinations and vomiting. The sufferer should be moved to a cool place and drink salty water to replace moisture and salt lost in perspiration.

Heatstroke: When the body's cooling mechanism stops, the body becomes dry and temperature rises. The symptoms are burning sensations and dry skin followed by feverishness, sometimes developing into headache and confusion. Immediate medical attention is essential as heatstroke may be fatal. The patient should be cooled as fast as possible, preferably put in a cool place, splashed with cold or iced water, wrapped in a wet sheet with a fan directed on the body. Vigorous massage can also help. *Prevention:* In a very hot country do not over-exert until after about a week's acclimatisation, especially after air travel. (Air-conditioning delays the process of acclimatisation.) Drink plenty of liquid, not too much alcohol and take salt. Avoid sunburn and wear comfortable, light clothing.

Cold: Body heat can be generated by physical activity, and maintained by wearing suitable clothing. The danger occurs if one stops moving, becomes tired or if one remains in a strong wind below freezing point.

Hypothermia: Otherwise known as 'exposure'. The body temperature falls and this can be fatal. Risks of hypothermia usually occur through lack of adequate clothing in mountainous regions or at sea, especially at night and if clothes become wet (evaporation from wet clothing causes the body to lose heat more rapidly). Rain and snow with a strong wind increase the danger. Old people are particularly susceptible. Hypothermia becomes critical at a very low level of body temperature, around 25-28°C (77-82°F). The body should be rewarmed rapidly, preferably in a bath of 40-45°C (104-113°F). Artificial respiration and cardiac massage are required if breathing has stopped.

Frostbite: Affects flesh exposed to extreme cold, usually the face, hands and feet. The flesh freezes and this can result in the loss of limbs. The affected parts should be rewarmed slowly though as soon as possible, preferably in water no hotter than 40-44°C (104-111°F). Do not bandage, massage or rub frostbitten skin.

CLIMATE CONVERSIONS

Easy to use and informative climate charts are provided at the end of each country's entry. Very occasionally a climate chart from a nearby country will be used. Below is an example of these, giving the conversions between Centigrade/Celsius and Fahrenheit, and between millimetres and inches. The former measures have been used in the charts in the text.

EXAMPLE CLIMATE GRAPH FOLLOWS

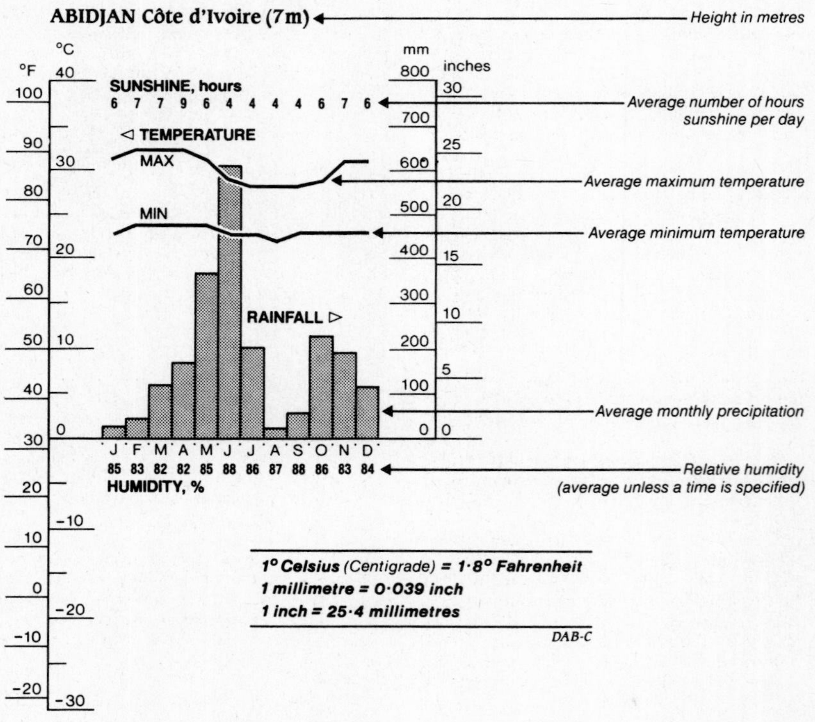

COMPUTER RESERVATIONS SYSTEMS

By Mike Swindell

For many people of a certain age, the computer represents the twilight zone of technical terror. At a pinch, if driven to it by what are often regarded as the unreasonable demands of a lunatic employer, those people might, like mice in a maze, ultimately learn the simple functions of keyboard and screen. They might even come to value the equipment as a labour-saving, if somewhat mysterious device.

Fortunately for the travel industry, most of the people charged with the task of creating the countless reservations and itineraries for people on the move are not of that age. The industry is fed by school-leavers who, these days, have grown up with the computer and who are therefore comfortable and knowledgeable users. It is doubly fortunate for the travel industry as 1993 has shaped up as the year of a new technical explosion in the UK marketplace.

In 1992 it was estimated that more than 60 per cent of the technology being used in UK travel agencies relied on the so-called dumb viewdata terminals. By the end of this year, it was expected that as many as 80 per cent of the terminals in use were likely to be personal computers (PCs) capable of highly sophisticated functions.

The fact that the prediction came from a supplier of terminals to the travel industry may lead one to suspect that an element of wishful thinking was involved in the calculation. But certainly, developments in a number of key areas makes it inevitable that the PC, with all its advantages of flexibility and functional flair, will quickly triumph over the viewdata equipment.

While smaller travel agents, caught in the vice of economic recession, are likely to continue to use their cheap viewdata terminals as long as they can, the cost of maintaining older equipment is steadily rising while the cost of hiring or buying new PCs is falling.

Ultimately, there will be no contest between the two, especially now that so many PC-based functions are being brought on line by the CRS companies. Further impetus to the switch to smart terminals is given by the development of the GTI project in the UK which aimed to launch pilot trials of a revolutionary leisure booking format.

Formed by *Galileo*, *Thomson* and *Istel* – hence the name GTI – the technology initiative wants to offer the package holiday sector what the CRS companies already provide for airlines and to a lesser degree, hotels and car hire companies – a fast, efficient and comprehensive booking system. The problem for viewdata users is that it will work only with PC technology.

With *Galileo's* intimate involvement in the GTI project, cries of protest have come from rival CRS camps SABRE and *Worldspan*, both of whom have strong interests in the UK travel market and who are concerned that *Galileo* will lead the march into the huge leisure travel market while remaining dominant in the business travel field.

All the GTI partners have tried to allay those fears, especially *Istel* which has links with all three CRS companies. *Istel* says its role was to defend the neutrality of the system and promote it as an industry solution for any supplier that wanted access. While recognising that its involvement with GTI would give it a high profile in the leisure market, *Galileo* insists that it does not expect to be the exclusive CRS vehicle for access.

SABRE'S protest at GTI could be considered a shade hollow considering the company was developing its own leisure development project at the same time, called *European Local Vendor Access (Elva)*. Elva was due to undergo trials around the same time as GTI and aimed to use SABRE as the vehicle to display the wares of the top set of tour operators, charter airlines, ferry firms and railways in each European country. Considering that *Thomson, Airtours and Owners Abroad* were all involved in the development of GTI, it seemed that SABRE'S aspirations for Elva in the UK would be more than a little hampered.

Galileo's strength in the UK market is a by-product of *British Airways'* involvement and the fact that the system made its entry into travel agents' shops via *Travicom*, which used to be the industry standard for airline booking. After a long build-up to the fully fledged *Galileo* CRS, about half the company's customers had been switched over to the new *Central System* by the end of 1992, with full transition due by the summer of 1993.

Early users of the *Central System* were plagued by problems as the database struggled to cope with the rush of demand. By January, some 1300 travel agents were on line with the new system and *Galileo* had promised that its teething problems were over. The company had loaded a new message-handling software package called *Comms Integrator* and introduced a second reservations processing system.

Yet a third reservations processor was planned to act as a back-up and ensure no further capacity problems. At the same time, *Galileo* signed a definitive agreement with US-based *Covia* to merge the main functions of the two systems and rivals once again waited for teething troubles with this process to exploit and turn into increased market share.

British travel agents in general, however, prefer to remain with systems they have grown used to and while sales for *Worldspan* and SABRE increased, *Galileo* remained well in the lead. The creation of *Galileo* International allowed *Amadeus*, *Galileo's* European rival, to claim it is now the only truly European system for European agents.

In truth, however, the combination of *Galileo* and *Covia*, which operates the *Apollo* CRS in the USA, has created an extremely powerful tool for retailers looking increasingly at global markets. By integrating the databases of the three CRS partners in the alliance, *Galileo*, *Apollo* and *Gemini* in Canada, the new company is able to promote *Global Access*, a 'translator' which allows agents easy access to any one of the three CRSs.

This means that agencies can form international business alliances and offer services worldwide, satisfying the needs of international travel clients. A *Galileo*-automated agency in London, for example, can retrieve a reservation created by their associated agency, an *Apollo* user in Chicago, and make any changes required by a traveller en route.

But while *Galileo International* offers obvious advantages of common access, they remain fundamentally distinct. This is a reflection of the reason why *Galileo* was originally created as a separate CRS - the demand by non-US carriers and travel agencies for a truly international CRS designed to meet their unique needs for local functionality and vendor presentation. The new *Galileo International* is pledged to preserve *Galileo's* local product and participation with local databases.

While *Amadeus* might try to make capital out of its perceived independence as a stand-alone European CRS dedicated to its local markets, it has moved to hedge its bets in the global market with technical alliances with *Worldspan* and the Worldspan affiliate, Singapore-based *Abacus* reservations system. The three had planned to interconnect their respective CRSs by the first quarter of 1993 to allow access by users to information in any of the systems.

Although this falls far short of *Galileo International's Global Access* facility which allows partner agents in different parts of the world to alter the other's bookings, it at least offers affiliated agents access to each other's passenger name records to provide better en route service to customers.

Amadeus and *Worldspan* have announced that they are studying the possibility of enhancing the access levels to allow modification by one agent of another's bookings, and maintain that the current technical link is the first step in what could evolve into a wide range of co-operative efforts.

Amadeus, while claiming the high ground in continental European markets with a 60 per cent share of automated travel agencies, is nevertheless a minnow in the UK. Having taken up residence in the UK with offices large enough to mount training programmes, the CRS had, a year on, managed to attract 14 customers. This compared with 2222 locations for *Galileo*, 700 for SABRE and 550 for *Worldspan*. For the time being at least, *Galileo* counts the two US systems as its main rivals in its home market. With an increase of 300 UK subscribers in 1992, *Worldspan* set out to notch up a further 200 locations by the end of 1993.

While *Galileo* was working to bring on its new CRS to replace *Travicom*, *Worldspan* and *Sabre* were able to work in the UK market with systems that were demonstrably better than the old British technology. *Worldspan* in particular have made an art of supplying quality products at low prices. Its easy-to-use *World Dial Link*, which allows agents to dial up the CRS without needing expensive leased lines, was a prime example. *Worldspan's World Solutions* is another demonstration of the company's ability to find cheaper ways of connecting agents to its CRS.

World Solutions allows companies to use existing computer hardware which *Worldspan* claims can be as much as 50 per cent cheaper than alternatives which require an investment in replacement equipment. For those who want to upgrade to PC technology, *Worldspan* now has a low-cost answer in its IBM PS/1 Pro workstation which can be networked and expanded if necessary. Standard features include IBM-DOS and Microsoft Works which comes with spreadsheet and database.

The increasing sophistication of the hardware now available is mirrored in a new SABRE product which brings a Windows function to travel agents' workstations. Introduced in the first half of 1993, the Windows application offers the key advantage of being able to open and run several SABRE work areas concurrently, enabling users to conduct different transactions simultaneously.

This includes the ability, for example, to link into several multi-access hosts whist using different windows within one computer terminal at the same time.

Alternatively, users are able to work within several different areas of SABRE at once, allowing agents to work on different but interdependent aspects of a client's bookings.

With *Galileo's* conversion to *Central System*, the company started to stamp real authority on the UK market. In the first month of 1993 bookings through *Galileo* reached a record 1.8 million – nearly 30 per cent up on January 1992; of that total, more than 80 per cent were made through the *Galileo Central System*.

Also in January, bookings for *RoomMaster*, Galileo's hotels reservations function, and *CarMaster*, the equivalent car rental operation, had doubled over the previous month.

This said, the company was a good indication of the importance the industry was placing on PC technology.

Galileo, now fully in its stride, is developing and marketing a wide range of applications to be used within the CRS. They range from back office functions to the generation of new-style

Automated Ticket & Boarding passes which will act as the first step towards self-service check-in at airports and to *TravelLink*, a system which allows agents to access their *Galileo* workstation by means of a notebook PC or laptop computer hooked into a telephone line any time of the day or night.

The list continues with *FocalPoint UK* which is a sales and automation tool as well as a reservations system, as well as *TravelManager*, an agency management system that provides agents with a comprehensive Local Booking File database containing all services bookable for a passenger trip, including air, car, hotel, rail, ferry, cruises and theatre.

The tide of new functions flowing from the competing CRSs is now irresistible and if travel agents are not to be overwhelmed by competitors taking advantage of what is now on offer, they would be well advised to set aside any lingering Luddite tendencies and join the new-age technology.

Cōde-Link™

As you will have noticed, there are bar codes throughout the *World Travel Guide*. These bar codes have been specially developed for use in the travel industry and are known as Code-link™.
Codelink™ has been designed to help ease the operation of CRS (Computer Reservation Systems). Codelink™ locates the information or product you want with one stroke of a light-pen (sometimes called a 'wand'), or if you don't yet have your light-pen, Codelink™ can be used as a text prompt for keyboard input.
Codelink™ can access the information or product you want on screen quickly, accurately and, above all, easily.

DESTINATION INFORMATION

The *World Travel Guide* provides you with a wide range of accurate information on every country in the world. Much of the information, however, will change over the year; some of the information (eg visa or health) might change next week or even overnight.
Every single country section has a Codelink™ Factfinder matrix. Each matrix contains two rows: the upper row is dedicated for users of the **Galileo** or **Worldspan** system, the lower row is for users of the **SABRE** system.
Each of the two rows contains two Codelink™ symbols. These are clearly labelled **Health Regulations** and **Visa Regulations.** To get the latest information on screen using a Galileo, Worldspan or SABRE system simply use the appropriate Codelink™ symbol.

HOW TO USE CODELINK™

Simply wipe your light-pen over the Codelink™ symbol and the required information will appear on screen.

If you do not yet have a light-pen

Type in the keystrokes which are shown underneath the Codelink™ symbol.

LIGHT-PENS

Barcoding has changed the world of retailing and distribution. Codelink™, the barcode system for the travel industry, is destined to simplify all aspects of business and leisure product selection on screen. Just one wipe of a Codelink™ symbol can replace up to 20 keystrokes. With Codelink™ there is no need to memorise a complex keystroke formula to get the information or product you want on screen.
We have all seen bar codes being 'read' in shops, supermarkets, garages etc. Bar codes can be read by laser beam, contact pad or by a red beam light-pen. Laser guns are expensive, light-pens are not. All of the above devices are known as 'readers'.
Whichever reader you choose, it has to be plugged into a small box of electronics, a decoder. Decoders vary in size but are often not bigger than a small pocket dictionary. The decoder can be attached neatly to the side of your terminal.

How is a light-pen connected to a PC

Fitting a light-pen and decoder to your PC or terminal takes less than two minutes.
Plug the wire from your keyboard into the decoder, then from the decoder into the socket on your terminal where your keyboard wire used to fit.
Finally, plug the reader into the free socket on the decoder. You are now ready for action.
The keyboard will operate as normal whilst fitted to the decoder.
Prices for the reader and decoder vary considerably. As a rough guide expect to pay upwards of £100 (US$150) for a complete unit.

CODELINK™ AND CRS

The box labelled **Health** is programmed to deliver, on screen, the full health text for the given country. If there are more details to be checked than can be shown on a single screen then move down to the next screen.
The box labelled **Visa** is programmed to deliver, on screen, the full visa display for the given country. If there are more details to be checked than can be shown on a single screen then move down to the next screen.

THE COLUMBUS HOTEL-FINDER

'The Hotel Finder For The Age of IT.'

The Columbus Hotel-Finder™ is markedly different from existing hotel directories. It is the only travel publication in the world to incorporate the established technology of barcoding.
The advent of CRS as a hotel-booking medium has created a new selection and reservation environment in which the traditional hotel reference works are clearly unsuited. It is against this background that the Columbus Hotel-Finder™ has been developed.
The 'at a swipe' simplicity which Codelink™ gives to the retrieval of essential country information can now be used to bring a chosen or preferred hotel on screen.

The page opposite is from the Columbus Hotel-Finder™.

The Columbus Hotel-Finder™ lists the CRS codes for up to six different systems. In addition, a number of selected properties have Codelink™ features. For the sake of clarity, only five hotel properties are to be featured on a page. Each of the individual property features includes the following details:

Location Address	**CRS Reference Codes**
Description	**Telephone Number**
Price Guide	**Fax Number**
Locator Map	**Codelink™ symbol**

All hotels within the Columbus Hotel-Finder™ are chain hotels and are ordered in the following way:
Alphabetically by location (country by county, city by city). Each hotel is entered within its own chain grouping. For example, turn to a country section (Germany), then to a given city (Hamburg). The principle chain hotels are shown, grouped within branded sections, with their direct access CRS reference codes clearly displayed. Notice that the two Queens Hotels in Hamburg and Hamm have Codelink™ features.

With the Columbus Hotel-Finder™ you can get your chosen hotel on screen with the minimal amount of keystrokes or at the speed of light, just with a wipe!

'Codelink™ Welcomes You To The International Travel Supermarket'

COUNTRY	HEALTH REGULATIONS	VISA REGULATIONS
GALILEO/WORLDSPAN	TI-DFT/LON/HE	TI-DFT/LON/VI
SABRE	TIDFT/LON/HE	TIDFT/LON/VI

Code-Link

To access this information on your CRS, swipe the barcode with a light pen or type in the text under the barcode.

• Queens Hotel Hamburg •

Mexikoring 60, W-2000 Hamburg 60, Germany.
Location: Business District • Airport.
Accommodation: 185 rooms • 2 Restaurants • 2 Bars.
Facilities: Business Centre • Cable TV • Conference Centre • Hairdresser • Health Club • Sauna • Solarium • Steam Bath • Fitness Centre • Bike Hire.
Rates (Sgl/Dbl): DM215-304/DM260-304 • **Comm:** 10%.
Tel: (0)40 632-940 • **Fax:** (0)40 632-2472 • **Tlx:** 2174155 • **Rep:** QMH/UIN • **DATAS 2:** UI5523 • **AMEX:** B095.

APOLLO: HOA 29MAY-31MAY **17734**

PARS: HN-**UI05523** 29MAY31MAY

SABRE: HRD **UI21041***RAC/29MAY-2NT

SYS ONE: HA **UIHAMQUE** 29MAY31MAY

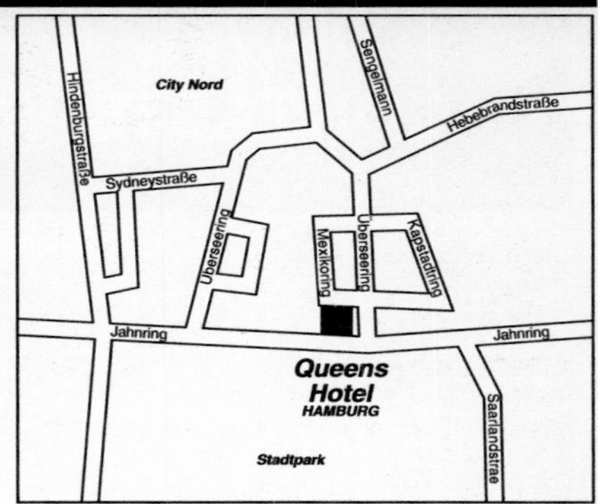

NAME	APOLLO	DATAS 2	PARS	SABRE	SYSTEM ONE	AMEX	Telephone	Fax
HAMBURG (Continued)								
Hotel Ibis								
Hamburg An Der Alster	RT23808	-	RTIBHAD	RT29524	-	-	(0)40 652 4001	(0)40 652 6603
Hamburg Wandsbek	RT32699	-	RTIBHAM	RT25845	-	-	(0)40 682 9021	(0)40 652 6603
Inter Continental Hotels								
Hamburg	IC19208	-	UI08899	IC1159	ICHAMICA	I133	(0)40 41415-0	(0)40 41415-186
Inter Europe Hotels								
Hotel Monopol	UI31874	UI14778	UI14778	UI25764	UIHAMMON	-	(0)40 31177-0	(0)40 31177-151
Hotel Panorama	UI11731	UI8840	UI08840	UI11748	UIHAMPMA	-	(0)40 73359-0	(0)40 73359-950
Kempinski Hotels								
Atlantic Hotel	KE9700	-	KIHAM01	KI4795	-	K203	(0)40 28880	(0)40 247 129
Maritim Hotels								
Maritim Hotel Reichsof	-	OM21499	OM02189	OM2348	OMHAMRIM	M612	(0)40 24833-0	(0)40 24833-488
Queens Hotels								
• Hamburg	UI17734	UI5523	UI05523	UI21041	UIHAMQUE	B095	(0)40 632-940	(0)40 632-2472
Ramada International								
Renaissance	RA123	RAHAMRN	RAHAMRN	RA123	RAHAM123	R129	(0)40 34918-0	(0)40 34918-431
SAS International Hotels								
Plaza	SK27618	-	UI11324	SK18409	UIHAMSAS	X618	(0)40 3502-0	(0)40 3502-3333
HAMM (MSR)								
Queens Hotels								
• Hamm	UI22056	UI8519	UI08519	UI22393	UIMSRQUE	B115	(0)2381 130-60	(0)2381 130-79
HANNOVER (HAJ)								
Independent								
Kastens Hotel Luisenhof	SR21456	SRHAJKA	SRHAJKA	SR13117	SRHAJKAS	X526	(0)511 3044-0	(0)511 3044-807
Best Western								
Hotel Föhrenhof	BW11337	-	UI03505	BW11686	BWHAJ012	-	(0)511 61721	(0)511 619 719
Parkhotel Kronsberg	BW13099	-	BW95013	BW11665	BWHAJ013	-	(0)511 861 086	(0)511 867 112
Forte Hotels								
Crest Hannover/Hildesheim	FE5790	FE0314	FE00314	FE18412	FEHAJ314	-	(0)5121 300-0	(0)5121 300-444

• Queens Hotel Hamm •

Neue Bahnhofstraße 3, W-4700 Hamm 1, Germany.
Location: City Centre.
Accommodation: 142 rooms • 2 Restaurants • Bar.
Facilities: Cable TV • Conference Centre • Health Club • Non-smoking rooms • Bowling • Swimming Pool • Sauna • Solarium.
Rates (Sgl/Dbl): DM205/DM245 • **Comm:** 10%.
Tel: (0)2381 130-60 • **Fax:** (0)2381 130-79 • **Tlx:** 828886 • **Rep:** QMH/UIN • **DATAS 2:** UI8519 • **AMEX:** B115.

APOLLO: HOA 29MAY-31MAY **22056**

PARS: HN-**UI08519** 29MAY31MAY

SABRE: HRD **UI22393***RAC/29MAY-2NT

SYS ONE: HA **UIMSRQUE** 29MAY31MAY

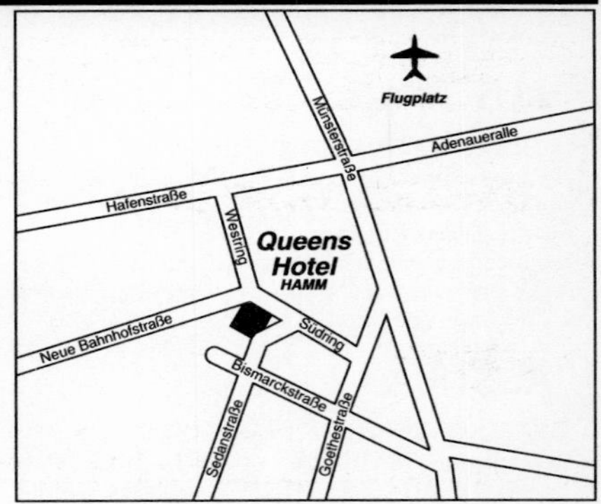

TRAVEL CONTACTS

Travel Contacts Limited
45 Idmiston Road
London SE27 9HL
Tel: +44 (81) 766 7868. Fax: +44 (81) 766 6123.
Australasian Representative:
Philip Thorniley
Thorncross
PO Box 126
BERRY, NSW 2535
Australia
Tel & Fax: +61 (44) 642 198.

Travel Contacts, established in 1980, publishes annually a *Directory of Destination Management Companies* (Ground Handling Agents) worldwide. The companies are carefully chosen for their efficiency and stability. They specialise in Incentive and Conference Group Traffic but most are also happy to handle individual business and holiday travellers.

The complete Directory is available free on request from the above address. A full Profile (continuously up-dated) of each company is available free by fax on request.

Where the information has been available at the time of going to press, tours in the Special Interest section are followed by numbers in brackets: these indicate the best (and in some cases the only) months in which the respective activities are available. Please bear in mind that such information is included only as a guide, as arrangements may change at short notice.

ANTIGUA

ANTOURS
BWIA Sunjet House, PO Box 508, Long & Thames Streets, ST JOHN'S.
Tel: +1 (809) 462 4788/9. Fax: 462 4799. Tlx: 2168 ANTOURS AK.
Contact: Mrs Alwyn Fletcher.
Established: 1982.
Associations: Caribbean Hotels Assn, Caribbean Tourist Assn.
Languages: Eng, Fr, Ger, It, Sp.

ARGENTINA

TURYTRAVEL SA
Viamonte 524 – 3rd, (1053) BUENOS AIRES.
Tel: +54 (1) 311 1553/1489/1105/313 0173. Fax: 313 0177. Tlx: 33-18364 TURY A.
Contacts: Mr Harry Uryson, Ms Maria Virginia del Rio, Ms Mabel Taranto.
Established: 1980; 15 employees.
Languages: Eng, Fr, Ger, It, Polish, Port, Sp.
Associations: ASTA, IATA, IDMA, SITE, WATA, AVIABUE/AAAVYT, Internet, Intralink.
Special Interest: animal breeding, gourmet eating, wildlife (1-12); hunting (3-7); whale-watching (6-11); fishing (8-9); horse breeding (8-12); dairy farming (9-12); diving, mountaineering, trekking (11-3); agriculture (12-5).

ARUBA

ECO DESTINATION MANAGEMENT SERVICES OF ARUBA
Ponton 36 F, ORANJESTAD.
Tel: +297 (8) 26034. Fax: 31078.
Contact: Mrs Wichita M Every.
Established: 1989; 20 employees.
Languages: Eng, Dutch, Fr, Ger, It, Sp.
Associations: SITE.
Special Interest: caves, coral reefs, deep-sea fishing, diving, fishing, gambling, golf, sailing, tennis, water-skiing, windsurfing (1-12); carnivals (2-3); jazz festival (6).

AUSTRALIA

I.D. TOURS SOUTH PACIFIC LTD
30 Atchison Street, St Leonards, SYDNEY NSW 2065
Tel: +61 (2) 965 4343. Fax: 906 1955.
Contact: Belinda Walls.
Special Interest: agriculture, botany, cattle breeding, coral reefs, cruises, gemstones, golf, horse breeding, ornithology, all sports, wildlife, wines, vineyards (1-12).

AUSTRIA

AUSTROBUS WELCOME TOURISTIC
Lueger-Ring 8, 1014 VIENNA.
Tel: +43 (1) 53411-0. Fax: 53411-203. Tlx: 114239 AUBU A.
Contacts: Mr Bernhard Henhapel, General Manager, Inbound and Ms Nicole Zaar, Manager, Sales & Operations.
Established: 1932; 15 employees (Inbound Dept).
Languages: Eng, Fr, It, Sp.
Associations: ASTA, NETWORLD, UFTAA, ITP, IATA, WATA, SITE.
Special Interest: architecture, art, castles, cathedrals, history, medicine, museums (1-12); bicycle touring, walking (spring/autumn); opera (9-7); wines & vineyards (autumn); skiing (11-3).

BAHAMAS – NASSAU

MAJESTIC TOURS LTD
PO Box 1401, Hillside Manor, Cumberland Street, NASSAU.
Tel: +1 (809) 322 2606/7. Fax: 328 2712/326 5785. Tlx: 20176 REGAL.
Contact: William A Saunders.
Associations: ASTA, IATA, WATA.
Special Interest: coral reefs, deep-sea fishing, diving, gambling, game fishing, golf, sailing, sub-aqua sport (1-12); carnivals (6-9, 12).

BARBADOS

SUNLINC BARBADOS
Bulkeley Great House, Bulkeley, ST GEORGE.
Tel: +1 (809) 436 1710. Fax: 436 1715.
Contact: Helen Schur-Parris, Vice President, Sales & Marketing.
Established: 1983; 26 employees.
Languages: Eng, Fr, Ger, Sp, Swiss-Ger.
Associations: SITE Intl, SITE Caribbean.
Special Interest: caves, flowers/horticulture, sub-aqua sport, history, zoos, underwater marine park, museums, house tours, watersports, yachting, driving tours, shopping, deep-sea fishing (1-12).

BELGIUM

BRUSSELS INTERNATIONAL TRAVEL SERVICE
30 rue Arthur Diderich, 1060 BRUSSELS.
Tel: +32 (2) 537 8766. Fax: 538 1294. Tlx: 22066 BRUINT B.
Contacts: Mr Marc Dans, Mr Igor Korn and Mr Yves Dubus.
Established: 1988; 4 employees.
Languages: Dutch, Eng, Fr, Ger, Polish, Russ, Sp.
Associations: CMT, API.
Special Interest: architecture, art, breweries, food, gourmet eating, museums, pharmaceuticals (1-12); flowers (4-6); history (4-10); caves (5-9); educational visits.

BERMUDA

PENBOSS DESTINATION MANAGEMENT
PO Box 510, 35 Church Street, HAMILTON HM, CX.
Tel: +1 (809) 295 9733. Fax: 292 8251/4823. Tlx: 3361 MEYER BA
Contact: Ms Carla Fountain.
Established: 1948; 50 employees.
Languages: Eng, Ger, Port, Sp.
Associations: ASTA, IATA, SITE, IFWTO.
Special Interest: deep-sea fishing, gourmet eating (1-12); golf, tennis (10-6); sailing (4-11); coral reefs (5-11).

BOLIVIA

TURISMO BALSA LTDA
PO Box 5889, Avenida 16 de Julio 1650, LA PAZ.
Tel: +591 (2) 357 817/354 049. Fax: 391 310. Tlx: 2358 BALTOUR.
Contact: Mr Jean-Jacques Valloton.
Associations: IATA, COTAL, ASTA, UFTAA.
Special Interest: agriculture, anthropology, architecture, carnivals, golf, photography, steamboats, pilgrimages; mountaineering (4-9).

BOPHUTHATSWANA

BOPHUTHATSWANA TOURISM COUNCIL
PO Box 4488, MMABATHO 8681.
Tel: +27 (140) 84 30 40 03.
Contact: Mr Chris More.
London Office:
Bophuthatswana International Affairs, Piccadilly House, 33 Regent Street, London SW1Y 4NE.
Tel: +44 (71) 439 8611. Fax: 734 0346.
Contact: Mr Ian Findlay.
Special Interest: birdwatching, casinos, different cultures, entertainment, fishing, game viewing, golf, horseriding, hunting, safaris, watersports, wildlife (1-12).

BRAZIL

G B INTERNACIONAL
Rua Capitao Salomao 40, 22271 RIO DE JANEIRO.
Tel: +55 (21) 286 9697. Fax: 286 9484. Tlx: 21-31575 GBIT BR/21-21113.
Contact: Mr Roberto Dultra.
Established: 1972; 22 employees.
Languages: Eng, Fr, Ger, Jap, Port, Sp.
Associations: ABAV, IATA, SITE, ASTA.
Special Interest: agriculture, architecture, art gemstones, golf, hydroelectrics, textiles (1-12); cattle breeding, fishing (3-11); deep-sea fishing, diving (12-3).

BURMA (UNION OF MYANMAR)

BURMA CULTURAL TOURS CO LTD
Skyline General Consultancy Services, No 64, 1st Floor, 32nd Street, YANGON (= Rangoon).
Tel: +95 (1) 82022/85534. Tlx: 21201 TELBOX BM SKYLINE RGN/ST 404.
Thailand Office:
2nd Floor, 491/39-40 Silom Plaza, Silom Road, BANGKOK 10500.
Tel: +66 (2) 235 9780-1/236 6583-4. Fax: 236 6585/237 6696. Tlx: 82243 SKYLIPS TH.
Contact: Mr Aung Khin.
Special Interest: religion, cultural visits (1-12); archaeology, pilgrimages, history, museums (11-3).

CANADA – EAST

GROUP SPECIALISTS CANADA
Suite 200, 980 Yonge Street, TORONTO, M4W 2J5.
Tel: +1 (416) 323 9090. Fax: 323 3980. Tlx: 06-218776 CISS.
Contact: Joan Cooper, Director.

CANADA – WEST

CONTACTS PACIFIC SERVICES INC
Suite 600, 1090 W Georgia St, VANCOUVER, BC. V6E 3V7.
Tel: +1 (604) 683 2174. Fax: 688 6972. Tlx: 04-55434.
Contact: Mr George Bartel.
Established: 1973; 15 employees.
Languages: Eng, Fr, Ger, It.
Special Interest: anthropology, aquaculture, mining, sports, ornithology (1-12); whale-watching (3-4); forestry, hydroelectrics, ranching (4-10); skiing (12-4).

CAYMAN ISLANDS

MAJESTIC TOURS
PO Box 298, GRAND CAYMAN.
Tel: +1 (809) 949 7773. Fax: 949 8647. Tlx: 4304 MAJESTIC.
Contact: Murray J Mitten.
Associations: Cayman Is Hotel Assn, American Sightseeing International.
Special Interest: coral reefs, deep-sea fishing, diving, game fishing, golf, museums, sailing, sub-aqua sport (1-12).

CHANNEL ISLANDS

STAR TRAVEL LTD
Grenville House, Grenville St, ST HELIER.
Tel: +44 (534) 78605. Fax: 66441.
Contacts: Iain MacFirbhisigh, Director; and Ms Sue Gillen, Manager.
Established: 1980; 6 employees.
Languages: Eng, Fr, Ger, Norw, Swed.
Associations: ABTA, IATA, CITOG, Avis.
Special Interest: bicycling, boating & boat races, bowls, castles, deep-sea fishing, finance, flowers & horticulture, food & gourmet eating, golf, military history, insect life, museums, ornithology, sailing, walking, yachting, zoo.

CHILE

TURISMO COCHA
PO Box 1001, Agustinas 1173, SANTIAGO DE CHILE.
Tel: +56 (2) 698 3341. Fax: 699 3290. Tlx: 441228 *or* 341099 COCHA.
Contacts: Mario Fuenzalida, President and Jorge Guazzini, Inbound Manager.
Associations: IATA, COTAL, ASTA, USTOA, WOODSIDE.
Special Interest: canal cruising (3-11); fishing, geology (4-8); hot springs (4-10); flowers, horse breeding (9-1); botany, diving (9-3); ornithology (9-4); wildlife (10-3); forestry (9-3); wines & vineyards (11-4).

CIS – RUSSIAN FEDERATION

ONE EUROPE TRAVEL LTD
Bolshaya Naberezhnaya Ul. 5-233, 123362 MOSCOW.
Tel: +7 (095) 490 5195. Fax: 490 5195.
Contact: Sergey Kholdenko, General Manager.
Sub-offices:
ST PETERSBURG. Tel & Fax: +7 (0812) 552 9032.
Contact: Anton.
TASHKENT. Tel & Fax: +7 (093172) 687 262.
Contact: Shamil Bakhtiarov.
London Office:

Research House, Fraser Road, PERIVALE UB6 7AQ.
Tel: +44 (81) 566 9424. Fax: 566 8845. Tlx: 918439 RPTLON G.
Other offices in: KIEV, MINSK, IRKUTSK, ALMA-ATA, TBILISI, EREVAN, VLADIVOSTOK, SAMARKAND & ULAAN BAATAR (Mongolia); but all enquiries to Moscow or London.
Special Interest: trans-Siberian express itineraries, opera, ballet, music, trekking, bicycling, rafting, kayaking, religious groups, Central Asia cities routes, private home stays, camel trekking, horseriding.

CROATIA

ATLAS TRAVEL AGENCY
Pile 1, 5000 DUBROVNIK.
Tel: +38 (50) 442 2222. Fax: 411 100/28342. Tlx: 27515/27583 ATLAS.
Contact: Mr Tonko Kolendic.
Established: 1923; 1200 employees.
Languages: Dutch, Eng, Fr, Ger, It, Sp, Swed.
Associations: UFTAA, IATA, JATA, DRV, USTOA, ICCA, COTAL, ACTA, ASTA, ABTA.
Special Interest: archaeology, art, history, tennis, pilgrimages, ornithology, naturism, rafting, canoeing, sailing, wines & vineyards, skiing.

CYPRUS

CYDEM TOURS LTD
PO Box 4134, 20 Stassicrates Street, NICOSIA.
Tel: +357 (2) 451 223. Fax: 457 297. Tlx: 2706.
Contacts: Aristos Demetriou, Panikos Apeyitos.
Associations: IATA, ACTA, SITE, ITA UK.
Special Interest: archaeology, botany, bicycle touring, diving (5-10); geology, horticulture, ornithology, pilgrimages, trekking, walking, wines & wineyards (8-11); skiing (2).

CZECH REPUBLIC

WELCOME TOURISTIC PRAHA
Havlickova 11, 11000 PRAGUE.
Tel: +42 (2) 232 6733/6534. Fax: 232 7193. Tlx: 122480.
Contacts: Mr Vaclav Dvorak, Mrs Ingrid Kent.
Established: 1990; 10 employees.
Languages: Czech, Eng, Ger.
Special Interest: architecture, art, castles, cathedrals, history, museums, opera, wines & vineyards, beer-brewing, hunting, china/porcelain/crystal (1-12).

DENMARK

RITZAU SPECIAL TOURS
PO Box 825, Ostbanegade 39, 2100 COPENHAGEN O.
Tel: +45 35 26 48 88/30 88. Fax: 35 26 34 45. Tlx: 22946 LETH DK.
Contacts: Mrs Majken Ritzau, Mrs Turid Johansen.
Associations: SITE, ASTA, DRF.
Special Interest: architecture, art, agriculture, cattle/dairy, gourmet cooking & eating, textile design (1-12); medicine (1-6, 9-12); antiques/appraisals, opera (4-5, 9-11); ornithology (4-8); horticulture & gardens (4-10); sailing & cruising (5-9)

DOMINICA

WHITCHURCH TRAVEL AGENCY
PO Box 71, Old Street, ROSEAU.
Tel: +1 (809) 445 2181/3121/3122. Fax: 448 5787. Tlx: 8650 WHITRVL DO.
Contact: Gerry Aird.
Associations: IATA, WTO, CHA.

DOMINICAN REPUBLIC

TURINTER S.A.
Leopoldo Navarro 4, SANTO DOMINGO.
Tel: +1 (809) 686 4020/685 4020. Fax: 688 3890. Tlx: (326) 0554/4536 TURITER.
Contact: Felix A Jimenez.
Established: 1976; 110 employees.
Languages: Eng, Fr, It, Sp.
Special Interest: baseball, caves, driving tours, gambling, golf, real estate, underwater marine parks, watersports, yachting, handicraft, cable cars, whale watching.
Branch Offices:
Plaza Jose Augusto Puig, PUERTO PLATA.
Tel: +1 (809) 586 3911/586 2315. Fax: 586 4755. Tlx: (346) 2034.
Jose El Julian No 2, Higuey, PUNTA CANA.
Tel: +1 (809) 554 5565.

ECUADOR

METROPOLITAN TOURING
PO Box 2542, Avenida Amazonas 239, QUITO.
Tel: +593 (2) 560 550. Fax: 564 655. Tlx: 2482 METOUR ED.
Contact: Mr Eduardo Proano, Director General.
Associations: ASTA, WATA, ICCA, COTAL, SATA, USTOA.
Special Interest: agriculture & farming, archaeology, art (colonial & modern), ethnic culture, fishing, gardens, jungle cruises, ornithology, wildlife cruises (Galapagos), religion (1-12).

EGYPT

MENATOURS TRAVEL & TOURIST AGENCY
PO Box 46, El Nasr Building, El Nil Street, GIZA.
Tel: +20 (2) 349 0168/348 2387/348 2231. Fax: 348 4016. Tlx: 93889/ 21176 MENAT UN.
Contacts: Mr Badran Kamel, Managing Director; and Mr Samy Khalil, Marketing Director.
Luxor Office:
Salah el Din Square, LUXOR.
Tel: +20 (95) 385 660. Fax: 384 724.
Contact: Mr Sarwat Agamy.
Associations: ASTA, ACTA, IATA, UFTAA, COTAL, DRV, PATA.
Established: 1956; 265 employees.
Languages: Arab, Eng, Fr, Ger, It.
Special Interest: diving, gambling, sub-aqua sport, surfing, water-skiing, windsurfing (1-12); horse breeding (2), archaeology (10-2); Nile cruises (10-5)

ESTONIA & BALTIC STATES

VIRONE TRAVEL BUREAU
Pronksi 11, TALLINN EE0007.
Tel: +7 (0142) 443 992/425 398. Fax: 448 960. Tlx: 64-173824 VIRON.
(dialling access codes, currently CIS, will soon change: consult *Travel Contacts* if you have difficulties.)
Contacts: Mrs Eno Truusa, Incoming Manager & Mr Enn Vilgo, Managing Director.

FIJI

I.D. TOURS SOUTH PACIFIC LTD
c/o Rosies The Travel Service, PO Box 9268, NADI AIRPORT.
Tel: +679 722 155. Fax: 722 607. Tlx: 5143 FJ.
Contact: Tony Whitton.
Special Interest: agriculture, coral reefs, deep-sea fishing, scuba-diving, gamefishing, golf, horticulture, squash, tennis (1-12); cricket (10-5); rugby (5-10); charter yachting (5-11

FINLAND

FINLAND TRAVEL BUREAU LTD: INCOMING & INCENTIVE DEPT
PO Box 319, Kaivokatu 10A, 00100 HELSINKI.
Tel: +358 (0) 18261. Fax: 612 1547. Tlx: 124626 FTBHK SF.
Contact: Ms Sari Viljamaa, Manager.
Established: 1909; 15 employees (Incoming Dept).
Languages: Eng, Fin, Fr, Ger, It.
Associations: ASTA, AFTA, Hickory Europe, Networld, SITE, UFTAA.
Special Interest: architecture (1-12); hospitals (1-6, 8-12); safaris (2-10); ornithology (5-7); music festivals/jazz/opera (5-8); forestry, paper, trekking (5-10); agriculture, canoeing, fishing (6-9).

FRANCE – PARIS & THE NORTH

HOLT PARIS WELCOME SERVICE SA
12 rue du Helder, 75009 PARIS.
Tel: +33 (1) 45 23 08 14. Fax: 42 47 19 89. Tlx: 660195 HOLT F.
Contacts: Mr Alan Holt and Mrs Susan Holt.
Associations: IDMA, SNAV.
Special Interest: art, architecture, food, horseracing, medicine, museums, railways, wines (1-12); cookery, religion theatre (1-6, 9-12).

– THE RIVIERA & MONACO

VIP RIVIERA SERVICE
PO Box 152, 205 Promenade des Anglais, 06203 NICE Cedex 3.
Tel: +33 93 44 22 33. Fax: 93 37 49 93. Tlx: 461483.
Contact: Mr Ralph Holt.
Established: 1979; 8 employees.
Languages: Dutch, Eng, Fr, Ger, It, Jap, Port.
Associations: Welcome People, SITE, SKAL, UFTAA, FUAVV.
Special Interest: cruises, golf, museums, opera, railways, tennis (1-12); carnivals (2-3); flowers, gardens (4-8); yachting (4-10); Grand Prix (5); jazz (7); horse-racing, submarine harbour cruise.

GAMBIA

GAMBIA NATIONAL TOURS CO LTD (GAMTOURS)
PO Box 101, BANJUL.
Tel: +220 92259/92505. Fax: 91013. Tlx: 2215 GV.
Contact: Mr Sammy Lai Mboge.
Associations: ATA (African Travel Assoc).
Special Interest: cattle breeding, fishing, gambling, golf, hunting, pottery (1-12); butterflies (5-9); insect life (7-9); safaris (10-5); deep-sea fishing, river cruises (11-5); ornithology (11-12).

GERMANY– BERLIN

CONFERENCE & TOURING GFB BERLIN
PO Box 1207, Kaiserdamm 30, W-1000 BERLIN 19.
Tel: +49 (30) 301 7027. Fax: 301 9625. Tlx: 182834.
Contact: Peter Antoni.
Established: 1981; 9 employees.
Languages: Eng, Fr, Ger, Russ, Sp.
Associations: SITE, UFTAA, BTC.
Special Interest: museums & galleries, architecture, WWII & Cold War relics, fashion shows, opera & cabaret, ballooning, history.

– DRESDEN

CLASSIC TOURS
Schaeferstrasse 49, O-8010 DRESDEN.
Tel & Fax: +49 (351) 496 2166. Fax: 496 2166.
Contact: Katja Samberg.
Established: 1990; 4 employees.
Languages: Eng, Fr, Ger, Jap.
Associations: SITE.
Branch Office:
Rauentalstrasse 6, O-8250 MEISSEN.
Tel: +49 (3521) 2260. Fax: 2260.
Contact: Elvira Beyer.

– DÜSSELDORF & COLOGNE

HARTMANN INCOMING & INCENTIVE SERVICE
Parsevalstrasse 7a, W-4000 DÜSSELFDORF 30.
Tel: +49 (211) 9078-03. Fax: 9078-399.
Contact: Ms Sabine Hakvoort, Sales Manager Incoming.
Branch Office:
Ebert Platz 9, W-5000 COLOGNE 1.
Tel: +49 (221) 771 0440. Fax: 771 0427.
Associations: DRV, American Ch of Commerce.
Special Interest: funfairs (7); carnivals (2); breweries, museums, castles, monorail, cathedrals (1-12).

– FRANKFURT

GTS – GRIMM TRAVEL SERVICE
Max-Planck-Strasse 21, W-6382 FRIEDRICHSDORF.
Tel: +49 (6172) 75011. Fax: 77372.
Contact: Mr Walter Dierks.
Established: 1990; 3 employees.
Languages: Eng, Ger.
Special Interest: cattle breeding, dolls, museums, wines (4-10); castles, cruises, disabled tours, military history, railways (5-9).

– HAMBURG

COLUMBUS TOURS
Ost-West-Strasse 59, W-2000 HAMBURG 11.
Tel: +49 (40) 37 05 23 85. Fax: 37 05 25 17. Tlx: 21321660 HS D.
Contact: Klaus Schneider.
Established: 1978; 8 employees.
Languages: Eng, Fr, Ger, Sp.
Associations: SITE, DRV, IATA.
Special Interest: architecture, gourmet eating, history, public transport, universities, zoo (1-12); sailing (4-9); agriculture, horticulture, cattle breeding/dairy farming (4-10); tennis (5-6); butterflies (5-9); horse-racing (6-7).

– MUNICH

WELCOME DESTINATION MANAGEMENT GmbH
Mauerkircherstrasse 4, W-8000 MUNICH 80.
Tel: +49 (89) 988 835. Fax: 980 208. Tlx: 524602 WELC D.
Contact: Mr Gunter H Roleff, CITE.
Established: 1968; 10 employees.
Languages: Eng, Fr, Ger.
Associations: ICCA, SITE, MPI, IDMA.
Special Interest: architecture, art, beer festivals, castles, cookery, food, museums, music festivals, universities, zoos (1-12); skiing (1-4); photography (4-10).

– STUTTGART & THE SW

REISEBÜRO ROMINGER GmbH
Stephanstrasse 33, 7000 STUTTGART 1.
Tel: +49 (711) 208 6300. Fax: 208 6298. Tlx: 722888.
Contact: Ms Andrea Koehler.
Established: 1842; 400 employees.
Associations: IATA, AIR.

GHANA

BLACK BEAUTY TOURS LIMITED
PO Box 2189, The Loom Building, Samlotte House, Kwame Nkrumah Ave, Adabraka, ACCRA.
Tel: +233 (21) 227 078/220 384. Fax: 220 062. Tlx: 3033 GH BLACK BEAUTY.
Contacts: Joseph K Ankumah, MBA (Managing Director) and

Mrs Elizabeth E Ankumah (Tour Manager).
Established: 1969; 10 employees.
Languages: Eng.
Associations: IATA, ASTA, American Sightseeing Intl.
Special Interest: cruises, golf, pilgrimages, pottery (1-12); safari (4-9); gardens, history, museums, religion, universities (6-9); castles, music festivals (6, 7, 9).

GIBRALTAR

BLAND LIMITED
Cloister Building, GIBRALTAR.
Tel: +350 79200. Fax: 76189. Tlx: 2118 BLAND.
Contact: Ms Jane Tickle.
Special Interest: birdwatching, sailing, dolphin safari, shark fishing, historical sites, museums, apes' den, castles, caves & galleries, casino, changing of the guards.

GREECE

ARVANITIS TOURIST AND TRAVEL BUREAU
36 Voulis Street, ATHENS 10557.
Tel: +30 (1) 323 2375/322 0383. Fax: 323 2340. Tlx: 215781 ARDI GR.
Contact: Mr Michael Wheen.
Established: 1950; 15 employees.
Languages: Eng, Fr, Ger, Greek, Jap, Port.
Associations: HATA, COTAL, CMT, FIYTO, FIAV, IATA, EUROMIC, ASTA, SITE, MPI, AIR, IDMA, ASATA (Assoc), AFTA (non-resident), TAANZ (allied).
Special Interest: history, religion, spas (1-12); botany (4-6); insect life (4-7); agriculture (5-6); cruises, ornithology, yachting (spring/autumn); wines & vineyards (9); archaeology (winter).

GRENADA

ELEGANT CARIBBEAN HOLIDAY SERVICES
PO Box 32, ST GEORGE'S.
Tel: +1 (809) 440 7997. Fax: 440 6605.
Contacts: Edward Frederick, Managing Director; or Andrea Redhead-Frederick, Operations Director.
Established: 1991; 3 employees.
Associations: SITE Intl, Grenada Hotel Assn.
Special Interest: bicycling, boating & boat races, driving tours, game fishing, horseriding, sailing, yachting (1-12); cricket (12-6).

HONG KONG

THE TRAVEL ADVISERS LTD
Room 1006, Silvercord, Tower 1, Canton Road, KOWLOON.
Tel: +852 375 8321. Fax: 375 1078. Tlx: 44430.
Contact: Mr H Y Loo.
Established: 1932; 50 employees.
Languages: Chin, Eng, Fr.
Special Interest: arts/cultural festivals, China tours, cruises, food/gourmet eating, golf, rugby (7); shopping (1-12); watersports (5-11); Macau Grand Prix (9).

HUNGARY

IBUSZ – HUNGARIAN TRAVEL COMPANY LIMITED
Felszabadulas ter 5, 1364 BUDAPEST.
Tel: +36 (1) 186 866. Fax: 118 9161. Tlx: 61-224976/224999.
Contact: Tomas Bekassy.
UK Sales Office:
Danube Travel Ltd, 6 Conduit Street, LONDON W1R 9TG.
Tel: +44 (71) 493 0263. Fax: 493 6963. Tlx: 23541 DNBTVL G.
Contact: Mr Balazs Orosz.

ICELAND

URVAL/UTSYN TRAVEL
Alfabakka 16, 109 REYKJAVIK.
Tel: +354 (1) 699 300. Fax: 71233. Tlx: 2036 UTSYN IS.
Contact: Mr Godi Sveinsson.
Associations: IATA, UFTAA, TIA.
Established: 1970; 45 employees.
Languages: Dan, Eng, Fr, Ger, Ice, Norw, Swed.
Special Interest: geology, photography, ornithology, fishing, horseriding, golf, rafting, volcano visits, gourmet eating, hot springs, jeep safaris, glacier trips, whale-watching.

INDIA

TRADE-WINGS LTD
30K Dubash Marg, Fort, BOMBAY 400 023.
Tel: +91 (22) 244 334. Fax: 204 4223. Tlx: 11 85470/82494 TWBB IN.
Contacts: Mr Vinoo Ubhayakar and Mr Arvind Mantri.
Established: 1949; 250 employees.
Languages: Eng, Fr, Ger.
Associations: ACTA, USTOA, IATA, UFTAA, ASTA, TAAI, PATA, AFTA.
Special Interest: agriculture, archaeology, cricket, fishing, gourmet eating, houseboats, jungle expeditions, pilgrimages, railways, textiles, trekking, wildlife (10-3).

IRELAND

THE O'MARA TRAVEL COMPANY LIMITED
37 Main Street, Donnybrook, DUBLIN 4.
Tel: +353 (1) 269 6033. Fax: 269 6705. Tlx: 91342.
Contacts: Ms Stephanie Byrne, Ms Susanne Monks.
Established: 1978; 11 employees.
Languages: Dan, Eng, Fr, Sp.
Associations: ITAA, ITOA, ASTA, IATA.
Special Interest: heritage, golf, country pursuits, castles & gardens, incentive, theatre, music.

ISRAEL

PALEX TOURS LTD
59 Ha'atzmaut Road, 33033 HAIFA.
Tel: +972 (4) 524 254-9. Fax: 522 491. Tlx: 46745 PALEX IL.
Contacts: Mrs Tamar Brenner, Director and Mrs Maya Rotter.
Established: 1937.
Associations: DRV, ASTA.
Special Interest: hot springs, medicine, pilgrimages, universities (1-12); agriculture, dairy farming, irrigation (spring); disabled tours (spring/autumn); wines & vineyards (8); health fitness (11).

ITALY

CLEMENTSON TRAVEL OFFICE
PO Box 412, Castello 4709, VENICE.
Tel: +39 (41) 520 0466. Fax: 523 1203. Tlx: 410496 CLEMVE I.
Contact: Mr Corrado Spalazzi.
Established: 1946; 8 employees.
Languages: Eng, Fr, Ger, It.
Associations: FIAVET, SITE, UFTAA, MPI.
Special Interest (Venice itself): architecture, art, carnivals, gourmet eating, museums, opera, painting, theatre.
Special Interest (Italy): archaeology, botany, canoeing, car racing, cruises, film festivals, gardens, golf, rowing, skiing, tennis, volcanoes, wines & vineyards.

JAMAICA

XAYMACA TOURS
PO Box 1381, MONTEGO BAY.
Tel: +1 (809) 952 3274-6. Fax: 952 9270. Tlx: 2001 MOBAY JA.
Contact: Linda Leslie, General Manager.
Special Interest: caves, deep-sea fishing, diving, golf, rafting, sailing, tennis (1-12).

JAPAN

TOPPAN TRAVEL SERVICE CORPORATION
Central PO Box 1948.Toppan Yaesu Building, 2-2-7, Yaesu, Chuo-ku, TOKYO 104.
Tel: +81 (3) 32 76 81 13. Fax: 32 71 76 70. Tlx: 2228464 TOPTRV J.
Contacts: Mr Ken Kato and Mr R Wittwer.
Associations: IATA, JATA, PATA, ASTA.
Special Interest: architecture, railways, religion (1-12); spas/hot springs (5-10); botany, flowers, gardens, horticulture, pottery (5 & 10); mountaineering (5-9); skiing (12-3); music festival (11).

JORDAN

BISHARAT TOURS CORPORATION
PO Box 35010, AMMAN.
Tel: +962 (6) 41350. Fax: 659 330. Tlx: 21363 BTC JO.
Contact: Dr Faik Bisharat.
Associations: IATA, UFTAA, ASTA, ISTA, COTAL, American Sightseeing Intl, WTA, PATA.

KENYA

ABERCROMBIE & KENT LTD
PO Box 59749, Bruce House, Standard Street, NAIROBI.
Tel: +254 (2) 334 955/919/355. Fax: 215 752. Tlx: 22853/ 25574 KENTOURS.
Contact: Julian Hutton.
London Office:
A & K Overseas, Sloane Square House, Holbein Place, LONDON SW1W 8NS.
Tel: +44 (71) 730 9600. Fax: 973 0478.
Contact: George Morgan-Grenville.
Established: 1962; 75 employees.
Languages: Eng, Fr, Ger, Jap, Sp.
Associations: KATO.
Special Interest: anthropology, botany, film sets, golf, mountaineering, safaris, sub-aqua sport, trekking, wildlife, deep-sea fishing, migration.

LUXEMBOURG

WEZENBERG INCENTIVE TRAVEL SERVICES
75 rue Michel Gehrend, 1619 LUXEMBOURG.
Tel: +352 402 332. Fax: 481 801.
Contact: Mr Han Wezenberg.
Languages: Dan, Dutch, Eng, Fr, Ger.
Special Interest: art & painting, ballooning, castles, cycling, fishing, gambling, golf, gourmet eating, music festivals, squash, tennis, wines & vineyards, walking, war history.

MALAYSIA

WORLD EXPRESS
2-14 Angkasa Raya, Jalan Ampang, KUALA LUMPUR 50450.
Tel: +60 (3) 243 5412. Fax: 242 1129. Tlx: 31132.
Contact: Mr Ronnie Phuah.
Penang Office:
Penang Plaza (Unit 203), 126 Jalan Burmah, PENANG 10050.
Tel: +60 (4) 361 910. Fax: 369 654. Tlx: 40793.
Contact: Lau Ee Bee.
Established: 1970; 20 employees.
Languages: Chin, Eng, Fr, Ger, It.
Special Interest: agriculture/botany, festivals, gourmet eating, golf, horseracing, jungle expeditions, museums, pottery, railways, religion, shopping, zoos.

MALTA

SPECIAL INTEREST TRAVEL LTD
103, Archbishop Street, VALLETTA.
Tel: +356 233 121. Fax: 235 145. Tlx: 1278 OJAMED MW.
Contacts: Mr Jose Calleja, Mr Michael Kamsky.
Established: 1977; 12 employees.
Languages: Eng, Fr, Ger, It.
Associations: Conference & Incentive Travel Bureau, Malta.
Special Interest: archaeology, architecture, fortresses, cathedrals, history, museums, religion, coral reefs, military history (1-12); diving, windsurfing (4-11); carnival (pre-Lent).

MAURITIUS

MAUTOURCO
MAURITIUS TOURING CO LTD/TRANSMAURICE LTD
Gustave Colin Street, FOREST SIDE.
Tel: +230 674 3695/6. Fax: 674 3720. Tlx: 4435 HERMCO IW.
Contact: Mr Jacques de Speville.
Established: 1955; 100 employees.
Languages: Eng, Fr.
Associations: Hertz franchise.
Special Interest: coral reefs, folk-dancing, gardens, golf, history, religion, scuba diving, water-skiing, wildlife (1-12); horseracing (5-11); yacht cruises, deep-sea fishing.

MEXICO

M P V – MEXICANOS PROFESIONALES EN VIAJES
Timaulipas 30, Pisos 2 y 3, Col. Hipodromo Condesa, MEXICO DF 06140.
Tel: +52 (5) 256 0075/4505/5505. Fax: 256 1255/0225. Tlx: 1776302 VIMAME.
Contacts: Jaime Ocampo or Penny Longsworth.
Cancun Office:
Lobby Hotel Fiesta Americana, Coral Beach Blvd, Kukulkan, Zona Hoteliera, CANCUN, Quintana Roo, 77500.
Tel: +52 (988) 32900, ext 4700 *or* 30705. Fax: 30705.
Contact: Helene Herrmann.
Established: 1973; 50 employees.
Associations: IATA, ASTA, SITE.
Special Interest: archaeology, folk-dancing, food, history, museums, pottery, textiles (1-12); car racing (5); deep-sea fishing).

MOROCCO

OLIVE BRANCH TOURS, SA
35 rue El Oraibi Jilali, CASABLANCA 01.
Tel: +212 226 4203/ 226 1416/ 222 3919. Fax: 226 0976. Tlx: 21651/23953.
Contacts: Mr Clive Chandler and Mr B Akli.
Established: 1958; 16 employees.
Languages: Arabic, Berber, Eng, Fr, Ger, It, Port.
Associations: ASTA, USTOA, UFTAA, API, FNAVM (MOROCCO).
Special Interest: agriculture, archaeology, architecture, folklore, golf, history, kasbahs, pottery (1-12); ornithology (spring/autumn); wines & vineyards (summer); university (term).

NEPAL

YETI TRAVELS PVT LTD
PO Box 76, Dubarg Marg, KATHMANDU.
Tel: +977 (1) 22 1234/ 22 1739/ 22 1754/ 22 2285. Fax: 22 6153. Tlx: 2204 YETI NP/2303 AMXREP NP/2648 YETI NP.
Contact: Mr J L Khanna.
Established: 1966; 350 employees.
Languages: Eng, Fr, Ger, It, Jap, Sp.
Associations: IATA, WATA, PATA, AFTA, ASTA, UFTAA, USTOA, ISTA, COTAL, JATA, NATA, TAAI (non-resident), IATO, ICCA.
Special Interest: folk-dancing, gambling, hospitals, museums, photography, pottery, rafting, safaris, wildlife (1-12); golf (9-6); mountaineering (2-4, 8-9); trekking (10-6).

NETHERLANDS

BEUK TRAVEL CONSULTANTS
Strawinskylaan 911, 1077 XX AMSTERDAM.
Tel: +31 (20) 662 6277/ 662 6322. Fax: 662 9826. Tlx: 18321.
Contacts: Mr John Brandenburg, Managing Director; Mr Marc Beuk, Sales Manager; and Mr Jan Kuipers, Operations Manager.
Established: 1974; 6 employees (incoming dept).
Languages: Dutch, Eng, Fr, Ger, Sp.
Associations: ANVR, ASTA, UFTAA, PATA, VNC (Congress Organisers).
Special Interest: agriculture, architecture, cattle breeding, flowers, food, hospitals, medicine, museums, public transport (1-12); dairy farming (3-10); gardens, horticulture (4-9).

NEW ZEALAND

I.D. TOURS SOUTH PACIFIC LTD
Private Bag 92-171, Level 9, Quay Tower, 29 Customs Street West, AUCKLAND.
Tel: +64 (9) 302 5074. Fax: 309 4156.
Contact: Barry J Huston.
Special Interest: agriculture, golf, hydro-electrics (1-12); wines & vineyards (1-4); rugby (5-9); skiing (8-9); dairy farming, cattle & horse breeding (10-4); sea fishing, yachting (11-4)

NORWAY

PERFECTION
Engelgarden, Bryggen, N-5003 BERGEN.
Tel: +47 (5) 318 899 (531 8899 from Sep 10 '93). Fax: 327 032 (532 7032 from Sep 10 '93).
Contact: Ms Eli Lilleheim Aamodt.
Established: 1987; 3 employees.
Languages: Eng, Fr, Ger, Norw.
Associations: SITE.
Special Interest: fjord cruises, seaplane flights (glaciers, fjords), midnight sun, Arctic winter, fishing, rafting, medieval wood architecture; heritage (Viking & Hanseatic), industrial themes (fisheries, oil gas)

OMAN

GRAY MACKENZIE TRAVEL – GULF VENTURES
PO Box 3985, MUSCAT.
Tel: +968 700 326. Fax: 793 390. Tlx: 3215 OUA ON.
Contact: Mr Pradip Hazaldar.
Special Interest: archaeology, coral reefs, birdwatching, sailing, deep-sea fishing, desert & mountain safaris.

PAKISTAN

SITARA TRAVEL CONSULTANTS (PVT) LTD
PO Box 63, Sitara House, 232 Khadim Hussain Road, RAWALPINDI.
Tel: +92 (51) 564 750-1/566 272. Fax: 584 958. Tlx: 5751 STARA PK.
Contact: Mr Shiraz M Poonja.
International Sales Office:
203-1774 West 5th Avenue, VANCOUVER, BC V6J 1P2.
Tel: +1 (604) 732 4131. Fax: 732 9744. Tlx: 0455768.
Established: 1974; 35 employees.
Languages: Eng.
Associations: ASTA, TAAP, PATA, USTOA, JATA.
Special Interest: museums, squash (1-12); botany (2-4, 9-11); gemstones (3-11); bicycle touring, mountaineering, trekking (5-10); safaris (6-10); archaeology, military history (9-4); gardens, steam trains (11-3).

PAPUA NEW GUINEA

TRANS NIUGINI TOURS
PO Box 371, MT HAGEN.
Tel: +675 521 438. Fax: 522 470. Tlx: 52012.
Contact: Mr R E Bates.
Established: 1976; 50 employees.
Languages: Eng.
Associations: PATA, ASTA, AFTA, TAPNG, USTOA.
Special Interest: anthropology, botany, butterflies, canoeing, diving, flowers, jungle expeditions, ornithology, rafting, safaris (adventure), trekking, war relics (1-12).

PARAGUAY

INTER-EXPRESS
Yegros 690, ASUNCION.
Tel: +595 (21) 490 111/5. Fax: 449 156. Tlx: 264 IE PY.
Contact: Mr Ronald Birks, Partner/Manager, Incoming Dept.
Associations: ASTA, WATA, COTAL.
Special Interest: agriculture, cattle breeding, fishing, gambling, history, hydroelectricity, wild orchids, old trains (1-12).

PERU

DASATOUR SA
Jose Llana Zapata 331 – Suite 901/3 Miraflores, LIMA 18; PO Box 649, LIMA 100.
Tel: +51 (14) 415 045/ 401 750. Fax: 422 970. Tlx: 21002 PE PB HCSAR FOR DASATOUR/20053 PE PB LIMT FOR DASATOUR.
Contact: Mr Jose Lemor.
Associations: IATA, ASTA, COTAL, ICCA, SATA, PATA, USTOA.
Special Interest: anthropology, archaeology, museums, railways, canoeing, jungle expeditions, pottery, golf, rafting, wildlife (1-12); trekking (5-11); mountaineering (5-8).

PHILIPPINES

INTAS TRAVEL AND TOURS, INC.
Ground Floor, Philippine Village Hotel, Nayong Pilipino Park, Mia Road, Pasay City, MANILA; PO Box 7054, ADC PASAY.
Tel: +63 (2) 832 3161/2, 831 2997, 831 2965, 833 8081. Fax: 831 0021. Tlx: 45255 INTAS PM/63683 INTAS PN.
Contact: Ms Sonia Teresita Henderson.
Branch Office:
Shangri-La's EDSA Plaza Hotel, 1 Garden Way, Ortigas Center, Mandaluyong, METRO MANILA.
Tel: +63 (2) 633 6550/8888.
Special Interest: agriculture, caves, coral reefs, diving, jungle expeditions, mountaineering, safaris, volcano visits, wind surfing (1-12).

POLAND

ONE EUROPE TRAVEL
Ul. Nowolipki 21, 01-006 WARSAW.
Tel: +48 (22) 383 231. Tlx: 813991.
Contact: Jacek Robak, Office Manager.
London Office:
Research House, Fraser Road, PERIVALE UB6 7AQ.
Tel: +44 (81) 566 9424. Fax: 566 8845. Tlx: 935309 FRT G.
Contact: Neil McGowan.
Special Interest: arts & culture, 'new Europe', castles, religion, Jewish heritage, opera, ballet, business and political introductions.

PORTUGAL – LISBON & OPORTO

GOLDEN GROUP TRAVEL
Avenida de Berna 35-2o-Dto., 1000 LISBON.
Tel: +351 (1) 793 5428. Fax: 793 5777. Tlx: 65873 GOLDEN P.
Contact: Mr Jose Luis G Sousa.
Established: 1985; 12 employees.
Languages: Eng, Fr, Ger, Port, Sp.
Associations: IATA, ASTA, ACTA, Lisbon Conv Bureau.
Special Interest: art, castles, folk-dancing, gardens, golf, history, museums, pottery, wines & vineyards (1-12); religion/pilgrimages (5,9,10); watersports (6-9); Grand Prix car racing (9).

– ALGARVE

GOLDEN GROUP TRAVEL
Rua Santo Antonio, 129-1o, 8000 FARO.
Tel: +351 (89) 803 712. Fax: 803 715. Tlx: 56743 GOLDEN P.
Contact: Mr Jose Luis G Sousa.
Associations: APAVT, IATA, ASTA, ACTA, SITE.
Special Interest: art, castles, folk-dancing, gardens, golf, history, museums, pottery, wines & vineyards (1-12); religion, pilgrimages (5, 9, 10); watersports (9).

– MADEIRA

GOLDEN GROUP TRAVEL
Rua Dr. Joao Brito Camara 26-A, 1o Esq., 9000 FUNCHAL.
Tel: +351 (91) 743 707. Fax: 743 709. Tlx: 72298 GOLDEN P.
Contact: Mr Samorano Pina.
Associations: ASTA, ACTA.
Special Interest: botanical gardens, flowers, deep-sea fishing, handicrafts, ornithology, walking tours, wines & vineyards.

QATAR

QATAR TRAVELS
PO Box 747, DOHA.
Tel: +974 428 001-2. Fax: 428 004.
Contact: Mr Saleem Zafar.
Established: 1980; 5 employees.
Languages: Arabic, Bengali, Eng, Hindi, Urdu.
Associations: IATA, ASTA.

ROMANIA

FRIENDLY TRAVEL LTD
Suite 101, Hotel Majestic, Str. Academiei, BUCHAREST.
Tel: +40 (0) 155 985 ext. 101. Fax: 840 671.
London Office:
Research House, Fraser Road, PERIVALE UB6 7AQ.
Tel: +44 (81) 566 9040. Fax: 566 8494. Tlx: 935309.
Contact: Mike Laculeanu.

SAINT LUCIA

CONFERENCE & INCENTIVE SERVICES LTD
PO Box 1235, CASTRIES.
Tel: +1 (809) 452 7058/31652. Fax: 453 1780. Tlx: 6201 CISLC.
Contact: David Coathup.
Special Interest: natural beauty, watersports (windsurfing, water-skiing, diving), yachting, ethnic culture, golf, tennis, walking, carnivals & festivals.

SAINT MARTIN (SINT MAARTEN)

ST MARTIN EVASION
B P 1144, Galisbay Road, MARIGOT 97150.
Tel: +590 877 301. Fax: 877 547. Tlx: 919161 GL.
Contact: Isabelle Patry.
Languages: Dutch, Eng, Fr.
Special Interest: deep-sea fishing, helicopter rides, horseriding.

SAINT VINCENT & THE GRENADINES

BAREFOOT HOLIDAYS
PO Box 39, Blue Lagoon, ST VINCENT.
Tel: +1 (809) 456 9334. Fax: 456 9238. Tlx: 7506.
Contacts: Martin and Mary Barnard.
Special Interest: yachting, volcano, nature trails, botanical gardens, museums, waterfall, forts, handicrafts, cathedrals.

SARDINIA

SARDINIAN WELCOME SERVICES
Corso Vittorio Emanuele 45, 08013 BOSA (Nuoro), SARDINIA.
Tel: +39 (785) 374 391. Fax: 374 473. Tlx: 792060 SWS I.
Contact: Mr Pino Masia.
Associations: USAV/FIAVET Italy.
Special Interest: archaeology, folk-dancing, rowing, trekking, wildlife, wines & vineyards (1-12); horseriding, caves (4-10)

SEYCHELLES

NATIONAL TRAVEL AGENCY
PO Box 611, Kingsgate House, Victoria, MAHE.
Tel: +248 24900-7. Fax: 25111. Tlx: 2356 NTA SZ.
Contact: Mr Hugh Payet.
Special Interest: coral reefs, deep-sea fishing, diving, fishing, flowers, game fishing, golf, ornithology, sailing, surfing, walking, water-skiing, windsurfing (1-12).

SINGAPORE

WORLD EXPRESS Pte LTD
114 Middle Road, SINGAPORE 0718.
Tel: +65 336 3877. Fax: 339 8625. Tlx: 33372 WXPSIN RS.
Contact: Mr Tan Chee Chye.
Established: 1969; 50 employees.
Languages: Chin, Eng, Fr, Ger, It.
Associations: ASTA, SITE, ICCA, PATA, AFTA, TAANZ.
Special Interest: architecture, art/painting, gardens, golf, gourmet eating, horseracing, hospitals, museums, religion, wet market & other shopping, windsurfing, zoos (1-12).

SOUTH AFRICA

WALTHERS TOURS (PTY) LTD
60 Harley Street, Ferndale, Randburg, JOHANNESBURG 2125; PO Box 7979, JOHANNESBURG 2000.
Tel: +27 (11) 789 3624. Fax: 789 5255. Tlx: 427238.
Contact: Mr Klaus Walther.
Established: 1981; 11 employees.
Languages: Afrikaans, Eng, Fr, Ger, It, Sp.
Associations: SITE, SATSA, ASATA, WATA, USTOA.
Special Interest: agriculture, cattle breeding, dairy farming, ethnic cultures, flowers/horticulture, fishing, gemstones, golf, mining, photography, wildlife, wines & vineyards.

SPAIN – BALEARIC ISLANDS

C I C (CONVENTIONS, INCENTIVES & CONGRESSES) SA
San Miguel 30-4 D-bis, 07002 PALMA DE MALLORCA.
Tel: +34 (71) 724 934. Fax: 713 545. Tlx: 69127 CICP E.
Contact: Mr Tomeu Bosch.
Established: 1977.
Associations: ITP, MTB.
Special Interest: cycling, folk-dancing, photography, textiles, windsurfing (1-12); cruises, sailing, yachting (4-10); golf (9-5).

– BARCELONA & COSTA BRAVA

LATITUD 4 DESTINATION MANAGEMENT
Diputacion 279, 08007 BARCELONA.
Tel: +34 (3) 488 2220. Fax: 488 2361. Tlx: 98934.
Contact: Mr Eduardo Subirats, Managing Director.
Special Interest: archaeology, architecture, art, cathedrals, gourmet eating, museums, pharmaceuticals, pottery, wines & vineyards (1-12); fashions (4-5, 10-11); opera (10-5).

– COSTA DEL SOL & ANDALUCIA

VIAJES APOLO XII, SA
Centro Commercial Fuensalud, Local 4, BENALMADENA COSTA, Malaga.
Tel: +34 (52) 442 673-4-1. Fax: 441 310. Tlx: 77420 APOL E.
Contact: Mr Jose Puig, President.
Established: 1971; 12 employees.
Languages: Eng, Fr, Sp.
Special Interest: history, gourmet eating, architecture, beaches, golf, historic sites, gambling.

– GRAND CANARY

VIAJES CORPHI
Edificio Bayuca, Calle Alfereces Provisionales 36, PLAYA DEL INGLES.
Tel: +34 (28) 763 254/763 831. Fax: 761 601. Tlx: 95609 LTRA E.
Contact: Paul Leleux.
Established: 1985; 15 employees.
Languages: Dutch, Eng, Fr, Ger, Sp.

– BILBAO

LATITUD 4 DESTINATION MANAGEMENT
Colon de Larreatequi, 35, 1a 3a, 48009 BILBAO.
Tel: +34 (4) 423 6093. Fax: 463 2666.
Contact: Patricio Arana.
Established: 1984.
Special Interest: art, climbing, gourmet eating, history, museums, music, opera, theatre, walking.

– LANZAROTE

VIAJES CORPHI
Please contact our head office on Grand Canary:
Edificio Bayuca, Calle Afereces Provisionales 36, PLAYA DEL INGLES.
Tel: +34 (28) 763 254/763 831. Fax: 761 601. Tlx: 95609 LTRA E.
Contact: Paul Leleux.
Established: 1985; 15 employees.
Languages: Dutch, Eng, Fr, Ger, Sp.
Special Interest: golf & tennis tournaments, go-kart & windsurfing championships, island cruises.

– MADRID

LATITUD 4 DESTINATION MANAGEMENT
Po. de la Castellana, 121, 28046 MADRID.
Tel: +34 (1) 597 0822. Fax: 556 2326. Tlx: 49008 LTD E.
Contact: Eugenia Gomez, Manager.
Special Interest: art, gourmet eating, history, museums, opera.

– TENERIFE

VIAJES LIDER CANARIAS SA
Calle La Hoya 58, 38400 PUERTO DE LA CRUZ.
Tel: +34 (22) 382 100. Fax: 380 768/371 832. Tlx: 92398/92772 LIDE E.
Contact: Mr Jose Alonso.
Branch Offices:
Edificio Veronica II, 38660 PLAYA DE LAS AMERICAS.
Tel: +34 (22) 790 813-4. Fax: 796 520. Tlx: 92394 LIDE E.
Chaparral Shopping Centre, 38630 COSTA DE SILENCIO.
Tel: +34 (22) 785 957.
Established: 1987; 29 employees.
Languages: Eng, Fr, Sp.

SRI LANKA

QUICKSHAWS LTD
PO Box 1830, 3 Kallinga Place, COLOMBO 5.
Tel: +94 (1) 583 133-5. Fax: 587 613. Tlx: 21267 QUIKTUR CE.
Contacts: Ms Nirmala de Mel and Mr I N de Silva.
Associations: ASTA, IATA, PATA, AFTA.
Special Interest: herbal medicine, meditation & oriental religions; cricket, tennis, sailing, golf; gems & jewellery; processions with dancing, handicrafts; agricultural schemes, free trade zones & environmental programmes.

SWEDEN

RISBECKER INTERNATIONAL
PO Box 5128, 4th Floor, Drottninggatan 71a, S-102 43 STOCKHOLM.
Tel: +46 (8) 214 707. Fax: 214 873.
Contact: Tom Risbecker.
Established: 1977; 5 employees.
Associations: SITE, MPI, HSMA, ASTA, DRV.
Special Interest: agriculture, canal cruising, folk-dancing, forestry, golf, gourmet eating, hospitals, hunting, museums, rafting.

SWITZERLAND

WELCOME SWISS TOURS
PO Box 4133, Avenue Benjamin Constant 7, 1002 LAUSANNE.
Tel: +41 (21) 206 821. Fax: 231 366. Tlx: 454803 WST CH.
Contacts: Gerry Boyle, Andrew Done.
Associations: SITE, ITA UK, ACE.

TAHITI

TAHITI TOURS
PO Box 627, rue Jeanne d'Arc, PAPEETE.
Tel: +689 427 870. Fax: 425 050. Tlx: 299 SETOUR FP.
Contact: Ms Diana Chin Choi, General Director.
Established: 1958; 12 employees.
Languages: Chin, Eng, Fr, Ger, It, Port, Sp, Tahitian.
Associations: IATA, ATAF, PATA.
Special Interest: scuba diving, cruises, charter yachting, deep-sea fishing, golfing, nature walks, trekking, horseriding, helicopter tours.

TAIWAN, R.O.C.

INTER-ASIA HOLIDAYS
PO Box 81-278, TAIPEI.
Tel: +886 (2) 511 6341. Fax: 563 0028/511 9204. Tlx: 13385/20450 CHRISLAW.
Contact: Christopher Law.
Established: 1970.
Languages: Chin, Eng.
Associations: UFTAA, USTOA, PATA, ASTA, SITE.

TANZANIA

ABERCROMBIE & KENT LTD
PO Box 427, Arusha International Conference Centre, ARUSHA.
Tel: +255 (57) 8347. Fax: 8273. Tlx: 42005 TZ.
Contact: Mr Sandy Evans.
Established: 1985; 150 employees.
Languages: Eng, Fr, Ger, It.
Special Interest: agriculture, anthropology, botany, gemstones, hospitals, ornithology, photography, safaris, wildlife (1-12); mountaineering, walking (1-3, 6-12).

THAILAND

DIETHELM TRAVEL
Kian Gwan II Building, 140/1 Wireless Road, BANGKOK 10330.
Tel: +66 (2) 255 9150/9160/9170. Fax: 256 0248-9.
Tlx: 81183/21763/227001 DIETRAV TH.
Contact: Mr Chaladol Ussamarn.
Associations: ASTA, ICCA, PATA, USTOA, TICA, TTI, Networld.
Special Interest: archaeology, cruises, gemstones (1-12); jungle expeditions, ornithology, rafting, trekking, walking (11-4); diving (12-3); bicycling, conoeing, golf, sailing, watersports.

TRINIDAD & TOBAGO

THE TRAVEL CENTRE, LTD
Level 2, Uptown Mall, Edward Street, PORT OF SPAIN.
Tel: +1 (809) 625 1636/4266, 623 5096. Fax: 623 5101.
Contact: Catherine de Gannes-Martin, Director.
Established: 1988; 8 employees.
Languages: Eng.
Associations: IATA, TAATT, T&T Hotel & Tourism Assoc.
Special Interest: carnivals, coral reefs, scuba diving, sailing, golf, nature, sports, squash, food, flowers, ornithology.

TURKEY
– ISTANBUL & ANTALYA

VIP TOURISM DESTINATION MANAGEMENT COMPANY
Cumhuriyet Caddesi 269/2, Harbiye, 80230 ISTANBUL.
Tel: +90 (1) 241 6514/230 1331. Fax: 241 1995. Tlx: 27089 VIP TR.
Contact: Mr Ceylan Pirinccioglu.
Established: 1968.
Languages: Eng, Fr, Ger, Greek, Jap, Russ, Sp, Turk.
Branch Offices:
Halici Sokak No 8/3 Gaziosmanpasa, ANKARA.
Tel: +90 (4) 467 6505/467 0210. Fax: 467 01 04.
30 Agustos Cad. Kahramanlar Apt. No. 43/2, ANTALYA.
Tel: +90 (31) 474 376/7. Fax: 412 144.
Associations: ASTA, IATA, ICCA, Internet, JATA, SITE, DRV, UFTAA, USTOA.
Special Interest: food, gourmet eating, museums (1-12); archaeology, spas, religion (4-6, 9-10); ornithology (4/5, 10/11); yachting (5-10); music festivals, agriculture (6-9); art (9-6); universities (10-6).

– IZMIR & AEGEAN COAST

TURCEM TOURISM AND TRAVEL LTD
858 Sokak No. 2, Cakiroglu is Hani 301, 35250 KONAK, IZMIR.
Tel: +90 (51) 257 657. Fax: 144 511. Tlx: 53775 TCMT TR.
Contacts: Mr Nazmi Buldanlioglu and Mrs Beria Buldanlioglu.
Established: 1988; 5 employees.
Languages: Eng, Ger, Turk.
Associations: TURSAB, UFTAA, ATTO.
Special Interest: folk-dancing, food, walking (1-12); flowers, religion (4-5); steam trains (4-5, 9-10); cruises, sailing, spas/hot springs, yachting (4-10); agriculture, diving (5-9).

UNITED ARAB EMIRATES

MMI – GULF VENTURES
PO Box 70, DUBAI.
Tel: +971 (4) 346 838. Fax: 345 029. Tlx: 45425 GRAY EM.
Contact: Mrs Paddy Paul.
Special Interest: archaeology, coral reefs, deep-sea fishing, sailing, (1-12); camel races (10-2); cricket, diving, golfing, safaris (10-5).

UNITED KINGDOM

ALASTAIR SAWDAY'S TOURS LTD
44 Ambra Vale East, BRISTOL BS8 4RE.
Tel: +44 (272) 299 921. Fax: 254 712.
Contacts: Annie Shillito and Alastair Sawday.
Languages: Fr, It, Sp.
Special Interest: music festivals, cooking, country dancing, gardens, golf, cycling, walking, church groups, choirs, bargeing.

ANGLO AMERICAN TRAVEL LTD
35 Spencer Road, LONDON SW20 OQN.
Tel: +44 (81) 947 3416. Fax: 947 1175.
Contact: Roger Stevens.
Associations: BITOA.

EUROPA TRAVEL INTERNATIONAL
71 Crouch Street, COLCHESTER, Essex CO3 3EY.
Tel: +44 (206) 763 737. Fax: 763 420.
Contact: Michael Wheeler.
Associations: BITOA, IATA, ABTA, LTD.

EVENTS INTERNATIONAL LTD
53 St Owen Street, HEREFORD HR1 2JQ.
Tel: +44 (432) 263 263. Fax: 342 323.
Contact: Paul Terry, Managing Director.
Established: 1985; 6 employees.
Languages: Fr.
Special Interest: corporate market.

JOURNEYS (Journeys Abroad Ltd)
Bro Dyffryn, Llwynmawr, LLANGOLLEN, Clwyd LL20 7BH.
Tel & Fax: +44 (691) 728 919 (to change during 1993 to 718 919).
Contact: Hugh Jordan, Managing Director.
Languages: Eng, Fr, Ger, Pol, Russ, Welsh.
Special Interest: schools/colleges, railway enthusiasts, country sports.

SPORTSWORLD GROUP PLC
New Abbey Court, Stert Street, ABINGDON OX14 3JZ.
Tel: +44 (235) 554 844. Fax: 550 428.
Contacts: Jonathan Callow or Sarah Furness.
Languages: Fr, Ger, It, Pol, Port, Sp.

TRAVEL TALK
31 Load Street, BEWDLEY DY12 2AS.
Tel: +44 (299) 400 754. Fax: 403 032.
Contacts: Roger Hunstone, Richard Crosby, Joan Appleton.
Languages: Eng, Fr, Ger, Greek, It, Russ, Sp.
Associations: SITE, ITMA, ABTA, IATA, ATOL

USA – ARIZONA & SOUTHWEST

SOUTHWEST ARRANGERS LTD
4520 East Grant Road, TUCSON, AZ 85712.
Tel: +1 (602) 881 4474. Fax: 881 8165.
Contact: Stephen Spitzer.

– CALIFORNIA

DESTINATION RESOURCES
5435 Balboa Blvd, Suite 106, ENCINO, CA 91316.

Tel: +1 (818) 995 7915. Fax: 990 6129.
Contact: Ruth Pash.
Established: 1985; 4 employees.
Languages: Eng, Fr, Ger, It, Sp.
Associations: SITE, MPI, HSMA.
Special Interest: ballooning, fashions, film studios, gourmet eating, horseracing, museums, rafting, spas/hot springs (1-12); whale-watching (spring); film festivals (summer); parades (11-1).

– COLORADO

ORGANIZERS, ETC
7373 South Alton Way, Suite B100, ENGLEWOOD, CO 80112.
Tel: +1 (303) 771 1178. Fax: 771 1157.
Contact: Craig Cook.
Established: 1981; 12 employees.
Languages: Fr, Ger, It, Sp.
Special Interest: skiing (11-4).

– FLORIDA

SUNCOAST DESTINATION MGT SCES (INCENTIVE MEETING PLANNERS)
Suite 700, 6149 Chancellor Drive, ORLANDO, FL 32809.
Tel: +1 (407) 859 0027. Fax: 855 1092/5547. Tlx: 510-601-3341.
Contact: Graydon Hall.
Branch offices:
Suite 301, 150, 153rd Avenue, MADEIRA BEACH, FL 33708.
Suite 266, 17070 Collins Avenue, N MIAMI BEACH, FL 33160.
Established: 1980; 350 employees.
Languages: Dutch, Eng, Fr, Ger, It, Jap, Sp.
Associations: SITE, MPI, CFCSA.
Special Interest: car racing, cruising, food/gourmet eating, golf, horse breeding, yachting.

– GEORGIA

ATLANTA ARRANGEMENTS
Suite 652, 2964 Peachtree Road NW, ATLANTA, GA 30305.
Tel: +1 (404) 262 7660. Fax: 233 2426.
Contact: Pamela Thompson, Executive Director & General Manager.
Languages: Eng, Fr, Ger, It, Sp.
Associations: MPI, NTA, ASAE, NAEM, PCMA, HCEA, ISES, SITE.
Special Interest: private homes, historic locales, architecture, gardens, museums, gourmet eating, Afro-American heritage, gospel music, sports events, golf, tennis; rafting (6-8).

– HAWAII

MARY CHARLES & ASSOCIATES, INC.
Suite 205, 2334 South King Street, HONOLULU HI 96826.
Tel: +1 (808) 942 9655. Fax: 949 1273. Tlx: (743) 1705 MCAHI.
Contacts: Mary Charles and Ipo Minniear.
Associations: SITE, MPI, Intralink, HSMAI.
Special Interest: rugby (6-8); history, surfing, volcano visits, windsurfing, yachting (1-12).

– ILLINOIS

CHICAGO WELCOMES, INC.
Suite 2010, 100, North LaSalle Street, CHICAGO, IL 60602.
Tel: +1 (312) 641 6633. Fax: 641 6641. Tlx: 4955963.
Contact: Mr Rex Fritschi.
Associations: ASTA, NATA, SITE, IATAN.
Special Interest: architecture (world centre for modern architecture), financial, jazz & blues (1-12); railways (4-10); agriculture (4-11); music (6-8, 10-3); opera (11-3).

– INDIANA

ACCENT ON INDIANAPOLIS, INC
Suite 1200, 55 Monument Circle, INDIANAPOLIS, IN 46204.
Tel: +1 (317) 632 8687. Fax: 632 5848.
Associations: MPI, ASAE, ICVA, IAEP, The Network.
Special Interest: architecture, historic homes, museums, sports – car racing, basketball, football, golf, tennis.

– LOUISIANA

CUSTOM CONVENTIONS OF NEW ORLEANS
PO Box 50958, NEW ORLEANS, LA 70150.
Tel: +1 (504) 944 0814. Fax: 944 0815.
Contact: Carling Dinkler.
Associations: GNOTCC, HSMA, ASTA.
Special Interest: architecture, beaches, Cajun culture, cruises, river and swamplands cruises, cuisine, Southern plantations.

– MASSACHUSETTS & NEW ENGLAND

DESTINATION MANAGEMENT
86 Pleasant Street, MARLBOROUGH, MA 01752.
Tel: +1 (508) 460 0900. Fax: 460 9996.
Contact: Jonathan P. Danforth, Exec Vice President.
Associations: PCMA, ASAE, SITE, MPI.
Special Interest: cruises, dining, museums, shopping, sightseeing, theatre.

– MINNESOTA

METRO CONNECTIONS, INC
Suite 110, 1219 Marquette Avenue, MINNEAPOLIS, MN 55403.
Tel: +1 (612) 333 8687. Fax: 333 4169.
Contact: Mr Sam Thompson.
Associations: MPI, HSMA, Tour Managers' Assn.
Special Interest: hospitals, medicine (1-12); fishing (5-9); agriculture, forestry, mining (5-10); sailing (6-8); canoeing (6-9); dairy farming (summer); hunting (9-11); ice skating (10-3).

– NEVADA (LAS VEGAS)

SUNCOAST DESTINATION MGT SCES (INTERNATIONAL MEETING PLANNERS)
3750-60 S Jones Boulevard, LAS VEGAS, NV 89103.
Tel: +1 (702) 221 8812. Fax: 228 0559.
Contacts: Joanne Ballard.
Languages: Eng.
Special Interest: snow skiing, water skiing, boating, canyons, river rafting, fishing, cruising, ghost towns, golf, mountain climbing, houseboating, gambling.

– NEW YORK

MANHATTAN PASSPORT
236 East 47th Street, NEW YORK, NY 10017.
Tel: +1 (212) 832 9010. Fax: 750 9285/ 570 2391. Tlx: 6972498.
Contact: Ms Ina Lee Selden, President.
Associations: SITE, NY CVB.
Special Interest: gourmet eating, jazz, museums, theatre (1-12); ballet (2-5); gardens (4-8); baseball (4-9); tennis (9); opera (9-4); autumn foliage (10-11); football (10-1); basketball (10-4).

– OHIO

ACCENT ON CINCINNATI, INC
Suite 1017, 105 West Fourth Street, CINCINNATI, OH 45202.
Tel: +1 (513) 721 8687. Fax: 721 1542.
Contact: David Freeman.
Associations: MPI, ASAE, GCCVB, HCEA, OTA, The Network.
Special Interest: historic homes, horse farms, museums, river boats, sports – baseball, football, golf, horseracing, tennis.

– PUERTO RICO

TRAVEL SERVICES, INC
PO Box 4606, 1052 Ashford Avenue, Condado, SAN JUAN, PR 00905.
Tel: +1 (809) 724 6281. Fax: 725 6245. Tlx: RCA 3252687.
Contact: Mr Paul Ferguson, President.
Established: 1955; 30 employees.
Languages: Eng, Fr, Sp.
Associations: ASTA, American Sightseeing, PR Hotel Assn, PR Conv Bureau, SITE, CHA, IATAN, CAREY.
Special Interest: art, deep-sea fishing, food, gambling, horseriding, museums, sailing, tennis, water-skiing, windsurfing (1-12).

– TENNESSEE

HELEN L MOSKOVITZ & ASSOCIATES
Suite 500, 95 White Bridge Road, NASHVILLE, TN 37205.
Tel: +1 (615) 352 6900. Fax: 356 9285.
Contacts: Helen L Moskovitz and Rhonda Marko.
Established: 1979; 12 employees.
Associations: MPI, ASAE, HSMA, NV&CB, PCMA, HCEA, PRSA.
Special Interest: antebellum mansions, country music, historic homes (eg President Andrew Jackson), private homes, river boats, sports – golf, tennis etc.

– TEXAS

WILD WEST TOURS
16903 Lilly Crest, SAN ANTONIO, TX 78232.
Tel: +1 (210) 494 6133. Fax: 490 7490.
Contact: Mr Bob Marsh.
Established: 1970; 5 employees.
Languages: Eng, Fr. Ger, It, Sp.
Special Interest: agriculture, carnivals & parades, cookouts, dairy farming, rafting, ranching, cattle breeding, caves, country music, golf, deep-sea fishing, trail riding, Wild West life.

– VIRGIN ISLANDS: ST THOMAS

TROPIC TOURS
PO Box 1855, The Guardian Building, Havensight, ST THOMAS, , 00803-1855.
Tel: +1 (809) 774 1855. Fax: 776 9597. Tlx: 49573862.
Contact: Ms Brooks Reid Brown, Manager.
Special Interest: coral reefs, deep-sea fishing, diving, golf, shopping, sailing, sightseeing, submarine helicopters, underwater marine parks, tennis (1-12); carnival (April).

– VIRGINIA (FOR WASHINGTON DC)

NATO – North American Tour Organization
8249 Honeysuckle Road, MANASSAS, VA 22111.
Tel: +1 (703) 791 5930. Fax: 791 3513.
Contact: Mr Ingo Blondal, Managing Director.
Established: 1989; 6 employees.
Languages: Dan, Eng, Fr, Ger, Swed.
Special Interest: autumn foliage, civil war, gardens, golf, gourmet eating, history, horse-breeding, museums, performing arts, photography, sailing & boating, shopping, wines & vineyards.

– WASHINGTON (STATE) & PACIFIC NW

WORLD TRAVELERS, INC.
6612 SE 24th Street, Mercer Island, SEATTLE, WA 98040.
Tel: +1 (206) 236 8747. Fax: 232 6311.
Contact: Malte Klutz.
Associations: IATA, ASTA, ARC.
Special Interest: art & architecture, bicycling, walking, nature tours, wine & vineyards, gourmet-eating, whale watching, adventure tours, river-rafting, fishing, volcano tours.

VENEZUELA

CANDES TURISMO CA
PO Box 61142, Edificio Roraima, Avenida Francisco de Miranda, CARACAS 1060.
Tel: +58 (2) 335 773/74. Fax: 328 219. Tlx: 23330 CANDE VC.
Contact: Mr Richard Falsone.
Established: 1950; 30 employees.
Languages: Eng, Fr, Ger, It.
Special Interest: cable car, coral reefs, diving, driving tours, game fishing, hydroelectrics, jungle expeditions, ornithology, sailing, yachting, waterfalls, wildlife (1-12).

YEMEN, REPUBLIC OF

UNIVERSAL TRAVEL & TOURISM
PO Box 10473, Saif Bin Dhi Yezen Street, SANA'A.
Tel: +967 (1) 275 028-30/129-30. Fax: 274 150/275 134. Tlx: 2688/2369 ALAMIA YE.
Contacts: Marco Livadiotti and Mahmood Al Shaibani.

YUGOSLAVIA

See *Croatia*.

ZIMBABWE

WILD AFRICA SAFARIS
PO Box 1737, HARARE.
Tel: +263 (4) 738 329-0. Fax: 737 956. Tlx: 26641.
Contacts: David Ballantyne.
UK Office:
Castle Bank House, Oak Road, LEATHERHEAD, KT22 7PT.
Tel: +44 (372) 362 288. Fax: 360 147.
Associations: ABTA.
Branch Offices:
Horizons Sauvages, La Boursidiere, Boite 101, Route Nationale 186, 92357 LE PLESSIS ROBINSON, France.
Tel: +33 (1) 39 75 49 07. Fax: 39 75 64 14.
Suite 508, 402 West Pender St, VANCOUVER, BC, V6B 1T6.
Tel: +1 (604) 682 1610. Fax: 682 1615.
PO Box 68132, BRYANSTON 2021, South Africa.
Tel: +27 (11) 792 2353. Fax: 792 2833/793 7054.
c/o Sheraton Hotel, Postbag BR 158, GABARONE, Botswana.
Tel: +267 371 096. Fax: 304 281.
Special Interest: wildlife, canoeing, rafting, photography, fishing, ornithology, botany, golf, bowls, tennis, ballooning, archaeology.

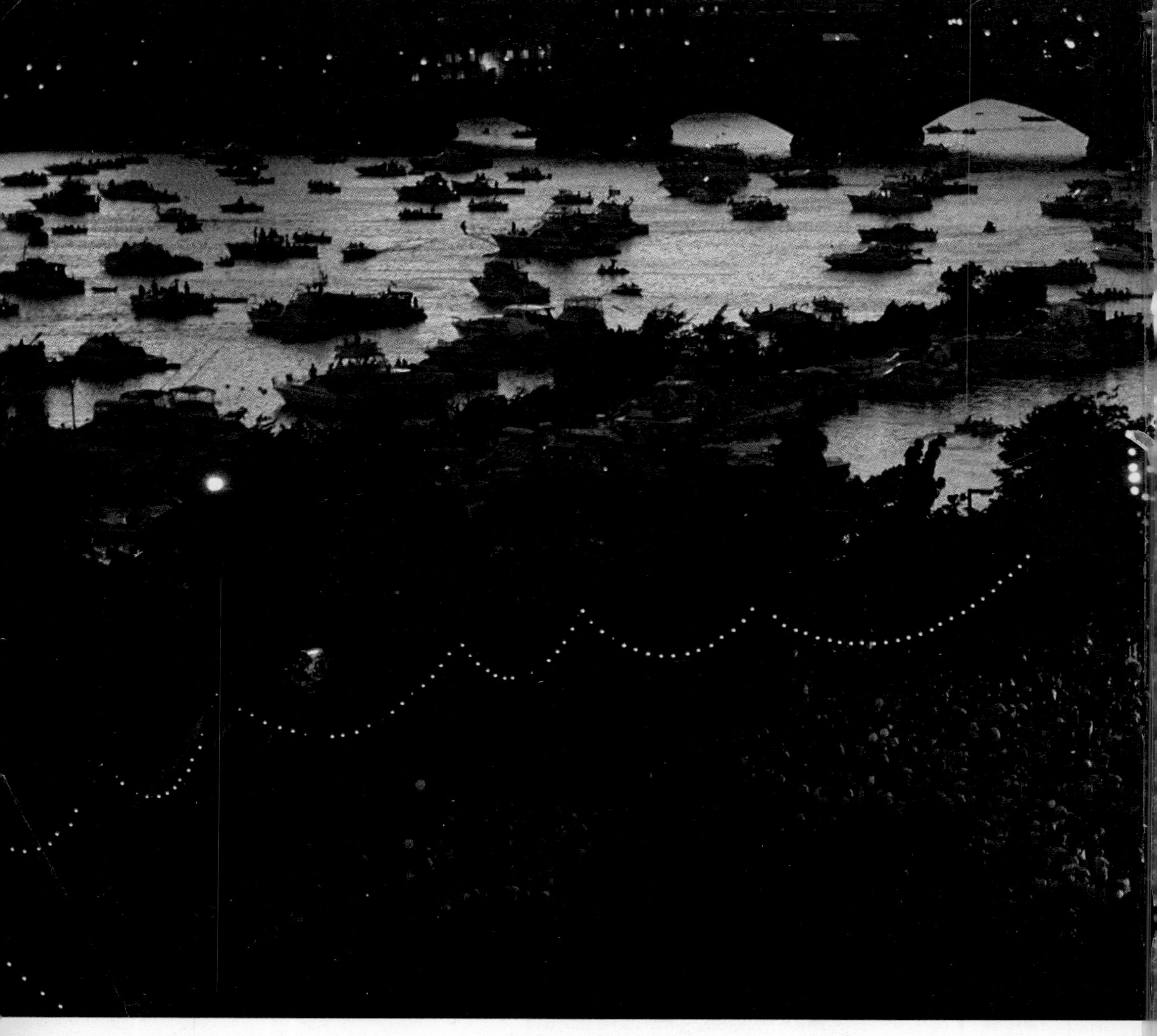